£58.42

YEARBOOK OF THE
UNITED NATIONS
1985

Volume 39

YEARBOOK
OF THE
UNITED
NATIONS
1985

Volume 39

Department of Public Information
United Nations, New York

Martinus Nijhoff Publishers
DORDRECHT / BOSTON / LONDON

Published by Martinus Nijhoff Publishers
P.O. Box 163, 3300 AD Dordrecht, The Netherlands

Kluwer Academic Publishers incorporates the
publishing programmes of Martinus Nijhoff Publishers

Sold and distributed in the U.S.A. and Canada
by Kluwer Academic Publishers,
101 Philip Drive, Norwell, MA 02061, U.S.A.

In all other countries, sold and distributed
by Kluwer Academic Publishers Group,
P.O. Box 322, 3300 AH Dordrecht, The Netherlands

S/D

Yearbook of the United Nations, 1985
Vol. 39
ISBN: 0-7923-0503-5
ISSN: 0082-8521

Printed in the United States of America

Foreword

I T has been said that a fact is the sweetest dream labour knows. The *Yearbook of the United Nations*, a summary of the actions of the world Organization within a single year, is a book of facts. It is also a book of dreams; not vacuous or ephemeral ones but practical visions for a secure life in a world of freedom with justice, where human dignity is honoured, where economic and social progress are sustainable, where natural and human resources are not squandered on weapons, and where peoples fulfil their determination, in the words of the United Nations Charter, "to practice tolerance and live together in peace with one another as good neighbours".

The *Yearbook* is also a reflection of labour in pursuit of the dream of a world at harmony with itself. It is the record of multilateral efforts to deal with the pressing concerns of our times, such as disarmament, human rights, the settlement of regional conflicts, economic and social development, international trade, the environment, drug abuse control, adequate shelter and health care, humanitarian assistance for refugees and disaster relief.

In 1985, the United Nations commemorated the fortieth anniversary of its founding. In looking back over four decades of activity, there was general agreement that the world body was an essential instrument through which the international community could make a collective effort to solve common problems.

As nations return to the precepts of multilateralism, and interest in the United Nations rekindles, the *Yearbook of the United Nations* continues to be an invaluable reference work.

Javier PÉREZ DE CUÉLLAR
Secretary-General

Contents

FOREWORD, by SECRETARY-GENERAL JAVIER PÉREZ DE CUÉLLAR   v

ABOUT THE 1985 EDITION OF THE *YEARBOOK*   xv

ABBREVIATIONS COMMONLY USED IN THE *YEARBOOK*   xvi

EXPLANATORY NOTE ON DOCUMENTS   xvii

Part One: *United Nations*

REPORT OF THE SECRETARY-GENERAL ON THE WORK
OF THE ORGANIZATION   3

POLITICAL AND SECURITY QUESTIONS

I. DISARMAMENT   13
COMPREHENSIVE APPROACHES TO DISARMAMENT, 13: Follow-up to the General
Assembly's special sessions on disarmament, 15; General and complete disarmament, 25; Proposed world disarmament conference, 32; Proposed comprehensive
programme of disarmament, 33. NUCLEAR DISARMAMENT, 35: Prevention of
nuclear war, 35; Climatic effects of nuclear war, 39; Nuclear-arms limitation and
disarmament, 40; Cessation of nuclear-weapon tests, 47; Proposed nuclear-weapon
freeze, 53; Nuclear non-proliferation, 56; Strengthening the security of non-
nuclear-weapon States, 67. PROHIBITION OR RESTRICTION OF OTHER WEAPONS,
70: Chemical and biological weapons, 70; New weapons of mass destruction, including radiological weapons, 74; Conventional weapons, 76; Arms race in outer
space, 78. OTHER DISARMAMENT ISSUES, 82: Reduction of military budgets, 82;
Information on military matters, 85; Military research and development, 86; Disarmament and development, 87; Economic and social consequences of the arms race,
88; Declaration of the Indian Ocean as a Zone of Peace, 89. INFORMATION AND
STUDIES, 91: World Disarmament Campaign, 92; Disarmament Week, 95; UN
fellowship programme, 97; Disarmament research, 98; Parties and signatories to ·
disarmament agreements, 100.

II. PEACEFUL USES OF OUTER SPACE   101
SCIENCE, TECHNOLOGY AND LAW, 101: Space science and technology, 101; Space
law, 104. SPACECRAFT LAUNCHINGS, 108.

III. LAW OF THE SEA   109
UN Convention on the Law of the Sea, 109; Preparatory Commission, 110; Functions of the Secretary-General, 112.

IV. INTERNATIONAL PEACE AND SECURITY   116
IMPLEMENTATION OF THE 1970 DECLARATION ON INTERNATIONAL SECURITY, 116.
IMPLEMENTATION OF THE SECURITY PROVISIONS OF THE UN CHARTER, 119. SET-
TLING DISPUTES THROUGH NEGOTIATIONS, 121. REVIEW OF PEACE-KEEPING
OPERATIONS, 122. INTERNATIONAL YEAR OF PEACE (1986), 122: Right of peoples to
peace, 125.

V. AFRICA   126
SOUTH AFRICA AND *APARTHEID*, 126: General aspects, 127; Relations with South
Africa, 135; Situation in South Africa, 152; Aid programmes and inter-agency co-
operation, 169; Other aspects, 172. SOUTH AFRICA AND THE FRONT-LINE STATES OF
SOUTHERN AFRICA, 178: Angola–South Africa armed incidents and South African
occupation of Angola, 180; Botswana–South Africa armed incidents, 189; Lesotho–
South Africa dispute, 193; Mozambique–South Africa relations, 196. CHAD-LIBYAN
ARAB JAMAHIRIYA DISPUTE, 196. BURKINA FASO-MALI DISPUTE, 198. ETHIOPIA-
SOMALIA DISPUTE, 198. COMORIAN ISLAND OF MAYOTTE, 198. MALAGASY ISLANDS
QUESTION, 200. UN EDUCATIONAL AND TRAINING PROGRAMME FOR SOUTHERN
AFRICA, 200. CO-OPERATION BETWEEN OAU AND THE UN SYSTEM, 201.

VI. AMERICAS   205
CENTRAL AMERICA SITUATION, 205: Nicaragua situation, 208.

VII. ASIA AND THE PACIFIC   220
EAST ASIA, 220: Korean question, 220. SOUTH-EAST ASIA, 221: Kampuchea situation, 221; International security in South-East Asia, 229; China–Viet Nam dispute,
231; Lao People's Democratic Republic–Thailand dispute, 231. WESTERN AND SOUTH-
WESTERN ASIA, 232: Afghanistan situation and Afghanistan-Pakistan armed incidents,
232; Iran-Iraq armed conflict, 239.

VIII. MEDITERRANEAN   251
CYPRUS QUESTION, 251: Peace-keeping and humanitarian assistance, 256. OTHER
QUESTIONS CONCERNING THE MEDITERRANEAN REGION, 258: Questions concern-
ing the Libyan Arab Jamahiriya, 258; Security in the Mediterranean, 259.

IX. MIDDLE EAST   261
MIDDLE EAST SITUATION, 263. PALESTINE QUESTION, 272: Jerusalem, 280; Assistance
to Palestinians, 281; Related questions, 285. INCIDENTS AND DISPUTES BETWEEN ARAB
COUNTRIES AND ISRAEL, 293: Iraq and Israel, 293; Lebanon situation, 295; Israel
and the Syrian Arab Republic, 313. FINANCING OF PEACE-KEEPING FORCES, 316:
UNDOF financing, 316; UNIFIL financing, 320; Review of reimbursement rates to
troop contributors, 324. TERRITORIES OCCUPIED BY ISRAEL, 326: Fourth Geneva
Convention, 334; Palestinian detainees, 335; Israeli settlements policy, 338; Golan
Heights, 340; Palestinian officials, 343; Living conditions of the Palestinians, 344;
Israeli measures against educational institutions, 349; Mediterranean–Dead Sea canal
project, 351. PALESTINE REFUGEES, 353: UN Agency for Palestine refugees, 353;
Other aspects, 357.

X. OTHER POLITICAL QUESTIONS   369
INFORMATION, 369: Mass communication, 369; UN public information, 374; Depart-
mental News Service, 387. RADIATION EFFECTS, 388. ANTARCTICA, 389. ANNIVER-
SARY OF THE EMANCIPATION OF SLAVES IN THE BRITISH EMPIRE, 391.

XI. INSTITUTIONAL MACHINERY   392
UN MEMBERS, 392. SECURITY COUNCIL, 392. GENERAL ASSEMBLY, 394. SECRETARY-
GENERAL, 398. CO-OPERATION WITH OTHER INTERGOVERNMENTAL ORGANIZA-
TIONS, 398. OTHER INSTITUTIONAL QUESTIONS, 403.

ECONOMIC AND SOCIAL QUESTIONS

I. DEVELOPMENT POLICY AND INTERNATIONAL ECONOMIC
CO-OPERATION   409
INTERNATIONAL ECONOMIC RELATIONS, 410: Development and economic co-
operation, 410; Economic rights and duties of States, 424; Economic co-operation
among developing countries, 425. ECONOMIC AND SOCIAL TRENDS AND POLICY, 427.
DEVELOPMENT PLANNING, EDUCATION AND ADMINISTRATION , 430. RURAL DEVEL-
OPMENT, 432. SPECIAL ECONOMIC AREAS, 433: Developing countries, 433.

II. OPERATIONAL ACTIVITIES FOR DEVELOPMENT   456
GENERAL ASPECTS, 456: Financing of operational activities, 458; Inter-agency co-operation, 463. TECHNICAL CO-OPERATION THROUGH UNDP, 464: UNDP operational activities, 467; Programme planning and management, 473; Financing, 475; Staff-related matters, 483; Other administrative matters, 484. OTHER TECHNICAL CO-OPERATION, 485: UN programmes, 485; United Nations Volunteers, 486; Technical co-operation among developing countries, 488. UN CAPITAL DEVELOPMENT FUND, 493.

III. ECONOMIC ASSISTANCE, DISASTERS AND EMERGENCY RELIEF   496
ECONOMIC ASSISTANCE, 497: Africa and the critical economic situation, 498; Countries in other regions, 527. DISASTERS, 534: Office of the United Nations Disaster Relief Co-ordinator, 534; Co-ordination in the UN system, 536; Disaster relief, 537; Disaster preparedness and prevention, 546. EMERGENCY RELIEF AND ASSISTANCE, 547.

IV. INTERNATIONAL TRADE AND FINANCE   551
INTERNATIONAL CO-OPERATION IN TRADE AND FINANCE, 552. INTERNATIONAL TRADE, 554: Trade policy, 554; Trade promotion and facilitation, 560; Commodities, 565; Consumer protection, 571. FINANCE, 575: Financial policy, 575; Trade-related finance, 579; Taxation, 580. PROGRAMME AND FINANCES OF UNCTAD, 581; UNCTAD programme, 581; Organizational questions, 583.

V. TRANSPORT AND TOURISM   585
TRANSPORT, 585: Maritime transport, 585; Transport of dangerous goods, 588. TOURISM, 590.

VI. INDUSTRIAL DEVELOPMENT   591
CONVERSION OF UNIDO TO A SPECIALIZED AGENCY, 591: Programme and finances of UNIDO, 597; Programme policy, 597; Financial questions, 599. INDUSTRIAL DEVELOPMENT ACTIVITIES, 600: Technical co-operation, 600; Industrial co-operation, 603; Industrial development of LDCs, 605; Redeployment of industrial production to developing countries, 605; Industrial financing, 606; Industrial management, 606; Industrial planning, 607; Industrial studies, 608; Industrial technology, 608. DEVELOPMENT OF SPECIFIC INDUSTRIES, 609: Agro-industries, 609; Chemical industries, 610; Engineering industries, 612; Metallurgical and mineral industries, 614; Other industrial categories, 615.

VII. TRANSNATIONAL CORPORATIONS   616
DRAFT CODE OF CONDUCT, 616. STANDARDS OF ACCOUNTING AND REPORTING, 617. CENTRE ON TNCs, 618.

VIII. REGIONAL ECONOMIC AND SOCIAL ACTIVITIES   624
REGIONAL CO-OPERATION, 624. AFRICA, 625: Economic and social trends, 625; Activities in 1985, 626; Programme, organizational and administrative questions, 640. ASIA AND THE PACIFIC, 644: Economic and social trends, 645; Activities in 1985, 645; Programme, organizational and administrative questions, 651. EUROPE, 653: Economic trends, 653; Activities in 1985, 654. LATIN AMERICA AND THE CARIBBEAN, 660: Economic trends, 660; Activities in 1985, 661; Programme, organizational and administrative questions, 664. WESTERN ASIA, 665: Economic and social trends, 665; Activities in 1985, 666.

IX. NATURAL RESOURCES AND CARTOGRAPHY   669
GENERAL ASPECTS OF NATURAL RESOURCES, 669: Exploration, 669; Permanent sovereignty over natural resources, 672; Committee on Natural Resources, 673; Co-ordination of UN activities, 674; Other aspects, 674. MINERAL RESOURCES, 675: Technical co-operation, 675; Exploitation and processing, 675; Evaluation, 677. WATER AND MARINE RESOURCES, 677: Water resources development, 677; Marine resources, 681. CARTOGRAPHY, 683: Third UN Regional Cartographic Conference for the Americas, 683.

X.   ENERGY RESOURCES   684
GENERAL ASPECTS, 684: Energy resources development, 685; Energy resources in
industry, 690. NEW AND RENEWABLE ENERGY SOURCES, 691: Implementation of the
1981 Nairobi Programme of Action, 691. NUCLEAR ENERGY, 693: IAEA report, 693;
Preparations for the Conference on nuclear energy, 694.

XI.   FOOD   697
FOOD PROBLEMS, 697. FOOD AID, 701: World Food Programme, 701.

XII.   SCIENCE AND TECHNOLOGY   707
IMPLEMENTATION OF THE VIENNA PROGRAMME OF ACTION, 708: Mid-decade review,
708; Information systems for science and technology, 709. FINANCING, 711: UN
Financing System, 711. INSTITUTIONAL ARRANGEMENTS, 714: National focal points,
714; Intergovernmental Committee, 714; Advisory Committee, 715; Centre for science
and technology, 716; Co-ordination in the UN system, 716. TECHNOLOGY TRANSFER,
717: Draft code of conduct, 718. BRAIN DRAIN, 719.

XIII.   SOCIAL AND CULTURAL DEVELOPMENT   721
SOCIAL DEVELOPMENT AND WELFARE, 721: World social situation, 721; Social aspects
of development, 725; Social welfare, 731; Institutional machinery, 736. CRIME
PREVENTION, 738: Seventh UN Congress, 738; Questions related to criminal justice,
742; UN Trust Fund for Social Defence, 757. CULTURAL DEVELOPMENT, 757.

XIV.   POPULATION   760
FOLLOW-UP TO THE 1984 CONFERENCE ON POPULATION, 760. UN FUND FOR POPULA-
TION ACTIVITIES, 762. OTHER POPULATION ACTIVITIES, 769.

XV.   HEALTH AND HUMAN RESOURCES   773
HEALTH, 773: Human and environmental health, 773; Disabled persons, 775. HUMAN
RESOURCES, 780: Human resources development, 780; UN Institute for Training
and Research, 781; UN University, 785.

XVI.   ENVIRONMENT   788
PROGRAMME AND FINANCES OF UNEP, 788: Programme policy, 789; Regional activities, 793; Co-ordination, 794; UNEP Fund, 796; Other administrative and
organizational questions, 798. ENVIRONMENTAL ACTIVITIES, 799: Environmental
monitoring, 799; Protection against harmful products and pollutants, 801; Ecosystems,
804; Environmental aspects of political, economic and other issues, 817.

XVII.   HUMAN SETTLEMENTS   822
PROGRAMME AND FINANCES OF UNCHS, 822: Programme policy, 822; Financing, 824.
HUMAN SETTLEMENTS ACTIVITIES, 825: UNCHS (Habitat), 825; International Year
of Shelter for the Homeless (1987), 827; Political, economic and social issues, 830.
ORGANIZATIONAL QUESTIONS, 831: Co-ordination in the UN system, 831; Commis-
sion on Human Settlements, 833.

XVIII.   HUMAN RIGHTS   835
DISCRIMINATION, 835: Racial discrimination, 835; Other aspects of discrimination,
845. CIVIL AND POLITICAL RIGHTS, 852: Covenant on Civil and Political Rights and
Optional Protocol, 853; Self-determination of peoples, 854; Rights of detained persons, 862; Disappearance of persons, 869; Other aspects of civil and political rights,
871. ECONOMIC, SOCIAL AND CULTURAL RIGHTS, 874: Covenant on Economic, Social
and Cultural Rights, 876; Right to development, 879; Right to food, 881; Popular
participation and human rights, 881. ADVANCEMENT OF HUMAN RIGHTS, 882: UN
machinery, 886; Public information activities, 887; Regional arrangements, 889; International human rights instruments, 889; Advisory services, 893; Technical assistance
to strengthen legal institutions, 896; Responsibility to promote and protect human
rights, 896; Proposed establishment of a new international humanitarian order,
896. HUMAN RIGHTS VIOLATIONS, 898: Africa, 898; Asia and the Pacific, 905;

HUMAN RIGHTS *(cont.)*
Europe and the Mediterranean area, 912; Latin America, 912; Middle East, 925; Mass exoduses, 927; Genocide, 928. OTHER HUMAN RIGHTS QUESTIONS, 929: Rights of the child, 929; Youth and human rights, 930; Human rights of disabled persons, 931; Human rights of the individual and international law, 931; Human rights and science and technology, 932; Human rights and peace, 933; Non-interference in States' internal affairs, 935.

XIX. WOMEN   936
CONFERENCE ON THE DECADE FOR WOMEN, 937. WOMEN AND DEVELOPMENT, 944: UN Development Fund for Women, 949. STATUS OF WOMEN, 952. CONVENTION ON DISCRIMINATION AGAINST WOMEN, 960.

XX. CHILDREN, YOUTH AND AGING PERSONS   962
CHILDREN, 962: UN Children's Fund, 962; Draft declaration on adoption and foster placement, 976. YOUTH, 976: Activities of the UN system, 977; International Youth Year, 978; Strengthening communication between youth and the United Nations, 980; Integrating youth in development and society, 982. AGING PERSONS, 984: Implementation of the Plan of Action, 984.

XXI. REFUGEES AND DISPLACED PERSONS   990
PROGRAMME AND FINANCES OF UNHCR, 991: Programme policy, 991; Financial and administrative questions, 992. ACTIVITIES FOR REFUGEES, 994: Assistance, 994; Refugee protection, 1009. INTERNATIONAL CO-OPERATION TO AVERT NEW REFUGEE FLOWS, 1011.

XXII. DRUGS OF ABUSE   1012
Drug abuse and international control, 1013; Supply and demand, 1019; Conventions, 1028; Organizational questions, 1029.

XXIII. STATISTICS   1031

XXIV. INSTITUTIONAL ARRANGEMENTS   1038
CO-ORDINATION IN THE UN SYSTEM, 1038. ECONOMIC AND SOCIAL COUNCIL, 1045; Co-operation with other organizations, 1046; Other organizational matters, 1055. OTHER INSTITUTIONAL ARRANGEMENTS, 1057: Work programme of the Second Committee, 1058.

TRUSTEESHIP AND DECOLONIZATION

I. GENERAL QUESTIONS RELATING TO COLONIAL COUNTRIES   1059
THE 1960 DECLARATION ON COLONIAL COUNTRIES, 1059. OTHER GENERAL QUESTIONS CONCERNING NSGTs, 1082.

II. INTERNATIONAL TRUSTEESHIP SYSTEM   1084
TRUST TERRITORY OF THE PACIFIC ISLANDS, 1084. OTHER ASPECTS OF THE INTERNATIONAL TRUSTEESHIP SYSTEM, 1088.

III. NAMIBIA   1090
NAMIBIA QUESTION, 1091. ECONOMIC AND SOCIAL CONDITIONS, 1122. INTERNATIONAL ASSISTANCE, 1127.

IV. OTHER COLONIAL TERRITORIES   1132
FALKLAND ISLANDS (MALVINAS), 1132. EAST TIMOR, 1136. WESTERN SAHARA, 1137. OTHER TERRITORIES, 1141.

LEGAL QUESTIONS

I.   INTERNATIONAL COURT OF JUSTICE   1155
     Judicial work of the Court, 1155; Organizational questions, 1157.

II. LEGAL ASPECTS OF INTERNATIONAL POLITICAL RELATIONS   1160
     Peaceful settlement of disputes between States, 1160; Good-neighbourliness between
     States, 1161; Non-use of force in international relations, 1162; Draft Code of Offences
     against peace and security, 1163; Draft convention against mercenaries, 1165; Preven-
     tion of terrorism, 1166; Draft articles on non-navigational uses of international water-
     courses, 1170.

III. STATES AND INTERNATIONAL LAW   1172
     DIPLOMATIC RELATIONS, 1172. STATE IMMUNITIES, LIABILITY AND RESPONSIBILITY,
     1175.

IV. INTERNATIONAL ORGANIZATIONS AND INTERNATIONAL LAW   1177
     STRENGTHENING THE ROLE OF THE UNITED NATIONS, 1177. HOST COUNTRY RELA-
     TIONS, 1180. DRAFT STANDARD RULES OF PROCEDURE FOR CONFERENCES, 1181.

V.   TREATIES AND AGREEMENTS   1182

VI. INTERNATIONAL ECONOMIC LAW   1191
     GENERAL ASPECTS, 1191: Report of UNCITRAL, 1191. INTERNATIONAL TRADE LAW,
     1192: Unification of trade law, 1192; Most-favoured-nation clauses, 1193; Training and
     assistance, 1194. LEGAL ASPECTS OF THE NEW INTERNATIONAL ECONOMIC ORDER, 1195.

VII. OTHER LEGAL QUESTIONS   1197
     International Law Commission, 1197; UN Programme for the teaching and study of
     international law, 1198; Co-operation between the United Nations and the Asian-African
     Legal Consultative Committee, 1200.

ADMINISTRATIVE AND BUDGETARY QUESTIONS

I.   UNITED NATIONS FINANCING   1201
     UN BUDGET, 1201: Budget for 1984-1985, 1201; Budget for 1986-1987, 1204. ASSESS-
     MENT OF CONTRIBUTIONS, 1213: Scale of assessments, 1213; Budget contributions
     in 1985, 1217. FINANCIAL SITUATION, 1220: Financial emergency, 1220; Impact of
     inflation and monetary instability, 1222. ACCOUNTS AND AUDITING, 1222: Accounts
     for 1984, 1222.

II. UNITED NATIONS PROGRAMMES   1224
     PROGRAMME PLANNING AND BUDGETING, 1224. PROGRAMME EVALUATION, 1227.
     ADMINISTRATIVE AND BUDGETARY CO-ORDINATION IN THE UN SYSTEM, 1230.

III. UNITED NATIONS OFFICIALS   1233
     PERSONNEL MANAGEMENT, 1233: Staff composition, 1234; Job classification, 1241;
     Staff representation, 1242; Field staff, 1243; Travel, 1243; Staff Rules, 1244; Privileges
     and immunities, 1244. STAFF COSTS, 1245: Salaries and allowances, 1245; Pensions,
     1247. UN ADMINISTRATIVE TRIBUNAL, 1251: Appeals system for staff, 1251. OTHER
     UN OFFICIALS, 1252: Conditions of service and compensation, 1252; Experts and con-
     sultants, 1253.

IV. OTHER ADMINISTRATIVE AND MANAGEMENT QUESTIONS   1254
     REVIEW OF UN ADMINISTRATIVE AND FINANCIAL MATTERS, 1254. CONFERENCES AND
     MEETINGS, 1256. DOCUMENTS AND PUBLICATIONS, 1261. UN PREMISES, 1262. IN-
     FORMATION SYSTEMS, COMPUTERS AND TELECOMMUNICATION, 1263. UN POSTAL
     ADMINISTRATION, 1266.

Part Two: *Intergovernmental organizations related to the United Nations*

I.	INTERNATIONAL ATOMIC ENERGY AGENCY (IAEA)	1271
II.	INTERNATIONAL LABOUR ORGANISATION (ILO)	1278
III.	FOOD AND AGRICULTURE ORGANIZATION OF THE UNITED NATIONS (FAO)	1287
IV.	UNITED NATIONS EDUCATIONAL, SCIENTIFIC AND CULTURAL ORGANIZATION (UNESCO)	1295
V.	WORLD HEALTH ORGANIZATION (WHO)	1302
VI.	INTERNATIONAL BANK FOR RECONSTRUCTION AND DEVELOPMENT (WORLD BANK)	1309
VII.	INTERNATIONAL FINANCE CORPORATION (IFC)	1317
VIII.	INTERNATIONAL DEVELOPMENT ASSOCIATION (IDA)	1323
IX.	INTERNATIONAL MONETARY FUND (IMF)	1330
X.	INTERNATIONAL CIVIL AVIATION ORGANIZATION (ICAO)	1337
XI.	UNIVERSAL POSTAL UNION (UPU)	1342
XII.	INTERNATIONAL TELECOMMUNICATION UNION (ITU)	1345
XIII.	WORLD METEOROLOGICAL ORGANIZATION (WMO)	1350
XIV.	INTERNATIONAL MARITIME ORGANIZATION (IMO)	1356
XV.	WORLD INTELLECTUAL PROPERTY ORGANIZATION (WIPO)	1359
XVI.	INTERNATIONAL FUND FOR AGRICULTURAL DEVELOPMENT (IFAD)	1365
XVII.	INTERIM COMMISSION FOR THE INTERNATIONAL TRADE ORGANIZATION (ICITO) AND THE GENERAL AGREEMENT ON TARIFFS AND TRADE (GATT)	1370

Appendices

I.	ROSTER OF THE UNITED NATIONS	1377
II.	CHARTER OF THE UNITED NATIONS AND STATUTE OF THE INTERNATIONAL COURT OF JUSTICE	1379
	Charter of the United Nations, 1379; Statute of the International Court of Justice, 1388.	
III.	STRUCTURE OF THE UNITED NATIONS	1393
	General Assembly, 1393; Security Council, 1409; Economic and Social Council, 1410; Trusteeship Council, 1420; International Court of Justice, 1421; Other United Nations-related bodies, 1421; Principal members of the Secretariat, 1423.	

IV. AGENDA OF UNITED NATIONS PRINCIPAL ORGANS IN 1985   1426
     General Assembly, 1426; Security Council, 1432; Economic and Social Council, 1432;
     Trusteeship Council, 1434.

 V. UNITED NATIONS INFORMATION CENTRES AND SERVICES   1435

Indexes

USING THE SUBJECT INDEX   1440

SUBJECT INDEX   1441

INDEX OF NAMES   1482

INDEX OF RESOLUTIONS AND DECISIONS   1491

HOW TO OBTAIN PREVIOUS VOLUMES OF THE *YEARBOOK*   1494

About the 1985 edition of the *Yearbook*

The 1985 *YEARBOOK OF THE UNITED NATIONS* has been designed as a reference tool for use by all who might need readily available information on a particular activity of the United Nations system. It covers, during a calendar year, the main activities of the United Nations (Part One) and those of each related organization in the United Nations system (Part Two).

The book is subject-oriented. Part One, containing 50 chapters, is divided into five major sections: political and security questions, economic and social questions, trusteeship and decolonization, legal questions, and administrative and budgetary questions.

Each chapter is divided into a hierarchy of topics. The assignment of headings implies no editorial judgement about the relative importance of a topic.

Structure and scope of articles

Presented under each topical heading is a summary of pertinent United Nations activities, including those of intergovernmental and expert bodies, major reports, Secretariat activities, and the views of States in written communications. The 1985 edition also gives the position of those States explaining their votes in the principal organs of the Organization. Such explanations are generally given when a recorded vote was taken. At the end of each chapter or subchapter is a list of REFERENCES, linked by numerical indicators to the text. These references indicate document symbols, previous *Yearbook* volumes supplying additional information, and previous resolutions and/or decisions by the principal United Nations organs. The *Yearbook* covers the following:

Activities of United Nations bodies. All resolutions, decisions and other major activities of the principal organs and, where applicable, those of subsidiary bodies are either reproduced or summarized in the respective articles. The texts of all resolutions adopted by the General Assembly, the Security Council, the Economic and Social Council and the Trusteeship Council, with information on their adoption, are reproduced under the relevant topic. Where mention is made of other resolutions and decisions, highlighted in bold-face type, the full text or summary can be found by using the INDEX OF RESOLUTIONS AND DECISIONS at the end of this volume.

Major reports. Most 1985 reports of the Secretary-General, along with selected reports from other United Nations sources such as seminars and working groups, are summarized briefly. The document symbols of all reports cited appear in the REFERENCES.

Secretariat activities. The operational activities of the United Nations for development and humanitarian assistance are described under the relevant topics. For all major activities financed outside the United Nations regular budget, information is given on contributions by individual countries and on expenditures. Financial data are generally obtained from the audited accounts prepared for each fund, and cover the 1985 calendar year unless otherwise specified.

Views of States. Written communications sent to the United Nations by Member States and circulated as documents of the principal organs have been summarized under the most relevant topic.

All substantive debates in the Security Council have been analysed and their main points can be found under the pertinent topic(s). Users wishing details on the position of individual States in the principal organs of the United Nations or any of their main/sessional committees should refer to the meeting numbers to be found at the end of the summaries of procedural action following resolution/decision texts.

Related intergovernmental organizations. Part Two of the *Yearbook* describes the 1985 activities of each specialized agency, the International Atomic Energy Agency and the General Agreement on Tariffs and Trade, based on information prepared by them. Included are data on budgets, contributions by member States, and principal officials.

Texts

The *Yearbook* reproduces the texts of all resolutions and decisions of a substantive nature adopted in 1985 by the General Assembly, the Security Council, the Economic and Social Council and the Trusteeship Council. These texts are followed by the procedural details giving: date of adoption, meeting number and vote totals (in favour-against-abstaining); information on their approval by a sessional or subsidiary body prior to final adoption, with document symbols of drafts, approved amendments and committee reports; and a list of sponsors. Also given are the document symbols of any financial implications and all relevant meeting numbers of the General Assembly's Main Committees. Details of any recorded or roll-call vote on the resolution/decision as a whole also follow the text. The texts of resolutions and decisions of a purely procedural nature are not reproduced, but are summarized and their numbers given in bold type.

Terminology

Formal titles of bodies, organizational units, conventions, declarations and officials are given in full on first mention in an article or sequence of articles. They are also used in resolution/decision texts, and in the SUBJECT INDEX under the key word of the title. Short titles may be used in subsequent references; they have no official standing.

How to find information in the *Yearbook*

The 1985 edition has been designed to enable the user to locate information on United Nations activities in a number of ways.

By subject: Broad subjects may be located in the table of contents on pages vii-xiv. Each chapter opens with an introduction highlighting the main developments. Where a main topic is subdivided, shorter introductions may precede such subchapters. Cross-references give chapters for related information. The SUBJECT INDEX may be used to locate individual topics and specific references to the bodies dealing with each.

By body: Although the *Yearbook* is oriented by subject rather than by body, surveys of the work of many bodies appear under the topic of their main concern. For the principal organs, APPENDIX IV gives the 1985 agenda for each session. The members, officers, and date and place of sessions of each body are given in APPENDIX III. The SUBJECT INDEX lists bodies by the key word(s) of their formal title: "*Apartheid*, Special Committee against".

By resolution and decision number: A numerical list of all resolutions and substantive decisions adopted in 1985 by the principal organs, with page numbers for their text, appears in the final pages of this volume.

Resolution/decision texts appear in an article together with the circumstances of their adoption. Summaries of relevant provisions of other resolutions or decisions may also be added where applicable.

Other information: The 1985 report of the Secretary-General on the work of the Organization is reproduced, beginning on page 3. A list of Member States, with their dates of admission to the United Nations, comprises APPENDIX I. The Charter of the United Nations, including the Statute of the International Court of Justice, is in APPENDIX II. An INDEX OF NAMES follows the SUBJECT INDEX.

ABBREVIATIONS COMMONLY USED IN THE *YEARBOOK*

ACABQ	Advisory Committee on Administrative and Budgetary Questions
ACC	Administrative Committee on Co-ordination
ACPAQ	Advisory Committee on Post Adjustment Questions
AMS	Administrative Management Service
ANC	African National Congress of South Africa
ASEAN	Association of South-East Asian Nations
CCAQ	Consultative Committee on Administrative Questions
CCISUA	Co-ordinating Committee for Independent Staff Unions and Associations of the United Nations System
CCSQ	Consultative Committee on Substantive Questions
CDP	Committee for Development Planning
CEDAW	Committee on the Elimination of Discrimination against Women
CERD	Committee on the Elimination of Racial Discrimination
CFA	Committee on Food Aid Policies and Programmes
CILSS	Permanent Inter-State Committee on Drought Control in the Sahel
CMEA	Council for Mutual Economic Assistance
COPUOS	Committee on the Peaceful Uses of Outer Space
CPC	Committee for Programme and Co-ordination
CSDHA	Centre for Social Development and Humanitarian Affairs [DIESA]
DIEC	Development and International Economic Co-operation
DIESA	Department of International Economic and Social Affairs
DPI	Department of Public Information
DTCD	Department of Technical Co-operation for Development
EC	European Community
ECA	Economic Commission for Africa
ECDC	economic co-operation among developing countries
ECE	Economic Commission for Europe
ECLAC	Economic Commission for Latin America and the Caribbean
ECOWAS	Economic Community of West African States
ECWA	Economic Commission for Western Asia
EEC	European Economic Community
ESC	Economic and Social Council
ESCAP	Economic and Social Commission for Asia and the Pacific
ESCWA	Economic and Social Commission for Western Asia
FAO	Food and Agriculture Organization of the United Nations
FICSA	Federation of International Civil Servants' Associations
GA	General Assembly
GATT	General Agreement on Tariffs and Trade
GDP	gross domestic product
GNP	gross national product
IAEA	International Atomic Energy Agency
ICAO	International Civil Aviation Organization
ICITO	Interim Commission for the International Trade Organization
ICJ	International Court of Justice
ICRC	International Committee of the Red Cross
ICSC	International Civil Service Commission
IDA	International Development Association
IDB	Industrial Development Board [UNIDO]
IDDA	Industrial Development Decade for Africa
IEFR	International Emergency Food Reserve
IFAD	International Fund for Agricultural Development
IFC	International Finance Corporation
ILC	International Law Commission
ILO	International Labour Organisation
IMF	International Monetary Fund
IMO	International Maritime Organization
INCB	International Narcotics Control Board
INSTRAW	International Research and Training Institute for the Advancement of Women
IPF	indicative planning figure [UNDP]
ITC	International Trade Centre [UNCTAD/GATT]
ITO	International Trade Organization
ITU	International Telecommunication Union
IUCN	International Union for Conservation of Nature and Natural Resources
IYDP	International Year of Disabled Persons
IYY	International Youth Year
JAG	Joint Advisory Group on the International Trade Centre
JIU	Joint Inspection Unit
JUNIC	Joint United Nations Information Committee
LDC	least developed country
NATO	North Atlantic Treaty Organization
NGO	non-governmental organization
NPT	Treaty on the Non-Proliferation of Nuclear Weapons
NRSE	new and renewable sources of energy
NSGT	Non-Self-Governing Territory
OAS	Organization of American States
OAU	Organization of African Unity
ODA	official development assistance
OECD	Organisation for Economic Co-operation and Development
OPEC	Organization of Petroleum Exporting Countries
PAC	Pan Africanist Congress of Azania
PLO	Palestine Liberation Organization
SC	Security Council
SDR	special drawing right
S-G	Secretary-General
SNPA	Substantial New Programme of Action for the 1980s for the Least Developed Countries
SPC	Special Political Committee
SWAPO	South West Africa People's Organization [Namibia]
TC	Trusteeship Council
TCDC	technical co-operation among developing countries
TDB	Trade and Development Board [UNCTAD]
TNC	transnational corporation
UN	United Nations
UNCDF	United Nations Capital Development Fund
UNCHS	United Nations Centre for Human Settlements (Habitat)
UNCITRAL	United Nations Commission on International Trade Law
UNCTAD	United Nations Conference on Trade and Development
UNDOF	United Nations Disengagement Observer Force [Golan Heights]
UNDP	United Nations Development Programme
UNDRO	Office of the United Nations Disaster Relief Co-ordinator
UNEF	United Nations Emergency Force
UNEP	United Nations Environment Programme
UNESCO	United Nations Educational, Scientific and Cultural Organization
UNFDAC	United Nations Fund for Drug Abuse Control
UNFICYP	United Nations Peace-keeping Force in Cyprus
UNFPA	United Nations Fund for Population Activities
UNFSSTD	United Nations Financing System for Science and Technology for Development
UNHCR	Office of the United Nations High Commissioner for Refugees
UNIC	United Nations Information Centre
UNICEF	United Nations Children's Fund
UNIDF	United Nations Industrial Development Fund [UNIDO]
UNIDIR	United Nations Institute for Disarmament Research
UNIDO	United Nations Industrial Development Organization
UNIFIL	United Nations Interim Force in Lebanon
UNITAR	United Nations Institute for Training and Research
UNRFNRE	United Nations Revolving Fund for Natural Resources Exploration
UNRISD	United Nations Research Institute for Social Development
UNRWA	United Nations Relief and Works Agency for Palestine Refugees in the Near East
UNSCEAR	United Nations Scientific Committee on the Effects of Atomic Radiation
UNSDRI	United Nations Social Defence Research Institute
UNSO	United Nations Sudano-Sahelian Office
UNTAG	United Nations Transition Assistance Group
UNTSO	United Nations Truce Supervision Organization [Israel and neighbouring States]
UNU	United Nations University
UNV	United Nations Volunteers
UPU	Universal Postal Union
WFC	World Food Council
WFP	World Food Programme
WHO	World Health Organization
WIPO	World Intellectual Property Organization
WMO	World Meteorological Organization
WTO	World Tourism Organization
YUN	*Yearbook of the United Nations*

EXPLANATORY NOTE ON DOCUMENTS

References at the end of each article in Part One of this volume give the symbols of the main documents issued in 1985 on the topic, arranged in the order in which they are referred to in the text. The following is a guide to the principal document symbols:

A/- refers to documents of the General Assembly, numbered in separate series by session. Thus, A/40/- refers to documents issued for consideration at the fortieth session, beginning with A/40/1. Documents of special and emergency special sessions are identified as A/S- and A/ES-, followed by the session number.

A/C.- refers to documents of six of the Assembly's Main Committees, e.g. A/C.1/- is a document of the First Committee, A/C.6/-, a document of the Sixth Committee. The symbol for documents of the seventh Main Committee, the Special Political Committee, is A/SPC/-. A/BUR/- refers to documents of the General Committee. A/AC.- documents are those of the Assembly's *ad hoc* bodies and A/CN.-, of its commissions; e.g. A/AC.105/- identifies documents of the Assembly's Committee on the Peaceful Uses of Outer Space, A/CN.4/-, of its International Law Commission. Assembly resolutions and decisions since the thirty-first (1976) session have been identified by two arabic numerals: the first indicates the session of adoption; the second, the sequential number in the series. Resolutions are numbered consecutively from 1 at each session. Decisions of regular sessions are numbered consecutively, from 301 for those concerned with elections and appointments, and from 401 for all other decisions. Decisions of special and emergency special sessions are numbered consecutively, from 11 for those concerned with elections and appointments, and from 21 for all other decisions.

E/- refers to documents of the Economic and Social Council, numbered in separate series by year. Thus, E/1985/- refers to documents issued for consideration by the Council at its 1985 sessions, beginning with E/1985/1. E/AC., E/C.- and E/CN.-, followed by identifying numbers, refer to documents of the Council's subsidiary *ad hoc* bodies, committees and commissions. For example, E/C.1/-, E/C.2/- and E/C.3/- refer to documents of the Council's sessional committees, namely, the First (Economic), Second (Social) and Third (Programme and Co-ordination) Committees, respectively; E/CN.5/- refers to documents of the Council's Commission for Social Development, E/CN.7/-, to documents of its Committee on Natural Resources. E/ICEF/- documents are those of the United Nations Children's Fund (UNICEF). Symbols for the Council's resolutions and decisions, since 1978, consist of two arabic numerals: the first indicates the year of adoption and the second, the sequential number in the series. There are two series: one for resolutions, beginning with 1 (resolution 1985/1); and one for decisions, beginning, since 1983, with 101 (decision 1985/101).

S/- refers to documents of the Security Council. Its resolutions are identified by consecutive numbers followed by the year of adoption in parentheses, beginning with resolution 1(1946).

T/- refers to documents of the Trusteeship Council. Its resolutions are numbered consecutively, with the session at which they were adopted indicated by Roman numerals, e.g. resolution 2179(LII) of the fifty-second session. The Council's decisions are not numbered.

ST/-, followed by symbols representing the issuing department or office, refers to documents of the United Nations Secretariat.

Documents of certain bodies bear special symbols, including the following:

ACC/-	Administrative Committee on Co-ordination
CD/-	Conference on Disarmament
CERD/-	International Convention on the Elimination of All Forms of Racial Discrimination
DC/-	Disarmament Commission
DP/-	United Nations Development Programme
HS/-	Commission on Human Settlements
ID/-	United Nations Industrial Development Organization
ITC/-	International Trade Centre
LOS/PCN/-	Preparatory Commission for the International Sea-Bed Authority and for the International Tribunal for the Law of the Sea
TD/-	United Nations Conference on Trade and Development
UNEP/-	United Nations Environment Programme
UNITAR/-	United Nations Institute for Training and Research

Many documents of the regional commissions bear special symbols. These are sometimes preceded by the following:

E/CEPAL/-	Economic Commission for Latin America and the Caribbean
E/CN.14/-, E/ECA/-	Economic Commission for Africa
E/ECE/-	Economic Commission for Europe
E/ECWA/-	Economic Commission for Western Asia*
E/ESCAP/-	Economic and Social Commission for Asia and the Pacific

"L" in a symbol refers to documents of limited distribution, such as draft resolutions; "CONF." to documents of a conference; "INF." to those of general information. Summary records are designated by "SR.", verbatim records by "PV.", each followed by the meeting number.

United Nations sales publications each carry a sales number with the following components separated by periods: a capital letter indicating the language(s) of the publication; two arabic numerals indicating the year; a Roman numeral indicating the subject category; a capital letter indicating a subdivision of the category, if any; and an arabic numeral indicating the number of the publication within the category. Examples: E.85.V.7; E/F/R.85.II.E.8; E.85.IX.3.

*ECWA, on 26 July 1985, became ESCWA (Economic and Social Commission for Western Asia).

PART ONE

United Nations

Report of the Secretary-General on the work of the Organization

Following is the text of the report of the Secretary-General on the work of the Organization, submitted to the General Assembly and dated 4 September 1985. The Assembly took note of the report on 9 December 1985 when it adopted **decision 40/417**.

We face today a world of almost infinite promise which is also a world of potentially terminal danger. The choice between these alternatives is ours. The question is whether the Governments and peoples of the world are capable, without the spur of further disasters, of together making the right choice; for the choice and its implementation will, in many important ways, have to be collective. I believe that the United Nations and the way in which its Members decide to use it is—and will be—an essential element in this historic choice. The question I shall consider in my annual report on this fortieth anniversary of our Organization is, therefore, not so much the future of the United Nations as the future of humanity and of our planet and the role of the United Nations in that future.

The world which confronts us would certainly surprise the statesmen who produced the Charter of the United Nations 40 years ago. In those 40 years vast and fundamental changes have occurred in the map of our world and our scientific understanding of it, in international relations, in the nature of war and in the way we live. We are all, in one way or another, engaged in a search for new landmarks, better systems and effective adjustments.

We are living in a time of flux and uncertainty. This situation becomes particularly clear when the world is suddenly faced with a desperate problem, be it a new conflict, a great humanitarian disaster or the temporary paralysis caused by a premeditated act of violence.

There can be no question that, at the global level, between the poles of the massive and sophisticated nuclear weaponry of the major Powers and the desperation of the underprivileged or the dispossessed, there often lies a great vacuum of legitimacy and respected authority. Our most urgent challenge is to fill that vacuum through determined efforts to build a working international political system in which all participate—a system which will not only guarantee survival and order, but will make our planet run more evenly in the interests of all of its inhabitants.

It seems to me important to examine the concept of international authority, a concept which remains elusive in the present world. The only authority that existed in international affairs before the founding of the League of Nations and its successor, the United Nations, was the actual power of the strongest States or Empires. It was mainly the abuse of this power which led to two world wars in this century. It was to replace this state of affairs that the United Nations was founded. The founding of the United Nations, President Roosevelt stated after the Crimean Conference, "spells—and it ought to spell—the end of the system of unilateral action, exclusive alliances, and spheres of influence, and balances of power, and all the other expedients which have been tried for centuries and have always failed".

What has happened since falls far short of that vision. It is certainly true that the two world wars, and the immense changes of the past 40 years, have clearly shown that the world cannot return to its old ways and that the system set forth in the Charter is a logical answer to the question of the maintenance of international peace and security and the joint promotion of economic development and social progress in the actual circumstances of our time. But the fact is that we have so far failed to achieve the political conditions, and in particular the requisite relationships among the most powerful States, in which this noble concept can be made to function for the benefit of all.

An illustration of this issue is the current difficulty in addressing the problem of terrorism. Much of the public discussion of this problem seems to assume that there are no existing international conventions on the subject. I need only mention here the three conventions adopted under the auspices of the International Civil Aviation Organization and the International Convention against the Taking of Hostages, adopted by the General Assembly in 1979, as providing at least some legal framework for much more effective action in combating hijacking and hostage-taking. The difficulty that does arise is the incapacity, or the unwillingness, of Governments to implement these conventions in specific cases. Once again the essential political conditions, the sense of solidarity and mutual confidence, that could make international instruments *work* is largely lacking.

The best place where those conditions could be cultivated and a sense of international solidarity developed is the United Nations. Indeed, that was one of the main original purposes of the Organization. Only when the minimum positive conditions exist in the relations between States will the concept of international authority begin to assume its rightful place in human affairs.

* * *

The United Nations cannot—and was not intended to—solve *all* the problems of the international community, but it is the best place to avoid the worst and to strive for improvement. And it *has* made a good start—far better, in fact, than is often recognized. Let me briefly substantiate this assertion.

After 40 years we have, for the first time in history, a virtually universal world Organization. We have, also for the first time in history, a world of independent sovereign States. Although there have been all too many conflicts since 1945, we have so far escaped a third world war and have perhaps learned more than we realize about techniques and expedients for avoiding such a terminal disaster. We have achieved unprecedented economic growth and social progress, in which developing countries have shared, although not yet in sufficient measure. We are making collective efforts to respond to the new generation of global problems which mostly stem from the need to protect the planet and its resources while providing for all of its people. There is a greater international responsiveness to humanitarian challenges wherever they occur. The protection of human rights, for all the violations that still persist, is becoming a world-wide concern. More international law affecting virtually all areas of human activity has been codified in the past 40 years than in all the previous years of recorded history. Much of it has been done under the auspices of the General Assembly.

The world is still, admittedly, a very imperfect, insecure, unjust, dangerous and, in all too many regions, impoverished place, but in the achievements I have mentioned above—and in many others— we have a foundation to build on. It is mainly up to Governments to decide if they wish to co-operate in building on this foundation a useful, coherent, effective institution, or whether they choose the alternative that may sometimes seem easier in the short run, each taking its own short-sighted and self-interested course. In that case, the promising foundations, established with so much thought and hard work, will end up surmounted by a rambling, contentious slum, the breeding ground of endless new troubles and disasters. Surely the first alternative is the one which must be chosen.

* * *

There are two basic functions which make the United Nations an essential enterprise. The first is to provide an instrument through which a collective effort can be made to meet emergencies and deal with current problems. These vary from international conflicts, through disputes among States, to humanitarian emergencies and sudden economic and social crises affecting millions of people.

The second function is of a more long-term nature and is related to the complex phase of political and economic development in which our world now finds itself. Throughout history there has been a natural political progression from small groups to larger ones—from family to tribe, to town, to city, to province, to nation state. This progression has taken place more or less spontaneously at different times in different regions, as economic life has become more complex, specialized and interdependent. Thus we have arrived at a world which is almost entirely composed of nation states. The sovereign independent State is the largest political entity and the main unit of the structure of the United Nations.

There are now, however, a number of problems and realities with which only a larger unity can effectively deal and where the requisite security or common interest can only be achieved through a collective effort of sovereign States. Many of these problems lend themselves best to subregional or regional co-operation in groups of nations with common interests, but many others already transcend the regional dimension. We have, whether we like it or not, created a world which is in many respects one world. On some major problems affecting all humanity we have reached a global stage where interdependence is a fact of life.

A basic role of the United Nations, therefore, is to serve as the foundation on which to build the international system of the future, a system fully recognizing national sovereignty but also recognizing that some of our present realities and concerns call urgently for something more.

Anyone who contemplates the prospects for the future of humanity must conclude that the two functions to which I have referred will become increasingly urgent, perhaps even indispensable to survival. In the 40 years since 1945 the population of the world has more than doubled. In the next 15 years it will increase by one third. Some of the strains and stresses in the world community will certainly stem from the pressure on institutions and resources resulting from this population explosion.

But we must also consider the many precarious balances of the claims and ambitions of nations: the unresolved disputes we carry with us into the future; the many smouldering conflicts of ideas, beliefs and interests in this world; the dizzy pace of the technological revolution both in production and in weapons; the widening gulf between abundance and absolute poverty; the web of economic ties which locks all parts of the world together; and the steadily increasing danger of deep harm to the biosphere on which life depends. Such a list—and it could easily be made longer—makes it clear that international co-operation, however complex and difficult to organize, is not a choice for the nations of the world, but a necessity.

However, if the United Nations is fully to play the role I have indicated in the development of the international system, it has to become a more effective institution. I should like to discuss this problem in the context of the principal responsibilities laid down in the Charter.

*   *   *

In terms of its first basic function of meeting emergencies and dealing with current problems, the maintenance of international peace and security is the primary purpose of the United Nations. In the minds of the writers of the Charter it was closely linked with progress in arms limitation and disarmament. Indeed, Article 26 of the Charter gives the Security Council a leading role in the establishment of a system for the regulation of armaments.

Forty years ago, with the lessons of the disastrous period leading up to the Second World War still vividly in mind, it was concluded that the old idea of achieving national security through a competitive armaments race led only to increasing general insecurity. That concept was therefore to be replaced by a collective system of international peace and security, involving in particular the most powerful nations, which would play a key role in the United Nations Security Council. In carrying out its duties the Security Council would, if necessary, and with the support of its members, use the whole range of measures set out in Chapters VI and VII of the Charter. With such a system in place and respected, it was believed that arms limitation and disarmament would naturally follow.

This noble and logical concept has not been realized for many practical and political reasons, not least the lack of that unanimity of the permanent members which was to have been its main driving force. How has the United Nations reacted to the problems posed by the absence of the key prerequisite of its system of international peace and security?

Obviously where international peace is concerned, the ultimate priority is the avoidance of a global conflagration. That is, of course, a main concern of the nuclear Powers themselves, but great dangers remain for all. These include accident, misapprehension or an unexpected concatenation of events involving the nuclear Powers in a way which they cannot evade. This latter situation could most likely develop from the escalation of a regional conflict.

If this brief analysis is valid, insurance against nuclear war requires measures to slow down the onrush of events in such a way as to allow Governments not to take irrevocable decisions and to gain time by substituting deliberation for force. Such expedients also include formulas which allow Governments to change policies that are bound to lead to confrontation. They include stabilizing mechanisms and negotiating processes by which crucial conflicts, if they cannot be resolved, can at least be contained and prevented from escalating. In the case of regional conflicts, especially in sensitive areas, forms of conflict control are often desirable. And overall, a central forum where opposing views can be freely expressed and third-party assistance is available is an important part of keeping the peace.

The Security Council has time and again slowed the onrush of events, gained time for vital changes in direction, produced face-saving mechanisms and substituted talk for violent action. It has striven for cease-fires and truces to prepare the way for negotiation. It has set important guidelines for the solution of complex problems and provided, with the co-operation of the Secretary-General, all manner of forms of conciliation, mediation, good offices, fact-finding, truce observation and quiet diplomacy. It has managed often to isolate regional conflicts from the area of confrontation of the nuclear Powers. It has provided a repository for the most dangerous of problems even though it could not solve them. It has frequently provided the framework for important combinations of bilateral and multilateral effort. It has acted as a safety net, a last resort to be used by Governments as the alternative to falling into the abyss of unconfined war. Finally, in the absence of the political conditions in which Chapter VII could be used, a system of conflict control has been pioneered, now known as peace-keeping, which has shown considerable promise and effectiveness in 13 separate operations.

Succeeding Secretaries-General have been intensively involved in all these efforts, and the role of the Secretary-General in peace and security matters has developed accordingly. I shall be dealing with this subject later on in relation to the future.

In a changeable and often unfavourable international climate, I believe the Council's record in its primary task stands up better and is a good deal more central and relevant than is sometimes recognized. Of course it is in no way up to the expectations of a chastened but hopeful world 40 years ago, and it does not include a full and effective use of the range of actions suggested by the Charter. But in the unfavourable political conditions in which the Security Council has mostly had to operate, it represents a considerable effort to find alternative ways for the maintenance of peace.

There is no denying that in the present circumstances the peace and security system of the United Nations has many weaknesses and many shortcomings. It suffers from lack of unanimity and collegial spirit in the Security Council. It suffers from a lack of respect for, and failure to co-operate with, the Council's decisions. It often suffers from a reluctance to pre-empt, or even to foresee, dangerous situations and to use the powers of the Council at a stage when problems might be more susceptible of treatment. It suffers from the Council's incapacity to approach some problems at all. But I maintain that in the real conditions of international life these 40 years—as opposed to various rhetorical versions of the same events—the Security Council has played an essential and often central role in providing stability and limiting conflict.

The question is how to enhance that role and bring the Council closer to the position prescribed for it in the Charter. It would obviously be extremely desirable to see that change in relationships among the permanent members that above all might restore the Council to the position it was originally intended to occupy. But surely, in the mean while, there are ways in which the Council could improve its capacity along the lines on which it has been working for many years.

In my previous annual reports, and especially in the report for 1982, I have made a number of suggestions on this score. I shall not repeat such suggestions here, although I hope that Governments will see fit to act on some of them. On the occasion of the fortieth anniversary, however, I shall make a simpler set of suggestions.

First, I would suggest that a determined and conscious effort be made by members of the Security Council, and especially the permanent members, to use their membership to make the Council more the guardian of peace it was set up to be and less the battleground on which to fight out political and ideological differences which are not directly relevant to the issue under discussion—in other words, to give matters of international peace and security priority over bilateral differences.

Secondly, I suggest that the Security Council should, in the near future, make a deliberate and concerted effort to solve one or two of the major problems before it by making fuller use of the measures available to it under the Charter.

Thirdly, the membership as a whole might reaffirm Charter obligations, especially those relating to the non-use of force or the threat of force, the peaceful settlement of disputes, resort to the mechanism set out in the Charter for the settlement of disputes and respect for the decisions of the Security Council.

In the present circumstances these suggestions may to some seem simplistic. But in our nuclear age there is nothing more dangerous than failing to make the collective system of international peace and security *work.* The United Nations is in no way a super-State. It is an organization of sovereign independent States. The Organization has no sovereignty of its own. Sovereignty remains entirely vested in the individual Member States unless they decide otherwise. The Organization's function, and hence that of the Secretary-General, is therefore to harmonize, to encourage and to initiate. But the implementation, the drive, must come from the Members. When this drive does come, it can achieve remarkable results. I would like to see this drive, this collective will, directed to the key function of the United Nations, the maintenance of international peace and security. Next year, 1986, has been designated the International Year of Peace. Let us try to make this designation a call for serious reflection and action.

*   *   *

Without collective determination and the acknowledgement of a minimum common interest in survival, there can be no meaningful progress in disarmament. International insecurity and the arms race, with the fear of its possible extension to new areas, create a relentless vicious spiral. Where the arms race is concerned, it cannot be sufficiently emphasized that the quest for advantage is illusory. In the nuclear era it also places all people at risk and puts in doubt the lives of future generations.

Governments have to find the courage to take the first steps. We should recall the vision that led to such advances as the Partial Test-Ban Treaty some 20 years ago. Today, a clear and vital signal of humanity's willingness to confront the nuclear challenge would be through agreement on a comprehensive test-ban treaty. Impeding as it would the ceaseless technological refinement of nuclear weapons, its adoption would help to break the sequence that threatens our very existence. There are other areas deserving of urgent attention—nuclear-weapon-free zones, for example.

While the fear of nuclear weapons is pervasive because of their potentially global devastating effects, it is conventional weapons that every day claim countless lives. Those who engage in and fuel the arms trade bear a particularly heavy responsibility. The conventional arms race, moreover, squanders precious economic resources. We must push for practical measures for multilateral disarmament, including regional plans, bearing in mind the link between disarmament and development.

Bilateral negotiations between the great Powers are clearly of crucial importance to the future of all peoples as well as their own. In this connection, I am sure that we all share the profound hope that the forthcoming meeting between the leaders of the Soviet Union and the United States will contribute to a reduction of tension and to progress on disarmament, as well as on other important matters.

At the same time, I wish to emphasize that the United Nations can and must contribute to progress in disarmament. The Conference on Disarmament affords a unique multilateral arena for discussions on arms limitation and disarmament. Indeed the Organization has a comprehensive responsibility for restraining dangerous trends in this field—for example, in regard to chemical weapons.

I believe that the Organization's ability to assist in verification and compliance arrangements should also be actively explored. The International Atomic Energy Agency has unique experience in monitoring non-proliferation compliance and ensuring the peaceful uses of nuclear energy. This expertise could be built on and expanded to provide a monitoring capability for nuclear-arms agreements. Suggestions have also been made, and should be further considered, for the United Nations to verify compliance through seismic stations, through on-site inspection or through satellite observation.

* * *

Many of the greatest hopes of mankind focus on economic and social progress, which must remain a primary goal of the United Nations system. Much progress has been made in the past 40 years, but many worries and uncertainties now prevail about risks of stagnation or even regression in some parts of the world.

There is no denying that for some time now the world economy has been functioning in an uneven and unsatisfactory way. In industrial countries the wave of high technology promises great affluence but also causes overcapacity, obsolescence and unemployment. Many developing countries, apart from basic problems of development, are crippled by their debt burdens which have been compounded by the rise in international interest rates. But all these difficulties, which are these days often euphemistically described as adjustment problems, seem to be part of one great process of global adjustment which is made rather more difficult by the inclination of many countries to resort to protectionism or unilateral exchange rate policies to solve their own problems at the expense of other countries.

It was this kind of short-sighted economic nationalism that brought the world economy to a collapse in the 1930s. This was why, along with the foundation of the United Nations, a great effort was made to set up a system of specialized organizations in the areas of money, finance and trade.

The deliberations in the United Nations on world economic affairs are seldom conducted among those who are ultimately responsible for these issues within their own Governments. Finance ministries and central banks are represented in other international forums, such as the World Bank and the International Monetary Fund, whose functions are exclusively the consideration of economic, financial and monetary issues.

And yet it has become increasingly clear in recent years that economic, financial, monetary and trade issues are so interrelated and are of such profound political and social importance that they can only be dealt with effectively as part of a wider political process. In the case of international development this was recognized in the creation of the United Nations Conference on Trade and Development as well as the call for a new international economic order, but it is now true of an even broader range of issues. This development must be reflected in the approach of the United Nations and in the nature of governmental representation in it if the efforts on problems which affect virtually all humanity are to be relevant and well conceived.

The need for international co-operation in economic affairs more and more cuts across traditional sectoral boundaries as represented nationally by different ministries and internationally by different specialized agencies. What is required in many cases is a more effective and pragmatic use of the United Nations as a forum for integrating practical effort. This in no sense detracts from the importance of the work of the specialized agencies—on the contrary, it should enhance their effectiveness and relevance. A parallel co-ordinating effort is necessary at the national level. There is a need for governmental ministries to act in concert with each other towards agreed objectives, if the international system is to perform effectively.

The Economic and Social Council should have a useful function to serve in exploring new needs and opportunities for joint international action. An effort is being made by its members to make the Council more effective, and by the Secretariat to enhance the quality of support. While some progress has been made, much remains to be done if the Council is to fulfil the great task allotted to it in the Charter and to indicate with clarity the directions and the spirit in which we should all act together.

We are facing economic changes of such magnitude and complexity that no country can adjust to them in isolation. We see this, for example, in attempts to protect domestic jobs from import competition, which result in the exporting of unemployment. What is clearly required is a wider vision and more dynamic understanding of the global nature of the problems we are facing. Such a vision has to be based on the open recognition of interdependence and the practical necessity of a fair sharing of burdens and of the accommodation of others. The ultimate rewards of such a system, for example, fuller use of resources, less unemployment and greater economic efficiency and social justice, would be immense. Unfortunately, the difficulty of getting such an approach generally accepted is also immense.

The international debt situation is particularly alarming. Many of the debtor countries are now again facing very weak export markets. Commodity prices are lower in real terms than they have been since the 1930s and are still declining. But interest rates remain high, and there seems to be no tendency for new lending to resume; if anything, the opposite. To adjust to the drying-up of bank lending, many debtor countries are cutting their imports, their living standards and their development programmes to the point where social, and even political, consequences have become extremely serious. Furthermore, the loss of markets weakens the fragile recovery in the industrial countries.

There is a strong mutual interest in resolving the debt crisis. However, the debt problem illustrates the inconsistencies which short-circuit attempts to move in a positive direction. While efforts are being made to reschedule debts over longer periods to alleviate the burdens, elsewhere protectionist measures are being taken which nullify those efforts. I see a strong need for a joint, comprehensive and speedy examination of all aspects of this situation, including the political ones.

The promotion of better understanding of world economic and social problems is an essential task of the United Nations and other international agencies. There are some encouraging experiences in this field. The series of conferences on global problems sponsored by the United Nations over the past 15 years has certainly been an innovation in raising knowledge and consciousness of problems and trying to develop a concerted approach to them. Current international efforts to come to grips with the problems of Africa also show a willingness to apply the skill and resources of the international community to a particular series of problems.

In the economic as in the political sphere, we are faced with the necessity of making our institutions relevant and effective in the realities of our time. We have to learn to manage our increasing economic interdependence. This is an enormous and daunting task. But the failure to face up to it can have results in terms of economic and social decline and chaos, which, in their own way and in the circumstances of our time, can be just as serious and debilitating as a failure to evolve a collective system of international peace and security in a nuclear age.

*   *   *

Today international co-operation is recognized as indispensable even in matters where not long ago it was thought to be Utopian. In social and economic development, the achievements of United Nations programmes and agencies are universally recognized. The force of necessity has made the United Nations system a global source of advice and assistance, co-operation and co-ordination in all areas where Governments, whatever their philosophical differences, have to act together.

It is ironic that, as we enter a phase in history in which the practical necessity of co-operative internationalism is so patent, there should, in some quarters at least, be a retreat from it. Questioning of international organizations striving to create greater order in the world polity and economy is widespread, and the United Nations is the subject of especially heavy criticism. We need to examine this phenomenon and try to understand it. Surely the fortieth anniversary is a good time to take a collective look at this problem and the role of Member States in addressing it.

There is no question that the difficulties of making the United Nations work to their satisfaction have an important bearing on the attitude of some Governments towards the Organization. Certainly the new complexity of the expanded membership and new voting patterns, as well as instances where division and conflict have been highlighted at the expense of broad areas of agreement and common interest, have had an impact. In these circumstances there has been a tendency to make the United Nations a scapegoat for current problems and confusions and to see it as the symbol of a lack of international authority and responsibility, rather than as an instrument for co-operation in addressing the current problems of a newly global society.

It is the General Assembly, the main representative organ of the United Nations, which inevitably carries the weight of much of the criticism of the United Nations. Only in the General Assembly can the world be seen in its full variety, and it is there that differences and conflicts are highlighted in a particularly dramatic way. The General Assembly, when all is said and done, is the first approximation of a town meeting of the world. Far less well known is the painstaking work carried on within the framework of the Assembly in codifying international law and standards of behaviour and in focusing and maintaining attention on vital issues.

Many efforts have been made over the years to reform the General Assembly and to streamline and rationalize its procedures. The truth is that the Assembly represents the universality of the membership and has a very broad and diverse agenda. It is therefore difficult to streamline it without losing its main point. There are certainly, however, ways in which the performance of the General Assembly could be progressively improved.

It seems to me that essential steps in improving the political process in the General Assembly should include a much greater degree of intergovernmental consultation before each session, and a determined attempt to hammer out consensus on important issues and to avoid divisive rhetoric. Otherwise the quality of the political process in the General Assembly will deteriorate.

* * *

The responsibilities and duties which are inherent in the functions of the Secretary-General or are delegated to him represent a high challenge. The functions of the Secretary-General and the Secretariat have evolved to a notable extent in the first 40 years of the Organization. Both are based on the concept of independent and objective international service.

I wish only to make one observation about the evolution of the Secretary-Generalship and its relation to the overall development of international institutions. While greatly appreciative of the co-operation and understanding extended to the Secretary-General and the trust bestowed on him, I am sometimes concerned that the delegation of responsibility to the Secretary-General may, in certain instances, have the effect of diminishing the effort that is expected of Member States under the Charter. This will not serve the effective development of the United Nations as a political institution.

That being said, I nevertheless believe that it would be in the interests of the Organization as a whole if the Secretary-General's capacity to serve as an objective third party were to be further developed. There is much, of course, to be said for quiet diplomacy, but sometimes more is required. I am thinking in particular of a wider and earlier use of fact-finding and observation. I am also thinking of the need to survey more regularly and systematically the world-wide state of international peace and security—a task in which the Security Council and the Secretary-General should be jointly involved. The best radar in the world is not reliable or effective unless it makes systematic surveys of the surrounding space. The same applies, it seems to me, to the task of maintaining international peace.

The basic elements of the international civil service—independence from national pressures, efficiency, competence and integrity—must remain the guiding tenets of the Secretariat. Their validity has been proven over the years, especially in critical and controversial situations. The Secretariat must continually strive to be the dependable arm required to implement the evolving needs of the Organization.

I am, however, concerned with the question of what policies and methods can best achieve the standards of efficiency and integrity which are required for the international civil service. The development of such a service using personnel from well-over 100 Member States is no easy task. I am certainly not satisfied that we have in all cases found the right solutions, the right rules or the most effective organization for the Secretariat. I am in favour of pursuing our efforts to improve the existing administrative, personnel and budgetary practices of the United Nations. However, I believe that the best results can, and should, be achieved within the framework of the Secretary-General's authority under Chapter XV of the Charter. This is essential both for proper management and in the interests of the Organization as a whole.

I have repeatedly emphasized the need for the Secretariat to explore all avenues for utilizing the Organization's resources in the most efficient manner, and to provide an equitable role for women in the Secretariat. I have initiated a series of management-improving measures, and this is a process that will be pursued on a continuing basis. It is particularly essential, in times of change, constantly to evaluate and reassess programmes and structures and to institute such reforms as may be required.

In the preparation of my proposals for the current and forthcoming biennial programme budgets, I have endeavoured to reassure all Member States of my commitment to achieve the delivery of programmes entrusted to the Secretariat in the most cost-effective way possible. I am bound, however, to express my deep concern at the practice of certain Member States of selectively withholding their duly assessed contributions. This can only have a most detrimental effect on the future viability of our Organization.

* * *

In thinking of the future of the Organization, one is struck by the fact that the United Nations is almost unique among political institutions in having little direct contact with its basic constituency, "the peoples of the United Nations" who address us in the first words of the Charter. This is a delicate matter, since the independent national sovereignty of Member States is a primary prerequisite of the Charter.

Nevertheless the United Nations deals with more and more issues which are important internationally and also have strong domestic implications. Only the support of national domestic constituencies in each Member State can assure the necessary follow-up which will lead to effective action on such issues. Here a far greater involvement with non-governmental organizations in the broadest sense of the term could go a long way towards a solution. We have had an indication of their enormous direct value and influence in a series of global conferences as well as in the remarkable world-wide efforts by voluntary agencies, entertainers and others in support of relief in Africa and elsewhere.

We also need to encourage the concept of practical international service in a manner broader and more systematic than has yet been the case. In particular more effort should be made to devise ways of engaging young people directly in matters of concern to the world community.

* * *

I have, in a series of other reports to the General Assembly and the Security Council, commented in detail on the major political issues with which the United Nations is concerned, in many of which the Secretary-General has particular responsibilities. I shall not, therefore, repeat myself here nor deal with the specific situations covered by those reports.

I should like, however, to mention certain other great issues of our time which have an important bearing on the future. Perhaps the broadest and most complex of these issues is the question of human rights, which affects everyone.

The Universal Declaration of Human Rights, adopted nearly 37 years ago, must be counted as one of the great achievements of the United Nations. The Declaration and the Covenants and conventions that grew out of it provided the world, for the first time, with an international code of human rights which establishes as norms of international law the way in which the State must treat individuals. Specific mechanisms have also been established by the United Nations to monitor compliance with these agreements, and we are increasingly providing advisory services and technical assistance to Governments in the field of human rights.

Yet we must recognize that, despite these advances, there is a continuing need to keep a close watch over the way the rights and freedoms of the individual are respected by States. Massive violations of human rights continue to take place, often of tragic proportions. Many States have not yet ratified the relevant international conventions, nor brought their laws or institutions into conformity with the international standards proclaimed by the United Nations. Persecution for political, religious or racial reasons continues. Minorities and indigenous populations are often inadequately protected. There are also instances in which the co-operation of Governments with the United Nations and its organs leaves much to be desired.

Let us in this fortieth anniversary year rededicate ourselves, jointly and individually, to the task of achieving the unimpeded application of the Universal Declaration and the International Covenants. To this end, I appeal to those States that have not yet ratified the Covenants to do so. I appeal to *all* States to support, strengthen and take part in the procedures which have been established to examine violations of human rights, and assure their protection.

A particularly important aspect of human rights is racial discrimination, which should have no place in any form in our society and which represents the most dangerous of social and political poisons. In one particular and extreme instance, the policy of *apartheid* in South Africa, the unwillingness to undertake timely, remedial measures has now produced an ominous and violent situation, on which the Security Council has recently pronounced itself. I need hardly reiterate my strongly held views on the abhorrent system of *apartheid* and the massive human tragedy which has resulted from it. I hope that, even at this very late hour, steps can be taken and contacts established which may avert the worst. I feel obliged to add here that the failure to bring Namibia to independence through the United Nations Plan is, together with *apartheid,* a fundamental reason for the tension and suffering in southern Africa.

An immense and widespread social evil is the burgeoning problem of narcotic drugs, which ruins the lives of uncounted millions of individuals, and even undermines the integrity and stability of Governments. In large areas of the world the plague of drug abuse and illicit trafficking, fuelled by the immense profits which they generate, has reached an emergency stage. As this problem increases in magnitude, despite the growing efforts of Governments to deal with it, even more attention must be given to improving the co-ordination of efforts so that an effective range of strategies may be developed to meet the new challenges posed. Clearly, the drug problem can no longer be regarded as a merely social, and largely domestic, concern.

It is against this background that I have proposed that the first global conference should be convened to deal with all aspects of drug abuse and illicit trafficking. I trust that such a conference would be action-oriented. It should serve to raise the level of world-wide awareness of the escalating problems of drug abuse, mobilize the full potential of the United Nations system, and result in a programme of action at the international, regional and national levels. The moment has arrived for the international community to expand its efforts in a global undertaking to meet this deadly peril.

Acts of terrorism have now spread to virtually all parts of the globe. They are exceptionally difficult to cope with since they involve desperate acts by desperate people willing to violate national and international law regardless of the risk to their own lives. The most tragic aspect of this problem is the increasing loss of innocent civilian lives, which I have repeatedly condemned. As indicated earlier, some of the necessary international legal instruments are in place, and it is time for concerted efforts to be made by Governments to implement them. In this context, Governments may wish to consider what further measures of international co-operation could be effectively devised.

I believe that in concerting an international response to great common problems we may also begin to develop the kind of social and political solidarity and mutual confidence which will eventually serve well in the more traditional field of political problems. Several encouraging examples of such responses do exist, and I want to recall some of them very briefly:

International efforts for the relief of refugees and their voluntary return or resettlement represent one of the most practical expressions of international solidarity;

The steps taken to create more adequate food security for all countries have brought us forward in the struggle to free the world from hunger;

The great endeavour to bring immunization to all children in the world by 1990 now seems capable of realization if there is a will to make the final effort. I urge the leaders of the world to give full support to this vital and universal enterprise with the potential for saving countless young lives.

In these fields and many others the range of the possible has steadily widened as international co-operation has taken its place as a permanent element in the governance of the world.

In another important instance, the World Conference of the United Nations Decade for Women, which was held at Nairobi to review the achievements of the United Nations Decade for Women, completed its work with greater success than some had anticipated and, to my satisfaction, adopted by consensus an important set of propositions for the future. Evidently, the enormous importance of the subject finally carried the day. It is hard as yet to judge the full significance and impact of this dynamic and widely representative gathering. One thing is certain: the full and equal participation of women in all aspects of human endeavour, which throughout history has been obscured and suppressed, has assumed an importance and a vitality which can give an irresistible momentum to the various practical efforts by which the Nairobi Conference must be followed up. I hope it will also add a healthy new dimension to political thinking and action world-wide.

* * *

I have previously mentioned international responsiveness to human disasters. Although the African continent today attracts our most urgent attention, the international community was slow to respond to the initial alarms signalling the drought-induced crises that were affecting several African nations. For many thousands of people, it responded too late.

But for the vast majority of the 30 million Africans who have suffered from the most widespread, devastating drought in memory, a unique partnership between the Governments of affected African countries and the international community has brought life and hope. This partnership has managed to arrest a disaster of unprecedented proportions that would otherwise have occurred and has almost certainly saved several million lives. The United Nations has played, and will in various ways continue to play, a central—indeed indispensable—role in this great example of international humanitarian co-operation.

Millions of Africans still face a difficult and uncertain future, a future which could be more hopeful if the partnership that has been forged in response to Africa's emergency needs is maintained through the critically important recovery period now at hand. We must be prepared to plan and carry through sustained development assistance programmes designed to prevent the recurrence of such tragedies and deal with their fundamental causes.

* * *

In our journey of 40 years we have had many experiences, some encouraging, others frustrating, and many that have been deeply enlightening. We have taken on many activities and some excess baggage. In looking forward let us decide which activities are really useful and what baggage we can well do without.

Let us remember that we have created the means to destroy ourselves, and that a great effort of will and intelligence is going to be needed to build a system which will effectively preserve peace and which will work in the interests of all the peoples of this Earth. Let us look at the future as an opportunity, not as a potential disaster. Let us remember all the things we have in common as human beings, all the marvels that the human mind has created and all the splendid diversity of our world.

Let us above all, on this occasion, look at the United Nations as its founders looked at it, as the practical hope for the future and not merely as the unhappy bearer of the burdens of the past. We must be realistic about our difficulties and the dangers that we face. But let us also resolve to find the ways by which, together, we can surmount them.

Javier PÉREZ DE CUÉLLAR
Secretary-General

Political and security questions

Disarmament

The General Assembly, at its 1985 regular session, adopted a record number of 66 resolutions on arms limitation and disarmament, reflecting, in most part, the persisting differences of approach to substantive issues. While preparatory work began earlier in the year for the International Conference on the Relationship between Disarmament and Development, scheduled for mid-1986, the Assembly decided that it would, in that year, set the date of its third special session on disarmament and establish a United Nations Regional Centre for Peace and Disarmament in Africa. Further, it requested the Secretary-General to prepare two studies—one on climatic effects of nuclear war, including nuclear winter, and the other, an update on economic and social consequences of the arms race and of military expenditures.

The Conference on Disarmament—the 40-nation negotiating body at Geneva—continued working towards a future chemical-weapons convention, prevention of an arms race in outer space, nuclear-war prevention and related issues, and a ban on radiological weapons. The United Nations Disarmament Commission, a deliberative body composed of all United Nations Member States, considered three new substantive items—review of the role of the United Nations in disarmament, curbing the naval arms race, and review and appraisal of the implementation of the Declaration of the 1980s as the Second Disarmament Decade.

Among other developments, the Third Review Conference of the Parties to the Treaty on the Non-Proliferation of Nuclear Weapons took place in August/September at Geneva. Outside the United Nations framework, the USSR and the United States began, at Geneva in March, bilateral negotiations on both strategic and intermediate-range space and nuclear arms; and the heads of the respective Governments, at a November summit meeting, agreed to accelerate the work. The South Pacific Nuclear-Free Zone Treaty, prepared by the South Pacific Forum, was opened for signature.

Topics related to this chapter. Peaceful uses of outer space. Law of the sea. International peace and security: implementation of the 1970 Declaration. Arms race and the environment.

PUBLICATIONS
Disarmament: Unilateral Nuclear Disarmament Measures, Sales No. E.85.IX.2. *Disarmament: A Periodic Review by the United Nations*, vol. VIII: No. 1, Sales No. E.85.IX.3; No. 2, Sales No. E.85.IX.5; No. 3, Sales No. E.85.IX.8. *The United Nations Disarmament Yearbook*, vol. 10: *1985*, Sales No. E.86.IX.7. *The United Nations General Assembly and Disarmament, 1985*, Sales No. E.86.IX.11.

Comprehensive approaches to disarmament

The commitment to general and complete disarmament was reaffirmed in 1985 by all Member States, which acknowledged, at the same time, that tangible measures towards that aim had been at best partial and modest.

In addition to following up on the recommendations adopted at the two disarmament special sessions in 1978 and 1982, the General Assembly examined the general question of disarmament and international security, and the progress made in implementing the Declaration of the 1980s as the Second Disarmament Decade. The Assembly requested the Disarmament Commission to continue its review, begun in 1985, of the United Nations role in disarmament, and its consideration of naval arms reduction. Further, it urged the Conference on Disarmament to continue consideration of measures to prevent an arms race on the sea-bed, and to submit, in 1986, a draft comprehensive programme of disarmament.

Different approaches persisted in 1985 on a proposal to hold a world disarmament conference. Studies were completed by two governmental expert groups—one on the naval arms race, naval forces and naval arms systems, and the other on concepts of security.

Report of the Secretary-General. In his 1985 annual report to the General Assembly on the work of the Organization (see p. 3), the Secretary-General emphasized that, in the nuclear age, the quest for military advantage not only was illusory but also endangered the entire human race and its future, and that only collective determination and the acknowledgement of a minimum common interest in survival could lead to progress in disarmament. He expressed hope that the bilateral talks between the USSR and the United States would contribute to such progress, called for agreement on a comprehensive test-ban treaty, and urged exploration of the United Nations ability to assist in verification and compliance arrangements, including the possibility of expanding the expertise of the International Atomic Energy Agency to provide a monitoring capability for nuclear-arms agreements. Noting that, against the looming fear of global nuclear devastation, it was conventional weapons that daily claimed countless lives, the Secretary-General called for practical measures for multilateral disarmament, including regional plans, bearing also in mind the link between disarmament and development.

Communications. In 1985, the Secretary-General received several communications, from countries in groups or individually, calling for arms control and disarmament.

In a declaration transmitted by Bulgaria,[1] the Political Consultative Committee of the States parties to the 1955 Warsaw Treaty of Friendship, Co-operation and Mutual Assistance (Sofia, 22 and 23 October) called for, among other things, reducing nuclear weapons and eliminating chemical weapons in Europe and freezing, at the 1 January 1986 level, the armed forces of the USSR and the United States, including those outside their national territories.

On 9 May,[2] Czechoslovakia transmitted a statement delivered to the Disarmament Commission by a group of Eastern European socialist countries and Mongolia, calling for practical results in that body on the fortieth anniversary of the victory over nazism and fascism.

The United Kingdom transmitted a communiqué issued by the Ministers for Foreign Affairs of the North Atlantic Council (Brussels, Belgium, 12 and 13 December),[3] in which they expressed their commitment to substantive progress in arms control, based on the criteria of strengthened stability, equitable and significant reductions, and effective verification, and expressed their concern over chemical weapons.

Indonesia transmitted the Declaration of the Commemorative Meeting in Observance of the Thirtieth Anniversary of the Asian-African Conference (Bandung, 24 and 25 April),[4] in which the participants, among other things, expressed concern at the accelerated arms race and the escalation of global military expenditures, and

urged the nuclear-weapon States to cease all nuclear-weapon tests and production and to negotiate on nuclear disarmament.

In the Final Political Declaration adopted by the Conference of Foreign Ministers of Non-Aligned Countries (Luanda, Angola, 4-7 September),[5] transmitted by Angola on 5 November, the participants called for a wide range of disarmament measures and underlined the central role and primary responsibility of the United Nations regarding disarmament.

On 14 October,[6] Togo transmitted two documents adopted at the Ministerial Regional Conference on Security, Disarmament and Development in Africa (Lomé, 13-16 August)—the Lomé Declaration on Security, Disarmament and Development in Africa, and a Programme of Action for Peace, Security and Co-operation in Africa. The Declaration noted that the current security requirements of African States imposed extremely heavy burdens to the detriment of their social and economic development.

Romania transmitted two appeals for peace and disarmament: a 29 March appeal[7] by its Grand National Assembly to the legislative bodies of the USSR, the United States, all European countries and Canada; and a 23 May appeal[8] from its Socialist Democracy and Unity Front to the peoples of Europe, Canada and the United States.

On 24 June,[9] China transmitted extracts of speeches made that month by the Chairman of its Central Military Commission and by the General Secretary of the Communist Party Central Committee, stressing China's opposition to the arms race and announcing reductions in its armed forces by 1 million men. On 21 October,[10] China transmitted to the Chairman of the General Assembly's First Committee proposals for measures to promote disarmament and reduce the danger of war, focusing on nuclear and conventional disarmament, outer space and chemical weapons.

The USSR transmitted several statements by the General Secretary of the Central Committee of the Communist Party, among them a 13 November statement[11] to a delegation of the Nobel Prize winners' congress, in which reference was made to disarmament issues, including an arms race in outer space and chemical weapons; and a 27 November statement on domestic and foreign policy,[12] at a Supreme Soviet session, in which he appraised the results and significance of the USSR–United States summit meeting at Geneva.

Some communications submitted under the item on general and complete disarmament also dealt with specific conflicts or with the Assembly's annual review of its 1970 Declaration on the Strengthening of International Security (see p. 116).

Follow-up to the General Assembly's special sessions on disarmament

In 1985, the General Assembly adopted 27 resolutions and one decision under the two agenda items concerning follow-up to its two special sessions devoted to disarmament: the first held in 1978 as the Assembly's tenth special session,[13] and the second held in 1982 as the twelfth special session.[14] At the 1978 session, the Assembly had adopted a Final Document,[15] and in 1982, a Concluding Document.[16]

This section deals with resolutions concerning: the Disarmament Commission (40/152 F); the Conference on Disarmament (40/152 M); implementation of the recommendations of the tenth special session (40/152 J and N); international co-operation for disarmament (40/152 I); implementation of the Declaration of the 1980s as the Second Disarmament Decade (40/152 L); verification (40/152 O); and the convening of a third special session on disarmament (40/151 I). Others dealing with various specific issues are discussed elsewhere in the chapter.

Disarmament Commission

The Disarmament Commission, composed of all United Nations Member States, at its 1985 session in New York, held 17 plenary meetings between 6 and 31 May.[17] It also met on 2 December to organize its work and elect officers for 1986.

Its agenda included items on aspects of the arms race, particularly the nuclear-arms race and nuclear disarmament; reduction of military budgets; and South Africa's nuclear capability. It also considered three new substantive items—review of the role of the United Nations in disarmament, curbing the naval arms race, and review and appraisal of the implementation of the Declaration of the 1980s as the Second Disarmament Decade.[18]

The Commission established a Committee of the Whole, which in turn set up a contact group to deal with aspects of the arms race and elaboration of a general approach to disarmament negotiations. In addition, a working group was established for each of the other agenda items, except for the naval arms race and review of the implementation of the Declaration of the 1980s as the Second Disarmament Decade, to which the Commission devoted two plenary meetings each. Work on substantive items, other than on the review of the Declaration's implementation, remained inconclusive, and the groups recommended that the Commission either pursue its efforts to reach agreement or refer the questions concerned to the General Assembly's 1985 session. Details on the Commis-sion's discussion of these questions can be found elsewhere in this chapter.

GENERAL ASSEMBLY ACTION

On the recommendation of the First Committee, the General Assembly, on 16 December, adopted **resolution 40/152 F** without vote.

Report of the Disarmament Commission
The General Assembly,

Having considered the report of the Disarmament Commission,

Emphasizing again the importance of an effective follow-up to the relevant recommendations and decisions contained in the Final Document of the Tenth Special Session of the General Assembly, the first special session devoted to disarmament,

Taking into account the relevant sections of the Concluding Document of the Twelfth Special Session of the General Assembly, the second special session devoted to disarmament,

Considering the role that the Disarmament Commission has been called upon to play and the contribution that it should make in examining and submitting recommendations on various problems in the field of disarmament and in the promotion of the implementation of the relevant decisions of the tenth special session,

Desirous of strengthening the effectiveness of the Disarmament Commission as the deliberative body in the field of disarmament,

Recalling its resolutions 33/71 H of 14 December 1978, 34/83 H of 11 December 1979, 35/152 F of 12 December 1980, 36/92 B of 9 December 1981, 37/78 H of 9 December 1982, 38/183 E of 20 December 1983 and 39/148 R of 17 December 1984,

1. *Takes note* of the report of the Disarmament Commission;

2. *Notes* that the Disarmament Commission has yet to conclude its consideration of some items on its agenda;

3. *Requests* the Disarmament Commission to continue its work in accordance with its mandate, as set forth in paragraph 118 of the Final Document of the Tenth Special Session of the General Assembly, and with paragraph 3 of resolution 37/78 H, and to that end to make every effort to achieve specific recommendations, at its 1986 substantive session, on the outstanding items on its agenda, taking into account the relevant resolutions of the General Assembly as well as the results of its 1985 substantive session;

4. *Requests* the Disarmament Commission to meet for a period not exceeding four weeks during 1986 and to submit a substantive report, containing specific recommendations on the items included in its agenda, to the General Assembly at its forty-first session;

5. *Requests* the Secretary-General to transmit to the Disarmament Commission the report of the Conference on Disarmament, together with all the official records of the fortieth session of the General Assembly relating to disarmament matters, and to render all assistance that the Commission may require for implementing the present resolution;

6. *Decides* to include in the provisional agenda of its forty-first session the item entitled "Report of the Disarmament Commission".

General Assembly resolution 40/152 F
16 December 1985　　　Meeting 117　　　Adopted without vote

Approved by First Committee (A/40/877/Add.1) without vote, 14 November (meeting 37); 12-nation draft (A/C.1/40/L.41); agenda item 65 *(a)*.
Sponsors: Bahamas, Byelorussian SSR, Cameroon, Ecuador, German Democratic Republic, Greece, Iran, Mexico, Morocco, Pakistan, Romania, Spain.
Meeting numbers. GA 40th session: 1st Committee 3-32, 37; plenary 117.

In another 16 December resolution (**40/152 N**), the Assembly called on the Disarmament Commission to intensify and improve its work with a view to making recommendations on specific items on its agenda. In addition, the Assembly instructed the Commission on certain topics, among them: South Africa's nuclear capability (**40/89 B**), reduction of military budgets (**40/91 A**), the naval arms race (**40/94 F** and **I**), review of the United Nations role in disarmament (**40/94 O**), and implementation of the Declaration of the 1980s as the Second Disarmament Decade (**40/152 L**).

Conference on Disarmament

In 1985, the Conference on Disarmament, the 40-member multilateral negotiating body, met at Geneva from 5 February to 23 April and from 11 June to 30 August.[19] Holding 48 formal plenary meetings and 29 informal meetings, it considered a nuclear-test ban, cessation of the nuclear-arms race and nuclear disarmament, prevention of nuclear war, chemical weapons, prevention of an arms race in outer space, security assurances to non-nuclear-weapon States, radiological weapons, and the proposed comprehensive programme of disarmament.

The Conference re-established *ad hoc* committees—on chemical weapons, on 7 February; radiological weapons, on 14 March; and security assurances to non-nuclear-weapon States, on 1 August—and established, on 29 March, a new subsidiary body on preventing an arms race in outer space. On 7 February, the Conference President noted that no subsidiary body need be re-established on the comprehensive programme of disarmament, on which work would begin at an appropriate time.

As regards the possibility of increasing its membership by four additional States, the Conference decided to continue consultations with a view to reporting its decision to the General Assembly in 1986. Consideration of its improved and effective functioning, to which one informal meeting was devoted in 1985, was to continue in 1986.

GENERAL ASSEMBLY ACTION

On 16 December, the General Assembly, on the recommendation of the First Committee, adopted two resolutions on the work of the Conference on Disarmament: one on its report (**40/152 M**) and the other on participation in its work by non-members (**40/152 J**).

The Assembly adopted **resolution 40/152 M** by recorded vote.

Report of the Conference on Disarmament
The General Assembly,

Recalling its resolutions 34/83 B of 11 December 1979, 35/152 J of 12 December 1980, 36/92 F of 9 December 1981, 37/78 G of 9 December 1982, 38/183 I of 20 December 1983 and 39/148 N of 17 December 1984,

Recalling also the Final Document of the Tenth Special Session of the General Assembly, the first special session devoted to disarmament, and the Concluding Document of the Twelfth Special Session of the General Assembly, the second special session devoted to disarmament,

Having considered the report of the Conference on Disarmament,

Convinced that the Conference on Disarmament, as the single multilateral negotiating body on disarmament, should play the central role in substantive negotiations on priority questions of disarmament and on the implementation of the Programme of Action set forth in section III of the Final Document of the Tenth Special Session,

Reaffirming that the establishment of *ad hoc* committees offers the best available machinery for the conduct of multilateral negotiations on items on the agenda of the Conference on Disarmament and contributes to the strengthening of the negotiating role of the Conference,

Expressing its satisfaction at the establishment within the Conference on Disarmament of an *Ad Hoc* Committee on the prevention of an arms race in outer space,

Deploring the fact that, despite the repeated requests of the General Assembly and the expressed wish of the great majority of members of the Conference on Disarmament, the establishment of an *ad hoc* committee on the cessation of the nuclear-arms race and on nuclear disarmament was once again prevented during the 1985 session of the Conference,

Deploring also the fact that the Conference on Disarmament has not been enabled to set up *ad hoc* committees under item 1 of its agenda, entitled "Nuclear-test ban", and on the prevention of nuclear war,

Noting that some progress has been made in the negotiations on the elaboration of a draft convention on the prohibition of the development, production and stockpiling of all chemical weapons and on their destruction,

1. *Expresses its deep concern and disappointment* that the Conference on Disarmament has not been enabled, this year either, to reach concrete agreements on any disarmament issues to which the United Nations has assigned greatest priority and urgency and which have been under consideration for a number of years;

2. *Calls upon* the Conference on Disarmament to intensify its work, to further its mandate more earnestly through negotiations and to adopt concrete measures on the specific priority issues of disarmament on its agenda, in particular those relating to nuclear disarmament;

3. *Once again urges* the Conference on Disarmament to continue or to undertake, during its 1986 session, substantive negotiations on the priority questions of disarmament on its agenda, in accordance with the provisions of the Final Document of the Tenth Special Session of the General Assembly and other resolutions of the Assembly on those questions;

4. *Calls upon* the Conference on Disarmament to provide the existing *ad hoc* committees, including the *Ad Hoc* Committee on the prevention of an arms race in outer space, with appropriate negotiating mandates and to establish, as a matter of urgency, the *ad hoc* committees under item 1 of its agenda, entitled "Nuclear-test ban", on the cessation of the nuclear-arms race and nuclear disarmament and on the prevention of nuclear war;

5. *Urges* the Conference on Disarmament to undertake, without further delay, negotiations with a view to elaborating a draft treaty on a nuclear-test ban;

6. *Also urges* the Conference on Disarmament to intensify further its work on the elaboration of a draft convention on the prohibition of the development, production and stockpiling of all chemical weapons and on their destruction;

7. *Once again calls upon* the Conference on Disarmament to organize its work in such a way as to concentrate most of its attention and time on substantive negotiations on priority issues of disarmament;

8. *Requests* the Conference on Disarmament to submit a report on its work to the General Assembly at its forty-first session;

9. *Decides* to include in the provisional agenda of its forty-first session the item entitled "Report of the Conference on Disarmament".

General Assembly resolution 40/152 M

16 December 1985   Meeting 117   133-2-18 (recorded vote)

Approved by First Committee (A/40/877/Add.1) by recorded vote (116-2-17), 18 November (meeting 40); 28-nation draft (A/C.1/40/L.57), orally revised; agenda item 65 *(b)*.

Sponsors: Algeria, Argentina, Bangladesh, Bolivia, Brazil, Burma, Colombia, Cuba, Ecuador, Egypt, Ethiopia, India, Indonesia, Iran, Madagascar, Mexico, Morocco, Nigeria, Pakistan, Peru, Romania, Sri Lanka, Sudan, Swaziland, Sweden, Venezuela, Viet Nam, Yugoslavia.

Meeting numbers. GA 40th session: 1st Committee 3-32, 35, 38, 40; plenary 117.

Recorded vote in Assembly as follows:

In favour: Afghanistan, Algeria, Angola, Antigua and Barbuda, Argentina, Austria, Bahamas, Bahrain, Bangladesh, Barbados, Benin, Bhutan, Bolivia, Botswana, Brazil, Brunei Darussalam, Bulgaria, Burkina Faso, Burma, Burundi, Byelorussian SSR, Cameroon, Cape Verde, Central African Republic, Chad, Chile, China, Colombia, Comoros, Congo, Costa Rica, Cuba, Cyprus, Czechoslovakia, Democratic Kampuchea, Democratic Yemen, Djibouti, Dominican Republic, Ecuador, Egypt, El Salvador, Equatorial Guinea, Ethiopia, Fiji, Finland, Gabon, Gambia, German Democratic Republic, Ghana, Greece, Guatemala, Guinea, Guinea-Bissau, Guyana, Haiti, Honduras, Hungary, India, Indonesia, Iran, Iraq, Ireland, Ivory Coast, Jamaica, Jordan, Kenya, Kuwait, Lao People's Democratic Republic, Lebanon, Lesotho, Liberia, Libyan Arab Jamahiriya, Madagascar, Malawi, Malaysia, Maldives, Mali, Malta, Mauritania, Mauritius, Mexico, Mongolia, Morocco, Mozambique, Nepal, Nicaragua, Niger, Nigeria, Oman, Pakistan, Panama, Papua New Guinea, Paraguay, Peru, Philippines, Poland, Qatar, Romania, Rwanda, Saint Lucia, Saint Vincent and the Grenadines, Samoa, Sao Tome and Principe, Saudi Arabia, Senegal, Seychelles, Sierra Leone, Singapore, Somalia, Sri Lanka, Sudan, Suriname, Swaziland, Sweden, Syrian Arab Republic, Thailand, Togo, Trinidad and Tobago, Tunisia, Uganda, Ukrainian SSR, USSR, United Arab Emirates, United Republic of Tanzania, Uruguay, Vanuatu, Venezuela, Viet Nam, Yemen, Yugoslavia, Zaire, Zambia, Zimbabwe.

Against: France, United States.

Abstaining: Australia, Belgium, Canada, Denmark, Germany, Federal Republic of, Grenada, Iceland, Israel, Italy, Japan, Luxembourg, Netherlands, New Zealand, Norway, Portugal, Spain, Turkey, United Kingdom.

In the First Committee, Ireland orally proposed—and subsequently withdrew after an oral revision had been made by the draft's sponsors—amending the reference to a draft treaty in paragraph 5 from the original wording of "nuclear-weapon test ban" to "complete cessation of nuclear-test explosions".

Several States explained their abstention in the vote. The Netherlands held that the draft lacked

impartiality and showed little respect for the rule of consensus by which the Conference operated and, by implication, for positions held by some delegations. The United Kingdom regretted that the sponsors had not sought to negotiate the draft's language to arrive at a consensus. While agreeing with a number of points covered in the text, Denmark found the procedure proposed for achieving nuclear disarmament hardly realistic, and Australia believed that the Geneva bilateral negotiations should be given a chance to succeed, before the Conference on Disarmament considered establishing an *ad hoc* committee on nuclear disarmament.

Brazil, one of the draft's sponsors, believed that Member States should not try to solve the substantive problems of the scope of a nuclear-test-ban treaty by Assembly resolutions; efforts should focus on negotiations of a treaty banning ongoing nuclear-weapon tests rather than curbing tests which were not currently carried out.

The Assembly adopted **resolution 40/152 J** by recorded vote.

Implementation of the recommendations and decisions of the tenth special session

The General Assembly,

Recalling its resolution 39/148 L of 17 December 1984,

Noting with concern that the problem identified in the above-mentioned resolution has not been alleviated,

Firmly convinced that all States have a vital interest in the success of disarmament negotiations,

Bearing in mind paragraph 28 of the Final Document of the Tenth Special Session of the General Assembly, in which it affirmed that all States have the duty to contribute to the efforts in the field of disarmament and that all States have the right to participate in disarmament negotiations,

Recalling further its resolution 38/183 F of 20 December 1983, in which it called upon the Governments of all States to contribute substantially, *inter alia*, to halting and reversing the arms race, particularly in the nuclear field, and thus to reducing the danger of nuclear war,

1. *Reiterates once more* the right of all States not members of the Conference on Disarmament to participate in the work of the plenary sessions of the Conference on substantive questions;

2. *Urges* States members of the Conference on Disarmament not to misuse the rules of procedure of the Conference so as to prevent States not members from participating in the work of the Conference.

General Assembly resolution 40/152 J

16 December 1985   Meeting 117   128-0-20 (recorded vote)

Approved by First Committee (A/40/877/Add.1) by recorded vote (111-0-17), 14 November (meeting 38); 2-nation draft (A/C.1/40/L.51); agenda item 65 *(m)*.

Sponsors: Iraq, Jordan.

Meeting numbers. GA 40th session: 1st Committee 3-32, 35, 38; plenary 117.

Recorded vote in Assembly as follows:

In favour: Afghanistan, Algeria, Angola, Antigua and Barbuda, Argentina, Australia, Bahamas, Bahrain, Bangladesh, Barbados, Benin, Bhutan, Bolivia, Botswana, Brazil, Bulgaria, Burkina Faso, Burundi, Byelorussian SSR, Cameroon, Cape Verde, Central African Republic, Chad, Chile, China, Colombia, Comoros, Congo, Costa Rica, Cuba, Cyprus, Czechoslovakia, Democratic Kampuchea,

Democratic Yemen, Denmark, Djibouti, Dominican Republic, Ecuador, Egypt, El Salvador, Equatorial Guinea, Fiji, Finland, France, Gabon, Gambia, German Democratic Republic, Ghana, Greece, Guatemala, Guinea, Guinea-Bissau, Guyana, Haiti, Honduras, Hungary, Iceland, Iraq, Ireland, Israel, Ivory Coast, Jamaica, Japan, Jordan, Kenya, Kuwait, Lao People's Democratic Republic, Lebanon, Lesotho, Liberia, Libyan Arab Jamahiriya, Madagascar, Malawi, Malaysia, Maldives, Mali, Malta, Mauritania, Mauritius, Mexico, Mongolia, Morocco, Mozambique, Nicaragua, Niger, Norway, Oman, Panama, Papua New Guinea, Peru, Poland, Portugal, Qatar, Romania, Rwanda, Saint Lucia, Saint Vincent and the Grenadines, Samoa, Sao Tome and Principe, Saudi Arabia, Senegal, Seychelles, Sierra Leone, Somalia, Spain, Sri Lanka, Sudan, Suriname, Swaziland, Syrian Arab Republic, Togo, Trinidad and Tobago, Tunisia, Turkey, Uganda, Ukrainian SSR, USSR, United Arab Emirates, United Republic of Tanzania, Uruguay, Vanuatu, Venezuela, Viet Nam, Yemen, Yugoslavia, Zaire, Zambia, Zimbabwe.
Against: None.
Abstaining: Austria, Belgium, Burma, Canada, Ethiopia, Germany, Federal Republic of, Grenada, India, Iran, Italy, Luxembourg, Nepal, Netherlands, New Zealand, Nigeria, Pakistan, Paraguay, Sweden, United Kingdom, United States.

The recorded vote in the Committee was requested by the United States.

Iraq, introducing the draft, stated that the previous year's resolution with the same thrust[20] had not been implemented and that the right to speak or reply had been denied at the Conference's 1985 session because one member objected.

The United Kingdom wished to see all States participate in the disarmament process, but considered—as did Sweden—that participation in the Conference should be decided by that body based on its rules of procedure. Iran recalled that the Conference was a negotiating forum rather than a deliberative body.

France cautioned that paragraph 2 could be interpreted as an invitation to Conference members to reject its rules concerning adoption of decisions, and added that it would have preferred the Assembly to have expressed the hope that the Conference would respond favourably to non-members' requests to speak.

In 1985, the Assembly adopted a number of other resolutions concerning the Conference on Disarmament. It called on the Conference to take up specific topics, such as: cessation of nuclear-weapon test explosions (**40/80 A**), a comprehensive nuclear-test-ban treaty (**40/81**), strengthening the security of non-nuclear-weapon States (**40/85, 40/86**), an arms race in outer space (**40/87**), banning nuclear-weapon tests (**40/88**), new types of weapons of mass destruction (**40/90**), chemical weapons (**40/92 A-C**), radiological weapons (**40/94 D**), a convention banning the use of nuclear weapons (**40/151 F**), non-use of nuclear weapons and prevention of nuclear war (**40/152 A**), nuclear weapons in all aspects (**40/152 C**), a comprehensive programme of disarmament (**40/152 D**), prohibition of the nuclear neutron weapon (**40/152 H**), implementation of the Declaration of the 1980s as the Second Disarmament Decade (**40/152 L**), implementation of the recommendations of the tenth special session (**40/152 N**), cessation of the nuclear-arms race and nuclear disarmament (**40/152 P**) and the prevention of nuclear war (**40/152 Q**).

Implementation of the recommendations of the 1978 special session

The General Assembly adopted 17 resolutions and one decision in 1985 relating to the implementation of the recommendations and decisions adopted in 1978 at its tenth special session[13]— the first devoted to disarmament. They dealt with the non-use of nuclear weapons and prevention of nuclear war (**40/152 A**); bilateral nuclear-arms and space-arms negotiations (**40/152 B**); nuclear weapons in all aspects (**40/152 C**); a comprehensive programme of disarmament (**40/152 D**); Disarmament Week (**40/152 E**); the Disarmament Commission's report (**40/152 F**); climatic effects of nuclear war, including nuclear winter (**40/152 G**); prohibiting the nuclear neutron weapon (**40/152 H**), international co-operation for disarmament (**40/152 I**), implementing the 1978 special session's recommendations (**40/152 J** and **N**); United Nations disarmament studies (**40/152 K**); review and appraisal of the implementation of the Declaration of the 1980s as the Second Disarmament Decade (**40/152 L**); the Conference on Disarmament's report (**40/152 M**); verification (**40/152 O**); cessation of the nuclear-arms race and nuclear disarmament (**40/152 P**); and prevention of nuclear war (**40/152 Q**). The decision (**40/428**) dealt with the work of the Advisory Board on Disarmament Studies.

In November, the Secretary-General submitted to the Assembly a note[21] containing information received from the German Democratic Republic and the USSR, which had responded to an invitation in a 1984 Assembly resolution,[22] on implementation of the recommendations and decisions adopted at the 1978 special session, to supply information concerning disarmament and arms limitation negotiations outside the framework of the United Nations.

GENERAL ASSEMBLY ACTION

The General Assembly adopted on 16 December, on the recommendation of the First Committee, **resolution 40/152 N** by recorded vote.

Implementation of the recommendations and decisions of the tenth special session

The General Assembly,

Having reviewed the implementation of the recommendations and decisions adopted by the General Assembly at its tenth special session, the first special session devoted to disarmament, as well as the Concluding Document of the Twelfth Special Session of the General Assembly, the second special session devoted to disarmament,

Recalling its resolutions S-10/2 of 30 June 1978, 34/83 C of 11 December 1979, 35/46 of 3 December 1980, 35/152 E of 12 December 1980, 36/92 M of 9 December 1981, 37/78 F of 9 December 1982, 38/183 H of 20 December 1983 and 39/148 O of 17 December 1984 and its decision S-12/24 of 10 July 1982,

Deeply concerned that no concrete results regarding the implementation of the recommendations and decisions of the tenth special session have been realized in the course of more than seven years since that session, that in the mean time the arms race, particularly in its nuclear aspect, has gained in intensity, that there has been further deployment of nuclear weapons in some parts of the world, that annual global military expenditures are estimated to have reached the staggering figure of $1,000 billion, that mankind is faced with a real danger of spreading the arms race into outer space, that urgent measures to prevent nuclear war and for disarmament have not been adopted and that continued colonial domination and foreign occupation, open threats, pressures and military intervention against independent States and violations of the fundamental principles of the Charter of the United Nations have taken place, posing the most serious threat to international peace and security,

Convinced that the renewed escalation of the nuclear-arms race, in both the quantitative and the qualitative dimensions, as well as reliance on nuclear deterrence and on the use of nuclear weapons, has heightened the risk of the outbreak of nuclear war and led to greater insecurity and instability in international relations,

Further convinced that international peace and security can only be ensured through general and complete disarmament under effective international control and that one of the most urgent tasks is to halt and reverse the arms race and to undertake concrete measures of disarmament, particularly nuclear disarmament, and that, in this respect, the nuclear-weapon States and other militarily significant States have the primary responsibility,

Believing that the preservation of the existing bilateral, regional and global system of arms limitation and disarmament agreements and the strict observance of such agreements by their parties are important elements of disarmament efforts at all levels,

Noting with great concern that no real progress in disarmament negotiations has been achieved in the course of several years, which has rendered the current international situation even more dangerous and insecure,

Expressing the desire that the launching of negotiations between the United States of America and the Union of Soviet Socialist Republics would produce agreements on preventing an arms race in outer space and on significant reductions in their strategic and intermediate-range nuclear-weapon systems, as well as that the results of these negotiations would lead to a relaxation of tension in their mutual relations and in the world at large,

Considering that bilateral negotiations should not in any way diminish the urgent need to initiate and pursue multilateral negotiations in the Conference on Disarmament on the cessation of the nuclear-arms race and nuclear disarmament and on the prevention of an arms race in outer space,

Stressing that it is more than ever imperative in the present circumstances to give a new impetus to negotiations on disarmament, in particular nuclear disarmament, at all levels and to achieve genuine progress in the immediate future and that all States should refrain from any actions which have or may have negative effects on the outcome of disarmament negotiations,

Reaffirming that the United Nations has a central role and primary responsibility in the sphere of disarmament,

Stressing that the Final Document of the Tenth Special Session of the General Assembly, which was unanimously and categorically reaffirmed by all Member States at the twelfth special session as the comprehensive basis for efforts towards halting and reversing the arms race, retains all its validity and that the objectives and measures contained therein still represent one of the most important and urgent goals to be achieved,

1. *Expresses its grave concern* over the acceleration and intensification of the arms race, particularly the nuclear-arms race, which threaten international peace and security and increase the danger of nuclear war;

2. *Calls upon* all States, in particular nuclear-weapon States and other militarily significant States, to take urgent measures in order to promote international security on the basis of disarmament, to halt and reverse the arms race and to launch a process of genuine disarmament;

3. *Invites* all States, particularly nuclear-weapon States and especially those among them which possess the most important nuclear arsenals, to take urgent measures with a view to implementing the recommendations and decisions contained in the Final Document of the Tenth Special Session of the General Assembly, as well as to fulfilling the priority tasks set forth in the Programme of Action contained in section III of the Final Document;

4. *Calls upon* great Powers to pursue their negotiations in a constructive and accommodating spirit and taking into account the interest of the entire international community in order to halt the arms race, particularly the nuclear-arms race, and to achieve disarmament;

5. *Calls upon* the Conference on Disarmament to proceed urgently to negotiations on the cessation of the nuclear-arms race and nuclear disarmament and on the prevention of nuclear war, to undertake and intensify negotiations on the prevention of an arms race in outer space and to elaborate drafts of treaties on a nuclear-weapon-test ban and on a complete and effective prohibition of the development, production and stockpiling of all chemical weapons and on their destruction;

6. *Calls upon* the Disarmament Commission to intensify its work in accordance with its mandate and to continue improving its work with a view to making concrete recommendations on specific items on its agenda;

7. *Invites* all States engaged in disarmament and arms limitation negotiations outside the framework of the United Nations to keep the General Assembly and the Conference on Disarmament informed on the status and/or results of such negotiations, in conformity with the relevant provisions of the Final Document of the Tenth Special Session;

8. *Decides* to include in the provisional agenda of its forty-first session the item entitled "Implementation of the recommendations and decisions of the tenth special session".

General Assembly resolution 40/152 N

16 December 1985   Meeting 117   135-13-5 (recorded vote)

Approved by First Committee (A/40/877/Add.1) by recorded vote (113-13-6), 20 November (meeting 44); 27-nation draft (A/C.1/40/L.58/Rev.1); agenda item 65 *(m)*.

Sponsors: Algeria, Bahamas, Bangladesh, Bolivia, Burma, Colombia, Cuba, Ecuador, Egypt, Ethiopia, German Democratic Republic, Ghana, India, Indonesia, Iran, Madagascar, Nigeria, Pakistan, Peru, Poland, Romania, Sri Lanka, Sudan, Tunisia, Venezuela, Viet Nam, Yugoslavia.
Meeting numbers. GA 40th session: 1st Committee 3-32, 36, 43, 44; plenary 117.

Recorded vote in Assembly as follows:

In favour: Afghanistan, Algeria, Angola, Antigua and Barbuda, Argentina, Austria, Bahamas, Bahrain, Bangladesh, Barbados, Benin, Bhutan, Bolivia, Botswana, Brazil, Brunei Darussalam, Bulgaria, Burkina Faso, Burma, Burundi, Byelorussian SSR, Cameroon, Cape Verde, Central African Republic, Chad, Chile, China, Colombia, Comoros, Congo, Costa Rica, Cuba, Cyprus, Czechoslovakia, Democratic Kampuchea, Democratic Yemen, Denmark, Djibouti, Dominican Republic, Ecuador, Egypt, El Salvador, Equatorial Guinea, Ethiopia, Fiji, Finland, Gabon, Gambia, German Democratic Republic, Ghana, Greece, Grenada, Guatemala, Guinea, Guinea-Bissau, Guyana, Haiti, Honduras, Hungary, India, Indonesia, Iran, Iraq, Ireland, Ivory Coast, Jamaica, Jordan, Kenya, Kuwait, Lao People's Democratic Republic, Lebanon, Lesotho, Liberia, Libyan Arab Jamahiriya, Madagascar, Malawi, Malaysia, Maldives, Mali, Malta, Mauritania, Mauritius, Mexico, Mongolia, Morocco, Mozambique, Nepal, Nicaragua, Niger, Nigeria, Oman, Pakistan, Panama, Papua New Guinea, Paraguay, Peru, Philippines, Poland, Qatar, Romania, Rwanda, Saint Lucia, Saint Vincent and the Grenadines, Samoa, Sao Tome and Principe, Saudi Arabia, Senegal, Seychelles, Sierra Leone, Singapore, Somalia, Sri Lanka, Sudan, Suriname, Swaziland, Sweden, Syrian Arab Republic,[a] Thailand, Togo, Trinidad and Tobago, Tunisia, Uganda, Ukrainian SSR, USSR, United Arab Emirates, United Republic of Tanzania, Uruguay, Vanuatu, Venezuela, Viet Nam, Yemen, Yugoslavia, Zaire, Zambia, Zimbabwe.
Against: Belgium, Canada, France, Germany, Federal Republic of, Iceland, Israel, Luxembourg, Netherlands, Norway, Portugal, Turkey, United Kingdom, United States.
Abstaining: Australia, Italy,[b] Japan, New Zealand, Spain.

[a]Later advised the Secretariat it had intended to abstain.
[b]Later advised the Secretariat it had intended to vote against.

Norway voted against the draft as it objected to the fourth preambular paragraph. Similarly, Denmark, not sharing the security perception endorsed in that paragraph, would have voted against the paragraph, had a separate vote been taken; it voted in favour of the text as a whole, however, since it subscribed to the draft's main thrust.

France, abstaining in the Committee and subsequently voting against in the plenary Assembly, concluded that it could not support a text challenging nuclear deterrence, which formed part of its defence and security policy.

Implementation of the recommendations of the 1982 special session

In 1985, the Assembly adopted nine resolutions concerning the implementation of the Concluding Document[16] of its 1982 second special session devoted to disarmament. They were on: disarmament and international security (**40/151 A**), the World Disarmament Campaign (**40/151 B** and **D**), a nuclear-arms freeze (**40/151 C**), a nuclear-weapons freeze (**40/151 E**), a convention banning the use of nuclear weapons (**40/151 F**), a United Nations Regional Centre for Peace and Disarmament in Africa (**40/151 G**), the United Nations disarmament fellowship programme (**40/151 H**) and a third special session on disarmament (**40/151 I**).

Third special session

The Assembly, which had agreed in 1984 to set the date in 1985 for its third special session on disarmament,[23] postponed its decision on the date for another year.

On the recommendation of the First Committee, the Assembly, on 16 December, adopted **resolution 40/151 I** without vote.

Convening of the third special session of the General Assembly devoted to disarmament

The General Assembly,

Bearing in mind the decision adopted at its twelfth special session, the second special session devoted to disarmament, concerning the convening of the third special session devoted to disarmament,

Recalling its resolution 38/73 I of 15 December 1983, in which it decided that the third special session devoted to disarmament should be held not later than 1988,

Recalling also its resolution 39/63 I of 12 December 1984,

Desiring to contribute to the furthering and broadening of positive processes initiated through the laying down of the foundations of an international disarmament strategy at its tenth special session, the first special session devoted to disarmament,

Decides to set, at its forty-first session, the date of the third special session of the General Assembly devoted to disarmament and to establish the Preparatory Committee for the third special session.

General Assembly resolution 40/151 I

16 December 1985   Meeting 117   Adopted without vote

Approved by First Committee (A/40/946) without vote, 14 November (meeting 37); 26-nation draft (A/C.1/40/L.59); agenda item 61 *(g)*.
Sponsors: Algeria, Argentina, Bahamas, Bangladesh, Bolivia, Cameroon, Colombia, Cuba, Ecuador, Egypt, Ethiopia, Ghana, India, Indonesia, Madagascar, Mexico, Nigeria, Pakistan, Peru, Romania, Sri Lanka, Sudan, Tunisia, Venezuela, Viet Nam, Yugoslavia.
Meeting numbers. GA 40th session: 1st Committee 3-32, 35, 37; plenary 117.

International co-operation for disarmament

As it had done annually since 1981,[24] the General Assembly, in 1985, again called for implementation of its 1979 Declaration on International Co-operation for Disarmament.[25]

On 16 December, the Assembly, as recommended by the First Committee, adopted **resolution 40/152 I** by recorded vote.

International co-operation for disarmament

The General Assembly,

Stressing again the urgent need for an active and sustained effort to expedite the implementation of the recommendations and decisions unanimously adopted at its tenth special session, the first special session devoted to disarmament, as contained in the Final Document of that session and confirmed in the Concluding Document of the Twelfth Special Session of the General Assembly, the second special session devoted to disarmament,

Recalling the Declaration on International Co-operation for Disarmament of 11 December 1979 and its resolutions 36/92 D of 9 December 1981, 37/78 B of 9 December 1982, 38/183 F of 20 December 1983 and 39/148 M of 17 December 1984,

Stressing the vital importance of eliminating the danger of a nuclear war, halting the arms race and attaining disarmament, particularly in the nuclear field, for the preservation of peace and the strengthening of international security,

Deeply concerned over the continued nuclear-arms race, the initiation of a quantitatively and qualitatively more dangerous round of that race and the danger of the extension of the arms race to outer space, which has an immediate negative impact on the development of the international situation and international relations and which will destabilize the situation and lead to a multiple increase of the danger of a nuclear conflict,

Bearing in mind the vital interest of all States in the adoption of concrete effective disarmament measures which would release considerable financial and material resources to be used for the economic and social development of all States, in particular developing countries,

Stressing the topicality of the Delhi Declaration issued on 28 January 1985 by the heads of State or Government of six States Members of the United Nations,[26]

Considering the increased activity of peace and anti-war movements in the struggle for peace, against the arms race and for disarmament,

Convinced of the need to strengthen constructive international co-operation based on the political goodwill of States for successful negotiations on disarmament, in accordance with the Final Document of the Tenth Special Session of the General Assembly,

Emphasizing the duty of States to co-operate for the preservation of international peace and security, as set forth in the Charter of the United Nations and confirmed in the Declaration on Principles of International Law concerning Friendly Relations and Co-operation among States in accordance with the Charter of the United Nations, of 24 October 1970, the obligation to co-operate actively and constructively for the attainment of the aims of disarmament being an indispensable part of that duty,

Stressing that, within the framework of international co-operation for the attainment of the aims of disarmament, it is necessary to avert nuclear war by means of preventing an arms race in outer space and halting it on Earth, and limiting and reducing nuclear armaments up to the complete elimination of nuclear weapons everywhere on the basis of the principle of equal security,

Underlining the need to halt both qualitative improvement and quantitative buildup of nuclear weapons so as to take the first step towards their radical reduction,

Believing that the two nuclear-weapon States which possess the most important nuclear arsenals should take the lead and show a good example in curbing the arms race and preventing its spread to outer space,

Stressing that proposals, relatively simple in their execution and at the same time effective, and agreements aimed at eliminating the use or the threat of use of force, be it on a world-wide or regional scale, would contribute considerably to that end,

Bearing in mind that the United Nations bears primary responsibility and plays a central role in unifying efforts to maintain and to develop active co-operation among States in order to resolve disarmament issues,

1. *Calls upon* all States, in implementing the Final Document of the Tenth Special Session of the General Assembly, to make active use of the principles and ideas contained in the Declaration on International Co-operation for Disarmament by actively participating in disarmament negotiations, with a view to achieving concrete results, and by conducting them on the basis of the principles of reciprocity, equality, undiminished security and the non-use of force in international relations, and to refrain at the same time from developing new channels of the arms race;

2. *Stresses* the importance of strengthening the effectiveness of the United Nations in fulfilling its responsibility for maintaining international peace and security in accordance with the Charter of the United Nations;

3. *Emphasizes* the necessity of refraining from war propaganda, in particular from propaganda for a nuclear war—global or limited—and from the elaboration and dissemination of any doctrines and concepts endangering international peace and justifying the unleashing of nuclear war, which lead to deterioration of the international situation and to further intensification of the arms race and which are detrimental to the generally recognized necessity of international co-operation for disarmament;

4. *Declares* that the use of force in international relations as well as in attempts to prevent the full implementation of the Declaration on the Granting of Independence to Colonial Countries and Peoples constitutes a phenomenon incompatible with the idea of international co-operation for disarmament;

5. *Expresses the firm conviction* that for effective international co-operation for the attainment of the aims of disarmament it is inevitable that the policy of States, primarily of those which dispose of nuclear weapons, be directed to averting a nuclear war;

6. *Demands* that the arms race not be extended into other spheres of human activity, such as outer space, that should be used for peaceful purposes, exclusively for the benefit of mankind;

7. *Appeals* to States which are members of military groupings to promote, on the basis of the Final Document of the Tenth Special Session and in the spirit of international co-operation for disarmament, the gradual mutual limitation of military activities of these groupings, thus creating conditions for their dissolution;

8. *Calls upon* all Member States to continue to cultivate and disseminate, particularly in connection with the World Disarmament Campaign, launched by the General Assembly at its twelfth special session, the ideas of international co-operation for disarmament, in particular through their educational systems, mass media and cultural policies;

9. *Calls upon* the United Nations Educational, Scientific and Cultural Organization to continue to consider, in order further to mobilize world public opinion on behalf of disarmament, measures aimed at strengthening the ideas of international co-operation for disarmament through research, education, information, communication and culture;

10. *Calls upon* the Governments of all States to contribute substantially, while observing the principle of undiminished security, to halting and reversing the arms race, particularly in the nuclear field, and thus to reducing the danger of nuclear war.

General Assembly resolution 40/152 I

16 December 1985　　Meeting 117　　109-19-17 (recorded vote)

Approved by First Committee (A/40/877/Add.1) by recorded vote (91-19-14), 14 November (meeting 38); 17-nation draft (A/C.1/40/L.48); agenda item 65.
Sponsors: Afghanistan, Angola, Congo, Cuba, Czechoslovakia, Democratic Yemen, German Democratic Republic, Guyana, Hungary, Indonesia, Lao People's

Democratic Republic, Mongolia, Mozambique, Poland, Syrian Arab Republic, Ukrainian SSR, Viet Nam.
Meeting numbers. GA 40th session: 1st Committee 3-32, 36, 38; plenary 117.

Recorded vote in Assembly as follows:

In favour: Afghanistan, Algeria, Angola, Antigua and Barbuda, Argentina, Bahrain, Bangladesh, Barbados, Benin, Bhutan, Bolivia, Botswana, Bulgaria, Burkina Faso, Burma, Burundi, Byelorussian SSR, Cameroon, Cape Verde, Comoros, Congo, Costa Rica, Cuba, Cyprus, Czechoslovakia, Democratic Yemen, Djibouti, Dominican Republic, Ecuador, Egypt, El Salvador, Equatorial Guinea, Ethiopia, Gabon, Gambia, German Democratic Republic, Ghana, Guatemala, Guinea, Guinea-Bissau, Guyana, Honduras, Hungary, India, Indonesia, Iran, Iraq, Ivory Coast, Jordan, Kenya, Kuwait, Lao People's Democratic Republic, Lebanon, Lesotho, Liberia, Libyan Arab Jamahiriya, Madagascar, Malawi, Malaysia, Maldives, Mali, Mauritius, Mexico, Mongolia, Mozambique, Nepal, Nicaragua, Niger, Nigeria, Oman, Pakistan, Panama, Papua New Guinea, Peru, Poland, Qatar, Romania, Rwanda, Saint Lucia, Samoa, Sao Tome and Principe, Saudi Arabia, Senegal, Seychelles, Sierra Leone, Somalia, Sri Lanka, Sudan, Suriname, Swaziland, Syrian Arab Republic, Thailand, Togo, Trinidad and Tobago, Tunisia, Uganda, Ukrainian SSR, USSR, United Arab Emirates, United Republic of Tanzania, Uruguay, Vanuatu, Venezuela, Viet Nam, Yemen, Yugoslavia, Zaire, Zambia, Zimbabwe.

Against: Australia, Belgium, Canada, Denmark, France, Germany, Federal Republic of, Iceland, Israel, Italy, Japan, Luxembourg, Netherlands, New Zealand, Norway, Portugal, Spain, Turkey, United Kingdom, United States.

Abstaining: Austria, Bahamas, Brazil, Central African Republic, Chad, Chile, Colombia, Fiji, Finland, Greece, Grenada, Haiti, Ireland, Morocco, Paraguay, Saint Vincent and the Grenadines, Sweden.

Under the same agenda item, a draft resolution by the German Democratic Republic, on obligations of States to contribute to effective disarmament negotiations,[27] was submitted to the First Committee and subsequently withdrawn. The draft would have had the Assembly express the conviction that all States, particularly the nuclear-weapon ones and other militarily significant States, had the foremost obligation to conduct serious negotiations based on equality, reciprocity and undiminished security to halt and reverse the arms race.

Implementation of the Declaration of the 1980s as the Second Disarmament Decade

Disarmament Commission consideration. The 1980 General Assembly Declaration of the 1980s as the Second Disarmament Decade[18] had stipulated that the Assembly would review and appraise, through the Disarmament Commission in 1985, progress in implementing the measures identified in that document. In that connection, the Commission had before it a working paper submitted by India and Nigeria,[28] which suggested that, since the Decade's goals were far from being achieved, the Commission should call on the Assembly to urge States to reaffirm their commitment to the Decade's objectives. Eighteen Governments and the 10 States members of the European Community (EC)[29] submitted their views in response to a 1984 Assembly request.[30]

Following two plenary meetings on the topic, the Commission adopted on 29 May, and annexed to its annual report to the Assembly,[17] a summary of its review of the Declaration, as prepared by its Chairman based on consultations among interested delegations. It was noted that no substantial progress had been made even on highest-priority disarmament questions and that the threat

to humanity's survival had not diminished since the beginning of the Decade. The Commission recommended that the Assembly call on all States, particularly the nuclear-weapon ones, to reaffirm their commitment to attaining the ultimate objective of general and complete disarmament under effective international control.

GENERAL ASSEMBLY ACTION

On 16 December, the Assembly, on the recommendation of the First Committee, adopted **resolution 40/152 L** without vote.

Review and appraisal of the implementation of the Declaration of the 1980s as the Second Disarmament Decade

The General Assembly,

Recalling its resolution 35/46 of 3 December 1980, by which it adopted the Declaration of the 1980s as the Second Disarmament Decade,

Recalling also its resolution 39/148 Q of 17 December 1984, by which it decided to review and appraise at its fortieth session, in 1985, the implementation of the Declaration,

Noting with concern that half-way through the Second Disarmament Decade its goals are far from being achieved and that no substantial progress has been made even on items of highest priority,

Alarmed at the continued escalation of the arms race, particularly the nuclear-arms race,

Also alarmed at the recent findings of the possible consequences of a nuclear war under present circumstances, as documented by competent scientists,

Deeply concerned at the continued dissipation of ever-increasing human and material resources on the arms race,

Taking note of the views of Member States and suggestions made by them on the implementation of the Declaration,

Taking note with satisfaction of the part of the report of the Disarmament Commission on the item entitled "Review and appraisal of the implementation of the Declaration of the 1980s as the Second Disarmament Decade: preliminary assessment and suggestions to ensure progress",

Welcoming the bilateral negotiations between the Union of Soviet Socialist Republics and the United States of America in accordance with the joint statement issued by the two Governments on 8 January 1985,

1. *Decides* to adopt the relevant part of the report of the Disarmament Commission;

2. *Requests* the Conference on Disarmament to accelerate the implementation of the activities elaborated in the Declaration of the 1980s as the Second Disarmament Decade, as enumerated in the report of the Disarmament Commission;

3. *Calls upon* all States, particularly the nuclear-weapon States:

   (*a*) To reaffirm their commitment to the Declaration of the 1980s as the Second Disarmament Decade;

   (*b*) To reaffirm their commitment to the attainment of the ultimate objective of general and complete disarmament under effective international control;

(c) To adopt concrete and practical measures for preventing the outbreak of war, in particular nuclear war;

(d) To take appropriate steps to halt and reverse the nuclear-arms race with a view to improving the international climate and enhancing the efficacy of disarmament negotiations;

(e) To exert greater efforts in the implementation of the World Disarmament Campaign;

4. *Requests* the Secretary-General to report annually to the General Assembly on the implementation of the Declaration of the 1980s as the Second Disarmament Decade.

General Assembly resolution 40/152 L

16 December 1985   Meeting 117   Adopted without vote

Approved by First Committee (A/40/877/Add.1) without vote, 14 November (meeting 37); 11-nation draft (A/C.1/40/L.55), orally revised; agenda item 65 *(n)*.
Sponsors: Algeria, Argentina, Bangladesh, Cameroon, India, Indonesia, Nigeria, Pakistan, Romania, Tunisia, Yugoslavia.
Meeting numbers. GA 40th session: 1st Committee 3-32, 34, 37; plenary 117.

Compliance and verification

GENERAL ASSEMBLY ACTION

In December 1985, the General Assembly, on the recommendation of the First Committee, adopted two resolutions relating to compliance—compliance with arms limitation and disarmament agreements (**40/94 L**) and verification of compliance (**40/152 O**). (See also p. 100 for a listing and status of ratification of existing disarmament agreements.)

On 12 December, the Assembly adopted **resolution 40/94 L** by recorded vote.

Compliance with arms limitation and disarmament agreements

The General Assembly,

Conscious of the abiding concern of all Member States for preserving respect for rights and obligations arising from treaties and other sources of international law,

Convinced that observance of the Charter of the United Nations, relevant treaties and other sources of international law is essential for the strengthening of international security,

Mindful in particular of the fundamental importance of full implementation and strict observance of agreements on arms limitation and disarmament if individual nations and the international community are to derive enhanced security from them,

Stressing that any violation of such agreements not only adversely affects the security of States parties but can also create security risks for other States relying on the constraints and commitments stipulated in those agreements,

Stressing further that any weakening of confidence in such agreements diminishes their contribution to global or regional stability and to further disarmament and arms limitation efforts and undermines the credibility and effectiveness of the international legal system,

Believing that compliance with arms limitation and disarmament agreements by States parties is, therefore, a matter of interest and concern to the international community, and noting the role that the United Nations could play in that regard,

1. *Urges* all States parties to arms limitation and disarmament agreements to implement and comply with the entirety of the provisions subscribed to;

2. *Calls upon* all Member States to give serious consideration to the implications of non-compliance with those obligations for international security and stability, as well as for the prospects for further progress in the field of disarmament;

3. *Appeals* to all Member States to support efforts aimed at the resolution of non-compliance questions, with a view towards encouraging strict observance of the provisions subscribed to and maintaining or restoring the integrity of arms limitation or disarmament agreements;

4. *Requests* the Secretary-General to provide Member States with assistance that may be necessary in this regard.

General Assembly resolution 40/94 L

12 December 1985   Meeting 113   131-0-16 (recorded vote)

Approved by First Committee (A/40/976) by recorded vote (99-0-23), 19 November (meeting 42); 9-nation draft (A/C.1/40/L.66/Rev.1); agenda item 68.
Sponsors: Costa Rica, Denmark, France, Greece, Iceland, Italy, New Zealand, Norway, United States.
Meeting numbers. GA 40th session: 1st Committee 3-33, 42; plenary 113.

Recorded vote in Assembly as follows:

In favour: Antigua and Barbuda, Argentina, Australia, Austria, Bahamas, Bahrain, Bangladesh, Barbados, Belgium, Bhutan, Bolivia, Botswana, Brazil, Brunei Darussalam, Bulgaria, Burma, Burundi, Byelorussian SSR, Cameroon, Canada, Cape Verde, Central African Republic, Chad, Chile, China, Colombia, Comoros, Congo, Czechoslovakia, Democratic Kampuchea, Denmark, Djibouti, Dominican Republic, Ecuador, El Salvador, Equatorial Guinea, Fiji, Finland, France, Gabon, German Democratic Republic, Germany, Federal Republic of, Ghana,[a] Greece, Grenada, Guatemala, Guinea, Guinea-Bissau, Guyana, Haiti, Honduras, Hungary, Iceland, Iran, Iraq, Ireland, Israel, Italy, Ivory Coast, Jamaica, Japan, Jordan, Kenya, Lao People's Democratic Republic, Lebanon, Lesotho, Liberia, Luxembourg, Malawi, Malaysia, Maldives, Mali, Malta, Mauritania, Mauritius, Mexico, Mongolia, Morocco, Mozambique, Nepal, Netherlands, New Zealand, Niger, Norway, Oman, Pakistan, Panama, Papua New Guinea, Paraguay, Peru, Philippines, Poland, Portugal, Qatar, Romania, Rwanda, Saint Christopher and Nevis, Saint Lucia, Saint Vincent and the Grenadines, Samoa, Sao Tome and Principe, Saudi Arabia, Senegal, Seychelles, Sierra Leone, Singapore, Solomon Islands, Somalia, Spain, Sudan, Suriname, Swaziland, Sweden, Thailand, Togo, Trinidad and Tobago, Tunisia, Turkey, Ukrainian SSR, USSR, United Arab Emirates, United Kingdom, United Republic of Tanzania, United States, Uruguay, Vanuatu, Venezuela, Yemen, Zaire, Zambia, Zimbabwe.

Against: None.

Abstaining: Afghanistan, Algeria, Benin, Burkina Faso, Cuba, Cyprus, Egypt, Ethiopia, India, Indonesia, Nicaragua, Nigeria, Sri Lanka, Uganda, Viet Nam, Yugoslavia.

[a]Later advised the Secretariat it had intended to abstain.

Egypt asserted that separate consideration of the compliance question was undesirable and redundant, given the existence of paragraphs on compliance in all disarmament agreements—a view shared by others abstaining, among them, India, Indonesia, Nigeria, Sri Lanka and Yugoslavia. India believed that treating compliance as a separate issue could impede progress in concluding disarmament agreements, and Yugoslavia felt such an approach could be used to derail negotiations whenever it suited one side or the other. Sweden, voting in favour, asserted that compliance should not become a politically controversial issue of a general character.

Sri Lanka observed that the text would enable the Assembly to discuss cases of non-compliance, when treaty compliance was a matter for the parties concerned to legislate. Indonesia said obligation to comply with agreements or treaties to which a country had become a party of its own volition was self-evident; it added that widening the scope of the non-compliance issue outside the parties to the agreement or treaty, as called for in paragraph 3, would not achieve the paragraph's purported objective. Nigeria and Sweden believed that possible concern about non-compliance should be dealt with on a case-by-case basis and directly in the context of the obligations in question. Egypt, Sri Lanka and Sweden also urged the nuclear-weapon States to demonstrate their commitment to the 1968 Treaty on the Non-Proliferation of Nuclear Weapons.[31]

The USSR, while supporting the proposal in general, condemned what it called the practice of using the compliance question as a pretext for breaking off ongoing negotiations or for postponing the entry into force of international agreements; it also condemned unfounded assertions of non-compliance as a means of covering up negative attitude to arms limitation and disarmament agreements. Brazil said its positive vote was made possible by the sponsors' willingness to accommodate certain suggestions which, it believed, had improved the text. Morocco and Venezuela understood that the draft embraced both bilateral and multilateral treaties.

In the plenary Assembly, Mexico explained its affirmative vote by saying that the validity and pertinence of a series of provisions in the text were irrefutable; it had abstained in the First Committee simply to emphasize the irony it saw in the fact that the draft had been introduced by the United States which, it said, had for a number of years voted against Assembly resolutions on disarmament agreements such as those dealing with halting all nuclear-weapon tests.

On 16 December, the Assembly adopted **resolution 40/152 O** without vote.

Verification in all its aspects

The General Assembly,

Conscious of the urgent need to reach agreements on arms limitation and disarmament measures capable of contributing to the maintenance of peace and security,

Convinced that, if such measures are to be effective, they must be fair and balanced, acceptable to all parties, their substance must be clear and compliance with them must be evident,

Reaffirming its conviction, as expressed in paragraph 91 of the Final Document of the Tenth Special Session of the General Assembly, adopted by consensus at that session, its first special session devoted to disarmament, that in order to facilitate the conclusion and effective implementation of disarmament agreements and to create confidence, States should accept appropriate provisions for verification in such agreements,

Reiterating its view that:

(a) Disarmament and arms limitation agreements should provide for adequate measures of verification satisfactory to all parties concerned in order to create the necessary confidence and to ensure that they are being observed by all parties,

(b) The form and modalities of the verification to be provided for in any specific agreement depend upon and should be determined by the purposes, scope and nature of the agreement,

(c) Agreements should provide for the participation of parties directly or through the United Nations system in the verification process,

(d) Where appropriate, a combination of several methods of verification as well as other compliance procedures should be employed,

Recalling that:

(a) In the context of international disarmament negotiations, the problem of verification should be further examined and adequate methods and procedures in this field should be considered,

(b) Every effort should be made to develop appropriate methods and procedures that are non-discriminatory and that do not unduly interfere with the internal affairs of other States or jeopardize their economic and social development,

Believing that verification techniques should be developed as an objective means of determining compliance with agreements and appropriately taken into account in the course of disarmament negotiations,

1. *Calls upon* Member States to intensify their efforts towards achieving agreements on balanced, mutually acceptable, verifiable and effective arms limitation and disarmament measures;

2. *Invites* all Member States, bearing in mind the Final Document of the Tenth Special Session of the General Assembly, to communicate to the Secretary-General, not later than 15 April 1986, their views and suggestions on verification principles, procedures and techniques for promoting the inclusion of adequate verification in arms limitation and disarmament agreements and on the role of the United Nations in the field of verification;

3. *Requests* the Secretary-General to prepare and submit to the General Assembly at its forty-first session a report containing the views and suggestions of Member States;

4. *Decides* to include in the provisional agenda of its forty-first session an item entitled "Verification in all its aspects" under the item entitled "Review of the implementation of the recommendations and decisions adopted by the General Assembly at its tenth special session: implementation of the recommendations and decisions of the tenth special session".

General Assembly resolution 40/152 O

16 December 1985   Meeting 117   Adopted without vote

Approved by First Committee (A/40/877/Add.1) without vote, 22 November (meeting 47); 11-nation draft (A/C.1/40/L.62/Rev.1); agenda item 65.
Sponsors: Australia, Belgium, Cameroon, Canada, Costa Rica, Germany, Federal Republic of, Italy, Japan, New Zealand, Turkey, United Kingdom.
Meeting numbers. GA 40th session: 1st Committee 3-32, 34, 47; plenary 117.

In explanation of position, the USSR stated its readiness to supplement national technical measures, when necessary, with additional mutually agreed measures, including international verification. It stressed that the essential point of any agreement was the actual means of limiting and reducing the arms themselves; verification abstracted from specific steps to limit arms was senseless. Czechoslovakia opposed attempts to deal with verification separately from disarmament or as a pre-condition for negotiations.

Brazil understood the expression "fair and balanced, acceptable to all parties" in the text to mean that verification measures included in specific disarmament agreements must be universal and non-discriminatory among the parties to such agreements. India, Mexico and Yugoslavia stressed that there could be no verification in the abstract and that verification had to be related to individual disarmament agreements. India, accordingly, was unable to understand the need to restate the obvious in a general way and believed that the verification aspect was being exploited to frustrate progress on disarmament negotiations. Mexico believed that there was no perfect verification, but in most cases imperfect verification was preferable to none at all; its participation in the consensus should not be construed as a change in its position that verification should not be used as a pretext to prevent the conclusion of disarmament agreements.

In related action, the Assembly called on all States to comply with and implement all provisions of disarmament and arms limitation agreements and to negotiate for the conclusion of additional treaties and conventions (**resolution 40/94 N**).

General and complete disarmament

As requested by the General Assembly in 1984,[32] the Disarmament Commission began in 1985 a comprehensive review of the United Nations role in disarmament, and the Assembly agreed that the work should continue (resolution 40/94 O). It also called for achieving the principles and priorities for disarmament as agreed in the 1978 Final Document[15] (40/94 N), and called again on the Security Council to initiate procedures, under the United Nations Charter, for halting the arms race (40/151 A).

The Assembly reaffirmed the need to start negotiations on naval arms reduction and requested the Disarmament Commission to continue consideration of that question as a matter of priority (40/94 I); it also asked the Conference on Disarmament to continue consideration of further measures to prevent an arms race on the sea-bed (40/94 J).

Studies were completed in 1985 by two groups of governmental experts—one on the naval arms race, naval forces and naval arms systems (40/94 F) and the other on concepts of security (40/94 E).

Those who engaged in and fuelled the arms trade bore a heavy responsibility for the daily loss of countless lives, the Secretary-General emphasized (see p. 8).

Disarmament Commission activities. The contact group of the Committee of the Whole, set up by the Commission[17] to deal with a two-tiered agenda item—on various aspects of the arms race, particularly the nuclear-arms race and nuclear disarmament, and elaboration of a general approach to negotiations on nuclear and conventional disarmament—held four meetings between 15 and 24 May, basing its work on the 1984 compilation of proposals for recommendations on the topic.[33] It also considered two working papers submitted in 1985—one by the German Democratic Republic and the other by Belgium, Canada, Denmark, France, the Federal Republic of Germany, Italy, Japan, the Netherlands, Norway, Portugal, Spain, Turkey and the United Kingdom. Again unable to agree on a consensus on a complete set of recommendations, the Group suggested that the Commission continue its efforts to reach agreed formulations on recommendations on the topic.

UN role in disarmament

Disarmament Commission consideration. Responding to a 1984 General Assembly request[32] that the Disarmament Commission carry out a comprehensive review of the United Nations role in disarmament, the Commission established, on 17 May 1985,[17] Working Group III to consider the topic. In connection with its work, the Group had before it views on strengthening the Organization's role, submitted in response to the Assembly's invitation, by 22 individual States and jointly by the 10 EC members.[34]

The Working Group held seven formal and additional informal meetings between 21 and 28 May under the chairmanship of Paul Bamela Engo (Cameroon). It examined the Chairman's paper on topics for appropriate recommendations, which was subsequently annexed to the Commission's 1985 report to the Assembly.[17] Unable to conclude the discussions for lack of time, the Group recommended that the work be continued as a priority in 1986.

GENERAL ASSEMBLY ACTION

On 12 December, the General Assembly, on the recommendation of the First Committee, adopted **resolution 40/94 O** without vote.

Review of the role of the United Nations in the field of disarmament

The General Assembly,

Recalling its resolution 39/151 G of 17 December 1984,

Bearing in mind that the primary purpose of the United Nations is to maintain international peace and security,

Reaffirming its conviction that genuine and lasting peace can be created only through the effective implementation of the security system provided for in the Charter of the United Nations and the speedy and substantial reduction of arms and armed forces, by international agreement and mutual example, leading ultimately to general and complete disarmament under effective international control,

Reaffirming further that the United Nations, in accordance with its Charter, has a central role and primary responsibility in the sphere of disarmament,

Regretting that, especially in recent years, no substantive progress has been made in the field of disarmament,

Recognizing the need for the United Nations, in discharging its central role and primary responsibility in the sphere of disarmament, to play a more active role in the field of disarmament in accordance with its primary purpose under the Charter to maintain international peace and security,

Taking into account the part of the report of the Disarmament Commission relating to this question,

1. *Requests* the Disarmament Commission to continue its consideration of the role of the United Nations in the field of disarmament as a matter of priority at its next substantive session, in 1986, with a view to the elaboration of concrete recommendations and proposals, as appropriate, taking into account, *inter alia*, the views and suggestions of Member States as well as the aforementioned documents on the subject;

2. *Requests further* the Disarmament Commission to submit its report on the subject, including findings, recommendations and proposals, as appropriate, to the General Assembly at its forty-first session;

3. *Decides* to include in the provisional agenda of its forty-first session the item entitled "Review of the role of the United Nations in the field of disarmament: report of the Disarmament Commission".

General Assembly resolution 40/94 O

12 December 1985   Meeting 113   Adopted without vote

Approved by First Committee (A/40/976) without vote, 14 November (meeting 37); 44-nation draft (A/C.1/40/L.72); agenda item 68 *(g)*.

Sponsors: Australia, Bahamas, Belgium, Burundi, Cameroon, Canada, Cape Verde, Central African Republic, Chad, Colombia, Comoros, Congo, Costa Rica, Djibouti, Dominican Republic, Ecuador, Equatorial Guinea, Fiji, Gabon, Germany, Federal Republic of, Ghana, Greece, Guinea, Guyana, Jamaica, Japan, Kenya, Liberia, Madagascar, Malaysia, Mali, Mauritius, Oman, Rwanda, Samoa, Sierra Leone, Singapore, Sudan, Suriname, Thailand, Togo, Trinidad and Tobago, Zaire, Zambia.

Meeting numbers. GA 40th session: 1st Committee 3-32, 36, 37; plenary 113.

Disarmament and international security

Various ways of maintaining international peace and security remained a priority for the United Nations in 1985 (see also Chapter IV of this section).

In December 1985, the General Assembly declared the urgent need for achieving the principles and priorities for disarmament as agreed in the 1978 Final Document[15] (**resolution 40/94 N**), and reiterated its 1984 call to the Security Council[35] to initiate due procedures, in accordance with the United Nations Charter, for halting the arms race (**40/151 A**).

In February 1985,[36] the Secretary-General had drawn the Council's attention to the Assembly's 1984 call.

On the recommendation of the First Committee, the General Assembly, on 12 December, adopted **resolution 40/94 N** by recorded vote. Paragraph 24 of the 1978 Final Document,[15] mentioned in the resolution's preamble, called for measures that would help create favourable conditions for adopting additional disarmament measures and relaxing international tension.

Disarmament and the maintenance of international peace and security

The General Assembly,

Recognizing the occasion of the fortieth anniversary of the founding of the United Nations,

Solemnly reaffirming the common recognition of Member States of the unique importance of the United Nations and the Charter of the United Nations through which they are all committed "to practice tolerance and live together in peace" and "to unite our strength to maintain international peace and security", as well as "to ensure . . . that armed force shall not be used, save in the common interest",

Further determined to implement the provisions of the Charter to ensure the maintenance of international peace and security, in particular the common commitments of Member States to "settle international disputes by peaceful means" and to "refrain in their international relations from the threat or use of force against the territorial integrity or political independence of any State",

Affirming the critical relationship described in the Charter between the maintenance of international peace and security and the principles governing disarmament and the regulation of armaments,

Reaffirming that the promotion of fundamental human rights, the equal rights of nations large and small and the promotion of social progress and better standards of life in larger freedom remain irreducible goals of the United Nations,

Deeply concerned that the arms race directly threatens the right of people to better standards of life and economic and social advancement,

Recognizing once again the validity of, and reaffirming the commitment of Member States to, the Final Document of the Tenth Special Session of the General Assembly,

Noting that disarmament and arms limitation is necessarily a matter for negotiation and carefully worked out agreements which take account of all the concerns of all participating Governments,

Reaffirming the statement contained in paragraph 13 of the Final Document that genuine and lasting peace can be created only through the effective implementation of the security system provided for in the Charter and the speedy and substantial reduction of arms and armed forces, leading ultimately to general and complete disarmament under effective international control,

Taking into account the existence of negotiations in multilateral, regional and bilateral forums,

Convinced of the need for all States to work to achieve general and complete disarmament, including the conclusion of arms limitation and disarmament agreements wherever feasible,

Further convinced that adequate verification is an essential ingredient if confidence is to be placed in arms limitation or disarmament measures,

Mindful of the provisions of paragraph 24 of the Final Document,

1. *Declares* the urgent need for effective measures to ensure achievement of the principles and priorities for disarmament as agreed upon by consensus at the tenth special session of the General Assembly, to be supported by the following objectives:

(*a*) Avoidance of war, in particular nuclear war;

(*b*) Cessation of existing armed conflicts and military threats of all kinds;

(*c*) Cessation of the arms race in all its manifestations:

(i) In nuclear weapons and other weapons of mass destruction, as well as conventional weapons;

(ii) In qualitative as well as quantitative terms;

(iii) On the regional as well as global scale;

(*d*) Prevention of an arms race in space;

(*e*) Deep reductions in nuclear arsenals ultimately leading to the complete elimination of nuclear weapons under effective, legally binding and verifiable arrangements;

(*f*) The prevention of proliferation of nuclear weapons or other nuclear explosive devices;

(*g*) Elimination of chemical weapons and effective, legally binding and verifiable measures against the development, production, stockpiling and use of biological or chemical weapons;

(*h*) Reduction in arms of all types by all States to levels consistent with their right of self-defence as recognized by Article 51 of the Charter of the United Nations;

(*i*) The exercise of responsibility by exporters of weapons and suppression of the clandestine or illegal traffic in weapons;

(*j*) Application of the physical and intellectual resources of humankind for peaceful purposes;

2. *Calls upon* all States to conduct their relations and to refrain from the use or threat of force in accordance with the provisions of the Charter of the United Nations;

3. *Calls upon* all States to undertake measures specifically designed to build confidence in order to contribute to the creation of favourable conditions for the adoption of additional disarmament measures and to further relaxation of international tension;

4. *Calls upon* all States faithfully to comply with and implement all provisions of multilateral, regional and bilateral disarmament and arms limitation agreements to which they are a party and to negotiate in good faith for the conclusion of additional treaties and conventions, multilateral, regional or bilateral as appropriate, taking into account the need for strict observance of an acceptable balance of mutual responsibilities and obligations for nuclear and non-nuclear-weapon States;

5. *Also calls upon* all States, including those with significant military arsenals as well as those which have special responsibilities as recognized by consensus in the Final Document of the Tenth Special Session of the General Assembly, to exercise their responsibilities regarding disarmament and arms limitation in good faith and according to the provisions of the Final Document, in order to facilitate the achievement of meaningful disarmament and arms limitation measures.

General Assembly resolution 40/94 N

12 December 1985   Meeting 113   99-0-53 (recorded vote)

Approved by First Committee (A/40/976) by recorded vote (80-0-50), 22 November (meeting 47); 6-nation draft (A/C.1/40/L.70/Rev.2); agenda item 68.

Sponsors: Australia, Bolivia, Cameroon, Fiji, Greece, Samoa.

Meeting numbers. GA 40th session: 1st Committee 3-32, 35, 47; plenary 113.

Recorded vote in Assembly as follows:

In favour: Australia, Austria, Bahamas, Bahrain, Barbados, Belgium, Bolivia, Botswana, Brunei Darussalam, Burundi, Cameroon, Canada, Cape Verde, Central African Republic, Chad, Chile, China, Colombia, Comoros, Democratic Kampuchea, Denmark, Djibouti, Dominican Republic, El Salvador, Equatorial Guinea, Ethiopia, Fiji, Finland, Gabon, Germany, Federal Republic of, Ghana, Greece, Grenada, Guatemala, Guinea, Guinea-Bissau, Guyana, Haiti, Honduras, Iceland, Iran, Iraq, Ireland, Israel, Italy, Ivory Coast, Japan, Jordan, Kenya, Kuwait, Lebanon, Lesotho, Liberia, Luxembourg, Malawi, Malaysia, Maldives, Mali, Malta, Mauritania, Mauritius, Morocco, Mozambique, Nepal, Netherlands, New Zealand, Niger, Nigeria, Norway, Oman, Papua New Guinea, Paraguay, Portugal, Qatar, Rwanda, Saint Lucia, Saint Vincent and the Grenadines, Samoa, Sao Tome and Principe, Saudi Arabia, Senegal, Seychelles, Sierra Leone, Singapore, Solomon Islands, Somalia, Spain, Sudan, Swaziland, Sweden, Thailand, Togo, Trinidad and Tobago, Turkey, United Kingdom, United Republic of Tanzania, Uruguay, Yemen, Zambia.

Against: None.

Abstaining: Afghanistan, Algeria, Angola, Antigua and Barbuda, Argentina, Bangladesh, Benin, Bhutan, Brazil, Bulgaria, Burkina Faso, Burma, Byelorussian SSR, Congo, Cuba, Cyprus, Czechoslovakia, Democratic Yemen, Ecuador, Egypt, France, German Democratic Republic, Hungary, India, Indonesia, Jamaica, Lao People's Democratic Republic, Libyan Arab Jamahiriya, Madagascar, Mexico, Mongolia, Nicaragua, Pakistan, Panama, Peru, Poland, Romania, Saint Christopher and Nevis, Sri Lanka, Suriname, Syrian Arab Republic, Tunisia, Uganda, Ukrainian SSR, USSR, United Arab Emirates, United States, Vanuatu, Venezuela, Viet Nam, Yugoslavia, Zaire, Zimbabwe.

In explanation of vote, India said the text was a disturbing attempt at reversing the achievement of the 1978 special session, which, it said, had shifted the international community's focus from the amorphous dialectical interdependence of disarmament and international security to disarmament *per se;* thus paragraph 1 placed on the same level such vital issues as preventing nuclear war and ceasing the nuclear-arms race with other less important objectives. Indonesia similarly feared that the text would undermine the 1978 Final Document[15] and added, as regards the eighth preambular paragraph, that disarmament agreements must take account of the concerns of all countries, not just those of the participating Governments. The USSR felt that the text did not contain a number of important ideas it had proposed.

The Libyan Arab Jamahiriya, changing its affirmative vote in the Committee to an abstention in the plenary Assembly, said it did so in view of the special circumstances prevailing in Africa and the Middle East, caused by the presence of what it called two racist régimes.

On 16 December, the Assembly, also on the recommendation of the First Committee, adopted **resolution 40/151 A** by recorded vote.

Disarmament and international security

The General Assembly,

Deeply concerned over the continuing escalation of the arms race, particularly in nuclear weapons,

Considering that resolution 39/63 K of 12 December 1984 calls upon the Security Council to give consideration to the escalating arms race—particularly the nuclear-arms race—with a view to initiating due procedures, in accordance with Article 26 of the Charter of the United Nations, for bringing it to a halt,

Having regard to the existing reality that the Security Council has not yet given any consideration to the question of the escalating arms race, as provided for in the aforesaid resolution,

1. *Calls upon* the Security Council, and particularly its permanent members, to initiate due procedures in conformity with the provisions of the aforesaid resolution;

2. *Requests* the Secretary-General to report thereon to the General Assembly at its forty-first session.

General Assembly resolution 40/151 A

16 December 1985   Meeting 117   123-1-23 (recorded vote)

Approved by First Committee (A/40/946) by recorded vote (108-1-22), 19 November (meeting 42); draft by Cyprus (A/C.1/40/L.9/Rev.1); agenda item 61 *(h)*.
Meeting numbers. GA 40th session: 1st Committee 3-32, 42; plenary 117.

Recorded vote in Assembly as follows:

In favour: Afghanistan, Algeria, Angola, Antigua and Barbuda, Argentina, Bahamas, Bahrain, Bangladesh, Benin, Bhutan, Bolivia, Botswana, Brazil, Brunei Darussalam, Bulgaria, Burkina Faso, Burma, Burundi, Byelorussian SSR, Cameroon, Cape Verde, Central African Republic, Chad, Chile, China, Colombia, Comoros, Congo, Costa Rica, Cuba, Cyprus, Czechoslovakia, Democratic Kampuchea, Democratic Yemen, Djibouti, Dominican Republic, Ecuador, Egypt, El Salvador, Equatorial Guinea, Ethiopia, Fiji, Gabon, Gambia, German Democratic Republic, Ghana, Greece, Guatemala, Guinea, Guinea-Bissau, Guyana, Haiti, Honduras, Hungary, India, Indonesia, Iran, Iraq, Ivory Coast, Jamaica, Jordan, Kenya, Kuwait, Lao People's Democratic Republic, Lebanon, Lesotho, Liberia, Libyan Arab Jamahiriya, Madagascar, Malaysia, Maldives, Mali, Mauritania, Mauritius, Mexico, Mongolia, Morocco, Mozambique, Nepal, Nicaragua, Niger, Nigeria, Oman, Pakistan, Panama, Papua New Guinea, Paraguay, Peru, Philippines, Poland, Qatar, Romania, Rwanda, Saint Lucia, Saint Vincent and the Grenadines, Samoa, Sao Tome and Principe, Saudi Arabia, Senegal, Seychelles, Sierra Leone, Singapore, Somalia, Sri Lanka, Sudan, Suriname, Swaziland, Syrian Arab Republic, Thailand, Togo, Trinidad and Tobago, Tunisia, Uganda, Ukrainian SSR, USSR, United Arab Emirates, United Republic of Tanzania, Uruguay, Vanuatu, Venezuela, Viet Nam, Yugoslavia, Zambia.

Against: United States.

Abstaining: Australia, Austria, Belgium, Canada, Denmark, Finland, France, Germany, Federal Republic of, Grenada, Iceland, Ireland, Israel, Italy, Japan, Luxembourg, Malta, Netherlands, New Zealand, Norway, Portugal, Spain, Sweden, United Kingdom.

The Assembly adopted a number of other texts on security issues relating to disarmament, among them resolutions on strengthening security and co-operation in the Mediterranean region (**40/157**), implementing the 1970 Declaration on strengthening international security (**40/158**) and implementing the collective security provisions of the United Nations Charter (**40/159**).

The Assembly also adopted three resolutions (**40/156 A-C**) on the question of Antarctica.

Study on concepts of security

The Group of Governmental Experts to Carry Out a Comprehensive Study of Concepts of Security, established following a 1983 Assembly request,[37] completed its work and submitted the study to the Secretary-General in July 1985.[38]

The Group—13 experts from Algeria, Argentina, Australia, China, the German Democratic Republic, India, the Philippines, Romania, Sweden, Uganda, the USSR, Venezuela and Yugoslavia—which had held one session in 1984,[39] held three sessions in New York in 1985 (7-18 January, 8-19 April and 8-19 July) under the chairmanship of Anders Ferm (Sweden) and adopted the study by consensus.

The study contained five chapters: introduction, overview of security concepts, problems and threats in international security, measures to promote international peace and security, and conclusions and recommendations. It defined security as a condition in which States considered that there was no danger of military attack, political pressure or economic coercion, so that they were able to pursue freely their own development and progress. Noting the universal threat posed by the nuclear-arms race, the Group recognized that all nations had not only the right to defend their own security but also the responsibility to ensure that national policies did not jeopardize global security. It stressed that nations should move towards common security, and recommended actions towards: renewed disarmament efforts to reduce the risk of war, in particular nuclear war; maintenance of the rule of law in international relations through the strict observance of the United Nations Charter and effective application of the collective security concept; decolonization and elimination of *apartheid;* and political and economic co-operation for development and security.

GENERAL ASSEMBLY ACTION

On the recommendation of the First Committee, the General Assembly, on 12 December, adopted **resolution 40/94 E** without vote.

Comprehensive study of concepts of security
The General Assembly,

Recalling its resolution 38/188 H of 20 December 1983, by which it requested the Secretary-General to carry out, with the assistance of qualified governmental experts, a comprehensive study of concepts of security,

Having examined the report of the Secretary-General transmitting the study undertaken by the Group of Governmental Experts to Carry Out a Comprehensive Study of Concepts of Security,

1. *Takes note* of the comprehensive study on concepts of security;

2. *Expresses its appreciation* to the Secretary-General and to the Group of Governmental Experts to Carry Out a Comprehensive Study of Concepts of Security, which assisted him in the preparation of the study;

3. *Commends* the study and its conclusions to the attention of all Member States;

4. *Invites* all Member States to inform the Secretary-General, no later than 30 April 1986, of their views regarding the study;

5. *Requests* the Secretary-General to make the necessary arrangements for the reproduction of the study as a United Nations publication and to give it the widest possible distribution;

6. *Requests* the Secretary-General to prepare for the General Assembly at its forty-first session a report containing the views of Member States received regarding the study.

General Assembly resolution 40/94 E

12 December 1985   Meeting 113   Adopted without vote

Approved by First Committee (A/40/976) without vote, 14 November (meeting 37); 17-nation draft (A/C.1/40/L.29); agenda item 68 *(c)*.

Sponsors: Algeria, Argentina, Australia, Austria, Bahamas, Bolivia, China, Colombia, Ecuador, Finland, Morocco, Philippines, Romania, Sweden, Uganda, Venezuela, Yugoslavia.
Meeting numbers. GA 40th session: 1st Committee 3-32, 37; plenary 113.

In explanation of position, the Federal Republic of Germany, Italy, Japan and the USSR stated that they had certain reservations about the study and would communicate their full views later. The Federal Republic of Germany added that it considered the Group's membership to have been insufficiently balanced.

Study on deterrence

In pursuance of a 1984 General Assembly decision,[40] the Secretary-General appointed a group of governmental experts—from Argentina, Egypt, the German Democratic Republic, the Federal Republic of Germany, India, Sweden, the USSR and the United States—to carry out a study on "Deterrence: its implications for disarmament and the arms race, negotiated arms reductions and international security and other related matters". The eight-member Group held two sessions in 1985—29 April to 3 May in New York, and 7 to 18 October at Geneva—under the chairmanship of K. Subrahmanyam (India). At its first session, it agreed on an outline for the draft study and exchanged views on specific points that should be reflected in each chapter; at the second, it considered individual contributions and outlined its future work. Its third and final session was scheduled for March 1986 in New York.

Naval arms race

Proposed negotiations

Disarmament Commission consideration. The Disarmament Commission[17] devoted two plenary meetings in 1985 to the question of curbing the naval arms race, having before it a working paper by Bulgaria, the German Democratic Republic and the USSR,[41] listing a number of areas the Commission might consider with a view to negotiating on naval disarmament. In response to a 1984 Assembly resolution,[42] 15 Governments submitted, in 1985, their views regarding the holding of negotiations aimed at limiting and reducing naval armaments.[43]

Divergent views on the topic were expressed in the Commission. Some delegations called for paving the way for negotiations, while others deemed it inappropriate to consider the question in view of what they felt was the imbalanced nature of the 1984 resolution[42] and in advance of the finalization of the study being prepared by the Secretary-General (see p. 30). Some further expressed their concern at the nuclear aspect of the naval arms race. In the absence of a consensus, the Commission decided to refer the question to the Assembly.

GENERAL ASSEMBLY ACTION

On 12 December, the General Assembly, on the recommendation of the First Committee, adopted **resolution 40/94 I** by recorded vote.

Curbing the naval arms race: limitation and reduction of naval armaments and extension of confidence-building measures to seas and oceans

The General Assembly,

Recalling its resolutions 38/188 F of 20 December 1983 and 39/151 I of 17 December 1984,

Convinced that all channels of the arms race, in particular the nuclear-arms race, should be effectively covered by the efforts to halt and reverse it,

Disturbed by the growing threat to peace, international security and global stability posed by the continuing escalation of the naval arms race,

Alarmed by the even more frequent use of naval fleets or other naval formations for demonstrations or use of force and as an instrument to exert pressure against sovereign States, especially developing countries, to interfere in their internal affairs, to commit acts of armed aggression and intervention and to preserve the remnants of the colonial system,

Aware that the growing presence of naval fleets and the intensification of the naval activities of some States in conflict areas or far from their own shores increase tensions in those areas and could adversely affect the security of the international sea lanes there, the freedom of navigation and the exploitation of maritime resources,

Firmly convinced that the undertaking of urgent steps to curb military confrontation at sea would be a significant contribution to preventing war, especially nuclear war, and to strengthening peace and international security,

Aware of the numerous initiatives and concrete proposals to undertake effective measures aimed at limiting naval activities, limiting and reducing naval armaments and extending confidence-building measures to seas and oceans,

Convinced that such measures should be worked out and implemented with due regard to the principle of not harming the legitimate security interests of any State concerned,

Stressing once again the importance of relevant measures of a regional character, such as the implementation of the Declaration of the Indian Ocean as a Zone of Peace and the transformation of the Mediterranean into a zone of peace, security and co-operation,

Reaffirming once again that seas and oceans, being of vital importance to mankind, should be used exclusively for peaceful purposes in accordance with the régime established by the United Nations Convention on the Law of the Sea,

Taking note of the report of the Secretary-General[44] and other documents, submitted in pursuance of resolutions 38/188 F and 39/151 I, which contain the replies of Member States, including a major naval Power, on the modalities for negotiations, as well as various specific ideas and new proposals for joint measures on curbing the naval arms race and naval activities,

Noting with satisfaction that the prevailing view expressed in these replies strongly favours an early commencement of negotiations aimed at curbing the naval arms race and naval activities, strengthening confidence and security at sea and reducing naval armaments,

Taking note of the study on the naval arms race[45] carried out by the Secretary-General with the assistance of the Group of Governmental Experts to Carry Out a Comprehensive Study on the Naval Arms Race, Naval Forces and Naval Arms Systems,

Considering that the discussion on the subject that has taken place at the 1985 substantive session of the Disarmament Commission constitutes a valuable initial step in the common search for ways and means which could ensure proper conditions for more detailed and thorough consideration of the issue of curbing the naval arms race, with a view to holding appropriate negotiations,

1. *Appeals once again* to all Member States, in particular to nuclear-weapon States and other major naval Powers, to refrain from enlarging their naval presence and activities in areas of conflict or tension, or far from their own shores;

2. *Reaffirms once again its recognition* of the urgent need to start negotiations with the participation of the major naval Powers, in particular the nuclear-weapon States, and other interested States on the limitation of naval activities, the limitation and reduction of naval armaments and the extension of confidence-building measures to seas and oceans, especially to areas with the busiest international sea lanes or to regions where the probability of conflict situations is high;

3. *Invites* Member States, particularly the major naval Powers, including the nuclear-weapon States, to consider the possibility of holding direct consultations, bilateral and/or multilateral, with a view to preparing the opening at an early date of such negotiations;

4. *Also invites* Member States, especially those that have not yet done so, to communicate to the Secretary-General not later than April 1986 their views concerning the modalities for holding the multilateral negotiations referred to above, including the possibilities for holding them at the Conference on Disarmament at Geneva;

5. *Requests* the Disarmament Commission to continue the consideration of this question as a matter of priority in an appropriate subsidiary body, taking due account of the proposals made and the views expressed on the subject-matter contained in the replies of Member States to the Secretary-General, in the verbatim records of the Disarmament Commission, in the working papers and the study on the naval arms race, as well as of future initiatives, with a view to submitting its recommendations to the General Assembly at its forty-first session;

6. *Decides* to include in the provisional agenda of its forty-first session the item entitled "Curbing the naval arms race: limitation and reduction of naval armaments and extension of confidence-building measures to seas and oceans".

General Assembly resolution 40/94 I

12 December 1985   Meeting 113   71-19-59 (recorded vote)

Approved by First Committee (A/40/976) by recorded vote (56-19-56), 18 November (meeting 40); 8-nation draft (A/C.1/40/L.46/Rev.1); agenda item 68 *(i)*.
Sponsors: Bulgaria, Democratic Yemen, German Democratic Republic, Lao People's Democratic Republic, Libyan Arab Jamahlrlya, Poland, Syrian Arab Republic, Viet Nam.
Meeting numbers. GA 40th session: 1st Committee 3-33, 40; plenary 113.

Recorded vote in Assembly as follows:

In favour: Afghanistan, Algeria, Angola, Argentina, Bahrain, Benin, Bolivia, Botswana, Brazil, Bulgaria, Burkina Faso, Byelorussian SSR, Cape Verde, Chad,[a] Congo, Cuba, Cyprus, Czechoslovakia, Democratic Yemen, El Salvador, Ethiopia, German Democratic Republic, Ghana, Grenada, Guinea, Guinea-Bissau, Guyana, Hungary, Indonesia, Iran, Iraq, Jordan, Kenya, Kuwait, Lao People's Democratic

Republic, Lebanon, Lesotho, Liberia, Libyan Arab Jamahiriya, Madagascar, Malawi, Mali, Malta, Mexico, Mongolia, Mozambique, Nicaragua, Nigeria, Poland, Qatar, Romania, Rwanda, Saudi Arabia, Seychelles, Swaziland, Syrian Arab Republic, Togo, Tunisia, Uganda, Ukrainian SSR, USSR, United Arab Emirates, United Republic of Tanzania, Uruguay,[a] Venezuela, Viet Nam, Yemen, Yugoslavia, Zaire, Zambia, Zimbabwe.
Against: Australia, Belgium, Canada, Denmark, France, Germany, Federal Republic of, Iceland, Israel, Italy, Japan, Luxembourg, Netherlands, New Zealand, Norway, Portugal, Spain, Turkey, United Kingdom, United States.
Abstaining: Antigua and Barbuda, Austria, Bahamas, Bangladesh, Barbados, Bhutan, Brunei Darussalam, Burma, Central African Republic, Chile, China, Colombia, Comoros, Democratic Kampuchea, Djibouti, Dominican Republic, Ecuador, Egypt, Equatorial Guinea, Fiji, Finland, Gabon, Greece, Guatemala, Haiti, Honduras, India, Ireland, Ivory Coast, Jamaica, Malaysia, Maldives, Mauritania, Mauritius, Nepal, Niger, Oman, Pakistan, Panama, Papua New Guinea, Paraguay, Peru, Philippines, Saint Christopher and Nevis, Saint Lucia, Saint Vincent and the Grenadines, Samoa, Senegal, Sierra Leone, Singapore, Solomon Islands, Somalia, Sri Lanka, Sudan, Suriname, Sweden, Thailand, Trinidad and Tobago, Vanuatu.
[a]Later advised the Secretariat it had intended to abstain.

The United Kingdom considered the initiative flawed and irrelevant, and asserted that the USSR had unilaterally proposed limiting naval deployments only in areas used extensively by Western navies. Pointing, as did the United Kingdom, to the existing geographical disparities between major naval Powers, the Netherlands believed the text to be superfluous in view of a draft resolution on the naval arms study (see below), and that some notions in the preamble and paragraphs 1 and 2 were an insufficient basis for fruitful consideration of the issues in the Conference on Disarmament.

India, also explaining its vote on the naval arms study (see below), stated that detaching the naval arms race from the wider issues of the nuclear-arms race and of general and complete disarmament distorted established priorities regarding disarmament. Colombia supported the curbing of the naval arms race, but could not accept many of the text's formulations.

Benin stressed that African States had not been pressured to vote in favour. Democratic Yemen felt the United Kingdom was crying over the loss of its historical colonialism. Argentina supported the request for the nuclear-weapon States to refrain from increasing their naval activities in areas of conflict or tension or far from their own shores, such as in the South Atlantic. The USSR said the draft was non-discriminatory and rightly expressed alarm at the use of naval forces to exert pressure against sovereign States.

Experts' study

In July 1985, the Group of Governmental Experts to Carry Out a Comprehensive Study on the Naval Arms Race, Naval Forces and Naval Arms Systems—which had held two sessions in 1984[44] and two in 1985 since it was set up in response to a 1983 General Assembly request[46]—completed and adopted its study by consensus, which the Secretary-General submitted to the Assembly in September.[45] The Group—seven experts from China, France, Gabon, Indonesia, the Netherlands, Peru and Sweden—held its third and fourth sessions in New York, from 4 to 15 March and from 17 to 26 July 1985, under the chairmanship of Ali Alatas (Indonesia).

The study comprised eight chapters: general background and setting, development of naval capabilities, naval forces and naval arms systems, applications and uses of naval capabilities, maritime legal context, implications for security and the peaceful uses of the seas, possible measures of disarmament and confidence-building, and summary and conclusions. It examined, as possible disarmament and confidence-building measures, restraints—of quantitative, qualitative or technological, geographic and/or mission nature—as well as verification, and modernization of the laws of sea warfare. Noting that some 71 per cent of the earth's surface was sea and over two thirds of the world's human population lived within 300 kilometres of a sea coast, the Group noted the need for more effective internationally accepted ocean-management policies, and warned that the widened national responsibilities under the United Nations Convention on the Law of the Sea[47] should not be misused to justify expanding and utilizing naval force.

After summarizing their findings, the experts identified two basic objectives for action: achieving, by negotiation, measures of naval arms limitation and reduction—both nuclear and conventional—in the overall context of halting and reversing the arms race in general; and exploring ways in which naval organization, capabilities and experience might contribute to establishing improved ocean-management policies for the peaceful uses of the world's seas.

GENERAL ASSEMBLY ACTION

On 12 December, the General Assembly, on the recommendation of the First Committee, adopted **resolution 40/94 F** by recorded vote.

Study on the naval arms race

The General Assembly,

Recalling its resolution 38/188 G of 20 December 1983, by which it requested the Secretary-General, with the assistance of qualified governmental experts, to carry out a comprehensive study on the naval arms race,

Reaffirming its concern about the naval buildup and the development of naval arms systems,

Having examined the report of the Secretary-General transmitting the study carried out by the Group of Governmental Experts to Carry Out a Comprehensive Study on the Naval Arms Race, Naval Forces and Naval Arms Systems,

1. *Takes note with satisfaction* of the study on the naval arms race;

2. *Expresses its appreciation* to the Secretary-General and to the Group of Governmental Experts to Carry Out a Comprehensive Study on the Naval Arms Race,

Naval Forces and Naval Arms Systems which assisted him in the preparation of the study;

3. *Commends* the study and its conclusions to the attention of all Member States;

4. *Invites* all Member States to inform the Secretary-General, no later than 5 April 1986, of their views concerning the study;

5. *Requests* the Secretary-General to make the necessary arrangements for the reproduction of the study as a United Nations publication and to give it the widest possible distribution;

6. *Requests* the Secretary-General to prepare for the Disarmament Commission at its substantive session in May 1986 a compilation of the views received from Member States regarding this issue;

7. *Requests* the Disarmament Commission to consider, at its forthcoming session in 1986, the issues contained in the study on the naval arms race, both its substantive content and its conclusions, taking into account all other relevant present and future proposals, with a view to facilitating the identification of possible measures in the field of naval arms reductions and disarmament, pursued within the framework of progress towards general and complete disarmament, as well as confidence-building measures in this field, and to report on its deliberations and recommendations to the General Assembly at its forty-first session;

8. *Decides* to include in the provisional agenda of its forty-first session an item entitled "Naval armaments and disarmament".

General Assembly resolution 40/94 F

12 December 1985   Meeting 113   146-1-3 (recorded vote)

Approved by First Committee (A/40/976) by recorded vote (131-1-3), 18 November (meeting 40); 14-nation draft (A/C.1/40/L.36); agenda item 68 *(b)*.

Sponsors: Australia, Austria, China, Finland, France, Gabon, Iceland, Indonesia, Mexico, Netherlands, Peru, Sri Lanka, Sweden, Yugoslavia.

Meeting numbers. GA 40th session: 1st Committee 3-32, 36, 40; plenary 113.

Recorded vote in Assembly as follows:

In favour: Afghanistan, Algeria, Angola, Antigua and Barbuda, Argentina, Australia, Austria, Bahamas, Bahrain, Bangladesh, Barbados, Belgium, Benin, Bhutan, Bolivia, Botswana, Brazil, Brunei Darussalam, Bulgaria, Burkina Faso, Burma, Burundi, Byelorussian SSR, Canada, Cape Verde, Central African Republic, Chad, Chile, China, Comoros, Congo, Cuba, Cyprus, Czechoslovakia, Democratic Kampuchea, Democratic Yemen, Denmark, Djibouti, Dominican Republic, Ecuador, Egypt, El Salvador, Equatorial Guinea, Ethiopia, Fiji, Finland, France, Gabon, German Democratic Republic, Germany, Federal Republic of, Ghana, Greece, Guatemala, Guinea, Guinea-Bissau, Guyana, Haiti, Honduras, Hungary, Iceland, Indonesia, Iran, Iraq, Ireland, Israel, Italy, Ivory Coast, Jamaica, Japan, Jordan, Kenya, Kuwait, Lao People's Democratic Republic, Lebanon, Lesotho, Liberia, Libyan Arab Jamahiriya, Luxembourg, Madagascar, Malawi, Malaysia, Maldives, Mali, Malta, Mauritania, Mauritius, Mexico, Mongolia, Morocco, Mozambique, Nepal, Netherlands, New Zealand, Nicaragua, Niger, Nigeria, Norway, Oman, Pakistan, Panama, Papua New Guinea, Paraguay, Peru, Philippines, Poland, Portugal, Qatar, Romania, Rwanda, Saint Lucia, Saint Vincent and the Grenadines, Samoa, Sao Tome and Principe, Saudi Arabia, Senegal, Sierra Leone, Singapore, Solomon Islands, Somalia, Spain, Sri Lanka, Sudan, Suriname, Swaziland, Sweden, Syrian Arab Republic, Thailand, Togo, Trinidad and Tobago, Tunisia, Turkey, Uganda, Ukrainian SSR, USSR, United Arab Emirates, United Kingdom, United Republic of Tanzania, Uruguay, Vanuatu, Venezuela, Viet Nam, Yemen, Yugoslavia, Zaire, Zambia, Zimbabwe.

Against: United States.

Abstaining: Grenada, India, Saint Christopher and Nevis.

Explaining its vote, the United States asserted that any study that focused on naval forces in isolation, ignoring the geographical factors and threats which made maritime forces necessary in the first place, would be skewed against those nations and groups of States with vital maritime interests to defend; referring the study to the Commission, it added, diverted that body's attention from more appropriate pursuits. India explained its vote in conjunction with the text that became resolution 40/94 I (see p. 30).

The USSR said the study, while reflecting many of its proposals, contained unbalanced arguments, unjustified attempts to blame the USSR, and inaccurate statistics; the study having been completed, it was unwarranted further to delay negotiations on curbing naval armaments. Bulgaria expressed reservations regarding some of the study's conclusions. The United Kingdom, while not sharing all the views expressed on the topic, believed that the resolution, supported by a broadly-based group of countries, offered a reasonable basis for the Commission's work. Argentina said the study confirmed the views of those who had wanted the subject of the naval arms race to be dealt with.

Prevention of an arms race on the sea-bed

Consideration by the Conference on Disarmament. In its 1985 consideration of further disarmament measures for preventing an arms race on the sea-bed, the Conference on Disarmament[19] heard the view that the scope of the Treaty on the Prohibition of the Emplacement of Nuclear Weapons and Other Weapons of Mass Destruction on the Sea-Bed and the Ocean Floor and in the Subsoil Thereof[48] should be broadened, that its provisions governing procedures for verification and compliance should be improved and that access to information on relevant technological developments should be facilitated. It was also stated that the continuing deployment of nuclear weapons throughout the seas threatened all coastal States and it was, therefore, necessary to begin negotiations on the question. The Treaty, which had entered into force in May 1972, had 75 parties as at the end of 1985. The delegation of one of the three depositary States—the USSR, the United Kingdom and the United States— considered the Treaty to be fulfilling its objectives, while another depositary State expressed readiness to negotiate on the full demilitarization of the sea-bed.

GENERAL ASSEMBLY ACTION

On 12 December, the General Assembly adopted **resolution 40/94 J** without vote, as recommended by the First Committee.

Further measures in the field of disarmament for the prevention of an arms race on the sea-bed, the ocean floor and in the subsoil thereof

The General Assembly,

Recalling its resolution 38/188 B of 20 December 1983, in which it reiterated its hope for the widest possible adherence to the Treaty on the Prohibition of the Emplacement of Nuclear Weapons and Other Weapons of Mass Destruction on the Sea-Bed and the Ocean Floor and in the Subsoil Thereof, called again upon all States to refrain from any action which might lead to the extension of the arms race to the sea-bed and ocean floor, and also requested the Conference on Disarmament to proceed promptly with consideration of further measures in the field of disarmament for the prevention of an arms race on the sea-bed, the ocean floor and in the subsoil thereof,

Taking note of the part of the report of the Conference on Disarmament on its consideration of further measures in the field of disarmament for the prevention of an arms race on the sea-bed, the ocean floor and in the subsoil thereof,

Noting that the Third United Nations Conference on the Law of the Sea had concluded and that the United Nations Convention on the Law of the Sea was opened for signature on 10 December 1982,

Emphasizing the interest of all States, including specifically the interest of developing countries, in the progress of the exploration and use of the sea-bed and the ocean floor and its resources for peaceful purposes,

Requests the Conference on Disarmament, in consultation with the States parties to the Treaty on the Prohibition of the Emplacement of Nuclear Weapons and Other Weapons of Mass Destruction on the Sea-Bed and the Ocean Floor and in the Subsoil Thereof, taking into account existing proposals and any relevant technological developments, to continue its consideration of further measures in the field of disarmament for the prevention of an arms race on the sea-bed, the ocean floor and in the subsoil thereof.

General Assembly resolution 40/94 J

12 December 1985   Meeting 113   Adopted without vote

Approved by First Committee (A/40/976) without vote, 18 November (meeting 40); 5-nation draft (A/C.1/40/L.53/Rev.2); agenda item 68 *(a)*.

Sponsors: Cameroon, Canada, Poland, Romania, Ukrainian SSR.

Meeting numbers. GA 40th session: 1st Committee 3-32, 40; plenary 113.

Proposed world disarmament conference

The General Assembly continued discussion in 1985, as it had done annually since 1971, of the proposal for convening a world disarmament conference—an idea it first endorsed in 1965[49]—but made no further progress, as the basic positions of nuclear-weapon States remained largely unchanged.

In December, the Assembly renewed the mandate of the 40-member *Ad Hoc* Committee on the World Disarmament Conference (resolution 40/154).

***Ad Hoc* Committee consideration.** The *Ad Hoc* Committee on the World Disarmament Conference held two sessions in New York in 1985: four meetings each between 22 and 25 April and between 15 and 19 July. Its annual report to the Assembly[50] contained the updated views of the five nuclear-weapon States regarding the holding of such a conference. The Committee, which had been discussing the question since it first met in 1974,[51] also informed the Assembly that, through its Chairman, it had maintained close contact with those States so as to remain currently informed of their attitudes.

According to the report, the USSR continued to support the convening of a conference and expressed readiness to promote the adoption of a decision on preparations for it, including the dates.

China remained ready to support the idea, if the majority of Member States favoured a conference to discuss how the two super-Powers should take the lead in drastically reducing their armaments.

In view of the continuing deadlock on the question, France said it had no objection to the *Ad Hoc* Committee's studying the possibility of spacing its meetings. The United Kingdom maintained that, in the current international climate, no useful purpose would be served by preparing for a conference and doubted the usefulness of further Committee meetings. That view continued to be expressed by the United States, which again felt it premature to convene a conference, in view of insufficient political agreement on the conditions for, and on the disarmament issues central to, such a conference.

In its conclusions, the *Ad Hoc* Committee reiterated that the idea of a world disarmament conference had wide support, though with varying degrees of emphasis and differences regarding conditions and aspects related to its convening, including the deteriorating international situation; and that no consensus on convening a conference under current conditions had been reached among the nuclear-weapon States, whose participation was widely deemed essential. It suggested that the Assembly might renew the Committee's mandate and request it to maintain close contact with the nuclear-weapon and all other States and to consider any comments and observations which might be made to the Committee.

GENERAL ASSEMBLY ACTION

On the recommendation of the First Committee, the General Assembly, on 16 December, adopted **resolution 40/154** without vote, thereby renewing the *Ad Hoc* Committee's mandate.

World Disarmament Conference

The General Assembly,

Recalling its resolutions 2833(XXVI) of 16 December 1971, 2930(XXVII) of 29 November 1972, 3183(XXVIII) of 18 December 1973, 3260(XXIX) of 9 December 1974, 3469(XXX) of 11 December 1975, 31/190 of 21 December 1976, 32/89 of 12 December 1977, 33/69 of 14 December 1978, 34/81 of 11 December 1979, 35/151 of 12 December 1980, 36/91 of 9 December 1981, 37/97 of 13 December 1982, 38/186 of 20 December 1983 and 39/150 of 17 December 1984,

Reiterating its conviction that all the peoples of the world have a vital interest in the success of disarmament negotiations and that all States should be in a position to contribute to the adoption of measures for the achievement of this goal,

Stressing anew its conviction that a world disarmament conference, adequately prepared and convened at an appropriate time, could provide the realization of such an aim and that the co-operation of all nuclear-weapon Powers would considerably facilitate its attainment,

Taking note of the report of the *Ad Hoc* Committee on the World Disarmament Conference,

Recalling that, in paragraph 122 of the Final Document of the Tenth Special Session of the General Assembly, it decided that, at the earliest appropriate time, a world disarmament conference should be convened with universal participation and with adequate preparation,

Recalling also that, in paragraph 23 of the Declaration of the 1980s as the Second Disarmament Decade, contained in the annex to its resolution 35/46 of 3 December 1980, the General Assembly considered it pertinent also to recall that in paragraph 122 of the Final Document of the Tenth Special Session it had stated that at the earliest appropriate time a world disarmament conference should be convened with universal participation and with adequate preparation,

1. *Notes with satisfaction* that, in paragraph 14 of its report to the General Assembly, the *Ad Hoc* Committee on the World Disarmament Conference stated the following:

"Having regard for the important requirements of a world disarmament conference to be convened at the earliest appropriate time, with universal participation and with adequate preparation, the General Assembly should take up the question at its fortieth session for further consideration, bearing in mind the relevant provisions of resolution 36/91, adopted by consensus, in particular paragraph 1 of that resolution, and resolution 39/150, also adopted by consensus";

2. *Renews* the mandate of the *Ad Hoc* Committee;

3. *Requests* the *Ad Hoc* Committee to continue to maintain close contact with the representatives of the nuclear-weapon States in order to remain currently informed of their positions, as well as with all other States, and to consider any relevant comments and observations which might be made to the Committee, especially bearing in mind paragraph 122 of the Final Document of the Tenth Special Session of the General Assembly;

4. *Requests* the *Ad Hoc* Committee to report to the General Assembly at its forty-first session;

5. *Decides* to include in the provisional agenda of its forty-first session the item entitled "World Disarmament Conference".

General Assembly resolution 40/154

16 December 1985   Meeting 117   Adopted without vote

Approved by First Committee (A/40/947) without vote, 14 November (meeting 37); 5-nation draft (A/C.1/40/L.50); agenda item 67.
Sponsors: Burundi, Peru, Poland, Spain, Sri Lanka.
Financial implications. ACABQ, A/40/7/Add.15; 5th Committee, A/40/1019; S-G, A/C.1/40/L.76, A/C.5/40/53.
Meeting numbers. GA 40th session: 1st Committee 3-33, 37; 5th Committee 56; plenary 117.

Proposed comprehensive programme of disarmament

Little progress was made in 1985 in the Conference on Disarmament[19] towards agreeing on a comprehensive programme of disarmament. Envisaged in paragraph 109 of the Final Document[15] of the General Assembly's first (1978) special session devoted to disarmament, the proposed programme had been considered annually since 1980—by the Committee on Disarmament until 1984, when it was renamed the Conference on Disarmament, and by the latter since 1984. In December 1985, the Assembly urged the Conference to continue its work in 1986 with the firm intention of submitting a draft programme to the Assembly later that year (resolution 40/152 D).

Consideration by the Conference on Disarmament. In 1985, the *Ad Hoc* Committee on the Comprehensive Programme of Disarmament, of the Conference on Disarmament,[19] held 25 meetings between 7 March and 15 August under the chairmanship of Alfonso García Robles (Mexico). It based its work on a text produced by the 1983 *Ad Hoc* Working Group[52] and discussed, for the first time, a draft introduction, which the Committee's Chairman (in his capacity as the Working Group's Chairman) had proposed at the second (1982) disarmament special session. It also had before it a draft text of the programme proposed by France, the Federal Republic of Germany, Norway, the United Kingdom and the United States, along with nine other new proposals, submitted, respectively, by Argentina (two), France (two), Morocco, the USSR, the United States, Yugoslavia and a group of socialist countries on various aspects of the programme. Contact groups were established to elaborate sections of the programme dealing with measures and stages of implementation and with machinery and procedures. In addition, consultations were held among concerned delegations to reconcile differences on other points.

Despite intensive efforts, progress remained modest. While it was possible to agree on some texts, others reflected points of difference or remained pending; it was understood that delegations could not take final positions until agreement was reached on outstanding points of difficulty and until the document was complete. The *Ad Hoc* Committee concluded that work should resume and conclude in 1986 with a view to enabling the Conference to submit a draft programme to the Assembly that year.

In comparison with the corresponding 1983 text, the new version of the draft programme contained a number of changes, mostly additions concerning questions such as the nuclear-test ban, USSR–United States negotiations on nuclear and space arms, conventional weapons and armed forces in Europe, prevention of an arms race in outer space, zones of peace in the Indian Ocean and the Mediterranean regions, verification problems, and the programme's machinery and procedures.

The *Ad Hoc* Committee's report was adopted by the Conference on 29 August as part of its report to the Assembly.[19]

On the recommendation of the First Committee, the General Assembly, on 16 December, adopted **resolution 40/152 D** without vote.

Comprehensive programme of disarmament

The General Assembly,

Recalling that in paragraph 109 of the Final Document of the Tenth Special Session of the General Assembly, the Assembly called for the elaboration of a comprehensive programme of disarmament encompassing all measures thought to be advisable in order to ensure that the goal of general and complete disarmament under effective international control becomes a reality in a world in which international peace and security prevail and in which the new international economic order is strengthened and consolidated,

Recalling also its resolution 38/183 K of 20 December 1983, in which it urged the Conference on Disarmament, as soon as it considered that the circumstances were propitious for that purpose, to renew its work on the elaboration of the comprehensive programme of disarmament previously requested, to submit to the General Assembly at its thirty-ninth session a progress report on the matter and to submit to the Assembly, not later than at its forty-first session, a complete draft of such a programme,

Recalling further its resolution 39/148 I of 17 December 1984, in which it urged that all efforts be made so that the Conference on Disarmament might resume its work on the elaboration of the comprehensive programme of disarmament early in its 1985 session with a view to submitting to the General Assembly at its forty-first session a complete draft of such a programme,

Having examined the report of the *Ad Hoc* Committee on the Comprehensive Programme of Disarmament concerning its work during the 1985 session of the Conference on Disarmament, which is an integral part of the report of the Conference,

1. *Notes* that in its report the *Ad Hoc* Committee on the Comprehensive Programme of Disarmament stated that during the 1985 session, despite intensive efforts, only modest progress was achieved;

2. *Urges* the Conference on Disarmament to resume the work on the elaboration of the comprehensive programme of disarmament at the beginning of its 1986 session with the firm intention of concluding that task and submitting to the General Assembly at its forty-first session a complete draft of the programme;

3. *Decides* to include on the provisional agenda of its forty-first session the item entitled "Comprehensive programme of disarmament: report of the Conference on Disarmament".

General Assembly resolution 40/152 D

16 December 1985   Meeting 117   Adopted without vote

Approved by First Committee (A/40/877/Add.1) without vote, 14 November (meeting 37); 13-nation draft (A/C.1/40/L.19); agenda item 65 *(k)*.
Sponsors: Algeria, Argentina, Bangladesh, Ecuador, Indonesia, Mexico, Pakistan, Romania, Sri Lanka, Sweden, Togo, Uruguay, Yugoslavia.
Meeting numbers. GA 40th session: 1st Committee 3-32, 37; plenary 117.

REFERENCES

[1]A/C.1/40/7. [2]A/CN.10/72. [3]A/41/58. [4]A/40/276-S/17138. [5]A/40/854-S/17610 & Corr.1. [6]A/40/761-S/17573. [7]A/40/228. [8]A/40/362. [9]A/40/411. [10]A/C.1/40/6. [11]A/40/900. [12]A/40/987-S/17670. [13]YUN 1978, p. 17.

(14)YUN 1982, p. 12. (15)YUN 1978, p. 39, GA res. S-10/2, 30 June 1978. (16)YUN 1982, p. 18, GA dec. S-12/24, 10 July 1982. (17)A/40/42. (18)YUN 1980, p. 102, GA res. 35/46, annex, 3 Dec. 1980. (19)A/40/27 & Corr.1. (20)YUN 1984, p. 15, GA res. 39/148 L, 17 Dec. 1984. (21)A/40/842. (22)YUN 1984, p. 17, GA res. 39/148 O, 17 Dec. 1984. (23)*Ibid.*, p. 18, GA res. 39/63 I, 12 Dec. 1984. (24)YUN 1981, p. 25, GA res. 36/92 D, 9 Dec. 1981. (25)YUN 1979, p. 86, GA res. 34/88, 11 Dec. 1979. (26)A/40/114-S/16921. (27)A/C.1/40/L.6. (28)A/CN.10/75. (29)A/CN.10/68 & Add.1-7. (30)YUN 1984, p. 20, GA res. 39/148 Q, 17 Dec. 1984. (31)YUN 1968, p. 17, GA res. 2373(XXII), annex, 12 June 1968. (32)YUN 1984, p. 98, GA res. 39/151 G, 17 Dec. 1984. (33)*Ibid.*, p. 22. (34)A/CN.10/69 & Add.1-8 & A/CN.10/71. (35)YUN 1984, p. 82, GA res. 39/63 K, 12 Dec. 1984. (36)S/16932. (37)YUN 1983, p. 83, GA res. 38/188 H, 20 Dec. 1983. (38)*Concepts of Security* (A/40/553), Sales No. E.86.IX.1. (39)YUN 1984, p. 82. (40)*Ibid.*, p. 92, GA dec. 39/423, 17 Dec. 1984. (41)A/CN.10/73 & Corr.1. (42)YUN 1984, p. 67, GA res. 39/151 I, 17 Dec. 1984. (43)A/CN.10/70 & Add.1-5. (44)YUN 1984, p. 67. (45)*The Naval Arms Race* (A/40/535), Sales No. E.86.IX.3. (46)YUN 1983, p. 68, GA res. 38/188 G, 20 Dec. 1983. (47)YUN 1982, p. 181. (48)YUN 1970, p. 18, GA res. 2660(XXV), annex, 7 Dec. 1970. (49)YUN 1965, p. 62, GA res. 2030(XX), 29 Nov. 1965. (50)A/40/28. (51)YUN 1974, p. 52. (52)YUN 1983, p. 12.

Nuclear disarmament

The Disarmament Commission, the Conference on Disarmament and the General Assembly continued to discuss in 1985 proposals for nuclear-war prevention, without reaching a consensus on how to deal with the issue at the multilateral level. As in the past, the Assembly called for efforts aimed at freezing or banning nuclear weapons, prohibiting nuclear-weapons testing, and strengthening the security of non-nuclear-weapon States, while supporting the call for nuclear non-proliferation through the establishment of nuclear-weapon-free zones.

The Assembly adopted more than two dozen resolutions in 1985 on nuclear questions, including two on bilateral negotiations (40/18 and 40/152 B) that began earlier in the year between the USSR and the United States on strategic and intermediate-range nuclear weapons. It also recommended that States parties to the 1963 Treaty Banning Nuclear Weapon Tests in the Atmosphere, in Outer Space and under Water[1] consult among themselves on the advisability of converting that Treaty into a comprehensive nuclear-test-ban treaty (40/80 B), and requested that the climatic effects of nuclear war, including nuclear winter, be studied (40/152 G).

Throughout 1985, the Secretary-General received communications calling for nuclear disarmament and other general disarmament measures (see p. 14). He also received letters referring specifically to the negotiations on reducing nuclear weapons, begun in January 1985 between the USSR and the United States (see p. 45).

The Third Review Conference of the Parties to the Treaty on the Non-Proliferation of Nuclear Weapons (NPT),[2] meeting at Geneva in mid-1985, confirmed the continuing validity of the fundamental aims of the Treaty.

Prevention of nuclear war

In the light of little progress achieved in 1985 in the Conference on Disarmament on the issue of nuclear-war prevention and non-use of nuclear weapons, the General Assembly reiterated its request that the Conference negotiate with a view to agreeing on practical measures to prevent nuclear war (resolution 40/152 Q) and on an international convention prohibiting the use or threat of use of nuclear weapons (40/151 F), and to consider elaborating an international legal instrument laying down the obligation of non-first-use of nuclear weapons (40/152 A).

The 1985 Nobel Peace Prize was awarded to the International Physicians for the Prevention of Nuclear War.

Consideration by the Conference on Disarmament. In 1985, the Conference on Disarmament[3] had before it working papers submitted by Australia, listing the responsibilities of nuclear-weapon States and those of all States with respect to preventing nuclear war; the Federal Republic of Germany, suggesting issues for consideration; and Romania, specifying topics to facilitate negotiations.

As again requested by the Assembly in 1984,[4] the Conference held consultations on an appropriate organizational arrangement to deal with the item, including proposals for setting up a subsidiary body, but no agreement could be reached. On 30 July, the group of 21 (the non-aligned and neutral States within the Conference—Algeria, Argentina, Brazil, Burma, Cuba, Egypt, Ethiopia, India, Indonesia, Iran, Kenya, Mexico, Morocco, Nigeria, Pakistan, Peru, Sri Lanka, Sweden, Venezuela, Yugoslavia, Zaire) put forward a draft mandate for an *ad hoc* committee, which would consider all proposals on preventing nuclear war. The draft mandate was supported by the group of socialist countries and by China. The Western delegations, however, stated that they were not in a position to associate themselves with a consensus on the proposed mandate.

Disarmament Commission consideration. Eliminating the danger of nuclear war was considered by the Disarmament Commission in 1985 in conjunction with a general approach to negotiations on nuclear and conventional disarmament (see p. 25).

Report of the Secretary-General. In response to a 1984 Assembly request,[4] the Secretary-General submitted—to the Conference in June

1985[5] and to the Assembly in August[6]—a report on suitable steps to expedite effective action for preventing nuclear war. In addition to the replies received from 35 Governments containing their views on such steps, the report contained an introduction summarizing the relevant paragraphs of the 1978 Final Document of the Assembly's tenth special session[7] and the views held on the question, respectively, by non-aligned and neutral, socialist, and Western countries, as well as by China; the report also included a survey of relevant developments since 1961. It concluded that removing the threat of nuclear war was the highest-priority task facing the international community, and that the most effective guarantee against the danger of nuclear war was nuclear disarmament which would eventually lead to agreements on eliminating nuclear weapons under effective international control.

GENERAL ASSEMBLY ACTION

In December 1985, the Assembly adopted two resolutions—**40/152 A** and **Q**—on nuclear-war prevention and non-use of nuclear weapons. It also again took up the question of a proposed convention to prohibit nuclear-weapon use (see p. 38).

Two other proposals on preventing nuclear war were withdrawn at the request of their sponsors. A draft by Cyprus[8] would have had the Assembly outlaw nuclear weapons and prohibit their future development or production. The other draft, on preventing war in the nuclear age, sponsored by Canada, Denmark, the Federal Republic of Germany, Italy, Japan, Norway, Portugal, Turkey and the United Kingdom,[9] was a follow-up to another Western-country text submitted and withdrawn in 1984.[10] It covered renunciation of force, restraint, balanced disarmament measures and confidence-building, and added the importance of regional efforts at peace-keeping. It would also have had the Assembly reject policies aimed at achieving military superiority in the place of balance, stability and undiminished security for all States; and declare that a nuclear war could not be won and that a conventional war might involve the risk of escalation to nuclear war.

On the recommendation of the First Committee, the General Assembly, on 16 December, adopted **resolution 40/152 A** by recorded vote.

Non-use of nuclear weapons and prevention of nuclear war

The General Assembly,

Alarmed by the threat to the survival of mankind posed by the existence of nuclear weapons and the continuing arms race, in particular in the nuclear field,

Recalling that, in accordance with paragraph 20 of the Final Document of the Tenth Special Session of the General Assembly, the first special session devoted to disarmament, effective measures of nuclear disarmament and the prevention of nuclear war have the highest priority,

Recalling also that this commitment was reaffirmed by the General Assembly at its twelfth special session, the second special session devoted to disarmament,

Bearing in mind its relevant resolutions on this subject,

Reaffirming that the most effective guarantee against the danger of nuclear war and the use of nuclear weapons is nuclear disarmament and the complete elimination of nuclear weapons,

Recalling that, in paragraph 58 of the Final Document of the Tenth Special Session, it is stated that all States should actively participate in efforts to bring about conditions in international relations among States in which a code of peaceful conduct of nations in international affairs could be agreed upon and which would preclude the use or threat of use of nuclear weapons,

Reaffirming also that the nuclear-weapon States have the primary responsibility for nuclear disarmament and for undertaking measures aimed at preventing the outbreak of nuclear war, *inter alia*, by establishing corresponding norms regulating relations between them,

Commemorating the fortieth anniversary of the end of the Second World War, the most destructive and bloody war in the history of mankind, and also commemorating the fortieth anniversary of the founding of the United Nations,

Reaffirming its conviction that removing the threat of a world war—a nuclear war—is the most acute and urgent task of the present time,

Convinced that the renunciation of the first use of nuclear weapons is a most important and urgent measure for the prevention of nuclear war, and taking note of the broad, positive international reaction to the concept of non-first use of nuclear weapons,

1. *Considers* that the solemn declarations by two nuclear-weapon States made or reiterated at the twelfth special session of the General Assembly, concerning their respective obligations not to be the first to use nuclear weapons, offer an important avenue to decrease the danger of nuclear war;

2. *Expresses the hope* that those nuclear-weapon States that have not yet done so would consider making similar declarations with respect to not being the first to use nuclear weapons;

3. *Requests* the Conference on Disarmament to consider under its relevant agenda item, *inter alia*, the elaboration of an international instrument of a legally binding character laying down the obligation not to be the first to use nuclear weapons;

4. *Decides* to include in the provisional agenda of its forty-first session the item entitled "Non-use of nuclear weapons and prevention of nuclear war".

General Assembly resolution 40/152 A

16 December 1985   Meeting 117   123-19-7 (recorded vote)

Approved by First Committee (A/40/877/Add.1) by recorded vote (98-19-8), 20 November (meeting 44); 4-nation draft (A/C.1/40/L.7); agenda item 65 *(f)*.
Sponsors: Cuba, German Democratic Republic, Hungary, Romania.
Meeting numbers. GA 40th session: 1st Committee 3-32, 34, 44; plenary 117.

Recorded vote in Assembly as follows:

In favour: Afghanistan, Algeria, Angola, Antigua and Barbuda, Argentina, Bahamas, Bahrain, Bangladesh, Barbados, Benin, Bhutan, Bolivia, Botswana, Brunei Darussalam, Bulgaria, Burkina Faso, Burma, Burundi, Byelorussian SSR, Cameroon, Cape Verde, Central African Republic, Chad, Comoros, Congo, Cuba, Cyprus, Czechoslovakia, Democratic Yemen, Djibouti, Dominican Republic, Ecuador, Egypt, El Salvador, Equatorial Guinea, Ethiopia, Fiji, Finland, Gabon, Gambia, German Democratic Republic, Ghana, Greece, Grenada, Guatemala, Guinea, Guinea-Bissau, Guyana, Haiti, Honduras, Hungary, India, Indonesia, Iran, Iraq, Ireland, Ivory Coast, Jamaica, Jordan, Kenya, Kuwait, Lao People's Democratic Republic, Lebanon, Lesotho, Liberia, Libyan Arab Jamahiriya, Madagascar, Malawi, Malaysia, Maldives, Mali, Mauritania, Mauritius, Mexico, Mongolia, Morocco, Mozambique, Nepal, Nicaragua, Niger, Nigeria, Oman, Pakistan, Panama, Papua New Guinea, Peru, Poland, Qatar, Romania, Rwanda, Saint Lucia, Saint Vincent and the Grenadines, Samoa, Sao Tome and Principe, Saudi Arabia, Senegal, Seychelles, Sierra Leone, Somalia, Sri Lanka, Sudan, Suriname, Swaziland, Sweden, Syrian Arab Republic, Thailand, Togo, Trinidad and Tobago, Tunisia, Uganda, Ukrainian SSR, USSR, United Arab Emirates, United Republic of Tanzania, Uruguay, Vanuatu, Venezuela, Viet Nam, Yemen, Yugoslavia, Zaire, Zambia, Zimbabwe.

Against: Australia, Belgium, Canada, Denmark, France, Germany, Federal Republic of, Iceland, Israel, Italy, Japan, Luxembourg, Netherlands, New Zealand, Norway, Portugal, Spain, Turkey, United Kingdom, United States.

Abstaining: Austria, Brazil, Chile, China, Colombia, Costa Rica, Paraguay.

Explaining its vote, Norway, while fully supportive of efforts to reduce the importance of and dependence on nuclear weapons, viewed the draft as directed at the defensive strategy of the alliance to which it belonged.

Austria stressed that an obligation of non-first-use, to be credible, had to lead to a modification of military doctrines and structures, and it had to be verifiable; an agreement on non-first-use of nuclear weapons would be realistic only if the nuclear Powers ensured stability by reaching an understanding on conventional weapons.

Finland stressed that nuclear weapons should never be used under any circumstances. Similarly, Indonesia maintained that all use, not only first use, must be prohibited. Asserting that what was required was improved compliance with existing prohibitions and the obligation under the United Nations Charter for peaceful settlement of disputes, Sweden said that an international instrument by which the nuclear-weapon States would pledge non-first-use should deal exclusively with that concept without bringing in any further elements. Ireland continued to have some reservations it had voiced previously, and emphasized that the nuclear-weapon Powers needed to consider seriously what methods or agreements they might work out to provide against first use.

On 16 December, the General Assembly, on the recommendation of the First Committee, adopted **resolution 40/152 Q** by recorded vote.

Prevention of nuclear war

The General Assembly,

Alarmed by the threat to the survival of mankind posed by the existence of nuclear weapons and the continuing nuclear-arms race,

Deeply concerned by an increased danger of nuclear war as a result of the intensification of the nuclear-arms race and the serious deterioration of the international situation,

Conscious that removal of the threat of nuclear war is the most acute and urgent task of the present day,

Reiterating that it is the shared responsibility of all Member States to save succeeding generations from the scourge of another world war, which would inevitably be a nuclear war,

Recalling the provisions of paragraphs 47 to 50 and 56 to 58 of the Final Document of the Tenth Special Session of the General Assembly, regarding the procedures designed to secure the avoidance of nuclear war,

Recalling also that at the Seventh Conference of Heads of State or Government of Non-Aligned Countries, held at New Delhi from 7 to 12 March 1983, it was stated that nuclear weapons were more than weapons of war, they were instruments of mass annihilation, and that at the Conference of Ministers of Foreign Affairs of Non-Aligned Countries held at Luanda from 4 to 7 September 1985, it was stated that measures for the prevention of nuclear war and for nuclear disarmament must take into account the security interests of nuclear-weapon and non-nuclear-weapon States alike and ensure that the survival of mankind is not endangered,

Recalling further its resolutions 36/81 B of 9 December 1981, 37/78 I of 9 December 1982, 38/183 G of 20 December 1983 and, in particular, its resolution 39/148 P of 17 December 1984, in which it expressed its conviction that, in view of the urgency of this matter and the inadequacy or insufficiency of existing measures, it is necessary to devise suitable steps to expedite effective action for the prevention of nuclear war, and again requested the Conference on Disarmament to undertake, as a matter of the highest priority, negotiations with a view to achieving agreement on appropriate and practical measures for the prevention of nuclear war,

Having considered the report of the Conference on Disarmament on its 1985 session,

Noting with grave concern that the Conference on Disarmament was once again unable to start negotiations on the question during its 1985 session,

Taking into account the deliberations on this item at its fortieth session,

Convinced that the prevention of nuclear war and the reduction of the risk of nuclear war are matters of the highest priority and of vital interest to all peoples of the world,

Also convinced that the prevention of nuclear war is a problem too important to be left to the nuclear-weapon States alone,

Taking note of the report of the Secretary-General,

1. *Notes with regret* that, despite the fact that the Conference on Disarmament has discussed the question of the prevention of nuclear war for several years, it has been unable even to establish a subsidiary body to consider appropriate and practical measures to prevent it;

2. *Reiterates its conviction* that, in view of the urgency of this matter and the inadequacy or insufficiency of existing measures, it is necessary to devise suitable steps to expedite effective action for the prevention of nuclear war;

3. *Again requests* the Conference on Disarmament to undertake, as a matter of the highest priority, negotiations with a view to achieving agreement on appropriate and practical measures for the prevention of nuclear war and to establish for that purpose an *ad hoc* committee on the subject at the beginning of its 1986 session;

4. *Decides* to include in the provisional agenda of its forty-first session the item entitled "Prevention of nuclear war".

General Assembly resolution 40/152 Q

16 December 1985   Meeting 117   136-3-14 (recorded vote)

Approved by First Committee (A/40/877/Add.1) by recorded vote (110-3-15), 21 November (meeting 46); 22-nation draft (A/C.1/40/L.65/Rev.1); agenda item 65 *(h)*.

Sponsors: Algeria, Argentina, Bangladesh, Brazil, Cameroon, Colombia, Congo, Ecuador, Egypt, German Democratic Republic, India, Indonesia, Mexico, Morocco, Nigeria, Oman, Pakistan, Romania, Sudan, Uruguay, Viet Nam, Yugoslavia.

Meeting numbers. GA 40th session: 1st Committee 3-32, 36, 46; plenary 117.

Recorded vote in Assembly as follows:

In favour: Afghanistan, Algeria, Angola, Antigua and Barbuda, Argentina, Australia, Austria, Bahamas, Bahrain, Bangladesh, Barbados, Benin, Bhutan, Bolivia, Botswana, Brazil, Brunei Darussalam, Bulgaria, Burkina Faso, Burma, Burundi, Byelorussian SSR, Cameroon, Cape Verde, Central African Republic, Chad, Chile, China, Colombia, Comoros, Congo, Costa Rica, Cuba, Cyprus, Czechoslovakia, Democratic Kampuchea, Democratic Yemen, Djibouti, Dominican Republic, Ecuador, Egypt, El Salvador, Equatorial Guinea, Ethiopia, Fiji, Finland, Gabon, Gambia, German Democratic Republic, Ghana, Greece, Grenada, Guatemala, Guinea, Guinea-Bissau, Guyana, Haiti, Honduras, Hungary, India, Indonesia, Iran, Iraq, Ireland, Ivory Coast, Jordan, Kenya, Kuwait, Lao People's Democratic Republic, Lebanon, Lesotho, Liberia, Libyan Arab Jamahiriya, Madagascar, Malawi, Malaysia, Maldives, Mali, Malta, Mauritania, Mauritius, Mexico, Mongolia, Morocco, Mozambique, Nepal, New Zealand, Nicaragua, Niger, Nigeria, Oman, Pakistan, Panama, Papua New Guinea, Paraguay, Peru, Philippines, Poland, Qatar, Romania, Rwanda, Saint Lucia, Saint Vincent and the Grenadines, Samoa, Sao Tome and Principe, Saudi Arabia, Senegal, Seychelles, Sierra Leone, Singapore, Solomon Islands, Somalia, Sri Lanka, Sudan, Suriname, Swaziland, Sweden, Syrian Arab Republic, Thailand, Togo, Trinidad and Tobago, Tunisia, Uganda, Ukrainian SSR, USSR, United Arab Emirates, United Republic of Tanzania, Uruguay, Vanuatu, Venezuela, Viet Nam, Yemen, Yugoslavia, Zaire, Zambia, Zimbabwe.

Against: France, United Kingdom, United States.

Abstaining: Belgium, Canada, Denmark, Germany, Federal Republic of, Iceland, Israel, Italy, Japan, Luxembourg, Netherlands, Norway, Portugal, Spain, Turkey.

In explanation of vote, the United Kingdom said the call for negotiations in the Conference on nuclear-war prevention overlooked the fact that a number of practical measures had already been taken in that regard; respect for the Charter's provisions was the best way to prevent all war.

Proposed convention

GENERAL ASSEMBLY ACTION

On 16 December, the General Assembly adopted, by recorded vote, **resolution 40/151 F** on a proposed convention prohibiting the use of nuclear weapons. A draft convention, as annexed to a 1982[11] Assembly resolution and resubmitted in 1983[12] and 1984,[13] was again annexed to the resolution, as a basis for negotiations in the Conference on Disarmament.

Convention on the Prohibition of the Use of Nuclear Weapons

The General Assembly,

Alarmed by the threat to the survival of mankind and to the life-sustaining system posed by nuclear weapons and by their use, inherent in concepts of deterrence,

Conscious of an increased danger of nuclear war as a result of the intensification of the nuclear-arms race and the serious deterioration of the international situation,

Convinced that nuclear disarmament is essential for the prevention of nuclear war and for the strengthening of international peace and security,

Further convinced that a prohibition of the use or threat of use of nuclear weapons would be a step towards the complete elimination of nuclear weapons leading to general and complete disarmament under strict and effective international control,

Recalling that, in paragraph 58 of the Final Document of the Tenth Special Session of the General Assembly, it is stated that all States should actively participate in efforts to bring about conditions in international rela-

tions among States in which a code of peaceful conduct of nations in international affairs could be agreed upon and that would preclude the use or threat of use of nuclear weapons,

Reaffirming that the use of nuclear weapons would be a violation of the Charter of the United Nations and a crime against humanity, as declared in its resolutions 1653(XVI) of 24 November 1961, 33/71 B of 14 December 1978, 34/83 G of 11 December 1979, 35/152 D of 12 December 1980 and 36/92 I of 9 December 1981,

Noting with regret that the Conference on Disarmament, during its session in 1985, was not able to undertake negotiations with a view to achieving agreement on an international convention prohibiting the use or threat of use of nuclear weapons under any circumstances, taking as a basis the text annexed to General Assembly resolution 39/63 H of 12 December 1984,

1. *Reiterates its request* to the Conference on Disarmament to commence negotiations, as a matter of priority, in order to achieve agreement on an international convention prohibiting the use or threat of use of nuclear weapons under any circumstances, taking as a basis the text of the draft Convention on the Prohibition of the Use of Nuclear Weapons annexed to the present resolution;

2. *Further requests* the Conference on Disarmament to report to the General Assembly at its forty-first session on the results of those negotiations.

ANNEX
Draft Convention on the Prohibition of the Use of Nuclear Weapons

The States Parties to this Convention,

Alarmed by the threat to the very survival of mankind posed by the existence of nuclear weapons,

Convinced that any use of nuclear weapons constitutes a violation of the Charter of the United Nations and a crime against humanity,

Convinced that this Convention would be a step towards the complete elimination of nuclear weapons leading to general and complete disarmament under strict and effective international control,

Determined to continue negotiations for the achievement of this goal,

Have agreed as follows:

Article 1

The States Parties to this Convention solemnly undertake not to use or threaten to use nuclear weapons under any circumstances.

Article 2

This Convention shall be of unlimited duration.

Article 3

1. This Convention shall be open to all States for signature. Any State that does not sign the Convention before its entry into force in accordance with paragraph 3 of this article may accede to it at any time.

2. This Convention shall be subject to ratification by signatory States. Instruments of ratification or accession shall be deposited with the Secretary-General of the United Nations.

3. This Convention shall enter into force on the deposit of instruments of ratification by twenty-five Governments, including the Governments of the five nuclear-weapons States, in accordance with paragraph 2 of this article.

4. For States whose instruments of ratification or accession are deposited after the entry into force of this Convention, it shall enter into force on the date of the deposit of their instruments of ratification or accession.

5. The depositary shall promptly inform all signatory and acceding States of the date of each signature, the date of deposit of each instrument of ratification or accession and the date of the entry into force of this Convention, as well as of the receipt of other notices.

6. This Convention shall be registered by the depositary in accordance with Article 102 of the Charter of the United Nations.

Article 4

This Convention, of which the Arabic, Chinese, English, French, Russian and Spanish texts are equally authentic, shall be deposited with the Secretary-General of the United Nations, who shall send duly certified copies thereof to the Governments of the signatory and acceding States.

In witness whereof the undersigned, being duly authorized thereto by their respective Governments, have signed this Convention, opened for signature at _____ on the _____ day of _____ one thousand nine hundred and _____.

General Assembly resolution 40/151 F

16 December 1985   Meeting 117   126-17-6 (recorded vote)

Approved by First Committee (A/40/946) by recorded vote (106-17-5), 20 November (meeting 44); 15-nation draft (A/C.1/40/L.26); agenda item 61 *(f)*.
Sponsors: Algeria, Argentina, Bahamas, Bangladesh, Bhutan, Ecuador, Egypt, Ethiopia, India, Indonesia, Madagascar, Nigeria, Romania, Viet Nam, Yugoslavia.
Meeting numbers. GA 40th session: 1st Committee 3-33, 44; plenary 117.

Recorded vote in Assembly as follows:

In favour: Afghanistan, Algeria, Angola, Antigua and Barbuda, Argentina, Bahamas, Bahrain, Bangladesh, Barbados, Benin, Bhutan, Bolivia, Botswana, Brazil, Brunei Darussalam, Bulgaria, Burkina Faso, Burma, Burundi, Byelorussian SSR, Cameroon, Cape Verde, Central African Republic, Chad, Chile, China, Colombia, Comoros, Congo, Costa Rica, Cuba, Cyprus, Czechoslovakia, Democratic Kampuchea, Democratic Yemen, Djibouti, Dominican Republic, Ecuador, Egypt, El Salvador, Equatorial Guinea, Ethiopia, Fiji, Finland, Gabon, Gambia, German Democratic Republic, Ghana, Guatemala, Guinea, Guinea-Bissau, Guyana, Haiti, Honduras, Hungary, India, Indonesia, Iran, Iraq, Ivory Coast, Jordan, Kenya, Kuwait, Lao People's Democratic Republic, Lebanon, Lesotho, Liberia, Libyan Arab Jamahiriya, Madagascar, Malawi, Malaysia, Maldives, Mali, Malta, Mauritania, Mauritius, Mexico, Mongolia, Morocco, Mozambique, Nepal, Nicaragua, Niger, Nigeria, Oman, Pakistan, Panama, Papua New Guinea, Paraguay, Peru, Poland, Qatar, Romania, Rwanda, Saint Lucia, Saint Vincent and the Grenadines, Samoa, Sao Tome and Principe, Saudi Arabia, Senegal, Seychelles, Sierra Leone, Singapore, Somalia, Sri Lanka, Sudan, Suriname, Swaziland, Sweden, Syrian Arab Republic, Thailand, Togo, Trinidad and Tobago, Tunisia, Uganda, Ukrainian SSR, USSR, United Arab Emirates, United Republic of Tanzania, Uruguay, Vanuatu, Venezuela, Viet Nam, Yugoslavia, Zaire, Zambia.

Against: Australia, Belgium, Canada, Denmark, France, Germany, Federal Republic of, Iceland, Italy, Luxembourg, Netherlands, New Zealand, Norway, Portugal, Spain, Turkey, United Kingdom, United States.

Abstaining: Austria, Greece, Grenada, Ireland, Israel, Japan.

In explanation of vote, Greece said it believed the Conference on Disarmament was the place where a draft convention should be drawn up. Sweden expressed reservations as to the draft resolution's interpretation, in the sixth preambular paragraph, of the United Nations Charter; it added that if the use of nuclear weapons violated the Charter, there would be no obvious need for another international legal instrument in that respect.

Climatic effects of nuclear war

In December 1985, the General Assembly requested the Secretary-General, with the help of experts, to study the climatic and potential physical effects of nuclear war, including nuclear winter (resolution 40/152 G).

Report of the Secretary-General. Pursuant to the Assembly's 1984 request,[14] the Secretary-General submitted in September 1985 a report containing excerpts of all national and international scientific studies, published before 31 July, on the climatic effects of nuclear war, including nuclear winter.[15] The report had eight chapters, dealing with introduction; background; methodology, baseline cases and models, and their critique; fires and effects of smoke; dust and soot; chemical changes in the atmosphere; effects and consequences on atmosphere and climate—nuclear winter; and conclusions of various studies. An appendix contained a selective bibliography.

GENERAL ASSEMBLY ACTION

On 16 December, on the recommendation of the First Committee, the General Assembly adopted **resolution 40/152 G** by recorded vote.

Climatic effects of nuclear war, including nuclear winter

The General Assembly,

Recalling that in the Final Document of the Tenth Special Session of the General Assembly, after referring specifically to "the threat to the very survival of mankind" posed by the existence of nuclear weapons, it declared, in paragraph 18, that removing the threat of a world war—a nuclear war—is the most acute and urgent task of the present day,

Having examined the report of the Secretary-General transmitting the compilation, requested in General Assembly resolution 39/148 F of 17 December 1984, of appropriate excerpts of all national and international scientific studies on the climatic effects of nuclear war, including nuclear winter, published so far,

Noting that the conclusions of some of those studies confirm that nuclear winter and other climatic effects of nuclear war pose an unprecedented peril to all nations, even those far removed from the nuclear explosions, which would add immeasurably to the previously known dangers of nuclear war, without excluding the possibility of all the Earth being transformed into a darkened, frozen planet, where conditions would be conducive to mass extinction,

Noting also that from those conclusions and from various sections of the studies themselves it clearly follows that international efforts to carry out further systematic research are necessary,

1. *Expresses its appreciation* to the Secretary-General for the compilation of excerpts of scientific studies on the climatic effects of nuclear war, including nuclear winter, prepared in accordance with the request made in its resolution 39/148 F;

2. *Requests* the Secretary-General, with the assistance of a group of consultant experts* chosen by him, bearing in mind the advisability of wide geographical

representation and of their qualifications in a broad range of scientific fields, to carry out a study on the climatic and potential physical effects of nuclear war, including nuclear winter, which will examine, *inter alia*, its socio-economic consequences and would take into account the Secretary-General's report and the source documents from which the compilation was prepared, together with any other relevant scientific studies;

3. *Also requests* the Secretary-General to transmit the study to the General Assembly in due time for consideration at its forty-second session, in 1987;

4. *Decides* to include in the provisional agenda of its forty-second session an item entitled: "Climatic effects of nuclear war, including nuclear winter: report of the Secretary-General".

———————

*Subsequently referred to as the Group of Consultant Experts to Carry Out a Study on the Climatic and Potential Physical Effects of Nuclear War, including Nuclear Winter.

General Assembly resolution 40/152 G

16 December 1985   Meeting 117   141-1-10 (recorded vote)

Approved by First Committee (A/40/877/Add.1) by recorded vote (118-1-10), 20 November (meeting 44); 7-nation draft (A/C.1/40/L.43), orally revised; agenda item 65.
Sponsors: Bangladesh, Ecuador, India, Mexico, Pakistan, Sweden, Yugoslavia.
Financial implications. ACABQ, A/40/7/Add.15; 5th Committee, A/40/1019; S-G, A/C.1/40/L.78, A/C.5/40/57.
Meeting numbers. GA 40th session: 1st Committee 3-32, 44; 5th Committee 56; plenary 117.

Recorded vote in Assembly as follows:

In favour: Afghanistan, Algeria, Angola, Antigua and Barbuda, Argentina, Australia, Austria, Bahamas, Bahrain, Bangladesh, Barbados, Benin, Bhutan, Bolivia, Botswana, Brazil, Brunei Darussalam, Bulgaria, Burkina Faso, Burma, Burundi, Byelorussian SSR, Cameroon, Canada, Cape Verde, Central African Republic, Chad, Chile, China, Colombia, Comoros, Congo, Costa Rica, Cuba, Cyprus, Czechoslovakia, Democratic Kampuchea, Democratic Yemen, Denmark, Djibouti, Dominican Republic, Ecuador, Egypt, El Salvador, Equatorial Guinea, Ethiopia, Fiji, Finland, Gabon, Gambia, German Democratic Republic, Ghana, Greece, Guatemala, Guinea, Guinea-Bissau, Guyana, Haiti, Honduras, Hungary, Iceland, India, Indonesia, Iran, Iraq, Ireland, Ivory Coast, Jamaica, Japan, Jordan, Kenya, Kuwait, Lao People's Democratic Republic, Lebanon, Lesotho, Liberia, Libyan Arab Jamahiriya, Madagascar, Malawi, Malaysia, Maldives, Mali, Malta, Mauritania, Mauritius, Mexico, Mongolia, Morocco, Mozambique, Nepal, New Zealand, Nicaragua, Niger, Nigeria, Norway, Oman, Pakistan, Panama, Papua New Guinea, Paraguay, Peru, Philippines, Poland, Portugal, Qatar, Romania, Rwanda, Saint Lucia, Saint Vincent and the Grenadines, Samoa, Sao Tome and Principe, Saudi Arabia, Senegal, Seychelles, Sierra Leone, Singapore, Somalia, Spain, Sri Lanka, Sudan, Suriname, Swaziland, Sweden, Syrian Arab Republic, Thailand, Togo, Trinidad and Tobago, Tunisia, Uganda, Ukrainian SSR, USSR, United Arab Emirates, United Republic of Tanzania, Uruguay, Vanuatu, Venezuela, Viet Nam, Yugoslavia, Zaire, Zambia, Zimbabwe.
Against: United States.
Abstaining: Belgium, France, Germany, Federal Republic of, Grenada, Israel, Italy, Luxembourg, Netherlands, Turkey, United Kingdom.

The United States in explaining its vote believed that the issue merited intensive study by highly qualified scientists, shielded from an emotionally and politically charged atmosphere—which, it felt, would be impossible in the study proposed in the draft; further, the text had financial implications.

The United Kingdom, also concerned about the study's cost, said it would duplicate work done elsewhere, that the international community should devote its full attention to ways of ensuring that a nuclear war would not take place, and that it had doubts about the terms of reference, especially the socio-economic aspect, of the study.

Japan felt it would be more appropriate to have that part of the draft which was basically a technical matter subjected to full scientific consideration rather than have the Assembly directly and hastily involve itself.

Nuclear-arms limitation and disarmament

In November and again in December 1985, the General Assembly expressed support for the bilateral negotiations, begun earlier in the year between the USSR and the United States, on strategic and intermediate-range nuclear weapons (resolutions 40/18 and 40/152 B). In addition, the Assembly called on the Conference on Disarmament: to begin multilateral negotiations on, and elaborate practical measures for, the cessation of the nuclear-arms race and nuclear disarmament (40/152 C and P), to discuss the question of adequately verified cessation and prohibition of the production of fissionable material for nuclear weapons and other nuclear explosive devices (40/94 G), and to initiate negotiations with a view to concluding a convention banning the nuclear neutron weapon (40/152 H).

The Secretary-General also stressed the crucial importance to all peoples of the bilateral talks between the two super-Powers (see p. 8).

Consideration by the Conference on Disarmament. The Conference on Disarmament[3] again considered in 1985, but failed to agree on, the possibility of establishing a subsidiary body to negotiate on nuclear disarmament. Two formal proposals made in 1984[16] concerning a mandate for such a body were reiterated, respectively, by a group of socialist States members of the Conference and by the group of 21. The former had envisaged a committee to begin elaborating practical measures for the cessation of the arms race and for nuclear disarmament, while the latter had suggested that the proposed body elaborate on paragraph 50 of the 1978 Final Document,[7] dealing with multilateral agreements and adequate verification measures, and identify substantive issues for multilateral negotiations. The Western States, however, remained unconvinced of the merit of creating a subsidiary body.

Disarmament Commission consideration. As in previous years, the Disarmament Commission[17] considered, under a two-tiered agenda item, various aspects of the nuclear-arms race and nuclear disarmament in order to expedite negotiations aimed at eliminating the dangers of nuclear war; and a general approach to negotiations on nuclear and conventional disarmament in accordance with priorities established at the Assembly's 1978 special session[7] (see p. 25).

GENERAL ASSEMBLY ACTION

On 16 December, the Assembly adopted by recorded vote **resolution 40/152 C**, as recommended by the First Committee.

Nuclear weapons in all aspects

The General Assembly,

Recalling that at its twelfth special session, the second special session devoted to disarmament, it expressed its profound preoccupation over the danger of war, in particular nuclear war, the prevention of which remains the most acute and urgent task of the present day,

Reaffirming that nuclear weapons pose the most serious threat to mankind and its survival and that it is therefore essential to proceed with nuclear disarmament and the complete elimination of nuclear weapons,

Reaffirming also that all nuclear-weapon States, in particular those which possess the most important nuclear arsenals, bear a special responsibility for the fulfilment of the task of achieving the goals of nuclear disarmament,

Stressing again that existing arsenals of nuclear weapons alone are more than sufficient to destroy all life on Earth, and bearing in mind the devastating results which nuclear war would have on belligerents and non-belligerents alike,

Recalling that at its tenth special session, the first special session devoted to disarmament, it decided that effective measures of nuclear disarmament and the prevention of nuclear war had the highest priority and that it was essential to halt and reverse the nuclear-arms race in all its aspects in order to avert the danger of war involving nuclear weapons,

Stressing that any expectation of winning a nuclear war is senseless and that such a war would inevitably lead to the destruction of nations, to enormous devastation and to catastrophic consequences for civilization and life itself on Earth,

Convinced of the necessity of rejecting any military doctrine and concept that might lead to the unleashing of a nuclear war and might impede measures to halt the nuclear-arms race,

Stressing the urgent need for a halt to the nuclear-arms race as a step on the road to nuclear disarmament,

Stressing again that priority in disarmament negotiations should be given to nuclear weapons, and referring to paragraphs 49 and 54 of the Final Document of the Tenth Special Session of the General Assembly,

Recalling its relevant resolutions on this subject,

Welcoming the negotiations between the Union of Soviet Socialist Republics and the United States of America on a complex of questions concerning space and nuclear arms—both strategic and intermediate-range—aimed at preventing an arms race in space and terminating it on Earth,

Noting the belief expressed by the Union of Soviet Socialist Republics and the United States of America that ultimately their negotiations, just as efforts in general to limit and reduce arms, should lead to the complete elimination of nuclear arms everywhere,

Welcoming the Delhi Declaration issued on 28 January 1985 by the heads of State or Government of six States Members of the United Nations, as well as the positive response this Declaration has met with in many States,

Taking note of the Final Political Declaration adopted by the Conference of Foreign Ministers of Non-Aligned Countries, held at Luanda from 4 to 7 September 1985, in which is stressed, *inter alia*, the urgent need to initiate multilateral negotiations in the Conference on Disarmament on the cessation of the nuclear-arms race and nuclear disarmament,

Taking note also of the relevant deliberations of the Disarmament Commission in 1985 with regard to item 4 of its agenda, as contained in its report,

Noting that the Conference on Disarmament, at its 1985 session, discussed the question of the cessation of the nuclear-arms race and nuclear disarmament, including the establishment of an *ad hoc* committee for negotiations on that question,

Regretting, however, that the Conference on Disarmament was unable to reach agreement on the establishment of an *ad hoc* committee for the purpose of undertaking multilateral negotiations on the question of the cessation of the nuclear-arms race and nuclear disarmament,

Considering that efforts will continue to be made in order to enable the Conference on Disarmament to fulfil its negotiating role with regard to the cessation of the nuclear-arms race and nuclear disarmament, and that for this purpose all members of the Conference should display a constructive approach to such negotiations, bearing in mind the high priority they have accorded to this question in the Final Document of the Tenth Special Session,

Convinced that the Conference on Disarmament is the most suitable forum for the preparation and conduct of multilateral negotiations on nuclear disarmament,

1. *Calls upon* the Conference on Disarmament to proceed without delay to negotiations on the cessation of the nuclear-arms race and nuclear disarmament and especially to begin the elaboration of practical measures for the cessation of the nuclear-arms race and for nuclear disarmament in accordance with paragraph 50 of the Final Document of the Tenth Special Session of the General Assembly, including a nuclear-disarmament programme, and to establish for this purpose an *ad hoc* committee;

2. *Decides* to include in the provisional agenda of its forty-first session the item entitled "Cessation of the nuclear-arms race and nuclear disarmament: report of the Conference on Disarmament".

General Assembly resolution 40/152 C

16 December 1985   Meeting 117   117-19-11 (recorded vote)

Approved by First Committee (A/40/877/Add.1) by recorded vote (99-19-10), 20 November (meeting 43); 15-nation draft (A/C.1/40/L.13/Rev.1); agenda item 65 *(e)*.

Sponsors: Afghanistan, Angola, Bulgaria, Byelorussian SSR, Cuba, Czechoslovakia, German Democratic Republic, Hungary, Lao People's Democratic Republic, Mongolia, Poland, Romania, Ukrainian SSR, USSR, Viet Nam.

Meeting numbers. GA 40th session: 1st Committee 3-32, 34, 36, 43; plenary 117.

Recorded vote in Assembly as follows:

In favour: Afghanistan, Algeria, Antigua and Barbuda, Argentina, Austria, Bahrain,[a] Bangladesh, Barbados, Benin, Bhutan, Botswana, Brazil, Brunei Darussalam, Bulgaria, Burma, Byelorussian SSR, Cameroon, Cape Verde, Central African Republic, Chile, China, Colombia, Comoros, Congo,[b] Costa Rica, Cuba, Cyprus, Czechoslovakia, Democratic Yemen, Djibouti, Dominican Republic, Ecuador, Egypt, El Salvador, Equatorial Guinea, Ethiopia, Fiji, Finland, Gabon, Gambia, German Democratic Republic, Ghana, Greece, Grenada, Guatemala, Guinea, Guinea-Bissau, Guyana, Haiti, Honduras, Hungary, India, Indonesia, Iran, Iraq, Ivory Coast, Jamaica, Jordan, Kenya, Kuwait, Lao People's Democratic Republic, Lebanon, Lesotho, Liberia, Libyan Arab Jamahiriya, Luxembourg,[b] Madagascar, Malawi, Maldives, Mali, Mauritania, Mauritius, Mexico, Mongolia, Morocco, Mozambique, Nepal, Nicaragua, Nigeria, Oman, Pakistan, Panama, Papua New Guinea, Peru, Philippines, Poland, Romania, Rwanda, Saint Lucia, Samoa, Saudi Arabia, Senegal, Seychelles, Sierra Leone, Singapore, Somalia, Sri Lanka, Sudan, Suriname, Syrian Arab Republic, Thailand, Togo, Trinidad and Tobago, Tunisia, Uganda, Ukrainian SSR, USSR, United Republic of Tanzania, Uruguay, Vanuatu, Venezuela, Viet Nam, Yemen, Yugoslavia, Zaire, Zambia, Zimbabwe.

Against: Australia, Belgium, Canada, Denmark, France, Germany, Federal Republic of, Iceland, Israel, Italy, Japan, Netherlands, New Zealand, Norway, Portugal, Spain, Swaziland, Turkey, United Kingdom, United States.

Abstaining: Angola,[c] Bahamas, Bolivia,[c] Burkina Faso, Chad, Ireland, Malaysia, Niger, Paraguay, Saint Vincent and the Grenadines, Sweden.

[a]Later advised the Secretariat it had intended to abstain.

[b]Later advised the Secretariat it had intended to vote against.

[c]Later advised the Secretariat it had intended to vote in favour.

The Bahamas said it had abstained on a number of other draft resolutions because of their redundancy; while in agreement with many aspects of those proposals, it was disappointed that the similar elements could not be extracted and combined into a positive whole. Finland said that because it concurred with the draft's main thrust of ending the nuclear-arms race, it cast an affirmative vote despite reservations about certain parts of the preamble.

Also on 16 December, the Assembly, on the recommendation of the First Committee, adopted **resolution 40/152 P** by recorded vote.

Cessation of the nuclear-arms race and nuclear disarmament

The General Assembly,

Recalling that, in paragraph 11 of the Final Document of the Tenth Special Session of the General Assembly, the first special session devoted to disarmament, the Assembly stated that the nuclear-arms race, far from contributing to the strengthening of the security of all States, on the contrary weakens it and increases the danger of the outbreak of a nuclear war and that existing arsenals of nuclear weapons are more than sufficient to destroy all life on Earth,

Recalling also that, in paragraph 47 of the Final Document, the Assembly expressed the belief that nuclear weapons pose the greatest danger to mankind and to the survival of civilization, that it is essential to halt and reverse the nuclear-arms race in all its aspects in order to avert the danger of war involving nuclear weapons, and that the ultimate goal in this context is the complete elimination of nuclear weapons,

Noting that, in the Political Declaration adopted by the Seventh Conference of Heads of State or Government of Non-Aligned Countries, held at New Delhi from 7 to 12 March 1983, it was stated that the renewed escalation of the nuclear-arms race, as well as reliance on doctrines of nuclear deterrence, had heightened the risk of the outbreak of nuclear war and led to greater insecurity and instability in international relations, and that it was also stated that nuclear weapons were more than weapons of war, that such weapons were instruments of mass annihilation,

Noting further that, in the Final Political Declaration adopted by the Conference of Foreign Ministers of Non-Aligned Countries held at Luanda from 4 to 7 September 1985, it was stated that doctrines of nuclear deterrence, far from contributing to the maintenance of international peace and security, lay at the root of the continuing escalation in quantitative and qualitative development of nuclear weapons,

Believing that all nations have a vital interest in negotiations on nuclear disarmament because the existence of nuclear weapons in the arsenals of a handful of States directly and fundamentally jeopardizes the vital security interests of both nuclear and non-nuclear-weapon States alike,

Considering that it is necessary to halt all testing, production and deployment of nuclear weapons and their delivery systems as a first step in the process which should lead to the achievement of substantial reductions

in nuclear forces, and welcoming in this context the Joint Declaration issued on 22 May 1984 by the heads of State or Government of six States Members of the United Nations, which was reaffirmed in the Delhi Declaration issued by those States on 28 January 1985,

Convinced of the imperative need to take constructive action towards halting and reversing the nuclear-arms race,

1. *Takes note* of the initiation of bilateral negotiations on nuclear and space arms and affirms that such negotiations in no way diminish the urgent need to initiate multilateral negotiations in the Conference on Disarmament on the cessation of the nuclear-arms race and nuclear disarmament;

2. *Believes* that efforts should be intensified with a view to initiating, as a matter of the highest priority, multilateral negotiations in accordance with the provisions of paragraph 50 of the Final Document of the Tenth Special Session of the General Assembly;

3. *Again requests* the Conference on Disarmament to establish an *ad hoc* committee at the beginning of its 1986 session to elaborate on paragraph 50 of the Final Document and to submit recommendations to the Conference as to how it could best initiate multilateral negotiations of agreements, with adequate measures of verification, in appropriate stages for:

   (*a*) Cessation of the qualitative improvement and development of nuclear-weapon systems;

   (*b*) Cessation of the production of all types of nuclear weapons and their means of delivery, and of the production of fissionable material for weapons purposes;

   (*c*) Substantial reduction in existing nuclear weapons with a view to their ultimate elimination;

4. *Requests* the Conference on Disarmament to report to the General Assembly at its forty-first session on its consideration of this subject;

5. *Decides* to include in the provisional agenda of its forty-first session the item entitled "Cessation of the nuclear-arms race and nuclear disarmament".

General Assembly resolution 40/152 P

16 December 1985   Meeting 117   131-16-6 (recorded vote)

Approved by First Committee (A/40/877/Add.1) by recorded vote (112-16-5), 20 November (meeting 43); 11-nation draft (A/C.1/40/L.64); agenda item 65 *(e)*.
Sponsors: Argentina, Bangladesh, German Democratic Republic, Greece, India, Indonesia, Mexico, Oman, Romania, Sweden, United Republic of Tanzania.
Meeting numbers. GA 40th session: 1st Committee 3-32, 36, 43; plenary 117.

Recorded vote in Assembly as follows:

In favour: Afghanistan, Algeria, Angola, Antigua and Barbuda, Argentina, Austria, Bahrain, Bangladesh, Barbados, Benin, Bhutan, Bolivia, Botswana, Brazil, Brunei Darussalam, Bulgaria, Burkina Faso, Burma, Burundi, Byelorussian SSR, Cameroon, Cape Verde, Central African Republic, Chad, Chile, China, Colombia, Comoros, Congo, Costa Rica, Cuba, Cyprus, Czechoslovakia, Democratic Kampuchea, Democratic Yemen, Djibouti, Dominican Republic, Ecuador, Egypt, El Salvador, Equatorial Guinea, Ethiopia, Fiji, Finland, Gabon, Gambia, German Democratic Republic, Ghana, Greece, Guatemala, Guinea, Guinea-Bissau, Guyana, Haiti, Honduras, Hungary, India, Indonesia, Iran, Iraq, Ireland, Ivory Coast, Jamaica, Jordan, Kenya, Kuwait, Lao People's Democratic Republic, Lebanon, Lesotho, Liberia, Libyan Arab Jamahiriya, Madagascar, Malawi, Malaysia, Maldives, Mali, Malta, Mauritania, Mauritius, Mexico, Mongolia, Morocco, Mozambique, Nepal, Nicaragua, Niger, Nigeria, Oman, Pakistan, Panama, Papua New Guinea, Paraguay, Peru, Philippines, Poland, Qatar, Romania, Rwanda, Saint Lucia, Saint Vincent and the Grenadines, Samoa, Sao Tome and Principe, Saudi Arabia, Senegal, Seychelles, Singapore, Somalia, Sri Lanka, Sudan, Suriname, Swaziland, Sweden, Syrian Arab Republic, Thailand, Togo, Trinidad and Tobago, Tunisia, Uganda, Ukrainian SSR, USSR, United Arab Emirates, United Republic of Tanzania, Uruguay, Vanuatu, Venezuela, Viet Nam, Yemen, Yugoslavia, Zaire, Zambia, Zimbabwe.

Against: Australia, Belgium, Canada, France, Germany, Federal Republic of, Iceland, Israel, Italy, Luxembourg, Netherlands, New Zealand, Norway, Portugal, Turkey, United Kingdom, United States.

Abstaining: Bahamas, Denmark, Grenada, Japan, Sierra Leone, Spain.

In explanation of vote, France stated that the text ran directly counter to a doctrine which was at the root of its security and defence policy. The United Kingdom believed that bilateral negotiations between the two major Powers—possessing the greatest military capability in space and some 95 per cent of the world's nuclear weapons—offered the most realistic hope of halting the nuclear-arms race and initiating the process of reducing nuclear armaments; it added that multilateral negotiations on the subject in the Conference on Disarmament would be unrealistic and premature, and could prove harmful to the prospects for the bilateral negotiations.

China regretted the text's failure to mention the special responsibility to be shouldered by the countries with the largest nuclear arsenals.

Prohibition of nuclear weapons

In 1985, the General Assembly requested the Conference on Disarmament to pursue consideration of adequately verified cessation and prohibition of the production of fissionable material for nuclear weapons and other nuclear explosive devices (**resolution 40/94 G**). In addition, for the fifth consecutive year, the Assembly requested the Conference to start without delay negotiations aimed at concluding a convention prohibiting the development, production, stockpiling, deployment and use of nuclear neutron weapons, also known as enhanced radiation weapons (**40/152 H**).

Fissionable material

GENERAL ASSEMBLY ACTION

On 12 December, the Assembly, on the recommendation of the First Committee, adopted **resolution 40/94 G** by recorded vote.

Prohibition of the production of fissionable material for weapons purposes

The General Assembly,

Recalling its resolutions 33/91 H of 16 December 1978, 34/87 D of 11 December 1979, 35/156 H of 12 December 1980, 36/97 G of 9 December 1981, 37/99 E of 13 December 1982, 38/188 E of 20 December 1983 and 39/151 H of 17 December 1984, in which it requested the Committee on Disarmament, at an appropriate stage of the implementation of the Programme of Action set forth in section III of the Final Document of the Tenth Special Session of the General Assembly, and of its work on the item entitled "Nuclear weapons in all aspects", to consider urgently the question of adequately verified cessation and prohibition of the production of fissionable material for nuclear weapons and other nuclear explosive devices and to keep the Assembly informed of the progress of that consideration,

Noting that the agenda of the Conference on Disarmament for 1985 included the item entitled "Nuclear weapons in all aspects" and that the programme of work of the Conference for both parts of its session held in 1985 contained the item entitled "Cessation of the nuclear-arms race and nuclear disarmament",

Recalling the proposals and statements made in the Conference on Disarmament on those items,

Considering that the cessation of production of fissionable material for weapons purposes and the progressive conversion and transfer of stocks to peaceful uses would be a significant step towards halting and reversing the nuclear-arms race,

Considering that the prohibition of the production of fissionable material for nuclear weapons and other explosive devices also would be an important measure in facilitating the prevention of the proliferation of nuclear weapons and explosive devices,

Requests the Conference on Disarmament, at an appropriate stage of its work on the item entitled "Nuclear weapons in all aspects", to pursue its consideration of the question of adequately verified cessation and prohibition of the production of fissionable material for nuclear weapons and other nuclear explosive devices and to keep the General Assembly informed of the progress of that consideration.

General Assembly resolution 40/94 G

12 December 1985   Meeting 113   145-1-7 (recorded vote)

Approved by First Committee (A/40/976) by recorded vote (127-0-7), 20 November (meeting 43); 22-nation draft (A/C.1/40/L.37); agenda item 68 *(h)*.

Sponsors: Australia, Austria, Bahamas, Bangladesh, Cameroon, Canada, Chad, Denmark, Finland, Greece, Indonesia, Ireland, Japan, Netherlands, New Zealand, Norway, Philippines, Romania, Samoa, Singapore, Sweden, Uruguay.

Meeting numbers. GA 40th session: 1st Committee 3-32, 36, 43; plenary 113.

Recorded vote in Assembly as follows:

In favour: Afghanistan, Algeria, Angola, Antigua and Barbuda, Australia, Austria, Bahamas, Bahrain, Bangladesh, Barbados, Belgium, Benin, Bhutan, Bolivia, Botswana, Brunei Darussalam, Bulgaria, Burkina Faso, Burma, Burundi, Byelorussian SSR, Cameroon, Canada, Cape Verde, Central African Republic, Chad, Chile, Colombia, Comoros, Congo, Cuba, Cyprus, Czechoslovakia, Democratic Kampuchea, Democratic Yemen, Denmark, Djibouti, Dominican Republic, Ecuador, Egypt, El Salvador, Equatorial Guinea, Ethiopia, Fiji, Finland, Gabon, German Democratic Republic, Germany, Federal Republic of, Ghana, Greece, Grenada, Guatemala, Guinea, Guinea-Bissau, Guyana, Haiti, Honduras, Hungary, Iceland, Indonesia, Iran, Iraq, Ireland, Israel, Italy, Ivory Coast, Jamaica, Japan, Jordan, Kenya, Kuwait, Lao People's Democratic Republic, Lebanon, Lesotho, Liberia, Libyan Arab Jamahiriya, Luxembourg, Madagascar, Malawi, Malaysia, Maldives, Mali, Malta, Mauritania, Mauritius, Mexico, Mongolia, Morocco, Mozambique, Nepal, Netherlands, New Zealand, Nicaragua, Niger, Nigeria, Norway, Oman, Pakistan, Panama, Papua New Guinea, Paraguay, Peru, Philippines, Poland, Portugal, Qatar, Romania, Rwanda, Saint Lucia, Saint Vincent and the Grenadines, Samoa, Sao Tome and Principe, Saudi Arabia, Senegal, Seychelles, Sierra Leone, Singapore, Solomon Islands, Somalia, Spain, Sri Lanka, Sudan, Suriname, Swaziland, Sweden, Syrian Arab Republic, Thailand, Togo, Trinidad and Tobago, Tunisia, Turkey, Uganda, Ukrainian SSR, USSR, United Arab Emirates, United Republic of Tanzania, Uruguay, Vanuatu, Venezuela, Viet Nam, Yemen, Yugoslavia, Zaire, Zambia, Zimbabwe.

Against: France.

Abstaining: Argentina, Brazil, China, India, Saint Christopher and Nevis, United Kingdom, United States.

France, which had abstained in the First Committee, cast a negative vote in the plenary Assembly, stating that the prohibition of the production of fissionable material for weapons purposes could be conceived of realistically only within the context of an effective process of nuclear disarmament, and not as a pre-condition for such a process. Argentina shared that view, as did the USSR, which added that it supported the draft on the understanding that "its work" in the operative paragraph referred to practical negotiations in the Conference. For India, the draft embodied a one-sided approach inconsistent with that of the 1978 Final Document,[7] notably its paragraph 50.

The Assembly, in **resolution 40/151 E**, called on all nuclear-weapon States to agree to a freeze on nuclear weapons, which would, among other things, provide for a simultaneous total stoppage of any further production of nuclear weapons and a complete cut-off in the production of fissionable material for weapons purposes.

Nuclear neutron weapon

GENERAL ASSEMBLY ACTION

On 16 December, the General Assembly adopted **resolution 40/152 H** by recorded vote, on the recommendation of the First Committee.

Prohibition of the nuclear neutron weapon
The General Assembly,

Recalling paragraph 50 of the Final Document of the Tenth Special Session of the General Assembly, in which it is stated that the achievement of nuclear disarmament will require urgent negotiation of agreements, *inter alia,* for the cessation of the qualitative improvement and development of nuclear-weapon systems, which is especially emphasized in paragraph 50 *(a)* of that Document,

Recalling also that in paragraph 50 of the Final Document it is also underlined that in the course of negotiations consideration can be given to mutual and agreed limitation or prohibition, without prejudice to the security of any State, of any types of nuclear armaments,

Stressing that the development and production of the nuclear neutron weapon is a dangerous consequence of the continuing qualitative arms race in the field of nuclear weapons, especially through the qualitative improvement and development of new nuclear warheads by enhancing specific characteristics of nuclear weapons,

Reaffirming its relevant resolutions on the prohibition of the nuclear neutron weapon,

Sharing the world-wide concern expressed by Member States, as well as by non-governmental organizations, about the continued and expanded production and introduction of the nuclear neutron weapon in military arsenals, which escalates the nuclear-arms race and significantly lowers the threshold of nuclear war,

Aware of the inhuman effects of that weapon, which constitutes a grave threat, particularly to the unprotected civilian population,

Noting the consideration by the Conference on Disarmament at its 1985 session of issues connected with the cessation of the nuclear-arms race and nuclear disarmament, as well as the prohibition of the nuclear neutron weapon,

Regretting that the Conference on Disarmament was prevented from reaching agreement on the commencement of negotiations on the cessation of the nuclear-arms race and nuclear disarmament, including the prohibition of the nuclear neutron weapon, in an appropriate organizational framework,

1. *Reaffirms its request* to the Conference on Disarmament to start without delay negotiations within an appropriate organizational framework, with a view to concluding a convention on the prohibition of the development, production, stockpiling, deployment and use of nuclear neutron weapons as an organic element of negotiations, as envisaged in paragraph 50 of the Final

Document of the Tenth Special Session of the General Assembly;

2. *Requests* the Secretary-General to transmit to the Conference on Disarmament all documents relating to the consideration of this question by the General Assembly at its fortieth session;

3. *Requests* the Conference on Disarmament to submit a report on this question to the General Assembly at its forty-first session;

4. *Decides* to include in the provisional agenda of its forty-first session the item entitled "Prohibition of the nuclear neutron weapon".

General Assembly resolution 40/152 H

16 December 1985   Meeting 117   70-11-65 (recorded vote)

Approved by First Committee (A/40/877/Add.1) by recorded vote (62-11-56), 20 November (meeting 43); 18-nation draft (A/C.1/40/L.47); agenda item 65 *(g)*.
Sponsors: Afghanistan, Angola, Bulgaria, Byelorussian SSR, Cuba, Czechoslovakia, Democratic Yemen, Ethiopia, German Democratic Republic, Hungary, Lao People's Democratic Republic, Mongolia, Mozambique, Poland, Romania, Syrian Arab Republic, Ukrainian SSR, Viet Nam.
Meeting numbers. GA 40th session: 1st Committee 3-32, 34, 43; plenary 117.

Recorded vote in Assembly as follows:

In favour: Afghanistan, Algeria, Angola, Antigua and Barbuda, Bahrain, Benin, Bolivia, Botswana, Bulgaria, Burkina Faso, Burundi, Byelorussian SSR, Cameroon, Cape Verde, Congo, Cuba, Cyprus, Czechoslovakia, Democratic Yemen, Ethiopia, Fiji, Finland, German Democratic Republic, Ghana, Guinea, Guinea-Bissau, Hungary, India, Indonesia, Iran, Iraq, Jordan, Kenya, Kuwait, Lao People's Democratic Republic, Lebanon, Lesotho, Liberia, Libyan Arab Jamahiriya, Madagascar, Malawi, Mali, Mauritius, Mexico, Mongolia, Mozambique, Nicaragua, Nigeria, Papua New Guinea, Poland, Qatar, Romania, Samoa, Saudi Arabia, Seychelles, Swaziland, Syrian Arab Republic, Tunisia, Uganda, Ukrainian SSR, USSR, United Arab Emirates, United Republic of Tanzania, Vanuatu, Viet Nam, Yemen, Yugoslavia, Zaire,[a] Zambia, Zimbabwe.
Against: Belgium, Canada, France, Germany, Federal Republic of, Israel, Italy, Japan, Portugal, Turkey, United Kingdom, United States.
Abstaining: Argentina, Australia, Austria, Bahamas, Bangladesh, Barbados, Bhutan, Brazil, Brunei Darussalam, Burma, Central African Republic, Chad, Chile, China, Colombia, Comoros, Costa Rica, Democratic Kampuchea, Denmark, Djibouti, Dominican Republic, Ecuador, Egypt, El Salvador, Equatorial Guinea, Gabon, Gambia, Greece, Grenada, Guatemala, Guyana, Haiti, Honduras, Iceland, Ireland, Ivory Coast, Jamaica, Luxembourg, Malaysia, Maldives, Morocco, Nepal, Netherlands, New Zealand, Niger, Norway, Oman, Pakistan, Panama, Paraguay, Peru, Philippines, Rwanda, Saint Vincent and the Grenadines, Senegal, Sierra Leone, Singapore, Spain, Sri Lanka, Sudan, Suriname, Sweden, Trinidad and Tobago, Uruguay, Venezuela.

[a]Later advised the Secretariat it had intended to abstain.

Argentina, Australia, Bangladesh and Oman opposed singling out the nuclear neutron weapon, saying that the question should be discussed within the general framework of nuclear disarmament.

USSR—United States negotiations

In accordance with an agreement reached in January 1985, the USSR and the United States began, at Geneva in March, new bilateral negotiations on strategic and intermediate-range nuclear weapons. The heads of the respective Governments, at a summit meeting at Geneva from 19 to 21 November, agreed to accelerate the work.

The Assembly adopted two resolutions wishing success in the bilateral talks—one in November, as proposed by a group of non-aligned countries (**40/18**), and the other in December, based on a draft by Western and other countries (**40/152 B**). In other action, the Assembly made numerous calls to the two States to address various specific aspects of nuclear disarmament (see under related subject headings).

Communications. A number of 1985 communications addressed to the Secretary-General were on the USSR–United States talks. On 30 January,[18] Argentina, Greece, India, Mexico, Sweden and the United Republic of Tanzania transmitted the 28 January Delhi Declaration by the leaders of the six countries, welcoming the 8 January agreement between the USSR and the United States to negotiate on strategic and intermediate-range nuclear weapons and calling for a halt to all nuclear-weapons testing and for the early conclusion of a comprehensive test-ban treaty. In February, the German Democratic Republic[19] and Mongolia[20] expressed support for the Declaration. In connection with the November Geneva summit meeting, the six leaders, by a joint message of 24 October,[21] called on the USSR and the United States to suspend all nuclear tests for a 12-month period and offered their assistance in verifying compliance with the proposed moratorium. In response, the General Secretary of the Central Committee of the Communist Party of the USSR, on 6 November,[22] reiterated his country's willingness to extend its unilateral moratorium on nuclear explosions, begun on 6 August (see p. 47), beyond 1 January 1986 if the United States joined in it, and to conclude a treaty prohibiting all nuclear-weapon tests indefinitely.

Hopes for the bilateral summit's success were expressed by Brazil, which on 18 November[23] transmitted the messages its President had sent to the heads of the two Governments, and by Uganda in a 20 November Foreign Ministry communiqué.[24]

By a letter of 16 December,[25] the USSR and the United States forwarded their 21 November joint statement, issued at Geneva, in which their leaders emphasized the importance of preventing wars between them and agreed to accelerate arms control and disarmament negotiations.

GENERAL ASSEMBLY ACTION

On the recommendation of the First Committee, the General Assembly, on 18 November, adopted **resolution 40/18** by recorded vote.

Bilateral nuclear-arms negotiations

The General Assembly,

Noting the agreement between the Union of Soviet Socialist Republics and the United States of America to begin negotiations on "a complex of questions concerning space and nuclear arms—both strategic and intermediate-range—" with the objective "to work out effective agreements aimed at preventing an arms race in space and terminating it on Earth", which negotiations ultimately "should lead to the complete elimination of nuclear arms everywhere",

Deeply concerned by the fact that humanity is confronted today with an unprecedented threat to its survival arising from the massive and competitive accumulation of the most destructive weapons ever produced, especially nuclear weapons more than sufficient to destroy all life on Earth,

Conscious that such a situation is all the more difficult to justify if one takes into account that there already exists an international consensus that a nuclear war cannot be won and must never be fought,

1. *Expresses its hope* that the forthcoming meeting between the two leaders of the Union of Soviet Socialist Republics and the United States of America will give a decisive impetus to their current bilateral negotiations so that these negotiations produce early and effective agreements on the halting of the nuclear-arms race with its negative effects on international security as well as on social and economic development, reduction of their nuclear arsenals, prevention of an arms race in outer space and the use of outer space for peaceful purposes;

2. *Invites* the two negotiating parties to keep the General Assembly duly informed of the progress of their negotiations;

3. *Reaffirms* that in these negotiations the vital interests of all peoples, including those of the two negotiating parties, are at stake;

4. *Further reaffirms* that bilateral negotiations do not in any way diminish the urgent need to initiate and pursue multilateral negotiations on the cessation of the nuclear-arms race and nuclear disarmament and on the prevention of an arms race in outer space;

5. *Requests* the Secretary-General to convey this resolution to the leaders of the Union of Soviet Socialist Republics and the United States of America before their meeting at Geneva on 19 and 20 November 1985.

General Assembly resolution 40/18

18 November 1985   Meeting 80   76-0-12 (recorded vote)

Approved by First Committee (A/40/877) by recorded vote (117-0-16), 14 November (meeting 38); 20-nation draft (A/C.1/40/L.60); agenda item 65 *(i)*.

Sponsors: Algeria, Bahamas, Bangladesh, Colombia, Cuba, Ecuador, Egypt, Ghana, India, Indonesia, Madagascar, Mexico, Nigeria, Pakistan, Peru, Romania, Sri Lanka, Yemen, Yugoslavia, Zimbabwe.

Meeting numbers. GA 40th session: 1st Committee 3-32, 34, 38; plenary 80.

Recorded vote in Assembly as follows:

In favour: Algeria, Antigua and Barbuda, Argentina, Bahamas, Bangladesh, Bolivia, Botswana, Bulgaria, Burkina Faso, Burundi, Byelorussian SSR, Canada, Cape Verde, Chad, Chile, China, Colombia, Congo, Cuba, Cyprus, Czechoslovakia, Democratic Kampuchea, Democratic Yemen, Denmark, Djibouti, Ecuador, El Salvador, Finland, German Democratic Republic, Greece, Guyana, Hungary, Indonesia, Iran, Ireland, Jordan, Lao People's Democratic Republic, Lebanon, Libyan Arab Jamahiriya, Madagascar, Mali, Malta, Mauritania, Mongolia, Morocco, Mozambique, New Zealand, Niger, Oman, Pakistan, Panama, Peru, Poland, Qatar, Romania, Samoa, Senegal, Somalia, Spain, Sri Lanka, Sweden, Syrian Arab Republic, Thailand, Togo, Trinidad and Tobago, Tunisia, Uganda, Ukrainian SSR, USSR, United Republic of Tanzania, Uruguay, Venezuela, Viet Nam, Yugoslavia, Zaire, Zambia.

Against: None.

Abstaining: Australia, Belgium, Germany, Federal Republic of, Iceland, Israel, Italy, Japan, Luxembourg, Portugal, Turkey, United Kingdom, United States.

The United States could not support the text as agreement could not be reached on language neither promoting nor prejudicing the viewpoints of anyone, including the participants in the Geneva meeting.

Abstaining in the Committee, France stated that it had difficulties with paragraph 4; it asserted that the Geneva talks, important as they were, could not by themselves solve all the problems; further, it was inappropriate for the Assembly to appear to be giving a general mandate to the two parties.

The Netherlands abstained to express its disappointment over the failure to reach a consensus on an important issue.

Canada, which supported the text's overall thrust, thought it was imperfect and that paragraph 4, in particular, was susceptible to different interpretations; its vote did not indicate support of immediate negotiations on outer space in the Conference on Disarmament. The USSR agreed that bilateral and multilateral negotiations should complement one another.

Albania did not participate in the voting, saying the illusion that humanity's problems would be solved by agreements between the two superPowers was fraught with grave consequences.

On 16 December, the General Assembly, on the recommendation of the First Committee, adopted **resolution 40/152 B** by recorded vote.

Bilateral nuclear-arms and space-arms negotiations

The General Assembly,

Recalling its resolutions 38/183 P of 20 December 1983 and 39/148 B of 17 December 1984,

Welcoming warmly the resumption on 12 March 1985 of the bilateral negotiations at Geneva between the Union of Soviet Socialist Republics and the United States of America,

Noting that in their joint statement of 8 January 1985 the two Governments agreed that the subject of these negotiations is a complex of questions concerning space and nuclear arms—both strategic and intermediate-range—with all these questions considered and resolved in their interrelationship,

Noting that the agreed objective of these negotiations is to work out effective agreements aimed at preventing an arms race in space and terminating it on Earth, at limiting and reducing nuclear arms and at strengthening strategic stability,

Noting also that the two sides believe that ultimately these negotiations, just as efforts in general to limit and reduce arms, should lead to the complete elimination of nuclear weapons everywhere,

Noting further that both the Union of Soviet Socialist Republics and the United States of America have expressed their readiness to keep the other States Members of the United Nations duly informed of progress in their bilateral negotiations, in accordance with paragraph 114 of the Final Document of the Tenth Special Session of the General Assembly,

Convinced that, through negotiations pursued in a spirit of flexibility and with full account taken of the security interests of all States, it is possible to reach agreement,

Firmly convinced that an early agreement in these negotiations, in accordance with the principle of undiminished security at the lowest possible level of armaments, would be of crucial importance for the strengthening of international peace and security,

1. *Calls upon* the Government of the Union of Soviet Socialist Republics and the Government of the United States of America to spare no effort in seeking the attainment of their agreed objective in the negotiations, in accordance with the security interests of all States and the universal desire for progress towards disarmament;

2. *Urges* the Governments of the two States concerned to work actively towards the achievement of that objective in order to enable the negotiations to make substantial progress;

3. *Expresses its firmest possible encouragement and support* for these negotiations and their successful conclusion.

General Assembly resolution 40/152 B

16 December 1985   Meeting 117   107-0-40 (recorded vote)

Approved by First Committee (A/40/877/Add.1) by recorded vote (71-0-51), 22 November (meeting 47); 15-nation draft (A/C.1/40/L.8), amended by Argentina, Ecuador and Mexico (A/C.1/40/L.80); agenda item 65 *(i)*.

Sponsors: Australia, Belgium, Canada, Denmark, Germany, Federal Republic of, Italy, Japan, Netherlands, New Zealand, Norway, Portugal, Rwanda, Swaziland, Turkey, United Kingdom.

Meeting numbers. GA 40th session: 1st Committee 3-32, 47; plenary 117.

Recorded vote in Assembly as follows:

In favour: Angola,[a] Antigua and Barbuda, Australia, Austria, Bahrain,[a] Belgium, Benin,[a] Bolivia, Botswana, Brunei Darussalam, Burkina Faso, Burundi, Cameroon, Canada, Cape Verde, Chile, China, Colombia, Congo,[a] Costa Rica, Democratic Kampuchea, Denmark, Djibouti, Dominican Republic, Ecuador, Egypt, El Salvador, Equatorial Guinea, Ethiopia, Fiji, Finland, France, Gambia, Germany, Federal Republic of, Ghana, Greece, Grenada, Guatemala, Guinea, Guinea-Bissau, Guyana, Iceland, Iran, Iraq,[a] Ireland, Israel, Italy, Ivory Coast, Jamaica, Japan, Jordan, Kenya, Lebanon, Lesotho, Liberia, Luxembourg, Malawi, Malaysia, Maldives, Mali, Mauritania, Mauritius, Morocco, Nepal, Netherlands, New Zealand, Niger, Nigeria, Norway, Papua New Guinea, Paraguay, Philippines, Portugal, Qatar, Rwanda, Saint Lucia, Saint Vincent and the Grenadines, Samoa, Saudi Arabia, Seychelles, Sierra Leone, Singapore, Somalia, Spain, Sri Lanka,[a] Sudan, Suriname, Swaziland, Sweden, Syrian Arab Republic, Thailand, Togo, Trinidad and Tobago, Tunisia, Turkey, Uganda, United Arab Emirates, United Kingdom, United Republic of Tanzania, United States, Uruguay, Vanuatu, Venezuela,[a] Yemen, Zaire, Zambia, Zimbabwe.

Against: None.

Abstaining: Afghanistan, Algeria, Argentina, Bahamas, Bangladesh, Barbados,[b] Bhutan, Brazil, Bulgaria, Burma, Byelorussian SSR, Central African Republic, Chad, Cuba, Cyprus, Czechoslovakia, Democratic Yemen, Gabon, German Democratic Republic, Haiti, Hungary, India, Indonesia, Lao People's Democratic Republic, Libyan Arab Jamahiriya, Madagascar, Mexico, Mongolia, Nicaragua, Oman, Pakistan, Panama, Peru, Poland, Romania, Senegal,[b] Ukrainian SSR, USSR, Viet Nam, Yugoslavia.

[a] Later advised the Secretariat it had intended to abstain.
[b] Later advised the Secretariat it had intended to vote in favour.

Prior to approving the text as a whole, the First Committee approved—by a recorded vote of 61 to 24, with 23 abstentions—a three-nation amendment which deleted from paragraph 2, after "to work actively", the phrase "and without preconditions". Voting against the amendment, the United Kingdom said the draft's sponsors felt that the amendment would give the impression that the Committee favoured imposing pre-conditions on the progress of negotiations. The United States shared that misgiving, while France feared that prior conditions might complicate, or lead to failure in, the negotiations. For Nigeria, however, the phrase's deletion facilitated its support of the text.

Six countries explained their abstentions on the amended text. The USSR said it distorted the actual state of affairs, for instance in the second preambular paragraph, by describing the bilateral negotiations as having been resumed, rather than commenced as a new round as mentioned in the USSR–United States agreement of November 1984;[(26)] the draft also referred to the 1983 and 1984 Assembly resolutions which it had opposed.

For the same reasons, the Ukrainian SSR would have opposed the first and second preambular paragraphs had they been voted on separately. Hungary also pointed out that it had voted against some resolutions mentioned in the preamble, which, it added, had been overtaken by events since then. Yugoslavia felt that the text expressed the view of only one group of countries. Mexico said the amended text—which was not more acceptable, only less unacceptable, than the unamended version—remained unbalanced and did not help the negotiating Powers in any way. Sri Lanka was unconvinced of what it regarded as the extravagant hopes reflected in the text, in the light of the record of the previous three rounds of bilateral negotiations. That view was shared by Argentina, which added that the text reflected neither the way in which multilateral mechanisms could participate in disarmament negotiations nor the role of the United Nations in them.

France stressed that the bilateral talks could deal only with the weapons of the two parties concerned and could not take into account the nuclear forces of third parties; it added that the total elimination of nuclear weapons would be accomplished only through general and complete disarmament.

The Assembly's call on major Powers to pursue their negotiations on arms limitation and disarmament were repeated in a number of 1985 resolutions, notably, **40/152 N** and **P**.

Cessation of nuclear-weapon tests

In December 1985, the General Assembly adopted three resolutions in which it called again on the Conference on Disarmament to negotiate on a nuclear-weapon test-ban treaty (40/80 A, 40/81, 40/88) and to establish an *ad hoc* committee to that end. By another resolution, the Assembly recommended that States parties to the 1963 Treaty Banning Nuclear Weapon Tests in the Atmosphere, in Outer Space and under Water,[1] also known as the partial test-ban treaty, consult among themselves as to the advisability and most appropriate method of converting that Treaty into a comprehensive nuclear-test-ban treaty (40/80 B).

Outside the United Nations framework, the USSR announced, on 29 July, its unilateral decision to halt all nuclear explosions from 6 August 1985 until 1 January 1986. Also on 29 July, the United States announced that it had invited Soviet experts to visit a test site with the equipment they deemed necessary to measure the yield of a test.

Consideration by the Conference on Disarmament. In 1985, the Conference on Disarmament,[3] which had again been asked by the Assembly in 1984[27] to proceed to negotiations on a nuclear-weapon test-ban treaty, failed to agree on the mandate of an *ad hoc* committee on the topic.

In addition to previous proposals, updated by the group of 21[28] and by the socialist States,[29] for an *ad hoc* committee to initiate the multilateral negotiation of a treaty, the Conference received in 1985 a proposal by Brazil[30] urging it to establish a subsidiary body. Bulgaria and the German Democratic Republic[31] submitted a joint working paper proposing a list of subjects for consideration by an *ad hoc* committee, while a draft programme of work for a subsidiary body[32] was suggested by Australia, Belgium, Canada, the Federal Republic of Germany, Italy, Japan, the Netherlands, Norway, the United Kingdom and the United States.

In the Conference, the Western countries held that a subsidiary body should resume its substantive examination of specific issues—such as verification, compliance and scope of a future treaty—with a view to negotiating a treaty, adding that, in a spirit of flexibility, it had proposed a revised broader mandate to enable practical work to continue. The group of 21, on the other hand, asserted that the limited mandate it had agreed for a subsidiary body in 1982 and 1983 had become outdated.

The USSR transmitted its views on the test ban, including a statement by its General Secretary[33] on its announcement of a unilateral moratorium starting on 6 August 1985.

Working papers on seismic monitoring were submitted to the Conference in 1985 by: the Federal Republic of Germany—one on an international monitoring and verification system based on current technology, without awaiting the conclusion of a comprehensive test-ban treaty or other contractual arrangements,[34] and the other on a system design for improving the seismic monitoring and verification capabilities of a comprehensive nuclear-test ban;[35] by Japan,[36] on measures for, and estimated costs of, realizing an international seismic data exchange system; and by the United Kingdom,[37] on the possibility of establishing, and likely capabilities of, a global monitoring network. Norway, a non-member of the Conference, submitted the report of a workshop (Oslo, 4-7 June) it had sponsored on seismological verification of a comprehensive test ban, which was attended by 84 participants from 41 countries.[38]

The *Ad Hoc* Group of Scientific Experts to Consider International Co-operative Measures to Detect and Identify Seismic Events held its nineteenth (25-29 March)[39] and twentieth (15-19 July)[40] sessions at Geneva under the chairmanship of Ola Dahlman (Sweden), submitting progress reports on each session.

Communications. Nuclear-weapon tests were the subject of several 1985 communications to the Secretary-General. By letters dated 30 July[41] and 15 August,[42] the USSR transmitted statements made by its General Secretary on that country's decision to proclaim a unilateral moratorium on nuclear-weapon tests from 6 August 1985 to 1 January 1986, and his call to the United States to do likewise; provided the United States did so, the moratorium would remain in effect, he stated. On 26 December,[43] the Libyan Arab Jamahiriya welcomed the USSR decision and expressed concern over the danger posed by continued tests.

On 19 September,[44] Papua New Guinea forwarded the South Pacific Forum communiqué (Rarotonga, Cook Islands, 5 and 6 August) (see also p. 58), in which the Forum reaffirmed its opposition to French nuclear testing at Mururoa Atoll and to the dumping of radioactive waste in the oceans of the region.

GENERAL ASSEMBLY ACTION

In addition to the four draft texts relating to the cessation of nuclear-weapon tests and a test-ban treaty (see below), a draft on notification of nuclear tests[45] was submitted to the First Committee. Sponsored by Australia, Fiji, Ireland, New Zealand, Papua New Guinea, Samoa and Sweden, the draft would have had the Assembly call on States concerned to provide data to the Secretary-General within one week of each nuclear explosion, and express its conviction that such a full and open accounting would help improve independent monitoring capabilities and thereby facilitate the early conclusion of a verifiable comprehensive test-ban treaty. Since the sponsors subsequently ascertained that other considerations had to be addressed before the procedure could be implemented, they requested that no action be taken on the text.

On 12 December 1985, the General Assembly adopted four resolutions concerning a nuclear-test-ban treaty, on the recommendation of the First Committee, where several delegations explained in single statements their votes on two or more texts (see p. 53).

The Assembly adopted **resolution 40/80 A** by recorded vote.

The General Assembly,

Bearing in mind that the complete cessation of nuclear-weapon tests, which has been examined for more than twenty-five years and on which the General Assembly has adopted nearly fifty resolutions, is a basic objective of the United Nations in the sphere of disarmament, to the attainment of which it has repeatedly assigned the highest priority,

Stressing that on eight different occasions it has condemned such tests in the strongest terms and that, since 1974, it has stated its conviction that the continuance of nuclear-weapon testing will intensify the arms race, thus increasing the danger of nuclear war,

Reiterating the assertion made in several previous resolutions that, whatever may be the differences on the question of verification, there is no valid reason for delaying the conclusion of an agreement on a comprehensive test ban,

Recalling that as early as 1972 the Secretary-General declared that all the technical and scientific aspects of the problem have been so fully explored that only a political decision is now necessary in order to achieve final agreement, that when the existing means of verification are taken into account it is difficult to understand further delay in achieving agreement on an underground-test ban, and that the potential risks of continuing underground nuclear-weapon tests would far outweigh any possible risks from ending such tests,

Recalling also that the Secretary-General, addressing a plenary meeting of the General Assembly on 12 December 1984, after appealing for a renewed effort towards a comprehensive test-ban treaty, emphasized that no single multilateral agreement could have a greater effect on limiting the further refinement of nuclear weapons and that a comprehensive test-ban treaty is the litmus test of the real willingness to pursue nuclear disarmament,

Taking into account that the three nuclear-weapon States which act as depositaries of the Treaty Banning Nuclear Weapon Tests in the Atmosphere, in Outer Space and under Water undertook in article I of that Treaty to conclude a treaty resulting in the permanent banning of all nuclear-test explosions, including all those explosions underground, and that such an undertaking was reiterated in 1968 in the preamble to the Treaty on the Non-Proliferation of Nuclear Weapons, article VI of which further embodies their solemn and legally binding commitment to take effective measures relating to the cessation of the nuclear-arms race at an early date and to nuclear disarmament,

Bearing in mind that the same three nuclear-weapon States, in the report they submitted on 30 July 1980 to the Committee on Disarmament after four years of trilateral negotiations, stated, *inter alia*, that they were "mindful of the great value for all mankind that the prohibition of all nuclear-weapon test explosions in all environments will have" as well as "conscious of the important responsibility placed upon them to find solutions to the remaining problems", adding furthermore that they were "determined to exert their best efforts and necessary will and persistence to bring the negotiations to an early and successful conclusion",

Noting that the Third Review Conference of the Parties to the Treaty on the Non-Proliferation of Nuclear Weapons, in its Final Declaration adopted on 21 September 1985, called upon the nuclear-weapon States parties to the Treaty to resume trilateral negotiations in 1985 and called upon all the nuclear-weapon States to participate in the urgent negotiation and conclusion of a comprehensive nuclear-test-ban treaty, as a matter of the highest priority, in the Conference on Disarmament,

Bearing in mind that the multilateral negotiation of such a treaty in the Conference on Disarmament must cover all the various interrelated problems which it will be necessary to solve in order that the Conference may transmit a complete draft treaty to the General Assembly,

1. *Reiterates once again its grave concern* that nuclear-weapon tests have not yet stopped, in spite of the wishes of the overwhelming majority of Member States;

2. *Reaffirms its conviction* that a treaty to achieve the prohibition of all nuclear-test explosions by all States for all time is a matter of the highest priority;

3. *Reaffirms also its conviction* that such a treaty would constitute a contribution of the utmost importance to the cessation of the nuclear-arms race and that the commencement of negotiations on such a treaty is an indispensable element of the obligations of States parties to the Treaty on the Non-Proliferation of Nuclear Weapons under article VI of that Treaty;

4. *Urges once more* the three depositary Powers of the Treaty Banning Nuclear Weapon Tests in the Atmosphere, in Outer Space and under Water and of the Treaty on the Non-Proliferation of Nuclear Weapons to abide strictly by their undertakings to seek to achieve the early discontinuance of all test explosions of nuclear weapons for all time and to expedite negotiations to this end;

5. *Appeals* to all States members of the Conference on Disarmament, in particular to the three depositary Powers of the Treaty Banning Nuclear Weapon Tests in the Atmosphere, in Outer Space and under Water and of the Treaty on the Non-Proliferation of Nuclear Weapons, to promote the establishment by the Conference at the beginning of its 1986 session of an *ad hoc* committee to carry out the multilateral negotiation of a treaty on the complete cessation of nuclear-test explosions;

6. *Recommends* to the Conference on Disarmament that it instruct such an **ad hoc** committee to establish two working groups which will deal, respectively, with the following interrelated questions:

(a) Working Group I—Structure and scope of the treaty;

(b) Working Group II—Compliance and verification;

7. *Calls upon* the States depositaries of the Treaty Banning Nuclear Weapon Tests in the Atmosphere, in Outer Space and under Water and the Treaty on the Non-Proliferation of Nuclear Weapons, by virtue of their special responsibilities under those two Treaties and as a provisional measure, to bring to a halt without delay all nuclear-test explosions, either through a trilaterally agreed moratorium or through three unilateral moratoria, for which they would then proceed to negotiate the establishment of appropriate means of verification;

8. *Decides* to include in the provisional agenda of its forty-first session an item entitled "Cessation of all nuclear-test explosions".

General Assembly resolution 40/80 A

12 December 1985   Meeting 113   124-3-21 (recorded vote)

Approved by First Committee (A/40/941) by recorded vote (111-2-25), 21 November (meeting 45); 12-nation draft (A/C.1/40/L.35/Rev.1); agenda item 50.
Sponsors: Austria, Ecuador, Finland, Indonesia, Ireland, Kenya, Mexico, Pakistan, Peru, Sri Lanka, Sweden, Yugoslavia.
Meeting numbers. GA 40th session: 1st Committee 3-32, 45; plenary 113.

Recorded vote in Assembly as follows:

In favour: Afghanistan, Algeria, Angola, Argentina, Austria, Bahamas, Bahrain, Bangladesh, Barbados, Benin, Bhutan, Bolivia, Botswana, Brunei Darussalam, Bulgaria, Burkina Faso, Burma, Burundi, Byelorussian SSR, Cameroon, Cape Verde, Central African Republic, Chad, Chile, Colombia, Comoros, Congo, Cuba, Cyprus, Czechoslovakia, Democratic Kampuchea, Democratic Yemen, Djibouti, Dominican Republic, Ecuador, Egypt, El Salvador, Equatorial Guinea, Ethiopia, Fiji, Finland, Gabon, German Democratic Republic, Ghana, Greece, Guatemala, Guinea, Guinea-Bissau, Guyana, Haiti, Honduras, Hungary, India, Indonesia, Iran, Iraq, Ireland, Ivory Coast, Jamaica, Jordan, Kenya, Kuwait, Lao People's Democratic Republic, Lebanon, Lesotho, Liberia, Libyan Arab Jamahiriya, Madagascar, Malaysia, Maldives, Mali, Malta, Mauritania, Mauritius, Mexico, Mongolia, Morocco, Mozambique, Nepal, Nicaragua, Niger, Nigeria, Oman, Pakistan, Panama, Paraguay, Peru, Philippines, Poland, Qatar, Romania, Rwanda, Saint Christopher and Nevis, Saint Lucia, Saint Vincent and the Grenadines, Sao Tome and Principe, Saudi Arabia, Senegal, Seychelles, Sierra Leone, Singapore, Somalia, Sri Lanka, Sudan, Suriname, Swaziland, Sweden, Syrian Arab Republic, Thailand, Togo, Trinidad and Tobago, Tunisia, Uganda, Ukrainian SSR, United Arab Emirates, United Republic of Tanzania, Uruguay, Venezuela, Viet Nam, Yemen, Yugoslavia, Zaire, Zambia.
Against: France, United Kingdom, United States.
Abstaining: Australia, Belgium, Brazil, Canada, China, Denmark, Germany, Federal Republic of, Grenada, Iceland, Israel, Italy, Japan, Luxembourg, Netherlands, New Zealand, Norway, Papua New Guinea, Portugal, Samoa, Spain, Turkey.

In explanation of its negative vote, France, which had abstained in the First Committee, said the cessation of tests formed part of, and was not a precondition to, the process of nuclear disarmament.

Brazil said the draft implied a judgement of NPT,[2] with which it did not agree, nor did the text distinguish between nuclear explosions for peaceful purposes and nuclear-weapon explosions. For Canada, the draft called for a moratorium without any acceptable verification measures and seemed to ignore the necessity of all five major nuclear-weapon States participating in the work towards a comprehensive test ban. Similarly, New Zealand could not understand why the draft's call was directed only to the three nuclear-weapon States and not to China and France as well.

The USSR said the envisaged treaty should contain provisions preventing the circumvention of a comprehensive ban by means of nuclear explosions for peaceful purposes.

The Assembly adopted **resolution 40/80 B**, also by recorded vote.

The General Assembly,

Bearing in mind the determination, proclaimed since 1963 in the Treaty Banning Nuclear Weapon Tests in the Atmosphere, in Outer Space and under Water, to seek to achieve the discontinuance of all test explosions of nuclear weapons for all time and to continue negotiations to this end,

Bearing also in mind that in 1968 the Treaty on the Non-Proliferation of Nuclear Weapons recalled such determination and included in its article VI an undertaking by each of its parties to pursue negotiations in good faith on effective measures relating to cessation of the nuclear-arms race at an early date,

Recalling that in its resolution 2028(XX) of 19 November 1965, adopted unanimously, it had stressed that one of the basic principles on which the treaty to prevent the proliferation of nuclear weapons should be based was that such treaty, which was then to be negotiated, should embody an acceptable balance of mutual responsibilities and obligations of the nuclear and non-nuclear Powers,

Recalling also that the Third Review Conference of the Parties to the Treaty on the Non-Proliferation of Nuclear Weapons, in its Final Declaration adopted by consensus on 21 September 1985, expressed its deep regret that a comprehensive multilateral nuclear-test-ban treaty had not been concluded so far and called for the urgent negotiation and conclusion of such a treaty as a matter of the highest priority,

Noting that article II of the Treaty Banning Nuclear Weapon Tests in the Atmosphere, in Outer Space and under Water provides a procedure for the consideration and eventual adoption of amendments to the Treaty by a conference of its parties,

Recommends that States parties to the Treaty Banning Nuclear Weapon Tests in the Atmosphere, in Outer Space and under Water carry out urgent consultations among themselves as to the advisability and most appropriate method of taking advantage of the provisions of its article II for the conversion of the partial nuclear-test-ban treaty into a comprehensive nuclear-test-ban treaty.

General Assembly resolution 40/80 B

12 December 1985   Meeting 113   121-3-24 (recorded vote)

Approved by First Committee (A/40/941) by recorded vote (108-3-26), 21 November (meeting 45); 7-nation draft (A/C.1/40/L.49); agenda item 50.
Sponsors: Ecuador, Indonesia, Kenya, Mexico, Peru, Sri Lanka, Yugoslavia.
Meeting numbers. GA 40th session: 1st Committee 3-32, 45; plenary 113.

Recorded vote in Assembly as follows:

In favour: Afghanistan, Algeria, Angola, Antigua and Barbuda, Bahamas, Bahrain, Bangladesh, Barbados, Benin, Bhutan, Bolivia, Botswana, Brazil, Brunei Darussalam, Bulgaria, Burkina Faso, Burma, Burundi, Byelorussian SSR, Cameroon, Cape Verde, Central African Republic, Chad, Chile, Colombia, Comoros, Congo, Cuba, Cyprus, Czechoslovakia, Democratic Kampuchea, Democratic Yemen, Djibouti, Dominican Republic, Ecuador, Egypt, El Salvador, Equatorial Guinea, Ethiopia, Fiji, Gabon, German Democratic Republic, Ghana, Greece, Guatemala, Guinea, Guinea-Bissau, Guyana, Haiti, Honduras, Hungary, India, Indonesia, Iran, Iraq, Ivory Coast, Jamaica, Jordan, Kenya, Kuwait, Lao People's Democratic Republic, Lebanon, Lesotho, Liberia, Libyan Arab Jamahiriya, Madagascar, Malaysia, Maldives, Mali, Malta, Mauritania, Mauritius, Mexico, Mongolia, Morocco, Mozambique, Nepal, Nicaragua, Niger, Nigeria, Oman, Pakistan, Panama, Papua New Guinea, Paraguay, Peru, Philippines, Poland, Qatar, Romania, Rwanda, Saint Christopher and Nevis, Saint Lucia, Saint Vincent and the Grenadines, Sao Tome and Principe, Saudi Arabia, Senegal, Seychelles, Sierra Leone, Singapore, Somalia, Sri Lanka, Sudan, Suriname, Swaziland, Syrian Arab Republic, Thailand, Togo, Trinidad and Tobago, Tunisia, Uganda, Ukrainian SSR, USSR, United Arab Emirates, United Republic of Tanzania, Uruguay, Venezuela, Viet Nam, Yemen, Yugoslavia, Zaire.

Against: France, United Kingdom, United States.

Abstaining: Argentina, Australia, Austria, Belgium, Canada, Denmark, Finland, Germany, Federal Republic of, Grenada, Iceland, Ireland, Israel, Italy, Japan, Luxembourg, Netherlands, New Zealand, Norway, Portugal, Samoa, Spain, Sweden, Turkey, Zambia.

France, a non-party to the Treaties mentioned in the text, asserted that a test ban must be realized in the framework of a nuclear disarmament process, the prerequisite for which remained reductions in the arsenals of the two major Powers. The United Kingdom declared that it did not support a meeting of States parties for the purposes put forward in the text.

Australia and New Zealand did not feel the draft promised the best way to achieve a negotiated, verifiable comprehensive test-ban treaty. Australia added that the problem was not finding an appropriate treaty format for a comprehensive test ban but overcoming the outstanding verification problem and the national security policy objections of the nuclear-weapon and some other States. Argentina said the five nuclear Powers would not be represented in the mechanism envisaged in the proposal.

The USSR said it supported strengthening the 1963 Treaty, and hoped that China and France would join in a nuclear-weapon test ban.

The United States could not support the texts that became resolutions 40/80 A and B for what it felt was their erroneous implication that the

Third Review Conference of the parties to NPT (see p. 56) had reached consensus on a call for immediate negotiations on a comprehensive test ban.

Also on 12 December, the General Assembly adopted, by recorded vote, **resolution 40/88**.

Implementation of General Assembly resolution 39/60 on the immediate cessation and prohibition of nuclear-weapon tests

The General Assembly,

Deeply concerned about the intensification of the nuclear-arms race and the growing threat of nuclear war,

Recalling that over the past three decades the need for cessation and prohibition of nuclear-weapon testing has been in the focus of attention of the General Assembly,

Reaffirming its conviction that the conclusion of a multilateral treaty on the prohibition of nuclear-weapon tests by all States would constitute an indispensable element of efforts to halt and reverse the nuclear-arms race and the qualitative improvement of nuclear weapons, and to prevent the expansion of existing nuclear arsenals and the spread of nuclear weapons to additional countries, thus contributing to the achievement of the final goal of the complete elimination of nuclear weapons under appropriate verification,

Stressing once again that the elaboration of such a treaty is the task of the highest priority and should not be made dependent on the attainment of any other measure in the field of disarmament,

Welcoming the proposals contained in the Delhi Declaration issued on 28 January 1985 by the heads of State or Government of six States Members of the United Nations—Argentina, Greece, India, Mexico, Sweden and the United Republic of Tanzania—and their joint message of 24 October 1985 addressed to the leaders of the United States of America and the Union of Soviet Socialist Republics,

Recalling its previous resolutions on this subject, in particular resolutions 39/52 and 39/60 of 12 December 1984, by which it called for a moratorium or moratoria on all nuclear-test explosions and for the negotiation of a treaty for the prohibition of all nuclear-weapon tests,

Deeply deploring that the Conference on Disarmament has been unable to carry out negotiations with a view to reaching agreement on such a treaty,

1. *Urges* the Conference on Disarmament to proceed promptly to negotiations on all aspects of this matter, including adequate measures of verification, with the aim of preparing without delay a draft treaty that would effectively ban all test explosions of nuclear weapons by all States everywhere and would contain provisions, acceptable to all, preventing the circumvention of this ban by means of nuclear explosions for peaceful purposes;

2. *Resolutely urges* all States, and especially all nuclear-weapon States, to exert maximum efforts and exercise political will for the elaboration and conclusion without delay of such a treaty;

3. *Welcomes* the unilateral cessation by one major nuclear-weapon State of all its nuclear explosions, effective 6 August 1985, as well as the proposal for the suspension of all nuclear tests for a period of 12 months, with the possibility of its extension, contained in the joint message of 24 October 1985 addressed to the leaders of the United States of America and the Union of Soviet

Socialist Republics by the heads of State or Government of six States Members of the United Nations;

4. *Expresses its hope* that all other nuclear-weapon States will also consider joining in such a moratorium;

5. *Decides* to include in the provisional agenda of its forty-first session an item entitled "Implementation of General Assembly resolution 40/88 on the immediate cessation and prohibition of nuclear-weapon tests".

General Assembly resolution 40/88

12 December 1985   Meeting 113   120-3-29 (recorded vote)

Approved by First Committee (A/40/944) by recorded vote (107-3-26), 21 November (meeting 45); 13-nation draft (A/C.1/40/L.42); agenda item 58.

Sponsors: Afghanistan, Angola, Bulgaria, Byelorussian SSR, Czechoslovakia, German Democratic Republic, Hungary, Lao People's Democratic Republic, Mongolia, Poland, Ukrainian SSR, USSR, Viet Nam.

Meeting numbers. GA 40th session: 1st Committee 3-32, 36, 45; plenary 113.

Recorded vote in Assembly as follows:

In favour: Afghanistan, Algeria, Angola, Argentina, Austria, Bahamas, Bahrain, Bangladesh, Barbados, Benin, Bhutan, Bolivia, Botswana, Brunei Darussalam, Bulgaria, Burkina Faso, Burma, Burundi, Byelorussian SSR, Cameroon, Cape Verde, Central African Republic, Chad, Chile, Colombia, Comoros, Congo, Cuba, Cyprus, Czechoslovakia, Democratic Yemen, Djibouti, Dominican Republic, Ecuador, Egypt, El Salvador, Equatorial Guinea, Ethiopia, Fiji, Gabon, German Democratic Republic, Ghana, Greece, Guatemala, Guinea, Guinea-Bissau, Guyana, Honduras, Hungary, India, Indonesia, Iran, Iraq, Ivory Coast, Jordan, Kenya, Kuwait, Lao People's Democratic Republic, Lebanon, Lesotho, Liberia, Libyan Arab Jamahiriya, Madagascar, Malawi, Malaysia, Maldives, Mali, Malta, Mauritania, Mauritius, Mexico, Mongolia, Morocco, Mozambique, Nepal, Nicaragua, Niger, Nigeria, Oman, Pakistan, Panama, Peru, Philippines, Poland, Qatar, Romania, Rwanda, Saint Christopher and Nevis, Saint Vincent and the Grenadines, Sao Tome and Principe, Saudi Arabia, Senegal, Seychelles, Sierra Leone, Singapore, Somalia, Sudan, Suriname, Swaziland, Sweden, Syrian Arab Republic, Thailand, Togo, Trinidad and Tobago, Tunisia, Uganda, Ukrainian SSR, USSR, United Arab Emirates, United Republic of Tanzania, Uruguay, Vanuatu, Venezuela, Viet Nam, Yemen, Yugoslavia, Zaire, Zambia, Zimbabwe.

Against: France, United Kingdom, United States.

Abstaining: Antigua and Barbuda, Australia, Belgium, Brazil, Canada, China, Democratic Kampuchea, Denmark, Germany, Federal Republic of, Grenada, Haiti, Iceland, Ireland, Israel, Italy, Jamaica, Japan, Luxembourg, Netherlands, New Zealand, Norway, Papua New Guinea, Paraguay, Portugal, Saint Lucia, Samoa, Solomon Islands, Spain, Turkey.

France said it did not accept the appeal in the text to all nuclear-weapon States to join in a test moratorium, because such a measure would help enshrine the qualitative and quantitative advantages currently held by the two main nuclear Powers. Stating that some agreement on verification must precede negotiations, the United Kingdom said an unverifiable ban or moratorium would be worse than useless.

Brazil regretted that the text highlighted views which it considered were not directly pertinent to the actual negotiation of a ban. Canada had reservations about the value of a declaratory, unverifiable moratorium. New Zealand saw contradiction in paragraphs 1 and 5, and stressed that an unverified moratorium could not substitute for a properly verifiable and legally binding treaty.

The Assembly adopted **resolution 40/81** by recorded vote on 12 December.

Urgent need for a comprehensive nuclear-test-ban treaty

The General Assembly,

Convinced of the urgent need for a comprehensive nuclear-test-ban treaty capable of attracting the widest possible international support and adherence,

Reaffirming its conviction that an end to all nuclear testing by all States in all environments for all time would be a major step towards ending the qualitative improvement, development and proliferation of nuclear weapons, a means of relieving the deep apprehension concerning the harmful consequences of radioactive contamination for the health of present and future generations and a measure of the utmost importance in bringing the nuclear-arms race to an end,

Recalling that the parties to the Treaty Banning Nuclear Weapon Tests in the Atmosphere, in Outer Space and under Water undertook not to carry out any nuclear-weapon-test explosion, or any other nuclear explosion, in the environments covered by that Treaty, and that in that Treaty the parties expressed their determination to continue negotiations to achieve the discontinuance of all test explosions of nuclear weapons for all time,

Recalling also that the parties to the Treaty on the Non-Proliferation of Nuclear Weapons recalled the determination expressed by the parties to the Treaty Banning Nuclear Weapon Tests in the Atmosphere, in Outer Space and under Water in its preamble to seek to achieve the discontinuance of all test explosions of nuclear weapons for all time and to continue negotiations to that end, declaring their intention to achieve at the earliest possible date the cessation of the nuclear-arms race and to undertake effective measures in the direction of nuclear disarmament,

Noting that in the Final Declaration of the Third Review Conference of the Parties to the Treaty on the Non-Proliferation of Nuclear Weapons, regret was expressed that a comprehensive multilateral nuclear-test-ban treaty banning all nuclear tests by all States in all environments for all time had not been concluded and that all nuclear-weapon States were called on to participate in the urgent negotiation and conclusion of such a treaty, as a matter of the highest priority, in the Conference on Disarmament,

Recalling further its previous resolutions on this subject,

Taking into account that part of the report of the Conference on Disarmament relating to consideration of the item entitled "Nuclear-test ban" during its session in 1985,

Also taking into account relevant proposals and initiatives put forward in the Conference on Disarmament during its session in 1985 and other proposals and actions advanced in 1985 concerning efforts to promote an end to nuclear testing,

Expressing its profound regret that, in spite of strenuous efforts, the Conference on Disarmament was unable to reach agreement on the re-establishment at its session in 1985 of an *ad hoc* committee under item 1 of its agenda, entitled "Nuclear-test ban",

Recognizing the important role of the Conference on Disarmament in the negotiation of a comprehensive nuclear-test-ban treaty,

Recognizing the importance to such a treaty of the work on a global seismic detection network, assigned by the Conference on Disarmament to the *Ad Hoc* Group of Scientific Experts to Consider International Cooperative Measures to Detect and Identify Seismic Events,

Recalling paragraph 31 of the Final Document of the Tenth Special Session of the General Assembly, the first special session devoted to disarmament, relating to verification of disarmament and arms control agreements, which stated that the form and modalities of the verification to be provided for in any specific agreement depend on, and should be determined by, the purposes, scope and nature of the agreement,

1. *Reiterates its profound concern* that, despite the express wishes of the majority of Member States, nuclear testing continues;

2. *Reaffirms its conviction* that a treaty to achieve the prohibition of all nuclear-test explosions by all States in all environments for all time is a matter of greatest importance;

3. *Expresses the conviction* that such a treaty would constitute a vital element for the success of efforts to halt and reverse the nuclear-arms race and the qualitative improvement of nuclear weapons and to prevent the expansion of existing nuclear arsenals and the spread of nuclear weapons to additional countries;

4. *Urges* the Conference on Disarmament to establish at the beginning of its session in 1986 an *ad hoc* committee under item 1 of its agenda, entitled "Nuclear-test ban", to begin negotiations on a comprehensive nuclear-test-ban treaty in accordance with the following programme of work:

(a) Scope:
(i) Comprehensive ban on nuclear explosions in all environments;
(ii) Question of nuclear explosions for peaceful purposes;
(b) Verification:
(i) Central importance of verification of a comprehensive test ban;
(ii) Factors affecting verification needs;
(iii) Means for monitoring compliance:
    a. National technical means;
    b. International seismic monitoring network:
      i. Determination of capabilities for monitoring compliance;
      ii. Steps for establishment and improvement;
      iii. Institutional, administrative and financial arrangements for establishment, testing and operation;
      iv. Relationship to an effective verification system;
    c. Other means, including an international atmospheric radioactivity monitoring network;
    d. On-site inspection;
(iv) Specific verification problems and their solutions, including:
    a. Monitoring large land masses;
    b. Methods of possible evasion;
    c. Chemical explosions;
(c) Compliance:
(i) Procedures and mechanisms for consultation and co-operation;
(ii) Co-ordinating body, e.g. committee of experts;
(iii) Consultative committee;
(iv) Series of actions triggered by suspicion or violation, including complaints procedures;

5. *Further urges* the Conference on Disarmament:

(a) To take immediate steps for the establishment, with the widest possible participation, of an international seismic monitoring network to determine the capabilities of such a network for monitoring and verifying compliance with a comprehensive nuclear-test-ban treaty,

taking into account the work performed by the *Ad Hoc* Group of Scientific Experts to Consider International Co-operative Measures to Detect and Identify Seismic Events;

(b) To initiate detailed investigation of other measures to monitor and verify compliance with such a treaty, including an international network to monitor atmospheric radioactivity;

6. *Urges* all members of the Conference on Disarmament, in particular the nuclear-weapon States, to co-operate within the Conference in fulfilling these tasks as called for, *inter alia*, in the Final Declaration of the Third Review Conference of the Parties to the Treaty on the Non-Proliferation of Nuclear Weapons;

7. *Calls upon* the Conference on Disarmament to report on progress to the General Assembly at its forty-first session;

8. *Decides* to include in the provisional agenda of its forty-first session the item entitled "Urgent need for a comprehensive nuclear-test-ban treaty".

General Assembly resolution 40/81

12 December 1985　　　Meeting 113　　　116-4-29 (recorded vote)

Approved by First Committee (A/40/942) by recorded vote (103-3-32), 21 November (meeting 45); 20-nation draft (A/C.1/40/L.73); agenda item 51.
Sponsors: Australia, Austria, Bahamas, Denmark, Fiji, Finland, Iceland, Ireland, Jamaica, Kenya, New Zealand, Norway, Papua New Guinea, Philippines, Samoa, Singapore, Solomon Islands, Sweden, Thailand, Vanuatu.
Meeting numbers. GA 40th session: 1st Committee 3-32, 34, 45; plenary 113.

Recorded vote in Assembly as follows:

In favour: Algeria, Antigua and Barbuda, Australia, Austria, Bahamas, Bahrain, Bangladesh, Barbados, Benin, Bhutan, Bolivia, Botswana, Brunei Darussalam, Burkina Faso, Burma, Burundi, Cameroon, Canada, Cape Verde, Central African Republic, Chad, Chile, Colombia, Comoros, Congo, Cyprus, Democratic Kampuchea, Democratic Yemen, Denmark, Djibouti, Dominican Republic, Ecuador, Egypt, El Salvador, Equatorial Guinea, Ethiopia, Fiji, Finland, Gabon, Ghana,[a] Greece, Guatemala, Guinea, Guinea-Bissau, Guyana, Haiti, Honduras, Iceland, Indonesia, Iran, Iraq, Ireland, Ivory Coast, Jamaica, Japan, Jordan, Kenya, Kuwait, Lesotho, Liberia, Libyan Arab Jamahiriya, Malawi, Malaysia, Maldives, Mali, Malta, Mauritania, Mauritius, Morocco, Mozambique, Nepal, Netherlands, New Zealand, Niger, Nigeria, Norway, Oman, Pakistan, Panama, Papua New Guinea, Paraguay, Peru, Philippines, Qatar, Romania, Rwanda, Saint Christopher and Nevis, Saint Lucia, Saint Vincent and the Grenadines, Samoa, Sao Tome and Principe, Saudi Arabia, Senegal, Seychelles, Sierra Leone, Singapore, Somalia, Spain, Sri Lanka, Sudan, Suriname, Swaziland, Sweden, Syrian Arab Republic, Thailand, Togo, Trinidad and Tobago, Tunisia, Turkey, Uganda, United Arab Emirates, United Republic of Tanzania, Uruguay, Yemen, Yugoslavia, Zaire.
Against: France, Grenada, United Kingdom, United States.
Abstaining: Afghanistan, Angola, Argentina, Belgium, Brazil, Bulgaria, Byelorussian SSR, China, Cuba, Czechoslovakia, German Democratic Republic, Germany, Federal Republic of, Hungary, India, Israel, Italy, Lao People's Democratic Republic, Luxembourg, Madagascar, Mexico, Mongolia, Nicaragua, Poland, Portugal, Ukrainian SSR, USSR, Venezuela, Viet Nam, Zambia.

[a] Later advised the Secretariat it had intended to abstain.

Prior to adopting the text as a whole, the Assembly adopted paragraph 4 by a recorded vote of 84 to 4 (France, Grenada, United Kingdom, United States), with 55 abstentions; it also adopted paragraph 5 by a recorded vote, requested by the USSR, of 94 to 12 (including the Eastern European States except Romania), with 35 abstentions. The First Committee had approved paragraphs 4 and 5 by recorded votes, respectively, of 70 to 3 (France, United Kingdom, United States), with 60 abstentions, and of 80 to 12 (including the Eastern European States except Romania), with 40 abstentions.

In explanation of vote, the propriety of the Assembly's dictating a programme of work to the

Conference on Disarmament was questioned by many, among them Brazil, Bulgaria, France, India, Italy, Morocco, the USSR and Venezuela. Brazil felt the programme could prejudge the scope and outcome of the negotiations, and would depart from the guidelines on the topic set forth in the 1978 Final Document. Bulgaria feared that the programme, unbalanced in its view, could set back negotiations for a number of years. France further reiterated its position regarding a test ban outside a nuclear disarmament process, and India emphasized that the text did not support its approach of principle in the matter. Italy believed that progress towards a ban could be better accomplished through a gradual approach based on comprehensive consideration of the issue in its proper perspective. The USSR felt the programme placed excessive stress on the verification issue, and Venezuela added that the programme would force the *ad hoc* committee into focusing on issues relating to scope and verification. The United Kingdom observed that the work programme for an *ad hoc* committee which a group of Western and other States had submitted to the Conference on Disarmament in 1985 remained on the table.

Argentina approved the negotiating mandate on the nuclear-weapon test ban given to the Conference, but remained unconvinced that the Assembly should make a detailed statement on technical aspects of the topic. In Canada's view, the draft not only outlined a realistic and detailed programme of work but also highlighted the importance of establishing an international seismic monitoring network; it added that, while it shared the broad objective of the text, it was not entirely satisfied that the proposed way of achieving that objective was realistic.

As regards paragraph 5, Bulgaria and the USSR said they voted negatively as they could not support setting up verification mechanisms apart from or prior to the conclusion of a treaty. Bulgaria considered such mechanisms superfluous in the absence of a treaty, and added that an overemphasis on verification could prolong negotiations while tests continued unabated. Venezuela shared those views. The United States supported the development and improvement of a seismic monitoring network and the efforts of the *Ad Hoc* Group of Scientific Experts.

Speaking on the series of resolutions, Australia said it could not support the texts that became resolutions 40/80 A and 40/88, viewing them to be limited in scope and not providing for the development of adequate means of compliance verification. Zambia had no choice but to abstain on the texts that became resolutions 40/80 A, 40/80 B and 40/81 because of their reference to NPT, to which it was not a party. Similarly,

Burma, a non-party to NPT, dissociated itself from the reference to that Treaty in paragraph 3 of resolution 40/80 A, while welcoming the prospect it detected in all four texts for the commencement of negotiations. Denmark also supported the gist of the four drafts, but considered more realistic the one it had sponsored (40/81).

Proposed nuclear-weapon freeze

GENERAL ASSEMBLY ACTION

In December 1985, the General Assembly adopted, on the recommendation of the First Committee, three resolutions (**40/151 C, 40/151 E** and **40/94 H**) calling for a freeze on nuclear armaments. A number of States explained in single statements their positions on these texts (see p. 56).

The Assembly, on 16 December, adopted **resolution 40/151 C** by recorded vote.

Nuclear-arms freeze

The General Assembly,

Recalling that in the Final Document of the Tenth Special Session of the General Assembly, the first special session devoted to disarmament, adopted in 1978 and unanimously and categorically reaffirmed in 1982 during the twelfth special session of the General Assembly, the second special session devoted to disarmament, the Assembly expressed deep concern over the threat to the very survival of mankind posed by the existence of nuclear weapons and the continuing arms race,

Recalling also that, on those occasions, it pointed out that existing arsenals of nuclear weapons are more than sufficient to destroy all life on Earth and stressed that mankind is therefore confronted with a choice: halt the arms race and proceed to disarmament, or face annihilation,

Noting that in the Political Declarations adopted by the Seventh Conference of Heads of State or Government of Non-Aligned Countries, held at New Delhi from 7 to 12 March 1983 and the Conference of Foreign Ministers of Non-Aligned Countries held at Luanda from 4 to 7 September 1985, it was stated that the renewed escalation in the nuclear-arms race, both in its quantitative and qualitative dimensions, as well as reliance on doctrines of nuclear deterrence, had heightened the risk of the outbreak of nuclear war and led to greater insecurity and instability in international relations,

Bearing in mind that in their Joint Declaration, issued on 22 May 1984, the heads of State or Government of six States Members of the United Nations, coming from five different continents, urged the nuclear-weapon States as a necessary first step to halt all testing, production and deployment of nuclear weapons and their delivery systems, and that in the Delhi Declaration issued on 28 January 1985 they reiterated: "A halt to the nuclear arms race is at the present moment imperative. Only thus can it be ensured that nuclear arsenals do not grow while negotiations proceed.",

Believing that it is a matter of the utmost urgency to stop any further increase in the awesome arsenals of the two major nuclear-weapon States, which already have ample retaliatory power and a frightening overkill capacity,

Welcoming the start of negotiations between the Union of Soviet Socialist Republics and the United States of America on a complex of questions concerning space and nuclear arms—both strategic and intermediate-range—with all these questions considered and resolved in their interrelationship,

Considering that a nuclear-arms freeze, while not an end in itself, would constitute the most effective first step to prevent the continued increase and qualitative improvement of existing nuclear weaponry during the period when the negotiations take place,

Firmly convinced that at present the conditions are most propitious for such a freeze, since the Union of Soviet Socialist Republics and the United States of America are now equivalent in nuclear military power and it seems evident that there exists between them an overall rough parity,

Conscious that the application of the systems of surveillance, verification and control already agreed upon in some previous cases would be sufficient to provide a reasonable guarantee of faithful compliance with the undertakings derived from the freeze,

Convinced that it would be to the benefit of all other States possessing nuclear weapons to follow the example of the two major nuclear-weapon States,

1. *Urges once more* the Union of Soviet Socialist Republics and the United States of America, as the two major nuclear-weapon States, to proclaim, either through simultaneous unilateral declarations or through a joint declaration, an immediate nuclear-arms freeze, which would be a first step towards the comprehensive programme of disarmament and whose structure and scope would be the following:

(*a*) It would embrace:

(i) A comprehensive test ban of nuclear weapons and of their delivery vehicles;

(ii) The complete cessation of the manufacture of nuclear weapons and of their delivery vehicles;

(iii) A ban on all further deployment of nuclear weapons and of their delivery vehicles;

(iv) The complete cessation of the production of fissionable material for weapons purposes;

(*b*) It would be subject to appropriate measures and procedures of verification, such as those that have already been agreed by the parties in the case of the SALT I and SALT II treaties, and those agreed upon in principle by them during the preparatory trilateral negotiations on the comprehensive test ban held at Geneva;

(*c*) It would be of an initial five-year duration, subject to prolongation when other nuclear-weapon States join in such a freeze, as the General Assembly urges them to do;

2. *Requests* the above-mentioned two major nuclear-weapon States to submit a joint report or two separate reports to the General Assembly, prior to the opening of its forty-first session, on the implementation of the present resolution;

3. *Decides* to include in the provisional agenda of its forty-first session an item entitled "Implementation of General Assembly resolution 40/151 C on a nuclear-arms freeze".

General Assembly resolution 40/151 C

16 December 1985   Meeting 117   131-10-8 (recorded vote)

Approved by First Committee (A/40/946) by recorded vote (113-11-6), 20 November (meeting 43); 8-nation draft (A/C.1/40/L.18); agenda item 61 *(c)*.

Sponsors: Ecuador, Indonesia, Mexico, Pakistan, Peru, Romania, Sweden, Uruguay.

Meeting numbers. GA 40th session: 1st Committee 3-32, 43; plenary 117.

Recorded vote in Assembly as follows:

In favour: Afghanistan, Algeria, Angola, Antigua and Barbuda, Argentina, Australia, Austria, Bahrain, Bangladesh, Barbados, Benin, Bhutan, Bolivia, Botswana, Brazil, Brunei Darussalam, Bulgaria, Burkina Faso, Burma, Burundi, Byelorussian SSR, Cameroon, Cape Verde, Central African Republic, Chad, Chile, Colombia, Comoros, Congo, Costa Rica, Cuba, Cyprus, Czechoslovakia, Democratic Yemen, Denmark, Djibouti, Dominican Republic, Ecuador, Egypt, El Salvador, Equatorial Guinea, Ethiopia, Fiji, Finland, Gabon, Gambia, German Democratic Republic, Ghana, Greece, Guatemala, Guinea, Guinea-Bissau, Guyana, Haiti, Honduras, Hungary, India, Indonesia, Iran, Iraq, Ireland, Ivory Coast, Jamaica, Jordan, Kenya, Kuwait, Lao People's Democratic Republic, Lebanon, Lesotho, Liberia, Libyan Arab Jamahiriya, Madagascar, Malawi, Malaysia, Maldives, Mali, Malta, Mauritania, Mauritius, Mexico, Mongolia, Morocco, Mozambique, Nepal, New Zealand, Nicaragua, Niger, Nigeria, Norway, Oman, Pakistan, Panama, Papua New Guinea, Paraguay, Peru, Poland, Qatar, Romania, Rwanda, Saint Lucia, Saint Vincent and the Grenadines, Samoa, Sao Tome and Principe, Saudi Arabia, Senegal, Seychelles, Sierra Leone, Singapore, Somalia, Sri Lanka, Sudan, Suriname, Swaziland, Sweden, Syrian Arab Republic, Thailand, Togo, Trinidad and Tobago, Tunisia, Uganda, Ukrainian SSR, USSR, United Arab Emirates, United Republic of Tanzania, Uruguay, Vanuatu, Venezuela, Viet Nam, Yugoslavia, Zaire, Zambia.

Against: Belgium, Canada, France, Israel, Italy, Japan, Portugal, Turkey, United Kingdom, United States.

Abstaining: Bahamas, China, Germany, Federal Republic of,[a] Grenada, Iceland, Luxembourg, Netherlands, Spain.

[a]Later advised the Secretariat it had intended to vote against.

The Netherlands asserted that the declaratory approach to the freeze concept fell short of meeting verification needs, and that only negotiations could lead to acceptable solutions to the verification issues.

Norway did not believe that reliance on nuclear deterrence had heightened the risk of nuclear war; its vote should not be considered as criticism of the countries which were implementing the decisions of NATO, whose defensive strategy it supported. New Zealand said a nuclear-arms freeze should be based on a balance of deterrence at the lowest possible level of nuclear arsenals, encompass a comprehensive test-ban treaty, and be accompanied by negotiations to reduce drastically nuclear arms leading to their complete elimination, and that it must be balanced, mutual and verifiable. Sharing those views, Australia said nuclear deterrence was the only option currently available to avoid serious nuclear instability and conflict, although it should be regarded as only an interim step leading to the goal of complete disarmament.

The USSR said it had proposed to the United States, among other things, to freeze nuclear weapons at current levels and limit their modernization, and to halt testing and deployment of new types of such weapons.

On 16 December, the Assembly adopted **resolution 40/151 E** by recorded vote.

Freeze on nuclear weapons

The General Assembly,

Recalling its resolutions 37/100 A of 13 December 1982, 38/73 B of 15 December 1983 and 39/63 G of 12 December 1984 concerning a freeze on nuclear weapons,

Convinced that in this nuclear age lasting world peace can be based only on the attainment of the goal of general and complete disarmament under effective international control,

Further convinced that the highest priority objectives in the field of disarmament have to be nuclear disarmament and the elimination of all weapons of mass destruction,

Recognizing the urgent need to halt the arms race, particularly in nuclear weapons,

Recognizing further the urgent need for a negotiated reduction of nuclear-weapon stockpiles leading to their complete elimination,

Noting with deep concern that nuclear-weapon States have not so far taken any action in response to the call made in resolutions 37/100 A, 38/73 B and 39/63 G,

1. *Once again calls upon* all nuclear-weapon States to agree to a freeze on nuclear weapons, which would, *inter alia*, provide for a simultaneous total stoppage of any further production of nuclear weapons and a complete cut-off in the production of fissionable material for weapons purposes;

2. *Decides* to include in the provisional agenda of its forty-first session the item entitled "Freeze on nuclear weapons".

General Assembly resolution 40/151 E

16 December 1985   Meeting 117   126-12-10 (recorded vote)

Approved by First Committee (A/40/946) by recorded vote (110-12-8), 20 November (meeting 43); draft by India (A/C.1/40/L.25); agenda item 61 *(e)*.
Meeting numbers. GA 40th session: 1st Committee 3-33, 43; plenary 117.

Recorded vote in Assembly as follows:

In favour: Afghanistan, Algeria, Angola, Antigua and Barbuda, Argentina, Austria, Bahrain, Bangladesh, Benin, Bhutan, Bolivia, Botswana, Brazil, Brunei Darussalam, Bulgaria, Burkina Faso, Burma, Burundi, Byelorussian SSR, Cameroon, Cape Verde, Central African Republic, Chad, Chile, Colombia, Comoros, Congo, Costa Rica, Cuba, Cyprus, Czechoslovakia, Democratic Yemen, Denmark, Djibouti, Dominican Republic, Ecuador, Egypt, El Salvador, Equatorial Guinea, Ethiopia, Fiji, Finland, Gabon, Gambia, German Democratic Republic, Ghana, Greece, Guatemala, Guinea, Guinea-Bissau, Guyana, Haiti, Honduras, Hungary, India, Indonesia, Iran, Iraq, Ireland, Ivory Coast, Jordan, Kenya, Kuwait, Lao People's Democratic Republic, Lebanon, Lesotho, Liberia, Libyan Arab Jamahiriya, Madagascar, Malawi, Malaysia, Maldives, Mali, Malta, Mauritania, Mauritius, Mexico, Mongolia, Mozambique, Nepal, Nicaragua, Niger, Nigeria, Oman, Pakistan, Panama, Papua New Guinea, Paraguay, Peru, Philippines, Poland, Qatar, Romania, Rwanda, Saint Lucia, Saint Vincent and the Grenadines, Samoa, Sao Tome and Principe, Saudi Arabia, Senegal, Seychelles, Sierra Leone, Singapore, Somalia, Sri Lanka, Sudan, Suriname, Swaziland, Sweden, Syrian Arab Republic, Thailand, Togo, Trinidad and Tobago, Tunisia, Uganda, Ukrainian SSR, USSR, United Arab Emirates, United Republic of Tanzania, Uruguay, Vanuatu, Venezuela, Viet Nam, Yugoslavia, Zaire, Zambia.

Against: Belgium, Canada, France, Germany, Federal Republic of, Israel, Italy, Luxembourg, Netherlands, Portugal, Turkey, United Kingdom, United States.

Abstaining: Australia, Bahamas, Barbados, China, Grenada, Iceland, Japan, New Zealand, Norway, Spain.

The Netherlands said the text ignored aspects of verification and its scope was imprecise and arbitrary.

Honduras expressed reservations, stating that a reduction and eventual elimination of nuclear arsenals, rather than a freeze, would produce the results mentioned in the preamble. The USSR said the last preambular paragraph did not reflect accurately its unilateral moratorium on nuclear explosions and on the deployment of medium-range nuclear missiles in Europe.

The Assembly adopted **resolution 40/94 H** by recorded vote on 12 December.

Nuclear-weapon freeze

The General Assembly,

Expressing its deep alarm over the continuation and intensification of the nuclear-arms race, which seriously increases the threat of nuclear war,

Taking into account the great responsibility of nuclear-weapon States for the preservation of universal peace and the prevention of nuclear war,

Recalling its previous resolutions calling for a nuclear-weapon freeze both in quantitative and in qualitative terms,

Recalling also that on several occasions it has expressed the firm conviction that at present the conditions are most propitious for such a freeze,

Convinced that a nuclear-weapon freeze would raise the level of trust among States, ease international tension and diminish the threat of nuclear war,

Convinced also that compliance with the obligations of the freeze could be verified by national technical means as well as through some additional verification measures based on co-operation, taking into account previous nuclear-arms limitation negotiations,

Noting the wide support for the Joint Declaration issued on 22 May 1984 and the Delhi Declaration issued on 28 January 1985, by the heads of State or Government of six States Members of the United Nations, which contained an appeal to the nuclear-weapon States to halt testing, production and deployment of nuclear weapons and their means of delivery,

Deeply regretting that some nuclear Powers have not responded positively to its relevant appeals or to appeals and proposals by other States made repeatedly during the last three years,

1. *Reaffirms its appeal* to all nuclear-weapon States to freeze, from a specific date, their nuclear arsenals on a global scale and under appropriate verification as a first step to their reduction with the view to their complete elimination;

2. *Urges once again* the Union of Soviet Socialist Republics and the United States of America, which possess the largest nuclear arsenals, to freeze, in the first place and simultaneously, their nuclear weapons on a bilateral basis by way of example to the other nuclear-weapon States;

3. *Strongly believes* that all the other nuclear-weapon States should subsequently and as soon as possible freeze their nuclear weapons.

General Assembly resolution 40/94 H

12 December 1985   Meeting 113   120-17-10 (recorded vote)

Approved by First Committee (A/40/976) by recorded vote (101-17-8), 20 November (meeting 43); 13-nation draft (A/C.1/40/L.44); agenda item 68.
Sponsors: Afghanistan, Angola, Bulgaria, Byelorussian SSR, Czechoslovakia, Ethiopia, German Democratic Republic, Hungary, Mongolia, Poland, Romania, Ukrainian SSR, USSR.
Meeting numbers. GA 40th session: 1st Committee 3-32, 36, 43; plenary 113.

Recorded vote in Assembly as follows:

In favour: Afghanistan, Algeria, Angola, Antigua and Barbuda, Argentina, Austria, Bahamas, Bahrain, Bangladesh, Barbados, Benin, Bhutan, Bolivia, Botswana, Brazil, Brunei Darussalam, Bulgaria, Burkina Faso, Burma, Burundi, Byelorussian SSR, Cameroon, Cape Verde, Central African Republic, Chad, Chile, Colombia, Comoros, Congo, Cuba, Cyprus, Czechoslovakia, Democratic Yemen, Djibouti, Dominican Republic, Ecuador, Egypt, El Salvador, Equatorial Guinea, Ethiopia, Fiji, Finland, Gabon, German Democratic Republic, Ghana, Greece, Grenada, Guatemala, Guinea, Guinea-Bissau, Guyana, Haiti, Honduras, Hungary, India, Indonesia, Iran, Iraq, Ireland, Ivory Coast, Jordan, Kenya, Kuwait, Lao People's Democratic Republic, Lebanon, Lesotho, Liberia, Libyan Arab Jamahiriya, Madagascar, Malawi, Mali, Mauritius, Mexico, Mongolia, Mozambique, Nepal, Nicaragua, Niger, Nigeria, Oman, Pakistan, Panama, Papua New Guinea, Peru, Philippines, Poland, Qatar, Romania, Rwanda, Saint Vincent and the Grenadines,

Samoa, Saudi Arabia, Senegal, Seychelles, Singapore, Solomon Islands, Somalia, Sri Lanka, Sudan, Suriname, Swaziland, Sweden, Syrian Arab Republic, Togo, Trinidad and Tobago, Tunisia, Uganda, Ukrainian SSR, USSR, United Arab Emirates, United Republic of Tanzania, Uruguay, Vanuatu, Venezuela, Viet Nam, Yemen, Yugoslavia, Zaire, Zambia, Zimbabwe.
Against: Belgium, Canada, Denmark, France, Germany, Federal Republic of, Iceland, Israel, Italy, Japan, Luxembourg, Netherlands, Norway, Portugal, Spain, Turkey, United Kingdom, United States.
Abstaining: Australia, China, Democratic Kampuchea, Malaysia, Maldives, New Zealand, Saint Christopher and Nevis, Saint Lucia, Sierra Leone, Thailand.

A number of delegations explained in single statements their positions on the texts which became resolutions 40/151 C, 40/151 E and 40/94 H.

France, the Federal Republic of Germany, Japan and the Netherlands asserted that a nuclear-weapon freeze under current circumstances would establish the advantage of one party over another and sanction a destabilizing imbalance, especially in Europe.

The Federal Republic of Germany added that a freeze left existing nuclear arsenals in place, so that the threat emanating from them would endure; efforts should focus rather on a disarmament process leading to a much lower level of armaments and military forces, taking into account the requirement of undiminished security for all States in accordance with paragraph 29 of the 1978 Final Document.[7] Stating that the surest path to nuclear-arms reductions should begin with the two super-Powers' defining and establishing a satisfactory military balance and proceeding with negotiations, France said a freeze would be difficult to verify and the negotiations necessary to ensure conditions for verification would be as complex as verification of actual reductions; further, to the extent that it could benefit a given Power, a freeze would risk reducing that Power's interest in negotiations and in reducing its weaponry. Japan questioned the practicability and meaningfulness of the three proposals, saying that realistic disarmament should be predicated on the balance of military strength and on deterrence. Referring to the text which became resolution 40/94 H, the Netherlands said it failed to define the scope of the requested freeze, thus leaving its implications unclear. Also speaking on that text and the one that became resolution 40/151 E, Norway saw no important changes compared with previous years.

Abstaining on all three texts, China reiterated that the two Powers with the largest nuclear arsenals should discharge their special responsibility by halting the testing, improvement and production of nuclear weapons, and by drastically reducing their arsenals; other nuclear-weapon States should subsequently follow suit. The Bahamas was disappointed that the similar elements of the three drafts could not be combined into one comprehensive proposal.

Bulgaria considered a freeze to be fully realistic and practical, and stated that verification of compliance posed no problem, given the presence of political will.

Nuclear non-proliferation

NPT Review Conference

The Third Review Conference of the Parties to the Treaty on the Non-Proliferation of Nuclear Weapons (NPT)[2] was held at Geneva from 27 August to 21 September 1985, with the following 86 States parties participating: Afghanistan, Australia, Austria, Bangladesh, Belgium, Bhutan, Bolivia, Brunei Darussalam, Bulgaria, Burundi, Cameroon, Canada, Cyprus, Czechoslovakia, Democratic Yemen, Denmark, Ecuador, Egypt, Ethiopia, Finland, German Democratic Republic, Germany, Federal Republic of, Ghana, Greece, Guatemala, Holy See, Honduras, Hungary, Iceland, Indonesia, Iran, Iraq, Ireland, Italy, Ivory Coast, Japan, Jordan, Kenya, Lebanon, Libyan Arab Jamahiriya, Liechtenstein, Luxembourg, Malaysia, Maldives, Malta, Mauritius, Mexico, Mongolia, Morocco, Nauru, Nepal, Netherlands, New Zealand, Nicaragua, Nigeria, Norway, Panama, Papua New Guinea, Peru, Philippines, Poland, Portugal, Republic of Korea, Romania, Rwanda, San Marino, Senegal, Seychelles, Somalia, Sri Lanka, Sudan, Sweden, Switzerland, Syrian Arab Republic, Thailand, Tunisia, Turkey, Uganda, USSR, United Kingdom, United States, Uruguay, Venezuela, Viet Nam, Yugoslavia, Zaire.[46]

Three signatories (Colombia, Kuwait, Yemen) participated without taking part in decision-making, and another 10 States attended as observers (Algeria, Argentina, Bahrain, Brazil, Chile, Cuba, Israel, Pakistan, Spain, United Republic of Tanzania). Also attending as observers were the Agency for the Prohibition of Nuclear Weapons in Latin America, the League of Arab States, the Organization of African Unity (OAU) and the Organization of American States, as well as the Palestine Liberation Organization. The International Atomic Energy Agency (IAEA) and the United Nations were also represented, as were 48 non-governmental organizations.

The Review Conference adopted by consensus a Final Document,[46] containing a Final Declaration comprising a solemn preambular statement and a detailed article-by-article review of the operation of the Treaty and recommendations. The Final Document also contained a Declaration and two draft resolutions—on a nuclear-test-ban moratorium and a nuclear-arms freeze—submitted to the Conference, but not pressed to a vote, by the group of non-aligned and neutral States; a third draft by the group, on a comprehensive nuclear-test ban, was incorporated in essence in the Conference Final Declaration. In addition, the Final Document contained statements by Iran and Iraq, the latter having asked the Conference to discuss attacks against peaceful nuclear facilities.

The Treaty, which opened for signature on 1 July 1968 and entered into force on 5 March 1970 upon ratification by 40 non-nuclear-weapon States, had 132 States parties as at 31 December 1985, including the three nuclear-weapon States depositories of the Treaty—the USSR, the United Kingdom and the United States. The other nuclear-weapon States, China and France, had not signed the Treaty. Previous quinquennial review conferences had been held in 1975[47] and 1980.[48]

The Preparatory Committee for the Conference, which had held two sessions in 1984,[49] held a final session at Geneva from 22 April to 1 May 1985 to discuss substantive and organizational matters, focusing on the Conference's final documentation.

GENERAL ASSEMBLY ACTION

On 7 November, Mexico transmitted to the Chairman of the General Assembly's First Committee the texts of the Final Declaration adopted by the Review Conference and of the Declaration and two draft resolutions submitted to the Conference by the group of non-aligned and neutral States.[50]

On the recommendation of the First Committee, the General Assembly, on 12 December, adopted **resolution 40/94 M** by recorded vote.

Third Review Conference of the Parties to the Treaty on the Non-Proliferation of Nuclear Weapons

The General Assembly,

Recalling its resolution 38/74 of 15 December 1983, in which, *inter alia*, it noted that in the Final Document of the Second Review Conference of the Parties to the Treaty on the Non-Proliferation of Nuclear Weapons, held at Geneva from 11 August to 7 September 1980, the Conference had proposed to the depositary Governments that a third conference to review the operation of the Treaty be convened in 1985 and that there appeared to be a consensus among the parties that the Third Review Conference should be held at Geneva in August/September of that year,

Recalling that States parties to the Treaty met at Geneva from 27 August to 21 September 1985 to review the operation of the Treaty with a view to assuring that the purposes of the preamble and the provisions of the Treaty were being realized,

Notes with satisfaction that on 21 September 1985, the Third Review Conference of the Parties to the Treaty on the Non-Proliferation of Nuclear Weapons adopted by consensus a Final Declaration.

General Assembly resolution 40/94 M

12 December 1985   Meeting 113   138-0-11 (recorded vote)

Approved by First Committee (A/40/976) by recorded vote (119-0-11), 19 November (meeting 42); 48-nation draft (A/C.1/40/L.67); agenda item 68.

Sponsors: Australia, Austria, Bahamas, Bangladesh, Belgium, Bulgaria, Burkina Faso, Cameroon, Canada, Czechoslovakia, Denmark, Ecuador, Egypt, Ethiopia,

Finland, German Democratic Republic, Germany, Federal Republic of, Greece, Hungary, Indonesia, Ireland, Italy, Ivory Coast, Japan, Kenya, Luxembourg, Malaysia, Mexico, Mongolia, Nepal, Netherlands, New Zealand, Norway, Poland, Romania, Samoa, Senegal, Sri Lanka, Sudan, Swaziland, Sweden, Turkey, USSR, United Kingdom, United States, Venezuela, Yugoslavia, Zaire.

Meeting numbers. GA 40th session: 1st Committee 3-32, 36, 42; plenary 113.

Recorded vote in Assembly as follows:

In favour: Afghanistan, Antigua and Barbuda, Australia, Austria, Bahamas, Bahrain, Bangladesh, Barbados, Belgium, Benin, Bhutan, Bolivia, Botswana, Brunei Darussalam, Bulgaria, Burkina Faso, Burundi, Byelorussian SSR, Cameroon, Canada, Cape Verde, Central African Republic, Chad, Chile, Colombia, Comoros, Congo, Cyprus, Czechoslovakia, Democratic Kampuchea, Democratic Yemen, Denmark, Djibouti, Dominican Republic, Ecuador, Egypt, El Salvador, Equatorial Guinea, Ethiopia, Fiji, Finland, Gabon, German Democratic Republic, Germany, Federal Republic of, Ghana, Greece, Grenada, Guatemala, Guinea, Guinea-Bissau, Guyana, Haiti, Honduras, Hungary, Iceland, Indonesia, Iran, Iraq, Ireland, Italy, Ivory Coast, Jamaica, Japan, Jordan, Kenya, Kuwait, Lao People's Democratic Republic, Lebanon, Lesotho, Liberia, Libyan Arab Jamahiriya, Luxembourg, Madagascar, Malawi, Malaysia, Maldives, Mali, Malta, Mauritania, Mauritius, Mexico, Mongolia, Morocco, Mozambique, Nepal, Netherlands, New Zealand, Nicaragua, Nigeria, Norway, Oman, Panama, Papua New Guinea, Paraguay, Peru, Philippines, Poland, Portugal, Qatar, Romania, Rwanda, Saint Christopher and Nevis, Saint Lucia, Saint Vincent and the Grenadines, Samoa, Sao Tome and Principe, Saudi Arabia, Senegal, Seychelles, Sierra Leone, Singapore, Solomon Islands, Somalia, Sri Lanka, Sudan, Suriname, Swaziland, Sweden, Syrian Arab Republic, Thailand, Togo, Trinidad and Tobago, Tunisia, Turkey, Uganda, Ukrainian SSR, USSR, United Arab Emirates, United Kingdom, United States, Uruguay, Vanuatu, Venezuela, Viet Nam, Yemen, Yugoslavia, Zaire, Zimbabwe.

Against: None.

Abstaining: Argentina, Brazil, Burma, Cuba, France, India, Israel, Niger, Spain, United Republic of Tanzania, Zambia.

Nine States non-parties to the Treaty explained their abstentions. Burma, France, the Niger, Spain and Zambia said their votes were determined by the fact that they were not parties. France said that, by abstaining rather than not participating in the vote, it intended to make clear its reservations about a number of points in the Final Declaration; it added, as did the Niger, that a document adopted at a review conference among the signatories to a Treaty did not apply to non-signatories.

Brazil continued to believe that effective means to prevent nuclear-weapons proliferation must be based on the 1965 Assembly resolution on the topic,[51] and emphasized that disarmament agreements must not be used to legitimize exclusive possession, or to condone vertical or geographical proliferation, of nuclear weapons by the existing nuclear-weapon Powers. India declared that the nuclear-weapon States had failed to comply with their commitments to halt and reverse vertical proliferation and to conclude a comprehensive test-ban treaty, that their concern was limited to preventing horizontal proliferation of nuclear weapons, and that the discriminatory nature of NPT was not highlighted at the Third Review Conference. While also supporting the principle of non-proliferation, Israel had serious reservations regarding what it considered politically motivated and unfounded references to Israel, and rejected specific references singling it out in the Final Document. Cuba asserted that the hostile policy of the United States and its illegal occupation of part of Cuban territory impeded Cuba's adherence to the Treaty.

Sweden urged the nuclear-weapon States parties to demonstrate their commitment to NPT's article VI, under which each party was to negotiate effective measures for halting the nuclear-arms race and for achieving nuclear disarmament.

Nuclear-weapon-free zones

As in previous years, the international community continued to discuss the establishment of nuclear-weapon-free zones in Africa, the Middle East and South Asia, as well as implementation of a treaty establishing such a zone in Latin America. References were also made to informal proposals for such zones in the Balkans and northern and central Europe. The South Pacific Nuclear-Free Zone Treaty, prepared by the South Pacific Forum, was opened for signature in 1985 (see below).

Among a number of resolutions on nuclear-weapon-free zones, the Assembly took note with regret that the Group of Governmental Experts on Nuclear-Weapon-Free Zones, set up in 1982 to update a 1975 expert study on the topic, could not complete that task (**resolution 40/94 B**).

Communications. By a note verbale of 11 March 1985 to the Secretary-General,[52] Yemen transmitted documents adopted at the Fifteenth Islamic Conference of Foreign Ministers (Sanaa, 18-22 December 1984), among them a number of resolutions, calling on all States to respond positively to the proposals for establishing nuclear-weapon-free zones in Africa, the Middle East and South Asia, and welcoming the decision of the States members of the Association of South-East Asian Nations to work towards realizing the subregion as a nuclear-free zone.

On 19 September,[44] Papua New Guinea transmitted to the Secretary-General the South Pacific Forum communiqué (Rarotonga, Cook Islands, 5 and 6 August), in which the Forum announced that it had opened for signature the South Pacific Nuclear-Free Zone Treaty and that Australia, Cook Islands, Fiji, Kiribati, New Zealand, Niue, Samoa and Tuvalu had signed it on that occasion. The Treaty prohibited the use, testing or stationing of nuclear explosive devices, or ocean dumping of nuclear wastes, in the South Pacific. There were three protocols to the Treaty: the first invited France, the United Kingdom and the United States to apply key provisions of the Treaty to their South Pacific territories, while the other two invited the five major nuclear-weapon States not to use or threaten to use such weapons against the Treaty's parties and not to test nuclear explosive devices within the zone. In addition to the Treaty's signatories (see above), the Forum in 1985 was made up of Nauru, Papua New Guinea, Solomon Islands, Tonga and Vanuatu, with the Federated States of Micronesia as an observer.

Study by group of experts

The 21-member Group of Governmental Experts on Nuclear-Weapon-Free Zones, set up in accordance with a 1982 General Assembly resolution[53] to review and supplement a 1975 expert study on the topic,[54] held one session in 1985 (21 January–8 February) in an attempt to complete its study for submission to the Assembly. The Group had been given a one-year extension of its mandate in 1984,[55] when it was unable to conclude its work that year.

In a 9 February 1985 letter annexed to the Secretary-General's report to the Assembly,[56] the Group's Chairman, Klaus Törnudd (Finland), stated that the Group had made considerable progress, but had been unable to agree on the study as a whole and, in particular, on its conclusions. The Group transmitted to the Secretary-General the draft text of the study as it stood at the closure of its final session, with paragraphs still under discussion indicated in brackets together with proposed alternative or additional text.

GENERAL ASSEMBLY ACTION

On 12 December, the General Assembly, on the recommendation of the First Committee, adopted **resolution 40/94 B** without vote.

Study of the question of nuclear-weapon-free zones in all its aspects

The General Assembly,

Recalling its resolution 37/99 F of 13 December 1982, in which it decided that a study should be undertaken to review and supplement the *Comprehensive Study of the Question of Nuclear-Weapon-Free Zones in All Its Aspects* in the light of information and experience accumulated since 1975,

Recalling also that it requested the Secretary-General, with the assistance of an *ad hoc* group of qualified governmental experts, to carry out the study and to submit it to the General Assembly at its thirty-ninth session,

Recalling further its resolution 39/151 B of 17 December 1984, in which it took note of the report of the Secretary-General to the effect that the Group of Governmental Experts on Nuclear-Weapon-Free Zones had not been able to conclude the study within the time available and requested therefore the Secretary-General to continue the study and to submit the report to the General Assembly at its fortieth session,

Reaffirming its resolutions 3472 A (XXX) of 11 December 1975 and 31/70 of 10 December 1976, in which it expressed its conviction that the establishment of nuclear-weapon-free zones could contribute to the security of members of such zones, to the prevention of proliferation of nuclear weapons and to the goals of general and complete disarmament,

Having received the report of the Secretary-General, to which is annexed a letter from the Chairman of the Group of Governmental Experts on Nuclear-Weapon-Free Zones,

Appreciating the efforts made by the Group of Governmental Experts,

1. *Takes note* of the report of the Secretary-General and regrets that the Group of Governmental Experts on Nuclear-Weapon-Free Zones was unable to complete the study;

2. *Conveys its thanks* to the Secretary-General, the Director-General of the International Atomic Energy Agency and the Secretary-General of the Agency for the Prohibition of Nuclear Weapons in Latin America for the assistance they have given for the preparation of the study.

General Assembly resolution 40/94 B

12 December 1985　　　Meeting 113　　　Adopted without vote

Approved by First Committee (A/40/976) without vote, 18 November (meeting 41); draft by Finland (A/C.1/40/L.3/Rev.1); agenda item 68 *(d)*.
Meeting numbers. GA 40th session: 1st Committee 3-32, 41; plenary 113.

In explanation of position, Brazil said it had joined the consensus, hoping that the study would be completed in the near future based on all the views expressed. France outlined what it saw as the two main reasons for the difficulties encountered: the impossibility of transporting the experience of the Treaty for the Prohibition of Nuclear Weapons in Latin America (Treaty of Tlatelolco) to other regions, and the attempt by the Group to draw up a general theory of denuclearized zones.

Africa

In 1985, the General Assembly had on its agenda, as it had had annually since 1964, the question of implementing the Declaration on the Denuclearization of Africa,[57] adopted in 1964 by OAU. In addition to a resolution on implementing the Declaration (**40/89 A**), the Assembly, in 1985 as in previous years, adopted a text on the nuclear capability of South Africa (**40/89 B**).

Throughout 1985, South Africa's military and nuclear relations with other States were kept under consideration by various other United Nations bodies (see p. 141).

Consideration by the Disarmament Commission. As in the past, the Disarmament Commission[17] established in 1985 Working Group II to consider, in response to a 1984 Assembly request,[58] South Africa's nuclear capability. Under the chairmanship of Davidson L. Hepburn (Bahamas), the Group held seven meetings as well as informal consultations between 13 and 24 May, using as a basis for discussion its 1984 working paper.[59] Unable to agree on draft conclusions and recommendations on the issue, the Group recommended that the Commission refer the question to the Assembly later in 1985.

Reports by the Secretary-General. In February 1985,[60] the Secretary-General drew the Security Council's attention to the Assembly's 1984 resolution[58] on South Africa's nuclear capability, in which the Assembly requested the Council to take action aimed at, among other things, prohibiting

all forms of nuclear collaboration with South Africa. In an August report,[61] prepared in accordance with the same resolution,[58] the Secretary-General stated that he had followed South Africa's nuclear activities closely but had received no information to add to his 1984 report on the question.[59]

Communications. Among communications relating to the topic, the Assembly had before it the Declaration and Programme of Action adopted at the Ministerial Regional Conference on Security, Disarmament and Development in Africa (Lomé, Togo, 13-16 August),[62] by which the Conference expressed concern over the continued development of South Africa's nuclear-weapon capability, called for a legal instrument that would define Africa as a nuclear-free zone, and expressed concern over what it called continued military and nuclear collaboration between South Africa and certain Western countries and Israel. Such collaboration was condemned in the Final Political Declaration adopted by the Conference of Foreign Ministers of Non-Aligned Countries (Luanda, Angola, 4-7 September).[63]

GENERAL ASSEMBLY ACTION

In December 1985, the Assembly adopted two resolutions relating to the denuclearization of Africa—**40/89 A**, on implementation of the 1964 Declaration, and **40/89 B**, on the nuclear capability of South Africa—on the recommendation of the First Committee.

A number of States explained in single statements their positions on the texts that became resolutions 40/89 A and B, while others made general explanations on several of the texts on nuclear-weapon-free zones (see p. 62).

Resolution 40/89 A was adopted by recorded vote on 12 December.

Implementation of the Declaration

The General Assembly,

Bearing in mind the Declaration on the Denuclearization of Africa adopted by the Assembly of Heads of State and Government of the Organization of African Unity at its first ordinary session, held at Cairo from 17 to 21 July 1964,

Recalling its resolution 1652(XVI) of 24 November 1961, its earliest on the subject, as well as its resolutions 2033(XX) of 3 December 1965, 31/69 of 10 December 1976, 32/81 of 12 December 1977, 33/63 of 14 December 1978, 34/76 A of 11 December 1979, 35/146 B of 12 December 1980, 36/86 B of 9 December 1981, 37/74 A of 9 December 1982, 38/181 A of 20 December 1983 and 39/61 A of 12 December 1984, in which it called upon all States to consider and respect the continent of Africa and its surrounding areas as a nuclear-weapon-free zone,

Recalling that in its resolution 33/63 it vigorously condemned any overt or covert attempt by South Africa to introduce nuclear weapons into the continent of Africa and demanded that South Africa refrain forthwith from conducting any nuclear explosion in the continent or elsewhere,

Taking note of the report of the United Nations Institute for Disarmament Research entitled "South Africa's nuclear capability",[59] undertaken in co-operation with the Department for Disarmament Affairs of the Secretariat and in consultation with the Organization of African Unity, as well as the report of the Disarmament Commission,

Expressing regret that despite the threat South Africa's nuclear capability constitutes to international peace and security and, in particular, to the realization of the objective of the Declaration on the Denuclearization of Africa, the Disarmament Commission has, once again, in 1985, failed to reach a consensus on this important item on its agenda,

1. *Strongly renews its call* upon all States to consider and respect the continent of Africa and its surrounding areas as a nuclear-weapon-free zone;

2. *Reaffirms* that the implementation of the Declaration on the Denuclearization of Africa adopted by the Assembly of Heads of State and Government of the Organization of African Unity would be an important measure to prevent the proliferation of nuclear weapons and to promote international peace and security;

3. *Expresses once again its grave alarm* at South Africa's possession and continued development of nuclear-weapon capability;

4. *Condemns* South Africa's continued pursuit of a nuclear capability and all forms of nuclear collaboration by any State, corporation, institution or individual with the racist régime that enable it to frustrate the objective of the Declaration on the Denuclearization of Africa, which seeks to keep Africa free from nuclear weapons;

5. *Calls upon* all States, corporations, institutions and individuals to desist from further collaboration with the racist régime that may enable it to frustrate the objective of the Declaration on the Denuclearization of Africa;

6. *Demands once again* that the racist régime of South Africa refrain from manufacturing, testing, deploying, transporting, storing, using or threatening to use nuclear weapons;

7. *Appeals* to all States that have the means to do so to monitor South Africa's research on and development and production of nuclear weapons, and to publicize any information in that regard;

8. *Demands once again* that South Africa submit forthwith all its nuclear installations and facilities to inspection by the International Atomic Energy Agency;

9. *Requests* the Secretary-General to render all necessary assistance that the Organization of African Unity may seek towards the implementation of its solemn Declaration on the Denuclearization of Africa;

10. *Decides* to include in the provisional agenda of its forty-first session the item entitled "Implementation of the Declaration on the Denuclearization of Africa".

General Assembly resolution 40/89 A

12 December 1985   Meeting 113   148-0-6 (recorded vote)

Approved by First Committee (A/40/931) by recorded vote (130-0-5), 18 November (meeting 41); draft by Mauritius, for African Group (A/C.1/40/L.38); agenda item 59.

Meeting numbers. GA 40th session: 1st Committee 3-32, 35, 41; plenary 113.

Recorded vote in Assembly as follows:

In favour: Afghanistan, Albania, Algeria, Angola, Antigua and Barbuda, Argentina, Australia, Austria, Bahamas, Bahrain, Bangladesh, Barbados, Benin, Bhutan, Bolivia, Botswana, Brazil, Brunei Darussalam, Bulgaria, Burkina Faso, Burma, Burundi, Byelorussian SSR, Cameroon, Canada, Cape Verde, Central African Republic, Chad, Chile, China, Colombia, Comoros, Congo, Cuba, Cyprus, Czechoslovakia, Democratic Kampuchea, Democratic Yemen, Denmark, Djibouti, Dominican Republic, Ecuador, Egypt, El Salvador, Equatorial Guinea, Ethiopia, Fiji, Finland, Gabon, German Democratic Republic, Germany, Federal Republic of, Ghana, Greece, Grenada, Guatemala, Guinea, Guinea-Bissau, Guyana, Haiti, Honduras, Hungary, Iceland, India, Indonesia, Iran, Iraq, Ireland, Italy, Ivory Coast, Jamaica, Japan, Jordan, Kenya, Kuwait, Lao People's Democratic Republic, Lebanon, Lesotho, Liberia, Libyan Arab Jamahiriya, Luxembourg, Madagascar, Malaysia, Maldives, Mali, Malta, Mauritania, Mauritius, Mexico, Mongolia, Morocco, Mozambique, Nepal, Netherlands, New Zealand, Nicaragua, Niger, Nigeria, Norway, Oman, Pakistan, Panama, Papua New Guinea, Paraguay, Peru, Philippines, Poland, Portugal, Qatar, Romania, Rwanda, Saint Christopher and Nevis, Saint Lucia, Saint Vincent and the Grenadines, Samoa, Sao Tome and Principe, Saudi Arabia, Senegal, Seychelles, Sierra Leone, Singapore, Solomon Islands, Somalia, Spain, Sri Lanka, Sudan, Suriname, Swaziland, Sweden, Syrian Arab Republic, Thailand, Togo, Trinidad and Tobago, Tunisia, Turkey, Uganda, Ukrainian SSR, USSR, United Arab Emirates, United Republic of Tanzania, Uruguay, Vanuatu, Venezuela, Viet Nam, Yemen, Yugoslavia, Zaire, Zambia, Zimbabwe.

Against: None.

Abstaining: Belgium, France, Israel, Malawi, United Kingdom, United States.

While voting in favour, the Federal Republic of Germany said it gave the strictest possible interpretation to the clause "surrounding areas" because of its continued difficulties with the text's ambiguous definition of the confines of the future zone. Japan said it did not fully agree with the assertions contained in some paragraphs which, it felt, lacked conclusive evidence. Norway, speaking also on behalf of Denmark, Finland, Iceland and Sweden, expressed reservations on certain formulations in the draft, particularly paragraph 7. Italy wished to record its specific reservations on the last preambular paragraph and on paragraphs 1 and 3.

Also on 12 December, the Assembly adopted **resolution 40/89 B** by recorded vote.

Nuclear capability of South Africa

The General Assembly,

Recalling its resolutions 34/76 B of 11 December 1979, 35/146 A of 12 December 1980, 36/86 A of 9 December 1981, 37/74 B of 9 December 1982, 38/181 B of 20 December 1983 and 39/61 B of 12 December 1984,

Bearing in mind the Declaration on the Denuclearization of Africa adopted by the Assembly of Heads of State and Government of the Organization of African Unity at its first ordinary session, held at Cairo from 17 to 21 July 1964,

Recalling that, in paragraph 12 of the Final Document of the Tenth Special Session of the General Assembly, it noted that the accumulation of armaments and the acquisition of armaments technology by racist régimes, as well as their possible acquisition of nuclear weapons, presented a challenging and increasingly dangerous obstacle to the world community, faced with the urgent need to disarm,

Recalling also that in its resolution 33/63 of 14 December 1978, it vigorously condemned any overt or covert attempt by South Africa to introduce nuclear weapons into the continent of Africa and demanded that South Africa refrain forthwith from conducting any nuclear explosion in the continent or elsewhere,

Taking note of resolution GC(XXIX)/RES/442 on South Africa's nuclear capabilities, adopted on 27

September 1985 by the General Conference of the International Atomic Energy Agency during its twenty-ninth regular session,

Having taken note of the report of the United Nations Institute for Disarmament Research entitled "South Africa's nuclear capability",[59] undertaken in co-operation with the Department for Disarmament Affairs of the Secretariat and in consultation with the Organization of African Unity,

Expressing regret that despite the threat South Africa's nuclear capability constitutes to international peace and security and, in particular, to the realization of the objective of the Declaration on the Denuclearization of Africa, the Disarmament Commission has, once again, in 1985, failed to reach a consensus on this important item on its agenda,

Gravely concerned that South Africa, in flagrant violation of the principles of international law and the relevant provisions of the Charter of the United Nations, has continued its acts of aggression and subversion against the peoples of the independent States of southern Africa,

Strongly condemning the continued military occupation by South African troops of parts of the territory of Angola in violation of its national sovereignty, independence and territorial integrity, and urging the immediate and unconditional withdrawal of South African troops from Angolan soil,

Expressing its grave disappointment that, despite repeated appeals by the international community, certain Western States and Israel have continued to collaborate with the racist régime of South Africa in the military and nuclear fields and that some of the same Western States have, by a ready recourse to the use of the veto, consistently frustrated every effort in the Security Council to deal decisively with the question of South Africa,

Recalling its decision taken at the tenth special session that the Security Council should take appropriate effective steps to prevent the frustration of the implementation of the decision of the Organization of African Unity for the denuclearization of Africa,

Stressing the need to preserve peace and security in Africa by ensuring that the continent is a nuclear-weapon-free zone,

1.   *Condemns* the massive buildup of South Africa's military machine, in particular its frenzied acquisition of nuclear-weapon capability for repressive and aggressive purposes and as an instrument of blackmail;

2.   *Expresses its full support* for the African States faced with the danger of South Africa's nuclear capability;

3.   *Reaffirms* that the acquisition of nuclear-weapon capability by the racist régime constitutes a very grave danger to international peace and security and, in particular, jeopardizes the security of African States and increases the danger of the proliferation of nuclear weapons;

4.   *Condemns* all forms of nuclear collaboration by any State, corporation, institution or individual with the racist régime of South Africa, in particular the decision by some Member States to grant licences to several corporations in their territories to provide equipment and technical and maintenance services for nuclear installations in South Africa;

5.   *Demands* that South Africa and all other foreign interests put an immediate end to the exploration for and exploitation of uranium resources in Namibia;

6.   *Calls upon* all States, corporations, institutions and individuals to terminate forthwith all forms of military and nuclear collaboration with the racist régime;

7.   *Requests* the Disarmament Commission to consider as a matter of priority during its session in 1986 South Africa's nuclear capability, taking into account, *inter alia*, the findings of the report of the United Nations Institute for Disarmament Research on South Africa's nuclear capability;

8.   *Requests* the Security Council, for the purposes of disarmament and to fulfil its obligations and responsibility, to take enforcement measures to prevent any racist régime from acquiring arms or arms technology;

9.   *Further requests* the Security Council to conclude expeditiously its consideration of the recommendations of its Committee established by resolution 421(1977) concerning the question of South Africa, with a view to blocking the existing loopholes in the arms embargo so as to render it more effective, and prohibiting, in particular, all forms of co-operation and collaboration with the racist régime of South Africa in the nuclear field;

10.   *Demands once again* that South Africa submit forthwith all its nuclear installations and facilities to inspection by the International Atomic Energy Agency;

11.   *Requests* the Secretary-General to follow very closely South Africa's evolution in the nuclear field and to report thereon to the General Assembly at its forty-first session.

General Assembly resolution 40/89 B

12 December 1985   Meeting 113   135-4-14 (recorded vote)

Approved by First Committee (A/40/931) by recorded vote (117-4-12), 18 November (meeting 41); draft by Mauritius, for African Group (A/C.1/40/L.40); agenda item 59.

Meeting numbers. GA 40th session: 1st Committee 3-32, 35, 41; plenary 113.

Recorded vote in Assembly as follows:

In favour: Afghanistan, Albania, Algeria, Angola, Antigua and Barbuda, Argentina, Austria, Bahamas, Bahrain, Bangladesh, Barbados, Benin, Bhutan, Bolivia, Botswana, Brazil, Brunei Darussalam, Bulgaria, Burkina Faso, Burma, Burundi, Byelorussian SSR, Cameroon, Cape Verde, Central African Republic, Chad, Chile, China, Colombia, Comoros, Congo, Cuba, Cyprus, Czechoslovakia, Democratic Kampuchea, Democratic Yemen, Denmark, Djibouti, Dominican Republic, Ecuador, Egypt, El Salvador, Equatorial Guinea, Ethiopia, Fiji, Finland, Gabon, German Democratic Republic, Ghana, Greece, Guatemala, Guinea, Guinea-Bissau, Guyana, Honduras, Hungary, Iceland, India, Indonesia, Iran, Iraq, Ireland, Ivory Coast, Jamaica, Jordan, Kenya, Kuwait, Lao People's Democratic Republic, Lebanon, Lesotho, Liberia, Libyan Arab Jamahiriya, Madagascar, Malaysia, Maldives, Mali, Malta, Mauritania, Mauritius, Mexico, Mongolia, Morocco, Mozambique, Nepal, Nicaragua, Niger, Nigeria, Norway, Oman, Pakistan, Panama, Papua New Guinea, Peru, Philippines, Poland, Qatar, Romania, Rwanda, Saint Christopher and Nevis, Saint Lucia, Saint Vincent and the Grenadines, Sao Tome and Principe, Saudi Arabia, Senegal, Seychelles, Sierra Leone, Singapore, Solomon Islands, Somalia, Spain, Sri Lanka, Sudan, Suriname, Swaziland, Sweden, Syrian Arab Republic, Thailand, Togo, Trinidad and Tobago, Tunisia, Turkey, Uganda, Ukrainian SSR, USSR, United Arab Emirates, United Republic of Tanzania, Uruguay, Vanuatu, Venezuela, Viet Nam, Yemen, Yugoslavia, Zaire, Zambia, Zimbabwe.

Against: France, Israel, United Kingdom, United States.

Abstaining: Australia, Belgium, Canada, Germany, Federal Republic of, Grenada, Haiti, Italy, Japan, Luxembourg, Malawi, Netherlands, New Zealand, Paraguay, Portugal.

Israel declared that it had no nuclear collaboration with South Africa, as did the United Kingdom which added that the right of all States to the peaceful uses of nuclear energy should not be limited in individual cases for political reasons.

Australia, France and the Netherlands objected to the call on the Security Council to take enforcement measures, saying it was not in keeping with the provisions of the United Nations Charter regarding allocation of responsibilities among the main organs. Norway—speaking for the Nordic States—expressed similar reservations, and added that they objected, as did Australia, to the singling out of individual or groups of countries for condemnation. The Netherlands, which agreed that the arms embargo should be strengthened, asserted that the language in paragraph 1 was in sharp contrast to the 1984 report by the United Nations Institute for Disarmament Research[59] which, it said, provided no new information regarding South Africa's capability to manufacture nuclear weapons. Italy said it would have voted against the tenth preambular paragraph, had there been a separate vote.

A number of delegations spoke, in single statements, on the texts that became resolutions 40/89 A and B. Albania said its affirmative votes for them, and the text on Israeli nuclear armament (see p. 65), were in keeping with its support of the struggle of the peoples of the regions against South Africa and against Israel, without prejudice to its stand regarding establishing zones of peace or nuclear-weapon-free zones. Brazil said it went along with a consensus on both texts, taking into account the specific features of the African continent. France concurred with the basic aims of the drafts, but objected that they did not distinguish between peaceful and military uses of nuclear energy.

The United States gave a general explanation of vote on several of the drafts on nuclear-weapon-free zones. It supported the concept of such zones as a non-proliferation measure when consistent with a number of criteria: among others, zonal arrangements should provide for adequate verification and compliance, uphold existing security arrangements, prohibit parties from developing any nuclear explosive device, honour the exercise of rights recognized under international law, and preclude the conduct of any nuclear explosions. Japan also reiterated that the arrangement should be based on the initiatives of the countries in the region and freely agreed upon by all concerned, including a nuclear-weapon State as the case might be; it also considered it desirable that all the countries in the region adhere to NPT. The USSR stated that the creation of such a zone should be in keeping with international law, in particular the principle of freedom of navigation on the high seas.

The question of nuclear weapons and South Africa was also dealt with by the Assembly in **resolutions 40/56, 40/64 A, 40/64 E, 40/64 I** and **40/158**. The Assembly also condemned military and nuclear collaboration with South Africa in several resolutions, among them **40/52,** **40/57, 40/97 A** and **40/97 D**, and in **decision 40/415**.

Latin America

Since the signature and ratification of Additonal Protocol II of the Treaty for the Prohibition of Nuclear Weapons in Latin America (Treaty of Tlatelolco) by five nuclear-weapon States by 1979,[64] only one item concerning that Treaty remained on the General Assembly's agenda: the signature and ratification of Additional Protocol I, concerning the application of the Treaty to territories in the region for which outside States had *de jure* or *de facto* responsibility, such as the colonial Powers.

GENERAL ASSEMBLY ACTION

On the recommendation of the First Committee, the General Assembly, on 12 December, adopted **resolution 40/79** by recorded vote.

Implementation of General Assembly resolution 39/51 concerning the signature and ratification of Additional Protocol I of the Treaty for the Prohibition of Nuclear Weapons in Latin America (Treaty of Tlatelolco)

The General Assembly,

Recalling its resolutions 2286(XXII) of 5 December 1967, 3262(XXIX) of 9 December 1974, 3473(XXX) of 11 December 1975, 32/76 of 12 December 1977, S-10/2 of 30 June 1978, 33/58 of 14 December 1978, 34/71 of 11 December 1979, 35/143 of 12 December 1980, 36/83 of 9 December 1981, 37/71 of 9 December 1982 and 38/61 of 15 December 1983 concerning the signature and ratification of Additional Protocol I of the Treaty for the Prohibition of Nuclear Weapons in Latin America (Treaty of Tlatelolco),

Taking into account that within the zone of application of that Treaty, to which twenty-three sovereign States are already parties, there are some territories which, in spite of not being sovereign political entities, are nevertheless in a position to receive the benefits deriving from the Treaty through its Additional Protocol I, to which the four States that *de jure* or *de facto* are internationally responsible for those territories may become parties,

Considering that it would not be fair if the peoples of some of those territories were deprived of such benefits without being given the opportunity to express their opinion in this connection,

Recalling that three of the States to whom Additional Protocol I is opened—the United Kingdom of Great Britain and Northern Ireland, the Kingdom of the Netherlands and the United States of America—became parties to the Protocol in 1969, 1971 and 1981, respectively,

1. *Deplores* that the signature of Additional Protocol I by France, which took place on 2 March 1979, has not yet been followed by the corresponding ratification, notwithstanding the time already elapsed and the pressing invitations which the General Assembly has addressed to it;

2. *Once more urges* France not to delay any further such ratification, which has been requested so many

times and which appears all the more advisable, since it is the only one of the four States to which the Protocol is open that is not yet party to it;

3. *Decides* to include in the provisional agenda of its forty-first session an item entitled "Implementation of General Assembly resolution 40/79 concerning the signature and ratification of Additional Protocol I of the Treaty for the Prohibition of Nuclear Weapons in Latin America (Treaty of Tlatelolco)".

General Assembly resolution 40/79

12 December 1985   Meeting 113   139-0-7 (recorded vote)

Approved by First Committee (A/40/919) by recorded vote (126-0-7), 18 November (meeting 41); 18-nation draft (A/C.1/40/L.61); agenda item 49.

Sponsors: Bahamas, Bolivia, Colombia, Costa Rica, Dominican Republic, Ecuador, El Salvador, Guatemala, Haiti, Honduras, Jamaica, Mexico, Nicaragua, Panama, Paraguay, Suriname, Trinidad and Tobago, Uruguay.

Meeting numbers. GA 40th session: 1st Committee 3-32, 41; plenary 113.

Recorded vote in Assembly as follows:

In favour: Afghanistan, Algeria, Angola, Australia, Austria, Bahamas, Bahrain, Bangladesh, Barbados, Belgium, Benin, Bhutan, Bolivia, Botswana, Brazil, Brunei Darussalam, Bulgaria, Burkina Faso, Burma, Burundi, Byelorussian SSR, Cameroon, Canada, Cape Verde, Chad, Chile, China, Colombia, Comoros, Congo, Cyprus, Czechoslovakia, Democratic Kampuchea, Democratic Yemen, Denmark, Dominican Republic, Ecuador, Egypt, El Salvador, Equatorial Guinea, Ethiopia, Fiji, Finland, Gabon, German Democratic Republic, Germany, Federal Republic of, Ghana, Greece, Grenada, Guatemala, Guinea, Guinea-Bissau, Haiti, Honduras, Hungary, Iceland, India, Indonesia, Iran, Iraq, Ireland, Israel, Jamaica, Japan, Jordan, Kenya, Kuwait, Lao People's Democratic Republic, Lebanon, Lesotho, Liberia, Libyan Arab Jamahiriya, Luxembourg, Madagascar, Malaysia, Maldives, Malta, Mauritania, Mauritius, Mexico, Mongolia, Morocco, Mozambique, Nepal, Netherlands, New Zealand, Nicaragua, Niger, Nigeria, Norway, Oman, Pakistan, Panama, Papua New Guinea, Paraguay, Peru, Philippines, Poland, Portugal, Qatar, Romania, Rwanda, Saint Christopher and Nevis, Saint Lucia, Saint Vincent and the Grenadines, Samoa, Saudi Arabia, Senegal, Seychelles, Sierra Leone, Singapore, Somalia, Spain, Sri Lanka, Sudan, Suriname, Swaziland, Sweden, Syrian Arab Republic, Thailand, Togo, Trinidad and Tobago, Tunisia, Turkey, Uganda, Ukrainian SSR, USSR, United Arab Emirates, United Kingdom, United Republic of Tanzania, United States, Uruguay, Venezuela, Viet Nam, Yemen, Yugoslavia, Zaire, Zambia.

Against: None.

Abstaining: Argentina, Central African Republic, Cuba, France, Guyana, Ivory Coast, Mali.

France could not accept being singled out when some countries in the Treaty's area of application had not signed, ratified or adhered to the instrument, and said it would take an appropriate decision in due course, taking into account the status of ratification of the Treaty itself. Cuba said it chose to use whatever means appropriate to defend its territory, since the only nuclear Power on the continent maintained a climate of threat and pressure in the zone and occupied part of Cuban territory with a naval base.

In the plenary Assembly, Peru explained that it did not sponsor the 1985 text for reasons involving full compliance with the stipulation set forth in article 28, paragraph 1, of the Treaty; it reiterated its understanding that since Additional Protocol I was silent on the question of reservations it permitted their being entered—as distinct from Protocol II which explicitly prohibited them—but that a reservation could in no way contravene the object and purpose of the Treaty.

Middle East

In response to a 1984 Assembly request,[65] the Secretary-General submitted to the Assembly in July 1985 a report, with a later addendum,[66] containing the views received from 10 Member States—seven States of the region, as well as China, France and the USSR—on establishing a nuclear-weapon-free zone in the Middle East.

Israel, in a 13 June letter,[67] reiterated its serious reservations as to the ways and means for establishing a nuclear-weapon-free zone in the Middle East, adding that the modalities that had led to the conclusion of the Treaty of Tlatelolco should serve as a model; the 1984 Assembly resolution,[65] it stated, had omitted mention of the direct negotiating process between the States of the region, without which a zonal arrangement was unlikely.

GENERAL ASSEMBLY ACTION

On the recommendation of the First Committee, the General Assembly, on 12 December, adopted **resolution 40/82** without vote.

Establishment of a nuclear-weapon-free zone in the region of the Middle East

The General Assembly,

Recalling its resolutions 3263(XXIX) of 9 December 1974, 3474(XXX) of 11 December 1975, 31/71 of 10 December 1976, 32/82 of 12 December 1977, 33/64 of 14 December 1978, 34/77 of 11 December 1979, 35/147 of 12 December 1980, 36/87 of 9 December 1981, 37/75 of 9 December 1982, 38/64 of 15 December 1983 and 39/54 of 12 December 1984 on the establishment of a nuclear-weapon-free zone in the region of the Middle East,

Recalling also the recommendations for the establishment of such a zone in the Middle East consistent with paragraphs 60 to 63, and in particular paragraph 63 *(d)*, of the Final Document of the Tenth Special Session of the General Assembly,

Emphasizing the basic provisions of the above-mentioned resolutions, which call upon all parties directly concerned to consider taking the practical and urgent steps required for the implementation of the proposal to establish a nuclear-weapon-free zone in the region of the Middle East and, pending and during the establishment of such a zone, to declare solemnly that they will refrain, on a reciprocal basis, from producing, acquiring or in any other way possessing nuclear weapons and nuclear explosive devices and from permitting the stationing of nuclear weapons on their territory by any third party, to agree to place all their nuclear facilities under International Atomic Energy Agency safeguards and to declare their support for the establishment of the zone and deposit such declarations with the Security Council for consideration, as appropriate,

Reaffirming the inalienable right of all States to acquire and develop nuclear energy for peaceful purposes,

Emphasizing further the need for appropriate measures on the question of the prohibition of military attacks on nuclear facilities,

Bearing in mind the consensus reached by the General Assembly at its thirty-fifth session that the establishment of a nuclear-weapon-free zone in the region of the Middle East would greatly enhance international peace and security,

Desirous to build on that consensus so that substantial progress can be made towards establishing a nuclear-weapon-free zone in the region of the Middle East,

Emphasizing the essential role of the United Nations in the establishment of a nuclear-weapon-free zone in the region of the Middle East,

Having examined the report of the Secretary-General,

1. *Urges* all parties directly concerned to consider seriously taking the practical and urgent steps required for the implementation of the proposal to establish a nuclear-weapon-free zone in the region of the Middle East in accordance with the relevant resolutions of the General Assembly and, as a means of promoting this objective, invites the countries concerned to adhere to the Treaty on the Non-Proliferation of Nuclear Weapons;

2. *Calls upon* all countries of the region that have not done so, pending the establishment of the zone, to agree to place all their nuclear activities under International Atomic Energy Agency safeguards;

3. *Invites* those countries, pending the establishment of a nuclear-weapon-free zone in the region of the Middle East, to declare their support for establishing such a zone, consistent with the relevant paragraph of the Final Document of the Tenth Special Session of the General Assembly, and to deposit those declarations with the Security Council;

4. *Further invites* those countries, pending the establishment of the zone, not to develop, produce, test or otherwise acquire nuclear weapons or permit the stationing on their territories, or territories under their control, of nuclear weapons or nuclear explosive devices;

5. *Invites* the nuclear-weapon States and all other States to render their assistance in the establishment of the zone and at the same time to refrain from any action that runs counter to both the letter and spirit of the present resolution;

6. *Extends its thanks* to the Secretary-General for his report containing the views of parties concerned regarding the establishment of a nuclear-weapon-free zone in the region of the Middle East;

7. *Takes note* of the above-mentioned report;

8. *Requests* those parties that have not yet communicated their views to the Secretary-General to do so;

9. *Welcomes* any further comments from those parties that have already communicated their views to the Secretary-General;

10. *Requests* the Secretary-General to submit a report to the General Assembly at its forty-first session on the implementation of the present resolution;

11. *Decides* to include in the provisional agenda of its forty-first session the item entitled "Establishment of a nuclear-weapon-free zone in the region of the Middle East".

General Assembly resolution 40/82

12 December 1985   Meeting 113   Adopted without vote

Approved by First Committee (A/40/905) without vote, 14 November (meeting 37); draft by Egypt (A/C.1/40/L.5); agenda item 52.
Meeting numbers. GA 40th session: 1st Committee 3-32, 36, 37; plenary 113.

A number of delegations spoke in explanation of position.

Iraq declared that the stockpiling of nuclear weapons by Israel prevented the establishment of a zone in the region, and that repetition of armed attacks against peaceful nuclear facilities should be prevented. The Syrian Arab Republic said Israel should be obliged to place its nuclear facilities under IAEA safeguards and to accede to NPT; it asserted that the Treaty of Tlatelolco came into being under circumstances different from those prevailing in the Middle East, where Israel occupied certain territories and violated the rights of the Arab Palestinian people. Israel said the zone's establishment should be based on arrangements directly and freely arrived at among the States of the region.

Argentina and India said their joining the consensus on the text was without prejudice to their stance on NPT and the application of full-scale IAEA safeguards, with India also pointing to what it called the inefficacy of partial measures in nuclear disarmament. Brazil stated that the creation of a zone should not be related to adherence to NPT which, it felt, was not only discriminatory and unbalanced, but had allowed nuclear proliferation by nuclear-weapon States to proceed unchecked; it added that the particular situation and characteristics of the region deserved a specific approach, and noted that the text had the support of the States directly concerned. Argentina said that specific circumstances in a region might justify proposals being addressed to and accepted by the countries of the region, but such proposals might not prove to be as timely or appropriate for other regions or countries.

Israeli nuclear armament

In February 1985,[68] the Secretary-General drew the Security Council's attention to those paragraphs of a 1984 General Assembly resolution[69] in which it requested the Council to ensure that Israel placed all its nuclear facilities under IAEA safeguards, and to investigate Israel's nuclear activities and the collaboration of other parties in those activities.

On 16 May,[70] the Libyan Arab Jamahiriya informed the Council President of what it said was Israel's deployment, with United States support, of nuclear missiles in the Golan Heights and the Negev Desert.

UNIDIR report. In August 1985, the Secretary-General transmitted to the Assembly a study on Israeli nuclear armament,[71] prepared by the United Nations Institute for Disarmament Research (UNIDIR) in pursuance of a 1984 Assembly resolution.[69] Prepared in co-operation with the United Nations Department for Disarmament Affairs and in consultation with the League of Arab States and OAU, the study comprised four chapters: introduction, United Nations concern with the question, Israel's nuclear development, and summary. The chapter on

Israel's nuclear development dealt with research activities and with nuclear weapon potential in the context of availability of nuclear explosive materials, the capability to design and produce nuclear explosives, and the available means of delivery of those weapons.

The report concluded that the publicly available information used for the study confirmed the assessment and conclusions in the 1981 report by an expert group on the topic;[72] the 1981 findings, reproduced in the 1985 study, were that the quantity and quality of available reliable information on the subject was such that it was difficult to draw definitive conclusions, but that Israel had the capability to manufacture nuclear weapons. The 1985 study also pointed out that Israel had not acceded to requests from the Security Council and the General Assembly to place all its nuclear activities under international safeguards.

GENERAL ASSEMBLY ACTION

On 12 December, the General Assembly, on the recommendation of the First Committee, adopted **resolution 40/93** by recorded vote.

Israeli nuclear armament

The General Assembly,

Bearing in mind its previous resolutions on Israeli nuclear armament, the latest of which is 39/147 of 17 December 1984,

Recalling resolution 39/54 of 12 December 1984, in which, *inter alia*, it called upon all countries of the Middle East, pending the establishment of a nuclear-weapon-free zone in the Middle East, to agree to place all their nuclear activities under International Atomic Energy Agency safeguards,

Recalling further Security Council resolution 487(1981) of 19 June 1981 in which, *inter alia*, the Council called upon Israel urgently to place its nuclear facilities under International Atomic Energy Agency safeguards,

Noting with grave concern Israel's persistent refusal to commit itself not to manufacture or acquire nuclear weapons, despite repeated calls by the General Assembly, the Security Council and the International Atomic Energy Agency, and to place its nuclear facilities under Agency safeguards,

Aware of the grave consequences that endanger international peace and security as a result of Israel's development and acquisition of nuclear weapons and Israel's collaboration with South Africa to develop nuclear weapons and their delivery systems,

1. *Takes note* of the report of the United Nations Institute for Disarmament Research on this question;

2. *Reiterates its condemnation* of Israel's refusal to renounce any possession of nuclear weapons;

3. *Requests once more* the Security Council to take urgent and effective measures to ensure that Israel complies with Security Council resolution 487(1981) and places all its nuclear facilities under International Atomic Energy Agency safeguards;

4. *Reiterates its request* to the Security Council to investigate Israel's nuclear activities and the collaboration of other States, parties and institutions in these activities;

5. *Calls upon* all States and organizations that have not yet done so to discontinue co-operating with and giving assistance to Israel in the nuclear field;

6. *Reaffirms its condemnation* of the continuing nuclear collaboration between Israel and South Africa;

7. *Requests* the Secretary-General to follow closely Israeli nuclear activities and to report thereon as appropriate to the General Assembly.

General Assembly resolution 40/93

12 December 1985   Meeting 113   101-2-47 (recorded vote)

Approved by First Committee (A/40/933) by recorded vote (92-2-40), 18 November (meeting 41); 24-nation draft (A/C.1/40/L.63); agenda item 64.

Sponsors: Afghanistan, Algeria, Bahrain, Bangladesh, Democratic Yemen, Djibouti, Iraq, Jordan, Kuwait, Lebanon, Libyan Arab Jamahiriya, Malaysia, Mali, Mauritania, Morocco, Oman, Qatar, Saudi Arabia, Somalia, Sudan, Syrian Arab Republic, Tunisia, United Arab Emirates, Yemen.

Meeting numbers. GA 40th session: 1st Committee 3-32, 36, 41; plenary 113.

Recorded vote in Assembly as follows:

In favour: Afghanistan, Albania, Algeria, Angola, Argentina, Bahrain, Bangladesh, Barbados, Benin, Bhutan, Botswana, Brazil, Brunei Darussalam, Bulgaria, Burkina Faso, Burundi, Byelorussian SSR, Cameroon, Cape Verde, Central African Republic, Chad, China, Comoros, Congo, Cuba, Cyprus, Czechoslovakia, Democratic Kampuchea, Democratic Yemen, Djibouti, Egypt, Equatorial Guinea, Ethiopia, Gabon, German Democratic Republic, Ghana, Greece, Guinea, Guinea-Bissau, Guyana, Hungary, India, Indonesia, Iran, Iraq, Jordan, Kenya, Kuwait, Lao People's Democratic Republic, Lebanon, Lesotho, Liberia, Libyan Arab Jamahiriya, Madagascar, Malaysia, Maldives, Mali, Malta, Mauritania, Mexico, Mongolia, Morocco, Mozambique, Nicaragua, Niger, Nigeria, Oman, Pakistan, Peru, Philippines, Poland, Qatar, Romania, Rwanda, Sao Tome and Principe, Saudi Arabia, Senegal, Seychelles, Sierra Leone, Somalia, Sri Lanka, Sudan, Swaziland, Syrian Arab Republic, Thailand, Trinidad and Tobago, Tunisia, Turkey, Uganda, Ukrainian SSR, USSR, United Arab Emirates, United Republic of Tanzania, Vanuatu, Venezuela, Viet Nam, Yemen, Yugoslavia, Zambia, Zimbabwe.

Against: Israel, United States.

Abstaining: Antigua and Barbuda, Australia, Austria, Bahamas, Belgium, Bolivia, Burma, Canada, Chile, Colombia, Denmark, Dominican Republic, Ecuador, El Salvador, Fiji, Finland, France, Germany, Federal Republic of, Grenada, Guatemala, Haiti, Honduras, Iceland, Ireland, Italy, Ivory Coast, Jamaica, Japan, Luxembourg, Malawi, Nepal, Netherlands, New Zealand, Norway, Panama, Papua New Guinea, Paraguay, Portugal, Saint Christopher and Nevis, Saint Lucia, Saint Vincent and the Grenadines, Solomon Islands, Spain, Sweden, United Kingdom, Uruguay, Zaire.

The Assembly adopted, by separate recorded votes, paragraph 4 by 91 to 24, with 28 abstentions, and paragraph 5 by 89 to 22, with 32 abstentions. The First Committee had likewise approved those paragraphs: paragraph 4 by 85 to 23, with 19 abstentions, and paragraph 5 by 86 to 23, with 19 abstentions.

In explanation of vote, Israel, reiterating that it would not be the first to introduce nuclear weapons into the Middle East, said that: it had been singled out for investigation from among all the countries which were advanced in nuclear technology and non-parties to NPT and that no country could accept to be told how best to serve the cause of non-proliferation; the expert team had been enjoined to consult with the League of Arab States; paragraph 4 called for applying one standard to Israel and not to other non-NPT States; paragraph 5 was an attempt by the sponsors to make Member States and organizations downgrade relations with Israel; it had no nuclear collaboration with South Africa; and the United Nations should challenge the sponsors to take up negotiations for the creation of a nuclear-weapon-free zone in the region. Similarly, the United States characterized the text as discriminatory, adding that it would welcome a balanced resolution calling for all non-nuclear-weapon States which had not done so to place their nuclear facilities under IAEA safeguards.

Australia felt that the Security Council was being asked to take action beyond its competence, that paragraph 5 could have implications for Israel's rights and privileges of IAEA membership, and that, in its view, the assumption of the continuing collaboration between Israel and South Africa had not been substantiated. Brazil abstained in the votes on the paragraphs because it believed the actions requested of the Council went beyond its constitutional powers.

In related 1985 action, the Assembly took up the question of armed Israeli aggression against Iraqi nuclear installations (**resolution 40/6**), and condemned nuclear collaboration between Israel and South Africa (**40/168 A**).

South Asia

In a July 1985 report,[73] the Secretary-General stated that he had been in contact with the States of South Asia with regard to the Assembly's 1984 request[74] that he assist in promoting a nuclear-weapon-free zone in the region, but that there had been no request by the States concerned for his assistance. In the course of those contacts, a view had been expressed that he should continue to be available for that purpose.

GENERAL ASSEMBLY ACTION

On 12 December, the General Assembly, on the recommendation of the First Committee, adopted **resolution 40/83** by recorded vote.

Establishment of a nuclear-weapon-free zone in South Asia

The General Assembly,

Recalling its resolutions 3265 B (XXIX) of 9 December 1974, 3476 B (XXX) of 11 December 1975, 31/73 of 10 December 1976, 32/83 of 12 December 1977, 33/65 of 14 December 1978, 34/78 of 11 December 1979, 35/148 of 12 December 1980, 36/88 of 9 December 1981, 37/76 of 9 December 1982, 38/65 of 15 December 1983 and 39/55 of 12 December 1984 concerning the establishment of a nuclear-weapon-free zone in South Asia,

Reiterating its conviction that the establishment of nuclear-weapon-free zones in various regions of the world is one of the measures which can contribute most effectively to the objectives of non-proliferation of nuclear weapons and general and complete disarmament,

Believing that the establishment of a nuclear-weapon-free zone in South Asia, as in other regions, will strengthen the security of the States of the region against the use or threat of use of nuclear weapons,

Noting the declaration issued at the highest level by Governments of South Asian States reaffirming their undertaking not to acquire or manufacture nuclear weapons and to devote their nuclear programmes exclusively to the economic and social advancement of their peoples,

Recalling that in the above-mentioned resolutions it called upon the States of the South Asian region, and such other neighbouring non-nuclear-weapon States as might be interested, to make all possible efforts to establish a nuclear-weapon-free zone in South Asia and to refrain, in the mean time, from any action contrary to this objective,

Further recalling that, in its resolution 3265 B (XXIX), it requested the Secretary-General to convene a meeting for the purpose of the consultations mentioned therein and to render such assistance as might be required to promote the efforts for the establishment of a nuclear-weapon-free zone in South Asia,

Bearing in mind the provisions of paragraphs 60 to 63 of the Final Document of the Tenth Special Session of the General Assembly regarding the establishment of nuclear-weapon-free zones, including in the region of South Asia,

Taking note of the report of the Secretary-General,

1. *Reaffirms* its endorsement, in principle, of the concept of a nuclear-weapon-free zone in South Asia;

2. *Urges once again* the States of South Asia, and such other neighbouring non-nuclear-weapon States as may be interested, to continue to make all possible efforts to establish a nuclear-weapon-free zone in South Asia and to refrain, in the mean time, from any action contrary to this objective;

3. *Calls upon* those nuclear-weapon States that have not done so to respond positively to this proposal and to extend the necessary co-operation in the efforts to establish a nuclear-weapon-free zone in South Asia;

4. *Requests* the Secretary-General to render such assistance as may be required to promote the efforts for the establishment of a nuclear-weapon-free zone in South Asia and to report on the subject to the General Assembly at its forty-first session;

5. *Decides* to include in the provisional agenda of its forty-first session the item entitled "Establishment of a nuclear-weapon-free zone in South Asia".

General Assembly resolution 40/83

12 December 1985   Meeting 113   104-3-41 (recorded vote)

Approved by First Committee (A/40/916) by recorded vote (90-3-40), 18 November (meeting 41); draft by Pakistan (A/C.1/40/L.10); agenda item 53.

Meeting numbers. GA 40th session: 1st Committee 3-32, 41; plenary 113.

Recorded vote in Assembly as follows:

In favour: Antigua and Barbuda, Australia, Bahrain, Bangladesh, Barbados, Belgium, Bolivia, Botswana, Brunei Darussalam, Burundi, Cameroon, Canada, Central African Republic, Chad, Chile, China, Colombia, Comoros, Democratic Kampuchea, Djibouti, Dominican Republic, Ecuador, Egypt, El Salvador, Equatorial Guinea, Finland, Gabon, Germany, Federal Republic of, Ghana, Greece, Grenada, Guatemala, Guinea, Guinea-Bissau, Guyana, Haiti, Honduras, Iran, Iraq, Ireland, Israel, Ivory Coast, Jamaica, Japan, Jordan, Kenya, Kuwait, Lebanon, Lesotho, Liberia, Libyan Arab Jamahiriya, Luxembourg, Malawi, Malaysia, Maldives, Mali, Malta, Mauritania, Mexico, Morocco, Nepal, Netherlands, New Zealand, Niger, Nigeria, Oman, Pakistan, Panama, Papua New Guinea, Paraguay, Peru, Philippines, Portugal, Qatar, Romania, Rwanda, Saint Christopher and Nevis, Saint Lucia, Saint Vincent and the Grenadines, Samoa, Saudi Arabia, Senegal, Sierra Leone, Singapore, Solomon Islands, Somalia, Spain, Sri Lanka, Sudan, Swaziland, Thailand, Togo, Trinidad and Tobago, Tunisia, Turkey, Uganda, United Arab Emirates, United Republic of Tanzania, United States, Uruguay, Venezuela, Yemen, Zaire, Zambia.

Against: Bhutan, India, Mauritius.

Abstaining: Afghanistan, Algeria, Angola, Argentina, Austria, Bahamas, Benin, Brazil, Bulgaria, Burkina Faso, Burma, Byelorussian SSR, Cape Verde, Congo, Cuba, Cyprus, Czechoslovakia, Democratic Yemen, Denmark, Ethiopia, Fiji, France, German Democratic Republic, Hungary, Iceland, Indonesia, Italy, Lao People's Democratic Republic, Madagascar, Mongolia, Mozambique, Nicaragua,

Norway, Poland, Suriname, Sweden, Ukrainian SSR, USSR, United Kingdom, Viet Nam, Yugoslavia.

India said no consensus existed among the region's States for establishing a nuclear-weapon-free zone, and that, in areas immediately adjacent to the proposed zone, nuclear weapons existed and continued to proliferate both on land and at sea.

Brazil abstained as in the past because the proposal failed to attract unanimous support in the region. Denmark and Sweden spoke in like manner as did Indonesia, which added that the proposal should be initiated by the States in the region, based on voluntary participation, with all arrangements being freely arrived at.

Also stressing the importance of full consent and co-operation, Bangladesh hoped that consultations would be held to define the limits of the zone and to deal with other related issues, and Sri Lanka emphasized the need to take into account the region's inherent characteristics, adding that no model of such a zone anywhere else could be transplanted. Japan also reiterated its view on a number of conditions required for the zone's success (see p. 62).

Strengthening the security of non-nuclear-weapon States

Little progress was made in 1985 in reaching agreements on effective international assurances for non-nuclear-weapon States against the use or threat of use of nuclear weapons—arrangements also known as negative security assurances. The General Assembly adopted two resolutions in December (40/85 and 40/86), reflecting differing approaches to the question and calling for the resumption of discussion on the issue in the Conference on Disarmament in 1986.

Consideration by the Conference on Disarmament. The Conference on Disarmament[3] again considered negative security assurances, from 8 to 12 April and from 29 July to 2 August 1985. In addition, an *Ad Hoc* Committee, re-established on 1 August to deal with the item, held three meetings between 12 and 22 August under the chairmanship of Mansur Ahmad (Pakistan). Because of the time constraint imposed by the Committee's late establishment, the Chairman held consultations on the most efficacious way to deal with the question, concluding that the nuclear-weapon States' previous positions remained unchanged. Most delegations expressed readiness to engage in substantive discussion, while some considered such action futile in the absence of a nuclear disarmament process; others felt some progress might have been possible had the *Ad Hoc* Committee been established earlier.

The Committee recommended that the Conference continue exploring ways to overcome the difficulties.

In December 1985, the General Assembly, on the recommendation of the First Committee, adopted two resolutions on negative security assurances.

On 12 December, it adopted **resolution 40/86** by recorded vote.

Conclusion of effective international arrangements to assure non-nuclear-weapon States against the use or threat of use of nuclear weapons

The General Assembly,

Bearing in mind the need to ally the legitimate concern of the States of the world with regard to ensuring lasting security for their peoples,

Convinced that nuclear weapons pose the greatest threat to mankind and to the survival of civilization,

Deeply concerned at the continuing escalation of the arms race, in particular the nuclear-arms race, and the possibility of the use or threat of use of nuclear weapons,

Convinced that nuclear disarmament and the complete elimination of nuclear weapons are essential to remove the danger of nuclear war,

Taking into account the principle of the non-use of force or threat of force enshrined in the Charter of the United Nations,

Deeply concerned about the possibility of the use or threat of use of nuclear weapons,

Recognizing that the independence, territorial integrity and sovereignty of non-nuclear-weapon States need to be safeguarded against the use or threat of use of force, including the use or threat of use of nuclear weapons,

Considering that, until nuclear disarmament is achieved on a universal basis, it is imperative for the international community to develop effective measures to ensure the security of non-nuclear-weapon States against the use or threat of use of nuclear weapons from any quarter,

Recognizing that effective measures to assure the non-nuclear-weapon States against the use or threat of use of nuclear weapons can constitute a positive contribution to the prevention of the spread of nuclear weapons,

Recalling its resolutions 3261 G (XXIX) of 9 December 1974 and 31/189 C of 21 December 1976,

Bearing in mind paragraph 59 of the Final Document of the Tenth Special Session of the General Assembly, in which it urged the nuclear-weapon States to pursue efforts to conclude, as appropriate, effective arrangements to assure non-nuclear-weapon States against the use or threat of use of nuclear weapons,

Desirous of promoting the implementation of the relevant provisions of the Final Document of the Tenth Special Session,

Recalling its resolutions 33/72 B of 14 December 1978, 34/85 of 11 December 1979, 35/155 of 12 December 1980, 36/95 of 9 December 1981, 37/81 of 9 December 1982, 38/68 of 15 December 1983 and 39/58 of 12 December 1984,

Further recalling paragraph 12 of the Declaration of the 1980s as the Second Disarmament Decade, contained in the annex to its resolution 35/46 of 3 December 1980, which states, *inter alia*, that all efforts should be exerted by the Committee on Disarmament urgently to negotiate with a view to reaching agreement on effective international arrangements to assure non-nuclear-weapon States against the use or threat of use of nuclear weapons,

Noting the in-depth negotiations undertaken in the Conference on Disarmament and its *Ad Hoc* Committee on Effective International Arrangements to Assure Non-Nuclear-Weapon States against the Use or Threat of Use of Nuclear Weapons, with a view to reaching agreement on this item,

Noting the proposals submitted under this item in the Conference on Disarmament, including the drafts of an international convention,

Taking note of the decision of the Seventh Conference of Heads of State or Government of Non-Aligned Countries, held at New Delhi from 7 to 12 March 1983, as well as the relevant recommendations of the Organization of the Islamic Conference reiterated in the Final Communiqué of the Fifteenth Islamic Conference of Foreign Ministers, held at Sanaa from 18 to 22 December 1984, calling upon the Conference on Disarmament to reach an urgent agreement on an international convention to assure non-nuclear-weapon States against the use or threat of use of nuclear weapons,

Further noting the support expressed in the Conference on Disarmament and in the General Assembly for the elaboration of an international convention to assure non-nuclear-weapon States against the use or threat of use of nuclear weapons, as well as the difficulties pointed out in evolving a common approach acceptable to all,

1. *Reaffirms* the urgent need to reach agreement on effective international arrangements to assure non-nuclear-weapon States against the use or threat of use of nuclear weapons;

2. *Notes with satisfaction* that in the Conference on Disarmament there is no objection, in principle, to the idea of an international convention to assure non-nuclear-weapon States against the use or threat of use of nuclear weapons, although the difficulties as regards evolving a common approach acceptable to all have also been pointed out;

3. *Appeals* to all States, especially the nuclear-weapon States, to demonstrate the political will necessary to reach agreement on a common approach and, in particular, on a common formula which could be included in an international instrument of a legally binding character;

4. *Recommends* that further intensive efforts should be devoted to the search for such a common approach or common formula and that the various alternative approaches, including in particular those considered in the Conference on Disarmament, should be further explored in order to overcome the difficulties;

5. *Recommends* that the Conference on Disarmament should actively continue negotiations with a view to reaching early agreement and concluding effective international arrangements to assure non-nuclear-weapon States against the use or threat of use of nuclear weapons, taking into account the widespread support for the conclusion of an international convention and giving consideration to any other proposals designed to secure the same objective;

6. *Decides* to include in the provisional agenda of its forty-first session the item entitled "Conclusion of effective international arrangements to assure non-nuclear-weapon States against the use or threat of use of nuclear weapons".

General Assembly resolution 40/86

12 December 1985   Meeting 113   142-0-6 (recorded vote)

Approved by First Committee (A/40/930) by recorded vote (122-0-5), 18 November (meeting 41); draft by Pakistan (A/C.1/40/L.11); agenda item 56.

Meeting numbers. GA 40th session: 1st Committee 3-32, 41; plenary 113.

Recorded vote in Assembly as follows:

In favour: Afghanistan, Algeria, Angola, Antigua and Barbuda, Australia, Austria, Bahamas, Bahrain, Bangladesh, Barbados, Belgium, Benin, Bolivia, Botswana, Brunei Darussalam, Burkina Faso, Burma, Burundi, Byelorussian SSR, Cameroon, Canada, Cape Verde, Central African Republic, Chad, Chile, China, Colombia, Comoros, Congo, Cuba, Cyprus, Czechoslovakia, Democratic Kampuchea, Democratic Yemen, Denmark, Djibouti, Dominican Republic, Ecuador, Egypt, El Salvador, Equatorial Guinea, Ethiopia, Fiji, France, Gabon, German Democratic Republic, Germany, Federal Republic of, Ghana, Greece, Guatemala, Guinea, Guinea-Bissau, Guyana, Haiti, Honduras, Hungary, Iceland, Indonesia, Iran, Iraq, Ireland, Israel, Italy, Ivory Coast, Jamaica, Japan, Jordan, Kenya, Kuwait, Lao People's Democratic Republic, Lebanon, Lesotho, Liberia, Libyan Arab Jamahiriya, Luxembourg, Madagascar, Malawi, Malaysia, Maldives, Mali, Malta, Mauritania, Mauritius, Mexico, Mongolia, Morocco, Mozambique, Nepal, Netherlands, New Zealand, Nicaragua, Niger, Nigeria, Norway, Oman, Pakistan, Panama, Papua New Guinea, Paraguay, Peru, Philippines, Poland, Portugal, Qatar, Romania, Rwanda, Saint Lucia, Saint Vincent and the Grenadines, Samoa, Sao Tome and Principe, Saudi Arabia, Senegal, Seychelles, Sierra Leone, Singapore, Solomon Islands, Somalia, Spain, Sri Lanka, Sudan, Suriname, Swaziland, Sweden, Syrian Arab Republic, Thailand, Togo, Trinidad and Tobago, Tunisia, Turkey, Uganda, Ukrainian SSR, USSR, United Arab Emirates, United Kingdom, United Republic of Tanzania, Uruguay, Venezuela, Viet Nam, Yemen, Yugoslavia, Zaire, Zambia.

Against: None.

Abstaining: Argentina, Brazil, Grenada, India, Saint Christopher and Nevis, United States.

Japan said it had voted in favour—despite reservations about a specific modality of assurances mentioned in paragraphs 2, 3 and 5—because the text reflected better than the other one (see below) the work of the Conference on Disarmament and because it expected continued efforts in the *Ad Hoc* Committee in line with the common approach referred to in the text. Sweden supported the draft for giving consideration to proposals not confined to an international convention.

Other States explained their abstentions in conjunction with the other text on negative security assurances (see p. 69).

Also on 12 December, the Assembly adopted **resolution 40/85** by recorded vote.

Conclusion of an international convention on the strengthening of the security of non-nuclear-weapon States against the use or threat of use of nuclear weapons

The General Assembly,

Convinced of the need to take effective measures for the strengthening of the security of States and prompted by the desire shared by all nations to eliminate war and prevent nuclear conflagration,

Taking into account the principle of non-use of force or threat of force enshrined in the Charter of the United Nations and reaffirmed in a number of United Nations declarations and resolutions,

Considering that, until nuclear disarmament is achieved on a universal basis, it is imperative for the international community to develop effective measures to ensure the security of non-nuclear-weapon States against the use or threat of use of nuclear weapons from any quarter,

Recognizing that effective measures to assure non-nuclear-weapon States against the use or threat of use of nuclear weapons can constitute a positive contribution to the prevention of the spread of such weapons,

Noting with satisfaction the determination of non-nuclear-weapon States in various parts of the world to prevent nuclear weapons from being introduced into their territories and to ensure the complete absence of such weapons in their respective regions, including through the establishment of nuclear-weapon-free zones on the basis of arrangements freely arrived at among the States of the region concerned, and being anxious to encourage and contribute to the attainment of this objective,

Concerned at the continuing escalation of the arms race, in particular the nuclear-arms race having entered a qualitatively new stage, and the possibility of the use or threat of use of nuclear weapons and the danger of nuclear war,

Desirous of promoting the implementation of paragraph 59 of the Final Document of the Tenth Special Session of the General Assembly, the first special session devoted to disarmament, in which it urged the nuclear-weapon States to pursue efforts to conclude, as appropriate, effective arrangements to assure non-nuclear-weapon States against the use or threat of use of nuclear weapons,

Recalling its numerous resolutions on this subject as well as the relevant part of the special report of the Committee on Disarmament submitted to the General Assembly at its twelfth special session, the second special session devoted to disarmament,

Noting that the Conference on Disarmament considered in 1985 the item entitled "Effective international arrangements to assure non-nuclear-weapon States against the use or threat of use of nuclear weapons", and the work done by its *Ad Hoc* Committee on this item, as reflected in the report of the Conference on Disarmament,

Noting further that this consideration revealed that an overwhelming number of delegations, including those of the nuclear-weapon States, stressed the importance of that item and their readiness to engage in a substantive dialogue on the issue,

Recalling the proposals submitted on this subject to the General Assembly and in the Conference on Disarmament, including the drafts of an international convention, and the widespread international support for the conclusion of such a convention,

Further recalling that the idea of interim arrangements as a first step towards the conclusion of such a convention has also been considered in the Conference on Disarmament,

Welcoming once again the solemn declarations made by some nuclear-weapon States concerning non-first use of nuclear weapons, and convinced that, if all nuclear-weapon States were to assume obligations not to be the first to use nuclear weapons, that would be tantamount in practice to banning the use of nuclear weapons against all States, including all non-nuclear-weapon States,

Considering that the non-nuclear-weapon States having no nuclear weapons on their territories have every right to receive reliable international legal guarantees against the use or threat of use of nuclear weapons,

Being aware that unconditional guarantees by all nuclear-weapon States not to use or threaten to use nuclear weapons under any circumstances against the non-nuclear-weapon States having no nuclear weapons on their territories should constitute an integral element of a mandatory system of norms regulating the relations between the nuclear-weapon States, which bear the primary responsibility for preventing a nuclear war, thus sparing mankind from its devastating consequences,

1. *Reaffirms once again* the urgent need to reach agreement on effective international arrangements to assure non-nuclear-weapon States against the use or threat of use of nuclear weapons and to find a common approach acceptable to all, which could be included in an international instrument of a legally binding character;

2. *Considers* that the Conference on Disarmament should continue to explore ways and means of overcoming the difficulties encountered in carrying out negotiations on this question;

3. *Requests* the Conference on Disarmament to continue active consideration on this subject, including through re-establishment of the *Ad Hoc* Committee on Effective International Arrangements to Assure Non-Nuclear-Weapon States against the Use or Threat of Use of Nuclear Weapons as soon as practicable, at its 1986 session, with a view to concluding an international instrument of a legally binding character to assure non-nuclear-weapon States against the use or threat of use of nuclear weapons;

4. *Decides* to include in the provisional agenda of its forty-first session an item entitled "Conclusion of effective international arrangements on the strengthening of the security of non-nuclear-weapon States against the use or threat of use of nuclear weapons".

General Assembly resolution 40/85

12 December 1985   Meeting 113   101-19-25 (recorded vote)

Approved by First Committee (A/40/929) by recorded vote (83-19-17), 18 November (meeting 41); 10-nation draft (A/C.1/40/L.34); agenda item 55.
Sponsors: Afghanistan, Angola, Bulgaria, Byelorussian SSR, Czechoslovakia, Democratic Yemen, Ethiopia, Mongolia, USSR, Viet Nam.
Meeting numbers. GA 40th session: 1st Committee 3-33, 41; plenary 113.

Recorded vote in Assembly as follows:

In favour: Afghanistan, Algeria, Angola, Bahrain, Bangladesh, Barbados, Benin, Bolivia, Botswana, Bulgaria, Burkina Faso, Burundi, Byelorussian SSR, Cameroon, Cape Verde, Central African Republic, Chad, Chile, Comoros, Congo, Cuba, Cyprus, Czechoslovakia, Democratic Yemen, Djibouti, Dominican Republic, Ecuador, Egypt, El Salvador, Equatorial Guinea, Ethiopia, Fiji, Finland, Gabon, German Democratic Republic, Ghana, Guatemala, Guinea, Guinea-Bissau, Guyana, Hungary, Indonesia, Iran, Iraq, Jordan, Kenya, Kuwait, Lao People's Democratic Republic, Lebanon, Lesotho, Liberia, Libyan Arab Jamahiriya, Madagascar, Malawi, Malaysia, Maldives, Mali, Malta, Mauritius, Mexico, Mongolia, Morocco, Mozambique, Nepal, Nicaragua, Niger, Nigeria, Oman, Pakistan, Panama, Papua New Guinea, Peru, Poland, Qatar, Romania, Rwanda, Saudi Arabia, Senegal, Seychelles, Sierra Leone, Somalia, Sri Lanka, Sudan, Suriname, Swaziland, Syrian Arab Republic, Thailand, Togo, Trinidad and Tobago, Tunisia, Uganda, Ukrainian SSR, USSR, United Arab Emirates, United Republic of Tanzania, Venezuela, Viet Nam, Yemen, Yugoslavia, Zaire, Zambia.
Against: Australia, Belgium, Canada, Denmark, France, Germany, Federal Republic of, Iceland, Israel, Italy, Japan, Luxembourg, Netherlands, New Zealand, Norway, Portugal, Spain, Turkey, United Kingdom, United States.
Abstaining: Antigua and Barbuda, Argentina, Austria, Bahamas, Brazil, Burma, China, Colombia, Democratic Kampuchea, Greece, Grenada, Haiti, Honduras, India, Ireland, Ivory Coast, Jamaica, Paraguay, Saint Christopher and Nevis, Saint Lucia, Saint Vincent and the Grenadines, Samoa, Solomon Islands, Sweden, Uruguay.

France asserted that the text gave a distorted view of the assurances by linking the granting of negative assurances and nuclear-weapon deployment on the territory of the State concerned, and by proposing that such assurances be included in a mandatory system that would govern relations between nuclear-weapon States, rather than be given by each nuclear-weapon State on an individual basis. In particular, France deplored the demand for non-deployment, which, it believed, had impeded the harmonization of the various formulae for negative security guarantees since 1978. Japan considered the text unbalanced and lacking in objectivity, in that the preambular part contained one-sided assertions and the reference in the operative part to specific modalities of assurances prejudged the work of the Conference on Disarmament.

Sweden abstained because the idea of an international convention seemed to imply the imposition of obligations on non-nuclear-weapon States beyond their declared choice to be and to stay nuclear-weapon free.

Argentina, Brazil and India explained, in single statements, their abstentions on the two drafts on negative security assurances. Argentina continued to have reservations about the value and credibility of negative assurances which, it added, would be achieved only through nuclear disarmament and the elimination of nuclear weapons. Sharing that view, India considered it futile for the non-nuclear-weapon States to expect assurances from the nuclear Powers while the latter continued to predicate their security policies on nuclear-weapon use. Brazil also stated that no progress could be made in multilateral consideration of the topic as long as the nuclear Powers continued to approach it from the narrow point of view of their own security perceptions; with but one exception, unilateral declarations of assurances contained qualifications and conditions, thus rendering them instruments of the interests of the nuclear-weapon Powers themselves.

In 1985, a safeguards agreement between the USSR and IAEA entered into force in June and the first inspections under that agreement were carried out in August. In September, China announced its intention to place some of its civilian nuclear facilities under IAEA safeguards.

REFERENCES

[1]YUN 1963, p. 137. [2]YUN 1968, p. 17, GA res. 2373(XXII), annex, 12 June 1968. [3]A/40/27 & Corr.1. [4]YUN 1984, p. 28, GA res. 39/148 P, 17 Dec. 1984. [5]CD/603. [6]A/40/498. [7]YUN 1978, p. 39, GA res. S-10/2, 30 June 1978. [8]A/C.1/40/L.23/Rev.1. [9]A/C.1/40/L.74. [10]YUN 1984, p. 29. [11]YUN 1982, p. 53, GA res. 37/100 C, annex, 13 Dec. 1982. [12]YUN 1983, p. 34, GA res. 38/73 G, annex, 15 Dec. 1983. [13]YUN 1984, p. 31, GA res. 39/63 H, annex, 12 Dec. 1984. [14]*Ibid.*, p. 29, GA res. 39/148 F, 17 Dec. 1984. [15]A/40/449 & Corr.2. [16]YUN 1984, p. 22. [17]A/40/42. [18]A/40/114-S/16921. [19]A/40/130-S/16958. [20]A/40/125. [21]A/40/825-S/17596. [22]A/40/888-S/17629. [23]A/C.1/40/10. [24]A/C.1/40/14. [25]A/40/1070. [26]YUN 1984, p. 24. [27]*Ibid.*, p. 48, GA res. 39/60, 12 Dec. 1984. [28]CD/520/Rev.1. [29]CD/522/Rev.1. [30]CD/602. [31]CD/629. [32]CD/621. [33]CD/625. [34]CD/612. [35]CD/624. [36]CD/626. [37]CD/610 & Corr.1. [38]CD/599. [39]CD/583. [40]CD/616. [41]A/40/522. [42]A/40/558. [43]A/41/66 & Corr.1. [44]A/40/672-S/17488. [45]A/C.1/40/L.71/Rev.1. [46]NPT/CONF.III/64/I-III. [47]YUN 1975, p. 27. [48]YUN 1980, p. 51. [49]YUN 1984, p. 47. [50]A/C.1/40/9. [51]YUN 1965, p. 72, GA res. 2028(XX), 19 Nov. 1965. [52]A/40/173-S/17033. [53]YUN 1982, p. 64, GA res. 37/99 F, 13 Dec. 1982. [54]*Comprehensive Study of the Question of Nuclear-Weapon-Free Zones in All Its Aspects*, Sales No. E.76.I.7. [55]YUN 1984, p. 38, GA res. 39/151 B, 17 Dec. 1984. [56]A/40/379. [57]YUN 1964, p. 69. [58]YUN 1984, p. 40, GA res. 39/61 B, 12 Dec. 1984. [59]*Ibid.*, p. 39. [60]S/16930. [61]A/40/510. [62]A/40/761-S/17573. [63]A/40/854-S/17610 & Corr.1. [64]YUN 1979, p. 46. [65]YUN 1984, p. 43, GA res. 39/54, 12 Dec. 1984. [66]A/40/442 & Add.1. [67]A/40/383. [68]S/16934. [69]YUN 1984, p. 44, GA res. 39/147, 17 Dec. 1984. [70]S/17195. [71]A/40/520. [72]YUN 1981, p. 51. [73]A/40/473. [74]YUN 1984, p. 46, GA res. 39/55, 12 Dec. 1984.

OTHER PUBLICATIONS

Unilateral Nuclear Disarmament Measures (A/39/516), Sales No. E.85.IX.2. *Prevention of Nuclear War: A United States Approach* (UNITAR/RR/32), Sales No. E.85.XV.RR/32.

Prohibition or restriction of other weapons

Chemical and biological weapons

In 1985, the General Assembly again adopted three resolutions (40/92 A-C), reflecting the persisting differences in approach to an envisaged convention banning chemical and bacteriological (biological) weapons, but all urging the Conference on Disarmament to intensify its negotiations on a convention.

Consideration by the Conference on Disarmament. The Conference on Disarmament[1] continued negotiations on a convention banning chemical and biological weapons, from 25 March to 5 April and from 15 to 26 July 1985.

A number of new documents on verification problems were submitted by Australia, the German Democratic Republic, the Federal Republic of Germany, Japan, Spain, the United Kingdom and Yugoslavia, as well as by Finland and Norway, non-members of the Conference. In addition, China submitted a document on destroying chemical weapons, France on eliminating chemical-weapons stocks, the United Kingdom on the structure of an envisaged organization for implementing a convention, and Sweden on a comprehensive approach for elaborating régimes for chemicals in a convention. The USSR submitted a TASS statement on the approval by the United States Congress of appropriations for binary chemical-weapons production.

The Conference President received communications from Iran on the alleged use of chemical weapons in its conflict with Iraq (see Chapter VII of this section), and one requesting the distribution in the Conference of the 1984 report of the specialists appointed to investigate Iran's allegations of chemical-weapons use.[2]

As agreed in 1984,[3] the *Ad Hoc* Committee on Chemical Weapons, established that year by the Conference on Disarmament, resumed work from 14 January to 1 February 1985 to discuss, among other things, the issues of permitted activities and verification on challenge.

At its 1985 session, the Conference re-established on 7 February the *Ad Hoc* Committee, which, under the chairmanship of Stanislaw Turbanski (Poland), held 12 meetings between 27 February and 19 August; in addition, the Chairman held a number of informal consultations. The Committee set up three working groups on the envisaged convention: Working Group A, on scope, definitions, non-production and permitted activities; Working Group B, on elimination of stocks and production facilities; and Working Group C, on compliance. The prohibition of chemical-weapons use and the problem of herbicides were considered in open-ended consultations. Some progress was made in those groups in formulating certain aspects of the convention, including those covering plans for eliminating chemical weapons; on the other hand, some controversial questions remained unresolved, such as verification by challenge, definition of some basic concepts, eliminating the existing stocks and production facilities, and the so-called permitted activities.

The report of the *Ad Hoc* Committee—later incorporated into that of the Conference[1] to the General Assembly—appended a preliminary structure of a convention, indicating the stage reached in the negotiations during the 1985 session, and the reports of the working groups and of the Chairman of the open-ended consultations. The basic structure of the convention, as formulated in 1984,[3] was retained by the Committee.

The Conference accepted the recommendations of the *Ad Hoc* Committee to use the appendices, together with other existing and future Conference documents, in elaborating the convention. It also agreed that the *Ad Hoc* Committee resume work under the current mandate for a session of limited duration in January 1986, that the Chairman hold informal consultations on specific issues in preparation for the resumed session, and that the *Ad Hoc* Committee be re-established with its 1985 mandate before the end of the second week of the Conference's 1986 session.

Communications. In 1985, the United Nations received a number of communications on various aspects of the question of chemical weapons, some of which also dealt with general and complete disarmament (see p. 14). In addition, the Secretary-General received a series of communications from Iran on the alleged use of chemical weapons by Iraq in their ongoing conflict (see Chapter VII of this section).

On 20 September,[4] Czechoslovakia and the German Democratic Republic transmitted identic letters that their heads of Government had sent on 12 September to their counterpart in the Federal Republic of Germany, officially proposing that they jointly establish a chemical-weapon-free zone in Europe. On 25 October,[5] the Federal Republic of Germany transmitted the identical replies it had sent on 27 September to the two countries, suggesting that all concerned enter into talks within the framework of the Conference on Disarmament on a treaty for a world-wide ban on chemical weapons. On 20 November,[6] the two countries transmitted their 8 November letters to the Federal Republic of Germany, proposing that, parallel to the latter's September proposal, representatives of their Foreign Ministries should hold consultations.

GENERAL ASSEMBLY ACTION

On 12 December 1985, the General Assembly, on the recommendation of the First Committee, adopted three resolutions (**40/92 A-C**)—one (**40/92 B**) without vote—on prohibiting chemical and bacteriological weapons. Some States explained in single statements their positions on the three texts (see p. 73).

The Assembly adopted **resolution 40/92 A** by recorded vote.

Prohibition of chemical and bacteriological weapons
The General Assembly,
Recalling paragraph 75 of the Final Document of the Tenth Special Session of the General Assembly, which states that the complete and effective prohibition of the development, production and stockpiling of all chemical weapons and their destruction represents one of the most urgent measures of disarmament,
Recalling its previous resolutions relating to the complete and effective prohibition of the development, production and stockpiling of all chemical weapons and to their destruction,
Convinced of the need for the earliest conclusion of a convention on the prohibition of the development, production and stockpiling of all chemical weapons and on their destruction, which would significantly contribute to general and complete disarmament under effective international control,
Stressing the continuing importance of the Protocol for the Prohibition of the Use in War of Asphyxiating, Poisonous or Other Gases, and of Bacteriological Methods of Warfare, signed sixty years ago at Geneva,
Determined, for the sake of all mankind, to exclude completely the possibility of the use of chemical weapons, through the earliest conclusion and implementation of a convention on the prohibition of the development, production and stockpiling of all types of chemical weapons and on their destruction, thereby complementing the obligations assumed under the Geneva Protocol of 17 June 1925,
Taking into consideration the work of the Conference on Disarmament during its session in 1985 regarding the prohibition of chemical weapons and, in particular, highly appreciating the work of its *Ad Hoc* Committee on Chemical Weapons,
Expressing profound concern at recent decisions on the production of binary chemical weapons, as well as at their intended deployment,

Deeming it desirable for States to refrain from taking any action that could delay or further complicate negotiations and to display a constructive approach to such negotiations and the political will to reach an early agreement on the chemical weapons convention,

Aware that the qualitative improvement and development of chemical weapons complicate ongoing negotiations on the prohibition of chemical weapons,

Taking note of proposals on the creation of chemical-weapon-free zones aimed at facilitating the complete prohibition of chemical weapons and at contributing to the achievement of stable regional and international security,

1. *Reaffirms* the necessity of the speediest elaboration and conclusion of a convention on the prohibition of the development, production and stockpiling of all chemical weapons and on their destruction;

2. *Appeals* to all States to facilitate in every possible way the conclusion of such a convention;

3. *Urges* the Conference on Disarmament to intensify the negotiations in the *Ad Hoc* Committee on Chemical Weapons with a view to achieving accord on a chemical weapons convention at the earliest possible date and, for this purpose, to intensify the drafting process of such a convention for submission to the General Assembly at its forty-first session;

4. *Reaffirms its call* to all States to conduct serious negotiations in good faith and to refrain from any action that could impede negotiations on the prohibition of chemical weapons and specifically to refrain from the production and deployment of binary and other new types of chemical weapons, as well as from stationing chemical weapons on the territory of other States;

5. *Calls upon* all States that have not yet done so to become parties to the Protocol for the Prohibition of the Use in War of Asphyxiating, Poisonous or Other Gases, and of Bacteriological Methods of Warfare, signed at Geneva on 17 June 1925.

General Assembly resolution 40/92 A

12 December 1985   Meeting 113   93-15-41 (recorded vote)

Approved by First Committee (A/40/932) by recorded vote (81-13-38), 15 November (meeting 39); 12-nation draft (A/C.1/40/L.15/Rev.1); agenda item 63.

Sponsors: Afghanistan, Angola, Bulgaria, Byelorussian SSR, Czechoslovakia, German Democratic Republic, Hungary, Mongolia, Poland, Ukrainian SSR, USSR, Viet Nam.

Meeting numbers. GA 40th session: 1st Committee 3-32, 36, 39; plenary 113.

Recorded vote in Assembly as follows:

In favour: Afghanistan, Algeria, Angola, Antigua and Barbuda, Bahrain, Bangladesh, Barbados, Benin, Bhutan, Bolivia, Botswana, Bulgaria, Burkina Faso, Burundi, Byelorussian SSR, Cameroon, Cape Verde, Chad, Colombia, Congo, Cuba, Cyprus, Czechoslovakia, Democratic Yemen, Egypt, El Salvador, Equatorial Guinea, Ethiopia, Fiji, German Democratic Republic, Ghana, Guinea, Guinea-Bissau, Guyana, Hungary, Indonesia, Iran, Iraq, Jamaica, Jordan, Kenya, Kuwait, Lao People's Democratic Republic, Lebanon, Lesotho, Liberia, Libyan Arab Jamahiriya, Madagascar, Malawi, Malaysia, Maldives, Mali, Mauritius, Mexico, Mongolia, Mozambique, Nepal, Nicaragua, Niger, Nigeria, Oman, Pakistan, Panama, Papua New Guinea, Peru, Poland, Qatar, Romania, Samoa, Saudi Arabia, Seychelles, Singapore,[a] Solomon Islands, Somalia, Swaziland, Syrian Arab Republic, Thailand, Togo, Trinidad and Tobago, Tunisia, Uganda, Ukrainian SSR, USSR, United Arab Emirates, United Republic of Tanzania, Vanuatu, Venezuela, Viet Nam, Yemen, Yugoslavia, Zaire, Zambia, Zimbabwe.

Against: Belgium, France, Germany, Federal Republic of, Grenada, Iceland, Italy, Luxembourg, Netherlands, Norway, Portugal, Saint Christopher and Nevis, Spain, Turkey, United Kingdom, United States.

Abstaining: Argentina, Australia, Austria, Bahamas, Brazil, Brunei Darussalam, Burma, Canada, Central African Republic, Chile, China, Comoros, Democratic Kampuchea, Denmark, Djibouti, Dominican Republic, Ecuador, Finland, Gabon, Greece, Guatemala, Haiti, Honduras, India, Ireland, Israel, Ivory Coast, Japan, Mauritania, Morocco, New Zealand, Paraguay, Rwanda, Saint Lucia, Saint Vincent and the Grenadines, Senegal, Sierra Leone, Sri Lanka, Suriname, Sweden, Uruguay.

[a]Later advised the Secretariat it had intended to abstain.

In explanation of vote, the Netherlands, viewing the draft as superfluous in view of the consensus adoption of resolution 40/92 B (see below), said the text criticized the intended resumption of chemical-weapons production by the United States which, it said, had unilaterally observed a freeze for over 15 years while the USSR continued to stockpile such weapons.

Australia, Brazil, Jamaica and Pakistan considered the draft deficient in that it singled out one particular kind of chemical weapon, and did not believe that the concept of chemical-weapon-free zones would facilitate the negotiation of a convention. Further, Australia felt that negotiating an equitable and verifiable treaty establishing such a zone would be no less difficult than negotiating a comprehensive ban on chemical weapons.

Cuba welcomed the proposals to create a chemical-weapon-free zone in Europe, but believed that in the case of Latin America and the Caribbean account would have to be taken of extra-regional nearby countries, which had colonial Territories in the region and which possessed chemical weapons.

The Assembly adopted **resolution 40/92 B** without vote.

Chemical and bacteriological (biological) weapons

The General Assembly,

Recalling its previous resolutions relating to the complete and effective prohibition of the development, production and stockpiling of all chemical weapons and to their destruction,

Reaffirming the urgent necessity of strict observance by all States of the principles and objectives of the Protocol for the Prohibition of the Use in War of Asphyxiating, Poisonous or Other Gases, and of Bacteriological Methods of Warfare, signed at Geneva on 17 June 1925, and of the adherence by all States to the Convention on the Prohibition of the Development, Production and Stockpiling of Bacteriological (Biological) and Toxin Weapons and on Their Destruction, signed in London, Moscow and Washington, on 10 April 1972,

Having considered the part of the report of the Conference on Disarmament on chemical weapons, in particular the report of its *Ad Hoc* Committee on Chemical Weapons,

Convinced of the necessity that all efforts be exerted for the continuation and successful conclusion of negotiations on the prohibition of the development, production and stockpiling of all chemical weapons and on their destruction,

1. *Takes note* of the work of the Conference on Disarmament during its session in 1985 regarding the prohibition of chemical weapons and, in particular, appreciates the work of its *Ad Hoc* Committee on Chemical Weapons on that question and the progress recorded in its report;

2. *Expresses again its regret and concern* that an agreement on the complete and effective prohibition of the development, production and stockpiling of all chemical weapons and on their destruction has not yet been elaborated;

3. *Urges again* the Conference on Disarmament, as a matter of high priority, to intensify, during its session in 1986, the negotiations on such a convention and to reinforce further its efforts, *inter alia*, by increasing the time during the year that it devotes to such negotiations, taking into account all existing proposals and future initiatives, with a view to the final elaboration of a convention at the earliest possible date, and to re-establish its *Ad Hoc* Committee on Chemical Weapons for this purpose with the 1985 mandate;

4. *Requests* the Conference on Disarmament to report to the General Assembly at its forty-first session on the results of its negotiations.

General Assembly resolution 40/92 B

12 December 1985   Meeting 113   Adopted without vote

Approved by First Committee (A/40/932) without vote, 15 November (meeting 39); 22-nation draft (A/C.1/40/L.24); agenda item 63.
Sponsors: Argentina, Australia, Belgium, Canada, Denmark, German Democratic Republic, Germany, Federal Republic of, Greece, Indonesia, Ireland, Japan, Kenya, Mongolia, Netherlands, Norway, Poland, Rwanda, Spain, Ukrainian SSR, United Kingdom, Uruguay, Viet Nam.
Meeting numbers. GA 40th session: 1st Committee 3-32, 36, 39; plenary 113.

The Assembly adopted **resolution 40/92 C** by recorded vote.

Chemical and bacteriological (biological) weapons

The General Assembly,

Reaffirming the urgent necessity of strict observance by all States of the principles and objectives of the Protocol for the Prohibition of the Use in War of Asphyxiating, Poisonous or Other Gases, and of Bacteriological Methods of Warfare, signed at Geneva on 17 June 1925, and of the adherence by all States to the Convention on the Prohibition of the Development, Production and Stockpiling of Bacteriological (Biological) and Toxin Weapons and on Their Destruction, signed in London, Moscow and Washington, on 10 April 1972,

Noting with concern reports that chemical weapons have been used, as well as indications of their emergence in an increasing number of national arsenals,

Expressing concern at the increasing risk that chemical weapons may be resorted to again,

Noting international efforts to strengthen relevant international prohibitions, including efforts to develop appropriate fact-finding mechanisms,

Recalling its resolution 39/65 A of 12 December 1984,

Rededicating its efforts to protect mankind from chemical and biological warfare,

1. *Reaffirms* the need for strict observance of existing international obligations regarding prohibitions on chemical and biological weapons and condemns all actions that contravene those obligations;

2. *Welcomes* the ongoing efforts to ensure the most effective prohibitions possible on chemical and biological weapons;

3. *Urges* the Conference on Disarmament to accelerate its negotiations on a multilateral convention on the complete and effective prohibition of the development, production and stockpiling of chemical weapons and on their destruction;

4. *Calls upon* all States, pending the conclusion of such a comprehensive ban, to co-operate in efforts to prevent the use of chemical weapons.

General Assembly resolution 40/92 C

12 December 1985   Meeting 113   112-16-22 (recorded vote)

Approved by First Committee (A/40/932) by recorded vote (96-16-21), 15 November (meeting 39); 26-nation draft (A/C.1/40/L.31); agenda item 63.
Sponsors: Australia, Belgium, Canada, Colombia, Costa Rica, Denmark, Ecuador, France, Germany, Federal Republic of, Greece, Iceland, Italy, Japan, Kenya, Netherlands, New Zealand, Norway, Portugal, Samoa, Sierra Leone, Spain, Sweden, Thailand, United Kingdom, United States, Uruguay.
Meeting numbers. GA 40th session: 1st Committee 3-32, 39; plenary 113.

Recorded vote in Assembly as follows:

In favour: Antigua and Barbuda, Argentina, Australia, Austria, Bahamas, Bangladesh, Barbados, Belgium, Bhutan, Bolivia, Botswana, Brazil, Brunei Darussalam, Burkina Faso, Burma, Burundi, Cameroon, Canada, Cape Verde, Central African Republic, Chad, Chile, China, Colombia, Comoros, Democratic Kampuchea, Denmark, Djibouti, Dominican Republic, Ecuador, Egypt, El Salvador, Equatorial Guinea, Fiji, Finland, France, Gabon, Germany, Federal Republic of, Ghana, Greece, Guatemala, Guinea, Guinea-Bissau, Guyana, Haiti, Honduras, Iceland, Indonesia, Iran, Ireland, Israel, Italy, Ivory Coast, Jamaica, Japan, Kenya, Lesotho, Liberia, Luxembourg, Malawi, Malaysia, Maldives, Mali, Malta, Mauritania, Mauritius, Morocco, Nepal, Netherlands, New Zealand, Niger, Nigeria, Norway, Pakistan, Panama, Papua New Guinea, Paraguay, Peru, Philippines, Portugal, Romania, Rwanda, Saint Christopher and Nevis, Saint Lucia, Saint Vincent and the Grenadines, Samoa, Sao Tome and Principe, Senegal, Sierra Leone, Singapore, Solomon Islands, Somalia, Spain, Sri Lanka, Sudan, Suriname, Swaziland, Sweden, Thailand, Togo, Trinidad and Tobago, Tunisia, Turkey, United Kingdom, United Republic of Tanzania, United States, Uruguay, Vanuatu, Venezuela, Zaire, Zambia, Zimbabwe.

Against: Afghanistan, Bulgaria, Byelorussian SSR, Cuba, Czechoslovakia, Democratic Yemen, German Democratic Republic, Hungary, Lao People's Democratic Republic, Libyan Arab Jamahiriya, Mongolia, Poland, Syrian Arab Republic, Ukrainian SSR, USSR, Viet Nam.

Abstaining: Algeria, Angola, Bahrain, Benin, Congo, Cyprus, Ethiopia, Grenada, India, Iraq, Jordan, Lebanon, Madagascar, Mexico, Nicaragua, Oman, Qatar, Saudi Arabia, Uganda, United Arab Emirates, Yemen, Yugoslavia.

Democratic Yemen held that the text reflected a one-sided view and would not be conducive to achieving the common goal. The USSR believed that the text would create additional obstacles to eliminating chemical weapons, by inventing artificial issues about setting up verification machinery outside the Geneva multilateral negotiations, and would be tantamount to revising the 1925 Protocol. Asserting that it had been a victim of unprecedented chemical warfare from 1960 to 1971, involving nearly 100,000 tons of various chemical agents, Viet Nam said all efforts should focus on the ongoing negotiations on a convention, a position shared by the Lao People's Democratic Republic, which stated that its negative vote was in line with its previous stand.

Yugoslavia felt that the draft constituted a continuation of the action it had not supported in 1984; it called for the establishment of an effective system of verification of compliance.

Speaking in support of all three texts on a chemical-weapons ban, Bangladesh said it did so even though it considered some parts to contain one-sided and contradictory positions. Voting in like manner, Romania believed that a unilateral or common undertaking to renounce the development and production of new chemical weapons and their deployment on the territories of other countries would have a positive impact on the successful conclusion of negotiations. Venezuela declared that such abhorrent weapons of mass destruction should be totally eliminated.

New weapons of mass destruction, including radiological weapons

As in the past, no tangible progress was achieved in 1985, due to divergent approaches, on prohibiting the development and manufacture of new types of weapons of mass destruction.

In December, the General Assembly requested the Conference on Disarmament, with the assistance of a periodically convened group of experts, to keep the question under constant review with a view to recommending specific negotiations on the identified types of such weapons (resolution 40/90). As regards radiological weapons, the Conference was requested to continue, and conclude promptly, its negotiations on prohibiting such weapons (40/94 D).

Earlier in 1985, in February,[7] the Secretary-General had drawn the Security Council's attention to the Assembly's 1984 call[8] to the Council's permanent members and other militarily significant States to declare their refusal to create new types of weapons of mass destruction, as a first step towards concluding a comprehensive agreement on the topic.

Consideration by the Conference on Disarmament. The Conference on Disarmament[1] considered the item "New types of weapons of mass destruction and new systems of such weapons; radiological weapons" from 15 to 19 April and from 5 to 9 August 1985. It re-established, on 14 March, an *Ad Hoc* Committee on Radiological Weapons with a view to reaching agreement on a convention prohibiting the development, production, stockpiling and use of such weapons. At the same time, the question of new types and systems of weapons of mass destruction continued to be considered in plenary and informal meetings.

The *Ad Hoc* Committee held 16 meetings between 19 April and 16 August, under the chairmanship of Richard Butler (Australia), who also held a number of informal consultations. As in the past, it continued examining questions relating to "traditional" radiological weapons and those relating to prohibition of attacks against nuclear facilities. Among the documents before the Committee in 1985 were a compendium, submitted by Canada, of Conference verbatim records and working papers on radiological weapons, and a paper by a group of socialist States, on prohibition of radiological weapons and of attacks against nuclear facilities.

The Committee discussed the Chairman's suggestions for elements of a draft treaty; a compilation of draft provisions, subsequently prepared by him and annexed to the report, reflected the state of deliberations on the two major questions. The Committee recommended that it be re-established at the beginning of the Conference's 1986 session

and that the annex to its report be considered as a basis for further work. On 29 August, the Conference adopted the report of the *Ad Hoc* Committee as part of its own report to the General Assembly.

As regards the question of new types and systems of weapons of mass destruction, the Eastern European and a number of other States supported a proposal made in the Conference plenary by the USSR, aimed at starting negotiations on the prohibition of any new kind of weapon of mass destruction immediately after it had been identified, and the simultaneous introduction of a moratorium on its development; the proposal also stipulated that the Conference on Disarmament, with the assistance of a group of experts periodically convened, should keep the question under review in order to make recommendations on issues that required concrete negotiations.

Western and other States maintained that since no new types of weapons of mass destruction had been identified or were expected to emerge imminently, the Conference could continue to hold informal meetings from time to time, with the participation of experts as appropriate, in order to monitor the situation.

GENERAL ASSEMBLY ACTION

On 12 December, the General Assembly, on the recommendation of the First Committee, adopted two resolutions aimed at banning new weapons of mass destruction.

The Assembly adopted **resolution 40/90** by recorded vote.

Prohibition of the development and manufacture of new types of weapons of mass destruction and new systems of such weapons

The General Assembly,

Recalling its resolutions 3479(XXX) of 11 December 1975, 31/74 of 10 December 1976, 32/84 A of 12 December 1977, 33/66 B of 14 December 1978, 34/79 of 11 December 1979, 35/149 of 12 December 1980, 36/89 of 9 December 1981, 37/77 A of 9 December 1982, 38/182 of 20 December 1983 and 39/62 of 12 December 1984 concerning the prohibition of new types of weapons of mass destruction,

Bearing in mind the provisions of paragraph 39 of the Final Document of the Tenth Special Session of the General Assembly, according to which qualitative and quantitative disarmament measures are both important for halting the arms race and efforts to that end must include negotiations on the limitation and cessation of the qualitative improvement of armaments, especially weapons of mass destruction, and the development of new means of warfare,

Recalling the decision contained in paragraph 77 of the Final Document to the effect that, in order to help to prevent a qualitative arms race and so that scientific and technological achievements might ultimately be used solely for peaceful purposes, effective measures should be taken to prevent the emergence of new types of weapons of mass destruction based on new scientific principles and achievements, and that efforts aiming at the prohibition of such new types and new systems of weapons of mass destruction should be appropriately pursued,

Expressing once again its firm belief, in the light of the decisions adopted at the tenth special session, in the importance of concluding an agreement or agreements to prevent the use of scientific and technological progress for the development of new types of weapons of mass destruction and new systems of such weapons,

Noting that in the course of its session in 1985 the Conference on Disarmament considered the item entitled "New types of weapons of mass destruction and new systems of such weapons; radiological weapons",

Convinced that all ways and means should be utilized to prevent the development and manufacture of new types of weapons of mass destruction and new systems of such weapons,

Taking into consideration the part of the report of the Conference on Disarmament relating to this question,

1. *Reaffirms* the necessity of prohibiting the development and manufacture of new types of weapons of mass destruction and new systems of such weapons;

2. *Requests* the Conference on Disarmament, in the light of its existing priorities, to keep constantly under review, with the assistance of a periodically convened group of experts, the question of the prohibition of the development and manufacture of new types of weapons of mass destruction and new systems of such weapons with a view to making, when necessary, recommendations on undertaking specific negotiations on the identified types of such weapons;

3. *Calls upon* all States to contribute, immediately following the identification of any new type of weapon of mass destruction, to the commencement of negotiations on its prohibition with the simultaneous introduction of a moratorium on its practical development;

4. *Once again urges* all States to refrain from any action that could adversely affect the efforts aimed at the prevention of the emergence of new types of weapons of mass destruction and new systems of such weapons;

5. *Calls again upon* all States to undertake efforts to ensure that ultimately scientific and technological achievements may be used solely for peaceful purposes;

6. *Requests* the Secretary-General to transmit to the Conference on Disarmament all documents relating to the consideration of this item by the General Assembly at its fortieth session;

7. *Requests* the Conference on Disarmament to submit a report on the results achieved to the General Assembly for consideration at its forty-first session;

8. *Decides* to include in the provisional agenda of its forty-first session the item entitled "Prohibition of the development and manufacture of new types of weapons of mass destruction and new systems of such weapons: report of the Conference on Disarmament".

General Assembly resolution 40/90

12 December 1985   Meeting 113   128-1-21 (recorded vote)

Approved by First Committee (A/40/945) by recorded vote (106-1-23), 19 November (meeting 42); 24-nation draft (A/C.1/40/L.33); agenda item 60.

Sponsors: Afghanistan, Angola, Benin, Bulgaria, Burkina Faso, Byelorussian SSR, Congo, Cuba, Czechoslovakia, Democratic Yemen, Ethiopia, German Democratic Republic, Ghana, Hungary, Lao People's Democratic Republic, Libyan Arab Jamahiriya, Mongolia, Mozambique, Poland, Romania, Syrian Arab Republic, Ukrainian SSR, USSR, Viet Nam.

Meeting numbers. GA 40th session: 1st Committee 3-32, 36, 42; plenary 113.

Recorded vote in Assembly as follows:

In favour: Afghanistan, Algeria, Angola, Antigua and Barbuda, Argentina, Austria, Bahamas, Bahrain, Bangladesh, Barbados, Benin, Bhutan, Bolivia, Botswana, Brazil, Brunei Darussalam, Bulgaria, Burkina Faso, Burma, Burundi, Byelorussian SSR, Cameroon, Cape Verde, Central African Republic, Chad, Chile, Colombia, Comoros, Congo, Cuba, Cyprus, Czechoslovakia, Democratic Yemen, Djibouti, Dominican Republic, Ecuador, Egypt, El Salvador, Equatorial Guinea, Ethiopia, Fiji, Finland, Gabon, German Democratic Republic, Ghana, Grenada, Guatemala, Guinea, Guinea-Bissau, Guyana, Haiti, Honduras, Hungary, India, Indonesia, Iran, Iraq, Ivory Coast, Jordan, Kenya, Kuwait, Lao People's Democratic Republic, Lebanon, Lesotho, Liberia, Libyan Arab Jamahiriya, Madagascar, Malawi, Malaysia, Maldives, Mali, Malta, Mauritania, Mauritius, Mexico, Mongolia, Morocco, Mozambique, Nepal, Nicaragua, Niger, Nigeria, Oman, Pakistan, Panama, Papua New Guinea, Peru, Philippines, Poland, Qatar, Romania, Rwanda, Saint Christopher and Nevis, Saint Lucia, Saint Vincent and the Grenadines, Samoa, Sao Tome and Principe, Saudi Arabia, Senegal, Seychelles, Sierra Leone, Singapore, Solomon Islands, Somalia, Sri Lanka, Sudan, Suriname, Swaziland, Sweden, Syrian Arab Republic, Thailand, Togo, Trinidad and Tobago, Tunisia, Uganda, Ukrainian SSR, USSR, United Arab Emirates, United Republic of Tanzania, Uruguay, Vanuatu, Venezuela, Viet Nam, Yemen, Yugoslavia, Zaire, Zambia, Zimbabwe.

Against: United States.

Abstaining: Australia, Belgium, Canada, China, Denmark, France, Germany, Federal Republic of, Greece, Iceland, Ireland, Israel, Italy, Japan, Luxembourg, Netherlands, New Zealand, Norway, Portugal, Spain, Turkey, United Kingdom.

In explaining the abstentions of the 10 EC members, Portugal and Spain, the Netherlands stated, on their behalf, that only when the possibility of the manufacture of weapons of mass destruction based on new scientific principles had been clearly established would it be possible to enter into negotiations aimed at an adequately verifiable prohibition of them. They believed that a consensus resolution could have been possible if the draft had not specified the procedural form by which the Conference on Disarmament should acquire expert assistance; further, they considered that setting up such an expert group would be premature, since it would have no real work to do in the existing situation.

The Assembly adopted **resolution 40/94 D** without vote.

Prohibition of the development, production, stockpiling and use of radiological weapons

The General Assembly,

Recalling its resolution 39/151 J of 17 December 1984,

1. *Takes note* of that part of the report of the Conference on Disarmament on the question of radiological weapons, in particular the report of the Ad Hoc Committee on Radiological Weapons;

2. *Takes note also* of the recommendation of the Conference on Disarmament that the *Ad Hoc* Committee on Radiological Weapons should be re-established at the beginning of its 1986 session and that the annex to the report of the *Ad Hoc* Committee should be considered as a basis for further work;

3. *Recognizes* that the work accomplished by the *Ad Hoc* Committee on Radiological Weapons in 1985 made a further contribution to the solution of the issues entrusted to it;

4. *Requests* the Conference on Disarmament to continue its negotiations on the subject with a view to a prompt conclusion of its work, taking into account all proposals presented to the Conference to this end, the result of which should be submitted to the General Assembly at its forty-first session;

5. *Also requests* that the Secretary-General transmit to the Conference on Disarmament all relevant documents relating to the discussion of all aspects of the issue by the General Assembly at its fortieth session;

6. *Decides* to include in the provisional agenda of its forty-first session the item entitled "Prohibition of the development, production, stockpiling and use of radiological weapons".

General Assembly resolution 40/94 D

12 December 1985   Meeting 113   Adopted without vote

Approved by First Committee (A/40/976) without vote, 14 November (meeting 37); 4-nation draft (A/C.1/40/L.27); agenda item 68 *(j)*.
Sponsors: Australia, Czechoslovakia, Japan, Sweden.
Meeting numbers. GA 40th session: 1st Committee 3-32, 37; plenary 113.

Conventional weapons

While fear of nuclear weapons was pervasive because of their potential for global devastation, it was conventional weapons that daily claimed countless lives, the Secretary-General stressed (see p. 6).

In December 1985, the General Assembly endorsed recent regional and subregional initiatives directed towards limiting armaments and reducing military expenditures, and requested the Secretary-General to provide Governments so requesting with technical services and assistance in regional conventional-disarmament measures (resolution 40/94 A). Inviting further comments on the 1984 expert study on conventional disarmament,[9] the Assembly decided to include, for the first time, an item on conventional disarmament in its 1986 agenda (40/94 C). In addition, the Assembly called for wider adherence to the 1980 Convention on Prohibitions or Restrictions on the Use of Certain Conventional Weapons Which May Be Deemed to Be Excessively Injurious or to Have Indiscriminate Effects, and its three Protocols[10] (40/84).

GENERAL ASSEMBLY ACTION

On 12 December, the General Assembly, on the recommendation of the First Committee, adopted **resolution 40/94 A** by recorded vote.

Conventional disarmament on a regional scale
The General Assembly,

Reaffirming the determination to save succeeding generations from the scourge of war that is expressed in the Preamble to the Charter of the United Nations,

Again recognizing the urgent need for the harmonizing of political wills in order to promote initiatives aimed at reducing expenditure on armaments so that the resources thus released can be devoted to the social and economic development of all peoples,

Recalling paragraph 2 of the Final Document of the Tenth Special Session of the General Assembly, in which it is stated, *inter alia*, that the nuclear and conventional arms buildup threatens to stall the efforts aimed at reaching the goals of development, to become an obstacle on the road of achieving the new international economic order and to hinder the solution of other vital problems facing mankind,

Recalling further paragraphs 45 and 46 of the Final Document of the Tenth Special Session, in which it declared, *inter alia*, that priorities in disarmament negotiations should be: nuclear weapons; other weapons of mass destruction, including chemical weapons; conventional weapons, including any which may be deemed to be excessively injurious or to have indiscriminate effects; and reduction of armed forces; and that nothing should preclude States from conducting negotiations on all priority items concurrently,

Recognizing that unilateral measures to limit or reduce armaments can make a contribution to the attainment of disarmament,

Recalling its resolution 37/100 F of 13 December 1982 on regional disarmament, in which it stressed, *inter alia*, the importance of the regional measures already adopted, as well as of efforts of a regional nature undertaken in the field of nuclear and conventional disarmament,

Recalling also its resolutions 38/73 J of 15 December 1983 and 39/63 F of 12 December 1984 on regional disarmament,

1. *Urges* Governments, where the regional situation so permits and on the initiative of the States concerned, to consider and adopt appropriate measures at the regional level with a view to strengthening peace and security at a lower level of forces through the limitation and reduction of armed forces and conventional weapons, under strict and effective international control, taking into account the need of States to protect their security, bearing in mind the inherent right of self-defence enshrined in the Charter of the United Nations and without prejudice to the principle of equal rights and of the self-determination of peoples, in conformity with the Charter, and taking into account the need to ensure balance in each phase and to avoid impairing the security of any State;

2. *Expresses its most firm support* for recent unilateral measures, adopted by some Governments, which are intended to limit conventional armaments and reduce military expenditures and which contribute to the creation of an atmosphere favourable to the realization of conventional disarmament on a regional scale;

3. *Endorses most emphatically* the recent regional and subregional initiatives directed towards the conclusion of agreements to limit armaments and reduce military expenditures;

4. *Reaffirms* the primary responsibility of the militarily significant States, especially the nuclear-weapon States, for halting and reversing the arms race, and the priority assigned to nuclear disarmament in the context of the advances towards general and complete disarmament;

5. *Requests* all States to facilitate progress towards regional disarmament by strictly honouring their commitment to refrain from the threat or use of force and to contribute to the creation of an atmosphere favourable to the realization of conventional disarmament on a regional scale;

6. *Urges also* countries which are suppliers of conventional weapons to co-operate with regional efforts;

7. *Requests* the Secretary-General to provide interested Governments, upon request, with such technical services and assistance as may be useful in measures of conventional disarmament on a regional scale and also requests him to submit a report on the situation with

regard to this matter to the General Assembly at its forty-first session;

8. *Decides* to include in the provisional agenda of its forty-first session an item entitled "Conventional disarmament on a regional scale".

General Assembly resolution 40/94 A

12 December 1985   Meeting 113   128-0-8 (recorded vote)

Approved by First Committee (A/40/976) by recorded vote (107-0-8), 14 November (meeting 38); 20-nation draft (A/C.1/40/L.2/Rev.2); agenda item 68 *(e)*.
Sponsors: Bangladesh, Bolivia, Cameroon, Central African Republic, Chad, Chile, Colombia, Costa Rica, Ecuador, Ivory Coast, Pakistan, Paraguay, Peru, Romania, Sudan, Thailand, Togo, Uruguay, Yugoslavia.
Meeting numbers. GA 40th session: 1st Committee 3-33, 38; plenary 113.

Recorded vote in Assembly as follows:

In favour: Antigua and Barbuda, Argentina, Australia, Austria, Bahamas, Bangladesh, Barbados, Belgium, Benin, Bhutan, Bolivia, Botswana, Brazil, Brunei Darussalam, Bulgaria, Burkina Faso, Burma, Burundi, Byelorussian SSR, Cameroon, Canada, Cape Verde, Central African Republic, Chad, Chile, China, Colombia, Comoros, Congo, Cuba, Cyprus, Czechoslovakia, Democratic Kampuchea, Denmark, Dominican Republic, Ecuador, El Salvador, Equatorial Guinea, Fiji, Finland, France, Gabon, German Democratic Republic, Germany, Federal Republic of, Greece, Grenada, Guatemala, Guinea, Guinea-Bissau, Guyana, Haiti, Honduras, Hungary, Iceland, Indonesia, Iran, Ireland, Israel, Italy, Ivory Coast, Jamaica, Japan, Kenya, Lebanon, Lesotho, Liberia, Libyan Arab Jamahiriya,[a] Luxembourg, Madagascar, Malawi, Malaysia, Maldives, Mali, Malta, Mauritania, Mauritius, Mexico, Mongolia, Morocco, Nepal, Netherlands, New Zealand, Nicaragua, Niger, Nigeria, Norway, Pakistan, Panama, Papua New Guinea, Paraguay, Peru, Philippines, Poland, Portugal, Romania, Rwanda, Saint Christopher and Nevis, Saint Lucia, Saint Vincent and the Grenadines, Samoa, Sao Tome and Principe, Senegal, Seychelles, Sierra Leone, Singapore, Solomon Islands, Spain, Sri Lanka, Sudan, Suriname, Swaziland, Sweden, Thailand, Togo, Trinidad and Tobago, Turkey, Ukrainian SSR, USSR, United Kingdom, United Republic of Tanzania, United States, Uruguay, Vanuatu, Venezuela, Yugoslavia, Zaire, Zambia, Zimbabwe.
Against: None.
Abstaining: Afghanistan, Angola, Ethiopia, Ghana, India, Lao People's Democratic Republic, Uganda, Viet Nam.
[a]Later advised the Secretariat it had intended not to participate in the vote.

India felt that the text's main thrust was considerably at variance with the 1978 Final Document:[11] neither the global perspective of paragraph 81 of the Document, which envisaged limiting and gradually reducing conventional weapons within the framework of progress towards general and complete disarmament, nor the priority assigned to nuclear disarmament in paragraph 55 was reflected adequately. While agreeing that conventional armaments imposed a burden on the economies of developing countries, Cuba said that, in its case, the scope of regional measures to attain security through limiting armed forces and conventional weapons would have to be broader than merely the Caribbean region, because of what it described as the United States policy of hostility towards Cuba. Similarly, the Lao People's Democratic Republic did not feel that the regional approach was acceptable in areas where nuclear-weapon States carried out policies hostile to their neighbours. Viet Nam was alarmed at attempts to take advantage of the legitimate concern over conventional weapons to divert attention from the prevention of nuclear war. In the plenary Assembly, Ethiopia stated that the resolution would shift the focus of attention from the primary goal of nuclear disarmament, and that it did not take into account the situation of countries which were vulnerable to attacks by South Africa.

Venezuela considered the twice-revised text to be an important supplement to efforts to contain the arms race in areas such as nuclear and other weapons of mass destruction. Belgium considered the draft to be a significant initiative in the regional approach to disarmament, based on the 1984 Assembly resolution on the topic.[12] Australia did not agree that unilateral disarmament measures were effective in halting the arms race, but supported the text because of the need to halt and reverse the conventional arms race, and because of the text's emphasis on limiting conventional arms transfers and reducing military budgets and on the role of regional initiatives in realizing conventional disarmament on a regional scale.

Follow-up on the 1984 study

In an August 1985 report, with a later addendum,[13] the Secretary-General transmitted to the General Assembly the replies received from 23 Member States in response to its 1984 request[14] for views on the 1984 expert study[9] on all aspects of the conventional arms race and on disarmament relating to conventional weapons and armed forces.

GENERAL ASSEMBLY ACTION

The General Assembly, on 12 December, adopted **resolution 40/94 C** without vote, as recommended by the First Committee.

Study on conventional disarmament

The General Assembly,

Recalling its resolution 39/151 C of 17 December 1984, in which the Secretary-General was requested to prepare a report for the General Assembly at its fortieth session containing the views of Member States received regarding the study on all aspects of the conventional arms race and on disarmament relating to conventional weapons and armed forces,

Further recalling paragraph 81 and other relevant paragraphs of the Final Document of the Tenth Special Session of the General Assembly, in which the importance also of conventional disarmament measures is stressed,

Taking note of the report of the Secretary-General on the work of the Organization in which it is stated that "while the fear of nuclear weapons is pervasive because of their potentially global devastating effect, it is conventional weapons that every day claim countless lives", and further that "the conventional arms race, moreover, squanders precious economic resources",

Bearing in mind the immense drain on human, economic and technological resources caused by the conventional arms race,

Further noting the link between disarmament and development and the forthcoming International Conference on the Relationship between Disarmament and Development,

Having examined the report of the Secretary-General containing the views received from Member States regarding the *Study on Conventional Disarmament,*

1. *Appeals* to all Member States to make the widest use of the *Study* and its conclusions and recommendations;

2. *Invites* Member States that have not yet informed the Secretary-General of their views regarding the *Study* to do so no later than 31 May 1986;

3. *Requests* the Secretary-General to prepare a report for the General Assembly at its forty-first session containing further views of Member States received regarding the *Study;*

4. *Decides* to include in the provisional agenda of its forty-first session an item entitled "Conventional disarmament".

General Assembly resolution 40/94 C

12 December 1985   Meeting 113   Adopted without vote

Approved by First Committee (A/40/976) without vote, 14 November (meeting 38); draft by Denmark (A/C.1/40/L.14); agenda item 68 *(e)*.
Meeting numbers. GA 40th session: 1st Committee 3-32, 35, 38; plenary 113.

Ratification of the 1980 Convention and Protocols

The Secretary-General, as depositary of the 1980 Convention on Prohibitions or Restrictions on the Use of Certain Conventional Weapons Which May Be Deemed to Be Excessively Injurious or to Have Indiscriminate Effects, and its three Protocols,[10] reported to the General Assembly on the status of ratification as at 31 July 1985.[15]

The Convention and Protocols, which had entered into force in December 1983,[16] provided new rules of protection from injury or attack by means of incendiary weapons, land-mines, booby traps and other devices, as well as fragments that cannot be easily detected in the human body by X-rays.

As at 31 December 1985, there were 25 States parties to the Convention, Pakistan having ratified it during the year.[17] Those States had also accepted the three Protocols dealing with non-detectable fragments; mines, booby traps and other devices; and incendiary weapons.

GENERAL ASSEMBLY ACTION

On 12 December, the General Assembly, on the recommendation of the First Committee, adopted **resolution 40/84** without vote.

Convention on Prohibitions or Restrictions on the Use of Certain Conventional Weapons Which May Be Deemed to Be Excessively Injurious or to Have Indiscriminate Effects

The General Assembly,

Recalling its resolutions 32/152 of 19 December 1977, 35/153 of 12 December 1980, 36/93 of 9 December 1981, 37/79 of 9 December 1982, 38/66 of 15 December 1983 and 39/56 of 12 December 1984,

Recalling with satisfaction the adoption, on 10 October 1980, of the Convention on Prohibitions or Restrictions on the Use of Certain Conventional Weapons Which May Be Deemed to Be Excessively Injurious or to Have Indiscriminate Effects, together with the Protocol on Non-Detectable Fragments (Protocol I), the Protocol on Prohibitions or Restrictions on the Use of Mines, Booby Traps and Other Devices (Protocol II) and the Protocol on

Prohibitions or Restrictions on the Use of Incendiary Weapons (Protocol III),

Reaffirming its conviction that general agreement on the prohibition or restriction of use of specific conventional weapons would significantly reduce the suffering of civilian populations and of combatants,

Taking note with satisfaction of the report of the Secretary-General,

1. *Notes with satisfaction* that an increasing number of States have either signed, ratified, accepted or acceded to the Convention on Prohibitions or Restrictions on the Use of Certain Conventional Weapons Which May Be Deemed to Be Excessively Injurious or to Have Indiscriminate Effects, which was opened for signature in New York on 10 April 1981;

2. *Further notes with satisfaction* that, consequent upon the fulfilment of the conditions set out in article 5 of the Convention, the Convention and the three Protocols annexed thereto entered into force on 2 December 1983;

3. *Urges* all States that have not yet done so to exert their best endeavours to become parties to the Convention and the Protocols annexed thereto as early as possible, so as ultimately to obtain universality of adherence;

4. *Notes* that, under article 8 of the Convention, conferences may be convened to consider amendments to the Convention or any of the annexed Protocols, to consider additional protocols relating to other categories of conventional weapons not covered by the existing annexed Protocols, or to review the scope and operation of the Convention and the Protocols annexed thereto and to consider any proposal for amendments to the Convention or to the existing Protocols and any proposals for additional protocols relating to other categories of conventional weapons not covered by the existing Protocols;

5. *Requests* the Secretary-General as depositary of the Convention and its three annexed Protocols to inform the General Assembly from time to time of the state of adherence to the Convention and its Protocols;

6. *Decides* to include in the provisional agenda of its forty-first session the item entitled "Convention on Prohibitions or Restrictions on the Use of Certain Conventional Weapons Which May Be Deemed to Be Excessively Injurious or to Have Indiscriminate Effects".

General Assembly resolution 40/84

12 December 1985   Meeting 113   Adopted without vote

Approved by First Committee (A/40/943) without vote, 14 November (meeting 37); 19-nation draft (A/C.1/40/L.32); agenda item 54.
Sponsors: Austria, Belgium, Cuba, Denmark, Ecuador, Finland, France, German Democratic Republic, Greece, Ireland, Italy, Mongolia, Netherlands, New Zealand, Nigeria, Norway, Sweden, Viet Nam, Yugoslavia.
Meeting numbers. GA 40th session: 1st Committee 3-32, 37; plenary 113.

The United States explained that it did not consider the text's approval as prejudging any State's decision regarding adherence or ratification of the Convention, and that its support of the consensus was not indicative of any such decision by the United States.

Arms race in outer space

With the initiation, in 1985, of bilateral negotiations between the USSR and the United States (see p. 44) on nuclear and space arms, the Assembly urged them to negotiate in a constructive spirit, and asked all Member States for their views on the possibility of enhancing international co-operation in preventing an arms race in, and promoting the peaceful uses of, outer space, including the desirability of establishing machinery for that purpose (resolution 40/87). (See also Chapter II of this section.)

Consideration by the Conference on Disarmament. In 1985, the Conference on Disarmament[1] considered the item on prevention of an arms race in outer space, from 4 to 15 March and from 1 to 5 July. An *Ad Hoc* Committee, established on 29 March in pursuance of a 1984 General Assembly request,[18] held 20 meetings between 24 June and 26 August under the chairmanship of Saad Alfarargi (Egypt) to examine relevant issues through substantive and general consideration.

The documents before the Conference included two submissions by Canada—a two-volume compendium of verbatim records and working papers on the item submitted to the Conference, and a survey of international law relevant to arms control and outer space; one by China outlining its basic position; a working paper by a group of socialist countries; a document by the United Kingdom on international agreements applicable or relevant to outer space; and two submissions from the USSR—the comments, published on 6 July, of its General Secretary to the Union of Concerned Scientists, and documents connected with its proposal entitled "The basic directions and principles of international co-operation in the peaceful exploration of outer space under conditions of its non-militarization" (see below).

Different views persisted on the mandate of the *Ad Hoc* Committee. The group of 21 maintained that the initial stage of substantive and general consideration of the issues should end with the 1985 session of the Committee, and that negotiations should begin in 1986 to conclude an agreement or agreements on the topic. Similarly, the socialist States advocated re-establishing the Committee in 1986 with a mandate enabling it to start negotiations on concrete practical measures. Other delegations held that the 1985 mandate was realistic and should not expire at the end of the current session if the Committee had not completed the kind of exploratory work envisaged in it. Still others expressed the need for further consultations to examine the matter.

On 29 August, the Conference adopted the report of the *Ad Hoc* Committee as part of its own report to the General Assembly.

Consideration by the Committee on outer space. In accordance with a 1984 General Assembly resolution,[19] the Committee on the Peaceful Uses of Outer Space (New York, 17-28 June 1985)[20] discussed as a priority ways of maintaining outer space for peaceful purposes. However, as in previous years, divergent views persisted on the competence of the Committee, as against the Conference on Disarmament, in addressing issues of arms control in outer space.

The General Assembly, in **resolution 40/162**, again requested the Committee to consider the subject as a priority and urged all States to help prevent an arms race in outer space.

UNIDIR study. As decided in 1984 by the Advisory Board on Disarmament Studies acting as the Board of Trustees of UNIDIR, the Institute began in 1985 its study on the limitation of military uses of outer space, by establishing a group of experts from Argentina, Brazil, France, the Federal Republic of Germany, India, Poland, the USSR and the United States to guide its preparation. Two sessions were held during the year (22-24 April and 9-13 December), with the initial draft of the study being considered in detail at the second; the study was to be published in 1986 after consideration by the Board.

The General Assembly, in **resolution 40/87**, invited Member States to submit their views on the study no later than 1 April 1986.

GENERAL ASSEMBLY ACTION

In addition to an agenda item on the report of the Conference on Disarmament[1] as it related to preventing an arms race in outer space, the General Assembly took up in 1985 a new item proposed by the USSR, on international co-operation in the peaceful exploitation of outer space under conditions of its non-militarization.

In submitting that request by a 15 August letter,[21] the USSR stated that there was a growing possibility of outer space becoming a source of great military danger due to plans to develop and deploy what it termed "space strike weapons". A draft resolution, appended to the letter, would have had the Assembly convene not later than 1987 an international conference to consider all aspects of international co-operation in the peaceful exploitation and use of outer space and of establishing a world space organization. Details of the USSR's proposals were provided in what it called main lines and principles, annexed to the letter, and which were again submitted to the First Committee on 9 October,[22] and to the Special Political Committee on 13 November.[23]

Taken up in the First Committee, the draft was subsequently revised[24] to delete specifics regarding the conference, and instead would have had the Assembly call on States to examine the possibility of holding such a conference at a proper stage, and request the Committee on the Peaceful Uses of Outer Space to study the proposal.

At the request of the sponsor, no action was taken on the draft resolution, and the General Assembly, by **decision 40/424** of 12 December, took note of the report of the First Committee[25] on its consideration of the USSR-proposed agenda item.

Along with the USSR proposal, three other draft resolutions—submitted to the First Committee, respectively, by China, a group of Western countries and Poland—were also not put to a vote at the request of the sponsors.

The draft by China,[26] on prevention of an arms race in outer space, would have had the Assembly request the Conference on Disarmament to initiate negotiations without delay for concluding an agreement(s) on prohibiting and destroying all outer-space weapon systems. It also would have had the Assembly urge the USSR and the United States to negotiate on preventing an arms race in outer space and to keep the Conference informed of progress.

Also entitled the prevention of an arms race in outer space, the proposal by Belgium, Canada, the Federal Republic of Germany, Italy, Japan, the Netherlands, Norway and the United Kingdom[27] would have had the Assembly stress the importance of continued substantive work in the Conference as well as of upholding the relevant existing treaties, and welcome the initiation of bilateral negotiations between the USSR and the United States on strategic and intermediate-range space and nuclear arms.

The draft by Poland,[28] on a study of the various consequences of the militarization of outer space, would have had the Assembly request the Secretary-General to prepare a comprehensive study—based on accessible material, with the assistance of eminent consultant experts of various nationalities appointed by him—to be submitted by 1 July 1987. The Secretary-General subsequently submitted a statement of the draft's financial implications.[29]

On 12 December, the General Assembly, on the recommendation of the First Committee, adopted, by recorded vote, a 22-nation draft as **resolution 40/87**.

Prevention of an arms race in outer space

The General Assembly,

Inspired by the great prospects opening up before mankind as a result of man's entry into outer space,

Recognizing the common interest of all mankind in the exploration and use of outer space for peaceful purposes,

Reaffirming that the exploration and use of outer space, including the Moon and other celestial bodies, shall be carried out for the benefit and in the interest of all countries, irrespective of their degree of economic or scientific development, and shall be the province of all mankind,

Reaffirming further the will of all States that the exploration and use of outer space, including the Moon and other celestial bodies, shall be for peaceful purposes,

Recalling that the States parties to the Treaty on Principles Governing the Activities of States in the Explora-

tion and Use of Outer Space, including the Moon and Other Celestial Bodies,[30] have undertaken, in article III, to carry on activities in the exploration and use of outer space, including the Moon and other celestial bodies, in accordance with international law and the Charter of the United Nations, in the interest of maintaining international peace and security and promoting international co-operation and understanding,

Reaffirming, in particular, article IV of the above-mentioned Treaty, which stipulates that States parties to the Treaty undertake not to place in orbit around the Earth any objects carrying nuclear weapons or any other kinds of weapons of mass destruction, install such weapons on celestial bodies or station such weapons in outer space in any other manner,

Reaffirming also paragraph 80 of the Final Document of the Tenth Special Session of the General Assembly, the first special session devoted to disarmament, in which it is stated that, in order to prevent an arms race in outer space, further measures should be taken and appropriate international negotiations held in accordance with the spirit of the Treaty,

Recalling its resolutions 36/97 C and 36/99 of 9 December 1981, as well as resolutions 37/83 of 9 December 1982, 37/99 D of 13 December 1982, 38/70 of 15 December 1983 and 39/59 of 12 December 1984,

Gravely concerned at the danger posed to all mankind by an arms race in outer space and in particular by the impending threat of the exacerbation of the current state of insecurity by developments that could further undermine international peace and security, retard the pursuit of general and complete disarmament, and risk creating obstacles to the development of international co-operation in the peaceful uses of outer space,

Mindful of the widespread interest expressed by Member States in the course of the negotiations on and following the adoption of the above-mentioned Treaty in ensuring that the exploration and use of outer space should be for peaceful purposes, and taking note of proposals submitted to the General Assembly at its tenth special session and at its regular sessions and to the Conference on Disarmament,

Noting the grave concern expressed by the Second United Nations Conference on the Exploration and Peaceful Uses of Outer Space at the extension of an arms race into outer space and the recommendations made to the competent organs of the United Nations, in particular the General Assembly, and also to the Committee on Disarmament,*

Convinced that further measures are needed for the prevention of an arms race in outer space,

Recognizing that, in the context of multilateral negotiations for preventing an arms race in outer space, bilateral negotiations between the Union of Soviet Socialist Republics and the United States of America could make a significant contribution to such an objective, in accordance with paragraph 27 of the Final Document of the Tenth Special Session,

Noting with satisfaction that bilateral negotiations between the Union of Soviet Socialist Republics and the United States of America have begun in 1985, on a complex of questions concerning space and nuclear arms, both strategic and intermediate-range, and in their interrelationship, with the declared objective of working out effective agreements aimed, *inter alia*, at preventing an arms race in outer space,

Anxious that concrete results should emerge from these negotiations as soon as possible, as was urged in resolution 39/59,

Taking note of the part of the report of the Conference on Disarmament relating to this question,

Welcoming the establishment of an *Ad Hoc* Committee on the prevention of an arms race in outer space during the 1985 session of the Conference on Disarmament, in the exercise of the negotiating responsibilities of this sole multilateral negotiating body on disarmament, to examine, as a first step at this stage, issues relevant to the prevention of an arms race in outer space,

Mindful that consensus had not yet been reached in the Conference on Disarmament on concrete proposals for re-establishing the *ad hoc* committee on this question during the 1986 session of the Conference on Disarmament,

1. *Recalls* the obligation of all States to refrain from the threat or use of force in their space activities;

2. *Reaffirms* that general and complete disarmament under effective international control warrants that outer space shall be used exclusively for peaceful purposes and that it shall not become an arena for an arms race;

3. *Emphasizes* that further measures with appropriate and effective provisions for verification to prevent an arms race in outer space should be adopted by the international community;

4. *Calls upon* all States, in particular those with major space capabilities, to contribute actively to the objective of the peaceful use of outer space and to take immediate measures to prevent an arms race in outer space in the interest of maintaining international peace and security and promoting international co-operation and understanding;

5. *Requests* the Secretary-General to invite Member States to submit their views on the possibility of enhancing international co-operation in the field of preventing an arms race in outer space and the peaceful uses of outer space, including the desirability of establishing relevant machinery for that purpose, and to submit a report to the General Assembly at its forty-first session;

6. *Reiterates* that the Conference on Disarmament, as the single multilateral disarmament negotiating forum, has the primary role in the negotiation of a multilateral agreement or agreements, as appropriate, on the prevention of an arms race in outer space in all its aspects;

7. *Requests* the Conference on Disarmament to consider as a matter of priority the question of preventing an arms race in outer space;

8. *Also requests* the Conference on Disarmament to intensify its consideration of the question of the prevention of an arms race in outer space in all its aspects, taking into account all relevant proposals including those presented in the *Ad Hoc* Committee on the prevention of an arms race in outer space at the 1985 session of the Conference and at the fortieth session of the General Assembly;

9. *Further requests* the Conference on Disarmament to re-establish an *ad hoc* committee with an adequate mandate at the beginning of its session in 1986, with a view to undertaking negotiations for the conclusion of an agreement or agreements, as appropriate, on the prevention of an arms race in outer space in all its aspects;

10. *Urges* the Union of Soviet Socialist Republics and the United States of America to pursue intensively their bilateral negotiations in a constructive spirit aimed at reaching early agreement for preventing an arms race in outer space, and to advise the Conference on Disarmament periodically of the progress of their bilateral sessions so as to facilitate its work;

11. *Calls upon* all States, especially those with major space capabilities, to refrain, in their activities relating to outer space, from actions contrary to the observance of the relevant existing treaties or to the objective of preventing an arms race in outer space;

12. *Invites* Member States to transmit to the Secretary-General, not later than 1 April 1986, their views on the scope and content of the study being undertaken by the United Nations Institute for Disarmament Research on disarmament problems relating to outer space and the consequences of extending the arms race into outer space, and requests the Secretary-General to convey the views of the Member States to the Advisory Board on Disarmament Studies for consideration in order to enable it, in its capacity of Board of Trustees of the Institute, to give the Institute such possible guidance with respect to the elaboration of its study as it may derive from those views;

13. *Requests* the Conference on Disarmament to report on its consideration of this subject to the General Assembly at its forty-first session;

14. *Requests* the Secretary-General to transmit to the Conference on Disarmament all documents relating to the consideration of this subject by the General Assembly at its fortieth session;

15. *Decides* to include in the provisional agenda of its forty-first session the item entitled "Prevention of an arms race in outer space".

---

*The Committee on Disarmament was redesignated the Conference on Disarmament as from 7 February 1984.

General Assembly resolution 40/87

12 December 1985   Meeting 113   151-0-2 (recorded vote)

Approved by First Committee (A/40/964) by recorded vote (131-0-1), 22 November (meeting 47); 22-nation draft (A/C.1/40/L.68/Rev.1); agenda item 57.
Sponsors: Algeria, Bangladesh, Brazil, Cameroon, China, Egypt, Ethiopia, German Democratic Republic, Ghana, India, Indonesia, Ireland, Malaysia, Mexico, Pakistan, Romania, Sri Lanka, Sudan, Sweden, Venezuela, Yugoslavia, Zimbabwe.
Meeting numbers. GA 40th session: 1st Committee 3-32, 35, 47; plenary 113.

Recorded vote in Assembly as follows:

In favour: Afghanistan, Algeria, Angola, Antigua and Barbuda, Argentina, Australia, Austria, Bahamas, Bahrain, Bangladesh, Barbados, Belgium, Benin, Bhutan, Bolivia, Botswana, Brazil, Brunei Darussalam, Bulgaria, Burkina Faso, Burma, Burundi, Byelorussian SSR, Cameroon, Canada, Cape Verde, Central African Republic, Chad, Chile, China, Colombia, Comoros, Congo, Cuba, Cyprus, Czechoslovakia, Democratic Kampuchea, Democratic Yemen, Denmark, Djibouti, Dominican Republic, Ecuador, Egypt, El Salvador, Equatorial Guinea, Ethiopia, Fiji, Finland, France, Gabon, German Democratic Republic, Germany, Federal Republic of, Ghana, Greece, Guatemala, Guinea, Guinea-Bissau, Guyana, Haiti, Honduras, Hungary, Iceland, India, Indonesia, Iran, Iraq, Ireland, Israel, Italy, Ivory Coast, Jamaica, Japan, Jordan, Kenya, Kuwait, Lao People's Democratic Republic, Lebanon, Lesotho, Liberia, Libyan Arab Jamahiriya, Luxembourg, Madagascar, Malawi, Malaysia, Maldives, Mali, Malta, Mauritania, Mauritius, Mexico, Mongolia, Morocco, Mozambique, Nepal, Netherlands, New Zealand, Nicaragua, Niger, Nigeria, Norway, Oman, Pakistan, Panama, Papua New Guinea, Paraguay, Peru, Philippines, Poland, Portugal, Qatar, Romania, Rwanda, Saint Christopher and Nevis, Saint Lucia, Saint Vincent and the Grenadines, Samoa, Sao Tome and Principe, Saudi Arabia, Senegal, Seychelles, Sierra Leone, Singapore, Solomon Islands, Somalia, Spain, Sri Lanka, Sudan, Suriname, Swaziland, Sweden, Syrian Arab Republic, Thailand, Togo, Trinidad and Tobago, Tunisia, Turkey, Uganda, Ukrainian SSR, USSR, United Arab Emirates, United Kingdom, United Republic of Tanzania, Uruguay, Vanuatu, Venezuela, Viet Nam, Yemen, Yugoslavia, Zaire, Zambia, Zimbabwe.

Against: None.

Abstaining: Grenada, United States.

The Assembly adopted paragraphs 5 and 9 by recorded votes, respectively, of 123 to 2 (Grenada, United States), with 21 abstentions, and 136 to 2 (Grenada, United States), with 11 abstentions. The First Committee had also approved those paragraphs by recorded votes of 105 to 1 (United States), with 21 abstentions, and 118 to 1 (United States), with 11 abstentions, respectively.

Explaining its opposition to the two paragraphs and its abstention on the text as a whole, the United States felt it inappropriate for the First Committee to consider the peaceful uses of outer space, because such action denigrated the functions of the Special Political Committee—where it believed the item belonged—the Committee on outer space, and a 25-year tradition of consensus in the United Nations on matters relating to co-operation in that area; further, it felt that paragraph 5 had been included to give some recognition to subjects associated with the new USSR-proposed agenda item (see p. 79), and that the language of paragraph 9 lacked balance, in contrast to that of the Western draft which, it felt, had avoided intervening in the internal consultations and decision-making of the Conference on Disarmament and was consistent with the conclusions of that body's *Ad Hoc* Committee at its 1985 session.

Several other delegations explained their support for the text as a whole and their abstentions on the paragraphs. Australia and Canada, voicing objections to paragraph 5, felt that maintaining the current institutional division of labour, whereby the Committee on outer space focused on peaceful co-operation and the Conference on Disarmament on arms-control measures, was the best way of ensuring that those issues remained separate. Sharing that view and the United States objections to paragraphs 5 and 9, Italy—speaking also on behalf of Belgium, the Federal Republic of Germany, Japan, Luxembourg, the Netherlands, Portugal, Turkey and the United Kingdom—expressed support for maintaining in the Conference on Disarmament an approach which, they believed, had already produced useful work. France, abstaining on the paragraphs for similar reasons, also considered it essential that the *Ad Hoc* Committee continue its work with a mandate similar to that of 1985, and announced a $30,000 contribution towards the financing of the UNIDIR study mentioned in paragraph 12.

In other 1985 action, the Assembly, in **resolution 40/152 E**, again expressed concern at the danger of the arms race extending into outer space.

REFERENCES

[1]A/40/27 & Corr.1. [2]YUN 1984, p. 232. [3]*Ibid.*, p. 60. [4]A/C.1/40/2. [5]A/C.1/40/8. [6]A/C.1/40/11. [7]S/16931. [8]YUN 1984, p. 63, GA res. 39/62, 12 Dec. 1984. [9]*Ibid.*, p. 65. [10]YUN 1980, p. 76. [11]YUN 1978, p. 39, GA res. S-10/2, 30 June 1978. [12]YUN 1984, p. 78, GA res. 39/63 F, 12 Dec. 1984. [13]A/40/486 & Add.1. [14]YUN 1984, p. 66, GA res. 39/151 C, 17 Dec. 1984. [15]A/40/550. [16]YUN 1983, p. 66. [17]*Multilateral Treaties Deposited with the Secretary-General: Status as at 31 December 1985* (ST/LEG/SER.E/4), Sales No. E.86.V.3. [18]YUN 1984, p. 76, GA res. 39/59, 12 Dec. 1984. [19]*Ibid.*, p. 104, GA res. 39/96, 14 Dec. 1984. [20]A/40/20 & Corr.1. [21]A/40/192. [22]A/C.1/40/4. [23]A/SPC/40/3. [24]A/C.1/40/L.1/Rev.1. [25]A/40/965. [26]A/C.1/40/L.4. [27]A/C.1/40/L.22/Rev.1. [28]A/C.1/40/L.45/Rev.1. [29]A/C.1/40/L.81. [30]YUN 1966, p. 41, GA res. 2222(XXI), annex, 19 Dec. 1966.

Other disarmament issues

In the continuing debate on measures to reduce military budgets and expenditures and to reallocate the resources thus released for economic and social development, the General Assembly, in 1985, requested the Disarmament Commission to finalize the governing principles for freezing and reducing military expenditures (resolution 40/91 A); requested the Secretary-General to update a 1982 report on economic and social consequences of the arms race and military expenditures (40/150); and stressed the importance of a better information flow on military capabilities (40/94 K). Also in 1985, the Group of Experts on the Reduction of Military Budgets completed its report (40/91 B), while the Group of Governmental Experts on Military Research and Development was unable to do likewise.

As preparatory work began for the International Conference on the Relationship between Disarmament and Development, the Assembly decided that the Conference should meet in Paris from 15 July to 2 August 1986 (40/155).

In another development, the Assembly requested the *Ad Hoc* Committee on the Indian Ocean to complete preparatory work during 1986 for the long-envisaged Conference on the Indian Ocean (40/153).

Reduction of military budgets

In 1985, at a time when estimated global military expenditures hovered around $1 trillion, the General Assembly requested the Disarmament Commission to finalize in 1986 the principles that should govern the actions of States in freezing and reducing military expenditures (resolution 40/91 A); and invited them to comment on an expert report on reducing military budgets (40/91 B).

Disarmament Commission consideration. In May 1985, the Disarmament Commission[1] again considered two aspects of reducing military budgets: harmonizing views on their gradual, agreed reduction and reallocating resources being used for military purposes to economic and social development; and examining and identifying ways to achieve agreements to freeze, reduce or otherwise restrain military expenditures in a balanced manner.

Working Group I, re-established by the Commission to consider the question for the fifth consecutive year, held eight meetings between 10 and 24 May under the chairmanship of Gheorghe Tinca (Romania), who also held informal consultations. The Group based its discussions on a 1984 working paper,[2] containing a synopsis of the texts on principles that should govern the actions of States in freezing and reducing military expenditures. While the Group broadened the area of agreement on many principles, there were still divergences of views on others; following the discussion, the Group annexed to its report a new working paper, reflecting the latest stage of its work.

On 29 May, the Commission adopted by consensus the Working Group's report, in which it was suggested that the Commission finalize the principles in 1986, and that the Assembly urge all Member States, in particular the most heavily armed, to co-operate in reaching agreements to freeze, reduce or otherwise restrain military expenditures.

Communications. On 12 August, Peru transmitted to the Secretary-General the 29 July Lima Declaration signed by 20 Latin American and Caribbean countries on the occasion of Peru's presidential inauguration,[3] in which they condemned the arms race as a threat to international peace and security and a further obstacle to development, and considered as timely the balanced reduction of military expenditures and the allocation of greater resources for development. In addition, Peru submitted to the President of the Conference on Disarmament a proposal, made by its new President in his 28 July inaugural address, for a regional agreement on reducing arms expenditure and freezing arms acquisitions.[4]

GENERAL ASSEMBLY ACTION

Acting on the First Committee's recommendation, the General Assembly, on 12 December, adopted **resolution 40/91 A** without vote.

The General Assembly,

Deeply concerned about the ever-spiralling arms race and growing military expenditures, which constitute a heavy burden for the economies of all nations and have extremely harmful effects on world peace and security,

Reaffirming once again the provisions of paragraph 89 of the Final Document of the Tenth Special Session of the General Assembly, the first special session devoted to disarmament, according to which the gradual reduction of military budgets on a mutually agreed basis, for example, in absolute figures or in terms of percentage,

particularly by nuclear-weapon States and other militarily significant States, would contribute to curbing the arms race and would increase the possibilities for the reallocation of resources now being used for military purposes to economic and social development, particularly for the benefit of the developing countries,

Convinced that the freezing and reduction of military budgets would have favourable consequences on the world economic and financial situation and might facilitate efforts made to increase international assistance for the developing countries,

Recalling that at its twelfth special session, the second special session devoted to disarmament, all Member States unanimously and categorically reaffirmed the validity of the Final Document of the Tenth Special Session, as well as their solemn commitment to it,

Recalling also that, in the Declaration of the 1980s as the Second United Nations Disarmament Decade, it is provided that during this period renewed efforts should be made to reach agreement on the reduction of military expenditures and the reallocation of resources thus saved to economic and social development, especially for the benefit of developing countries,

Recalling further the provisions of its resolution 34/83 F of 11 December 1979, subsequently reaffirmed in its resolutions 35/142 A of 12 December 1980, 36/82 A of 9 December 1981, 37/95 A of 13 December 1982, 38/184 A of 20 December 1983 and 39/64 A of 12 December 1984, in which it considered that a new impetus should be given to the endeavours to achieve agreements to freeze, reduce or otherwise restrain, in a balanced manner, military expenditure, including adequate measures of verification satisfactory to all parties concerned,

Aware of the various proposals submitted by Member States and of the activities carried out so far within the framework of the United Nations in the field of the reduction of military budgets,

Considering that the identification and elaboration of the principles that should govern further actions of States in freezing and reducing military budgets and the other current activities within the framework of the United Nations related to the question of the reduction of military budgets should be regarded as having the fundamental objective of reaching international agreements on the reduction of military expenditures,

Taking note of the report of the Disarmament Commission on the work accomplished during its session in 1985 on the item entitled "Reduction of military budgets",

1. *Declares again its conviction* that it is possible to achieve international agreements on the reduction of military budgets without prejudice to the right of all States to undiminished security, self-defence and sovereignty;

2. *Appeals* to all States, in particular to the most heavily armed States, pending the conclusion of agreements on the reduction of military expenditures, to exercise self-restraint in their military expenditures with a view to reallocating the funds thus saved to economic and social development, particularly for the benefit of developing countries;

3. *Reaffirms* that the human and material resources released through the reduction of military expenditures could be reallocated for economic and social development, particularly for the benefit of the developing countries;

4. *Requests* the Disarmament Commission to continue the consideration of the item entitled "Reduction of military budgets" and, in this context, to finalize, at its substantive session in 1986, the principles that should govern the actions of States in the field of freezing and reduction of military expenditures on the basis of the working paper annexed to its report, as well as other proposals and ideas on the subject;

5. *Draws anew the attention* of Member States to the fact that the identification and elaboration of the principles which should govern further actions of States in freezing and reducing military budgets could contribute to harmonizing the views of States and creating confidence among them conducive to international agreements on the reduction of military budgets;

6. *Urges* all Member States, in particular the most heavily armed States, to reinforce their readiness to cooperate in a constructive manner with a view to reaching agreements to freeze, reduce or otherwise restrain military expenditures;

7. *Decides* to include in the provisional agenda of its forty-first session the item entitled "Reduction of military budgets".

General Assembly resolution 40/91 A

12 December 1985   Meeting 113   Adopted without vote

Approved by First Committee (A/40/950) without vote, 14 November (meeting 37); 15-nation draft (A/C.1/40/L.12); agenda item 62.
Sponsors: Austria, Bangladesh, Colombia, Ecuador, Indonesia, Ireland, Ivory Coast, Nigeria, Peru, Romania, Rwanda, Senegal, Sudan, Sweden, Uruguay.
Meeting numbers. GA 40th session: 1st Committee 3-32, 37; plenary 113.

While joining in the consensus, India held that the onus of reductions lay almost exclusively with the few militarily significant States, which, it said, accounted for 80 per cent of global military expenditure.

Report of the Group of Experts

In August 1985, the Secretary-General submitted to the General Assembly a report prepared by the Group of Experts on the Reduction of Military Budgets.[5] The Group—experts appointed in 1983 in pursuance of a 1982 Assembly request,[6] from Indonesia, Italy, Nigeria, Peru, Romania, Sweden and the United States—held six sessions beginning in March 1983, including two in 1985 (19 February–9 March and 10-14 June), under the chairmanship of Hans Christian Cars (Sweden). Australia, Austria, Finland, Italy, Norway, Sweden, the United Kingdom and the United States participated in the exercise, in response to the Secretary-General's invitation to States for their voluntary co-operation.

In its report, which covered the construction of military price indexes and purchasing-power parities for comparison of military expenditures, the Group concluded, among other things, that the construction of useful instruments for comparing military expenditures was feasible, given a sufficient availability of statistics. It recommended that all Member States be invited to express their views on the report, including the prospects of

wider participation, in particular by countries with different budgeting and accounting systems and at very different levels of economic development, and to suggest further measures for promoting and facilitating international agreements.

GENERAL ASSEMBLY ACTION

In addition to the expert report, the Secretary-General submitted to the Assembly in May 1985, with later addenda, his annual report on military expenditures in standardized form reported by 24 States.[7] As in previous years, a majority of the responding States had used the standard reporting instrument, consisting of a matrix designed to show how much each force group (such as land, naval and air forces) spent in each resource category (such as personnel, procurement and operations).

On 12 December, the General Assembly adopted **resolution 40/91 B** by recorded vote, as recommended by the First Committee.

The General Assembly,

Deeply concerned about the arms race and present tendencies to increase further the rate of growth of military expenditures, the deplorable waste of human and economic resources and the potentially harmful effects on world peace and security,

Considering that a gradual reduction of military expenditures on a mutually agreed basis would be a measure that would contribute to curbing the arms race and would increase the possibilities of reallocating resources now being used for military purposes to economic and social development, particularly for the benefit of the developing countries,

Convinced that such reductions could and should be carried out on a mutually agreed basis without detriment to the national security of any country,

Reaffirming its conviction that provisions for defining, reporting, comparing and verifying military expenditures will have to be basic elements of any international agreement to reduce such expenditures,

Recalling that an international system for the standardized reporting of military expenditures has been introduced in pursuance of General Assembly resolution 35/142 B of 12 December 1980, and that national reports on military expenditures have been received from a number of Member States belonging to different geographic regions and having different budgeting and accounting systems,

Considering that a wider participation in the reporting system of States from different geographic regions and representing different budgeting systems would promote its further refinement and would, by contributing to greater openness in military matters, increase confidence between States,

Emphasizing that the above-mentioned activities and initiatives, as well as other ongoing activities within the United Nations related to the reduction of military budgets, have the objective of facilitating future negotiations aimed at the conclusion of international agreements on the reduction of military expenditures,

Recalling its resolution 37/95 B of 13 December 1982, in which it requested the Secretary-General, with the assistance of a group of qualified experts and with the voluntary co-operation of States, to undertake the task of constructing price indices and purchasing-power parities for the military expenditures of participating States,

Having examined the report of the Secretary-General containing the report of the Group of Experts on the Reduction of Military Budgets,

1. *Takes note with appreciation* of the report of the Group of Experts on the Reduction of Military Budgets;

2. *Expresses its appreciation* to the Secretary-General and to the Group of Experts that assisted him in the preparation of the report;

3. *Commends* the report and its conclusions and recommendations to the attention of all Member States;

4. *Requests* the Secretary-General to make the necessary arrangements for the reproduction of the report as a United Nations publication;

5. *Invites* all Member States to submit to the Secretary-General, no later than 15 April 1986, their views regarding the report and to suggest further measures with a view to facilitating future international agreements to reduce military expenditures;

6. *Requests* the Secretary-General to submit a report containing the views of Member States received concerning this issue to the General Assembly at its forty-first session;

7. *Also takes note with appreciation* of the report of the Secretary-General containing the replies received in 1985 from Member States in the framework of the above-mentioned reporting system;

8. *Stresses* the need to increase the number of reporting States with a view to the broadest possible participation from different geographic regions and representing different budgeting systems;

9. *Reiterates its recommendation* that all Member States should report annually, by 30 April, to the Secretary-General, using the reporting instrument, their military expenditures for the latest fiscal year for which data are available;

10. *Decides* to include in the provisional agenda of its forty-first session the item entitled "Reduction of military budgets".

General Assembly resolution 40/91 B

12 December 1985   Meeting 113   113-13-15 (recorded vote)

Approved by First Committee (A/40/950) by recorded vote (96-13-15), 14 November (meeting 37); 21-nation draft (A/C.1/40/L.16), orally revised; agenda item 62.
Sponsors: Australia, Austria, Bangladesh, Belgium, Colombia, Costa Rica, Denmark, Finland, France, Germany, Federal Republic of, Iceland, Ireland, Italy, Malta, New Zealand, Norway, Romania, Samoa, Sudan, Sweden, Uruguay.
Meeting numbers. GA 40th session: 1st Committee 3-32, 37; plenary 113.

Recorded vote in Assembly as follows:

In favour: Antigua and Barbuda, Argentina, Australia, Austria, Bahamas, Bangladesh, Barbados, Belgium, Benin, Bhutan, Bolivia, Botswana, Brunei Darussalam, Burundi, Cameroon, Canada, Cape Verde, Central African Republic, Chad, Chile, Colombia, Comoros, Cyprus, Democratic Kampuchea, Denmark, Djibouti, Dominican Republic, Ecuador, Egypt, El Salvador, Equatorial Guinea, Fiji, Finland, France, Gabon, Germany, Federal Republic of, Ghana, Greece, Grenada, Guatemala, Guinea, Guinea-Bissau, Guyana, Haiti, Honduras, Iceland, Indonesia, Ireland, Israel, Italy, Ivory Coast, Jamaica, Japan, Kenya, Lebanon, Liberia, Luxembourg, Madagascar, Malawi, Malaysia, Maldives, Mali, Malta, Mauritania, Mauritius, Mexico, Morocco, Nepal, Netherlands, New Zealand, Niger, Nigeria, Norway, Pakistan, Panama, Papua New Guinea, Paraguay, Peru, Philippines, Portugal, Romania, Rwanda, Saint Christopher and Nevis, Saint Lucia, Saint Vincent and the Grenadines, Samoa, Sao Tome and Principe, Senegal, Sierra Leone, Singapore, Solomon Islands, Somalia, Spain, Sri Lanka, Sudan, Suriname, Swaziland, Sweden, Syrian Arab Republic, Thailand, Togo, Trinidad and Tobago, Tunisia, Turkey, Uganda, United Kingdom, United States, Uruguay, Vanuatu, Venezuela, Yugoslavia, Zaire, Zimbabwe.

Against: Afghanistan, Bulgaria, Byelorussian SSR, Cuba, Czechoslovakia, German Democratic Republic, Hungary, Lao People's Democratic Republic, Mongolia, Poland, Ukrainian SSR, USSR, Viet Nam.
Abstaining: Algeria, Angola, Brazil, Burkina Faso, Burma, China, Congo, Ethiopia, India, Lesotho, Nicaragua, Saudi Arabia, United Republic of Tanzania, Yemen, Zambia.

Explaining its vote, the USSR, which considered the text a diversion from the actual task of reducing military expenditures, recalled the 1984[8] and 1985 (see p. 14) proposals by the Warsaw Treaty States members for achieving practical agreement with NATO counterparts on, among other things, freezing nuclear expenditures, or for the USSR and the United States to freeze their military budgets.

Brazil said there had been a marked decline in arms expenditures in South America, in contrast to those of nuclear-weapon States; the text, however, did not reflect the fact that those Powers and their allies had to first reduce their own military budgets. In a similar vein, India said that in the absence of political will on the part of those Powers, exercises such as the one recommended might not only prove futile but also divert attention from nuclear disarmament.

Information on military matters

In December 1985, the General Assembly urged all States to facilitate the flow of information on military capabilities, stating that such action could contribute to the building of confidence among States and to the halting and reversal of the arms race.

GENERAL ASSEMBLY ACTION

On 12 December, the General Assembly, on the recommendation of the First Committee, adopted **resolution 40/94 K** by recorded vote.

Objective information on military matters
The General Assembly,

Noting that misperceptions of the military capabilities and the intentions of potential adversaries, which could be caused, *inter alia*, by a lack of objective information, could induce States to undertake armaments programmes leading to the acceleration of the arms race, in particular the nuclear-arms race, and to heightened international tensions,

Recalling paragraph 105 of the Final Document of the Tenth Special Session of the General Assembly, which encourages Member States to ensure a better flow of information with regard to the various aspects of disarmament to avoid dissemination of false and tendentious information concerning armaments and to concentrate on the danger of escalation of the arms race and on the need for general and complete disarmament under effective international control,

Recognizing that the adoption of practical, confidence-building measures on a global, regional or subregional level would greatly contribute to a reduction in international tension,

Aware that objective information on the military capabilities, in particular of nuclear-weapon States and other militarily significant States, could contribute to the building of confidence among States and to the conclusion of concrete disarmament agreements, and thereby help to halt and reverse the arms race,

Recalling its resolutions 37/99 G of 13 December 1982 and 38/188 C of 20 December 1983,

Aware of the existence, under the auspices of the United Nations, of an international system for the standardized reporting of military expenditures, and that annual reports on military expenditures are now being received from an increasing number of States,

1. *Expresses its conviction* that a better flow of objective information on military capabilities could help relieve international tension and contribute to the building of confidence among States on a global, regional or subregional level and to the conclusion of concrete disarmament agreements;

2. *Urges* all States, in particular nuclear-weapon States and other militarily significant States, to consider implementing additional measures based on the principles of openness and transparency such as, for example, the international system for the standardized reporting of military expenditures, with the aim of facilitating the availability of objective information on, as well as objective assessment of, military capabilities;

3. *Invites* all Member States to communicate to the Secretary-General before 30 April 1986 the measures they have adopted to contribute to greater openness in military matters in general and in particular to improve the flow of objective information on military capabilities;

4. *Requests* the Secretary-General to report to the General Assembly at its forty-first session on the implementation of the provisions of the present resolution;

5. *Decides* to include in the provisional agenda of its forty-first session an item entitled "Objective information on military matters".

General Assembly resolution 40/94 K

12 December 1985   Meeting 113   107-13-16 (recorded vote)

Approved by First Committee (A/40/976) by recorded vote (88-13-16), 19 November (meeting 42); 11-nation draft (A/C.1/40/L.56); agenda item 68.
Sponsors: Australia, Belgium, Canada, Denmark, France, Iceland, Italy, New Zealand, Norway, Turkey, United Kingdom.
Meeting numbers. GA 40th session: 1st Committee 3-32, 36, 42; plenary 113.

Recorded vote in Assembly as follows:

In favour: Antigua and Barbuda, Argentina, Australia, Austria, Bahamas, Bangladesh, Barbados, Belgium, Bhutan, Bolivia, Botswana, Brunei Darussalam, Burundi, Cameroon, Canada, Cape Verde, Central African Republic, Chad, Chile, Colombia, Comoros, Democratic Kampuchea, Denmark, Djibouti, Dominican Republic, Ecuador, Egypt, El Salvador, Equatorial Guinea, Fiji, Finland, France, Gabon, Germany, Federal Republic of, Greece, Grenada, Guatemala, Guinea, Guinea-Bissau, Guyana, Haiti, Honduras, Iceland, Indonesia, Ireland, Israel, Italy, Ivory Coast, Jamaica, Japan, Kenya, Lebanon, Lesotho, Liberia, Luxembourg, Malawi, Malaysia, Maldives, Mali, Malta, Mauritania, Mauritius, Nepal, Netherlands, New Zealand, Niger, Nigeria, Norway, Pakistan, Panama, Papua New Guinea, Paraguay, Peru, Philippines, Portugal, Romania, Rwanda, Saint Christopher and Nevis, Saint Lucia, Saint Vincent and the Grenadines, Samoa, Sao Tome and Principe, Senegal, Sierra Leone, Singapore, Solomon Islands, Somalia, Spain, Sri Lanka, Sudan, Suriname, Swaziland, Sweden, Thailand, Togo, Trinidad and Tobago, Turkey, Uganda, United Kingdom, United States, Vanuatu, Venezuela, Yemen, Yugoslavia, Zaire, Zambia, Zimbabwe.

Against: Afghanistan, Bulgaria, Byelorussian SSR, Cuba, Czechoslovakia, German Democratic Republic, Hungary, Lao People's Democratic Republic, Mongolia, Poland, Ukrainian SSR, USSR, Viet Nam.

Abstaining: Algeria, Benin, Brazil, Burkina Faso, Burma, China, Congo, Cyprus, Ethiopia, Ghana, India, Iran, Madagascar, Mexico, Nicaragua, United Republic of Tanzania.

The USSR asserted that no flow of disarmament information nor any survey on comparing military data could replace real efforts to limit the arms race; information exchange, it added, should take place along with concrete disarmament measures and not in isolation or as a pre-condition for the holding of negotiations. Sharing those views, Bulgaria felt that the text exaggerated the importance of information. Yugoslavia spoke in similar vein and added that one should not overestimate the effects of a lack of objective information on the acceleration of the arms race, as it felt the text did. Brazil felt that the text was based on concepts pertaining to the climate of confrontation and suspicion between the two super-Powers and their respective military alliances and would not contribute to the adoption of real disarmament measures.

Military research and development

The Group of Governmental Experts on Military Research and Development, which had been given an extra year by the General Assembly in 1984[9] to complete a study due that year, failed to agree on a report in 1985.

Established by the Secretary-General in 1983[10] in response to a 1982 Assembly request,[11] the Group—experts from Argentina, China, Czechoslovakia, Egypt, France, the German Democratic Republic, Ghana, India, Japan, Peru, Sweden, the USSR, the United Kingdom and the United States—was to prepare a comprehensive study covering the scope, role and direction of the military use of research and development, the mechanisms involved, its role in the arms race, and its impact on arms limitation and disarmament, with a view to preventing a qualitative arms race and to ensuring that scientific and technological achievements might ultimately be used solely for peaceful purposes. It had held two sessions in 1983 and three in 1984.

In a 10 May 1985 letter annexed to the Secretary-General's report to the Assembly,[12] the Group's Chairman, Rolf Björnerstedt (Sweden), stated that the Group, meeting from 22 April to 4 May 1985, could not reach consensus on the draft report due to one outstanding sentence. The basic problem of an imbalance in the availability of official information and data concerning military use of research and development, the Chairman stated, stemmed from existing differences of opinion regarding the need to provide such information, and that basic difficulty proved in the end to be insurmountable. After the Chairman's letter was received, the Secretary-General stated, further ways had been explored to reach a solution but they had not led to generally acceptable results.

Sweden told the First Committee that the success of expert studies depended on the co-operation of all Governments and experts involved; the draft report on military research and development contained a wealth of information, and there was every reason for the United Nations to return to that crucial subject.

Disarmament and development

Preparations began in 1985 for the International Conference on the Relationship between Disarmament and Development, which the General Assembly had decided in 1984[13] to convene in order to review the implications of that relationship and consider ways of releasing additional resources, through disarmament measures, for development purposes.

In December, the Assembly took note of the work of the Conference's Preparatory Committee[14] and decided that the Conference would be held in Paris from 15 July to 2 August 1986 (resolution 40/155).

Reports of the Secretary-General. In his August 1985 report to the Assembly on the overall socio-economic perspective of the world economy to the year 2000[15] (see p. 415), the Secretary-General stated that the arms race had major economic and social consequences, in that military expenditures used up large amounts of real resources (such as skilled labour, industrial capacity and essential raw materials) and deprived the civilian economy of much-needed expertise. He noted that world-wide military expenditures had almost doubled between 1960 and 1980, growing at an average annual rate of about 3.2 per cent and reaching $649 billion (in 1980 prices) in 1984. It was estimated that in 1980 about 50 million people, or over 4 per cent of the world's working population, were engaged in producing military goods and services. The Secretary-General asserted that the pursuit of disarmament measures would result in global gains, including increases in world gross national product and in capital stocks.

In addition, the Assembly had before it an October report of the Secretary-General,[16] containing information received from 12 Member States, and from within the United Nations system, on measures they had taken in accordance with the recommendations of a 1981 expert study on the relationship between disarmament and development.[17]

Conference preparations

Work of the Preparatory Committee. The Preparatory Committee for the International Conference on the Relationship between Disarmament and Development (New York, 29 July–9 August 1985)[14] held 11 meetings, including five informal open-ended meetings, to formulate recommendations on the provisional agenda, procedure, place, date and duration of the Conference.

The Committee adopted by consensus, and submitted to the Assembly, a number of recommendations, among them, that the Conference be held for three weeks in June/July 1986 in Paris—in response to France's indication of preparedness to host it; and that the Assembly renew the Committee's mandate and authorize it to hold one more session to make substantive preparations, with the possibility of its deciding to convene, if necessary, a resumed session immediately before the Conference. Other recommendations included that a Conference Secretary-General be named as early as possible, and that a panel of eminent personalities in the disarmament field, drawn from different regions and covering a wide range of views, might be convened to contribute to the preparatory process.

GENERAL ASSEMBLY ACTION

On 16 December, on the recommendation of the First Committee, the General Assembly adopted **resolution 40/155** without vote.

Relationship between disarmament and development

The General Assembly,

Recalling its resolutions 38/71 B of 15 December 1983 and 39/160 of 17 December 1984,

Recalling, in particular, its decision to convene an International Conference on the Relationship between Disarmament and Development, which should be preceded by thorough preparation and should take decisions by consensus, and to set up a Preparatory Committee for the Conference, which should formulate and submit, by consensus, to the General Assembly, at its fortieth session, recommendations as to the provisional agenda, procedure, place, date and duration of the Conference,

1. *Takes note with satisfaction* of the report of the Preparatory Committee for the International Conference on the Relationship between Disarmament and Development and approves the recommendations contained therein;

2. *Recommends* for adoption by the International Conference on the Relationship between Disarmament and Development the following provisional agenda drawn up by the Preparatory Committee:

1.   Opening of the Conference
2.   Election of the President
3.   Adoption of the rules of procedure
4.   Election of the other officers
5.   Credentials of the representatives to the Conference:
    (a) Appointment of the Credentials Committee;
    (b) Report of the Credentials Committee
6.   Adoption of the agenda
7.   Organization of work
8.   Consideration of the relationship between disarmament and development in all its aspects and dimensions with a view to reaching appropriate conclusions
9.   Consideration of the implications of the level and magnitude of military expenditures, in particular those of nuclear-weapon States and other militarily important States, for the world economy and the

international economic and social situation, particularly for the developing countries, and formulation of appropriate recommendations for remedial measures

10. Consideration of ways and means of releasing additional resources, through disarmament measures, for development purposes, in particular for the benefit of developing countries

11. Adoption of the final document of the Conference

12. Adoption of the report of the Conference to the General Assembly;

3. *Also recommends* for adoption by the Conference the proposals relating to procedure contained in the report of the Preparatory Committee;

4. *Expresses its appreciation* to the Government of France for its invitation to act as host to the Conference, and accordingly decides that the Conference shall be held in Paris from 15 July to 2 August 1986;

5. *Requests* the Secretary-General to invite all States to participate in the Conference and to apply, as regards other participants and observers, the provisions of section XI of the provisional rules of procedure for the Conference, annexed to the report of the Preparatory Committee;

6. *Authorizes* the Preparatory Committee to hold one or, if necessary, two additional sessions, each of two weeks' duration, open to all States and devoted to consideration of the substantive questions included in the agenda for the Conference;

7. *Decides* that the second session of the Preparatory Committee shall be held in New York from 1 to 11 April 1986 and that, if necessary, a third session shall be held in New York in June, taking into account all relevant factors, including the need for minimizing costs and for adequate representation;

8. *Requests* the Secretary-General to appoint the Secretary-General of the Conference;

9. *Requests* the Secretary-General of the Conference to assist in the tasks provided for in paragraph 19 of the report of the Preparatory Committee and to ensure implementation of the recommendations contained in paragraphs 20 (documentation), 21 (convening of a panel of eminent personalities qualified in the field of disarmament and development*), 22 (appropriate information to the General Assembly on the preparatory process) and 23 (dissemination of information relating to the Conference and its preparatory work);

10. *Requests* the organizations of the United Nations system and the International Atomic Energy Agency to contribute fully to the preparatory work in the field of documentation, in conformity with the recommendations contained in paragraph 20 of the report of the Preparatory Committee.

---

*Subsequently referred to as the Panel of Eminent Personalities on the Relationship between Disarmament and Development.

General Assembly resolution 40/155

16 December 1985   Meeting 117   Adopted without vote

Approved by First Committee (A/40/896) without vote, 15 November (meeting 39); 52-nation draft (A/C.1/40/L.69); agenda item 69.

Sponsors: Australia, Austria, Bahamas, Bangladesh, Burkina Faso, Cameroon, Canada, Central African Republic, China, Colombia, Congo, Costa Rica, Cuba, Denmark, Djibouti, Dominican Republic, Ecuador, Egypt, France, Gabon, German Democratic Republic, Ghana, Greece, India, Indonesia, Italy, Ivory Coast, Kenya, Mali, Mauritania, Mexico, Morocco, Nepal, Nigeria, Norway, Pakistan, Peru, Romania, Samoa, Senegal, Spain, Sri Lanka, Sudan, Swaziland, Sweden, Togo, Trinidad and Tobago, Tunisia, Uruguay, Venezuela, Yugoslavia, Zaire.

Financial implications. ACABQ, A/40/7/Add.15; Committee on Conferences, A/C.5/40/52/Add.1; 5th Committee, A/40/1019; S-G, A/C.1/40/L.75, A/C.5/40/52. *Meeting numbers.* GA 40th session: 1st Committee 3-32, 34, 39; 5th Committee 56; plenary 117.

On 17 December, the Secretary-General reported on further preparations for the Conference.[18] He announced the appointment of Jan Martenson (Sweden), Under-Secretary-General for Disarmament Affairs, as the Conference Secretary-General; proposed the convening of the panel of eminent persons from 16 to 18 April 1986, in New York; and discussed the preparation of documentation for the Conference.

Economic and social consequences of the arms race

In 1985, the General Assembly took up an item on the economic and social consequences of the arms race and its extremely harmful effects on world peace and security, as agreed in 1982,[19] and called for the updating of the 1982 report entitled *Economic and Social Consequences of the Arms Race and of Military Expenditures*,[20] which, in turn, had updated a 1977 report on the topic.[21]

Among communications the Secretary-General received in 1985 was a 28 May letter from Czechoslovakia on behalf of a group of socialist countries, transmitting a declaration on the situation in the International Labour Organisation, criticizing various aspects of its activities, including the role in disarmament matters (see ECONOMIC AND SOCIAL QUESTIONS, Chapter XXIV).

GENERAL ASSEMBLY ACTION

On the recommendation of the First Committee, the General Assembly, on 16 December, adopted **resolution 40/150** by recorded vote.

Economic and social consequences of the armaments race and its extremely harmful effects on world peace and security

The General Assembly,

Having considered the item entitled "Economic and social consequences of the armaments race and its extremely harmful effects on world peace and security",

Recalling its resolutions 2667(XXV) of 7 December 1970, 2831(XXVI) of 16 December 1971, 3075(XXVIII) of 6 December 1973, 32/75 of 12 December 1977, 35/141 of 12 December 1980 and 37/70 of 9 December 1982,

Deeply concerned that the arms race, particularly in nuclear armaments and military expenditures, has continued to increase at an alarming speed, absorbing enormous material and human resources, which represents a heavy burden for the peoples of all countries and constitutes a grave danger for world peace and security,

Convinced that, as disarmament is a matter of universal concern, there is a pressing need for all Governments and peoples to be informed about and be aware of the problems created by the armaments race and of the need for disarmament, and that the United Nations has a central role in this connection,

Recalling also paragraph 93 *(c)* of the Final Document of the Tenth Special Session of the General Assembly, in which it is provided that the Secretary-General shall periodically submit reports to the Assembly on the economic and social consequences of the armament race and its extremely harmful effects on world peace and security,

Noting that, since the preparation of the updated report of the Secretary-General entitled *Economic and Social Consequences of the Arms Race and of Military Expenditures*, new developments have taken place in the fields covered by the report that are of particular relevance in the present economic and political conditions of the world,

Considering that the elaboration of such reports should be viewed as a measure aimed at building confidence among States,

Recalling further its resolution 39/160 of 17 December 1984, in which it decided to convene an International Conference on the Relationship between Disarmament and Development, at which inevitably the issue of the economic and social consequences of the arms race and of military expenditures would be discussed,

1. *Requests* the Secretary-General to bring up to date, with the assistance of a group of qualified consultant experts* appointed by him and making appropriate use of the capabilities of the United Nations Institute for Disarmament Research in a consultant capacity, the report entitled *Economic and Social Consequences of the Arms Race and of Military Expenditures*, taking into account the significant developments that have taken place since the preparation of that report;

2. *Invites* all Governments to extend to the Secretary-General their support and full co-operation so as to en-sure that the study will be carried out in the most effec-tive way;

3. *Calls upon* the specialized agencies, other inter-national organizations and institutions as well as non-governmental organizations to co-operate with the Secretary-General, upon his request, in the preparation of the report;

4. *Requests* the Secretary-General to submit the report to the General Assembly at its forty-second session;

5. *Decides* to include in the provisional agenda of its forty-second session the item entitled "Economic and social consequences of the armaments race and its ex-tremely harmful effects on world peace and security".

---

*Subsequently referred to as the Group of Consultant Ex-perts on the Economic and Social Consequences of the Arms Race and of Military Expenditures.

General Assembly resolution 40/150

16 December 1985   Meeting 117   139-1-7 (recorded vote)

Approved by First Committee (A/40/915) by recorded vote (126-1-6), 19 November (meeting 42); 21-nation draft (A/C.1/40/L.30); agenda item 48.

Sponsors: Bahamas, Bangladesh, Bolivia, Cameroon, Colombia, Cuba, Czecho-slovakia, Ecuador, Egypt, Greece, Indonesia, Ireland, Mexico, Peru, Romania, Rwanda, Samoa, Sweden, Uruguay, Venezuela, Yugoslavia.

Financial implications. ACABQ, A/40/7/Add.15; 5th Committee, A/40/1019; S-G, A/C.1/40/L.77, A/C.5/40/56.

Meeting numbers. GA 40th session: 1st Committee 3-32, 35, 42; 5th Committee 56; plenary 117.

Recorded vote in Assembly as follows:

In favour: Afghanistan, Algeria, Angola, Antigua and Barbuda, Argentina, Australia, Austria, Bahamas, Bahrain, Bangladesh, Benin, Bhutan, Bolivia, Bo-tswana, Brazil, Brunei Darussalam, Bulgaria, Burkina Faso, Burma, Burundi, Byelorussian SSR, Cameroon, Canada, Cape Verde, Central African Republic, Chad, Chile, China, Colombia, Comoros, Congo, Costa Rica, Cuba, Cyprus, Czechoslovakia, Democratic Kampuchea, Democratic Yemen, Djibouti, Dominican Republic, Ecuador, Egypt, El Salvador, Equatorial Guinea, Ethiopia, Fiji, Finland, Gabon, Gambia, German Democratic Republic, Ghana, Greece, Guatemala, Guinea, Guyana, Haiti, Honduras, Hungary, Iceland, India, Indonesia, Iran, Iraq, Ireland, Israel, Italy, Ivory Coast, Jamaica, Japan, Jordan, Kenya, Kuwait, Lao People's Democratic Republic, Lebanon, Lesotho, Liberia, Libyan Arab Jamahiriya, Madagascar, Malaysia, Maldives, Mali, Malta, Mauritania, Mauritius, Mexico, Mongolia, Morocco, Mozambique, Nepal, New Zealand, Nicaragua, Niger, Nigeria, Norway, Oman, Pakistan, Panama, Papua New Guinea, Paraguay, Peru, Philippines, Poland, Portugal, Qatar, Romania, Rwanda, Saint Lucia, Saint Vincent and the Grenadines, Samoa, Sao Tome and Principe, Saudi Arabia, Senegal, Seychelles, Sierra Leone, Singapore, Somalia, Spain, Sri Lanka, Sudan, Suriname, Swaziland, Sweden, Syrian Arab Republic, Thailand, Togo, Trinidad and Tobago, Tunisia, Turkey, Uganda, Ukrainian SSR, USSR, United Arab Emirates, United Republic of Tanzania, Uruguay, Vanuatu, Venezuela, Viet Nam, Yugoslavia, Zambia.

Against: United States.

Abstaining: Belgium, France, Germany, Federal Republic of, Grenada, Lux-embourg, Netherlands, United Kingdom.

Explaining its vote, the United States said it did not believe another report was warranted, in terms of developments since the last report in 1982 or of the cost estimate for a new report, involving an additional appropriation of $150,000 to the pro-posed 1986-1987 programme budget.

France and the United Kingdom also expressed misgivings about the financial implications. France added that implementing the recommen-dation in paragraph 1 would duplicate the preparatory work for the International Conference on the Relationship between Disarmament and Development (see p. 87). The United Kingdom believed it would have been preferable to delay commissioning the report until the Assembly's forty-first (1986) session, when the documentation and the results of the Conference could be used to avoid possible duplication and limit costs.

Declaration of the Indian Ocean as a Zone of Peace

In 1985, the General Assembly requested the *Ad Hoc* Committee on the Indian Ocean to com-plete preparatory work for the Conference on the Indian Ocean during 1986 in order to enable its convening at Colombo, Sri Lanka, at an early date and no later than 1988 (resolution 40/153).

Activities of the Committee on the Indian Ocean. The *Ad Hoc* Committee on the Indian Ocean, established by the General Assembly in 1972[22] to study practical measures for achieving the objectives of the 1971 Declaration of the In-dian Ocean as a Zone of Peace,[23] held three ses-sions in 1985 (New York, 28 January–8 February, 25 March–4 April, 1-12 July), with two additional meetings on 19 November and 5 December.[24]

In the course of 30 formal and a number of in-formal meetings, the Committee discussed the Conference's provisional agenda, rules of pro-cedure, participation, stages, level of representa-tion and draft final document. In July, it set up an open-ended working group to identify, expand and facilitate agreement on substantive issues relating to the establishment of a zone of peace, with a view to recommending to the *Ad Hoc* Committee elements which might be taken into account during the subsequent preparation of a draft final document of the Conference.

Two divergent views persisted on the convening of the Conference. Most non-aligned and Eastern European States maintained that the Committee should proceed expeditiously with its preparatory work in order to facilitate the opening of the Conference in the first half of 1986. The Western States, on the other hand, stressed the need, prior to convening a Conference, for a clearer understanding of some fundamental issues, such as the scope and definition of the zone-of-peace concept, and for improving the political and security climate in the region.

On 12 July, the Committee adopted by consensus parts I and II of its report; part III, containing a draft resolution prepared by an open-ended working group for consideration by the Assembly, and the report as a whole were similarly adopted on 5 December. The draft resolution, as approved by the Committee, differed in a number of ways from a draft text submitted in July by Sri Lanka on behalf of the non-aligned members of the Committee.[25] The non-aligned text would have had the Assembly request the *Ad Hoc* Committee to complete preparatory work in the early part of 1986, thus facilitating the convening of the Conference at Colombo thereafter at the earliest date in the first half of 1986.

Communications. Bulgaria[26] transmitted to the Chairman of the *Ad Hoc* Committee, on 8 February, a 23 May 1984 letter from its Foreign Minister to the Secretary-General, giving Bulgaria's views on limitation of naval activities and naval armaments.

In a Political Declaration, the Conference of Foreign Ministers of Non-Aligned Countries (Luanda, Angola, 4-7 September)[27] asserted that the convening of the Conference on the Indian Ocean had been inordinately delayed due to the unhelpful attitude of some States, and pledged their continued efforts to ensure that it would be held at Colombo during the first half of 1986. Regret that the Conference had not been convened was also expressed by Seychelles, in a resolution adopted by its People's Progressive Front (sixth annual congress, Victoria, Mahé, 27 and 28 September).[28]

GENERAL ASSEMBLY ACTION

On 16 December, the General Assembly adopted without vote **resolution 40/153**, the draft of which had been recommended by the *Ad Hoc* Committee on the Indian Ocean and approved by the First Committee.

Implementation of the Declaration of the Indian Ocean as a Zone of Peace

The General Assembly,

Recalling the Declaration of the Indian Ocean as a Zone of Peace, contained in its resolution 2832(XXVI) of 16 December 1971, and recalling also its resolutions 2992(XXVII) of 15 December 1972, 3080(XXVIII) of 6 December 1973, 3259 A (XXIX) of 9 December 1974, 3468(XXX) of 11 December 1975, 31/88 of 14 December 1976, 32/86 of 12 December 1977, S-10/2 of 30 June 1978, 33/68 of 14 December 1978, 34/80 A and B of 11 December 1979, 35/150 of 12 December 1980, 36/90 of 9 December 1981, 37/96 of 13 December 1982, 38/185 of 20 December 1983 and 39/149 of 17 December 1984, and other relevant resolutions,

Recalling further the report of the Meeting of the Littoral and Hinterland States of the Indian Ocean,

Reaffirming its conviction that concrete action for the achievement of the objectives of the Declaration of the Indian Ocean as a Zone of Peace would be a substantial contribution to the strengthening of international peace and security,

Recalling its decision, taken at its thirty-fourth session in resolution 34/80 B, to convene a Conference on the Indian Ocean at Colombo during 1981,

Recalling also its decision to make every effort, in consideration of the political and security climate in the Indian Ocean area and progress made in the harmonization of views, to finalize, in accordance with its normal methods of work, all preparations for the Conference, including the dates for its convening,

Recalling further its decision, taken at its thirty-ninth session in resolution 39/149, concerning the convening of the Conference in the first half of 1986,

Recalling the exchange of views in the *Ad Hoc* Committee on the Indian Ocean in 1985,

Noting the exchange of views on the adverse political and security climate in the region,

Noting further the various documents before the *Ad Hoc* Committee,

Convinced that the continued military presence of the great Powers in the Indian Ocean area, conceived in the context of their confrontation, gives urgency to the need to take practical steps for the early achievement of the objectives of the Declaration of the Indian Ocean as a Zone of Peace,

Considering that any other foreign military presence in the area, whenever it is contrary to the objectives of the Declaration of the Indian Ocean as a Zone of Peace and the purposes and principles of the Charter of the United Nations, gives greater urgency to the need to take practical steps towards the early achievement of the objectives of the Declaration,

Considering further that the creation of a zone of peace requires co-operation and agreement among the States of the region to ensure conditions of peace and security within the area, as envisaged in the Declaration of the Indian Ocean as a Zone of Peace, and respect for the independence, sovereignty and territorial integrity of the littoral and hinterland States,

Calling for the renewal of genuinely constructive efforts through the exercise of the political will necessary for the achievement of the objectives of the Declaration of the Indian Ocean as a Zone of Peace,

Deeply concerned at the danger posed by the grave and ominous developments in the area and the resulting sharp deterioration of peace, security and stability which particularly seriously affect the littoral and hinterland States, as well as international peace and security,

Convinced that the continued deterioration of the political and security climate in the Indian Ocean area is an important consideration bearing on the question of the urgent convening of the Conference and that the easing of tension in the area would enhance the prospect of success being achieved by the Conference,

1. *Takes note* of the report of the *Ad Hoc* Committee on the Indian Ocean and the exchange of views in the Committee;

2. *Emphasizes* its decision to convene the Conference on the Indian Ocean at Colombo as a necessary step for the implementation of the Declaration of the Indian Ocean as a Zone of Peace, adopted in 1971;

3. *Notes* that the *Ad Hoc* Committee has been unable, during 1985, to complete preparatory work relating to the convening of the Conference on the Indian Ocean and urges the Committee to continue its work with vigour and determination;

4. *Requests* the *Ad Hoc* Committee, taking into account the political and security climate in the region, to complete preparatory work relating to the Conference on the Indian Ocean during 1986 in order to enable the opening of the Conference at Colombo at an early date soon thereafter, but not later than 1988, to be decided by the Committee in consultation with the host country;

5. *Emphasizes* that the Conference called for in its resolution 34/80 B and subsequent resolutions and the establishment and maintenance of the Indian Ocean as a zone of peace require the full and active participation and co-operation of all the permanent members of the Security Council, the major maritime users and the littoral and hinterland States;

6. *Decides* that preparatory work would comprise organizational matters and substantive issues, including the provisional agenda for the Conference, rules of procedure, participation, stages of the Conference, level of representation, documentation, consideration of appropriate arrangements for any international agreements that may ultimately be reached for the maintenance of the Indian Ocean as a zone of peace and the preparation of the draft final document of the Conference;

7. *Requests* the *Ad Hoc* Committee at the same time to seek the necessary harmonization of views on remaining relevant issues;

8. *Requests* the Chairman of the *Ad Hoc* Committee to consult the Secretary-General, at the appropriate time, on the establishment of a secretariat for the Conference;

9. *Renews* the mandate of the *Ad Hoc* Committee as defined in the relevant resolutions, and requests the Committee to intensify its work with regard to the implementation of its mandate;

10. *Requests* the *Ad Hoc* Committee to hold three preparatory sessions in 1986 of a duration of two weeks each, for completion of the preparatory work;

11. *Requests* the *Ad Hoc* Committee to submit to the Conference a report on its preparatory work;

12. *Requests* the Chairman of the *Ad Hoc* Committee to continue his consultations on the participation in the work of the Committee by States Members of the United Nations that are not members of the Committee, with the aim of resolving this matter at the earliest possible date;

13. *Requests* the *Ad Hoc* Committee to submit to the General Assembly at its forty-first session a full report on the implementation of the present resolution;

14. *Requests* the Secretary-General to continue to render all necessary assistance to the *Ad Hoc* Committee, including the provision of summary records, in recognition of its preparatory function.

General Assembly resolution 40/153

16 December 1985   Meeting 117   Adopted without vote

Approved by First Committee (A/40/1018) without vote, 6 December (meeting 62); draft by Committee on Indian Ocean (A/40/29); agenda item 66.
Financial implications. 5th Committee, A/40/1053; S-G, A/C.1/40/L.90, A/C.5/40/89.
Meeting numbers. GA 40th session: 1st Committee 3-32, 62; 5th Committee 62; plenary 117.

Speaking as co-ordinator of the *Ad Hoc* Committee's non-aligned group of countries, Sri Lanka stressed the importance of paragraphs 4 and 5, and said that the approval of the text assured the active participation in the Conference of the permanent members of the Security Council along with the major maritime users; that the group had resigned itself to another postponement of the Conference in order to maintain consensus and to ensure the participation of all concerned; and that it was its understanding that, once the preparatory work was completed in 1986, convening the Conference in 1987 would not be precluded. Sharing the last point, the USSR considered unsatisfactory the formulations relating to the Conference's convening and its timetable. Bulgaria said it was disappointed that the lack of political will of one group of countries impeded the achievement of mutually acceptable agreement on all issues related to the Conference.

Canada, expressing its commitment to the idea of a Conference, asserted, however, that few of the items in paragraph 6 had been debated fully and openly, and that little of significance had been achieved in the *Ad Hoc* Committee.

REFERENCES

[1]A/40/42. [2]YUN 1984, p. 69. [3]A/40/544. [4]CD/631. [5]*Reduction of Military Budgets* (A/40/421), Sales No. E.86.IX.2. [6]YUN 1982, p. 119, GA res. 37/95 B, 13 Dec. 1982. [7]A/40/313 & Add.1-3. [8]YUN 1984, p. 114. [9]*Ibid.*, p. 73, GA res. 39/151 F, 17 Dec. 1984. [10]YUN 1983, p. 86. [11]YUN 1982, p. 135, GA res. 37/99 J, 13 Dec. 1982. [12]A/40/533. [13]YUN 1984, p. 84, GA res. 39/160, 17 Dec. 1984. [14]A/40/51. [15]A/40/519. [16]A/40/618 & Corr.1. [17]YUN 1981, p. 96. [18]A/40/913. [19]YUN 1982, p. 147, GA res. 37/70, 9 Dec. 1982. [20]*Economic and Social Consequences of the Arms Race and of Military Expenditures*, Sales No. E.83.IX.2. [21]YUN 1977, p. 57. [22]YUN 1972, p. 29, GA res. 2992(XXVII), 15 Dec. 1972. [23]YUN 1971, p. 34, GA res. 2832(XXVI), 16 Dec. 1971. [24]A/40/29. [25]A/AC.159/L.68. [26]A/AC.159/L.66. [27]A/40/854-S/17610 & Corr.1. [28]A/C.1/40/13.

Information and studies

As the World Disarmament Campaign entered its fourth year in 1985, the General Assembly reaffirmed the importance of following the priorities set in its 1978 Final Document (resolution 40/151 D). For 1986, it decided to establish the United Nations Regional Centre for Peace and Disarmament in Africa (40/151 G) and to hold, as in 1985, a pledging conference for the Campaign (40/151 B); and recommended that all States observe Disarmament Week in 1986 in close connection with the celebration of the International Year of Peace (40/152 E).

The Assembly also expanded the assistance to Member States under the United Nations disarmament fellowships programme to include training and advisory services (40/151 H). With several United Nations disarmament studies under way in 1985, including some by the United Nations Institute for Disarmament Research (UNIDIR), the Assembly reaffirmed their value and invited proposals from Member States for improving the Organization's work in that area (40/152 K).

World Disarmament Campaign

Entering its fourth year of implementation, the World Disarmament Campaign—launched by the General Assembly on 7 June 1982, at the start of its second special session devoted to disarmament[1]—continued to inform, educate and generate public understanding and support for the disarmament objectives of the United Nations.

Report of the Secretary-General. In an October 1985 report,[2] submitted in response to a 1984 Assembly request,[3] the Secretary-General discussed various 1985 activities by the United Nations system to promote the Campaign's objectives, including diversified production of information materials; interpersonal communication, seminars and training; special events; a publicity programme; and the roles played by United Nations information centres and other field offices.

The 1985 programme for the Campaign included a regional conference for Africa (Cairo, Egypt, 9-14 February), where 26 African countries were represented, and a subregional conference for constituencies of the Campaign in the Nordic countries (Jönköping, Sweden, 15-19 April). The United Nations Department for Disarmament Affairs and UNIDIR jointly organized, in co-operation with OAU, a Meeting of Experts on Security, Disarmament and Development in Africa (Lomé, Togo, 11 and 12 August). The Department also co-operated with the Inter-Parliamentary Union in a symposium on disarmament relating to conventional weapons (Mexico City, 28-31 May).

Among other activities, the Department published a quarterly newsletter of the Campaign.

On 16 December, the General Assembly, on the recommendation of the First Committee, adopted **resolution 40/151 D** by recorded vote.

World Disarmament Campaign: actions and activities

The General Assembly,

Aware of the growing public concern at the dangers of the arms race, particularly the nuclear-arms race, and its negative social and economic consequences,

Noting with satisfaction the successful implementation of the World Disarmament Campaign and its positive impact on the mobilization on a large scale of world public opinion on behalf of peace and disarmament,

Recalling its resolutions 36/92 J of 9 December 1981, 37/100 H of 13 December 1982, 38/73 F of 15 December 1983 and 39/63 A of 12 December 1984,

Welcoming the voluntary contributions made to the World Disarmament Campaign Voluntary Trust Fund to carry out the objectives of the Campaign,

Taking into account the report of the Secretary-General on the progress and implementation of the programme of activities of the World Disarmament Campaign,

Convinced that the United Nations system, Member States, with respect for their sovereign rights, and other bodies, in particular non-governmental organizations, all have their role to play in achieving the objectives of the Campaign,

Taking into account the great number of various activities carried out within the framework of the Campaign, including actions for collecting signatures in support of measures to prevent nuclear war, to curb the arms race and for disarmament,

1. *Reaffirms* the usefulness of further carrying out actions and activities that are an important manifestation of the will of world public opinion and contribute effectively to the achievement of the objectives of the World Disarmament Campaign and thus to the creation of a favourable climate for making progress in the field of disarmament with a view to achieving the goal of general and complete disarmament under effective international control;

2. *Urges* the Governments of all States, especially the nuclear-weapon States and other militarily significant States, in formulating their policies in the field of disarmament, to take into account the main demands of the mass peace and disarmament movements, in particular, with regard to the prevention of nuclear war and curbing the nuclear-arms race;

3. *Reaffirms* the importance of carrying out the Campaign in accordance with the priorities in the field of disarmament established in the Final Document of the Tenth Special Session of the General Assembly, taking into account that the adoption of effective measures for nuclear disarmament and the prevention of nuclear war has the highest priority;

4. *Recommends* that, in carrying out the Campaign, due regard should be given to the proclamation by the General Assembly of 1986 as the International Year of Peace, as well as to other important dates and anniversaries related to international peace and security, with a view to intensifying the actions and activities in support of effective measures to prevent nuclear war, to curb the arms race and for disarmament;

5. *Invites once again* Member States to co-operate with the United Nations to ensure a better flow of accurate information with regard to the various aspects of disarmament, as well as actions and activities of the world public in support of peace and disarmament, and to avoid dissemination of false and tendentious information;

6. *Requests* the Secretary-General, in implementing the programme of activities of the Campaign, to give wider publicity to the work of the General Assembly in the field of disarmament, paying due attention, in particular, to the proposals of Member States and the action taken thereon;

7. *Also requests* the Secretary-General to report annually to the General Assembly on the implementation of the provisions of the present resolution.

General Assembly resolution 40/151 D

16 December 1985   Meeting 117   114-0-34 (recorded vote)

Approved by First Committee (A/40/946) by recorded vote (99-0-33), 15 November (meeting 39); 7-nation draft (A/C.1/40/L.21); agenda item 61 *(a)*.
Sponsors: Bulgaria, Byelorussian SSR, German Democratic Republic, Mongolia, Romania, Ukrainian SSR, Viet Nam.
Meeting numbers. GA 40th session: 1st Committee 3-33, 39; plenary 117.

Recorded vote in Assembly as follows:

In favour: Afghanistan, Algeria, Angola, Antigua and Barbuda, Argentina, Australia, Bahrain, Bangladesh, Barbados, Benin, Bhutan, Bolivia, Botswana, Brunei Darussalam, Bulgaria, Burkina Faso, Burundi, Byelorussian SSR, Cameroon, Cape Verde, Central African Republic, Chad, China, Comoros, Congo, Cuba, Cyprus, Czechoslovakia, Democratic Yemen, Djibouti, Dominican Republic, Ecuador, Egypt, Equatorial Guinea, Ethiopia, Fiji, Gabon, Gambia, German Democratic Republic, Ghana, Guatemala, Guinea, Guinea-Bissau, Guyana, Haiti, Honduras, Hungary, India, Indonesia, Iran, Iraq, Ivory Coast, Jordan, Kenya, Kuwait, Lao People's Democratic Republic, Lebanon, Lesotho, Liberia, Libyan Arab Jamahiriya, Madagascar, Malawi, Malaysia, Maldives, Mali, Malta, Mauritania, Mauritius, Mexico, Mongolia, Morocco, Mozambique, Nepal, Nicaragua, Niger, Nigeria, Pakistan, Panama, Papua New Guinea, Peru, Philippines, Poland, Qatar, Romania, Rwanda, Saint Lucia, Saint Vincent and the Grenadines, Samoa, Sao Tome and Principe, Saudi Arabia, Senegal, Seychelles, Sierra Leone, Somalia, Sri Lanka, Sudan, Suriname, Swaziland, Syrian Arab Republic, Thailand, Togo, Trinidad and Tobago, Tunisia, Uganda, Ukrainian SSR, USSR, United Arab Emirates, United Republic of Tanzania, Vanuatu, Venezuela, Viet Nam, Yugoslavia, Zaire, Zambia.
Against: None.
Abstaining: Austria, Bahamas, Belgium, Brazil, Burma, Canada, Chile, Colombia, Costa Rica, Denmark, El Salvador, Finland, France, Germany, Federal Republic of, Greece, Grenada, Iceland, Ireland, Israel, Italy, Jamaica, Japan, Luxembourg, Netherlands, New Zealand, Norway, Paraguay, Portugal, Spain, Sweden, Turkey, United Kingdom, United States, Uruguay.

Japan found the text's overall tone to be more alarmist and emotional than others on the same subject. The United Kingdom found the concept in paragraph 5 repugnant, as it could not accept that anyone had the right to decide what was accurate and suppress what was judged false and tendentious.

In related action, the Assembly declared that the Campaign should give full consideration to the mass media's role as the most effective way to promote understanding, confidence and co-operation conducive to peace and disarmament; it asked the United Nations Department of Public Information to assist in furthering the objectives of the Campaign and Disarmament Week (**resolution 40/164 A**).

Financing

The Third United Nations Pledging Conference for the World Disarmament Campaign was held at United Nations Headquarters on 31 October, during the 1985 Disarmament Week, with 58 delegations participating.

Either during the Conference or in the course of the year, the following pledges were made: Australia ($A 50,000, of which $A 20,000 was earmarked for UNIDIR), Austria ($10,000), Canada ($Can 100,000, of which $50,000 was earmarked for production and more global distribution of *The United Nations Disarmament Yearbook*, $40,000 for UNIDIR research on verification, and $10,000 for the International Year of Peace (1986) Voluntary Trust Fund), China (60,000 yuan renminbi), Denmark (50,000 kroner), German Democratic Republic (100,000 marks), Greece ($10,000), Indonesia ($5,000), Kuwait ($5,000), Norway ($10,000) and Sweden (100,000 kronor). Cameroon (1,000,000 CFA francs), Senegal ($1,000) and Togo (25,000,000 CFA francs) announced that their pledges were earmarked for the United Nations Regional Centre for Peace and Disarmament in Africa (see below), for which a Trust Fund was established after the Third Pledging Conference.

GENERAL ASSEMBLY ACTION

On 16 December, the General Assembly, on the recommendation of the First Committee, adopted **resolution 40/151 B** by recorded vote.

World Disarmament Campaign

The General Assembly,

Recalling that in paragraph 15 of the Final Document of the Tenth Special Session of the General Assembly, the first special session devoted to disarmament, it declared that it was essential that not only Governments but also the peoples of the world recognize and understand the dangers in the present situation and stressed the importance of mobilizing world public opinion on behalf of disarmament,

Recalling also its resolutions 35/152 I of 12 December 1980, 36/92 C of 9 December 1981, 37/100 I of 13 December 1982, 38/73 D of 15 December 1983 and 39/63 D of 12 December 1984, as well as the reports of the Secretary-General of 17 September 1981, 11 June 1982, 3 November 1982, 30 August 1983 and 4 October 1985,

Having examined the report of the Secretary-General of 4 October 1985 on the implementation of the programme of activities of the World Disarmament Campaign by the United Nations system during 1985 and the activities contemplated for 1986, as well as its main financial aspects,

Having also examined the part of the report of the Secretary-General of 15 October 1985 dealing with the activities of the Advisory Board on Disarmament Studies relating to the implementation of the World Disarmament Campaign, as well as the Final Act of the 1985 United Nations Pledging Conference for the Campaign, held on 31 October 1985,

1. *Commends* the manner in which, as described in the above-mentioned reports, the World Disarmament Campaign has been geared by the Secretary-General in order to guarantee "the widest possible dissemina-

tion of information and unimpeded access for all sectors of the public to a broad range of information and opinions on questions of arms limitation and disarmament and the dangers relating to all aspects of the arms race and war, in particular nuclear war";

2. *Recalls* that, as was also agreed by consensus in the Concluding Document of the Twelfth Special Session of the General Assembly, the second special session devoted to disarmament, it is likewise an essential requisite for the universality of the World Disarmament Campaign that it receive "the co-operation and participation of all States";

3. *Endorses once more* the statement made by the Secretary-General on the occasion of the 1984 United Nations Pledging Conference for the World Disarmament Campaign to the effect that such co-operation implies that adequate funds be made available and that consequently the criterion of universality also applies to pledges, since a campaign without world-wide participation and funding will have difficulty in reflecting this principle in its implementation;

4. *Reiterates its regret* that most of the States that have the largest military expenditures have not so far made any financial contribution to the World Disarmament Campaign;

5. *Decides* that at its forty-first session there should be a fourth United Nations Pledging Conference for the World Disarmament Campaign, and expresses the hope that on that occasion all those Member States that have not yet announced any voluntary contribution will do so;

6. *Reiterates its recommendation* that the voluntary contributions made by Member States to the World Disarmament Campaign Voluntary Trust Fund should not be earmarked for specific activities inasmuch as it is most desirable that the Secretary-General enjoy full freedom to take the decisions he deems fit within the framework of the Campaign previously approved by the General Assembly and in exercise of the powers vested in him in connection with the Campaign;

7. *Notes with appreciation* that the Secretary-General has given permanent character to his instructions to the United Nations information centres and regional commissions to give wide publicity to the World Disarmament Campaign and, whenever necessary, to adapt, as far as possible, United Nations information materials to local languages;

8. *Requests* the Secretary-General to submit to the General Assembly at its forty-first session a report covering both the implementation of the programme of activities of the World Disarmament Campaign by the United Nations system during 1986 and the programme of activities contemplated by the system for 1987;

9. *Decides* to include in the provisional agenda of its forty-first session the item entitled "World Disarmament Campaign".

General Assembly resolution 40/151 B

16 December 1985   Meeting 117   139-0-11 (recorded vote)

Approved by First Committee (A/40/946) by recorded vote (125-0-11), 15 November (meeting 39); 10-nation draft (A/C.1/40/L.17); agenda item 61 *(a)*.
Sponsors: Bangladesh, Egypt, Indonesia, Mexico, Pakistan, Romania, Sri Lanka, Sweden, Togo, Yugoslavia.
Meeting numbers. GA 40th session: 1st Committee 3-32, 39; plenary 117.

Recorded vote in Assembly as follows:

In favour: Afghanistan, Algeria, Angola, Antigua and Barbuda, Argentina, Australia, Austria, Bahamas, Bahrain, Bangladesh, Barbados, Benin, Bhutan, Bolivia, Botswana, Brazil, Brunei Darussalam, Bulgaria, Burkina Faso, Burma,

Burundi, Byelorussian SSR, Cameroon, Canada, Cape Verde, Central African Republic, Chad, Chile, China, Colombia, Comoros, Congo, Costa Rica, Cuba, Cyprus, Czechoslovakia, Democratic Kampuchea, Democratic Yemen, Denmark, Djibouti, Dominican Republic, Ecuador, Egypt, El Salvador, Equatorial Guinea, Ethiopia, Fiji, Finland, Gabon, Gambia, German Democratic Republic, Ghana, Greece, Guatemala, Guinea, Guinea-Bissau, Guyana, Haiti, Honduras, Hungary, Iceland, India, Indonesia, Iran, Iraq, Ireland, Ivory Coast, Jamaica, Japan, Jordan, Kenya, Kuwait, Lao People's Democratic Republic, Lebanon, Lesotho, Liberia, Libyan Arab Jamahiriya, Madagascar, Malawi, Malaysia, Maldives, Mali, Malta, Mauritania, Mauritius, Mexico, Mongolia, Morocco, Mozambique, Nepal, New Zealand, Nicaragua, Niger, Nigeria, Norway, Oman, Pakistan, Panama, Papua New Guinea, Paraguay, Peru, Philippines, Poland, Portugal, Qatar, Romania, Rwanda, Saint Lucia, Saint Vincent and the Grenadines, Samoa, Sao Tome and Principe, Saudi Arabia, Senegal, Seychelles, Sierra Leone, Singapore, Somalia, Spain, Sri Lanka, Sudan, Suriname, Swaziland, Sweden, Syrian Arab Republic, Thailand, Togo, Trinidad and Tobago, Tunisia, Uganda, Ukrainian SSR, USSR, United Arab Emirates, United Republic of Tanzania, Uruguay, Vanuatu, Venezuela, Viet Nam, Yugoslavia, Zambia.

Against: None.

Abstaining: Belgium, France, Germany, Federal Republic of, Grenada, Israel, Italy, Luxembourg, Netherlands, Turkey, United Kingdom, United States.

The recorded vote in the First Committee was requested by the United States. In explanation of vote, Canada, while agreeing in principle with paragraph 6, felt that earmarking funds might be warranted where activities particularly interested Member States.

The Federal Republic of Germany said the text again failed to confirm the principles of universality and voluntariness which underlay the Campaign. France, pointing out that it had contributed $1 million to UNIDIR since its founding, considered it inappropriate to accuse certain States of lack of support. Similarly, the United Kingdom stated that part of its contribution—of over $200 million during the current financial year—to the United Nations regular budget would be used for the Campaign, and it had also devoted substantial sums to its own disarmament information activities.

Establishment of a regional centre in Africa

The Secretary-General reported to the General Assembly in November 1985[4] that, following the Assembly's 1984 request[5] that he assist Member States in establishing regional and institutional arrangements for implementing the Campaign, he had concluded consultations on a specific request received from OAU States members.

The OAU Assembly of Heads of State and Government (twenty-first ordinary session, Addis Ababa, Ethiopia, 18-20 July) and the OAU Ministerial Regional Conference on Security, Disarmament and Development in Africa (Lomé, 13-16 August) had requested the United Nations Secretary-General to create a regional centre in Africa for peace and disarmament in order to promote co-ordination and harmonization of the research, study, documentation and information activities of the region on peace, security, disarmament and development, in co-operation with related United Nations institutions. In so doing, OAU had welcomed Togo's offer to host the proposed centre and to provide, at no cost, office space for it.

The Secretary-General proposed that the centre be established initially under the Department for Disarmament Affairs, within the framework of the World Disarmament Campaign. He pointed out that, because existing resources were limited, voluntary contributions were needed for staff and basic operating and administrative costs.

GENERAL ASSEMBLY ACTION

On the recommendation of the First Committee, the Assembly, on 16 December, adopted **resolution 40/151 G** without vote, thus establishing the United Nations Regional Centre for Peace and Disarmament in Africa as of 1 January 1986.

United Nations Regional Centre for Peace and Disarmament in Africa

The General Assembly,

Recalling its resolution 39/63 J of 12 December 1984 in which it requested the Secretary-General to provide assistance to such Member States in the regions concerned as may request it with a view to establishing regional and institutional arrangements for the implementation of the World Disarmament Campaign, on the basis of existing resources and of voluntary contributions that Member States may make to that end,

Bearing in mind resolution AHG/Res.138(XXI) adopted by the Assembly of Heads of State and Government of the Organization of African Unity at its twenty-first ordinary session, held at Addis Ababa from 18 to 20 July 1985, in which the African leaders requested the Secretary-General of the United Nations to take the necessary measures to establish a regional office in Africa to promote the objectives of peace, disarmament and development in the region,

Reaffirming its resolutions 37/100 F of 13 December 1982, 38/73 J of 15 December 1983 and 39/63 F of 12 December 1984 on regional disarmament,

Taking into account the Lomé Declaration and Programme of Action adopted at the Ministerial Regional Conference on Security, Disarmament and Development in Africa, held at Lomé from 13 to 16 August 1985 under the auspices of the Organization of African Unity,

Taking into account the report of the Secretary-General entitled "United Nations regional centre for peace and disarmament in Africa",

1. *Decides* to establish as at 1 January 1986, within the framework of the Secretariat, the United Nations Regional Centre for Peace and Disarmament in Africa on the basis of existing resources and of voluntary contributions that Member States may make to that end;

2. *Decides further* that the Centre shall provide, upon request, substantive support for initiatives and other efforts of Member States of the African region towards the realization of measures of peace, arms limitation and disarmament in the region, in co-operation with the Organization of African Unity, as well as co-ordinate the implementation of regional activities in Africa under the World Disarmament Campaign;

3. *Requests* the Secretary-General to take the necessary administrative measures to ensure the establishment and functioning of the Centre;

4. *Invites* Member States to make voluntary contributions to the Centre;

5. *Requests* the Secretary-General to report to the General Assembly at its forty-first session on the implementation of the present resolution.

General Assembly resolution 40/151 G

16 December 1985   Meeting 117   Adopted without vote

Approved by First Committee (A/40/946) without vote, 15 November (meeting 39); draft by Mauritius, for African Group (A/C.1/40/L.39); agenda item 61.
Meeting numbers. GA 40th session: 1st Committee 3-32, 35, 39; plenary 117.

The Federal Republic of Germany, Japan, the United Kingdom and the United States, while welcoming the goals of the Centre, expressed reservations about its funding, stating their understanding that it would be financed from existing resources and voluntary contributions and not place burdens on the United Nations regular budget. Should that not be the case, the Federal Republic of Germany and the United Kingdom reserved the right to re-examine their positions; they both regarded the Centre's creation as a singular event that would not result in a world network of disarmament centres. The United States said that if in later years requests were made for funds from the regular budget, it would not expect to be able to support them.

Disarmament Week

Disarmament Week—observed annually since it was proclaimed by the General Assembly in 1978[6] to start on United Nations Day, 24 October—was observed at United Nations Headquarters on 31 October 1985 at a special meeting of the Assembly's First Committee, where statements were made by the Assembly President, the Secretary-General and representatives of regional groups. It was also observed at the United Nations Office at Geneva in the context of the fortieth anniversary of the Organization.

In his message, the President called for renewed efforts to prevent the proliferation of nuclear weapons, urged support for regional efforts to reduce conventional weapons, and stressed the primary responsibility and central role of the United Nations in disarmament.

The Secretary-General stated that disarmament endeavours and a search for better international relations—based on common interest rather than on fear and arms competition—must be sustained with a force and conviction that neither partial successes nor temporary set-backs could diminish.

In September, the Secretary-General submitted a report to the Assembly[7] containing information supplied by 14 Governments, the United Nations system and international non-governmental organizations on their activities to promote the objectives of Disarmament Week.

GENERAL ASSEMBLY ACTION

On 16 December, on the recommendation of the First Committee, the General Assembly adopted **resolution 40/152 E** by recorded vote.

Disarmament Week

The General Assembly,

Gravely concerned over the escalating arms race, especially the nuclear-arms race, which represents a serious threat to the very existence of mankind,

Stressing the vital importance of eliminating the threat of a nuclear war, ending the nuclear-arms race and bringing about disarmament for the maintenance of world peace,

Emphasizing anew the urgent need for and the importance of wide and continued mobilization of world public opinion in support of halting and reversing the arms race, especially the nuclear-arms race, in all its aspects,

Mindful of the world-wide mass anti-war and anti-nuclear movement,

Recognizing the important role of the mass media in mobilizing world public opinion in support of disarmament,

Noting with satisfaction the broad and active support by Governments and international and national organizations of the decision taken by the General Assembly at its tenth special session, the first special session devoted to disarmament, regarding the proclamation of the week starting 24 October, the day of the foundation of the United Nations, as a week devoted to fostering the objectives of disarmament,

Recalling the recommendations concerning the World Disarmament Campaign contained in annex V to the Concluding Document of the Twelfth Special Session of the General Assembly, the second special session devoted to disarmament, in particular the recommendation that Disarmament Week should continue to be widely observed,

Recalling also its resolutions 33/71 D of 14 December 1978, 34/83 I of 11 December 1979, 37/78 D of 9 December 1982, 38/183 L of 20 December 1983 and 39/148 J of 17 December 1984,

1. *Takes note with satisfaction* of the report of the Secretary-General on the follow-up measures undertaken by governmental and non-governmental organizations in holding Disarmament Week;

2. *Expresses its appreciation* to all States and international and national governmental and non-governmental organizations for their energetic support of and active participation in Disarmament Week, in particular in holding the 1985 Disarmament Week in close connection with the celebrations of the fortieth anniversary of the end of the Second World War and of the foundation of the United Nations and the International Youth Year;

3. *Expresses serious concern* over the continued escalation of the arms race, especially the nuclear-arms race, and the imminent danger of its extension into outer space, which gravely jeopardizes international peace and security and increases the danger of outbreak of a nuclear war;

4. *Stresses* the important role of the mass media in acquainting the world public with the aims of Disarmament Week and measures undertaken within its framework;

5. *Recommends* to all States that they observe Disarmament Week in 1986 in close connection with the celebration of the International Year of Peace;

6. *Invites* all States, in carrying out appropriate measures at the local level on the occasion of Disarmament Week, to take into account the elements of the model programme for Disarmament Week, prepared by the Secretary-General;

7. *Invites* the relevant specialized agencies and the International Atomic Energy Agency to intensify activities, within their areas of competence, to disseminate information on the consequences of the arms race, especially the nuclear-arms race, and requests them to inform the Secretary-General accordingly;

8. *Also invites* international non-governmental organizations to take an active part in Disarmament Week and to inform the Secretary-General of the activities undertaken;

9. *Further invites* the Secretary-General to use the United Nations mass media as widely as possible to promote better understanding among the world public of disarmament problems and the objectives of Disarmament Week;

10. *Requests* Governments to continue, in accordance with General Assembly resolution 33/71 D, to inform the Secretary-General of activities undertaken to promote the objectives of Disarmament Week;

11. *Requests* the Secretary-General, in accordance with paragraph 4 of resolution 33/71 D, to submit to the General Assembly at its forty-first session a report on the implementation of the provisions of the present resolution.

General Assembly resolution 40/152 E

16 December 1985   Meeting 117   129-0-22 (recorded vote)

Approved by First Committee (A/40/877/Add.1) by recorded vote (110-0-22), 15 November (meeting 39); 12-nation draft (A/C.1/40/L.20); agenda item 65 *(l)*.

Sponsors: Afghanistan, Angola, Bulgaria, Byelorussian SSR, Cuba, Czechoslovakia, German Democratic Republic, Lao People's Democratic Republic, Mongolia, Mozambique, Ukrainian SSR, Viet Nam.

Meeting numbers. GA 40th session: 1st Committee 3-32, 34, 39; plenary 117.

Recorded vote in Assembly as follows:

In favour: Afghanistan, Algeria, Angola, Antigua and Barbuda, Argentina, Austria, Bahamas, Bahrain, Bangladesh, Barbados, Benin, Bhutan, Bolivia, Botswana, Brazil, Brunei Darussalam, Bulgaria, Burkina Faso, Burma, Burundi, Byelorussian SSR, Cameroon, Cape Verde, Central African Republic, Chad, Chile, China, Colombia, Comoros, Congo, Costa Rica, Cuba, Cyprus, Czechoslovakia, Democratic Kampuchea, Democratic Yemen, Djibouti, Dominican Republic, Ecuador, Egypt, El Salvador, Equatorial Guinea, Ethiopia, Fiji, Finland, Gabon, Gambia, German Democratic Republic, Ghana, Guatemala, Guinea, Guinea-Bissau, Guyana, Haiti, Honduras, Hungary, India, Indonesia, Iran, Iraq, Ivory Coast, Jamaica, Japan, Jordan, Kenya, Kuwait, Lao People's Democratic Republic, Lebanon, Lesotho, Liberia, Libyan Arab Jamahiriya, Madagascar, Malawi, Malaysia, Maldives, Mali, Malta, Mauritania, Mauritius, Mexico, Mongolia, Morocco, Mozambique, Nepal, Nicaragua, Niger, Nigeria, Pakistan, Panama, Papua New Guinea, Peru, Philippines, Poland, Qatar, Romania, Rwanda, Saint Lucia, Saint Vincent and the Grenadines, Samoa, Sao Tome and Principe, Saudi Arabia, Senegal, Seychelles, Sierra Leone, Somalia, Sri Lanka, Sudan, Suriname, Swaziland, Sweden, Syrian Arab Republic, Thailand, Togo, Trinidad and Tobago, Tunisia, Uganda, Ukrainian SSR, USSR, United Arab Emirates, United Republic of Tanzania, Uruguay, Vanuatu, Venezuela, Viet Nam, Yemen, Yugoslavia, Zaire, Zambia, Zimbabwe.

Against: None.

Abstaining: Australia, Belgium, Canada, Denmark, France, Germany, Federal Republic of, Greece, Grenada, Iceland, Ireland, Israel, Italy, Luxembourg, Netherlands, New Zealand, Norway, Paraguay, Portugal, Spain, Turkey, United Kingdom, United States.

Australia, France and the Federal Republic of Germany objected to paragraph 7, stating that the United Nations should not invite the specialized agencies to conduct activities outside their competence. Australia added that the role of mass media was to transmit, without restriction, views on disarmament issues to ensure that individuals and groups had the freest possible access to a wide range of opinions and factual material.

Japan, which had expressed concern on the 1984 text for its alarmist overtones, said if the negative trend continued it would be forced to change its vote in the future.

UN fellowship programme

The Secretary-General reported to the General Assembly in October[8] that the 1985 United Nations programme of fellowships on disarmament had started at Geneva during the June-August session of the Conference on Disarmament and was scheduled to end in New York by 30 November after the First Committee concluded consideration of its disarmament items. Twenty-five fellows from as many countries participated in the programme, which consisted of lectures, seminars, research, observing the Conference and the First Committee, and a visit to IAEA at Vienna. The fellows also visited Bulgaria, the Federal Republic of Germany, Japan, Sweden and the United States, at the invitation of those Governments.

Since its establishment by the Assembly in 1978 at the first special session on disarmament,[6] the programme had trained 155 public officials from 88 countries in developing expertise relating to disarmament.

The Secretary-General also reported that, in pursuance of a 1984 Assembly resolution,[9] he had established a Steering Board, chaired by the Co-ordinator of the disarmament fellowship programme and composed of senior officers of the Department for Disarmament Affairs, to evaluate the fellows' research papers; outstanding papers were to appear in a new series of annual publications. In further response to the 1984 Assembly invitation for proposals regarding training, the Secretary-General suggested that courses might be offered at the regional or subregional level to benefit government officials.

GENERAL ASSEMBLY ACTION

On the recommendation of the First Committee, the General Assembly, on 16 December, adopted **resolution 40/151 H** by recorded vote.

United Nations programme of fellowships on disarmament

The General Assembly,

Recalling its decision, contained in paragraph 108 of the Final Document of the Tenth Special Session of the General Assembly, the first special session devoted to disarmament, to establish a programme of fellowships on disarmament, as well as its decisions contained in annex IV to the Concluding Document of the Twelfth Special Session of the General Assembly, the second special session devoted to disarmament, in which it decided, *inter alia*, to continue the programme and to increase the number of fellowships from twenty to twenty-five as from 1983,

Recalling also its resolution 39/63 B of 12 December 1984,

Noting with satisfaction that the programme has already trained one hundred and fifty-five public officials from eighty-eight countries, most of whom are now in positions of responsibility in the field of disarmament within their Governments or permanent missions to the United Nations, or representing their Governments at international disarmament meetings,

Recognizing that the programme of studies and activities as outlined in the report of the Secretary-General on the United Nations programme of fellowships on disarmament has continued to expand and intensify,

Taking account of the fact that in recent years developing countries have shown increased interest in disarmament items, which has been reflected in the initiatives taken by them,

Considering that the forms of assistance available to Member States, particularly developing countries, under the United Nations programme of fellowships on disarmament can be further expanded by way of advisory services and training programmes arranged for participants in various countries on request, in view of the increasing and specific needs of Member States,

1. *Takes note with satisfaction* of the report of the Secretary-General and the view that the expansion of the programme of fellowships has brought with it higher responsibilities, including planning, implementation, co-ordination, servicing, follow-up work and supervision of all activities relating to the programme;

2. *Further takes note* of the view of the Secretary-General on the possibilities for additional services;

3. *Decides* to expand the forms of assistance available to Member States under the United Nations programme of fellowships on disarmament to include training programmes and advisory services in the field of disarmament and security, all the programmes to be consolidated under the Department for Disarmament Affairs of the Secretariat, at the appropriate level, bearing in mind the savings that can be made within the existing overall budgetary appropriations for the programme of fellowships; such advisory services should include the organization of training courses at the regional or subregional level, in co-operation with the Governments and/or intergovernmental organizations concerned for the benefit of government officials whose duties involve the implementation of arms limitation and disarmament measures, as well as the promotion of disarmament efforts;

4. *Further decides* that the Secretary-General should make provision for advisory services in the field of disarmament on the basis of requests received from Governments and/or governmental organizations in accordance with the following policies:

(a) The kind of service to be rendered to Governments and/or governmental organizations shall be determined by the Governments and/or organizations concerned in consultation with the Secretary-General;

(b) The amount of service and the conditions under which it is to be rendered shall be decided by the Secretary-General, with due regard to the needs of States, in particular the developing countries, and in conformity with the principle that the requesting Governments and/or governmental organizations shall be expected to assume responsibility for a considerable part of the expenses connected with the services rendered, either by making a contribution in cash, or by providing supporting staff services and defraying the local costs of carrying out the programme;

(c) The service shall be applicable to any subject in the field of disarmament;

5. *Expresses its appreciation* to the Governments of Bulgaria, the Federal Republic of Germany, Japan, Sweden and the United States of America for inviting fellows to their countries in 1985 to study selected activities in the field of disarmament, thereby contributing to the fulfilment of the overall objectives of the programme;

6. *Requests* the Secretary-General to report to the General Assembly at its forty-first session on the operations of the programme of fellowships and on the implementation of the provisions of the present resolution and to develop modalities for implementation of the training programmes and advisory services.

General Assembly resolution 40/151 H

16 December 1985   Meeting 117   148-1-1 (recorded vote)

Approved by First Committee (A/40/946) by recorded vote (127-1), 20 November (meeting 44); 24-nation draft (A/C.1/40/L.54/Rev.1); agenda item 61 *(b)*.

Sponsors: Bahamas, Bangladesh, Bolivia, Dominican Republic, Ecuador, Greece, Indonesia, Kenya, Mali, Mauritania, Mauritius, Morocco, Mozambique, Nigeria, Senegal, Somalia, Sudan, Swaziland, Tunisia, Uganda, Venezuela, Zaire, Zambia, Zimbabwe.

Financial implications. ACABQ, A/40/7/Add.15; 5th Committee, A/40/1019; S-G, A/C.1/40/L.79, A/C.5/40/62.

Meeting numbers. GA 40th session: 1st Committee 3-32, 34, 44; 5th Committee 56; plenary 117.

Recorded vote in Assembly as follows:

In favour: Afghanistan, Algeria, Angola, Antigua and Barbuda, Argentina, Australia, Austria, Bahamas, Bahrain, Bangladesh, Barbados, Belgium, Benin, Bhutan, Bolivia, Botswana, Brazil, Brunei Darussalam, Bulgaria, Burkina Faso, Burma, Burundi, Byelorussian SSR, Cameroon, Canada, Cape Verde, Central African Republic, Chad, Chile, China, Colombia, Comoros, Congo, Costa Rica, Cuba, Cyprus, Czechoslovakia, Democratic Kampuchea, Democratic Yemen, Denmark, Djibouti, Dominican Republic, Ecuador, Egypt, El Salvador, Equatorial Guinea, Ethiopia, Fiji, Finland, France, Gabon, Gambia, German Democratic Republic, Germany, Federal Republic of, Greece, Guatemala, Guinea, Guinea-Bissau, Guyana, Haiti, Honduras, Hungary, Iceland, India, Indonesia, Iran, Iraq, Ireland, Israel, Italy, Ivory Coast, Jamaica, Japan, Jordan, Kenya, Kuwait, Lao People's Democratic Republic, Lebanon, Lesotho, Liberia, Libyan Arab Jamahiriya, Luxembourg, Madagascar, Malawi, Malaysia, Maldives, Mali, Malta, Mauritania, Mauritius, Mexico, Mongolia, Morocco, Mozambique, Nepal, Netherlands, New Zealand, Nicaragua, Niger, Nigeria, Norway, Oman, Pakistan, Panama, Papua New Guinea, Paraguay, Peru, Philippines, Poland, Portugal, Qatar, Romania, Rwanda, Saint Lucia, Saint Vincent and the Grenadines, Samoa, Sao Tome and Principe, Saudi Arabia, Senegal, Seychelles, Sierra Leone, Singapore, Somalia, Spain, Sri Lanka, Sudan, Suriname, Swaziland, Sweden, Syrian Arab Republic, Thailand, Togo, Trinidad and Tobago, Tunisia, Turkey, Uganda, Ukrainian SSR, USSR, United Arab Emirates, United Kingdom, United Republic of Tanzania, Uruguay, Vanuatu, Venezuela, Viet Nam, Yugoslavia, Zaire, Zambia.

Against: United States.

Abstaining: Grenada.

Explaining its vote, the United States said that, despite its support for the programme, it opposed increased spending; it wished that consultations had taken place earlier, in order to enable it to join in a consensus.

The USSR said its vote should not be interpreted as approving the proposed additional appropriations of $63,700 for 1986-1987. Japan and the United Kingdom said their votes were without prejudice to the report which the Secretary-General was being asked to prepare on the matter. Japan added that the proposals for expanding the programme had not been sufficiently discussed beforehand, and the United Kingdom felt that the resources required for preparing the report should be found within the

initially proposed appropriations. France interpreted paragraph 3 to mean that the programme would be administered within the existing structures, without creating new posts.

Disarmament research

Disarmament studies

In 1985, the General Assembly initiated two new studies—one on climatic and potential physical effects of nuclear war, including nuclear winter (see p. 39), and the other on the economic and social consequences of the arms race and of military expenditures (see p. 88). Work began, as requested by the Assembly based on the 1984 recommendation of the Advisory Board on Disarmament Studies,[10] on a study on deterrence and its implications for disarmament and the arms race, negotiated arms reductions and international security and other related matters (see p. 29).

Chairmen of the expert groups entrusted with studies—one on the military use of research and development (see p. 86) and the other on nuclear-weapon-free zones (see p. 58)—reported to the Secretary-General that the groups had concluded their work without reaching agreement on their final reports.

In the course of the year, three studies—on the concepts of security (see p. 28), on the naval arms race (see p. 30) and on the reduction of military budgets (see p. 84)—were concluded, as was a compilation, by the Secretary-General, of national and international scientific studies on the climatic effects of nuclear war, including nuclear winter (see p. 39).

GENERAL ASSEMBLY ACTION

On 16 December, the General Assembly, on the recommendation of the First Committee, adopted **resolution 40/152 K** without vote.

United Nations disarmament studies

The General Assembly,

Recalling that, in paragraph 96 of the Final Document of the Tenth Special Session of the General Assembly, the Assembly stated that:

"Taking further steps in the field of disarmament and other measures aimed at promoting international peace and security would be facilitated by carrying out studies by the Secretary-General in this field with appropriate assistance from governmental or consultant experts.",

Recalling also the relevant parts of the United Nations study on the institutional arrangements relating to the process of disarmament,

Aware that a number of United Nations studies have been concluded satisfactorily in the field of disarmament, and that the reports on them presented to the General Assembly have contributed significantly to the clarification of certain issues,

Noting that, even where diverse views have been reflected, the final reports elaborated by United Nations expert groups so far have stimulated wider-ranging discussions on a variety of issues,

Noting the recent non-completion of final reports on two studies, despite renewal of the mandate in both cases by the General Assembly,

Noting the discussions that have taken place in the Advisory Board on Disarmament Studies,

Believing that a thorough appraisal of the subject, including the methods of work to be adopted by United Nations expert groups, could enhance the value and relevance of United Nations studies in the field of disarmament,

1. *Reaffirms* the value of United Nations studies, prepared with appropriate assistance from governmental or consultant experts, as a useful means by which important issues in the field of arms limitation and disarmament can be addressed in a comprehensive and detailed manner;

2. *Invites* Member States to communicate to the Secretary-General, by 1 April 1986, their views and proposals on how the work of the United Nations in the field of disarmament studies can be further improved;

3. *Requests* the Secretary-General to transmit the replies of Member States to the General Assembly at its forty-first session and to the Advisory Board on Disarmament Studies;

4. *Also requests* the Secretary-General to invite the Advisory Board on Disarmament Studies to prepare a comprehensive report on these matters for submission to the General Assembly at its forty-second session;

5. *Decides* to include in the provisional agenda of its forty-first session an item entitled "United Nations disarmament studies".

General Assembly resolution 40/152 K

16 December 1985   Meeting 117   Adopted without vote

Approved by First Committee (A/40/877/Add.1) without vote, 19 November (meeting 42); 2-nation draft (A/C.1/40/L.52/Rev.1); agenda item 65 *(d)*.
Sponsors: France, United Kingdom.
Meeting numbers. GA 40th session: 1st Committee 3-32, 34, 42; plenary 117.

In explanation of position, Bulgaria said the preparation of studies should not become an end in itself or divert attention from practical measures. Sweden said that given the great variety of subjects in United Nations disarmament studies, it was difficult to see general guidelines serving any meaningful purpose; it understood that the text was not intended to limit Governments in taking new initiatives on such studies.

Advisory Board on Disarmament Studies

The 24-member Advisory Board on Disarmament Studies—established in 1978[11] to advise the Secretary-General on various aspects of United Nations studies on disarmament and arms limitation—held its twelfth session from 6 to 10 May in New York and its thirteenth from 23 to 27 September at Geneva.[12]

The Board discussed the United Nations studies on disarmament, implementation of the World Disarmament Campaign and the current disarma-

ment situation, focusing on nuclear winter (see p. 39). Following examination of a Secretariat paper on experience gained from the completion of 22 disarmament studies since 1979, the Board reaffirmed that, while it could not censor study proposals by Member States, it should be in a position to examine them before submission to the Assembly and to advise on matters such as possible directions or scope, priorities and approaches, if so requested by the initiators of proposals.

In its capacity as the Board of Trustees of UNIDIR (see also below), the Advisory Board also examined UNIDIR's budget estimates and proposed 1986 work programme. In so doing, the Board noted that the comments and recommendations of the Advisory Committee on Administrative and Budgetary Questions, which it was required to take into account in considering budgetary matters, would not be available before the commencement of the regular 1986 Assembly session. Under the circumstances, the Board was obliged to seek Assembly authorization to reschedule and hold the second of its biannual sessions at Headquarters at a time when subsidiary bodies were not normally allowed to meet.

GENERAL ASSEMBLY ACTION

On 16 December, the General Assembly adopted **decision 40/428** without vote.

Advisory Board on Disarmament Studies

At its 117th plenary meeting, on 16 December 1985, the General Assembly, on the recommendation of the First Committee:

(a) Decided that, in order to give timely consideration to the recommendations of the Advisory Committee on Administrative and Budgetary Questions regarding the proposed annual budget of the United Nations Institute for Disarmament Research, the Advisory Board on Disarmament Studies should be authorized to hold its second session of 1986 during the early weeks of the forty-first session of the Assembly, in the light of the request of the Advisory Board contained in paragraph 38 of the report of the Secretary-General;

(b) Requested the Committee on Conferences at its 1986 substantive session to consider the pattern of future meetings of the Advisory Board on Disarmament Studies.

General Assembly decision 40/428

Adopted without vote

Approved by First Committee (A/40/877/Add.1) without vote, 14 November (meeting 37); 9-nation draft (A/C.1/40/L.28); agenda item 65 *(d)*.
Sponsors: Cameroon, Cuba, Ecuador, Egypt, Mexico, Nigeria, Sri Lanka, Sweden, Yugoslavia.
Financial implications. ACABQ, A/40/7/Add.9; S-G, A/C.5/40/33.
Meeting numbers. GA 40th session: 1st Committee 3-32, 37; 5th Committee 49; plenary 117.

UN Institute for Disarmament Research

The Director of UNIDIR, in his report approved by the Advisory Board and transmitted to the Assembly by the Secretary-General in October,[13] stated that the Assembly's adoption in 1984[14] of the UNIDIR statute had created better conditions for the further development of the Institute, but that the growing complexity of tasks before it required further strengthening of its scientific capacity and resources.

In the period covered by the report (September 1984–August 1985), the Institute carried out a number of disarmament activities. Among its publications was a reference book aimed as a guide to basic disarmament information sources[15] for non-experts. It also completed a study on Israeli nuclear armament, in response to a 1984 Assembly request[16] (see p. 64). Among ongoing studies or projects were those concerning disarmament and outer space (see also p. 79), international law of disarmament, international nuclear commerce and the NPT régime, verification, subjective factors in disarmament, arms transfer dependence, security of States and lowering of the levels of armament, and security and prospects for disarmament in Europe.

Parties and signatories to disarmament agreements

In August 1985, the Secretary-General submitted to the General Assembly his annual report on the status of multilateral disarmament agreements,[17] based on information received from the States depositories of those agreements. Listing the parties to and signatories of agreements as at 31 July 1985, the report also contained similar information on the Convention on the Prohibition of Military or Any Other Hostile Use of Environmental Modification Techniques, the Agreement Governing the Activities of States on the Moon and Other Celestial Bodies, and the Convention on Prohibitions or Restrictions on the Use of Certain Conventional Weapons Which May Be Deemed to Be Excessively Injurious or to Have Indiscriminate Effects (see p. 78), of which the Secretary-General was the depositary.

As at 31 December 1985, the following numbers of States had become parties to the multilateral agreements covered in the Secretary-General's report (listed in chronological order, with the years in which they were initially signed or opened for signature).[18]

(Geneva) Protocol for the Prohibition of the Use in War of Asphyxiating, Poisonous or Other Gases, and of Bacteriological Methods of Warfare (1925): 107 parties

The Antarctic Treaty (1959): 32 parties

Treaty Banning Nuclear Weapon Tests in the Atmosphere, in Outer Space and under Water (1963): 114 parties

Treaty on Principles Governing the Activities of States in the Exploration and Use of Outer Space, including the Moon and Other Celestial Bodies (1967):[19] 84 parties

Treaty for the Prohibition of Nuclear Weapons in Latin America (1967): 31 parties

Treaty on the Non-Proliferation of Nuclear Weapons (1968):[20] 132 parties

Treaty on the Prohibition of the Emplacement of Nuclear Weapons and Other Weapons of Mass Destruction on the Sea-Bed and the Ocean Floor and in the Subsoil Thereof (1971):[21] 75 parties

Convention on the Prohibition of the Development, Production and Stockpiling of Bacteriological (Biological) and Toxin Weapons and on Their Destruction (1972):[22] 102 parties (see also p. 70)

Convention on the Prohibition of Military or Any Other Hostile Use of Environmental Modification Techniques (1977):[23] 48 parties

Agreement Governing the Activities of States on the Moon and Other Celestial Bodies (1979):[24] 5 parties

Convention on Prohibitions or Restrictions on the Use of Certain Conventional Weapons Which May Be Deemed to Be Excessively Injurious or to Have Indiscriminate Effects (1981): 25 parties

REFERENCES

[1]YUN 1982, p. 31. [2]A/40/443. [3]YUN 1984, p. 89, GA res. 39/63 D, 12 Dec. 1984. [4]A/40/443/Add.1. [5]YUN 1984, p. 88, GA res. 39/63 J, 12 Dec. 1984. [6]YUN 1978, p. 39, GA res. S-10/2, 30 June 1978. [7]A/40/552 & Corr.1. [8]A/40/816. [9]YUN 1984, p. 96, GA res. 39/63 B, 12 Dec. 1984. [10]*Ibid.*, p. 92, GA dec. 39/423, 17 Dec. 1984. [11]YUN 1978, p. 109. [12]A/40/744. [13]A/40/725. [14]YUN 1984, p. 93, GA res. 39/148 H, 17 Dec. 1984. [15]*Disarmament—A Short Guide to United Nations and Other Sources of Information*, Sales No. GV.E.84.O.6. [16]YUN 1984, p. 44, GA res. 39/147, 17 Dec. 1984. [17]A/40/551. [18]*The United Nations Disarmament Yearbook*, vol. 10, *1985*, Sales No. E.86.IX.7. [19]YUN 1966, p. 41, GA res. 2222(XXI), annex, 19 Dec. 1966. [20]YUN 1968, p. 17, GA res. 2373(XXII), annex, 12 June 1968. [21]YUN 1970, p. 18, GA res. 2660(XXV), annex, 7 Dec. 1970. [22]YUN 1971, p. 19, GA res. 2826(XXVI), annex, 16 Dec. 1971. [23]YUN 1976, p. 45, GA res. 31/72, annex, 10 Dec. 1976. [24]YUN 1979, p. 111, GA res. 34/68, annex, 5 Dec. 1979.

Chapter II

Peaceful uses of outer space

Issues concerning international co-operation in the peaceful uses of outer space continued to be discussed in 1985 by the Committee on the Peaceful Uses of Outer Space (Committee on outer space), by its two sub-committees—the Scientific and Technical Sub-Committee and the Legal Sub-Committee—and by the General Assembly.

The Committee on outer space held its twenty-eighth session in New York from 17 to 28 June 1985. Its recommendations were endorsed in December by the Assembly (resolution 40/162), which also urged States to prevent an arms race in outer space, and invited those not parties to international treaties governing the use of outer space to ratify them.

Topics related to this chapter. Disarmament: arms race in outer space. Other administrative and management questions: communications satellite. International Telecommunication Union.

Science, technology and law

Space science and technology

The Scientific and Technical Sub-Committee of the Committee on outer space held its twenty-second session in New York from 11 to 22 February 1985.[1] It recommended approval of the 1986 United Nations Programme on Space Applications, reviewed the co-ordination of space activities in the United Nations system, and noted the urgency of implementing the recommendations of the Second (1982) United Nations Conference on the Exploration and Peaceful Uses of Outer Space (UNISPACE-82),[2] as emphasized in 1984 by the General Assembly.[3] It again considered the use of nuclear power sources in outer space and related safety requirements, examined technical aspects of the geostationary orbit, and reviewed progress in remote sensing of the Earth by satellites and space transportation systems.

The Sub-Committee's recommendations were acted upon by the Committee on outer space in June.[4] The Committee also decided to grant, at their request, permanent observer status to the International Telecommunications Satellite Organization (INTELSAT) and to the International System and Organization of Space Communications (INTERSPUTNIK).

UN Programme on Space Applications

As part of the United Nations Programme on Space Applications, in 1985 training courses, seminars and workshops were given, fellowships were awarded and technical advisory missions were carried out.[5]

Two international training courses were conducted. The tenth United Nations/Food and Agriculture Organization of the United Nations (FAO) international training course (Rome, Italy, and Feldafing, Federal Republic of Germany, 6-31 May) examined the application of remote sensing to monitoring of forest land. Held in co-operation with the host Governments, it was attended by 20 senior technical personnel from 18 countries in Africa, Asia and Latin America. The course focused on aerial and satellite sensor systems, forest monitoring, detection of changes in forest conditions, forest management, data bases and geographic information systems.

The second international training course on remote-sensing applications to operational agrometeorology and hydrology (Nairobi, Kenya, 16 April–2 May) was attended by 25 senior technical personnel from 19 countries in Africa and Western Asia. Jointly organized by the United Nations, the World Meteorological Organization, the European Space Agency (ESA) and FAO and co-sponsored by Sweden, the course included presentations on the fundamentals of remote sensing using aerial and space platforms, the use of various sensors, and the methodologies of image interpretation.

An international seminar on satellite communications, co-sponsored by the USSR (Moscow, 20-31 May), was attended by 24 senior technical personnel from 20 countries. Presentations focused on the development of satellite communication systems in the USSR, satellite television distribution systems and other satellite communications topics.

Three workshops were held in co-operation with the respective Governments. A workshop in Bulgaria (Sofia, 29 April–10 May) dealt with remote-sensing instrumentation, data acquisition and analysis, and was attended by 23 senior technical personnel from 18 countries. In China (Beijing, 21-29 October), a workshop on advances in space science and technology and its applications was attended by 57 high-level scientists and technicians from 16 countries and four international organizations. A workshop in India (Ahmedabad, 4-8 November) on space science and technology and its applications in educational systems was attended by 48 high-level national planners of space-related activities, education administrators and educators from technical institutions and universities; they were from 11 countries and three international organizations.

To promote co-operation in space science and technology among developed and developing countries, the Programme co-sponsored with ESA and the Pan-African Telecommunication Union two symposia for decision-makers on space telecommunications in Africa (Lomé, Togo, 18-22 March; Harare, Zimbabwe, 14-18 October).

A technical advisory service mission, dealing with space-applications-related activities, was carried out in Malaysia, Pakistan and the Syrian Arab Republic, in response to their requests. Assistance was also provided to the development of a remote-sensing programme at the University of Ife, Ile-Ife, Nigeria; a three-day workshop and a three-week national training course were held.

Two one-year fellowships in microwave technology were offered by Austria at the Technical University of Graz. Ten fellowships, each for six years, were offered by the USSR for studies in geodesy, cartography, aerial photography and aerial photogeodesy at the Moscow Engineering Institute for Geodesy, Cartography and Air Photography. Three one-year fellowships were offered by ESA at the European Space Research and Technology Centre, Noordwijk, Netherlands; the European Space Research Institute, Frascati, Italy; and the European Space Operations Centre, Darmstadt, Federal Republic of Germany. Ten long-range fellowships in remote-sensing technology were offered by Brazil at the Instituto de Pesquisas Espaciais, São José dos Campos, São Paulo.

Based on responses received from Member States and their agencies, a directory of education, training, research and fellowship opportunities in space science and technology was published, and was to be updated every three years.

An evaluation of the effectiveness of the 1983 Programme was carried out in 1985, based on 65 replies to a questionnaire sent in June to 169 individuals who had taken part in 1983 seminars and training courses. The replies indicated that a high percentage of the respondents had continued to work in aspects of remote sensing, meteorology and communications. The majority's subsequent activities in research and development and in the initiation of regional and international co-operation indicated that they had gained through the seminars a measure of relevant knowledge.

In his report on implementing the recommendations of UNISPACE-82 (see p. 103), the Secretary-General[6] listed activities (training courses, workshops, seminars, fellowships, meetings of experts, advisory missions) carried out in 1984 and 1985 under the Programme.

Responding to questions by the Scientific and Technical Sub-Committee, the Expert on Space Applications pointed out in April[7] that the Programme's long-range activities focused on space science disciplines that met developing countries' specific requests. Technical advisory services were undertaken based on various criteria, such as the possibility for funding or the promotion of regional co-operation. The costs of Programme activities amounted to allocations of $202,800 from the 1984-1985 regular budget. A budget proposal of $207,700 had been submitted for 1986-1987.

Voluntary contributions in cash and kind to the Programme were received in 1985 from Austria, Brazil, Chile, Cyprus, the Dominican Republic and Pakistan.[8]

The Committee on outer space endorsed the Programme for 1986 as proposed by the Expert on Space Applications[9] and recommended by the Sub-Committee. The Assembly also endorsed it in **resolution 40/162**. Among activities planned for 1986 were a long-range fellowship programme for in-depth training, technical advisory services and provision of space information to Member States, training courses and meetings of experts, and the promotion of increased co-operation in space science and technology.

Co-ordination in the UN system

Noting the progress in co-ordinating programmes on space activities among organizations within the United Nations system, the Scientific and Technical Sub-Committee stressed the need for effective consultation to avoid duplication of activities.[1] The Committee on outer space[4] stated that the reports submitted by United Nations bodies, specialized agencies and other organizations had helped the Committee and its subsidiary bodies to fulfil their role as a focal point for international co-operation, especially in the practical applications of space science and technology in developing countries.

The seventh Inter-Agency Meeting on Outer Space Activities (Paris, 30 September–2 October),[10] convened by the Administrative Committee on Co-ordination, felt that the co-ordinating machinery had worked satisfactorily and that there were no major questions to be addressed. It examined a draft report of the Secretary-General on co-ordination of outer space activities for 1986 and 1987 and future years, prepared at the request of the Scientific and Technical Sub-Committee and subsequently submitted to the Committee on outer space in October 1985.[11] The report listed United Nations outer space activities, which comprised remote sensing, communications, meteorology, air navigation and maritime communications. Planned activities ranged from education and training to expert services, survey missions and information dissemination. The Meeting recommended that the next such Meeting be held in the latter part of 1986.

Implementation of the recommendations of the 1982 Conference on outer space

Action to carry out the recommendations made by UNISPACE-82[2] continued. The draft final versions of three studies, recommended by that conference and conducted by the United Nations with the assistance of expert groups in 1984,[12] were considered by the Scientific and Technical Sub-Committee in 1985. The studies concerned assistance to countries in studying their remote-sensing needs and assessing appropriate systems for meeting such needs;[13] the feasibility of obtaining closer spacing of satellites in the geostationary orbit;[14] and the feasibility of using direct broadcasting satellites for educational purposes and of internationally or regionally owned space segments.[15]

After considering the draft final studies, the Sub-Committee[1] forwarded them, with comments and amendments proposed by Member States,[16] to its parent Committee. It also noted the activities under way to establish an international space information service. It urged Member States to provide additional voluntary contributions to implement the UNISPACE-82 recommendations, and reaffirmed that the United Nations, in implementing them, should continue to seek the support of the United Nations Development Programme and other international funding institutions.

The Committee on outer space[4] recommended that the three studies and the related comments be called to the attention of Member States, specialized agencies and other United Nations bodies. It also recommended that the Sub-Committee consider carrying out further studies on projects of international space co-operation.

In his September report on implementing the UNISPACE-82 recommendations,[6] submitted pursuant to the General Assembly's 1984 request,[3] the Secretary-General summarized inter-agency co-operation and described action carried out and planned under the Programme on Space Applications (see p. 101).

Two other studies were carried out and submitted to the Committee on outer space in 1985: the Committee on Space Research (COSPAR) of the International Council of Scientific Unions considered the environmental effects of space activities[17] and the International Astronautical Federation (IAF) studied the implications to international co-operation of large-scale space systems.[18]

Remote sensing of the Earth by satellites

The Scientific and Technical Sub-Committee[1] continued considering remote sensing of the Earth by satellites, stating that it should be carried out taking into account the fundamental need to provide assistance to developing countries. Regarding a list of remote-sensing applications[19] being compiled by the Secretariat, the Sub-Committee restated that its updating should be continued and that more Member States should provide information.

The Committee on outer space[4] endorsed those views, and agreed that the Sub-Committee should continue to give the item priority in 1986.

Nuclear power sources and safety in spacecraft

The use of nuclear devices as sources of power for spacecraft was given further consideration by the Scientific and Technical Sub-Committee, which adopted the report of its Working Group on the subject.[1]

The Group (fifth session, New York, 11-15 February) reviewed working papers by Canada, the Federal Republic of Germany, Indonesia, Poland and Sweden and reaffirmed its previous conclusions, particularly those of 1983.[20] It discussed criteria for safe use of nuclear power sources; method, form and frequency of notification; emergency procedures in case of unplanned re-entry of those sources; and accumulation of radioactive material dispersed in the upper atmosphere as a consequence of such re-entry. Some delegations felt that the working papers were of great use, that important work remained to be carried out, and that the Group should be reconvened in 1986. Others noted that the Group's session was ineffective because it used an insignificant part of the time allocated to its meetings and carried out its work only by presenting papers without a scientific discussion; accordingly, there was no need to continue the Group's work.

After similar views were expressed in the Committee on outer space,[4] the Committee endorsed the Sub-Committee's view that in future work on nuclear power sources in space more attention should be given to the needs of developing countries, and endorsed its recommendation that the item be kept as a priority in 1986.

Space transportation

Progress made in space transportation systems was considered by the Scientific and Technical Sub-Committee,[1] which noted space activities by

China, India, Japan, the USSR, the United States and ESA. The Committee on outer space[4] endorsed a Sub-Committee decision that it continue considering those systems in 1986.

Technical aspects of the geostationary orbit

The Scientific and Technical Sub-Committee[1] continued to examine the physical nature and technical attributes of the geostationary orbit, in which satellites for communications and other purposes maintain a position some 36,000 kilometres above a selected location on the Equator. The Sub-Committee noted the preparatory work being done by the International Telecommunication Union (ITU) to establish scientific and technical criteria on the use of the orbit for the World Administrative Radio Conferences (WARCs) of 1985 (see PART TWO, Chapter XII) and 1988. The Sub-Committee recommended that it examine the question again in 1986, a recommendation endorsed by the Committee on outer space.[4]

Other questions

The Scientific and Technical Sub-Committee[1] recommended that at its 1986 session, in addition to the items examined above, it should consider life sciences, including space medicine; that COSPAR and IAF be invited to submit reports and arrange a presentation on progress in the geosphere-biosphere programme; and that a theme be fixed well in advance for special attention at each meeting of the Sub-Committee. COSPAR and IAF might be invited to arrange a symposium on the selected theme, during the first week of the Sub-Committee's session.

The Committee on outer space[4] endorsed those recommendations, noted a proposal that the Sub-Committee's 1986 theme be remote sensing for developing countries, and called for informal consultations to select that theme by consensus. In December, these suggestions were endorsed by the General Assembly in **resolution 40/162**.

The Committee also took note of a working paper,[21] submitted by Australia, Belgium, the Federal Republic of Germany, Japan, the Netherlands, Turkey, the United Kingdom and the United States, on its revitalization. Among the paper's proposals was the establishment of an informal open-ended working group to review the organization and work methods of the Committee and its Sub-Committees to make them as effective as possible. The paper also suggested adding to the agenda of the Scientific and Technical Sub-Committee items on advances in space life science research, including space medicine; international co-operation in space science through geophysical and biophysical research programmes; advances in space science and applications particularly relevant to developing countries; and spin-offs from outer space programmes.

For General Assembly action regarding space science and technology, see **resolution 40/162**, on p. 106.

Space law

The Legal Sub-Committee of the Committee on outer space held its twenty-fourth session in New York from 18 March to 4 April 1985.[22] It continued to consider three items: legal implications of remote sensing of the Earth from space, with the aim of formulating draft principles; the possibility of supplementing the norms of international law relevant to the use of nuclear power sources in outer space; and matters relating to the definition and delimitation of outer space and to the character and utilization of the geostationary orbit.

Legal aspects of remote sensing from satellites

On 19 March 1985, the Legal Sub-Committee re-established a Working Group, which continued, from then until 3 April, to consider the legal implications of remote sensing of the Earth from outer space, with the aim of formulating draft principles. The Group considered working papers submitted by Brazil, Chile, France and Kenya. It reviewed the 17 draft principles as they appeared at the conclusion of the Sub-Committee's 1984 session,[23] and then discussed principles I to IV, VI, VII and XII, concerning definitions of terms (I), objectives of remote sensing (II), international law (III), international co-operation (IV), technical assistance (VI), the United Nations role (VII) and access to data by a State whose territory was sensed (XII). The Chairman of the Working Group then presented a working document on the principles, as a basis for an agreement by consensus.

The Committee on outer space[4] held consultations with a view to finalizing the principles and, based on those consultations, Austria submitted a further working document[24] which the Committee felt could provide a basis for a future consensus agreement. The Chairman of the Group of 77 stated that, while that Group could not conclude consideration of Austria's document due to time constraints, it could be the basis for further consultations, and recommended that it be considered by the Legal Sub-Committee in 1986.

The Committee recommended that the item be retained on the Sub-Committee's 1986 agenda.

Legal aspects of nuclear power sources in spacecraft

A Working Group, re-established by the Legal Sub-Committee on 18 March 1985, continued to consider, from then until 4 April, supplementing the norms of international law relevant to the use of nuclear power sources in outer space.[22] The Group discussed two themes: notification prior to re-entry of a space object with nuclear power sources on board, and assistance to States. On the first topic, the Group formulated the principle that data distribution should commence with the notification of malfunctioning, and the updating frequency should increase as the time of the expected re-entry approached.

On assistance to States, the Group agreed on a formulation stating that upon notification of an expected re-entry of a space object with nuclear power sources on board, all States with space monitoring facilities should co-operate in monitoring that object. Additional information should be made available promptly to allow potentially affected States to assess the situation and take precautionary measures. After re-entry, the launching State should provide assistance to eliminate harmful effects; other States and international organizations should also assist. The Group felt that these formulations on the two themes could provide a basis for agreement by consensus in the near future.

The Committee on outer space[4] recommended that work on the agenda item be continued in 1986 and endorsed the Sub-Committee's recommendation to reformulate the item's title as the elaboration of draft principles relevant to the use of nuclear power sources in outer space.

Legal aspects of the geostationary orbit and definition of outer space

The Legal Sub-Committee continued to consider matters relating to the definition and delimitation of outer space and to the character and utilization of the geostationary orbit. On 18 March 1985, it re-established a Working Group, which examined the subject until 4 April.[22] The Group agreed to consider the two aspects of the item (definition and delimitation of outer space, and geostationary orbit) separately, but also to allow time to consider the item as a whole.

Discussing definition and delimitation of outer space, some delegations felt a multilateral agreement establishing a specific altitude as the upper limit of airspace and the commencement of outer space was the appropriate course. Some delegations referred to a 1983 USSR working paper,[25] proposing such an agreement, and noted the paper's proposals to establish the commencement of outer space at an altitude not exceeding 110 kilometres above sea-level. Other delegations said that establishing a boundary between airspace and outer space would be arbitrary; the lack of such a definition or delimitation had not given rise to difficulties, and its establishment might create problems for the development of space activities and

the existing smooth relationship between activities in airspace and outer space; and space activities were being conducted in a way entirely compatible with State sovereignty, and it was incorrect to consider a definition or delimitation of outer space as necessary for securing that sovereignty. It was also suggested that, as the positions of delegations on the topic had not moved closer for many years, it might be useful to consider whether a definition of space activities, rather than of outer space, would not be the appropriate course. It was stated, however, that seeking both definitions was not incompatible.

On the geostationary orbit, some delegations felt it was a limited natural resource and a special legal régime should be established for it. Current ITU arrangements provided for the allocation of orbital positions and related frequencies on an unacceptable first come, first served basis. The orbit and related frequencies were approaching saturation, with positions and frequencies occupied by only a few countries. Thus, the United Nations should establish principles governing its equitable use by all countries. Some delegations emphasized that the equatorial countries had special rights and responsibilities with respect to the orbit, as it was on the equatorial plane and was a unique natural resource. Others disagreed, stating that the geostationary orbit as part of outer space was the common heritage of mankind.

It was also said that, while a legal régime for utilizing the geostationary orbit was necessary, discussions should be based on four points: the orbit was a part of outer space, subject to international law and not subject to national appropriation; all States had equal rights of utilization, and the positioning of a space object in the orbit created no right of ownership over that particular orbital segment; utilization should not be detrimental to the interests of other States, and account should be taken of developing countries' special needs; and States should co-operate in placing communications satellites in the orbit with due regard to ITU decisions on frequency utilization.

Still other delegations felt the 1985 and 1988 WARCs should formulate principles and that it was necessary to regulate the matter juridically, since ITU regulations could no longer cope with certain technological trends and monopolistic tendencies. Other delegations disagreed.

The Committee on outer space[4] recommended that the item be retained on the agenda of the Sub-Committee for further consideration in 1986.

GENERAL ASSEMBLY ACTION

On 16 December 1985, the General Assembly, on the recommendation of the Special Political Committee, adopted **resolution 40/162** without vote.

International co-operation in the peaceful uses of outer space

The General Assembly,

Recalling its resolution 39/96 of 14 December 1984,

Deeply convinced of the common interest of mankind in promoting the exploration and use of outer space for peaceful purposes and in continuing efforts to extend to all States the benefits derived therefrom, and of the importance of international co-operation in this field, for which the United Nations should continue to provide a focal point,

Reaffirming the importance of international co-operation in developing the rule of law, including the relevant norms of space law, for the advancement and preservation of the exploration and peaceful uses of outer space,

Gravely concerned at the extension of an arms race into outer space,

Recognizing that all States, in particular those with major space capabilities, should contribute actively to the goal of preventing an arms race in outer space as an essential condition for the promotion of international co-operation in the exploration and uses of outer space for peaceful purposes,

Aware of the need to increase the benefits of space technology and its applications and to contribute to an orderly growth of space activities favourable to the socio-economic advancement of mankind, in particular the peoples of developing countries,

Taking note of the progress achieved in the further development of peaceful space exploration and application as well as in various national and co-operative space projects, which contribute to international co-operation in this field,

Taking note also of the report of the Secretary-General on the implementation of the recommendations of the Second United Nations Conference on the Exploration and Peaceful Uses of Outer Space,

Having considered the report of the Committee on the Peaceful Uses of Outer Space on the work of its twenty-eighth session,

1. *Endorses* the report of the Committee on the Peaceful Uses of Outer Space;

2. *Invites* States that have not yet become parties to the international treaties governing the uses of outer space* to give consideration to ratifying or acceding to those treaties;

3. *Notes* that the Legal Sub-Committee of the Committee on the Peaceful Uses of Outer Space at its twenty-fourth session, in its working groups, continued:

(a) Its detailed consideration of the legal implications of remote sensing of the Earth from space, with the aim of formulating draft principles relating to remote sensing;

(b) Its consideration of the possibility of supplementing the norms of international law relevant to the use of nuclear power sources in outer space;

(c) Its consideration of matters relating to the definition and delimitation of outer space and to the character and utilization of the geostationary orbit, including consideration of ways and means to ensure the rational and equitable use of the geostationary orbit, without prejudice to the role of the International Telecommunication Union;

4. *Endorses* the recommendations of the Committee on the Peaceful Uses of Outer Space that the Legal Sub-Committee at its twenty-fifth session should, taking into account the concerns of all countries, particularly those of developing countries, in its working groups:

(a) Continue its detailed consideration of the legal implications of remote sensing of the Earth from space, with the aim of finalizing the draft set of principles;

(b) Undertake the elaboration of draft principles relevant to the use of nuclear power sources in outer space;

(c) Continue its consideration of matters relating to the definition and delimitation of outer space and to the character and utilization of the geostationary orbit, including consideration of ways and means to ensure the rational and equitable use of the geostationary orbit, without prejudice to the role of the International Telecommunication Union;

5. *Notes* that the Scientific and Technical Sub-Committee on the Peaceful Uses of Outer Space at its twenty-second session continued:

(a) Its consideration of the following items on a priority basis:

(i) United Nations Programme on Space Applications and the co-ordination of space activities within the United Nations system;

(ii) Implementation of the recommendations of the Second United Nations Conference on the Exploration and Peaceful Uses of Outer Space; In this context, it was noted that it was particularly urgent to implement the following recommendations:

a. All countries should have the opportunity to use the techniques resulting from medical studies in space;

b. Data banks at the national and regional levels should be strengthened and expanded and an international space information service should be established to function as a centre of co-ordination;

c. The United Nations should support the creation of adequate training centres at the regional level, linked, whenever possible, to institutions implementing space programmes; necessary funding for the development of such centres should be made available through financial institutions;

(iii) Questions relating to remote sensing of the Earth by satellites;

(iv) Use of nuclear power sources in outer space;

(b) Its consideration of the following items:

(i) Questions relating to space transportation systems and their implications for future activities in space;

(ii) Examination of the physical nature and technical attributes of the geostationary orbit;

6. *Endorses* the recommendations of the Committee on the Peaceful Uses of Outer Space that the Scientific and Technical Sub-Committee at its twenty-third session, taking into account the concerns of all countries, particularly those of developing countries, should:

(a) Consider the following items on a priority basis:

(i) United Nations Programme on Space Applications and the co-ordination of space activities within the United Nations system;

(ii) Implementation of the recommendations of the Second United Nations Conference on the Exploration and Peaceful Uses of Outer Space;

In this context, it is particularly urgent to implement the following recommendations:

a. All countries should have the opportunity to use the techniques resulting from medical studies in space;

b. Data banks at the national and regional levels should be strengthened and expanded and an international space information service should be established to function as a centre of co-ordination;

c. The United Nations should support the creation of adequate training centres at the regional level, linked, whenever possible, to institutions implementing space programmes; necessary funding for the development of such centres should be made available through financial institutions;

d. The United Nations should organize a fellowship programme through which selected graduates or post-graduates from developing countries should get in-depth, long-term exposure to space technology or applications; it is also desirable to encourage the availability of opportunities for such exposures on other bilateral and multilateral bases outside the United Nations system;

(iii) Questions relating to remote sensing of the Earth by satellites;

(iv) Use of nuclear power sources in outer space;

(b) Consider the following items:

(i) Questions relating to space transportation systems and their implications for future activities in space;

(ii) Examination of the physical nature and technical attributes of the geostationary orbit;

7. *Endorses also* the recommendations of the Committee on the Peaceful Uses of Outer Space:

(a) That there should be a continued consideration in the Scientific and Technical Sub-Committee of the item relating to life sciences, including space medicine;

(b) That, for the twenty-third session of the Scientific and Technical Sub-Committee, the Committee on Space Research and the International Astronautical Federation should be invited to submit reports and arrange a special presentation on progress in the geosphere-biosphere programme;

(c) That the Scientific and Technical Sub-Committee should, at its twenty-third session, give special attention to the theme "Remote sensing for developing countries" selected in accordance with the procedure recommended by the Sub-Committee at its twenty-second session and that the Committee on Space Research and the International Astronautical Federation should be invited to make presentations in accordance with this theme;

8. *Endorses* the United Nations Programme on Space Applications for 1986, as proposed to the Committee on the Peaceful Uses of Outer Space by the Expert on Space Applications;

9. *Emphasizes* the urgency and importance of implementing fully the recommendations of the Second United Nations Conference on the Exploration and Peaceful Uses of Outer Space as early as possible;

10. *Reaffirms* its approval of the recommendation of the Conference regarding the establishment and strengthening of regional mechanisms of co-operation and their promotion and creation through the United Nations system;

11. *Expresses its appreciation* to all Governments that made or expressed their intention to make contributions towards carrying out the recommendations of the Conference;

12. *Invites* all Governments to take effective action for the implementation of the recommendations of the Conference;

13. *Urges* all States, in particular those with major space capabilities, to contribute actively to the goal of preventing an arms race in outer space as an essential condition for the promotion of international co-operation in the exploration and uses of outer space for peaceful purposes;

14. *Takes note* of the views expressed and documents circulated during the twenty-eighth session of the Committee on the Peaceful Uses of Outer Space and during the fortieth session of the General Assembly concerning ways and means of maintaining outer space for peaceful purposes;

15. *Requests* the Committee on the Peaceful Uses of Outer Space to continue to consider, as a matter of priority, ways and means of maintaining outer space for peaceful purposes and to report thereon to the General Assembly at its forty-first session;

16. *Endorses* the recommendation of the Committee on the Peaceful Uses of Outer Space that the following three studies proposed by the Second United Nations Conference on the Exploration and Peaceful Uses of Outer Space should, together with the comments made thereon during the twenty-second session of the Scientific and Technical Sub-Committee, be called to the attention of Governments of all Member States, specialized agencies and other organizations of the United Nations system:

(a) Assistance to countries in studying their remote-sensing needs and assessing appropriate systems for meeting such needs;

(b) The feasibility of using direct broadcasting satellites for educational purposes and of internationally or regionally owned space segments;

(c) The feasibility of obtaining closer spacing of satellites in the geostationary orbit and their satisfactory coexistence, including a closer examination of techno-economic implications, particularly for developing countries, in order to ensure the most effective utilization of this orbit in the interest of all countries;

17. *Also endorses* the recommendation of the Committee on the Peaceful Uses of Outer Space with regard to possible further studies as set out in paragraph 48 of the report of the Committee, bearing in mind in particular the needs of the developing countries;

18. *Endorses* the decision of the Committee on the Peaceful Uses of Outer Space to grant, at their request, permanent observer status to the International Telecommunications Satellite Organization (INTELSAT) and to the International System and Organization of Space Communications (INTERSPUTNIK);

19. *Affirms* that the interference that satellite systems to be newly established may cause to systems already registered with the International Telecommunication Union shall not exceed the limits specified in the relevant provision of the International Telecommunication Union Radio Regulations applicable to space services;

20. *Requests* all organs, organizations and bodies of the United Nations system and other intergovernmental organizations working in the field of outer space or on space-related matters to co-operate in the implementation of the recommendations of the Conference;

21. *Requests* the Secretary-General to report to the General Assembly at its forty-first session on the implementation of the recommendations of the Conference;

22. *Requests* the specialized agencies and other international organizations to continue and, where appropriate, enhance their co-operation with the Committee on the Peaceful Uses of Outer Space and to provide it with progress reports on their work relating to the peaceful uses of outer space;

23. *Requests* the Committee on the Peaceful Uses of Outer Space to continue its work, in accordance with the present resolution, to consider, as appropriate, new projects in outer space activities and to submit a report to the General Assembly at its forty-first session, including its views on which subjects should be studied in the future.

---

*Treaty on Principles Governing the Activities of States in the Exploration and Use of Outer Space, including the Moon and Other Celestial Bodies (resolution 2222(XXI), annex); Agreement on the Rescue of Astronauts, the Return of Astronauts and the Return of Objects Launched into Outer Space (resolution 2345(XXII), annex); Convention on International Liability for Damage Caused by Space Objects (resolution 2777(XXVI), annex); Convention on Registration of Objects Launched into Outer Space (resolution 3235(XXIX), annex); Agreement Governing the Activities of States on the Moon and Other Celestial Bodies (resolution 34/68, annex).

General Assembly resolution 40/162

16 December 1985   Meeting 118   Adopted without vote

Approved by SPC (A/40/1023) without vote, 6 December (meeting 46); draft by Austria, for SPC working group (A/SPC/40/L.30); agenda item 76.
Meeting numbers. GA 40th session: SPC 37-46; plenary 118.

Following approval of the text in the Special Political Committee, the United States said it was gratified that paragraph 14 reflected the proposals by the United States and other Western countries to revitalize the Committee on outer space.[21]

The USSR interpreted the draft resolution as requiring the Committee on outer space to consider establishing an international arrangement, and referred to a proposal submitted by it to the Special Political Committee[26] on main lines and principles of international co-operation in the peaceful exploitation of outer space under conditions of its non-militarization.

The Assembly considered that question as a supplementary agenda item (see p. 79).

REFERENCES

[1]A/AC.105/351. [2]YUN 1982, p. 162. [3]YUN 1984, p. 104, GA res. 39/96, 14 Dec. 1984. [4]A/40/20 & Corr.1. [5]A/AC.105/364. [6]A/40/621 & Corr.1. [7]A/AC.105/348/-Add.1. [8]A/AC.105/L.135/Add.3 & 4. [9]A/AC.105/348. [10]ACC/1985/PG/14. [11]A/AC.105/359. [12]YUN 1984, p. 102. [13]A/AC.105/339 & Corr.1. [14]A/AC.105/340 & Corr.1, 2. [15]A/AC.105/341 & Corr.1. [16]A/AC.105/339/Rev.1, A/AC.105/340/Rev.1 & A/AC.105/341/Rev.1. [17]A/AC.105/344. [18]A/AC.105/349. [19]A/AC.105/297/Add.1-4. [20]YUN 1983, p. 98. [21]A/AC.105/L.154. [22]A/AC.105/352. [23]YUN 1984, p. 103. [24]A/AC.105/L.158. [25]YUN 1983, p. 100. [26]A/SPC/40/3.

PUBLICATIONS

Maintaining Outer Space for Peaceful Uses, Sales No. E.85.III.A.11.
Space Activities of the United Nations and International Organizations, 1975-1985 (A/AC.105/358), Sales No. E.86.I.2.

Spacecraft launchings

In 1985, four countries and an intergovernmental organization provided information to the United Nations on the launching of objects into orbit or beyond, in accordance with a 1961 General Assembly resolution[1] and the Convention on Registration of Objects Launched into Outer Space.[2]

Eighteen notifications of objects launched during 1985 and the latter part of 1984, and on the status of other spacecraft, were received in 1985 and distributed as United Nations documents.[3] Information was submitted by Japan on 3 launchings, by the USSR on 74, by the United Kingdom on 3, by the United States on 31 and by ESA on 2. (Some launchings involved multiple space objects sent aloft by a single carrier rocket. Launchings during 1985 but not reported to the United Nations until 1986 are excluded from the above count.)

Convention on registration of launchings

As at 31 December 1985, there were 33 States parties to the Convention on Registration, including Mongolia which ratified it on 10 April.[4]

REFERENCES

[1]YUN 1961, p. 35, GA res. 1721 B (XVI), 20 Dec. 1961. [2]YUN 1974, p. 63, GA res. 3235(XXIX), annex, 12 Nov. 1974. [3]ST/SG/SER.E/119-122, 123 & Corr.1, 124-136. [4]*Multilateral Treaties Deposited with the Secretary-General: Status as at 31 December 1985* (ST/LEG/SER.E/4), Sales No. E.86.V.3.

Chapter III

Law of the sea

Ratifications to the 1982 United Nations Convention on the Law of the Sea increased to 25 during 1985.

The Preparatory Commission, which had been mandated to set up the Convention's two major institutions—the International Sea-Bed Authority and the International Tribunal for the Law of the Sea—continued its work. It declared that the only régime for exploring and exploiting the international sea-bed "Area" (the sea-bed beyond national jurisdiction) was that established by the Convention and other resolutions adopted in 1982 by the Third United Nations Conference on the Law of the Sea.

In resolution 40/63, the General Assembly called on States to observe the Convention's provisions when enacting national legislation and called for early adoption of the rules for registration of pioneer investors.

Topics related to this chapter. Disarmament: naval arms race. Transport: maritime transport. Natural resources: marine resources. Environment: marine ecosystems. International Court of Justice: continental shelf delimitation (Libyan Arab Jamahiriya/Tunisia, Libyan Arab Jamahiriya/Malta).

UN Convention on the Law of the Sea

Signatures and ratifications

The number of ratifications to the United Nations Convention on the Law of the Sea increased to 25 during 1985,[1] with the addition of Bahrain, Cameroon, Guinea, Iceland, Iraq, Mali, Saint Lucia, the Sudan, Togo, Tunisia and the United Republic of Tanzania. The Convention, adopted by the Third United Nations Conference on the Law of the Sea in April 1982,[2] was to enter into force 12 months after receipt of the sixtieth instrument of ratification or accession.

The Convention had closed for signature on 9 December 1984. At that time, 159 signatures had been received.[3]

Developments relating to the Convention

In response to a 1984 General Assembly resolution,[4] the Secretary-General reported on developments relating to the Convention and on implementation of that resolution.[5] He declared that even before its entry into force, the Convention was exerting a considerable influence on all aspects of the law of the sea, as well as on marine affairs in general.

The report was divided into two parts: part one contained an overview of the Convention's impact on State practice and on the mandates and activities of international organizations concerned with marine affairs, decisions of the International Court of Justice and other tribunals, and information on other developments relating to the law of the sea; part two outlined the activities of the Office of the Special Representative of the Secretary-General for the Law of the Sea in the discharge of its mandate (see p. 112).

A number of States had adopted national legislation dealing with a variety of marine issues, particularly on determining baselines, breadth and status of the territorial sea, establishing exclusive economic zones, defining the continental shelf and delimiting maritime boundaries between States with opposite or adjacent coasts.

A large number of States had agreed to a 12-mile territorial sea as embodied in the Convention. Currently, 89 had a territorial sea of 12 nautical miles in breadth, while 22 had legislation establishing the limits of the territorial sea beyond 12 nautical miles. Seventy-nine States had promulgated laws or decrees establishing exclusive economic zones or exclusive fishery zones of up to 200 nautical miles.

With respect to the continental shelf, 16 nations had enacted legislation incorporating the concept of natural prolongation as embodied in the Convention.

Coastal States' expanded jurisdiction over adjacent maritime areas, a distinctive feature of the new legal régime for the seas, had created several potential conflicts among States. By providing a legal order for the seas, the Convention promoted the peaceful resolution of such disputes.

Several problems with respect to maritime delimitation had been resolved either by delimitation agreements or by international adjudication or other forms of peaceful settlement. Recent cases included the dispute between Argentina and Chile in the Beagle Channel, the delimitation of maritime boundaries between Guinea and Guinea-Bissau and the delimitation of the continental shelf between the Libyan Arab Jamahiriya and Malta.

Among other developments relating to the law of the sea and reviewed in the Secretary-General's report were: peaceful uses; maritime law; environmental law; fisheries management and development; marine science, technology and ocean services; and marine resource development.

Throughout 1985, the International Maritime Organization (IMO) continued working towards preventing marine pollution and improving maritime safety (see PART TWO, Chapter XIV). It continued work on, among other things, amending the 1974 International Convention for the Safety of Life at Sea, the 1966 International Convention on Load Lines and a new convention to replace one of 1910 on salvage and assistance at sea. The first two projects were to be considered at a conference in 1988. The IMO Legal Committee continued preparing a draft revision of the Convention on salvage, which involved both private and public law. The 1979 International Convention on Maritime Search and Rescue entered into force on 22 June 1985, 12 months after 15 States had become parties to it. The Ninth Consultative Meeting of Contracting Parties to the 1972 Convention on the Prevention of Marine Pollution by Dumping of Wastes and Other Matter (London, 23-27 September 1985) adopted revised criteria for the allocation of substances to the Convention's annexes.

Other 1985 developments included the adoption on 21 June of a Convention to protect, manage and develop the marine and coastal environment of eastern Africa (see ECONOMIC AND SOCIAL QUESTIONS, Chapter XVI); and in July, the reaching by the United Nations Conference on Conditions for Registration of Ships of an agreed text on the contentious issues of national participation and management, manning and ownership of ships (see ECONOMIC AND SOCIAL QUESTIONS, Chapter V).

GENERAL ASSEMBLY ACTION

For General Assembly action with regard to the Convention, see **resolution 40/63** on p. 113.

Preparatory Commission

The Preparatory Commission for the International Sea-Bed Authority and for the International Tribunal for the Law of the Sea met twice during 1985.[5] It held its third session at Kingston, Jamaica, from 11 March to 4 April and meetings at Geneva from 12 August to 4 September.

The Commission received a letter from the USSR dated 10 June 1985,[6] in which it stated that the Soviet enterprise Yuzhmorgeologiya had received a letter from the consortium Ocean Mining Associates declaring that the National Oceanic and Atmospheric Administration of the United States Department of Commerce on 29 August 1984 had issued the consortium a licence to explore part of the international sea-bed Area of the Pacific Ocean. The licence granted the consortium exclusive rights to manganese nodules in the Area and priority in regard to other resources. Similar licences had been issued by the United States to other consortia. The Soviet enterprise had replied to Ocean Mining Associates that it did not recognize the validity of the licence, that its issuance was unlawful, and that it attempted to appropriate the powers of the Commission and to undermine the Convention on the Law of the Sea. Annexed were a TASS statement of 5 June and the Yuzhmorgeologiya reply.

On 30 August, the Commission, taking note of the USSR letter, adopted without vote a Declaration, by which it asserted that the Convention and related resolutions adopted by the Third United Nations Conference on the Law of the Sea[2] established the only régime for exploring and exploiting the Area and that any claim, agreement or action regarding the Area which was incompatible with them was illegal and should not be recognized.

At the time of its adoption, the Chairman stated that, after consulting delegations, it was his understanding that the Declaration commanded a large majority in the Commission; however, he noted, a number of delegations could not support it because of concerns about some aspects of its substance and effect.

In the light of the Declaration's adoption, the Group of Eastern European States did not press for a decision on its draft on the same subject.[7] By that text, the Commission would have rejected as illegal an agreement on sea-bed matters concluded in August 1984 by eight Western Governments[8] and would have decided not to recognize it.

The Chairman characterized the Commission's third session as encouraging, in that it had settled down to work on all substantive matters. The Commission was mandated to prepare for the establishment of the International Sea-Bed Authority (Assembly, Council, Legal and Technical Commission, Economic Planning Commission) and the Enterprise (mining arm); draft a mining code; study the possible impact of production of sea-bed minerals on developing countries which were land-based producers; prepare for the establishment of the international disputes settlement Tribunal; and administer the régime for registration of pioneer investors, under resolution II adopted by the Third United Nations Conference on the Law of the Sea.[9] Pioneer investors were States and private consortia interested in exploring the Area before the Convention's entry into force; resolution II set out a scheme to enable them to qualify for registration by the Commission as pioneer investors and to protect investments made by them.

The Commission began its second reading of the draft rules of procedure of the Assembly of the Authority; the major outstanding issue was the status of observers. Another important issue was a proposal to establish a finance committee in the Assembly which would assist the Secretary-General of the Authority in preparing the budget and oversee financial affairs.

Consultations were undertaken informally by the Chairman among three pioneer investors—France, Japan and the USSR—whose claims overlapped in the north-east Pacific Ocean. (Four nations had submitted applications for registration as pioneer investors, the USSR in 1983,[10] and France, Japan and India in 1984.[11]) While it was possible to resolve provisionally the overlap between Japan and the USSR (see below), the overlap between France and the USSR created particular problems in that it was difficult to find a solution which would meet all the conditions of resolution II, paragraph 3, which provided that each application should cover a total area which need not be a single continuous area, sufficiently large and of sufficient estimated commercial value to allow two mining operations, a part of which was to be reserved for the Authority.

On 28 February 1985,[12] France, Japan and the USSR stated that negotiations (Paris, 11-16 January; Tokyo, 1-6 February; and Moscow, 22-28 February) had provisionally resolved the overlapping claims between the Japanese and USSR application areas. That solution would be finalized simultaneously with, and depending on, the outcome of the conflict between France and the USSR.

During the Geneva meetings, consultations continued on the overlapping issue and it was decided that they would be pursued during the inter-sessional period.

Also at Geneva, the Commission completed the second reading of the Assembly's draft rules of procedure and examined more than two thirds of those of the Council. The following issues remained outstanding: the question of subsidiary organs (whether main committees should be institutionalized in the rules of the Assembly); the status and extent of participation by States observers to the Authority; control over financial and budgetary matters (including a proposal by six industrialized countries to have a key role in a finance committee whose membership was to include the Authority's four largest contributors); and the majority required to elect the Authority's Secretary-General.

Other communications. A number of other communications were addressed to the Commission's Chairman on the subjects of the sea-bed mining régime and registration of pioneer investors. (No applications for registration as pioneer investors were submitted in 1985.)

On 19 March,[13] the Federal Republic of Germany pointed out that it had not signed the Convention because of its objections to specific elements of the sea-bed mining régime; however, it did not reject the Convention *in toto* and it was prepared to explore all avenues which might lead to general consensus on a mining régime.

Several States declared that overlapping claims among applicants for registration as pioneer investors could be satisfactorily solved only by agreements encompassing all potential claimants. Such statements were made by Belgium (2 April),[14] Canada (3 April),[15] Italy (2 April)[16] and the Netherlands (28 March).[17] In connection with those statements, the USSR on 28 June[18] and 10 July[19] said that the demand for resolving disputes among all potential applicants, irrespective of whether they had signed the Convention, was contrary to resolution II and could only be seen as reflecting a desire to nullify the Commission's work in implementing that resolution. France, in letters of 31 July,[20] also stated that it was unable to accept the views of the four States on solving overlapping claims, which would make Commission decisions subject to the goodwill of commercial undertakings unable or unwilling to benefit from resolution II.

On 15 August,[21] China, pointing out that a certain country had unilaterally issued licences to explore the resources of the international sea-bed, declared that any action which violated the Convention was illegal and would never be recognized by the international community.

In a 25 October letter,[22] referring to the August 1985 Declaration, the Federal Republic of Germany stated that, while parts of the Convention reflected already existing law, that was not the case with the part relating to deep sea-bed mining; pending its entry into force, the Convention could not create contractual rights and obligations for any country, and even when it came into force it would be binding only on States which had ratified or acceded to it.

The United Kingdom, in a letter of 4 November,[23] referred to the Commission Chairman's statement at the time the Declaration was adopted (see above) and said that, since that statement had not been followed by discussion, it wished to assert that, in the absence of a generally accepted deep sea-bed mining régime, a State must retain its rights and might exercise its freedom of action relating to deep sea-bed activities and resources.

Special Commissions

The Commission's four Special Commissions continued their work in accordance with their respective mandates. Special Commission 1 considered the problems of land-based producer States which would be most seriously affected by sea-bed mining production. Special Commission 2 took up a project profile for a deep sea-bed mining operation. Special Commission 3 examined draft regulations on the use of terms, scope, prospecting and procedure for submission and approval of plans for exploring and exploiting sea-bed minerals. Special Commission 4 studied draft rules of procedure for the International Tribunal for the Law of the Sea.

Developing land-based producer States

Special Commission 1 held 10 meetings during the Preparatory Commission's Kingston session, seeking to identify the developing land-based producer States likely to be most seriously affected by sea-bed mining. The Chairman of Special Commission 1 told the plenary Commission that substantial progress had been made in identifying the States, the possible effects and possible remedial measures.[24] In addition, a better understanding was reached of the studies that should be carried out in the following few years before the International Sea-Bed Authority came into being and of studies to be pursued by the Authority in the relatively long period that might be required before sea-bed production began.

The Enterprise

Special Commission 2, preparing for establishment of the Enterprise (the Authority's operational arm) which was to conduct sea-bed activities, had before it a project profile for a deep sea-bed mining operation, prepared by the secretariat, which marked a new phase in the work of the Preparatory Commission. That paper provided a basis for more concrete discussion of a mining operation compared to the somewhat philosophical discussions that had taken place at previous meetings. It indicated the various steps in establishing a sea-bed mining operation, spanning 14 years, before commercial production could begin. It outlined a number of operational options open to the Enterprise as well as the financial requirements under each option. The Chairman of Special Commission 2 informed the Preparatory Commission[25] that secretariat papers on an *ad hoc* expert group to assist in planning for the operation of the Enterprise and on the training needs and requirements of the Enterprise also had been considered. Special Commission 2 held 11 meetings.

Sea-bed mining code

Special Commission 3, charged with drafting the mining code, began to consider a draft regulation on prospecting, exploration and exploitation of polymetallic nodules in the Area. It particularly discussed the question of notification of prospecting and the submission of reports by prospectors to the Authority, the right to apply, the time of sub-mission of approval of plans of work, the submission of applications and their form. The Chairman of Special Commission 3, which held 11 meetings during the Preparatory Commission's Kingston session, stated[26] that it had completed an article-by-article first reading of the provisions on scope and prospecting and began considering regulations on nationality of applicant, sponsorship and control by the sponsoring State.

International Tribunal

Special Commission 4, which was considering practical arrangements for setting up the International Tribunal for the Law of the Sea, examined the Tribunal's draft rules of procedure. It held 12 meetings. The Chairman of Special Commission 4, addressing the Preparatory Commission, said[27] it had taken up the draft rules article by article, including such matters as who might represent parties before the Tribunal, privileges, immunities and facilities that should be accorded to representatives of parties, agent and counsel, preliminary procedures intended to safeguard coastal States' exercise of resource rights in the exclusive economic zone against abuse by vexatious litigation, official languages of the Tribunal, provision of information by international organizations and provisional measures to protect parties' rights and to prevent damage to the marine environment. The Special Commission also considered draft rules dealing with procedure for the prompt release by a detaining State of vessels and crews; the procedure was of immediate concern to fishing States and maritime States.

GENERAL ASSEMBLY ACTION

For General Assembly action concerning the work of the Preparatory Commission, see **resolution 40/63** on p. 113.

Functions of the Secretary-General

Office of the Special Representative

The Office of the Special Representative of the Secretary-General was responsible for executing the central programme on law of the sea affairs and was the core office of the Organization for the law of the sea.[5]

In 1985, the demand from Governments, intergovernmental organizations, academic institutions and scholars for information on law of the sea developments continued to increase. There was a corresponding increase in requests for specialized information and technical advice on the content and effect of different provisions of the Convention and the significance of interrelationships between its provisions, particularly as regards the rights and obligations of States.

Several States sought advice on the implications of ratifying the Convention. Matters of concern included environmental protection, regional and subregional co-operation and finance. The secretariat was preparing a study on the financial implications of establishing the Authority and Tribunal.

Increased interest was noted in marine affairs at the regional and intergovernmental levels. For example, the Office was requested to be represented at a meeting of the Economic and Social Commission for Asia and the Pacific (ESCAP) natural resources committee and also its expert group on maritime legislation; an expert group on marine surveying technologies of ESCAP and the Ocean Economics and Technology Branch of the Department of International Economic and Social Affairs; an Indian Ocean conference on marine affairs co-operation; a United Nations conference on nickel; and an African intergovernmental expert meeting on exploring and exploiting sea-bed resources. In each case, the objective was to provide information on various aspects of the Convention and to promote its uniform application.

The Office proposed to supplement the advice and assistance already being given by it on purely legal and management aspects through the mechanism of technical advisory groups which would provide advice and assistance on technical matters, such as the continental shelf delineation in accordance with the Convention, the drawing of different types of baselines referred to in the Convention, and the establishment of guidelines on scales, geodetic system, projections and symbols in maritime charts for which the Secretary-General was the depositary.

Considerable effort was made to evaluate and strengthen the law of the sea information system, and to convert it from manual to electronic operation. Priority was given to the processing and entry of information on State practice in matters covered by the Convention, particularly national legislation and policy as well as international agreements and arrangements.

A list of multilateral treaties relevant to the law of the sea was published[28] as were further issues of the *Law of the Sea Bulletin*, and the law of the sea reference library continued to be updated. The *Bulletin* included extracts of national legislation, treaties and other multilateral instruments, recent decisions of international courts and tribunals and other modes for peaceful settlement of disputes; information required by States pertaining to the Convention; and developments in marine activities at all levels. The reference library collection was strengthened to include meeting and symposia working papers and proceedings, articles in journals from developing countries, and unpublished working papers of various institutions which were in the public domain.

The Office represented the Secretary-General in meetings and symposia of government officials, scholars and citizens to explain the Convention and its contribution to the rule of law and to international peace.

GENERAL ASSEMBLY ACTION

On 10 December, the General Assembly adopted **resolution 40/63** by recorded vote.

Law of the sea

The General Assembly,

Recalling its resolutions 37/66 of 3 December 1982, 38/59 A of 14 December 1983 and 39/73 of 13 December 1984, regarding the law of the sea,

Taking note of the increasing and overwhelming support for the United Nations Convention on the Law of the Sea, as evidenced, *inter alia*, by the one hundred and fifty-nine signatures as of 9 December 1984, the closing date for signature, and twenty-four of the sixty ratifications or accessions required for entry into force of the Convention,

Considering that, in its resolution 2749(XXV) of 17 December 1970, it proclaimed that the sea-bed and ocean floor, and the subsoil thereof, beyond the limits of national jurisdiction, as well as the resources of the area, are the common heritage of mankind,

Recalling that the Convention provides the régime to be applied to the Area and its resources,

Further recalling the Declaration adopted by the Preparatory Commission for the International Sea-Bed Authority and for the International Tribunal for the Law of the Sea on 30 August 1985,

Seriously concerned at any attempt to undermine the Convention and the related resolutions adopted at the Third United Nations Conference on the Law of the Sea,

Recognizing that, as stated in the third preambular paragraph of the Convention, the problems of ocean space are closely interrelated and need to be considered as a whole,

Convinced that it is important to safeguard the unified character of the Convention and related resolutions adopted therewith and to refrain from any action to apply their provisions selectively, in a manner inconsistent with their object and purpose,

Emphasizing the need for States to ensure consistent application of the Convention, as well as the need for harmonization of national legislation with the provisions of the Convention,

Recognizing also the need for co-operation in the early and effective implementation by the Preparatory Commission of resolution II of the Third United Nations Conference on the Law of the Sea,

Noting the increasing needs of countries, especially developing countries, for information, advice and assistance in the implementation of the Convention and in their developmental process for the full realization of the benefits of the comprehensive legal régime established by the Convention,

Noting also that the Preparatory Commission has decided to hold its fourth regular session at Kingston from 17 March to 11 April 1986 and its summer meeting in 1986 at Geneva, Kingston or New York as it may decide,

Taking note of activities carried out in 1985 under the major programme on marine affairs, set forth in chapter

25 of the medium-term plan for the period 1984-1989, in accordance with the report of the Secretary-General as approved in General Assembly resolution 38/59 A,

Recognizing that the United Nations Convention on the Law of the Sea encompasses all uses and resources of the oceans and that all related activities within the United Nations system need to be implemented in a manner consistent with it,

Recalling its approval of the financing of the expenses of the Preparatory Commission from the regular budget of the United Nations,

Taking special note of the report of the Secretary-General prepared in response to paragraph 10 of General Assembly resolution 39/73,

1. *Recalls* the historic significance of the United Nations Convention on the Law of the Sea as an important contribution to the maintenance of peace, justice and progress for all peoples of the world;

2. *Expresses its satisfaction* at the increasing number of ratifications deposited with the Secretary-General;

3. *Calls upon* all States that have not done so to consider ratifying or acceding to the Convention at the earliest possible date to allow the effective entry into force of the new legal régime for the uses of the sea and its resources;

4. *Calls upon* all States to safeguard the unified character of the Convention and related resolutions adopted therewith;

5. *Takes note* of the Declaration adopted by the Preparatory Commission for the International Sea-Bed Authority and for the International Tribunal for the Law of the Sea on 30 August 1985;

6. *Calls upon* States to desist from taking actions which undermine the Convention or defeat its object and purpose;

7. *Calls upon* States to observe the provisions of the Convention when enacting their national legislation;

8. *Calls* for an early adoption of the rules for registration of pioneer investors in order to ensure the effective implementation of resolution II of the Third United Nations Conference on the Law of the Sea, including the registration of pioneer investors;

9. *Expresses its appreciation* for the effective execution by the Secretary-General of the central programme in law of the sea affairs under chapter 25 of the medium-term plan for the period 1984-1989;

10. *Further expresses its appreciation* for the report of the Secretary-General prepared in response to General Assembly resolution 39/73 and requests him to continue to carry out the activities outlined therein, as well as those aimed at the strengthening of the new legal régime of the sea, special emphasis being placed on the work of the Preparatory Commission for the International Sea-Bed Authority and for the International Tribunal for the Law of the Sea, including the implementation of resolution II of the Third United Nations Conference on the Law of the Sea;

11. *Approves* the programme of meetings of the Preparatory Commission for 1986;

12. *Calls upon* the Secretary-General to continue to assist States in the implementation of the Convention and in the development of a consistent and uniform approach to the new legal régime thereunder, as well as in their national, subregional and regional efforts towards the full realization of the benefits therefrom and invites the organs and organizations of the United Na-

tions system to co-operate and lend assistance in these endeavours;

13. *Requests* the Secretary-General to report to the General Assembly at its forty-first session on developments relating to the Convention and on the implementation of the present resolution;

14. *Decides* to include in the provisional agenda of its forty-first session the item entitled "Law of the sea".

General Assembly resolution 40/63

10 December 1985   Meeting 110   140-2-5 (recorded vote)

56-nation draft (A/40/L.33 & Add.1); agenda item 36.

Sponsors: Algeria, Angola, Antigua and Barbuda, Australia, Bahamas, Barbados, Brazil, Cameroon, Cape Verde, Chile, Colombia, Congo, Cuba, Djibouti, Egypt, Ethiopia, Fiji, Gabon, Gambia, Grenada, Guinea-Bissau, Guyana, Honduras, Iceland, India, Indonesia, Ireland, Ivory Coast, Jamaica, Kenya, Kuwait, Madagascar, Malaysia, Mexico, Morocco, New Zealand, Nigeria, Oman, Pakistan, Qatar, Saint Lucia, Saint Vincent and the Grenadines, Senegal, Seychelles, Sierra Leone, Singapore, Sri Lanka, Sudan, Thailand, Trinidad and Tobago, Tunisia, Uganda, United Republic of Tanzania, Uruguay, Vanuatu, Yugoslavia.

Meeting numbers. GA 40th session: plenary 110, 111.

Recorded vote in Assembly as follows:

In favour: Afghanistan, Algeria, Angola, Antigua and Barbuda, Argentina, Australia, Austria, Bahamas, Bahrain, Bangladesh, Barbados, Belgium, Benin, Bhutan, Bolivia, Botswana, Brazil, Brunei Darussalam, Bulgaria, Burkina Faso, Burma, Burundi, Byelorussian SSR, Cameroon, Canada, Cape Verde, Central African Republic, Chad, Chile, China, Colombia, Comoros, Congo, Costa Rica, Cuba, Cyprus, Czechoslovakia, Democratic Kampuchea, Democratic Yemen, Denmark, Djibouti, Dominican Republic, Egypt, El Salvador, Ethiopia, Fiji, Finland, France, Gabon, Gambia, German Democratic Republic, Ghana, Greece, Grenada, Guinea, Guinea-Bissau, Guyana, Haiti, Honduras, Hungary, Iceland, India, Indonesia, Iran, Iraq, Ireland, Italy, Ivory Coast, Jamaica, Japan, Jordan, Kenya, Kuwait, Lao People's Democratic Republic, Lebanon, Lesotho, Liberia, Libyan Arab Jamahiriya, Luxembourg, Madagascar, Malawi, Malaysia, Maldives, Mali, Malta, Mauritania, Mauritius, Mexico, Mongolia, Morocco, Mozambique, Nepal, Netherlands, New Zealand, Nicaragua, Niger, Nigeria, Norway, Oman, Pakistan, Panama, Paraguay, Philippines, Poland, Portugal, Qatar, Romania, Saint Lucia, Saint Vincent and the Grenadines, Samoa, Saudi Arabia, Senegal, Seychelles, Sierra Leone, Singapore, Solomon Islands, Somalia, Spain, Sri Lanka, Sudan, Suriname, Swaziland, Sweden, Thailand, Togo, Trinidad and Tobago, Tunisia, Uganda, Ukrainian SSR, USSR, United Arab Emirates, United Republic of Tanzania, Uruguay, Vanuatu, Viet Nam, Yemen, Yugoslavia, Zaire, Zambia, Zimbabwe.

Against: Turkey, United States.

Abstaining: Germany, Federal Republic of, Israel, Peru, United Kingdom, Venezuela.

Two States explained their non-participation in the vote: Albania said that the text contained the same provisions it had rejected in previous resolutions; Ecuador noted that it had not signed the Convention because it did not reflect its rights and interests.

Turkey gave the same reason for its negative vote, while the United States maintained that part XI of the Convention, governing exploitation of sea-bed resources beyond national jurisdiction, ran contrary to its policy; both States opposed including the costs of the Preparatory Commission in the United Nations regular budget as they believed those costs should be borne by the Convention's signatories. The United States, moreover, felt that the Commission's Declaration was not in accord with international law.

Peru said its abstention did not prevent it from recognizing the Convention's historical value, and stated that its accession was still being studied. The Federal Republic of Germany declared that neither the resolution nor the Declaration was conducive to efforts to find consensus solutions to unresolved issues in the law of the sea. The United Kingdom spoke in like manner, adding that although it had been unable to accept the Convention's régime for deep sea-bed mining, it had continued to work for a universally acceptable régime.

Argentina interpreted the sixth preambular paragraph and paragraph 4 of the resolution to be in accordance with the statement made by it when it signed the Convention. Belgium said it was not entirely satisfied with the text which, it felt, contained elements likely to make the Commission's work more difficult. Canada agreed, citing the Declaration which it did not support and the reference to registering pioneer investors. Italy found that both the resolution and the Declaration contained divisive elements which would not encourage ratification of the Convention. Although strongly supporting the law of the sea régime, the Netherlands felt that the Declaration did not accurately reflect current international law.

Among other related actions, the Assembly, in **resolution 40/19**, invited Member States seeking to recover artistic treasures from the sea-bed to facilitate the participation of States having a historical link with those treasures; in **resolution 40/94 J**, requested that further measures be taken to prevent an arms race on the sea-bed; and in **resolution 40/97 A**, endorsed a decision by the United Nations Council for Namibia proclaiming an exclusive economic zone for Namibia with a 200-mile outer limit.

ECONOMIC AND SOCIAL COUNCIL ACTION

The Economic and Social Council, in **resolution 1985/75**, acknowledged that ocean resources represented an important contribution to the developmental process of States, and requested the Secretary-General to report to it in 1987 on the specific needs and problems encountered by countries, particularly developing ones, in managing and developing ocean resources in their exclusive economic zones.

REFERENCES

[1]*Multilateral Treaties Deposited with the Secretary-General: Status as at 31 December 1985* (ST/LEG/SER.E/4), Sales No. E.86.V.3. [2]YUN 1982, p. 178. [3]YUN 1984, p. 108. [4]*Ibid.*, p. 112, GA res. 39/73, 13 Dec. 1984. [5]A/40/923. [6]LOS/PCN/64. [7]LOS/PCN/L.7/Rev.2. [8]YUN 1984, p. 110. [9]YUN 1982, p. 216. [10]YUN 1983, p. 107. [11]YUN 1984, p. 112. [12]LOS/PCN/56. [13]LOS/PCN/57. [14]LOS/PCN/61. [15]LOS/PCN/63. [16]LOS/PCN/62. [17]LOS/PCN/60. [18]LOS/PCN/65. [19]LOS/PCN/66. [20]LOS/PCN/67-70. [21]LOS/PCN/71. [22]LOS/PCN/73. [23]LOS/PCN/74. [24]LOS/PCN/L.18. [25]LOS/PCN/L.20. [26]LOS/PCN/L.16. [27]LOS/PCN/L.17. [28]*The Law of the Sea: Multilateral Treaties Relevant to the United Nations Convention on the Law of the Sea*, Sales No. E.85.V.11.

OTHER PUBLICATIONS

Law of the Sea: A Select Bibliography (LOS/LIB/1), Sales No. E.85.V.2. *The Law of the Sea: Status of the United Nations Convention on the Law of the Sea*, Sales No. E.85.V.5. *The Law of the Sea: Master File Containing References to Official Documents of the Third United Nations Conference on the Law of the Sea*, Sales No. E.85.V.9. *The Law of the Sea: National Legislation on the Exclusive Economic Zone, the Economic Zone and the Exclusive Fishery Zone*, Sales No. E.85.V.10. *The Law of the Sea: Pollution by Dumping*, Sales No. E.85.V.12.

Chapter IV

International peace and security

Ways of maintaining international peace and security continued to be the primary objective of the United Nations during 1985.

Expressing concern over the increasing recourse to the use of force, the General Assembly took action to try to improve the situation. It urged all States, particularly the Security Council's permanent members, to prevent the further deterioration of the international situation (resolution 40/158) and, in a solemn appeal to conflicting States to settle disputes peacefully, it invited the Council to act promptly in such cases (40/9). As the *Ad Hoc* Committee on the Implementation of the Collective Security Provisions of the Charter of the United Nations had still not been formed, the Assembly urged that 54 States be appointed as members (40/159).

On United Nations Day, 24 October, the Assembly proclaimed 1986 as the International Year of Peace (40/3), subsequently adopted a programme for the Year and decided to convene a second pledging conference for contributions to it (40/10). The Assembly also called for the implementation of its 1984 Declaration on the Right of Peoples to Peace (40/11) and renewed the mandate of its Special Committee on Peace-keeping Operations (40/163).

In his annual report to the Assembly (see p. 3), the Secretary-General recalled that 40 years previously it had been concluded that the old idea of achieving national security through a competitive armaments race led only to increasing general insecurity. Therefore, that concept was to be replaced by a collective system, involving particularly the most powerful nations, which would play a key role in the Security Council. Although that had not been realized for many reasons, the Council had time and again slowed the onrush of events, gained time for vital changes in direction, produced face-saving mechanisms and substituted talk for violent action. A system of conflict control, known as peace-keeping, had been pioneered, which had shown considerable effectiveness in 13 separate operations. Urging States to direct their will to the key function of maintaining international peace and security, the Secretary-General stressed that in the nuclear age, there was nothing more dangerous than failing to make the system work.

All aspects of the maintenance of international peace and security were also discussed by the Special Committee on the Charter of the United Nations and on the Strengthening of the Role of the Organization (see LEGAL QUESTIONS, Chapter IV).

Topics related to this chapter. Disarmament. Human rights: human rights and peace. Legal aspects of international political relations: peaceful settlement of disputes between States; good-neighbourliness between States; non-use of force in international relations; draft Code of Offences against peace and security; draft convention against mercenaries; prevention of terrorism. International organizations and international law: strengthening the role of the United Nations.

Implementation of the 1970 Declaration on international security

The General Assembly, in December 1985, after its annual review of the implementation of the 1970 Declaration on the Strengthening of International Security,[1] urged all States to prevent the further deterioration of the international situation and stated that the gradual military disengagement of the great Powers and their military alliances should be promoted.

In connection with the item, the Secretary-General submitted several documents to the Assembly. In an August report and subsequent addenda,[2] submitted pursuant to a 1984 request,[3] he forwarded 10 substantive replies to the Assembly's invitation to Member States for their views concerning the Declaration's implementation. Responding to a further 1984 Assembly request,[4] for him to report on its recommendation that the Security Council give priority consideration to the need for strengthening the collective security system provided for in the United Nations Charter, the Secretary-General stated that he had no further information to report.[5]

Communications. Letters were received from Member States during the year, concerning the review of the implementation of the Declaration.

On 17 June,[6] the United Kingdom transmitted a communiqué by the Ministers for Foreign Affairs of the North Atlantic Council (Lisbon, Portugal, 6 and 7 June), setting out the Council's policy on East-West relations and calling on the new USSR leadership to join the Ministers in seeking tangible improvements in those relations.

On 6 May,[7] Poland forwarded a communiqué adopted at a summit meeting of the States parties to the 1955 Warsaw Treaty of Friendship, Co-operation and Mutual Assistance (Warsaw, 26 April); participants signed a Protocol extending the Treaty for the coming 20 years, emphasized its importance in preserving peace in Europe, and declared that they favoured developing equitable and mutually advantageous international co-operation. In connection with the Protocol's signing, Mongolia, on 29 April,[8] stated that the current world situation required the continuance of the Warsaw Treaty Organization (WTO), although its members opposed dividing the world into military blocs and advocated the simultaneous dissolution of WTO and NATO.

The German Democratic Republic and the USSR in a joint communication of 2 April[9] gave the details of a visit to the USSR on 19 and 20 March by the German Democratic Republic Foreign Minister, and declared that the negotiations started at Geneva between the USSR and the United States could lead to reducing the threat of war.

An interview on international affairs with Mikhail S. Gorbachev, General Secretary of the Central Committee of the Communist Party of the USSR, published on 8 April in *Pravda* (USSR), was transmitted by the USSR on 17 April,[10] while extracts from a statement also relating to foreign policy made by Mr. Gorbachev at Dnepropetrovsk, USSR, on 26 June were forwarded on 4 July.[11] In the interview, Mr. Gorbachev declared that there were possibilities for improving Soviet-American relations and the international situation; at Dnepropetrovsk, he stated that the task of the Geneva negotiations was to halt the arms race.

Four communications concerned the fortieth anniversary of the end of the Second World War. Madagascar, in an 8 May message,[12] stressed the need to strengthen the United Nations. Czechoslovakia transmitted on 17 May[13] a joint statement made at the Economic and Social Council's May/June session by Bulgaria, the Byelorussian SSR, Cuba, Czechoslovakia, the German Democratic Republic, Hungary, Mongolia, Poland, the Ukrainian SSR, the USSR and Viet Nam, declaring that in memory of those who gave their lives for peace, it was necessary to improve the international situation. On 20 May,[14] Mongolia forwarded a 17 May statement by the Central Committee of the Mongolian People's Revolutionary Party, declaring that Mongolia joined with the USSR in a resolve to prevent another war. The USSR conveyed on 9 May[15] an address from the Central Committee of the

Communist Party, the Presidium of the Supreme Soviet and the Council of Ministers of the USSR appealing to peoples, parliaments and Governments to bar the way to another war.

On 19 July,[16] the USSR transmitted a message of greeting to the twenty-first session of the Assembly of Heads of State and Government of the Organization of African Unity (Addis Ababa, Ethiopia, 18-20 July) in which it wished success to those participating, in the interests of peace and international security.

Other 1985 letters received under this subject heading dealt with disarmament (see p. 14) or specific situations, such as: Afghanistan, Angola-South Africa dispute, Central America, China-Viet Nam, Ethiopia–Somalia, Iran-Iraq, Kampuchea and Lao People's Democratic Republic-Thailand (see SUBJECT INDEX).

GENERAL ASSEMBLY ACTION

On 16 December, the General Assembly, on the recommendation of the First Committee, adopted **resolution 40/158** by recorded vote.

Review of the implementation of the Declaration on the Strengthening of International Security

The General Assembly,

Having considered the item entitled "Review of the implementation of the Declaration on the Strengthening of International Security",

Taking note of the fifteenth anniversary of the adoption of the Declaration on the Strengthening of International Security and the important role it has played in international life in strengthening and consolidating peace and security, as well as promoting co-operation among States on the basis of the purposes and principles of the United Nations,

Noting with concern that the provisions of the Declaration on the Strengthening of International Security have not been fully implemented,

Noting further with concern that the United Nations system of collective security has not been used effectively,

Recalling the duty of States not to intervene in the internal or external affairs of any State, in accordance with the purposes and principles of the Charter of the United Nations,

Recalling the provisions of the Declaration on Principles of International Law concerning Friendly Relations and Co-operation among States in accordance with the Charter of the United Nations,

Bearing in mind the provisions of the Declaration on the Inadmissibility of Intervention and Interference in the Internal Affairs of States,

Recalling the Manila Declaration on the Peaceful Settlement of International Disputes,

Concerned by the continued escalation of tension in the world, accompanied by the policy of competition for spheres of influence, domination and exploitation in more and more parts of the world, the escalation to new levels of the arms race, particularly in nuclear weapons, and the danger of its extension into outer space, all of which pose a grave threat to global peace and security,

Profoundly disturbed by the increasing recourse to the use or threat of use of force, military intervention and interference, aggression and foreign occupation, by the aggravation of existing crises in the world, by the continued infringement of the independence, sovereignty and territorial integrity of countries, by the denial of the right to self-determination of peoples under colonial and foreign occupation and by attempts to characterize erroneously the struggles of peoples for independence and human dignity as falling within the context of East-West confrontation, thus denying them the right to self-determination, to decide their own destiny and realize their legitimate aspirations, by the persistence of colonialism, racism and *apartheid* supported by the growing use of military force, by the intensification and expansion of the scope and frequency of manœuvres and other military activities conceived within the context of big-Power confrontation and used as means of pressure, threat and destabilization, and by the lack of solutions to the world economic crisis in which the deeper underlying problems of a structural nature have been compounded by cyclical factors and which has further aggravated the inequalities and injustices in international economic relations,

Aware of the increasing interdependence among nations and of the fact that in the present-day world there is no alternative to a policy of peaceful coexistence, détente and co-operation among States on the basis of equality, irrespective of their economic or military power, political and social systems or size and geographic location,

Reaffirming the role of the United Nations as an indispensable forum for negotiations and reaching agreements on measures to promote and strengthen international peace and security,

Stressing the need for the main organs of the United Nations responsible for the maintenance of peace and security, particularly the Security Council, to contribute more effectively to the promotion of international peace and security by seeking solutions to unresolved problems and crises in the world,

Expressing its satisfaction with the resolute support for the purposes and principles of the Charter of the United Nations, which have proved to be of universal validity, and for the ideals of the United Nations, expressed in the context of the commemoration of the fortieth anniversary of the Organization with the participation of a large number of heads of States or Government,

1. *Reaffirms* the validity of the Declaration on the Strengthening of International Security and calls upon all States to contribute effectively to its implementation;

2. *Urges once again* all States to abide strictly, in their international relations, by their commitment to the Charter of the United Nations and, to this end:

(a) To refrain from the use or threat of use of force, intervention, interference, aggression, foreign occupation and colonial domination or measures of political and economic coercion which violate the sovereignty, territorial integrity, independence and security of other States as well as the permanent sovereignty of peoples over their natural resources;

(b) To refrain from supporting or encouraging any such act for any reason whatsoever and to reject and refuse recognition of situations brought about by any such act;

3. *Calls upon* all States, in particular the nuclear-weapon States and other militarily significant States, to take immediate steps aimed at:

(a) Promoting and using effectively the system of collective security as envisaged in the Charter;

(b) Halting effectively the arms race and achieving general and complete disarmament under effective international control and, to this end, to start serious, meaningful and effective negotiations with a view to implementing the recommendations and decisions contained in the Final Document of the Tenth Special Session of the General Assembly, and to fulfilling the priority tasks listed in the Programme of Action set forth in section III of the Final Document;

4. *Invites* all States, in particular the major military Powers and States members of military alliances, to refrain, especially in critical situations and in crisis areas, from actions, including military activities and manœuvres, conceived within the context of big-Power confrontation and used as a means of pressure on, threat to and destabilization of other States and regions;

5. *Expresses its conviction* that the gradual military disengagement of the great Powers and their military alliances from various parts of the world should be promoted;

6. *Urges* all States, in particular the permanent members of the Security Council, to take all necessary measures to prevent the further deterioration of the international situation and, to this end:

(a) To seek, through more effective utilization of the means provided for in the Charter, the peaceful settlement of disputes and the elimination of the focal points of crisis and tension which constitute a threat to international peace and security;

(b) To proceed without delay to a global consideration of ways and means for bringing about a revival of the world economy and for the restructuring of international economic relations within the framework of the global negotiations with a view to establishing the new international economic order;

(c) To accelerate the economic development of developing countries, particularly the least developed ones;

(d) To implement urgently measures agreed upon to ameliorate the critical economic situation in Africa which is the result, *inter alia*, of persistent inclement climatic factors;

7. *Emphasizes* the role that the United Nations has in the maintenance of peace and security and in economic and social development and progress for the benefit of all mankind;

8. *Calls upon* all States, taking into account the views expressed at the commemorative session of the fortieth anniversary of the United Nations, to promote the role of the General Assembly and the Secretary-General in the strengthening of international security, in accordance with the Charter;

9. *Stresses* that there is an urgent need to enhance the effectiveness of the Security Council in discharging its principal role of maintaining international peace and security and, to that end, emphasizes the need to examine mechanisms and working methods on a continued basis in order to enhance the authority and enforcement capacity of the Council, in accordance with the Charter;

10. *Emphasizes* that the Security Council should consider holding periodic meetings in specific cases to consider and review outstanding problems and crises, thus enabling the Council to play a more active role in preventing conflicts;

11. *Reiterates* the need for the Security Council, in particular its permanent members, to ensure the effective implementation of its decisions in compliance with the relevant provisions of the Charter;

12. *Considers* that respect for and promotion of human rights and fundamental freedoms in their civil, political, economic, social and cultural aspects, on the one hand, and the strengthening of international peace and security, on the other, mutually reinforce each other;

13. *Reaffirms* the legitimacy of the struggle of peoples under colonial domination, foreign occupation or racist régimes and their inalienable right to self-determination and independence, and urges Member States to increase their support for and solidarity with them and their national liberation movements and to take urgent and effective measures for the speedy completion of the implementation of the Declaration on the Granting of Independence to Colonial Countries and Peoples and for the final elimination of colonialism, racism and *apartheid;*

14. *Calls upon* all States, particularly the members of the Security Council, to take appropriate and effective measures to promote the fulfilment of the objective of the denuclearization of Africa in order to avert the serious danger which the nuclear capability of South Africa constitutes to the African States, in particular the front-line States, as well as to international peace and security;

15. *Welcomes* the continuation of the process within the framework of the Conference on Security and Co-operation in Europe and expresses the hope that the Stockholm Conference on Confidence- and Security-building Measures and Disarmament in Europe, the continent with the greatest concentration of armaments and military forces, will achieve significant and positive results;

16. *Reaffirms* that the democratization of international relations is an imperative necessity enabling, under the conditions of interdependence, the full development and independence of all States as well as the attainment of genuine security, peace and co-operation in the world, and stresses its firm belief that the United Nations offers the best framework for the promotion of these goals;

17. *Invites* Member States to submit their views on the question of the implementation of the Declaration on the Strengthening of International Security, and requests the Secretary-General to submit a report to the General Assembly at its forty-first session on the basis of the replies received;

18. *Decides* to include in the provisional agenda of its forty-first session the item entitled "Review of the implementation of the Declaration on the Strengthening of International Security".

General Assembly resolution 40/158

16 December 1985   Meeting 117   127-0-26 (recorded vote)

Approved by First Committee (A/40/1028) by recorded vote (102-0-25), 6 December (meeting 61); 21-nation draft (A/C.1/40/L.88), orally revised; agenda item 72.

Sponsors: Algeria, Bahamas, Bangladesh, Congo, Egypt, Ghana, Guyana, India, Indonesia, Madagascar, Mali, Nigeria, Pakistan, Romania, Senegal, Sri Lanka, Sudan, Tunisia, Uganda, Yugoslavia, Zambia.

Meeting numbers. GA 40th session: 1st Committee 55-61; plenary 117.

Recorded vote in Assembly as follows:

In favour: Afghanistan, Algeria, Angola, Antigua and Barbuda, Argentina, Bahamas, Bahrain, Bangladesh, Barbados, Benin, Bhutan, Bolivia, Botswana, Brazil, Brunei Darussalam, Bulgaria, Burkina Faso, Burma, Burundi, Byelorussian SSR, Cameroon, Cape Verde, Central African Republic, Chad, Chile, China, Colombia, Comoros, Congo, Costa Rica, Cuba, Cyprus, Czechoslovakia, Democratic Kampuchea, Democratic Yemen, Djibouti, Dominican Republic, Ecuador, Egypt, El Salvador, Equatorial Guinea, Ethiopia, Fiji, Gabon, Gambia, German Democratic Republic, Ghana, Guatemala, Guinea, Guinea-Bissau, Guyana, Haiti, Honduras, Hungary, India, Indonesia, Iran, Iraq, Ivory Coast, Jamaica, Jordan, Kenya, Kuwait, Lao People's Democratic Republic, Lebanon, Lesotho, Liberia, Libyan Arab Jamahiriya, Madagascar, Malawi, Malaysia, Maldives, Mali, Malta, Mauritania, Mauritius, Mexico, Mongolia, Morocco, Mozambique, Nepal, Nicaragua, Niger, Nigeria, Oman, Pakistan, Panama, Papua New Guinea, Paraguay, Peru, Poland, Qatar, Romania, Rwanda, Saint Lucia, Saint Vincent and the Grenadines, Samoa, Sao Tome and Principe, Saudi Arabia, Senegal, Seychelles, Sierra Leone, Singapore, Somalia, Sri Lanka, Sudan, Suriname, Swaziland, Syrian Arab Republic, Thailand, Togo, Trinidad and Tobago, Tunisia, Uganda, Ukrainian SSR, USSR, United Arab Emirates, United Republic of Tanzania, Uruguay, Vanuatu, Venezuela, Viet Nam, Yemen, Yugoslavia, Zaire, Zambia, Zimbabwe.

Against: None.

Abstaining: Australia, Austria, Belgium, Canada, Denmark, Finland, France, Germany, Federal Republic of, Greece, Grenada, Iceland, Ireland, Israel, Italy, Japan, Luxembourg, Netherlands, New Zealand, Norway, Portugal, Solomon Islands, Spain, Sweden, Turkey, United Kingdom, United States.

France abstained because the paragraph mentioning military disengagement dealt exclusively with the great Powers; it believed there were cases in which disengagement would be just as desirable where those Powers were not involved; also, the paragraphs concerning the roles of the Assembly and Security Council created thorny legal problems that should have been studied more carefully.

The United States felt that the text strayed into contentious regional issues, took positions prejudicing the outcome of negotiations, and blamed the deterioration of the international security climate exclusively on the super-Powers, ignoring other conflicts; noting that the text favoured the gradual military disengagement of those Powers from various parts of the world, it said it interpreted the language as calling again for withdrawal of the 118,000 USSR troops currently occupying Afghanistan.

REFERENCES

[1]YUN 1970, p. 105, GA res. 2734(XXV), 16 Dec. 1970. [2]A/40/506 & Add.1-3. [3]YUN 1984, p. 115, GA res. 39/155, 17 Dec. 1984. [4]*Ibid.*, p. 121, GA res. 39/154, 17 Dec. 1984. [5]A/40/823. [6]A/40/388. [7]A/40/292-S/17164. [8]A/40/304. [9]A/40/221. [10]A/40/238. [11]A/40/460. [12]A/40/308. [13]A/40/320-E/1985/82. [14]A/40/322. [15]A/40/302. [16]A/40/497.

Implementation of the security provisions of the UN Charter

Pursuant to a 1984 Assembly resolution,[1] the Secretary-General reported in August 1985[2] that five Member States had replied to his request for comments on implementing the collective security provisions of the United Nations Charter.

In accordance with the same resolution, the Assembly President consulted the Chairmen of the regional groups on the constitution of the *Ad Hoc* Committee on the subject, to be set up under a 1983 Assembly resolution.[3] However, differing views as to the distribution of seats prevented establishment of the Committee, the Secretary-General stated.[2]

GENERAL ASSEMBLY ACTION

On 16 December 1985, on the recommendation of the First Committee, the General Assembly adopted **resolution 40/159** by recorded vote.

Implementation of the collective security provisions of the Charter of the United Nations for the maintenance of international peace and security

The General Assembly,

Recalling its resolutions 37/119 of 16 December 1982, 38/191 of 20 December 1983 and 39/158 of 17 December 1984 on the implementation of the collective security provisions of the Charter of the United Nations for the maintenance of international peace and security,

Reaffirming that the primary function of the United Nations, in particular through the Security Council, is the maintenance of international peace and security,

Stressing that the purposes of the United Nations can be achieved only under conditions in which States comply fully with their obligations assumed under the Charter,

Alarmed over the growing tendency of States to resort to the use of force, intervention and interference in the internal affairs of States, thus ignoring the Charter and the Declaration on Principles of International Law concerning Friendly Relations and Co-operation among States in accordance with the Charter of the United Nations,

Concerned that the Security Council has not always been able to take decisive action for the maintenance of international peace and for resolving international problems,

Recognizing that fundamental approaches to genuine security include, *inter alia*, the strengthening of the Charter system of collective security,

Conscious of the important role with which the Security Council is entrusted in enhancing the collective security provisions of the Charter for the promotion of peace and security in the world in accordance with the Charter,

Regretting that the provisions of the Charter relating to collective security measures have not been fully implemented,

Taking into account, in this connection, the reports of the Secretary-General on the work of the Organization to the General Assembly at its thirty-seventh, thirty-eighth, thirty-ninth and fortieth sessions,

Also taking into account the statement by the President of the Security Council at the commemorative session of the Council on 26 September 1985,

Recalling the Final Political Declaration adopted by the Conference of Foreign Ministers of Non-Aligned Countries, held at Luanda from 4 to 7 September 1985,

Also recalling the views of the Governments of the five Nordic countries on the strengthening of the United Nations,

Taking note of the note by the Secretary-General on the implementation of the collective security provisions of the Charter of the United Nations for the maintenance of international peace and security,

Having considered the item entitled, "Implementation of the collective security provisions of the Charter of the

United Nations for the maintenance of international peace and security",

1. *Regrets* that the *Ad Hoc* Committee on the Implementation of the Collective Security Provisions of the Charter of the United Nations which the General Assembly, by its resolution 38/191, decided to establish for the purpose of exploring ways and means of implementing the said provisions has not been constituted;

2. *Requests* the President of the General Assembly, as a matter of urgency, to appoint fifty-four Member States and on the basis of consultation already conducted to constitute the membership of the *Ad Hoc* Committee on the basis of equitable geographical representation and including the permanent members of the Security Council;

3. *Requests* the Secretary-General urgently to invite those Member States that have not yet done so to communicate to him not later than 30 April 1986 their views and comments on the matter and to transmit those views and comments to the *Ad Hoc* Committee as soon as possible;

4. *Requests* the *Ad Hoc* Committee, in considering the matter, to take due account of the views and comments of Member States, including their recommendations, and to submit a progress report to the Security Council for its consideration and comments and to the General Assembly at its forty-first session, and a final report to the Assembly at its forty-second session;

5. *Decides* to include in the provisional agenda of its forty-first session the item entitled "Implementation of the collective security provisions of the Charter of the United Nations for the maintenance of international peace and security".

General Assembly resolution 40/159

16 December 1985   Meeting 117   114-21-16 (recorded vote)

Approved by First Committee (A/40/1029) by recorded vote (91-21-16), 6 December (meeting 61); 5-nation draft (A/C.1/40/L.87), orally revised; agenda item 73.
Sponsors: Ghana, Malaysia, Mali, Nigeria, Trinidad and Tobago.
Financial implications. 5th Committee, A/40/1054; S-G, A/C.1/40/L.89, A/C.5/40/88.
Meeting numbers. GA 40th session: 1st Committee 55-61; 5th Committee 62; plenary 117.

Recorded vote in Assembly as follows:

In favour: Algeria, Angola, Antigua and Barbuda, Argentina, Australia, Bahamas, Bahrain, Bangladesh, Barbados, Benin, Bhutan, Bolivia, Botswana, Brazil, Brunei Darussalam, Burkina Faso, Burma, Burundi, Cameroon, Cape Verde, Central African Republic, Chad, Chile, China, Colombia, Comoros, Congo, Costa Rica, Cyprus, Democratic Kampuchea, Djibouti, Dominican Republic, Ecuador, Egypt, El Salvador, Equatorial Guinea, Ethiopia, Fiji, Gabon, Gambia, Ghana, Greece, Guatemala, Guinea, Guinea-Bissau, Guyana, Haiti, Honduras, India, Indonesia, Iran, Iraq, Ivory Coast, Jamaica, Jordan, Kenya, Kuwait, Lebanon, Lesotho, Liberia, Libyan Arab Jamahiriya, Madagascar, Malawi, Malaysia, Maldives, Mali, Mauritania, Mauritius, Mexico, Morocco, Mozambique, Nepal, Nicaragua, Niger, Nigeria, Oman, Pakistan, Panama, Paraguay, Peru, Philippines, Qatar, Romania, Rwanda, Saint Lucia, Saint Vincent and the Grenadines, Samoa, Sao Tome and Principe, Saudi Arabia, Senegal, Seychelles, Sierra Leone, Singapore, Solomon Islands, Somalia, Sri Lanka, Sudan, Suriname, Swaziland, Thailand, Togo, Trinidad and Tobago, Tunisia, Uganda, United Arab Emirates, United Republic of Tanzania, Uruguay, Vanuatu, Venezuela, Yemen, Yugoslavia, Zaire, Zambia, Zimbabwe.

Against: Afghanistan, Belgium, Bulgaria, Byelorussian SSR, Cuba, Czechoslovakia, France, German Democratic Republic, Germany, Federal Republic of, Hungary, Italy, Luxembourg, Mongolia, Netherlands, Poland, Portugal, Turkey, Ukrainian SSR, USSR, United Kingdom, United States.

Abstaining: Austria, Canada, Denmark, Finland, Grenada, Iceland, Ireland, Israel, Japan, Lao People's Democratic Republic, New Zealand, Norway, Papua New Guinea, Spain, Sweden, Viet Nam.

The USSR declared that in its provisions calling for the constitution of the *Ad Hoc* Committee, the text ran counter to the United Nations Charter, under which collective security questions fell within the purview of the Security Council.

The United States opposed establishing a committee to perform activities already provided for in the mandate of the Special Committee on the Charter of the United Nations and on the Strengthening of the Role of the Organization, whose progress could only be dangerously complicated by institutional duplication; expenditure of funds for that purpose was neither wise nor necessary.

The responsibility of the Council for maintaining international peace and security and its operations was the subject of a statement made by its President on its behalf at a 26 September Council meeting commemorating the United Nations fortieth anniversary (see Chapter XI of this section).

REFERENCES
[1]YUN 1984, p. 119, GA res. 39/158, 17 Dec. 1984. [2]A/40/454. [3]YUN 1983, p. 113, GA res. 38/191, 20 Dec. 1983.

Settling disputes through negotiations

Under a new agenda item, requested by Romania on 6 September 1985,[1] the General Assembly solemnly appealed to States in conflict to end armed action and settle their disputes peacefully and through negotiations. Annexed to Romania's request was a draft which became the basis for the resolution adopted by the Assembly.

Meanwhile, work continued on legal measures for the peaceful settlement of disputes and on the non-use of force in international relations (see LEGAL QUESTIONS, Chapter II).

GENERAL ASSEMBLY ACTION

On 8 November, the General Assembly adopted **resolution 40/9** without vote.

Solemn appeal to States in conflict to cease armed action forthwith and to settle disputes between them through negotiations, and to States Members of the United Nations to undertake to solve situations of tension and conflict and existing disputes by political means and to refrain from the threat or use of force and from any intervention in the internal affairs of other States

The General Assembly,

Deeply concerned at the persistence of armed conflicts, acts of aggression and situations of tension in different parts of the world, at the emergence of new sources of conflict and tension in international life and at the danger to the independence and security of States and to international peace and security posed by the threat or use of force in relations between States,

Convinced that all States should exert the utmost efforts to settle any conflict or dispute between them exclusively by peaceful means and that resorting to the threat or use of force against other States can only aggravate the international situation and make more difficult the solution of problems,

Considering that it is in the interest both of States involved in conflict and other States, and of the general cause of world peace and security, to put an end to armed conflicts and to encourage and assist the solution of problems through peaceful means,

Solemnly reaffirming, on the occasion of the fortieth anniversary of the United Nations, the resolute commitment of Member States to the purposes and principles of the Charter of the United Nations and the obligations which they assumed as Members of the Organization, in particular their commitment to refrain in international relations from the threat or use of force against the sovereignty, territorial integrity and political independence of any other State,

Reaffirming that all States shall settle their international disputes by peaceful means in such a manner that international peace and security, and justice, are not endangered,

Recalling the inherent right of all States to individual or collective self-defence, as enshrined in Article 51 of the Charter,

Reaffirming the Manila Declaration on the Peaceful Settlement of International Disputes, approved by the General Assembly in its resolution 37/10 of 15 November 1982,

Considering that the question of the peaceful settlement of disputes should constitute a central concern of all States and of the United Nations,

1. *Addresses a solemn appeal* to States in conflict to put an end to armed action forthwith and to proceed to the settlement of their disputes by negotiations and other peaceful means;

2. *Calls upon* all States to comply fully and consistently with the obligations they have assumed, in accordance with the purposes and principles of the Charter of the United Nations, to resolve conflicts and disputes by peaceful means and to refrain from the threat or use of force and from any intervention in the internal affairs of other States;

3. *Invites* the Security Council, which has the primary responsibility for the maintenance of international peace and security, to act promptly in accordance with its functions under the Charter, in cases of conflict and dispute in different regions of the world, by recommending appropriate procedures or methods of adjustment, including designation of representatives of the United Nations, with a view to settling disputes between States by peaceful means, eliminating situations of tension and conflict, and establishing relations based on understanding, co-operation and peace among all the States of the world;

4. *Reaffirms* the important role as conferred by the Charter on the General Assembly in the areas of the peaceful settlement of disputes and the maintenance of international peace and security;

5. *Encourages* the Secretary-General to play an active role within the scope of his functions under the Charter with a view to promoting efforts for the peaceful settlement of disputes and conflicts between States;

6. *Calls upon* Member States to make full use, in accordance with the Charter, of the framework provided by the United Nations for the peaceful settlement of disputes and international problems;

7. *Appeals* to Member States to act resolutely, in view of the purposes and principles of the Charter and in accordance with their duties as Members, in order that the Organization may harmonize the combined efforts of States aimed at strengthening world peace and security, solving the major issues confronting humanity and ensuring conditions for the free and independent development of all peoples.

General Assembly resolution 40/9

8 November 1985   Meeting 69   Adopted without vote

Draft by Romania (A/40/L.12); agenda item 146.

Iran felt that political realism should have led to a solemn appeal acknowledging that there was a link between justice and peace; it supported the principle of peaceful settlement of disputes, but maintained that the concept made no sense after aggression had been launched.

REFERENCE

(1)A/40/241.

Review of peace-keeping operations

The Special Committee on Peace-keeping Operations, established by the General Assembly in 1965,(1) did not meet in 1985. United Nations peace-keeping forces continued to operate in Cyprus and Lebanon and on the Golan Heights between Israel and the Syrian Arab Republic (see Chapters VIII and IX of this section).

On 19 December,(2) the Netherlands informed the Secretary-General that it had decided to make the following units available as stand-by forces for United Nations peace-keeping operations: within 48 hours, a marine corps unit, a liaison unit and a reinforced infantry company, comprising in all some 300 men, one frigate, three light reconnaissance helicopters, one transport aircraft, and a 30-man military police unit; within a week, a second marine corps unit of 300 men, a number of frigates and one support vessel. Those units would be available, in general, for up to six months, while for long-term participation, other units would be designated in the light of circumstances and availability.

GENERAL ASSEMBLY ACTION

On 16 December, the General Assembly, on the recommendation of the Special Political Committee, adopted **resolution 40/163** without vote.

Comprehensive review of the whole question of peace-keeping operations in all their aspects
The General Assembly,
Recalling its resolutions 2006(XIX) of 18 February 1965, 2053 A (XX) of 15 December 1965, 2249(S-V) of 23 May 1967, 2308(XXII) of 13 December 1967, 2451(XXIII) of 19 December 1968, 2670(XXV) of 8 December 1970, 2835(XXVI) of 17 December 1971, 2965(XXVII) of 13 December 1972, 3091(XXVIII) of 7 December 1973, 3239(XXIX) of 29 November 1974, 3457(XXX) of 10 December 1975, 31/105 of 15 December 1976, 32/106 of 15 December 1977, 33/114 of 18 December 1978, 34/53 of 23 November 1979, 35/121 of 11 December 1980, 36/37 of 18 November 1981, 37/93 of 10 December 1982, 38/81 of 15 December 1983 and 39/97 of 14 December 1984,
Awaiting the issuance of the report of the Special Committee on Peace-keeping Operations to the General Assembly at its forty-first session,
1. *Reaffirms and renews* the mandate given to the Special Committee on Peace-keeping Operations by the relevant resolutions of the General Assembly;
2. *Decides* to include in the provisional agenda of its forty-first session the item entitled "Comprehensive review of the whole question of peace-keeping operations in all their aspects".

General Assembly resolution 40/163

16 December 1985   Meeting 118   Adopted without vote

Approved by Special Political Committee (A/40/807) without vote, 10 October (meeting 7); draft by Chairman (A/SPC/40/L.5) following informal consultations; agenda item 77.
Meeting numbers. GA 40th session: SPC 5-7; plenary 118.

REFERENCES
(1)YUN 1964, p. 59, GA res. 2006(XIX), 18 Feb. 1965.
(2)A/41/56-S/17688.

PUBLICATION
The Blue Helmets: A Review of United Nations Peace-keeping (DPI/850), Sales No. E.85.I.18.

International Year of Peace (1986)

At the conclusion of its special commemorative session on the United Nations fortieth anniversary (see Chapter XI of this section), the General Assembly on 24 October 1985—United Nations Day—proclaimed 1986 as the International Year of Peace (IYP).

Preparations for IYP, which was first declared by the Assembly in 1982,(1) continued throughout 1985. On 11 November, the Assembly adopted a programme for the Year.

Reports of the Secretary-General. Responding to a 1984 Assembly request,(2) the Secretary-General in August 1985(3) gave details of four regional seminars held to promote IYP objectives: African region (8-14 January 1985, Addis Ababa); Latin America and Caribbean region (25 February–5 March, New York); European region (6-10 May, Vienna, Austria); and Asia and the Pacific and Western Asia regions (20-24 May, Bangkok, Thailand). Participants included experts designated by 95 Member States and two non-member States as well as representatives of 20 United Nations organizations and of 76 non-governmental organizations (NGOs). The

Secretary-General pointed out that a consensus had emerged at each seminar on the adoption of a final statement; participants at all seminars had called for effective measures to stop the arms race, particularly the nuclear arms race, recognized the importance of preparing for life in peace, agreed that international economic co-operation was essential for the achievement of peace, and declared that IYP could contribute to peace-building on a truly global basis.

In September and November,[4] the Secretary-General summarized the preparations and outlined the draft programme for observance of IYP. As at 5 November, 29 States had responded to his request for comments, information and proposals. A pledging conference had taken place (1 March, New York), attended by 49 Member States. As at 31 December 1985, pledges totalled $334,457. The Secretary-General concluded that IYP provided a basis for renewed efforts to promote peace and that the potential of the United Nations must be fully utilized to resolve problems inhibiting the co-operation needed for the betterment of the human condition. A draft programme for the Year, including guidelines for activities and a calendar of events, and a list of 252 organizations that had expressed interest in the programme, were annexed to the report.

Planned activities of the United Nations system in 1986 included a meeting of the heads of all organizations at the first regular session of the Administrative Committee on Co-ordination (ACC) in April; preparation of special bulletins, articles and reports; holding special meetings, seminars and lectures; organizing research projects, studies, international exhibits and competitions; presentation of awards to organizations and institutions making significant contributions to the observance of IYP; and issuing a peace medal. NGOs were to hold a conference, "Together for Peace", at Geneva from 20 to 24 January 1986.

Communications. A number of communications were received during 1985 regarding IYP. The majority also dealt with the observance of 1985 as the Year of the United Nations, as decided by the Assembly in 1984[5] in connection with the fortieth anniversary of the Organization (see Chapter XI of this section).

The USSR, on 27 March,[6] named the members of a commission established for both the Year of the United Nations and IYP, and on 5 April,[7] described the activities planned in observance of the Years.

The composition of similar bodies and activities for both Years were outlined by Mongolia on 26 April,[8] 3 June[9] and 30 August;[10] by the Byelorussian SSR on 26 April[11] and 3 May;[12] by Afghanistan on 9 May,[13] 11 September[14] and 23 December;[15] by Hungary on 30 May;[16] by the Ukrainian SSR on 5 June;[17] by the German

Democratic Republic on 12 June;[18] and by Czechoslovakia on 20 June.[19]

China, on 10 June,[20] listed the members of its committee for IYP, and Democratic Yemen, on 15 November,[21] detailed the formation of a similar body.

Other communications received in connection with IYP also dealt with other topics. They included letters from: the German Democratic Republic[22] and the Philippines[23] on the fortieth anniversary of the signing of the Charter; the Federal Republic of Germany,[24] transmitting a political declaration by seven Western nations on the fortieth anniversary of the end of the Second World War; and Poland[25] on the fortieth anniversary of the United Nations.

ACC consideration. ACC reported[26] that from May 1984 to April 1985 the IYP secretariat had maintained contact with all organizations of the United Nations system, and that at the second regular session of 1984 of the ACC Consultative Committee on Substantive Questions (Programme Matters), agency representatives had confirmed their support for the Year.

GENERAL ASSEMBLY ACTION

In 1985, the General Assembly adopted two resolutions on IYP.

On 24 October, it adopted **resolution 40/3** without vote.

International Year of Peace

The General Assembly,

Recalling resolution 37/16 of 16 November 1982, in which it declared 1986 to be the International Year of Peace,

Recognizing that the importance of the International Year of Peace, which has been linked with the fortieth anniversary of the United Nations, requires that the Year be devoted to concentrate the efforts of the United Nations and its Member States on the promotion and achievement of the ideals of peace by all possible means, which constitutes a fundamental purpose of the Charter of the United Nations,

Considering that efforts and activities to achieve positive results in international co-operation for the promotion of peace must be intensified during the Year and for ever,

1. *Approves* the Proclamation of the International Year of Peace, the text of which is annexed to the present resolution;

2. *Invites* all States, all organizations of the United Nations system and interested non-governmental organizations, educational, scientific, cultural and research organizations and the communications media to co-operate with the Secretary-General in achieving the objectives of the International Year of Peace;

3. *Requests* the Secretary-General to ensure the widest possible dissemination of this Proclamation.

Annex
Proclamation of the International Year of Peace

Whereas the General Assembly has decided unanimously to proclaim solemnly the International Year of Peace on 24 October 1985, the fortieth anniversary of the United Nations,

Whereas the fortieth anniversary of the United Nations provides a unique opportunity to reaffirm the support for and commitment to the purposes and principles of the Charter of the United Nations,

Whereas peace constitutes a universal ideal and the promotion of peace is the primary purpose of the United Nations,

Whereas the promotion of international peace and security requires continuing and positive action by States and peoples aimed at the prevention of war, removal of various threats to peace—including the nuclear threat—respect for the principle of non-use of force, the resolution of conflicts and the peaceful settlement of disputes, confidence-building measures, disarmament, the maintenance of outer space for peaceful uses, development, the promotion and exercise of human rights and fundamental freedoms, decolonization in accordance with the principle of self-determination, the elimination of racial discrimination and *apartheid*, the enhancement of the quality of life, satisfaction of human needs and the protection of the environment,

Whereas peoples must live together in peace and practise tolerance, and it has been recognized that education, information, science and culture can contribute to that end,

Whereas the International Year of Peace provides a timely impetus for initiating renewed thought and action for the promotion of peace,

Whereas the International Year of Peace offers an opportunity to Governments, intergovernmental, non-governmental organizations and others to express in practical terms the common aspiration of all peoples for peace,

Whereas the International Year of Peace is not only a celebration or commemoration, but an opportunity to reflect and act creatively and systematically in fulfilling the purposes of the United Nations,

Now, therefore,

The General Assembly

Solemnly proclaims 1986 to be the International Year of Peace and calls upon all peoples to join with the United Nations in resolute efforts to safeguard peace and the future of humanity.

General Assembly resolution 40/3

24 October 1985   Meeting 49   Adopted without vote

56-nation draft (A/40/L.6/Rev.1 & Rev.1/Add.1); agenda item 27.

Sponsors: Antigua and Barbuda, Argentina, Australia, Bahamas, Bangladesh, Barbados, Belize, Bolivia, Cameroon, Canada, Central African Republic, Chile, China, Colombia, Comoros, Congo, Costa Rica, Cuba, Cyprus, Dominican Republic, Ecuador, Egypt, El Salvador, Equatorial Guinea, Gabon, Gambia, German Democratic Republic, Ghana, Guatemala, Honduras, Jamaica, Kenya, Lebanon, Maldives, Malta, Mauritius, Mongolia, Morocco, Nepal, New Zealand, Nicaragua, Nigeria, Pakistan, Panama, Paraguay, Peru, Philippines, Poland, Romania, Saint Lucia, Samoa, Senegal, Thailand, Togo, Uruguay, Venezuela.

On 11 November, the Assembly adopted **resolution 40/10** without vote.

Programme of the International Year of Peace

The General Assembly,

Recalling its resolutions 37/16 of 16 November 1982, 38/56 of 7 December 1983 and 39/10 of 8 November 1984 on the International Year of Peace,

Recalling also the solemn Proclamation of the International Year of Peace approved on 24 October 1985, the fortieth anniversary of the United Nations, by which it called upon all peoples to join with the United Na-

tions in resolute efforts to safeguard peace and the future of humanity,

Aware that in the nuclear age the establishment of a lasting peace on Earth constitutes the primary condition for the preservation of civilization and the survival of mankind,

Welcoming the contributions made to the Voluntary Fund for the Programme of the International Year of Peace,

Taking note of the report of the Secretary-General on the regional seminars, which served to increase awareness in each region of the need to take effective steps to promote peace and also contributed towards the preparations for the Year,

Taking note also of the report of the Secretary-General on the activities undertaken in the implementation of General Assembly resolution 39/10 and the final version of the draft programme of the International Year of Peace annexed thereto,

1.   *Welcomes* the efforts of Member States to achieve substantive results in fulfilling the objectives of the International Year of Peace and to express the common aspiration of peoples for peace;

2.   *Invites* Member States, as well as organs and subsidiary bodies of the United Nations, intergovernmental and non-governmental organizations, educational, scientific, cultural and research institutions and the communication media to commemorate the International Year of Peace in the most appropriate form, highlighting, *inter alia*, the role of the United Nations in the promotion and maintenance of international peace and security;

3.   *Decides* to convene a second pledging conference during the first quarter of 1986 so that Member States which have not yet announced their contributions may have an opportunity to do so;

4.   *Requests* the Secretary-General, on the basis of the Voluntary Fund for the Programme of the International Year of Peace, to assist in the commemoration of the Year and to ensure the widest possible dissemination of information about the Year and its objectives;

5.   *Emphasizes* the importance of continuing the co-ordination and co-operation established among United Nations programmes and activities related to the promotion of the International Year of Peace;

6.   *Requests* the Secretary-General to report to the General Assembly at its forty-first session on the implementation of the programme of the International Year of Peace;

7.   *Decides* to include in the provisional agenda of its forty-first session the item entitled "International Year of Peace".

General Assembly resolution 40/10

11 November 1985   Meeting 70   Adopted without vote

53-nation draft (A/40/L.13/Rev.1 & Rev.1/Add.1), orally revised; agenda item 27.

Sponsors: Antigua and Barbuda, Argentina, Australia, Bahamas, Bangladesh, Barbados, Bolivia, Brunei Darussalam, Cameroon, Canada, Central African Republic, Chile, China, Colombia, Comoros, Congo, Costa Rica, Cuba, Cyprus, Dominica, Dominican Republic, Ecuador, El Salvador, Equatorial Guinea, Gambia, German Democratic Republic, Guatemala, Guyana, Honduras, Indonesia, Ivory Coast, Jamaica, Lebanon, Mongolia, Nepal, New Zealand, Nicaragua, Pakistan, Panama, Papua New Guinea, Paraguay, Philippines, Poland, Romania, Samoa, Senegal, Singapore, Sri Lanka, Thailand, Togo, Trinidad and Tobago, Uruguay, Venezuela.

In related action, the Assembly, in **resolution 40/151 D**, recommended that, in carrying out the World Disarmament Campaign, due regard be given to IYP, and in **resolution 40/152 E**, recommended that States observe Disarmament Week in 1986 in connection with the celebration of the Year.

Right of peoples to peace

In November 1985, States and international organizations were asked to implement the General Assembly's 1984 Declaration on the Right of Peoples to Peace.[27]

On 17 January 1985,[28] Mongolia transmitted a 12 December 1984 statement by its Great People's Khural, approving the Declaration, declaring that the primordial right to peace must be guaranteed everywhere, and drawing particular attention to the Assembly's appeal to Governments to assist in implementing that right through national and international measures.

GENERAL ASSEMBLY ACTION

On 11 November 1985, the General Assembly adopted **resolution 40/11** by recorded vote.

Right of peoples to peace

The General Assembly,

Bearing in mind that the year 1986 was proclaimed the International Year of Peace,

Recalling that the principal aim of establishing the United Nations forty years ago, as enshrined in the Charter, was to save succeeding generations from the scourge of war,

Reaffirming the strong resolve of peoples to maintain and strengthen international peace and security,

Recalling its Declaration on the Right of Peoples to Peace, approved on 12 November 1984,

Recalling further that, pursuant to the Declaration, all States and international organizations are urged to do their utmost to contribute to the implementation of the right of peoples to peace,

Bearing in mind that peace is an inalienable right of every human being and that, in the Proclamation of the International Year of Peace approved on 24 October 1985, the General Assembly, having reaffirmed that peace constitutes a universal ideal, called upon all peoples to join with the United Nations in resolute efforts to safeguard peace and the future of humanity,

Taking note of the programme for the International Year of Peace,

1. *Calls upon* all States and international organizations to do their utmost to implement the provisions of the Declaration on the Right of Peoples to Peace;

2. *Requests* the Secretary-General, when submitting his report on the implementation of the programme for the International Year of Peace, to report on the measures taken by Member States and international organizations in the implementation of the Declaration on the Right of Peoples to Peace.

General Assembly resolution 40/11

11 November 1985   Meeting 70   109-0-29 (recorded vote)

13-nation draft (A/40/L.14); agenda item 27.

Sponsors: Angola, Bulgaria, Cuba, German Democratic Republic, Lao People's Democratic Republic, Libyan Arab Jamahiriya, Madagascar, Mali, Mauritania, Mauritius, Mongolia, Nicaragua, Viet Nam.

Recorded vote in Assembly as follows:

In favour: Afghanistan, Algeria, Angola, Antigua and Barbuda, Argentina, Bahamas, Bahrain, Bangladesh, Barbados, Belize, Benin, Bhutan, Bolivia, Brazil, Bulgaria, Burma, Burundi, Byelorussian SSR, Cameroon, Cape Verde, Chad, Chile, China, Colombia, Comoros, Congo, Costa Rica, Cuba, Cyprus, Czechoslovakia, Democratic Yemen, Djibouti, Dominican Republic, Ecuador, Egypt, El Salvador, Equatorial Guinea, Ethiopia, Gambia, German Democratic Republic, Ghana, Guatemala, Guinea, Guinea-Bissau, Guyana, Haiti, Hungary, India, Indonesia, Iran, Iraq, Ivory Coast, Jamaica, Jordan, Kenya, Kuwait, Lao People's Democratic Republic, Lebanon, Lesotho, Libyan Arab Jamahiriya, Madagascar, Maldives, Mali, Malta, Mauritania, Mauritius, Mexico, Mongolia, Mozambique, Nepal, Nicaragua, Niger, Nigeria, Oman, Pakistan, Panama, Papua New Guinea, Peru, Poland, Qatar, Romania, Rwanda, Sao Tome and Principe, Saudi Arabia, Senegal, Seychelles, Sierra Leone, Somalia, Sri Lanka, Sudan, Suriname, Syrian Arab Republic, Thailand, Togo, Trinidad and Tobago, Tunisia, Uganda, Ukrainian SSR, USSR, United Arab Emirates, United Republic of Tanzania, Uruguay, Venezuela, Viet Nam, Yemen, Yugoslavia, Zaire, Zambia, Zimbabwe.

Against: None.

Abstaining: Australia, Austria, Belgium, Canada, Central African Republic, Denmark, Finland, France, Gabon, Germany, Federal Republic of, Greece, Iceland, Ireland, Israel, Italy, Japan, Luxembourg, Netherlands, New Zealand, Norway, Paraguay, Philippines, Portugal, Spain, Swaziland, Sweden, Turkey, United Kingdom, United States.

Albania, which did not participate in the vote, felt that the resolution did not say enough, since it did not indicate the sources of the tense world situation, which, it said, were the super-Powers' hegemonistic and military policies, including the militarization of outer space.

REFERENCES

[1]YUN 1982, p. 254, GA res. 37/16, 16 Nov. 1982. [2]YUN 1984, p. 124, GA res. 39/10, 8 Nov. 1984. [3]A/40/524. [4]A/40/669. [5]YUN 1984, p. 383, GA res. 39/161 A, 17 Dec. 1984. [6]A/40/211. [7]A/40/227. [8]A/40/271 & Corr.1. [9]A/40/358. [10]A/40/598. [11]A/40/275. [12]A/40/285. [13]A/40/297-S/17173. [14]A/40/627. [15]A/41/62-S/17695. [16]A/40/356 & Corr.1. [17]A/40/357. [18]A/40/397. [19]A/40/457. [20]A/40/400. [21]A/40/898. [22]A/40/415. [23]A/40/566. [24]A/40/306. [25]A/40/326. [26]E/1985/57. [27]YUN 1984, p. 119, GA res. 39/11, annex, 12 Nov. 1984. [28]A/40/90.

Chapter V

Africa

The United Nations considered in 1985 a number of political questions concerning Africa, and, as in previous years, focused on South Africa's *apartheid* policies and its aggression against neighbouring States.

In regard to *apartheid*, the General Assembly adopted nine resolutions and, as the situation in South Africa deteriorated rapidly, repeatedly condemned that Government's mass arrests and violence against defenceless people, as did the Security Council in two resolutions.

Of special note in 1985 was the Assembly's adoption of the International Convention against *Apartheid* in Sports, preparations for which had begun in 1976.

In addition to the Assembly and the Council, the Special Committee against *Apartheid*, the United Nations Council for Namibia, the Special Committee on the Situation with regard to the Implementation of the Declaration on the Granting of Independence to Colonial Countries and Peoples (Committee on colonial countries), the Commission on Human Rights and the Commission on Transnational Corporations were the main bodies concerned with *apartheid* and the related issue of South Africa's relations with its neighbours. On several occasions, those bodies condemned South Africa's aggression against the so-called front-line States.

Following repeated South African aggression against and continued occupation of Angola during 1985, the Security Council adopted four resolutions condemning that action—in June, September, October and December. The Council also sent an investigative commission to Angola to assess the damage resulting from South Africa's invasion. It adopted two resolutions concerning Botswana's complaint that South Africa had attacked the capital city of Gaborone. In June, it condemned the attack and decided to send a Secretariat mission to assess the damage and make proposals on assistance; it endorsed the mission's report in September.

After Lesotho complained of aggression by South Africa, the Council in December condemned the violence and requested the Secretary-General to establish a civilian presence in Maseru to report any further development affecting the territorial integrity of Lesotho. Mozambique also complained of aggression by South Africa.

In January, the Council met at the request of Chad, which said that the Libyan Arab Jamahiriya was attempting to overthrow its Government, a

charge the Jamahiriya denied. In September, Somalia complained that Ethiopia was occupying part of its territory, but Ethiopia replied that Somalia's problems were due to an internal conflict.

The Assembly reaffirmed the sovereignty of the Comoros over the Indian Ocean island of Mayotte, appealed for contributions to the United Nations Educational and Training Programme for Southern Africa which provided scholarships for students from the region, and called for continued co-operation with the Organization of African Unity.

Topics related to this chapter. Disarmament: nuclear-weapon-free zones—Africa. Mediterranean: Egypt–Libyan Arab Jamahiriya relations; Libyan Arab Jamahiriya–United States relations. Economic assistance, disasters and emergency relief: critical economic situation in Africa. Regional economic and social activities: Africa. Environment: environmental aspects of *apartheid*. Human rights: human rights violations in South Africa and Namibia. Women: women under *apartheid*. Refugees and displaced persons: Africa. Namibia. International Court of Justice: frontier dispute between Burkina Faso and Mali.

South Africa and *apartheid*

Apartheid—South Africa's enforced system of racial separation—remained a major concern of the United Nations throughout 1985, with various bodies voicing particular concern about rising tensions, repression and violence in that country, as documented by the Special Committee against *Apartheid*.

On three occasions, the Security Council protested that repression as the situation deteriorated. On 12 March (resolution 560(1985)), it condemned the Pretoria régime for the killing of defenceless indigenous Africans protesting their forced removal from Crossroads township, near Cape Town, and other places, as well as for the arbitrary arrests of members of mass organizations opposed to *apartheid*. On 26 July (569(1985)), the Council condemned the mass arrests and detentions by South Africa and the murders which had been committed, as well as the imposition of the state of emergency in 36 districts where blacks resided. It called on Member States to adopt certain measures against South Africa, including suspending all new investment there, restricting sports and cultural relations, prohibiting new nuclear co-operation, and banning sales of computer equipment that could be used by the military and police. In a 21 August statement, the Council, alarmed at the worsening situation of the black majority since the imposition of the state of emergency, condemned the continued killings and the arbitrary mass arrests and called for the freeing of all political prisoners and detainees.

Citing the policy of *apartheid* in South Africa as an extreme instance of racial discrimination, the Secretary-General urged that the ominous and violent situation be averted through contacts and timely action (see p. 10).

Expressing shock over the situation, the General Assembly, in addition to condemning South Africa's oppression and violence, called for its isolation. In the first of a series of nine resolutions on *apartheid* adopted on 10 December, it condemned certain States' collaboration with the *apartheid* régime (resolution 40/64 A) and reiterated its call for comprehensive mandatory sanctions, particularly regarding military and nuclear collaboration, an oil embargo, prohibiting loans and investment, and a trade ban; pending action by the Council, States were asked to take such action individually.

Condemning Israel's collaboration with South Africa, especially military and nuclear co-operation (40/64 E), the Assembly demanded that Israel desist and called on those in a position to do so to try to influence it in that regard. The Assembly decided to organize, in co-operation with the Organization of African Unity (OAU) and the Movement of Non-Aligned Countries, a World Conference on Sanctions against Racist South Africa, in June 1986 (40/64 C).

The Assembly reaffirmed its support for South African national liberation movements as the people's authentic representatives (40/64 B) and appealed for increased support for them in their just struggle for self-determination. To avert further tension and conflict, the Assembly requested the Council to consider the situation emanating from the imposition of the so-called new constitution and the state of emergency, demanding the latter's immediate lifting. It condemned the Pretoria régime for the killing of defenceless people protesting their forced removal from their homes as well as the arbitrary arrests of members of opposition organizations; it demanded that South Africa drop trumped-up charges and release those members, as well as all political prisoners and detainees. The Assembly again condemned the authorities for the killings, arbitrary arrests and detention of those opposing *apartheid* and demanded the immediate abrogation of discriminatory laws (40/64 I). It encouraged the Committee

against *Apartheid* and the Secretariat's Centre against *Apartheid* to inform world public opinion of the South African situation; requested the United Nations system to disseminate information on the evils of *apartheid*, and appealed to others to join in the effort; and called for intensification of the international campaign for the release of political prisoners (40/64 D).

The Assembly also endorsed the recommendations of the Committee against *Apartheid* relating to its work programme (40/64 F) and adopted and opened for signature the International Convention against *Apartheid* in Sports (40/64 G).

It appealed for contributions to the United Nations Trust Fund for South Africa and for direct contributions to the voluntary agencies assisting *apartheid* victims in South Africa and Namibia (40/64 H).

The Security Council issued two statements—on 20 August and 17 October—urging South Africa to rescind the death sentence imposed on Malesela Benjamin Maloise, a member of the African National Congress of South Africa. The Assembly condemned his execution, carried out on 18 October (40/64 B).

As part of its attempt to isolate South Africa, the United Nations continued trying to reduce the activities of transnational corporations (TNCs) in that country. In September and October, public hearings on TNCs in South Africa and Namibia were held by an 11-member panel appointed by the Secretary-General which made recommendations on further limiting TNC activities, particularly in the military and nuclear fields, on monitoring those activities and on employment practices for TNCs remaining in the region. The Economic and Social Council welcomed the actions of certain home countries of TNCs to restrict further investments in and loans to South Africa (resolution 1985/72). Aspects of *apartheid* were considered also by the Commission on Human Rights, the Council for Namibia, the Committee on colonial countries and the Commission on TNCs.

General aspects

Activities of the Committee against *Apartheid*. The Special Committee against *Apartheid*, in its annual report to the General Assembly and the Security Council adopted unanimously on 7 October,[1] described the situation in South Africa and the Committee's activities to intensify the international campaign against *apartheid*. The report, which included recommendations for further action and outlined the Committee's future work, covered the 12-month period beginning in October 1984; October-December 1985 was covered by its 1986 report.[2] The Committee proposed international action to eliminate *apartheid*, called for economic and trade sanctions and boycotts against South Africa and an end to military and nuclear relations, and urged the banning of foreign investment there and loans to Pretoria. The Committee also issued four special reports in 1985: on implementing the arms embargo against South Africa;[3] on developments concerning Israel–South Africa relations;[4] on further action to inform world public opinion and encourage public action in support of the oppressed people of South Africa;[5] and on international action to eliminate *apartheid*.[6] (For details on these subjects, see below, under relevant subject headings.)

According to the Committee, 1985 was marked by increased repression characterized by mass detentions, arrests and the banning of mass gatherings. Following increased opposition to the "constitution" put into effect by South Africa in 1984,[7] the régime on 21 July 1985 imposed a state of emergency on 36 magisterial districts where blacks lived, thereby empowering security forces to search homes without warrants, detain persons and declare curfews.

The Committee expanded its activities regarding consultations with Governments and organizations, dissemination of information on the situation in South Africa and the region, promotion of boycotts of South Africa, support for the liberation of political prisoners, and encouragement of artists, writers, sportspersons, religious leaders and others contributing to the campaign against *apartheid*. In the Committee's view, the effectiveness of the United Nations had been undermined by a minority of Governments that had failed to implement sanctions against South Africa as called for by the Assembly, and, in many cases, had increased their economic relations with that country. The Committee's purpose was to promote efforts to persuade those Governments, TNCs and others to desist from those policies.

The Committee urged States to denounce the manœuvres of those who advocated so-called reforms by the *apartheid* régime or so-called power sharing or other arrangements that did not involve the total eradication of *apartheid*. Calling on the United Nations to affirm that no acceptable solution could be attained without the participation of the national liberation movements and *apartheid* opponents, it stated that South Africa's attempts to consult elements that had colluded in the implementation of *apartheid* should be denounced.

Noting the current grave situation, the Committee intended to intensify its activities in accordance with its mandate and to give particular attention to consultations with Governments and organizations in order to promote international support of the legitimate struggle of the South African people for a non-racial society, to promote

assistance to the oppressed people and their national liberation movements and to increase public awareness of the situation.

Action by the Commission on Human Rights. On 26 February,[8] the Commission on Human Rights reaffirmed the legitimacy of the struggle of the oppressed people of South Africa and its national liberation movements by all available means, including armed struggle, for the elimination of the *apartheid* system and the exercise of the right of self-determination. The Commission urged States to provide moral and material assistance to the oppressed people of South Africa and Namibia.

On the same day,[9] the Commission reaffirmed the inalienable right of those people to self-determination, independence and enjoyment of the natural resources of their territories, as well as their right to dispose of the resources for their greater well-being and to obtain just reparation for their exploitation.

Communications. During the year, the following countries addressed letters to the Secretary-General, or forwarded messages from organizations, expressing their opposition to *apartheid*: Indonesia, on 1 May, transmitting the Declaration of the Commemorative Meeting in Observance of the Thirtieth Anniversary of the Asian-African Conference (Bandung, 24 and 25 April);[10] Madagascar, on 13 May;[11] Morocco, on 19 August, transmitting the final communiqué of an extraordinary Summit Conference of Arab States (Casablanca, 7-9 August);[12] the USSR, on 28 and 30 August;[13] Viet Nam, on 30 August;[14] Cuba, on 3 September;[15] Israel, on 4 September;[16] Canada, on 17 September;[17] the Ukrainian SSR, on 17 September;[18] the Byelorussian SSR, on 1 October;[19] Brazil, on 11 October;[20] Yemen, on 15 October, forwarding the communiqué of a co-ordination meeting of the Ministers for Foreign Affairs of the Organization of the Islamic Conference (New York, 9 October);[21] Togo, on 14 October, transmitting the Declaration and Programme of Action of the Ministerial Regional Conference on Security, Disarmament and Development in Africa (Lomé, 13-16 August);[22] Canada, on 15 October, forwarding the resolutions adopted by the seventy-fourth Inter-Parliamentary Conference (Ottawa, 2-7 September);[23] the Bahamas, on 28 October, forwarding the communiqué adopted by heads of Government of Commonwealth States (Nassau, 16-22 October);[24] Democratic Yemen, on 1 November;[25] and Egypt, on 4 December, forwarding the resolutions adopted by the Conference of African Ministers of Information at its first extraordinary session (Cairo, 23-25 November).[26]

In those letters, the African Information Ministers, the Asian-African Conference, the

Inter-Parliamentary Conference, the Islamic Conference, the Byelorussian SSR, the Ukrainian SSR and the USSR called for the adoption of mandatory sanctions against South Africa. The Islamic Conference, the Byelorussian SSR, Canada, Cuba, the USSR and Viet Nam denounced the increased repression against protesters, and the Commonwealth States, the Byelorussian SSR and the USSR demanded an end to the state of emergency. Israel called for an end to the *apartheid* system. The African Information Ministers, the Commonwealth States, the Inter-Parliamentary Conference, Canada and the USSR demanded freedom for political prisoners. Among those condemning the United States policy of "constructive engagement" with Pretoria were the Inter-Parliamentary Conference, the Byelorussian SSR, Cuba, the Ukrainian SSR and the USSR. The Asian-African Conference, the Byelorussian SSR, the Ukrainian SSR and the USSR expressed support for the struggle of the national liberation movements.

Canada listed steps it had taken to foster peaceful change in South Africa, including a halt to all official support for trade and investment there. Brazil stressed that the participation of the leaders imprisoned by the régime was indispensable in negotiating a solution to the plight of the South African majority.

According to the African security conference, South Africa's policies were a leading cause for insecurity, aggression, economic destabilization and an arms race in Africa, and the collaboration between South Africa, Israel and some Western Powers in the development of the South African nuclear-weapon capability worsened the explosive situation in the region. The Commonwealth States called for further economic measures, such as a ban on all government loans to the South African Government, a ban on the sale of computer equipment capable of use by its forces, a halt on the export of nuclear technology to South Africa, and embargoes on oil and on all military co-operation.

Algeria and Burkina Faso stated that they would not participate in the commemoration of the United Nations fortieth anniversary since the South West Africa People's Organization (SWAPO) and the Palestine Liberation Organization (PLO) had been excluded (see p. 403).

GENERAL ASSEMBLY ACTION

On 10 December 1985, the General Assembly adopted nine resolutions on the *apartheid* policies of South Africa. Two of these dealt with the broader aspects—**resolution 40/64 A** on sanctions and **resolution 40/64 I** on international action to eliminate *apartheid*. Both were adopted by recorded vote.

Comprehensive sanctions against the racist régime of South Africa

The General Assembly,

Recalling and reaffirming its resolution 39/72 A of 13 December 1984,

Recalling its relevant resolutions and those of the Security Council calling for concerted international action to force the racist régime to start eliminating *apartheid* by putting an immediate end to repressive practices against the black majority, releasing all political prisoners, abrogating all racist laws and regulations, dismantling bantustans and finding a political solution to the crisis in South Africa through the full participation of the black majority in determining their future,

Taking note of the declarations adopted at the following meetings organized by the Special Committee against *Apartheid:*

(a) The special session of the Committee in commemoration of the twenty-fifth anniversary of the Sharpeville massacre, held at Headquarters on 22 March 1985,

(b) The International Conference on Women and Children under *Apartheid,* held at Arusha, United Republic of Tanzania, from 7 to 10 May 1985,

(c) The International Conference on Sports Boycott against South Africa, held in Paris from 16 to 18 May 1985,

(d) The International Seminar on Racist Ideologies, Attitudes and Organizations Hindering Efforts for the Elimination of *Apartheid* and on Means to Combat Them, held at Siofok, Hungary, from 9 to 11 September 1985,

Gravely concerned about the breaches of peace and the threat to international peace and security resulting from the escalation of violence against the oppressed people of South Africa by the *apartheid* régime, its acts of aggression against neighbouring African independent States and its continued occupation of Namibia,

Deeply shocked by the policy of extermination carried out by the racist régime towards the black civilian population of South Africa,

Reaffirming that *apartheid* is a crime against humanity, which should be eliminated without any further delay, and that the United Nations has a primary responsibility to assist in efforts to eliminate this threat to international peace and security,

Reaffirming its support to the struggle of the people of South Africa for the exercise of their right to self-determination and for the establishment of a democratic, united and non-racial South Africa where all the people participate freely to determine their destiny,

Reaffirming its conviction that comprehensive and mandatory sanctions imposed by the Security Council under Chapter VII of the Charter of the United Nations, universally applied, would be the most appropriate and effective and peaceful means by which the international community can assist the legitimate struggle of the oppressed people of South Africa and discharge its responsibilities for the maintenance of international peace and security,

Considering that political, economic, military, cultural and other forms of collaboration with the racist régime of South Africa bolster the régime in its attempt to break its international isolation, thus encouraging it to persist in its defiance of the world public opinion and to escalate its repression, aggression and destabilization,

Considering also that collaboration with the racist régime of South Africa, in particular in the political, economic, military and cultural fields, displays an utter insensitivity towards the prolonged suffering of the oppressed people of South Africa resulting from the criminal acts and policies of the racist régime of South Africa,

Expressing its grave concern at the continued violation of the arms embargo as well as nuclear collaboration by certain Western States and Israel with the racist régime of South Africa,

Deploring the attitude of those Western permanent members of the Security Council that have so far prevented the Council from adopting comprehensive and mandatory sanctions against South Africa under Chapter VII of the United Nations Charter,

Commending the Secretary-General for his efforts to ensure concerted action against *apartheid* by organizations within the United Nations system,

Taking note with appreciation of the resolution adopted on 27 September 1985 by the General Conference of the International Atomic Energy Agency on South Africa's nuclear capability,

Expressing its appreciation to Governments that have adopted measures and policies against collaboration with the *apartheid* régime of South Africa,

Welcoming action taken by legislators, municipalities and other government institutions as well as universities, churches, labour unions, student and women's groups and anti-*apartheid* movements to divest from corporations and financial institutions that are collaborating with South Africa,

Commending the decisions of those banks, financial institutions and other corporations that have withdrawn from South Africa and decided not to extend any loans or credits to it,

Urging Member States that have not yet done so to adopt legislative and other measures to ensure the total isolation of the racist régime of South Africa in political, military, nuclear, economic, cultural and other fields,

Commending athletes, entertainers and others who have demonstrated solidarity with the oppressed people of South Africa by complying with the boycotts of South Africa,

1. *Endorses* the report of the Special Committee against *Apartheid;*

2. *Commends* to the attention of all Governments and organizations the declarations adopted at the conferences and seminars organized or co-sponsored by the Special Committee;

3. *Strongly condemns* the racist régime of South Africa for its brutal oppression, repression and violence against the people of South Africa, its illegal occupation of Namibia and its repeated acts of aggression, subversion, terrorism and destabilization against independent African States;

4. *Condemns* the policies of "constructive engagement" and active collaboration with the *apartheid* régime followed by the Governments of certain Western and other States which give encouragement to the racist régime in its repression of the people's legitimate struggle, aggression against neighbouring States and defiance of the decisions and resolutions of the United Nations, and appeals to those Governments to abandon such policies and join in the concerted efforts to bring a speedy end to *apartheid;*

5. *Condemns* the activities of those transnational corporations and financial institutions that have continued political, economic, military and nuclear collaboration with the racist minority régime of South Africa ignoring repeated appeals by the General Assembly;

6. *Again declares* that it is the responsibility of the United Nations and the international community as a whole to assist the people of South Africa in eliminating *apartheid* through cessation of any form of collaboration with the régime;

7. *Again calls upon* the Security Council urgently to take action under Chapter VII of the Charter of the United Nations with a view to applying comprehensive and mandatory sanctions against South Africa and, in particular:

   (a) To review the implementation of and to re-enforce the mandatory arms embargo against South Africa adopted by its resolution 418(1977) of 4 November 1977;

   (b) To strengthen the voluntary embargo on the imports of arms from South Africa adopted by its resolution 558(1984) of 13 December 1984 by rendering it mandatory and extending it to cover the imports of related materials in addition to arms and ammunitions;

   (c) To prohibit all co-operation with South Africa, particularly in the military and nuclear fields, by Governments, corporations, institutions and individuals;

   (d) To impose a total ban on all forms of nuclear collaboration with South Africa, including effective embargoes on the imports of South African and Namibian uranium and on the export and supply of nuclear material, equipment or technology to South Africa;

   (e) To impose an effective embargo on the supply of oil and oil products to South Africa and on all assistance to the oil industry in South Africa, particularly to the oil from coal industry;

   (f) To prohibit financial loans and credits to and investment in South Africa;

   (g) To ban all trade with South Africa;

8. *Requests* all States, individually and collectively, to take all appropriate measures to facilitate such action by the Security Council;

9. *Requests* all States that have not yet done so, pending action by the Security Council, to adopt legislative and/or other comparable measures to ensure the following:

   (a) Strict implementation of the arms embargo against South Africa, including the prohibition of imports of arms from South Africa and the enactment of appropriate legislation to ensure such a ban;

   (b) Prohibition of any form of collaboration with South Africa in the military and nuclear fields;

   (c) Effective implementation of a ban on all trade with South Africa, in particular, the sale of krugerrands and the import of gold, uranium, coal and other minerals;

   (d) Prohibition of the supply of oil and oil products to South Africa as well as technology to its oil industry;

   (e) Prohibition of financial loans and investments as well as the withdrawal of investment in South Africa;

   (f) Speedy accession to or ratification of the International Convention on the Suppression and Punishment of the Crime of *Apartheid;*

   (g) Observance of sports, cultural, academic, consumer, tourism and other boycotts of South Africa;

10. *Requests* all States concerned to take action against corporations and other interests that violate the mandatory arms embargo against South Africa and those that are involved in the illicit supply to South Africa of oil and oil products in spite of the embargo imposed on the supply of oil and oil products to South Africa, as well as those who persist in collaboration with the *apartheid* régime;

11. *Calls upon* States and organizations to support United Nations action for total isolation of the *apartheid* régime of South Africa and to co-operate with the Special Committee against *Apartheid* for the achievement of this goal;

12. *Calls upon* all organizations within the United Nations system as well as other international organizations that have not yet done so to exclude forthwith the South African régime from their membership;

13. *Calls upon* the Economic Commission for Europe to discontinue all contacts with the racist régime of South Africa and to terminate all co-operation with it;

14. *Calls once again upon* the International Monetary Fund urgently to terminate credit and other assistance to the racist régime of South Africa;

15. *Calls upon* all organizations within the United Nations system to take all necessary measures:

(*a*) To withhold any facilities from or investments of any funds in banks, financial institutions and corporations that are doing business with South Africa;

(*b*) To refrain from purchasing directly or indirectly products of South African origin;

(*c*) To deny any contracts or facilities to corporations collaborating with South Africa and not to invest any money in them;

(*d*) To prohibit any official travel by South African Airways or South African shipping lines;

16. *Strongly supports* the movement against conscription into the armed forces of the racist régime of South Africa;

17. *Invites* all Governments and organizations to assist, in consultation with the liberation movements, persons genuinely compelled to leave South Africa because of their objection on the ground of conscience to serving in the military or police force of the *apartheid* régime;

18. *Further commends* anti-*apartheid* movements, religious bodies, trade unions, student and women's organizations and other groups engaged in campaigns for the isolation of the *apartheid* régime and for assistance to the South African liberation movements recognized by the Organization of African Unity;

19. *Requests and authorizes* the Special Committee against *Apartheid* to redouble its efforts and intensify its activities for the total isolation of the *apartheid* régime, for promoting comprehensive and mandatory sanctions against South Africa and for mobilizing public opinion and encouraging public action against collaboration with South Africa;

20. *Further requests* the Special Committee to keep the matter of collaboration between South Africa and Israel and between South Africa and any other State under constant review and to report to the General Assembly and the Security Council as appropriate.

General Assembly resolution 40/64 A

10 December 1985   Meeting 111   122-18-14 (recorded vote)

48-nation draft (A/40/L.26 & Corr.1); agenda item 35.

Sponsors: Afghanistan, Algeria, Angola, Benin, Burkina Faso, Burundi, Byelorussian SSR, Cameroon, Congo, Cuba, Democratic Yemen, Egypt, Equatorial Guinea, Ethiopia, German Democratic Republic, Ghana, Guinea, Guinea-Bissau, Guyana, India, Iran, Iraq, Kenya, Lao People's Democratic Republic, Lebanon, Liberia, Libyan Arab Jamahiriya, Madagascar, Malaysia, Mali, Mauritania, Mauritius, Mongolia, Morocco, Nicaragua, Nigeria, Papua New Guinea, Senegal, Sierra Leone, Sudan, Syrian Arab Republic, Tunisia, Uganda, Ukrainian SSR, United Republic of Tanzania, Viet Nam, Zaire, Zambia.

Financial implications. 5th Committee, A/40/1022; S-G, A/C.5/40/76.

Meeting numbers. GA 40th session: 5th Committee 58; plenary 51-57, 111.

Recorded vote in Assembly as follows:

In favour: Afghanistan, Albania, Algeria, Angola, Antigua and Barbuda, Argentina, Bahamas, Bahrain, Bangladesh, Barbados, Belize, Benin, Bhutan, Bolivia, Brazil, Brunei Darussalam, Bulgaria, Burkina Faso, Burma, Burundi, Byelorussian SSR, Cameroon, Cape Verde, Central African Republic, Chad, China, Colombia, Comoros, Congo, Costa Rica, Cuba, Cyprus, Czechoslovakia, Democratic Kampuchea, Democratic Yemen, Djibouti, Dominican Republic, Ecuador, Egypt, El Salvador, Equatorial Guinea, Ethiopia, Gabon, Gambia, German Democratic Republic, Ghana, Guatemala, Guinea, Guinea-Bissau, Guyana, Haiti, Honduras, Hungary, India, Indonesia, Iran, Iraq, Jamaica, Jordan, Kenya, Kuwait, Lao People's Democratic Republic, Lebanon, Liberia, Libyan Arab Jamahiriya, Madagascar, Malaysia, Maldives, Mali, Malta, Mauritania, Mauritius, Mexico, Mongolia, Morocco, Mozambique, Nepal, Nicaragua, Niger, Nigeria, Oman, Pakistan, Panama, Papua New Guinea, Peru, Philippines, Poland, Qatar, Romania, Rwanda, Saint Lucia, Saint Vincent and the Grenadines, Sao Tome and Principe, Saudi Arabia, Senegal, Seychelles, Sierra Leone, Singapore, Somalia, Sri Lanka, Sudan, Suriname, Syrian Arab Republic, Thailand, Togo, Trinidad and Tobago, Tunisia, Turkey, Uganda, Ukrainian SSR, USSR, United Arab Emirates, United Republic of Tanzania, Uruguay, Vanuatu, Venezuela, Viet Nam, Yemen, Yugoslavia, Zaire, Zambia, Zimbabwe.

Against: Belgium, Canada, Denmark, France, Germany, Federal Republic of, Grenada, Iceland, Ireland, Israel, Italy, Japan, Luxembourg, Netherlands, Norway, Portugal, Spain, United Kingdom, United States.

Abstaining: Australia, Austria, Botswana, Fiji, Finland, Greece, Ivory Coast, Lesotho, Malawi, New Zealand, Samoa, Solomon Islands, Swaziland, Sweden.

Concerted international action for the elimination of *apartheid*

The General Assembly,

Alarmed by the further aggravation of the situation in South Africa caused by the policy of *apartheid*, and lately in particular by the imposition of the state of emergency,

Convinced that the root-cause of the grave situation in southern Africa is the policy of *apartheid*,

Noting with grave concern that in order to perpetuate *apartheid* in South Africa the authorities there have committed acts of aggression and breaches of the peace,

Convinced that only the total eradication of *apartheid* and the establishment of majority rule on the basis of the free and fair exercise of universal adult suffrage can lead to a peaceful and lasting solution in South Africa,

Noting that the so-called reforms in South Africa, including the so-called "new constitution", have the effect of further entrenching the *apartheid* system and further dividing the people of South Africa,

Recognizing that the policy of bantustanization deprives the majority of the people of their citizenship and makes them foreigners in their own country,

Recognizing the responsibility of the United Nations and the international community to take all necessary action for the eradication of *apartheid*, and, in particular, the need for increased and effective pressure on the South African authorities as a peaceful means of achieving the abolition of *apartheid*,

Encouraged, in this context, by the growing international consensus to this end, as demonstrated by the adoption of Security Council resolution 569(1985) of 26 July 1985 and the increase in and expansion of national and regional measures,

Convinced of the vital importance of the strict observance of Security Council resolution 418(1977) of 4 November 1977, by which the Council instituted a mandatory arms embargo against South Africa, and Security

Council resolution 558(1984) of 13 December 1984 concerning the import of arms, ammunition and military vehicles produced in South Africa, and of the need to make these embargoes fully effective,

Commending the decisions of oil-exporting countries that have declared it their policy not to sell and export oil to South Africa,

Considering that measures to ensure effective and scrupulous implementation of such embargoes through international co-operation are essential and urgent,

Noting with deep concern that, through a combination of military and economic pressures, in violation of international law, the South African authorities have sought to destabilize the front-line and other neighbouring States,

Considering that contacts between *apartheid* South Africa and the front-line and other neighbouring States, necessitated by geography, colonial legacy and other reasons, should not be used by other States as a pretext for legitimizing the *apartheid* system or justifying attempts to break the international isolation of that system,

Convinced that the existence of *apartheid* will continue to lead to ever-increasing resistance by the oppressed people, by all possible means, and increased tension and conflict that will have far-reaching consequences for southern Africa and the world,

Convinced that policies of collaboration with the *apartheid* régime, instead of respect for the legitimate aspirations of the genuine representatives of the great majority of the people, will encourage its repression and aggression against neighbouring States and defiance of the United Nations,

Expressing its full support for the legitimate aspiration of African States and peoples, and of the Organization of African Unity, for the total liberation of the continent of Africa from colonialism and racism,

1. *Strongly condemns* the policy of *apartheid* which deprives the majority of the South African population of their citizenship, fundamental freedoms and human rights, in particular the right to self-determination;

2. *Strongly condemns* the South African authorities for the killings, arbitrary mass arrests and the detention of members of mass organizations as well as individuals, the overwhelming majority of whom belong to the majority population, for opposing the *apartheid* system, the so-called "new constitution" and the state of emergency;

3. *Further condemns* the overt and the covert aggressive actions of South Africa directed at the destabilization of neighbouring States, and those aimed against refugees from South Africa and Namibia;

4. *Demands* that the South African authorities:

(a) Release immediately and unconditionally Nelson Mandela and all other political prisoners, detainees and restrictees;

(b) Immediately lift the state of emergency;

(c) Abrogate discriminatory laws and lift bans on all organizations, news media and individuals opposing *apartheid;*

(d) Grant freedom of association and full trade union rights to all workers of South Africa;

(e) Initiate without pre-conditions a political dialogue with genuine leaders of the majority population with a view to dismantling *apartheid* without delay and establishing a representative government;

(f) Dismantle the bantustan structures;

(g) Immediately withdraw all their troops from southern Angola and end the destabilization of front-line and other States;

5. *Urges* the Security Council to consider without delay the adoption of effective mandatory sanctions against South Africa;

6. *Further urges* the Security Council to take steps for the strict implementation of the mandatory arms embargo instituted by its resolution 418(1977) and of the arms embargo requested in its resolution 558(1984) and, within the context of the relevant resolutions, to secure an end to military and nuclear co-operation with South Africa and the import of military equipment or supplies from South Africa;

7. *Appeals* to all States that have not yet done so, pending mandatory sanctions by the Security Council, to consider national legislative or other appropriate measures to increase the pressure on the *apartheid* régime of South Africa, such as:

(a) Cessation of further investments in, and financial loans to, South Africa;

(b) An end to all promotion of and support for trade with South Africa;

(c) Prohibition of the sale of krugerrands and all other coins minted in South Africa;

(d) Cessation of all forms of military, police or intelligence co-operation with the South African authorities, in particular the sale of computer equipment;

(e) An end to nuclear collaboration with South Africa;

(f) Cessation of export and sale of oil to South Africa;

8. *Appeals* to all States, organizations and institutions:

(a) To increase humanitarian, legal, educational and other such assistance to the victims of *apartheid;*

(b) To increase support for the liberation movements recognized by the Organization of African Unity and to all those struggling against *apartheid* and for a non-racial, democratic society in South Africa;

(c) To increase assistance to the front-line States and the Southern African Development Co-ordination Conference in order to increase their economic strength and independence from South Africa;

9. *Appeals* to all Governments and organizations to take appropriate action for the cessation of all academic, cultural, scientific and sports relations that would support the *apartheid* régime of South Africa, as well as relations with individuals, institutions and other bodies endorsing or based on *apartheid;*

10. *Commends* those States that have already adopted voluntary measures against the *apartheid* régime of South Africa in accordance with General Assembly resolution 39/72 G of 13 December 1984 and invites those that have not yet done so to follow their example;

11. *Reaffirms* the legitimacy of the struggle of the oppressed people of South Africa for the total eradication of *apartheid* and for the establishment of a non-racial, democratic society in which all the people, irrespective of race, colour or creed, enjoy human rights and fundamental freedoms;

12. *Pays tribute to and expresses solidarity with* organizations and individuals struggling against *apartheid* and for a non-racial, democratic society in accordance with the principles of the Universal Declaration of Human Rights;

13. *Requests* the Secretary-General to report to the General Assembly at its forty-first session on the implementation of the present resolution.

General Assembly resolution 40/64 I

10 December 1985   Meeting 111   149-2-4 (recorded vote)

19-nation draft (A/40/L.40 & Add.1); agenda item 35.

Sponsors: Australia, Austria, Denmark, Egypt, Finland, Gambia, Ghana, Greece, Iceland, Ireland, Madagascar, Malaysia, New Zealand, Nigeria, Norway, Sweden, United Republic of Tanzania, Zambia, Zimbabwe.

Meeting numbers. GA 40th session: plenary 51-57, 111.

Recorded vote in Assembly as follows:

In favour: Afghanistan, Albania, Algeria, Angola, Antigua and Barbuda, Argentina, Australia, Austria, Bahamas, Bahrain, Bangladesh, Barbados, Belgium, Belize, Benin, Bhutan, Bolivia, Botswana, Brazil, Brunei Darussalam, Bulgaria, Burkina Faso, Burma, Burundi, Byelorussian SSR, Cameroon, Canada, Cape Verde, Central African Republic, Chad, Chile, China, Colombia, Comoros, Congo, Costa Rica, Cuba, Cyprus, Czechoslovakia, Democratic Kampuchea, Democratic Yemen, Denmark, Djibouti, Dominican Republic, Ecuador, Egypt, El Salvador, Equatorial Guinea, Ethiopia, Fiji, Finland, France, Gabon, Gambia, German Democratic Republic, Ghana, Greece, Guatemala, Guinea, Guinea-Bissau, Guyana, Haiti, Honduras, Hungary, Iceland, India, Indonesia, Iran, Iraq, Ireland, Italy, Ivory Coast, Jamaica, Japan, Jordan, Kenya, Kuwait, Lao People's Democratic Republic, Lebanon, Lesotho, Liberia, Libyan Arab Jamahiriya, Luxembourg, Madagascar, Malaysia, Maldives, Mali, Malta, Mauritania, Mauritius, Mexico, Mongolia, Morocco, Mozambique, Nepal, Netherlands, New Zealand, Nicaragua, Niger, Nigeria, Norway, Oman, Pakistan, Panama, Papua New Guinea, Peru, Philippines, Poland, Portugal, Qatar, Romania, Rwanda, Saint Lucia, Saint Vincent and the Grenadines, Samoa, Sao Tome and Principe, Saudi Arabia, Senegal, Seychelles, Sierra Leone, Singapore, Solomon Islands, Somalia, Spain, Sri Lanka, Sudan, Suriname, Swaziland, Sweden, Syrian Arab Republic, Thailand, Togo, Trinidad and Tobago, Tunisia, Turkey, Uganda, Ukrainian SSR, USSR, United Arab Emirates, United Republic of Tanzania, Uruguay, Vanuatu, Venezuela, Viet Nam, Yemen, Yugoslavia, Zaire, Zambia, Zimbabwe.

Against: United Kingdom, United States.

Abstaining: Germany, Federal Republic of, Grenada, Israel, Malawi.

The other seven resolutions in the series dealt with the situation in South Africa and assistance to liberation movements (**40/64 B**), the World Conference on Sanctions against Racist South Africa (**40/64 C**), public information and public action against *apartheid* (**40/64 D**), relations between Israel and South Africa (**40/64 E**), the work programme of the Special Committee against *Apartheid* (**40/64 F**), the International Convention against *Apartheid* in Sports (**40/64 G**) and the United Nations Trust Fund for South Africa (**40/64 H**) (see below, under relevant subject headings).

When the Assembly adopted the nine resolutions on *apartheid*, some States explained their votes on all of them, while others cited the individual texts.

In explaining their votes on the resolutions in general, several countries expressed opposition to arbitrary or selective singling out of Member States for criticism. Austria, Belgium, Luxembourg (speaking for the 10 European Community (EC) countries, Portugal and Spain), the Netherlands, Norway (speaking for the five Nordic countries) and Turkey voiced such opposition. Belgium, for example, felt that treatment of the issue must not be influenced by East-West confrontations. Turkey did not approve of express mention when it was difficult to make definitive determinations of respective responsibilities.

Austria, Belgium, Luxembourg (for the EC countries, Portugal and Spain), the Netherlands and Norway (for the Nordic countries) affirmed their preference for a peaceful solution to the South African situation or expressed reservations on provisions endorsing the use of force or armed struggle.

According to Austria, Luxembourg (for the EC countries, Portugal and Spain) and Norway (for the Nordic countries), imposing sanctions was the prerogative of the Security Council not the Assembly. They also upheld the principle of universal membership in the United Nations system.

In regard to the call for comprehensive mandatory sanctions, Canada, Ireland, the United Kingdom and the United States questioned the wisdom of taking such action at the current juncture. Ireland reiterated its preference for the imposition of carefully chosen, graduated, mandatory sanctions by the Council; Canada also called for sustained pressure. The United Kingdom considered that mandatory sanctions would probably delay the abolition of *apartheid*, and the United States doubted that sanctions could contribute to a peaceful resolution of *apartheid*. Luxembourg (for EC, Portugal and Spain) said channels of communication should remain open so that the outside world could pressure South Africa for a democratic society. Due to their geographic situation, Botswana and Lesotho could not support mandatory sanctions against South Africa. However, Botswana was prepared to suffer the consequences if in the end a new South Africa could be brought into being with a minimum of violence; Lesotho asserted that its stand should not be used as an excuse for inaction against *apartheid*.

Belgium, Israel and the Netherlands said they would have preferred consensus texts to demonstrate international support for the cause. According to Israel, only consensus could give the resolutions the moral and international support that the struggle against *apartheid* deserved. France and Portugal regretted some wording of the texts. For the Netherlands and Portugal, South Africa was not a decolonization issue; the Netherlands regarded the African National Congress of South Africa (ANC) and the Pan Africanist Congress of Azania (PAC) as anti-*apartheid* movements, not liberation movements.

As to the report of the Committee against *Apartheid*, Belgium and Luxembourg (for EC, Portugal and Spain) regretted its depiction of the steps taken by the EC members to pressure South Africa and to promote the rights of the South African majority. Luxembourg said Western European countries regretted that the report questioned their determination to contribute to the abolition of *apartheid*.

In regard to resolution 40/64 A, Costa Rica, Israel and Turkey disagreed with singling out individual countries or groups of countries. Israel said *apartheid* was too great an evil to be manipulated as a tool of hatred for Israel. Costa Rica also had difficulties with such references. In Turkey's view, the eleventh and twelfth preambular paragraphs and paragraph 4 had not been drafted in a balanced way. The United States said it made no apology for its constructive engagement policy, which it believed had contributed to the limited improvements in the lives of oppressed South Africans; on that basis, it also opposed resolution 40/64 I.

Ireland and the Netherlands preferred graduated, selective measures by the Security Council rather than South Africa's total isolation through comprehensive mandatory sanctions. Ireland would have been able to support many of the specific measures in paragraph 7, but doubted the wisdom of comprehensive sanctions at that point.

Some countries expressed reservations about the Committee's report as endorsed by the Assembly in paragraph 1. France regretted the arbitrary and systematic criticism of countries, particularly the EC members. Italy said the report failed to reflect adequately EC's efforts, and presented in a misleading manner the EC mission to Pretoria, which had led to the adoption at Luxembourg on 10 September of certain restrictive economic measures against South Africa (see p. 135). The Netherlands felt the report contained unwarranted criticism of a particular group of countries. The United Kingdom rejected the report's distortion and criticism of the policy of the EC members, of the Luxembourg measures, of the visit to South Africa by three European Foreign Ministers and of the EC code of conduct for businesses operating in South Africa.

New Zealand questioned the wisdom of excluding South Africa from all international organizations, and of asserting that every country with any relationship with South Africa was guilty of aiding human rights violations.

Several countries also had reservations about sanctions as proposed in resolution 40/64 I. Italy and the Netherlands said that such mandatory action was within the exclusive competence of the Security Council. France agreed, adding that its support for the resolution should not be interpreted as a questioning of that competence; moreover, the voluntary measures recommended in paragraph 7 did not necessarily cover national ones which France might take to pressure South Africa. The Netherlands could not endorse certain aspects of that paragraph, such as subparagraphs *(a)* and *(e)*, but believed that collective international action to curtail investment in South Africa could contribute to increasing pressure on that Government; to be effective, such action must be based on a mandatory decision of the Council. For Italy, the paragraph did not take account of the negative effect that the measures could have on victims of *apartheid* and on neighbouring States. Canada rejected the premise that individual relations supported *apartheid* and did not interpret paragraph 9 as endorsing termination of all contacts, which might make change more difficult. Portugal had reservations on formulations such as those in paragraphs 5 and 7, and in particular

paragraph 1, since it did not consider the problem to be one of decolonization.

Italy and the Netherlands welcomed the efforts of the resolution's drafters to avoid controversial elements and to gain as broad a base of support as possible.

The Assembly took related action in **resolution 40/25**, in which it reaffirmed the legitimacy of the struggle of peoples for their liberation from *apartheid* by all means, including armed struggle. In **resolution 40/28**, the Assembly condemned *apartheid* in South Africa and Namibia as a crime against humanity and urged Member States to adopt political, economic and other measures in conformity with the resolutions of the Assembly, the Council and other United Nations bodies. The Assembly commended the Committee on the Elimination of Racial Discrimination for its endeavours towards eliminating discrimination and welcomed a Committee decision on *apartheid* (see p. 159).

In accordance with an Assembly decision that organizations and individuals having a special interest in the item on *apartheid* would, at their request, be heard by the Special Political Committee, the following addressed the Committee in October.[27]

Beyers Naudé, South African Council of Churches; Wendell Foster, Council of the City of New York; Beatrice von Roemer, International Confederation of Free Trade Unions; Reverend Noel Enuma El-Mahmud-Okereke, El-Mahmud Mass Communication of Nigeria; Karen Talbot, World Peace Council; Vinie Burrows, Women's International Democratic Federation; Evelyn Lowery, Southern Christian Leadership Conference; Roger Green, State Assembly of New York; Jeanne M. Woods, Afro-Asian Peoples' Solidarity Organization; Gora Ibrahim, PAC; Reverend Simangaliso Mkhatshwa, South African Catholic Bishops Conference; Yvonne Ismail, People's Organization for Progress; Lawrence Hamm, Commission for Racial Justice of the United Church of Christ; Frank Chapman, National Alliance against Racial and Political Repression.

The Committee also convened to hear Bishop Desmond Tutu, the 1984 Nobel Peace Laureate.

On 28 October, by **decision 40/407**, the Assembly, on an oral proposal by the President, took note of the Committee's report.

International action to eliminate *apartheid*

The Special Committee against *Apartheid* continued promoting an international campaign against South Africa's racial policies.[1]

In February, the Chairman commended the action by non-governmental organizations (NGOs) in the United States and the Netherlands for their divestment from companies with South African holdings and the prohibition of the sale of kruger-rands. Among those cited were New York organizations and municipalities, the Bank of Boston and Morgan Guaranty Trust, and the Danish Occupational Therapists' Association for its refusal to accept delegates from South Africa to a 1986 international congress.

In connection with the intensified international campaign in Western Europe and North America for divestment, the Committee, in a 17 April statement, welcomed steps further to isolate South Africa, noting that anti-*apartheid* movements, parliaments, local legislators, trade unions, religious organizations, political parties, students, academicians and individuals were effectively exposing the *apartheid* system to the public.

In the United States, concerted action had led to divestment, legislative action and other measures by states, cities and universities, and several anti-*apartheid* bills were introduced in the Congress. Seven states and more than 20 cities enacted divestment legislation, committing themselves to sell their holdings in companies operating in South Africa. In September, the President issued an executive order banning computer sales to South African security agencies, barring some types of loans to South Africa and terminating krugerrand imports to the United States. As a result of an anti-*apartheid* campaign in the Netherlands, its three major banks decided to stop the sale of krugerrands in February. On 10 September, the European Economic Community (EEC) adopted limited sanctions against South Africa, including an embargo on oil, arms and law enforcement equipment; a ban on military and nuclear co-operation; measures to discourage cultural and scientific links; and withdrawal of military attachés. In May, the Danish Parliament prohibited new investments in South Africa and Namibia, and the Swedish Parliament enacted a law limiting further Swedish investments. In addition, a Swedish law forbade the sale of vehicles and computer equipment to the South African military and police forces. Canada announced in July that it was curtailing trade with South Africa through such measures as ending export and investment incentives for Canadian companies doing business with South Africa and restrictions on high-technology sales.

While noting the advance in the world-wide movement of solidarity with the struggle for liberation in South Africa, the Committee urged that international action be comprehensive, rather than piecemeal, and considered that voluntary, unilateral and limited sanctions by individual Western Governments were inadequate. The Committee urged, pending the imposition of comprehensive and mandatory sanctions against South Africa, that national action be taken by Western countries (see below).

In an October addendum[6] to its annual report, the Committee issued replies it had received from 26 Governments and the 10 EC members in response to the Assembly's 1984 appeal[28] for consideration of national measures to increase pressure on the *apartheid* régime (see p. 138).

GENERAL ASSEMBLY ACTION

In **resolution 40/64 A**, the General Assembly commended anti-*apartheid* movements, religious bodies, trade unions, student and women's organizations and other groups engaged in campaigns to isolate the *apartheid* régime and to assist South African liberation movements recognized by OAU. The Assembly requested and authorized the Committee to intensify its activities to isolate the régime totally, to promote comprehensive and mandatory sanctions against South Africa and to mobilize public opinion and encourage public action against collaboration with South Africa.

Relations with South Africa

The General Assembly and the Special Committee against *Apartheid* continued in 1985 to lead United Nations efforts to have States and organizations break off all relations with South Africa as a means of pressuring it to abandon its *apartheid* policies.

Activities of the Committee against *Apartheid*. The Committee monitored relations with South Africa in several areas, including military and nuclear relations (see p. 141), economic and trade relations (see p. 145) and cultural ties, and made recommendations concerning such relations.[1] It reported that anti-*apartheid* groups, trade unions, local authorities and cultural personalities had encouraged others not to perform in that country and to support the cultural boycott; there was a significant decline in the number of artists visiting South Africa during the year. Most of those who had visited it came from Europe, in particular the United Kingdom. Since the publication in December 1984 of the second register of entertainers, actors and others who had performed in South Africa during the previous four years,[29] many on the register had written to the Committee undertaking not to appear there again.

Anti-*apartheid* organizations and other NGOs had been effective in deterring entertainers from visiting South Africa and specific actions to that end were reported taken in a number of countries. Artists taking action to draw attention to the cultural boycott or the situation in South Africa included Stevie Wonder, a United States musician and singer, who accepted his Oscar Award in March in the name of Nelson Mandela, the imprisoned South African opposition leader; Woody Allen, a United States actor and director, who decided not to allow the release of his films in South Africa; and Albert Finney, a British actor, who directed and acted in

The Biko Inquest, a film based on the 1977 death of Steve Biko from head injuries while in the custody of the South African police. In a ceremony on 10 October, "Artists United against *Apartheid*", a group of popular musicians who worked together on a record, presented the first pressing of the record "Sun City" to the United Nations. It was produced in co-operation with the Committee and its message was that South Africa should be boycotted as long as *apartheid* prevailed.

Despite these developments, the Committee reported that there was some collaboration in the cultural field, and it named three musicians who had contacts with South Africa.

The Committee followed with particular attention the United States response to the calls for isolating the *apartheid* régime, because of the importance of its role as a major trading partner of South Africa and as a leader of the Western alliance (see p. 135). It noted that the United States reaffirmed its policy of "constructive engagement" with the régime and asserted that the executive order issued by the President in September demonstrated the Administration's opposition to legislative measures against *apartheid* under consideration by the United States Congress, and was designed to avoid pressure on the régime. The Committee called the measures announced by EEC in September (see p. 135) limited and ineffective. The Committee considered it essential that the international community persuade the United States, as well as the United Kingdom and the Federal Republic of Germany, to co-operate with the United Nations in international action against *apartheid* and desist from fraternizing with the régime.

Action by the Council for Namibia. In its Vienna Declaration and Programme of Action adopted in June,[30] the Council for Namibia deplored, and called for an immediate end to, the assistance rendered to South Africa by the major Western countries and Israel in the political, economic, military and other areas. In particular, the Council condemned and rejected the United States policy of so-called constructive engagement for having emboldened the *apartheid* régime to intensify its repression of the peoples of Namibia and South Africa, to escalate aggression against the front-line States, and to continue its intransigence over the independence of Namibia. The Council urged those States that co-operated with South Africa to cease any form of collaboration with it and called on the international community to reject the United States policy.

Action by the Commission on Human Rights. On 26 February,[8] the Commission on Human Rights condemned all collaboration, particularly nuclear, military and economic,

with South Africa and called on the States concerned to cease forthwith.

The Commission, on the same date,[9] condemned the increased assistance rendered by the major Western countries and Israel to South Africa, particularly military assistance, stating that it constituted a hostile action against the peoples of South Africa, Namibia and the neighbouring States since it was bound to strengthen the régime's military capability, and demanded that such assistance be immediately terminated. The Commission called on Governments that had not done so to ensure that trading, manufacturing and investing activities in South Africa and Namibia were stopped.

Action by the Committee on colonial countries. On 16 May,[31] the Committee on colonial countries deplored the collaboration of certain Western and other countries with South Africa in the political, economic, military and nuclear fields, and reiterated that such collaboration undermined international solidarity against the *apartheid* régime and helped to perpetuate its illegal occupation of Namibia.

On 7 August,[32] the Committee condemned countries, as well as TNCs, which continued investments in, and supply of armaments and oil and nuclear technology to, South Africa, thus buttressing it and aggravating the threat to world peace. It called on States, in particular certain Western States, to terminate that collaboration and to refrain from entering into other relations in violation of United Nations and OAU resolutions. On the same day,[33] the Committee reiterated its call for the termination of all collaboration with South Africa.

GENERAL ASSEMBLY ACTION

The General Assembly repeatedly called for termination of all relations with South Africa in 1985.

In **resolution 40/25**, it condemned the policy of those Western States, Israel and other States whose political, economic, military, nuclear, strategic, cultural and sports relations with South Africa encouraged that régime to persist in suppressing the aspirations of peoples to self-determination and independence.

In **resolution 40/64 A**, the Assembly condemned the policies of "constructive engagement" and active collaboration with the *apartheid* régime followed by certain Western and other States which encouraged the régime in its repression of the people's legitimate struggle, aggression against neighbouring States and defiance of United Nations decisions. It also condemned the activities of those TNCs and financial institutions that continued collaboration with South Africa, and again declared that it was the responsibility of the international community to assist the people of South

Africa in eliminating *apartheid* through cessation of any form of collaboration with the régime.

In **resolution 40/64 I**, the Assembly appealed to Governments and organizations to cease academic, cultural, scientific and sports relations that would support the *apartheid* régime, as well as relations with individuals, institutions and other bodies endorsing or based on *apartheid*.

Similar calls for an end to relations in a wide variety of areas were also made by the Assembly when it dealt with the questions of decolonization and Namibia. These calls were contained mainly in **resolutions 40/52, 40/56** and **40/97 A** and in **decision 40/415**.

ECONOMIC AND SOCIAL COUNCIL ACTION

By **resolution 1985/59**, the Economic and Social Council requested the specialized agencies and other United Nations organizations to isolate the *apartheid* régime totally.

Communications. Throughout the year, a number of countries forwarded letters to the Secretary-General regarding their relations with and policy concerning South Africa.

On 13 February,[34] the USSR rejected South Africa's 1984 "new constitution";[7] condemned the military and political support of the United States and other members of the North Atlantic Treaty Organization (NATO) for South Africa; expressed support for the African countries' demand that the Security Council impose comprehensive and mandatory sanctions against South Africa; and affirmed its continued support to the national liberation movements in southern Africa. Expressing the same views on 26 February,[35] the Byelorussian SSR said it had no relations with South Africa and called on the United Nations to ensure the implementation of its decisions concerning *apartheid*. Similarly, the Ukrainian SSR affirmed on 5 March[36] that it had no relations with South Africa, denounced the policies of a number of NATO countries and Israel in regard to it, and supported the call for comprehensive and mandatory sanctions.

Iran on 17 April[37] stated that it had broken all ties with South Africa; had refused to issue trade permits to nationals dealing with it; had prohibited all cultural and economic relations; did not permit its nationals to travel there, nor had granted South African nationals visas to enter Iran; and had cut all air and sea transport between the two countries.

In a policy statement of 6 July on its relations with South Africa,[38] Canada announced additional measures as a response to the situation in that country, such as strengthening its voluntary code of conduct and employment practices for Canadian companies operating in South Africa, tightening the arms embargo by restricting exports

of sensitive equipment such as computers for military and police use, banning the import of arms manufactured there, and terminating a number of official measures which lent support to trade with and investment in South Africa. Brazil forwarded a 9 August decree by its President[39] prohibiting: cultural, artistic or sports exchanges; the export of petroleum and its by-products to that country; the supply of arms to it, including sales or transfers of arms and ammunition, military vehicles and equipment, police equipment, or spare parts for those items; and shipment of such equipment through Brazilian territory.

On 19 August,[40] Australia announced measures taken against South Africa following its review of recent developments there. It affirmed its intention to work for the imposition of mandatory economic sanctions and announced it would close the Trade Commission in Johannesburg in September. It would prohibit exports of petroleum and petroleum products to South Africa, request Australian financial institutions to suspend new loans to South Africa and prohibit direct investment in Australia by the South African Government. Affirming that it had voluntarily imposed trade sanctions against South Africa since 1978, Thailand, on 29 August,[41] added that it had issued regulations prohibiting bilateral trade.

Madagascar transmitted on 18 September[42] the resolutions adopted by the forty-second OAU Council of Ministers (Addis Ababa, Ethiopia, 10-17 July). Noting recent action in the anti-*apartheid* campaign, OAU proposed convening a World Conference on Sanctions against Racist South Africa in collaboration with the Non-Aligned Movement and the United Nations (see p. 140), to coincide with the tenth anniversary of the Soweto uprising of June 1976; supported the campaign for an oil embargo against South Africa; mandated the Group of African States at the United Nations to step up the campaign for the isolation of South Africa, especially through the convening of the Security Council to consider sanctions; condemned the United States policy of constructive engagement; and called on the international community to take measures against South Africa, including a ban on new investments, cessation of maritime and air links, the prohibition of the sale of South African coins, and a total boycott of sporting and cultural relations.

Japan stated on 9 October[43] that, in view of recent developments, it had taken additional measures against South Africa on top of the strict measures already in operation (no diplomatic relations, restricted investment and financing, limited sporting, cultural and educational interchanges, a ban on arms exports to South Africa); new measures included prohibiting the export of computers that could be used by the armed forces and the police, urging a voluntary halt in importing South African gold coins, and calling on companies with offices in South Africa to follow fair employment practices.

Denmark, Finland, Iceland, Norway and Sweden forwarded their 18 October Programme of Action against South Africa,[44] adopted as a follow-up to their 1978 Programme. In the new Programme, they stated their intention to work for the adoption by the Security Council of mandatory sanctions, and described their national measures, including prohibition or discouragement of new investments in South Africa, negotiations to restrict Nordic enterprises' production in South Africa, recommendations to reduce trade, implementation of Council resolution 558(1984)[45] on refraining from importing arms from South Africa, prohibition of the importation of krugerrands, of new nuclear contracts and of the exportation of computer equipment which might be used by the armed forces and police, and a halt of government support for promoting trade with South Africa.

The Bahamas transmitted the Commonwealth Accord on Southern Africa, adopted by the heads of Government of Commonwealth States (Nassau, 16-22 October).[24] Calling on South Africa to dismantle *apartheid*, they outlined a programme of action opposing that system, including recommendations for: strict enforcement of the mandatory arms embargo against South Africa and a commitment to prosecute violators; reaffirmation of the 1977 Gleneagles Declaration, which called on Commonwealth members to discourage sporting contacts; a ban on new government loans; halting government funding for trade missions; a ban on the export of computer equipment; and discouragement of cultural and scientific events.

Democratic Yemen stated on 1 November[25] that imperialist circles, particularly the United States, continued to support South Africa in violation of international covenants and resolutions; it saw dangers arising from the close relations between South Africa and Israel and from their military co-operation, which extended to the nuclear field.

Sanctions and boycotts

Activities of the Committee against *Apartheid*. The Special Committee against *Apartheid*[1] noted with satisfaction that the Security Council, for the first time, had urged Member States, in resolution 566(1985) of 19 June on Namibia (see TRUSTEESHIP AND DECOLONIZATION, Chapter III) and in resolution 569(1985) of 26 July on South Africa (see p. 158), to impose specific economic sanctions against South Africa. While recognizing that several Western countries had taken significant action, however limited, in the previous year, the Committee expressed disappointment that a number of Western Governments

had failed to do so despite pressure by public opinion; in particular, it expressed distress that the United States, the United Kingdom and the Federal Republic of Germany, with a large responsibility for the situation in South Africa, had failed to take meaningful measures in response to Assembly and Council requests to isolate the *apartheid* régime and support the struggle of the oppressed people.

Since any delay in action would likely lead to wider conflict, the Committee said, it was essential that the United Nations ensure comprehensive mandatory sanctions without delay. It asserted that the economic difficulties encountered by South Africa owing to loss of confidence in Western financial circles should not cause complacency, and that pressure on South Africa should be sustained through effective governmental action to prevent foreign economic interests from resuming financial support.

The Committee expressed satisfaction at the increasing recognition by Western public opinion of the need for economic sanctions against South Africa as the main component of international action to eliminate *apartheid*. It rejected the arguments of those profiting from *apartheid* that sanctions would involve great sacrifice by the oppressed people and it denounced the use of "codes of conduct" for employment practices—which included those of the United States, known as the Sullivan Principles—as a means of justifying continued collaboration with *apartheid*.

With regard to sports, cultural, consumer and other boycotts, the Committee noted with satisfaction significant advances and called for their promotion. It welcomed the actions of local authorities, trade unions, anti-*apartheid* movements and others against those who continued to play or perform in South Africa, and called for public opposition to *apartheid* collaborators, such as denial of facilities and patronage to them. It hoped that the General Assembly would adopt a draft instrument prepared by the *Ad Hoc* Committee on the Drafting of an International Convention against *Apartheid* in Sports (see p. 165).

In an October addendum[6] to its annual report, the Committee issued the replies it had received—to its Chairman's request for information on the implementation of the Assembly's 1984 appeal for measures to increase pressure on South Africa[28]— from Australia, Austria, China, Cyprus, Czechoslovakia, Denmark, the German Democratic Republic, Greece, Haiti, Ireland, Japan, Norway, Panama, Romania, Saint Lucia, Seychelles, Solomon Islands, Sweden, the Syrian Arab Republic, Thailand, Turkey, the Ukrainian SSR, the USSR, the United States, Yugoslavia and Zambia; a reply was also received from the 10 EC members. Czechoslovakia, Haiti, Solomon Islands, the Syrian Arab Republic and Yugoslavia said they had no relations with South Africa. Similarly, no relations were maintained by China, Czechoslovakia, the German Democratic Republic, the Ukrainian SSR and the USSR, which were joined by Norway in adding that they provided support to the South African liberation movements.

Australia referred to a statement of 18 April[46] (see p. 146), in which it introduced a voluntary code of conduct for Australian companies and subsidiaries operating in South Africa which applied the principle of equality of treatment in employment practices; it had placed an embargo on all new government dealings with majority-owned South African firms for contracts of more than $20,000. Australia also mentioned the actions it had outlined on 19 August.[40]

Cyprus said that since 1964 it had imposed comprehensive sanctions.

Denmark, a sponsor of the 1984 Assembly resolution,[28] said it had implemented the suggested measures, in co-operation with the other Nordic countries, as well as national legislative and executive steps to pressure South Africa to abandon *apartheid*; individual measures included the Government's request that companies importing coal from South Africa gradually liquidate such imports before 1990, discouraging Danish oil companies and shipowners from trading or transporting oil to South Africa, prohibiting new Danish investment there and in Namibia, and terminating air agreements with South Africa. Norway also adopted measures to reduce commercial and other relations, such as banning the sale of Norwegian-produced oil to South Africa, prohibiting Norwegian investments there, and denying credit guarantees for export to South Africa. The members of EC had also applied the mandatory measures decided on by the United Nations and they considered that their code of conduct for European enterprises having subsidiaries in South Africa was playing an important role towards the elimination of racial discrimination in work places. Ireland said it did not maintain diplomatic relations with South Africa, and had no companies with subsidiaries and no public investment there.

The German Democratic Republic expressed support for comprehensive and mandatory sanctions against South Africa, and urged the Committee to analyse the implementation of the Assembly's 1984 resolution. Norway, Sweden, the Syrian Arab Republic, the Ukrainian SSR and the USSR also advocated such sanctions.

Greece said it had no collaboration in the military field, while Ireland said it would support a mandatory ban on imports of arms and related equipment.

Japan's policy included no diplomatic relations, no direct investment in South Africa and Namibia by Japanese nationals or corporations, and no military co-operation. Panama announced that in

May it had ordered the closure of the South African Consulate in Panama and had severed consular relations.

Saint Lucia had adopted legislation to deny facilities to South African aircraft and vessels flying the South African flag, to prohibit transport companies registered in Saint Lucia from connecting with South Africa, and to deny entry to Saint Lucia of holders of South African passports. Seychelles had revoked South African Airways' landing rights in 1980 and had found alternative trading partners for most of its imported domestic goods. In addition to banning companies from expanding business in South Africa, Sweden in 1985 had prohibited loans and credits, financial transactions and financial leasing to it, and banned export of data processing equipment and cross-country vehicles. Thailand had imposed trade sanctions.

The United States said that in addition to the Sullivan Principles, followed by most of its companies in South Africa, many national and local laws and executive actions regulated its economic relations with South Africa.

Action by the Council for Namibia. The Council for Namibia, in its June 1985 Vienna Declaration and Programme of Action,[30] asserted that comprehensive mandatory sanctions under Chapter VII of the United Nations Charter were the most effective means of ensuring South Africa's compliance with United Nations resolutions and decisions on Namibia. The Council resolved to promote the imposition of such sanctions by the Security Council, in order to ensure South Africa's compliance with the 1978 United Nations independence plan for Namibia,[47] and urged those permanent members of the Security Council that had shielded South Africa to display the necessary political will in that regard. It called on all States to apply voluntary sanctions unilaterally and collectively and urged NGOs, including in particular trade unions, to campaign in their countries in support of a comprehensive programme of sanctions and to monitor that programme.

Action by the Committee on colonial countries. On 16 May,[31] the Committee on colonial countries recommended that the Security Council act decisively against any dilatory manoeuvres of the illegal occupation régime of Namibia, and that the Council, which had been prevented from discharging its responsibilities for maintaining international peace and security in the region owing to the opposition of certain Western permanent members, respond to the demand of the international community by imposing comprehensive mandatory sanctions against South Africa. The Committee noted with satisfaction the pressures being exerted by NGOs in a number of Western countries to promote the severance of links with South Africa, and urged Member States to encourage those organizations to work for mandatory sanctions, as well as to impose voluntary ones. It called on those Governments which had not taken measures aimed at isolating South Africa to take action, pending the imposition of mandatory sanctions.

On 7 August,[32] the Committee called on States to terminate investments in Namibia or loans to South Africa, and to end financial and military assistance to South Africa—which used the assistance to repress the Namibian people and their national liberation movement—to isolate it and to discontinue relations with it concerning Namibia.

Action by the Commission on Human Rights. The Commission on Human Rights, on 26 February,[9] welcomed the Assembly's request that the Security Council consider complete and mandatory sanctions, particularly in the military and financial field. On the same day,[8] the Commission called for the application of sanctions as set out by the 1983 International Conference in Support of the Struggle of the Namibian People for Independence[48] and the 1981 International Conference on Sanctions against South Africa.[49]

SECURITY COUNCIL ACTION

In two 1985 resolutions, the Security Council, reacting to South Africa's installation of a so-called interim government in Windhoek (see TRUSTEESHIP AND DECOLONIZATION, Chapter III) and to the increased repression in South Africa (see p. 152), made recommendations concerning sanctions against that country.

In **resolution 566(1985)** of 19 June, the Council, demanding that South Africa rescind its installation of the so-called interim government, warned that failure to do so would compel the Council to consider measures under the Charter, including Chapter VII (which deals with action with respect to threats to the peace, breaches of the peace and acts of aggression). The Council urged Member States to consider in the mean time voluntary measures against South Africa, including suspending new investments and applying disincentives to that end, re-examining maritime and aerial relations with South Africa, prohibiting the sale of South African coins, and restricting sports and cultural relations.

On 26 July, the Council, in **resolution 569(1985)**, again urged the adoption of measures against South Africa, such as those specified in June, as well as suspending guaranteed export loans, and prohibiting new contracts in the nuclear field and sales of computer equipment that might be used by its forces.

GENERAL ASSEMBLY ACTION

On 10 December, the General Assembly adopted **resolution 40/64 C** by recorded vote.

World Conference on Sanctions against Racist South Africa

The General Assembly,

Gravely concerned about the deteriorating situation in South Africa,

Recalling its resolutions concerning economic and other sanctions against South Africa,

Recalling also Security Council resolution 569(1985) of 26 July 1985,

Noting with regret, however, that the Security Council has thus far failed to take action under Chapter VII of the Charter of the United Nations,

Taking note of the resolution adopted by the Council of Ministers of the Organization of African Unity at its forty-second ordinary session, held at Addis Ababa from 10 to 17 July 1985, and of the statement by the current Chairman of the Assembly of Heads of State and Government of that organization of 21 October 1985, *inter alia,* for the convening of a World Conference on Sanctions against Racist South Africa,

1. *Decides* to organize, in co-operation with the Organization of African Unity and the Movement of Non-Aligned Countries, a World Conference on Sanctions against Racist South Africa in June 1986;

2. *Authorizes* the Special Committee against *Apartheid,* in co-operation with the Organization of African Unity and the Movement of Non-Aligned Countries, to make all necessary arrangements for the organization of the Conference;

3. *Requests* the Secretary-General to provide all necessary assistance to the Special Committee in the organization of the Conference;

4. *Invites* all appropriate United Nations organs, the specialized agencies and other intergovernmental and non-governmental organizations to co-operate with the Special Committee in the implementation of the present resolution;

5. *Requests* the Secretary-General to report on the Conference to the General Assembly at its forty-first session.

General Assembly resolution 40/64 C

10 December 1985   Meeting 111   137-6-10 (recorded vote)

59-nation draft (A/40/L.28/Rev.1 & Rev.1/Corr.1); agenda item 35.

Sponsors: Afghanistan, Algeria, Angola, Antigua and Barbuda, Benin, Burkina Faso, Burundi, Cameroon, Cape Verde, Comoros, Congo, Cuba, Democratic Yemen, Djibouti, Egypt, Equatorial Guinea, Ethiopia, Gambia, German Democratic Republic, Ghana, Guinea, Guinea-Bissau, Guyana, India, Indonesia, Iran, Iraq, Kenya, Lao People's Democratic Republic, Lebanon, Liberia, Libyan Arab Jamahiriya, Madagascar, Malaysia, Mali, Mauritania, Mauritius, Mongolia, Morocco, Nicaragua, Niger, Nigeria, Papua New Guinea, Romania, Rwanda, Senegal, Sierra Leone, Somalia, Sudan, Syrian Arab Republic, Tunisia, Uganda, Ukrainian SSR, United Republic of Tanzania, Viet Nam, Yugoslavia, Zaire, Zambia, Zimbabwe.

Financial implications. 5th Committee, A/40/1022; S-G, A/C.5/40/76.

Meeting numbers. GA 40th session: 5th Committee 58; plenary 51-57, 111.

Recorded vote in Assembly as follows:

In favour: Afghanistan, Albania, Algeria, Angola, Antigua and Barbuda, Argentina, Australia, Bahamas, Bahrain, Bangladesh, Barbados, Benin, Bhutan, Bolivia, Botswana, Brazil, Brunei Darussalam, Bulgaria, Burkina Faso, Burma, Burundi, Byelorussian SSR, Cameroon, Cape Verde, Central African Republic, Chad, China, Colombia, Comoros, Congo, Costa Rica, Cuba, Cyprus, Czechoslovakia, Democratic Kampuchea, Democratic Yemen, Denmark, Djibouti, Dominican Republic, Ecuador, Egypt, El Salvador, Equatorial Guinea, Ethiopia, Fiji, Finland, Gabon, Gambia, German Democratic Republic, Ghana, Greece, Guatemala, Guinea, Guinea-Bissau, Guyana, Haiti, Honduras, Hungary, Iceland, India, Indonesia, Iran, Iraq, Ireland, Jamaica, Japan, Jordan, Kenya, Kuwait, Lao People's Democratic Republic, Lebanon, Lesotho, Liberia, Libyan Arab Jamahiriya, Madagascar, Malaysia, Maldives, Mali, Malta, Mauritania, Mauritius, Mexico, Mongolia, Morocco, Mozambique, Nepal, New Zealand, Nicaragua, Niger, Nigeria, Norway, Oman, Pakistan, Panama, Papua New Guinea, Peru, Philippines, Poland, Qatar, Romania, Rwanda, Saint Lucia, Saint Vincent and the Grenadines,

Samoa, Sao Tome and Principe, Saudi Arabia, Senegal, Seychelles, Sierra Leone, Singapore, Solomon Islands, Somalia, Sri Lanka, Sudan, Suriname, Swaziland, Sweden, Syrian Arab Republic, Thailand, Togo, Trinidad and Tobago, Tunisia, Turkey, Uganda, Ukrainian SSR, USSR, United Arab Emirates, United Republic of Tanzania, Uruguay, Vanuatu, Venezuela, Viet Nam, Yemen, Yugoslavia, Zaire, Zambia, Zimbabwe.

Against: Belgium, Germany, Federal Republic of, Italy, Portugal, United Kingdom, United States.

Abstaining: Austria, Belize, Canada, France, Grenada, Israel, Luxembourg, Malawi, Netherlands, Spain.

Explaining their votes, Austria and Canada believed that the Security Council was the appropriate forum for discussing sanctions. Canada and New Zealand regarded the proposed cost of the Conference to be higher than necessary; the United Kingdom agreed, pointing out that the Assembly had devoted seven days to discussing sanctions, and views had also been expressed in the Special Political Committee, the Fourth Committee and the Security Council. Similarly, the Netherlands doubted that the Conference could contribute to the imposition of selective mandatory sanctions by the Council. The United States assumed that the Conference would focus on the unacceptable goal of mandatory sanctions and would be destined to condemn unfairly the United States and other permanent Council members; it believed that each State should be free to impose the peaceful measures it deemed most appropriate for bringing about change in South Africa.

The Assembly called for sanctions against South Africa in several other 1985 resolutions.

It called on the Council to take action under Chapter VII of the Charter with a view to applying sanctions, in particular, to re-enforce the arms embargo; and requested States, individually and collectively, to take measures to facilitate such action by the Council (**40/64 A**). The Assembly urged the Council to consider without delay the adoption of mandatory sanctions and commended States that had already adopted voluntary measures in accordance with the Assembly's 1984 request[28] (**40/64 I**). It also called for the application of sanctions as called for by the 1981 Conference on Sanctions against South Africa[49] (**40/25**).

Resolutions dealing with South Africa's occupation of Namibia also included calls for sanctions. The Assembly, in **resolution 40/97 A**, called on the Council to implement the recommendations contained in the 1980 report[50] of the Council Committee established in pursuance of resolution 421(1977),[51] which dealt with strengthening the Council's 1977 mandatory arms embargo.[52] In view of South Africa's refusal to comply with United Nations resolutions on Namibia, the Assembly urged the Council to impose comprehensive mandatory sanctions. In **resolution 40/97 B**, the Assembly condemned the use of the veto by the two Western permanent members of the Council on 15 November (see TRUSTEESHIP AND DECOLONIZATION, Chapter

III), resulting in the Council's being prevented from taking measures under Chapter VII of the Charter, and appealed to them to desist from further misuse of the veto.

The Assembly requested United Nations organizations to withhold from South Africa any form of financial, economic and technical assistance and to discontinue support to that régime until the people of Namibia had exercised their right to self-determination and independence in a united Namibia and until *apartheid* had been eradicated and a non-racial, united and democratic State had been established (**40/52**).

Military and nuclear relations

Activities of the Committee against *Apartheid*. The Special Committee against *Apartheid*, citing various press and other reports, stated that South Africa continued its military buildup in 1985, its 1984/85 military spending went up by 21.4 per cent over 1983/84, and the 1985/86 figures increased by 8.1 per cent over the previous year. South Africa continued to develop new weapons, such as a semi-automatic grenade launcher for use in close combat situations and riot control weapons, and was proceeding with plans for the Overberg Missile Testing Range at De Hoop.

According to a British Anti-*Apartheid* Movement memorandum of July 1985, South Africa used "front" companies, fraud and falsehoods to sabotage the Security Council's 1977 arms embargo against it.[52] The memorandum added that the United Kingdom continued to supply South Africa with nuclear technology and personnel, radar equipment and computers, codified information from NATO, and aircraft and arms through third countries. South Africa had been able to circumvent the arms embargo because of loopholes in United Kingdom arms controls.

According to press reports, United States strategic exports to South Africa had risen steadily since it had lifted the ban on sales of commercial goods to the military and police and relaxed restrictions on sales of computers and aircraft in 1982 and 1983. Licences issued in 1984 for exporting aircraft, computers and communications equipment had increased by almost 100 per cent over the average of the three previous years. Nationals and corporations of the Federal Republic of Germany were also known to have violated the arms embargo in recent years, the Committee said. A French newspaper reported in November that South Africa was setting up a helicopter industry with French co-operation and five aerospatial engineers were reported to have gone to South Africa for that purpose.

In the nuclear field, the Uranium Enrichment Corporation of South Africa announced that South Africa would expand the number of its nuclear reactors rapidly by the end of the century because the country's coal resources were limited. In January, the Electricity Supply Commission of South Africa (ESCOM) disclosed that it had recruited United States personnel to operate the nuclear power station in Koeberg. Approximately 20 United States citizens were working directly for ESCOM and an undisclosed number for United States–based companies that had contracted to work for ESCOM. In the same month, the South African Atomic Energy Corporation announced that the country would be self-sufficient in enriched uranium by 1987 when its first processing plant would become operative. Until then, South Africa would continue receiving supplies from abroad.

Noting the developments of the past year— particularly the use of armed forces in Angola and Botswana and repression against the people of South Africa—the Committee said that any form of assistance to the military, police, intelligence or other forces in South Africa constituted complicity in the crimes of the *apartheid* régime. It considered that Governments that opposed the strengthening and effective monitoring of the mandatory arms embargo, as well as corporations that supplied equipment and expertise for military and police use in South Africa, bore a grave responsibility. The Committee urged the Security Council to strengthen the arms embargo, prohibit all nuclear co-operation with South Africa and ensure the effective monitoring of such measures. In that connection, it attached special importance to the prohibition of supply of "dual purpose" equipment, such as computers and technology that could be put to military and police use. Furthermore, the Committee considered that an effective embargo on the supply of petroleum, petroleum products and other strategic supplies should be instituted without delay as an essential reinforcement of the arms embargo.

Report of the Secretary-General. In an August report to the Commission on Transnational Corporations,[53] the Secretary-General described the development of the military and nuclear sectors in the South African economy and the role played by TNCs in those areas.

The report identified some specific activities undertaken by TNCs, both before and after the mandatory arms embargo was imposed by the Security Council in 1977,[52] prohibiting the provision to South Africa of military supplies and licensing arrangements for their manufacture, as well as co-operation in the manufacture and development of nuclear weapons. It pointed to the wide range of essential ancillary inputs that were provided to the two sectors through the activities of foreign enterprises in other sectors. The report concluded that, while the various measures may

have reduced the arms flow to South Africa considerably, they had not had any noticeable impact on the system of *apartheid* or on reducing the threat of war in the region.

According to the report, South Africa had developed the capacity to manufacture light aircraft, fast attack patrol boats and a range of land-based armaments (armoured personnel carriers, artillery, ammunition and electronic surveillance and communications systems); however, it was unable to produce sophisticated jet aircraft, helicopters or large naval vessels. If South Africa continued to be denied the assistance it needed to modernize and service its jet aircraft and to build helicopters, it could be left with an obsolete air force in a few years. However, South Africa continued to make clandestine purchases and was able to buy weaponry on the world market.

Activities of the Council for Namibia. In its annual report to the General Assembly,[30] the United Nations Council for Namibia said the support that South Africa received from Western TNCs and other financial interests that were collaborating with it in exploiting the natural and human resources of Namibia had helped it to entrench its illegal occupation there and to strengthen its military domination and *apartheid* system. To retain its occupation and to further its aggression, South Africa had continued to increase its military spending. The Council referred to the 1985/86 budget presented in March 1985 by the South African Minister of Finance, noting that spending had increased by 8.1 per cent over the previous year, to 4,274 million rand ($1.00 = R 1.98). It pointed out that the exact extent of military spending was unclear, since military and security costs were spread over a number of departments.

The acquisition and production of arms by South Africa were carried out under the aegis of the State-owned Armaments Development and Production Corporation (ARMSCOR), which relied heavily on manufacturing licences obtained from foreign entities. Besides its own production facilities, ARMSCOR depended on about 800 private sector contractors, including many local subsidiaries of United States and Western European companies, which produced a range of weapons, including naval equipment, armoured vehicles and heavy artillery, and operated under secrecy laws that covered military matters.

The Council, in its Vienna Declaration and Programme of Action adopted in June,[30] condemned the continuing military collaboration with and assistance to South Africa by certain Western States and Israel, which it considered a breach of the 1977 arms embargo.[52] It called for the scrupulous observance of the 1984 Security Council resolution requesting States not to import armaments from South Africa.[45] The Council said the acquisition of a nuclear-weapons capability by South Africa had added another dangerous dimension to the grave situation, and condemned the collaboration of Israel and certain Western States, particularly the United States, with South Africa in the nuclear sector. It called on States to refrain from supplying South Africa, directly or indirectly, with installations that might enable it to use uranium, plutonium or other nuclear materials and reactors for military purposes. Furthermore, it called on the Security Council to ensure the total cessation of nuclear collaboration and contacts with South Africa.

Action by the Commission on Human Rights. The Commission on Human Rights, on 26 February,[9] condemned the continuing nuclear collaboration of certain Western States, Israel and other States with South Africa and urged them to cease. It called on Governments to end all technological assistance in the manufacture of arms and military supplies in South Africa and Namibia, in particular to cease all nuclear collaboration. The Commission welcomed the Assembly's request that the Security Council consider complete and mandatory sanctions against South Africa, including the cessation of all nuclear collaboration.

Action by the Committee on colonial countries. The Committee on colonial countries, on 7 August,[33] considered that South Africa's acquisition of nuclear-weapons capability constituted an effort to terrorize and intimidate regional States while posing a threat to all mankind. The continuing assistance rendered to South Africa by certain Western and other countries in the military and nuclear fields belied their stated opposition to its racist practice. The Committee called on those countries to end the nuclear co-operation.

On the same date,[32] the Committee again condemned the nuclear collusion of certain countries and called on Governments to refrain from supplying South Africa, directly or indirectly, with installations that might enable it to produce uranium, plutonium and other nuclear materials, reactors or military equipment.

Communications. In a letter of 3 July to the Secretary-General,[54] Iran stated that Iraq had purchased heavy artillery from South Africa, which had been developed by ARMSCOR and the American Space Research Corporation, and added that the co-operation between South Africa and the United States violated the 1977 mandatory arms embargo against South Africa and that the Iraqi purchase contravened the Security Council's 1984 request that States refrain from importing South African arms.[45] Two days later,[55] Iran forwarded an article from the magazine *Africa Confidential* of 10 April, reporting the alleged military

transaction. On 26 July,[56] Iraq stated that the allegations were false.

On three occasions in 1985, the Security Council called for an end to military or nuclear collaboration with South Africa.

In **resolution 569(1985)**, it urged Member States to adopt measures against South Africa, such as prohibiting new contracts in the nuclear sector and sales of computer equipment that might be used by its forces. **Resolutions 571(1985)** and **574(1985)** included the Council's call for States to implement fully the 1977 arms embargo.

The General Assembly took similar action in numerous 1985 resolutions.

It called on the Security Council to apply mandatory sanctions, including a total ban on all forms of nuclear collaboration, and embargoes on the imports of South African and Namibian uranium and on the export and supply of nuclear material, equipment or technology (**40/64 A**). It again called for Council sanctions, including the cessation of all forms of military, police or intelligence co-operation, in particular the sale of computer equipment, and an end to nuclear collaboration (**40/64 I**).

The Assembly, in **resolution 40/97 A**, declared that the acquisition of nuclear-weapons capability by South Africa constituted a threat to peace and security in Africa and a danger to all mankind. It called for an end to the military and nuclear collaboration, including refraining from supplying South Africa with materials that might enable it to produce uranium, plutonium or other nuclear materials or reactors. A similar request was also made in **resolution 40/52**. Similarly, in **resolution 40/57**, the Assembly condemned all such collaboration and asked that it cease.

In **decision 40/415**, the Assembly considered that South Africa's nuclear-weapons capability was an effort to terrorize and intimidate regional States.

In **resolution 40/158** on strengthening international security, the Assembly called on States, particularly Security Council members, to fulfil the objective of the denuclearization of Africa. In resolutions dealing with the Declaration on the Denuclearization of Africa (**40/89 A** and **B**), the Assembly: condemned nuclear collaboration with South Africa and called for its end, in particular the granting of licences by some Member States to corporations to provide equipment and technology for nuclear installations in South Africa; demanded that South Africa refrain from manufacturing, testing, threatening to use or using nuclear weapons; and appealed to States to monitor South Africa's development of nuclear weapons.

Arms embargo

Activities of the Committee against *Apartheid*.
The Special Committee against *Apartheid* continued to emphasize the importance of an effective and comprehensive arms embargo and again urged the Security Council to strengthen it.[1] In an October addendum[3] to its 1985 annual report, the Committee provided information on legislation and other measures adopted by Governments to enforce the Security Council's 1977 arms embargo against South Africa.[52] As of 30 August 1985, information was provided by 25 Governments (Australia, Brazil, China, Czechoslovakia, Denmark, German Democratic Republic, Greece, Iceland, Ireland, Japan, Lesotho, Libyan Arab Jamahiriya, Mexico, Netherlands, Norway, Romania, Saint Lucia, Sweden, Thailand, Togo, Turkey, Ukrainian SSR, USSR, United States, Yugoslavia) in response to the Committee's request of 6 June.

Australia said that its recent measures included prohibiting exports to South Africa of petroleum and petroleum products, computer hardware and any other products of use to the security forces. By a Presidential decree, Brazil banned the supply of arms and related *matériel* to South Africa, including military and paramilitary police equipment. Denmark said its compliance with the embargo was based on a royal decree on certain measures against South Africa of 1978, as amended in 1982, which included the prohibition of licensing agreements for the manufacture or maintenance of military and paramilitary equipment. Greece said that it strictly enforced the embargo and had no military collaboration with South Africa. Iceland reported that no Icelandic citizen or firm had taken part in any sale or transport of arms to South Africa, which Iceland had banned in 1969.

Irish legislation on the control of exports was embodied in a 1983 law which empowered its trade minister to approve the export of certain goods, including arms and related goods; since 1963 Ireland had voluntarily observed the embargo on the sale of arms and military equipment to South Africa. Lesotho stated it would not assist or facilitate arms acquisition by South Africa. Mexico had banned the sale of weapons and related equipment to South Africa and did not purchase such military materials originating there. The Netherlands had banned transactions involving military goods for South Africa. By royal decree of 1977, Norway had prohibited export or delivery of war material to South Africa. Saint Lucia said it fully supported the arms embargo. Together with the other Nordic countries, Sweden supported strict compliance with and a strengthening of the embargo, and it had prohibited exports of data processing equipment and related software, cross-country vehicles and fuel for the South African military or police authorities.

Thailand had issued regulations prohibiting trade with South Africa, which also applied to arms. Concerning the question of legislative measures adopted to uphold the arms embargo, the United States said it observed it fully and co-operated with the Committee established pursuant to the embargo.

China, Czechoslovakia, the German Democratic Republic, Romania, Togo, Turkey, the Ukrainian SSR, the USSR and Yugoslavia said that they had no relations with South Africa. Japan said it had no military co-operation with it and had never extended any kind of nuclear co-operation. The Libyan Arab Jamahiriya said it opposed any relations with the régime.

Communication. On 15 January,[57] Denmark informed the Chairman of the Security Council Committee established by resolution 421(1977)[51] that its police authorities were investigating alleged violations of the arms embargo by a merchant vessel owned by a Danish citizen and the results of the investigations would be reported to the Committee; the owner and others involved in the shipments had been charged with offences against the 1978 royal decree.

Activities of the Council for Namibia. In its June Vienna Declaration and Programme of Action,[30] the Council for Namibia considered the continuing military collaboration with and assistance to South Africa by certain Western States and Israel to be a breach of the arms embargo, and called for all States to observe the 1984 Security Council request that they not import armaments from South Africa.[45]

Action by the Committee on colonial countries. Similarly, the Committee on colonial countries, on 7 August,[33] condemned the continued military, nuclear and intelligence collaboration between South Africa and certain countries, as a violation of the arms embargo and a threat to international peace and security.

Report of the Secretary-General. In December,[58] the Secretary-General reported on the implementation of the 1984 Security Council resolution requesting States not to import South African arms.[45] His report included the responses, some of which were also issued as separate documents, to a letter he had sent a year earlier to Governments. Australia, Belgium, Bolivia, Botswana, Bulgaria, the Byelorussian SSR,[59] Canada, Chile, China,[60] Cuba, Czechoslovakia,[61] Denmark,[62] Ethiopia,[63] the German Democratic Republic,[64] Ghana, Greece, India,[65] Indonesia,[66] Iran,[37] Iraq, Ireland, Luxembourg, Madagascar,[67] Mexico, Mongolia,[68] the Netherlands, New Zealand, Norway, Papua New Guinea, Peru,[69] the Philippines, Qatar, the Syrian

Arab Republic, Sierra Leone, Spain, Suriname, Thailand,[70] Togo, Turkey, Uganda, the Ukrainian SSR,[71] the USSR[72] and the United Kingdom indicated that they complied with the terms of the resolution. Austria intended not to grant any requests to import South African military material. Brunei Darussalam said it did not wish to import arms produced in South Africa. Support was expressed for the implementation of the provisions of the resolution by the Dominican Republic. By ordinances issued in 1983, Sweden had prohibited the import of most arms and military material.[73] The United States enclosed documents detailing its measures taken in compliance with the resolution.

GENERAL ASSEMBLY ACTION

The General Assembly again demanded the immediate application of the mandatory arms embargo by all countries and more particularly by those that maintained military and nuclear co-operation with South Africa and supplied it with related *matériel* (**resolution 40/25**). It called on States to implement the embargo fully and to comply with Security Council resolution 558(1984) (requesting States to refrain from importing South African arms),[45] and on the Council to adopt measures to tighten the embargo and to ensure strict compliance (**40/97 A**). It called for the Council to apply comprehensive mandatory sanctions, including re-enforcing the 1977 mandatory arms embargo, strengthening the 1984 voluntary embargo[45] by making it mandatory and extending it to cover imports of related materials in addition to arms and ammunition, and prohibiting all military and nuclear co-operation. Pending Council action, States were requested to ensure strict implementation of the arms embargo and prohibition of all military and nuclear collaboration. States were also requested to take action against corporations and others that violated the embargo and those involved in supplying South Africa with oil, as well as those who persisted in collaborating with the régime (**40/64 A**). The Assembly again urged the Council to take steps for the strict implementation of the 1977 and 1984 embargoes and to secure an end to military and nuclear co-operation with South Africa and the import of South African military equipment (**40/64 I**).

The Assembly requested the Council to conclude its consideration of the 1980 recommendations[50] of its Committee established by resolution 421(1977) with a view to blocking the existing loopholes in the embargo so as to render it more effective, and prohibiting, in particular, nuclear collaboration (**40/89 B**). In **decision 40/415**, the Assembly urged that the Council consider, as a matter of urgency, the Committee's 1980 report, which contained recommendations on tightening the arms embargo, and suggested that it adopt further measures to widen the embargo's scope. The Assembly also called for the scrupulous observance of Council resolution 558(1984).

Economic relations

Activities of the Committee against *Apartheid*. The Special Committee against *Apartheid* reported that South Africa was going through a severe recession, which began in 1984 and, as a result of the deterioration of the political environment and other factors, took a downturn in mid-1985.[1] The economic performance could also be attributed to the defiance by the country's growing black trade union movement and the régime's failure to contain the opposition. South Africa's imposition of the state of emergency in mid-1985 led to the loss of international confidence in the economy, sparking the worst financial crisis since South Africa was established in 1948. Major international banks did not renew their short-term lines of credit to the Government, causing the worst devaluation of the rand and prompting the régime to declare a moratorium on debt servicing. Even before this happened, the country's financial system was experiencing difficulties. In May, foreigners sold South African securities worth $40 million, and another $70 million was sold in July. The capital flight affected the economy by substantially reducing South Africa's foreign-exchange reserves and causing inflation to rise. To curb the capital flight and to attract more foreign investment, South Africa gradually reduced the prime rate from an all-time high of 25 per cent to 15.5 per cent.

In 1985, of the total foreign trade ($16.3 billion) excluding gold, arms and oil, South Africa's main trading partners were: the United States, with 21.3 per cent; the United Kingdom, 16.6 per cent; Japan, 16.3 per cent; the Federal Republic of Germany, 16.3 per cent; France, 6.3 per cent; and Italy, 6 per cent. Despite fluctuations in its price, gold remained the most important export; in 1985, it constituted 75 per cent of the aggregate exports. Nevertheless, gold exports were not able to pay for all of South Africa's imports, so the régime continued to rely on international financing. Platinum, coal and iron ore were also important exports. Foreign investments represented approximately 10 per cent of all investments, with the United Kingdom being the largest foreign investor.

Action by the Commission on Human Rights. On 26 February,[9] the Commission on Human Rights called on Governments that had not done so to take measures in respect of their nationals and companies under their jurisdiction that owned and operated enterprises in South Africa and Namibia, in order to stop their activities there. The Commission welcomed the General Assembly's request that the Security Council consider prohibiting loans to, and investments in, South Africa and demanding the cessation of trade with it.

Communication. Australia transmitted to the Secretary-General an 18 April statement by its Foreign Minister,[46] introducing a code of conduct for Australian companies with commercial interests in South Africa; the code was based on the principle of equality of treatment in the work place irrespective of race.

GENERAL ASSEMBLY ACTION

In **resolution 40/64 A**, the General Assembly called on the Security Council to ban trade with South Africa and, pending such action, requested States to ensure such a ban, particularly on the sale of krugerrands and the import of gold, uranium, coal and other minerals. United Nations organizations were called on to refrain from purchasing South African products, to deny contracts or facilities to corporations collaborating with South Africa and not to invest any money in them, and to prohibit any official travel by South African Airways or South African shipping lines. The Assembly, in **resolution 40/64 I**, appealed to States, pending mandatory sanctions, to consider national measures to increase pressure on South Africa, such as an end to promoting and supporting trade with it and prohibiting the sale of its coins. In **resolution 40/52**, the Assembly again called on States to refrain from promoting trade or other economic relations.

Oil embargo

The International Conference of Maritime Trade Unions on the Implementation of the United Nations Oil Embargo against South Africa adopted on 31 October a declaration which was transmitted to the Secretary-General by the Chairman of the Committee against *Apartheid*.[74] Convened on the initiative of seafarers' and dockers' unions and organized by the Maritime Trade Unions against *Apartheid* in co-operation with the Committee, the Conference (London, 30 and 31 October) commended those Governments which had supported the United Nations oil embargo and called on others to implement it. It condemned shipowners and shipping management companies (including flag-of-convenience operators), shipping agents and oil companies violating the oil embargo, called for compliance with it, and warned them that, until assurance was received of their compliance, their vessels were liable to trade union action, including boycott.

The Conference resolved that seafarers and port, dock and other transport workers would urge Governments to make it illegal to supply or transport oil to South Africa, and take action against the vessels of companies involved. The Conference requested the United Nations to organize a conference of oil producers and transporters, with the participation of Governments, shipowners and trade unions, to lay down specific mandatory procedures to make the oil embargo effective.

On 26 February,[9] the Commission on Human Rights welcomed the request of the General Assembly that the Security Council consider an embargo on the supply of petroleum, petroleum products and other strategic goods to South Africa.

The Committee on colonial countries, on 7 August,[32] called on those oil-producing and oil-exporting countries that had not done so to take measures against the companies concerned so as to stop such supplies.

GENERAL ASSEMBLY ACTION

The General Assembly, in **resolution 40/64 A**, called on the Security Council to apply an embargo on oil and oil products and on all assistance to the oil industry in South Africa, particularly to the oil-from-coal industry. Pending such action, States were requested to ensure prohibition of the supply of oil and oil products as well as related technology. States were also requested to take action against those involved in supplying South Africa with oil and oil products in spite of the embargo. Likewise, in **resolution 40/64 I**, the Assembly appealed to States, pending the Council's action, to increase pressure on South Africa by ceasing the export and sale of oil to it.

In **resolution 40/52**, the Assembly called on those oil-producing and oil-exporting countries that had not done so to act against the companies concerned so as to terminate supplies of crude oil and petroleum products to South Africa.

Foreign investments and loans

South Africa's total foreign liabilities, according to the Committee against *Apartheid*,[1] were around $60 billion in 1985, two thirds of which was in short-term loans repayable within the year. Loans by United States banks to the South African private sector increased to $4.2 billion in 1984 from $1 billion in 1980. United States investments in South Africa totalled approximately $2.3 billion, around 1 per cent of all United States overseas investment. Seventy per cent of the South African computer industry, 50 per cent of the petroleum industry and 30 per cent of the automobile industry were controlled by United States companies operating in and exporting to South Africa. United Kingdom interests continued to expand in South Africa despite the international campaign for divestment, and its investments were approximately 7 per cent of the total United Kingdom overseas portfolio. Short-term and medium-term South African stocks were marketed in the United Kingdom, and South African business groups were expanding their investments in the United Kingdom.

Citing South African press reports, the Committee said that the profitability of investments in South Africa had declined from 31 per cent in 1980 to 7 per cent in 1982 and to a loss of 9 per cent in 1985. In 1985, United States banks decided not to renew their short-term credit lines to South Africa, which amounted to $14 billion; British and other Western European banks followed suit. The largest creditors were British banks with a $5.5 billion exposure, United States banks with a $4.5 billion exposure and a group of banks from the Federal Republic of Germany, France and Switzerland with an aggregate short-term exposure of $4 billion to the South African private and public sector.

In October and November, South Africa met with representatives of 30 major banks for negotiations on rescheduling all short-term payments for five years and to start repayment of capital in 1990. On 22 October, the Chairman of the Committee sent a message to Fritz Leutwiler, the mediator of the banks, urging them to refuse the régime's request for an extension of its loans. He appealed for the withdrawal of existing loans and an end to new ones.

The Committee noted with satisfaction that the United Nations Joint Staff Pension Board had divested from corporations operating in South Africa. Acknowledging the contribution made by several United Nations agencies in this regard, it suggested that the General Assembly call on the Secretary-General and the specialized agencies to end any other deposits or investments in, or any contracts with or the provision of facilities to, any banks or corporations operating in South Africa. It recommended that the International Monetary Fund cease all forms of assistance to that country (see p. 150).

The Commission on Human Rights, on 26 February,[9] welcomed the Assembly's request that the Security Council prohibit loans to, and investments in, South Africa.

GENERAL ASSEMBLY ACTION

In **resolution 40/64 A**, the General Assembly called on the Security Council to prohibit financial loans and credits to and investment in South Africa. Pending that action, States were requested to ensure such prohibition, as well as the withdrawal of investment in South Africa. United Nations organizations were called on to withhold any facilities from or investments of any funds in banks, financial institutions and corporations doing business in South Africa. Pending Council sanctions, the Assembly, in **resolution 40/64 I**, appealed to States to increase pressure on South Africa by ceasing further investments in and financial loans to it. In **resolution 40/52**, the Assembly called on States to terminate, or cause to have terminated, any investments in Namibia or loans to South Africa.

SECURITY COUNCIL ACTION

Reacting to the deteriorating situation and repression in South Africa, the Security Council in **resolution 569(1985)** also urged States to suspend new investment and guaranteed export loans.

Transnational corporations

Commission on TNCs. The Commission on Transnational Corporations, at its eleventh session in April 1985, considered several reports on the activities of TNCs in South Africa and Namibia.[75]

In January, the Secretary-General, responding to a 1984 request of the Economic and Social Council,[76] submitted a report,[77] briefly describing recent economic developments there, with emphasis on direct foreign investment and the involvement of TNCs. The report, which contained a list of TNCs operating in South Africa and Namibia, said South Africa had a relatively open economy in that its exports constituted nearly 30 per cent of its gross domestic product (GDP). The industrial countries were the major buyers of South Africa's merchandise exports, with Western Europe accounting for nearly half of its total export market and the United States for over 15 per cent. Although all exports to South Africa of internationally traded crude oil were under embargo, it was estimated that approximately 15 million tons of crude oil, valued at about $3 billion, were not reported in world trade statistics because they were sold and shipped to South Africa, whose economy depended heavily on oil imports.

Gold, the most important South African export, accounted for nearly half of total exports and constituted more than 80 per cent of South Africa's international reserves. Other exports were chromite, manganese, platinum, diamonds and maize. Since 1981, weak external demand for non-gold exports, falling international gold prices and severe drought had devastated South Africa's economy, leading to a sharp depreciation of the rand *vis-à-vis* all major currencies and to a significant acceleration of inflation. Following a weak economic recovery in 1983, the rate of growth of real GDP for 1984 was estimated at 3 per cent, as against 4.75 per cent for the developed market economies for the year. The growth rate of real output was expected to be under 2 per cent in 1985 and business fixed investment was expected to continue to decline in real terms well into the year.

TNCs continued to play a key role, and major divestments in 1983 and 1984 were overwhelmed by the significant and growing presence of several hundred TNCs in the South African economy.

In February, the Secretariat issued a report[78] updating that of 1984[79] on the responsibilities of home countries with respect to TNCs operating in South Africa and Namibia in violation of United Nations decisions. In addition to the measures taken by the United Nations and others, the report analysed codes of conduct adopted by home countries concerning employment practices of TNCs and found them to have had only limited positive effects. The Secretariat noted that the home countries had in general affirmed their commitment to enforcing the mandatory arms embargo, and some had adopted national legislation to implement it; however, the operations of TNCs in strategic sectors of the South African economy, such as electronics and computers, energy including nuclear energy and petroleum, and machinery and equipment, had continued.

Having considered the reports, the Commission on TNCs adopted a draft resolution on TNCs and their collaboration with South Africa and a draft decision on organization of public hearings on TNC activities, which were then submitted to and subsequently adopted by the Economic and Social Council (see below).

The Commission also continued trying to resolve the main outstanding issues of a draft code of conduct on TNCs (see ECONOMIC AND SOCIAL QUESTIONS, Chapter VII).

Action by the Commission on Human Rights. The Commission on Human Rights, on 26 February,[9] called on Governments that had not done so to take measures in respect of their nationals and the companies under their jurisdiction that owned and operated enterprises in South Africa and Namibia, with a view to stopping their trading, manufacturing and investing activities there. The Commission welcomed the 1984 General Assembly decision[80] to invite the Special Rapporteur of the Sub-Commission on Prevention of Discrimination and Protection of Minorities to continue to update, subject to annual review, the list of banks, TNCs and other organizations assisting South Africa (see ECONOMIC AND SOCIAL QUESTIONS, Chapter XVIII). The Sub-Commission, in August,[81] welcomed the Commission's appeal.

ECONOMIC AND SOCIAL COUNCIL ACTION

On 26 July, the Economic and Social Council, acting on the recommendation of its First (Economic) Committee, adopted **resolution 1985/72** by vote.

Activities of transnational corporations in South Africa and Namibia and collaboration of such corporations with the racist minority régime of South Africa
The Economic and Social Council,
Recalling Security Council resolution 560(1985) of 12 March 1985,
Recalling also General Assembly resolutions 39/72 A to G of 13 December 1984, in particular resolution 39/72 G on concerted international action for the elimination of *apartheid,*
Reaffirming previous resolutions of the Economic and Social Council on the activities of transnational corporations in South Africa and Namibia and the collaboration of such corporations with the racist minority régime of South Africa,

Having considered the report of the Secretary-General on the activities of transnational corporations in South Africa and Namibia and the collaboration of such corporations with the racist minority régime in that area and the report of the Secretariat on the responsibilities of home countries with respect to the transnational corporations operating in South Africa and Namibia in violation of the relevant resolutions and decisions of the United Nations,
Noting with grave concern the deterioration of the situation in South Africa as evidenced by the recent increased brutality, indiscriminate killings and mass arrests of innocent persons, including children, by the authorities of the racist minority régime of South Africa,
Regretting that the inflows of foreign direct investment to South Africa have risen significantly in recent years,
Affirming the need for intensified action at the international level by all Governments and non-governmental organizations, including trade unions, academic institutions, parliamentarians and public officials in various countries,
1.   *Takes note* of the report of the Secretary-General on the activities of transnational corporations in South Africa and Namibia and the collaboration of such corporations with the racist minority régime in that area, in particular the list of transnational corporations operating in that area, and the report of the Secretariat on the responsibilities of home countries with respect to the transnational corporations operating in South Africa and Namibia in violation of the relevant resolutions and decisions of the United Nations;
2.   *Condemns* the racist minority régime of South Africa and its brutal perpetuation of the inhuman system of *apartheid* and the illegal occupation of Namibia;
3.   *Reaffirms* that the activities of transnational corporations in South Africa reinforce the racist minority régime in its perpetuation of the system of *apartheid* and its illegal occupation of Namibia;
4.   *Notes with appreciation* the actions of those non-governmental organizations and academic institutions that have exerted pressure on transnational corporations collaborating with the racist minority régime for disinvestment of their assets and the proposals for legislative and other regulatory measures put forward by some parliamentarians and other public officials in various countries with a view to terminating the activities of transnational corporations in South Africa and Namibia, and requests the Secretariat to transmit the text of the present resolution to all such organizations, parliamentarians and public officials;
5.   *Welcomes* as a positive first step the measures taken by certain home countries of transnational corporations to place restrictions on further investments in South Africa and on bank loans to the racist minority régime;
6.   *Urges* all transnational corporations to terminate their investments in South Africa and to end all forms of collaboration with the racist minority régime;
7.   *Reaffirms* Security Council resolution 301(1971) of 20 October 1971, in which the Council called upon States to abstain from entering into economic relations with South Africa in respect of Namibia and declared that rights, titles or contracts granted to individuals or corporations by South Africa after the termination of the mandate were not subject to protection or espousal by their States against the claims of a future lawful Government of Namibia;

8. *Invites* all States, non-governmental organizations and all transnational corporations operating in South Africa and Namibia to co-operate with the United Nations in organizing public hearings on the activities of transnational corporations in South Africa and Namibia so as to facilitate the conduct of fair, objective and balanced hearings on such activities with regard to the topics set out in Economic and Social Council resolution 1982/70 of 27 October 1982;

9. *Requests* the Secretary-General:

(a) To continue the useful work of the Secretariat on the activities of transnational corporations in South Africa and Namibia through the collection and dissemination of information;

(b) To provide more detailed information on the profiles of transnational corporations operating in South Africa and Namibia;

(c) To update, for submission to the Commission on Transnational Corporations at its twelfth session, the report of the Secretary-General on the activities of transnational corporations in South Africa and Namibia and the report of the Secretariat on the responsibilities of home countries with respect to the transnational corporations operating in South Africa and Namibia in violation of the relevant resolutions and decisions of the United Nations.

Economic and Social Council resolution 1985/72

| 26 July 1985 | Meeting 52 | 35-2-8 |

Approved by First Committee (E/1985/146) by vote (34-2-8), 24 July (meeting 28); draft by Commission on TNCs (E/1985/28); agenda item 9.

Paragraphs 3 and 6 were approved by the Committee by votes of 28 to 5, with 8 abstentions, and of 28 to 3, with 10 abstentions, respectively. In the Council, paragraph 3 was adopted by a roll-call vote, requested by Zimbabwe, of 32 to 5, with 9 abstentions, and paragraph 6 was adopted by 32 votes to 3, with 10 abstentions.

In explanation of vote, Sweden, also on behalf of Finland and Iceland, said they had voted in favour of the draft but abstained in the vote on the paragraphs because their wording went beyond what the delegations could currently endorse. For similar reasons, Spain voted against paragraph 3 and abstained on the text as a whole. Luxembourg, speaking also on behalf of France, the Federal Republic of Germany, the Netherlands and the United Kingdom, said they had been unable to support the draft; they remained convinced that the progress made by European firms in applying the provisions of the EC Code of Conduct would contribute to solving the *apartheid* problem, thus encouraging, by means of existing economic relations, the possibility of a peaceful change in South African society.

Hearings on TNC activities in South Africa and Namibia

The *Ad Hoc* Committee on the Preparations for the Public Hearings on the Activities of TNCs in South Africa and Namibia met from 16 to 18 January and on 14 and 15 February 1985,[82] and submitted to the Commission on TNCs revised guidelines on the organization of the hearings as well as suggestions as to persons and organizations to be invited. The Committee recommended that the hearings should identify measures to bring about the eradication of *apartheid* and the cessation of South Africa's occupation of Namibia; promote greater awareness of the support by TNCs for South Africa and its *apartheid* system; and endeavour to identify TNCs involved in such collaboration and seek divestment of their investments in South Africa and Namibia. The recommendations were approved by the Economic and Social Council by **decision 1985/127** of 28 May.

Also in accordance with the Committee's recommendations, the Secretary-General and the Chairman of the Commission jointly appointed an 11-member Panel of eminent international personalities to conduct the hearings. The hearings were held in New York from 16 to 20 September and the Panel, which reconvened on 10 and 11 October to consider its report, submitted its unanimously adopted report and recommendations to the Commission.[83]

In preparation for the hearings, the Centre on TNCs prepared reports issued by the Secretary-General on measures regarding TNC activities in South Africa and Namibia,[84] TNC activities and operations in South Africa and their contribution to *apartheid*,[85] the role of TNCs in the military and nuclear sectors of South Africa and Namibia[53] (see p. 142), employment practices of TNCs and their socio-economic impact, including effects on housing and family life-styles,[86] and TNC activities in Namibia[87] (see TRUSTEESHIP AND DECOLONIZATION, Chapter III).

In the first of the reports,[84] the Centre provided a compilation of action proposed in resolutions of the United Nations and other intergovernmental organizations, and legislation adopted by Member States, as well as measures by institutional investors (such as colleges, universities and pension funds), NGOs and TNCs. They included measures restricting economic, military and nuclear collaboration, and steps to establish an oil embargo. The Centre, in the second report,[85] described the role of TNCs in the South African economy and its key sectors (the automotive industry, banking, energy, mining, chemicals and electronics), assessed the importance of foreign investment in the economy, and discussed whether disinvestment or continued involvement of TNCs in South Africa would bring more rapid progress towards eradication of *apartheid*.

The report on TNC employment practices[86] reviewed the situation regarding the terms and conditions of employment of the black majority, pointing to measures by the Government to control the market for them. It also examined the codes of conduct that had been formulated in certain home countries to improve the terms and conditions of employment for black workers employed by South African affiliates of companies based in those home countries (EC, Australia, Canada and the United States had put forward such codes), and the employment practices in Namibia, where the codes did not apply. The Centre concluded that the impact of the employment practices of TNCs in South Africa, even where they had sought to improve the socio-economic conditions of the black majority, had been marginal at best. Ultimately, an assessment of the impact of TNCs would have to go beyond employment practices and focus on their contribution to the survival of *apartheid*. In Namibia, pressure from the home countries had compelled some TNCs, particularly the three large mining corporations operating there, to make concessions to black labour, including greater trade union freedom, better wages and improvements in housing, training and job advancement.

In preparation for the hearings, the Secretary-General outlined, in April,[88] a publicity programme to promote greater awareness on the part of Governments, particularly those of home countries of TNCs operating in South Africa and Namibia, of the support by TNCs to South Africa and *apartheid*.

The Panel determined that there were 1,068 TNCs operating in South Africa, 406 of them based in the United States, 364 from the United Kingdom, 142 from the Federal Republic of Germany and the remaining 156 from 16 other States or territories. TNCs transferred capital and technology to South Africa, provided markets for its exports and supplied imports, making a major contribution to its economy. Within South Africa, TNCs accounted for approximately one tenth of the country's capital stock and up to a quarter of its GDP.

While recognizing the steps that the business community had made to promote change, the Panel did not consider that the actions matched their public condemnation of *apartheid*. It recommended that all TNCs producing for the military, police and security sector disinvest immediately and that the mandatory arms embargo (see p. 144) be expanded to include dual-use items—items serving military and civilian purposes. The Panel also recommended that: all nuclear co-operation with South Africa and Namibia be prohibited; TNCs refuse to comply with South African legislation providing for the establishment of company militia that could be put under the authority of the Government; the voluntary oil embargo be made mandatory; loans to and investment in South Africa be banned; multilateral financial arrangements be conditional on the abolition of *apartheid;* new licensing of technology be banned; and imports of South African gold be prohibited. The Panel also recommended that TNCs remain-

ing in South Africa adhere to certain standards of behaviour, such as not supplying the security forces with equipment that could be used to enforce *apartheid*. TNCs were urged to desegregate all work facilities, apply the principle of equal pay and benefits, allow their workers to live permanently with their families and ensure housing for all workers within a reasonable distance of the workplace, and pay an acceptable minimum wage. In addition, the Panel made suggestions for implementing its recommendations, monitoring the situation and follow-up to its report. The Secretary-General was called on to assume overall responsibility for monitoring the implementation, and the United Nations was urged to publicize a list of TNCs that did not comply.

GENERAL ASSEMBLY ACTION

By **decision 40/433** of 17 December, the General Assembly noted that the Commission on TNCs and the Economic and Social Council would in 1986 consider the Panel's recommendations and propose appropriate action.

In **resolution 40/64 A**, the Assembly condemned the activities of those TNCs and financial institutions that had continued collaborating with South Africa ignoring repeated Assembly appeals. By **resolution 40/52**, it condemned the TNCs which continued their investments in, and supply of armaments and oil and nuclear technology to, South Africa. The Assembly, in **resolution 40/27**, took note of the report of the Group of Three of the Commission on Human Rights, established in accordance with the 1973 International Convention on the Suppression and Punishment of the Crime of *Apartheid*,[89] and drew the attention of all States to the Group's opinion that article III of the Convention could apply to the actions of TNCs operating in South Africa.

IMF and World Bank relations with South Africa

In 1985, several United Nations bodies called on the International Monetary Fund (IMF) and the World Bank to terminate relations with South Africa.

On 26 February,[9] the Commission on Human Rights urgently requested all specialized agencies, particularly IMF and the World Bank, to refrain from granting any financial aid to South Africa.

The Committee on colonial countries took similar action on 16 May[31] and 9 August,[90] as did the Council for Namibia in its 7 June[30] Vienna Declaration and Programme of Action. The Committee regretted that the World Bank and IMF continued to maintain links with Pretoria, as exemplified by the participation of South Africa in the work of both agencies, and called on IMF to end such collaboration and not to grant new loans. The Committee recommended that the Assembly reiterate its proposal, under the Agreement between the

United Nations and IMF, for the inclusion in the agenda of the IMF Board of Governors of an item on the IMF–South Africa relationship; the Fund was urged to discuss the subject in September 1985 and to report to the Secretary-General on any action.

The Committee's concerns and recommendations were incorporated into General Assembly **resolution 40/53** and **resolution 40/64 A**, by which it called on IMF to terminate credit and other assistance to South Africa. It took similar action in **resolution 40/97 A**, calling on all specialized agencies, in particular IMF, to terminate collaboration with, and assistance to, South Africa, since such assistance served to augment its military capability, thus enabling it not only to continue the repression in Namibia and South Africa but also to commit aggression against neighbouring States.

Similarly, in **resolution 1985/59**, the Economic and Social Council deplored the persistent collaboration of IMF with South Africa and urgently called on the Fund to put an end to it.

Israel–South Africa relations

The Special Committee against *Apartheid*, in October 1985,[4] described recent developments concerning relations between Israel and South Africa. It said that over the previous 10 years, there had been increasing collaboration which threatened peace and security in southern Africa, the Middle East and the rest of the world; the two countries had always concealed the extent of their relationship and particularly their nuclear and military collaboration.

Since 1977, when the South African Prime Minister had visited Israel, officials of the two countries had frequently exchanged visits, including a November 1984 visit of the South African Foreign Minister to Israel for consultations with the Prime Minister and his Israeli counterpart.

Nuclear collaboration had been reported since 1977 when South Africa was spotted preparing a nuclear-test site in the Kalahari desert. Israel helped South Africa develop the technical expertise for nuclear weapons, and there was evidence that they had tested a nuclear bomb on 22 September 1979 in the South Atlantic. As for military collaboration, Israel supplied arms and ammunition, served as a conduit for arms supplies to South Africa and assisted in developing South Africa's arms industry. Although accurate statistics were unavailable, it appeared that South Africa had been acquiring as much as 35 per cent of Israeli arms exports in recent years, including gunboats and missiles.

Israeli–South African economic co-operation was increasing, and bilateral trade (excluding oil, arms, gold and diamonds) reached a record 280 million rand in the first 11 months of 1984, according to the South African press. South African investment in Israel also increased in spite of an economic crisis in Israel. Israel was one of the few countries that maintained political, military, economic and cultural relations with the bantustans; in 1984, for example, Ciskei opened the first of six Israeli factories due to be set up there.

The Committee called for international action against the collaboration, in particular the military and nuclear co-operation. It recommended to the General Assembly that there should be closer co-operation between the Department of Public Information and the Centre against *Apartheid* in disseminating information on that collaboration. It also recommended to the Assembly that all States, particularly Western ones, withhold assistance that enhanced collaboration between Israel and South Africa.

GENERAL ASSEMBLY ACTION

On 10 December, the General Assembly adopted **resolution 40/64 E** by recorded vote.

Relations between Israel and South Africa

The General Assembly,

Reaffirming its resolutions on relations between Israel and South Africa,

Having considered the special report of the Special Committee against *Apartheid* on recent developments concerning relations between Israel and South Africa,

Noting with appreciation the efforts of the Special Committee to expose the increasing and continuing collaboration between Israel and South Africa,

Reiterating that the increasing collaboration by Israel with the racist régime of South Africa, especially in the military and nuclear fields, in defiance of resolutions of the General Assembly and the Security Council is a serious hindrance to international action for the eradication of *apartheid*, an encouragement to the racist régime of South Africa to persist in its criminal policy of *apartheid* and a hostile act against the oppressed people of South Africa and the entire African continent and constitutes a threat to international peace and security,

1. *Commends* the Special Committee against *Apartheid* for publicizing the growing relations between Israel and South Africa and promoting public awareness of the grave dangers of the alliance between Israel and South Africa;

2. *Again strongly condemns* the continuing and increasing collaboration of Israel with the racist régime of South Africa, especially in the military and nuclear fields;

3. *Demands* that Israel desist from and terminate all forms of collaboration with South Africa forthwith, particularly in the military and nuclear fields, and abide scrupulously by the relevant resolutions of the General Assembly and the Security Council;

4. *Calls upon* all Governments and organizations in a position to do so to exert their influence to persuade Israel to desist from such collaboration;

5. *Requests* the Special Committee to continue to publicize, as widely as possible, information on the relations between Israel and South Africa;

6. *Again requests* the Secretary-General to render, through the Department of Public Information and the Centre against *Apartheid* of the Secretariat, all possible assistance to the Special Committee in disseminating information relating to the collaboration between Israel and South Africa;

7. *Further requests* the Special Committee to keep the matter under constant review and to report to the General Assembly and the Security Council as appropriate.

General Assembly resolution 40/64 E

10 December 1985   Meeting 111   102-20-30 (recorded vote)

51-nation draft (A/40/L.30 & Corr.2); agenda item 35.

Sponsors: Afghanistan, Algeria, Angola, Benin, Burkina Faso, Burundi, Byelorussian SSR, Comoros, Cuba, Democratic Yemen, Djibouti, Egypt, Equatorial Guinea, Ethiopia, German Democratic Republic, Ghana, Guinea, Guinea-Bissau, Guyana, India, Indonesia, Iran, Iraq, Kenya, Lao People's Democratic Republic, Lebanon, Libyan Arab Jamahiriya, Madagascar, Malaysia, Mali, Mauritania, Mongolia, Morocco, Mozambique, Nicaragua, Niger, Nigeria, Rwanda, Sao Tome and Principe, Senegal, Sierra Leone, Sudan, Syrian Arab Republic, Tunisia, Uganda, Ukrainian SSR, United Republic of Tanzania, Viet Nam, Yugoslavia, Zambia, Zimbabwe.

Financial implications. 5th Committee, A/40/1022; S-G, A/C.5/40/76.

Meeting numbers. GA 40th session: 5th Committee 58; plenary 51-57, 111.

Recorded vote in Assembly as follows:

In favour: Afghanistan, Albania, Algeria, Angola, Argentina, Bahrain, Bangladesh, Benin, Bhutan, Bolivia, Botswana, Brazil, Brunei Darussalam, Bulgaria, Burkina Faso, Burundi, Byelorussian SSR, Cape Verde, Central African Republic, Chad, China, Comoros, Congo, Cuba, Cyprus, Czechoslovakia, Democratic Kampuchea, Democratic Yemen, Djibouti, Ecuador, Egypt, Ethiopia, Gabon, Gambia, German Democratic Republic, Ghana, Guinea, Guinea-Bissau, Guyana, Haiti, Hungary, India, Indonesia, Iran, Iraq, Jordan, Kenya, Kuwait, Lao People's Democratic Republic, Lebanon, Lesotho, Libyan Arab Jamahiriya, Madagascar, Malaysia, Maldives, Mali, Malta, Mauritania, Mauritius, Mongolia, Morocco, Mozambique, Nicaragua, Niger, Nigeria, Oman, Pakistan, Papua New Guinea, Peru, Philippines, Poland, Qatar, Romania, Rwanda, Sao Tome and Principe, Saudi Arabia, Senegal, Seychelles, Sierra Leone, Singapore, Somalia, Sri Lanka, Sudan, Suriname, Syrian Arab Republic, Thailand, Togo, Tunisia, Turkey, Uganda, Ukrainian SSR, USSR, United Arab Emirates, United Republic of Tanzania, Vanuatu, Venezuela, Viet Nam, Yemen, Yugoslavia, Zambia, Zimbabwe.

Against: Australia, Austria, Belgium, Canada, Denmark, Finland, France, Germany, Federal Republic of, Grenada, Iceland, Ireland, Israel, Italy, Luxembourg, Netherlands, New Zealand, Norway, Sweden, United Kingdom, United States.

Abstaining: Bahamas, Barbados, Belize, Burma, Cameroon, Chile, Colombia, Costa Rica, Dominican Republic, Equatorial Guinea, Fiji, Greece, Guatemala, Honduras, Ivory Coast, Jamaica, Japan, Liberia, Malawi, Nepal, Panama, Portugal, Saint Lucia, Saint Vincent and the Grenadines, Samoa, Solomon Islands, Spain, Swaziland, Uruguay, Zaire.

Israel said the false accusation of its support for *apartheid* was propagated by Arab States, which enjoyed immunity from public exposure of their trade with South Africa; according to Israel, Arab oil exports to South Africa reached $2.2 billion per year.

Costa Rica, stating that it would have voted against paragraphs 2 and 3, had separate votes been taken, did not favour singling out specific States in connection with situations where others were co-operating with South Africa. Austria and Ireland also opposed selective singling out of one Member State for condemnation. The United States agreed, adding that many African countries continued to co-operate with South Africa, especially in trade matters.

The Assembly took related action in **resolution 40/64 A**, requesting the Committee against *Apartheid* to keep the matter of collaboration between South Africa and Israel under review and to report to the

Assembly and the Security Council as appropriate. In **resolution 40/25**, the Assembly denounced the collusion between the two and expressed support for the Declaration of the 1983 International Conference on the Alliance between South Africa and Israel.[91] By **resolution 40/168 A**, it condemned the increasing collaboration, especially in the economic, military and nuclear areas, which constituted a hostile act against the African and Arab States. The Assembly's condemnation of the continuing nuclear collaboration between the two countries was restated in **resolution 40/93**.

Situation in South Africa

Activities of the Committee against *Apartheid*. South Africa's repression of the oppressed people increased dramatically in 1985 as the Government attempted to suppress the growing resistance to *apartheid*. According to the Special Committee against *Apartheid*,[1] the régime resorted to large-scale killings, detained thousands of people and subjected scores of its leading opponents to political trials in order to destroy opposition organizations. In February, South Africa attempted forcibly to remove thousands of blacks from Crossroads township near Cape Town to the newly created black township, Khayelitsha, situated in sand dunes several miles away. At least 23 people were killed and more than 200 injured when police fought with demonstrators protesting the removal of 65,000 inhabitants. Forced removals continued, and the Government announced in September that 42,000 blacks would be forcibly moved to the bantustan of KwaZulu.

South Africa deployed the army in and around 36 black townships and declared a state of emergency on 21 July. About 700 people were killed in clashes with the security forces. Deaths in detention and the torture of detainees continued, and assassinations, disappearances and banning of meetings were intensified. South Africa continued its policies of bantustanization (confining the homes of black people to certain areas known as bantustans), forced population removals and influx control under the "pass laws". Resistance to *apartheid* grew after the imposition in 1984 of the so-called new constitution,[7] under which the black majority was ignored in the new parliamentary procedures and merely advisory and segregated chambers were created for the so-called coloureds (South Africa's term for people of mixed race) and those of Indian origin.

The state of emergency did not bring peace or restore order, but heightened the unrest. By that proclamation, the Government gave unlimited powers to the army and the police in 36 magisterial districts to enter homes and search without warrant, detain persons, declare curfews and shoot at will. No one was allowed to enter or leave a township proclaimed a "demarcated area". The Commissioner of Police was empowered to impose total press censorship, and the police were allowed to seize property and move people from one location to another. Within six weeks of the proclamation, over 2,500 persons were detained and over 140 were killed. Despite the international protest, South Africa continued its repression of opponents of *apartheid*, including arrests, detentions and killings. Furthermore, in July South Africa banned outdoor funerals for victims of black unrest and forbade political speeches at the funerals, the last remaining legal forum for black meetings.

On 15 August, President P. W. Botha made a policy speech, confirming the régime's intention of not only perpetuating but further entrenching the *apartheid* system. He rejected the principle of one person, one vote and political rights for blacks in a democratic and unitary State, and threatened stronger measures against opponents of *apartheid*. With regard to the question of citizenship, he described the Government's intention of considering dual citizenship for blacks in the so-called "independent homelands" or bantustans and South African citizenship for all other blacks who would "be accommodated within political institutions" within South Africa. Mr. Botha did not, however, define those institutions other than referring to "participation in institutions on a regional and/or group basis". According to the Committee, this statement meant that blacks were expected to become South African citizens but without full citizenship and political rights. The statement was deplored even by South Africa's trading partners and friends. On 16 August, the Secretary-General stated that his concerns had not been allayed by the President's speech, which did not address the main issues raised in Security Council resolution 569(1985) (see p. 158).

In addition to police and army violence, the assassination and disappearance of *apartheid* opponents increased. Three leaders of the Port Elizabeth Black Civic Organization, an affiliate of the United Democratic Front (UDF), disappeared on their way to the airport in May. On 26 June, eight young Africans, most of them members of the Congress of South African Students, were killed in suspicious circumstances in three townships near Johannesburg. Also in June, four leading anti-*apartheid* activists and UDF members left Port Elizabeth by car but never arrived at their destination. UDF claimed that 27 of its members had disappeared in mysterious circumstances and that 11 others were assassinated. In August, riot police hurled tear-gas grenades into the house of Winnie Mandela, wife of ANC leader Nelson Mandela, who had been imprisoned for more than 20 years. Later, her house was burnt down during the night, an act she said was the work of the security forces. (The Committee against *Apartheid*

collected $116,450 from countries and individuals for Mrs. Mandela and presented it to the Secretary-General on 30 October.) Under the state of emergency, hundreds of schoolchildren, some as young as eight years old, were arrested and taken to court on charges of boycotting their schools.

In October, police hid in containers on the back of a decoy truck and shot dead three youths in Athlone township, Cape Town. The next month they killed 19 people, including a baby, in Mamelodi township of Pretoria, when they fired on a crowd of women.

Resistance reached a new level, with blacks starting to boycott white-owned shops, and school boycotts by black students continued. The campaign to boycott the elections to the coloured and Indian Houses of Parliament was effective—as a result, only 17 per cent of the electorate voted and the régime-instituted local government system in African townships collapsed after many councillors resigned and several others were killed. Other anti-*apartheid* actions included rent and bus-fare strikes. From September 1984 to May 1985, about 1,500 cases of violent demonstrations took place, according to the police.

In March, a three-month ban, later extended to the end of the year, was imposed on all meetings by 28 organizations.

To ease domestic and international pressures for change, the Government announced its intention to consider so-called reforms, repealed some discriminatory laws of no real consequence to blacks and made a policy statement reaffirming its commitment to *apartheid*. After opening the new tricameral Parliament in January, the President announced his intention to establish an "informal" forum for blacks, who were excluded from the Parliament. Later, the régime repealed the Prohibition of Mixed Marriages Act and legislation which prohibited political parties from recruiting members of more than one racial group. Despite the change in the marital law, the lives of those involved would not be improved since, by law, a husband and wife of different races could not live in the same place and the schooling of the children would still be governed by other *apartheid* laws.

On 24 July,[92] the Committee against *Apartheid* issued a statement drawing the attention of Governments and organizations to the explosive situation in South Africa and the need for urgent action by the international community. It condemned the imposition of a state of emergency as a desperate act by the *apartheid* régime, which had been unable to control rising popular resistance against oppression despite continuous killings and arrests. The constitutional fraud had only led, in the previous two years, to a greater mobilization of the people against the Government. The responsibility for the loss of life rested not only on the Pretoria régime, but also on those Powers that had continued to hinder international action to force it to abandon *apartheid* and repression, abrogate the racist Constitution and negotiate with the genuine leaders of the people for the establishment of a democratic State. In view of the situation, the United Nations had a responsibility to take all necessary action under the Charter to avert a wider conflict. As a first step, the Security Council must demand that South Africa end the state of emergency, cease its police and military terror, release all detainees, abrogate the Constitution and comply with United Nations resolutions. The Committee urged all Governments and organizations to exert their influence on those Governments, particularly the United States and the United Kingdom, that had frustrated attempts to impose sanctions.

Action by the Commission on Human Rights and its subsidiary bodies. The Commission on Human Rights, in a 26 February resolution[93] on human rights violations in South Africa (see ECONOMIC AND SOCIAL QUESTIONS, Chapter XVIII), condemned *apartheid*, the bantustanization policy, the forced removals of the black population, the policy of denationalization, the suppression of *apartheid* opponents, the use of violence in dealing with protests, and the inferior quality of education for blacks. It reaffirmed its rejection of the so-called constitutional arrangements in South Africa, as they served to perpetuate *apartheid* and denied the black population their full citizenship rights. The Commission called on South Africa to respect international standards on trade union rights in respect of black trade unions and to desist from maltreating black trade union leaders.

In related action, the Commission's *Ad Hoc* Working Group of Experts on southern Africa reported on allegations of infringements of trade union rights in South Africa, and, by **resolution 1985/43**, the Economic and Social Council took action on those rights.

Also on 26 February,[8] the Commission again rejected the so-called new constitution as null and void. It condemned South Africa for its repression, torture and killing of workers, schoolchildren and other opponents of *apartheid*, the imposition of death sentences on freedom fighters (see p. 163), and the policy of bantustanization.

The Sub-Commission on Prevention of Discrimination and Protection of Minorities, on 30 August,[94] condemned South Africa for the terrorism carried out to suppress the mass movement for the human rights of the black majority and demanded the immediate lifting of the state of emergency and the cessation of brutality by South African police and military forces.

SECURITY COUNCIL ACTION (March)

In 1985, as tension in South Africa mounted, the Security Council took action by adopting two resolutions—**resolution 560(1985)**, on 12 March, and the second, **resolution 569(1985)**, on 26 July—on the question of South Africa. In addition, the Council issued two statements—on 22 March and 21 August—expressing alarm at the continuing deterioration of the situation.

Egypt, on behalf of the Group of African States, on 28 February,[95] requested the President of the Council to convene a meeting to consider the situation in South Africa resulting from the murder of demonstrators protesting forced removals, the arrests and high treason charges against UDF officials and the continued repression. At the two meetings held, on 8 and 12 March, the Council invited, at their request, Democratic Yemen, Guinea, South Africa, the Syrian Arab Republic, the United Republic of Tanzania and Viet Nam to participate, without the right to vote, in the discussion. The Council also invited, under rule 39[a] of its provisional rules of procedure, the Acting Chairman of the Special Committee against *Apartheid*.

South Africa said that the convening of the Council contravened the provisions of the United Nations Charter which precluded intervention in a Member State's domestic affairs. The February events at Crossroads township occurred because population drift to the cities had resulted in squatter camps and their concomitant problems, and, instead of bulldozing the camps or consigning the squatters to so-called re-education camps, as had been done elsewhere, South Africa was trying to alleviate the inhabitants' problems in a compassionate way through an urban renewal programme and orderly development. Those arrested were subject to due legal process and were arrested not for their political beliefs but for specific acts committed in contravention of the law.

Most speakers condemned the so-called constitutional reforms, massive repression, arbitrary arrests, detention without trial, killings and the forced removal of the inhabitants of Crossroads and other black townships. They were Australia, Burkina Faso, China, Democratic Yemen, Denmark, Egypt, Guinea, India, Madagascar, Peru, Thailand, Trinidad and Tobago, the Ukrainian SSR, the USSR and the United Republic of Tanzania. France, Madagascar and Thailand saw the forced removals as part of the policy of bantustanization.

Guinea, speaking for the African Group, condemned any collusion with the South African

---

[a]Rule 39 of the Council's provisional rules of procedure states: "The Security Council may invite members of the Secretariat or other persons, whom it considers competent for the purpose, to supply it with information or to give other assistance in examining matters within its competence."

régime. India stated that the Co-ordinating Bureau of the Movement of Non-Aligned Countries had met urgently on 6 March in New York and had condemned South Africa's actions of forced removal of defenceless people and called on the Council to implement its resolutions pertaining to *apartheid*. China fully supported the Non-Aligned Movement's position. Stating that in addition to the 4 million people already banished to the homelands, some 2 million more were threatened with being uprooted, the United Republic of Tanzania called for action under Chapter VII of the Charter. Democratic Yemen, the Ukrainian SSR and the USSR also called for such action. According to Trinidad and Tobago, those with influence over South Africa ought not only to indicate their disapproval of the régime's policies but to pressure it to ensure an end to *apartheid*.

Australia hoped that recent statements of the South African Government concerning its intention to give leasehold rights to black people would be carried out. Egypt stressed that South Africa must withdraw the charges of high treason against UDF officials. While expressing disappointment at South Africa's statement, especially in view of the universal condemnation of its actions at Crossroads, the United Kingdom took heart at what it said were some significant developments taking place in South Africa, particularly the recent speech by its President indicating greater flexibility and commitment to a fuller dialogue between the Government and black opinion there. Denmark said the President's speech did not correspond with the latest wave of violence. Burkina Faso saw nothing in the current attitude of the Pretoria Government to suggest any hope of evolution in South Africa's internal situation.

The Acting Chairman of the Special Committee against *Apartheid* read a message from Bishop Desmond Tutu, who hoped that the Council would express abhorrence of South Africa's reactions to peaceful opposition and urged the Council not to remain indifferent to the serious threat to peace.

On 12 March, the Council unanimously adopted **resolution 560(1985)**.

The Security Council,

Recalling its resolutions 473(1980), 554(1984) and 556(1984), which, *inter alia*, demanded the cessation of the uprootings, relocation and denationalization of the indigenous African people,

Noting with deep concern the aggravation of the situation in South Africa resulting from repeated killings of defenceless opponents of *apartheid* in various townships all over South Africa and, most recently, the killing of African demonstrators against forced removals at Crossroads,

Gravely concerned by the arbitrary arrests of members of the United Democratic Front and other mass organizations opposed to the *apartheid* régime,

Deeply concerned by the preferment of charges of "high treason" on Mrs. Albertina Sisulu, Mr. Archie Gumede,

Mr. George Sewpershad, Mr. M. J. Naidoo, the Reverend Frank Chikana, Professor Ismael Mohammed, Mr. Mewa Ramgobin, Mr. Cassim Saloojee, Mr. Paul David, Mr. Essop Jasset, Mr. Curtis Nkondo, Mr. Aubrey Mokoena, Mr. Thomazile Qweta, Mr. Sisa Njikelana, Mr. Sam Kikine and Mr. Isaac Ngcobo, officials of the United Democratic Front and other opponents of *apartheid* for their participation in the non-violent campaign for a united non-racial and democratic South Africa,

Aware that racist South Africa's intensified repression and charges of "high treason" against leading opponents of *apartheid* constitute an effort further to entrench racist minority rule,

Concerned that repression further undermines the possibilities of a peaceful solution of the South African conflict,

Concerned over racist South Africa's policy of the uprooting, denationalization and dispossession of three and a half million indigenous African people to date, thus swelling the ranks of the other millions already doomed to permanent unemployment and starvation,

Noting with indignation that South Africa's policy of bantustanization is also aimed at the creation of internal bases for the fomenting of fratricidal conflict,

1. *Strongly condemns* the Pretoria régime for the killing of defenceless African people protesting against their forced removal from Crossroads and other places;

2. *Strongly condemns* the arbitrary arrests by the Pretoria régime of members of the United Democratic Front and other mass organizations opposed to South Africa's policy of *apartheid;*

3. *Calls upon* the Pretoria régime to release unconditionally and immediately all political prisoners and detainees, including Nelson Mandela and all other black leaders with whom it must deal in any meaningful discussion of the future of the country;

4. *Also calls upon* the Pretoria régime to withdraw the charges of "high treason" instituted against the United Democratic Front officials, and calls for their immediate and unconditional release;

5. *Commends* the massive united resistance of the oppressed people of South Africa against *apartheid*, and reaffirms the legitimacy of their struggle for a united, non-racial and democratic South Africa;

6. *Requests* the Secretary-General to report to the Security Council on the implementation of the present resolution;

7. *Decides* to remain seized of the matter.

Security Council resolution 560(1985)

12 March 1985   Meeting 2574   Adopted unanimously

6-nation draft (S/17013/Rev.1).
Sponsors: Burkina Faso, Egypt, India, Madagascar, Peru, Trinidad and Tobago.
Meeting numbers. SC 2571, 2574.

Speaking after the vote, the United States, stressing its abhorrence of *apartheid* and the need for change in South Africa, expressed reservations on formulations in the resolution which, it felt, prejudged the South African judicial process and neglected to call for observance of judicial due process, including speedy trial and access to legal counsel; it also regretted the deviations from language proper to a Council resolution.

As the situation continued to deteriorate in South Africa, the President of the Council, on 22 March, issued the following statement:[96]

"The members of the Security Council have entrusted me to express on their behalf their grave concern over the rapid deterioration of the situation in South Africa resulting from the spate of violence against defenceless opponents of *apartheid* throughout the country and most recently in the town of Uitenhage on 21 March 1985, where the South African police opened fire on innocent people proceeding to a funeral, killing and wounding scores of them.

"The members of the Council strongly deplore such acts of violence, which can only further aggravate the situation in South Africa and make more difficult the search for a peaceful solution of the South African conflict.

"The members of the Council recall the provisions of resolution 560(1985), adopted unanimously on 12 March 1985, in which the Council noted with deep concern the intensification of repression in South Africa, commended the massive united resistance of the oppressed people of South Africa against *apartheid*, and reaffirmed the legitimacy of their struggle for a united, non-racial and democratic South Africa.

"The members of the Council urge the Government of South Africa to end violence and repression against the black people and other opponents of *apartheid* and to take urgent measures to eliminate *apartheid*."

Referring to the Council President's statement, South Africa, in a letter to the Secretary-General of 22 March,[97] expressed regret at the loss of life resulting from the 21 March events. It said the organizers of the march, on the anniversary of the Sharpeville incidents, bore heavy responsibility for what occurred. Describing the sequence of events, South Africa said a 19-man police unit had fired in self-defence after trying to halt the unlawful march of some three to four thousand people, armed with stones, petrol bombs and bricks. The President had appointed a commission to investigate the incident.

SECURITY COUNCIL ACTION (July/August)

On 24 July, France, concerned at the continuance and worsening of the human suffering in South Africa, requested that the Council convene immediately.[98] The next day, Mali, on behalf of the African Group, made a similar request.[99] The Council debated the question at three meetings, on 25 and 26 July; at their request, it invited the Central African Republic, Cuba, Ethiopia, the German Democratic Republic, Kenya, Mali, Senegal, South Africa, the Syrian Arab Republic, Yugoslavia and Zaire to participate without vote. It also invited, under rule 39 of the provisional rules of procedure,[b] the Chairman of the Special Committee against *Apartheid*.

During the debate, Burkina Faso, Egypt, India, Madagascar, Peru and Trinidad and Tobago submitted an amendment[100] to a revised draft resolution sponsored by Denmark and France, which was eventually adopted as **resolution 569(1985)**. By the proposed amendment, a paragraph would have been inserted, after paragraph 5, by which the Council would have warned South Africa that failure to eliminate *apartheid* would compel it to consider measures under the United Nations Charter, including Chapter VII, as additional pressure to ensure compliance with United Nations decisions. The amendment was not adopted, owing to the negative votes of two permanent members of the Council. The vote was 12 to 2 (United Kingdom, United States), with 1 abstention (France).

France believed that the provisions of Chapter VII of the Charter did not apply to the question before the Council.

Speaking on behalf of the amendment's sponsors, Burkina Faso regretted that permanent members had weakened the Council's position by sending Pretoria a false message.

Addressing the Council, South Africa said it was committed to political reform which would involve all the South African communities, was seeking to create structures of government without domination, and was ready to negotiate with representatives of black opinion to find an equitable solution satisfying the reasonable aspiration of all its peoples. South Africa urged that violence be forsworn as a means to achieve political ends. The unrest was intended to frustrate the reform process, and moderate black leaders were being intimidated by acts of assassination, murder, arson and threats to their lives to prevent their becoming involved in the negotiating process. The emergency measures were introduced to protect the lives and property of blacks and they would be lifted as soon as the violence diminished.

Nearly all speakers condemned the imposition of the state of emergency and said it only added to the tension and further violence. Many— including Australia, Cuba, Denmark, France, Mali (for the African Group) and the United Kingdom—said that the root cause of the tension was the *apartheid* system which must be eliminated. Australia said the introduction of the state of emergency had revealed how far South Africa was prepared to go to shore up the *apartheid* system; that situation would not provide a permanent end to violence but would more likely encourage people to feel that the only way to achieve progress was through confrontation. Thailand said the state of emergency would aggravate the sufferings of the black majority and exacerbate tension as well as

[b]See footnote a on p. 154.

threaten international peace and security. For India, the state of emergency amounted to a declaration of war on the oppressed. In China's view, the double tactic of deception and suppression exposed further the false nature of so-called reforms by South Africa, which was only trying to defend the *apartheid* system. The genocide of South African blacks had to be stopped, Cuba said, and there had to be a united effort to bring about the final elimination of *apartheid*.

Madagascar believed the state of emergency was intended to legalize the terror perpetrated by South Africa's forces, and reflected the disarray of the régime in the face of the increasing turbulence and the growing fervour of the demonstrators. Asserting that the non-aligned countries had consistently called for the elimination of *apartheid*, Yugoslavia said that to support the liberation struggle and the liberation movements in southern Africa was the most efficient way to eliminate *apartheid*.

Burkina Faso, China, Cuba, Egypt, Ethiopia, the German Democratic Republic, India, Kenya, Madagascar, the Syrian Arab Republic, Trinidad and Tobago, the Ukrainian SSR, the USSR and Yugoslavia explicitly called on the Council to adopt comprehensive, mandatory sanctions under Chapter VII of the Charter. The Syrian Arab Republic said the Council had to support the revolution going on in South Africa by imposing mandatory sanctions; to argue that sanctions would adversely affect the black masses belittled their struggle.

Burkina Faso, Denmark and Peru called for increased international pressure against South Africa as a means to force it to abandon *apartheid*. Burkina Faso said it was time to use the only language that South Africa understood—the language of force.

Affirming that the latest manifestation of the policy of repression demonstrated the need for increased international pressure against *apartheid*, Denmark stressed that South Africa must be made to understand that the system had to be abolished while it was still possible through peaceful means.

Peru stated that a combined force of both internal and external pressure—the latter in the form of specific measures—would have a decisive influence on South Africa and bring about conditions more favourable to the struggling people.

Mali, for the African Group, said South Africa's actions were encouraged by certain Western allies, and stressed that the Group condemned the policy of constructive engagement and all other collaboration with *apartheid*.

Kenya, Trinidad and Tobago, the Ukrainian SSR and the USSR made similar statements about the support of certain countries for South Africa. According to Trinidad and Tobago, policies of constructive dialogue had not only produced intransigence by South Africa, but had given the régime moral support for its violence. The Ukrainian SSR

said South Africa had been able to act so brutally because it relied on its co-operation with the United States and several other Western countries and Israel, and felt secure that they would protect it from sanctions. The USSR condemned such support and the United States policy of "constructive engagement".

Australia, Denmark, Egypt, Kenya, the United Kingdom and the United States stressed the need for negotiations or peaceful means in order to achieve progress in eliminating *apartheid*. Australia said that only the removal of the grievances and the introduction of genuine reform, through consultation with the real representatives of the black community, could offer the prospect of lasting and peaceful solutions. Egypt said the Council ought to demand that South Africa embark unconditionally on a dialogue with the true leaders of the black majority to lay the foundations for a democratic, authentic government. Similarly, Kenya called on South Africa to embark on an immediate dialogue between the different races with a view to instituting a democratic system and to free all detainees, including Nelson Mandela.

Although supporting most elements of the resolution, the United Kingdom and the United States expressed reservations about certain measures against South Africa. The United Kingdom said it could not vote for the resolution and had voted against the proposed amendment because it would not be responsible to call for measures, such as those under Chapter VII of the Charter, that would not achieve the changes all sought in South Africa and which might prove counter-productive. The United States said totally isolating South Africa economically and politically would lead to more bloodshed, to increased autarky of the South African economy, to a curtailment of external influence to effect change, and to greater suffering for the very people all were trying to help; it added that it would maintain its policy of constructive engagement with South Africa.

India warned that, if the Council did not act decisively, the oppressed South Africans would act on their own through mass popular mobilization, and that the cycle of violence and bloodshed would intensify.

France announced that it was recalling its Ambassador to South Africa and suspending new investment there. France's decisions were welcomed by Zaire. The Central African Republic spoke in like manner and was joined by Ethiopia and Senegal in praising France for having requested the meeting.

The Chairman of the Committee against *Apartheid* believed that the minimum required of the Council was a determination that the situation in South Africa constituted a threat to international peace and security under Chapter VII of the Charter; he said the Council's previous failure to discharge its responsibility was due to the protection of the *apartheid* régime by certain permanent members.

On 26 July, the Security Council adopted **resolution 569(1985)**.

The Security Council,

Deeply concerned at the worsening of the situation in South Africa and at the continuance of the human suffering that the *apartheid* system, which the Council strongly condemns, is causing in that country,

Outraged at the repression, and condemning the arbitrary arrests of hundreds of persons,

Considering that the imposition of the state of emergency in thirty-six districts of the Republic of South Africa constitutes a grave deterioration of the situation in that country,

Considering as totally unacceptable the practice by the South African Government of detention without trial and of forcible removal, as well as the discriminatory legislation in force,

Acknowledging the legitimacy of the aspirations of the South African population as a whole to benefit from all civil and political rights and to establish a united non-racial and democratic society,

Acknowledging further that the very cause of the situation in South Africa lies in the policy of *apartheid* and the practices of the South African Government,

1. *Strongly condemns* the *apartheid* system and all the policies and practices deriving therefrom;

2. *Strongly condemns* the mass arrests and detentions recently carried out by the Pretoria Government and the murders which have been committed;

3. *Strongly condemns* the establishment of the state of emergency in the thirty-six districts in which it has been imposed and demands that it be lifted immediately;

4. *Calls upon* the South African Government to set free immediately and unconditionally all political prisoners and detainees, first of all, Mr. Nelson Mandela;

5. *Reaffirms* that only the total elimination of *apartheid* and the establishment in South Africa of a free, united and democratic society on the basis of universal suffrage can lead to a solution;

6. *Urges* States Members of the United Nations to adopt measures against South Africa, such as the following:

   (a) Suspension of all new investment in South Africa;

   (b) Prohibition of the sale of krugerrands and all other coins minted in South Africa;

   (c) Restrictions on sports and cultural relations;

   (d) Suspension of guaranteed export loans;

   (e) Prohibition of all new contracts in the nuclear field;

   (f) Prohibition of all sales of computer equipment that may be used by the South African army and police;

7. *Commends* those States which have already adopted voluntary measures against the Pretoria Government and urges them to adopt new provisions, and invites those which have not yet done so to follow their example;

8. *Requests* the Secretary-General to report to the Security Council on the implementation of the present resolution;

9. *Decides* to remain seized of the matter and to reconvene as soon as the Secretary-General has issued his report, with a view to considering the progress made in the implementation of the present resolution.

Security Council resolution 569(1985)

26 July 1985   Meeting 2602   13-0-2

Draft by Denmark and France (S/17354/Rev.1).
Meeting numbers. SC 2600-2602.

Vote in Council as follows:

In favour: Australia, Burkina Faso, China, Denmark, Egypt, France, India, Madagascar, Peru, Thailand, Trinidad and Tobago, Ukrainian SSR, USSR.

Against: None.

Abstaining: United Kingdom, United States.

Speaking after the resolution's adoption, France said the vote was the gravest condemnation of South Africa for racial discrimination and violation of human rights.

On 21 August, the Council held a meeting at which the President stated that, as a result of consultations among members, he had been authorized to make the following statement on their behalf:[101]

Meeting number. SC 2603.

"The members of the Security Council, deeply alarmed by the worsening and deteriorating situation of the oppressed black majority population in South Africa since the imposition of the state of emergency on 21 July 1985, express once again their profound concern at this deplorable situation.

"The members of the Council condemn the Pretoria régime for its continued failure to heed the repeated appeals made by the international community, including Security Council resolution 569(1985) and, in particular, the demand made in that resolution for the immediate lifting of the state of emergency.

"The members of the Council strongly condemn the continuation of killings and the arbitrary mass arrests and detentions carried out by the Pretoria Government. They call, once again, upon the South African Government to set free immediately and unconditionally all political prisoners and detainees, first of all, Mr. Nelson Mandela, whose home has lately been subjected to an act of arson.

"The members of the Council believe that a just and lasting solution in South Africa must be based on the total eradication of the system of *apartheid* and the establishment of a free, united and democratic society in South Africa. Without concrete action towards such a just and lasting solution in South Africa, any pronouncements of the Pretoria régime can represent nothing more than a reaffirmation of its attachment to *apartheid* and underline its continuing intransigence in the face of mounting domestic and international opposition to the continuation of this thoroughly unjustified political and social system. In this context, the members of the Council express their grave concern at the latest pronouncements of the President of the Pretoria régime."

The Foreign Minister of South Africa, in a letter to the Secretary-General of 28 August,[102] referring to resolution 569(1985) and the Council's declaration of 21 August, stated that those actions violated the principle of non-interference in a Member State's internal affairs and that the criteria applied in the resolution were suspect in so far as the demand for a democratic society on the basis of universal suffrage was a test that could not be met by many United Nations Members. In addition, punitive measures called for could have damaging effects on the economy and stability of South Africa's neighbours. South Africa rejected the charge that the imposition of a state of emergency in certain areas constituted a grave deterioration of the situation. It was imposed to combat lawlessness of every kind in black townships, including large-scale intimidation by blacks against blacks.

Action by Committee on the Elimination of Racial Discrimination. On 20 August,[103] the Committee on the Elimination of Racial Discrimination condemned South Africa for crimes against the black people and appealed to States parties to the International Convention on the Elimination of All Forms of Racial Discrimination[104] to implement resolution 569(1985).

Communications. Throughout the year, States addressed letters to the Secretary-General or the President of the Security Council expressing concern about the South Africa situation—India, on 6 March,[105] 27 July[106] and 27 August,[107] all forwarding communiqués adopted by the Co-ordinating Bureau of the Movement of Non-Aligned Countries; China, on 23 March,[108] 29 July[109] and 24 December;[110] Saint Lucia, on 28 March;[111] Spain, on 29 March;[112] Italy, on 3 April[113] and 2 May,[114] forwarding declarations of 25 March and 29 April of EC ministerial meetings on European political co-operation; the USSR, on 9 April,[115] forwarding a statement by TASS; Argentina, on 3 June[116] and 30 July;[117] Australia, on 24 July;[118] Luxembourg, on 25 July[119] and 26 August,[120] forwarding a declaration adopted by an EC ministerial meeting and an EC press release, respectively; Brazil, on 26 July;[121] Tunisia, on 26 July;[122] Democratic Kampuchea, on 29 July;[123] Burkina Faso, on 29 July,[124] transmitting a letter from Oliver Tambo, President of ANC; Japan, on 5 August[125] and 27 December;[126] Senegal, on 5 August[127] and 16 August;[128] Indonesia, on 9 August;[129] Uruguay, on 12 August;[130] Thailand, on 19 August;[131] Jamaica, on 22 August;[132] Nicaragua, on 22 August;[133] Antigua and Barbuda, on 23 December;[134] and the Libyan Arab Jamahiriya, on 31 December.[135]

Argentina, China, Democratic Kampuchea, the Libyan Arab Jamahiriya, Nicaragua, Saint Lucia, Senegal, Spain, Thailand, Uruguay, EC and the Non-Aligned Movement denounced the violence by the South African authorities. Some mentioned, in particular, the killing of demonstrators at Uitenhage, Crossroads and other places. Spain condemned the large-scale uprooting and relocation of black people, as did the Non-Aligned Movement, which demanded that South Africa put an immediate and unconditional end to banishing the black people to artificially created "bantustans".

The Movement condemned South Africa for the arbitrary arrests of UDF members and other *apartheid* opponents and for "high treason" charges against a number of UDF officials; reiterated its call for the unconditional release of all South African political prisoners, including Nelson Mandela, and for the release of Allan Boesak, a UDF leader; and admired Mr. Mandela's rejection of an offer of conditional release made by South Africa (see p. 162). EC also called for Mr. Mandela's release, ending detention without trial, discontinuing forcible removal, and abolishing discriminatory legislation, including the pass laws and the Group Areas Act. Democratic Kampuchea demanded the release of all political prisoners and detainees. Antigua and Barbuda, China and the Libyan Arab Jamahiriya deplored the arrest of Winnie Mandela on 23 December. Antigua and Barbuda called on Governments which were able to influence South Africa and especially the United States to do all possible to secure her release.

The Movement, Senegal (for OAU) and the USSR urged the Security Council to deal with the grave situation by imposing sanctions against South Africa. Argentina appealed to the international community to halt all direct or indirect support for South Africa. Indonesia called for implementation of voluntary economic sanctions and the embargo on military supplies. Saint Lucia said the world must find the political will to act against South Africa. EC called for a dialogue leading to substantial reforms, with a view to responding to the legitimate aspirations of the black population. Also calling for comprehensive sanctions, ANC said that mere condemnation of the *apartheid* system would only serve to convince South Africa that the international community was unable to take firm action.

The imposition of the state of emergency was condemned by Argentina, Australia, Brazil, China, Democratic Kampuchea, Indonesia, Japan, Nicaragua, Senegal, Thailand, Tunisia, EC and the Non-Aligned Movement. Argentina said the problem's definitive solution involved, at that time, lifting the state of emergency and halting repression. Australia was concerned that the state of emergency would encourage people to feel that the only way to achieve progress was through confrontation; Australia recognized that only the removal of grievances and genuine political reforms through consultation with the real representatives of the black community would offer prospects of lasting and peaceful solutions. In Brazil's view, the emergency measures only aggravated the deplorable situation. Noting world outrage over those events, Tunisia was gratified at France's response (see p. 157) and considered the United States attitude and actions as being of particular significance.

According to the USSR, the United States or imperialist circles that collaborated with South Africa also bore responsibility for its actions.

The Non-Aligned Movement condemned the 15 August policy statement by the South African

President, which, it said, constituted further proof of the régime's refusal to renounce *apartheid*. Asserting that the statement did not meet their expectations, EC, joined by Spain and Portugal, urged South Africa to open a real dialogue with the authentic representatives of the black population; EC would undertake a mission to South Africa from 30 August to 1 September to appeal to it to do so.

In the current circumstances, the Libyan Arab Jamahiriya said, armed struggle had become the sole means of liberating the people in South Africa and of securing their rights and freedom.

By a letter of 14 November,[(136)] the Chairman of the Committee against *Apartheid* forwarded a statement from the Executive Committee of the InterAction Council—26 former heads of Government—on proposals for the rapid abolition of *apartheid*, including termination of the state of emergency, release of political prisoners, equal rights for all South Africans and elimination of media censorship.

GENERAL ASSEMBLY ACTION

On 10 December, the General Assembly adopted **resolution 40/64 B** by recorded vote.

Situation in South Africa and assistance to the liberation movements

The General Assembly,

Having considered the report of the Special Committee against *Apartheid*,

Recalling its resolution 39/2 of 28 September 1984, in which, *inter alia*, it stated that South Africa's continued defiance of United Nations resolutions and its imposition of the rejected so-called "new constitution" will inevitably lead to further escalation of the already explosive situation in South Africa and will have far-reaching consequences for southern Africa and the world,

Recalling Security Council resolutions 473(1980) of 13 June 1980, 554(1984) of 17 August 1984, 556(1984) of 23 October 1984 and 569(1985) of 26 July 1985, in which it demanded, *inter alia*, the cessation of the uprootings, relocation and denationalization of the indigenous African people, and demanded the immediate lifting of the state of emergency in thirty-six districts in South Africa,

Recalling, in particular, its resolution 3411 C (XXX) of 28 November 1975, in which it proclaimed that the United Nations and the international community had a special responsibility towards the oppressed people of South Africa and their national liberation movements,

Gravely concerned about the situation in South Africa, and in southern Africa as a whole, resulting from the policies and actions of the *apartheid* régime, in particular, its efforts to perpetuate and consolidate racist domination in the country, its policy of "bantustanization", its brutal repression of opponents of *apartheid* and its constant acts of aggression against neighbouring States,

Noting with indignation that South Africa's policy of bantustanization is aimed at further dispossessing the African majority of its inalienable rights and depriving it of citizenship and fomenting fratricidal conflict,

Gravely concerned at the continuing massacres, killings and other atrocities against defenceless opponents of *apartheid* perpetrated by the racist régime in Sharpeville, Soweto, Sebokeng and other black townships,

Alarmed at the massive arrests and detentions of leaders and activists of liberation organizations inside the country as well as the increasing number of deaths resulting from police brutality and torture during detentions, which have been confirmed by reports of international humanitarian organizations, and the Detainees Parent Support Committee in South Africa and the Institute of Criminology of the University of Cape Town,

Reaffirming the legitimacy of the struggle of the oppressed people of South Africa and their liberation movements by all available means, including armed struggle, for the elimination of *apartheid*, which is declared as a crime against humanity, and seriously violating international peace and security,

1. *Again proclaims* its full support of the national liberation movements of South Africa as the authentic representatives of the South African people in its just struggle for freedom;

2. *Strongly condemns* the illegitimate minority racist régime of South Africa for its policies and actions, in particular the imposition of the state of emergency in that country;

3. *Condemns* the South African racist régime for defying resolutions of the United Nations and persisting with the further entrenchment of *apartheid*, a system declared a crime against humanity and a threat to international peace and security;

4. *Strongly condemns* the Pretoria régime for the killing of defenceless African people protesting against their forced removal from Crossroads and other places as well as the arbitrary arrests of members of the United Democratic Front, National Forum and other mass organizations opposed to *apartheid;*

5. *Condemns* the execution of Benjamin Maloise in defiance of international calls for rescinding his execution order;

6. *Reaffirms* that freedom fighters of South Africa should be treated as prisoners of war in accordance with Additional Protocol I to the Geneva Conventions of 12 August 1949;

7. *Demands* that the Pretoria régime withdraw the trumped up charges of "high treason" instituted against members of the United Democratic Front and other organizations and immediately and unconditionally release all of them;

8. *Further demands* that the Pretoria régime release unconditionally and immediately all political prisoners and detainees, including Nelson Mandela and Zephania Mothopeng;

9. *Commends* the massive united resistance of the oppressed people of South Africa against *apartheid*, and reaffirms the legitimacy of their struggle for a united, non-racial and democratic South Africa;

10. *Demands* the immediate lifting of the state of emergency in South Africa;

11. *Demands* that the racist régime:

(*a*) Withdraw all its troops immediately and unconditionally from Angola;

(*b*) Put an end to its illegal occupation of Namibia;

(*c*) Strictly observe the independence, sovereignty and territorial integrity of independent African States;

12. *Appeals* to all States, intergovernmental and non-governmental organizations, anti-*apartheid* and solidarity movements, trade unions, religious bodies, student and

other public organizations, mass media as well as city and other local authorities and individuals urgently to provide increased political, economic, educational, legal and other forms of support to the oppressed people of South Africa, as well as humanitarian and all other necessary assistance to the national liberation movements of South Africa in their just struggle for the exercise of the right of self-determination by the oppressed people of South Africa;

13. *Reaffirms* that only the total eradication of *apartheid* and the establishment of a non-racial democratic society based on majority rule, through the full and free exercise of adult suffrage by all the people in a united and unfragmented South Africa, can lead to a just and lasting solution of the explosive situation in South Africa;

14. *Decides* to continue the authorization of adequate financial provision in the regular budget of the United Nations to enable the South African liberation movements recognized by the Organization of African Unity—namely, the African National Congress of South Africa and the Pan Africanist Congress of Azania—to maintain offices in New York in order to participate effectively in the deliberations of the Special Committee against *Apartheid* and other appropriate bodies;

15. *Requests* the Security Council, as a matter of urgency, to consider the serious situation in South Africa emanating from the imposition of the so-called "new constitution" and the state of emergency and to take all necessary measures, in accordance with Chapter VII of the Charter of the United Nations, to avert the further aggravation of tension and conflict in South Africa and in southern Africa as a whole.

General Assembly resolution 40/64 B

10 December 1985   Meeting 111   128-8-18 (recorded vote)

60-nation draft (A/40/L.27 & Corr.1); agenda item 35.

Sponsors: Afghanistan, Algeria, Angola, Antigua and Barbuda, Benin, Burkina Faso, Burundi, Byelorussian SSR, Cameroon, Cape Verde, Comoros, Congo, Cuba, Democratic Yemen, Djibouti, Egypt, Equatorial Guinea, Ethiopia, Gambia, German Democratic Republic, Ghana, Guinea, Guinea-Bissau, Guyana, India, Indonesia, Iran, Iraq, Kenya, Lao People's Democratic Republic, Lebanon, Liberia, Libyan Arab Jamahiriya, Madagascar, Malaysia, Mali, Mauritania, Mauritius, Mongolia, Morocco, Mozambique, Nicaragua, Niger, Nigeria, Romania, Rwanda, Sao Tome and Principe, Senegal, Sierra Leone, Sudan, Syrian Arab Republic, Tunisia, Uganda, Ukrainian SSR, United Republic of Tanzania, Viet Nam, Yugoslavia, Zaire, Zambia, Zimbabwe.

Financial implications. 5th Committee, A/40/1022; S-G, A/C.5/40/76.

Meeting numbers. GA 40th session: 5th Committee 58; plenary 51-57, 111.

Recorded vote in Assembly as follows:

In favour: Afghanistan, Albania, Algeria, Angola, Antigua and Barbuda, Argentina, Bahamas, Bahrain, Bangladesh, Barbados, Belize, Benin, Bhutan, Bolivia, Botswana, Brazil, Brunei Darussalam, Bulgaria, Burkina Faso, Burma, Burundi, Byelorussian SSR, Cameroon, Cape Verde, Central African Republic, Chad, China, Colombia, Comoros, Congo, Costa Rica, Cuba, Cyprus, Czechoslovakia, Democratic Kampuchea, Democratic Yemen, Djibouti, Dominican Republic, Ecuador, Egypt, El Salvador, Equatorial Guinea, Ethiopia, Fiji, Gabon, Gambia, German Democratic Republic, Ghana, Greece, Guinea, Guinea-Bissau, Guyana, Haiti, Hungary, India, Indonesia, Iran, Iraq, Ivory Coast, Jamaica, Jordan, Kenya, Kuwait, Lao People's Democratic Republic, Lebanon, Lesotho, Liberia, Libyan Arab Jamahiriya, Madagascar, Malaysia, Maldives, Mali, Malta, Mauritania, Mauritius, Mexico, Mongolia, Morocco, Mozambique, Nepal, Nicaragua, Niger, Nigeria, Oman, Pakistan, Panama, Papua New Guinea, Peru, Philippines, Poland, Qatar, Romania, Rwanda, Saint Lucia, Saint Vincent and the Grenadines, Samoa, Sao Tome and Principe, Saudi Arabia, Senegal, Seychelles, Sierra Leone, Singapore, Solomon Islands, Somalia, Sri Lanka, Sudan, Suriname, Swaziland, Syrian Arab Republic, Thailand, Togo, Trinidad and Tobago, Tunisia, Turkey, Uganda, Ukrainian SSR, USSR, United Arab Emirates, United Republic of Tanzania, Uruguay, Vanuatu, Venezuela, Viet Nam, Yemen, Yugoslavia, Zaire, Zambia, Zimbabwe.

Against: Belgium, France, Germany, Federal Republic of, Italy, Luxembourg, Portugal, United Kingdom, United States.

Abstaining: Australia, Austria, Canada, Denmark, Finland, Grenada, Guatemala, Honduras, Iceland, Ireland, Israel, Japan, Malawi, Netherlands, New Zealand, Norway, Spain, Sweden.

Speaking in explanation of vote, Canada, Ireland, the Netherlands and New Zealand expressed reservations about the affirmation of the legitimacy of armed struggle although they supported such demands as the release of political prisoners and detainees and the lifting of the state of emergency. New Zealand added that it objected to some of the extravagant rhetoric in the resolution. The Netherlands said it could not subscribe to its general thrust, which postulated the existence of a colonial situation in South Africa. Uruguay agreed with the resolution in general, but its policy was to support the peaceful settlement of disputes.

The United States opposed the resolution because it failed to understand how the imposition of sanctions would lessen tension or promote dialogue and negotiations.

In **resolution 40/64 I**, the Assembly took similar action, condemning the South African authorities for the killings, arbitrary mass arrests and the detention of members of mass organizations as well as individuals for opposing *apartheid*, the so-called new constitution and the state of emergency. The Assembly demanded, among other things, that the authorities immediately lift the state of emergency; initiate a political dialogue with genuine leaders of the majority population with a view to establishing a representative government; and dismantle the bantustan structures. Similar provisions were contained in **resolution 40/25**, in which the Assembly also condemned the policy of "bantustanization" and reiterated support for the oppressed people of South Africa in its just and legitimate struggle against the racist minority régime.

In **resolution 40/64 A**, the Assembly supported the movement against conscription into the armed forces of South Africa, and invited all Governments and organizations to assist, in consultation with the liberation movements, persons compelled to leave South Africa for conscientious objection.

Political prisoners and other detained persons

Activities of the Committee against *Apartheid*. The Special Committee against *Apartheid* continued to campaign for the release of political prisoners in South Africa and for an end to repression against the opponents of *apartheid*.[1] It reported that thousands of such opponents were arrested in 1985 on various charges under security legislation and the state of emergency regulations; over 11,000 people were detained without charge or trial, many were tortured, and 12 persons, including three children, died in detention.

Police arrested seven prominent black leaders in February and three more in April, mostly UDF leaders. South African authorities arrested more than 200 people on 26 March, as they marched to the South African Parliament in Cape Town to present a list of democratic demands. In June, hundreds were arrested in townships in the Eastern Cape and Orange Free State, and many community leaders of Port Elizabeth were detained under security laws. From July to mid-September, about 3,500 people were detained under the emergency measures, most of them leaders of political and community organizations such as UDF, the Azanian People's Organization, and youth, student and trade groups.

In a statement issued on 20 February, at the time South Africa was attempting to remove blacks forcibly from Crossroads township, the Committee's Chairman expressed alarm at the deterioration of the situation. He called on the international community to oblige South Africa to stop the violence and to ensure the immediate release of UDF leaders and other political prisoners. On 18 July, the Acting Chairman sent a message of greetings to Nelson Mandela on his sixty-seventh birthday and pledged intensified efforts towards the unconditional release of political prisoners.

At a special meeting held on 24 July, the Committee concluded that the state of emergency imposed on 36 communities constituted a declaration of war against the oppressed people and other opponents of *apartheid*, and called on the Security Council to demand that South Africa end the state of emergency, cease its police and military terror and release all detainees.

On 27 August, the Chairman issued a statement condemning the South African authorities for the arrest of Allan Boesak, President of the World Alliance of Reformed Churches and a UDF supporter, who was to have led a mass protest march on Pollsmoor prison to present a message of solidarity to Mr. Mandela. The Chairman urged the international community to pressure South Africa for the release of those two men and all other political prisoners.

Some provisions of the Internal Security Act authorized detention without trial indefinitely, while others authorized periods specified in the order of the Minister of Law and Order, who could extend detention for an unlimited period by a review of the case. The detainee had no right to legal representation before the review committee. Reliable information on detention conditions was difficult to obtain, but the Committee against *Apartheid* stated in October that over the past year nine detainees had died in or as a result of detention. Amnesty International reported on 13 August that detainees—including students, trade unionists and clerics—held since the state of emergency was declared were being tortured by security forces. In September, a judge granted an order restraining the police from assaulting detainees after a Port Elizabeth district surgeon, Dr. Wendy Orr, told

the court that she had found evidence of systematic abuse and assault. Dr. Orr was immediately transferred to another office where she would have no contact with detainees.

The number of political trials—on charges such as contravening the Internal Security Act, belonging to an unlawful organization, terrorism, subversion, treason or possessing ANC literature—increased in 1985, as did the number of political detentions. On 26 February, two ANC members, Sipho Bridget Xulu and Clarence Lucky Payi, were sentenced to death. In August, 48 people were awaiting trial for treason, a crime punishable by death. In December, six Sharpeville residents were sentenced to death in connection with the murder of the so-called Deputy Mayor of Sharpeville.

The Co-ordinating Bureau of the Non-Aligned Movement, in a 23 December communiqué,[137] condemned South Africa for passing death sentences on the six—Mojalefa Reginald Sefatsa, Oupa Moses Diniso, Reid Melebu Mokoena, Theresa Ramashamula, Duma Joshua Khumalo and Francis Don Mokgesi—and sentencing two others to eight years' imprisonment each. It also condemned the sentencing of five alleged members of PAC to a total of 33 years' imprisonment for furthering the aims and objectives of PAC and supplying its members with weapons and equipment.

Early in 1985, South Africa offered Mr. Mandela release from prison on condition that he renounce violence and accept the citizenship of Transkei. He refused, asking that South Africa itself renounce violence. Zephania Mothopeng, a PAC leader who was also offered conditional amnesty, rejected it and opted to serve his entire 15-year sentence.

The Committee against *Apartheid* held meetings in observance of the Day of Solidarity with South African Political Prisoners on 11 October.

Action by the Council for Namibia. The Council for Namibia, in its June Vienna Declaration and Programme of Action,[30] demanded the immediate and unconditional release of all Namibian political prisoners, including those imprisoned or detained under the so-called internal security laws, martial law, or any other arbitrary measures, whether they had been charged or tried, or were being held without charge in Namibia or South Africa.

Action by the Committee on colonial countries. The Council's demand had also been made by the Committee on colonial countries in May.[31] The Committee further demanded that captured Namibian freedom fighters be accorded prisoner-of-war status under the August 1949 Geneva Conventions relating to the protection of victims of armed conflicts and Additional Protocol I,[138] pending their release, and that South Africa ensure that all Namibians in exile for political reasons be able to return without risk of arrest, detention, intimidation, imprisonment or loss of life.

Action by the Commission on Human Rights and its Sub-Commission. On 26 February,[8] the Commission on Human Rights condemned South Africa for its repression and torture and killing of opponents of *apartheid*, and the imposition of death sentences on freedom fighters. It demanded that South Africa immediately release all people detained or imprisoned as a result of their struggle for self-determination and independence, and demanded full respect for their rights and the observance of article 5 of the Universal Declaration of Human Rights,[139] under which no one was to be subjected to torture or to cruel, inhuman or degrading treatment.

Also on that date,[93] the Commission expressed indignation at the continued violations in South Africa, including arrests and torture, violence in dealing with legitimate protests and demonstrations against *apartheid* policies, and the killing, torture and other ill-treatment of captured freedom fighters and others, including those held by the so-called independent homelands. It called for the unconditional release of all political prisoners and renewed its request to South Africa to allow the Commission's *Ad Hoc* Working Group of Experts to make on-the-spot investigations of conditions in the prisons in South Africa and Namibia and the treatment of prisoners.

The Sub-Commission on Prevention of Discrimination and Protection of Minorities, in August,[94] demanded the immediate lifting of the state of emergency, cessation of all brutality by South Africa and the immediate release of all political prisoners.

Communications. Letters were addressed to the Secretary-General appealing for the release of Nelson Mandela, who had been in solitary confinement for 23 years in a South African prison. On 19 August,[140] India forwarded an appeal by its Prime Minister, stating that the only way South Africa could be made to release Mr. Mandela was to isolate that country totally, and urging Governments to sever all contacts with Pretoria. On 11 October,[141] the Day of Solidarity with South African Political Prisoners, Brazil stated its belief that no effective negotiation for a solution to the plight of the South African majority could be held without the participation of its imprisoned leaders, and again requested Mr. Mandela's liberation.

SECURITY COUNCIL ACTION

In 1985, the Security Council again called for the unconditional and immediate release of all South African political prisoners and detainees. In March (**resolution 560(1985)**), it condemned the arbitrary arrests of members of UDF and other mass organizations opposing *apartheid*, and called

on South Africa to release them, including Mr. Mandela. The Council called on the régime to withdraw "high treason" charges instituted against UDF officials, and called for their release.

In **resolution 569(1985)**, the Council in July again condemned South Africa's mass arrests and detentions and the murders which had been committed and called for the freeing of all political prisoners and detainees, first of all Mr. Mandela. On 21 August, the Council issued a statement with a similar thrust,[101] after Mr. Mandela's home had been subjected to an act of arson.

In addition, the Council in October called on South Africa not to carry out the death sentence on an ANC member (see below).

GENERAL ASSEMBLY ACTION

The General Assembly also made numerous demands for the unconditional and immediate release of the political prisoners and detainees. In **resolution 40/64 B**, it reaffirmed that freedom fighters of South Africa should be treated as prisoners of war in accordance with Additional Protocol I[138] to the 1949 Geneva Conventions. It demanded that the régime withdraw the trumped-up charges of "high treason" against members of UDF and other organizations, and release them as well as Nelson Mandela and Zephania Mothopeng. In **resolution 40/64 D**, the Assembly appealed for the intensification of the campaign for their release and that of all South African political prisoners and detainees—a demand repeated in **resolutions 40/64 I** and **40/25**. In **resolution 40/97 A**, the Assembly demanded the immediate release of all Namibian political prisoners, including those imprisoned or detained under the so-called internal security laws, martial law or any other arbitrary measures, whether such Namibians had been charged or tried or were being held without charge.

Capital punishment of ANC members

Malesela Benjamin Maloise, an ANC member who had been sentenced to death in June 1983 for killing a policeman,[142] was scheduled to be hanged on 21 August 1985, after the South African President rejected his clemency appeal in mid-August. In a 16 August press release, OAU appealed to the international community to intervene and, on 19 and 20 August, respectively, the Committee against *Apartheid* and the Security Council issued statements in which they urged the South African authorities to rescind the death sentence.[1] Mr. Maloise was granted a 21-day stay of execution to allow new evidence to be brought before the court. In the mean time, ANC issued a press statement on 20 August, claiming responsibility for the act and stating that Mr. Maloise had not been involved in the crime. On

18 October, he was executed, despite another appeal by the Council on 17 October and other international calls for clemency.

SECURITY COUNCIL ACTION

On 20 August, after consultations with the Security Council's members, its President issued the following statement on their behalf:[143]

"The members of the Security Council have learned with great concern the intention of the South African authorities to carry out shortly the death sentence imposed upon Mr. Malesela Benjamin Maloise.

"The members of the Council recall Council resolution 547(1984), which, *inter alia*, called upon the South African authorities not to carry out the execution of Mr. Maloise.

"The members of the Security Council once again urge the South African authorities to rescind the death sentence imposed on Mr. Maloise, convinced that the carrying out of the execution, apart from being a direct defiance of the above-mentioned Council resolution, will result in the further deterioration of an already extremely grave situation."

The carrying out of the sentence was postponed until 18 October. At a Council meeting on 17 October, the President issued another statement on behalf of the members, as follows:[144]

Meeting number. SC 2623.

"The members of the Security Council have learned with indignation and the gravest concern of the South African authorities' intention to implement the death sentence imposed on Malesela Benjamin Maloise, in spite of the Council's appeals in this regard.

"The members of the Council once again draw the attention of the South African authorities to the Council President's statement of 20 August 1985 and Council resolution 547(1984), which, *inter alia*, called upon the South African authorities not to carry out the execution of Mr. Maloise.

"The members of the Council are convinced that the carrying out of the execution will only result in a further worsening of an extremely grave situation.

"Once again, the members of the Council strongly urge the South African Government to extend clemency to Mr. Maloise and to rescind his death sentence."

GENERAL ASSEMBLY ACTION

In **resolution 40/64 B**, the General Assembly condemned the execution of Mr. Maloise in defiance of international calls.

Communications. A number of countries addressed letters to the Secretary-General concerning the death sentence.

On 20 August,[145] the President of Senegal said that South Africa was planning to take a new step in its repression by carrying out the execution of Mr. Maloise, who had been falsely convicted of murder. Mexico, on 16 October,[146] expressed support for the efforts to persuade South Africa to commute the sentence. On behalf of the Non-Aligned

Movement, India, on 17 October,[147] urging executive clemency, stated that executing the South African patriot would be a grave miscarriage of justice that would exacerbate the already explosive situation.

The next day,[148] India, again on behalf of the Movement, expressed indignation at the execution, which, it said, made a mockery of all norms of law and justice and constituted another instance of South Africa's defiance of international opinion. On 19 October,[149] Egypt condemned the execution in similar terms. Calling South Africa's action merciless, Israel, on 21 October,[150] reiterated its opposition to the racist ideology of *apartheid*. Expressing on 22 October[151] its regret that South Africa had carried out the execution, Japan appealed to South Africa to eliminate *apartheid* as early as possible so that such an incident would not happen again.

Apartheid in sports

The Special Committee against *Apartheid* continued to report on sports contacts with South Africa.[1] It said that, under international pressure, *apartheid* sport was further isolated in 1985 although contacts with South Africa by some individual sportspersons and teams occurred. The Committee continued to publish a semi-annual *Register* of such sports contacts, which included a list of sportspersons who participated in events in South Africa. Names of those who pledged not to engage in further sports events there were deleted from the *Register*. The *Register* showed that South Africa had lured some individuals and teams with international standing by paying large fees. South Africa continued its generous funding of *apartheid* in sports through tax concessions to private sector sponsors. Nevertheless, it continued to have limited access to international sports exchanges.

Among the signs of the growing international resolve to end *apartheid* in sports, the Committee noted that Australia and Canada informed the South African Women's Bowling Association in February that its representative would not be given a visa to either country. In July, Canada announced guidelines curtailing sports contacts with South Africa.

In April, the Chairman of the Committee, having learned of a proposed tour to South Africa by the All Blacks, a New Zealand rugby team, stated that the tour represented insensitivity to the great majority of South Africans and an encouragement to racist sports organizations, and could be used by the régime to boost its international image. He expressed appreciation to New Zealand for a Parliamentary resolution and statements by its Prime Minister and other officials affirming opposition to the proposed tour. Because of mounting opposition and following an interim injunction granted by the High Court of New Zealand, the New Zealand

Rugby Football Union cancelled its tour. The national rugby team of the Federal Republic of Germany, under pressure from anti-*apartheid* groups, cancelled in July a planned 1986 tour of South Africa.

Another significant development in the campaign was the decision of the Association of National Olympic Committees in November 1984 to urge international federations to exclude South Africa from membership, in line with the policy of the International Olympic Committee (IOC) until that country renounced *apartheid*, a policy contravening the Olympic Charter.

The Committee, in co-operation with the Supreme Council for Sport in Africa and the South Africa Non-Racial Olympic Committee, organized the International Conference on Sports Boycott against South Africa (Paris, 16-18 May).[152] At the Conference, the Committee presented citations to athletes who participated in the struggle against *apartheid*. The Conference adopted a declaration[153] in which it appealed to States to bring the International Convention against *Apartheid* in Sports into force by speedy ratification, following its adoption by the General Assembly (see below). It supported the IOC position that South Africa should not be readmitted to the Olympic Movement until *apartheid* was ended, and it urged IOC to adopt a code of conduct to discourage sports contacts with South Africa and to take the disciplinary actions necessary to deal with any of its affiliates that transgressed the international campaign. The Conference welcomed the IOC rejection of a proposal that a commission of inquiry be sent to South Africa, on the basis that as long as *apartheid* existed there could be no normal sport in that country for a commission to investigate.

The Conference congratulated the Association of National Olympic Committees on its declaration of intent to campaign for the exclusion of South Africa from all remaining international sports federations. Associations of non-Olympic sports, particularly cricket and rugby because of their popularity, were urged to play a full part in the international campaign. The Conference applauded those cricketing countries which had disciplined cricketers for playing in South Africa. It welcomed the effects of the United Nations *Register of Sports Contacts* with South Africa which had resulted in a number of countries and sports organizations taking action against teams and individuals who had competed there, thus discouraging others from participating in South African sports events.

Convention against *apartheid* in sports

The *Ad Hoc* Committee on the Drafting of an International Convention against *Apartheid* in Sports, established in 1976,[154] submitted its final draft of the Convention to the General Assembly in August 1985.[155]

In order to hold follow-up discussions on the draft, the Committee's Chairman undertook a mission from 3 to 19 May to the USSR, China and the Philippines; while attending the Paris Conference (see above), he held further discussions on article 10, dealing with compliance with the Convention, and an understanding was reached which formed the basis for debate in New York by the Committee's Working Group. The Group, open to all Committee members, convened from 1 to 5 July. After further amendments, the text was circulated to Governments. Ireland and the Netherlands[156] informed the Committee that they would not be able to accept the Convention because it conflicted with their respective constitutions. After meetings on 10 July and 7, 12, 15 and 21 August, the Working Group completed its consideration and submitted the final draft to the *Ad Hoc* Committee, which forwarded it to the Assembly for approval.

GENERAL ASSEMBLY ACTION

Acting on the *Ad Hoc* Committee's recommendation, the General Assembly, on 10 December, adopted **resolution 40/64 G** by recorded vote, thereby adopting the Convention.

International Convention against *Apartheid* in Sports

The General Assembly,

Recalling its resolution 32/105 M of 14 December 1977, by which it adopted the International Declaration against *Apartheid* in Sports,

Recalling also its resolution 39/72 D of 13 December 1984, by which it requested the *Ad Hoc* Committee on the Drafting of an International Convention against *Apartheid* in Sports to continue its work with a view to submitting the draft Convention to the General Assembly at its fortieth session,

Recalling further that the International Convention on the Suppression and Punishment of the Crime of *Apartheid* declares that *apartheid* is a crime violating principles of international law, in particular the purposes and principles of the Charter of the United Nations,

Mindful of the special responsibility of the United Nations to eliminate *apartheid* and racial discrimination in sports and in society,

Convinced that *apartheid* still dominates sports and the society as a whole in South Africa and that all so-called reforms have not led to any meaningful change in sports and the society in that country,

Reaffirming its unqualified support for the Olympic principle that no discrimination be allowed on the grounds of race, religion or political affiliation and its belief that merit should be the sole criterion in sport activities,

Reaffirming the necessity to ensure an international concerted action to isolate the racist régime of South Africa from the field of international sports as well as all other fields,

Commending the efforts of the Special Committee against *Apartheid* to ensure the total isolation of *apartheid* in sports and, in particular, the publication of the *Register of Sports Contacts* with South Africa, and urging Member States, pending the entry into force of the Convention, to co-operate with the Special Committee on matters relating to the isolation of *apartheid* in sports,

Commending all sports bodies, teams and individual sportsmen that have declared their determination not to engage in sports contacts with South Africa until the evil system of *apartheid* is abolished,

Convinced that the Convention would be an important instrument towards the isolation of the racist régime of South Africa and the elimination of *apartheid* in sports and that it should be signed and ratified by States at the earliest possible date and its provisions implemented without delay,

Considering that the text of the Convention should be made known throughout the world,

1. *Adopts* and opens for signature and ratification the International Convention against *Apartheid* in Sports, the text of which is annexed to the present resolution;

2. *Appeals* to all States to sign and ratify the Convention as soon as possible;

3. *Requests* all Governments and intergovernmental and non-governmental organizations to acquaint the public as widely as possible with the text of the Convention, using all the information media at their disposal;

4. *Requests* the Secretary-General to ensure the urgent and wide dissemination of the Convention and, for that purpose, to publish and circulate its text;

5. *Commends* the efforts of the Special Committee against *Apartheid* and requests it to continue to publish the *Register of Sports Contacts* with South Africa until the establishment of the Commission against *Apartheid* in Sports.

ANNEX
International Convention against *Apartheid* in Sports

The States Parties to the present Convention,

Recalling the provisions of the Charter of the United Nations, in which all Members pledged themselves to take joint and separate action, in co-operation with the Organization, for the achievement of universal respect for, and observance of, human rights and fundamental freedoms for all without distinction as to race, sex, language or religion,

Considering that the Universal Declaration of Human Rights proclaims that all human beings are born free and equal in dignity and rights and that everyone is entitled to all the rights and freedoms set forth in the Declaration without distinction of any kind, particularly in regard to race, colour or national origin,

Observing that, in accordance with the International Convention on the Elimination of All Forms of Racial Discrimination, States Parties to that Convention particularly condemn racial segregation and *apartheid* and undertake to prevent, prohibit and eradicate all practices of this nature in all fields,

Observing that the General Assembly of the United Nations has adopted a number of resolutions condemning the practice of *apartheid* in sports and has affirmed its unqualified support for the Olympic principle that no discrimination be allowed on the grounds of race, religion or political affiliation and that merit should be the sole criterion for participation in sports activities,

Considering that the International Declaration against *Apartheid* in Sports, which was adopted by the General Assembly on 14 December 1977, solemnly affirms the necessity for the speedy elimination of *apartheid* in sports,

Recalling the provisions of the International Convention on the Suppression and Punishment of the Crime of *Apartheid* and recognizing, in particular, that participation in sports exchanges with teams selected on the basis of *apartheid* directly abets and encourages the commission of the crime of *apartheid*, as defined in that Convention,

Resolved to adopt all necessary measures to eradicate the practice of *apartheid* in sports and to promote international sports contacts based on the Olympic principle,

Recognizing that sports contact with any country practising *apartheid* in sports condones and strengthens *apartheid* in violation of the Olympic principle and thereby becomes the legitimate concern of all Governments,

Desiring to implement the principles embodied in the International Declaration against *Apartheid* in Sports and to secure the earliest adoption of practical measures to that end,

Convinced that the adoption of an International Convention against *Apartheid* in Sports would result in more effective measures at the international and national levels, with a view to eliminating *apartheid* in sports,

Have agreed as follows:

Article 1

For the purposes of the present Convention:

(a) The expression *"apartheid"* shall mean a system of institutionalized racial segregation and discrimination for the purpose of establishing and maintaining domination by one racial group of persons over another racial group of persons and systematically oppressing them, such as that pursued by South Africa, and *"apartheid* in sports" shall mean the application of the policies and practices of such a system in sports activities, whether organized on a professional or an amateur basis;

(b) The expression "national sports facilities" shall mean any sports facility operated within the framework of a sports programme conducted under the auspices of a national government;

(c) The expression "Olympic principle" shall mean the principle that no discrimination be allowed on the grounds of race, religion or political affiliation;

(d) The expression "sports contracts" shall mean any contract concluded for the organization, promotion, performance or derivative rights, including servicing, of any sports activity;

(e) The expression "sports bodies" shall mean any organization constituted to organize sports activities at the national level, including national Olympic committees, national sports federations or national governing sports committees;

(f) The expression "team" shall mean a group of sportsmen organized for the purpose of participating in sports activities in competition with other such organized groups;

(g) The expression "sportsmen" shall mean men and women who participate in sports activities on an individual or team basis, as well as managers, coaches, trainers and other officials whose functions are essential for the operation of a team.

Article 2

States Parties strongly condemn *apartheid* and undertake to pursue immediately by all appropriate means the policy of eliminating the practice of *apartheid* in all its forms from sports.

Article 3

States Parties shall not permit sports contact with a country practising *apartheid* and shall take appropriate action to ensure that their sports bodies, teams, and individual sportsmen do not have such contact.

Article 4

States Parties shall take all possible measures to prevent sports contact with a country practising *apartheid* and shall ensure that effective means exist for bringing about compliance with such measures.

Article 5

States Parties shall refuse to provide financial or other assistance to enable their sports bodies, teams and individual sportsmen to participate in sports activities in a country practising *apartheid* or with teams or individual sportsmen selected on the basis of *apartheid*.

Article 6

Each State Party shall take appropriate action against its sports bodies, teams and individual sportsmen that participate in sports activities in a country practising *apartheid* or with teams representing a country practising *apartheid*, which in particular shall include:

(a) Refusal to provide financial or other assistance for any purpose to such sports bodies, teams and individual sportsmen;

(b) Restriction of access to national sports facilities by such sports bodies, teams and individual sportsmen;

(c) Non-enforceability of all sports contracts which involve sports activities in a country practising *apartheid* or with teams or individual sportsmen selected on the basis of *apartheid;*

(d) Denial and withdrawal of national honours or awards in sports to such teams and individual sportsmen;

(e) Denial of official receptions in honour of such teams or sportsmen.

Article 7

States Parties shall deny visas and/or entry to representatives of sports bodies, teams and individual sportsmen representing a country practising *apartheid*.

Article 8

States Parties shall take all appropriate action to secure the expulsion of a country practising *apartheid* from international and regional sports bodies.

Article 9

States Parties shall take all appropriate measures to prevent international sports bodies from imposing financial or other penalties on affiliated bodies which, in accordance with United Nations resolutions, the provisions of the present Convention and the spirit of the Olympic principle, refuse to participate in sports with a country practising *apartheid*.

Article 10

1. States Parties shall use their best endeavours to ensure universal compliance with the Olympic principle of non-discrimination and the provisions of the present Convention.

2. Towards this end, States Parties shall prohibit entry into their countries of members of teams and individual sportsmen participating or who have participated in sports competitions in South Africa and shall prohibit entry into their countries of representatives of sports bodies, members of teams and individual sportsmen who invite on their own initiative sports bodies, teams and sportsmen officially representing a country practising *apartheid* and participating under its flag. States Parties may also prohibit entry of representatives of sports bodies, members of teams or individual sportsmen who maintain sports contacts with sports bodies, teams or sportsmen representing a country practising *apartheid* and participating under its flag. Prohibition of entry should not violate the regulations of the relevant sports federations which support the elimination of *apartheid* in sports and shall apply only to participation in sports activities.

3. States Parties shall advise their national representatives to international sports federations to take all possible and practical steps to prevent the participation of the sports bodies, teams and sportsmen referred to in paragraph 2 above in international sports competitions and shall, through their representatives in international sports organizations, take every possible measure:

(a) To ensure the expulsion of South Africa from all federations in which it still holds membership as well as to deny South Africa reinstatement to membership in any federation from which it has been expelled;

(b) In case of national federations condoning sports exchanges with a country practising *apartheid*, to impose sanctions against such national federations including, if necessary, expulsion from the relevant international sports organization and exclusion of their representatives from participation in international sports competitions.

4. In cases of flagrant violations of the provisions of the present Convention, States Parties shall take appropriate action as they deem fit, including, where necessary, steps aimed at the exclusion of the responsible national sports governing bodies, national sports federations or sportsmen of the countries concerned from international sports competition.

5. The provisions of the present article relating specifically to South Africa shall cease to apply when the system of *apartheid* is abolished in that country.

Article 11

1. There shall be established a Commission against *Apartheid* in Sports (hereinafter referred to as "the Commission") consisting of fifteen members of high moral character and committed to the struggle against *apartheid*, particular attention being paid to participation of persons having experience in sports administration, elected by the States Parties from among their nationals, having regard to the most equitable geographical distribution and the representation of the principal legal systems.

2. The members of the Commission shall be elected by secret ballot from a list of persons nominated by the States Parties. Each State Party may nominate one person from among its own nationals.

3. The initial election shall be held six months after the date of the entry into force of the present Convention. At least three months before the date of each election, the Secretary-General of the United Nations shall address a letter to the States Parties inviting them to submit their nominations within two months. The Secretary-General shall prepare a list in alphabetical order of all persons thus nominated, indicating the States Parties which have nominated them, and shall submit it to the States Parties.

4. Elections of the members of the Commission shall be held at a meeting of States Parties convened by the Secretary-General at United Nations Headquarters. At that meeting, for which two thirds of the States Parties shall constitute a quorum, the persons elected to the Commission shall be those nominees who obtain the largest number of votes and an absolute majority of the votes of the representatives of States Parties present and voting.

5. The members of the Commission shall be elected for a term of four years. However, the terms of nine of the members elected at the first election shall expire at the end of two years; immediately after the first election, the names of these nine members shall be chosen by lot by the Chairman of the Commission.

6. For the filling of casual vacancies, the State Party whose national has ceased to function as a member of the Commission shall appoint another person from among its nationals, subject to the approval of the Commission.

7. States Parties shall be responsible for the expenses of the members of the Commission while they are in performance of Commission duties.

Article 12

1. States Parties undertake to submit to the Secretary-General of the United Nations, for consideration by the Commission, a report on the legislative, judicial, administrative or other measures which they have adopted to give effect to the provisions of the present Convention within one year of its entry into force and thereafter every two years. The Commission may request further information from the States Parties.

2. The Commission shall report annually through the Secretary-General to the General Assembly of the United Nations on its activities and may make suggestions and general recommendations based on the examination of the reports and information received from the States Parties. Such suggestions and recommendations shall be reported to the General Assembly together with comments, if any, from States Parties concerned.

3. The Commission shall examine, in particular, the implementation of the provisions of article 10 of the present Convention and make recommendations on action to be undertaken.

4. A meeting of States Parties shall be convened by the Secretary-General at the request of a majority of the States Parties to consider further action with respect to the implementation of the provisions of article 10 of the present Convention. In cases of flagrant violation of the provisions of the present Convention, a meeting of States Parties shall be convened by the Secretary-General at the request of the Commission.

Article 13

1. Any State Party may at any time declare that it recognizes the competence of the Commission to receive and examine complaints concerning breaches of the provisions of the present Convention submitted by States Parties which have also made such a declaration. The Commission may decide on the appropriate measures to be taken in respect of breaches.

2. States Parties against which a complaint has been made, in accordance with paragraph 1 of the present article, shall be entitled to be represented and take part in the proceedings of the Commission.

Article 14

1. The Commission shall meet at least once a year.

2. The Commission shall adopt its own rules of procedure.

3. The secretariat of the Commission shall be provided by the Secretary-General of the United Nations.

4. The meetings of the Commission shall normally be held at United Nations Headquarters.

5. The Secretary-General shall convene the initial meeting of the Commission.

Article 15

The Secretary-General of the United Nations shall be the depositary of the present Convention.

Article 16

1. The present Convention shall be open for signature at United Nations Headquarters by all States until its entry into force.

2. The present Convention shall be subject to ratification, acceptance or approval by the signatory States.

Article 17

The present Convention shall be open for accession by all States.

Article 18

1. The present Convention shall enter into force on the thirtieth day after the date of deposit with the Secretary-General of the United Nations of the twenty-seventh instrument of ratification, acceptance, approval or accession.

2. For each State ratifying, accepting, approving or acceding to the present Convention after its entry into force, the Convention shall enter into force on the thirtieth day after the date of deposit of the relevant instrument.

Article 19

Any dispute between States Parties arising out of the interpretation, application or implementation of the present Convention which is not settled by negotiation shall be brought before the International Court of Justice at the request and with the mutual consent of the States Parties to the dispute, save where the Parties to the dispute have agreed on some other form of settlement.

Article 20

1. Any State Party may propose an amendment or revision to the present Convention and file it with the depositary. The Secretary-General of the United Nations shall thereupon communicate the proposed amendment or revision to the States Parties with a request that they notify him whether they favour a conference of States Parties for the purpose of considering and voting upon the proposal. In the event that at least one third of the States Parties favour such a conference, the Secretary-General shall convene the conference under the auspices of the United Nations. Any amendment or revision adopted by the majority of the States Parties present and voting at the conference shall be submitted to the General Assembly of the United Nations for approval.

2. Amendments or revisions shall come into force when they have been approved by the General Assembly and accepted by a two-thirds majority of the States Parties, in accordance with their respective constitutional processes.

3. When amendments or revisions come into force, they shall be binding on those States Parties which have accepted them, other States Parties still being bound by the provisions of the present Convention and any earlier amendment or revision which they have accepted.

Article 21

A State Party may withdraw from the present Convention by written notification to the depositary. Such withdrawal shall take effect one year after the date of receipt of the notification by the depositary.

Article 22

The present Convention has been concluded in Arabic, Chinese, English, French, Russian and Spanish, all texts being equally authentic.

General Assembly resolution 40/64 G

10 December 1985   Meeting 111   125-0-24 (recorded vote)

60-nation draft (A/40/L.32 & Corr.1); agenda item 35.

Sponsors: Afghanistan, Algeria, Angola, Antigua and Barbuda, Barbados, Benin, Burkina Faso, Burundi, Cameroon, Cape Verde, Comoros, Congo, Cuba, Democratic Yemen, Djibouti, Egypt, Equatorial Guinea, Ethiopia, Gambia, German Democratic Republic, Ghana, Guinea, Guinea-Bissau, Guyana, India, Indonesia, Iran, Iraq, Jamaica, Kenya, Lebanon, Liberia, Libyan Arab Jamahiriya, Madagascar, Malaysia, Mali, Mauritania, Mauritius, Mongolia, Morocco, Nicaragua, Niger, Nigeria, Papua New Guinea, Rwanda, Sao Tome and Principe, Senegal, Sierra Leone, Somalia, Sudan, Syrian Arab Republic, Tunisia, Uganda, Ukrainian SSR, United Republic of Tanzania, Viet Nam, Yugoslavia, Zaire, Zambia, Zimbabwe.

Financial implications. 5th Committee, A/40/1022; S-G, A/C.5/40/76.

Meeting numbers. GA 40th session: 5th Committee 58; plenary 51-57, 111.

Recorded vote in Assembly as follows:

In favour: Afghanistan, Albania, Algeria, Angola, Antigua and Barbuda, Argentina, Bahamas, Bahrain, Bangladesh, Barbados, Belize, Benin, Bhutan, Bolivia, Botswana, Brazil, Brunei Darussalam, Bulgaria, Burkina Faso, Burma, Burundi, Byelorussian SSR, Cameroon, Cape Verde, Central African Republic, Chad, China, Colombia, Comoros, Congo, Costa Rica, Cuba, Cyprus, Czechoslovakia, Democratic Kampuchea, Democratic Yemen, Djibouti, Dominican Republic, Ecuador, Egypt, El Salvador, Equatorial Guinea, Ethiopia, Gabon, Gambia, German Democratic Republic, Ghana, Grenada, Guatemala, Guinea, Guinea-Bissau, Guyana, Haiti, Honduras, Hungary, India, Indonesia, Iran, Iraq, Israel, Jamaica, Jordan, Kenya, Kuwait, Lao People's Democratic Republic, Lebanon, Lesotho, Liberia, Libyan Arab Jamahiriya, Madagascar, Malaysia, Maldives, Mali, Malta, Mauritania, Mauritius, Mexico, Mongolia, Morocco, Mozambique, Nepal, Nicaragua, Niger, Nigeria, Oman, Pakistan, Panama, Papua New Guinea, Peru, Philippines, Poland, Qatar, Romania, Rwanda, Saint Lucia, Sao Tome and Principe, Saudi Arabia, Senegal, Seychelles, Sierra Leone, Singapore, Somalia, Sri Lanka, Sudan, Swaziland, Syrian Arab Republic, Thailand, Togo, Trinidad and Tobago, Tunisia, Turkey, Uganda, Ukrainian SSR, USSR, United Arab Emirates, United Republic of Tanzania, Uruguay, Vanuatu, Venezuela, Viet Nam, Yemen, Yugoslavia, Zaire, Zambia, Zimbabwe.

Against: None.

Abstaining: Australia, Austria, Belgium, Canada, Denmark, Finland, France, Germany, Federal Republic of, Greece, Iceland, Ireland, Italy, Japan, Luxembourg, Malawi, Netherlands, New Zealand, Norway, Portugal, Solomon Islands, Spain, Sweden, United Kingdom, United States.

Speaking in explanation of vote, Austria, Belgium, Canada, France, Greece, Ireland, Italy, Luxembourg (for the EC members, Portugal and Spain), the Netherlands, New Zealand, Norway (for the Nordic States), the United Kingdom and the United States said that, although they supported the broad objectives of the Convention, they would be unable to vote for the resolution or accede to the Convention due to various legal or constitutional difficulties. Austria explained that it had taken measures aimed at further limiting sports relations with South Africa. Belgium stressed that its authorities would continue discouraging sports contacts and banning the entry into Belgium of South African sportspersons

wishing to participate in competitions. Canada expressed support for the principle of sporting boycotts against South Africa. France pointed out that it had discouraged the sports contacts in question. Greece objected to certain elements of the resolution owing to constitutional constraints. Stating its intention to continue to discourage sports contacts, Italy found some unacceptable elements in the Convention, in particular articles 3, 4, 6, 7 and 10, but it would recommend that its national organizations implement articles 2, 5 and 9. Ireland, which had supported the drafting of a Convention and intended to prevent international sporting contacts, said articles 3, 6 and 10 were incompatible with the Irish Constitution.

Luxembourg (for EC, Portugal and Spain) observed that sports activities were organized in their respective countries on private initiative. The Netherlands believed that a sports boycott was an effective instrument towards eradicating *apartheid* and it had introduced visa requirements for South Africans to control their participation in sports events. New Zealand spoke similarly, adding that it had discouraged its sportspersons from having contacts with South Africa. Norway (speaking for the Nordic countries) noted their strict policy against sports contacts with South Africa. The United Kingdom also discouraged such contacts. The United States said it could not support a resolution that urged States to adopt legal measures contrary to its own laws.

Costa Rica said signature and ratification of the Convention would be subject to approval by its Legislative Assembly.

In **resolution 40/64 A**, the Assembly requested States that had not done so, pending action by the Security Council, to take legislative or other measures to ensure isolation of South Africa, including the observance of a sports boycott.

Aid programmes and inter-agency co-operation

United Nations aid to victims of *apartheid* was provided through national liberation movements or directly to individuals for educational and training purposes. The United Nations Trust Fund for South Africa provided legal assistance, relief and education grants to persons persecuted under repressive and discriminatory legislation of South Africa. Other assistance was provided for education by the United Nations Educational and Training Programme for Southern Africa.

National liberation movements

In 1985, several United Nations organizations continued to provide assistance to national liberation movements, particularly the United Nations

Development Programme (UNDP) and the United Nations Industrial Development Organization (UNIDO). The United Nations Commission on Human Settlements also provided aid to victims of *apartheid* and colonialism in Africa (see ECONOMIC AND SOCIAL QUESTIONS, Chapter XVII), and educational assistance was provided by the United Nations Educational and Training Programme for Southern Africa (see p. 200).

UNDP action. In March 1985, the UNDP Administrator submitted a report to the Governing Council,[157] describing UNDP's 1984 assistance programmes to national liberation movements of southern Africa recognized by OAU—ANC and PAC of South Africa and SWAPO of Namibia—worth $2.9 million.[158] On 28 June 1985,[159] the Council endorsed the Administrator's plans to evaluate ongoing assistance projects to determine the thrust of development assistance over the 1987-1991 programming cycle. It requested him to continue to assist the movements flexibly, to ensure that such assistance was delivered expeditiously and that quality and effectiveness were maintained, and to report on trends and developments relating to the administration, management and effectiveness of the assistance.

UNDP in 1985 provided $2.4 million for technical assistance to national liberation movements recognized by OAU.[160] Nine of the 16 projects under way in 1985 were for education and training, accounting for 76 per cent of total expenditure. Other projects were designed to promote self-reliance in agriculture, health and education.

UNIDO action. UNIDO continued to provide technical assistance to the South African national liberation movements recognized by OAU (ANC and PAC), as reported by the Executive Director to the Industrial Development Board.[161] In 1985, assistance was provided for two projects— establishment in the United Republic of Tanzania of a mechanical workshop organized by ANC at Mazimbu, and of a women's garment manufacturing workshop for the benefit of PAC members located in Botswana, Lesotho, the United Republic of Tanzania and Zimbabwe.

On 31 May,[162] the Board, mindful of the low level of UNDP resources during 1982-1984, which led to the exclusion of some UNIDO projects for assistance to the movements from the priority list of UNDP-funded projects, urged the UNDP Governing Council to ensure adequate funds for UNIDO projects. It appealed to member States, United Nations organizations and NGOs to provide assistance through the South African national liberation movements for the establishment and development of technical co-operation projects in the industrial sector aimed at enhancing the self-reliance of the oppressed black majority of South Africa. The UNIDO secretariat was requested to increase its technical assistance to those movements recognized by OAU and to report on technical assistance to them.

Activities of the Committee against *Apartheid*. The Special Committee against *Apartheid* also appealed for more assistance to the oppressed people of South Africa and the South African liberation movements recognized by OAU, emphasizing the need for all possible political, moral, humanitarian, educational, material and other assistance.[1] It said there was an urgent need for direct assistance, as a demonstration, by action, of support to their legitimate struggle. The Committee urged the General Assembly to address an urgent appeal for such assistance.

Action by the Commission on Human Rights. On 26 February,[9] the Commission on Human Rights appealed to States, specialized agencies and NGOs to extend all possible co-operation to the liberation movements of southern Africa recognized by the United Nations and OAU.

Action by the Committee on colonial countries. The Committee on colonial countries, on 9 August,[90] expressed concern that the assistance extended so far by United Nations organizations to colonial peoples, particularly the people of Namibia and their national liberation movement, SWAPO, was inadequate.

ECONOMIC AND SOCIAL COUNCIL ACTION

In **resolution 1985/59** of 26 July, the Economic and Social Council requested United Nations organizations, in view of the deteriorating situation in South Africa and the acts of aggression and destabilization by the régime against States in the region (see p. 178), to increase assistance to the liberation movements in South Africa. The Council noted with satisfaction the arrangements made by several United Nations bodies which enabled representatives of the movements recognized by OAU to participate as observers during discussions of matters concerning their respective countries, and called on those international institutions which had not done so to make the necessary arrangements, including defraying the costs of their participation.

GENERAL ASSEMBLY ACTION

The General Assembly took action on many occasions in 1985 on assistance to the national liberation movements recognized by OAU.

It decided to continue authorizing financial provisions in the regular United Nations budget to enable the South African liberation movements— ANC and PAC—to maintain New York offices in order to participate in appropriate deliberations (**resolution 40/64 B**).

The Assembly reiterated its appeal to States, organizations and institutions for increased support for those movements (**resolution 40/64 I**) and called for an increase in assistance to the victims of *apartheid* through their movements (**40/25**).

United Nations organizations were urged to continue to expand their co-operation with OAU and, through it, their assistance to the movements it recognized (**40/20**). The Assembly recommended that a separate item on such assistance be included in the agenda of high-level meetings between the OAU General Secretariat and the secretariats of United Nations organizations with a view to strengthening co-ordination to ensure the best use of available resources for assistance to colonial peoples; it noted with satisfaction the arrangements made by several such organizations enabling representatives of the liberation movements recognized by OAU to participate as observers in matters concerning their countries, and called on those organizations that had not done so to follow that example (**40/53**).

UN Trust Fund for South Africa

In October 1985,[163] the Secretary-General reported that the United Nations Trust Fund for South Africa, established in 1965[164] to provide voluntary assistance to persons persecuted under discriminatory legislation in South Africa and Namibia, made eight grants totalling $2,115,000 in 1985. The Fund received $2,309,081 in 1985 (see table below). As at 15 October, total income to the Fund since its inception, including private donations and interest, was $22,204,868 and the total amount of grants was $21,615,627, leaving a balance of $589,241.

CONTRIBUTIONS TO THE UNITED NATIONS TRUST FUND
FOR SOUTH AFRICA, 1985

(as at 31 December 1985, in US dollar equivalent)

Country	Amount
Algeria	10,000
Australia	49,014
Austria	37,200
Barbados	500
Brazil	20,000
Bulgaria	1,000
Cameroon	3,763
Canada	21,492
China	30,000
Cyprus	(39)
Denmark	280,047
Egypt	2,834
Finland	106,050
France	69,892
Germany, Federal Republic of	49,912
Greece	4,500
Hungary	2,500
India	2,000
Indonesia	3,000
Iran	4,400
Ireland	25,288
Italy	15,258
Jamaica	2,000
Japan	20,000
Kuwait	4,000
Malaysia	1,000
Maldives	1,000
Netherlands	73,099

Country	Amount
New Zealand	5,260
Norway	402,685
Pakistan	2,495
Sri Lanka	1,000
Sweden	340,716
Thailand	1,000
Trinidad and Tobago	1,250
Turkey	1,500
United States	686,000
Venezuela	1,000
Yugoslavia	4,000
Zimbabwe	22,465
Total	2,309,081

SOURCE: Accounts for the 12-month period of the biennium 1984-1985 ended 31 December 1985—schedules of individual trust funds.

GENERAL ASSEMBLY ACTION

On 10 December, the General Assembly adopted **resolution 40/64 H** without vote.

United Nations Trust Fund for South Africa
The General Assembly,

Having considered the report of the Secretary-General on the United Nations Trust Fund for South Africa, to which is annexed the report of the Committee of Trustees of the Trust Fund,

Alarmed by the increasing number of political trials and detentions and the harsh sentences, including the death penalty, imposed on opponents of *apartheid*,

Gravely concerned at the imposition of the state of emergency in South Africa and the increased repression of thousands of opponents of *apartheid*, including leaders of democratic political mass organizations, community and church leaders, students and trade unionists,

Reaffirming that increased humanitarian and legal assistance by the international community to those persecuted under repressive and discriminatory legislation in South Africa and Namibia is appropriate and essential,

Recognizing that increased contributions to the Trust Fund and to the voluntary agencies concerned are necessary to enable them to meet the growing needs for humanitarian and legal assistance,

1. *Commends* the Secretary-General and the Committee of Trustees of the United Nations Trust Fund for South Africa for their persistent efforts to promote humanitarian and legal assistance to persons persecuted under repressive and discriminatory legislation in South Africa and Namibia, as well as assistance to their families and to refugees from South Africa;

2. *Expresses its appreciation* to the Governments, organizations and individuals that have contributed to the Trust Fund and to the voluntary agencies engaged in rendering humanitarian and legal assistance to the victims of *apartheid* and racial discrimination;

3. *Appeals* for generous and increased contributions to the Trust Fund;

4. *Also appeals* for direct contributions to the voluntary agencies engaged in assistance to the victims of *apartheid* and racial discrimination in South Africa and Namibia.

General Assembly resolution 40/64 H

10 December 1985	Meeting 111	Adopted without vote

45-nation draft (A/40/L.39 & Add.1); agenda item 35.

Sponsors: Argentina, Australia, Austria, Brazil, Canada, Cape Verde, China, Congo, Denmark, Egypt, Finland, France, Gambia, Germany, Federal Republic of, Greece, Guinea, Guyana, Iceland, India, Indonesia, Ireland, Italy, Japan, Kenya, Lesotho,

Madagascar, Malaysia, Malta, Mozambique, Netherlands, Nicaragua, Nigeria, Norway, Pakistan, Sierra Leone, Sweden, Syrian Arab Republic, Togo, Trinidad and Tobago, Tunisia, Turkey, United Republic of Tanzania, Venezuela, Yugoslavia, Zambia.

Meeting numbers. GA 40th session: plenary 51-57, 111.

Other aspects

Public information

The Special Committee against *Apartheid*, in response to a 1984 request of the General Assembly,[165] issued in October 1985 a special report on its efforts to inform world public opinion and encourage wider action in support of the struggle of the oppressed people of South Africa.[5]

The Committee noted that over the years it had organized hearings with media representatives and other events to generate an understanding of the true character of *apartheid*. Further public information activities were needed since South Africa had been devoting more resources to propaganda, directed primarily at the United States and the United Kingdom. Because those two States had veto power in the Security Council, their continued support had been regarded by South Africa as crucial in its campaign against the imposition of economic sanctions. South Africa had been trying to convince public opinion, particularly in Western countries, that white-ruled South Africa was a valuable strategic ally of the West. Furthermore, South Africa had attempted to portray black South Africans as culturally, ethnically and politically fragmented into mutually hostile and diverse "tribes" and therefore unable to govern themselves. It had attempted to convince public opinion that the liberation movements were "Communist dominated" and that any political change in South Africa would endanger the West's sea route around the Cape and the supply of strategically important minerals.

The Committee's activities to counteract South Africa's efforts included publication of a biannual *Register of Sports Contacts* with South Africa (see p. 164) and an annual register of entertainers, actors and others who had performed in South Africa (see p. 135), as part of the sports and cultural boycotts. In May 1985, the Centre against *Apartheid* initiated an occasional *News Digest* to inform organizations of United Nations–related activities against *apartheid*, and to promote an exchange of information on the international campaign against it. Other Secretariat activities included the dissemination of information, including audio-visual material, by the Department of Public Information (DPI).

The Committee made a number of recommendations for further information activities. It called for co-operative arrangements with UNDP and specialized agencies for information distribution wherever United Nations information centres had not been established. DPI was called on to prepare, in co-operation with the Centre against *Apartheid*, special information kits on *apartheid* for use by the media and organizations. The Centre was urged to produce more information material for use by special groups, such as trade unions, churches, and women's, student and youth organizations, relating to specific aspects of the international campaign. The Committee recommended that DPI, the Centre and other Secretariat bodies produce and disseminate audio-visual material on *apartheid*. It stressed the need to expand liaison with the media, and suggested that a special supplement be prepared for insertion in wide-circulation newspapers during the observance of international days related to the struggle against *apartheid*. The Committee found that concerts and other events of a promotional nature involving prominent cultural and sports personalities and entertainers had been effective in drawing media attention. It suggested that the United Nations Postal Administration, as well as Member States, issue commemorative postage stamps publicizing the struggle against *apartheid*.

In the Committee's view, the Centre should be provided with greater resources to strengthen its dissemination activities. In order to carry out its recommendations, the Committee urged Member States to make larger contributions to the Trust Fund for Publicity against *Apartheid*.

On 7 November,[2] the Acting Chairman of the Committee condemned the restrictions imposed by South Africa to curb the reporting of unrest and repression, and called on journalists, academicians, liberation movements, Governments, organizations and individuals to combat South African attempts in that regard.

The Committee and the secretariat of the Commonwealth countries organized a Media Workshop on Countering *Apartheid* Propaganda (London, 20-22 May).[166] Participants, including representatives of Commonwealth Governments, the media, anti-*apartheid* and other organizations and liberation movements, as well as experts, discussed the nature and objective of *apartheid* propaganda, impediments to exposure of the truth about *apartheid* and possible future action. Among a number of recommendations, the Workshop called on the Commonwealth secretariat and the Centre against *Apartheid* to assist third world media in establishing direct access to news and events in southern Africa. It also recommended that an *apartheid* monitoring unit be set up within the Commonwealth secretariat, that a study be commissioned on how selected Western media handled South African and Namibian issues, and that educational exchanges be instituted between Commonwealth trade unions and emerging black trade unions in South Africa.

On 2 and 3 December, the Committee against *Apartheid* met with the Commonwealth Committee on Southern Africa to review their respective activities, and agreed on measures to generate and request increased television and radio coverage of resistance in South Africa and to counter propaganda. Further, they decided to co-sponsor events designed to promote media coverage of developments in southern Africa and international action against *apartheid*.

Other United Nations bodies also called for dissemination of information on *apartheid*. In its June Vienna Declaration,[30] the Council for Namibia noted with satisfaction the pressures being exerted by parliamentarians, NGOs and individuals in Western countries to promote the severance of economic and other links with South Africa as part of a concerted public campaign against *apartheid*. It urged the campaign to work for comprehensive mandatory sanctions against South Africa (see p. 138).

The Committee on colonial countries, on 7 August,[32] appealed to mass media, trade unions and other NGOs, as well as individuals, to coordinate and intensify their efforts to mobilize international public opinion against the policy of the *apartheid* régime and to work for the enforcement of sanctions and for systematic divestment in corporations doing business in South Africa.

On 26 February,[9] the Commission on Human Rights called on States, specialized agencies, intergovernmental organizations and NGOs to intensify their campaign to mobilize public opinion for the enforcement of economic and other sanctions.

The Conference of African Ministers of Information (Cairo, Egypt, 23-25 November) adopted a number of resolutions,[26] including one on the responsibilities of the Pan African News Agency (PANA) and the African press in the struggle against *apartheid*. By that text, it urged the African media, particularly PANA, to include among their priority objectives the sensitization of African and international public opinion to the struggle for freedom waged by the national liberation movements and the peoples of South Africa and Namibia; it directed the PANA Director General to assign competent journalists in southern Africa to inform Africa and the world about the struggle against *apartheid*.

GENERAL ASSEMBLY ACTION

On 10 December, the General Assembly adopted **resolution 40/64 D** by recorded vote.

Public information and public action against *apartheid*

The General Assembly,

Reaffirming its resolutions on public information and public action against *apartheid*, including in particular resolution 39/72 E of 13 December 1984,

Having considered the special report of the Special Committee against *Apartheid* on concerted international action for the elimination of *apartheid*,

Recognizing the inescapable moral challenge by the inhuman system of *apartheid* in South Africa,

Reaffirming its solidarity with the just struggle of the people of South Africa for the elimination of *apartheid* and the exercise of the right of self-determination by that people as a whole, irrespective of race, colour or creed,

Recognizing the important role of public information and public involvement in international efforts for the elimination of *apartheid*,

Condemning the racist régime of South Africa and its collaborators for their nefarious propaganda to confuse and divert public attention from the evils of *apartheid*,

Considering that the United Nations has a special responsibility to disseminate as widely as possible information on the inhumanity of *apartheid*, including the escalation of racist violence by the régime against the black majority, the just struggle of the oppressed people of South Africa and the action by the international community for the elimination of *apartheid*,

Recognizing the importance of contributions by Governments, non-governmental organizations, information media and individuals towards such efforts,

Welcoming and commending the relevant activities of many trade unions, artists, athletes and other individuals committed to freedom and human dignity,

Noting with concern the recent measure imposed by the racist régime further to restrict the freedom of the press and information media to report on the situation prevailing in South Africa,

1. *Commends* the efforts of the Special Committee against *Apartheid* and endorses the recommendations contained in its special report to further enhance the dissemination of information on the evils of *apartheid;*

2. *Encourages* the Special Committee and the Centre against *Apartheid* of the Secretariat to intensify their activities designed to inform world public opinion of the situation in South Africa, and promote public action in support of the just struggle of the oppressed people and the objectives of the United Nations;

3. *Requests* the Secretary-General, as a matter of high priority, to take all appropriate steps to ensure full cooperation by the Department of Public Information of the Secretariat and all organizations within the United Nations system with the Special Committee and the Centre against *Apartheid* in dissemination of information on the evils of *apartheid;*

4. *Requests* the Department of Public Information to ensure the widest dissemination of information on atrocities and crimes committed by the *apartheid* régime;

5. *Appeals* to all Governments, information media, non-governmental organizations and individuals to lend their co-operation to the United Nations in disseminating information against *apartheid;*

6. *Appeals* to all Governments, information media, non-governmental organizations and individuals to intensify further the international campaign for the release of Nelson Mandela, Zephania Mothopeng and all South African political prisoners and detainees;

7. *Appeals* to all Governments to contribute generously to the Trust Fund for Publicity against *Apartheid* and to information activities of non-governmental organizations engaged in programmes against *apartheid;*

8. *Launches an appeal* to all information media, intellectuals and other public leaders to contribute to efforts to arouse the conscience of the world against *apartheid;*

9. *Fully supports* the efforts of the information media to continue, in the face of great difficulty, danger and official curbs, to keep the world informed of the truth.

General Assembly resolution 40/64 D
10 December 1985   Meeting 111   150-0-5 (recorded vote)

62-nation draft (A/40/L.29 & Corr.1); agenda item 35.
Sponsors: Afghanistan, Algeria, Angola, Antigua and Barbuda, Benin, Burkina Faso, Burundi, Byelorussian SSR, Cameroon, Cape Verde, Comoros, Congo, Cuba, Democratic Yemen, Djibouti, Egypt, Equatorial Guinea, Ethiopia, Gambia, German Democratic Republic, Ghana, Guinea, Guinea-Bissau, Guyana, India, Indonesia, Iran, Iraq, Kenya, Lao People's Democratic Republic, Lebanon, Liberia, Libyan Arab Jamahiriya, Madagascar, Malaysia, Mali, Mauritania, Mauritius, Mongolia, Morocco, Mozambique, Nicaragua, Niger, Nigeria, Papua New Guinea, Romania, Rwanda, Sao Tome and Principe, Senegal, Sierra Leone, Somalia, Sudan, Syrian Arab Republic, Tunisia, Uganda, Ukrainian SSR, United Republic of Tanzania, Viet Nam, Yugoslavia, Zaire, Zambia, Zimbabwe.
Financial implications. 5th Committee, A/40/1022; S-G, A/C.5/40/76.
Meeting numbers. GA 40th session: 5th Committee 58; plenary 51-57, 111.

Recorded vote in Assembly as follows:

In favour: Afghanistan, Albania, Algeria, Angola, Antigua and Barbuda, Argentina, Australia, Austria, Bahamas, Bahrain, Bangladesh, Barbados, Belgium, Belize, Benin, Bhutan, Bolivia, Botswana, Brazil, Brunei Darussalam, Bulgaria, Burkina Faso, Burma, Burundi, Byelorussian SSR, Cameroon, Canada, Cape Verde, Central African Republic, Chad, Chile, China, Colombia, Comoros, Congo, Costa Rica, Cuba, Cyprus, Czechoslovakia, Democratic Kampuchea, Democratic Yemen, Denmark, Djibouti, Dominican Republic, Ecuador, Egypt, El Salvador, Equatorial Guinea, Ethiopia, Fiji, Finland, France, Gabon, Gambia, German Democratic Republic, Germany, Federal Republic of, Ghana, Greece, Guatemala, Guinea, Guinea-Bissau, Guyana, Haiti, Honduras, Hungary, Iceland, India, Indonesia, Iran, Iraq, Ireland, Italy, Ivory Coast, Jamaica, Japan, Jordan, Kenya, Kuwait, Lao People's Democratic Republic, Lebanon, Lesotho, Liberia, Libyan Arab Jamahiriya, Luxembourg, Madagascar, Malaysia, Maldives, Mali, Malta, Mauritania, Mauritius, Mexico, Mongolia, Morocco, Mozambique, Nepal, Netherlands, New Zealand, Nicaragua, Niger, Nigeria, Norway, Oman, Pakistan, Panama, Papua New Guinea, Peru, Philippines, Poland, Portugal, Qatar, Romania, Rwanda, Saint Lucia, Saint Vincent and the Grenadines, Samoa, Sao Tome and Principe, Saudi Arabia, Senegal, Seychelles, Sierra Leone, Singapore, Solomon Islands, Somalia, Spain, Sri Lanka, Sudan, Suriname, Swaziland, Sweden, Syrian Arab Republic, Thailand, Togo, Trinidad and Tobago, Tunisia, Turkey, Uganda, Ukrainian SSR, USSR, United Arab Emirates, United Republic of Tanzania, Uruguay, Vanuatu, Venezuela, Viet Nam, Yemen, Yugoslavia, Zaire, Zambia, Zimbabwe.

Against: None.

Abstaining: Grenada, Israel, Malawi, United Kingdom, United States.

Speaking in explanation of vote, the United States said it did not believe that States' reactions to *apartheid* should be mandated by the Assembly. Ireland considered it important that information about *apartheid* practices have wide dissemination, and it expressed concern at the current restrictions on the media in South Africa in relation to their reporting of the situation there. Belgium voted for the resolution despite serious reservations on some paragraphs.

The Assembly took related action in **resolution 40/64 E**, in which it requested the Secretary-General to render, through DPI and the Centre against *Apartheid*, assistance to the Committee against *Apartheid* in disseminating information on the collaboration between Israel and South Africa. In **resolution 40/52**, it appealed to mass media, trade unions and other NGOs, as well as individuals, to intensify efforts to mobilize international public opinion against *apartheid* and to work for the enforcement of economic and other sanctions against South Africa and for systematic divestment in corporations doing business there.

By **resolution 40/164 A**, the Assembly urged DPI and the mass media world-wide to intensify their dissemination of *apartheid* information, taking account of recent measures and official censorship imposed on the media. The Assembly also

approved the recommendations of the Committee on Information, among them a proposal that the Secretary-General be requested to intensify his efforts, within existing resources, to disseminate information on the struggle of the oppressed people of South Africa; another called for DPI to ensure a more coherent coverage of the United Nations, especially in its priority areas, including the struggle against *apartheid*.

Non-governmental organizations

The Special Committee against *Apartheid* reported that non-governmental organizations, in particular anti-*apartheid* movements, had intensified their activities in support of the liberation struggle in South Africa.[1] On 25 and 26 November 1985, the Committee invited several NGOs and anti-*apartheid* organizations to discuss the programme of action against *apartheid*. Their representatives and those of national liberation movements and some individuals concerned with the situation in southern Africa participated in the strategy session and adopted a statement setting out recommendations for action by NGOs.[167] The session agreed on the necessity for the Committee, in co-operation with anti-*apartheid* movements, to intensify the campaign to secure the imposition by the United Nations of mandatory comprehensive sanctions against South Africa in order to eradicate *apartheid*, halt South Africa's aggression against the front-line States, and compel it to end its occupation of Namibia. The session believed that the campaign should be aimed at exposing the role of the United States and the United Kingdom, which had blocked the adoption of sanctions, to end their support of the régime.

In addition to enforcing the mandatory arms embargo, the session called for mandatory embargoes on oil, nuclear collaboration and high technology exports, including computers and electronic equipment. It recommended a campaign to stop all air links with South Africa and Namibia, as well as sports, cultural, academic and similar boycotts. It requested the Committee to ensure monitoring and to develop co-operation with anti-*apartheid* movements.

GENERAL ASSEMBLY ACTION

The General Assembly, in **resolution 40/64 D**, appealed to NGOs, among others, to co-operate with the United Nations in disseminating information against *apartheid*, and to intensify the international campaign for the release of all South African political prisoners and detainees (see p. 161).

Meetings, missions and observances

As part of its work to promote the international campaign against *apartheid*, the Special

Committee against *Apartheid* organized or co-sponsored a number of meetings, missions and observances in 1985.[1] It was also represented at conferences, meetings and events throughout the world.

Meetings. The Committee, in co-operation with the Hungarian Solidarity Committee, organized the International Seminar on Racist Ideologies, Attitudes and Organizations Hindering Efforts for the Elimination of *Apartheid* and Means to Combat Them (Siofok, 9-11 September).[168] The Seminar adopted a declaration[169] in which it considered comprehensive mandatory sanctions against South Africa to be one of the most effective and the only peaceful means to eradicate *apartheid*, and recommended joint action by Member States, intergovernmental organizations and NGOs to expose and combat *apartheid* and racism.

The Committee helped organize three international meetings in May—the International Conference on Women and Children under *Apartheid* (Arusha, United Republic of Tanzania) (see ECONOMIC AND SOCIAL QUESTIONS, Chapter XIX), the International Conference on Sports Boycott against South Africa (Paris) (see p. 165), and the Media Workshop on Countering *Apartheid* Propaganda (London) (see p. 172).

On 7 May, the Committee invited several student leaders from the United States to discuss action against *apartheid*, and many made statements.

Missions. In preparation for the International Conference on Women and Children under *Apartheid*, the Committee sent a mission to Angola, Zambia and the United Republic of Tanzania from 3 to 16 April to evaluate the needs of assistance to women and children refugees as well as to the front-line States. Besides holding talks with representatives of those Governments and of ANC, PAC and SWAPO, it visited various projects operated by the national liberation movements: a settlement operated by SWAPO at Kwanza-Sul, an ANC construction site at Viana, near Luanda, and a SWAPO transit camp at Viana, all in Angola; a SWAPO transit camp, an ANC day-care centre, a printing shop and a farm at Lusaka, Zambia; and an ANC settlement at Morogoro and a PAC temporary work centre at Dar es Salaam, both in the United Republic of Tanzania.

On-the-spot inspection of the settlements revealed the intolerable conditions under which thousands of women, children and elderly refugees were living as a result of the invasions and aggression by South Africa. The mission found, however, that the settlements, in particular those of SWAPO and ANC, were efficiently run and well organized. Angola had been particularly affected, since occupation by South African forces had resulted in an increased movement of displaced persons towards the north. The mission commended Governments, in particular the Nordic and socialist countries, for having provided material support to the oppressed people of South Africa and Namibia. It called for increased assistance to the national liberation movements for their women's programmes and for opportunities to be made available for training women, listing specific assistance needs for those programmes.

In its report,[170] the mission concluded that women and children fleeing *apartheid*, who constituted the majority of the refugee population from South Africa and Namibia in the neighbouring countries, needed durable asylum, food, medical care and legal protection as well as education, training and employment. Short-term or emergency assistance was the first priority. There was an increasing need to mobilize public opinion on the plight of those refugees from South Africa and Namibia. The mission suggested that the International Conference on Women and Children under *Apartheid* urge the World Conference to Review and Appraise the Achievements of the United Nations Decade for Women (see ECONOMIC AND SOCIAL QUESTIONS, Chapter XIX) to give priority to the question of assistance to women in southern Africa.

The Committee Chairman undertook three missions in 1985 to hold discussions with governmental leaders on international action against *apartheid*. He visited New Zealand, Vanuatu and India from 19 February to 8 March; the USSR and France from 24 to 30 May; and the Republic of Korea, Japan and China from 4 to 12 November.

The Chairman informed the Prime Minister of New Zealand of the Committee's appreciation for his Government's position in regard to *apartheid*, and particularly for breaking consular relations with South Africa and its statements of opposition to the impending tour of the All Blacks rugby team to South Africa (see p. 164). In Vanuatu, the Chairman was informed that the Government was mobilizing the support of the States of the South Pacific Forum for further action against South Africa. At New Delhi, the Prime Minister said that India would contribute to mobilizing the international community towards eliminating *apartheid*. The Supreme Soviet and the Foreign Ministry of the USSR expressed support for the Committee's activities in seeking comprehensive and mandatory sanctions against South Africa. In France, the Minister for External Relations and the Chairman agreed that there had been no meaningful change in South Africa and the Minister pledged his Government's support for the Committee's work. In the Republic of Korea, the Chairman called for the establishment of an anti-*apartheid* movement there. In Japan, he gave interviews to major media networks and met with anti-*apartheid* organizations to review their strategies for public action. After talks with Government officials in China, the Chairman addressed the Chinese People's Institute for Foreign Affairs under the sponsorship of the China United Nations Association.

Observances. In 1985, as in previous years, the Committee held solemn meetings in observance of the International Day for the Elimination of Racial Discrimination (21 March), the International Day of Solidarity with the Struggling People of South Africa (16 June), the International Day of Solidarity with the Struggle of Women of South Africa and Namibia (9 August), and the Day of Solidarity with South African Political Prisoners (11 October).

In addition, the Committee held a special session on 22 March to commemorate the twenty-fifth anniversary of the Sharpeville massacre, with the theme "Sharpeville, Soweto and Sebokeng: Struggle for Liberation in South Africa and International Response". In a declaration adopted at the conclusion of the session on 28 March,[171] the Committee condemned the killings and other atrocities against unarmed demonstrators by the régime, and the attack on mourners at the funeral procession in Uitenhage on 21 March. Pending the imposition by the Security Council of comprehensive mandatory sanctions, it called on States to adopt measures on boycotts and sanctions against South Africa. Furthermore, it rejected South Africa's attempt to create the illusion that it was introducing change and reform, for example, by creating the so-called new constitution.[7] The Committee reaffirmed the legitimacy of the struggle of the oppressed people of South Africa and their liberation movements by all available means, including armed struggle. It declared that freedom fighters captured during the struggle for national liberation were entitled to prisoner-of-war status and treatment in accordance with Additional Protocol I to the Geneva Conventions of 12 August 1949. The Committee condemned policies of "constructive engagement" and active collaboration with the régime followed by the United States and certain Western States.

On 26 June, the Committee held a special meeting in observance of the thirtieth anniversary of the Freedom Charter of South Africa; the Acting Chairman pointed out that the Freedom Charter had served to foster in the international community a better understanding of the struggle of the oppressed people for their just cause.

Work programme of the Committee against *Apartheid*

In its annual report,[1] the Special Committee against *Apartheid* outlined its programme of work, stating its intention to give particular attention to consultations with Governments, intergovernmental organizations and NGOs in order to promote international action in support of the legitimate struggle of the South African people for a non-racial society, to promote increased assistance to the oppressed people of South Africa and their national liberation movements and to increase public

awareness of the situation. It would continue to promote action by the public in all countries in the campaign against *apartheid*. Among its activities, the Committee would send missions, organize and support conferences and seminars, hold hearings and other events and commission and publicize expert studies. It would seek the advice and assistance of leaders of campaigns against *apartheid*, as well as of publicists and other experts, as special consultants. The Committee requested a special allocation of $500,000 from the regular United Nations budget for 1986 for special projects to be decided by it, as well as adequate resources for other activities.

GENERAL ASSEMBLY ACTION

On 10 December, the General Assembly adopted **resolution 40/64 F** by recorded vote.

Programme of work of the Special Committee against *Apartheid*

The General Assembly,

Having considered the report of the Special Committee against *Apartheid,*

1. *Commends* the Special Committee against *Apartheid* for its vigorous efforts to promote concerted international action in support of the legitimate aspirations of the oppressed people of South Africa and in implementation of relevant United Nations resolutions;

2. *Endorses* the recommendations contained in paragraphs 400 to 404 of the report of the Special Committee relating to its programme of work and activities to promote the international campaign against *apartheid;*

3. *Authorizes* the Special Committee to organize or co-sponsor conferences, seminars or other events, to send missions to Governments, organizations and conferences and to assist campaigns against *apartheid* as it may deem necessary in the discharge of its responsibilities, within the financial resources allocated under the present resolution, and requests the Secretary-General to provide the necessary staff and services for such activities;

4. *Decides* to make a special allocation of $500,000 to the Special Committee for 1986 from the regular budget of the United Nations for the cost of special projects to be decided upon by the Committee in order to promote the international campaign against *apartheid;*

5. *Again requests* Governments and organizations to make voluntary contributions or provide other assistance for the special projects of the Special Committee and to make generous contributions to the Trust Fund for Publicity against *Apartheid.*

General Assembly resolution 40/64 F

10 December 1985   Meeting 111   141-2-12 (recorded vote)

56-nation draft (A/40/L.31 & Corr.1); agenda item 35.

Sponsors: Afghanistan, Algeria, Angola, Benin, Burkina Faso, Burundi, Cameroon, Comoros, Congo, Cuba, Democratic Yemen, Djibouti, Egypt, Equatorial Guinea, Ethiopia, Gambia, German Democratic Republic, Ghana, Guinea, Guinea Bissau, Guyana, India, Indonesia, Iran, Iraq, Kenya, Lebanon, Liberia, Libyan Arab Jamahiriya, Madagascar, Malaysia, Mali, Mauritania, Mauritius, Mongolia, Morocco, Mozambique, Nicaragua, Niger, Nigeria, Papua New Guinea, Romania, Rwanda, Sao Tome and Principe, Senegal, Sierra Leone, Somalia, Sudan, Syrian Arab Republic, Tunisia, Uganda, Ukrainian SSR, United Republic of Tanzania, Zaire, Zambia, Zimbabwe.

Financial implications. 5th Committee, A/40/1022; S-G, A/C.5/40/76.

Meeting numbers. GA 40th session: 5th Committee 58; plenary 51-57, 111.

Recorded vote in Assembly as follows:

In favour: Afghanistan, Albania, Algeria, Angola, Antigua and Barbuda, Argentina, Australia, Austria, Bahamas, Bahrain, Bangladesh, Barbados, Benin, Bhutan, Bolivia, Botswana, Brazil, Brunei Darussalam, Bulgaria, Burkina Faso, Burma, Burundi, Byelorussian SSR, Cameroon, Canada, Cape Verde, Central African Republic, Chad, Chile, China, Colombia, Comoros, Congo, Costa Rica, Cuba, Cyprus, Czechoslovakia, Democratic Kampuchea, Democratic Yemen, Denmark, Djibouti, Dominican Republic, Ecuador, Egypt, El Salvador, Equatorial Guinea, Ethiopia, Fiji, Finland, Gabon, Gambia, German Democratic Republic, Ghana, Greece, Guatemala, Guinea, Guinea-Bissau, Guyana, Haiti, Honduras, Hungary, Iceland, India, Indonesia, Iran, Iraq, Ireland, Ivory Coast, Jamaica, Japan, Jordan, Kenya, Kuwait, Lao People's Democratic Republic, Lebanon, Lesotho, Liberia, Libyan Arab Jamahiriya, Madagascar, Malaysia, Maldives, Mali, Malta, Mauritania, Mauritius, Mexico, Mongolia, Morocco, Mozambique, Nepal, New Zealand, Nicaragua, Niger, Nigeria, Norway, Oman, Pakistan, Panama, Papua New Guinea, Peru, Philippines, Poland, Qatar, Romania, Rwanda, Saint Lucia, Saint Vincent and the Grenadines, Samoa, Sao Tome and Principe, Saudi Arabia, Senegal, Seychelles, Sierra Leone, Singapore, Solomon Islands, Somalia, Sri Lanka, Sudan, Suriname, Swaziland, Sweden, Syrian Arab Republic, Thailand, Togo, Trinidad and Tobago, Tunisia, Turkey, Uganda, Ukrainian SSR, USSR, United Arab Emirates, United Republic of Tanzania, Uruguay, Vanuatu, Venezuela, Viet Nam, Yemen, Yugoslavia, Zaire, Zambia, Zimbabwe.

Against: United Kingdom, United States.

Abstaining: Belgium, Belize, France, Germany, Federal Republic of, Grenada, Israel, Italy, Luxembourg, Malawi, Netherlands, Portugal, Spain.

Speaking in explanation of vote, the Netherlands was concerned that the allocation for the Committee had been increased in spite of the pressing need for budgetary restraint. New Zealand expressed reservations about some aspects of the work programme and the funding approved. The United Kingdom regretted that the Committee had failed to heed the chorus of disapproval which had been expressed in the Assembly over the past few years and which led to the United Kingdom's inability to approve the Committee's work programme—the Committee's report was an example of that tendency. The United States opposed the text because it was unable to support a resolution that commended the work of a committee advocating mandatory sanctions; furthermore, it did not believe it was desirable to increase the allocation for the Committee's work programme during the current financial difficulties.

In other resolutions, the Assembly endorsed the Committee's 1985 report;[1] requested it to intensify its activities for the total isolation of the *apartheid* régime, for promoting comprehensive and mandatory sanctions against South Africa and for mobilizing public opinion and encouraging public action against collaboration with South Africa; and requested it to keep the matter of collaboration between South Africa and Israel and between South Africa and other States under review and to report to the Assembly and the Security Council as appropriate (**40/64 A**). The Assembly requested the Committee, with the assistance of DPI and the Centre against *Apartheid*, to continue to publicize information on Israel–South Africa relations (**40/64 E**).

The Assembly endorsed the Committee's recommendations to enhance the dissemination of information on *apartheid* and encouraged the Committee and the Centre to intensify their activities to inform world public opinion and promote action in support of the struggle of the oppressed people and United Nations objectives; United Nations organizations, and DPI in particular, were requested to co-operate with the Committee and the Centre in disseminating information on *apartheid*'s evils (**40/64 D**).

REFERENCES

[1]A/40/22-S/17562. [2]A/41/22-S/18360. [3]A/40/22/Add.1-S/17562/Add.1. [4]A/40/22/Add.2-S/17562/Add.2. [5]A/40/22/Add.3-S/17562/Add.3. [6]A/40/22/Add.4-S/17562/Add.4. [7]YUN 1984, p. 157. [8]E/1985/22 (res. 1985/6). [9]*Ibid.* (res. 1985/9). [10]A/40/276-S/17138. [11]A/40/308. [12]A/40/564 & Corr.1. [13]A/40/592-S/17425, A/40/594-S/17430. [14]A/40/593. [15]A/40/601-S/17436 & Corr.1. [16]A/40/602-S/17437. [17]A/40/651-S/17470. [18]A/40/661-S/17478. [19]A/40/733-S/17546. [20]A/40/749. [21]A/40/758-S/17570. [22]A/40/761-S/17573. [23]A/40/837. [24]A/40/817. [25]A/40/840-S/17605. [26]A/40/980. [27]A/40/805. [28]YUN 1984, p. 133, GA res. 39/72 G, 13 Dec. 1984. [29]*Ibid.*, p. 138. [30]A/40/24. [31]A/40/23 (A/AC.109/830). [32]*Ibid.* (A/AC.109/840). [33]*Ibid.* (A/AC.109/841). [34]S/16957. [35]S/16986. [36]S/17006. [37]S/17108. [38]A/40/475-S/17336. [39]A/40/555-S/17402. [40]A/40/565-S/17411. [41]S/17429. [42]A/40/666. [43]A/40/745-S/17563. [44]A/40/784-S/17583. [45]YUN 1984, p. 143, SC res. 558(1984), 13 Dec. 1984. [46]A/40/265-S/17125. [47]YUN 1978, p. 915, SC res. 435(1978), 29 Sep. 1978. [48]YUN 1983, p. 1045. [49]YUN 1981, p. 165. [50]YUN 1980, p. 200. [51]YUN 1977, p. 162, SC res. 421(1977), 9 Dec. 1977. [52]*Ibid.*, p. 161, SC res. 418(1977), 4 Nov. 1977. [53]E/C.10/AC.4/1985/4. [54]A/40/455-S/17322 & Corr.1. [55]A/40/464-S/17326. [56]S/17368. [57]S/AC.20/37. [58]S/AC.20/38 & Add.1-6. [59]S/16966. [60]S/16947. [61]S/17061. [62]S/17053. [63]S/17113. [64]S/17076. [65]S/17040. [66]S/17183. [67]S/17056. [68]S/17048. [69]S/16924. [70]S/17429. [71]S/16950. [72]S/16918. [73]S/17140 & Add.1. [74]A/40/892-S/17632. [75]E/1985/28. [76]YUN 1984, p. 147, ESC res. 1984/53, 25 July 1984. [77]E/C.10/1985/7 & Corr.1. [78]E/C.10/1985/9. [79]YUN 1984, p. 146. [80]*Ibid.*, p. 857, GA res. 39/15, 23 Nov. 1984. [81]E/CN.4/1986/5 (res. 1985/3). [82]E/C.10/1985/8. [83]E/C.10/1986/9. [84]E/C.10/AC.4/1985/2 & Add.1. [85]E/C.10/AC.4/1985/3. [86]E/C.10/AC.4/1985/5. [87]E/C.10/AC.4/1985/6. [88]E/C.10/1985/18 & Corr.1. [89]YUN 1973, p. 103, GA res. 3068(XXVIII), annex, 30 Nov. 1973. [90]A/40/23 (A/AC.109/843). [91]YUN 1983, p. 147. [92]A/AC.115/L.627. [93]E/1985/22 (res. 1985/8). [94]E/CN.4/1986/5 (res. 1985/36). [95]S/16991. [96]S/17050. [97]S/17051. [98]S/17351. [99]S/17356. [100]S/17363. [101]S/17413. [102]S/17426. [103]A/40/18 (dec. 1(XXXII)). [104]YUN 1965, p. 440, GA res. 2106 A (XX), annex, 21 Dec. 1965. [105]A/40/164-S/17009. [106]A/40/514-S/17367. [107]A/40/585-S/17421. [108]S/17065. [109]A/40/518-S/17372. [110]A/41/63-S/17696. [111]A/40/217. [112]S/17071. [113]A/40/222-S/17079. [114]A/40/280-S/17145. [115]A/40/229-S/17092. [116]A/40/355. [117]A/40/521. [118]A/40/502-S/17355. [119]A/40/508-S/17362. [120]A/40/577-S/17419. [121]S/17364. [122]S/17360. [123]A/40/515-S/17369. [124]S/17374. [125]A/40/532-S/17384. [126]A/41/67-S/17699. [127]A/40/530-S/17382. [128]A/40/557-S/17405. [129]A/40/539-S/17391. [130]A/40/547-S/17398. [131]A/40/559-S/17406. [132]A/40/574-S/17418. [133]A/40/571-S/17415. [134]A/41/59-S/17691. [135]A/41/72-S/17709. [136]A/40/1026-S/17678 & Corr.1. [137]A/41/60-S/17693. [138]YUN 1977, p. 706. [139]YUN 1948-49, p. 535, GA res. 217 A (III), 10 Dec. 1948. [140]A/40/560 (S/17407). [141]A/40/749. [142]YUN 1984, p. 156. [143]S/17408. [144]S/17575. [145]A/40/572-S/17416. [146]A/40/763. [147]A/40/767-S/17577. [148]A/40/744-S/17580. [149]A/40/799-S/17589. [150]A/40/804. [151]A/40/820-S/17593. [152]A/AC.115/L.624 & Corr.1. [153]A/40/343-S/17224. [154]YUN 1976, p. 136, GA res. 31/6 F, 9 Nov. 1976. [155]A/40/36. [156]A/AC.192/L.4. [157]DP/1985/17. [158]YUN 1984, p. 168. [159]E/1985/32 (dec. 1985/14). [160]DP/1986/21. [161]ID/B/344. [162]A/40/16 (conclusion 1985/14). [163]A/40/780. [164]YUN 1965, p. 115, GA res. 2054 B (XX), 15 Dec. 1965. [165]YUN 1984,

p. 171, GA res. 39/72 E, 13 Dec. 1984. [166]A/40/696-S/17511.
[167]A/AC.115/L.633.   [168]A/AC.115/L.634.   [169]A/40/660-
S/17477. [170]A/AC.115/L.621. [171]A/40/213 & Corr.1 (S/17142).

South Africa and the front-line and other States of southern Africa

In 1985, South Africa carried out aggression against some neighbouring States, for which it was condemned by several United Nations bodies. The States of southern Africa which shared security concerns—Angola, Botswana, Mozambique, the United Republic of Tanzania, Zambia and Zimbabwe—were known as the front-line States. South Africa's aggression particularly against Angola, Botswana and Lesotho was condemned by the Security Council in several 1985 resolutions.

The situation in Angola was particularly serious, and the Council took action on South Africa's attacks against and occupation of that country on four occasions during the year—on 20 June, 20 September, 7 October and 6 December. It demanded that South Africa withdraw all its forces and decided to send a commission to evaluate the damage resulting from the invasion. After the commission visited Angola and made recommendations for assistance, the Council endorsed its report, demanded that South Africa compensate Angola for the damage to life and property, and requested Member States and international organizations to provide assistance for its reconstruction.

The Council reacted similarly on 21 June following South Africa's attack on Gaborone, the capital of Botswana. It demanded that South Africa pay compensation and requested the Secretary-General to send a mission to assess the damage. On 30 September, the Council endorsed the mission's report and called for assistance to Botswana.

Lesotho also complained about an attack by South Africa during which six South African refugees and three Lesotho nationals were killed. Condemning the violence for which it held South Africa responsible, the Council, on 30 December, demanded that it pay compensation, reaffirmed Lesotho's right to receive victims of *apartheid*, called on the parties to use established channels of communication on matters of mutual concern, and requested Member States to give economic assistance to Lesotho so that it could receive South African refugees.

In October, Mozambique complained that South Africa was assisting bandits in Mozambique, in contravention of a 1984 bilateral agreement to improve relations. South Africa responded that it was only acting to help Mozambique resist opposition forces.

Activities of the Committee against *Apartheid*.
In its annual report to the General Assembly issued in October 1985,[1] the Special Committee against *Apartheid* said that South Africa, despite accords and understandings with some of its neighbouring States, had committed acts of aggression and destabilization against them, in its effort to counter the national liberation movements of South Africa and to extract the acquiescence of the neighbouring States to its policies. South Africa claimed that the unrest in South Africa was the work of revolutionary elements who were returning to the country illegally after undergoing military training in neighbouring countries, and that it was trying to ensure that the countries concerned refused bases to those fighters. According to the Committee, the agreements brought no peace, as they were ignored by South Africa; peace in southern Africa was not possible unless *apartheid* was eliminated and Namibia achieved independence.

Since gaining independence a decade earlier, Angola had been invaded more than 12 times by South Africa, which also supported the forces of the União Nacional para a Independência Total de Angola (UNITA), concentrated in southern Angola. Although Angola and South Africa had reached agreement in February 1984 on the withdrawal of South African forces from Angola (an agreement known as the Lusaka Understanding),[2] South Africa withdrew its forces only after a long delay, leaving behind about 60 soldiers, and continued to support UNITA forces.

In May 1985, Angolan troops killed two South African commandos and captured another during their attempt to sabotage oil installations at Malonga, Cabinda province, in southern Angola. The captured commando confessed that his unit had carried out several other attacks on strategic installations in Angola. In the same month, Angolan authorities intercepted two South African night parachute drops of weapons to UNITA in the northern part of the country. As a result, Angola called off scheduled talks with South Africa. South Africa sent ground and air forces into Angola on 16 September to support UNITA forces against an effective drive of Angolan troops towards southern Angola. It admitted that it had provided aid to UNITA. Further acts of aggression by South Africa took place in October and December.[3]

In Gaborone, Botswana, two South African refugees were injured in February when their house was bombed, and a leader of a black South African trade union was killed in a car bomb explosion in May. South African forces raided Gaborone on 14 June, allegedly to attack ANC bases; 12 persons were killed. The aggression was condemned by the Commonwealth Committee on Southern Africa at an emergency meeting on 24 June.

South Africa's destabilization efforts continued against Mozambique, despite a non-aggression agreement, known as the Nkomati Accord, signed with that country in March 1984.[2] Mozambique claimed that South African agents continued to supply the rebel National Resistance Movement (MNR) with arms and ammunition. Although South Africa denied giving support to MNR after signing the accord, Mozambique obtained evidence of South African involvement when its forces destroyed camps of the MNR forces. On 13 June 1985, the Presidents of Mozambique, the United Republic of Tanzania and Zimbabwe held a one-day meeting at Harare, Zimbabwe, to discuss Mozambique's security situation and to explore ways of increasing co-operation with it. The South African Foreign Minister said at a press conference on 19 September that South Africa maintained radio links with MNR, had constructed a landing strip for its forces, and dropped supplies.

South Africa also supported rebels in Lesotho—the so-called Lesotho Liberation Army. In October, Lesotho was shelled from South African territory. South African soldiers in December killed six recently exiled members of ANC and three Lesotho citizens in an attack against Maseru, Lesotho.

Action by the Committee on colonial countries. On 16 May,[4] the Committee on colonial countries paid tribute to the front-line and other African States for their commitment to an independent Namibia. It deemed it imperative that the international community increase its support to the front-line States to enable them to resolve their own economic difficulties, which were a consequence of South Africa's policies of aggression and subversion, and to defend themselves against South Africa's attempts to destabilize them. The Committee urged States to assist the Southern African Development Co-ordination Conference (SADCC) in its efforts to promote regional economic co-operation and development and to reduce the economic dependence of countries of the area on South Africa.

The Committee, on 7 August,[5] noted that South Africa had repeatedly committed armed aggression against neighbouring countries, particularly Angola and Botswana, causing extensive loss of human lives and destruction of the economic infrastructure.

On 9 August,[6] the Committee urged United Nations organizations to extend, as a matter of priority, material assistance to the front-line States to enable them to support the Namibian people's struggle for independence and to resist the violation of their territorial integrity by South Africa, directly or, as in Angola and Mozambique, through puppet traitor groups in the service of Pretoria.

Action by the Commission on Human Rights and its Sub-Commission. The Commission on Human Rights also condemned South Africa's ag-

gression against front-line and other neighbouring States. On 26 February, it called the acts wanton and unprovoked,[7] condemned South Africa for its military pressure on front-line States and for its support to bandits who sought to destabilize the States in question,[8] and demanded that South Africa cease its aggression aimed at undermining the economies and destabilizing the political institutions of its neighbours.[9]

On 30 August,[10] the Sub-Commission on Prevention of Discrimination and Protection of Minorities condemned South Africa for continued acts of international terrorism against those States.

Activities of the Council for Namibia. The United Nations Council for Namibia, in its 1985 report to the General Assembly,[11] said that the increased militarization of southern Africa and the aggression and destabilization perpetrated by South Africa had impeded the development of the front-line States. In its efforts to intimidate the people of Namibia and South Africa and their national liberation movements recognized by OAU, South Africa had subjected Angola, Botswana, Lesotho, Mozambique, Zambia and Zimbabwe to subversion, military aggression, incursions and other forms of destabilization. Furthermore, South Africa had recruited, trained, financed and equipped mercenaries to cause instability, and supplied puppet groups with military hardware and funds.

In its Vienna Declaration and Programme of Action adopted on 7 June,[12] the Council condemned South Africa's latest act of aggression against Angola and reaffirmed that the support of the front-line States for Namibia continued to be an important factor in efforts to bring about independence. It called on Governments to assist the States to enable them to defend themselves, and to support SADCC, with a view to reducing their economic dependence on South Africa and to enable them to resist its aggression and destabilization efforts.

Communications. A number of countries addressed communications to the Secretary-General in 1985 on South Africa's aggression (for letters dealing with aggression against a particular State, see also pp. 181, 183, 189, 193 and 196).

Spain forwarded its Foreign Ministry's 19 June communiqué on events in southern Africa.[13] Noting the 1984 Lusaka and Nkomati agreements, Spain condemned South Africa's covert mission to capture oil installations in Angola's Cabinda province as well as its military incursion into Gaborone, Botswana, and urged South Africa to settle disputes peacefully. The Libyan Arab Jamahiriya, on 15 July,[14] called attention to the dangers arising from South Africa's aggression, particularly against Angola, in violation of the United Nations Charter and Security Council resolutions. On 18 September,[15] Madagascar forwarded the resolutions adopted by the OAU Council of Ministers

(Addis Ababa, 10-17 July). In one, the Council condemned South Africa for the aggression against Angola and Botswana, during which scores of innocent civilians and refugees were killed under the pretext of hot pursuit of ANC and SWAPO fighters and the elimination of non-existent military bases; it commended the front-line States and Lesotho for their commitment and readiness to sacrifice for Namibia's independence and majority rule in South Africa.

The Bahamas forwarded a communiqué adopted by heads of Commonwealth Governments on 22 October.[16] Recalling that South Africa had entered into pacts with Angola and Mozambique in 1984, they said that South Africa had nevertheless continued to occupy Angolan territory, to launch attacks against it and to support rebel movements in those two countries; they condemned South Africa's attacks on those neighbouring countries which had refused to enter into pacts with it, and especially deplored the June attack against Botswana. The President of Senegal, current OAU Chairman, in a statement of 5 November,[17] condemned the attacks on Angola, Botswana and Mozambique, said UNITA had become a movement serving South African policies, and appealed to Governments to denounce South Africa's moves.

Angola, on 5 November,[18] forwarded the Final Political Declaration adopted by the Conference of Foreign Ministers of Non-Aligned Countries (Luanda, 4-7 September). They stressed the positive role played by the front-line States, condemned South Africa for the continued military occupation of Angola, decided to increase material support to Angola, expressed concern about the concentration of South African troops along the Angolan-Namibian border as well as destabilization efforts against Mozambique, condemned the repeal by the United States Congress of the 1975 Clark Amendment which was designed to terminate United States involvement in Angola's internal affairs, condemned the June 1985 meeting in Angola of subversive renegades and mercenary groups under the auspices of the United States which constituted interference in Angola's internal affairs, condemned the use of South African territory for the infiltration into Mozambique of armed bandits which attacked the defenceless population, called for assistance to Mozambique for defence purposes, and condemned the aggression against Botswana and Lesotho.

On 23 December,[19] China condemned the recent South African invasion of southern Angola and commando raid of Lesotho, which showed the régime's continued hostility towards the black masses.

ECONOMIC AND SOCIAL COUNCIL ACTION

In **resolution 1985/59**, the Economic and Social Council requested United Nations organizations, in view of the deteriorating situation in South Africa and the acts of aggression and destabilization against States in the region, to increase assistance to the front-line and neighbouring States and to the liberation movements in South Africa.

GENERAL ASSEMBLY ACTION

In numerous 1985 resolutions, the General Assembly condemned South Africa's aggression, subversion, terrorism and destabilization against African States. It did so in **resolutions 40/56, 40/64 A and 40/64 I**, and in the last also condemned those actions aimed against refugees from South Africa and Namibia, demanded that South Africa immediately withdraw its troops from southern Angola and end the destabilization of front-line and other States, and appealed to States, organizations and institutions to increase assistance to the front-line States and SADCC in order to increase their economic strength and independence from South Africa.

The Assembly again urged the international community to increase support to the front-line States to enable them to resolve their own economic difficulties, caused largely by Pretoria's policies of aggression and to defend themselves better against South Africa's persistent destabilization attempts; Member States were also urged to assist Angola and other front-line States in strengthening their defence capacity, and South Africa was condemned for its use of Namibia as a springboard for perpetrating acts of aggression against neighbouring States (**40/97 A**). Similar condemnations were contained in **resolution 40/25** and the Assembly also condemned South Africa's use of armed terrorist groups with a view to pitting them against the national liberation movements and destabilizing the Governments of southern Africa; it called on the international community to increase assistance to the countries so that they could defend their sovereignty and rebuild and develop.

The Assembly again urged United Nations organizations to assist the front-line States to enable them to resist attacks by South African forces (**40/53**). Noting with concern that a critical situation prevailed in southern Africa, the Assembly stated that the régime had resorted to desperate measures in order to suppress by force the legitimate aspirations of the people of southern Africa and had repeatedly committed acts of armed aggression against neighbouring States, particularly Angola and Botswana, causing extensive loss of human lives and destruction of the economic infrastructure (**decision 40/415**).

Angola–South Africa armed incidents and South African occupation of Angola

Following increased South African aggression against and occupation of Angola in 1985, the

Security Council adopted four resolutions condemning that action—on 20 June (567(1985)), 20 September (571(1985)), 7 October (574(1985)) and 6 December (577(1985)). The Council also sent an investigative commission to Angola to assess damage resulting from South Africa's invasion; it endorsed the commission's report in December.

The Commission on Human Rights, the Council for Namibia and the General Assembly similarly condemned South Africa's aggression against Angola.

Action by the Commission on Human Rights. On 26 February, the Commission on Human Rights demanded that South Africa put an immediate, total and unconditional end to its unprovoked acts of aggression and withdraw its forces from Angola,[7] and condemned South Africa for its persistent acts of subversion and aggression against Angola, including the continued occupation of parts of its territory in violation of Angolan sovereignty and all norms of international law.[20] Again on that day,[9] the Commission similarly condemned South Africa for aggression against Angola.

Action by the Council for Namibia. The Council for Namibia, in its June Vienna Declaration,[12] condemned South Africa's latest act of aggression against Angola, which it said exposed Pretoria's duplicity and bad faith, and rejected Pretoria's arrogated right to transgress the borders of front-line States. It also rejected the attempts by the United States and South Africa to establish a "linkage" between Namibia's independence and the withdrawal of Cuban forces from Angola (see TRUSTEESHIP AND DECOLONIZATION, Chapter III).

Communications (April-June). In a letter of 15 April 1985 to the Secretary-General,[21] South Africa said that it remained ready, as had been agreed in November 1984 with Angola, to move the office of the Joint Monitoring Commission (Angola, Cuba, South Africa) to the Angola/Namibia border area, in order to complete the disengagement process. Ministerial talks on that move had not taken place; the move had recently been delayed due to the SWAPO annual rainy season offensive. Despite these activities, South Africa had instructed its forces to withdraw from southern Angola within a week; it trusted that this would be conducive to the withdrawal of Cuban forces from Angola, thus paving the way for a peaceful resolution of regional problems, including Namibia's independence. Over the previous 16 months, South Africa said, it had established a working relationship with Angola, having held five bilateral ministerial meetings, and it hoped the relationship would help in achieving a peaceful resolution of the problems in the region.

Angola addressed three letters to the President of the Security Council in June, reporting a deterioration in the situation. In a 6 June message,[22] Angola stated that on 21 May its forces had captured South African commandos intending to sabotage the Cabinda Gulf Oil Company compound at Malongo; their objective was to destroy the credibility of the Angolan Government with the Western Governments with which it had economic relations, and to destabilize Angola's economy and make those Governments believe that the UNITA puppet group was a valid party in a peaceful solution in southern Africa. The South African action was particularly reprehensible as it was in violation of the 1984 Lusaka Understanding.[2]

On 12 June,[23] Angola said that over the previous fortnight there had been an increased violation of its airspace as well as a concentration of South African motorized brigades and battalions along the Angolan border, leading Angola to surmise that the increased activity at the beginning of the dry season was a sign that a new invasion was being prepared.

The following day,[24] Angola requested that the Council convene to deal with the continuous acts of aggression and violence perpetuated by South African forces, resulting in the violation of Angolan territorial integrity and sovereignty.

On 20 June,[25] Brazil transmitted a 6 June telegram it had sent to Angola repudiating the South African incursion and the 8 June reply by Angola acknowledging Brazil's support.

SECURITY COUNCIL ACTION (June)

In response to Angola's complaint against South Africa, the Security Council held two meetings on 20 June. It invited Angola, Argentina, the Bahamas, the Congo, Cuba, the German Democratic Republic, Liberia, Pakistan, Sao Tome and Principe, South Africa, the Sudan, the United Republic of Tanzania and Yugoslavia, at their request, to participate without the right to vote.

Angola recapitulated the May events surrounding the capture of the South African commandos, who it said were planning to attack the Cabinda Gulf Oil compound at Malongo, more than 2,000 kilometres from the Namibian border. The arms seized by Angola, including explosives, incendiary bombs and land-mines, showed the absurdity of South Africa's claim that the operation was intended to locate SWAPO and ANC bases. Some weeks earlier, even as Angola and South Africa were preparing a ministerial-level meeting on re-establishing peace in southern Africa, plans were being made for the commando operation and South Africa was funnelling military aid to UNITA rebels. Despite South Africa's statements about withdrawing its troops from Angola, its forces remained there.

South Africa said the Angolan Government was providing facilities for thousands of ANC terrorists, actively assisting ANC in training, arming and planning for terrorism against the people of South Africa. South Africa had sought a peaceful resolution of its dispute with Angola, and had repeatedly urged it to remove ANC terrorists from its territory and to cease assisting them, but Angola had failed to respond. South Africa, which had acted in accordance with international law, would not apologize for having taken appropriate action to counteract the threat and would take whatever action was necessary to defend itself. South Africa had not recognized the Angolan régime because, among other things, it was not in control of the greater part of Angola, and because it would be incapable of maintaining itself without the support of foreign troops. South Africa called on all Council members to join it in calling for an international agreement for the withdrawal of all foreign forces from Angola.

All speakers condemned South Africa's aggression against Angola. Many countries—Burkina Faso, China, the Congo, Cuba, Egypt, the German Democratic Republic, India, Liberia, Madagascar, Pakistan, Sao Tome and Principe (on behalf of African countries whose official language was Portuguese), the Ukrainian SSR, the USSR and Yugoslavia—urged the Council to adopt effective sanctions against South Africa to deter it from its acts of aggression. India, Peru and Thailand endorsed Angola's right to compensation for the losses it had suffered.

A number of countries said South Africa's attack was a threat to regional and international security and an attempt to destabilize neighbouring States. For example, the Bahamas (on behalf of the Latin American and Caribbean Group) said that for this reason, South Africa's unconstrained behaviour ought not to be tolerated by the international community. China said South Africa remained the root of the trouble in the region, and Denmark said its conduct not only threatened regional stability but had wider implications for international peace and security. The Sudan joined those condemning the acts as a threat to international peace and security. Sao Tome and Principe, speaking also on behalf of Cape Verde, Guinea-Bissau and Mozambique, said South Africa was a permanent source of destabilization in the region as proved by its terrorist acts against Angola and Botswana. Asserting that South Africa was pursuing a policy of brutal pressure against regional countries and striving to weaken their already shaky economies, France condemned such destabilization efforts.

According to Madagascar, South Africa was responsible for repressing democratic liberation movements, the illegal occupation of an international territory and acts of aggression against States in the region.

In view of South Africa's persistent aggression, Trinidad and Tobago believed that Angola would have to continue to rely on international support to preserve its sovereignty and territorial integrity.

Yugoslavia perceived the aggression against Angola as pressure against all non-aligned countries.

Some countries, such as Australia, condemned South Africa's actions as a violation of international law. Egypt said South Africa had decided to challenge the entire international community by its raids on sovereign States, and Peru described its actions as colonialist and racist.

Some States believed that South Africa's conduct had been encouraged by the support of certain countries. Among those expressing such a view, Burkina Faso said support came from countries which had opposed sanctions against South Africa. Cuba, as well as the German Democratic Republic on behalf of the Group of Eastern European States, spoke similarly. The latter added that South Africa's actions in Angola showed that its declarations of peace were null and void. The USSR said the provocative conduct and the challenging statements made by South Africa in the Council were the result of the support given to it by Western countries, particularly the United States and the United Kingdom, and of the alliance between Pretoria and the authors of the policy of so-called constructive engagement.

The United Kingdom regarded the involvement of South African military personnel in Cabinda as illegal and an unjustifiable act of force; however, it did not endorse every formulation in the resolution before the Council (see below). Also deploring the South African action, the United States was particularly disturbed by evidence that the action had threatened the lives and property of United States citizens and companies, and it added that such instances of violence in the region underscored the importance of moving rapidly to a negotiated settlement.

Liberia, on behalf of the African Group, deplored the fact that South Africa arrogated to itself the right to transgress the borders of front-line States in violation of the 1984 Lusaka Understanding. Argentina said South Africa's actions challenged the credibility of the United Nations, while the Congo perceived them as attempts to extend of bantustanization outside South Africa.

At the conclusion of the second meeting on 20 June, the Council unanimously adopted **resolution 567(1985)**.

The Security Council,
Having heard the statement of the Minister for External Relations of the People's Republic of Angola,
Recalling its resolutions 387(1976), 418(1977), 428(1978), 447(1979), 454(1979), 475(1980), 545(1983) and 546(1984),
Gravely concerned at the renewed escalation of unprovoked and persistent acts of aggression committed by the racist régime of South Africa in violation of the sovereignty, airspace and territorial integrity of Angola, as evidenced by the recent military attack in the province of Cabinda,

Conscious of the need to take effective steps for the prevention and removal of all threats to international peace and security posed by South Africa's military attacks,

1. *Strongly condemns* South Africa for its recent act of aggression against the territory of Angola in the province of Cabinda as well as for its renewed intensified, premeditated and unprovoked acts of aggression, which constitute a flagrant violation of the sovereignty and territorial integrity of that country and seriously endanger international peace and security;

2. *Further strongly condemns* South Africa for its utilization of the international Territory of Namibia as a springboard for perpetrating its armed attacks as well as sustaining its occupation of parts of the territory of Angola;

3. *Demands* that South Africa should unconditionally withdraw forthwith all its occupation forces from the territory of Angola, cease all acts of aggression against that State and scrupulously respect the sovereignty and territorial integrity of the People's Republic of Angola;

4. *Considers* that Angola is entitled to appropriate redress and compensation for any material damage it has suffered;

5. *Requests* the Secretary-General to monitor the implementation of the present resolution and report to the Security Council;

6. *Decides* to remain seized of the matter.

Security Council resolution 567(1985)

20 June 1985	Meeting 2597	Adopted unanimously

6-nation draft (S/17286).
Sponsors: Burkina Faso, Egypt, India, Madagascar, Peru, Trinidad and Tobago.
Meeting numbers. SC 2596, 2597.

Communications (September-November). In late 1985, a number of countries addressed letters to either the President of the Security Council or the Secretary-General concerning South African aggression against Angola.

Angola, on 18 September,[26] said that South African forces had again crossed into Angola on 16 September and engaged in acts of destruction and brutality, under the pretext of countering non-existent pre-emptive strikes by Namibians. The next day,[27] Angola requested that the Council convene, in view of the South African invasion and its threat to regional and international peace and security. After the Council took action on 20 September (see below), Angola made a similar request on 1 October.[28]

Brazil transmitted a telegram it had sent to Angola on 17 September[29] expressing its solidarity with Angola following South Africa's latest aggression. On 19 September,[30] Botswana expressed concern over press reports about South Africa's land and air attack, condemned the invasion, called on South Africa to withdraw immediately from Angola and appealed to the United States to continue efforts to restrain South Africa from such aggression. Mongolia, on 20 September,[31] also demanded that South Africa withdraw its troops immediately, and called on the Council to put an end to the aggression and to condemn the States which encouraged South Africa in such acts.

Also condemning the South African aggression, the USSR, in a statement of 21 September,[32] said that South Africa, by its incursion into Angola, was attempting to save UNITA—the puppet organization used by South Africa and its Western supporters to destabilize the Government—from inevitable defeat. Noting that the invading forces had penetrated up to 190 kilometres into Angola, Viet Nam made a similar statement on 20 September,[33] demanding that South Africa immediately halt its aggression, which was aimed at aiding UNITA.

India forwarded a special communiqué adopted on 1 October by the Meeting of Ministers and Heads of Delegation of Non-Aligned Countries to the 1985 session of the General Assembly in which they condemned South Africa for its latest aggression against Angola.[34] Similarly, India forwarded a communiqué adopted on 25 November[35] by the Coordinating Bureau of the Movement of Non-Aligned Countries regarding the situation in southern Africa following the repeal of the 1975 Clark Amendment by the United States Congress. Noting that the Amendment was designed to terminate United States involvement in Angola's internal affairs, the Bureau expressed concern that its repeal indicated that the United States was contemplating assistance to Angolan rebels, and it urged the United States to refrain from assisting South Africa and rebels aided by it to subvert or overthrow Governments of southern Africa. Earlier, in September, the Conference of Foreign Ministers of Non-Aligned Countries had also condemned the repeal of the Clark Amendment (see p. 180).

Angola forwarded on 20 November[36] a statement made by the Political Bureau of the Central Committee of the MPLA/Workers' Party (Movimento Popular de Libertação de Angola–Partido do Trabalho) on the tenth anniversary of Angola's independence. The Bureau said that the developments in Angola, with direct South African intervention in support of puppet insurgent groups, were evidence of the imperialist forces' intention of thwarting Angola's revolution through South Africa to preserve their interests in the region. Encouraged by the United States, South Africa was developing a policy of open confrontation with and destabilization of countries in the region. The repeal of the Clark Amendment had neutralized any chance of success for the United States policy of "constructive engagement" towards South Africa.

SECURITY COUNCIL ACTION (September-December)

September. On 20 September, the Security Council held two meetings on Angola's complaint.[27] At their request, the Council invited Angola, Argentina, Brazil, Cuba, Cyprus, Greece, Guyana, Qatar, Senegal, South Africa, Sri Lanka and Zambia to participate, without vote, in the discussion. The Chairman of the Special Committee against *Apartheid* was also invited, under rule 39 of the Council's provisional rules of procedure.[c]

Opening the debate, Angola said that on 17 September South African armed forces had launched a massive invasion of Angola, including air raids and attacks on Angolan military units in the provinces of Cunene, Cuando Cubango and Moxico, 275 kilometres from the border with Namibia. The attack was directed against Angola's forces which were advancing towards the UNITA rebel base in Cuando Cubango. On 19 September, South African Mirage jets had bombed the Mavinga area and vast quantities of arms, weapons and other military equipment had been airdropped by the South African forces in the Cazombo area in eastern Angola. There were no SWAPO bases in Cuando Cubango and Moxico and South Africa's actions were intended exclusively to save the UNITA rebels who could not survive without such assistance. The attack was part of a pattern of similar aggression against Botswana and Mozambique. Appealing to the Council for assistance, Angola asserted that the continuation of such attacks might force it to take recourse under Article 51 of the United Nations Charter, granting States the right to individual or collective self-defence against armed attack.

South Africa said that since the disengagement of its forces as it had announced on 18 April, SWAPO forces had returned to the southern Angola border area in ever-larger numbers and had stated their intention to increase attacks on civilian targets in Namibia. Information was obtained from two SWAPO terrorists, part of a reconnaissance and sabotage team, and the tracks of some 30 others were followed to the border with Angola; South Africa then launched an operation into southern Angola, where further large arms caches for use in Namibia had been found. The contingents involved in that operation had been ordered to commence their withdrawal. South Africa remained willing to enter into discussions with Angola as soon as possible, since that dialogue was essential to resolve the region's problems, particularly the volatile Angola-Namibia border situation. According to South Africa, Cuban and Soviet combat elements were directly involved in fighting against opposition groups in southern Angola.

Several speakers rejected South Africa's justification of hot pursuit for its incursions. Burkina Faso said South Africa's pretext was fallacious. Also rejecting South Africa's pretext, France said its operations were linked to its illegal presence in Namibia and its refusal to accept the United Nations plan for Namibia's independence. India said South Africa had no business in Namibia in the first place. Madagascar, speaking on behalf of the African Group, said that South Africa's theory of preventive action was unacceptable in the framework of positive international law since South Africa was occupying Namibia illegally. Speaking for OAU, Senegal said South Africa's act of destabilization constituted undeniable aggression. Thailand said South Africa's incursions into a neighbouring country, on any pretext whatsoever, constituted a gross violation of international law and the United Nations Charter. Trinidad and Tobago said the international community should send a strong signal to South Africa that it would not allow Namibia to be used as a springboard for armed attacks against Angola. The United States said it was not sympathetic to South Africa's assertion of its right to pursuit stemming from its illegal occupation of Namibia. The USSR said South Africa was concocting inventions about a Cuban-Soviet danger in the area and it would not have the temerity to counter the will of the overwhelming majority of States without the support of a number of Western powers, primarily the United States. The Ukrainian SSR expressed a similar view. Australia, Brazil, Cyprus, Qatar (on behalf of the Arab Group) and Zambia also rejected South Africa's pretext of preventive attacks.

Brazil, Burkina Faso, China, Cuba, Egypt, Madagascar, Peru, Qatar, Senegal, Sri Lanka, Trinidad and Tobago, the Ukrainian SSR, the USSR and Zambia called for strong measures by the Council against South Africa.

Touching on other aspects of the issue, Australia questioned South Africa's proclaimed wish for good relations in southern Africa in view of its policies of destabilization in Angola, Botswana and Mozambique. Burkina Faso and Egypt said South Africa's attack on Angola was an act of defiance against the Council. Asserting that South Africa had no intention of solving the problem of southern Africa through peaceful talks, China said it had to be compelled to implement all Council resolutions. Denmark expressed satisfaction that, within the white minority in South Africa itself, the country's policy of aggression against Angola was being questioned.

Peru said the source of weapons with which South Africa carried out its attacks had to be determined. Thailand stressed that Angola had to be fully compensated for the attack. Calling on South Africa to withdraw its troops immediately, the United Kingdom stressed that it did not accept paragraph 5 of the text before the Council (see below) as endorsing the intervention of combat troops from other countries in the region, since that risked widening the conflict and exacerbating regional problems. The United States cautioned all parties to act with restraint and urged South Africa to withdraw immediately its forces from Angola.

[c]See footnote a on p. 154.

The Chairman of the Committee against *Apartheid* said South Africa, under the pretext of self-defence, was subverting and destabilizing the Angolan Government, and called on the Council to act under Chapter VII of the United Nations Charter.

At the conclusion of the second meeting on 20 September, the Council, at the request of the United States, voted on paragraph 5 of the draft resolution before it. The paragraph was adopted by 14 votes to none, with 1 abstention (United States). The Council then unanimously adopted **resolution 571(1985)**.

The Security Council,

Having considered the request by the Permanent Representative of the People's Republic of Angola to the United Nations, contained in document S/17474,

Having heard the statement of the Permanent Representative of Angola,

Recalling its resolutions 387(1976), 428(1978), 447(1979), 454(1979), 475(1980), 545(1983), and 567(1985), in which it, *inter alia*, condemned South Africa's aggression against the People's Republic of Angola and demanded that South Africa scrupulously respect the independence, sovereignty and territorial integrity of Angola,

Gravely concerned at the further renewed escalation of hostile, unprovoked and persistent acts of aggression and sustained armed invasions committed by the racist régime of South Africa, in violation of the sovereignty, airspace and territorial integrity of the People's Republic of Angola,

Convinced that the intensity and timing of these acts of armed invasions are intended to frustrate efforts at negotiated settlements in southern Africa, particularly in regard to the implementation of Security Council resolutions 385(1976) and 435(1978),

Grieved at the tragic loss of human life, mainly that of civilians, and concerned about the damage and destruction of property, including bridges and livestock, resulting from the escalated acts of aggression and armed incursions by the racist régime of South Africa against the People's Republic of Angola,

Gravely concerned that these wanton acts of aggression by South Africa form a consistent and sustained pattern of violations and are aimed at weakening the unrelenting support of front-line States for the movements for freedom and national liberation of the peoples of Namibia and South Africa,

Conscious of the need to take effective steps for the prevention and removal of all threats to international peace and security posed by South Africa's military attacks,

1. *Strongly condemns* the racist régime of South Africa for its premeditated, persistent and sustained armed invasions of the People's Republic of Angola, which constitute a flagrant violation of the sovereignty and territorial integrity of that country, as well as a serious threat to international peace and security;

2. *Strongly condemns also* South Africa for its utilization of the international Territory of Namibia as a springboard for perpetrating armed invasions and destabilization of the People's Republic of Angola;

3. *Demands* that South Africa withdraw forthwith and unconditionally all its military forces from the territory of the People's Republic of Angola, cease all acts of aggression against that State and scrupulously respect the sovereignty and territorial integrity of Angola;

4. *Calls upon* all States to implement fully the arms embargo imposed against South Africa in resolution 418(1977);

5. *Requests* Member States urgently to extend all necessary assistance to the People's Republic of Angola and other front-line States, in order to strengthen their defence capacity against South Africa's acts of aggression;

6. *Calls* for payment of full and adequate compensation to the People's Republic of Angola for the damage to life and property resulting from those acts of aggression;

7. *Decides* to appoint and send immediately to Angola a commission of investigation, comprising three members of the Security Council, in order to evaluate the damage resulting from the invasion by South African forces and to report to the Council not later than 15 November 1985;

8. *Urges* Member States, pending the report of the Commission of Investigation, to take prompt, appropriate and effective action to bring pressure to bear upon the Government of South Africa to comply with the provisions of the present resolution and of the Charter of the United Nations, to respect the sovereignty and territorial integrity of Angola, and to desist from all acts of aggression against neighbouring States;

9. *Decides* to remain seized of the matter.

Security Council resolution 571(1985)

20 September 1985   Meeting 2607   Adopted unanimously

6-nation draft (S/17481), orally revised.
Sponsors: Burkina Faso, Egypt, India, Madagascar, Peru, Trinidad and Tobago.
Meeting numbers. SC 2606, 2607.

On 30 September,[37] the Council President reported that agreement had been reached in consultations with Council members that the Commission of Investigation would be composed of Australia, Egypt and Peru.

October. Meeting again at the request of Angola,[28] the Security Council held four meetings on 3, 4 and 7 October. It invited, at their request, Afghanistan, Algeria, Angola, Botswana, Cameroon, Cuba, Ethiopia, Ghana, Iran, Kuwait, Morocco, Mozambique, Nicaragua, Nigeria, Senegal, South Africa, Tunisia, the United Arab Emirates, the United Republic of Tanzania, Viet Nam, Yugoslavia, Zambia and Zimbabwe to participate, without voting rights. Under rule 39 of the provisional rules of procedure,[d] the Council invited, at Burkina Faso's request,[38] Peter Mueshihange of SWAPO and, at the request of Burkina Faso, Egypt and Madagascar,[39] Mfanafuthi J. Makatini of ANC.

South Africa on 3 October put forward a draft resolution,[40] by which the Council would have demanded that all foreign military forces withdraw unconditionally from Angola, called on all States to respect the sovereignty and territorial integrity of Angola, requested the various Angolan factions

[d]See footnote a on p. 154.

to settle their differences through peaceful negotiation, and requested Member States not to intervene in the domestic affairs of Angola. No action was taken on South Africa's draft.

Angola said that from 28 to 30 September South African planes had violated Angola's airspace. Eight planes had bombed Angolan troops near Mavinga, 250 kilometres from the Namibian border, incurring more than 65 casualties, wounding hundreds and destroying six Angolan helicopters. The South African action had taken place just as Angola's armed forces were breaking through the last defensive position of UNITA.

South Africa said some Soviet pilots were flying Angolan planes and that the USSR was militarily involved in Angola, that it was commanding the current MPLA offensive, and that it was seeking to expand its influence in Africa. SWAPO was sending units southward as part of its terrorist campaign against the people of Namibia. South Africa would not shed its responsibilities for the region or for the security of the South African and Namibian people.

The other speakers called for the withdrawal of South African troops from Angola. Nigeria, speaking for the African Group, said there was no reason or circumstances that could justify South Africa's unprovoked aggression. It called on the Council to apply without delay comprehensive and mandatory sanctions and consider other measures against South Africa, including those specified in Article 42 of the Charter. Also calling for the application of mandatory sanctions were Burkina Faso, China, Cuba, Egypt, Ethiopia, Ghana, India, Madagascar, Nicaragua, Trinidad and Tobago, the Ukrainian SSR, the USSR, the United Arab Emirates, the United Republic of Tanzania, Viet Nam, Yugoslavia, Zambia and Zimbabwe.

Egypt, saying South Africa had proved it would not abide by Council resolutions until the Council took the steps provided for in the Charter, urged the Council to act decisively. Nicaragua, while welcoming unilateral measures adopted by certain countries to increase pressure on South Africa, said that was not enough and urged the Council to act more forcefully. Peru said that while the draft resolution before the Council (see below) was significant, it was more important for the Council to adopt a qualitatively different position and make effective use of all recourse measures available under the Charter. Zambia urged the Council to go beyond passing resolutions of mere condemnation and adopt tougher, action-oriented resolutions.

A number of speakers agreed with Angola that South Africa's attack was aimed primarily at saving the UNITA rebels. They were Cuba, Denmark, Mozambique, Nigeria, the Ukrainian SSR, the USSR, Viet Nam and Zimbabwe (for the African Group). Mozambique noted that South Africa had abandoned its justification of hot pursuit and had

acknowledged that its aggression against Angola and Mozambique was aimed at propping up its puppets in those countries.

The USSR accused the United States of preparing to provide open support to the UNITA rebels and encouraging South Africa's aggressive behaviour in the region by adopting a policy of so-called constructive engagement with South Africa. According to Viet Nam, South Africa's actions resulted from the comfort it enjoyed from its North American ally.

The United States rejected claims that it was supplying arms to South Africa and reminded the Council that it had placed an embargo on such sales; it accused certain forces outside the region of fuelling the conflict to further their own interests at the expense of peace and security in the region.

Among those condemning South Africa for its aggression, Australia said it could not condone the doctrine of tutorial or punitive aggression. Ghana took issue with some Council members' definition of South Africa's aggression as mere cross-border violence, and said those actions were a deliberate, systematic pattern of aggression aimed at destabilizing Angola. Thailand said South Africa, by maintaining forces in Angola, was defying the Council. The United Arab Emirates rejected South Africa's invoking the justification of the right of self-defence in attacking Angola as contrary to international law and called it nothing but a flagrant act of aggression.

Some countries saw South Africa's actions as a threat to international peace and security. Cameroon stated that South Africa had acquired a nuclear capability, thereby increasing the chances of escalating the arms race in the subregion and further endangering international peace and security. According to Madagascar, South Africa's latest incursion into Angola unquestionably constituted aggression as defined by the General Assembly.[(41)]

Botswana and Denmark emphasized the regional aspects of the issue. Botswana asserted that the problem in southern Africa was not the presence of Cuban forces in Angola but the illegal occupation of Namibia by South Africa and the tyranny of *apartheid*. Denmark, while urging Member States to take prompt and effective action to force South Africa to comply with Council resolutions, said the problem had to be approached not in an East-West context but in a regional one.

The United Kingdom said Angolans should resolve their internal affairs without intervention by foreign troops, and condemned South Africa's action as improper, illegitimate and counterproductive.

Several countries mentioned their support for Angola in resisting South Africa. Algeria said the non-aligned countries had consistently lent their support to southern Africa, as shown by holding their recent ministerial meeting in Luanda and by deciding to meet in 1986 in Zimbabwe at the highest level. China urged the Council to strengthen its support and assistance to Angola. According to Ethiopia, the front-line States could not alone cope with South Africa's repeated aggression and destabilization schemes and had to be assisted by nations committed to maintaining peace and security. India reassured Angola of its support and that of the Non-Aligned Movement in the face of continuing South African aggression.

Trinidad and Tobago called on the Council to reaffirm Angola's right, under Article 51 of the Charter, to defend itself.

Both Mr. Mueshihange of SWAPO and Mr. Makatini of ANC stated that certain permanent Council members had blocked the adoption of effective enforcement measures by the Council. The former singled out the United States for co-operating with South Africa to protect the UNITA rebels.

At the conclusion of the debate on 7 October, the Council, at the request of the United States, voted on paragraph 6 of the draft resolution before it; the paragraph was adopted by 14 votes to none, with 1 abstention (United States). **Resolution 574(1985)** as a whole was then adopted unanimously.

The Security Council,

Having considered the request of the Permanent Representative of the People's Republic of Angola to the United Nations contained in document S/17510,

Having heard the statement of the Permanent Representative of Angola,

Bearing in mind that all Member States are obliged to refrain in their international relations from the threat or use of force against the sovereignty, territorial integrity or political independence of any State and from acting in any other manner inconsistent with the principles and purposes of the United Nations,

Recalling its resolutions 387(1976), 428(1978), 447(1979), 454(1979), 475(1980), 545(1983), 546(1984), 567(1985) and 571(1985), which, *inter alia*, condemned South Africa's aggression against the People's Republic of Angola and demanded that South Africa should scrupulously respect the independence, sovereignty and territorial integrity of Angola,

Gravely concerned at the persistent, hostile and unprovoked acts of aggression and sustained armed invasions committed by the racist régime of South Africa in violation of the sovereignty, airspace and territorial integrity of the People's Republic of Angola and, in particular, the armed invasion of Angola carried out on 28 September 1985,

Conscious of the need to take effective steps for the prevention and removal of all threats to international peace and security posed by South Africa's acts of aggression,

1. *Strongly condemns* the racist régime of South Africa for its latest premeditated and unprovoked aggression against the People's Republic of Angola, as well as its continuing occupation of parts of the territory of that State, which constitute a flagrant violation of the sovereignty and territorial integrity of Angola and seriously endanger international peace and security;

2. *Strongly condemns also* South Africa for its utilization of the illegally occupied Territory of Namibia as a springboard for perpetrating acts of aggression against the People's Republic of Angola, as well as sustaining its occupation of part of the territory of that country;

3. *Demands once again* that South Africa cease immediately all acts of aggression and unconditionally withdraw forthwith all military forces occupying Angolan territory, as well as scrupulously respect the sovereignty, airspace, territorial integrity and independence of the People's Republic of Angola;

4. *Reaffirms* the right of the People's Republic of Angola, in accordance with the relevant provisions of the Charter of the United Nations, in particular Article 51, to take all the measures necessary to defend and safeguard its sovereignty, territorial integrity and independence;

5. *Calls upon* all States to implement fully the arms embargo imposed against South Africa in Security Council resolution 418(1977);

6. *Renews* its request to Member States to extend all necessary assistance to the People's Republic of Angola in order to strengthen its defence capability in the face of South Africa's escalating acts of aggression and the occupation of parts of its territory by the South African military forces;

7. *Requests* the Security Council Commission of Investigation established in pursuance of resolution 571(1985), consisting of Australia, Egypt and Peru, to report urgently on its evaluation of the damage resulting from South African aggression, including the latest bombings;

8. *Decides* to meet again in the event of non-compliance by South Africa with the present resolution in order to consider the adoption of more effective measures in accordance with the appropriate provisions of the Charter;

9. *Decides* to remain seized of the matter.

Security Council resolution 574(1985)

7 October 1985	Meeting 2617	Adopted unanimously

6-nation draft (S/17531).

Sponsors: Burkina Faso, Egypt, India, Madagascar, Peru, Trinidad and Tobago.
Meeting numbers. SC 2612, 2614, 2616, 2617.

November/December. On 15 November,[42] the Security Council President stated that the Chairman of the Council's Commission of Investigation had requested an extension of the deadline for submission of its report by one week, until 22 November. Following informal consultations among Council members, the request was granted.

The Commission stated in its report[43] that it had visited Angola from 13 to 23 October, stopping in six provinces including Cazombo in Moxico province (eastern Angola) where military operations had occurred in September. Because of ongoing hostilities, it was unable to visit Mavinga in Cuando Cubango province (southeastern Angola), which had also been the subject of Angola's complaint. The Commission's reconstruction of the events surrounding the reported South African interventions in September and October was based mainly on accounts of Angolan government and military officials. As far as possible, they were verified against personal observation, individual interviews and other available information.

As a result of its observations in Cazombo, the Commission estimated that material damage attributed to the September events amounted to $604,000, which took into account damage to buildings, plants and equipment, the cost of repairing a bridge over the Zambezi River, restoring electricity and water supplies and repairing an airstrip. The Angolan Government provided information about losses in the Mavinga region, where South African forces had been engaged in September and October. The Government assessed the losses at $36,084,508, and the Commission believed that the assessment accurately reflected the situation.

The Commission stressed that the estimates did not fully reflect the extent of damage suffered by Angola and did not include compensation for losses to human life and injuries, as called for in Security Council resolution 571(1985). According to Angolan figures, 86 military personnel were killed and 83 wounded in the Mavinga region. Furthermore, the estimates did not include the consequences of the latest fighting because of lack of data, or the costs of maintaining displaced persons; therefore, the real cost of damage was substantially higher than the total estimate. The Commission believed international assistance was needed to alleviate the suffering of the people affected by South African aggression, as well as refugees from Namibia, South Africa and elsewhere. International organizations, including UNDP and UNICEF, had contributed, but further assistance was needed for rehabilitation and reconstruction. The UNDP Resident Representative in Angola submitted a list of the most urgently needed items for displaced persons, which the Commission annexed to its report.

South Africa, in a 27 November statement by its Foreign Minister,(44) rejected the Commission's report as one-sided and as misrepresenting the facts, and stated that it was part of the United Nations and Angola's propaganda against South Africa. According to South Africa, the situation in Angola was the result of the civil war being waged between MPLA and UNITA; instead of allowing the people to decide their own future, MPLA had imported more than 35,000 Cuban troops and thousands of Soviet surrogates. The Commission should have reported on the suffering inflicted on the Angolan people and the exploitation of its natural resources by those elements, and should have assessed the damage done in Namibia by SWAPO terrorists operating from bases in Angola. South Africa said it was regrettable that the Council did not send a fact-finding mission to the area to establish who was fighting whom, who was directing the operations, what armaments were being used and what the Angolans wanted for their country.

The Council, meeting on 6 December to consider the Commission's report, invited Angola, Burundi and South Africa, at their request, to participate in the discussion without vote.

Presenting the report, the Commission's Chairman, Egypt, said the Commission had interviewed some hospitalized Angolan military personnel whose helicopters had been shot down by South African planes at Mavinga, as well as refugees who had fled from there. The Commission concluded that the plight of the civilian population was one of the more tragic aspects of the situation, which called for further humanitarian assistance by the international community without prejudice to South Africa's obligation to pay compensation.

Rejecting the report, South Africa again asserted that the situation in Angola was the result of civil war and that the Commission's report was nothing more than an attempt to lend credence to Angolan propaganda against South Africa. It said the Commission had ignored the presence of thousands of foreign troops in Angola and the suffering they had inflicted. Furthermore, the Council had ignored South Africa's suggestion that a fact-finding mission be sent to the area (see above).

Angola urged the Council to demand that South Africa make full and immediate reparation to Angola and to indict, punish and penalize the aggressor; failure to do so would only embolden the South African régime to continue its aggression and to undermine all that the United Nations Charter stood for.

India and Burundi concurred with the Commission's conclusion that there was need for international aid without diminishing South Africa's responsibility fully to compensate Angola.

The United Kingdom said it supported the draft resolution before the Council (see below) because it condemned South Africa's incursions into Angola, but it did not interpret anything in the text as endorsing the intervention of foreign troops, as encouraging a policy of armed struggle or as falling within the provisions of Chapter VII of the United Nations Charter. Similarly, the United States also could not support any request for assistance to strengthen Angola's military structure.

At the conclusion of the meeting on 6 December, the Council voted on paragraph 6, at the United States request. The paragraph was adopted by 14 votes to none, with 1 abstention (United States). The Council then unanimously adopted **resolution 577(1985)**.

The Security Council,

Having examined the report of the Security Council Commission of Investigation established under resolution 571(1985),

Having considered the statement of the Permanent Representative of the People's Republic of Angola to the United Nations,

Gravely concerned at the numerous hostile and unprovoked acts of aggression committed by the racist régime of South Africa violating the sovereignty, airspace and territorial integrity of the People's Republic of Angola,

Grieved at the tragic loss of human life and concerned about the damage to and destruction of property resulting from repeated acts of aggression committed by the South African racist régime,

Convinced that these wanton acts of aggression by the minority racist régime in South Africa form a consistent and sustained pattern of violations aimed at destroying the economic infrastructure of the People's Republic of Angola and weakening its support of the struggle of the people of Namibia for freedom and national liberation,

Recalling its resolutions 571(1985) and 574(1985) by which it, inter alia, strongly condemned South Africa's armed invasion perpetrated against the People's Republic of Angola and demanded that South Africa should scrupulously respect the independence, sovereignty and territorial integrity of Angola,

Reaffirming that the pursuance of these acts of aggression against Angola constitutes a threat to international peace and security,

Conscious of the need to take immediate and effective steps for the prevention and removal of all threats to international peace and security,

1. *Endorses* the report of the Security Council Commission of Investigation established under resolution 571(1985) and expresses its appreciation to the members of the Commission;

2. *Strongly condemns* the racist South African régime for its continued, intensified and unprovoked acts of aggression against the People's Republic of Angola, which constitute a flagrant violation of the sovereignty and territorial integrity of Angola;

3. *Strongly condemns* South Africa's utilization of the international Territory of Namibia as a springboard for armed invasions and destabilization of the People's Republic of Angola;

4. *Demands once again* that South Africa cease immediately all acts of aggression against the People's Republic of Angola and unconditionally withdraw forthwith all forces occupying Angolan territory as well as scrupulously respect the sovereignty, airspace, territorial integrity and independence of Angola;

5. *Commends* the People's Republic of Angola for its steadfast support for the people of Namibia in their just and legitimate struggle against the illegal occupation of their territory by South Africa and for the enjoyment of their inalienable rights to self-determination and national independence;

6. *Requests* Member States urgently to extend all necessary assistance to the People's Republic of Angola, in order to strengthen its defence capacity;

7. *Demands* that South Africa pay full and adequate compensation to the People's Republic of Angola for the damage to life and property resulting from the acts of aggression;

8. *Requests* Member States and international organizations urgently to extend material and other forms of assistance to the People's Republic of Angola

in order to facilitate the immediate reconstruction of its economic infrastructure;

9. *Requests* the Secretary-General to monitor developments in this situation and report to the Security Council as necessary, but no later than 30 June 1986, on the implementation of the present resolution and, in particular, of paragraphs 7 and 8 thereof;

10. *Decides* to remain seized of the matter.

Security Council resolution 577(1985)

6 December 1985   Meeting 2631   Adopted unanimously

6-nation draft (S/17667).

Sponsors: Burkina Faso, Egypt, India, Madagascar, Peru, Trinidad and Tobago.

GENERAL ASSEMBLY ACTION

On several occasions in 1985, the General Assembly condemned the repeated acts of aggression and the continued occupation of southern Angola and demanded the immediate and unconditional withdrawal of the South African troops. It did so in **resolutions 40/25, 40/64 B, 40/64 I and 40/97 A**.

Botswana–South Africa armed incidents

In 1985, the Security Council adopted two resolutions after Botswana complained that South Africa had attacked its capital, Gaborone. In June (resolution 568(1985)), the Council condemned the attack and requested the Secretary-General to send a mission to assess the damage and to propose how to strengthen Botswana's capacity to receive South African refugees. The Council endorsed the mission's report in September (resolution 572(1985)).

Communications. On 14 June,[45] Botswana informed the President of the Security Council that, during an attack on Gaborone that morning by South African forces, 12 persons were killed, including three women and a five-year-old child, and six injured, and four houses were demolished. The raiders apparently entered the country by road. Such violence was particularly deplorable considering Botswana's repeated assurances that it did not permit its territory to be used to launch attacks against neighbouring countries. On 17 June,[46] Botswana requested that the Council convene to consider the situation arising from the attack.

In a statement of 14 June,[47] South Africa provided its version of the events. It said it had repeatedly warned Botswana to curtail the activities of ANC members inside Botswana and in particular their planning and execution of terrorist activities in South Africa, and had provided Botswana with information on such activities. South Africa had no alternative but to protect itself from the increasing terrorist attacks emanating from Botswana.

Several letters were sent to the Council President or the Secretary-General condemning the attack. On 14 June,[48] Zimbabwe said the raid, following closely on the raid into Angola (see p. 180), showed that South Africa was ready to intensify its military aggression against and destabilization of regional

States and also showed the culpability of those nations which continued to support Pretoria. Democratic Kampuchea, on 17 June,[49] said the attack was another premeditated crime by South Africa and demanded that it end its aggression, destabilization and intimidation against its neighbours. Italy forwarded a 19 June EC declaration,[50] stating that South Africa's action ran counter to the continuation of a dialogue aimed at seeking peaceful solutions to the region's problems. Liberia transmitted a 20 June letter[51] from Oliver Tambo, President of ANC, stating that South Africa had undertaken the raid under the pretext of dealing with so-called terrorism, when all Botswana had done was to provide refuge to people in accordance with international law and morality; ANC urged the Council to impose comprehensive mandatory sanctions against South Africa. Brazil expressed solidarity with Botswana on 20 June,[52] as did the Sudan, on 21 June;[53] the latter also called on the Council to take deterrent measures such as comprehensive mandatory sanctions.

SECURITY COUNCIL ACTION (June)

The Council held two meetings on 21 June to consider Botswana's complaint. It invited the Bahamas, Benin, Botswana, the German Democratic Republic, Lesotho, Liberia, Seychelles, South Africa, the Sudan, Swaziland and the United Republic of Tanzania, at their request, to participate without vote in the discussion. It also invited, under rule 39 of its provisional rules of procedure,[e] a Vice-Chairman of the Special Committee against *Apartheid.*

Opening the debate, Botswana said that the invasion was the culmination of a progressively aggressive South African attitude towards Botswana that had intensified as agitation for change had grown inside South Africa. Botswana had never allowed and would not allow its territory to be used as a base for ANC guerrilla operations against South Africa, and South African commandos had not found one military camp or centre in Gaborone. However, Botswana gave political asylum to South African refugees and would continue to do so regardless of the consequences. Botswana believed that a solution to the region's problems lay solely in ending *apartheid* in South Africa.

South Africa said it had sent a message to Botswana expressing regret at the loss of innocent life in the operation against ANC targets. The operation was begun after repeated requests to Botswana to curtail ANC's terrorist activities against South Africa originating from its territory went unheeded. Botswana's failure to do so left South Africa no alternative but to take steps to prevent such acts from being planned and executed from Botswana and other neighbouring States. South Africa said that although it was committed to resolving differences with its neighbours

peacefully, it would not hesitate to take whatever action was necessary for its defence.

All other speakers condemned South Africa's attack and several urged the Council to act effectively. They were Benin, Burkina Faso, China, Denmark, Egypt, France, the German Democratic Republic, India, Lesotho, Liberia, the Sudan, the Ukrainian SSR, the USSR and the United Republic of Tanzania.

Some countries drew a parallel between South Africa's attack against Botswana and other conflicts in the region. The Bahamas, for example, said South Africa's actions in Namibia, Angola and Botswana proved that it could not be coaxed into peaceful change. France said the attack, which coincided with developments in Namibia, underlined the close interconnection of the problems of southern Africa. According to the USSR, the events in Botswana and Angola showed that they formed an inseparable part of South Africa's policy of force and destabilization of the sovereign States of the region, to preserve *apartheid* at any cost. However, Australia believed that notwithstanding the coincidence of three consecutive Council debates in the previous few days on developments in Namibia, Angola and Botswana, the issues had to be stated clearly and unequivocally in response to each specific situation.

A number of countries raised questions about South Africa's sincerity in explaining its reasons for the attack. Denmark said South Africa's assertion that its attack against Botswana had been carried out after careful deliberations and calculations confirmed South Africa's hypocrisy when it declared its willingness to co-operate with its neighbours in controlling cross-border violations. Egypt saw it as ironic for South Africa to call on Botswana, which had no army, to enter into a non-aggression pact. Lesotho observed that the reasons given by South Africa for its attack were nearly identical to the reasons advanced for the attacks against its other neighbours. The Sudan said all military operations undertaken by national liberation movements were being planned and executed from within South Africa itself and not from the territory of front-line States. India rejected South Africa's invoking international law to justify its attack on Botswana, and Swaziland rejected its invoking Article 51 of the Charter which recognized the right of self-defence.

Benin criticized the lack of political will on the part of some Powers to act firmly in the face of South Africa's aggressive actions. Similarly, Liberia criticized certain permanent Council members for tolerating those actions. The German Democratic Republic accused imperialist circles of collaboration with the South African régime. The Ukrainian SSR believed that certain Western Powers shared responsibility for South Africa's

[e] See footnote a on p. 154.

acts. The United Republic of Tanzania called on countries providing support to South Africa to cease appeasing it.

While recognizing the complexities of the internal situation in South Africa, the United Kingdom remained convinced that *apartheid* had to be dismantled from within, not from without. Thailand agreed with Botswana's assertion that the region's salvation lay solely in dismantling *apartheid*.

China said South Africa's invasion, at a time when the Council was considering the question of Namibia, not only violated Botswana's sovereignty but also constituted an open provocation of the international community. Peru expressed concern that South Africa's repeated actions jeopardized the legitimate right of the countries of southern Africa to live in peace, independently and in equality.

Madagascar hoped that the mission to be dispatched by the Secretary-General to Botswana, as envisaged in the draft resolution before the Council, would enable the international community to provide assistance to Botswana to defend itself and to harbour refugees fleeing South Africa. Trinidad and Tobago said South Africa must make full reparation for its attack.

Pointing out that Botswana and South Africa had affirmed their willingness to control cross-border violence, the United States hoped that mechanisms already in place would be utilized and that the dialogue which had been under way before the raid would be resumed; it added that the draft resolution contained inappropriate language and reiterated the view that nothing in the text implied that action under Chapter VII of the Charter was contemplated. The United Kingdom said it did not interpret the text as falling within those Charter provisions or as a decision which had specific consequences under the Charter.

The Vice-Chairman of the Committee against *Apartheid* called on the Western Powers to join in the demands for effective, punitive action against South Africa, asserting that the Council's failure to adopt mandatory sanctions had encouraged South Africa's defiance of the United Nations and world opinion.

On 21 June, the Council unanimously adopted **resolution 568(1985)**.

The Security Council,
Taking note of the letter dated 17 June 1985 from the Permanent Representative of Botswana to the United Nations and having heard the statement of the Minister for External Affairs of Botswana concerning the recent acts of aggression by the racist régime of South Africa against the Republic of Botswana,
Expressing its shock and indignation at the loss of human life, the injuries inflicted, and the extensive damage as a result of that action,

Affirming the urgent need to safeguard the territorial integrity of Botswana and maintain peace and security in southern Africa,
Reaffirming the obligation of all States to refrain in their international relations from the threat or use of force against the sovereignty and territorial integrity of any State,
Expressing its profound concern that the racist régime resorted to the use of military force against the defenceless and peace-loving nation of Botswana,
Gravely concerned that such acts of aggression can only serve to aggravate the already volatile and dangerous situation in southern Africa,
Bearing in mind that this latest incident is one in a series of provocative actions carried out by South Africa against Botswana and that the racist régime has declared that it will continue and escalate such attacks,
Commending Botswana for its unflagging adherence to the conventions relating to the status of refugees and of stateless persons and for the sacrifices it has made and continues to make in giving asylum to victims of *apartheid*,
1. *Strongly condemns* South Africa's recent unprovoked and unwarranted military attack on the capital of Botswana as an act of aggression against that country and a gross violation of its territorial integrity and national sovereignty;
2. *Further condemns* all acts of aggression, provocation and harassment, including murder, blackmail, kidnapping and destruction of property committed by the racist régime of South Africa against Bostwana;
3. *Demands* the immediate, total and unconditional cessation of all acts of aggression by South Africa against Botswana;
4. *Denounces and rejects* racist South Africa's practice of "hot pursuit" to terrorize and destabilize Botswana and other countries in southern Africa;
5. *Demands* full and adequate compensation by South Africa to Botswana for the damage to life and property resulting from such acts of aggression;
6. *Affirms* Botswana's right to receive and give sanctuary to the victims of *apartheid* in accordance with its traditional practice, humanitarian principles and international obligations;
7. *Requests* the Secretary-General to enter into immediate consultation with the Government of Botswana and the relevant United Nations agencies on measures to be undertaken to assist the Government of Botswana in ensuring the safety, protection and welfare of the refugees in Botswana;
8. *Requests* the Secretary-General to send a mission to visit Botswana for the purpose of:
(*a*) Assessing the damage caused by South Africa's unprovoked and premeditated acts of aggression;
(*b*) Proposing measures to strengthen Botswana's capacity to receive and provide assistance to South African refugees;
(*c*) Determining the consequent level of assistance required by Botswana;
and to report thereon to the Security Council;
9. *Requests* all States and relevant agencies and organizations of the United Nations system urgently to extend all necessary assistance to Botswana;
10. *Requests* the Secretary-General to monitor developments related to this question and to report to the Security Council as the situation demands;
11. *Decides* to remain seized of the matter.

Security Council resolution 568(1985)
21 June 1985   Meeting 2599   Adopted unanimously
6-nation draft (S/17291).
Sponsors: Burkina Faso, Egypt, India, Madagascar, Peru, Trinidad and Tobago.
Meeting numbers. SC 2598, 2599.

Report of the mission. In response to the Council's request, the Secretary-General sent a mission to Botswana from 27 July to 2 August. In its report,[54] the mission stated that the unprovoked military attack on Gaborone had resulted in the death of 12 people and injury to 7 others; several houses, believed by the South African attackers to be occupied by ANC members, had also been blown up. The mission underlined the precarious security situation of Botswana.

Under the circumstances, the Government felt it essential to increase its defence capacity to permit it to patrol its borders. It estimated its immediate defence needs at $5.9 million. In addition, as a result of the 14 June events, there was a pressing need to improve Botswana's capacity to receive, process and administer its refugee community. Botswana had proposed at the Second (1984) International Conference on Assistance to Refugees in Africa[55] to strengthen its administrative, technical and logistic support to facilitate the reception and screening of refugees, which was later revised in the light of changing circumstances. The revised proposal estimated the cost of strengthening that support to $5,885,000, which would cover needs for housing, education and vocational training, communication equipment, transport and health facilities.

In spite of the circumstances, Botswana was determined to keep its doors open to South African refugees. The mission said the international community should enhance its assistance to Botswana in order to ensure the refugees' safety, protection and welfare. It concluded that the right of refugee-asylum countries to be secure from attack or coercion by refugee-producing countries—a principle of international agreements on refugees—was at stake.

SECURITY COUNCIL ACTION (September)

On 26 September,[56] Botswana requested that the Council convene to consider and adopt the report. Meeting on 30 September, the Council invited Botswana, at its request, to participate without the right to vote.

Addressing the Council, Botswana said the mission's report confirmed Botswana's 21 June charges and also that the attack was unprovoked and unwarranted. The fact that a state of emergency had been declared in South Africa proved that South Africa's problems were internal and not a consequence of external conspiracy. Botswana had a right to demand compensation for the damage caused to life and property. The 14 June attack was not only a serious challenge to Botswana but to the international community as a whole. Botswana called

for international assistance in strengthening its security, if it was expected to provide security for the refugees residing there.

Madagascar, speaking for the African Group, expressed satisfaction with the mission's report and praised Botswana for providing assistance to refugees from South Africa despite its economic problems and geographical situation. In this connection, Madagascar emphasized Botswana's commitment to continue, as a party to the 1951 Convention relating to the Status of Refugees[57] and a signatory to the 1969 OAU Convention on specific aspects of the problems of African refugees, to honour its obligations as a State of asylum. Madagascar also welcomed the co-operation between the United Nations High Commissioner for Refugees (UNHCR) and Botswana.

At the conclusion of the meeting on 30 September, the Council unanimously adopted **resolution 572(1985)**.

The Security Council,
Recalling its resolution 568(1985),
Having considered the report of the mission to Botswana appointed by the Secretary-General in accordance with resolution 568(1985),
Having heard the statement of the Permanent Representative of Botswana to the United Nations expressing the deep concern of his Government over the attack by South Africa against the territorial integrity of Botswana,
Deeply concerned that the attack by South Africa resulted in the loss of life and casualties to many residents and refugees in Gaborone as well as the destruction of and damage to property,
Noting with satisfaction the policy which Botswana follows in regard to the granting of asylum to people fleeing from the oppression of *apartheid* as well as its respect for and adherence to the international conventions on the status of refugees,
Reaffirming its opposition to the system of *apartheid* and the right of all countries to receive refugees fleeing from the oppression of *apartheid*,
Noting further the urgent needs of Botswana to provide adequate shelter and facilities to refugees seeking asylum in Botswana,
Convinced of the importance of international support for Botswana,
1. *Commends* the Government of Botswana for its steadfast opposition to *apartheid* and for the humanitarian policies it is following in regard to refugees;
2. *Expresses its appreciation* to the Secretary-General for having arranged to send a mission to Botswana to assess the damage caused by South Africa's unprovoked and premeditated acts of aggression and for proposing measures to strengthen Botswana's capacity to receive and provide assistance to South African refugees as well as for determining the level of assistance required by Botswana to cope with the situation resulting from the attack;
3. *Endorses* the report of the mission to Botswana under resolution 568(1985);
4. *Demands* that South Africa pay full and adequate compensation to Botswana for the loss of life and damage to property resulting from its act of aggression;

5. *Requests* Member States, international organizations and financial institutions to assist Botswana in the fields identified in the report of the mission to Botswana;

6. *Requests* the Secretary-General to give the matter of assistance to Botswana his continued attention and to keep the Security Council informed;

7. *Decides* to remain seized of the situation.

Security Council resolution 572(1985)

30 September 1985   Meeting 2609   Adopted unanimously

7-nation draft (S/17503).

Sponsors: Botswana, Burkina Faso, Egypt, India, Madagascar, Peru, Trinidad and Tobago.

Referring to resolution 572(1985) in a letter to the Secretary-General of 21 October,[58] South Africa said it did not accept that it was under any obligation to pay compensation to Botswana, and rejected inferences in the resolution that it had carried out aggression against that country or that terrorist groups established in and operating from Botswana were synonymous with "refugees". South Africa had made its position clear as recently as 25 September during talks between the Foreign Ministers of Botswana and South Africa. South Africa added that it had exercised its right of self-defence in order to curtail further imminent violence in South Africa.

GENERAL ASSEMBLY ACTION

The General Assembly, in **resolution 40/25**, condemned the unprovoked and unwarranted military attack on the capital of Botswana and demanded that South Africa pay full and adequate compensation for the loss of life and damage to property. In **decision 40/415**, the Assembly also called for the scrupulous observance of Security Council resolution 572(1985).

Lesotho–South Africa dispute

On several occasions in 1985, Lesotho complained of aggression or destabilization attempts by South Africa. Acting on such a complaint in December, the Security Council adopted resolution 580(1985), by which it condemned the violence and requested the Secretary-General to establish a civilian presence in Maseru to report any development affecting Lesotho's territorial integrity.

In its first 1985 complaint, made to the Council President on 9 September,[59] Lesotho expressed concern over statements broadcast from South Africa that Lesotho's general elections scheduled for 17 and 18 September had been cancelled. The facts were that the ruling Basotho National Party's candidates had been returned unopposed because opposition parties had failed to field or nominate candidates on 14 August, the day declared for their nomination. Lesotho also protested a South African radio broadcast by the leader of a splinter group of the Basutoland Congress Party of Lesotho that he would continue his acts of sabotage, murder and

destruction in Lesotho; in addition, Lesotho accused South Africa of involvement in the subsequent murder of a Basotho National Party candidate, his wife, daughter-in-law and and four others. Lesotho denied South African charges that it had allowed Oliver Tambo, President of ANC, to speak over Radio Lesotho.

Further letters were addressed to the Secretary-General. On 7 October,[60] Lesotho stated that the day before, Maseru had been attacked by mortar fire from South Africa which damaged property. Responding on 18 October,[61] South Africa said it had investigated Lesotho's claim and had determined that the attack did not originate from South African territory; it appeared that the attack was carried out by persons intending to harm relations between the two countries.

A series of telexes exchanged between South Africa and Lesotho from 13 to 19 December were transmitted by the latter.[62] As background, Lesotho said that the number of South African refugees flowing into Lesotho had increased as a result of growing unrest in South Africa. A plane carrying some refugees from Lesotho to Zambia was forced to return to Lesotho by South African authorities, but later they left on four smaller charter flights, under arrangements made by UNHCR. On 4 December, bandits entered Lesotho from South Africa and murdered seven innocent nationals before returning. Lesotho requested the Secretary-General to use his good offices to stop South Africa from carrying out a threatened armed attack against it.

By the first telex, South Africa requested clarification about claims that it was involved in the recent murders and responsible for supplying arms to Lesotho opposition forces. In reply, Lesotho said it had evidence of the murders being committed by terrorists from South Africa, who had been seen crossing the border. South Africa charged that ANC had a large number of trained terrorists in Lesotho, which indicated that it had not carried out its undertaking to prevent its territory from being used as a springboard for terrorist activities against South Africa; Lesotho's failure to address South Africa's security concerns was impeding South Africa's efforts to promote good relations between the two countries. Lesotho replied that it was not aware of the existence of any ANC organizations, and that political refugees were the responsibility of UNHCR. Rejecting that response as unacceptable, South Africa again urged Lesotho to ensure that its territory was not used for terrorist attacks, and added that if such actions took place, South Africa reserved the right to take whatever action might be necessary. Lesotho said it could not take meaningful action because South Africa had not provided sufficient information, such as who and where ANC terrorists were, nor had Lesotho learned of any planned attacks from Lesotho; furthermore, Lesotho reiterated that refugees who misused the privilege of asylum would not be allowed to remain. In regard to South Africa's reserving the right to take action, Lesotho said it preferred negotiation and exchange of information on all matters of mutual concern.

Lesotho, on 23 December,[63] requested that the Council convene to deal with the situation created by unprovoked armed aggression by South Africa on 19 December, when its forces invaded Maseru and murdered four registered refugees, two South Africans and three Lesotho nationals, all with ANC affiliation, who were lured into a would-be party and killed.

Cuba, condemning the attack on 24 December,[64] said Pretoria was attempting to intimidate the countries of the region and to make international public opinion believe that the difficult internal situation was due to external causes.

SECURITY COUNCIL ACTION

The Security Council considered Lesotho's complaint against South Africa at two meetings on 30 December. At their request, the Council invited Burundi, Lesotho, Senegal and South Africa to participate in the debate, without vote. At the request of Burkina Faso, Egypt and Madagascar,[65] the Council invited Neo Mnumzana, ANC representative to the United Nations, under rule 39 of its provisional rules of procedure.[f]

Speaking about the December 1985 attack, Lesotho reminded the Council that in December 1982 South Africa had carried out a similar attack. Despite the Council's action,[66] South Africa had continued its destabilization campaign through the so-called Lesotho Liberation Army, which was based, trained and armed in South Africa. Prior to the 1985 attack, South Africa had alleged that ANC members were planning attacks from Lesotho and had stated that if such action took place, it reserved the right to defend itself; however, South Africa had no tangible evidence. Acknowledging that it received refugees from South Africa, Lesotho explained that UNHCR made arrangements for moving them to second countries of asylum. Due to the situation in South Africa, Lesotho believed it likely that more would arrive in the neighbouring countries, and unless South Africa was checked there was a risk that it would behave with increasing lawlessness towards the refugees and its neighbours. By creating transit problems for people and goods, South Africa was placing Lesotho's security and economic development in jeopardy. Stating its willingness to resolve differences through negotiation, Lesotho called on the Council to pronounce the unacceptability of South Africa's conduct.

Rejecting the charges, South Africa said Lesotho was attempting to deflect attention from its internal instability and from the alienation of part of its population from the Government, which had spawned armed resistance inside the country. There was also resentment at the presence of an organization funded, sponsored and organized by the USSR and imposed on the Lesotho people by their Government. Furthermore, elements within Lesotho's security forces were sympathizers and collaborators with ANC, and dissident groups in Lesotho viewed those pro-ANC elements as their enemies. Lesotho was endeavouring to exploit the situation by addressing appeals for financial aid to the international community. South Africa had on numerous occasions sought Lesotho's co-operation to address mutual security problems and had proposed a joint monitoring mechanism, but Lesotho was unwilling. South Africa had experienced terrorist violence emanating from Lesotho, where ANC was given sanctuary under the guise of refugee status. The real question at issue, according to South Africa, concerned terrorists operating from Lesotho. It called on the Council to prevail on Lesotho to co-operate with South Africa in order to eliminate terrorism in the region.

All other speakers condemned South Africa's aggression. A number of countries, including Burundi, China, Egypt, India, Madagascar, Peru, Senegal, the Ukrainian SSR, the USSR and the United Kingdom, remarked on the recent aggression against other neighbouring States, such as Angola (see p. 180). According to India, South Africa had been engaged in a series of actions of State terrorism under the pretext of hot pursuit of ANC activists and, on the basis of such arguments, justifying them in terms of its own security, but in reality it was another instance to pursue its policy of destabilizing Governments in front-line and other neighbouring States. Madagascar noted that to date the Council had adopted seven resolutions in 1985 condemning South Africa for maintaining *apartheid* and for its aggression against neighbouring countries, but South Africa continued to ignore United Nations resolutions; Madagascar did not recognize that South Africa had a right to justify its aggression against neighbouring States by alleging that terrorist activities had been launched from them.

Burkina Faso, Burundi, China, India, Madagascar and the USSR said that South Africa's action was a violation of international law and/or the United Nations Charter. In the view of Burundi, China and Senegal, that action was a threat to international peace and security.

Among those calling for the Council to demand compensation for Lesotho were Burundi, China, Egypt, India, Madagascar, Senegal and Thailand. Senegal, for example, said that Africa called for a mission to be sent to Lesotho to assess the damage resulting from the attack, and it added that

[f]See footnote a on p. 154.

compensation to Lesotho and the victims was the very minimum that the Council could determine. In addition to calling on the Council to demand adequate compensation, Burundi, speaking for the African Group, called on the international community to provide economic assistance to Lesotho, to resist South African aggression and to strengthen its ability to receive refugees.

China, India, Senegal, the Ukrainian SSR and the USSR believed that the Council should adopt comprehensive and mandatory sanctions against South Africa. The Ukrainian SSR said that two permanent members of the Council had blocked effective measures provided for in the Charter, thereby supporting and encouraging South Africa to continue its repression, aggression and State terrorism. Similarly, the USSR said that if the protection of the *apartheid* régime in the Council continued through use of the veto by certain Western permanent members, then South Africa would continue to threaten neighbouring States and to widen the scope of its terrorism against them. Burkina Faso said that despite repeated Council warnings, South Africa continued to ignore it due to those whose aid permitted it to defy the Council's resolutions without fear of punishment.

China said South Africa, in order to cover up its own crimes, was attempting to divert public opinion and to subvert right and wrong by drawing a parallel between the South African people against *apartheid* and the acts of terrorism elsewhere in the world.

India and Thailand praised Lesotho for its policy of accepting refugees. Thailand added that any humanitarian policy regarding refugees from *apartheid* could be maintained by the neighbouring States only at the risk of border incursions and armed attacks by South Africa. Egypt supported Lesotho's view that South Africa had implicitly and explicitly threatened Lesotho, and added that the Council had a responsibility to protect Lesotho and help it receive refugees.

Both the United Kingdom and the United States called for a dialogue as a means of finding a solution. The United Kingdom said it was clear that Lesotho harboured no aggressive designs against South Africa and therefore there could be no excuse for the violation of its sovereignty and territorial integrity; the United Kingdom and the other Commonwealth countries, as stated in the Bahamas in October, appealed for initiation of dialogue and the suspension of violence. The United States said it had made clear to South Africa that it could not accept the idea that South Africa might dispatch troops for military actions beyond its borders; the solution to South Africa's problems lay rather in the elimination of *apartheid* and in strengthening its dialogue with its neighbours through all channels and at all levels.

On 30 December, the Council unanimously adopted **resolution 580(1985)**.

The Security Council,

Taking note of the letter dated 23 December 1985 from the Permanent Representative of the Kingdom of Lesotho to the United Nations addressed to the President of the Security Council,

Having heard the statement by the Honourable Minister for Foreign Affairs of the Kingdom of Lesotho, Mr. M.V. Makhele,

Bearing in mind that all Member States must refrain in their international relations from the threat or use of force against the territorial integrity or political independence of any State, or acting in any other manner inconsistent with the purposes of the Charter of the United Nations,

Recalling its resolution 527(1982),

Gravely concerned at the recent unprovoked and premeditated killings for which South Africa is responsible, in violation of the sovereignty and territorial integrity of the Kingdom of Lesotho, and their consequences for peace and security in southern Africa,

Gravely concerned that this act of aggression is aimed at weakening the determined and unrelenting humanitarian support given by Lesotho to South African refugees,

Grieved at the tragic loss of life of six South African refugees and three nationals of Lesotho resulting from this act of aggression committed against Lesotho,

Alarmed at the fact that the continued existence of *apartheid* in South Africa is the root cause of increased violence both within South Africa and from South Africa against neighbouring countries,

1. *Strongly condemns* these killings and recent acts of unprovoked and premeditated violence, for which South Africa is responsible, against the Kingdom of Lesotho in flagrant violation of the sovereignty and territorial integrity of that country;

2. *Demands* the payment by South Africa of full and adequate compensation to the Kingdom of Lesotho for the damage and loss of life resulting from this act of aggression;

3. *Calls upon* all parties to normalize their relations and to employ established channels of communication on all matters of mutual concern;

4. *Reaffirms* Lesotho's right to receive and give sanctuary to the victims of *apartheid* in accordance with its traditional practice, humanitarian principles and its international obligations;

5. *Requests* Member States to extend urgently all necessary economic assistance to Lesotho in order to strengthen its capacity to receive, maintain and protect South African refugees in Lesotho;

6. *Calls upon* the South African Government to resort to peaceful means in resolving international problems in accordance with the Charter of the United Nations and the Declaration on Principles of International Law concerning Friendly Relations and Co-operation among States in accordance with the Charter of the United Nations;

7. *Further calls* upon South Africa to live up to its commitment not to destabilize neighbouring countries nor to allow its territory to be used as a springboard for attacks against neighbouring countries and to declare publicly that it will, in future, comply with provisions

of the Charter of the United Nations and that it will not commit acts of violence against Lesotho, either directly or through its proxies;

8. *Demands* that South Africa forthwith take meaningful steps towards the dismantling of *apartheid;*

9. *Requests* the Secretary-General to establish, in consultation with the Government of Lesotho, an appropriate presence comprising one or two civilians in Maseru, for the purpose of keeping him informed of any development affecting the territorial integrity of Lesotho;

10. *Further requests* the Secretary-General, through appropriate means, to monitor the implementation of the present resolution and the prevailing situation and to report to the Security Council as the situation demands;

11. *Decides* to remain seized of the matter.

Security Council resolution 580(1985)

30 December 1985   Meeting 2639   Adopted unanimously

6-nation draft (S/17701).
Sponsors: Burkina Faso, Egypt, India, Madagascar, Peru, Trinidad and Tobago.
Meeting numbers. SC 2638, 2639.

GENERAL ASSEMBLY ACTION

The General Assembly, by **resolution 40/25**, condemned South Africa for its acts of destabilization, armed aggression and economic blockade against Lesotho and urged the international community to extend maximum assistance to Lesotho to enable it to fulfil its international humanitarian obligations towards refugees and to use influence on South Africa so that it would desist from such terrorist acts.

Mozambique-South Africa relations

In 1985, Mozambique complained of South Africa's attempts to destabilize the Mozambique Government by aiding opposition forces.

On 31 October,[67] it submitted photocopies of extracts from documents it said were seized from armed bandits at Gorongoza, in Sofala province of Mozambique, which confirmed the continuing support the bandits were receiving from South Africa in violation of the Agreement on Non-Aggression and Good Neighbourliness (the Nkomati Accord) signed by Mozambique and South Africa in March 1984.[68] South Africa, responding on 6 December 1985,[69] reaffirmed its commitment to the Nkomati Accord. South Africa said that at a meeting of the Foreign Ministers of the two countries at Maputo on 16 September, Mozambique had submitted a list of alleged South African violations of the Accord, which South Africa had investigated. The allegations were in general correct, but they had arisen from South Africa's efforts, at Mozambique's request, to bring about a possible cease-fire between Mozambique and a rebel group. The results of the investigation were conveyed to Mozambique at a meeting at Komatipoort on 19 September; since then, Mozambique had not communicated to South Africa any further allegations.

The Non-Aligned Movement condemned South Africa's use of armed bandits against Mozambique on 7 September[18] (see p. 180).

REFERENCES

[1]A/40/22-S/17562. [2]YUN 1984, p. 178. [3]A/41/22-S/18360. [4]A/40/23 (A/AC.109/830). [5]*Ibid.* (A/AC.109/841). [6]*Ibid.* (A/AC.109/843). [7]E/1985/22 (res. 1985/6). [8]*Ibid.* (res. 1985/8). [9]*Ibid.* (res. 1985/9). [10]E/CN.4/1986/5 (res. 1985/6). [11]A/40/24. [12]A/40/375-S/17262. [13]A/40/395-S/17288. [14]A/40/485-S/17341. [15]A/40/666. [16]A/40/817. [17]A/40/857. [18]A/40/854-S/17610 & Corr.1. [19]A/41/63-S/17696. [20]E/1985/22 (res. 1985/7). [21]A/40/233-S/17101. [22]S/17246. [23]S/17263. [24]S/17267. [25]S/17294. [26]S/17472. [27]S/17474. [28]S/17510. [29]A/40/658-S/17475. [30]A/40/665-S/17480. [31]S/17487. [32]A/40/676-S/17491. [33]A/40/683-S/17498. [34]A/40/699-S/17518. [35]A/40/951-S/17656. [36]S/17645. [37]S/17506. [38]S/17525. [39]S/17541. [40]S/17522. [41]YUN 1974, p. 847, GA res. 3314((XXIX), annex, 14 Dec. 1974. [42]S/17635. [43]S/17648. [44]S/17662. [45]S/17274. [46]S/17279. [47]S/17282. [48]S/17278. [49]S/17283. [50]A/40/396-S/17289. [51]S/17290. [52]S/17314. [53]A/40/418-S/17310. [54]S/17453. [55]YUN 1984, p. 943. [56]S/17497. [57]YUN 1951, p. 520. [58]S/17586. [59]S/17454. [60]S/17547. [61]S/17579. [62]S/17689. [63]S/17692. [64]A/41/68-S/17704. [65]S/17700. [66]YUN 1982, p. 317, SC res. 527(1982), 15 Dec. 1982. [67]A/40/839-S/17604. [68]YUN 1984, p. 184. [69]A/40/1004-S/17677.

Chad-Libyan Arab Jamahiriya dispute

The territorial dispute between Chad and the Libyan Arab Jamahiriya was again brought before the United Nations in 1985 (for other questions concerning the Libyan Arab Jamahiriya, see p. 258 and LEGAL QUESTIONS, Chapter I). The two States again made charges against each other through letters to the President of the Security Council and at a Council meeting. In January, the Council met at Chad's request but took no action.

On 25 January,[1] Chad called for a Council meeting to resume consideration of its August 1983 complaint against the Libyan Arab Jamahiriya,[2] charging that the Jamahiriya was occupying 550,000 square kilometres of Chadian territory, that it refused to follow the terms of the Council's April 1983 statement[3] in which the two countries were called on to settle their differences quickly and peacefully, and that the Libyan Government was planning an attack on Chad's President, Hissein Habré. Three days later, Chad again called for a Council meeting to consider the situation,[4] reiterating its charges and adding that the Tripoli régime had plotted to eliminate physically the President and all members of the Chadian Government.

These claims were denied by the Libyan Arab Jamahiriya on 28 January.[5] It stated that it had no forces in Chad and that it did not wish to deal with the so-called Government of Hissein Habré, since it considered him a rebel with no right to speak for Chad, who was leading the opposition in a civil war against the legal Government there.

On 30 January, the Council met to consider Chad's complaint.

Meeting number. SC 2567.

The Council invited Chad and the Libyan Arab Jamahiriya to participate in the discussion without the right to vote.

Chad said that over the previous 20 years the Libyan Arab Jamahiriya had attempted to annex Chad. Currently, the entire prefecture of Borkou-Ennedi-Tibesti was occupied. The Jamahiriya based its claim on the 1935 Laval-Mussolini Treaty, which had no legal validity since there had never been an exchange of instruments of ratification between France and Italy. Suffering from drought and hunger, Chad had limited resources and could ill afford the war imposed on it by the Tripoli régime. In Chad's view, President Habré was the main obstacle to the Jamahiriya's expansionist designs. Chad appealed to Member States to condemn the assassination plot fomented by the Jamahiriya. Chad hoped that its providing data on the plot, supported by a video tape showing what it described as an attempt to place an explosive device in the Chamber of Commerce in N'Djamena, would contribute to international efforts to foil terrorism.

Rejecting the allegations, the Libyan Arab Jamahiriya said it did not interfere in Chad and had no presence on its territory. What had been described by some as a presence of Libyan forces were only forces of the legitimate Government which controlled northern Chad and were present throughout the country. The purpose of Mr. Habré in convening the Council meeting was to slander the Jamahiriya by depicting it as an aggressor; to belittle the military power of the legitimate Government of Chad, headed by Goukouni Weddey; and to create justification for Mr. Habré to obtain more weapons, foreign forces and mercenaries to use against his opponents. Mr. Habré had impeded conciliation efforts between the warring factions in Chad by insisting on his being recognized as head of State. The only solution to the civil war was national reconciliation in accordance with the Lagos Accord signed by the 11 Chadian parties on 18 August 1979, under OAU supervision. The Libyan Arab Jamahiriya remained ready to contribute again to reconciliation efforts within the OAU framework to achieve peace and security in Chad. The Jamahiriya asserted that the so-called Aouzou Strip was an integral part of its territory which it had inherited from Italian colonialism.

The President of the Council pointed out that the complaint under consideration came from the internationally recognized Government of Chad, whose legitimacy could not be challenged in the Council. It was at that Government's request that the Council President, speaking on behalf of its members, had made known in April 1983[3] the recommendations of the Council regarding the settlement of the dispute between Chad and the Libyan Arab Jamahiriya.

At the end of the meeting, the President stated that the date of the next Council meeting to consider Chad's complaint would be decided during consultations with Council members. No further meetings on the subject were held in 1985.

The Libyan Arab Jamahiriya, in a letter of 1 February,[6] stated that the remarks made by the Council's January President (France) at the conclusion of the meeting represented the viewpoint of France alone. The Jamahiriya noted with regret that this was the second occasion on which a Council President has exceeded his/her power and used the presidency to express the view of his/her country. In that connection the Jamahiriya cited the April 1983 statement[3] made by the then Council President (United States). In response, France requested the Office of Legal Affairs of the Secretariat to give its opinion on the question, which France transmitted on 5 February.[7] The Office noted that the Credentials Committee of the 1984 General Assembly session had accepted, without dissent, credentials for Chad signed by President Hissein Habré, and therefore the Assembly had recognized the right of the Government concerned to represent Chad in the United Nations at that time.

On 4 February,[8] Chad transmitted a White Paper entitled "Kadhafi's terrorism in Chad", describing alleged attacks against it by the Libyan Arab Jamahiriya.

The OAU Assembly of Heads of State and Government (Addis Ababa, Ethiopia, 18-20 July) adopted a resolution[9] renewing the mandate of the President of the Congo, in close collaboration with the current OAU Chairman, to pursue the search for peace and national reconciliation in Chad and appealing to all conflicting parties to co-operate fully. In the Final Political Declaration adopted by the Conference of Foreign Ministers of Non-Aligned Countries (Luanda, Angola, 4-7 September),[10] the Conference expressed support for OAU efforts for national reconciliation and the establishment of a lasting peace in Chad without foreign interference, and urged the international community to contribute to Chad's national reconstruction.

REFERENCES

(1)S/16906. (2)YUN 1983, p. 184. (3)*Ibid.*, p. 183. (4)S/16911. (5)S/16912. (6)S/16922. (7)S/16942. (8)S/16923. (9)A/40/666. (10)A/40/854-S/17610 & Corr.1.

Burkina Faso-Mali dispute

On 31 December 1985,[1] Senegal transmitted to the Secretary-General an appeal that its President, in his capacity as current Chairman of OAU, had sent to Burkina Faso and Mali, asking them to order an immediate cease-fire following serious developments on 25 December in the ongoing frontier dispute between the two countries. It was noted in the appeal that the International Court of Justice was already seized of the legal aspect of the dispute (see LEGAL QUESTIONS, Chapter I) and that the OAU Council of Ministers of the Agreement on Non-Aggression and Assistance in Matters of Defence was scheduled to meet on 28 December in order to take practical measures required in the disputed area.

REFERENCE
[1]A/41/71.

Ethiopia-Somalia dispute

Somalia, in a 20 September letter to the Secretary-General,[1] said that on 15 and 16 September Ethiopian forces had carried out artillery and aerial attacks on the populated areas of Audal, Mudugh, Abud-Waaq and north-west regions of Somalia, killing 23 people, wounding 36, and destroying houses. Ethiopia responded on 25 September,[2] rejecting the charges and stating that the people of Somalia who were opposed to the dictatorial régime of Siad Barre were engaged in armed rebellion; the reasons for the baseless allegations against Ethiopia could be understood only in the context of Somalia's attempts to divert world attention from its internal difficulties arising from the ongoing civil war.

REFERENCES
[1]A/40/671-S/17484. [2]A/40/680-S/17495.

Comorian island of Mayotte

The question of Mayotte—one of a group of four islands in the Indian Ocean Comoro Archipelago—remained before the United Nations in 1985. The issue was raised after a 1974 referendum, followed by France granting independence to the other three islands but not to Mayotte, whose inhabitants had voted to remain associated with France.

Secretary-General's report. The Secretary-General, as requested by the General Assembly in 1984,[1] reported in October 1985[2] on developments concerning Mayotte. In June, he had requested the Com-

oros and France, as well as OAU, to provide him with information and their responses were included in his report.

The Comoros stated that, despite its many contacts with France, including consultative meetings at the highest level as recommended by the Assembly, no positive result had been achieved. Although it was willing to participate in a dialogue to find a speedy solution, the Comoros said that it had been confronted by a barrier of incomprehension on the French side and that the situation in Mayotte was deteriorating and affecting national unity.

In its reply, France said that since December 1976, Mayotte had been a territorial community (*collectivité territoriale*) of the French Republic. On 20 December 1984, France had submitted to the French Parliament a bill stating that the population of Mayotte would be consulted on whether or not it wished to remain part of France. France's policy continued to take into account the regional context of Mayotte; thus, it encouraged the development and normalization of relations between Mayotte and neighbouring States, particularly the Comoros. Action had been taken to establish good-neighbourly relations between the Comoros and Mayotte and to promote complementarity of aid supplied for the development of the two communities.

OAU responded that its Council of Ministers, in July 1985[3] had requested the OAU *Ad Hoc* Committee of Seven, in co-operation with the Comoros, to consider ways of implementing the Committee's 1981 recommendations on returning the island to the Comoros[4] and of accelerating the negotiation process between France and the Comoros, with a view to reaching a peaceful solution. No date or venue had been fixed for the Committee meeting, OAU reported, but Gabon, the Committee's Chairman, was consulting on the matter.

Communications. In 1985, three intergovernmental organizations conveyed to the Secretary-General their policy on Mayotte. OAU put forward its position in a July resolution (see above), included with others forwarded by Madagascar on 18 September.[3] The Organization of the Islamic Conference's policy, as stated in a resolution adopted by its Foreign Ministers (Sanaa, 18-22 December 1984), was forwarded by Yemen on 11 March.[5] The Conference reaffirmed the territorial unity of the Comoros and its sovereignty over Mayotte, reaffirmed support for a global application of the results of the 1974 referendum to the whole of the Comoro territory, rejected any proposal to carry out a referendum in Mayotte, urged France to reinstate Mayotte in the Comorian entity, and called on Islamic Conference members to urge France to engage in a dialogue with the Comoros. The non-aligned countries expressed their position in a Political Declaration adopted by their Conference of Foreign

Ministers (Luanda, 4-7 September) and transmitted by Angola on 5 November.[6] They considered the island to be an integral part of the Comoros which was still under French occupation and regretted that France had not taken any initiative that could lead to an acceptable solution.

GENERAL ASSEMBLY ACTION

On 9 December, the General Assembly adopted **resolution 40/62** by recorded vote.

Question of the Comorian island of Mayotte

The General Assembly,

Recalling its resolutions 1514(XV) of 14 December 1960, containing the Declaration on the Granting of Independence to Colonial Countries and Peoples, and 2621(XXV) of 12 October 1970, containing the programme of action for the full implementation of the Declaration,

Recalling also its previous resolutions, in particular resolutions 3161(XXVIII) of 14 December 1973, 3291(XXIX) of 13 December 1974, 31/4 of 21 October 1976, 32/7 of 1 November 1977, 34/69 of 6 December 1979, 35/43 of 28 November 1980, 36/105 of 10 December 1981, 37/65 of 3 December 1982, 38/13 of 21 November 1983 and 39/48 of 11 December 1984, in which it, *inter alia*, affirmed the unity and territorial integrity of the Comoros,

Recalling, in particular, its resolution 3385(XXX) of 12 November 1975 on the admission of the Comoros to membership in the United Nations, in which it reaffirmed the necessity of respecting the unity and territorial integrity of the Comoro Archipelago, composed of the islands of Anjouan, Grande-Comore, Mayotte, and Mohéli,

Recalling further that, in accordance with the agreements between the Comoros and France, signed on 15 June 1973, concerning the accession of the Comoros to independence, the results of the referendum of 22 December 1974 were to be considered on a global basis and not island by island,

Convinced that a just and lasting solution to the question of Mayotte is to be found in respect for the sovereignty, unity and territorial integrity of the Comoro Archipelago,

Convinced further that a speedy solution of the problem is essential for the preservation of the peace and security which prevail in the region,

Bearing in mind the wish expressed by the President of the French Republic to seek actively a just solution to the problem,

Taking note of the repeated wish of the Government of the Comoros to initiate as soon as possible a frank and serious dialogue with the French Government with a view to accelerating the return of the Comorian island of Mayotte to the Islamic Federal Republic of the Comoros,

Taking note of the report of the Secretary-General,

Bearing in mind the decisions of the Organization of African Unity, the Movement of Non-Aligned Countries and the Organization of the Islamic Conference on this question,

1. *Reaffirms* the sovereignty of the Islamic Federal Republic of the Comoros over the island of Mayotte;

2. *Invites* the Government of France to honour the commitments entered into prior to the referendum on the self-determination of the Comoro Archipelago of 22 December 1974 concerning respect for the unity and territorial integrity of the Comoros;

3. *Calls* for the translation into practice of the wish expressed by the President of the French Republic to seek actively a just solution to the question of Mayotte;

4. *Urges* the Government of France to open negotiations with the Government of the Comoros with a view to ensuring the effective and prompt return of the island of Mayotte to the Comoros;

5. *Requests* the Secretary-General of the United Nations to maintain continuous contact with the Secretary-General of the Organization of African Unity with regard to this problem and to make available his good offices in the search for a peaceful negotiated solution to the problem;

6. *Further requests* the Secretary-General to report on this matter to the General Assembly at its forty-first session;

7. *Decides* to include in the provisional agenda of its forty-first session the item entitled "Question of the Comorian island of Mayotte".

General Assembly resolution 40/62

9 December 1985   Meeting 109   117-1-22 (recorded vote)

34-nation draft (A/40/L.38 & Add.1); agenda item 32.

Sponsors: Bahrain, Benin, Botswana, Burkina Faso, Comoros, Cuba, Ecuador, Equatorial Guinea, Ethiopia, Gambia, Ghana, Guinea-Bissau, Guyana, Kenya, Lesotho, Libyan Arab Jamahiriya, Madagascar, Mauritania, Mauritius, Morocco, Nigeria, Oman, Papua New Guinea, Qatar, Senegal, Sierra Leone, Somalia, Sudan, Swaziland, Uganda, United Arab Emirates, United Republic of Tanzania, Yemen, Zambia.

Recorded vote in Assembly as follows:

In favour: Afghanistan, Albania, Algeria, Angola, Antigua and Barbuda, Argentina, Bahamas, Bahrain, Bangladesh, Barbados, Benin, Bhutan, Bolivia, Botswana, Brazil, Brunei Darussalam, Bulgaria, Burkina Faso, Burma, Burundi, Byelorussian SSR, Cameroon, Cape Verde, Central African Republic, Chad, Chile, China, Colombia, Comoros, Cuba, Czechoslovakia, Democratic Kampuchea, Democratic Yemen, Djibouti, Dominican Republic, Ecuador, Egypt, El Salvador, Equatorial Guinea, Ethiopia, Fiji, Finland, Gabon, German Democratic Republic, Guinea, Guinea-Bissau, Guyana, Haiti, Honduras, Hungary, India, Indonesia, Iran, Iraq, Ivory Coast, Jamaica, Jordan, Kenya, Kuwait, Lao People's Democratic Republic, Lesotho, Liberia, Libyan Arab Jamahiriya, Madagascar, Malawi, Malaysia, Maldives, Mali, Malta, Mauritania, Mauritius, Mexico, Mongolia, Morocco, Mozambique, Nepal, Niger, Nigeria, Oman, Pakistan, Panama, Papua New Guinea, Philippines, Poland, Qatar, Romania, Saint Vincent and the Grenadines, Sao Tome and Principe, Saudi Arabia, Senegal, Sierra Leone, Singapore, Somalia, Sri Lanka, Sudan, Suriname, Swaziland, Sweden, Syrian Arab Republic, Thailand, Togo, Trinidad and Tobago, Tunisia, Turkey, Ukrainian SSR, USSR, United Arab Emirates, United Republic of Tanzania, Uruguay, Venezuela, Viet Nam, Yemen, Yugoslavia, Zaire, Zambia, Zimbabwe.

Against: France.

Abstaining: Australia, Austria, Belgium, Canada, Cyprus, Denmark, Germany, Federal Republic of, Greece, Grenada, Iceland, Ireland, Israel, Japan, Luxembourg, Netherlands, New Zealand, Norway, Portugal, Saint Lucia, Spain, United Kingdom, United States.

The Comoros called on France to honour its commitment to the unity of the Archipelago made prior to granting independence to the Comoros. In the view of the Comoros, the solution was not to be found in the repeated organization of a referendum in Mayotte; it could only be the result of dialogue between France and the Comoros.

France, stating that it shared with the Comoros a readiness for agreement on the question, said that it would consult with the population of Mayotte by referendum to ascertain whether or not it wished the island to remain a part of France. France did not exclude any development that was in keeping with international law and the French Constitution and respected the rights of the population concerned.

The United Kingdom said it had abstained in the vote because the resolution was silent on the rights of the inhabitants of Mayotte to self-determination and therefore implied that they should be considered an exception to the universal principle that all peoples have that right.

The Assembly took related action in **resolution 40/25**, by which it noted the contacts between the Comoros and France in the search for a just solution to the problem of the integration of Mayotte into the Comoros, in accordance with the resolutions of OAU and the United Nations. In **resolution 40/223**, the Assembly called for special economic assistance for the Comoros, a least developed country.

REFERENCES
[1]YUN 1984, p. 188, GA res. 39/48, 11 Dec. 1984. [2]A/40/619. [3]A/40/666. [4]YUN 1981, p. 223. [5]A/40/173-S/17033. [6]A/40/854-S/17610 & Corr.1.

Malagasy islands question

In 1985, the General Assembly did not debate the question of the Malagasy islands of Glorieuses, Juan de Nova, Europa and Bassas da India (islands north and west of Madagascar), but decided to include the item in its provisional agenda for the following year. The Assembly had postponed debate in each of the previous four years, and had not taken action since 1980[1] when it reaffirmed its first action on the question (in 1979),[2] inviting France to negotiate with Madagascar on reintegrating the islands with Madagascar.

The Conference of Foreign Ministers of Non-Aligned Countries (Luanda, 4-7 September),[3] in its Final Political Declaration, reaffirmed the need to preserve the national unity and territorial integrity of Madagascar and urged all parties concerned to initiate immediate negotiations in conformity with the resolutions of the United Nations, OAU and the Movement of Non-Aligned Countries.

GENERAL ASSEMBLY ACTION

The Chairman of the Special Political Committee informed its members on 4 December that he had held consultations with the interested parties, in particular France and Madagascar. In view of discussions being held by the two countries, he proposed that the Assembly postpone consideration of the item until 1986. Subsequently, the Committee recommended that action to the Assembly[4] which, in turn, by **decision 40/429** adopted without vote on 16 December, decided to include the item in the provisional agenda of its 1986 session.

REFERENCES
[1]YUN 1980, p. 262, GA res. 35/123, 11 Dec. 1980. [2]YUN 1979, p. 270, GA res. 34/91, 12 Dec. 1979. [3]A/40/854-S/17610 & Corr.1. [4]A/40/992.

UN Educational and Training Programme for Southern Africa

The United Nations Educational and Training Programme for Southern Africa, financed by a trust fund made up of voluntary contributions from States, organizations and individuals, granted scholarships to 929 persons in 1984/85. The Secretary-General described the Programme's activities in a report covering the period from 1 October 1984 to 15 October 1985.[1] Scholarships were given to 766 South Africans, 145 Namibians (see TRUSTEESHIP AND DECOLONIZATION, Chapter III) and 18 Zimbabweans. The Programme granted new scholarships only to students from South Africa and Namibia, but assistance was continued to students from Zimbabwe for a transitional period, while they completed courses for which grants had been made previously. During the reporting period, 318 new awards were granted while 611 awards were extended. New awards went to 218 South Africans and 100 Namibians. In addition to cash contributions, the Programme received offers of scholarships for training in their own countries from 29 States. The awards were granted for general university studies as well as a wide variety of professional, commercial and technical training programmes in 26 countries. Those receiving scholarships attended schools in the following regions: Africa (467 students), North America (276), Asia (155), Europe (30), and Latin America and the Caribbean(1).

The Secretary-General stated that due to inflation and rising scholarship costs, the 1985 contributions and pledges (totalling $3,124,430) represented, in real terms, a drastic decrease in resources over the previous year when they totalled $3,303,064. Given the worsening political situation and believing that there would be larger outflows of South African and Namibian refugees in search of educational and training opportunities, the Programme's Advisory Committee made recommendations to promote the expansion and development of the Programme. It proposed that arrangements should be made with the Commonwealth Fund for Technical Assistance to take advantage of Commonwealth countries' offer to provide placement facilities and administer scholarship awards at no cost to the Programme, and to expand a programme for South Africans in the United Republic of Tanzania. Other proposals included the use of the World University Service's large counselling network in Africa; co-operation with scholarship agencies in fund-raising, the search for applicants, and administration of scholarship awards; and promotion of co-financing and tuition waivers by universities.

Financial contributions

In 1985, 37 States contributed $3,246,427 to the Programme (see table following), as compared with $3,276,925 in 1984.

CONTRIBUTIONS TO THE UN EDUCATIONAL AND TRAINING
PROGRAMME FOR SOUTHERN AFRICA, 1985

(as at 31 December 1985; in US dollars)

Country	1985 payment
Algeria	10,000
Argentina	10,000
Australia	73,521
Austria	37,200
Bahamas	1,000
Brazil	10,000
Burma	1,000
Cameroon	2,070
Canada	254,156
Cyprus	(39)
Denmark	326,721
Egypt	2,834
Finland	106,050
France	78,947
Germany, Federal Republic of	49,912
Greece	9,000
Haiti	2,000
India	2,000
Indonesia	3,000
Ireland	25,288
Italy	34,178
Japan	200,000
Kuwait	1,000
Malaysia	1,000
Netherlands	58,480
New Zealand	10,520
Norway	626,398
Republic of Korea	5,000
Spain	18,138
Sweden	113,572
Switzerland	71,531
Trinidad and Tobago	1,250
Turkey	1,500
United Kingdom	60,825
United States	1,000,000
Venezuela	5,000
Yugoslavia	2,000
Zimbabwe	31,375
Total	3,246,427

NOTE: Figure in parentheses indicates a loss due to changes in exchange rates.

SOURCE: Accounts for the 12-month period of the biennium 1984-1985 ended 31 December 1985—schedules of individual trust funds.

GENERAL ASSEMBLY ACTION

On 2 December, the General Assembly, on the recommendation of the Fourth Committee, adopted **resolution 40/54** without vote.

United Nations Educational and Training Programme for Southern Africa

The General Assembly,

Recalling its earlier resolutions on the United Nations Educational and Training Programme for Southern Africa, in particular resolution 39/44 of 5 December 1984,

Having considered the report of the Secretary-General containing an account of the work of the Advisory Committee on the United Nations Educational and Training Programme for Southern Africa and the administration of the Programme for the period from 1 October 1984 to 15 October 1985,

Recognizing the valuable assistance rendered by the Programme to the peoples of South Africa and Namibia,

Noting with satisfaction that educational and technical assistance for southern Africa has become a growing concern of the international community,

Fully recognizing the need at this critical juncture in southern Africa to provide educational opportunities and counselling to a greater number of student refugees in a wide variety of professional, cultural and linguistic disciplines, as well as opportunities for vocational and technical training and for advanced studies at graduate and post-graduate levels in the priority fields of study,

Strongly convinced that the continuation and expansion of the Programme is essential in order to meet the increasing demand for educational and training assistance to students from South Africa and Namibia,

1. *Endorses* the report of the Secretary-General on the United Nations Educational and Training Programme for Southern Africa;

2. *Commends* the Secretary-General and the Advisory Committee on the United Nations Educational and Training Programme for Southern Africa for their continued efforts to promote generous contributions to the Programme and to enhance co-operation with governmental, intergovernmental and non-governmental agencies involved in educational and technical assistance for southern Africa;

3. *Expresses its appreciation* to all those that have supported the Programme by providing contributions, scholarships or places in their educational institutions;

4. *Appeals* to all States, institutions, organizations and individuals to offer greater financial and other support to the Programme in order to secure its continuation and steady expansion.

General Assembly resolution 40/54

2 December 1985   Meeting 99   Adopted without vote

Approved by Fourth Committee (A/40/886) without vote, 8 November (meeting 20); 43-nation draft (A/C.4/40/L.5); agenda item 112.

Sponsors: Australia, Bangladesh, Brazil, Burkina Faso, Burundi, Byelorussian SSR, Canada, Colombia, Cyprus, Denmark, Egypt, Finland, France, Germany, Federal Republic of, Guinea, Guinea-Bissau, Guyana, Iceland, India, Indonesia, Ireland, Italy, Japan, Kenya, Lesotho, Mali, Mauritania, Netherlands, Nicaragua, Nigeria, Norway, Papua New Guinea, Romania, Sweden, Tunisia, Turkey, United Kingdom, United Republic of Tanzania, United States, Venezuela, Zaire, Zambia, Zimbabwe.

Meeting numbers. GA 40th session: 4th Committee 11, 12, 15-20; plenary 99.

REFERENCE

[1]A/40/781.

Co-operation between OAU and the UN system

Co-operation between the United Nations and the Organization of African Unity continued in 1985, as requested by the General Assembly in 1984.[1] The Secretary-General, in an August report to the Assembly,[2] described that co-operation.

The Secretary-General addressed the Assembly of Heads of State and Government of OAU (Addis

Ababa, 18-20 July). The declarations and resolutions adopted at that meeting were forwarded to the Secretary-General by Madagascar on 18 September.[3] On 19 July, the USSR also forwarded its message to the OAU summit,[4] in which it stressed support for OAU efforts to strengthen its members' political independence and economic self-sufficiency.

At the meeting, the Secretary-General said that only through co-ordinated measures and international co-operation would it be possible to avert economic catastrophe and relaunch the process of long-term development in Africa. He described some activities undertaken by the United Nations Office for Emergency Operations in Africa (see ECONOMIC AND SOCIAL QUESTIONS, Chapter III), including ascertaining the critical needs of each country concerned and then mobilizing international aid. The March 1985 International Conference on the Emergency Situation in Africa had been successful in mobilizing additional resources for relief operations, although they were insufficient to meet the considerable needs. He emphasized that priority attention should be given to food and agriculture and called for the mobilization of additional resources to rehabilitate the devastated economies of Africa. As to the situation in southern Africa, he said that States there had to contend with externally supported acts of sabotage and destabilization and with violations of their territorial integrity. The interim government installed in Namibia by South Africa would not be recognized by the United Nations or any Member State, he added (see TRUSTEESHIP AND DECOLONIZATION, Chapter III).

In October, the OAU Chairman and its Secretary-General met with the United Nations Secretary-General in New York.

The proposed meeting between the United Nations system and OAU, as called for by the Assembly in 1984,[1] was postponed at the request of OAU due to unforeseen developments. Co-operation continued between OAU and United Nations organizations, including the Economic Commission for Africa, the Centre for Human Rights, DPI, FAO, IFAD, IMO, ITU, UNCTAD, UNIDO, UNCHS, UNHCR, UNESCO, UPU, the World Bank, WFP and WHO. UNDP provided assistance to the national liberation movements recognized by OAU (see p. 170).

ECONOMIC AND SOCIAL COUNCIL ACTION

The Economic and Social Council, in **resolution 1985/59**, recommended that an item on assistance to national liberation movements recognized by OAU be included in the agenda of high-level meetings of the OAU General Secretariat and the secretariats of the United Nations and other organizations within the system, with a view to strengthening existing co-ordination measures to ensure the best use of available resources for assistance to the peoples of colonial territories.

GENERAL ASSEMBLY ACTION

On 21 November, the General Assembly adopted **resolution 40/20** without vote.

Co-operation between the United Nations and the Organization of African Unity

The General Assembly,

Having considered the report of the Secretary-General on co-operation between the United Nations and the Organization of African Unity,

Recalling its previous resolutions on the promotion of co-operation between the United Nations and the Organization of African Unity and the practical measures taken for their implementation, in particular resolution 39/8 of 8 November 1984, and its resolution 39/29 of 3 December 1984 on the critical economic situation in Africa and the Declaration annexed thereto,

Taking note of the relevant resolutions, decisions and declarations adopted by the Council of Ministers of the Organization of African Unity at its forty-second ordinary session and by the Assembly of Heads of State and Government of that organization at its twenty-first ordinary session, which were held at Addis Ababa from 10 to 17 July and from 18 to 20 July 1985, respectively,

Taking note also of the resolutions, decisions and declarations adopted by the Organization of African Unity on the promotion of co-operation between the United Nations and the Organization of African Unity,

Noting, in particular, the Declaration on the Economic Situation in Africa and Africa's Priority Programme for Economic Recovery 1986-1990, annexed thereto, adopted by the Assembly of Heads of State and Government of the Organization of African Unity at its twenty-first session, which was devoted mainly to the critical economic situation in Africa,

Considering the important statement by the current Chairman of the Assembly of Heads of State and Government of the Organization of African Unity of 21 October 1985, particularly with regard to the critical economic situation in Africa as well as other matters of concern to the two organizations,

Gravely concerned about the serious and deteriorating economic situation in Africa, in particular the effects of the prolonged drought, desertification and the adverse effects of the international economic environment on the African States,

Recalling, in this connection, the Lagos Plan of Action for the Implementation of the Monrovia Strategy for the Economic Development of Africa, adopted by the Assembly of Heads of State and Government of the Organization of African Unity at its second extraordinary session, held at Lagos on 28 and 29 April 1980,

Recognizing the need for closer co-operation between the Organization of African Unity and all specialized agencies, organizations and bodies of the United Nations system in realizing the goals and objectives set forth in the Lagos Plan of Action,

Gravely concerned at the deteriorating situation in southern Africa arising from the continued domination of the peoples of the area by the minority racist régime of South Africa and conscious of the need to provide increased assistance to the peoples of the region and to their liberation movements in their struggle against colonialism, racial discrimination and *apartheid,*

Conscious of its responsibilities to provide economic, material and humanitarian assistance to independent States in southern Africa to help them cope with the situation caused by the acts of aggression committed against their territories by the *apartheid* régime of South Africa,

Deeply concerned at the gravity of the situation of the refugees in Africa and the urgent need for increased international assistance to help African countries of asylum cope with the heavy social, economic and administrative burden imposed on their fragile economies,

Recognizing the important role which the various information units and departments of the United Nations system can play in disseminating information to bring about a greater awareness of the grave situation prevailing in southern Africa as well as the social and economic problems and the needs of African States and their regional and subregional institutions,

Aware of the need for continuous liaison, consultations on matters of common concern, exchange of information at the secretariat level and technical co-operation on such matters as training and research between the Organization of African Unity and the United Nations,

1. *Takes note* of the report of the Secretary-General on co-operation between the United Nations and the Organization of African Unity and commends his efforts to strengthen such co-operation;

2. *Notes with appreciation* the increasing and continued participation of the Organization of African Unity in the work of the United Nations and the specialized agencies and its constructive contribution to that work;

3. *Commends* the continued efforts of the Organization of African Unity to promote multilateral co-operation among African States and to find solutions to African problems of vital importance to the international community and notes with satisfaction the increased collaboration of various organizations of the United Nations system in support of those efforts;

4. *Reaffirms* the determination of the United Nations to work closely with the Organization of African Unity towards the establishment of the new international economic order in accordance with the resolutions adopted by the General Assembly and, in that regard, to take full account of the Lagos Plan of Action for the Implementation of the Monrovia Strategy for the Economic Development of Africa and Africa's Priority Programme for Economic Recovery 1986-1990, adopted by the Assembly of Heads of State and Government of the Organization of African Unity at its twenty-first session, in the implementation of the International Development Strategy for the Third United Nations Development Decade;

5. *Calls upon* all Member States and regional and international organizations, in particular those of the United Nations system, to implement fully General Assembly resolution 39/29 on the critical economic situation in Africa and the Declaration annexed thereto;

6. *Also calls upon* all Member States, and regional and international organizations, in particular those of the United Nations system, to give their maximum support to Africa's Priority Programme for Economic Recovery 1986-1990;

7. *Requests* the Secretary-General to draw the attention of the specialized agencies and other organizations of the United Nations system to the need to give increasingly wide publicity to all matters relating to the social and economic development of Africa, in particular to General Assembly resolution 39/29 on the critical economic situation in Africa and the Declaration annexed thereto;

8. *Expresses its appreciation* to the Secretary-General for the timely initiative he has taken to alert the international community to the critical economic and social situation in Africa and welcomes the measures he has taken to facilitate international co-operation and co-ordination to assist Africa, in particular through the establishment of the Office for Emergency Operations in Africa;

9. *Commends* the Office for Emergency Operations in Africa for its efforts to sensitize the international community to the emergency situation in Africa, to co-ordinate the efforts of the international community and to monitor the situation in the affected African countries;

10. *Expresses its appreciation* to donor countries, the European Economic Community and other intergovernmental and non-governmental organizations for their participation in the round-table and consultative groups and for their response to the emergency food situation in Africa;

11. *Expresses its appreciation also* to the United Nations Development Programme, the Office of the United Nations Disaster Relief Co-ordinator, the World Food Programme, the Food and Agriculture Organization of the United Nations, the World Health Organization, the United Nations Children's Fund and the United Nations High Commissioner for Refugees for the assistance so far rendered to the African States in dealing with the emergency situation as well as with the critical economic problems that exist on the African continent;

12. *Calls upon* all Member States and organizations of the United Nations system to increase their assistance to the African States affected by serious economic problems, in particular problems of displaced persons resulting from natural and other disasters, by implementing fully General Assembly resolution 39/29 and Africa's Priority Programme for Economic Recovery 1986-1990;

13. *Invites* the Secretary-General to continue his commendable efforts in alerting and sensitizing the international community to the plight of African countries, in mobilizing additional assistance to Africa, in co-ordinating the activities of the United Nations system in Africa, and in monitoring the situation and presenting periodic reports thereon;

14. *Reiterates its appreciation* to the Secretary-General for his efforts, on behalf of the international community, to organize and mobilize special programmes of economic assistance for African States experiencing grave economic difficulties, as well as for the front-line States and other independent States of southern Africa, to help them cope with the situation caused by the acts of aggression committed against their territories by the *apartheid* régime of South Africa;

15. *Expresses its appreciation* to the World Bank, the United Nations Development Programme and other interested international financial institutions for their response to the critical economic situation in Africa as well as their assistance in the organization of round-table and donor conferences in favour of the least developed countries of Africa, as well as in the implementation of those special programmes of economic assistance;

16. *Requests* the Secretary-General to continue to keep the Organization of African Unity informed periodically of the response of the international community to those special programmes of economic assistance and to continue to co-ordinate efforts with all similar programmes initiated by that organization;

17. *Calls upon* the international community to provide generous assistance on a long-term basis to all African States affected by the economic crisis, particularly those suffering calamities such as drought and flood, in accordance with General Assembly resolution 39/29 and Africa's Priority Programme for Economic Recovery 1986-1990;

18. *Reiterates* the determination of the United Nations, in co-operation with the Organization of African Unity, to intensify its efforts to eliminate colonialism, racial discrimination and *apartheid* in southern Africa;

19. *Requests* the Secretary-General to take the necessary measures to strengthen co-operation at the political, economic, cultural and administrative levels between the United Nations and the Organization of African Unity in accordance with the relevant resolutions of the General Assembly, particularly with regard to the provision of assistance to the victims of colonialism and *apartheid* in southern Africa, and, in this connection, draws once again the attention of the international community to the need to contribute to the Assistance Fund for the Struggle against Colonialism and *Apartheid* established by the Organization of African Unity;

20. *Urges* the specialized agencies and other organizations concerned within the United Nations system to continue to expand their co-operation with the Organization of African Unity and, through it, their assistance to the liberation movements recognized by that organization;

21. *Reaffirms* its willingness to co-operate with the Organization of African Unity and its organs in the implementation of resolutions and decisions of mutual concern;

22. *Calls upon* the competent organs, specialized agencies and other organizations of the United Nations system to continue to ensure that their personnel and recruitment policies provide for the just and equitable representation of Africa at all levels at their respective headquarters and in their regional and field operations;

23. *Urges* all Member States and regional and international organizations, in particular those of the United Nations system, and non-governmental organizations to provide material and economic assistance to help African countries of asylum cope with the heavy burden imposed on their limited resources and weak infrastructures by the presence of large numbers of refugees;

24. *Invites* Member States and regional and international organizations, in particular those of the United Nations system, and non-governmental organizations to contribute generously and effectively to the implementation of the Declaration and Programme of Action of the Second International Conference on Assistance to Refugees in Africa;

25. *Calls upon* United Nations organs—in particular the Security Council, the Economic and Social Council, the Special Committee on the Situation with regard to the Implementation of the Declaration on the Granting of Independence to Colonial Countries and Peoples, the Special Committee against *Apartheid* and the United Nations Council for Namibia—to continue to associate closely the Organization of African Unity with all their work concerning Africa;

26. *Requests* the Secretary-General to ensure that adequate facilities continue to be made available to facilitate continued liaison and consultations on matters of common interest as well as for the provision of technical assistance to the General Secretariat of the Organization of African Unity, as required;

27. *Also requests* the Secretary-General, in consultation with the Secretary-General of the Organization of African Unity, to arrange the date and venue for the next meeting between representatives of the General Secretariat of that organization and the secretariats of the United Nations and other organizations of the United Nations system;

28. *Further requests* the Secretary-General to report to the General Assembly at its forty-first session on the implementation of the present resolution and on the development of co-operation between the Organization of African Unity and the organizations concerned within the United Nations system.

General Assembly resolution 40/20

21 November 1985   Meeting 87   Adopted without vote

49-nation draft (A/40/L.17 & Add.1); agenda item 25.

Sponsors: Algeria, Angola, Benin, Botswana, Burkina Faso, Burundi, Cameroon, Cape Verde, Central African Republic, Chad, Comoros, Congo, Djibouti, Egypt, Equatorial Guinea, Ethiopia, Gabon, Gambia, Ghana, Guinea, Guinea-Bissau, Ivory Coast, Kenya, Lesotho, Liberia, Libyan Arab Jamahiriya, Madagascar, Malawi, Mali, Mauritania, Mauritius, Mozambique, Niger, Nigeria, Rwanda, Sao Tome and Principe, Senegal, Seychelles, Sierra Leone, Somalia, Sudan, Swaziland, Togo, Tunisia, Uganda, United Republic of Tanzania, Zaire, Zambia, Zimbabwe.

Meeting numbers. GA 40th session: plenary 42, 87.

The Assembly called for United Nations–OAU co-operation in other 1985 resolutions. In **resolution 40/53**, it echoed the action recommended by the Economic and Social Council (see p. 202) on assistance to the movements recognized by OAU. The Assembly welcomed the efforts of the OAU Chairman and the United Nations Secretary-General to promote a solution to the Western Sahara problem, and called on them to persuade the conflicting parties to negotiate a cease-fire and referendum (**40/50**). It requested the Secretary-General to publicize United Nations work in decolonization and to maintain a close working relationship with OAU by consulting periodically and by exchanging information (**40/58**).

The Assembly requested the Secretary-General to assist OAU to implement the 1964 Declaration on the Denuclearization of Africa (**40/89 A**). It decided to establish a United Nations Regional Centre for Peace and Disarmament in Africa to support disarmament efforts in the region, in co-operation with OAU, as well as to co-ordinate the implementation of regional activities in Africa under the World Disarmament Campaign (**40/151 G**).

The Assembly decided to organize, in co-operation with OAU and the Movement of Non-Aligned Countries, a World Conference on Sanctions against Racist South Africa (**40/64 C**). Noting the interest of African States in Antarctica as shown by the OAU Council of Ministers July meeting,[3] the Assembly viewed with concern the continued status of South Africa as a Consultative Party to the Antarctic Treaty (**40/156 C**).

REFERENCES

[1]YUN 1984, p. 192, GA res. 39/8, 8 Nov. 1984. [2]A/40/536. [3]A/40/666. [4]A/40/497.

Chapter VI

Americas

The situation in Central America was considered by the Security Council and the General Assembly in 1985. Both bodies addressed specific disputes between countries.

The Council held two series of meetings at Nicaragua's request regarding allegations of aggression against it. In May, the Council adopted resolution 562(1985) calling on all States to refrain from supporting any actions against any State in the region which might impede the peace objectives of the Contadora Group (Colombia, Mexico, Panama and Venezuela). In December, the Council considered what Nicaragua called the escalation of acts of aggression against it, but took no action.

The General Assembly, in December, adopted resolution 40/188 calling for an end to a United States trade embargo against Nicaragua. In an October report to the Assembly, the Secretary-General expressed regret that, despite the efforts of the Contadora Group, whose political initiative for peace and co-operation in Central America had begun in 1983, the situation in Central America had steadily deteriorated during the year. He urged the countries with interests in the region to support with deeds the Contadora Group's efforts.

An agenda item on the observance of the quincentenary of the discovery of America was not considered at the Assembly's 1985 regular session, but was among the items deferred, by decision 40/470, to its resumed session in 1986.

Topics related to this chapter. Disarmament: nuclear-weapon-free zones—Latin America. Regional economic and social activities: Latin America. Human rights: Latin America. Refugees and displaced persons: Americas. Other colonial Territories: Falkland Islands (Malvinas). International Court of Justice: military and parliamentary activities in and against Nicaragua.

Central America situation

Communications. The majority of communications addressed to the Secretary-General in 1985 on the situation in Central America concerned the Contadora Group's activities. These included either communiqués from the Group or comments on those communiqués by the Central American States. The meetings of the Contadora Group as well as joint meetings with the Central American countries were held at Panama City; the communications relating to such meetings were transmitted by Panama. Other communications dealt with a situation concerning political asylum and disputes between Nicaragua and several other States (see below under the relevant subject heading).

On 10 January,[1] Panama transmitted the text of a declaration issued by the Ministers for Foreign Affairs of the Contadora Group at their meeting on 8 and 9 January. The declaration noted the accomplishments of the Group in establishing regional political machinery to facilitate dialogue and negotiations among the Central American Governments.

By a letter of 15 February,[2] Honduras transmitted the text of a joint communiqué issued at San José, Costa Rica, on 14 February by the Foreign Ministers of Honduras, El Salvador and Costa Rica. They stated that they had decided not to participate in a proposed February meeting of the Contadora Group, in support of Costa Rica's defence of the right of asylum violated by Nicaragua (see p. 208). On the same day,[3] Nicaragua conveyed a government communiqué asserting that the Contadora negotiating process was jeopardized by the United States policy of imposing its will through military force and that the negotiating process depended on countries being able to take decisions based on their national interests without intervention from third States. In a letter of 20 February,[4] Costa Rica stated that the joint communiqué of 14 February constituted a categorical reply to the unfounded statements of Nicaragua. In a further letter of 22 February,[5] Costa Rica transmitted the text of a communiqué it had issued the day before recounting the dispute between it and Nicaragua and stating its willingness to negotiate bilateral or multilateral agreements with any country that fulfilled its international legal obligations. A letter of 2 April[6] conveyed the text of a joint declaration by the Presidents of Costa Rica and Panama, issued after an 18/19 March meeting, in which the Presidents appealed to countries with interests in Central America to refrain from actions that would jeopardize the culmination of the Contadora peace effort.

The text of the "Statute of the Verification and Control Mechanism for Security Matters under the Contadora Act on Peace and Co-operation in Central America", drafted by representatives of the Governments of Costa Rica, El Salvador and Honduras during meetings in Costa Rica and Honduras in February and March, was forwarded to the Secretary-General on 15 April.[7] A bulletin issued at the end of a high-level meeting of the plenipotentiaries of the Contadora Group members and Central American countries in Panama City on 11 and 12 April was transmitted by Panama on 15 April.[8] The bulletin described an agreement reached to establish an *Ad Hoc* Committee for Evaluation and Follow-up of Commitments concerning Political and Refugee Matters, a Verification and Control Commission for Security Matters and an *Ad Hoc* Committee for Evaluation and Follow-up of Commitments concerning Economic and Social Matters.

On 9 May,[9] El Salvador conveyed an excerpt from the text of the "Declaration of San Salvador" issued on 7 May by the Foreign Ministers of Costa Rica, El Salvador and Honduras and the Deputy Minister for External Relations of Guatemala. The Ministers declared that to achieve peace in Central America it was indispensable to strengthen the political undertakings contained in the Contadora Act and to improve the verification mechanisms and rules of application that would ensure their strict observance.

By letters of 20 May[10] and 20 June,[11] Panama transmitted information bulletins issued following plenipotentiary meetings of the Contadora Group members and the Central American countries (Panama City, 14-16 May and 18 and 19 June). The first bulletin stated that all the working documents previously submitted to the Group were examined with a view to achieving balanced solutions to the different issues in the negotiations. The second contained the view of Nicaragua, expressed at the meeting, that there was an urgent need for the Group to concentrate first and foremost on containing the escalation of aggression against Nicaragua and against peace in the region. Honduras, on 24 June,[12] forwarded a press release it issued on 21 June expressing regret at the obstructionist attitude of Nicaragua at the plenipotentiary meeting in June.

Honduras, on 26 June,[13] transmitted a letter of 24 June to the Foreign Ministers of the Contadora Group, inviting them to send observers to witness the Honduran electoral process which would culminate in general elections on 24 November. Honduras and El Salvador, on 17 July,[14] transmitted a joint statement issued following meetings of their Presidents in Honduras on 10 and 11 July in which they expressed their grave concern over the deterioration of the Central American situation and called on Nicaragua to abandon its policy of confrontation and return to multilateral negotiations. A 22 July[15] letter from Honduras transmitted a note to the Foreign Ministers of the Contadora Group countries on the occasion of their 21 July meeting. Directed at stimulating the renewal of the Contadora negotiating process, which it said had been obstructed by Nicaragua's attitude at the plenipotentiaries' June meeting in Panama City, Honduras said three principal items depended on a clear reply from Nicaragua: commitments relating to security, commitments on national reconciliation and verification and supervision machinery.

On 23 July,[16] Panama conveyed a communiqué issued at the conclusion of the 21/22 July meeting of the Foreign Ministers of the Contadora Group, outlining steps they had decided to take to finalize the Contadora Act for Peace and Co-operation in Central America. On 2 August,[17] Honduras forwarded a letter of 1 August from its Acting Minister for Foreign Affairs and the Deputy Ministers for External Relations of Costa Rica and of El Salvador to the Foreign Ministers of the Contadora Group countries. Having met at Tegucigalpa on 1 August to appraise the negotiation process, the Ministers expressed their support for the Contadora process and urged other States to make fresh efforts to accelerate and conclude the negotiations.

Peru, on 10 August,[18] transmitted a communiqué of 29 July from Argentina, Brazil, Peru and Uruguay, in which they said they were at the disposal of the Contadora Group for consultations on matters with which they might be helpful. On 12 August,[19] Peru transmitted the text of the Lima Declaration, signed on 29 July by Argentina, Bolivia, Brazil, Chile, Colombia, Costa Rica, Cuba, the Dominican Republic, Ecuador, El Salvador, Guatemala, Haiti, Honduras, Mexico, Nicaragua, Panama, Paraguay, Peru, Uruguay and Venezuela. It stated that the crisis in Central America must be settled by peaceful and negotiated means. On 12 August,[20] Panama circulated the text of a bulletin issued on 9 August by the Deputy Foreign Ministers of the Contadora Group countries after their visit to the five countries of Central America between 3 and 8 August to seek views of Governments on pending matters in the Contadora Act. They stated that the visit made possible a more precise understanding of the regional situation and helped the Ministers gather comments useful for their efforts at diplomatic harmonization.

Panama, on 27 August,[21] forwarded a 25 August communiqué by the Foreign Ministers of the Contadora Group and the Support Group, composed of Argentina, Brazil, Peru and Uruguay, following a 24/25 August meeting at Cartagena de Indias, Colombia. The communiqué said the meeting had confirmed the serious concern among the Latin American countries regarding the Central American crisis and the decision to strengthen, in regional unity, the efforts at diplomatic negotiation promoted by the Contadora Group, and outlined the tasks of the Support Group to facilitate the conclusion of the Contadora Act.

On 5 September,[22] Costa Rica transmitted a joint declaration adopted on 4 September by the Foreign Ministers of Costa Rica, El Salvador and Honduras, giving notice of their intention to attend a 12/13 September meeting in Panama City of the Contadora Group and Central American countries to appraise the peace negotiations. On 16 September,[23] Panama transmitted a press release issued by the Foreign Ministers of the Contadora Group and Central American countries at the end of their September meeting. The Group had given the Central American Ministers the final draft of the Act on Peace and Co-operation in Central America, and decided to convene again in October to discuss armaments control and reduction, implementation and follow-up matters, military manœuvres, and operational questions such as entry into force and budget. In appendices to the press release, the Ministers condemned the recent kidnapping of the daughter of the President of El Salvador and acknowledged the importance of the process towards democratic constitutionality taking place in Guatemala.

A letter from Nicaragua of 13 November[24] conveyed a note of 11 November from its President to the Presidents of the Contadora and Support Group countries, with an appendix of 8 November stating Nicaragua's position on the draft Contadora Act of 12 September. It insisted that minimum security conditions guarantee that any commitments entered into would not endanger its sovereignty. These minimum conditions implied the immediate cessation of aggression against Nicaragua and a commitment by the United States to desist from such acts.

Panama, on 22 November,[25] transmitted a communiqué issued by the Deputy Foreign Ministers of the Contadora Group countries at the conclusion of plenipotentiary meetings held from 19 to 21 November, stating that their views had been heard at meetings held from 7 to 10 and 17 to 19 October; at the November meetings, they had made new proposals to their Central American counterparts designed to reconcile differences and make negotiations possible.

On 5 December,[26] Nicaragua transmitted a letter of the same date from its President stating that, as long as conditions guaranteeing its survival did not exist, the Contadora Group should suspend until May 1986 plenipotentiary meetings to negotiate pending aspects of the Contadora Act and take action to persuade the United States to

end its aggression, the principal factor in the regional crisis, in order to create conditions for negotiation among the Central American countries.

On 13 December,[27] Luxembourg, on behalf of the 10 member States of the European Community (EC), and Spain and Portugal, transmitted the text of the Final Act of the Conference of Ministers for Foreign Affairs of the States members of EC, of Spain and of Portugal, and of Ministers for External Relations of the States of Central America and of the Contadora Group (Luxembourg, 11 and 12 November). Also forwarded were the texts of joint political and economic communiqués issued on that occasion. The political communiqué stated that the participants held a common conviction that their political dialogue and economic co-operation, particularly among the Central American States in the context of the Contadora initiative, would help support efforts to put an end to violence and instability in the region.

Report of the Secretary-General (October). Pursuant to a 1983 request by the Security Council[28] and resolution 562(1985) of 10 May (see p. 212), the Secretary-General, in October 1985,[29] reported on the Central America situation. He stated that since his December 1984 report[30] to the General Assembly he had maintained contact with the Contadora Group countries as well as the five Central American countries and other States with interests in the region. The Contadora Foreign Ministers had delivered the final draft of the Contadora Act on Peace and Co-operation in Central America to him on 26 September, after their Central American counterparts received it at the Panama City meeting on 12 and 13 September. The Ministers had told the Secretary-General that the final draft incorporated comments by some Central American Governments on the original draft of September 1984[31] as well as new proposals. The plenipotentiaries of the nine countries would meet in Panama beginning on 7 October for 45 days or less to discuss unresolved aspects of the Act, after which a conference would be convened to sign it.

The Secretary-General expressed admiration to the Contadora Group for its persistent efforts to find a comprehensive, negotiated solution to the crisis in Central America. He also expressed satisfaction at the creation of the Contadora Support Group, an action which reflected strong Latin American concern and would strengthen the political action of Contadora.

The Secretary-General regretted that, despite the efforts of the Contadora Group, the situation in Central America had steadily deteriorated during the year. There had been an increase in bilateral incidents between countries which hindered the Group's work. He deplored the border incidents, threats, instances of foreign intervention and the continued presence of military forces from outside the region, especially those involving loss of life.

The Secretary-General noted that although elections were held in El Salvador in March, armed conflict continued, while talks between the Government and the Frente Democrático Revolucionario–Frente Farabundo Martí para la Liberación Nacional remained stalled. Talks between the United States and Nicaragua were also suspended. He reiterated his view that the roots of the Central American crisis could be found in unjust socio-economic structures and domestic policies and that the solution depended on the political will of the States in the region. It was imperative for countries with interests in the region to support with deeds the Contadora Group's efforts.

Annexed to the Secretary-General's report was a letter of 26 September from the Foreign Ministers of Colombia, Mexico, Panama and Venezuela to the Secretary-General recounting the peace efforts made by their Governments since the Secretary-General's December 1984 report. A second annex contained a bulletin issued in Panama on 13 February 1985 explaining the Ministers' decision to postpone a scheduled 14/15 February meeting of plenipotentiaries of the Contadora Group and to seek to create more favourable conditions for political understanding on peace and co-operation in Central America. A 28 June report of a fact-finding committee established by the Permanent Council of the Organization of American States (OAS) to investigate a complaint by Costa Rica of a border incident on 31 May, in which it said its civil guard was fired upon by Nicaraguan troops, resulting in the death of two Costa Rican guards, comprised a third annex. A fourth annex contained a resolution adopted by the OAS Permanent Council on 11 July following the investigation; Costa Rica and Nicaragua were urged to fulfil commitments undertaken in bilateral treaties. The Contadora Act on Peace and Co-operation in Central America was also annexed to the report.

GENERAL ASSEMBLY ACTION

On 16 September 1985, at the close of its resumed thirty-ninth (1984) session, the General Assembly decided, by **decision 39/462**, adopted without vote on an oral proposal by its President, to include the item on the situation in Central America in the agenda of its fortieth (1985) session, which opened the next day.

The Assembly discussed the item at five meetings on 22, 25 and 27 November. It had before it two draft resolutions on the subject. One of them[32] was sponsored by Argentina, Brazil, Colombia, Mexico, Panama, Peru, Uruguay and Venezuela, the other[33] by Costa Rica, El Salvador and Honduras. Both texts would have urged Governments of the region to continue negotiations on unresolved issues in the Contadora Act to achieve its early entry into force, urged the United States and Nicaragua to renew their dialogue with the aim of normalizing their relations, and urged Central American States to resolve their bilateral differences peacefully through mechanisms conducive to normalizing their relations.

On 18 December, the two sets of sponsors requested that the texts not be put to a vote at that time but that the item be kept on the agenda. Suspending its 1985 regular session on that day, the Assembly, by **decision 40/470**, decided to retain the item among those to be considered when its session resumed in 1986.

Nicaragua situation

Costa Rica–Nicaragua dispute and armed incidents

Costa Rica and Nicaragua continued to accuse each other of aggressive acts at various times throughout the year. A number of communications regarding the situation between the two States were addressed to the Secretary-General. The communications mainly transmitted letters exchanged between the respective Foreign Ministers or Deputies.

Communications. A charge was made that a citizen of Costa Rica who, in August 1984, was granted asylum in his country's Embassy in Managua, Nicaragua, was wounded in being taken from the Embassy on 24 December by Nicaraguan authorities. On 21 January 1985,[34] Costa Rica transmitted the text of a speech by its Ambassador to the Permanent Council of OAS saying that Nicaragua had been asked to return the political refugee to Costa Rica's diplomatic mission and Costa Rica would request the Council to appoint a special commission to investigate the incident. Nicaragua, on 4 February,[35] stated its willingness to discuss, within the framework of the Commission for Supervision and Prevention established at the request of the Contadora Group on 15 May 1984, any issues or incidents which the two Governments might wish to raise regarding the right of asylum in the two countries.

Nicaragua, by a letter of 15 June,[36] transmitted a letter to the Contadora Group Ministers asking them to appoint a delegation to conduct an on-site inspection of Nicaragua's frontier area with Costa Rica. A critical situation had arisen there, Nicaragua said, as a consequence of the presence of irregular forces as part of the interventionist policy of the United States. On 21 June,[37] Nicaragua transmitted a letter of 18 June to the

Contadora Group Ministers describing a meeting held on 17 June at Liberia, Costa Rica, by the Deputy Minister for External Relations of Nicaragua with representatives of the Contadora Group countries and the Secretary-General of OAS, who made up a fact-finding commission in Costa Rica at that time. Nicaragua had stated at the meeting that tensions with Costa Rica arose from the presence of mercenary forces there and from their use of Costa Rican territory to launch military actions against Nicaragua.

On 21 June,[38] Nicaragua transmitted a 19 June letter it sent to Costa Rica referring to the deportation by Costa Rica of a captured mercenary, an action, Nicaragua said, that seemed to indicate that the capture had been a public relations stunt aimed at refurbishing the country's image of neutrality. On 26 June,[39] Nicaragua transmitted a letter of 25 June from its President to the Chairman of the Permanent Council of OAS formally inviting the OAS commission established on 7 June to carry out an on-site inspection of the Nicaraguan side of the border with Costa Rica in the area where the incident of 31 May occurred (see p. 208). On 27 June,[40] Nicaragua conveyed a note of 26 June by its President to the President of Costa Rica stating that Nicaragua considered it timely and necessary for both Governments to attempt to set up a demilitarized zone on their border and announcing that Nicaragua had decided to establish a neutralized zone under international supervision in its territory along the border.

In a letter of 27 June,[41] Costa Rica called for restraint on the part of Nicaragua in asking the Secretary-General to circulate statements, notes and official press communiqués.

In a letter of 5 July,[42] Nicaragua transmitted a note of 3 July to Costa Rica's Minister for External Relations and Worship protesting Costa Rica's open support for mercenaries attacking Nicaraguan territory. On the same date,[43] Nicaragua transmitted a note written on 4 July to Costa Rica protesting an attack on Nicaraguan troops that day by 200 mercenaries said to be operating from Costa Rican territory. Nicaragua, on 5 August,[44] forwarded a note of 2 August urgently requesting that Costa Rica immediately prevent attacks on Nicaragua from Costa Rican territory and capture the mercenaries responsible.

Also on 5 August,[45] Costa Rica transmitted a letter of 31 July from its President to the President of Nicaragua, following an alleged attack on Costa Rica by Nicaraguan aircraft on 26 July. The letter expressed indignation at what it termed Nicaragua's repeated attempts to extend into Costa Rican territory military activities aimed at ending its civil war.

On 28 August,[46] Nicaragua transmitted the texts of two notes verbales from its Acting Minister for External Relations. One, dated 23 August, was to the Costa Rican Foreign Minister and protested alleged attacks on frontier posts in Nicaragua on 21 and 22 August by mercenaries based in Costa Rica. The second, dated 27 August, was to the Minister for Foreign Affairs of Honduras (see p. 210).

Further charges of attacks on Nicaragua by mercenaries based in Costa Rica constituted the subject of a number of notes from Nicaragua's Foreign Minister or Deputy Foreign Minister to their Costa Rican counterpart. On 30 August,[47] Nicaragua transmitted a note verbale of 29 August protesting an alleged mercenary attack from Costa Rican territory that day and calling on Costa Rica to give the Contadora Group the support needed to bring the peace initiative to fruition. Nicaragua transmitted another note verbale, dated 2 September, by a letter of 5 September,[48] in which it expressed concern at Costa Rican assertions that on 27 August the Sandinist People's Army had directed an attack against Costa Rica, a charge contradicted by a statement by the Commander of Costa Rica's civil guard that he did not know the source of the incident. Nicaragua affirmed that the Sandinist People's Army had at no time directed attacks against Costa Rican territory. Alleged attacks by rifle, machine-gun and mortar fire on 7, 8 and 9 September were protested in a letter by Nicaragua of 9 September, transmitted the following day.[49] A protest note dated 28 September charging three attacks on frontier posts on 27 September from Costa Rican territory was transmitted by Nicaragua on 30 September.[50] On 4 October,[51] Nicaragua transmitted a note of protest dated 3 October concerning alleged mercenary attacks on a Sandinist air force helicopter and on army troops on 2 and 3 October, respectively. A letter of 9 October[52] by Nicaragua transmitted a 7 October note protesting an alleged border-post attack that day by mercenaries operating from Costa Rica. The use of 57-millimetre cannon was an escalation of the aggression against Nicaragua, the note said.

On 9 October,[53] Nicaragua transmitted a note of 7 October protesting an alleged attack earlier that day against it in which artillery, rocket launchers, cannon and mortars were said to have been used. Nicaragua said the incident reflected the absolute necessity for the Costa Rican authorities to deter constant attacks against Nicaragua. In a letter of 10 October,[54] Nicaragua transmitted a note of 8 October protesting an alleged attack on 7 October against its troops from Costa Rican territory. The fact that a Costa Rican civil guard post was located at the very place where the incident occurred, the note said, clearly demonstrated tolerance by Costa Rican authorities of counter-revolutionary groups quartered in the area. On 4

November,[55] Nicaragua conveyed a note of 1 November alleging two attacks on Nicaragua from Costa Rica on 30 October that were carried out, it said, despite the presence of a Costa Rican civil guard post.

Honduras-Nicaragua dispute and armed incidents

Letters were received from both Honduras and Nicaragua, throughout 1985, on alleged armed incidents between the countries. The letters were addressed to the Secretary-General or the Security Council President and generally contained communications exchanged between the Foreign Ministers of the two countries.

Communications. On 8 January,[56] Nicaragua transmitted the text of a note of 6 January to Honduras attaching a list of bases in Honduran territory which it said were operated by mercenary groups, known as Misura and Fuerza Democrática Nicaragüense, conducting attacks against Nicaragua. The note referred to a press conference statement by the Foreign Minister of Honduras that such forces should be expelled from its territory. On 2 April,[57] Honduras conveyed a note of the same date to Nicaragua protesting an alleged violation of Honduran national territory by 17 Nicaraguan soldiers and an army officer who crossed the border by truck. On 9 April,[58] Honduras circulated a protest note of 8 April describing an alleged incident in a Honduran village on 4 March during which two Honduran citizens were killed and two peasants of Nicaraguan origin were abducted. A letter of 19 April[59] transmitted a note sent by Honduras to Nicaragua that day protesting a reported Nicaraguan coastguard vessel attack on a Honduran ship in Honduran waters. Two notes of 19 April were transmitted by Nicaragua in a letter of 22 April.[60] One described an attack on two Nicaraguan coastguard vessels on 18 April by three Honduran air force fighter planes; the other referred to the presence of counter-revolutionary forces in Honduran territory dressed in uniforms similar to those of the Sandinist People's Army.

In a letter of 13 May,[61] Honduras conveyed a note of protest sent to Nicaragua on 10 May charging that the Nicaraguan army had been committing aggressive attacks with heavy weapons along the eastern border between the two countries. In response, Nicaragua transmitted on 13 May[62] the text of a letter dated 11 May to Honduras rejecting those charges and proposing that the two countries' armed forces draw up a joint plan to reduce and remove mercenary forces from the border areas. Honduras transmitted, on 15 May,[63] a press release stating that the deteriorating situation along the border with Nicaragua was a result of that country's internal political and armed conflict, which had spilt over

to its neighbouring countries. On 17 May,[64] Nicaragua conveyed the text of a note it had sent on 16 May to the Contadora Group Ministers expressing serious concern about the critical situation existing in the Honduras/Nicaragua border areas and bringing to their attention Nicaragua's proposal that the Group establish a special commission to consider the situation in the area and carry out on-site inspections. It sent a letter on 17 May[65] containing a communiqué of 16 May issued by the Office of the President in which Nicaragua reiterated that proposal, made at a 15 May meeting of the Contadora Group.

On 6 June,[66] Nicaragua transmitted a protest note of 3 June charging that helicopters coming from Honduran territory that day had penetrated Nicaraguan airspace and attacked an observation post of the Sandinist People's Army. Honduras responded on 10 and 12 June,[67] in letters to the President of the Security Council and the Secretary-General, respectively, transmitting a note of 4 June rejecting the Nicaraguan protest as unfounded.

A letter of 5 July[68] from Nicaragua transmitted a 4 July note to Honduras rejecting reports broadcast by a Honduran radio station that the Sandinist People's Army had launched an artillery attack that day on Honduran territory. Honduras sent a letter dated 8 July[69] containing a note of 4 July stating that the broadcasting station was a private one, and that the Government had not and would not accuse Nicaragua without proof. Honduras, on 11 July,[70] transmitted a note of 10 July informing Nicaragua that its investigation had confirmed that an artillery attack had been launched against Honduras on 4 July.

On 12 July,[71] Honduras transmitted a note of 11 July describing a bombing attack the day before, during which a Honduran home was reportedly destroyed, and protesting Nicaragua's dangerous policy of provoking and harassing its neighbours. It transmitted on 24 July[72] a note sent to Nicaragua on 23 July protesting a series of seven alleged attacks on Honduran territory between 4 and 19 July by the Sandinist People's Army. On 16 August,[73] it transmitted letters of 15 and 16 August to Nicaragua alleging incursions into Honduran territory by troops of that Army on 12 and 14 August. The second annex of a letter of 28 August[46] was a note verbale from Nicaragua to Honduras in which Nicaragua denied Honduran allegations of entry into its territory by troops of the Sandinist People's Army.

Honduras, on 14 September,[74] transmitted two protest notes sent to Nicaragua on 13 September alleging a mortar attack on Honduran territory that day, killing one person and wounding eight, and four separate attacks on 6, 7, 9 and 10 September. Also annexed were press releases by Honduras issued on 13 and 14 September announcing the 13 September incident and others which occurred on 12 and 13 September along the border.

Nicaragua, on 19 September,[75] transmitted two notes dated 18 September to Honduras. In one, Nicaragua expressed concern about the presence of armed mercenaries in Honduras and called on that country to dismantle the force. The second note alleged an attempt by mercenary forces to infiltrate Nicaragua through Honduras on 18 September, supported by Honduran army artillery fire. Honduras responded on 19 September,[76] annexing two notes, one informing Nicaragua that it was forwarding its information on mercenaries to the military authorities for appropriate action, the other rejecting Nicaragua's charges as an incident artificially contrived for propaganda purposes.

On 3 October,[77] Nicaragua transmitted a note of 1 October containing the names of 17 of its citizens allegedly abducted and still missing after mercenaries from Honduras infiltrated into Nicaragua on 17 September. In a second letter of 3 October,[78] Nicaragua transmitted a note of 2 October charging that about 2,500 armed mercenaries were massing in Honduran territory near the Nicaraguan border. Honduras, on 4 October,[79] conveyed a note of 2 October rejecting Nicaragua's accusations as being part of a propaganda campaign and calling on Nicaragua to devote its energies to the Contadora Group negotiations.

In a letter of 3 October,[80] Nicaragua transmitted a note of 1 October to the Contadora Group Ministers calling on them to investigate the frontier areas between Nicaragua and Honduras where, Nicaragua said, a 2,500-man mercenary force was preparing to provoke a hostile confrontation between the two countries.

On 16 October,[81] Honduras transmitted a note of the previous day protesting an alleged attack on 10 October against a Honduran patrol by the Sandinist People's Army. On 23 October,[82] Honduras transmitted a note of the same day charging that that Army's troops had fired on a Honduran border patrol on 18 October, conducted raids into Honduras on 18 and 19 October, and attacked a patrol on 20 October. On 30 October,[83] Honduras forwarded a note it had sent to Nicaragua on 29 October recounting incidents it said involved the Sandinist Army, including the placing of a mine inside Honduras that killed a Honduran soldier on 28 October, attacks on a Honduran helicopter that day and firing on a patrol boat on 18 October.

Nicaragua, on 21 November,[84] transmitted a note of 20 November protesting a violation of Nicaraguan airspace and sea space in an attack on two coastguard patrols by aircraft and vessels coming from Honduran territory. In a letter of 30 November,[85] Nicaragua protested what it described as attacks by Honduran army soldiers on 23 and 25 November on Nicaraguan army positions. On 6 December,[86] Nicaragua transmitted a note sent to Honduras that day alleging that on 2 December a Sandinist air force helicopter was shot down by a surface-to-air missile fired from Honduras by mercenaries in the service of the United States, killing 14 soldiers.

Nicaragua-United States dispute

Deteriorating relations between Nicaragua and the United States during 1985 were reflected in the exchange of communications between the countries and those addressed to the United Nations. Communications to the Secretary-General and/or the Security Council President mainly transmitted texts which had been exchanged between the Nicaraguan Minister for External Relations and the United States Secretary of State. Several other countries also transmitted communications expressing general concern about the situation. The Council met in May and December to consider Nicaragua's complaints of aggression against it. In May, the Council adopted a resolution which called on all States to refrain from carrying out or supporting political, economic or military actions against any State in the region which might impede the peace objectives of the Contadora Group. In December, the Council considered a Nicaraguan complaint about the escalation of acts of aggression against it but did not receive any proposal for action.

Communications (February-May). Nicaragua, on 5 February,[87] transmitted the text of a 30 January note to the United States Secretary of State protesting the joint military manoeuvres called "Big Pine III", scheduled to be carried out from 11 February to 3 May by the armed forces of the United States and Honduras. Nicaragua charged that the exercise was aimed at intimidating and pressuring Nicaragua and constituted a direct attack on the Contadora peace negotiations. On 28 February,[88] Nicaragua transmitted a statement of 27 February by its President asserting Nicaragua's non-aligned status and announcing its intention to return 100 military instructors to Cuba beginning in May, declaring an indefinite moratorium on the acquisition of new weapons systems and fighter aircraft, and inviting a United States congressional delegation to visit the country and assess the defensive nature of its armed forces.

Cuba, on 5 March,[89] transmitted a government statement supporting the initiatives announced by Nicaragua on 27 February and stating that it would refrain, in March and April, from sending additional military and security collaborators to Nicaragua and would withdraw 100 such personnel from that country in May. However, if the United States persisted in its aggression against Nicaragua, Cuba would feel free to dispatch more advisers if Nicaragua requested it.

Nicaragua, on 12 April,[90] transmitted a letter sent on 11 April by its President to the heads of State of the Contadora Group countries and other countries stating that it could not agree to any ultimatum, such as the one it said the President of the United States had made public on 4 April, to bring its policies into line with the dictates of that country. Nicaragua reiterated its support for the Contadora negotiating process and its demand that the United States resume bilateral talks begun in Manzanillo, Mexico, in 1984, which the United States had unilaterally suspended in January 1985.

Mongolia, on 25 April,[91] transmitted the text of a 22 April statement by its Ministry of Foreign Affairs supporting Nicaragua's struggle to defend its independence and demanding that the United States stop what it said amounted to an undeclared war against Nicaragua.

Several communications pertained to an announcement on 1 May by the United States of a suspension of its trade relations with Nicaragua and of air and sea transport between the two countries, effective 7 May.

On 7 May,[92] India forwarded a communiqué adopted that day by the Co-ordinating Bureau of the Movement of Non-Aligned Countries strongly condemning the embargo and other coercive economic measures against Nicaragua, which undermined the efforts of the Contadora Group. It emphasized the need for political and negotiated solutions to the region's problems.

Uruguay on 7 and 9 May[93] transmitted to the Secretary-General and the President of the Security Council, respectively, a press release issued on 6 May by the Office of its President deploring recent economic sanctions by the United States against Nicaragua and calling for the reopening of the Manzanillo bilateral talks. Bolivia, in a note verbale of 9 May,[94] transmitted a government statement of 8 May stating that the decision of the United States to impose a trade embargo against Nicaragua was an additional obstacle to the efforts of the Contadora Group and the international community in their search for solutions to the Central American crisis. Brazil, in a note verbale of 8 May,[95] submitted a government statement of 6 May declaring that it did not support unilateral sanctions, which were against international law, and calling for the States involved in the Central American crisis to seek a negotiated settlement. On 9 May,[96] Suriname forwarded to the Security Council President a memorandum stating that the international community should appeal to the United States to nullify its trade embargo against Nicaragua and resume the Manzanillo dialogue. Venezuela on 10 May[97] forwarded a government communiqué of 6 May stating that it found the United States trade embargo against Nicaragua disturbing. However, Venezuela also felt that a recent trip by the President of Nicaragua to the Soviet Union had added to existing antagonisms and did not help promote understanding.

Democratic Yemen on 9 May[98] transmitted a statement of 8 May condemning the trade embargo which, it said, constituted a new escalation in attempts by the United States to destroy the Nicaraguan revolution and to interfere with the Contadora peace efforts.

SECURITY COUNCIL CONSIDERATION (May)

On 6 May,[99] Nicaragua requested an urgent meeting of the Security Council to consider what it called the extremely serious situation facing the Central American region.

The Council considered the situation at four meetings between 8 and 10 May. At their request, Algeria, Argentina, Bolivia, Brazil, Colombia, Costa Rica, Cuba, Cyprus, the Dominican Republic, Ecuador, Ethiopia, the German Democratic Republic, Guatemala, Guyana, Honduras, Iran, the Lao People's Democratic Republic, Mexico, Mongolia, Nicaragua, Poland, Spain, the Syrian Arab Republic, the United Republic of Tanzania, Viet Nam, Yugoslavia and Zimbabwe were invited to take part in the proceedings without the right to vote.

On 10 May 1985, the Security Council unanimously adopted **resolution 562(1985)**.

The Security Council,

Having heard the statement of the Permanent Representative of Nicaragua to the United Nations,

Having also heard the statements of representatives of various States Members of the United Nations in the course of the debate,

Recalling resolution 530(1983), which reaffirms the right of Nicaragua and of all the other countries of the area to live in peace and security, free from outside interference,

Recalling also General Assembly resolution 38/10, which reaffirms the inalienable right of all the peoples to decide on their own form of government and to choose their own economic, political and social system free from all foreign intervention, coercion, or limitation,

Recalling also General Assembly resolution 39/4, which encourages the efforts of the Contadora Group and appeals urgently to all the interested States in and outside the region to co-operate fully with the Group through a frank and constructive dialogue, so as to achieve solutions to the differences between them,

Recalling General Assembly resolution 2625(XXV), in the annex of which the Assembly proclaims the principle that no State may use or encourage the use of economic, political or any other type of measures to coerce another State in order to obtain from it the subordination of the exercise of its sovereign rights and to secure from it advantages of any kind,

Reaffirming the principle that all members shall fulfil in good faith the obligations assumed by them in accordance with the Charter of the United Nations,

1. *Reaffirms* the sovereignty and inalienable right of Nicaragua and other States freely to decide their own political, economic and social systems, to develop their international relations according to their people's interests free from outside interference, subversion, direct or indirect coercion or threats of any kind;

2. *Reaffirms once again* its firm support to the Contadora Group and urges it to intensify its efforts; it also expresses its conviction that only with genuine political support from all interested States will those peace efforts prosper;

3. *Calls upon* all States to refrain from carrying out, supporting or promoting political, economic or military actions of any kind against any State in the region which might impede the peace objectives of the Contadora Group;

4. *Calls upon* the Governments of the United States of America and Nicaragua to resume the dialogue they had been holding in Manzanillo, Mexico, with a view to reaching accords favourable for normalizing their relations and regional détente;

5. *Requests* the Secretary-General to keep the Security Council apprised of the development of the situation and the implementation of the present resolution;

6. *Decides* to remain seized of this matter.

Security Council resolution 562(1985)

10 May 1985   Meeting 2580   Adopted unanimously

Draft by Nicaragua (S/17172), amended by vote.
Meeting numbers. SC 2577-2580.

The resolution was adopted after a paragraph-by-paragraph vote requested by the United States. The first, second, third, fourth, fifth and seventh preambular paragraphs were adopted unanimously; the sixth preambular paragraph was adopted by 14 votes to none, with 1 abstention (United Kingdom). An eighth preambular paragraph, which would have had the Council express serious concern about increased tensions in Central America, recently aggravated by the trade embargo and other coercive economic measures against Nicaragua that endangered the stability of the region and undermined the Contadora Group's efforts, received 13 votes to 1 (United States), with 1 abstention (United Kingdom), and was not adopted because of the negative vote by a permanent member of the Council.

The first two operative paragraphs of the Nicaraguan draft were not adopted, receiving, respectively, 11 votes to 1 (United States), with 3 abstentions (Egypt, Thailand, United Kingdom), and 13 votes to 1 (United States), with 1 abstention (United Kingdom). These paragraphs would have had the Council: express regret over the recent trade embargo and other coercive economic measures against Nicaragua which were inconsistent with the principle of non-interference in the internal affairs of States and represented a danger to the stability of the region, and call for an immediate end to those measures; and call on the interested States to refrain from any action or intention to destabilize or undermine other States or their institutions, including the imposition of trade embargoes or other measures incompatible with the

United Nations Charter, and in violation of commitments contracted multilaterally or bilaterally.

Votes were also taken on the provisions which became operative paragraphs 1 and 4, adopted, respectively, by 14 votes to none, with the United Kingdom abstaining, and 13 votes to none, with the United Kingdom and the United States abstaining. Paragraphs 2, 3, 5 and 6 were adopted unanimously.

Before the vote on the draft resolution, Thailand explained that, while it regretted the recent trade embargo and other coercive economic measures against Nicaragua as being inconsistent with the Contadora process, it could not go as far as to agree with the wording of operative paragraph 1 of the draft and would abstain in the vote on it.

After the vote, the United Kingdom explained that it had abstained on the sixth preambular paragraph and on what became operative paragraph 1 on the ground that the right to self-determination was one that belonged to peoples and not to States, and it deplored the distortion of that principle in the first paragraph. Nicaragua expressed satisfaction that the overwhelming majority of speakers had spoken out against the coercive measures taken by a major Power against a small non-aligned State and voiced the hope that the United States would comply with the terms of the resolution and allow Central Americans to find solutions to the problems confronting their region.

Debate on the item centred on the policies of the United States towards Nicaragua, particularly the imposition of the total trade embargo that went into effect on 7 May.

Nicaragua expressed concern that the United States had continued to present Nicaragua as a danger to United States security and had publicly avowed its intention to overthrow the Nicaraguan Government. The latest step towards this goal was the decision by the United States President to impose a total trade embargo. Nicaragua said that it was not and could never be a threat to the United States; rather, the contrary was true. The United States actions against Nicaragua were illegal, violating fundamental norms governing political and economic relations between States and the principle of non-interference in the internal affairs of other States and of the peaceful settlement of disputes between States, and affected the peace process in Central America. Nicaragua stressed that a central pillar of its foreign policy, which was based on the tenet of non-alignment, was its complete support for the efforts of the Contadora Group.

The United States rejected the charge that Nicaragua was a victim of American aggression and asserted that the Sandinists were intent on converting Nicaragua into another totalitarian satellite of the Soviet Union; they were bent on intimidating, destabilizing and subverting their neighbours. The

United States argued that its trade embargo did not violate the United Nations Charter, the OAS Charter, the United States–Nicaragua Friendship, Commerce and Navigation Treaty or the General Agreement on Tariffs and Trade (GATT); such economic measures were commonly recognized and frequently used as legitimate instruments of foreign policy. Although the United States continued to support the Contadora process, it expressed scepticism about Nicaragua's commitment to the Contadora objectives because Nicaragua continued to increase its war-making potential and develop anti-democratic governmental structures.

Virtually every other speaker in the debate expressed the view that the problems in the Central American region could be resolved only through a peaceful, negotiated settlement based on the principles of international law and in conformity with the United Nations Charter. They expressed full support for the efforts of the Contadora Group.

India expressed the position of the Co-ordinating Bureau of the Movement of Non-Aligned Countries, which had condemned the trade embargo and other coercive measures against Nicaragua as contrary to the norms governing the international legal and economic order and which saw the measure as part of a larger plan to destabilize and overthrow the Nicaraguan Government, endangering peace and security in the region. The Ukrainian SSR agreed that the embargo was a violation of international law and Algeria added that it ran counter to the Contadora spirit of harmony. Zimbabwe said the embargo only aggravated tension in Central America and vitiated the efforts of the Contadora Group.

Many other States expressed the view that coercive economic measures were proscribed by international law and violated its fundamental principles. Among them were the German Democratic Republic, Guyana, Madagascar and the Syrian Arab Republic. Mexico said it had offered its own territory, at Manzanillo, for dialogue between the United States and Nicaragua and urged that this diplomatic activity be resumed. China agreed that the trade embargo violated the principles of the United Nations Charter and said the Central American question should be settled by the countries themselves through negotiations. The USSR condemned the imposition of a trade embargo as the latest link in a chain of lawless actions against Nicaragua and asserted that a solution to the problem in Central America would be found only through a peaceful, negotiated settlement which respected the sovereignty of the countries of the region. Bolivia cited a number of charters that prohibited the use of measures against a sovereign State that had chosen its own political and economic system. Mongolia asked the Security Council to condemn vigorously the illegal acts of

the United States and demand an immediate end to all its aggressive acts against Nicaragua.

Viet Nam drew a parallel between the cases of Nicaragua and Viet Nam in the escalation of coercive measures and force by the United States and urged the Council to compel the United States to end its hostile acts.

Ethiopia deplored the embargo because it believed that it was inconceivable that Nicaragua, a small, developing country, could pose a threat to its neighbours, especially a super-Power. The Lao People's Democratic Republic saw the embargo as part of the United States intention, which it had expressed since Nicaragua's revolution, to topple that Government.

Costa Rica said it had concluded that it was legally impossible for it to participate in the economic measures against Nicaragua.

India believed that the cause of tension in the region lay in historical factors which had resulted in deep-rooted economic and social ills; peace would not be brought about by intervention, interference or intimidation. Several other States shared the view that long-existing economic and social imbalances were the root cause of the problems in Central America. Guatemala felt that the economic situation made the region particularly vulnerable to outside influences. Peru believed that to insist on attributing the conflicts in Central America solely to the East-West confrontation was detrimental to a more realistic view of the hemisphere that would enable proper assessment of the obstacles to the development of its peoples, which included a profound economic imbalance and the political corollary of instability generated by the accumulation of unsatisfied needs. Poland expressed a similar view and added that instability in the region was exacerbated by the intensified policy of interference and intervention through increased United States military activity in the region. Brazil stated that transplanting problems pertaining to the East-West confrontation to Central America could only postpone the establishment of peace and tranquillity there.

Among other countries which cited economic inequality as the main problem in the region and felt that the region's difficulties should not be drawn into the East-West context were Trinidad and Tobago and Yugoslavia. Argentina and Costa Rica saw East-West conflict as affecting the regional crisis. Guyana believed that the struggles of the people of Central America were aimed at improving their quality of life and at fuller participation in the political process, rather than securing a strategic advantage for outside Powers or proving or disproving any ideological world view. Colombia said that everything at this moment in history was subordinated to the need to ensure economic development in the region.

Honduras agreed that the crisis in Central America had its origins in economic backwardness and a lack of political, democratic and pluralistic development, but added that Nicaragua had not stayed within the boundaries of the legitimate exercise of its sovereign powers.

Cuba, which said it had been a victim of a 26-year blockade policy that had caused it great suffering, stated that the United States was using the Nicaraguan President's visit to the Soviet Union as the pretext for its criminal embargo.

Denmark asserted that just and durable solutions to social inequalities and economic underdevelopment, which were at the root of the situation in Central America, could not be achieved by armed force or any other form of coercion and expressed the view that economic sanctions, although not violating general international law, would not help solve the problems and reduce tensions in the region. France stated that economic measures would affect the lives of populations that had already been sorely tried and bore the seeds of further internal tensions.

While expressing understanding for United States concerns in the region, Australia did not consider the imposition of trade sanctions to be an appropriate action in the circumstances.

Ecuador said the principles of self-determination of peoples and non-intervention, which were the corner-stone of the international law system, could serve as a guide in the search for solutions to the problem. The Dominican Republic called for respect for those principles.

Colombia believed that it was of the utmost importance for the Government of Nicaragua to undertake a frank and open dialogue with the democratic opposition in its country to bring about national reconciliation, and urged the United States and Nicaragua to resume their talks.

The United Republic of Tanzania stated that, to remove tension in Central America in general and in Nicaragua in particular, it was important to end all interference and threats from outside.

Communications (May-December). On 10 May,[100] Nicaragua transmitted the text of a message issued by the National Command of the Sandinist National Liberation Front and the Nicaraguan Government on the occasion of its National Dignity Day, 4 May 1985, in which it asserted that the United States economic boycott against Nicaragua was a step towards direct military intervention in Nicaragua. The text of a decision adopted by the Latin American Economic System urging the United States to rescind its trade embargo was conveyed by Nicaragua in a letter of 17 May.[101] On 20 May,[102] Nicaragua transmitted the text of a note verbale of 17 May to the United States Embassy in Managua proposing the resumption of bilateral talks at Manzanillo. Transmitted in a letter of 30 May[103] was a response to Nicaragua

sent on 28 May by the United States stating that when, in January 1985, it had informed Nicaragua of its decision not to schedule further meetings at Manzanillo at that time, while making it clear it was not terminating the talks, it had described the circumstances under which it would consider it useful to schedule additional meetings.

Letters from Nicaragua of 13 and 14 June[104] to the Council President and the Secretary-General, respectively, circulated a 13 June Declaration by the Government of Nicaragua and the National Command of the Sandinist National Liberation Front expressing concern at what they called the successful efforts of the United States Administration to induce Congress to approve budget appropriations to finance mercenary forces which were launching terrorist attacks against Nicaragua under the direction of the Central Intelligence Agency (CIA). The Declaration outlined steps Nicaragua had taken to deal with the situation.

On 21 June,[105] Nicaragua transmitted a communiqué issued on 17 June concerning a recent decision by the United States Congress to approve $27 million to support what Nicaragua called mercenary forces trained, armed and directed by the United States Government. Nicaragua said this represented a decision to escalate the aggression and obliged it to suspend measures it had taken unilaterally as a gesture of good faith and willingness to comply with agreements that might be reached in the Contadora process. A letter of the same day[106] conveyed a communiqué of 20 June concerning what it said was an attack that day on Nicaragua's diplomatic mission in Washington, D.C., which Nicaragua saw as a result of the warlike rhetoric directed against it.

Responsibility for disrupting the Contadora peace negotiations was placed on Nicaragua by the United States in a State Department statement of 20 June, transmitted on 26 June,[107] which said it deplored Nicaragua's refusal to consider a Contadora Group proposal for agreement on key security issues at a meeting in Panama on 18 and 19 June.

On 22 July,[108] Nicaragua transmitted the text of a communication of 17 July from the United States Ambassador in Managua to the Nicaraguan Government and Nicaragua's reply to that communication in a note verbale of 18 July. The Ambassador's communication warned of serious repercussions if United States citizens were subjected to terrorist attacks supported by Nicaragua, as the United States said had been the case when six of its citizens were killed in El Salvador on 19 June. Nicaragua rejected the communication, which it said contained false accusations and intolerable threats, and confirmed its total condemnation of all forms of terrorism.

On 26 July,[109] India forwarded a communiqué adopted that day by the Co-ordinating Bureau of the Movement of Non-Aligned Countries, expressing grave concern at the deterioration of the situation in the region stemming from grave new threats against Nicaragua, including financial aid to counter-revolutionary forces. It called on all States to refrain from action that might exacerbate the situation and reaffirmed its support for the Contadora Group's efforts. On 29 July,[110] Nicaragua circulated a note of the same day to the United States Secretary of State charging that, on 27 July, a group of mercenaries in the service of the United States Government had ambushed two trucks, killing nine civilians and wounding 18 others.

On 8 August,[111] Nicaragua transmitted a communiqué of 7 August concerning the alleged kidnapping that day, by a mercenary organization in Costa Rica, of about 50 people, including 29 United States citizens and approximately 18 Nicaraguan and foreign journalists travelling along the San Juan River on a Christian organization peace mission. A note of 12 August to the United States Secretary of State was transmitted by Nicaragua the same day,[112] calling on the United States to cease its support for mercenary organizations such as the one that had allegedly kidnapped the Witness for Peace mission travellers on 7 August, releasing the United States citizens the following day. In a letter dated 16 September,[113] Nicaragua circulated a presidential communiqué of 13 September charging that mercenary groups, supported by the United States, were engaging that day in new aggressive actions against Nicaragua from Costa Rican and Honduran territory with the aim of provoking a confrontation between the Central American Governments that would involve the participation of United States troops.

A letter by Nicaragua of 31 October[114] contained a government communiqué of the same date in which Nicaragua said it deplored the attitude of the United States in insisting that direct talks with Nicaragua were conditional upon its National Assembly being dissolved, and condemned its insistence that Nicaragua recognize as negotiating partners those directed by the CIA. Nicaragua proposed a high-level meeting in November between the two countries to discuss an agenda for subsequent meetings. Nicaragua, on 4 November,[115] transmitted a note of 2 November from its Minister for External Relations to the Foreign Ministers of the Contadora Group countries explaining that Nicaragua had recently proclaimed a state of emergency to give it the necessary legal instruments to defend itself in the face of the United States trade embargo and support for mercenaries.

The United States, on 6 November,[116] transmitted a report, " 'Revolution Beyond Our Borders': Sandinista Intervention in Central America", which it said described chronologically and geographically unlawful Nicaraguan activities directed against the neighbouring States of Central America and the collective response to Nicaraguan aggression. Nicaragua, in a letter of 19 November,[117] said the United States report was an attempt to justify military intervention in Nicaragua with a peculiar interpretation of Article 51 of the Charter, which speaks of the right of individual or collective self-defence. Annexed to the letter was: documentation relating to the case before the International Court of Justice (ICJ) concerning military and paramilitary activities in and against Nicaragua (see p. 1156); a section of a document concerning the intervention of Nicaragua before the Court on 30 April; the verbatim record of the testimony of David MacMichael, a United States citizen; and letters from the President of the United States National Committee for Peace in Central America. On 23 November,[118] Nicaragua transmitted the text of a letter of 20 November to the United States stating that a decision of the United States Administration to use additional funds, or to find new ways of applying those already approved, for directly supplying military equipment to the counter-revolutionary forces it supported was further evidence that the United States was preparing direct military intervention against Nicaragua.

On 6 December,[119] Nicaragua transmitted the text of a note sent the same day to the United States charging that the crash of a Sandinist helicopter on 2 December and the death of 14 soldiers was caused by surface-to-air missiles fired by mercenary forces supplied and supported by the United States.

SECURITY COUNCIL CONSIDERATION (December)

On 6 December,[120] Nicaragua requested an urgent meeting of the Security Council to consider what it called the extremely serious situation created by the escalation of acts of aggression, repeated threats and new acts of provocation directed against it by the United States.

The Council held three meetings, on 10, 11 and 12 December, to consider the Nicaraguan complaint. Invited to participate, at their request, without the right to vote, were Costa Rica, Cuba, Honduras, Iran, the Libyan Arab Jamahiriya, Mexico, Nicaragua, the Syrian Arab Republic, Viet Nam and Zimbabwe.

Meeting numbers. SC 2633, 2634, 2636.

Opening the debate, Nicaragua asserted that, in the weeks immediately preceding the Council meetings, United States involvement in the war in Central America had escalated. Characteristic of that situation was the holding of joint military manœuvres in Honduras and the supply to the counter-revolutionary forces of further sophisticated equipment. Nicaragua noted in particular the use by those forces of surface-to-air missiles supplied by the United States Government to bring down a Nicaraguan helicopter. That action, Nicaragua said, confirmed the disdain of the United States for international law and for the 10 May 1984 decision[121] of ICJ calling on the United States to halt its aggression against Nicaragua. The United States also continued to refuse to respond to the request of the Contadora Group to end its aggression against Nicaragua.

The United States said that the Nicaraguan Government continued to ignore the central fact that there was much domestic opposition to its policies and, instead, portrayed democratic armed resistance to its attempt to impose a totalitarian régime as a reactionary mercenary force organized by the United States. Rejecting Nicaraguan allegations concerning the supply of missiles, the United States asserted that it was the Sandinists who had upset the military equilibrium in Central America by receiving the sophisticated attack helicopter from the Soviet Union, and that Nicaragua's neighbours and its own people had suffered from Sandinist threats and intimidation. Regarding Nicaragua's reference to ICJ, the United States said that of the 15 Judges on that Court, 10 of the countries to which those Judges belonged, including some of Nicaragua's close friends, rejected the compulsory authority of the Court. Stating that Nicaragua had declined to attend OAS meetings in Cartagena, Colombia, to discuss the future of the Contadora negotiations, the United States said it continued to believe that the Contadora negotiating process offered the best prospect for achieving peace in Central America.

The majority of countries participating in the debate expressed concern at the deteriorating situation in Central America and deplored the coercive measures against Nicaragua as well as overt and covert attempts to interfere in its affairs. Costa Rica and Honduras joined other countries, including China, India, Madagascar, Peru, the Syrian Arab Republic, Trinidad and Tobago and the USSR, in expressing the conviction that the tensions in the region could be resolved only through negotiations among all concerned and through support for the efforts of the Contadora Group.

Honduras said the Sandinist Government had halted the Contadora negotiating process and continued to disregard the internal Central American causes of the conflict, trying to make them out to be foreign factors because Nicaragua believed its ideological and party interests were more important than the needs of the other peoples of Central America.

Costa Rica rejected the assertion by Nicaragua that counter-revolutionary groups were operating on Costa Rican territory, stating that it was neutral, had no armed forces and sought the establishment of peaceful and stable standards of coexistence with all countries of Central America regardless of their political or economic system.

In its capacity as Chairman of the Movement of Non-Aligned Countries, India reaffirmed its solidarity with the Government and people of Nicaragua, affirmed the sovereign right of every country to pursue its political, social and economic system, rejected policies of intervention and intimidation and called for further efforts by the Contadora Group and the Support Group.

Peru stated that it was untenable to try to bend by force the will of a people recently emerged from a genuine struggle for freedom and that imposing domination and dependence from outside was dangerous to third world peoples because attempts by the super-Powers to settle exclusively regional conflicts in the third world would repudiate the system of multilateral relations. The Libyan Arab Jamahiriya saw the intervention by the United States as an attempt to impose hegemony on small nations struggling for freedom.

The USSR said that the main reason for the aggravation of the situation in Central America was the further escalation of the aggressive policy of interference and destabilization by the United States against Nicaragua.

Trinidad and Tobago deplored the use of force or the threat of force in the resolution of disputes and was concerned about the prospect of an arms race in Central America and the competitive use of increasingly sophisticated weapons. China opposed intimidation, interference and infiltration carried out by any outside force against the Central American countries and held that the sovereignty and territorial integrity of those countries, including Nicaragua, should be respected. Mexico reiterated its opposition to any violation of the sovereignty, independence and territorial integrity of States and advocated the establishment of dialogue and the adoption of constructive agreements. Repudiation of the use of force was also expressed by Burkina Faso and Madagascar.

Cuba and Viet Nam regarded the supply of surface-to-air missiles by the United States to the *contras* as a clear violation of the Charter and the norms of international law, and demanded an end to all assistance to the mercenary forces.

Zimbabwe stated that the way the United States had handled the Contadora and Manzanillo talks showed that it was not sincere about finding a settlement with Nicaragua, and that Nicaragua could not feel safe when military manœuvres planned by the United States would put in place the necessary infrastructure for an invasion of Nicaragua.

The Syrian Arab Republic called on the Security Council to promote a peaceful settlement of the dispute and to persuade the United States to resume the dialogue with Nicaragua and cease its acts of aggression against that country.

Iran said that if the Contadora Group did not take timely and determined action it could be rendered ineffective because of the danger that the United States might try to influence the Group and its Support Group, consequently damaging the credibility and effectiveness of the Contadora process.

GENERAL ASSEMBLY ACTION

On 17 December 1985, the General Assembly, on the recommendation of the Second (Economic and Financial) Committee, adopted **resolution 40/188** by recorded vote.

Trade embargo against Nicaragua

The General Assembly,

Recalling the relevant purposes and principles set forth in the Charter of the United Nations,

Reaffirming the fundamental principles that govern relations among the States of the international community,

Recalling the Universal Declaration of Human Rights,

Recalling Security Council resolution 562(1985) of 10 May 1985,

Recalling also General Assembly resolution 2625(XXV) of 24 October 1970, in particular the principle concerning the duty not to intervene in matters within the domestic jurisdiction of any State, in accordance with the Charter of the United Nations,

Reaffirming that each country has the sovereign right to choose its own development policies and strategies,

Recalling all relevant articles of the General Agreement on Tariffs and Trade,

Recalling also General Assembly resolution 39/4 of 26 October 1984, in which the Assembly encouraged the efforts of the Contadora Group and all interested States, in particular those with ties to and interests in the region, to respect fully the purposes and principles of the Contadora Act on Peace and Co-operation in Central America of 7 September 1984,

Concerned that the unilateral trade embargo and other measures imposed on Nicaragua on 1 May 1985, which have been extended and broadened as from 1 November 1985, adversely affect the economy of the country, specifically its trade, and consequently its development plans,

Deeply concerned that the said measures will not contribute to the economic and social development of Nicaragua and to the goals and objectives of the Contadora process,

Recalling the widespread concern expressed by the international community about the situation in Central America, aggravated by the trade embargo against Nicaragua,

Considering that the international community is unanimous in contributing to the economic and social progress of the countries of the area and to the reinforcing of the process of economic integration of the area, in order to contribute to the quest for a negotiated political solution to the regional crisis,

Reaffirming the sovereignty and inalienable right of Nicaragua and the rest of the States in the region to decide freely on their own political, economic and social systems, to develop their international relations according to their peoples' interests, free from outside interference, subversion, direct or indirect coercion or threats of any kind,

Deeply concerned that the said trade embargo jeopardizes the principles of free trade and non-discrimination that should prevail among nations,

1. *Regrets* the recent trade embargo and other measures imposed against Nicaragua and requests that those measures be immediately revoked;

2. *Invites* all States to promote and take concrete actions of co-operation in the economic and technological spheres in Central America, in particular to help reduce the negative effects of the trade embargo and other measures imposed against Nicaragua and to contribute to economic and social development and to regional economic integration;

3. *Requests* the Secretary-General to report to the General Assembly at its forty-first session on the implementation of the present resolution.

General Assembly resolution 40/188

17 December 1985   Meeting 119   91-6-49 (recorded vote)

Approved by Second Committee (A/40/989/Add.3) by recorded vote (84-4-37), 5 December (meeting 48); 4-nation draft (A/C.2/40/L.89/Rev.1); agenda item 84 *(c)*.

Sponsors: Algeria, Mexico, Nicaragua, Peru.

Meeting numbers. GA 40th session: 2nd Committee 45-48; plenary 119.

Recorded vote in Assembly as follows:

In favour: Afghanistan, Albania, Algeria, Angola, Argentina, Australia, Austria, Bahamas, Benin, Bolivia, Botswana, Brazil, Bulgaria, Burkina Faso, Burma, Burundi, Byelorussian SSR, Cameroon, Cape Verde, China, Colombia, Comoros, Congo, Costa Rica, Cuba, Cyprus, Czechoslovakia, Democratic Yemen, Denmark, Dominican Republic, Ethiopia, Finland, France, German Democratic Republic, Ghana, Greece, Guinea, Guinea-Bissau, Guyana, Haiti, Hungary, Iceland, India, Indonesia, Iran, Iraq, Kenya, Lao People's Democratic Republic, Lesotho, Liberia, Libyan Arab Jamahiriya, Madagascar, Malaysia, Maldives, Mali, Malta, Mexico, Mongolia, Mozambique, New Zealand, Nicaragua, Nigeria, Norway, Panama, Papua New Guinea, Peru, Poland, Qatar, Romania, Sao Tome and Principe, Seychelles, Spain, Sri Lanka, Suriname, Sweden, Syrian Arab Republic, Trinidad and Tobago, Tunisia, Uganda, Ukrainian SSR, USSR, United Arab Emirates, United Republic of Tanzania, Uruguay, Vanuatu, Venezuela, Viet Nam, Yemen, Yugoslavia, Zambia, Zimbabwe.

Against: Gambia, Grenada, Israel, Saint Christopher and Nevis, Sierra Leone, United States.

Abstaining: Antigua and Barbuda, Bangladesh, Barbados, Belgium, Brunei Darussalam, Canada, Central African Republic, Chad, Chile, Dominica, Ecuador, Egypt, El Salvador, Equatorial Guinea, Fiji, Gabon, Germany, Federal Republic of, Guatemala, Ireland, Italy, Ivory Coast, Jamaica, Japan, Jordan, Kuwait, Luxembourg, Malawi, Nepal, Netherlands, Niger, Oman, Pakistan, Paraguay, Philippines, Portugal, Rwanda, Saint Lucia, Saint Vincent and the Grenadines, Samoa, Saudi Arabia, Senegal, Singapore, Somalia, Swaziland, Thailand, Togo, Turkey, United Kingdom, Zaire.

The United States introduced several amendments[122] to the sponsor-revised version of the draft resolution, which incorporated some of the earlier amendments[123] by the United States and subamendments[124] by the sponsors. By the amendments to the operative provisions, in paragraph 1 the word "that" would have been inserted after the word "regrets" and the words "were considered necessary" would have been inserted after "Nicaragua"; the words "immediately revoked" would have been replaced with "kept under constant review with the view to their eventual revocation".

Paragraph 2 would have ended with the words "Central America" and paragraph 3 would have been replaced by one recommending that Nicaragua continue to receive treatment appropriate to its special needs until the economic situation returned to normal.

The United States proposed that a separate vote be taken on each of the amendments. Nicaragua counter-proposed that no action be taken on the United States amendments and that a decision be taken immediately on the revised draft resolution.

The Nicaraguan motion was carried by a recorded vote of 50 to 40, with 33 abstentions. Saint Lucia then proposed that no action be taken on the resolution, a motion rejected by a recorded vote of 73 to 25, with 27 abstentions.

The United States said it regretted that no discussion was permitted in the Second Committee on its amendments, aimed at creating a more balanced text. The resolution was potentially damaging to the Central American peace process and was an attempt by Nicaragua to achieve there what it had been unable to achieve in any other United Nations or hemispheric forum.

Honduras said the text dealt only with effects without treating causes, and went beyond the competence of the Second Committee and the bilateral approach that should be taken. It attempted to make the economic integration of the developing countries in the subregion subject to the interpretation of only one of them. Moreover, documentation, in the form of reports by the Contadora Group countries and the final Act of 1985, was ignored and only the Act of 1984 mentioned. Thus, it had not participated in the vote.

While it voted in favour, Costa Rica said it did not support certain elements of the text, which did not adequately reflect the subject or its implications for the critical situation in Central America.

Speaking on behalf of the EC members, France said they regretted the procedures followed in the Second Committee, a view also expressed by Australia, Barbados, Canada, Denmark, Greece, India, Norway, Papua New Guinea, Solomon Islands and the United Kingdom.

The Federal Republic of Germany and Israel felt the text was one-sided and regarded the Second Committee as not the appropriate forum for considering highly political texts. The latter view was shared by Australia, Barbados, Canada, the Philippines, Singapore, the United Kingdom and the United States.

France added that the resolution drew attention to only one aspect of a complex situation. Canada, Egypt, Singapore and Trinidad and Tobago also felt that it took a selective approach to a complex problem which should have been dealt with as a whole. Belize said its support of the text in no way reflected its policies in relation to the situation in Central America, but only in relation to the principle of embargo. Norway regretted the embargo, believing it would not help solve the problems or reduce the conflicts in the region. Pakistan considered unilateral trade embargoes to be in contravention of GATT principles; by its abstention, however, it did not wish to convey a lack of confidence in the Contadora process. Austria said the embargo went against the Contadora Group's efforts and would have preferred a bilateral solution.

Bulgaria, speaking on behalf of the Eastern European States, opposed the trade embargo and fully supported the Latin American countries' struggle for social and economic independence, as well as their right to choose their economic and social policy. Cuba said its affirmative vote was not only in solidarity with Nicaragua but also because Cuba had been the victim of a quarter-century blockade by the United States. The Libyan Arab Jamahiriya said the embargo and coercive measures used against developing countries were contrary to the Charter and threatened international peace. Nicaragua believed the adoption of the resolution represented a triumph for justice, peace and reason and would enable developing and developed countries to have more equitable economic relations.

REFERENCES

[1]A/39/856-S/16889. [2]A/39/866-S/16959. [3]A/39/868 (S/16961). [4]A/39/871-S/16973. [5]A/39/873-S/16977. [6]A/40/220. [7]A/39/889-S/17104. [8]A/40/235-S/17103. [9]A/39/898 (S/17174). [10]A/40/330-S/17208. [11]A/40/401-S/17301. [12]A/39/920-S/17302. [13]A/39/922-S/17308. [14]A/40/495. [15]A/39/935. [16]A/40/499-S/17350. [17]A/39/939-S/17380. [18]A/39/943-S/17394. [19]A/40/544. [20]A/40/545-S/17395. [21]A/40/582-S/17420. [22]A/39/949-S/17446. [23]A/40/640-S/17468. [24]A/40/894-S/17634. [25]A/40/922-S/17651. [26]A/40/993-S/17674. [27]A/40/1034-S/17681. [28]YUN 1983, p. 206, SC res. 530(1983), 19 May 1983. [29]A/40/737-S/17549. [30]YUN 1984, p. 200. [31]*Ibid.*, p. 198. [32]A/40/L.34. [33]A/40/L.36. [34]A/39/857. [35]A/39/861. [36]A/39/914 (S/17277). [37]A/39/916-S/17295. [38]A/39/918-S/17297. [39]A/39/923-S/17309. [40]A/39/924-S/17312. [41]A/39/925-S/17315. [42]A/39/927-S/17327. [43]A/39/928-S/17328. [44]A/39/940-S/17381. [45]A/39/941-S/17386. [46]A/39/946-S/17423. [47]A/39/947-S/17428. [48]A/39/948-S/17440. [49]A/39/950-S/17449. [50]A/40/693-S/17508. [51]A/40/731-S/17544. [52]A/40/738-S/17550. [53]A/40/739-S/17551. [54]A/40/742-S/17561. [55]A/40/851-S/17608. [56]A/39/855-S/16886. [57]A/39/882-S/17077. [58]A/39/885-S/17091. [59]A/39/890-S/17115. [60]A/39/891 (S/17122). [61]A/39/900 (S/17178). [62]S/17188. [63]A/39/901 (S/17193). [64]A/39/904 (S/17201). [65]A/39/903 (S/17199). [66]A/39/908 (S/17245). [67]A/39/910(S/17252). [68]A/39/929-S/17329. [69]A/39/930-S/17331. [70]A/39/932-S/17337. [71]A/39/933-S/17338. [72]A/39/936-S/17353. [73]A/39/945-S/17404. [74]A/39/952-S/17466 & Corr.1. [75]A/40/659-S/17476. [76]A/40/670-S/17485. [77]A/40/710-S/17528. [78]A/40/711-S/17529. [79]A/40/719-S/17537. [80]A/40/712-S/17530. [81]A/40/760-S/17572. [82]A/40/794-S/17587. [83]A/40/828-S/17598. [84]A/40/924-S/17652. [85]S/17664. [86]A/40/995-S/17676. [87]A/39/863-S/16939. [88]A/39/875-S/16993. [89]A/39/876. [90]A/39/888 (S/17098). [91]A/40/269. [92]A/39/896-S/17163. [93]A/39/894 (S/17169). [94]S/17189. [95]S/17166. [96]S/17171. [97]S/17175. [98]A/39/897-S/17170. [99]S/17156. [100]A/39/899-S/17179. [101]A/40/321 (S/17200). [102]A/39/905-S/17203. [103]A/39/906-S/17235. [104]A/39/913 (S/17275). [105]A/39/917-S/17296. [106]A/39/919-S/17300. [107]A/39/926-S/17321. [108]A/39/934-S/17349. [109]A/39/937-S/17366. [110]A/39/938-S/17373. [111]A/39/942-S/17388. [112]A/39/944-S/17396. [113]A/40/641-S/17469. [114]A/40/835-S/17602. [115]A/40/850-S/17607. [116]A/40/858-S/17612. [117]A/40/907-S/17639. [118]A/40/925-S/17654. [119]A/40/994-S/17675. [120]S/17671. [121]YUN 1984, p. 1084. [122]A/C.2/-40/L.115. [123]A/C.2/40/L.95. [124]A/C.2/40/L.102/Rev.1.

Chapter VII

Asia and the Pacific

Matters relating to Korea, the situation in Afghanistan and that in Kampuchea, as well as the Iran-Iraq conflict, were prominent concerns in Asia brought before the United Nations in 1985.

The United Nations Command continued to monitor the 1953 Armistice Agreement between the Democratic People's Republic of Korea and the Republic of Korea. A relief operation from North Korea to flood victims in South Korea was the first such co-operative effort since 1948.

In South-East Asia, the situation in Kampuchea and border incidents affecting that country, China, the Lao People's Democratic Republic, Thailand and Viet Nam occupied the attention of the United Nations. The Secretary-General and his Special Representative visited the area in pursuit of a peaceful solution to the problems of the region. The *Ad Hoc* Committee of the International Conference on Kampuchea dispatched three missions to seven countries in pursuance of its mandate to assist in seeking a settlement of the situation. The General Assembly, in November (resolution 40/7), reiterated that a just and lasting solution required the withdrawal of all foreign forces, restoration and preservation of the country's independence, sovereignty and territorial integrity, the exercise of the people's right to determine its destiny, and a commitment by all States to non-interference in Kampuchea's internal affairs.

Armed incidents affecting Afghanistan and Pakistan continued to be reported, while the Secretary-General's Personal Representative maintained his contacts with the parties involved in the situation in Afghanistan in a format of separate, high-level "proximity" talks regarding a political settlement. The Assembly, in November, called on all parties concerned to work for the achievement of a political solution and expressed its support for the Secretary-General's efforts to that end (resolution 40/12).

Missions to investigate the treatment of prisoners of war in both Iran and Iraq and a mission to European hospitals to examine Iranian patients suffering from the effects of chemical weapons allegedly used by Iraq were undertaken in connection with the continuing conflict between Iran and Iraq. The Security Council considered the question of chemical weapons use and, in a declaration, appealed to both countries to cease violations of a 1984 undertaking not to attack purely civilian populations.

East Asia

Korean question

During 1985, the President of the Security Council received the report of the United Nations Command (UNC) concerning maintenance of the 1953 Korean Armistice Agreement. The Council President also received a communication from the Democratic People's Republic of Korea concerning the report.

Report of the United Nations Command. A report of UNC concerning the maintenance in 1984 of the 1953 Korean Armistice Agreement[1] was submitted by a letter[2] of 13 June 1985 from the United States on behalf of the Unified Command established pursuant to a 1950 Security Council resolution.[3]

The report stated that in 1984 the Korean People's Army (KPA) and the Chinese People's Volunteers (CPV) continued to conduct hostile acts against UNC and the Republic of Korea. These totalled more than 2,000 violations of the Agreement. An appendix gave details of two incidents which occurred in 1984 and were discussed by the Military Armistice Commission (MAC). The first one involved the recovery, on 9 April, of a boat of the Democratic People's Republic of Korea which had been sunk by the Republic of Korea navy after allegedly infiltrating two North Korean armed agents into the Republic on 3 December 1983, thus substantiating, the report said, a charge made that month of a violation of the Agreement.

The second incident, occurring on 23 November, involved what was described as an unprovoked North Korean armed attack on UNC security guards and a Soviet defector in the Joint Security Area. As a result of the incident, one UNC guard was killed, another wounded, and three North Korean guards were killed and an unknown number wounded. Subsequently, at a MAC meeting, UNC demanded from the KPA/CPV side the institution of control measures and procedures to preclude the recurrence of similar incidents.

UNC also reported taking a number of initiatives to reduce military tensions on the Korean peninsula. Among them was a proposal that mutual notification be given about major training exercises. UNC also invited the five members of the KPA/CPV component of MAC to observe the training exercise "Team Spirit–84" held from early February to mid-April, and proposed that closed-door meetings of MAC secretaries be convened to find mutually agreeable actions to reduce military tensions. According to the report, these proposals were ignored by the other party.

The report also mentioned an unprecedented humanitarian event which started on 8 September when the North Korean Red Cross Society offered relief goods to flood victims in South Korea. The deliveries of relief goods took place between 29 September and 3 October 1984. The multi-site relief transfer operation was a historical first since the 1948 establishment of the two opposing Governments in North and South Korea. Upon completion of this operation and at the suggestion of the heads of the respective Red Cross Societies, seven North-South meetings were held to discuss a variety of issues. Among these was the first North-South government-to-government–level economic meeting which took place on 15 November. UNC provided security, facilities and administrative support for these talks as well as for the relief goods–transfer operation.

The report asserted that North Korea had been unwilling to co-operate in enabling MAC to carry out its mission by refusing to investigate jointly violations of the Armistice Agreement and by disavowing responsibility for violations.

. **Communication.** By a letter of 19 September 1985[4] to the President of the Security Council, the Democratic People's Republic of Korea described the UNC report as full of distortions and fabrications designed to veil the aggressive policy of the United States in South Korea. The letter stated that it was the United States which aggravated tension and increased the danger of a new war by introducing into South Korea various kinds of weapons of mass destruction, including nuclear weapons and means of nuclear delivery, in gross violation of the Armistice Agreement. The United States had also worked to introduce medium-range nuclear "Cruise" and "Pershing-2" missiles into South Korea.

The letter stated that during 1984 there were more than 21,500 violations of the Armistice Agreement by the United States and South Korea; during the period from 1 January to 31 June 1985, there were over 10,800 cases. "Team Spirit–85" was termed a combined preliminary war and nuclear war test aimed at attacking the Democratic People's Republic of Korea from the ground, sea and sky.

To remove the danger of war and ease tension in Korea, the Democratic People's Republic said it had proposed on 10 January 1984 that tripartite talks be held between it, the United States and South Korea.

Appended to the letter was an appeal dated 6 September 1985 to the Governments of all countries of the world actively to prevent war in Korea and realize at the earliest date Korea's independent and peaceful reunification after the withdrawal of United States troops.

REFERENCES

[1]YUN 1953, p. 136, GA res. 725(VIII), annex, 7 Dec. 1953. [2]S/17447. [3]YUN 1950, p. 230, SC res. 84(1950), 7 July 1950. [4]S/17483.

South-East Asia

Kampuchea situation

The situation in and around Kampuchea—particularly border incidents, attacks which endangered refugees and civilians, escalation of tensions along the Thai-Kampuchean border and the possibility for peace negotiations, as well as Kampuchea's representation in the United Nations—continued to occupy the attention of the United Nations in 1985.

The *Ad Hoc* Committee of the International Conference on Kampuchea dispatched three missions in April, June and July to seven countries in pursuance of its mandate to assist in seeking a settlement of the situation. In November (resolution 40/7), the General Assembly reiterated that a just and lasting solution required the withdrawal of all foreign forces, restoration and preservation of the country's independence, sovereignty and territorial integrity, the exercise of the people's right to determine its destiny, and a commitment by all States to non-interference in Kampuchea's internal affairs.

Communications. Among the numerous communications received by the Secretary-General during the year on various aspects of the situation in Kampuchea and related issues, a number related to incidents on the common borders of Democratic Kampuchea, Thailand and Viet Nam.

In a letter of 3 January 1985,[1] Thailand charged that on 31 December 1984 a group of Vietnamese troops supported by heavy artillery entered Thai territory and ambushed Thai paramilitary troops on routine patrol near the Thai-Kampuchean border, killing four Thai soldiers and wounding two others. The Government condemned this act and reaffirmed its legitimate right to take measures to safeguard Thailand's sovereignty and territorial integrity.

The Viet Nam News Agency, in a statement of 5 January transmitted on 7 January,[2] rejected what it called Thailand's recent false news that Vietnamese army volunteers in Kampuchea crossed the border into Thai territory. Viet Nam declared that the slanderous contention was intended to cover Thailand's collusion with China against the revival of the Kampuchean people.

On 9 January,[3] Thailand transmitted a message from its Minister for Foreign Affairs, noting that the Government found it impossible to participate in a forthcoming plenary session of the Interim Mekong Committee to be held at Hanoi, Viet Nam, on 10 January because of sustained incursions into Thai territory by Vietnamese forces operating in Kampuchea.

In a second letter of 9 January,[4] Thailand condemned a series of acts of aggression allegedly perpetrated by Vietnamese forces in Kampuchea against Thailand from 4 to 8 January. These acts involved incursions into and shelling of Thai territory, border partrol clashes and firing on aircraft, and resulted in several deaths, injuries and the dislocation of villagers.

On 15 January,[5] Democratic Kampuchea transmitted excerpts from the New Year's message by its Vice-President in Charge of Foreign Affairs. The statement surveyed the military, political and international situation and condemned an alleged Vietnamese attack on a Kampuchean refugee camp on 25 December 1984. In a second letter of 15 January,[6] Democratic Kampuchea transmitted a telegram dated 12 January from its President, Norodom Sihanouk, asking the Secretary-General to prevail upon Viet Nam to end the frequent attacks by its army he said were mounted against the Khmer civilian population living in the refugee camps on the Thai-Kampuchean border. He also appealed to the rich and liberal-minded countries throughout the world to take a larger number of Khmer refugees.

A letter from Democratic Kampuchea of 24 January[7] annexed a statement of 20 January by the Ministry of Foreign Affairs of the Coalition Government of Democratic Kampuchea asserting the right of the people of Kampuchea to fight the Vietnamese aggressors and the right of the world to support the just struggle of the people of Kampuchea. Hanoi authorities, it said, must unconditionally withdraw their forces from Kampuchea. Democratic Kampuchea, to a letter of 29 January,[8] annexed a statement of 25 January from the Foreign Ministry condemning what it said was Viet Nam's deliberate policy of starving the people of Kampuchea so as to supply its forces.

Vietnamese attacks against Kampuchean refugee encampments along the Thai-Kampuchean border were addressed in a 9 January statement, transmitted on 30 January,[9] by Malaysia's Foreign Minister in his capacity as current Chairman of the Standing Committee of the Association of South-East Asian Nations (ASEAN). The ASEAN countries (Brunei Darussalam, Indonesia, Malaysia, the Philippines, Singapore and Thailand) deplored the escalation of fighting along the border, which had led to the exodus of tens of thousands of Kampuchean refugees into Thailand. They called on Viet Nam to heed the desire of the international community for an early and comprehensive political settlement of the Kampuchean problem through negotiation and to abandon its policy of military occupation of Kampuchea.

On 5 February,[10] Democratic Kampuchea circulated a communiqué of 3 February from the Council of Ministers of its Coalition Government reviewing the subjects discussed at its meeting that day and condemning Viet Nam's manœuvres to split the tripartite coalition and other actions, including genocide through its policy of starvation and levy of the population to clear jungles, attacks against the border refugee camps and the policy of "Vietnamization" through the massive influx of Vietnamese settlers.

Italy, on behalf of the 10 States members of the European Community (EC), circulated, in a letter of 31 January,[11] an EC Declaration on Viet Nam's offensive in Kampuchea and incursions into Thailand, adopted at a meeting on European political co-operation (Rome, 23 January). The States condemned violations of human rights and the principles of the United Nations Charter resulting from the increasingly intensive attacks by Vietnamese troops on refugee camps in the area, and appealed for a halt to military activities on the border and a political settlement.

Viet Nam responded on 15 February,[12] rejecting as fabrication the allegations by the EC States, which Viet Nam said only repeated the slanders by China and Thailand—the supporters of the Pol Pot gang who were destroying and sabotaging the Kampuchean people's revival.

Thailand, in a letter of the same day,[13] reviewed what it described as recent acts of aggression by Vietnamese forces in violation of Thailand's sovereignty and territorial integrity, including border incursions, clashes with troops inside Thailand and shelling; it demanded that Viet Nam immediately cease its hostile actions. On 19 February,[14] Thailand circulated a letter detailing alleged attacks on its territory by Viet Nam on 6 February, when it said four rounds of rocket shells containing toxic chemicals were fired into Thailand by Vietnamese forces; on 16 February, when five Thai villagers were killed and seven wounded by artillery shells; and on 16 and 17 February, when Vietnamese troops attacked a military position, killing three soldiers and wounding 16. On 29 March,[15] Thailand circulated eight photographs of the Thai villagers reportedly wounded or killed on 16 February.

Viet Nam, in a letter of 22 February,[16] rejected Thailand's allegations as slanderous fabrications.

In a letter of 20 February,[17] Democratic Kampuchea transmitted excerpts from the Directives of the High Command of its National Army to military units in all fronts in Kampuchea on 31 January. These reviewed and assessed the current military situation of the Vietnamese during the current dry season as well as Kampuchea's line of action.

China annexed to a letter of 19 February[18] statements of 6 and 18 February by its Ministry of Foreign Affairs on the situation in Kampuchea and on relations between China and Viet Nam. China saw no sincerity in the professed intention of the Vietnamese to settle the Kampuchean question, believed that the Coalition Government was expanding its political influence and military strength, and stated that tension along the Sino-Vietnamese border was solely the making of the Vietnamese authorities. China named Viet Nam the aggressor in Kampuchea and announced its intention to continue to support and assist the Kampuchean people in their just struggle against the Vietnamese invaders.

Democratic Kampuchea, on 7 March,[19] transmitted information on the situation in Kampuchea as at the end of February, as described in excerpts from the Directives of its National Army's High Command to all its military units.

On 8 March,[20] Thailand described alleged attacks on its territory by Vietnamese forces in Kampuchea: on 28 February, when three Thai soldiers were killed and several wounded by artillery shells, which also fell on 1 March; on 4 March, when a Thai soldier was killed in a clash inside Thai territory; and on 5 March, when 800 to 1,000 Vietnamese soldiers launched attacks. Thailand stated that it drove away the troops on 6 March, inflicting heavy casualties.

A letter of 12 March[21] transmitted a communiqué of 1 March following a meeting of the Co-ordination Committee for Defence of the Coalition Government of Democratic Kampuchea, attended by the Ministers of the Co-ordination Committee of the party of Norodom Sihanouk, the Khmer People's National Liberation Front and the party of Democratic Kampuchea, as well as military personnel of the three parties. The Committee stated its assessment of the politico-military situation in the field following the latest series of offensives by Vietnamese forces; it had also discussed maximum use of resources, especially in logistics and military intelligence. It observed that Viet Nam was still faced with enormous problems six years after its invasion of Kampuchea.

China, in a letter of 11 March,[22] condemned alleged attacks by Viet Nam on border towns and villages inside China, forcing counter-attacks. It demanded that Viet Nam cease infringing the ter-ritorial sovereignty of Thailand, withdraw its troops from Kampuchea and stop military provocations against China.

On 13 March,[23] Viet Nam forwarded the text of an 11 March statement by its Foreign Ministry rejecting what it called the slanderous charge that Vietnamese army volunteers crossed the Kampuchean-Thai border and trespassed on Thailand's territory. Viet Nam said the charge was a customary trick of Thai ruling circles aimed at covering their collusion with China in backing the genocidal Pol Pot clique and other Khmer reactionary forces.

On 14 March,[24] Thailand described alleged attacks by Vietnamese forces: on 4 March some 100 Vietnamese troops invaded and captured 62 Thai villagers; more than 7,500 Thai villagers had to be evacuated when threatened by heavy cross-border artillery fire from 5 to 10 March; and on 11 March Vietnamese forces resumed incursions into Thai territory, resulting in the deaths of 11 Thai soldiers and the wounding of 68. Responding on 25 March,[25] Viet Nam rejected the allegations as fabrications and claimed that Thailand was teaming up with China to sabotage Kampuchea's rebirth. Viet Nam also circulated on 26 March[26] a Foreign Ministry statement of the previous day on what it called the bellicose statements of Thai authorities, in particular references to the right of "hot pursuit". Viet Nam said the situation required urgent measures to establish immediately a safety zone under international supervision on either side of the Thai-Kampuchean border.

Democratic Kampuchea, on 2 April,[27] transmitted a statement of 29 March by the Ministry of Foreign Affairs of its Coalition Government stating that a recent announcement by Viet Nam of a partial troop withdrawal from Kampuchea was deceitfully designed to mislead international public opinion. To a letter of 8 April,[28] Democratic Kampuchea annexed a communiqué of 3 April following a meeting in Kampuchea of members of all Co-ordination Committees of the Coalition Government, at which it was decided to set up a joint body to reinforce co-ordination among the three participating parties of that Government; they noted the increasing activities of their resistance forces around the capital, Phnom Penh. A letter of 19 April[29] from Democratic Kampuchea described the situation in Kampuchea as of mid-April through excerpts from an address by its Vice-President on 13 April, the tenth anniversary of the founding of Democratic Kampuchea. On 25 April,[30] Democratic Kampuchea transmitted a document prepared by the Office of the Prime Minister of the Coalition Government alleging crimes committed by Viet Nam against the civilian population of Dangrek, one of several civilian encampments along the Kampuchea-Thailand border, on 24 January.

Seven alleged acts of aggression—incursions, mine-laying, rocket and mortar fire—by Viet Nam against Thailand between late April and 10 May, resulting in the deaths of nine Thai soldiers, were described in a Thai letter of 13 May.[31]

Viet Nam, on 8 May,[32] transmitted a statement of 6 May by the Viet Nam News Agency rejecting as false Thailand's recent news that Viet Nam had used helicopters to attack Thai fishing boats in international waters.

Information on the situation in Kampuchea from October 1984 to April 1985 (the seventh dry season), excerpted from the 30 April 1985 communiqué of its army High Command, was circulated by Democratic Kampuchea on 21 May.[33]

Viet Nam, on 20 May,[34] forwarded a statement of 17 May by its Foreign Ministry on what it termed serious violations of the territory of the People's Republic of Kampuchea by Thai troops, recounting airspace, sea space and troop intrusions, bombardments and firing incidents between 1 and 17 May. In response, Thailand, on 24 May,[35] transmitted a 22 May Foreign Ministry statement rejecting as groundless the accusation made by Viet Nam on behalf of what it called its puppet régime in Phnom Penh.

On 23 May,[36] the Lao People's Democratic Republic transmitted a 20 May statement by the People's Republic of Kampuchea recounting alleged bomb, rocket and artillery attacks on it by Thai aircraft on 1, 7, 8, 9 and 11 May and demanding that Thailand put an immediate end to its dangerous violations of Kampuchea's territorial integrity.

On 18 June,[37] a letter from Thailand described alleged acts of aggression against Thailand's sovereignty by Viet Nam on 7 and 10 June, charging troop incursions and clashes and the wounding of two Thai soldiers. Viet Nam rejected these accusations on 27 June,[38] questioning Thailand's rejection of initiatives by the People's Republic of Kampuchea, especially the proposal to establish a safe zone along the Thai-Kampuchean border.

On 19 June,[39] Democratic Kampuchea transmitted a 14 June statement by its Foreign Ministry condemning Viet Nam for creating a shortage of food in Kampuchea in 1985.

A joint communiqué issued by the ASEAN Foreign Ministers on 9 July was annexed to a letter of 17 July[40] from the Philippines. The Ministers expressed deep concern at what they termed the continued illegal occupation of Kampuchea by Vietnamese forces, deplored Viet Nam's recent dry-season border offensive and aggression, and were of the view that Viet Nam's partial withdrawal of troops in April was mere troop rotation. They also reaffirmed the validity of their appeal of September 1983[41] for Kampuchean in-

dependence and reiterated their call for a political settlement and their support for the Coalition Government.

Democratic Kampuchea, on 25 July,[42] transmitted a declaration of 6 July of the Democratic Kampuchea Party, following a 5/6 July meeting of cadres of the National Army and cadres of Democratic Kampuchea. The Party reaffirmed its position on several issues, including: the solution to the Kampuchea problem; the rounding up of several hundred thousand Kampucheans and the plundering of Kampuchean lands by Vietnamese settlers; Kampuchea's union of national forces against Viet Nam; the nature of the future régime in Kampuchea; its policy of independence, peace, neutrality and non-alignment; future relations between Kampuchea and Viet Nam; and relations between Kampuchea, the Soviet Union and other countries of the Warsaw Pact. On 26 July,[43] Democratic Kampuchea transmitted the transcript of a radio interview on 10 July by a spokesman for the Department of National Defence of the Democratic Kampuchea Party commenting on a statement by Viet Nam's Foreign Minister on the Kampuchean problem.

On 21 August,[44] Thailand condemned alleged acts of aggression against it by Vietnamese forces on 18 August which involved troop incursions with heavy weapons, resulting in the deaths of three villagers, the wounding of six others and four soldiers, and property damage.

On 13 September,[45] Democratic Kampuchea transmitted a memorandum, comprising excerpts from official statements and the media on the situation in Kampuchea in 1985, outlining the military situation, the strengthening of national unity within Kampuchea's Coalition Government, what it described as Viet Nam's manœuvres and the real objective of its aggression, and proposals for a solution. On 23 September,[46] Democratic Kampuchea transmitted a document entitled "The Vietnamization of Kampuchea: a process of absorption of a people and a nation"—a discussion using the same sources.

Thailand, in a letter of 26 September,[47] drew attention to alleged acts of aggression by Viet Nam: on 17 September, when mortar shells killed one Thai paramilitary person; on 19 September, when shelling was resumed; on 21 September, when a Thai military unit was attacked; and on 22 September, when mortar shells seriously wounded two Thai military personnel.

The Lao People's Democratic Republic, on 4 October,[48] circulated an 18 September message from the Chairman of the Council of Ministers for Foreign Affairs of the People's Republic of Kampuchea on the occasion of the fortieth anniversary of the United Nations. He referred to possibilities for solving the problems of that country mentioned at the tenth conference of the Foreign Ministers of Kampuchea,

Laos and Viet Nam in January 1985 and reiterated at the eleventh conference at Phnom Penh in August: if the concerned parties could not reach a political solution, Viet Nam would continue its gradual withdrawal from Kampuchea and complete its total pull-out in 1990, or withdraw sooner if the parties could reach a political solution.

Democratic Kampuchea, on 14 October,[49] transmitted a document entitled "Vietnamese genocidal crimes in Kampuchea: a new process of extermination of the people of Kampuchea", which contained accusations that, to maintain its occupation at all costs, Viet Nam was employing increasingly barbarous methods against Kampuchea's civilian population.

On 5 November,[50] Angola forwarded the Final Political Declaration and the Final Economic Declaration adopted by the Conference of Foreign Ministers of Non-Aligned Countries (Luanda, 4-7 September). In the Political Declaration, the Ministers warned that there was a danger of the tensions in and around Kampuchea escalating over a wider area and urged that the tensions be de-escalated through a comprehensive political solution which would provide for the withdrawal of all foreign forces. They reaffirmed the right of the Kampuchean people to determine their own destiny free from foreign interference and hoped that a climate conducive to exercising that right would be created through negotiations.

Democratic Kampuchea, in a letter of 19 November,[51] transmitted a situation report on Kampuchea during the seventh rainy season (May-September), excerpted from a communiqué of its National Army High Command. On 25 November,[52] it brought to the Secretary-General's attention its latest information on the situation in the country at the beginning of the 1985/86 dry season, from late October to mid-November.

ECONOMIC AND SOCIAL COUNCIL ACTION

On 30 May 1985, the Economic and Social Council, by **decision 1985/155** on the right of peoples to self-determination, endorsed a February resolution of the Commission on Human Rights and expressed concern at the activities of the foreign forces in Kampuchea, particularly the continuing attacks on Kampuchean civilian encampments along the Thai-Kampuchean border.

Activities of the Committee of the Conference on Kampuchea. The 10-member *Ad Hoc* Committee of the International Conference on Kampuchea met in 1985 pursuant to a 1984 Assembly resolution,[53] and dispatched a mission to Beijing, China, and Bangkok, Thailand, in the second half of April, another to Buenos Aires, Argentina, Lima, Peru, and Port of Spain, Trinidad, from 2 to 11 June and a third to Amman, Jordan, and Kuala Lumpur,

Malaysia, from 2 to 8 July. These consultations underscored the continuing concern of the international community over the Kampuchean issue, seeking the widest possible support for the efforts towards a comprehensive political solution.

The report[54] on its 1984-1985 activities noted that the first two meetings of the *Ad Hoc* Committee in 1985 were devoted to considering the situation along the Thai-Kampuchean border. The Committee issued statements on 17 January and 15 February expressing serious concern at the escalation of hostilities along the border, and deploring and calling for an immediate end to the military attacks by foreign forces against Kampuchean encampments in the area and their incursions into Thailand. It reiterated its conviction that the problem could be solved only through peaceful means in accordance with the Declaration[55] adopted by the 1981 International Conference on Kampuchea and the relevant General Assembly resolutions, and appealed to all parties to join efforts to create an atmosphere conducive to constructive dialogue and negotiations.

The missions, during their visits, held consultations with the Governments on prospects for a political settlement of the problem in the light of developments following the adoption of the most recent General Assembly resolution, particularly the hostilities along the Thai-Kampuchean border during the 1985 dry-season offensive.

The missions restated that a just and lasting settlement must be based on withdrawal of all foreign forces and the right of the Kampuchean people to determine their own destiny, and should take account of the legitimate security concerns of the States of the region, including a commitment by all to non-interference and non-intervention in Kampuchea's internal affairs.

In the discussions with the Governments, China said that the key to the solution was the withdrawal of Viet Nam's troops from Kampuchea and restated its position as set out in its five-point proposal of 1 March 1983.[41] Thailand emphasized the united and continued determination of ASEAN to pursue its efforts towards a political settlement based on the total withdrawal of foreign forces, national reconciliation and self-determination for the Kampuchean people. Argentina, Peru and Jordan expressed support for the Committee's work and the principles laid down in the Declaration on Kampuchea, and indicated their willingness to contribute towards achieving a negotiated settlement. Trinidad and Tobago also supported the Committee's efforts and reaffirmed its commitment to the principle of non-intervention. Jordan viewed the problem as stemming from a violation of Charter principles, which could not be applied selectively; it would seek their implementation in the case of Kampuchea and other conflicts.

ASEAN Foreign Ministers in Kuala Lumpur urged the Committee to continue its consultations to keep alive public awareness and foster a better understanding of the problems involved.

The Committee again appealed to Member States which had not participated in the Conference to co-operate in efforts to attain the goals of the Declaration on Kampuchea and Assembly resolutions on the question. All parties concerned were called upon to pursue dialogue and refrain from action that would further complicate the situation.

Report of the Secretary-General. In an October report[56] to the General Assembly, submitted pursuant to a 1984 request,[53] the Secretary-General stated that he had continued, within the framework of his good offices, to seek ways of achieving progress towards a peaceful resolution to the problem and had paid official visits to Thailand, Viet Nam, Malaysia and Indonesia in January/February 1985 for that purpose. Discussions with the leaders of those countries had enabled him to assess the situation and obtain clarifications on the positions and concerns of the countries of the region. He reiterated his conviction that differences could only be bridged by a sustained dialogue on the basic elements for a comprehensive settlement.

The serious tension and hostilities which had developed along the Thai-Kampuchean border before the Secretary-General's visit and which continued throughout the dry season prevented any immediate progress towards that goal. However, all the interlocutors had expressed support and asked him to persevere in his efforts towards a political solution.

In July, on the Secretary-General's behalf, his Special Representative, Rafeeuddin Ahmed, attended the eighteenth annual ASEAN meeting at Kuala Lumpur, and subsequently visited Hanoi (10-12 July) for consultations with the Vietnamese authorities. Since then the Secretary-General had further discussions in New York with the President of Democratic Kampuchea, the Prime Minister of Thailand, the Deputy Prime Minister and Minister for Foreign Affairs of the Lao People's Democratic Republic, the Deputy Prime Minister of Malaysia, the Foreign Ministers of China and of Indonesia, the Acting Foreign Minister of the Philippines, and the Minister Member of the Council of Ministers of Viet Nam.

The discussions that the Secretary-General and his Special Representative had held during the year suggested that there was a reasonable degree of agreement on the main elements of a comprehensive political settlement, including: withdrawal of all foreign forces from Kampuchea; non-return to the universally condemned policies of a recent past; promotion of national reconcilia-tion; exercise by the Kampuchean people of the right to determine their own destiny; respect for the independence, territorial integrity and non-aligned status of Kampuchea; ensuring the security and sanctity of all States in the region; international guarantees for and supervision of the implementation of the agreements reached; and establishment of a zone of peace, freedom and neutrality in South-East Asia. Significant differences still existed, however, on the interpretation of those goals and the modalities for achieving them.

A limited international conference involving parties concerned, the five permanent members of the Security Council and other mutually acceptable countries had been found implicitly acceptable among the various alternatives for the dialogue format, the Secretary-General said, preceded by exploratory discussions aimed at achieving a common understanding on the above elements. The main difficulty with proximity talks lay in designating mutually acceptable participants. He stood ready to assist in promoting the dialogue process.

The Secretary-General stated that he had continued to implement the programmes of humanitarian assistance to the Kampuchean people. Funded largely by voluntary contributions, they consisted mainly of operations within Kampuchea, at the border, and within Thailand. He noted with gratification that the number of Kampuchean refugees in Thailand had been reduced from the peak of some 175,000 in 1980 to some 21,000 as of 1 October 1985. He reiterated deep appreciation to the international community for its generous support of these humanitarian assistance programmes.

The Secretary-General remarked that recent diplomatic exchanges had improved the chances for progress towards the initiation of negotiations. He urged that those exchanges be pursued with a renewed vigour and sense of urgency and reiterated his own determination to continue exercising his good offices towards that end.

GENERAL ASSEMBLY ACTION

The General Assembly, on 5 November 1985, adopted by recorded vote **resolution 40/7**.

The situation in Kampuchea

The General Assembly,

Recalling its resolutions 34/22 of 14 November 1979, 35/6 of 22 October 1980, 36/5 of 21 October 1981, 37/6 of 28 October 1982, 38/3 of 27 October 1983 and 39/5 of 30 October 1984,

Recalling further the Declaration on Kampuchea and resolution 1(I) adopted by the International Conference on Kampuchea, which offer the negotiating framework for a comprehensive political settlement of the Kampuchean problem,

Taking note of the report of the Secretary-General on the implementation of General Assembly resolution 39/5,

Deploring that foreign armed intervention and occupation continue and that foreign forces have not been withdrawn from Kampuchea, thus causing continuing hostilities in that country and seriously threatening international peace and security,

Noting the continued and effective struggle waged against foreign occupation by the Coalition with Samdech Norodom Sihanouk as President of Democratic Kampuchea,

Taking note of Economic and Social Council decision 1985/155 of 30 May 1985 on the right of peoples to self-determination and its application to peoples under colonial or alien domination or foreign occupation,

Greatly disturbed that the continued fighting and instability in Kampuchea have forced an additional large number of Kampucheans to flee to the Thai-Kampuchean border in search of food and safety,

Recognizing that the assistance extended by the international community has continued to reduce the food shortages and health problems of the Kampuchean people,

Emphasizing that it is the inalienable right of the Kampuchean people who have sought refuge in neighbouring countries to return safely to their homeland,

Emphasizing further that no effective solution to the humanitarian problems can be achieved without a comprehensive political settlement of the Kampuchean conflict,

Seriously concerned about reported demographic changes being imposed in Kampuchea by foreign occupation forces,

Convinced that, to bring about lasting peace in South-East Asia and reduce the threat to international peace and security, there is an urgent need for the international community to find a comprehensive political solution to the Kampuchean problem that will provide for the withdrawal of all foreign forces and ensure respect for the sovereignty, independence, territorial integrity and neutral and non-aligned status of Kampuchea, as well as the right of the Kampuchean people to self-determination free from outside interference,

Reiterating its conviction that, after the comprehensive political settlement of the Kampuchean question through peaceful means, the States of the South-East Asian region can pursue efforts to establish a zone of peace, freedom and neutrality in South-East Asia so as to lessen international tensions and to achieve lasting peace in the region,

Reaffirming the need for all States to adhere strictly to the principles of the Charter of the United Nations, which call for respect for the national independence, sovereignty and territorial integrity of all States, non-intervention and non-interference in the internal affairs of States, non-recourse to the threat or use of force and peaceful settlement of disputes,

1. *Reaffirms* its resolutions 34/22, 35/6, 36/5, 37/6, 38/3 and 39/5 and calls for their full implementation;

2. *Reiterates its conviction* that the withdrawal of all foreign forces from Kampuchea, the restoration and preservation of its independence, sovereignty and territorial integrity, the right of the Kampuchean people to determine their own destiny and the commitment by all States to non-interference and non-intervention in the internal affairs of Kampuchea are the principal components of any just and lasting resolution of the Kampuchean problem;

3. *Takes note with appreciation* of the report of the *Ad Hoc* Committee of the International Conference on Kampuchea on its activities during 1984-1985 and requests that the Committee continue its work, pending the reconvening of the Conference;

4. *Authorizes* the *Ad Hoc* Committee to convene when necessary and to carry out the tasks entrusted to it in its mandate;

5. *Reaffirms* its decision to reconvene the Conference at an appropriate time, in accordance with Conference resolution 1(I);

6. *Renews its appeal* to all States of South-East Asia and others concerned to attend future sessions of the Conference;

7. *Requests* the Conference to report to the General Assembly on its future sessions;

8. *Requests* the Secretary-General to continue to consult with and assist the Conference and the *Ad Hoc* Committee and to provide them on a regular basis with the necessary facilities to carry out their functions;

9. *Expresses its appreciation once again* to the Secretary-General for taking appropriate steps in following the situation closely and requests him to continue to do so and to exercise his good offices in order to contribute to a comprehensive political settlement;

10. *Expresses its deep appreciation once again* to donor countries, the United Nations and its agencies and other humanitarian organizations, national and international, that have rendered relief assistance to the Kampuchean people, and appeals to them to continue to provide emergency assistance to those Kampucheans who are still in need, especially along the Thai-Kampuchean border and in the holding centres in Thailand;

11. *Reiterates its deep appreciation* to the Secretary-General for his efforts in co-ordinating humanitarian relief assistance and in monitoring its distribution, and requests him to intensify such efforts as are necessary;

12. *Urges* the States of South-East Asia, once a comprehensive political solution to the Kampuchean conflict is achieved, to exert renewed efforts to establish a zone of peace, freedom and neutrality in South-East Asia;

13. *Reiterates the hope* that, following a comprehensive political solution, an intergovernmental committee will be established to consider a programme of assistance to Kampuchea for the reconstruction of its economy and for the economic and social development of all States in the region;

14. *Requests* the Secretary-General to report to the General Assembly at its forty-first session on the implementation of the present resolution;

15. *Decides* to include in the provisional agenda of its forty-first session the item entitled "The situation in Kampuchea".

General Assembly resolution 40/7

5 November 1985   Meeting 63   114-21-16 (recorded vote)

58-nation draft (A/40/L.4); agenda item 22.
Sponsors: Antigua and Barbuda, Bangladesh, Belgium, Brunei Darussalam, Cameroon, Canada, Central African Republic, Chad, Chile, Colombia, Comoros, Costa Rica, Denmark, Dominica, Dominican Republic, Ecuador, Equatorial Guinea, Fiji, Gambia, Germany, Federal Republic of, Haïti, Honduras, Iceland, Indonesia, Italy, Japan, Liberia, Luxembourg, Malaysia, Maldives, Mauritania, Mauritius, Nepal, Netherlands, New Zealand, Niger, Nigeria, Norway, Oman, Pakistan, Papua New Guinea, Paraguay, Philippines, Saint Lucia, Saint Vincent and the Grenadines, Samoa, Senegal, Sierra Leone, Singapore, Solomon Islands, Somalia, Swaziland, Thailand, Togo, Turkey, United Kingdom, Uruguay, Zaire.
Financial implications. 5th Committee, A/40/846; S-G, A/C.5/40/35.
Meeting numbers. GA 40th session: 5th Committee 25; plenary 60-63.

Recorded vote in Assembly as follows:

In favour: Antigua and Barbuda, Argentina, Australia, Austria, Bahamas, Bahrain, Bangladesh, Barbados, Belgium, Belize, Bhutan, Bolivia, Botswana, Brazil, Brunei Darussalam, Burkina Faso, Burma, Burundi, Cameroon, Canada, Central African Republic, Chad, Chile, China, Colombia, Comoros, Costa Rica, Democratic Kampuchea, Denmark, Djibouti, Dominica, Dominican Republic, Ecuador, Egypt, El Salvador, Equatorial Guinea, Fiji, France, Gabon, Gambia, Germany, Federal Republic of, Ghana, Greece, Grenada, Guatemala, Guinea, Haiti, Honduras, Iceland, Indonesia, Ireland, Israel, Italy, Ivory Coast, Jamaica, Japan, Jordan, Kenya, Kuwait, Lesotho, Liberia, Luxembourg, Malaysia, Maldives, Mali, Malta, Mauritania, Mauritius, Morocco, Nepal, Netherlands, New Zealand, Niger, Nigeria, Norway, Oman, Pakistan, Panama, Papua New Guinea, Paraguay, Peru, Philippines, Portugal, Qatar, Rwanda, Saint Christopher and Nevis, Saint Lucia, Saint Vincent and the Grenadines, Samoa, Saudi Arabia, Senegal, Sierra Leone, Singapore, Solomon Islands, Somalia, Spain, Sri Lanka, Sudan, Suriname, Swaziland, Sweden, Thailand, Togo, Trinidad and Tobago, Tunisia, Turkey, United Arab Emirates, United Kingdom, United States, Uruguay, Venezuela, Yugoslavia, Zaire, Zambia.

Against: Afghanistan, Albania, Angola, Bulgaria, Byelorussian SSR, Congo, Cuba, Czechoslovakia, Democratic Yemen, Ethiopia, German Democratic Republic, Hungary, Lao People's Democratic Republic, Libyan Arab Jamahiriya, Mongolia, Nicaragua, Poland, Syrian Arab Republic, Ukrainian SSR, USSR, Viet Nam.

Abstaining: Algeria, Benin, Cape Verde, Finland, Guyana, India, Iraq, Lebanon, Madagascar, Malawi, Mexico, Sao Tome and Principe, Uganda, United Republic of Tanzania, Vanuatu, Zimbabwe.

In explanation of vote, Burkina Faso said that it had voted for the draft resolution, in keeping with its opposition to intervention by foreign forces in the internal affairs of another State and because of its desire to see peace restored among the South-East Asian States, but had reservations about the content of the fifth preambular paragraph. Ireland agreed with the general thrust of the resolution but said its vote did not imply agreement with the wording of that paragraph or a change in its position regarding Kampuchean representation. Brazil recorded reservations to the same paragraph because it could not subscribe to language that it said prejudged the outcome of the Kampuchean people's exercise of their right to determine their own destiny. Trinidad and Tobago and Sweden also expressed reservations about elements of the preambular paragraphs but agreed with the confirmation of the principles of sovereignty, self-determination and the withdrawal of foreign forces as the basis for a settlement to the Kampuchean conflict.

In consideration of its recognition of a clear need at the current juncture to give maximum support and encouragement to any genuine movement towards a political negotiated solution, Guyana said it would abstain.

Cuba held that the resolution was invalid since it was adopted without the presence in the United Nations of the genuine representative of the People's Republic of Kampuchea. The Lao People's Democratic Republic found the text a distortion of reality aimed at imposing on the People's Republic of Kampuchea a one-sided settlement. There was no fighting taking place in Kampuchea, it said, simply hotbeds of tension on the border due to terrorist activities of reactionary Khmer groups; nothing was said about the assistance being provided to those groups by certain circles hostile to the Kampuchean people, and the allegations of demographic change

imposed on Kampuchea were based on dubious hearsay.

Morocco said its affirmative vote reaffirmed its support for the people of Democratic Kampuchea and other States of the region working to bring about a comprehensive solution with respect for basic Charter principles.

Participation and representation of Democratic Kampuchea in UN bodies

The question of Democratic Kampuchea's representation in United Nations bodies was again raised in 1985.

On 18 October, the Lao People's Democratic Republic conveyed a 17 October statement[57] from the Ministry of Foreign Affairs of the People's Republic of Kampuchea, protesting the decision by the United Nations to allow what it called the genocidal Pol Pot clique, masquerading in the guise of the so-called "Coalition Government of Democratic Kampuchea", illegally to retain Kampuchea's seat in the United Nations by including in the agenda the so-called "Question of Kampuchea". The statement said the Pol Pot régime had been condemned by Kampucheans and all mankind, had no right to represent the Kampuchean people and should be expelled from the United Nations. The People's Republic said it was the sole genuine and legal representative of the Kampuchean people and any discussion at the United Nations without its presence constituted gross interference in its internal affairs and a flagrant violation of its independence and sovereignty.

The Lao People's Democratic Republic and Viet Nam issued a joint statement on 28 October, transmitted in a joint letter of the same day,[58] in which the two countries reaffirmed their position on the General Assembly's debate on the situation in Kampuchea, including their non-participation partly because of their support of the stand of the People's Republic of Kampuchea that discussions without its participation constituted interference in its internal affairs.

The validity of Democratic Kampuchea's credentials to the 1985 General Assembly was also questioned at an October meeting of the Credentials Committee.

The USSR opposed accepting the credentials of the representatives of what it termed so-called Democratic Kampuchea—a political ghost to which certain circles were attempting to give some semblance of material existence by allowing it to be represented. The Government of the People's Republic of Kampuchea, formed as a result of general elections, was exercising effective control over the entire country and its legitimate rights should be restored, the USSR said.

China felt that the General Assembly had taken correct decisions on the legitimacy of the credentials of Democratic Kampuchea, since the Coalition Government, headed by Norodom Sihanouk, was the sole legitimate Government of Kampuchea. Any attempt to bring the Heng Samrin régime, propped up by Viet Nam following its invasion of Kampuchea, into the United Nations would be an attempt to legalize aggression.

The United States stated that the credentials of the representatives of Democratic Kampuchea were in order and that the substance of the situation in the country would be debated at a later stage in an appropriate forum. The reference to popular elections could not obscure the fact that those elected were merely those brought in by Viet Nam when it had invaded the country. Canada believed that the Credentials Committee should concern itself with the technical aspects of documents; whatever it felt concerning the Coalition Government, the credentials of Democratic Kampuchea appeared to be in order.

Democratic Kampuchea's credentials were approved by virtue of General Assembly **resolution 40/2 A**, approving the first report[59] of the Credentials Committee.

International security in South-East Asia

A number of letters received by the United Nations in 1985 dealt with the general aspects of relations among the countries of South-East Asia.

In a letter of 18 January,[60] Viet Nam transmitted a communiqué issued at the close of the tenth conference of the Foreign Ministers of the Lao People's Democratic Republic, the People's Republic of Kampuchea and the Socialist Republic of Viet Nam (Ho Chi Minh City, 17 and 18 January). The countries reiterated their willingness to enter into negotiations for a solution encompassing: the withdrawal of Vietnamese volunteers from Kampuchea paired with exclusion of the Pol Pot clique, respect for the Kampuchean people's right to self-determination and the right to return to a life free from the threat of genocide, the holding by the Kampucheans of free general elections in the presence of foreign observers, building South-East Asia into a zone of peace and stability, respect by all external States of the national rights of South-East Asian countries, and the establishment of international guarantees and supervision of the implementation of the agreements.

Referring to their proposal to convene an international conference on peace in South-East Asia, to be attended by all States in the region and those outside directly concerned, the Ministers considered the best solution to be a negotiated one. They stated that the tension prevailing on the Kampuchean-Thai and Lao-Thai borders stemmed from the Thai expansionist policy and supported the policy of national unity of the People's Republic of Kampuchea. On 25 January,[61] Viet Nam forwarded a transcript of an interview by the Viet Nam News Agency with the country's Foreign Minister on 19 January on the results of the conference.

Malaysia, on 22 February,[62] transmitted a statement issued in Bangkok at an 11 February meeting of the ASEAN Foreign Ministers deploring the continuing military offensive launched by Viet Nam along the Thai-Kampuchean border which had resulted in renewed hardship and suffering for tens of thousands of displaced Kampucheans and Thai villagers. The Ministers reiterated their call on Viet Nam to seek a political settlement and for a direct dialogue between Viet Nam and the Coalition Government of Democratic Kampuchea.

On 15 February,[63] Viet Nam transmitted a statement of 14 February by a Foreign Ministry spokesman commenting on the ASEAN statement. Viet Nam said the ASEAN demand that Viet Nam talk with the Coalition Government was an attempt to legalize the country's disguised Pol-Potist leaders. Viet Nam believed that Kampuchea's internal affairs must be decided by the Kampuchean people. Viet Nam, Laos and Kampuchea, the spokesman said, supported dialogue with the ASEAN countries based on equality, mutual respect and consideration of each other's stand.

The Lao People's Democratic Republic transmitted several statements by the Minister for Foreign Affairs of the People's Republic of Kampuchea or its spokesman. On 22 February,[64] it transmitted a statement of 20 February describing as a dangerous new step the appeal it said was made by the Thai Foreign Minister on 11 February calling on the United States, China and Western countries to increase military aid to the Pol Pot clique. The statement also rejected the Thai authorities' charges of violations of Thai territory and use of chemical weapons.

On 16 May,[65] Viet Nam transmitted a statement of 10 May by its Foreign Ministry rejecting as slanderous a statement attributed to Thai authorities that Viet Nam was planning to annex 17 Thai provinces in the north-east.

On 21 May,[66] the Lao representative transmitted a People's Republic of Kampuchea statement of 15 May also rejecting those allegations by the Thai authorities as part of an unremitting campaign of slander against Kampuchea and Viet Nam. A 19 June statement, transmitted by the Lao representative on 15 July,[67] demanded that Thai authorities end their misleadingly termed "repatriation" of refugees who, it said, were used by Thai authorities, seasonally opening their borders to Pol Pot supporters and other reactionaries in the dry season, and driving them back in the rainy season to perpetrate crimes. Thailand, it added, should respond positively to the People's Republic of Kampuchea's proposals for direct or indirect negotiations. On 23 July,[68] the Lao People's Democratic Republic transmitted a 13 July message from the Prime Minister and Minister for Foreign Affairs of the People's Republic of Kampuchea denouncing what was described as Thai authorities' manipulation of the Kampuchean refugee situation for their own strategic and pecuniary ends.

Viet Nam, on 8 July,[69] forwarded a statement of 5 July by its Foreign Ministry saying that a 3 July proposal by Thailand for indirect negotiations between Viet Nam and the Coalition Government of Democratic Kampuchea was put forth when world public opinion was demanding elimination of that régime and was welcoming the proposal for dialogue, which Viet Nam supported, put forth on 18 January by the three Indo-Chinese countries.

The Philippines, in a letter of 17 June[70] on behalf of the Permanent Missions to the United Nations of the States members of ASEAN, transmitted a joint statement issued on 8 July at Kuala Lumpur by the ASEAN Foreign Ministers in which it was reported that the Coalition Government of Democratic Kampuchea had informed them that it was ready to enter into exploratory indirect or "proximity" talks with Viet Nam, which could also be attended by representatives of the Vietnamese-installed Heng Samrin régime as part of the Vietnamese delegation, to discuss the basic elements of a comprehensive, political settlement: withdrawal of foreign forces from Kampuchea; establishment of a United Nations control and supervisory commission; national recognition; and organization of United Nations–supervised elections/exercise of self-determination. It called on Viet Nam to respond positively.

Thailand, on 26 July,[71] transmitted a statement of the same day by its Foreign Ministry urging Viet Nam to heed the ASEAN countries' call to respond positively to its proposal for indirect or proximity talks—and denying that its Foreign Minister had made a similar separate proposal—and to accept the reality of the Coalition Government of Democratic Kampuchea. Viet Nam's rejection of the proposal before it was delivered, the statement said, demonstrated its inflexibility.

Democratic Kampuchea, on 3 September,[72] transmitted a 28 August declaration of the Coalition Government's Council of Ministers endorsing the ASEAN proposal for proximity talks and urging Viet Nam not to delay in accepting it.

On 21 October,[73] Democratic Kampuchea transmitted a communiqué of 20 October, issued following a New York meeting of the Inner Cabinet of the Coalition Government, reaffirming the Cabinet's readiness to accept the ASEAN formula of proximity talks with Viet Nam and appealing to all peace-loving countries to continue to support the struggle of the Khmer people.

The Philippines, on behalf of the ASEAN countries, transmitted on 31 October[74] a letter of 9 October from the Chairman of ASEAN's Standing Committee reporting that Viet Nam had not responded positively to ASEAN's proposal for proximity talks with Democratic Kampuchea and calling for consistent and continued efforts by the United Nations to bring about a comprehensive political settlement.

The Lao People's Democratic Republic on 19 August[75] transmitted the text of a communiqué of the eleventh conference of the Foreign Ministers of Kampuchea, Laos and Viet Nam (Phnom Penh, 15 and 16 August), noting that a general understanding had emerged whereby a genuine dialogue had to be initiated to solve the question of peace and stability in South-East Asia and their proposals of 18 January provided a basis for such a dialogue. Regarding the ASEAN proposal for direct or indirect talks, the conference held it important to know who the interlocutors would be. It noted that the ASEAN States had nominated Indonesia as their representative and Indo-China had selected Viet Nam. It considered that Malaysia's proposal on proximity talks deserved examination. The conference also considered the time had come to resume China–Viet Nam talks towards normalizing relations. It was prepared to negotiate a treaty with Thailand based on mutual non-aggression, non-interference in internal affairs, respect for each other's sovereignty within existing borders, refusal to let one's territory be used against other countries, and peaceful coexistence.

By a letter of 6 December,[76] the Lao People's Democratic Republic transmitted copies of a book entitled *Undeclared War against the People's Republic of Kampuchea*, published by that country's Foreign Ministry in November.

On 9 December,[77] Thailand transmitted a statement of 22 November by its Foreign Ministry expressing the view that Viet Nam's claims that purported to subject the sea areas in the Gulf of Thailand and the Gulf of Tonkin to the régime of internal waters could not be justified on the basis of the applicable principles and rules of international law. Viet Nam's 1982 definition[78] of the baseline from which it measured its territorial sea and other maritime zones was also at variance with well-established rules of international law, it said, and claims[79] seeking to assert sovereignty over so-called "historical waters" in the two Gulfs and within the baselines were likewise rejected.

GENERAL ASSEMBLY ACTION

Following a discussion of the subject at two plenary meetings on 6 November, the General Assembly adopted that day, without vote, **decision 40/408**, by which it decided to include in the provisional agenda of its forty-first (1986) session the agenda item "Question of peace, stability and co-operation in South-East Asia".

China-Viet Nam dispute

Between January and March 1985, the Secretary-General received several communications from China and Viet Nam, each charging the other with policies of annexation and aggressive acts along their common border and elsewhere.

China on 24 January[80] transmitted a Foreign Ministry statement of the day before asserting that since November Viet Nam had intensified its military provocations and incursions along the Sino-Vietnamese border, involving shelling, sneak attacks and armed incursions. In an appended background paper, China charged that Viet Nam was attempting to occupy Chinese territory, was causing heavy losses to local people's lives and property, and was dispatching spies to carry out sabotage activities.

On 10 January,[81] Viet Nam forwarded a communiqué of 25 December 1984 by the Commission for Investigation of Chinese Expansionists' and Hegemonists' War Crimes against Viet Nam which described alleged land-nibbling and shelling incidents along Viet Nam's northern border in November and December of that year, resulting in the killing and wounding of dozens of people and the destruction of houses and crops. In a statement of 18 January transmitted two days later,[82] Viet Nam's Ministry of Foreign Affairs described alleged land-grabbing attacks on Vietnamese territory between 15 and 17 January by Chinese troops. On 2 February, the Vietnamese Foreign Ministry issued a statement, forwarded on 4 February,[83] condemning alleged acts of aggression—massing troops close to the border, stepped-up armed provocations—and warlike statements by China against Viet Nam.

China, on 19 February,[18] circulated Foreign Ministry statements of 6 and 18 February on the situation in Kampuchea and relations between China and Viet Nam. China stated that border tension would be relaxed only when Vietnamese troops stopped their armed provocation and intrusions (see also p. 223).

Viet Nam, in a letter of 4 March,[84] described the tense situation on the Sino-Vietnamese border as due to China's intensification of war preparations against Viet Nam; it asked the Secretary-General to exert his influence to contribute to halting these actions and to promote dialogue between the parties. On 11 March,[85] it forwarded an 8 March communiqué by its Commission for Investigation of Chinese Expansionists' and Hegemonists' War Crimes, charging that in 1984 China had reinforced its border garrisons, had escalated land-grabbing operations, and, together with the United States, had intensified spying, armed activities and

psychological warfare to incite rebellions in Viet Nam. China, in a letter of 11 March,[86] stated that, while launching a frenzied offensive on the Thai-Kampuchean border, Viet Nam had intensified its military provocations along the Sino-Vietnamese border, bombarding villages inside China, shooting and kidnapping border inhabitants and dispatching secret agents into China's territory to sabotage production and economic installations.

Lao People's Democratic Republic-Thailand dispute

The Lao People's Democratic Republic and Thailand, between January and June 1985, transmitted to the Secretary-General a number of communications on their border dispute.

The Lao People's Democratic Republic, on 7 January,[87] transmitted a 5 January statement by its Ministry of Foreign Affairs, charging that Thai troops, stationed inside Lao territory, on 2 and 3 January, launched an attack aimed at encroaching on the area of three villages in Lao territory—proof, it said, that Thailand's 1984 statement[88] that it was undertaking to withdraw from the area of the villages was a cunning manoeuvre. On 30 April,[89] Viet Nam forwarded a Foreign Ministry statement of 20 April regarding Thailand's alleged hostile activities against the three villages since the beginning of April. Thailand's Ministry of Foreign Affairs issued a statement on 7 May,[90] denying the Vietnamese allegation that Thai troops violated Lao territory; such false charges, it said, could be refuted by the fact that Lao troops had opened fire against and made incursions into Thailand on 2 and 13 March and 3 April.

In letters sent on 31 May and 3 June[91] to the President of the Security Council and the Secretary-General, respectively, the Lao People's Democratic Republic rejected the 7 May charges as slanderous allegations, and charged that Thai police gunboats had entered Lao territorial waters on 18 and 19 May. Expressing scorn for manoeuvres aimed at camouflaging criminal activities by Thailand's ultra-rightists, the Lao letter attached a Foreign Ministry statement of 25 April charging acts of aggression committed on 3, 9, 14, 18 and 22 April in the area of the three disputed villages and in other districts.

The Lao Foreign Ministry, by a 6 June statement transmitted the following day,[92] proposed to Thailand that it appoint a delegation to resume talks with the Lao Government delegation in Bangkok or Vientiane to solve problems of mutual concern, in order to improve and develop friendly relations between the two countries, including issues of guaranteeing security along the border, promoting implementation of agreements between them, and discussing economic, cultural, trade and other relations. The proposal was supported by Viet Nam in a Foreign Ministry statement of 8 June transmitted on 13 June,[93] which also demanded that Thailand respond positively.

Thailand, on 14 June,[94] observed that the Lao proposal for resuming talks was accompanied by slanderous accusations against Thailand. The Thai Government was always prepared to respond positively to a serious proposal for talks to promote economic, social and cultural relations, but the introduction of extraneous issues into the proposed bilateral talks cast serious doubt on the sincerity and readiness of the Lao Government to engage in meaningful talks. Thailand said that the machinery for promoting Thai-Lao relations had been available since a proposal by Thailand in a note by the Foreign Minister of December 1984, reaffirming that since 13 October 1984 there had been no Thai armed forces in the area of the three villages, and stating that, in order for the two countries to co-operate in normalizing their relations, the response from the Lao Government had to be continuously positive, forsaking efforts to intervene in Thailand's internal affairs through attempts to divide the Thai leaders, to create division between the Government and people, and to destroy its image through false accusation. Cessation of such activities would help create an atmosphere which would lead to normalization of relations.

REFERENCES

[1]A/40/66-S/16881. [2]A/40/68. [3]A/40/74-S/16887. [4]A/40/75-S/16888. [5]A/40/88-S/16898. [6]A/40/89-S/16899. [7]A/40/96-S/16905. [8]A/40/109-S/16914. [9]A/40/112-S/16917. [10]A/40/117-S/16940. [11]A/40/122-S/16945. [12]A/40/153. [13]A/40/131-S/16960. [14]A/40/136-S/16965. [15]A/40/214-S/17068. [16]A/40/149. [17]A/40/139-S/16969. [18]A/40/140-S/16970. [19]A/40/166-S/17010. [20]A/40/169-S/17015. [21]A/40/171-S/17022 & Corr.1. [22]A/40/172-S/17023. [23]A/40/175. [24]A/40/180-S/17038. [25]A/40/206-S/17057. [26]A/40/210-S/17064. [27]A/40/218-S/17074. [28]A/40/226-S/17087. [29]A/40/259-S/17118. [30]A/40/267-E/1985/69. [31]A/40/309-S/17185. [32]A/40/296. [33]A/40/331-S/17209. [34]A/40/333-S/17211. [35]A/40/338-S/17218. [36]A/40/335. [37]A/40/391-S/17285. [38]A/40/419-S/17311. [39]A/40/393-E/1985/128. [40]A/40/492-S/17365. [41]YUN 1983, p. 226. [42]A/40/505-S/17359. [43]A/40/507-S/17361. [44]A/40/568-S/17414. [45]A/40/636-S/17464. [46]A/40/678-S/17492. [47]A/40/685-S/17499. [48]A/40/723. [49]A/40/750-S/17565. [50]A/40/854-S/17610 & Corr.1. [51]A/40/903-S/17638. [52]A/40/937-S/17655. [53]YUN 1984, p. 218, GA res. 39/5, 30 Oct. 1984. [54]A/CONF.109/9. [55]YUN 1981, p. 242. [56]A/40/759. [57]A/40/776. [58]A/40/814. [59]A/40/747. [60]A/40/91. [61]A/40/98. [62]A/40/147-S/16981. [63]A/40/133. [64]A/40/146. [65]A/40/316-S/17194. [66]A/40/332. [67]A/40/484. [68]A/40/501. [69]A/40/466-S/17330. [70]A/40/491-S/17344. [71]A/40/512-S/17365. [72]A/40/599-S/17432. [73]A/40/786-S/17584. [74]A/40/832. [75]A/40/561. [76]A/40/1005. [77]A/40/1033. [78]YUN 1982, p. 345. [79]YUN 1984, p. 216. [80]A/39/858-S/16908. [81]A/40/76. [82]A/40/93. [83]A/40/116. [84]A/40/161. [85]A/40/170. [86]A/40/172-S/17023. [87]A/40/70 (S/16884). [88]YUN 1984, p. 222. [89]A/40/278-S/17139. [90]A/40/293-S/17165. [91]A/40/351 (S/17231). [92]A/40/364-S/17247. [93]A/40/378-S/17269. [94]A/40/382-S/17276.

Western and south-western Asia

Afghanistan situation and Afghanistan-Pakistan armed incidents

The General Assembly, in November 1985, again took up the situation in Afghanistan and its implications for international peace and security. By resolution 40/12, it again called for the immediate withdrawal of foreign troops, reaffirmed the Afghan people's right to determine their own form of government, renewed its appeal for relief assistance for the Afghan refugees and requested the Secretary-General to continue his efforts to promote a political solution.

The Secretary-General's Personal Representative travelled to the area in May and met with officials from Afghanistan and Pakistan. In June and August, the Foreign Ministers of both countries met with the Personal Representative in Geneva in proximity talks and established grounds for negotiating a solution to the situation.

Communications. The majority of communications addressed to the Secretary-General during 1985 relating to the situation in Afghanistan concerned allegations by both Pakistan and Afghanistan of violations of airspace and territory, shellings and other attacks by one against the other. Many of Afghanistan's communications reported on meetings between its Director or Officer-in-Charge of the First Political Department or the Deputy Minister for Foreign Affairs and the Chargé d'affaires of Pakistan's Embassy in Kabul when the latter was summoned to Afghanistan's Ministry of Foreign Affairs.

In a letter of 2 January,[1] Afghanistan said that claims[2] by Pakistan authorities that Afghan aircraft entered Pakistan's airspace on 22 and 25 December 1984 were false. In a Foreign Ministry statement of 2 January, transmitted on 4 January,[3] Afghanistan accused Pakistan of conducting shellings from 24 to 29 December on its Barikot region, wounding 11 soldiers and eight civilians. Afghanistan warned that if such aggressions were not stopped immediately its security forces would resort to firm and reciprocal action. Afghanistan, in a letter of 7 January,[4] described a protest lodged that day of an armed band, 250 strong, including 50 Pakistan militia, which had entered Afghanistan from Pakistan on 28 December and repeatedly shelled a village and a frontier post, leaving a number of victims.

Pakistan, on 7 January,[5] reported that on 6 January four Afghan aircraft had intruded into Pakistan airspace, dropping bombs and firing rockets. Pakistan also rejected as baseless the allegations that there had been firing across the border towards Barikot from 24 to 29 December.

In a letter of 10 January,[6] Afghanistan transmitted a Foreign Ministry statement protesting three alleged shellings of the Barikot region on 5 and 6 January which resulted in the deaths of six civilians and three military personnel and the injuring of 14. In a letter of 14 January,[7] Afghanistan reported its formal denial the day before of Pakistan's charge of an Afghan air attack on 6 January and charged that on 10 January personnel wearing Pakistan frontier militia uniforms had participated in shellings on the residential areas in Chamkani and Bangash resulting in civilian and military loss of life.

Pakistan, on 10 January,[8] reported what it called two serious violations of its airspace and territory on 7 and 8 January, when it said three Afghan aircraft dropped two bombs which failed to explode in the Domandi area and four bombs in the Chitral district. Pakistan also rejected as false Afghanistan's allegations of a 28 December incursion. Pakistan's charges were rejected and condemned in an Afghan Foreign Ministry announcement of 15 January.[9] Pakistan, on 15 January,[10] claimed that on 11 January seven Afghan aircraft violated Pakistan's airspace in the Chitral district, dropping 12 bombs and firing rockets. At the same time, it rejected Afghanistan's charges of attacks by Pakistan on 5, 6 and 10 January. Afghanistan, in a 19 January statement transmitted on 22 January,[11] denied what it called Pakistan's imaginary and baseless claims.

On 24 and 29 January,[12] Pakistan charged that on 21, 22 and 23 January Afghan aircraft had dropped six bombs in the Arandu area, at the same time rejecting as baseless an allegation by Afghanistan, whose protest was reported in a letter of 29 January,[13] that Pakistan armed forces had fired across the border towards Barikot between 19 and 21 January, resulting in 16 deaths and considerable damage to dwellings and two helicopters.

A letter from Afghanistan of 7 February[14] transmitted a note that had been presented to China on 31 January, protesting China's provision of arms and arms training to counter-revolutionary bands in Afghanistan and in counter-revolutionary camps, some in Pakistan, some of which had been moved to China. Afghanistan demanded that China stop its hostile actions, armed aggression and intervention in Afghanistan's internal affairs. China, on 19 February,[15] rejected the contents of Afghanistan's protest note as sheer fabrication. The Afghan question was entirely the result of the invasion and occupation of the country by foreign troops, it said. Afghan authorities were attempting to shift onto China and other countries responsibility for the continued presence of those troops which had impeded the implementation of resolutions on the issue adopted at six sessions of the General Assembly.

Pakistan, on 7 February,[16] charged that on 5 February four Afghan aircraft violated Pakistan airspace in the Arandu area and fired 20 rockets.

Afghanistan, on 12 February,[17] rejected the charges, and those of a 23 January air attack, as groundless accusations designed to conceal Pakistan's own repeated aggressions. Afghanistan, in a letter of 14 February,[18] reported delivery of a protest note the day before condemning the continuing and escalating number of raids against the residential areas of Barikot (where a helicopter was fired on on 7 February), Bangash (hit by some 200 rounds on 5, 7 and 8 February) and Chamkani, which had resulted in the deaths of a large number of people, including women and children, as well as in material losses.

Pakistan, on 19 February,[19] rejected as false Afghanistan's charges of raids by Pakistan armed forces from 5 to 8 February and reported what it termed a serious violation of its airspace and territory on 11 February when, it charged, two bombs were dropped on its territory near Kharlachi from three Afghan aircraft. Afghanistan rejected those charges on 19 February.[20] Afghanistan, on 27 February,[21] submitted a protest note it had lodged on 25 February, charging that Pakistan had recently expanded its aggression, and that, in addition to repeated shellings—on the Barikot area on 18 February, for instance—it had armed and dispatched murderous bandits for raids into Afghanistan, including a 400-man attack on the Barikot garrison on 23 February.

Pakistan, on 1 March,[22] rejected Afghanistan's 25 February protest, saying that the frequent repetition of baseless charges reflected Afghanistan's attempt to blame developments within the country on Pakistan. On 13 March,[23] Pakistan alleged two violations of its airspace on 7 and 12 March.

Afghanistan charged, on 18 March,[24] expanded armed raids and provocations by Pakistan military units, including heavy-weapons firing and an attack on 6 March on the Barikot garrison. It rejected on 18 March an allegation that it had bombed and rocketed Pakistan territory on 12 and 13 March, reported in a letter of 19 March.[25]

Pakistan, on 19 March,[26] reported violations of its airspace and territory on 13 March, when Afghan aircraft were said to have dropped 37 bombs and fired rockets in the Arandu area; on 14 March when five bombs were reported dropped and one Afghan refugee and one Pakistani were killed; and on 16 March when two bombs were dropped. Concurrently, Pakistan rejected as baseless Afghanistan's charge of firing on Barikot on 6 March. Further such violations were reported by Pakistan in a letter of 25 March,[27] referring to bombing incidents said to have occurred near Arandu on 18 and 19 March. Pakistan noted its rejection, conveyed on 23 March to Afghan authorities, of charges of shelling attacks on 12, 13 and 14 March near Barikot and attacks on an Afghan border post at Torkham on 8, 14 and 15 March, described in a 25 March letter from Afghanistan.[28] That letter conveyed a 20 March protest against continued heavy-weapons firing on Afghan frontier residential localities by frontier forces of Pakistan, resulting in a number of deaths. In recent months, it charged, the residential areas of the Barikot district had sustained attacks 29 times. Afghanistan also rejected as groundless Pakistan's allegations concerning the 14 March air attacks.

A letter from Afghanistan of 28 March[29] transmitted a statement of 25 March protesting Pakistan's expansion of its propaganda against Afghanistan, levelling baseless charges of bombing on 16, 18 and 19 March, it said.

Afghanistan, on 15 April,[30] charged that from 15 March to 9 April, residential areas of the Barikot district came under heavy fire 13 times. Women and children were killed in the attacks on 8 and 9 April, among others, residential property was destroyed and crops lost. Afghanistan again warned of the dangerous consequences if Pakistan did not stop its interference. It called Pakistan's charges of a bombing south-east of Arandu on 11 April groundless, a rejection it reiterated on 18 April.[31] Also on 15 April,[32] Afghanistan reported a protest it had lodged the day before of a Pakistan violation of its airspace in the Torkham area on 12 April and denied charges of an Afghan bombing in the Arandu and Darah areas on 14 and 15 April, rejecting the claims as malicious and groundless. On 18 April,[33] Pakistan charged that: on 10 April four Afghan aircraft dropped nine bombs in the Arandu area; on 11 April six aircraft dropped two bombs in the same area; on 14 April two more; on 15 April four more bombs and 20 rockets; and on 16 April two aircraft dropped two more bombs. Pakistan rejected as false Afghanistan's charges in its letters of 15 April.

Afghanistan, on 22 April,[34] reported its rejection on 20 April of Pakistan's charge of a 16 April attack as baseless and designed to increase tensions. In a letter of 25 April,[35] Afghanistan reported its denouncement on 22 April of a violation of its airspace by a Pakistan military aircraft on 17 April. On 29 April,[36] Afghanistan transmitted a message of its *Loya Jirgah*, or Grand Assembly, held in Kabul from 23 to 25 April. The message declared that the traditional friendly Afghan-Soviet relations were in full accord with national interests and expressed the Assembly's determination to defend Afghanistan from counter-revolutionary forces, trained by United States, Iranian, Chinese and Pakistan instructors, through mobilizing all of Afghanistan's people, strengthening its armed forces and safeguarding its borders.

Pakistan, on 26 April,[37] reported a violation of its airspace on 23 April by four Afghan aircraft which it said dropped two bombs south-east of Arandu. Pakistan also rejected as totally false Afghanistan's allegation of a 17 April airspace violation. On 2 May,[38] Pakistan alleged intrusions and bombings of the area around Chitral on 25, 26 and 29 April. These were denied by Afghanistan on 30 April, as reported in a letter of 1 May,[39] and on 6 May.[40] Allegations by Pakistan of an Afghan overflight on 3 May were rejected by Afghanistan on 8 May.[41]

Pakistan, on 9 May,[42] reported that on 3 May four Afghan aircraft dropped a bomb and 20 rockets in the Arandu area and that on 5 May six aircraft, in two separate incidents, committed similar violations.

Afghanistan charged on 9 May, as reported in a letter of 13 May,[43] that 12 Afghan and 12 Soviet military personnel were kidnapped by Afghan counter-revolutionaries and were imprisoned in a military camp in Pakistan controlled by Pakistan authorities. In an escape attempt towards the end of April, they had taken over the camp's ammunition depot and asked to be returned to Afghanistan or to their embassies in Islamabad. After refusing to surrender, all the captives were killed in an explosion of the depot during an attack on the camp by Afghan counter-revolutionaries, in which, Afghanistan said, Pakistan soldiers participated. Afghanistan protested this incident and the imprisonment of Afghan military personnel and citizens in Pakistan as contrary to international law, and demanded that Pakistan punish those responsible.

In a letter of 14 May,[44] Afghanistan reported charges it made the day before of repeated shellings by Pakistan with heavy weapons of the residential area of Barikot district on 8, 19 and 21 April, which resulted in death or injury to military personnel and local residents; it also rejected Pakistan's charges of overflights on 5 May.

On 20 May,[45] Afghanistan reported delivery of a note verbale of 12 May to the Kabul Embassy of the Federal Republic of Germany, bringing to its attention that an organization based in the Federal Republic had set up a short-wave radio station in Pakistan called the "Voice of Free Afghanistan" to support the Afghan counter-revolution. Afghanistan lodged a strong complaint against what it called open interference in its internal affairs.

Pakistan, in a letter of 23 May,[46] reported that it had, on 14 May, rejected as baseless Afghan allegations that it had carried out shellings against Barikot on 9, 10 and 11 May. Afghanistan, on 3 June,[47] said it had rejected on 2 June charges of airspace violations on 21, 26, 27 and 28 May and shelling of the Landikotal area on 24 May. Pakistan, on 4 June,[48] reported that, on 29 May, four Afghan jet aircraft allegedly fired rockets at and dropped two bombs near a refugee camp at

Badini, and, on 31 May, Afghan aircraft dropped 15 bombs on a village, killing 11 persons and 25 livestock, wounding 32 persons and destroying houses. Afghanistan, on 10 June,[49] reported charges lodged on 6 June that Pakistan was responsible for shellings on 1 June on residential areas of Barikot, killing two and wounding three others, and, on the same day, firing on Afghan helicopters. The following day,[50] Afghanistan denied that Afghan aircraft had violated airspace over Chitral and Quetta on 3 and 4 June.

In a letter of 11 June,[51] Pakistan charged that on 7 June four Afghan aircraft intruded into the Arandu area dropping four bombs, firing rockets and seriously injuring one person. It rejected as false allegations that it had fired on Barikot on 31 May resulting in two deaths and a damaged helicopter. Afghanistan, on 24 June,[52] reported that Pakistan had been informed on 22 June that it considered Pakistan's allegations of airspace violations on 7 and 9 June and firing on the Spinboldak frontier post as devoid of truth. Pakistan, on 25 June,[53] reported a 22 June incident in which Afghanistan allegedly fired artillery from across the border, killing three civilians in Chamman, injuring four and starting fires. Afghanistan rejected this allegation on 30 June, as it noted in a letter of 1 July.[54]

A letter of 9 July[55] contained a Pakistan charge that from Afghanistan on 2 July four rounds of artillery were fired, killing one Afghan refugee girl.

Afghanistan, in a letter of 11 July,[56] reported a 10 July charge that the Spinboldak district was fired on on 3 July and on the next day Pakistan fired 300 artillery shells at the Khima area, killing one person and injuring three. It also rejected Pakistan's claim of an attack on 2 July. Pakistan, on 16 July,[57] rejected as baseless Afghanistan's charge of responsibility for those attacks. Afghanistan reported on 23 July[58] that on 21 July it had rejected claims by Pakistan of air aggression at Parachinar on 12 July and rocket firing on Landikotal on 16 July. In a letter of 31 July,[59] Afghanistan noted its protest lodged on 29 July that Pakistan had machine-gunned the Arandu residential area on 25 July which resulted in one death; two persons were injured. It also denied that an Afghan aircraft had violated airspace over Waziristan on 16 July. According to a 5 August letter from Pakistan,[60] charges by Afghanistan of attacks on Barikot the last week in July had been rejected on 4 August as false. Those charges, having been lodged by Afghanistan on 3 August, were contained in a letter of 9 August,[61] which reported that on 26 July four aircraft of the Pakistan air force overflew Afghan territory and that on 26, 27 and 29 July Pakistan military forces opened fire on residential areas of Barikot, killing

three persons, injuring four and destroying several homes. Pakistan, on 14 August,[62] reported that on 10 August 13 rounds of artillery were allegedly fired into Pakistan south of Parachinar, killing one Afghan refugee; a protest had been lodged on 11 August. Afghanistan rejected these charges on 14 August, as it reported on 16 August.[63]

Pakistan, on 20 August,[64] charged that, on the day before, four Afghan aircraft dropped eight bombs on Khewas village in the Parachinar area, killing eight nationals and injuring 12. Afghanistan rejected these charges as false on 21 August, as noted in a letter of 22 August.[65] Pakistan described in a letter of 30 August[66] Afghan shelling on 26 August of Kurram Agency and south of Arawali, killing two persons. On 4 September,[67] Pakistan noted its protest lodged the day before charging that on 24 August Afghan shelling of the Teri Mangal area killed one person, and on 27 August shells fired into the Pewar Kotal area injured another. Afghanistan, on 8 September, as reported in a letter of 11 September,[68] rejected Pakistan's 30 August and 4 September allegations and called on it to end its fallacious charges.

According to Pakistan on 13 September,[69] four Afghan aircraft fired on the village of Faqiran Kalli on 9 September killing two and injuring 10, and on 11 September dropped six bombs and fired rockets at the border post of Punnu; a strong protest was lodged. Afghanistan rejected the allegations as provocative on 19 September.[70] On 23 September,[71] Afghanistan said attacks had taken place on 7 and 8 September south of Khost during which it said 50 members of the Pakistan militia forces were killed and 80 injured.

Transmitted in a letter of 23 September[72] was a message to the Secretary-General from the representatives who participated in the High *Jirgah* (Assembly) of the frontier tribes (Kabul, 14 September), stating that the Pashtun tribes wanted peace and security in their areas and supported the peaceful policies of the Democratic Republic of Afghanistan, and attaching great hopes to the results of the sixth round of the Geneva peace talks on Afghanistan; the message said that they would foil the expansionist plans of the United States and China in the area as well as the reactionary régimes of Pakistan and Iran.

On 30 September,[73] Afghanistan charged that, on 22 September, 150 Pakistan militia penetrated into the area of Zhorah; on the same day, the residential areas of Barikot district received mortar and machine-gun fire, injuring three residents and destroying four houses. On 24 September heavy shellings there left four dead and five houses destroyed; on the same day firing on the frontier posts of Shamshad left two soldiers dead and two injured. Pakistan, on 30

September,[74] said it had rejected as baseless, on 17 and 24 September, an Afghan charge that on 6, 7 and 8 September Pakistan militia had attacked areas south of Khost. Afghanistan, on 7 October,[75] said that on 30 September the residential area of the Barikot district was subjected to heavy fire, leaving eight civilians dead and six houses destroyed. Pakistan, in a letter of 11 October,[76] noted that it had rejected as false, on 1 and 7 October, Afghanistan's allegations of attacks on 23, 25 and 30 September on Zhawara, Barikot and Shamshad Picquet. Afghanistan, on 14 October,[77] charged that from 1 to 4 October heavy shelling was conducted on the Barikot district; 14 residents died and 11 were injured.

On 15 October,[78] Iran stated that while its Government supported an early solution to the situation in Afghanistan that would meet the legitimate aspirations and interests of the Afghan people, it held that an active participation of the true representatives of the Afghan people was an inherent factor in the validity and legitimacy of such negotiations.

Pakistan, on 28 October,[79] reported protests lodged on 15, 20 and 28 October charging that on 14 October an Afghan round of artillery landed near Teri Mangal killing a woman, and that mortar shells were also fired towards the frontier corps of Havildar Picquet and Koh-E-Noor village. Pakistan also alleged that on 19 October artillery in the Chakhai district killed a woman and injured a man and that on 27 October Afghan artillery landed near Teri Mangal killing nine Afghan refugees and injuring three. Pakistan rejected as totally false the allegations of firing from the Pakistan side on the Barikot area on 1 and 4 October.

Shellings on the Barikot district on 16 October, which resulted in the death of one person and injury to 13, were brought to Pakistan's attention on 20 October, as stated in a 21 October letter from Afghanistan.[80] It rejected as baseless Pakistan's charges of shelling in its Mangal district and Koh-E-Noor area.

Afghanistan, in a letter of 28 October,[81] transmitted a statement by its Minister for Foreign Affairs commenting on a 24 October speech by the President of the United States to the United Nations. Afghanistan said the speech was meant to provoke further and instigate acts of armed aggression perpetrated against it from Pakistan while putting additional hurdles in the way of negotiations between the two countries. In a letter of 6 November,[82] Afghanistan transmitted a statement from its Government in reaction to the United States speech. The statement protested what it called malicious interpretations of the events and realities in Afghanistan and accused the United States of supporting aggression towards

Afghanistan, including the allocation of more than $1.5 billion in recent years for training and equipping counter-revolutionaries. Afghanistan said that it enjoyed the support of its people and declared that normalization of the situation in the country was possible only through cessation by the United States and its followers of assistance to the counter-revolutionaries and through the guaranteed termination of the undeclared war and all forms of intervention in Afghanistan's internal affairs.

Afghanistan, on 8 November,[83] forwarded information on aspects of Pakistan's policy regarding Afghan fugitives in Pakistan. Afghanistan said that Pakistan was inflating their numbers, using their camps to recruit bandits, and using the fugitive question to receive so-called humanitarian assistance in the form of weapons, equipment and money from reactionary countries and some organizations. It condemned the efforts of the Pakistan authorities to create obstacles to the return of Afghans residing in Pakistan in violation of international law.

Pakistan, in a letter of 15 November,[84] reported that its protests had been lodged on 7 and 13 November that on 6 November Afghan small-arms fire towards Arandu resulted in injury to one civilian, and on 12 November artillery fire in the Shilman area killed one girl. Pakistan said its rejection as totally false of an Afghan allegation that on 16 October its troops had fired rockets and missiles on the Barikot area had been conveyed on 21 October. Afghanistan rejected Pakistan's charges on 11 and 19 November, as noted in letters of 15 November[85] and 20 November.[86]

Afghanistan, in a letter of 29 November,[87] transmitted the text of a 19 November Declaration of its Revolutionary Council in which, among other policies, the goals of the Democratic Republic of Afghanistan were elaborated. These included defending Afghanistan's independence, national sovereignty and territorial integrity, consolidation of the achievements of its revolution and ensuring vast participation of the people in the anti-imperialist national democratic transformations and the transformation of the country into a developed State.

Pakistan, in a 17 December letter,[88] reported that on 12 December Afghan artillery landed in the Nawa Pass area and on 13 December Afghan artillery near Pewar Pass killed four women and injured a child, against which a protest was lodged on 15 December. In a letter of 24 December,[89] Afghanistan said it had charged on 22 December that on 11 and 14 December helicopters and reconnaissance aircraft penetrated into the Ganjgul Pass area, and on 12 December two more helicopters flew over the Nawah Pass and opened fire on Sarkani.

On 31 December,[90] Afghanistan transmitted a translation of a resolution adopted on 21 November at the sixteenth plenum of the Central Committee of the People's Democratic Party of Afghanistan. It assigned various tasks to party organs and government departments towards expanding the social pillars of the revolution, strengthening the armed forces, developing the economy and normalizing the situation in the country.

Report of the Secretary-General. Pursuant to a 1984 General Assembly resolution,[91] the Secretary-General submitted in October 1985 a report[92] regarding the Afghanistan situation. He stated that he had pursued with determination his efforts to promote the search for a political solution to the situation because he had received repeated assurances that these were strongly supported by the international community. There was also a growing conviction on both sides that a negotiated settlement was the only possible way to achieve peace in Afghanistan.

Pakistan had requested postponement of the round of talks scheduled for February, as elections had been scheduled in that country. The Secretary-General's Personal Representative, Diego Cordovez, travelled to the area from 25 to 31 May. He met with Pakistan's President, Prime Minister and Foreign Minister at Islamabad and with Afghanistan's President and Foreign Minister at Kabul. Upon his return, he briefed the Permanent Representative of Iran in New York.

As a result of the negotiations conducted during these visits, an understanding had been reached between the parties concerned that a political settlement should include a bilateral agreement on non-interference and non-intervention; a declaration on international guarantees; a bilateral agreement on the voluntary return of refugees; an instrument setting out the interrelationships between each of those instruments; and the solution of the question of the withdrawal of foreign troops in accordance with an agreement to be concluded between Afghanistan and the USSR.

A subsequent round of talks was held at Geneva from 20 to 24 June. During these talks, the formulation of two draft bilateral agreements was virtually completed. One covered the principles of mutual relations, in particular non-interference and non-intervention, and the other contained arrangements for the voluntary return of refugees. A declaration on international guarantees was also concluded and the texts sent to the Governments of the United States and the USSR, the designated guarantors, for their comments.

The interlocutors met again at Geneva from 27 to 30 August. The Secretary-General noted that Afghanistan's position was that the instrument on interrelationships should be negotiated in direct talks between the parties, while Pakistan considered that a change in the format of the negotiations was not yet justified. The Secretary-General stated that the matter could not be resolved and a draft instrument on interrelationships could not be considered. The interlocutors agreed, however, to hold another round of talks from 16 to 20 December.

On 9 September, the written comments received from each of the designated guarantors were transmitted to the other. The Government of Iran was kept informed of the discussions.

The Secretary-General observed that the political import underlying the position of each side could not be underestimated. He hoped that the parties involved would bear in mind the overriding advantages for the peoples of the region of an effective settlement.

GENERAL ASSEMBLY ACTION

The General Assembly, on 13 November 1985, adopted **resolution 40/12** by recorded vote.

The situation in Afghanistan and its implications for international peace and security

The General Assembly,

Having considered the item entitled "The situation in Afghanistan and its implications for international peace and security",

Recalling its resolutions ES-6/2 of 14 January 1980, 35/37 of 20 November 1980, 36/34 of 18 November 1981, 37/37 of 29 November 1982, 38/29 of 23 November 1983 and 39/13 of 15 November 1984,

Reaffirming the purposes and principles of the Charter of the United Nations and the obligation of all States to refrain in their international relations from the threat or use of force against the sovereignty, territorial integrity and political independence of any State,

Reaffirming further the inalienable right of all peoples to determine their own form of government and to choose their own economic, political and social system free from outside intervention, subversion, coercion or constraint of any kind whatsoever,

Gravely concerned at the continuing foreign armed intervention in Afghanistan, in contravention of the above principles, and its serious implications for international peace and security,

Noting the increasing concern of the international community over the continued and serious sufferings of the Afghan people and over the magnitude of social and economic problems posed to Pakistan and Iran by the presence on their soil of millions of Afghan refugees, and the continuing increase in their numbers,

Deeply conscious of the urgent need for a political solution of the grave situation in respect of Afghanistan,

Taking note of the report of the Secretary-General, and the status of the diplomatic process initiated by him,

Recognizing the importance of the initiatives of the Organization of the Islamic Conference and the efforts of the Movement of Non-Aligned Countries for a political solution of the situation in respect of Afghanistan,

1. *Reiterates* that the preservation of the sovereignty, territorial integrity, political independence and non-aligned character of Afghanistan is essential for a peaceful solution of the problem;

2. *Reaffirms* the right of the Afghan people to determine their own form of government and to choose their economic, political and social system free from outside intervention, subversion, coercion or constraint of any kind whatsoever;

3. *Calls* for the immediate withdrawal of the foreign troops from Afghanistan;

4. *Calls upon* all parties concerned to work for the urgent achievement of a political solution, in accordance with the provisions of the present resolution, and the creation of the necessary conditions which would enable the Afghan refugees to return voluntarily to their homes in safety and honour;

5. *Renews its appeal* to all States and national and international organizations to continue to extend humanitarian relief assistance with a view to alleviating the hardship of the Afghan refugees, in co-ordination with the United Nations High Commissioner for Refugees;

6. *Expresses its appreciation and support* for the efforts and constructive steps taken by the Secretary-General, especially the diplomatic process initiated by him, in the search for a solution to the problem;

7. *Requests* the Secretary-General to continue those efforts with a view to promoting a political solution, in accordance with the provisions of the present resolution, and the exploration of securing appropriate guarantees for the non-use of force, or threat of force, against the political independence, sovereignty, territorial integrity and security of all neighbouring States, on the basis of mutual guarantees and strict non-interference in each other's internal affairs and with full regard for the principles of the Charter of the United Nations;

8. *Requests* the Secretary-General to keep Member States and the Security Council concurrently informed of progress towards the implementation of the present resolution and to submit to Member States a report on the situation at the earliest appropriate opportunity;

9. *Decides* to include in the provisional agenda of its forty-first session the item entitled "The situation in Afghanistan and its implications for international peace and security".

General Assembly resolution 40/12

13 November 1985   Meeting 74   122-19-12 (recorded vote)

46-nation draft (A/40/L.11); agenda item 28.
Sponsors: Antigua and Barbuda, Bahrain, Bangladesh, Brunei Darussalam, Chile, Colombia, Comoros, Costa Rica, Djibouti, Dominica, Egypt, Fiji, Gambia, Guatemala, Guinea, Haiti, Honduras, Jamaica, Jordan, Kuwait, Malaysia, Maldives, Mauritania, Morocco, Nepal, Niger, Oman, Pakistan, Papua New Guinea, Paraguay, Philippines, Qatar, Saint Lucia, Saint Vincent and the Grenadines, Samoa, Saudi Arabia, Senegal, Singapore, Solomon Islands, Somalia, Thailand, Tunisia, Turkey, United Arab Emirates, Uruguay, Zaire.
Financial implications. 5th Committee, A/40/867; S-G, A/C.5/40/43.
Meeting numbers. GA 40th session: 5th Committee 30; plenary 71-74.

Recorded vote in Assembly as follows:

In favour: Albania, Antigua and Barbuda, Argentina, Australia, Austria, Bahamas, Bahrain, Bangladesh, Barbados, Belgium, Belize, Bolivia, Botswana, Brazil, Brunei Darussalam, Burkina Faso, Burma, Burundi, Cameroon, Canada, Central African Republic, Chad, Chile, China, Colombia, Comoros, Costa Rica, Democratic Kampuchea, Denmark, Djibouti, Dominica, Dominican Republic, Ecuador, Egypt, El Salvador, Equatorial Guinea, Fiji, France, Gabon, Gambia, Germany, Federal Republic of, Ghana, Greece, Grenada, Guatemala, Guinea, Guyana, Haiti, Honduras, Iceland, Indonesia, Iran, Ireland, Israel, Italy, Ivory Coast, Jamaica, Japan, Jordan, Kenya, Kuwait, Lebanon, Lesotho, Liberia, Luxembourg, Malawi, Malaysia, Maldives, Malta, Mauritania, Mauritius, Mexico, Morocco,

Nepal, Netherlands, New Zealand, Niger, Nigeria, Norway, Oman, Pakistan, Panama, Papua New Guinea, Paraguay, Peru, Philippines, Portugal, Qatar, Rwanda, Saint Christopher and Nevis, Saint Lucia, Saint Vincent and the Grenadines, Samoa, Saudi Arabia, Senegal, Sierra Leone, Singapore, Solomon Islands, Somalia, Spain, Sri Lanka, Sudan, Suriname, Swaziland, Sweden, Thailand, Togo, Trinidad and Tobago, Tunisia, Turkey, Uganda, United Arab Emirates, United Kingdom, United Republic of Tanzania, United States, Uruguay, Vanuatu, Venezuela, Yugoslavia, Zaire, Zambia, Zimbabwe.
Against: Afghanistan, Angola, Bulgaria, Byelorussian SSR, Cuba, Czechoslovakia, Democratic Yemen, Ethiopia, German Democratic Republic, Hungary, Lao People's Democratic Republic, Libyan Arab Jamahiriya, Madagascar, Mongolia, Poland, Syrian Arab Republic, Ukrainian SSR, USSR, Viet Nam.
Abstaining: Algeria, Benin, Cape Verde, Congo, Cyprus, Finland, Guinea-Bissau, India, Iraq, Mali, Nicaragua, Sao Tome and Principe.

The Libyan Arab Jamahiriya said it voted against the resolution because it did not believe it would help in solving the problem. Rather, it believed that the Afghan people should have an opportunity to choose the régime they wanted and needed without foreign intervention. The Syrian Arab Republic voted against the text on the basis of the principle of non-interference in the internal affairs of States; the current discussion, it said, implied interference in Afghanistan's internal affairs.

Iran said it had reservations about the eighth preambular paragraph; no matter how successful the talks might be, they were devoid of validity because of the absence of the Afghan people, the main party to the negotiations. What were usually described in oversimplified terms as the internal affairs of Afghanistan, Iran said, did not seem to be so internal; 2 million Afghans who had taken refuge in Iran indicated that the overflow of these internal affairs had been affecting others considerably.

Because it considered the principle that States must refrain from the threat or use of force against any other State to be of universal validity and not subject to interpretations or exceptions, Mexico said it firmly supported the resolution and hoped that foreign troops would be speedily withdrawn.

The USSR said some countries had tried to use the discussion to camouflage the undeclared war they had been waging against Afghanistan, passing over in silence what their Governments were doing to undermine and overthrow the people's revolutionary system, arming and directing those who were destroying schools and were responsible for the deaths of hundreds of civilians, and preventing the Government from developing the economy and raising the standards of living of the people. They were trying to use the United Nations to interfere in the internal affairs of that country, the USSR said.

Afghanistan said it had consistently objected to the inclusion of the artificial question of Afghanistan on the agenda, firmly rejected any discussion of its internal matters in any international forum, and held that the resolution, whose submission was a gross violation of the Charter, would in no way be binding on Afghanistan. The sponsors had arrogated to themselves the right to advise Afghanistan on its form of socio-economic and political system and had fabricated numbers of refugees grossly at variance with the real ones. Afghanistan stated emphatically that the limited military contingent of the Soviet Union in Afghanistan was there at the explicit request and wish of its lawful Government. The debate and resolution could have harmful consequences for the prospects of negotiation, it said.

REFERENCES
[1]A/40/63-S/16879. [2]YUN 1984, p. 225. [3]A/40/67-S/16882. [4]A/40/69-S/16883. [5]A/40/71-S/16885. [6]A/40/79-S/16890. [7]A/40/80-S/16891; A/40/81-S/16892. [8]A/40/82-S/16893. [9]A/40/83-S/16894. [10]A/40/86-S/16895. [11]A/40/94-S/16902. [12]A/40/95-S/16904; A/40/110-S/16951. [13]A/40/111-S/16916. [14]A/40/120-S/16944. [15]A/40/138-S/16968. [16]A/40/124-S/16951. [17]A/40/126-S/16952. [18]A/40/129-S/16955. [19]A/40/151-S/16985. [20]A/40/134-S/16964. [21]A/40/155-S/16988. [22]A/40/157-S/16995 & Corr.1. [23]A/40/178-S/17030. [24]A/40/181-S/17041. [25]A/40/182-S/17042. [26]A/40/186-S/17045. [27]A/40/204-S/17054. [28]A/40/208-S/17060. [29]A/40/212-S/17066. [30]A/40/234-S/17102. [31]A/40/255-S/17112. [32]A/40/240-S/17109; A/40/257-S/17116. [33]A/40/258-S/17117. [34]A/40/264-S/17126. [35]A/40/268-S/17131. [36]A/40/273-S/17135. [37]A/40/274-S/17136. [38]A/40/282-S/17149. [39]A/40/287-S/17155. [40]A/40/288-S/17158. [41]A/40/294-S/17167. [42]A/40/300-S/17176. [43]A/40/310-S/17186 & Corr.1. [44]A/40/311-S/17187. [45]A/40/324-S/17204. [46]A/40/337-S/17214. [47]A/40/352-S/17236. [48]A/40/354-S/17238. [49]A/40/368-S/17250. [50]A/40/371-S/17256. [51]A/40/376-S/17268. [52]A/40/403-S/17303. [53]A/40/412-S/17305. [54]A/40/424-S/17318. [55]A/40/472-S/17333. [56]A/40/479-S/17339. [57]A/40/488-S/17343. [58]A/40/500-S/17352. [59]A/40/526-S/17377. [60]A/40/531-S/17383. [61]A/40/538-S/17390. [62]A/40/554-S/17401. [63]A/40/556-S/17403. [64]A/40/562-S/17409. [65]A/40/573-S/17417. [66]A/40/595-S/17431. [67]A/40/609-S/17441. [68]A/40/630-S/17458. [69]A/40/639-S/17465. [70]A/40/664-S/17479. [71]A/40/674-S/17489. [72]A/40/675-S/17490. [73]A/40/690-S/17504. [74]A/40/691-S/17505. [75]A/40/732-S/17545. [76]A/40/748-S/17564. [77]A/40/753-S/17568. [78]A/40/755-S/17569. [79]A/40/822-S/17595. [80]A/40/782-S/17582. [81]A/40/821-S/17594. [82]A/40/859-S/17613. [83]A/40/866-S/17615. [84]A/40/899-S/17636. [85]A/40/902-S/17637. [86]A/40/908-S/17641. [87]A/40/958-S/17660. [88]A/41/57-S/17690. [89]A/41/64-S/17697. [90]A/41/70-S/17708. [91]YUN 1984, p. 227, GA res. 39/13, 15 Nov. 1984. [92]A/40/709-S/17527.

Iran-Iraq armed conflict

In the continuing hostilities between Iran and Iraq, communications from the two countries focused on violations of a 12 June 1984 undertaking[1] to refrain from attacks on purely civilian populations, the treatment of prisoners of war and interference with navigation. Iran also charged use of chemical weapons and an attack on its nuclear power plant.

In January, the Secretary-General dispatched a mission to investigate the conditions in prisoner-of-war camps in both countries; the mission's report was considered by the Security Council in March. He dispatched a medical specialist to hospitals in Europe to examine Iranian patients who were suffering from injuries allegedly caused by chemical weapons. The Security Council issued a declaration deploring the use of such weapons.

The Secretary-General reported on a visit he made to both countries in April and on efforts to promote a negotiated settlement to the conflict.

The General Assembly did not discuss at its 1985 session the agenda item on the consequences of the prolongation of the conflict, but deferred consideration to its resumed session in 1986.

The Assembly, the Economic and Social Council and the Commission on Human Rights expressed deep concern over the situation of human rights in Iran.

Communications (January–9 April). United Nations inspection teams stationed in Teheran and Baghdad were asked by the respective countries in January to investigate incidents of alleged violations of the 12 June 1984 undertaking to refrain from deliberate military attacks on purely civilian population centres. The teams had been set up in the two capitals to verify compliance. Charges of violations of this agreement drew several exchanges of communications during the year.

On 5 January 1985, the head of the inspection team in Teheran was requested by the Government to inspect the villages of Bardieh, Dehlavieh and Alavaneh, which Iran said had been subjected to Iraqi air attacks the day before. The Secretary-General forwarded the report[2] of the inspection carried out on 7 and 8 January, reviewing the procedures and findings of the team. The team concluded that Iran's allegations were credible. All three villages, which were civilian population centres, appeared to have been subjected to an aerial attack on the claimed date, although, in view of the relative proximity to Alavaneh of a military installation, the team was unable to determine whether that village itself had been the intended target.

What it described as Iraq's repeated violations of the June 1984 agreement were denounced in a 24 January letter from the Foreign Minister of Iran,[3] in which Iran also stated that it remained committed to full observance of the agreement.

Iraq requested an inspection of alleged shellings on the villages of Al-Jawaber and Saregah by Iranian forces on 26 January. The inspection was carried out on 28 January by the team in Baghdad and its report was contained in a note by the Secretary-General.[4] On the basis of the evidence examined, the team was unable to state that a deliberate attack on a purely civilian population centre occurred on 26 January.

Iran's Foreign Minister, by a letter of 9 February,[5] said Iraq's resort to unsubstantiated claims against Iran, in addition to manipulation of the United Nations inspection team in Baghdad, could not be considered as an excuse for the full-fledged violation of the June 1984 agreement, and charged Iraq with air attacks on civilian areas on 3 and 5 February.

On 8 February,[6] Iraq's Foreign Ministry rejected allegations made that day by Iran's President that Iraq was shelling Iranian cities. Iraq said it would not resort to shelling civilian centres except to retaliate for such actions. Iran responded on 19 February,[7] saying that Iraq's charges, which the investigation teams had proved to be lies, had disclosed the country's true criminal nature. If Iraq continued shelling Iranian civilian centres, Iran was left with no option but to retaliate strongly. Iraq, in a letter of the same day,[8] said it remained committed to the letter and spirit of the June 1984 agreement.

Iraq commented on the 7/8 January inspection of the team in Teheran in a letter of 21 February.[9] Despite the team's conclusion that the villages of Bardieh and Dehlavieh were purely civilian centres, Iran had been using these and other villages as assembly areas for concentrating its forces as a point of departure for attacks on Iraq, in violation of the 1984 agreement and the 1949 (fourth) Geneva Convention relative to the Protection of Civilian Persons in Time of War.

The Security Council President, on 5 March,[10] after consultations with Council members, issued the following statement:

> "As President of the Security Council, I feel it my duty to express alarm over reports that the Governments of the Islamic Republic of Iran and of Iraq are attacking or preparing to attack civilian areas. I appeal to both Governments to exercise restraint and to continue to honour their undertakings to the Secretary-General, made last June, not to attack civilian targets which, until now, have saved thousands of innocent lives."

Iraq's Deputy Prime Minister and Minister for Foreign Affairs responded to the Council President's appeal in a letter of 6 March.[11] Iraq offered its assurance that it had adhered to the June agreement and charged that Iran had violated it in attacks on the city of Basra on 5 March, carried out on the grounds that Iraq had bombed areas within Iran; Iraq said the bombarded areas were not covered by the June agreement. In a letter of 5 March,[12] Iraq had accused Iran of shelling Basra that day with concentrated artillery fire. Iran's Foreign Minister, the same day,[13] said that on 4 March two Iraqi jet fighters had attacked Ahwaz, leaving 11 civilians dead and 25 injured. An aerial attack on Bushehr on the same day had resulted in damage to the nuclear reactor installation in that city. In spite of its sincere attempts to preserve the authority of the June 1984 agreement, Iran said, as of that moment it would assume a retaliatory stance _vis-à-vis_ all such Iraqi attacks, although the inhabitants of Iraqi cities would be informed prior to retaliation so they might evacuate.

On 6 March,[14] Iraq said it had requested the United Nations mission stationed in Iraq to visit Basra to investigate the crimes of the Iranian bombardment, but had been informed that Iranian authorities were hindering the mission's task.

Iran, on 8 March,[15] transmitted a message from its Foreign Minister in response to an appeal by the Secretary-General of 6 March to Iran and Iraq to refrain from violating the June 1984 agreement. Iran charged that Iraq had recently intensified its attacks against civilian areas, for instance, Ahwaz and Bushehr on 4 March. Expecting international organizations to take effective measures to stop these attacks, Iran had refrained from retaliating, it said. However, in view of the absence of such international action, after the lapse of a 24-hour warning period, Iran was forced to target the cities of Dezful, Abadan, Sar-e-Pol-e Zahab and Masjid Solayman from the air and by missiles in a limited action intended to forewarn Iraq from continuing its attacks.

The Secretary-General, in a message[16] of 9 March to the Presidents of Iran and Iraq, declared that he was dismayed that an appeal he had made on 6 March had not brought a halt to the waves of attacks on both sides, each claiming to be acting in retaliation. Whatever the provocation, he said, the attacks must stop to spare further bloodshed of innocent civilians, and he called on both Governments to cease all attacks on purely civilian populations by 2359 hours GMT on 11 March 1985.

Iraq, on 10 March,[17] transmitted a letter from its Deputy Prime Minister and Minister for Foreign Affairs setting forth its view with respect to the Secretary-General's message. Based on Iran's conduct in the situation, Iraq said that, in spite of its desire to comply with the Secretary-General's appeal, it could not leave matters ambivalent and fluid so that violations might recur. Iraq urged the Secretary-General to establish direct contacts with authorized representatives of the two parties to draw up agreed principles, rules and guarantees for an agreement to prevent deliberate bombardment of purely civilian population centres and for establishing a modality for tackling other matters. Iran responded to the Secretary-General's message in a letter of 10 March,[18] stating that the appeal came at a time when Iraq had continued its missile attacks, aerial bombardments and artillery fire against several cities, inflicting great loss of life and property among Iran's civilian population. Iran said that, as always, it was willing to respect its June 1984 commitment and comply with the Secretary-General's latest appeal provided that Iraq also withheld attacks against Iranian civilians; it pointed to the need for effective measures against a violation of the renewed agreement.

On 12 March,[19] Iraq claimed that on that day Iran began to launch an attack across the Hur-Al-Hoveizeh marsh. Iran, in a letter of the same day,[20] stated that, while it had complied with the Secretary-General's appeal, Iraqi forces had continued attacks against civilians by bombarding Marivan and Piranshahr and conducting aerial attacks on Ghassemabad, Hamadan and Bostan, where 16 people were killed, leaving Iran no choice but to retaliate. In a second letter of the same day,[21] Iran stated that Iraq's attacks had resulted in the deaths of 773 people and injuries to 2,747 between 5 and 11 March, and annexed to its letter a list of such attacks and casualties for that period.

Iran, in a letter of 14 March,[22] stated that after Iraqi bombing attacks on several cities, including Teheran and Isfahan, on 13 March, Iran was obliged to retaliate, after giving warning, by striking certain economic and industrial centres of Baghdad, launching a missile in a strike timed and targeted to cause the smallest number of casualties possible. Iran appealed to the Secretary-General to reiterate his appeal for the immediate cessation of military operations against purely civilian areas.

Security Council members again expressed their concern over the renewed hostilities between Iran and Iraq in a statement[23] issued on their behalf on 15 March by the Security Council President, following consultations:

> "The members of the Security Council express their deep concern over the scale of the renewed hostilities in the conflict between Iran and Iraq, which have led to an alarming aggravation of the situation between the two countries, to the detriment of peace and security in the region.
>
> "They believe that combatants and civilians will continue to suffer as long as the conflict, which has already imposed great sacrifices on the two countries in terms of human life and material resources, lasts. They emphasize anew the urgent necessity for a cessation of hostilities commencing with the implementation of the moratorium on attacks against purely civilian population centres with a view to finding a peaceful settlement to the conflict in conformity with the Charter of the United Nations and international law and acceptable to both parties.
>
> "The members of the Security Council have decided to remain actively seized of the question and to pursue consultations with the two parties and with the Secretary-General with a view to finding an end to this tragic conflict, which has already lasted far too long."

Iraq welcomed the substance of the Council's statement in a letter of 16 March.[24] Charging that a large-scale act of aggression launched by Iran on 12 March was still continuing, Iraq proposed that the United Nations, and the Security Council in particular, take the necessary measures to bring about a comprehensive settlement by: arranging an immediate cease-fire and withdrawal of forces to internationally recognized frontiers, verified by a United Nations observer group; direct contacts by the Secretary-General or the Council with the two parties to put those arrangements into effect; negotiations between the two parties, under his or the Council's auspices, to reach a comprehensive and just settlement; finding a speedy solution to the prisoner-of-war issue; and proceeding to consider arrangements for abstaining from attacks on purely civilian population centres.

The Libyan Arab Jamahiriya, on 19 March,[25] transmitted a telegram from the Secretary of the People's Committee of the People's Bureau for Foreign Liaison reporting that the Libyan President had called on the leaders of Iran and Iraq to halt immediately the bombardment of civilian installations and populated areas. The telegram said Iran responded by affirming its readiness to cease attacking towns and civilian installations immediately upon Iraq's ceasing to do so.

Iran, on 21 March,[26] said that in the face of the silence of the international community regarding Iraq's announced intention to annihilate Ahwaz within 72 hours of its ultimatum to evacuate it, it was likely that Iran would be forced to retaliate. On 25 March,[27] Iran said it had been obliged to launch a surface-to-surface missile on Baghdad that day, following the resumption of Iraqi attacks on Iranian civilian population centres and commercial vessels. Iran, on 27 March,[28] declared that it would immediately stop the retaliatory measures it had been forced to take as soon as Iraq ceased its violation of international conventions concerning the conduct of hostilities, which it was the duty of the Council and other competent international bodies to condemn. On 1 April,[29] Iran said it had made it clear that the Iraqi holy cities of Karbala, Najaf, Kazemain and Samera would be spared from any retaliatory measures despite the fact that it had been informed that Iraq was planning sabotage activities in those cities that it would blame on Iran.

In retaliation for what it said were bombardments of its cities and civilian areas by Iraq on 31 March, Iran, on 1 April,[30] said it had launched two surface-to-surface missiles on Baghdad. On 3 April,[31] Iran announced that, the day before, its armed forces were instructed immediately to halt all retaliatory measures against Iraqi cities, inasmuch as Iraq had stopped its attacks against civilian quarters in Iran's larger cities. Iran would maintain this policy as long as Iraq continued to refrain from attacking civilian quarters, merchant shipping and civil aviation. Iran warned, on 4 April,[32] that it would have to take defensive retaliatory actions against Iraq after Iraq had resumed its attacks against Iranian civilian areas following a two-day interruption.

Iran maintained, in a letter of 4 April,[33] that the Security Council, with such a dark record of indifference and lack of commitment to its constitutional duties, had undermined the basis for its legitimacy to intervene in the conflict. Iran could not legally and constitutionally be deprived of its right to self-defence by the Council because of that body's failure to discharge its duties with regard to the Iraqi-imposed war of aggression.

Iran, on 9 April,[34] transmitted a letter it had sent to the Director-General of the United Nations Educational, Scientific and Cultural Organization urgently requesting him to send a mission to Iran to verify the damage caused to its cultural heritage by aerial bombardments on the historic city of Isfahan on 13 March.

Report of the Secretary-General. The Secretary-General travelled to Teheran on 7 and 8 April and to Baghdad on 8 and 9 April to pursue proposals he had presented to the Foreign Ministers of both parties in New York in March, designed to reduce the level of conflict and promote an end to hostilities. In a report of 12 April,[35] the Secretary-General said that during his visits both Governments reaffirmed their desire for peace. However, it was clear that each harboured profound distrust of the other. Iran felt that since the beginning of the conflict the Security Council had not acted impartially or justly, particularly in failing to condemn Iraq as the aggressor and to counter violations of international humanitarian law, especially Iraq's use of chemical weapons. Iran felt that in order to start a process towards peace, the Security Council should rectify its past actions. The Secretary-General said he had reported these views to Iraq, and stressed that Iran should explain its position to the Council directly.

Discussions had also been held in both capitals on an eight-point proposal the Secretary-General had first presented to both parties in New York on 28 March. The underlying premise of the proposals was that, as Secretary-General, he was responsible under the Charter to seek an end to the conflict and, until that was achieved, to try to mitigate its effects. The proposals envisaged that both parties would enter into sustained discussion in all those respects with him.

He reported that Iran believed that the application of specific conventions and protocols to mitigate the effects of war could not be conditional upon a cease-fire. It was prepared to accept a comprehensive cessation of hostilities provided that two conditions were met: condemnation of the aggressor and payment of reparations. Iraq believed that specific mitigating measures must be linked to a comprehensive cease-fire within a timetable; measures envisaged should include a mutual withdrawal of troops, a comprehensive exchange of prisoners of war, and reactivation of all ports, reiterating that all issues must be dealt with in an integrated framework. Both parties agreed that his proposals could serve as a basis for further discussion.

The Secretary-General concluded that, although the positions of both parties remained wide apart, there existed a real basis for pursuing efforts to bring the prospect of peace closer. As a first step, the Security Council should extend an invitation to both parties to renew examination of all aspects of the conflict.

The Council considered the report at the same time it considered a report of a medical specialist dispatched to Europe to look into charges that Iranian patients there were suffering from the effects of chemical weapons and, on 25 April, adopted a declaration on the subject (see p. 248).

Communications (12 April–December). On 12 April,[36] Iraq forwarded a statement of 11 April by the spokesman for the Supreme Command of the Iraqi armed forces, saying that Iran was preparing a new attack against it. In a letter of 13 April,[37] Iraq said that a 12 April sermon by Iran's President, annexed to the letter, made it clear that Iran believed that the only means of settling the conflict was through the use of force and the continuation of the war.

On 22 April,[38] Iran rejected what it said were baseless allegations by Iraq that Mandali and Ghazanieh had been the targets of artillery fire by Iran. Iran warned that these allegations were pretexts for Iraq to resume its attacks against civilian areas in Iran.

Iraq responded to the Council's declaration of 25 April on 27 April.[39] It regretted that the Council had been dwelling on questions which it felt were secondary. Some members of the Council, it said, were attempting to attract the party that was boycotting it; contrary to the notion in some circles, the Council had not displayed a bias in favour of Iraq. Iran would negotiate with the Council and the United Nations only for propaganda purposes; it had never concealed its aim of invading Iraq or belief that force was the only means of settling the conflict. While the declaration called on the parties to co-operate with the Council, those who issued it were well aware that from the outset Iraq had consistently done so, while Iran not only failed to co-operate but constantly flouted and accused it. Despite its reservations about certain parts of the declaration, Iraq accepted the appeals contained therein because they constituted an indivisible whole, especially the appeals for an honourable settlement, if Iran accepted them on the same basis.

Iran, on 7 May,[40] said it was evident from a statement of 24 April by Iraq's President that Iraq was planning to resume its attacks against Iran's civilian populations after such action had been halted for 20 days as a gesture of respect for the Secretary-General's presence in Baghdad. Iran hoped it would not be forced to take retaliatory measures. On 13 May,[41] Iran rejected as baseless a claim by Iraq that Iran had shelled Mandali, the Shahabi district and the village of Ghazanieh on 9 and 10 May. Iran urgently forewarned, in a letter of 25 May,[42] that Iraq had announced on radio and television that it was about to resume strikes against various cities, including Teheran; Iran reserved the right to retaliate. The following day,[43] Iran charged that, as predicted, Iraq had bombarded Teheran and had made aerial attacks on Ilam, Gilan-e-Gharb, Karand and Baneh and missile attacks on Bakhtaran and Islam Abad, leaving many killed and injured and damaging property. Iran again called on the United Nations to condemn Iraq and take measures to stop these violations of international humanitarian law. On 28 May,[44] Iran charged that during strikes on Teheran that day, an Iraqi aeroplane attacked a prisoner-of-war camp, causing damage and casualties, failing to spare even Iraqi prisoners in its violations of international law.

A new dimension had been added to Iraq's violations of international law, the Iranian Foreign Minister charged in a letter of 29 May:[45] Iran said Iraq was using an abortive attempt on the life of the Emir of Kuwait, which it blamed on Iran, as a pretext to resume its attacks on Iran's civilian populations. On 3 June,[46] Iran announced that it had launched a second missile attack against Baghdad, contrary to its desire, but it was forced to by the inaction of the Security Council.

Iran charged, on 10 June,[47] that Iraq, on 9 June, had bombarded the Ziveh refugee camp, which housed Iraqi Kurdish refugees, killing 142 people, including 79 children, and wounding 300 others. Iran said it had asked the United Nations team in Iran to visit the site. Iran asked the Secretary-General, in a letter of 20 June,[48] to guard against Iraq's grave breach of the fourth Geneva Convention by ending the long years of detention and captivity of Khuzistanis (Arabic-speaking Iranians) and other civilian Iranians in Iraqi refugee camps and arranging their voluntary repatriation to Iran. On 13 August,[49] Iraq said that allegations that it was detaining civilian Iranians in captivity were false; those civilians had left their villages in Iran either from fear of oppression or in flight from combat, Iraq said; they had been given asylum in Iraq and were considered as refugees with absolute freedom of movement and action. Allegations by Iran on 23 June (see p. 246) that Iraq had executed certain repatriated Iraqi prisoners of war and had not handed others over to their families were also groundless.

In a message to diplomatic representatives at Teheran, transmitted on 25 June,[50] the Speaker for the Islamic Consultative Assembly and spokesman for the Supreme Defence Council of Iran deplored attacks against civilian targets, the use of chemical weapons and threats against civilian aviation, and stated that massive demonstrations which took place on 14 June, the day of Al-Quds, despite threats of increased attacks on cities by Iraq, proved that the Government enjoyed the resolute support of its people. If nations and international forums sought the implementation of justice and the observance of international law, and confessed their lack of responsible action in the past and thus gained the trust of the Iranian people, then the establishment of an international tribunal to determine the punishment of the aggressor and compensation for the victims would become possible and so would paving the way for ending the war. The lowest estimate of casualties resulting from Iraqi attacks on gathering places and demonstrations on the day of Al-Quds was 600, Iran charged in a letter from its Foreign Minister, transmitted on 27 June.[51]

Iraq, in a letter of 18 July,[52] recalled that on 14 June it had reported to Iran its decision to stop bombing selected targets inside Iranian cities; instead of taking the opportunity to scale down the fighting and prepare for peace, Iran had continued making statements announcing its intention to continue the war. Iraq charged that Iran had also launched continuous attacks against various points across the Iran-Iraq border and was entirely responsible for the escalation of the fighting.

Iraq's Foreign Minister, in a letter of 10 September,[53] said Iran had launched a new hostile action in the northern border area against Iraqi territory on 9 September in an attempt to violate Iraq's sovereignty and occupy its territory by force. On 15 September,[54] Iran reported that two of its jet fighters attacked an Iraqi tobacco factory outside Soleymanieh. Claiming that Iran had attacked civilian areas, Iraq had used this excuse to open artillery fire on population centres in Piranshahr, inflicting loss of life and property on civilians. Iran, on 30 October,[55] charged that on 29 October Iraq had air-raided areas of the city of Ilam. On 8 November,[56] it charged that Iraq had bombarded Ahwaz on 6 November, killing 30 and wounding 100 civilians. In a second letter of 8 November,[57] Iran said it had denied an Iraqi accusation that it had shelled the city of Al-Qurna on 5 November, an allegation Iran said Iraq had offered to pave the ground for its escalation of indiscriminate attacks on civilians in Iran. Iran reported on 10 December[58] that Iraqi forces had air-raided Hoveyzeh with cluster bombs that day, leaving 12 dead and 28 injured and destroying 13 residential units. Iran said Iraq would be severely punished for levelling the newly reconstructed city.

Iraq charged in a letter of 19 December[59] that Iran was planning to launch a large-scale offensive with the intention of occupying Iraqi territory; it appealed to the Secretary-General to induce Iran to enter, without pre-conditions, into negotiations for peace under his or the Security Council's auspices. On 31 December,[60] Iraq alleged that on 30 December Iranian aircraft attacked the town of Djuarta, causing the death of 21 civilians, wounding 15 others and destroying 38 dwellings, and, on the same day, attacked populated areas of Meisan, causing three deaths and the wounding of six others.

Treatment of prisoners of war

Communications (January–16 February). A number of communications to the Secretary-General from January through early March 1985 contained charges by both Iran and Iraq concerning the treatment of prisoners of war (POWs).

Iraq, on 22 January,[61] transmitted a report on what it described as the savage treatment of Iraqi POWs by Iran, accusing Iran of using threats of physical and psychological torture, sectarian isolation, coercive measures, hiding large numbers of prisoners from the International Committee of the Red Cross (ICRC), changing the prisoners' locations, employing solitary confinement, placing agents among the prisoners' ranks, intimidating pilots, poisoning food, encouraging sexual assaults, conducting night raids and withholding letters.

Iran, on 31 January,[62] rejected Iraq's charges and regretted that such unfounded allegations by Iraq were circulated in the United Nations on the day that a mission sent by the Secretary-General to investigate the conditions of POWs in both countries had concluded its visits. Iran said Iraq was trying to divert the world's attention from the contents of the forthcoming report.

In a letter of 19 February,[63] Iran requested that the Secretary-General ensure the placement among their families of 31 handicapped Iraqi POWs whom, three weeks before, Iran had said it was ready to free, inasmuch as Iraq had not announced it was ready to accept them. In response, Iraq declared, in a Foreign Ministry statement of 16 February transmitted on 24 February,[64] that Iran was distorting the facts; Iraq had given consent to Turkey, as an intermediary, to receive 30 handicapped POWs, and delivered a list of 20 Iranian prisoners to be handed over to Iran in return.

Report of the mission on POWs. Late in 1984,[65] Iraq had requested that the Secretary-General send a mission to Iran to investigate an incident which Iraq alleged took place on 10 October 1984 at a POW camp in Gorgan, Iran, when Iranian military authorities were said to have opened fire on prisoners, killing or injuring many. Iran had agreed to receive the mission on the condition that it also investigate Iran's concerns regarding Iranian POWs in Iraq. The Secretary-General stated, in a note of 19 February[66] transmitting the mission's report to the

Security Council, that as an extraordinary measure and in the light of his humanitarian responsibility under the Charter he had decided to dispatch a mission to Iran and Iraq. The mission, composed of three qualified specialists constituted as an independent body, was mandated to inquire into the 10 October incident and to report to him on other concerns that the Governments of both Iran and Iraq had expressed regarding the situation of POWs and civilian detainees.

The mission visited Iraq from 11 to 17 January and Iran from 18 to 25 January and submitted its report on 9 February to the Secretary-General. He expressed dismay and concern that the unanimous findings of the mission indicated that the fundamental purposes the international community had set itself in adopting the 1949 (third) Geneva Convention relative to the Treatment of Prisoners of War were not being fulfilled, and said that respect for its provisions must be restored. That could best be achieved if ICRC were enabled to continue the functions envisaged in that Convention for humanitarian organizations, on the basis of mutually agreed arrangements, in close co-operation with and under the scrutiny of Protecting Powers vested with the task of ensuring the observance of the terms of the Convention. He felt that an exchange of at least certain defined categories of POWs should be sought on the basis of understandings to be promoted with the two Governments concerned.

The mission had observed that in neither country were POWs treated as badly as alleged by the Government of the other country, nor as well as claimed by the detaining Power. Prolonged captivity was the prisoners' greatest hardship. The mission said that the situation on both sides was cause for serious concern, and stated that it was not in a position to form definite conclusions about allegations regarding missing persons or mass killings of POWs. It concluded that the Gorgan incident had caused the death of at least nine prisoners, with 47 hospitalized and others less severely injured.

The mission offered recommendations that: prisoners' rights under the third Geneva Convention should be respected; corporal or collective punishment should be prohibited; living conditions should be improved; rights to send and receive mail should be given full effect; officers should be treated according to their rank; freedom of thought, religion and conscience should be respected; opposing groups of prisoners should be physically separated; ICRC should be enabled to carry out all its functions under the Geneva Conventions; information on the wounded, sick or dead should be provided to each Government by the other; lists of POWs and their state of health should be exchanged; consideration should be given to releasing as many prisoners as possible; and prisoners should not be used for propaganda purposes.

Communications (24 February–4 March). Iraq's Ministry of Foreign Affairs responded to the mission's report in a 24 February statement,[67] indicating that Iraq would request a meeting of the Security Council during the first week of March to discuss the report. Iraq said the mission had overlooked the fact that ICRC had been working in Iraq without interruption, while Iran had prevented it from working in Iran. Iraq also believed that the mission's recommendations regarding the conditions of POWs should be implemented.

Iran, on 26 February,[68] said Iraq was attempting to take advantage of the Security Council in order to divert attention from the country's crimes against the POWs in its custody. Iran questioned Iraq's sincerity in accepting the mission's recommendations, and set forth the objectives it felt should be pursued in the investigation of the situation of the POWs: extension of the mission's mandate; investigation of, and a framework for disclosing, the fate of missing persons; measures towards repatriation of civilian POWs and civilians forcibly removed from Iran to Iraq; guarantees to end physical and psychological ill-treatment of Iranian POWs; investigation into the situation of Iran's Minister of Oil; examination of the treatment of the injured, particularly in the war fronts, and their immediate release; measures to improve conditions in the camps; guarantee of religious freedom; uncovering clandestine camps in Iraq; and putting forward proposals for repatriation.

Iraq forwarded on 4 March[69] detailed observations on the mission's report, holding the view that the Security Council must establish means to put the recommendations into effect. On the same day,[70] Iran transmitted a report on the conditions of Iranian POWs in Iraqi camps prepared by the War Information Headquarters of its Supreme Defence Council. The report accused Iraq of, among other offences, ill-treatment of prisoners, improper care of the sick and wounded, providing inadequate living conditions, food, sanitation, work conditions and training and communications facilities, abandoning wounded Iranians to die, and hiding from ICRC the fact that numerous Iranian doctors, nurses, Red Crescent Society personnel and female relief workers had been captured.

SECURITY COUNCIL CONSIDERATION (March)

The Security Council met on 4 March in response to a 24 February request[71] by Iraq that the President of the Council convene a meeting during the first week of March to discuss the report of the mission that investigated the conditions of POWs in Iran and Iraq.

Invited, at their request, to participate in the discussion without the right to vote were Iraq, Jordan, Saudi Arabia and Yemen. The Secretary-General of the League of Arab States was also invited to

participate under rule 39[a] of the Council's provisional rules of procedure, at the request of Qatar, in a letter of 28 February,[72] as Chairman of the Arab Group of States at the United Nations.
Meeting number. SC 2569.

Addressing the Council, Iraq stated that Iran's treatment of POWs was based on its primary political objective regarding Iraq: to change the country's political and social system. This was manifested in the murder of POWs who the Iranian authorities believed were affiliated with the legitimate political institutions in their country, in persecutions aimed at forcing the prisoners to renounce their political beliefs and commit treason, in dividing POWs according to their religious beliefs and subjecting them to intensive psychological indoctrination, and in entrusting the prisoners' supervision to political groups acting as agents of the régime. All these tactics forced the prisoners to choose between treason and death. Iraq, on the other hand, had no political objectives motivating it to mistreat prisoners.

Iraq said that, unlike Iran, it had always co-operated with ICRC. It had also handed over large numbers of prisoners without reciprocity. The United Nations mission, which visited all the POW camps in Iraq, was not able to visit all the camps in Iran and discover all the facts. Iraq said the mission's report reflected diplomatic considerations designed to encourage Iran to co-operate with the Security Council and participate in its discussions; thus, in an attempt to balance the report more emphasis was placed on elements relating to Iraq. Iraq was ready to implement all the recommendations of the mission. The Council should also adopt a clear resolution to ensure their implementation. Iraq urged the Council to force Iran to allow ICRC to resume its work there. The best way to put an end to the prisoners' sufferings, it said, was to exchange all prisoners.

The Secretary-General of the League of Arab States urged the Council to ensure strict implementation of the proposals put forward by the mission and to adopt a resolution that would speed measures likely to improve the condition of the POWs in accordance with international law and, particularly, the third Geneva Convention.

Yemen supported the resolutions of the League of Arab States calling for the establishment of a committee of seven to be charged with finding a just and honourable solution to the conflict, as well as the good-offices committee created in 1984 by the Organization of the Islamic Conference. Yemen, which endorsed the recommendations of the fact-

[a]Rule 39 of the Council's provisional rules of procedure states: "The Security Council may invite members of the Secretariat or other persons, whom it considers competent for the purpose, to supply it with information or to give other assistance in examining matters within its competence."

finding mission, hoped the Council would adopt measures to force Iran to end military operations and turn to peaceful efforts to end its war with Iraq. Jordan agreed that there should be strict respect for the Geneva Convention and the role of ICRC, stressed that the freedom of thought, religion and conscience of the prisoners must be respected and called for a complete and comprehensive exchange of all POWs. Jordan called on the Council to adopt the recommendations of the mission, create a practical mechanism for their implementation and adopt a timetable for the release of all POWs. Egypt also called for a complete exchange of POWs and hoped that the recommendations of the mission would be implemented without delay.

Saudi Arabia expressed satisfaction with Iraq's positive response to the mission's recommendations and hoped that Iran would respond positively to the POW issue and to efforts aimed at putting an end to the war and all its tragedies. Saudi Arabia called on the Council to take a clear stand to secure implementation of the recommendations.

Communications (9 March–December). The issue of POWs was the subject of an Iraqi letter of 9 March, transmitted on 11 March,[73] responding to a letter to Iraq by the Secretary-General of 7 March. Iraq said it considered that the exchange of POWs should be full, comprehensive and without exceptions. It should take place either on a proportional basis, in accordance with the number of prisoners present in each country, over a maximum period of six months, or in stages with exchanges of, first, sick, disabled, elderly and child prisoners, second, prisoners who had spent two or more years in captivity, and third, the remaining prisoners. Iraq would welcome the Secretary-General's playing a role in the process in co-operation with ICRC.

On 1 May,[74] Iran asked the Secretary-General to pursue the answers Iran had asked of ICRC concerning POWs Iraq claimed it had released on 7 April. Iran asked if the prisoners were actually freed and had been handed over to ICRC, when Iran would be informed of their return to Iran and their identities, and what measures ICRC had taken to save their lives. On 2 May,[75] Iran said it had handed over to the Turkish Red Crescent 48 more disabled POWs on 29 April, in addition to the 27 repatriated through the same channel on 2 March. Despite Iraq's earlier announcements that 52 Iranian POWs would be released, Iraq had taken no such action, Iran said. Iran asked the Secretary-General to persuade Iraq to heed international principles concerning POWs, particularly relating to their repatriation.

Iraq, in a letter of 20 May,[76] circulated a summary of reports by ICRC on the situation of Iraqi prisoners in Iran after the ICRC mission in Teheran had visited a number of POW camps from 19 May to 18 October 1984. Iraq said Iran was to be con-

demned for the mistreatment of prisoners, including suspicious deaths, disciplinary punishment with electricity and beatings, insufficient hospital beds, mattresses and food, inadequate sanitation, religious and political indoctrination, solitary confinement, non-delivery of letters and preventing the sending of letters. Iran, on 30 May,[77] said that by publicizing the summary of the reports of ICRC, whose work and impartiality Iran had occasionally questioned, Iraq was trying to mislead public opinion and justify its crimes. It considered the report of the Secretary-General's mission to be a more valid and up-to-date account.

Iran, in a letter of 23 May,[78] urgently requested that the United Nations take measures to stop the continued subjugation of Iranian POWs to Iraqi violence and torture. For its part, Iran said, it had unilaterally repatriated two groups of prisoners and was preparing to repatriate 50 more. It had also unilaterally implemented visits by the families of POWs.

Iraq, on 30 May,[79] said Iran's letters were sent for propaganda purposes and self-praise and to release spurious statements against Iraq. Iraq recalled that it had handed over to Iran some 430 prisoners since August 1981, some without reciprocation, and planned in the next few days to hand over 89 more. These facts, Iraq said, proved the deception in Iran's statement that it had released prisoners unilaterally.

Iran reported on 12 June[80] that it had transmitted to the Turkish Red Crescent a list of 56 disabled Iraqi prisoners for their return to Iraq and another group was being prepared for repatriation. Iran drew the Secretary-General's attention on 23 June[81] to a report by the Islamic Republic News Agency from Damascus that repatriated Iraqi POWs who refused to say false things about Iran were liable to be executed by Iraq and that some of the recently released disabled POWs had not yet been handed over to their families. Iran asked the Secretary-General to investigate the matter to protect the lives of repatriated prisoners and those scheduled to be repatriated.

On 4 September,[82] Iraq denied a statement, said to have been made by an official of Iran's War Information Commission at a press conference on 11 August, that there were secret POW camps in Iraq for Iranian prisoners. Iraq also denied a charge that it did not hand over wounded who were taken behind the front and that there were civilians among the POWs, including women; it said that if Iran was truly concerned about its prisoners, it would comply with Iraq's 9 March suggestions for their release.

Iran, on 11 November,[83] transmitted a list of 199 Iraqi teen-age POWs being held there, prepared, it said, for the information of the Secretary-General and the peace of mind of their families.

On 12 November,[84] Iraq transmitted a letter of the same day from its Deputy Prime Minister and Minister for Foreign Affairs concerning a newspaper report that Iran had put seven Iraqis taken prisoner on 24 May 1982 on trial for inciting prisoners to rise up against guards in the Gorgan camp. Iraq said no accurate information was available regarding the fate of prisoners and requested the Secretary-General to use his good offices to obtain such information.

Iraq, on 20 November,[85] supplied information provided by returning POWs on the practices of Iran towards its prisoners. Iraq charged that Iran had employed physical and psychological torture, and ideological, religious, factional and racial pressure, deliberately neglected prisoners' health and maintained poor sanitary conditions in prison camps, applied unethical practices, and obstructed the work of ICRC.

Iraq reported, on 22 November,[86] that it had released to ICRC 17 Iranian prisoners on 20 November, bringing the total number of Iranian prisoners released unilaterally by Iraq to 592.

Use of chemical weapons

Communications (February–11 April). Allegations over the use of chemical weapons by Iraq in the conflict were forwarded in a series of communications from Iran to the Secretary-General.

Iran's Foreign Minister, in a letter of 5 February,[87] asked the Secretary-General to deal with the fact that, seven months after his appeal to the Governments of Iran and Iraq to refrain from using chemical weapons,[88] Iraq continued to use them while Iran did not. Iran, in a letter of 27 February,[89] asked the Secretary-General to provide it and the entire international community with any response that may have been received from Iraq concerning his 1984 appeal.

On 12 March,[90] Iran charged that Iraq was about to resume chemical attacks on a large scale. Iran warned the United Nations that unless it prevented the recurrence of such violations of international and humanitarian norms, the international body, along with Iraq, would be held responsible for the consequences. On 13 March,[91] Iran transmitted a letter by its Foreign Minister charging that, as predicted, Iraq had again resorted to the use of chemical weapons on the war front. Iran urgently requested the Secretary-General to take steps immediately to stop this gross violation of, in particular, the Geneva Protocol of 1925, and expressed regret that the United Nations had not agreed to its request for the stationing of a permanent expert mission in Teheran to investigate the use of such weapons by Iraq. Iran alleged on 14 March[92] that chemical agents were used against its forces on two occasions in the southern war-front of Hur-Al-Hoveizeh, bringing the number injured as a result to 180. The President of Iran, in a letter forwarded on 18 March,[93] noted that more than a year had passed since Iraq began its deployment of chemical weapons. Iran had been the victim of two such attacks recently, and he questioned why the Secretary-General did not commission a team of experts to investigate these attacks. Iran warned that the continued use of chemical weapons and attacks on civilian populations would require retaliation.

In a letter of 20 March,[94] Iran reported that on 16 March a number of Iraqi planes allegedly dropped at least six large capsules on an Iranian position east of Majnoon Island. Iran believed these capsules contained cyanide, phosphorus and mustard gases. It charged that the attack had been preceded by four others since 11 March, leaving 200 Iranian combatants hospitalized. In a letter of 26 March,[95] Iran stated that international bodies concerned with upholding the authority of the relevant international instrument on the use of chemical weapons and those obliged to maintain international peace and security had been irresponsibly reticent since Iraq began using these weapons against Iran. It annexed to its letter a list of alleged chemical-weapon attacks and casualties.

In a letter of 8 April,[96] Iran claimed that that day the Iraqi régime used mustard and nerve gases at four points in the Badr operation region, including the Hur-Al-Hoveizeh area, despite Iraq's claim of a unilateral cease-fire during the Secretary-General's visit there. On 9 April,[97] Iran charged that Iraqi use of chemical weapons the day before had left 15 people dead and 200 wounded. Iran invited the Secretary-General to return to Teheran for further consultations on the issue, to visit the latest victims and immediately to dispatch an expert team to examine the evidence. In a letter of 11 April,[98] Iran charged that on 8 April mustard gas delivered through Iraqi artillery shelling was used in the Kushk area, killing and injuring more than 11 people, and on 8 and 9 April in the Gofair area, killing and injuring more than 28 people. Iran transmitted on 11 April[99] a table of chemical attacks that allegedly occurred between 13 and 20 March and resulted in the deaths of 32 people and injury to 2,231. Iran said the ease with which Iraq continued its campaign reflected the callousness and indifference of the Security Council in its unwillingness to take appropriate preventive measures against Iraq.

Specialist's report. The Secretary-General, in a letter to the President of the Security Council of 17 April,[100] transmitted a report of a medical expert, Dr. Manuel Domínguez, a specialist in atomic, biological and chemical weapons, whom he had dispatched to visit from 1 to 5 April Iranian patients hospitalized in Belgium, the Federal Republic of Germany and the United Kingdom. The patients were allegedly suffering from the effects of chemical weapons. The report detailed symptoms affecting the patients, including lesions, blackened and detached skin, and bronchial pneumonia. Following his examination of the patients and their records, the expert concluded that chemical weapons were used during March 1985 in the war between Iran and Iraq, that yperite was used, affecting Iranian soldiers, and possibly hydrocyanic gas, and that the attacks were made by means of bombs dropped from aircraft, according to patients' statements. In an addendum to the report, Dr. Domínguez stated that some patients were poisoned by organophosphorated agents not used in agriculture.

SECURITY COUNCIL CONSIDERATION (April)

With the Secretary-General's 12 April report[35] (see p. 242) and medical expert's report before it, the Security Council met on 25 April. The Council President stated that he was authorized to make the following declaration:[101]

Meeting number. SC 2576.

"The members of the Security Council, seized with the continuing conflict between Iran and Iraq, are appalled that chemical weapons have been used against Iranian soldiers during the month of March 1985 in the war between the two countries, as concluded in the report of the medical specialist appointed by the Secretary-General.

"They recall the statement of 30 March 1984[102] by the President of the Security Council on behalf of the members. They strongly condemn the renewed use of chemical weapons in the conflict and any possible future use of such weapons. They again urge the strict observance of the Geneva Protocol of 1925, according to which the use in war of chemical weapons is prohibited and has been justly condemned by the world community.

"The members of the Council condemn all violations of international humanitarian law and urge both parties to observe the generally recognized principles and rules of international humanitarian law which are applicable to armed conflicts and their obligations under international conventions designed to prevent or alleviate the human suffering of warfare. At the same time, they urge a cessation of hostilities and remain convinced that a prompt, comprehensive, just and honourable settlement acceptable to both sides is essential and in the interest of international peace and security.

"The members of the Council express their full appreciation and support to the Secretary-General for his report contained in document S/17097. They are ready to issue at the appropriate moment an invitation to both parties to take part in a renewed examination of all aspects of the conflict. They call on the parties to co-operate with the Security Council and with the Secretary-General in their efforts to restore peace to the peoples of Iran and Iraq."

Communications (25 April–December). Iran claimed, in a letter of 25 April,[103] that on 17 April Iraq shelled the city of Khorramshahr with a chemical cannon-ball, causing eye and throat irritation to a number of people. Iran said the international community was looking to the Council to condemn Iraq for its repeated use of chemical weapons.

In a letter of 2 May,[104] Iran reported that the total number of people injured in three Iraqi chemical attacks against Iranian soldiers on 8 and 9 April had increased to 201. On 13 May,[105] it charged that Iraq had again resorted to chemical warfare, using mustard gas in attacks on the north-western parts of Fakkeh and Sardasht on 7 and 8 May.

Iran's Foreign Minister, in a letter transmitted on 24 May,[106] said the work of the Security Council and the United Nations could not be confined to issuing statements and resolutions; they must mobilize all international means in their power to stop immediately violations of international regulations, such as Iraq's use of chemical weapons, which continued despite the Council's condemnation. In response to that letter, Iraq, on 30 May,[107] stated that Iran's position involved a gross inconsistency, on the one hand calling on the Council and the United Nations to take steps to maintain international peace and security, and on the other rejecting the jurisdiction of the Council and the United Nations in the conflict and their competence to pass judgement on it.

Iran, on 16 July,[108] called on the Secretary-General to take further necessary action to end the Iraqi use of chemical weapons, reporting that Iraq had allegedly shelled with chemical cannon-balls the north-east of Basra on 7 May and the Kenareh region on 8 May. On 4 November,[109] Iran charged that on 2 November Iraq had shelled Minou Island with chemical cannon-balls leaving eight people severely injured.

Iraq, in a letter of 6 November,[110] stated that on 5 November it had firmly rejected the charge that Iranian troops had been killed by chemical artillery shells. The purpose of Iran's allegations, Iraq said, was to justify continued Iranian shelling of Iraqi border towns. Iran, on 11 November,[111] pointed out that it had charged Iraq with injuring and not killing its troops with chemical weapons.

Other communications. Interference with commercial shipping and commercial air traffic was the subject of several communications.

On 25 January,[112] Iran transmitted a letter from its Foreign Minister expressing to the Secretary-General a shared concern over attacks, which Iran attributed to Iraq, on neutral mercantile ships in the Gulf. Iraq, on 20 February,[113] said the concern expressed by Iran was surprising since it was common knowledge that Iran had prevented by military might the exercise by Iraq of its legitimate right to free navigation in the Gulf. It had no alternative but to defend itself on the basis of the provisions of international law which authorized a State party to an armed conflict to impose a blockade on the ports of the adversary State in order to induce it to accept peace. Iraq said the activity of the so-called "neutral mercantile ships" was tantamount to supplying the Iranian military machine.

Iran had taken it upon itself to declare Iran's airspace unsafe for commercial aircraft, Iran said in a letter of 18 March,[114] asking all nations to condemn the act. On 25 March,[115] Iran said that, in the light of threats made by Iraq against innocent passengers, while it could not conceivably resort to retaliatory measures against civilian aircraft, should a civilian aircraft be shot down over its airspace, Iran would level the airport in Baghdad.

Kuwait and Iran exchanged charges stemming from the interception of a Kuwaiti commercial vessel in June. Kuwait, in a letter of 10 July[116] to the President of the Security Council, reported that on 20 June the Iranian navy had intercepted the commercial vessel *Al-Muharraq* in international waters south of the Strait of Hormuz and ordered a diversion of its course to the Iranian port of Bandar Abbas, where it was impounded. The Gulf Co-operation Council, Kuwait said, had adopted a resolution on 9 July stating that the Iranian action constituted a flagrant violation of international law concerning navigation on the high seas as well as freedom of navigation in international waterways. Annexed to the letter was a communiqué from the United Arab Shipping Company, owner of the vessel, describing the commercial cargo and route of the vessel, as well as the events which overtook it.

Iran, in a letter of 19 July,[117] said its authorities had been informed that the Kuwaiti vessel carried logistical goods destined for Iraq. The Iranian navy had intercepted it on the basis of the 1907 Hague Convention respecting the Rights and Duties of Neutral Powers in Naval War and directed it to Bandar Abbas where it was inspected, 4,500 tons of logistical goods destined for Iraq were seized, and it was released.

Kuwait, on 20 September,[118] circulated a letter of 19 September from its Deputy Prime Minister and Minister for Foreign Affairs recounting the detaining by Iran of four Kuwaiti ships in 1984 and 1985, as well as, in September, an Italian ship and a Chinese ship chartered by Kuwait—all intercepted in international waters. Kuwait said it had called on Iran to end such acts. Iran, on 25 September,[119] said it had repeatedly announced that it would not allow the transport of arms from Gulf waters to the Iraqi aggressors and that, contrary to the principles of good-neighbourly relations, cargo ships destined for Kuwait had carried logistical goods and arms headed for Iraq via Kuwait. Iran said it would continue to inspect ships in the Gulf suspected of carrying arms to Iraq.

Iran expressed concern over alleged repeated military attacks by Iraq on its Bushehr nuclear power plant in several communications. An alleged attack on the power plant on 12 February by two Iraqi missiles, which killed one Iranian worker and caused significant damage, was the subject of a letter of 14 February,[120] in which the President of the Atomic Energy Organization of Iran requested that the Director General of the International Atomic Energy Agency (IAEA) give his personal attention to the incident. Iran asked that the Director General's representative inspect the site to verify the losses. Iraq, in a statement by a military spokesman on 14 February conveyed on 24 February,[121] denied Iran's allegations of the attack; the statement said the spokesman had stated on 12 February that the Iraqi air force had attacked only two maritime targets near Kharg Island and troop concentrations on the Iraqi border.

On 26 April,[122] Iran circulated a letter of 17 March from the President of its Atomic Energy Organization to the IAEA Director General, stating that IAEA was either impotent in implementing its own resolutions or strongly biased in its dealings with the affairs of member States, because it had done nothing to halt Iraq from attacking Iran's nuclear power plant in March 1985, had not sent a mission to inspect the site as Iran had requested, and had not expelled Iraq from IAEA. Iran considered itself discriminated against by IAEA's argument that the plant was not completed and therefore not covered by Agency safeguards, since there was no fissionable material present, the release of which could be dangerous.

The Secretary-General, on 6 May,[123] circulated a 26 March reply to Iran by the IAEA Director General reiterating that the verification of reported war damage and losses in respect of a plant still under construction, not containing radioactive material and not yet subject to safeguards, was not appropriately a mission to be undertaken by him. The Agency's statute contained no provisions for the expulsion of a member State.

General comments about the conflict were recorded in several communications.

Iran, in a letter of 3 July,[124] charged that, according to reliable sources, Iraq had recently purchased 100 G-5 155-millimetre howitzers (heavy artillery) from South Africa, in blatant contravention of the Security Council's 1984 resolution[125] requesting Member States to refrain from importing arms produced in South Africa. In a letter of 5 July,[126] Iran transmitted the text of an article from the magazine *Africa Confidential* of 10 April about the weapons purchase. Iraq responded in a letter of 26 July,[127] in which it stated that Iran's charges had no factual basis.

On 25 September,[128] Iraq transmitted the text of an article from *The Times* of London of 20 September containing statements by an Iranian military intelligence officer, which Iraq said proved that Iran had sent children to fight its battles against Iraq and thousands had died.

Iran, on 22 October,[129] expressed objection to the address by the Iraqi Vice-President before the General Assembly on 18 October, which, Iran said, contained fallacious allegations against it.

Iraq, on 12 November,[130] announced that, on 6 November, 30 of its fighter aircraft destroyed the Noward iron and steel complex and the shipbuilding centre for Iranian warships.

Italy, on behalf of the 10 EC member States, transmitted on 6 May[131] a declaration on the Iran-Iraq conflict, adopted by the Ministers for Foreign Affairs of the Ten at the fifty-seventh Ministerial Meeting on European Political Co-operation (Luxembourg, 29 April). The Ten viewed with utmost concern the aggravation of the conflict, the escalation in military activities against civilian targets, the continued loss of life among the civilian population and the serious damage to the economy of both countries. They urged Iran and Iraq to agree to an immediate cease-fire, start a negotiating process and comply with the 12 June 1984 agreement.[1] They condemned the use of chemical weapons, whenever and wherever it occurred.

Morocco, on 19 August,[132] transmitted the final communiqué of an Extraordinary Summit Conference of Arab States (Casablanca, 7-9 August). The Conference noted with deep concern and great pain the continuance of the war and expressed strong disapproval at Iran's insistence on continuing it and launching attacks against Iraq aimed at violating the country's border and occupying territory, which could impel the Arab States to reconsider their relations with Iran.

Yemen, as Chairman of the Organization of the Islamic Conference, transmitted on 15 October[133] a communiqué of the co-ordination meeting of the Ministers for Foreign Affairs of the Conference (New York, 9 October), expressing appreciation for the efforts being undertaken by the Islamic Peace Committee during two sessions at Jeddah, Saudi Arabia, in May and September to bring about an honourable and just peace based on Islamic principles and international law.

Oman, on 20 November,[134] as President of the sixth session of the Ministerial Council of the Gulf Co-operation Council (GCC), enclosed the final communiqué adopted by the GCC Supreme Council (Oman, 3-6 November). The Council called on Iran to abide by the principles laid down in Security Council resolutions of 1983[135] and 1984[136] which expressed the attitude of the international community with regard to the freedom of navigation in international waterways and freedom of passage to and from the ports of the GCC States. These States reiterated assurances that they were prepared to pursue efforts with the parties concerned to bring an end to the war.

GENERAL ASSEMBLY ACTION

On 16 September 1985, at the close of its resumed thirty-ninth (1984) session, the General Assembly adopted **decision 39/466**, by which it decided to include the item "Consequences of the prolonga-tion of the armed conflict between Iran and Iraq" on the draft agenda of its fortieth (1985) session, which opened the following day. The item was not taken up at that session before year's end; however, when the session was suspended on 18 December, by **decision 40/470**, the Assembly decided to consider the item, among others, at its resumed session in 1986 at a date to be announced. These decisions were adopted without vote, on oral proposals by the Assembly President.

Other action. The Commission on Human Rights, in March 1985, expressed deep concern at alleged violations of human rights in Iran and urged it to respect and ensure the rights recognized in the International Covenant on Civil and Political Rights. Subsequently, the Economic and Social Council, by **decision 1985/148**, approved the Commission's decision to extend the mandate of its Special Representative on the human rights situation in Iran.

The General Assembly, in **resolution 40/141** of 13 December, expressed deep concern over the allegations of human rights violations in Iran reported by the Commission's Special Representative and decided to continue examining the human rights situation in that country. (See ECONOMIC AND SOCIAL QUESTIONS, Chapter XVIII.)

REFERENCES

[1]YUN 1984, p. 236. [2]S/16897. [3]S/16907. [4]S/16920. [5]S/16949. [6]A/39/864 (S/16948). [7]A/39/870-S/16967. [8]S/16971. [9]A/39/872-S/16976. [10]S/17004. [11]S/17005. [12]S/16999. [13]A/39/877 (S/17002). [14]S/17016. [15]S/17017. [16]S/17018. [17]S/17019. [18]S/17020. [19]S/17024. [20]A/39/878 (S/17025). [21]A/39/879 (S/17026). [22]S/17029. [23]S/17036. [24]S/17037. [25]A/39/880-S/17044. [26]S/17049. [27]S/17058. [28]S/17063. [29]S/17070. [30]S/17073. [31]S/17078. [32]S/17083. [33]S/17084. [34]S/17090. [35]S/17097. [36]S/17094. [37]S/17099. [38]S/17121. [39]A/39/892 (S/17134). [40]S/17160. [41]S/17180. [42]S/17220. [43]S/17221. [44]S/17223. [45]S/17226. [46]S/17237. [47]S/17257. [48]S/17299. [49]S/17397. [50]S/17307. [51]S/17313. [52]S/17347. [53]S/17450. [54]S/17467. [55]A/40/829-S/17599. [56]S/17616. [57]A/40/868-S/17617. [58]S/17679. [59]S/17687. [60]S/17706. [61]A/39/859-S/16909. [62]A/39/860-S/16919. [63]A/39/869-S/16963. [64]A/39/874-S/16982. [65]YUN 1984, p. 238. [66]S/16962. [67]S/16978. [68]S/16992 & Corr.1. [69]S/16996. [70]S/16998. [71]S/16980. [72]S/16994. [73]S/17021. [74]S/17137. [75]S/17144. [76]S/17212. [77]S/17248. [78]S/17216. [79]S/17230. [80]S/17258. [81]S/17306. [82]S/17435. [83]A/40/872-S/17622. [84]S/17626. [85]S/17640. [86]S/17649. [87]A/40/118-S/16941. [88]YUN 1984, p. 237. [89]A/40/154-S/16987. [90]S/16998. [91]A/40/176-S/17028. [92]S/17031. [93]S/17039. [94]A/40/189-S/17046. [95]A/40/209 (S/17059). [96]S/17088. [97]S/17089. [98]S/17095 & Corr.1. [99]A/40/231 (S/17096). [100]S/17127 & Add.1. [101]S/17130. [102]YUN 1984, p. 232. [103]S/17129. [104]S/17143. [105]S/17181. [106]S/17217. [107]S/17225. [108]A/40/487-S/17342. [109]A/40/849-S/17606. [110]S/17611. [111]A/40/873-S/17623. [112]S/16910. [113]S/16972. [114]S/17047. [115]S/17052. [116]S/17335. [117]S/17348. [118]S/17482. [119]S/17496. [120]A/39/865-S/16956. [121]S/16979. [122]S/17133. [123]S/17157. [124]A/40/455-S/17322 & Corr.1. [125]YUN 1984, p. 143, SC res. 558(1984), 13 Dec. 1984. [126]A/40/464-S/17326. [127]S/17368. [128]S/17500. [129]A/40/785. [130]S/17625. [131]A/39/895-S/17161. [132]A/40/564 & Corr.1. [133]A/40/758-S/17570. [134]A/40/911-S/17644. [135]YUN 1983, p. 239, SC res. 540(1983), 31 Oct. 1983. [136]YUN 1984, p. 234, SC res. 552(1984), 1 June 1984.

Chapter VIII

Mediterranean

Political issues in the Mediterranean during 1985 continued to centre on Cyprus and the deteriorating relations between the Libyan Arab Jamahiriya and other States, principally Egypt and the United States. With regard to security and co-operation in the Mediterranean, the General Assembly expressed concern over the increasing tension there and urged all States to reduce it and promote peace in the area.

Concerning Cyprus, the Secretary-General continued his contacts at the highest level with the Greek Cypriot and Turkish Cypriot communities, and after noting in February that the search for a solution had never been so narrow, at year's end he said he believed it possible to resolve the remaining issues provided both sides were willing to agree on a framework for an overall agreement.

Expressing its strong support for the Secretary-General's good offices mission, the Security Council twice extended the stationing of the United Nations Peace-keeping Force in Cyprus (UNFICYP).

Topics related to this chapter. Africa: Chad–Libyan Arab Jamahiriya dispute. International Court of Justice: continental shelf delimitation (Tunisia/Libyan Arab Jamahiriya, Libyan Arab Jamahiriya/Malta).

Cyprus question

Owing in good part to the activities of UNFICYP, the situation in Cyprus continued to be calm in 1985.

The Security Council twice extended the mandate of UNFICYP—on 14 June (resolution 565(1985)) and on 12 December (resolution 578(1985))—which continued its peace-keeping and humanitarian tasks.

Throughout the year the Secretary-General continued his mission of good offices, entrusted to him by the Council. In January, a joint high-level meeting between President Spyros Kyprianou of Cyprus and Rauf R. Denktas of the Turkish Cypriot community was held under his auspices. The Turkish Cypriot side accepted a draft agreement contained in documentation presented by the Secretary-General. The Greek Cypriot side would accept the documentation only as a basis for negotiations.

To overcome those difficulties, the Secretary-General worked out a consolidated draft agreement with the incorporated components of the documentation prepared for the January meeting. He discussed the consolidated draft during a meeting with President Kyprianou in March and subsequently received an affirmative reply from the Greek Cypriot side. The Turkish Cypriot side informed the Secretary-General that due to a "referendum" and "elections" to be held in May and June it could not discuss the matter until that process was over.

In September, the Security Council President made a statement on behalf of its members expressing strong support for the Secretary-General's mission and calling on all parties to co-operate with him to reach an early agreement.

In December, the Secretary-General stressed that unless both sides were willing to work to an overall solution within an agreed framework, no further progress could be expected.

Although the Cyprus question was on the agenda of the General Assembly in 1985, it was not discussed.

Cyprus and Turkey addressed letters to the Secretary-General on various aspects of the situation throughout 1985. Those from Turkey forwarded letters from the Turkish Cypriot community signed by Rauf R. Denktas as "President of the Turkish Republic of Northern Cyprus", by Necati Munir Ertekun as "Minister for Foreign Affairs and Defence" or by Ozer Koray as "representative" of that "Republic".

Report of the Secretary-General (February). On 2 February,[1] the Secretary-General reported to the Security Council on the results of the joint meeting between President Kyprianou and Mr. Denktas, which took place in New York from 17 to 20 January 1985.

The parties considered the documentation for a draft agreement, presented by the Secretary-General and resulting from the 1984 separate high-level "proximity talks".[2] The Secretary-General noted that he made every effort to assist the parties in resolving their differences. He said that certain aspects of the substance of the draft agreement were touched upon and the gap between the respective positions in some cases appeared to be narrowing. He noted that the Turkish Cypriot side fully accepted the draft, while the Greek Cypriot side accepted the documentation as a basis for negotiations in accordance with the integrated whole approach aiming at a comprehensive and overall solution to the Cyprus problem.

Commenting that the gap in the search for a solution had never been so narrow, the Secretary-General appealed to both sides and to all those concerned with the future of Cyprus to ensure that nothing was done in the island or elsewhere that would make that search more difficult.

Communications (3 May–13 June). On 3 May,[3] Cyprus protested a decision by the Turkish Cypriot side to hold a so-called referendum for what was termed a constitution of the illegal entity calling itself the Turkish Republic of Northern Cyprus. Replying on 17 May,[4] Mr. Ertekun said the allegations of illegality were an attempt to discredit Turkish Cypriot actions in the eyes of the world.

Referring again to illegalities in the northern occupied territory, Cyprus, on 5 June,[5] drew attention to the colonization of that part of the island by Turks from the Turkish mainland which, according to Turkish Cypriot sources, had brought the total of such settlers in 1985 to between 60,000 and 65,000 in occupied Cyprus.

On 10 June,[6] Cyprus, stating that the Turkish side had held so-called elections the previous day for a "president" of its "Republic", said the illegal action had taken place in an area from which some 82 per cent of the indigenous population had been expelled. Responding on 12 June,[7] Mr. Koray stated that the alleged settlers from Turkey were Turkish Cypriots, forced over the years to leave because of Greek Cypriot oppression, who had returned after the north's liberation in 1974; the few thousand mainland Turkish workers were a normal importation of labour in a developing economy.

Mr. Denktas, in a 13 June press statement,[8] said that what hampered the solution of the Cyprus problem was not the elections by the Turkish Cypriots but the crisis of authority in the Greek Cypriot community following the January New York meeting.

Report of the Secretary-General (May/June). In a report to the Security Council on the United Nations operation in Cyprus covering 13 December 1984 to 31 May 1985, the Secretary-General gave details of UNFICYP activities[9] (see p. 256) and his good offices mission.[10] After summarizing the results of the January high-level meeting (see above), he said that, in order to overcome the difficulties which had arisen at that time, he had incorporated components of the documentation into a single consolidated draft agreement, which included clarifications of its elements and possible follow-up procedures.

During a meeting with the President of Cyprus on 11 March and then with its Foreign Minister on 3 April, the Secretary-General stated that he had sought the Greek Cypriot side's views on the consolidated draft and had subsequently received an affirmative reply. On 12 April, he had written to Mr. Denktas to seek his views, but was informed that due to the referendum and elections which his community intended to conduct in May and June, the Turkish Cypriot side was not in a position to engage in substantive discussions until that process was complete.

Concerning the so-called electoral process, the Secretary-General pointed out that on 6 May his spokesman had stated that the United Nations recognized no Cypriot State other than the Republic of Cyprus and therefore the Secretary-General could not condone any action at variance with that position.

Even though he was unable to report that the two sides had reached an agreement, the Secretary-General believed the documentation's substance, worked out through 10 months of strenuous effort, represented the formula for a just and lasting solution, which, provided both sides showed the necessary good will, could be arrived at without further delay. He intended to intensify his diplomatic action to that end.

In the search for a peaceful solution, the continued presence of UNFICYP remained indispensable. The Secretary-General therefore recommended that the Council extend the Force's mandate for a further six months. The Governments of Cyprus, Greece and the United Kingdom concurred with his recommendation, while Turkey and the Turkish Cypriot community indicated that their stand would be expounded in the Council.[11]

The Secretary-General also stated that, at his request, the United Nations High Commissioner for Refugees (UNHCR) was continuing to help the needy in the island (see p. 257). Details were also given about the Force's growing financial problems (see p. 258). With regard to the Committee on Missing Persons in Cyprus, the Secretary-General appointed, effective 28 April 1985, Paul Wurth (Switzerland) to succeed the late Claude Pilloud; the three-member Committee, established in 1981,[12] was expected to resume work in the near future (see p. 255).

SECURITY COUNCIL ACTION (June)

The Security Council met on 14 June to consider the Secretary-General's report and recommendation to extend UNFICYP's mandate. Cyprus, Greece and Turkey were invited, at their request, to participate in the discussion without the right to vote. The Council also extended an invitation, under rule 39[a] of its provisional rules of procedure, to Ozer Koray.

---

[a]Rule 39 of the Council's provisional rules of procedure states: "The Security Council may invite members of the Secretariat or other persons, whom it considers competent for the purpose, to supply it with information or to give other assistance in examining matters within its competence."

On that day, the Council unanimously adopted **resolution 565(1985)**.

The Security Council,

Taking note of the report of the Secretary-General on the United Nations operation in Cyprus of 31 May and 14 June and of 11 June 1985,

Noting the recommendation by the Secretary-General that the Security Council should extend the stationing of the United Nations Peace-keeping Force in Cyprus for a further period of six months,

Noting also that the Government of Cyprus has agreed that in view of the prevailing conditions in the island it is necessary to keep the Force in Cyprus beyond 15 June 1985,

Reaffirming the provisions of its resolution 186(1964) and other relevant resolutions,

1. *Extends once more* the stationing in Cyprus of the United Nations Peace-keeping Force established under resolution 186(1964) for a further period, ending on 15 December 1985;

2. *Requests* the Secretary-General to continue his mission of good offices, to keep the Security Council informed of the progress made and to submit a report on the implementation of the present resolution by 30 November 1985;

3. *Calls upon* all the parties concerned to continue to co-operate with the Force on the basis of the present mandate.

Security Council resolution 565(1985)

14 June 1985   Meeting 2591   Adopted unanimously

Draft prepared in consultations among Council members (S/17266).

After the vote, Cyprus pointed out that the peace-keeping functions of UNFICYP were made imperative by the situation prevailing in Cyprus and by the Secretary-General's delicate ongoing initiative for which Cyprus assured its full co-operation and support. Its voluntary contribution to UNFICYP, together with the assessed contribution for its maintenance, would exceed $1 million for 1985.

The January high-level meeting, Cyprus said, had not produced any progress, because of the negative attitude of the Turkish Cypriot side and its premeditated plans to ruin the meeting in order to proceed with further partitionist acts. According to the interpretation of the Greek Cypriot side, Cyprus noted, the meeting was to entail constructive discussion based on documentation presented by the Secretary-General. However, Mr. Denktas had insisted that the texts should be signed without discussion and that outstanding matters—such as the withdrawal of non-Cypriot forces, the questions of guarantees and freedom of movement and settlement, and the territorial aspect—be referred to working groups.

Cyprus said that after four days of intensive efforts to salvage the meeting, Mr. Denktas had not agreed to discuss anything and had left, having rejected a proposal by the Secretary-General for a new high-level meeting and after stating that none

of the documents prepared in the three rounds of talks, even the non-papers, which included shifts in Turkish positions, was any longer valid.

Referring to the so-called referendum and presidential elections, Cyprus called them a mockery of democratic principles which violated United Nations resolutions on the island. It emphasized that the principle of self-determination could not be interpreted in such a way as to impair the unity of the people and the territorial integrity of any State. The results of the referendum showed that without the "votes" of the Turkish settlers, a majority in favour of the new "constitution" would not have been secured. In May, President Kyprianou had stated that there could be no solution of the Cyprus problem without the withdrawal of all occupation troops and all settlers, Cyprus stated.

Greece considered it imperative that the Force should remain with its current strength and noted that it had become an important component of a delicate balance. Greece observed that Cyprus had displayed political restraint and statesmanship, having accepted, with onerous sacrifices, all of the Secretary-General's proposals; it said the so-called referendum and elections ran counter to and defied United Nations resolutions. A viable solution to secure the territorial integrity and unity of Cyprus, based on justice and respect for human rights, should be found soon, Greece said, adding that any solution would be totally incompatible with the presence of any occupation or other foreign troops.

Speaking on behalf of the Turkish Cypriot community, Mr. Koray said that the Greek Cypriot side did not want a solution to the problem, based on bicommunal, bi-zonal federal principles, as envisaged by the draft agreement presented in January. He also stressed the necessity to ensure the continuation of the Turkish guarantee, which was indispensable for Turkish Cypriots.

Referring to the resolution, Mr. Koray said that it contained elements unacceptable to the Turkish Cypriot side and thus rejected it *in toto*. The text referred to the Government of Cyprus, which Turkish Cypriots considered illegal since the legitimate Government had been destroyed in 1963 by its Greek Cypriot wing. The Turkish Cypriot side had also previously rejected, or accepted with reservations, the other relevant resolutions mentioned in the current one. Further, Mr. Koray said, reference was made to the "present mandate" which his community believed was incompatible with the radically changed conditions. He reiterated Turkish Cypriot support for the good offices mission of the Secretary-General and his side's readiness to contact him after the 23 June elections.

Turkey, speaking of the January meeting, stressed that the Turkish Cypriot side had fully accepted the draft agreement while the Greek Cypriot side regarded the documentation as a basis for negotiations only, which meant that it was not ready to enter into reciprocal commitments with its counterpart. After the collapse of that meeting, a new situation had emerged in which both parties were free to re-formulate their negotiating positions and therefore a new negotiating process had to be initiated.

Turkey reiterated that the Greek Cypriots had never had any constitutional or legal right to represent Turkish Cypriots and hence the whole of Cyprus. In the absence of a joint federal Government, it was the inalienable right of the Turkish Cypriot people to be represented only by the authorities elected by them. Turkey pointed out that the Turkish Cypriot side had left the door open to a bicommunal and bi-zonal federal solution to be negotiated between the two sides with the purpose of establishing a partnership. It also stressed that the absolute prerequisite of the good offices mission was that the two sides be treated as equal political authorities representing the two peoples of the island.

With regard to the Council's resolution, Turkey gave similar reasons to those given by Mr. Koray as its objections, adding that the text did not rest on a legally or politically valid foundation and therefore did not enjoy the support of all the directly interested parties. However, Turkey would continue its traditional role of moderation and strive to facilitate the search for a bi-zonal federal solution.

Australia thought an early solution to the problem could be achieved only through negotiation and dialogue, and said it supported Council resolutions 541(1983)[13] and 550(1984),[14] which it felt outlined the path towards a just and lasting settlement. The Secretary-General's mission of good offices continued to present the best means of progress, and the international community should support further diplomatic activity; while those efforts continued, it was essential that no side should jeopardize them, Australia stated, adding that it would continue its contingent of civilian policemen in UNFICYP, and urging Member States to increase substantially their voluntary contributions to the Force.

Communications (18-25 June). In a letter of 18 June,[15] Sri Lanka expressed concern over the so-called presidential elections of 9 June, terming them but one in a series of secessionist measures which could only aggravate the situation in the island.

Cyprus, on 25 June,[16] drew attention to the "parliamentary elections" held two days earlier in the north of the island, which it said aimed at consolidating the illegalities created by the use of force; the Turkish side was continuing its negative at-

titude at a time when the Secretary-General's mission had reached a delicate and important phase.

SECURITY COUNCIL CONSIDERATION (September)

On 8 August the Secretary-General received a reply to his 12 April letter from Mr. Denktas, setting out the views of the Turkish Cypriot side on specific aspects of the Secretary-General's efforts. After the two had further discussions on 12 and 13 September, the Secretary-General reported orally to the Security Council.

On 20 September 1985, the Council President made the following statement on its behalf:[17]

Meeting number. SC 2607.

> The Security Council has been seized with the Cyprus question since 1964. The members of the Council have been kept informed of the efforts begun by the Secretary-General in August 1984 as part of the mission of good offices entrusted to him by the Council.
>
> On 20 September 1985, the members of the Council heard an oral report from the Secretary-General, in the course of which he conveyed his assessment that his initiative had brought the positions of the two sides closer than ever before and expressed his conviction that what had been achieved so far should lead to an early agreement on the framework for a just and lasting settlement of the Cyprus question in accordance with the principles of the Charter. Recalling their support for the sovereignty, independence, territorial integrity, unity and non-alignment of the Republic of Cyprus, members of the Council expressed strong support for the mission of the Secretary-General under his mandate from the Council.
>
> The members of the Security Council, therefore, called upon all parties to make a special effort in co-operation with the Secretary-General to reach an early agreement.

Communications (September-November). On 7 November,[18] Cyprus protested several violations of its airspace by fighter-planes of the Turkish air force which, it said, took place on 5 November. Responding on 20 November,[19] Mr. Koray stated that the overflights had taken place with prior notification to UNFICYP, within what he called the sovereign borders and airspace of the Turkish Republic of Northern Cyprus.

In its Final Political Declaration, the Conference of Foreign Ministers of Non-Aligned Countries (Luanda, Angola, 4-7 September)[20] deplored the separatist actions by the Turkish Cypriot leadership, including the so-called referendum and elections. A similar position was taken by the heads of Governments of Commonwealth States (Nassau, Bahamas, 16-22 October),[21] who noted that no other country besides Turkey had recognized the illegal entity.

Report of the Secretary-General (November/December). In a report to the Security Council on the operation in Cyprus covering 1 June to 30 November 1985, the Secretary-General updated

UNFICYP activities[22] (see p. 256) and recapitulated events related to his good offices mission,[23] adding that he had met with President Kyprianou in October. During his discussions with the community leaders, he had stressed the vital importance of preserving what had been achieved since August 1984, since he believed that the two sides were within reach of an agreement whose details would have to be negotiated to their satisfaction. However, unless both were willing to agree on the framework for an overall agreement, no further progress could be expected. With an important opportunity at hand, the Secretary-General believed it possible to resolve the few remaining issues by working in co-operation with him. Referring to his recommendation that the Council extend the mandate of UNFICYP for a further six months,[22] he stated that Cyprus, Greece and the United Kingdom concurred, while Turkey and the Turkish Cypriot community would expound their position before the Council.[24]

Concerning the Committee on Missing Persons, the Secretary-General reported that it resumed its substantive work in June and had held two sessions of four and five meetings, respectively. Its investigatory work had reached an advanced stage in nearly one quarter of the cases before it, while initial work had been completed on nearly half of the cases.

SECURITY COUNCIL ACTION (December)

The Security Council met on 12 December to consider the Secretary-General's report and his recommendation to extend the UNFICYP mandate. Austria, Cyprus, Greece and Turkey were invited, at their request, to participate without the right to vote. Mr. Koray was also invited to participate under rule 39[b] of the provisional rules of procedure.

The Council then unanimously adopted **resolution 578(1985)**.

The Security Council,

Taking note of the report of the Secretary-General on the United Nations operation in Cyprus of 30 November and 11 December and of 9 December 1985,

Noting the recommendation by the Secretary-General that the Security Council should extend the stationing of the United Nations Peace-keeping Force in Cyprus for a further period of six months,

Noting also that the Government of Cyprus has agreed that in view of the prevailing conditions in the island it is necessary to keep the Force in Cyprus beyond 15 December 1985,

Reaffirming the provisions of its resolution 186(1964) and other relevant resolutions,

1. *Extends once more* the stationing in Cyprus of the United Nations Peace-keeping Force established under resolution 186(1964) for a further period, ending on 15 June 1986;

2. *Requests* the Secretary-General to continue his mission of good offices, to keep the Security Council informed of the progress made and to submit a report on the implementation of the present resolution by 31 May 1986;

3. *Calls upon* all the parties concerned to continue to co-operate with the Force on the basis of the present mandate.

Security Council resolution 578(1985)
12 December 1985   Meeting 2635   Adopted unanimously
Draft prepared in consultations among Council members (S/17680).

After the vote, Austria expressed on behalf of the countries contributing troops and civilian police—Australia, Austria, Canada, Denmark, Finland, Ireland, Sweden and the United Kingdom—deep concern over the financial situation of UNFICYP (see p. 258), emphasizing that the widening gap between voluntary contributions and the operation's real costs placed an ever heavier burden on those countries, which had always borne a large portion of UNFICYP's expenses; they appealed to States to increase or begin making contributions, to alleviate the serious financial situation.

Cyprus reiterated that a basic pre-condition for solving the island's problems was the withdrawal of Turkish occupation troops before the establishment of an interim Government. It recalled that the United Nations, in mandatory resolutions on Cyprus, had urged the speedy withdrawal of all foreign forces, the return of all refugees to their homes and lands, respect for the sovereignty and unity of Cyprus and non-interference in its affairs. Cyprus pointed out that Turkey had voted in favour of a 1974 General Assembly resolution,[25] subsequently endorsed by the Council,[26] containing such calls, but Turkey's record towards implementing those resolutions had been dismal; Turkish troops in Cyprus posed an insurmountable obstacle to genuine negotiations. The continued Turkish policy of militarization and expansion against Cyprus explained the positions taken by the Turkish Cypriot community in the intercommunal talks. Cyprus charged Turkey and Mr. Denktas with having admitted that the withdrawal of troops was non-negotiable and that they would remain in perpetuity.

Cyprus noted that after the high-level meeting's failure to produce results because of the refusal of Mr. Denktas to engage in meaningful dialogue and his rejection of compromise efforts, the Greek Cypriot side had accepted the Secretary-General's idea for a new high-level meeting. Cyprus accused Mr. Denktas of a series of illegal acts aimed at entrenching the unilateral declaration of independence. It was anxious, however, to reach a negotiated settlement in the framework of the Secretary-General's initiative.

Having emphasized that Greece was one of the guarantors of the Republic of Cyprus, Greece

[b]See footnote a on p. 252.

agreed that no solution to the question could be envisaged if it did not provide for withdrawing the Turkish army before any transitional machinery was set up in Cyprus; furthermore, a system of effective guarantees should be agreed upon.

Greece quoted its Prime Minister, who had said that Greece could not accept a transitional period or provisional Government before the last Turkish soldier had withdrawn; if Turkey became a guarantor Power, Greece would not agree to act likewise, since Greece's idea was to have guarantees from a group of States from East, West and the third world.

It would be dangerous for Greece to guarantee a constitutionally unworkable solution, providing for the Turkish army presence in the island under one form or the other, Greece explained; such a structure would probably collapse, leading to a major crisis threatening peace in the area. Reaffirming support for the Secretary-General's initiative and pointing to the important concessions made by President Kyprianou—which, in Greece's opinion, had gone beyond the safety limit for the Greek Cypriot community and the State of Cyprus—Greece stated that it was time for Turkey to take a decisive step.

Mr. Koray felt it was ironic that the side which had tried to destroy the bicommunal independence of the 1960 Republic of Cyprus and make it a colony of Greece was claiming to be the Government of Cyprus, capable of representing both sides. He believed that the choice was between peace through negotiations on an equal footing with the elected representatives of the Turkish people of Cyprus or the pursuit of unrealistic, one-sided, condemnatory resolutions harmful to reconciliation. Pointing out that the Greek Cypriot leadership had rejected the 1984 draft agreement in January 1985, he referred to the positions taken by the non-aligned countries[20] and the Commonwealth States[21] (see p. 252) and charged that the Greek Cypriot leaders had tried to internationalize the conflict further. Mr. Koray stressed that the Turkish guarantee had proved effective in bringing his community from the brink of destruction and colonization; the only element capable of safeguarding a Cyprus settlement was the establishment of a bicommunal, bi-zonal federal republic with guarantees of equal political status and the legitimate rights of both sides.

With regard to the current resolution, Mr. Koray stated that the Turkish Cypriot side rejected it completely because it would not help bridge the gap between the conflicting parties but would increase the intransigence of the other side. However, his community favoured the presence of UNFICYP on what he said was its territory. He reiterated that all aspects of co-operation between the "Turkish Republic of Northern Cyprus" and UNFICYP should be based only on decisions taken by that "Government". The Turkish Cypriot side had preserved its faith in the Secretary-General's initiative and continued to give it full support, Mr. Koray added.

Turkey pointed out that UNFICYP's continued presence after 21 years had to be viewed in the light of the radically changed circumstances in the island and in the context of its role in support of peace-making efforts. Because of this role in particular, Turkey would have wished that the current resolution on UNFICYP enjoyed the support of all the directly interested parties. Turkey completely agreed with the position outlined by Mr. Koray, and had consistently supported the Secretary-General's mission. Stressing its support of an agreed settlement between the two communities, which had to reconcile their differences through negotiations in a manner which satisfied their legitimate concerns on the basis of political equality, Turkey added that it was incumbent upon Turkey and Greece to facilitate an agreement between the two through the good offices mission. Turkey emphasized that it would not support any other negotiating process and accused Greece of actively intervening in that process, with the objective of disrupting it.

GENERAL ASSEMBLY CONSIDERATION

On 16 September 1985, at the closing meeting of its resumed thirty-ninth session, the General Assembly adopted **decision 39/464** without vote. By this decision, orally proposed by its President, the Assembly deferred consideration of the question of Cyprus and included it in the agenda of its fortieth (1985) session.

On 18 December, the Assembly, in **decision 40/470** on the suspension of its fortieth session, again deferred the item, together with other agenda items, to its resumed fortieth session, at a date to be announced.

Other action. The Commission on Human Rights on 13 March postponed its debate on human rights in Cyprus to 1986 (see ECONOMIC AND SOCIAL QUESTIONS, Chapter XVIII).

Peace-keeping and humanitarian assistance

The United Nations Peace-keeping Force in Cyprus, established by the Security Council in 1964,[27] continued throughout 1985 to supervise the cease-fire lines of the Cyprus National Guard and of the Turkish and Turkish Cypriot forces. It also provided security for civilians in the area between the lines; discharged its functions with regard to the security, welfare and well-being of the Greek Cypriots living in northern Cyprus; regularly visited Turkish Cypriots residing in the south; and supported United Nations relief operations.

The area between the cease-fire lines was kept under constant surveillance by UNFICYP through a system of 141 observation posts, 60 of which were permanently manned. The number of cease-fire violations remained at a low level; the frequency of shooting incidents had decreased slightly and there were no exchanges of fire between opposing forces. UNFICYP continued to be successful in restoring the *status quo ante*. In Nicosia, however, the troops of both sides continued to be exposed to each other at dangerously close range, which continued to be of great concern to the Force since the overwhelming majority of cease-fire violations and other related incidents occurred in that area. Following an earlier UNFICYP initiative to abate the risk of destabilization of the cease-fire in Nicosia, the Force Commander had put forward to both sides on 10 July a proposal aimed at establishing mutually agreed military deconfrontation of the area of Nicosia on both sides of the so-called Green Line, where no operational and observation activities would be permitted and where no military-oriented construction or renovation work would take place. Further discussions of the proposal were envisaged during the mandate period from 16 December 1985 to 15 June 1986.

After new civilian construction projects close to the lines in Nicosia were protested by both sides, UNFICYP monitored the projects to confirm their civilian nature and alleviate concerns.

In the Famagusta area, a maritime security line restricting boat movement in the seaward extension of the United Nations buffer zone was accepted by both sides.

Overflights of the buffer zone continued, with 26 such flights by Turkish forces or civilian aircraft and 26 from the south; all overflights were protested.

Temporary visits by Greek Cypriots living in the north to the south continued through the good offices of UNFICYP and 1,236 such visits were made for family or medical reasons. Thirty-three Greek Cypriots transferred permanently to the south leaving 727 residing in the north. UNFICYP continued visiting Turkish Cypriots living in the south and contacting their relatives in the north; 10 reunions involving 38 persons were arranged. Two Turkish Cypriots moved permanently from the south to the north. Frequent contacts between members of the Maronite community residing on opposite sides of the lines continued and four Maronites transferred to the south; the number remaining in the north was 365. It was verified that all transfers were voluntary.

Emergency medical service was provided to both civilian communities. Turkish Cypriots were escorted to the south for treatment and medicines were delivered to them in the north. UNFICYP distributed 616 tons of food and other related items provided by Cyprus and the Cyprus Red Cross to Greek Cypriots in the north. Food continued to be provided by the World Food Programme to 22,000 children and to social welfare institutions on both sides.

As Co-ordinator of humanitarian assistance for Cyprus, UNHCR continued to assist the displaced and needy. The 1985 programme, providing for $7.5 million to finance 22 projects and co-ordinated by the Cyprus Red Cross Society, involved constructing a general hospital, overseas procurement of equipment and supplies for health, education and agriculture, and professional training. UNFICYP supported the programme by delivering 312.9 tons of supplies in the 12-month period.

Joint activities continued between the Greek Cypriot and the Turkish Cypriot communities in the framework of ongoing projects, assisted by the United Nations Development Programme, with the second phase of the joint Nicosia Master Plan project due to end on 31 December.

The UNFICYP Civilian Police continued to support UNFICYP military units and operated in liaison with both the Cyprus and the Turkish Cypriot police, contributing to the protection and movement of civilians between the cease-fire lines.

This information on UNFICYP was contained in two reports by the Secretary-General to the Security Council, covering 13 December 1984 to 31 May 1985,[9] and until 30 November 1985.[22] In both, he recommended that the Force's mandate be extended. The Council twice in 1985 extended the mandate for a six-month period, first until 15 December 1985 and then until 15 June 1986 (see pp. 252 and 255).

Composition of UNFICYP. As at 30 November 1985, UNFICYP had a strength of 2,328, including 36 civilian police, and was composed of contingents from eight States (see table below).

During the year ended 30 November 1985, five members of the Force died, bringing total fatalities to 138 since UNFICYP's inception in 1964.

CONTINGENTS OF UNFICYP
(by country of origin, as at 30 November 1985)

Military personnel	
Austria	301
Canada	515
Denmark	341
Finland	10
Ireland	8
Sweden	376
United Kingdom	741
Total	2,292
Civilian police	
Australia	20
Sweden	16
Total	36
Grand total	2,328

UNFICYP financing

UNFICYP continued to be financed by voluntary contributions and by troop-contributing Governments. Contributions received in 1985 from 28 countries totalled $16,565,800 (see table below). Estimated costs, including United Nations operational costs and reimbursement of extra costs to Governments providing contingents, totalled some $28 million. The full 12-month cost was approximately $100.5 million, of which troop-contributing Governments absorbed some $72.5 million for such items as regular pay and allowances and normal *matériel* expenses.

As at 15 December 1985, the accumulated deficit since the operation's inception in 1964 was of the order of $133.9 million, an increase of some $12 million in 12 months. Consequently, the claims of the troop contributors had been met only through June 1978.

CONTRIBUTIONS RECEIVED IN 1985 FOR UNFICYP

(as at 31 December 1985; in US dollars)

Country	Amount
Australia	100,000
Austria	125,000
Bahamas	2,000
Barbados	3,000
Brunei Darussalam	5,000
Cameroon	2,000
Cyprus	500,000
Denmark	120,000
Finland	37,500
Germany, Federal Republic of	815,700
Greece	860,800
Iceland	20,000
India	10,000
Japan	800,000
Kuwait	25,000
Lebanon	1,000
Luxembourg	10,600
Malta	3,900
Nigeria	30,300
Norway	305,000
Pakistan	3,000
Sri Lanka	2,000
Sweden	200,000
Thailand	1,000
United Kingdom	3,576,200
United States	8,995,300
Venezuela	10,000
Zimbabwe	1,500
Total	16,565,800

SOURCE: A/42/11/Add.1.

On 18 February[28] and 4 November 1985,[29] the Secretary-General made renewed appeals to States for voluntary contributions to finance UNFICYP. He again stressed its indispensable contribution in support of his efforts to promote a just and lasting settlement, and expressed his concern over its precarious financial situation, which continued to place an unfair burden on the troop-contributing countries. Annexed to his appeals were details on the Force's financing.

REFERENCES

[1]S/16858/Add.2. [2]YUN 1984, p. 249. [3]A/39/893-S/17150. [4]A/39/902-S/17198. [5]A/39/907-S/17241. [6]A/39/909-S/17260. [7]A/39/11-S/17261. [8]A/39/912-S/17273. [9]S/17227. [10]S/17227/Add.1. [11]S/17227/Add.2. [12]YUN 1981, p. 345. [13]YUN 1983, p. 254, SC res. 541(1983), 18 Nov. 1983. [14]YUN 1984, p. 243, SC res. 550(1984), 11 May 1984. [15]A/39/915-S/17280. [16]A/39/921-S/17304. [17]S/17486. [18]A/40/862-S/17614. [19]A/40/920-S/17650. [20]A/40/854-S/17610 & Corr.1. [21]A/40/817. [22]S/17657. [23]S/17657/Add.1. [24]S/17657/Add.2. [25]YUN 1974, p. 295, GA res. 3212(XXIX), 1 Nov. 1974. [26]*Ibid.*, p. 296, SC res. 365(1974), 13 Dec. 1974. [27]YUN 1964, p. 165, SC res. 186(1964), 4 Mar. 1964. [28]S/17032. [29]S/17620.

Other questions concerning the Mediterranean region

Tensions remained high in the Mediterranean region in 1985, particularly with regard to relations between Egypt and the Libyan Arab Jamahiriya and between the latter and the United States. Letters sent by those States to the President of the Security Council or the Secretary-General concerned various aspects of the situation, and in December the General Assembly, by resolution 40/157, again urged all States to reduce tension and promote peace in the area.

Questions concerning the Libyan Arab Jamahiriya

Libyan Arab Jamahiriya–United States relations

On 4 April,[1] the Libyan Arab Jamahiriya referred to what it said were aggressive statements by United States officials against the Jamahiriya, specifically threats to commit military aggression. It also suggested that the symmetry between those threats and an announcement by Egypt of an alleged conspiracy against it hatched by the Libyan Arab Jamahiriya showed that there was a United States plan for military action against the Jamahiriya.

On 28 June,[2] the Jamahiriya denied United States allegations that it had been involved in hijacking a United States civilian aircraft at Athens airport (see p. 304) and condemned international terrorism.

Directives issued by the United States President and published in *Newsweek* on 8 July showed, according to the Libyan Arab Jamahiriya, that the United States intended to attack civilian targets in several countries including the Jamahiriya, it stated on 3 July;[3] and, on 10 July,[4] it claimed that the United States President had two days earlier threatened the Jamahiriya militarily.

Egyptian–United States military manœuvres currently being carried out in Egypt, the

Jamahiriya stated on 6 August,[5] were a provocative act. That charge was rejected by Egypt on 11 August[6] when it said that the exercises had the goal of training its armed forces in defence of the country. Agreeing, the United States on 14 August[7] added that the training exercises, in which it was participating at Egypt's request, would enable both States to benefit from each other's expertise.

According to the Libyan Arab Jamahiriya on 5 November,[8] an item in the *The Washington Post* on 3 November had quoted informed United States Government sources to the effect that the United States President had authorized the Central Intelligence Agency to undertake a new terrorist operation against the Libyan people. On 31 December,[9] the Jamahiriya charged that an attack was being prepared by Israel and the United States.

Egypt-Libyan Arab Jamahiriya relations

On 20 August,[10] Egypt claimed that a large number of its nationals, working in the Libyan Arab Jamahiriya, were being arbitrarily expelled, having their funds and property confiscated or were being forced to adopt Libyan citizenship to remain there. Egypt said it reserved the right to safeguard its nationals' rights. Such language, the Libyan Arab Jamahiriya countered on 23 August,[11] confirmed Egypt's involvement in continued aggressive acts against the Jamahiriya; it rejected Egypt's charges as slander, stating that no one had been treated arbitrarily.

On 29 November,[12] the Jamahiriya stated that Egypt had intensified its political, media and military provocations—particularly along the common frontier—further evidence that Egypt and the United States were collaborating to attack the Jamahiriya. Terming the charges propaganda, Egypt, on 12 December,[13] cited what it said were several examples of Libyan terrorist operations against Egypt, and said it would not relinquish its right to repel destabilization attempts.

For other questions relating to the Libyan Arab Jamahiriya, see p. 196 and LEGAL QUESTIONS, Chapter I.

Security in the Mediterranean

The views of 11 States on strengthening security and co-operation in the Mediterranean region were forwarded to the General Assembly on 21 August.[14] They had been submitted in reply to the Assembly's 1984 invitation for States' ideas on their potential contribution to strengthening peace in the area.[15]

The Final Political Declaration adopted by the Conference of Foreign Ministers of Non-Aligned Countries (Luanda, Angola, 4-7 September)[16] contained a call to States to respect the non-aligned Movement's 1984 Valletta Final Declaration,[17] particularly regarding adherence to non-use or threat of force.

GENERAL ASSEMBLY ACTION

Acting on the recommendation of the First Committee, the General Assembly adopted **resolution 40/157** without vote on 16 December.

Strengthening of security and co-operation in the Mediterranean region

The General Assembly,

Recalling its resolutions 36/102 of 9 December 1981, 37/118 of 16 December 1982, 38/189 of 20 December 1983 and 39/153 of 17 December 1984,

Recognizing the importance of promoting peace, security and co-operation in the Mediterranean region and of strengthening further the economic, commercial and cultural links in the region,

Expressing concern over persistent and increasing tension in parts of the Mediterranean region and the consequent threat to peace,

Deeply concerned at the recent extension of military operations to new areas of the Mediterranean and the grave dangers which these create for peace, security and general equilibrium in the region,

Considering, in this regard, the urgency for all States to conform in their actions to the purposes and principles of the Charter of the United Nations, as well as to the provisions of the Declaration on Principles of International Law concerning Friendly Relations and Co-operation among States in accordance with the Charter of the United Nations,

Reaffirming the need to promote security and to strengthen co-operation in the region, as provided for in the Mediterranean chapter of the Final Act of the Conference on Security and Co-operation in Europe, signed at Helsinki on 1 August 1975,

Recalling the declarations of successive meetings of non-aligned countries concerning the Mediterranean, as well as official declarations on, and contributions to, peace and security in the Mediterranean region made by individual countries,

Reaffirming the primary role of Mediterranean countries in the promotion of security and co-operation in the Mediterranean region,

Recalling, in this connection, the Final Declaration adopted at Valletta on 11 September 1984 by the Mediterranean members of the Movement of Non-Aligned Countries, and the commitments assumed by the participants with the objective of contributing to peace and security in the region,

Taking note of the fact that a meeting of economic experts of the Mediterranean members of the Movement of Non-Aligned Countries was held at Valletta on 13 and 14 November 1985, in the context of their efforts to strengthen regional co-operation in various fields,

Taking note of the debate on this item during the various sessions of the General Assembly,

Taking note also of the note by the Secretary-General and of the replies contained therein received in 1985 from Governments in accordance with General Assembly resolution 39/153,

1. *Reaffirms*:

(a) That the security of the Mediterranean is closely linked with European security and with international peace and security;

(b) That further efforts are necessary for the reduction of tension and of armaments and for the creation of conditions of security and fruitful co-operation in all fields for all countries and peoples of the Mediterranean, on the basis of the principles of sovereignty, independence, territorial integrity, security, non-intervention and non-interference, non-violation of international borders, non-use of force or threat of use of force, the inadmissibility of the acquisition of territory by force, peaceful settlement of disputes and respect for permanent sovereignty over natural resources;

(c) The need for just and viable solutions of existing problems and crises in the area on the basis of the provisions of the Charter and of relevant resolutions of the United Nations, the withdrawal of foreign forces of occupation and the right of peoples under colonial or foreign domination to self-determination and independence;

2. *Welcomes* any further communication to the Secretary-General, from all States, of proposals, declarations and recommendations on strengthening peace, security and co-operation in the Mediterranean region;

3. *Urges* all States to co-operate with the Mediterranean States in the further efforts required to reduce tension and promote peace, security and co-operation in the region in accordance with the purposes and principles of the Charter and with the provisions of the Declaration on Principles of International Law concerning Friendly Relations and Co-operation among States in accordance with the Charter of the United Nations;

4. *Encourages once again* efforts to intensify existing forms and to promote new forms of co-operation in various fields, particularly those aimed at reducing tension and strengthening confidence and security in the region;

5. *Renews its invitation* to the Secretary-General to give due attention to the question of peace, security and co-operation in the Mediterranean region and, if requested to do so, to render advice and assistance to concerted efforts by Mediterranean countries in promoting peace, security and co-operation in the region;

6. *Invites* the member States of the relevant regional organizations to lend their support and to submit to the Secretary-General concrete ideas and suggestions on their potential contribution to the strengthening of peace and co-operation in the Mediterranean region;

7. *Requests* the Secretary-General to submit to the General Assembly at its forty-first session, on the basis of all replies received and notifications submitted in the implementation of the present resolution and, taking into account the debate on this question during its fortieth session, an updated and comprehensive report on the strengthening of security and co-operation in the Mediterranean region;

8. *Decides* to include in the provisional agenda of its forty-first session the item entitled "Strengthening of security and co-operation in the Mediterranean region".

General Assembly resolution 40/157

16 December 1985   Meeting 117   Adopted without vote

Approved by First Committee (A/40/1027) without vote, 6 December (meeting 61); 8-nation draft (A/C.1/40/L.86); agenda item 71.
Sponsors: Algeria, Cyprus, Libyan Arab Jamahiriya, Malta, Morocco, Romania, Tunisia, Yugoslavia.
Meeting numbers. GA 40th session: 1st Committee 55-61; plenary 117.

In the First Committee, several States explained their position on the text. The United States said it had reservations, for example with regard to paragraph 1 *(c)* referring to previous United Nations resolutions, since it did not support all of those texts; it also considered the 1984 Valletta Declaration unacceptable. Despite reservations on textual inadequacies and references, Israel said it had joined the consensus to emphasize its commitment to strengthening regional security and cooperation. Bulgaria felt that the text would have gained substance by dealing more directly with the region's main security issue—curbing the arms race.

The Security Council also expressed grave concern at the threat to Mediterranean peace and security when it considered a 1 October 1985 Israeli bombing attack on Tunisia (see p. 285).

(For other questions concerning peace and security in the area brought before the United Nations in 1985, see next chapter.)

REFERENCES

[1]A/40/224-S/17081. [2]A/40/422-S/17317. [3]A/40/456-S/17323. [4]A/40/474. [5]S/17387. [6]S/17393. [7]S/17400. [8]A/40/853-S/17609. [9]A/41/69-S/17707 & Corr.2. [10]A/40/569. [11]A/40/578. [12]A/40/959-S/17661 & Corr.1. [13]A/40/1038-S/17682. [14]A/40/448 & Corr.1. [15]YUN 1984, p. 255, GA res. 39/153, 17 Dec. 1984. [16]A/40/854-S/17610 & Corr.1. [17]YUN 1984, p. 255.

Chapter IX

Middle East

The search for a peaceful settlement to the conflict in the Middle East and its key issue, the Palestine problem, continued in 1985. The General Assembly, the Security Council and several other United Nations bodies considered various aspects of the situation, including the Palestine question—seen as the core of the conflict—incidents and disputes between individual Arab States and Israel, the situation in Lebanon and in the territories occupied by Israel, and Palestine refugees. The United Nations continued to maintain two major peace-keeping operations in the region, the United Nations Disengagement Observer Force (UNDOF) in the Golan Heights and the United Nations Interim Force in Lebanon (UNIFIL).

The Assembly again endorsed the call for an International Peace Conference on the Middle East, stressing the need to convene it without delay.

The question of Palestine continued in 1985 to be a concern of the Assembly and its Committee on the Exercise of the Inalienable Rights of the Palestinian People (Committee on Palestinian rights). The Assembly adopted resolutions asking for the situation relating to the question to be kept under review, inviting co-operation with the Committee and the Secretariat's Division for Palestinian Rights, and requesting the Department of Public Information to continue its special information programme on the question.

The Assembly also again dealt with the status of Jerusalem.

The Middle East situation, with particular emphasis on the Palestine question, was also considered by the Security Council at four meetings in October.

In July, a meeting of various United Nations bodies and funds assessed progress towards a co-ordinated assistance programme for Palestinians. Both the Economic and Social Council and the Assembly requested that the United Nations system intensify its efforts, in co-operation with the Palestine Liberation Organization (PLO), to provide economic and social assistance.

PLO was accused by some Members of being involved in several terrorist attacks that took place during the year. In what it said was a retaliatory action, Israel bombed PLO headquarters in Tunisia on 1 October, killing and wounding many persons. The act was condemned by the Security Council. Palestinians, said to be members of a

PLO faction, on 7 October hijacked the Italian cruise ship *Achille Lauro*, during which incident a passenger was killed and thrown overboard. Council members condemned the hijacking and all acts of terrorism.

Throughout the year, the Secretary-General continued consultations with the Lebanese Government and other parties involved in the ongoing conflict in Lebanon. Despite those efforts, the positions of the parties remained far apart. In January, Israel announced a three-phase plan for unilateral redeployment and withdrawal of its forces. During the third phase in May/June, Israel Defence Forces (IDF) withdrew progressively, handing their positions over to the "South Lebanon Army" (SLA), which was supported by IDF, in an area to be maintained as a "security zone"—a strip of land north of the international border.

During and after the withdrawal, both the number and intensity of attacks by Lebanese resistance groups against Israeli forces and Lebanese irregulars armed and controlled by them increased sharply. In part of its area of deployment, UNIFIL was confronted with many positions which overlapped those manned by IDF and/or local Lebanese forces, mainly SLA, in the security zone. Attacks by Lebanese groups gave rise to countermeasures by Israeli and associated forces and led to frequent and dangerous confrontations between those forces and UNIFIL.

The Security Council considered the situation in Lebanon in February/March and again in May. It called for an end to the violence against civilians and for measures to alleviate their suffering. During the year, the Council extended the mandate of UNIFIL twice, in April and October, each time for six months.

The 1981 bombing by Israeli aircraft of a nuclear research centre near Baghdad, Iraq, was again taken up in 1985. The Assembly requested the International Atomic Energy Agency (IAEA) to consider additional measures to ensure that Israel undertook not to attack or threaten to attack peaceful nuclear facilities, and reaffirmed that Iraq was entitled to compensation. The IAEA General Conference, in September, noted that Israel had committed itself not to attack peaceful nuclear facilities.

The Assembly, as well as the Commission on Human Rights, dealt with the situation in the Syrian Golan Heights since Israel's December 1981 decision to impose its laws, jurisdiction and administration on that territory. The Assembly again declared that decision to be illegal and that the decision and Israel's occupation constituted an act of aggression. UNDOF continued to supervise the observance of the cease-fire between Israel and the Syrian Arab Republic in the Golan Heights area. The Security Council twice in 1985 extended UNDOF's mandate for six months, in May and November.

The Assembly approved appropriations for UNDOF for operations from 1 June 1985 to 31 May 1986 totalling more than $36 million, and appropriated some $142 million for UNIFIL's operations from 19 April 1985 to 18 April 1986. It also authorized suspension of certain provisions of the Financial Regulations of the United Nations that would otherwise have required surrender of some funds to States.

The Secretary-General reviewed the rates of reimbursement to troop-contributing States. The Assembly retained the current rates, last revised in 1980, but asked him to review them at least every two years.

The United Nations Truce Supervision Organization continued to assist the two peace-keeping forces in the Middle East—UNDOF and UNIFIL—in the performance of their tasks, and maintained two observation groups of its own in Beirut, Lebanon, and in Egypt.

The situation in the territories occupied by Israel as a result of previous armed conflicts was again considered by the Assembly and its Special Committee to Investigate Israeli Practices Affecting the Human Rights of the Population of the Occupied Territories (Committee on Israeli practices). The Committee observed that there was a continuing deterioration in the respect for the civil, political, economic, social and cultural rights of the population of the territories.

The Assembly adopted seven resolutions dealing with specific aspects of the Committee's report. It condemned and demanded that Israel desist from a number of policies and practices, among them action that would change the legal status and composition of the Palestinian and other Arab territories occupied since 1967, including the Syrian Golan Heights, and demanded that Israel comply with the 1949 Geneva Convention relative to the Protection of Civilian Persons in Time of War, that it release Ziyad Abu Eain and other Palestinian prisoners, that it rescind the measures taken expelling Palestinians and that it ensure the freedom of educational institutions.

The Security Council considered the situation in the occupied territories during two meetings in September, but did not adopt any formal decisions.

In March, the Secretary-General organized a seminar on remedies for the deterioration of the economic and social conditions of the Palestinians in the territories. Affirming that Israeli occupation was contradictory to the basic requirements for their development, the Assembly requested the Secretary-General to organize by April 1987 a seminar on development projects to improve their living conditions.

In June 1985, the Secretary-General submitted a study on Israeli economic practices in the territories and a progress report on lifting Israeli restrictions and on projects to facilitate the territories' economic development. The Assembly and the Economic and Social Council requested a report on Israeli financial and trade practices in the territories, and called for the lifting of Israeli restrictions and facilitation of the establishment of a seaport and citrus and cement plants.

The Secretary-General reported that in June Israel had ceased all work on a planned canal linking the Mediterranean Sea and the Dead Sea. The Assembly requested that he monitor any new development relating to the project.

Emergency operations in Lebanon dominated relief efforts in 1985 of the United Nations Relief and Works Agency for Palestine Refugees in the Near East (UNRWA). In addition, UNRWA continued to assist Palestinian refugees in Jordan, the Syrian Arab Republic, the West Bank and the Gaza Strip, providing education, health and relief services.

UNRWA activities and various aspects of the Palestine refugee problem were addressed by the Assembly, which adopted 11 resolutions on assistance to Palestine refugees, the Working Group on the Financing of UNRWA, assistance to displaced persons, scholarships for higher education and training, Palestine refugees in the Gaza Strip, ration distribution, return of refugees displaced since 1967, revenues derived from refugee properties, refugee protection, refugees in the West Bank, and a proposed University of Jerusalem for Palestine refugees.

Topics related to this chapter. Disarmament: Israeli nuclear armament. International peace and security: review of peace-keeping operations. Mediterranean: other related questions. Institutional machinery: other institutional questions—fortieth anniversary of the United Nations. Economic assistance, disasters and emergency relief: emergency relief and assistance—Lebanon. Human rights: human rights violations—Middle East. Human settlements: political, economic and social issues—human settlements in the territories occupied by Israel. Women: status of women—Palestinian women. Legal aspects of international political relations—prevention of terrorism.

Middle East situation

The situation in the Middle East continued to be unstable and the search for a peaceful settlement of the conflict there remained elusive despite intensive efforts by the United Nations and individual Member States, the Secretary-General stated in an October 1985 report.[1] While the positions of the various parties to the conflict remained far apart, there was wide acceptance of Security Council resolution 242(1967)[2] which spelt out two important principles for a settlement: the withdrawal of Israel's forces from territories it occupied, and respect for and acknowledgement of the sovereignty, territorial integrity and political independence of every State in the area and their right to live in peace within secure and recognized boundaries. There was also wide agreement that there must be a satisfactory resolution of the Palestine problem based on recognition of the legitimate rights of the Palestinian people, including self-determination.

Various peace proposals made in 1985 and in previous years contained important elements that could contribute to the formulation of a common approach, the Secretary-General stated. There were also some signs of flexibility with regard to the negotiating process. He believed that a new and determined effort should be made to explore and use United Nations machinery to enhance the search for a settlement in the Middle East.

The convening of an International Peace Conference on the Middle East was widely seen as one of these possibilities. The Secretary-General, in March,[3] reported on Security Council consultations on the question. The Committee on Palestinian rights, in its annual report to the General Assembly,[4] expressed the conviction that a conference would provide an opportunity for all the parties to participate in negotiations which should lead to a just and lasting solution.

By resolution 40/168 A, the Assembly dealt with a variety of issues related to the Middle East situation. Reaffirming its conviction that the question of Palestine was the core of the conflict in the region, it declared once more that peace in the Middle East was indivisible and must be based on a comprehensive, just and lasting solution under United Nations auspices and on the basis of United Nations resolutions. By resolution 40/96 D, it again endorsed the call for the convening of a peace conference, stressing the need for additional constructive efforts to convene it without delay.

Communications. In connection with the Middle East situation, communications were addressed during the year to the Presidents of the General Assembly and of the Security Council and to the Secretary-General. By letters of 10 January[5] and 2 December,[6] Israel drew the Secretary-General's attention to what it called some of the extreme examples of anti-Semitic rhetoric in United Nations forums during November and December 1984, among them statements made before the Assembly by Iran, Jordan and Saudi Arabia, and by Bahrain and Iraq in committee. There was a trend emerging at the United Nations, Israel said, allowing such rhetoric to be practised with ever-growing impunity, traceable to the 1975 Assembly resolution[7] equating zionism with racism. Israel urged the Secretary-General to condemn the recurrent outbreaks of anti-Semitic rhetoric and consider ways of preventing those breaches of the Charter of the United Nations and of the 1948 Universal Declaration of Human Rights.[8]

On 6 May,[9] Italy transmitted a declaration on the Arab-Israeli conflict, adopted by the Ministers for Foreign Affairs of the 10 member States of the European Community (EC) at the fifty-seventh Ministerial Meeting on European Political Co-operation (Luxembourg, 29 April). The Ministers stated that they welcomed recent moves towards a reactivation of the negotiation process in the search for a solution to the conflict, notably an agreement reached at Amman on 11 February between Jordan and the Palestinians which contained a commitment to negotiations in accordance with United Nations resolutions. Such initiatives, in their opinion, deserved encouragement and a positive response; no effort should be spared to facilitate a dialogue between all the parties. The Ten reconfirmed their willingness to contribute to a comprehensive settlement on the basis of the principles of recognition of the rights of all States in the region, including Israel, to existence and security, and the right of the Palestinians to self-determination.

On 16 May,[10] the Libyan Arab Jamahiriya transmitted to the Security Council President a letter of 15 May from the Secretary of the People's Committee of the People's Bureau for Foreign Liaison of the Libyan Arab Jamahiriya. It charged Israeli deployment of nuclear missiles in the Syrian Golan and Negev Desert areas. That deployment, the Libyan Arab Jamahiriya stated, was a serious threat to peace and security in the region and the world. It signalled an escalation in aggression against the Arab nation, laid the groundwork for occupation operations and posed the threat of attack against Arab cities and vital installations. The act was a flagrant violation of international treaties and United Nations resolutions, flouted repeated appeals to States to accede to the 1968 Treaty on the Non-Proliferation of Nuclear Weapons,[11] heightened tension in the region, and placed the Arab nation in a position obliging it to exercise its right of self-defence under the United Nations Charter, as long as the Security Council did not take immediate steps to remove the threat of those missiles. The Libyan Arab Jamahiriya reserved the right to request the convening of the Council.

On 19 August,[12] Morocco transmitted to the Secretary-General the Final Communiqué of the Extraordinary Summit Conference of Arab States (Casablanca, 7-9 August), which stressed the need for Arab solidarity and continued collective Arab commitment to the principles of the 1982 Twelfth Arab Summit Conference at Fez, Morocco.[13] By a letter of 28 August,[14] the Syrian Arab Republic pointed out that the Casablanca Communiqué did not express a unanimous Arab position owing to the fact that five Arab States, including itself, had not participated in the Conference and more than half of the Arab heads of State had been absent from it.

On 18 September,[15] Madagascar transmitted a number of resolutions adopted by the Council of Ministers of the Organization of African Unity (OAU) at its forty-second ordinary session (Addis Ababa, Ethiopia, 10-17 July). By one of them, OAU affirmed total support for the Arab countries, victims of Israeli aggression; it recommended that member States renew their firm determination not to establish or re-establish diplomatic ties with Israel and urgently appealed to the international community to exert effective pressure on Israel in all fields to coerce it to comply with OAU decisions.

In a communiqué of the co-ordination meeting of the Ministers for Foreign Affairs of the Organization of the Islamic Conference (New York, 9 October), Israel's rejection of United Nations decisions was condemned. The meeting demanded that the international community take the necessary measures, including sanctions, to ensure that Israel abided by the Charter and international law. The communiqué was transmitted by Yemen on 15 October.[16]

Reports of the Secretary-General. In an October report,[1] the Secretary-General said that in recent contacts with leaders of the parties concerned, he had gained the impression that they were fully conscious of the dangers a further delay in finding an agreed settlement of the Middle East problem could entail for the region and beyond.

While the positions of the various parties to the conflict remained far apart, the Secretary-General noted that there was general acceptance of Security Council resolution 242(1967)[2] and wide agreement that the Palestine problem must be resolved satisfactorily, based on recognition of the legitimate rights of the Palestinian people, including self-determination.

During recent years, a number of peace proposals had been put forward by Governments. They included the proposals made in September 1982 by the United States President,[17] by the USSR,[13] and by the Fez Summit Conference in its Declaration,[13] as well as the proposals of the USSR made in July 1984.[18] In addition, there was the peace initiative of Jordan's King Hussein based on an agreement reached in February 1985 with PLO Chairman Yasser Arafat, under which Jordan and PLO would move together towards a just and peaceful settlement and towards the termination of Israeli occupation of Arab territories. Although those proposals for various reasons were so far unacceptable to one or another of the parties, they all contained important elements that could contribute to the formulation of a common approach.

The Secretary-General also noted signs of flexibility with regard to the negotiating process. To enable the parties to embark on such a process, a generally acceptable procedure had to be found, with the full support of Governments in a position to help. He felt that, despite the existing difficulties, a new and determined effort should be made to explore the various possibilities of the United Nations machinery to promote progress in the Middle East peace process.

In this context, the Secretary-General reported that he had pursued his contacts with the parties and others concerned regarding the search for a peaceful settlement, including the convening of an international conference as recommended by the Assembly (see p. 268). In the evolution of a settlement, the Security Council could play a vital role, but other avenues of the United Nations could also be explored.

The Secretary-General annexed to another report[19] replies from 13 countries, received by 18 October 1985, on their implementation of three 1984 Assembly resolutions: in two of them,[20] the Assembly had called on States to adopt a number of measures concerning military, economic, diplomatic and cultural relations with Israel; by the third,[21] it had called again on States that had transferred their diplomatic missions to Jerusalem to abide by United Nations resolutions.

GENERAL ASSEMBLY ACTION

On 16 December 1985, the General Assembly adopted, by recorded vote, **resolution 40/168 A** on the situation in the Middle East.

The General Assembly,

Having discussed the item entitled "The situation in the Middle East",

Reaffirming its resolutions 36/226 A and B of 17 December 1981, ES-9/1 of 5 February 1982, 37/123 F of 20 December 1982, 38/58 A to E of 13 December 1983, 38/180 A to D of 19 December 1983 and 39/146 A to C of 14 December 1984,

Recalling Security Council resolutions 425(1978) of 19 March 1978, 497(1981) of 17 December 1981, 508(1982)

of 5 June 1982, 509(1982) of 6 June 1982, 511(1982) of 18 June 1982, 512(1982) of 19 June 1982, 513(1982) of 4 July 1982, 515(1982) of 29 July 1982, 516(1982) of 1 August 1982, 517(1982) of 4 August 1982, 518(1982) of 12 August 1982, 519(1982) of 17 August 1982, 520(1982) of 17 September 1982, 521(1982) of 19 September 1982 and 555(1984) of 12 October 1984,

Taking note of the reports of the Secretary-General of 11 March 1985,[3] 24 September 1985[19] and 22 October 1985,[1]

Reaffirming the need for continued collective support for the resolutions adopted by the Twelfth Arab Summit Conference, held at Fez, Morocco, on 25 November 1981 and from 6 to 9 September 1982, reiterating its previous resolutions regarding the Palestinian question and its support for the Palestine Liberation Organization as the sole, legitimate representative of the Palestinian people, and considering that the convening of an International Peace Conference on the Middle East, under the auspices of the United Nations, in accordance with General Assembly resolution 38/58 C and other relevant resolutions related to the question of Palestine, would contribute to the promotion of peace in the region,

Welcoming all efforts contributing towards the realization of the inalienable rights of the Palestinian people through the achievement of a comprehensive, just and lasting peace in the Middle East, in accordance with the United Nations resolutions relating to the question of Palestine and to the situation in the Middle East,

Welcoming the world-wide support extended to the just cause of the Palestinian people and the other Arab countries in their struggle against Israeli aggression and occupation in order to achieve a comprehensive, just and lasting peace in the Middle East and the full exercise by the Palestinian people of its inalienable national rights, as affirmed by previous resolutions of the General Assembly relating to the question of Palestine and to the situation in the Middle East,

Gravely concerned that the Palestinian and other Arab territories occupied since 1967, including Jerusalem, still remain under Israeli occupation, that the relevant resolutions of the United Nations have not been implemented and that the Palestinian people is still denied the restoration of its land and the exercise of its inalienable national rights in conformity with international law, as reaffirmed by resolutions of the United Nations,

Reaffirming the applicability of the Geneva Convention relative to the Protection of Civilian Persons in Time of War, of 12 August 1949, to all the occupied Palestinian and other Arab territories, including Jerusalem,

Reaffirming also all relevant United Nations resolutions which stipulate that the acquisition of territory by force is inadmissible under the Charter of the United Nations and the principles of international law and that Israel must withdraw unconditionally from all the Palestinian and other Arab territories occupied by Israel since 1967, including Jerusalem,

Reaffirming further the imperative necessity of establishing a comprehensive, just and lasting peace in the region, based on full respect for the Charter and the principles of international law,

Gravely concerned also at the continuing Israeli policies involving the escalation and expansion of the conflict in the region, which further violate the principles of

international law and endanger international peace and security,

Stressing once again the great importance of the time factor in the endeavours to achieve an early comprehensive, just and lasting peace in the Middle East,

1. *Reaffirms its conviction* that the question of Palestine is the core of the conflict in the Middle East and that no comprehensive, just and lasting peace in the region will be achieved without the full exercise by the Palestinian people of its inalienable national rights and the immediate, unconditional and total withdrawal of Israel from all the Palestinian and other occupied Arab territories;

2. *Reaffirms further* that a just and comprehensive settlement of the situation in the Middle East cannot be achieved without the participation on an equal footing of all the parties to the conflict, including the Palestine Liberation Organization, the representative of the Palestinian people;

3. *Declares once more* that peace in the Middle East is indivisible and must be based on a comprehensive, just and lasting solution of the Middle East problem, under the auspices and on the basis of the relevant resolutions of the United Nations, which ensures the complete and unconditional withdrawal of Israel from the Palestinian and other Arab territories occupied since 1967, including Jerusalem, and which enables the Palestinian people, under the leadership of the Palestine Liberation Organization, to exercise its inalienable rights, including the right to return and the right to self-determination, national independence and the establishment of its independent sovereign State in Palestine, in accordance with the resolutions of the United Nations relevant to the question of Palestine, in particular General Assembly resolutions ES-7/2 of 29 July 1980, 36/120 A to F of 10 December 1981, 37/86 A to D of 10 December 1982, 37/86 E of 20 December 1982, 38/58 A to E of 13 December 1983 and 39/49 A to D of 11 December 1984;

4. *Considers* the Arab Peace Plan adopted unanimously at the Twelfth Arab Summit Conference, held at Fez, Morocco, on 25 November 1981 and from 6 to 9 September 1982, and reiterated by the Extraordinary Summit Conference of the Arab States held at Casablanca, Morocco, from 7 to 9 August 1985, as well as relevant efforts and action to implement the Fez Plan, as an important contribution towards the realization of the inalienable rights of the Palestinian people through the achievement of a comprehensive, just and lasting peace in the Middle East;

5. *Condemns* Israel's continued occupation of the Palestinian and other Arab territories, including Jerusalem, in violation of the Charter of the United Nations, the principles of international law and the relevant resolutions of the United Nations, and demands the immediate, unconditional and total withdrawal of Israel from all the territories occupied since 1967;

6. *Rejects* all agreements and arrangements which violate the inalienable rights of the Palestinian people and contradict the principles of a just and comprehensive solution to the Middle East problem to ensure the establishment of a just peace in the area;

7. *Deplores* Israel's failure to comply with Security Council resolutions 476(1980) of 30 June 1980 and 478(1980) of 20 August 1980 and General Assembly resolutions 35/207 of 16 December 1980 and 36/226 A

and B of 17 December 1981; determines that Israel's decision to annex Jerusalem and to declare it as its "capital" as well as the measures to alter its physical character, demographic composition, institutional structure and status are null and void and demands that they be rescinded immediately; and calls upon all Member States, the specialized agencies and all other international organizations to abide by the present resolution and all other relevant resolutions and decisions;

8. *Condemns* Israel's aggression, policies and practices against the Palestinian people in the occupied Palestinian territories and outside these territories, including expropriation, the establishment of settlements, annexation and other terrorist, aggressive and repressive measures, which are in violation of the Charter and the principles of international law and the relevant international conventions;

9. *Strongly condemns* the imposition by Israel of its laws, jurisdiction and administration on the occupied Syrian Golan Heights, its annexationist policies and practices, the establishment of settlements, the confiscation of lands, the diversion of water resources and the imposition of Israeli citizenship on Syrian nationals, and declares that all these measures are null and void and constitute a violation of the rules and principles of international law relative to belligerent occupation, in particular the Geneva Convention relative to the Protection of Civilian Persons in Time of War, of 12 August 1949;

10. *Considers* that the agreements on strategic co-operation between the United States of America and Israel, signed on 30 November 1981, and the continued supply of modern arms and *matériel* to Israel, augmented by substantial economic aid, including the recently concluded Agreement on the Establishment of a Free Trade Area between the two Governments, have encouraged Israel to pursue its aggressive and expansionist policies and practices in the Palestinian and other Arab territories occupied since 1967, including Jerusalem, have had adverse effects on efforts for the establishment of a comprehensive, just and lasting peace in the Middle East and threaten the security of the region;

11. *Calls once more upon* all States to put an end to the flow to Israel of any military, economic, financial and technological aid, as well as of human resources, aimed at encouraging it to pursue its aggressive policies against the Arab countries and the Palestinian people;

12. *Strongly condemns* the continuing and increasing collaboration between Israel and the racist régime of South Africa, especially in the economic, military and nuclear fields, which constitutes a hostile act against the African and Arab States and enables Israel to enhance its nuclear capabilities, thus subjecting the States of the region to nuclear blackmail;

13. *Reaffirms its call* for the convening of an International Peace Conference on the Middle East under the auspices of the United Nations and on the basis of its relevant resolutions—as specified in paragraph 5 of the Geneva Declaration on Palestine and endorsed by General Assembly resolution 38/58 C of 13 December 1983;

14. *Requests* the Secretary-General to report to the Security Council periodically on the development of the situation and to submit to the General Assembly at its forty-first session a comprehensive report covering the developments in the Middle East in all their aspects.

General Assembly resolution 40/168 A

16 December 1985   Meeting 118   98-19-31 (recorded vote)

24-nation draft (A/40/L.43 & Add.1); agenda item 38.

Sponsors: Afghanistan, Bahrain, Bangladesh, Cuba, Djibouti, India, Indonesia, Iraq, Kuwait, Malaysia, Mauritania, Mongolia, Morocco, Oman, Pakistan, Qatar, Saudi Arabia, Somalia, Sudan, Tunisia, United Arab Emirates, Viet Nam, Yemen, Yugoslavia.

Meeting numbers. GA 40th session: plenary 104-107, 118.

Recorded vote in Assembly as follows:

In favour: Afghanistan, Albania, Algeria, Argentina, Bahrain, Bangladesh, Benin, Bhutan, Bolivia, Botswana, Brazil, Brunei Darussalam, Bulgaria, Burkina Faso, Burundi, Byelorussian SSR, Cape Verde, Central African Republic, Chad, China, Congo, Cuba, Cyprus, Czechoslovakia, Democratic Kampuchea, Democratic Yemen, Djibouti, Ecuador, Egypt, Equatorial Guinea, Ethiopia, Gabon, Gambia, German Democratic Republic, Ghana, Greece, Guinea, Guinea-Bissau, Guyana, Hungary, India, Indonesia, Iran, Iraq, Jordan, Kenya, Kuwait, Lao People's Democratic Republic, Lebanon, Lesotho, Libyan Arab Jamahiriya, Madagascar, Malaysia, Maldives, Mali, Malta, Mauritania, Mexico, Mongolia, Morocco, Mozambique, Nepal, Nicaragua, Niger, Nigeria, Oman, Pakistan, Peru, Philippines, Poland, Qatar, Romania, Rwanda, Sao Tome and Principe, Saudi Arabia, Senegal, Singapore, Somalia, Sri Lanka, Sudan, Syrian Arab Republic, Thailand, Togo, Trinidad and Tobago, Tunisia, Turkey, Uganda, Ukrainian SSR, USSR, United Arab Emirates, United Republic of Tanzania, Vanuatu, Venezuela, Viet Nam, Yemen, Yugoslavia, Zambia, Zimbabwe.

Against: Australia, Belgium, Canada, Costa Rica, Denmark, El Salvador, France, Germany, Federal Republic of, Iceland, Ireland, Israel, Italy, Luxembourg, Netherlands, New Zealand, Norway, Portugal, United Kingdom, United States.

Abstaining: Antigua and Barbuda, Austria, Bahamas, Barbados, Burma, Cameroon, Chile, Colombia, Dominica, Dominican Republic, Fiji, Finland, Grenada, Guatemala, Haiti, Honduras, Ivory Coast, Jamaica, Japan, Liberia, Malawi, Panama, Paraguay, Saint Lucia, Saint Vincent and the Grenadines, Samoa, Spain, Swaziland, Sweden, Uruguay, Zaire.

Before adopting the text as a whole, the Assembly adopted paragraph 10 by a recorded vote of 64 to 33, with 41 abstentions.

Reservations on that paragraph were voiced by several speakers. The United States found it particularly repugnant and regarded it as unwarranted interference in its internal affairs, totally outside the Assembly's jurisdiction; it rejected the allegation that its co-operation with and assistance to Israel threatened the security of the region and had an adverse effect on peace efforts. Turkey found the reference to the free-trade-area agreement unhelpful and stressed that its positive vote did not mean that it fully agreed with the paragraph's contents. Democratic Yemen, on the other hand, believed that the paragraph merely mentioned facts; among those facts was that the strategic co-operation agreements had encouraged Israel to commit acts of aggression. Democratic Yemen believed that the free-trade-area agreement encouraged Israel not to heed the international will on negotiations.

Strong reservations on paragraph 10, as well as on paragraph 11, were also voiced by Sweden. Peru objected to the interpretation that might be given to those paragraphs and to paragraph 6, none of which, it said, recognized the relevance of all the peace efforts initiated. Reservations on the same three paragraphs were expressed by Argentina.

Mexico reserved its position in particular on paragraph 6, Greece on paragraph 12. Albania had reservations on paragraph 13, as well as on the second and fifth preambular paragraphs. General reservations on some of the wording and provisions of the text were voiced by Ecuador and the Philippines; the latter added that resolutions on the Middle East situation should be balanced and should not prejudice the sovereign rights of States to conduct their own international affairs as they saw fit.

Nepal felt that elements in the text ran counter to the guiding principles for its Middle East policy, reflected in Security Council resolutions 242(1967)[2] and 338(1973).[22] Austria could not support elements in the text which, it felt, not only aggravated the existing situation but impeded the search for peace.

The Syrian Arab Republic stated that it had not joined the sponsors because it objected to the mention of the August Summit Conference of the Arab States in paragraph 4; at the same time, it emphasized its full support of the decisions taken at the 1982 Fez Summit.[13]

The Libyan Arab Jamahiriya stressed its strong reservations against anything in the text that could be interpreted as recognition of the Zionist entity or of a *fait accompli* imposed by force in the territories.

Israel said that, rather than address in the resolution the real issues and major conflicts of the Middle East, the sponsors had averted any initiative towards their solution or even discussion and instead repeated false accusations.

Seeking to place the entire blame on one party to the Arab-Israeli conflict, said the United States, tended to widen rather than to reconcile the differences among the parties, thus making any peace process even more difficult.

New Zealand regretted that the text did not reflect the balance of principles embodied in Security Council resolutions and the measured approach essential to secure the co-operation of all parties.

Speaking on behalf of the 10 members of the European Economic Community (EEC), as well as Portugal and Spain, Luxembourg stated their serious reservations on the text, saying it contained aspects which were not in accord with their common stand on the principles for a comprehensive settlement; they could not accept formulations levelling criticisms against a permanent Security Council member for having exercised its rights in accordance with the United Nations Charter. Expressing agreement with that view, Greece declared its attachment to the Charter principle proscribing the threat or use of force, and to the Helsinki Final Act.

Peru would have liked explicit mention of Security Council resolutions 242(1967) and 338(1973), which it considered an acceptable and just basis for an agreement. Mexico believed that a general framework for a Middle East solution might be found in Security Council and Assembly resolutions. It considered it urgent and necessary for the parties to take positions promoting accord on agreements; the possibility of negotiating an agreement under international auspices would be progress towards normalizing political relations in the area.

Brazil warned that the possibilities of achieving a solution should not be reduced by diplomatic isolation of one of the parties to the conflict, even if that party had been acting in a manner incompatible with international law; Israel should not be offered further excuses to act, because of its isolation, in further disregard for that law.

Singapore said it supported all efforts aimed at restoring the rights of the Palestinians and a return to a just and durable peace in the Middle East; however, it could not support texts that did not recognize the legitimate rights of Israel, were selective and unbalanced in their condemnation or impinged on the sovereign right of third countries having diplomatic relations with Israel.

In Egypt's view, the text included many principles for a settlement to which it adhered, foremost among them the inadmissibility of the occupation of the territory of others by force, the applicability of the 1949 Geneva Convention to the occupied Arab territories and the condemnation of the establishment of Israeli settlements in those territories.

Introducing the draft resolution on behalf of the sponsors, India stated that recent months had witnessed a deterioration in the Middle East situation resulting in further acts of aggression and intimidation by Israel; it was important to find an early solution on the basis of internationally recognized guidelines and principles and to support the early convening of an international peace conference under United Nations auspices.

Also on 16 December, the Assembly adopted under the agenda item on the Middle East **resolution 40/168 B** dealing mainly with the Israeli-occupied Golan Heights. In that resolution, the Assembly determined once more that Israel's policies and actions confirmed that it was not a peace-loving Member State, that it had persistently violated the Charter principles, and that it had carried out neither its obligations under the Charter nor its commitments as a United Nations Member. The Assembly called on all Member States to refrain from supplying Israel with any weapons and related equipment and to suspend any military assistance to it; to refrain from acquiring weapons or military equipment from Israel; to suspend economic, financial and technological assistance to and co-operation with it; and to cease, individually and collectively, all dealings with Israel in order totally to isolate it. It also urged non-member States to act in accordance with the resolution, and made a similar call on the specialized agencies and other international organizations.

In **resolution 40/5**, the Assembly requested the Secretary-General to continue to strengthen co-operation with the General Secretariat of the League of Arab States for the purpose of implementing United Nations resolutions relating to the Palestine question and the Middle East situation, in order to achieve a just, comprehensive and durable solution.

Proposed peace conference

In 1985, the General Assembly stressed the urgent need for constructive efforts by all Governments for the convening of an International Peace Conference on the Middle East, as called for by the 1983 International Conference on the Question of Palestine.[23] The Secretary-General reported on ongoing consultations concerning the proposed conference, including the question of participants, and the Committee on Palestinian rights expressed the conviction that a conference provided an opportunity for all the parties concerned to participate in negotiations.

Communication. On 15 October 1985,[16] Yemen, as Chairman of the Organization of the Islamic Conference, transmitted to the Secretary-General a communiqué of the co-ordination meeting of the Ministers for Foreign Affairs of that organization (New York, 9 October). Among other matters, the communiqué condemned Israel's rejection of the Assembly's decision to hold an International Peace Conference on the Middle East, with the participation of all parties concerned, including PLO.

Reports of the Secretary-General. In March,[3] the Secretary-General reported on his continued efforts, in consultation with the Security Council, with regard to the convening of an International Peace Conference on the Middle East, as the General Assembly had requested in 1984.[24] He stated that in January 1985 he had asked for the Council's views. The President had replied that he had held bilateral talks with all members, almost all of which were in favour of the principle of holding such a conference. Many felt that it should be convened as early as possible; others considered that the conditions for such a step had not yet been met. The Secretary-General said he intended to pursue consultations, as he had been invited to do by the Council members, and would inform the Assembly and the Council of any new developments.

In his October report[1] on the situation in the Middle East, the Secretary-General stated that he had pursued his contacts with the parties to the Middle East conflict and with others concerned regarding the search for a peaceful settlement, including the convening of an international conference. In commenting on the difficulties encountered, he had suggested on several occasions that the machinery of the Security Council be used to enhance that search. He had been kept informed of efforts made by Jordan's King Hussein to bring about negotiations within the framework of an international conference.

Recommendations of the Committee on Palestinian rights. In its annual report to the Assembly,[4] the Committee on Palestinian rights (see p. 273) expressed its conviction that an international conference would provide a comprehensive opportunity for all the parties concerned to participate in negotiations which should lead to a just and lasting solution of the Palestine question. The Committee was encouraged by the responses it had received in the course of its official visits so far to the capitals of a number of Security Council members. The Committee recommended that the Assembly renew the Secretary-General's mandate for contacts regarding preparations with a sense of urgency, and appealed to all countries to exert their best efforts for a successful outcome.

Also at the seminars and symposia of non-governmental organizations (NGOs) held under United Nations aegis (see p. 273), the view was strongly held that the convening of an international conference was a priority which offered the best and most comprehensive approach to a just and lasting solution to the Palestine question.

GENERAL ASSEMBLY ACTION

On 12 December 1985, under the agenda item on the question of Palestine, the General Assembly adopted **resolution 40/96 D** by recorded vote.

The General Assembly,

Recalling its resolutions 38/58 C of 13 December 1983 and 39/49 D of 11 December 1984, in which it, *inter alia*, endorsed the convening of an International Peace Conference on the Middle East,

Reaffirming its resolution 39/49 D, in which it, *inter alia*, requested the Secretary-General, in consultation with the Security Council, to continue his efforts with a view to convening the Conference,

Having considered the reply of the President of the Security Council to the Secretary-General, dated 26 February 1985, in which he, *inter alia*, stated on the subject of the Conference: "In this context, members of the Council invite the Secretary-General to continue consultations on the subject in any manner he deems appropriate in the light of General Assembly resolution 39/49 D.",

Having considered again the reports of the Secretary-General of 13 March 1984 and 13 September 1984, in which he stated, *inter alia*, that it was clear from the replies of the Governments of Israel and the United States of America that they were not prepared to participate in the proposed Conference, and regretting the continued negative response of these two Governments and the lack of willingness to reconsider their position towards the Conference,

Having considered the reports of the Secretary-General of 11 March 1985 and 22 October 1985, in which he, *inter alia,* referred to the difficulties experienced in his efforts made the previous year with a view to convening the Conference,

Having heard the constructive statements made by numerous representatives, including that of the Palestine Liberation Organization,

Taking note of the positive positions of the concerned parties, including the Palestine Liberation Organization, and of other States on the convening of the Conference,

Taking note also of the position of the Palestine Liberation Organization which condemns all acts of terrorism, whether committed by States or individuals, including acts of terrorism committed by Israel against the Palestinian people and the Arab nation,

Reiterating once again its conviction that the convening of the Conference would constitute a major contribution by the United Nations towards the achievement of a comprehensive, just and lasting solution to the Arab-Israeli conflict,

1. *Takes note with appreciation* of the reports of the Secretary-General;

2. *Reaffirms again* its endorsement of the call for convening the International Peace Conference on the Middle East in conformity with the provisions of its resolution 38/58 C;

3. *Stresses* the urgent need for additional constructive efforts by all Governments in order to convene the Conference without further delay and for the achievement of its peaceful objectives;

4. *Determines* that the question of Palestine is the root-cause of the Arab-Israeli conflict in the Middle East;

5. *Calls upon* the Governments of Israel and the United States of America to reconsider their positions towards the attainment of peace in the Middle East through the convening of the Conference;

6. *Requests* the Secretary-General, in consultation with the Security Council, to continue his efforts with a view to convening the Conference and to report thereon to the General Assembly not later than 15 March 1986;

7. *Decides* to consider at its forty-first session the report of the Secretary-General on the implementation of the present resolution.

General Assembly resolution 40/96 D

12 December 1985   Meeting 114   107-3-41 (recorded vote)

14-nation draft (A/40/L.41 & Add.1); agenda item 33.
Sponsors: Afghanistan, Cuba, German Democratic Republic, India, Indonesia, Lao People's Democratic Republic, Madagascar, Malaysia, Mongolia, Pakistan, Senegal, Ukrainian SSR, Viet Nam, Yugoslavia.
Meeting numbers. GA 40th session: plenary 98, 100-103, 114.

Recorded vote in Assembly as follows:

In favour: Afghanistan, Algeria, Angola, Argentina, Bahamas, Bahrain, Bangladesh, Barbados, Benin, Bhutan, Bolivia, Botswana, Brazil, Brunei Darussalam, Bulgaria, Burma, Burundi, Byelorussian SSR, Cameroon, Cape Verde, Central African Republic, Chad, China, Comoros, Congo, Cuba, Cyprus, Czechoslovakia, Democratic Kampuchea, Democratic Yemen, Djibouti, Egypt, Equatorial Guinea, Ethiopia, Fiji, Gabon, Gambia, German Democratic Republic, Ghana, Guinea, Guinea-Bissau, Guyana, Hungary, India, Indonesia, Iraq, Jamaica, Jordan, Kenya, Kuwait, Lao People's Democratic Republic, Lebanon, Lesotho, Libyan Arab Jamahiriya, Madagascar, Malaysia, Maldives, Mali, Malta, Mauritania, Mauritius, Mexico, Mongolia, Morocco, Mozambique, Nepal, Nicaragua, Niger, Nigeria, Oman, Pakistan, Peru, Philippines, Poland, Qatar, Romania, Rwanda, Samoa, Sao Tome and Principe, Saudi Arabia,

Senegal, Seychelles, Sierra Leone, Singapore, Somalia, Sri Lanka, Sudan, Suriname, Syrian Arab Republic, Thailand, Togo, Trinidad and Tobago, Tunisia, Turkey, Uganda, Ukrainian SSR, USSR, United Arab Emirates, United Republic of Tanzania, Uruguay, Vanuatu, Venezuela, Viet Nam, Yemen, Yugoslavia, Zambia, Zimbabwe.
Against: Canada, Israel, United States.
Abstaining: Antigua and Barbuda, Australia, Austria, Belgium, Chile, Colombia, Denmark, Dominican Republic, Ecuador, El Salvador, Finland, France, Germany, Federal Republic of, Greece, Grenada, Guatemala, Haiti, Honduras, Iceland, Ireland, Italy, Ivory Coast, Japan, Liberia, Luxembourg, Malawi, Netherlands, New Zealand, Norway, Panama, Papua New Guinea, Paraguay, Portugal, Saint Lucia, Saint Vincent and the Grenadines, Solomon Islands, Spain, Swaziland, Sweden, United Kingdom, Zaire.

Before voting on the text as a whole, the Assembly adopted paragraphs 2 and 5 by recorded votes of 111 to 6, with 29 abstentions, and 89 to 22, with 33 abstentions, respectively. Recorded votes were also taken on the fourth and eighth preambular paragraphs: the former was adopted by 84 votes to 22, with 38 abstentions; the latter, by 79 to 33, with 32 abstentions.

The United States found unacceptable the critical references to its opposition to an international conference as being an intrusion on government policy decisions and harmful to peace efforts. A conference as envisaged would neither yield a constructive examination of the Middle East question nor contribute to a lasting solution; instead, it would be an ideological and propagandistic exercise directed against Israel. The parties to the conflict should resolve the issues in direct negotiations among themselves. The United States also categorically rejected the charge in the eighth preambular paragraph which it said equated Israel with the perpetrators of the vicious acts of terrorism that marked the Middle East.

The one sure and tested road to peace, said Israel, was through direct negotiations, and it would welcome a genuine expression of support for that course by the international community; those who were not genuinely concerned with peace and who would like to arrange an international conference were actually defeating their own purposes, because they called for a conference with Israel and at the same time condemned it as a non-peace-loving State.

In Canada's view, a renewed appeal in constructive terms for a conference could have held promise of positive impact. The text, however, contained extraneous and unacceptable language; the inclusion of unsubstantiated controversial accusations and intemperate language would not contribute to an atmosphere propitious for peace talks.

Finland said it could not support the text as a whole because it contained new elements and unacceptable formulations. Similarly, Sweden believed that elements, particularly in the sixth, seventh and eighth preambular paragraphs, had created a bias which limited the constructive role the text might have played otherwise. In addition, Sweden felt that it could not be the intention of a resolution to force Governments to a conference or to convene one without their agreement. Austria reiterated its support in principle for convening a conference; however, it had difficulties with paragraph 5 and the wording of some preambular paragraphs and objected to the singling out of countries for criticism.

New Zealand was disappointed that the text failed to take cognizance of recent positive developments and did not reflect accurately the balance of principles in resolution 242(1967)[2] or provide a basis for the realistic settlement of the Palestinian problem; although it saw merit in the idea of a conference, it did not consider it timely to convene one until the parties demonstrated the will to resolve the dispute by peaceful means.

Norway said it could support the proposal to convene a conference if that was acceptable to all the parties that were supposed to take part in the negotiations. The text adopted, however, was unconstructive; paragraph 5 and the fourth preambular paragraph did not reflect the constructive steps taken by the United States and Israel during the preceding months, and the eighth preambular paragraph did not mention some of the most serious terrorist activities in the Middle East.

Speaking on behalf of the 10 EC member States, as well as Portugal and Spain, Luxembourg said that, although they had no objection in principle to the holding of an international conference, considerable preparatory work remained. Moreover, the text adopted seemed to lack balance, particularly because of the weight it placed on the views of one of the parties to the conflict. The eighth preambular paragraph was unacceptable as it did not reflect the balanced position adopted by all United Nations Members on terrorism in resolution 40/61 (see LEGAL QUESTIONS, Chapter II); the language in the fourth preambular paragraph and in paragraph 5 would isolate and criticize two of the proposed conference participants and was therefore not productive.

Reservations, especially on those provisions, were also expressed by Zaire. Malawi regarded the eighth preambular paragraph as provocative and the insinuation in paragraph 5 as not constructive. It believed that, as one of the parties to the dispute was not prepared to participate, another agreed method should be adopted. Haiti said the holding of a conference presupposed the co-operation of all parties, which meant a halt to rhetoric; the eighth preambular paragraph merely added grist to the mill of those who believed it was not currently appropriate to hold a conference.

Reservations on paragraph 5, as well as on the fourth and eighth preambular paragraphs, were also voiced by several others, among them Bolivia, Malawi, Peru and Venezuela. In Peru's opinion,

they were not conducive to creating the best possible conditions to bring about a conference. Argentina felt that certain ideas in the fourth and eighth preambular paragraphs were not specifically relevant to the substance of the resolution; the former tended to prejudge the future attitude of two sovereign States. With regard to the eighth preambular paragraph, Venezuela felt that one particular State should not be singled out as being solely responsible for the terrorist activities in the region and that a more general statement of the problem was called for. It believed that a conference could contribute to peace, provided a number of conditions were met. Uruguay reiterated reservations previously expressed in connection with the documents adopted by the 1983 International Conference on the Question of Palestine.

Singapore suggested mutual recognition of Israel and PLO and said the international community should urge them to pursue a course of compromise.

Albania, which did not participate in the vote, felt the two super-Powers would try to manipulate the conference for their own interests, in rivalry with each other.

Iran took exception to the use of the term "Government of Israel".

Senegal, as Chairman of the Committee on Palestinian rights, introduced the draft resolution on behalf of the sponsors, stating that the international community acknowledged that an international conference was the best way to achieve a comprehensive, just and lasting solution to the Middle East problem and the Palestine question. In its work, the Committee had given priority to efforts to bring about the conference, and it was strongly encouraged by the positive replies from Governments.

In a statement after the vote, PLO remarked that Israel's terrorist acts against the Palestinians continued. Those who objected to the eighth preambular paragraph refused to take note of PLO's position, and those who were speaking about direct negotiations had it very clear in their minds that the Palestinians did not exist and that they had no right to self-determination.

Other action. Both the Commission on Human Rights and its Sub-Commission on Prevention of Discrimination and Protection of Minorities, in resolutions on the Israeli-occupied territories adopted, respectively, on 26 February[25] and 29 August,[26] welcomed the call to convene an international peace conference under United Nations auspices with the participation of all parties on an equal footing and with equal rights.

United Nations Truce Supervision Organization

In his October 1985 report[1] on the Middle East situation, the Secretary-General provided an overview of the three peace-keeping operations in the Middle East: the two peace-keeping forces— UNDOF and UNIFIL (see below, under "Incidents and disputes between Arab countries and Israel")—and one observer mission, the United Nations Truce Supervision Organization (UNTSO). Apart from assisting UNDOF and UNIFIL in their tasks, UNTSO maintained two observation groups of its own, the Observer Group in Beirut, set up in 1982[27] (see p. 297), and the Observer Group in Egypt, where about 50 observers have remained since 1979 with the agreement of the Government. In addition to a liaison office at Cairo, the Observer Group in Egypt maintained five observation posts in the Sinai.

Credentials of Israel

By a letter of 15 October 1985 to the General Assembly President,[28] 50 States conveyed their reservations on the credentials of Israel, citing instances where, they charged, Israel was continuing its flagrant and persistent violation of the United Nations Charter and international law, and its defiance of United Nations resolutions. The signatories cited the fact that Israel's credentials had been issued in Jerusalem, although the Assembly had determined that the 1980 proclamation of the city as the capital of Israel, among other Israeli legislative and administrative actions, was null and void (see p. 280). The Assembly had stated in 1982[29] that Israel's measures and actions confirmed that it was not a peace-loving State and that it had fulfilled neither its Charter obligations nor its commitments under the 1949 Assembly resolution[30] admitting it to United Nations membership. The Ministers for Foreign Affairs of the Organization of the Islamic Conference, by a communiqué adopted in New York on 9 October 1985, had requested all Islamic countries to sign the letter.[16]

On 18 October,[31] Israel responded that the attack on its credentials—which had been found in due form and accepted by the Credentials Committee—was an attempt to abuse the credentials procedure. By trying to deny acceptance of Israel's credentials in the Assembly, the signatories persisted in efforts to violate the letter and spirit of the Charter and the Assembly's rules of procedure; Israel was pleased that the overwhelming majority of Member States recognized and rejected that irresponsible action.

Before adopting **resolution 40/2 A** approving the first report of the Credentials Committee,[32] the Assembly, by a recorded vote of 80 to 41, with 20 abstentions, decided not to act on an amendment to that report by Algeria, Bahrain, Democratic Yemen, Djibouti, Iraq, Kuwait, Lebanon, the Libyan Arab Jamahiriya, Mauritania, Morocco, Qatar, Saudi Arabia, Somalia, the Sudan, the Syrian Arab Republic, Tunisia, the United Arab Emirates and Yemen[33] to reject the credentials of Israel. The motion to take no action was tabled by Sweden on behalf also of Denmark, Finland, Iceland and Norway (see p. 396).

Voting procedures

Referring to a motion by the United States[34] in connection with the vote on a 1984 General Assembly resolution on the Middle East,[35] the United Arab Emirates, in a letter of 8 January 1985[36] to the Secretary-General, rejected the United States interpretation of the applicability to the resolution of Article 18, paragraph 2, of the United Nations Charter. According to Article 18(2), Assembly decisions on important questions—including those on the maintenance of international peace and security—were to be adopted by a two-thirds majority. On the basis of the two precedents cited by the Legal Counsel of the United Nations, the United Arab Emirates said, the impression might have been created that the Assembly's practice on resolutions dealing with the question of Palestine in all its aspects required a two-thirds majority, since they fell within the purview of Article 18(2). However, it said, there were contrary precedents emphasizing the applicability of paragraph 3 of Article 18, which stipulated that decisions on "other questions, including the determination of additional categories of questions to be decided by a two-thirds majority", should be made by a simple majority of Members present and voting. The trend of the Assembly's general practice with regard to resolutions on the Palestine question had been adoption by a simple, rather than two-thirds, majority.

Replying on 11 January,[37] the Secretary-General recalled that the opinion given by the Legal Counsel did not contain an explicit or implicit statement to the effect that under Assembly practice all resolutions dealing with the Palestine question required a two-thirds majority. The practice had varied, a note attached to the letter said; many of the resolutions relating to the Middle East situation had received a two-thirds majority, so that the question had not arisen as to whether or not they had been adopted under Article 18(2). In other cases, decisions had been taken that individual resolutions came under that provision.

REFERENCES

[1]A/40/779-S/17581 & Corr.1. [2]YUN 1967, p. 257, SC res. 242(1967), 22 Nov. 1967. [3]A/40/168-S/17014. [4]A/40/35. [5]A/40/77. [6]A/40/966-S/17665. [7]YUN 1975, p. 599, GA res. 3379(XXX), 10 Nov. 1975. [8]YUN 1948-49, p. 535, GA res. 217 A (III), 10 Dec. 1948. [9]A/40/291-S/17162. [10]S/17195. [11]YUN 1968, p. 17, GA res. 2373(XXII), annex, 12 June 1968. [12]A/40/564 & Corr.1. [13]YUN 1982, p. 388. [14]A/40/584. [15]A/40/666. [16]A/40/758-S/17570. [17]YUN 1982, p. 387. [18]YUN 1984, p. 259. [19]A/40/668 & Add.1. [20]YUN 1984, pp. 260 & 323, GA res. 39/146 A & B,

14 Dec. 1984. [21]*Ibid.*, p. 273, GA res. 39/146 C, 14 Dec. 1984. [22]YUN 1973, p. 213, SC res. 338(1973), 22 Oct. 1973. [23]YUN 1983, p. 274. [24]YUN 1984, p. 266, GA res. 39/49 D, 11 Dec. 1984. [25]E/1985/22 (res. 1985/4). [26]E/CN.4/1986/5 (res. 1985/16). [27]YUN 1982, p. 475, SC res. 516(1982), 1 Aug. 1982. [28]A/40/752/Rev.1 & Rev.1/Corr.1. [29]YUN 1982, p. 515, GA res. ES-9/1, 5 Feb. 1982. [30]YUN 1948-49, p. 405, GA res. 273(III), 11 May 1949. [31]A/40/775. [32]A/40/747. [33]A/40/L.3. [34]YUN 1984, p. 261. [35]*Ibid.*, p. 260, GA res. 39/146 A, 14 Dec. 1984. [36]A/40/73. [37]A/40/85.

Palestine question

The question of Palestine continued in 1985 to be a concern of the General Assembly and its Committee on Palestinian rights. The Assembly, in December, adopted four resolutions on the question. By the first (resolution 40/96 A), it requested the Committee to keep under review the situation relating to the Palestine question as well as the implementation of the Programme of Action for the Achievement of Palestinian Rights, adopted by the 1983 International Conference on the Question of Palestine.[1] By the second resolution (40/96 B), the Assembly invited co-operation with the Committee and the United Nations Secretariat's Division for Palestinian Rights. By the third (40/96 C), it requested the United Nations Department of Public Information (DPI) to continue its special information programme on the Palestine question, and by the fourth (40/96 D), it reaffirmed its endorsement of the call for an International Peace Conference on the Middle East (see p. 268). The Assembly, in resolution 40/168 C, again dealt with the status of Jerusalem, having determined that Israel's 1980 decision to impose its laws, jurisdiction and administration on the Holy City was null and void.

The Middle East situation, with particular emphasis on the Palestine question, was also considered by the Security Council during four meetings in October.

United Nations bodies continued to examine the situation in the Israeli-occupied territories (see p. 326) and to provide and encourage assistance to Palestinians (see p. 281). To assess progress towards a co-ordinated assistance programme and plan future activities in that regard, the Secretary-General convened in July a meeting of various United Nations programmes, organizations, agencies, funds and organs. Both the Economic and Social Council (resolution 1985/57) and the Assembly (resolution 40/170) requested that the United Nations system intensify its efforts, in co-operation with PLO, to provide assistance to the Palestinians, and that the Secretary-General take all necessary steps to finalize a co-ordinated programme.

PLO was charged with being involved in several terrorist attacks that took place during the year. In what it said was in retaliation for the murder of three Israeli citizens in Cyprus, allegedly carried out by PLO, Israel bombed PLO headquarters in Tunisia on 1 October, killing and wounding scores of people. The Security Council, in resolution 573(1985), condemned the bombing as an act of aggression and demanded that Israel refrain from such acts. Four Palestinians, said to be members of a PLO faction, hijacked the Italian cruise ship *Achille Lauro* on 7 October; during the incident, an American citizen, Leon Klinghoffer, was killed and thrown overboard. The members of the Security Council, by a statement of 9 October, condemned the hijacking and all acts of terrorism.

Communications. Throughout the year, Israel, in letters to the Secretary-General, accused PLO of attacks against its citizens. On 26 April,[2] it said that, on 19 April, an Israeli naval vessel on patrol had fired warning shots at an unidentified ship approaching Israel's coast. When the ship opened fire and tried to escape, the patrol boat sank it. One body was recovered and 19 apparently drowned. The eight crewmen rescued said they had set out from an Algerian port where they had received special training. They had been ordered by a Fatah deputy commander to attack civilian targets in Israel. The aborted attack was merely one of several recent PLO attacks, Israel said. With these acts, it added, PLO continued to espouse terror as its *modus operandi* and its *raison d'être*.

Charging another PLO attempt to attack Israeli cities from the sea, in a letter of 10 May,[3] Israel said that on the night of 8/9 May an Israel Defence Force (IDF) patrol boat had sighted a rubber dinghy painted in camouflage colours approaching Israel's coast from Tyre, Lebanon. Trying to escape, the boat was fired upon and sank. PLO, Israel said, had claimed "credit" for this act. Israel added that it would continue to defend its coast and citizens.

Two similar incidents, reported to have taken place during the night of 25/26 August and on 31 August, were described by Israel on 4 September.[4]

On 17 June,[5] Israel brought to the Secretary-General's attention a message made public by the PLO Chairman on 25 April at Bandung, Indonesia, in which he had praised two Palestinian leaders whom Israel described as notorious Nazi collaborators.

On 20 May,[6] Egypt transmitted a letter of 15 May from PLO, annexed to which was a 16 April memorandum by 35 Palestinians to the United States Assistant Secretary of State for Middle Eastern Affairs, calling for a change in the United States position with regard to the Palestine question and demanding that all dealings related to that question be conducted through PLO.

On 20 June,[7] Israel transmitted a summary of several PLO statements on activities of PLO constituent groups pertaining to attacks on civilian targets between 31 March and 19 June. The fact that most of those attacks either failed or were never launched was irrelevant, Israel said; what was significant was PLO's boasting of murdering, bombing and rocketing innocents on buses and in cars, hospitals, villages and cities.

The Acting Chairman of the Committee on Palestinian rights, by a letter of 8 August,[8] expressed concern about reports of reinstated Israeli policies of detention without trial, censorship, and new legislation submitted to the Israeli Knesset which reportedly sought to bar any contacts between Israeli citizens and PLO, under penalty of gaol and fine.

On 21 August,[9] Israel drew attention to the murders of three women and the stabbing of five children which had taken place between October 1984 and the end of July 1985—acts for which PLO had boasted of its responsibility, Israel said.

On 9 September[10] and 27 September,[11] Israel charged further attacks by PLO against Israeli citizens in and outside Israel. During the previous 45 days, it said in its 27 September letter, there had been 32 PLO terrorist attacks on Israeli civilians, resulting in the murder of eight persons and the wounding of 25 women and children. One of the examples cited was the murder of three Israelis vacationing aboard a private yacht at Larnaca, Cyprus (see p. 285). In its 9 September letter, Israel charged that recently PLO had escalated its terror campaign by infiltrating terrorists and smuggling weapons and explosives from Jordan.

Jordan, by a letter of 12 September,[12] refuted that allegation; Palestinian resistance—carried out mainly with stones and knives originating in the occupied territories—was escalating as a natural reaction to Israel's occupation practices (see p. 328). The meaning of Israel's allegation was to sow confusion with regard to Jordan's efforts to consolidate with all parties concerned its February agreement with PLO.

On 6 November,[13] under the Assembly's agenda item on terrorism, Israel submitted a document which it called a record of the PLO terror campaign since its expulsion from Lebanon (see LEGAL QUESTIONS, Chapter II). On 5 December,[14] Israel submitted what it titled a "Calendar of Middle Eastern violence", listing bombings, kidnappings, assassinations, executions, coups, hijackings and border incursions during 1985, which Israel said had been taken mostly from Arab press reports.

Two further examples of what Israel termed PLO's unrestricted policy of murder were cited in a 2 December letter,[15] in which Israel also stated that PLO's admitted aim remained the liquidation of Israel, all of which it considered occupied territory.

On 12 December,[16] Yemen transmitted a 1 December statement by its Ministry of Foreign Affairs, rejecting what it called lies and allegations in Israeli information media according to which Palestinians had attacked a number of Yemeni citizens of Jewish faith.

Support for PLO was expressed by some States through protests or expressions of regret that PLO was not invited to address the United Nations fortieth anniversary commemorative ceremonies (see p. 403).

Activities of the Committee on Palestinian rights. The Committee on Palestinian rights continued in 1985 to follow developments in the Israeli-occupied territories and actions by Israel which the Committee regarded as violations of international law or of United Nations resolutions. The Committee brought such actions—including Israeli settlements in the occupied territories, exploitation by Israeli authorities of Arab-owned lands and other matters affecting the rights of the Palestinians (for details, see below, under "Territories occupied by Israel")—to the attention of the General Assembly and the Security Council.

In its annual report to the Assembly,[17] the Committee pointed out that the Palestine question had reached a critical phase; it urged a renewed, concentrated and collective effort to end the plight of the Palestinians and find a just solution under United Nations auspices on the basis of United Nations resolutions. It said its 1976 recommendations,[18] endorsed by the Assembly,[19] were designed to achieve that goal, as were the guidelines adopted by the 1983 Conference on the question of Palestine.[1] The Committee supported the convening of an international peace conference on the Middle East (see p. 268). It believed that it should continue its efforts to increase awareness and understanding of the Palestine question and of its recommendations, and was encouraged by the favourable reaction of non-governmental and other organizations through which public opinion was manifested.

Annexed to the Committee's report were its 1976 recommendations, as well as the Geneva Declaration on Palestine and the Programme of Action for the Achievement of Palestinian Rights adopted by the 1983 Conference on Palestine.[1]

With the Committee's participation, the tenth (Beijing, China, 22-26 April 1985), eleventh (Georgetown, Guyana, 17-20 June) and twelfth (New York, 8 and 9 July) United Nations seminars on the question of Palestine were held. Under the Committee's guidance, the Division for Palestinian Rights organized three regional NGO symposia on the question—for NGOs in Asia (New Delhi, India, 1-3 May), in North America (New York, 10-12 July) and in Africa (Dakar, Senegal, 5-7 August)—and an international NGO meeting (Geneva, 9-12 September). The reports of the seminars and the declarations of the NGO meetings were annexed to the Committee's report.

SECURITY COUNCIL CONSIDERATION (October)

During four meetings held on 10 and 11 October, the Security Council considered the situation in the Middle East, including the Palestinian question. The Council met in response to a request from India of 30 September,[20] made in accordance with a decision of the Conference of Foreign Ministers of Non-Aligned Countries (Luanda, Angola, 4-8 September). Twenty-three speakers participated in the debate. The Council did not take formal action on the question at these meetings.

Meeting numbers. SC 2619-2622.

The Council invited Afghanistan, Algeria, Bangladesh, Cuba, Czechoslovakia, Democratic Yemen, the German Democratic Republic, Indonesia, Israel, Jordan, Kuwait, Morocco, Pakistan, the Syrian Arab Republic and Yugoslavia, at their request, to participate in the discussion without the right to vote. It also invited the Permanent Observer of the League of Arab States, at Kuwait's request,[21] the Secretary-General of the Organization of the Islamic Conference, at Egypt's request,[22] and the Chairman of the Committee on Palestinian rights, at his request, to participate, under rule 39[a] of the Council's provisional rules of procedure.

At Egypt's request in a letter of 9 October,[23] the Council decided, by 10 votes to 1 (United States), with 4 abstentions (Australia, Denmark, France, United Kingdom), that an invitation to participate be accorded to PLO. The President stated that Egypt's proposal was not made pursuant to rule 37[b] or rule 39 of the Council's provisional rules of procedure, but, if approved, the invitation would confer on PLO the same rights as those conferred on Member States when invited to participate pursuant to rule 37.

Before the vote, the United States reiterated its consistent position that the only legal basis on which the Council might grant a hearing to persons speaking on behalf of non-governmental entities was rule 39. It opposed special *ad hoc* departures from orderly procedure and consequently opposed extending to PLO the same rights as if it represented a Member State. The Council appeared selectively to try to enhance the prestige of those who wished to speak there, through a departure from the rules of procedure, a practice

which the United States considered to be without legal foundation and an abuse of the rules.

Opening the debate, India said the Council meeting should provide an opportunity for an in-depth discussion of all aspects of the Palestine question and the tense situation in the Middle East, with a view to analysing the major obstacles to a comprehensive, just and lasting solution, an essential element of which would be the establishment of an independent Palestinian State in Palestine. Israel's efforts to bring about permanent geopolitical and demographic changes at the expense of the Palestinians must be prevented. Israel should discontinue its settlements policy and withdraw unconditionally from Lebanon, as well as from all Arab and Palestinian territories occupied since 1967. The only viable course to achieve a comprehensive settlement was the early convening of an international peace conference in accordance with well-established guidelines endorsed by the United Nations.

Support for the convening of such a conference (see p. 268) was also expressed by Algeria, Bangladesh, China, the German Democratic Republic, Indonesia, Jordan, Morocco, Pakistan, Peru, the Syrian Arab Republic, Thailand, the USSR and Yugoslavia.

The United States said the serious situation in the Middle East was not improving and grew more violent daily. Terrorism, but one aspect of the situation, dominated all others and made the quest for peace even more elusive. The just and lasting peace in the Middle East that all desired would not be achieved by terrorists or through their actions, but only at the negotiating table.

According to Egypt, the United Nations should support the positions and initiatives taken by King Hussein of Jordan and the PLO Chairman, and continue to encourage any dialogue or negotiation aimed at reaching a just and lasting settlement. Peace required the affirmation of the right of all in the region to live in peace and security, recognition of the Palestinians' national rights, including their right to self-determination, Israel's withdrawal from all occupied territories, and establishment of normal relations between all parties to the conflict on the basis of equality and good-neighbourliness.

[a]Rule 39 of the Council's provisional rules of procedure states: "The Security Council may invite members of the Secretariat or other persons, whom it considers competent for the purpose, to supply it with information or to give other assistance in examining matters within its competence."

[b]Rule 37 of the Council's provisional rules of procedure states: "Any Member of the United Nations which is not a member of the Security Council may be invited, as the result of a decision of the Security Council, to participate, without vote, in the discussion of any question brought before the Security Council when the Security Council considers that the interests of that Member are specially affected, or when a Member brings a matter to the attention of the Council in accordance with Article 35(1) of the Charter."

The increase in terrorist acts on the one hand and in legitimate resistance on the other reaffirmed the seriousness of the absence of a comprehensive, just peace, Jordan believed, and made time a critical factor. In its search for the best path to peace, Jordan, in co-operation with its Arab brothers and in particular the Palestinians, had advocated the political option to solve the conflict on the basis of the principle that had become the foundation of international unanimity—that of territory in return for peace, an approach also manifested in the resolutions of the 1982 Fez Summit.[24] The 11 February 1985 Palestinian-Jordanian accord was an appropriate mechanism for fulfilling the Arab peace aspirations expressed in those resolutions. It affirmed the wish of the Palestinians to achieve self-determination, while maintaining relations of unity; it also dealt with the way in which the major Powers and the international community would participate in the achievement of peace and called for an international conference to be attended by all parties concerned, in addition to the Council's permanent members.

The situation in the region was developing in an unprecedented manner due to Israel's persistence in escalating its aggression and terrorism against the Arab people, the Syrian Arab Republic charged. Though pretending to advocate peace, Israel rejected true peace efforts and continued to expand at the expense of other peoples. Stressing the need for Arab solidarity and for a just, lasting and comprehensive peace, the Syrian Arab Republic rejected partial solutions, such as the 11 February Jordan-PLO agreement which it felt was tantamount to eliminating Palestinian rights; the renunciation of an independent Palestinian State would make the concept of self-determination devoid of meaning.

In Australia's view, a comprehensive settlement would prove possible only on the basis of a series of compromises, including Israeli withdrawal from the occupied territories, recognition by the States of the region and by PLO of Israel's right to exist, their acceptance of Council resolutions 242(1967)[25] and 338(1973),[26] as well as the acknowledgement of the right of self-determination for the Palestinians, including their right to independence and the possibility of their own independent State.

Similar conditions for a settlement were enumerated by other speakers. Peru considered it impossible to envisage a solution that did not take into account the Palestinians' rights and Israel's withdrawal from all occupied territories, and ensure the right of all States to exist within secure and internationally recognized borders. Thailand similarly supported Palestinian rights, including the right to statehood. Without a settlement, it warned, the cycle of violence would continue and might worsen. Resolution 242(1967) remained the agreed basis for achieving a lasting peace.

Pakistan said demand for the recognition of Palestinian rights was seen by Israel as a threat to its expansionist ambitions. Responsibility for Israel's intransigence must be shared by its powerful allies, it added; failure to persuade Israel to accept the conditions for a just and durable peace would intensify the conflict and its attendant violence.

Whatever pretexts Israel might use to justify its acts of murder, aggression and invasion, said Morocco, the logic behind them was to subjugate the Palestinians and create a "Greater Israel" from the Nile to the Euphrates. The doors to peace were still closed because of Israel's flouting of international resolutions and its pursuance of a policy of *fait accompli* based on power, displacement and military occupation.

Pending a just settlement of the Palestinian issue, and as long as Israel continued its aggression, expansion and occupation of Arab territories by relying on the support and connivance of a certain big Power, there would be no chance for a comprehensive and durable Middle East settlement, China said.

The circle of the crisis continued to widen because of essentially centrifugal Israeli violence, said Algeria; it was a dangerous illusion to believe that the conflict could be kept within limits acceptable in the concept of world peace, when each new Israeli act of aggression was a threatening step towards the conflict's globalization.

It was Israel's incessant aggression against its neighbours, its stepped-up repression of the Palestinians in the occupied territories and its systematic attempts to destroy PLO, in the vain hope of extinguishing Palestinian nationalism and obliterating Palestinian national identity, that had kept the cauldron of enmity stirring, Indonesia believed. Terrorist acts against innocent civilians had grown into a menace of alarming proportions, it added, impeding the search for a just and comprehensive solution.

The Palestinians had been exposed to the most brutal acts of colonization and even annihilation, Yugoslavia stated, but the exercise of their sovereign will could not be thwarted; the right to existence could not be secured by force which denied that same right to others.

In the face of growing international consensus in favour of the Palestinian cause, said Bangladesh, Israel had again resorted to force to heighten tension in the region, with a view to frustrating current international efforts to resolve the Middle East problem peacefully.

Israel's policy of aggression formed the main obstacle to a comprehensive settlement, the German Democratic Republic stated; in defiance of

United Nations resolutions, Israel denied the Palestinians their rights, especially the right to establish a State of their own, and its policy of State terrorism against the Palestinians had been escalating. The USSR proposals of July 1984,[27] which coincided with the 1982 Fez peace plan,[24] were the way to a comprehensive, just and durable solution to the Palestinian problem.

Israel was trying to thwart any United Nations decision to create two States in Palestine and was attempting forcibly to remove the Palestine question from the agenda, the USSR alleged; it had raised to the level of State policy terror, violence and the flouting of the rights of other peoples. Attempts to prompt the Arabs to undertake separate agreements with the aggressor was a myopic policy and fraught with the danger of further complicating the situation. It was essential that the Palestinians were guaranteed their rights and that all States in the area, including Israel, were guaranteed a secure and independent existence and development; international safeguards should be provided for settling the problem.

The Chairman of the Committee on Palestinian rights believed that the possibility of a just and lasting Middle East peace would be increased if the Council adopted measures to implement the Committee's 1976 recommendations.[18]

In the opinion of the Permanent Observer of the League of Arab States, the Middle East was at the boiling-point and every incident in any part of the Arab world was used by Israel to gloss over the central issue: the denial of the Palestinians' right to self-determination. If the Middle East conflict were resolved within the United Nations framework, it would no longer feed on an undermining of relations between the two super-Powers.

In the view of the Secretary-General of the Organization of the Islamic Conference, the cycle of violence was a symptom rather than the cause of the conflict; the symptoms could not be removed without touching on the basic cause: the denial of Palestinian rights, including the rights to return, to self-determination and to establish an independent State in Palestine.

Attempts to deny the Palestinians their inalienable rights would never lead to the desired peace, PLO said. PLO's sincere and constructive efforts towards achieving peace had met only with further denial of Palestinian rights and with more suppression, murder and displacement. Allowing Israel's occupation to continue and maintaining the *status quo* could only worsen the situation; the right path to peace was the convening of an international peace conference. The

Palestinian revolution would continue until the Palestinians—now totalling 5 million—returned to their homeland.

GENERAL ASSEMBLY ACTION (December)

Following consideration of the report of the Committee on Palestinian rights, the General Assembly, in December 1985, adopted four resolutions on the question of Palestine, dealing with the Committee and its recommendations (**resolution 40/96 A**), the Division for Palestinian Rights (**40/96 B**), public information activities (**40/96 C**) and the convening of an International Peace Conference on the Middle East (**40/96 D**, see p. 268).

Resolution 40/96 A was adopted on 12 December by recorded vote.

The General Assembly,

Recalling its resolutions 3376(XXX) of 10 November 1975, 31/20 of 24 November 1976, 32/40 of 2 December 1977, 33/28 of 7 December 1978, 34/65 A and B of 29 November 1979 and 34/65 C and D of 12 December 1979, ES-7/2 of 29 July 1980, 35/169 of 15 December 1980, 36/120 of 10 December 1981, ES-7/4 of 28 April 1982, ES-7/5 of 26 June 1982, ES-7/9 of 24 September 1982, 37/86 A of 10 December 1982, 38/58 A of 13 December 1983 and 39/49 A of 11 December 1984,

Having considered the report of the Committee on the Exercise of the Inalienable Rights of the Palestinian People,

1. *Expresses its appreciation* to the Committee on the Exercise of the Inalienable Rights of the Palestinian People for its efforts in performing the tasks assigned to it by the General Assembly;

2. *Endorses* the recommendations contained in paragraphs 163 to 172 of the report of the Committee and draws the attention of the Security Council to the fact that action on the Committee's recommendations, as repeatedly endorsed by the General Assembly at its thirty-first session and subsequently, is still awaited;

3. *Requests* the Committee to continue to keep under review the situation relating to the question of Palestine as well as the implementation of the Programme of Action for the Achievement of Palestinian Rights and to report and make suggestions to the General Assembly or the Security Council, as appropriate;

4. *Authorizes* the Committee to continue to exert all efforts to promote the implementation of its recommendations, including representation at conferences and meetings and the sending of delegations where such activities would be considered by it to be appropriate, and to report thereon to the General Assembly at its forty-first session and thereafter;

5. *Requests* the Committee to continue to extend its co-operation to non-governmental organizations in their contribution towards heightening international awareness of the facts relating to the question of Palestine and in creating a more favourable atmosphere for the full implementation of the Committee's recommendations, and to take the necessary steps to expand its contacts with those organizations;

6. *Requests* the United Nations Conciliation Commission for Palestine, established under General Assembly resolution 194(III) of 11 December 1948, as well as other United Nations bodies associated with the question of Palestine, to co-operate fully with the Committee and to make available to it, at its request, the relevant information and documentation which they have at their disposal;

7. *Decides* to circulate the report of the Committee to all the competent bodies of the United Nations and urges them to take the necessary action, as appropriate, in accordance with the Committee's programme of implementation;

8. *Requests* the Secretary-General to continue to provide the Committee with all the necessary facilities for the performance of its tasks.

General Assembly resolution 40/96 A

12 December 1985   Meeting 114   128-2-22 (recorded vote)

13-nation draft (A/40/L.23 & Add.1); agenda item 33.

Sponsors: Afghanistan, Cuba, Cyprus, Gambia, India, Indonesia, Lao People's Democratic Republic, Madagascar, Malaysia, Pakistan, Senegal, Viet Nam, Yugoslavia.

Financial implications. ACABQ, A/40/7/Add.18; 5th Committee, A/40/1032; S-G, A/C.5/40/81.

Meeting numbers. GA 40th session: 5th Committee 60; plenary 98, 100-103, 114.

Recorded vote in Assembly as follows:

In favour: Afghanistan, Albania, Algeria, Angola, Antigua and Barbuda, Argentina, Bahamas, Bahrain, Bangladesh, Barbados, Benin, Bhutan, Bolivia, Botswana, Brazil, Brunei Darussalam, Bulgaria, Burma, Burundi, Byelorussian SSR, Cameroon, Cape Verde, Central African Republic, Chad, Chile, China, Colombia, Comoros, Congo, Cuba, Cyprus, Czechoslovakia, Democratic Kampuchea, Democratic Yemen, Djibouti, Dominican Republic, Ecuador, Egypt, El Salvador, Equatorial Guinea, Ethiopia, Fiji, Gabon, Gambia, German Democratic Republic, Ghana, Greece, Guatemala, Guinea, Guinea-Bissau, Guyana, Haiti, Honduras, Hungary, India, Indonesia, Iraq, Ivory Coast, Jamaica, Jordan, Kenya, Kuwait, Lao People's Democratic Republic, Lebanon, Lesotho, Liberia, Libyan Arab Jamahiriya, Madagascar, Malaysia, Maldives, Mali, Malta, Mauritania, Mauritius, Mexico, Mongolia, Morocco, Mozambique, Nepal, Nicaragua, Niger, Nigeria, Oman, Pakistan, Panama, Papua New Guinea, Paraguay, Peru, Philippines, Poland, Qatar, Romania, Rwanda, Saint Lucia, Saint Vincent and the Grenadines, Samoa, Sao Tome and Principe, Saudi Arabia, Senegal, Seychelles, Sierra Leone, Singapore, Somalia, Spain, Sri Lanka, Sudan, Suriname, Swaziland, Syrian Arab Republic, Thailand, Togo, Trinidad and Tobago, Tunisia, Turkey, Uganda, Ukrainian SSR, USSR, United Arab Emirates, United Republic of Tanzania, Uruguay, Vanuatu, Venezuela, Viet Nam, Yemen, Yugoslavia, Zaire, Zambia, Zimbabwe.

Against: Israel, United States.

Abstaining: Australia, Austria, Belgium, Canada, Denmark, Finland, France, Germany, Federal Republic of, Grenada, Iceland, Ireland, Italy, Japan, Luxembourg, Malawi, Netherlands, New Zealand, Norway, Portugal, Solomon Islands, Sweden, United Kingdom.

Israel said that by its calculation more than $6 million of the United Nations budget was allocated for services involving the issue of Palestine, while for the question of *apartheid* only about $1.5 million was allocated. Arab oil producers, which had earned an estimated $100 billion in 1985, had thereby hijacked United Nations resources that could otherwise have been channelled to end hunger, to combat *apartheid* or to finance a number of other worthy causes.

The United States opposed the text, saying it endorsed the work of a body which propagated partial, partisan views of the Palestine issue; the United States had consistently opposed the Committee's work because of its inherent and blatant bias.

In Finland's view, the text failed to represent the prerequisite balance for a comprehensive, just and lasting Middle East settlement.

New Zealand deplored that for too long, and unjustly, the Palestinians had been denied their legitimate rights, in particular their right to self-determination and to national independence; at the same time, it recognized Israel's right to live in peace within secure and recognized boundaries. Security Council resolution 242(1967)[25] established the principles for a just and lasting peace that would be achieved only through discussion, negotiation and conciliation.

Singapore appealed to both Israel and PLO to recognize each other's legitimate rights. It considered that Council resolutions 242(1967) and 338(1973)[26] established the fundamental basis for a stable and lasting Middle East peace, a view shared by Norway, which added that it must be up to the parties to the conflict themselves to determine which negotiating formula would serve progress towards such peace. Spain felt that those resolutions, a sound point of departure in the search for a solution, should be supplemented with a formulation expressing clear and unequivocal recognition of the rights of the Palestinians.

Zaire expressed support for the Palestinians' struggle to recover their right to independence and freedom and to have a State, in conformity with those two resolutions and the 1947 General Assembly resolution on the partition of Palestine.[28]

Bolivia believed that in order to achieve the exercise of Palestinian rights, including the right to self-determination, it was important that Israel and the Palestinians pursue steps towards peace through negotiation and without resorting to the use of force.

Uruguay voted in favour in view of its continuing concern for the achievement of a peaceful, just and lasting solution, but reiterated its reservations in connection with the Declaration and the Programme of Action adopted at the 1983 Conference on Palestine[1] which, it said, had essentially inspired the text. Such reservations were also reiterated by Peru.

Also on 12 December, the Assembly adopted **resolution 40/96 B** by recorded vote.

The General Assembly,

Having considered the report of the Committee on the Exercise of the Inalienable Rights of the Palestinian People,

Noting the particularly relevant information contained in paragraphs 135 to 150 of that report,

Recalling its resolutions 32/40 B of 2 December 1977, 33/28 C of 7 December 1978, 34/65 D of 12 December 1979, 35/169 D of 15 December 1980, 36/120 B of 10 December 1981, 37/86 B of 10 December 1982, 38/58 B of 13 December 1983 and 39/49 B of 11 December 1984,

1. *Takes note with appreciation* of the action taken by the Secretary-General in compliance with General Assembly resolution 39/49 B;

2. *Requests* the Secretary-General to ensure that the Division for Palestinian Rights of the Secretariat continues to discharge the tasks detailed in paragraph 1 of General Assembly resolution 32/40 B, paragraph 2 (*b*) of resolution 34/65 D, paragraph 3 of resolution 36/120 B and paragraphs 2 and 3 of resolution 38/58 B, in consultation with the Committee on the Exercise of the Inalienable Rights of the Palestinian People and under its guidance;

3. *Also requests* the Secretary-General to provide the Division for Palestinian Rights with the necessary resources to accomplish its tasks and to expand its work programme, particularly through additional meetings for nongovernmental organizations, in order to heighten awareness of the facts relating to the question of Palestine and to create a more favourable atmosphere for the full implementation of the recommendations of the Committee on the Exercise of the Inalienable Rights of the Palestinian People;

4. *Further requests* the Secretary-General to ensure the continued co-operation of the Department of Public Information and other units of the Secretariat in enabling the Division for Palestinian Rights to perform its tasks and in covering adequately the various aspects of the question of Palestine;

5. *Invites* all Governments and organizations to lend their co-operation to the Committee on the Exercise of the Inalienable Rights of the Palestinian People and the Division for Palestinian Rights in the performance of their tasks;

6. *Takes note with appreciation* of the action taken by Member States to observe annually on 29 November the International Day of Solidarity with the Palestinian People and the issuance by them of special postage stamps for the occasion.

General Assembly resolution 40/96 B

12 December 1985   Meeting 114   129-3-20 (recorded vote)

13-nation draft (A/40/L.24 & Add.1); agenda item 33.
Sponsors: Afghanistan, Cuba, Cyprus, Gambia, India, Indonesia, Lao People's Democratic Republic, Madagascar, Malaysia, Pakistan, Senegal, Viet Nam, Yugoslavia.
Financial implications. ACABQ, A/40/7/Add.18; 5th Committee, A/40/1032; S-G, A/C.5/40/81.
Meeting numbers. GA 40th session: 5th Committee 60; plenary 98, 100-103, 114.

Recorded vote in Assembly as follows:

In favour: Afghanistan, Albania, Algeria, Angola, Antigua and Barbuda, Argentina, Bahamas, Bahrain, Bangladesh, Barbados, Benin, Bhutan, Bolivia, Botswana, Brazil, Brunei Darussalam, Bulgaria, Burma, Burundi, Byelorussian SSR, Cameroon, Cape Verde, Central African Republic, Chad, Chile, China, Colombia, Comoros, Congo, Cuba, Cyprus, Czechoslovakia, Democratic Kampuchea, Democratic Yemen, Djibouti, Dominican Republic, Ecuador, Egypt, El Salvador, Equatorial Guinea, Ethiopia, Fiji, Gabon, Gambia, German Democratic Republic, Ghana, Greece, Guatemala, Guinea, Guinea-Bissau, Guyana, Haiti, Honduras, Hungary, India, Indonesia, Iraq, Ivory Coast, Jamaica, Jordan, Kenya, Kuwait, Lao People's Democratic Republic, Lebanon, Lesotho, Liberia, Libyan Arab Jamahiriya, Madagascar, Malawi, Malaysia, Maldives, Mali, Malta, Mauritania, Mauritius, Mexico, Mongolia, Morocco, Mozambique, Nepal, Nicaragua, Niger, Nigeria, Oman, Pakistan, Panama, Papua New Guinea, Paraguay, Peru, Philippines, Poland, Qatar, Romania, Rwanda, Saint Lucia, Saint Vincent and the Grenadines, Samoa, Sao Tome and Principe, Saudi Arabia, Senegal, Seychelles, Sierra Leone, Singapore, Somalia, Spain, Sri Lanka, Sudan, Suriname, Swaziland, Syrian Arab Republic, Thailand, Togo, Trinidad and Tobago, Tunisia, Turkey, Uganda, Ukrainian SSR, USSR, United Arab Emirates, United Republic of Tanzania, Uruguay, Vanuatu, Venezuela, Viet Nam, Yemen, Yugoslavia, Zaire, Zambia, Zimbabwe.
Against: Canada, Israel, United States.
Abstaining: Australia, Austria, Belgium, Denmark, Finland, France, Germany, Federal Republic of, Grenada, Iceland, Ireland, Italy, Japan, Luxembourg, Netherlands, New Zealand, Norway, Portugal, Solomon Islands, Sweden, United Kingdom.

The United States said it opposed the work of the Division because of its inherent and blatant biases; the text called for activities which in addition to being costly propagated partial and partisan views of the Palestine issue. Israel objected to what it felt was a misallocation of resources for matters relating to the Palestine question.

Speaking on behalf of the 10 EC member States, Portugal and Spain, Luxembourg said it regretted that the supplementary expenditures were several times the amounts reflected in the draft programme budget; given the difficult financial situation, all efforts should be made not to impose unnecessary burdens on the budget. In Finland's view, the text failed to represent the balance necessary for a comprehensive, just and lasting settlement. According to New Zealand, it did not represent the balance of principles in resolution 242(1967) or provide a basis for a realistic settlement of the Palestinian problem.

Uruguay said the text was essentially inspired by the Declaration and the Programme of Action adopted by the 1983 Conference, on which it had reservations.

In **resolution 40/25**, the Assembly strongly condemned the constant and deliberate violations of the rights of the Palestinians, as well as Israel's expansionist activities, which it considered an obstacle to the achievement of Palestinian self-determination and independence and a threat to peace and stability in the region. The Assembly called for immediate implementation of the declarations and programmes of action on Palestine adopted by international conferences. It urged States and international organizations to support the Palestinian people through PLO in struggling to regain their right to self-determination and independence.

Other action. The Sub-Commission on Prevention of Discrimination and Protection of Minorities, in a resolution of 29 August 1985[29] on the situation in the Israeli-occupied territories (see ECONOMIC AND SOCIAL QUESTIONS, Chapter XVIII), affirmed its support for the Declaration adopted by the 1983 Conference on Palestine[1] and expressed deep concern that, until a just and equitable solution to the Palestine problem had been implemented, the Palestinians would be exposed to grave dangers.

Public information activities

The Committee on Palestinian rights, in its 1985 annual report,[17] examined implementation of a 1984 General Assembly resolution[30] requesting DPI, in co-operation with the Committee, to continue and expand information activities relating to the Palestine question.

The Department's information programme included publications, audio-visual coverage, a fact-finding mission for journalists, and a series of national and regional journalists' encounters. DPI coverage of the Palestine question included radio news programmes broadcast in all the official United Nations languages, as well as in many others, and preparations for the production of a short film on the subject were under way.

A fact-finding mission to the Middle East, comprising a team of prominent media persons from around the world, visited Tunisia, Egypt, Jordan and the Syrian Arab Republic from 1 to 18 April, meeting with leading personalities and visiting refugee camps.

In 1985, DPI again organized two regional journalists' encounters, bringing together high-level journalists and experts on the Palestine question. An encounter for 15 such journalists from the North American–Caribbean region was held at Bridgetown, Barbados, in February, and another for 15 Asian journalists at Jakarta, Indonesia, in May.

As requested by the Assembly in 1984,[30] DPI began in 1985 to organize national encounters in which a team of expert panelists held in-depth press conferences with national journalists in various countries. Three African journalists' encounters were held between 24 July and 7 August, in Egypt, Madagascar and Senegal. European encounters were held in the United Kingdom, France and Czechoslovakia, between 21 and 29 August. United Nations information centres throughout the world continued to carry out information activities in connection with the question and disseminate United Nations publications; they also helped organize the world-wide observance of the International Day of Solidarity with the Palestinian People on 29 November.

DPI's coverage of policies and practices that frustrated the attainment and exercise of Palestinian rights, submitted pursuant to another 1984 Assembly resolution,[31] was summarized in a Secretariat note submitted to the Committee on Information in April.[32]

GENERAL ASSEMBLY ACTION

On 12 December 1985, the Assembly adopted **resolution 40/96 C** by recorded vote.

The General Assembly,

Having considered the report of the Committee on the Exercise of the Inalienable Rights of the Palestinian People,

Noting, in particular, the information contained in paragraphs 151 to 162 of that report,

Recalling its resolutions 38/58 E of 13 December 1983 and 39/49 C of 11 December 1984,

Convinced that the world-wide dissemination of accurate and comprehensive information and the role of non-governmental organizations and institutions remain of vital importance in heightening awareness of and support for the inalienable rights of the Palestinian people to self-determination and to the establishment of an independent sovereign Palestinian State,

1. *Takes note with appreciation* of the action taken by the Department of Public Information of the Secretariat in compliance with General Assembly resolutions 38/58 E and 39/49 C;

2. *Requests* the Department of Public Information, in full co-operation and co-ordination with the Committee on the Exercise of the Inalienable Rights of the Palestinian People, to continue its special information programme on the question of Palestine for the biennium 1986-1987 and, in particular:

(a) To disseminate information on all the activities of the United Nations system relating to the question of Palestine;

(b) To continue to update publications on the facts and developments pertaining to the question of Palestine;

(c) To publish brochures and booklets on the various aspects of the question of Palestine, including Israeli violations of the human rights of the Arab inhabitants of the occupied territories;

(d) To expand its audio-visual material on the question of Palestine, including the production of a new film, special series of radio programmes and television broadcasts;

(e) To organize fact-finding news missions to the area for journalists;

(f) To organize regional and national encounters for journalists.

General Assembly resolution 40/96 C

12 December 1985   Meeting 114   131-3-18 (recorded vote)

13-nation draft (A/40/L.25 & Add.1); agenda item 33.

Sponsors: Afghanistan, Cuba, Cyprus, India, Indonesia, Lao People's Democratic Republic, Madagascar, Malaysia, Pakistan, Senegal, Viet Nam, Yugoslavia.

Financial implications. ACABQ, A/40/7/Add.18; 5th Committee, A/40/1032; S-G, A/C.5/40/81.

Meeting numbers. GA 40th session: 5th Committee 60; plenary 98, 100-103, 114.

Recorded vote in Assembly as follows:

In favour: Afghanistan, Albania, Algeria, Angola, Antigua and Barbuda, Argentina, Austria, Bahamas, Bahrain, Bangladesh, Barbados, Benin, Bhutan, Bolivia, Botswana, Brazil, Brunei Darussalam, Bulgaria, Burma, Burundi, Byelorussian SSR, Cameroon, Cape Verde, Central African Republic, Chad, Chile, China, Colombia, Comoros, Congo, Cuba, Cyprus, Czechoslovakia, Democratic Kampuchea, Democratic Yemen, Djibouti, Dominican Republic, Ecuador, Egypt, El Salvador, Equatorial Guinea, Ethiopia, Fiji, Finland, Gabon, Gambia, German Democratic Republic, Ghana, Greece, Guatemala, Guinea, Guinea-Bissau, Guyana, Haiti, Honduras, Hungary, India, Indonesia, Iraq, Ivory Coast, Jamaica, Jordan, Kenya, Kuwait, Lao People's Democratic Republic, Lebanon, Lesotho, Liberia, Libyan Arab Jamahiriya, Madagascar, Malawi, Malaysia, Maldives, Mali, Malta, Mauritania, Mauritius, Mexico, Mongolia, Morocco, Mozambique, Nepal, Nicaragua, Niger, Nigeria, Oman, Pakistan, Panama, Papua New Guinea, Paraguay, Peru, Philippines, Poland, Qatar, Romania, Rwanda, Saint Lucia, Saint Vincent and the Grenadines, Samoa, Sao Tome and Principe, Saudi Arabia, Senegal, Seychelles, Sierra Leone, Singapore, Somalia, Spain, Sri Lanka, Sudan, Suriname, Swaziland, Sweden, Syrian Arab Republic, Thailand, Togo, Trinidad and Tobago, Tunisia, Turkey, Uganda, Ukrainian SSR, USSR, United Arab Emirates, United Republic of Tanzania, Uruguay, Vanuatu, Venezuela, Viet Nam, Yemen, Yugoslavia, Zambia, Zimbabwe.

Against: Canada, Israel, United States.

Abstaining: Australia, Belgium, Denmark, France, Germany, Federal Republic of, Grenada, Iceland, Ireland, Italy, Japan, Luxembourg, Netherlands, New Zealand, Norway, Portugal, Solomon Islands, United Kingdom, Zaire.

In the opinion of the United States, the text called for activities by DPI which—in addition to being costly—invariably propagated partial, partisan views of the Palestine issue which did not advance negotiated solutions.

Israel pointed to what it called the distorted nature of the material, symposia and forums recommended in the text, and deplored what it felt was a misallocation of resources, including $1 million for public information on the question.

Luxembourg, on behalf of the 10 EC members, Portugal and Spain, hoped that DPI would continue to base itself on the principle of impartiality and would stick to its usual decision-making process. Luxembourg also objected to the budgetary implications of the resolution.

Zaire had reservations on paragraph 2 *(c)*. Malawi said it realized the importance of disseminating information on Palestine, but hoped that the information would be as objective as possible.

Introducing the draft resolution, the Chairman of the Committee on Palestinian rights said it enumerated the activities DPI had been performing for two years and of which the Committee, in its annual report, took note with satisfaction. The only new parts of the 1985 and 1984 texts were those regarding the production of new films and radio and television broadcasts on the Palestine question.

In **resolution 40/164 A**, the Assembly requested DPI to cover adequately those policies and practices which frustrated the attainment and exercise of Palestinian rights.

Jerusalem

In an October report[33] on the situation in the Middle East (see p. 264), the Secretary-General informed the General Assembly about implementation by 13 responding States of its 1984 resolution[34] deploring the transfer by some States of their diplomatic missions to Jerusalem and calling on them to abide by the relevant United Nations resolutions. The Assembly, by resolution 40/168 C, again determined that Israel's 1980 decision to impose its laws and administration on the city was illegal and null and void.

The closing of the Medical Facility Hospice in the Old City of Jerusalem, which had provided services to nearly 150,000 Arab patients, was the subject of several communications (see p. 281). The Assembly, in resolution 40/161 D, called on Israel to allow its reopening.

In several communications, Israel charged PLO with attacks on Israeli civilians in Jerusalem.

Communications. On 14 May 1985,[35] Israel brought to the Secretary-General's attention a bomb explosion at a hospital bus stop in Jerusalem on 12 May, adding that another bomb was left at the entrance to a park and two more were found that day at bus stops on busy streets in the town of Beth Shemesh. Two different terrorist groups, Israel said, had claimed respon-

sibility. From whichever faction of PLO the would-be killers were sent, Israel added, their aim was the same—the deliberate murder of innocent civilians.

On 23 July,[36] Israel reported that on 19 July a young Arab man from Hebron had stabbed five children and their day-camp counsellor on their way to a swimming pool in Jerusalem. According to Israeli police, PLO had said that it was part of an "entrance examination" for PLO recruits.

On 27 September,[11] Israel cited a booby-trapped car in the Mea Sharim neighbourhood of Jerusalem and a bomb explosion at a bus station near Hadassah Hospital, injuring two, as further examples of PLO terrorist attacks against innocent Israelis.

GENERAL ASSEMBLY ACTION

On 16 December, under the agenda item on the Middle East, the General Assembly adopted **resolution 40/168 C** by recorded vote.

The General Assembly,

Recalling its resolutions 36/120 E of 10 December 1981, 37/123 C of 16 December 1982, 38/180 C of 19 December 1983 and 39/146 C of 14 December 1984, in which it determined that all legislative and administrative measures and actions taken by Israel, the occupying Power, which had altered or purported to alter the character and status of the Holy City of Jerusalem, in particular the so-called "Basic Law" on Jerusalem and the proclamation of Jerusalem as the capital of Israel, were null and void and must be rescinded forthwith,

Recalling Security Council resolution 478(1980) of 20 August 1980, in which the Council, *inter alia*, decided not to recognize the "Basic Law" and called upon those States that had established diplomatic missions at Jerusalem to withdraw such missions from the Holy City,

Having considered the report of the Secretary-General of 22 October 1985,

1. *Determines* that Israel's decision to impose its laws, jurisdiction and administration on the Holy City of Jerusalem is illegal and therefore null and void and has no validity whatsoever;

2. *Deplores* the transfer by some States of their diplomatic missions to Jerusalem in violation of Security Council resolution 478(1980) and their refusal to comply with the provisions of that resolution;

3. *Calls once again upon* those States to abide by the provisions of the relevant United Nations resolutions, in conformity with the Charter of the United Nations;

4. *Requests* the Secretary-General to report to the General Assembly at its forty-first session on the implementation of the present resolution.

General Assembly resolution 40/168 C

16 December 1985   Meeting 118   137-2-10 (recorded vote)

32-nation draft (A/40/L.45 & Add.1); agenda item 38.

Sponsors: Afghanistan, Algeria, Bahrain, Bangladesh, Cuba, Democratic Yemen, Djibouti, Egypt, India, Indonesia, Iraq, Jordan, Kuwait, Lebanon, Libyan Arab Jamahiriya, Malaysia, Mauritania, Mongolia, Morocco, Oman, Pakistan, Qatar,

Saudi Arabia, Somalia, Sri Lanka, Sudan, Syrian Arab Republic, Tunisia, United Arab Emirates, Viet Nam, Yemen, Yugoslavia.
Meeting numbers. GA 40th session: plenary 104-107, 118.

Recorded vote in Assembly as follows:

In favour: Afghanistan, Albania, Algeria, Argentina, Australia, Austria, Bahamas, Bahrain, Bangladesh, Barbados, Belgium, Benin, Bhutan, Bolivia, Botswana, Brazil, Brunei Darussalam, Bulgaria, Burkina Faso, Burma, Burundi, Byelorussian SSR, Cameroon, Canada, Cape Verde, Central African Republic, Chad, Chile, China, Colombia, Comoros, Congo, Cuba, Cyprus, Czechoslovakia, Democratic Kampuchea, Democratic Yemen, Denmark, Djibouti, Dominican Republic, Ecuador, Egypt, Equatorial Guinea, Ethiopia, Fiji, Finland, France, Gabon, Gambia, German Democratic Republic, Germany, Federal Republic of, Ghana, Greece, Guinea, Guinea-Bissau, Guyana, Honduras, Hungary, Iceland, India, Indonesia, Iran, Iraq, Ireland, Italy, Ivory Coast, Jamaica, Japan, Jordan, Kenya, Kuwait, Lao People's Democratic Republic, Lebanon, Lesotho, Libyan Arab Jamahiriya, Luxembourg, Madagascar, Malaysia, Maldives, Mali, Malta, Mauritania, Mauritius, Mexico, Mongolia, Morocco, Mozambique, Nepal, Netherlands, New Zealand, Nicaragua, Niger, Nigeria, Norway, Oman, Pakistan, Panama, Peru, Philippines, Poland, Portugal, Qatar, Romania, Rwanda, Saint Lucia, Saint Vincent and the Grenadines, Samoa, Sao Tome and Principe, Saudi Arabia, Senegal, Singapore, Somalia, Spain, Sri Lanka, Sudan, Suriname, Sweden, Syrian Arab Republic, Thailand, Togo, Trinidad and Tobago, Tunisia, Turkey, Uganda, Ukrainian SSR, USSR, United Arab Emirates, United Kingdom, United Republic of Tanzania, Uruguay, Vanuatu, Venezuela, Viet Nam, Yemen, Yugoslavia, Zambia, Zimbabwe.

Against: Costa Rica, Israel.

Abstaining: Antigua and Barbuda, Dominica, Grenada, Guatemala, Liberia, Malawi, Paraguay, Swaziland, United States, Zaire.

In the view of the United States, the status of Jerusalem could only be determined through negotiations among the concerned parties in the framework of an overall peace settlement; repeated resolutions on the question served no useful purpose.

Luxembourg, speaking for the 10 EEC members, Portugal and Spain, recalled the importance they attached to the 1980 Security Council decision[37] not to recognize the "Basic Law" enacted by Israel that year proclaiming a change in the character and status of Jerusalem.

New Zealand reaffirmed that it did not recognize the validity of Israel's annexation of East Jerusalem.

Introducing the text, India said that Israel's total and unconditional withdrawal from all Arab territories occupied since 1967, including the Holy City of Jerusalem, should be a part of a just and comprehensive solution to the problems of West Asia.

Closing of the Hospice hospital

Communications. By a letter of 18 July,[38] the Acting Chairman of the Committee on Palestinian rights informed the Secretary-General of news reports of action taken by the Israeli authorities to close at the end of the month the Roman Catholic Medical Facility Hospice in occupied East Jerusalem—the only government hospital in the Arab part of Jerusalem caring for the poor. In the Committee's view, this was further evidence of Israel's failure to provide medical services in a manner acceptable to the local population.

The closing of the hospital was cited by the Committee on Israeli practices[39] (see p. 328) as an example of Israel's policy to de-Arabize Jerusalem. To protest the closing, all shops in Arab East Jerusalem were closed on 24 July.

The evacuation of the hospital was also the subject of a cablegram from the Minister for Foreign Affairs of Jordan, transmitted to the Secretary-General on 29 July.[40] The hospital had been caring especially for patients from Jerusalem and the West Bank of Jordan who for financial reasons had not been admitted to other hospitals, Jordan said. Israel had deliberately adopted certain measures against the hospital, including the withholding of funds, which had led to a deterioration of services. Jordan regarded those measures as illegal and called for immediate action by the international community.

Israel, on 2 August,[41] categorically rejected the allegations that the closure of the hospital was the result of a political decision. The reasons for its action, it said, was that the medical equipment was out of date, resulting in inadequate medical care, and the building structure did not allow room for a suitable elevator, so that patients had to be carried to and from the operating room by hand-held stretchers. The decision was in line with the Ministry of Health's policy of closing small hospitals and those with one category of patient (such as women), Israel continued. The assertions that its closure would deprive the residents of proper medical care was unfounded; they would receive care at Jerusalem's other hospitals. At the Hospice building, a first-aid station would continue to operate. Moreover, Israel added, increased medical supervision in Arab schools and municipal assistance to first-aid stations, along with health insurance and hospitalization, enabled Arab residents of Jerusalem to receive medical care on a par with that of the rest of Israel and far superior to that found elsewhere in the Middle East.

GENERAL ASSEMBLY ACTION

In a separately adopted paragraph of **resolution 40/161 D** on the occupied territories, the General Assembly called on Israel to allow the reopening of the Hospice so that it could continue to provide health and medical services to the Arab population in the city.

Assistance to Palestinians

Report of the Secretary-General. In June 1985,[42] the Secretary-General submitted a report on United Nations assistance to the Palestinians currently being carried out by United Nations bodies, as well as planned or proposed activities. As requested by the General Assembly in 1984,[43] United Nations efforts to provide economic and social assistance to the Palestinians, in co-operation with PLO and with the consent of Arab host Governments, had been intensified. Also as requested, the Secretary-General had utilized an inter-agency mechanism, the Consultative Committee on Substantive Questions (Programme Matters) (CCSQ (PROG)) of the Administrative Committee on Co-ordination, for consultations with the organizations of the system towards developing a co-ordinated assistance programme. CCSQ (PROG) considered the question in April 1985, agreeing to group future activities into three main categories: development activities; education and training; and health.

The Secretary-General convened a meeting of 21 United Nations programmes, organizations, agencies, funds, organs and Secretariat departments, in which PLO, the Arab host countries and inter- and non-governmental organizations participated (Geneva, 5 and 8 July). The meeting discussed current, future and proposed activities of the United Nations system. It noted that some progress had been made towards a co-ordinated programme and that the Secretary-General's report represented a modest advance in that direction, providing fuller information on proposed activities in a thematic framework. However, it was felt that the proposals before the meeting did not constitute such a programme in its final form as envisaged by the Assembly; given the complexity of the issues and circumstances, it was difficult to provide specific information on all aspects of the activities, with a detailed assessment of financial requirements. The meeting concluded that there was a need to ensure continuing review of the progress made in implementing the various activities and programmes, and that further efforts were needed to finalize the programme of assistance.

UNDP action. The United Nations Development Programme (UNDP) programme of assistance to the Palestinians became operational in 1980. In accordance with 1983 Economic and Social Council[44] and Assembly resolutions,[45] UNDP set up a special programme to help the Palestinians improve their social and economic conditions. The programme was centred in the West Bank and the Gaza Strip, except for one project in the Syrian Arab Republic. It was the only intergovernmental development programme with large-scale, continuing operations in those territories. The UNDP Administrator was directly responsible for the programme.

As of 1 March 1985, UNDP had 20 projects at various stages of implementation; 8 were already completed. Projects included development and strengthening of health institutions, health manpower development and training, agricultural training, and community services for youth.

After considering an April 1985 report on UNDP assistance to the Palestinians,[46] the Governing Council, in June,[47] reaffirmed UNDP's commitment to assist the Palestinians in their economic and social development. Expressing gratitude to

Governments and funds which had made additional special contributions, the Council noted that unless further contributions were received it would not be possible to undertake effectively basic development projects for the West Bank and the Gaza Strip. It authorized an additional $2 million for assistance to the Palestinians.

UNIDO action. The Industrial Development Board of the United Nations Industrial Development Organization (UNIDO), on 31 May 1985,[48] took note with appreciation of the 1984 report of the UNIDO Executive Director on technical assistance to the Palestinians[49] and of implementation of technical co-operation projects. The Board affirmed that Israel's occupation was detrimental to the basic requirements for the economic development of the Palestinians in the West Bank and Gaza Strip. Additionally, its restrictive policies inhibited the development of the Palestinian industrial sector in those territories. The Board expressed its rejection of the Israeli settlements there and of the exploitation of Palestinian resources by the occupation authorities. It called for urgent repeal of the restrictions impeding the development of the Palestinian national economy, and regretted Israel's refusal to give UNIDO staff and experts access to the territories. The Board requested UNIDO to identify priority industrial development projects and to intensify its efforts, in co-operation with PLO, to provide technical assistance to the Palestinians. A further progress report on such assistance was requested.

UNICEF activities. The programme of the United Nations Children's Fund (UNICEF) to assist Palestinian children and mothers in Jordan, Lebanon, the Syrian Arab Republic and the occupied Arab territories focused on child survival and development, pre-school services, promotion of income-generating activities for women, and water supply and sanitation. A programme coordinator, based at Amman, Jordan, was appointed.

In Jordan, the main thrust of the programme related to reducing infant and child mortality and enhancing institutional and non-institutional approaches to child care. UNICEF assisted in establishing five new kindergartens in various camps and in giving refresher courses to 20 kindergarten teachers. It also provided furniture and knitting- and sewing-machines for pre-vocational workshops.

In Lebanon, UNICEF supported the maternal and child health network run by the Palestinian Red Crescent Society and UNRWA by providing vaccines, oral rehydration salts, medical equipment and essential drugs. In co-operation with UNRWA and the Norwegian People's Relief Association, UNICEF had started a field survey to identify disabled Palestinians in the Beirut area, with a view to establishing small-scale physiotherapy centres and vocational training workshops and developing educational programmes.

A programme for assistance to Palestinian children and mothers in the Syrian Arab Republic, approved in 1984, supported child health, preschool services, non-formal education, and water supply and sanitation.

A $1.7 million, three-year project (1984-1987) to be financed by the Federal Republic of Germany sought to enhance the survival, growth and development of Palestinian children, with particular emphasis on those up to 6 years of age. It concentrated on maternal and child health services, oral rehydration therapy, immunization, breast-feeding, early childhood stimulation, prevention and treatment of childhood disabilities, and rehabilitation. In addition, UNICEF supported preschool activities and teacher training courses in the occupied territories.

Other activities. The Economic Commission for Western Asia (ECWA), on 24 April 1985, adopted a resolution[50] calling for the updating of a study it had commissioned in 1976[51] on the economic and social situation and potential of the Palestinians. A regional review concerning implementation of the 1979 Vienna Programme of Action on Science and Technology for Development,[52] undertaken by ECWA in co-operation with the Secretariat's Centre for Science and Technology for Development (Baghdad, 17-20 February 1985), led to the adoption of recommendations to enhance the ability of the Palestinians in developing their capacity for the application of science and technology.

The Food and Agriculture Organization of the United Nations continued to provide training assistance, including an agricultural training centre project for refugee camps in the Syrian Arab Republic, and fellowships for specialized training in agricultural development. The World Health Organization provided technical advice for the review of existing environmental health facilities and programmes in the West Bank; work was also under way on the first of three planned health centres in the occupied territories, at Ramallah.

ECONOMIC AND SOCIAL COUNCIL ACTION

On 25 July, on the recommendation of its Third (Programme and Co-ordination) Committee, the Economic and Social Council adopted **resolution 1985/57** by roll-call vote.

Assistance to the Palestinian people

The Economic and Social Council,

Recalling General Assembly resolution 39/224 of 18 December 1984,

Recalling also Council resolution 1984/56 of 25 July 1984,

Recalling further the Programme of Action for the Achievement of Palestinian Rights, adopted by the International Conference on the Question of Palestine,

Noting the need to provide economic and social assistance to the Palestinian people,

1. *Takes note* of the report of the Secretary-General on assistance to the Palestinian people;

2. *Notes* the meeting on assistance to the Palestinian people which was held at Geneva on 5 and 8 July 1985 in response to General Assembly resolution 39/224;

3. *Expresses its thanks* to the Secretary-General for convening the meeting on assistance to the Palestinian people;

4. *Regards* such a meeting as a valuable opportunity to assess progress in economic and social assistance to the Palestinian people and to explore ways and means of enhancing such assistance;

5. *Draws the attention* of the international community, the United Nations system and intergovernmental and non-governmental organizations to the need to disburse their aid to the occupied Palestinian territories only for the benefit of the Palestinian people;

6. *Requests* the Secretary-General:

(a) To review the progress made in the implementation of the proposed activities and projects described in the report of the Secretary-General on assistance to the Palestinian people;

(b) To take all necessary steps to finalize the programme of economic and social assistance to the Palestinian people requested in General Assembly resolution 38/145 of 19 December 1983;

(c) To convene in 1986 a meeting of the relevant programmes, organizations, agencies, funds and organs of the United Nations system to consider economic and social assistance to the Palestinian people;

(d) To provide for the participation in the meeting of the Palestine Liberation Organization, the Arab host countries and relevant intergovernmental and non-governmental organizations;

7. *Requests* the relevant programmes, organizations, agencies, funds and organs of the United Nations system to intensify their efforts, in co-operation with the Palestine Liberation Organization, to provide economic and social assistance to the Palestinian people;

8. *Also requests* that United Nations assistance to the Palestinians in the Arab host countries should be rendered in co-operation with the Palestine Liberation Organization and with the consent of the Arab host Government concerned;

9. *Requests* the Secretary-General to report to the General Assembly at its forty-first session, through the Economic and Social Council, on the progress made in the implementation of the present resolution.

Economic and Social Council resolution 1985/57

25 July 1985	Meeting 52	44-1 (roll-call vote)

Approved by Third Committee (E/1985/138) by roll-call vote (43-1), 12 July (meeting 10); 14-nation draft (E/1985/C.3/L.2); agenda item 21.

Sponsors: Algeria, Bangladesh, China, India, Indonesia, Libyan Arab Jamahiriya, Malaysia, Morocco, Pakistan, Saudi Arabia, Somalia, Sri Lanka, Syrian Arab Republic, Yugoslavia.

Roll-call vote in Council as follows:

In favour: Algeria, Argentina, Bangladesh, Botswana, Brazil, Bulgaria, Canada, China, Congo, Ecuador, Finland, France, German Democratic Republic, Germany, Federal Republic of, Iceland, India, Indonesia, Japan, Luxembourg, Malaysia, Mexico, Morocco, Netherlands, New Zealand, Nigeria, Poland, Romania, Rwanda, Saudi Arabia, Senegal, Sierra Leone, Somalia, Spain, Suriname, Sweden,

Thailand, Turkey, Uganda, USSR, United Kingdom, Venezuela, Yugoslavia, Zaire, Zimbabwe.
Against: United States.

If the text's objective was truly to promote the interests and well-being of the Palestinians, the United States said, it would also have been necessary to refer to the attacks committed—and not by Israel—against Palestinian refugees in Lebanon. It did not believe, however, that such an essentially political question should be raised in the Council. The text could not provide a solution to the Palestinian problem but was in fact part of it.

Israel remarked that the text drew attention to the need for assistance to the Palestinians only; it should be noted that UNDP had stated in a 1985 report[46] that mobilization of additional funds was urgent, since the project pipeline approved by all parties concerned contained some $50 million worth of potential activities.

Jordan considered the text extremely important; it would provide an occasion for assistance particularly to the Palestinians in the Israeli-occupied territories whose authorities would not otherwise allow the channelling of any aid to that people. Canada said it favoured assistance designed to promote the Palestinians' economic and social development.

Speaking on behalf of the EEC members, Luxembourg said they attached great importance to humanitarian assistance to the Palestinians through tried and tested complementary instruments, i.e. food and emergency supplies as well as co-financing in collaboration with NGOs. The EEC members would continue, both directly and through the United Nations system, to provide the best possible response to the Palestinians' emergency needs.

GENERAL ASSEMBLY ACTION

On 17 December 1985, on the recommendation of the Second (Economic and Financial) Committee, the General Assembly adopted **resolution 40/170** by recorded vote.

Assistance to the Palestinian people

The General Assembly,

Recalling its resolution 39/224 of 18 December 1984,

Recalling also Economic and Social Council resolution 1985/57 of 25 July 1985,

Recalling further the Programme of Action for the Achievement of Palestinian Rights, adopted by the International Conference on the Question of Palestine,

Noting the need to provide economic and social assistance to the Palestinian people,

1. *Takes note* of the report of the Secretary-General on assistance to the Palestinian people;

2. *Notes* the meeting on assistance to the Palestinian people that was held at Geneva on 5 and 8 July 1985 in response to General Assembly resolution 39/224;

3. *Expresses its thanks* to the Secretary-General for convening the meeting on assistance to the Palestinian people;

4. *Regards* such a meeting as a valuable opportunity to assess progress in economic and social assistance to the Palestinian people and to explore ways and means of enhancing such assistance;

5. *Draws the attention* of the international community, the United Nations system and intergovernmental and non-governmental organizations to the need to disburse their aid to the occupied Palestinian territories only for the benefit of the Palestinian people;

6. *Requests* the Secretary-General:

(a) To review the progress made in the implementation of the proposed activities and projects described in his report on assistance to the Palestinian people;

(b) To take all necessary steps to finalize the programme of economic and social assistance to the Palestinian people requested in General Assembly resolution 38/145 of 19 December 1983;

(c) To convene in 1986 a meeting of the relevant programmes, organizations, agencies, funds and organs of the United Nations system to consider economic and social assistance to the Palestinian people;

(d) To provide for the participation in the meeting of the Palestine Liberation Organization, the Arab host countries and relevant intergovernmental and non-governmental organizations;

7. *Requests* the relevant programmes, organizations, agencies, funds and organs of the United Nations system to intensify their efforts, in co-operation with the Palestine Liberation Organization, to provide economic and social assistance to the Palestinian people;

8. *Also requests* that United Nations assistance to the Palestinians in the Arab host countries should be rendered in co-operation with the Palestine Liberation Organization and with the consent of the Arab host Government concerned;

9. *Requests* the Secretary-General to report to the General Assembly at its forty-first session, through the Economic and Social Council, on the progress made in the implementation of the present resolution.

General Assembly resolution 40/170

17 December 1985   Meeting 119   145-2-1 (recorded vote)

Approved by Second Committee (A/40/1009/Add.1) by recorded vote (131-2), 11 November (meeting 30); 10-nation draft (A/C.2/40/L.17); agenda item 12.
Sponsors: Algeria, Bangladesh, Gambia, Indonesia, Madagascar, Pakistan, Senegal, Tunisia, Yemen, Yugoslavia.
Meeting numbers. GA 40th session: 2nd Committee 22, 30; plenary 119.

Recorded vote in Assembly as follows:

In favour: Afghanistan, Albania, Algeria, Angola, Antigua and Barbuda, Argentina, Australia, Austria, Bahamas, Bahrain, Bangladesh, Barbados, Belgium, Benin, Bhutan, Bolivia, Botswana, Brazil, Brunei Darussalam, Bulgaria, Burkina Faso, Burma, Burundi, Byelorussian SSR, Cameroon, Canada, Cape Verde, Central African Republic, Chad, Chile, China, Colombia, Comoros, Congo, Cuba, Cyprus, Czechoslovakia, Democratic Kampuchea, Democratic Yemen, Denmark, Djibouti, Dominica, Dominican Republic, Ecuador, Egypt, Equatorial Guinea, Ethiopia, Fiji, Finland, France, Gabon, German Democratic Republic, Germany, Federal Republic of, Ghana, Greece, Guatemala, Guinea, Guinea-Bissau, Guyana, Haiti, Honduras, Hungary, Iceland, India, Indonesia, Iran, Iraq, Ireland, Italy, Ivory Coast, Jamaica, Japan, Jordan, Kuwait, Lao People's Democratic Republic, Lebanon, Lesotho, Liberia, Libyan Arab Jamahiriya, Luxembourg, Madagascar, Malawi, Malaysia, Maldives, Mali, Malta, Mauritania, Mauritius, Mexico, Mongolia, Morocco, Mozambique, Nepal, Netherlands, New Zealand, Nicaragua, Niger, Nigeria, Norway, Oman, Pakistan, Panama, Papua New Guinea, Paraguay, Peru, Philippines, Poland, Portugal, Qatar, Romania, Rwanda, Saint Christopher and Nevis, Saint Vincent and the Grenadines, Samoa, Sao Tome and Principe, Saudi Arabia, Senegal, Sierra Leone, Singapore, Somalia, Spain, Sri Lanka, Sudan, Suriname, Swaziland, Sweden, Syrian Arab Republic, Thailand, Togo, Trinidad and Tobago, Tunisia, Turkey, Uganda, Ukrainian SSR, USSR, United Arab Emirates, United Kingdom, United Republic of Tanzania, Uruguay, Venezuela, Viet Nam, Yemen, Yugoslavia, Zaire, Zambia.
Against: Israel, United States.
Abstaining: Grenada.

Before the Committee vote, Israel said the text was motivated by political rather than humanitarian concerns, was repetitious and was based on false pretences; it ignored the fact that Israel was currently promoting the well-being and socio-economic development of the Palestinian Arabs whose position, under its administration, was better than that of the people in most of the neighbouring countries. The ritual resolutions submitted each year were an effort to present Israel as opposing international assistance to the Palestinians. It opposed assistance to PLO, but welcomed assistance for constructive purposes through the proper channels, co-operated with UNDP and other international organizations and made every effort to assist the Palestinians while the countries that were most vociferous gave them little or no aid.

In the opinion of the United States, the text was not likely to advance the goal of peace or benefit the people of the area; the improvement in the quality of life that Israel had brought to the Palestinians should be acknowledged. The United States was opposed to channelling assistance through PLO, which it did not recognize as the sole legitimate representative of the Palestinians.

Speaking for the EEC members, Luxembourg said they would continue to provide assistance to the Palestinians, including food aid and projects co-financed with NGOs, directly and through United Nations channels. Though voting in favour, Japan reiterated its general position on aid to national liberation movements.

Jordan was convinced that the Palestinians had suffered under Israeli occupation and needed support to help them recover their legitimate rights; however, it had reservations on paragraphs 7 and 8, on the grounds that all activities and operations on Jordanian territory must be undertaken with Jordan's approval.

The USSR, speaking also on behalf of Bulgaria, the Byelorussian SSR, Czechoslovakia, the German Democratic Republic, Hungary, Mongolia, Poland and the Ukrainian SSR, reiterated their support for Palestinian rights and stressed that all parties to the conflict, including PLO, should be allowed to participate in efforts to find a solution.

Related questions

Israeli air raid on PLO headquarters in Tunisia

The murder of three of its citizens in Cyprus, allegedly carried out by a PLO group, was cited by Israel as the reason for its bombing of PLO headquarters in Tunisia on 1 October 1985, killing or wounding a number of Palestinian refugees and Tunisians. The Security Council, by resolution 573(1985) of 4 October, condemned the bomb-

ing as an act of aggression and demanded that Israel refrain from carrying out or threatening such acts.

The Council of the International Civil Aviation Organization, by a resolution of 18 October,[53] condemned the violation of Tunisian airspace by Israel which endangered international civil aviation.

Communications. By a letter of 27 September,[11] Israel charged that during the preceding 45 days PLO had carried out 32 terrorist attacks, among them a 10-hour siege of three Israelis vacationing aboard a yacht moored at Larnaca, Cyprus, who were then murdered on 25 September. Initial reports, Israel said, indicated that the act had been carried out by a personal bodyguard unit of PLO Chairman Yasser Arafat.

On 1 October,[54] Tunisia reported to the President of the Security Council that on that day six Israeli military aircraft had penetrated Tunisian airspace and at 10.07 a.m. had bombed the civilian locality of Borj-Cedria, called Hammam Plage, in the southern suburbs of Tunis, dropping five 1,000-pound bombs. The operation, for which it said Israel had officially claimed responsibility, had resulted in the loss of many lives and material damage and destruction on a wide scale. Contrary to Israel's claims, Tunisia stated, the target was situated in an exclusively residential urban area which traditionally had been home to Tunisian families and a small number of Palestinian civilians who had fled from Lebanon following Israel's invasion of that country.

Tunisia regarded the raid as a blatant act of aggression against its territorial integrity, sovereignty and independence, and a flagrant violation of international law and the principles of the United Nations Charter. It requested an immediate meeting of the Security Council, calling on it to condemn the act in the strongest terms, to require fair and full compensation for all the damage and to take measures to prevent such acts from recurring.

A number of communications sent between 1 October and 20 November to the President of the Council or to the Secretary-General expressed solidarity with the Tunisian Government and people and condemned the air raid.

According to Democratic Yemen,[55] the attack confirmed once again Israel's policy of aggression and terrorism against the Palestinians in particular and the Arab people in general.

A special communiqué adopted by a 1 October Meeting of Ministers and Heads of Delegation of Non-Aligned Countries to the General Assembly at its current session, transmitted by India,[56] expressed grave concern at the act, the target of which, it said, had been the premises of PLO in a vain attempt to destroy Palestinian resistance.

The United Republic of Tanzania[57] charged that the attack had been premeditated to decimate the PLO leadership and to intimidate countries like Tunisia that extended humanitarian assistance and political solidarity to the Palestinians. It called on the international community to respond immediately to the humanitarian needs of the victims and demanded that those countries which had in multiple ways abetted Israel's policy of aggression prevail on it to cease such genocidal acts.

Viet Nam[58] said the criminal act challenged the Arab, African and non-aligned countries and peace-loving forces throughout the world; with the connivance of the United States and other reactionary forces, Israel was further intensifying its terrorism against PLO and its policy of threat and pressure designed to prevent the Arab countries from supporting the just struggle of the Palestinians for their national rights.

In Mongolia's view,[59] the provocative action proved that the United States and Israel were continuing to interfere in the internal affairs of the Arab States, and were attempting to undermine a political settlement in the Middle East and to annihilate PLO.

Spain[60] said the brutal attack on a sovereign State served only to aggravate tension and seriously undermine efforts to bring about a Middle East peace. Similarly, Brazil[61] saw no justification for such acts, which served only to increase tension and make more distant the day when all the nations in the Middle East would coexist peacefully.

A declaration adopted on 1 October by the Ministers for Foreign Affairs of the 10 EC member States, and of Spain and Portugal, transmitted by Luxembourg,[62] characterized the bombing as a new factor in the cycle of violence and counter-violence in the Middle East; terrorist acts committed against Israeli citizens, which they condemned, did not justify the action.

Argentina[63] affirmed that solutions to international problems must be sought through dialogue and negotiation and not through force. Yemen[64] said the international community demanded a halt to Israel's actions and the imposition of a boycott and deterrent sanctions; the attack on PLO headquarters, which threatened all Arab territories designated as targets for Israel's expansionist intentions, made it essential that the Arab States stand together. The United Arab Emirates[65] also believed that the Arab community must confront the aggression with a decisive and united stand.

In a statement of 1 October, transmitted by Kuwait,[66] an Extraordinary Ministerial Meeting of the Arab Group at the United Nations called on the international community to assist Tunisia in facing up to the Israeli aggression and its consequences and, supporting Tunisia's request for a Council meeting, urged the Council to adopt the necessary resolutions to condemn and curb that aggression.

Oman[67] called on the international community to stand firm against such acts. Peru[68] transmitted a motion of order of its Senate dated 2 October, protesting the aggression and placing on record its agreement that such aggression should be punished. Burundi[69] called on the Security Council to take measures to prevent such behaviour, and reaffirmed the need to find an equitable solution to the Palestinian problem, in particular through the establishment of a Palestinian State.

A statement by the Deputy Prime Minister and Minister for Foreign Affairs of Yemen, on behalf of the heads of delegation and the Ministers for Foreign Affairs of the members of the Organization of the Islamic Conference participating in the current session of the General Assembly,[70] categorically rejected a statement issued by the United States which, the statement said, justified the bombing as an act of self-defence, and called for international support for Tunisia and for its right to just and equitable compensation.

To Malta,[71] it seemed impossible that the act was carried out by Israel alone from its own territory; everyone should help to apprehend the perpetrators. Malta wished to ensure that similar acts of international piracy were not repeated.

The President of Senegal,[72] as current OAU Chairman, expressed in messages to the Tunisian President and the PLO Chairman Africa's support and solidarity. The Supreme Council of the Gulf Co-operation Council, in the Final Communiqué adopted at its sixth session (Oman, 3-6 November),[73] also affirmed its support and solidarity with Tunisia and PLO.

In a letter of 16 November, transmitted by Yemen on 20 November,[74] the Secretary-General of the Organization of the Islamic Conference noted that the Conference's Governing Board, at its eighth session (Sanaa, 26-28 October), had approved a telegram to the United Nations Secretary-General characterizing Israel's action as a criminal act against Tunisia, against justice and against all mankind. The Board denounced the crime and condemned the Israeli authorities and those that had supported them.

In a statement of 24 October, transmitted to the Secretary-General the next day,[75] the Minister for Foreign Affairs of Tunisia, on the occasion of the fortieth anniversary of the United Nations, said Israel's aggression was an undeserved blow against a country which had been the first to advocate dialogue in the Middle East conflict; the unanimous condemnation of the act by the international community revived Tunisia's hope in the United Nations as the custodian of international law and morality. Israel's aggression could only strengthen further Tunisia's support for the struggle of the Palestinians.

SECURITY COUNCIL ACTION

The Security Council considered Tunisia's complaint at four meetings between 2 and 4 October. Afghanistan, Algeria, Bangladesh, Cuba, the German Democratic Republic, Greece, Indonesia, Iran, Israel, Jordan, Kuwait, Lesotho, the Libyan Arab Jamahiriya, Malta, Mauritania, Morocco, Nicaragua, Nigeria, Pakistan, Saudi Arabia, Senegal, the Syrian Arab Republic, Tunisia, Turkey, Viet Nam, Yemen and Yugoslavia were invited, at their request, to participate in the discussion without the right to vote. Invitations under rule 39[c] of the Council's provisional rules of procedure were extended to the Permanent Observer of the League of Arab States[76] and to the Under-Secretary-General for Political and International Affairs of that organization,[77] both at Kuwait's request in its capacity as Chairman of the Arab Group, and to the Secretary-General of the Organization of the Islamic Conference, at Egypt's request.[78]

Also at the request of Egypt,[79] the Council decided, by 10 votes to 1 (United States), with 4 abstentions (Australia, Denmark, France, United Kingdom), that an invitation to participate be accorded to PLO. The President stated that Egypt's proposal was not made pursuant to rule 37[d] or rule 39 of the provisional rules of procedure, but, if approved, the invitation would confer on PLO the same rights as those conferred on Member States when invited to participate pursuant to rule 37.

Before the vote on that decision, the United States reiterated its opposition (see p. 274) to conferring such rights on non-governmental entities.

On 4 October, the Council adopted **resolution 573(1985)**.

The Security Council,

Having considered the letter dated 1 October 1985, in which Tunisia made a complaint against Israel following the act of aggression which the latter committed against the sovereignty and territorial integrity of Tunisia,

Having heard the statement by the Minister for Foreign Affairs of Tunisia,

Having noted with concern that the Israeli attack has caused heavy loss of human life and extensive material damage,

Considering that, in accordance with Article 2, paragraph 4, of the Charter of the United Nations, all States Members shall refrain in their international relations from the threat or use of force against the territorial integrity or political independence of any State, or acting in any other manner inconsistent with the purposes of the United Nations,

Gravely concerned at the threat to peace and security in the Mediterranean region posed by the air raid perpetrated on 1 October by Israel in the area of Hammam Plage, situation in the southern suburb of Tunis,

Drawing attention to the serious effect which the aggression carried out by Israel and all acts contrary to the Charter cannot but have on any initiative designed to establish an overall, just and lasting peace in the Middle East,

Considering that the Israeli Government claimed responsibility for the attack as soon as it had been carried out,

1. *Condemns vigorously* the act of armed aggression perpetrated by Israel against Tunisian territory in flagrant violation of the Charter of the United Nations, international law and norms of conduct;

2. *Demands* that Israel refrain from perpetrating such acts of aggression or from threatening to do so;

3. *Urges* Member States to take measures to dissuade Israel from resorting to such acts against the sovereignty and territorial integrity of all States;

4. *Considers* that Tunisia has the right to appropriate reparations as a result of the loss of human life and material damage which it has suffered and for which Israel has claimed responsibility;

5. *Requests* the Secretary-General to report to the Security Council on the implementation of the present resolution by 30 November 1985 at the latest;

6. *Decides* to remain seized of the matter.

Security Council resolution 573(1985)

| 4 October 1985 | Meeting 2615 | 14-0-1 |

6-nation draft (S/17535).
Sponsors: Burkina Faso, Egypt, India, Madagascar, Peru, Trinidad and Tobago.
Meeting numbers. SC 2610, 2611, 2613, 2615.
Vote in Council as follows:
　In favour: Australia, Burkina Faso, China, Denmark, Egypt, France, India, Madagascar, Peru, Thailand, Trinidad and Tobago, Ukrainian SSR, USSR, United Kingdom.
　Against: None.
　Abstaining: United States.

The real threat all civilized peoples were facing was terrorism, said the United States in explaining its vote; the failure adequately to address the subject prevented it from supporting the text, which placed all the blame for the latest round of the rising spiral of violence in the Middle East on only one set of shoulders, while not also holding at fault those responsible for the terrorist acts which provoked it. The principle that a State subjected to continuing terrorist attacks might respond with appropriate force to defend itself against further attacks was an aspect of the inherent right of self-defence recognized in the Charter. It was the collective responsibility of sovereign States to see that terrorism enjoyed no sanctuary and that those who practised it had no immunity from the responses their acts warranted; moreover, it was the responsibility of each State to take appropriate steps to prevent persons or groups within its sovereign territory from perpetrating such acts. The incident should be an impetus for renewed efforts towards successful completion of the peace process.

[c]See footnote a on p. 274.
[d]See footnote b on p. 274.

Despite legal reservations that it felt stemmed from the concept of acts of aggression in the text, France said it had voted in favour not only because of its traditional friendly relations with Tunisia but also because it condemned all acts of violence, whatever their origin, that would compromise the search for a comprehensive, just and lasting Middle East peace.

Thailand remarked that no matter how deplorable and regrettable the situation in Tunisia, there was no state of war between the two countries involved; while the loss suffered by the Tunisian Government and people must be made good by those who had attacked them, the word "compensation" should have been used instead of "reparations" in paragraph 4.

Speaking before the vote, Israel said the resolution would propagate the notion that the victim could not defend itself and that the terrorist deserved sanctuary. The Council had been convened to attack a legitimate act of self-defence, Israel said. The allegation that Israel had engaged in an aggressive act against another country was a perversion of the truth. If anything could be defined as aggression, it was the actions against Israel; for the past year, PLO headquarters in Tunisia had organized and launched hundreds of terrorist attacks against Israel, Israeli targets and Jews everywhere. According to irrefutable evidence, the butchery at Larnaca had been perpetrated by "Force 17", the personal bodyguard unit of Yasser Arafat.

Israel's forces had taken special care to pinpoint the target—three buildings housing PLO headquarters. Any civilian casualties had been inadvertent and were the result of PLO's deliberate tactic of planting its bases among civilians. Israel could not accept the notion that the headquarters of terrorist killers should enjoy immunity anywhere, any time, and Tunisia, which knowingly harboured PLO and allowed it complete freedom of action, bore considerable responsibility. If the Council were to adhere to its true purposes, it would convene to find ways to combat international terrorism as the major threat to the international order.

Tunisia refuted the charge that it had become a terrorist base; no act of terrorism had been perpetrated from its territory and no Tunisian had been implicated in any such act. As for "Force 17", its headquarters were not on Tunisian territory. Contrary to what Israel claimed, Israel had attacked a clearly defined residential urban area, killing 68 civilians and wounding more than 100. Any attempt to justify that act could only set the seal of approval on and encourage aggression. The crime was particularly reprehensible because it was aimed at jeopardizing efforts to bring about a peaceful settlement of the Palestinian problem;

everyone was aware that the hospitality extended by Tunisia to the Palestinian leadership fell within that framework. Tunisia called for firm condemnation of the illegitimate and unwarranted use of force by Israel, a clear affirmation of the firm will of the international community to prevent the repetition of such terrorist acts, and reparations for damage caused.

Virtually every speaker in the debate agreed that Tunisia's sovereignty and territorial integrity had been violated and that the attack was against international law and Charter principles. Israel had blatantly flouted the most fundamental tenets of the Charter, Indonesia said, namely, respect for the territorial integrity and sovereignty of States, the non-use of force, non-intervention and non-interference. In the opinion of the USSR, the events again showed the essence of Israel's policy against Arab States and peoples for almost four decades: a cynical disregard for the fundamental provisions of the Charter, international law and United Nations resolutions; a studied undermining of the recognized bases for inter-State relations; reliance on terror and naked force; and the complete absence of respect for elementary human rights, primarily the right to life. Burkina Faso said that, by violating the Charter once again, Israel had made it clear that it would never be prepared to fulfil its obligations thereunder or abide by United Nations decisions. Israel's flagrant violation of international law and Charter principles was all the more striking in view of the fact that it had struck against a country whose peace-loving nature was universally recognized, Cuba said.

Most speakers did not accept the justification given by Israel that the attack had been carried out in self-defence. It could not be justified as a reprisal raid, Turkey said. The United Kingdom said it could not accept the reasons put forward by Israel for its action. Under the Charter, Members committed themselves to settle their international disputes by peaceful means; arbitrary and disproportionate violence, even in retaliation, was a clear breach of that obligation. Bangladesh also rejected Israel's argument that it had the right to attack any State at any time on the basis of its self-conceived self-defence.

According to Australia, even if one were to accept Israel's version of the events, two wrongs did not make a right. It was a new and disproportionate application of the principle of an eye for an eye, carried out with arrogant disregard of others, Peru said. Denmark also did not believe that acts of terrorism against Israeli citizens justified the raid on Tunisia. Madagascar found it difficult to find a sufficient justification for that aggression, planned and carried out in cold blood. The slaying of Israeli nationals in Cyprus could in no way serve as an excuse for an attack on a third country, Greece stressed. There could be no justification for any country to take the law into its own hands in such a manner, or for any other to condone or excuse such aggression, Malta stated. The attack was illegal on all counts and could not be legitimized on the basis of any legal or moral criteria, Pakistan said. Wanton reprisals against innocent civilians had always been condemned by the international community since the Second World War, Morocco added; if self-defence consisted of bombing all territories where Palestinians lived, no country would be safe from Israel's destructive folly.

Madagascar rejected the argument that since Tunisia harboured PLO headquarters, it bore a responsibility for all hostile acts against Israel and its citizens, even if they were carried out by individuals and responsibility was not claimed by PLO; according to that reasoning, Israel could arrogate to itself the right to destroy all PLO offices wherever they could be found. Even if one were to entertain Israel's lame justifications, in the opinion of Indonesia, the magnitude of the action was wholly disproportionate to the so-called provocation. Despite one isolated opinion, Viet Nam said, international opinion unanimously viewed the act as criminal aggression and terrorism.

Egypt charged that the Israeli raid had been organized long before the incident in Cyprus. The Under-Secretary-General for Political and International Affairs of the League of Arab States also considered that the attack had been premeditated and carefully planned, in full awareness that it would inflict a heavy toll on innocent Tunisians and Palestinians. The USSR believed that the facts set forth by Tunisia demonstrated convincingly that Israel had carefully planned the action and executed it in cold blood.

Israel's crime fell into the category of official State terrorism, said Kuwait, speaking on behalf of the Group of Arab States. This view was shared by several other speakers, among them Afghanistan, Bangladesh, the German Democratic Republic, Indonesia, Lesotho, Nicaragua and Yugoslavia.

The attack was seen by many as one more link in a chain of repeated acts of Israeli aggression against Arab countries and as part of its expansionist designs. That position was held by the Libyan Arab Jamahiriya, the Syrian Arab Republic, the Ukrainian SSR, Yemen and Yugoslavia, among others. Speaking as Chairman of the Group of African States, Nigeria said the attack did not set a precedent; Israel had previously unleashed violence, terror and naked force not only against the Palestinians but also against its Arab neighbours under the pretext that they provided refuge to individuals and groups opposed to its existence. Malta warned of the dangers of allowing the conflict to spread to North Africa.

India described the attack as yet another glaring entry in the lengthy catalogue of Israel's aggressive policies and as one more manifestation of its desire to eliminate Palestinian resistance. In Indonesia's opinion, the assault on PLO headquarters must be viewed in the context of Israel's avowed war of annihilation against the Palestinians. Zionism, which meant desire for expansion and endless hegemony and the genocide of the Palestinians, had broadened its sphere of aggression, according to Algeria. Israel's expansionist designs could be realized only by destroying the institutions of the Palestinians, said Kuwait, speaking for the Arab Group.

Many speakers expressed the view that Israel's attack was an attempt to sabotage the Middle East peace process. The underlying motive for Israel's attack was undoubtedly to destroy recently improved peace prospects, Pakistan said, timed to take place when important proposals for negotiations involving the Palestinians were taking shape. It was not unreasonable to say that Israel's aggression was a preventive action against peace, Madagascar added.

According to the Secretary-General of the Organization of the Islamic Conference, peace would foreclose Israel's expansionist designs and endanger the massive assistance it currently received; therefore, it systematically rejected and defeated every effort to promote peace in the Middle East. In Jordan's opinion, Israel was trying to delay a solution to the Arab-Israeli conflict as long as possible. In the face of growing international consensus in favour of the Arab and Palestinian cause, said Bangladesh, Israel had once again resorted to force to heighten tension and frustrate current international efforts to resolve the problems in the Middle East peacefully. Similarly, Yugoslavia believed that the attack was calculated to thwart efforts to seek a solution to the Middle East crisis and the Palestine question. A similar view was held by Indonesia, Morocco and Saudi Arabia. Nigeria, speaking for the African Group, believed that the raid reversed fruitful peace prospects that had just begun to glimmer. Trinidad and Tobago, holding a similar view, added that the attack could only militate against attempts to secure a just and lasting peace. By committing such a crime, PLO said, Israel reaffirmed its insistence on undermining international peace efforts; by justifying the attack, the United States revealed its lack of credibility in playing a constructive role in those endeavours.

Madagascar felt only one conclusion was possible, namely, that Israel wished to eliminate PLO physically in order to impose its own peace. The United States and Israel were attempting to impose on the Arabs their military and political diktat and to draw them into separate deals, said the

Ukrainian SSR. Decisive action by the United States, Israel's principal ally, to ensure the fruition of current Arab peace initiatives and promote an international peace conference on the Middle East (see p. 268) was necessary to dispel the shadow cast on peace prospects by Israel's action, said Pakistan.

France expressed concern at the disastrous consequences the action would inevitably have on current efforts to bring about a resumption of the peace process. The United Kingdom called on Israel and all the parties concerned to reaffirm their commitment to seeking a peaceful solution and to abstain completely from violent and provocative actions which imperilled that objective.

Sanctions against Israel and measures under the Charter were called for by many speakers, among them the Libyan Arab Jamahiriya, Nicaragua and the Secretary-General of the Organization of the Islamic Conference. Afghanistan, Cuba and Morocco said the Council should adopt mandatory sanctions under Chapter VII of the Charter, with a view to restraining Israel. The Syrian Arab Republic added that such sanctions were necessary to eliminate the effects of aggression and punish the aggressor. Viet Nam called on the Council to adopt the measures at its disposal to prevent Israel from committing similar crimes in the future, a position also taken by Bangladesh, Mauritania and Pakistan. It was for the Council to make sure that Israel took account of its obligations under international law and the Charter and of United Nations resolutions, said Senegal. The Eastern European States, said the Group's current Chairman, the Ukrainian SSR, favoured the adoption of stern measures in conformity with the Charter. Saudi Arabia also hoped that the Council members would take a firm stand that complied with the Charter.

Madagascar and Burkina Faso wondered whether the time had not come, in view of Israel's repeated use or threat of force and its refusal to comply with its Charter obligation to accept Council decisions, to consider the adoption of measures provided for in the Charter. In line with the call by the non-aligned countries for comprehensive mandatory sanctions under Chapter VII, Yugoslavia said, the Council had to act and bring about respect for Charter principles and see to it that Israel's aggressive acts were met with adequate measures. Israel's perverted sense of immunity from international accountability was related to the Council's inability adequately to enforce its decisions, Indonesia believed; the Council should move beyond mere words to an effective exercise of its authority under the Charter.

China also called on the Council to adopt strong measures under the Charter and to see to it that Tunisia's demands were met: Israel should be con-

demned, should compensate Tunisia for the losses, and pledge not to commit any further similar crimes. It was imperative that Israel be compelled to give up its policy of aggression and expansion. Given the Council's limitations, Pakistan said, the least to be expected was that it condemn the attack, adopt a decision to prevent recurrence of such acts, and promote the Arab initiatives for peace, especially those within the United Nations context. The victims also deserved to be fully compensated.

That Israel must pay compensation to Tunisia and the Palestinians for the loss of life and for the damages was a view shared by many, including Burkina Faso, Cuba and Yemen. Jordan said if the Council strongly condemned the raid and held Israel responsible for the losses, its prestige and credibility would be restored. A strong and unanimous condemnation of Israel, according to PLO, could convey the message that the international community would no longer tolerate its crimes and acts of aggression. The representative of the League of Arab States warned that failure to take the necessary measures would mean further disintegration of the Organization. Iran believed that any political action would remain impotent unless all Moslem nations, particularly in the Arab world, joined in a united Islamic front.

Report of the Secretary-General. As called for by the Security Council, the Secretary-General submitted in November, and revised in December, a report[80] on implementation of resolution 573(1985). He had transmitted the resolution to Israel, Tunisia and all United Nations Member States, drawing particular attention to paragraph 3. As of 30 November, he had received replies from Israel, Oman and Tunisia, substantive parts of which were reproduced in an annex to his report.

Israel, in its reply of 21 November, had categorically rejected all allegations that its action constituted an act of aggression, or that it had been directed against Tunisia's territorial integrity or political independence; it had been directed against PLO. Israel added that the 1970 Declaration on Principles of International Law concerning Friendly Relations and Co-operation among States in accordance with the Charter of the United Nations,[81] reaffirmed in the 1974 Definition of Aggression,[82] clearly spelt out that an act of aggression occurred when a country failed to fulfil its duty to refrain from organizing or encouraging the organization of irregular forces or armed bands for incursion into the territory of another State; they also required that States must not acquiesce in organized activities within its territory directed towards the commission of terrorist acts. Tunisia directly violated both instruments. To Israel, the Council resolution was unacceptable in its entirety, and it rejected in particular the improper use of the terms "acts of aggression" and "act of armed aggression".

Tunisia, by a reply of 27 November, had submitted a governmental commission report investigating the consequences of, and evaluating the damage caused by, Israel's aggression, as a basis for claim for reparations. It stated that the assessment was not complete, either in respect of individuals or corporate losses or in respect of property destroyed. In addition to the material damage, the effects of the feeling of insecurity engendered by the attack were bound to make themselves felt, in particular in the tourism industry and foreign investment. Tunisia reserved its right to return to the question when it had sufficient evidence to claim damages for violation of its sovereignty and impairment of its economic and social development.

Oman, by a reply of 13 November, said it considered that the Council was required to adopt more serious resolutions in order to prevent or halt repeated Israeli acts of aggression against Arab territories. With regard to paragraph 3, Oman believed that certain super-Powers with which Israel had special relationships were the States most qualified to play a greater role.

Hijacking of the *Achille Lauro*

On 7 October 1985, the Italian cruise ship *Achille Lauro*, with several hundred persons aboard, was hijacked and one of its passengers, the American citizen Leon Klinghoffer, was killed and thrown overboard. The Secretary-General, in a statement of 8 October, endorsed by the members of the Security Council the next day, condemned all acts of terrorism and noted that the hijacking was another escalation of violence in the Middle East; he urged those responsible to understand that their act was criminal and unjustifiable and should be ended without delay in a manner that would avoid further suffering by the innocent victims.

Communications. By a letter of 8 October,[83] Italy requested, following the events which led to the hijacking, that the matter be brought to the attention of the Security Council, with a view to condemning firmly such an act and appealing for prompt liberation of the hostages. On the same date,[84] Austria appealed to the Council President to undertake every effort to contribute to an early end of the tragedy; Greece, on 9 October,[85] also said it hoped that the act might be resolved as quickly as possible without loss of human life. Both countries understood that some of their citizens were aboard. On the same date,[86] Italy asked the Council President to inform the Council members that the hijackers had abandoned the *Achille Lauro* and released the hostages; therefore, no further consideration of the matter appeared necessary.

SECURITY COUNCIL ACTION

On 9 October, the Council President made a statement on behalf of the Council members:[87]

"The members of the Security Council welcome the news of the release of the passengers and the crew of the cruise ship *Achille Lauro* and deplore the reported death of a passenger.

"They endorse the Secretary-General's statement of 8 October 1985, which condemns all acts of terrorism.

"They resolutely condemn this unjustifiable and criminal hijacking as well as other acts of terrorism, including hostage-taking.

"They also condemn terrorism in all its forms, wherever and by whomever committed."

Meeting numbers. SC 2618-2620, 2622.

During a Council meeting the following day on the Middle East situation, including the Palestine question, Israel gave an account of the killing of Leon Klinghoffer, saying he had been singled out from other passengers on the ship because he was Jewish, there being no Israelis aboard. The facts showed, Israel said, that the hijacking had been carried out by the Abul Abbas faction of PLO's Palestine Liberation Front (PLF), with the full prior approval of the PLO Chairman.

It had not been planned originally as a hijacking, Israel believed; the PLF men were to have travelled on the ship to the Israeli port of Ashdod, to have staged there a hostage-taking and then demanded the release of Al Fatah terrorists held in Israeli jails. However, when the terrorists were discovered, they hijacked the ship, demanded the release of 50 Palestinian terrorists and then shot Klinghoffer. Then, on orders from Arafat, acting through a lieutenant, the hijackers gave themselves up to Egyptian authorities, Israel said.

The Secretary-General of the Organization of the Islamic Conference said the hijacking was an act of terrorism by individuals, which could not be condoned. Since then, he added, the aircraft carrying the four hijackers out of Egypt had been intercepted by the United States Air Force and forced to land at a United States military base in Sicily; they were currently in custody.

PLO contended that there was no proof that Klinghoffer was murdered. PLO had intervened in the hijacking, at the request of the Italian Government, to save the lives of the almost 400 passengers and crew. Its endeavours had helped put an end to the operation and saved the vessel and those on board from dire consequences. The hijackers were on their way to a Palestinian court, PLO went on; Chairman Arafat, who had expressed PLO's condemnation of the operation, had declared that PLO would interrogate them in co-ordination with the Egyptian and Italian authorities. The arrest of the four Palestinians would not put an end to violence and terrorism in the Middle East, because Israel was its primary source.

The United States said it felt relief—tinged with sadness and anger about the murder of Leon Klinghoffer—that the passengers and crew of the ship had been released and that the latest act of terrorism and violence had ended, and urged all peoples and Governments to renounce terrorism as inimical to the norms of civilization.

Australia considered Klinghoffer yet another innocent victim of the cycle of violence afflicting the Middle East.

Attack against the offices of the American-Arab Anti-Discrimination Committee

During an attack on 11 October against the offices of the American-Arab Anti-Discrimination Committee (ADC) at Santa Ana, California, the west coast Regional Director of ADC, Alex Odeh, an American of Palestinian origin, was killed and six Americans were injured. By a letter of 17 October,[88] Kuwait, as Chairman of the Arab Group, expressed members' concern over the climate of anti-Arab hostility in the United States which, it believed, had encouraged the attack. The Arab Group hoped that the perpetrators would be identified and brought to justice. Annexed to the letter was a telegram from the Secretary-General of the League of Arab States to the National Chairman of ADC stating that the murder of Mr. Odeh had shocked the Arab world; his work in fighting discrimination and his defence of Palestinian rights in particular had earned him high esteem. The Arab world hoped that the tragic episode would only lead ADC to redouble its endeavours.

The United States, on 18 October,[89] said its authorities were investigating the incident fully so that all responsible parties would be brought to justice. Annexed to its letter was a White House statement of 12 October deeply deploring the event and condemning in the strongest possible terms the criminal use of violence and terrorism to achieve political ends.

Hijacking of an Egyptian aircraft

On 23 November 1985, an Egyptian airliner bound from Athens to Cairo was hijacked to Malta by four Palestinians; during the incident, 60 people died. By a letter of 25 November, transmitted by Egypt on 27 November,[90] PLO said its Palestine Central Council, currently meeting at Baghdad, had issued a statement on 24 November expressing strong disapproval of the hijacking and condemning the perpetrators and parties behind it. The Council considered that the act gave the enemies of the Arab nation an opportunity to slander its reputation and damage it in the eyes of world public opinion. PLO announced that it was placing all of its capacities at Egypt's disposal so that it might take appropriate measures to cope with the situation and protect the lives of the passengers.

A spokesman for the Secretary-General, in a statement of 25 November, expressed deep sadness at the heavy loss of innocent life in the hijacking, adding that such tragedies reinforced the necessity for Governments to make concerted efforts to implement existing international agreements and consider what further measures could be effectively devised.

The hijacking was listed by Israel in its "Calendar of Middle Eastern violence, 1985", annexed to a 5 December letter[14] cataloguing press reports of violence in the area.

Attacks at Rome and Vienna airports

On 27 December 1985, terrorist attacks were carried out in the passenger terminals at the airports of Rome, Italy and Vienna, Austria; the perpetrators were said to be Palestinians.

A spokesman for the Secretary-General, in a statement of the same date, expressed shock at the news of the attacks, which had resulted in the loss of innocent human lives; the Secretary-General hoped that the unanimous position on terrorism adopted by the United Nations membership—General Assembly **resolution 40/61** (see LEGAL QUESTIONS, Chapter II)—would be followed up by determined efforts by all Governments and authorities concerned, so that all acts, methods and practices of terrorism might be brought to an end.

SECURITY COUNCIL ACTION

Following consultations with the members of the Security Council, its President, on 30 December, read out a statement on their behalf,[91] strongly condemning the attacks at the Rome and Vienna airports as unjustifiable and criminal; they urged that those responsible for the killings be brought to trial and called on all concerned to exercise restraint and refrain from taking any action inconsistent with their obligations under the Charter and other relevant rules of international law. (For further details, see LEGAL QUESTIONS, Chapter II.)

Communication. Commenting in a letter of 31 December[92] on the events which had led to the Security Council President's statement of the day before, Israel said the Palestinian terror, inspired directly by PLO, constantly prided itself on its "armed struggle" against Israel and its citizens; in the most recent atrocities, that terror had resulted in the ruthless and deliberate killing of women, children and babies, intentionally during the holidays in order to maximize civilian casualties. Attacks on civilian air transportation had become PLO's trade mark. There was a blatant contradiction between the stance many countries had adopted against international terrorism and the permission some of them gave to the world's central terrorist organization to operate "missions" in their capitals, Israel stated. The Libyan Arab Jamahiriya had become the world centre of international terrorism, but criminal gangs also found shelter and backing in Iraq and the Syrian Arab Republic, it said. It was imperative that all countries which opposed acts of international terrorism united and took decisive action to fight that cancerous evil.

REFERENCES

[1]YUN 1983, p. 274. [2]A/40/270-S/17132 & Corr.1. [3]A/40/301-S/17182. [4]A/40/603-S/17438. [5]A/40/398-S/17292. [6]S/17210. [7]A/40/399-S/17293. [8]A/40/540-S/17392. [9]A/40/567-S/17412. [10]A/40/620 (S/17448). [11]A/40/688-S/17502. [12]A/40/634-S/17462. [13]A/C.6/40/9. [14]A/40/985-S/17668. [15]A/40/967-S/17666. [16]A/40/105î. [17]A/40/35. [18]YUN 1976, p. 235. [19]*Ibid.*, p. 245, GA res. 31/20, 24 Nov. 1976. [20]S/17507. [21]S/17558. [22]S/17560. [23]S/17552. [24]YUN 1982, p. 388. [25]YUN 1967, p. 257, SC res. 242(1967), 22 Nov. 1967. [26]YUN 1973, p. 213, SC res. 338(1973), 22 Oct. 1973. [27]YUN 1984, p. 259. [28]YUN 1947-48, p. 247, GA res. 181 A (II), 29 Nov. 1947. [29]E/CN.4/1986/5 (res. 1985/16). [30]YUN 1984, p. 274, GA res. 39/49 C, 11 Dec. 1984. [31]*Ibid.*, p. 356, GA res. 39/98 A, 14 Dec. 1984. [32]A/AC.198/85. [33]A/40/668 & Add.1. [34]YUN 1984, p. 273, GA res. 39/146 C, 14 Dec. 1984. [35]A/40/314-S/17192. [36]A/40/503-S/17357. [37]YUN 1980, p. 426, SC res. 478(1980), 20 Aug. 1980. [38]A/40/494-S/17346. [39]A/40/702. [40]A/40/517-S/17371. [41]A/40/528-S/17379. [42]A/40/353-E/1985/115 & Corr.1 & Add.1 & Add.1/Corr.1. [43]YUN 1984, p. 278, GA res. 39/224, 18 Dec. 1984. [44]YUN 1983, p. 282, ESC res. 1983/43, 25 July 1983. [45]*Ibid.*, p. 284, GA res. 38/145, 19 Dec. 1983. [46]DP/1985/18. [47]E/1985/32 (dec. 85/15). [48]A/40/16 (conclusion 1985/13). [49]YUN 1984, p. 276. [50]E/1985/35 (res. 141(XII)). [51]YUN 1976, p. 504. [52]YUN 1979, p. 636. [53]*Action of the Council, 116th Session, Montreal, 13 September–20 December 1985* (Doc. 9480-C/1092). [54]S/17509. [55]A/40/697-S/17517. [56]A/40/699-S/17518. [57]A/40/705-S/17523. [58]A/40/729-S/17542. [59]S/17533. [60]S/17516. [61]A/40/713-S/17532. [62]A/40/700-S/17520. [63]S/17519. [64]A/40/715-S/17534. [65]A/40/721-S/17540. [66]S/17514. [67]A/40/716-S/17536. [68]S/17566. [69]A/40/722-S/17538. [70]A/40/720-S/17539. [71]S/17553. [72]A/40/741-S/17559. [73]A/40/911-S/17644. [74]A/40/917-S/17647. [75]A/40/812-S/17591. [76]S/17513. [77]S/17515. [78]S/17524. [79]S/17512. [80]S/17659/Rev.1. [81]YUN 1970, p. 789, GA res. 2625(XXV), annex, 24 Oct. 1970. [82]YUN 1974, p. 847, GA res. 3314(XXIX), annex, 14 Dec. 1974. [83]S/17548. [84]S/17574. [85]S/17555. [86]S/17556. [87]S/17554. [88]S/17576. [89]S/17578. [90]A/40/960-S/17663. [91]S/17702. [92]S/17703.

Incidents and disputes between Arab countries and Israel

Iraq and Israel

Armed incident involving Iraqi nuclear facilities

The 1981 bombing by Israeli aircraft of a nuclear research centre near Baghdad[1] was the subject of a 1985 report by the Secretary-General

and a General Assembly request (resolution 40/6) that IAEA consider additional measures to ensure that Israel undertook not to attack or threaten peaceful nuclear facilities. The IAEA General Conference, in September, noted that Israel had committed itself not to attack peaceful nuclear facilities.

Communications. On 3 May 1985,[2] Iraq transmitted to the Secretary-General a statement made by the Israeli Minister of Industry and Trade, at a press conference at Haifa, Israel, on 26 March, saying that Israel had the right to strike against any nuclear reactor built by Iraq which constituted a danger to Israel's security.

In a letter of 15 May,[3] Israel stated that no one but the Prime Minister and the Foreign Minister and their appointed representatives expressed authorized government policy on the issue. It reiterated its position stated in July 1984[4] declaring its support for international arrangements to ensure the status and inviolability of peaceful nuclear facilities, as restated recently to IAEA.

IAEA action. The General Conference of IAEA, on 27 September,[5] adopted a resolution taking note of Israel's declaration that it would not attack or threaten to attack peaceful nuclear facilities in Iraq or anywhere else.

Report of the Secretary-General. In October 1985,[6] the Secretary-General reported to the Assembly on steps taken with regard to implementation of a 1981 Security Council resolution[7] calling on Israel to refrain from attacks on nuclear facilities devoted to peaceful purposes and to place its nuclear facilities under IAEA safeguards. By a note of 7 February 1985, the Secretary-General had requested Israel to inform him of action it had taken or envisaged in response to the Council's demand, reiterated by the Assembly in 1984.[8] In reply, Israel transmitted on 24 October a 26 September statement by the Director-General of the Israel Atomic Energy Commission, according to which Israel held that all States must refrain from attacking or threatening to attack peaceful nuclear facilities, and that the IAEA safeguards system brought evidence of the peaceful operation of a facility. Israel reconfirmed that it would not attack or threaten any nuclear facilities devoted to peaceful purposes, in the Middle East or elsewhere, and that it would support action in competent forums convened to work out binding agreements protecting such installations from attack and threat of attack.

GENERAL ASSEMBLY ACTION

On 1 November 1985, the General Assembly adopted **resolution 40/6** by recorded vote.

Armed Israeli aggression against the Iraqi nuclear installations and its grave consequences for the established international system concerning the peaceful uses of nuclear energy, the non-proliferation of nuclear weapons and international peace and security \

The General Assembly,

Having considered the item entitled "Armed Israeli aggression against the Iraqi nuclear installations and its grave consequences for the established international system concerning the peaceful uses of nuclear energy, the non-proliferation of nuclear weapons and international peace and security",

Recalling the relevant resolutions of the Security Council and the General Assembly,

Taking note of the relevant resolutions of the International Atomic Energy Agency,

Viewing with deep concern Israel's refusal to comply with Security Council resolution 487(1981) of 19 June 1981,

Noting with deep concern the threatening statement made by an Israeli cabinet member on 26 March 1985, in which he stated, *inter alia,* "We are prepared to strike against any nuclear reactor built by Iraq in the future",

Deeply alarmed by Israel's failure to state without ambiguity its acceptance of the internationally recognized criteria for the definition of a peaceful nuclear facility and to acknowledge the effectiveness of the safeguards system of the International Atomic Energy Agency as a reliable means of verifying the peaceful operation of nuclear facilities,

Concerned that armed attacks against nuclear facilities raise fears about the safety of present and future nuclear installations,

Aware that all States developing nuclear energy for peaceful purposes need assurances against armed attacks on nuclear facilities,

1. *Strongly condemns* all military attacks on all nuclear installations dedicated to peaceful purposes, including the military attacks by Israel on the nuclear facilities of Iraq;

2. *Considers* that Israel has not yet committed itself not to attack or threaten to attack nuclear facilities in Iraq or elsewhere, including facilities under International Atomic Energy Agency safeguards;

3. *Requests* the Security Council to take urgent and effective measures to ensure that Israel complies without further delay with the provisions of resolution 487(1981);

4. *Requests* the International Atomic Energy Agency to consider additional measures effectively to ensure that Israel undertakes not to attack or threaten to attack peaceful nuclear facilities in Iraq or elsewhere, in violation of the Charter of the United Nations and in disregard of the safeguards system of the International Atomic Energy Agency;

5. *Calls upon* Israel urgently to place all its nuclear facilities under International Atomic Energy Agency safeguards in accordance with resolution 487(1981) adopted unanimously by the Security Council;

6. *Reaffirms* that Iraq is entitled to compensation for the damage it has suffered as a result of the Israeli armed attack on 7 June 1981;

7. *Urges* all Member States to provide necessary technical assistance to Iraq to restore its peaceful nuclear programme and to overcome the damage caused by the Israeli attack;

8. *Calls upon* all States and organizations that have not yet done so to discontinue co-operating with and giving assistance to Israel in the nuclear field;

9. *Requests* the Conference on Disarmament to continue negotiations with a view to an immediate conclusion of the agreement on the prohibition of military attacks on nuclear facilities as a contribution to promoting and ensuring the safe development of nuclear energy for peaceful purposes;

10. *Decides* to include in the provisional agenda of its forty-first session the item entitled "Armed Israeli aggression against the Iraqi nuclear installations and its grave consequences for the established international system concerning the peaceful uses of nuclear energy, the non-proliferation of nuclear weapons and international peace and security".

General Assembly resolution 40/6

1 November 1985	Meeting 59	88-13-39 (recorded vote)

26-nation draft (A/40/L.9/Rev.1), amended by Iran (A/40/L.10); agenda item 29.

Sponsors: Afghanistan, Algeria, Bahrain, Bangladesh, Cuba, Cyprus, Democratic Yemen, Djibouti, Indonesia, Iraq, Jordan, Kuwait, Lebanon, Libyan Arab Jamahiriya, Malaysia, Mauritania, Morocco, Oman, Qatar, Saudi Arabia, Somalia, Sudan, Tunisia, United Arab Emirates, Yemen, Yugoslavia.

Meeting numbers. GA 40th session: plenary 58, 59.

Recorded vote in Assembly as follows:

In favour: Afghanistan, Albania, Algeria, Angola, Bahrain, Bangladesh, Benin, Bhutan, Brazil, Brunei Darussalam, Bulgaria, Burkina Faso, Burundi, Byelorussian SSR, Cape Verde, Central African Republic, Chad, China, Comoros, Congo, Cuba, Cyprus, Czechoslovakia, Democratic Kampuchea, Democratic Yemen, Djibouti, Egypt, Gabon, German Democratic Republic, Ghana, Guinea, Guinea-Bissau, Guyana, Hungary, India, Indonesia, Iran, Iraq, Jordan, Kenya, Kuwait, Lao People's Democratic Republic, Lebanon, Lesotho, Libyan Arab Jamahiriya, Madagascar, Malaysia, Maldives, Mali, Malta, Mauritania, Mauritius, Mongolia, Morocco, Mozambique, Nepal, Nicaragua, Niger, Nigeria, Oman, Pakistan, Peru, Philippines, Poland, Qatar, Romania, Rwanda, Saudi Arabia, Senegal, Seychelles, Somalia, Sri Lanka, Sudan, Syrian Arab Republic, Togo, Trinidad and Tobago, Tunisia, Turkey, Uganda, Ukrainian SSR, USSR, United Arab Emirates, United Republic of Tanzania, Viet Nam, Yemen, Yugoslavia, Zambia, Zimbabwe.

Against: Belgium, Canada, Denmark, Finland, Germany, Federal Republic of, Iceland, Israel, Luxembourg, Netherlands, Norway, Sweden, United Kingdom, United States.

Abstaining: Antigua and Barbuda, Argentina, Australia, Austria, Barbados, Bolivia, Cameroon, Chile, Colombia, Costa Rica, Dominican Republic, Ecuador, Equatorial Guinea, Fiji, France, Greece, Grenada, Guatemala, Haiti, Ireland, Italy, Ivory Coast, Jamaica, Japan, Liberia, Malawi, Mexico, New Zealand, Panama, Papua New Guinea, Paraguay, Portugal, Saint Vincent and the Grenadines, Samoa, Solomon Islands, Spain, Uruguay, Venezuela, Zaire.

The Assembly adopted by a recorded vote of 79 to 2, with 50 abstentions, an amendment by Iran, adding what became paragraph 1.

The United States said it strongly believed that the issue the text purported to address had been decisively resolved by the IAEA General Conference in September, after four years of difficult and painstaking consideration; the attempt to reopen the issue flouted the clear intention of the majority of the IAEA members.

In Canada's view, the IAEA resolution had fully responded to many of the points raised, yet this text did not take account of that and sought to have the issue taken up again in IAEA. Canada also could not support the request in paragraph 3 which, it said, implied the imposition of further restrictive measures against Israel, nor could it support the call in paragraph 7 which would have the effect of preventing organizations such as IAEA from co-operating with all their member States, including Israel.

Canada and Sweden supported the call on Israel to place its nuclear facilities under IAEA safeguards. Nevertheless, Sweden felt that the main thrust of paragraphs 3 and 5 and the sixth preambular paragraph, in particular, was in contradiction of the IAEA resolution.

Though strongly condemning Israel's 1981 attack, Austria said it did not consider the changes in the 1985 resolution made in comparison to the one adopted in 1984[8] to be conducive to achieving its aims.

Mexico said it regretted that the IAEA resolution was not properly reflected in the text. In Australia's opinion, the text called on IAEA to become involved in matters outside its area of competence. Ecuador believed that the text should not have been silent with regard to Israel's positive statements, such as the one contained in the Secretary-General's report; moreover it would not appear appropriate to reopen the question in IAEA, where it had been closed. Bolivia noted certain technical flaws pertaining to IAEA and no mention of the Secretary-General's report. Argentina said the question of safeguards was not covered to its satisfaction.

Brazil and Peru would have preferred mention of the Secretary-General's report. Peru also reserved its position with respect to certain technical concepts which, it believed, were not in conformity with IAEA resolutions. Brazil doubted whether anyone could tell what the internationally recognized criteria mentioned in the sixth preambular paragraph were. Paragraph 4 seemed to disregard the fact that the matter had been withdrawn from the IAEA agenda; paragraph 8 deserved some examination in connection with IAEA decisions; and paragraph 9 was imprecise.

The item under consideration was Israeli aggression against the Iraqi nuclear installations, Iraq stressed, and what happened in IAEA was a very small part of that. Israel refused to put its nuclear installations under the IAEA safeguards system, while there was never a question about Iraq's compliance with the system. If the United Nations did not make Israel commit itself not to repeat its act of aggression and perhaps submit its own facilities to international inspection, it was driving nails into the coffin of the 1968 Treaty on the Non-Proliferation of Nuclear Weapons[9] and the safeguards system.

Lebanon situation

Reports of the Secretary-General. As requested by the Security Council in 1984,[10] the Secretary-General reported on activities of the United Nations Interim Force in Lebanon from 10 October 1984 to 11 April 1985.[11] He had continued consultations with the Lebanese Government and other parties involved in the ongoing conflict in Lebanon. Following consultations with the Governments of Lebanon and Israel, their military representatives met, beginning on 8 November 1984,[12] for a conference which took place at UNIFIL headquarters at Naqoura. From the outset of the conference, Lebanon insisted on the full withdrawal of Israeli forces from Lebanese territory and the subsequent deployment of the Lebanese army together with UNIFIL down to the international boundary, in accordance with Security Council resolution 425(1978) establishing the Force.[13] Israel took the position that UNIFIL should be deployed in the entire area to be evacuated by the Israeli forces, with the positioning of the main forces of UNIFIL between the Zahrani and Awali rivers up to the border between Lebanon and the Syrian Arab Republic. Israel would accept a limited UNIFIL presence further south, but maintained that local forces should be responsible for security arrangements in the southernmost part of Lebanon. The Secretary-General said there was little change in those basic positions and the Naqoura conference, which lasted into January 1985 and adjourned *sine die*, had produced no result.

On 14 January, Israel announced a plan, formally presented to the conference on 22 January, for a unilateral redeployment of its forces in southern Lebanon in three phases. During the first phase, the Israel Defence Forces would evacuate the Sidon area and deploy in the Litani-Nabatiyah region in the western sector. In the second phase, IDF would deploy in the Hasbaiya area in the eastern sector, and in the third, they would deploy along the Israel-Lebanon international border while maintaining a zone where local forces, i.e. the South Lebanon Army (SLA), would function with IDF backing. The first phase would be carried out within five weeks of the Israeli Government's decision. The timing of the subsequent phases, tentatively scheduled to be completed in the spring and summer of 1985, would be decided by Israel. Throughout all the phases, efforts to achieve political arrangements would continue.

On 24 January, at the conference, Lebanon announced that the Israeli redeployment plan did not satisfy its demand for a detailed plan and timetable for complete Israeli withdrawal from Lebanese territory.

The Secretary-General observed that, as a result of increasing confrontation between Israeli forces and Lebanese resistance groups, the situation in southern Lebanon deteriorated. Both the number and the intensity of attacks by resistance groups against the Israeli forces and Lebanese irregulars armed and controlled by IDF increased sharply after IDF started preparing for its evacuation from the Sidon area, which was completed on

16 February. IDF carried out frequent cordon-and-search operations in villages in the UNIFIL area—assembling the men in a village for interrogation and searching houses for weapons and ammunition, sometimes demolishing them if they were thought to serve as shelter for members of resistance groups or if weapons were found in them. From February on, 32 such operations had been carried out and the demolition of 33 houses was recorded. Fourteen bodies were found after such operations, a number of persons were injured, and more than 700 persons were arrested.

On 18 February, the report continued, IDF had imposed restrictions on the movement of civilians, including a curfew, restrictions on the movement of vehicles, a ban on motorcycles, and prohibition of parking along major routes. On 4 March, an explosion in a meeting hall at Ma'rakah (south of the Litani River near Tyre) had killed 12 Lebanese and injured more than 30 (see also p. 298). Since then, villagers had frequently asked UNIFIL to search their houses for explosives following Israeli cordon-and-search operations. UNIFIL had reported that the economy of the area also suffered severely owing to the spreading violence as well as restrictions affecting the movement of people and goods.

In a statement of 27 February (see below), the Secretary-General had referred to the new situation that had developed in southern Lebanon since early February as the result of the restrictions imposed on civilians and the increasing number of attacks on the Israeli forces by Lebanese resistance groups, leading to strong countermeasures, including new cordon-and-search operations reported in the UNIFIL area since 6 February.

The Secretary-General noted in his report that in recent weeks, there had been indications that the Israeli withdrawal programme was being speeded up. His efforts and those of his colleagues had been directed to trying to bring together Israel's and Lebanon's positions. The main problem, he concluded, was to reach a situation in Lebanon south of the Litani after the Israeli withdrawal in which peace and security could be assured and normal conditions progressively restored. The best means of achieving that, the Secretary-General believed, would be an orderly take-over from the Israeli forces, perhaps in the first instance by UNIFIL with elements of the Lebanese army, with the ultimate aim of restoring the complete authority of the Lebanese Government and army. Some form of consultative mechanism under United Nations auspices would be essential. If the Naqoura talks or the 1949 Israel-Lebanon General Armistice Agreement[14] were not acceptable to the parties, for one reason or another, he would be prepared to consider convoking a new conference of military representatives of the two Governments.

Lebanon, in a 27 March 1985 letter,[15] stated its understanding of UNIFIL's role; the whole of southern Lebanon should be under the exclusive authority of the Lebanese army, assisted in its task solely by UNIFIL, since Lebanon would not assign any role to any military force which was not a legal force, nor would it accept buffer zones or security zones of any kind. UNIFIL's deployment area should not become a disengagement zone between illegal armed forces on Lebanese territory and UNIFIL posts would be determined by agreement with the Lebanese Government alone.

Israel had stated, according to the Secretary-General's report, that it had two principal objectives—complete withdrawal of its forces from Lebanon and security for Israel's northern border. Those objectives, it believed, could be achieved either by agreement with the Lebanese authorities or, failing that, by unilateral security arrangements made by Israel.

The second phase of redeployment of IDF, carried out gradually during March and April, was described in the Secretary-General's report covering the period from 12 April to 10 October.[16] The Israeli forces withdrew from the Nabatiyah area on 11 March, while the Jezzine area and north-eastern sector, including the Bekaa valley and the strategic position at Jebal Baruk, were evacuated on 14 April. On 29 April, they withdrew from the Tyre pocket and from positions they had established in the western sector of the UNIFIL area. At the end of the second phase, they were redeployed in a strip of land north of the international border extending from the Mediterranean Sea to the Hasbaiya area with a depth varying between about 2 and 10 kilometres. In accordance with the Israeli plan, that strip of land, which extended into part of the UNIFIL area, was to be maintained as a "security zone" where SLA and other local militias armed and controlled by the Israeli forces were to function after completion of the third and last phase of Israeli redeployment.

After the Security Council in April (**resolution 561(1985)**) asked him to continue consultations, the Secretary-General initiated new efforts through his personal representatives and the Commander of UNIFIL to work out, in consultation with the Lebanese and Israeli authorities, arrangements leading to the full withdrawal of the Israeli forces, the deployment of UNIFIL to the international border and the establishment of peace and security in the area. Those efforts were inconclusive, however, and IDF proceeded with the third phase of its redeployment, without change, in May and early June. During that period, the Israeli forces withdrew progressively from positions in the security zone, handing them over to SLA. By 10 June, Israel announced that the third phase had been completed. It indicated that, while all combat units had been withdrawn from Lebanese territory, some Israeli troops would continue to operate in the security zone for an unspecified period of time and act as advisers to SLA. Part of the security zone overlapped with UNIFIL's area of deployment, which led to frequent and dangerous confrontations between the irregulars and UNIFIL personnel. There were three positions manned by IDF, 16 by SLA and two jointly (SLA withdrew from three positions in July following negotiations with Israel by the UNIFIL Commander). In the remaining part of the security zone, which included the former enclave and the Hasbaiya area, Israeli forces had continued to operate with elements of SLA and other local forces controlled by them.

The situation in the security zone was very tense, the Secretary-General said. Lebanese resistance groups had launched 250 attacks since May on Israeli troops and the Lebanese irregulars associated with them throughout that zone, both within and outside the UNIFIL area of deployment, as well as a number of suicide bomb attacks. IDF and SLA elements carried out a number of cordon-and-search operations against Shiite villages, nine of them in the UNIFIL area, during which 16 houses were demolished and 73 persons arrested. On some occasions, SLA also shelled Shiite villages; following two June attacks, about 2,000 persons sought temporary refuge near Qana where the Fijian battalion of UNIFIL was headquartered. Leaders of Amal—the Shiite organization—and other Lebanese resistance groups had generally cooperated with UNIFIL in the area Israeli forces had evacuated.

The Secretary-General continued his contacts with Israel and Lebanon concerning security arrangements following completion of the Israeli withdrawal and to promote a steady return to normality, pointing out that the security zone manned by SLA assisted by IDF elements contravened Security Council resolutions and violated Lebanon's sovereignty and was certain to give rise to increasing opposition and a new round of violence.

After the Council renewed UNIFIL's mandate for six months in October (**resolution 575(1985)**), the Secretary-General held discussions with the parties concerned, including the Lebanese President and the Prime Minister and Minister of Defence of Israel. In addition, Jean-Claude Aimé, Director in the Office of the Under-Secretaries-General for Special Political Affairs, undertook a mission to the area for discussions with those concerned.

In spite of those efforts, the Secretary-General noted in a December interim report,[17] the positions of the parties remained far apart. Israel announced that it would continue to rely on the security zone to ensure the security of its northern settlements and that UNIFIL would not be allowed

to deploy to the border. Lebanon was strongly opposed to Israel's continuing presence and the concept of the security zone, and insisted that UNIFIL should deploy to the border and fully implement Security Council resolution 425(1978).[13] The situation was not acceptable, the Secretary-General continued, and could well deteriorate; he noted that the leader of Amal had recently stated his intention to step up activities against SLA and Israel if there was no change in the situation by the end of the year.

The situation in and around Beirut, with particular emphasis on developments involving Israeli forces and Palestinians, was monitored by the Observer Group in Beirut, with observers from UNTSO, set up in 1982[18] following the first incursion of Israeli troops into West Beirut. The Secretary-General reported in October 1985[19] that, since the withdrawal of the Israeli forces from the Beirut area in September 1983, the Group's strength had been brought down from 50 to 18.

Communications (January-March). By a letter of 16 January 1985, transmitted by Egypt on 17 January,[20] PLO characterized Israel's plan to withdraw from Lebanon as a unilateral decision that did not take into consideration the 1978 Security Council resolutions on the establishment of UNIFIL[21] or its 1982 resolutions calling for immediate cessation of all military activities in Lebanon[22] and withdrawal of Israeli forces to the internationally recognized boundaries of Lebanon.[23]

On 12 February,[24] Lebanon informed the Secretary-General that that morning the Israeli army had attacked the village of Toura, in UNIFIL's area of operation, surrounding it with more than 90 tanks and military vehicles. Lebanon feared that a massacre could take place. The Israeli army had prevented the International Committee of the Red Cross (ICRC) from entering the village and was preventing all citizens from leaving it. Lebanon considered it necessary to intervene quickly.

On 21 February,[25] Lebanon protested Israeli practices in southern Lebanon, the western Bekaa and the Rashaya district, which it said included a series of raids, arrests, killings and repression that had resulted in many casualties. Recent information from the area indicated that a great number of Israeli soldiers in military vehicles and bulldozers had made their way to the villages of Deir Kanoun and Tair Dibbah, north-east of Tyre. Annexed to the letter was a listing entitled "Report on the abusive practices of Israel in southern Lebanon: 12 to 20 February 1985". On 25 February,[26] Lebanon transmitted two further reports for the periods 21 to 23 February and 23 to 25 February, and, on 26 February,[27] another covering 25 and 26 February.

By a letter of 4 March,[28] Lebanon informed the Secretary-General of what it charged was a massacre perpetrated by over 800 Israeli soldiers in the village of Ma'rakah on 4 March. On 2 March, 350 citizens had been locked up in the village school after being interrogated, Lebanon said; 17 of them were later taken away to an unknown destination. Before leaving the village, the Israeli forces had planted explosives at the mosque and blew it up when as many as 200 villagers gathered there on 4 March; the number of victims had not yet been determined. Israeli forces had prevented ambulances and other emergency vehicles from entering the village; they surrounded the hospital in Jebel Aamel, the village closest to Ma'rakah, and prevented the wounded from being taken inside. Lebanon condemned the act as criminal and reiterated its call for condemnation of Israel's abusive operations and practices and for an immediate end to them.

Israel rejected those charges on 6 March,[29] stating that it had no involvement in the explosion near the mosque and that there were no IDF units in the village at the time of the incident. It appeared that the explosion had taken place when terrorists mishandled the triggering device and caused it to detonate. Also, IDF had not prevented emergency vehicles from entering the hospital; on the contrary, they had cleared a path and assured access by dispersing a violent demonstration in front of it and apprehending some demonstrators who had fled inside. Israel had acted responsibly to prevent further terrorism; IDF had uncovered large caches of weapons and explosives, whose use would have killed many Lebanese civilians in the south as well as Israeli forces. Lebanon not only attacked Israel for defending its own forces as they were leaving the country, but had fallen into the habit of blaming Israel for every outbreak of internal violence, which reflected its inability to enforce law and order.

On 6 March,[30] India transmitted a communiqué adopted that day at an urgent session of the Co-ordinating Bureau of the Movement of Non-Aligned Countries regarding the situation in the Israeli-occupied areas in southern Lebanon, the western Bekaa and the Rashaya district. The Bureau condemned Israel's practices and measures against the civilian population there as a violation of international law, in particular the Geneva Convention relative to the Protection of Civilian Persons in Time of War (fourth Geneva Convention) of 12 August 1949, and demanded that Israel desist from those practices and immediately lift all restrictions and obstacles to the restoration of normal conditions in the areas under its occupation. The Bureau called on the Security Council to ensure Israel's immediate and unconditional withdrawal to the internationally recognized borders.

On 23 March,[31] Lebanon informed the Secretary-General of what it called further inhuman acts of aggression by Israel against the inhabitants of southern Lebanon, citing, among other operations, an incident of 21 March when Israeli forces bombarded two villages and besieged 10 in the district of Zahrani. Israeli forces advanced to within 7 kilometres of Sidon, besieging, on their way, three Lebanese army posts in areas they had previously evacuated, leaving 22 people killed and several wounded and causing material damage. In other towns, they destroyed houses and police posts and took prisoners. Lebanon emphatically condemned those acts of aggression, drawing the Security Council's attention to their gravity and inhuman character. Because the Council was unable to perform its tasks, Israel was tacitly encouraged to pursue its inhuman policy towards the population of the Lebanese territory it occupied.

In a letter of 28 March,[32] the 10 countries contributing troops to UNIFIL (see p. 305) took note of Israel's declaration that it would fully implement the withdrawal of IDF from Lebanese territory. They called for strict observance of the fourth Geneva Convention and deplored all acts of violence in the area.

SECURITY COUNCIL ACTION (February/March)

Following a request from Lebanon dated 25 February,[33] the Security Council considered the situation in southern Lebanon at four meetings on 28 February and 7, 11 and 12 March.

Meeting numbers. SC 2568, 2570, 2572, 2573.

In addition to Israel and Lebanon, the Council invited Afghanistan, Algeria, Bangladesh, Cuba, Cyprus, Czechoslovakia, Democratic Yemen, the German Democratic Republic, Indonesia, Iran, Jordan, Nicaragua, Nigeria, Pakistan, Poland, Qatar, Saudi Arabia, Senegal, the Sudan, the Syrian Arab Republic, the United Arab Emirates, Viet Nam and Yugoslavia, at their request, to participate in the discussion without the right to vote. The Council also invited the Permanent Observer of the League of Arab States, at Qatar's request,[34] to participate under rule 39[e] of its provisional rules of procedure.

At the request of Democratic Yemen,[35] the Council decided on 11 March, by 10 votes to 1 (United States), with 4 abstentions (Australia, Denmark, France, United Kingdom), that an invitation to participate be accorded to PLO. The President stated that the proposal was not made pursuant to rule 37[f] or rule 39 of the provisional rules of procedure, but the invitation would confer on PLO the same rights as those conferred on Member States when invited to participate pursuant to rule 37.

[e]See footnote a on p. 274.
[f]See footnote b on p. 274.

Before the vote, the United States reiterated its opposition (see p. 274) to granting such rights to non-governmental entities.

Denmark said the procedure followed, designed to grant PLO a status similar to that of a Member State, did not reflect PLO's true relationship to the United Nations. In Australia's view, PLO should properly be invited to participate on the same basis as other organizations or bodies which were not States.

On 12 March, the Council voted on a draft resolution by Lebanon.[(36)] The vote was 11 to 1, with 3 abstentions.

> *In favour:* Burkina Faso, China, Egypt, France, India, Madagascar, Peru, Thailand, Trinidad and Tobago, Ukrainian SSR, USSR.
> *Against:* United States.
> *Abstaining:* Australia, Denmark, United Kingdom.

Owing to the negative vote of a permanent member, the draft was not adopted.

By the draft, the Council would have: (1) condemned Israeli practices and measures against the civilian population in southern Lebanon, the western Bekaa and the Rashaya district; (2) reaffirmed the urgent need to implement Council resolutions on Lebanon,[(37)] which demanded that Israel withdraw all its military forces unconditionally to the internationally recognized boundaries; (3) reiterated its call for strict respect for Lebanon's sovereignty, independence, unity and territorial integrity; (4) affirmed that the provisions of the fourth Geneva Convention applied to the Israeli-occupied territories in southern Lebanon, the western Bekaa and the Rashaya district, and that the occupying Power was duty-bound to respect and uphold those provisions and other norms of international law; (5) demanded that Israel as the occupying Power desist from its practices against the civilian population in those territories and immediately lift all restrictions and obstacles to the restoration of normal conditions in the area under its occupation; (6) requested the Secretary-General to establish a fact-finding mission to report to the Council on Israel's practices and measures there; and (7) asked him to keep the situation under review, to consult with the Lebanese Government and to report to the Council.

The United States said the text was unbalanced, applied double standards and did not accord Israel fair treatment. It would have preferred a consensus resolution committing the Council to a sincere effort to deal with Lebanon's problems while respecting the rights of all United Nations Members; it was ready to join in a statement reflecting the Council's dismay at the escalation of violence in the country, expressing sympathy to the victims, urging restraint on all parties, affirming the application of the fourth Geneva Convention to the occupied areas, and reaffirming the commitment of all Members to full restoration of Lebanon's sovereignty, independence, territorial integrity and unity. The United States supported the withdrawal of all foreign troops from Lebanon and the enjoyment of full sovereignty by Lebanon, but did not currently believe that a Council resolution was the best way of achieving the common objective of confirming the Lebanese Government's authority.

Despite the draft's positive aspects, such as paragraphs 2 to 4 and 7, the United Kingdom believed that the text took insufficient account of the need to dampen the cycle of violence and to promote the peaceful diplomatic solution so urgently needed. In particular, there was no mention of the role of UNIFIL or of the need to assist the Secretary-General's efforts in pursuance of Council resolution 555(1984)[(10)] and encourage the immediate return to the Naqoura talks.

Israel said adoption of the text would not stop it from defending its citizens against terrorist attacks, but would encourage the forces of fanaticism and extremism in southern Lebanon.

Lebanon said if some Council members had been true to themselves, they would have condemned the arbitrary and inhumane practices of the occupying army, which were inevitable results of the Israeli invasion they had condemned. By failing to meet its obligations, the Council left the population of Beirut, the Rashaya district and western Bekaa victims of that army and encouraged Israel to proceed with its brutal policies and defiance of the Council. However, that stand would not affect Lebanon's insistence on liberating the parts of the country occupied by Israel.

Trinidad and Tobago, noting that Israel had approved the second phase of its withdrawal, expressed concern over reports of increased violence accompanying that withdrawal. It would have liked to see incorporated in the text an appeal to all parties to exercise restraint and refrain from violence during the withdrawal, as well as an appeal to demonstrate some mutual forbearance. It believed that Israel and Lebanon could usefully engage in consultations aimed at ensuring a peaceful withdrawal—consultations which might also yield insights into requirements for maintaining law and order in the evacuated areas and indicate possibilities for an enhanced role for United Nations peace-keeping operations.

Thailand regretted that the text did not refer to the initiatives of the Secretary-General and his representative, as well as their good offices to have the Naqoura talks resumed, and noted with regret the absence of a reference to UNIFIL. In paragraph 1, all practices and measures against the civilian population which violated international law and the fourth Geneva Convention should have been condemned.

Peru believed that if there had been a specific reference to the objective of finding the minimal machinery to stabilize and systematize the withdrawal of the occupying forces, the text would have been less narrow. Also, it felt that condemnations should be in keeping with facts that were suitably corroborated at the international level.

Algeria, Democratic Yemen, India and the Syrian Arab Republic fully supported Lebanon's demand as outlined in the draft resolution. India said the Council must act decisively to halt Israeli aggression and intransigence and to put an end to the tragedy of Lebanon. Democratic Yemen said the Council would thereby affirm the credibility of its resolutions and its responsibility for the maintenance of international peace and security.

Cyprus said adoption of the draft would demonstrate a clear determination by the international community to ensure respect for Lebanon's sovereignty, independence, territorial integrity and unity and profound solidarity with and sympathy for its much-tormented people.

Saudi Arabia felt that a draft reinforcing the Council's 1982 resolutions on Lebanon represented the minimum the Council could adopt to keep its credibility. Senegal believed that the draft contained all elements to restore peace to Lebanon and enable it to regain its independence and territorial integrity. Pakistan said the least the Council could do was to remind Israel of its demand for immediate and unconditional withdrawal and strict compliance with the 1949 Geneva Conventions; adoption of the text would serve that purpose and send a clear message.

Speaking as Chairman of the Arab Group, Qatar said the Council should reaffirm its 1982 resolutions calling for respect for the rights of the civilian population and an end to acts of violence against them;[38] Israel must be compelled to commit itself to respect the Charter, the Universal Declaration of Human Rights[39] and other international agreements, especially the fourth Geneva Convention. The Council's resolution must include provisions ending Israel's determination to disregard Council resolutions.

Iran said the draft contained two very important points: condemnation of the Zionist aggressor for its recent crimes and its illegal occupation of Lebanese territory; and immediate and unconditional withdrawal of Israeli forces from all the occupied territories.

Czechoslovakia and the Syrian Arab Republic called on the United States not to stand in opposition to the other Council members and all peace-loving forces. Obstruction of the draft resolution would not protect Israel from rising resistance to its occupation, Pakistan cautioned, but would only deal a blow to the current peace effort.

Opening the debate, Lebanon charged that Israel's military operations and inhuman practices in the areas under its occupation were daily becoming more severe; if Israel had committed itself to comply with the Council's resolutions, the situation would not have deteriorated to such an extent. The third stage of redeployment, in accordance with the decision of the Israeli Government, did not constitute a true withdrawal as long as it set out a security belt in which Israel arrogated to itself the right to maintain nominal forces and re-enter any region from which it had withdrawn. Lebanon declared it had sincerely attempted to bring about a successful outcome to the Naqoura talks; however, despite repeated demands for a detailed timetable for withdrawal, Israel refused to present one or to give any role to the legitimate Lebanese army.

Israel stated that it had agreed to meet at Naqoura to negotiate security arrangements which, among other things, would facilitate its withdrawal, but Lebanon, under Syrian pressure, refused. After that last Lebanese abrogation of responsibility, Israel had chosen to act on its own. It had decided to withdraw its forces in three phases to the international border; now, entering the second phase, it was seeking the widest co-operation to complete it in as orderly and peaceful a manner as possible. The Lebanese Government had not agreed to arrange an orderly transfer of authority as a way of minimizing violence in the areas evacuated by Israel; after unusual restraint in the face of countless provocations during its withdrawal, Israel had taken action necessary to protect its soldiers and prevent terrorists from attacking them and organizing a safe haven for future attacks. The withdrawal was expected to take from six to nine months; specifying a more exact timetable was not practical, since conditions changed with each phase and terrorist attacks might require modifications in timing and procedures.

There was almost unanimous agreement among the countries speaking in the Council that Israel's practices and measures against the civilian population in Lebanon violated international law, in particular the fourth Geneva Convention. Like all States that signed the Convention, France said, Israel must scrupulously implement its provisions. Implementation of Council resolutions on Lebanon—especially those[37] mentioned in paragraph 2 of the Lebanese draft, calling for a cessation of all military activity and demanding Israel's unconditional withdrawal to the internationally recognized boundaries—was seen by most as necessary and a pre-condition for normalization of the situation. Poland and the USSR, for example, saw in the immediate and unconditional implementation of the 1982 resolutions the only reliable key to a solution of the Lebanese problem.

The United Arab Emirates believed that the current situation in southern Lebanon was a direct result of their non-implementation. Others, including Algeria, Bangladesh, Egypt, Indonesia, Jordan, Madagascar, Nicaragua and Nigeria, specifically mentioned in this respect the 1978 resolution[13] establishing UNIFIL, which called for strict respect for Lebanon's territorial integrity, sovereignty and independence.

Egypt regarded as the only option Israel's complete and unconditional withdrawal, in order to enable Lebanon to regain true sovereignty over all its territory, protect its population and restore security and order. China said that under no pretext should Israel continue its occupation, pursue its "iron-fist" policy and bully the local inhabitants. In Yugoslavia's opinion, any other approach but Israel's immediate and unconditional withdrawal undermined the basis of international peace and security envisaged in the Charter. Australia observed that it had consistently called for withdrawal of all foreign forces, except those in Lebanon at the Government's request.

Many other speakers viewed Israel's practices as a threat not only to Lebanon but to the Middle East as a whole, endangering even international peace and security. Among them were Czechoslovakia and Qatar on behalf of the Arab Group. The escalation of Israel's aggression, Cuba said, greatly increased the danger that another war would break out in the region. Considering the Lebanese problem in isolation from the general explosive situation in the region was impossible, according to Bangladesh, the German Democratic Republic, India, Senegal and the Ukrainian SSR. Viet Nam added that the problems in Lebanon could be solved only through a comprehensive Middle East settlement which guaranteed Palestinian rights and respect for the legitimate interests of all countries in the region, including an independent State of Palestine.

The increase in violence in Lebanon made it necessary to ensure that there was a new movement towards peace, said Senegal, which also noted recent diplomatic developments that could make such a movement possible.

The necessity to resume the Naqoura talks was widely recognized. To find practical ways to implement the second and third stages of Israel's withdrawal, the United States urged that both countries return to Naqoura; the violence accompanying the withdrawal and the counter-reaction to it only worked against Lebanon's interest. Burkina Faso said resumption of the talks, under the Secretary-General's auspices, had become necessary. Thailand joined in the appeal for their resumption as soon as possible, hoping for an agreement to enable Israel to withdraw unimpeded, with an expeditious timetable; while

the withdrawal was under way, the civilian population and refugees must be spared from repressive measures. Denmark urged Lebanon and Israel to show flexibility in establishing security arrangements in southern Lebanon. For Peru, it was a matter of greatest priority to make use of the machinery existing for a dialogue between the parties and to work for the speedy resumption of contacts.

A clearly spelt-out timetable had become absolutely necessary for the success of resumed talks, the representative of the League of Arab States said. Israel's refusal to provide a time-frame for its withdrawal to the international borders and its practices against the people in the area were proof that it wanted them to leave their lands so that it might usurp those territories, the Syrian Arab Republic charged. Israel's actions were genocidal and an alarming indication that it was planning to perpetuate its control and create a "buffer State", as originally envisaged in its plans for the 1982 invasion of Lebanon, Cuba stated.

Measures to compel Israel to comply with the Council's resolutions and completely withdraw from Lebanon were called for by many speakers. Among them, the Sudan said it was incumbent on the Council to live up to its duties enshrined in the Charter and to put an end to Israel's persistent aggressive practices. In the search for suitable measures, Czechoslovakia believed, each Council member must be guided by the fact that Israel was an aggressor in the terms of the 1974 Definition of Aggression.[40] The Syrian Arab Republic called on the Council to take measures to eliminate acts of aggression against Lebanese territory and restore it to its rightful owners.

Communications (April/May). By a letter of 4 April,[41] Lebanon informed the Secretary-General that on 3 April Israel had transferred 1,131 Lebanese and Palestinian prisoners from the Al-Ansar detention camp in Israeli-occupied Lebanese territory to some prisons inside Israel, in violation of the fourth Geneva Convention. At the same time, Israel had released 752 prisoners to palliate the reaction of international public opinion, which was unanimous in condemning the transfer. Information from ICRC indicated, it said, that Israel intended to retransfer the prisoners to a detention camp within Lebanon's borders and inside the security zone. Lebanon vehemently condemned Israel's action, saying that it violated international law and custom and endangered the lives and future of the prisoners; it was incumbent on the international community to bring Israel's persistent violations to an immediate halt.

In its reply of 17 April 1985,[42] Israel said Lebanon had totally misrepresented the truth concerning the transfer. The 752 detainees had been released because they no longer represented a danger to IDF units currently withdrawing from south Lebanon. The temporary transfer to Israel of detainees who still constituted a danger to the security of IDF had become imperative because of the particular circumstances in south Lebanon. That such a temporary transfer violated the fourth Geneva Convention was equally groundless, since the Convention authorized such measures when for material reasons it was impossible to avoid such displacement. Keeping the detainees at Ansar would have complicated and prolonged Israel's ongoing withdrawal; releasing them would have added to the instability and bloodshed and the likelihood of attacks against IDF; and building alternative detention facilities in the area being evacuated had not been possible in the time-frame of the ongoing withdrawal. Efforts were being made to establish a smaller facility at Majidiyah, in south Lebanon, to hold some of the detainees pending withdrawal from the area. The detainees temporarily transferred to Israel were given suitable facilities and medical care, access to ICRC representatives and entitlement to petition an Appeals Board. Several had already been released.

On 12 April[43] and 16 April,[44] the United Arab Emirates, as Chairman of the Group of Arab States, transmitted three letters from PLO, dated 10, 11 and 15 April, charging Israeli occupation forces and their allies with heavy bombing on 10 April of the city and area of Tyre, including three Palestinian refugee camps. Israeli tanks and armoured vehicles had supported what PLO called Fascist isolationist elements in the assaults; hundreds of civilians, including Palestinians, had been arrested and taken to Israel. For the twelfth consecutive day, Israeli occupation forces and their allies had shelled two Palestinian refugee camps; four children and three men had been killed that day and 15 others had been seriously injured. Daily life in Tyre had been brought to a standstill by an endless artillery barrage. PLO believed the objective was to impose a military siege by land and sea against the Palestinian refugee camps at Sidon and Tyre to uproot the Palestinians as a pre-condition for the success of Israel's plan to establish a so-called safe-border zone—the fulfilment of its aspiration to establish a sectarian, Fascist mini-State in south Lebanon. On 11 April, PLO said, Israeli troops in south Lebanon and their allies had resumed heavy artillery bombardment of Palestinian refugee camps in the Sidon area. On 15 April, it said that, for the past few days, Israeli occupation forces in the Tyre area had besieged four Palestinian refugee camps and had conducted house-to-house searches, arresting 270 Palestinian civilians and taking them to unknown destinations. PLO deemed it clear that the Israeli occupation forces were hoping through terror and panic to facilitate the mass exodus of Palestinians from the Tyre area, as they had attempted in the Sidon area. Israel's strategy aimed at emptying southern Lebanon of all Palestinian presence. PLO reiterated its call on the United Nations for adequate measures to end Israel's crimes immediately and provide protection for the Palestinians in southern Lebanon.

On 3 May,[45] Italy transmitted a declaration adopted on 29 April by the Ministers for Foreign Affairs of the 10 EC member States, stating that they continued to view with concern the deterioration of the situation in Lebanon, in particular the consequences for the civilians in the south subjected to unjustifiable acts of violence. They looked for the early, orderly and complete withdrawal of Israeli and other forces which were not in Lebanon at the Government's request. They considered it important that appropriate security arrangements be reached between Israel and Lebanon, and appealed to all the parties to facilitate the restoration of Lebanon's sovereignty, unity, territorial integrity and independence. They expressed deep concern for the suffering of the Lebanese and the kidnapping of foreign nationals, and called on all parties to co-operate fully with UNIFIL.

On 8 May,[46] the Secretary-General submitted to the Security Council a 7 May letter by Pope John Paul II warning that the ever more tragic events in Lebanon could become fatal for the survival of the country, and that a widening gap between the different communities— Christians and Moslems—could lead to a disappearance of all national identity. The Pope was confident that the United Nations would do everything in its power to co-ordinate the initiatives that such a complex crisis demanded; it was a particularly suitable forum for appealing to all nations not to abandon Lebanon and to help its people lay the foundations of a dialogue aimed at building a renewed country.

On 14 May,[47] Australia transmitted an 8 May statement by its Prime Minister expressing concern at the continued violence in Lebanon, particularly in Beirut, and at the recent events in the southern part of the country where as many as 20,000 Christians were reported to have sought refuge in Jezzine and other towns in the area. The Prime Minister lamented that Lebanon should have become the battleground on which foreign forces conducted their battles openly or by proxy. Australia called for maximum restraint by all parties and for an end to all external interference in the country's affairs; agreement among the warring factions was the only basis on which Lebanon's independence and sovereignty would be respected.

SECURITY COUNCIL ACTION (May)

On 24 May, after consultations with the Council members, the Security Council President issued the following statement on their behalf:[48]

"The members of the Security Council express their serious concern at the heightened violence in certain parts of Lebanon in the past few days.

"They take note of and fully support the statement issued on 22 May 1985 by the Secretary-General, which also refers to the situation in and around the Palestinian refugee camps, and his appeal to all concerned to make every possible effort to put an end to violence involving the civilian population.

"They reaffirm that the sovereignty, independence and territorial integrity of Lebanon must be respected.

"In response to their humanitarian concern, they strongly appeal for restraint, in order to alleviate the sufferings of civilians in Lebanon."

Following Egypt's request of 30 May,[49] the Council met on 31 May to consider the situation created by the continued escalation of violence involving the civilian population in and around Beirut, affecting the safety and security of the Palestinians in the refugee camps.

The Council invited Lebanon, Malta and the Syrian Arab Republic, at their request, to participate in the discussion without the right to vote. It also decided, by 10 votes to 1 (United States), with 4 abstentions (Australia, Denmark, France, United Kingdom), that an invitation should be accorded to PLO.

The President stated that an Egyptian proposal to invite PLO[50] was not made pursuant to rule 37[g] or rule 39[h] of the Council's provisional rules of procedure, but the invitation would confer on PLO the same rights as those conferred on Member States when invited to participate pursuant to rule 37.

Before the vote, the United States reiterated its position of principle (see p. 274) opposing granting such rights to non-governmental entities.

On 31 May, without prior debate, the Council unanimously adopted **resolution 564(1985)**.

The Security Council,

Recalling the statement made by the President on 24 May 1985 on behalf of the members of the Council on the heightened violence in certain parts of Lebanon,

Alarmed at the continued escalation of violence involving the civilian population, including Palestinians in refugee camps, resulting in grievous casualties and material destruction on all sides,

1. *Expresses anew* its deepest concern at the heavy costs in human lives and material destruction affecting the civilian population in Lebanon, and calls on all concerned to end acts of violence against the civilian population in Lebanon and, in particular, in and around Palestinian refugee camps;

2. *Reiterates* its calls for respect for the sovereignty, independence and territorial integrity of Lebanon;

3. *Calls upon* all parties to take necessary measures to alleviate the suffering resulting from acts of violence, in particular by facilitating the work of United Nations agencies, especially the United Nations Relief and Works Agency for Palestine Refugees in the Near East, and non-governmental organizations, including the Inter-national Committee of the Red Cross, in providing humanitarian assistance to all those affected and emphasizes the need to ensure the safety of all the personnel of these organizations;

4. *Appeals* to all interested parties to co-operate with the Lebanese Government and the Secretary-General with a view to ensuring the implementation of this resolution, and requests the Secretary-General to report to the Security Council thereon;

5. *Reaffirms* its intention to continue to follow the situation closely.

Security Council resolution 564(1985)

31 May 1985   Meeting 2582   Adopted unanimously

Draft prepared in consultations among Council members (S/17232).

Egypt said the United Nations bore a clear historical responsibility for the safety and welfare of the Palestinians; there was a need to look for practical means to ensure their protection, security, tranquillity and welfare in the context of full sovereignty of Lebanon. The unanimous adoption of the resolution was evidence of the continued United Nations commitment to the search for a comprehensive and just Middle East settlement, in all its political and humanitarian aspects.

Lebanon opposed the Council's meeting without its consent and on what it considered interference in its internal affairs; the Palestinian camps were on its territory and it could not agree to give up its sovereignty over a single inch. The convening of the Council was a dangerous precedent that could at any time affect any State in whose territory conflicts between local groups took place; the Council's mandate was confined to situations threatening international peace and security and it was not useful for it to consider internal situations that were dealt with on both the regional and internal levels.

Though expressing understanding of Lebanon's concerns, France said the international community had, for humanitarian reasons, a particular responsibility in the light of the human tragedies stemming from the conflict; the victims were again piling up inside and around the Sabra and Shatila camps in Beirut which had been the scene of massacres in 1982.[51] The resolution attested to the determination of the Council and its concern fully to assume its responsibilities.

Proceeding from humanitarian concerns, the USSR stated that it regretted that Lebanon's position was not taken into account by the initiators of the meeting. The situation in Lebanon was an integral part and a direct result of Israeli occupation and the continuing Middle East conflict. Events in Lebanon once again confirmed the urgent need to attain a just and comprehensive Middle East settlement in the context of which the

[g]See footnote b on p. 274.
[h]See footnote a on p. 274.

Palestinians would be able to exercise their right to self-determination and establish their own State.

In the opinion of the Syrian Arab Republic, the resolution would not help Lebanon. Instead of maintaining its sovereignty and independence, it would do exactly the opposite and might even lead to an escalation of the fighting in the camps. The Council's consideration of an internal Lebanese question was interference in its affairs and, in the light of Lebanon's objection, in direct contravention of the Charter. Egypt's move to internationalize an internal problem was aimed at thwarting Syrian-Lebanese efforts to restore peace and security and was motivated by a desire to divert attention from surrender agreements imposed by Washington, from Israeli practices in the occupied territories and from the fact that Israel was trying to perpetuate its occupation.

Malta appealed to all to desist from further fighting and hoped that reconciliation would follow. It pledged to assist in any humanitarian way and to continue working to convince all concerned that an overdue solution could be delayed only at the expense of the chances for a lasting Middle East peace.

The urgency of the situation in Beirut demanded no less of the Council than unanimous adoption of the resolution, the United States said; it hoped the Council's humanitarian calls would be heeded as well as its call to honour Lebanon's sovereignty, independence and territorial integrity.

What was happening in Beirut was not strictly a domestic issue, but affected the fate of Palestinian refugees whose safety and welfare were a historic responsibility of the United Nations, PLO said. The vindictive bombardment had the clear aim of eliminating the Palestinian presence in the Beirut area and probably the rest of Lebanon. Expressing appreciation at the adoption of the resolution, PLO added that the immediate task was to rebuild the destroyed houses and buildings; it appealed to the Council members to authorize immediate action to provide shelter for the refugees. The Lebanese Government and PLO could reach an agreement, as they had in the past; the current main concern was the security and safety of the inhabitants, including those in the camps.

Australia believed that the meeting was an appropriate response to the sombre situation in Lebanon which had caused widespread loss of life and property. It hoped that the Council resolution would be respected and adhered to and would contribute to strengthening Lebanon's hand in dealing with its difficulties.

Communications (June-December). By a letter of 1 July,[52] Israel again rejected the assertion that the transfer of detainees from southern Lebanon to Israel in April (see p. 301) violated the fourth Geneva Convention; their detention as well

as their displacement, which had been necessary because they had participated in acts of violence against IDF, were permitted under the Convention's articles 78 and 49, respectively. Since the transfer, several hundred detainees had been released and those remaining would be released as soon as the conditions in southern Lebanon enabled IDF to do so.

On 5 July,[53] Lebanon transmitted to the Secretary-General a government note concerning a United States announcement on 2 July that it had decided to take measures to isolate Beirut International Airport, to call on foreign airlines to suspend their flights to Beirut, to prevent Lebanese aircraft from using American airports and to urge other States to take similar measures; the United States Government had justified this action on grounds that it represented a response to the recent hijacking of a Trans World Airlines (TWA) aircraft. Lebanon regretted that course of action as a step that would have negative consequences for both countries and that might further complicate matters. The following should be taken into consideration, Lebanon said: the hijacking was only another manifestation of ongoing conflicts in Lebanese territory; for more than 10 years, the Lebanese had been subjected to suffering and hardship which in ferocity and impact went far beyond the seizure of an aircraft or the kidnapping of passengers. Though condemning interference with civil aircraft and the kidnapping of innocent people, Lebanon nevertheless considered that the TWA hijacking had political roots and underpinnings and was not merely a criminal or terrorist act. The most successful way of confronting such acts lay in understanding those roots and dealing with them on that basis. The hijackers' demands stemmed from positions which were part of Lebanese and Middle East political reality; the demand for release of Lebanese civilians detained by Israel without legal cause was a legitimate demand. Isolating Lebanon and preventing its national airlines from operating normally was not proportionate to the damage caused and punished not the perpetrators but a Government that had condemned the hijacking and a people and companies that had not been involved; the kidnapping and the introduction of weapons into the aircraft had not taken place at Beirut airport, and the aircraft landed there in spite of the opposition of the Lebanese authorities. Lebanon stated that it was making efforts to control the security at the airport and was prepared to take part in any international initiative aimed at combating acts contrary to international law. It also considered violation of that law by States to be more serious than by irregular groups. It requested the international community to bolster Lebanon's sovereignty and not to support decisions adverse to it. It reserved the right, if necessary, to call for a Security Council meeting.

In a letter of 24 July,[54] the United States said Lebanon's note revealed a serious misunderstanding of United States policies and goals. The aim in bringing the problem to the attention of the world community was not to punish Lebanon. Beirut International Airport had become a haven for hijackers. In 1985 alone, there had been six hijackings involving that airport; in the past 15 years, 36. Nowhere else had air pirates enjoyed such a permissive atmosphere, moving with total freedom to and from hijacked aircraft that landed there. Though encouraged by actions recently announced by Lebanon to meet those deficiencies, the necessary measures went beyond those announced to date. Although Lebanon was party to international conventions setting standards of behaviour towards hijackings, it had not demonstrated that it could enforce its commitments. The United States initiative should be understood as a first step in the corrective process.

The Chairman of the Committee on Palestinian rights, by a letter of 31 July,[55] brought to the Secretary-General's attention newspaper reports that tanks had been delivered that might affect the rights and lives of the Palestinian refugees living in Lebanon and amplify tension in the area. Lebanon, on 9 August,[56] stated that the subject dealt with in the Chairman's letter was entirely outside the Committee's competence.

On 5 December,[57] Lebanon transmitted what it said was a list of Israeli acts of aggression against Lebanese territory since the withdrawal of Israeli forces from Sidon to south of the Litani River, as well as supplementary information on such acts in southern Lebanon between 28 November and 4 December. Lebanon said Israel's expansionist policy and continual arbitrary practices were contributing to the worsening of the situation in southern Lebanon in particular, were hampering peace efforts and were the cause of an explosion of violence which threatened peace and security regionally and internationally.

Israel, on 26 December,[58] characterized Lebanon's letter as yet another attempt to divert attention from its inability to enforce law and order. It appeared that the fate of the country—which was controlled by the Syrian Arab Republic—was of concern to the Lebanese Government only when southern Lebanon was involved. Israel's activity along the border was carried out entirely in self-defence, it said; its only aim was to guarantee the safety and welfare of its citizens living in northern Israel and it would continue to defend its people. Since June 1985, 790 attacks and attempted attacks had been carried out by terrorist elements in Lebanon against targets in southern Lebanon and Israel. One day's violence in the streets of Beirut or Tripoli

accounted for a considerably higher number of casualties than the total casualties from incidents in the border area since then. Unlike the civilians in Beirut or Tripoli, the people of southern Lebanon lived under normal conditions, free from the endless cycle of violence that was destroying the rest of the country. Israel had consistently attempted to guarantee peace and security to its citizens through mutual arrangements with Lebanon. In November 1985, another attempt had been made to renew contacts through a special emissary of the Secretary-General; Lebanon, initially showing interest, had retracted again under Syrian pressure. Israel continued to be willing to negotiate with any Lebanese element that could guarantee suitable security arrangements for northern Israel.

By a letter of 26 December,[59] the Syrian Arab Republic stated that overflight of Lebanese territory by Israeli fighter aircraft was not only a violation of the sovereignty of a fraternal United Nations Member but also a direct threat to the Syrian forces in Lebanon at its request and in accordance with a decision of the League of Arab States. Any threat to the security of the Syrian forces in Lebanon also constituted a threat to the security of the Syrian Arab Republic (see also p. 313).

Other action. Both the Commission on Human Rights and the Economic and Social Council asked the Secretary-General to monitor the human rights situation in southern Lebanon (see ECONOMIC AND SOCIAL QUESTIONS, Chapter XVIII).

Peace-keeping operation

In 1985, the Security Council twice extended the mandate of UNIFIL, on 17 April and 17 October, each time for six months. The Force, which was deployed in southern Lebanon, was established by the Council in 1978.[13] Its terms of reference were to confirm the withdrawal of the Israeli forces as called for by the Council, to restore international peace and security, and to assist the Lebanese Government in ensuring the return of its effective authority in the area.

The authorized strength of UNIFIL was 7,000, but because of its reduced activities it had in October 1985 some 5,700 troops, provided by Fiji, Finland, France, Ghana, Ireland, Italy, Nepal, the Netherlands, Norway and Sweden. A group of UNTSO observers assisted the Force in the performance of its tasks.

Communications. By a letter of 27 March 1985,[60] Lebanon requested the Security Council to extend UNIFIL's mandate, due to expire on 19 April, for another six months, without a change of its mandate as laid down by Council resolutions. In Lebanon's understanding, UNIFIL's area of deployment extended from the Litani River southward to the internationally recognized boundaries of Lebanon; that area should be under the exclusive authority of the Lebanese army, assisted solely by UNIFIL. In no circumstance would Lebanon accept "buffer zones" or "security cordons" of any kind inside its territory; the area of deployment of UNIFIL should not become a disengagement zone between illegal armed forces within Lebanese territory, and the posts which the United Nations forces were to occupy would be determined by agreement with the Lebanese Government alone. In spite of the difficult conditions in south Lebanon, Lebanon added, UNIFIL's presence continued to be a necessary and important factor of stability and an international commitment to upholding Lebanon's independence, sovereignty and territorial integrity.

On 29 March,[32] the Secretary-General transmitted to the Security Council President a letter of the previous day from the 10 troop-contributing countries, expressing deep concern at the recent events in southern Lebanon which, they said, not only had made it more difficult for UNIFIL to fulfil its mandate but also posed serious security risks to its members. For more than two years, they added, UNIFIL had carried out interim tasks entrusted to it following the 1982 Israeli invasion of Lebanon,[61] when the Force had been unable to carry out its original mandate. In spite of the difficulties under which UNIFIL operated, the troop contributors were convinced that it had had a stabilizing effect on the situation in southern Lebanon and had played a useful humanitarian role.

Recalling the Force's original mandate, approved by the Council in 1978,[62] which spoke of three essential conditions[63] that must be met for UNIFIL to be effective, the troop contributors considered it incumbent on the Council to insist that all parties respect the Force's integrity, and stressed that UNIFIL could hope to fulfil its mandate only on the basis of an understanding between the parties on the role of the Force in an area that formed an uninterrupted whole up to the international boundary.

The troop-contributing countries urgently called on Israel and Lebanon to meet the requirements necessary to ensure security in the area in the wake of a full Israeli withdrawal and continued to support the Secretary-General's efforts to that end. They indicated their willingness to continue to support UNIFIL on the basis of their expectation that events in the near future would allow UNIFIL to play its originally envisaged role.

Report of the Secretary-General (April). On 11 April,[11] the Secretary-General reported on the activities of UNIFIL since 10 October 1984 (see also p. 295). During that period, it had continued to operate check-points and conduct patrols with a view to maintaining order and ensuring the security of the local population. The deteriorating situation in Lebanon was reflected also in the UNIFIL area of deployment, where attacks were carried out almost daily against IDF fixed positions. Roadside bombs and car-bomb attacks had inflicted heavy casualties on IDF. The activities by the Lebanese resistance against the Israeli forces and Israeli countermeasures had created a difficult situation for UNIFIL.

UNIFIL closely monitored the movements of IDF within its area, the Secretary-General reported. During the cordon-and-search operations carried out by IDF in villages in the UNIFIL area, it was present to prevent, within its means, acts of violence against the population and the destruction of property. The Force also continued its efforts to contain the activities of Lebanese irregulars armed and controlled by IDF. There had been a number of incidents in which such irregulars fired close to UNIFIL positions, and in a few cases fire was returned; there had also been a few incidents, protested to the Israeli authorities, in which Israeli troops fired close to UNIFIL personnel.

During the period under review, UNIFIL had maintained contact with the Lebanese Government, Lebanese regional authorities and Israeli authorities. It co-operated with the Lebanese authorities, UNRWA, UNICEF and ICRC in assisting the local population. A number of Lebanese civilians were treated in UNIFIL medical centres.

In a statement of 27 February on the role of the Force, the Secretary-General had said that, owing to the restrictions imposed on the civilians in southern Lebanon by the Israeli occupation, the increasing number of attacks on Israeli forces and strong Israeli countermeasures, UNIFIL's position was becoming increasingly difficult. For obvious reasons, UNIFIL had no right to impede Lebanese acts of resistance, nor did it have the mandate or means to prevent countermeasures. To withdraw UNIFIL would not be in the interest of Lebanon, while to involve it actively in the current violence would further complicate an already difficult situation. It seemed that the only course for UNIFIL was to maintain its presence and continue within its limited means to carry out its functions, while efforts continued to put an end to the current difficulties.

Following Israel's announcement in January that it intended to withdraw from Lebanon in three phases, the report continued, the Secretary-General's representatives had held extensive discussions with the Lebanese Government, which, however, had not agreed to any role for UNIFIL in the Israeli withdrawal process north of the Litani River. Brian Urquhart, Under-Secretary-General for Special Political Affairs, visited the area and discussed matters relating to UNIFIL's future; he also visited Lebanon and Israel in April, as well as the Syrian Arab

Republic. During the consultations, he stressed the importance of securing a speedy, orderly and complete withdrawal of Israeli forces, of the establishment of peace and security in southern Lebanon, and of a proper context and basis for the future functioning of UNIFIL. The best means of achieving such conditions after Israel's withdrawal would be, in the Secretary-General's opinion, an orderly take-over from the Israeli forces, perhaps in the first instance by UNIFIL with elements of the Lebanese army, with the ultimate aim of restoring the complete authority of the Lebanese Government and army.

It was essential to establish, under the authority of the Security Council, conditions in which UNIFIL could function effectively in co-operation with the Lebanese authorities and army. There had to be a clear understanding that no armed military or paramilitary personnel of any kind could be allowed to operate in the area, other than the Lebanese army and UNIFIL, and that all parties and elements publicly declare their co-operation with the Lebanese authorities and UNIFIL.

The Secretary-General believed that the presence of UNIFIL was essential in the current circumstances and recommended an extension taking into account Lebanon's request;[60] he stressed again that it was essential to secure at least the minimum conditions for the Force's effective future work.

SECURITY COUNCIL ACTION (April)

The Security Council met on 17 April to consider Lebanon's request and the Secretary-General's report. The Council invited Israel and Lebanon, at their request, to participate in the discussion without the right to vote.

On the same date, the Council adopted **resolution 561(1985)**.

The Security Council,

Recalling its resolutions 425(1978), 426(1978), 501(1982), 508(1982), 509(1982) and 520(1982), as well as all its resolutions on the situation in Lebanon,

Having studied the report of the Secretary-General on the United Nations Interim Force in Lebanon of 11 April 1985, and taking note of the observations expressed therein,

Taking note of the letter of the Permanent Representative of Lebanon addressed to the Secretary-General of 27 March 1985,

Responding to the request of the Government of Lebanon,

1. *Decides* to extend the present mandate of the United Nations Interim Force in Lebanon for a further interim period of six months, that is, until 19 October 1985;

2. *Reiterates* its strong support for the territorial integrity, sovereignty and independence of Lebanon within its internationally recognized boundaries;

3. *Re-emphasizes* the terms of reference and general guidelines of the Force as stated in the report of the Secretary-General of 19 March 1978, approved by resolution 426(1978), and calls upon all parties concerned to co-operate fully with the Force for the full implementation of its mandate;

4. *Reiterates* that the Force should fully implement its mandate as defined in resolutions 425(1978), 426(1978) and all other relevant resolutions;

5. *Requests* the Secretary-General to continue consultations with the Government of Lebanon and other parties directly concerned on the implementation of the present resolution and to report to the Council thereon.

Security Council resolution 561(1985)

| 17 April 1985 | Meeting 2575 | 13-0-2 |

Draft prepared in consultations among Council members (S/17100).

Vote in Council as follows:

In favour: Australia, Burkina Faso, China, Denmark, Egypt, France, India, Madagascar, Peru, Thailand, Trinidad and Tobago, United Kingdom, United States.

Against: None.

Abstaining: Ukrainian SSR, USSR.

The USSR emphasized that it was the Council's duty to ensure respect for UNIFIL; it would be desirable for the Secretary-General to continue his practice of informing the Council of any instances when the forces could not perform their functions. Though not objecting to the renewal of UNIFIL's mandate, in the light of Lebanon's request, the USSR reiterated its fundamental position with regard to the Force, including the method of its financing.

Australia declared itself to be a strong supporter of the United Nations peace-keeping role. It recognized the dangers and difficulties under which UNIFIL operated, and hoped that the parties involved could create the conditions necessary for the Force's effective operation. Australia would support new consultations between the two parties to consider UNIFIL's future role as Israel withdrew from southern Lebanon, and hoped that they would agree to such discussions.

Denmark believed that UNIFIL should be assigned important tasks during the take-over from the Israeli forces, with the ultimate aim of restoring the Lebanese Government's and army's complete authority, taking into account the security interests of all parties, and thus finally allowing the Force to play the role originally envisaged for it. UNIFIL had demonstrated its ability to reduce considerably the violence in its area of operation, and even to bring about complete quiet when all parties supported and co-operated with it.

The United Kingdom agreed that the best means of achieving peace and security in the area and restoring Lebanon's authority and sovereignty up to the international border was an orderly take-over from the withdrawing Israeli forces by UNIFIL, with units of the Lebanese army. All concerned, particularly the Lebanese and Israeli authorities and the population of the area, had a duty to support and co-operate with UNIFIL to ensure its effective operation. No armed military or paramilitary personnel other than UNIFIL or the Lebanese army should be allowed to operate in UNIFIL's area. The United Kingdom believed that the Council should be prepared during the next six months to give further thought to UNIFIL's mandate; for the time being, the Force could continue to play a helpful role in the area while a way was sought for it to fulfil its original mandate.

France also agreed that despite the difficulties it had encountered, UNIFIL had been able to limit the scope of incidents; however, it must as soon as possible be put in a position fully to carry out its mandate. France wished by its vote to demonstrate again its commitment to Lebanon's unity, territorial integrity and independence; it hoped that the Secretary-General would continue to study and foster all necessary measures to ensure the full discharge of that mandate.

The United States believed that UNIFIL could help create stable conditions in southern Lebanon if all the parties agreed to co-operate. It strongly supported the Secretary-General's suggestion that a consultative mechanism be created under United Nations auspices—such as perhaps renewal of the Naqoura talks—to effect the needed co-operation of the parties. As UNIFIL's current restricted role was both inappropriate and unsatisfactory, a clarification of that role, agreed upon by the parties concerned, must be achieved soon to adapt to the situation after Israel's withdrawal. The United States urged all parties to redouble efforts during the coming mandate period to achieve an agreed role for UNIFIL which utilized its potential and assigned to it an important task in the continuing international effort to restore Lebanon's sovereignty and peaceful conditions in the south.

Trinidad and Tobago firmly believed that UNIFIL's presence could be an essential factor of stability in the region, contributing to the maintenance of Lebanon's sovereignty and political independence and the return of effective State authority. However, to attain the objectives of UNIFIL's original mandate, full implementation of resolution 425(1978)[13] was necessary. Israel's withdrawal to the international borders, currently under way, was an essential prerequisite to peace. In addition, the security of the peace-keeping forces and all United Nations personnel in the area must be safeguarded, all parties had to co-operate and acts of violence had to cease.

Lebanon reiterated its position on UNIFIL, as expressed in its 27 March letter (see p. 305). It was convinced that the Force's presence was an essential and basic factor for stability in southern Lebanon and that a minimum degree of security for UNIFIL's work was also basic and necessary. Israel, which had consistently refused to assign any role to UNIFIL, must abide by the Council's resolutions to allow UNIFIL to carry out its mandated tasks.

Israel said it welcomed the Secretary-General's call to reconvene a forum of consultations. With regard to a suggestion that UNIFIL fulfil the police function of stopping cross-border attacks that the Lebanese army was not equipped to do, Israel pointed out that the task of policing a border strip was not merely a peace-keeping function but a peace-enforcing function, which an international force by its very nature and inherent structure was not organized to carry out. Israel did not expect others to take upon them the security of northern Israel and the prevention of terrorist attacks; that function would be assumed by IDF.

Communications (April-October). In a declaration on Lebanon (see p. 302), adopted on 29 April and transmitted on 3 May,[45] the Ministers for Foreign Affairs of the 10 EC member States reaffirmed their support for UNIFIL and called on all parties to the conflict in Lebanon to respect the Force's role, avoiding all incidents, co-operating fully with it and ensuring the safety of its personnel.

The 10 troop-contributing States, by a letter of 10 June to the Secretary-General,[64] expressed deepest concern at recent developments in southern Lebanon, in particular the taking as prisoner of members of the Force. They supported the use of the Secretary-General's good offices to arrange their immediate release, and appealed to Governments to exert their influence so that the prisoners would be released without delay and unharmed.

On 3 October,[65] Lebanon requested that the Security Council extend UNIFIL's mandate, due to expire on 19 October, for another six months. Despite the current circumstances in the southern part of the country, UNIFIL continued to be an important factor in providing stability, Lebanon said; at the same time, increased efforts were needed to allow it fully to implement its mandate.

Report of the Secretary-General (October). On 10 October,[16] the Secretary-General reported on the activities of UNIFIL since 12 April (see also p. 296). He stated that the greater part of the UNIFIL area had been relatively quiet since its evacuation by the Israeli forces. UNIFIL had continued to maintain liaison with the local leaders of Amal and other Lebanese groups, which had generally co-operated with the Force. The leaders, however, had made it clear that the Lebanese resistance would continue to attack the Israeli forces and associated Lebanese irregulars in the security zone where the situation had been very tense. IDF and SLA carried out a number of cordon-and-search operations against Shiite villages in the UNIFIL area. UNIFIL monitored them closely with a view to preventing acts of violence and destruction of property, and dispensed humanitarian assistance, providing emergency food, supplies and bedding to displaced persons and later facilitating their return. UNIFIL strongly protested demolitions, arrests and other incidents as well as the indiscriminate shelling of population centres.

The activities of SLA and other irregulars armed and controlled by IDF were limited essentially to the security zone. Where that zone extended into the UNIFIL area of deployment, the Force continued its efforts to contain those activities, which led to frequent and dangerous confrontations. Most of the incidents related to firing at or near UNIFIL positions and attempts to break through UNIFIL check-points, at times using tanks and armoured personnel carriers. At check-points controlling entry to the security zone, SLA and other irregulars from time to time imposed on UNIFIL personnel restrictions of movement, which were usually of short duration and lifted after negotiations. The increasing number of attacks by Lebanese resistance groups on those check-points led to their frequent closure to all traffic, including that of UNIFIL, and indiscriminate firing at approaching vehicles, including ambulances. On 1 October, a French officer had been shot and wounded at an SLA check-point. A number of confrontations occurred when UNIFIL denied passage through its check-points to unauthorized armed personnel.

On 7 June, following the defection of 11 SLA personnel, 23 members of the Finnish battalion were detained by SLA. After lengthy negotiations between the Force Commander and the Secretary-General on one side and Israel on the other, they were released unharmed on 15 June.

Following Israel's withdrawal and establishment of a security zone, UNIFIL had not been able to extend its deployment to the border. In the part of its area that overlapped with the zone, it was confronted with 21 positions manned by IDF or SLA or both. After completion of Israel's redeployment in June, the UNIFIL Commander continued negotiations with the Israeli authorities, only partly successful, to get IDF and SLA to evacuate those positions.

During the period under review, the UNIFIL Commander and staff maintained contact with the Government of Lebanon and the Lebanese regional authorities, as well as with Israeli authorities on matters pertaining to the functioning of the Force. Under-Secretary-General Urquhart held discussions with government officials in the region in June and October.

UNIFIL continued to treat Lebanese civilians in UNIFIL medical centres and to co-operate with the Lebanese authorities, UNRWA, UNICEF and ICRC in assisting the local population.

The Secretary-General believed that the level of violence in southern Lebanon had been limited to some extent because of UNIFIL's presence. However, the current situation was not only unsatisfactory but dangerous, as UNIFIL found itself once again between hostile forces and was precluded from deploying right up to the international border in accordance with its mandate. Also, Israel's continued presence in the security zone could lead to escalating and spreading violence. Such a situation could well develop into a new and serious international crisis, he warned.

The Secretary-General hoped that the Israeli authorities would conclude that, of all the options available, the effective implementation of UNIFIL's mandate would in the long run be the least hazardous for all concerned. In the light especially of Lebanon's request, he recommended a further extension of UNIFIL's mandate. However, extending the mandate must not be understood to mean that UNIFIL would be allowed to become an open-ended commitment for the troop-contributing countries and for the United Nations if the requisite conditions for its effective operation continued to be absent.

SECURITY COUNCIL ACTION (October)

The Security Council met on 17 October to consider the Secretary-General's report. It invited Israel and Lebanon, at their request, to participate in the discussion without the right to vote.

On the same date, the Council adopted **resolution 575(1985)**.

The Security Council,

Recalling its resolutions 425(1978), 426(1978), 501(1982), 508(1982), 509(1982) and 520(1982), as well as all its resolutions on the situation in Lebanon,

Having studied the report of the Secretary-General on the United Nations Interim Force in Lebanon of 10 October 1985 and taking note of the observations expressed therein,

Taking note of the letter of the Permanent Representative of Lebanon addressed to the Secretary-General of 3 October 1985,

Responding to the request of the Government of Lebanon,

1. *Decides* to extend the present mandate of the United Nations Interim Force in Lebanon for a further interim period of six months, that is, until 19 April 1986;

2. *Reiterates* its strong support for the territorial integrity, sovereignty and independence of Lebanon within its internationally recognized boundaries;

3. *Re-emphasizes* the terms of reference and general guidelines of the Force as stated in the report of the Secretary-General of 19 March 1978, approved by resolution 426(1978), and calls upon all parties concerned to co-operate fully with the Force for the full implementation of its mandate;

4. *Reiterates* that the Force should fully implement its mandate as defined in resolutions 425(1978), 426(1978) and all other relevant resolutions;

5.   *Requests* the Secretary-General to continue consultations with the Government of Lebanon and other parties directly concerned on the implementation of the present resolution and to report to the Council thereon.

Security Council resolution 575(1985)

17 October 1985   Meeting 2623   13-0-2

Draft prepared in consultations among Council members (S/17567).

Vote in Council as follows:

In favour: Australia, Burkina Faso, China, Denmark, Egypt, France, India, Madagascar, Peru, Thailand, Trinidad and Tobago, United Kingdom, United States.

Against: None.

Abstaining: Ukrainian SSR, USSR.

The USSR said that if Israel would withdraw and cease its interference in Lebanon's affairs, that would create conditions in which UNIFIL could carry out its mandate; with that in mind and taking into consideration Lebanon's request and the Secretary-General's recommendations, the USSR said it did not object to extending the Force's mandate for a further interim period.

China said it hoped that in the coming six months UNIFIL's situation would be fundamentally improved. The elimination of the aftermath of the Israeli invasion of Lebanon, including the dismantling of the security zone and the total withdrawal of Israeli troops from Lebanese territory, was a prerequisite for the normal functioning of the Force, the recovery of Lebanese sovereignty and the restoration of peace and security. China shared the Secretary-General's position that UNIFIL's extension should not be allowed to become an open-ended commitment, a view also shared by France, which insisted on comprehensive application as soon as possible of resolutions 425(1978)[13] and 427(1978)[66] through negotiations with the parties.

The United Kingdom also agreed with the Secretary-General that the balance of advantage lay in renewing the mandate, but that the current situation was both unsatisfactory and dangerous; by maintaining a security zone and preventing UNIFIL from carrying out its mandate, Israel's policy damaged the chances of restoring stable and peaceful conditions in southern Lebanon.

Denmark pointed out that the so-called security zone was contrary to Council resolutions and meant that UNIFIL found itself in the midst of mutually hostile forces. It hoped Israel would conclude that the effective implementation of UNIFIL's mandate would in the long run be the least hazardous for all. The Force should be allowed to carry out its mandate.

Lebanon believed that UNIFIL was an important expression of the Council's commitment to helping it cope with continuing violations of its sovereignty and restore its authority over all its territory.

In Israel's view, the purpose of UNIFIL was to ensure that there was no cross-border violence and no continuous problem involving international peace and security, namely, the problem of terrorist attacks continuously launched against Israel. UNIFIL could not stop terrorism, because it could only serve as a buffer between two Governments and there was no sufficiently strong Government on one side.

Report of the Secretary-General (December). In an interim report of 16 December on UNIFIL[17] (see also p. 297), the Secretary-General stated that the situation in the UNIFIL area of deployment had remained basically the same since October. The part that the Israeli forces had evacuated in the spring had remained quiet and the Shiite organization, Amal, and other Lebanese resistance groups had generally co-operated with the Force. But the other part, the security zone, had been very tense. That zone overlapped UNIFIL's area and included the whole Norwegian battalion sector in the east, areas adjacent to the border and the Christian enclave around Marjayoun. In those areas, UNIFIL had only isolated positions and was restricted in its freedom of movement. Access to the zone was controlled by fortified positions, road-blocks and check-points, manned by IDF and local Lebanese forces it armed and controlled, mainly SLA.

During the previous two months, the Secretary-General continued, Lebanese resistance groups had launched almost daily attacks, usually at night, against Israeli troops and associated local forces in the security zone. The attacks had been particularly frequent in the southern parts of the Nepalese and Irish battalion. On the night of 14/15 November, a building billeting UNIFIL personnel was seriously damaged by an errant rocket. Military observer teams of UNTSO also received evidence of attacks in the border area south of the UNIFIL deployment area.

IDF and associated local forces carried out a number of search operations in the overlapping security zone. The most important ones took place on 22 and 25 November at Chebaa, where five persons were arrested, and on 28 November, when an IDF unit sealed off and searched Yatar and its vicinity, following reports that two rockets had impacted on Israeli territory.

UNIFIL continued its efforts to contain the activities of SLA and other irregulars in its area, which led to frequent confrontations. The irregulars often attempted to break through UNIFIL check-points. From time to time, SLA and other irregulars restricted the movement of UNIFIL personnel, affecting in particular the Norwegian battalion. Incidents of firing close to UNIFIL positions continued, although their number decreased and all incidents were protested to the Israeli authorities.

Since May 1985, the Secretary-General and his colleagues had been trying to promote agreement on security arrangements in southern Lebanon which would be in line with UNIFIL's mandate and take into account Lebanon's and Israel's concerns. However, the positions of the parties remained far apart: Israel announced that it would continue to rely on the security zone to safeguard its northern settlements and that UNIFIL would not be allowed to deploy to the border; Lebanon insisted that the Force should deploy to the border and fully implement its mandate.

Despite UNIFIL's stabilizing presence, the current situation was not acceptable and could well deteriorate. In the case of further escalation of violence, UNIFIL would find itself in a difficult position. The Secretary-General shared the concern of the troop-contributing countries at probable developments if conditions were allowed to persist.

The most effective means to minimize risks and preserve the Force's credibility would be a change in Israel's position. Were UNIFIL withdrawn, the Secretary-General had no doubt that there would be a disastrous increase in violence in southern Lebanon and that the concept of United Nations peace-keeping would be weakened. On the other hand, if the Force remained in place in a deteriorating situation, it would become increasingly difficult for it to limit violence, assist and protect the civilians and establish peace and security in the area.

The Secretary-General did not make any recommendations to the Council for future action, but expressed the hope that the Council members would ponder on what action they might take, individually or collectively, to implement resolutions on UNIFIL and bring about peace and normality in southern Lebanon.

Palestinian refugees in Lebanon

While much of the violence in Lebanon affected Palestinians and Lebanese citizens indiscriminately, in many instances Palestinians were the specific target, according to the UNRWA Commissioner-General in reports covering the periods 1 July 1984 to 30 June 1985[67] and 1 July 1985 to 30 June 1986.[68]

The lives of Palestinian refugees continued to be threatened everywhere in Lebanon. In the year preceding 30 June 1985, the UNRWA field office in Lebanon reported over 800 violent deaths, over 2,500 woundings, 500 arrests, 27 kidnappings and nine disappearances.

Until February 1985, all Palestinian refugee camps in the southern part of the country were subject to searches as the Israeli army reacted to attacks from local groups. After the Israeli withdrawal from Saida on 16 February to the Litani River, the frequency and severity of the searches intensified in the Tyre area. Many refugees left the camps and sought refuge elsewhere.

Fighting erupted on 18 March, during which the Ein el-Hilweh and Mieh Mieh camps suffered extensive damage from shelling by militias in the surrounding hills; 60 refugees were killed, 314 were wounded and some 40,000 people were displaced.

During fighting in April, almost all shelters at Mieh Mieh camp were destroyed or damaged, as well as many at Ein el-Hilweh.

Fierce fighting in and around Beirut camps rapidly escalated from 19 May. Violent clashes between Amal militiamen and Palestine refugees resulted in heavy loss of life, as did sporadic Israeli air raids. In the Saida area, at Tripoli and at Beirut, the refugee camps of Shatila and Burj el-Barajneh were the targets of repeated attacks, with an estimated toll of 635 dead and 2,500 wounded.

As a result of fighting around and in the Beirut camps in June, some 18,000 refugees fled to other parts of Lebanon. In spite of intensive efforts sponsored by the Lebanese Government, including the formation of a special force to take charge of security in West Beirut, fighting continued in and around the two main Beirut camps. In mid-September, fierce fighting broke out at Tripoli and lasted three weeks. In spite of these difficulties, UNRWA continued to function in Lebanon.

The situation of Palestine refugees in Lebanon was also dealt with in a report of the Secretary-General on refugee protection (see p. 358).

Communications. By a letter of 16 January, transmitted by Egypt the next day,[20] PLO reiterated its view that, in view of Israel's planned withdrawal, the United Nations was fully responsible for providing adequate protection and safety to the Palestinians in southern Lebanon and specifically in the refugee camps.

By a letter of 6 February, transmitted by Qatar as Chairman of the Arab Group,[69] PLO charged that Israeli occupation troops had opened fire on Palestinians near the Burj Ash-Shamali refugee camp on 5 February, wounding several, sealing the camp off, cutting off electricity, imposing a curfew and carrying out mass arrests. On 6 February, PLO alleged, Israeli troops in an armoured vehicle passing through the Tyre area opened fire and seriously wounded six Palestinian civilians in a car. The situation in and around the camps in southern Lebanon was extremely tense, PLO said, with mounting anxiety that it was Israel's aim to liquidate or terrify into flight the remaining Palestinian civilians there. PLO insisted that the United Nations do everything in its power to guarantee their safety and security.

The Chairman of the Committee on Palestinian rights, by a letter of 12 February,[70] called attention to those and other incidents and expressed utmost concern at the mounting tension in the refugee camps in southern Lebanon and the West Bank (see also p. 327).

By letters of 1 and 3 April, transmitted by the United Arab Emirates as Chairman of the Arab Group,[71] PLO gave an account of shelling by Israeli artillery and Lebanese elements, beginning on 29 March, of the camps of Ein el-Hilweh and Mieh Mieh, resulting in a number of casualties, and forcing 75,000 Palestinians (25,000 of them from the camps), most of them women and children, to leave the area. Meanwhile, the Israeli navy had imposed a sea blockade on Sidon and Beirut and abducted six Palestinians from a Lebanese ship. PLO called again on the United Nations and specifically the Security Council to take the necessary measures to put an end to such criminal acts.

Heavy artillery bombardment of Palestinian refugee camps in Lebanon was reported in two other letters from PLO, dated 10 and 11 April, also transmitted by the United Arab Emirates.[43] In bombarding three camps in the Tyre area on 9 and 10 April, several houses were destroyed and hundreds of civilians, including Palestinians, were arrested and taken to Israel (see p. 302). For the twelfth consecutive day, Israeli forces and their allies had shelled Ein el-Hilweh and Mieh Mieh; on 10 April, seven persons were killed and 15 injured. On 11 April, bombardment of and search-and-arrest operations in camps in the Sidon area were carried out. The aim, PLO believed, was to uproot the Palestinian presence in south Lebanon to establish a so-called "safe border zone" and a sectarian, Fascist mini-State in south Lebanon.

The United Arab Emirates, again for the Arab Group, transmitted another PLO letter, dated 15 April,[44] informing the Secretary-General that for the past few days Israeli occupation forces in the Tyre area had besieged four camps and arrested 270 Palestinian civilians, taking them to unknown destinations. PLO said it was clear that the Israeli forces were attempting to break the will of the Palestinians, create an atmosphere of terror and panic, and facilitate their mass exodus. PLO called again on the United Nations to take adequate measures to end Israel's crimes and protect the Palestinians.

The Chairman of the Committee on Palestinian rights, on 23 May,[72] expressed profound concern at the tragic developments in and around the camps of Sabra, Shatila and Burj el-Barajneh in Beirut, the object of armed attacks. He urged the Secretary-General to do all in his power to put an end to the violence against the camps and promote a durable solution of the Palestinian question.

On 31 July,[55] the Committee Chairman brought to the Secretary-General's attention newspaper reports that tanks had been delivered that might affect the rights and lives of the Palestin-

ian refugees living in Lebanon and that amplified tension in the area. Lebanon, on 9 August,[56] stated that the subject was outside the Committee's competence, having nothing to do with the Palestinians' exercise of their inalienable rights.

UNRWA activities

Emergency operations

For most of 1985, emergency operations launched in the aftermath of the 1982 invasion of Lebanon[61] continued to predominate in UNRWA's relief efforts. The year brought widespread hardship for tens of thousands of refugee families in Lebanon, the Commissioner-General stated.[67] Due to the fighting that persisted almost without interruption in one part of Lebanon or another, thousands of refugees were displaced and lost their homes and possessions; many were killed or injured. The programme of reconstruction, begun in previous years, had to be postponed because of continuing hostilities.

Despite the difficulties, the Agency continued to function, distributing food, water, medical supplies and other benefits. Normal education, health and welfare programmes were carried out to the extent that circumstances permitted.

Following the fighting around and in the Beirut camps in June 1985, UNRWA provided food, blankets and household items to the 18,000 refugees who had fled the camps and to those who remained, numbering some 25,000 altogether. Later in the year, the Agency gave some $1,406,233 in direct cash aid to the residents of those camps to help them repair their shelters.

Due to prevailing security conditions, supplies could be transported from Beirut to south Lebanon only with great difficulty and after much negotiation, despite an agreement that had been reached between UNRWA and Israel.

The chaotic situation in Beirut had an increasingly serious impact on UNRWA's ability to supervise certain operations from its field office. In an effort to ease that problem, the Commissioner-General decided to open a small sub-office at Larnaca, Cyprus, with two international and 12 area staff, to improve the carrying out of basic administrative and financial services for refugees in Lebanon.

Relief measures

Like its emergency measures, UNRWA's relief operations in Lebanon continued with great difficulty. Discontinuation of emergency food rations in March 1984[73] still caused consternation among the refugees, many of whom were unable to find steady work and were cut off from other sources of income. In Tyre, refugees refused to accept special-hardship-case assistance in support of their contention that all refugees should be so classified; they began to accept assistance again in May 1985 after withdrawal of the Israeli forces. Similar protests had been made in the Saida area and part of the Bekaa sub-area in January and February, so rations were issued only in the Beirut and Tripoli areas.

Rations to special hardship families were disrupted in the Beirut camps when fierce fighting broke out on 19 May and continued for three weeks; supplies were finally allowed into the camps the second week of June. UNRWA assisted thousands of refugees to obtain or renew travel documents issued by the host Governments through close co-operation between its staff and government offices.

Economic problems, particularly loss of employment, continued to have particularly severe impact on the refugees, though the economic situation in the south improved marginally after the Israeli withdrawals, which allowed for a precarious restoration of the agricultural economy. UNRWA continued its co-operative efforts with the Young Men's Christian Association and UNESCO to alleviate the unemployment situation.

Restoration of regular services

The difficulty of travel in Lebanon compelled UNRWA to change some of its hospital arrangements, referring to the Syrian Arab Republic some patients who normally would have been referred to the American University Hospital in Beirut, and subsidizing private hospitals in south Lebanon that treated patients who could not be referred out of that area. The Agency and the Norwegian Refugee Council agreed to continue operating jointly a rehabilitation centre in Tyre when the situation permitted.

Agreements effective 1 January 1985 were concluded with the Hammoud Hospital (25 beds) in Saida and the al-Sahel Hospital (20 beds) in Beirut for the hospitalization of refugees, and two with Sidon hospitals were cancelled in February; one centre in Saida became inaccessible after April.

As health services inside the camps were often paralysed by the heavy fighting in March/April in Saida and in May/June in Beirut, UNRWA launched emergency medical services and established mobile medical teams. Due to local clashes, the UNRWA polyclinic at Beirut was closed on 29 April and the staff were relocated to the Mar Elias camp. An agreement between UNRWA and the International Rescue Committee, which had a health care unit in Saida, was extended to the end of June. Two dental units were installed at Ein el-Hilweh. Some 20 refugee patients were receiving haemodialysis in local hospitals at UNRWA expense.

UNRWA schools were able to operate for much of the 1984/85 school year, although their reopen-

ing was delayed in the north and in Beirut. Schools in the Sabra Quarter and Mar Elias and three schools in the Shatila camp remained inoperative for long periods and were unable to complete their curriculum until well into the following school year. From July to November 1985, Agency schools at Beirut were inoperative, seven of them occupied by displaced refugee families. Elsewhere in the country, interruptions in school operations during the second half of 1985 were mainly due to local strikes.

Food and other benefits were distributed to special hardship cases, damaged Agency buildings were repaired, roads relaid, water supply installations repaired or replaced and electricity supplies restored.

SECURITY COUNCIL ACTION

The Security Council met on 31 May to consider the escalation of violence in and around Beirut, affecting also the safety and security of the Palestinians in the refugee camps (see p. 303). By **resolution 564(1985)**, the Council called for an end to acts of violence against the civilian population in Lebanon, in particular in and around Palestinian refugee camps. It also called on all parties to facilitate the work of United Nations agencies, in particular UNRWA.

GENERAL ASSEMBLY ACTION

In **resolution 40/165 I** on the protection of Palestine refugees, the General Assembly urged the Commissioner-General to provide housing, in consultation with the Lebanese Government, to those refugees whose houses had been demolished or razed by the Israeli forces. It called again on Israel to compensate UNRWA for the damage to its property and facilities resulting from Israel's invasion of Lebanon, without prejudice to its responsibility for all damages resulting from that invasion.

Israel and the Syrian Arab Republic

In 1985, the General Assembly and the Commission on Human Rights dealt with the situation in the Syrian Golan Heights in the light of Israel's 1981 decision[74] to impose its laws, jurisdiction and administration on the Israeli-occupied territory (see p. 340).

The United Nations Disengagement Observer Force, with some 1,300 troops in October 1985, provided by Austria, Canada, Finland and Poland, was deployed between the Israeli and Syrian forces on the Golan Heights in accordance with the Agreement on Disengagement of Forces between Israel and the Syrian Arab Republic, concluded between the two countries in 1974.[75] A group of observers from UNTSO assisted UNDOF in its tasks.

The main functions of UNDOF continued to be to supervise the observance of the cease-fire between Israel and the Syrian Arab Republic in the Golan Heights area and ensure that there were no military forces in the area of separation. The Security Council extended UNDOF's mandate twice during the year, in May and November, by resolutions 563(1985) and 576(1985). The Force's headquarters was at Damascus.

In a September report[76] on the Middle East situation (see p. 264), the Secretary-General transmitted replies from 13 States regarding their implementation of the General Assembly's 1984 resolution[77] on Israeli policies in the Golan Heights, by which Member States were called on to refrain from supplying Israel with weapons, to refrain from acquiring weapons from Israel, to suspend economic, financial and technological co-operation with Israel and to sever diplomatic, trade and cultural relations with it.

Communications. In a letter of 6 November 1985 to the Secretary-General,[78] Israel stated that a reporter for a magazine published in the Federal Republic of Germany had interviewed and photographed a Nazi war criminal, Alois Brunner, who, Israel charged, the Syrian Arab Republic had sheltered for 30 years. When asked on 30 October to explain Syria's action, a Syrian representative to the Assembly's Third (Social, Humanitarian and Cultural) Committee had claimed no such person lived in Syria, Israel said. Despite being a party to the 1948 Convention on the Prevention and Punishment of the Crime of Genocide,[79] the Syrian Arab Republic refused to try or extradite Brunner; if it continued to do so, Israel said, the international community should demand that he be handed over to an impartial international tribunal.

On 20 November,[80] the Syrian Arab Republic charged that on the previous day two Israeli fighter aircraft had violated Syrian airspace. They clashed with Syrian aircraft before withdrawing. That provocative act, it stated, was one further element in a series of acts of aggression in which Israel persisted in violating international law with serious consequences for international peace and security.

On 26 December,[59] the Syrian Arab Republic stated that it regarded overflight of Lebanese territory by Israeli fighters as a flagrant violation of the sovereignty of a fraternal United Nations Member and a deliberate threat to the Syrian forces in Lebanon at that country's request and in accordance with a decision of the League of Arab States; any threat to the security of the Syrian forces in Lebanon also constituted a threat to the security of the Syrian Arab Republic. Israel's threats were designed to sabotage Syrian efforts to contribute to national reconciliation and restoration of normal life in Lebanon. The Syrian

Arab Republic reaffirmed its determination to exercise its legitimate right to defend its security and protect its armed forces. The international community must adopt a firmer position in the face of Israel's provocations.

Peace-keeping operation

UNDOF activities

Reports of the Secretary-General. Prior to the expiration of the six-month extensions of the mandate of UNDOF, on 31 May and 30 November 1985, the Secretary-General submitted reports on the activities of the Force for the periods from 17 November 1984 to 13 May 1985[81] and from 14 May to 13 November 1985.[82]

In both reports, the Secretary-General stated that UNDOF had continued to fulfil its tasks, with the co-operation of the parties and facilitated by the close contact maintained by the Force Commander and his staff with the military liaison staffs of Israel and the Syrian Arab Republic. The cease-fire had been maintained and no complaints concerning the UNDOF area of operation had been lodged by either party.

Supervision of the area of separation was carried out through static positions and observation posts manned 24 hours a day, patrols operating at irregular intervals on predetermined routes, and temporary outposts. Under a Syrian programme, civilians had been returning to the area of separation.

UNDOF continued fortnightly inspections of armament and forces in the area of limitation, assisted by liaison officers from the parties. It received the co-operation of both parties, although restricted in movement and inspection in certain areas by both sides.

Because mines posed a threat to the Force and the growing population, UNDOF continued its efforts, in consultation with the parties, to make the area mine-free. Intensified patrolling and a security fence had helped prevent or reduce incidents involving Syrian shepherds. UNDOF also assisted ICRC with facilities for handing over mail and prisoners of war and for the passage of students across the area.

Despite the quiet in the sector, the Secretary-General stated, the situation in the Middle East as a whole continued to be potentially dangerous. He hoped that determined efforts would be made to tackle the problem in all its aspects, with a view to arriving at a just and durable peace settlement, as called for by the Security Council in 1973.[83]

In the circumstances, he considered the continued presence of UNDOF to be essential and recommended—the Syrian Arab Republic having given its assent and Israel having expressed agreement—in each report that the Council extend its mandate for a further six months.

SECURITY COUNCIL ACTION

On 21 May 1985, without debate, the Security Council unanimously adopted **resolution 563(1985)**, extending UNDOF's mandate until 30 November.

The Security Council,
Having considered the report of the Secretary-General on the United Nations Disengagement Observer Force,
Decides:

(a) To call upon the parties concerned to implement immediately Security Council resolution 338(1973);

(b) To renew the mandate of the United Nations Disengagement Observer Force for another period of six months, that is, until 30 November 1985;

(c) To request the Secretary-General to submit, at the end of this period, a report on the developments in the situation and the measures taken to implement resolution 338(1973).

Security Council resolution 563(1985)

21 May 1985   Meeting 2581   Adopted unanimously

Draft prepared in consultations among Council members (S/17202).

On 21 November, again without debate, the Council unanimously adopted **resolution 576(1985)**, extending UNDOF's mandate until 31 May 1986.

The Security Council,
Having considered the report of the Secretary-General on the United Nations Disengagement Observer Force,
Decides:

(a) To call upon the parties concerned to implement immediately Security Council resolution 338(1973);

(b) To renew the mandate of the United Nations Disengagement Observer Force for another period of six months, that is, until 31 May 1986;

(c) To request the Secretary-General to submit, at the end of this period, a report on the developments in the situation and the measures taken to implement resolution 338(1973).

Security Council resolution 576(1985)

21 November 1985   Meeting 2630   Adopted unanimously

Draft prepared in consultations among Council members (S/17642).

After adoption of each resolution, the President made the following statement on behalf of the Council:[84]

"As is known, the report of the Secretary-General on the United Nations Disengagement Observer Force states, in paragraph 26 [25 in the November report]: 'Despite the present quiet in the Israel-Syria sector, the situation in the Middle East as a whole continues to be potentially dangerous and is likely to remain so, unless and until a comprehensive settlement covering all aspects of the Middle East problem can be reached.' That statement of the Secretary-General reflects the view of the Security Council."

Composition

As at 13 November 1985, the composition of UNDOF was as follows:

Austria	533
Canada	226
Finland	411
Poland	153
United Nations military observers (detailed from UNTSO)	8
Total	1,311

In addition, UNTSO observers assigned to the Israel-Syria Mixed Armistice Commission assisted UNDOF as required.

Change of Commander

In April,[85] the Secretary-General informed the Security Council that the Commander of UNDOF, Major-General Carl-Gustav Stahl (Sweden), was resigning and that he intended, subject to consultations, to appoint Major-General Gustav Hägglund (Finland) as Commander, effective 1 June. Major-General Stahl had assumed command of the Force in June 1982.[86]

The President of the Council responded on 3 May.[87]

"I wish to inform you that your letter dated 29 April 1985 concerning your intention to appoint Major-General Gustav Hägglund of Finland to the post of Commander of the United Nations Disengagement Observer Force has been brought to the attention of the members of the Security Council. They considered the matter in informal consultations on 1 May and agreed with the proposal contained in your letter."

Major-General Hägglund assumed command of the Force on 1 June.

REFERENCES

[1]YUN 1981, p. 275. [2]A/40/283. [3]A/40/315. [4]YUN 1984, p. 281. [5]GC(XXIX)/RESOLUTIONS(1985) (res. 443). [6]A/40/783. [7]YUN 1981, p. 282, SC res. 487(1981), 19 June 1981. [8]YUN 1984, p. 281, GA res. 39/14, 16 Nov. 1984. [9]YUN 1968, p. 17, GA res. 2373(XXII), annex, 12 June 1968. [10]YUN 1984, p. 302, SC res. 555(1984), 12 Oct. 1984. [11]S/17093. [12]YUN 1984, p. 283. [13]YUN 1978, p. 312, SC res. 425(1978), 19 Mar. 1978. [14]YUN 1948-49, p. 185. [15]S/17062. [16]S/17557. [17]S/17684. [18]YUN 1982, p. 475, SC res. 516(1982), 1 Aug. 1982. [19]A/40/779-S/17581 & Corr.1. [20]S/16900. [21]YUN 1978, p. 312, SC res. 425(1978) & 426(1978), 19 Mar. 1978. [22]YUN 1982, p. 450, SC res. 508(1982), 5 June 1982. [23]*Ibid.*, SC res. 509(1982), 6 June 1982. [24]A/40/127-S/16953. [25]A/40/148 (S/16974). [26]A/40/178/Add.1 (S/16974/Add.1). [27]A/40/156-S/16990. [28]A/40/158-S/16997. [29]A/40/165 (S/17007). [30]A/40/163-S/17008. [31]A/40/205-S/17055 & Corr.1. [32]S/17067. [33]S/16983. [34]S/16989. [35]S/17011. [36]S/17000. [37]YUN 1978, p. 312, SC res. 425(1978), 19 Mar. 1978; YUN 1982, p. 450, SC res. 508(1982) & 509(1982), 5 & 6 June 1982. [38]YUN 1982, pp. 451 & 452, SC res. 512(1982) & 513(1982), 19 June & 4 July 1982. [39]YUN 1948-49, p. 535, GA res. 217 A (III), 10 Dec. 1948. [40]YUN 1974, p. 847, GA res. 3314(XXIX),

annex, 14 Dec. 1974. [41]A/40/223-S/17080. [42]A/40/253-S/17110. [43]A/40/236-S/17106. [44]A/40/254-S/17111. [45]A/40/286-S/17153. [46]S/17168. [47]S/17191. [48]S/17215. [49]S/17228. [50]S/17234. [51]YUN 1982, p. 481. [52]A/40/427-S/17320. [53]A/40/462-S/17325 & Corr.1. [54]A/40/504-S/17358. [55]A/40/523-S/17375. [56]A/40/537-S/17389. [57]A/40/986-S/17669. [58]A/41/65-S/17698. [59]A/41/61-S/17694. [60]S/17062. [61]YUN 1982, p. 433. [62]YUN 1978, p. 312, SC res. 426(1978), 19 Mar. 1978. [63]*Ibid.*, p. 301. [64]S/17251. [65]S/17526. [66]YUN 1978, p. 312, SC res. 427(1978), 3 May 1978. [67]A/40/13 & Corr.1. [68]A/41/13. [69]A/40/123-S/16946. [70]A/40/128-S/16954. [71]A/40/219-S/17075, A/40/225-S/17085. [72]A/40/339-S/17219. [73]YUN 1984, p. 335. [74]YUN 1981, p. 308. [75]YUN 1974, p. 198. [76]A/40/668 & Add.1. [77]YUN 1984, p. 323, GA res. 39/146 B, 14 Dec. 1984. [78]A/C.3/40/9. [79]YUN 1948-49, p. 959, GA res. 260 A (III), annex, 9 Dec. 1948. [80]A/40/909-S/17643. [81]S/17177. [82]S/17628. [83]YUN 1973, p. 213, SC res. 338(1973), 22 Oct. 1973. [84]S/17206, S/17653. [85]S/17147. [86]YUN 1982, p. 497. [87]S/17148.

Financing of peace-keeping forces

United Nations peace-keeping operations in the Middle East comprised two peace-keeping forces—UNDOF and UNIFIL—and one observer mission, UNTSO.

The General Assembly, following the recommendations of the Advisory Committee on Administrative and Budgetary Questions (ACABQ) and the Fifth (Administrative and Budgetary) Committee, approved appropriations for UNDOF for operations from 1 June 1985 to 31 May 1986 totalling more than $36 million (resolution 40/59 A), and for UNIFIL's operations from 19 April 1985 to 18 April 1986, some $142 million (40/246 A).

In each case, the Assembly apportioned the expenses for the Forces among all Member States in accordance with a special scale used for this purpose[1] since the establishment of the second United Nations Emergency Force (UNEF II) in 1973. According to that arrangement, the permanent members of the Security Council were assessed more than they would have been under the scale of assessments for the United Nations regular budget, while most developing countries were assessed 80 per cent less and the least developed countries 90 per cent less than under the regular scale.

In view of the difficult financial situation of the two Forces, the Assembly authorized suspension of certain provisions of the Financial Regulations of the United Nations to enable UNDOF and UNIFIL to retain a "surplus balance" of about $3 million and $9 million, respectively (40/59 B and 40/246 B).

Although the last revision of standard rates of reimbursement to countries which contributed troops to the Forces had taken place in 1980, the Assembly decided to retain the current rates of reimbursement (40/247).

UNDOF financing

Report of the Secretary-General. In an October 1985 report on the financing of UNDOF,[2] the Secretary-General noted that, as at 30 September, $665.1 million in contributions for UNDOF together with UNEF II had been received since the latter's inception in 1973 to 30 November 1985. The unpaid balance due from Member States was $73 million, of which $30.8 million represented amounts apportioned among Member States which had stated that they did not intend to pay, and $36 million in contributions due from China which had been transferred to a special account in accordance with a 1981 Assembly resolution.[3]

According to the Secretary-General, there was a shortfall of approximately $7.2 million in the UNDOF Special Account for the period from 25 October 1979 to 30 November 1985. The shortfall for periods prior to 24 October 1979 together with UNEF II until its liquidation in 1980 was some $59.6 million. In the circumstances, troop contributors had not been paid on time, nor had they been reimbursed fully in accordance with the rates agreed upon; they had again conveyed to the Secretary-General their serious concern over the situation which, they said, placed a heavy burden on them.

For the operation of UNDOF from 1 December 1985 on, the Secretary-General estimated monthly costs of $3,047,000 gross ($2,989,083 net). For the period 1 June to 30 November 1985, an appropriation of $17,852,496 gross ($17,592,000 net) would be required.

ACABQ recommendations. ACABQ, in November 1985,[4] recommended that the Secretary-General's estimates be approved and that he be permitted the usual flexibility to transfer credits between items of expenditure, should it be necessary for good management and efficiency.

ACABQ also recommended acceptance of the Secretary-General's proposal to establish one new Field Service post for property and inventory control which would bring the total UNDOF posts to 155 (8 at the Professional level and above, 10 General Service, 31 Field Service and 106 local level). The Committee noted his statement that the Force continued to explore the possibility of relocating UNDOF headquarters to just outside Damascus; should additional funds be required, the matter would be brought to the Committee's attention for action.

ACABQ also noted information that the 1984-1985 interim accounts indicated a "surplus" balance of $3,250,131 in the Special Account for

UNEF and UNDOF as at 31 December 1984, representing an excess of income over expenditure due to interest and miscellaneous credits which had accrued. However, "income" included "assessed contributions" irrespective of collectability. In consequence of the withholding of contributions by certain Member States, the "surplus" had in effect been drawn upon to its full extent.

Introducing ACABQ's report in the Fifth Committee, the Chairman of ACABQ added that it also approved UNDOF costs from 1 December 1983 to 30 November 1985, as detailed by the Secretary-General.

GENERAL ASSEMBLY ACTION

In December 1985, the General Assembly, acting on the recommendation of the Fifth Committee, adopted two resolutions—40/59 A and B—dealing with the financing of UNDOF.

On 2 December, it adopted **resolution 40/59 A** by recorded vote.

The General Assembly,

Having considered the report of the Secretary-General on the financing of the United Nations Disengagement Observer Force, as well as the related report of the Advisory Committee on Administrative and Budgetary Questions,

Bearing in mind Security Council resolutions 350(1974) of 31 May 1974, 363(1974) of 29 November 1974, 369(1975) of 28 May 1975, 381(1975) of 30 November 1975, 390(1976) of 28 May 1976, 398(1976) of 30 November 1976, 408(1977) of 26 May 1977, 420(1977) of 30 November 1977, 429(1978) of 31 May 1978, 441(1978) of 30 November 1978, 449(1979) of 30 May 1979, 456(1979) of 30 November 1979, 470(1980) of 30 May 1980, 481(1980) of 26 November 1980, 485(1981) of 22 May 1981, 493(1981) of 23 November 1981, 506(1982) of 26 May 1982, 524(1982) of 29 November 1982, 531(1983) of 26 May 1983, 543(1983) of 29 November 1983, 551(1984) of 30 May 1984, 557(1984) of 28 November 1984, 563(1985) of 21 May 1985 and 576(1985) of 21 November 1985,

Recalling its resolutions 3101(XXVIII) of 11 December 1973, 3211 B (XXIX) of 29 November 1974, 3374 C (XXX) of 2 December 1975, 31/5 D of 22 December 1976, 32/4 C of 2 December 1977, 33/13 D of 8 December 1978, 34/7 C of 3 December 1979, 35/44 of 1 December 1980, 35/45 A of 1 December 1980, 36/66 A of 30 November 1981, 37/38 A of 30 November 1982, 38/35 A of 1 December 1983 and 39/28 A of 30 November 1984,

Reaffirming its previous decisions regarding the fact that, in order to meet the expenditures caused by such operations, a different procedure is required from that applied to meet expenditures of the regular budget of the United Nations,

Taking into account the fact that the economically more developed countries are in a position to make relatively larger contributions and that the economically less developed countries have a relatively limited capacity to contribute towards peace-keeping operations involving heavy expenditures,

Bearing in mind the special responsibilities of the States permanent members of the Security Council in the financing of such operations, as indicated in General Assembly resolution 1874(S-IV) of 27 June 1963 and other resolutions of the Assembly,

I

Decides to appropriate to the Special Account referred to in section II, paragraph 1, of General Assembly resolution 3211 B (XXIX) the amount of $17,852,496 gross ($17,592,000 net) authorized and apportioned by section III of Assembly resolution 39/28 A for the operation of the United Nations Disengagement Observer Force for the period from 1 June to 30 November 1985, inclusive;

II

1. *Decides* to appropriate to the Special Account an amount of $18,282,000 for the operation of the United Nations Disengagement Observer Force for the period from 1 December 1985 to 31 May 1986, inclusive;

2. *Decides further*, as an *ad hoc* arrangement, without prejudice to the positions of principle that may be taken by Member States in any consideration by the General Assembly of arrangements for the financing of peace-keeping operations, to apportion the amount of $18,282,000 among Member States in accordance with the scheme set out in Assembly resolution 3101(XXVIII) and the provisions of section II, paragraphs 2 *(b)* and 2 *(c)*, and section V, paragraph 1, of resolution 3374 C (XXX), section V, paragraph 1, of resolution 31/5 D, section V, paragraph 1, of resolution 32/4 C, section V, paragraph 1, of resolution 33/13 D, section V, paragraph 1, of resolution 34/7 C, section V, paragraph 1, of resolution 35/45 A, section V, paragraph 1, of resolution 36/66 A, section V, paragraph 1, of resolution 37/38 A and section V, paragraphs 1 and 2, of resolution 39/28 A; the scale of assessments for the years 1983, 1984 and 1985 shall be applied against a portion thereof, that is $3,047,000, being the amount pertaining on a *pro rata* basis to the month of December 1985, and the scale of assessments for the years 1986, 1987 and 1988 shall be applied against the balance, that is $15,235,000, for the period thereafter;

3. *Decides* that there shall be set off against the apportionment among Member States, as provided in paragraph 2 above, their respective share in the estimated income of $10,000 other than staff assessment income approved for the period from 1 December 1985 to 31 May 1986, inclusive;

4. *Decides* that, in accordance with the provisions of its resolution 973(X) of 15 December 1955, there shall be set off against the apportionment among Member States, as provided for in paragraph 2 above, their respective share in the Tax Equalization Fund of the estimated staff assessment income of $337,500 approved for the period from 1 December 1985 to 31 May 1986, inclusive;

III

Authorizes the Secretary-General to enter into commitments for the United Nations Disengagement Observer Force at a rate not to exceed $3,047,000 gross ($2,989,083 net) per month for the period from 1 June to 30 November 1986, inclusive, should the Security Council decide to continue the Force beyond the period of six months authorized under its resolution 576(1985), the said amount to be apportioned among Member States in accordance with the scheme set out in the present resolution;

IV

1. *Stresses* the need for voluntary contributions to the United Nations Disengagement Observer Force, both in cash and in the form of services and supplies acceptable to the Secretary-General;

2. *Requests* the Secretary-General to take all necessary action to ensure that the United Nations Disengagement Observer Force is conducted with a maximum of efficiency and economy.

General Assembly resolution 40/59 A

2 December 1985   Meeting 99   96-2-13 (recorded vote)

Approved by Fifth Committee (A/40/957) by recorded vote (78-2-18), 2 December (meeting 51); 9-nation draft (A/C.5/40/L.4, part A); agenda item 126 *(a)*.
Sponsors: Australia, Austria, Canada, Denmark, Finland, Ireland, New Zealand, Norway, Sweden.
Meeting numbers. GA 40th session: 5th Committee 50, 51; plenary 99.

Recorded vote in Assembly as follows:

In favour: Argentina, Australia, Austria, Bahrain, Bangladesh, Barbados, Belgium, Bhutan, Bolivia, Botswana, Brazil, Burkina Faso, Burma, Burundi, Cameroon, Canada, Central African Republic, Chad, Chile, China, Colombia, Congo, Cyprus, Denmark, Dominican Republic, Ecuador, Egypt, El Salvador, Ethiopia, Fiji, Finland, France, Germany, Federal Republic of, Greece, Guyana, Honduras, Iceland, India, Indonesia, Ireland, Italy, Ivory Coast, Japan, Jordan, Kenya, Kuwait, Madagascar, Malaysia, Mauritania, Mauritius, Mexico, Nepal, Netherlands, New Zealand, Niger, Nigeria, Norway, Oman, Pakistan, Panama, Papua New Guinea, Peru, Philippines, Poland, Portugal, Qatar, Romania, Rwanda, Saint Lucia, Samoa, Saudi Arabia, Senegal, Sierra Leone, Singapore, Somalia, Spain, Sri Lanka, Sudan, Suriname, Swaziland, Sweden, Thailand, Togo, Trinidad and Tobago, Tunisia, Turkey, Uganda, United Arab Emirates, United Kingdom, United States, Uruguay, Venezuela, Viet Nam,[a] Zaire, Zambia, Zimbabwe.

Against: Albania, Syrian Arab Republic.

Abstaining: Afghanistan, Algeria, Benin, Bulgaria, Byelorussian SSR, Cuba, Czechoslovakia, German Democratic Republic, Hungary, Iraq, Morocco, USSR, Yemen.

[a]Later advised the Secretariat it had intended to abstain.

Iraq and Yemen said the aggressor alone, not Member States, should pay for UNDOF's operations. Iran did not participate in the vote for similar reasons. Maldives also announced its non-participation. The United Arab Emirates, expressing a similar view, said it cast a positive vote out of solidarity with the international community and support for international peace and security. Jordan emphasized that its vote in favour did not mean that it condoned Israel's continuing occupation of Arab territories; peace-keeping operations should play a temporary role only and the United Nations should go beyond that and bring about a lasting peace in the Middle East. Albania said its negative vote was cast not out of financial considerations but out of respect for certain principles.

Since Israel's aggression had been identified clearly in United Nations resolutions, Israel, not Member States, should finance UNDOF; funding should at best be voluntary, Algeria believed. Since UNDOF had proved incapable of halting the Zionist aggression, a more appropriate solution was required.

The USSR said it could not understand why the costs of peace-keeping forces in the Middle East were so high, and agreed with ACABQ on the need

to economize and make expenditures more cost-effective.

Peace-keeping operations could not be a substitute for peaceful settlement, Israel said. The prolongation of such operations in the Middle East reflected the complexity of the problems there.

Introducing the text, Canada said the success of peace-keeping operations was linked to respect for the principle of collective responsibility for their financing, and the permanent members of the Security Council had a special responsibility in that connection.

The Controller, in response to an inquiry by Canada on the approaching end of the authorized expenditure period for UNDOF, said that even if, according to the regulations, financing for UNDOF should cease on 30 November, steps could be taken to ensure uninterrupted financing until the following week.

Also on 2 December, the Assembly adopted **resolution 40/59 B** by recorded vote.

The General Assembly,

Having regard to the financial position of the Special Account for the United Nations Emergency Force and the United Nations Disengagement Observer Force, as set forth in the report of the Secretary-General, and referring to paragraph 5 of the report of the Advisory Committee on Administrative and Budgetary Questions,

Mindful of the fact that it is essential to provide the United Nations Disengagement Observer Force with the necessary financial resources to enable it to fulfil its responsibilities under the relevant resolutions of the Security Council,

Concerned that the Secretary-General is continuing to face growing difficulties in meeting the obligations of the Forces on a current basis, particularly those due to the Governments of troop-contributing States,

Recalling its resolutions 33/13 E of 14 December 1978, 34/7 D of 17 December 1979, 35/45 B of 1 December 1980, 36/66 B of 30 November 1981, 37/38 B of 30 November 1982, 38/35 B of 1 December 1983 and 39/28 B of 30 November 1984,

Recognizing that, in consequence of the withholding of contributions by certain Member States, the surplus balances in the Special Account for the United Nations Emergency Force and the United Nations Disengagement Observer Force have, in effect, been drawn upon to the full extent to supplement the income received from contributions for meeting expenses of the Forces,

Concerned that the application of the provisions of regulations 5.2 *(b)*, 5.2 *(d)*, 4.3 and 4.4 of the Financial Regulations of the United Nations would aggravate the already difficult financial situation of the Forces,

Decides that the provisions of regulations 5.2 *(b)*, 5.2 *(d)*, 4.3 and 4.4 of the Financial Regulations of the United Nations shall be suspended in respect of the amount of $3,250,131, which otherwise would have to be surrendered pursuant to those provisions, this amount to be entered into the account referred to in the operative part of General Assembly resolution 33/13 E and held in suspense until a further decision is taken by the Assembly.

General Assembly resolution 40/59 B

2 December 1985   Meeting 99   93-10-6 (recorded vote)

Approved by Fifth Committee (A/40/957) by recorded vote (75-11-8), 2 December (meeting 51); 9-nation draft (A/C.5/40/L.4, part B); agenda item 126 *(a)*.
Sponsors: Australia, Austria, Canada, Denmark, Finland, Ireland, New Zealand, Norway, Sweden.
Meeting numbers. GA 40th session: 5th Committee 50, 51; plenary 99.

Recorded vote in Assembly as follows:

In favour: Argentina, Australia, Austria, Bahrain, Bangladesh, Barbados, Belgium, Bhutan, Bolivia, Botswana, Brazil, Burkina Faso, Burma, Burundi, Cameroon, Canada, Central African Republic, Chad, Chile, China, Colombia, Congo, Cyprus, Denmark, Dominican Republic, Ecuador, Egypt, El Salvador, Ethiopia, Fiji, Finland, France, Germany, Federal Republic of, Greece, Guyana, Honduras, Iceland, India, Indonesia, Ireland, Italy, Ivory Coast, Japan, Jordan, Kenya, Kuwait, Madagascar, Malaysia, Mauritania, Mauritius, Mexico, Nepal, Netherlands, New Zealand, Niger, Nigeria, Norway, Oman, Pakistan, Panama, Papua New Guinea, Peru, Philippines, Poland, Portugal, Qatar, Rwanda, Saint Lucia, Samoa, Saudi Arabia, Senegal, Sierra Leone, Somalia, Spain, Sri Lanka, Sudan, Suriname, Swaziland, Sweden, Thailand, Togo, Trinidad and Tobago, Tunisia, Turkey, Uganda, United Arab Emirates, United Kingdom, United States, Uruguay, Venezuela, Zaire, Zambia, Zimbabwe.

Against: Afghanistan, Albania, Bulgaria, Byelorussian SSR, Cuba, Czechoslovakia, German Democratic Republic, Hungary, Syrian Arab Republic, USSR.

Abstaining: Algeria, Benin, Iraq, Morocco, Romania, Yemen.

Explaining its vote, the USSR said it could not countenance any violation of the Financial Regulations which provided that the balance of unutilized funds should be returned to Member States.

CONTRIBUTIONS TO UNDOF

(as at 31 December 1985; in US dollars)

Member State	Assessment in 1985	Paid in 1985	Total contribution outstanding*	Member State	Assessment in 1985	Paid in 1985	Total contributions outstanding*
Afghanistan	176	—	3,879	Gabon	703	—	11,377
Albania	352	—	22,346	Gambia	352	352	—
Algeria	4,572	—	65,098	German Democratic Republic	244,430	729,045	1,395,170
Angola	176	—	2,293	Germany, Federal Republic of	1,501,757	3,003,464	—
Antigua and Barbuda	176	—	1,360	Ghana	703	1,407	—
Argentina	24,971	39,592	49,963	Greece	14,068	28,148	—
Australia	276,084	581,595	—	Grenada	176	—	1,196
Austria	131,887	263,770	—	Guatemala	703	—	3,470
Bahamas	352	704	—	Guinea	176	176	315
Bahrain	352	704	—	Guinea-Bissau	176	—	868
Bangladesh	528	528	528	Guyana	352	—	1,050
Barbados	352	1,044	6	Haiti	176	—	10,318
Belgium	225,088	450,684	—	Honduras	352	—	352
Belize	176	—	352	Hungary	8,089	60,000	91,392
Benin	176	—	10,982	Iceland	5,276	10,552	—
Bhutan	176	352	—	India	12,661	25,333	—
Bolivia	352	—	14,378	Indonesia	4,572	4,576	4,572
Botswana	176	176	176	Iran	20,399	—	253,210
Brazil	48,885	257,570	97,813	Iraq	4,220	—	116,904
Brunei Darussalam	1,055	2,322	—	Ireland	31,653	63,305	—
Bulgaria	6,331	65,177	73,270	Israel	8,089	16,735	32
Burkina Faso	176	176	3,177	Italy	657,677	1,303,928	657,677
Burma	352	698	352	Ivory Coast	1,055	4,183	—
Burundi	176	—	10,982	Jamaica	703	1,470	—
Byelorussian SSR	63,306	233,657	652,986	Japan	1,814,768	3,598,006	1,814,768
Cameroon	352	1,050	—	Jordan	352	1,050	—
Canada	541,617	1,083,216	—	Kenya	352	352	698
Cape Verde	176	5,870	352	Kuwait	8,792	17,592	—
Central African Republic	352	298	21,823	Lao People's Democratic Republic	176	—	2,830
Chad	176	10,806	176	Lebanon	703	21,103	1,407
Chile	2,462	4,926	—	Lesotho	176	—	352
China	188,278	376,543	—	Liberia	352	—	15,200
Colombia	3,869	3,872	3,869	Libyan Arab Jamahiriya	9,144	—	242,205
Comoros	176	—	7,581	Luxembourg	10,551	21,102	—
Congo	352	—	22,346	Madagascar	352	474	2,538
Costa Rica	703	352	351	Malawi	176	175	176
Cuba	3,165	—	24,365	Malaysia	3,165	3,165	—
Cyprus	352	704	—	Maldives	176	—	1,173
Czechoslovakia	133,646	396,298	717,081	Mali	176	—	499
Democratic Kampuchea	352	—	22,346	Malta	352	698	352
Democratic Yemen	176	—	6,062	Mauritania	352	—	12,613
Denmark	131,887	263,770	—	Mauritius	352	—	1,000
Djibouti	176	—	2,037	Mexico	30,949	92,337	—
Dominica	176	—	2,747	Mongolia	352	704	8,441
Dominican Republic	1,055	—	13,719	Morocco	1,758	—	13,881
Ecuador	703	1,347	440	Mozambique	176	—	9,127
Egypt	2,462	4,926	—	Nepal	176	176	176
El Salvador	352	—	7,679	Netherlands	313,012	313,001	313,012
Equatorial Guinea	352	—	16,113	New Zealand	45,721	91,441	—
Ethiopia	176	1,355	—	Nicaragua	352	—	2,390
Fiji	352	352	352	Niger	176	—	1,656
Finland	84,408	168,813	—	Nigeria	6,682	—	27,208
France	1,392,832	1,392,735	1,392,832				

Member State	Assessment in 1985	Paid in 1985	Total contribution outstanding*	Member State	Assessment in 1985	Paid in 1985	Total contribution outstanding*
Norway	89,683	178,808	555	Sudan	176	—	687
Oman	352	704	346	Suriname	176	1,260	176
Pakistan	2,110	4,222	—	Swaziland	352	—	22,346
Panama	703	680	21,099	Sweden	232,122	464,237	—
Papua New Guinea	176	176	176	Syrian Arab Republic	1,055	—	33,361
Paraguay	352	—	22,346	Thailand	2,814	5,630	—
Peru	2,462	—	36,840	Togo	352	—	2,378
Philippines	3,165	6,418	6,092	Trinidad and Tobago	1,055	1,056	1,055
Poland	126,612	253,220	—	Tunisia	1,055	2,112	1,035
Portugal	6,331	6,336	12,291	Turkey	11,254	26,328	456
Qatar	1,055	—	10,615	Uganda	176	—	8,056
Romania	6,682	—	123,679	Ukrainian SSR	232,122	856,744	2,436,645
Rwanda	176	176	349	USSR	2,255,062	8,320,833	21,744,460
Saint Christopher and Nevis	176	176	530	United Arab Emirates	5,627	—	27,754
Saint Lucia	176	606	176	United Kingdom	999,159	1,998,249	—
Saint Vincent and the Grenadines	176	173	352	United Republic of Tanzania	176	—	8,186
Samoa	176	1,482	525	United States	5,424,976	10,841,910	7,666
Sao Tome and Principe	176	—	2,112	Uruguay	1,407	9,048	2,397
Saudi Arabia	30,245	29,720	60,517	Vanuatu	176	—	1,187
Senegal	176	—	176	Venezuela	19,343	141,471	—
Seychelles	176	—	698	Viet Nam	703	—	20,233
Sierra Leone	352	—	13,308	Yemen	176	—	10,582
Singapore	3,165	6,333	—	Yugoslavia	16,178	15,625	79,561
Solomon Islands	176	—	2,577	Zaire	352	—	5,801
Somalia	176	—	1,355	Zambia	352	352	—
South Africa	72,098	—	3,145,478	Zimbabwe	352	686	704
Spain	67,877	270,529	—				
Sri Lanka	352	704	—	Total	17,668,157	38,476,036	36,168,735

*Includes contributions due for UNDOF from its inception on 31 May 1974 through 30 November 1985, as at 31 December 1985, and those due for UNEF II (1973-1979); between 1974 and 1979 there was a single account for the two Forces.
SOURCE: ST/ADM/SER.B/283.

UNIFIL financing

Report of the Secretary-General. In a November 1985 report[5] on the financing of UNIFIL, the Secretary-General stated that, as at 30 September, he had received $833.6 million for the operation of UNIFIL, out of $1,084.8 million apportioned among Member States for the periods from the inception of the Force in March 1978 to 18 October 1985. The balance due—$251.2 million—included $204.4 million that Members said they did not intend to pay and $19.6 million due from China, transferred to a special account in accordance with a 1981 General Assembly resolution.[3] Only $27.2 million of the unpaid balance was considered collectable, leaving a shortfall of $224 million.

This situation posed a serious problem for the financial management of the Force, the Secretary-General said. Obligations could not be met on a current basis, particularly those due to troop-contributing countries, payments to which had never been made in full in accordance with agreed rates. Voluntary contributions to a Suspense Account established in 1979[6] to alleviate the financial burden on the troop contributors amounted to only $18,356.

For UNIFIL operations from 19 April to 18 October 1985, commitments amounted to $70,446,000 gross ($69,445,998 net), as authorized in 1984;[7] the costs for the period 19 October 1985 to 18 April 1986 were estimated at $71,745,000 gross ($70,575,000 net), based on an average Force strength of 5,860. The Secretary-General requested ACABQ concurrence for commitments of $23,482,000 gross ($23,148,666 net) for the period 19 October to 18 December 1985. From 19 April to 18 December 1986, should the Security Council renew UNIFIL's mandate, appropriations of $11,957,500 gross ($11,762,500 net) a month would be required.

Expressing extreme concern about the shortfall burden on troop-contributing countries, particularly on the less wealthy ones, and which might jeopardize UNIFIL's functioning, the Secretary-General appealed in the strongest terms to all Member States to pay their assessments without delay; he also appealed for voluntary contributions to the UNIFIL Suspense Account.

ACABQ recommendations. ACABQ, also in November 1985,[8] recommended approval of commitments entered into from 19 April to 18 October 1985. It also recommended appropriations of the amount of the commitments for 19 October to 18 December, and of $48,263,000 gross ($47,426,334 net) for the remaining four months of the mandate, 19 December 1985 to 18 April 1986, with the Secretary-General having the usual flexibility to revise apportionments between objects of expenditure.

ACABQ also recommended that, for the period from 19 April to 18 December 1986, the Secretary-General be authorized to enter into commitments at a rate not to exceed $11,957,500 gross ($11,762,500 net) per month.

The Committee said it had been informed that, as a consequence of the increase in estimated average Force strength (5,550 in April 1985; 5,860 for April 1986), with no increase in the authorized commitment, it would be necessary to allocate increased resources for such items as reimbursement to troop contributors, daily allowance to troops and rotation costs, while at the same time, in order to remain within the limits set by the Assembly in 1984,[7] to reduce and defer expenditures in other areas, particularly construction, adaptation of premises and purchase of transportation equipment. Bearing this in mind, and noting that the estimate for the October 1985–April 1986 period was 1.6 per cent more than that for each of the two previous mandates, ACABQ had no objection to the estimate.

ACABQ said it had been informed that the interim accounts for 1984-1985 indicated a "surplus" balance of $8,868,174 for the UNIFIL Special Account as at 31 December 1984, representing excess of income over expenditure due to interest and miscellaneous credits. "Income" included assessed contributions irrespective of collectability. In consequence of States' withholding contributions, the "surplus" had, in effect, been drawn upon to its full extent.

GENERAL ASSEMBLY ACTION

In December 1985, the General Assembly adopted two resolutions—40/246 A and B—on the financing of UNIFIL.

On 18 December, it adopted **resolution 40/246 A** by recorded vote.

The General Assembly,

Having considered the report of the Secretary-General on the financing of the United Nations Interim Force in Lebanon and the related report of the Advisory Committee on Administrative and Budgetary Questions,

Bearing in mind Security Council resolutions 425(1978) and 426(1978) of 19 March 1978, 427(1978) of 3 May 1978, 434(1978) of 18 September 1978, 444(1979) of 19 January 1979, 450(1979) of 14 June 1979, 459(1979) of 19 December 1979, 474(1980) of 17 June 1980, 483(1980) of 17 December 1980, 488(1981) of 19 June 1981, 498(1981) of 18 December 1981, 501(1982) of 25 February 1982, 511(1982) of 18 June 1982, 519(1982) of 17 August 1982, 523(1982) of 18 October 1982, 529(1983) of 18 January 1983, 536(1983) of 18 July 1983, 538(1983) of 18 October 1983, 549(1984) of 19 April 1984, 555(1984) of 12 October 1984, 561(1985) of 17 April 1985 and 575(1985) of 17 October 1985,

Recalling its resolutions S-8/2 of 21 April 1978, 33/14 of 3 November 1978, 34/9 B of 17 December 1979, 35/44 of 1 December 1980, 35/115 A of 10 December 1980, 36/138 A of 16 December 1981, 36/138 C of 19 March 1982, 37/127 A of 17 December 1982, 38/38 A of 5 December 1983 and 39/71 A of 13 December 1984,

Reaffirming its previous decisions regarding the fact that, in order to meet the expenditures caused by such

operations, a different procedure from the one applied to meet expenditures of the regular budget of the United Nations is required,

Taking into account the fact that the economically more developed countries are in a position to make relatively larger contributions and that the economically less developed countries have a relatively limited capacity to contribute towards peace-keeping operations involving heavy expenditures,

Bearing in mind the special responsibilities of the States permanent members of the Security Council in the financing of peace-keeping operations decided upon in accordance with the Charter of the United Nations,

I

Decides to appropriate to the Special Account referred to in section I, paragraph 1, of General Assembly resolution S-8/2 an amount of $70,446,000 gross ($69,446,000 net), being the amount authorized with the prior concurrence of the Advisory Committee on Administrative and Budgetary Questions and apportioned under the provisions of section IV of Assembly resolution 39/71 A for the operation of the United Nations Interim Force in Lebanon from 19 April to 18 October 1985, inclusive;

II

Decides to appropriate to the Special Account an amount of $23,482,000 gross ($23,148,666 net), being the amount authorized with the prior concurrence of the Advisory Committee on Administrative and Budgetary Questions and apportioned under the provisions of section IV of Assembly resolution 39/71 A for the operation of the United Nations Interim Force in Lebanon from 19 October to 18 December 1985, inclusive;

III

1. *Decides* to appropriate to the Special Account an amount of $48,263,000 for the operation of the United Nations Interim Force in Lebanon for the period from 19 December 1985 to 18 April 1986, inclusive;

2. *Decides further*, as an *ad hoc* arrangement, without prejudice to the positions of principle that may be taken by Member States in any consideration by the General Assembly of arrangements for the financing of peace-keeping operations, to apportion the amount of $48,263,000 among Member States in accordance with the scheme set out in Assembly resolution 33/14 and the provisions of section V, paragraph 1, of resolution 34/9 B, section VI, paragraph 1, of resolution 35/115 A, section VI, paragraph 1, of resolution 36/138 A, section IX, paragraph 1, of resolution 37/127 A and section VII, paragraphs 1 and 2, of resolution 39/71 A; the scale of assessments for the years 1983, 1984 and 1985 shall be applied against a portion thereof, that is $5,185,281, being the amount pertaining on a *pro rata* basis to the period from 19 to 31 December 1985, inclusive, and the scale of assessments for the years 1986, 1987 and 1988 shall be applied against the balance, that is $43,077,719, for the period thereafter;

3. *Decides* that there shall be set off against the apportionment among Member States, as provided for in paragraph 2 above, their respective share in the estimated income of $13,333 other than staff assessment income approved for the period from 19 December 1985 to 18 April 1986, inclusive;

4. *Decides* that, in accordance with the provisions of its resolution 973(X) of 15 December 1955, there shall

be set off against the apportionment among Member States, as provided for in paragraph 2 above, their respective share in the Tax Equalization Fund of the estimated staff assessment income of $823,333 approved for the period from 19 December 1985 to 18 April 1986, inclusive;

IV

Authorizes the Secretary-General to enter into commitments for the operation of the United Nations Interim Force in Lebanon at a rate not to exceed $11,957,500 gross ($11,762,500 net) per month for the period from 19 April to 18 December 1986, inclusive, should the Security Council decide to continue the Force beyond the period of six months authorized under its resolution 575(1985), subject to obtaining the prior concurrence of the Advisory Committee on Administrative and Budgetary Questions for the actual level of commitments to be entered into for each mandate period that may be approved subsequent to 19 April 1986, the said amount to be apportioned among Member States in accordance with the scale of assessments for the years 1986, 1987 and 1988;

V

1. *Renews its invitation* to Member States to make voluntary contributions to the United Nations Interim Force in Lebanon both in cash and in the form of services and supplies acceptable to the Secretary-General;

2. *Invites* Member States to make voluntary contributions in cash to the Suspense Account established in accordance with its resolution 34/9 D of 17 December 1979;

VI

Requests the Secretary-General to take all necessary action to ensure that the United Nations Interim Force in Lebanon shall be administered with a maximum of efficiency and economy.

General Assembly resolution 40/246 A

18 December 1985   Meeting 121   124-15-4 (recorded vote)

Approved by Fifth Committee (A/40/1037) by recorded vote (97-12-4), 12 December (meeting 60); 21-nation draft (A/C.5/40/L.5, part A); agenda item 126 *(b)*.

Sponsors: Austria, Canada, Denmark, Fiji, Finland, France, Germany, Federal Republic of, Ghana, Iceland, Ireland, Italy, Lebanon, Nepal, Netherlands, New Zealand, Norway, Panama, Papua New Guinea, Samoa, Sweden, Thailand.

Recorded vote in Assembly as follows:

In favour: Antigua and Barbuda, Argentina, Australia, Austria, Bahamas, Bahrain, Bangladesh, Barbados, Belgium, Belize, Benin, Bhutan, Bolivia, Botswana, Brazil, Brunei Darussalam, Burkina Faso, Burma, Burundi, Cameroon, Canada, Cape Verde, Central African Republic, Chad, Chile, China, Colombia, Congo, Costa Rica, Cyprus, Democratic Kampuchea, Denmark, Djibouti, Dominican Republic, Ecuador, Egypt, El Salvador, Equatorial Guinea, Ethiopia, Fiji, Finland, France, Gabon, Gambia, Germany, Federal Republic of, Ghana, Greece, Grenada, Guatemala, Guyana, Honduras, Iceland, India, Indonesia, Ireland, Israel, Italy, Ivory Coast, Jamaica, Japan, Jordan, Kenya, Kuwait, Lebanon, Lesotho, Liberia, Luxembourg, Madagascar, Malawi, Malaysia, Malta, Mauritania, Mauritius, Mexico, Morocco, Nepal, Netherlands, New Zealand, Nicaragua, Niger, Nigeria, Norway, Oman, Pakistan, Panama, Papua New Guinea, Peru, Philippines, Portugal, Qatar, Romania, Rwanda, Saint Lucia, Saint Vincent and the Grenadines, Samoa, Sao Tome and Principe, Saudi Arabia, Senegal, Sierra Leone, Singapore, Solomon Islands, Somalia, Spain, Sri Lanka, Sudan, Suriname, Swaziland, Sweden, Thailand, Togo, Trinidad and Tobago, Tunisia, Turkey, Uganda, United Arab Emirates, United Kingdom, United Republic of Tanzania, United States, Uruguay, Venezuela, Yugoslavia, Zaire, Zambia, Zimbabwe.

Against: Afghanistan, Albania, Bulgaria, Byelorussian SSR, Cuba, Czechoslovakia, German Democratic Republic, Hungary, Lao People's Democratic Republic, Mongolia, Poland, Syrian Arab Republic, Ukrainian SSR, USSR, Viet Nam.

Abstaining: Democratic Yemen, Iraq, Maldives, Yemen.

Introducing the text, Ireland called on all Member States to look to their responsibilities for maintaining peace and to support the peace-keeping efforts. No operation could be expected to function efficiently if it was deprived of nearly a quarter of its revenue, regarded as uncollectable. The extent to which the troop-contributing countries could continue to absorb an unacceptable proportion of the cost of UNIFIL was not unlimited; the responsibility for funding rested on all Member States and any shortfall must be shared by all.

Lebanon said it had always regarded as incontrovertible the principle of collective financial responsibility; the withholding of contributions was particularly unfair, both to those developing countries which contributed and to the countries which supplied troops and assumed the financial burden of UNIFIL as well. The Member States which had participated in the vote on Assembly resolution 181 A (II) in 1947,[9] to which the current tragedy in Lebanon could largely be ascribed, bore a heavy responsibility. UNIFIL's mission was the most urgent and challenging: its function was not merely to observe, but also to assist the Lebanese Government in ensuring the return of its effective authority.

The USSR explained that it did not participate in the financing of UNIFIL because of its position of principle that the consequences of the armed aggression against Lebanon should be borne by the aggressor. The view that the aggressor should bear the financial burden was shared by several others, including Democratic Yemen, Iraq and the Syrian Arab Republic.

Iran did not participate in the vote because it said it believed that the cost of United Nations activities in the Middle East should be borne by the Zionist entity and its supporters. Benin voted in favour for essentially humanitarian reasons, but considered that UNIFIL ought in fact to be financed by those responsible for the situation.

Among those which did not take part in the vote for similar reasons were Algeria and the Libyan Arab Jamahiriya. Algeria added that it hoped that the financial arrangements for all peace-keeping operations could be reviewed in the near future since it had serious doubts as to their usefulness and the propriety of financing them from the regular budget.

Jordan stressed that its vote in favour should not be interpreted as condoning or accepting the continued Israeli occupation of Lebanon.

Also on 18 December, the Assembly adopted **resolution 40/246 B** by recorded vote.

The General Assembly,

Having regard to the financial position of the Special Account for the United Nations Interim Force in Lebanon, as set forth in the report of the Secretary-General, and referring to paragraph 7 of the report of the Advisory Committee on Administrative and Budgetary Questions,

Mindful of the fact that it is essential to provide the United Nations Interim Force in Lebanon with the necessary financial resources to enable it to fulfil its responsibilities under the relevant resolutions of the Security Council,

Concerned that the Secretary-General is continuing to face growing difficulties in meeting the obligations of the United Nations Interim Force in Lebanon on a current basis, particularly those due to the Governments of troop-contributing States,

Recalling its resolutions 34/9 E of 17 December 1979, 35/115 B of 10 December 1980, 36/138 B of 16 December 1981, 37/127 B of 17 December 1982, 38/38 B of 5 December 1983 and 39/71 B of 13 December 1984,

Recognizing that, in consequence of the withholding of contributions by certain Member States, the surplus balances in the Special Account for the United Nations Interim Force in Lebanon have, in effect, been drawn upon to the full extent to supplement the income received from contributions for meeting expenses of the Force,

Concerned that the application of the provisions of regulations 5.2 *(b)*, 5.2 *(d)*, 4.3 and 4.4 of the Financial Regulations of the United Nations would aggravate the already difficult financial situation of the United Nations Interim Force in Lebanon,

Decides that the provisions of regulations 5.2 *(b)*, 5.2 *(d)*, 4.3 and 4.4 of the Financial Regulations of the United Nations shall be suspended in respect of the amount of $8,868,174, which otherwise would have to be surrendered pursuant to those provisions, this amount to be entered in the account referred to in the operative part of General Assembly resolution 34/9 E and held in suspense until a further decision is taken by the Assembly.

General Assembly resolution 40/246 B

18 December 1985   Meeting 121   122-14-5 (recorded vote)

Approved by Fifth Committee (A/40/1037) by recorded vote (97-12-5), 12 December (meeting 60); 21-nation draft (A/C.5/40/L.5, part B); agenda item 126 *(b)*.

Sponsors: Austria, Canada, Denmark, Fiji, Finland, France, Germany, Federal Republic of, Ghana, Iceland, Ireland, Italy, Lebanon, Nepal, Netherlands, New Zealand, Norway, Panama, Papua New Guinea, Samoa, Sweden, Thailand.

Recorded vote in Assembly as follows:

In favour: Antigua and Barbuda, Argentina, Australia, Austria, Bahamas, Bahrain, Bangladesh, Barbados, Belgium, Belize, Bhutan, Bolivia, Botswana, Brazil, Brunei Darussalam, Burkina Faso, Burma, Burundi, Cameroon, Canada, Cape Verde, Central African Republic, Chad, Chile, China, Colombia, Congo, Costa Rica, Cyprus, Democratic Kampuchea, Denmark, Djibouti, Dominican Republic, Ecuador, Egypt, El Salvador, Equatorial Guinea, Ethiopia, Fiji, Finland, France, Gabon, Gambia, Germany, Federal Republic of, Ghana, Greece, Grenada, Guatemala, Guyana, Honduras, Iceland, India, Indonesia, Ireland, Israel, Italy, Ivory Coast, Jamaica, Japan, Jordan, Kenya, Kuwait, Lebanon, Lesotho, Liberia, Luxembourg, Madagascar, Malawi, Malaysia, Malta, Mauritania, Mauritius, Mexico, Morocco, Nepal, Netherlands, New Zealand, Nicaragua, Niger, Nigeria, Norway, Oman, Pakistan, Panama, Papua New Guinea, Peru, Philippines, Poland,[a] Portugal, Qatar, Rwanda, Saint Lucia, Saint Vincent and the Grenadines, Samoa, Saudi Arabia, Senegal, Sierra Leone, Singapore, Solomon Islands, Somalia, Spain, Sri Lanka, Sudan, Suriname, Swaziland, Sweden, Thailand, Togo, Trinidad and Tobago, Tunisia, Turkey, Uganda, United Arab Emirates, United Kingdom, United Republic of Tanzania, United States, Uruguay, Venezuela, Yugoslavia, Zaire, Zambia, Zimbabwe.

Against: Afghanistan, Albania, Bulgaria, Byelorussian SSR, Cuba, Czechoslovakia, German Democratic Republic, Hungary, Lao People's Democratic Republic, Mongolia, Syrian Arab Republic, Ukrainian SSR, USSR, Viet Nam.

Abstaining: Democratic Yemen, Iraq, Maldives, Romania, Yemen.

[a]Later advised the Secretariat it had intended to vote against.

Algeria emphasized that, out of solidarity with Lebanon, it had refrained from participating in the vote instead of voting against the text; it reiterated its reservations regarding the usefulness of UNIFIL.

Cuba also doubted the usefulness of UNIFIL which, it said, was not respected by Israel and its supporters; the cost of the operations should be borne by the aggressor.

Jordan reiterated that its vote in favour should not be interpreted as condoning or accepting the continued Israeli occupation of Lebanon.

CONTRIBUTIONS TO UNIFIL

(as at 31 December 1985; in US dollars)

Member State	Assessment in 1985	Paid in 1985	Total contribution outstanding*	Member State	Assessment in 1985	Paid in 1985	Total contribution outstanding*
Afghanistan	680	—	9,440	Burma	1,385	1,389	1,385
Albania	1,385	—	21,620	Burundi	680	—	10,428
Algeria	18,012	—	258,703	Byelorussian SSR	250,006	—	4,139,925
Angola	680	—	9,562	Cameroon	1,385	4,756	5,051
Antigua and Barbuda	680	—	6,002	Canada	2,138,937	4,277,231	—
Argentina	98,372	8,921	475,490	Cape Verde	680	4,746	1,375
Australia	1,090,302	2,260,925	—	Central African Republic	1,385	—	17,907
Austria	520,845	1,041,533	—	Chad	680	9,748	680
Bahamas	1,385	2,774	—	Chile	9,698	19,421	—
Bahrain	1,385	4,164	—	China	743,122	1,486,288	—
Bangladesh	2,040	—	6,210	Colombia	15,241	46,128	390
Barbados	1,385	4,164	3,293	Comoros	680	—	10,428
Belgium	888,909	1,777,551	—	Congo	1,385	—	21,620
Belize	680	—	2,243	Costa Rica	2,771	—	34,673
Benin	680	—	10,428	Cuba	12,469	—	221,570
Bhutan	680	1,375	—	Cyprus	1,385	2,774	—
Bolivia	1,385	—	21,620	Czechoslovakia	527,790	—	8,713,530
Botswana	680	1,375	695	Democratic Kampuchea	1,385	—	21,620
Brazil	192,586	910,117	585,660	Democratic Yemen	680	—	10,428
Brunei Darussalam	4,156	7,827	—	Denmark	520,845	1,041,533	—
Bulgaria	24,940	—	353,296	Djibouti	680	—	7,892
Burkina Faso	680	695	9,733	Dominica	680	—	10,720

Member State	Assessment in 1985	Paid in 1985	Total contribution outstanding*	Member State	Assessment in 1985	Paid in 1985	Total contribution outstanding*
Dominican Republic	4,156	—	56,096	Niger	680	—	8,321
Ecuador	2,771	4,585	2,249	Nigeria	26,325	—	117,039
Egypt	9,698	9,723	9,698	Norway	354,175	708,243	—
El Salvador	1,385	—	20,593	Oman	1,385	2,774	—
Equatorial Guinea	1,385	—	21,620	Pakistan	8,313	17,147	—
Ethiopia	680	8,549	—	Panama	2,771	3,563	32,188
Fiji	1,385	—	2,774	Papua New Guinea	680	2,070	—
Finland	333,341	666,581	—	Paraguay	1,385	—	21,620
France	5,497,410	5,497,742	5,497,410	Peru	9,698	—	131,417
Gabon	2,771	—	35,670	Philippines	12,469	10,541	55,442
Gambia	1,385	—	21,620	Poland	500,011	—	11,630,215
German Democratic Republic	965,299	—	14,898,566	Portugal	24,940	74,958	—
Germany, Federal Republic of	5,930,688	11,859,592	—	Qatar	4,156	—	12,031
Ghana	2,771	5,549	—	Romania	26,325	—	425,229
Greece	55,421	110,981	—	Rwanda	680	—	3,049
Grenada	680	—	5,113	Saint Christopher and Nevis	680	—	2,657
Guatemala	2,771	—	12,319	Saint Lucia	680	—	8,294
Guinea	680	—	4,713	Saint Vincent and the Grenadines	680	695	1,375
Guinea-Bissau	680	—	7,814	Samoa	680	4,463	2,070
Guyana	1,385	—	2,774	Sao Tome and Principe	680	—	8,961
Haiti	680	—	10,428	Saudi Arabia	119,154	—	358,123
Honduras	1,385	—	7,543	Senegal	680	1,651	6,733
Hungary	31,867	—	632,268	Seychelles	680	—	2,915
Iceland	20,834	41,660	—	Sierra Leone	1,385	—	21,424
India	49,880	99,884	—	Singapore	12,469	24,970	—
Indonesia	18,012	36,124	18,012	Solomon Islands	680	—	10,719
Iran	80,360	—	1,194,863	Somalia	680	—	6,125
Iraq	16,627	—	241,742	South Africa	284,729	—	4,501,264
Ireland	125,003	125,003	—	Spain	267,402	834,961	—
Israel	31,867	63,158	656	Sri Lanka	1,385	2,774	—
Italy	2,597,280	6,795,300	—	Sudan	680	—	3,472
Ivory Coast	4,156	36,518	—	Suriname	680	2,373	695
Jamaica	2,771	3,970	2,771	Swaziland	1,385	—	21,620
Japan	7,166,827	14,335,624	7,166,827	Sweden	916,687	1,833,097	—
Jordan	1,385	2,774	—	Syrian Arab Republic	4,156	—	60,438
Kenya	1,385	1,385	10,600	Thailand	11,084	22,196	—
Kuwait	34,638	69,363	—	Togo	1,385	2,622	10,300
Lao People's Democratic Republic	680	—	10,428	Trinidad and Tobago	4,156	4,167	4,156
Lebanon	2,771	—	5,171	Tunisia	4,156	10,155	4,156
Lesotho	680	—	1,375	Turkey	44,337	84,300	34,404
Liberia	1,385	—	21,620	Uganda	680	—	9,647
Libyan Arab Jamahiriya	36,025	—	490,637	Ukrainian SSR	916,687	—	15,374,955
Luxembourg	41,668	83,323	—	USSR	8,900,569	—	142,711,130
Madagascar	1,385	2,005	14,302	United Arab Emirates	22,169	—	98,561
Malawi	680	—	1,375	United Kingdom	3,943,611	7,086,123	4,113,777
Malaysia	12,469	24,970	—	United Republic of Tanzania	680	—	10,428
Maldives	680	—	4,294	United States	21,409,288	42,795,836	23,848
Mali	680	—	4,496	Uruguay	5,542	—	38,280
Malta	1,385	1,389	1,385	Vanuatu	680	—	6,002
Mauritania	1,385	—	21,620	Venezuela	76,203	625,537	—
Mauritius	1,385	—	4,825	Viet Nam	2,771	—	56,742
Mexico	121,925	488,745	—	Yemen	680	—	10,428
Mongolia	1,385	—	21,620	Yugoslavia	63,734	27,877	376,144
Morocco	6,927	—	75,138	Zaire	1,385	—	27,098
Mozambique	680	—	12,493	Zambia	1,385	2,693	—
Nepal	680	1,153	680	Zimbabwe	1,360	3,231	6,523
Netherlands	1,236,139	2,471,905	—				
New Zealand	180,560	361,066	—	Total	69,743,881	110,313,073	225,960,079
Nicaragua	1,385	—	10,249				

*Covers the period from the inception of UNIFIL (19 March 1978) to 18 October 1985, as at 31 December 1985.
SOURCE: ST/ADM/SER.B/283.

Review of reimbursement rates to troop contributors

Report of the Secretary-General. In a November 1985 report,[10] the Secretary-General reviewed the rates of reimbursement to troop-contributing States, as requested by the General Assembly in 1984.[11] Standard rates had been first established in 1974[12] and were revised twice, in 1977[13] and 1980.[14]

The two main factors that could change the level of compensation based on the reimbursement rates effective December 1980 were inflation and currency exchange-rate fluctuations. At the end of 1984, the value of the United States dollar—the currency of reimbursement—in relation to the national currencies of the 13 troop contributors had increased by an overall average of 50.4 per cent. With regard to troop costs, the Secretary-General for various reasons considered it not possible to determine their escalation.

Concluding, the Secretary-General stated that the changes in the currency exchange rates had been such that in most cases they had offset the adverse effects of inflation; it appeared that the current standard rates continued to provide a fair and reasonable compensation to troop contributors for troop costs and that a basis did not exist to warrant for the time being an adjustment to the rates of reimbursement.

At the time of the initial establishment of standard rates, it was recognized that certain States would not be fully reimbursed for their entire expenses of providing troops; all troop contributors, however, should receive at least that portion paid to their troops as actual overseas allowances. Based on the data provided by the 11 troop contributors included in the review, 10 were currently absorbing between 11.7 and 72.2 per cent, for an average of 34.3 per cent, in respect of pay and allowances.

The Secretary-General proposed that a review of the rates be undertaken as and when changes in the currency exchange and/or inflation rates drastically affected compensation for troop costs.

ACABQ consideration. In its November 1985 report[8] on UNIFIL (see p. 320), ACABQ noted the Secretary-General's conclusion that it would appear that the current standard rates were fair and reasonable and that currently no basis existed to warrant an adjustment. It also noted his statement proposing a review of the rates as and when changes dictated.

GENERAL ASSEMBLY ACTION

On 18 December, the General Assembly adopted **resolution 40/247** by recorded vote.

Review of the rates of reimbursement to the Governments of troop-contributing States

The General Assembly,

Having considered the report of the Secretary-General on the review of the rates of reimbursement to the Governments of troop-contributing States, submitted pursuant to General Assembly resolution 39/70 of 13 December 1984, as well as the related report of the Advisory Committee on Administrative and Budgetary Questions,

Recalling its decision of 29 November 1974, taken at its twenty-ninth session, by which it established, as from 25 October 1973, standard rates of reimbursement to the Governments of troop-contributing States for pay and allowances of their troops serving in the United Nations Emergency Force and the United Nations Disengagement Observer Force, and its decision 32/416 of 2 December 1977, by which it revised those rates of reimbursement as from 25 October 1977,

Recalling also its resolution S-8/2 of 21 April 1978, by which it applied the same standard rates of reimbursement in effect for the United Nations Emergency Force and the United Nations Disengagement Observer Force to those Governments of States contributing troops to the United Nations Interim Force in Lebanon,

Recalling further its resolution 35/44 of 1 December 1980, by which it established new standard rates of reim-

bursement to the Governments of troop-contributing States of $950 per person per month for all ranks, plus $280 per person per month for a limited number of specialists (up to 25 per cent of logistics contingents and up to 10 per cent of other contingents), with effect from 1 December 1980 in the case of the United Nations Disengagement Observer Force and from 19 December 1980 in the case of the United Nations Interim Force in Lebanon,

Recalling further its decision of 15 December 1975, taken at its thirtieth session, by which it approved the principle of reimbursing the troop-contributing States for the usage factor for personal clothing, gear and equipment and personal weaponry, including ammunition, issued by Governments to their troops for service in the United Nations peace-keeping forces and in which it requested the Secretary-General to negotiate a settlement thereof, pursuant to which a reimbursement rate of $70 per person per month was agreed upon,

Recognizing that, in consequence of the shortfall of financial contributions, troop-contributing States are not being reimbursed to the full extent of the established rates and are thus bearing considerably larger portions of the costs for their troops serving in the United Nations peace-keeping forces than those indicated by the Secretary-General in his report,

1.   *Takes note* of the conclusions and recommendations of the Secretary-General as outlined in paragraphs 12 to 15 of his report;

2.   *Decides* to retain the current rates of reimbursement of $950 per person per month for all ranks, plus the specialists' allowance of $280 per person per month for 25 per cent of logistics contingents and 10 per cent of other contingents, as well as $65 per person per month for the usage factor for personal clothing, gear and equipment and $5 per person per month for personal weaponry, including ammunition;

3.   *Also decides* that the rates of reimbursement to the Governments of troop-contributing States shall be reviewed by the Secretary-General, in consultation with the troop-contributing States, and requests the Secretary-General to report thereon to the General Assembly, at least once every two years, if, in the light of inflation and currency-exchange fluctuations or other factors brought to the attention of the Secretary-General, these rates appreciably affect the absorption factor of two or more of the troop-contributing States.

General Assembly resolution 40/247

18 December 1985   Meeting 121   120-14-7 (recorded vote)

Approved by Fifth Committee (A/40/1037) by recorded vote (97-11-7), 12 December (meeting 60); 18-nation draft (A/C.5/40/L.6); agenda item 126 *(c)*.

Sponsors: Austria, Canada, Denmark, Fiji, Finland, France, Ghana, Iceland, Ireland, Italy, Lebanon, Nepal, Netherlands, New Zealand, Norway, Papua New Guinea, Samoa, Sweden.

Recorded vote in Assembly as follows:

In favour: Antigua and Barbuda, Argentina, Australia, Austria, Bahamas, Bahrain, Bangladesh, Barbados, Belgium, Belize, Bhutan, Bolivia, Botswana, Brazil, Brunei Darussalam, Burkina Faso, Burma, Burundi, Cameroon, Canada, Central African Republic, Chad, Chile, China, Colombia, Congo, Costa Rica, Cyprus, Democratic Kampuchea, Denmark, Djibouti, Dominican Republic, Ecuador, Egypt, El Salvador, Equatorial Guinea, Ethiopia, Fiji, Finland, France, Gabon, Gambia, Germany, Federal Republic of, Ghana, Greece, Grenada, Guatemala, Guyana, Honduras, Iceland, India, Indonesia, Ireland, Israel, Italy, Ivory Coast, Jamaica, Japan, Jordan, Kenya, Kuwait, Lebanon, Lesotho, Liberia, Luxembourg, Madagascar, Malawi, Malaysia, Malta, Mauritania, Mauritius, Mexico, Morocco, Nepal, Netherlands, New Zealand, Nicaragua, Niger, Nigeria, Norway, Oman, Pakistan, Panama, Papua New Guinea, Peru, Philippines, Poland, Portugal, Qatar, Rwanda, Saint Lucia, Saint Vincent and the Grenadines, Samoa, Saudi Arabia, Senegal, Sierra Leone, Singapore, Solomon Islands, Somalia,

Spain, Sri Lanka, Sudan, Suriname, Swaziland, Sweden, Thailand, Togo, Trinidad and Tobago, Tunisia, Turkey, Uganda, United Arab Emirates, United Republic of Tanzania, United States, Uruguay, Venezuela, Yugoslavia, Zaire, Zambia, Zimbabwe.

Against: Afghanistan, Albania, Bulgaria, Byelorussian SSR, Cuba, Czechoslovakia, German Democratic Republic, Hungary, Lao People's Democratic Republic, Mongolia, Syrian Arab Republic, Ukrainian SSR, USSR, Viet Nam.

Abstaining: Algeria, Benin, Democratic Yemen, Iraq, Maldives, Romania, Yemen.

Explaining its vote, the USSR said it considered that the position in regard to the expenses borne by the United Nations for peace-keeping troops and reimbursement was not clear-cut; there was a considerable element of increase in those expenditures.

Introducing the text, Sweden said the established standard rates of reimbursement consisted of average figures, per person per month for all ranks, used as factors to determine the troop costs, which constituted approximately half of the budgets for UNDOF and UNIFIL. They were also meant to correspond to certain portions of the troop-contributing countries' national costs for maintaining their troops in the service of the United Nations. Since 1980, those costs had increased significantly, in some cases by more than 40 per cent.

REFERENCES

[1]YUN 1973, p. 222, GA res. 3101(XXVIII), 11 Dec. 1973. [2]A/40/754. [3]YUN 1981, p. 1299, GA res. 36/116 A, 10 Dec. 1981. [4]A/40/948. [5]A/40/844. [6]YUN 1979, p. 352, GA res. 34/9 D, 17 Dec. 1979. [7]YUN 1984, p. 310, GA res. 39/71 A, 13 Dec. 1984. [8]A/40/954. [9]YUN 1947-48, p. 247, GA res. 181 A (II), 29 Nov. 1947. [10]A/40/845. [11]YUN 1984, p. 314, GA res. 39/70, 13 Dec. 1984. [12]YUN 1974, p. 215. [13]YUN 1977, p. 281, GA dec. 32/416, 2 Dec. 1977. [14]YUN 1980, p. 369, GA res. 35/44, 1 Dec. 1980.

Territories occupied by Israel

During 1985, the situation in the territories occupied by Israel as a result of previous armed conflicts in the Middle East was again considered by the General Assembly and its Special Committee to Investigate Israeli Practices Affecting the Human Rights of the Population of the Occupied Territories (Committee on Israeli practices). The Committee observed that there was a continuing deterioration in the respect for the human—civil and political, as well as economic, social and cultural—rights of the civilian population of the territories, which comprised the West Bank of the Jordan River (including East Jerusalem), the Golan Heights and the Gaza Strip.

The Assembly, in December, adopted seven resolutions dealing with specific aspects of the Committee's report: it demanded that Israel desist from certain policies and practices in the territories (40/161 D); that it comply with the 1949 Geneva Convention relative to the Protection of Civilian Persons in Time of War (fourth Geneva Convention) (40/161 B); that it desist from any action which would change the legal status and composition of the Palestinian and other Arab territories occupied since 1967 (40/161 C), including the Syrian Golan Heights (40/161 F); that it release Ziyad Abu Eain and other Palestinian prisoners (40/161 A); that it rescind the expulsion of Palestinians, some of whom had been in public office (40/161 E); and that it ensure the freedom of educational institutions (40/161 G).

The Security Council considered the situation in the occupied territories at two meetings on 12 and 13 September. It voted on a draft resolution in which it would have called on Israel to stop repressive measures against the civilian Palestinian population and abide by the fourth Geneva Convention. The draft was not adopted owing to the negative vote of a permanent member of the Council.

In March, the Secretary-General organized a seminar on remedies for the deterioration of the economic and social conditions of the Palestinians in the occupied territories. Affirming that Israeli occupation was contradictory to the basic requirements for the social and economic development of the Palestinians, the Assembly, by resolution 40/201, requested the Secretary-General to organize by April 1987 a seminar on priority development projects to improve their living conditions.

In June 1985, the Secretary-General submitted a study on Israeli economic practices in the territories and a report on progress made in the lifting of Israeli restrictions on their economy and on projects to facilitate their economic development. The Assembly (decision 40/432), as earlier the Economic and Social Council had done (decision 1985/177), asked him to report on Israeli financial and trade practices in the territories. The Council (resolution 1985/58) and the Assembly (resolution 40/169) called for the urgent lifting of Israeli restrictions on the territories' economy, and called on all concerned to facilitate the establishment of a seaport and a citrus plant in the Gaza Strip, as well as of a cement plant in the West Bank.

The Secretary-General reported that in June Israel had given instructions to cease all work related to a planned canal linking the Mediterranean and the Dead Sea. The Assembly, by resolution 40/167, requested him to monitor any new development relating to the project.

Communications. By a letter of 5 February,[1] the Chairman of the Committee on Palestinian rights brought to the Secretary-General's attention what he termed another instance of intensification of the planned policy of annexation of the occupied territories of the West Bank by Israel. According to December 1984 reports in Israeli papers, a plan for the establishment of a national road grid for the entire West Bank had been promulgated, greatly increasing the integration of the West Bank road system into that of Israel. According to a recent study, the road system would serve none of the 20 major Palestinian towns and cities in the West Bank. About 78 million square metres of private Palestinian land would have to be expropriated. The Chairman expressed utmost concern at the plan which, in the Committee's view, had ominous implications for the future of the territories and international peace efforts.

On 12 February,[2] the Chairman expressed the Committee's concern at the growing tension in and around Palestinian refugee camps in southern Lebanon (see above, under "Lebanon situation") and in the West Bank. It was reported that at Dheisheh, near Bethlehem, all roads into the camp had been blocked, affecting the provision of services to the camp and aggravating the atmosphere of living under siege caused by almost daily incidents of provocation and harassment against the camp residents by Israeli settlers. On 1 February, the police, reinforced by military troops, had arrested scores of residents in the camp and villages in the vicinity.

By a letter of 6 March, transmitted by Democratic Yemen,[3] PLO charged that on 5 March Israeli troops had surrounded the Palestinian town of Saeer in the Al-Khalil (Hebron) area, breaking into several Palestinian homes, razing two of them, and injuring about 30 persons. Those injured could not be transferred to hospitals as a curfew was imposed and the area declared an Israeli military zone. The troops also arrested a number of Palestinians and took them away for interrogation. A request by the Red Cross to visit the area was denied. PLO called on the United Nations to assume its full responsibility, spelt out in General Assembly resolutions calling for adequate protection of Palestinians living under Israeli military occupation and for a guarantee of their safety and security and their human and legal rights.

Renewed acts of Israeli repression against Palestinians in the West Bank were charged by the Chairman of the Committee on Palestinian rights in a letter of 19 March;[4] the Committee expressed profound concern at news reports of measures against Bir Zeit University, the treatment of student detainees and the continued establishment of Israeli settlements in the occupied territories (for details, see p. 338).

By a letter of 11 April, transmitted by the United Arab Emirates,[5] PLO accused Israel of implementing exceptional military measures, among them curfews, collective punishments, and attacks on students and refugee camps. The PLO Chairman called for international condemnation of the continued Zionist aggression, to deter Israel from further crimes against the Palestinians.

The Acting Chairman of the Committee on Palestinian rights, on 2 May,[6] brought to the Secretary-General's attention further incidents in the territories which, in his view, indicated a continuing pattern of repression by Israel aimed at stifling Palestinian opposition. Demonstrations and strikes between 30 March and 21 April had been met by hundreds of arrests, the forcible reopening of shops, heavy censorship of Arabic language newspapers, the closing of schools, and the shooting of demonstrators. As long as the Palestinians were prevented from exercising their rights and their territory remained illegally occupied, tension and violence would continue, the Acting Chairman stated; the Committee remained convinced that a peaceful solution under United Nations auspices was possible and continued to call on all concerned to co-operate.

On 12 July,[7] the Acting Chairman called attention to press reports that Israeli forces had demolished on 18 June seven villages in the Hebron area, displacing some 200 families, in order to convert their land into a military training zone. The press also had reported proposed new laws to allow for rapid deportation of Palestinians who took part in "anti-Israeli activity" and for imprisonment without trial or charges for an unlimited period. Such proposed action, the Acting Chairman stated, directly contravened basic human rights principles and could not but aggravate tension; positive action by the Security Council on the Committee's 1976 recommendations[8] and on the proposed international peace conference on the Middle East (see p. 268) would advance peace prospects and help preclude such inequities.

On 8 August,[9] he quoted further press reports, according to which the Israeli Cabinet on 4 August had decided to reinstate its policies of "administrative detention" (see p. 336) and deportation of those considered security risks, and to authorize the closing down of newspapers which violated censorship regulations or were considered to have incited terrorist attacks. New legislation was also reported to have been submitted to the Knesset to bar contacts between Israeli citizens and PLO, under penalty of gaol and a fine. The Acting Chairman also reported the recent temporary closing of Al-Najah University at Nablus, repeated closings of a theatre in East Jerusalem, and a decision to dismiss all Arab employees of the town of Kiryat and accord preference to businesses employing Jews only. Those measures, he said, were designed to stifle political, economic and cultural activity, and to pressure the Palestinians into emigrating with a view to annexation of their land.

Qatar, as Chairman of the Arab Group, transmitted letters of 6, 9 and 10 September from PLO.[10] PLO reported the arrest of Palestinians under the reimposed administrative detention law and other repressive measures by Israeli forces which, it was charged, had blown up several Palestinian homes at Al-Khalil (Hebron), placed the town under curfew, declared the area a military zone, and fired on Palestinians, injuring several. In the opinion of PLO, such acts and the continued deportation of Palestinians only exacerbated an already explosive situation, and required an immediate practical response from the Secretary-General and the Security Council. Alleging that Israeli repression had intensified in recent days and that additional military forces had been deployed throughout the territories, PLO also charged that Israeli officials had threatened to take military action against PLO offices at Amman and elsewhere if Palestinians continued to challenge the Israeli occupation. Israeli paratroopers, employed instead of the regular border guards who had been withdrawn, had rampaged through Jenin and Nablus, indiscriminately beating up Palestinian men, women and children. At Al-Khalil, they had shot and wounded four children.

The Chairman of the Committee on Palestinian rights, by a letter of 11 September,[11] charged that Israel, according to press reports, had engaged in a massive campaign of detention of Palestinians, holding over 50 in the West Bank and several others in Gaza. Curfews were imposed in a number of towns and refugee camps. At least three Palestinians were threatened with deportation from the West Bank. Those and other actions, the Chairman said, were taking place in an atmosphere of growing provocation by Jewish settlers in the territories, clearly aimed at pressuring the local population to emigrate.

On 12 September,[12] Jordan refuted an allegation made by Israel on 9 September[13] (see p. 273) that PLO had recently escalated its campaign of terror on innocent civilians by infiltrating terrorists and smuggling weapons and explosives from Jordan. That accusation, Jordan said, was contrary to the truth, as the resistance arose from within the territories and was escalating as a natural reaction to Israeli practices, involving oppression, injustice, suppression of freedoms, detention of innocent people, expulsion and deportation, confiscation of land and property, the establishment of settlements and the bringing in of immigrants.

In a 23 September letter, transmitted by Qatar,[14] PLO reported that Israeli occupation authorities had deported 29 Palestinians, had closed the Palestinian newspaper *Al-Darb* and had

issued a three-day closure notice for another, *Al Sha'b*. Israeli demonstrators outside the Jerusalem offices of *Al-Fajr* had demanded that the paper be immediately closed, and threats had been made against the newspaper's employees.

In a 24 October letter, transmitted by Kuwait,[15] PLO reported an attack on 13 Palestinians by Israeli settlers, increased detentions, destruction of houses, expropriation of land, and closure of the Palestinian weekly *Al-Bayader Al-Siyassiya*. The PLO Chairman called on the Secretary-General to use his good offices to take immediate measures to end the intolerable and inhuman situation in the territories.

Kuwait transmitted a 30 October letter from PLO,[16] apprising the Secretary-General of the arrest on 28 October and probable deportation of four Palestinians. The alarming number of Palestinians being deported, PLO said, raised the possibility that Israel intended to eliminate forcibly all Palestinian presence from the territories, and required an immediate practical response by the Secretary-General and the Security Council.

On 13 November,[17] the Chairman of the Committee on Palestinian rights quoted press reports that on 25 October Israeli forces had placed the town of Yatta under a 60-hour curfew, conducted searches, destroyed two houses and arrested several people. Also in October, there had been reports of a two-week ban on the distribution of *Al-Bayader*, the closure of the Al-Manar press office and the newspaper *Al-Darb* and the administrative detention or town arrest of eight journalists. In the Committee's view, such measures were in violation of human rights instruments and United Nations resolutions, and posed a serious obstacle to international efforts to achieve a just and lasting solution to the Palestinian question. Other charges made in the letter related to the detention of Palestinians (see p. 336).

Referring to reports of PLO's alleged intention to limit terrorist attacks to the occupied territories, Israel said in a letter of 2 December[18] that nothing justified terrorism, and that PLO's definition of "occupied territory" meant all of Israel, the liquidation of which remained PLO's admitted aim.

Several communications dealt with the closing of the Medical Facility Hospice in East Jerusalem, which served the Arab population of the city and the West Bank (see p. 281).

Action by the Commission on Human Rights and its Sub-Commission. Violations of human rights in the occupied territories were the subject of four resolutions[19] adopted by the Commission on Human Rights in February 1985. By the first, it condemned a number of specific practices; by the second, it condemned Israel's failure to acknowledge the applicability the fourth Geneva

Convention; by the third, it called on Israel to rescind its decision to impose its laws and administration on the Syrian Golan Heights and to cease its acts of terrorism against Syrian citizens; and by the fourth, it condemned Israel's occupation of the Palestinian and other Arab territories, and reaffirmed Palestinian rights.

The Sub-Commission on Prevention of Discrimination and Protection of Minorities, by a resolution of 29 August,[20] also reiterated elements that it considered Palestinian rights should include, and strongly affirmed that the perpetuation of the Israeli occupation of the Palestinian and other Arab territories, including Jerusalem, could only be a source of increasing human rights violations and increasing tension. It also recommended that the Commission adopt a resolution condemning Israel for its continued occupation of the Palestinian and other Arab territories, for its persistence in colonizing them and for its policies against the inhabitants, and calling for immediate withdrawal from those territories. (For details, see ECONOMIC AND SOCIAL QUESTIONS, Chapter XVIII.)

Report of the Committee on Israeli practices. In its annual report to the General Assembly,[21] approved on 30 August 1985, the Committee on Israeli practices, established in 1968,[22] presented information on Israeli policy in the occupied territories and on various aspects of the situation there, including information on annexation and settlements, treatment of civilians and detainees, prison conditions, and judicial remedies sought by the population.

To examine information on the situation since adoption of its previous report in September 1984,[23] the Committee held three series of meetings: from 21 to 25 January at Geneva to review its mandate, examine communications and decide on its organization of work; between 13 and 31 May at Geneva, Damascus, Amman and Cairo to undertake hearings for recording information or evidence; and from 22 to 30 August at Geneva to examine information on the situation in the territories between May and August.

The Committee had before it a number of communications addressed to it by Governments, organizations and individuals; it also heard testimony from persons living in the West Bank, the Gaza Strip and the Golan Heights. At Damascus, the Committee was presented with an updated report on the human rights situation in occupied Syrian territory by an official of the Syrian Ministry of Foreign Affairs. At Amman, it was presented with ministry reports on the situation in the occupied territories, discussed various aspects of its mandate, and met with PLO Chairman Yasser Arafat. In the Syrian Arab Republic, the Committee observed the occupied village of Majdal Shams and met with a number of persons

from the Golan Heights. At Cairo, it met with PLO officials and the Chairman of the Palestine Red Crescent Society.

On the basis of the information and evidence before it, the Committee concluded that Israel continued to follow the same policy in the territories as in previous years, based on the concept that the territories constituted a part of Israel. Measures affecting the security of person and property and, in general, every aspect of life continued to be taken. New settlements continued to be established and planned, and considerable funds allocated for that purpose. The conditions for some 3,000 Palestinians in overcrowded Israeli prisons gave rise to much suffering.

The Committee observed that there was a continuing deterioration in respect for the human—civil and political, as well as economic, social and cultural—rights of the civilian population. The relevant provisions of the fourth Geneva Convention continued to be disregarded and all sectors of life were constantly pervaded by Israel's relentless annexation and settlements policy. At the same time, hundreds of thousands of Palestinians outside the territories were denied the right to return and their property was taken over for the establishment of Israeli settlements.

Confirming the view that the cycle of violence was bound to continue and that the grave situation would remain explosive, the Committee stated that the international community must adopt measures to reverse the deterioration. The parties must change their attitude in regard to the overall political aspects of the problem and give priority to safeguarding fundamental rights.

Report of the Secretary-General. In August 1985,[24] the Secretary-General reported to the General Assembly on the implementation of its 1984 requests[25] that he provide the Committee on Israeli practices with necessary facilities and staff, and ensure widest circulation of its reports and of information on its activities and findings. The Secretary-General stated that, as in previous years, he had provided the facilities and additional staff required by the Committee. Its report was given coverage in various United Nations publications, press releases and radio and television programmes and disseminated through United Nations information centres, whose Geneva and Cairo offices provided press coverage and other assistance during the Committee meetings there.

SECURITY COUNCIL ACTION (September)

The Security Council held meetings on 12 and 13 September 1985 to consider the situation in the occupied territories, as requested by Qatar on behalf of the Group of Arab States at the United Nations.[26]

Meeting numbers. SC 2604, 2605.

The Council invited Iran, Israel, Jordan, Qatar and the Syrian Arab Republic, at their request, to participate in the discussion without the right to vote. Also invited to participate, under rule 39[i] of the Council's provisional rules of procedure, were the Chairman of the Committee on Palestinian rights, at his request, and the Permanent Observer of the League of Arab States, at Qatar's request on behalf of the Arab Group.[27]

Also at Qatar's request in a letter of 12 September,[28] the Council decided, by 10 votes to 1 (United States), with 4 abstentions (Australia, Denmark, France, United Kingdom), that an invitation to participate be accorded to a representative of PLO. The invitation, though not made pursuant to rule 37[j] or rule 39 of the rules of procedure, conferred on PLO the same rights as those conferred on Member States when invited to participate pursuant to rule 37.

Before the vote, the United States restated its position in opposition to the granting of hearings to persons speaking on behalf of non-governmental entities, except on the basis of rule 39 (see p. 274).

On 13 September, the Council voted on a draft resolution,[29] submitted by Burkina Faso, Egypt, India, Madagascar, Peru, and Trinidad and Tobago, by which it would have: (1) deplored Israel's repressive measures since 4 August 1985 against the civilian Palestinian population, especially in the West Bank and Gaza, and expressed concern that persistence in applying such measures would lead to further deterioration of the situation; (2) called on Israel to stop those measures, release all detainees and refrain from further deportations; and (3) abide scrupulously by the provisions of the fourth Geneva Convention. The voting was as follows:

In favour: Burkina Faso, China, Egypt, India, Madagascar, Peru, Thailand, Trinidad and Tobago, Ukrainian SSR, USSR.
Against: United States.
Abstaining: Australia, Denmark, France, United Kingdom.

Owing to the negative vote of a permanent Council member, the draft was not adopted.

The United States said it could not support a text which singled out for condemnation Israeli policies in the West Bank and Gaza without equally condemning and calling for a halt to the terrorist acts against Israeli civilians and officials there which had provoked those policies. One-sided resolutions encouraged the spiral of violence by hardening attitudes; the draft undercut the Council's ability to play a positive role in resolving the problems by exacerbating an already volatile situation.

Australia would have preferred recognition in the draft of the regrettable escalation of violence in the territories rather than a focus solely on the actions of one party. The draft also contained unbalanced and in some cases less than fully accurate reflections of the situation in its relation to the fourth Geneva Convention.

Denmark feared that the draft might hamper moves towards negotiations on the Arab-Israeli conflict; in its view, it did not take adequately into account that a continuation of the cycle of violence and countermeasures could only undermine the necessary basis of dialogue and trust essential for constructive negotiations.

The United Kingdom indicated that, although it was unhappy about certain aspects of Israel's conduct, it was not satisfied that paragraph 2 conformed with the occupying Power's legal obligations and would have welcomed a balanced reference calling for an end to violence by all parties. Only if calm was restored to the West Bank would it be possible to move the peace process forward; however, suggestions on those lines, it said, were not taken up.

France deplored the constraints which the revived special legislation dating from the time of the British Mandate imposed on the population of the territories; nevertheless, only a cessation of violence, from whatever source, would make it possible to restore the climate of confidence indispensable to dialogue. France also remarked that, according to information at its disposal, some of the recent Israeli measures were not in keeping with the fourth Geneva Convention; the draft, however, suggested that all those measures were contrary to the Convention.

The USSR rejected any attempt to equate the occupiers with the inhabitants of the territories who were resisting occupation; any talk of a cycle of violence was out of place. It was Israel that had established conditions of terror, opening fire on defenceless Palestinians, carrying out mass arrests, imposing curfews and threatening deportation. It was high time that the Council took the strictest measures to put an end to such activities.

Although the draft had failed of adoption, stated Qatar for the Arab Group, it had given support to the Palestinians in the territories and would encourage them.

The Syrian Arab Republic stressed that the right to struggle for liberation was legitimate and enshrined in the Charter; all countries under occupation were obliged to use that right. The draft resolution was not commensurate with the gravity of the situation; it should have explicitly condemned Israel for its acts of individual terrorism, mass punishment and killing of innocent people.

The measures called for in the draft were the least the Council could expect of any State,

[i]See footnote a on p. 274.
[j]See footnote b on p. 274.

Burkina Faso and Jordan believed. Adoption of the text should be a reflection of the Council's concern over the worsening of security in the area, Peru said.

PLO said the occupied territories had been witnessing a marked escalation of Israel's "iron fist" policy, designed to suppress Palestinian mass resistance since 4 August, when Israel had adopted a set of oppressive laws and procedures. The deportation law gave the military governor absolute authority to deport whomever he wanted and for any reason he deemed fit. Although additions to those laws granted appeal rights before the military courts, they were not binding on the military governor, and invoking them so far had failed to have rescinded any expulsion decisions. Since 28 August, administrative detention had been imposed on dozens of Palestinians, especially trade unionists and university students. Most of the territories were subjected to a curfew and armed settlers intensified their aggression against Palestinians, destroying their homes and property. At Al-Khalil (Hebron) and Gaza, groups of Palestinians had been fired on and large numbers attacked, beaten and arrested. That escalation was preceded by Israeli statements threatening PLO headquarters and offices, including those at Amman and in Tunisia. The occupation authorities also closed down a press office in Jerusalem, and on 12 September the Israeli Supreme Court expelled freedom fighters. A legislative bill was soon introduced to execute Palestinian freedom fighters. Israel's recent oppressive practices called not only for condemnation and denunciation by the Council but for measures to end them and redress their consequences.

In Israel's view, the Council had been convened not merely for an absolutely preposterous and irrelevant reason, but with a distortion, because those very people who had been engaged in mass killings and attacks, in deliberate and systematic murder, were usurping its meaning and purpose. It was not a mighty Israel attacking defenceless Palestinians, but it was defenceless Israeli civilians who were being remorselessly attacked by PLO terrorists, Israel responded. In the past year, PLO murderers had attempted dozens of times to blow up, shoot, stab and mutilate Israeli citizens. Israel had made it clear that it would not tolerate the establishment of new terror bases on its borders; it had taken steps to apprehend the killers and their collaborators and to prevent them from committing further atrocities. The steps included the detention of suspected terrorists and, in a few cases, selective deportation; contrary to the allegations, those actions were fully legal under the fourth Geneva Convention.

Opening the Council debate, Qatar, for the Arab Group, charged that Israel's recent practices—which Israel justified as a response to Palestinian resistance—were but one link in a chain of crimes against the Palestinians, aimed at emptying their territories in order to create a Jewish State on Palestinian soil.

Several speakers, among them Egypt, India, Madagascar, Qatar for the Arab Group, Thailand, Trinidad and Tobago, and the Ukrainian SSR, believed that Israel's "iron fist" policy was responsible for the worsening situation in the territories and that it was not in accordance with international law, in particular the fourth Geneva Convention. They called for Council action to end that policy which, they believed, threatened international peace and security. Persistence in that policy, Egypt, Jordan and others warned, obstructed peace efforts under way and would lead to even more tension and turmoil.

India said the situation could assume tragic proportions unless the international community restrained Israel and made it discharge its obligations under international conventions that dictated civilized behaviour for occupying Powers towards the people of occupied territories.

Rather than implement its avowed intention to respond to the activities of Israeli extremists, Egypt said, Israel expelled, arrested, oppressed and persecuted the peaceful inhabitants of the territories. Israel must punish the settlers for their actions and remove them from the territories. One of the basic conditions for a settlement of the problem was a feeling of trust among the Palestinians; unfortunately, the conduct of the occupying authorities failed to provide the framework for such a settlement.

Recent Israeli actions could frustrate the attainment of a settlement, Trinidad and Tobago feared; if those actions were considered within the context of expropriation of land and the establishment of settlements, that would seem to indicate that the Israeli authorities were instituting a programme to change the very character of the territories and further frustrate the just aspirations of the Palestinians.

Israel's decision to carry out administrative detentions and deportations was in violation of the fourth Geneva Convention and should be repealed immediately, said China. Israel must stop its repression and intimidation against the Palestinians and other Arab peoples and ensure them their right to existence, and the Council should support them in that regard.

The Syrian Arab Republic called on the Council to reaffirm that, under the fourth Geneva Convention, expulsion and deportation, whether individual or collective, were war crimes, as was, under the Convention and its Additional Protocol I, the transfer of foreign settlers to the occupied territories.

With its repressive measures in the territories and threats of military action against countries harbouring PLO offices, Burkina Faso said, Israel was seeking totally to destroy the will of the population to resist.

The escalating provocation against the Palestinians had reached such a level that groups of Israeli fanatics, led by a member of the Knesset, had called publicly for the expulsion of all Palestinians from the West Bank and the Gaza Strip, Jordan stated; the only solution to their suffering was an end to occupation and the establishment of a just and comprehensive peace.

Madagascar said the Israeli authorities, rather than confining themselves to police measures to keep peace and maintain order, chose—faithful to their policies of escalation and expansion— military or paramilitary operations. No imperatives of security or public order could legitimize Israel's practices, since the incidents invoked to justify those practices derived from Israel's persistence in intensifying its settlements policy; Palestinian opposition to military occupation could not be described as terrorism except by the occupying Power itself.

Peru urged an end to the measures against the civilian population and called on the occupying forces strictly to observe the fourth Geneva Convention.

In Thailand's opinion, the burden of proof should not rest on the territories' population, but on the occupying authorities; Israel had to prove beyond doubt that no measure prohibited by the fourth Geneva Convention had been taken against the Palestinians. The prolonged occupation was responsible for the actions cited by Israel as the cause for its repressive measures.

Of the adult population in Palestinian refugee camps, 87 per cent had been subject to arrest or detention, the Ukrainian SSR charged; the most recent wave of repression was aimed at creating an atmosphere of terror among the Palestinians, forcing them to leave their ancestral homes to create so-called living space for the Israeli settlers.

Iran called for a united Islamic front to defeat the Zionist enemy.

The Permanent Observer of the League of Arab States said the prospects for a just and comprehensive peace in the area were undermined if there was a certain level of permissiveness for one single settler. Inherent in the situation were incalculable dangers, with crisis-management becoming more and more difficult and ultimately impossible, and with polarization reaching acute dimensions which could threaten not only peace in the region, but the basic rights of peoples everywhere.

Israel's measures were taken in an atmosphere of growing provocation by Jewish settlers, provocation that had even been denounced by some of the occupying authorities and was clearly aimed at forcing the local population to emigrate, said the Chairman of the Committee on Palestinian rights. Violence would only increase and the situation would continue to deteriorate until the rights of the Palestinians had been fully recognized. The United Nations had the responsibility to ensure the fulfilment of those rights, as well as the physical protection of the Palestinians and other peoples of the region. It was up to the Council to give effect to the Committee's 1976 recommendations[8] and the recommendations adopted at the 1983 International Conference on the Question of Palestine.[30]

GENERAL ASSEMBLY ACTION

On 16 December 1985, on the recommendation of the Special Political Committee, the General Assembly adopted, by recorded vote, **resolution 40/161 D** on the report of the Committee on Israeli practices.

The General Assembly,

Guided by the purposes and principles of the Charter of the United Nations and by the principles and provisions of the Universal Declaration of Human Rights,

Bearing in mind the provisions of the Geneva Convention relative to the Protection of Civilian Persons in Time of War, of 12 August 1949, as well as of other relevant conventions and regulations,

Recalling all its resolutions on the subject, in particular, resolutions 32/91 B and C of 13 December 1977, 33/113 C of 18 December 1978, 34/90 A of 12 December 1979, 35/122 C of 11 December 1980, 36/147 C of 16 December 1981, 37/88 C of 10 December 1982, 38/79 D of 15 December 1983 and 39/95 D of 14 December 1984,

Recalling also the relevant resolutions adopted by the Security Council, by the Commission on Human Rights, in particular its resolutions 1983/1 of 15 February 1983, 1984/1 of 20 February 1984, 1985/1 A and B of 19 February 1985, and 1985/2 of 19 February 1985, and by other United Nations organs concerned and by the specialized agencies,

Having considered the report of the Special Committee to Investigate Israeli Practices Affecting the Human Rights of the Population of the Occupied Territories, which contains, *inter alia*, self-incriminating public statements made by officials of Israel, the occupying Power,

Taking note of the letter dated 29 July 1985 from the Permanent Representative of Jordan addressed to the Secretary-General, concerning the closing down of the Roman Catholic Medical Facility Hospice at Jerusalem,

1.   *Commends* the Special Committee to Investigate Israeli Practices Affecting the Human Rights of the Population of the Occupied Territories for its efforts in performing the tasks assigned to it by the General Assembly and for its thoroughness and impartiality;

2.   *Deplores* the continued refusal by Israel to allow the Special Committee access to the occupied territories;

3.   *Demands* that Israel allow the Special Committee access to the occupied territories;

4. *Reaffirms* the fact that occupation itself constitutes a grave violation of the human rights of the civilian population of the occupied Arab territories;

5. *Condemns* the continued and persistent violation by Israel of the Geneva Convention relative to the Protection of Civilian Persons in Time of War, of 12 August 1949, and other applicable international instruments, and condemns in particular those violations which the Convention designates as "grave breaches" thereof;

6. *Declares once more* that Israel's grave breaches of that Convention are war crimes and an affront to humanity;

7. *Reaffirms*, in accordance with the Convention, that the Israeli military occupation of the Palestinian and other Arab territories is of a temporary nature, thus giving no right whatsoever to the occupying Power over the territorial integrity of the occupied territories;

8. *Strongly condemns* the following Israeli policies and practices:

   (a) Annexation of parts of the occupied territories, including Jerusalem;

   (b) Imposition of Israeli laws, jurisdiction and administration on the Syrian Golan Heights, which has resulted in the effective annexation of the Syrian Golan Heights;

   (c) Illegal imposition and levy of heavy and disproportionate taxes and dues;

   (d) Establishment of new Israeli settlements and expansion of the existing settlements on private and public Arab lands, and transfer of an alien population thereto;

   (e) Eviction, deportation, expulsion, displacement and transfer of Arab inhabitants of the occupied territories and denial of their right to return;

   (f) Confiscation and expropriation of private and public Arab property in the occupied territories and all other transactions for the acquisition of land involving the Israeli authorities, institutions or nationals on the one hand and the inhabitants or institutions of the occupied territories on the other;

   (g) Excavation and transformation of the landscape and the historical, cultural and religious sites, especially at Jerusalem;

   (h) Pillaging of archaeological and cultural property;

   (i) Destruction and demolition of Arab houses;

   (j) Collective punishment, mass arrests, administrative detention and ill-treatment of the Arab population;

   (k) Ill-treatment and torture of persons under detention;

   (l) Interference with religious freedoms and practices as well as family rights and customs;

   (m) Interference with the system of education and with the social and economic and health development of the population in the occupied Palestinian and other Arab territories;

   (n) Interference with the freedom of movement of individuals within the occupied Palestinian and other Arab territories;

   (o) Illegal exploitation of the natural wealth, resources and population of the occupied territories;

9. *Condemns also* the Israeli repression against and closing of the educational institutions in the occupied Syrian Golan Heights, particularly the prohibition of Syrian textbooks, Syrian educational system, the deprivation of Syrian students from pursuing their higher education in Syrian universities, the denial of the right to return to Syrian students receiving their higher education in the Syrian Arab Republic, the forcing of Hebrew on Syrian students, the imposition of courses that promote hatred, prejudice and religious intolerance and the dismissal of teachers, all in clear violation of the Geneva Convention;

10. *Strongly condemns* the arming of Israeli settlers in the occupied territories to commit acts of violence against Arab civilians and the perpetration of acts of violence by these armed settlers against individuals, causing injury and death and wide-scale damage to Arab property;

11. *Reaffirms* that all measures taken by Israel to change the physical character, demographic composition, institutional structure or legal status of the occupied territories, or any part thereof, including Jerusalem, are null and void, and that Israel's policy of settling parts of its population and new immigrants in the occupied territories constitutes a flagrant violation of the Geneva Convention and of the relevant resolutions of the United Nations;

12. *Demands* that Israel desist forthwith from the policies and practices referred to in paragraphs 8, 9 and 10 above;

13. *Calls upon* Israel, the occupying Power, to take immediate steps for the return of all displaced Arab and Palestinian inhabitants to their homes or former places of residence in the territories occupied by Israel since 1967, in implementation of Security Council resolution 237(1967) of 14 June 1967;

14. *Urges* international organizations, including the specialized agencies, in particular the International Labour Organisation, to examine the conditions of Arab workers in the occupied Palestinian and other Arab territories, including Jerusalem;

15. *Reiterates its call* upon all States, in particular those States parties to the Geneva Convention, in accordance with article 1 of that Convention, and upon international organizations, including the specialized agencies, not to recognize any changes carried out by Israel in the occupied territories and to avoid actions, including those in the field of aid, which might be used by Israel in its pursuit of the policies of annexation and colonization or any of the other policies and practices referred to in the present resolution;

16. *Requests* the Special Committee, pending early termination of Israeli occupation, to continue to investigate Israeli policies and practices in the Arab territories occupied by Israel since 1967, to consult, as appropriate, with the International Committee of the Red Cross in order to ensure the safeguarding of the welfare and human rights of the population of the occupied territories and to report to the Secretary-General as soon as possible and whenever the need arises thereafter;

17. *Requests* the Special Committee to continue to investigate the treatment of civilians in detention in the Arab territories occupied by Israel since 1967;

18. *Condemns* Israel's refusal to permit persons from the occupied territories to appear as witnesses before the Special Committee and to participate in conferences and meetings held outside the occupied territories;

19. *Requests* the Secretary-General:

   (a) To provide all necessary facilities to the Special Committee, including those required for its visits to the occupied territories, with a view to investigating the

Israeli policies and practices referred to in the present resolution;

(b) To continue to make available additional staff as may be necessary to assist the Special Committee in the performance of its tasks;

(c) To ensure the widest circulation of the reports of the Special Committee and of information regarding its activities and findings, by all means available through the Department of Public Information of the Secretariat and, where necessary, to reprint those reports of the Special Committee that are no longer available;

(d) To report to the General Assembly at its forty-first session on the tasks entrusted to him in the present paragraph;

20. *Requests* the Security Council to ensure Israel's respect for and compliance with all the provisions of the Geneva Convention relative to the Protection of Civilian Persons in Time of War, of 12 August 1949, in the Palestinian and other Arab territories occupied since 1967, including Jerusalem, and to initiate measures to halt Israeli policies and practices in those territories;

21. *Calls upon* Israel, the occupying Power, to allow the reopening of the Roman Catholic Medical Facility Hospice at Jerusalem in order to continue to provide needed health and medical services to the Arab population in the city;

22. *Decides* to include in the provisional agenda of its forty-first session the item entitled "Report of the Special Committee to Investigate Israeli Practices Affecting the Human Rights of the Population of the Occupied Territories".

General Assembly resolution 40/161 D

16 December 1985   Meeting 118   109-2-34 (recorded vote)

Approved by SPC (A/40/890) by recorded vote (90-3-27), 8 November (meeting 27); draft by Afghanistan, Bangladesh, Cuba, Egypt, India, Indonesia, Kuwait for the Arab Group, Madagascar, Malaysia, Mali, Nicaragua, Pakistan, Qatar, Senegal (A/SPC/40/L.11); agenda item 75.
Financial implications. 5th Committee, A/40/972; S-G, A/C.5/40/46, A/SPC/40/L.15.
Meeting numbers. GA 40th session: SPC 16-23, 27; 5th Committee 51; plenary 118.

Recorded vote in Assembly as follows:

In favour: Afghanistan, Albania, Algeria, Antigua and Barbuda, Argentina, Bahrain, Bangladesh, Benin, Bhutan, Bolivia, Botswana, Brazil, Brunei Darussalam, Bulgaria, Burkina Faso, Burma, Burundi, Byelorussian SSR, Cape Verde, Central African Republic, Chad, China, Colombia, Congo, Cuba, Cyprus, Czechoslovakia, Democratic Kampuchea, Democratic Yemen, Djibouti, Ecuador, Egypt, Equatorial Guinea, Ethiopia, Gabon, Gambia, German Democratic Republic, Greece, Guatemala, Guinea, Guinea-Bissau, Guyana, Hungary, India, Indonesia, Iran, Iraq, Jamaica, Jordan, Kenya, Kuwait, Lao People's Democratic Republic, Lebanon, Lesotho, Libyan Arab Jamahiriya, Madagascar, Malaysia, Maldives, Mali, Malta, Mauritania, Mauritius, Mexico, Mongolia, Morocco, Mozambique, Nepal, Nicaragua, Niger, Nigeria, Oman, Pakistan, Panama, Peru, Philippines, Poland, Qatar, Romania, Rwanda, Samoa, Sao Tome and Principe, Saudi Arabia, Senegal, Seychelles, Sierra Leone, Singapore, Spain, Sri Lanka, Sudan, Suriname, Syrian Arab Republic, Thailand, Togo, Trinidad and Tobago, Tunisia, Turkey, Uganda, Ukrainian SSR, USSR, United Arab Emirates, United Republic of Tanzania, Uruguay, Vanuatu, Venezuela, Viet Nam, Yemen, Yugoslavia, Zambia, Zimbabwe.
Against: Israel, United States.
Abstaining: Australia, Austria, Bahamas, Belgium, Cameroon, Canada, Costa Rica, Denmark, Dominica, Dominican Republic, El Salvador, Fiji, Finland, France, Germany, Federal Republic of, Grenada, Iceland, Ireland, Italy, Ivory Coast, Japan, Liberia, Luxembourg, Malawi, Netherlands, New Zealand, Norway, Portugal, Saint Lucia, Saint Vincent and the Grenadines, Swaziland, Sweden, United Kingdom, Zaire.

Paragraphs 6 and 21 were adopted by separate recorded votes both in plenary meeting and in Committee. The Assembly adopted paragraph 6 by 85 votes to 19, with 37 abstentions, and paragraph 21 by 136 to 1, with 7 abstentions; the respective Committee votes were 79 to 18, with 23 abstentions, and 117 to 1, with 3 abstentions.

Israel said the charges in the text were unfounded and in certain cases mere figments of imagination. Paragraph 9, for example, gave a wholly distorted picture of the educational system in the Golan Heights. The most shocking aspect of the whole text was paragraph 6; breaches that were war crimes and an affront to humanity might be the proper terms for PLO crimes but to use them against the Israeli people was an abominable offence.

The United States considered that such unbalanced texts served only to widen differences and inflame an already embittered situation. The United States also objected to the expense imposed on the budget as an unwise diversion of scarce resources. Paragraph 21, on which it had abstained, lacked due regard for the fact that the Hospice was the property of the Austrian Catholic Church, whose wish to return it to its original function as a pilgrims' hostel had been one of the factors in the decision to close it.

Austria supported particularly paragraph 21, but could not accept certain formulations in the text overall, though it agreed with its basic thrust.

Sweden believed that the text went beyond the Assembly's competence, and it was not convinced that all the formulations in paragraph 8 were fully justified by proven facts.

Since Israel had challenged what had been stated in the Special Committee's report, Mexico believed it would be a good idea for it to grant the Committee all the facilities necessary to discharge its duties in an impartial and objective way, and permit it to visit the territories.

Fourth Geneva Convention

The General Assembly and the Commission on Human Rights reaffirmed in 1985 that the Geneva Convention relative to the Protection of Civilian Persons in Time of War, of 12 August 1949 (fourth Geneva Convention), was applicable to the Israeli-occupied territories.

Action by the Commission on Human Rights. In a 19 February 1985 resolution on human rights violations in the occupied territories,[31] the Commission on Human Rights condemned Israel's failure to acknowledge the applicability of the Convention to the occupied territories, including Jerusalem, expressed deep concern at the consequences and urged all States parties to ensure Israel's compliance.

On 16 December, on the recommendation of the Special Political Committee, the General Assembly adopted, by recorded vote, **resolution 40/161 B** on the report of the Committee on Israeli practices.

The General Assembly,

Recalling Security Council resolution 465(1980) of 1 March 1980, in which, *inter alia,* the Council affirmed that the Geneva Convention relative to the Protection of Civilian Persons in Time of War, of 12 August 1949, is applicable to the Arab territories occupied by Israel since 1967, including Jerusalem,

Recalling also its resolutions 3092 A (XXVIII) of 7 December 1973, 3240 B (XXIX) of 29 November 1974, 3525 B (XXX) of 15 December 1975, 31/106 B of 16 December 1976, 32/91 A of 13 December 1977, 33/113 A of 18 December 1978, 34/90 B of 12 December 1979, 35/122 A of 11 December 1980, 36/147 A of 16 December 1981, 37/88 A of 10 December 1982, 38/79 B of 15 December 1983 and 39/95 B of 14 December 1984,

Considering that the promotion of respect for the obligations arising from the Charter of the United Nations and other instruments and rules of international law is among the basic purposes and principles of the United Nations,

Bearing in mind the provisions of the Geneva Convention,

Noting that Israel and the Arab States whose territories have been occupied by Israel since June 1967 are parties to that Convention,

Taking into account that States parties to the Convention undertake, in accordance with article 1 thereof, not only to respect but also to ensure respect for the Convention in all circumstances,

1. *Reaffirms* that the Geneva Convention relative to the Protection of Civilian Persons in Time of War, of 12 August 1949, is applicable to the Palestinian and other Arab territories occupied by Israel since 1967, including Jerusalem;

2. *Condemns once again* the failure of Israel, the occuping Power, to acknowledge the applicability of that Convention to the territories it has occupied since 1967, including Jerusalem;

3. *Strongly demands* that Israel acknowledge and comply with the provisions of that Convention in the Palestinian and other Arab territories it has occupied since 1967, including Jerusalem;

4. *Urgently calls upon* all States parties to that Convention to exert all efforts in order to ensure respect for and compliance with its provisions in the Palestinian and other Arab territories occupied by Israel since 1967, including Jerusalem;

5. *Requests* the Secretary-General to report to the General Assembly at its forty-first session on the implementation of the present resolution.

General Assembly resolution 40/161 B

16 December 1985   Meeting 118   137-1-6 (recorded vote)

Approved by SPC (A/40/890) by recorded vote (114-1-5), 8 November (meeting 27); draft by Afghanistan, Bangladesh, Cuba, Egypt, India, Indonesia, Kuwait for the Arab Group, Madagascar, Malaysia, Mali, Nicaragua, Pakistan, Qatar, Senegal (A/SPC/40/L.9); agenda item 75.

Meeting numbers. GA 40th session: SPC 16-23, 27; plenary 118.

Recorded vote in Assembly as follows:

In favour: Afghanistan, Albania, Algeria, Antigua and Barbuda, Argentina, Australia, Austria, Bahamas, Bahrain, Bangladesh, Belgium, Benin, Bhutan, Bolivia, Botswana, Brazil, Brunei Darussalam, Bulgaria, Burkina Faso, Burma, Burundi, Byelorussian SSR, Canada, Cape Verde, Central African Republic, Chad, Chile, China, Colombia, Congo, Costa Rica, Cuba, Cyprus, Czechoslovakia, Democratic Kampuchea, Democratic Yemen, Denmark, Djibouti, Dominica, Dominican Republic, Ecuador, Egypt, El Salvador, Equatorial Guinea, Ethiopia, Fiji, Finland, France, Gabon, Gambia, German Democratic Republic, Germany, Federal Republic of, Greece, Grenada, Guatemala, Guinea, Guinea-Bissau, Guyana, Hungary, Iceland, India, Indonesia, Iraq, Ireland, Italy, Jamaica, Japan, Jordan, Kenya, Kuwait, Lao People's Democratic Republic, Lebanon, Lesotho, Libyan Arab Jamahiriya, Luxembourg, Madagascar, Malaysia, Maldives, Mali, Malta, Mauritania, Mauritius, Mexico, Mongolia, Morocco, Mozambique, Nepal, Netherlands, New Zealand, Nicaragua, Niger, Nigeria, Norway, Oman, Pakistan, Panama, Peru, Philippines, Poland, Portugal, Qatar, Romania, Rwanda, Saint Vincent and the Grenadines, Samoa, Sao Tome and Principe, Saudi Arabia, Senegal, Seychelles, Sierra Leone, Singapore, Spain, Sri Lanka, Sudan, Suriname, Swaziland, Sweden, Syrian Arab Republic, Thailand, Togo, Trinidad and Tobago, Tunisia, Turkey, Uganda, Ukrainian SSR, USSR, United Arab Emirates, United Kingdom, United Republic of Tanzania, Uruguay, Vanuatu, Venezuela, Viet Nam, Yemen, Yugoslavia, Zambia, Zimbabwe.

Against: Israel.

Abstaining: Cameroon, Ivory Coast, Liberia, Malawi, United States, Zaire.

Paragraph 1 was adopted separately in the plenary Assembly and in Committee, by a recorded vote of 139 to 1, with 4 abstentions, and of 117 to 1, with 2 abstentions, respectively.

The United States said it had requested a separate vote to reiterate its view that the Convention, a landmark in ameliorating for civilian populations some of the rigours of war and military occupation, applied to the Israeli-occupied territories; the Convention's provisions must be fairly and consistently applied, without regard to the nature and causes of the underlying conflict that had resulted in the occupation. With regard to the text as a whole, however, the United States believed it to be another instance where condemnation of Israel retarded rather than promoted a solution; in addition, it considered the phrase "Palestinian and other Arab territories occupied by Israel since 1967, including Jerusalem", which appeared also in the other texts under the agenda item, as being merely demographically and geographically descriptive, and not indicative of sovereignty.

Israel said its position concerning the applicability of the Convention had been made clear; it abided by its humanitarian provisions and by the Hague Regulations annexed to the Hague Convention of 1907 respecting the laws and customs of war on land.

Sweden expressed the firm conviction that the fourth Geneva Convention was fully applicable to all Israeli-occupied territories.

Iran noted that the text contained certain phrases implying recognition of the Zionist base occupying Palestine which were inconsistent with its official position.

Palestinian detainees

Communications. In a letter of 16 January 1985 mainly dealing with Israel's plan to withdraw from Lebanon (see p. 297), transmitted by Egypt,[32]

PLO expressed grave concern for the future of the detainees at the Al-Ansar detention camp in southern Lebanon, where Israeli occupation forces were detaining more than 300 Palestinians.

In a letter of 19 March[33] charging Israel with acts of repression against Palestinians in the occupied territories, the Chairman of the Committee on Palestinian rights expressed concern at reports of the continued detention and treatment of 35 youths arrested on 31 January during a raid on the Dheisheh refugee camp in the West Bank. In addition, some 300 Palestinians from the West Bank had been detained at Fara's prison since January.

By a letter of 1 April[34] dealing mainly with attacks on the Palestinian refugee camps Ein el-Hilweh and Mieh Mieh in Lebanon (see p. 312), transmitted by the United Arab Emirates, PLO charged that on 30 March six Palestinians on board a Lebanese ship had been abducted and taken to Israel.

By a letter of 4 April,[35] Lebanon condemned the recent transfer of more than 1,000 Lebanese and Palestinian prisoners from the Al-Ansar detention camp to some prisons inside Israel (see p. 301). Concern about the transfer was also expressed by PLO in a letter of 3 April, transmitted by the United Arab Emirates.[36] The PLO Chairman stated that he would appreciate hearing from the Secretary-General about the fate of the six Palestinians abducted from the Lebanese vessel.

By a letter of 8 August,[9] the Acting Chairman of the Committee on Palestinian rights expressed utmost concern at recent Israeli policies affecting the rights of the Palestinians. According to press reports, the Israeli Cabinet had voted on 4 August to reinstate administrative detention without trial and deportation of persons considered "security risks". The Cabinet also had decided to expand prisons in the occupied territories.

Qatar, as Chairman of the Arab Group, transmitted letters of 3, 6 and 10 September from PLO,[37] charging that since 28 August Israel had been carrying out a massive campaign of arrests against Palestinians from all areas of the territories. Three of the 56 arrested as of 3 September—two trade unionists and a student leader—had been served with deportation notices. By 6 September, the number of Palestinians arrested under the reimposed detention law was well beyond 100, among them 50 trade unionists, with 15 facing detention, PLO said. On 9 September, 20 more had been detained. If 15 others who had been served with deportation notices were deported, it would be in flagrant violation of the 1948 Universal Declaration of Human Rights,[38] the 1949 Geneva Conventions and United Nations resolutions. It was all part of Israel's 4 August decision to reintroduce administrative detention without

trial and deportations to maximize repression of the Palestinians. Such laws were in contravention of international law and civilized behaviour, PLO said.

By a letter of 11 September,[11] the Chairman of the Committee on Palestinian rights stated that, according to recent press reports, Israel had engaged in a massive detention campaign, holding over 50 persons in the West Bank and several in the Gaza Strip. At least three were threatened with deportation. Four Arab youths had been shot and wounded by Israeli soldiers at Hebron. Curfews had been imposed in a number of towns and refugee camps. Those developments, the Chairman stated, could not but further exacerbate tensions and obstruct international efforts to achieve a comprehensive, just and lasting solution to the Palestine question.

Qatar for the Arab Group transmitted a PLO letter of 23 September[39] listing 29 Palestinians deported by Israel; 11 of them had appealed to the Supreme Court which, however, had upheld a decision of the military governor. The 18 others were deported without recourse.

Further cases of administrative detention of and deportation orders for Palestinians were reported by the Chairman of the Committee on Palestinian rights on 13 November.[17] He said an estimated 104 people were being detained without charge. Protesting such detention, all Palestinian administrative detainees had gone on hunger strike on 14 October, according to press reports, and on 25 October their relatives had held sit-in protests at three Red Cross offices in various towns, expressing concern over prison conditions and demanding that the orders be cancelled; those complaints were supported by four Knesset members.

Kuwait transmitted letters of 24 October[15] and 30 October[16] from PLO, reporting that currently there were 186 Palestinians in various Israeli prisons, that Israel had carried out wide-scale arrests in the Bethlehem area and that four more Palestinians had received deportation orders.

Action by the Commission on Human Rights. The Commission on Human Rights, in a 19 February resolution on human rights violations in the occupied territories,[40] strongly condemned Israeli practices such as annexation, mass arrests, establishing new settlements, collective punishments, administrative detention, deportation, expropriation, torture under detention and the inhuman conditions in prisons. It called on Israel to release all Arabs detained as a result of their struggle for liberation of their territories and, pending their release, to accord them protection under international instruments concerning treatment of prisoners of war, and to cease torture and ill-treatment of Arab detainees and prisoners.

Condemning Israel for its continued detention of Ziyad Abu Eain, the Commission called on Israel to implement fully an agreement concluded in 1983 between ICRC and Israel for the exchange of prisoners between PLO and Israel, and to release Ziyad Abu Eain and others it continued to detain at Al-Ansar camp, which must be closed under the 1983 agreement.

Report of the Secretary-General. In a September 1985 report on Ziyad Abu Eain and other Palestinians detained by Israel,[41] the Secretary-General said that on 29 March he had requested information from Israel concerning implementation of a 1984 General Assembly resolution[42] demanding that prisoners registered with ICRC be freed immediately. On 1 July, Israel had replied that in the light of recent developments, it considered any reference to that resolution as not being pertinent to the Special Political Committee's work.

As reported by the international press, the Secretary-General added, Abu Eain was released on 20 May 1985. According to further reports, he was taken into custody on 31 July and issued with an order of administrative detention.

Report of the Committee on Israeli practices. The annual report[21] of the Committee on Israeli practices also contained information relating to the treatment of detainees, including information on prison conditions and individual prisoners. As an illustration of detention conditions over the entire period of Israeli occupation, the Committee cited the case of Abdul Aziz Shahin from the Gaza Strip who had spent 15 years in Israeli prisons; upon completion of his sentence, he was released but put under house arrest and eventually expelled while proceedings were still under way in an effort to protect his right to live in his homeland.

The Committee also examined the situation resulting from the release of 1,150 prisoners in May 1985, a large number of which were Palestinians held in Israeli prisons. Some 600 of those released remained in the occupied territories, which provoked a concentrated campaign of violence and harassment by Israeli settlers.

Following a series of attacks on Jewish civilians in Israel and in the territories, the Attorney General was asked on 25 July to consider ways of imposing harsher penalties on persons responsible for terrorist acts against civilians. Among the measures considered were increased patrols and road-blocks, searches of suspects' homes and special actions by security services, police and civil defence units. On 29 July, the Israeli Cabinet set up a ministerial team headed by the Defence Minister to examine legal aspects of the possibility of imposing the death penalty on terrorist-murderers, deporting inciters and resorting again to administrative arrests.

GENERAL ASSEMBLY ACTION

On 16 December 1985, on the recommendation of the Special Political Committee, the General Assembly adopted resolution 40/161 A on the report of the Committee on Israeli practices, by recorded vote.

The General Assembly,

Recalling its resolutions 38/79 A of 15 December 1983 and 39/95 A of 14 December 1984,

Taking note of the report of the International Committee of the Red Cross of 13 December 1983,

Taking note also of the report of the Secretary-General of 30 September 1985,

Taking note further of the report of the Special Committee to Investigate Israeli Practices Affecting the Human Rights of the Population of the Occupied Territories,

1. *Calls upon* Israel to release all Arabs arbitrarily detained and/or imprisoned as a result of their struggle for self-determination and for the liberation of their territories;

2. *Notes* the initial release of Ziyad Abu Eain, among others, from prison on 20 May 1985;

3. *Deplores* the Israeli subsequent arbitrary detention of Ziyad Abu Eain and others;

4. *Demands* that the Government of Israel, the occupying Power, rescind its action against Ziyad Abu Eain and others and release them immediately;

5. *Requests* the Secretary-General to report to the General Assembly as soon as possible and not later than the beginning of its forty-first session on the implementation of the present resolution.

General Assembly resolution 40/161 A

16 December 1985   Meeting 118   95-2-37 (recorded vote)

Approved by SPC (A/40/890) by recorded vote (77-2-29), 8 November (meeting 27); 28-nation draft (A/SPC/40/L.8); agenda item 75.

Sponsors: Afghanistan, Algeria, Bahrain, Bangladesh, Cuba, Democratic Yemen, Djibouti, Egypt, India, Indonesia, Iraq, Kuwait, Lebanon, Madagascar, Malaysia, Mali, Mauritania, Morocco, Nicaragua, Pakistan, Qatar, Saudi Arabia, Senegal, Sudan, Syrian Arab Republic, Tunisia, United Arab Emirates, Yemen.

Meeting numbers. GA 40th session: SPC 16-23, 27; plenary 118.

Recorded vote in Assembly as follows:

In favour: Afghanistan, Albania, Algeria, Argentina, Bahrain, Bangladesh, Benin, Bhutan, Bolivia, Botswana, Brazil, Brunei Darussalam, Bulgaria, Burkina Faso, Burundi, Byelorussian SSR, Cape Verde, Central African Republic, Chad, China, Congo, Cuba, Cyprus, Czechoslovakia, Democratic Kampuchea, Democratic Yemen, Djibouti, Dominican Republic, Ecuador, Egypt, El Salvador, Ethiopia, Gabon, Gambia, German Democratic Republic, Guinea, Guinea-Bissau, Guyana, Hungary, India, Indonesia, Iraq, Jordan, Kenya, Kuwait, Lao People's Democratic Republic, Lebanon, Lesotho, Libyan Arab Jamahiriya, Madagascar, Malaysia, Maldives, Mali, Malta, Mauritania, Mauritius, Mexico, Mongolia, Morocco, Mozambique, Nicaragua, Niger, Nigeria, Oman, Pakistan, Panama, Peru, Poland, Qatar, Romania, Rwanda, Sao Tome and Principe, Saudi Arabia, Senegal, Seychelles, Sierra Leone, Sri Lanka, Sudan, Suriname, Syrian Arab Republic, Togo, Tunisia, Turkey, Uganda, Ukrainian SSR, USSR, United Arab Emirates, United Republic of Tanzania, Vanuatu, Venezuela, Viet Nam, Yemen, Yugoslavia, Zambia, Zimbabwe.

Against: Israel, United States.

Abstaining: Antigua and Barbuda, Australia, Austria, Bahamas, Belgium, Cameroon, Canada, Costa Rica, Denmark, Dominica, Fiji, Finland, France, Germany, Federal Republic of, Greece, Grenada, Iceland, Ireland, Italy, Ivory Coast, Jamaica, Japan, Liberia, Luxembourg, Malawi, Nepal, Netherlands, New Zealand, Norway, Portugal, Saint Lucia, Samoa, Spain, Swaziland, Sweden, United Kingdom, Zaire.

Israel said the text deserved nothing but rejection. Abu Eain was a convicted murderer who, after his release on 20 May within the framework of the 1983 agreement between PLO and ICRC, had been placed under administrative detention for plotting to commit new criminal acts. Furthermore, under paragraph 1, convicted criminals, even murderers, should be released if they claimed to have fought for self-determination.

Austria also expressed reservations on the wording of paragraph 1, as did Canada and Sweden.

The United States felt that the text appeared implicitly to condone violence; though opposing practices such as administrative detention, it could not support the effort made in the text to excuse acts of terrorism.

Greece and Spain believed that the wording of paragraphs 1 and 4 was vague and could lead to misinterpretation incompatible with international law.

Iran remarked that certain paragraphs contained phrases which implied recognition of the Zionist philosophy on recognition of Israel and, therefore, was inconsistent with its position.

The Libyan Arab Jamahiriya had reservations about any reference that could be interpreted as implying a willingness to recognize Israel or its occupation of the territories.

Argentina expressed concern that some references could give rise to erroneous interpretations. Mexico also believed some paragraphs might have been better worded.

Introducing the text, the Sudan said the increased number of detainees, a large number of whom were held in custody for long periods without charge or arraignment in court, and the circumstances under which they lived made it imperative that the international community attach due importance to the issue.

Israeli settlements policy

Israel's policy of establishing settlements in the occupied territories and incidents involving Israeli settlers were the subject of several communications. According to information before the Committee on Israeli practices, Israelis continued to establish settlements, expropriate Palestinian property and encourage directly or indirectly the Palestinian population to leave the territories. A number of speakers during the Security Council's consideration in September of the situation in the occupied territories (see p. 329) held the settlements policy, among other Israeli practices, to a large degree responsible for the escalation of violence.

Communications. On 15 January 1985,[43] the Chairman of the Committee on Palestinian rights brought to the Secretary-General's attention reports of action taken by Israel aimed at annexing the occupied territories of the West Bank. On 10 January, Israel had approved sites for six new Jewish settlements, each said to cost $1 million,

in the northern part of the West Bank, the Hebron area, the Jordan Valley and the Jerusalem area. As on previous occasions, the Committee noted, there had been public and parliamentary questioning of the decision within Israel itself. In December 1984, the Deputy Prime Minister and Foreign Minister of Israel reportedly had requested the establishment of 20 others. During the previous six years, the Committee noted, some 100 new settlements had been established in the territories notwithstanding their illegality and the censure of numerous United Nations resolutions.

By a letter of 15 March,[44] Jordan informed the Secretary-General of Israeli settlement activity, including confiscation of Arab lands, in the occupied territories during the last three months of 1984. Jordan reported such activity from January to May 1985 in a 9 July letter;[45] during that period, nine settlements were established in the West Bank and the Gaza Strip and some 40.3 million square metres of land were confiscated. According to published information, settlers in the West Bank amounted to 42,600 by the end of 1984, distributed over 114 settlements.

By a letter of 19 March charging Israel with renewed acts of repression against Palestinians,[4] the Chairman of the Committee on Palestinian rights also expressed grave concern at the continued establishment of Israeli settlements in the occupied territories. According to a press report, the Israeli Housing Ministry had begun the construction of three permanent settlements: Azmona, on the Gaza shore; Kaddim, in the northern West Bank; and Na'an, in the Jordan Rift Valley. Settlers were already living in all three.

By a letter of 29 March,[46] the Committee Chairman drew attention to statements by Israeli officials concerning settlements in the West Bank and Gaza, as reported in the Israeli press. On 21 March, the Defence Minister had assured Jewish settlers in the Katif area in the Gaza Strip that the area must remain an inseparable part of Israel, having been always part of the biblical Land of Israel. A similar statement with regard to the Jordan Valley was attributed to the Israeli Prime Minister. Such statements, the Committee said, were yet a further confirmation of Israel's annexation policy which violated its Charter obligations and the fourth Geneva Convention, endangered peace and security, and undermined international peace efforts.

Kuwait transmitted a letter of 24 October from PLO,[15] charging that Israeli settlers on 22 October had attacked 13 Palestinian motorists between the Gaza Strip and the West Bank. In the Gaza Strip, 16 Palestinian homes were destroyed under the pretext of having been built without planning permission and 20 acres of agricultural land belonging to Palestinians had been expropriated in Khan Younis to establish a new settlement; a government decision disclosed plans to do the same with lands from the village of Bidya in the West Bank.

Report of the Committee on Israeli practices.
Israel's settlements policy and the activities of its settlers in the occupied territories were also dealt with by the Committee on Israeli practices.[21] According to information before the Committee, measures continued to be taken to establish settlements, expropriate Palestinian property and encourage directly or indirectly the Palestinian population to leave the territories. Among those actions, the Committee cited the occupation during August 1985 by Israeli government members of a Palestinian house at Hebron, with the express purpose of asserting the pretended Israeli right to settle and take over the occupied territory. Considerable amounts continued to be allocated: in May, the Finance Committee of the Knesset set aside approximately $146 million for the creation of two new settlements in the West Bank and about $375 million to strengthen the infrastructure of existing ones in the West Bank and the Gaza Strip. The Israeli trade union, Histadrut, up to May, had invested $100 million for construction and infrastructure in West Bank settlements. It had been reported that, by April 1985, Israeli authorities had gained control over 52 per cent of the land in the West Bank.

GENERAL ASSEMBLY ACTION

On 16 December, on the recommendation of the Special Political Committee, the General Assembly adopted, by recorded vote, **resolution 40/161 C** on the report of the Committee on Israeli practices.

The General Assembly,

Recalling Security Council resolution 465(1980) of 1 March 1980,

Recalling also its resolutions 32/5 of 28 October 1977, 33/113 B of 18 December 1978, 34/90 C of 12 December 1979, 35/122 B of 11 December 1980, 36/147 B of 16 December 1981, 37/88 B of 10 December 1982, 38/79 C of 15 December 1983 and 39/95 C of 14 December 1984,

Expressing grave anxiety and concern at the present serious situation in the occupied Palestinian and other Arab territories, including Jerusalem, as a result of the continued Israeli occupation and the measures and actions taken by Israel, the occupying Power, designed to change the legal status, geographical nature and demographic composition of those territories,

Confirming that the Geneva Convention relative to the Protection of Civilian Persons in Time of War, of 12 August 1949, is applicable to all Arab territories occupied since June 1967, including Jerusalem,

1. *Determines* that all such measures and actions taken by Israel in the Palestinian and other Arab territories occupied since 1967, including Jerusalem, are in violation of the relevant provisions of the Geneva Convention relative to the Protection of Civilian Persons in Time of War, of 12 August 1949, and constitute a serious

obstacle to the efforts to achieve a comprehensive, just and lasting peace in the Middle East and therefore have no legal validity;

2. *Strongly deplores* the persistence of Israel in carrying out such measures, in particular the establishment of settlements in the Palestinian and other occupied Arab territories, including Jerusalem;

3. *Demands* that Israel comply strictly with its international obligations in accordance with the principles of international law and the provisions of the Geneva Convention;

4. *Demands once more* that Israel, the occupying Power, desist forthwith from taking any action which would result in changing the legal status, geographical nature or demographic composition of the Palestinian and other Arab territories occupied since 1967, including Jerusalem;

5. *Urgently calls upon* all States parties to the Geneva Convention to respect and to exert all efforts in order to ensure respect for and compliance with its provisions in all Arab territories occupied by Israel since 1967, including Jerusalem;

6. *Requests* the Secretary-General to report to the General Assembly at its forty-first session on the implementation of the present resolution.

General Assembly resolution 40/161 C

16 December 1985   Meeting 118   138-1-6 (recorded vote)

Approved by SPC (A/40/890) by recorded vote (118-1-2), 8 November (meeting 27); draft by Afghanistan, Bangladesh, Cuba, Egypt, India, Indonesia, Kuwait for the Arab Group, Madagascar, Malaysia, Mali, Nicaragua, Pakistan, Qatar, Senegal (A/SPC/40/L.10); agenda item 75.

Meeting numbers. GA 40th session: SPC 16-23, 27; plenary 118.

Recorded vote in Assembly as follows:

In favour: Afghanistan, Albania, Algeria, Antigua and Barbuda, Argentina, Australia, Austria, Bahamas, Bahrain, Bangladesh, Belgium, Benin, Bhutan, Bolivia, Botswana, Brazil, Brunei Darussalam, Bulgaria, Burkina Faso, Burma, Burundi, Byelorussian SSR, Cameroon, Canada, Cape Verde, Central African Republic, Chad, Chile, China, Colombia, Congo, Cuba, Cyprus, Czechoslovakia, Democratic Kampuchea, Democratic Yemen, Denmark, Djibouti, Dominica, Dominican Republic, Ecuador, Egypt, El Salvador, Equatorial Guinea, Ethiopia, Fiji, Finland, France, Gabon, Gambia, German Democratic Republic, Germany, Federal Republic of, Greece, Guatemala, Guinea, Guinea-Bissau, Guyana, Hungary, Iceland, India, Indonesia, Iraq, Ireland, Italy, Jamaica, Japan, Jordan, Kenya, Kuwait, Lao People's Democratic Republic, Lebanon, Lesotho, Liberia, Libyan Arab Jamahiriya, Luxembourg, Madagascar, Malaysia, Maldives, Mali, Malta, Mauritania, Mauritius, Mexico, Mongolia, Morocco, Mozambique, Nepal, Netherlands, New Zealand, Nicaragua, Niger, Nigeria, Norway, Oman, Pakistan, Panama, Peru, Philippines, Poland, Portugal, Qatar, Romania, Rwanda, Saint Vincent and the Grenadines, Samoa, Sao Tome and Principe, Saudi Arabia, Senegal, Seychelles, Sierra Leone, Singapore, Spain, Sri Lanka, Sudan, Suriname, Swaziland, Sweden, Syrian Arab Republic, Thailand, Togo, Trinidad and Tobago, Tunisia, Turkey, Uganda, Ukrainian SSR, USSR, United Arab Emirates, United Kingdom, United Republic of Tanzania, Uruguay, Vanuatu, Venezuela, Viet Nam, Yemen, Yugoslavia, Zaire, Zambia, Zimbabwe.

Against: Israel.

Abstaining: Costa Rica, Grenada, Ivory Coast, Malawi, Saint Lucia, United States.

In Israel's view, it was fully entitled to enhance the security of the territories through the establishment of agricultural and urban centres; there was no legal justification for prohibiting Jews from living in the territories of the former British Mandate or in other areas.

The United States believed that the text diverted attention from the basic question of whether the settlements advanced or hindered a just and lasting peace.

Sweden believed that Israel could improve peace prospects by dismantling the settlements.

Iran had reservations about certain phrases in the text, which, it felt, implied recognition of Israel.

Golan Heights

In 1985, developments in the Golan Heights—a part of the Syrian Arab Republic occupied by Israel since 1967—brought action by the General Assembly and the Commission on Human Rights.

Action by the Commission on Human Rights. By a resolution of 19 February 1985,[47] the Commission on Human Rights declared that Israel's 1981 decision[48] to impose its laws, jurisdiction and administration on the occupied Golan Heights, which had resulted in effective annexation, was null and void and gravely violated international law and the United Nations Charter, and called on Israel to rescind it. The Commission strongly deplored the negative vote and pro-Israeli position of a permanent Security Council member which had prevented the Council from adopting appropriate measures against Israel. It deplored the practices against Syrian citizens in the Golan Heights and called on Israel to cease its acts of terrorism against them in order to impose Israeli citizenship on them and force them to carry Israeli identity cards. The Commission reaffirmed its request to Member States not to recognize any jurisdiction, laws or measures by Israel in respect of occupied Syrian and other Arab territories. It emphasized the necessity of total and unconditional Israeli withdrawal from all Palestinian and Syrian territories as an essential prerequisite for the establishment of a Middle East peace.

Report of the Secretary-General. In September,[49] the Secretary-General reported on action taken pursuant to a 1984 Assembly resolution[50] calling on Israel to desist from repressive measures against the population of the Syrian Arab Golan Heights. In a 1 July reply to a note verbale he had sent on 29 March asking Israel what steps it had taken or envisaged to implement the resolution, Israel referred to its stated position as set out in a letter of 29 December 1981.[51] In addition, replies to a note verbale of 9 April 1985 to other Member States asking for information on measures they might have taken in implementation of the 1984 resolution, received from Czechoslovakia, Gabon, Poland, the Ukrainian SSR and the USSR, were annexed to the Secretary-General's report.

GENERAL ASSEMBLY ACTION

On 16 December, on the recommendation of the Special Political Committee, the General Assembly adopted, by recorded vote, **resolution 40/161 F** on the report of the Committee on Israeli practices.

The General Assembly,

Deeply concerned that the Arab territories occupied since 1967 have been under continued Israeli military occupation,

Recalling Security Council resolution 497(1981) of 17 December 1981,

Recalling also its resolutions 36/226 B of 17 December 1981, ES-9/1 of 5 February 1982, 37/88 E of 10 December 1982, 38/79 F of 15 December 1983 and 39/95 F of 14 December 1984,

Having considered the report of the Secretary-General of 18 September 1985,

Recalling its previous resolutions, in particular resolutions 3414(XXX) of 5 December 1975, 31/61 of 9 December 1976, 32/20 of 25 November 1977, 33/28 and 33/29 of 7 December 1978, 34/70 of 6 December 1979 and 35/122 E of 11 December 1980, in which it, *inter alia*, called upon Israel to put an end to its occupation of the Arab territories and to withdraw from all those territories,

Reaffirming once more the illegality of Israel's decision of 14 December 1981 to impose its laws, jurisdiction and administration on the Syrian Golan Heights, which has resulted in the effective annexation of that territory,

Reaffirming that the acquisition of territory by force is inadmissible under the Charter of the United Nations and that all territories thus occupied by Israel must be returned,

Recalling the Geneva Convention relative to the Protection of Civilian Persons in Time of War, of 12 August 1949,

1. *Strongly condemns* Israel, the occupying Power, for its refusal to comply with the relevant resolutions of the General Assembly and the Security Council, particularly Council resolution 497(1981), in which the Council, *inter alia*, decided that the Israeli decision to impose its laws, jurisdiction and administration on the occupied Syrian Golan Heights was null and void and without international legal effect and demanded that Israel, the occupying Power, should rescind forthwith its decision;

2. *Condemns* the persistence of Israel in changing the physical character, demographic composition, institutional structure and legal status of the occupied Syrian Arab Golan Heights;

3. *Determines* that all legislative and administrative measures and actions taken or to be taken by Israel, the occupying Power, that purport to alter the character and legal status of the Syrian Golan Heights are null and void and constitute a flagrant violation of international law and of the Geneva Convention relative to the Protection of Civilian Persons in Time of War, of 12 August 1949, and have no legal effect;

4. *Strongly condemns* Israel for its attempts and measures to impose forcibly Israeli citizenship and Israeli identity cards on the Syrian citizens in the occupied Syrian Arab Golan Heights and calls upon it to desist from its repressive measures against the population of the Syrian Arab Golan Heights;

5. *Calls once again upon* Member States not to recognize any of the legislative or administrative measures and actions referred to above;

6. *Requests* the Secretary-General to submit to the General Assembly at its forty-first session a report on the implementation of the present resolution.

General Assembly resolution 40/161 F

16 December 1985   Meeting 118   136-1-10 (recorded vote)

Approved by SPC (A/40/890) by recorded vote (114-1-6), 8 November (meeting 27); draft by Afghanistan, Bangladesh, Cuba, Egypt, India, Indonesia, Kuwait for the Arab Group, Madagascar, Malaysia, Mali, Nicaragua, Pakistan, Qatar, Senegal (A/SPC/40/L.13); agenda item 75.

Meeting numbers. GA 40th session: SPC 16-23, 27; plenary 118.

Recorded vote in Assembly as follows:

In favour: Afghanistan, Albania, Algeria, Antigua and Barbuda, Argentina, Australia, Austria, Bahamas, Bahrain, Bangladesh, Belgium, Benin, Bhutan, Bolivia, Botswana, Brazil, Brunei Darussalam, Bulgaria, Burkina Faso, Burma, Burundi, Byelorussian SSR, Canada, Cape Verde, Central African Republic, Chad, Chile, China, Colombia, Congo, Cuba, Cyprus, Czechoslovakia, Democratic Kampuchea, Democratic Yemen, Denmark, Djibouti, Dominica, Dominican Republic, Ecuador, Egypt, El Salvador, Equatorial Guinea, Ethiopia, Fiji, Finland, France, Gabon, Gambia, German Democratic Republic, Germany, Federal Republic of, Greece, Guatemala, Guinea, Guinea-Bissau, Guyana, Hungary, Iceland, India, Indonesia, Iran, Iraq, Ireland, Italy, Jamaica, Japan, Jordan, Kenya, Kuwait, Lao People's Democratic Republic, Lebanon, Lesotho, Libyan Arab Jamahiriya, Luxembourg, Madagascar, Malaysia, Maldives, Mali, Malta, Mauritania, Mauritius, Mexico, Mongolia, Morocco, Mozambique, Nepal, Netherlands, New Zealand, Nicaragua, Niger, Nigeria, Norway, Oman, Pakistan, Panama, Peru, Philippines, Poland, Portugal, Qatar, Romania, Rwanda, Saint Vincent and the Grenadines, Samoa, Sao Tome and Principe, Saudi Arabia, Senegal, Seychelles, Sierra Leone, Singapore, Somalia, Spain, Sri Lanka, Sudan, Suriname, Sweden, Syrian Arab Republic, Thailand, Togo, Trinidad and Tobago, Tunisia, Turkey, Uganda, Ukrainian SSR, USSR, United Arab Emirates, United Kingdom, United Republic of Tanzania, Uruguay, Vanuatu, Venezuela, Viet Nam, Yemen, Yugoslavia, Zambia, Zimbabwe.

Against: Israel.

Abstaining: Cameroon, Costa Rica, Grenada, Ivory Coast, Liberia, Malawi, Saint Lucia, Swaziland, United States, Zaire.

Israel found the text unacceptable, adding that under Syrian administration the Golan area had been a peripheral region with no local judicial system; the application of Israeli laws endowed the area with normal legal guarantees and due process, thus favouring its development.

The United States felt that the text went beyond the 1981 Security Council resolution,[52] which was the authoritative United Nations action on Israel's decision to impose its laws, jurisdiction and administration in the Golan Heights.

Sweden pointed out that its support of the text did not alter its negative stand on the 1982 Assembly resolution on the Golan Heights and other Israeli-occupied territories.[53]

Also on 16 December, under the agenda item on the Middle East, the General Assembly adopted **resolution 40/168 B** by recorded vote.

The General Assembly,

Having discussed the item entitled "The situation in the Middle East",

Taking note of the report of the Secretary-General of 22 October 1985,

Recalling Security Council resolution 497(1981) of 17 December 1981,

Reaffirming its resolutions 36/226 B of 17 December 1981, ES-9/1 of 5 February 1982, 37/123 A of 16 December 1982, 38/180 A of 19 December 1983 and 39/146 B of 14 December 1984,

Recalling its resolution 3314(XXIX) of 14 December 1974, in which it defined an act of aggression, *inter alia*, as "the invasion or attack by the armed forces of a State of the territory of another State, or any military occupation, however temporary, resulting from such invasion or attack, or any annexation by the use of force of the territory of another State or part thereof" and provided that "no consideration of whatever nature, whether political, economic, military or otherwise, may serve as a justification for aggression",

Reaffirming the fundamental principle of the inadmissibility of the acquisition of territory by force,

Reaffirming once more the applicability of the Geneva Convention relative to the Protection of Civilian Persons in Time of War, of 12 August 1949, to the occupied Palestinian and other Arab territories, including Jerusalem,

Noting that Israel's record, policies and actions establish conclusively that it is not a peace-loving Member State and that it has not carried out its obligations under the Charter of the United Nations,

Noting further that Israel has refused, in violation of Article 25 of the Charter, to accept and carry out the numerous relevant decisions of the Security Council, in particular resolution 497(1981), thus failing to carry out its obligations under the Charter,

1. *Strongly condemns* Israel for its failure to comply with Security Council resolution 497(1981) and General Assembly resolutions 36/226 B, ES-9/1, 37/123 A, 38/180 A and 39/146 B;

2. *Declares once more* that Israel's continued occupation of the Golan Heights and its decision of 14 December 1981 to impose its laws, jurisdiction and administration on the occupied Syrian Golan Heights constitute an act of aggression under the provisions of Article 39 of the Charter of the United Nations and General Assembly resolution 3314(XXIX);

3. *Declares once more* that Israel's decision to impose its laws, jurisdiction and administration on the occupied Syrian Golan Heights is illegal and therefore null and void and has no validity whatsoever;

4. *Declares* all Israeli policies and practices of, or aimed at, annexation of the occupied Palestinian and other Arab territories, including Jerusalem, to be illegal and in violation of international law and of the relevant United Nations resolutions;

5. *Determines once more* that all actions taken by Israel to give effect to its decision relating to the occupied Syrian Golan Heights are illegal and invalid and shall not be recognized;

6. *Reaffirms its determination* that all relevant provisions of the Regulations annexed to the Hague Convention IV of 1907, and the Geneva Convention relative to the Protection of Civilian Persons in Time of War, of 12 August 1949, continue to apply to the Syrian territory occupied by Israel since 1967, and calls upon the parties thereto to respect and ensure respect for their obligations under these instruments in all circumstances;

7. *Determines once more* that the continued occupation of the Syrian Golan Heights since 1967 and their annexation by Israel on 14 December 1981, following Israel's decision to impose its laws, jurisdiction and administration on that territory, constitute a continuing threat to international peace and security;

8. *Strongly deplores* the negative vote by a permanent member of the Security Council which prevented the Council from adopting against Israel, under Chapter VII of the Charter, the "appropriate measures" referred to in resolution 497(1981) unanimously adopted by the Council;

9. *Further deplores* any political, economic, financial, military and technological support to Israel that encourages Israel to commit acts of aggression and to consolidate and perpetuate its occupation and annexation of occupied Arab territories;

10. *Firmly emphasizes once more* its demand that Israel, the occupying Power, rescind forthwith its illegal decision of 14 December 1981 to impose its laws, jurisdic-

tion and administration on the Syrian Golan Heights, which resulted in the effective annexation of that territory;

11. *Reaffirms once more* the overriding necessity of the total and unconditional withdrawal by Israel from all the Palestinian and other Arab territories occupied since 1967, including Jerusalem, which is an essential prerequisite for the establishment of a comprehensive and just peace in the Middle East;

12. *Determines once more* that Israel's record, policies and actions confirm that it is not a peace-loving Member State, that it has persistently violated the principles contained in the Charter and that it has carried out neither its obligations under the Charter nor its commitment under General Assembly resolution 273(III) of 11 May 1949;

13. *Calls once more upon* all Member States to apply the following measures:

(*a*) To refrain from supplying Israel with any weapons and related equipment and to suspend any military assistance that Israel receives from them;

(*b*) To refrain from acquiring any weapons or military equipment from Israel;

(*c*) To suspend economic, financial and technological assistance to and co-operation with Israel;

(*d*) To sever diplomatic, trade and cultural relations with Israel;

14. *Reiterates its call* to all Member States to cease forthwith, individually and collectively, all dealings with Israel in order totally to isolate it in all fields;

15. *Urges* non-member States to act in accordance with the provisions of the present resolution;

16. *Calls upon* the specialized agencies and other international organizations to conform their relations with Israel to the terms of the present resolution;

17. *Requests* the Secretary-General to report to the General Assembly at its forty-first session on the implementation of the present resolution.

General Assembly resolution 40/168 B

16 December 1985   Meeting 118   86-23-37 (recorded vote)

30-nation draft (A/40/L.44 & Add.1); agenda item 38.

Sponsors: Afghanistan, Algeria, Bahrain, Bangladesh, Cuba, Democratic Yemen, Djibouti, India, Indonesia, Iraq, Jordan, Kuwait, Lebanon, Libyan Arab Jamahiriya, Malaysia, Mauritania, Mongolia, Morocco, Oman, Pakistan, Qatar, Saudi Arabia, Somalia, Sudan, Syrian Arab Republic, Tunisia, United Arab Emirates, Viet Nam, Yemen, Yugoslavia.

Meeting numbers. GA 40th session: plenary 104-107, 118.

Recorded vote in Assembly as follows:

In favour: Afghanistan, Albania, Algeria, Argentina, Bahrain, Bangladesh, Barbados,[a] Benin, Bhutan, Botswana, Brunei Darussalam, Bulgaria, Burkina Faso, Burundi, Byelorussian SSR, Cape Verde, Chad, China, Comoros, Congo, Cuba, Cyprus, Czechoslovakia, Democratic Kampuchea, Democratic Yemen, Djibouti, Ethiopia, Gabon, Gambia, German Democratic Republic, Ghana, Greece, Guinea, Guinea-Bissau, Guyana, Hungary, India, Indonesia, Iran, Iraq, Jordan, Kenya, Kuwait, Lao People's Democratic Republic, Lebanon, Lesotho, Libyan Arab Jamahiriya, Madagascar, Malaysia, Maldives, Mali, Malta, Mauritania, Mexico, Mongolia, Morocco, Mozambique, Nicaragua, Niger, Nigeria, Oman, Pakistan, Poland, Qatar, Rwanda, Sao Tome and Principe, Saudi Arabia, Senegal, Somalia, Sri Lanka, Sudan, Syrian Arab Republic, Togo, Trinidad and Tobago, Tunisia, Turkey, Uganda, Ukrainian SSR, USSR, United Arab Emirates, United Republic of Tanzania, Viet Nam, Yemen, Yugoslavia, Zambia, Zimbabwe.

Against: Australia, Belgium, Canada, Costa Rica, Denmark, El Salvador, Finland, France, Germany, Federal Republic of, Haiti, Iceland, Ireland, Israel, Italy, Japan, Luxembourg, Netherlands, New Zealand, Norway, Portugal, Sweden, United Kingdom, United States.

Abstaining: Antigua and Barbuda, Austria, Bahamas, Bolivia, Brazil, Burma, Cameroon, Colombia, Dominica, Dominican Republic, Ecuador, Egypt, Equatorial Guinea, Fiji, Grenada, Guatemala, Honduras, Ivory Coast, Jamaica, Liberia, Malawi, Nepal, Panama, Paraguay, Peru, Philippines, Saint Lucia, Saint

Vincent and the Grenadines, Samoa, Sierra Leone, Singapore, Spain, Swaziland, Thailand, Uruguay, Venezuela, Zaire.

[a]Later advised the Secretariat it had intended to abstain.

In the opinion of the United States, the declaration that Israel was not a peace-loving Member State and accusing it of an act of aggression was another polemic which did not advance peace and was not consistent with Security Council resolutions 242(1967)[54] and 338(1973);[55] the charges purported to engage the Assembly in matters which under the Charter were expressly reserved to the Council.

Sweden had strong objections in particular to paragraphs 12 to 16, with regard to their substantive content as well as to the fact that they could not be reconciled with the division of responsibilities between the Assembly and the Council. New Zealand regretted the absence in the text of the balance of principles embodied in Council resolutions and of a measured approach essential for securing the co-operation of all parties.

Nepal believed that the diplomatic isolation and economic boycott of Israel, as called for in paragraph 13, could be counter-productive. The Philippines and Singapore said they were unable to support a text that was unbalanced in its condemnation or impinged on the sovereign right of third countries to conduct their own international affairs as they saw fit. In Ecuador's opinion, certain paragraphs affected the principle of the universality of the United Nations and decisions flowing from State sovereignty, which in no circumstances should be subordinated to any decision or urgings of third countries or international organizations.

Bolivia did not agree with certain provisions which, it felt, did not contribute to a Middle East solution. Egypt also found certain elements which it could not approve. The measures proposed in the text, Peru believed, were not liable to prejudice efforts for achieving a solution within the United Nations framework. Implicit in the text was the danger of infringing some of the principles of international law and of an increasing erosion of the Organization's authority and effectiveness. Brazil and Austria did not believe that measures aimed at breaking relations with Israel and leading to its isolation would bring a solution any closer. Brazil added that Israel should not be offered excuses because of its isolation to disregard further the rules of international law.

Turkey found it difficult to reconcile paragraphs 13 and 14 with efforts under way to initiate a long-overdue negotiating process aimed at working out a solution. Argentina and Mexico had serious reservations on paragraphs 12 to 14; paragraph 9 and the eighth preambular paragraph as well, Argentina said, were not compatible with its foreign policy or with the objective of a comprehensive negotiated solution. Greece, although voting in favour, dissociated itself from paragraphs 8, 13(c), 13(d) and 14.

In **resolution 40/161 D**, the Assembly condemned Israeli repression against and closing of the educational institutions in the Golan Heights, particularly the prohibition of Syrian textbooks, Syrian educational system, the deprivation of Syrian students from pursuing their higher education in Syrian universities, the denial of the right to return to Syrian students receiving their higher education in the Syrian Arab Republic, the forcing of Hebrew on Syrian students, the imposition of courses promoting hatred, prejudice and religious intolerance, and the dismissal of teachers.

Palestinian officials

Expulsion of Palestinian leaders

In 1985, the General Assembly and the Commission on Human Rights again called on Israel to allow the return of three West Bank officials so that they could resume their functions. Israel had deported the three Palestinian officials in 1980,[56] on the ground that they had systematically engaged in inciting the local Arab population to acts of violence and subversion, abusing their public offices.

Report of the Secretary-General. In August 1985,[57] the Secretary-General reported on implementation of a 1984 Assembly resolution[58] demanding that Israel rescind the expulsion of and release from imprisonment the Mayors of Hebron and Halhul, rescind the expulsion of the Sharia Judge of Hebron and facilitate their immediate return.

In its 1 July reply to his note verbale of 29 March 1985, the Secretary-General stated, Israel had reiterated its previously stated position.[59]

GENERAL ASSEMBLY ACTION

On 16 December 1985, on the recommendation of the Special Political Committee and in connection with the report of the Committee on Israeli practices, the General Assembly adopted **resolution 40/161 E** by recorded vote.

The General Assembly,

Recalling Security Council resolutions 468(1980) of 8 May 1980, 469(1980) of 20 May 1980 and 484(1980) of 19 December 1980,

Recalling also its resolutions 36/147 D of 16 December 1981, 37/88 D of 10 December 1982, 38/79 E of 15 December 1983 and 39/95 E of 14 December 1984,

Taking note of the report of the Secretary-General of 14 August 1985,

Deeply concerned at the expulsion by the Israeli military occupation authorities of the Mayor of Halhul, the Mayor of Hebron who has since died, the Sharia Judge of Hebron and, in 1985, other Palestinians,

Alarmed by the decision of the Israeli military occupation authorities on 26 October 1985 to expel four Palestinian leaders,

Recalling the Geneva Convention relative to the Protection of Civilian Persons in Time of War, of 12 August 1949, in particular article 1 and the first paragraph of article 49, which read as follows:

"*Article 1*

"The High Contracting Parties undertake to respect and to ensure respect for the present Convention in all circumstances."

"*Article 49*

"Individual or mass forcible transfers, as well as deportations of protected persons from occupied territory to the territory of the occupying Power or to that of any other country, occupied or not, are prohibited, regardless of their motive . . .",

Reaffirming the applicability of the Geneva Convention to the Palestinian and other Arab territories occupied by Israel since 1967, including Jerusalem,

1. *Strongly condemns* Israel, the occupying Power, for its persistent refusal to comply with the relevant resolutions of the Security Council and the General Assembly;

2. *Demands* that the Government of Israel, the occupying Power, rescind the illegal measures taken by the Israeli military occupation authorities in expelling the Mayor of Halhul, the Sharia Judge of Hebron and, in 1985, other Palestinians and that it facilitate the immediate return of the expelled Palestinians so that they can, *inter alia*, resume the functions for which they were elected and appointed;

3. *Calls upon* Israel, the occupying Power, to rescind its illegal decision taken on 26 October 1985 and refrain from deporting the four Palestinian leaders;

4. *Further calls upon* Israel, the occupying Power, to cease forthwith the expulsion of Palestinians and to abide scrupulously by the provisions of the Geneva Convention relative to the Protection of Civilian Persons in Time of War, of 12 August 1949;

5. *Requests* the Secretary-General to report to the General Assembly as soon as possible and not later than the beginning of its forty-first session on the implementation of the present resolution.

General Assembly resolution 40/161 E

16 December 1985   Meeting 118   126-1-19 (recorded vote)

Approved by SPC (A/40/890) by recorded vote (106-1-14), 8 November (meeting 27); draft by Afghanistan, Bangladesh, Cuba, Egypt, India, Indonesia, Kuwait for the Arab Group, Madagascar, Malaysia, Mali, Nicaragua, Pakistan, Qatar, Senegal (A/SPC/40/L.12/Rev.1); agenda item 75.

Meeting numbers. GA 40th session: SPC 16-23, 27; plenary 118.

Recorded vote in Assembly as follows:

In favour: Afghanistan, Albania, Algeria, Antigua and Barbuda, Argentina, Australia, Austria, Bahamas, Bahrain, Bangladesh, Benin, Bhutan, Bolivia, Botswana, Brazil, Brunei Darussalam, Bulgaria, Burkina Faso, Burma, Burundi, Byelorussian SSR, Cape Verde, Central African Republic, Chad, Chile, China, Colombia, Congo, Cuba, Cyprus, Czechoslovakia, Democratic Kampuchea, Democratic Yemen, Djibouti, Dominica, Dominican Republic, Ecuador, Egypt, El Salvador, Equatorial Guinea, Ethiopia, Fiji, Finland, France, Gabon, Gambia, German Democratic Republic, Greece, Guatemala, Guinea, Guinea-Bissau, Guyana, Hungary, India, Indonesia, Iran, Iraq, Ireland, Italy, Jamaica, Japan, Jordan, Kenya, Kuwait, Lao People's Democratic Republic, Lebanon, Lesotho, Libyan Arab Jamahiriya, Madagascar, Malaysia, Maldives, Mali, Malta, Mauritania, Mauritius, Mexico, Mongolia, Morocco, Mozambique, Nepal, New Zealand, Nicaragua, Niger, Nigeria, Oman, Pakistan, Panama, Peru, Philippines, Poland, Portugal, Qatar, Romania, Rwanda, Saint Vincent and the Grenadines, Samoa, Sao Tome and Principe, Saudi Arabia, Senegal, Seychelles, Sierra Leone, Singapore, Spain, Sri Lanka, Sudan, Suriname, Sweden, Syrian Arab Republic,

Thailand, Togo, Trinidad and Tobago, Tunisia, Turkey, Uganda, Ukrainian SSR, USSR, United Arab Emirates, United Republic of Tanzania, Uruguay, Vanuatu, Venezuela, Viet Nam, Yemen, Yugoslavia, Zambia, Zimbabwe.

Against: Israel.

Abstaining: Belgium, Cameroon, Canada, Costa Rica, Denmark, Germany, Federal Republic of, Grenada, Iceland, Ivory Coast, Liberia, Luxembourg, Malawi, Netherlands, Norway, Saint Lucia, Swaziland, United Kingdom, United States, Zaire.

Before voting on the text as a whole, the Assembly and the Committee adopted paragraph 1, by recorded votes of 110 to 2, with 33 abstentions, and 98 to 2, with 22 abstentions, respectively.

In Israel's view, the text was unjustified and unacceptable. The authority for expulsion orders flowed from the Defence (Emergency) Regulations of 1945, which had been in force under the British and Jordanian administrations. The expulsions had taken place to protect public order and safety.

The United States faulted the text for not containing a reference to the factors that had contributed to the deportation of the individuals in question; however, it believed that the deportations were contrary to the 1949 fourth Geneva Convention and the deportees should be allowed to return.

Canada said it could not support the language used in paragraph 1.

Prosecution in assassination attempts

In August 1985,[60] the Secretary-General reported to the General Assembly on implementation of a 1984 Assembly demand[61] that Israel inform him of the results of the investigations and prosecution relative to the 1980 assassination attempts against the Mayors of Nablus, Ramallah and Al Bireh.[62]

In reply to the Secretary-General's request of 29 March 1985 for relevant information, Israel stated on 1 July that its position concerning the attempts on the lives of the three officials had been fully set out in various statements; recent developments had made any further consideration of the subject inappropriate. On 22 August, Israel had transmitted a summary of an Israeli press bulletin dated 22 July noting that, on 10 July, 15 men had been convicted of terrorism and that the sentences were handed down on 22 July; of those 15 men, 10 were charged with activities leading to the attacks against the mayors. Of the 10, one received life imprisonment and nine received terms from 3 to 10 years, the varying lengths due to charges of additional violations.

Living conditions of the Palestinians

In June 1985,[63] the Secretary-General reported on a seminar on remedies for the deterioration of the economic and social conditions of the Palestinian people in the occupied territories (Vienna, 25-29 March), which he had organized pursuant

to a 1984 General Assembly request.[64] The seminar examined, among other topics, agriculture, industry, trade, the monetary situation, fiscal policies, housing and basic facilities, higher education and welfare. Among the participants were 12 experts, and representatives of PLO, United Nations bodies and the World Health Organization (WHO).

The Economic and Social Council, by **decision 1985/174** of 25 July, took note of the Secretary-General's report.

ECWA action. On 24 April, the Economic Commission for Western Asia (ECWA) adopted a resolution[65] on the economic and social conditions of the Palestinian people under occupation, calling on the Executive Secretary to ensure that all available data on the occupied territories were included in all ECWA studies and statistical abstracts. It also called on him to include studies on economic and social conditions in the territories in the 1986-1987 work programme, and to prepare studies on the population situation, on Israel's settlements policy and on support for the industrial sector, particularly existing industries and the solution of problems from which they suffered, such as those of marketing, finance, manpower and raw materials. ECWA appealed to international and Arab organizations to assist in their preparation and execution.

GENERAL ASSEMBLY ACTION

On 17 December, on the recommendation of the Second Committee, the General Assembly adopted **resolution 40/201** by recorded vote.

Living conditions of the Palestinian people in the occupied Palestinian territories

The General Assembly,

Recalling the Vancouver Declaration on Human Settlements, 1976, and the relevant recommendations for national action adopted by Habitat: United Nations Conference on Human Settlements,

Recalling also its resolution 39/169 of 17 December 1984,

Taking note of Commission on Human Settlements resolution 8/3 of 10 May 1985,

Gravely alarmed by the continuation of the Israeli settlement policies, which have been declared null and void and a major obstacle to peace,

Recognizing the need to identify priority development projects needed for improving the living conditions of the Palestinian people in the occupied Palestinian territories,

1. *Takes note with concern* of the report of the Secretary-General on the living conditions of the Palestinian people in the occupied Palestinian territories;

2. *Takes note also* of the statement made on 25 October 1985 by the observer of the Palestine Liberation Organization;

3. *Rejects* the Israeli plans and actions intended to change the demographic composition of the occupied Palestinian territories, particularly the increase and expansion of the Israeli settlements, and other plans and actions creating conditions leading to the displacement

and exodus of Palestinians from the occupied Palestinian territories;

4. *Expresses its alarm* at the deterioration, as a result of the Israeli occupation, in the living conditions of the Palestinian people in the Palestinian territories occupied since 1967;

5. *Affirms* that the Israeli occupation is contradictory to the basic requirements for the social and economic development of the Palestinian people in the occupied Palestinian territories;

6. *Requests* the Secretary-General:

(a) To organize, by April 1987, a seminar on priority development projects needed for improving the living conditions of the Palestinian people in the occupied Palestinian territories, including a comprehensive general housing programme, as recommended in resolution 8/3 of the Commission on Human Settlements;

(b) To make the necessary preparations for the seminar, providing for the participation of the Palestine Liberation Organization;

(c) To invite experts to present papers to the seminar;

(d) To invite also relevant intergovernmental and non-governmental organizations;

(e) To report to the General Assembly at its forty-first session, through the Economic and Social Council, on the preparations for the seminar;

(f) To report to the General Assembly at its forty-second session, through the Economic and Social Council, on the seminar.

General Assembly resolution 40/201

17 December 1985   Meeting 119   153-2-1 (recorded vote)

Approved by Second Committee (A/40/989/Add.7) by recorded vote (133-2), 11 November (meeting 30); 5-nation draft (A/C.2/40/L.13), orally amended by Vice-Chairman based on informal consultations and by Luxembourg, for EEC; agenda item 84(g).

Sponsors: Bangladesh, Democratic Yemen, Madagascar, Morocco, Tunisia.

Financial implications. 5th Committee, A/40/973; S-G, A/C.2/40/L.26, A/C.5/40/47 & Add.1.

Meeting numbers. GA 40th session: 2nd Committee 17, 22, 30; 5th Committee 51; plenary 119.

Recorded vote in Assembly as follows:

In favour: Afghanistan, Albania, Algeria, Angola, Antigua and Barbuda, Argentina, Australia, Austria, Bahamas, Bahrain, Bangladesh, Barbados, Belgium, Belize, Benin, Bhutan, Bolivia, Botswana, Brazil, Brunei Darussalam, Bulgaria, Burkina Faso, Burma, Burundi, Byelorussian SSR, Cameroon, Canada, Cape Verde, Central African Republic, Chad, Chile, China, Colombia, Comoros, Congo, Costa Rica, Cuba, Cyprus, Czechoslovakia, Democratic Kampuchea, Democratic Yemen, Denmark, Djibouti, Dominica, Dominican Republic, Ecuador, Egypt, El Salvador, Equatorial Guinea, Ethiopia, Fiji, Finland, France, Gabon, Gambia, German Democratic Republic, Germany, Federal Republic of, Ghana, Greece, Guatemala, Guinea, Guinea-Bissau, Guyana, Haiti, Honduras, Hungary, Iceland, India, Indonesia, Iran, Iraq, Ireland, Italy, Ivory Coast, Jamaica, Japan, Jordan, Kenya, Kuwait, Lao People's Democratic Republic, Lebanon, Lesotho, Liberia, Libyan Arab Jamahiriya, Luxembourg, Madagascar, Malawi, Malaysia, Maldives, Mali, Malta, Mauritania, Mauritius, Mexico, Mongolia, Morocco, Mozambique, Nepal, Netherlands, New Zealand, Nicaragua, Niger, Nigeria, Norway, Oman, Pakistan, Panama, Papua New Guinea, Paraguay, Peru, Philippines, Poland, Portugal, Qatar, Romania, Rwanda, Saint Christopher and Nevis, Saint Lucia, Saint Vincent and the Grenadines, Samoa, Sao Tome and Principe, Saudi Arabia, Senegal, Sierra Leone, Singapore, Somalia, Spain, Sri Lanka, Sudan, Suriname, Swaziland, Sweden, Syrian Arab Republic, Thailand, Togo, Trinidad and Tobago, Tunisia, Turkey, Uganda, Ukrainian SSR, USSR, United Arab Emirates, United Kingdom, United Republic of Tanzania, Uruguay, Vanuatu, Venezuela, Viet Nam, Yemen, Yugoslavia, Zaire, Zambia, Zimbabwe.

Against: Israel, United States.

Abstaining: Grenada.

The United States believed that the text would perpetuate unproductive, if not counter-productive, activities which would in no way resolve the problems or improve the well-being of the Palestinians. It also felt the Secretary-General's report was slanted. Further, the United States expressed concern about the financial implications of the text which, it felt, would be better spent on helping the Palestinians directly.

Australia also had some misgivings concerning the financial implications; it hoped that the seminar would be held at a time when conference-servicing costs could be kept to a minimum.

Speaking for the EEC member States, Luxembourg said that the budget implications should have been more specific and, as far as possible, the funds should be drawn from existing resources; initiatives to hold seminars should be carefully co-ordinated in order to avoid multiplication and efforts must be made to have United Nations bodies meet at their headquarters.

The USSR, in explanation of vote also on behalf of Bulgaria, the Byelorussian SSR, Czechoslovakia, the German Democratic Republic, Hungary, Mongolia, Poland and the Ukrainian SSR, said they strongly condemned any Israeli action which hindered the attainment of Palestinian rights. Those who gave the Israelis protection were also obstructing peace. All parties to the conflict, including PLO, should be allowed to participate in efforts to find a solution to the Middle East problem.

Iraq stated that the United Nations had been responsible for the partitioning of Palestine; as a result, the Palestinians were living under alien occupation and were threatened with genocide.

Introducing the draft, Democratic Yemen said the living conditions of the Palestinians continued to deteriorate because Israel had been changing the demographic composition of the territories, thus increasing Palestinian emigration. The Palestinians not only lacked full control over land and water, but were subject to constraints on self-generating development.

If Israel was indeed helping the Palestinians and living conditions had improved, PLO remarked, it was not clear why Palestinians were demonstrating and being killed. Progress and development would not be possible until Palestine had been liberated.

PLO said the Secretary-General's report was based partly on Israeli statistics that did not show the real level of deterioration of the Palestinians' living conditions. The occupying authorities had been destroying the Palestinian national economy and making it dependent on Israel. Despite a high birth rate, the population in the West Bank and the Gaza Strip had declined. Expulsion, imprisonment, the suppression of human rights and the denial of permits for the reunification of families, against a background of economic decline, prompted the young and educated to leave.

Israel had appropriated more than 60 per cent of the land and monopolized 90 per cent of the water resources. Restrictions on Palestinian farming, the dumping of subsidized Israeli agricultural products on the Palestinian market, restrictions on imports and the blocking of several industrial development projects had caused further damage to both the agricultural and industrial sectors. Industrial employment opportunities were quite limited and many Palestinians had to seek employment in the Israeli economy or emigrate.

External trade was also subject to Israeli domination. The territories were a captive market, with 92 per cent of their imports originating in Israel. Israel refused to allow the establishment of Palestinian financial institutions. Inflation had diminished the real value of earnings, discouraged investment and increased unemployment. Taxes imposed by Israel amounted to approximately 33 per cent of the territories' income, and external aid was restricted or prevented, PLO said.

The Secretary-General's report, Israel said, had been prepared in implementation of a resolution referring to the deterioration of the economic and social conditions of the Palestinians, which was tantamount to condemning Israel in advance of any investigation. It was based on the wilful suppression and misuse of statistical data, presenting Israel's policy of socio-economic promotion as cruel oppression. The statistics that it purported to quote revealed that, unlike the rest of the Middle East, the areas under consideration had undergone unparalleled economic and social development.

Israel's comments refuting a number of statements in the report were reproduced in the annex to a 5 November 1985 letter to the Secretary-General.[(66)]

Israeli economic practices

Report of the Secretary-General. In June 1985,[(67)] the Secretary-General submitted a comparative study on Israeli economic practices in the occupied territories and its obligations under international law, as requested by the General Assembly in 1984,[(68)] when it had asked him to elaborate on a 1983 report by a legal expert.[(69)] In particular, he had been asked to cover in detail the resources exploited by the Israeli settlements and the Israeli-imposed regulations and policies hampering the territories' economic development, including a comparison between Israel's practices and its obligations under international law. As it had not been possible to send a fact-finding mission to the territories, the report had to rely on information from other United Nations reports and available sources. The report covered in particular the land and water resources exploited by Israeli settlements.

With regard to land resources, up to January 1984 Israel had appropriated 40 per cent of the land in the West Bank and 31 per cent of that of the Gaza Strip; 26 per cent of the West Bank area had been used for Israeli settlements. International law would seem to require that Israel as the occupying Power should not hinder the right of the local population to use freely, control and dispose of their land resources. Israel was also prohibited from taking any lands in the territories for establishing Israeli settlements.

Similar rules applied to water resources, the report stated. Water supply and water resources management in the territories had been under the direct control of the Israeli Water Commission through its Department of Water Allocation and Certification. Israel's policy included measures based on claims of national security requirements, restrictive measures aimed at controlling the search for, and the development and use of, water by the Arab population, and practices resulting in quantitative reduction of and qualitative damage to the water made available to that population. Drilling new artesian wells or deepening existing ones was forbidden without special permits; on no account were Arab inhabitants permitted to drill wells near Israel's borders. In many areas of the West Bank, Arab wells had run dry because Israeli wells had been dug too close to them; similar problems had occurred in the Golan Heights and the Gaza Strip.

ECONOMIC AND SOCIAL COUNCIL ACTION

In July 1985, the Economic and Social Council adopted **decision 1985/177** by roll-call vote.

Israeli economic practices in the occupied Palestinian and other Arab territories

At its 52nd plenary meeting, on 25 July 1985, the Council:

(a) Took note, with concern, of the report of the Secretary-General prepared in pursuance of General Assembly decision 39/442 of 18 December 1984;

(b) Requested the Secretary-General to prepare a report on the financial and trade practices of the Israeli occupation authorities in the occupied Palestinian and other Arab territories;

(c) Invited the Secretary-General to utilize the services of competent United Nations bodies in preparing the report requested in paragraph (b) above;

(d) Requested the Secretary-General to submit the report to the General Assembly at its forty-first session, through the Economic and Social Council.

Economic and Social Council decision 1985/177

49-1 (roll-call vote)

10-nation draft (E/1985/L.50); agenda item 6.
Sponsors: Bangladesh, India, Indonesia, Jordan, Libyan Arab Jamahiriya, Malaysia, Pakistan, Saudi Arabia, Syrian Arab Republic, Yugoslavia.
Meeting numbers. ESC 43-45, 52.

Roll-call vote in Council as follows:

In favour: Algeria, Argentina, Bangladesh, Botswana, Brazil, Bulgaria, Canada, China, Colombia, Congo, Ecuador, Finland, France, German Democratic Republic, Germany, Federal Republic of, Guinea, Haiti, Iceland, India, Indonesia, Japan, Lebanon, Luxembourg, Malaysia, Mexico, Morocco, Netherlands, New Zealand, Nigeria, Poland, Romania, Rwanda, Saudi Arabia, Senegal, Sierra Leone, Somalia,

Spain, Sri Lanka, Suriname, Sweden, Thailand, Turkey, Uganda, USSR, United Kingdom, Venezuela, Yugoslavia, Zaire, Zimbabwe.
Against: United States.

The United States would have liked to have had a balanced and impartial report, submitted to the competent authority, on the financial and trade practices of the Israeli occupation authorities. Unfortunately, the mandate given to the Secretary-General in the decision would not allow him to prepare such a report.

Jordan considered that the practices of the occupying Power called for the study requested; there were abundant instances in which that Power sought to choke off all economic activity in the territories.

The reason for the decision, said Saudi Arabia in introducing it, was the lack of information in the Secretary-General's report on Israel's financial and trade practices in the territories.

Israel wondered whether it was useful to ask for another report which could be as repetitive as the preceding ones. With regard to its obligations under international law, it stated that the only principle recognized and binding in the circumstances was set out in article 55 of the Hague Regulations annexed to the Hague Convention of 1907 respecting the laws and customs of war on land, under which the occupying State would be regarded as usufructuary of the properties situated in the occupied country.

PLO said that article 55 of the Hague Regulations expressly stated that the occupying State should be regarded only as administrator of the occupied territories, and article 53 of the fourth Geneva Convention prohibited the occupying Power from destroying real or personal property belonging to private persons in the territories. Under no circumstances did international law authorize the occupying Power to arrogate to itself the right to dispose as it pleased of those territories.

UNCTAD report. In July 1985, the Special Economic Unit of the United Nations Conference on Trade and Development (UNCTAD), set up in 1983,[70] submitted to the Trade and Development Board a report[71] reviewing the economic conditions of the Palestinians in the occupied territories and the effects of policies by the occupying authorities which appeared to hinder their economic development. The report gave an overview of population movements in the territories, water resources, agriculture, industrial development, the labour market and tourism since 1967.

GENERAL ASSEMBLY ACTION

In December 1985, on the recommendation of the Second Committee, the Assembly adopted **decision 40/432** by recorded vote.

Israeli economic practices in the occupied Palestinian and other Arab territories

At its 119th plenary meeting, on 17 December 1985, the General Assembly, on the recommendation of the Second Committee:

(a) Took note, with concern, of the report of the Secretary-General prepared in pursuance of Assembly decision 39/442;

(b) Requested the Secretary-General to prepare a report on the financial and trade practices of the Israeli occupation authorities in the occupied Palestinian and other Arab territories;

(c) Invited the Secretary-General to utilize the services of competent United Nations bodies in preparing the report;

(d) Requested the Secretary-General to submit the report to the General Assembly at its forty-first session, through the Economic and Social Council.

General Assembly decision 40/432

147-2-2 (recorded vote)

Approved by Second Committee (A/40/1009/Add.1) by recorded vote (126-2), 11 November (meeting 30); 11-nation draft (A/C.2/40/L.14); agenda item 12.
Sponsors: Bangladesh, Gambia, Indonesia, Madagascar, Malaysia, Pakistan, Saudi Arabia, Senegal, Syrian Arab Republic, Tunisia, Yemen.
Meeting numbers. GA 40th session: 2nd Committee 22, 30; plenary 119.

Recorded vote in Assembly as follows:

In favour: Afghanistan, Albania, Algeria, Angola, Antigua and Barbuda, Argentina, Australia, Austria, Bahamas, Bahrain, Bangladesh, Barbados, Belgium, Benin, Bhutan, Bolivia, Botswana, Brazil, Brunei Darussalam, Bulgaria, Burkina Faso, Burma, Burundi, Byelorussian SSR, Cameroon, Canada, Cape Verde, Central African Republic, Chad, Chile, China, Colombia, Comoros, Congo, Costa Rica, Cuba, Cyprus, Czechoslovakia, Democratic Kampuchea, Democratic Yemen, Denmark, Djibouti, Dominica, Dominican Republic, Ecuador, Egypt, El Salvador, Equatorial Guinea, Ethiopia, Fiji, Finland, France, Gabon, German Democratic Republic, Germany, Federal Republic of, Ghana, Greece, Guatemala, Guinea, Guinea-Bissau, Guyana, Haiti, Honduras, Hungary, Iceland, India, Indonesia, Iran, Iraq, Ireland, Italy, Ivory Coast, Jamaica, Japan, Jordan, Kuwait, Lao People's Democratic Republic, Lebanon, Lesotho, Liberia, Libyan Arab Jamahiriya, Luxembourg, Madagascar, Malawi, Malaysia, Maldives, Mali, Malta, Mauritania, Mauritius, Mexico, Mongolia, Morocco, Mozambique, Nepal, Netherlands, New Zealand, Nicaragua, Niger, Nigeria, Norway, Oman, Pakistan, Panama, Papua New Guinea, Paraguay, Peru, Philippines, Poland, Portugal, Qatar, Romania, Rwanda, Saint Lucia, Saint Vincent and the Grenadines, Samoa, Sao Tome and Principe, Saudi Arabia, Senegal, Sierra Leone, Singapore, Somalia, Spain, Sri Lanka, Sudan, Suriname, Swaziland, Sweden, Syrian Arab Republic, Thailand, Togo, Trinidad and Tobago, Tunisia, Turkey, Uganda, Ukrainian SSR, USSR, United Arab Emirates, United Kingdom, United Republic of Tanzania, Uruguay, Venezuela, Viet Nam, Yemen, Yugoslavia, Zaire, Zambia.
Against: Israel, United States.
Abstaining: Grenada, Saint Christopher and Nevis.

Israel said it was evident that the motives behind the text were political and that the main purpose was to advance the cause of the so-called PLO rather than improve the well-being of the Palestinians.

Iraq stated that it was fitting that the United Nations, which had created the Palestinian problem by deciding to partition the land without the right to do so, should be responsible for taking care of the Palestinians.

Introducing the text, Pakistan explained that a fact-finding mission had not been able to make an in-depth analysis because of Israel's attitude. Israel had systematically tried to dismantle any indigenous economic institutions; it had closed Palestinian banking institutions, forcing Palestinians and other Arab residents to conduct business exclusively through Israeli banks and in Hebrew. A report such as the one requested, combined with the information already available, would provide a true picture of Israeli policies.

Economic development projects

Report of the Secretary-General. In June 1985,[72] the Secretary-General reported on progress made in implementing the General Assembly's 1984 resolution[73] calling for the urgent lifting of Israeli restrictions on the economy of the occupied territories and for the carrying out of projects to facilitate economic development there. In reply to his note verbale of 2 May 1985 requesting information from Israel, Israel had stated by a letter of 24 May (annexed to the Secretary-General's report) that it considered the resolution biased and politically motivated, falsely accusing Israel of imposing arbitrary restrictions and deliberately disregarding the improved economic and social welfare of the inhabitants of the territories, as well as Israel's actions to foster economic growth there. The ports of Ashdod and Haifa were fully open to the inhabitants of the territories and products from there thus had free access to external markets. All development projects, Israel added, were considered solely on the basis of their economic merit.

The Secretary-General also drew attention to information on projects carried out by UNIDO, contained in his report[74] on assistance to the Palestinians (see p. 281). UNIDO was carrying out for the Palestinians a project to identify problems of the plastics industry and make recommendations with particular emphasis on capacity utilization, and a feasibility study on a canning plant for citrus fruits.

ECONOMIC AND SOCIAL COUNCIL ACTION

On 26 July 1985, by **decision 1985/187**, the Economic and Social Council took note of the Secretary-General's report.

On 25 July, on the recommendation of its Third Committee, the Council adopted **resolution 1985/58** by roll-call vote.

Economic development projects in the occupied Palestinian territories

The Economic and Social Council,

Aware of the Israeli restrictions imposed on the foreign trade of the occupied Palestinian territories,

Aware also of the imposed domination of the Palestinian market by Israel,

Taking into account the need to give Palestinian firms and products direct access to external markets without Israeli interference,

Noting the lack of progress in the implementation of General Assembly resolution 39/223 of 18 December 1984, as reflected in the report of the Secretary-General on economic development projects in the occupied Palestinian territories,

1. *Calls* for the urgent lifting of the Israeli restrictions imposed on the economy of the occupied Palestinian territories;

2. *Recognizes* the Palestinian interest in establishing a seaport in the occupied Gaza Strip to give Palestinian firms and products direct access to external markets;

3. *Calls upon* all concerned to facilitate the establishment of a seaport in the occupied Gaza Strip;

4. *Also calls upon* all concerned to facilitate the establishment of a cement plant in the occupied West Bank and a citrus plant in the occupied Gaza Strip;

5. *Requests* the Secretary-General to continue his efforts to facilitate the establishment of the above-mentioned projects and to report to the General Assembly at its forty-first session, through the Economic and Social Council, on the progress made in the implementation of the present resolution.

Economic and Social Council resolution 1985/58

25 July 1985	Meeting 52	41-1-4 (roll-call vote)

Approved by Third Committee (E/1985/138) by roll-call vote (40-1-4), 12 July (meeting 10); 10-nation draft (E/1985/C.3/L.3), orally revised; agenda item 21.
Sponsors: Algeria, Bangladesh, Djibouti, India, Morocco, Pakistan, Saudi Arabia, Somalia, Syrian Arab Republic, Yugoslavia.

Roll-call vote in Council as follows:

In favour: Algeria, Argentina, Bangladesh, Botswana, Brazil, Bulgaria, China, Congo, Ecuador, France, German Democratic Republic, Germany, Federal Republic of, Haiti, India, Indonesia, Japan, Luxembourg, Malaysia, Mexico, Morocco, Netherlands, New Zealand, Nigeria, Poland, Romania, Rwanda, Saudi Arabia, Senegal, Sierra Leone, Somalia, Spain, Suriname, Thailand, Turkey, Uganda, USSR, United Kingdom, Venezuela, Yugoslavia, Zaire, Zimbabwe.
Against: United States.
Abstaining: Canada, Finland, Iceland, Sweden.

In the view of the United States, the text could not provide a solution to the Palestinian problem but was part of it. The Council had been established to discuss questions of international cooperation and promote economic and social development, not to lose time in making political statements.

Canada considered that the Council was not an appropriate place to discuss such projects; it would have been sufficient to indicate to the competent organizations that emphasis should be placed on the economic and social development of the Palestinians.

Luxembourg, speaking also for France, the Federal Republic of Germany, the Netherlands and the United Kingdom, said their positive votes implied no commitment on their part; economic development projects should be economically and technically viable so that they could contribute to the region's economic prosperity, in the interest of all.

Israel said the text was based on false premises, particularly in regard to the call for a seaport in the Gaza Strip. Trade in the occupied territories was being restricted not by Israel but by its Arab neighbours. The Director-General of the International Labour Organisation (ILO), reporting on his mission to the territories, had stated that the situation in the Gaza Strip, where 40 per cent of agricultural production consisted of citrus fruits, faced permanent difficulties because of the closures of the Egyptian markets and intermittent closures of Jordanian markets. The establishment of a citrus plant had in fact been approved, and a cement plant in the West Bank depended on fuel-supply security, which would be no problem if the Arab States lifted the oil boycott imposed on the territory.

PLO remarked that the Israeli authorities had stated that the citrus plant could be established on condition that it was obtained from Israel, that the produce was not marketed in Israel and that Israel's produce should have access to Arab markets. Consultants from the Federal Republic of Germany had undertaken a feasibility study on the cement plant and had concluded that it was viable. With regard to port outlets, Israel controlled 90 per cent of the occupied territories' foreign trade; world public opinion had reiterated that Palestinian trade should be completely free from Israeli restrictions. Since 1979, UNDP—which could provide only what Israel allowed—had spent less than $4 million there, PLO added.

GENERAL ASSEMBLY ACTION

On 17 December 1985, on the recommendation of the Second Committee, the General Assembly adopted **resolution 40/169** by recorded vote.

Economic development projects in the occupied Palestinian territories

The General Assembly,

Aware of the Israeli restrictions imposed on the foreign trade of the occupied Palestinian territories,

Aware also of the imposed domination of the Palestinian market by Israel,

Taking into account the need to give Palestinian firms and products direct access to external markets without Israeli interference,

Noting with regret the lack of progress in the implementation of General Assembly resolution 39/223 of 18 December 1984, as reflected in the report of the Secretary-General on economic development projects in the occupied Palestinian territories,

1. *Calls* for the urgent lifting of the Israeli restrictions imposed on the economy of the occupied Palestinian territories;

2. *Recognizes* the Palestinian interest in establishing a seaport in the occupied Gaza Strip to give Palestinian firms and products direct access to external markets;

3. *Calls upon* all concerned to facilitate the establishment of a seaport in the occupied Gaza Strip;

4. *Also calls upon* all concerned to facilitate the establishment of a cement plant in the occupied West Bank and a citrus plant in the occupied Gaza Strip;

5. *Requests* the Secretary-General to continue his efforts to facilitate the establishment of the above-mentioned projects and to report to the General Assembly at its forty-first session, through the Economic and Social Council, on the progress made in the implementation of the present resolution.

General Assembly resolution 40/169

17 December 1985   Meeting 119   138-2-7 (recorded vote)

Approved by Second Committee (A/40/1009/Add.1) by recorded vote (125-2-6), 11 November (meeting 30); 10-nation draft (A/C.2/40/L.15); agenda item 12.
Sponsors: Bangladesh, Gambia, Lebanon, Madagascar, Malaysia, Pakistan, Somalia, Sudan, Tunisia, Yemen.
Meeting numbers. GA 40th session: 2nd Committee 22, 30; plenary 119.
Recorded vote in Assembly as follows:

In favour: Afghanistan, Albania, Algeria, Angola, Antigua and Barbuda, Argentina, Austria, Bahamas, Bahrain, Bangladesh, Barbados, Belgium, Benin, Bhutan, Bolivia, Botswana, Brazil, Brunei Darussalam, Bulgaria, Burkina Faso, Burma, Burundi, Byelorussian SSR, Cameroon, Cape Verde, Central African Republic, Chad, Chile, China, Colombia, Comoros, Congo, Cuba, Cyprus, Czechoslovakia, Democratic Kampuchea, Democratic Yemen, Denmark, Djibouti, Dominica, Dominican Republic, Ecuador, Egypt, El Salvador, Equatorial Guinea, Ethiopia, Fiji, France, Gabon, German Democratic Republic, Germany, Federal Republic of, Ghana, Greece, Guatemala, Guinea, Guinea-Bissau, Haiti, Honduras, Hungary, India, Indonesia, Iran, Iraq, Ireland, Italy, Ivory Coast, Jamaica, Japan, Jordan, Kuwait, Lao People's Democratic Republic, Lebanon, Lesotho, Liberia, Libyan Arab Jamahiriya, Luxembourg, Madagascar, Malawi, Malaysia, Maldives, Mali, Malta, Mauritania, Mauritius, Mexico, Mongolia, Morocco, Mozambique, Nepal, Netherlands, New Zealand, Nicaragua, Niger, Nigeria, Oman, Pakistan, Panama, Papua New Guinea, Paraguay, Peru, Philippines, Poland, Portugal, Qatar, Romania, Rwanda, Saint Vincent and the Grenadines, Samoa, Sao Tome and Principe, Saudi Arabia, Senegal, Sierra Leone, Singapore, Somalia, Spain, Sri Lanka, Sudan, Suriname, Swaziland, Syrian Arab Republic, Thailand, Togo, Trinidad and Tobago, Tunisia, Turkey, Uganda, Ukrainian SSR, USSR, United Arab Emirates, United Kingdom, United Republic of Tanzania, Uruguay, Venezuela, Viet Nam, Yemen, Yugoslavia, Zaire, Zambia.
Against: Israel, United States.
Abstaining: Australia, Canada, Finland, Grenada, Iceland, Norway, Sweden.

Israel said the ports of Ashdod and Haifa were entirely at the disposal of the inhabitants of Judaea, Samaria and the Gaza district. Products originating there had free access to external markets, and development projects were considered solely on their merits.

Though agreeing on the desirability of ensuring the territories' economic development, Sweden, speaking also on behalf of Finland, Iceland and Norway, said the text implied that the Assembly would have to pronounce itself in favour of specific proposals which had not been discussed or scrutinized by any relevant United Nations body and had no assurance of their technical and financial viability. The same reasons were cited by Australia and Canada for their abstentions.

Speaking for the EC members, Luxembourg reiterated their positions on the need for projects to be economically and technically sound, and observed that their positive votes implied no specific commitment.

Introducing the draft, Bangladesh said it had the full support of the Group of 77 and sought to ensure that the necessary facilities and opportunities were made available for development projects; in view of the overwhelming support the resolution had received in the Economic and Social Council, it hoped that the Committee would adopt it by consensus.

Israeli measures against educational institutions

Communications. By a letter of 5 March 1985, transmitted by Democratic Yemen as Chairman of the Arab Group,[75] PLO brought to the Secretary-General's attention charges that on 1 March several students were badly injured when units from the occupation army and border guards stormed both campuses of Bir Zeit University in the West Bank to stop the opening of a Palestinian cultural exhibit. Israel then declared the University a military zone, suspended classes, stormed student houses and arrested scores of students and faculty members. On 3 March, Israeli reinforcements were sent to the University to crush a student protest demanding their immediate release; it remained closed and under siege. Also in the West Bank, Al-Najah University was surrounded by Israeli army units on 2 March. PLO called on the United Nations to end such Fascist and inhuman acts.

Grave concern at the raids on Bir Zeit University was also expressed by the Chairman of the Committee on Palestinian rights in a letter of 19 March.[4] According to press reports, he said, 53 students and their guests had been detained and further detentions were expected.

UNESCO action. The Executive Board of the United Nations Educational, Scientific and Cultural Organization (UNESCO), at its May/June 1985 session,[76] noting with grave apprehension that Israel continued to obstruct the functioning of educational, cultural and training institutions, deplored any obstruction and harassment of such institutions in the occupied territories, which, it said, could imperil their existence. It called on the occupying authority to comply with the 1949 fourth Geneva Convention and the 1954 Hague Convention for the Protection of Cultural Property in the Event of Armed Conflict by rescinding all measures and military orders against educational and cultural institutions, and to safeguard their academic freedoms. The Board invited the UNESCO Director-General to appoint a mission of academics to study the conditions in which academic freedoms were guaranteed and exercised in the territories.

Report of the Secretary-General. In August 1985,[77] the Secretary-General reported on Israeli policies and practices against Palestinian students and faculties in schools, universities and other educational institutions in the territories. He stated that, by a note verbale of 29 March, he had requested Israel to inform him of any steps taken or envisaged to implement the Assembly's 1984 resolution[78] demanding that Israel rescind all actions and measures against educational institutions.

By a note verbale of 1 July 1985, annexed to the report, Israel had categorically rejected the accusations made against it in the 1984 resolution. The school system in the occupied territories had grown considerably during the years of Israeli administration, it stated; in Judaea and Samaria, the number of pupils and classes in 1984/85 had doubled since 1967/68, and in the Gaza district it had increased

by over 209 per cent. With regard to higher education, there had been no university in Judaea and Samaria in June 1967; the Israeli administration had enabled the establishment of five universities. Teachers' seminars, agricultural, technical and paramedical institutions, mostly operating since 1967, also provided higher education and their students had increased to 4,680 in 1984/85 from 2,599 in 1980/81.

Academic activity on the campuses was conducted without its interference, Israel went on. The curricula were, in Judaea and Samaria, those of the Jordanian educational system and, in the Gaza district, those of the Egyptian educational system. Academic freedom, however, did not subsume disruption of public order by incitement, threats or violence, Israel added.

The March 1985 seminar[63] on the living conditions of the Palestinians (see p. 344) also examined the question of higher education in the territories. In its view, the establishment of a Palestinian system of higher education, which included six universities serving more than 10,000 students, was a singular achievement in a society under occupation, all the more remarkable in that it was an indigenous effort that had received no encouragement from the occupying authorities. However, owing to military occupation and the practices of the occupying Power, the further development of the Palestinian system of higher education was severely hindered and suffered from three serious problems: constraints on the autonomy and freedom of academic institutions; absence of an effective local Palestinian authority to plan, co-ordinate and support higher education; and scarcity of resources.

The seminar's working group on the topic proposed that all measures of collective punishment imposed on academic institutions should cease, as should those curtailing their autonomy and restricting their academic functions and freedoms. Restrictions imposed on the work of the Council for Higher Education should be removed and it should be recognized as the local Palestinian authority. Israeli restrictions on the entry of funds to Palestinian higher education should be lifted; universities and higher-education bodies abroad should be encouraged to establish links with Palestinian institutions. International assistance was of the utmost importance for further progress in higher education in the territories. Various United Nations organizations and bodies as well as other international and non-governmental organizations could provide such assistance and co-operation.

GENERAL ASSEMBLY ACTION

On 16 December 1985, on the recommendation of the Special Political Committee, the General

Assembly adopted **resolution 40/161 G**, on the report of the Committee on Israeli practices, by recorded vote.

The General Assembly,

Bearing in mind the Geneva Convention relative to the Protection of Civilian Persons in Time of War, of 12 August 1949,

Deeply concerned at the continued harassment by Israel, the occupying Power, against educational institutions in the occupied Palestinian territories,

Recalling its resolutions 38/79 G of 15 December 1983 and 39/95 G of 14 December 1984,

Taking note of the report of the Secretary-General of 14 August 1985,

Taking note of the relevant decisions adopted by the Executive Board of the United Nations Educational, Scientific and Cultural Organization concerning the educational and cultural situation in the occupied territories,

1. *Reaffirms* the applicability of the Geneva Convention relative to the Protection of Civilian Persons in Time of War, of 12 August 1949, to the Palestinian and other Arab territories occupied by Israel since 1967, including Jerusalem;

2. *Condemns* Israeli policies and practices against Palestinian students and faculties in schools, universities and other educational institutions in the occupied Palestinian territories, especially the policy of opening fire on defenceless students, causing many casualties;

3. *Condemns* the systematic Israeli campaign of repression against and closing of universities and other educational and vocational institutions in the occupied Palestinian territories, restricting and impeding the academic activities of Palestinian universities by subjecting the selection of courses, textbooks and educational programmes, the admission of students and the appointment of faculty members to the control and supervision of the military occupation authorities, in clear contravention of the Geneva Convention;

4. *Demands* that Israel, the occupying Power, comply with the provisions of that Convention, rescind all actions and measures against all educational institutions, ensure the freedom of those institutions and refrain forthwith from hindering the effective operation of the universities and other educational institutions;

5. *Requests* the Secretary-General to report to the General Assembly as soon as possible and not later than the beginning of its forty-first session on the implementation of the present resolution.

General Assembly resolution 40/161 G

16 December 1985   Meeting 118   112-2-32 (recorded vote)

Approved by SPC (A/40/890) by recorded vote (92-2-26), 8 November (meeting 27); draft by Afghanistan, Bangladesh, Cuba, Egypt, India, Indonesia, Kuwait for the Arab Group, Madagascar, Malaysia, Mali, Nicaragua, Pakistan, Qatar, Senegal (A/SPC/40/L.14); agenda item 75.
Meeting numbers. GA 40th session: SPC 16-23, 27; plenary 118.

Recorded vote in Assembly as follows:

In favour: Afghanistan, Albania, Algeria, Antigua and Barbuda, Argentina, Austria, Bahamas, Bahrain, Bangladesh, Benin, Bhutan, Bolivia, Botswana, Brazil, Brunei Darussalam, Bulgaria, Burkina Faso, Burundi, Byelorussian SSR, Cape Verde, Central African Republic, Chad, China, Colombia, Congo, Cuba, Cyprus, Czechoslovakia, Democratic Kampuchea, Democratic Yemen, Djibouti, Dominican Republic, Ecuador, Egypt, Equatorial Guinea, Ethiopia, Fiji, Gabon, Gambia, German Democratic Republic, Greece, Guinea, Guinea-Bissau, Guyana, Hungary, India, Indonesia, Iran, Iraq, Jamaica, Jordan, Kenya, Kuwait, Lao People's Democratic Republic, Lebanon, Lesotho, Libyan Arab Jamahiriya, Madagascar, Malaysia, Maldives, Mali, Malta, Mauritania, Mauritius, Mexico, Mongolia, Morocco, Mozambique, Nepal, Nicaragua, Niger, Nigeria, Oman, Pakistan, Peru, Philippines, Poland, Qatar, Romania, Rwanda, Samoa, Sao Tome and Principe, Saudi Arabia, Senegal, Seychelles, Sierra Leone, Singapore, Somalia, Spain, Sri Lanka, Sudan, Suriname, Sweden, Syrian Arab Republic, Thailand, Togo, Trinidad and Tobago, Tunisia, Turkey, Uganda, Ukrainian SSR, USSR, United Arab Emirates, United Republic of Tanzania, Uruguay, Vanuatu, Venezuela, Viet Nam, Yemen, Yugoslavia, Zambia, Zimbabwe.

Against: Israel, United States.

Abstaining: Australia, Belgium, Cameroon, Canada, Chile, Costa Rica, Denmark, Dominica, El Salvador, Finland, France, Germany, Federal Republic of, Grenada, Guatemala, Iceland, Ireland, Italy, Ivory Coast, Japan, Liberia, Luxembourg, Malawi, Netherlands, New Zealand, Norway, Panama, Portugal, Saint Lucia, Saint Vincent and the Grenadines, Swaziland, United Kingdom, Zaire.

Before voting on the text as a whole, the Assembly and the Committee adopted paragraph 2 by recorded vote, by 96 to 2, with 45 abstentions, and 84 to 2, with 34 abstentions, respectively.

Israel said although it did not subscribe to many of the observations in the Secretary-General's report on the Vienna seminar, the picture presented there was totally different from that portrayed by the resolution, which spoke of a systematic Israeli campaign of repression against and closing of universities; the truth was that the six Palestinian universities functioned normally and satisfactorily as long as foreign elements did not stir up the student body to disturbance and violence.

The United States said it strongly defended academic freedom and had made its views known when Israeli practices towards academic institutions were open to criticism, but it could not support broad condemnatory and inflammatory language seeking to condemn indiscriminately without regard to the facts or actual policies.

Though supporting the text as a whole with some hesitation, Sweden abstained on paragraph 2 because of what it felt were very categorical and sweeping formulations not totally borne out by the facts.

Mediterranean-Dead Sea canal project

Israel's 1981 plan[79] to build a 67-mile canal linking the Mediterranean Sea to the Dead Sea for electric power generation was the subject of a 1985 General Assembly resolution (40/167) and a decision of the United Nations Environment Programme (UNEP). The Secretary-General reported that, in June, Israel had given instruction to cease all work on the project.

UNEP Council action. On 23 May,[80] the UNEP Governing Council deplored Israel's noncompliance with Assembly resolutions on the subject and requested the UNEP Executive Director to facilitate the Secretary-General's work in monitoring and assessing all aspects, especially ecological ones, of the adverse effects on Jordan and on the occupied territories arising from the implementation of the Israeli decision, and to report on the matter in 1987.

Report of the Secretary-General. Pursuant to a 1984 General Assembly request,[81] the

Secretary-General submitted in November 1985 a report[82] on the adverse—including juridical, political, economic, ecological and demographic—effects of Israel's decision to construct a canal linking the Mediterranean and Dead Seas. By letters of 10 May, the Under-Secretary-General for Technical Co-operation for Development had requested Israel and Jordan to make available relevant information, give a small team of experts access to sites and arrange contacts with officials concerned.

Jordan replied on 21 May that it would be glad to receive the experts, facilitate their work and forward any information available. Israel, on 29 May, stated that it believed that the canal project would benefit the population of the entire area and had repeatedly sought to discuss and co-ordinate the matter with Jordan. Jordan had not responded to those offers. As the report to be prepared was on the "adverse" effects of the canal project, the report's outcome would thus be predetermined and Israel believed that no useful purpose would be served by an additional visit of experts. On 1 July, Israel informed the Secretary-General that on 11 June its Minister of Energy and Industry had instructed the Mediterranean–Dead Sea Corporation to cease all work related to the canal.

A United Nations mission visited Jordan from 19 to 25 September 1985; its report annexed to the Secretary-General's report, assessed effects of a canal on agricultural development, mineral production, tourism and recreation, and the environment, along the lines of the 1984 report.[83]

GENERAL ASSEMBLY ACTION

On 16 December 1985, on the recommendation of the Special Political Committee, the General Assembly adopted **resolution 40/167** by recorded vote:

Israel's decision to build a canal linking the Mediterranean Sea to the Dead Sea

The General Assembly,

Recalling its resolutions 36/150 of 16 December 1981, 37/122 of 16 December 1982, 38/85 of 15 December 1983 and 39/101 of 14 December 1984,

Taking note of the report of the Secretary-General,

1. *Requests* the Secretary-General to monitor on a continuing basis any new development relating to the proposed canal linking the Mediterranean Sea to the Dead Sea and to report all findings in this regard to the General Assembly;

2. *Decides* to resume consideration of this item in case activities by Israel relating to the said canal are resumed.

General Assembly resolution 40/167

16 December 1985   Meeting 118   150-1 (recorded vote)

Approved by SPC (A/40/1025) by recorded vote (118-1), 6 December (meeting 46); 22-nation draft (A/SPC/40/L.31); agenda item 81.

Sponsors: Algeria, Bahrain, Bangladesh, Democratic Yemen, Djibouti, Iraq, Jordan, Kuwait, Lebanon, Libyan Arab Jamahiriya, Mauritania, Morocco, Oman, Pakistan, Qatar, Saudi Arabia, Somalia, Sudan, Syrian Arab Republic, Tunisia, United Arab Emirates, Yemen.

Meeting numbers. GA 40th session: SPC 45, 46; plenary 118.

Recorded vote in Assembly as follows:

In favour: Afghanistan, Albania, Algeria, Argentina, Australia, Austria, Bahamas, Bahrain, Bangladesh, Barbados, Belgium, Benin, Bhutan, Bolivia, Botswana, Brazil, Brunei Darussalam, Bulgaria, Burkina Faso, Burma, Burundi, Byelorussian SSR, Cameroon, Canada, Cape Verde, Central African Republic, Chad, Chile, China, Colombia, Congo, Costa Rica, Cuba, Cyprus, Czechoslovakia, Democratic Kampuchea, Democratic Yemen, Denmark, Djibouti, Dominica, Dominican Republic, Ecuador, Egypt, El Salvador, Equatorial Guinea, Ethiopia, Fiji, Finland, France, Gabon, Gambia, German Democratic Republic, Germany, Federal Republic of, Ghana, Greece, Grenada, Guatemala, Guinea, Guinea-Bissau, Guyana, Haiti, Honduras, Hungary, Iceland, India, Indonesia, Iran, Iraq, Ireland, Italy, Ivory Coast, Jamaica, Japan, Jordan, Kenya, Kuwait, Lao People's Democratic Republic, Lebanon, Lesotho, Liberia, Libyan Arab Jamahiriya, Luxembourg, Madagascar, Malawi, Malaysia, Maldives, Mali, Malta, Mauritania, Mauritius, Mexico, Mongolia, Morocco, Mozambique, Nepal, Netherlands, New Zealand, Nicaragua, Niger, Nigeria, Norway, Oman, Pakistan, Panama, Paraguay, Peru, Philippines, Poland, Portugal, Qatar, Romania, Rwanda, Saint Lucia, Saint Vincent and the Grenadines, Samoa, Sao Tome and Principe, Saudi Arabia, Senegal, Seychelles, Sierra Leone, Singapore, Somalia, Spain, Sri Lanka, Sudan, Suriname, Swaziland, Sweden, Syrian Arab Republic, Thailand, Togo, Trinidad and Tobago, Tunisia, Turkey, Uganda, Ukrainian SSR, USSR, United Arab Emirates, United Kingdom, United Republic of Tanzania, United States, Uruguay, Vanuatu, Venezuela, Viet Nam, Yemen, Yugoslavia, Zaire, Zambia, Zimbabwe.

Against: Israel.

Israel saw no valid reason for the United Nations to take a stand on a plan which was still at the stage of feasibility studies. Israel had stopped all work related to the canal in June; it had not been resumed. In addition to maligning Israel and distorting the nature of a *bona fide* development blueprint, the text dealt with an irrelevant inquiry after all work had been terminated and asked the Secretary-General to monitor hypothetical future activities, putting a purposeless strain on personnel and finances. Israel also considered that its territory and operations should not be subject to any United Nations surveillance and objected to such monitoring as a matter of principle.

The United States regarded the text as a positive step towards solving a difficult problem, but did not alter its opposition to previous resolutions on the subject.

Introducing the text, Jordan emphasized that work on the canal could be resumed when the reasons which had led Israel to suspend that work no longer existed.

REFERENCES

[1]A/40/119-S/16943. [2]A/40/128-S/16954. [3]A/40/167-S/17012. [4]A/40/183-S/17043. [5]A/40/237-S/17107. [6]A/40/281-S/17146. [7]A/40/480-S/17340. [8]YUN 1976, p. 235. [9]A/40/540-S/17392. [10]A/40/610-S/17445, A/40/625-S/17452, A/40/624-S/17451. [11]A/40/628-S/17455. [12]A/40/634-S/17462. [13]A/40/620 (S/17448). [14]A/40/679-S/17493. [15]A/40/833-S/17600. [16]A/40/834-S/17601. [17]A/40/889-S/17630. [18]A/40/967-S/17666. [19]E/1985/22 (res. 1985/1 A, 1985/1 B, 1985/2, 1985/4). [20]E/CN.4/1986/5 (res. 1985/16). [21]A/40/702. [22]YUN 1968, p. 555, GA res. 2443(XXIII), 19 Dec. 1968. [23]YUN 1984, p. 316. [24]A/40/575. [25]YUN 1984, p. 317, GA res. 39/95 D, 14 Dec. 1984. [26]S/17456. [27]S/17461. [28]S/17460. [29]S/17459. [30]YUN 1983, p. 274. [31]E/1985/22 (res. 1985/1 B). [32]S/16900. [33]A/40/183-S/17043. [34]A/40/219-S/17075. [35]A/40/223-S/17080. [36]A/40/225-S/17085. [37]A/40/608-S/17439, A/40/610-S/17445, A/40/624-S/17451. [38]YUN 1948-49, p. 535, GA res. 217 A (III), 10 Dec. 1948. [39]A/40/679-S/17493. [40]E/1985/22 (res. 1985/1 A). [41]A/40/686. [42]YUN 1984, p. 280, GA res. 39/95 A, 14 Dec. 1984. [43]A/40/84-S/16896. [44]A/40/179-S/17035. [45]A/40/470-S/17332.

(46)A/40/215-S/17069. (47)E/1985/22 (res. 1985/2). (48)YUN 1981, p. 309. (49)A/40/649 & Add.1. (50)YUN 1984, p. 322, GA res. 39/95 F, 14 Dec. 1984. (51)YUN 1981, p. 312. (52)*Ibid.*, SC res. 497(1981), 17 Dec. 1981. (53)YUN 1982, p. 515, GA res. ES-9/1, 5 Feb. 1982. (54)YUN 1967, p. 257, SC res. 242(1967), 22 Nov. 1967. (55)YUN 1973, p. 213, SC res. 338(1973), 22 Oct. 1973. (56)YUN 1980, p. 411. (57)A/40/541. (58)YUN 1984, p. 326, GA res. 39/95 E, 14 Dec. 1984. (59)YUN 1980, p. 424; YUN 1981, p. 313; YUN 1982, p. 538. (60)A/40/583. (61)YUN 1984, p. 326, GA res. 39/95 H, 14 Dec. 1984. (62)YUN 1980, p. 413. (63)A/40/373-E/1985/99. (64)YUN 1984, p. 328, GA res. 39/169, 17 Dec. 1984. (65)E/1985/35 (res. 139(XII)). (66)A/C.2/40/9. (67)A/40/381-E/1985/105. (68)YUN 1984, p. 330, GA dec. 39/442, 18 Dec. 1984. (69)YUN 1983, p. 339. (70)*Ibid.*, p. 282. (71)TD/B/1065 & Corr.1. (72)A/40/367-E/1985/116. (73)YUN 1984, p. 330, GA res. 39/223, 18 Dec. 1984. (74)A/40/353-E/1985/115 & Corr.1 & Add.1 & Add.1/Corr.1. (75)A/40/162-S/17003. (76)121 EX/Decisions (dec. 5.1.3). (77)A/40/542. (78)YUN 1984, p. 333, GA res. 39/95 G, 14 Dec. 1984. (79)YUN 1981, p. 318. (80)A/40/25 (dec. 13/8). (81)YUN 1984, p. 332, GA res. 39/101, 14 Dec. 1984. (82)A/40/803. (83)YUN 1984, p. 331.

Palestine refugees

UN Agency for Palestine refugees

In 1985, the United Nations Relief and Works Agency for Palestine Refugees in the Near East continued to assist 2,093,545 refugees in Jordan, Lebanon (see p. 311), the Syrian Arab Republic and the Israeli-occupied territories of the West Bank and the Gaza Strip, providing quasi-governmental education, health and relief services to refugees living in and outside camps. Less than a third of the refugees were registered as living in camps. The Agency maintained its own schools, training institutions, clinics and health centres, and procured and distributed food rations to needy refugees. It employed more than 16,500 schoolteachers, doctors, nurses, sanitation labourers, relief workers and others. Its operations were administered from its headquarters at Vienna and Amman and from five field offices in Jordan, Lebanon, the Syrian Arab Republic, the West Bank and the Gaza Strip, with liaison offices in New York and Cairo.

UNRWA activities and various aspects of the Palestine refugee problem were addressed by the General Assembly, which in December adopted 11 resolutions on: assistance to Palestine refugees (40/165 A); the Working Group on the Financing of UNRWA (40/165 B); assistance to displaced persons (40/165 C); scholarships for higher education and vocational training (40/165 D); Palestine refugees in the Gaza Strip (40/165 E); ration distribution to Palestine refugees (40/165 F); refugees displaced since 1967 (40/165 G); revenues derived from refugee properties (40/165 H); refugee protection (40/165 I); Palestine refugees in

the West Bank (40/165 J); and a proposed University of Jerusalem for Palestine refugees (40/165 K).

The Agency's activities and its staff were particularly affected by the events in Lebanon (see p. 295). Following the kidnapping of two British subjects in mid-March, the United Kingdom Embassy at Beirut advised all British citizens to leave; three of the five British staff members of the Lebanon field office were transferred to duties outside Beirut. On 25 March, Alec Collett, a British journalist working under contract with UNRWA, was kidnapped by unidentified gunmen south of Beirut. The Commissioner-General ordered the remaining British nationals working for UNRWA, including the field office Director, to leave Lebanon. On 15 May, the UNRWA Deputy Director in Lebanon, an Irish citizen, was abducted by armed men, to be released 37 hours later. During two incidents in April/May, armed militiamen intruded into UNRWA's central warehouse in Beirut and searched the premises. On 7 June, the Director of UNRWA Affairs, Lebanon, who was leading a relief convoy to Burj el-Barajneh camp, was forced with others to leave his vehicle but was released on the intervention of the Lebanese Minister for Justice. In the West Bank and the Gaza Strip, Israeli authorities continued to summon Agency staff for interrogation during office hours without adequate notice, causing disruption especially of UNRWA school programmes.

In the Gaza Strip, there was a marked deterioration of the security situation resulting in an increasing number of incidents. Numerous incidents also characterized the situation of refugees in the West Bank, including confrontations with Israeli settlers (see p. 338). No solution was reached to the problem of the Palestinian refugees, numbering approximately 5,000, on the Egyptian side of the border between the Gaza Strip and the Sinai, to whom UNRWA continued to provide limited assistance.

The process of issuing individual registration cards for all Palestine refugees—intended to facilitate provision of services and to reassure the refugees that certain rights acknowledged by the General Assembly would not be affected because UNRWA had suspended the basic ration—as requested by the Assembly in 1982,(1) was stopped in March 1985 in the Gaza Strip at the request of the Israeli authorities, although most of the refugees there had received them. The Syrian and Jordanian Governments also prevailed upon UNRWA to stop issuing them in the Syrian Arab Republic, Jordan and the West Bank; no attempt was made to issue cards in Lebanon because of the security situation there. Instead of individual cards, family registration cards were again being issued in all fields.

UNRWA activities and its financial situation in 1985 were described by the Commissioner-General in reports covering the periods 1 July 1984 to 30 June 1985[2] and 1 July 1985 to 30 June 1986.[3] Introducing in the General Assembly's Special Political Committee the 1984/85 report, the Commissioner-General stated that it described one of the most difficult years in the Agency's 35-year history.

On 1 November 1985, Giorgio Giacomelli (Italy) succeeded Olof Rydbeck (Sweden) as Commissioner-General.

GENERAL ASSEMBLY ACTION

On 16 December 1985, on the recommendation of the Special Political Committee, the General Assembly adopted **resolution 40/165 A**, by recorded vote.

Assistance to Palestine refugees

The General Assembly,

Recalling its resolution 39/99 A of 14 December 1984 and all its previous resolutions on the question, including resolution 194(III) of 11 December 1948,

Taking note of the report of the Commissioner-General of the United Nations Relief and Works Agency for Palestine Refugees in the Near East, covering the period from 1 July 1984 to 30 June 1985,

1. *Notes with deep regret* that repatriation or compensation of the refugees as provided for in paragraph 11 of General Assembly resolution 194(III) has not been effected, that no substantial progress has been made in the programme endorsed by the Assembly in paragraph 2 of its resolution 513(VI) of 26 January 1952 for the reintegration of refugees either by repatriation or resettlement and that, therefore, the situation of the refugees continues to be a matter of serious concern;

2. *Expresses its thanks* to the Commissioner-General and to all the staff of the United Nations Relief and Works Agency for Palestine Refugees in the Near East, recognizing that the Agency is doing all it can within the limits of available resources, and also expresses its thanks to the specialized agencies and private organizations for their valuable work in assisting the refugees;

3. *Expresses its deep appreciation* to the former Commissioner-General, Mr. Olof Rydbeck, for his many years of effective service to the Agency and his dedication to the welfare of the refugees;

4. *Reiterates its request* that the headquarters of the Agency should be relocated to its former site within its area of operations as soon as practicable;

5. *Notes with regret* that the United Nations Conciliation Commission for Palestine has been unable to find a means of achieving progress in the implementation of paragraph 11 of General Assembly resolution 194(III), and requests the Commission to exert continued efforts towards the implementation of that paragraph and to report to the Assembly as appropriate, but no later than 1 September 1986;

6. *Directs attention* to the continuing seriousness of the financial position of the Agency, as outlined in the report of the Commissioner-General;

7. *Notes with profound concern* that, despite the commendable and successful efforts of the Commissioner-General to collect additional contributions, this increased level of income to the Agency is still insufficient to cover essential budget requirements in the present year and that, at currently foreseen levels of giving, deficits will recur each year;

8. *Calls upon* all Governments, as a matter of urgency, to make the most generous efforts possible to meet the anticipated needs of the Agency, particularly in the light of the budgetary deficit projected in the report of the Commissioner-General, and therefore urges non-contributing Governments to contribute regularly and contributing Governments to consider increasing their regular contributions.

General Assembly resolution 40/165 A

16 December 1985   Meeting 118   149-0-1 (recorded vote)

Approved by SPC (A/40/921) by recorded vote (123-0-1), 15 November (meeting 34); draft by United States (A/SPC/40/L.16); agenda item 79.
Meeting numbers. GA 40th session: SPC 22-28, 31, 34; plenary 118.

Recorded vote in Assembly as follows:

In favour: Afghanistan, Algeria, Antigua and Barbuda, Argentina, Australia, Austria, Bahamas, Bahrain, Bangladesh, Barbados, Belgium, Benin, Bhutan, Bolivia, Botswana, Brazil, Brunei Darussalam, Bulgaria, Burkina Faso, Burma, Burundi, Byelorussian SSR, Cameroon, Canada, Cape Verde, Central African Republic, Chad, Chile, China, Colombia, Congo, Costa Rica, Cuba, Cyprus, Czechoslovakia, Democratic Kampuchea, Democratic Yemen, Denmark, Djibouti, Dominica, Dominican Republic, Ecuador, Egypt, El Salvador, Equatorial Guinea, Ethiopia, Fiji, Finland, France, Gabon, Gambia, German Democratic Republic, Germany, Federal Republic of, Ghana, Greece, Grenada, Guatemala, Guinea, Guinea-Bissau, Guyana, Haiti, Honduras, Hungary, Iceland, India, Indonesia, Iran, Iraq, Ireland, Italy, Ivory Coast, Jamaica, Japan, Jordan, Kenya, Kuwait, Lao People's Democratic Republic, Lebanon, Lesotho, Liberia, Libyan Arab Jamahiriya, Luxembourg, Madagascar, Malawi, Malaysia, Maldives, Mali, Malta, Mauritania, Mauritius, Mexico, Mongolia, Morocco, Mozambique, Nepal, Netherlands, New Zealand, Nicaragua, Niger, Nigeria, Norway, Oman, Pakistan, Panama, Peru, Philippines, Poland, Portugal, Qatar, Romania, Rwanda, Saint Lucia, Saint Vincent and the Grenadines, Samoa, Sao Tome and Principe, Saudi Arabia, Senegal, Seychelles, Sierra Leone, Singapore, Somalia, Spain, Sri Lanka, Sudan, Suriname, Swaziland, Sweden, Syrian Arab Republic, Thailand, Togo, Trinidad and Tobago, Tunisia, Turkey, Uganda, Ukrainian SSR, USSR, United Arab Emirates, United Kingdom, United Republic of Tanzania, United States, Uruguay, Vanuatu, Venezuela, Viet Nam, Yemen, Yugoslavia, Zaire, Zambia, Zimbabwe.
Against: None.
Abstaining: Israel.

Israel said the ritual expression of deep regret for non-implementation of the Assembly's stipulation in paragraph 11 of the 1948 resolution on the partition of Palestine[4]—that the refugees should be permitted to return to their homes and live at peace with their neighbours and that compensation should be paid for the property of those choosing not to return and for loss of or damage to property—which had been adopted in entirely different historical circumstances, was unacceptable.

The Libyan Arab Jamahiriya emphasized that, though voting in favour of the texts under the agenda item, that did not imply its recognition of Israel or its practices in the occupied territories.

Iran had reservations concerning all references to the Zionist régime as "Israel". It also stressed that the relief programmes should not be considered a permanent solution to the Palestinian question.

UNRWA financing

Total income received by UNRWA for all funds, in cash and in kind, in 1985 was $182 million, including about $16 million received in response to an appeal by the Commissioner-General. Expenditure in 1985 by all funds was $187.4 million, $3.9

million less than in 1984. The excess of expenditure over income was reduced from $10.1 million in 1984 to $5.4 million in 1985, $1.2 million of which was in respect of the General Fund.

In a special report, annexed to a May 1985 note by the Secretary-General,[5] the Commissioner-General drew attention to the critical state of the Agency's finances and outlined the efforts he had made to overcome the difficulties as well as the measures that would have to be taken—including major cuts in services to refugees—unless additional funding could be obtained at an early date; those measures, he pointed out, could adversely affect stability in the Middle East and be harmful to the search for a just and lasting peace.

In his report for the period ended 30 June 1985,[2] the Commissioner-General again stressed UNRWA's grave financial situation, in spite of strenuous efforts to reduce expenditure while avoiding major cuts in services, and to raise additional funds. He warned that the Agency still faced a shortfall of several million dollars which, if not covered by additional contributions or programme reductions, would lead to a further drawdown of UNRWA's already low capital. The minimum budget for 1986 would require some $20 million more than Governments had pledged as their regular contributions; there was no way to reduce projected expenses without depriving refugees of basic education and health services. In the light of those potentially serious consequences, the Commissioner-General urged Governments to discuss a rational approach to the Agency's financial problems.

In 1985, by cancelling all construction, slashing maintenance deeply, denying area staff pay raises and making other reductions, the budget gap was reduced from $67 million to $27 million. At that point, the Commissioner-General again addressed Governments stating that he had reduced the budget as far as possible without mass reductions in staff or directly cutting vital services. Although several countries—Australia, Canada, Japan, the United States and the Nordic countries—responded generously, he said, the overall response from Member States was disappointing and further cuts had to be made, which had a direct impact on services to refugees. On the positive side, UNRWA benefited from some reduced costs because of exchange rate gains. With those savings and with continuing austerity measures, the Agency was still $8 million short of the estimated needed income to cover 1985's already reduced programme.

The Commissioner-General's decision to implement austerity measures was a matter of great concern to the refugees and to host Governments. Although continuing to press their view that UNRWA should do more for the refugees and should restore the basic ration programme suspended in 1982 due to financial constraints, those Governments were helpful in assisting UNRWA to overcome its difficulties. For example, when the Agency experienced a critical shortage of flour in late 1985, Jordan loaned it sufficient stocks to maintain distribution to special hardship cases in the country until new supplies could be obtained.

Working Group on UNRWA financing

Report of the Working Group (March). At the end of February 1985, the Commissioner-General urgently requested the Working Group on the Financing of the United Nations Relief and Works Agency for Palestine Refugees in the Near East to hold a meeting as soon as possible so that it could be informed about UNRWA's alarming financial situation. The Group met on 1 March and discussed an oral report of the UNRWA Comptroller on the acute budgetary crisis. On 26 March, it adopted a special report[6] and authorized its Chairman to take whatever steps he might find possible to assist the Commissioner-General and the Secretary-General in their fund-raising efforts.

The Comptroller reported that contributions had declined from $190.6 million in 1980 to an estimated $177.9 million in 1984, while pledged and expected contributions for 1985 amounted to only $164.4 million, of which $138.3 million was in cash for the General Fund. As expenditure to maintain the programmes in 1985 amounted to $231.6 million, including a $205.1 million cash expenditure, there was a shortfall of some $67 million.

Austerity measures introduced by the Commissioner-General—reductions in personnel costs ($13.9 million), postponement of construction, maintenance and replacement of equipment ($19.4 million), reductions in provisions for administrative services, supplies and reserves ($6.4 million)—totalled some $40 million, leaving an unfunded balance of some $27 million.

The $27 million represented the minimum needed to maintain education, health and relief programmes until the end of 1985. By a letter of 19 February, the Commissioner-General appealed to Governments and selected intergovernmental organizations for additional pledges by the end of May.

Concluding, the Working Group expressed deep concern at UNRWA's financial outlook. It expressed its appreciation to the Commissioner-General for his efforts to reduce expenditure, but noted that a major portion of his austerity measures related to the deferral of payments due to area staff for salary increases and cost-of-living adjustments which would have to be met in the future; also, deferred construction and maintenance would probably be more costly in the long run. Nevertheless, the Group agreed that in the circumstances he had had no other alternative.

The Group reiterated its conviction that the international community should not allow UNRWA to collapse for want of funds. Noting that many Governments which supported UNRWA in their votes in the General Assembly did not contribute to it, the Group urged them to do so and invited those that were contributing to make additional special contributions.

As an initial step, the Group authorized its Chairman to address a letter to the Secretary-General underlining the critical financial situation, endorsing the Commissioner-General's appeal and emphasizing the need for Governments to respond generously. The Chairman did so on 27 March,[7] warning that services would have to be reduced, inevitably affecting the education programme, and that the continued employment of many of the 17,000 locally recruited Palestinian staff would be jeopardized.

Report of the Working Group (October). At a meeting on 1 October, the Working Group examined a report with up-to-date information on UNRWA's financial situation in 1985 and on the outlook for 1986.[8] Since March 1985, estimated income had increased by some $13 million as a result of additional contributions pledged by Australia ($260,000), Canada ($2.2 million), Denmark ($451,000), Finland ($170,000), Norway ($562,000), Sweden ($1.2 million) and the United States ($8 million), reducing the shortfall from $27 million to $14 million. Additional austerity measures could further reduce the estimated shortfall to about $5 million by the end of the year.

Based on those projections and the possibility that further additional contributions would be pledged, the Commissioner-General expected to be able to maintain Agency services at the current levels until the end of 1985; he warned, however, that the shortfall would have to be met by drawing on UNRWA's precariously low working capital, thus seriously affecting the Agency's ability to finance its operations until contributions were paid in 1986.

The outlook for 1986 was not encouraging; even if the level of expenditures did not exceed that of the severely reduced 1985 budget, some $20 million more than the 1985 regular contributions would be required.

In the concluding remarks of its October report,[9] the Working Group paid tribute to the Commissioner-General for his efforts to raise income and again underlined that his austerity measures involved deferments providing only temporary relief; postponed items would have to be funded in the future. It also noted that, despite strenuous efforts, income in 1985 was not expected to exceed that of 1984.

The Group shared the Commissioner-General's concern about the magnitude of the task of soliciting an additional $20 million to fund the programme in 1986. It continued to believe that a solution to UNRWA's chronic financial problems lay not so much in economy, postponement and reduction as in finding ways to assure required resources.

As UNRWA services for refugees remained indispensable until a Middle East settlement was reached, it was incumbent on the international community to ensure that the Agency was provided with the means to continue its work. The Group welcomed the Commissioner-General's suggestion for a meeting to discuss ways of placing UNRWA's finances on a more rational footing; it encouraged him to pursue that matter with a view to holding the meeting as soon as possible in 1986. The Group also welcomed a suggestion by the Advisory Commission (see below) for special fund-raising missions to current and prospective donor countries to solicit greater 1986 contributions.

The Group urged all Governments to recognize the seriousness of UNRWA's financial difficulties and match their political support with financial support, and urged payment of contributions as early as possible.

UNRWA Advisory Commission

The UNRWA Advisory Commission met on 30 May 1985 at Vienna to consider the critical financial situation and its implications for the Agency's ability to maintain services if the shortfall was not overcome. In a statement to the Commissioner-General, transmitted to the Secretary-General on the same date,[10] the Commission members unanimously commended and declared support for the Commissioner-General's efforts to obtain additional contributions. They shared his disappointment that responses had been inadequate and noted with deep concern his statement that UNRWA faced the imminent prospect of having to reduce services already at a minimum level. They urged UNRWA to take steps to avoid such action. They endorsed the view that the Member States which expressed support for UNRWA should help provide it with needed funds. More programme cut-backs, the Advisory Commission believed, would have profoundly disturbing consequences for stability in the area and for prospects of reaching a peaceful settlement of the Middle East conflict.

The Commission called on all Member States to contribute to ensure UNRWA's survival and ability to carry out its mandate.

At a regular meeting on 29 August, the Commission endorsed the suggestion for a gathering of concerned Governments early in 1986 for informal consultations on the Agency's financial plight.

GENERAL ASSEMBLY ACTION

On 16 December 1985, on the recommendation of the Special Political Committee, the General Assembly adopted **resolution 40/165 B**, without vote.

Working Group on the Financing of the United Nations Relief and Works Agency for Palestine Refugees in the Near East

The General Assembly,

Recalling its resolutions 2656(XXV) of 7 December 1970, 2728(XXV) of 15 December 1970, 2791(XXVI) of 6 December 1971, 2964(XXVII) of 13 December 1972, 3090(XXVIII) of 7 December 1973, 3330(XXIX) of 17 December 1974, 3419 D (XXX) of 8 December 1975, 31/15 C of 23 November 1976, 32/90 D of 13 December 1977, 33/112 D of 18 December 1978, 34/52 D of 23 November 1979, 35/13 D of 3 November 1980, 36/146 E of 16 December 1981, 37/120 A of 16 December 1982, 38/83 B of 15 December 1983 and 39/99 B of 14 December 1984,

Recalling also its decision 36/462 of 16 March 1982, whereby it took note of the special report of the Working Group on the Financing of the United Nations Relief and Works Agency for Palestine Refugees in the Near East and adopted the recommendations contained therein,

Having considered the report of the Working Group on the Financing of the United Nations Relief and Works Agency for Palestine Refugees in the Near East,

Taking into account the report of the Commissioner-General of the United Nations Relief and Works Agency for Palestine Refugees in the Near East, covering the period from 1 July 1984 to 30 June 1985,

Gravely concerned at the critical financial situation of the Agency, which has already reduced the essential minimum services being provided to the Palestine refugees and which threatens even greater reductions in the future,

Emphasizing the urgent need for extraordinary efforts in order to maintain, at least at their present minimum level, the activities of the Agency,

1. *Commends* the Working Group on the Financing of the United Nations Relief and Works Agency for Palestine Refugees in the Near East for its efforts to assist in ensuring the Agency's financial security;

2. *Takes note with approval* of the report of the Working Group;

3. *Requests* the Working Group to continue its efforts, in co-operation with the Secretary-General and the Commissioner-General, for the financing of the Agency for a further period of one year;

4. *Requests* the Secretary-General to provide the necessary services and assistance to the Working Group for the conduct of its work.

General Assembly resolution 40/165 B

16 December 1985   Meeting 118   Adopted without vote

Approved by SPC (A/40/921) without vote, 15 November (meeting 34); 16-nation draft (A/SPC/40/L.17); agenda item 79.

Sponsors: Austria, Canada, Denmark, Germany, Federal Republic of, India, Indonesia, Liberia, Malaysia, Netherlands, New Zealand, Nigeria, Pakistan, Philippines, Spain, Sweden, Yugoslavia.
Financial implications. S-G, A/SPC/40/L.27.
Meeting numbers. GA 40th session: SPC 22-28, 31, 34; plenary 118.

Claims for compensation

According to the Commissioner-General, UNRWA had received no response to a 1984 claim against Israel for $4,381,867 as compensation for loss and damage caused to Agency property and facilities as a result of the invasion of Lebanon in 1982. The General Assembly had called for such compensation in 1983[11] and 1984.[12] A separate claim had also been made for $194,901 for loss and damage caused by Israeli military action in Lebanon before June 1982. There had also been no response from Israel or any indication as to when it expected to complete its examination of UNRWA's claims, lodged in 1969, arising out of the 1967 hostilities.

No progress had been made over claims amounting to $675,000 against Jordan, despite an understanding reached in October 1984 that it would nominate representatives to a joint UNRWA/Government committee to study the claims, which included those arising out of the 1967 hostilities and the disturbances of 1970 and 1971.

Other aspects

Displaced persons

Humanitarian assistance

In addition to relief services, which included the provision of basic food commodities, blankets, clothing, shelter repair and cash grants, UNRWA continued to provide in 1985 a small measure of humanitarian assistance for persons displaced as a result of the June 1967 and subsequent hostilities in the Middle East but who were not registered with UNRWA as refugees.

In Jordan, UNRWA continued to distribute rations on the Government's behalf to some 193,000 persons, and to provide schooling, supplementary feeding, milk, medical, sanitation and other camp services to people living in the post-1967 refugee camps; the Government reimbursed the Agency for the cost of supplies used in the supplementary feeding and milk programmes and the cost of distributing basic rations to displaced persons.

In Egypt, UNRWA provided elementary and preparatory schooling and basic health care to 1,200 refugee children. With the co-operation of the Israeli and Egyptian Governments, UNRWA distributed food, blankets and clothing to 4,350 refugees left stranded in the Egyptian sector of Rafah as a result of the withdrawal of Israeli forces in April 1982 to the international border between the Sinai and the Gaza Strip.

GENERAL ASSEMBLY ACTION

On 16 December 1985, on the recommendation of the Special Political Committee, the General Assembly adopted **resolution 40/165 C**, without vote.

Assistance to persons displaced as a result of the June 1967 and subsequent hostilities

The General Assembly,

Recalling its resolution 39/99 C of 14 December 1984 and all its previous resolutions on the question,

Taking note of the report of the Commissioner-General of the United Nations Relief and Works Agency for Palestine Refugees in the Near East, covering the period from 1 July 1984 to 30 June 1985,

Concerned about the continued human suffering resulting from the hostilities in the Middle East,

1. *Reaffirms* its resolution 39/99 C and all its previous resolutions on the question;

2. *Endorses,* bearing in mind the objectives of those resolutions, the efforts of the Commissioner-General of the United Nations Relief and Works Agency for Palestine Refugees in the Near East to continue to provide humanitarian assistance as far as practicable, on an emergency basis and as a temporary measure, to other persons in the area who are at present displaced and in a serious need of continued assistance as a result of the June 1967 and subsequent hostilities;

3. *Strongly appeals* to all Governments and to organizations and individuals to contribute generously for the above purposes to the United Nations Relief and Works Agency for Palestine Refugees in the Near East and to the other intergovernmental and non-governmental organizations concerned.

General Assembly resolution 40/165 C

16 December 1985   Meeting 118   Adopted without vote

Approved by SPC (A/40/921) without vote, 15 November (meeting 34); 22-nation draft (A/SPC/40/L.18); agenda item 79.
Sponsors: Australia, Austria, Belgium, Canada, Cyprus, Denmark, Finland, Germany, Federal Republic of, Greece, India, Indonesia, Ireland, Italy, Japan, Malaysia, Mali, Netherlands, Norway, Pakistan, Philippines, Sri Lanka, Sweden.
Meeting numbers. GA 40th session: SPC 22-28, 31, 34; plenary 118.

Repatriation of refugees

Report of the Secretary-General. In accordance with a 1984 General Assembly resolution,[13] the Secretary-General submitted in September 1985 a report[14] on population and refugees displaced since 1967. In response to his request in a note verbale of 22 March 1985 for information on Israeli steps to facilitate the return of displaced inhabitants, Israel on 12 August had referred to its position as set out in successive annual replies in recent years, most recently in June 1984.[15] The total number of persons who had returned since 1967 stood at approximately 65,000, Israel added.

The Secretary-General also had obtained information from the UNRWA Commissioner-General on the return of refugees registered with the Agency; since UNRWA was not involved in arrangements for return, the data was based on requests by returning refugees for transfer of their entitlements for services to the areas to which they had returned. Between 1 July 1984 and 30 June 1985, 234 registered refugees (including family members) had returned to the West Bank and 70 to the Gaza Strip. The number of displaced registered refugees known to have returned to the occupied territories since June 1967 was some 10,725.

Report of the Commissioner-General. The Commissioner-General stated[2] that in the Agency's understanding, Israel and Egypt had reached an agreement in principle on the return of refugees to the Gaza Strip, following the withdrawal of Israeli forces in April 1982 to the international border between the Sinai and Gaza. He had been informed by Israel that, in recent discussions between the two Governments, it had been agreed that the refugees would return, perhaps commencing at an early date. The Commissioner-General said UNRWA would welcome the implementation of such an agreement and would facilitate the refugees' relocation and provide schooling, health care and welfare services, similar to its assistance prior to April 1982.

Report of the Conciliation Commission. The thirty-ninth report of the United Nations Conciliation Commission for Palestine covering the period from 1 September 1984 to 31 August 1985[16] was transmitted to the General Assembly by the Secretary-General in September 1985. In 1984,[17] the Assembly had requested the Commission to continue efforts towards implementation of paragraph 11 of its 1948 resolution[4] on the partition of Palestine, stipulating that the Palestine refugees should be permitted to return to their homes and live at peace with their neighbours and that compensation should be paid for the property of those choosing not to return and for loss of or damage to property. The Commission stated that events in the region had further complicated the situation and the circumstances which limited its possibilities of action had remained essentially unchanged. Nevertheless, it continued to hope that the situation would improve towards achievement of a comprehensive, just and lasting peace in the Middle East, thus enabling it to carry forward its work.

GENERAL ASSEMBLY ACTION

On 16 December 1985, on the recommendation of the Special Political Committee, the General Assembly adopted **resolution 40/165 G** by recorded vote.

Population and refugees displaced since 1967

The General Assembly,

Recalling Security Council resolution 237(1967) of 14 June 1967,

Recalling also General Assembly resolutions 2252(ES-V) of 4 July 1967, 2452 A (XXIII) of 19 December 1968,

2535 B (XXIV) of 10 December 1969, 2672 D (XXV) of 8 December 1970, 2792 E (XXVI) of 6 December 1971, 2963 C and D (XXVII) of 13 December 1972, 3089 C (XXVIII) of 7 December 1973, 3331 D (XXIX) of 17 December 1974, 3419 C (XXX) of 8 December 1975, 31/15 D of 23 November 1976, 32/90 E of 13 December 1977, 33/112 F of 18 December 1978, 34/52 E of 23 November 1979, ES-7/2 of 29 July 1980, 35/13 E of 3 November 1980, 36/146 B of 16 December 1981, 37/120 G of 16 December 1982, 38/83 G of 15 December 1983 and 39/99 G of 14 December 1984,

Having considered the report of the Commissioner-General of the United Nations Relief and Works Agency for Palestine Refugees in the Near East, covering the period from 1 July 1984 to 30 June 1985, and the report of the Secretary-General,

1. *Reaffirms* the inalienable right of all displaced inhabitants to return to their homes or former places of residence in the territories occupied by Israel since 1967, and declares once more that any attempt to restrict, or to attach conditions to, the free exercise of the right to return by any displaced person is inconsistent with that inalienable right and inadmissible;

2. *Considers* any and all agreements embodying any restriction on, or condition for, the return of the displaced inhabitants as null and void;

3. *Strongly deplores* the continued refusal of the Israeli authorities to take steps for the return of the displaced inhabitants;

4. *Calls once more upon* Israel:

(a) To take immediate steps for the return of all displaced inhabitants;

(b) To desist from all measures that obstruct the return of the displaced inhabitants, including measures affecting the physical and demographic structure of the occupied territories;

5. *Requests* the Secretary-General, after consulting with the Commissioner-General of the United Nations Relief and Works Agency for Palestine Refugees in the Near East, to report to the General Assembly before the opening of its forty-first session on Israel's compliance with paragraph 4 above.

General Assembly resolution 40/165 G

16 December 1985   Meeting 118   127-2-23 (recorded vote)

Approved by SPC (A/40/921) by recorded vote (106-2-19), 15 November (meeting 34); 9-nation draft (A/SPC/40/L.22); agenda item 79.
Sponsors: Afghanistan, Bangladesh, Cuba, Egypt, India, Indonesia, Malaysia, Pakistan, Yugoslavia.
Meeting numbers. GA 40th session: SPC 22-28, 31, 34; plenary 118.

Recorded vote in Assembly as follows:

In favour: Afghanistan, Albania, Algeria, Antigua and Barbuda, Argentina, Bahamas, Bahrain, Bangladesh, Barbados, Benin, Bhutan, Bolivia, Botswana, Brazil, Brunei Darussalam, Bulgaria, Burkina Faso, Burma, Burundi, Byelorussian SSR, Cameroon, Cape Verde, Central African Republic, Chad, Chile, China, Colombia, Congo, Cuba, Cyprus, Czechoslovakia, Democratic Kampuchea, Democratic Yemen, Djibouti, Dominica, Dominican Republic, Ecuador, Egypt, El Salvador, Equatorial Guinea, Ethiopia, Fiji, Gabon, Gambia, German Democratic Republic, Ghana, Greece, Guatemala, Guinea, Guinea-Bissau, Guyana, Haiti, Honduras, Hungary, India, Indonesia, Iran, Iraq, Ivory Coast, Jamaica, Japan, Jordan, Kenya, Kuwait, Lao People's Democratic Republic, Lebanon, Lesotho, Liberia, Libyan Arab Jamahiriya, Madagascar, Malaysia, Maldives, Mali, Malta, Mauritania, Mauritius, Mexico, Mongolia, Morocco, Mozambique, Nepal, Nicaragua, Niger, Nigeria, Oman, Pakistan, Panama, Peru, Philippines, Poland, Portugal, Qatar, Romania, Rwanda, Saint Lucia, Saint Vincent and the Grenadines, Samoa, Sao Tome and Principe, Saudi Arabia, Senegal, Seychelles, Sierra Leone, Singapore, Somalia, Spain, Sri Lanka, Sudan, Suriname, Syrian Arab Republic, Thailand, Togo, Trinidad and Tobago, Tunisia, Turkey, Uganda, Ukrainian SSR, USSR, United Arab Emirates, United Republic of Tanzania, Uruguay, Vanuatu, Venezuela, Viet Nam, Yemen, Yugoslavia, Zambia, Zimbabwe.

Against: Israel, United States.

Abstaining: Australia, Austria, Belgium, Canada, Costa Rica, Denmark, Finland, France, Germany, Federal Republic of, Grenada, Iceland, Ireland, Italy, Luxembourg, Malawi, Netherlands, New Zealand, Norway, Paraguay, Swaziland, Sweden, United Kingdom, Zaire.

The United States regarded the text as highly polemical, one-sided and harshly condemnatory. In stating that inhabitants of the occupied territories had an inalienable right to return, Israel said, the text was based not on consideration of the interests of those inhabitants but on the policy of rejection.

In Sweden's opinion, the text appeared to rule out negotiations or discussions on the means by which the displaced Palestinians might return to their homes.

Iran said all practices which prevented the Palestine refugees from exercising their right to voluntary repatriation to their homeland should be condemned.

In **resolution 40/165 A**, the Assembly, noting with regret that the Conciliation Commission had been unable to achieve progress in implementing paragraph 11 of the 1948 resolution on Palestine,[4] requested the Commission to exert continued efforts in that direction and to report by 1 September 1986. That paragraph was unacceptable to Israel (see p. 354).

Food aid

The General Assembly, in December 1985, again called for resumption of the general ration distribution to Palestine refugees which had been suspended in September 1982,[18] except in Lebanon, where it had ceased in March 1984.[19] Distribution of food rations was currently confined to special hardship cases which comprised about 5 per cent of the refugee population. Particularly in the Gaza Strip and the West Bank, where unemployment and underemployment were on the rise, UNRWA faced increasing pressure from refugees applying for special hardship assistance; many did not qualify because the criteria for granting such assistance was based on a family's capacity for employment rather than on actual employment. As a result, refugee community leaders had been pressing for more flexibility, which would require a substantial increase in resources. In the West Bank, refugees in some camps refused to allow rations to be distributed to hardship cases on the ground that all refugees were in need of food aid and unless they all received it, none would be permitted to do so.

By the end of June 1985, according to the Commissioner-General,[2] assistance to hardship cases was benefiting 103,857 persons: 25,044 in Gaza; 23,693 in the West Bank; 22,717 in Lebanon; 19,686 in Jordan; and 12,717 in the Syrian Arab Republic.

Given the lack of sufficient resources and of responses from Governments, it had not been possible to comply with the Assembly's 1984 request to resume the general ration distribution.[20]

Report of the Secretary-General. In October 1985,[21] the Secretary-General reported that the response to the Assembly's repeated appeals for contributions had not been encouraging; contributions had declined from $154 million in 1982 to $136 million in 1984. It was clear that income for 1985 was insufficient to maintain existing programmes at desired levels. Without additional resources, it had not been possible to resume the general distribution of basic food rations.

GENERAL ASSEMBLY ACTION

On 16 December 1985, on the recommendation of the Special Political Committee, the General Assembly adopted **resolution 40/165 F** by recorded vote.

Resumption of the ration distribution to Palestine refugees

The General Assembly,

Recalling its resolutions 36/146 F of 16 December 1981, 37/120 F of 16 December 1982, 38/83 F of 15 December 1983, 39/99 F of 14 December 1984 and all its previous resolutions on the question, including resolution 302(IV) of 8 December 1949,

Having considered the report of the Commissioner-General of the United Nations Relief and Works Agency for Palestine Refugees in the Near East, covering the period from 1 July 1984 to 30 June 1985, and the report of the Secretary-General,

Deeply concerned at the interruption by the Agency, owing to financial difficulties, of the general ration distribution to Palestine refugees in all fields,

1. *Regrets* that its resolutions 37/120 F, 38/83 F and 39/99 F have not been implemented;

2. *Calls once again upon* all Governments, as a matter of urgency, to make the most generous efforts possible and to offer the necessary resources to meet the needs of the United Nations Relief and Works Agency for Palestine Refugees in the Near East, particularly in the light of the interruption by the Agency of the general ration distribution to Palestine refugees in all fields, and therefore urges non-contributing Governments to contribute regularly and contributing Governments to consider increasing their regular contributions;

3. *Requests* the Commissioner-General to resume on a continuing basis the interrupted general ration distribution to Palestine refugees in all fields;

4. *Requests* the Secretary-General, in consultation with the Commissioner-General, to report to the General Assembly at its forty-first session on the implementation of the present resolution.

General Assembly resolution 40/165 F

16 December 1985   Meeting 118   127-20-4 (recorded vote)

Approved by SPC (A/40/921) by recorded vote (105-19-3), 15 November (meeting 34); 7-nation draft (A/SPC/40/L.21); agenda item 79.
Sponsors: Afghanistan, Bangladesh, Egypt, Indonesia, Malaysia, Pakistan, Yugoslavia.
Meeting numbers. GA 40th session: SPC 22-28, 31, 34; plenary 118.

Recorded vote in Assembly as follows:

In favour: Afghanistan, Algeria, Antigua and Barbuda, Argentina, Bahamas, Bahrain, Bangladesh, Barbados, Benin, Bhutan, Bolivia, Botswana, Brazil, Brunei Darussalam, Bulgaria, Burkina Faso, Burma, Burundi, Byelorussian SSR, Cameroon, Cape Verde, Central African Republic, Chad, Chile, China, Colombia, Congo, Cuba, Cyprus, Czechoslovakia, Democratic Kampuchea, Democratic Yemen, Djibouti, Dominica, Dominican Republic, Ecuador, Egypt, El Salvador, Equatorial Guinea, Ethiopia, Fiji, Gabon, Gambia, German Democratic Republic, Ghana, Greece, Guatemala, Guinea, Guinea-Bissau, Guyana, Haiti, Honduras, Hungary, India, Indonesia, Iran, Iraq, Ivory Coast, Jamaica, Jordan, Kenya, Kuwait, Lao People's Democratic Republic, Lebanon, Lesotho, Liberia, Libyan Arab Jamahiriya, Madagascar, Malawi, Malaysia, Maldives, Mali, Malta, Mauritania, Mauritius, Mexico, Mongolia, Morocco, Mozambique, Nepal, Nicaragua, Niger, Nigeria, Oman, Pakistan, Panama, Paraguay, Peru, Philippines, Poland, Qatar, Romania, Rwanda, Saint Lucia, Saint Vincent and the Grenadines, Samoa, Sao Tome and Principe, Saudi Arabia, Senegal, Seychelles, Sierra Leone, Singapore, Somalia, Sri Lanka, Sudan, Suriname, Swaziland, Syrian Arab Republic, Thailand, Togo, Trinidad and Tobago, Tunisia, Turkey, Uganda, Ukrainian SSR, USSR, United Arab Emirates, United Republic of Tanzania, Uruguay, Vanuatu, Venezuela, Viet Nam, Yemen, Yugoslavia, Zaire, Zambia, Zimbabwe.

Against: Australia, Belgium, Canada, Denmark, Finland, France, Germany, Federal Republic of, Iceland, Ireland, Israel, Italy, Japan, Luxembourg, Netherlands, New Zealand, Norway, Portugal, Sweden, United Kingdom, United States.

Abstaining: Austria, Costa Rica, Grenada, Spain.

Israel remarked that the wealthy Arab States which had sponsored the text had reduced their contributions to UNRWA. Without sufficient financial resources, said Sweden, the resumption of the general ration distribution would endanger the most important activities of the Agency. The United States strongly supported the Commissioner-General's efforts to make the most efficient use of UNRWA's scarce resources, and said the text was aimed at narrowing his discretionary powers in that regard.

Education and training services

Schools and teacher training centres

UNRWA activities. Under an agreement between UNRWA and UNESCO, the latter provided technical and professional advice to the Commissioner-General on aspects of the UNRWA education programme which included schooling for some 350,000 Palestine refugee children. Nine grades of elementary and preparatory (lower secondary) education were provided in some 635 Agency schools.

The curriculum followed that of the host country, and that of Jordan and Egypt for the West Bank and the Gaza Strip, respectively. With some UNRWA assistance, many refugee children were able to continue at the upper secondary level in government or private schools.

In addition, UNRWA provided vocational and pre-service teacher training at Agency centres, in-service teacher training and a university scholarship programme (see below). Pre-service training was given to some 1,000 trainees at three training centres in Jordan and at Ramallah in the West Bank, and a variety of in-service training courses was conducted through education development centres located in the five field office areas of UNRWA operations. The number of places available to refugees in vocational and technical courses conducted in eight UNRWA training centres was 3,812; in addition, the Agency sponsored the vocational training of 40 refugees in private institutions. It also organized pre-school education programmes, youth activities, adult training in crafts, and medical and paramedical education and training.

The general education programme continued as the largest single Agency activity in 1984/85. Seven school buildings were constructed during that period and work began on another six.

Of the 16,500 UNRWA employees, over 12,000 were in education, and over 90 per cent of those were schoolteachers. UNRWA's teacher training programme aimed primarily at providing qualified teachers for the Agency's schools.

Proposed University of Jerusalem "Al-Quds"

Report of the Secretary-General. As requested by the General Assembly in 1984,[22] the Secretary-General reported in August 1985[23] on the latest efforts to establish a university for Palestine refugees at Jerusalem, first considered by the Assembly in 1980.[24] In order to complete the feasibility study requested of him, he had contacted the Rector of the United Nations University, who designated an expert to carry out the study. The expert was to meet with Israeli officials, bearing in mind that the co-operation of Israel, which was in effective control of Jerusalem, was a prerequisite for establishing the university.

In a note verbale of 1 April 1985, the Secretary-General requested that Israel facilitate the visit of the expert at a mutually convenient date. In its reply of 2 May, Israel referred to its statements made in 1983[25] and 1984;[26] the 1984 resolution[22] was an attempt to use the field of higher education for transparent political ends, totally extraneous to genuine academic pursuits. Israel also pointed out that higher academic institutions in Judaea and Samaria were meeting the requirements in the area while continuing to improve education standards; until substantive clarifications were provided, it was unable to help in taking the matter further.

In view of Israel's position, the Secretary-General concluded, it had not been possible to complete the feasibility study as planned.

GENERAL ASSEMBLY ACTION

On 16 December 1985, on the recommendation of the Special Political Committee, the General Assembly adopted **resolution 40/165 K** by recorded vote.

University of Jerusalem "Al-Quds" for Palestine refugees

The General Assembly,

Recalling its resolutions 36/146 G of 16 December 1981, 37/120 C of 16 December 1982, 38/83 K of 15 December 1983 and 39/99 K of 14 December 1984,

Having examined the report of the Secretary-General on the question of the establishment of a university at Jerusalem,

Having also examined the report of the Commissioner-General of the United Nations Relief and Works Agency for Palestine Refugees in the Near East, covering the period from 1 July 1984 to 30 June 1985,

1.	*Commends* the constructive efforts made by the Secretary-General, the Commissioner-General of the United Nations Relief and Works Agency for Palestine Refugees in the Near East, the Council of the United Nations University and the United Nations Educational, Scientific and Cultural Organization, which worked diligently towards the implementation of General Assembly resolution 38/83 D of 15 December 1983 and other relevant resolutions;

2.	*Further commends* the close co-operation of the competent educational authorities concerned;

3.	*Emphasizes* the need for strengthening the educational system in the Arab territories occupied since 5 June 1967, including Jerusalem, and specifically the need for the establishment of the proposed university;

4.	*Requests* the Secretary-General to continue to take all necessary measures for establishing the University of Jerusalem, "Al-Quds", in accordance with General Assembly resolution 35/13 B of 3 November 1980, giving due consideration to the recommendations consistent with the provisions of that resolution;

5.	*Calls upon* Israel, the occupying Power, to co-operate in the implementation of the present resolution and to remove the hindrances which it has put in the way of establishing the University of Jerusalem;

6.	*Requests* the Secretary-General to report to the General Assembly at its forty-first session on the progress made in the implementation of the present resolution.

General Assembly resolution 40/165 K

16 December 1985   Meeting 118   149-2-1 (recorded vote)

Approved by SPC (A/40/921) by recorded vote (126-2), 15 November (meeting 34); 9-nation draft (A/SPC/40/L.26); agenda item 79.

Sponsors: Afghanistan, Bangladesh, Egypt, India, Indonesia, Jordan, Malaysia, Pakistan, Yugoslavia.

Financial implications. 5th Committee, A/40/975; S-G, A/C.5/40/51, A/SPC/40/L.28.

Meeting numbers. GA 40th session: 5th Committee 51; SPC 22-28, 31, 34; plenary 118.

Recorded vote in Assembly as follows:

In favour: Afghanistan, Albania, Algeria, Antigua and Barbuda, Argentina, Australia, Austria, Bahamas, Bahrain, Bangladesh, Barbados, Belgium, Benin, Bhutan, Bolivia, Botswana, Brazil, Brunei Darussalam, Bulgaria, Burkina Faso, Burma, Burundi, Byelorussian SSR, Cameroon, Canada, Cape Verde, Central African Republic, Chad, Chile, China, Colombia, Congo, Costa Rica, Cuba, Cyprus, Czechoslovakia, Democratic Kampuchea, Democratic Yemen, Denmark, Djibouti, Dominica, Dominican Republic, Ecuador, Egypt, El Salvador, Equatorial Guinea, Ethiopia, Fiji, Finland, France, Gabon, Gambia, German Democratic Republic, Germany, Federal Republic of, Ghana, Greece, Guatemala, Guinea, Guinea-Bissau, Guyana, Haiti, Honduras, Hungary, Iceland, India, Indonesia, Iran, Iraq, Ireland, Italy, Ivory Coast, Jamaica, Japan, Jordan, Kenya, Kuwait, Lao People's Democratic Republic, Lebanon, Lesotho, Liberia, Libyan Arab Jamahiriya, Luxembourg, Madagascar, Malawi, Malaysia, Maldives, Mali, Malta, Mauritania, Mauritius, Mexico, Mongolia, Morocco, Mozambique, Nepal, Netherlands, New Zealand, Nicaragua, Niger, Nigeria, Norway, Oman, Pakistan, Panama, Paraguay, Peru, Philippines, Poland, Portugal, Qatar, Romania, Rwanda, Saint Lucia, Saint Vincent and the Grenadines, Samoa, Sao Tome and Principe, Saudi Arabia, Senegal, Seychelles, Sierra Leone, Singapore, Somalia, Spain, Sri Lanka, Sudan, Suriname, Swaziland, Sweden, Syrian Arab Republic, Thailand, Togo, Trinidad and Tobago, Tunisia, Turkey, Uganda, Ukrainian SSR, USSR, United Arab Emirates, United Kingdom, United Republic of Tanzania, Uruguay, Vanuatu, Venezuela, Viet Nam, Yemen, Yugoslavia, Zaire, Zambia, Zimbabwe.

Against: Israel, United States.

Abstaining: Grenada.

The United States considered the university a purely political project which would not meet the educational needs of the refugees. Israel said the request for its establishment was absurd, in view of the existence of a large number of renowned educational institutions, both Jewish and Arab, in Jerusalem.

In **resolution 40/165 D**, the Assembly appealed for generous contributions to Palestinian universities in the occupied territories, including, in due course, the proposed University of Jerusalem.

Scholarships

UNRWA activities. During the 1984/85 academic year, UNRWA awarded 353 scholarships to Palestine refugees for study at Arab universities, 271 of them continuing and 82 new. Scholarships, partly funded from special contributions, were awarded for one year, but were renewable from year to year for the duration of a course of study. In addition, UNESCO annually provided fellowships for short training courses for UNRWA's senior education staff.

Report of the Secretary-General. In a September 1985 report,[27] submitted in accordance with a 1984 General Assembly resolution,[28] the Secretary-General provided information on responses to the Assembly's numerous appeals for special allocations for grants and scholarships to Palestine refugees, for which UNRWA acted as recipient and trustee.

In 1985, the Federal Republic of Germany granted six fellowships to Palestine refugee graduates from UNRWA vocational training centres, all from Jordan. Japan offered five training scholarships for UNRWA's vocational training instructors in the West Bank and Gaza.

Among United Nations organizations and agencies, the Food and Agriculture Organization of the United Nations had two programmes for Palestinians, one providing specialized training in agricultural development and awarding three fellowships to university graduates, the other helping Palestine families of the Gilline and Ramadan refugee camps in the Syrian Arab Republic to improve production and efficiency in crop and livestock farming. On the invitation of the World Intellectual Property Organization (WIPO), UNRWA proposed eight candidates for WIPO training fellowships. ILO was involved in two UNDP-sponsored projects: one to increase facilities for vocational training by UNRWA centres, governmental services and private institutions; the other, implemented in the second half of 1984, to provide vocational and technical refresher courses for 19 Palestinians. An ILO expert assisted a project to help Palestinian women's institutions promote vocational training. UNESCO granted four fellowships for overseas training of UNRWA education staff. During the 1985/86 academic year, EC agreed to finance 5 to 10 scholarships for Palestinians from Gaza for studies in Europe, the West Bank or Arab countries.

On 16 December 1985, on the recommendation of the Special Political Committee, the General Assembly adopted **resolution 40/165 D** by recorded vote.

Offers by Member States of grants and scholarships for higher education, including vocational training, for Palestine refugees

The General Assembly,

Recalling its resolution 212(III) of 19 November 1948 on assistance to Palestine refugees,

Recalling also its resolutions 35/13 B of 3 November 1980, 36/146 H of 16 December 1981, 37/120 D of 16 December 1982, 38/83 D of 15 December 1983 and 39/99 D of 14 December 1984,

Cognizant of the fact that the Palestine refugees have, for the last three decades, lost their lands and means of livelihood,

Having examined the report of the Secretary-General,

Having also examined the report of the Commissioner-General of the United Nations Relief and Works Agency for Palestine Refugees in the Near East, covering the period from 1 July 1984 to 30 June 1985,

1. *Urges* all States to respond to the appeal contained in General Assembly resolution 32/90 F of 13 December 1977 in a manner commensurate with the needs of Palestine refugees for higher education and vocational training;

2. *Strongly appeals* to all States, specialized agencies and non-governmental organizations to augment the special allocations for grants and scholarships to Palestine refugees in addition to their contributions to the regular budget of the United Nations Relief and Works Agency for Palestine Refugees in the Near East;

3. *Expresses its appreciation* to all Governments, specialized agencies and non-governmental organizations that responded favourably to General Assembly resolution 39/99 D;

4. *Invites* the relevant specialized agencies and other organizations of the United Nations system to continue, within their respective spheres of competence, to extend assistance for higher education to Palestine refugee students;

5. *Appeals* to all States, specialized agencies and the United Nations University to contribute generously to the Palestinian universities in the territories occupied by Israel since 1967, including, in due course, the proposed University of Jerusalem "Al-Quds" for Palestine refugees;

6. *Also appeals* to all States, specialized agencies and other international bodies to contribute towards the establishment of vocational training centres for Palestine refugees;

7. *Requests* the United Nations Relief and Works Agency for Palestine Refugees in the Near East to act as the recipient and trustee for such special allocations and scholarships and to award them to qualified Palestine refugee candidates;

8. *Requests* the Secretary-General to report to the General Assembly at its forty-first session on the implementation of the present resolution.

General Assembly resolution 40/165 D

16 December 1985   Meeting 118   147-0-1 (recorded vote)

Approved by SPC (A/40/921) by recorded vote (126-0-1), 15 November (meeting 34); 8-nation draft (A/SPC/40/L.19); agenda item 79.

Sponsors: Afghanistan, Bangladesh, Egypt, Indonesia, Jordan, Malaysia, Pakistan, Yugoslavia.
Meeting numbers. GA 40th session: SPC 22-28, 31, 34; plenary 118.

Recorded vote in Assembly as follows:

In favour: Afghanistan, Algeria, Antigua and Barbuda, Argentina, Australia, Austria, Bahamas, Bahrain, Bangladesh, Barbados, Belgium, Benin, Bhutan, Bolivia, Botswana, Brazil, Brunei Darussalam, Bulgaria, Burkina Faso, Burma, Burundi, Byelorussian SSR, Cameroon, Canada, Central African Republic, Chad, Chile, China, Colombia, Congo, Costa Rica, Cuba, Cyprus, Czechoslovakia, Democratic Kampuchea, Democratic Yemen, Denmark, Djibouti, Dominica, Ecuador, Egypt, El Salvador, Equatorial Guinea, Ethiopia, Fiji, Finland, France, Gabon, Gambia, German Democratic Republic, Germany, Federal Republic of, Ghana, Greece, Grenada, Guatemala, Guinea, Guinea-Bissau, Guyana, Haiti, Honduras, Hungary, Iceland, India, Indonesia, Iran, Iraq, Ireland, Italy, Ivory Coast, Jamaica, Japan, Jordan, Kenya, Kuwait, Lao People's Democratic Republic, Lebanon, Lesotho, Liberia, Libyan Arab Jamahiriya, Luxembourg, Madagascar, Malawi, Malaysia, Maldives, Mali, Malta, Mauritania, Mauritius, Mexico, Mongolia, Morocco, Mozambique, Nepal, Netherlands, New Zealand, Nicaragua, Niger, Nigeria, Norway, Oman, Pakistan, Panama, Peru, Philippines, Poland, Portugal, Qatar, Romania, Rwanda, Saint Lucia, Saint Vincent and the Grenadines, Samoa, Sao Tome and Principe, Saudi Arabia, Senegal, Seychelles, Sierra Leone, Singapore, Somalia, Spain, Sri Lanka, Sudan, Suriname, Swaziland, Sweden, Syrian Arab Republic, Thailand, Togo, Trinidad and Tobago, Tunisia, Turkey, Uganda, Ukrainian SSR, USSR, United Arab Emirates, United Kingdom, United Republic of Tanzania, United States, Uruguay, Vanuatu, Venezuela, Viet Nam, Yemen, Yugoslavia, Zaire, Zambia, Zimbabwe.

Against: None.

Abstaining: Israel.

In the opinion of the United States, the text provided a practical way of meeting some of the needs of the refugees. Israel said it was unable to support it because it contained a reference to the proposed university of Jerusalem for Palestine refugees.

Property rights

Report of the Secretary-General. In September 1985,[29] the Secretary-General reported on revenues derived from Palestine refugee properties, as requested in a 1984 Assembly resolution[30] which he had brought to Israel's attention, asking for any information regarding its implementation, preferably by 30 June 1985. In a reply of 12 August, Israel stated that its position had been set out in 1981 before the Special Political Committee.[31] With regard to the resolution's request for information from other States on Arab property, assets and property rights in Israel, no replies had been received.

GENERAL ASSEMBLY ACTION

On 16 December 1985, on the recommendation of the Special Political Committee, the General Assembly adopted **resolution 40/165 H** by recorded vote.

Revenues derived from Palestine refugee properties

The General Assembly,

Recalling its resolutions 35/13 A to F of 3 November 1980, 36/146 C of 16 December 1981, 37/120 H of 16 December 1982, 38/83 H of 15 December 1983, 39/99 H of 14 December 1984 and all its previous resolutions on the question, including resolution 194(III) of 11 December 1948,

Taking note of the report of the Secretary-General,

Taking note also of the report of the United Nations Conciliation Commission for Palestine, covering the period from 1 September 1984 to 31 August 1985,

Recalling that the Universal Declaration of Human Rights and the principles of international law uphold the principle that no one shall be arbitrarily deprived of his or her private property,

Considering that the Palestine Arab refugees are entitled to their property and to the income derived from their property, in conformity with the principles of justice and equity,

Recalling, in particular, its resolution 394(V) of 14 December 1950, in which it directed the United Nations Conciliation Commission for Palestine, in consultation with the parties concerned, to prescribe measures for the protection of the rights, property and interests of the Palestine Arab refugees,

Taking note of the completion of the programme of identification and evaluation of Arab property, as announced by the United Nations Conciliation Commission for Palestine in its twenty-second progress report, and of the fact that the Land Office had a schedule of Arab owners and file of documents defining the location, area and other particulars of Arab property,

1. *Requests* the Secretary-General to take all appropriate steps, in consultation with the United Nations Conciliation Commission for Palestine, for the protection and administration of Arab property, assets and property rights in Israel, and to establish a fund for the receipt of income derived therefrom, on behalf of the rightful owners;

2. *Calls once again upon* Israel to render all facilities and assistance to the Secretary-General in the implementation of the present resolution;

3. *Calls upon* all other Governments of Member States concerned to provide the Secretary-General with any pertinent information in their possession concerning Arab property, assets and property rights in Israel, which would assist the Secretary-General in the implementation of the present resolution;

4. *Deplores* Israel's refusal to co-operate with the Secretary-General in the implementation of the resolutions on the question;

5. *Requests* the Secretary-General to report to the General Assembly at its forty-first session on the implementation of the present resolution.

General Assembly resolution 40/165 H

16 December 1985   Meeting 118   122-2-26 (recorded vote)

Approved by SPC (A/40/921) by recorded vote (103-2-23), 15 November (meeting 34); 8-nation draft (A/SPC/40/L.23); agenda item 79.
Sponsors: Afghanistan, Bangladesh, Cuba, Egypt, India, Indonesia, Malaysia, Pakistan.
Meeting numbers. GA 40th session: SPC 22-28, 31, 34; plenary 118.

Recorded vote in Assembly as follows:

In favour: Afghanistan, Albania, Algeria, Antigua and Barbuda, Argentina, Bahamas, Bahrain, Bangladesh, Barbados, Benin, Bhutan, Bolivia, Botswana, Brazil, Brunei Darussalam, Bulgaria, Burkina Faso, Burma, Burundi, Byelorussian SSR, Cameroon, Cape Verde, Central African Republic, Chad, Chile, China, Colombia, Congo, Cuba, Cyprus, Czechoslovakia, Democratic Kampuchea, Democratic Yemen, Djibouti, Dominica, Dominican Republic, Ecuador, Egypt, El Salvador, Equatorial Guinea, Ethiopia, Fiji, Gabon, Gambia, German Democratic Republic, Ghana, Greece, Guatemala, Guinea, Guinea-Bissau, Guyana, Honduras, Hungary, India, Indonesia, Iran, Iraq, Jamaica, Jordan, Kenya, Kuwait, Lao People's Democratic Republic, Lebanon, Lesotho, Libyan Arab Jamahiriya, Madagascar, Malaysia, Maldives, Mali, Malta, Mauritania, Mauritius, Mexico, Mongolia, Morocco, Mozambique, Nepal, Nicaragua, Niger, Nigeria, Oman, Pakistan, Panama, Peru, Philippines, Poland, Portugal, Qatar, Romania, Rwanda, Saint Lucia, Saint Vincent and the Grenadines, Samoa, Sao Tome and Principe, Saudi Arabia, Senegal, Seychelles, Sierra Leone, Singapore, Spain, Sri Lanka, Sudan, Suriname, Syrian Arab Republic, Thailand, Togo, Trinidad and Tobago, Tunisia, Turkey, Uganda, Ukrainian SSR, USSR, United Arab Emirates, United Republic of Tanzania, Uruguay, Vanuatu, Venezuela, Viet Nam, Yemen, Yugoslavia, Zambia, Zimbabwe.

Against: Israel, United States.
Abstaining: Australia, Austria, Belgium, Canada, Costa Rica, Denmark, Finland, France, Germany, Federal Republic of, Grenada, Iceland, Ireland, Italy, Ivory Coast, Japan, Liberia, Luxembourg, Malawi, Netherlands, New Zealand, Norway, Paraguay, Swaziland, Sweden, United Kingdom, Zaire.

In the opinion of the United States, the text prejudged the issues of refugee repatriation and compensation which, it felt, could be best settled through direct negotiations among the parties. In Israel's view, the text ran counter to the basic tenets of international law, since property rights within the borders of a sovereign State were exclusively subject to domestic law. Sweden believed that claims by Palestine refugees in respect of property or compensation should be dealt with in the context of a comprehensive Middle East solution.

Refugee protection

Protection of Palestine refugees, especially those in southern Lebanon, was again the subject in 1985 of a General Assembly resolution. The Secretary-General reported on steps taken to ensure their protection, as did the Commissioner-General in his annual report. When introducing his report[2] in the Assembly's Special Political Committee, the Commissioner-General stated that the refugees in Lebanon had been affected by almost uninterrupted fighting (see above, under "Lebanon situation"), and the living conditions for refugees in the West Bank and the Gaza Strip had deteriorated.

Report of the Secretary-General. In October 1985,[32] the Secretary-General reported on the implementation of a 1984 General Assembly resolution[12] calling for protection of Palestine refugees, especially those in refugee camps in Lebanon. Responding on 12 August 1985 to the Secretary-General's request for information on steps taken or envisaged in compliance with the resolution, Israel stated that it deemed the resolution not relevant, since its troops had completed their withdrawal from southern Lebanon in June and were currently deployed along the international border.

The UNRWA Commissioner-General continued his efforts in consultation with the Secretary-General to do all that was feasible to contribute to the safety and security of the refugees in all the territories under occupation.

Palestine refugees in southern Lebanon resided in the vicinity of Saida and Tyre. The Israeli forces withdrew from those areas in February and April 1985, respectively. Up to the dates of their withdrawal, the UNRWA field office in Lebanon reported the following incidents involving Palestine refugees: in southern Lebanon as a whole from July 1984 to the end of February 1985, there were 51 violent deaths, 27 explosions and 2 kidnappings; in the Tyre area in March and April, there were 6 violent deaths and 5 explosions. UNRWA

officials drew the attention of the Israeli military authorities to such incidents and, when necessary, lodged protests, with a view to having them investigated and to reminding Israel of its responsibility for the safety and security of the civilian population.

By a note verbale of 28 February to Israel, UNRWA had expressed deep concern about the security of Palestine refugees in southern Lebanon, pointing out that it had been obliged at times to close its schools in the Tyre area to avoid possible injury from stray bullets and requesting adequate and urgent steps to prevent further such incidents. UNRWA had also referred to difficulties in moving personnel and supplies through Israeli checkpoints and in obtaining access to Israeli military officials in a position to deal with such problems.

UNRWA continued to provide education, health and relief services to Palestine refugees in southern Lebanon. Continuing disturbances throughout the area and delays at IDF check-points and those of local forces armed and controlled by IDF adversely affected access to UNRWA clinics and subsidized hospitals.

GENERAL ASSEMBLY ACTION

On 16 December, on the recommendation of the Special Political Committee, the General Assembly adopted **resolution 40/165 I** by recorded vote.

Protection of Palestine refugees
The General Assembly,

Recalling Security Council resolutions 508(1982) of 5 June 1982, 509 (1982) of 6 June 1982, 511(1982) of 18 June 1982, 512(1982) of 19 June 1982, 513(1982) of 4 July 1982, 515(1982) of 29 July 1982, 517(1982) of 4 August 1982, 518(1982) of 12 August 1982, 519(1982) of 17 August 1982, 520(1982) of 17 September 1982 and 523(1982) of 18 October 1982,

Recalling General Assembly resolutions ES-7/5 of 26 June 1982, ES-7/6 and ES-7/8 of 19 August 1982, ES-7/9 of 24 September 1982, 37/120 J of 16 December 1982, 38/83 I of 15 December 1983 and 39/99 I of 14 December 1984,

Having considered the report of the Secretary-General,

Having also considered the report of the Commissioner-General of the United Nations Relief and Works Agency for Palestine Refugees in the Near East, covering the period from 1 July 1984 to 30 June 1985,

Referring to the humanitarian principles of the Geneva Convention relative to the Protection of Civilian Persons in Time of War, of 12 August 1949, and to the obligations arising from the Regulations annexed to the Hague Convention IV of 1907,

Taking into consideration the marked deterioration in the security situation experienced by the refugees living in the Gaza Strip as reported by the Commissioner-General in his statement of 4 November 1985,

Deeply concerned at the lack of security for the Palestine refugees in the Palestinian and other Arab territories occupied since 1967, including Jerusalem, resulting in scores of violent deaths, woundings, kidnappings, disappearances, evictions in the face of threats, explosions and arsons,

Deeply distressed at the sufferings of the Palestinians resulting from the Israeli invasion of Lebanon,

Reaffirming its support for the sovereignty, unity and territorial integrity of Lebanon, within its internationally recognized boundaries,

1. *Urges* the Secretary-General, in consultation with the United Nations Relief and Works Agency for Palestine Refugees in the Near East, to undertake effective measures to guarantee the safety and security and the legal and human rights of the Palestine refugees in all the territories under Israeli occupation in 1967 and thereafter;

2. *Holds* Israel responsible for the security of the Palestine refugees in the Palestinian and other Arab territories occupied since 1967, including Jerusalem, and calls upon it to fulfil its obligations as the occupying Power in this regard, in accordance with the pertinent provisions of the Geneva Convention relative to the Protection of Civilian Persons in Time of War, of 12 August 1949;

3. *Calls once again upon* Israel, the occupying Power, to release forthwith all detained Palestine refugees, including the employees of the United Nations Relief and Works Agency for Palestine Refugees in the Near East;

4. *Urges* the Commissioner-General to provide housing, in consultation with the Government of Lebanon, to the Palestine refugees whose houses were demolished or razed by the Israeli forces;

5. *Calls once again upon* Israel to compensate the Agency for the damage to its property and facilities resulting from the Israeli invasion of Lebanon, without prejudice to Israel's responsibility for all damages resulting from that invasion;

6. *Requests* the Secretary-General, in consultation with the Commissioner-General, to report to the General Assembly, before the opening of its forty-first session, on the implementation of the present resolution.

General Assembly resolution 40/165 I

16 December 1985   Meeting 118   116-2-33 (recorded vote)

Approved by SPC (A/40/921) by recorded vote (96-2-28), 15 November (meeting 34); 8-nation draft (A/SPC/40/L.24); agenda item 79.
Sponsors: Afghanistan, Bangladesh, Cuba, Egypt, Indonesia, Malaysia, Pakistan, Yugoslavia.
Meeting numbers. GA 40th session: SPC 22-28, 31, 34; plenary 118.

Recorded vote in Assembly as follows:

In favour: Afghanistan, Albania, Algeria, Antigua and Barbuda, Argentina, Bahamas, Bahrain, Bangladesh, Barbados, Benin, Bhutan, Bolivia, Botswana, Brazil, Brunei Darussalam, Bulgaria, Burkina Faso, Burma, Burundi, Byelorussian SSR, Cameroon, Cape Verde, Central African Republic, Chad, Chile, China, Colombia, Congo, Cuba, Cyprus, Czechoslovakia, Democratic Kampuchea, Democratic Yemen, Djibouti, Dominica, Dominican Republic, Ecuador, Egypt, Equatorial Guinea, Ethiopia, Fiji, Gabon, Gambia, German Democratic Republic, Ghana, Guinea, Guinea-Bissau, Guyana, Honduras, Hungary, India, Indonesia, Iran, Iraq, Jamaica, Jordan, Kenya, Kuwait, Lao People's Democratic Republic, Lebanon, Lesotho, Libyan Arab Jamahiriya, Madagascar, Malaysia, Maldives, Mali, Malta, Mauritania, Mauritius, Mexico, Mongolia, Morocco, Mozambique, Nepal, Nicaragua, Niger, Nigeria, Oman, Pakistan, Peru, Philippines, Poland, Qatar, Romania, Rwanda, Saint Lucia, Saint Vincent and the Grenadines, Samoa, Sao Tome and Principe, Saudi Arabia, Senegal, Seychelles, Sierra Leone, Singapore, Somalia, Sri Lanka, Sudan, Syrian Arab Republic, Thailand, Togo, Trinidad and Tobago, Tunisia, Turkey, Uganda, Ukrainian SSR, USSR, United Arab Emirates, United Republic of Tanzania, Uruguay, Vanuatu, Venezuela, Viet Nam, Yemen, Yugoslavia, Zambia, Zimbabwe.
Against: Israel, United States.
Abstaining: Australia, Austria, Belgium, Canada, Costa Rica, Denmark, El Salvador, Finland, France, Germany, Federal Republic of, Greece, Grenada, Guatemala, Haiti, Iceland, Ireland, Italy, Ivory Coast, Japan, Liberia, Luxembourg, Malawi, Netherlands, New Zealand, Norway, Panama, Paraguay, Portugal, Spain, Swaziland, Sweden, United Kingdom, Zaire.

The seventh preambular paragraph was adopted, by recorded votes of 101 to 16, with 29 abstentions, in plenary and 91 to 17, with 18 abstentions, in Committee.

In the opinion of the United States, the text included an unacceptable, one-sided condemnation of Israel in complete disregard of the truth; such exercises in empty polemics only aggravated the problems facing UNRWA. Also, charging the Secretary-General with guaranteeing the safety, security and rights of the Palestine refugees in the occupied territories would raise practical and legal problems with the possibility of conflicting jurisdictional authorities.

Israel said the text contained identical opening paragraphs to the previous year's unjustified and unwarranted resolution, and despite the fact that Israeli forces had meanwhile left Lebanon. The subsequent paragraphs referred not to the situation in Lebanon, but to that in Palestine and other occupied territories. Both the Chairman of the Committee on Palestinian rights and the Security Council had expressed concern over tragic developments in and around the camps at Beirut after Israel's withdrawal from the area, Israel said. There was little doubt that the principal cause of such concern was action by the Syrian Arab Republic, whose forces, in conjunction with Lebanese forces, had killed some 2,000 refugees and wounded over 6,000 in camps in Lebanon. However, the seventh preambular paragraph merely substituted the phrase "in the Palestinian and other Arab territories occupied since 1967, including Jerusalem", for "in occupied southern Lebanon", used in the 1984 text. It was clear to the many visitors to Judaea, Samaria and Gaza that the outrages which had allegedly occurred in southern Lebanon during the previous year were not being re-enacted in exactly the same way in those territories.

Lebanon responded that the Palestinian civilian and military presence in Lebanon and the violence which had involved Palestinians and Lebanese together had resulted from Israeli acts of aggression. Lebanon hoped that the talks currently being held under Syrian sponsorship would lead to a stable and lasting peace in Lebanon and make it possible to restore the rule of law throughout the country. Despite Israel's claim to have withdrawn its forces from southern Lebanon, United Nations forces and the Lebanese Government continued to consider that no such withdrawal had taken place.

In Sweden's view, the language of several paragraphs was sweeping and contradictory and the text did not appear to address the security situation of the refugees most in need of protection; Sweden and Finland felt it was inappropriate to demand that the Secretary-General should guarantee the safety of refugees when he had no means to do so. Finland said the seventh preambular paragraph and paragraph 3 were inaccurate and overlooked the serious security problems of Palestine refugees in parts of Lebanon that were not occupied. It was Finland's understanding that the damage referred to in paragraph 5 was that specified in UNRWA's claim of approximately $4.4 million submitted to Israel.

Speaking for the 10 EC member States, Luxembourg said they had difficulty in understanding why a text which had been traditionally related to the specific situation of Palestine refugees in Lebanon now appeared to have a more general application. The impression given was that their situation was less grave than that in other occupied territories, although reports demonstrated that the opposite was true. With regard to paragraph 1, the EC members felt that it was important not to detract from Israel's responsibility, as the occupying Power, to provide protection to the civilian population; they also had difficulty in supporting certain other passages in the text which in their view contained extreme generalizations.

In a similar vein, Austria remarked that previous resolutions on the subject had referred to the situation of refugees in Lebanon; the new text, however, applied in general to the territories occupied by Israel since 1967.

Turkey reserved its position on paragraph 1 and on the seventh preambular paragraph.

Palestine refugees in the Gaza Strip

The living conditions of refugees and the security situation in the Gaza Strip had deteriorated, the Commissioner-General stated when introducing his annual report[2] in the General Assembly's Special Political Committee. There was a serious shortage of adequate housing and increasing numbers of refugees were finding it difficult to obtain employment, which added to other hardships. As a consequence, there was heightened demand for special hardship assistance and help in finding employment. Unhealthy environmental conditions and continued settlement activity further compounded unsatisfactory living conditions, by reducing the amount of land available for agriculture and by increasing the pressure on already insufficient water supply and waste disposal facilities. In addition, no solution had been reached to the problem of the approximately 5,000 Palestinian refugees on the Egyptian side of the border between the Gaza Strip and the Sinai, to whom UNRWA continued to provide limited assistance, the Commissioner-General said.

Report of the Secretary-General. In September 1985,[33] the Secretary-General submitted a report on Palestine refugees in the Gaza Strip, in accordance with a 1984 General Assembly resolution[34] demanding that Israel desist from removing and resettling Palestine refugees in the Gaza Strip and destroying their shelters. In reply to a note verbale of 22 March 1985 by the Secretary-General, Israel stated on 12 August that its position on the matter had been set out in successive annual replies, the latest in June 1984.[35] To date, Israel said, it had provided housing for more than 9,500 families and, during 1985, another 620 families were to be housed under the refugee voluntary rehabilitation programme.

The Secretary-General reported that, following a shooting incident in Gaza town on 17 April when an Israeli soldier was wounded by a Palestine refugee, Israeli authorities had partially demolished the refugee's father's shelter in Bureij camp. In response to UNRWA's protest that the demolition amounted to collective punishment contrary to the fourth Geneva Convention, the authorities stated that the demolition had been limited to extensions that contravened building regulations.

UNRWA was following up with the Israeli authorities the rehousing of refugees who remained affected by the demolitions in 1971 in the Gaza Strip.[36] Of 87 families previously categorized as living in hardship conditions, 19 were still in hardship, 18 were inadequately and 37 adequately housed, and 13 had purchased houses in Israeli-sponsored projects. The authorities stated that the 19 families living in hardship conditions were being rehoused.

Several refugee families living on the northern perimeter of Jabalia camp had been told by Israeli authorities to remove some of their shelter extensions on the ground that they had been built without proper authority on State land outside camp boundaries; the families had taken the matter to the High Court of Israel where proceedings were continuing. Some of the families concerned were understood to have accepted an Israeli offer to move to a housing project at Beit Lahiya, demolishing their shelters at Jabalia as a pre-condition. Israeli authorities had also levelled boundary walls and gardens at that camp on the grounds that they were in contravention of building regulations.

The 35 families whose shelters on the perimeter of Beach camp had been demolished in 1983[37] had still not been rehoused; 28 of them were living in temporary shelters on or near the same site, 2 had moved in with relatives and 5 had left. Israel had stated that arrangements were being made to provide alternative accommodation.

In the year under review, according to information available, 326 refugee families, comprising 2,075 persons, moved to 194 plots of land in Israeli-sponsored housing projects; in addition, three refugee families comprising 14 persons moved to completed housing units. As a pre-condition, 501 shelter rooms had to be demolished, of which 245 had been built by UNRWA and 27 had been assisted by it. In requiring such demolitions,

Israel maintained that it was to relieve congestion in the camps and that material from demolished shelters was used in new construction. UNRWA believed such demolitions added to the acute housing crisis in the Gaza Strip.

The Israeli authorities had to date allocated a total of 3,714 plots of land in the Gaza Strip for housing projects. Houses had been built by 2,816 refugee families of 17,316 persons on 2,067 plots, and construction was continuing on 361 plots. The remaining plots were either vacant or belonged to non-refugee families. In addition, 2,809 refugee families consisting of 17,649 persons and 14 non-refugee families comprising 65 persons had moved into 2,665 completed housing units.

Refugee families were continuing to purchase plots of land at subsidized rates for constructing houses in projects developed by Israel in the Beit Lahiya, Naslah and Tel el-Sultan areas. Israel had also started recently to expand the al-Amal and Sheikh Radwan housing projects.

GENERAL ASSEMBLY ACTION

On 16 December 1985, on the recommendation of the Special Political Committee, the General Assembly adopted **resolution 40/165 E** by recorded vote.

Palestine refugees in the Gaza Strip

The General Assembly,

Recalling Security Council resolution 237(1967) of 14 June 1967,

Recalling also General Assembly resolutions 2792 C (XXVI) of 6 December 1971, 2963 C (XXVII) of 13 December 1972, 3089 C (XXVIII) of 7 December 1973, 3331 D (XXIX) of 17 December 1974, 3419 C (XXX) of 8 December 1975, 31/15 E of 23 November 1976, 32/90 C of 13 December 1977, 33/112 E of 18 December 1978, 34/52 F of 23 November 1979, 35/13 F of 3 November 1980, 36/146 A of 16 December 1981, 37/120 E of 16 December 1982, 38/83 E of 15 December 1983 and 39/99 E of 14 December 1984,

Having considered the report of the Commissioner-General of the United Nations Relief and Works Agency for Palestine Refugees in the Near East, covering the period from 1 July 1984 to 30 June 1985, and the report of the Secretary-General,

Recalling the provisions of paragraph 11 of its resolution 194(III) of 11 December 1948 and considering that measures to resettle Palestine refugees in the Gaza Strip away from the homes and property from which they were displaced constitute a violation of their inalienable right of return,

Alarmed by the reports received from the Commissioner-General that the Israeli occupying authorities, in contravention of Israel's obligation under international law, persist in their policy of demolishing shelters occupied by refugee families,

1. *Reiterates strongly its demand* that Israel desist from the removal and resettlement of Palestine refugees in the Gaza Strip and from the destruction of their shelters;

2. *Requests* the Secretary-General, after consulting with the Commissioner-General of the United Nations Relief and Works Agency for Palestine Refugees in the Near East, to report to the General Assembly, before the opening of its forty-first session, on Israel's compliance with paragraph 1 above.

General Assembly resolution 40/165 E

16 December 1985   Meeting 118   146-2-2 (recorded vote)

Approved by SPC (A/40/921) by recorded vote (126-2), 15 November (meeting 34); 9-nation draft (A/SPC/40/L.20); agenda item 79.

Sponsors: Afghanistan, Bangladesh, Cuba, Egypt, India, Indonesia, Malaysia, Pakistan, Yugoslavia.

Meeting numbers. GA 40th session: SPC 22-28, 31, 34; plenary 118.

Recorded vote in Assembly as follows:

In favour: Afghanistan, Albania, Algeria, Antigua and Barbuda, Argentina, Australia, Austria, Bahamas, Bahrain, Bangladesh, Barbados, Belgium, Benin, Bhutan, Bolivia, Botswana, Brazil, Brunei Darussalam, Bulgaria, Burkina Faso, Burma, Burundi, Byelorussian SSR, Cameroon, Canada, Cape Verde, Central African Republic, Chad, Chile, China, Colombia, Congo, Costa Rica, Cuba, Cyprus, Czechoslovakia, Democratic Kampuchea, Democratic Yemen, Denmark, Djibouti, Dominica, Dominican Republic, Ecuador, Egypt, El Salvador, Equatorial Guinea, Ethiopia, Fiji, Finland, France, Gabon, Gambia, German Democratic Republic, Germany, Federal Republic of, Ghana, Guatemala, Guinea, Guinea-Bissau, Guyana, Haiti, Honduras, Hungary, Iceland, India, Indonesia, Iran, Iraq, Ireland, Italy, Ivory Coast, Jamaica, Japan, Jordan, Kenya, Kuwait, Lao People's Democratic Republic, Lebanon, Lesotho, Liberia, Libyan Arab Jamahiriya, Luxembourg, Madagascar, Malawi, Malaysia, Maldives, Mali, Malta, Mauritania, Mauritius, Mexico, Mongolia, Morocco, Mozambique, Nepal, Netherlands, New Zealand, Nicaragua, Niger, Nigeria, Norway, Oman, Pakistan, Panama, Paraguay, Peru, Philippines, Poland, Portugal, Qatar, Romania, Rwanda, Saint Lucia, Saint Vincent and the Grenadines, Samoa, Sao Tome and Principe, Saudi Arabia, Senegal, Seychelles, Sierra Leone, Singapore, Spain, Sri Lanka, Sudan, Suriname, Swaziland, Sweden, Syrian Arab Republic, Thailand, Togo, Trinidad and Tobago, Tunisia, Turkey, Uganda, Ukrainian SSR, USSR, United Arab Emirates, United Kingdom, United Republic of Tanzania, Uruguay, Vanuatu, Venezuela, Viet Nam, Yemen, Yugoslavia, Zambia, Zimbabwe.

Against: Israel, United States.

Abstaining: Grenada, Zaire.

Israel declared that it would continue to provide better-quality accommodation to refugees in the Gaza Strip, despite the demand in the text that it should abandon its efforts to do so. The United States regarded the text as highly polemical, one-sided and harshly condemnatory.

Palestine refugees in the West Bank

The living conditions of refugees in the West Bank had deteriorated, the UNRWA Commissioner-General stated when introducing his annual report in the Special Political Committee. The situation had been characterized by numerous incidents, including confrontations between Israeli settlers and the local population; occasional curfews had been decreed in the camps and there had been disruptions in schools.

Communications. By a letter of 12 February 1985,[38] the Chairman of the Committee on Palestinian rights brought to the Secretary-General's attention the grave situation and growing tension in and around Palestinian refugee camps, both in southern Lebanon (see p. 311) and in the West Bank. At Dheisheh, near Bethlehem, all roads into the camp had been blocked, the Chairman said; only one narrow pedestrian entrance had remained open, affecting services to the camp and aggravating the atmosphere of living under siege. On 1 February, he added, police reinforced by military troops had arrested scores of residents in the camp and villages in the vicinity.

In a letter of 19 March,[39] the Chairman expressed the Committee's profound concern that, on 12 March, the press had reported that 35 youths from the Dheisheh camp, arrested during a night raid on the camp on 31 January, were still being detained for interrogation without charges.

Report of the Secretary-General. Of the 357,704 Palestine refugees in the West Bank registered with UNRWA, 266,473 lived outside camps, the Secretary-General noted in a September 1985 report.[40] He also reported that, in reply to a note verbale of 22 March requesting Israel to inform him of any steps taken to implement the General Assembly's 1984 resolution[41] calling on Israel to refrain from removing and resettling refugees in the West Bank, Israel had stated on 12 August 1985 that its position had been set out in 1984.[42] The views of the UNRWA Commissioner-General remained also as stated in 1984.[42] The Agency did not envisage being involved in removing and resettling refugees; while it did not oppose measures voluntarily accepted by them to improve their living conditions, it would strongly object to any attempt to force them to comply with any particular scheme. The mere fact of relocation did not affect eligibility for UNRWA services, the Secretary-General added.

GENERAL ASSEMBLY ACTION

On 16 December 1985, on the recommendation of the Special Political Committee, the General Assembly adopted **resolution 40/165 J**, by recorded vote.

Palestine refugees in the West Bank

The General Assembly,

Recalling Security Council resolution 237(1967) of 14 June 1967,

Recalling also General Assembly resolutions 38/83 J of 15 December 1983 and 39/99 J of 14 December 1984,

Having considered the report of the Secretary-General,

Having also considered the report of the Commissioner-General of the United Nations Relief and Works Agency for Palestine Refugees in the Near East, covering the period from 1 July 1984 to 30 June 1985,

Alarmed by Israel's plans to remove and resettle the Palestine refugees of the West Bank and to destroy their camps,

Recalling the provisions of paragraph 11 of its resolution 194(III) of 11 December 1948 and considering that measures to resettle Palestine refugees in the West Bank away from the homes and property from which they were displaced constitute a violation of their inalienable right of return,

1. *Calls once again upon* Israel to abandon its plans and to refrain from the removal, and from any action that may lead to the removal and resettlement, of Palestine refugees in the West Bank and from the destruction of their camps;

2. *Requests* the Secretary-General, in co-operation with the Commissioner-General of the United Nations Relief and Works Agency for Palestine Refugees in the Near East, to keep the matter under close supervision and to report to the General Assembly, before the opening of its forty-first session, on any developments regarding this matter.

General Assembly resolution 40/165 J

16 December 1985   Meeting 118   146-2-2 (recorded vote)

Approved by SPC (A/40/921) by recorded vote (126-2), 15 November (meeting 34); 9-nation draft (A/SPC/40/L.25); agenda item 79.

Sponsors: Afghanistan, Bangladesh, Cuba, Egypt, India, Indonesia, Malaysia, Pakistan, Yugoslavia.

Meeting numbers. GA 40th session: SPC 22-28, 31, 34; plenary 118.

Recorded vote in Assembly as follows:

In favour: Afghanistan, Albania, Algeria, Antigua and Barbuda, Argentina, Australia, Austria, Bahamas, Bahrain, Bangladesh, Barbados, Belgium, Benin, Bhutan, Bolivia, Botswana, Brazil, Brunei Darussalam, Bulgaria, Burkina Faso, Burma, Burundi, Byelorussian SSR, Cameroon, Canada, Cape Verde, Central African Republic, Chad, Chile, China, Colombia, Congo, Costa Rica, Cuba, Cyprus, Czechoslovakia, Democratic Kampuchea, Democratic Yemen, Denmark, Djibouti, Dominica, Dominican Republic, Ecuador, Egypt, El Salvador, Equatorial Guinea, Ethiopia, Fiji, Finland, France, Gabon, Gambia, German Democratic Republic, Germany, Federal Republic of, Ghana, Greece, Guatemala, Guinea, Guinea-Bissau, Guyana, Haiti, Honduras, Hungary, Iceland, India, Indonesia, Iran, Iraq, Ireland, Italy, Ivory Coast, Jamaica, Japan, Jordan, Kenya, Kuwait, Lao People's Democratic Republic, Lebanon, Lesotho, Liberia, Libyan Arab Jamahiriya, Luxembourg, Madagascar, Malaysia, Maldives, Mali, Malta, Mauritania, Mauritius, Mexico, Mongolia, Morocco, Mozambique, Nepal, Netherlands, New Zealand, Nicaragua, Niger, Nigeria, Norway, Oman, Pakistan, Panama, Paraguay, Peru, Philippines, Poland, Portugal, Qatar, Romania, Saint Lucia, Saint Vincent and the Grenadines, Samoa, Sao Tome and Principe, Saudi Arabia, Senegal, Seychelles, Sierra Leone, Singapore, Spain, Sri Lanka, Sudan, Suriname, Swaziland, Sweden, Syrian Arab Republic, Thailand, Togo, Trinidad and Tobago, Tunisia, Turkey, Uganda, Ukrainian SSR, USSR, United Arab Emirates, United Kingdom, United Republic of Tanzania, Uruguay, Vanuatu, Venezuela, Viet Nam, Yemen, Yugoslavia, Zaire, Zambia, Zimbabwe.

Against: Israel, United States.

Abstaining: Grenada, Malawi.

The United States said it could not support paragraph 1 of the text as it would exclude any programmes which might seek to improve the refugees' quality of life pending an overall political settlement; such programmes might include the construction of new housing outside existing camps, undertaken voluntarily by the refugees themselves and in co-ordination with UNRWA.

REFERENCES

[1]YUN 1982, p. 558, GA res. 37/120 I, 16 Dec. 1982. [2]A/40/13 & Corr.1. [3]A/41/13. [4]YUN 1948-49, p. 174, GA res. 194(III), 11 Dec. 1948. [5]A/40/299. [6]A/40/207. [7]A/40/216-S/17072. [8]A/40/13/Add.1 & Add.1/Corr.1. [9]A/40/736. [10]A/40/350. [11]YUN 1983, p. 354, GA res. 38/83 I, 15 Dec. 1983. [12]YUN 1984, p. 344, GA res. 39/99 I, 14 Dec. 1984. [13]*Ibid.*, p. 347, GA res. 39/99 G, 14 Dec. 1984. [14]A/40/614. [15]YUN 1984, p. 346. [16]A/40/580. [17]YUN 1984, p. 336, GA res. 39/99 A, 14 Dec. 1984. [18]YUN 1982, p. 560. [19]YUN 1984, p. 335. [20]*Ibid.*, p. 343, GA res. 39/99 F, 14 Dec. 1984. [21]A/40/766. [22]YUN 1984, p. 341, GA res. 39/99 K, 14 Dec. 1984. [23]A/40/543. [24]YUN 1980, p. 443, GA res. 35/13 B, 3 Nov. 1980. [25]YUN 1983, p. 351. [26]YUN 1984, p. 341. [27]A/40/612. [28]YUN 1984, p. 342, GA res. 39/99 D, 14 Dec. 1984. [29]A/40/616. [30]YUN 1984, p. 346, GA res. 39/99 H, 14 Dec. 1984. [31]YUN 1981, p. 336. [32]A/40/756. [33]A/40/613. [34]YUN 1984, p. 348, GA res. 39/99 E, 14 Dec. 1984. [35]*Ibid.*, p. 347. [36]YUN 1971, p. 198. [37]YUN 1983, p. 358. [38]A/40/128-S/16954. [39]A/40/183-S/17043. [40]A/40/615. [41]YUN 1984, p. 349, GA res. 39/99 J, 14 Dec. 1984. [42]*Ibid.*, p. 349.

Chapter X

Other political questions

In 1985, the General Assembly considered various aspects of information questions, adopting two resolutions—on public information activities and policies (resolution 40/164 A) and on mass communication development (40/164 B). Both called for promoting the establishment of a new world information and communication order.

The Assembly also reviewed work on two other questions: radiation from all sources, and Antarctica. Concerning the first, the Assembly called for the continued pursuit of knowledge of the levels, effects and risks of radiation (40/160). Regarding the second, it asked mainly for information on the management, exploration and use of Antarctica's resources (40/156 A-C).

Topics related to this chapter. Disarmament: public information. Africa: South Africa and *apartheid*—public information. Middle East: Palestine question—public information. Institutional machinery: other institutional questions—fortieth anniversary of the United Nations. General questions relating to colonial countries: the 1960 Declaration on colonial countries—information dissemination. Namibia: information dissemination. Other administrative and management questions: information systems, computers and telecommunication.

Information

Information activities of the United Nations fell into two broad categories. One was mass communication co-operation and development, in particular activities designed to develop, through programmes of the United Nations Educational, Scientific and Cultural Organization (UNESCO) and the International Telecommunication Union (ITU), the communication capacities of developing countries. The other was public information, aimed at publicizing the work and goals of the United Nations, among them the free and balanced flow of information. Co-operation and co-ordination in public information activities throughout the United Nations system continued to be promoted by the Joint United Nations Information Committee (JUNIC), which also adopted recommendations for a common information strategy for the system.

The 69-member Committee on Information, established by the General Assembly in 1978 as the Committee to Review United Nations Public Information Policies and Activities,[1] continued to monitor the Organization's information and communication activities—executed principally by the Secretariat's Department of Public Information (DPI)—and to promote the establishment of a new world information and communication order. The Committee made 70 recommendations concerning these matters at its seventh substantive session, held in New York from 17 June to 5 July and on 29 August 1985. The session was preceded by an organizational session, also in New York, from 19 to 21 March.[2]

The Committee's recommendations were approved in December by Assembly **resolution 40/164 A**, to which they were annexed.

Mass communication

UNESCO and ITU activities. In 1985, UNESCO continued efforts to implement its International Programme for the Development of Communication (IPDC)—a programme to help developing countries build communication infrastructure—and to establish a new world information and communication order (see p. 373); it also continued its studies on the social, economic and cultural effects of the accelerated development of communication technologies. Details of these efforts, including related activities of ITU, were described by the UNESCO Director-General in a report submitted to the General Assembly in response to its 1984 request[3] and transmitted by the Secretary-General in September 1985.[4]

The report noted several trends in the progress of IPDC, among them an increase in the number of projects submitted for financing and in the number of national projects, with greater emphasis on audio-visual media, book development and training. Having achieved a geographical balance in projects from developing countries, IPDC was giving priority support to projects from the least developed countries. Emphasis was being placed on training, i.e. special training projects and enhancement of the training component of projects. IPDC had also established a good working relationship with United Nations organizations concerned with communication.

At its sixth session (Paris, March 1985), the IPDC Intergovernmental Council approved for funding

39 projects, of which 13 (11 regional, 2 national) were for refinancing and 26 were new. Those for refinancing were providing assistance for: training professional and technical communication personnel, including journalists, broadcasting personnel, graphic artists and postal administrators; news agency consultants' services, equipment and computerization; and the strengthening of regional mass communication activities. The new projects included support for: rural broadcasting studies and training on media and the changing family in Africa; development of sound broadcasting in Latin America; and information exchanges among Arab, Latin American and European news agencies. Two special projects were also approved: one on communication training and career development for women in Africa, the other for preliminary work on a report on the state of communication in the world.

Field-based development projects in Africa, the Arab States, Asia and the Pacific, and Latin America and the Caribbean totalled 125. A major activity of UNESCO's communication programme, they represented more than $26 million in ongoing projects (including those financed by IPDC). About 50 per cent of this amount was funds-in-trust, the largest contributors of which were the Arab Gulf Programme for United Nations Development Organizations, the Federal Republic of Germany, the Netherlands and the Scandinavian countries; about 6 per cent came from the United Nations Development Programme.

Large-scale extrabudgetary projects in Africa, Asia and the Caribbean were providing assistance for a mass communications institute, to develop educational radio and broadcasting, rural press and news agency services, and to train radio, film and video personnel.

The Intergovernmental Council of IPDC adopted a budget of $2.5 million for 1985-1986 to be paid from the IPDC Special Account. As of the reporting date, $7,034,645 had been paid to that Account, out of $8,603,670 pledged. The USSR offered 30 additional fellowships for professional training, and the Republic of Korea offered training facilities for producing radio and television programmes valued at $300,000. Commitment of funds-in-trust support had also been received from Canada, France, the Federal Republic of Germany, the Netherlands, Sweden and the United States.

As requested by the Assembly in 1984,[3] UNESCO, in its 1986-1987 draft programme and budget, provided for periodic studies to identify new technological trends in information, communication, telematics and informatics and to assess their socio-economic and cultural impact on development. As a first step, a series of regionally based consultations had been organized, the first by Florida State University (United States, December 1984) to discuss possible areas of collaboration in North America,

Latin America and the Caribbean. The second was held in Ahmedabad (India, December 1985), which brought together researchers and institution representatives from Asia and the Pacific, Africa and the Arab States.

Related activities of ITU included holding the first of a series of preparatory meetings for a World Administrative Telegraph and Telephone Conference, scheduled for 1988, to draw up new regulations governing the use and operation of international public telecommunications. Also, in keeping with a recommendation of the Independent Commission for World-wide Telecommunication Development set up by ITU in 1982, the ITU Administrative Council, at its fortieth session (Geneva, 1-17 July 1985), took steps towards establishing a Centre for Telecommunications Development. In addition, ITU[5] laid the foundation-stone of the Multinational School of Advanced Telecommunication Studies at Dakar, Senegal. This project, launched in 1981 as part of a global effort to achieve fuller control of telecommunication network management, was serving eight West African States. In December 1985, ITU completed the translation into Arabic of ITU's provisional glossary of telecommunication terms and terms relating to space telecommunications.

The UNESCO General Conference, at its twenty-third session (Sofia, Bulgaria, 8 October–9 November), adopted a resolution on its programme on communication in the service of man, renewing its appeal for increased contributions to IPDC, calling for a balance between research and operational activities in implementing the service-of-man programme, and setting forth guidelines for studies on communication, for promoting the free flow and balanced dissemination of information and increased news exchanges, and for the development of communication. The resolution also called for close co-operation with other United Nations and non-governmental organizations (NGOs) dealing with communication.

Activities of the Committee on Information. The Committee on Information,[2] recognizing the contribution that the mass media world-wide could make to promoting development and other objectives, recommended that the General Assembly appeal to the media to support international efforts towards global development, in particular the efforts of developing countries to achieve economic, social and cultural progress, and to the United Nations system to promote, through its information services, development activities on behalf of those countries. The Committee recommended that developing countries be assured access to communication technology to enable them to improve their communication systems. The United Nations system and the developed countries should be urged to co-operate with them towards strengthening their information and communication infrastructures, and to give full support to IPDC in this connection.

DPI likewise should be urged to monitor meetings of the Movement of Non-Aligned Countries and of regional intergovernmental bodies devoted to information and communication issues; and should co-operate with UNESCO to prepare and implement a plan of integrated communication network and regional data and communication centres and to provide facilities for data and communication exchange for non-aligned countries.

The foregoing recommendations were part of a series of Committee recommendations for the establishment of a new, more just and effective world information and communication order (see p. 373), which were approved by Assembly **resolution 40/164 A**.

Communications. A number of resolutions or declarations adopted by intergovernmental bodies and transmitted to the Secretary-General in 1985 dealt with, among other matters, the question of a more objective and balanced presentation of information to the international community.

The Fifteenth Islamic Conference of Foreign Ministers (Sanaa, 18-22 December 1984), by a resolution among those transmitted by Yemen on 11 March 1985,[6] called for stronger co-operation among its members in the field of information and for implementation of an information plan to counter propaganda against Islam and Moslems.

By the Declaration of the Commemorative Meeting in Observance of the Thirtieth Anniversary of the Asian-African Conference (Bandung, 24 and 25 April), transmitted by Indonesia on 1 May,[7] the participating countries declared that, to preserve cultural heritage and national identity and to ensure a more balanced flow of information among the international community, it was imperative to realize a new international information and communication order, initiated by UNESCO.

The Conference of Foreign Ministers of Non-Aligned Countries (Luanda, 4-7 September), by its Final Political Declaration transmitted by Angola on 5 November,[8] requested the non-aligned countries to continue efforts towards the establishment of a new information order, asked all States to strengthen the role of UNESCO in this endeavour, and agreed to support DPI activities to increase information dissemination and ensure coherent coverage of priority issues.

The Conference of African Ministers of Information, by a resolution adopted at its first extraordinary session (Cairo, 23-25 November) and among those transmitted on 4 December by Egypt,[9] invited UNESCO to intensify efforts to assist the Organization of African Unity (OAU) to set up a new African information order that was fairer and more balanced, as a prelude to the establishment of a new world information order.

Argentina, India, Italy and Nigeria transmitted on 10 April[10] the conclusions and recommendations of a study week on the impact of space exploration on mankind (Vatican, 1-5 October 1984), which fell under three headings: telecommunication satellites, space technology, and the future uses of space. The participants considered it desirable that the tools of space technology be used to improve the conditions of life, to promote greater harmony among humankind, to permit the sharing of cultures and knowledge, and to use and care for the world's resources for the common good of all.

By a letter of 20 May,[11] Cuba conveyed to the Secretary-General a message it wished to transmit to the United States, protesting that Government's decision to inaugurate broadcasts to Cuba through Radio Martí, a decision Cuba said would damage the foundations for communications and relations between citizens of Cuban origin in the United States and citizens of Cuba.

GENERAL ASSEMBLY ACTION

Acting on the recommendation of the Special Political Committee on 16 December 1985, the General Assembly adopted by recorded vote **resolution 40/164 B** on questions relating to information.

The General Assembly,

Recalling its resolutions 34/181 and 34/182 of 18 December 1979, 35/201 of 16 December 1980, 36/149 A of 16 December 1981, 37/94 A and B of 10 December 1982, 38/82 A of 15 December 1983 and 39/98 A and B of 14 December 1984,

Taking note of the ongoing efforts of the United Nations Educational, Scientific and Cultural Organization to contribute to the clarification, elaboration and application of the concept of a new world information and communication order,

Recalling the relevant provisions of the Declarations of the Sixth and Seventh Conferences of Heads of State or Government of Non-Aligned Countries held at Havana from 3 to 9 September 1979 and at New Delhi from 7 to 12 March 1983 as well as the Final Documents of the Conference of the Ministers of Information of Non-Aligned Countries held at Jakarta from 26 to 30 January 1984, and the relevant provisions of the Final Political Declaration of the Conference of Ministers for Foreign Affairs of Non-Aligned Countries, held at Luanda from 4 to 7 September 1985, in which the importance of the establishment of a new world information and communication order was stressed anew,

Recalling the relevant resolutions adopted by the Assembly of Heads of State and Government of the Organization of African Unity at its eighteenth ordinary session, held at Nairobi from 24 to 27 June 1981, the Conference of Ministers of Information of States members of the Organization of African Unity at its third ordinary session, held at Addis Ababa in March 1985 and at its first extraordinary session, held at Cairo in November 1985, especially those encouraging regional co-operation in the field of information and promoting the establishment of a new world information and communication order,

Recalling article 19 of the Universal Declaration of Human Rights, which provides that everyone has the right to freedom of opinion and expression and that this right includes freedom to hold opinions without interference and to seek, receive and impart information and ideas through any media and regardless of frontiers, and article 29, which stipulates that these rights and freedoms may in no case be exercised contrary to the purposes and principles of the United Nations,

Recalling the relevant provisions of the Final Act of the Conference on Security and Co-operation in Europe, signed at Helsinki on 1 August 1975, and those of the Concluding Document of the meeting of representatives of the participating States of the Conference on Security and Co-operation in Europe, held at Madrid from 11 November 1980 to 9 September 1983,

Recalling resolution 4/21 of 27 October 1980, adopted by the General Conference of the United Nations Educational, Scientific and Cultural Organization at its twenty-first session, and resolution 2/03 of 3 December 1982, adopted by the General Conference at its fourth extraordinary session,

Recalling also resolutions 4/19 of 27 October 1980, 3.1 of 25 November 1983 and 3.1 of 8 November 1985 adopted by the General Conference of the United Nations Educational, Scientific and Cultural Organization, and, in this context, expressing anew the wish that that organization should contribute to the clarification, elaboration and application of the concept of a new world information and communication order,

Recalling the Declaration on Fundamental Principles concerning the Contribution of the Mass Media to Strengthening Peace and International Understanding, to the Promotion of Human Rights and to Countering Racialism, *Apartheid* and Incitement to War, adopted on 28 November 1978 by the General Conference of the United Nations Educational, Scientific and Cultural Organization,

Recalling also the relevant provisions of the Declaration on the Preparation of Societies for Life in Peace,

Considering that international co-operation in the field of communication development should take place on the basis of equality, justice, mutual advantage and the principles of international law so as to remedy existing imbalances by strengthening and intensifying the development of human and material resources, communication networks and infrastructures, particularly in developing countries, and thus encourage a wider and better balanced dissemination of information,

Emphasizing its full support for the International Programme for the Development of Communication of the United Nations Educational, Scientific and Cultural Organization, which constitutes an essential instrument for the development of human and material resources and communication infrastructures in the developing countries and the establishment of a new world information and communication order,

Conscious that diverse solutions to information and communication problems are required because political, economic, cultural and social problems differ from one country to another,

Recognizing the central role of, and the progress accomplished by, the United Nations Educational, Scientific and Cultural Organization in the field of information and communication within its mandate, and that the United Nations system as a whole and all others concerned should give that organization adequate support and assistance in the field of information and communication,

1. *Takes note with satisfaction* of the report of the Director-General of the United Nations Educational, Scientific and Cultural Organization on the implementation of the International Programme for the Development of Communication, on the activities relating to the establishment of a new world information and communication order and on the social, economic and cultural impact of the new communication technologies;

2. *Appeals* to the mass media world-wide to explore all possible avenues for more equitable international co-operation in the field of information and communication and to respond in a positive way to the exceptional opportunities now available to them in the field of international relations, in order to open new vistas of progress for the world community;

3. *Underlines* the importance of efforts made to implement the principles set forth in the Declaration on Fundamental Principles concerning the Contribution of the Mass Media to Strengthening Peace and International Understanding, to the Promotion of Human Rights and to Countering Racialism, *Apartheid* and Incitement to War;

4. *Reiterates its appeal* to all Member States and all organizations of the United Nations system, international, governmental and non-governmental organizations and professional organizations in the field of communication to exert every effort to make better known through all means at their disposal the issues underlying the need for the development of communication capacities in developing countries as a step towards the establishment of a new world information and communication order;

5. *Considers* that the International Programme for the Development of Communication represents a significant step towards the development of conditions for the establishment of a new world information and communication order, and welcomes the decisions adopted by the Intergovernmental Council of the Programme at its fifth and sixth sessions, held in Paris in 1984 and 1985;

6. *Notes with satisfaction* the co-operation existing between the United Nations, the United Nations Educational, Scientific and Cultural Organization and all other organizations of the United Nations system, particularly the International Telecommunication Union, the Food and Agriculture Organization of the United Nations and the Universal Postal Union, whose projects have been approved by the Intergovernmental Council of the International Programme for the Development of Communication;

7. *Expresses its appreciation* to all Member States that have made or pledged a contribution towards the implementation of the International Programme for the Development of Communication;

8. *Reiterates its requests* to Member States and organizations and bodies of the United Nations system as well as other international governmental and non-governmental organizations and concerned public and private enterprises to respond to the appeals of the Director-General of the United Nations Educational, Scientific and Cultural Organization to make an increased contribution to the International Programme

for the Development of Communication by making greater financial resources available, as well as more training resources, equipment, technologies and staff;

9. *Appeals* to Member States to respond positively and effectively to resolution 4/22 of 27 October 1980 concerning the reduction of telecommunication tariffs for news exchanges, adopted by the General Conference of the United Nations Educational, Scientific and Cultural Organization, and to take the necessary steps to implement that resolution;

10. *Notes with satisfaction* that a second Round Table on a New World Information and Communication Order will be organized jointly by the United Nations and the United Nations Educational, Scientific and Cultural Organization at Copenhagen in April 1986;

11. *Reaffirms* its strong support for the United Nations Educational, Scientific and Cultural Organization, its Constitution, the ideals reflected in it, its activities and for its efforts to further enhance its capabilities with a view to promoting the establishment of a new world information and communication order;

12. *Encourages* the Director-General of the United Nations Educational, Scientific and Cultural Organization to continue the chronological survey of the documents dealing with the establishment of a new world information and communication order and the analysis of the evolution of this concept, and to keep the Committee informed on developments in this area;

13. *Encourages* the United Nations Educational, Scientific and Cultural Organization to continue and intensify its studies, programmes and activities with a view to identifying new technological trends in information, communication, telematics and informatics and assess their socio-economic and cultural impact on the development of peoples, and in this context requests it to provide, whenever necessary, periodic studies relevant to these topics;

14. *Invites* the Director-General of the United Nations Educational, Scientific and Cultural Organization to continue his efforts in the information and communication field and to submit to the General Assembly, at its forty-first session, a detailed report on the implementation of the International Programme for the Development of Communication and the activities relating to the establishment of a new world information and communication order as well as on the social, economic and cultural effects of the accelerated development of communication technologies.

General Assembly resolution 40/164 B

16 December 1985   Meeting 118   122-16-9 (recorded vote)

Approved by SPC (A/40/1024) by recorded vote (96-15-9), 6 December (meeting 46); draft by Yugoslavia for Group of 77 (A/SPC/40/L.29/Rev.1); agenda item 78.
Meeting numbers. GA 40th session: SPC 29-39, 45, 46; plenary 118.

Recorded vote in Assembly as follows:

In favour: Afghanistan, Algeria, Antigua and Barbuda, Argentina, Bahamas, Bahrain, Bangladesh, Barbados, Benin, Bhutan, Bolivia, Botswana, Brazil, Brunei Darussalam, Bulgaria, Burkina Faso, Burma, Burundi, Byelorussian SSR, Cameroon, Cape Verde, Central African Republic, Chad, Chile, China, Colombia, Congo, Costa Rica, Cuba, Cyprus, Czechoslovakia, Democratic Kampuchea, Democratic Yemen, Djibouti, Dominica, Dominican Republic, Ecuador, Egypt, El Salvador, Equatorial Guinea, Ethiopia, Fiji, Gabon, German Democratic Republic, Guatemala, Guinea, Guinea-Bissau, Guyana, Haiti, Honduras, Hungary, India, Indonesia, Iran, Iraq, Ivory Coast, Jamaica, Jordan, Kenya, Kuwait, Lao People's Democratic Republic, Lebanon, Lesotho, Liberia, Libyan Arab Jamahiriya, Madagascar, Malawi, Malaysia, Maldives, Mali, Malta, Mauritania, Mauritius, Mexico, Mongolia, Morocco, Mozambique, Nepal, Nicaragua, Niger, Nigeria, Oman, Pakistan, Panama, Peru, Philippines, Poland, Qatar, Romania, Rwanda, Saint Lucia, Saint Vincent and the Grenadines, Sao Tome and Principe, Saudi Arabia, Senegal, Seychelles, Sierra Leone, Singapore, Somalia, Sri Lanka, Sudan, Suriname, Swaziland, Syrian Arab Republic, Thailand, Togo, Trinidad and Tobago, Tunisia, Uganda, Ukrainian SSR, USSR, United Arab Emirates, United Republic of Tanzania, Uruguay, Vanuatu, Venezuela, Viet Nam, Yemen, Yugoslavia, Zaire, Zambia, Zimbabwe.

Against: Belgium, Canada, Denmark, Finland, Germany, Federal Republic of, Grenada, Iceland, Israel, Japan, Luxembourg, Netherlands, Norway, Portugal, Sweden, United Kingdom, United States.

Abstaining: Australia, Austria, France, Greece, Ireland, Italy, New Zealand, Spain, Turkey.

Explaining its vote in the Special Political Committee, Canada said the text did not reflect the important progress made at the UNESCO General Conference held at Sofia and that it voted negatively precisely because it was determined to work towards strengthening UNESCO. Canada and others referred to the absence in the text of words qualifying a new world information and communication order as an "evolving and continuous process", reached by consensus at the General Conference. (For the views of other States on this matter, see p. 383.) Canada added that the Assembly should strengthen the basis of the compromise established by UNESCO to enable the Committee on Information to focus its work on the activities of DPI. The United States said that since it had withdrawn from UNESCO, it would be illogical for it to endorse a resolution which supported that organization.

Austria regretted that it had had to abstain, in view of the text's encouraging elements, in particular the second preambular paragraph noting UNESCO's efforts. It expressed reservations on paragraphs 11 to 14, which it said contained formulations that seemed to call into question the consensus reached at the UNESCO Conference concerning the treatment of communication questions.

Proposed new world information and communication order

UNESCO activities. UNESCO, its Director-General reported,[4] continued to consolidate knowledge and experience regarding the concept of a new world information and communication order, seen as an evolving and continuous process. Its interest in defining alternative forms of communication focused on case-studies in Asia, Africa and Latin America, utilizing traditional and interpersonal modes, including small-scale media, and encouraging self-expression by minorities or disadvantaged groups. Case-studies on the information and communication situation of migrant workers included research carried out in Australia, Austria, Denmark, Finland, Norway, the United Kingdom, the United States and the Arab States. Also explored were the questions of: access to and participation in communication, particularly the uses of new communication technologies, with special attention to case-studies affecting rural populations in developing countries, especially rural women; the right to communicate; and the media's contribution to mutual respect, international understanding, human rights, peace and the elucidation of major world problems.

A first series of studies—on plurality of information, obstacles to a balanced and free flow of information, including censorship, and the role of the press in scrutinizing abuses of power—was under way. A synthesis was also undertaken of past studies on various aspects of the democratization of communication (greater public participation, more numerous and significant means, wider access, more extensive information exchanges, two-way communication, reduction in discrimination and domination, greater awareness of differences of opinion and diverging interpretation of facts, and plurality of sources, opinion and content).

Publications issued in 1985 relating to the concept included "International flow of information, a global report and analysis", "The new international economic order: links between economics and communications", and "Mass communication and the advertising industry". Preparations for a historical survey of documents dealing with a new information order were in progress, as were preparations for a second (1986) round table on the topic to be organized jointly by the United Nations and UNESCO.

UNESCO continued to play an important role in the investigation of information flow, particularly between industrialized and developing countries, a situation considered central to the concept of a new information order. Three case-studies were initiated to provide basic data on methodology, and three studies were published: "Global report on international flow of information", "International bibliography on the flow in international news", and "International flow of TV news and programmes". Financial and technical assistance was provided for the development of news collection and dissemination through regional news networks in Africa, Asia, and Latin America and the Caribbean. Technical missions to Africa, Asia and the Arab States investigated ways of improving news agency operations through enhanced telecommunications facilities and computers. In Latin America and the Caribbean, two conferences were held at San José, Costa Rica (15-18 January and 20-22 July): the first reformulated the concept of the Latin American State Radio and Television Association and proposed the creation of a broadcasting union for the region; the second approved the basic documents for launching the Association's activities.

Activities of the Committee on Information. The Committee on Information, in its 1985 report to the General Assembly,[2] submitted a set of recommendations on promoting a new world information order, reiterating its call on all countries, the United Nations system and all others concerned to collaborate in establishing a new order based on the free circulation and wider and better balanced dissemination of information and guaranteeing the diversity of sources of information and free access to it. Observing that the principle of sovereign equality among nations extended to information and communication, the Committee stressed the urgent need to change the dependent status of developing countries in that field.

GENERAL ASSEMBLY ACTION

By **resolution 40/164 A**, the General Assembly approved the recommendations of the Committee on Information, annexed them to the resolution, and urged their full implementation. It requested the Committee, in keeping with its mandate to promote a new information order, to continue to seek the active participation of the United Nations system, in particular UNESCO and ITU, while avoiding overlapping activities.

By **resolution 40/164 B**, the Assembly, noting that a second round table was being organized by the United Nations and UNESCO for 1986, reaffirmed its strong support for UNESCO and for its efforts to enhance its capabilities to promote the establishment of a new order. It encouraged the UNESCO Director-General to continue the chronological survey of documents dealing with that order and his efforts in the area of information and communication.

UN public information

The fortieth anniversary of the United Nations was prominent among United Nations public information activities in 1985. To observe the occasion, DPI and United Nations information centres around the world mounted a wide-ranging information programme to publicize the goals and accomplishments of the Organization to help solve the world's major problems (see p. 403). Also in 1985, the Secretary-General reported to the Committee on Information on his decision against a United Nations–owned satellite system in favour of an enhanced communications system through leased satellite facilities, expected to have a major impact on United Nations information activities (see ADMINISTRATIVE AND BUDGETARY QUESTIONS, Chapter IV).

Among the 70 recommendations submitted in 1985 by the Committee on Information[2] for General Assembly approval were those calling for reiteration of 1984 recommendations approved by the Assembly[12] on public information matters and renewal of the Committee's mandate. They also included several on mass communication (see p. 369) and on the proposed new world information and communication order (see above), as well as guidelines on public information policies and activities to be carried out by DPI and its radio and visual services and information centres (see p. 385). Other recommendations concerned JUNIC activities (see p. 386), information exchange between the Committee on Information and the Commission on Transnational Corporations, as well as public information on the critical economic situation in Africa (see ECONOMIC AND SOCIAL QUESTIONS, Chapter III), United Nations decisions on acts of terrorism, the World Disarmament Campaign, human rights violations in the occupied Arab territories, the illegal occupation of Namibia and *apartheid* policies.

GENERAL ASSEMBLY ACTION

On 16 December 1985, acting on the recommendation of the Special Political Committee, the General Assembly adopted **resolution 40/164 A,** by recorded vote.

The General Assembly,

Recalling its resolutions 3535(XXX) of 17 December 1975, 31/139 of 16 December 1976, 33/115 A to C of 18 December 1978, 34/181 and 34/182 of 18 December 1979, 35/201 of 16 December 1980, 36/149 B of 16 December 1981, 37/94 B of 10 December 1982, 38/82 B of 15 December 1983 and 39/98 A of 14 December 1984, on questions relating to information,

Recalling article 19 of the Universal Declaration of Human Rights, which provides that everyone has the right to freedom of opinion and expression and that this right includes freedom to hold opinions without interference and to seek, receive and impart information and ideas through any media and regardless of frontiers, and article 29, which stipulates that these rights and freedoms may in no case be exercised contrary to the purposes and principles of the United Nations,

Recalling also articles 19 and 20 of the International Covenant on Civil and Political Rights,

Recalling the relevant provisions of the Declarations of the Sixth and Seventh Conferences of Heads of State or Government of Non-Aligned Countries held at Havana from 3 to 9 September 1979 and at New Delhi from 7 to 12 March 1983 as well as the Final Documents of the Conference of the Ministers of Information of Non-Aligned Countries, held at Jakarta from 26 to 30 January 1984, and the relevant provisions of the Final Political Declaration adopted by the Conference of Ministers for Foreign Affairs of Non-Aligned Countries, held at Luanda from 4 to 7 September 1985, in which the importance of the establishment of a new world information and communication order was stressed anew,

Recalling its resolutions 3201(S-VI) and 3202(S-VI) of 1 May 1974, containing the Declaration and the Programme of Action on the Establishment of a New International Economic Order, 3281(XXIX) of 12 December 1974, containing the Charter of Economic Rights and Duties of States, and 3362(S-VII) of 16 September 1975 on development and international economic co-operation,

Recalling the Declaration on Fundamental Principles concerning the Contribution of the Mass Media to Strengthening Peace and International Understanding, to the Promotion of Human Rights and to Countering Racialism, *Apartheid* and Incitement to War, adopted on 28 November 1978 by the General Conference of the United Nations Educational, Scientific and Cultural Organization, as well as the resolutions on information and mass communications adopted by the General Conference at its nineteenth, twentieth, twenty-first, twenty-second and twenty-third sessions,

Recalling the relevant provisions of the Final Act of the Conference on Security and Co-operation in Europe, signed at Helsinki on 1 August 1975, and those of the Concluding Document of the meeting of representatives of the participating States of the Conference on Security and Co-operation in Europe, held at Madrid from 11 November 1980 to 9 September 1983,

Recalling also the relevant provisions of the Declaration on the Preparation of Societies for Life in Peace,

Conscious of the need for all countries, the United Nations system as a whole and all others concerned to collaborate in the establishment of a new world information and communication order based, *inter alia*, on the free circulation and wider and better balanced dissemination of information, guaranteeing diversity of sources of information and free access to information, and, in particular, the urgent need to change the dependent status of the developing countries in the field of information and communication, as the principle of sovereign equality among nations extends also to this field, and intended also to strengthen peace and international understanding, enabling all persons to participate effectively in political, economic, social and cultural life and promoting understanding and friendship among all nations and human rights,

Noting the ongoing efforts of the United Nations Educational, Scientific and Cultural Organization to contribute to the clarification, elaboration and application of the concept of a new world information and communication order and recalling resolutions 4/19 of 27 October 1980, 3.1 of 25 November 1983 and 3.1 of 8 November 1985 adopted by consensus by its General Conference,

Reaffirming that the establishment of a new world information and communication order is linked to the new international economic order and is an integral part of the international development process, and that public information plays an important role in promoting understanding of and support for international co-operation for development,

Emphasizing the role that public information plays in promoting support for universal disarmament and in increasing awareness of the relationship between disarmament and development among as broad a public as possible,

Reaffirming the primary role which the General Assembly is to play in elaborating, co-ordinating and harmonizing United Nations policies and activities in the field of information, and recognizing the central and important role of the United Nations Educational, Scientific and Cultural Organization in the field of information and communication, and that the United Nations system as a whole and all others concerned should give that organization adequate support and assistance in the field of information and communication,

Recognizing the importance of the co-ordination and co-operation between the Department of Public Information of the Secretariat, the United Nations Development Programme, the United Nations Educational, Scientific and Cultural Organization and its International Programme for the Development of Communication in the promotion of the establishment of a new world information and communication order,

Fully aware and cognizant of the important contribution which the mass media world-wide can make in enhancing and strengthening peace, deepening international understanding, promoting justice, equality, national independence, development, the exercise of human rights and the establishment of a new world information and communication order,

Noting with satisfaction that, during the observance of the fortieth anniversary of the United Nations, the lasting values of the purposes and principles of the Charter of the United Nations were reconfirmed as a reflection of the high hopes which peoples of the world continue to repose in the United Nations as the most appropriate framework for multilateral co-operation and the pursuit of shared objectives,

Recalling with satisfaction the resolution adopted by the General Assembly, acting as United Nations World Conference for the International Youth Year,

Emphasizing its full support for the International Programme for the Development of Communication, which constitutes an important contribution in the development of the infrastructures of communication in the developing countries,

Conscious that the transfer of technology in the field of information and communication to developing countries is vital for the acceleration of efforts towards the establishment of a new world information and communication order based on justice, freedom and equity,

Expressing its satisfaction with the successful co-ordination and co-operation displayed by the Department of Public Information with the Pool of Non-Aligned News Agencies, as well as with news agencies of other developing and developed countries, and convinced that such efforts have contributed significantly to progress towards a new world information and communication order,

Taking note of the implementation by the Department of Public Information of those parts relevant to public information of the Paris Declaration on Namibia and the Programme of Action on Namibia, as well as those of the Declaration and the Programme of Action contained in the Final Document adopted by the United Nations Council for Namibia at its extraordinary plenary meetings, held at Vienna from 3 to 7 June 1985, in order to develop and further strengthen the dissemination of information regarding the struggle for independence of the people of Namibia, with a view to reaching the broadest possible public by means of more systematic and better co-ordinated information,

Taking note also of the implementation by the Department of Public Information of those parts of the Programme of Action for the Achievement of Palestinian Rights relevant to information, in accordance with General Assembly resolution 39/49 C of 11 December 1984,

Expressing its satisfaction with the work of the Committee on Information as reflected in its report,

Taking note with satisfaction of the report of the Secretary-General on questions relating to information,

Taking note with satisfaction of the report of the Director-General of the United Nations Educational, Scientific and Cultural Organization,

1. *Approves* the report of the Committee on Information and the recommendations contained in paragraph 139 of that report and annexed to the present resolution, as adopted, and affirms the requests and appeals reproduced therein as well as the provisions of General Assembly resolution 39/98 A and urges their full implementation;

2. *Reaffirms* the mandate given to the Committee on Information by the General Assembly in its resolution 34/182;

3. *Requests* the Committee on Information, keeping in mind its mandate, the essential tasks of which are to continue to examine the policies and activities of the Department of Public Information of the Secretariat, and to continue to promote the establishment of a new, more just and effective world information and communication order, to continue to seek the co-operation and active participation of all organizations of the United Nations system, particularly the United Nations Educational, Scientific and Cultural Organization and the International Telecommunication Union, while taking all possible steps to avoid any overlapping of activities on this subject;

4. *Reaffirms* its strong support for the United Nations Educational, Scientific and Cultural Organization, its Constitution and the ideals reflected therein, its activities and for its efforts to further enhance its capabilities with a view to promoting the establishment of a new world information and communication order;

5. *Reiterates its appeal* to Member States, to the information and communication media, both public and private, as well as to non-governmental organizations, to disseminate more widely objective and better balanced information about the activities of the United Nations and, *inter alia*, about the efforts of the developing countries towards their economic, social and cultural progress and about the efforts of the international community to achieve international social justice and economic development, international peace and security, the promotion of disarmament and the progressive elimination of international inequities and tensions; and the promotion of human rights and fundamental freedoms and the right of peoples to self-determination; such dissemination being aimed at achieving a more comprehensive and realistic image of the activities and potential of the United Nations system in all its purposes and endeavours;

6. *Calls upon* the Department of Public Information to continue to give, as a matter of high priority, its full support in promoting and publicizing the noble goals and accomplishments of the United Nations, as the most appropriate forum for multilateral co-operation and for pooling efforts of States to contribute to the quest for a climate of mutual trust, political dialogue and negotiated solutions to the outstanding problems;

7. *Urges* the Department of Public Information to give the widest possible dissemination of information pertaining to the acute world economic problems, particularly to the critical economic situation in Africa, the severe economic difficulties of the least developed countries and the external debt of developing countries, as well as to the adverse effect of the international economic environment on these countries, taking into account the views expressed during the fortieth session on these issues;

8. *Urges* the Department of Public Information to strengthen its co-operation with the Pool of Non-Aligned News Agencies and, in particular, to ensure that its daily dispatches are received by the United Nations Office at Geneva and the United Nations Headquarters in New York;

9. *Urges* the Department of Public Information to take all necessary measures to ensure the dissemination of

appropriate information on the guidelines for further planning and suitable follow-up in the field of youth;

10. *Urges* the Department of Public Information to adequately disseminate in its programmes and information activities the positive results of the World Conference to Review and Appraise the Achievements of the United Nations Decade for Women: Equality, Development and Peace, aimed at the elimination of discrimination and the promotion of the role of women world-wide;

11. *Requests* the Department of Public Information to continue its follow-up programmes in further implementation of those parts relevant to public information of the Paris Declaration on Namibia and the Programme of Action on Namibia, as well as of the Declaration and Programme of Action contained in the Final Document adopted by the United Nations Council for Namibia, and to report thereon to the Committee on Information at its substantive session in 1986;

12. *Requests* the Department of Public Information to cover adequately policies and practices which violate the principles of international law relative to belligerent occupation, in particular the Geneva Convention relative to the Protection of Civilian Persons in Time of War, of 12 August 1949, wherever they occur, especially those policies and practices which frustrate the attainment and exercise of the inalienable and national legitimate rights of the Palestinian people in accordance with the relevant resolutions of the United Nations, and to report thereon to the Committee on Information at its substantive session in 1986;

13. *Urges* the Department of Public Information and the mass media world-wide, pursuant to General Assembly resolutions 34/182 and 35/201, to intensify their activities of dissemination of information with regard to the policies and practices of *apartheid*, taking due account of recent measures and official censorship imposed upon the local and international media related to all aspects of this issue;

14. *Reiterates* the recommendation contained in its resolution 35/201 that additional resources for the Department of Public Information should be commensurate, as appropriate, with the increase in the activities of the United Nations which the Department covers for the purpose of public information, and that the Secretary-General should provide such resources to the Department to this end where needed;

15. *Requests* the Department of Public Information to contribute more effectively, through its training programmes, to the development of human, managerial and technical resources of the mass media from developing countries;

16. *Reaffirms* the importance of the rapidly increasing role of the United Nations public information programmes in fostering public understanding and support of United Nations activities and requests the Department of Public Information to consider the recommendations contained in the report of the Joint Inspection Unit on publications policy and practice in the United Nations system and to report to the Committee on Information at its substantive session in 1986;

17. *Requests* the Secretary-General to report to the Committee on Information, at its substantive session in 1986, on the implementation of all the recommendations contained in the Committee's report and annexed to the present resolution;

18. *Also requests* the Secretary-General to report to the General Assembly at its forty-first session on the implementation of the present resolution and, in particular, on the implementation of all the recommendations contained in the annex to the present resolution;

19. *Takes note* of the report of the Secretary-General on the restructuring of the Radio and Visual Services Division of the Department of Public Information, and requests that additional information be submitted to the Committee on Information at its substantive session in 1986;

20. *Requests* the Committee on Information to report to the General Assembly at its forty-first session;

21. *Decides* to include in the provisional agenda of its forty-first session the item entitled "Questions relating to information".

ANNEX
Recommendations of the Committee on Information

1. The recommendations of the Committee on Information approved by the General Assembly in resolution 39/98 A of 14 December 1984, as well as all the provisions of the resolution, should be reiterated, taking into account the views expressed by delegations at the 100th plenary meeting of the thirty-ninth session of the Assembly on 14 December 1984. Those recommendations should be implemented in full, and the Secretary-General should be requested to report to the Committee on Information at its substantive session in 1986 on measures taken for the implementation of those recommendations and provisions pending implementation.

2. The mandate of the Committee on Information, as set forth in General Assembly resolution 34/182 of 18 December 1979 and reaffirmed in Assembly resolutions 35/201 of 16 December 1980, 36/149 B of 16 December 1981, 37/94 B of 10 December 1982, 38/82 B of 15 December 1983 and 39/98 A of 14 December 1984, should be renewed.

Promotion of the establishment of a new, more just and more effective world information and communication order intended to strengthen peace and international understanding and based on the free circulation and wider and better balanced dissemination of information

3. All countries, the United Nations system as a whole, and all others concerned, should collaborate in the establishment of a new world information and communication order based, *inter alia*, on the free circulation and wider and better balanced dissemination of information, guaranteeing diversity of sources of information and free access to information and, in particular, the urgent need to change the dependent status of the developing countries in the field of information and communication, as the principle of sovereign equality among nations extends also to this field, and intended also to strengthen peace and international understanding, enabling all persons to participate effectively in political, economic, social and cultural life and promoting understanding and friendship among all nations and human rights.

4. The ongoing efforts of the United Nations Educational, Scientific and Cultural Organization to contribute to the clarification, elaboration and application of the concept of a new world information and communication order should be noted. In this regard, resolutions 4/19 of 27 October 1980 and 3.1 of 25 November

1983, which the General Conference of the United Nations Educational, Scientific and Cultural Organization adopted by consensus, should be recalled.

5.   Under the current international climate of political conflicts and economic disorders, the Committee on Information, fully aware and cognizant of the important contribution which the mass media world-wide can make in enhancing and strengthening peace, deepening international understanding, promoting justice, equality, national independence, development, the exercise of human rights and the establishment of a new world information and communication order, recommends that the General Assembly address appeals to the following:

(*a*)   The international media, in order to obtain their support for the efforts of the international community towards global development and, in particular, for the efforts of the developing countries to achieve economic, social and cultural progress;

(*b*)   The United Nations system as a whole to co-operate in a concerted manner, through its information services, in promoting the development activities of the United Nations and, in particular, the improvement of the conditions of the lives of the peoples of the developing countries.

Such appeals should be aimed at achieving a more comprehensive and realistic image of the activities and potential of the United Nations system in all its endeavours, in accordance with the purposes of the Charter of the United Nations.

6.   Article 19 of the Universal Declaration of Human Rights, which provides that everyone has the right to freedom of opinion and expression and that this right includes freedom to hold opinions without interference and to seek, receive and impart information and ideas through any media and regardless of frontiers, and article 29, which stipulates that these rights and freedoms may in no case be exercised contrary to the purposes and principles of the United Nations, should be recalled.

7.   Aware of the existence of structural imbalance in the international distribution of news affecting the two-way flow of news, the Committee on Information recommends that urgent attention should be given to the elimination of existing inequalities in and all other obstacles to the free flow and wider and better balanced dissemination of information, ideas and knowledge by, *inter alia*, diversifying the sources of information as a step towards free and more balanced information and the promotion of the establishment of a new world information and communication order.

8.   The Committee on Information recommends that the need be stressed to ensure and promote the access of the developing countries to communication technology, including communication satellites, modern electronic information systems, informatics and other advanced information and communication facilities with a view to improving their own information and communication systems corresponding to the specific conditions prevailing in each country.

9.   The Committee on Information, while expressing satisfaction with the successful co-ordination and co-operation displayed by the Department of Public Information of the Secretariat with the Pool of Non-Aligned News Agencies, as well as with regional news agencies of developing countries, recommends that the Department of Public Information continue to strengthen this co-operation as it constitutes a concrete step towards a more just and equitable world flow of information, thus

contributing to the establishment of a new world information and communication order.

10.   The Department of Public Information should be urged to monitor, as appropriate, important meetings of the Movement of Non-Aligned Countries, as well as of regional intergovernmental organizations devoted to information and communication questions, in particular the fourth Conference of the Pool of Non-Aligned News Agencies to be held at Havana in 1986.

11.   With regard to its co-operation with the Pool of Non-Aligned News Agencies as well as with the regional news agencies in developing countries, the Department of Public Information should co-operate, as appropriate, with the United Nations Educational, Scientific and Cultural Organization in assisting that organization, within existing resources, in the following activities:

(*a*)   Preparation and implementation of a plan of integrated communication network and regional data and communication centres;

(*b*)   Provision of facilities for meetings on data and communication exchange of the public information bodies of the non-aligned countries.

12.   The United Nations system as a whole, as well as the developed countries, should be urged to co-operate in a concerted manner with the developing countries towards strengthening the information and communication infrastructures of the latter countries, in accordance with the priorities attached to such areas by the developing countries, with a view to enabling them to develop their own information and communication policies freely and independently and in the light of their history, social values and cultural traditions. In this regard, full support for the International Programme for the Development of Communication, which constitutes an important step in the development of these infrastructures, should always be emphasized.

13.   The United Nations system should constantly promote the creation of a climate of confidence in relations among States, as a means of easing tension and facilitating the establishment of a new world information and communication order.

14.   Reaffirming the primary role that the General Assembly is to play in elaborating, co-ordinating and harmonizing United Nations policies and activities in the field of information and recognizing the central and important role of the United Nations Educational, Scientific and Cultural Organization in the field of information and communication, the Committee on Information recommends that the United Nations system as a whole and all others concerned should be urged to give that organization adequate support and assistance in the field of information and communication. The Department of Public Information, in particular, should co-operate more regularly with the United Nations Educational, Scientific and Cultural Organization, especially at the working level, with a view to maximizing the contributions of the Department to the efforts of that organization in promoting the establishment of a new world information and communication order and to disseminating as widely as possible information on the activities of that organization in this respect.

15.   The consolidated study contained in the report of the Secretary-General on the contributions, effects and levels of co-ordination between the United Nations Development Programme, the United Nations Educational,

Scientific and Cultural Organization, its International Programme for the Development of Communication and the International Telecommunication Union in support of the development of information and communication infrastructures in the developing countries should be noted.

16. Recalling its recommendation, as endorsed by the General Assembly in its resolution 39/98 A, the Committee on Information recommends that the Secretary-General should be requested to expedite the convening, jointly with the United Nations Educational, Scientific and Cultural Organization, of a Round Table on a New World Information and Communication Order.

17. The United Nations system, particularly the United Nations Educational, Scientific and Cultural Organization, should aim at providing all possible support and assistance to the developing countries, within existing resources, with regard to their interests and needs in the field of information and to actions already adopted within the United Nations system, including, in particular:

(a) Assistance to developing countries in training journalists and technical personnel and in setting up appropriate educational institutions and research facilities;

(b) Granting of favourable conditions to provide access to developing countries to such communication technology as is requisite for the establishment of a national information and communication system and corresponding to the specific situation of the country concerned;

(c) Creation of conditions that will gradually enable the developing countries to produce the communication technology suited to their national needs, as well as the necessary programme material, specifically for radio and television broadcasting, by using their own resources;

(d) Assistance in establishing telecommunication links at subregional, regional and interregional levels, especially among developing countries, free from conditions of any kind.

18. All the information activities of the Department of Public Information should be guided by and carried out in conformity with the principles of the Charter of the United Nations and the aspiration for a new world information and communication order, as well as conform to the consensus reached among States in resolutions 4/19, 4/21 and 4/22 of 27 October 1980, adopted by the General Conference of the United Nations Educational, Scientific and Cultural Organization and 3.1 of 25 November 1983 adopted by the General Conference on Major Programme III.

19. The Secretary-General should be requested to ensure that the activities of the Department of Public Information, as the focal point of the public information tasks of the United Nations, are strengthened, keeping in view the principles of the Charter of the United Nations and along the lines established in the pertinent resolutions of the General Assembly and the recommendations of the Committee on Information, so as to ensure a more coherent coverage of and a better knowledge about the United Nations and its work, especially in its priority areas, such as those stated in section III, paragraph 1, of Assembly resolution 35/201, including international peace and security, disarmament, peace-keeping and peace-making operations, decolonization, the promotion of human rights, the struggle against *apartheid* and racial discrimination, economic, social and development issues, the integration of women in the struggle for peace and development, the establishment of the new international economic order

and of a new world information and communication order, the work of the United Nations Council for Namibia and programmes on women and youth.

20. The relevant provisions of the Final Act of the Conference on Security and Co-operation in Europe, signed at Helsinki on 1 August 1975, and those of the Concluding Document of the meeting of representatives of the participating States of the Conference on Security and Co-operation in Europe, held at Madrid from 11 November 1980 to 9 September 1983, should be recalled.

21. The Final Documents of the Conference of Ministers of Information of Non-Aligned Countries, held at Jakarta from 26 to 30 January 1984, should be recalled.

22. The Department of Public Information should be requested to continue its co-operation with the Movement of Non-Aligned Countries as well as with intergovernmental organizations and regional organizations with a view to promoting a new world information and communication order.

23. The Conference of Ministers of Information of States members of the Organization of African Unity, held at Addis Ababa in March 1985, which expressed its conviction of the importance of a new world information and communication order, should be noted.

24. In the light of the grave economic situation prevailing in Africa, the Secretary-General should be requested to ensure that the Department of Public Information does its utmost in bringing to the attention of the international community the real dimensions of the plight of the African people and the tremendous efforts of the African countries, with a view to increasing its contribution towards alleviating this human tragedy.

25. The relevant resolution on the question relating to information of the Fourth Islamic Summit Conference, held at Casablanca from 16 to 19 January 1984, should be recalled.

Continuation of examination of United Nations public information policies and activities in the light of the evolution of international relations, particularly during the past two decades, and of the imperatives of the establishment of the new international economic order and of a new world information and communication order

26. In connection with the celebration of the fortieth anniversary of the United Nations, the Department of Public Information should be urged to give appropriate support to the Preparatory Committee for the Fortieth Anniversary of the United Nations in promoting and publicizing the noble goals and accomplishments of the United Nations as a major forum for pooling efforts of States to contribute to the solution of vital world problems.

27. The Committee on Information again stresses that the Department of Public Information should maintain editorial independence and accuracy in all material produced by the Department and should promote, to the greatest extent possible, an informed understanding of the work and purposes of the United Nations among the peoples of the world. The Department should ensure that its output contains objective and equitable information about issues before the Organization, reflecting divergent opinions where they occur.

28. The Department of Public Information should continue to ensure that the daily dispatches of the Pool of Non-Aligned News Agencies that it receives are appropriately utilized in the performance of the public information tasks of the United Nations:

(a) With a view to further promotion and development of functional and mutually beneficial co-operation between the Department and the Pool, the existing arrangements in the Department for the conduct of this co-operation should be established on a more regular basis;

(b) In view of the successful joint coverage by the Pool and the Department of important conferences and other events within the United Nations system, this practice should be continued and further strengthened;

(c) The Department should consider the possibility of utilizing the dispatches received from the Pool to establish a data base on the information and communication facilities in the non-aligned countries.

29. In connection with its annual training programme for journalists and broadcasters from developing countries, the Department of Public Information should continue to allocate the last week of the programme for a visit by them to one of the developing countries that expresses readiness to receive them for the purpose of acquainting themselves with the ways in which information on the United Nations is received and utilized.

30. The Secretary-General should be requested once again to make available to the Committee on Information, as soon as possible, a comprehensive report on the outcome of the activities of the International Telecommunication Union with regard to the World Communications Year.

31. The exchange of information between the Committee on Information and the Commission on Transnational Corporations on matters pertaining to the mandate of the Committee should again be encouraged.

32. The assessment contained in the report of the Secretary-General relating to the acquisition by the United Nations of its own communications satellite in conformity with recommendation 36 made by the Committee on Information to the General Assembly at its thirty-seventh session should be noted, and it would be appropriate to re-examine the question of the acquisition of such a satellite should circumstances permit.

33. The attention of the pertinent organs of the General Assembly and of the United Nations system as a whole should be drawn to the findings of the International Telecommunication Union set forth in its report, especially as concerns the problem of the geostationary orbit reflected, *inter alia*, in paragraphs 33 and 49 of that report, taking into account the needs of the developing countries.

34. The Committee on Information recommends the rejection of the use of the mass media, especially radio broadcasting, to disseminate false or distorted reports as an instrument of hostile propaganda against the sovereignty of other States. In this regard, it stresses that the media should contribute to the fostering of peace, mutual respect, non-interference and self-determination.

35. With regard to the improvement of communication infrastructures, the Committee on Information draws attention to the success attained by the ARABSAT, BRASILSAT, INSAT-1B, MORELOS and PALAPA satellite systems, designed to promote national and regional integration. In this connection, it endorses the execution of satellite projects such as CONDOR by the Andean group of countries. The United Nations and the specialized agencies, in particular those in the financial sector, should support such activities and initiatives.

36. The Department of Public Information should co-operate closely with the United Nations Educational, Scientific and Cultural Organization and the Pool of Non-Aligned News Agencies to organize a workshop, within existing resources, in 1985 for the familiarization of news agencies of developing countries with modern technology of relevance to news agencies and for the standardization of teaching methods and syllabuses and to produce training manuals in various languages for the training centres of the Pool, and should report to the Committee on Information at its substantive session in 1986 on progress made to this effect.

37. In order to enhance awareness and understanding of the lofty objectives of the United Nations, the Department of Public Information should endeavour to promote teaching in the educational institutions of Member States about the structure, principles and aims of the Organization in conformity with the relevant resolutions of the General Assembly and the Economic and Social Council. In order to implement this recommendation, the Department should continue to organize, on a yearly basis, a fellowship programme for educators.

38. The Department of Public Information should be requested, in accordance with the relevant United Nations resolutions, to continue to cover adequately the Israeli policies and practices which violate and affect the human rights of the populations in Arab territories occupied since June 1967, including Jerusalem and the Golan Heights, especially those policies and practices which impede the attainment and exercise of the inalienable national rights of the Palestinian people, and to report thereon to the Committee on Information at its substantive session in 1986.

39. The Secretary-General should be requested once again to maintain the functions of the Middle East/Arabic Unit as the producer of Arabic television and radio programmes, to strengthen and expand this unit to enable it to function in an effective manner and to report to the Committee on Information at its substantive session in 1986 on the measures taken in implementation of this recommendation.

40. In view of the importance of United Nations broadcasting for the European region, further steps should be taken to maintain and enhance the functions of the European Unit in the Radio Service, within existing resources.

41. Taking into account the needs of numerous radio producers and journalists who use French as a working language, and the role of the "blue notes" in the preparation of radio programmes of the United Nations, the Committee on Information requests the Secretary-General to instruct the Radio and Visual Services Division of the Department of Public Information to produce a daily edition, in French, of the messages concerning the activities of the United Nations.

42. The Department of Public Information should be requested anew to use the official languages of the General Assembly adequately in its documents and audio-visual documentation and to arrange accordingly for an appropriate number of staff in order better to inform the public about the activities of the United Nations. It should also make available to the French Language Production Section of the Press and Publications Division of the Department, within existing resources, the means that will allow it consistently to distribute press releases in sufficient quantity to satisfy the needs of the numerous journalists and delegations that use French as a working language.

43. United Nations information centres should continue to assist press and information media in their respective countries in accordance with the mandate given by the General Assembly and, *inter alia*, promote the establishment of a new world information and communication order.

44. While the co-operation between the Department of Public Information and the United Nations Development Programme in the field should be promoted to the maximum extent, it is also important to bear in mind the intrinsic functions of the United Nations information centres as distinct from those of the United Nations development activities. The information centres should redouble their efforts to publicize the activities and achievements of operational activities for development, including those of the United Nations Development Programme, taking into account the priorities determined by the General Assembly.

45. The report of the Secretary-General concerning measures to improve the effectiveness of United Nations information centres should be further noted and the Secretary-General should be encouraged to implement the proposals made by him therein, within existing resources.

46. The United Nations information centres should intensify direct and systematic communication exchange with local information and educational communities in a mutually beneficial way, in accordance with the priorities of the General Assembly and taking into account the areas of particular interest to host countries.

47. In accordance with General Assembly resolution 39/98 A, by which the Assembly acceded to the request of the Government of Benin for the opening of a United Nations information centre at Cotonou, the Secretary-General should be requested to continue negotiations with the authorities in Benin for the rapid opening of the centre, within existing resources, and to report thereon to the Committee on Information at its substantive session in 1986.

48. Taking into account the request of the Government of Poland for the opening of a United Nations information centre at Warsaw, the Secretary-General should be requested to continue to take appropriate steps for the establishment of the centre, within existing resources, and to report thereon to the Committee on Information at its substantive session in 1986.

49. The Department of Public Information should disseminate information concerning the decisions of the United Nations dealing with acts of terrorism in all its forms. In this regard, all the relevant United Nations resolutions and the statement made by the Secretary-General at San Francisco on 26 June 1985 should be recalled.

50. The Department of Public Information should focus on and give wider coverage to the economic, social and development activities of the United Nations system aimed at achieving a more comprehensive image of the activities and potential of the system, taking into account the priorities set by the General Assembly, particularly in the light of the fortieth anniversary of the United Nations.

51. Note should be taken of the assessment contained in the report of the Secretary-General of the experimental daily short-wave radio broadcasts from Headquarters, pending the submission to the Committee on Information of the final report on the results of the experiment.

52. The Secretary-General should continue his efforts to develop a system for monitoring and evaluating the effectiveness of the activities of the Department of Public Information, particularly in the priority areas determined by the General Assembly.

53. Future reports of the Department of Public Information to the Committee on Information, in particular on new programmes or on the expansion of existing programmes, should contain:

(a) More adequate information on the output of the Department in respect of each topic included in its work programme, which forms the basis of its programme budget;

(b) The costs of the activities undertaken in respect of each topic;

(c) More adequate information on target audiences, end-use of the Department's products and analysis of feedback data received by the Department;

(d) The Department's evaluation of the effectiveness of its different programmes and activities;

(e) A statement detailing the priority level that the Secretary-General has attached to current or future activities of the Department in documents dealing with such activities.

54. The Department of Public Information should improve, within existing resources, its data-collection procedures with regard to the actual use made by redisseminators of materials distributed by the Department and its information centres and submit a report to the Committee on Information at its substantive session in 1986 on progress made in this area.

55. The steps taken by the Department of Public Information in redressing the imbalance in its staff should be noted. The Department should continue to intensify its efforts to that end and the Secretary-General should be requested to take urgent steps to increase the representation of underrepresented developing countries and of other underrepresented groups of countries, especially at the senior levels, in conformity with the relevant provisions of the Charter of the United Nations, and to submit a report to the Committee on Information at its substantive session in 1986.

56. Member States should be called upon once again to make voluntary contributions to the United Nations Trust Fund for Economic and Social Information.

57. The assessment contained in the report of the Secretary-General on the present system of charging Member States and the media for video tapes, audio tapes and news photographs of important United Nations events should be noted, and the Department of Public Information should report to the Committee on Information at its substantive session in 1986 on that subject with a view to reducing appropriately the final cost of these materials and spreading overtime charges legitimately incurred in an equitable way so as to enable the media in the Member States, particularly in the developing countries, to give wider publicity to the aims and activities of the United Nations.

58. The interim report of the Secretary-General entitled "The Department of Public Information as the Focal Point for the Formulation and Implementation of Information Activities of the United Nations" should be noted and the Secretary-General should be requested to submit his final report in the light of the ongoing consultations within the Secretariat on the role of the Department with respect to all information activities of the United

Nations. The Committee on Information once again recommends that the proliferation of information units in the Secretariat independent of the Department should be discouraged.

59.   The Committee on Information takes note of the report on the review of the distribution of taped radio programmes produced by the Department of Public Information in New York and requests the Department to take steps to improve their distribution and to report to the Committee at its substantive session in 1986 on the implementation of the recommendations contained in that report.

60.   The operations of the Non-Governmental Liaison Services (Geneva and New York) as voluntarily funded inter-agency projects reaching specific target audiences in the industrialized countries on international development issues should be continued on a stable financial basis through United Nations participation in these services. As with *Development Forum*, it is essential that United Nations financial participation, from the regular budget, should be ensured in the next biennium. Furthermore, the Secretary-General should be requested to urge all specialized agencies to make long-term contributions to the financing of these services, thereby stressing their inter-agency character.

61.   The Joint United Nations Information Committee, as the essential instrument for inter-agency co-ordination and co-operation in the field of public information, should be further strengthened and given more responsibility for the public information activities of the entire United Nations system.

62.   The quality, usefulness and coverage of the daily press release and the weekly news summary issued by the Department of Public Information in all working languages should be further enhanced and improved in view of the important public information tasks that they can perform. Services provided at the Press Section of the Department both for the media and the delegations should be improved. The Department should continue to co-operate closely with and provide assistance to the United Nations Correspondents Association.

63.   The Department of Public Information should improve, within existing resources, the timely distribution of its materials to subscribers and United Nations information centres, particularly the *UN Chronicle*, in all languages, a major source of information on the United Nations to its recipients.

64.   The report on the programme and activities of the Joint United Nations Information Committee should be noted, particularly in regard to *Development Forum* as the only inter-agency publication of the United Nations system that concentrates on development issues, and the Secretary-General should, while continuing his efforts to secure a sound and independent basis for the periodical, make such arrangements as necessary, through the regular budget, to ensure its continued publication. The resources of the United Nations system should be pooled in support of *Development Forum* and *Development Business* and any attempt in the United Nations system to duplicate the functions performed by these publications should be avoided. All specialized agencies and other organizations of the United Nations system should be urged to contribute to the financing of these system-wide publications, thereby recognizing their inter-agency character.

65.   The Secretary-General should continue to ensure that *Development Forum* retains its editorial policy of intellectual independence, thus enabling this publication to continue to serve as a world-wide forum in which diverse opinions on issues related to economic and social development can be freely expressed.

66.   The Secretary-General should be encouraged to continue and intensify his efforts to explore all possibilities of securing the adequate resources for the continuation of the *World Newspaper Supplement* project.

67.   The World Disarmament Campaign should give full consideration to the role of the mass media as the most effective way to promote in world public opinion a climate of understanding, confidence and co-operation conducive to peace and disarmament, the enhancement of human rights and development. Within the World Disarmament Campaign and Disarmament Week, the Department of Public Information should fulfil the role assigned to it by the General Assembly by utilizing its expertise and resources in public information to ensure its maximum effectiveness.

68.   The Department of Public Information should be requested to implement fully, within existing resources, the provisions of General Assembly resolution 38/82 B relating to the work programme of the Caribbean Unit and the Secretary-General should be requested to report to the Committee on Information at its substantive session in 1986 on the measures taken in implementation of this recommendation.

69.   The conclusions and recommendations adopted by the Special Committee on the Situation with regard to the Implementation of the Declaration on the Granting of Independence to Colonial Countries and Peoples at its extraordinary session, held at Tunis from 13 to 17 May 1985 to celebrate the twenty-fifth anniversary of the Declaration, should be noted. In this regard, the Secretary-General should be requested to intensify his efforts, within existing resources, in order to alert world public opinion against the illegal occupation of Namibia and the policies of *apartheid* of the régime of South Africa and to continue to disseminate as widely as possible information relating to the struggle of the oppressed peoples of South Africa and Namibia.

70.   In view of the concerns expressed by several delegations regarding the possible implications on productivity and effectiveness of the proposed restructuring of the Radio and Visual Services Division and taking into account the necessity of strengthening the Professional staff, the Committee on Information recommends that the Secretary-General be requested to submit a written report on the subject to the General Assembly at its fortieth session. Pending submission of the report and a decision thereon, action on the proposed restructuring should be postponed.

General Assembly resolution 40/164 A

16 December 1985   Meeting 118   121-19-8 (recorded vote)

Approved by Special Political Committee (A/40/1024) by recorded vote (96-18-6), 6 December (meeting 46); draft by Yugoslavia for Group of 77 (A/SPC/40/L.29/Rev.1); agenda item 78.

Meeting numbers. GA 40th session: SPC 29-39, 45, 46; plenary 118.

Recorded vote in Assembly as follows:

In favour: Afghanistan, Algeria, Antigua and Barbuda, Argentina, Bahamas, Bahrain, Bangladesh, Benin, Bhutan, Bolivia, Botswana, Brazil, Brunei Darussalam, Bulgaria, Burkina Faso, Burma, Burundi, Byelorussian SSR, Cameroon, Cape Verde, Central African Republic, Chad, Chile, China, Colombia, Congo, Costa Rica, Cuba, Cyprus, Czechoslovakia, Democratic Kampuchea, Democratic Yemen, Djibouti, Dominica, Dominican Republic, Ecuador, Egypt, El Salvador, Equatorial Guinea, Ethiopia, Fiji, Gabon, Gambia, German Democratic Republic, Guatemala, Guinea, Guinea-Bissau, Guyana, Honduras, Hungary, India, Indonesia, Iran, Iraq, Ivory

Coast, Jamaica, Jordan, Kenya, Kuwait, Lao People's Democratic Republic, Lebanon, Lesotho, Liberia, Libyan Arab Jamahiriya, Madagascar, Malawi, Malaysia, Maldives, Mali, Malta, Mauritania, Mauritius, Mexico, Mongolia, Morocco, Mozambique, Nepal, Nicaragua, Niger, Nigeria, Oman, Pakistan, Panama, Peru, Philippines, Poland, Qatar, Romania, Rwanda, Saint Lucia, Saint Vincent and the Grenadines, Sao Tome and Principe, Saudi Arabia, Senegal, Seychelles, Sierra Leone, Singapore, Somalia, Sri Lanka, Sudan, Suriname, Swaziland, Syrian Arab Republic, Thailand, Togo, Trinidad and Tobago, Tunisia, Uganda, Ukrainian SSR, USSR, United Arab Emirates, United Republic of Tanzania, Uruguay, Vanuatu, Venezuela, Viet Nam, Yemen, Yugoslavia, Zaire, Zambia, Zimbabwe.

Against: Australia, Belgium, Canada, Denmark, Finland, France, Germany, Federal Republic of, Grenada, Iceland, Israel, Italy, Japan, Luxembourg, Netherlands, Norway, Portugal, Sweden, United Kingdom, United States.

Abstaining: Austria, Barbados, Greece, Haiti, Ireland, New Zealand, Spain, Turkey.

Most of the States that explained their votes in the Special Political Committee either found the resolution unacceptable or regretted that it did not qualify the references to a new world information and communication order with a phrase that it was seen as "an evolving and continuous process". These included Australia, Austria, Canada, Japan, Luxembourg (for the 10 European Community members, Portugal and Spain), Norway (on behalf also of Denmark, Finland, Iceland and Sweden) and the United States. That qualification, Norway said, had been reached by consensus and used in resolutions adopted by the UNESCO General Conference in 1983 and 1985. The United States regarded it as essential to an understanding of the concept of a new order that was not static and could not be codified. While Uruguay felt that the tenth preambular paragraph citing the UNESCO resolutions was a tacit admission of the qualification, Luxembourg said that that single reference would not suffice to make up for the omission. Austria would have liked inclusion of the qualification, whereas Mexico had not, solely to facilitate a consensus.

Paragraphs 1 and 14 also elicited objections. Besides reiterating the Nordic countries' reservations on article 20 of the International Covenant on Civil and Political Rights, cited in the third preambular paragraph, Norway said they could not support paragraph 1, as it took no account of the views they had expressed in the Committee on Information, thus tilting the resolution against their fundamental constitutional and political principles. Paragraph 1 was for the same reason unacceptable to Luxembourg, as was paragraph 14, given the repeated calls for economy measures. Through restraint and imagination, rather than additional resources, DPI could achieve maximum efficiency and ensure the wisest possible use of the considerable resources already at its disposal, Luxembourg added. Japan made similar observations. Canada, which also objected to the two paragraphs, pointed out that the Assembly had stated on several occasions that UNESCO played the main role in establishing a new information and communication order; it could thus not support attempts to reopen the debate on that subject when UNESCO had already succeeded in laying the groundwork for a compromise.

The United States said it objected to paragraph 1, calling for implementation of recommendations against which it had voted, as well as paragraph 14. It believed, moreover, that divisive political issues had no place in a resolution on information and therefore could not accept the paragraph on Palestine. It observed that the considerable increase in negative votes indicated that, despite efforts by the Group of 77 developing countries to overcome differences, there had been no real accommodation of the Western countries' main concerns. Argentina, whose vote in favour was without reservation, observed that comparing the voting results with those of 1984 on the same subject could be misleading, for while the current numbers might seem less positive, constructive efforts had nevertheless been made. Turkey said that although it had not been possible to do more to overcome the difficulties encountered, it hoped the spirit of co-operation that prevailed during the negotiations would be demonstrated in the future.

While Austria found encouraging elements in the resolution's tenth preambular paragraph, it could not accept recommendation 34. Uruguay called that recommendation incompatible with the right to freedom of opinion and expression—the corner-stone of all other freedoms.

Albania said its non-participation in the voting was based on its position on the principle of sovereign equality of nations in the field of information and on its support of developing countries' efforts to establish information and communication systems independent of the media of the two super-Powers. It had reservations on the paragraphs referring to the Conference on Security and Co-operation in Europe, which it characterized as a farce mounted by the super-Powers to strengthen their zones of influence in Europe.

In the plenary, Colombia expressed its concern that a consensus resolution had not been achieved. It called for greater efforts towards consensus in the next year, saying that in such a delicate matter as a new information order, genuine international co-operation, rather than confrontation, should be sought.

The Assembly took various actions on information dissemination in 1985. It noted that the Secretary-General had made permanent his instructions to the information centres and regional commissions to give wide publicity to the World Disarmament Campaign and to adapt as far as possible United Nations materials to local languages (**resolution 40/151 B**). It requested that DPI and the United Nations system fully co-operate with the Special Committee against *Apartheid* and the United Nations Centre against *Apartheid* in disseminating information on the evils of *apartheid*, and appealed to Governments, the media, NGOs and individuals to co-operate with the United Nations in that endeavour (**40/64 D**). The Secretary-General was asked to assist the Special Committee, through DPI and the Centre, in disseminating information on Israeli–South African collaboration (**40/64 E**). He was also asked to ensure DPI's co-operation with the Division for Palestinian Rights to enable it to cover adequately the various aspects of the Palestine question (**40/96 B**). DPI was asked, in co-operation with the Committee on the Exercise of the Inalienable Rights of the Palestinian People, to continue its special information programme on the question for 1986-1987 (**40/96 C**).

The Assembly asked the Secretary-General to ensure that DPI, in disseminating information on Namibia, followed the policy guidelines laid down by the United Nations Council for Namibia; it asked that DPI assist the Council in implementing its information dissemination programme, in particular specific activities for 1986, so as to mobilize public support for Namibia's independence (**40/97 D**). It also requested the Secretary-General to continue, through the media at his disposal, to give wide and continuous publicity to the United Nations work on decolonization (**40/58**). Finally, the Assembly asked him to continue, through DPI, an intensified publicity campaign to inform world public opinion of the military activities in colonial Territories that were impeding implementation of the Declaration on the Granting of Independence to Colonial Countries and Peoples (**decision 40/415**).

DPI activities

In 1985, DPI continued to act as a focal point for formulating and implementing United Nations information activities, enhancing and co-ordinating the work of the various media at its disposal, including radio, visual and publications services, and information centres (for details, see below under the respective headings). Conscious of the Committee on Information's concern for the need to underline that role, the Under-Secretary-General for Public Information, in an oral report to the Committee,[2] stated that consultations were continuing in the Secretariat that might eventually lead to a Secretariat-wide meeting to consider DPI's role with respect to all United Nations information activities and to editorial policy with respect to intergovernmental bodies.

A number of written reports on improvements to various aspects of DPI operations were before the Committee in response to its 1984 recommendations that had been approved by the General Assembly.[12]

The reports included an April 1985 Secretariat note,[13] stating that the current system of charging Member States and the media for video tapes, audio tapes and news photographs of important United Nations events was under review by DPI. The exercise was aimed at reducing the costs of those materials to enable the media, particularly in developing countries, to give wider publicity to such events. Another report[14] dealt with the improvement of data-collection procedures to monitor and evaluate use made by redisseminators (the media, NGOs, government agencies, schools and universities) of DPI materials—such as taped radio programmes, the *World Chronicle* television programme, daily short-wave radio programmes, the bimonthly *Development Forum* and its fortnightly business edition, *Development Business*—as well as with evaluation of the annual editors' round table and the 1975-1981 fellowship programme for educators. The Secretariat also reported[15] on progress made to redress the geographical imbalance in DPI staffing by the recruitment of nationals from developing countries.

As requested by the Assembly in 1984,[12] DPI undertook extensive programmes to publicize the World Disarmament Campaign and Disarmament Week (see pp. 92 and 95), the Organization's fortieth anniversary (see p. 403) and the twenty-fifth anniversary of the Declaration on the Granting of Independence to Colonial Countries and Peoples (see TRUSTEESHIP AND DECOLONIZATION, Chapter I). It continued its public information activities relating to the Palestine question (see p. 272), the African crisis (see p. 499) and Namibia (see TRUSTEESHIP AND DECOLONIZATION, Chapter III). For the participants of its 1985 training programme for journalists and broadcasters, DPI scheduled a one-week field visit (Belgrade, Yugoslavia, 27 October–2 November) to acquaint them with how United Nations information was received and utilized. DPI took other action in response to recommendations relating to radio services and information centres (see below).

The foregoing activities were outlined by the Secretary-General in a September report to the Assembly.[16]

Following its review of United Nations public information policies and activities, the Committee on Information, in its 1985 recommendations to the General Assembly,[2] stressed anew that DPI should maintain editorial independence and accuracy, promote an informed understanding of the United Nations work and purposes, ensure appropriate use of daily dispatches from the Pool of Non-Aligned News Agencies, and acquaint journalists and broadcasters with how United Nations information was received and used. The Secretary-General should continue efforts to develop a system for monitoring and evaluating DPI activities, especially in priority areas. DPI reports were to contain information on: output and costs for each programme element, target audiences and end-use of products, programme evaluation, and priority levels attached to current and future activities. DPI was to continue to improve data-collection procedures on the use of its materials, to correct the geographical imbalance in its staffing, and to establish a final pricing policy for its audio and video tapes and news photographs.

Recommendations called for a final report on the role of DPI as a focal point for all United Nations information activities and discouraged the proliferation of independent information units within the Secretariat. Others called for improvement of the daily press releases and the weekly news summary, of services to the media and the delegations in general, and of the timely distribution of materials, particularly the *UN Chronicle*, to subscribers and information centres.

Radio and visual services

In 1985, a proposal was put forward to the General Assembly to restructure the Radio and Visual Services Division of DPI into two divisions, the Visual Services Division and the Radio Services Division. The restructuring was proposed in view of the differences in technique of the two media involved. The operations of the two services were essentially separate, and, as a rule, their staffs were not easily interchangeable. It was envisaged that the proposed restructuring would enable DPI better to complement national and international broadcasting in the production of radio and audio-visual materials, and to ensure more effective management of each of these two expanding activities.

The proposal was included in the proposed programme budget for the 1986-1987 biennium, and was described in a report by the Secretary-General[17] submitted in response to a 1985 recommendation of the Committee on Information, later approved by the General Assembly in **resolution 40/164 A**.

The Advisory Committee on Administrative and Budgetary Questions (ACABQ) had no objection to the financial consequences of the restructuring, provided that the proposal was accepted by the Assembly.[18] The Committee for Programme and Co-ordination (CPC)[19] recommended that the Secretary-General, in arriving at a decision, should take into account the views expressed by CPC members.

As requested by CPC in 1983[20] and by the Committee on Information in 1984,[21] the Secretary-General submitted to the Committee a report[22] reviewing the distribution of United Nations taped radio programmes to determine their timeliness and utilization, covering 49 radio programmes (in 20 languages) distributed on tape to 1,156 addresses in some 160 countries; an average of 11,434 tapes and cassettes had been sent out each month. Of the questionnaires sent, 351 were returned in time for use in the review. About 66 per cent of respondents reported receiving their programmes regularly and on time for broadcasting. Of the 49 taped programmes, 27 were reported as being broadcast in their entirety; most of the remainder were excerpted for broadcast. No mention was made at all of 12 programmes.

The survey revealed the need for: a rational global pattern for distribution; procedures for changing or introducing programme titles, and notifying users; a centralized and computerized mailing list; and systems for determining the speediest channel of delivery, for marking each reel or cassette as to content and specifications, and for expediting dispatch. There was need for co-ordination between the information centres, as channels for distribution, and with the Radio Service, and for close liaison with users, including promotion.

As called for by the Committee in 1984,[12] the Secretariat, in an April 1985 note,[23] reported that DPI was conducting an experiment to determine whether daily short-wave radio programmes from United Nations Headquarters could attract a significant number of listeners during the inter-Assembly period. Begun on 4 February for six months, the experiment was limited to Africa (except for the southern region). Using rented facilities from the Voice of America, news and documentary feature programmes were being broadcast in English and French for half an hour each, five days a week. To stimulate feedback, the experiment had been preceded by a broad publicity effort in the pilot region. The results of the experiment were to to be submitted to the Committee in 1986.

Also, as recommended by the Committee in 1983,[24] the Secretary-General reported[16] that the Asian Unit of the Radio Service had undertaken radio programming in Bengali and Indonesian on a weekly basis.

In its 1985 recommendations approved by Assembly **resolution 40/164 A**, the Committee[2] renewed its request to maintain the functions of the Middle East and Arabic Unit as the producer of Arabic television and radio programmes, and to strengthen and expand the Unit. It called for further enhancing the European Unit in the Radio Service and for the production of a daily edition in French of messages concerning United Nations activities. DPI should be requested anew to use adequately the official languages of the Assembly in its documents and audio-visual documentation and be given the means to distribute sufficient press releases in French to meet the needs of journalists and delegations that use French.

UN information centres and services

In 1985, the Secretary-General reported[16] that DPI, in response to a 1984 General Assembly request,[12] had begun consultations with Benin and Poland on the opening of information centres at Cotonou and Warsaw through redeployment of resources. In response to 1983 requests,[24] it reopened the Centre at Jakarta, Indonesia, on 20 August, and pursued consultations with Cameroon and Burundi on their requests for full-time directors for the centres in their capitals.

The Committee on Information made a series of recommendations in 1985[2] concerning information centres. These called for the centres to continue to assist press and information media in promoting the establishment of a new world information and communication order, to redouble efforts to publicize the achievements of United Nations operational activities for development, and to intensify communication exchange with local information and educational communities. The Secretary-General should continue negotiations for opening centres at Cotonou and Warsaw. The Committee also recommended that the 1984 report of the Secretary-General on measures to improve the centres' effectiveness[25] should be further noted and that he should be encouraged to implement them within existing resources.

These recommendatons were approved by Assembly **resolution 40/164 A**.

Yearbook of the United Nations

ACABQ consideration. In 1985, ACABQ[18] examined a provision for continued temporary assistance to reduce the backlog in the publication of the *Yearbook of the United Nations*, included in the proposed programme budget for the biennium 1986-1987 for DPI. The provision called for continuation of 24 work-months each of general temporary assistance at the P-3 and General Service levels.

ACABQ noted that a report on adherence to the production schedule outlined by the Secretary-General in 1983[26] revealed a failure to reduce the backlog; moreover, delay in production had increased, due mainly to the decision to have the *Yearbook* staff draft the texts (beginning with the 1981 edition), instead of editing and revising departmental submissions, and to widening the scope of dcbatc coverage. ACABQ regarded these initiatives as premature. Noting that the backlog would not be entirely eliminated until June 1995, ACABQ said such delay was unacceptable and felt that the *Yearbook* must be issued on a timely basis if it was to be used more widely by the general public.

ACABQ therefore recommended that DPI issue abbreviated editions until the backlog had been eliminated. It was of the opinion that neither the quality nor the value of the *Yearbook* as an objective reference work need be diminished as a result, provided that care was taken, *inter alia*, to supply sufficient references to more detailed sources of information. Subject to its observations, ACABQ recommended acceptance of the request for temporary assistance and asked the Secretary-General to submit to it in 1987 a further report on the implementation of its recommendation for abbreviated editions.

Report of the Secretary-General. In a November 1985 report,[27] the Secretary-General reviewed the current format of the *Yearbook* with a view to developing a new format to make the book more usable and accessible. Submitted in response to a 1983 General Assembly request,[28] the report examined the purposes which the *Yearbook* was intended to serve, analysed four different formats to determine which would best fulfil those purposes and discussed possible changes of content and presentation within the selected format. The report also described several changes introduced on an experimental basis in the 1981 edition and those retained for the 1982 edition.

The review led to the following conclusions. The three guiding elements of the format—organization of information to permit ready retrieval, comprehensiveness implying objective recording of United Nations activities, and comprehensibility for a non-specialist—remained valid. A format essentially similar to the current one should be retained, and the submission of texts by substantive departments should be reinstituted.

The Secretary-General proposed that the ACABQ recommendation for abbreviated editions be carried out, beginning with the 1983 edition, until the backlog was eliminated, while retaining a format similar to that of the 1982 edition.

GENERAL ASSEMBLY ACTION

On 18 December 1985, acting without vote on the recommendation of the Fifth (Administrative and Budgetary) Committee, the General Assembly adopted **section I of resolution 40/252** on questions relating to the proposed programme budget for the 1986-1987 biennium.

> *Yearbook of the United Nations*
> [*The General Assembly*,]
> *Having considered* the report of the Secretary-General and the relevant observations of the Advisory Committee on Administrative and Budgetary Questions as contained in paragraphs 27.35 to 27.43 of chapter II of its first report on the proposed programme budget for the biennium 1986-1987,
> 1. *Takes note* of the report of the Secretary-General;
> 2. *Concurs* with the observations of the Advisory Committee as contained in paragraphs 27.42 and 27.43 of its report;
> 3. *Decides* that the *Yearbook of the United Nations* shall be issued in abbreviated editions until such time as the backlog in its publication has been eliminated;
> . . .

General Assembly resolution 40/252, section I

18 December 1985   Meeting 122   Adopted without vote

Approved by Fifth Committee (A/40/1069) without objection, 18 November (meeting 39); oral proposal by ACABQ Chairman; agenda item 116.

Co-ordination in the UN system

JUNIC activities. The Joint United Nations Information Committee, the essential instrument for inter-agency co-ordination and co-operation in public information in the United Nations system—charged also with elaborating longer-term indicative planning and joint action—held its twelfth session at Rome, Italy, from 16 to 19 April 1985.[29]

At that session, JUNIC discussed the work of the Committee on Information in 1984 and subsequent developments in the General Assembly on information questions, reviewed the public information aspects of the critical situation in Africa and approved several recommendations aimed at coordinating information activities and ceremonies in observance of the fortieth anniversary of the United Nations (see p. 403). It decided to inform the World Bank of its concern over the Bank's decision to launch a new subscription service, the International Business Opportunities Service, which could compete with *Development Business*, the business edition of *Development Forum*.

The role, function and place of the Non-Governmental Liaison Services (Geneva and New York) were examined, with a view to strengthening their institutional framework. JUNIC approved most of the recommendations of the Administrative Committee on Co-ordination (ACC) for a common information strategy for the United Nations system.

Other topics discussed concerned: JUNIC participation in Expo '85 (Tsukuba, Japan) and Expo '86 (Vancouver, Canada); the possibility of incorporating special training courses/seminars on development issues in the 1986 United Nations Staff Development Programme; the recommendations of the JUNIC *Ad Hoc* Working Group on Audio-Visual Matters at its 15 April meeting and the continued publication of the newsletter on audio-visual matters, *Playback*; recent and planned meetings of a consortium of some 26 national broadcasting networks on "Agenda for a Small Planet", a series of television films on subjects of special importance to the international community; continuance of reportage missions; and improvement of the roster of journalists taking part in United Nations-organized media events.

JUNIC approved its plan of action for 1986-1987, excepting a proposal that, from 1986, members commit 1 per cent of their public information budgets to finance agreed joint projects.

The action plan included such projects as publication of *Development Forum;* maintenance of the Non-Governmental Liaison Services; development education; meetings to agree on co-operative actions with information services of industrialized countries; ensuring a unified United Nations presence at international expositions; audio-visual activities; assistance in development-support communication planning and activities; and system-wide public information on international years and special events. Other projects concerned joint inter-agency activities on the emergency situation in Africa; development of the third phase of "Agenda for a Small Planet", addressing disarmament; follow-up of the recommendations of the 1982 JUNIC report on public perceptions of the United Nations system,[30] as endorsed by the Committee on Information,[31] aimed at improving monitoring and response to the media; implementation of a common strategy to reinvigorate support for development assistance and United Nations operational activities; and joint reportage missions.

Action by the Committee on Information. The main issues dealt with by JUNIC at its April session were reviewed by the Committee on Information[2] in June. The Committee recommended to the General Assembly that JUNIC be given more responsibility for the public information activities of the entire United Nations system, and that operation of the Non-Governmental Liaison Services and of *Development Forum* be ensured through support from the regular budget and through a pooling of system-wide resources. The Committee also called for securing adequate resources for the continuation of the *World Newspaper Supplement* project.

These recommendations were approved by the Assembly in **resolution 40/164 A**.

ACC decision. Following consideration of the JUNIC report, ACC, on 29 October,[32] expressed the wish that consultations be pursued with the World Bank with a view to continuing assistance for the production of *Development Forum*, while obviating competition for subscriptions to the Bank's International Business Opportunities Service and to *Development Business*, the main source of financial support for *Development Forum*.

REFERENCES

[1]YUN 1978, p. 1043, GA res. 33/115 C, 18 Dec. 1978. [2]A/40/21. [3]YUN 1984, p. 352, GA res. 39/98 B, 14 Dec. 1984. [4]A/40/667. [5]A/41/582/Add.1. [6]A/40/173-S/17033. [7]A/40/276-S/17138. [8]A/40/854-S/17610 & Corr.1. [9]A/40/980. [10]A/40/272. [11]A/40/323. [12]YUN 1984, p. 356, GA res. 39/98 A, 14 Dec. 1984. [13]A/AC.198/87. [14]A/AC.198/90. [15]A/AC.198/86. [16]A/40/617. [17]A/40/841. [18]A/40/7. [19]A/40/38. [20]YUN 1983, p. 383. [21]YUN 1984, p. 365. [22]A/AC.198/99. [23]A/AC.198/88. [24]YUN 1983, p. 366, GA res. 38/82 B, 15 Dec. 1983. [25]YUN 1984, p. 364. [26]YUN 1983, p. 380. [27]A/C.5/40/37. [28]YUN 1983, p. 381, GA res. 38/234, sect. VI, 20 Dec. 1983. [29]ACC/1985/16. [30]YUN 1982, p. 575. [31]YUN 1983, p. 385. [32]ACC/1985/DEC/16-29 (dec. 1985/25).

Departmental News Service

On 18 December 1985, the General Assembly adopted, without vote, on the Fifth Committee's recommendation, **section XI of resolution 40/252**.

News Service of the Department of Political and Security Council Affairs

[*The General Assembly . . .*]

Decides to maintain for 1986 the current staffing resources of the News Service of the Department of Political and Security Council Affairs pending consideration by the Committee for Programme and Co-ordination and the General Assembly of the Secretary-General's report on the evaluation of the News Service;

. . .

General Assembly resolution 40/252, section XI
18 December 1985   Meeting 122   Adopted without vote

Approved by Fifth Committee (A/40/1069) without objection, 14 December (meeting 65); oral proposal by Trinidad and Tobago, orally amended by Sweden; agenda item 116.
Meeting numbers. GA 40th session: 5th Committee 28, 62, 65; plenary 122.

The oral amendment by Sweden limited the action to 1986.

Earlier, an oral proposal by the United Kingdom—that the staff allocated to the News Service revert to the original level of seven posts pending consideration by CPC and the Assembly in 1986 of a study currently under way—was rejected by a recorded vote of 38 to 19, with 27 abstentions. The Committee did not take action on an oral proposal by Nigeria to request the Secretary-General to ensure the editorial integrity, objectivity, balanced reflection of developments relevant to the maintenance of international peace and security, and operational efficiency of the News Service by including more information sources from developing countries, and to provide guidelines for the operation of the Service.

Radiation effects

Pursuant to a 1984 General Assembly request,[1] the United Nations Scientific Committee on the Effects of Atomic Radiation continued its work, including its co-ordinating activities, to increase knowledge of the levels, effects and risks of ionizing radiation from all sources. It also continued to review the main problems in the field of radiation.

At its thirty-fourth session (Vienna, Austria, 10-14 June 1985),[2] the Committee's discussions were based on a number of scientific documents on topics in three main areas: physics, biology and genetics. The topics in physics were on natural radiation sources including those technologically modified; exposures from nuclear explosions and from the production of nuclear-weapon materials; current exposures received globally from the production of nuclear power and the predicted radiological impact of the nuclear fuel cycle up to the year 2050; and medical irradiation. In biology, they included radiation-induced cancer; biological effects of pre-natal irradiation; early effects of high radiation doses; and scientific uncertainties associated with the assessment of radiation risk per unit dose, mostly somatic. The various topics in genetics were related to the hereditary effects of radiation.

The discussions aimed at improving the documents that were to serve as background material for future Committee reports to the Assembly. Since the reports' quality and completeness depended on the availability of information on the topics dealt with, the Committee renewed its call on Member

States, United Nations organizations and other international and national scientific bodies to make such information available.

In carrying out its activities, the Committee continued to receive co-operation from the United Nations Environment Programme, the International Atomic Energy Agency and the World Health Organization, as well as from two scientific organizations: the International Commission on Radiation Units and Measurements, and the International Commission on Radiological Protection.

GENERAL ASSEMBLY ACTION

On 16 December 1985, acting without vote on the recommendation of the Special Political Committee, the General Assembly adopted **resolution 40/160**.

Effects of atomic radiation
The General Assembly,

Recalling its resolution 913(X) of 3 December 1955, by which it established the United Nations Scientific Committee on the Effects of Atomic Radiation, and its subsequent resolutions on the subject, including resolution 39/94 of 14 December 1984, by which it, *inter alia*, requested the Scientific Committee to continue its work,

Taking note with appreciation of the report of the United Nations Scientific Committee on the Effects of Atomic Radiation,

Reaffirming the desirability of the Scientific Committee continuing its work,

Concerned about the potentially harmful effects on present and future generations, resulting from the levels of radiation to which man is exposed,

Conscious of the continued need to examine and compile information about atomic and ionizing radiation and to analyse its effects on man and his environment,

Bearing in mind the decision of the Scientific Committee to submit, as soon as the relevant studies are completed, shorter reports with scientific supporting documents on the specialized topics mentioned by the Committee,

1. *Commends* the United Nations Scientific Committee on the Effects of Atomic Radiation for the valuable contribution it has been making in the course of the past thirty years, since its inception, to wider knowledge and understanding of the levels, effects and risks of atomic radiation and for fulfilling its original mandate with scientific authority and independence of judgement;

2. *Notes with satisfaction* the continued and growing scientific co-operation between the Scientific Committee and the United Nations Environment Programme;

3. *Requests* the Scientific Committee to continue its work, including its important co-ordinating activities, to increase knowledge of the levels, effects and risks of ionizing radiation from all sources;

4. *Endorses* the Scientific Committee's intentions and plans for its future activities of scientific review and assessment on behalf of the General Assembly;

5. *Requests* the Scientific Committee to continue at its next session the review of the important problems in the field of radiation and to report thereon to the General Assembly at its forty-first session;

6. *Requests* the United Nations Environment Programme to continue providing support for the effective conduct of the Scientific Committee's work and for the dissemination of its findings to the General Assembly, the scientific community and the public;

7. *Expresses its appreciation* for the assistance rendered to the Scientific Committee by Member States, the specialized agencies, the International Atomic Energy Agency and non-governmental organizations, and invites them to increase their co-operation in this field;

8. *Invites* Member States, the organizations of the United Nations system and non-governmental organizations concerned to provide further relevant data about doses, effects and risks from various sources of radiation, which would greatly help in the preparation of the Scientific Committee's future reports to the General Assembly.

General Assembly resolution 40/160

16 December 1985   Meeting 118   Adopted without vote

Approved by SPC (A/40/806) without vote, 7 October (meeting 4); 30-nation draft (A/SPC/40/L.2); agenda item 74.
Sponsors: Argentina, Australia, Austria, Canada, Chile, Colombia, Czechoslovakia, Denmark, Ecuador, Egypt, France, Germany, Federal Republic of, India, Indonesia, Japan, Libyan Arab Jamahiriya, Netherlands, New Zealand, Nigeria, Oman, Peru, Poland, Samoa, Sri Lanka, Swaziland, Sweden, USSR, United Kingdom, United States, Uruguay.
Meeting numbers. GA 40th session: SPC 3, 4; plenary 118.

REFERENCES
[1]YUN 1984, p. 369, GA res. 39/94, 14 Dec. 1984. [2]A/40/417.

Antarctica

In 1985, the General Assembly again took up the question of Antarctica, considering developments that had emerged from an October 1984 study by the Secretary-General[1] and from previous discussions of specific features of the 1959 Antarctic Treaty system. Notable among them were non-militarization, non-nuclearization and the prohibition of nuclear waste disposal; freedom of scientific research; open access to the area covered by the Treaty; and protection of the environment and of the living resources of the continent.

Communications. A resolution on Antarctica, adopted by the Council of Ministers of OAU (Addis Ababa, Ethiopia, 10-17 July) and transmitted by Madagascar on 18 September,[2] declared Antarctica to be the common heritage of mankind and called on all OAU members to take appropriate steps at the 1985 General Assembly session to seek its recognition as such. In a Final Political Declaration adopted by the Conference of Foreign Ministers of Non-Aligned Countries (Luanda, 4-7 September) and transmitted by Angola on 5 November,[3] the Ministers reaffirmed their conviction that Antarctica should be used exclusively for peaceful purposes and be accessible to all nations and not become the object of international discord; they felt that the Assembly should remain seized of the question of Antarctica and expressed hope that the Secretary-General's 1984 study[1] would contribute to a more

comprehensive examination by the Assembly in 1985, taking into account the concerns of the Movement of Non-Aligned Countries.

On 25 November, Belgium transmitted an English version of the final report of the Thirteenth Antarctic Treaty Consultative Meeting (Brussels, 7-18 October).[4]

GENERAL ASSEMBLY ACTION

On 16 December 1985, the General Assembly, acting on the recommendation of the First Committee, adopted three texts—**resolutions 40/156 A, B** and **C**—each by roll-call vote, on the question of Antartica.

A

The General Assembly,
Recalling its resolutions 38/77 of 15 December 1983 and 39/152 of 17 December 1984,
Having considered the item entitled "Question of Antarctica",
Welcoming the increasing international awareness of and interest in Antarctica,
Bearing in mind the Antarctic Treaty and the significance of the system it has developed,
Taking into account the debate on this item at its fortieth session,
Convinced of the advantages of a better knowledge of Antarctica,
Affirming the conviction that, in the interest of all mankind, Antarctica should continue for ever to be used exclusively for peaceful purposes and that it should not become the scene or object of international discord,
Recalling the relevant paragraphs of the Economic Declaration adopted by the Seventh Conference of Heads of State or Government of Non-Aligned Countries, held at New Delhi from 7 to 12 March 1983, and of the Final Political Declaration adopted by the Conference of Foreign Ministers of Non-Aligned Countries, held at Luanda from 4 to 7 September 1985, as well as the resolution on Antarctica adopted by the Council of Ministers of the Organization of African Unity at its forty-second ordinary session, held at Addis Ababa from 10 to 17 July 1985,
Conscious of the significance of Antarctica to the international community in terms, *inter alia*, of international peace and security, economy, environment, scientific research and meteorology,
Recognizing, therefore, the interest of mankind as a whole in Antarctica,
Bearing in mind the United Nations Convention on the Law of the Sea,
Noting once again with appreciation the study on the question of Antarctica,
Convinced that it would be desirable to examine further certain issues affecting Antarctica,
1. *Requests* the Secretary-General to update and expand the study on the question of Antarctica by addressing questions concerning the availability to the United Nations of information from the Antarctic Treaty Consultative Parties on their respective activities in and their deliberations regarding Antarctica, the involvement of the relevant specialized agencies and intergovernmental organizations in the Antarctic Treaty system and the significance

of the United Nations Convention on the Law of the Sea in the southern ocean;

2. *Requests* the Secretary-General to seek the co-operation of all Member States and the relevant specialized agencies, organs, organizations and bodies of the United Nations system, as well as the relevant intergovernmental and non-governmental bodies, in the preparation of the updated study by inviting them to transmit, as appropriate, their views and any information they may wish to provide;

3. *Requests* the Secretary-General to submit the study to the General Assembly at its forty-first session;

4. *Decides* to include in the provisional agenda of its forty-first session the item entitled "Question of Antarctica".

General Assembly resolution 40/156 A

16 December 1985   Meeting 117   96-0-11 (roll-call vote)

Approved by First Committee (A/40/996 & Corr.1) by roll-call vote (80-0-9), 2 December (meeting 55); 13-nation draft (A/C.1/40/L.82), orally revised; agenda item 70.
Sponsors: Bangladesh, Brunei Darussalam, Cameroon, Ghana, Indonesia, Malaysia, Mali, Nigeria, Oman, Pakistan, Philippines, Rwanda, Sri Lanka.
Meeting numbers. GA 40th session: 1st Committee 48-55; plenary 117.

Roll-call vote in Assembly as follows:

In favour: Algeria, Angola, Antigua and Barbuda, Bahamas, Bahrain, Bangladesh, Benin, Bhutan, Bolivia, Botswana, Brunei Darussalam, Burkina Faso, Burma, Burundi, Cameroon, Cape Verde, Central African Republic, Chad,[a] Comoros, Congo, Costa Rica, Cyprus, Democratic Kampuchea, Djibouti, Dominican Republic, Egypt, El Salvador, Equatorial Guinea, Ethiopia, Gabon, Gambia, Ghana, Guatemala, Guinea, Guinea-Bissau, Guyana, Haiti, Honduras, Indonesia, Iran, Iraq, Ivory Coast, Jamaica, Jordan, Kenya, Kuwait, Lebanon, Lesotho, Liberia, Libyan Arab Jamahiriya, Madagascar, Malawi, Malaysia, Maldives, Mali, Malta, Mauritania, Mauritius, Mexico, Morocco, Mozambique, Nepal, Niger, Nigeria, Oman, Pakistan, Panama, Peru, Philippines, Qatar, Romania, Rwanda, Sao Tome and Principe, Saudi Arabia, Senegal, Sierra Leone, Singapore, Somalia, Sri Lanka, Sudan, Suriname, Swaziland, Thailand, Togo, Trinidad and Tobago, Tunisia, Uganda, United Arab Emirates, United Republic of Tanzania, Vanuatu, Venezuela, Yemen, Yugoslavia, Zaire, Zambia, Zimbabwe.
Against: None.
Abstaining: Austria, Canada, China, Fiji, Ireland, Luxembourg, Portugal, Saint Lucia, Saint Vincent and the Grenadines, Solomon Islands, Turkey.
[a]Later advised the Secretariat it had intended to abstain.

B

The General Assembly,

Recalling its resolutions 38/77 of 15 December 1983 and 39/152 of 17 December 1984,

Having considered the item entitled "Question of Antarctica",

Recalling the relevant paragraphs of the Economic Declaration adopted by the Seventh Conference of Heads of State or Government of Non-Aligned Countries, held at New Delhi from 7 to 12 March 1983, and of the Final Political Declaration adopted by the Conference of Foreign Ministers of Non-Aligned Countries held at Luanda from 4 to 7 September 1985, as well as the resolution on Antarctica adopted by the Council of Ministers of the Organization of African Unity at its forty-second ordinary session, held at Addis Ababa from 10 to 17 July 1985,

Recognizing that the management, exploration and use of Antarctica should be conducted in accordance with the purposes and principles of the Charter of the United Nations and in the interest of maintaining international peace and security and of promoting international co-operation for the benefit of mankind as a whole,

Aware that negotiations are in progress among the Antarctic Treaty Consultative Parties, with the non-Consultative Parties as observers, to which other States are not privy, with a view to establishing a régime regarding Antarctic minerals,

1. *Affirms* that any exploitation of the resources of Antarctica should ensure the maintenance of international peace and security in Antarctica, the protection of its environment, the non-appropriation and conservation of its resources and the international management and equitable sharing of the benefits of such exploitation;

2. *Invites* the Antarctic Treaty Consultative Parties to inform the Secretary-General of their negotiations to establish a régime regarding Antarctic minerals;

3. *Requests* the Secretary-General to submit to the General Assembly for consideration at its forty-first session a report containing the replies received from Consultative Parties;

4. *Decides* to include in the provisional agenda of its forty-first session the item entitled "Question of Antarctica".

General Assembly resolution 40/156 B

16 December 1985   Meeting 117   92-0-14 (roll-call vote)

Approved by First Committee (A/40/996 & Corr.1) by roll-call vote (78-0-10), 2 December (meeting 55); 13-nation draft (A/C.1/40/L.83); agenda item 70.
Sponsors: Bangladesh, Brunei Darussalam, Cameroon, Ghana, Indonesia, Kenya, Malaysia, Mali, Nigeria, Oman, Pakistan, Rwanda, Sri Lanka.
Meeting numbers. GA 40th session: 1st Committee 48-55; plenary 117.

Roll-call vote in Assembly as follows:

In favour: Algeria, Angola, Antigua and Barbuda, Bahrain, Bangladesh, Benin, Bhutan, Bolivia, Botswana, Brunei Darussalam, Burkina Faso, Burma, Burundi, Cameroon, Cape Verde, Central African Republic, Chad,[a] Comoros, Congo, Costa Rica, Cyprus, Democratic Kampuchea, Djibouti, Dominican Republic, Egypt, El Salvador, Equatorial Guinea, Ethiopia, Gabon, Gambia, Ghana, Guatemala, Guinea, Guinea-Bissau, Guyana, Haiti, Indonesia, Iran, Iraq, Ivory Coast, Jamaica, Jordan, Kenya, Kuwait, Lebanon, Lesotho, Liberia, Libyan Arab Jamahiriya, Madagascar, Malawi, Malaysia, Maldives, Mali, Malta, Mauritania, Mauritius, Mexico, Mozambique, Nepal, Niger, Nigeria, Oman, Pakistan, Panama, Philippines, Qatar, Romania, Rwanda, Sao Tome and Principe, Saudi Arabia, Senegal, Sierra Leone, Singapore, Somalia, Sri Lanka, Sudan, Suriname, Thailand, Togo, Trinidad and Tobago, Tunisia, Uganda, United Arab Emirates, United Republic of Tanzania, Vanuatu, Venezuela, Yemen, Yugoslavia, Zaire, Zambia, Zimbabwe.
Against: None.
Abstaining: Austria, Bahamas, Canada, China, Fiji, Grenada, Ireland, Luxembourg, Peru, Portugal, Saint Lucia, Saint Vincent and the Grenadines, Solomon Islands, Turkey.
[a]Later advised the Secretariat it had intended to abstain.

C

The General Assembly,

Having considered the item entitled "Question of Antarctica",

Noting with regret that the racist *apartheid* régime of South Africa, which has been suspended from participation in the General Assembly of the United Nations, is a Consultative Party to the Antarctic Treaty,

Recalling the interest of African States in Antarctica as shown by the resolution adopted by the Council of Ministers of the Organization of African Unity at its forty-second ordinary session, held at Addis Ababa from 10 to 17 July 1985,

Recalling further that the Antarctic Treaty is, by its terms, intended to further the purposes and principles embodied in the Charter of the United Nations,

1. *Views with concern* the continued status of the *apartheid* régime of South Africa as a Consultative Party to the Antarctic Treaty;

2. *Urges* the Antarctic Treaty Consultative Parties to exclude the racist *apartheid* régime of South Africa from participation in the meetings of the Consultative Parties at the earliest possible date;

3. *Invites* the States parties to the Antarctic Treaty to inform the Secretary-General on the actions taken regarding the provisions of the present resolution.

General Assembly resolution 40/156 C

16 December 1985   Meeting 117   100-0-12 (roll-call vote)

Approved by First Committee (A/40/996 & Corr.1) by roll-call vote (81-0-9), 2 December (meeting 55); draft by Mauritius for African Group (A/C.1/40/L.85); agenda item 70.
Meeting numbers. GA 40th session: 1st Committee 48-55; plenary 117.

In favour: Albania, Algeria, Angola, Antigua and Barbuda, Bahamas, Bahrain, Bangladesh, Barbados, Benin, Bhutan, Bolivia, Botswana, Brunei Darussalam, Burkina Faso, Burma, Burundi, Cameroon, Cape Verde, Central African Republic, Chad, China, Colombia, Comoros, Congo, Costa Rica, Cyprus, Democratic Kampuchea, Democratic Yemen, Djibouti, Dominican Republic, Ecuador, Egypt, El Salvador, Equatorial Guinea, Ethiopia, Gabon, Gambia, Ghana, Guatemala, Guinea, Guinea-Bissau, Guyana, Haiti, India, Indonesia, Iran, Iraq, Jamaica, Jordan, Kenya, Kuwait, Lebanon, Lesotho, Liberia, Libyan Arab Jamahiriya, Madagascar, Malaysia, Maldives, Mali, Malta, Mauritania, Mexico, Morocco, Mozambique, Nepal, Nicaragua, Niger, Nigeria, Oman, Pakistan, Panama, Peru, Qatar, Romania, Rwanda, Sao Tome and Principe, Saudi Arabia, Senegal, Sierra Leone, Singapore, Somalia, Sri Lanka, Sudan, Suriname, Syrian Arab Republic, Thailand, Togo, Trinidad and Tobago, Tunisia, Uganda, United Arab Emirates, United Republic of Tanzania, Vanuatu, Venezuela, Viet Nam, Yemen, Yugoslavia, Zaire, Zambia, Zimbabwe.

Against: None.

Abstaining: Austria, Canada, Fiji, Ireland, Luxembourg, Malawi, Portugal, Saint Lucia, Saint Vincent and the Grenadines, Solomon Islands, Swaziland, Turkey.

Before the Assembly voted on the resolutions, Australia, on behalf of the Antarctic Treaty Consultative Parties, requested that the Assembly records reflect the non-participation of countries so announcing in the roll-call votes. The parties were firmly of the view, Australia noted, that consensus offered the only realistic basis for Assembly consideration of Antarctica; therefore, unless consensus could be restored, they would be compelled to reconsider their further participation in the consideration of the item.

States which announced their intention not to participate in the roll-call vote on resolution 40/156 A were: Afghanistan, Albania, Argentina, Australia, Barbados, Belgium, Brazil, Bulgaria, Byelorussian SSR, Chile, Colombia, Cuba, Czechoslovakia, Denmark, Ecuador, Finland, France, German Democratic Republic, Germany, Federal Republic of, Greece, Hungary, Iceland, India, Israel, Italy, Japan, Lao People's Democratic Republic, Netherlands, New Zealand, Nicaragua, Norway, Paraguay, Poland, Samoa, Spain, Sweden, Ukrainian SSR, USSR, United Kingdom, United States, Uruguay.

The same 41 States, plus Honduras and Morocco, similarly announced non-participation in the vote on resolution 40/156 B; most of the 41 did likewise in the vote on 40/156 C, excepting Afghanistan, Albania, Barbados, Colombia, Cuba, Ecuador, India and Nicaragua, but including Grenada, Honduras, the Ivory Coast and Mauritius.

Explaining their abstention on all three texts in the First Committee were Canada and Turkey. Canada reiterated the importance of basing any resolution relating to Antarctica on general agreement. The inability to reach agreement on the appropriate way to deal with the question, Canada said, did not enhance the functioning of the Treaty, whose contribution to international peace and security, to scientific co-operation, to the preservation of Antarctic resources and to the protection of its environment was widely recognized. Turkey said that, while it agreed that the Treaty was valid, it none the less felt that the Antarctic régime needed to be adapted to the international community's interests—a need that could not be served by resolutions not reflecting consensus. Nor could Turkey—despite its abhorrence for the South Africa régime—support a United Nations recommendation concerning the Treaty's membership.

Expressing deep regret at the lack of consensus, China said its vote on resolution 40/156 C was based on its support of the African people's struggle against *apartheid*. Its abstentions, however, reflected its consistent stand that Antarctica should be used to serve the cause of peace, science and mankind's common interests and not be an arena of international disputes. Pending a consensus, it felt its actions on the question should be as helpful as possible in creating a harmonious atmosphere, avoiding confrontation and seeking continued dialogue.

Peru's vote for resolution 40/156 A was based on its belief that all United Nations Members had a natural interest in Antarctica, and that the text neither interfered with the purposes and objectives of the Antarctic Treaty nor attempted to undermine its validity and implementation.

Italy, speaking also on behalf of Denmark, Finland, the Netherlands, Spain and Sweden, expressed deep concern that consensus could not be obtained, the reason why they had not found it possible to participate in the votes.

Proposed as a compromise text to enable the Committee to proceed by consensus but later withdrawn on behalf of the Treaty parties was a draft sponsored by Australia.[5] Although it included a request similar to that in resolution 40/156 A for a supplement to the Secretary-General's 1984 study,[1] the Australian text did not call for inclusion in that report of the significance of the United Nations Convention on the Law of the Sea in the southern ocean; it asked for presentation of the study in 1987, instead of 1986 when only a progress report was to be made; its preambular section also differed in several respects from that of the resolution adopted.

REFERENCES

[1]YUN 1984, p. 369. [2]A/40/666. [3]A/40/854-S/17610 & Corr.1. [4]A/C.1/40/12. [5]A/C.1/40/L.84.

Anniversary of the emancipation of slaves in the British Empire

In 1985, there were no speakers on the agenda item "Celebration of the one-hundred-and-fiftieth anniversary of the emancipation of slaves in the British Empire". The General Assembly, by **decision 40/461**, adopted without vote on 18 December, on an oral proposal by its President, included the item in the provisional agenda of its forty-first (1986) session.

Chapter XI

Institutional machinery

The year 1985 marked the fortieth anniversary of the United Nations. Its theme was "United Nations for a better world".

The Security Council, apart from considering its agenda, held a commemorative session at ministerial level to review the international situation and, in the context of the anniversary's theme, to continue examining possibilities for improving its effectiveness in discharging its principal role of maintaining international peace and security.

The General Assembly resumed and concluded its thirty-ninth session and held the major part of its fortieth session, considering 140 items of a 149-item agenda. A special significance attached to the Assembly in 1985, which also held a commemorative session, from 14 to 24 October, at which Member States reflected on the performance of the United Nations during its 40 years of existence, on its accomplishments and failures, and on how it could be improved. Not the least of those accomplishments was the achievement of near universality in its membership, which had risen from 51 Member States in 1945 to 159 in 1984, remaining at that number in 1985.

On the occasion of the anniversary, the Secretary-General considered humanity's future and the United Nations role in it (see p. 3). The choice between a world of infinite promise and one of potentially terminal danger was ours to make, he said, and the United Nations and the use to which its Members put it was an essential element in that choice. The Secretary-General, who suggested further development of his capacity to serve as an objective third party, continued to exercise his good offices towards resolving the situations involving the questions of Afghanistan, Cyprus, the Falkland Islands (Malvinas), Iran and Iraq, and Kampuchea.

Also during the year, the Assembly adopted six resolutions on co-operation between the United Nations and intergovernmental organizations.

Topics related to this chapter. Africa: co-operation between OAU and the UN system. Regional economic and social activities: Africa—co-operation between the Southern African Development Co-ordination Conference and the United Nations. Institutional arrangements: Economic and Social Council—co-operation with other organizations. International organizations and international law: draft standard rules of procedure for conferences. Other legal questions: co-operation between the United Nations and the Asian-African Legal Consultative Committee. Other administrative and management questions: calendar of meetings.

UN Members

As there were no new admissions to the United Nations during 1985, its membership remained at 159.

Côte d'Ivoire

On 6 November 1985,[1] the Ivory Coast drew attention to a decision taken by the Parti Démocratique de Côte d'Ivoire at its eighth Congress (Abidjan, 9-12 October) that the designation Côte d'Ivoire, the country's proper name, should no longer be considered a geographical term and that the practice of translating it into the different languages be stopped. Aware, however, of the practical difficulties for implementing the decision during the current General Assembly session, the Ivory Coast requested the Secretary-General to make the decision fully effective within the Secretariat of the United Nations and applicable to all of the Organization's related bodies by 1 January 1986.

REFERENCE

[1]A/40/860.

Security Council

The Security Council held 74 meetings in 1985 and adopted 21 resolutions.

Meeting numbers. SC: 2566-2639.

In accordance with a decision taken during informal consultations on 29 August,[1] the Council held a commemorative meeting on 26 September to celebrate the United Nations fortieth anniversary. At that meeting, the President said he had been authorized by Council members to make the following statement on their behalf:[2]

"The Security Council met in public at the Headquarters of the United Nations in New York on Thursday, 26 September 1985, at the level of Foreign

Ministers, to celebrate the fortieth anniversary of the Organization.

"The meeting was chaired by the Minister for Foreign Affairs of the United Kingdom of Great Britain and Northern Ireland as the President of the Security Council for September. Statements were made by the Ministers for Foreign Affairs of the Union of Soviet Socialist Republics, the Ukrainian Soviet Socialist Republic, Trinidad and Tobago, Thailand and Peru; by the Permanent Representative of Madagascar; by the Minister of State for Commerce of India; and by the Ministers for Foreign Affairs of France, Egypt, Denmark, China, Burkina Faso, Australia, the United States of America and the United Kingdom of Great Britain and Northern Ireland, as well as by the Secretary-General.

"The agenda for the commemorative meeting was: 'United Nations for a better world and the responsibility of the Security Council in maintaining international peace and security'.

"The members of the Council welcomed the opportunity provided by the fortieth anniversary of the United Nations to reaffirm at a high level their obligations under the Charter and their continued commitment to its purposes and principles. They conducted a wide-ranging review of the international situation. They expressed their deep concern at the existence of various threats to peace, including the nuclear threat. While acknowledging that it had not always proved possible for the Organization to eradicate those threats, they underlined the continuing relevance of the United Nations as a positive force for peace and human advancement. They welcomed the continuing growth of the membership of the Organization to a point where the objective of universality of membership, which they endorsed, had almost been achieved.

"The members of the Council were cognizant of the primary responsibility for the maintenance of international peace and security conferred by the Charter on the Security Council and of the special rights and responsibilities of its permanent members. They stressed that a collegial approach within the Council was desirable to facilitate considered and concerted action by the Council as the main instrument for international peace. They acknowledged that the high hopes placed in the Organization by the international community had not been fully met and undertook to fulfil their individual and collective responsibility for the prevention and removal of threats to the peace with renewed dedication and determination. They agreed to employ appropriate measures available under the Charter when considering international disputes, threats to the peace, breaches of the peace and acts of aggression. They recognized the valuable contribution made on many occasions by the United Nations peace-keeping forces. They called again upon the entire membership of the United Nations to abide by their obligations under the Charter to accept and carry out decisions of the Security Council.

"They agreed that there was an urgent need to enhance the effectiveness of the Security Council in discharging its principal role of maintaining international peace and security. Accordingly, they resolved to continue the examination of the possibilities for further improvement of the functioning of the Security Council in carrying out its work in accordance with the Charter. In this context, they paid special attention to the suggestions addressed to the members of the Council in the Secretary-General's annual reports on the work of the Organization. They thanked the Secretary-General for those reports and encouraged him to play an active role within the scope of his functions under the Charter."

Also on the occasion of the Organization's fortieth anniversary, the Secretary-General, referring to the question of how to enhance the Council's role in providing stability and limiting conflict, made what he called a simpler set of suggestions than those he had put forward previously (see p. 6). These included a determined and conscious effort by Council members, especially the permanent ones, to give matters of international peace and security priority over bilateral differences; a deliberate and concerted effort to solve one or two of the major problems before the Council by making fuller use of the measures available to it under the Charter; and a reaffirmation by the United Nations membership as a whole of Charter obligations, especially those relating to the non-use or threat of force, peaceful settlement of disputes, resort to the mechanism set out in the Charter for such settlement, and respect for Council decisions.

The General Assembly, in stressing the urgent need to enhance the effectiveness of the Council's principal role of maintaining international peace and security, emphasized, by **resolution 40/158** on implementing the 1970 Declaration on the Strengthening of International Security, that the Council should consider holding periodic meetings in specific cases to review outstanding problems and crises, thus enabling it to play a more active role in preventing conflicts. The Assembly reiterated the need for the Council, in particular its permanent members, to ensure implementation of its decisions in compliance with relevant Charter provisions.

That same role continued to be considered in 1985 by the Special Committee on the Charter of the United Nations and on the Strengthening of the Role of the Organization. Discussion centred on a revised working paper containing proposals for preventive measures to be applied by the Council, among other principal organs of the United Nations, in situations which might lead to international friction (see LEGAL QUESTIONS, Chapter IV).

Agenda

During 1985—its fortieth year—the Security Council considered 19 agenda items. It continued the practice of adopting at each meeting the agenda for that meeting. (For list of agenda items, see APPENDIX IV.)

Eight of the items were included for the first time in the Council's agenda.[3] They concerned complaints by Chad against the Libyan Arab Jamahiriya (one item), by Nicaragua against the United States (two items), by Botswana against South Africa (two items) and by Tunisia against Israel (one item); the situation created by hostage-taking and abduction; and United Nations for a better world and the Council's responsibility in maintaining international peace and security (in celebration of the fortieth anniversary of the United Nations).

In a 16 September note,[4] the Secretary-General notified the General Assembly, in accordance with Article 12, paragraph 2, of the United Nations Charter, of 12 matters relative to the maintenance of international peace and security that the Council had discussed since his previous annual notification.[5] He listed 108 other matters not discussed during the period but of which the Council remained seized. The Assembly took note of these matters on 9 December by **decision 40/416**.

During the year, the Assembly also asked the Council to take certain specific actions in fulfilment of its responsibilities for the maintenance of peace and security. It reiterated its 1984 call[6] on the Council to initiate procedures in accordance with the Charter for bringing the escalating arms race to a halt (**resolution 40/151 A**). It requested the Council to act to prevent any racist régime from acquiring arms or arms technology and to conclude consideration of recommendations aimed at blocking existing loopholes in the arms embargo against South Africa (**resolution 40/89 B**). It again called on the Council urgently to take action under Chapter VII of the Charter with a view to applying comprehensive and mandatory sanctions against that country (**resolution 40/64 A**)—a call the Assembly repeated when it asked the Council to exercise its authority in the implementation of its various resolutions to bring about Namibia's independence without further delay (**resolution 40/97 B**).

The Assembly urged the Council to act decisively in fulfilment of United Nations responsibility over Namibia, as well as against schemes to frustrate the legitimate struggle of the Namibian people, and to ensure full implementation of the United Nations independence plan for the Territory and strict compliance with the arms embargo against South Africa; and urged implementation of the recommendations of the Council Committee established in 1977 to monitor the embargo (**resolution 40/97 A**).

Members

In 1985 as in the previous year, the question of equitable representation on the Security Council and increase in its membership was not considered. Thus, on 18 December, the General Assembly, acting without vote on an oral proposal by its President, adopted **decision 40/460** by which it decided to include the item in the provisional agenda of its forty-first (1986) session.

Reports for 1983/84 and 1984/85

At two meetings held in private in 1985, on 29 January and on 15 November, the Security Council considered its draft annual reports to the General Assembly covering the periods 16 June 1983 to 15 June 1984[7] and 16 June 1984 to 15 June 1985,[8] respectively, and unanimously adopted them. The Assembly took note of the first report on 9 April by **decision 39/457** and of the second on 9 December by **decision 40/418**.

At the 29 January meeting, the Council President stated[9] that members, in preparing the 1983/84 report, were of the opinion that it could be shortened without changing its general format. Accordingly, they agreed that the report would no longer summarize documents addressed to the Council President or to the Secretary-General and circulated as Council documents, the full text of which was available elsewhere. Also, the report would simply indicate the subject-matter of those documents relating to the Council's procedure, such as requests for meetings or requests to take part in discussions.

REFERENCES

[1]S/17424. [2]S/17501. [3]*Resolutions and Decisions of the Security Council, 1985*, S/INF/41. [4]A/40/642. [5]YUN 1984, p. 373. [6]*Ibid.*, p. 82, GA res. 39/63 K, 12 Dec. 1984. [7]A/39/2. [8]A/40/2. [9]S/16913.

OTHER PUBLICATION
Index to Proceedings of the Security Council, Fortieth Year—1985 (ST/LIB/SER.B/S.22), Sales No. E.86.I.9.

General Assembly

The General Assembly met in two sessions during 1985, to resume and conclude its thirty-ninth regular session and to hold the major part of its fortieth.

The first part of the thirty-ninth session had been held from 18 September to 18 December 1984.[1] The session resumed in 1985 from 9 to 12 April and on 16 September, when it was declared closed after consideration of the remaining items on its agenda was concluded.

The fortieth regular session was opened on 17 September and continued until its suspension on 18 December. During the general debate, from 23 September to 11 October, the Assembly heard 137 statements by heads of State or Government and heads or members of delegations.

GENERAL ASSEMBLY ACTION

Following a statement by its President that, with the exception of nine items and four sub-items, consideration of the agenda had been concluded, the General Assembly adopted **decision 40/470** without vote.

Suspension of the fortieth session

At its 122nd plenary meeting, on 18 December 1985, the General Assembly decided to resume its fortieth session, at a date to be announced, for the sole purpose of considering the following agenda items:

Item 16 *(a)*: Election of two members of the Governing Council of the United Nations Environment Programme;

Item 17 *(h)*: Appointment of members of the Consultative Committee on the United Nations Development Fund for Women;

Item 17 *(l)*: Appointment of a member of the Special Committee on the Situation with regard to the Implementation of the Declaration on the Granting of Independence to Colonial Countries and Peoples;

Item 21: The situation in Central America: threats to international peace and security and peace initiatives;

Item 41: Launching of global negotiations on international economic co-operation for development;

Item 43: Observance of the quincentenary of the discovery of America;

Item 44: Question of Cyprus;

Item 45: Implementation of the resolutions of the United Nations;

Item 46: Consequences of the prolongation of the armed conflict between Iran and Iraq;

Item 84 and 84 *(c)*: Development and international economic co-operation; trade and development;

Item 116: Proposed programme budget for the biennium 1986-1987;

Item 123: Personnel questions.

General Assembly decision 40/470

Adopted without vote

Oral proposal by President; agenda item 8.

Agenda

As the General Assembly had decided in December 1984,[1] it resumed its thirty-ninth session in 1985 to consider 11 items and two sub-items remaining on that session's agenda. In addition, it reopened three sub-items to consider a request for the appointment of one member of the Joint Inspection Unit (JIU) (item 17 *(g)*) and another for the resumption of the United Nations Conference on Conditions for Registration of Ships for two weeks in July (item 80 *(c)*); and to consider a draft decision by which the Assembly would ask the Commission on the Status of Women, acting as the preparatory body for the July 1985 World Conference to Review and Appraise the Achievements of the United Nations Decade for Women, to resume its third (March 1985) session in April in order to complete its preparatory work (item 93 *(b)*). The items involving the resumption of meetings were also considered under the related item on the programme budget.

With the exception of the item on global negotiations on international economic co-operation for development, consideration of all the other items was concluded, including the appointment of a JIU member (see APPENDIX III).

On 16 September, the Assembly, by a series of decisions, included several items in the agenda of its fortieth session on: the confirmation of the appointment of the Secretary-General of the United Nations Conference on Trade and Development (UNCTAD) (**decision 39/324 B**), the launching of global negotiations on international economic co-operation for development (**decision 39/454 C**), the situation in Central America (**decision 39/462**), the observance of the quincentenary of the discovery of America (**decision 39/463**), the Cyprus question (**decision 39/464**), implementation of United Nations resolutions (**decision 39/465**), the Iran-Iraq conflict (**decision 39/466**), and the celebration of the one-hundred-and-fiftieth anniversary of the emancipation of slaves in the British Empire (**decision 39/467**).

In 1985, the fortieth session had 149 items on its agenda, of which 146 were adopted by the Assembly on 20 September and three were added to the list on 23 September, 29 October and 15 November.[2] Inclusion of the items in the agenda, as well as their allocation to the Assembly's Main Committees or directly to plenary meetings,[3] was recommended by the General Committee.[4] On 18 September, it approved a 146-item agenda on the basis of preliminary[5] and annotated[6] lists of items, a 144-item provisional agenda,[7] a two-item supplementary list,[8] and two requests for inclusion of additional items: on settlement of disputes through negotiation[9] (see p. 121) and on an election to fill a vacancy on the International Court of Justice[10] (see APPENDIX III). The Committee also recommended that the item concerning East Timor (see TRUSTEESHIP AND DECOLONIZATION, Chapter IV) be deferred to the forty-first (1986) session. On 23 September, 29 October and 15 November, it recommended approval of three additional items proposed during the fortieth session: on international relief to Mexico[11] (see p. 543), on a draft declaration relating to the protection of children[12] (see ECONOMIC AND SOCIAL QUESTIONS, Chapter XX) and on international relief to Colombia[13] (see p. 545).

GENERAL ASSEMBLY ACTION

Following examination of the recommendations of the General Committee, the General Assembly adopted **decision 40/402** without vote.

Adoption of the agenda and allocation of agenda items

At its 3rd, 5th, 53rd, 78th, 123rd and 124th plenary meetings, on 20 and 23 September, 29 October and 15 November 1985 and on 28 April 1986, the General Assembly, on the recommendations of the General Committee as set forth in its first, second, third, fourth and fifth reports and on the proposal of the Secretary-General, adopted the agenda and the allocation of agenda items for the fortieth session.

At its 3rd plenary meeting, on 20 September 1985, the General Assembly, on the recommendation of the

General Committee, decided to include in the provisional agenda of its forty-first session the item entitled "Question of East Timor".

General Assembly decision 40/402

Adopted without vote

Approved by General Committee (A/40/250 & Add.1-4) without vote, 18 and 23 September, 29 October and 15 November 1985 and 28 April 1986 (meetings 1-5); agenda item 8.

Organization of work

In its first and third reports, dated 18 September[14] and 29 October,[15] the General Committee made recommendations concerning the organization of the fortieth session, based on suggestions by the Secretary-General[16] and on letters from the Committee on Conferences.[17]

The recommendations provided for a schedule of daily meetings, including a commemorative session in observance of the fortieth anniversary of the United Nations, fixed the duration of the general debate and set 17 December as the session's closing date. Other recommendations drew attention to provisions embodied in a 1979 decision on the rationalization of the Assembly's procedures and organization,[18] such as early agreement among regional groups on the distribution of Main Committee chairmanships for the following session, limiting explanations of vote and meeting records and, in general, dispensing with concluding statements. Attention was also drawn to the mandatory deadline of 1 December for submitting draft resolutions with financial implications and to setting deadlines for submitting reports requiring consideration by the Fifth (Administrative and Budgetary) Committee, as well as to the 48-hour interval between the submission of and voting on a proposal involving expenditure. The Assembly was neither to debate nor to adopt resolutions on reports unless requested to do so by the reporting bodies. Maximum restraint was to be exercised in requests for the circulation of material as official documents.

In addition to recommending that the Main Committees review the number of special conferences already scheduled before scheduling additional ones, the General Committee also recommended authorization for a number of subsidiary organs to meet during the session, which was later granted by Assembly **decision 40/403**.

GENERAL ASSEMBLY ACTION

Acting on the General Committee's recommendations, the General Assembly adopted **decision 40/401** without vote.

Organization of the fortieth session

At its 3rd and 53rd plenary meetings, on 20 September and 29 October 1985, the General Assembly, on the recommendations of the General Committee as set forth in its first and third reports, adopted a number of provisions concerning the organization of the fortieth session.

General Assembly decision 40/401

Adopted without vote

Approved by General Committee (A/40/250 & Add.2) without vote, 18 September and 29 October (meetings 1,3); agenda item 8.

Representatives' credentials

At its first meeting, on 9 October 1985, the Credentials Committee examined a memorandum of the previous day from the Secretary-General indicating that formal credentials to the fortieth session of the General Assembly had been submitted by 120 Member States. At that meeting, the Legal Counsel provided supplementary information that credentials had subsequently been received from two other Member States.

The Committee also heard statements in connection with the credentials of Afghanistan, Chile and Democratic Kampuchea.

China reiterated its position that allowing Afghanistan to participate in the current Assembly session should not be interpreted as acquiescence to the situation created in that country by foreign armed invasion and occupation. The United States, saying it had raised no objection to those credentials out of respect for the technical nature of the credentials exercise, expressed a similar reservation. Such assertions, the USSR said, were an attempt to distort historical and political reality and were contrary to the interests of normalizing the situation in south-west Asia and ensuring favourable conditions for the ongoing talks on Afghanistan.

The USSR reiterated its opposition to acceptance of the credentials of Chile and of Democratic Kampuchea. The United States, on the other hand, considered those credentials to be in order and saw no basis for questioning their acceptance. The guiding principle, Canada said, was concern solely with the technical aspects of such documents, which, in the case of those under challenge including Afghanistan's, appeared to be fully in accord with the relevant rule of the Assembly's rules of procedure, based on information provided to the Committee. Canada stressed that their acceptance and those of others was not intended to imply any foreign policy position.

Acting on an oral proposal by its Chairman, the Committee adopted without vote a resolution by which it accepted the credentials received, taking into account the various reservations expressed. It also recommended for adoption a draft resolution by which the Assembly would approve the Committee's first report.[19]

On 12 December, at its second meeting, the Committee examined a further memorandum from the Secretary-General reporting that, since the Committee's first meeting and as of 11

December, formal credentials from 36 other Member States, including Grenada, had been received.

The USSR reaffirmed its non-recognition of the credentials of what it called the puppet régime established by the United States in Grenada. The United States said the credentials complied with the Assembly's rules of procedure and were therefore in order.

Acting without vote on an oral proposal by its Chairman, the Committee adopted a resolution by which it accepted the credentials received, taking into account the reservations expressed. It also submitted a draft resolution recommending Assembly approval of its second report.[20]

GENERAL ASSEMBLY ACTION

Acting on the recommendations of the Credentials Committee, the General Assembly adopted two resolutions on credentials of representatives to its fortieth session.

On 16 October, it adopted **resolution 40/2 A** without vote.

The General Assembly
Approves the first report of the Credentials Committee.

General Assembly resolution 40/2 A

16 October 1985   Meeting 37   Adopted without vote

Approved by Credentials Committee (A/40/747) without vote, 9 October (meeting 1); draft orally proposed by Chairman; agenda item 3.

Before adopting the resolution, the Assembly, by a recorded vote of 80 to 41, with 20 abstentions, decided not to act on an amendment sponsored by 18 States to reject the credentials of Israel. That decision was taken on a motion by Sweden, also on behalf of Denmark, Finland, Iceland and Norway. Reservations concerning those credentials had been entered by 50 States (see p. 271).

Explaining their positions following adoption of the resolution, Egypt said it voted for the Swedish motion because it related to a procedural matter that in no way changed the situation in the Middle East; that the credentials of Israel had been issued in Jerusalem, Egypt added, did not detract from the illegal character of that city's annexation. Iran said it wanted its reservations on those credentials to be made part of Assembly official records.

Referring to Afghanistan's credentials, Belgium, along with the Federal Republic of Germany and the United Kingdom, stated that not objecting to those credentials was not to be interpreted as recognition of the current Afghan régime, which had been imposed from outside.

Afghanistan characterized the reservations made on its credentials in the Credentials Committee as impertinent, and entered its own reservations on the credentials of what it termed the so-called Government of Democratic Kampuchea;

the only authority that could speak for the Kampucheans, it asserted, was the People's Republic of Kampuchea. Democratic Kampuchea on the other hand expressed gratitude for the recognition of and support for its sovereignty and independence.

On 17 December, the Assembly adopted **resolution 40/2 B** without vote.

The General Assembly
Approves the second report of the Credentials Committee.

General Assembly resolution 40/2 B

17 December 1985   Meeting 120   Adopted without vote

Approved by Credentials Committee (A/40/747/Add.1) without vote, 12 December (meeting 2); draft orally proposed by Chairman; agenda item 3.

The representation of Kampuchea in the United Nations was also challenged in two communications (see p. 228).

Likewise, the legitimacy of Chad's representation under its current Government was challenged by the Libyan Arab Jamahiriya, at a Security Council meeting on 30 January. The legal opinion on that question, sought and obtained on 4 February by France, as Council President at the time, noted General Assembly acceptance, without dissent, of Chad's credentials as presented by that Government (see p. 197).

Rationalization of UN procedures

As requested by the General Assembly in 1984,[21] the Special Committee on the Charter of the United Nations and on the Strengthening of the Role of the Organization kept the question of the rationalization of United Nations procedures under review, devoting two meetings to the topic during its March 1985 session[22] (see LEGAL QUESTIONS, Chapter IV). A working paper was presented by France and the United Kingdom as containing a clearer formulation of various items previously considered but deserving further consideration.

While it was generally recognized that the topic was a useful and important one, two main views emerged during the Committee's discussion. In the light of the Committee's 1984 conclusions,[23] which the Assembly had approved for reproduction as an annex to its rules of procedure,[24] the view was expressed that there was nothing to add to those conclusions at the current stage, nor would the time be ripe to resume consideration of the new proposals at the Committee's 1986 session. The view was also expressed, however, that the 1984 conclusions did not respond sufficiently to all the problems of rationalization, nor did they rule out further Committee consideration of the topic.

In **resolution 40/78** on the report of the Special Committee's March session, the Assembly again requested the Committee to keep the topic under review.

Recommendations for the rationalization of the Assembly's procedures were made by Presidents of the General Assembly at a June meeting held in commemoration of the United Nations fortieth anniversary (see p. 403).

The Secretary-General pointed to the difficulty in streamlining the Assembly and rationalizing its procedures, which he attributed to the universality of its membership and to its diverse agenda; he suggested, however, that improving the political process in the Assembly should include a much greater degree of intergovernmental consultation before each session, and a determined attempt to hammer out consensus on important issues and to avoid divisive rhetoric (see pp. 8 and 9).

REFERENCES

[1]YUN 1984, p. 374. [2]A/40/251 & Add.1-3. [3]A/40/252 & Add.1-3. [4]A/40/250 & Add.1-3. [5]A/40/50/Rev.1. [6]A/40/100 & Add.1. [7]A/40/150. [8]A/40/200. [9]A/40/241. [10]A/40/242. [11]A/40/243. [12]A/40/244. [13]A/40/245. [14]A/40/250. [15]A/40/250/Add.2. [16]A/BUR/40/1. [17]A/40/632 & A/40/648. [18]YUN 1979, p. 440, GA dec. 34/401, 21 Sep., 25 Oct., 29 Nov. & 12 Dec. 1979. [19]A/40/747. [20]A/40/747/Add.1. [21]YUN 1984, p. 1101, GA res. 39/88 A, 13 Dec. 1984. [22]A/40/33 & Corr.1. [23]YUN 1984, p. 376. [24]*Ibid.*, GA res. 39/88 B, 13 Dec. 1984.

PUBLICATIONS

Index to Proceedings of the General Assembly, Fortieth Session—1985/1986: Part I—Subject Index; Part II—Index to Speeches (ST/LIB/SER.B/A.39 (Parts I & II)), Sales No. E.86.I.15 (Parts I & II). *Resolutions and Decisions adopted by the General Assembly during its fortieth session, 17 September–18 December 1985, 28 April–9 May and 20 June 1986, A/40/53; and Addendum, 15 September 1986.*

Secretary-General

In his 1985 annual report on the work of the United Nations (see p. 3), the year of its fortieth anniversary, the Secretary-General focused on the future of humanity and the United Nations role in that future. Noting the general lack of the essential political conditions, the sense of solidarity and mutual confidence that could make international instruments work towards addressing some of the major problems confronting the international community, he asserted that the United Nations was the best place where such conditions and solidarity could be developed. While it could not solve all those problems, it was the best place to avoid the worst and to strive for improvement.

Of his own office, the Secretary-General said its responsibilities and duties were a high challenge. While appreciative of the trust bestowed on him, he had been concerned that delegation of responsibility to the Secretary-General might, in certain instances, have the effect of diminishing the effort expected of Member States. It would be in the Organization's interest, he suggested, if the Secretary-General's capacity to serve as an objective third party were to be further developed by the wider and earlier use of fact-finding and observation, and by regular, systematic surveys of the state of international peace and security—a task in which both the Security Council and the Secretary-General should be involved.

Good offices

During 1985, the Secretary-General continued the missions of good offices entrusted to him either by the Security Council or by the General Assembly. These missions concerned Afghanistan, Cyprus, the Falkland Islands (Malvinas), the Iran-Iraq conflict and Kampuchea.

The Secretary-General's determined efforts to promote the search for a political solution to the Afghanistan situation continued in contacts with the principals and in two rounds of talks during the year through the intermediary of his Personal Representative (see p. 232). With regard to Cyprus, he continued his high-level meetings with the Greek Cypriot and Turkish Cypriot communities in order to seek their agreement on a framework for an overall solution to the Cyprus problem (see p. 251). Apart from maintaining contacts with representatives of Iran and Iraq in New York on his proposals for a cease-fire between them, the Secretary-General visited the capitals of both countries, conveying his personal commitment to continue trying to bring closer the prospect of peace (see p. 242).

Likewise, he renewed his efforts to assist Argentina and the United Kingdom to resume negotiations towards a peaceful solution to their sovereignty dispute over the Falkland Islands (Malvinas). Those efforts included meetings with the respective leaders of both countries aimed at promoting a dialogue between the two sides (see TRUSTEESHIP AND DECOLONIZATION, Chapter IV). Also, with the assistance of his Special Representative, the Secretary-General continued his exchanges with all concerned towards a solution of the Kampuchea situation (see p. 226).

Co-operation with other intergovernmental organizations

Co-operation between the United Nations and other intergovernmental organizations was the subject of six 1985 General Assembly resolutions. Those organizations were the League of Arab States and the Organization of the Islamic Conference (see below); the Organization of African

Unity (see p. 201); the Southern African Development Co-ordination Conference and the Agency for Cultural and Technical Co-operation (see ECONOMIC AND SOCIAL QUESTIONS, Chapters VIII and XXIV, respectively); and the Asian-African Legal Consultative Committee (see LEGAL QUESTIONS, Chapter IV).

League of Arab States

The Secretary-General submitted in July 1985 a report[1] concerning progress in implementing, since the beginning of the year, a 1984 General Assembly resolution[2] on enhancing political, economic, social and cultural co-operation between the United Nations and the League of Arab States.

The report described consultations between the two organizations at various levels and summarized progress achieved on the proposals for co-operation as had been agreed by them in 1983.[3] Twenty-four multilateral proposals involving two or more bodies of the United Nations system were on such matters as disarmament, education and training for the handicapped and on human rights, energy, the environmental aspects of agricultural and industrial development and in planning human settlements, health care, maritime transport, natural resources (water, land, minerals), informatics and computer sciences, and regional technical co-operation projects.

The report also summarized action taken and planned for the future, as described by the United Nations agencies, programmes and bodies concerned, on bilateral proposals in six main areas of co-operation. These included political matters, in particular the maintenance of international peace and security in the Middle East and in the Gulf area, and co-operation in the struggle against *apartheid;* economic, financial and technical co-operation for development; food and agriculture; social development, labour, human resources and cultural affairs; refugees, disaster prevention and emergency relief, and human rights; and information and communication.

In September,[4] the Secretary-General reported that the United Nations and the League had held a sectoral meeting on social development (Amman, Jordan, 19-21 August) (see ECONOMIC AND SOCIAL QUESTIONS, Chapter XIII).

In 1985, the League's Secretary-General, its Under-Secretary-General for Political and International Affairs and its Permanent Observer to the United Nations made statements at seven Security Council meetings, to which they had been invited to participate in accordance with rule 39[a] of the Council's provisional rules of procedure. Those meetings dealt with the situation between Iran and Iraq, the Middle East situation including the Palestine question, the situation in Namibia, and a complaint by Tunisia of an Israeli air attack on Tunis.

The final communiqué of the Extraordinary Summit Conference of Arab States (Casablanca, Morocco, 7-9 August) was transmitted on 19 August and issued as an official document of the General Assembly.[5] Its circulation as such was viewed with deep regret by the Syrian Arab Republic, which stated on 28 August[6] that, together with four other Arab States, it had not participated in the Conference and that, therefore, the communiqué did not accurately express the true nature of the Arab position on the topics discussed: the Middle East situation, the Iran-Iraq conflict and the situation in the Horn of Africa.

GENERAL ASSEMBLY ACTION

On 25 October, the General Assembly adopted **resolution 40/5** by recorded vote.

Co-operation between the United Nations and the League of Arab States

The General Assembly,

Recalling its previous resolutions on the promotion of co-operation between the United Nations and the League of Arab States, in particular resolutions 36/24 of 9 November 1981, 37/17 of 16 November 1982, 38/6 of 28 October 1983 and 39/9 of 8 November 1984,

Having considered the report of the Secretary-General on co-operation between the United Nations and the League of Arab States,

Having heard the statement by the Permanent Observer of the League of Arab States on co-operation between the United Nations and the League of Arab States of 25 October 1985 and having noted the emphasis placed therein on follow-up projects, actions and procedures on the recommendations adopted at the meeting between representatives of the General Secretariat of the League of Arab States and its specialized organizations and the secretariats of the United Nations and other organizations of the United Nations system, held at Tunis from 28 June to 1 July 1983, as well as on various sectoral activities related to development priorities in the Arab region,

Recalling the relevant Articles of the Charter of the United Nations which encourage activities through regional arrangements for the promotion of the purposes and principles of the United Nations,

Noting with appreciation the desire of the League of Arab States to consolidate and develop the existing ties with the United Nations in all areas relating to the maintenance of international peace and security, and to co-operate in every possible way with the United

---

[a]Rule 39 of the Council's provisional rules of procedure states: "The Security Council may invite members of the Secretariat or other persons, whom it considers competent for the purpose, to supply it with information or to give other assistance in examining matters within its competence."

Nations in the implementation of United Nations resolutions relating to the question of Palestine and the situation in the Middle East,

Aware of the vital importance for the countries members of the League of Arab States of achieving a just, comprehensive and durable solution to the Middle East conflict and the question of Palestine, the core of the conflict,

Realizing that the strengthening of international peace and security is directly related, *inter alia*, to disarmament, decolonization, self-determination and the eradication of all forms of racism and racial discrimination,

Convinced that the maintenance and further strengthening of co-operation between the United Nations and the organizations of the United Nations system and the League of Arab States contribute to the work of the United Nations system and to the promotion of the purposes and principles of the United Nations,

Recalling that at the meeting held at Tunis the framework of co-operation between the United Nations and the League of Arab States in certain priority sectors was defined, and proposals that could lend themselves to joint implementation were recommended,

Recognizing the need for closer co-operation between the United Nations system and the League of Arab States and its specialized organizations in realizing the goals and objectives set forth in the Strategy for Joint Arab Economic Development adopted by the Eleventh Arab Summit Conference, held at Amman from 25 to 27 November 1980,

1. *Takes note with satisfaction* of the report of the Secretary-General;

2. *Expresses its appreciation* to the Secretary-General for the follow-up action taken by him on the proposals adopted at the meeting between representatives of the General Secretariat of the League of Arab States and its specialized organizations and the secretariats of the United Nations and other organizations of the United Nations system, held at Tunis, as well as to the specialized agencies and other organizations of the United Nations system for their efforts to facilitate the implementation of the proposals;

3. *Notes with satisfaction* the results achieved at the sectoral meeting on social development in the Arab region, held at Amman from 19 to 21 August 1985;

4. *Requests* the Secretary-General to continue to strengthen co-operation with the General Secretariat of the League of Arab States for the purpose of implementing United Nations resolutions relating to the question of Palestine and the situation in the Middle East in order to achieve a just, comprehensive and durable solution to the Middle East conflict and the question of Palestine, the core of the conflict;

5. *Requests* the Secretariat of the United Nations and the General Secretariat of the League of Arab States, within their respective fields of competence, further to intensify their co-operation towards the realization of the purposes and principles of the Charter of the United Nations, the strengthening of international peace and security, disarmament, decolonization, self-determination and the eradication of all forms of racism and racial discrimination;

6. *Requests* the Secretary-General to continue his efforts to strengthen co-operation and co-ordination between the United Nations and the organizations of the United Nations system and the League of Arab States and its specialized organizations in order to enhance their capacity to serve the mutual interests of the two organizations in the political, economic, social and cultural fields;

7. *Requests* the Secretary-General to continue the follow-up action to facilitate the implementation of the proposals of a multilateral nature adopted at the meeting held at Tunis in 1983, and to take appropriate action regarding the multilateral proposals relating to social development adopted at the meeting held at Amman in 1985, including the following measures:

(a) Promotion of contacts and consultations between the counterpart programmes, organizations and agencies concerned;

(b) Setting up of joint sectoral inter-agency working groups;

(c) Consultation with the Secretary-General of the League of Arab States regarding the convening in 1987 of the joint sectoral meeting on development of human resources in the Arab region;

8. *Calls upon* the specialized agencies, and other organizations and programmes of the United Nations system:

(a) To continue to co-operate with the Secretary-General and the programmes, organizations and agencies concerned within the United Nations system and the League of Arab States and its specialized organizations in the follow-up of multilateral proposals aimed at strengthening and expanding co-operation in all fields between the United Nations system and the League of Arab States and its specialized organizations;

(b) To maintain and increase contacts and consultations with the counterpart programmes, organizations and agencies concerned regarding projects of a bilateral nature in order to facilitate their implementation;

(c) To inform the Secretary-General, not later than 15 May 1986, of the progress of their co-operation with the League of Arab States and its specialized organizations, in particular, the follow-up action taken on the multilateral and bilateral proposals adopted at the meetings held at Tunis and Amman;

9. *Requests* the Secretary-General, in close co-operation with the Secretary-General of the League of Arab States, to hold periodic consultations as and when appropriate between representatives of the Secretariat of the United Nations and of the General Secretariat of the League of Arab States on follow-up policies, projects, actions and procedures;

10. *Further requests* the Secretary-General to submit to the General Assembly, at its forty-first session, a progress report on the implementation of the present resolution;

11. *Decides* to include in the provisional agenda of its forty-first session the item entitled "Co-operation between the United Nations and the League of Arab States".

General Assembly resolution 40/5

25 October 1985   Meeting 50   133-2-2 (recorded vote)

20-nation draft (A/40/L.7); agenda item 26.

Sponsors: Algeria, Bahrain, Democratic Yemen, Djibouti, Iraq, Jordan, Kuwait, Lebanon, Libyan Arab Jamahiriya, Mauritania, Morocco, Oman, Qatar, Saudi Arabia, Somalia, Sudan, Syrian Arab Republic, Tunisia, United Arab Emirates, Yemen.

Recorded vote in Assembly as follows:

In favour: Albania, Algeria, Argentina, Australia, Austria, Bahrain, Bangladesh, Belgium, Benin, Bolivia, Botswana, Brazil, Brunei Darussalam, Bulgaria, Burkina Faso, Burma, Burundi, Byelorussian SSR, Cameroon, Canada, Central African Republic, Chad, Chile, China, Colombia, Comoros, Congo, Costa Rica, Cuba, Cyprus, Czechoslovakia, Democratic Kampuchea, Democratic Yemen, Denmark, Djibouti, Dominican Republic, Ecuador, Egypt, El Salvador, Equatorial Guinea, Fiji, Finland, France, Gabon, German Democratic Republic, Germany, Federal Republic of, Ghana, Greece, Guatemala, Guinea, Guinea-Bissau, Guyana, Haiti, Hungary, Iceland, India, Indonesia, Iran, Iraq, Ireland, Italy, Ivory Coast, Jamaica, Japan, Jordan, Kenya, Kuwait, Lao People's Democratic Republic, Lebanon, Liberia, Libyan Arab Jamahiriya, Luxembourg, Madagascar, Malaysia, Maldives, Mali, Malta, Mauritania, Mauritius, Mexico, Mongolia, Morocco, Mozambique, Nepal, Netherlands, New Zealand, Nicaragua, Niger, Nigeria, Norway, Oman, Pakistan, Panama, Peru, Philippines, Poland, Portugal, Qatar, Romania, Rwanda, Samoa, Sao Tome and Principe, Saudi Arabia, Senegal, Seychelles, Sierra Leone, Singapore, Somalia, Spain, Sri Lanka, Sudan, Suriname, Sweden, Syrian Arab Republic, Thailand, Togo, Trinidad and Tobago, Tunisia, Turkey, Uganda, Ukrainian SSR, USSR, United Arab Emirates, United Kingdom, United Republic of Tanzania, Uruguay, Venezuela, Viet Nam, Yemen, Yugoslavia, Zaire, Zambia, Zimbabwe.

Against: Israel, United States.

Abstaining: Ethiopia, Grenada.

Israel explained that its negative vote was because of the League's disregard of the principles of peace and security on which the United Nations was based, the League's history having been dedicated to united Arab action aimed at Israel's eradication. The United States could not but vote against, it stated, due to paragraph 4, which it saw as opposing many of its fundamental policies; it voiced concern that the costs of the joint sectoral meeting envisaged in paragraph 7 *(c)* needed to be absorbed within existing United Nations financial resources.

Ethiopia abstained because the League had adopted resolutions detrimental to Ethiopia's national unity and territorial integrity. Grenada's difficulties were with the provisions of paragraph 4.

Also voicing reservations on that paragraph were: Australia; Canada, which did not support all the resolutions referred to; Finland, also on behalf of Denmark, Iceland, Norway and Sweden, which held that the elements with political implications could not prejudice their positions on the substantive matter; and Luxembourg, for the 10 members of the European Community (EC), which recalled that they had not supported all the resolutions mentioned and stressed their preference for dealing with the co-operation issue in terms avoiding divisive elements. The Libyan Arab Jamahiriya said its vote did not mean recognition of Israel.

Organization of the Islamic Conference

In 1985, co-operation continued between the United Nations system and the Organization of the Islamic Conference. The Secretary-General, responding to a 1984 General Assembly request,[7] reported in September 1985[8] on measures taken to strengthen the mechanism for co-operative activities of the two organizations, as provided for by the Assembly in 1982.[9]

The report gave a brief account of the consultations between the two organizations and their representation at meetings, as well as of a co-ordination meeting of the focal points of their lead agencies (Geneva, 30 and 31 July). It outlined developments concerning co-operation between the organizations in political and security-related matters and in economic, social and cultural questions.

The July meeting evaluated progress achieved in the five priority areas of co-operation: food security and agriculture, science and technology, investment mechanisms and joint ventures, eradication of illiteracy and assistance to refugees. The meeting concluded that co-operation should be further strengthened and the emerging modalities systematized through regular and more frequent contacts. Information collection and dissemination was to be intensified and, in view of financial constraints especially in respect of the Conference, emphasis should be on consolidation of selected programmes rather than expansion into new ones.

Political and security activities focused on the situation in Afghanistan and in the Middle East, the Iran-Iraq conflict, decolonization and *apartheid*, and outer space. With respect to economic, social and cultural development, activities in co-operation with some 18 agencies and other entities in the United Nations system were reviewed. The latest such entity to sign a memorandum of co-operation with the Conference was UNCTAD, on 27 June 1985. Discussions with other bodies in the system for concluding similar agreements were under way.

On 11 March,[10] Yemen transmitted the final communiqué and resolutions adopted by the Fifteenth Islamic Conference of Foreign Ministers (Sanaa, 18-22 December 1984[11]), together with reports on those resolutions. Yemen also transmitted, on 15 October 1985,[12] a communiqué of the co-ordination meeting of the Ministers for Foreign Affairs of the Conference (New York, 9 October), dealing with, among other matters, the Middle East situation, South Africa and Namibia, Afghanistan, the Iran-Iraq conflict and the drought in the African Sahel.

During 1985, the Chairman of the Conference participated at one Security Council meeting and its Secretary-General at two meetings, under rule 39[b] of the Council's provisional rules of procedure. Those meetings dealt with a complaint by Tunisia of an Israeli air attack on

---

[b]See footnote a on p. 399.

Tunis; and with the Middle East problem, including the Palestine question.

GENERAL ASSEMBLY ACTION

On 25 October, the General Assembly adopted without vote **resolution 40/4**.

Co-operation between the United Nations and the Organization of the Islamic Conference

The General Assembly,

Having considered the report of the Secretary-General on co-operation between the United Nations and the Organization of the Islamic Conference,

Taking into account the desire of both organizations to co-operate more closely in their common search for solutions to global problems, such as questions relating to international peace and security, disarmament, self-determination, decolonization, fundamental human rights and the establishment of a new international economic order,

Recalling the Articles of the Charter of the United Nations which encourage activities through regional co-operation for the promotion of the purposes and principles of the United Nations,

Noting the strengthening of co-operation between the specialized agencies and other organizations of the United Nations system and the Organization of the Islamic Conference,

Noting the convening of the co-ordination meeting of the focal points of the lead agencies of the United Nations system and the Organization of the Islamic Conference, held at Geneva on 30 and 31 July 1985 in compliance with General Assembly resolution 39/7, which afforded an opportunity to evaluate the progress achieved in the five priority areas of co-operation identified by the first annual meeting between representatives of the secretariats of the United Nations and other organizations of the United Nations system and the secretariat of the Organization of the Islamic Conference, held at Geneva on 15 July 1983,

Taking note of the encouraging results obtained in the evaluation of the progress achieved in the five priority areas of co-operation as well as in the exchange of views on preparatory work and other details for the second general meeting between the two organizations as provided for in General Assembly resolution 37/4,

Convinced that the strengthening of co-operation between the United Nations and other organizations of the United Nations system and the Organization of the Islamic Conference contributes to the promotion of the purposes and principles of the United Nations,

Recalling its resolutions 36/23 of 9 November 1981, 37/4 of 22 October 1982, 38/4 of 28 October 1983 and 39/7 of 8 November 1984,

1. *Takes note with satisfaction* of the report of the Secretary-General;

2. *Approves* the conclusions and recommendations of the co-ordination meeting of the focal points of the lead agencies of the United Nations system and the Organization of the Islamic Conference;

3. *Notes with satisfaction* the active participation of the Organization of the Islamic Conference in the work of the United Nations towards the realization of the purposes and principles of the Charter of the United Nations;

4. *Requests* the United Nations and the Organization of the Islamic Conference to continue co-operation in their common search for solutions to global problems, such as questions relating to international peace and security, disarmament, self-determination, decolonization, fundamental human rights and the establishment of a new international economic order;

5. *Encourages* the specialized agencies and other organizations of the United Nations system to continue to expand their co-operation with the Organization of the Islamic Conference, particularly by negotiating co-operation agreements, and invites them to multiply the contacts and meetings of focal points for co-operation in priority areas of interest to the United Nations and the Organization of the Islamic Conference;

6. *Requests* the Secretary-General to strengthen co-operation and co-ordination between the United Nations and other organizations of the United Nations system and the Organization of the Islamic Conference to serve the mutual interests of the two organizations in the political, economic, social and cultural fields;

7. *Recommends* that the second general meeting between representatives of the secretariats of the United Nations and other organizations of the United Nations system and the secretariat of the Organization of the Islamic Conference as provided for in General Assembly resolution 37/4 should be organized in 1986 at a date and place to be determined through consultations with the organizations concerned;

8. *Expresses its appreciation* for the efforts of the Secretary-General in the promotion of co-operation between the United Nations and the Organization of the Islamic Conference, and expresses the hope that he will continue to strengthen the mechanisms of co-operation between the two organizations;

9. *Requests* the Secretary-General to report to the General Assembly at its forty-first session on the state of co-operation between the United Nations and the Organization of the Islamic Conference;

10. *Decides* to include in the provisional agenda of its forty-first session the item entitled "Co-operation between the United Nations and the Organization of the Islamic Conference".

General Assembly resolution 40/4

25 October 1985   Meeting 50   Adopted without vote

Draft by Yemen (A/40/L.5); agenda item 24.

Other intergovernmental organizations

At the request of the host Governments of several intergovernmental conferences, the main documents of those meetings were transmitted to the Secretary-General in 1985 for circulation as documents of the General Assembly, the Security Council or both, as follows:

—Declaration of the Commemorative Meeting in Observance of the Thirtieth Anniversary of the Asian-African Conference (Bandung, Indonesia, 24 and 25 April).[13]

—Final Political and Economic Declarations adopted by the Conference of Foreign Ministers of

Non-Aligned Countries (Luanda, Angola, 4-7 September);[14] final communiqué adopted by the Meeting of Ministers and Heads of Delegation of Non-Aligned Countries to the fortieth session of the General Assembly (New York, 1 October).[15]

—Communiqué adopted at a meeting of heads of Government of Commonwealth States (Nassau, Bahamas, 16-22 October).[16]

—Final communiqué adopted by the sixth session of the Supreme Council of the Gulf Co-operation Council (Oman, 3-6 November).[17]

—Resolutions adopted by the first extraordinary session of the Conference of African Ministers of Information (Cairo, Egypt, 23-25 November).[18]

REFERENCES
[1]A/40/481 & Corr.1. [2]YUN 1984, p. 378, GA res. 39/9, 8 Nov. 1984. [3]YUN 1983, p. 394. [4]A/40/481/Add.1. [5]A/40/564 & Corr.1. [6]A/40/584. [7]YUN 1984, p. 381, GA res. 39/7, 8 Nov. 1984. [8]A/40/657. [9]YUN 1982, p. 588, GA res. 37/4, 22 Oct. 1982. [10]A/40/173-S/17033. [11]YUN 1984, p. 381. [12]A/40/758-S/17570. [13]A/40/276-S/17138. [14]A/40/854-S/17610 & Corr.1. [15]A/40/704-S/17521. [16]A/40/817. [17]A/40/911-S/17644. [18]A/40/980.

Other institutional questions

Fortieth anniversary of the United Nations

The year 1985 marked the fortieth anniversary of the United Nations, whose theme was "United Nations for a better world", and was also observed as the Year of the United Nations in accordance with the General Assembly's 1984 decision.[1]

Notable among the commemorative activities was the meeting of former and current Presidents of the General Assembly, under the auspices of the United Nations Institute for Training and Research, held in New York from 6 to 10 June 1985. The meeting, whose purpose was to contribute to the debate on improving the impact of the United Nations, centred on two issues: the crisis of multilateralism as it affected the United Nations and the improvement of the General Assembly. The main conclusions and the recommendations of the 11 Presidents for the rationalization of the Assembly's procedures were transmitted by the President of the thirty-ninth session of the Assembly to the Secretary-General on 12 June[2] for circulation to Member States.

Within the context of the anniversary's theme, the Security Council held a commemorative meeting on 26 September, at which it considered its responsibilities for maintaining international peace and security (see p. 392).

In accordance with **decision 40/404** (see p. 406), the Assembly held a commemorative session from 14 to 24 October, the last day coinciding with the proclamation of 1986 as the International Year of Peace (IYP) (see p. 122). Statements made and messages delivered during the proceedings were later published in a compendium.[3] Because the Palestine Liberation Organization (PLO) and the South-West Africa People's Organization (SWAPO)—two organizations with observer status—were not invited to address the commemorative session, Algeria[4] and Burkina Faso,[5] on 17 and 22 October, respectively, advised of their intention not to participate in the proceedings. For the same reason, Iran on 23 October[6] conveyed its deep regret and that of the Muslim people.

In his 24 October concluding address, the Secretary-General said that the commemoration assumed the importance that it did because international relations had reached a critical stage; he emphasized the need—amidst a world seething with tensions and racked by violence—to strengthen that structure of international co-operation which was the United Nations. The Assembly President followed with a restatement of the concerns voiced during the ceremonies, of those areas in which the United Nations had achieved a satisfactory measure of success but where work remained to be done, and of the gravest problems, concluding by appealing to Member States to muster the necessary political will to solve existing conflicts and prevent new ones from arising.

Meeting numbers. GA 40th session: plenary 34, 35, 40-49.

As mandated by the Assembly in 1984,[7] the Department of Public Information of the United Nations Secretariat mounted a wide-ranging information programme aimed at providing an overall perspective of United Nations achievements. Various publications were issued, including two books—one surveying the work of the United Nations in its first 40 years[8] and the other reviewing its peace-keeping operations;[9] a brochure highlighting United Nations–related events in those years;[10] a special issue of the periodical *Objective: Justice*, featuring a history of decolonization;[11] a newsletter on the anniversary;[12] and a booklet giving an overview of United Nations work in development.[13] A special anniversary issue of the magazine *UN Chronicle* was also issued.[14]

The Department produced films and television programmes carrying the anniversary message, among them a film entitled "Why", examining the United Nations and its prospects for the future, and another reflecting young people's aspirations for the Organization. It organized book and photographic exhibitions, an international poster competition on the anniversary, seminars, and meetings with professional groups to promote teaching about the United Nations. A press kit for the occasion was prepared, and special events and activities were conducted at United Nations information centres around the world.

Numerous communications concerning the anniversary were received and circulated (see p. 406), a number of them dealing also with IYP (see p. 123).

ACC activities. Observance of the anniversary was of primary concern to the Administrative Committee on Co-ordination (ACC) in view of the significant contribution of the United Nations specialized agencies and programmes to the betterment of world conditions and to increased international co-operation during the past 40 years. Activities included the designation of focal points by organizations, an assessment of the work of the United Nations system during those years and of its further potentialities, and joint measures to convey effectively to the public information and knowledge about that work. In its annual overview report for 1984/85,[15] ACC said the anniversary provided an opportunity to reassess the United Nations role in international economic co-operation, reverse certain negative trends in multilateralism and renew commitment to the Charter.

Responding to a 1984 Economic and Social Council recommendation[16] and to a General Assembly invitation of the same year,[7] ACC members provided information on their plans and programmes, which ACC submitted in February 1985 to the Preparatory Committee for the anniversary (see below).

On 23 April, during its first 1985 session, ACC requested its Organizational Committee to make recommendations and prepare material to enable it to contribute appropriately to the anniversary's observance.[17] Accordingly, at a special meeting on 25 October, the Committee approved a draft declaration for ACC consideration at its second (October) session. However, no action was taken on the draft.

Activities of the Preparatory Committee. The Preparatory Committee for the Fortieth Anniversary of the United Nations held eight meetings between 19 February and 11 September 1985. The Committee of 117 members (as at 11 September), under the chairmanship of the President of the thirty-ninth session of the General Assembly, made recommendations concerning procedural and organizational arrangements for commemorating the anniversary. Those recommendations were approved by the Assembly when it acted on the Preparatory Committee's report,[18] and embodied them in **decision 40/404.**

As to participation in the ceremonies of organizations with observer status, the Committee stated its understanding that, in accordance with established Assembly practices, representatives of such organizations could address the Assembly under the items of direct relevance to them and could refer to the fortieth anniversary under those items.

The Committee, which had been requested to draw up a suitable text for a final document for signature or adoption by the Assembly as a high point of the commemorative session,[1] had before it two draft declarations. The main draft under consideration was sponsored by the non-aligned countries of Algeria, Democratic Yemen, India, Iraq, the Syrian Arab Republic, Yemen and Yugoslavia.[19] Amendments to that draft were proposed by the United States.[20] By a letter of 18 December,[21] India clarified that the draft represented a consensus text—rather than a proposal by the sponsors—which had evolved as a result of informal consultations, and pointed out that the draft had been transmitted to the Committee on 22 October, at which time there were several unresolved issues remaining. The second draft was put forward by the 10 EC members, Portugal and Spain.[22]

The Committee met once more, on 24 October, to resolve the remaining points of contention, including one on the question of Palestine. The Committee failed to reach agreement on a final text, however, so that, at the sponsors' request, the two drafts and the proposed amendments were circulated as official documents. Thus, the Assembly was unable, on 24 October, to adopt a declaration in honour of the anniversary.

By the first draft, United Nations States Members, having considered the Organization's 40 years' experience, would have declared that it had helped prevent another global war and had achieved significant progress in such endeavours as peace-keeping, promoting human rights and enhancing awareness of the need for disarmament and co-operation for development. They would have acknowledged the Organization's invaluable contribution to decolonization, improving the quality of human life and assisting developing countries; its significant role in the development of international law; and its indispensability as a forum for negotiations for the political, economic, social and humanitarian benefit of humankind.

Members would have also acknowledged, however, that the purposes of the Charter had not been fully realized, and its principles and provisions not universally respected; that the world situation continued to be characterized by confrontation and conflicts, intervention and occupation, threat or use of force, terrorism, violations of human rights and fundamental freedoms, and grave economic and social problems; and that the most destructive weapons ever produced threatened the survival of humanity.

Members would have reiterated their commitment to respect the Charter without reservation and determination to promote the rule of law in international affairs. They would have resolved to promote friendly relations among States based on sovereign equality, to give effect to the principles of sovereignty, independence and territorial integrity of States, to reverse the arms race through genuine disarmament and to redeploy arms resources for economic and social development. They would have stressed the need to address the critical economic situation and famine in Africa and the United Nations role in enhancing international co-operation in science and technology. They would also have: declared their intention to strengthen the United Nations role in maintaining international peace and security and in promoting economic and social development and human rights; emphasized the importance of the Assembly's role under the Charter; agreed to enhance the Security Council's effectiveness; reaffirmed the Secretary-General's responsibilities; and pledged to work together in the United Nations for a better world, through multilateral co-operation.

Other provisions concerned peoples' right to self-determination, early independence for Namibia, eradication of *apartheid*, an end to situations caused by foreign aggression and occupation, disasters, children, youth and the advancement of women.

The amendments proposed by the United States were to three paragraphs. By the first, Members would have declared that all people should have access to basic requirements of life through national efforts supported and strengthened by a just international economic system, to which end they would have reaffirmed their determination to work for the establishment of a new international economic order. The United States amendment would, among other changes, have stated that, while developing countries recognized that ultimate responsibility for their development rested on themselves, industrialized countries would stress their commitment to strengthen support of the developing countries by, *inter alia*, endeavouring to ensure a stable and equitable international environment conducive to development; a collective endeavour to promote a system of just and mutually beneficial international economic relations would contribute to establishing a new international economic order.

By the second paragraph, Members would have pointed to the need urgently and comprehensively to solve the interrelated issues of money, finance, debt and trade, and to the need to address the international debt crisis through a dialogue involving debtor and creditor countries, international private banks and multilateral financial institutions. The amendment would have stated that those issues needed to be resolved urgently with full recognition of their interrelationship and that progress towards resolving the international debt problem should encompass, *inter alia*, pursuit of the dialogue mentioned.

By the third paragraph, Members would have expressed concern that, although the United Nations agenda had included the question of Palestine since 1947, the problem remained unresolved; they would have reaffirmed their commitment to work together, under the auspices of the United Nations, to ensure a just, comprehensive and lasting settlement of the Middle East problem in all its aspects, encompassing the right to self-determination of the Palestinian people and the principle of the inadmissibility of acquisition of territory by force which required termination of the occupation. The United States amendment would have referred instead to the Arab-Israeli dispute and the Palestinian issue, and would have reaffirmed commitment to working together under appropriate auspices for a just, comprehensive and lasting settlement of the Middle East problem in all its aspects, omitting reference to what those aspects encompassed.

The second draft text embodied many elements of the first, adding crisis management as a United Nations achievement. Its provision on the world economic crisis would have had Members recognize the need to reinforce and further develop United Nations activities designed to bring about the economic and social progress of all countries, in the first instance that of the developing countries, and to accentuate the convergence of the economic policies of all States within the framework of a long-term development strategy. The draft spoke of peaceful settlement of disputes without, however, referring to any specific dispute. It also spoke of reinforcing international co-operation for the consolidation of peace and security for all; of the Organization's capacity to promote the ideals of peace and co-operation; and of the current era as offering unprecedented possibilities for mankind to become master of its destiny and to forge a better world by making the forces of reason prevail over those of division and destruction.

A note by the Secretariat with later addenda[23] updated information on action taken or contemplated in observance of the anniversary by: Member States; the Secretariat, specialized agencies and other bodies of the United Nations system; and intergovernmental and non-governmental organizations. Another such note, also with later addenda,[24] summarized information received from Governments in response to the Assembly's 1984 invitation[7] to organize appropriate observances.

In September, acting on the recommendations of the Preparatory Committee, the General Assembly adopted **decision 40/404** without vote.

Commemoration of the fortieth anniversary of the United Nations

At its 3rd plenary meeting, on 20 September 1985, the General Assembly, on the recommendations of the Preparatory Committee for the Fortieth Anniversary of the United Nations, decided that:

(a) All statements made by Heads of State or Government and special envoys during the entire fortieth session of the General Assembly in 1985 should be considered part of the commemoration;

(b) The general debate should be held as usual for a three-week period, from 23 September to 11 October, on the clear and explicit understanding that statements made by Heads of State or Government and special envoys during that period would also be considered part of the commemoration;

(c) Between the conclusion of the general debate and the commemorative ceremony, to be held on 24 October, Heads of State or Government and special envoys might address the General Assembly in connection with the fortieth anniversary celebration;

(d) The culmination of this period should be on 24 October, with a solemn ceremony to hear statements by the Secretary-General and the President of the General Assembly and to adopt a final declaration by consensus;

(e) During the commemorative proceedings between 14 and 24 October, Heads of State or Government should be seated in the General Assembly Hall and escorted to the podium from the floor and, following the practice already approved by the Assembly, delegations should refrain from expressing their congratulations in the Assembly Hall after a speech had been delivered; to this end, Heads of State or Government should be advised of such arrangements and the President of the General Assembly should be requested to draw the attention of representatives to those arrangements;

(f) Delegations should be informed that the number of speakers per day on 21, 22 and 23 October could not exceed twenty-one during regular morning and afternoon meetings, that this number could only be accommodated on the assumption that statements did not exceed fifteen minutes and that any additional speakers on those days would have to be heard at an extended afternoon meeting or at a night meeting;

(g) Heads of State or Government should be advised of the arrangements referred to in subparagraph *(f)* above and the President of the General Assembly should be requested to draw the attention of representatives to those arrangements;

(h) A compendium of the statements delivered by or received from Heads of State or Government with duly accredited delegations and the statements made by their special envoys should be issued as a United Nations publication as part of the commemoration of the fortieth anniversary of the United Nations;

(i) Member States might consider including in their delegations to the fortieth session of the General Assembly those dignitaries who were actively involved in the work of the United Nations, particularly those who had signed the Charter of the United Nations and/or former Presidents of the Assembly.

General Assembly decision 40/404

Adopted without vote

Draft by Preparatory Committee (A/40/49); agenda item 39.

On 14 October, at the beginning of the commemorative session, the Assembly had before it a revised draft resolution on PLO and SWAPO participation, sponsored by India, Iraq, Kuwait, Nigeria, Senegal and Yemen.[25] However, the sponsors did not press the draft to a vote. By the draft, the Assembly would have invited both organizations to address it during the session. The Assembly President stated that the sponsors' major concern related to the Preparatory Committee's interpretation of the participation of such organizations (see above). He explained that the Assembly, in acting on the Committee's report on 20 September, did so without prejudice to its 1974[26] and 1976[27] resolutions granting observer status to PLO and SWAPO, respectively.

Under the agenda item on the commemoration of the anniversary, the Assembly also adopted **resolution 40/237** on the review of the efficiency of the administrative and financial functioning of the United Nations.

Communications. Throughout 1985, the Secretary-General received many letters transmitting statements, messages, appeals, declarations and resolutions, issued officially by Governments in observance of the anniversary. The majority recalled the purposes for which the United Nations had been founded and underscored its achievements and the contribution of States in bringing them about. They also pointed to areas for improvement and to tasks that lay ahead, and called for actions to be taken.

Several letters annexed a description of commemorative activities, such as an 8 April letter from Yugoslavia[28] mentioning special publications and commemorative stamps, children and youth activities, streets and squares named after the United Nations, and special sessions held by United Nations associations. On 14 June, Bulgaria[29] listed such activities as solemn meetings and mass gatherings, popular scientific activities, lectures, publications, film and broadcast documentaries, photo exhibits, newspaper and magazine features, and special school programmes including the awarding of scholarships for 1985/86 to students from developing countries and national liberation movements. Similarly, the Foreign Minister of the Byelorussian SSR, in a 28 June letter,[30] spoke of special press, radio and television programmes, as well as photo and poster exhibits.

A number of communications called for united action to avert the threat of nuclear war and to halt the arms race. They included a 9 May letter from the Foreign Minister of Poland,[31] a statement issued by Czechoslovakia jointly with Bulgaria, the Byelorussian SSR, Cuba, the German Democratic Republic, Hungary, Mongolia, Poland, the Ukrainian SSR, the USSR and Viet Nam,[32] a 17 May statement from Mongolia[33] and a 24 June message from the German Democratic Republic.[34]

Venezuela, on 24 June,[35] transmitted a message by its Foreign Minister expressing confidence that the commemoration would strengthen joint action towards attaining Charter ideals. A 24 October[36] communication by its President expressed pride in United Nations accomplishments and stated that without the Organization mankind would be living in a less hopeful world.

In a 24 June telegram,[37] the Foreign Minister of the USSR underscored the anniversary's significance in terms of United Nations accomplishments and its potential for preserving peace and improving the economic and social well-being of all; it affirmed USSR readiness to ensure that the democratic principles on which the Organization had been founded became firmly established in international relations.

Several communications used the occasion to reaffirm a commitment to the Charter's purposes and principles and to the United Nations. These included a 26 June[38] joint appeal by the heads of State or Government of Argentina, Austria, Canada, Jordan, Malaysia, Senegal, Spain, Sweden and the United Republic of Tanzania; a 22 June letter[39] from the Foreign Minister of the Ukrainian SSR; the 29 July Lima Declaration signed by 20 Latin American States;[40] and a declaration from Bulgaria,[41] a resolution by the Ivory Coast,[42] a message from Mongolia[43] and a message from the President of Guinea,[44] all issued in October.

The President of Brazil issued two messages: on 26 June,[45] he reiterated his confidence in the Organization's ability to strengthen its role in the peaceful solution of conflicts; and on 23 October,[46] he stated that renewed dedication to the Charter was indispensable for realizing the ideals that had inspired the United Nations.

The Foreign Minister of Uruguay, on 25 October,[47] stated that existing conflicts and the accelerating arms race committed the international community more than ever to redoubling its efforts towards the peaceful settlement of disputes. A motion adopted by the Senate of Peru on 22 October[48] voiced hope that United Nations influence would make possible the attainment of peace, the survival of the human race and its harmonious coexistence.

A 24 October message[49] by the President of Afghanistan cited not only United Nations achievements but also the obstacles to its functioning—such as the activities of the imperialist Powers and their industrial-military complexes; elimination of those obstacles, the message said, required total observance of the Organization's aspirations.

United Nations reform was called for in two statements. On 16 August,[50] the Philippines made a series of recommendations, among them a more efficient, institutionalized system of evaluation, programme policies and priorities reflecting national priorities, retrenchment measures and greater utilization of the network concept. On 29 October,[51] Egypt reiterated its call to amend the Charter to enable the Organization to keep pace with developments and to perform its functions in such manner as to realize the purposes for which it had been created.

The indispensability of the United Nations as an instrument of co-operation and understanding among its Members and as the best forum for solving complex problems was stressed by Yugoslavia on 5 July.[52] That there was no alternative to the Organization was equally stressed by a declaration adopted by Austria's Socialist International (Vienna, 15 October),[53] which also suggested measures for reform. A 24 October statement[54] by the Foreign Minister of Tunisia stated that, criticism of its detractors notwithstanding, the United Nations remained mankind's greatest hope, the last resort of small nations, and the instrument without which law and justice would go into oblivion.

A 26 June statement[55] by the Foreign Minister of the Federal Republic of Germany attributed the weaknesses of the United Nations principally to the lack of political determination of its Members to act in accordance with its purposes and principles. A message of 23 October[56] by the Prime Minister of Malaysia said the anniversary provided the opportunity for the international community to redirect its political will towards overcoming the Organization's shortcomings. Also on 23 October,[57] the President of the Lao People's Democratic Republic pointed to the need for a demonstration of such will.

The Chairman of the Council of Ministers of Viet Nam, in a 23 October message,[58] expressed appreciation to the Secretary-General for his contribution to the cause of world peace and to building a South-East Asia of peace, stability, friendship and co-operation; Viet Nam highly valued United Nations economic and technical assistance for the country's reconstruction. Bolivia's President, by a message of 24 October,[59] paid tribute to the Organization and cited its outstanding achievements, in particular the multinational co-operation it had begun in support of his country's economic recovery.

A 28 September statement[60] by Argentina's Senate expressed hope that United Nations action on behalf of justice, peace and development of all peoples would continue to guide all nations and that Members would contribute towards strengthening the Organization.

Communications were also received from intergovernmental and non-governmental organizations. The Asian-African Legal Consultative Committee transmitted,[61] as its contribution to the anniversary's observance, a study it had prepared on strengthening the United Nations role through rationalization of functional modalities with special reference to the Assembly (see LEGAL QUESTIONS, Chapter VII). The final communiqué of the Meeting of Ministers and Heads of Delegation of Non-Aligned Countries (see p. 403) reaffirmed the Movement's support to the United Nations; the Political Declaration of the Movement's ministerial Conference (see also p. 403) stated that the anniversary should give impetus to strengthening the Organization so that multilateral negotiations might bring about political solutions, and so that equality and independence of all countries and principles of coexistence might become the basis of international relations.

A statement by the World Federation of United Nations Associations (WFUNA) (thirtieth plenary assembly, Geneva, October), transmitted by Canada on 17 October,[62] affirmed WFUNA's determination to work towards United Nations objectives and called on all Member States to intensify efforts to strengthen its authority and on all non-governmental organizations (NGOs) to support those efforts. A 13 September message[63] by the Conference of Non-Governmental Organizations reconfirmed NGO commitment to the Charter and underscored that strict adherence to its provisions was indispensable for the maintenance of international peace and security and for creating conditions necessary for economic, social and cultural development and for safeguarding human rights.

Several communications related to addresses made before the Assembly during the commemorative session.

On 24 October,[64] Ethiopia, referring to the speech made that day by the United States President, called baseless his allegation that 1,700 USSR advisers and 2,500 Cuban troops were in Ethiopia; there were but few foreign advisers and no combat troops, it said, and its bilateral relations with any country were determined solely by Ethiopia.

Referring to the same address, Afghanistan, on 28 October,[65] accused the United States President of evading serious consideration of global questions by fabricating artificial issues in his references to Afghanistan. On 6 November,[66] Afghanistan further accused him of putting regional conflicts at the centre of his speech and protested against what it labelled ill-intentioned interpretations of the realities in that country.

On 18 October,[67] Iran stated that Iraq, in its address that day, had repeated its fallacious allegations against Iran.

On 8 November,[68] Bulgaria, referring to what it called unwarranted accusations made against it by Turkey when that country spoke on 22 October, stated that the existence of a Turkish minority in Bulgaria was fictitious; Turkey's attempts to destabilize the Balkans were intended to divert world attention from Turkey's own domestic problems. Replying on 18 November,[69] Turkey insisted that a Muslim Turkish minority, numbering 1.5 million and suffering from a campaign of terror, existed in Bulgaria; Turkey quoted excerpts from the world's press giving accounts of clashes between ethnic Turks and the Bulgarian authorities during the first half of 1985.

A number of the communications received in connection with the anniversary also dealt with the observance of 1985 as the International Year of Peace (see p. 123).

Composition of UN organs

In 1985, as in previous years since 1979, consideration of the question of the composition of the relevant organs of the United Nations was deferred, based on a recommendation of the Special Political Committee, which reported that none of its members had requested to speak on the substance of the item.[70] Acting without vote on that recommendation, the General Assembly, on 16 December, adopted **decision 40/430**, by which it included the item in the provisional agenda of its forty-first (1986) session.

REFERENCES

[1]YUN 1984, p. 383, GA res. 39/161 A, 17 Dec. 1984. [2]A/40/377. [3]*Commemoration of the Fortieth Anniversary of the United Nations: Statements and Messages*, Sales No. E.86.I.6. [4]A/40/797-S/17588. [5]A/40/787-S/17585. [6]A/40/796. [7]YUN 1984, p. 383, GA dec. 39/425, 17 Dec. 1984. [8]*The United Nations at Forty: A Foundation to Build On* (DPI/865), Sales No. E.85.I.24. [9]*The Blue Helmets: A Review of United Nations Peace-keeping* (DPI/850), Sales No. E.85.I.18. [10]*UN for a Better World*, DPI/849. [11]*Objective: Justice*, vol. XVII, No. 1, June 1985. [12]*Fortieth Anniversary Newsletter*. [13]*Aid through the UN System: Questions and Answers*. [14]*UN Chronicle*, vol. XXII, No. 9, Oct. 1985. [15]E/1985/57. [16]YUN 1984, p. 382, ESC res. 1984/82, 27 July 1984. [17]ACC/1985/DEC/1-13 (dec. 1985/3). [18]A/40/49. [19]A/AC.222/L.5 & Corr.1. [20]A/AC.222/L.7. [21]A/40/1071. [22]A/AC.222/L.6. [23]A/AC.222/9 & Add.1,2. [24]A/AC.222/10 & Add.1-9 & Add.9/Corr.1 & Add.10,11. [25]A/40/L.2/Rev.1. [26]YUN 1974, p. 227, GA res. 3237(XXIX), 22 Nov. 1974. [27]YUN 1976, p. 790, GA res. 31/152, 20 Dec. 1976. [28]A/40/230. [29]A/40/387. [30]A/40/490. [31]A/40/326. [32]A/40/320-E/1985/82. [33]A/40/322. [34]A/40/415. [35]A/40/408. [36]A/40/813. [37]A/40/428. [38]A/40/402. [39]A/40/413. [40]A/40/544. [41]A/40/746. [42]A/40/810. [43]A/40/795. [44]A/40/878. [45]A/40/483. [46]A/40/800. [47]A/40/875. [48]A/40/836-S/17603. [49]A/40/811-S/17590. [50]A/40/566. [51]A/40/824. [52]A/40/467. [53]A/40/765. [54]A/40/812-S/17591. [55]A/40/414. [56]A/40/819. [57]A/40/792. [58]A/40/793. [59]A/40/802. [60]A/40/1030. [61]A/40/726. [62]A/40/764. [63]A/40/912. [64]A/40/801. [65]A/40/821-S/17594. [66]A/40/859-S/17613. [67]A/40/785. [68]A/40/869. [69]A/40/904. [70]A/40/809.

Economic and social questions

Chapter I

Development policy and international economic co-operation

The need for the developing countries to advance at an acceptable pace against the background of the debt crisis was discussed in several United Nations bodies throughout 1985. During discussions on the world economic situation and in major economic reports, it was stressed that, despite the significant expansion of world output and international trade, the legacy of the global recession of the early 1980s was still affecting a large number of developing countries and the middle years of the decade would continue to be characterized by high unemployment and inadequate progress against world poverty. Particular attention was given to the seriousness of the plight of the least developed countries and of sub-Saharan Africa.

In his annual report on the work of the Organization (see p. 3), the Secretary-General also noted the uneven functioning of the world economy, stating that high technology in industrial countries promised great affluence but also caused overcapacity, obsolescence and unemployment, while many developing countries, in addition to basic development problems, were crippled by debt burdens. Since the need for international economic co-operation increasingly cut across traditional sectoral boundaries, what was required was more effective use of the United Nations as a forum for integrating practical effort which should also increase the effectiveness of the specialized agencies. There was a parallel need for governmental ministries to act in concert with each other towards agreed objectives if the international system was to perform effectively.

The mid-term review and appraisal of the implementation of the International Development Strategy for the Third United Nations Development Decade (the 1980s) was completed in 1985 by the Committee established to carry out that process. Although the Strategy's growth and assistance targets had not been met, the continuing validity of its goals and objectives were reaffirmed.

The mid-term global review of the implementation of the Substantial New Programme of Ac-

tion for the 1980s for the Least Developed Countries (LDCs) was carried out in October by the United Nations Conference on Trade and Development (UNCTAD) Intergovernmental Group on LDCs. The General Assembly emphasized that they needed urgent and special attention from the international community and added Vanuatu to the list of officially designated LDCs, bringing the total number of countries so listed to 37. Country review meetings continued to be organized for individual LDCs by the United Nations Development Programme (UNDP), which also administered the special fund for them.

After the implementation of the Charter of Economic Rights and Duties of States was reviewed by an *Ad Hoc* Committee, the Assembly urged States to examine further the Charter's implementation, thereby contributing to the establishment of the new international economic order.

Following discussions in the Economic and Social Council on conducting constructive international economic negotiations, the Assembly urged Member States to continue negotiations initiated in the United Nations system on international economic issues and to bring them to a successful end.

Informal discussions continued throughout the year on the launching of global negotiations on international economic co-operation for development, originally scheduled to start in 1980; in suspending its 1985 session, the Assembly decided to consider the issue when it resumed the session in 1986. The Assembly also felt that a common endeavour to promote just and mutually beneficial international economic relations would contribute to the economic well-being of States and to the establishment of a new international economic order.

During the year, the question of economic co-operation among developing countries was considered in UNCTAD, while activities in the United Nations system regarding economic and technical co-operation among those countries were discussed in the Assembly, the Council, the Committee for Programme Co-ordination (CPC) and Joint Meetings of CPC and the Administrative Committee on Co-ordination (ACC).

The *World Economic Survey 1985*, which analysed current trends and policies in the world economy, was the background document for the Council's annual discussion of international economic and social policy. UNCTAD produced its fifth annual report on trade and development issues, the *Trade and Development Report, 1985*, which, in addition to analysing the world economy, focused on the problem of debt and development. A further assessment of the world economic situation was carried out by the Committee for Development Planning (CDP) which stated that effective multilateral economic co-operation was particularly necessary in four areas—the trading system, the monetary and financial system, debt and development finance, and the crisis in sub-Saharan Africa.

The Assembly again considered the specific problems and geographical handicaps of landlocked developing countries and called for assistance to help them with their transport and transit infrastructures. The United Nations Special Fund for Land-locked Developing Countries was dissolved by the Assembly because of the low level of contributions.

The Assembly decided that the Secretary-General should continue reporting on the overall socio-economic perspective of the world economy to the year 2000 and it singled out areas for special attention in 1987. In other actions, the Assembly again deplored the application of coercive economic measures by developed countries, and requested Member States to submit additional comments on a proposed new international human order: moral aspects of development.

Broad areas of economic and social development were considered in several United Nations forums during the year. The improvement of various aspects of development planning, education and administration continued to be studied, while the work of the United Nations system in rural development continued to be reviewed.

Topics related to this chapter. Disarmament: disarmament and development. Operational activities for development. Economic assistance, disasters and emergency relief: Africa and the critical economic situation. International trade and finance. Regional economic and social activities: economic and social trends—Africa, Asia and the Pacific, Europe, Latin America and the Caribbean, Western Asia; development policy and regional economic co-operation—Africa, Asia and the Pacific, Europe, Latin America and the Caribbean, Western Asia. Social and cultural development: social aspects of development; crime prevention. Human rights: right to development. Women: women and development. Statistics: economic statistics. International economic law: legal aspects of the new international economic order.

International economic relations

Development and economic co-operation

Several United Nations bodies, including the General Assembly and the Economic and Social Council, continued to follow aspects of development and economic co-operation during 1985. In resolution 40/178, the Assembly urged Member States to continue, in good faith, negotiations initiated in the United Nations system on international economic issues, stressing the willingness of those States to strengthen that system as a framework for solving economic, scientific-technological and social problems. Having considered a report on the overall socio-economic perspective of the world economy to the year 2000, the Assembly identified topics for special attention in 1987 (resolution 40/207). It considered that promoting just and mutually beneficial international economic relations would contribute to each State's economic well-being and to establishing a new international economic order (40/173). The Assembly again deplored the use of coercive economic measures by some developed countries and their impact on international economic relations (40/185). In other action, the Assembly considered the moral aspects of development contained in the proposed international human order (40/206).

The mid-term review and appraisal of the implementation of the International Development Strategy for the Third United Nations Development Decade (the 1980s) was concluded by the Committee established for that purpose and the Assembly endorsed the Committee's agreed conclusions (decision 40/438). A review of the implementation of the 1974 Charter of Economic Rights and Duties of States was carried out by an *Ad Hoc* Committee and the Assembly urged States to examine further the Charter's implementation (resolution 40/182).

Economic co-operation among developing countries (ECDC) was widely discussed in various United Nations forums, with the UNCTAD Committee on ECDC holding its fourth session in 1985.

Several United Nations bodies expressed concern over the economic situation in Africa, particularly in the sub-Sahara.

Informal contacts on global economic negotiations continued throughout the year, with no agreement being reached.

CDP activities. At its twenty-first session, held in two parts, the first in November 1984[1] and the second in April 1985,[2] CDP had multilateral economic co-operation as its central theme. Noting that the contribution of multilateralism to post-war economic progress had been impressive but that major changes in the world economy had created new challenges, CDP expressed concern at the strains facing multilateral co-operation and the resulting danger of a drift away from order, stability, predictability and rules, which posed a threat to the international community, especially its weakest members.

In view of the growing economic interdependence of national economies and dramatic changes taking place in the world's industrial and financial structures, and in order to cope more effectively with demographic momentum and the ecological impact of economic activity, CDP proposed a strengthening of multilateralism. Effective multilateral co-operation would be particularly necessary to meet four immediate challenges to the world economy, namely: the risk of disintegration of the world trading system; the instability and uncertainty in the international monetary and financial system; debt and development finance (see also Chapter IV of this section); and the crisis in sub-Saharan Africa (see Chapter III of this section).

CDP noted that the primary focus on multilateral economic co-operation did not indicate lack of concern for the appropriateness of national policies, in both developing and industrialized countries; in many developing ones, there could be little prospect of future development unless there was major domestic policy reform to complement a more supportive international environment.

A CDP working group on capital requirements of developing countries met in New York from 9 to 11 December 1985.

ACC activities. In its annual overview report to the Economic and Social Council,[3] ACC stated that, in reviewing the world economy, it had noted the recovery from recession in industrialized countries and the resumption of growth in a great number of developing countries. Recovery, however, had been accompanied by increasing protectionist pressures and moves away from multilateral trade agreements, while weaknesses persisted in commodity prices. ACC noted that the fortieth anniversary of the United Nations in 1985 provided an opportunity to reassess the Organization's role in international economic co-operation, reverse negative trends in multilateralism and renew commitment to the Charter of the United Nations.

At its first regular 1985 session (Geneva, 22 and 23 April),[4] ACC took note of a 1984 report by its Task Force on Long-Term Development Objectives on medium- and long-term perspectives and problems of employment and development,[5] and requested the Task Force to continue assessing the world economic situation, taking into account the views expressed in ACC, the coherence of the United Nations system's long-term development objectives and issues such as employment and social aspects of development, including the social cost of adjustment.

At its second regular session of the year (New York, 28 and 29 October),[6] ACC decided to undertake at its first regular 1986 session an in-depth review of issues related to conditions for fostering economic growth and asked the Task Force to prepare for it, focusing on the economic and social implications of growth strategies and the impact of adjustment policies and measures. ACC took note of the intention of the Director-General for Development and International Economic Co-operation to undertake a study, in consultation with ACC members, on strengthening co-operation and co-ordination in selected economic and social areas.

World Economic Survey 1985. During its annual discussion of international economic and social policy, which took place in July (see below), the Economic and Social Council had before it the *World Economic Survey 1985*,[7] prepared by the United Nations Department of International Economic and Social Affairs (DIESA) and based on information available as at 1 April 1985.

After analysing trends and prospects in the world economy (see p. 428), the *Survey* listed key policy issues for international and national action: the adoption by industrial countries of standstill provisions on trade barriers and a gradual dismantling of non-tariff barriers and discriminatory trade restrictions; gradually reducing the United States budget deficit combined with relaxing cautious fiscal stances in those developed countries in a position to do so, to avoid deceleration of world economic growth; more effective consultations among developed countries to further exchange rate stability; use of the centrally planned economies' five-year plans (1986-1990) to consolidate recent progress, lay the foundations for more balanced long-term growth and expand economic relations with developing countries; effective policies in developing countries to increase domestic savings and to attract official and private capital from abroad; an improvement in the mix of internal adjustment efforts and external financial support for countries facing balance-of-payments difficulties and a more supportive stance by the International Monetary Fund in that regard, particularly the restoration of the orginal character of its extended fund and compensatory financing facilities; increased exports and a return to more normal interest rates to restore creditworthiness to many developing countries and arrest further negative resource transfers from them, with further debt renegotiations required in the mean time; an increased inflow of official development assistance (ODA), as well as debt relief, to LDCs and other low-income countries which continued to be afflicted by stagnation or declines in per capita incomes and still faced weak primary commodity markets; an increase in the capital base of the World Bank and regional development banks, which faced resource constraints precluding a normal increase in lending activities; close attention to the emergency food situation in sub-Saharan Africa and further international and domestic efforts to rehabilitate the social and productive infrastructure; and the strengthening of existing trade arrangements and the enactment of more comprehensive ones.

The Economic and Social Council's general discussion of international economic and social policy[8] focused on international co-operation in the interrelated areas of money, finance, debt and trade and the United Nations role in promoting such co-operation in an increasingly interdependent world. The Council had decided, in 1984,[9] that in 1985 it would give special attention to the Organization's role in that regard. Shared concern about future world economic prospects prompted most delegations to stress the need for enhanced international co-operation in those interrelated areas. Of immediate concern was the prospective deceleration in growth in certain industrialized countries and the possible concomitant slow-down in world trade. Averting a new global recession required sustained non-inflationary growth in those countries, greater monetary stability, enlarged market access for exports of developing countries and larger resource flows to them. It also required sustained adjustment efforts by those countries to redress external and internal imbalances and improve allocative efficiency in their economies.

In the longer term, concerted efforts were necessary to redress fundamental inequities and deficiencies in the international monetary, financial and trading systems, including restoration of the multilateral character of the trading régime, improved mechanisms for creating and distributing international liquidity and ensuring adequate financial resources for developing countries in support of their development efforts.

On 25 July, the Council took note of the *Survey* (**decision 1985/182**) and decided to transmit a summary of its discussion to the General Assembly (**decision 1985/183**); it was transmitted on 5 August as a statement by the Council President.[10]

Report of the Secretary-General. In his September 1985 report to the General Assembly on the Organization's work (see p. 3), the Secretary-General stated that it had become increasingly clear that economic, financial, monetary and trade issues were so interrelated and of such profound political and social importance that they could be dealt with effectively only as part of a wider political process. The need for international co-operation in economic affairs more and more cut across traditional sectoral boundaries, as represented nationally by different ministries and internationally by different specialized agencies. What was required was more effective and pragmatic use of the United Nations as a forum for integrating practical effort which should enhance the effectiveness of the specialized agencies. At the national level, there was need for governmental ministries to act in concert with each other if the international system was to perform effectively.

Communications. During 1985, communications dealing with general aspects of international economic relations were received by the Secretary-General. Among these were: an 11 March[11] note verbale from Yemen transmitting documents of the Fifteenth Islamic Conference of Foreign Ministers (Sanaa, 18-22 December 1984); an 18 March[12] letter from Uruguay transmitting the final communiqué of the Third Ministerial Meeting of the Consultation and Follow-up Machinery of the Cartagena Consensus (Santo Domingo, Dominican Republic, 7 and 8 February); a 2 April[13] letter from Costa Rica and Panama transmitting a joint declaration signed by their heads of State on 19 March; a 1 May letter[14] from Indonesia transmitting the Declaration of the Commemorative Meeting in Observance of the Thirtieth Anniversary of the Asian-African Conference (Bandung, 24 and 25 April); a 9 May letter[15] from the USSR transmitting a document on its economic assistance to developing countries; a 9 May[16] letter from the Federal Republic of Germany transmitting the Bonn Economic Declaration entitled "Towards sustained growth and higher employment", issued at the Bonn Economic Summit (2-4 May) which was attended by the heads of State or Government of seven major industrialized countries (Canada, France, Federal Republic of Germany, Italy, Japan, United Kingdom, United States) and the President of the Commission of the European Communities; a 24 June[17] note verbale from the USSR transmitting a document giving its position on problems of development and international economic co-operation; a 4 July[18] letter from Poland transmitting the communiqué of the fortieth session of the Council for Mutual Economic Assistance (Warsaw, 25-27 June); a 9 July[19] letter from the Federal Republic of Germany, Japan, the United Kingdom and the United States concerning contributions to the development activities of the United Nations system; a 12 July[20] letter from Bulgaria transmitting a statement delivered on behalf of the socialist countries to the Economic and Social Council on 9 July; a 12 August[21] letter from Peru transmitting the Lima Declaration signed on 29 July by the heads of State of Argentina, Bolivia, Colombia, the Dominican Republic, Panama, Uruguay and Peru, and by the special representatives of 13 other Latin American countries; a 19 September[22] letter from Papua New Guinea transmitting the Sixteenth South Pacific Forum communiqué (Rarotonga, Cook Islands, 5 and 6 August); a 1 October[23] letter from the German Democratic Republic transmitting a communication on its assistance to developing countries and national liberation movements in 1984; an 8 October[24] letter from Japan transmitting information on its new medium-term target for expanding ODA; a 17 October[25] letter from Egypt transmitting a declaration adopted by the Group of 77 developing countries at their annual meeting (New York, 4 October); a 28 October[26] letter from the Bahamas transmitting a communiqué adopted by heads of Government of Commonwealth States at their summit (Nassau, 16-22 October); a 15 October[27] note verbale from Canada transmitting the resolutions of the Seventy-fourth Inter-Parliamentary Conference (Ottawa, 2-7 September); a 30 October[28] letter from Czechoslovakia transmitting a report on its economic assistance to developing countries and national liberation movements in 1984; a 5 November[29] letter from Kuwait transmitting data on its contributions to a number of African countries since January 1984; a 5 November[30] letter from Angola transmitting the Final Political Declaration and Final Economic Declaration of the Conference of Foreign Ministers of Non-Aligned Countries (Luanda, 4-7 September); and a 20 November[31] letter from the USSR transmitting a document on its economic co-operation with developing countries.

ECONOMIC AND SOCIAL COUNCIL ACTION

In July, the Economic and Social Council adopted **decision 1985/181** without vote.

Conducting constructive and action-oriented international economic negotiations

At its 52nd plenary meeting, on 25 July 1985, the Council, recalling its resolution 1984/82 of 27 July 1984 on the fortieth anniversary of the United Nations in 1985, having devoted special attention to an assessment of the role of the United Nations in promoting international economic and social co-operation and to the consideration of ways of strengthening the role of the Organization and of further enhancing its effectiveness in this regard, and noting the importance of the ideas contained in the draft resolution entitled "Conducting constructive and

action-oriented international economic negotiations", annexed to the present decision, and the extensive discussion held thereon, decided to transmit the draft resolution to the General Assembly at its fortieth session for further consideration and appropriate action.

ANNEX
Conducting constructive and action-oriented international economic negotiations

The General Assembly,

Reaffirming the fundamental purposes of the United Nations as laid down in its Charter,

Recalling that the United Nations should promote, *inter alia,* higher standards of living, full employment, and conditions of economic and social progress and development, as well as solutions of international economic, social and related problems,

Bearing in mind that conditions of stability and well-being are necessary for peaceful and friendly relations among nations based on respect for the principle of equal rights and self-determination of peoples,

Particularly concerned at the deterioration in the international economic environment, especially at the very grave economic situation suffered by developing countries,

Alarmed about the growing tendency to solve internal economic problems at the expense of other countries and to undermine normal economic and scientific-technological co-operation among nations,

Concerned also at the impasse in international economic negotiations within the United Nations on nearly all substantial issues as a result of a retreat from multilateral co-operation by certain developed countries,

Noting the important role and historic responsibility of Governments, statesmen and politicians for promoting international economic co-operation and for conducting fruitful multilateral negotiations to this end,

Stressing that the purposes of the United Nations can be achieved only under conditions in which States comply fully with their obligations assumed under the Charter,

Expressing the hope and desire that the year 1985—the fortieth anniversary of the establishment of the United Nations—will mark the beginning of an era of durable and global economic and social co-operation, of strengthening the role of the Organization and of further enhancing its effectiveness in this regard,

1. *Reaffirms* that co-operation among all nations should be based on respect for the independence, sovereignty and territorial integrity of each State, including the right of each people to choose freely its own socio-economic and political system and to exercise full sovereignty over its wealth and natural resources;

2. *Appeals* to all States Members of the United Nations to reaffirm their solemn pledge to take joint and separate action in co-operation with the Organization for the achievement of the purposes set forth in the Charter of the United Nations on international economic and social co-operation and to contribute their genuine share of efforts to this end;

3. *Emphasizes* the urgency for all Member States to contribute actively to creating an atmosphere favourable to fruitful and constructive negotiations on international economic problems within the United Nations;

4. *Stresses* the willingness of the Member States to strengthen the United Nations Organization as a forum

for constructive dialogue and joint efforts in solving international economic problems, especially problems confronting the developing countries, on the basis of the principle of equality, mutual benefit and respect for the legitimate interests and rights of all peoples, and with due regard for the real situation in the world;

5. *Urges* all Member States to conduct in good faith the negotiations initiated in recent years in the United Nations on international economic problems and to bring them to a successful end by reaching mutually acceptable and just solutions in accordance with the objectives agreed upon;

6. *Invites* the Secretary-General to report to the General Assembly at its forty-first session, through the Economic and Social Council, on the progress achieved in this regard and to make conclusions as appropriate.

Economic and Social Council decision 1985/181

Adopted without vote

Draft by Vice-President (E/1985/L.56), based on informal consultations on draft by German Democratic Republic (E/1985/L.48); agenda item 3.
Meeting numbers. ESC 44, 52.

GENERAL ASSEMBLY ACTION

After considering the draft transmitted by the Council, the General Assembly on 17 December adopted **resolution 40/178** without vote, as recommended by the Second (Economic and Financial) Committee.

Strengthening the role of the United Nations in the field of international economic, scientific-technological and social co-operation

The General Assembly,

Reaffirming the fundamental purposes of the United Nations as laid down in its Charter,

Recognizing that the creation of conditions of stability and well-being is necessary for peaceful and friendly relations among nations based on respect for the principle of equal rights and self-determination of peoples,

Reaffirming that the United Nations, with a view to the creation of such conditions, should promote higher standards of living, full employment, conditions of economic and social progress and development, solutions of international economic, social, health and related problems, international cultural and educational co-operation, and universal respect for, and observance of, human rights and fundamental freedoms for all without distinction as to race, sex, language or religion,

Recalling its resolutions 3201(S-VI) and 3202(S-VI) of 1 May 1974, containing the Declaration and the Programme of Action on the Establishment of a New International Economic Order, 3281(XXIX) of 12 December 1974, containing the Charter of Economic Rights and Duties of States, 3362(S-VII) of 16 September 1975 on development and international economic co-operation and 35/56 of 5 December 1980, the annex to which contains the International Development Strategy for the Third United Nations Development Decade,

Aware of the current state of international economic relations which calls for renewed efforts to promote international economic co-operation and to create a more favourable environment for advancing the economic and social development of all countries, in particular the developing countries,

Stressing the importance of multilateral economic negotiations in the United Nations system,

Noting the important role and historic responsibility of Governments for promoting international economic co-operation and for conducting fruitful multilateral negotiations to this end,

Stressing that the purposes of the United Nations can be achieved only under conditions in which its Members comply fully with their obligations assumed under the Charter,

Expressing the hope and desire that the year 1985 will mark the beginning of a new era of durable and global economic and social co-operation, of strengthening the role of the United Nations system and of further enhancing its effectiveness in this regard,

1. *Reaffirms* that co-operation among all nations should be based on respect for the independence, sovereignty and territorial integrity of each State, including the right of each people to choose freely its own socio-economic and political system;

2. *Appeals* to all Member States to reaffirm their solemn pledge to take joint and separate action in co-operation with the Organization for the achievement of the purposes set forth in the Charter on international economic co-operation and to contribute genuinely their share of efforts to this end;

3. *Emphasizes* the important contribution of the United Nations system in responding to the particular needs of the developing countries, and stresses in this context the need to strengthen multilateral co-operation for development, including increased voluntary contributions to operational activities for development of the United Nations system;

4. *Emphasizes also* the urgent need for all Member States to intensify their contribution to creating an atmosphere favourable to fruitful and constructive negotiations on international economic problems within the United Nations system;

5. *Stresses* the willingness of Member States to strengthen the United Nations system as a framework for constructive dialogue and joint efforts in solving international economic, scientific-technological and social problems, especially problems confronting the developing countries;

6. *Urges* all Member States to continue in a constructive spirit and in good faith the negotiations initiated in the United Nations system on international economic issues and to bring them to a successful end by reaching mutually acceptable and just solutions in accordance with the objectives agreed upon;

7. *Invites* the Secretary-General to report to the General Assembly, in his annual reports, on the progress achieved in the implementation of the present resolution.

General Assembly resolution 40/178

17 December 1985   Meeting 119   Adopted without vote

Approved by Second Committee (A/40/1009/Add.2) without vote, 11 December (meeting 50); draft by Vice-Chairman (A/C.2/40/L.118), based on informal consultations on draft annexed to Economic and Social Council decision 1985/181 (A/C.2/40/L.3); agenda item 12.
Meeting numbers. GA 40th session: 2nd Committee 36, 39, 48-50; plenary 119.

The Second Committee devoted a major part of its work during the Assembly's 1985 regular session to development and international economic co-operation, making recommendations on a large number of topics (see APPENDIX IV, agenda item 84). A list of pertinent documents was included in part I of the Committee's report on that item,[32] which the Assembly took note of on 17 December when it adopted without vote **decision 40/437**, as orally proposed by its President.

Long-term trends in economic development

Report of the Secretary-General. In accordance with a 1982 General Assembly request,[33] the Secretary-General in August 1985 submitted to the Assembly a comprehensive report on the overall socio-economic perspective of the world economy to the year 2000.[34] A summary of that report[35] was considered by the Economic and Social Council at its July 1985 session.

Analytical work on long-term trends in economic development had been initiated by the Assembly in 1975[36] and the perspective had been updated periodically since first prepared in 1982.[37] The perspective was intended as a framework for examining long-term economic policy and reviewing implementation of the policy measures in the International Development Strategy for the Third United Nations Development Decade (the 1980s)[38] (see p. 418).

The report, supplemented by statistical annexes, discussed world economic prospects and gave alternative development scenarios for the balance of the 1980s. A section dealing with longer-term projections to the year 2000 compared a baseline scenario, reflecting the extrapolation to the year 2000 of existing trends, with both a lower-growth and a higher-growth scenario.

From the higher-growth scenario, in which investment effort and capital effectiveness in developing countries gradually moved in the direction of the targets of the International Development Strategy, the general conclusion emerged that 7 per cent real growth for developing countries was achievable but not until the 1990s. It also became apparent that achieving the Strategy's target growth rates required a supportive world economy and international economic system. While the scenario indicated that it was feasible to finance the projected capital requirements from domestic resources, together with ODA and other private capital flows, it also indicated that performance was likely to falter if ODA was not forthcoming or if private capital flows ceased at each short-run crisis.

A section of the report devoted to socio-economic perspectives compared the implications of macro-economic aspects of the higher- and lower-growth scenarios for several social or socio-economic aspects of development, including employment, literacy, school enrolment, nutrition and the availability of drinking-water and sanitation. The major conclusion from the comparison

was that social aspects would improve significantly faster from 1985 to 2000 with higher economic growth. However, since even with high growth there would be large gaps between the levels achieved and the Strategy's goals, major policy initiatives and institutional developments would be needed to increase the quantity and efficiency of public and private expenditure.

Although forward-looking, the perspective also attempted to place recent trends in a longer-term historical context by reviewing briefly the 25-year experience from 1960 to the mid-point of the Third Development Decade.

Among selected critical issues also considered in the report were: the crisis in Africa, highlighting the broader problems affecting LDCs, many of which were in sub-Saharan Africa (see p. 498); and military expenditures and various aspects of the relationship between disarmament and development (see p. 87).

ECONOMIC AND SOCIAL COUNCIL ACTION

Following its consideration of the summary of the perspective,[35] the Economic and Social Council adopted **decision 1985/178** without vote.

Long-term trends in economic development

At its 52nd plenary meeting, on 25 July 1985, the Council decided to transmit the draft resolution annexed to the present decision to the General Assembly at its fortieth session, for consideration and appropriate action.

ANNEX
Long-term trends in economic development
The General Assembly,

Recalling its resolution 3508(XXX) of 15 December 1975, by which it initiated ten years ago the examination, within the United Nations system, of long-term trends in world economic and social development,

Recalling also its resolution 37/249 of 21 December 1982, by which it decided, *inter alia*, that the overall socio-economic perspective of the world economy to the year 2000 should be revised and updated,

Convinced that a better knowledge of long-term trends in economic and social development can form a sound basis for policies determining development strategies and economic co-operation on a national, regional and global scale,

Noting that, despite certain improvements in the world economic situation, the long-term trends and prospects for many countries and regions remain uncertain, with persistent underdevelopment and growing social insecurity,

Conscious of the urgent necessity of reversing the growing arms race, which absorbs resources that might otherwise satisfy acute social and economic development requirements, especially those of the developing countries,

Considering that the examination of long-term trends in global socio-economic development should contribute to confidence-building in international economic relations and greater economic security for all countries,

1. *Takes note with appreciation* of the report of the Secretary-General on the overall socio-economic perspective of the world economy to the year 2000;

2. *Decides* to retain the practice of the submission of comprehensive reports every five years, the next to be prepared in time for the deliberations on the international development strategy for the fourth United Nations development decade;

3. *Commends* Member States and United Nations organizations, organs and bodies for their contributions to the implementation of General Assembly resolution 37/249 and calls upon them to continue to give all possible support in this endeavour;

4. *Requests* the Secretary-General, when preparing the updated version of the overall socio-economic perspective, to focus on conclusions pertaining to possible domains, mechanisms and forms of international economic co-operation designed to facilitate structural adjustment within the world economy and bring closer a new international economic order;

5. *Decides* to include in the provisional agenda of its forty-fifth session an item entitled "Long-term trends in social and economic development" and requests the Secretary-General to submit to it at that session the report referred to in paragraph 4 above.

Economic and Social Council decision 1985/178

Adopted without vote

Draft by Vice-President (E/1985/L.51), based on informal consultations on draft by
  Poland (E/1985/L.46); agenda item 3.
Meeting numbers. ESC 44, 52.

Also on 25 July, the Council adopted **decision 1985/179** by which it noted that the full report on the perspective could not be submitted to it as requested in 1982[33] and asked the Secretary-General to submit the full report to the Assembly's 1985 regular session.

GENERAL ASSEMBLY ACTION

On 17 December, on the recommendation of the Second Committee, the General Assembly adopted by recorded vote **resolution 40/207**.

Long-term trends in economic development
The General Assembly,

Recalling its resolutions 3201(S-VI) and 3202(S-VI) of 1 May 1974, containing the Declaration and the Programme of Action on the Establishment of a New International Economic Order, 3281(XXIX) of 12 December 1974, containing the Charter of Economic Rights and Duties of States, 3362(S-VII) of 16 September 1975 on development and international economic co-operation and 35/56 of 5 December 1980, the annex to which contains the International Development Strategy for the Third United Nations Development Decade,

Recalling also its resolutions 3508(XXX) of 15 December 1975, by which it initiated the analytical work relating to the examination within the United Nations system of long-term trends in world economic and social development, and 37/249 of 21 December 1982, by which it decided, *inter alia*, that the overall socio-economic perspective of the world economy to the year 2000 should be revised and updated,

Recalling further its resolution 32/197 of 20 December 1977 on the restructuring of the economic and social sectors of the United Nations system, by which it decided, *inter alia*, to undertake in-depth intersectoral analyses

and syntheses of development issues and to identify and bring to the attention of Governments emerging economic and social issues of international concern,

Affirming the need for an effective and timely response to unforeseen international economic problems,

Taking into account that 1985 marks the fortieth anniversary of the founding of the United Nations and that the implementation of Article 55 of the Charter will contribute to the creation of the conditions of sustained growth, stability and well-being which are necessary for peaceful and friendly relations among nations,

Mindful that the maintenance of peace and security, the promotion of disarmament, mutual trust and the strengthening of international co-operation would contribute to the improvement of the overall socio-economic perspective of all countries,

Concerned that low growth rates would have serious repercussions for the world economy, in particular for the developing countries,

Noting with grave concern that Africa is the only continent in which standards of living have declined over the past decade and that, as underscored by all forecasts, the real economic growth per capita will remain near zero or will be negative, on average, until the year 2000 unless drastic action is taken,

Reaffirming the relevance of long-term perspectives for providing impetus to policies and decision-making processes in relation to development strategies and economic co-operation on a national, regional and global scale,

1. *Takes note* of the report of the Secretary-General on the overall socio-economic perspective of the world economy to the year 2000;

2. *Decides*, subject to review of the next report at the forty-second session of the General Assembly, to continue the submission of reports on the overall socio-economic perspective of the world economy to the year 2000, which should be prepared so that they contribute to the identification of potential problem areas and critical issues in the world economy;

3. *Requests* the Secretary-General, when preparing the report, to give special attention to the impact on economic and social development of trends and prospective changes in, *inter alia*, international trade, financial flows and debt problems, including the net outflow of resources from developing to developed countries, technological change and the transfer of technology to developing countries, capital formation and investment patterns, development of human resources, the allocation of public resources between developmental and non-developmental purposes, environmental issues, economic co-operation and integration among developing countries, the implications of different economic and development policies, special problems faced by the least developed countries and the critical economic situation in Africa;

4. *Also requests* the Secretary-General, in preparing the report, to take into account socio-economic analyses that give special attention to mechanisms and forms of international economic co-operation aimed at facilitating structural adjustment within the world economy towards the new international economic order;

5. *Further requests* the Secretary-General to convene, if necessary, a meeting of a group of experts, acting in their personal capacity, to elaborate on the elements of the report specified above, and invites the Committee

for Development Planning to review progress in the preparation of the report;

6. *Calls upon* the relevant organs, organizations and bodies of the United Nations system, including the Administrative Committee on Co-ordination Task Force on Long-term Development Objectives, to contribute, in their respective areas of competence, to the preparation of the report;

7. *Decides* to include in the provisional agenda of its forty-second session an item entitled "Long-term trends in social and economic development", and requests the Secretary-General to submit to it at that session, through the Economic and Social Council, the report on the overall socio-economic perspective of the world economy to the year 2000, together with the views and recommendations of the Committee for Development Planning.

General Assembly resolution 40/207

17 December 1985   Meeting 119   141-1-13 (recorded vote)

Approved by Second Committee (A/40/989/Add.12) by recorded vote (105-1-11), 13 December (meeting 51); draft by Poland, and Yugoslavia for Group of 77 (A/C.2/40/L.22/Rev.1), orally revised; agenda item 84 *(l)*.
Financial implications. S-G, A/C.2/40/L.32.
Meeting numbers. GA 40th session: 2nd Committee 24, 51; plenary 119.

Recorded vote in Assembly as follows:

In favour: Afghanistan, Algeria, Angola, Antigua and Barbuda, Argentina, Australia, Austria, Bahamas, Bahrain, Bangladesh, Barbados, Belize, Benin, Bhutan, Bolivia, Botswana, Brazil, Brunei Darussalam, Bulgaria, Burkina Faso, Burma, Burundi, Byelorussian SSR, Cameroon, Cape Verde, Central African Republic, Chad, Chile, China, Colombia, Comoros, Congo, Costa Rica, Cuba, Cyprus, Czechoslovakia, Democratic Kampuchea, Democratic Yemen, Denmark, Djibouti, Dominica, Dominican Republic, Ecuador, Egypt, El Salvador, Equatorial Guinea, Ethiopia, Fiji, Finland, Gabon, Gambia, German Democratic Republic, Ghana, Greece, Guatemala, Guinea, Guinea-Bissau, Guyana, Haiti, Honduras, Hungary, Iceland, India, Indonesia, Iran, Iraq, Ireland, Ivory Coast, Jamaica, Jordan, Kenya, Kuwait, Lao People's Democratic Republic, Lebanon, Lesotho, Liberia, Libyan Arab Jamahiriya, Madagascar, Malawi, Malaysia, Maldives, Mali, Malta, Mauritania, Mauritius, Mexico, Mongolia, Morocco, Mozambique, Nepal, Netherlands, New Zealand, Nicaragua, Niger, Nigeria, Norway, Oman, Pakistan, Panama, Papua New Guinea, Paraguay, Peru, Philippines, Poland, Qatar, Romania, Rwanda, Saint Lucia, Saint Vincent and the Grenadines, Samoa, Sao Tome and Principe, Saudi Arabia, Senegal, Sierra Leone, Singapore, Somalia, Sri Lanka, Sudan, Suriname, Swaziland, Sweden, Syrian Arab Republic, Thailand, Togo, Trinidad and Tobago, Tunisia, Turkey, Uganda, Ukrainian SSR, USSR, United Arab Emirates, United Republic of Tanzania, Uruguay, Vanuatu, Venezuela, Viet Nam, Yemen, Yugoslavia, Zaire, Zambia, Zimbabwe.

Against: United States.

Abstaining: Belgium, Canada, France, Germany, Federal Republic of, Grenada, Israel, Italy, Japan, Luxembourg, Portugal, Saint Christopher and Nevis, Spain, United Kingdom.

Yugoslavia orally revised the Group of 77's draft to insert in paragraph 3 "including the net outflow of resources from developing to developed countries", and to include in paragraph 4 the reference to the new international economic order. Yugoslavia explained that the revisions were made because Belgium had asked for a vote on the Group's text. The recorded vote was taken at the request of those two States.

The United States said it could have accepted the call for another report in 1987 despite misgivings about frequent analyses of long-term economic trends but had voted against the draft because of its sixth preambular paragraph and the oral revisions.

The United Kingdom, also on behalf of Belgium, France, the Federal Republic of Germany, Italy, Luxembourg, Portugal and Spain, said they had abstained because the requested report would duplicate documentation available from other United Nations sources; they also stressed the inappropriateness of the reference to disarmament in the sixth preambular paragraph, as did Canada which, too, objected to the revisions.

Turkey voted in favour but did not support the preambular text in question. Bulgaria, also on behalf of the Byelorussian SSR, Czechoslovakia, the German Democratic Republic, Hungary, Mongolia, Poland, the Ukrainian SSR and the USSR, stated that the socialist countries attached great importance to United Nations studies on long-term trends and outlined areas on which the Secretariat should concentrate in its 1987 report; any study should take account of the potential for implementing disarmament measures and using resources made available for peaceful purposes, including economic development of developing countries. Yugoslavia, for the Group of 77, said it was hard to understand why the reference to disarmament was not acceptable, since it was closely linked to development and was in the interest of all; it stressed that no report had provided details on the net outflow of resources from developing to developed countries and its implications for the development process.

Proposed global economic negotiations

Informal consultations on launching a round of global negotiations on international economic co-operation for development, originally scheduled to begin in 1980,[39] continued throughout 1985.

GENERAL ASSEMBLY ACTION

Reporting to the General Assembly's resumed thirty-ninth session on 12 April 1985, its President stated that nothing substantive had emerged from the informal consultations which had taken place since the suspension of the session in December 1984.[40] On his oral proposal, the Assembly adopted **decision 39/454 B**, by which it decided to keep the item open in order to allow further informal, but intensive, consultations after the session's suspension and to reconvene on short notice to consider any decisions or agreements that might emerge.

When the Assembly again resumed its thirty-ninth session on 16 September 1985, the President once more reported a lack of progress; therefore, he proposed, and the Assembly adopted, **decision 39/454 C**, by which it included the item in the draft agenda of its fortieth session.

At that session in December, the President again proposed that the matter be kept open to allow for the continuation of informal consultations. The Assembly accepted his proposal in adopting **decision 40/459** on 18 December without vote.

Also on that day, the Assembly decided to resume its fortieth session, at a date to be announced, to consider several agenda items, one of which was on the launching of the global negotiations (**decision 40/470**).

International Development Strategy for the Third UN Development Decade

During 1985, the review and appraisal of the implementation of the International Development Strategy for the Third United Nations Development Decade (the 1980s) continued. That exercise, provided for in the Strategy adopted by the General Assembly in 1980,[38] had commenced in 1984[41] through a Committee of universal membership set up in 1982[42] to carry out the review and appraisal. Since the Committee had been unable to complete its task, the Economic and Social Council decided that it should resume its work in 1985.

ECONOMIC AND SOCIAL COUNCIL ACTION (February)

In accordance with a 1984 Assembly resolution,[43] the Council in February 1985 considered the question of a resumed session of the Committee and, on the proposal of its President, adopted **decision 1985/103** without vote.

Resumed session of the Committee on the Review and Appraisal of the Implementation of the International Development Strategy for the Third United Nations Development Decade

At its 5th plenary meeting, on 8 February 1985, the Council:

(a) Decided that the Committee on the Review and Appraisal of the International Development Strategy for the Third United Nations Development Decade should hold a resumed session beginning with a formal meeting on 6 May 1985, to be followed by up to nine formal or informal meetings ending on 17 May 1985, drawing on the facilities provided for the first regular session of 1985 of the Council, as available;

(b) Requested the Bureau of the Council, in preparing the organization of the work of the first regular session of the Council, to take into account the requirements of the resumed session of the Committee, without adversely affecting the work of the Council;

(c) Requested the Secretary-General to prepare a report on the status of the implementation of the International Development Strategy, focusing on the achievement of the goals and objectives of the Strategy;

(d) Decided further that an annotated outline of the Secretary-General's report should be submitted to the Committee at its resumed session in May 1985;

(e) Recommended that informal consultations should be held among delegations or groups of delegations, with the assistance of the Bureau of the Committee, to consider the procedural and organizational aspects of the work of the Committee at its resumed session;

(f) Decided to consider future arrangements for the work of the Committee at its first regular session of 1985, on the basis of the recommendations of the Committee.

Economic and Social Council decision 1985/103

Adopted without vote

Oral proposal by President; agenda item 4.
Meeting numbers. ESC 1, 5.

Committee on the Strategy. At the first part of its resumed session (New York, 6-14 May 1985), the Committee on the Review and Appraisal of the Implementation of the International Development Strategy for the Third United Nations Development Decade requested its Chairman to prepare a new text as a basis for its work.

At the second part of the session (New York, 9-24 September), the Committee had before it the Secretary-General's report[44] on the status of the Strategy's implementation—as requested by the Council (see above)—updating a 1984 report[41] which had assessed progress made in the Decade's first years. It was noted that, since the earlier report, the world economic recovery had spread to Western Europe and to some developing countries. The strong recovery in the United States had checked the slide in the world economy but was associated with internal and external imbalances that did not appear sustainable.

International bank lending had been further curtailed, especially to developing countries, and the debt service burden had again increased. In 1984 the total resource outflow from developing countries exceeded all inflows and was expected to be similar in 1985. Improvements in output growth and in their external positions had been achieved through major sacrifices in real income and consumption, unemployment and social dislocation. In sub-Saharan Africa, the situation remained critical.

Concern, which had earlier centred on the pace and breadth of the recovery, had turned to the need for long-term growth for all countries. In that context, there was also concern about the patterns of exchange rates and trade balances.

Also before the Committee were its informal conclusions as compiled by the Chairman. On 24 September, the Committee adopted by consensus those conclusions, which were subsequently incorporated in its October report to the General Assembly.[45] They confirmed the validity of the Strategy, noting that it: represented the broadest consensus on international co-operation for development; provided a major instrument for collaboration both among States and within the United Nations system; set goals for the Decade and beyond, linking economic, social and political issues, short- and long-term perspectives, and domestic and international policy measures; and represented both a reaffirmation that the ultimate responsibility for their development rested with the developing countries themselves, and a commitment from other countries to support those efforts through the improvement of the international political and economic environment.

The conclusions outlined developments in the world economy since the Strategy's adoption and compared its targets with the performance of the developing countries. Although key targets had not been met there had been some modest progress.

Neither the critical economic situation in sub-Saharan Africa nor the international debt crisis had been foreseen at the time of the Strategy's adoption. Therefore the review and appraisal process had provided an occasion not only to assess the past and identify and appraise the causes of shortfalls, but also to consider the requirements of the collective endeavour to promote the economic and social development of each country in a more favourable external environment.

The assessment had resulted in some convergence of views on the processes that had brought about the prevailing situation, particularly the close interrelationships between money, finance, debt and trade, and the need to enhance economic co-operation among nations. A continuing analysis was required of the policy implications of the large imbalances in the world economy, including current account disequilibria among major developed countries, the transfer of resources from developing to developed countries and the implications of different development policies.

Each developing country would continue to determine objectives and endeavour to fulfil development plans; the commitment of developed countries was to strengthen support of developing countries' efforts by ensuring a stable and equitable international environment. Improvements were therefore needed in the international economic system through reform and strengthening of the framework governing trade, monetary and financial relations.

With regard to trade relations, countries remained committed to improving the system, to strengthening its open and universal character and to the continued expansion of world trade, giving particular attention to the development needs of developing countries. They reiterated that the system should be characterized by generally accepted rules, norms and principles.

With regard to commodity trade, countries agreed that efforts should continue to improve the effectiveness of export earnings stabilization schemes and to seek agreement on more effective co-operation in international commodity policy.

In connection with the international monetary and financial system, countries reiterated the Strategy's call to provide participation of developing countries in its decision-making processes, taking into account their growing role in the world economy. Ways to make the system more stable and effective should be explored, with efforts being made to: reduce exchange rate instabilities;

strengthen multilateral surveillance focusing on the promotion of sound economic policies aimed at achieving sustained real growth in the world economy; conclude without delay deliberations on a new allocation of special drawing rights; and pay due regard to the application of conditionality to domestic social and political objectives, economic priorities and the circumstances of countries with a view towards sound long-term development. The Strategy assigned a key role to an effective, symmetrical and equitable adjustment process consistent with high sustainable employment and growth, price stability and the dynamic expansion of trade; countries agreed on the need for an appropriate mix of adjustments and financing to achieve an orderly transition to the medium- and long-term goals of growth and development.

With respect to international debt, countries agreed that, although there had been some positive developments, the problem was far from being solved. Countries would intensify efforts towards solving the debt problems of developing countries by pursuing a dialogue involving debtor and creditor countries, international private banks, and multilateral financial institutions.

Access to external resources was an essential requirement for the accelerated development of developing countries. In that connection, developed countries reaffirmed commitments undertaken under the Strategy regarding the 0.7 per cent target of gross national product (GNP) as ODA. Donor countries were urged to attain 0.15 per cent of their GNP in ODA to LDCs in line with commitments undertaken under the Substantial New Programme of Action (SNPA) for LDCs (see p. 434). Every effort would be made to provide the resources required by the United Nations system and other international organizations to allow them to discharge their tasks as called for in the Strategy.

Other issues on which countries agreed to focus attention included: support of capital formation in developing countries; strengthening their industrial capacities; eradicating hunger and malnutrition; and commitment to the Strategy's basic social goals, notably in employment, health, education, population, environment, shelter and the full integration of women, youth and vulnerable population groups in development. It was reaffirmed that special attention should be given to fulfilling the objectives of SNPA, and countries agreed that promoting peace, security, disarmament, mutual trust and co-operation was indispensable to achieving the goals of economic and social development.

Annexed to the Committee's report[45] was a statement by the Chairman analysing the Committee's discussions on key policy issues, giving particular attention to areas of divergence.

During its consideration in May 1985 of future arrangements for the work of the Committee on the Review and Appraisal, the Council—after hearing an oral progress report by the Committee Chairman in which he conveyed the Committee's recommendation that it should meet in September—adopted **decision 1985/116** without vote.

Resumed session of the Committee on the Review and Appraisal of the Implementation of the International Development Strategy for the Third United Nations Development Decade

At its 15th plenary meeting, on 15 May 1985, the Council:

(a) Took note with appreciation of the oral report made at that meeting by the Chairman of the Committee on the Review and Appraisal of the Implementation of the International Development Strategy for the Third United Nations Development Decade and endorsed the recommendations of the Committee;

(b) Decided that the Committee should resume its session from 6 to 16 September 1985 and endorsed the Committee's request to its Chairman to prepare a new text on the review and appraisal of the Strategy to enable the Committee to further its work with a view to its completion at that session.

Economic and Social Council decision 1985/116

Adopted without vote

Oral proposal by President; agenda item 1.

With regard to the social goals and objectives of the Strategy, the Council on 29 May, on the recommendation of the Second (Social) Committee, adopted **resolution 1985/25** without vote.

International Development Strategy for the Third United Nations Development Decade

The Economic and Social Council,

Recalling that the Declaration on Social Progress and Development, contained in General Assembly resolution 2542(XXIV) of 11 December 1969, emphasized the interdependence of economic and social development and the wider process of growth and change, as well as the importance of a strategy of integrated development which takes full account, at all stages, of its social aspects,

Recalling also that the International Development Strategy for the Third United Nations Development Decade, annexed to General Assembly resolution 35/56 of 5 December 1980, called, *inter alia*, for the elimination of hunger and malnutrition, the achievement of full employment by the year 2000, health for all by the year 2000, appropriate population policies, the reduction of the infant mortality rate, the availability of safe water and adequate sanitary facilities by 1990, the attainment of a life expectancy of 60 years as a minimum by the year 2000, universal primary school enrolment by the year 2000, and the securing of the full participation of women in all sectors and at all levels of the development process,

Recalling further its resolution 1983/9 of 26 May 1983,

Bearing in mind General Assembly resolution 39/162 of 17 December 1984, in which the Assembly expressed

concern that the first review and appraisal of the implementation of the International Development Strategy had not been successfully carried out,

1. *Urges* the Committee on the Review and Appraisal of the Implementation of the International Development Strategy for the Third United Nations Development Decade, while carrying out the review and appraisal of the implementation of the Strategy, to examine fully the progress made towards the achievement of the social goals and objectives of the Strategy;

2. *Invites* Governments to carry out the adjustment, intensification or reformulation of the policy measures for achieving the social goals and objectives of the International Development Strategy;

3. *Requests* the Committee for Development Planning, at its twenty-second session, to give due attention to the social dimensions relevant to the formulation of both economic and social policy measures designed to achieve the continuous raising of the material, spiritual and living standards of all members of society, and to make available its contribution to the Commission for Social Development at its thirtieth session;

4. *Requests* the Secretary-General to submit the results of the review and appraisal to the Commission for Social Development at its thirtieth session.

Economic and Social Council resolution 1985/25

29 May 1985   Meeting 23   Adopted without vote

Approved by Second Committee (E/1985/96 & Corr.1) without vote, 17 May (meeting 8); draft by Commission for Social Development (E/1985/24 & Corr.1); agenda item 17.

By **decision 40/438** of 17 December, the General Assembly endorsed the Committee's agreed conclusions and took note of the Chairman's statement annexed to its report. The Assembly welcomed the co-operation displayed by all delegations in adopting the conclusions by consensus.

Several General Assembly and Economic and Social Council resolutions on various topics also called for full implementation of the goals and objectives of the Strategy.

Proposed new international economic order

During 1985, aspects of a new international economic order, called for by the General Assembly in 1974,[46] continued to be discussed in several United Nations bodies.

In June, the United Nations Commission on International Trade Law considered reports by its Working Group on the New International Economic Order which was continuing to draft a legal guide on drawing up contracts for the supply and construction of industrial works. In December, the Assembly, by **resolution 40/67**, again urged States to comment on a 1984 study by the United Nations Institute for Training and Research on international law relating to the new order. (See LEGAL QUESTIONS, Chapter VI.)

In other action, the Assembly in **resolution 40/20** reaffirmed the United Nations determination to work closely with the Organization of African Unity towards establishing the new international economic order, and in **resolution 40/158** States were urged to revive the world economy and restructure international economic relations to establish the new order.

International economic security

At the July session of the Economic and Social Council, the USSR introduced a draft decision entitled "International economic security: a major condition for accelerating the economic decolonization of developing countries".[47] By that text, the Council would have recommended to the General Assembly the adoption of a draft resolution, by which it would have called for the elimination from international economic relations of inequality, exploitation, colonialism and neocolonialism, economic aggression and blackmail, boycott, and trade, credit and technological blockade, of any forms of interference in the domestic affairs of sovereign States, and of the use of economic relations as an instrument of political pressure. The Secretary-General would have been asked to prepare a report containing information provided by Governments on the use of measures constituting a threat to economic security and impeding the economic development of States, for submission in 1986.

Following informal consultations on that draft, the Council on 25 July adopted without vote **decision 1985/180,** by which it recommended that the Assembly consider the issues in the draft resolution.

GENERAL ASSEMBLY ACTION

In November, the USSR submitted to the Assembly's Second Committee a further draft on international economic security which took into account the Council's discussions as well as proposals made during consultations. Subsequently, the USSR revised that text to incorporate delegations' suggested proposals, and made further oral revisions as suggested by Egypt.

On 17 December, on the Committee's recommendation, the Assembly adopted **resolution 40/173** by recorded vote.

International economic security

The General Assembly,

Recalling its resolutions 1514(XV) of 14 December 1960, containing the Declaration on the Granting of Independence to Colonial Countries and Peoples, 3201(S-VI) and 3202(S-VI) of 1 May 1974, containing the Declaration and the Programme of Action on the Establishment of a New International Economic Order, 3281(XXIX) of 12 December 1974, containing the Charter of Economic Rights and Duties of States, 3362(S-VII) of 16 September 1975 on development and international economic co-operation, and 35/56 of 5

December 1980, the annex to which contains the International Development Strategy for the Third United Nations Development Decade,

Recalling also the purposes and principles set forth in the Charter of the United Nations, in particular that of achieving international co-operation in solving international problems of an economic, social, cultural or humanitarian character and the inadmissibility of the threat or use of force in international relations,

Referring to Economic and Social Council resolution 1911(LVII) of 2 August 1974,

Considering that ever-increasing interdependence between States and regions is an inevitable condition of world economic development, which determines the mutuality of interest of all countries in promoting development in a secure world environment,

Convinced that all countries would benefit from a more stable economic, trade, monetary and financial situation and from equitable solutions of the existing problems in these areas,

Further convinced that alleviation of the urgent economic problems of developing countries and elimination of the gap in the levels of economic development are major factors of international economic stability and a better political climate,

Recognizing the need to promote international economic security aimed at the economic and social development and progress of each country, in particular developing countries, through international economic co-operation and utilizing the potential of multilateral and regional organizations,

1. *Considers* that a common endeavour to promote just and mutually beneficial international economic relations would contribute to the economic well-being of each State and to the establishment of a new international economic order;

2. *Requests* the Secretary-General, taking into account the relevant previous studies, to prepare a comprehensive analytical report on a concept of international economic security, including ways and means of its attainment, with emphasis on the development interests of developing countries, for submission through the Economic and Social Council to the General Assembly at its forty-second session;

3. *Calls upon* all Governments and organizations, organs and bodies of the United Nations system to contribute to the implementation of the present resolution.

General Assembly resolution 40/173

17 December 1985   Meeting 119   96-19-28 (recorded vote)

Approved by Second Committee (A/40/1009/Add.1) by recorded vote (85-19-25), 25 November (meeting 43); draft by USSR (A/C.2/40/L.28/Rev.1), orally revised; agenda item 12.

Meeting numbers. GA 40th session: 2nd Committee 22, 23, 29, 30, 34, 36, 39, 42, 43; plenary 119.

Recorded vote in Assembly as follows:

In favour: Afghanistan, Algeria, Angola, Argentina, Bahrain, Bangladesh, Benin, Bhutan, Bolivia, Botswana, Brazil, Brunei Darussalam, Bulgaria, Burkina Faso, Burma, Burundi, Byelorussian SSR, Cameroon, Cape Verde, Colombia, Comoros, Congo, Cuba, Cyprus, Czechoslovakia, Democratic Yemen, Dominican Republic, Ecuador, Egypt, El Salvador, Equatorial Guinea, Ethiopia, Fiji, German Democratic Republic, Ghana, Guatemala, Guinea, Guinea-Bissau, Guyana, Haiti, Hungary, India, Indonesia, Iran, Iraq, Jordan, Kuwait, Lao People's Democratic Republic, Lebanon, Lesotho, Liberia, Libyan Arab Jamahiriya, Madagascar, Malawi, Maldives, Mali, Malta, Mauritania, Mauritius, Mexico, Mongolia, Morocco, Mozambique, Nepal, Nicaragua, Niger, Nigeria, Oman, Pakistan, Panama, Papua New Guinea, Peru, Poland, Qatar, Romania, Sao Tome and Principe, Saudi Arabia, Somalia, Sri Lanka, Sudan, Suriname, Syrian Arab Republic, Togo, Trinidad and Tobago, Tunisia, Uganda, Ukrainian SSR, USSR, United Arab Emirates, United Republic of Tanzania, Uruguay, Venezuela, Viet Nam, Yemen, Yugoslavia, Zambia.

Against: Australia, Belgium, Canada, Denmark, France, Germany, Federal Republic of, Iceland, Ireland, Israel, Italy, Japan, Luxembourg, Netherlands, New Zealand, Norway, Portugal, Spain, United Kingdom, United States.

Abstaining: Antigua and Barbuda, Austria, Bahamas, Barbados, Central African Republic, Chad, Chile, China, Dominica, Finland, Gabon, Greece, Grenada, Ivory Coast, Jamaica, Malaysia, Paraguay, Rwanda, Saint Christopher and Nevis, Saint Vincent and the Grenadines, Samoa, Senegal, Sierra Leone, Singapore, Swaziland, Sweden, Turkey, Zaire.

In the Second Committee, the United States stated that it had voted against because it felt it had been impossible to define the concept of international economic security. Similarly, Canada questioned the obscurity of that concept, as did Japan which queried the need for a report. Luxembourg said the European Economic Community (EEC) would have preferred a text based on the concept of international economic co-operation.

Chile said that, although the text contained positive elements, international economic security could be ensured only by launching constructive negotiations.

China felt that the text was too vague and gave rise to political controversies. Sweden questioned the logic whereby the Assembly would recognize the need for a concept that the Secretary-General would endeavour to define. Finland stressed that greater attention should have been paid to the existing multilateral framework and arrangements which were crucial for the stability of trade and other international economic transactions. Zaire stated that a decision of such importance should have been taken by consensus and that some parts of the text could have been included in other drafts before the Committee.

Liberia thought that a consensus would have avoided politicizing the issue. Argentina, Cameroon and Indonesia also would have preferred a consensus and hoped that the forthcoming report would help create it. India spoke in like manner and was joined by Egypt and Pakistan in adding that consultations should continue on the concept before putting a text to a vote.

The USSR hoped that those which could not support the draft would still contribute to the report.

Venezuela, which voted in favour in the Assembly, did not participate in the Committee's vote because it considered that more thorough consultations should have taken place to clarify the text and to obtain the widest possible consensus.

Coercive economic measures against developing countries

In response to a 1984 General Assembly request,[48] the Secretary-General in October 1985 submitted a report on economic measures taken by developed countries for coercive purposes, including their impact on international economic relations.[49] The report was based on information provided by 22 Member States and by UNCTAD, ECA, ESCAP and ECLAC.

Most of the Governments that replied to the Secretariat's request for information strongly condemned the use of economic coercion and reaffirmed their support for the 1983[50] and 1984[48] Assembly resolutions on the issue. The replies received addressed the scope and type of coercive economic measures, their impact and their incompatibility with various international principles, including the Charter of the United Nations.

The replies from Governments and inputs from UNCTAD and the regional commissions highlighted the following: firmer international measures were needed to denounce and ban economic coercion; the promotion of international economic co-operation and application of Assembly resolutions on establishing a new international economic order and on the Charter of Economic Rights and Duties of States would contribute towards ending economic coercion; the possibility of organizing international action against such measures in appropriate forums should be further explored; developed countries should refrain from threatening or applying trade restrictions, blockades, embargoes or other economic sanctions; and the work of the United Nations, particularly UNCTAD, on this issue should be undertaken universally and should take account of the interests of all countries against which such measures were employed.

GENERAL ASSEMBLY ACTION

On 17 December, on the recommendation of the Second Committee, the General Assembly adopted by recorded vote **resolution 40/185**.

Economic measures as a means of political and economic coercion against developing countries

The General Assembly,

Recalling the relevant principles set forth in the Charter of the United Nations,

Recalling also its resolutions 2625(XXV) of 24 October 1970, containing the Declaration on Principles of International Law concerning Friendly Relations and Co-operation among States in accordance with the Charter of the United Nations, 3201(S-VI) and 3202(S-VI) of 1 May 1974, containing the Declaration and the Programme of Action on the Establishment of a New International Economic Order, and 3281(XXIX) of 12 December 1974, containing the Charter of Economic Rights and Duties of States,

Reaffirming article 32 of the Charter of Economic Rights and Duties of States, which declares that no State may use or encourage the use of economic, political or any other type of measures to coerce another State in order to obtain from it the subordination of the exercise of its sovereign rights,

Bearing in mind the general principles governing international trade and trade policies for development contained in its resolution 1995(XIX) of 30 December 1964, United Nations Conference on Trade and Development resolution 152(VI) of 2 July 1983 entitled "Rejection of coercive economic measures", and the principles and rules of the General Agreement on Tariffs and Trade and paragraph 7 (iii) of the Ministerial Declaration adopted on 29 November 1982 by the Contracting Parties to the General Agreement on Tariffs and Trade at their thirty-eighth session,

Reaffirming its resolutions 38/197 of 20 December 1983 and 39/210 of 18 December 1984,

Taking note of the report of the Secretary-General on the effects of economic measures taken by developed countries for coercive purposes, including their impact on international economic relations, and considering that further work should be undertaken in order to implement resolutions 38/197 and 39/210,

Gravely concerned that the use of coercive measures adversely affects the economies and development efforts of developing countries and that, in some cases, those measures have been intensified, creating a negative impact on international economic co-operation,

1. *Deplores* the fact that some developed countries continue to apply and, in some cases, have increased the scope and magnitude of economic measures that have the purpose of exerting, directly or indirectly, coercion on the sovereign decisions of developing countries subject to those measures;

2. *Reaffirms* that developed countries should refrain from threatening or applying trade restrictions, blockades, embargoes and other economic sanctions, incompatible with the provisions of the Charter of the United Nations and in violation of undertakings contracted, multilaterally and bilaterally, against developing countries as a form of political and economic coercion which affects their economic, political and social development;

3. *Requests* the Secretary-General to prepare a comprehensive, in-depth report on the economic measures mentioned in paragraph 2 above, taken by developed countries for coercive purposes, including their impact on international economic relations, with a view to appraising the economic effects of such measures on the development and development prospects of affected developing countries and with a view to assisting in concrete international action against those measures, and to submit that report to the General Assembly at its forty-first session;

4. *Also requests* the Secretary-General, in preparing the comprehensive in-depth report, to request further comments from Governments and inputs from competent organizations of the United Nations system, particularly the United Nations Conference on Trade and Development, the regional commissions and those specialized agencies that have received information on the application of economic coercive measures against developing countries;

5. *Appeals* to Governments and to the pertinent international organizations to provide the necessary information to the Secretary-General, as requested in paragraph 4 above.

General Assembly resolution 40/185

17 December 1985   Meeting 119   128-19-7 (recorded vote)

Approved by Second Committee (A/40/989/Add.3) by recorded vote (114-19-6), 3 December (meeting 46); draft by Yugoslavia, for Group of 77 (A/C.2/40/L.83); agenda item 84 *(c)*.
Meeting numbers. GA 40th session: 2nd Committee 31, 36, 41, 45, 46; plenary 119.
Recorded vote in Assembly as follows:

In favour: Afghanistan, Albania, Algeria, Angola, Antigua and Barbuda, Argentina, Bahamas, Bahrain, Bangladesh, Barbados, Belize, Benin, Bhutan, Bolivia,

Botswana, Brazil, Brunei Darussalam, Bulgaria, Burkina Faso, Burma, Burundi, Byelorussian SSR, Cameroon, Cape Verde, Central African Republic, Chad, Chile, China, Colombia, Comoros, Congo, Costa Rica, Cuba, Cyprus, Czechoslovakia, Democratic Kampuchea, Democratic Yemen, Djibouti, Dominica, Dominican Republic, Ecuador, Egypt, El Salvador, Equatorial Guinea, Ethiopia, Fiji, Gabon, German Democratic Republic, Ghana, Guatemala, Guinea, Guinea-Bissau, Guyana, Haiti, Honduras, Hungary, India, Indonesia, Iran, Iraq, Jamaica, Jordan, Kenya, Kuwait, Lao People's Democratic Republic, Lebanon, Lesotho, Liberia, Libyan Arab Jamahiriya, Madagascar, Malawi, Malaysia, Maldives, Mali, Malta, Mauritania, Mauritius, Mexico, Mongolia, Morocco, Mozambique, Nepal, Nicaragua, Niger, Nigeria, Oman, Pakistan, Panama, Papua New Guinea, Paraguay, Peru, Philippines, Poland, Qatar, Romania, Rwanda, Saint Christopher and Nevis, Saint Lucia, Saint Vincent and the Grenadines, Samoa, Sao Tome and Principe, Saudi Arabia, Senegal, Sierra Leone, Somalia, Sri Lanka, Sudan, Suriname, Swaziland, Syrian Arab Republic, Thailand, Togo, Trinidad and Tobago, Tunisia, Uganda, Ukrainian SSR, USSR, United Arab Emirates, United Republic of Tanzania, Uruguay, Vanuatu, Venezuela, Viet Nam, Yemen, Yugoslavia, Zaire, Zambia, Zimbabwe.

Against: Australia, Belgium, Canada, Denmark, France, Germany, Federal Republic of, Iceland, Ireland, Israel, Italy, Japan, Luxembourg, Netherlands, New Zealand, Norway, Portugal, Turkey, United Kingdom, United States.

Abstaining: Austria, Finland, Greece, Grenada, Ivory Coast, Spain, Sweden.

Speaking in explanation of vote in the Second Committee, Luxembourg said that the EEC States were against using coercion but could not accept a text aimed solely at actions taken by developed countries. Turkey's position was that the question was not within UNCTAD's competence.

Austria was also opposed to coercive measures but was unable to support the draft as it lacked universal application, a view shared by Sweden.

Proposed new international human order

Responding to a 1983 General Assembly resolution,[51] the Secretary-General in September 1985 submitted a report[52] summarizing the views of Member States on a draft declaration on a new international human order: moral aspects of development, which had been transmitted to the Assembly by the Economic and Social Council in 1983.[53]

The report noted that substantive comments had been received from only one State in response to the 1983 Assembly resolution, although 10 countries had submitted comments earlier in response to a 1982 request.[54]

Most comments noted that there already existed a large number of United Nations instruments and recommendations covering the same ground addressed by the new proposal. It was stressed that what mattered most was the strict observance by all Member States of existing decisions rather than the adoption of new ones. Other States recognized the importance of existing instruments but considered that they needed further elaboration, stressing that proposals concerning economic solutions were insufficient and should be extended to include social and cultural issues.

GENERAL ASSEMBLY ACTION

On 17 December, on the recommendation of the Second Committee, the Assembly adopted **resolution 40/206** without vote.

New international human order: moral aspects of development

The General Assembly,

Recalling its resolutions 37/225 of 20 December 1982 and 38/170 of 19 December 1983 entitled "New international human order: moral aspects of development", as well as the report of the Economic and Social Council on its consideration of this question and Council decision 1983/171 of 25 July 1983,

Having considered the report of the Secretary-General containing the responses of Governments concerning the question,

Taking into account the views expressed on the question in the Second Committee,

1. *Requests* Member States to submit to the Secretary-General additional comments and suggestions on the question;

2. *Decides* to consider the question at its forty-second session on the basis of a report of the Secretary-General taking into account suggestions of Member States.

General Assembly resolution 40/206

17 December 1985   Meeting 119   Adopted without vote

Approved by Second Committee (A/40/989/Add.11) without vote, 11 November (meeting 30); 6-nation draft (A/C.2/40/L.21); agenda item 84 *(k)*.

Sponsors: Burkina Faso, Costa Rica, Malaysia, Paraguay, Philippines, Thailand.

Meeting numbers. GA 40th session: 2nd Committee 24, 30; plenary 119.

Economic rights and duties of States

In accordance with a 1984 General Assembly resolution,[55] the *Ad Hoc* Committee of the Whole to Review the Implementation of the Charter of Economic Rights and Duties of States met in New York from 25 March to 18 April 1985.[56]

The Committee had before it a report of the Secretary-General[57] explaining the significance of the 1974 Charter,[58] discussing its implementation, and reflecting on the modalities for future reviews of its implementation.

The report noted that a number of reviews of the Charter's implementation had been carried out in the United Nations system, either periodically or on an *ad hoc* basis, and that those reviews indicated that certain steps had been taken to implement it. However, the fact that only 25 Member States had responded to a request for information on their application of the Charter's provisions indicated that there were obstacles to implementing the instrument's articles, some of which had been adopted after intensive negotiations. Some Governments had referred to specific articles of the Charter, while others spoke of a general lack of progress towards the objectives in its preamble.

The report stated that the Charter's objectives and principles remained valid and important, and each Government and the international community would continue to find it a source of inspiration to advance development and international political and economic co-operation.

Also before the *Ad Hoc* Committee were communications from Italy,[59] forwarding a statement by the EEC member States, Japan[60] and the United States,[61] indicating that they would not participate in the Committee's work since they had had reservations at the time the 1974 Charter was adopted[62] and on the establishment of the Committee.

The agreed conclusions of the *Ad Hoc* Committee, annexed to its report to the Assembly,[56] stated that the Charter remained relevant to the international community's efforts to establish the new international economic order. Ten years after its adoption, the Charter remained largely unimplemented, with the international economic structure being inadequate to achieve the stability and sustained growth of the world economy envisaged in it. Developing countries continued to be confronted with an adverse external environment seriously affecting their development, with the crisis in Africa particularly illustrating the basic problems facing them.

The world community faced an impasse in international economic negotiations as a result of a retreat from multilateralism, a situation aggravated by heightened tensions and the arms race. It was imperative to improve the climate for genuine international economic co-operation. Extraneous considerations should not influence international economic and financial co-operation, which should be based on universal respect for each State's right to determine its own economic and political system. Developed countries should refrain from applying coercive measures against developing countries.

All States were called on to eliminate colonialism, *apartheid*, racial discrimination, neo-colonialism and foreign aggression, occupation and domination. It was regretted that some States continued to support South Africa and the policies of Israel in the occupied Palestinian and other Arab territories. Foreign investments in Namibia gave economic strength to the occupation forces there.

Governments should implement the Charter so as to contribute to eliminating the adverse effects of the international economic crisis on developing countries. The United Nations had an important responsibility as it provided the multilateral framework for considering and promoting the Charter's implementation. To that end, its role should be enhanced with a view to exploring ways to broaden areas of agreement of international economic co-operation for development.

Efforts towards implementing the Charter were taking place when interdependence between the economies of countries should lead to co-operative endeavours to eliminate the widening gap between developing and developed countries. Accordingly, that required changes in the international economic system to enable developing countries to play their role in the world economy and to participate fully in decision-making in order to contribute to establishing a more just and equitable international economic system. The international community was urged to work collectively towards the Charter's full implementation.

After the *Ad Hoc* Committee concluded its work on 18 April, a joint statement was issued by the Eastern European socialist countries and Mongolia, and transmitted to the Secretary-General by Czechoslovakia on 21 May.[63] They said that the review had confirmed the Charter's importance and the increasing need to democratize international economic relations and promote mutually advantageous economic co-operation among all States irrespective of their economic systems.

GENERAL ASSEMBLY ACTION

On 17 December, on the recommendation of the Second Committee, the Assembly adopted by recorded vote **resolution 40/182**.

Charter of Economic Rights and Duties of States

The General Assembly,

Recalling its resolutions 3201(S-VI) and 3202(S-VI) of 1 May 1974, containing the Declaration and the Programme of Action on the Establishment of a New International Economic Order, 3281(XXIX) of 12 December 1974, containing the Charter of Economic Rights and Duties of States, and 3362(S-VII) of 16 September 1975 on development and international economic co-operation, which laid the foundations of the new international economic order,

Recalling also its resolution 37/204 of 20 December 1982 on the review of the implementation of the Charter of Economic Rights and Duties of States,

Recalling further its resolution 39/163 of 17 December 1984, in which it decided to establish an *Ad Hoc* Committee of the Whole to Review the Implementation of the Charter of Economic Rights and Duties of States,

1. *Takes note* of the report of the *Ad Hoc* Committee of the Whole to Review the Implementation of the Charter of Economic Rights and Duties of States;

2. *Urges* all States to examine further the implementation of the Charter of Economic Rights and Duties of States, thereby contributing to the establishment of the new international economic order;

3. *Requests* the Secretary-General to submit to the General Assembly at its forty-fourth session, through the Economic and Social Council at its second regular session of 1989, a comprehensive and analytical report, in order to ensure systematic and comprehensive consideration of the implementation of the Charter of Economic Rights and Duties of States, in accordance with the provisions of article 34 thereof;

4. *Invites* the organs, organizations and bodies of the United Nations system to facilitate the implementation of the Charter of Economic Rights and Duties of States in their respective spheres of action.

General Assembly resolution 40/182

17 December 1985   Meeting 119   134-1-19 (recorded vote)

Approved by Second Committee (A/40/989/Add.2) by recorded vote (122-1-19), 25 November (meeting 43); draft by Yugoslavia, for Group of 77 (A/C.2/40/L.20/Rev.1); agenda item 84 *(b)*.

Meeting numbers. GA 40th session: 2nd Committee 24, 43; plenary 119.

Recorded vote in Assembly as follows:

In favour: Afghanistan, Algeria, Angola, Antigua and Barbuda, Argentina, Australia, Bahamas, Bahrain, Bangladesh, Barbados, Belize, Benin, Bhutan, Bolivia, Botswana, Brazil, Brunei Darussalam, Bulgaria, Burkina Faso, Burma, Burundi, Byelorussian SSR, Cameroon, Cape Verde, Central African Republic, Chad, Chile, China, Colombia, Comoros, Congo, Costa Rica, Cuba, Cyprus, Czechoslovakia, Democratic Kampuchea, Democratic Yemen, Djibouti, Dominica, Dominican Republic, Ecuador, Egypt, El Salvador, Equatorial Guinea, Ethiopia, Fiji, Finland, Gabon, Gambia, German Democratic Republic, Ghana, Guatemala, Guinea, Guinea-Bissau, Guyana, Haiti, Honduras, Hungary, India, Indonesia, Iran, Iraq, Ivory Coast, Jamaica, Jordan, Kenya, Kuwait, Lao People's Democratic Republic, Lebanon, Lesotho, Liberia, Libyan Arab Jamahiriya, Madagascar, Malawi, Malaysia, Maldives, Mali, Malta, Mauritania, Mauritius, Mexico, Mongolia, Morocco, Mozambique, Nepal, New Zealand, Nicaragua, Niger, Nigeria, Oman, Pakistan, Panama, Papua New Guinea, Paraguay, Peru, Philippines, Poland, Qatar, Romania, Rwanda, Saint Christopher and Nevis, Saint Lucia, Saint Vincent and the Grenadines, Samoa, Sao Tome and Principe, Saudi Arabia, Senegal, Sierra Leone, Singapore, Somalia, Sri Lanka, Sudan, Suriname, Swaziland, Sweden, Syrian Arab Republic, Thailand, Togo, Trinidad and Tobago, Tunisia, Turkey, Uganda, Ukrainian SSR, USSR, United Arab Emirates, United Republic of Tanzania, Uruguay, Venezuela, Viet Nam, Yemen, Yugoslavia, Zaire, Zambia, Zimbabwe.

Against: United States.

Abstaining: Austria, Belgium, Canada, Denmark, France, Germany, Federal Republic of, Greece, Grenada, Iceland, Ireland, Israel, Italy, Japan, Luxembourg, Netherlands, Norway, Portugal, Spain, United Kingdom.

Speaking in explanation of vote in the Second Committee, the United States pointed out that, having rejected several of the Charter's provisions and having voted against it as a whole, it did not envisage any steps towards its implementation.

Luxembourg said the EEC member countries reaffirmed their previous position on the substance of the matter and had abstained in order to show the importance they attached to a compromise approach. Austria maintained its reservations regarding the Charter and doubted the usefulness of a review of its implementation.

Australia voted in favour in order to show its attachment to the Charter, although the reservations it had expressed in 1974 still applied; the use of a special review procedure was not to be recommended as it entailed high costs.

Economic co-operation among developing countries

During 1985, the United Nations continued to promote ECDC, mainly through UNCTAD. Technical co-operation among developing countries (TCDC) received the support of UNDP (see next chapter).

UNCTAD activities. The Working Party on Trade Expansion and Regional Economic Integration among Developing Countries (third session, Geneva, 28 January–1 February 1985),[64] established by the Committee on ECDC of UNCTAD in 1978,[65] met to carry out an overall review of progress in integration and economic co-operation programmes, adjust the work programme for co-operation between secretariats of economic co-operation and integration groupings, and draw up a new work programme.

In its conclusions and recommendations, the Working Party expressed satisfaction with progress achieved in implementing certain activities of the programme for co-operation among economic co-operation and integration groupings of developing countries, which it had established in 1982,[66] but noted that there remained scope for action in all the programme's areas. The Working Party focused its attention on issues of special concern, particularly the problems for the trade within groupings and co-operation mechanisms arising from balance-of-payments difficulties of member countries.

With regard to institutional arrangements for implementing the programme for co-operation, the Working Party stressed its importance as the main forum setting out objectives and orientations for mutual co-operation. It considered it essential that it be regarded as a forum of the executive heads of such groupings and it recommended that its name be changed to Meeting of Heads of Secretariats of Economic Co-operation and Integration Groupings of Developing Countries.

At its fourth session (Geneva, 18-29 November), the Committee on ECDC reiterated the need for continued UNCTAD secretariat support to ECDC and called on the UNCTAD Secretary-General to take action in the areas of trade expansion and promotion and of money and financial co-operation among developing countries, and requested him to continue trying to raise additional extrabudgetary resources for ECDC activities. In implementing its ECDC work programme, the secretariat was asked to maintain close co-operation with other United Nations bodies and interregional financial institutions.[67]

Co-ordination in the UN system

CPC activities. In response to a 1984 General Assembly resolution,[68] the Secretary-General submitted to the 1985 session of the Committee for Programme and Co-ordination (CPC) (New York, 29 April-1 June)[69] a report on the cross-organizational programme analysis (COPA) of the activities of the United Nations system in the area of economic and technical co-operation among developing countries.[70] In line with the Assembly's recommendation,[68] the COPA report drew on a 1984 report,[71] which had analysed the mandates of and problems addressed by the system in ECDC and TCDC, and also incorporated a cross-organizational review of such co-operation in the medium-term plans of United Nations organizations which was to be considered by the Economic and Social Council in 1985.

The 1985 COPA report[70] concluded that there were no significant gaps or overlaps in programme terms. The organizations' plans did not reflect adequately their real work, which was much more comprehensive than the plans indicated. However, when seen as a whole, the individual plans were not a complete response to the range of mandates which guided the system in support of ECDC and TCDC. Organizations should ensure that their planning documents paid more explicit attention to the subject and showed the underlying work more clearly. Intergovernmental guidance was required regarding programmatic objectives and strategies to be pursued by the system as a whole, as existing intergovernmental decisions did not set relative priorities among sectors. The report stated that CPC might suggest to the Economic and Social Council that specific areas be given increased relative emphasis in work programmes.

With regard to resource availability, the COPA noted that some $160 million had been devoted to ECDC and TCDC during 1982-1983, a major increase from 1978-1979. However, since total resources available to the system had shown little growth in recent years, there was an overall constraint on formulating new activities, a factor which CPC could take into account when reviewing programme budget proposals.

As to the distinction between ECDC and TCDC and the respective relative competences of UNCTAD and UNDP, the analysis showed that the lead agency functions as assigned derived from their unique and distinct roles in promoting co-operation among developing countries. Increased trade between developing countries was the centrepiece of promoting ECDC and UNCTAD was responsible for issues of trade and development, while UNDP was the major funding source for technical co-operation activities. Both organizations reported that adequate arrangements existed for co-operation and co-ordination between them.

Noting that the bulk of United Nations efforts in support of ECDC and TCDC remained concentrated at regional and subregional levels, the report suggested that ACC and CPC might recommend strengthening action at those levels. It was pointed out that there was also considerable scope for rationalizing the collection of information on the system's activities in ECDC and TCDC, including maintenance of the data base compiled for preparation of the current COPA report.

Following consideration of the report, CPC stated that it was too descriptive and lacked a critical and analytical assessment of the United Nations role and the relationship between its activities and mandates; the information in the report did not justify a positive conclusion concerning the effectiveness of existing co-ordination arrangements and it too frequently recorded uncritically the views on their work of United Nations Secretariat units that were active in ECDC and TCDC.

CPC stated that a recommendation in the 1978 Buenos Aires Plan of Action for Promoting and Implementing TCDC[72] on internal secretariat arrangements for ECDC and TCDC should be implemented, and that the medium-term plans of United Nations organizations should reflect a commitment to carrying out their mandates in the area. CPC decided to consider the question at a future session based on a follow-up report which should contain a response to its criticisms. It concluded that efforts should also be made to ensure that information was collected on United Nations activities in ECDC and TCDC.

CPC/ACC Joint Meetings. The 1985 Joint Meetings of CPC and ACC (Geneva, 2 and 3 July)[73] also considered the COPA report[70] and had before them an extract from the CPC report[69] on its consideration of the issue.

It was generally agreed by the Joint Meetings that ECDC and TCDC should be viewed as an instrument for enhancing the endogenous capacities of developing countries and assisting them to meet problems caused by the world economic situation, but not as a substitute for North-South co-operation.

It was recognized that responsibility for carrying out ECDC and TCDC lay primarily with the developing countries but that the United Nations system had an important role to play. It was agreed that the system's organizations should reinforce their catalytic and promotional role and activities in ECDC and TCDC respectively and that the dimension of intergovernmental mandates in the area should be reflected in their programmes and medium-term plans. CPC members stressed the importance of co-ordination between organizations to avoid duplicating activities.

It was generally stressed that attention should focus on the mutually supportive character of ECDC and TCDC rather than on problems of definition; it was noted, however, that a proper definition of those activities would have to be developed in due course.

Members of CPC reiterated their comments made during the 1985 CPC session.

ECONOMIC AND SOCIAL COUNCIL ACTION

On 26 July 1985, the Economic and Social Council, in **resolution 1985/76**, stressed the importance of effectively implementing CPC's recommendations and, in **resolution 1985/77**, took note of the report on the Joint Meetings.

GENERAL ASSEMBLY CONSIDERATION

In further follow-up to the 1984 General Assembly resolution,[68] the Secretary-General submitted to that body in September 1985 a report on economic and technical co-operation among developing countries,[74] giving a brief review of major developments in ECDC since his previous report on the subject in 1979,[75] and dealing with action taken within the framework of the COPA and review, as well as inter-secretariat co-

ordination within the system. An account was also given of the 1984-1985 activities of individual United Nations organizations in response to the Assembly's request[68] to intensify their activities in support of ECDC.

The 1985 report was considered by the Assembly's Second Committee when it took up the subject of TCDC (see p. 488).

REFERENCES

[1]YUN 1984, p. 407. [2]E/1985/29. [3]E/1985/57. [4]ACC/1985/DEC/1-13 (dec. 1985/1). [5]YUN 1984, p. 387. [6]ACC/1985/DEC/16-29 (dec. 1985/16). [7]*World Economic Survey 1985: Current Trends and Policies in the World Economy* (E/1985/54), Sales No. E.85.II.C.1. [8]A/40/3/Rev.1. [9]YUN 1984, p. 382, ESC res. 1984/82, 27 July 1984. [10]A/40/525. [11]A/40/173-S/17033. [12]A/40/184-E/1985/61. [13]A/40/220. [14]A/40/276-S/17138. [15]A/40/303-E/1985/76. [16]A/40/305. [17]A/40/407-E/1985/131. [18]A/40/459-E/1985/133. [19]A/40/476-E/1985/137. [20]A/40/477-E/1985/136. [21]A/40/544. [22]A/40/672-S/17488. [23]A/C.2/40/2. [24]A/C.2/40/5. [25]A/40/762. [26]A/40/817. [27]A/40/837. [28]A/C.2/40/8. [29]A/40/852. [30]A/40/854-S/17610 & Corr.1. [31]A/40/910 & Corr.1. [32]A/40/989. [33]YUN 1982, p. 606, GA res. 37/249, 21 Dec. 1982. [34]A/40/519. [35]E/1985/102. [36]YUN 1975, p. 539, GA res. 3508(XXX), 15 Dec. 1975. [37]YUN 1982, p. 604. [38]YUN 1980, p. 503, GA res. 35/56, annex, 5 Dec. 1980. [39]YUN 1979, p. 468, GA res. 34/138, 14 Dec. 1979. [40]YUN 1984, p. 391. [41]*Ibid.*, p. 392. [42]YUN 1982, p. 608, GA res. 37/202, 20 Dec. 1982. [43]YUN 1984, p. 394, GA res. 39/162, 17 Dec. 1984. [44]A/AC.219/36. [45]A/40/48. [46]YUN 1974, p. 324, GA res. 3201(S-VI), 1 May 1974. [47]E/1985/L.47. [48]YUN 1984, p. 397, GA res. 39/210, 18 Dec. 1984. [49]A/40/596. [50]YUN 1983, p. 412, GA res. 38/197, 20 Dec. 1983. [51]*Ibid.*, p. 411, GA res. 38/170, 19 Dec. 1983. [52]A/40/591. [53]YUN 1983, p. 410, ESC dec. 1983/171, 25 July 1983. [54]YUN 1982, p. 597, GA res. 37/225, 20 Dec. 1982. [55]YUN 1984, p. 399, GA res. 39/163, 17 Dec. 1984. [56]A/40/52. [57]A/AC.226/2. [58]YUN 1974, p. 403, GA res. 3281(XXIX), 12 Dec. 1974. [59]A/40/185. [60]A/40/202. [61]A/40/203. [62]YUN 1974, p. 394. [63]A/40/334. [64]TD/B/C.7/72. [65]YUN 1978, p. 432. [66]YUN 1982, p. 600. [67]TD/B/1083 (res. 3(IV)). [68]YUN 1984, p. 402, GA res. 39/216, 18 Dec. 1984. [69]A/40/38 & Corr.1. [70]E/1985/53. [71]YUN 1984, p. 400. [72]YUN 1978, p. 467. [73]E/1985/112. [74]A/40/581. [75]YUN 1979, p. 487.

Economic and social trends and policy

The uneven spread of the recovery under way in the world economy was highlighted in economic reports prepared by the United Nations Secretariat in 1985, which also noted that the recovery had bypassed a large part of the developing world. Two major reports, submitted as background to the annual discussion of international economic and social policy in the Economic and Social Council and the UNCTAD Trade and Development Board, focused on the effect of the uneven international trade performance and the debt crisis on the development prospects of developing countries (see Chapter IV of this section).

Economic surveys and trends

The *World Economic Survey 1985*,[1] prepared by DIESA, stated that the significant expansion of world output and international trade in 1984 was giving way to more modest growth rates in 1985 and there was the prospect of a further deceleration in 1986.

The *Survey*, which was based on information available as at 1 April 1985, reported that, while the average rate of world economic growth for the middle years of the 1980s seemed likely to be more than twice the rate of the period 1980-1983 and was a much welcomed recovery from the worst international recession of the post-war era, it fell short of global needs. The middle years would continue to be characterized by unusually high rates of unemployment and inadequate progress against world poverty.

The impulses that led to a strong recovery in North America and to a dramatic rise in its imports weakened in the second half of 1984. In 1985, the rate of increase in North America's gross domestic product (GDP) was expected to be only about half the nearly 7 per cent achieved in 1984, which should produce a slow-down in the global economy since no substantial acceleration of growth was likely to occur elsewhere.

The growth momentum recently achieved by most of the developing economies in Asia was maintained in 1984 and Latin American countries experienced a slight rebound in economic activity from depressed 1982-1983 levels, partly as a consequence of increased exports. Growth in sub-Saharan Africa, however, continued to be constrained by the weak expansion in agriculture in most of the region. Since domestic and external impulses for growth in developing countries were not going to change markedly in the near future, growth rates would remain generally weak. Even by the second half of the decade, the majority of developing countries would not have recovered fully from the dramatic set-back suffered in the early 1980s.

The Japanese economy, largely on account of buoyant exports, had experienced robust growth since mid-1983, while the economies of Western Europe were gradually achieving a somewhat higher rate of growth in GDP, but still insufficient to make a dent in unemployment. The centrally planned economies of Eastern Europe maintained, especially in industry, the growth momentum reached in the second half of 1983. Domestic impulses for growth remained strong in China and its rapid economic expansion continued in 1984 and 1985.

The rate of growth of aggregate global output rose from less than 3 per cent in 1983 to an estimated 4 per cent in 1984-1985, as growth in both the developed market and developing countries accelerated. For the developing countries as a whole, the average growth rate of real GDP in 1984, although substantially higher than in 1983, was only 3 per cent, 2 percentage points below those countries' average growth in the late 1970s. Real GDP in the energy exporters and energy importers grew on average by about 2 and 3.5 per cent respectively, representing a significant decline in comparison to their average growth rates in the latter half of the 1970s.

Within the group of developed market economies, there was considerable diversity in economic performance. Although the variation in growth rates had narrowed somewhat since the latter part of 1984, North America and the developed countries of the Pacific region, particularly Japan, were continuing to grow at rates that were 1 to 2 percentage points higher than Western Europe's average annual growth rate of 2.5 per cent.

In the Eastern European countries, the 5 per cent pace of economic activity in 1984, although below post-war trends, represented a substantial acceleration compared with 1979-1982, when output stagnated. In contrast to the upturn witnessed in Eastern Europe, economic growth in the Soviet Union in 1984 slowed from 4.2 to about 3 per cent, which was below planned levels. The deceleration stemmed mostly from the stagnation in agriculture, where grain output was below plan for the sixth year in a row.

The strong output growth registered in China during the first three years of the decade continued in 1984, when the economy expanded by about 12 per cent, well above the already very high 9 per cent growth achieved in 1983.

With regard to the short-term outlook for the world economy, the *Survey* noted that there were some encouraging signals pointing to an upswing after 1986. According to those signals, the post-1986 upturn, as distinct from the recent recovery, could be characterized by some convergence in the growth rates of the developed countries, less instability in key economic variables, and a resumption of development in a less restricted number of developing countries. However, the world economy had proved to be fragile and, if current problems were not tackled, it was likely that a significant upswing would not occur in 1987. Persistent protectionist pressures and the possibility of more restrictive trade measures, the considerable fiscal deficit and trade imbalance in the United States, protracted adjustment in the European economies that prevented them from attaining high rates of growth in domestic product and in import demand, slow progress in resolving the debt problem, and critical economic conditions in sub-Saharan countries, all indicated how hazardous the path towards a strong and broad-based world recovery remained.

The *Survey* stated that changes in policies to deal with those problems could significantly affect events in the second half of the 1980s. Joint actions to halt and roll back protectionism, to support more decisively the multilateral financial institutions and to harmonize macro-economic policies among large developed countries would go a long way towards improving the international economic environment. Even in the event of such an improvement, however, many low-income countries would still have to put in place more effective policies to expand agricultural production rapidly and to increase savings and investment, which could prove difficult to achieve without worsening their already depressed consumption levels. Some inflation-ridden countries also confronted difficult choices, since indexation mechanisms and expectations of continuing high inflation rates had become entrenched. For developed countries, it was still necessary to consolidate recent gains in the fight against inflation and to create jobs at a faster pace.

Two chapters of the *Survey* concentrated on major developments and policy needs in international trade and financial relations (see Chapter IV of this section), while others dealt with selected policy responses and adjustment to economic disequilibria, and summarized conclusions and recommendations for possible action on some key issues (see p. 411).

In its account of current and short-term prospects for the world economy, the *Trade and Development Report, 1985*[(2)] noted the weak and uneven influence on the developing countries of the economic revival in the industrialized countries. The recovery in the latter, which was losing momentum, left many parts of the developing world still in straitened economic circumstances and estimates of performance in 1985 indicated no significant acceleration in growth.

Disparities in performance among industrialized countries partly accounted for the pattern of economic trends in developing ones, as the expansionary fiscal policy of the United States gave rise to an upsurge of economic activity there, as well as to an acceleration in Japan, while restrictive fiscal policies in Western Europe restrained its pace of recovery. This favoured developing countries with close trade links with the former countries, especially those which were substantial exporters of manufactures. The sluggish economic performance of Western Europe was also a major reason for the weak prices of primary commodities used as industrial raw materials. Other primary commodity markets, including that for petroleum, had also been weak.

The *Report* did not foresee any marked improvement in the performance prospects for developing countries in the near future; the external environment was unlikely to bring significant relief to pressures on their balance of payments on current account. Since economic growth in the industrialized countries was slowing down and expected to continue at a lower rate, the growth in demand for exports from developing countries would probably decelerate and primary commodity prices might weaken further. Although interest rates had been declining, they remained high and their course was uncertain. The rate of increase in gross borrowing on international capital markets continued to decline, and no appreciable change was expected in ODA. A further increase in imports was likely, but the improvement in rates of growth in total output was expected to be marginal in 1985, though modestly better in 1986.

Among the developed market-economy countries, rates of expansion in economic activity were likely to converge, with Japan and the United States approaching the lower pace of growth in Western Europe. In the United States, however, the combination of an expansionary fiscal policy with a stringent monetary policy, which was instrumental in bringing about a strong recovery, had also given rise to high interest rates and a misalignment of the dollar exchange rate. The combination of the worsening United States balance of payments, the financing of the deficit through large capital inflows attracted mainly by high interest rates and the strong dollar, and intensified calls for protection as domestic demand was diverted from domestic production to imports did not make for a stable situation.

While Western Europe and Japan had also been pursuing tight monetary policies, their fiscal policies remained restrictive. However, the absence of a strong stimulus to aggregate domestic demand had disadvantageous consequences. Among the close trading partners of the United States, especially Japan, the foreign demand for exports had outpaced the domestic demand for imports, and large surpluses on current account had accumulated. For Western Europe, it was widely recognized that greater investment and a higher economic growth rate were fundamental to alleviating the high rate of unemployment. Actions on the supply side could contribute to promoting investment, but maintaining a high level of aggregate demand was an essential prerequisite.

Recovery in Eastern Europe continued in 1984 although individual countries experienced varying growth patterns. For the group, other than the Soviet Union, the annual growth rate of net material product (NMP) reached 5.1 per cent in 1984 against 3.9 in 1983. In fact, in 1984, NMP growth rates in almost all socialist countries of Eastern Europe exceeded not only the previous year's level, but also the 1984 annual plans' targets. The economy of the Soviet Union continued to expand in accordance with its annual and five-year plans, although at a slower pace than in 1983. The NMP growth rate reached 3 per cent in 1984 (3.1 was planned), against 4.2 in 1983 and 3.9 in 1982.

The economy of China continued to surge with growth in national income being led by the exceedingly good performance of agriculture, which expanded by 14.5 per cent, giving an average real growth of 9.2 per cent over the period 1980-1984.

A large section of the *Report* was devoted to problems of debt, development and the world economy (see Chapter IV of this section).

Resources, environment, people and development

During 1985, the ACC Consultative Committee on Substantive Questions (Programme Matters) (CCSQ(PROG)) continued to deal with inter-agency co-ordination of the programme of work on interrelationships between resources, environment, people and development, and to screen projects proposed for financing under the general trust fund for the programme, established in June 1981.[3]

At its first regular session of 1985 (Geneva, 1-4 April),[4] CCSQ(PROG) was briefed by the Food and Agriculture Organization of the United Nations (FAO) and the United Nations Educational, Scientific and Cultural Organization on a carrying capacity (ability to support growing populations at increasing standards of living) project in Kenya, which had been completed and tested. Kenya wished to use it as a basis for long-term planning but further technical assistance was needed to install the model and modify it for the Government's specific needs. Several other countries were interested in using the model in their development planning.

The United Nations Environment Programme (UNEP) informed CCSQ(PROG) of progress relating to a project on deforestation of the Himalayan foothills, stating that a meeting was planned to develop regional co-operation and to agree on specific case-studies.

The Committee was further informed that UNEP would develop an approach for a project in the Sudano-Sahelian region, for which continued inter-agency consultations would be necessary.

The Committee recalled that the programme was designed to develop policy approaches which Governments could integrate into national policies and was not intended to finance major development projects. Funding for extending the carrying-capacity approach to other countries would need to be sought from traditional funding sources rather than from the interrelationships trust fund.

It was agreed that CCSQ(PROG) would consider the question of interrelationships only when specific project proposals were put forward or when there had been developments in approved activities.

In **resolution 40/179** of 17 December 1985, the General Assembly requested the Secretary-General to continue implementing a 1974 Assembly resolution[5] in order to assist States, particularly developing countries, and United Nations organs in their efforts to advance knowledge on the interrelated issues of resources, population, environment and development.

REFERENCES

[1]*World Economic Survey 1985: Current Trends and Policies in the World Economy* (E/1985/54), Sales No. E.85.II.C.1. [2]*Trade and Development Report, 1985* (UNCTAD/TDR/5), Sales No. E.85.II.D.16. [3]YUN 1981, p. 391. [4]ACC/1985/4. [5]YUN 1974, p. 560, GA res. 3345(XXIX), 17 Dec. 1974.

Development planning, education and administration

Improving development planning, education and administration continued to be a focus of several United Nations bodies during 1985, among them CDP which studied development issues against the background of a general lack of commitment to multilateral economic co-operation. The Economic and Social Council reviewed the findings of the Seventh (1984) Meeting of Experts on the United Nations Programme in Public Administration and Finance and set the agenda for the Eighth (1987) Meeting. The Joint United Nations Information Committee (JUNIC) continued to co-ordinate preparation of United Nations educational materials.

Development planning

CDP activities. The Committee for Development Planning resumed its twenty-first session in New York from 20 to 23 April 1985,[1] having held the first part in 1984.[2] Meetings of CDP working groups were cancelled by the Economic and Social Council to finance the resumed session (see below).

Composed of 24 experts appointed by the Council, CDP examined the challenges to multilateral co-operation created by post-war changes in the world economy and called for a renewed commitment to multilateralism (see p. 411). It also considered the risk of disintegration of the trading system, the instability in the international monetary and financial system and the debt crisis (see Chapter IV of this section). The crisis in sub-Saharan Africa was also addressed, as was the eligibility of Kiribati, Tuvalu and Vanuatu for inclusion in the list of LDCs (see p. 433).

With regard to its future work, the Committee decided to revert to a single-session work programmc and proposed convening a representative working group to review the state of world development and identify themes for its 1986 report.

On 8 February 1985, the Council adopted **decision 1985/108** in which it recalled its 1984 resolution[3] regarding the CDP meeting schedule and authorized it to resume its session, bearing in mind that CDP working groups for 1984-1985 would be cancelled to finance the resumed session within existing resources. On 25 July it took note, by **decision 1985/182**, of the report on CPC's regular (1984) and resumed (1985) sessions.

Development administration

In 1985, the United Nations Department of Technical Co-operation for Development (DTCD) implemented 179 projects to assist developing countries in improving the performance of their public administration, public finance and public enterprises. The programme continued to emphasize the strengthening of government capabilities for evaluation, which was an integral part of projects and seminars in such areas as policy analysis, government budget and audit, personnel performance, management control and public enterprises. During the year, DTCD, whose main source of funds was UNDP, delivered $11.8 million, 39 per cent of which was spent in Africa, 23 per cent in Asia and the Pacific, 13 per cent in Latin America, and 25 per cent in the Middle East, the Mediterranean and Europe and for interregional projects.[4]

ECONOMIC AND SOCIAL COUNCIL ACTION

In May 1985, the Economic and Social Council had before it a report of the Secretary-General[5] commenting on the discussions and major recommendations of the Seventh Meeting of Experts on the United Nations Programme in Public Administration and Finance, held in 1984.[6] The Secretary-General believed that the priorities identified for developing countries deserved serious national consideration. He also agreed with the analysis of the crisis in the sub-Saharan African countries and recommended that both matters be brought to international attention.

With regard to suggestions on aspects of the United Nations programme in public administration and finance, he stated that he would take them into account and requested that recommendations on allocating resources for public administration and finance be considered a priority area under the new indicative planning figure (IPF) cycle of UNDP.

In the light of the Meeting's recommendation, and subject to Council approval, the Secretary-General had included a proposal for the next (1987) review of the public administration and finance programme in the 1986-1987 budget.

On 28 May, the Council, on the recommendation of its First (Economic) Committee, adopted **resolution 1985/10** without vote.

Public administration and finance for development

The Economic and Social Council,

Recalling General Assembly resolutions 35/56 of 5 December 1980, the annex to which contains the International Development Strategy for the Third United Nations Development Decade, 36/194 of 17 December 1981 on the United Nations Conference on the Least Developed Countries, particularly paragraph 3 thereof, 34/137 of 14 December 1979 on the role of the public sector in promoting the economic development of developing countries, and 35/80 of 5 December 1980 and 39/219 of 18 December 1984 on the role of qualified national personnel in the social and economic development of developing countries,

Recalling also Council resolutions 1978/6 of 4 May 1978, 1978/75 of 8 November 1978, 1980/12 of 28 April 1980 and 1982/44 of 27 July 1982, concerning public administration and finance for development in the 1980s, and 1981/45 of 20 July 1981 and 1983/61 of 28 July 1983 on the role of the public sector in promoting the economic development of developing countries,

Reiterating the importance of effective and responsive public administration systems for the economic and social development of developing countries,

Reiterating also the critical importance of developing and strengthening the public administration and finance capabilities of developing countries, in particular improving the performance of existing institutions, personnel and policies,

Concerned about the critical economic situation in Africa and the need for increased urgent assistance to African countries, *inter alia*, in the fields of institutional, managerial and financial resource development,

1. *Takes note* of the report of the Seventh Meeting of Experts on the United Nations Programme in Public Administration and Finance, held at Geneva from 17 to 26 October 1984, and the report of the Secretary-General thereon;

2. *Takes note* of the recommendations made by the Seventh Meeting of Experts and requests the Secretary-General to transmit them to the States Members of the United Nations for their review and appropriate action at the national level;

3. *Requests* the Secretary-General to further strengthen, taking into account the recommendations of the Seventh Meeting of Experts, the catalytic role of the United Nations programme in public administration and finance to assist developing countries in the improvement of their systems of public administration and finance for development;

4. *Invites* all organs, agencies and organizations of the United Nations system and the international community to take into account the Action Programme in Public Administration for Sub-Saharan Africa proposed by the Seventh Meeting of Experts, in formulating their programmes of assistance for countries in Africa;

5. *Invites* the United Nations Development Programme, in formulating its regional and interregional programmes, to bear in mind the need for improving the administrative and managerial capabilities of developing countries, especially the least developed among them, in the field of public administration and finance;

6. *Notes* the recommendation of the Seventh Meeting of Experts that its next meeting should be convened in 1987, and requests the Secretary-General to make the necessary preparations for that meeting, which, in reviewing the United Nations programme in public administration and finance in accordance with its mandate, should also deal in particular with:

(a) Challenges and constraints in public administration and finance in the developing countries;

(b) Development of computer-based management information systems in public administration and finance;

(c) The specific needs of the least developed countries, especially in the field of training;

(d) Strategies and measures for improving the performance of public enterprises and their contribution to national development;

(e) Support and assistance by the United Nations system for the developing countries in this field, including technical co-operation among developing countries;

(f) Progress in the implementation of the proposals and recommendations made by the Seventh Meeting of Experts.

Economic and Social Council resolution 1985/10

28 May 1985	Meeting 22	Adopted without vote

Approved by First Committee (E/1985/93) without vote, 17 May (meeting 6); 12-nation draft (E/1985/C.1/L.1); agenda item 14.

Sponsors: Algeria, Argentina, Bangladesh, China, Congo, India, Indonesia, Nigeria, Romania, Senegal, Yugoslavia, Zaire.

Development education

At its April 1985 session,[7] JUNIC (see p. 387) reviewed the work of its *Ad Hoc* Working Group on Development Education, whose Chairman stated that implementation of the JUNIC Development Education Programme of Action continued to depend largely on the United Nations Non-Governmental Liaison Services (NGLS). JUNIC members were invited to think of areas and themes which their organizations considered priorities for development education and to which they could contribute.

JUNIC felt that the Working Group at its next session should consider development education in the United Nations system, the system's relationship with the non-governmental community in terms of development education, and a revised concept paper on the role of NGLS. The results of those discussions were to be reviewed at a special 1986 meeting of JUNIC.

In **resolution 40/164 A**, the General Assembly urged the United Nations Department of Public Information to disseminate widely information on acute world economic problems, particularly the critical situation in Africa, the severe difficulties of LDCs and the external debt of developing countries, as well as on the adverse effect of the international economic environment on those countries.

REFERENCES

[1]E/1985/29. [2]YUN 1984, p. 407. [3]*Ibid.*, p. 408, ESC res. 1984/83, 27 July 1984. [4]DP/1986/48 & Add.1. [5]E/1985/39. [6]YUN 1984, p. 409. [7]ACC/1985/16.

PUBLICATIONS

Challenge to Multilateralism: A Time for Renewal (views and recommendations of the Committee for Development Planning) (ST/ESA/169), Sales No. E.85.II.C.2. *Modern Management and Information Systems for Public Administration in Developing Countries* (ST/ESA/SER.E/3), Sales No. E.85.II.H.1. *Economic Performance of Public Enterprises: Major Issues and Strategies for Action* (ST/TCD/SER.E/2), Sales No. E.85.II.H.4.

Rural development

ACC action. The ACC Task Force on Rural Development (New York, 6-8 March 1985)[1] reviewed work accomplished since its 1984 meeting[2] in three areas: joint action at the country and regional levels; people's participation in rural development; and monitoring and evaluation. The Task Force considered progress reports from individual agencies and organizations, describing their activities since the 1984 meeting, which showed that they continued to focus on alleviating rural poverty, joint action between agencies and organizations at the country level, people's participation and women in rural development, and monitoring and evaluation at the project/programme and national levels.

The progress report by FAO, the lead agency in the rural development area, presented a positive assessment of change and progress towards rural poverty alleviation, increased decentralization in project planning, preparation and implementation, and increased regional attention on Africa. It was noted that there was a lack of institutional infrastructure at the national level to carry out effectively national programmes of poverty alleviation, combined with a lack of trained manpower.

A discussion by the Task Force on the impact of international economic recession on rural development at the country level and on resources available to the United Nations system highlighted the following: the change in income distribution in rural sectors due to the recession; the effect on rural employment; and the effect on infant mortality and malnutrition, and other socio-economic conditions of the rural population. It was noted that the recession had also led to possible long-term effects on international commodity prices. The Task Force's discussion focused on domestic adjustments taking place at the country level, such as lower rates of foreign exchange earnings in developing countries and cut-backs in domestic service programmes available to rural populations, thus exacerbating rural poverty. It was agreed that in future the Task Force would discuss new policy issues or developments bearing on the rural economy, and that studies on the effects of the recession on poverty and the standard of living prepared within the United Nations system should be circulated to Task Force members.

In April 1985,[3] CCSQ(PROG) heard an oral account of the Task Force's meeting and in October[4] took note of its report.

Other action. During the mid-term global review of the implementation of SNPA for the 1980s for LDCs (see p. 434), several conclusions and recommendations were made by UNCTAD's Intergovernmental Group on LDCs regarding food and agriculture and rural development in those countries. Those findings were endorsed by the General Assembly when it adopted **resolution 40/205**.

In May, the Economic and Social Council considered a report on social aspects of rural development[5] (see Chapter XIII of this section).

REFERENCES

[1]ACC/1985/PG/6. [2]YUN 1984, p. 410. [3]ACC/1985/4. [4]ACC/1985/20. [5]E/1985/8.

Special economic areas

In 1985, the General Assembly again considered measures being taken by the international community in favour of developing countries and called for action to deal with the specific problems of particular groups of them. By resolution 40/205, it endorsed the conclusions and recommendations of the UNCTAD Intergovernmental Group on the Least Developed Countries on the mid-term global review of the Substantial New Programme of Action for the 1980s for LDCs, and in resolution 40/233 added Vanuatu to the list of that group of countries, as recommended by CDP. By resolution 40/183, the Assembly again urged increased assistance to land-locked developing countries. However, due to the very low level of pledges and the declining trend in contributions, the Assembly, by decision 40/448 A, requested the Secretary-General to dissolve the United Nations Special Fund for Land-locked Developing Countries, as recommended by the UNDP Governing Council.

Developing countries

In response to a 1984 General Assembly resolution,[1] the Secretary-General submitted in September 1985 a report, prepared in co-operation with the heads of other United Nations bodies, on progress made in implementing immediate measures in favour of the developing countries.[2]

The report noted that United Nations entities had been endeavouring to develop specific proposals and to expedite the implementation of immediate measures in five areas identified by the Assembly in 1983,[3] namely: food and agriculture, money and finance, trade and raw materials, energy resources, and LDCs.

The conclusion that emerged from the system-wide review was that, although accomplishments had been significant in certain areas, they had generally been limited. The system had operated under stringent resource constraints and deliberative bodies found it difficult to agree on policy measures; action by the system required the consensus of the international community.

The Assembly took note of the report on 17 December by **decision 40/443**.

Least developed countries

The problems of the States officially designated as LDCs were considered in several United Nations forums during 1985, including the UNCTAD Intergovernmental Group on LDCs, the Governing Council of UNDP, ACC and the General Assembly.

With the General Assembly deciding in December to act on a CDP recommendation to include Vanuatu in the United Nations list of LDCs, the number rose to 37. The others were: Afghanistan, Bangladesh, Benin, Bhutan, Botswana, Burkina Faso, Burundi, Cape Verde, Central African Republic, Chad, Comoros, Democratic Yemen, Djibouti, Equatorial Guinea, Ethiopia, Gambia, Guinea, Guinea-Bissau, Haiti, Lao People's Democratic Republic, Lesotho, Malawi, Maldives, Mali, Nepal, Niger, Rwanda, Samoa, Sao Tome and Principe, Sierra Leone, Somalia, Sudan, Togo, Uganda, United Republic of Tanzania, Yemen.

Identification of LDCs

CDP action. Responding to 1984 requests contained in a General Assembly resolution on economic assistance to Vanuatu[4] and in an Economic and Social Council resolution[5] on including Kiribati and Tuvalu in the list of LDCs, CDP, at its April 1985 session,[6] considered their eligibility for inclusion in the list.

Based on data supplied by the Secretariat on the three criteria for determination of eligibility—per capita GDP, share of manufacturing output in GDP, and adult literacy rate—CDP concluded that Vanuatu qualified for inclusion. It decided to withhold its decision regarding the other two countries until a new set of criteria was established. The Committee was sceptical of the existing criteria and considered that new criteria should involve a clear definition of the purposes that the list of LDCs was meant to serve.

ECONOMIC AND SOCIAL COUNCIL ACTION

In February 1985, the Economic and Social Council considered an 11 January letter from El Salvador[7] transmitting a 1984 resolution of the Committee of the Whole of the Economic Commission for Latin America and the Caribbean,[8] by which it recommended that El Salvador be accorded treatment equivalent to that given to LDCs until its adverse economic situation returned to normal.

On 8 February, the Council adopted **decision 1985/110** without vote.

Resolution of the Committee of the Whole of the Economic Commission for Latin America and the Caribbean concerning El Salvador

At its 5th plenary meeting, on 8 February 1985, the Council:

(a) Took note of the fact that the Committee of the Whole of the Economic Commission for Latin America and the Caribbean adopted, on 28 June 1984, resolution 472(PLEN.17), concerning assistance to El Salvador, without signifying any agreement on the part of the Council with the contents of paragraph 2 thereof regarding the treatment of countries as least developed countries;

(b) Emphasized, in this connection, that as a general practice the existing procedures for the inclusion of countries in the list of the least developed countries should be followed by all the organs, organizations and bodies of the United Nations system.

Economic and Social Council decision 1985/110

Adopted without vote

Draft by President (E/1985/L.18), based on informal consultations; agenda item 2. *Meeting numbers.* ESC 1, 5.

In **resolution 1985/63** of 26 July, the Council called for measures to ensure the effective and accelerated implementation of SNPA in the African LDCs during the second half of the 1980s.

GENERAL ASSEMBLY ACTION

In **resolution 40/233** of 17 December 1985 on economic assistance to Vanuatu, the General Assembly decided to include Vanuatu in the list of LDCs.

Programme of Action for the 1980s

In 1985, United Nations bodies continued to monitor the implementation of the Substantial New Programme of Action for the 1980s for LDCs, adopted in 1981 by a United Nations Conference[9] and endorsed later that year by the General Assembly.[10] After the UNCTAD Intergovernmental Group on LDCs completed a global mid-term review of SNPA, the Group's conclusions and recommendations (see below) were endorsed by the Assembly. Meanwhile, ACC held three consultations during the year to co-ordinate preparations and facilitate a common understanding on the approach of the United Nations system to the review.

UNCTAD action. In accordance with a 1984 Assembly resolution,[11] a high-level meeting of the UNCTAD Intergovernmental Group on LDCs met (sixth session, Geneva, 30 September–12 October 1985)[12] to carry out the mid-term global review of the implementation of SNPA for the 1980s for LDCs.

On 12 October, the Intergovernmental Group adopted a resolution by which it reaffirmed the objective of SNPA as the basis for continuing co-operation between LDCs, submitted to the Assembly the conclusions and recommendations of its review of SNPA implementation—inviting the Assembly to endorse them—and the conclusions of its consideration of measures to ensure SNPA implementation over the second half of the decade, and called on Governments and organizations to take account of the conclusions and recommendations in their efforts to implement SNPA, to enable each LDC to achieve a minimum standard of performance in socio-economic development.

In a further resolution, also adopted on 12 October, the Group recommended that the Assembly at its 1985 session decide that a global review and appraisal of SNPA implementation should take place in 1990 at a high level, and invited the Assembly at its 1987 session to decide on the precise level, mandate, date and venue for such a review as well as on the preparatory process.

The Group's main background document was the second UNCTAD annual report on LDCs,[13] containing an assessment of their socio-economic development since 1980, a review of international support provided to them and of developments in the economies of individual LDCs since then, and a chapter setting forth conclusions and recommendations. An addendum to the report contained basic data in tabular form.

In addition to contributions by United Nations and other organizations describing their action to implement SNPA, the Group had before it the report of a Meeting of Governmental Experts of Donor Countries and Multilateral and Bilateral Financial and Technical Assistance Institutions with Representatives of LDCs (Geneva, 1-10 May 1985),[14] which was held in preparation for the mid-term review and in accordance with a 1984 UNCTAD Trade and Development Board decision.[15]

On 10 May, the experts adopted conclusions presented by the Chairman which reflected the informal discussions on issues relating to the mid-term review. The conclusions were on: national measures taken or to be undertaken by LDCs with international support for their accelerated progress and full and expeditious implementation of SNPA; ways of better adapting the implementation of development assistance programmes to the specific needs of LDCs; and measures to improve the co-ordination of assistance programmes.

ACC action. Also pursuant to the Assembly's 1984 resolution[11] and a 1981 ACC decision,[16] three inter-agency consultations on SNPA follow-up were held at Geneva during 1985 (11 and 12

February, 29 April, and 29 and 30 July). In February,[17] the consultation discussed the follow-up of the 1984 resolution on implementation of SNPA,[11] preparations for the mid-term review, both by the United Nations system and by UNC-TAD, and an overview by UNDP of experience gained from country meetings, including proposed changes in the format of round tables. The consultation also annexed to its report directions for the organizations of the United Nations system for the mid-term review and for the implementation of SNPA during the second half of the decade, and agreed to finalize them in April.

In April,[18] the consultation reviewed and adopted the directions, exchanged views on issues to be considered by the Meeting of Governmental Experts of Donor Countries and Multilateral and Bilateral Financial and Technical Institutions with Representatives of LDCs (see above), and discussed ways of assisting LDCs in preparing for the mid-term review.

At the July meeting,[19] the last before the review, the inter-agency consultation discussed preparations of the United Nations system, including facilitation of a common understanding on the system's approach, and exchanged views on the UNCTAD 1985 LDC report[13] and on policy proposals for the review.

UNDP action. During 1985, UNDP, together with the World Bank, continued to serve as lead agency in organizing country review meetings at which individual LDCs could consult with their aid partners on the recipient country's economic situation, on progress in SNPA implementation, on aid conditions and on needs for additional assistance. During 1985,[20] round-table-related activities were held with UNDP assistance for Benin, Chad, the Gambia, Guinea-Bissau, Lesotho, Mali, Rwanda, Sao Tome and Principe, and Togo. Other countries elected to have the World Bank assist them with review meetings.

Funding for the round-table process and for other activities benefiting LDCs was provided by the UNDP Special Measures Fund for LDCs. Contributions to the Fund in 1985 totalled $10.5 million and 11 countries pledged $11.5 million for 1986. Expenditures on round-table conferences were limited to $100,000 for each LDC. Resources from a trust fund established in 1983[21] for a special contribution from the Netherlands for LDCs were used to prepare round-table conferences and to finance follow-up activities to conferences held in recent years.

(For 1985 payments and 1986 pledges to the Special Measures Fund, see next chapter: table "Contributions to UNDP, 1985 and 1986".)

During 1985, UNDP continued to give highest priority to assisting the poorest countries (for UNDP IPFs and project expenditures, see next

chapter). Assistance to LDCs was also provided by the United Nations Capital Development Fund (UNCDF), the United Nations Sudano-Sahelian Office and the United Nations Volunteers programme.

In response to a 1984 UNDP Governing Council decision,[15] the UNDP Administrator submitted to the Council in 1985 an evaluation report on the role of UNDP in implementing SNPA.[22] The report reviewed UNDP involvement with LDCs and its response to the special action programmes introduced since the designation of the first group of LDCs in 1971[23] and particularly since the adoption of SNPA. The report contained proposals for revitalizing the Special Measures Fund for LDCs and described an improved format which had been introduced for the round-table process. The improved process would not focus on a single conference but would constitute a continuing process with multi-purpose functions of consultation, information and negotiation with the donor community over a period of time, with the round-table conference being followed by sectoral and other special programme consultations.

Noting that, with few exceptions, round-table conferences had exceeded the $100,000 allocated from the Special Measures Fund and that the estimated average cost of the improved format of the round-table process was $300,000, plus $200,000 for follow-up consultations, the report stated that ways of raising additional funds needed to be found, most appropriately by financing the process for the fourth programming cycle (1987-1991) from Special Programme Resources (SPR). An estimated ceiling of $500,000 per LDC per round-table cycle would ensure adequate support to the country concerned as well as a reasonable measure of control over SPR spending. UNDP was exploring alternative sources of funding in order to bridge the intervening period.

On 29 June,[24] the UNDP Governing Council endorsed the Administrator's proposals for revitalizing the Special Measures Fund, requested him to report in 1986 on arrangements made for utilizing and managing the Fund's resources, and urged Governments to contribute or increase contributions to the Fund and to UNCDF. The Council welcomed the improved format for the round-table process, requested the Administrator to ensure that the process provided an effective instrument for implementing SNPA, particularly in promoting a dialogue between LDCs and bilateral and multilateral donors on policy guidelines, and requested him to review periodically the round-table mechanism to ensure that it responded to the needs of LDCs and donors in efforts to achieve effective aid co-ordination. The Administrator was also requested to present to the mid-term review of SNPA a comprehensive report on UNDP efforts in favour of LDCs, particularly since the 1981 Conference on LDCs,[9] and to assess the results of round-table conferences since 1981 and present his views on how UNDP, donors and LDCs might contribute to the success of UNDP initiatives towards improved development co-operation with LDCs. The Council agreed in principle to the proposal for financing the round-table process from SPR and requested him to make the necessary recommendations to the Council in 1986, including an indication of the types of expenses that UNDP expected to incur.

Report of the Secretary-General. For its 1985 consideration of the implementation of SNPA, the General Assembly had before it the report of the UNCTAD Intergovernmental Group on LDCs (see p. 434), forwarded by the Secretary-General on 1 November,[25] and his 31 October report on the mid-term global review,[26] describing the United Nations system's preparations and summarizing the outcome of the review.

The latter report pointed out that the review had focused on issues of crucial importance to the development of LDCs and that Governments agreed on measures to expedite progress in implementing SNPA. Much attention was given to national policies of LDCs and priority areas for domestic action by LDCs were identified, such as food and agriculture, education, training, health and population policies. Particular attention was given to integrating women into the development process and their participation in the benefits therefrom. Important steps taken by many LDCs in adjusting their policies and programmes were acknowledged. On the other hand, it was repeatedly stressed that without substantially increased international support, progress in achieving SNPA objectives could not be made. Apart from urging increased aid flows, the review focused on ways that the international community could further strengthen the economies of LDCs through debt relief and commercial policy measures. Considerable attention was paid to the co-ordination and monitoring of SNPA.

It was noted that, although increased aid flows through fulfilment of SNPA targets could result by 1990 in a level of aid 30 per cent higher than in 1983, it might not be sufficient to allow LDCs to resume and accelerate economic growth. UNCTAD secretariat projections of capital requirements of LDCs implied an increase in ODA to those countries ranging from 34 to 300 per cent. The base scenario corresponded to continuing current trends, while the higher allowed LDCs to achieve a 7.2 per cent annual rate of growth by 1990.

To assist LDCs to improve their economic situation, substantially higher amounts of external financial resources were required, and fulfilment as soon as possible of commitments with regard to financial aid by all developed countries was extremely important. Urgent steps should be taken to provide substantially more resources through development banks and multilateral agencies and enhanced efforts would be needed to improve the quality and effectiveness of aid.

With regard to debt of LDCs, the mid-term review not only considered debt in the the the context of ODA debt to bilateral developed donors, but also invited creditors for official and officially guaranteed loans to LDCs and to multilateral assistance institutions to consider the debtor country's adjustment measures for restoring its debt-servicing capacity and long-term growth when concluding debt rescheduling arrangements.

With regard to trade policy, a wide range of measures had been set out in the mid-term review to expand the export earnings of LDCs. A number of developed countries had announced measures to improve access to their markets for the exports of LDCs.

GENERAL ASSEMBLY ACTION

On 17 December 1985, on the recommendation of the Second Committee, the Assembly adopted resolution 40/205 without vote.

Implementation of the Substantial New Programme of Action for the 1980s for the Least Developed Countries

The General Assembly,

Recalling its resolutions 3201(S-VI) and 3202(S-VI) of 1 May 1974, containing the Declaration and the Programme of Action on the Establishment of a New International Economic Order, 3281(XXIX) of 12 December 1974, containing the Charter of Economic Rights and Duties of States, and 3362(S-VII) of 16 September 1975 on development and international economic co-operation,

Recalling also its resolution 39/174 of 17 December 1984,

Reaffirming the provisions of the International Development Strategy for the Third United Nations Development Decade relating to the least developed countries, and the agreed conclusions concerning those countries of the Committee on the Review and Appraisal of the Implementation of the International Development Strategy for the Third United Nations Development Decade,

Reaffirming the Substantial New Programme of Action for the 1980s for the Least Developed Countries, whose objective is to transform the economies of the least developed countries so that they may achieve self-sustained development, and to enable them to provide at least internationally accepted minimum standards of nutrition, health, transport and communications, housing, education, and job opportunities to all their citizens, particularly the rural and urban poor,

Reaffirming the need to respect the socio-political and economic system of each least developed country in the implementation of the Substantial New Programme of Action,

Deeply concerned at the continued deterioration of the socio-economic conditions of the least developed countries despite national and international efforts to achieve the goals and objectives of the Substantial New Programme of Action,

Seriously concerned at the critical economic situation faced particularly by the least developed countries in Africa,

Recognizing the specific problems of the land-locked and island countries among the least developed countries, as reflected in United Nations Conference on Trade and Development resolutions 137(VI) and 138(VI) of 2 July 1983 and Trade and Development Board resolution 319(XXXI) of 27 September 1985,

Recalling paragraph 119 of the Substantial New Programme of Action in which it was recommended that the Intergovernmental Group on the Least Developed Countries of the United Nations Conference on Trade and Development, while carrying out the mid-term review, should consider the possibility of holding at the end of the decade a global review on the implementation of the Substantial New Programme of Action which might, *inter alia*, take the form of a United Nations conference on the least developed countries,

Taking note of the report of the Secretary-General on the mid-term global review of progress towards the implementation of the Substantial New Programme of Action, carried out by the Intergovernmental Group at its sixth session,

1. *Emphasizes* that the least developed countries, in view of their deteriorating socio-economic situation, need the urgent and special attention of the international community and its large-scale support on a continuous basis to enable them to progress towards self-reliant development, consistent with the plans and programmes of each least developed country;

2. *Reaffirms* the Substantial New Programme of Action for the 1980s for the Least Developed Countries as the basis for continuing co-operation between the least developed countries and their development partners, as well as the commitment to the full and effective implementation of the Programme;

3. *Endorses* the conclusions and recommendations contained in the report of the Intergovernmental Group on the Least Developed Countries on the mid-term global review of the Substantial New Programme of Action, as annexed hereto, which are designed to ensure the full implementation of the Substantial New Programme of Action over the second half of the decade;

4. *Calls upon* all Governments, intergovernmental and multilateral institutions, the organs, organizations and bodies of the United Nations system, non-governmental organizations and all others concerned to take immediate, concrete and adequate steps to implement the Substantial New Programme of Action for the Least Developed Countries, taking full account of the conclusions and recommendations of the mid-term global review so as to enable each least developed country to achieve a minimum standard of performance in socio-economic development;

5. *Reaffirms* that the least developed countries have primary responsibility for their overall development and that, although international support measures are vitally important, the domestic policies those countries pursue will be of importance for the success of their development efforts, and urges the least developed countries to continue their efforts to implement the provisions of the Substantial New Programme of Action at the national level;

6. *Calls upon* donor countries to continue to make every effort to increase their contributions in view of the important role that official development assistance plays in helping the least developed countries to achieve the objectives of their country programmes within the framework of the Substantial New Programme of Action, and urges those donor countries that have not yet attained 0.15 per cent of their gross national product, or have not yet doubled their official development assistance to least developed countries, to make every effort necessary to attain those targets as set out in United Nations Conference on Trade and Development resolution 142(VI) of 2 July 1983, as adopted;

7. *Urges* the least developed countries to create an appropriate policy framework (pricing policies, institutional reform, rationalization of public expenditures and public sector management, and measures to mobilize domestic savings through taxation, domestic financial institutions and the rural sector), in order to increase the mobilization of domestic resources and then ensure their effective use, and to strengthen their national financial and planning institutions and, in this regard, urges all concerned to support the least developed countries with appropriate technical and financial assistance;

8. *Stresses* the critical importance of multilateral assistance to the least developed countries through channels such as the International Development Association, the International Fund for Agricultural Development, regional development banks and their funds, the United Nations Development Programme, including its Special Measures Fund for the Least Developed Countries, the United Nations Capital Development Fund and the United Nations Volunteers programme;

9. *Calls upon* donor countries and institutions urgently to improve further the quality and effectiveness of official development assistance to increase its responsiveness to the requirements of the least developed countries, as called for in paragraph 70 of the Substantial New Programme of Action and in section XIII of part two of the annex to the present resolution;

10. *Reaffirms* the importance of co-ordination, follow-up and monitoring at the national, regional and global levels, as outlined in section XVII of part two of the annex to the present resolution, as crucial to the implementation of the Substantial New Programme of Action and requests the international community and the multilateral agencies to ensure that the country review meetings for the least developed countries facilitate understanding and dialogue between those countries and their development partners aimed at effective and expeditious implementation of the plans and programmes of the least developed countries with a view to achieving an accelerated growth rate and structural transformation of their economies, and invites the least developed countries to convene such meetings on a regular basis;

11. *Renews the invitation* to the governing bodies of appropriate organs, organizations and bodies of the United Nations system, including the United Nations Development Programme, to take the necessary and appropriate measures for effective implementation, monitoring and follow-up of the Substantial New Programme of Action and the conclusions and recommendations adopted by the Intergovernmental Group on the Least Developed Countries at its sixth session within their respective spheres of competence and mandates, and requests the

Secretary-General of the United Nations Conference on Trade and Development and the Director-General for Development and International Economic Co-operation to continue to undertake their responsibilities as specified in paragraphs 121 and 123, respectively, of the Substantial New Programme of Action;

12. *Decides* to carry out a global review and appraisal of the implementation of the Substantial New Programme of Action at a high level in 1990;

13. *Decides further* that the precise level, mandate, date and venue for such a review, as well as the preparatory process, should be determined by the General Assembly at its forty-second session, in the light of the consultations that will take place under the auspices of the United Nations Conference on Trade and Development, including those of the seventh session of the Conference;

14. *Requests* the Secretary-General to submit to the General Assembly at its forty-second session a report on the implementation of the present resolution.

ANNEX
Mid-term global review of progress towards the implementation of the Substantial New Programme of Action for the 1980s for the Least Developed Countries: conclusions and recommendations submitted by the Intergovernmental Group on the Least Developed Countries of the United Nations Conference on Trade and Development

Part One
Review of progress in implementation of the Substantial New Programme of Action at the country level and of progress in international support measures

Introduction

1. It was noted with serious concern that since the adoption in 1981 of the Substantial New Programme of Action for the 1980s for the Least Developed Countries there has been a significant deterioration in the overall socio-economic situation of the least developed countries, the causes of which were both external and domestic. The economic crisis had a depressing effect on the three major sources of foreign exchange of the least developed countries: export earnings, concessional capital flows and private transfers. The exceptionally high real interest rates prevailing during the past years have increased the interest obligations on their external debt. This situation was worsened by very adverse climatic conditions in many least developed countries, particularly in Africa, which have caused declines in agricultural and food production. There has also been uneven implementation of domestic policy changes that were required for social and economic development.

2. Thus, as a result of all these factors, after growing at a low average annual rate of close to 4 per cent in the 1970s and by 3 per cent in the first year of the present decade, the least developed countries as a group recorded a growth rate in gross domestic product (GDP) in 1982 and 1983 of only 2 per cent. Since population increased at the high rate of 2.6 per cent, in 1982 and 1983 their GDP per capita declined. Provisional indicators show a poor picture for 1984 when the African crisis came to a climax, affecting almost all the least developed countries in Africa. Preliminary estimates for 1985 point towards a virtual stagnation or decline of GDP for the group of least developed countries as a whole, which would mean a considerable reduction per capita. However, it is encouraging to note that, despite

this very poor development for the group as a whole, a few individual least developed countries did perform particularly well, some of them exceeding an annual GDP growth of 7.2 per cent, the rate required to double national income in a decade. This is evidence of the fact that the target of the Substantial New Programme of Action is not entirely beyond reach, although its attainment has become more difficult during the first half of the decade owing to the convulsions that have affected the world economic scene and to the vagaries of weather. Such an achievement requires an intelligent combination of measures undertaken by the least developed countries, on the one hand, and of the volume, conditions and structure of international assistance on the other.

3. Unless urgent measures are taken to implement fully and adequately the Substantial New Programme of Action, this declining trend in the socio-economic situation of the least developed countries will be even more acute in future, with serious and stark repercussions for their populations.

I. General situation and national measures

A. Food and agriculture

4. Among the essential social and economic priorities for the development of the least developed countries, both as a means of satisfying the most fundamental human needs and as a basis for economic growth, agriculture and food production were given the highest priority in the Substantial New Programme of Action. Specific recommendations were made in paragraphs 9-19 of the Programme and more especially in paragraph 13. Indeed, the weight of the agricultural sector within the overall economies of the least developed countries, supporting the overwhelming majority of the population and providing raw materials for industry and export revenues, establishes a clear and close link between progress in this sector and overall economic growth. These recommendations called for giving a high priority in the national development plans, programmes and policies of the least developed countries to the agricultural sector, with particular attention to food production and distribution. Agricultural and food strategies were to include among their objectives:

(*a*) The attainment of greater food self-sufficiency as soon as possible and at the latest by 1990;

(*b*) The attainment or surpassing of the 4 per cent growth rate in agricultural production;

(*c*) Achievement of food security through food supplies readily accessible at affordable prices.

5. During the first four years of the 1980s agricultural production in the least developed countries continued to be a source of continuing concern in terms both of growth rates and of the ability of the least developed countries to meet the food and nutritional needs of their growing populations. During this period the average rate of growth of agricultural output not only fell far short of the target of 4 per cent but also was lower than that recorded in the 1960s and 1970s. This implied a serious deterioration in per capita terms, given that population increased at the rate of 2.6 per cent per annum.

6. The goal of food self-sufficiency was even further from fulfilment, inasmuch as food production per capita fell even more than overall agricultural production. Food insecurity has worsened further, particularly at the

household level. The decline of per capita food production worsened, dropping from -0.5 per cent per annum in the 1970s to -1.4 per cent in 1980-1984. However, 7 among the 36 least developed countries did record positive growth rates in food output per capita, proving the realism of the targets set by the Substantial New Programme of Action.

7. Non-food agricultural production, destined largely for export, performed relatively better for the least developed countries as a group during the early 1980s.

8. The causes of the disappointing performance in agriculture and in food production in the least developed countries during the period under review are complex and vary from country to country. But in general, among them are the disastrous climatic conditions in most of those countries during the 1980s, which not only reduced agricultural production and negated the effects of the very substantial efforts made by many of them to increase production in this sector, but also caused severe ecological damage to the environment.

9. The importance accorded to food strategies has proven to be correctly placed. Such strategies enable donors and the least developed countries to deal with the problems of production, marketing and consumption in an integrated and comprehensive manner. Courageous and important steps have been taken by several least developed countries, with the support of the international community, to define and introduce food strategies. Success in these cases was the result of the political will of Governments to introduce changes. These measures have yet to produce full and tangible benefits but represent the principal achievement in this sector.

10. Failure in some cases to adopt appropriate food sector strategies and to implement appropriate reforms has contributed to the lack of progress in agricultural development. Difficulties have been encountered in such key areas as: full participation of the rural population in rural development programmes; appropriate pricing policies for both agricultural products and inputs to serve as incentives for increased production; institutional and agrarian reforms; the development of the required infrastructure; meeting the basic needs of rural societies; and overcoming the inequalities between men and women in participation in and benefiting from rural development programmes.

11. During recent years the particular dynamism of the rural sector has increased and shown itself in various forms, particularly in that of village groupings. It often developed in collaboration with non-governmental organizations. Several least developed countries have taken steps to support this dynamism using donor assistance, both bilateral and multilateral.

12. It was noted that there is a need to bring about an appropriate balance between food production for domestic consumption and cash crops for export. There are some positive examples for overcoming this potential dilemma, providing that the two objectives need not conflict with each other. For example, the development of agricultural export products may facilitate the introduction of new techniques and facilities that can also be used by traditional farmers to improve their production. Appropriate policies and development of infrastructures supporting export production may also benefit food production for local consumption.

13. Insufficient infrastructure in rural areas not only is a serious constraint to agricultural production, manufacturing and processing, but also serves to discourage linkages with other economic sectors.

14. While food aid has been useful in the short term, it has sometimes served to discourage moves towards increasing food self-sufficiency in the least developed countries by depressing prices and delaying urgent investments in the rural sector. However, ways have been found to use food aid as a tool for financing development projects in general and in the agricultural sector in particular.

15. Co-ordination in the agricultural sector at both the local and the international levels has been insufficient, priorities sometimes conflict, and the dialogue has not always been as comprehensive as might have been desired.

16. Severe price fluctuations on the international markets and uncertainties caused by natural factors have compounded problems facing the agricultural sector. The difficult economic conditions that faced many developed and developing countries in the early 1980s depressed demand for the major agricultural exports of the least developed countries, upon which they depend for a major part of their foreign exchange earnings, and further complicated their efforts to use agriculture as a means of improving their overall economic performance.

17. Support measures to help offset the shortfalls in export earnings arising from declining primary commodity prices were noted with satisfaction. However, many countries felt that the insufficient availability of such support, coupled with delays in bringing into operation the Common Fund for Commodities and the limited number of functioning commodity agreements, contributed to the difficulties of the least developed countries in overcoming the adverse consequences on their agricultural production.

B. Human resources and social development

18. On the issues of human resources and social development in the least developed countries there was general agreement that the recommendations of the Substantial New Programme of Action in this area remain valid. The development of human resources is an essential prerequisite for the development of the least developed countries, and therefore remains a priority. The scarcity of skilled manpower, particularly in an administrative and managerial capacity, hinders the development process in the least developed countries.

19. The progress achieved by some of the least developed countries in several areas, particularly declining infant mortality rates and increased literacy rates, was noted with satisfaction, while concern was expressed at the continued large discrepancy between male and female literacy rates. However, it was noted with concern that several other indicators reveal a declining trend in the education, health and nutrition status of the population of the least developed countries as a whole.

20. The scarcity of means available to accelerate the development of human resources in the least developed countries and efforts to overcome the situation were discussed. The need to consider public expenditure on education and health as investment from the point of view of the economy as a whole was stressed.

21. The reorientation of the educational system in some of the least developed countries in order to train

managers and technicians to better meet the needs of the economy was noted. There had been limited improvement in implementing training programmes meeting the priority needs of the rural populations. An important aspect has been increasing the prestige of manual work, especially in agriculture. The view was expressed that on-the-job training programmes have been more useful when integrated in development projects at an early stage and that they should be expanded and strengthened. Efforts to mobilize more domestic resources for education were highlighted. The necessity was stressed of maintaining and improving the quality of education in the context of the expansion of basic education.

22. It was emphasized that high priority for primary health care was still required. The contrast was noted in a general way between highly sophisticated medical care that was sometimes available only to a section of the urban population and the development of a widely decentralized preventive medicine which required simple methods, was relatively inexpensive and intended for as many people as possible. The efforts made by the least developed countries to achieve the target of "Health for All by the Year 2000" were also noted. The adaptation of the nomenclature of the essential drugs programme prepared by the World Health Organization forms part of these efforts.

23. Significant cuts in social expenditure have adversely affected the maintenance of physical facilities in both education and health in particular. Experience has shown that this difficulty can be overcome by flexibility on the part of both the least developed countries and donors. It was recognized that government funds were very limited in the least developed countries and experiences were reported where active participation of beneficiaries, *inter alia*, through user fees, contributed to covering the costs, to safeguarding the efficient use of existing facilities and to reducing dependency of vital services on external assistance. However, generally low income levels have resulted in some of the cases referred to in difficulties and limitations for such contributions. It was also stressed that universal access to basic education and health services was regarded as one of the major social aims of the least developed countries. Local and recurrent cost support in the aid programmes has in several cases been an essential complement of local efforts to keep physical facilities running.

24. The implementation of national population policies as recommended in the Substantial New Programme of Action was seen as an important factor for the success of development efforts by the least developed countries. It was noted that only a few least developed countries had vigorously encouraged population policies and family planning activities. Maternal and child care, including family planning, also bring general health benefits to mothers and children. The representatives of least developed countries explained that, while several least developed countries had adopted population programmes, the determinants of achieving lower fertility were not always favourable in their countries.

25. The significant contribution made by women in the development process of the least developed countries, especially in the agricultural sector, was highlighted.

26. Financial and technical assistance to the least developed countries plays an important part in support-ing their efforts in the sphere of human resources development. The linkage between both types of assistance and the right sequence to be followed in providing them was considered to be of crucial significance. The view was expressed by some donors that such assistance should have been provided on more flexible terms and should cover recurrent and local cost expenditures, as these have been identified as major constraints to the development of health and education.

27. It was observed that there is a lack of readily available data about the practical experience in human resources development that would permit analyses of past investment in and development of human resources. In this connection, the important role played by a number of partner countries of least developed countries and by the United Nations Development Programme in helping the least developed countries to develop their human resources and identify priorities was emphasized.

C. Natural resources and energy

28. In the sphere of natural resources and energy, the targets of the Substantial New Programme of Action remain entirely valid, despite the fact that they have not yet been achieved. The energy deficit experienced by most least developed countries often leads to their balances of payments being heavily mortgaged, as well as to destructive consequences on the environment. Most least developed countries have lacked the financial, human and material means to be able to assess and plan their traditional and other energy resources in a sufficiently comprehensive manner, with the result that the rational exploitation of these resources has so far been impeded.

29. Thus, the intensive use of fuelwood and charcoal has three consequences: a tendency towards the depletion of these resources, the degradation of the ecosystem and the weakening of the agricultural potential. Efforts to substitute the consumption of fuelwood by other resources have not yet yielded the results anticipated.

30. Despite the decline in real terms of the international price of energy, the cost of importing energy products remains heavy for the least developed countries.

31. For lack of financial and technical means, the hydroelectric resources of the least developed countries continue to be underexploited. Investments in this sector often have the twofold characteristic of requiring very considerable financial resources and of not invariably offering profitability sufficient to guarantee the covering of recurrent costs. The advantages afforded by small-scale hydroelectric schemes have not yet been fully exploited.

32. Although international aid has contributed to the efforts made in the energy sector, it has not solved the energy problems of the least developed countries, and modalities have not always been flexible enough to permit the full economic and social development of local potential.

D. Manufacturing industry

33. The industrialization targets of the Substantial New Programme of Action have not yet been achieved. In the majority of the least developed countries, the share of manufacturing in GDP is currently close to 9 per cent, while in a number of cases it does not even exceed 4 to 5 per cent.

34. The maintenance over a long period of unrealistic price structures and rates of exchange has sometimes exerted a negative impact on industrial development efforts.

35. In a number of least developed countries industrial policies, including the role to be played by the State in the industrial development sphere, have been redefined. In several least developed countries State enterprises continue to play an important role in this process.

36. In some cases industrial promotion mechanisms, mainly credit structures and technical training, as well as international aid, continue to be insufficient, and often entail severe conditions that the promoters are unable to fulfil.

37. In many cases in the past the choice of technologies, both by donors and by beneficiaries, has been inappropriate, leading to difficulties in maintenance and utilization of capacities.

38. The complementarity of the agricultural and industrial sectors has not always been fully taken into consideration, particularly in respect of linkage effects on employment. However, the least developed countries have endeavoured to promote the formulation of integrated strategies. Local capacities for on-the-spot processing of primary commodities have not yet been fully developed, owing to a lack of technical and financial means and of technology transfers to the least developed countries.

39. Although the situation varies considerably from country to country, the formulation of policies for the promotion of small- and medium-sized enterprises, as well as international assistance furnished for that purpose, are still inadequate. Industrial co-operation agreements between some enterprises of least developed countries and those of certain donor countries have been concluded.

40. Regional and subregional economic groupings have taken measures to exploit the opportunities offered by an expanding market in the regions concerned.

E. Physical and institutional infrastructure

41. The insufficiency, fragility and occasional ineffectiveness and inadequacy of the physical and institutional infrastructure continue to be one of the major obstacles to the structural transformation and economic development of the least developed countries.

42. The precarious situation of the physical infrastructure of the least developed countries is often aggravated by the inadequacy of maintenance services.

43. Institutional infrastructures are often insufficiently productive for various reasons, mainly the inadequacy of equipment and skilled staff and insufficient operating budgets.

44. In the case of land-locked least developed countries the inadequacy and the precarious situation of transport networks in adjoining countries, as well as occasional institutional instability in some of those countries, have formed an obstacle to the transportation of products coming from, or intended for, foreign countries.

F. Environment

45. The close interrelationship of poverty and environmental deterioration has become increasingly obvious in recent years. The lack of means and alternative energy resources compels the populations of the least developed countries to utilize resources that are becoming depleted, such as fuelwood, thus producing environmental deterioriation and an aggravation of the effects of drought and the desertification process. The deterioration of the ecosystem is thus the outcome of the joint impact of climatic conditions and human activity in a context of poverty and rapid population growth, which leads to the over-exploitation of the soil, water resources and vegetation. Consequently, climatic deterioration leading to drought and desertification may well become irreversible phenomena.

46. In some least developed countries, rural development policies have not yet always included specific measures designed to combat drought and desertification. Bearing in mind that fuelwood will continue to be the main source of energy for rural households in the least developed countries in the future, reforestation efforts have been inadequate. As they have been undertaken, activities, including international aid in this sphere, have frequently been geared to the short term and have neglected the need for long-term measures. Contemporary famines are the consequence of decades of unfavourable climatic factors but also of mistakes, inaction and a lack of foresight, both by the countries concerned and at the level of international aid.

47. In some cases political instability has made the efforts to combat desertification and drought hazardous. Similarly, population movements have sometimes constituted an aggravating factor.

48. Confronted with the seriousness of the situation, some least developed countries are beginning to implement policies associating local populations with measures to protect the environment.

G. Transformational investments

49. The number of major investment projects under preparation or under implementation in many least developed countries has decreased considerably since the adoption of the Substantial New Programme of Action, as a result of, *inter alia*, resource constraints, both internal and external, experienced by these countries, as mentioned in paragraphs 53 and 54 of the Programme. In the light of experience gained in design and implementation of projects, besides the capital needs, the following elements were considered important:

(*a*) A comprehensive approach for selecting major investment projects in accordance with national priorities;

(*b*) Carefully prepared pre-investment studies, including cost-benefit analysis;

(*c*) Pre-investment activities, with the necessary technical assistance;

(*d*) Human resources aspects, such as training of personnel, management capacity and participation of the local work force;

(*e*) Maintenance and rehabilitation, including preparedness to meet recurrent costs;

(*f*) A conducive atmosphere for investment.

H. Land-locked and island least developed countries

50. Paragraph 55 of the Substantial New Programme of Action, relating to the problems of land-locked and island least developed countries, was considered to retain its full pertinence. It was furthermore noted that the problems of those countries had been ag-

gravated in the recent period of recession. Attention was called to United Nations Conference on Trade and Development resolutions 137(VI) and 138(VI) of 2 July 1983 and Trade and Development Board resolution 319(XXXI) of 27 September 1985.

I.   Foreign trade

51.   The Intergovernmental Group reaffirmed the importance of paragraphs 56 to 58 of the Substantial New Programme of Action, which retain their full validity. The following factors were considered to be of special importance:

(*a*)   Horizontal and vertical diversification of production and exports;

(*b*)   The effects of the expansion of the network of intergovernmental long-term agreements on trade and economic co-operation, as well as the institutional framework, between the least developed countries and other countries;

(*c*)   Development of trade at the domestic and regional, as well as at the global level;

(*d*)   Trade promotion activities;

(*e*)   Adjustment efforts with regard to import programmes and policies of the least developed countries;

(*f*)   Development of institutional capabilities, including the training of personnel.

52.   It was recognized that, in carrying out their tasks in these fields, the least developed countries had benefited from, *inter alia*, the activities of the International Trade Centre UNCTAD/GATT and of the United Nations Conference on Trade and Development.

J.   Disaster assistance for the least developed countries

53.   The implementation of the Substantial New Programme of Action during the first four years has been impeded by natural disasters such as the drought in Africa and floods and cyclones in other countries, and man-made disasters such as internal and external conflicts that have affected a large number of the least developed countries and have considerably increased the number of refugees and displaced persons. The least developed countries, the industrialized countries and the international community, in particular the relevant specialized agencies of the United Nations system, are today in a position to draw some lessons from these dramatic experiences, which point to:

(*a*)   The need for creating conditions for improving the efficiency of emergency assistance, with the aim of reaching the target groups of the population;

(*b*)   The shortcomings relating to administrative structures for preventive purposes in the field regarding, *inter alia*, statistics, technology and various information networks and systems of monitoring the environment;

(*c*)   The relevance of using emergency assistance for measures improving the efficiency of the assistance, such as support for logistics and transport capacities;

(*d*)   The need for better co-ordination of efforts at both the national and the international level;

(*e*)   The value of the participation of non-governmental organizations;

(*f*)   The need for consideration of longer-term development objectives when providing emergency assistance, in particular with regard to production and distribution of food;

(*g*)   The special vulnerability of the least developed countries hosting refugees and persons affected by natural disasters.

54.   The Intergovernmental Group endorsed the conclusions relating to emergency assistance adopted by the Meeting of Governmental Experts of Donor Countries and Multilateral and Bilateral Financial and Technical Assistance Institutions with Representatives of the Least Developed Countries as Part of Preparation for the Mid-term Global Review of the Implementation of the Substantial New Programme of Action, which was held at Geneva from 1 to 10 May 1985.

II.   International support measures

A.   Transfer of financial resources

55.   The United Nations Conference on Least Developed Countries recognized that action by the least developed countries at the national level, including vigorous measures for the mobilization of domestic resources, should be complemented by international measures of support through both a substantial increase in financial resource transfers and policies and programmes affecting the modalities of assistance so that those countries might achieve the objectives of their country programmes within the framework of the Substantial New Programme of Action.

1.   *Volume of aid*

56.   The Substantial New Programme of Action envisaged that if all donors were to provide levels of net official development assistance consistent with one or other of the targets set out in paragraph 63 of the Programme, the level of such assistance to least developed countries would double by 1985 compared with the annual level of transfers to them during the period 1976-1980. On the basis of the data available up to 1984, it is anticipated that the actual level of assistance will fall substantially short of this amount in 1985. Nevertheless, a significant number of the donors who accepted one of the targets in 1981, either to provide official development assistance equivalent to 0.15 per cent of their gross national product (GNP) or to double the level of their assistance, have met or come close to reaching the target.

2.   *Multilateral programmes*

57.   The amount of multilateral aid, including flows from multilateral agencies financed by members of the Organization of Petroleum Exporting Countries, provided to least developed countries annually was 47 per cent higher in the period 1981-1983 than in 1976-1980. However, many countries expressed serious concern about the reduced level of funding for several important multilateral development agencies, in particular the International Development Association.

58.   It was noted, however, that several multilateral development agencies, mainly financed by countries members of the Development Assistance Committee, have adopted policies that emphasize the needs of the least developed countries. Although the share of flows from these agencies to the least developed countries has increased since 1981, the policy emphasis is yet to be fully reflected in aid disbursement patterns.

59.   Although the Special Facility for sub-Saharan Africa of the World Bank, established in 1985, is not specifically addressed to the least developed countries, it will increase financial flows to many least developed countries in Africa.

3.   *New mechanisms*

60.   No new initiatives have been taken since 1981 in respect of possible new mechanisms for increasing

financial transfers to the least developed countries. It was noted that the use by those countries of resources of the International Monetary Fund, designed to alleviate short-term balance-of-payments problems, which reached $2.2 billion in 1983, was now on the decline and that their net purchases from the Fund had been negative in 1984, despite their continuing serious balance-of-payments difficulties. It was further noted that the Task Force on Concessional Flows of the Development Committee of the World Bank had recently completed its work, which was considered at the 27th meeting of the Development Committee, held on 7 October 1985 at Seoul.

4. *Aid modalities*

61. The Substantial New Programme of Action urged donors and recipients to improve the quality and effectiveness of official development assistance by making improvements in aid practices and management. In this regard the following points were noted:

(a) Most donors have increasingly provided aid to the least developed countries on grant terms;

(b) The debt situation of many least developed countries remains serious and the amount of debt outstanding, including short-term debt and credits of the International Monetary Fund, had increased since 1981 to $35 billion by the end of 1983. Most donors members of the Development Assistance Committee had taken measures under Trade and Development Board resolution 165(S-IX) of 11 March 1978: the value of such measures in respect of least developed countries amounts to $4.0 billion, of which $2.9 billion is in the form of cancellation of official development assistance debt. Some donors have also rescheduled the official development assistance debt of least developed countries in several appropriate cases;

(c) Since 1981 there has been no general initiative by donors to increase the proportion of untied bilateral aid. Most bilateral aid, apart from local cost financing, has continued to be tied to procurement in the donor country. Representatives of least developed countries indicated that in their experience the tying of bilateral aid to their countries had increased since 1981;

(d) In the context of improved dialogue and understanding about domestic programmes and policies of the least developed countries, most donors have shown a greater willingness to provide aid in more flexible forms, in particular for balance-of-payments support, and at a sectoral level for rehabilitation and improved maintenance, as well as for longer-term development objectives. Representatives of some least developed countries pointed out that donors had continued, and in some cases increased, their preference for project aid, as compared to other forms of aid, which created difficulties in aid utilization in many least developed countries. The need was recognized for greater predictability in the provision of such assistance and for measures to be taken to reduce delays between commitments and disbursements;

(e) While most donors have been more willing to provide local cost financing, there remains a cautious attitude towards the funding of recurrent costs. It was noted that the provision of aid for the local costs of investments could facilitate the financing of recurrent costs from domestic resources, particularly in the social sectors. Nevertheless, the importance of aid for recurrent costs in appropriate cases was recognized, provided there was an understanding on the time-scale over which such costs could be increasingly financed from domestic resources;

(f) The donor Governments, and the public through voluntary contributions to non-governmental organizations in various countries, have responded to disasters, and in particular to the appalling famine in sub-Saharan Africa, with substantial emergency assistance.

B. Immediate action component of the Substantial New Programme of Action

62. The main issues concerning the immediate action component of the Substantial New Programme of Action were discussed in the context of aid modalities.

C. Technical assistance

63. Although the level of technical assistance to the least developed countries was substantially higher in the period 1981-1983 than in 1976-1980, it has remained at about $1.5 billion annually. The increased focus on technical assistance aimed at institution-building and training of manpower given by a number of donors, including the United Nations Development Programme, was noted.

64. Experience indicates that there is further scope for improving the effectiveness of technical co-operation, by establishing a closer link between technical co-operation and financial assistance and a further integration of different technical co-operation inputs, including the provision of equipment and highly qualified experts able to operate effectively in the environment of the least developed countries in association with appropriate counterpart staff.

D. Other economic policy measures at the international level

1. *Commercial policy measures*

65. The decline in dollar terms of the export earnings of the least developed countries, due particularly to the drop in the prices of primary commodities since 1979, is a source of serious concern. This, coupled with the deterioration in the terms of trade, has led to a reduction in essential imports and an increase in the external debt of the least developed countries, thus impeding their plans for trade expansion and diversification. In these circumstances, the efforts made by the industrialized countries in trade policy matters have not produced the desired effect.

(a) *Access to markets*

66. Some progress towards improved access for the products of the least developed countries to the markets of the industrialized countries has been noted. The persistence in certain cases of quantitative restrictions or of unduly severe rules of origin applied by certain countries was also noted.

67. Considerable improvements have been made by certain industrialized countries to their tariff preference schemes, although in many cases these schemes do not include all the export products that are of special relevance for the least developed countries. Moreover, the least developed countries do not or often could not take full advantage of the existing preference schemes for various reasons.

(b) *Export promotion*

68. A number of industrialized countries have set up offices to promote imports from developing countries, and more particularly imports from the least developed countries.

69. The technical assistance of the International Trade Centre UNCTAD/GATT and of the United Nations Conference on Trade and Development in formulating export strategies and trade promotion was considered to be constructive.

(c) Primary commodities

70. Little progress has been recorded in concluding commodity agreements. The successful conclusion of two new agreements for development purposes, the international agreements on jute and jute products and on tropical timber, was welcomed. The Agreement Establishing the Common Fund for Commodities, which would be advantageous for the least developed countries, has still not been implemented.

71. As far as compensation for shortfalls in export earnings is concerned, the extension of STABEX* to new products and the announcement of the implementation of a similar system for least developed countries that are not parties to the Lomé Convention were considered to be positive developments. However, there is still room for improvement in compensatory financing facilities. Reference was made to a plan for improving compensatory financing facilities that would provide for special treatment for the least developed countries and that is under discussion in the United Nations Conference on Trade and Development.

2. *Transport and communications*

72. Considerable difficulties continue to beset the least developed countries in respect of the upkeep and operation of transport and communications networks. These difficulties contribute to heavy losses in the event of natural disasters. The problems of land-locked and island least developed countries are particularly acute and require substantial investments in transport-transit infrastructure.

3. *Transfer and development of technology*

73. There has been a growing awareness of the importance of the transfer of technology for the social and economic transformation of the least developed countries. They continue to face difficulties in the acquisition and adaptation of appropriate technologies. A number of important measures taken by the least developed countries in effecting technological transformation were noted. Concern was expressed that the negotiations on an international code of conduct on the transfer of technology, the revision of the Paris Convention for the Protection of Industrial Property and the problem of the brain drain had not been concluded. The negative impact of reverse transfer of technology was mentioned.

III. Arrangements for implementation, follow-up and monitoring

74. The Substantial New Programme of Action recognized the importance of follow-up, implementation and monitoring at the national, regional and global levels.

A. National level

75. Co-ordination to ensure effectiveness of all development activities at the country level is a key responsibility of the least developed countries themselves and a crucial aspect of implementation, monitoring and follow-up of the Substantial New Programme of Action. Co-ordination needs differ from country to country, and mechanisms selected respond to the requirements of the individual country situation. The growing burden on the administrations of the least developed countries created by an increasing number of development activities, including measures to offset the consequences of natural disasters, has led to a stronger recognition by the least developed countries and the international community of the importance of co-ordination. In response, many least developed countries have established national focal points to co-ordinate external assistance. The United Nations Development Programme and other donors have contributed to strengthening the least developed countries' capabilities in this regard.

76. Since 1981 most of the least developed countries have established mechanisms in accordance with paragraph 111 of the Substantial New Programme of Action in the form of United Nations Development Programme round-table conferences and World Bank consultative groups or other arrangements. In response to the request from the least developed countries, the United Nations Development Programme has expanded its round-table conferences and the World Bank has increased the number of consultative groups, at the meetings of which the secretariat of the United Nations Conference on Trade and Development has played an active role. The initial results of the round-table conferences in terms of encouraging increased resource flows and a candid discussion of specific development issues were unsatisfactory. The meetings did not cover all the aspects suggested in paragraph 113 of the Programme but they provided a good basis for future development co-operation.

77. The United Nations Development Programme subsequently evaluated the round-table process and implemented a series of improvements, including co-operation with the World Bank and the European Economic Community on key aspects of macro-economic situations in conducting economic analyses. This is leading to a convergence of the types of issues dealt with at both forms of co-ordination meetings. Some donors have provided special assistance to the United Nations Development Programme for the purpose of conducting round-table conferences.

78. Although there is a general recognition that the United Nations Development Programme round-table conferences and World Bank consultative groups should be complemented by co-ordination at the local and sectoral levels, experience has shown that this has not been achieved in all cases.

79. Co-ordination of the activities of the United Nations system at the country level, as envisaged in paragraph 124 of the Substantial New Programme of Action, and under the aegis of the United Nations system resident co-ordinator has been insufficient and has scope for improvement as regards some reluctance to co-operate. In some least developed countries, at the specific request of the country concerned, the role of the system resident co-ordinator has assumed a broader focus. The activities undertaken by the regional commissions of the United Nations pursuant to paragraph 125 of the Programme were noted.

B. Global level

80. It was noted that the United Nations Conference on Trade and Development, in fulfilling the role of global monitoring of the Programme, had made a regular analysis of some aspects of the economic performance

of the least developed countries and the actions taken by the international community in implementing the Programme. The secretariat of the United Nations Conference on Trade and Development had also reported on a regular basis to the General Assembly on the implementation of the Substantial New Programme of Action. Furthermore, within the United Nations system the Director-General for Development and International Economic Co-operation, in close co-operation with the Secretary-General of the United Nations Conference on Trade and Development, has been convening interagency consultations on the least developed countries on a regular basis in order to ensure at the secretariat level the full mobilization and co-ordination of all regional commissions, organs, organizations and bodies of the United Nations system for the purpose of implementation and follow-up of the Programme.

Part Two
Measures for ensuring the implementation of the Substantial New Programme of Action over the second half of the Decade

The Intergovernmental Group on the Least Developed Countries,

I
Food and agriculture and rural development

Expressing concern that, although the Substantial New Programme of Action for the 1980s for the Least Developed Countries rightly attaches high priority to the agricultural sector, in particular to food production, progress in achievement of targets has been very slow, in many cases because of factors beyond the control of the least developed countries,

Recognizing that there is need to make further progress in developing and implementing food strategies in a co-ordinated and concentrated way,

1. *Concludes* that, while recognizing the individual situation of each least developed country, for an integrated policy in this area the following elements are of critical importance:

(a) Overall strategies, defining not only the goals of agricultural development and food security, but also the ways and means to reach those goals;

(b) Agricultural exports as a means to finance essential imports, notably for the agricultural sector, and to facilitate reinvestment in the sector;

(c) Improvement of research and development activities, adoption of appropriate technologies and study of possibilities for further processing of the main agricultural products;

(d) Promotion of co-operative development;

(e) Efficient structures and procedures to support the farmer in terms of, first, services (marketing and payment facilities, adequate agricultural extension, basic social services, such as primary health facilities and basic education, and ancillary services, such as repair shops and small-scale manufacturing); second, direct production inputs (for instance, an extended system of rural credit and seeds, fertilizers, pesticides, tools); and, third, infrastructures (for instance, storage and transport facilities, water supply);

(f) Appropriate pricing policies for agricultural inputs and products;

(g) Appropriate institutional and agrarian reforms, including more efficient and fairer distribution of the means of production;

(h) Measures to ensure the full participation of the rural population, with particular attention to women as regards the role they play and their share in the benefits received;

(i) Efficient management and utilization of forest resources based on the productive, protective and social potential of forests;

(j) Improved fisheries management and fisheries development strategy;

(k) Improvements in livestock breeding, disease control, including vaccine production, and provision of animal feed;

2. *Urges* that the least developed countries continue to take all necessary steps to allocate an appropriate share of domestic resources to rural development, as recommended, for example, by the Assembly of the Heads of State and Government of the Organization of African Unity at its twenty-first ordinary session, held at Addis Ababa from 18 to 20 July 1985;

3. *Urges* donors to support increasingly the least developed countries in devising and implementing the above-mentioned policies and programmes with technical and financial aid in order directly to improve agricultural production and living conditions in rural areas;

4. *Requests* donors to make clearer commitments for assistance, including food aid, which is to be integrated into longer-term agricultural and food strategies, so as to ensure that sufficient food is available to the least developed countries during the period in which the least developed countries concerned have not reached their objectives of self-reliance in food;

5. *Requests* the least developed countries and donors to recognize that their policies should be complementary in order to achieve the goals of sound agricultural development and complete food security;

II
Human resources and social development

Recognizing that for the least developed countries human resources and social development are of critical importance, noting that public expenditures on development of education, improvement of health services and population measures are investments for the future of the least developed countries, that rehabilitation and maintenance of existing facilities are essential and that involvement of local initiatives, support, motivation and participation of the people are crucial and noting further that many least developed countries have taken important initiatives in this regard,

1. *Urges* the least developed countries to devise and to implement, with the assistance of donors, concrete plans in the following areas:

(a) *Education and training*
(i) Universal primary education and universal adult literacy, bearing in mind the second Medium-Term Plan of the United Nations Educational, Scientific and Cultural Organization (1984-1989), emphasizing the need to narrow the disparities between men and women and to improve the quality of education;

(ii) Vocational training, including on-the-job training, for development projects;

(iii) Educational programmes geared to meet the priority needs of the rural population;

(iv) Special training of rural youth, also to limit further migration to urban areas;

(v) Labour-intensive and other appropriate technologies;

(vi) Increasing the availability of skilled manpower, particularly with administrative, managerial and development planning ability;

(vii) Raising the importance ascribed to productive activities and manual work, particularly in farming, at primary and higher levels of education;

(b) Health and nutrition

(i) Improved access to health services for the entire population, emphasizing primary health care, preventive medicine, supply of essential drugs and simple and less expensive techniques;

(ii) Strengthening the health infrastructure, including management, and establishing planning cycles for this purpose within the national development process of each least developed country;

(iii) Development of national health manpower;

(iv) Promotion and management of supply and storage of drugs, appropriate health technologies and basic health education;

(v) Integration of nutritional considerations into agricultural and health plans and policies;

(vi) Improved co-ordination in rural development programmes such as water supply and sanitation;

(c) Population

Integration of population policies into national development planning, emphasizing mother and child health care and family planning services as recommended by the International Conference on Population, 1984;

2. *Requests* increased support from donors and multilateral agencies for these highly important areas not only in terms of financial and technical aid but also in terms of a predictable and comprehensive package of aid measures including, as far as possible, local and recurrent costs in order to maintain existing facilities;

III
Position of women

1. *Urges* all countries to implement the conclusions and recommendations of the World Conference to Review and Appraise the Achievements of the United Nations Decade for Women: Equality, Development and Peace;

2. *Emphasizes* the need to ensure the full integration of women in all aspects of the development process in the least developed countries;

3. *Requests* the Governments of the least developed countries to show continuous awareness of the position of women as a critical factor for their development by strengthening their efforts to take the necessary steps to overcome cultural, legal and economic barriers that hamper the full participation of women in development and in the equitable sharing of the benefits of economic and social development;

4. *Urges* donors, in their support of development programmes and projects in the least developed countries, to give particular attention to their effect on the situation of women, including attention to ensuring that they do not inadvertently have negative consequences for women;

IV
Energy

1. *Calls upon* the least developed countries to include in their energy development plans measures for energy conservation and to assess the pattern of consumption of energy sources, including fuelwood, and its impact on the environment;

2. *Requests* developed donor countries and other countries in a position to do so to assist the least developed countries in the planning and implementation of these measures and to support as fully as possible measures to ensure energy supply and conservation, particularly through the development of renewable sources of energy as well as through reforestation;

V
Industrial development

Recognizing that industrial development is an important objective in overcoming under-development, in terms of employment and of the need for economic diversification,

Recognizing also that in many least developed countries the priority of agro-industry is reflected in policies for industrial development,

Noting resolution 6 adopted on 19 August 1984 by the Fourth General Conference of the United Nations Industrial Development Organization,

1. *Stresses* that the least developed countries should:

(a) Continue to give priority in their industrial development to agro-industry, industries producing agricultural inputs and industries based on local raw materials;

(b) Favour the development of national productive enterprises, in particular small and medium-scale, labour-intensive enterprises;

(c) Improve further the economic, legal and financial framework for industrial development and for all forms of international co-operation, including joint ventures between enterprises of least developed countries and those of other countries, within the context of national policies and priorities;

(d) Give priority to the maintenance and full use of existing industrial capacity;

(e) Seek appropriate technologies adapted to local needs and capacities for maintenance and repair;

(f) Use the full potential of the State, but also improve the incentives for entrepreneurship and support for local initiatives according to national policies;

2. *Calls upon* donor countries:

(a) To increase their effective support to the least developed countries in carrying out these measures in the light of the agreed priority noted above;

(b) To base their contributions firmly on local initiatives and involvement;

(c) To combine technical and management training with financial assistance;

(d) To provide assistance where possible on a multi-year basis;

(e) To assist in developing local sources of raw materials where necessary to make local industry less vulnerable to balance-of-payments problems;

VI
Physical and institutional infrastructures

Recognizing the primary importance for the least developed countries of overcoming bottle-necks in institutional and physical infrastructures,

Recognizing also that for the implementation of the Substantial New Programme of Action increased attention should be paid, in particular, to the strengthening of institutional capacity, which has an important bearing on, *inter alia*, effectiveness of development aid programmes, disaster relief and aid co-ordination,

1. *Requests* the least developed countries further to strengthen their planning, monitoring, evaluation and executing capacity, in particular so that it is geared to creating a policy framework that enables efficient and effective use of the possibilities for development in each country;

2. *Also requests* the least developed countries, with regard to physical infrastructure, to take steps to ensure that the existing capacity is fully used and that recurrent costs for maintenance and investments for balancing, modernization and replacement are covered, taking into account that foreign assistance will be needed in the short term in many least developed countries since in many cases it will not be possible to cover those costs fully from domestic resources;

3. *Calls upon* donors to support the least developed countries with technical and long-term financial assistance to improve their physical and institutional infrastructures;

4. *Further calls upon* donors to pay special attention to transport facilities and transit links of the least developed countries, in particular of the land-locked and island countries among them;

5. *Underlines* the special importance of feeder roads and tracks for opening up remote rural areas so as to increase accessibility to markets of their agricultural products and to facilitate delivery of emergency assistance;

VII
Environment

Recognizing the close interrelationship between poverty and the environment,

Further recognizing that conflict may exist between the immediate needs of people in the least developed countries and the need for environmental protection,

1. *Urges* all least developed countries and donors to take into account increasingly the environmental implications of development actions, notably the problem of desertification;

2. *Requests* donors to support actions by the least developed countries in terms of environmental protection, including, in particular, soil conservation, afforestation, reforestation and identification and conservation of water resources;

3. *Requests* the least developed countries to give increasing attention to the integration of environmental issues into development planning and to the active participation of the local population in all measures taken;

VIII
Land-locked and island countries among the least developed countries

Recognizing the specific problems of land-locked and island countries among the least developed countries, as reflected in United Nations Conference on Trade and Development resolutions 137(VI) and 138(VI) of 2 July 1983 and Trade and Development Board resolution 319(XXXI) of 27 September 1985,

1. *Calls upon* transit countries to intensify co-operation with the land-locked countries among the least developed countries in order to alleviate their transit-transport problems;

2. *Requests* donors to give attention to land-locked and island countries among the least developed countries in their technical and financial assistance, with particular focus on capital input in infrastructural development;

3. *Requests* the United Nations system, in particular the United Nations Development Programme, to continue to support those least developed countries in the solution of their specific transit-transport and communications problems;

IX
Disaster relief

Recognizing that natural and man-made disasters have seriously aggravated the already difficult situation of the least developed countries,

1. *Requests* the Governments of the least developed countries, within the context of their national policies and priorities, to increase their capacity to respond to disasters and to allow the free flow of relief materials to all those affected;

2. *Stresses* the need for better co-ordination of efforts at both the national and the international levels;

3. *Requests* donors to help the least developed countries, while fully respecting their sovereignty, to bring relief to the people affected by disaster by including in their assistance, *inter alia*, support for logistics and transport capacity;

4. *Urges* donors to assist the least developed countries not only in a situation when a disaster occurs, but also in strengthening the capacity of those countries to face disasters, including an extended early warning system for natural disasters as well as food storage facilities;

5. *Calls upon* all countries to ensure that food-aid and other supplies to relieve the suffering can reach the country in need in the fastest and most effective way;

6. *Calls upon* donors and the least developed countries to take into consideration longer-term development objectives when implementing emergency assistance measures, in particular with regard to production and distribution of food;

7. *Encourages* all countries to continue to promote the participation of non-governmental organizations and the general public in relief efforts;

X
Mobilization of domestic resources

1. *Urges* the least developed countries to create an appropriate policy framework (pricing policies, institutional reform, rationalization of public expenditures and public sector management, and measures to mobilize domestic savings through taxation, domestic financial institutions and the rural sector) in order to increase the mobilization of domestic resources and then ensure their effective use, and to strengthen their national financial and planning institutions;

2. *Urges* developed donor countries and multilateral institutions to support the least developed countries with

technical assistance to strengthen their planning and financial institutions and to assist by providing financial assistance for the purpose of stimulating the mobilization of domestic resources;

XI
Transfer of financial resources

Recognizing that action by the least developed countries at the national level, including vigorous measures for the mobilization of domestic resources, should be complemented by international measures of support both through a substantial increase in financial resource transfers and through policies and programmes affecting the modalities of assistance,

1. *Calls upon* the international community to continue to make special efforts to increase its contributions in view of the fact that only a substantial increase in official development assistance in real terms during the present decade will enable the least developed countries to achieve the objectives of their country programmes within the framework of the Substantial New Programme of Action;

2. *Reaffirms* United Nations Conference on Trade and Development resolution 142(VI) of 2 July 1983 as adopted, in which the Conference urged donor countries within the overall context of the Programme as adopted and of progress towards the 0.7 per cent target, to attain 0.15 per cent of their gross national product as official development assistance or to double their official development assistance to the least developed countries by 1985 or as soon as possible thereafter;

3. *Expresses* its appreciation that since 1981 several donor countries have reached 0.15 per cent of GNP as official development assistance or have doubled that assistance to least developed countries;

4. *Appeals* to those donor countries that have not yet contributed 0.15 per cent of their GNP, or have not yet doubled their official development assistance to least developed countries, to make every effort necessary to attain these targets as contained in resolution 142(VI);

5. *Stresses* the critical importance of multilateral assistance to the least developed countries through channels such as the International Development Association, the International Fund for Agricultural Development, regional development banks and their funds, the United Nations Development Programme, including its Special Measures Fund for the Least Developed Countries, the United Nations Capital Development Fund and the United Nations Volunteers programme;

6. *Calls upon* donor countries to channel a substantial part of their aid through multilateral development institutions and agencies, particularly those addressing the needs of the least developed countries, within the overall substantial increases of official development assistance to least developed countries;

7. *Stresses* the important role that the International Development Association plays in structural adjustment programmes of the least developed countries within the framework of the Substantial New Programme of Action, while noting with regret that the Seventh Replenishment of the Association was lower than the Sixth Replenishment and welcoming the fact that the Development Committee at its twenty-seventh meeting, held at Seoul on 7 October 1985, urged that a successful and adequate Eighth Replenishment be achieved by September 1986;

XII
Debt

Recognizing that the burden of debt and debt service has increased substantially for the least developed countries since the adoption of the Substantial New Programme of Action,

Recognizing also that it is in the interest of both creditors and debtors that the debt commitments of the least developed countries are met,

1. *Notes with satisfaction* that a number of donor countries have responded favourably to section A of Trade and Development Board resolution 165(S-IX) of 11 March 1978 by cancellation of official development assistance debt or other equivalent measures and firmly invites other donors that have not yet done so to implement fully commitments undertaken in pursuance of the resolution, keeping in mind paragraph 71 of the Substantial New Programme of Action;

2. *Further notes* that the repayment of debt to multilateral assistance institutions is one of the elements in the overall debt service burden of the least developed countries and invites those institutions to take this into account in their lending programmes for the least developed countries;

3. *Invites* creditors for official and officially guaranteed loans to the least developed countries when concluding a debt rescheduling arrangement for a least developed country, to give due consideration to, *inter alia*, the debtor country's adjustment measures for restoration of its debt-servicing capacity and long-term growth;

4. *Invites* donors and relevant international organizations to assist the least developed countries in strengthening their administrative structures in order to permit continuous monitoring and effective management of the debt of the least developed countries, its structures and service payment schedules;

5. *Recommends* that in the context of a review of the economic and financial situation of a least developed country, country review meetings may also take into account its debt situation;

XIII
Aid modalities

1. *Recognizes* that, in terms of aid modalities:

(a) Clear medium-term perspectives and greater predictability of the volume and forms of the resources available are important to the least developed countries and to the donor community to enable the latter to adapt assistance flexibly and effectively to the changing needs, objectives and priority of the least developed countries;

(b) In order to minimize delays in disbursement, advance payments should be made whenever appropriate and solutions to problems of disbursement should be sought by all parties;

2. *Urges* donors to take the necessary steps to ensure that:

(a) Bilateral official development assistance to the least developed countries is provided essentially in the form of grants, acknowledging, however, that increased flows may require a mixture of types of aid, such as grants, concessional loans and other forms of assistance;

(b) Multilateral development assistance agencies and institutions addressing the needs of the least developed countries provide credits to them on highly concessional terms, to the extent that their lending procedures permit;

(c) Aid to the least developed countries is untied to the maximum extent possible; when not possible, necessary steps should be taken to help offset the disadvantages of tying;

(d) Transactions financed by any type of associated financing are generally avoided for the least developed countries because of their relatively hard terms; if contracted, it should be ensured that such transactions with the least developed countries contain a high component of official development assistance;

3. *Recommends* with regard to different forms and types of aid, that:

(a) Particularly in support of domestic adjustment measures of the least developed countries, donors should provide aid in more flexible forms, in particular balance-of-payments support, and at a sectoral level, for rehabilitation and improved maintenance, as well as for longer-term development objectives;

(b) Donors should further increase, where appropriate, their participation in local and recurrent cost financing; adequate provisions should also be made for allowing a progressive take-over of recurrent costs by the least developed countries;

(c) Aid programmes should provide, as much as possible, for the use of local consultants and expertise;

4. *Concludes,* with regard to technical assistance, that:

(a) Because of the need for the development of human resources, technical assistance by donors is of primary importance and should accompany financial aid to the maximum extent possible;

(b) It is important further to integrate different technical co-operation inputs, including the provision of equipment;

(c) Appropriate co-ordination by the least developed countries of technical assistance is of primary importance; donors are requested to support the strengthening of aid administration and planning agencies in the least developed countries with a view to improving co-ordination capabilities at a national level;

(d) Increased attention should be paid by donors and the least developed countries to the appointment of suitable expatriate experts for the training of counterparts, to maintaining stability in their assignments, and to strengthening training institutions in the least developed countries;

XIV

Foreign trade and commercial policy measures

Noting with concern the problems facing the foreign trade sector of the least developed countries as referred to in paragraph 65 of the review, in part one above,

1. *Recognizes* the progress achieved in providing access for products of the least developed countries to the markets of industrialized countries, particularly under the Generalized System of Preferences;

2. *Notes* as a positive development the initiative of the European Economic Community in establishing a system similar to STABEX* for those least developed countries not parties to the Lomé Convention;

3. *Recommends* that the least developed countries give special attention to implementing the measures set out in paragraphs 56 to 58 of the Substantial New Programme of Action, giving particular emphasis to the factors identified in paragraph 51 of the review, in part one above;

4. *Invites* the least developed countries to utilize fully the opportunities that are already available in the field of market access, in particular under the Generalized System of Preferences;

5. *Calls upon* the international community to intensify efforts to strengthen and improve the open multilateral trading system aimed at benefiting all countries, keeping in view the specific needs of the least developed countries;

6. *Invites* all countries concerned to pursue action towards facilitating the trade of the least developed countries by reducing or eliminating tariff and non-tariff obstacles to their exports, in pursuance of paragraph 77 of the Substantial New Programme of Action and the Ministerial Declaration adopted on 29 November 1982 by the Contracting Parties of the General Agreement on Tariffs and Trade at their thirty-eighth session;

7. *Requests* the preference-giving countries that have not yet done so to make further improvements for the least developed countries on a non-discriminatory basis in their schemes under the Generalized System of Preferences through, *inter alia*, more flexible requirements for rules of origin, extension of the list of products that receive preferential treatment, and extension of the duration of these schemes for a reasonable period, in order to facilitate the fullest possible duty-free access to products of interest to the least developed countries;

8. *Calls upon* developed countries to provide the necessary resources to strengthen technical assistance facilities so that the least developed countries can fully benefit from the Generalized System of Preferences;

9. *Also calls upon* developed countries in a position to do so to explore the possibilities of promoting long-term arrangements for the sale of export products of the least developed countries, pursuant to paragraph 79 *(c)* of the Substantial New Programme of Action;

10. *Invites* developed countries and multilateral agencies, including the International Trade Centre UNCTAD/GATT and the United Nations Conference on Trade and Development, to provide appropriate technical and financial assistance to support export strategies and trade promotion efforts of the least developed countries;

11. *Calls upon* the developing countries in a position to do so to provide preferential treatment to imports of goods produced by the the least developed countries, pursuant to United Nations Conference on Trade and Development resolution 142(VI), paragraph 13 *(a)*;

12. *Invites* all countries to intensify their efforts for a broader utilization, where appropriate and feasible, of international commodity agreements for the stabilization of the export prices of the least developed countries;

13. *Requests* the international community to take appropriate steps to bring the Common Fund for Commodities into operation at an early date, which, once operational, should give due emphasis to commodities of interest to the least developed countries in determining its priorities for the use of resources of the Second Account;

14. *Invites* importing developed countries that have not yet done so to consider steps in the field of export earnings stabilization, in accordance with paragraph 83 of the Substantial New Programme of Action, and notes the establishment of an intergovernmental group of experts, as decided by Trade and Development Board decision 317(S-XIV) of 27 June 1985, to consider, *inter alia*, this matter;

15. *Invites* the International Monetary Fund to explore, within its existing rules, ways and means of improving the use of its compensatory financing facility by least developed countries;

XV
Economic co-operation among developing countries

1. *Calls upon* all developing countries to implement the recommendations on economic co-operation among developing countries, as contained in United Nations Conference on Trade and Development resolution 142(VI);

2. *Requests* all donor countries and multilateral organizations to support and strengthen economic co-operation among developing countries, in particular concerning the projects of special interest to the least developed countries, in order to ensure that the countries concerned will fully benefit from the results of such co-operation;

XVI
Role of non-governmental organizations

Recognizing that non-governmental organizations can contribute positively to the development of the least developed countries as well as provide valuable disaster relief,

1. *Calls upon* the Governments of the least developed countries and donors to encourage active participation of the local population, both women and men, through non-governmental entities;

2. *Calls upon* non-governmental organizations to comply with the national policies and legislation of the host countries and, while preserving their character, to contribute to the development priorities of the least developed countries, co-operating with appropriate authorities and organizations in order to implement effective development programmes;

3. *Invites* the non-governmental organizations of the donor countries to reinforce their role in consciousness-raising in their countries of origin and in mobilizing increased private and public resources for the benefit of the least developed countries;

XVII
Co-ordination and monitoring

1. *Reaffirms* the importance of co-ordination, follow-up and monitoring at the national, regional and global levels as crucial to the implementation of the Substantial New Programme of Action;

2. *Reaffirms also* the monitoring role of the United Nations Conference on Trade and Development at the global level and requests the Secretary-General of the United Nations Conference on Trade and Development to continue and intensify his work, as specified in paragraph 121 of the Substantial New Programme of Action;

3. *Welcomes* the growing attention to co-ordination at the national level;

4. *Recognizes* that effective co-ordination, monitoring and follow-up at the national level must be a continuous process;

5. *Endorses* the results concerning the co-ordination of assistance programmes of the Meeting of Governmental Experts of Donor Countries and Multilateral and Bilateral Financial and Technical Assistance Institutions with Representatives of the Least Developed Countries as part of Preparation for the Mid-term Global Review of the Substantial New Programme of Action, held at Geneva in May 1985;

6. *Welcomes* the steps taken by the World Bank and the United Nations Development Programme to improve the consultative groups and round-table meetings by, *inter alia*, enhancing co-operation among multilateral institutions and agencies, as well as efforts made with the help of the Special Measures Fund of the United Nations Development Programme and voluntary contributions and specific contributions of donor countries for the least developed countries;

7. *Emphasizes* the primary role of each least developed country in the co-ordination of aid activities;

8. *Further emphasizes* the importance of co-ordination in each least developed country at the sectoral level in order to ensure the greatest possible effectiveness of development activities;

9. *Requests* the Governments of the least developed countries to continue to strengthen their planning machinery and administrative capacity so as to improve the planning, negotiation and utilization of external assistance;

10. *Requests* the least developed countries, with the assistance of the lead agencies, to attend to the quality and early availability of preparatory documents for round-table conferences and meetings of consultative groups, which are essential for their success;

11. *Requests* the multilateral agencies to improve further the quality, coherence and timeliness of the background documentation they present at round-table conferences and meetings of consultative groups;

12. *Requests* donor countries and multilateral institutions to pay more attention to appropriate local representation and sectoral co-ordination;

13. *Urges* donors in a position to do so to support development plans or programmes of the least developed countries with multi-year, predictable and monitorable commitments and timely disbursements;

14. *Calls upon* the organizations of the United Nations system to co-operate closely in each least developed country under the aegis of the resident co-ordinator, as provided for in paragraph 124 of the Substantial New Programme of Action;

15. *Reiterates* paragraph 123 of the Substantial New Programme of Action, in which the Director-General for Development and International Economic Co-operation is called upon, in close collaboration with the Secretary-General of the United Nations Conference on Trade and Development, the executive secretaries of the regional commissions and the lead agencies for the aid groups, to ensure at the secretariat level the full mobilization and co-ordination of all organs, organizations and bodies of the United Nations system for the purpose of implementation and follow-up of the Programme;

16. *Urges* the resident co-ordinators of the United Nations system to respond constructively to requests by the Governments of the host countries to play a broader co-ordinating role in appropriate cases;

17. *Requests* the international community and the multilateral agencies:

(*a*) To ensure that review meetings result in facilitating an increased flow of external assistance through, *inter alia*, a better understanding and a candid dialogue between the least developed countries and their development partners;

(b) To harmonize terms and procedures of donors to the extent possible in order to achieve a co-ordinated approach conducive to the implementation of the development programmes of the least developed countries.

---

*System of stabilization of export earnings established by the first Lomé Convention, concluded between EEC and 46 ACP (African, Caribbean and Pacific) States on 28 February 1975, and reinforced by the second ACP-EEC Convention, concluded between EEC and 58 ACP States on 31 October 1979.

General Assembly resolution 40/205

17 December 1985   Meeting 119   Adopted without vote

Approved by Second Committee (A/40/989/Add.10) without vote, 13 December (meeting 51); draft by Vice-Chairman (A/C.2/40/L.131), based on informal consultations on draft by Yugoslavia, for Group of 77 (A/C.2/40/L.82); agenda item 84 *(j)*.

Meeting numbers. GA 40th session: 2nd Committee 45, 51; plenary 119.

Speaking in explanation of position in the Second Committee, Bulgaria, also on behalf of the Byelorussian SSR, Czechoslovakia, the German Democratic Republic, Hungary, Mongolia, Poland, the Ukrainian SSR and the USSR, said the socialist countries attached great importance to SNPA and had participated actively in the review; however, no recommendations had been made on the indebtedness and other financial problems of LDCs, eliminating protectionism and compensation for damage to their economies from the economic crisis, nor had any reference been made in the Intergovernmental Group's report[25] to the interrelationship between disarmament and development or to the need to establish a new international economic order.

The United States said it had been pleased to join the consensus but had difficulties with the reference to a global review of SNPA implementation at the end of the decade that might take the form of a conference, as the nature and scope of the review should not be prejudged until its purpose had been carefully assessed; paragraphs 12 and 13 were also of concern and it rejected the call in paragraph 6 for the setting of ODA targets. Similarly, the United Kingdom stressed that ODA to LDCs was subject to public-expenditure constraints and to the level of assistance it provided to other developing countries.

Land-locked developing countries

During 1985, the special needs and physical handicaps of land-locked developing countries were considered by UNCTAD and the General Assembly. On the recommendation of the UNDP Governing Council, the Assembly in December requested the Secretary-General to dissolve the United Nations Special Fund for Land-locked Developing Countries.

UNCTAD action. Responding to a 1984 UNCTAD Trade and Development Board decision,[27] the UNCTAD secretariat submitted to the Board (Geneva, 18-29 March 1985) the views and comments of Governments[28] on the report of the 1984 meeting of an *Ad Hoc* Group of Experts[29] which had studied ways of improving transit-transport infrastructures and services for land-locked developing countries.

It was concluded that the Group's report received the endorsement of most of the 30 Governments that responded to an UNCTAD note verbale on the subject. The report's recommendations were viewed as a basis for an approach by the international community towards solving the problems of land-locked developing countries. Although some Governments attached great importance to the role of international agencies as third parties in seeking solutions for land-locked and transit countries, the initiative to negotiate solutions should be taken by those countries. The need for intensified co-operation between land-locked countries and their transit neighbours was fully supported by all Governments and a special appeal was made to transit countries to ratify the 1965 Convention on Transit Trade of Land-locked States.[30] The importance of tackling transit-transport as part of national development plans was underlined and the Group's recommendations on co-operative subregional development were supported.

Some Governments commented that, although there were a number of common features characterizing the transit-transport problem, individual land-locked countries had their own peculiarities. Other issues on which some Governments had reservations included: the general question of recognizing land-locked developing countries as a special category; the questions of joint ownership and management of transit facilities; and issues pertaining to internal restructuring of the economies of land-locked countries with a view to reducing their dependency on transit routes and to institution building. Areas which should have been more adequately covered included: inter-modal co-ordination; pricing of transport services; diversity of problems facing individual countries; and the role of the regional commissions in work related to those countries.

On 29 March, the Board decided[31] to consider at its September session a draft resolution on specific action related to the particular needs and problems of land-locked developing countries.

On 27 September,[32] following consultations on the draft, the Board called on the international community to continue implementing UNCTAD resolutions 63(III),[33] 98(IV),[34] 123(V)[35] and 137(VI),[36] and on donors to provide assistance, including skilled manpower training, in assessing potentials for restructuring the economies of land-locked countries through the promotion of import substitution industries. The land-locked countries and their transit neighbours were invited to intensify transit-transport co-operative arrangements, including legal arrangements for the smooth flow of goods in transit.

International financial and technical assistance institutions were called on to give priority to programmes encouraging such co-operation as well as development schemes involving land-locked countries, and the Board urged that transit developing countries be given greater support in providing efficient transit-transport facilities. The international community was urged to consider positively the recommendations of the *Ad Hoc* Group[29] and the views of Governments thereon (see above).

The Board invited member States to ratify and implement international conventions on transit trade and requested the UNCTAD Secretary-General to provide technical assistance to land-locked developing countries and their transit neighbours to promote such ratification. He was also requested to pursue the work of UNCTAD technical advisory services as called for in UNCTAD resolution 137(VI),[36] to carry out studies recommended by the *Ad Hoc* Group, to seek extrabudgetary resources, including UNDP funds, to enable him to comply with requests contained in the resolution, and to report to the Board in 1986.

In resolution 137(VI),[36] the UNCTAD Secretary-General was called on to report annually to the General Assembly through the Trade and Development Board on progress in implementing specific action related to the needs and problems of the land-locked developing countries. The second such report prepared by the UNCTAD secretariat[37] was submitted to the Assembly in October 1985. It consisted of two parts, the first of which dealt with geographical handicaps and their impact on trade and development, as requested by the Assembly in 1984.[38]

The first part of the report discussed: basic considerations relating to the geographical handicaps of land-locked developing countries, including their remoteness from world markets and the need to ship goods through the territory of neighbouring States; the diversity of the 21 land-locked countries of Africa, Asia and Latin America; the need for alternative routes, such as air freight, should normal transit routes be disrupted; co-operative arrangements between land-locked and transit countries; international regulations for transit-transport operations; and the role of international assistance in support of transit-transport infrastructure development.

The report recommended: investment in transport infrastructure and improved management of transport facilities, complemented by domestic development strategies and international support measures; increasing local value added before export; and greater support to local production of low-value, high-bulk imports, particularly those increasing the utilization of local resources. The report stated that international support in developing alternative routes was a matter of high priority, as was co-operation between land-locked countries and their transit neighbours. Adherence to international conventions relevant to trade and transport was stressed as their ratification would significantly contribute to removing some bottle-necks restraining transit traffic.

The second part of the report contained information received from 26 countries and 24 international and intergovernmental organizations on specific action in favour of land-locked developing countries.

The report concluded that, although international support of land-locked developing countries continued to be inadequate to meet their growing requirements, it was widely recognized that they continued to face serious development problems because geographical handicaps were an additional burden on their weak and highly vulnerable economies. Sectoral diversification of assistance would, in the long run, help to restructure their economies and render them less vulnerable to their geographical handicaps. In the short run, however, increased resources were needed for the transit-transport sector where bottle-necks undermined development projects and threatened the survival of countries facing shortages of essentials. Particular attention was being given by some donors to subregional transport development, which encouraged close co-operation between land-locked countries and their neighbours.

GENERAL ASSEMBLY ACTION

On 17 December, on the recommendation of the Second Committee, the Assembly adopted resolution 40/183 by recorded vote.

Specific action related to the particular needs and problems of land-locked developing countries

The General Assembly,

Reiterating the specific actions related to the particular needs of the land-locked developing countries stated in United Nations Conference on Trade and Development resolutions 63(III) of 19 May 1972, 98(IV) of 31 May 1976, 123(V) of 3 June 1979 and 137(VI) of 2 July 1983 and Trade and Development Board resolution 319(XXXI) of 27 September 1985,

Recalling the provisions of its resolutions 31/157 of 21 December 1976, 32/191 of 19 December 1977, 33/150 of 20 December 1978, 34/198 of 19 December 1979, 35/58 of 5 December 1980, 36/175 of 17 December 1981 and 39/209 of 18 December 1984 and other resolutions of the United Nations relating to the particular needs and problems of land-locked developing countries,

Bearing in mind various other resolutions adopted by the General Assembly, its related organs and the specialized agencies emphasizing special and urgent measures in favour of land-locked developing countries,

Recalling the relevant provisions of the International Development Strategy for the Third United Nations Development Decade,

Recalling the United Nations Convention on the Law of the Sea, adopted on 10 December 1982,

Bearing in mind the report of the *Ad Hoc* Group of Experts to Study Ways and Means of Improving Transit-transport Infrastructures and Services for Land-locked Developing Countries,

Recognizing that the lack of territorial access to the sea, aggravated by remoteness and isolation from world markets, and the prohibitive transit, transport and trans-shipment costs impose serious constraints on the socio-economic development of land-locked developing countries,

Noting with concern that the measures taken thus far have not adequately addressed the problems of land-locked developing countries,

1. *Reaffirms* the right of access of land-locked countries to and from the sea and freedom of transit through the territory of transit States by all means of transport, in accordance with article 125 of the United Nations Convention on the Law of the Sea;

2. *Appeals* to all States, international organizations and financial institutions to implement, as a matter of urgency and priority, the specific actions related to the particular needs and problems of land-locked developing countries envisaged in resolutions 63(III), 98(IV), 123(V) and 137(VI) of the United Nations Conference on Trade and Development, in the International Development Strategy for the Third United Nations Development Decade, in the Substantial New Programme of Action for the 1980s for the Least Developed Countries and in other relevant resolutions of the United Nations;

3. *Urges* all concerned countries, as well as international organizations, to provide land-locked developing countries with appropriate financial and technical assistance in the form of grants or concessional loans for the construction, maintenance and improvement of their transport and transit infrastructures and facilities;

4. *Urges also* the international community and multilateral and bilateral financial institutions to intensify efforts in raising the net flow of resources to all land-locked developing countries to help offset the adverse effects of their disadvantageous geographical situation on their economic development efforts, in keeping with the overall development needs of each land-locked developing country;

5. *Invites* transit countries and the land-locked developing countries to co-operate effectively in harmonizing transport planning and in promoting other joint ventures in the field of transport at the regional, subregional and bilateral levels;

6. *Further invites* the international community to give financial, technical and other support to interested transit and land-locked developing countries in the construction of alternative routes to the sea;

7. *Commends* the United Nations Development Programme, the United Nations Conference on Trade and Development and other United Nations agencies for their work and the assistance they have provided to the land-locked developing countries, and invites them to continue to take appropriate and effective measures to respond to the specific needs of those countries;

8. *Recommends* continued and intensified activities relating to the conducting of necessary studies and the implementation of special actions and specific measures for the land-locked developing countries, including those in the area of economic co-operation among developing countries, as well as those that have been envisaged in the programme of work of the United Nations Conference on Trade and Development, the regional commissions and other programmes and activities at the regional and subregional levels;

9. *Once again requests* Member States to transmit to the Secretary-General of the United Nations Conference on Trade and Development their views and comments on the report of the *Ad Hoc* Group of Experts to Study Ways and Means of Improving Transit-transport Infrastructures and Services for Land-locked Developing Countries;

10. *Welcomes* the report of the Secretary-General of the United Nations Conference on Trade and Development on progress in the implementation of specific action related to the particular needs and problems of land-locked developing countries, submitted pursuant to resolution 39/209, and requests him to prepare another such report for submission to the General Assembly at its forty-second session.

General Assembly resolution 40/183

17 December 1985   Meeting 119   152-0-1 (recorded vote)

Approved by Second Committee (A/40/989/Add.3) by recorded vote (135-0-1), 3 December (meeting 46); 13-nation draft (A/C.2/40/L.38/Rev.1); agenda item 84 *(c)*.

Sponsors: Afghanistan, Bangladesh, Bolivia, Botswana, Burkina Faso, Burundi, Central African Republic, Lao People's Democratic Republic, Mongolia, Nepal, Paraguay, Rwanda, Zambia.

Meeting numbers. GA 40th session: 2nd Committee 31, 36, 41, 45, 46; plenary 119.

Recorded vote in Assembly as follows:

In favour: Afghanistan, Algeria, Angola, Antigua and Barbuda, Argentina, Australia, Austria, Bahamas, Bahrain, Bangladesh, Barbados, Belgium, Benin, Bhutan, Bolivia, Botswana, Brazil, Brunei Darussalam, Bulgaria, Burkina Faso, Burma, Burundi, Byelorussian SSR, Cameroon, Canada, Cape Verde, Central African Republic, Chad, Chile, China, Colombia, Comoros, Congo, Costa Rica, Cuba, Cyprus, Czechoslovakia, Democratic Kampuchea, Democratic Yemen, Denmark, Djibouti, Dominica, Dominican Republic, Ecuador, Egypt, El Salvador, Equatorial Guinea, Ethiopia, Fiji, Finland, France, Gabon, Gambia, German Democratic Republic, Germany, Federal Republic of, Ghana, Greece, Grenada, Guatemala, Guinea, Guinea-Bissau, Guyana, Haiti, Honduras, Hungary, Iceland, India, Indonesia, Iran, Iraq, Ireland, Israel, Italy, Ivory Coast, Jamaica, Japan, Jordan, Kenya, Kuwait, Lao People's Democratic Republic, Lebanon, Lesotho, Liberia, Libyan Arab Jamahiriya, Luxembourg, Madagascar, Malawi, Malaysia, Maldives, Mali, Malta, Mauritania, Mauritius, Mexico, Mongolia, Morocco, Mozambique, Nepal, Netherlands, New Zealand, Nicaragua, Niger, Nigeria, Norway, Oman, Pakistan, Panama, Papua New Guinea, Paraguay, Peru, Philippines, Poland, Portugal, Qatar, Romania, Rwanda, Saint Christopher and Nevis, Saint Vincent and the Grenadines, Samoa, Sao Tome and Principe, Saudi Arabia, Senegal, Sierra Leone, Singapore, Somalia, Spain, Sri Lanka, Sudan, Suriname, Swaziland, Sweden, Syrian Arab Republic, Thailand, Togo, Trinidad and Tobago, Tunisia, Turkey, Uganda, Ukrainian SSR, USSR, United Arab Emirates, United Kingdom, United Republic of Tanzania, Uruguay, Vanuatu, Venezuela, Viet Nam, Yemen, Yugoslavia, Zaire, Zambia, Zimbabwe.

Against: None.

Abstaining: United States.

Explaining its abstention, the United States said it believed that the category of land-locked countries was not meaningful and it opposed the institution of special categories other than that of least developed.

Prior to voting on the text as a whole, the Second Committee approved paragraph 1 by a recorded vote of 106 to none, with 26 abstentions. A number of States explained their abstentions on paragraph 1 relating to article 125 of the 1982 United Nations Convention on the Law of the Sea,[39] which assured land-locked States right of access and freedom of transit, under terms and modalities for transit agreed upon between the States concerned, and allowing transit States to ensure that their legitimate interests were not infringed.

Iran said the right of access to the sea and freedom of transit should be realized in compliance with subparagraphs 2 and 3 of article 125. Senegal said it also had reservations regarding the article and believed that the problems of land-locked countries could be better solved through bilateral arrangements, a position shared by Ghana, Liberia, Mauritania and India, which added that it could not understand the need for a detailed Assembly resolution paralleling that of 1984.[38] Mozambique stated that it had reservations on the article, as the issue in question should be agreed between the land-locked developing countries and transit States. The Federal Republic of Germany, speaking also on behalf of the United Kingdom, felt that matters regarding State sovereignty should be decided by consensus and that action in favour of land-locked countries should be related to their individual level of development.

Turkey said its vote in favour of the draft as a whole in no way implied that it had accepted the Convention on the Law of the Sea. Brazil said that its vote in favour of paragraph 1 and the draft as a whole was on the understanding that the text did not supersede existing bilateral arrangements. Peru voted in favour on the understanding that existing agreements between the concerned parties and the rights of transit States would be respected.

UN Special Fund for Land-locked Developing Countries

In a two-part report[40] to the UNDP Governing Council, the UNDP Administrator, responding to a 1981 Governing Council decision,[41] gave details of income, expenditure, programming and projects of the United Nations Special Fund for Land-locked Developing Countries for the 1983-1984 biennium, and, in accordance with a 1983 Council decision,[42] reviewed the Fund's history since its inception.

The Administrator stated that the decline in contributions continued during 1983-1984 when pledges amounted to some $88,000 and $55,000 respectively. As at March 1985, pledges for that year totalled some $38,000. (As at 31 December 1985, payments totalling $49,604 were received from 11 States, while 12 States pledged $15,116 for 1986—see table below.)

The Administrator noted that the 19 countries which abstained in the vote on the 1976 General Assembly resolution approving the Fund's statute[43] included virtually all the major donors to United Nations development activities. He said those countries were opposed to categorizing the

land-locked developing countries as a special group and preferred to assist them through bilateral programmes and through other multilateral programmes benefiting individual land-locked developing countries among others. Of the 115 countries which voted for the resolution, 27 had contributed to the Fund since its inception and 14 of those were themselves land-locked.

The Administrator concluded that the Fund would cease to be viable in 1985-1986 and stated that, if the UNDP Governing Council shared that conclusion, it might wish to recommend to the Assembly that the Fund be dissolved.

On 28 June,[44] the Council recommended to the Assembly that, in the absence of any prospect for increased contributions, the Fund should be dissolved and closed for further contributions as of 1 January 1986, and that, following completion of activities in respect of projects approved by that date, any uncommitted resources be transferred to UNDP general resources.

CONTRIBUTIONS TO THE UN SPECIAL FUND FOR LAND-LOCKED
DEVELOPING COUNTRIES, 1985 AND 1986

(as at 31 December 1985; in US dollar equivalent)

Country	1985 payment	1986 pledge
Bhutan	3,020	1,730
Brazil	20,000	—
Burundi	—	877
Lao People's Democratic Republic	2,000	1,000
Lesotho	765	575
Malawi	1,215	1,287
Nepal	2,000	2,000
Philippines	500	1,000
Rwanda	—	500
Senegal	—	1,000
Thailand	2,000	1,000
Togo	213	—
Tunisia	—	511
Zambia	14,163	—
Zimbabwe	3,728	3,636
Total	49,604	15,116

SOURCE: A/41/5/Add.1.

GENERAL ASSEMBLY ACTION

On 17 December, the Assembly adopted three decisions on the closure of the Special Fund. It adopted **decision 40/448 A** without vote, on the recommendation of the Second Committee.

At its 120th plenary meeting, on 17 December 1985, the General Assembly, on the recommendation of the Second Committee, having taken note of decision 85/32 of 28 June 1985 of the Governing Council of the United Nations Development Programme, requested the Secretary-General to take the necessary steps to dissolve the United Nations Special Fund for Land-locked Developing Countries in an orderly manner by 31 December 1986 and to transfer all uncommitted resources to the general resources of the Programme.

General Assembly decision 40/448 A

Adopted without vote

Approved by Second Committee (A/40/1041) without vote, 11 December (meeting 50); draft by Vice-Chairman (A/C.2/40/L.113); agenda item 85 *(b)*.
Meeting numbers. GA 40th session: 2nd Committee 35-42, 44, 46-50; plenary 120.

As a result of the adoption of the above decision, the Assembly, on the oral proposal of its President, adopted **decisions 40/448 B and C** without vote. It decided that there was no longer a need for the Assembly to elect members of the Fund's Board of Governors **(40/448 B)** or confirm the appointment of an Executive Director **(40/448 C)**.

REFERENCES

[1]YUN 1984, p. 412, GA res. 39/175, 17 Dec. 1984. [2]A/40/597 & Corr.1. [3]YUN 1983, p. 429, GA res. 38/200, 20 Dec. 1983. [4]YUN 1984, p. 498, GA res. 39/198, 17 Dec. 1984. [5]*Ibid.*, p. 417, ESC res. 1984/58, 26 July 1984. [6]E/1985/29. [7]E/1985/15. [8]YUN 1984, p. 638. [9]YUN 1981, p. 406. [10]*Ibid.*, p. 410, GA res. 36/194, 17 Dec. 1981. [11]YUN 1984, p. 415, GA res. 39/174, 17 Dec. 1984. [12]TD/B/1078. [13]*The Least Developed Countries 1985 Report* and *Addendum: Basic Data* (TD/B/1059 & Add.1), Sales No. E.86.II.D.2. [14]TD/B/1055 & Corr.1. [15]YUN 1984, p. 414. [16]YUN 1981, p. 408. [17]ACC/1985/8. [18]ACC/1985/24. [19]ACC/1985/25. [20]DP/1986/17. [21]YUN 1983, p. 431. [22]DP/1985/11 & Corr.1 & Add.1. [23]YUN 1971, p. 232. [24]E/1985/32 (dec. 85/11). [25]A/40/827. [26]A/40/826 & Corr.1. [27]YUN 1984, p. 419. [28]TD/B/1040 & Add.1,2. [29]YUN 1984, p. 418. [30]YUN 1965, p. 259. [31]A/40/15, vol. I. [32]*Ibid.*, vol. II (res. 319(XXXI)). [33]YUN 1972, p. 280. [34]YUN 1976, p. 398. [35]YUN 1979, p. 569. [36]YUN 1983, p. 435. [37]A/40/815. [38]YUN 1984, p. 419, GA res. 39/209, 18 Dec. 1984. [39]YUN 1982, p. 181. [40]DP/1985/53. [41]YUN 1981, p. 415. [42]YUN 1983, p. 436. [43]YUN 1976, p. 355, GA res. 31/177, 21 Dec. 1976. [44]E/1985/32 (dec. 85/32).

Chapter II

Operational activities for development

Total official development assistance (ODA) transferred through the United Nations system to developing countries in 1985 amounted to $5.1 billion. Total contributions for operational activities amounted to $5.5 billion, an overall decrease due to the drop in contributions to the World Bank and the International Fund for Agricultural Development (IFAD).

In its thirty-fifth anniversary year, the United Nations Development Programme (UNDP) received aggregate contributions of $863.7 million, of which $571.7 million was expended on field programme activities. In June, the UNDP Governing Council reached consensus on the target for annual resource growth for the Programme's fourth programming cycle (1987-1991), agreeing to average yearly increases in voluntary contributions of 8 per cent, on a basis of a target of $700 million anticipated for 1986. In November, at the annual United Nations Pledging Conference for Development Activities, recorded and estimated pledges for 1986 surpassed $700 million and were expected to exceed $745 million, the highest level in UNDP history.

The General Assembly in December, by resolution 40/211, called on States to make every effort to attain the planned funding levels for operational activities for development by the various organizations of the United Nations system.

The United Nations Department of Technical Co-operation for Development (DTCD) delivered $127.2 million in project expenditures, the largest programme since 1981. Special concerns addressed by DTCD during 1985 included the critical situation in Africa, pre-investment and investment follow-up, and women in development.

The United Nations Volunteers programme experienced sustained growth in 1985 with 1,128 volunteers in service as at 31 December. By resolution 40/212, the Assembly invited Governments to observe annually, on 5 December, an International Volunteer Day for Economic and Social Development.

In May/June, the High-level Committee on the Review of Technical Co-operation among Developing Countries (TCDC) held its fourth session and adopted decisions on a range of TCDC issues. The Assembly, by resolution 40/196, endorsed the Committee's decisions and requested United Nations organizations to ensure their implementation.

The United Nations Capital Development Fund (UNCDF) approved $37.5 million for 22 new projects and grant increases in existing project budgets. It continued to direct a large proportion of its resources to the least developed countries in Africa beset by critical economic and drought-related problems.

Topics related to this chapter. Africa: South Africa and *apartheid*—aid programmes and interagency co-operation. Middle East: aid programmes for Palestinians. Development policy and international economic co-operation: economic co-operation among developing countries. Economic assistance, disasters and emergency relief. International trade and finance: UNCTAD technical co-operation; development finance. Regional economic and social activities—technical co-operation. Natural resources and cartography: United Nations Revolving Fund for Natural Resources Exploration. Energy resources: energy resources development. Food: food aid. Science and technology: United Nations Financing System. Health and human resources: human resources. Women: women and development. Refugees: refugee assistance. Namibia: international assistance.

General aspects

In his annual report on United Nations operational activities for development,[1] the Director-General for Development and International Economic Co-operation (DIEC) stated that $5,147 million in ODA was transferred through all the organizations of the system to developing countries in 1985, amounting to about 15 per cent of net ODA received by those countries. Excluding the concessional funds provided by the International Development Association (IDA) and IFAD, which amounted to $2,601 million, the share of developing countries' net ODA receipts channelled through the system was a little over 7 per cent, almost the same percentage as in earlier years of the decade.

Grant-financed expenditures on field programmes totalled $2,546 million, an increase of about 7 per cent, part of which was the result of the stronger United States dollar, which might have had a depressive effect on contributions but had a beneficial effect on programme expenditures. The principal source of growth in expenditures was the World Food Programme (WFP); the United Nations Children's Fund (UNICEF), UNDP and the United Nations Fund for Population Activities (UNFPA) experienced less significant increases.

Total contributions to the operational activities of the United Nations system, including all funds and programmes of the United Nations and the operational activities of the specialized agencies and WFP, amounted to $5,490 million, a decrease compared with 1984 due to the drop in contributions to the World Bank and IFAD. Contributions were also received in respect of humanitarian, refugee, disaster relief and special economic assistance programmes, amounting to $593 million in 1985, an increase of 6 per cent over the 1984 level. This was mainly due to the response to the critical situation in Africa.

In response to a 1984 General Assembly resolution,[2] the Director-General included in his annual report to the 1985 Assembly[3] information on measures taken to strengthen co-ordination capabilities and national evaluation arrangements. Information was also included on co-operation with multilateral development banks and on the relationship between programme delivery and administrative and support costs. With regard to harmonization of administrative, financial, personnel, planning and procurement procedures, the report noted that some progress had been made in evaluation procedures, project proposals and procurement practices. As to bringing about greater use of the technical resources of DTCD, the Secretary-General had created a joint DTCD/UNDP task force to increase collaboration so as to promote the utilization of the comparative strengths of both organizations.

The question of co-ordination of external technical co-operation at the country level and steps taken by UNDP to strengthen co-ordination was also addressed in a report by the UNDP Administrator to the UNDP Governing Council (see p. 472).

ACC activities. In a preliminary exchange of ideas on the Director-General's report for the triennial policy review of operational activities for development to be undertaken by the Economic and Social Council and the General Assembly in 1986, the Consultative Committee on Substantive Questions (Operational Activities) (CCSQ(OPS)) (New York, 7-9 October)[4] of the Administrative Committee on Co-ordination (ACC) heard a representative of the Director-General's Office summarize possible topics to be considered to improve the coherence, impact and relevance of operational activities. Committee members would be consulted during preparation of the report and a paper on subjects to be included would be submitted to the Committee in 1986.

GENERAL ASSEMBLY ACTION

On 17 December 1985, on the recommendation of the Second (Economic and Financial) Committee, the General Assembly adopted **resolution 40/211** without vote.

Operational activities for development
The General Assembly,

Reaffirming the validity of its resolution 38/171 of 19 December 1983 on the comprehensive policy review of operational activities for development,

Reaffirming also its resolution 39/220 of 18 December 1984 on financing of operational activities for development, as well as its resolution 32/197 of 20 December 1977 on the restructuring of the economic and social sectors of the United Nations,

Reaffirming further its resolutions 2688(XXV) of 11 December 1970 on the capacity of the United Nations development system and 3405(XXX) of 28 November 1975 on new dimensions in technical co-operation,

Reaffirming the exclusive responsibility of the Government of the recipient country in formulating its national development plan, priorities and objectives, as set out in the consensus contained in the annex to resolution 2688(XXV), and emphasizing that the integration of the operational activities of the United Nations system with national programmes would enhance the impact and relevance of those activities,

Reaffirming also the responsibility of developing countries to co-ordinate development co-operation, including the determination of local co-ordination arrangements,

Reaffirming further the responsibilities of the resident co-ordinators on behalf of the United Nations system with respect to co-ordination of operational activities carried out by the United Nations system at the country level in accordance with their mandate,

Reaffirming the important contribution of operational activities for development of the United Nations system in support of the overall economic and social development of developing countries,

Reiterating its desire for a coherent and co-ordinated United Nations system in the field of operational activities for development and for effective leadership by the Director-General for Development and International Economic Co-operation in the co-ordination of the various components of the United Nations system and in exercising overall co-ordination within the system, as set forth in resolution 32/197, as well as its call for full co-operation with the Director-General by all organs, organizations and bodies of the United Nations system,

Noting the steps being taken by the United Nations Development Programme, the United Nations Fund for Population Activities, the United Nations Children's Fund and the World Food Programme, through the joint consultative group on policy to enhance their collaboration in programming and implementation,

Welcoming the decisions of the governing bodies of the relevant United Nations organizations to strengthen their efforts in response to the emergency situation in Africa, and welcoming the co-ordinated response of the United Nations organizations in support of relief operations in Africa and the co-ordination of such assistance through the United Nations Office for Emergency Operations in Africa, as well as the related arrangements at the country level,

Recognizing, in this regard, the need for additional financial resources to meet the urgent development needs of African countries,

Emphasizing the need for a significant, continuous and real increase in resources for operational activities to meet the growing requirements for development of the developing countries, in particular the least developed countries,

Expressing its appreciation to those Governments of both developed and developing countries that, at the 1985 United Nations Pledging Conference for Development Activities, announced increased contributions for operational activities for development for the year 1986, as well as to those Governments that have consistently maintained their contributions at a high level,

Having examined the report of the Director-General for Development and International Economic Co-operation on operational activities for development of the United Nations system,

1. *Requests* the Director-General for Development and International Economic Co-operation, within a general framework of broad objectives of operational activities in accordance with General Assembly resolution 32/197, to include the following in his report for the 1986 comprehensive policy review, in addition to the requests contained in General Assembly resolution 38/171 and the issues identified in paragraph 3 of the report of the Director-General for 1985 and to make recommendations, as appropriate, thereon:

(a) Measures to strengthen the existing mechanisms within the United Nations system, with a view to furthering the coherence and co-ordination of operational activities;

(b) An analysis of the relationship between the increasing responsibilities of the United Nations Development Programme in the area of co-ordination and its essential role in the provision of technical co-operation;

(c) An analysis of changing requirements for technical co-operation through multilateral channels and the responsiveness of the United Nations system to them;

(d) Further analysis of programme delivery and administrative and support costs;

(e) Developments regarding joint technical co-operation needs assessments;

(f) Steps taken by United Nations organizations engaged in operational activities to promote the participation of women in development;

(g) An analysis of the response of the United Nations system in assisting developing countries in the strengthening of their co-ordination capacity;

(h) Actions taken to increase programme effectiveness through, *inter alia*, evaluation;

(i) Efforts undertaken to expand the geographical distribution of the sources of supply, including in underutilized donor and developing countries, for the operational activities of the United Nations system;

2. *Emphasizes* the importance of the round-table country review process and other mechanisms for co-ordination at the country level in facilitating the effective implementation of the development programmes in the countries concerned;

3. *Takes note* of the report of the Governing Council of the United Nations Development Programme for the year 1985 and the decisions contained therein;

4. *Reaffirms* the central funding role of the United Nations Development Programme in the field of technical co-operation for development;

5. *Calls upon* all States to make every effort to attain the planned funding levels for operational activities for development by the various organizations of the United Nations system, and urges the successful completion of the current negotiations on the replenishment of the International Fund for Agricultural Development to enable it to maintain its effective contribution to agricultural and food development, as well as the early considera-

tion and completion of the eighth replenishment of the International Development Association at an adequate level;

6. *Expresses its deep concern* about the shortfall of resources of the United Nations Fund for Population Activities and the impact on its ability to carry out its planned programmes, and urges all countries to continue and increase their support for the Fund;

7. *Requests* the Director-General for Development and International Economic Co-operation to report on the results of the efforts to increase collaboration between the Department of Technical Co-operation for Development and the United Nations Development Programme;

8. *Requests* the Economic and Social Council, in discharging its responsibilities as defined in the annex to General Assembly resolution 32/197, to assist the Assembly in establishing overall strategies, policies and priorities for the system as a whole in respect of operational activities, and to formulate suggestions and recommendations at the time of its consideration of the 1986 comprehensive policy review;

9. *Invites* the governing bodies of the organizations of the United Nations system, where possible, to provide the Economic and Social Council at its second regular session of 1986 and the General Assembly at its forty-first session at the time of the 1986 comprehensive policy review of operational activities, their views on the system-wide policy issues affecting operational activities identified by the Assembly in its resolution 38/171 and in the present resolution, and also invites the organizations of the United Nations system to co-operate with the Director-General for Development and International Economic Co-operation in the preparation of his report for that review.

General Assembly resolution 40/211

17 December 1985   Meeting 120   Adopted without vote

Approved by Second Committee (A/40/1041) without vote, 13 December (meeting 51); draft by Vice-Chairman (A/C.2/40/L.132), based on informal consultations on draft by Canada, Denmark and Netherlands (A/C.2/40/L.103) and orally revised; agenda item 85 *(a)*.
Meeting numbers. GA 40th session: 2nd Committee 35-42, 48, 51; plenary 120.

By **decision 40/449** of 17 December, the Assembly took note of the report of the Secretary-General on United Nations technical co-operation activities in 1984.[5]

Financing of operational activities

In his 1985 report to the General Assembly,[3] the DIEC Director-General summarized the resource outlook for 1985-1988 for IDA, IFAD, UNDP, UNFPA, UNICEF and WFP. Estimates indicated that contributions to UNDP, UNFPA, UNICEF and WFP would amount to $1,900 million in 1985 compared to about $1,750 million actually received in 1984. For the period 1986-1988, the four organizations were planning for total contributions of $6,300 million compared to $5,437 million collected (estimated for 1985) for the immediate preceding three years, 1983-1985.

The seventh replenishment of IDA, amounting to $9 billion, represented a reduction of 25 per cent in nominal terms and 40 per cent in real terms over the sixth replenishment level of $12 billion. Effective 1 July 1985, the World Bank established a Special

1985 EXPENDITURES BY THE UN SYSTEM ON OPERATIONAL ACTIVITIES FOR DEVELOPMENT AND NON-DEVELOPMENT ASSISTANCE, BY RECIPIENT COUNTRY/TERRITORY AND REGION
(in thousands of US dollars)

RECIPIENT	Development assistance*	Other assistance†	RECIPIENT	Development assistance*	Other assistance†	RECIPIENT	Development assistance*	Other assistance†
Developing Member States			Hungary	136,910	—	Sri Lanka	93,223	—
			India	898,478	—	Sudan	89,422	103,988
Afghanistan	11,060	20	Indonesia	426,009	4,118	Suriname	953	—
Albania	3,394	—	Iran	(69,028)	12,169	Swaziland	(2,096)	1,195
Algeria	84,561	3,523	Iraq	(8,163)	—	Syrian Arab Republic	10,605	—
Angola	17,772	5,474	Ivory Coast	(47,945)	—	Thailand	74,471	28,475
Antigua and Barbuda	556	—	Jamaica	28,896	—	Togo	36,138	—
Argentina	35,144	2,386	Jordan	50,749	—	Trinidad and Tobago	(4,334)	—
Bahamas	1,006	—	Kenya	107,730	3,036	Tunisia	41,146	—
Bahrain	872	—	Kuwait	993	—	Turkey	243,068	768
Bangladesh	343,320	—	Lao People's			Uganda	153,769	—
Barbados	4,744	—	Democratic			United Arab Emirates	1,337	—
Belize	3,230	—	Republic	16,347	1,042	United Republic		
Benin	32,570	116	Lebanon	18,980	583	of Tanzania	69,826	4,080
Bhutan	11,334	—	Lesotho	24,176	740	Uruguay	2,421	—
Bolivia	4,077	82	Liberia	11,917	—	Vanuatu	1,156	10
Botswana	37,450	1,315	Libyan Arab			Venezuela	(22,512)	—
Brazil	(31,385)	—	Jamahiriya	2,176	—	Viet Nam	39,680	3,543
Bulgaria	1,640	—	Madagascar	61,369	57	Yemen	57,509	—
Burkina Faso	47,466	20	Malawi	35,469	—	Yugoslavia	53,998	1,947
Burma	64,706	16	Malaysia	(37,603)	6,588	Zaire	(41,337)	11,134
Burundi	35,844	855	Maldives	3,055	—	Zambia	75,896	2,373
Cameroon	24,536	2,030	Mali	59,633	1,362	Zimbabwe	35,735	1,398
Cape Verde	16,076	—	Malta	385	—			
Central African			Mauritania	15,848	862	Subtotal	6,276,887	415,499
Republic	18,775	3,178	Mauritius	19,332	—			
Chad	58,516	173	Mexico	187,098	12,157	*Developing non-member States/Territories*		
Chile	205,050	—	Mongolia	2,921	—			
China	659,670	3,805	Morocco	156,592	—	Bermuda	25	—
Colombia	293,443	140	Mozambique	41,098	3,542	Democratic People's		
Comoros	10,431	7	Nepal	69,795	25	Republic of Korea	5,162	—
Congo	13,230	—	Nicaragua	12,212	1,597	Hong Kong	113	4,277
Costa Rica	50,370	8,213	Niger	61,598	—	Namibia	2,815	—
Cuba	14,481	—	Nigeria	161,871	1,007	Republic of Korea	(156,263)	—
Cyprus	1,796	6,177	Oman	1,639	—	Tonga	1,673	15
Czechoslovakia	341	—	Pakistan	225,298	67,650	Other countries	20,884	—
Democratic			Panama	(6,649)	—			
Kampuchea	6,047	—	Papua New Guinea	13,751	—	Subtotal	(125,591)	4,292
Democratic Yemen	35,483	—	Paraguay	11,554	13			
Djibouti	11,085	3,217	Peru	64,513	418	Total	6,151,296	419,791
Dominica	2,058	—	Philippines	(22,714)	8,552			
Dominican Republic	284	—	Poland	1,048	—	*Developed countries*	(92,000)	10,335
Ecuador	(3,005)	139	Portugal	38,057	449			
Egypt	159,115	2,034	Qatar	1,300	—	TOTAL (all countries)	6,059,296	430,126
El Salvador	17,168	—	Romania	(223,524)	—			
Equatorial Guinea	8,586	—	Rwanda	49,349	5,384	*Intercountry*		
Ethiopia	135,272	24,583	Saint Lucia	634	—			
Fiji	(8,844)	47	Saint Vincent and			Regional Africa	184,243	3,238
Gabon	1,900	—	the Grenadines	1,610	—	Regional Americas	69,195	3,885
Gambia	12,261	—	Samoa	2,700	—	Regional Arab States	27,020	595
Ghana	(50,334)	30	Sao Tome and			Regional Asia	56,499	11,589
Greece	(10,204)	1,598	Principe	5,409	—	Regional Europe	14,295	847
Grenada	697	—	Saudi Arabia	11,550	—	Interregional	200,672	—
Guatemala	36,387	31	Senegal	35,396	1,297	Global	29,699	28,699
Guinea	24,885	148	Seychelles	2,976	—			
Guinea-Bissau	23,011	—	Sierra Leone	17,995	—	Total	581,623	48,853
Guyana	(2,442)	—	Singapore	(15,377)	—			
Haiti	32,918	—	Solomon Islands	2,513	—	*Not elsewhere classified*	4,137	165,401
Honduras	23,768	11,532	Somalia	92,227	42,031			
			Spain	(25,512)	1,020	GRAND TOTAL	6,645,056	644,380

*Represents the sum of operational activities financed under regular United Nations and agency budgets ($297.7 million), the UNDP main programme ($564.3 million), UNDP-administered funds ($77.1 million), UNFPA ($128.4 million), UNICEF ($278.6 million), other extrabudgetary funds ($327 million) and WFP ($778.9 million), plus net transfers from the World Bank ($1,496 million) and IDA ($2,410.3 million) and net disbursements from IFC ($93.8 million) and IFAD ($190.1 million).

†Represents expenditure financed by UNHCR, UNRWA and UNDRO.

NOTE: Figures in parentheses are negative.

SOURCE: A/42/207 & Corr.1.

Facility for sub-Saharan Africa, administered by IDA, of over $1.2 billion, to help countries of the region deal with their economic crisis.

The question of the second replenishment of IFAD resources was not resolved during 1985. In February, all but one important contributor reached a consensus on the minimum amount for the replenishment ranging from $500 million to $650 million, to be available for 1985-1987. The IFAD Executive Board approved the launching of a special programme for countries of sub-Saharan Africa affected by drought and desertification, targeted to mobilize $300 million over four years from contributors outside the formal second replenishment and aimed at stimulating the production of smallholder farmers in the region.

1985 CONTRIBUTIONS TO THE UN SYSTEM FOR OPERATIONAL ACTIVITIES FOR DEVELOPMENT
(in thousands of US dollars)

CONTRIBUTOR	Amount	CONTRIBUTOR	Amount	CONTRIBUTOR	Amount
Member States		Guinea-Bissau	31	Seychelles	29
		Guyana	178	Sierra Leone	54
Afghanistan	(3)	Haiti	310	Singapore	420
Albania	30	Honduras	2,049	Solomon Islands	23
Algeria	4,741	Hungary	10,184	Somalia	322
Angola	393	Iceland	746	South Africa	20,699
Antigua and Barbuda	27	India	38,900	Spain	52,620
Argentina	18,241	Indonesia	7,416	Sri Lanka	767
Australia	162,496	Iran	2,221	Sudan	505
Austria	63,915	Iraq	1,015	Suriname	89
Bahamas	85	Ireland	8,762	Swaziland	411
Bahrain	278	Israel	829	Sweden	226,787
Bangladesh	1,475	Italy	155,319	Syrian Arab Republic	457
Barbados	86	Ivory Coast	1,291	Thailand	1,733
Belgium	101,623	Jamaica	2,032	Togo	113
Belize	62	Japan	863,554	Trinidad and Tobago	313
Benin	48	Jordan	1,647	Tunisia	687
Bhutan	57	Kenya	5,015	Turkey	2,301
Bolivia	546	Kuwait	24,239	Uganda	19
Botswana	652	Lao People's Democratic Republic	43	Ukrainian SSR	3,958
Brazil	13,615	Lebanon	173	USSR	31,872
Bulgaria	1,480	Lesotho	161	United Arab Emirates	3,417
Burkino Faso	62	Liberia	33	United Kingdom	289,727
Burma	914	Libyan Arab Jamahiriya	3,724	United Republic of Tanzania	1,900
Burundi	44	Luxembourg	1,981	United States	653,007
Byelorussian SSR	1,152	Madagascar	450	Uruguay	891
Cameroon	1,806	Malawi	294	Vanuatu	23
Canada	438,686	Malaysia	4,857	Venezuela	4,410
Cape Verde	28	Maldives	33	Viet Nam	87
Central African Republic	32	Mali	145	Yemen	290
Chad	28	Malta	111	Yugoslavia	3,557
Chile	8,005	Mauritania	45	Zaire	107
China	10,383	Mauritius	90	Zambia	225
Colombia	26,507	Mexico	5,125	Zimbabwe	274
Comoros	28	Mongolia	194	*Not elsewhere classified*	12,475
Congo	1,636	Morocco	1,452		
Costa Rica	1,620	Mozambique	125	Total	5,110,056
Cuba	2,231	Nepal	1,268		
Cyprus	289	Netherlands	130,648	*Non-member States/Territories*	
Czechoslovakia	3,226	New Zealand	6,030		
Democratic Kampuchea	32	Nicaragua	272	Bermuda	6
Democratic Yemen	402	Niger	4,474	Democratic People's Republic of	
Denmark	148,209	Nigeria	15,926	Korea	189
Djibouti	263	Norway	188,388	Kiribati	29
Dominica	30	Oman	2,731	Republic of Korea	11,723
Dominican Republic	432	Pakistan	6,847	Switzerland	60,810
Ecuador	4,627	Panama	2,884	Tonga	334
Egypt	4,373	Papua New Guinea	1,176	Other	912
El Salvador	66	Paraguay	493		
Equatorial Guinea	28	Peru	1,685	Total	74,003
Ethiopia	200	Philippines	1,687		
Fiji	739	Poland	2,872	TOTAL (all countries)	5,184,059
Finland	252,033	Portugal	1,201		
France	113,710	Qatar	4,075	*Inter/non-governmental*	
Gabon	3,538	Romania	1,227		
Gambia	27	Rwanda	383	Arab Gulf Programme for	
German Democratic Republic	4,365	Saint Lucia	48	UN Development Organizations	8,463
Germany, Federal Republic of	816,872	Saint Vincent and the Grenadines	71	European Communities	87,026
Ghana	177	Samoa	191	Other intergovernmental	59,881
Greece	2,793	Sao Tome and Principe	111	Non-governmental	76,759
Grenada	37	Saudi Arabia	55,816		
Guatemala	235	Senegal	307	Total	232,129
Guinea	190			GRAND TOTAL	5,416,188

SOURCE: A/42/207 & Corr.1.

Expenditures

In his annual report on United Nations system technical co-operation expenditures,[6] the UNDP Administrator stated that 25 organizations and the five regional commissions had reported expenditures of almost $916 million financed from sources other than UNDP central funds in 1985, as against $841 million originally reported for 1984 (subsequently adjusted to $904 million, to take into account statistical differences arising from the World Health Organization (WHO) biennial budgeting and accounting system). This reflected a modest increase of 1.3 per cent as against about 7.4 per cent between 1983 and 1984. With data adjusted for WHO expenditures, regular technical co-operation expenditures rose by 5.9 per cent, while those funded by extraordinary sources other than UNDP, UNFPA and UNDP-administered funds decreased by 2.4 per cent. UNFPA-financed expenditures rose from $120 million in 1984 to $128 million, an increase of about 6.7 per cent. Those financed by UNDP-administered funds amounted to $77 million in 1985 against $81 million in 1984, a decrease of about 5 per cent.

The five larger agencies—the United Nations, the International Labour Organisation (ILO), the Food and Agriculture Organization of the United Nations (FAO), the United Nations Educational, Scientific and Cultural Organization (UNESCO) and WHO—accounted for some 71 per cent of total non-UNDP-financed technical co-operation expenditures, as against 70 per cent for 1984. Expenditures by the United Nations and ILO increased by almost 13.7 per cent, while WHO expenditures increased by 2.6 per cent. However, UNESCO's non-UNDP-funded expenditures declined by about 28 per cent. As in the past, the expenditure data for the smaller agencies produced no generally valid trends, although their total non-UNDP-financed technical co-operation expenditures continued to increase.

Because of the size of the WHO budget, the health sector had the highest concentration of expenditures not financed by UNDP central resources, accounting for 35.5 per cent of all non-UNDP-financed technical co-operation expenditures in 1985, about the same as in 1984. The second most important sector continued to be agriculture, forestry and fisheries, with about $145 million or some 15.8 per cent of total expenditures, followed by population (14 per cent), natural resources (6.7 per cent), transport and communications (4.5 per cent), industry (4.4 per cent), general development issues, policy and planning (3.6 per cent), employment (2.9 per cent) and science and technology (2.7 per cent).

Under regular budgets alone, the health sector accounted for some 71.3 per cent of total technical co-operation expenditures. Agriculture, forestry and fisheries occupied second place (7.8 per cent), followed by industry (4.2 per cent), general development issues, policy and planning (3.8 per cent) and natural resources (3.6 per cent).

Technical co-operation expenditures financed from extrabudgetary sources, including those funded by UNFPA- and UNDP-administered funds, reflected a less marked concentration of expenditures in a few sectors. As in previous years, the most important sector was population (24.5 per cent), followed by health (20.6 per cent), agriculture, forestry and fisheries (17 per cent) and natural resources (7.2 per cent).

UN SYSTEM TECHNICAL CO-OPERATION EXPENDITURES
IN 1985, BY EXECUTING BODY

(in thousands of US dollars)

Executing body	UNDP	Other sources	Total
UNCTAD	5,263	1,715	6,978
UN Centre on Transnational Corporations	—	581	581
ECA	3,550	6,103	9,653
ECE	292	251	543
ECLAC	1,227	6,874	8,101
ESCAP	5,685	8,530	14,215
ESCWA	422	1,888	2,310
UNCHS	10,959	4,063	15,022
Other UN	86,337	39,119	125,456
Subtotal UN	113,735	69,124	182,859
IAEA	1,736	32,064	33,800
ILO	37,972	51,554	89,526
FAO	115,908	180,618	296,526
UNESCO	33,575	45,804	79,379
WHO*	11,976	332,635	344,611
World Bank and IDA	31,406	3,259	34,665
ICAO	31,456	20,383	51,839
UPU	1,612	1,022	2,634
ITU	21,942	4,358	26,300
WMO	13,492	6,132	19,624
IMO	3,499	3,574	7,073
WIPO	1,723	2,447	4,170
ITC	5,867	9,768	15,635
UNDP	47,076†	34,779	81,855
UNFPA	—	21,319	21,319
UNICEF	—	5,524	5,524
UNIDO	61,171	31,591	92,762
Subtotal other UN system	420,411	786,831	1,207,242
World Tourism Organization	1,239	—	1,239
Asian Development Bank	4,549	—	4,549
Arab Fund for Economic and Social Development	81	—	81
Governments	24,315	45,193	69,508
Non-governmental organizations	—	14,654	14,654
Subtotal non-UN system	30,184	59,847	90,031
Total	564,330‡	915,802	1,480,132

*Including support costs.

†Representing expenditures by UN Volunteers and the Office for Projects Execution.

‡Excluding government cash counterpart expenditures of $7,340,000.

NOTE: Figures for UNDP are provisional data covering IPFs, Special Programme Resources, Special Measures Fund for Least Developed Countries, Special Industrial Services, cost-sharing and trust funds established by the Administrator, where applicable; UNDP-administered funds outside the Programme's central resources are included in the "Other sources" column.

SOURCE: DP/1986/68.

Unilateral "self-supporting" expenditures—those financed by the developing countries themselves—were concentrated in the agriculture, forestry and fisheries sector (35.7 per cent), followed by transport and communications (25 per cent), natural resources (13.5 per cent) and industry (7.6 per cent).

Total UNDP project expenditures for 1985 amounted to $564 million as against $527 million for 1984, an increase of almost 7 per cent compared with a decrease of about 5.8 per cent between 1984 and 1983. Non-UNDP-financed expenditures rose by about 1.2 per cent and amounted to $915 million compared with the adjusted figure of $904 million for 1984. The majority of the agencies continued to have the greater part of their technical co-operation expenditures financed by UNDP.

Total technical co-operation disbursements under World Bank loans and IDA credits for training and consultants reached almost $947 million in 1985, surpassing UNDP-financed technical co-operation expenditures.

Total grant assistance provided by the United Nations system, which continued at an annual level of $2.2 billion from 1982 to 1984, regained the 1981 level of $2.4 billion in 1985.

Contributions

In his annual report to the General Assembly,[1] the DIEC Director-General stated that total contributions to the operational activities of the United Nations system in 1985, including all the funds and programmes of the United Nations and the operational activities of the specialized agencies and WFP, amounted to $2,829 million, an increase of about 6 per cent over 1984. Although a number of countries increased the national currency value of their contributions, part of the increase was lost in accounting terms because of the movement of the United States dollar against most other currencies.

Contributions to UNDP, UNICEF and UNFPA totalled $1,316 million in 1985, an increase of 4 per cent over 1984. However, contributions to UNDP-administered trust funds and to other United Nations funds and programmes fell to $153 million from $165 million. Contributions to UNICEF began to increase after a drop in 1983-1984 and contributions to WFP increased by 21 per cent to $809 million.

Regular and extrabudgetary contributions for the technical co-operation activities of the specialized agencies and the International Atomic Energy Agency in 1985 reached $631 million. However, the increase in assessed contributions for technical co-operation (which totalled $290 million) was offset by a drop in funds-in-trust and other extrabudgetary contributions, to $340 million. Those figures included $40 million provided by the World Bank for programmes carried out by agencies of the system.

Contributions to IDA and IFAD and capital subscription payments to the World Bank and IFC amounted to $2,660 million in 1985, a further decline from levels attained in the earlier part of the decade.

Compared with previous years, there was a decrease in 1985 in overall contributions for operational activities, due to the drop in contributions to the World Bank and IFAD. Of the total contributions of $5,490 million to the system, about half was channelled through grant-financed operational activities and half on concessional terms through the World Bank and IFAD.

Contributions in respect of humanitarian, refugee, disaster relief and special economic assistance programmes amounted to $593 million in 1985, an increase of 6 per cent over the 1984 level, due in great part to the response to the critical situation in Africa.

Communications. During 1985, several communications concerning economic assistance to developing countries were received by the Secretary-General. Among them were: a 9 May letter[7] from the USSR transmitting a document on its economic assistance to developing countries; a 17 May letter[8] from Czechoslovakia containing a joint statement by Bulgaria, the Byelorussian SSR, Czechoslovakia, the German Democratic Republic, Hungary, Mongolia, Poland, the Ukrainian SSR and the USSR, which included information on assistance provided by them to developing countries and their views on obstacles to progress in the implementation of the International Development Strategy for the Third United Nations Development Decade (the 1980s);[9] and a 9 July letter[10] from the Federal Republic of Germany, Japan, the United Kingdom and the United States concerning their monetary contributions to the development activities of the United Nations system. These letters were, as requested by their authors, brought to the attention of the Committee on the Review and Appraisal of the Implementation of the International Development Strategy for the Third United Nations Development Decade (see p. 418).

In an 8 October letter,[11] Japan stated that it had adopted a third medium-term target for expanding its ODA disbursements for 1986-1992 to more than $40 billion.

General Assembly action. By **resolution 40/211,** the General Assembly called on all States to make every effort to attain the planned funding levels for operational activities for development by the organizations of the United Nations system, and urged successful completion of the negotiations on replenishing IFAD, as well as the early consideration and completion of the eighth replenishment of IDA at an adequate level. It also expressed deep concern about the shortfall of UNFPA resources and urged all countries to increase their support for the Fund.

During the mid-term global review of the implementation of the Substantial New Programme of Action for the 1980s for the Least Developed Countries (LDCs), several conclusions and recommendations were made by the Intergovernmental Group on LDCs of the United Nations Conference on Trade and Development (UNCTAD) regarding technical assistance to those countries (see p. 436). The

findings were endorsed by the Assembly in **resolution 40/205**.

UN Pledging Conference for Development Activities

The 1985 United Nations Pledging Conference for Development Activities was held at United Nations Headquarters on 14 and 15 November to receive government pledges for 1986 to United Nations funds and programmes concerned with development and related assistance.

Contributions to the funds and programmes participating in the Conference totalled $1,160 million in 1985. Pledges for 1986, as at 30 June 1986, amounted to $1,142 million, more than half of which was for UNDP.

CONTRIBUTIONS TO FUNDS AND PROGRAMMES INCLUDED IN THE
UN PLEDGING CONFERENCE FOR DEVELOPMENT ACTIVITIES, 1985 AND 1986
(1985, as at 31 December 1985; 1986, as at 30 June 1986;
in thousands of US dollars)

	1985 PAYMENT		1986 PLEDGE	
FUND OR PROGRAMME	Amount	Number of donor countries	Amount	Number of donor countries
International Year of Disabled Persons	NA	NA	70	9
International Year of Shelter for the Homeless	NA	NA	50	7
Special Voluntary Fund for the UN Volunteers	826	21	836	20
Trust Fund for the UN Centre on Transnational Corporations	501	NA	269	4
UN Capital Development Fund	21,877	36	24,907	40
UN Children's Fund	260,926	121	220,513	118
UN Development Fund for Women	2,014	32	3,482	45
UN Development Programme	662,780	132	697,756	116
Energy Account	40	1	63	1
Special Measures Fund for the Least Developed Countries	10,530	9	12,227	12
UN Environment Programme	29,258	92	24,790	64
UN Financing System for Science and Technology for Development	298	18	2,023	33
UN Fund for Drug Abuse Control	13,147	24	7,485	51
UN Fund for Population Activities	122,144	86	120,141	86
UN Habitat and Human Settlements Foundation	2,968	46	2,395	38
UN Industrial Development Fund	14,907	109	14,187*	67
UN Institute for Training and Research	1,263	46	1,274	45
UN Revolving Fund for Natural Resources Exploration	4,397	5	425	9
UN Special Fund for Land-locked Developing Countries	50	11	15	12
UN Trust Fund for African Development	3,023	NA	263	11
UN Trust Fund for Aging	19	7	8	3
UN Trust Fund for Social Defence	410	16	555	8
UN Trust Fund for Sudano-Sahelian Activities	5,735	10	5,328	15
UN Trust Fund for the International Research and Training Institute for the Advancement of Women	460	25	495	22
UN Trust Fund for the Transport and Communications Decade in Africa	104	NA	75	4
Voluntary Fund for the UN Decade for Women	2,823	NA	2,373	42
Total	1,160,500		1,142,005	

*Amount pledged for 1986, as at 31 December 1985.
NA = Not available.
SOURCES: For 1985, A/41/5/Add.1, Add.1/Corr.1, Add.2,4,6-9 and unpublished documents; for 1986, A/CONF.132/2.

Inter-agency co-operation

At its second session of 1985 (New York, 7-9 October),[4] CCSQ(OPS) expressed recognition that co-ordination was not an end in itself but a process designed to help both donors and recipients enhance the cost-effectiveness of external aid. It was emphasized that aid co-ordination

was a prerogative of the recipient country, and the primary contribution of the United Nations system should be to strengthen the capacity and commitment of recipient countries, particularly by assisting them to formulate a suitable macroeconomic and sectoral policy framework and strategy.

The Committee agreed: to request its substantive secretariat to identify and describe mechanisms and processes for sectoral and intersectoral co-ordination in use at the country level that could be more widely applied, and to provide details on measures taken by the United Nations system to strengthen the co-ordinating capacities of recipient countries; to invite its members to submit analyses of their arrangements for sectoral and intersectoral co-ordination in, for example, health, agriculture, manpower and employment, industry and education; to invite organizations to review their operationally oriented analytical work and means of encouraging both donors and recipients to make more effective use of their sectoral knowledge and experience in planning external assistance; and to request its substantive secretariat to explore, with the Office of the DIEC Director-General and member organizations, ways of pursuing aspects of collaboration with bilateral donors that were particularly important in enhancing overall co-ordination.

Programme evaluation

In a report on evaluation,[12] submitted to the UNDP Governing Council in April and taken note of by the Council on 29 June,[13] the UNDP Administrator discussed the development of measures taken to improve evaluation policies and procedures and summarized the status of harmonization in project evaluation and reporting throughout the United Nations using UNDP's proposed system as a frame of reference. The Administrator stated that preliminary reactions from the system were favourable to a proposal put to CCSQ(OPS) by UNDP and WHO in 1984 to apply new provisions in the UNDP Policies and Procedures Manual, jointly with the executing agencies, to all UNDP-financed projects. At a January meeting of an inter-agency working group on evaluation, it was agreed that the revised procedures would be so applied during a trial period extending to May 1986 and the experience gained would be analysed by both UNDP and the executing agencies. An analysis would be undertaken of experience gained with the new system in some 12 countries and the reaction of all Governments involved would be sought.

At its October meeting,[4] CCSQ(OPS) noted that the trial period for introducing new procedures for monitoring, evaluation and reporting for UNDP-financed projects was under way, with special emphasis being given to training. Several agencies had decided to apply the UNDP procedures to all their project monitoring, evaluation and reporting, regardless of the source of funds.

REFERENCES

[1]A/41/776 & Corr.1. [2]YUN 1984, p. 429, GA res. 39/220, 18 Dec. 1984. [3]A/40/698 & Corr.1. [4]ACC/1985/19. [5]YUN 1984, p. 425. [6]DP/1986/68. [7]A/40/303-E/1985/76. [8]A/40/327-E/1985/88. [9]YUN 1980, p. 503, GA res. 35/56, annex, 5 Dec. 1980. [10]A/40/476-E/1985/137. [11]A/C.2/40/5. [12]DP/1985/13. [13]E/1985/32 (dec. 85/48).

Technical co-operation through UNDP

In his annual report for 1985,[1] the UNDP Administrator said that a number of events in 1985 stood out as milestones in UNDP's transition to a new phase of operations. In June, the Governing Council reached consensus on the target for annual resource growth for the period 1987-1991 and Council members agreed to average yearly increases in voluntary contributions of 8 per cent, starting with a base of $700 million for 1986. It was also agreed that 80 per cent of resources earmarked for country programmes would flow to low-income nations.

Discussions at the second Global Meeting of UNDP Resident Representatives (Copenhagen, Denmark, October) centred on new trends in country programming, practices in country-level co-ordination, improvements in programme and project quality including monitoring and evaluation, methods for efficient programme delivery and UNDP's evolving financial structures. Based on that practical foundation, UNDP's management was currently developing revised strategies to enhance and diversify the Programme's operational capacity.

At the United Nations Pledging Conference for Development Activities (see above), recorded and estimated core pledges for 1986 surpassed the $700 million base figure set by the Council and were expected to exceed $745 million. That estimated total, the highest in UNDP history, would represent a 10.6 per cent increase over 1985 in dollar terms. Actual pledges of $487.4 million were announced by 102 countries to UNDP core resources for 1986.

The Administrator stated that trends discerned in several reappraisals of the first generation of development assistance were hopeful. He cited statistics on life expectancy, infant mortality, literacy and education demonstrating social advances made by developing countries since 1950 and stated that general economic indicators were equally encouraging. He also noted that events in sub-Saharan Africa in particular had put poverty high on the agenda for action. In other regions, the impact of recession and adjustment on disadvantaged segments of society showed that the poorest of the poor were no less vulnerable to reversals in national fortunes. In order to extend the fight against poverty, 41 per cent of all distributed country indicative planning figure (IPF) resources would be shared between the 37 countries designated by the General Assembly as LDCs (see p. 433). In other economically more advanced developing countries, specific poverty alleviation measures like urban renewal programmes and rural employment-creation schemes commanded an increasing share of country programme resources.

UNDP had found that past development policies had favoured the buildup of physical capacities over human resources and concluded that more attention needed to be given to the latter as the true agents and sole objects of development. Technical assistance could play a catalytic role in sustaining developing countries' newly formed linkages between universities, public and private research and development centres, and industry. Through such mechanisms as TCDC, UNDP could also support the exchange of technical information and experience between countries adopting similar strategies. UNDP's new focal point for short-term advisory services (STAS) concentrated on matching requests for assistance with expertise from the productive, commercial and service sectors of developed and developing countries (see p. 474), while the UNDP-supported programme for the transfer of knowledge through expatriate nationals was another mechanism to provide expertise to deal with immediate and specialized requirements.

In 1985, field programme expenditures supported by UNDP rose to $571.7 million from $532.6 million in 1984, an increase of 7.3 per cent. IPF expenditures of $482.1 million largely accounted for the improvement, which reversed a three-year trend towards lower levels of project spending. The total value and number of new project approvals during 1985 rose by 13.6 per cent and 33.7 per cent respectively. Supplementary contributions provided by developing and developed countries—the sources of which included programme and project cost-sharing, trust funds established under the authority of the Administrator, government cash counterpart contributions and contributions to the Special Measures Fund for the Least Developed Countries (SMF/LDCs)—in 1985 represented some 15 per cent of Programme resources, amounting to $137.2 million. (See also p. 475.)

Six new trust funds were established in 1985 with contributions amounting to $8.5 million (see p. 480). In addition, six sub-trust fund arrangements were established on behalf of UNCDF, the United Nations Financing System for Science and Technology for Development (UNFSSTD) and the United Nations Sudano-

Sahelian Office (UNSO), the value of which was some $12.6 million. Voluntary pledges for the numerous special-purpose funds administered by UNDP declined from $38.6 million in 1984 to $28.6 million in 1985. Income received by the special funds from cost-sharing and sub-trust fund arrangements amounted to about $25.5 million.

Total contributions to central resources, special-purpose funds and sub-trust fund and cost-sharing arrangements amounted to $863.7 million in 1985, an increase of 3.5 per cent over 1984.

Total expenditures from UNDP central resources in 1985 amounted to $778.1 million, of which $571.7 million was for field programme activities, while the balance was for agency, administrative and programme support costs and sectoral support and other field-level costs. Of the field programme expenditure, $482.1 million was delivered under IPF resources (see p. 475).

The number of new projects approved climbed to 1,436 in 1985 from 1,074 in 1984. New approvals by sector followed the pattern of the preceding year, with the three leading sectors in order of their numerical share of new approvals being industry, development policy and planning, and agriculture, forestry and fisheries.

Although the cultivation of staple foods rallied in several drought-stricken parts of the Africa region in 1985, in many countries social and economic conditions remained critical as rooted structural imbalances continued to affect recovery. For UNDP, the operational challenge remained twofold: to continue its support for immediate relief and rehabilitation measures, while assisting Governments to address the issues underlying the development crisis and sustain more durable, comprehensive and integrated solutions (see p. 500).

Management of the UNDP programme in Asia and the Pacific in 1985 concentrated on preparing country programmes, planning country and intercountry programme exercises, improving project preparation, strengthening monitoring and evaluation, preparing donor round-table meetings and producing studies. New commitments to the value of almost $200 million were entered into during the year so that, by the end of 1985, 95 per cent of third-programming-cycle (1982-1986) resources had been fully committed.

In Latin America and the Caribbean, UNDP concentrated on adapting country programming to new, debt-defined realities in technical cooperation by stepping up its support for national debt management and adjustment strategies. As part of its drive to enhance the impact of its assistance, UNDP intensified programme monitoring in the region during 1985; 167 tripartite reviews, 21 mid-term evaluations and 22 country-programme reviews were carried out. The 17 country-programmes to be submitted to the Governing Council in 1986 reflected the pre-occupations of Governments with economic reactivation, as well as the search for alternative development strategies for coping with adjustment measures and promoting growth with equity.

In partnership with UNDP, three Governments of the Arab States held formal annual reviews of their country programmes in 1985. A further 11 countries were assessed in preparation for the fourth programming cycle (1987-1991). Theme-oriented programming emerged as an appropriate form of UNDP support for intercountry co-operation, which had begun to concentrate on priority regional issues such as food security, human resources development, energy, promotion of advanced technologies and TCDC. The Sudan and Lebanon continued to experience acute drought- and security-related difficulties respectively, which severely affected UNDP assistance. In the Sudan, however, strong post-emergency efforts by the Government led to resumed UNDP-assisted rehabilitation and longer-term development activities. Cost-sharing rose by 40 per cent over 1984, indicating heightened interest by Governments in multilateral technical co-operation.

Other developments noted by the Administrator during 1985 concerned TCDC, project evaluation, inter-agency procurement, STAS, the Projects Annotated Listing (a compilation of project proposals), and staff development and training.

UNDP also administered the following special funds in 1985: UNCDF, UNSO, the UNDP Energy Account, the United Nations Volunteers (UNV) programme, the United Nations Revolving Fund for Natural Resources Exploration, the United Nations Development Fund for Women (formerly the Voluntary Fund for the United Nations Decade for Women, it was officially transferred from the United Nations Secretariat to autonomous association with UNDP on 1 July) and UNFSSTD.

In addition to its sizeable emergency and relief operations in Africa (see p. 500), UNDP collaborated with the Office of the United Nations Disaster Relief Co-ordinator and other agencies in responding to a number of natural disasters in other regions: a volcanic eruption in Colombia (see. p. 545); earthquakes in Mexico (see p. 543); cyclones in Vanuatu (see p. 532); and extensive flooding brought on by recurring typhoons in Viet Nam (see p. 541).

UNDP Council action. In New York, the UNDP Governing Council held organizational meetings on 19 and 22 February, a special meeting from 19 to 22 February on preparations for the fourth programming cycle, and its thirty-second session from 3 to 29 June.[2] At the session, the Council resolved itself into a Committee of the Whole,[3] which held meetings between 3 and 7 June to discuss country and intercountry programmes, projects and evaluation; it recommended that the Council take note of various reports and approved a number of programmes and projects it had reviewed. Financial, budgetary and administrative matters were considered by the Council's Budgetary and Finance Committee[4] between 3 and 29 June.

At its organizational meetings, the Council adopted[5] the schedule of meetings for its June session. The 46 decisions it adopted on 28 and 29 June, in addition to those mentioned in this chapter, dealt with assistance to the national liberation movements recognized by the Organization of African Unity (OAU) (see p. 169); assistance to the Palestinian people (see p. 281); implementation of the Substantial New Programme of Action (SNPA) for the 1980s for LDCs (see p. 435); the United Nations Special Fund for Land-locked Developing Countries (see p. 454); strengthening the response to the crisis in Africa (see p. 500); UNFPA and its 1986-1987 budget (see Chapter XIV of this section); the United Nations Revolving Fund for Natural Resources Exploration (see p. 670); information support to TCDC and to the International Drinking Water Supply and Sanitation Decade (see p. 680); programmes in energy development (see p. 686); UNFSSTD (see p. 712); human resources development (see p. 780) and a focal point for STAS (see p. 781); implementation of the Plan of Action to Combat Desertification in the Sudano-Sahelian Region and of the medium- and long-term recovery and rehabilitation programme in that region (see p. 810); and evaluation of the women-in-development programme, integration of issues relevant to women into promotional and operational activities for TCDC (see p. 946), and the United Nations Development Fund for Women (see p. 950).

By a decision of 3 June, the Council allocated agenda items and assigned tasks for the work of its 1985 session.[6] Three decisions of 29 June approved the provisional agenda and arrangements for its meetings in 1986[7] and took note of several reports.[8] By **decision 1985/186** of 25 July, the Economic and Social Council took note of an extract[9] of the report of the UNDP Governing Council covering its organizational and June meetings.

Having considered the Administrator's 1984 annual report,[10] the Governing Council on 29 June[11] expressed support for his efforts to improve UNDP's effectiveness, particularly measures to strengthen its technical capability and role in project development and to improve agency performance in project formulation and implementation. Governments and agencies were urged to streamline internal procedures and institutional mechanisms to ensure speedy implementation of UNDP-financed activities, and Governments and the Administrator were requested to use IPF resources in identifying requirements for technical assistance, with a view to mobilizing external resources. The Council took note of the Administrator's exceptional measures in response to the critical situation in Africa, particularly coordination of emergency assistance with longer-term rehabilitation and development measures, and of his efforts in managing residual funds transferred from the United Nations Emergency Operation Trust Fund for use in countries affected by natural disasters. He was encouraged to enhance the round-table consultation process in favour of LDCs and requested to consult with agencies to improve project budgeting practices and report on measures to improve programme and project quality. UNDP was urged to continue to respond to the changing technical co-operation requirements of developing countries.

By **resolution 40/211**, the General Assembly took note of the UNDP Governing Council's 1985 report[2] and decisions and reaffirmed UNDP's central funding role in technical co-operation for development. The Assembly requested the DIEC Director-General to report on efforts to increase collaboration between DTCD and UNDP, and on the relationship between UNDP's increasing co-ordination responsibilities and its essential role in providing technical co-operation.

UNDP operational activities

Country and intercountry programmes

In an April report[12] to the UNDP Governing Council, the Administrator analysed six (Bhutan, Fiji, Guatemala, India, Indonesia and Tonga) of the seven country programmes being submitted to the Council for approval. The Afghanistan programme, submitted to Council in 1984[13] on which a consensus was not reached, was not included. The report dealt with the timing of the programmes, preparatory work, financing, major development objectives and orientation, allocation of resources, pre-investment and investment support activities, and global and regional priorities.

In a section of his annual report for 1985[1] on project results of the global/interregional programme and special funds, the Administrator stated that agricultural research had retained its place as the first priority of UNDP's global programme. Under the joint sponsorship of UNDP, the World Bank and WHO, 3,000 scientists in 125 countries were planning and conducting research on six major diseases endemic in tropical countries. Also in collaboration with UNDP, a WHO-implemented diarrhoeal

diseases control programme had developed a world-wide research programme involving investigators in more than 80 countries. UNDP also supported global and interregional projects in energy, fisheries, water supply and sanitation, and human resources development.

Additional resources were mobilized and channelled to developing countries to meet the need for special efforts in specific areas through seven associated funds administered by UNDP or its Administrator: UNCDF (see p. 493); UNSO (see p. 810); the UNDP Energy Office (see p. 686); UNV (see p. 486); the United Nations Revolving Fund for Natural Resources Exploration (see p. 669); the United Nations Development Fund for Women (see p. 950); and UNFSSTD (see p. 711).

UNDP Council action. In June,[14] the Governing Council decided to convene, immediately after its 1986 organizational session, a special session to examine country programmes and programming matters and to consider the possibility of convening other sessions in accordance with information provided by the UNDP Administrator. It decided to establish, on an experimental basis, a 24-member working group of the Committee of the Whole to facilitate and expedite consideration of matters arising from the Committee's mandate, particularly programming matters, other than country and intercountry programmes. The 1986 review of the three-year trial period of the Committee of the Whole would be undertaken in the light of additional experience of the working group.

On 28 June,[15] the Council approved country programmes for Bhutan, Fiji, Guatemala, India, Indonesia and Tonga, and took note of extensions of country programmes for Bangladesh and Suriname. The Administrator was authorized to proceed with appraisal and approval of requests for UNDP assistance for projects falling within the outlines of each country programme, as long as expenditures were in conformity with IPFs, increased with governmental cost-sharing contributions but within available resources. In the absence of a country programme for Afghanistan, he was authorized to support ongoing projects there and to consider for approval new projects consistent with normal UNDP criteria.

Global projects on technology transfer on food and forage legumes in West Asia and North Africa, research and development of integrated resource recovery and West African sorghum and millet improvement were approved. The Council took note of the Administrator's steps, taken in consultation with the World Bank and FAO, to secure international status for agricultural research centres— including reconstitution of one each in Colombia and Mexico—of the Consultative Group on International Agricultural Research, under arrangements consistent with those worked out in setting up other agricultural research centres in India, the Netherlands and the Syrian Arab Republic, in agreement with host Governments.

Country programmes by region

Africa

In a report on implementation of selected country programmes in the Africa region during 1985,[16] the UNDP Administrator said that as at 31 December there were 45 approved programmes of assistance in 42 countries, including special programmes of assistance to Namibia and the national liberation movements recognized by OAU and the regional programme. From 1982 to 1986, some $1.2 billion was available though UNDP, excluding resources channelled through funds under the Administrator. Of the total resources available, $992 million was from the country and regional IPFs and the balance from SMF/LDCs, the Special Fund for Land-locked Developing Countries, Special Programme Resources, Special Industrial Services (SIS) of the United Nations Industrial Development Organization (UNIDO), cost sharing and a number of trust funds. Of total programmable resources for 1982-1986, $1.1 billion, or 91 per cent, was committed to approved projects by December 1985.

Each programme had been reviewed at headquarters and the majority had been the object of in-country reviews. The report gave examples of action taken by Governments and UNDP, following the reviews, to enhance the quality of the programmes. Countries whose commitment levels were not high enough and countries and individual projects with slow implementation rates were identified and measures initiated to rectify the shortcomings. During the year, the regional programme for Africa was subject to a series of evaluations of individual projects and clusters of projects such as the assistance programme to river basins. The reviews made it clear that the next regional programme should have sharper focus with fewer and more specific objectives aimed at addressing current and long-term African needs, should support fewer projects with larger size and should move away from institutional support to capacity-building and programme assistance; links should be forged and promoted between national activities and subregional and regional ones.

In a May report on co-ordination of external technical co-operation at the country level,[17] the Administrator said that most African countries had established formal consultation mechanisms in the form of round-table conferences or consultative group meetings, the latter convened under the auspices of the World Bank. UNDP was the lead agency for 19 round-table conferences and participated in the group meetings. Several Governments had left it to resident representatives to initiate and develop informal mechanisms for consultation with the local representatives of aid programmes outside the United Nations system. The principal outcome of such arrangements was a better flow of information among assistance programmes and a consequent avoidance of duplication.

Experience with co-ordination within the United Nations system was mixed; in a few cases a systematic attempt had been made at joint programming, while in others the resident representative had been unaware of projects negotiated directly between ministries and United Nations organizations using their own resources. The concept of aid co-ordination and the role of the resident co-ordinator was well received by a majority of Governments in the region; in two countries, major donors had requested monthly meetings for co-ordination.

Arab States

In a report on implementation of selected country programmes in the Arab States region during 1985,[18] the Administrator said that programmes there had started to take new shape by focusing UNDP assistance on certain developmental themes. Programme areas which were guiding project selection for regional co-operation were food security, human resources development, energy, promotion of advanced technologies and TCDC. As the most appropriate form of supporting the theme-oriented and often multisectoral technical assistance requirements, Governments often requested UNDP to provide assistance under "umbrella-type" projects which, in some countries, were Government-executed in association with United Nations agencies. Formal country programme reviews were conducted in the latter half of 1985 in the Libyan Arab Jamahiriya, Somalia and the Sudan.

Regional projects were geared to meeting manpower needs, with particular attention to LDCs. Assistance complemented national efforts in such sectors as development planning and statistics, public administration and education. Regional needs with regard to water resources and natural resources exploration and utilization were met by a number of projects; others addressed common problems in agriculture and fisheries and in the packaging and iron and steel sectors. In order to cover additional activities dealing with human resources development, water resources management, promotion of new and advanced technologies and TCDC activities, it was intended to strengthen co-operation with the World Bank's investment programmes and regional funding organizations.

The UNDP Regional Bureau for Arab States had 321 large-scale projects under implementation in 1985, almost all of which were reviewed on a continuing basis. Twenty in-depth evaluations were carried out, mostly for projects nearing completion and for which Governments had requested continuing UNDP assistance. Evaluators discerned a clear trend away from direct assistance for institutional management and organization towards technical support to institutional programmes and projects.

In his May report on co-ordination,[17] the Administrator said that co-ordination of external assistance in the Arab States region was undertaken through round-table conferences, consultative group meetings, and informal meetings between Governments, the donor community and multilateral assistance organizations. Emergency relief assistance was co-ordinated under the aegis of the United Nations. At a more informal level, many UNDP offices kept in touch with major donors to exchange information. Within the United Nations system, efforts were made to avoid overlaps through monthly consultations of local representatives of United Nations organizations. Co-operation with the World Bank was particularly strong in several countries. Governments had demonstrated an interest in improving their co-ordinating role in planning and monitoring external development aid. Some oil-exporting countries supported the principle of co-ordination of the international system's development and technical assistance activities, although one country, with a weakened central co-ordinating authority, had proposed that UNDP review its representation in the light of political and economic changes and activate a new dialogue with the Gulf Co-operation Council to cover socio-economic development responsibilities.

Asia and the Pacific

In a report on implementation of selected country programmes in the Asia and the Pacific region,[19] the Administrator stated that a principal activity during 1985 was the preparation of country programmes for the fourth programming cycle (1987-1991). Programmes for Bhutan, Fiji, India, Indonesia and Tonga, with a combined IPF of $230.4 million, were approved in June by the Governing Council[15] and a further 16 (Bangladesh, China, Cook Islands, Kiribati, Lao People's Democratic Republic, Mongolia, Nepal, Niue, Papua New Guinea, Philippines, Samoa, Solomon Islands, Tokelau, Tuvalu, Vanuatu, Viet Nam), with a combined IPF of $502.9 million, were prepared for submission to the Governing Council in 1986. Steps were taken to elaborate programmes for a further 11 countries for submission in 1987, by which time almost every country of the region would have been covered. The regional programme for the fourth cycle, to be submitted in 1987, also required substantial preparatory work during the year. Three special management studies were undertaken in 1985: on the use of national professional project personnel in the region; on government execution of projects in China; and on UNDP assistance over three cycles in Nepal.

At the end of 1985, commitments in the region totalled $1,029 million—95 per cent of the total programmable resources of $1,087 million available for the third cycle (1982-1986)—compared with $875 million at the end of 1984. Ongoing projects numbered 1,545, of which 1,385 were country and 160 were intercountry projects, with cumulative UNDP budgets of $1.2 billion. Agriculture, forestry and fisheries accounted for 22 per cent of total assistance, industry for 17 per cent, natural resources, 15 per cent, and transportation and communications, 12 per cent. There was an increase in training expenditures and a decrease in those for equipment; a content analysis of the regional programme also confirmed the increasing prominence given to human resources development.

Reporting on co-ordination of technical co-operation in the region,[17] the Administrator stated that formal arrangements included round-table conferences, consultative group meetings, the South Pacific Bureau for Economic Co-operation, the South Pacific Commission and the Pacific Operations Centre of the Economic and Social Commission for Asia and the Pacific. There were also informal local arrangements among Governments, inter-agency groups, international organizations and non-governmental organizations (NGOs).

It was UNDP's experience in the region that organizations of the United Nations system, particularly those with funding resources of their own, contributed to a weakening of central aid co-ordination by dealing directly with technical ministries on development co-operation activities.

The position of Governments on the focal-point role of resident co-ordinators in co-ordinating aid varied according to administrative capacity and the economic and political condition of each country. Although some countries strongly supported the concept, countries with sophisticated bureaucratic systems were anxious that links between the agencies and technical ministries should not be weakened. A close link had been developed at the regional level between UNDP and the World Bank, as well as with the Asian Development Bank and the International Monetary Fund (IMF).

Europe

In a report on implementation of country programmes in Europe during 1985,[20] the Administrator said that the majority of programmes were at an advanced stage of implementation in the third programming cycle. Apart from Cyprus and Portugal, where resident experts constituted the major component of projects, the majority of programmes emphasized specialized equipment and training.

During the year formal reviews were conducted in all countries except Albania, Cyprus, Czechoslovakia, Portugal and Romania. Several major projects were reviewed in those countries. A major objective of the reviews was to determine the effectiveness of third-cycle programmes before preparing country programmes for the fourth cycle. Governments were generally satisfied with the status of the regional programme and confirmed its priority areas: energy, environment, transport and communications, and science and technology. Several mentioned the possibility of utilizing in other regions the successful results of projects implemented in Europe. Governments viewed UNDP co-operation as an essential component of their overall development efforts and UNDP inputs were designed to fill technological gaps towards the attainment of specific economic goals.

The energy sector of the regional programme was strengthened in 1985 with the approval of projects for energy conservation in industry and for low-calorie coal utilization technology.

In his May report on co-ordination of external technical co-operation at the country level,[17] the Administrator said that, since the majority of the countries in Europe benefiting from IPF assistance were relatively high on the per capita income scale, bilateral and multilateral donors in the region were few in number and aid co-ordination was of limited significance. Only one country utilized the resident co-ordinator in a systematic way; most Governments had established their own co-ordinating bodies and did not require United Nations support. However, there were examples of resident co-ordinators playing effective roles, particularly in connection with disaster relief.

Latin America and the Caribbean

In a report on implementation of selected country programmes in Latin America and the Caribbean in 1985,[21] the Administrator said that in reviewing the country programmes for Barbados, Belize, the Cayman Islands, Cuba, El Salvador, Paraguay, and Trinidad and Tobago, and the regional programme, an attempt was made to illustrate varying conditions in which programmes were being implemented. The implementation rate was high and no major carry-over was foreseen for the fourth cycle. Programme and project cost-sharing resources were significant, with commitments reaching $19.7 million for the above programmes.

The principal characteristic of the regional programme was its coverage of objectives and sectors. During the period 1982-1986, 131 projects were implemented. Governments were aware that UNDP country programmes were an invaluable instrument for dealing with their economic difficulties and recapturing the pace of development.

In his report on country-level co-ordination of external technical co-operation,[17] the Administrator said that several resident co-ordinators had reported initiatives by Governments in requesting UNDP assistance to co-ordinate all technical co-operation, while others indicated that some weaknesses in the Governments' capacity to perform those functions were being corrected. A wide range of models for co-ordination were used in the region: formal structured mechanisms were used in one subregion, while informal *ad hoc* consultations took place in others. The support role played by many resident co-ordinators could be enhanced through periodic meetings of the entire donor community in the country and by strengthening co-ordination mechanisms in the host country. A model of co-ordination in the region was the Consultative Group for Economic Development in the Caribbean, for which UNDP provided support in the co-ordination of all technical co-operation and which was a full partner with the major donor institutions in all key phases of the co-ordination process.

Resource constraints had led to the involvement of resident co-ordinators in a variety of activities and approaches to assist Governments in mobilizing resources (most of which was realized through cost-sharing arrangements with UNDP), an approach that facilitated integration with the UNDP country programme. The United Nations system had been requested to support Governments in strengthening specific units of their planning institutions. UNDP and other United Nations organizations had become more active in training key policy-makers.

On 28 June,[22] the Governing Council accepted the recommendations of the Joint Inspection Unit regarding United Nations technical co-operation in Central America and the Caribbean (see p. 473).

Indicative planning figures

In a May note[23] to the Governing Council, the UNDP Administrator said that, in anticipation of a separate independent status for Aruba, the authorities of Aruba had informed him that, as of 1 January 1986, the island would no longer fall under the central Government of the Netherlands Antilles. They requested that he establish a separate illustrative IPF for Aruba as of that date. He informed the Council that he intended to do so by apportioning to Aruba $570,000 of the $1.5 million illustrative IPF for the Netherlands Antilles for 1982-1986; a separate IPF would also be calculated for the fourth programming cycle.

At the special February meeting of the Governing Council on preparations for the fourth programming cycle (see p. 473), the Administrator circulated a 19 February communication[24] from the Acting President of the United Nations Council for Namibia addressed to the Governing Council's President. The Acting President expressed concern that the proposed fourth cycle IPF for Namibia was some $900,000 lower than the third cycle amount. Drawing attention to a number of special circumstances that he felt needed to be taken into consideration when deciding on UNDP resources for Namibia, he appealed to the Governing Council to consider raising Namibia's IPF above that for the third cycle in order to provide comprehensive material assistance to the Namibian people.

On 28 June,[25] the Council approved the extension of an experimental arrangement of providing an add-on to IPFs for countries where government-executed projects were in operation (see p. 474); the next day[26] it increased the fourth cycle IPF for Namibia by 50 per cent with up to $3 million more to be provided following submission in 1986 of a report justifying that amount.

UNDP Council action. In a 29 June decision[26] on the fourth programming cycle (1987-1991), the UNDP Governing Council approved guidelines and criteria for allocating financial resources to the various programmes: of total resources allocated for IPFs, 19 per cent was to be for intercountry and 81 per cent for country IPFs; within the total IPF resources allocated to intercountry programmes, 79.5 per cent would be allocated to regional and 8 per cent to interregional programmes, and 12.5 per cent to the global programme; an additional $20 million would be allocated to the global programme from the Operational Reserve. Using 1983 per capita gross national product (GNP) as a base, 80 per cent of the amount available for country IPFs was to be allocated to countries with a per capita GNP of up to $750, weighted so as to be more advantageous to those with $375 and below, and the remaining 20 per cent to countries with per capita GNP of above $750, weighted to be advantageous to those between $751 and $1,500. Countries with a per capita GNP of under $3,000, and small island countries with populations of 1 million or less with a per capita GNP between $3,000 and $4,200, would have a fourth cycle supplement, if necessary, to receive no less than 100 per cent of their country IPFs for the third cycle; other countries would receive no less than 80 per cent. Each country with a per capita GNP of above $1,500 would receive an IPF amount not exceeding its third cycle IPF. The Council also indicated the weight ratio (75 to 25) between the basic criteria and supplementary criteria used in computing illustrative country IPFs, and stipulated a cap to limit the amount given for supplementary criteria to 50 per cent of the amount given for basic criteria.

Supplementary criteria were to be applied for countries with specific geographical and economic disadvantages, such as LDCs, land-locked or island

developing countries, newly independent countries, front-line States, those whose debt-service payments exceeded 20 per cent of export earnings in 1983, whose current account deficit exceeded 10 per cent of gross domestic product or national income for at least two of the years from 1981 to 1983, or whose terms of trade declined by more than 15 per cent in two of those years.

Countries were urged to increase their voluntary contributions to UNDP. Those with a per capita GNP of between $1,500 and $2,000 were urged to increase gradually their annual regular contributions to reimburse as great a proportion as possible of the UNDP-financed programme. Countries with a 1983 per capita GNP of between $2,000 and $3,000 and the island developing countries mentioned above were asked to do the same to reach from 1987 onwards a ratio of annual contributions of at least 75 per cent of the IPF expenditures, in addition to the cost of the UNDP field office, excluding the cost of the resident representative and the deputy. The Administrator was asked to negotiate with Governments an amendment to the Standard Basic Agreement or similar agreements incorporating measures to ensure contributions equivalent to the annual IPF expenditure and report thereon in 1986.

The Council also decided that: as of 1987, the Administrator should determine the difference between government contributions and the cost of the local office, on the one hand, and, on the other, the IPF delivered plus the cost of the UNDP field office, any deficiency being deducted from the IPF available for the rest of the cycle, beginning in 1989; monitoring should ensure that a country's deficiency never exceed its unspent IPF; and contributions above expenditures paid by UNDP in local currency should be paid in convertible currencies. The Administrator was to report at mid-term on the extent to which the above arrangements were fulfilled.

The Council decided that the IPF for national liberation movements should be increased in the same proportion as the increase for countries with per capita GNP below $750.

To maintain ongoing subregional projects to enhance multi-island co-operation, it allocated $2.5 million. It reconfirmed that 1.24 per cent of fourth cycle resources would be allocated to activities to be financed under Special Programme Resources, to which an additional $20 million would be allocated from resources set aside for increase in the Operational Reserve.

The Administrator was requested to keep programme commitments within foreseen resources and, if resources fell short, to make across-the-board percentage reductions.

Other consideration. In July, in the Third (Programme and Co-ordination) Committee of the Economic and Social Council, Bangladesh, India and Pakistan proposed a draft resolution,[27] subsequently withdrawn, by which the Council would have appealed to donor countries and others to increase their contributions to UNDP to the level of a 14 per cent growth rate agreed to in a 1970 consensus and reaffirmed in 1980.[28] It would have invited the Governing Council, at the review of UNDP resources in June 1989, to consider the continuing relevance of the supplementary criteria, including the need to make them more scientific and objective to ensure transparency, any increase in which should be distributed across the board in a percentage equal to the increase. It would have asked the Administrator for a report on total administrative and support costs, including the proportion of expenditure devoted to programmes, co-ordination activities and administration.

In October 1985,[29] CCSQ(OPS) discussed highlights of the 1985 UNDP Governing Council session, including fourth cycle resources, STAS, the project development facility and the process of round-table meetings.

Co-ordination at the country level

In response to a 1984 Governing Council decision,[13] the Administrator submitted to the Council's June 1985 session a report[17] on co-ordination of external technical co-operation at the country level. The report reviewed recent international dialogue among donors and recipients about the need to improve the effectiveness of development assistance and to strengthen the substantive foundations and processes which facilitated aid co-ordination. It examined the objectives and conditions for effective co-ordination of technical co-operation and discussed steps taken by UNDP to facilitate and participate in such co-ordination and measures taken by UNDP and resident co-ordinators to assist Governments to formulate programmes and prepare for and conduct consultations essential to effective aid co-ordination.

The report recommended that: all parties engaged in technical co-operation commit themselves to achieving greater aid co-ordination; the Governing Council affirm the central role and responsibilities of the resident co-ordinator in co-ordinating technical co-operation and reaffirm that such co-operation financed from UNDP's core and associated funds should be programmed within the framework of Governments' priorities and national technical co-operation programmes; developing countries be encouraged to establish national plans for priority technical co-operation, with resident co-ordinators providing leadership in assisting Governments to co-ordinate national programmes, with the assistance, upon request, of UNDP and other international agencies in their establishment; consultation arrangements be established for co-ordinating technical co-operation; and the Council advocate

consistent support for its co-ordination proposals in international forums and call on the international community to endorse and support UNDP measures to improve co-ordination of technical co-operation.

An addendum to the report contained information on aid co-ordination on a region-by-region basis (see above).

UNDP Council action. By a 28 June decision,[30] the Governing Council invited developing countries to ensure the best possible co-ordination of all external technical assistance, including establishing national programmes to identify priority needs, and to strengthen consultative arrangements. Bilateral aid agencies and multilateral organizations were encouraged to align their technical co-operation activities with those needs and Governments were invited to utilize the revised round-table process to attain maximum co-ordination. The Council urged the World Bank and regional development banks to continue their close collaboration with UNDP, especially in country and sectoral analysis and programming and in implementing technical co-operation. UNDP was to be ready to help developing countries strengthen their co-ordination capabilities and Governments were invited to continue co-ordinating national action on operational activities for development. The Council reaffirmed the resident co-ordinator's co-ordination responsibilities and urged United Nations organizations to co-operate with him. The Administrator was requested to report in 1987 on implementation of the decision.

ACC action. At its October session,[29] CCSQ(OPS) recognized that co-ordination was not an end in itself but a process designed to help both donors and recipients enhance the cost-effectiveness of external aid. Since aid co-ordination was a prerogative of the recipient countries, the primary contribution of the United Nations system was to strengthen their capacity and commitment. Assistance in formulating a suitable macro-economic and sectoral policy framework and strategy was particularly relevant. Further co-ordination efforts should focus on relieving recipient countries of some of the burden of aid-related procedures. Approaches at the country level should be pragmatic and flexible. The collaboration of bilateral donors was an important element in overall co-ordination efforts, since they accounted for a substantial part of the total aid flow. The Committee felt that there was scope for improving and making more effective use of sectoral and intersectoral inputs. Exchange of information, especially on sectoral programmes and projects, including their future orientation, was particularly important.

The Committee agreed to request its secretariat to describe mechanisms and processes for sectoral and intersectoral co-ordination in use at the country level that might be more widely applied, to provide information on measures taken by the United Nations system to strengthen recipient countries' co-ordination capacities, to explore with the Office of the DIEC Director-General and member organizations ways of pursuing collaboration with bilateral donors to enhance overall co-ordination, and to invite selected members to submit to it an analysis of their own co-ordination mechanisms in various sectors.

The Committee welcomed the draft guidelines for UNDP resident representatives, whereby agencies would be consulted on country programmes and their participation facilitated in the country-programming process, including the provision of funds under IPFs.

The Committee was informed that the UNDP Governing Council in June had reviewed the round-table meetings process in order to improve its effectiveness. Agencies would continue to play a major role in the process, particularly in the preparatory phase and in follow-up. Round-table meetings outside the country concerned would be attended only by major donors. UNCTAD would attend because of its special role in implementing SNPA (see p. 434).

JIU reports

In a February note,[31] the UNDP Administrator listed six Joint Inspection Unit (JIU) reports issued since the beginning of 1984 which were of interest to UNDP.

On 28 June,[22] the Governing Council took note of that information. It accepted JIU's recommendations on United Nations technical co-operation in Central America and the Caribbean and the comments of the Secretary-General thereon.[32] It noted with appreciation the Secretary-General's initiatives (see p. 1013) described in his comments on a 1984 JIU report on drug abuse control activities in the United Nations system,[33] and requested the Administrator to co-operate in enhancing system-wide co-ordination of drug abuse control projects and report regularly on UNDP activities in that area.

Programme planning and management

Programme evaluation

The Administrator reported[1] that, in 1985, the UNDP Central Evaluation Office concentrated on consolidating UNDP's new evaluation framework while broadening the base of the system. The Office joined in field evaluation activities with regional bureaux, carried out two regional studies on measures to strengthen monitoring and evaluation capacities of Governments and reviewed samples from 236 in-depth project evaluations conducted in 1983 and 1984.

Evaluations carried out in the forestry sector over two and a half years were examined to derive sectoral or programmatic conclusions, and thematic and *ex-post* evaluations were initiated with interested Governments and agencies.

A significant preliminary conclusion reached was that, as the traditional mix of project inputs and the priorities of technical co-operation changed, evaluation processes would need to evolve. An example was greater use of short-term experts and growing reliance on management by national personnel.

Two other conclusions which emerged echoed earlier findings and referred to the importance of information-sharing between agencies and to institution-building, which needed to be approached as a long-term endeavour. Accordingly, training of operational partners was stressed and, as a first step, UNDP launched a new round of training for its deputy resident representatives.

At its June 1985 session, the Council had before it the second report of the Administrator on evaluation,[34] prepared in response to a 1983 Council decision,[35] the first report having been submitted in 1984.[36] The report dealt with the development of measures taken to strengthen evaluation policies and procedures, and gave details of action being taken to harmonize evaluation and reporting throughout the United Nations system using UNDP's proposed system. The report included a summary of results of recent project evaluations and a status report on thematic and *ex-post* evaluations in progress. Also included was a section on follow-up action to the evaluation of UNDP-financed technical co-operation activities of UNIDO in manufactures (see Chapter VI of this section).

A separate report was submitted to the Council on an interorganizational assessment of women's participation in development (see Chapter XIX of this section).

ACC consideration. At its October 1985 session,[29] CCSQ(OPS) noted that the trial period for the new procedures for monitoring, evaluation and reporting for UNDP-financed projects was under way, with the system's main elements in place at the field level. Training courses for evaluation co-ordinators of UNDP field offices were being conducted in all regions to enable them to deal with operational problems in implementing the revised system and to advise field staff and Governments on appropriate action.

Preparations for the fourth programming cycle

In accordance with a 1984 Governing Council decision,[36] a special meeting of the Council on preparations for the fourth programming cycle (1987-1991) was held at United Nations Headquarters from 19 to 22 February 1985.

The Council had before it a note by the Administrator[37] which presented IPF values for each country/programme based on four different assumptions about resource levels for the fourth cycle. The note discussed that cycle in the perspective of estimated ODA for 1985-1991 and under four alternative resource-growth scenarios. Choices in the use of IPF resources and the proposed use of resources for purposes other than IPFs were also set out. The note's annex comprised statistical tables illustrating the actual IPFs that would result from each of the four resource-level scenarios presented.

UNDP Council action. In a 29 June decision,[26] the Governing Council decided to maintain for the fourth cycle a five-year planning period to cover the years 1987-1991. It also decided that World Bank data on population and per capita GNP for 1983, where available, would be used in the calculations; otherwise the best estimates available would be used. For forward planning purposes, an assumed average annual growth of voluntary contributions of at least 8 per cent on a basis of the $700 million target anticipated for 1986 would apply. In 1989 the Council was to review resources, plans and any further indications by contributors, taking into account the perceived needs of recipient countries, and determine whether higher IPFs should be established for the cycle's remaining years. The decision then set out the criteria on the basis of which any higher IPFs should be calculated (see p. 471).

Information activities

In response to a 1984 Governing Council request[38] for proposals for strengthening UNDP's Division of Information (DOI), the Administrator submitted in May 1985 a note[39] on measures to promote better understanding of the role, activities and resource needs of UNDP. It gave the history of UNDP's information capacity, analysed the nature of UNDP information and means of strengthening it, and described needed additional activities and resources to carry them out.

To increase DOI capacity, the Administrator recommended: the addition of three new Professional posts in New York with related support staff and operations costs and the reclassification of a post to the Professional level; one Professional and one support staff post at Geneva; the continued funding of information support programmes for TCDC and the International Drinking Water Supply and Sanitation Decade (see p. 680) during 1986; the sharing by certain UNDP-associated funds and programmes in the annual costs of a DOI special projects officer to give priority attention to their information needs; and the assignment of junior Professionals supplied by interested donor Governments, for project achievement reporting and other key roles. The 1986-1987

budget for DOI reflected an increase of $856,100 attributable to the proposals.

UNDP Council action. On 28 June,[40] the Council approved allocations of $319,200 from Special Programme Resources for the Decade and $150,000 for TCDC for continued information support in 1986. The Administrator was requested to report with his recommendations in 1986.

Short-term advisory services

In his annual report for 1985,[1] the UNDP Administrator noted that the Governing Council had approved in June the establishment on a two-year trial basis of the UNDP short-term advisory services programme (see p. 781) to perform clearing-house functions to help developing countries meet pressing needs for top-level technical and managerial advice on specific issues, such as immediate production and marketing problems. Drawn from largely untapped commercial and parastatal sectors of donor and developing countries alike, STAS advisers were made available for short-term assignments at minimal cost.

Initially, STAS was focusing its problem-specific assistance on requests from manufacturing, transportation and agro-business sectors in developing countries. Additional sectors would be added as demand grew.

The October meeting of CCSQ(OPS)[29] was informed that STAS would not impinge on the traditional role of the agencies, which would not normally deal with the particular types of expertise involved or use its modality of project financing, which was to cover only air fares and living costs.

Government execution

In an April 1985 report,[41] the UNDP Administrator reviewed progress in the execution of projects by Governments, with special reference to the add-on arrangement to IPFs approved by the Council in 1982[42] for an experimental period ending in June 1985. The report also described measures being taken to assist Governments in project execution and noted the role of United Nations agencies therein.

The Administrator concluded that difficulties related to a Government's ability to administer projects could be overcome with experience and with the assistance of UNDP field offices. He recommended that the role of field offices, and in some cases of the Office of Projects Execution (OPE), in assisting Governments should be strengthened and, in the case of substantive aspects of projects, the role of the specialized agencies should be emphasized at all stages.

The Administrator stated that the experimental period for the use of the add-on was not long enough to gain the necessary experience and requested the Council to extend the period. On 28

June,[25] the Council approved an extension until 31 December 1987 and requested the Administrator to monitor closely the use of the add-on in supporting government execution. The Council further requested that a review and assessment of government execution and the impact of the add-on, including special reference to cost-effectiveness, be presented to it in 1987.

Procurement

In his report on 1985 activities,[1] the Administrator said that during the year the Inter-Agency Procurement Services Unit (IAPSU) continued to emphasize standardization and preferential discounts for items of common use for the United Nations system. Technical bulletins facilitated direct ordering of items such as motor vehicles and office equipment, in line with UNDP's policy of delegating procurement to the field. IAPSU expanded its procurement from developing countries, and information on potential suppliers and manufacturers was entered into its computerized data bank for dissemination to participating and executing agencies. Studies had been undertaken on global insurance schemes, investigations were initiated into reducing transportation costs, and a special study was under way on implications of liability and ownership of equipment and related services for agencies acting as subcontractors mainly under trust-fund arrangements. IAPSU also chaired an inter-agency subgroup, which had unified procurement procedures in a document entitled "Common principles and practices", to be published in the General Business Guide.

By a 29 June decision,[43] the Governing Council noted with appreciation efforts to harmonize procurement practices and requested continued co-operation towards uniformity—reflecting common practices in the General Business Guide—and expansion of the geographical distribution of supply sources. The Council requested the Administrator to consult with the agencies on the production of a more specific analysis of replies to the questionnaire on their procurement practices[44] and to report orally to it in 1986.

Financing

In his annual review of the financial situation in 1985,[45] the Administrator stated that total income was $873 million ($34.8 million higher than forecast) and total expenditures $778.1 million ($51.5 million lower than forecast). As a result, UNDP general resources (previously known as the revenue reserve) increased from $116.5 million at the end of 1984 to $184.4 million at 31 December 1985. Income from voluntary contributions amounted to $662.8 million (lower than the forecast by $25.2 million, mainly due to the underpayment of a $33 million pledge). Miscellaneous income, mainly from placements of funds in short-term financial instruments and adjustments resulting from exchange-rate changes, amounted to $91.3 million, considerably higher than the $25 million forecast, reflecting the higher level of funds available for such investments and the weakening of the United States dollar in the latter part of 1985.

Field programme expenditure in 1985 was $571.7 million, of which $482.1 million represented expenditure against IPFs, $64.7 million against cost-sharing and $25 million against supplementary programmes—$5.3 million under Special Programme Resources, $2.7 million under SIS, $9.6 million under SMF/LDCs and $7.3 million in government cash counterpart funds. The 1985 IPF expenditures ($482.1 million) increased 10.4 per cent over 1984, but short 3.6 per cent of the $500 million forecast. The Administrator initiated in 1985 a joint study with the executing agencies on operational measures which could be taken to improve programme delivery.

In his annual report for 1985,[1] the Administrator stated that the outlook for supplementary contributions continued to be hopeful, amounting to $137 million in 1985 (see p. 465).

In the aggregate, contributions in 1985 to UNDP central resources, to the special-purpose funds under its administration, and to all cost-sharing and sub-trust fund arrangements amounted to $863.7 million, an increase of 3.5 per cent over the 1984 aggregate total of $834.5 million. Under government cash counterpart funds, expenditures rose by $2.2 million, while under SIS they increased by $900,000. Cost-sharing expenditures dropped by $8.8 million and SMF/LDCs expenditures by $700,000 from 1984 levels. Overall, the net increase in field expenditures in 1985 totalled $39.1 million, a 7.3 per cent advance over 1984.

The value of new projects approved rose by 13.6 per cent compared with 1984, going from $307.26 million to $349.05 million. The total number of new approvals increased by 33.7 per cent, rising from 1,074 in 1984 to 1,436.

Other expenditures from central resources in 1985 were $73 million on agency support costs, $127.7 million on UNDP administrative and programme support costs and $3 million on sectoral support and other field-level costs. A charge of $2.9 million arising from miscellaneous expenditures in previous years was also applied.

Project expenditures by OPE totalled $74.4 million in 1985, a 12.3 per cent increase over 1984. Expenditures from UNDP core funds amounted to approximately $40.2 million, an increase of 12.7 per cent over 1984. Expenditures from other funding sources increased by 28.7 per cent, amounting to some $34.2 million.

The report of the Board of Auditors for 1985[46] stated that the total of unexpended resources increased from $223.5 million in 1984 to $318.4 million as at 31 December 1985.

CONTRIBUTIONS TO UNDP, 1985 AND 1986
(as at 31 December 1985; in US dollar equivalent)

| CONTRIBUTOR | 1985 PAYMENT | | | | | 1986 PLEDGE | | |
	UNDP Account	Fund for LDCs	Government cost-sharing	Government cash counterpart	Total	UNDP Account*	Fund for LDCs	Total
Afghanistan	—	—	—	—	—	35,000	—	35,000
Albania	6,571	—	—	—	6,571	6,571	—	6,571
Algeria	834,000	—	2,600,647	208,205	3,642,852	834,000	—	834,000
Angola	—	—	350,000	—	350,000	—	—	—
Argentina	376,729	—	5,132,240	—	5,508,969	—	—	—
Australia	11,594,203	—	(120,975)	—	11,473,228	—	—	—
Austria	7,169,721	—	—	—	7,169,721	7,656,000	—	7,656,000
Bahamas	47,009	—	—	—	47,009	—	—	—
Bahrain	56,000	—	160,322	—	216,322	56,000	—	56,000
Bangladesh	228,000	—	—	—	228,000	250,800	—	250,800
Barbados	33,506	—	—	—	33,506	38,195	—	38,195
Belgium	10,161,290	—	—	—	10,161,290	12,607,843	—	12,607,843
Belize	55,556	—	56,660	—	112,216	—	—	—
Benin	—	—	—	—	—	1,500	1,000	2,500
Bermuda	6,056	—	—	—	6,056	—	—	—
Bhutan	10,700	3,020	—	—	13,720	6,550	1,730	8,280
Bolivia	—	—	501,835	—	501,835	60,000	—	60,000
Botswana	—	—	582,675	—	582,675	—	—	—
Brazil	4,944,203	—	3,838,793	522,177	9,305,173	2,503,394	—	2,503,394
British Virgin Islands	7,500	—	15,000	—	22,500	—	—	—
Brunei	50,000	—	—	—	50,000	—	—	—
Bulgaria	726,230	—	5,723	—	731,953	760,000	—	760,000
Burkina Faso	2,105	—	—	—	2,105	—	—	—
Burma	591,662	—	—	401	592,063	108,043	—	108,043
Burundi	—	—	(152)	—	(152)	13,158	877	14,035
Byelorussian SSR	153,409	—	—	—	153,409	174,870	—	174,870
Cameroon	—	—	1,401,391	267,395	1,668,786	130,548	—	130,548
Canada	43,462,691	—	1,628,787	—	45,091,478	46,376,812	—	46,376,812
Cayman Islands	5,700	—	15,005	—	20,705	—	—	—
Chile	820,000	—	574,780	13,455	1,408,235	820,000	—	820,000
China	1,880,000	—	2,584,902	—	4,464,902	2,040,000	—	2,040,000
Colombia	1,907,207	—	2,835,731	267,962	5,010,900	1,262,000	—	1,262,000
Congo	—	—	1,571,528	—	1,571,528	—	—	—
Cook Islands	8,866	—	55,812	—	64,678	5,000	—	5,000
Costa Rica	297,864	—	713,683	177,741	1,189,288	—	—	—
Cuba	827,874	—	—	—	827,874	923,109	—	923,109
Cyprus	199,000	—	22,420	—	221,420	209,000	—	209,000
Czechoslovakia	650,169	—	2,961	—	653,130	608,696	—	608,696
Democratic People's Republic of Korea	—	—	—	—	—	251,046	—	251,046
Democratic Yemen	12,100	—	45,970	—	58,070	13,800	—	13,800
Denmark	37,040,822	—	200,000	—	37,240,822	4,615,385	—	4,615,385
Djibouti	8,038	—	211,170	6,797	226,005	1,004	—	1,004
Dominica	1,500	—	—	—	1,500	37,037	—	37,037
Dominican Republic	33,333	—	140,000	21,940	195,273	—	—	—
Ecuador	567,033	—	976,367	4,530	1,547,930	254,000	—	254,000
Egypt	691,979	42,332	759,747	1,826,099	3,320,157	691,979	21,166	713,145
El Salvador	11,289	—	—	—	11,289	210,032	—	210,032
Ethiopia	144,928	—	—	—	144,928	144,928	—	144,928
Fiji	38,144	—	—	—	38,144	55,741	—	55,741
Finland	8,549,039	724,638	615,194	—	9,888,871	4,770,642	917,431	5,688,073
France	22,527,094	689,655	53,476	—	23,270,225	30,980,392	915,033	31,895,425
Gabon	—	—	3,461,651	—	3,461,651	—	—	—
Gambia	—	—	—	—	—	5,714	—	5,714
German Democratic Republic	325,851	—	—	—	325,851	400,000	—	400,000
Germany, Federal Republic of	40,426,394	—	387,468	—	40,813,862	47,200,000	—	47,200,000
Greece	905,071	—	106,340	—	1,011,411	1,037,400	—	1,037,400
Grenada	9,406	—	—	—	9,406	—	—	—
Guatemala	4,612	—	99,857	(50,000)	54,469	84,000	—	84,000
Guinea	—	—	(18,843)	—	(18,843)	—	—	—
Guinea-Bissau	—	—	2,828	—	2,828	—	—	—
Guyana	144,578	—	—	—	144,578	—	—	—
Haiti	9,500	—	167,900	—	177,400	—	—	—
Holy See	2,000	—	—	—	2,000	2,000	—	2,000
Honduras	62,500	—	1,662,547	235,651	1,960,698	62,500	—	62,500
Hong Kong	25,000	—	—	—	25,000	—	—	—
Hungary	636,500	—	—	27,798	664,298	680,413	—	680,413
Iceland	74,163	—	—	—	74,163	120,279	—	120,279
India	6,860,371	—	107,086	172,177	7,139,634	6,666,667	—	6,666,667
Indonesia	2,814,286	—	3,494,190	—	6,308,476	2,796,000	—	2,796,000
Iraq	—	—	651,700	—	651,700	—	—	—
Ireland	1,070,000	—	—	—	1,070,000	—	—	—
Israel	109,931	—	—	—	109,931	70,000	—	70,000
Italy	31,512,632	—	4,808,753	—	36,321,385	37,900,875	—	37,900,875

	1985 PAYMENT					1986 PLEDGE		
CONTRIBUTOR	UNDP Account	Fund for LDCs	Government cost-sharing	Government cash counterpart	Total	UNDP Account*	Fund for LDCs	Total
Ivory Coast	146,923	—	494,515	36,967	678,405	—	—	—
Jamaica	36,627	—	1,714,410	70,194	1,821,231	—	—	—
Japan	82,898,177	—	200,000	—	83,098,177	—	—	—
Jordan	293,520	—	1,043,852	—	1,337,372	280,000	—	280,000
Kenya	122,699	—	17,578	122,699	262,976	73,620	—	73,620
Kiribati	8,070	—	—	—	8,070	—	—	—
Kuwait	—	—	926,554	—	926,554	—	—	—
Lao People's Democratic Republic	—	—	—	—	—	19,600	—	19,600
Lebanon	100,000	—	—	(5,118)	94,882	—	—	—
Lesotho	119,248	—	—	—	119,248	17,241	—	17,241
Libyan Arab Jamahiriya	—	—	1,707,567	—	1,707,567	—	—	—
Luxembourg	56,591	—	—	—	56,591	95,098	—	95,098
Madagascar	300,715	—	97,866	—	398,581	12,898	—	12,898
Malawi	21,229	1,299	105,000	—	127,528	24,444	1,170	25,614
Malaysia	385,000	—	(514)	—	384,486	385,000	—	385,000
Maldives	1,800	—	—	—	1,800	2,000	—	2,000
Mali	—	—	100,000	—	100,000	—	—	—
Malta	74,011	—	—	—	74,011	—	—	—
Mauritania	13,296	—	—	—	13,296	—	—	—
Mauritius	40,700	—	—	3,399	44,099	—	—	—
Mexico	861,549	—	917,865	—	1,779,414	404,800	—	404,800
Monaco	3,316	—	—	—	3,316	4,706	—	4,706
Mongolia	157,789	—	—	—	157,789	173,027	—	173,027
Morocco	162,544	—	625,311	500,261	1,288,116	166,587	—	166,587
Mozambique	7,666	—	50,800	32,297	90,763	—	—	—
Nepal	57,300	—	763,904	—	821,204	57,500	—	57,500
Netherlands	43,511,893	—	2,759,290	—	46,271,183	52,464,286	—	52,464,286
Netherlands Antilles	—	—	309,244	—	309,244	—	—	—
New Zealand	1,052,000	—	—	—	1,052,000	1,052,000	—	1,052,000
Nicaragua	—	—	214,357	—	214,357	15,000	—	15,000
Nigeria	—	—	1,398,503	—	1,398,503	—	—	—
Niue	16,680	—	—	—	16,680	—	—	—
Norway	46,149,315	662,252	451,681	—	47,263,248	6,567,940	—	6,567,940
Oman	75,000	—	741,391	—	816,391	75,000	—	75,000
Pakistan	1,584,906	—	746,700	701,490	3,033,096	1,563,276	—	1,563,276
Panama	—	—	1,533,830	—	1,533,830	389,000	—	389,000
Papua New Guinea	282,236	—	858,852	4,805	1,145,893	25,253	—	25,253
Paraguay	81,473	—	334,932	—	416,405	30,000	—	30,000
Peru	477,624	—	442,062	—	919,686	—	—	—
Philippines	566,727	—	70,211	19,910	656,848	408,614	—	408,614
Poland	429,855	—	—	—	429,855	447,960	—	447,960
Portugal	104,363	—	127,980	—	232,343	140,625	—	140,625
Qatar	200,000	—	1,655,585	—	1,855,585	—	—	—
Republic of Korea	893,000	—	10,500	18,778	951,119	852,667	—	852,667
Romania	642,857	—	—	—	642,857	—	—	—
Rwanda	15,000	—	299,230	—	228,600	15,000	500	15,500
Saint Christopher and Nevis	18,520	—	—	—	18,520	—	—	—
Saint Lucia	19,334	—	—	—	19,334	—	—	—
Saint Vincent and the Grenadines	16,675	—	26,560	—	43,235	16,675	—	16,675
Samoa	6,250	—	60,000	—	66,250	—	—	—
Sao Tome and Principe	1,259	450	80,477	—	82,186	—	—	—
Saudi Arabia	3,500,000	—	13,815,949	318,009	17,633,958	3,500,000	—	3,500,000
Senegal	—	—	—	—	—	100,000	—	100,000
Seychelles	1,000	—	—	—	1,000	—	—	—
Sierra Leone	12,331	—	—	—	12,331	—	—	—
Singapore	120,000	—	55,407	—	175,407	—	—	—
Somalia	419	—	40,000	160,979	201,398	538	—	538
Spain	2,694,642	—	—	—	2,694,642	3,438,710	—	3,438,710
Sri Lanka	79,880	—	445,611	140,469	665,960	857,736	—	857,736
Sudan	—	—	151,229	218,367	369,596	—	—	—
Suriname	—	—	56,943	—	56,943	15,000	—	15,000
Swaziland	5,747	—	361,372	—	367,119	11,494	—	11,494
Sweden	48,367,507	5,965,909	352,069	—	54,685,485	9,150,327	6,535,948	15,686,275
Switzerland	17,662,714	2,440,711	1,868,114	—	21,971,539	3,157,895	3,110,048	6,267,943
Syrian Arab Republic	283,526	—	12,026	—	295,552	—	—	—
Thailand	1,001,394	—	152,197	—	1,153,591	1,001,030	—	1,001,030
Togo	2,340	—	8,511	61,728	72,579	—	—	—
Tokelau	2,850	—	8,165	—	11,015	3,078	—	3,078
Trinidad and Tobago	166,667	—	—	—	166,667	111,111	—	111,111
Trust Territory of the Pacific Islands	—	—	70,000	—	70,000	—	—	—
Tunisia	248,193	—	197,761	—	445,954	292,387	—	292,387
Turkey	155,103	—	576,374	19,883	751,360	946,000	—	946,000
Turks and Caicos Islands	25,802	—	—	—	25,802	—	—	—
Uganda	—	—	(14,355)	—	(14,355)	11,198	—	11,198
Ukrainian SSR	383,523	—	—	—	383,523	437,176	—	437,176
USSR	1,724,138	—	—	—	1,724,138	1,943,005	—	1,943,005
United Arab Emirates	—	—	1,446,957	—	1,446,957	—	—	—

| CONTRIBUTOR | 1985 PAYMENT | | | | | 1986 PLEDGE | | |
	UNDP Account	Fund for LDCs	Government cost-sharing	Government cash counterpart	Total	UNDP Account*	Fund for LDCs	Total
United Kingdom	24,410,679	—	—	—	24,410,679	31,157,270	—	31,157,270
United Republic of Tanzania	59,731	—	(1,102,283)	—	(1,042,552)	29,851	29,851	59,702
United States	135,439,781	—	3,345,000	55,584	138,840,365	—	—	—
Uruguay	600,000	—	349	1,778	602,127	—	—	—
Vanuatu	3,000	—	(5,543)	—	(2,543)	—	—	—
Venezuela	1,100,000	—	950,099	367,774	2,417,873	1,100,000	—	1,100,000
Viet Nam	13,000	—	—	—	13,000	15,000	—	15,000
Yemen	—	—	187,598	—	187,598	13,110	—	13,110
Yugoslavia	796,806	—	1,880	12,630	811,316	773,951	—	773,951
Zambia	111,588	—	—	—	111,588	—	—	—
Zimbabwe	62,112	—	—	—	62,112	61,818	—	61,818
Arab Fund for Economic and Social Development	—	—	33,474	—	33,474			
Arab Gulf Programme for UN Development Organizations	—	—	721,682	—	721,682	—	—	—
Arab Maritime Transport Academy	—	—	790,000	—	790,000	—	—	—
European Community	—	—	351,620	—	351,620	—	—	—
Inter-American Development Bank	—	—	514,712	—	514,712	—	—	—
IFAD	—	—	314,787	—	314,787	—	—	—
IMF	—	—	114,600	—	114,600	—	—	—
Latin American Institute for Economic and Social Planning	—	—	24,190	—	24,190	—	—	—
OPEC Special Fund	—	—	345,000	—	345,000	—	—	—
United Nations	—	—	2,900	—	2,900	—	—	—
UN Centre for Human Settlements (Habitat)	—	—	157,445	—	157,445	—	—	—
UNICEF	—	—	165,000	—	165,000	—	—	—
UNHCR	—	—	188,470	—	188,470	—	—	—
UNESCO	—	—	5,500	—	5,500	—	—	—
UN Fund for Drug Abuse Control (UNFDAC)	—	—	131,928	—	131,928	—	—	—
UNIDO	—	—	75,000	—·	75,000	—	—	—
UN Trust Fund for Sudano-Sahelian Activities	—	—	18,240	—	18,240	—	—	—
World Bank	—	—	183,250	—	183,250	—	—	—
WHO	—	—	138,385	—	138,385	—	—	—
Miscellaneous	—	—	1,423,171	—	1,423,171	—	—	—
Total	662,780,125	10,530,266	92,030,046†	6,565,211	771,848,859	340,446,425	11,534,754	351,981,179

*Includes only those pledges made in 1985.
†Does not include $545,000 in prior years' income from extrabudgetary resources.
SOURCE: A/41/5/Add.1.

Budgets

Revised 1984-1985 budget

The UNDP Administrator submitted to the Governing Council in May 1985 revised budget estimates for the biennium 1984-1985 and budget estimates for 1986-1987.[47] The revised estimates for UNDP core activities amounted to $224.5 million (net), a decrease of approximately $18.9 million compared with appropriations approved in 1984.[48] For the biennial budget as a whole, revised estimates amounted to $243.3 million (net) ($318.6 million (gross)), representing a decrease of some $19 million (net) ($14 million (gross)) compared with 1984 appropriations. The revised estimates embodied the introduction of the job classification scheme for both Professional and General Service posts in UNDP (see p. 483).

In its May report[49] on the same budget estimates, the Advisory Committee on Ad-

ministrative and Budgetary Questions (ACABQ) recommended approval of the revised 1984-1985 estimates proposed by the Administrator, subject to a reservation with regard to implementation of the General Service classification exercise.

UNDP Council action. On 29 June,[50] the Governing Council, noting the ACABQ report, approved revised appropriations of $318,552,200 (gross) to finance the 1984-1985 budget, offset by $75,212,100 in income estimates, i.e. $243,340,100 (net). The Administrator was authorized to implement the results of the job classification exercise and the new salary scale for UNDP General Service staff at headquarters at the same time as those for the United Nations (see ADMINISTRATIVE AND BUDGETARY QUESTIONS, Chapter III). An annex to the decision indicated the resources from which the appropriations were to be allocated.

1986-1987 budget

In his May report[47] on budget estimates, the Administrator proposed that the Council appropriate for the 1986-1987 biennium $348.9 million (gross) and $300 million (net). His budgetary proposals included a substantial programme, including 40 posts, to strengthen the operational capability of UNDP in Africa, which depended on the availability of extrabudgetary funding to complement provisions made in the core budget; extrabudgetary contributions pledged in cash or in kind had fallen short by $5.6 million of the projected $8.4 million required.

The Administrator also submitted to the Governing Council a consolidated report[51] on 1986-1987 budgetary and extrabudgetary expenditure estimates, which also included a brief description of activities supported.

ACABQ recommended that future budgets contain more precise information on methodology and on estimates for the Division of Management Information Services, including information on new and existing systems. It felt the 40 posts for increasing operational capacity in Africa should remain extrabudgetary and that the shortfall of voluntary contributions should be made up by a reimbursable subvention from the core budget.

Aside from staff costs, ACABQ stated, the most significant increase related to general operating expenses, including the field office network reflecting the programme to strengthen UNDP's operational capability in Africa and the proposed leasing of additional office space at headquarters. Several increases had also been proposed with regard to UNDP non-core units, to which ACABQ had no objection.

Since action was required by the Governing Council in connection with the redeployment of staff to strengthen activities related to Africa, ACABQ was not in a position to recommend specific appropriation amounts.

UNDP Council action. By a 29 June decision,[52] the Governing Council approved appropriations of $170,319,100 (gross) ($145,373,100 (net)) to finance the 1986 budget. Of that amount, $3 million was to be for "Africa strengthening" as a subvention to an extrabudgetary account for strengthening field offices there and reimbursed by contributions. United Nations organizations that benefited from those field offices were urged to make resources available—to be treated as a credit to the extrabudgetary account—to strengthen co-ordination and emergency functions in Africa. The Council called on member States to make further pledges to the extrabudgetary account to ensure that UNDP resources were devoted to their primary purpose—technical co-operation—to the maximum extent possible. The Administrator was requested to continue his efforts to secure system-wide co-operation. The Council requested the Department of Technical Co-operation for Development (DTCD) to submit to it in 1986 proposed adjustments to the technical co-operation guidelines endorsed by the Council, to enable DTCD to play a full part in addressing the emergency situation and long-term development needs in Africa. The issue of the closure of the Belgrade (Yugoslavia) field office would be reconsidered in 1986. The Council authorized implementation of the reclassification results for Professional posts effective 1 January 1986. An annex to the decision indicated the resources from which the 1986 budget would be financed.

Review of 1984 financial situation

In an April report,[53] the Administrator provided a comprehensive financial review of UNDP-financed activities during 1984 and of the financial position at the end of that year. The report included estimates of anticipated resources and expenditures for 1985 and 1986, and presented information on cost-sharing activities, SMF/LDCs, Special Programme Resources, placement of UNDP funds and the Operational Reserve and the use of accumulated non-convertible currencies. It also provided information on agency support costs, the Reserve for Construction Loans to Governments, and management and other support services.

In accordance with a 1984 Council decision,[54] the Administrator, in an addendum to his report, provided information on contributions to and payments from the UNDP system in respect of each participating Government.

By a 29 June decision,[55] the Council expressed concern at the decline in programme delivery in recent years, despite the availability of resources, and at the high level of financial holdings by UNDP. It urged the early implementation of measures to improve programme delivery and performance so as to achieve full delivery at the recognized programming targets for the third cycle. The Administrator was requested to report further on cash management. Member States were invited to expedite project-related actions awaiting their approval and concurrence, and Governments were urged to increase voluntary contributions to UNDP and promptly pay their pledges.

Special Programme Resources

The Administrator submitted to the Governing Council in April a report[56] proposing an increase in the resources allocated for Special Programme Resources (formerly Programme Reserve). The report traced the background of the programme and provided clarifications and justifications for the proposed increase.

The Administrator recommended that the purposes for which Special Programme Resources for the fourth programming cycle could be used be expanded to cover: assistance for emergency relief and medium-term rehabilitation and reconstruction of areas stricken by natural disasters; financing contingencies, including promotional and certain operational activities of TCDC; financing of a longer-term research and development programme in economic and social development and change; financing assistance for aid co-ordination activities, especially round-table meetings; and financing *ex-post* evaluation of projects.

On 29 June,[26] the Council reconfirmed that 1.24 per cent of total resources during the fourth cycle would be allocated to specific activities to be financed under Special Programme Resources, to which an additional $20 million would be allocated from resources set aside for increase in the Operational Reserve.

UNDP-administered funds

In 1985, six new trust funds were established under the authority of the Administrator on behalf of UNDP. Contributions to those funds received during the year amounted to $8.5 million. Six sub–trust fund arrangements were established on behalf of UNCDF, UNFSSTD and UNSO. The value of those arrangements was approximately $12.6 million.

Total voluntary contributions to the special-purpose funds in 1985 reflected a three-year pattern of decline: in 1983, the funds attracted pledges of $45.5 million; in 1984, $38.6 million; and only $28.58 million in 1985. In contrast, income received by the funds from cost-sharing and sub–trust fund arrangements amounted to about $25.5 million annually for the preceding two years.

In response to a 1984 Council decision,[57] the Administrator submitted in 1985 a report[58] on the financial structure of the UNDP-administered system. The report described the background of the different funds and programmes administered by UNDP and the types of financial contribution that could be made to them. It also described the concept of co-financing and UNDP's experience with it.

The Administrator noted that the analysis pointed to two complementary developments: the emergence of a wide range of programmes and funds under his authority, and the substantive or co-ordination role UNDP had been required to play in co-financing arrangements in which resources were not channelled centrally through it.

A report[59] on trust funds established by the Administrator in 1985 stated that the six trust funds established on behalf of UNDP were the Ethiopia-Italy Programme of Rehabilitation and Development, the UNDP Trust Fund for Support to the Programmes of the Ministry of Planning of Costa Rica, the UNDP Trust Fund for Assistance to the Technical Co-operation Fund between Peru and Argentina to Administer Food Aid, the Australian Development Assistance Bureau/UNDP Programme Trust Fund, the Fund for Assistance to the Centre for the Physically Handicapped (Bamako, Mali), and the Canadian International Development Agency/UNDP Trust Fund for the Caribbean Project Development Facility; two others were established on behalf of UNCDF, three on behalf of UNFSSTD and one on behalf of UNSO.

UNDP Council action. On 29 June,[60] the Council requested the Administrator to review current organizational arrangements for his management of funds and propose ways they could be made more effective and efficient. It noted his intention to make available to cost-sharing programmes the interest earned on cost-sharing balances after UNDP programme costs had been met. He was authorized to lower the support-cost reimbursement rate of a project financed by either a trust fund or cost-sharing if the agency concerned was willing to accept a lower rate. The Council recommended that the General Assembly endorse the Administrator's proposals that the Fund of the United Nations for the Development of West Irian, the United Nations Korean Reconstruction Agency—Residual Assets, the United Nations Relief Operations in Bangladesh and the Trust Fund Programme for the Republic of Zaire be formally closed.

By another decision of the same date,[61] the Council asked the Administrator to provide information on individual projects financed by trust funds restricted to use in the donor country, and on the status of all trust funds established by him since 1981 that were still financially active.

By **decision 40/446** of 17 December, the General Assembly requested the Secretary-General to take the necessary steps for the closure of the Fund for the United Nations Relief Operations in Bangladesh and the Trust Fund Programme for the Republic of Zaire, and to transfer any balances remaining as at 31 December 1985 as add-ons to the UNDP IPFs of the countries concerned.

By **decision 40/447** of the same date, the Assembly requested the Secretary-General to take steps to close, as of 31 December 1985, the Fund of the United Nations for the Development of West Irian and the United Nations Korean Reconstruction Agency—Residual Assets Fund.

Both decisions were approved without vote in the Assembly as well as in the Second Committee, which recommended them, based on texts submitted by a Committee Vice-Chairman.

Allocations from the
Emergency Operation Trust Fund

In accordance with a 1983 General Assembly resolution,[62] the United Nations Emergency Operation Trust Fund was liquidated and its remaining balance allocated to other United Nations funds and programmes. By **decision 39/458** adopted without vote on 9 April 1985, the Assembly, on the Second Committee's recommendation, took note of the 1984 report[63] of the Secretary-General on the liquidation and allocation of the remaining balance.

In October 1985, the Secretary-General submitted to the Assembly a progress report[64] on the subject. He stated that of the funds channelled through UNDP, some $34 million was used to establish the Trust Fund for Countries Afflicted by Famine and Malnutrition. As at 23 September 1985, the Administrator had approved 115 projects in 52 countries for a total value of some $36 million. An amount of $5.9 million was made available to the Trust Fund for Economic and Technical Co-operation among Developing Countries. The balance of the funds had been transferred to the United Nations Relief and Works Agency for Palestine Refugees in the Near East[65] and all monies had been fully disbursed by 31 December 1984.

By **decision 40/450** of 17 December 1985, the Assembly, on the Second Committee's recommendation, took note without vote of the Secretary-General's October report. It was orally proposed by the Chairman of the Second Committee, where it had been approved, also without vote.

Sectoral support

In response to a 1984 Governing Council decision,[48] the UNDP Administrator submitted in April 1985 a report[66] on the current and future development of sectoral support. The report also addressed the question of linkage between sectoral support and sectoral analysis and the need for improvements in the management of the sectoral support programme with smaller agencies. The question of UNDP support to the Senior Industrial Development Field Advisers (SIDFA) programme was postponed pending clarification of UNIDO's future status (see p. 603).

The Administrator recommended continuing allocations from central UNDP resources to smaller agencies for their sectoral support activities with improved management measures, through the fourth cycle. It was suggested that the Council might consider in 1986 the allocation level—in accordance with past practice, that would be approximately one third of the total sectoral support allocation—to be made to the smaller agencies in conjunction with the future of the SIDFA programme.

On 29 June,[67] the Governing Council endorsed the Administrator's proposals; it also addressed the question of UNDP support to the SIDFA programme.

Accounts and auditing

Accounts for 1984

The financial statements of UNDP for the year ended 31 December 1984, together with the report of the Board of Auditors, were submitted to the General Assembly in June 1985.[68] The statements also covered the trust funds for which the Administrator had responsibility.

The Board noted that the UNDP revenue reserve had increased again in 1984 to $116.5 million from $57.9 million as at 31 December 1983, while IPF expenditures continued to decrease and, as in 1983, fell short of the planned programme delivery targets by some $63 million. Unpaid pledges amounted to $43.2 million at the end of 1985, which compared unfavourably with $13.2 million in 1983. Factors contributing to the decline of expenditures included the strengthening of the United States dollar, cautious development planning in the face of uncertainty over resource availability, and often unfavourable conditions for project programming and delivery due to natural disasters or security-related problems.

Other findings included: a tendency to over-obligate funds, especially for travel; a lack of proper contractual arrangements and justification for temporary assistance; late submission and inadequate formulation of purchase requisitions; lack of consistency in adhering to recommendations and rules on standardization of equipment, on emergency procurement procedures for vehicle spare parts and on contractor-selection procedures for office supply procurement; delay in assessing staff for losses of or damage to UNDP property; the lack of timely reassignment or disposal of equipment of completed projects; problems in respect of title and ownership of rental income, fixing of rent levels and terms of loan reimbursement with regard to housing construction loan agreements with Governments; and shortcomings and deficiencies in basic agreements, preliminary planning and design, day-to-day supervision and follow-up with regard to construction of new United Nations common premises in a country.

In response, the Administration had stated that a joint study with the agencies had been initiated on measures to improve programme delivery, and IPF expenditure estimates for 1985 and 1986 had been revised to reflect more realistic delivery targets. Action had been taken or was planned in response to most of the Board's other recommendations.

Commenting on the Board's findings, ACABQ, in a September 1985 report,[69] said it had been informed that $25.5 million of the unpaid contributions had been collected by 30 June 1985. It noted that the UNDP Administrator had initiated measures to improve programme delivery, to update guidelines on contractual arrangements and to resolve the problems regarding loan agreements with Governments. With regard to procurement practices, ACABQ urged the Administration to ensure full compliance with all applicable rules.

By **resolution 40/238**, the General Assembly in December accepted the financial report, audited financial statements and audit opinion of the Board of Auditors, concurred with ACABQ's observations and comments, and renewed its invitation to the Governing Council to consider each year the remedial action taken by the Administrator in response to the Board's observations and comments.

Audit reports for 1983

In a 4 April note,[70] by which he submitted the audit reports of the participating and executing agencies for 1983 relating to funds allocated to them by UNDP, the Administrator stated that he had brought to the attention of the Panel of External Auditors the Council's 1984 decision[71] on the need for long-form narrative audit reports. The Panel had observed that the length of an audit report was determined by the size of the account being audited; the expenditures for certain executing agencies for UNDP were not enough for a long-form report to be produced. With regard to audits on the effectiveness of financial management, the Panel recalled that in 1982 it had indicated that the emphasis it placed on effectiveness auditing would be gradually increased and the findings reflected in the audit reports.

The Administrator noted that for 1983 the number and extent of long-form narrative reports from the agencies showed a significant increase and had covered such areas as project formulation, design, implementation, monitoring and evaluation and the results of field investigations of selected projects and programmes.

Included in the note was a brief summary of observations by the auditors and comments on them by the Administrator. As several of those observations related to project monitoring and evaluation systems, the Administrator also briefly noted action by UNDP and the agencies in that regard.

UNDP Council action. By a 29 June decision,[72] the Governing Council expressed its appreciation for the increasing emphasis given to long-form narrative audit reports with observations on financial management effectiveness. The Administrator was requested to bring the decision and members' views to the attention of the Panel of External Auditors, to continue to ensure submission of long-form narrative audit reports for every ex-

ecuting agency carrying out a significant volume of UNDP-financed activities, and to include in his comments on the audit reports a summary of the most significant observations in UNDP's and the United Nations' audit reports, as well as comments made and actions taken in response.

Financial regulations

In accordance with a 1984 Governing Council decision,[71] the Administrator submitted[73] to the Council's Budgetary and Finance Committee for consideration changes proposed in 1981 to the UNDP Financial Regulations, i.e. texts on which consensus was not reached at the 1984 session (mainly dealing with currencies of contributions and their utilization), and the text of two subparagraphs of a 1981 Council decision[74] on which consensus had also not been reached. The note also contained the Administrator's proposals that the Council adopt certain UNDP Financial Regulations that were identical, or nearly so, to corresponding old regulations that had remained in effect pending agreement on the new proposals, so long as the new regulations could replace their old counterparts without affecting the substance of the issues still under contention.

On 29 June,[75] the Council approved the Administrator's 1981 proposed texts for inclusion in the Financial Regulations in place of the former regulations that had remained in force pending agreement, and decided that the Budgetary and Finance Committee would consider in 1986 a draft text for regulation 4.6, proposing that a voluntary contribution would be deemed usable if previous accumulations of contributions from the donor amounted to less than the contribution itself, as well as other matters on which consensus was not achieved.

Currency exchange rates applicable to UNDP activities

In a June report,[76] the Administrator drew the attention of the Governing Council to the fact that UNDP had been involved in recent years in a number of differences with Governments on the question of the rate of exchange to be used for receipts from international organizations. The question typically arose in the context of economic adjustment programmes negotiated with IMF in which two or more exchange rates were authorized for different types of transactions. United Nations policy was that it was entitled to the most favourable legal rate of exchange in a country and that any advantage arising from multiple exchange rates should accrue to it. A dispute had arisen with a Government on UNDP's right to use the "market-determined" rate of exchange rather than the "official" rate, both authorized by the Central Bank, the practical effect being that UNDP was required to sell foreign exchange to the Central Bank at the official rate while having to buy import goods (other than fuel) at the market rate; local cost increases and salary and post allowances had to be adjusted accordingly. Negotiations to resolve the problem had not been successful and UNDP had advised the Government that if a settlement was not reached by 15 July 1985 it would invoke the arbitration procedure provided for in the Standard Basic Assistance Agreement, the basic legal instrument governing development assistance in most countries. UNDP would report further to the Council in 1986.

On 25 June, Somalia, in a statement[77] to the Governing Council, said the Arabic version of the Administrator's report had identified it as the country involved and confidential communications between the Secretary-General and Somalia had been leaked to the news media. Somalia wished to clarify its position for balanced understanding of the situation, as follows: the "favourable legal rate" referred to in the 1977 UNDP/Somalia Agreement meant the official rate applicable to international organizations, including UNDP, while the United Nations Office of Legal Affairs insisted that the open market system (applicable to individuals and commercial entities) was the rate to which UNDP was entitled; according to the 1969 Vienna Convention on the Law of Treaties,[78] agreements should be interpreted in the light of their purpose and content, and the appropriate interpretation of the word "legal" in the light of that purpose could only be the same as "official" as defined by the Central Bank; the functions that UNDP was performing were clearly governmental and not commercial.

On 29 June,[79] the Governing Council expressed the hope that further consultations on the issue would be fruitful.

ITU request for additional support-cost reimbursement

On 29 June,[80] the Governing Council, having considered information provided by the International Telecommunication Union (ITU) and UNDP concerning ITU's request for additional reimbursement of support costs for activities financed by UNDP, reaffirmed its 1984 decision[48] in which it had decided that support-cost reimbursement to executing agencies should be made in accordance with its 1980[81] and 1981[82] decisions on the subject.

Staff-related matters

Job classification

In his budget estimate report[47] for 1984-1985 and 1986-1987, the UNDP Administrator reported on the outcome of a job classification exercise for both Professional and General Service posts in UNDP. The scheme became effective for New York General Service posts in January 1985 and would go into effect for international Professional posts in January 1986. For General Service posts in field duty stations, UNDP was co-operating with the ACC Consultative Committee on Administrative Questions and the International Civil Service Commission in developing common classification standards. In budgetary terms, the total annual impact amounted to an increase of $200,000 for General Service and some $300,000 for Professionals.

In its related report,[49] ACABQ stated that, with respect to Professional posts, the Governing Council might wish to consider whether steps should be taken to correct the grading "pyramid", given the decreasing number of lower-level posts. ACABQ noted that new General Service salary scales had been implemented in February 1984 without its prior concurrence, the Secretary-General having implemented the new scale without waiting for the completion of the job classification exercise; the financial implication for UNDP in 1984-1985 was $1.5 million. Since the UNDP job classification exercise was virtually completed, the Council could decide on immediate implementation on an effective date the same as that for the United Nations.

On 29 June,[50] the Governing Council authorized the Administrator to implement the results of the job classification exercise and the new salary scale for UNDP General Service staff at headquarters when the results were implemented by the Secretary-General and with the same effective date.

Project personnel

In accordance with a 1983 Governing Council decision,[83] the Administrator submitted a report[84] in February 1985 on recent trends in the recruitment, cost and utilization of project personnel and other personnel working in development co-operation. The report concluded that the trend towards greater diversification of project personnel categories was intensifying. The United Nations system met many requirements of developing countries through a wide range of approaches which complemented the traditionally recruited experts and consultants. The fastest growing category of UNDP-financed personnel were nationally recruited project personnel. Since their salaries were tied to best prevailing local rates, their cost was much lower than for international recruits without any apparent loss in quality and impact. The UNV programme had become an essential source for middle- and upper-level positions and the Senior Executive Services programme provided retired experts for short-term assignments. TCDC personnel and the scheme for the transfer of knowledge through expatriate nationals (TOKTEN) could become other important sources for high-quality, short-term personnel at low cost. UNFSSTD permitted the employment of such personnel in science and technology from private and semi-private sources. Government execution of projects allowed Governments to recruit international personnel at rates they established, but not to exceed United Nations rates.

The Administrator recommended that the Governing Council: endorse his efforts to ensure greater use of the newer categories, such as nationally recruited project personnel; urge all agencies to ensure greater cost-effectiveness by focusing on project design and appraisal and by considering the full range of available personnel; endorse his initiatives to use a new form of operational personnel–type contract to facilitate the return of nationals working abroad; urge donor Governments to adopt flexible policies to meet short-term personnel shortages in the poorest countries; reaffirm the importance of UNV; endorse his efforts to strengthen data-collection systems and remedy problems in connection with implementing project personnel recruitment policies; reiterate that job descriptions for vacancies be widely circulated, including through national sources; and appeal to host Governments to speed up the clearance and government designation processes.

UNDP Council action. By a 28 June decision,[85] the Governing Council endorsed the Administrator's initiative to ensure more intensive use of nationally recruited project personnel, TOKTEN[84] and other initiatives mentioned in his report[84] with a view to achieving more cost-effectiveness, and endorsed his efforts to use operational assistance contracts facilitating the return of nationals. It urged that particular attention be paid at the project design stage to cost-effectiveness by identifying the most appropriate categories of personnel, taking into account also the potential role of UNV. Agencies were urged to ensure selection and nomination of the most suitable individuals for projects, to circulate job descriptions for vacancies promptly, making full use of national recruitment services, and to submit more than one candidate to Governments for each vacant post. Governments were urged to speed up personnel clearance and adhere to the schedule in assigning their staff. The Council endorsed the Administrator's efforts to improve data collection in order to monitor the quality and impact of categories of personnel and asked for a comparative report in 1987 on these aspects.

ACC consideration. At its October session,[29] ACC's CCSQ(OPS) noted the importance of inter-

national experts and national counterparts, especially in the context of trends in multilateral technical co-operation. It expressed the view that the basic consideration should be how to enhance cost-effectiveness in meeting projects' objectives through a mix of personnel inputs, rather than cost reduction as such. Noting that UNDP would prepare a comparative analysis of the cost, quality and impact of all categories of project personnel, the Committee suggested that it include qualitative evaluations to facilitate the determination of the optimal mix of project personnel. UNDP agreed to consult with the agencies in preparing the study and report on progress to a future Committee session. It was agreed that the role of national counterparts should be retained in the Committee's 1986 programme of work.

Other administrative matters

Governing Council documentation

In June,[86] the UNDP Administrator reported that, in response to a questionnaire to Governing Council members to ascertain the usefulness of documents issued for the 1984 session, 11 respondent countries (Argentina, Australia, Bahrain, Canada, Finland, Hungary, Poland, Saudi Arabia, Tunisia, United Kingdom, United States) agreed that the content and presentation of documents were useful. Most agreed that the frequency of issue was adequate but suggested that detailed reports on activities not receiving policy consideration no longer be issued. All agreed that reports currently written should not be presented orally; oral presentation should be shorter and some documents condensed; no documents were too short; and UNFPA documentation should not be prepared in a different manner in uneven years. Most felt that it was useful to categorize documents as either "main policy" or "support" papers. All except one respondent felt that suggested courses of action should continue to be included. Half felt that the Secretary-General's report on technical co-operation activities should focus on selected aspects in uneven years, and half felt that it should deal in uneven years with a specific theme.

UNDP Council action. By a 28 June decision,[87] the Governing Council requested those members that had not done so to respond to the questionnaire, on the basis of which the secretariat would prepare a report for examination in 1986. The Council strongly insisted that the Administrator take decisive action to solve the problems related to the preparation and timely distribution of Council documents and report in 1986 on measures taken, while continuing his efforts to improve the quality, reduce the quantity and accelerate the distribution of documentation.

The Council allocated up to $200,000 per biennium for the editing, translation, typing and production of its documents.

REFERENCES

[1]*Annual Report of the Administrator for 1985* (DP/1986/11 & Add.1-6), Sales No. E.86.III.B.3. [2]E/1985/32. [3]DP/1985/L.8. [4]DP/1985/70. [5]E/1985/32 (dec. 85/1). [6]*Ibid.* (dec. 85/2). [7]*Ibid.* (dec. 85/46 & 85/47). [8]*Ibid.* (dec. 85/48). [9]E/1985/L.42 & Corr.1. [10]YUN 1984, p. 434. [11]E/1985/32 (dec. 85/4). [12]DP/1985/21. [13]YUN 1984, p. 438. [14]E/1985/32 (dec. 85/17). [15]*Ibid.* (dec. 85/18). [16]DP/1986/26. [17]DP/1985/4 & Add.1. [18]DP/1986/27. [19]DP/1986/28. [20]DP/1986/29. [21]DP/1986/30. [22]E/1985/32 (dec. 85/6). [23]DP/1985/67. [24]DP/1985/INF/3. [25]E/1985/32 (dec. 85/9). [26]*Ibid.* (dec. 85/16). [27]E/1985/C.3/L.7. [28]YUN 1980, p. 587. [29]ACC/1985/19. [30]E/1985/32 (dec. 85/3). [31]DP/1985/6. [32]YUN 1984, p. 636. [33]*Ibid.*, p. 955. [34]DP/1985/13. [35]YUN 1983, p. 461. [36]YUN 1984, p. 441. [37]DP/1985/1 & Corr.1 & Annex & Annex/Corr.1. [38]YUN 1984, p. 447. [39]DP/1985/8. [40]E/1985/32 (dec. 85/8). [41]DP/1985/12. [42]YUN 1982, p. 643. [43]E/1985/32 (dec. 85/39). [44]YUN 1984, p. 452. [45]DP/1986/56. [46]A/41/5/Add.1 & Add.1/Corr.1. [47]DP/1985/57 & Corr.1 & Add.1. [48]YUN 1984, p. 448. [49]DP/1985/56. [50]E/1985/32 (dec. 85/35). [51]DP/1985/58 & Corr.1. [52]E/1985/32 (dec. 85/36). [53]DP/1985/54 & Add.1. [54]YUN 1984, p. 449. [55]E/1985/32 (dec. 85/34). [56]DP/1985/20. [57]YUN 1984, p. 450. [58]DP/1985/64. [59]DP/1986/61 & Add.1 & Add.1/Corr.1. [60]E/1985/32 (dec. 85/42). [61]*Ibid.* (dec. 85/37). [62]YUN 1983, p. 537, GA res. 38/201, 20 Dec. 1983. [63]YUN 1984. p. 451. [64]A/40/740. [65]YUN 1984, p. 337. [66]DP/1985/63. [67]E/1985/32 (dec. 85/41). [68]A/40/5/Add.1. [69]A/40/635. [70]DP/1985/62 & Add.1. [71]YUN 1984, p. 452. [72]E/1985/32 (dec. 85/40). [73]DP/1985/60. [74]YUN 1981, p. 456. [75]E/1985/32 (dec. 85/38). [76]DP/1985/7. [77]DP/1985/INF/5. [78]YUN 1969, p. 734. [79]E/1985/32 (dec. 85/44). [80]*Ibid.* (dec. 85/43). [81]YUN 1980, p. 592. [82]YUN 1981, p. 449. [83]YUN 1983, p. 474. [84]DP/1985/9. [85]E/1985/32 & Corr.1 (dec. 85/10). [86]DP/1985/69. [87]E/1985/32 (dec. 85/45).

OTHER PUBLICATIONS

Annual Report of the Administrator for 1984 (DP/1985/5), Sales No. E.85.III.B.1. *Generation: Portrait of the United Nations Development Programme, 1950-1985*, Sales No. E.85.III.B.2. *Compendium of Approved Projects as of September 1985* (UNDP/SER.A/16), Sales No. E.86.III.B.1.

Other technical co-operation

UN programmes

In 1985, the United Nations, mainly through its Department of Technical Co-operation for Development, continued to provide technical assistance to developing countries in the economic and social sectors. In a report[1] to the Governing Council, the Secretary-General addressed various policy matters and described the 1985 DTCD technical co-operation programme (see p. 488) and those of other entities of the United Nations Secretariat.

The report stated that in 1985 the United Nations delivered a technical co-operation programme of $273 million, compared to $254 million in 1984, a 7.5 per cent increase. The United Nations regular programme of technical co-operation financed activities totalling some $17 million through DTCD, the regional commissions, the Centre for Human Rights, the Division of Narcotic Drugs, the Office of Legal Affairs, the United Nations Centre for Human Settlements, the United Nations Centre on Transnational Corporations, UNCTAD, the United Nations Environment Programme and UNIDO. UNDP-financed projects carried out by those entities totalled some $177 million.

DTCD activities

In his report[1] on technical co-operation activities, the Secretary-General stated that the work of DTCD in 1985 was characterized by several positive developments: the delivery of $127.2 million in project expenditures, the largest programme since 1981; the elimination of the gap between administrative costs and programme support earnings; and the production of an operating surplus in the overhead account sizeable enough to eliminate much of the previous deficit. Those developments reflected greater mobilization of funds for technical co-operation, increased volume of project budgets available, a substantial improvement in programme delivery, and increased effectiveness in DTCD performance.

During the year, 1,352 projects were executed by DTCD in development planning, natural resources and energy, development administration and finance, statistics, population, ocean economics and technology, and social development and humanitarian affairs. Project expenditures were incurred against budgets of $165 million, giving an implementation rate of 77 per cent compared with 1984 budgets of $140 million, expenditures of $111 million, and an implementation rate of 79 per cent. By source of funds in 1985, expenditures were $87.9 million for UNDP-financed projects (69 per cent of the total), $13.7 million for UNFPA (11 per cent), $14.8 million under trust funds (12 per cent), $7.5 million under the United Nations regular programme of technical co-operation (6 per cent), and $3.2 million under the United Nations Educational and Training Programme for Southern Africa (UNETSPA).

By geographic area, delivery was $45.2 million for Africa, $36.1 million for Asia and the Pacific, $28.6 million for the Middle East, Mediterranean, European and interregional projects, and $17.3 million for the Americas.

By sector, natural resources and energy continued to account for the largest share of the programme: $59.7 million in expenditures (47 per cent), compared with $50 million (45 per cent) in 1984. Development planning was second, representing $21.7 million, or 17 per cent. The most notable change (a 43 per cent increase) was the statistics sector at $17.7 million, compared with $12 million in 1984.

Distribution of expenditures for other sectors was: public administration, $11.8 million; population, $7.1 million; social development, $4.8 million; UNETPSA, $3.2 million; and others, $1.2 million.

During the year, DTCD executed 254 development planning projects in 91 countries and 78 missions were undertaken by interregional advisers. Several new activities were launched, including assistance to Guinea in preparing an economic recovery programme, an umbrella project in Benin covering national accounts, planning and demography, a large planning project in Burkina Faso, including formulation of a macro-economic framework and the establishment of an investment data-bank cell, and the preparation of the first development plan for Zaire. In rural development, particular emphasis was placed on local grass-roots community development and on increasing the participation of women.

Activities in natural resources and energy included 147 minerals projects covering institution-building, general and targeted exploration, rehabilitation of mines, training, planning, mining legislation and contract negotiation, equipment supply and application of computer techniques. In energy, 142 projects were under execution in three main areas: conventional energy; electric power; and new and renewable energy. Assistance in water resources exploration, development and management was provided to 59 developing countries through some 175 field projects. In the sectors of remote sensing, public works and cartography, 68 projects were active and interregional advisers undertook four missions during the year.

DTCD assisted developing countries in public administration, public finance and public enterprises, implementing 179 projects. With regular programme support, it organized workshops and seminars to exchange experiences between developed and developing countries, to formulate guidelines for analysing public administration and finance issues and to implement development administration programmes.

With substantive support from the United Nations Statistical Office, DTCD provided technical co-operation in statistical organization, national accounts, and demographic and social statistics, including population censuses, surveys, civil registration and statistical data processing. There were 180 statistics and data-processing projects in 1985. DTCD executed 98 UNFPA-supported demographic projects, most of which were individual country projects, covering 62 developing countries.

Projects in social aspects of development covered assistance in crime prevention, criminal justice, youth, the aging and the disabled.

DTCD continued to help select and appoint personnel to advise Governments on various aspects of social and economic development; in 1985, 1,128 experts and consultants were appointed, compared with 1,020 in 1984. The Department implemented

a total of 3,670 awards for group training, study tours, workshops, seminars and in-service training, as well as for individual fellowships. Fellows and participants from 140 countries were trained in 101 host countries.

UNDP Council action. By a 29 June decision,[2] the UNDP Governing Council took note of the Secretary-General's report[3] on United Nations technical co-operation activities during 1984, commended DTCD for reducing its administrative costs and continuing to improve its procedures, and urged continued efforts to eliminate the deficit in its overhead income account. It reiterated its request that the Secretary-General cluster in a single organizational entity all technical, managerial and operational capabilities related to the Secretariat's technical co-operation activities, in pursuance of a 1977 Assembly resolution[4] on restructuring. The Secretary-General was requested to continue to explore and report on measures to increase DTCD's competitiveness as an executing agency. The Council endorsed DTCD's major role in setting in place a Special Action Programme for Africa to improve administrative and managerial capabilities in public administration and finance, for which there was a need for greater resources. It reaffirmed its support for the Department's use of regular programme of technical co-operation financing for country programming and to cover, on a cost-sharing and reimbursable basis, project identification, appraisal and formulation. The Council again requested financial and funding institutions to make full use of DTCD's capabilities and asked the Secretary-General to develop and present to the Council in 1986 an internal implementation strategy based on work already done to strengthen DTCD's capability to deal with issues of women in development. It invited the Department to co-operate fully with UNDP in that respect.

GENERAL ASSEMBLY ACTION

The General Assembly, without vote and on the recommendation of the Second Committee, also took note of the Secretary-General's report[3] on United Nations technical co-operation activities during 1984 by **decision 40/449** of 17 December 1985. The Second Committee had approved the action on 13 December on an oral proposal by its Chairman.

UN Volunteers

In 1985, the United Nations Volunteers programme experienced sustained growth, with 1,816 established posts and 1,128 volunteers in service at the end of the year, representing an increase of 13 per cent and almost 20 per cent, respectively, over the 1984 figures. There were 118 volunteers en route to their assignments, and nominations for 380 posts were pending clearance by Governments and agencies.

The African region remained the largest recipient of volunteer expertise, absorbing over 52 per cent of the volunteers in service in 1985, according to the Administrator's report[5] on 1985 UNV activities. A notable feature of its activities in the region was the implementation of the UNV project on emergency assistance to drought-affected countries in sub-Saharan Africa, which became fully operational in 1985 with 100 per cent of its budget—$1.5 million—committed and an implementation rate of 73 per cent. At year's end, 53 volunteers were in place in 24 African countries, 11 were en route to assignments and 13 awaited Government clearance.

The Asia and Pacific region was the second largest user of volunteers in 1985. As at 31 December, there were 335 volunteers in 26 countries of the region, representing 30 per cent of the total in the field.

UNV's presence in the Latin American region remained modest with 54 volunteers, although the number of recipient countries increased to 14. Nearly half of the volunteers were serving in Jamaica, mainly in the health sector.

There were over 150 volunteers assigned to projects and programmes in the Arab States and the Middle East region, with Somalia and Yemen absorbing over half of them. A regional project on assistance to LDCs in the Arab States, with activities in agriculture, communication, engineering and small-scale industries, became operational in 1985.

CONTRIBUTIONS TO THE SPECIAL VOLUNTARY FUND
FOR THE UN VOLUNTEERS, 1985 AND 1986

(as at 31 December 1985; in US dollar equivalent)

Country	1985 payment	1986 pledge*
Austria	10,000	10,000
Bangladesh	1,256	1,210
Belgium	150,943	235,294
Bhutan	1,720	990
Botswana	291	4,878
Brazil	20,000	10,000
China	20,000	20,000
Denmark	45,744	5,495
Germany, Federal Republic of	81,588	—
India	5,035	5,000
Italy	140,449	145,773
Lesotho	1,276	958
Netherlands	69,450	—
Norway	110,497	132,450
Papua New Guinea	—	1,515
Philippines	500	1,000
Republic of Korea	10,000	9,333
Sri Lanka	3,261	3,000
Switzerland	142,726	153,110
Syrian Arab Republic	5,064	—
Thailand	3,000	1,500
Tunisia	3,699	4,357
Zaire	—	500
Total	826,499	746,363

*Represents pledges made in 1985 only.
SOURCE: A/41/5/Add.1.

UNV PROJECT EXPENDITURES, 1985
(as at 31 December 1985; in thousands of US dollars)

Country/Territory	Amount	Country/Territory	Amount	Country/Territory	Amount
Afghanistan	13	Honduras	18	Sierra Leone	55
Angola	6	Indonesia	16	Singapore	5
Bangladesh	38	Ivory Coast	5	Solomon Islands	18
Benin	43	Jamaica	74	Somalia	151
Bhutan	42	Kenya	48	Sri Lanka	3
Botswana	64	Lao People's Democratic Republic	15	Sudan	46
Burkina Faso	15	Lesotho	107	Swaziland	17
Burundi	17	Liberia	8	Syrian Arab Republic	23
Cameroon	4	Malawi	12	Thailand	16
Central African Republic	87	Maldives	10	Togo	4
Chad	5	Mali	7	Tonga	3
China	1	Mauritania	10	Trinidad and Tobago	10
Colombia	3	Morocco	4	Trust Territory	
Comoros	48	Mozambique	44	of the Pacific Islands	66
Congo	15	Nepal	16	Turks and Caicos Islands	7
Cook Islands	56	Nicaragua	1	Tuvalu	12
Democratic Yemen	39	Niger	40	Uganda	62
Djibouti	10	Nigeria	3	United Arab Emirates	7
Dominica	9	Niue	10	United Republic of Tanzania	127
Dominican Republic	2	Oman	1	Vanuatu	9
El Salvador	1	Pakistan	6	Yemen	106
Equatorial Guinea	23	Papua New Guinea	25	Zimbabwe	19
Ethiopia	14	Paraguay	4	Other	1
Fiji	8	Rwanda	11		
Gabon	2	Saint Christopher and Nevis	18	Subtotal	2,116
Gambia	22	Saint Lucia	7		
Ghana	14	Saint Vincent		Global	80
Guatemala	1	and the Grenadines	2		
Guinea	11	Samoa	95	Interregional	30
Guinea-Bissau	67	Sao Tome and Principe	27	Subtotal	110
Guyana	13	Senegal	2		
Haiti	7	Seychelles	3	Total	2,226

SOURCE: DP/1986/11/Add.6.

UNDP Council action. By a 28 June decision,[6] the Governing Council took note of the Administrator's report[7] on the UNV programme for 1984 and noted the progress achieved in assisting the most severely affected African countries in effectively utilizing emergency relief assistance through volunteers. It urged the Administrator to provide such volunteers beyond the duration of the regional emergency project approved by the Council in 1984,[8] and urged donors and all United Nations organizations to consider the advantages of using volunteers when making allocations for emergencies and to increase their use in development projects, including design and preparation. That developing countries had recognized those advantages was manifested by the fact that the highest number of volunteers were serving in development projects since the programme's inception. The Council encouraged recipient Governments and the Administrator to consider allocating increased IPF resources for Domestic Development Service programmes aimed at helping the least advantaged communities participate more actively in their own development.

International Volunteer Day

In his report on 1984 UNV activities,[7] the Administrator had suggested that the Governing Council propose that the General Assembly designate 7 December, the anniversary of the date of adoption of the 1970 resolution establishing UNV,[9] for the annual observance of an International Volunteer Day.

On 29 June,[10] the Council recommended that the Assembly consider the question of designating an International Day for Volunteers for Economic and Social Development.

GENERAL ASSEMBLY ACTION

On 17 December, on the recommendation of the Second Committee, the General Assembly adopted **resolution 40/212**, without vote.

International Volunteer Day for Economic and Social Development

The General Assembly,

Taking note of the report of the Administrator of the United Nations Development Programme on the United Nations Volunteers programme, and the relevant decision of the Governing Council,

Considering that volunteer service, including that of the United Nations Volunteers, is making an important contribution to socio-economic development activities,

Recognizing the desirability of stimulating the work of all volunteers both in the field and in organizations—multilateral, bilateral or national, non-governmental or government-supported—and of giving encouragement to those volunteers, many of whom engage in volunteer service at considerable personal sacrifice,

1. *Invites* Governments to observe annually, on 5 December, an International Volunteer Day for Economic and Social Development, and urges them to take measures to heighten awareness of the important contribution of volunteer service, thereby stimulating more people in all walks of life to offer their services as volunteers, both at home and abroad;

2. *Invites also* specialized agencies, other organizations of the United Nations system and non-governmental organizations that provide, are affiliated with or benefit from volunteer service to undertake and promote activities to stimulate greater awareness of the contribution to their work made by volunteers;

3. *Requests* the Secretary-General to continue to promote world-wide publicity on the important role of volunteer service.

General Assembly resolution 40/212

17 December 1985   Meeting 120   Adopted without vote

Approved by Second Committee (A/40/1041) without vote, 9 December (meeting 49); draft by Vice-Chairman (A/C.2/40/L.107), based on informal consultations on draft by Algeria, Austria, Benin, Botswana, Cape Verde, Central African Republic, Chad, China, Comoros, Guinea-Bissau, Kenya, Lebanon, Lesotho, Liberia, Mauritania, Sri Lanka, Sudan, Swaziland, Tunisia, United States, Yemen and Zambia (A/C.2/40/L.68); agenda item 85 (d).

Meeting numbers. GA 40th session: 2nd Committee 35-37, 39, 40, 44, 49; plenary 120.

Technical co-operation among developing countries

In his annual report for 1985,[11] the Administrator said that considerable progress was registered during the year in operating and expanding the TCDC Information Referral System (INRES), which had launched its computerized inquiry service in 1984.[12] By the end of 1985, the INRES data bank contained information on more than 2,400 institutions in 101 developing countries. INRES processed 460 queries from 76 developing countries and international organizations, with each search resulting in the referral of about 20 to 50 developing-country institutions to would-be users in other developing countries.

In order to put INRES data to more effective use, the UNDP Special Unit for TCDC began reviewing projects at the formulation stage in order to identify institutions in other developing countries with the potential to assist in their implementation. In each of 45 selected developing countries, between 50 and 100 institutions were referred to resident representatives for review with host Governments and executing agencies to pinpoint sources of expertise or training relevant to 160 projects. The Special Unit continued to assist various action-oriented TCDC activities in developing countries and, by the end of 1985, 203 such activities at a cost of some $1.6 million had been supported: 49 in Africa; 26 in Asia and the Pacific; 16 in the Arab States; 9 in Europe; and 103 in Latin America and the Caribbean. The number of countries using TCDC modalities in implementing their IPF-financed projects increased from 17 to 19, with the umbrella project approach—under which multiple TCDC activities were covered by a single project—remaining the preferred modality.

Action by the Committee on TCDC. The fourth session of the High-level Committee on the Review of Technical Co-operation among Developing Countries was held in New York from 28 May to 3 June and on 5 June 1985.[13]

The Committee had before it a report[14] by the Administrator on progress in implementing the tasks entrusted to the United Nations development system by the 1978 Buenos Aires Plan of Action for Promoting and Implementing TCDC.[15] The report, which covered the period 1 November 1982 to 31 October 1984, contained information from 22 United Nations agencies and organizations on their activities in promoting TCDC and on the number of activities and financial support they provided for operational TCDC activities. Twelve of the organizations reported 197 TCDC promotional activities at some $28.4 million in expenditure. Support for 253 activities of a TCDC operational nature involved $24.1 million.

In a general assessment of experience over the reporting period, the Administrator stated that financial support for TCDC was rather evenly divided between promotional and operational activities. Promotional efforts were concentrated heavily on strengthening institutions and centres with TCDC potential and on linking bodies together in networks and associations. Less support had been required for identifying or formulating individual operational projects as the networks became fully operational and self-sustaining.

Financial constraints were cited as an obstacle to expanding support for TCDC activities. Main sources of finance had been agencies' regular and field programme budgets (39 per cent), UNDP funds (33 per cent) and funds-in-trust and other funds provided by Governments, mainly developed countries (28 per cent).

The Administrator noted that 12 of the 22 respondents had reported providing some $52.6 million for TCDC activities during the biennium, comparable to that of the previous biennium. Closer co-operative arrangements between NGOs and enterprises in different countries should be given more emphasis. Some progress had been made in that area in relation to women's organizations, co-operatives and other grass-roots developmental bodies and private enterprises. Some developing countries were slow in increasing their budget allocations for promoting and supporting TCDC and progress in using country IPFs for TCDC had also been slow. It was suggested that the Committee might wish to receive a short report assessing TCDC activities and information on those of the system.

An addendum to the Administrator's report contained chapters on maximization of use of capacities of developing countries and the problem of the "brain drain".

On 5 June, the Committee adopted eight decisions. By one,[16] it urged the United Nations development system to implement fully its decisions on TCDC to attain the goals of the Buenos Aires Plan of Action.[15] It called on United Nations organizations to identify more clearly the TCDC dimension in their projects, invited them to consider earmarking more resources for such projects and to make increasing use of equipment, services, experts and consultants available in developing countries, reviewing procurement policies in that regard. The Secretary-General was requested to increase United Nations procurement from those countries by disseminating information on their procurement potential and on procurement practices in the system. The UNDP Administrator was requested to report in 1986 on implementation of the decision and on obstacles faced. The Committee encourged TOKTEN as a useful experiment, and asked the Administrator to include a review and evaluation of it in a comprehensive progress report on the Buenos Aires Plan of Action to be submitted in 1987.

In another decision,[17] the Committee invited developing countries: to strengthen their focal points for TCDC with a view to promoting their TCDC activities in accordance with the 1978 Plan of Action; to review, analyse and transmit information on their TCDC activities annually, preferably by 31 January of the following year, to the Special Unit for TCDC, for preparation of the Administrator's report; to utilize opportunities for TCDC provided by the multilateral institutions set up by developing countries themselves; to make available information on their procurement potential; and to take full advantage of possibilities for financing TCDC activities under UNDP IPFs for the fourth programming cycle. The Council invited developed countries to continue supporting the Buenos Aires Plan of Action, applying the same annual reporting procedure for the Special Unit as the developing countries; their submission would be incorporated into the Committee's 1987 progress report.

By another decision,[18] the Committee recommended that the UNDP Governing Council allocate a specified amount on a continued and reliable basis for the fourth programming cycle to meet the increasing needs for promoting action-oriented TCDC activities, and requested the Administrator to report to its 1987 session on progress in implementing the interregional action-oriented TCDC project. By a further decision,[19] the Committee approved the provisional agenda for that session.

Other Committee decisions dealt with co-operative exchange of skills, staffing of the Special Unit for TCDC, TCDC activities under IPFs and use of UNDP Special Programme Resources for promoting TCDC.

UNDP Council action. In June,[20] the UNDP Governing Council took note of the decisions of the High-level Committee and approved the allocation of $1.5 million from Special Programme Resources for the promotion of action-oriented technical co-operation activities among developing countries.

On 29 June, the Council adopted a decision[21] on the integration of issues relevant to women into promotional and operational activities for TCDC (see Chapter XIX of this section).

Other action. On 25 July, by **decision 1985/186**, the Economic and Social Council took note of the report of the High-level Committee, on the recommendation of its Third (Programme and Co-ordination) Committee.

In September 1985, the Secretary-General submitted to the General Assembly a report[22] on economic co-operation among developing countries (ECDC) and TCDC (see p. 427), and to the April-June session of the Committee for Programme and Co-ordination a report[23] on the cross-organizational programme analysis of the activities of the United Nations system in ECDC/TCDC (see p. 426).

In a report[24] on liquidation of the United Nations Emergency Operation Trust Fund (see p. 481), the Secretary-General stated that $5,872,009 from the remaining balance of that Fund had been made available to the Trust Fund for Economic and Technical Co-operation among Developing Countries.

JIU report. In September, the Secretary-General submitted to the General Assembly a JIU report[25] on United Nations development system support to the implementation of the Buenos Aires Plan of Action on TCDC.

JIU stated that, although the Plan of Action had been unanimously endorsed throughout the system, support for TCDC had been uneven. There was insufficient grasp of the TCDC concept and of what made it distinct from "traditional" technical co-operation, or of the distinction between promotional TCDC activities (aimed at strengthening developing countries' capacities to initiate, organize and manage TCDC projects—i.e. workshops, study tours, seminars and training, on which emphasis had heretofore been placed) and operational TCDC activities (involving the actual sharing and exchange of technical resources and skills between two or more developing countries, which had so far received only limited support). While UNDP guidelines properly emphasized the primary role of Governments of developing countries with respect to TCDC projects, they omitted to spell out the supportive catalytic role expected from United Nations organizations in accordance with the recommendations of the Plan of Action. The traditionalist mentality on project delivery and the urge to protect vested interests of technical co-operation constituencies within and

outside the system represented a major obstacle to the Plan of Action's implementation and to the effective use of the growing capabilities of developing countries. The lucrative scale of expert remuneration under the traditional system was also a disincentive to applying TCDC techniques, since conditions of service for traditionally recruited experts were far more rewarding that those offered by Governments for TCDC experts. Despite those difficulties, field experience demonstrated that the TCDC concept was a viable and sound method of project delivery.

JIU offered recommendations that: (1) the Buenos Aires Plan of Action should be considered a binding legislative framework for TCDC activities, and governing bodies should address mandates and reporting and accountability requirements for ECDC and TCDC separately and at least every two years consider their organization's TCDC activities as a separate agenda item; (2) in supporting TCDC activities, the United Nations development system should be guided by the three main characteristics of typical TCDC projects—an agreement between two or more developing-country Governments participating in an activity and highlighting specific TCDC techniques to be employed, government execution arrangements with active United Nations participation in project initiation but whose role was limited to identifying solutions, bringing parties together and providing elements not available under TCDC arrangements, and limited United Nations financial support of financing foreign exchange components, such as travel expenses outside the host country or the cost of foreign equipment; (3) the TCDC focal points should be strengthened and the staffing strength of the Special Unit for TCDC should be upgraded; (4) UNDP country, regional, interregional and global programming should be given enhanced TCDC orientation and system-supported institutions should be used increasingly as executing agents of intercountry activities; and (5) no less than 10 per cent of technical co-operation resources should be earmarked for TCDC activities, and UNDP should review its 10 per cent limit on country IPFs for TCDC.

ACC felt that the report was particularly relevant because of its clear and concise summary of the status of mandates and concepts of the system's approach to TCDC, and because the assessment of TCDC and the report's recommendations had already resulted in a useful dialogue on TCDC within the system. Commenting on specific recommendations, ACC said it was in agreement with the thrust of recommendation 1 and noted that many agencies were already following the proposed course of action. The proposals in recommendation 2 were also acceptable. It endorsed recommendation 3, but noted that UNDP was constrained by the need to maintain zero growth in its staffing level. Addressing recommendation 4, ACC felt the most appropriate stage for considering TCDC modalities was during project formulation, rather than during the country programming exercise. As to recommendation 5, ACC felt that isolating TCDC into a separate subprogramme in the budget would be counterproductive to the need to integrate TCDC concepts with all the system's activities, and that the setting of financial quotas for specific activities would be undesirable.

In October,[26] ACC approved its comments[27] on the report.

GENERAL ASSEMBLY ACTION

On 17 December, on the recommendation of the Second Committee, the General Assembly adopted **resolution 40/196**, without vote.

Technical co-operation among developing countries
The General Assembly,

Recalling its resolutions 3201(S-VI) and 3202(S-VI) of 1 May 1974, containing the Declaration and the Programme of Action on the Establishment of a New International Economic Order, 3281(XXIX) of 12 December 1974, containing the Charter of Economic Rights and Duties of States, and 3362(S-VII) of 16 September 1975 on development and international economic co-operation,

Recalling also its resolution 35/56 of 5 December 1980, the annex to which contains the International Development Strategy for the Third United Nations Development Decade,

Recalling further its resolution 33/134 of 19 December 1978, in which it endorsed the Buenos Aires Plan of Action for Promoting and Implementing Technical Co-operation among Developing Countries, and its resolutions 34/117 of 14 December 1979 and 35/202 of 16 December 1980 on technical co-operation among developing countries,

Reaffirming that developing countries have the primary responsibility for promoting technical co-operation among themselves, that developed countries and the United Nations system should assist and support such activities, and that in addition the United Nations system should play a prominent role as promoter and catalyst of technical co-operation among developing countries, in accordance with the Buenos Aires Plan of Action,

Taking note of the report of the Secretary-General on economic and technical co-operation among developing countries,

Having considered the report of the High-level Committee on the Review of Technical Co-operation among Developing Countries,

Taking note with appreciation of the relevant decisions of the Governing Council of the United Nations Development Programme,

Taking note of the report of the Joint Inspection Unit on United Nations development system support to the implementation of the Buenos Aires Plan of Action and the comments of the Administrative Committee on Co-ordination thereon,

1. *Endorses* the decisions of the High-level Committee on the Review of Technical Co-operation among Developing Countries;

2. *Invites* the Governing Council of the United Nations Development Programme to give adequate and timely attention, preferably during its special session to be held from 19 to 22 February 1986, to relevant decisions of the High-level Committee, including decision 4/7 of 5 June 1985;

3. *Recognizes* the necessity for programmes of technical co-operation among developing countries to be fully integrated into the operational activities for development of the United Nations system;

4. *Takes note* of the recommendations of the Joint Inspection Unit on United Nations development system support to the implementation of the Buenos Aires Plan of Action for Promoting and Implementing Technical Co-operation among Developing Countries;

5. *Requests* the organizations of the United Nations system to take the necessary action, in their respective fields of activity, to ensure the implementation of the decisions of the High-level Committee;

6. *Requests* the Secretary-General to report to the General Assembly at its forty-second session on the implementation of the present resolution.

General Assembly resolution 40/196

17 December 1985   Meeting 119   Adopted without vote

Approved by Second Committee (A/40/989/Add.5) without vote, 9 December (meeting 49); draft by Vice-Chairman (A/C.2/40/L.116), based on informal consultations on draft by Yugoslavia, for Group of 77 (A/C.2/40/L.86); agenda item 84 *(e)*.
Meeting numbers. GA 40th session: 2nd Committee 45, 49; plenary 119.

Allocation from Special Programme Resources

In an April report[28] to the High-Level Committee on TCDC, the UNDP Administrator gave an account of the utilization of funds from Special Programme Resources for action-oriented promotional activities for TCDC during 1983-1985. He stated that, following the Governing Council's allocation in 1983 of $600,000,[29] he had approved an interregional project on promotion of action-oriented TCDC activities, with the following objectives: to provide direct support at the intercountry level through training and exchange of expertise and to promote the voluntary sharing and exchange of technical resources, skills and capacities through action-oriented TCDC activities; and to provide direct support to all developing countries and territories in strengthening their TCDC capacities and potentials. To accommodate the requests for assistance, the Council in 1984 approved a further allocation of $800,000.[12]

As at 15 February 1985, 133 action-oriented TCDC activities estimated at $1.28 million had been or were being financed. By region, 34 activities costing $649,500 were in Africa: 22, costing $173,500, were in Asia and the Pacific; 15, costing $75,500, were in the Arab States; 57, costing $328,900, were in Latin America and the Caribbean; and 5, costing $47,800, were in Europe. By component, $651,000 was requested for experts' services, $611,700 for training and $12,500 for equipment. Sectorally, the bulk of resources was utilized in agriculture, forestry and fisheries, general development issues, policy and planning, natural resources, transport and communications, and industry, while lesser resources were channelled into health, education, and international trade and development finance. Lesser amounts were used in science and technology, culture, social conditions and equity, human settlements and employment.

In addition to the UNDP contribution, which represented mainly the cost of airfare and/or partial or full daily subsistence and stipend, the project mobilized additional resources of some $4.2 million in cash and in kind from the co-operating countries.

The Administrator concluded that the project proved that, once the bottle-neck of scarce foreign exchange for travel, subsistence and equipment had been overcome, the developing countries were willing to contribute human resources, institutions, infrastructure and training to strengthen co-operation among themselves.

Other experiences gained from the project suggested that: UNDP had been able to mobilize resources in the form of expertise and training institutions to further the cause of TCDC; the appropriateness and cost-effectiveness of programming UNDP resources using TCDC in technical assistance programmes was viable; experts and trainees, exchanging experiences in developing countries with similar problems and aspirations, were also acquiring international experience while transferring their skills to the recipient countries; training under TCDC was likely to assist in stemming the brain-drain phenomenon; and the overall outcome of exchanging experts and training nationals among developing countries was a form of human resources facility.

By a 5 June decision,[30] the High-level Committee expressed concern that, without additional resources for the interregional project, UNDP promotion of action-oriented activities in support of TCDC for the remaining years of the 1982-1986 third programming cycle would be discontinued. It invited the UNDP Governing Council to consider making available up to $1.5 million to continue funding the project, including the possibility of increasing the interregional IPF by drawing from uncommitted Special Programme Resources. It requested the Administrator to report in 1987 on progress achieved in implementing the interregional project.

By a June decision[20] (see p. 490), the Governing Council approved the $1.5 million allocation as suggested by the High-level Committee.

Use of country IPFs for TCDC

At its special meeting on preparations for the fourth programming cycle (New York, 19-22 February 1985), the UNDP Governing Council had before it a report by the Administrator on the possibility of introducing greater flexibility in the use of country IPFs for TCDC activities. The report had been submitted to the Council in 1984[12] but was not reviewed at that time. The Council decided[31] to refer the matter to the May/June session of the High-level Committee on TCDC.

Transmitting his 1984 report to the High-level Committee in March,[32] the Administrator drew attention to two points: the consistency in the Committee's and the Council's position on placing the primary responsibility on the developing countries themselves for financing TCDC activities, with country IPFs being considered as a catalyst and supplementary contribution only; and the conflict between those positions and the Committee's 1983 request[33] that the Council allow country IPFs to cover fully the local currency expenditure on TCDC projects financed from those resources. A similar conflict had emerged regarding reimbursement of certain local costs associated with services and materials.

On 5 June,[34] the High-level Committee expressed concern that reduced IPFs during the third programming cycle had hampered UNDP's potential contribution to TCDC. It invited the Administrator to keep under review the existing procedures in order to guarantee optimal use of IPFs for TCDC activities during the fourth cycle, recommending that the greatest possible share of resources from IPFs in that cycle be devoted to TCDC projects in keeping with the Buenos Aires Plan of Action. The Administrator was asked to report to the Committee in 1987 on implementation.

Staffing of a Special Unit for TCDC

In an April note[35] to the High-level Committee on TCDC, the Administrator stated that, subsequent to a 1984 Governing Council request,[36] he had reviewed the staffing level of UNDP's Special Unit for TCDC in the context of the 1986-1987 budget. He had concluded that the essential staff was available in the Unit and did not recommend an increase in its staffing level for 1986-1987.

On 5 June,[37] the Committee reiterated its belief that strengthening the Special Unit would allow it to discharge fully its functions in support of TCDC and requested the Administrator to provide adequate staffing support to the Unit and report thereon to the UNDP Governing Council in 1986.

Skilled workers

In accordance with a 1984 UNCTAD Trade and Development Board (TDB) resolution,[36] a Meeting of Governmental Experts on Cooperative Exchange of Skills among Developing Countries was held at Geneva from 6 to 15 February 1985.[38]

The Meeting reaffirmed the important role of TCDC, particularly the exchange of skills among developing countries as an instrument for promoting ECDC and their general development. Governments were invited to promote the exchange of skills by providing technical assistance. Governments of developing countries were invited to integrate the development of skills in the context of national policy and ensure balance between training and development needs. The Meeting recommended that UNCTAD should contribute to implementing and strengthening a multisectoral information network on TCDC as an instrument for developing countries to exchange information on skills needed and available. It welcomed a proposal in an UNCTAD secretariat report[39] on creating or strengthening institutional linkages between national decision-making units concerned with education and manpower planning, and recommended that the UNCTAD Secretary-General be asked to support TCDC activities for establishing and strengthening national mechanisms for TCDC, including the co-operative exchange of skills. The Meeting also stressed the usefulness of a proposal relating to on-the-job training and the exchange of information on education activities which could be undertaken jointly by developing countries, welcomed a proposal calling for promotion of national, regional or interregional developing country–owned and –controlled consultancy agencies and private consulting offices, and stressed their usefulness for strengthening links between specialized agencies in developing countries and co-ordinating their activities. Governments of developing countries were invited to participate at all levels in making arrangements for the exchange of skills and it was recommended that the UNCTAD Secretary-General be asked to strengthen their technical and technological capacity by providing technical assistance. The Meeting recommended that a study be undertaken on the role of TCDC, particularly the exchange of skills in the transfer of technology, and that Governments and UNCTAD should support the accelerated development of the national skills of LDCs and enable them to benefit fully from the exchange of skills. TDB was invited to transmit the Meeting's report to the May/June session of the High-level Committee on TCDC.

On 29 March,[40] TDB endorsed the Meeting's agreed conclusions and recommendations and transmitted them to the High-level Committee. On 5 June,[41] the Committee expressed its satisfaction concerning those conclusions and recommendations and invited TDB to request the UNCTAD Secretary-General to prepare, in co-operation with United Nations organizations and particularly UNDP, the study mentioned therein for submission to the Committee's 1987 session.

REFERENCES

[1]DP/1986/48 & Add.1-3. [2]E/1985/32 (dec. 85/21). [3]YUN 1984, p. 454. [4]YUN 1977, p. 438, GA res. 32/197, 20 Dec. 1977. [5]DP/1986/49 & Add.1. [6]E/1985/32 (dec. 85/22). [7]YUN 1984, p. 456. [8]*Ibid.*, p. 458. [9]YUN 1970, p. 356, GA res. 2659(XXV), 7 Dec. 1970. [10]E/1985/32 (dec. 85/23). [11]DP/1986/11 & Add.1-6. [12]YUN 1984, p. 459. [13]A/40/39. [14]TCDC/4/2 & Corr.1 & Add.1. [15]YUN 1978, p. 467. [16]A/40/39 (dec. 4/1). [17]*Ibid.* (dec. 4/5). [18]*Ibid.* (dec. 4/7). [19]*Ibid.* (dec. 4/8). [20]E/1985/32 (dec. 85/26). [21]*Ibid.* (dec. 85/27). [22]A/40/581. [23]E/1985/53. [24]A/40/740. [25]A/40/656. [26]ACC/1985/DEC/16-29 (dec. 1985/27). [27]A/40/656/Add.1. [28]TCDC/4/6. [29]YUN 1983, p. 486. [30]A/40/39 (dec. 4/6). [31]E/1985/32 (dec. 85/1). [32]TCDC/4/9. [33]YUN 1983, p. 485. [34]A/40/39 (dec. 4/4). [35]TCDC/4/8. [36]YUN 1984, p. 460. [37]A/40/39 (dec. 4/3). [38]TD/B/1043. [39]TD/B/943 & Corr.1 & Add.1. [40]A/40/15, vol. I (dec. 306(XXX)). [41]A/40/39 (dec. 4/2).

UN Capital Development Fund

In his report on the United Nations Capital Development Fund for 1985,[1] the UNDP Administrator described project commitments and expenditures and programme developments, and provided information on the Fund's financial status.

In 1985, total UNCDF project approvals were $37.4 million: $29.2 million for 22 new projects and $8.2 million for grant increases in existing projects. At the beginning of the year, there were 182 ongoing projects totalling $122.4 million in outstanding commitments against general resources. The projects, located in 42 countries, were designed to be implemented by national executing agencies. Project expenditures in 1985 were $27 million and an additional $2 million was disbursed against trust fund and cost-sharing arrangements.

During the year, the Fund directed 54.5 per cent of its resources to LDCs in Africa, 30.6 per cent to Asian countries and the remaining 14.9 per cent to countries in Latin America or the Middle East. It continued to concentrate its assistance in rural areas, with projects in agriculture accounting for 43.4 per cent of total approvals.

The Fund continued to seek complementarity between capital assistance provided by it and other sources of financing, especially UNDP. Of 193 UNCDF-funded projects under way at the end of 1985, 82 were receiving technical assistance financed by UNDP through IPF resources, SMF/LDCs and UNSO. Joint-financing arrangements with bilateral donors or other multilateral agencies accounted for 24 of those projects, as well as a further 21 UNCDF-funded projects.

Contributions received during 1985 against pledges amounted to $21.4 million and an additional $500,000 was received against pledges from 1984

UNCDF PROJECT EXPENDITURES, 1985
(as at 31 December 1985; in thousands of US dollars)

Country	Amount*	Country	Amount*	Country	Amount*
Angola	303	Gambia	406	Sao Tome and Principe	35
Bangladesh	599	Guinea	209	Senegal	48
Benin	1,268	Guinea-Bissau	1,075	Sierra Leone	500
Bhutan	356	Haiti	380	Somalia	1,163
Bolivia	40	Lao People's		Sudan	28
Botswana	67	Democratic Republic	477	Togo	98
Burkina Faso	693	Lesotho	299	Tonga	114
Burundi	832	Malawi	586	Uganda	1,629
Cape Verde	306	Maldives	90	United Republic of Tanzania	1,267
Central African Republic	146	Mali	1,582	Viet Nam	456
Chad	158	Mauritania	202	Yemen	116
Comoros	452	Nepal	995		
Democratic Yemen	427	Nicaragua	521	Subtotal	22,758
Djibouti	33	Niger	272		
Equatorial Guinea	44	Rwanda	1,279	*Regional Africa*	(3)
Ethiopia	2,787	Samoa	420	Total	22,755†

*Figures are estimates not necessarily corresponding to audited figures given in the text.
†Excluding sub-trust fund expenditures of $1,842,000 and $82,000 from other charges.
SOURCE: DP/1986/11/Add.6.

CONTRIBUTIONS TO UNCDF, 1985 AND 1986
(as at 31 December 1985; in US dollar equivalent)

Country	1985 payment	1986 pledge	Country	1985 payment	1986 pledge
Algeria	37,000	37,000	Lesotho	1,276	958
Argentina	35,000	35,000	Malawi	5,484	5,146
Austria	13,636	16,949	Maldives	600	600
Bangladesh	4,441	4,617	Mauritius	816	—
Belgium	247,170	294,118	Nepal	1,250	1,250
Benin	—	500	Netherlands	3,549,159	4,142,857
Bhutan	3,460	1,990	Norway	3,017,607	3,973,510
Botswana	5,814	4,878	Sao Tome and Principe	450	—
Burkina Faso	1,053	—	Senegal	—	10,410
Burundi	—	2,632	Somalia	—	263
Cameroon	799	1,305	Sweden	3,818,182	5,228,758
China	—	94,044	Switzerland	1,841,304	2,153,110
Cuba	21,368	22,060	Tunisia	4,568	3,139
Cyprus	1,000	1,000	Turkey	140,918	75,000
Democratic Yemen	3,542	2,130	United Republic of Tanzania	1,194	1,194
Denmark	2,178,218	219,780	United States	1,988,000	—
Egypt	(21,166)	—	Viet Nam	1,000	—
Finland	956,522	1,284,404	Yemen	—	3,320
France	113,765	261,438	Yugoslavia	55,762	50,167
Greece	10,000	10,000	Zaire	—	500
Italy	2,332,362	2,448,980	Zimbabwe	3,728	3,636
Japan	1,500,000				
Lao People's Democratic Republic	1,500	1,500	Total	21,876,782	20,398,143

SOURCE: A/41/5/Add.1.

and prior years. Following the Pledging Conference in November 1985 (see p. 463), contributions to UNCDF general resources for 1986 were expected to total $24 million.

UNCDF continued to fund some projects through various joint-financing modalities. New joint-financing agreements for $4 million were concluded, bringing the total of such arrangements since 1981 to $32.1 million. During the year, $7.6 million was paid in against trust fund and cost-sharing arrangements. Two of the

trust funds concluded by UNCDF in 1985 had no conditions attached on procurement: Norway agreed to a $1 million untied trust fund for a project in Nicaragua, and Switzerland provided a $1 million fund for one in Bhutan. UNCDF also negotiated one new tied trust fund (conditioned on procurement in the donor country) of $700,000 from Belgium for a project in Mali.

In 1985, UNCDF concluded a cost-sharing agreement with the United States Child Survival Fund under which that Fund would provide

$660,000 for two projects in Somalia. It also obtained $700,000 for a portion of two water-development projects in drought-affected areas of Africa from the UNDP Trust Fund for Developing Countries Afflicted by Drought, Famine and Malnutrition.

UNDP Council action. The Administrator submitted a report on 1984 UNCDF activities[2] to the UNDP Governing Council in 1985. On 28 June,[3] the Council took note of it, noted the increase in project approvals made possible by joint-financing arrangements and noted especially the increased programme delivery. The Council agreed with the activation for a trial period of three years of a concessional loan facility for revenue-producing projects, requested the Administrator to keep it informed of such loan operations and their impact on the Fund's portfolio and resources, and decided to review the issue in 1988. It noted the emphasis being given to project evaluation activities and feedback to improve project quality, and considered it important that UNCDF views were presented in the round-table process. The Council called on Member States to provide adequate resources to allow the Fund to implement SNPA for LDCs, and encouraged UNCDF to make its programme better known to donors and potential donors.

REFERENCES

[1]DP/1986/50. [2]YUN 1984, p. 461. [3]E/1985/32 (dec. 85/24).

Chapter III

Economic assistance, disasters and emergency relief

The United Nations system continued in 1985 to provide special assistance to countries facing severe economic and financial difficulties and/or requiring aid for reconstruction, rehabilitation and development. Those problems were frequently aggravated by natural or man-made disasters. Many of those countries were among the least developed in the world and some were also geographically handicapped—that is, land-locked or island countries. Of particular concern was the critical economic situation in Africa, compounded by a prolonged drought, accelerating desertification and other disasters. The Secretary-General added his concern for the vast majority of the 30 million Africans who had suffered from an unprecedented drought, and assured that the United Nations would continue to play a central role in international humanitarian co-operation (see p. 11).

To deal more effectively with the situation, the Secretary-General established a United Nations Office for Emergency Operations in Africa (OEOA)—effective 1 January 1985—to co-ordinate and provide assistance to help ensure a broad yet concentrated international response to the continuing drought-related crisis in sub-Saharan Africa. In March, he convened, at Geneva, an International Conference on the Emergency Situation in Africa, followed by consultations in order to direct the general commitments made at the Conference to specific needs of individual countries.

Addressing the economic crisis in sub-Saharan Africa, the Committee for Development Planning (CDP), which met in New York in April 1985 (see p. 410), called on the international community to supplement the policy reform efforts of African Governments in order to rehabilitate seriously affected African countries and resume their economic growth. The Committee stressed that international assistance was crucial and urgent in sub-Saharan Africa.

The Economic and Social Council, in a July resolution on the critical economic situation in Africa, appealed to the international community for assistance (1985/80), and the General Assembly in December called for more effective special programmes of economic assistance (resolution 40/236), and dealt with the African crisis (40/40) and special economic assistance to Benin (40/222), Cape Verde (40/226), the Central African Republic (40/217), Chad (40/218), the Comoros

(40/223), Djibouti (40/227), Equatorial Guinea (40/216), the Gambia (40/224), Guinea (40/235), Guinea-Bissau (40/225), Mauritania (40/219), Mozambique (40/232) and Sierra Leone (40/220).

Economic assistance also continued for several countries in other regions. The Assembly adopted a decision on special assistance to Bolivia (40/452), and, by resolution 40/215, it requested the Secretary-General to continue mobilizing assistance to Democratic Yemen to help it overcome the damage caused by floods in 1981 and 1982. By resolution 40/234, it urged continued contributions to the reconstruction and development of Nicaragua. Following a conclusion by CDP, the Assembly, by resolution 40/233, included Vanuatu in the list of least developed countries (LDCs). To assess economic assistance needs, the Secretary-General arranged during the year for review missions to Haiti, Kiribati and Tuvalu.

The United Nations system, particularly the Office of the United Nations Disaster Relief Coordinator (UNDRO), continued to respond to emergency situations arising from natural disasters. UNDRO also promoted the study, prevention, control and prediction of natural disasters and provided Governments with assistance in pre-disaster planning. The Assembly called for assistance to the drought-stricken areas of Djibouti, Ethiopia, Kenya, Somalia, the Sudan and Uganda (resolution 40/221), as well as to Ethiopia alone (40/228) following a request by the Economic and Social Council (resolution 1985/1) that the Secretary-General continue efforts to mobilize resources for the drought victims there.

In the wake of cyclones in Bangladesh, the Assembly, in resolution 40/231, requested assistance to the country. Continuation of efforts to mitigate the damage caused previously by cyclones and floods in Madagascar was requested by Assembly resolution 40/230. Two earthquakes in September 1985 caused considerable destruction in Mexico, and the Assembly, by resolution 40/1, called for generous international relief. Assistance to Colombia, which suffered severe damage from a volcanic eruption in November, was called for by resolution 40/13.

Emergency humanitarian assistance and assistance for reconstruction and development continued to be provided to Lebanon, despite the lack of security which hampered United Nations efforts. Both the Council and the Assembly (resolutions 1985/56 and 40/229, respectively) called for continued assistance.

Topics related to this chapter. Development policy and international economic co-operation: special economic areas—developing countries. Regional economic and social activities: Africa—economic and social trends; Asia and the Pacific—typhoons. Food: food aid. Environment: Africa—environmental monitoring; desertification and drought control. Children—emergency relief. Refugees and displaced persons.

Economic assistance

In 1985, the United Nations continued to mobilize special economic assistance for a number of countries identified by the General Assembly as facing severe economic situations. While each country presented a unique set of problems, all of them shared a number of factors. Of the 24 countries benefiting from special economic assistance programmes, 15 were among the least developed, 7 were island developing countries, 5 were landlocked and 4 were also among those most affected by the drought-induced emergency in Africa. All countries had fragile economies which had been subjected to the external shocks experienced by developing countries in recent years. National economic policies had in some cases contributed to their precarious situation, but it appeared that the Governments concerned were fully aware of the need to review prior policies and make necessary changes.

The Assembly, in 1983 and 1984, had requested the Secretary-General to report in 1985 on the economic situation and on the progress made in organizing and implementing special economic assistance programmes. Each of the countries concerned was asked whether it would wish the report to be based on the findings of a review mission that would visit the country or whether it would prefer to provide information that would constitute the basis of a brief interim report to the Assembly. Sixteen of the countries concerned chose the latter; as of 12 August 1985, 14 had provided such information. Accordingly, the Secretary-General submitted in September[1] summary reports for Benin, Cape Verde, the Central African Republic, the Comoros, Djibouti, the Gambia, Ghana, Guinea, Lesotho, Mozambique, Sao Tome and Principe, Sierra Leone, Swaziland and Vanuatu, addressing the main developments in the respective economies and the status of the special economic assistance programmes.

In another September report,[2] the Secretary-General described United Nations assistance to 23

countries: Benin, Cape Verde, Central African Republic, Chad, Comoros, Djibouti, Equatorial Guinea, Gambia, Ghana, Guinea, Guinea-Bissau, Haiti, Kiribati, Lesotho, Liberia, Madagascar, Mozambique, Sao Tome and Principe, Sierra Leone, Swaziland, Tuvalu, Uganda, Vanuatu. The report was based on information from United Nations bodies that had provided technical and other forms of assistance (Department of Technical Co-operation for Development (DTCD), OEOA, UNCTAD, UNDP, UNDRO, UNFPA, UNHCR, UNICEF, UNIDO, WFC, WFP) and from specialized agencies such as ILO, FAO, UNESCO, the World Bank, IMF, ICAO, UPU, ITU, WMO, IMO, WIPO and IFAD. (See below for details on individual countries.)

Summaries of special economic assistance for various countries in 1985 were also given in later reports by the Secretary-General.[3, 4]

GENERAL ASSEMBLY ACTION

On 17 December 1985, the General Assembly, acting on the recommendation of the Second (Economic and Financial) Committee, adopted **resolution 40/236** without vote.

Special programmes of economic assistance
The General Assembly,
Reaffirming the need for the international community to respond to the needs of countries facing special economic problems,
Recognizing that, owing to their diverse nature, those problems require special and prompt responses,
Recognizing also the need for an adequate response by the international community to the specific measures identified in the special programmes of economic assistance, as well as the need for enhanced co-ordination within the United Nations system in that regard,
Taking into account the views expressed in the Second Committee on the rationalization of the work of the Committee,
1. *Requests* the Secretary-General to report to the General Assembly at its forty-first session, through the Economic and Social Council at its second regular session of 1986, on ways and means of enhancing efficiency and effectiveness in the implementation of decisions taken by intergovernmental bodies regarding the special programmes of economic assistance, including the mobilization of the resources necessary for the implementation of those programmes, taking into account available information provided by Governments and the related activities undertaken by the bodies of the United Nations system;
2. *Also requests* the Secretary-General to include in his report recommendations regarding the consideration of special programmes of economic assistance in the appropriate intergovernmental bodies.

General Assembly resolution 40/236

17 December 1985   Meeting 120   Adopted without vote

Approved by Second Committee (A/40/1043) without vote, 9 December (meeting 49); draft by Chairman (A/C.2/40/L.106), based on informal consultations; agenda item 87.

Meeting numbers. GA 40th session: 2nd Committee 31-34, 41-45, 47-49; plenary 120.

Africa and the critical economic situation

In 1985, the economic and social situation in Africa deteriorated. The devastating drought which had plagued some countries for the preceding three years persisted, even though it had abated to some degree in parts of western and southern Africa and in limited areas of eastern Africa. Population displacement became alarming. Out of the 150 million people living in drought-stricken countries, some 30 million were seriously affected, and it was estimated that over 10 million had had to abandon homes and lands in search of food, water and pasture for their herds.

In response to a 1984 resolution by which the General Assembly adopted the Declaration on the Critical Economic Situation in Africa,[5] the Secretary-General submitted a report in June/July 1985[6] which gave an overview of the situation with the objective of proposing action that would facilitate long-term development and economic growth in Africa and, at the same time, pursue effective action for relief and recovery, both for humanitarian and economic reasons.

The Secretary-General pointed out that since 1980 most African countries had sought to address the economic problems confronting them, and over the past three years had made some adjustments, often supported by financial assistance from IMF and the World Bank. To deal with their current accounts deficit, most countries in sub-Saharan Africa had had to curtail the import of capital goods, raw materials and spare parts, and some had had to devalue their currency. In many cases, arrangements were sought through the "Paris Club" (an informal group of officials from 16 industrialized nations who meet regularly on overdue loans owed by developing countries) to reschedule foreign debts by consolidating short-term liabilities and reducing debt service, which resulted in a decline of the current account deficit in Africa from $25 billion in 1981-1982 to $11 billion in 1984. Domestic efforts were also undertaken to restore internal balance, but all those measures to restore internal and external balances were carried out at a high economic and social cost and resulted in a decline in growth.

To provide the necessary financial assistance to African countries undertaking policy reforms, the World Bank established a special facility for Africa which, with initial resources of $1.1 billion, became operational in July 1985. Other funding organizations of the United Nations system also took action to support development efforts of concerned countries, and many donor countries increased their development assistance to sub-Saharan Africa. None the less, there had been a reduction in net financial flows to that area over the previous three years due to a drop in private capital flows

and repayment of loans, which weighed on the capacity of most African countries to finance their development.

The Secretary-General stressed that the coming five years would be crucial for sub-Saharan Africa which was faced with the double challenge of economic problems and severe drought; he felt that there was a need for more vigorous action to consolidate the response to the emergency situation and to relaunch the development process. Although there might appear to be a conflict between measures to deal with the emergency and the need to concentrate on activities for relaunching economic development, the two kinds of action were closely interrelated. The emergency was a result of both drought and economic hardships; dealing with it consisted not only of responding to famine problems but also of providing the foundation for resuming economic progress. The emergency situation was not a problem with solely a humanitarian dimension; the path towards resumption of growth and development passed through the solution of emergency problems.

The task of improving Africa's economic performance and building a better future for Africans was the prime responsibility of the Governments and peoples of Africa, the Secretary-General concluded, but the international community had the responsibility to help; it had committed itself to that task by adopting the 1984 Declaration on the Critical Economic Situation in Africa.

In June 1985,[7] the Secretary-General transmitted to the Economic and Social Council a Second Special Memorandum by the Economic Commission for Africa (ECA) Conference of Ministers on International Action for Relaunching the Initiative for Long-term Development and Economic Growth in Africa. The Memorandum was adopted by ECA at its twentieth session (Addis Ababa, Ethiopia, 25-29 April) (see p. 625). A first Special Memorandum on Africa's Economic and Social Crisis had been submitted in 1984.[8] The Ministers responsible for economic development and planning addressed for the second year the current crisis and its causes; the long-term measures for structural changes in the African economy along the lines of the Lagos Plan of Action for the Implementation of the Monrovia Strategy for the Economic Development of Africa and the Final Act of Lagos, both adopted by the Assembly of Heads of State and Government of the Organization of African Unity (OAU) in 1980;[9] and international action for development and economic growth in Africa, supported by regional and subregional action.

An International Conference on the Emergency Situation in Africa (Geneva, 11 March 1985)[10] was convened by the Secretary-General, who had launched an appeal for an additional $1.5 billion needed urgently to meet the requirements of 20 drought-stricken African countries—Angola, Botswana, Burkina Faso, Burundi, Cape Verde, Chad, Ethiopia, Kenya, Lesotho, Mali, Mauritania, Mozambique, the Niger, Rwanda, Senegal, Somalia, the Sudan, the United Republic of Tanzania, Zambia and Zimbabwe. Those requirements had been assessed by OEOA, which stated that the survival of some 30 million Africans was at risk.

The Conference affirmed the commitment of the international community to co-operate with and support the Governments and peoples of Africa affected by drought and famine. Priority continued to be accorded to identifying urgent human needs, monitoring and bringing them to the donors' attention, mobilizing additional resources and ensuring the delivery of emergency assistance on a timely basis in collaboration with the affected countries.

The Conference also affirmed the important role of the United Nations in addressing the emergency, co-ordinated through OEOA. It emphasized that concrete measures had to be taken to alleviate the emergency in order to facilitate the recovery, rehabilitation and long-term development of affected countries.

In a report on the activities of UNDRO[11] between 1 January 1984 and 31 December 1985, the Secretary-General reviewed efforts made to strengthen the capacity of the United Nations system to respond to disasters. He recalled that, during 1984-1985, UNDRO had been involved in some 98 disaster situations, a large number of which were major disasters calling for concerted relief programmes, within the framework of which bilateral donors, the United Nations system and non-governmental organizations (NGOs) provided assistance. Among those major disasters were tropical storms in Bangladesh, Madagascar, Mozambique and the Philippines; armed conflict in Lebanon (see p. 294); displaced persons in western Africa (see p. 1004); epidemics in Mali and Somalia; earthquakes in Mexico; a volcanic eruption in Colombia; and drought in Chad, Ethiopia, Mali, Mauritania, Mozambique, the Niger and the Sudan (see p. 805).

Referring to the unprecedented famine in Africa, the Secretary-General said that either partial or complete absence of seasonal rainfall, together with the deterioration of land through years of overgrazing and insufficient capital for agricultural inputs, had resulted in widespread crop failure and food shortages. Even before the establishment of OEOA, UNDRO was involved in 8 of the 20 drought-stricken African countries at their request. Massive humanitarian efforts were called for and put into operation by the world community, resulting in a major increase in contribu-

tions to UNDRO which amounted to over $2,149 million in 1984-1985, as compared to $700 million and $370 million in 1982-1983 and 1980-1981, respectively.

The twenty-first ordinary session of the Assembly of Heads of State and Government of OAU (Addis Ababa, 18-20 July) adopted three declarations and a series of resolutions which were transmitted to the Secretary-General by Madagascar on 18 September 1985.[12] By one declaration, the Assembly called on developed donor countries to implement urgently the 1984 General Assembly resolution on the critical economic situation in Africa,[5] asking for total or partial conversion of official development assistance (ODA) debts into grants. Annexed to the declaration was Africa's Priority Programme for Economic Recovery 1986-1990. The Assembly also called for an international conference to provide a forum for international creditors and African borrowers to discuss Africa's external debt with a view to arriving at emergency, short-, medium- and long-term solutions. By a resolution on the African economic situation, the OAU Assembly requested a special session of the General Assembly and asked the Secretary-General, in co-operation with the ECA Executive Secretary, to initiate the necessary preparations. In another resolution, on its Special Emergency Assistance Fund for Drought and Famine in Africa, the OAU Assembly expressed appreciation to member States and non-African Governments which had made or pledged contributions and appealed to others for generous contributions.

The critical situation in Africa was also discussed by the Joint United Nations Information Committee (JUNIC), responsible for co-ordinating information activities in the United Nations system (twelfth session, Rome, Italy, 16-19 April 1985).[13] JUNIC, reviewing efforts made to present the situation, agreed that certain themes should guide future work so that coherence of action was ensured. Information materials should present the emergency situation in the context of Africa's overall development needs, which, in turn, should be presented within the context of the international economic situation. JUNIC also stressed the importance of encouraging information which would provide a balance by emphasizing Africa's own self-help actions and presenting Africa's views on the nature of the crisis and possible solutions.

ACC and CPC activities. Reviewing the critical economic situation in Africa, the Administrative Committee on Co-ordination (ACC), at its April 1985 session,[14] adopted a decision[15] expressing appreciation to the Secretary-General for his initiative and actions taken for relief efforts in Africa through OEOA, and expressing support for all efforts by United Nations organizations. It reaffirmed its commitment towards a concerted response commensurate with the magnitude and gravity of the problem in respect of both its emergency and longer-term aspects. It decided that a drafting group under the chairmanship of Maurice F. Strong be convened on 24 April to prepare an outline of a background paper on the effectiveness and co-ordination of United Nations organs and agencies with regard to relief efforts in Africa.

The Consultative Committee on Substantive Questions (Operational Activities) of ACC discussed at its October session[16] the links between emergency relief, rehabilitation and longer-term development activities, with emphasis on the food crisis in Africa. The Committee was addressed by Mr. Strong in his capacity as Chairman of the Working Group on Emergency-Development Linkages set up by the Director-General for Development and International Economic Co-operation. It agreed that the Secretariat would submit a report in 1986 for possible recommendations to ACC on specific aspects of the Africa crisis.

At their July 1985 Joint Meetings (see Chapter XXIV of this section), the Committee for Programme and Co-ordination and ACC also discussed the effectiveness and co-ordination of United Nations organs and agencies in relief efforts in Africa.

UNDP activities. The Administrator of the United Nations Development Programme (UNDP), in his report for 1985,[17] described steps taken by UNDP to alleviate the crisis in Africa. As social and economic conditions remained critical and affected the recovery pace of many African countries, UNDP continued supporting immediate relief and rehabilitation measures while at the same time assisting Governments to address the issues underlying the crisis and sustain more durable, comprehensive and integrated solutions.

Aid co-ordination and specific inter-agency collaborative activities with other United Nations agencies—especially WFP, UNICEF and UNFPA—were among UNDP priority undertakings. Aware that co-ordinated action by all development partners was essential in assisting countries of the region, UNDP initiated in 1985 several measures to link the funds it programmed in sub-Saharan Africa to other resource flows, among them: supplementary guidelines for the preparation of new country programmes; support for activities aimed at building national capabilities in co-ordinating technical and capital assistance; and actions to evolve new mechanisms by which Governments could assess, identify and rank their most important technical co-operation requirements. Factors contributing to low rates of resource commitment and programme implementation in some 15 countries were reviewed to identify remedial measures.

In 1985, the United Nations Volunteers (UNV) programme launched its Domestic Development Services (DDS) and youth activities in Africa with the fielding of volunteers in Rwanda and Zambia and the endorsement of UNV-executed regional DDS and youth projects by 14 African countries. In addition, through a special allocation of $1.5 million, volunteers were recruited to enable the 24 countries most affected by the drought to participate in emergency relief aid operations mounted by both bilateral and multilateral donor agencies.

The UNDP Administrator, in a March 1985 report,[18] described programmes of assistance to 10 countries. In 1984, the General Assembly had invited UNDP and other United Nations organizations to bring to the attention of their governing bodies the specific needs of Benin,[19] Cape Verde,[20] the Central African Republic,[21] the Gambia,[22] Guinea,[23] Guinea-Bissau,[24] Lesotho,[25] Sierra Leone,[26] Uganda[27] and Vanuatu.[28]

In a report on implementation of selected country programmes,[29] the Administrator provided an overview of UNDP activities in Africa. As of December 1985, there were 45 approved assistance programmes in 42 countries, including special programmes to Namibia and national liberation movements recognized by OAU, and an intercountry (regional) programme. For 1982-1986, some $1.2 billion of programmable resources was available through UNDP, in addition to other resources through funds under the Administrator—the United Nations Capital Development Fund, the United Nations Sudano-Sahelian Office and the United Nations Financing System for Science and Technology for Development. Of the total programmable resources for that period, $1.1 billion (91 per cent) had been committed to approved projects by the end of 1985.

The Trust Fund to Combat Poverty and Hunger in Africa was established by the Administrator in November 1984. The Fund, which in 1985 totalled $569,180, was to be utilized to finance technical and/or capital assistance projects designed to combat poverty and hunger in Africa. By the end of 1985, the Fund had an excess of expenditures over income of $19,581.

In a report on United Nations technical co-operation activities for 1985,[30] the Secretary-General said the African crisis called for national efforts as well as international assistance on an unprecedented scale; several 1984 and 1985 UNDP Governing Council decisions on Africa provided the frame for special efforts by DTCD through projects executed on behalf of its funding partners or supported from Regular Programme resources.

To strengthen the response to the crisis in Africa, the Governing Council, on 29 June 1985,[31] encouraged the Administrator, in conjunction with recipient Governments and executing agencies, to orient UNDP programmes for the greatest impact on the priority needs of African countries, including assistance for the reinforcement of management capacities and the establishment of national strategies for rehabilitation, reconstruction and development. The Council requested the Administrator to ensure that all UNDP programmes played a supportive role *vis-à-vis* OEOA and supported his proposals for strengthening the capacity of field offices in sub-Saharan Africa.

Communications. Saudi Arabia, in communications of 31 January[32] and 7 June 1985[33] to the Secretary-General, outlined the assistance it was providing to drought-stricken African countries. On 17 May,[34] India transmitted a Plan of Action to meet the critical economic situation in Africa, adopted at an Extraordinary Ministerial Meeting of the Co-ordinating Bureau of Non-Aligned Countries on the question of Namibia (New Delhi, 19-21 April), and two reports of the Action Committee of the Co-ordinating Bureau on the situation in Africa. Both Senegal, on 22 July 1985,[35] and Madagascar, on 18 September,[12] forwarded the Declaration on the Economic Situation in Africa adopted by the OAU Assembly of Heads of State and Government in July (see p. 499). The Federal Republic of Germany, on 3 October,[36] submitted a report by a group of experts on aid to Africa, appointed by the "Bonn Economic Summit" (Bonn, 2-4 May) of the heads of State of seven industrialized nations (Canada, France, Federal Republic of Germany, Italy, Japan, United Kingdom, United States); the report was issued at Bonn on 30 September after its adoption in New York on 25 September by the Summit participants.

On 17 October,[37] Egypt, as Chairman of the Group of 77, transmitted a declaration of the Ministers for Foreign Affairs of the Group of 77 (ninth annual meeting, New York, 2-4 October), who expressed grave concern at the continuing deterioration of the economic and social situation in Africa, further exacerbated by famine, drought and desertification, which endangered the lives of millions of Africans.

On 5 November,[38] Kuwait forwarded a document on its contributions to a number of African countries since January 1984. The USSR transmitted on 20 November 1985[39] a document describing its economic co-operation with developing countries, including aid to African countries.

ECONOMIC AND SOCIAL COUNCIL ACTION

By a 21 June letter[40] to members of the Economic and Social Council, the Council President set out a possible framework for discussions to be held at the Council's July session regarding a review of the immediate and longer-term aspects of the critical economic situation in Africa and the follow-up of the response by the international community and the United Nations system.

On 26 July, the Council adopted **resolution 1985/80** by consensus.

Critical economic situation in Africa

The Economic and Social Council,

Recalling the Declaration on the Critical Economic Situation in Africa adopted by the General Assembly in its resolution 39/29 of 3 December 1984,

Gravely concerned at the continuing critical economic situation in Africa, which has been exacerbated by the unfavourable international economic environment,

Recognizing the impact of drought and desertification, and environmental and demographic factors on the critical economic situation,

Expressing its appreciation of the efforts and generous contributions of the international community—Governments, organizations of the United Nations system, the general public, intergovernmental and non-governmental organizations—in response to the emergency situation,

Welcoming all the initiatives undertaken by the Secretary-General in this connection,

Welcoming the resolve of African heads of State and Government and peoples to address in a coherent manner the economic and social problems facing the continent,

Welcoming in this context the declaration and resolutions on the economic situation in Africa, as well as on the Special Emergency Assistance Fund for Drought and Famine in Africa, adopted by the Assembly of Heads of State and Government of the Organization of African Unity at its twenty-first ordinary session, held at Addis Ababa from 18 to 20 July 1985, which was devoted essentially to economic issues,

Gravely concerned also at the continuing negative effects of the destabilization policy of South Africa on the economies of southern African States,

Considering that the responsibility for the development of Africa lies primarily with African Governments and peoples,

Stressing, however, the need for the international community as a whole to continue to give priority attention to the critical economic situation in Africa and, to that end, to increase its concrete support in addressing the immediate as well as the medium-term and long-term needs for the rehabilitation and sustained development of the African economies,

Concerned that, despite recent efforts undertaken by the donor community, the combined effects of a stagnation, over the past years, of overall official development assistance, higher levels of debt servicing and depressed commodity export earnings have led African countries to experience a negative flow of financial resources,

1. *Welcomes* the adoption of the priority programme for the economic recovery of Africa (1986-1990) by the Assembly of Heads of State and Government of the Organization of African Unity at its twenty-first ordinary session;

2. *Welcomes also* the high priority that African Governments individually and collectively have accorded to the improvement of the critical food situation in the

continent and to the rehabilitation and development of the food and agricultural sector;

3. *Strongly urges* the international community to intensify its efforts in order to increase substantially the flow of resources—particularly of a concessional character—to Africa and to address in a comprehensive manner the critical problem arising from negative or insufficient flows of resources due, *inter alia*, to the heavy debt burden and to the depressed commodity export earnings of African countries;

4. *Appeals* to the international community, in particular donor countries, to extend all necessary support to African regional and subregional institutions engaged in the process of implementation of economic recovery programmes and economic self-reliance for their member countries;

5. *Recognizes*, moreover, the urgent need to support the rehabilitation and development of the industrial, manufacturing, transport and communications sectors, as well as improved scientific and technological capabilities, health services and human resources development, which are crucial for a sustained and integrated process of development of African countries;

6. *Stresses* that the international community, while continuing to address the African emergency, should give greater focus to supporting the medium-term and longer-term development actions without which no lasting solutions to the emergency situation can be found;

7. *Appreciates and encourages* efforts by African Governments to ensure the effectiveness of development assistance by overseeing effective co-ordination and, to this end, stresses the importance of close co-ordination by the United Nations system of assistance provided under its auspices;

8. *Appeals* to donor countries, international organizations and non-governmental organizations to consider generous contributions to the Special Emergency Assistance Fund for Drought and Famine in Africa to enable affected countries to resist these calamities effectively;

9. *Stresses* the urgent need for concerted international measures aimed at mitigating the adverse economic effects on the economies of southern African States of destabilizing acts of aggression by South Africa;

10. *Fully recognizes* the importance of Africa's debt problems and, in this context, takes note of the appeal launched by African heads of State and Government calling for the urgent convening of an international conference on Africa's external debt;

11. *Takes note with interest* of the decision by the Assembly of Heads of State and Government of the Organization of African Unity by which it requested the convening as soon as possible of a special session of the General Assembly to consider the critical economic situation in Africa;

12. *Requests* the Secretary-General to report on the implementation of the present resolution, through the Economic and Social Council, to the General Assembly at its forty-first session.

Economic and Social Council resolution 1985/80

26 July 1985   Meeting 52   Adopted by consensus

Draft by Vice-President (E/1985/L.58)—based on informal consultations on draft by Algeria, for African Group, and Syrian Arab Republic (E/1985/L.53)—orally revised, withdrawn by Vice-President and reintroduced by Algeria for African Group; agenda item 4.

Meeting numbers. ESC 46-52.

In requesting a vote on paragraph 10 as orally revised, the United States said it wished to study further a number of points. Following the United States request, the Vice-President withdrew the draft resolution, stating that he had no other choice as it seemed not to be possible for the Council to adopt the text by consensus. Algeria resubmitted the draft on behalf of the African Group, saying that if a vote were requested, it would propose that paragraph 10 be replaced by a paragraph of the original draft, by which the Council would have invited the international community to consider favourably the appeal by the African heads of State and Government for the urgent convening of an international conference on Africa's external debt. Algeria stated that the text carried the political message of the recent OAU summit, renewing the expression of Africa's will to assume responsibility for its own destiny and of faith in international co-operation.

In the view of the United States, that stated objective would not be served by the proposed course of action; if the original paragraph were incorporated, the United States would be obliged to vote against it, an action which would rule out the possibility of the Council adopting the text as a whole by consensus.

Speaking also on behalf of the members of the European Economic Community (EEC), Luxembourg expressed the hope that the African Group would give very careful consideration to that point; a return to the original wording would be an obstacle to consensus. Canada saw a danger that the very attempt to achieve a consensus might result in some countries being forced to take up positions they would have preferred to avoid. The Federal Republic of Germany stressed that most of the countries that had difficulties in accepting paragraph 10 were the principal contributors of assistance to Africa.

Following a proposal by India and Pakistan, the Council decided, by 31 votes to 5, with 5 abstentions, to take no action on the United States request for a vote.

Following adoption of the resolution, the United States said the procedure adopted to prevent action on its request was a dangerous precedent; if a vote had been taken on paragraph 10, it would have abstained and it wished its vote against the proposal by India and Pakistan to be considered equivalent to such an abstention. It was convinced that the only productive method of dealing with debt problems was to ensure that they were given careful and expert consideration on a case-by-case basis in such appropriate forums as the Interim Committee of the International Monetary Fund (IMF), the Development Committees of the Fund and the World Bank, and the Paris Club.

Luxembourg declared on behalf of the EEC members that if there had been a vote on paragraph 10, they would not have been able to agree with its content; a constructive dialogue had developed in the competent international bodies, particularly IMF, the World Bank and the Paris Club, where strategies were being worked out for dealing with the debt problems of the African and other developing countries. A similar position was held by Canada.

Expressing its support for paragraph 10, the USSR said it had always co-operated constructively in the solution of the problems facing the peoples of Africa; the socialist countries would continue to provide every assistance to that end. China believed that adoption of the text would enable the momentum to be maintained in providing assistance to Africa.

Also on 26 July, on an oral proposal by its President, the Council, by **decision 1985/203**, took note of the Secretary-General's report on the critical economic situation in Africa[6] and the ECA Second Special Memorandum on International Action for Relaunching the Initiative for Long-term Development and Economic Growth in Africa.[7]

GENERAL ASSEMBLY ACTION

On 2 December, the Assembly adopted without vote **resolution 40/40.**

Critical economic situation in Africa
The General Assembly,

Recalling its resolution 39/29 of 3 December 1984, and the Declaration on the Critical Economic Situation in Africa annexed thereto,

Noting the Declaration on the Economic Situation in Africa and Africa's Priority Programme for Economic Recovery 1986-1990, annexed thereto, adopted by the Assembly of Heads of State and Government of the Organization of African Unity at its twenty-first ordinary session, held at Addis Ababa from 18 to 20 July 1985,

Noting further Economic and Social Council resolution 1985/80 of 26 July 1985,

Having considered the report of the Secretary-General on the critical economic situation in Africa,

Expressing its appreciation to the international community and the United Nations system for their positive response to the emergency situation in Africa and recognizing the need to continue to extend that support to fulfil unmet emergency needs,

Commending the Secretary-General for his continuing efforts in ensuring that the emergency assistance by the United Nations system and the international community is delivered to affected countries in a concerted manner,

Gravely concerned that, even if the current emergency situation is alleviated, the structural economic problems will continue to cripple African economies and might precipitate recurrent crises,

Alarmed by the forecasts that indicate for Africa stagnant or negative growth rates, declining per capita food production, escalating debt burden and the serious effects of drought and desertification,

Recognizing fully the need to focus attention and efforts on the rehabilitation and medium-term and long-term development problems of the African countries,

1. *Takes note* of the Declaration on the Economic Situation in Africa and Africa's Priority Programme for Economic Recovery 1986-1990, adopted by the Assembly of Heads of State and Government of the Organization of African Unity at its twenty-first session;

2. *Decides* to convene a special session of the General Assembly at the ministerial level to consider in depth the critical economic situation in Africa, to be held in New York from 27 to 31 May 1986;

3. *Decides also* that the special session of the General Assembly on the critical economic situation in Africa should focus, in a comprehensive and integrated manner, on the rehabilitation and medium-term and long-term development problems and challenges facing African countries, with a view to promoting and adopting action-oriented and concerted measures;

4. *Decides further* to establish a Preparatory Committee of the Whole for the Special Session of the General Assembly on the Critical Economic Situation in Africa that would undertake the necessary preparations to ensure the success of the session;

5. *Requests* the Secretary-General to take appropriate measures to facilitate the work of the Preparatory Committee;

6. *Further requests* the Secretary-General, in close co-operation with the relevant organs, organizations and bodies of the United Nations system, to submit to the Preparatory Committee and to the General Assembly at its special session reports containing action-oriented proposals to deal with the critical economic situation in Africa, particularly the major developmental areas identified in the Declaration on the Critical Economic Situation in Africa annexed to Assembly resolution 39/29, taking fully into account the priorities set by the Assembly of Heads of State and Government of the Organization of African Unity at its twenty-first session;

7. *Commends* the international community for its valuable support and positive response to the emergency situation in Africa, and appeals to it to continue these efforts and to give its support for the full implementation of resolution 39/29 and the Declaration annexed thereto;

8. *Commends* the Secretary-General for his valuable efforts in ensuring the co-ordinated response of the United Nations system and the international community to the emergency situation in Africa;

9. *Requests* the Secretary-General, in implementing resolution 39/29 and the Declaration annexed thereto, to continue to monitor the emergency situation, to assess the needs and responses, to maintain the system's capacity to respond to the continuing emergency in the affected countries, and to report to the General Assembly at its forty-first session.

General Assembly resolution 40/40

2 December 1985   Meeting 98   Adopted without vote

50-nation draft (A/40/L.15/Rev.1); agenda item 30.

Sponsors: Algeria, Angola, Benin, Botswana, Burkina Faso, Burundi, Cameroon, Cape Verde, Central African Republic, Chad, Comoros, Congo, Djibouti, Egypt, Equatorial Guinea, Ethiopia, Gabon, Gambia, Ghana, Guinea, Guinea-Bissau, Ivory Coast, Kenya, Lesotho, Liberia, Libyan Arab Jamahiriya, Madagascar, Malawi, Mali, Mauritania, Mauritius, Morocco, Mozambique, Niger, Nigeria, Rwanda, Sao Tome and Principe, Senegal, Seychelles, Sierra Leone, Somalia, Sudan, Swaziland, Togo, Tunisia, Uganda, United Republic of Tanzania, Zaire, Zambia, Zimbabwe.

Financial implications. 5th Committee, A/40/939; S-G, A/C.5/40/55 & Corr.1.
Meeting numbers. GA 40th session: 5th Committee 47; plenary 66, 67, 83, 98.

Introducing the text in the Assembly, Japan, which had been designated on 19 November as co-ordinator for the agenda item on the critical economic situation in Africa, said the unofficial consultations it had conducted had led to what it believed was a consensus.

In a statement of position following adoption of the resolution, Bulgaria, speaking also for the Byelorussian SSR, Czechoslovakia, the German Democratic Republic, Hungary, Mongolia, Poland, the Ukrainian SSR and the USSR, said they were deeply concerned at the further deterioration of the economic situation of Africa, despite the efforts made by the African countries themselves and assistance by the international community; the solution to Africa's economic and social problems was inextricably linked with the general problem of restructuring international economic relations on a just basis. Burundi, speaking on behalf of the African Group, stated again the commitment of the African heads of State or Government to take responsibility for Africa's development; they hoped that the text's adoption would establish a new basis for international co-operation and that the Assembly's special session would be crowned with success.

In separate action, the Assembly, in **resolution 40/20** on co-operation between the United Nations and OAU, called on member States and regional and international organizations to implement the 1984 Declaration on the Critical Economic Situation in Africa[5] and to give their maximum support to Africa's Priority Programme for Economic Recovery 1986-1990. The Assembly expressed its appreciation to the Secretary-General for his timely initiative in alerting the international community to the critical situation in Africa and welcomed the measures he had taken to facilitate international co-operation to assist Africa, particularly through the establishment of OEOA. It commended OEOA for its efforts to sensitize the international community, co-ordinate the community's efforts and monitor the situation in affected African countries. The Assembly also expressed its appreciation to UNDP, UNDRO, WFP, FAO, WHO, UNICEF and UNHCR, as well as the World Bank and other international financial institutions, for their assistance in dealing with the African emergency situation. It requested the Secretary-General to keep OAU informed periodically of the response of the international community to special economic assistance programmes, and called for generous assistance on a long-term basis to all African States affected by the economic crisis.

By **resolution 40/242**, the Assembly, noting with satisfaction that the project on the issue of special postage stamps on the social and economic crisis in Africa was well under way, decided to place half of the revenue from those stamps at the Secretary-General's disposal for implementation of objectives as detailed in the 1984 Declaration on the Critical Economic Situation in Africa.

By a 1985 recommendation of the Committee on Information, as approved by Assembly **resolution 40/164 A**, the Secretary-General was requested to ensure that the United Nations Department of Public Information did its utmost in bringing to the attention of the international community the real dimensions of the plight of the African people and the tremendous efforts of the African countries, with a view to increasing its contribution to alleviating that plight.

In **resolution 40/181**, the Assembly emphasized the need for priority attention at all levels to the timely delivery of food to those requiring assistance, especially in African countries. It appealed to the international community to provide urgently logistic agricultural inputs and fulfil the unmet aid needs of the drought- and famine-affected African countries.

In **resolution 40/100**, the Assembly noted with deep concern that the economic and social situation in Africa continued to be critical and had been exacerbated by world recession, famine, drought and desertification. It called for full implementation of its 1984 resolution on the critical economic situation in Africa.

In **resolution 40/158**, the Assembly urged all States to implement urgently measures to ameliorate the situation.

Benin

The Secretary-General, in his September 1985 report on special economic assistance programmes,[1] provided information on such assistance to Benin, as requested by the General Assembly in 1984.[19]

In 1985, Benin, classified by the United Nations as least developed, continued to suffer as a result of the international economic crisis which forced it to reduce its current and investment budget. In addition, following the expulsion of aliens from Nigeria in May, approximately 200,000 people passed through Benin. This displacement, on a massive scale and concentrated within a few days, resulted in road and plantation damage and had ecological consequences; some of the people who reached Benin's frontiers had no means of support or possessions, and a number of them remained illegally in the country causing serious food, shelter and logistic problems. In April, Benin appealed to international organizations for emergency aid. The encroachment of the desert, which had a negative impact on agricultural production and resulted in an immediate food deficit, remained a permanent concern; in that context, the Government organized a national seminar on desertification, at the end of which 1 June was declared "Tree Day".

In his report on United Nations assistance to individual countries,[2] the Secretary-General described the activities of United Nations bodies and agencies in Benin. In a later report,[4] he gave an account of such activities in 1985, when external assistance to Benin totalled over $100 million. Of that amount, $46.5 million was for technical assistance, of which the contribution of the United Nations system, including UNDP, was $10.5 million. Assistance for capital investment, provided by 15 donor agencies, totalled $53.5 million.

Addressing the Assembly's Second Committee on 12 November, Benin said its problems had been compounded by the damage caused by unusually heavy rain and floods in 1985, which had destroyed agricultural production and infrastructure and endangered lives; it appealed to the international community to mobilize additional resources for projects under the special economic assistance programme. It also welcomed the decision announced by the Federal Republic of Germany and the Netherlands to write off the debts of LDCs and hoped that other countries would follow their example.

GENERAL ASSEMBLY ACTION

On 17 December, the General Assembly, on the recommendation of the Second Committee, adopted **resolution 40/222** without vote.

Special economic assistance to Benin
The General Assembly,

Recalling its resolutions 35/88 of 5 December 1980, 36/208 of 17 December 1981, 37/151 of 17 December 1982, 38/210 of 20 December 1983 and 39/185 of 17 December 1984, in which it appealed to the international community to provide effective and continuous financial, material and technical assistance to Benin so as to help that country overcome its financial and economic difficulties,

Recalling also Security Council resolution 419(1977) of 24 November 1977, in which the Council appealed to all States and all appropriate international organizations, including the United Nations and its specialized agencies, to assist Benin,

Having heard the statement made by the representative of Benin on 12 November 1985, in which he described the serious economic and financial situation of his country and the action taken by his Government to tackle these difficulties,

Deeply concerned, nevertheless, by the fact that Benin continues to experience serious economic and financial difficulties, characterized by a marked balance-of-payments disequilibrium, heavy burdens of its external debt and a lack of the resources necessary for the implementation of its planned economic and social development programme,

Having considered the summary report of the Secretary-General,

Noting that the persisting unfavourable climatic conditions in the coastal and northern regions of Benin are still leading to losses in agriculture and livestock production, and threatening the lives of the population,

Considering that Benin is one of the least developed countries,

1. *Expresses its appreciation* to the Secretary-General for the steps he has taken to organize and mobilize support for the international programme of economic assistance to Benin;

2. *Takes note* of the summary report of the Secretary-General;

3. *Expresses its appreciation* for the assistance already provided or pledged to Benin by Member States, United Nations bodies and regional, interregional and intergovernmental organizations;

4. *Notes with satisfaction* the efforts undertaken by the Government of Benin to make structural adjustments in the economy of the country and to take other measures designed to help it to overcome its economic and financial difficulties;

5. *Notes with concern* that the assistance given to Benin has not been sufficient to cover all the country's pressing needs and that additional resources are still essential for the implementation of its recovery, reconstruction and development programme;

6. *Appeals* to Member States, international financial institutions, the specialized agencies and other United Nations bodies to respond generously and urgently to the needs of Benin;

7. *Urges* donor countries to provide financial assistance to help Benin to bear the counterpart costs of projects receiving external assistance, bearing in mind that it is one of the least developed countries;

8. *Appeals* to the international community to make contributions to the special account for Benin opened by the Secretary-General at United Nations Headquarters, for subsequent transfer to Benin;

9. *Invites* the programmes, specialized agencies and other organizations of the United Nations system—in particular the United Nations Development Programme, the United Nations Children's Fund, the World Food Programme, the Food and Agriculture Organization of the United Nations, the World Health Organization, the World Bank and the International Fund for Agricultural Development:

(a) To maintain and expand their programmes of assistance to Benin;

(b) To co-operate closely with the Secretary-General in organizing and promoting the special programme of economic assistance to Benin;

(c) To bring to the attention of their governing bodies, for their urgent consideration, the special needs of Benin;

(d) To report to the Secretary-General by 15 July 1986 on the measures they have taken and the resources they have made available, as well as the decisions of their governing bodies on assistance to Benin;

10. *Requests* the Secretary-General:

(a) To continue his efforts to mobilize the necessary resources for implementing the projects of the special programme of economic assistance to Benin;

(b) To evaluate, in consultation with the Government, the economic situation in Benin, the most urgent needs of the country and the implementation of the special programme of economic assistance;

(c) To keep the situation in Benin under constant review, in close collaboration with the Government of Benin, the specialized agencies, regional and intergovernmental organizations and international financial institutions, and to apprise the Economic and Social Council, at its second regular session of 1986, of the status of assistance to Benin;

(d) To report on the implementation of the present resolution to the General Assembly at its forty-first session.

General Assembly resolution 40/222

17 December 1985	Meeting 120	Adopted without vote

Approved by Second Committee (A/40/1043) without vote, 4 December (meeting 47); 34-nation draft (A/C.2/40/L.58), orally amended by Secretary following informal consultations; agenda item 87.

Sponsors: Algeria, Bangladesh, Benin, Bolivia, Botswana, Burkina Faso, Cape Verde, Central African Republic, Comoros, Democratic Yemen, Djibouti, Egypt, Equatorial Guinea, Ethiopia, Guinea, Guinea-Bissau, Haiti, Lesotho, Liberia, Libyan Arab Jamahiriya, Madagascar, Mali, Mauritania, Mongolia, Mozambique, Nicaragua, Niger, Pakistan, Senegal, Togo, United Republic of Tanzania, Vanuatu, Viet Nam, Zaire.

Meeting numbers. GA 40th session: 2nd Committee 32, 42, 47; plenary 120.

Cape Verde

As requested by the General Assembly in 1984,[20] the Secretary-General reported in September 1985 on special economic assistance to Cape Verde.[1] In his report on United Nations assistance to individual countries,[2] he stated that, at the March 1985 Conference on the Emergency Situation in Africa, total unmet emergency needs for Cape Verde had been estimated at $9.9 million. At a country-specific meeting held at Dakar, Senegal, on 1 April, those estimates were updated to $15.4 million—food aid requirements, including transport, $4.1 million; basic agricultural pastoral inputs, $4.4 million; water projects, $1.8 million; essential health action, $1.2 million; and additional logistics inputs, $3.9 million.

GENERAL ASSEMBLY ACTION

On 17 December, the General Assembly, on the recommendation of the Second Committee, adopted **resolution 40/226** without vote.

Assistance to Cape Verde

The General Assembly,

Recalling its resolutions on assistance to Cape Verde, in particular its resolution 39/189 of 17 December 1984, in which the international community was requested to provide an appropriate level of resources for the implementation of the programme of assistance for Cape Verde as envisaged in the reports of the Secretary-General,

Recalling United Nations Conference on Trade and Development resolutions 142(VI) and 138(VI) of 2 July 1983 on the progress made in the implementation of the Substantial New Programme of Action for the 1980s for the Least Developed Countries, and on activities in the field of island developing countries,

Noting that Cape Verde is one of the least developed countries and a small archipelagic State, with a fragile and open economy, aggravated by endemic and severe drought,

Reiterating that increased substantial, continuous and predictable assistance from the international community is needed for the effective completion of the First National Development Plan (1982-1985), which is still being implemented,

Gravely concerned at the critical food situation in Cape Verde resulting from the failure of seasonal rains, the continuing recurrence of drought and the spreading desertification,

Recognizing the strenuous efforts deployed by the Government and people of Cape Verde in the process of the economic and social development of their country despite existing constraints,

1. *Takes note* of the summary report of the Secretary-General;

2. *Expresses its appreciation* to the Secretary-General for the efforts deployed in mobilizing resources for the implementation of the programme of assistance for Cape Verde;

3. *Expresses its gratitude* to States and to international, regional and interregional organizations and other intergovernmental organizations for their contribution to the programme of assistance for Cape Verde;

4. *Reaffirms* the need for all Governments and international organizations to implement their commitments undertaken within the framework of the Substantial New Programme of Action for the 1980s for the Least Developed Countries, particularly those undertaken at the round-table conference of Cape Verde's partners in development, held at Praia in June 1982;

5. *Urges* Governments and international, regional and interregional organizations and other intergovernmental organizations to extend and intensify substantially their assistance for the early implementation of the programme of assistance for Cape Verde;

6. *Invites* the international community, in particular donor countries, to take appropriate and urgent measures to support the effective completion of the First National Development Plan (1982-1985) of Cape Verde;

7. *Calls upon* the international community to continue to contribute generously to all appeals for food and fodder assistance made by the Government of Cape Verde, or on its behalf by the specialized agencies and other organizations of the United Nations system, to help it cope with the critical situation in the country;

8. *Once again draws the attention* of the international community to the special account established at United Nations Headquarters by the Secretary-General, in accordance with General Assembly resolution 32/99 of 13 December 1977, for the purpose of facilitating the channelling of contributions to Cape Verde;

9. *Invites* the organs, organizations and bodies of the United Nations system, in particular the United Nations Children's Fund, the United Nations Conference on Trade and Development, the United Nations Development Programme, the United Nations Fund for Population Activities, the World Food Programme, the Food and Agriculture Organization of the United Nations, the World Health Organization, the World Bank, the International Fund for Agricultural Development and the United Nations Industrial Development Organization:

(a) To maintain and expand their programmes of assistance for Cape Verde;

(b) To co-operate closely with the Secretary-General in organizing and carrying out the special programme of economic assistance for Cape Verde;

(c) To bring to the attention of their governing bodies, for urgent consideration, the special needs of Cape Verde;

(d) To report the measures they have taken and the resources they have made available, as well as the decisions of their governing bodies regarding assistance to Cape Verde, to the Secretary-General by 15 July 1986;

10. *Requests* the Secretary-General:

(a) To continue his efforts to mobilize the necessary resources for implementing the programme of development assistance for Cape Verde;

(b) To arrange for a review of the economic situation in Cape Verde, in consultation with the Government of Cape Verde, to report thereon to the Economic and Social Council at its second regular session of 1986, and to make a substantive report on the implementation of the special programme of economic assistance for Cape Verde to be considered by the General Assembly at its forty-first session.

General Assembly resolution 40/226

17 December 1985   Meeting 120   Adopted without vote

Approved by Second Committee (A/40/1043) without vote, 4 December (meeting 47); 39-nation draft (A/C.2/40/L.62), orally amended by Secretary following informal consultations; agenda item 87.
Sponsors: Afghanistan, Algeria, Argentina, Bangladesh, Benin, Brazil, Cameroon, Canada, Cape Verde, China, Comoros, Cuba, Dominican Republic, Egypt, Ghana, Guinea-Bissau, India, Iraq, Ivory Coast, Jamaica, Japan, Liberia, Madagascar, Mali, Mozambique, Niger, Pakistan, Peru, Portugal, Sao Tome and Principe, Senegal, Sudan, Sweden, Trinidad and Tobago, United Republic of Tanzania, United States, Vanuatu, Viet Nam, Zambia.
Meeting numbers. GA 40th session: 2nd Committee 42, 47; plenary 120.

Central African Republic

In his September 1985 report on special economic assistance,[1] the Secretary-General, pursuant to a 1984 General Assembly resolution,[21] provided information on the Central African Republic—a land-locked LDC. Effects of the drought from November 1982 to the end of May 1983 were still being felt, he said, and 1985 had been a year of precarious stabilization, with a continued need for external assistance.

Efforts continued to implement a 1982-1985 national action plan for economic recovery, which, in January 1986, would be followed by a five-year plan for economic and social development. Under the 1982-1985 action plan, the budgetary deficit of the country was reduced. Between 1981 and 1985, recurrent revenues increased at an average annual rate of 14.3 per cent while recurrent expenditures increased by only 6.4 per cent per year; as a result, the recurrent revenues represented 13.2 per cent and expenditures 12.6 per cent of the gross domestic product (GDP) in 1985, compared with 11 per cent and 15.7 per cent in 1980. Agriculture remained the principal economic activity, accounting for one third of GDP, which increased by 2.7 per cent over 1984.

Total United Nations assistance to the Central African Republic reached $30.5 million in 1985.

Acting on the recommendation of the Second Committee, the General Assembly adopted on 17 December **resolution 40/217** without vote.

Assistance for the reconstruction, rehabilitation and development of the Central African Republic

The General Assembly,

Recalling its resolution 35/87 of 5 December 1980, in which it affirmed the urgent need for international action to assist the Government of the Central African Republic in its efforts for reconstruction, rehabilitation and development of the country and invited the international community to provide sufficient resources to carry out the programme of assistance to the Central African Republic,

Recalling also its resolutions 36/206 of 17 December 1981, 37/145 of 17 December 1982, 38/211 of 20 December 1983 and 39/180 of 17 December 1984, in which it noted with concern that the assistance provided had not been adequate to meet the urgent needs of the country,

Recalling further its resolution 38/195 of 20 December 1983 on the implementation of the Substantial New Programme of Action for the 1980s for the Least Developed Countries,

Considering that the Central African Republic is landlocked and is classified as one of the least developed countries,

Taking note of the statement made before the General Assembly by the Head of the Delegation of the Central African Republic on 11 October 1985, in which he described the economic problems of concern to the Central African Republic and stated that, because of the lack of financial means, external aid continued to be essential to the country,

Also taking note of the statement made by the representative of the Central African Republic on 13 November 1985, according to which, despite an incipient economic recovery, his country continued to be faced with enormous difficulties in implementing its socio-economic development programmes,

Particularly concerned that the Government of the Central African Republic is unable to provide the population with adequate health, educational and other essential social and public services because of an acute shortage of financial and material resources,

Taking account of the losses suffered by the Central African economy following the great drought of 1982-1983,

Noting with satisfaction the considerable efforts exerted by the Government and people of the Central African Republic for national reconstruction, rehabilitation and development, despite the limitations confronting them,

Taking note of the summary report of the Secretary-General,

Also taking note of table 12 of the report of the Secretary-General, according to which substantial additional assistance for the special programme of economic assistance is needed to finance projects which have only been implemented in part and others for which finance has not yet been obtained, including new high-priority projects specified therein,

1. *Expresses its appreciation* to the Secretary-General for the efforts he has made to mobilize resources for car-

rying out the programme of assistance to the Central African Republic;

2. *Reiterates its appreciation* to States, international, regional and interregional organizations and other intergovernmental organizations for their contribution to the programme of assistance to the Central African Republic;

3. *Notes with concern*, however, that the assistance provided under this heading continues to fall far short of the country's urgent needs;

4. *Urgently draws the attention* of the international community to table 12 of the Secretary-General's report, which indicates the projects still in need of financing;

5. *Reiterates its appeal* to all States to contribute generously, through bilateral or multilateral channels, to the reconstruction, rehabilitation and development of the Central African Republic;

6. *Invites* the appropriate programmes and organizations of the United Nations system—in particular the United Nations Development Programme, the World Bank, the International Monetary Fund, the Food and Agriculture Organization of the United Nations, the International Fund for Agricultural Development, the World Food Programme, the World Health Organization, the United Nations Children's Fund, the United Nations Fund for Population Activities and the United Nations Industrial Development Organization—to maintain their programmes of assistance to the Central African Republic, to co-operate closely with the Secretary-General in his efforts to organize an effective international programme of assistance and to report periodically to him on the steps they have taken and the resources they have made available to help that country;

7. *Invites also* regional and interregional organizations and other intergovernmental and non-governmental organizations to give urgent consideration to the establishment of a programme of assistance to the Central African Republic or, where one is already in existence, to the expansion and considerable strengthening of that programme with a view to its implementation as soon as possible;

8. *Urges* all States and relevant United Nations bodies—in particular the United Nations Development Programme, the World Food Programme, the United Nations Children's Fund, the World Health Organization, the United Nations Fund for Population Activities and the United Nations Industrial Development Organization—to provide all possible assistance to help the Government of the Central African Republic to cope with the critical humanitarian needs of the population and to provide, as appropriate, food, medicines and essential equipment for schools and hospitals, as well as to meet the emergency needs of the population in the drought-stricken areas of the country;

9. *Invites* the United Nations Development Programme, the United Nations Children's Fund, the World Food Programme, the World Health Organization, the United Nations Industrial Development Organization, the Food and Agriculture Organization of the United Nations, the World Bank and the International Fund for Agricultural Development to bring to the attention of their governing bodies, for their consideration, the special needs of the Central African Republic and to report the decisions of those bodies to the Secretary-General by 15 July 1986;

10. *Again draws the attention* of the international community to the special account opened by the Secretary-General at United Nations Headquarters, in accordance with General Assembly resolution 35/87, for the purpose of facilitating the channelling of contributions to the Central African Republic;

11. *Requests* the Secretary-General:

(a) To continue his efforts to organize a special emergency assistance programme with regard to food and health, especially medicaments, vaccines, hospital equipment, generating sets for field hospitals, water pumps and food products in order to help the vulnerable population;

(b) To continue also his efforts to mobilize necessary resources for an effective programme of financial, technical and material assistance to the Central African Republic;

(c) To ensure that the necessary financial and budgetary arrangements are made to continue the organization of the international programme of assistance to the Central African Republic and the mobilization of that assistance;

(d) To keep the situation in the Central African Republic under constant review, to maintain close contact with Member States, specialized agencies, regional and other intergovernmental organizations and the international financial institutions concerned and to apprise the Economic and Social Council, at its second regular session of 1986, of the status of the special programme of economic assistance for the Central African Republic;

(e) To report on the progress made in the economic situation of the Central African Republic and in organizing and implementing the special programme of economic assistance for that country in time for the matter to be considered by the General Assembly at its forty-first session.

General Assembly resolution 40/217

17 December 1985   Meeting 120   Adopted without vote

Approved by Second Committee (A/40/1043) without vote, 4 December (meeting 47); 32-nation draft (A/C.2/40/L.53), orally amended by Secretary following informal consultations; agenda item 87.

Sponsors: Bangladesh, Benin, Cameroon, Cape Verde, Central African Republic, Chad, China, Comoros, Congo, Cyprus, Democratic Kampuchea, Djibouti, Dominican Republic, Equatorial Guinea, Gabon, Guinea, Guinea-Bissau, Haiti, Lesotho, Liberia, Madagascar, Mali, Mauritania, Morocco, Nicaragua, Panama, Thailand, Uganda, United States, Vanuatu, Zaire, Zambia.

Meeting numbers. GA 40th session: 2nd Committee 33, 42, 47; plenary 33, 120.

Chad

Economic recovery in Chad—a land-locked LDC with an annual per capita gross national product (GNP) estimated at $110 or less—continued to be slow as a result of the devastating effects of war and recurring droughts. The situation was further aggravated by the drop in world commodity prices, especially that of cotton (the country's key cash crop), ecological problems such as desertification, and the nation's limited capacity to absorb economic inputs.

In his report on United Nations assistance,[2] the Secretary-General dealt with Chad, as requested by the General Assembly in 1984.[41] He stated that at the March 1985 Conference on the Emergency Situation in Africa, OEOA had estimated that unmet emergency needs for Chad totalled $113.9 million. Those estimates were reduced to $53.9 million at a country-specific meeting held at Geneva on 14 March to meet the most urgent requirements—food aid, including transport, $39.8 million; basic agricultural/pastoral inputs, $4.2 million; health action, $7.9 million; and water projects, $2 million.[6] Although rainfall in 1985 was normal, and the consensus among donors was that the emergency situation was over, there was a persistent basic food need among the disadvantaged parts of the population. From November 1984 to October 1985, an estimated 215,000 metric tons of food aid were brought to Chad, of which one third was handled through WFP projects.

Net flows of ODA, as reported by the Organisation for Economic Co-operation and Development (OECD), grew from $115 million in 1984 to $182 million in 1985, reflecting the strong response of the international community to Chad's emergency needs.

At a donors' round-table conference (Geneva, 4 and 5 December 1985), the Chadian Government presented an interim plan for 1986-1988 which outlined nearly 200 projects. In overall financial terms, commitments (actual and projected) made at the conference totalled $485 million, exceeding by some 20 per cent the total needs as presented in the plan.

GENERAL ASSEMBLY ACTION

On 17 December 1985, the Assembly, on the recommendation of the Second Committee, adopted **resolution 40/218** without vote.

Special economic assistance to Chad

The General Assembly,

Recalling its resolution 39/195 of 17 December 1984 and its previous resolutions on assistance in the reconstruction, rehabilitation and development of Chad, emergency humanitarian assistance to Chad and special economic assistance to that country,

Having considered the reports of the Secretary-General on special economic assistance to Chad, relating, *inter alia*, to the economic and financial situation of Chad, the status of assistance provided for the rehabilitation and reconstruction of the country and the progress made in organizing and executing the programme of assistance for that country,

Concerned by the unprecedented drought which is wreaking havoc in Chad, compounding the food and health situation that is already precarious because of the war and thus compromising all the country's efforts at reconstruction,

Considering that the war and the drought have occasioned a massive displacement of population and created enormous social problems,

Taking note of the numerous appeals launched by the Government of Chad and governmental and non-governmental organizations regarding the gravity of the food and health situation in Chad,

Recognizing the need for emergency humanitarian assistance to Chad,

Also recognizing the need for assistance in the reconstruction and development of Chad,

Welcoming the conference of donors and contributors of funds held in early December 1985, in accordance with the arrangements agreed upon at the International Conference on Assistance to Chad, held in November 1982,

1. *Expresses its gratitude* to the States and governmental and non-governmental organizations that responded and are continuing to respond generously to the appeals of the Government of Chad and of the Secretary-General by furnishing assistance to Chad;

2. *Expresses its appreciation* to the Secretary-General for his efforts to make the international community aware of the difficulties of Chad and to mobilize assistance for that country;

3. *Renews the request* made to States, appropriate organizations and programmes of the United Nations system and international economic and financial institutions:

(a) To continue to provide the necessary humanitarian assistance to the people of Chad who have suffered as a result of the war and the drought;

(b) To contribute to the rehabilitation and reconstruction of Chad;

4. *Notes with satisfaction* that the International Conference on Assistance to Chad was held at Geneva on 4 and 5 December 1985, and invites the States and agencies that participated in it to honour as early as possible the commitments they made at that Conference;

5. *Requests* the Secretary-General:

(a) To continue his efforts to implement the interim development plan submitted at Geneva;

(b) To assess, in close collaboration with the humanitarian agencies concerned, the humanitarian needs, particularly in the areas of food and health, of the people displaced by the war and the drought;

(c) To mobilize special humanitarian assistance for persons who have suffered as a result of the war and the drought and for the resettlement of displaced persons;

(d) To keep the situation in Chad under review and to report thereon to the General Assembly at its forty-first session.

General Assembly resolution 40/218

17 December 1985   Meeting 120   Adopted without vote

Approved by Second Committee (A/40/1043) without vote, 4 December (meeting 47); 51-nation draft (A/C.2/40/L.54); agenda item 87.

Sponsors: Algeria, Bangladesh, Botswana, Burkina Faso, Cameroon, Cape Verde, Central African Republic, Chad, Chile, China, Comoros, Congo, Cyprus, Dominican Republic, Djibouti, Egypt, Equatorial Guinea, Ethiopia, France, Gabon, Gambia, Ghana, Guinea, Guinea-Bissau, Haiti, Ivory Coast, Jamaica, Japan, Lesotho, Liberia, Madagascar, Mali, Mauritania, Morocco, Niger, Nigeria, Pakistan, Rwanda, Senegal, Sierra Leone, Somalia, Sudan, Swaziland, Togo, Tunisia, Turkey, Uganda, United Republic of Tanzania, United States, Vanuatu, Zaire.

Meeting numbers. GA 40th session: 2nd Committee 42, 47; plenary 120.

The Assembly, in **resolution 40/136**, reiterated its appeal to all States and organizations to support generously Chad's efforts to assist and resettle voluntary returnees and displaced persons. It also requested UNDRO and UNHCR to mobilize emergency humanitarian assistance to those persons.

Comoros

In 1985, the people of the Comoros—an LDC poor in natural resources, consisting of some 2,200 square kilometres of which less than half is suitable for agriculture or animal husbandry—suffered from widespread malnutrition and protein deficiency and continued to rely on rice imports of 20,000 to 25,000 metric tons annually. Over the past years, efforts had been made to encourage farmers to grow maize as a substitute for rice and to plant other food crops with a view to achieving food self-sufficiency, according to a September 1985 report of the Secretary-General.[1] He had been requested to report by the General Assembly in 1984.[42] With a population of less than half a million dispersed throughout the islands of the archipelago, the country's distance to principal world markets and major maritime routes adversely affected the competitiveness of its exports. In addition, the country was often hit by cyclones, and abundant rainfall was interspersed with drought. Its economy, which had slowed progressively in recent years, registered a growth rate of less than 3 per cent in 1985, compared with 4 per cent in 1984. As to the 1985 cyclone, total contributions reported to UNDRO as at mid-1985 amounted to $192,770, of which UNDRO itself provided $15,000.

The government budget was characterized by large deficits; in 1985, the overall deficit reached 39 per cent of GDP as compared with 26 per cent in 1982. Nearly all of that deficit had to be financed by external grants and loans. The balance of external trade also showed a deficit: imports amounted to $25.7 million, which exceeded the value of exports, consisting of three commodities (vanilla, cloves and ylang-ylang), by $10 million.

GENERAL ASSEMBLY ACTION

On the recommendation of the Second Committee, the General Assembly adopted **resolution 40/223** on 17 December without vote.

Assistance to the Comoros

The General Assembly,

Recalling its resolution 39/193 of 17 December 1984 and its previous resolutions on assistance to the Comoros, in which it appealed to the international community to provide effective and continuous financial, material and technical assistance to the Comoros in order to help that country overcome its financial and economic difficulties,

Taking note of the special problems confronting the Comoros as an island developing country and as one of the least developed countries,

Noting that the Government of the Comoros has given priority to the questions of infrastructure, transport and telecommunications,

Noting also the economic difficulties arising from the country's scarcity of natural resources, compounded by the recent drought and cyclones,

Noting further the grave budgetary and balance-of-payments problems facing the Comoros,

Bearing in mind the holding at Moroni, from 2 to 4 July 1984, of the first International Solidarity Conference for the Development of the Comoros,

Having examined the summary report of the Secretary-General,

1. *Expresses its appreciation* to the Secretary-General for the steps he has taken to mobilize assistance for the Comoros;

2. *Notes with satisfaction* the response by various Member States, organizations of the United Nations system and other organizations to its appeals and those of the Secretary-General for assistance to the Comoros;

3. *Notes with concern*, however, that the assistance thus far provided continues to fall short of the country's urgent requirements and that assistance is still urgently required in order to implement the projects described in the report of the Secretary-General;

4. *Appeals* to those States and organizations that participated in the first International Solidarity Conference for the Development of the Comoros to participate in the second Conference, to be held at Moroni towards the end of 1985, in order to put into effect as soon as possible their declarations of intent;

5. *Renews its appeal* to Member States, the appropriate organs, programmes and organizations of the United Nations system, regional and international organizations and other intergovernmental bodies and non-governmental organizations, as well as international financial institutions, to provide the Comoros with assistance to enable it to cope with its difficult economic situation and pursue its development goals;

6. *Invites* the appropriate programmes and organizations of the United Nations system to increase their current programmes of assistance to the Comoros, to cooperate closely with the Secretary-General in organizing an effective international programme of assistance and to report periodically to him on the steps they have taken and the resources they have made available to help that country;

7. *Requests* the Secretary-General:

(a) To continue his efforts to mobilize the necessary resources for an effective programme of financial, technical and material assistance to the Comoros;

(b) To keep the situation in the Comoros under constant review, to maintain close contact with Member States, the specialized agencies, the regional and other intergovernmental organizations and international financial institutions concerned, and to apprise the Economic and Social Council, at its second regular session of 1986, of the status of the special programme of economic assistance for the Comoros;

(c) To report on the evolution of the economic situation of the Comoros and the progress made in organizing and implementing the special programme of economic assistance for that country in time for the matter to be considered by the General Assembly at its forty-first session.

General Assembly resolution 40/223

17 December 1985   Meeting 120   Adopted without vote

Approved by Second Committee (A/40/1043) without vote, 4 December (meeting 47); 38-nation draft (A/C.2/40/L.59), orally amended by Secretary following informal consultations; agenda item 87.

Sponsors: Angola, Bangladesh, Benin, Burkina Faso, Cape Verde, Central African Republic, Chad, China, Colombia, Comoros, Democratic Kampuchea, Democratic Yemen, Djibouti, Egypt, Equatorial Guinea, Ethiopia, Gabon, Guinea, Guinea-Bissau, Japan, Lesotho, Liberia, Madagascar, Mali, Mauritania, Mauritius, Morocco, Niger, Oman, Rwanda, Senegal, Somalia, Sudan, Togo, Turkey, Uganda, United Republic of Tanzania, United States.

Meeting numbers. GA 40th session: 2nd Committee 42, 47; plenary 120.

Djibouti

Special economic assistance to Djibouti was among the programmes dealt with by the Secretary-General in a September 1985 report,[1] as he had been requested by the General Assembly in 1984.[43] An LDC with an arid environment providing little scope for agricultural production and a consequent dependence on food imports, Djibouti continued to rely on external assistance for budgetary and capital expenditures. By the end of 1984, the slowing down of its economy due to prolonged drought had come to a standstill; there had been no further depletion of foreign reserves and the budget deficit had narrowed. During 1985, it had rained in nearly all parts of the country, and the first generation of development programmes following a 1983 donors' conference[44] had got off the ground. Those improvements, however, did not significantly reduce the vulnerability of Djibouti's fragile economy, which remained dependent on external factors. There was an increased dependency on food aid. In addition, the year witnessed a new influx of refugees, primarily drought victims from Ethiopia and Somalia, estimated at 15,000 and representing nearly 5 per cent of Djibouti's population.

According to another September 1985 report of the Secretary-General,[2] DTCD continued to assist Djibouti in processing census data as a follow-up to its first population census in 1983, also carried out with DTCD assistance. An UNCTAD project funded by UNDP provided assistance to the port of Djibouti, at a total cost of $331,000 for 1984-1986; development and emergency operation projects were funded by WFP at a cost of $10.2 million and $2.7 million, respectively; and new loans by the World Bank and IDA totalled $10 million for education and urban projects.

GENERAL ASSEMBLY ACTION

On 17 December 1985, the Assembly, on the recommendation of the Second Committee, adopted **resolution 40/227** without vote.

Assistance to Djibouti

The General Assembly,

Recalling its resolution 39/200 of 17 December 1984 and its previous resolutions on assistance to Djibouti, in which it drew the attention of the international community to the critical economic situation confronting Djibouti and to the country's urgent need for assistance,

Deeply concerned at the lingering adverse effects of the drought on the economic and social development of Djibouti,

Bearing in mind its resolution 37/133 of 17 December 1982, in which it decided to include Djibouti in the list of the least developed countries,

Having examined the summary report of the Secretary-General,

Noting the critical economic situation of Djibouti and the list of urgent and priority projects formulated by the Government that require international assistance,

1. *Expresses its appreciation* to the Secretary-General for the steps he has taken to organize an international programme of economic assistance for Djibouti;

2. *Notes with appreciation* the assistance already provided or pledged to Djibouti by Member States, organizations of the United Nations system and other organizations;

3. *Draws the attention* of the international community to the difficult economic situation confronting Djibouti and to the severe structural constraints to its development;

4. *Renews its appeal* to Member States, the appropriate organs, organizations and programmes of the United Nations system, regional and international organizations and other intergovernmental and non-governmental organizations, as well as international financial institutions, to provide assistance bilaterally and multilaterally, as appropriate, to Djibouti in order to enable it to cope with its difficult economic situation and to implement its development strategies, including the programme of assistance that was presented at the round-table conference of development partners convened by the Government of Djibouti in November 1983;

5. *Requests* the appropriate specialized agencies and other organizations of the United Nations system to maintain and increase their current and future programmes of assistance to Djibouti, to co-operate closely with the Secretary-General in organizing an effective international programme of assistance and to report periodically to him on the steps they have taken and the resources they have made available to help that country;

6. *Requests* the Secretary-General:

(*a*) To continue his efforts to mobilize the necessary resources for an effective programme of financial, technical and material assistance to Djibouti;

(*b*) To keep the situation in Djibouti under constant review, to maintain close contact with Member States, the specialized agencies, regional and other intergovernmental organizations and the international financial institutions concerned, and to apprise the Economic and Social Council, at its second regular session of 1986, of the current status of the special programme of economic assistance for Djibouti;

(*c*) To report on the progress made in the economic situation of Djibouti and in organizing and implementing the special programme of economic assistance for that country in time for the matter to be considered by the General Assembly at its forty-first session.

General Assembly resolution 40/227

17 December 1985　　Meeting 120　　Adopted without vote

Approved by Second Committee (A/40/1043) without vote, 4 December (meeting 47); 24-nation draft (A/C.2/40/L.63); agenda item 87.

Sponsors: Bahrain, Bangladesh, Benin, Chad, Comoros, Democratic Yemen, Djibouti, Dominican Republic, Ethiopia, Guinea, Guinea-Bissau, Japan, Kuwait, Lebanon, Liberia, Libyan Arab Jamahiriya, Madagascar, Mauritania, Oman, Sierra Leone, Somalia, Sudan, Uganda, United Arab Emirates.

Meeting numbers. GA 40th session: 2nd Committee 42, 47; plenary 120.

Assistance to the drought-stricken areas of Djibouti was also called for by the Assembly in **resolution 40/221**.

Equatorial Guinea

The Secretary-General sent a mission to Equatorial Guinea from 7 to 14 May 1985, led by the Director of Special Economic Assistance Programmes, in response to a 1984 General Assembly request.[45] The report of the mission[46] described the economic and financial situation of the country, including a review of the more important economic sectors; discussed the implementation of the special economic assistance programme and the country's 1982-1984 programme on economic reactivation and development; and drew certain conclusions and recommendations with regard to support by the international community for the development efforts of the Government.

The mission noted that Equatorial Guinea, consisting of continental Guinea or Río Muni on the coast of west Africa and insular Guinea, was sparsely populated with a population of over 316,000 and an annual population growth rate of 2.7 per cent. Distances between various parts of the country rendered communications difficult and costly. Although classified by the United Nations as an LDC on the basis of its current economic performance, Equatorial Guinea had considerable potential and could produce enough to meet the basic food requirements of its population. It enjoyed a competitive advantage in the production of cocoa, which could be expanded considerably, as could its production of coffee, thus increasing foreign exchange earnings. The Gulf of Guinea and the waters around Annabón with their adequate fish resources could support both artisanal and commercial exploitation, and offshore exploration indicated the possibility of commercial gas and petroleum production.

During the period under review, however, agricultural production continued to stagnate at levels far below potential, and Equatorial Guinea faced major monetary and fiscal problems which overshadowed development efforts. On the external side, the financing of essential imports had become increasingly difficult and debt-service payments had grown to the point where the Government could not keep current.

Equatorial Guinea's GDP increased during 1980-1985 at an average annual rate of 1 per cent. On 1 January 1985, the country became a member of the Bank of Central African States and replaced the ekwele by the CFA franc as its monetary unit with a fixed rate *vis-à-vis* the French franc (F 1 = CFAF 50). It also decided at the end of 1984 to join the Central African Customs and Economic Union in association with Cameroon, the Central African Republic, the Congo and Gabon.

The country's external debt at the end of 1985 amounted to $133.2 million, according to data compiled by the World Bank, representing a 15 per cent increase compared with year-end 1984 and a 77 per cent increase compared with year-end 1980. Of that amount, $119.3 million was public and publicly guaranteed long-term debt,

while use of IMF credit amounted to $7.9 million and short-term debt to $6 million. To alleviate the heavy debt burden for the country, whose GNP was estimated at $85 million, an agreement was reached at a meeting of the Paris Club in June 1985 whereby repayment of a substantial proportion of the accumulated debt was put forward to 1991.

A government study of foreign assistance project implementation for 138 projects during 1983-1985 revealed that external assistance during that period was estimated at $220 million, corresponding to $700 per capita. Equatorial Guinea's contribution to the projects was $8.2 million and, of the total external assistance, some $96 million was in the form of grants and $125 million in loans. During the period under review, there was a decline in the grant component, from 42 per cent in 1984 to an estimated 15 per cent in 1985.

In view of the fact that the Government was in the process of formulating a new development programme, no specific priority projects were identified, but the mission made the following conclusions and recommendations. The international community was strongly urged to co-operate with the Government in its efforts to reschedule its debt; at the same time, there was a need for immediate concessional financing for essential imports, both to keep the economy functioning during the current transition period and to contribute to the more long-term development efforts. The need for ODA remained extremely important for national economic and social development; in that connection, the trend to a decline in grants should be reversed and multiyear commitments should be considered.

With regard to external assistance, harmonization of views between donors and the Government was a major problem; an improvement in the situation would require that the Government establish a clear framework reflecting development priorities and enhance its contribution to project implementation and monitoring. It also required support of those efforts by donors by undertaking projects consistent with national development priorities and consulting among themselves and with government authorities to ensure the most effective use of available resources.

Since Equatorial Guinea continued to face an acute shortage of skilled manpower at all levels, there was a continuing need for foreign technical assistance and donors should consider increasing the training component of projects. Assistance to agriculture as the basis of the national economy was essential if the country was to achieve a position where it could earn the foreign exchange necessary to finance its own growth; in addition to assisting in the promotion of food production for domestic consumption, the donor community was called upon to continue providing necessary food aid. The Government's revised policy to expand cocoa and timber production also required international technical and financial assistance.

In addition to supporting the formulation of a comprehensive national development strategy, donors were urged to consider ways to improve and utilize existing infrastructure more effectively. Concluding, the mission said the Government urged that assistance be continued and if possible enhanced in order to support its efforts to deal with its immediate and more long-term problems.

GENERAL ASSEMBLY ACTION

On the recommendation of the Second Committee, the General Assembly, on 17 December 1985, adopted **resolution 40/216** without vote.

Assistance to Equatorial Guinea

The General Assembly,

Recalling its resolutions 35/105 of 5 December 1980, 36/204 of 17 December 1981, 37/133 of 17 December 1982 and 38/224 of 20 December 1983,

Recalling also its resolution 39/181 of 17 December 1984, in which it earnestly called upon all Member States and international and regional organizations and other intergovernmental organizations, as well as international financial and development institutions and appropriate programmes of the United Nations system, especially the United Nations Development Programme and the United Nations Institute for Training and Research, to establish, maintain and expand their programmes of assistance to Equatorial Guinea, particularly in the areas of public administration and public finance in which a general transformation is required as a result of Equatorial Guinea's entry into the Central African Customs and Economic Union and the Bank of Central African States,

Recalling further that Equatorial Guinea is one of the least developed countries,

Having considered the report of the Secretary-General, submitted pursuant to General Assembly resolution 39/181,

Noting that Equatorial Guinea, despite the efforts made by its Government and people, continues to be beset by serious economic and financial difficulties,

Recognizing the essential role of short-term, medium-term and long-term international assistance in support of the efforts of the Government of Equatorial Guinea in the task of reconstruction and development of the country,

1. *Takes note* of the report of the Secretary-General;

2. *Expresses its thanks* to the international community for its interest in and assistance to Equatorial Guinea;

3. *Also expresses its thanks* for the efforts made by the Secretary-General to organize and mobilize the necessary resources for an effective programme of assistance to Equatorial Guinea;

4. *Reiterates its appeal* to all Member States to continue to respond generously, through bilateral or multilateral channels, so as to meet the needs indicated in the programme presented in 1982 at the International Conference of Donors for the Economic Reactivation and Development of Equatorial Guinea held at Geneva in April 1982;

5. *Invites* all Member States and international and regional organizations and other intergovernmental organizations, as well as international financial and development institutions, to participate in the round-table meeting of donors to be held in Equatorial Guinea in 1986 for the evaluation of the 1982-1984 three-year programme presented at the International Conference of Donors for the Economic Reactivation and Development of Equatorial Guinea;

6. *Requests* the Secretary-General:

(a) To intensify his efforts to mobilize the necessary resources for an effective programme of financial, technical and material assistance to Equatorial Guinea;

(b) To keep the situation in Equatorial Guinea under review, to maintain close contact with Member States, the specialized agencies, regional and other intergovernmental organizations and competent international financial institutions and to apprise the Economic and Social Council, at its second regular session of 1986, of the status of assistance to Equatorial Guinea;

(c) To submit to the General Assembly at its forty-first session a report on the economic situation of Equatorial Guinea and the progress made in implementing the present resolution;

7. *Requests* the Administrator of the United Nations Development Programme to ensure that the round-table conference to be held in Equatorial Guinea in 1986 receives the widest possible publicity among the bilateral and multilateral donors.

General Assembly resolution 40/216

17 December 1985   Meeting 120   Adopted without vote

Approved by Second Committee (A/40/1043) without vote, 4 December (meeting 47); 32-nation draft (A/C.2/40/L.50), orally amended by Secretary following informal consultations; agenda item 87.

Sponsors: Afghanistan, Argentina, Bangladesh, Benin, Bolivia, Cameroon, Central African Republic, Chad, Comoros, Congo, Costa Rica, Dominican Republic, Ecuador, Egypt, El Salvador, Equatorial Guinea, Ethiopia, Gabon, Guinea-Bissau, Honduras, Liberia, Libyan Arab Jamahiriya, Madagascar, Mauritania, Mexico, Morocco, Nigeria, Peru, Sierra Leone, Spain, Uruguay, Zaire.

Meeting numbers. GA 40th session: 2nd Committee 42, 47; plenary 120.

Gambia

Classified by the United Nations as an LDC, with per capita GDP well under $300, the Gambia was one of the world's poorest countries. With no known natural resources, the country's economy depended on one cash crop—groundnuts—as the main source of income for two thirds of its population and accounting for 85 to 90 per cent of domestic exports. With a decline in GDP in the 1980s and a doubling of its population between 1965 and 1985—currently estimated at 750,000—the Gambia's real per capita income fell by 16 per cent between 1970 and 1985. Unemployment, especially among young people, was high. Although involved in redressing its economic and financial problems, the Gambia had made significant advances in building up its economic and social infrastructure—schools, clinics, roads and public administration.

With a view to reversing the trend of economic deterioration, the Government launched a comprehensive economic recovery programme in mid-1985 with reforms in the exchange rate system, the financial sector, the civil service and parastatal institutions. The programme also aimed at raising agricultural productivity, promoting productive activities such as fishing, manufacturing and tourism, and included a restructuring of the public investment programme.

In his September report on special economic assistance,[1] the Secretary-General pointed out that in 1984/85 the Gambia's economic situation had deteriorated, with the production of groundnuts less than half of the previous year, resulting in an equivalent reduction in export earnings, and deficits persisting in the balance of payments and the government budget. Debt-service payments increased by 65 per cent and arrears had accumulated to about 50 per cent of GDP. Due partly to the country's inability to pay for rice imports, the food situation had become serious. To supplement its domestic production, the Gambia had to import annually over 30,000 tons of cereals, mainly rice. For the period from October 1984 to September 1985, the deficit to be met by rice imports was estimated at some 39,000 tons; the uncovered rice deficit for June to September 1985 reached 16,000 tons.

As at the end of June, the Gambia's medium- and long-term public debt was estimated at $312 million, representing about 200 per cent of GDP. External debt service due in 1984/85 was $18 million, which further eroded the deficit from 17 per cent of GDP in 1983/84 to 25 per cent in 1984/85.

Following the 1984 round-table donors' conference for assistance to the Gambia,[47] meetings on fisheries and on non-project financing were held in June and September 1985, respectively.

GENERAL ASSEMBLY ACTION

On 17 December, the General Assembly, on the recommendation of the Second Committee, adopted **resolution 40/224** without vote.

Assistance to the Gambia

The General Assembly,

Recalling its resolution 39/203 of 17 December 1984, in which it, *inter alia*, noted that the Gambia is a least developed country with acute economic and social problems arising from its weak economic infrastructure and that it also suffers from many of the serious problems common to countries of the Sahelian region, notably drought and desertification,

Having considered the summary report of the Secretary-General, in which the recent economic situation in the Gambia is described,

Concerned that the Gambia continues to encounter serious balance-of-payments and budgetary problems and noting that the lack of domestic resources is the most important constraint on development, since the Government lacks the funds to meet the counterpart costs of donor-assisted projects,

Noting that external assistance is still required to enable the Government of the Gambia to implement the

six projects recommended by the Secretary-General in his report submitted to the General Assembly at its thirty-ninth session,

Aware that a round-table conference of donors was held in the Gambia in November 1984, with the assistance of the United Nations Development Programme, to discuss the country's development needs and to consider ways and means of helping the Government in its efforts to meet those needs,

1. *Takes note* of the report of the Secretary-General;

2. *Expresses its appreciation* to the Secretary-General for the steps he has taken to mobilize assistance for the Gambia;

3. *Expresses its appreciation also* to those States and organizations that have provided assistance to the Gambia;

4. *Draws the attention* of the international community to the need for assistance for the projects and programmes identified by the Secretary-General in his report;

5. *Renews its urgent appeal* to Member States, the specialized agencies and other organizations of the United Nations system, regional and interregional organizations and other intergovernmental and nongovernmental organizations, as well as international development and financial institutions, to give generous assistance to the Gambia, through bilateral or multilateral channels, and to provide financial, technical and material assistance for the implementation of the projects and programmes recommended by the Secretary-General in his report;

6. *Urges* donors, as appropriate, to provide financial assistance to the Gambia to help meet the local counterpart costs of externally assisted projects, bearing in mind that the Gambia is classified as a least developed drought-stricken country;

7. *Urges* Member States, organizations and programmes of the United Nations system, regional and interregional bodies, financial and development institutions, as well as intergovernmental and nongovernmental organizations, to respond generously to the needs of the Gambia as discussed at the round-table conference of donors held in that country in November 1984;

8. *Invites* the appropriate organizations and programmes of the United Nations system—in particular the United Nations Development Programme, the United Nations Children's Fund, the World Food Programme, the World Health Organization, the Food and Agriculture Organization of the United Nations, the International Fund for Agricultural Development and the United Nations Industrial Development Organization—to increase their current and future programmes of assistance to the Gambia, to co-operate closely with the Secretary-General in organizing an effective international programme of assistance and to report periodically to him on the steps they have taken and the resources they have made available to assist that country;

9. *Invites also* the United Nations Development Programme, the United Nations Children's Fund, the World Food Programme, the World Health Organization, the Food and Agriculture Organization of the United Nations, the World Bank, the International Fund for Agricultural Development and the United Nations Industrial Development Organization to bring to the

attention of their governing bodies, for their consideration, the special needs of the Gambia and to report the decisions of those bodies to the Secretary-General by 15 July 1986;

10. *Requests* the Secretary-General:

(a) To continue his efforts to mobilize the necessary resources for an effective programme of financial, technical and material assistance to the Gambia;

(b) To keep the situation in the Gambia under constant review, to maintain close contact with Member States, the specialized agencies, regional and other intergovernmental organizations and the international financial institutions concerned and to apprise the Economic and Social Council, at its second regular session of 1986, of the status of the special programme of economic assistance for the Gambia;

(c) To report on the progress made in the economic situation of the Gambia and in organizing and implementing the special programme of economic assistance for that country in time for the matter to be considered by the General Assembly at its forty-first session.

General Assembly resolution 40/224

17 December 1985   Meeting 120   Adopted without vote

Approved by Second Committee (A/40/1043) without vote, 4 December (meeting 47); 16-nation draft (A/C.2/40/L.60), orally amended by Secretary following informal consultations; agenda item 87.

Sponsors: Algeria, Bangladesh, Chad, Ethiopia, Gambia, Ghana, Guinea-Bissau, Liberia, Madagascar, Mali, Mauritania, Niger, Nigeria, Senegal, Sudan, United States.

Meeting numbers. GA 40th session: 2nd Committee 42, 47; plenary 120.

Guinea

Classified by the United Nations as an LDC, Guinea continued to face serious economic difficulties despite initiation in 1984 of a special programme of economic assistance[48] and a national economic and financial recovery programme (1985-1987) launched by the Government in September 1985.

Apart from mining, Guinea's development was based solely on the public sector, according to a September 1985 report by the Secretary-General.[1] Despite investments, the public sector had declined since 1973 with the exception of the civil service. Public enterprises, which had been producing at less than 15 per cent of capacity, registered heavy losses, which led to a degree of liberalization from 1980 onwards and paved the way for an economic reform programme aimed at encouraging private sector development, which was at the core of the national programme.

In the rural sector, collective agriculture did not live up to expectations but small-scale peasant farming provided some supplies for the country despite adverse environmental conditions. Yet, agricultural output did not ensure food self-sufficiency, and the country continued to import an average of 70,000 tons of rice annually, including 30,000 tons of food aid. In the industrial sector, Guinea began to export diamonds—50,000 carats during the first four months of 1985—in addition to bauxite and aluminium, which accounted for 99 per cent of its export earnings. Agricultural exports—pineapple and coffee—were of marginal importance.

In its development planning process, the Government of Guinea was assisted by UNDP through a project aimed at streamlining the general organization of the national economy and strengthening the co-ordinating capacity for management and planning in sectors and subsectors crucial to economic recovery and growth, such as mining, processing industries, industrial fishing, feeder roads and foreign trade. To the same end, the World Bank was involved in a $9 million project of technical assistance for economic management to improve services responsible for the planning, evaluation and follow-up of the public investment programme, macro-economic and sectoral planning, and the management of the para-public sector; the restructuring of that sector was to result in the liquidation of non-profitable enterprises and the transfer of certain enterprises to the private sector. The policy of rehabilitating and revitalizing enterprises led to the granting of an $8 million IDA loan to improve the organization and management of the electricity sector and to overhaul installations for the production, conduction and supply of electricity. A donors' meeting was held at Conakry on the question of rehabilitating an initial 36-kilometre section and carrying out a diagnostic survey of Guinea's railways; among the participants were representatives of the World Bank, EEC and the Central Economic Co-operation Fund.

Other multilateral assistance included UNHCR emergency assistance to Guinean returnees amounting to $1.1 million from July 1984 to February 1985, to supply medical kits and vehicles, set up health care delivery systems and distribute food and agricultural inputs. In addition, the United Nations Emergency Operation Trust Fund provided $800,000 to finance the delivery in April 1985 of 6,000 ploughs following a December 1983 earthquake.

GENERAL ASSEMBLY ACTION

On 17 December 1985, the General Assembly, on the recommendation of the Second Committee, adopted **resolution 40/235** without vote.

Special economic assistance to Guinea

The General Assembly,

Recalling its resolution 39/202 of 17 December 1984, in which it appealed to the international community to contribute generously, through bilateral and multilateral channels, to the reconstruction, rehabilitation and development of Guinea,

Noting that the persistence of unfavourable climatic conditions in the northern part of the country has led to enormous losses in crop and livestock production,

Deeply concerned by the fact that Guinea continues to suffer serious economic and financial difficulties arising from a marked balance-of-payments deficit, onerous external debt charges and the massive return of formerly exiled persons,

Taking into consideration the objectives of Guinea's Interim Programme of National Rehabilitation for the period 1985-1987, whose implementation continues to be hampered by the lack of necessary resources,

Noting with satisfaction the considerable efforts made by the Government and people of Guinea to ensure the country's reconstruction, rehabilitation and development, despite existing constraints,

Noting that the Government of Guinea, in collaboration with the United Nations Development Programme, the World Bank, the International Monetary Fund and other international agencies concerned, is preparing a conference of donors for Guinea, which will be organized as soon as possible,

Considering that Guinea is one of the least developed countries,

Noting the statement made by the Minister of State for Foreign Affairs and International Co-operation of the Republic of Guinea on 4 October 1985, in which he described his country's economic problems,

Having considered the summary report of the Secretary-General,

1. *Expresses its appreciation* to the Secretary-General for his report and for the steps he has taken to mobilize assistance to Guinea;

2. *Expresses its gratitude* to the States and organizations that have provided assistance to that country;

3. *Again appeals* to the international community, including the specialized agencies and other United Nations bodies and organizations, to contribute generously, through bilateral or multilateral channels, to Guinea's economic and social development;

4. *Invites* all States and relevant organizations of the United Nations system to provide the Government of Guinea with all possible assistance with a view to meeting the population's critical humanitarian needs and to furnish it, as appropriate, with food, medicaments and essential hospital and school equipment;

5. *Also invites* the United Nations Development Programme, the United Nations Children's Fund, the World Food Programme, the United Nations Educational, Scientific and Cultural Organization, the United Nations Industrial Development Organization, the Food and Agriculture Organization of the United Nations, the World Bank and the International Fund for Agricultural Development to intensify and expand their assistance programmes in order to meet the needs of Guinea;

6. *Requests* the Secretary-General to continue and intensify his efforts to mobilize all possible assistance within the framework of the United Nations system in order to assist the Government of Guinea in its rehabilitation and development efforts;

7. *Also requests* the Secretary-General to report to the Economic and Social Council, at its second regular session of 1986, and to the General Assembly, at its forty-first session, on the progress achieved in the implementation of the present resolution.

General Assembly resolution 40/235

17 December 1985   Meeting 120   Adopted without vote

Approved by Second Committee (A/40/1043) without vote, 4 December (meeting 47); 60-nation draft (A/C.2/40/L.75), orally amended by Secretary following informal consultations; agenda item 87.

Sponsors: Afghanistan, Argentina, Bangladesh, Benin, Burkina Faso, Cameroon, Cape Verde, Central African Republic, Chad, China, Comoros, Congo, Cyprus, Democratic Kampuchea, Democratic Yemen, Djibouti, Ecuador, Egypt, Equatorial Guinea, Ethiopia, Gabon, Gambia, Ghana, Guatemala, Guinea, Guinea-Bissau, Guyana, Haiti, India, Iran, Iraq, Japan, Liberia, Madagascar, Mali, Mauritania, Mauritius, Morocco, Mozambique, Nepal, Nicaragua, Niger, Nigeria, Pakistan, Panama, Romania, Rwanda, Senegal, Sierra Leone, Somalia, Spain, Sudan, Suriname, Thailand, Togo, Tunisia, Uganda, United Republic of Tanzania, Yugoslavia, Zaire.

Meeting numbers. GA 40th session: 2nd Committee 44, 47; plenary 23, 120.

Addressing the Assembly on 4 October 1985, Guinea referred to its development plan for 1985-1987 which focused on agriculture, energy, education, transport and communication—basically the restructuring of the country's economy and administration. Efforts centred on finding ways to develop Guinea's natural resources, with an open-door policy enabling it to co-operate with other countries unconditionally and on the basis of equality and mutual interests. The new approach was to be supported within the country by a policy of freeing the economy and encouraging enterprises and private initiatives that had for a long time been stifled. Guinea also welcomed the importance attached by the United Nations to the integrated development plan for the Fouta Djallon massif to create a protective green belt against the progressive desertification of the region, thus making its hydroelectric potential available to all regional States.

Guinea-Bissau

The Secretary-General, in response to a 1984 request of the General Assembly,[24] arranged for a review mission to visit Guinea-Bissau from 16 to 23 April 1985 to consult with the Government. According to the mission's findings,[49] Guinea-Bissau's population was growing at an annual rate of 2.2 per cent. With a per capita income estimated at $190, life expectancy at birth at 42 years, the mortality rate among children aged 1 to 4 around 200 per 1,000 and 75 per cent of the population illiterate, Guinea-Bissau had been classified by the United Nations as an LDC.

The mission's report reviewed the economic situation in Guinea-Bissau taking into account recent developments, described the status of the special economic assistance programme and discussed the 1983-1986 national development plan. The mission found that the country continued to be beset by economic and financial difficulties but that the rigorous economic policy measures implemented by the Government in 1984 were beginning to have positive effects. For example, exports increased substantially following the progressive devaluation of the peso and adjustments to producer prices, and revenues rose noticeably in response to fiscal reforms and improved tax collection procedures. Nevertheless, the mission agreed with the Government that its planned stabilization programme would have to be continued beyond 1986.

The mission pointed out that agricultural production, which accounted for over 50 per cent of GDP, with rice as the main staple, could adequately ensure food self-sufficiency and increase export earnings, mainly from ground-nuts, palm kernels and cashew nuts. However, the country's output remained poor owing to lack of incentives, inadequate infrastructure and unfavourable weather.

Under the World Bank's sponsorship, representatives from the Bank, IMF, UNDP and EEC, as well as from France, the Federal Republic of Germany, the Netherlands, Portugal, Sweden, Switzerland and the United States, met with a delegation of Guinea-Bissau (Paris, 12 and 13 February 1985) to review ways in which the international assistance to Guinea-Bissau had been carried out. Guinea-Bissau indicated that its total requirements for 1985 amounted to $23.8 million ($7 million for food aid, $8 million for fuel import and $8.8 million for other essential imports); for 1986, it anticipated that exports of goods and services could reach $25 million, leaving a balance-of-payments deficit of about $30 million, including food aid, to be financed. The meeting acknowledged that the trend shown by some of the economic indicators was highly encouraging, and the countries supporting Guinea-Bissau promised that every effort would be made to meet the remaining balance-of-payments needs, through debt rescheduling, cancellation or rescheduling of commercial arrears and reconstitution of a minimum level of reserves.

The first round-table follow-up meeting to the 1984 donors' conference for assistance to Guinea-Bissau[50] was held at Bissau from 16 to 18 April 1985. Acknowledging the critical importance of external assistance to support the Government's economic and financial stabilization programme, the participants showed their readiness to consider favourably the financing of projects presented; the meeting recommended an extension of the stabilization programme to allow for consolidation of the results so far achieved. It also decided to hold a series of sectoral consultations.

The mission concluded that the international community had responded generously to and been supportive of the measures taken so far by Guinea-Bissau in its efforts to correct some of the fundamental structural imbalances in its economy. However, sustained external assistance would be required for the next few years, in particular the funding of the balance-of-payments deficit of about $53.8 million, including food aid, for 1985-1986; debt renegotiation and relief; and funding of some 22 development projects costing approximately $81.5 million.

GENERAL ASSEMBLY ACTION

On 17 December 1985, the General Assembly, on the recommendation of the Second Committee, adopted **resolution 40/225** without vote.

Special economic assistance to Guinea-Bissau
The General Assembly,

Recalling its resolution 35/95 of 5 December 1980, in which it reiterated its appeal to the international community to continue to provide effective financial, material and technical assistance to Guinea-Bissau to help it overcome its financial and economic difficulties and to permit the implementation of the projects and programmes recommended by the Secretary-General in his report submitted pursuant to General Assembly resolution 34/121 of 14 December 1979,

Recalling also its resolutions 36/217 of 17 December 1981 and 39/186 of 17 December 1984,

Noting, in particular, that Guinea-Bissau is one of the least developed countries,

Noting with concern that Guinea-Bissau continues to experience serious economic and financial difficulties, that the gross national product of Guinea-Bissau has decreased in real terms, that the balance-of-payments deficit continues to rise, that the external debt is imposing a heavy burden on the country's fragile economy and that the budget deficit has also grown substantially,

Noting also that Guinea-Bissau continues to have problems in supplying staple foodstuffs to satisfy the needs of its population,

Noting with satisfaction the main features of the first four-year development plan (1983-1986) of Guinea-Bissau and the implementation of the 1983-1984 economic and financial stabilization programme,

Also noting with satisfaction the prospects for co-operation stemming from the round-table conference of donors for Guinea-Bissau, held at Lisbon in May 1984,

Having considered the report of the Secretary-General on economic assistance to Guinea-Bissau,

1. *Expresses its appreciation* to the Secretary-General for the steps he has taken to mobilize assistance for Guinea-Bissau;

2. *Draws the attention* of the international community to the assistance required for implementing the projects and programmes submitted at the round-table conference;

3. *Expresses its gratitude* to the Member States and international organizations concerned for the food aid generously provided to Guinea-Bissau;

4. *Expresses its gratitude* to the States and organizations that have responded to the appeal of Guinea-Bissau and to the appeals of the Secretary-General by providing assistance to Guinea-Bissau;

5. *Renews its urgent appeal* to Member States, regional and interregional organizations and other intergovernmental and non-governmental organizations to continue to provide financial, material and technical assistance to Guinea-Bissau to help it overcome its economic and financial difficulties and to permit the implementation of the projects and programmes specified in its first four-year development plan;

6. *Urges* Member States, United Nations bodies, regional and interregional bodies and governmental

financing institutions to respond urgently to the needs of Guinea-Bissau in accordance with the dialogue held between Guinea-Bissau and its partners at the round-table conference of donors;

7. *Appeals* to the international community to contribute to the special account opened by the Secretary-General at United Nations Headquarters, in accordance with General Assembly resolution 32/100 of 13 December 1977, in order to facilitate the payment of contributions for Guinea-Bissau;

8. *Invites* the United Nations Development Programme, the United Nations Children's Fund, the World Food Programme, the World Health Organization, the Food and Agriculture Organization of the United Nations, the World Bank and the International Fund for Agricultural Development to bring to the attention of their governing bodies, for their consideration, the special and pressing needs of Guinea-Bissau and to report the decisions taken in that connection to the Secretary-General;

9. *Requests* the specialized agencies and other United Nations bodies to report periodically to the Secretary-General on the steps they have taken and the resources they have made available to assist Guinea-Bissau;

10. *Requests* the Secretary-General:

(a) To continue his efforts to mobilize the necessary resources for an effective programme of financial, technical and material assistance to Guinea-Bissau;

(b) To keep the situation in Guinea-Bissau under constant review, to maintain close contact with Member States, specialized agencies, regional and other intergovernmental organizations and the financial institutions concerned, and to apprise the Economic and Social Council, at its second regular session of 1986, of the status of the special programme of economic assistance for Guinea-Bissau;

(c) To report to the General Assembly at its forty-first session on the implementation of the present resolution.

General Assembly resolution 40/225

17 December 1985   Meeting 120   Adopted without vote

Approved by Second Committee (A/40/1043) without vote, 4 December (meeting 47); 53-nation draft (A/C.2/40/L.61); agenda item 87.

Sponsors: Algeria, Angola, Bangladesh, Benin, Bolivia, Brazil, Burkina Faso, Cape Verde, Central African Republic, Chad, China, Comoros, Congo, Cuba, Cyprus, Democratic Yemen, Djibouti, Equatorial Guinea, Ethiopia, Gabon, Gambia, Ghana, Guinea, Guinea-Bissau, Guyana, Haiti, India, Lesotho, Liberia, Madagascar, Mali, Mauritania, Mongolia, Mozambique, Nicaragua, Niger, Nigeria, Portugal, Rwanda, Sao Tome and Principe, Senegal, Sierra Leone, Sudan, Thailand, Togo, Trinidad and Tobago, Uganda, United States, Vanuatu, Viet Nam, Yugoslavia, Zaire, Zambia.

Meeting numbers. GA 40th session: 2nd Committee 42, 47; plenary 120.

Lesotho

The Secretary-General, as requested by the General Assembly in 1984,[25] reported in September 1985[1] on the current economic situation of Lesotho and the assistance requirements

of the 10 specific projects formulated in response to a 1982 Security Council request.[51]

Due to its unique geographical location and limited natural resources, Lesotho continued to depend economically on South Africa. One of the major features of its economy was the large difference between its GNP and its GDP which was accounted for by income from abroad, almost all of which represented remittances from the Basotho miners in South Africa. The implications of the difference reflected one of the principal characteristics of the economy, namely its great dependence on migrant labour and remittance which were the major sources of employment and purchasing power in Lesotho's economy. Recent developments in the labour market of South Africa indicated that there was an urgent need to reduce dependence on the migratory labour system. Recognizing that few job opportunities existed in Lesotho and that the labour force was growing rapidly, the Government had requested the ILO Southern African Team for Employment Promotion to prepare a long-term employment plan to help absorb the growing labour force and prepare contingency and emergency programmes for migrant workers.

Although agricultural production and productivity were very low, agriculture remained the main sector of the economy, providing some 50 per cent of exports. Of agricultural exports, 75 per cent came from livestock, a subsector whose contribution to GDP had grown over the years, surpassing that of crop farming. Industry and water resources—the latter one of the country's major resources—were still at the initial stages of development.

In response to the continuing adverse impact of drought, the Government evolved two kinds of remedial measures to alleviate and overcome its effects: projects addressing the emergency drought relief aspects; and projects aimed at resolving the continuous threat of drought in the medium- and long-term perspective. An appeal was made by Lesotho to the international community to deal with short-term implications of the drought. The emergency projects, totalling some $23 million, were aimed at assisting the country to overcome the devastating effects of the drought cycle. Several projects, or some of their aspects, were also to contribute to long-term measures to ensure against adverse drought effects in the future. In addition, Lesotho presented the international community with essential medium- to long-term structural reform projects totalling $159 million: watershed management, $99 million; destocking project, $33 million; and minor roads construction, $27 million.

In his June 1985 report on the critical economic situation in Africa,[6] the Secretary-General pointed to facts that had emerged from a country-specific meeting for Lesotho held at Lusaka, Zambia, on 11 April. In its third year of drought, Lesotho had been forced to increase cereal imports, using some of its foreign exchange reserves. Additional food aid for direct emergency purposes had not been requested, but it was indicated that support for supplementary feeding programmes would allow the Government to save foreign exchange reserves and channel more funds to drought-related activities. As a direct result of drought-induced hardships, there had been an increase in tuberculosis among vulnerable groups, and diarrhoeal and other gastro-intestinal diseases were spreading due to the lack of safe drinking-water supplies and basic sanitation. Additional medical supplies were therefore requested to help alleviate the severe health problems.

In another report,[2] the Secretary-General described assistance to Lesotho by the United Nations system. At the March 1985 Conference on the Emergency Situation in Africa, total unmet emergency needs for Lesotho were estimated at $2.1 million—basic agricultural/pastoral inputs, $1.4 million; essential health actions, $0.2 million; and additional logistics (capital inputs), $0.5 million.

Liberia

In response to a 1984 General Assembly request[52] that he report on the economic situation in and the special programme of economic assistance for Liberia, the Secretary-General arranged for a mission from 1 to 5 April 1985, led by the Under-Secretary-General for Special Political Questions. The mission's report,[53] described the country's economic and financial situation and made some recommendations. It indicated that Liberia was continuing to face economic and financial difficulties and that the situation had deteriorated to a critical point. There had been negative real economic growth, a decline in private consumption and overall savings, heavy external debt payments and problems of arrears, a substantial budget deficit, a weak balance-of-payments position with a large deficit on the current account, a tight liquidity situation which constrained economic activity in the country, and weak planning and implementation capacity.

By December 1984, Liberia's total public external debt was almost $960 million, of which $860.8 million represented national government debt and $98.6 million the recorded debt of public corporations. In 1982/83, debt servicing amounted to $62 million, or over 13 per cent of exports of goods and services in that year; by 1985, it had risen to $110 million and was expected to continue at that level for a few years, imposing a strain on Liberia's financial resources. Of that amount, $50 million

was not eligible for rescheduling, representing payments due to multilateral institutions and for other loans not eligible for debt relief. Following the Government's request for debt relief from bilateral donors, four rescheduling agreements were reached under the Paris Club, covering the period 1 January 1980 to 30 June 1985, under which $82.3 million was rescheduled. Under the "London Group" of commercial creditors, $26 million in commercial debt was refinanced in fiscal 1983/84 and further refinancing was under consideration. The mission recommended that the Government make the necessary arrangements for a timely payment of its external debt obligations. However, in view of the heavy burden which debt-service payments imposed on its budget and balance of payments and the Government's commitment to achieve a better balance in its internal and external accounts, financial assistance to Liberia on a grant basis or on highly concessional terms was suggested.

To improve its fiscal balance, the Government implemented measures to increase revenues and reduce outlays. Those measures curtailed its ability not only to provide basic health and other social services, but also to maintain the existing stock of capital and make the investments needed for the future growth of the economy. Increases in revenues were budgeted through the imposition of new taxes and the strengthening of the tax collection system; nevertheless, revenues continued to decline in fiscal year 1984/85.

In consultation with the World Bank, Liberia began in 1985 to implement a structural adjustment programme, supported by a Bank credit. The programme's main objectives were to reduce the size of the public enterprise sector through divestiture and/or restructuring, including partial privatization; improve the efficiency and financial health of enterprises remaining in the public sector through fiscal, financial and managerial reforms; and establish an institutional and policy environment for Government/enterprise relations that would clarify the objectives which enterprises were to pursue. Along those lines, the Government created a Bureau for State Enterprises.

The mission concluded that, although the Government continued to face severe economic and financial difficulties, it had to deal with the country's fundamental, longer-term problems. Despite its economic situation, Liberia had good potential in natural resources (iron ore, rubber, timber and diamonds) and cash crops (coffee, cocoa and oil palm). The mission supported rigorous and sustained implementation of the structural adjustment programme as a first step in addressing Liberia's problems, but stressed that the co-operation of the international community was essential for the programme to succeed.

The Secretary-General reported[2] that the United Nations provided to Liberia special economic assistance for: health, water supply and formal education (UNICEF); population statistics and development planning, water resources policy, natural resources development, training and equipment (DTCD); development projects (WFP); plant protection research, agricultural statistics, emergency rinder-pest vaccination, assistance to poultry farms, irrigation and forestry (FAO); agricultural development (IFAD); technical assistance (IMF); population data compilation and processing (UNFPA); maritime training (IMO); the Liberian Institute of Public Administration (UNDP/ILO); fellowships (ITU and UPU); civil aviation training (ICAO) and debt management (UNCTAD)—projects funded by UNDP; and loans for oil exploration and water supply projects (World Bank and IDA).

UNDP provided financial and technical support to several projects to assist Liberia with development planning, improve the managerial skills of various government officials and upgrade the professional capability of planning personnel.

GENERAL ASSEMBLY ACTION

By **decision 40/454** of 17 December, the General Assembly, on the recommendation of the Second Committee, took note of the Secretary-General's report on special economic assistance to Liberia.

Mauritania

By a letter of 25 September 1985 to the Secretary-General,[54] Mauritania appealed to the international community for assistance for the reconstruction, recovery, rehabilitation and development of the country and requested that the question be considered at the 1985 General Assembly session. Annexed to the letter was a memorandum proposing that Mauritania be classified as an LDC.

As in the past, the letter explained, Mauritania suffered from drought, desertification, the effects of war in Western Sahara and the international economic crisis. With an estimated annual population growth of 2.5 per cent, the economy employed in the modern sector—based on mining, fishing and administration—60,000 workers (30 per cent in the civil service and 20 per cent in public enterprises), while the majority of the potentially active population (540,000 workers) depended on traditional rural forms of the subsistence economy. The country lacked skilled personnel—some 70 per cent of all employees in small- and medium-scale enterprises had no training, and 50 per cent of them were illiterate.

The economic situation had deteriorated as a result of the cumulative effects of drought; over-population of livestock in grazing areas; the proliferation of wells; increasing deforestation to meet the population's firewood needs; the virtual disappearance of rain-fed agriculture and the decline of flood-plain agriculture; and the inadequacy of irrigated agriculture which, at best, was expected to increase from the 10,000 tons currently produced to 40,000 tons in 1990, although the annual demand for grain exceeded 250,000 tons.

Between 1975 and 1984, Mauritania's economy grew at an estimated 2.3 per cent annually, almost the same percentage as its population growth, meaning that real per capita income remained virtually constant. According to April 1985 World Bank figures, per capita GDP averaged $465 in 1982, $475 in 1983 and $430 in 1984. In 1984, the country's balance of payments was characterized by a persistent trade deficit (accounting for 34 per cent of GDP), and the external debt had risen to twice GDP. According to World Bank statistics, per capita GNP stood at $440 in 1983.

In his report on the critical economic situation in Africa,[6] the Secretary-General provided information on a country-specific meeting for Mauritania (Dakar, Senegal, 2 April), at which Mauritania had presented an emergency plan finalized by the new Government in January. The plan focused on two main actions: immediate relief operations for the population and livestock severely affected by continuing drought; and projects having a rapid development impact in the rural sector (agriculture, livestock development and environment protection), based on the concept of "food for work". The presentation was complemented by individual project data sheets included in four sector documents, relating to equipment for immediate operational needs of the Commission for Food Security, health requirements, water development programmes, and agriculture. Mauritania stressed the severe and profound impact of drought on the socio-economic situation, which included widespread malnutrition, drastic changes in the basic way of life of a largely nomadic population and increasing dependence on external assistance for survival. It emphasized national determination to reduce gradually the country's vulnerability through concurrent actions in water development, agriculture and animal husbandry, as well as by developing and improving the structures for food distribution and health.

At the meeting, donor countries made a number of commitments and firm pledges towards some of the programmes. Unmet needs for Mauritania, totalling $50.2 million, were specified: food aid requirements, including transport ($22.8 million), to which some 11 tons of butter oil and over 8 tons of dried skim milk should be added; basic agricultural/pastoral inputs

($1.1 million); essential health actions ($0.7 million); water projects ($10.2 million); and additional logistic (capital) inputs ($15.4 million), including the Government's project proposal to improve port handling and storage capacity as well as water projects.

GENERAL ASSEMBLY ACTION

On 17 December 1985, the General Assembly, on the recommendation of the Second Committee, adopted **resolution 40/219** without vote.

Assistance for the reconstruction, recovery, rehabilitation and development of Mauritania

The General Assembly,

Deeply concerned by the enormous devastation caused to woodlands and the serious damage suffered by the economic and social infrastructure of Mauritania over the last fifteen years of drought and desertification,

Deeply disturbed by the great economic and financial imbalances which have found expression in the paucity of overall growth and the magnitude of the budget deficit and the balance-of-payments deficit,

Aware of the fact that the deterioration of the productive economic base is caused by factors over which Mauritania has no control, such as drought, desertification, the current international economic situation and the fall in commodity prices,

Deeply concerned by the adverse consequences of those factors both at the socio-economic level, through a massive rural exodus and growing urban unemployment, and at the level of external indebtedness, which is reaching excessive proportions,

Asserting the urgent need for international action to help the Government of Mauritania in its efforts to overcome and control the effects of these devastating natural disasters,

Acknowledging that Mauritania, one of the countries most affected by drought and desertification, is in need of international assistance in order to overcome the hardships impeding its short-term and long-term development and hindering its efforts for reconstruction, recovery, rehabilitation and development,

Considering the serious social and human problems posed by the settlement and integration in urban centres of many vulnerable persons who, because of the rural exodus and the adverse effects of drought and desertification, are in need of immediate emergency aid,

Concerned by the persistent imbalances in the agricultural structure of the country and the fact that it is to a large extent dependent on food grants and totally dependent on imports in all sectors,

Concerned also that, in real terms, the projected volume of exports of iron ore for 1985 will be virtually two thirds lower than that of 1975, which will particularly hamper the development of the country,

Aware of the need to assist the country with a view to enabling it to develop and to exercise effective control over its fishing resources, its second source of foreign currency,

Noting with concern that, in addition to the country's demographic and geographical disadvantages, its only highway, constructed with outside financing, is constantly being covered by sand, thereby disrupting economic and social life in three quarters of the country,

Concerned further by the difficulties of all kinds encountered by the Government, Member States and international organizations in channelling food and relief to the afflicted population in the interior of the country because of the lack of a road network and of transport and communications,

Noting that the Government of Mauritania, by implementing a policy of economic austerity, devaluing its currency and raising producer prices, expects to succeed in 1985 in reducing the budget deficit that has accumulated over the preceding ten years,

Noting also that, despite the implementation by Mauritania of the harsh adjustment measures proposed by the International Monetary Fund and the World Bank, the country remains dependent on external sources for financing public and private investment,

Further noting with concern the deficit in the balance of payments from 1975 to 1984, the modest level of foreign-currency reserves and the accumulation from year to year of arrears in payments,

Bearing in mind the concern expressed by Member States and international organizations with regard to the catastrophic economic and social situation created in Mauritania by drought, desertification and war, and the particular interest that they take in the control of desertification with a view to the country's rapid return to normal living conditions and to its reconstruction and development,

Considering with satisfaction that the Government of Mauritania has, for the first time this year, succeeded in inducing several thousands of people to leave the urban centres and to return to their native soil in order to devote themselves to agriculture and stockraising,

Noting the urgent request addressed by the Government of Mauritania to the Secretary-General for the classification of Mauritania as one of the least developed countries,

1. *Expresses its appreciation* to the Secretary-General for the steps he has taken to mobilize humanitarian assistance for the countries affected by drought and desertification in general, and particularly for Mauritania as a country severely affected, and invites the international community to respond generously to the humanitarian needs of Mauritania;

2. *Also expresses its appreciation* to the countries, organizations of the United Nations system, other international organizations, the community commission, voluntary agencies and individuals whose generous assistance to the stricken population of Mauritania has never failed;

3. *Appeals urgently* to all Member States, specialized agencies and other United Nations bodies, as well as to international economic and financial institutions, to contribute generously, through bilateral or multilateral channels, towards meeting Mauritania's reconstruction, recovery, rehabilitation and development needs;

4. *Invites* the Economic and Social Council to request the Committee for Development Planning to examine, on a priority basis, the socio-economic situation of Mauritania and to consider including it in the list of the least developed countries;

5. *Requests* Member States, as well as United Nations programmes and organizations, to take special measures for Mauritania for the remainder of the Third United Nations Development Decade, pending examination of its situation by the Committee for Development Planning;

6. *Invites* the United Nations Development Programme, the Food and Agriculture Organization of the United Nations, the International Fund for Agricultural

Development, the World Food Programme, the World Health Organization, the United Nations Industrial Development Organization, the United Nations Children's Fund, the World Bank, the International Monetary Fund, the International Labour Organisation and the United Nations Educational, Scientific and Cultural Organization to maintain their current programmes and expand their future programmes of assistance and to report periodically to the Secretary-General on the steps they have taken and the resources they have made available to help Mauritania so that the General Assembly may consider them at its forty-first session;

7. _Requests_ the Secretary-General:

(a) To continue his efforts to mobilize international assistance for Mauritania and to ensure that the appropriate arrangements are made in order to establish an effective programme of special assistance;

(b) To open a special account under the United Nations Trust Fund for Special Economic Assistance Programmes, in order to facilitate payments of contributions for Mauritania, and urges Member States, non-governmental organizations and individuals to contribute generously to this account;

(c) To keep the situation in Mauritania constantly under review, to maintain contact with Member States, specialized agencies, regional and intergovernmental organizations and international financial institutions concerned, and to apprise the Economic and Social Council, at its second regular session of 1986, of the volume of economic assistance granted to Mauritania;

(d) To report on the progress achieved in remedying the economic situation of Mauritania and on the international assistance granted to the country in time for the matter to be considered by the General Assembly at its forty-first session.

General Assembly resolution 40/219

17 December 1985   Meeting 120   Adopted without vote

Approved by Second Committee (A/40/1043) without vote, 4 December (meeting 47); 88-nation draft (A/C.2/40/L.55), orally amended by Secretary following informal consultations; agenda item 87.

Sponsors: Algeria, Angola, Argentina, Austria, Bahrain, Barbados, Benin, Bolivia, Brazil, Burkina Faso, Cape Verde, Central African Republic, Chad, China, Colombia, Comoros, Cyprus, Democratic Kampuchea, Democratic Yemen, Djibouti, Dominican Republic, Ecuador, Egypt, Equatorial Guinea, Ethiopia, France, Gabon, Gambia, Ghana, Guinea, Guinea-Bissau, Guyana, Haiti, Honduras, India, Indonesia, Iran, Iraq, Ivory Coast, Japan, Jordan, Kenya, Kuwait, Lebanon, Lesotho, Liberia, Libyan Arab Jamahiriya, Madagascar, Mali, Mauritania, Mauritius, Mexico, Morocco, Nicaragua, Niger, Nigeria, Oman, Pakistan, Panama, Peru, Portugal, Qatar, Romania, Rwanda, Sao Tome and Principe, Saudi Arabia, Senegal, Sierra Leone, Singapore, Somalia, Spain, Sudan, Suriname, Swaziland, Syrian Arab Republic, Thailand, Togo, Tunisia, Turkey, Uganda, United Arab Emirates, United States, Uruguay, Venezuela, Yemen, Yugoslavia, Zaire, Zambia.

Meeting numbers. GA 40th session: 2nd Committee 42, 47; plenary 120.

Following approval of the text in the Committee, Belgium particularly welcomed paragraph 4; Mauritania deserved special attention, it believed.

Mozambique

In his September 1985 report[1] on special economic assistance to 14 African countries, the Secretary-General, as requested by the General Assembly in 1984,[55] reported on such assistance to Mozambique.

During the period under review, the country's economic and financial situation had not improved; if anything, the internal security situation

appeared to have deteriorated. On 23 March 1985, the Council of Ministers had announced measures to reinforce national defence and the introduction of a policy of maximum austerity, specifically in respect of fuel consumption, and policies to ensure improvement of economic and financial management.

In addition, Mozambique had continued to suffer from natural disasters. During the first two months of 1985, precipitation had been fair to good throughout most of the country, but the rain pattern had been irregular—heavy downpours had brought floods in the central and southern zones of the country which were expected to improve soil fertility in general, but summer crops had been lost. On 26 March, cyclonic winds with speeds of about 100 kilometres per hour had struck southern Maputo province, cutting off electrical supply to the capital, adversely affecting water supplies, hospitals, industrial activities, port operations, irrigation schemes, communications and public services. In spite of the difficulties, the Government had continued not only to deal with the immediate crises but also to establish a basis for long-term development.

By the end of 1984, the country's outstanding external debt totalled $2.4 billion, including arrears; of that amount, 92 per cent represented bilateral public debt owed to OECD members (36 per cent), centrally planned economies (30 per cent) and countries of the Organization of Petroleum Exporting Countries (OPEC) (16 per cent). At a Paris Club meeting in October 1984, agreement had been reached to provide debt relief on accumulated arrears as at 30 June 1984, as well as debt-service payments due between 1 July 1984 and 30 June 1985, leaving an estimated $550 million in payments due in 1984-1986. In spite of the debt relief, the debt-service ratio at the end of 1984 was equivalent to 174 per cent of the value of exports of goods, not including accumulated arrears.

Mozambique's emergency needs as presented at a country specific meeting (Geneva, 15 March 1985) totalled $88.5 million: food aid ($39.2 million), agricultural inputs ($17 million), essential health action ($10 million), relief survival items ($3.4 million), essential water projects ($10.9 million) and logistic inputs ($3.9 million). Those figures were under constant review and were revised in accordance with changing circumstances.

Even before the current emergency, Mozambique had relied on food aid to supplement domestic production and commercial imports to meet domestic food requirements. The Government reported that in 1984 food aid had totalled 308,451 tons. The country's cereal requirements (maize, wheat and rice) from 1 March to 31 December 1985 was estimated at 678,100 tons. The global supply forecast for that period was 408,400 tons (available stocks, 47,600 tons; planned market production, 103,800; commercial purchases, 103,700; WFP projects, 13,900; and food and commitments, 139,400), leaving a deficit of 269,700 tons.

In addition to emergency and food aid requirements, the Government called for a number of priority rehabilitation projects designed to link emergency assistance with development efforts. Those projects, totalling $84 million, included: rehabilitation of a rural commercial network ($22 million); support for a health network (medicines) ($4 million); water supply and construction ($5.3 million); rehabilitation of rural roads ($1.9 million); and irrigation schemes ($50.8 million).

In his report on the critical economic situation in Africa,[6] the Secretary-General gave an overview of the emergency situation in Mozambique as presented at the 15 March country-specific meeting. Government representatives had emphasized the need to give attention to rehabilitation as well as emergency needs, which included questions of food distribution, domestic market mechanisms, security aspects, accessibility of stricken populations in remote areas, structural measures, and relief and/or rehabilitation programmes.

GENERAL ASSEMBLY ACTION

On the recommendation of the Second Committee, the Assembly, on 17 December, adopted **resolution 40/232** without vote.

Assistance to Mozambique

The General Assembly,

Recalling Security Council resolution 386(1976) of 17 March 1976, in which the Council appealed to all States to provide financial, technical and material assistance to enable Mozambique to carry out its economic development programme, and requested the Secretary-General, in collaboration with the appropriate organizations of the United Nations system, to organize, with immediate effect, such assistance,

Recalling further its resolution 39/199 of 17 December 1984 and its earlier resolutions, in which it urged the international community to respond effectively and generously with assistance to Mozambique,

Having considered the report of the Secretary-General, submitted pursuant to its resolution 38/208, to which was annexed the report of the mission to Mozambique,

Deeply concerned at the loss of life and the destruction of essential infrastructures such as roads, railways, bridges, petroleum facilities, electricity supply, schools and hospitals, as identified in the reports of the Secretary-General,

Further concerned about the present difficult economic situation of Mozambique, as illustrated in the summary report of the Secretary-General, submitted pursuant to its resolution 39/199,

Noting with deep concern that Mozambique has continued to suffer from a prolonged drought causing heavy losses in human lives, food production and livestock and resulting in dislocation of its affected people,

Also noting with deep concern the extensive damage caused by the cyclone "Demoina" at the end of January 1984,

Noting that Mozambique faces an emergency food situation of an exceptional scale and needs imports of 638,000 tonnes of cereals in 1985/1986 to meet its food requirements, according to government estimates,

Recognizing that substantial international assistance is required for the implementation of a number of reconstruction and development projects,

1. *Strongly endorses* the appeals made by the Security Council and the Secretary-General for international assistance to Mozambique;

2. *Expresses its appreciation* to the Secretary-General for the measures he has taken to organize an international economic assistance programme for Mozambique;

3. *Also expresses its appreciation* for the assistance provided to Mozambique by various States and regional and international organizations and humanitarian institutions;

4. *Regrets*, however, that the total assistance provided to date falls far short of Mozambique's pressing needs;

5. *Appeals* to the international community to provide adequate food aid to Mozambique to prevent further starvation and malnutrition;

6. *Draws the attention* of the international community to the two areas for immediate action—the supply of crude oil and petroleum products and the supply of basic inputs and consumer goods for the agricultural sector—that are critical for the functioning of the economy;

7. *Also draws the attention* of the international community to the additional financial, economic and material assistance identified in the annex to the report of the Secretary-General as urgently required by Mozambique;

8. *Calls upon* Member States, regional and inter-regional organizations and other governmental and non-governmental organizations to provide financial, material and technical assistance to Mozambique, wherever possible in the form of grants, and urges them to give priority to the inclusion of Mozambique in their programmes of development assistance;

9. *Urges* Member States and organizations that are already implementing or negotiating assistance programmes for Mozambique to strengthen them;

10. *Strongly appeals* to the international community to contribute to the special account for Mozambique established by the Secretary-General for the purpose of facilitating the channelling of contributions to Mozambique;

11. *Invites* the appropriate organizations and programmes of the United Nations system—in particular the United Nations Development Programme, the Food and Agriculture Organization of the United Nations, the International Fund for Agricultural Development, the World Food Programme, the World Health Organization, the United Nations Children's Fund, the United Nations Fund for Population Activities and the United Nations Industrial Development Organization—to maintain and increase their current and future programmes of assistance to Mozambique, to co-operate closely with the Secretary-General in organizing an effective international programme of

assistance and to report periodically to him on the steps they have taken and the resources they have made available to help that country;

12. *Requests* the Secretary-General:

(a) To continue his efforts to mobilize the necessary financial, technical and material assistance to Mozambique;

(b) To keep the situation in Mozambique under constant review, to maintain close contact with Member States, the specialized agencies, regional and other intergovernmental organizations, international financial institutions and other bodies concerned, and to apprise the Economic and Social Council, at its second regular session of 1986, of the current status of the special programme of economic assistance for Mozambique;

(c) To prepare, on the basis of sustained consultations with the Government of Mozambique, a report on the development of the economic situation and the implementation of the special programme of economic assistance for that country in time for the matter to be considered by the General Assembly at its forty-first session.

General Assembly resolution 40/232

17 December 1985   Meeting 120   Adopted without vote

Approved by Second Committee (A/40/1043) without vote, 5 December (meeting 48); 44-nation draft (A/C.2/40/L.72), orally amended by Secretary following informal consultations; agenda item 87.

Sponsors: Afghanistan, Algeria, Angola, Austria, Bangladesh, Benin, Botswana, Brazil, Burkina Faso, Cape Verde, Congo, Cuba, Czechoslovakia, Democratic Yemen, Egypt, Ethiopia, Gambia, German Democratic Republic, Ghana, Guinea-Bissau, India, Lesotho, Liberia, Libyan Arab Jamahiriya, Madagascar, Malawi, Mexico, Mongolia, Mozambique, Nepal, Nicaragua, Nigeria, Pakistan, Panama, Peru, Portugal, Sao Tome and Principe, Sri Lanka, Swaziland, Sweden, United Republic of Tanzania, Viet Nam, Yugoslavia, Zambia.

Meeting numbers. GA 40th session: 2nd Committee 44, 48; plenary 120.

Sao Tome and Principe

In September 1985,[1] the Secretary-General, in response to a 1984 request by the General Assembly,[56] reported on economic assistance to Sao Tome and Principe, an archipelagic LDC with a population estimated at 104,000, affected by natural disasters—drought in some parts of the country combined with erratic rainfall in others, resulting in a disruption of the country's staple foods and cocoa production.

As indicated by the Government, the country's basic food requirements for 1985 were an estimated 14,000 tons of rice, sugar, wheat flour, beans, powdered skim milk and vegetable oil, of which some 4,000 tons were requested as food assistance.

The Secretary-General, also in September, reported[2] that special economic assistance to Sao Tome and Principe by the United Nations system included help in census analysis by DTCD, financed by UNFPA; port management by UNCTAD, funded by UNDP; health by UNICEF; industrial development by UNIDO; development and emergency operations projects by WFP; forestry, apiculture and crops by FAO, funded by UNDP, as well as equipment and pesticides for plant protection, financed by the United Nations Emergency Operation Trust Fund; and artisanal fisheries by

IFAD. In addition, UNDP supported various projects to increase agricultural production.

Sierra Leone

The Secretary-General, as requested by the General Assembly in 1984,[26] reported in September 1985[1] on special economic assistance to Sierra Leone, an LDC experiencing economic and financial difficulties, owing in part to structural imbalances in its economy and in part to the adverse impact of the slow-down in global economic activity. Average per capita GNP in 1982 was estimated at $390, with great disparities in income distribution.

However, Sierra Leone had the potential to achieve self-sustaining growth; it had natural resources and was suitable for agriculture, which provided employment to some 65 per cent of the work force and accounted for 30 per cent of GDP and 35 per cent of export earnings. The country was also endowed with mineral deposits, including diamonds, bauxite, rutile and iron ore, and there was a modest output of gold. The mining sector accounted for 65 per cent of export earnings. In addition, the country had excellent possibilities for hydropower development.

After growing at the rate of 4 per cent annually during the 1970s, Sierra Leone's economy became affected by the global recession of the early 1980s and had virtually stagnated since then. With an annual population growth rate of 2.7 per cent in 1974-1985, per capita income fell. A macro-economic environment typified by distortions and imbalances that were a disincentive to growth, as well as a decline in exports and export prices and capital outflow, resulted in a balance-of-payments crisis. Gross fiscal imbalance resulted in deficits in excess of 14 per cent of GDP, financed mainly by domestic bank credit, which resulted in the virtual doubling of the money supply between fiscal year 1984 and 1985 and was the principal cause of inflation. The fiscal deficit, due largely to declining revenue collection, affected development projects and project implementation became problematic. In an effort to redress the situation, the Government in December 1985 instituted a number of corrective measures.

The country's debt, amounting to $670 million at the end of 1985, was a question of concern. Discussions were under way between the Government and IMF about the possibility of a stand-by arrangement, and with the World Bank for a structural adjustment credit to support Sierra Leone's adjustment programme.

GENERAL ASSEMBLY ACTION

On 17 December, acting on the recommendation of the Second Committee, the General Assembly adopted **resolution 40/220** without vote.

Assistance to Sierra Leone

The General Assembly,

Recalling its resolutions 37/158 of 17 December 1982, 38/205 of 20 December 1983 and 39/192 of 17 December 1984, in which it appealed to all States, the specialized agencies and international development and financial institutions to provide all possible assistance for the development of Sierra Leone,

Further recalling its resolution 37/133 of 17 December 1982, in which it decided to include Sierra Leone in the list of the least developed countries,

Having considered the summary report of the Secretary-General,

Noting with concern that the economy of Sierra Leone is being undermined by severe scarcities of imported raw materials and spare parts for industry, a drying-up of trade and commercial credits, large commercial payment arrears and unmitigated strains on government finances,

Noting that the Government of Sierra Leone, in co-operation with the United Nations Development Programme, embarked upon preparations for a round table of partners in development of Sierra Leone, which was originally to be held early in 1985 but was deferred until early 1986,

Reiterating the need for effective mobilization of international assistance in order to implement fully the programme of development outlined in the report of the multi-agency mission,

1. *Expresses its appreciation* to the Secretary-General for the steps he has taken to mobilize assistance for Sierra Leone;

2. *Urgently reiterates its appeal* to the international community, including the specialized agencies and other organizations and bodies of the United Nations system, to contribute generously, through bilateral or multilateral channels, to the economic and social development of Sierra Leone;

3. *Urges* all States and relevant United Nations bodies—in particular the United Nations Development Programme, the World Food Programme, the United Nations Children's Fund, the World Health Organization, the United Nations Educational, Scientific and Cultural Organization and the United Nations Fund for Population Activities—to provide all possible assistance to help the Government of Sierra Leone meet the critical humanitarian needs of the population and to provide, as appropriate, food, medicines and essential equipment for hospitals and schools;

4. *Invites* the United Nations Development Programme, the United Nations Children's Fund, the World Food Programme, the World Health Organization, the Food and Agriculture Organization of the United Nations, the World Bank, the International Fund for Agricultural Development and the United Nations Industrial Development Organization to bring to the attention of their governing bodies, for their consideration, the special needs of Sierra Leone and to report the decisions of those bodies to the Secretary-General by 15 July 1986;

5. *Appeals* to all States and international organizations to participate at a high level in the round table of partners in development of Sierra Leone to be held early in 1986, and to contribute generously to the programme of action that will be presented by the Government of Sierra Leone;

6. *Requests* the Secretary-General:

(a) To continue his efforts to mobilize the necessary resources for an effective programme of financial, technical and material assistance to Sierra Leone;

(b) To apprise the Economic and Social Council, at its second regular session of 1986, of the assistance granted to Sierra Leone;

(c) To keep the situation regarding assistance to Sierra Leone under review and to report to the General Assembly at its forty-first session on the implementation of the present resolution.

General Assembly resolution 40/220

17 December 1985   Meeting 120   Adopted without vote

Approved by Second Committee (A/40/1043) without vote, 4 December (meeting 47); 13-nation draft (A/C.2/40/L.56); agenda item 87.
Sponsors: Algeria, Bangladesh, Chad, Ethiopia, Guinea, Japan, Madagascar, Nepal, Sao Tome and Principe, Sierra Leone, Singapore, Swaziland, Uganda.
Meeting numbers. GA 40th session: 2nd Committee 42, 47; plenary 120.

Swaziland

Swaziland, a land-locked developing country with a population of about 600,000 and an estimated per capita income of $880, continued to experience a difficult economic situation as a result of the 1981-1983 drought, the January 1984 cyclone Demoina, reduced investment and the world-wide recession which remained particularly severe in southern Africa, according to a September 1985 report of the Secretary-General.[1] Real growth of the economy remained negligible and per capita income fell as the population grew by 3.4 per cent annually. Opportunities existed for productive investment, but the slower growth of revenues and the burden of cyclone rehabilitation on the budget restricted government support of new investments.

The Fourth Development Plan (1984-1988), approved in late 1984, forecast that the economy would grow by 0.7 per cent per year during the remainder of the Plan period, implying a continuing annual fall in per capita income of 2.6 per cent. Government revenue was targeted to grow at 1.5 per cent annually and the trade deficit was expected to widen, mainly owing to poor prospects for the price of the sugar. The targets of the Plan included: greater efficiency and control over the use of public funds; stimulation of private investment; promotion of job creation; and establishment of productive agriculture employment opportunities in rural areas. The Government estimated it would take five years to complete the repair of damage caused by the 1984 cyclone; this was reflected in the 1985/86 budget by a shift in resource allocations from the social sector to the economic sector of some 10 per cent compared with 1984/85.

Although the balance of payments improved compared to previous years, the downward trend remained a matter of concern and indicated the need for overall restraint in public spending, diversification of exports and better promotion of private investment.

Agricultural production showed a marked improvement in the 1983/84 season with record crops in maize, sugar and pineapples. Maize production reached 110,000 tons as compared to 51,000 tons in 1982/83, and sugar production was 380,000 tons in 1983/84 and 402,000 tons in 1984/85. However, the falling price of sugar and the declining proportion of the crop being sold under quota or to protected markets resulted in a reduction in revenue. Pineapple production continued to grow and world prices improved owing to reduced supply from other areas. Citrus production, which had shown a downward trend in recent years, was seriously affected by the 1984 cyclone. Cotton, however, had made some recovery since the 1981-1983 drought, but production was still below earlier years; it was anticipated that a planned textile mill would stimulate production.

The manufacturing industry was dominated by processing local agricultural and forest products. Wood pulp—the second major export after sugar—was produced at a record 180,000 tons in 1984. Improvements were also recorded in the mining and transportation sectors. The Government signed an $8.6 million loan agreement with the World Bank for a road rehabilitation programme following cyclone Demoina. Other assistance came from the United States Agency for International Development (USAID) ($1.06 million) and the United Kingdom, which undertook the reconstruction of a principal bridge—Big Bend. The project for expanding Matsapha Airport was expected to be completed in 1986 and the northern rail link was scheduled to be opened late in 1985. The completion of the Luphohlo-Ezulwini hydroelectric scheme allowed Swaziland to become 70 per cent self-sufficient in electric-power generation.

To improve the funding of hospitals, especially in the area of drugs, the health sector budget was increased in 1985. Preventive health programmes continued to focus on the maternal and child health sector and on the control of infectious and water-borne diseases. Potable water supplies reached 80 per cent of the urban and 40 per cent of the rural populations. A recently approved UNDP project, financed from the United Nations Emergency Operation Trust Fund, made available $750,000 to provide potable water to an additional 25,000 people; the project was to focus particularly on the needs of drought-prone areas where surface water supplies had dried up during the 1981-1983 drought.

The special economic assistance programme aimed at repairing and reconstructing Swaziland's infrastructure resulting from cyclone and flood damage: nine projects were for road and bridge rehabilitation; five dealt with agriculture; two related to power; four were for water supply; and three concerned public facilities.

Assistance to Swaziland by United Nations bodies and agencies was summarized by the Secretary-General in another September 1985 report.[2] Among them, the World Bank/IDA made new loans totalling $8.6 million in fiscal 1985 for cyclone rehabilitation. Other projects included the repair of cyclone-damaged schools financed by UNESCO and vocational rehabilitation of the disabled by ILO, funded by UNDP.

Uganda

The Secretary-General had been requested in 1984[27] to report to the General Assembly in 1985 on the economic situation and on the progress made in organizing international assistance to Uganda. In September 1985,[1] he indicated that the Government had been asked whether it would wish the report to be based on the findings of a review mission or whether it would prefer to provide information for an interim report. Uganda requested a review mission, but asked that it be postponed.

In 1985, Uganda's economic situation continued to be precarious. Except for a period of recovery in 1981/82 to 1983/84, the country had been in economic decline since the early 1970s. Civil war had brought physical destruction, disruption of economic and social services, large-scale displacement of population within the country and flight of great numbers from it. The Luwera triangle, once among the richest areas in the country, was a wasteland. Transport bottle-necks were hindering the supply of foodstuffs to urban areas and the export of coffee, from which 95 per cent of export revenues were derived.

According to government estimates, Uganda's GDP fell between 1970 and 1985 by 11 per cent in real terms, while agricultural and manufacturing outputs declined by 30 and 50 per cent, respectively; the former exporter of sugar had come to import almost all its sugar requirements and, with the exception of staple foodstuffs, almost every essential commodity had to be imported. By the end of 1985, foreign exchange reserves had dwindled to the equivalent of less than two weeks of 1984/85 imports, and the shortage of raw materials, spare parts and equipment had idled industrial plants.

Assistance to Uganda by the United Nations system[2] included assistance in family planning by UNFPA; health and water supplies by UNICEF; development projects by UNIDO and WFP; livestock, dairy production, rehabilitation of national parks, emergency assistance for displaced persons, seeds and animal disease control by FAO; a project funded by UNDP and implemented by ICAO for pilot training and aircraft maintenance; agricultural development by IFAD and IDA; and a labour-intensive employment programme and assistance to a national manpower survey, carried out by ILO and funded by UNDP. In 1985, the World Bank/IDA granted new loans totalling $71.6 million for agricultural development, petroleum exploration and water supply projects.

UNCTAD continued its assistance to Uganda, with financial support from UNDP, as requested by the Trade and Development Board on 29 March 1985.[57] In December, UNCTAD reported[58] that, apart from its continuing technical support provided under a UNDP-financed project on external sector development, it had identified in Uganda the need for technical assistance in the area of external debt control; a project to be financed by UNDP at a cost of $89,000 was signed in 1985. Uganda also benefited from a regional transit-transport project, funded by UNDP and executed by UNCTAD, which covered the land-locked developing countries of East and Central Africa; assistance provided to Uganda under that project included advisory services in subregional transit-transport legal arrangements, the establishment of dry ports and other inland facilities for the trans-shipment of goods, the co-ordination of road and rail transport, the harmonization of transit-transport policies and the removal of non-physical barriers to transit-transport operations.

GENERAL ASSEMBLY ACTION

In December, the General Assembly adopted **decision 40/453** without vote.

Assistance to Uganda

At its 120th plenary meeting, on 17 December 1985, the General Assembly, on the recommendation of the Second Committee, having heard the statement of the representative of Uganda on 13 November 1985, and recalling its resolution 39/188 of 17 December 1984 on assistance to Uganda, decided to request the Secretary-General to continue to review the progress made in the economic situation in Uganda and in organizing international assistance for that country, to apprise the Economic and Social Council at its second regular session of 1986 of the situation and to report thereon to the Assembly at its forty-first session.

General Assembly decision 40/453

Adopted without vote

Approved by Second Committee (A/40/1043) without vote, 11 December (meeting 50); draft by Vice-Chairman (A/C.2/40/L.120), based on informal consultations; agenda item 87.
Meeting numbers. GA 40th session: 2nd Committee 34, 50; plenary 120.

In **resolution 40/221**, the Assembly dealt with relief to drought-stricken areas of East Africa, including Uganda.

Speaking on 13 November before the Second Committee, Uganda regretted that the Secretary-General had not submitted a report to the current Assembly session and that the section of his report[1] on special economic assistance dealing with Uganda contained no information on the country's situation in 1985. In view of its unchanged economic situation, Uganda would not submit a draft resolution on special assistance; it wished, however, to have an explicit statement from either the Committee Chairman or the Secretary-General as to whether resolution 39/188 still constituted a valid mandate and a directive to the Secretary-General. After two decades of anguish caused by political and moral decay and abuse of power by the previous authorities, Uganda was engaged in a determined effort to secure peace based on justice, law and order and economic and social prosperity for all Ugandans; the additional external assistance Uganda was requesting would supplement, rather than replace, national efforts.

Countries in other regions

Bolivia

On 17 December 1985, the General Assembly, on the recommendation of the Second Committee, adopted **decision 40/452** on special assistance to Bolivia. The Assembly decided, at the request of Venezuela, that the Secretary-General should transfer all remaining monies from the United Nations Special Fund, which consisted solely of contributions from Venezuela to that Fund, together with the interest accumulated over the years, to the Bolivia account in the Trust Fund for Special Economic Assistance Programmes.

Speaking on 25 November after the Committee's approval of the draft decision, Bolivia thanked Venezuela for its generous contribution to alleviate the effects of the serious economic crisis in Bolivia; the collapse of international prices for tin, which ranked second among Bolivia's export products, had had a negative effect on the Government's economic recovery programme.

Democratic Yemen

In July 1985,[59] the Secretary-General, in response to a 1984 General Assembly request,[60] reported on international assistance to Democratic Yemen, which had suffered serious damage from consecutive floods in 1981 and 1982, estimated at $950 million. According to the Disaster Relief Committee set up by the Government, the estimated losses were: loss of human life, 482; homeless, 12,000 families (about 50,000 people); houses destroyed, 25,000; and animals killed, 50,000 (sheep, goats, camels and cows).

Immediate action was taken by the international community to alleviate the devastating damages. According to information gathered by the UNDP Resident Representative in Democratic Yemen, assistance for relief operations was provided by 12 countries on a bilateral basis, 17 national or regional members of the Red Cross/Red Crescent and five United Nations organizations (UNDRO, UNICEF, UNDP, WFP and WHO).

Most of the rehabilitation and reconstruction programmes, which totalled $36.2 million in credits and grants, were either completed or nearing completion as of June 1985. For example, the reconstruction of flood-damaged roads in Abyan and Aden, a project funded by the World Bank, the Arab Fund for Economic and Social Development and the OPEC Fund, had achieved most of its objectives. However, a few projects were delayed, such as flood control of the Wadi Bana'a and the Wadi Hasan (FAO assistance) and Gabion flood protection (Netherlands Trust Fund assistance), which had begun in 1984 and were expected to be completed by mid-1986. A UNCDF-assisted project for the rehabilitation of crop production in the Abyan Delta started in January 1985 and was expected to be completed by the end of 1987. The reconstruction and rehabilitation of the Batais Dam by the USSR resulted in a new request from Democratic Yemen for the same kind of assistance for the Haiya Dam and canals. Operations under that project, also assisted by the USSR, started in January 1985.

GENERAL ASSEMBLY ACTION

On the recommendation of the Second Committee, the General Assembly, on 17 December 1985, adopted **resolution 40/215** without vote.

Assistance to Democratic Yemen

The General Assembly,

Recalling its resolution 39/184 of 17 December 1984 and Economic and Social Council resolutions 1982/6 of 28 April 1982 and 1982/59 of 30 July 1982 concerning the extensive devastation caused by the heavy floods in Democratic Yemen,

Recalling also resolution 107(IX) of 11 May 1982 of the Economic Commission for Western Asia, in which the Commission called for the urgent establishment of a programme for the rehabilitation and reconstruction of the flood-stricken areas of Democratic Yemen,

Having considered the report prepared by the Office of the United Nations Disaster Relief Co-ordinator on the extent and nature of the damage caused by the floods,

Taking note of the report of the Secretary-General on assistance to Democratic Yemen,

Recognizing that Democratic Yemen, as one of the least developed countries, is unable to bear the mounting burden of rehabilitation and reconstruction of the affected areas,

Recognizing also the efforts made by Democratic Yemen to alleviate the suffering of the victims of the floods,

1. *Expresses its appreciation* to the Secretary-General for the steps he has taken regarding assistance to Democratic Yemen;

2. *Expresses its gratitude* to those States and international, regional and intergovernmental organizations that have provided assistance to Democratic Yemen;

3. *Requests* the Secretary-General to continue to mobilize the necessary resources for an effective, comprehensive programme of financial, technical and material assistance to Democratic Yemen in order to help to mitigate the damage inflicted on it and implement its rehabilitation and reconstruction plans;

4. *Appeals* to Member States to contribute generously through bilateral or multilateral channels to the reconstruction and development process in Democratic Yemen;

5. *Invites* the appropriate organizations and programmes of the United Nations system—in particular the United Nations Development Programme, the World Bank, the World Food Programme, the Food and Agriculture Organization of the United Nations, the International Fund for Agricultural Development, the World Health Organization, the United Nations Fund for Population Activities, the United Nations Children's Fund and the United Nations Industrial Development Organization—to maintain and expand their programmes of assistance to Democratic Yemen and to cooperate closely with the Secretary-General in organizing an effective programme of assistance to that country;

6. *Calls upon* regional and interregional organizations and other intergovernmental and non-governmental organizations to continue their assistance to the development requirements of Democratic Yemen;

7. *Requests* the Secretary-General to keep the situation in Democratic Yemen under review and to report to the General Assembly at its forty-first session on the progress made in the implementation of the present resolution.

General Assembly resolution 40/215

17 December 1985   Meeting 120   Adopted without vote

Approved by Second Committee (A/40/1043) without vote, 4 December (meeting 47); 29-nation draft (A/C.2/40/L.45), orally amended by Secretary following informal consultations; agenda item 87.

Sponsors: Afghanistan, Algeria, Argentina, Bahrain, Bangladesh, China, Democratic Yemen, Djibouti, Ethiopia, India, Iraq, Jordan, Kuwait, Lebanon, Libyan Arab Jamahiriya, Madagascar, Mauritania, Oman, Pakistan, Qatar, Saudi Arabia, Sudan, Syrian Arab Republic, Tunisia, United Arab Emirates, United Republic of Tanzania, Vanuatu, Viet Nam, Yemen.

Meeting numbers. GA 40th session: 2nd Committee 42, 47; plenary 120.

Haiti

In response to a 1984 General Assembly request[61] that he consult with the Government of Haiti on its special assistance needs, the Secretary-General arranged for a mission to visit the country from 1 to 6 July and from 15 to 18 October 1985. The mission's report[62] reviewed the economic situation and key economic and social sectors, assessed development priorities, problems and critical issues, and presented for consideration by the international community priority programmes and projects requiring external assistance.

With a per capita GDP of $300, Haiti was the only country in the Americas to be classified by the United Nations as an LDC. Indications were that some 80 per cent of children under five years of age suffered from malnutrition. Infant mortality was reported at a high 120 per 1,000 live births. Sanitation was inadequate in both urban and rural areas. Under public education, only 17 per cent of children attended school. It was estimated that 77 per cent of the overall population was illiterate, with the percentage as high as 90 per cent in rural areas, where 75 per cent of Haiti's 5.3 million people lived. There was a strong exodus to principal cities, exacerbating unemployment and attendant social problems. Although the estimated population growth rate of 1.4 to 1.5 per cent was relatively low, it still exceeded increases in agricultural production. As a result of population pressure on available land and the general lack of alternative employment prospects, net emigration was high, averaging 25,000 annually in recent years.

It was estimated that only 70 to 80 per cent of the country's food requirements were grown locally. Virtually all requirements for wheat and wheat by-products (some 150,000 tons per annum) had to be imported. The annual deficit of locally produced grains ranged between 50,000 and 100,000 tons as compared to a local production of 400,000 tons. Food products accounted for almost 20 per cent of the value of all imports. The production of export crops (bananas, coffee, rice, maize and sugar cane) stagnated or declined.

Between 1980 and 1984, Haiti's external debt more than doubled, reaching $600 million by September 1984, and capital inflows were insufficient to offset the deficits, resulting in a drawing down of reserves and a chronically deficit government budget.

Following a government reform in 1982 of the educational system, which was to be restructured gradually into a 10-year programme of basic education, the number of students attending classes increased to 56 per cent in 1984/85, compared with 38 per cent in 1979/80.

Haiti benefited over the years from external development aid and technical assistance; Canada, France, Japan, the United States and, more recently, the Federal Republic of Germany had carried out active bilateral programmes. Grant and loan commitments in 1984 totalled some $83 million compared to $46.5 million in 1980.

The Inter-American Development Bank, EEC, the Organization of American States, WFP, IFAD and various United Nations agencies increased their grant commitments from $13.9 million in 1980 to $25.1 million in 1984. Concessional multilateral loan commitments on the other hand fell to $20.3 million in 1984 after reaching a peak of $80.1 million in 1983. The drop was primarily the result of IDA making no loan commitments to Haiti in 1984, reflecting difficulties encountered over the replenishment of its resources. In 1983, a stand-by agreement had been negotiated with IMF to continue stabilization efforts and to continue reducing the public sector deficit financed by Central Bank credit and non-concessional

resources. The programme called for further measures to increase revenues and tighten control over public sector expenditure, and emphasis was given to improving tax administration. In September 1984, IMF determined that Haiti's performance had fallen short of the agreed programme and the stand-by agreement was suspended.

Over 300 NGOs or private volunteer agencies also carried out programmes in Haiti, primarily financed externally, which were estimated to have exceeded the $14.8 million recorded by the World Bank in 1984. The Government was negotiating with the Inter-American Development Bank a series of projects to be initiated in 1985-1986, totalling about $145 million; they included rural education, drinking water, transportation infrastructure, rural development, health services and agricultural credit. Several of the projects were to be co-financed with other bilateral or multilateral donors.

The mission concurred in the Government's assessment that, while development efforts must continue in all areas, it must accord the highest priority to overcoming the critical problems of deforestation/soil erosion and illiteracy. The international community was urged to provide the necessary financial and technical assistance.

In addition, Haiti identified specific priority projects requiring external assistance that it wished to be called to the attention of the international community. The projects, amounting to $156 million, dealt with agriculture, industry, energy, potable water, transport, education, health, commerce and other sectors.

In a September 1985 report,[2] the Secretary-General described the activities of United Nations bodies and specialized agencies in Haiti, among them a UNDP-funded project on assistance in planning, carried out by UNCTAD; UNFPA support for the Government's maternal and child health care programme; emergency operations and development projects by WFP; rural development, livestock, crops, fisheries, forestry and fertilizers by FAO; fellowships and a consultancy mission by UPU; and projects to strengthen the national meteorological service and its observing equipment by WMO.

GENERAL ASSEMBLY ACTION

By **decision 40/454** on special economic assistance programmes, the General Assembly, on 17 December, took note of the mission's report on Haiti.

Kiribati

The Secretary-General, in response to a 1984 request of the Economic and Social Council,[63] arranged for a review mission to Kiribati from

28 January to 6 February 1985 to consult with the Government on priority sectors for development and its needs for external assistance.

Kiribati comprises 33 islands in the central Pacific Ocean. Among the main groups are the Gilbert Islands, which includes Tarawa, the centre of Government; the Line Islands, which include Kiritimati (or Christmas) Island, the largest island in the country; and the Phoenix Islands, of which only Kanton was inhabited in 1985. According to the mission's report, annexed to a report of the Secretary-General,[64] the country's population was estimated at 63,000 in 1982; its growth of about 2.2 per cent annually was accompanied by internal migration to the urban area of Bairiki in south Tarawa.

The atoll environment of the islands of Kiribati, with the exception of Banaba (in the Gilbert Islands), limited agricultural production. In addition, local production for inter-island and international trade was hampered by limited and relatively expensive transport. The principal food crops of the country were babai (swamp taro), pandanus and breadfruit, cultivated mainly for subsistence, and coconut palms, grown for both subsistence and trade. Chickens and pigs were raised mostly for subsistence. Ocean, lagoon and reef fishing were important subsistence activities. However, a high proportion of local food consumption, especially in areas of high population density, came from imports.

In its national development plan for 1983-1986, the Government attempted to deal with the critical effects on the economy of the termination of phosphate mining operations on Banaba in 1979, to sustain the survival, health, education and employment of the people, and to evolve towards economic self-sufficiency. Practically all development projects under the plan were financed from external sources. The largest donor, the United Kingdom, contributed some 52 per cent during the first two years of the plan. Other major sources of funding came from Australia, Japan, New Zealand and the European Development Fund. The Government also received substantial non-financial assistance from the same group, of which three fifths consisted of aid-in-kind.

In a September 1985 report,[2] the Secretary-General indicated that United Nations assistance to Kiribati included training fellowships by ICAO, ILO and UPU, all financed by UNDP, as well as financial support by UNFPA to the Tungara National Youth Council.

On 29 June 1985, in a decision on the allocation of resources for the fourth programming cycle (1987-1991),[65] the UNDP Governing Council took full account of the problems of island developing countries such as Kiribati and agreed to apply supplementary criteria to the determination of UNDP resources which would be made available to them.

UNDP assisted Kiribati with its Development Co-ordination Meeting of Donors, held in May/June 1985, designed, among other things, to review capital and technical assistance programmes and attract new donors.

On 19 September,[66] Papua New Guinea transmitted to the Secretary-General a South Pacific Forum communiqué of 6 August, which included a statement on smaller island countries, among them Kiribati. The Forum stressed the fact that characteristics of smallness, isolation, lack of resources and vulnerability gave rise to severe problems in terms of limited agricultural and manufacturing potential, diseconomies of scale and weak bargaining power, expensive and irregular transport links and inadequate communications. It recognized that special emphasis on meeting the needs of those countries should be given through support of their national development strategies and preferential treatment in regional programmes. To that end, it considered a series of proposals in the fields of fisheries, transport, tourism, agriculture, external employment, energy, water, culture, minerals, manufacturing, communications and education.

ECONOMIC AND SOCIAL COUNCIL
AND GENERAL ASSEMBLY ACTION

By **decision 1985/184** of 25 July, the Economic and Social Council took note of the mission's report on Kiribati,[64] and transmitted it to the General Assembly. The Assembly took note of it on 17 December, by **decision 40/454**.

Nicaragua

In October 1985,[67] the Secretary-General reported on assistance to Nicaragua, as requested by the General Assembly in 1984.[68] The report was based on information received from Nicaragua, nine Member States (Denmark, France, German Democratic Republic, Federal Republic of Germany, Ireland, Italy, Netherlands, Spain, Sweden), and United Nations bodies and agencies. In 1984, external bilateral assistance pledged to Nicaragua amounted to $341.7 million, bringing the total for the period from 1979 to 1984 to $2,109.5 million (Western Europe, 297.3 million; North America, 88.3 million; Latin America, $803.6 million; Africa and Asia, $139.8 million; and socialist countries, $780.5 million), while resources pledged by multilateral agencies for that period totalled $629.9 million. Non-reimbursable bilateral assistance and assistance from NGOs from 1980 to 1984 totalled $194.8 million; for the period from 1 January to 31 May 1985, that assistance reached $3.2 million. In addition, 201,870 tons of food—over 90 per cent in grain—was provided from January 1984 to July 1985 by 10 countries (Argentina, Austria, France, Federal Republic of Germany, Greece, Netherlands, Romania, Sweden, USSR, Yugoslavia), EEC and WFP.

Assistance approved by the United Nations system from 19 July 1979 to 1 April 1984 amounted to over $258.5 million, of which $149.6 million was financial and $108.9 million was technical. According to information provided by the resident co-ordinator of operational activities for development at Managua, co-operation and technical assistance approved between 1 April 1984 and 1 May 1985 totalled some $23.6 million.

GENERAL ASSEMBLY ACTION

On 17 December, the General Assembly, on the recommendation of the Second Committee, adopted **resolution 40/234** without vote.

Assistance to Nicaragua

The General Assembly,

Recalling its resolutions 34/8 of 25 October 1979, 35/84 of 5 December 1980, 36/213 of 17 December 1981, 37/157 of 17 December 1982, 38/223 of 20 December 1983 and 39/204 of 17 December 1984 concerning assistance for the reconstruction of Nicaragua,

Taking note of the report of the Secretary-General on assistance to Nicaragua,

Noting with satisfaction the support that Member States, the specialized agencies and other organizations of the United Nations system have given to the efforts of the Government of Nicaragua for the reconstruction of the country,

Bearing in mind that, in recent years, the Nicaraguan economy has been adversely affected by various events and natural disasters, such as drought, the intense rains and floods of 1982 and a sequence of natural disasters in June, July, October and November 1985,

Considering that, despite the efforts of the Government and people of Nicaragua, the economic situation has not returned to normal and continues to worsen,

Deeply concerned that Nicaragua is experiencing serious economic difficulties directly affecting its development efforts,

1. *Expresses its appreciation* to the Secretary-General for his efforts regarding assistance to Nicaragua;

2. *Expresses its appreciation also* to the States and organizations that have provided assistance to Nicaragua;

3. *Urges* all Governments to continue contributing to the reconstruction and development of Nicaragua;

4. *Invites* the organizations of the United Nations system to continue and to increase their assistance in this endeavour;

5. *Recommends* that Nicaragua should continue to receive treatment appropriate to the special needs of the country until the economic situation returns to normal;

6. *Requests* the Secretary-General to report to the General Assembly at its forty-first session on the progress made in the implementation of the present resolution.

General Assembly resolution 40/234

17 December 1985   Meeting 120   Adopted without vote

Approved by Second Committee (A/40/1043) without vote, 4 December (meeting 47); 66-nation draft (A/C.2/40/L.74), orally amended by Secretary following informal consultations; agenda item 87.

Sponsors: Afghanistan, Algeria, Angola, Argentina, Austria, Bangladesh, Barbados, Benin, Bolivia, Brazil, Bulgaria, Burkina Faso, Canada, Cape Verde, Central African Republic, China, Colombia, Congo, Costa Rica, Cuba, Cyprus, Czechoslovakia, Democratic Yemen, Denmark, Dominican Republic, Equatorial Guinea, Ethiopia, German Democratic Republic, Ghana, Guatemala, Guinea, Guinea-Bissau, Guyana, India, Lao People's Democratic Republic, Lebanon, Liberia, Libyan Arab Jamahiriya, Madagascar, Mali, Mauritania, Mexico, Mongolia, Mozambique, Nepal, Nicaragua, Niger, Norway, Pakistan, Panama, Peru, Romania, Sao Tome and Principe, Seychelles, Spain, Suriname, Sweden, Syrian Arab Republic, Trinidad and Tobago, United Republic of Tanzania, Uruguay, Vanuatu, Venezuela, Viet Nam, Yugoslavia, Zambia.

Meeting numbers. GA 40th session: 2nd Committee 44, 47; plenary 120.

Tuvalu

The Secretary-General, as requested by the Economic and Social Council in 1984,[63] arranged for a review mission to Tuvalu from 21 to 28 January 1985 to consult with the Government. According to the mission's report,[69] Tuvalu—consisting of nine widely dispersed coral atoll islands in the South Pacific—had a population of 8,364 in mid-1983, over a thousand more than in 1979. The rapid growth rate during that period, averaging 3.4 per cent annually, was the result of a significant inflow of returning Tuvaluans after the cessation of phosphate mining in 1979 on Banaba Island, Kiribati, and of repatriation from Nauru in 1982. It was accompanied by internal migration to and urbanization of the capital, Funafuti.

The mission reported that Tuvalu's atoll environment imposed serious constraints on its agricultural production, whose principal crops were coconuts, pandanus, swamp taro and toa, grown almost entirely for subsistence consumption. While chickens and pigs were raised, mostly on a subsistence basis, livestock development was limited by the inability to expand local feed production. Lagoon and reef fishing were important subsistence activities, but a high proportion of local food demand was met by imports, particularly in urban areas. Tourism was negligible and prospects for its development were limited owing to the remoteness of the country, infrequent and expensive air services, and limited tourist accommodations.

The mission stated that Tuvalu faced all of the constraints endemic to small island developing countries. The dispersion of islands and the remoteness of the country posed serious problems and costs in relation to both inter-island and international communication and commerce. In addition to unproductive soil which limited progress towards agricultural self-sufficiency, the absence of known mineral resources precluded economic activity in that area. Given its small size and open nature, Tuvalu's economy was highly vulnerable to external pressures whether in the form of commodity price movements (copra and tuna), financial developments, including imported inflation, or the general state of the world economy (demand for philatelic exports, on which Tuvalu's export receipts were dependent). Amid those constraints, the Government was called on to provide the basic services necessary for the welfare of its people.

As stated in its third development plan, for 1984-1987, the country's long-term objectives included strengthening and diversification of the Tuvalu economy as a means of achieving ultimate self-sufficiency, and continued improvement in the standard of living to reasonable levels that would ensure a secure, healthy and productive family life within the traditional social system and customs in all islands. To finance its development programme, Tuvalu was almost completely dependent on external assistance. Donor commitments for capital development programmes in 1985 totalled $3 million (4.5 million Australian dollars), with the United Kingdom and Australia as the main contributors. Other donors included Canada, the Federal Republic of Germany, Japan, New Zealand, Norway, the Republic of Korea, the United States (through Save the Children) and EEC, besides UNDP and other agencies.

A statement on smaller island countries, among them Tuvalu, was adopted by the South Pacific Forum in August. The statement was included in a communiqué transmitted to the Secretary-General on 19 September by Papua New Guinea (see p. 530).

ECONOMIC AND SOCIAL COUNCIL

AND GENERAL ASSEMBLY ACTION

The Economic and Social Council, by **decision 1985/184**, took note of the mission's report and transmitted it to the General Assembly. The Assembly took note of it by **decision 40/454** of 17 December.

Vanuatu

As requested by the General Assembly in 1984,[28] the Secretary-General reported in September 1985 on special economic and disaster relief assistance to Vanuatu,[1] an archipelago with an estimated population of 128,000, which became independent in 1980. About 87 per cent of the indigenous labour force was engaged in agricultural activities, although that sector contributed only 20 per cent to GDP, with government and other services making up 50 per cent of GDP, and offshore banking and tourism accounting for about 10 to 15 per cent of total output. The dualistic nature of Vanuatu's economy, its geographical fragmentation, demographic isolation and vulnerability to cyclones contributed to development problems.

At its April 1985 session (see p. 433), the Committee for Development Planning concluded that Vanuatu qualified for inclusion in the list of LDCs.

Damage from two cyclones in January necessitated unforeseen expenditures on relief and reconstruction. At the same time, reduced world prices caused a 52 per cent reduction in receipts from the country's principal export, copra, to which was added a substantial drop in tourism, the second most im-

portant foreign exchange earner. Vanuatu's balance of payments was characterized by a persistent trade deficit which, to a large extent, was offset by surpluses in the services account; in addition, international assistance helped the country maintain a favourable balance of payments. With no income tax, Vanuatu's tax system was heavily dependent on taxes on international trade, namely, commodity exports and imports of luxury items. Import duties remained the largest revenue source, their estimated share in total revenue for 1985 being 41 per cent, while expenditures for general administration, education and health continued to absorb a large share—over 75 per cent.

The Government reported on progress made in 35 special development projects, costing $74.6 million, which it had proposed for financing by the international donor community and which dealt with agriculture, transport, telecommunications, energy, social services, local government and natural disaster preparedness.

In his September report on assistance provided by the United Nations system,[2] the Secretary-General mentioned assistance to Vanuatu, including a UNDP-financed fisheries project operated by FAO.

The UNDP Administrator reported[17] that in 1985 a $30,000 disaster relief allocation had been made to Vanuatu from UNDP special programme resources to assist in clearing vital access roads following the January cyclones.

UNCTAD reported in December[58] that it had sent a mission to Port Vila in October for consultations with the Vanuatu authorities, and to the UNDP field office at Suva, Fiji, which also covered Vanuatu. The mission identified a number of areas where UNCTAD could be of assistance: in preparing documentation for a forthcoming meeting of Vanuatu with its development partners; import and distribution policy; review of investment incentives; and inter-island shipping. Subject to availability of resources, UNCTAD technical assistance to Vanuatu was to be provided in close collaboration, or jointly, with the Economic and Social Commission for Asia and the Pacific, which had established a Pacific Operations Centre in Port Vila in 1984.

GENERAL ASSEMBLY ACTION

On 17 December 1985, the General Assembly, on the recommendation of the Second Committee, adopted **resolution 40/233** without vote.

Economic assistance to Vanuatu

The General Assembly,

Recalling its resolution 39/198 of 17 December 1984 on economic assistance to Vanuatu, in which it requested the Secretary-General to continue his efforts to mobilize the necessary resources for an effective programme of financial, technical and material assistance to Vanuatu,

Recalling also its resolutions 31/156 of 21 December 1976, 32/185 of 19 December 1977, 34/205 of 19 December 1979,

35/61 of 5 December 1980, 37/206 of 20 December 1982 and 39/212 of 18 December 1984, relating to the special needs and problems of island developing countries,

Noting the difficult problems faced by island developing countries, owing mainly to their smallness, remoteness, constraints in transport, great distances from market centres, highly limited internal markets, lack of natural resources, heavy dependence on a few commodities, shortage of administrative personnel and heavy financial burdens,

Taking into account the fact that Vanuatu is an island developing country, that it is a geographically remote archipelago with a small population, that it has demographic disadvantages, that its dependence on imports is overwhelming and that it has a scarcity of adequate transportation and communications links, all of which pose special development problems, making the provision of services difficult and entailing very high overhead costs,

Noting that the Committee for Development Planning, as stated in its report on its twenty-first and resumed twenty-first sessions, of which the Economic and Social Council took note in its decision 1985/182 of 25 July 1985, reached the conclusion that Vanuatu qualified for inclusion in the list of the least developed countries on the basis of the existing criteria and in the light of the available data,

Noting further the damage caused by two major cyclones in January 1985 and the resulting additional constraints on the economic development of Vanuatu,

1. *Calls the attention* of the international community to the summary report of the Secretary-General;

2. *Also calls the attention* of the international community to the projects listed in the report of the Secretary-General to the General Assembly at its thirty-ninth session, endorsed by the Assembly in resolution 39/198, which still require funding;

3. *Expresses its appreciation* to the Secretary-General for the steps he has taken to mobilize assistance for Vanuatu;

4. *Also expresses its appreciation* to those States and organizations which have provided assistance to that country;

5. *Further calls the attention* of the international community to the special problems confronting Vanuatu as an island developing country with a small but rapidly growing and unevenly distributed population, a severe shortage of development capital and declining budgetary support from present donors;

6. *Invites* the appropriate organizations and programmes of the United Nations system to maintain and expand their current and future programmes of assistance to Vanuatu, to co-operate closely with the Secretary-General in organizing an effective international programme of assistance and to report periodically to him on the steps they have taken and the resources they have made available to help that country;

7. *Also invites* the Economic and Social Commission for Asia and the Pacific, the United Nations Conference on Trade and Development, the United Nations Industrial Development Organization, the United Nations Children's Fund, the United Nations Fund for Population Activities, the United Nations Development Programme, the World Food Programme, the International Labour Organisation, the Food and Agriculture Organisation of the United Nations, the United Nations Educational, Scientific and Cultural Organization, the International Civil Aviation Organization, the World Health Organization, the World Bank, the International Telecommunication Union, the World Meteorological Organization, the International Maritime Organization and the International Fund for Agricultural Development to bring to the attention of their governing bodies, for their consideration, the special needs of Vanuatu and to report the decisions of those bodies to the Secretary-General by 15 July 1986;

8. *Decides* to include Vanuatu in the list of the least developed countries;

9. *Requests* the Administrator of the United Nations Development Programme, in the light of the above decision and the desire of the Government of Vanuatu to organize a round-table conference of donors, to give all the necessary assistance to Vanuatu for the preparation and organization of that conference;

10. *Requests* the Secretary-General:

(a) To continue his efforts to mobilize the necessary resources for an effective programme of financial, technical and material assistance to Vanuatu;

(b) To keep the situation in Vanuatu under constant review, to maintain close contact with Member States, regional and other intergovernmental organizations, the specialized agencies and the international financial institutions concerned, and to apprise the Economic and Social Council, at its second regular session of 1986, of the current status of the special programme of economic assistance for Vanuatu;

(c) To report on the progress made in the economic situation in Vanuatu and in organizing international assistance for that country in time for the matter to be considered by the General Assembly at its forty-first session.

General Assembly resolution 40/233

17 December 1985   Meeting 120   Adopted without vote

Approved by Second Committee (A/40/1043) without vote, 4 December (meeting 47); 63-nation draft (A/C.2/40/L.73), orally amended by Secretary following informal consultations; agenda item 87.

Sponsors: Afghanistan, Algeria, Angola, Argentina, Australia, Bangladesh, Belize, Benin, Bolivia, Botswana, Cameroon, Cape Verde, Central African Republic, Chad, China, Cyprus, Democratic Yemen, Dominican Republic, Ecuador, Egypt, Ethiopia, Fiji, Gambia, Ghana, Greece, Guinea-Bissau, Guyana, India, Jamaica, Japan, Liberia, Madagascar, Maldives, Mozambique, New Zealand, Nicaragua, Nigeria, Pakistan, Panama, Papua New Guinea, Peru, Portugal, Romania, Rwanda, Samoa, Sao Tome and Principe, Senegal, Sierra Leone, Solomon Islands, Sri Lanka, Sudan, Syrian Arab Republic, Trinidad and Tobago, Uganda, United Kingdom, United Republic of Tanzania, United States, Uruguay, Vanuatu, Venezuela, Viet Nam, Yugoslavia, Zambia.

Meeting numbers. GA 40th session: 2nd Committee 44, 47; plenary 120.

REFERENCES

[1]A/40/441. [2]A/40/439. [3]A/41/592. [4]A/42/442. [5]YUN 1984, p. 470, GA res. 39/29, 3 Dec. 1984. [6]A/40/372-E/1985/104 & Add.1,2. [7]E/1985/122. [8]YUN 1984, p. 468. [9]YUN 1980, p. 548. [10]SG/CONF.2/1 & Corr.1,2. [11]A/41/295-E/1986/65. [12]A/40/666. [13]ACC/1985/16. [14]E/1985/57. [15]ACC/1985/DEC/1-13 (dec. 1985/2). [16]ACC/1985/19. [17]DP/1986/11/Add.1. [18]DP/1985/19. [19]YUN 1984, p. 473, GA res. 39/185, 17 Dec. 1984. [20]*Ibid.*, p. 474, GA res. 39/189, 17 Dec. 1984. [21]*Ibid.*, p. 476, GA res. 39/180, 17 Dec. 1984. [22]*Ibid.*, p. 482, GA res. 39/203, 17 Dec. 1984. [23]*Ibid.*, p. 484, GA res. 39/202, 17 Dec. 1984. [24]*Ibid.*, p. 485, GA res. 39/186, 17 Dec. 1984. [25]*Ibid.*, p. 487, GA res. 39/183, 17 Dec. 1984. [26]*Ibid.*, p. 493, GA res. 39/192, 17 Dec. 1984. [27]*Ibid.*, p. 494, GA res. 39/188, 17 Dec. 1984. [28]*Ibid.*, p. 498, GA res. 39/198, 17 Dec. 1984. [29]DP/1986/26. [30]DP/1986/48. [31]E/1985/32 (dec. 85/12). [32]A/40/115. [33]E/1985/124. [34]A/40/341. [35]E/1985/156. [36]A/40/724. [37]A/40/762. [38]A/40/852. [39]A/40/910 &

Corr.1. [40]E/1985/129. [41]YUN 1984, p. 478, GA res. 39/195, 17 Dec. 1984. [42]*Ibid.*, p. 479, GA res. 39/193, 17 Dec. 1984. [43]*Ibid.*, p. 480, GA res. 39/200, 17 Dec. 1984. [44]YUN 1983, p. 500. [45]YUN 1984, p. 480, GA res. 39/181, 17 Dec. 1984. [46]A/40/430. [47]YUN 1984, p. 482. [48]*Ibid.*, p. 483, ESC res. 1984/59, 26 July 1984. [49]A/40/423. [50]YUN 1984, p. 485. [51]YUN 1982, p. 317, SC res. 527(1982), 15 Dec. 1982. [52]YUN 1984, p. 489, GA res. 39/182, 17 Dec. 1984. [53]A/40/433. [54]A/C.2/40/3. [55]YUN 1984, p. 490, GA res. 39/199, 17 Dec. 1984. [56]*Ibid.*, p. 492, GA res. 39/187, 17 Dec. 1984. [57]A/40/15, vol. I (dec. 311(XXX)). [58]TD/B/1084. [59]A/40/435. [60]YUN 1984, p. 495, GA res. 39/184, 17 Dec. 1984. [61]*Ibid.*, p. 496, GA res. 39/196, 17 Dec. 1984. [62]A/40/432. [63]YUN 1984, p. 417, ESC res. 1984/58, 26 July 1984. [64]E/1985/67. [65]E/1985/32 (dec. 85/16). [66]A/40/672-S/17488. [67]A/40/436. [68]YUN 1984, p. 497, GA res. 39/204, 17 Dec. 1984. [69]E/1985/68.

Disasters

During 1985, the Office of the United Nations Disaster Relief Co-ordinator (UNDRO) was a focal point and clearing-house for information on relief needs arising from natural disasters and other disaster situations, such as drought, floods, storms, earthquakes and civil conflicts. It continued to mobilize and co-ordinate the relief assistance of the various organizations of the United Nations system and co-ordinated that assistance with what was given by others. It also promoted the study, prevention, control and prediction of natural disasters and provided Governments that requested it with assistance in pre-disaster planning.

The General Assembly called for assistance to deal with the special needs of countries afflicted by desertification and drought in certain areas of Africa (see p. 805), particularly East Africa (resolution 40/221) and the Sudano-Sahelian region (40/198 B); drought-stricken areas of Ethiopia (40/228), also addressed by the Economic and Social Council (resolution 1985/1); a cyclone in Bangladesh (40/231); cyclones and floods in Madagascar (40/230); a volcanic eruption in Colombia (40/13); and earthquakes in Mexico (40/1). In addition, the Assembly in resolution 40/205 recommended measures for the implementation of the Substantial New Programme of Action for the 1980s for the Least Developed Countries (see p. 434), which included assistance to countries impeded by natural disasters such as the drought in Africa and floods and cyclones in other countries, and man-made disasters such as internal and external conflicts that had considerably increased the number of refugees and displaced persons in a large number of LDCs.

Office of the United Nations Disaster Relief Co-ordinator

UNDRO activities

In 1985, as in previous years, UNDRO provided assistance at the request of Governments to reduce the economic and social impact of natural or man-made disasters. Its 1985 activities were described in reports of the Secretary-General of May 1985[1] and May 1986.[2]

During 1984-1985, UNDRO was involved in 98 disaster situations, including major disasters calling for concerted relief programmes, within the framework of which bilateral donors, the United Nations system and NGOs provided assistance to the stricken populations. Among the major disasters were tropical storms in Bangladesh, Madagascar, Mozambique and the Philippines; armed conflict in Lebanon (see p. 295); displaced persons in western Africa (see p. 1004); epidemics in Mali and Somalia; earthquakes in Mexico; a volcanic eruption in Colombia; and drought in Chad, Ethiopia, Mali, Mauritania, Mozambique, the Niger and the Sudan (see p. 805). All received wide attention and support from the world community.

The years 1984-1985 were marked by an unprecedented famine in Africa. Absence, either partial or complete, of seasonal rainfall, together with the deterioration of the land through years of overgrazing and insufficient capital for agricultural inputs resulted in widespread crop failure and food shortages. Apart from launching united appeals on behalf of the United Nations system for countries where UNDRO was involved, appeals were made also on behalf of OEOA (see above, under "Africa and the critical economic situation"), which was established by the Secretary-General effective 1 January 1985 to co-ordinate and provide assistance to help ensure a broad yet concentrated international response to the continuing drought-related crisis in sub-Saharan Africa. Regular in-depth monitoring of the situation in the emergency-stricken African countries was part of UNDRO's activities, and multisectoral overviews were published regularly to provide donors with a comprehensive picture.

Because of extensive humanitarian efforts that had been called for by the world community, contributions reported by UNDRO during 1984-1985 totalled $2,149 million ($347 million in 1984 and $1,802 million in 1985), as compared to over $700 million in 1982-1983 and under $370 million in 1980-1981.

UNDRO's direct relief assistance in Africa varied widely. For example, in Ethiopia—the most affected country—some $1.9 million received from Governments, intergovernmental organizations and individual donors was used to strengthen the Office of Emergency Operations in that country through field monitors and for operational projects requiring urgent cash payments, such as low-altitude air-dropping of food in inaccessible mountainous areas, local manufacturing of agricultural hand tools and of ovens for relief centres, provision of vehicle spare parts and procurement of fuel for the transportation of relief goods. In land-locked Mali, UNDRO and the Swiss Disaster Relief

Unit purchased and operated for one year a fleet of 18 medium-sized and 20 small-tonnage trucks to reach people in remote areas. Nutritional surveys of vulnerable groups were commissioned in the Niger and Mauritania where UNDRO, under an agreement with the European Communities, arranged for the transport and distribution of 14,000 tons of emergency food. In the wake of cyclone Demoina in Mozambique in January 1984, Italian grants of some $5.8 million enabled UNDRO to have a vital railway bridge reconstructed, purchase 11,000 tons of cement for dam projects, sub-contract emergency repairs to Maputo's principal electric power transmission line, and ensure the rebuilding of the Moamba-Sabie road as well as a bridge over the Incomati River. To transmit reliable information on developments in the affected regions, radio communications systems were provided to Chad, Mali and the Sudan. Emergency flights, transporting relief goods contributed by several donors, were also organized for Chad and Madagascar.

Other UNDRO assistance included the transport and installation of seismographic monitoring equipment within 48 hours after the destructive eruption of the Nevada del Ruiz volcano in Colombia in November, as well as cash contributions, including $36,000 collected from United Nations staff in New York and Geneva, to finance the procurement of water pumps for 50 rural localities, provide emergency shelter for the homeless and, in co-operation with the Pan-American Health Organization (PAHO), supply artificial limbs for disabled victims.

For the above and other relief operations, government donors entrusted UNDRO with the management of cash grants totalling $12.8 million. The latest technical information on disasters and on UNDRO-emergency-related activities was contained in the bimonthly *UNDRO News*.

UNDRO financing

In 1985, the activities of UNDRO continued to be financed mainly from the United Nations regular budget and voluntary contributions to the UNDRO Trust Fund. In addition, the United Nations Trust Fund for General Disaster Relief was used as a reserve and a revolving fund to guarantee and, if necessary, advance sums pledged by donors for particular relief operations, bridging the gap between the date of the pledge and actual receipt of the donation. For 1984-1985, the General Assembly by **resolution 40/239 A**, appropriated $5,176,800, i.e. $151,200 less than the previous biennium.

Expenditures under the Trust Funds totalled $11,271,592 in 1985, which included $10,251,113 as disaster relief assistance to 31 individual countries and the Caribbean. The UNDRO Trust Fund had

sub-accounts for strengthening UNDRO, emergency relief assistance earmarked for certain countries (see tables below), and technical assistance in disaster prevention and pre-disaster planning. Contributions from 22 Governments totalled $10,685,764 in 1985.

EXPENDITURES UNDER THE TRUST FUNDS FOR
DISASTER RELIEF ASSISTANCE, 1985
(as at 31 December 1985; in US dollars)

ACCOUNT/PURPOSE	AMOUNT
Disaster relief assistance	
Algeria	5,838
Angola	70,626
Benin	116,160
Bolivia	81,957
Botswana	80,176
Burma	15,551
Cape Verde	120
Caribbean	625,926
Chad	173,405
Colombia	139,740
Comoros	7,513
Ecuador	138,926
Ethiopia	2,754,162
Fiji	47,264
Guatemala	30,600
Guinea	(110)
Indonesia	2,632
Lebanon	11,804
Madagascar	56,842
Mali	1,196,876
Mauritania	862,067
Mozambique	2,897,476
Nicaragua	129,274
Niger	126,219
Peru	13,551
Philippines	18,892
Rwanda	89,459
Sudan	487,276
Tonga	14,991
Turkey	30,600
Vanuatu	10,000
Viet Nam	15,300
Subtotal	10,251,113
General disaster relief operations	14,371
Strengthening of UNDRO	807,300
UNDRO/UNEP projects	56,066
Disaster prevention and pre-disaster planning	142,742
Total	11,271,592

SOURCE: Accounts for the 12-month period ended 31 December 1985 of the 1984-1985 biennium — schedules of individual trust funds.

CONTRIBUTIONS TO THE TRUST FUNDS FOR
DISASTER RELIEF ASSISTANCE, 1985
(as at 31 December 1985; in US dollar equivalent)

PURPOSE/CONTRIBUTOR	AMOUNT PAID
Disaster relief in Algeria	
United Kingdom	10,000
Disaster relief in Benin	
Canada	7,176
Netherlands	103,188
Norway	127,000
United Kingdom	11,398
Subtotal	248,762
Disaster relief in Botswana	
United Kingdom	41,000

PURPOSE/CONTRIBUTOR	AMOUNT PAID
Disaster relief in Chad	
Canada	5,146
Netherlands	25,000
Switzerland	11,739
United Kingdom	10,000
United States	149,893
Subtotal	201,778
Disaster relief in Colombia	
Germany, Federal Republic of	39,582
Italy	(47,830)
Netherlands	51,458
Norway	50,000
Subtotal	93,210
Disaster relief in the Comoros	
Switzerland	(11,236)
Disaster relief in Ethiopia	
Australia	492,900
Canada	364,293
Finland	76,362
Maldives	5,000
Netherlands	50,000
Norway	66,000
Spain	15,600
Switzerland	14,200
United States	53,612
Subtotal	1,137,967
Disaster relief in Fiji	
Germany, Federal Republic of	20,000
Disaster relief in Ghana	
Switzerland	(6,967)
Disaster relief in Lebanon	
Italy	874,550
Disaster relief in Mali	
Canada	17,744
Germany, Federal Republic of	7,650
Netherlands	8,000
Norway	20,000
Subtotal	53,394
Disaster relief in Mauritania	
United Kingdom	85,725
Disaster relief in Mozambique	
Italy	5,722,265
Netherlands	16,000
Subtotal	5,738,265
Disaster relief in Nicaragua	
Italy	117,347
Disaster relief in Niger	
United Kingdom	260,000
Disaster relief in Sudan	
Canada	366,675
United Kingdom	101,850
Subtotal	468,525
Disaster relief in Viet Nam	
Australia	5,141
General disaster relief operations	
Cyprus	20,000
Strengthening of UNDRO	
Australia	98,028
Bahamas	1,500
Canada	182,482
Greece	10,000
Iceland	11,800
Indonesia	3,000
Italy	47,830
Japan	50,000

PURPOSE/CONTRIBUTOR	AMOUNT PAID
Strengthening of UNDRO (cont.)	
New Zealand	4,706
Portugal	7,000
Switzerland	65,217
Tunisia	5,625
Turkey	5,000
Subtotal	492,188
UNDRO Pan Caribbean Projects	
Canada	148,118
United States	221,525
Subtotal	369,643
Disaster prevention and pre-disaster planning	
Italy	466,472
Total	10,685,764

SOURCE: Accounts for the 12-month period ended 31 December 1985 of the 1984-1985 biennium—schedules of individual trust funds.

Co-ordination in the UN system

In his report covering the activities of UNDRO during 1984-1985,[2] the Secretary-General described the action taken on his 1984 recommendations for strengthening the capacity of the United Nations system to respond to natural and other disasters.[3]

To assess the emergency situation in affected countries, inter-agency missions were undertaken in 1984 to Benin, Mauritania and Mozambique, in 1985 to Chad and Mali, and in November 1985 a joint mission with OEOA to Mozambique. Major concerted relief programmes were developed for Chad, Colombia, Ethiopia, Mauritania, Nigeria, Somalia and the Sudan, and the respective united appeals were communicated to the international community. Out of a total of 102 appeals made by UNDRO during 1984-1985, 52 were united appeals launched after consultations with other relief agencies.

Concerning the delivery of relief supplies to and within disaster-stricken countries, the Secretary-General, who had proposed that steps be taken to expedite the provision of emergency assistance, reported that a recent agreement between UNDRO and Italy to use the United Nations Supply Depot at Pisa for commonly used relief supplies had gone some way to achieve that goal, and consultations were in progress with various donor Governments to place emergency relief supplies at the depot with an eventual sharing of storage costs.

With regard to the proposal calling on Governments and international relief organizations to transmit to UNDRO the names and specializations of qualified disaster experts who could be sent on assessment missions, a roster was compiled with information on over 200 experts; UNDRO was in contact with Governments and others with a view to increasing that number. Direct access to the system had also been provided to UNICEF and UNHCR.

Among the 1984 recommendations was an appeal to States to help increase the financial resources of the Trust Fund for General Disaster Relief (see p. 535), which provided a guarantee for some of UNDRO's cash advances in relation to disaster relief operations. It was estimated that $4 to $5 million needed to be set aside for that purpose. However, since no substantial contributions were received in response to the General Assembly's 1984 appeal,[4] the revolving fund showed a balance of only $970,900 as at 31 December 1985, i.e. $170,900 more than in 1984.

Disaster relief

Drought-stricken areas

In a preliminary June 1985 report[5] on countries stricken by desertification and drought (see p. 805), the Secretary-General stressed that the combination of drought and desertification had had far-reaching and disastrous consequences on economic and social life in the countries affected, especially in Africa. He recalled that in late 1983 and early 1984, over 150 million people had faced extreme hunger, malnutrition and in many cases shortages of potable water. Irregular or insufficient rainfall had resulted in major crop and livestock losses, and by April 1985 FAO had identified 21 African countries facing critical food shortages. By that time, massive movements of people within and between countries from drought-stricken to more favourable areas had started, causing additional strains on limited resources and aggravating environmental conditions. In addition to lowering water tables in rivers, lakes and aquifers, the prolonged drought resulted in serious implications for countries that were developing their hydroelectrical potential to lessen dependence on oil imports, and it also affected their productive capacities and basic social services. It was estimated that 30 million people were at risk and that drought-induced population displacements could reach well over 10 million people.

In March 1985, the UNDP Administrator reported[6] on UNDP action in favour of nine drought-affected countries—Benin, Cape Verde, the Central African Republic, the Gambia, Guinea, Guinea-Bissau, Lesotho, Uganda and Sierra Leone—and Vanuatu.[6] However, UNDP emergency and relief assistance extended beyond its continuing and sizeable activities in Africa. It continued to collaborate with UNDRO and other agencies in responding to natural disasters in other regions (see below).[7]

On 15 October, Yemen, as Chairman of the Organization of the Islamic Conference, transmitted to the Secretary-General a communiqué of a co-ordination meeting of the organization's Ministers for Foreign Affairs, held in New York on 9 October.[8] Addressing the continuing drought and famine in Africa, the meeting called on its members and the international community to increase emergency assistance to alleviate the sufferings of the drought-stricken people and provide long-term project aid to the African countries to prevent the recurrence of such disasters.

In **resolution 40/175**, the Assembly recommended that high priority be given in the development programmes of affected countries to the problem of desertification and the problems resulting from drought, and that the fight against desertification and drought be granted priority in bilateral and multilateral development aid programmes. Noting the generosity with which the international community had responded to the emergency in Africa, the Assembly appealed to the United Nations system, financial institutions and NGOs to provide full support to the development efforts of countries stricken by desertification and drought.

Sudano-Sahelian region

The United Nations Sudano-Sahelian Office (UNSO) continued in 1985 under the supervision of UNDP to assist in medium- and long-term rehabilitation and development programmes of the Sahel's eight drought-stricken countries—Burkina Faso, Cape Verde, Chad, the Gambia, Mali, Mauritania, the Niger and Senegal—members of the Permanent Inter-State Committee for Drought Control in the Sahel (CILSS). In 1978, UNSO's original mandate was expanded[9] to cover eventually 14 additional African countries—Benin, Cameroon, Djibouti, Ethiopia, Ghana, Guinea, Guinea-Bissau, Kenya, Nigeria, Somalia, the Sudan, Togo, Uganda and the United Republic of Tanzania—and the implementation of the 1977 Plan of Action to Combat Desertification (see Chapter XVI of this section).

UNSO's assistance during 1985 was aimed at mitigating the effects of past and future droughts; helping countries concerned in attaining self-sufficiency in staple food production; enhancing socio-economic development in areas subject to drought through sectoral or multisectoral activities geared at restoring or protecting the productive capacity of the land; and arresting and, as far as possible, reversing desertification.

The UNDP Administrator described the activities that UNSO, under its original recovery and rehabilitation mandate, carried out in 1985 in the eight member countries of CILSS.[10] It continued to give the highest priority to the construction, improvement and maintenance of a region-wide system of all-weather secondary roads in the Sahel, to permit food and medical supplies to be delivered to otherwise inaccessible areas and to bring the rural areas into effective contact with the socio-economic mainstream in the countries concerned. In 1985, operational construction projects were under way in Burkina Faso, Cape Verde, the Gambia, the Niger and Senegal. New programmes were formulated for the Gambia (83 kilometres) and the Niger (301 kilometres), and there were negotiations to use funds from regional development banks. For example, negotiations were started with the West African Development Bank to finance the construction of rural roads in Senegal, and the African Development Bank provided some $5 million for the construction of new feeder roads in the Niger. Total funds mobilized by UNSO in 1985 amounted to $87.8 million—$80.7 million for national projects and $7.1 million for regional projects.

UNSO provided financial and other support for an International Symposium on Drought and Desertification, held at Howard University (Washington, D.C., October 1985), which aimed to promote awareness of the need for long-term solutions to problems in Africa beyond the current emergency assistance. UNSO also contributed to the second ministerial conference for a joint policy to combat desertification and assisted in establishing the Intergovernmental Authority for Drought and Development (see below).

ECONOMIC AND SOCIAL COUNCIL
AND GENERAL ASSEMBLY ACTION

Activities supported in 1984 by UNSO[11] were described by the Secretary-General in a May 1985 report.[12] The Economic and Social Council took note of the report in **decision 1985/184** of 25 July.

In **resolution 40/198 B**, the General Assembly noted with concern the damage wrought by drought on the countries of Africa south of the Sahara, that insufficient financial resources continued to be a serious constraint in combating desertification, and that the struggle against desertification required financial and human resources beyond the means of the affected countries. It took note of the progress UNSO had made in assisting countries in combating desertification, under a joint UNEP/UNDP venture (see p. 809). The Assembly recommended that the UNEP and UNDP Governing Councils increase their support to UNSO. It drew the attention of the international community to the need for increased efforts to implement the Plan of Action to Combat Desertification in the Sudano-Sahelian region and urged it to contribute through appropriate means, including the United Nations Trust Fund for Sudano-Sahelian Activities.

UN Trust Fund for Sudano-Sahelian Activities

PROGRAMME EXPENDITURES UNDER THE UN TRUST FUND FOR SUDANO-SAHELIAN ACTIVITIES, 1985
(as at 31 December 1985; in thousands of US dollars)

Country/region	Amount
Benin	202
Burkina Faso	766
Cape Verde	1,395
Chad	8
Djibouti	145
Ethiopia	1,253
Gambia	181
Mali	122
Mauritania	2,181
Niger	3,636
Senegal	1,100
Somalia	329
Sudan	675
Subtotal	11,993
Regional Africa	474
Total	12,467

SOURCE: DP/1986/11/Add.6.

CONTRIBUTIONS TO THE UN TRUST FUND FOR SUDANO-SAHELIAN ACTIVITIES, 1985 AND 1986
(as at 31 December 1985; in US dollar equivalent)

Country	1985 payment	1985 pledge for 1986
Algeria	20,000	20,000
Benin	—	500
Cameroon	2,125	9,138
Chile	—	5,000
Denmark	168,067	219,780
Finland	86,232	183,486
Greece	10,000	—
Italy	561,798	641,399
Nigeria	—	10,000
Philippines	500	1,000
Portugal	10,000	10,000
Senegal	—	13,000
Sweden	4,873,188	2,614,379
Yugoslavia	2,788	8,361
Zaire	—	1,000
Total	5,734,698	3,737,043

SOURCE: A/41/5/Add.1.

East Africa

As requested by the General Assembly in 1984,[13] the Secretary-General issued in October 1985 a note on assistance to the drought-stricken areas of Djibouti, Ethiopia, Kenya, Somalia, the Sudan and Uganda, in East Africa.[14]

During 1984 and 1985, most regions of the East African countries had again experienced severe and extended drought. In response to the continued drought and to a decision by the East African countries to discuss the creation of an intergovernmental body, a ministerial meeting was held at Djibouti from 4 to 6 February 1985. The meeting, which was also attended by representatives of the Secretary-General and UNDP, adopted an agreement creating the Intergovernmental Authority for Drought and Development with headquarters at Djibouti. The agreement was formally signed during a second ministerial meeting at Djibouti on 7 and 8 May 1985. The first heads of State meeting was to take place in early January 1986. For that meeting, two consultants funded by UNSO and UNDP helped prepare a regional plan of action for the medium- and long-term recovery and rehabilitation of the stricken countries.

GENERAL ASSEMBLY ACTION

On 17 December, on the recommendation of the Second Committee, the General Assembly adopted **resolution 40/221** without vote.

Assistance to the drought-stricken areas of Djibouti, Ethiopia, Kenya, Somalia, the Sudan and Uganda

The General Assembly,

Recalling its resolutions 35/90 and 35/91 of 5 December 1980, 36/221 of 17 December 1981, 37/147 of 17 December 1982, 38/216 of 20 December 1983 and 39/205 of 17 December 1984 and Economic and Social Council resolution 1983/46 of 28 July 1983 on assistance to the drought-stricken areas of Djibouti, Ethiopia, Kenya, Somalia, the Sudan and Uganda,

Having considered the note by the Secretary-General on assistance to the drought-stricken areas of those countries,

Deeply concerned at the serious effects of the prolonged and persistent drought in the region, which precipitated food shortages and famine and hindered the development efforts of the countries members of the Intergovernmental Authority for Drought and Development,

Stressing the need for practical regional arrangements for co-operation to promote the rehabilitation, recovery, and medium-term to long-term development of the countries of the region,

Bearing in mind the imperative need for the international community to render assistance to Member States in the event of natural disasters,

1. *Reaffirms* its resolutions 35/90, 35/91, 36/221, 37/147, 38/216 and 39/205 on assistance to the drought-stricken areas of Djibouti, Ethiopia, Kenya, Somalia, the Sudan and Uganda;

2. *Takes note* of the note by the Secretary-General on assistance to the drought-stricken areas of those countries;

3. *Commends* the Governments of Djibouti, Ethiopia, Kenya, Somalia, the Sudan and Uganda for their decision to establish, in Djibouti, an Intergovernmental Authority for Drought and Development, as initially recommended by the General Assembly in its resolution 35/90;

4. *Notes with satisfaction* the decision taken by the Governments of Djibouti, Ethiopia, Kenya, Somalia, the Sudan and Uganda to meet in Djibouti at the level of head of State to endorse the agreement on the establishment of the Intergovernmental Authority and to adopt a regional plan of action for the implementation of medium-term and long-term recovery and rehabilitation programmes of the States members of the Authority;

5. *Notes with appreciation* the assistance provided by the Administrator of the United Nations Development Programme and by the United Nations Sudano-Sahelian Office in the effort to establish the Intergovernmental Authority, in line with the recommendations of the Secretary-General and pursuant to the resolutions of the General Assembly mentioned above;

6. *Requests* the Administrator of the United Nations Development Programme, pursuant to General Assembly resolution 37/147, to make the necessary arrangements to render operational, as soon as possible, the unit within the United Nations Sudano-Sahelian Office entrusted with the responsibility of assisting the countries members of the Intergovernmental Authority and to pay special attention to the unit so as to ensure that its responsibilities are discharged effectively;

7. *Appeals* to all Governments, organizations of the United Nations system and other intergovernmental and non-governmental organizations to contribute generously in order to provide the resources necessary for funding the operational costs of the unit and for implementing the projects and programmes in the countries members of the Intergovernmental Authority, and requests the Administrator of the United Nations Development Programme to intensify his efforts in this regard;

8. *Requests* the Secretary-General to submit a report to the Economic and Social Council at its second regular session of 1986 on the progress achieved in the implementation of the present resolution.

General Assembly resolution 40/221

17 December 1985   Meeting 120   Adopted without vote

Approved by Second Committee (A/40/1043) without vote, 11 December (meeting 50); draft by Vice-Chairman (A/C.2/40/L.119), based on informal consultations on draft by Bangladesh, Djibouti, Ethiopia, Kenya, Lebanon, Liberia, Somalia, Sudan and Uganda (A/C.2/40/L.57); agenda item 87.

Meeting numbers. GA 40th session: 2nd Committee 42, 50; plenary 120.

Speaking before the resolution's adoption by the Assembly, Djibouti said that successful implementation of the text would enhance the efforts of the countries concerned to overcome and guard themselves against future droughts and other natural disasters. They counted on UNDP to intensify its efforts in mobilizing the necessary financial, material and technical resources in support of the Intergovernmental Authority, which they hoped would enjoy the same status as CILSS. They appealed to the international community to recognize their basic needs and to support their efforts.

Assistance to Ethiopia

In October 1985, the Secretary-General issued a report on assistance to the drought-stricken areas of Ethiopia,[15] as requested by the General Assembly in 1984.[16] The report described the key supporting role played by OEOA in mobilizing, co-ordinating and delivering international assistance to the country. International relief efforts had begun with the first meeting of donors which the Secretary-General had called on 18 December 1984 in New York. On the basis of a report by the Assistant Secretary-General for Emergency Operations in Ethiopia, the meeting had agreed on the requirements for relief for the period December 1984 to December 1985 for a drought-affected population of about 7.9 million in need of emergency aid. The major targets were: food, 1,330,000 tons, including cereals, supplementary food and edible oil; seeds, 40,000 tons; medical supplies, estimated at $5.4 million; shelter, clothing and other related requirements, $5.2 million; and logistics to transport food and other relief goods of up to 120,000 tons per month, $139.2 million. The international community had responded generously to the appeal.

Pledges to date totalled some 1.3 million tons of food. A total of 26,000 tons of seed was distributed in time for the planting season. Targets for medical supplies, clothing and survival items for 1985 were largely reached. The donor community was slower in responding to the appeal for trucks, spare parts and tyres, resulting in transport problems of a considerable magnitude and affecting unloading at ports and food distribution throughout the country. To supplement transport by truck and in order to reach inaccessible areas, donors had provided the services of 55 aircraft since the beginning of the relief effort.

For the distribution of food, feeding centres, shelters and distribution points were established throughout Ethiopia. It was estimated that between December 1984 and September 1985, some 700,000 tons of grain and supplementary food were distributed. Figures prepared by the Relief and Rehabilitation Commission showed that 53.3 million monthly rations had been provided to 6.2 million beneficiaries per month, reaching at peak times 7.5 million people, with 45.7 per cent of the total food distribution handled by the Commission and the rest by NGOs.

Addressing the Economic and Social Council on 17 May 1985, the Commissioner for Relief and Rehabilitation of Ethiopia said that, owing to the goodwill and generosity of peoples and Governments, the emergency situation in Ethiopia appeared to be under control. The daily death tolls had been dramatically reduced and most parts of the country were receiving adequate rainfall; however, because they lacked the necessary agricultural inputs, the Ethiopians were unable to take full advantage of the rain. Therefore, disaster relief assistance was still urgently needed. The Government had taken wide-ranging institutional and financial measures to enhance and augment the relief and rehabilitation efforts. The Commissioner appealed to the international community to provide the resources needed for agricultural production, land reclamation, reforestation and water conservation.

Speaking before the Council on the same date, the OEOA Director said that although the situation regarding food pledges had improved considerably,

some 472,800 tons were still needed to reach the target of 1.5 million tons. Referring to the 50,000 tons of food being distributed monthly out of a target of 110,000, the Director explained that the distribution was slow due to inadequate logistic support (trucks and spare parts). However, some improvements were expected since several Governments had made commitments in cash or kind at the bilateral donors meeting earlier in May, and the Ethiopian Government was currently allocating 70 per cent of its national transport capacity to move relief supplies. A new technique of low-altitude air-dropping of emergency food in remote areas had been initiated in January and was to be extended to new locations in southern Wollo where access by road was impossible. Referring to the need for agricultural inputs (seeds, hand tools, draught oxen and veterinary drugs and vaccines), the Director pointed out that the situation was critical and that immediate requirements for 1985 had been estimated at $95 million. In view of the deterioration of health conditions of drought victims and the overcrowding in refugee camps, health needs had been reassessed and were currently estimated at $6 million; a further $4.8 million was needed for sanitation programmes.

ECONOMIC AND SOCIAL COUNCIL ACTION

The Economic and Social Council on 24 May adopted without vote **resolution 1985/1**.

Assistance to the drought-stricken areas of Ethiopia
The Economic and Social Council,

Recalling its resolution 1984/5 of 17 May 1984 and General Assembly resolution 39/201 of 17 December 1984 concerning emergency assistance to the drought victims in Ethiopia,

Noting with appreciation the statement made by the Director of the Office for Emergency Operations in Africa,

Having heard the statement made by the Commissioner for Relief and Rehabilitation of Ethiopia on the situation in the drought-stricken areas,

Aware of the presence of rain in Ethiopia after many years of prolonged drought,

Recognizing the necessity of sufficient agricultural inputs to take advantage of the good rains,

Disturbed by the lack of sufficient inputs which would help to expedite the rehabilitation of the drought victims and make them self-supporting,

Convinced that long-term solutions are imperative in order to avoid the recurrence of a tragic human drama such as the one that recently unfolded in the disaster-stricken areas,

1. *Commends* the generous response of the international community to the tragic situation in Ethiopia;

2. *Expresses its deep gratitude* to all States, governmental and non-governmental organizations and individuals that have provided emergency humanitarian assistance to Ethiopia;

3. *Urges* all Member States, organs and organizations of the United Nations system, specialized agencies and non-governmental organizations to assist the Government

of Ethiopia in its efforts to provide for the emergency needs of the drought victims and to deal with the problem of medium-term and long-term recovery and rehabilitation;

4. *Requests* the Secretary-General to continue his efforts to mobilize resources for relief and rehabilitation, including assistance for the victims of drought who either wish to return to their villages of origin or are willing to settle in areas less prone to drought, and to report to the General Assembly at its fortieth session on the response of the international community to those efforts.

Economic and Social Council resolution 1985/1

24 May 1985   Meeting 21   Adopted without vote

41-nation draft (E/1985/L.27); agenda item 7.

Sponsors: Afghanistan, Algeria, Argentina, Australia, Bangladesh, Botswana, Bulgaria, Burkina Faso, Canada, China, Congo, Costa Rica, Cuba, Cyprus, Djibouti, Egypt, Ethiopia, German Democratic Republic, Guinea, India, Japan, Kenya, Lebanon, Lesotho, Liberia, Mali, Mexico, Nicaragua, Nigeria, Norway, Pakistan, Rwanda, Senegal, Sudan, Swaziland, Sweden, Uganda, Uruguay, Yugoslavia, Zaire, Zimbabwe.

Meeting numbers. ESC 16, 17, 20, 21.

After adoption of the text, Ethiopia expressed deep gratitude to the United Nations for its sustained support which had saved millions of lives; Ethiopia was confident that the international community would undertake the needed long-term activities that would allow the Ethiopians to build a better future and never again experience such a disaster.

GENERAL ASSEMBLY ACTION

On 17 December, on the recommendation of the Second Committee, the Assembly adopted **resolution 40/228** without vote.

Assistance to the drought-stricken areas of Ethiopia

The General Assembly,

Recalling its resolution 39/201 of 17 December 1984 and Economic and Social Council resolutions 1984/5 of 17 May 1984 and 1985/1 of 24 May 1985 on emergency assistance to the drought victims in Ethiopia,

Taking note of the report of the Secretary-General on assistance to the drought-stricken areas of Ethiopia,

Noting with appreciation the unprecedented effort made by the Secretary-General to mobilize international humanitarian assistance for the drought victims in Ethiopia,

Noting further with satisfaction the able manner in which the Office for Emergency Operations in Africa has effectively handled its task of co-ordination and the admirable manner in which the organs and organizations of the United Nations system, including the specialized agencies, have carried out their roles,

Having heard the statement made by the Commissioner for Relief and Rehabilitation of Ethiopia on 12 November 1985 concerning the current situation in the drought-stricken areas,

Aware that, despite adequate rain, the emergency situation still exists in most parts of the country,

Recognizing that, owing to insufficient agricultural input, full advantage could not be taken of the rain,

Convinced that long-term solutions are imperative in dealing with the root causes of the tragic human drama that has recently unfolded in the disaster-stricken areas,

1. *Commends* the international community for its compassion, solidarity and generous response to the tragic situation in Ethiopia;

2. *Expresses its deep gratitude* to all States, intergovernmental and non-governmental organizations and individuals that have provided emergency humanitarian assistance to Ethiopia;

3. *Commends further* the relentless efforts made by the Secretary-General through the Office for Emergency Operations in Africa, in particular those of the Assistant Secretary-General for Emergency Operations in Ethiopia, in mobilizing and co-ordinating emergency humanitarian assistance for the drought victims in Ethiopia;

4. *Appreciates fully* the unprecedented role played by the organizations and programmes of the United Nations system—in particular, the Food and Agriculture Organization of the United Nations, the World Food Programme, the United Nations Children's Fund, the Office of the United Nations Disaster Relief Co-ordinator, the World Health Organization, the United Nations Development Programme, the World Bank and the International Labour Organisation—which they have carried out in a concerted and efficient manner to save the lives of millions of people in Ethiopia;

5. *Urges* all Member States, organs and organizations of the United Nations system, including the specialized agencies, and non-governmental organizations to assist the Government of Ethiopia in its efforts to provide for the emergency needs of the drought victims and to deal with the problem of medium-term and long-term recovery and rehabilitation;

6. *Requests* the Secretary-General to continue his efforts to mobilize international assistance for relief and rehabilitation, including assistance to the victims of drought who want either to return to their villages of origin or to settle in areas less prone to drought, and to report to the Economic and Social Council, at its first regular session of 1986, on the response of the international community to these efforts.

General Assembly resolution 40/228

17 December 1985   Meeting 120   Adopted without vote

Approved by Second Committee (A/40/1043) without vote, 4 December (meeting 47); 52-nation draft (A/C.2/40/L.64), orally amended by Secretary following informal consultations; agenda item 87.

Sponsors: Afghanistan, Algeria, Angola, Bangladesh, Benin, Bulgaria, Burkina Faso, Chad, Comoros, Cuba, Cyprus, Democratic Yemen, Djibouti, Dominican Republic, Egypt, Equatorial Guinea, Ethiopia, Gabon, Gambia, German Democratic Republic, Ghana, Guinea, Guinea-Bissau, India, Kenya, Lao People's Democratic Republic, Lesotho, Liberia, Madagascar, Malawi, Mali, Mongolia, Mozambique, Nicaragua, Nigeria, Pakistan, Panama, Poland, Rwanda, Sao Tome and Principe, Senegal, Sierra Leone, Sudan, Swaziland, Sweden, Togo, Uganda, United Republic of Tanzania, Vanuatu, Viet Nam, Zaire, Zambia.

Meeting numbers. GA 40th session: 2nd Committee 31, 42, 47; plenary 120.

Floods and storms

Generous assistance to Bangladesh and Madagascar, which had suffered from cyclones and floods, was called for by the General Assembly in December 1985. For Viet Nam, which had experienced extensive floods brought on by recurring typhoons, UNDP approved three relief efforts (medical supplies and other emergency assistance) and one rehabilitation project (flood control measures) at a total cost of $290,000.[7]

Cyclone in Bangladesh

In a 12 November 1985 statement before the General Assembly's Second Committee, Bangladesh said the cyclonic storms which had swept the country in 1985 had not only caused damage to life and property but also seriously impeded economic development. The first cyclone and tidal surge, which had struck the coast of Bangladesh in May, had affected over 1.3 million people in a 2,000-square-mile area; the second cyclone, which had hit the same area in October, had destroyed the harvest and property for the second time that year. Bangladesh had been able to handle the situation with the assistance of other nations and regional and international agencies. As a result of the latest calamities, the Government planned to enhance disaster preparedness and create an infrastructure to protect life and property in the event of other natural disasters; in that endeavour, Bangladesh was counting on the assistance of Member States, the United Nations system and other multilateral institutions.

GENERAL ASSEMBLY ACTION

On 17 December, the General Assembly, acting on the recommendation of the Second Committee, adopted **resolution 40/231** without vote.

Long-term and effective solution of the problems caused by natural disasters in Bangladesh

The General Assembly,

Aware of the grave devastation and substantial loss of life and property caused by the cyclone that struck large areas of Bangladesh on 25 May 1985,

Having heard the statement made on 12 November 1985 by the representative of Bangladesh, in which he enumerated the enormous losses suffered by Bangladesh in the cyclone as well as the adverse consequences of recurring natural disasters, particularly cyclones, tidal waves and floods, for the economic development of that country,

Concerned about the serious damage to infrastructure caused by such natural disasters, which has a far-reaching impact on the implementation of the national development plan in that country,

Considering that Bangladesh is one of the least developed countries, and that its situation has been worsened by the frequent recurrence of natural disasters having devastating consequences,

Aware that the coastal areas of Bangladesh are particularly vulnerable to natural calamity resulting in widespread human and material loss,

Recognizing the relief and rehabilitation efforts of the Government of Bangladesh to alleviate the sufferings of disaster victims, and its programmes for a more permanent solution,

Noting with appreciation the support and solidarity displayed by the countries of the South Asian region in assisting Bangladesh in the immediate aftermath of the cyclone of 25 May 1985,

Recognizing that natural disasters constitute a development problem of great magnitude, the solution of which calls for substantial resources, requiring national efforts to be supplemented by international financial and technical assistance,

Aware that considerable expertise and technical capabilities are available within the organizations of the United Nations system and other multilateral organizations to strengthen the preparedness and prevention capability of disaster-prone countries through the promotion of a long-term and effective solution of the problems caused by natural disasters,

1. *Expresses its appreciation* to the international community for its interest in and support to Bangladesh in its relief, rehabilitation and reconstruction efforts following the natural disaster;

2. *Also expresses its appreciation* to the Secretary-General for the support provided by him, particularly through the Office of the United Nations Disaster Relief Co-ordinator and other operational agencies of the United Nations system in Bangladesh;

3. *Appeals* to all Member States, specialized agencies, and other organs and bodies of the United Nations system, as well as international economic and financial institutions, to respond urgently and generously to assist Bangladesh in its plans and programmes to secure a long-term and effective solution of the problems caused by natural disasters;

4. *Requests* the relevant organs, organizations and bodies of the United Nations system and other multilateral organizations to take appropriate measures to provide assistance to Bangladesh for disaster preparedness and prevention programmes, taking into account the existing co-ordinated efforts of Member States;

5. *Requests* the Office of the United Nations Disaster Relief Co-ordinator to assist, in co-operation with other relevant agencies, the Government of Bangladesh in preparing a time-bound plan in this regard;

6. *Requests* the Secretary-General to report to the General Assembly at its forty-first session on the progress made in the implementation of the present resolution.

General Assembly resolution 40/231

17 December 1985   Meeting 120   Adopted without vote

Approved by Second Committee (A/40/1043) without vote, 11 December (meeting 50); draft by Vice-Chairman (A/C.2/40/L.121), based on informal consultations on draft by Argentina, Bangladesh, Benin, Bhutan, Bolivia, Botswana, Cape Verde, China, Colombia, Comoros, Democratic Yemen, Djibouti, Ecuador, Egypt, Equatorial Guinea, Ethiopia, Gambia, Ghana, Guyana, Honduras, Indonesia, Iran, Iraq, Jamaica, Japan, Lebanon, Lesotho, Liberia, Libyan Arab Jamahiriya, Madagascar, Malawi, Malaysia, Maldives, Mauritania, Mexico, Mongolia, Morocco, Mozambique, Nepal, Netherlands, Nicaragua, Nigeria, Pakistan, Panama, Peru, Philippines, Romania, Saudi Arabia, Senegal, Singapore, Somalia, Sri Lanka, Sudan, Suriname, Thailand, Togo, Turkey, United Kingdom, United States, Uruguay, Venezuela and Yugoslavia (A/C.2/40/L.70); agenda item 87.

Meeting numbers. GA 40th session: 2nd Committee 32, 44, 50; plenary 120.

Also on 17 December, by **decision 40/446**, the Assembly requested the Secretary-General to take the necessary steps for the closure of the Fund of the United Nations Relief Operations in Bangladesh and to transfer its balance remaining as at 31 December as add-on to the UNDP indicative planning figure of Bangladesh. In making that request, the Assembly followed a 29 June recommendation of the UNDP Governing Council (see p. 480).

Cyclones and floods in Madagascar

In the wake of a series of four cyclones and floods between December 1983 and April 1984,[17] the United Nations system provided special economic assistance to Madagascar, as reported by the

Secretary-General in September 1985.[18] The assistance included projects on development planning, transport and cartography by DTCD and debt monitoring by UNCTAD, funded by UNDP; disaster preparedness by UNDRO/UNDP; demographic and health statistics by UNFPA; health and education by UNICEF; industrial rehabilitation by UNIDO; food development assistance by WFP; civil aviation training by ICAO; vocational training, seminars and advisory services on working conditions and environment, hotel and tourism, and employment promotion by ILO; educational services and materials/equipment by UNESCO; fellowhips by IMO, ITU and UPU; and meteorological assistance by WMO. FAO operated six UNDP-financed projects in fisheries, agricultural census and seeds. It also assisted in projects dealing with forestry, crops, fisheries, fertilizers, use of audio-visual media, setting up of school compounds, reconstruction of cyclone-damaged irrigation networks and oceanographic research. In fiscal year 1985, the World Bank/IDA made new loans to Madagascar totalling $67.6 million for irrigation rehabilitation and the industry sector.

GENERAL ASSEMBLY ACTION

On 17 December, the General Assembly adopted **resolution 40/230** without vote, on the recommendation of the Second Committee.

Assistance to Madagascar

The General Assembly,

Recalling its resolution 39/191 of 17 December 1984 on assistance to Madagascar,

Recalling also Economic and Social Council resolution 1984/3 of 11 May 1984 on measures to be taken following the cyclones and floods in Madagascar in December 1983 and January and April 1984,

Concerned by the fact that the damage caused by these natural disasters is hampering the development efforts of that country,

Bearing in mind the special economic assistance programme prepared by the inter-agency mission which visited Madagascar from 24 May to 5 June 1984,

Taking note of the report of the Secretary-General,

Noting the efforts of the people and Government of Madagascar to deal with the emergency and to initiate a reconstruction and rehabilitation programme,

Noting also the emergency relief and assistance provided by several States, international and regional organizations, specialized agencies and voluntary agencies,

Reaffirming the need for concerted international action to assist the people and Government of Madagascar in carrying out the reconstruction and rehabilitation of the stricken regions and sectors,

1. *Expresses its gratitude* to the States, programmes and organizations of the United Nations system and to other organizations, intergovernmental, non-governmental and voluntary, which provided assistance to Madagascar;

2. *Urges* all States to participate or continue to participate generously through bilateral or multilateral channels in projects or programmes for the reconstruction and rehabilitation of Madagascar;

3. *Requests* the international and regional organizations, the specialized agencies and voluntary agencies to continue and increase their assistance in response to the reconstruction, rehabilitation and development needs of Madagascar;

4. *Invites* the programmes and organizations of the United Nations system, in particular the United Nations Development Programme, the World Bank, the Food and Agriculture Organization of the United Nations, the International Fund for Agricultural Development, the United Nations Industrial Development Organization, and all other international and regional financial institutions concerned, to give sympathetic and urgent consideration to requests for assistance submitted by the Government of Madagascar under its reconstruction, rehabilitation and development programmes;

5. *Requests* the Secretary-General:

(*a*) To continue his efforts, in collaboration with the programmes and organizations of the United Nations system, to mobilize the resources needed for implementing the reconstruction, rehabilitation and development programmes of Madagascar;

(*b*) To keep the question of assistance for the reconstruction and rehabilitation of Madagascar under constant review;

6. *Further requests* the Secretary-General to apprise the Economic and Social Council, at its second regular session of 1986, of the progress made in the implementation of the present resolution and to report thereon to the General Assembly at its forty-first session.

General Assembly resolution 40/230

17 December 1985   Meeting 120   Adopted without vote

Approved by Second Committee (A/40/1043) without vote, 4 December (meeting 47); 52-nation draft (A/C.2/40/L.69), orally amended by Secretary following informal consultations; agenda item 87.

Sponsors: Afghanistan, Algeria, Angola, Argentina, Bangladesh, Benin, Burkina Faso, Cape Verde, Central African Republic, Chad, China, Comoros, Congo, Democratic Yemen, Djibouti, Dominican Republic, Ecuador, Equatorial Guinea, Ethiopia, Gambia, Ghana, Guinea, Guinea-Bissau, Haiti, India, Japan, Lebanon, Lesotho, Liberia, Libyan Arab Jamahiriya, Malawi, Mali, Mauritania, Mauritius, Mozambique, Nicaragua, Nigeria, Pakistan, Romania, Rwanda, Sao Tome and Principe, Senegal, Seychelles, Sierra Leone, Sudan, Swaziland, Togo, Tunisia, Vanuatu, Viet Nam, Yugoslavia, Zaire.

Meeting numbers. GA 40th session: 2nd Committee 44, 47; plenary 120.

Introducing the text, Mauritius said that very little assistance had been received in response to the Assembly's 1984 appeal;[19] the international community was now called on to increase its assistance.

Earthquakes

Earthquakes in Mexico

On 19 and 20 September 1985, Mexico City and surrounding areas were shattered by two major earthquakes, which registered between 8 and 8.4 on the Richter scale, entailed considerable loss of life, damaged or destroyed houses, schools, hospitals and government buildings, and incapacitated the country's main telecommunications installations. The damage caused by the disaster and its repercussions on the country's economy—assessed also by the ECLAC secretariat in collaboration with the Mexican authorities[20]—was estimated at $4 billion.

The UNDP Administrator, in his annual report for 1985,[7] stated that the earthquakes had inflicted heavy human and material losses in metropolitan areas, affecting also the States of México, Jalisco, Michoacán, Guerro and Colima. It was estimated that over 4,000 people had died and some 20,000 homes, 3,000 commercial and 200 public buildings had been virtually destroyed. In addition, 761 schools had been damaged, and the capacity of two key social welfare hospitals and the National Medical Centre had been reduced by 5,000 beds. Essential utility services had also been disrupted.

The United Nations Disaster Relief Coordinator was immediately sent to Mexico to assess the extent of devastation and identify emergency requirements. UNDP allocated more than $2 million for relief and reconstruction activities. Projects approved or under development for financing from those funds included the buttressing of emergency health facilities at a hospital at Morelia, Michoacán; the reconstruction of health services in Mexico City; advisory services in seismography and reconstruction logistics; and the rebuilding of a damaged public training institution. Two additional projects in telecommunications and urban development were also under preparation.

The Secretary-General reported[21] that, following the adoption of General Assembly resolution 40/1 on 24 September (see below), the DTCD Assistant Secretary-General was designated as the focal point at United Nations Headquarters for identification of medium- and long-term needs for the reconstruction of affected areas and the co-ordination of multilateral assistance required, to be channelled through the United Nations system, while the United Nations resident co-ordinator had been named as the focal point in Mexico.

The Assistant Secretary-General went to Mexico (4-12 October) to work out, in consultation with the Mexican authorities, a strategy for the future through a framework of co-ordination within the National Reconstruction Commission set up by the President of Mexico, and to define the various operational stages and forms of assistance that might be expected, as well as the role of the United Nations. Agreement was reached with the authorities that the overall operation should be divided into three stages: an emergency phase; a rehabilitation phase, involving short-term action for the restoration of basic public services; and a reconstruction phase, involving longer-term action, taking into account the Government's decentralization policies. The role of the United Nations

system was twofold: direct contribution with its own resources, in the form of financial and technical co-operation; and indirect assistance that might be provided in mobilizing and co-ordinating international co-operation from other sources.

At an informal meeting in New York on 30 October, representatives of 34 countries spoke in support of Mexico and provided information on past and projected assistance, both in cash and in kind.

Assistance by the United Nations system in the reconstruction phase was directed towards the Government's priority sectors for international co-operation: health, education and communications (housing was to be dealt with mainly through national resources). Missions were undertaken and projects drawn up by UNDRO, UNEP, UNCHS, UNICEF, WFP, ILO, FAO, UNESCO, WHO/PAHO, ITU and UNIDO.

The Secretary-General indicated that loans of some $800 million from financial institutions, notably IMF, the World Bank and the Inter-American Development Bank, had been effected or were under negotiation, and contact had been established and maintained with NGOs, in both New York and Mexico, regarding their assistance. By the end of 1985, permanent missions to the United Nations had received a document prepared by the Mexican Government which provided a list of reconstruction projects eligible for international aid—in the priority sectors—totalling some $414 million, of which $375 million was requested from external sources.

GENERAL ASSEMBLY ACTION

By a letter of 22 September to the Secretary-General,[22] Nicaragua requested that the General Assembly include an item on international relief to Mexico in the agenda of its 1985 session, for consideration on a priority basis.

On 24 September, the Assembly adopted **resolution 40/1** wihout vote.

International relief to Mexico

The General Assembly,

Deeply distressed by the loss of lives, the number of afflicted persons and the enormous destruction wrought by the earthquakes which, on 19 and 20 September 1985, struck various regions of Mexico, especially its capital,

Conscious of the efforts of the Government and people of Mexico to save lives and alleviate the sufferings of the victims of the cataclysm,

Noting the enormous effort that will be required to alleviate the grave situation caused by this natural disaster, for which the Government of Mexico has established a National Reconstruction Trust Fund,

Conscious also of the prompt response of Governments, international agencies, non-governmental organizations and private individuals, which have contributed emergency disaster relief,

Recognizing that the magnitude of the catastrophe and its long-term effects will require, as a complement to the effort being made by the people and Government of Mexico, a demonstration of international solidarity and humanitarian concern to ensure broad multilateral co-operation in order to meet the immediate emergency situation in the affected areas, as well as to undertake the process of reconstruction,

1. *Expresses its solidarity and support* to the Government and people of Mexico;

2. *Expresses its appreciation* to the States, international and regional agencies, non-governmental organizations and private individuals that are providing emergency relief to that country;

3. *Requests* the Secretary-General to mobilize resources to contribute to the relief and reconstruction task undertaken by the Government of Mexico;

4. *Calls upon* all States to contribute generously to those relief and reconstruction efforts in the affected areas and, to the extent possible, to channel their assistance through the United Nations system;

5. *Requests* the Secretary-General to co-ordinate the multilateral assistance and, in consultation with the Government of Mexico, to identify the emergency and medium-term and long-term needs in order to contribute to the reconstruction of the affected areas.

General Assembly resolution 40/1

24 September 1985   Meeting 6   Adopted without vote

32-nation draft (A/40/L.1); agenda item 147.
Sponsors: Antigua and Barbuda, Argentina, Bahamas, Barbados, Belize, Bolivia, Brazil, Chile, Colombia, Costa Rica, Cuba, Dominica, Dominican Republic, Ecuador, El Salvador, Grenada, Guatemala, Guyana, Haiti, Honduras, Jamaica, Nicaragua, Panama, Paraguay, Peru, Saint Christopher and Nevis, Saint Lucia, Saint Vincent and the Grenadines, Suriname, Trinidad and Tobago, Uruguay, Venezuela.

Earthquake in Yemen

As requested by the General Assembly in 1984,[23] the Secretary-General reported in July 1985[24] on relief efforts and the reconstruction programme of Yemen, following the earthquake which had struck in 1982.[25] Preliminary statistics had shown that in addition to the people who had been killed or injured, there were 1,072 villages affected, and 21,000 damaged and 16,000 cracked houses. Survey teams, which collected data and information, formulated three main projects: building new houses by contracts; repairing cracked houses; and building new houses with the help of the affected inhabitants (self-help). Under the first project, the number of cracked and damaged houses was identified and then divided geographically into 17 groups. The number of houses to be constructed that way totalled 11,766 in 584 affected villages. The second project started at Dhamar city, since the type of construction of its houses and the materials used allowed the programme to be executed in a suitable way. It was expected that the experience in Dhamar—which had the largest number of cracked houses—would help in making a final decision on the other parts of the project.

The United Nations Capital Development Fund contributed $2.5 million towards the third project, to carry out work on 280 houses in the north-west

Dawran area with the assistance of UNDP which provided the engineers. A $2.5 million contribution of EEC to that programme was to be used in Maghrib Ans, together with a contribution by the Netherlands of some $8.5 million and a USAID loan of $3 million. A total of 570 houses were to benefit from those contributions. Other contributions to the financing of the reconstruction programme were made by Abu Dhabi, Japan, Kuwait, Oman, Saudi Arabia and Yemen. Aid of $15 million allocated by the Co-operative Council of Gulf States and paid by Saudi Arabia and Qatar was for building 44 schools, 10 medical centres, 30 mosques and roads in the affected areas. In addition, a loan of $145 million from the Council was to be used for road construction, $90 million; electrification of villages, $30 million; and the Dhamar water supply and sewage system, $10 million. The balance of $15 million was to be used to cover the deficit in the financing of houses.

GENERAL ASSEMBLY ACTION

By **decision 40/454** of 17 December, the General Assembly took note of the Secretary-General's report on Yemen.

Volcano eruption in Colombia

In his annual report for 1985,[7] the UNDP Administrator recalled that on 13 November, after a period of increased activity in the volcano Nevado del Ruiz during which the temperature of the permanent ice-cap rose, the snow melted and formed a mass of ash, rock and water which descended rapidly along the Lagunilla River, already swollen by heavy rains. On reaching level ground, the mass spread out to form a destructive layer of mud which completely covered the city of Armero and part of Chinchiná.

It was estimated that over 200,000 persons had been affected by the eruption. Out of a total of 67,000 persons living in the cities of Armero and Chinchiná, 22,000 died as a result of the floods that had levelled the former almost completely and destroyed some neighbourhoods of the latter. That figure represented nearly 90 per cent and 4 per cent respectively of the populations of the two cities. Damage to physical, social and economic infrastructure was extensive.

UNDP responded immediately, and the Resident Representative was designated UNDRO representative. In addition to performing co-ordination tasks, he led a United Nations team working with the Government to assess damage and prepare documentation which was presented to a Special Meeting on International Relief to Colombia, convened by the Secretary-General on 13 December 1985. The Secretary-General subsequently named the UNDP Assistant Administrator and Director of the Regional Bureau for Latin

America and the Caribbean as his representative to Colombia.

From its Special Programme Resources, UNDP approved two emergency allocations of $30,000 and $2 million for immediate technical co-operation needs and the provision of emergency salvage tools, medical supplies, water purification materials and transportation. The financing was also to assist the Government to develop and implement a major reconstruction plan for the installation of a permanent national disaster prevention and action system; the provision of new urban infrastructure; the restoration of agricultural productivity; and the creation of employment for resettled communities.

In two December 1985 reports prepared for the Special Meeting by the National Planning Department and the United Nations system,[26] it was estimated that the damage caused by the disaster totalled $211.8 million—$92.8 million in the social sectors (education, health, housing, employment and income, and others); $68.5 million in infrastructure services (water supply and sewage systems, transportation, telecommunications, electricity and urban infrastructure); and $50.6 million in production sectors (industry and trade, hydrocarbons, and agriculture and livestock production).

Immediately after the disaster, a day of national and international solidarity was launched, generating a massive flow of financial and material assistance, and teams of disaster-relief specialists, as well as equipment for monitoring seismic activity within the volcano, arrived in Colombia. At the same time, the Government began to study measures designed to facilitate the formulation of a plan for the rehabilitation, reconstruction and recovery of the affected areas.

The plan of action envisaged three phases for reconstruction programmes: after a transitional phase, a phase of infrastructure replacement, economic activity and establishment of prevention systems, and finally a phase of medium-term development and consolidation of prevention systems. An initial estimate of the most urgent and immediately viable reconstruction projects placed the cost at some $112 million—not counting the national counterpart contribution, which represented approximately 30 per cent of that amount—to repair damage and replace and strengthen infrastructure. That amount did not include the resources needed to repair indirect damage and consequences, rehabilitate areas affected by volcanic mud and, above all, create a production infrastructure based on the agricultural sector which would consolidate the economy of the area in question.

GENERAL ASSEMBLY ACTION

Bolivia, by a letter of 14 November to the Secretary-General,[27] requested that an item on international relief to Colombia be included in the agenda of the 1985 General Assembly session, on a priority basis.

On 15 November, the Assembly adopted **resolution 40/13** without vote.

International relief to Colombia

The General Assembly,

Deeply distressed by the loss of lives, the number of afflicted persons and the enormous destruction wrought by the volcanic activity of Nevado del Ruiz, affecting areas of the departments of Caldas, Tolima and Valle del Cauca in Colombia,

Noting the efforts of the Government and people of Colombia to save lives and alleviate the sufferings of the victims of this natural disaster,

Considering the enormous effort that will be required to alleviate the grave situation caused by this natural disaster,

Recognizing that the magnitude of the catastrophe and its effects will require, as a complement to the effort being made by the people and Government of Colombia, a demonstration of international solidarity to ensure the necessary multilateral co-operation in order to meet the immediate emergency in the affected areas, as well as to undertake the task of reconstruction,

1. *Expresses its solidarity and support* to the Government and people of Colombia in this tragedy;

2. *Expresses its appreciation* to the States, international and regional agencies, non-governmental organizations and individuals providing emergency relief to Colombia;

3. *Calls upon* the Governments of the Member States to contribute generously to the relief and reconstruction efforts in the affected areas and, to the extent possible, to channel their assistance through the United Nations system;

4. *Requests* the Secretary-General to mobilize resources in order to assist in the relief and reconstruction task of the Government of Colombia;

5. *Also requests* the Secretary-General to co-ordinate the multilateral assistance and, in consultation with the Government of Colombia, to determine the emergency and reconstruction needs of the affected areas.

General Assembly resolution 40/13

15 November 1985   Meeting 79   Adopted without vote

26-nation draft (A/40/L.16); agenda item 149.

Sponsors: Antigua and Barbuda, Argentina, Bahamas, Barbados, Bolivia, Brazil, Chile, Costa Rica, Cuba, Dominican Republic, Ecuador, El Salvador, Grenada, Guatemala, Guyana, Haiti, Honduras, Jamaica, Mexico, Nicaragua, Panama, Paraguay, Peru, Suriname, Uruguay, Venezuela.

Disaster preparedness and prevention

The international community was becoming increasingly aware of the relationship between development and two elements of pre-disaster planning—preparedness and prevention. There was an increased interest on the part of disaster-prone countries in including more disaster preparedness and prevention in UNDP projects. UNDRO encouraged that awareness by helping interested countries and regions to establish organizational structures to deal with potential disasters and emergency situations, the legal framework for such structures and training in disaster management.

The work of UNDRO in disaster preparedness and prevention was guided by an inter-branch committee established in February. Its responsibilities included: identification of priorities; development of regional programmes or national programmes that would benefit other countries of the same region; identification of project activities that would attract external funding; general guidance in carrying out projects; and evaluation of their effectiveness.

During 1985, the United Nations Supply Depot at Pisa, Italy, was expanded and UNDRO's warehouse became operational, thus ensuring a suitable pre-positioning of international relief supplies for immediate use.

Preparedness and prevention at the national level

Requests from disaster-prone countries for technical assistance in disaster preparedness had increased steadily since 1980. In 1985, the following requests were received and dealt with: Afghanistan (seismic hazard assessment and forecasting); Algeria (seismic microzoning of Ech Chlef (El Asnam)); Argentina (flood prevention in Buenos Aires); Central African Republic (bushfire preparedness and prevention); Madagascar (strengthening of intervention capacity); Egypt, El Salvador, Fiji, Indonesia, Mali, Nepal, Philippines, Tunisia, Vanuatu, Viet Nam and Zaire (national disaster preparedness and prevention planning).

At the Congo's request, two engineer hydrologists were sent in February to survey flood risks and advise the Government on flood protection and preparedness measures. In response to an urgent request from Argentina in March, UNDRO sent a glaciologist to advise on measures to avert the flood danger of a potential break in a glacier dam that had formed across the Rio Plomo owing to the advance of the glacier Grande del Nevado. In Honduras, a technical assistance mission took place in early March. A physical planning project for Montenegro, Yugoslavia, was completed in 1985.

Preparedness and prevention at the regional and international levels

Increasing emphasis was being put on regional approaches and methods to solve problems related to disaster prevention. Cases in point were the earthquake risk reduction projects in the Balkan region with the subsequent creation in April 1984 of a permanent intergovernmental committee[28] to oversee continuation of the work and its extension to the Mediterranean region; the Tropical Cyclone Committee for the South-West Indian Ocean and the WMO/ESCAP Panel on Tropical Cyclones; as well as the pan-Caribbean disaster

preparedness and prevention project—a multiagency project begun in 1981 covering 28 Caribbean island States and territories.

The project for the Mediterranean region as a whole, sponsored by UNEP jointly with UNDRO, UNCHS and UNESCO, was to be submitted to UNDP and the contracting parties to the 1978 Barcelona Convention for the Mediterranean Action Plan.

In co-operation with the Government of Italy, the Regional Authority of Umbria and the Polytechnic Institute of Milan, UNDRO established an international programme designed to train and inform both specialists and the public on measures to reduce earthquake losses in densely built urban areas. The first event of the programme was an international seminar on post-earthquake measures for structural engineering and physical planning (Perugia, Italy, 11-13 April 1985).

Preparedness for industrial accidents was another area of UNDRO activities; co-operation between UNDRO and IAEA was being further strengthened through participation in expert and advisory groups engaged in the preparation of handbooks dealing with various aspects of the effects of possible accidents in land-based nuclear facilities.

REFERENCES

[1]E/1985/75. [2]A/41/295-E/1986/65. [3]YUN 1984, p. 506. [4]*Ibid.*, p. 503, GA res. 39/207, 17 Dec. 1984. [5]A/40/392-E/1985/117. [6]DP/1985/19. [7]DP/1986/11/Add.1. [8]A/40/758-S/17570. [9]YUN 1978, p. 647. [10]DP/1986/82. [11]YUN 1984, p. 509. [12]E/1985/65. [13]YUN 1984, p. 514, GA res. 39/205, 17 Dec. 1984. [14]A/40/770. [15]A/40/431. [16]YUN 1984, p. 515, GA res. 39/201, 17 Dec. 1984. [17]YUN 1984, p. 516. [18]A/40/439. [19]YUN 1984, p. 517, GA res. 39/191, 17 Dec. 1984. [20]LC/G.1367. [21]A/41/369 & Corr.1. [22]A/40/243. [23]YUN 1984, p. 520, GA res. 39/190, 17 Dec. 1984. [24]A/40/440. [25]YUN 1984, p. 519. [26]SG/SM.1/1 & SG/SM.1/2. [27]A/40/245. [28]YUN 1984, p. 521.

Emergency relief and assistance

Trust Fund for Countries Afflicted by Famine and Malnutrition

Following the liquidation of the United Nations Emergency Operation Trust Fund at the end of 1983,[1] 70 per cent of the remaining balance, or some $34 million, was transferred to a UNDP-administered Trust Fund to finance urgently needed projects, primarily in the food and agricultural sectors in countries afflicted by famine and malnutrition as a result, particularly, of severe or prolonged drought, with special emphasis on African countries.

In an October 1985 report[2] on allocation of the emergency Fund's remaining balance (see

p. 481), the Secretary-General said that, as at 23 September, the UNDP Administrator had approved 115 projects in 52 countries totalling $36 million, of which 87 projects, amounting to $28.3 million, were in 34 African countries. While the implementation of some projects would continue beyond 31 December, the Secretary-General said he was confident that a large proportion of the Trust Fund resources would be expended in 1985 for the purposes for which they had been provided. He also indicated that the Administrator would provide a detailed report to that effect to the UNDP Governing Council in 1986.

Lebanon

The lack of security in Lebanon continued to affect the capability of the United Nations system to provide assistance for the reconstruction and development of the country. All aspects of life—especially the social and economic activities—were affected by the lack of security, and the situation worsened from October 1984 onwards, particularly in the Greater Beirut area, in spite of a security plan approved by the Government and the Parliament in June that year. Other security plans and cease-fires, approved in 1985, succeeded only temporarily in bringing some security to Beirut and other affected areas (see p. 295).

As requested by the General Assembly in 1984,[3] the Secretary-General, in October 1985,[4] reported that the general situation in Lebanon had produced extremely trying circumstances for the United Nations to provide assistance to the country in its reconstruction and development plans, as well as to implement relief programmes for those directly affected by hostilities. Most of the remaining international personnel had left Lebanon in 1985 for security reasons, particularly after a spate of kidnappings in March, which had a negative impact on the delivery of programmed United Nations technical assistance. Reconstruction and development would take longer than previously envisaged, as well as much larger resources; urgent steps must be taken to prevent the economy from deteriorating further.

With the increase in military activities, destruction and displacement of the civilian population, emergency humanitarian assistance had become an immediate and major concern. The United Nations co-ordinating Committee at Beirut, established in 1978[5] to promote reconstruction and development programmes, had evolved into the field of humanitarian relief assistance, emerging at every crisis as a central mechanism for assessing relief needs and developing co-ordinated response to them; it had become the only forum in Beirut for meetings of United Nations organizations and national as well as international NGOs, such as the International Committee of the Red Cross, donor countries and EEC. United Nations organizations contributed to the ongoing relief effort in a co-ordinated fashion, according to their mandates and in response to the Secretary-General's appeals for urgent assistance. That assistance was programmed and provided without discrimination towards any of the various Lebanese communities; in all cases it was negotiated in close consultation with the Lebanese Government.

The Trust Fund of the Secretary-General provided its resources, totalling $500,000, for emergency relief to needy displaced persons; $40,000 of that amount was being used to supplement UNICEF's ongoing water supply project for the displaced people of Beirut. The Lebanese High Relief Committee collaborated closely in the distribution of the relief items.

The regional office of UNHCR for the Middle East, located at Beirut, also continued to participate in providing emergency relief, over and above its traditional activities of legal protection and material assistance to refugees. The total amount allocated for those uprooted in Lebanon since 1976 had reached more than $10 million by the end of 1984. Since 1982, emergency aid had been provided in the Syrian Arab Republic to the displaced persons and refugees arriving from Lebanon, as well as to Lebanese in Europe and Africa; nearly $3 million had been obligated so far for that purpose. In April 1985, a contribution of $100,000 was approved for the populations affected in the Sidon area. Since June, the UNHCR Regional Representative had chaired the United Nations co-ordinating Committee, in the temporary absence of the United Nations Co-ordinator and the UNDP Resident Representative.

UNICEF continued to provide water, health and education services, launching a rehabilitation programme which extended the area of operations, covered by a 1980 agreement with the Government,[6] beyond south Lebanon and Beirut to include areas affected by the war in the Chouf, the High Metn, Beirut's southern suburbs and the Tripoli region. UNICEF had raised $40.8 million to complement funding by the Lebanese Council for Development and Reconstruction (CDR) for that programme. Although the programme was beset by delays due to the occupation of south Lebanon by foreign military forces and because of civil strife, it was largely successful in helping restore water, education and health services.

Emergency assistance to the local populations was also extended by the United Nations Interim Force in Lebanon and the United Nations Relief and Works Agency for Palestine Refugees in the Near East (see POLITICAL AND SECURITY QUESTIONS, Chapter IX).

In 1985, WFP decided to respond to the emergency needs in Lebanon by transferring from one of its development projects there an amount of $2.5 million for food commodities, which it distributed to the needy people affected by the most recent fighting; WFP commodities were stored and packaged in East and West Beirut and distributed according to the need of the population in all parts of the country, depending on the prevailing security situation.

Throughout the recent hostilities, WHO continued to support and co-ordinate medical and health-related assistance; its assistance to the development and rehabilitation of health services, however, was interrupted by the outbreak of armed conflict. In order to respond to the urgent needs of the population, WHO devised, with the Ministry of Public Health, a reprogramming of the WHO 1984-1985 budget amounting to $1,140,000: $220,000 was allocated to the purchase of essential drugs; $810,000 to technical assistance, through the appointment of national experts for strengthening the epidemiological services, health statistical services, primary health care, health manpower, public information and education, workers' health, and clinical, laboratory and radiological technology for health systems based on primary health care; and $110,000 to the planning unit of the Ministry of Public Health, a project for which USAID funding had stopped.

Apart from helping to implement, in co-operation with CDR, the Lebanon reconstruction programme, UNICEF implemented its own technical assistance projects in the fields of health, water supply, education and community self-help; $4.4 million was devoted to this programme. Other UNICEF activities included a basic services programme, assistance to Palestinians and child-care services.

Technical co-operation activities were also implemented by others, such as UNDP. For 1985, UNDP had authorized expenditure of $2.8 million, but those funds had only been partially used due to the security situation. During the first part of the year, UNDP resident experts ensured the implementation of FAO-executed projects outside Beirut; the remaining projects were supervised by short-term consultants and subcontractors. By mid-1985, the security risks became extremely severe and the remaining UNDP-funded experts and the Resident Representative had to be withdrawn from Lebanon.

In 1985, some 200,000 families, or 1 million persons, benefited from WFP assistance throughout the country at a cost of $4 million. The following development projects with WFP financial assistance were operational: a basic diet feeding programme for children and youth to reduce malnutrition ($21,940,800); integrated development of the Lebanese mountain areas to improve the economic and social conditions of the rural population, to benefit 109,000 persons ($18,523,200); and rehabilitation of sericulture to revive Lebanon's traditional silk industry, for 7,600 persons ($1,480,000). Total WFP assistance provided to Lebanon over 11 years was $94 million.

FAO made a special effort to support Lebanese agricultural sectors which had also been adversely affected. Until the first part of 1985, four FAO/UNDP projects were still operational; within the FAO regular programme, three projects were finalized during the year, while three new ones were approved. An FAO Trust Fund project providing 6,000 tons of fertilizers was completed in February; another project supporting agricultural and rural planning and development was operational, while a third, designed to strengthen the operational and technical capabilities of the Ministry of Agriculture, was suspended because of lack of security.

In July, a representative of the United Nations Co-ordinator of Assistance for the Reconstruction and Development of Lebanon gave an oral report to the Economic and Social Council's Third Committee.

Introducing the Secretary-General's report[4] in the General Assembly's Second Committee on 12 November, the Under-Secretary-General for Political and General Assembly Affairs said the increasing number of civilian victims of the hostilities and the physical destruction had led to a redirecting of relief and rehabilitation efforts. The displacement of the population constituted one of the major concerns of the Government, which had requested the international community's support.

Humanitarian assistance needs were constantly increasing and the United Nations had limited resources to meet them. The Secretary-General had dispatched a high-level mission from UNDRO which had visited Lebanon from 31 October to 4 November. According to the mission's findings, there were 500,000 displaced persons whose relief and rehabilitation needs were estimated at $51 million, in addition to health facility needs. The Under-Secretary-General pointed out that his Office, in collaboration with UNDRO in Geneva, had initiated a joint fund-raising effort. He was hoping that, after consideration of the Secretary-General's report on the subject, the Committee would decide to maintain the level of assistance provided in previous years.

ECONOMIC AND SOCIAL COUNCIL ACTION

On 25 July, the Economic and Social Council, on the recommendation of its Third Committee, adopted **resolution 1985/56** without vote.

Assistance for the reconstruction and development of Lebanon

The Economic and Social Council

1. *Takes note with interest* of the oral report made on 9 July 1985 by the representative of the United Nations Co-ordinator of Assistance for the Reconstruction and Development of Lebanon pursuant to General Assembly resolution 39/197 of 17 December 1984;

2. *Appeals* to all Member States and to organs, organizations and bodies of the United Nations system to continue and intensify their efforts to mobilize all possible assistance to the Government of Lebanon in its efforts for reconstruction and development, in accordance with the relevant resolutions and decisions of the General Assembly and the Economic and Social Council.

Economic and Social Council resolution 1985/56

25 July 1985   Meeting 52   Adopted without vote

Approved by Third Committee (E/1985/139) without vote, 15 July (meeting 12); 7-nation draft (E/1985/C.3/L.4); agenda item 17.
Sponsors: Algeria, Bangladesh, France, Morocco, Somalia, Syrian Arab Republic, Yugoslavia.

GENERAL ASSEMBLY ACTION

On 17 December, the General Assembly, acting on the recommendation of the Second Committee, adopted **resolution 40/229** without vote.

Assistance for the reconstruction and development of Lebanon

The General Assembly,

Recalling its resolutions 33/146 of 20 December 1978, 34/135 of 14 December 1979, 35/85 of 5 December 1980, 36/205 of 17 December 1981, 37/163 of 17 December 1982, 38/220 of 20 December 1983 and 39/197 of 17 December 1984 on assistance for the reconstruction and development of Lebanon,

Recalling also Economic and Social Council resolutions 1980/15 of 29 April 1980 and 1985/56 of 25 July 1985 and decisions 1983/112 of 17 May 1983 and 1984/174 of 26 July 1984,

Noting with deep concern the continuing heavy loss of life and the additional destruction of property, which have caused further extensive damage to the economic and social structures of Lebanon,

Also noting with concern the serious economic situation in Lebanon,

Welcoming the determined efforts of the Government of Lebanon in undertaking its reconstruction and rehabilitation programme,

Reaffirming the urgent need for further international action to assist the Government of Lebanon in its continuing efforts for reconstruction and development,

Considering that filling the vacant post of United Nations Co-ordinator of Assistance for the Reconstruction and Development of Lebanon would facilitate the normal operations of international assistance to Lebanon,

Taking note of the report of the Secretary-General and of the statement made on 12 November 1985 by the Under-Secretary-General for Political and General Assembly Affairs,

1. *Expresses its appreciation* to the Secretary-General for his report and for the steps he has taken to mobilize assistance to Lebanon;

2. *Commends* the Under-Secretary-General for Political and General Assembly Affairs for his co-ordination of system-wide assistance for Lebanon, as well as the staff of the Office of the United Nations Co-ordinator of Assistance for the Reconstruction and Development of Lebanon for their invaluable efforts in the discharge of their duties;

3. *Expresses its appreciation* for the relentless efforts undertaken by the Government of Lebanon in the implementation of the initial phase of reconstruction of the country, despite adverse circumstances, and for the steps it has taken to remedy the economic situation;

4. *Requests* the Secretary-General to continue and intensify his efforts to mobilize all possible assistance within the United Nations system to help the Government of Lebanon in its reconstruction and development efforts;

5. *Invites* the Secretary-General to consider arranging, under the terms of resolution 33/146, for the United Nations Co-ordinator of Assistance for the Reconstruction and Development of Lebanon to resume his functions in Lebanon;

6. *Requests* the organs, organizations and bodies of the United Nations system to intensify their programmes of assistance and to expand them in response to the needs of Lebanon, and to take the necessary steps to ensure that their offices in Beirut are adequately staffed at the senior level;

7. *Also requests* the Secretary-General to report to the General Assembly at its forty-first session on the progress achieved in the implementation of the present resolution.

General Assembly resolution 40/229

17 December 1985   Meeting 120   Adopted without vote

Approved by Second Committee (A/40/1043) without vote, 5 December (meeting 48); draft by Vice-Chairman (A/C.2/40/L.104), based on informal consultations on draft by Algeria, Australia, Austria, Bahrain, Bangladesh, Belgium, Canada, Cyprus, Democratic Yemen, Djibouti, France, India, Iraq, Italy, Japan, Jordan, Kuwait, Lebanon, Liberia, Libyan Arab Jamahiriya, Madagascar, Mauritania, Morocco, Nicaragua, Oman, Pakistan, Qatar, Saudi Arabia, Somalia, Spain, Sudan, Tunisia, United Arab Emirates, United Kingdom, United States, Uruguay and Yugoslavia (A/C.2/40/L.67); agenda item 87.
Meeting numbers. GA 40th session: 2nd Committee 31, 44, 48; plenary 120.

REFERENCES

[1]YUN 1983, p. 537, GA res. 38/201, 20 Dec. 1983. [2]A/40/740. [3]YUN 1984, p. 523, GA res. 39/197, 17 Dec. 1984. [4]A/40/434 & Add.1. [5]YUN 1978, p. 373, GA res. 33/146, 20 Dec. 1978. [6]YUN 1980, p. 447.

Chapter IV

International trade and finance

In 1985, several United Nations bodies focused on the interdependence of the world economy and the need to address international trade and finance issues in an interrelated manner, particularly in view of the serious debt servicing difficulties of many developing countries and the low price levels of their commodities. A significant part of the debate at both regular sessions in 1985 of the Trade and Development Board (TDB) of the United Nations Conference on Trade and Development (UNCTAD) dealt with the interdependence of problems of trade, development finance and the international monetary system, as did the general discussion at the second regular session of the Economic and Social Council in July. In December, the General Assembly decided to reconvene the Second (Economic and Financial) Committee for one week in early 1986 in order to consider ways in which international co-operation in the fields of money, finance, debt, resource flows, trade and development could be promoted (decision 40/445).

In his annual report on the work of the Organization (see p. 3), the Secretary-General stated that economic, financial, monetary and trade issues were so interrelated and were of such importance that they could be dealt with effectively only as part of a wider political process. The international debt situation was particularly alarming, with many debtor countries facing very weak export markets and commodity prices lower in real terms than they had been since the 1930s. Interest rates, however, remained high and there seemed to be no tendency for new lending to resume. Although there was a strong mutual interest in resolving the debt crisis and efforts were being made to reschedule debts over long periods, elsewhere protectionist measures were nullifying those efforts. The Secretary-General saw a strong need for a joint, comprehensive and speedy examination of all aspects of the situation, including the political ones.

Following its fourth annual review of protectionism and structural adjustment, TDB recommended that further efforts should be taken to liberalize the international trading system and outlined documentation to be prepared for the 1986 review.

The United Nations Conference to Review All Aspects of the Set of Multilaterally Agreed Equitable Principles and Rules for the Control of Restrictive Business Practices was held in November. Following consideration of the Conference's report, the General Assembly in December invited the UNCTAD Secretary-General and the Conference President to consult with regional groups and Governments on reconvening the Conference (resolution 40/192). The Intergovernmental Group of Experts on Restrictive Business Practices held its fourth session in April in preparation for the Conference.

During 1985, one additional State adhered to the 1980 Agreement Establishing the Common Fund for Commodities; by year's end it had not entered into force. With regard to individual commodities, the United Nations Cocoa Conference, 1984, and the United Nations Conference on Natural Rubber, 1985, held sessions in 1985. In both cases, progress was made towards preparing successor agreements to earlier agreements on those commodities and it was recommended that both Conferences be reconvened. Both the International Tropical Timber Agreement, 1983, and the International Sugar Agreement, 1984, entered into force in 1985. Meetings were held during the year to consider possible international measures on iron ore, nickel and tungsten.

In April 1985, at its resumed 1984 session, the Assembly adopted guidelines for consumer protection and asked the Secretary-General to disseminate them to Governments and other interested parties. All United Nations organizations were requested to distribute the guidelines to the appropriate bodies of individual States (resolution 39/248).

The serious debt problems of developing countries and development finance were taken up in a number of United Nations bodies, including the Committee for Development Planning (CDP), TDB, the Committee on Invisibles and Financing related to Trade, the Economic and Social Council and the General Assembly. These issues were also addressed in the Organization's major economic reports. A special session of TDB (the fourteenth) centred on the need for a compensatory financing facility to assist developing countries with their export earnings shortfalls. The first part of the 1985 session of Committee on Invisibles and Financing was devoted to insurance questions.

The place, date and duration of the seventh (1987) session of UNCTAD was discussed by TDB in September. In December (resolution 40/189), the Assembly called on Governments and international organizations to commence intensive and thorough preparations for that session.

In November, the Assembly confirmed the appointment of Kenneth K. S. Dadzie as Secretary-General of UNCTAD for a term of three years beginning on 1 January 1986 (decision 40/308).

Topics related to this chapter. Development policy and international economic co-operation. Economic assistance, disasters and emergency relief: Africa and the critical economic situation. Transport. Industrial development: manufactures. Regional economic and social activities: international trade and finance—Africa, Asia and the Pacific, Europe, Latin America and the Caribbean, Western Asia. Science and technology: technology transfer. International economic law: international trade law.

International co-operation in trade and finance

The Committee for Development Planning,[1] which met in April 1985 (see also Chapter I of this section), stated that it was increasingly recognized that trade issues were closely linked to the financial and monetary issues that loomed so large in the world's current economic disequilibria. Large swings in key currency-exchange rates subjected trading partners to uncertainties about long-run comparative advantage and appropriate investment strategies. To illustrate the close link between trade and finance, CDP observed that when currencies were over-valued, protectionist pressures increased and trade barriers tended to take the form of quantitative restrictions; when they were under-valued, inflationary pressures built up and uncompetitive industries were encouraged; when access to markets was denied them, debtors found difficulty in servicing their debts; when interest rates rose unexpectedly, export earnings were diverted from import demands to debt service with costly effects for both the local and the world economy. The proliferation of trade barriers, therefore, had to be seen in the context of the general need to restore international financial stability and sustained economic development.

The UNCTAD *Trade and Development Report, 1985*[2] stated that trade and financial policies needed to be made more supportive of development by fostering the spread of growth from developed to developing countries and meeting the needs of those parts of the developing world, such as sub-Saharan Africa, that would not be touched by faster growth in developed countries. Such policies would include: increasing lending by multilateral institutions; strengthening commodity export earnings beyond what would occur from more rapid growth in industrial countries; moving decisively towards meeting targets for official development assistance; ensuring greater access to markets in developed countries; and improving the functioning of the international monetary system. Policies in the developing countries themselves also required constant attention and improvement.

ACC activities. In its annual overview report to the Economic and Social Council for 1984/85,[3] the inter-agency Administrative Committee on Co-ordination (ACC) noted that deliberations in various forums of the United Nations system, including the Interim Committee of the International Monetary Fund (IMF) and the Development Committee of the World Bank and IMF, had recognized the need to address trade, money and finance in an interrelated manner.

ECONOMIC AND SOCIAL COUNCIL ACTION

By **decision 1985/159** of 31 May, the Economic and Social Council invited delegations at its July 1985 session, during the general discussion of international economic and social policy, to give special focus to international co-operation in the interrelated areas of money, finance, debt and trade.

During the discussion in July,[4] most delegations stressed the need for enhanced international co-operation in those areas. Of immediate concern was a prospective deceleration in growth in certain industrialized countries and the concomitant slow-down in world trade that that could entail. Averting a new global recession required sustained non-inflationary growth in industrialized countries, greater monetary stability, enlarged market access for exports of developing countries and a larger flow of resources to those countries. Sustained adjustment efforts by developing countries to redress external and internal imbalances and to improve allocative efficiency in their economies were also required. Concerted efforts were necessary to redress some fundamental inequities and deficiencies in the international monetary, financial and trading systems, including measures to restore the multilateral character of the trading régime, to improve mechanisms for creating and distributing international liquidity, and to ensure an adequate flow of financial resources to developing countries.

Commenting on the Council's general debate on 25 July, the President stated that the debt crisis had illustrated the need for greater insight into the interrelatedness of the issues in money, finance and trade, where policies had to be mutually reinforcing and not conflicting.

By **decision 1985/183** of 25 July, the Council decided to transmit the Council President's statement to the 1985 session of the General Assembly.

Report of the Secretary-General. In response to a 1984 General Assembly resolution,[5] the Secretary-General submitted to the Assembly in October 1985 a report on international co-operation in the fields of money, finance, debt, resource flows, trade and development.[6] A note verbale had been sent to consult all Member States and United Nations organizations and bodies, and a study was carried out of documents, statements, declarations, communiqués and reports, which articulated positions held by countries and groups of countries on the issues.

The report comprised two main sections: the first assessed major policy issues arising from the current international economic situation and examined the interrelatedness of those issues in the areas of money, finance, debt and trade in the light of consultations and the general state of international negotiations on those matters; the second detailed responses to the consultations and summarized the proposals raised in them.

GENERAL ASSEMBLY ACTION

In December, on the recommendation of the Second Committee, the Assembly adopted **decision 40/445**, by recorded vote.

International co-operation in the interrelated areas of money, finance, debt, resource flows, trade and development

At its 119th plenary meeting, on 17 December 1985, the General Assembly, on the recommendation of the Second Committee:

(a) Decided to reconvene the Second Committee immediately prior to the first regular session of the Economic and Social Council of 1986, for one week, in order to give in-depth consideration to ways in which international co-operation in the interrelated areas of money, finance, debt, resource flows, trade and development could be promoted effectively and to deal with unfinished business under agenda item 84, namely:

International Conference on Money and Finance for Development (draft resolution A/C.2/40/L.30);

External debt crisis and development (draft resolution A/C.2/40/L.52);

Commodities (draft resolution A/C.2/40/L.81);

Debt and related issues (draft resolution A/C.2/40/L.129);

(b) Requested the Secretary-General to provide all necessary information and documentation to support the work of the Committee, including an update of the report submitted under General Assembly resolution 39/218 of 18 December 1984, with a short summary of the relevant ideas and proposals put forward by the heads of State and Government and ministers for foreign affairs at the fortieth session of the General Assembly;

(c) Also requested the Secretary-General to invite the appropriate organs, organizations and bodies of the United Nations system to provide the Committee with information on their ongoing activities in the interrelated areas of money, finance, debt, resource flows, trade and development;

(d) Requested the Secretary-General of the United Nations Conference on Trade and Development to submit a report on the ongoing work of the Conference in the area of interdependence of trade, development, finance and the international monetary system.

General Assembly decision 40/445

133-1-20 (recorded vote)

Approved by Second Committee (A/40/989/Add.14) by recorded vote (88-1-19), 14 December (meeting 52); draft by Yugoslavia, for Group of 77 (A/C.2/40/L.51/Rev.1), orally revised; agenda item 84.
Financial implications. 5th Committee, A/40/1062; S-G, A/C.2/40/L.91, A/C.5/40/96.
Meeting numbers. GA 40th session: 2nd Committee 31, 41, 45, 52; 5th Committee 68; plenary 119.

Recorded vote in Assembly as follows:

In favour: Afghanistan, Algeria, Angola, Antigua and Barbuda, Argentina, Bahamas, Bahrain, Bangladesh, Barbados, Belize, Benin, Bhutan, Bolivia, Botswana, Brazil, Brunei Darussalam, Bulgaria, Burkina Faso, Burma, Burundi, Byelorussian SSR, Cameroon, Cape Verde, Central African Republic, Chad, Chile, China, Colombia, Comoros, Congo, Costa Rica, Cuba, Cyprus, Czechoslovakia, Democratic Kampuchea, Democratic Yemen, Djibouti, Dominica, Dominican Republic, Ecuador, Egypt, El Salvador, Equatorial Guinea, Ethiopia, Finland, Gabon, Gambia, German Democratic Republic, Ghana, Guatemala, Guinea, Guinea-Bissau, Guyana, Haiti, Honduras, Hungary, India, Indonesia, Iran, Iraq, Ivory Coast, Jamaica, Jordan, Kenya, Kuwait, Lao People's Democratic Republic, Lebanon, Lesotho, Liberia, Libyan Arab Jamahiriya, Madagascar, Malawi, Malaysia, Maldives, Mali, Malta, Mauritania, Mauritius, Mexico, Mongolia, Morocco, Mozambique, Nepal, Nicaragua, Niger, Nigeria, Norway, Oman, Pakistan, Panama, Papua New Guinea, Paraguay, Peru, Philippines, Poland, Qatar, Romania, Rwanda, Saint Christopher and Nevis, Saint Lucia, Saint Vincent and the Grenadines, Samoa, Sao Tome and Principe, Saudi Arabia, Senegal, Sierra Leone, Singapore, Somalia, Sri Lanka, Sudan, Suriname, Swaziland, Sweden, Syrian Arab Republic, Thailand, Togo, Trinidad and Tobago, Tunisia, Turkey, Uganda, Ukrainian SSR, USSR, United Arab Emirates, United Republic of Tanzania, Uruguay, Vanuatu, Venezuela, Viet Nam, Yemen, Yugoslavia, Zaire, Zambia, Zimbabwe.

Against: United States.

Abstaining: Australia, Austria, Belgium, Canada, Denmark, France, Germany, Federal Republic of, Greece, Grenada, Iceland, Ireland, Israel, Italy, Japan, Luxembourg, Netherlands, New Zealand, Portugal, Spain, United Kingdom.

The deferred draft resolutions referred to in the above decision are discussed elsewhere in this chapter. For the draft resolution on an international conference on money and finance for development, see p. 578; for that on commodities, see p. 567; for those on the external debt crisis and development and on debt and related issues, see p. 577.

Speaking in explanation of vote, Finland said it had voted in favour of the text although it considered that the Economic and Social Council would have been better suited to deal with the work envisaged. China regretted that the Committee had not been able to reach a consensus. Venezuela felt that refusal to take a decision on the draft on an international conference on money and finance for development, which it considered the most important draft submitted to the session, did not contribute to improving international co-operation or to the Committee's credibility. The German Democratic Republic was convinced that the draft decision would be implemented in the manner agreed by consensus among delegations before the vote.

Luxembourg, on behalf of the members of the European Community (EC), believed that resuming the Second Committee was not the best method to continue the debate; the Council had the competence to consider the issues.

Canada said it would have preferred an open-ended, deliberative discussion of the issues during the Council's second regular annual session. It saw a certain rigidity of position in regard to the locus for the discussions and wondered why one or another of several alternative proposals would not have been satisfactory.

The United States said it was actively seeking solutions to the problems discussed, but the principal forums for dealing with them were the interested Governments, other institutions within the United Nations family and private financial institutions. The Second Committee should move cautiously and methodically and its deliberations must promote the total effort on international financial problems. It should avoid special or reserved sessions without clearly defined procedures and objectives.

Poland attached special importance to the inter-related problems addressed in the text and considered that further consideration should be given to proposals that had been submitted during the Organization's fortieth anniversary session by heads of State or Government and by foreign ministers on, among other things, establishing an international debt and development research centre.

Yugoslavia, on behalf of the Group of 77 developing countries, said that although the Group had shown a constructive approach and a high degree of flexibility, it had not been possible to reach agreement on the drafts on an international conference on money and finance for development and on external debt because some developed countries insisted on maintaining their position and did not want the Assembly to be involved in the matter.

By **decision 40/470** of 18 December, the Assembly decided to resume its 1985 session at a date to be announced to consider a number of agenda items, including development and international economic co-operation, with specific reference to trade and development.

REFERENCES

[1]E/1985/29. [2]*Trade and Development Report, 1985* (UNCTAD/TDR/5), Sales No. E.85.II.D.16. [3]E/1985/57. [4]A/40/3/Rev.1. [5]YUN 1984, p. 542, GA res. 39/218, 18 Dec. 1984. [6]A/40/708.

International trade

In several United Nations bodies where international trade issues were discussed during 1985, including TDB and CDP, concern was expressed over the increasing tendency towards protectionism. The main conclusion of an UNCTAD report prepared for the Board's annual review of problems of protectionism and structural adjustment was that immediate action was required to deal with those problems on a simultaneous basis if there was to be any significant progress in expanding the share of developing countries in world production and trade.

In April, the Special Committee on Preferences reviewed the implementation of the generalized system of preferences and technical assistance activities in connection with the system. Governments were urged to make cash contributions to the UNCTAD trust fund so that technical co-operation activities could continue beyond 1985. The establishment of a global system of trade preferences among developing countries was discussed by the Committee on Economic Co-operation among Developing Countries in November.

Following discussions on trade relations among countries having different economic and social systems in September, TDB requested the UNCTAD Secretary-General to convene a group of experts to consider prospects for such trade, particularly between developing countries and socialist countries of Eastern Europe.

In the area of trade promotion and facilitation, the International Trade Centre (ITC)—operated jointly by UNCTAD and the General Agreement on Tariffs and Trade (GATT)—continued to serve as the focal point for United Nations assistance to developing countries in formulating and implementing trade promotion programmes. A United Nations Conference to Review All Aspects of the Set of Multilaterally Agreed Equitable Principles and Rules for the Control of Restrictive Business Practices was held in November and, in December, the General Assembly invited the UNCTAD Secretary-General to consult with regional groups and Governments on reconvening the Conference. The UNCTAD Intergovernmental Group of Experts on Restrictive Business Practices held its fourth session in 1985.

Several meetings on commodities were held under UNCTAD auspices during the year, including two special sessions of the Committee on Commodities, one regular session of that Committee, and a meeting of the Permanent Sub-Committee on Commodities. By 31 December, the Agreement Establishing the Common Fund for Commodities had still not been ratified by a sufficient number of countries for it to enter into force.

In April, the Assembly adopted guidelines for consumer protection and requested the Secretary-General to disseminate them to Governments and other interested parties.

Trade policy

Most developing countries participated in the significant improvement in world trade which took place in 1984, according to the UNCTAD *Trade and Development Report, 1985*.[1] Despite the increasing resort to restrictive trade measures, the volume of world exports grew by close to 9 per cent compared with an annual rate of increase of less than 2 per cent in 1983. However, it was not expected to grow at such a pace in 1985. Much of the increase reflected the strong performance of the United States economy supported by recovery in other industrial countries. While it had been instrumental in transmitting a measure of export-led expansion to economic activity in several parts of the developing world, the expansion in demand for traded goods had been very unevenly distributed among the developing countries. Countries with a relatively advanced manufacturing sector were more favoured by developments in trade than countries which relied more heavily on primary commodities, which constituted the majority of developing countries.

Among the developing countries, there were wide differences in the incidence of growth of United States import demand and in their ability to translate increased exports into increased output. A small group of developing countries, mainly in the Pacific basin, had not experienced debt-servicing crises and had seen their exports to the United States rise sharply. However, a large number of developing countries failed to register any appreciable increase in export earnings mainly because of the weakness of commodity markets, stemming largely from the slow rate of growth of demand in Western Europe. The group of countries that had experienced difficulty in servicing their debt—mainly Latin American countries—and that had sharply increased their exports to the United States in 1983 and 1984 could only improve their trade balance at the cost of massive cuts in imports. In 1984, imports rose only slightly. The pre-emption of export earnings by debt service thus prevented them from retransmitting to the rest of the world the demand impulses received from the United States.

Among developed countries, the United States trading partners in the Organisation for Economic Co-operation and Development had by their own policy stances failed to contribute significantly to demand growth, and had even dampened the demand expansion initiated by the United States. At the same time, they captured a sizeable share of the demand so generated.

The *Report* stated that the world-wide trade régime had been a source of difficulty on two counts: existing trade impediments had hampered the export efforts of developing countries, with over one third of their exports to developed market-economy countries subject to measures which constrained exports; and there was a tendency for impediments to increase in markets where developing countries were particularly successful.

Noting that the prevailing trends in trade imbalances could not continue for long, the *Report* stated that a unilateral shift by the United States towards a less expansionary fiscal stance would reduce the trade imbalance by reducing the disparity in demand-creation and might also lead to lower interest rates and a cheaper dollar, thereby improving United States competitiveness.

The *World Economic Survey 1985*[2] also devoted a chapter to the uneven international trade performance during 1984, echoing the view expressed in the *Trade and Development Report, 1985* that the major beneficiaries of the surge in trade were largely those countries in which manufactures provided a major share of export earnings and those with strong trade ties to the more rapidly growing markets. International commodity prices saw their cyclical recovery cut short in 1984, while the surge in exports in a number of sensitive sectors brought about a stiffening of protectionist barriers.

The *Survey* said that 1984 had witnessed: a further tightening in restrictions applied to already highly protected sectors, such as textiles, clothing and steel; continued proliferation of orderly market agreements, voluntary export restraints and other bilateral arrangements; a growing number of allegations of unfair trade prices, such as subsidies; increased trade restrictions imposed for balance-of-payments reasons; and escalating tensions surrounding agricultural trade.

To sustain the growth momentum in the world economy, to help reduce external and internal imbalances and, in particular, to improve the prospects of indebted countries, a continuous expansion of trading relations was critical, said the *Survey*. It was urgent that industrial countries adopt standstill provisions with regard to protectionist actions and start a gradual dismantling of non-tariff barriers and discriminatory restrictions on trade. Additional efforts should be made to carry forward the unfinished programme of work agreed upon at the 1982 GATT ministerial session,[3] since progress in its implementation should pave the way for a new round of trade negotiations with the broad-based participation of developed and developing countries.

Noting that bilateral agreements, in particular countertrade, and full use of regional and subregional clearing mechanisms had allowed for a significant increase in trade among developing countries, the *Survey* said there was a strong case for further enhancement of such mechanisms. Since many bilateral agreements tended to be of an *ad hoc* and temporary nature, the strengthening of existing arrangements and enactment of more comprehensive ones remained important; that process should take account of policies to encourage interaction among the private sectors of developing countries. In addition, more rapid progress was required in evolving a system of generalized trade preferences among developing countries (see p. 558).

In its 1985 report to the Economic and Social Council,[4] CDP stated that the seriousness of the slippage towards trade protectionism and discrimination could not be over-emphasized, as foreign trade and investment were at the core of the international economy. CDP supported the launching of a new round of GATT negotiations directed primarily towards strengthening the multilateral trading system and a further opening of world markets. Expansion of trade in services and exploration of whether multilateral rules could be devised for that sector were also important elements.

International trading system

In line with UNCTAD resolution 159(VI),[5] TDB at its September 1985 session discussed the organization of a review and in-depth study of the international trading system. The issue, together with an UNCTAD report on the subject, had also been discussed by the Board in 1984.[6]

On 27 September,[7] the Board, noting that recent developments had accentuated the need for improvement and strengthening of the international trading system and reversal of dangerous tendencies, decided to review and study, in depth, developments in that system; it requested the UNCTAD Secretary-General to submit appropriate documentation to assist the Board at its September 1986 session.

GENERAL ASSEMBLY ACTION

On 9 December, a draft resolution on international trade, sponsored by Australia, Canada and New Zealand,[8] was introduced in the Second Committee. By that text, the Assembly, welcoming the decision of the Contracting Parties to GATT to establish a preparatory committee to determine the objectives, subject-matter, modalities for and participation in the new round of multilateral trade negotiations (see PART TWO, Chapter XVII), would have urged all countries to oppose protectionist pressures, dismantle trade barriers and strengthen the open multilateral trading system.

At a meeting on 13 December, Yugoslavia, on behalf of the Group of 77 developing countries, submitted amendments[9] to replace the operative paragraph by five paragraphs, by which the Assembly would: reaffirm that the principle of preferential and more favourable treatment to developing countries should be fulfilled on a non-reciprocal basis; urge developed countries to implement commitments they undertook at the 1982 ministerial session of GATT and at UNCTAD VI on standstill and rollback of protectionism; recommend that urgent measures be taken to achieve greater stability in exchange rates; urge an end to developed countries' violation of the rules, norms and principles of the international trading system; and stress the need for a comprehensive agreement on safeguard measures to ensure their temporary nature.

At the same meeting, the sponsors withdrew their draft text and, consequently, the amendments were also withdrawn.

Protectionism and structural adjustment

In March 1985, TDB undertook its annual review of protectionism and structural adjustment. As requested by it in 1984,[10] the UNCTAD Secretary-General had asked member States to provide information on actions relevant to agreements and commitments in part I of UNC-TAD resolution 159(VI)[11] and on their experience with structural adjustment, in order to assist the Board's sessional committee in reviewing progress in structural adjustment and in assessing its implications for the trade and development of developing countries and for the world economy.

A secretariat note[12] reproduced information received from 18 countries (Australia, Austria, Chile, Cuba, Czechoslovakia, Ecuador, Finland, Federal Republic of Germany, Hungary, New Zealand, Norway, Qatar, Republic of Korea, Saudi Arabia, Spain, Sweden, Switzerland, Yugoslavia) and the European Economic Community (EEC); replies from France and the United Kingdom indicated that the information requested from them fell within EEC's competence. It was noted that Peru and the United States had provided information which was available for consultation in the secretariat files.

Also before TDB was a two-part secretariat report on problems of protectionism and structural adjustment. The first part of the report[13] discussed the role that a liberal trade régime could play in achieving structural adjustment, the role that effective adjustment could play in achieving a more liberal trade régime, and the connection between structural adjustment, economic growth and development, and a reversal of protectionist trends. Its main conclusion was that immediate action was required on a simultaneous basis to deal not only with protectionism but also with structural adjustment, if there was to be significant progress in expanding developing countries' share of world production and trade.

The second part of the report[14] described trends in production, employment and trade in agriculture, manufacturing and services, and some underlying factors in structural change. Its main conclusion was that the structural adjustment problem reached a new dimension as a result of difficulties experienced by the world economy. The 1970s had witnessed a retardation of structural adjustment when the need for such change was greatest because of the increased export competitiveness of a number of developing countries. Sluggish growth in the latter part of the 1970s, followed by prolonged recession, had made adjustment more difficult, particularly for certain major industries. A vicious circle between structural maladjustment and adverse growth conditions gradually emerged. The report stated that greater transparency of production and trade policies and of Governments' intentions would represent a step forward. It would provide guidance to prospective suppliers and remove the uncertainty which made correct investment decisions increasingly difficult. Greater transparency of the real cost involved in protectionist policies might help Governments resist pressure from interest groups and select more appropriate forms of intervention. If consumers were better informed about the indirect costs of protectionism brought about by higher prices, Governments would be in a better position to reconcile trade policies with policies to facilitate structural adjustment.

On 29 March,[15] TDB recommended: reaffirmation and full implementation of the commitments in UNCTAD resolution 159(VI);[11] liberalization efforts to strengthen the trading system and further expand trade; that developed countries fulfil their commitments on standstill and rollback and work towards eliminating quantitative restrictions and similar measures; and that developed countries provide more favourable treatment to developing countries in international trade and facilitate structural adjustment based on a dynamic pattern of comparative advantage, with special attention being paid to the problems of the least developed countries (LDCs).

To foster greater transparency, work on the UNCTAD Data Base on Trade Measures should continue and the information therein be circulated to UNCTAD member States, whose comments should be taken into account when updating it. An intergovernmental group of experts should be convened to focus on reaching a consensus on definitions and methodology employed in the Data Base. The work should assist the Board in addressing questions of dissemination of the inventory of non-tariff barriers, preferably at the 1986 annual review. For that review, the secretariat should intensify its analysis of structural adjustment, using information available from other organizations and considering the problem in the context of relevant factors, including a liberal trade régime. The need for improved access, especially for products of export interest to developing countries, should be borne in mind.

In preparing documentation for the 1986 review, attention should be given to problems of strengthening the participation of developing countries in agro-industrial production and trade. Special attention should also be given to the difficulties of the African countries and LDCs.

GENERAL ASSEMBLY ACTION

The Second Committee had before it a draft resolution[16] on protectionism and structural adjustment. The draft, originally submitted in 1980 on behalf of the Group of 77[17] and revised by the sponsors in 1981.[18] It was considered in 1982,[19] 1983[20] and 1984,[21] then referred to the Assembly's 1985 session.[22]

By the draft, the Assembly would have urged the developed countries to limit protectionist policies and facilitate measures to increase the share of developing countries in international trade. A table containing suggestions by some developed countries for changes in the draft was annexed to it.

On 17 December, by **decision 40/439** adopted without vote, the Assembly, on the recommendation of the Second Committee, as orally proposed by its Chairman on 9 December, deferred consideration of the draft resolution to its 1986 session.

Services

In accordance with part IV of UNCTAD resolution 159(VI),[23] which instructed the UNCTAD Secretary-General to continue studying the issues involved in trade in services and invited TDB to consider appropriate future work, the Board had considered the subject in 1984[24] and annexed to its report a draft decision submitted by the Group of 77. That draft was discussed at the Board's March 1985 session, where it was submitted to a contact group for consideration.

On 29 March,[25] the Board agreed that UNCTAD's contribution to future work in services should encompass the following four aspects: consideration of the definitional aspects of services; strengthening and refining the data base at the national, regional and international levels, together with methodological improvement; further in-depth studies of the role of services in the development process to enable countries to analyse the role of the services sector in their economies and its contribution to all aspects of development; and assisting interested member States in analysing the role of services in their economies. The UNCTAD Secretary-General was requested to invite the United Nations Development Programme (UNDP) and other sources to assist in meeting individual and joint requests in implementation of the decision.

In accordance with that decision, the UNCTAD secretariat transmitted to the Board's September 1985 session a report[26] describing UNCTAD's ongoing work in the four areas of services in the development process.

Trade preferences

In 1985, the Special Committee on Preferences reviewed changes and improvements in the generalized system of preferences (GSP). It urged Governments to contribute to the UNCTAD trust fund for technical co-operation activities. Discussions continued on a proposed global system of trade preferences among developing countries.

Generalized system of preferences

The Trade and Development Board's Special Committee on Preferences held its thirteenth session at Geneva from 10 to 19 April 1985,[27] having before it the UNCTAD secretariat's ninth general report on implementing GSP.[28] The report described changes and improvements in the system since the previous review in 1984.[24]

Improvements made in 1984 with respect to product coverage and tariff cuts could be characterized as modest, according to the report. Efforts continued towards improving the benefits of the system with respect to LDCs and towards making it more restrictive with respect to other beneficiaries considered to be more competitive—a twin policy aimed at bringing about greater differentiation among developing countries in the application of preferential treatment.

Notable developments in 1984 were the extensions by Canada and the United States of their respective schemes. Thus, all GSP schemes had been renewed beyond their initial 10-year period.

The Special Committee also considered a report[29] on technical co-operation activities in connection with GSP during 1984.[30]

On 19 April, the Special Committee adopted a set of agreed conclusions which it annexed to its report.[27] It recognized the important role of GSP in facilitating exports of developing countries and expanding international trade. The objectives and character of GSP were reaffirmed, but it was noted that the objectives had not been fully achieved. The Committee also recognized the important role of GSP in the development efforts of developing countries and its objectives, i.e. to increase their export earnings, to promote their industrialization and to accelerate their rates of economic growth. In that context, the crucial importance of the expansion of exports of the indebted countries was recognized. The Committee noted the requests of preference-receiving countries that preference-giving countries fully respect the generalized, non-discriminatory and non-reciprocal character of GSP and refrain from excluding beneficiary countries.

The Special Committee, noting that improvements in GSP had been relatively modest, urged the preference-giving countries to improve their schemes significantly. Developed countries should pay special attention to products not adequately covered in the agricultural and industrial sectors and to products of interest to LDCs. The interests of developing countries enjoying special advantages and the need to find ways of protecting their interests should be taken into account.

The Committee reaffirmed that the rules of origin should be further liberalized and harmonized and their operation simplified, and the rules of cumulative origin improved. It was noted that the adoption of the Harmonized Commodity Description and Coding System,[31] to be introduced in January 1987, in national tariff systems could lead to changes in tariff rates, product coverage, safeguard limitations and rules of origin. The Committee agreed that in changing to the new nomenclature, the overall level of GSP benefits should be maintained and the change in tariff schedules should not hinder preference-giving countries in examining ways to improve their schemes. Preference-giving countries modifying their schemes should afford an opportunity for prompt consultations; any modifications should take into account the development, financial and trade needs of the developing countries. Preference-giving countries should also provide detailed statistics on GSP imports from preference-receiving countries, in order to increase transparency and improve utilization of the schemes.

Special measures should be taken for LDCs to derive full benefits from GSP.

The Special Committee stressed the importance of continued financial support for GSP technical co-operation activities. It urged Governments, in particular those of preference-giving countries, to make cash contributions to the UNCTAD trust fund so that the multilateral nature of such technical co-operation could be continued beyond 1985. It also urged that future technical assistance be provided to all regions on an equitable basis.

On 27 September, TDB took note of the report of the Special Committee.

Technical co-operation

In 1985, the first full year in which the UNCTAD technical assistance programme on GSP functioned without any direct financial support from UNDP, extrabudgetary trust fund contributions from both developed and developing countries covered the operation of the project and its activities, but were insufficient to cover fully the costs of the Geneva focal point.

During 1985,[32] new trust fund contributions were received from Austria, Colombia and Sweden, and funds were pledged by the Netherlands and Norway. The financial position for 1986 was expected to be in the range of $173,000.

After three years of in-kind support by the Philippines, the UNDP/UNCTAD regional GSP project for Asia and the Pacific sought a new location for its office. Indonesia accepted to host the regional office at Jakarta for two years starting in July 1985 and donated facilities for the Japanese-financed expert stationed there.

Training activities undertaken under the project for Asia and the Pacific and the UNCTAD inter-regional GSP project included national GSP seminars for the Governments of China, Indonesia and Papua New Guinea, and four regional seminars on GSP and other trade laws for Asian countries, Latin American countries, Pacific basin countries, and member States of the Association of South-East Asian Nations. The seminars trained approximately 293 developing-country government officials who administered GSP as well as private-sector representatives from 34 countries.

During the year, project personnel updated GSP handbooks on the schemes of Austria, Finland, Japan, Norway, Sweden, Switzerland and the United States and supervised their translation into French and Spanish.

Rules of origin

In accordance with a 1984 recommendation of the Special Committee on Preferences,[30] the Working Group on Rules of Origin convened its tenth session at Geneva from 9 to 13 December 1985,[33] its previous session having been held in 1982.[34] To continue its consultations on proposals for improvements in the rules of origin, including greater harmonization and simplification, the Working Group had before it a compendium of replies[35] by member States to a secretariat questionnaire on their experiences in the use of the current rules and a secretariat study[36] on improvement in rules of origin, including harmonization and simplification, which gave a broad overview of the GSP origin systems and examined progress made in their improvement over the years.

On 13 December, the Group adopted a set of agreed conclusions stating that: a request by preference-receiving countries that measures be taken to liberalize the percentage criterion by increasing the permitted proportion of imported inputs could be considered further; preference-giving countries had indicated their willingness further to consider particular difficulties encountered by preference-receiving LDCs; concerning verification and control, it agreed on the continuing need for close administrative co-operation between the authorities of both preference-giving and -receiving countries, on the importance of feedback information within a reasonable time for receiving countries, particularly when the response to the verification request was open to differing interpretations and GSP treatment was refused, and on the importance of prompt and complete replies by preference-receiving countries to verification requests; and, with regard to goods exported from a preference-receiving country which reached a preference-giving country after passing through an intermediate country or being held there for customs control, the Group agreed that the certificate of origin should be accepted, provided that it corresponded to the requirements of the country of destination.

The Group recommended that, since its task had not been completed, it should be reconvened at a date to be decided by the Special Committee on Preferences at its 1986 session.

Global system of trade preferences among developing countries

The UNCTAD Committee on Economic Co-operation among Developing Countries (fourth session, Geneva, 18-29 November 1985)[37] (see also p. 426) considered the reports of meetings held in 1984 on the global system of trade preferences among developing countries (GSTP).[30] Also before the Committee was a secretariat report on issues bearing on the negotiation and application of tariff and non-tariff preferences under GSTP.[38] The report explained and reviewed the diversity of instruments used by developing countries to regulate their imports and their impact on trade, discussed issues relating to negotiation and application of tariff preferences, and addressed some related issues in the area of non-tariff preferences.

In a 29 November resolution, annexed to its report to TDB,[37] the Committee called on the UNCTAD Secretary-General to assist developing countries to expand trade among themselves and adopt adequate commercial policy measures at the national, regional and interregional levels by means of GSTP.

Trade among countries having different economic and social systems

In accordance with a 1984 TDB decision,[39] the secretariat submitted to the Board's September 1985 session a report[40] on trends and policies in trade and economic co-operation among countries having different economic and social systems, together with a statistical annex. The report outlined the world economic background and recent developments of policies in trade among countries having different economic and social systems, dealt briefly with the main developments in trade and economic relations, described the prospects for trade and economic relations among those countries, and explored policies and measures for the further expansion of trade among them.

The report's principal conclusion with respect to prospects for East-South trade was that it would grow more rapidly during the 1980s than world trade as a whole and, as in the past, significantly faster than the overall trade of the socialist countries of Eastern Europe.

Also in accordance with a 1984 Board decision,[39] the UNCTAD secretariat submitted a report[41] on consultative machinery for bilateral and multilateral consultations among countries having different economic and social systems. The report stated that, within the framework of UNC-TAD's consultative machinery established in 1969,[42] 360 bilateral and multilateral consultations between interested member States of UNCTAD had been organized. A hundred countries had availed themselves of those consultations to discuss issues pertaining to their mutual trade and economic relations, and a number of intergovernmental organizations had used the machinery for bilateral and/or multilateral consultations. UNCTAD's machinery had been particularly useful in assisting the socialist countries of Eastern Europe and developing countries in establishing trade-creative contacts and identifying possible areas for mutual commercial exchanges and economic co-operation.

Based on replies by UNCTAD member States to a note verbale inviting their suggestions and comments on measures to improve the consultative machinery, the report stated, efforts were required by both Governments and the UNCTAD secretariat to expand the machinery and make it more effective. The Board might wish to take action to make it more efficient and more responsive to countries' needs and to recommend measures for further utilizing the mechanism outside the framework of its sessions.

TDB action. Following discussions in a sessional committee, the Board on 27 September adopted a decision[43] by which it reiterated its request to the UNCTAD members and secretariat to implement further UNCTAD resolutions 15(II),[44] 53(III)[45] and 95(IV).[46] It invited the UNCTAD Secretary-General to report to it in 1986 on implementation and to prepare proposals for further promotion of trade and economic co-operation among countries having different economic and social systems, giving particular consideration to the interests of developing countries.

The UNCTAD Secretary-General was requested to prepare, prior to the September 1986 Board session, background studies on: modalities of payments arrangements and prospects for trade and economic co-operation among countries having different economic and social systems, with special consideration given to the interests of the developing countries; and trade and economic co-operation of African developing countries with the socialist countries of Eastern Europe. The Board confirmed its request for case-studies on this topic between LDCs and Eastern European countries.

The UNCTAD Secretary-General was requested to convene, before UNCTAD VII, an *ad hoc* group of experts to consider prospects for trade and economic co-operation among countries having different economic and social systems, particularly between developing and Eastern European countries, including ways to expand the volume and diversify the structure of such trade.

Members and the secretariat were called on to reinforce multilateral and bilateral consultations and to consider the secretariat suggestions on machinery for such consultations among countries having different economic and social systems.[41]

The Board requested the UNCTAD Secretary-General to ensure adequate support for UNCTAD's technical assistance projects and programmes in promoting trade and economic co-operation of developing countries, particularly the least developed, with the socialist countries of Eastern Europe; it invited him and the UNDP Administrator to hold consultations on their financing, and also invited voluntary contributions.

Also on 27 September, the Board decided[47] to remit to its September 1986 session for further negotiations the informal text on trade among countries having different economic and social systems, which was annexed to UNCTAD decision 145(VI).[48]

Technical co-operation

During 1985, the activities of UNCTAD's operational programme of technical assistance for developing trade between developing countries and socialist countries of Eastern Europe were financed mainly from a USSR/UNDP trust fund and to a lesser extent from a Bulgaria/UNDP trust fund. Contributions in kind were provided by several other Eastern European countries.

An interregional symposium in Moscow offered government officials and business representatives from 18 LDCs in Africa and Asia an opportunity to acquaint themselves with the foreign trade systems, trade policies, modalities and trading practices of the USSR and other socialist countries of Eastern Europe. In collaboration with the Economic Commission for Latin America and the Caribbean, a regional seminar on trade and economic relations between the countries of the two regions was held in Moscow and Sofia, Bulgaria, financed by the two UNDP-supported trust funds. Trade issues raised included credit, financing and exports of specific manufactured goods from Latin American countries.

Trade promotion and facilitation

During 1985, the United Nations continued to assist developing countries to promote exports and facilitate the movement of goods in international commerce. The main body responsible for technical co-operation projects in the area was ITC. The Intergovernmental Group of Experts on Restrictive Business Practices held its fourth session in April and the United Nations Conference to Review All Aspects of the Set of Multilaterally Agreed Equitable Principles and Rules for the Control of Restrictive Business Practices met in November.

International Trade Centre

During 1985, the International Trade Centre, under the joint sponsorship of UNCTAD and GATT, continued its technical co-operation activities, serving as the focal point for United Nations assistance to developing countries in the formulation and implementation of trade promotion programmes.[49]

ITC recorded a slight increase in its overall technical co-operation programme, despite constraints in financial resources resulting in particular from a decline in dollar values of trust fund contributions. The number of voluntary donors to ITC again increased over the previous year, including several new developing-country contributors.

In Africa, programme implementation dropped slightly from $3.7 million in 1984 to $3.4 million, although the number of national projects rose from 20 to 25 and regional projects from 14 to 16. In Asia and the Pacific, implementation was also down marginally from $4.5 million to $4.4 million while national projects increased from 32 to 36 and regional ones from 7 to 8. In Latin America and the Caribbean, implementation increased to $2 million from $1.8 million, with the number of country projects dropping from 21 to 15 while regional projects remained at 10. In Europe, the Mediterranean and the Middle East, ITC doubled its implementation, reaching $1 million with 14 national projects. Interregional activities declined from $4.5 million to $4.3 million.

ITC activities regarding institutional infrastructure for trade promotion at the national level in 1985 consisted primarily of advisory services, training, and research and development. Advisory missions were undertaken to Paraguay, Turkey and Uruguay to analyse the institutional set-up for export promotion, to Zambia to help prepare a law for creating a new promotional organization, and to Colombia to discuss improving the effectiveness of its five-year export promotion programme. ITC participated in multidisciplinary programming missions to Indonesia and Uganda to facilitate project design and in the organization of seminars in Sweden and Tunisia on a comprehensive approach to national export development programmes. A workshop was held in Ecuador for government officials on the design of a national export strategy and development programme, which had as an objective the dissemination of the results of the 1984 comparative analysis of trade promotion systems in Latin American countries.[50] Research on services, operating procedures, planning techniques and sources of finance of trade promotion organizations continued during 1985, and a first workshop was held at Geneva for senior trade promotion officials from developing countries on techniques for evaluating trade promotion programmes.

In 1985, ITC's export market development programme consisted of activities to develop and promote developing countries' exports of products and services through selected export sectors as well as with individual companies. In accordance with UNCTAD resolution 158(VI),[51] ITC continued to strengthen export market activities in commodities and in support of UNCTAD's Integrated Programme for Commodities. Proposals were made or being developed on market research, trade information, technical advisory services and training on technical co-operation needs relating to commodities, including cocoa, coconuts, coffee, jute, rubber, tea, tropical timber and vegetable oils. Proposals had also been prepared for silk and pepper products. Advisory services concentrated on selecting markets, planning marketing strategies, adapting products to buyers' requirements, organizing sales missions and planning promotional activities. Major market surveys published related to bicycles and components, builders' woodwork, technical consulting services, and sales possibilities in the Colombian and Hungarian markets. Seminars and consulting sessions were organized in developing countries to disseminate the findings of those and earlier studies.

Within its import-export contact programme, ITC provided trade information to exporters and importers in developing countries; at the end of 1985, the ITC computerized data base, "TRADERS", contained over 23,000 company profiles. Trade information was provided in response to approximately 1,300 requests, an increase of 7 per cent over 1984.

The ITC Market News Service expanded its operations during the year to 152 recipients in 82 developing countries regularly receiving information, such as prices and trends in supply and demand, on product groups of interest to them.

In the area of specialized national trade promotion services, ITC activities included: export packaging; export finance; export costing and pricing; trade information; trade fairs and commercial publicity; export quality control; national trade representation; legal aspects of foreign trade; and export co-operation schemes for small and medium-sized enterprises. During 1985, 60 advisory missions and 39 training events were undertaken in those areas.

In the multinational trade promotion programme, activities were concentrated on projects to strengthen the competitive position of jute and jute products in selected import markets, carried out at the request of the International Jute Organization. Promotional actions were undertaken in Western Europe for selected products, i.e. carpet backing, yarn, wall coverings, bags and jute geotextiles.

ITC's programme of manpower development for trade promotion focused on short- and long-term training activities, including workshops, seminars and individual study awards, organized at the national, subregional, regional and interregional levels. During 1985, ITC continued to strengthen its training activities in co-operation with other training institutions and provided technical staff and training materials to their programmes.

In 1985, ITC established a training materials working group to develop a programme to design new foreign-trade-development training materials in association with institutions in developed and developing countries. A new series of reference materials for administering training activities commenced in 1985 with the publication of: a revised world directory of institutions offering training programmes in export marketing and trade promotion; an index of training materials developed or adapted by training institutions in developing countries in export marketing and trade promotion; a compendium of training programmes; and a manual on organization, presentation and evaluation of training events.

Activities in national import operations and techniques in 1985 included projects in Angola, Burundi, Colombia, Egypt, Ethiopia, Mozambique and Rwanda; integrated country projects with import components were being implemented in Afghanistan, Benin, El Salvador, Lesotho, Madagascar, Mali, Mauritania and Morocco. Continued emphasis was placed on rationalizing import régimes and streamlining procedures, with advisory work concentrating on developing criteria for allocating import licences and guidelines for annual import programming, providing automatic import licences to industry, defining the information base needed within importing enterprises, establishing and monitoring national import programmes, setting up a system for registering importers, and establishing mechanisms for price monitoring of imported goods.

ITC's special programme of technical co-operation with LDCs included: pre-feasibility studies on potential export products to help diversify the export structure; high-level workshops with national development finance institutions to accelerate the flow of funds to export-oriented investments; joint venture studies to stimulate the flow of external capital and technology to the export sector; and the preparation of operational manuals to strengthen the management capability of small and inexperienced exporting firms in LDCs.

Technical co-operation with national chambers of commerce in 1985 included the organization of three seminars for chamber-of-commerce officials from developing countries: one workshop on computerized trade information services (Geneva), and two training programmes on chamber services in foreign trade matters (Austria and the Federal Republic of Germany). A technical advisory mission took place in Morocco for the federation of Moroccan chambers.

Total ITC expenditure in 1985 was $25.5 million. Of this amount, technical co-operation activities accounted for $15.1 million. Trust fund contributions furnished $8.5 million of the 1985 amount for technical co-operation; the remainder was provided by UNDP. The Centre's 1985 regular budget of $8.1 million, covering operations at its Geneva headquarters, was contributed in equal parts by the United Nations and GATT. As at 31 December, ITC had a headquarters-based staff of 76 Professionals and 129 in the General Service category. It assigned 621 experts to projects during the year.

JAG action. The Joint Advisory Group (JAG) on ITC (eighteenth session, Geneva, 15-22 April)[52] recommended that ITC should continue to try to increase both extrabudgetary resources and regular budget allocations and to establish closer collaboration with international organizations dealing with trade development and related fields, including expansion of training opportunities for businesswomen in developing countries, particularly in Africa. Among its other recommendations were that ITC should: assist Governments in evolving sound national institutional infrastructures and a favourable overall export climate; devote greater attention to assisting Governments in implementing export development strategies and generating export earnings through enterprise-level actions; scrutinize all possibilities of expanding and improving the production base, particularly in LDCs; intensify its involvement in marketing and distributing commodities; expand its technical co-operation in LDCs; analyse the feasibility of future action in international physical distribution of goods; and intensify its activities in expanding trade of developing countries with the socialist countries of Eastern Europe and make more use of experts from the latter countries.

On 25 September, TDB took note of the JAG report.

Trade facilitation

During 1985, the UNCTAD Special Programme on Trade Facilitation (FALPRO) continued to provide the focal point in an international network of national trade facilitation bodies and interested international organizations. In the absence of UNDP funding, advisory services in trade facilitation were financed through trust funds contributed by Finland and Sweden through government development agencies. Additional financial support was received from the Netherlands, the World Bank and EC. Advisory missions were carried out in Burundi, Ethiopia, Ghana, Kenya, Malawi,

Morocco, Nepal, the Sudan, the United Republic of Tanzania, Zambia and Zimbabwe. In co-operation with ITC, advisory missions were also carried out in Haiti, Lesotho and Mali, financed from national projects, and in the Ivory Coast, financed from the UNCTAD programme on training development in the field of maritime transport. A mission to Ghana was partly financed by the World Bank.

FALPRO staff conducted or lectured at three seminars financed by the Netherlands: a seminar on the Northern Corridor Transit System (Turin, Italy, February), partly financed by EEC; a port seminar (Barcelona, Spain, October); and a facilitation seminar (Bangkok, Thailand, December).

The Northern Corridor seminar was held as part of the implementation of the Northern Corridor Transit Agreement, signed in Bujumbura, Burundi, in February by Burundi, Kenya, Rwanda and Uganda. During the year, FALPRO prepared four annexes to the Agreement and participated in the final negotiations which, in November, led to the conclusion of the Agreement and the creation of a Transit Transport Co-ordination Authority, to which FALPRO lent continuing support.

Various manuals, directories and code systems in trade facilitation, established jointly by UNCTAD and the Economic Commission for Europe (ECE), were updated during the year; four issues of *Trade Facilitation News* were published by ECE and FALPRO.

Restrictive business practices

On 29 March 1985,[53] TDB took note of the report of the Intergovernmental Group of Experts on Restrictive Business Practices on its third (1984) session,[54] endorsed the resolution adopted at that session, and called on all States to ensure implementation of the Set of Multilaterally Agreed Equitable Principles and Rules for the Control of Restrictive Business Practices, adopted in 1980.[55]

At its fourth session (Geneva, 22-30 April 1985),[56] the Intergovernmental Group, acting as the preparatory meeting for the United Nations Conference to review the principles and rules, approved the provisional agenda for the Conference. It agreed that the UNCTAD Secretary-General should request States and regional groupings to supply information on steps taken to meet their commitment to the principles and rules and on the adoption and application of legislation, regulations and policies concerning restrictive business practices for submission to the Conference. The Group considered, but could not agree on, proposals by the Group of 77 (developing countries), Group B (developed market economies) and Group D (cen-

trally planned economies) for improving and developing the principles and rules. The proposals concerned their legal nature, establishment of a special committee to replace the Intergovernmental Group, technical assistance, a framework for multilateral consultations, and a further review conference in 1990.

In accordance with a 1983 request by the Intergovernmental Group,[57] the UNCTAD secretariat issued in June 1985 the 1983-1984 annual report on legislative and other developments in developed and developing countries in the control of restrictive business practices.[58] The report, which covered the period from early 1983 to January 1985, was based on information received from Governments and international organizations. It noted that the period under review had witnessed a reduction in the number of countries enacting new or amending existing legislation on restrictive business practices, compared with the period covered in the 1982 report.

United Nations Conference to review principles and rules to control restrictive business practices

In accordance with a 1980 General Assembly resolution,[59] a United Nations Conference to Review All Aspects of the Set of Multilaterally Agreed Equitable Principles and Rules for the Control of Restrictive Business Practices was held under UNCTAD auspices at Geneva from 4 to 15 November 1985.[60]

The Conference had before it a note by the UNCTAD secretariat[61] reviewing the application and implementation of the principles and rules and making proposals for their improvement and further development. The report concluded that they had not lived up to expectations; since their adoption, restrictive business practices had become an increasingly important component of international trade policy.

The report recommended that the Conference should urge all States to take action to eliminate restrictive business practices from international trade transactions and to avoid entering into arrangements in restraint of trade, and should strengthen control of restrictive practices at all levels by implementing the principles. Steps towards that end could include: establishing national or regional focal points for contacts with enterprises and other States to facilitate consultations on application, and assisting developing countries in establishing such focal points; establishing or improving States' notification procedures for enterprises on the use of restrictive business practices in import and export transactions; strengthening notification procedures among States regarding adverse effects of such practices on international trade; agreeing that, when a State decided to investigate a practice likely to affect adversely international trade and having implications for another State, it should consult that State before initiating judicial or administrative action); inviting States, particularly the developed ones, to contribute to technical assistance and advisory and training programmes on restrictive business practices, and to pursue in the UNDP Governing Council resources for implementing work in that area; requesting further studies on the link between restrictive business practice policies and governmental trade policies; establishing a special committee on restrictive business practices in place of the Intergovernmental Group to reflect properly the importance of the issue; and recommending a review conference for 1990.

Another secretariat note[62] contained extracts of replies to a request for information received from States and regional groupings on steps taken to meet their commitment to the principles and rules.

On 15 November, the Conference decided to transmit its report[60] to the General Assembly, together with proposals made by regional groups, and requested the Assembly, in the light of the positions reflected therein, to decide whether to convene a resumed session of the Conference in 1986.

The *proposal of the Group of 77* consisted of a draft declaration by which the Conference would have recommended that: developed countries should ensure a standstill and rollback on the use of restrictive business practices in international trade transactions, especially those affecting imports from developing countries, and should repeal measures permitting or encouraging such practices; States should make available details of all such practices affecting international trade transactions, establish notification procedures on their use by enterprises, including transnational corporations (TNCs), and establish within UNCTAD a registry of such information; States should establish national or regional focal points to strengthen their capacity to control such practices and facilitate contacts with enterprises to ensure full adherence to the principles and rules, and a special committee on restrictive business practices should be established within the UNCTAD framework to monitor their application and implementation; effective use should be made of the consultation procedure provided therein when investigating a practice likely to have adverse effects on international trade, and having implications for another State; multilateral consultations should be held at each session of the special committee to exchange experience on policy issues relating to the control of restrictive business practices in international trade transactions; States, particularly developed ones, should ensure resources for multilateral technical assistance activities; continued work should be directed at establishing a legally binding instrument to control restrictive business practices in international trade; and a further session of the Conference should be held in 1990.

The *proposal of Group B* comprised draft conclusions by which the Conference would have recommended that: the Intergovernmental Group should provide improved mechanisms for informal discussions and exchanges of views among experts (beginning in 1986 at least two such meetings, each on a subject of practical importance); the Group should develop proposals to further the implementation of technical assistance, advisory and training programmes on restrictive business practices in the United Nations system; the UNCTAD Secretary-General should maintain an inventory of such programmes, for assisting national agencies to identify available technical assistance; he should also submit recommendations on priorities for such programmes for the Group's consideration, following which the Group's comments could be transmitted to Governments, international organizations and financing programmes, particularly UNDP, for them to consider providing additional resources; delegations could inform the Group about national and regional developments in restrictive business practices control; and regional groupings of States should be enabled to participate fully in the work of the institutional machinery on the basis of procedures adopted by the Conference.

In draft *proposals submitted by Group D*, the Conference would have stated that the main cause of the principles' insufficient effectiveness lay in the unwillingness of some States, particularly those in which TNCs were based, to fulfil their obligations, particularly with regard to: improving and enforcing legislation and procedures to control restrictive business practices, including those of TNCs; adopting measures to prevent abuse by dominant corporations to limit access to markets; seeking measures against restrictive business practices adversely affecting international trade and development, particularly that of developing countries; and instituting procedures for obtaining from enterprises information necessary for effective control of restrictive business practices, including details of restrictive agreements, understandings and other arrangements. To increase the effectiveness of action foreseen in the principles, it was necessary to ensure their proper implementation, particularly in connection with the control and elimination of restrictive business practices by TNCs and cartels, which caused serious damage to international trade, and to make wider use of multilateral and bilateral consultations for studying and resolving issues concerning control of those practices. The draft also proposed that the

UNCTAD Secretary-General take measures to implement vigorously technical assistance, advisory and training programmes on restrictive business practices and ensure balance in using the experience available in both developed and developing countries. Finally, a further United Nations conference to review the principles should be convened in 1990.

GENERAL ASSEMBLY ACTION

In November,[63] the United Nations Secretary-General transmitted to the Assembly the texts of the Conference's decision and of the draft proposals submitted by the regional groups.

On 17 December, on the recommendation of the Second Committee, the Assembly adopted **resolution 40/192** without vote.

United Nations Conference to Review All Aspects of the Set of Multilaterally Agreed Equitable Principles and Rules for the Control of Restrictive Business Practices

The General Assembly,

Having considered the report of the United Nations Conference to Review All Aspects of the Set of Multilaterally Agreed Equitable Principles and Rules for the Control of Restrictive Business Practices, held at Geneva from 4 to 15 November 1985, together with the proposals made by regional groups,

Invites the Secretary-General of the United Nations Conference on Trade and Development and the President of the United Nations Conference to Review All Aspects of the Set of Multilaterally Agreed Equitable Principles and Rules for the Control of Restrictive Business Practices to undertake consultations, as appropriate, with regional groups and Governments on the reconvening of the Conference at Geneva and to report thereon to the General Assembly at the earliest opportunity.

General Assembly resolution 40/192

17 December 1985   Meeting 119   Adopted without vote

Approved by Second Committee (A/40/989/Add.3) without vote, 13 December (meeting 51); draft by Vice-Chairman (A/C.2/40/L.127), based on informal consultations on draft by Yugoslavia, for Group of 77 (A/C.2/40/L.92); agenda item 84(c).

Meeting numbers. GA 40th session: 2nd Committee 46, 51; plenary 119.

Commodities

The *World Economic Survey 1985*[2] stated that a marked softening of commodity prices, affecting energy prices as well as non-fuel commodities, was a major unexpected development of 1984. Although specific policy and market factors were important determinants of price trends in individual commodities, a number of general factors also accounted for the performance of different groups of commodities. For minerals and non-food agricultural products, the price recovery was aborted in early 1984 by a combination of factors. Suppliers reacted strongly to favourable market conditions after several lean years, contributing to a glut which caused prices to fall, and the stimulus to commodity demand arising from the world recovery was generally weak. In addition, the 1984 rebound in interest rates increased the actual financial cost of carry-over stocks, tending to lower target inventory levels, and the gathering strength of the dollar acted as a damper on import demand in local currencies for several commodities. In 1983, price increases in most food and beverage commodities stemmed less from demand-pull factors linked to the recovery than from supply deficiencies caused mainly by adverse weather. Likewise, the subsequent price decline was largely a reflection of actual and anticipated output gains in 1984/85 associated with improved weather.

The *Trade and Development Report, 1985*[1] noted that the overall outlook for commodities was not encouraging. With the deceleration of economic growth foreseen in Japan and the United States and good crop prospects in many agricultural commodities, prices were expected to decline in 1985. Evidence that monetary factors had become more pronounced in influencing primary-commodity markets did not necessarily mean that short-term reversals in trends of exchange rates and inflation would generate a considerable improvement in prices.

The issue of commodity trade was also addressed during the review and appraisal of the implementation of the International Development Strategy for the Third United Nations Development Decade (the 1980s) (see p. 418).

The Permanent Sub-Committee on Commodities (fourth session, Geneva, 14-22 January 1985)[64] considered studies issued by the UNCTAD secretariat in 1984[65] on the processing, marketing and distribution, including transportation, of individual commodities (bauxite/alumina/aluminium, cocoa, coffee, copper, hard fibres (sisal and henequen), iron ore, jute and jute products, manganese, phosphates, sugar, tea and tin). These studies had originally been called for by UNCTAD resolution 124(V).[66]

In a personal summary of the Permanent Sub-Committee's work, the Chairman said the debate revealed that a wide range of problems was involved in expanding developing countries' participation in processing, marketing and distribution of commodities and, while many of those problems were common to different commodities, they were often of varying applicability from commodity to commodity.

The debate on a commodity-by-commodity basis allowed a number of speakers to address problems facing developing countries in processing, marketing and distribution, such as redeployment of productive facilities, synthetics and substitutes, market outlets, market transparency, financial and technical assistance, finance, trade liberalization, contractual marketing, unfair competition, transportation and training.

In accordance with UNCTAD resolution 156(VI),[67] a special session (the second) of the UNCTAD Committee on Commodities (Geneva, 21-25 January 1985)[68] was held to discuss possible frameworks for international co-operation in processing, marketing and distribution, including transportation, of commodities of export interest to developing countries.

In addition to the report of its Permanent Sub-Committee (see above), the special session also had before it secretariat reports outlining possible elements of frameworks for international co-operation in the field of marketing and distribution of commodities of export interest to developing countries[69] and in the field of processing commodities.[70]

On 25 January,[71] the Committee decided to establish a sessional committee at its next regular session to continue elaborating the elements of the frameworks, recommending to TDB that that session be held in the second half of 1985. Annexed to the Committee's report were proposals submitted by the Group of 77 and by Group B on negotiating the frameworks.

In accordance with UNCTAD resolution 155(VI),[67] a further special session (the third) of the Committee on Commodities (Geneva, 3-7 June)[72] met to examine the role of international commodity agreements or arrangements, negotiated or renegotiated within UNCTAD, in attaining the objectives of the Integrated Programme for Commodities (IPC). In addition to a secretariat study on the subject,[73] the Committee also examined documents prepared by international commodity organizations on the operation of their respective agreements, i.e. cocoa, coffee, jute, olive oil, rubber, sugar, tin and wheat.

On 13 June,[74] the Committee decided to annex to its report proposed agreed recommendations submitted by the Group of 77 and the draft conclusions/summary submitted by Group B, and to resume consideration of those proposals at its next regular session.

By the *Group of 77 draft*, the Committee would have recommended: flexibility in the design and application of mechanisms over the life-span of a commodity agreement; that provisions on buffer stocks and/or export quotas be carefully formulated during negotiations; the immediate entry into force of the Common Fund for Commodities; the setting of price ranges for commodities compatible with dynamic market conditions; that universal producer and consumer participation be coupled with firm commitment to the objectives of an international commodity agreement by its members; avoidance of disruption in international commodity markets when Governments purchased for, and sold from, national non-commercial reserves and stockpiles; better

preparations for negotiations on international commodity agreements; that forthcoming negotiations or renegotiations of agreements include economic price stabilization clauses and other development measures; and improvement of the competitiveness of natural products competing with synthetics and substitutes.

The *Group B text* would have stated that the Committee identified the following elements as relevant for the success of international commodity agreements: price ranges for an international price stabilization scheme should be realistic and market-related; provisions for adjustment of price ranges in accordance with market-trend shifts should be adequate; where price stabilization measures were deemed feasible and desirable, it was important that economic provisions were effective and seen to be effective by market participants; and commodity agreements should receive the support and participation of as many important producing and consuming countries as possible. Also, when considering individual commodities, attention should be paid to measures other than price stabilization measures, including commodity development measures and those that fostered greater market transparency and improved information exchange, which might serve to improve commodity market conditions and achieve IPC objectives.

On 27 September, TDB took note of the reports of the Committee on Commodities on its second and third special sessions.

The Committee on Commodities held its eleventh regular session at Geneva from 2 to 13 December 1985.[75] In addition to the reports of its second and third special sessions, the Committee had before it a commodity survey prepared by the secretariat, covering the years 1980 to 1985.[76] The report gave the background to the current commodity crisis, discussed the reasons for the commodity price recession and its impact on developing countries, and explored the outlook for future commodity prices and exports.

On 13 December, the Committee adopted a resolution[77] requesting the UNCTAD Secretary-General to consult with producing and consuming countries of commodities included in the IPC indicative list and not covered by international commodity agreements or arrangements, with a view to convening review meetings on those commodities before the Committee's regular session in 1986 or in any event before the seventh session of UNCTAD (1987); he was also requested to include hides and skins in such consultations. The meetings were to: consider the situation in and problems of world markets for each commodity; review the status of intergovernmental work on that commodity within the context of IPC; and consider follow-up action to further international co-operation in conformity with IPC objectives. The Secretary-General was also requested to report to TDB in 1986 on the progress of those consultations, and to consult with the principal and other interested producing and consuming countries on the possibility of convening the Second Preparatory Meeting on Bananas.

Also on 13 December, the Committee decided[78] to adopt the following conclusions: where price stabilization measures were deemed feasible and desirable, producers and consumers could choose between measures, such as buffer stocks, export quotas and other supply management measures, to be applied singly or in combination, with the measures being effective and capable of defending both "floor" and "ceiling" prices; where measures included buffer stocks, financial resources for their operation should be assured, possibly through the First Account of the Common Fund for Commodities, when operational; measures that included export quotas or other supply management measures could be effective only if supported by the majority of important producing and consuming countries; in implementing the above measures, agreed price levels should be market-related and compatible with dynamic market conditions; in setting such levels, account should be taken of UNCTAD resolution 93(IV)[79] on IPC; price ranges should be structured to include discretionary zones to defend both "floor" and "ceiling" prices and provisions included for adjusting prices to take account of market conditions, including changes in exchange rates; in negotiating agreements, consideration could be given to price stabilization and other measures to attain IPC objectives, possibly including commodity development measures and measures for improving information exchange and market transparency; international commodity agreements should receive the support of as many important producing and consuming countries as possible and a major prerequisite of their functioning was the strict observance by participants of their rights and obligations; to facilitate negotiations on agreements, producing and consuming countries should co-operate fully and explain their objectives and concerns; Governments purchasing for and selling from national non-commercial reserves and stockpiles should avoid disruptions of international commodity markets; the potential importance of the Common Fund for Commodities for implementing IPC and progress in ratifying the Agreement Establishing the Common Fund were noted; and Committee members were urged to take the political decisions for the Agreement's entry into force as quickly as possible.

In an agreed conclusion on implementing IPC in the area of processing, marketing and distribution, including transportation, also adopted on 13 December,[80] the Committee agreed that the frameworks for those functions should be mutually acceptable global principles for international co-operation specific to the commodity sector, and should aim at expanding in developing countries the processing of primary commodities and their export and at increasing developing-country participation in their marketing and distribution, including transportation. The question of frameworks should be pursued on the basis of proposals by the regional groups at the Committee's second special session (see above), taking into account the views expressed during its current session. The Committee agreed to recommend establishing a working party to meet before its 1986 regular session, to continue examining technical assistance and human resources development.

GENERAL ASSEMBLY ACTION

A draft resolution on commodities[81] was submitted to the General Assembly's Second Committee on 27 November by Yugoslavia, on behalf of the Group of 77. By the text, the Assembly would have stressed the need for action to address the deteriorating situation of developing countries in the field of commodities, reaffirmed the importance of the Common Fund for Commodities and urged States to ratify the Agreement establishing it. It would have called on developed countries to refrain from raising barriers to the importation of commodities and to eliminate existing ones, as well as subsidies, to permit freer access to their markets of primary, semi-processed and processed commodities. It would also have called on producing and consuming countries facing constraints on the effective operation of international commodity agreements to meet to work out short- and medium-term solutions, including measures to restore prices to levels remunerative to producers and equitable to consumers, and appealed to those countries to promote trade co-operation in accordance with IPC. States would have been called on to co-operate towards greater participation of developing countries in commodity processing, distribution and marketing. The Assembly would have welcomed TDB's June 1985 decision (see p. 579) on compensatory financing of export earnings shortfalls and urged States to pursue its implementation. The UNCTAD Secretary-General would have been requested to examine long-term trends and prospects for primary commodities, recommend policy measures to support efforts by producer developing countries to maximize commodity trade in their development, continue monitoring movements in commodity trade and report in 1986 on progress in implementing the resolution.

By **decision 40/445**, the Assembly decided to reconvene the Second Committee immediately prior to the April/May 1986 session of the Economic and Social Council to consider ways in which international co-operation in money, finance, debt, resource flows, trade and development could be promoted, and to deal with unfinished business on several draft resolutions, including the one on commodities.

Common Fund for Commodities

During 1985, preparations continued on arrangements for the Common Fund for Commodities, a mechanism intended to stabilize the commodities market by helping to finance buffer stocks of specific commodities as well as commodity development activities such as research and marketing. Although six additional States adhered to the 1980 Agreement Establishing the Common Fund for Commodities,[82] by the end of the year it had not received the required 90 ratifications to enter into force.

Signatures and ratifications

As at 31 December 1985, the 1980 Agreement Establishing the Common Fund for Commodities had been signed by 113 States and EEC, and 88 States had formally adhered by ratifying, accepting, approving or acceding to it.[83] Of these, one State (Barbados) signed the Agreement during 1985 and six (Belgium, Djibouti, Federal Republic of Germany, Guatemala, Jamaica, Luxembourg) adhered to it.

Report of the Secretary-General. For the General Assembly's review of the situation regarding the entry into force of the Agreement establishing the Fund, the Secretary-General submitted in October 1985 a report[84] on the status of that Agreement. The report recalled that the Agreement was to enter into force after: ratification by at least 90 States, accounting for at least two thirds of the Fund's directly contributed capital of $470 million; and at least half of the $280-million target for pledges of voluntary contributions to the Second Account had been met. While the latter requirement had been met by 31 March 1982, the initial deadline for entry into force, the former had not, and it was not possible for the Fund to begin operations.

The UNCTAD Secretary-General was consulting with the States that had adhered to the Agreement to decide on a new period for fulfilment of requirements for its entry into force, while the process of signature and adherence continued.

On the Second Committee's recommendation, approving an oral proposal by the Chairman, the General Assembly adopted **decision 40/440** on 17 December, without vote, taking note of the Secretary-General's report.

Financial implications
for the 1986-1987 budget

In a December note[85] to the General Assembly on preparatory work for bringing the Common Fund into operation, the Secretary-General stated that no expenditures had been incurred in the 1984-1985 biennium from the advance appropriation of $942,000 made by the Assembly in 1983.[86] The Secretary-General anticipated that conditions for the Agreement's entry into force would be met during the 1986-1987 biennium and that the Fund's Preparatory Commission would meet in 1986; to service those meetings, the advance was expected to be fully utilized during that biennium. He recommended approval of a $942,000 appropriation for the biennium, representing the unspent advance approved for 1984-1985, to be fully reimbursed by the Common Fund once it was declared operational. Provision for staff assessment estimated at $49,700 would also be required.

On 9 December, the Assembly's Fifth (Administrative and Budgetary) Committee approved without vote the additional appropriations for 1986-1987.

Individual commodities

An UNCTAD secretariat report on international action in relation to commodities not covered by international commodity agreements or arrangements,[87] submitted to the December session of the Committee on Commodities (see p. 566), reviewed progress in implementing IPC for 11 commodities on the indicative list of UNCTAD resolution 93(IV),[88] which were not the subject of international agreements at the time. Those commodities comprised six agricultural commodities and five minerals and metals: bananas, cotton and cotton yarns, hard fibres and their products, meat, tea, vegetable oils and oilseeds, bauxite, copper, iron ore, manganese and phosphates.

The review showed that results varied from commodity to commodity. For some agricultural products (bananas, meat, some vegetable oils and oilseeds, and to a certain extent some hard fibres), limited progress had been achieved or soon seemed likely. Work was in progress on iron ore with the objective of promoting co-operation among producers and consumers, possibly within a standing body on the commodity. However, for copper, cotton, hard fibres and tea, international discussions had reached a deadlock, and for bauxite, manganese and phosphates, meaningful discussions had not even begun.

The report stated that early entry into force of the Agreement Establishing the Common Fund for Commodities would improve the climate for international co-operation in the commodity field. There was urgent need to reactivate intergovernmental work on the reviewed commodities and, given the lapse of time since many of them had been considered, it was suggested that Governments might convene general review meetings before UNCTAD VII (1987) for the seven commodities on which discussions were deadlocked or had not begun. It was suggested that Governments might also consider the case of minerals and metals, on which international co-operative action had been rather limited. While agreements and organizations had been established for eight agricultural commodities, there was only one such organization for a metal, namely tin. In addition, while intergovernmental specialized forums with participating producers and consumers existed for 10 agricultural commodities, there were only two such bodies for minerals and metals, namely the Tungsten Committee within UNCTAD and the International Lead and Zinc Study Group outside UNCTAD. It was suggested that Governments might study the possibility of setting up consultative bodies for individual minerals and metals, possibly linked by common administrative, statistical and meeting services.

Agricultural commodities

Cocoa. In 1985, the third part of the United Nations Cocoa Conference, 1984, was held (Geneva, 19 February–16 March) under the auspices of UNCTAD to negotiate a successor agreement to the 1980 International Cocoa Agreement.[89] The first two parts had been held in 1984.[90]

On 16 March, the Conference adopted a resolution[91] by which, welcoming progress in preparing a successor agreement, it adjourned, requesting the Conference President to consult exporting and importing countries on outstanding issues, particularly the price structure, the annual review and revision of prices, and the withholding scheme, to prepare a basis for successfully concluding the Conference. On the basis of those consultations, he was to make a recommendation to the UNCTAD Secretary-General with regard to resuming the Conference.

Rubber. In 1985, a United Nations Conference on Natural Rubber was held (Geneva, 22 April–8 May) under UNCTAD auspices to negotiate a successor agreement to the International Natural Rubber Agreement, 1979.[92] In a note dealing with policy issues,[93] the UNCTAD secretariat stated that the Conference provided an opportunity to review and improve the 1979 Agreement as an instrument of co-operation between the developing countries as the exporters and the developed countries as the predominant importers of an important raw material. The principal issues for negotiation were expected to be the initial level

of the reference price and the provisions governing possible revisions of that level under a new agreement. Price issues, however, were closely related to the means for ensuring that prices were stabilized within the agreed limits. A further issue, therefore, would be whether the existing practice of relying solely on a buffer stock should continue or be supplemented by additional measures to be brought into operation at times of weak prices.

The report concluded that lack of finances for projects had impeded progress in translating the Agreement's developmental objectives into concrete action and suggested that the Conference might wish to consider ways to raise funds for that purpose. If the predominant view of Governments was that a successor agreement should reflect market forces and price trends in order to minimize fluctuations in prices, then the essential features of the existing Agreement, loosened to permit more flexible adjustments in the reference and related prices, would be broadly appropriate. If, on the other hand, the predominant view was that a successor agreement should provide assurances of agreed minimum prices, consideration would have to be given to strengthening the means for effective intervention, including possible inclusion of the mechanism of supply management as a supplement to stocking measures. Since the existing Agreement fell between those two conceptions, although considerably nearer the first, whether there should be a further move in that direction or a change in the Agreement's character to incorporate the supply management concept at source was the key question.

The Conference also had before it a report[94] by the secretariat of the International Natural Rubber Organization which gave the historical development, status and operation of the 1979 Agreement.

On 8 May, the Conference adopted a resolution[95] by which, noting the progress made in preparing a successor agreement, it decided to adjourn, and requested the UNCTAD Secretary-General, in consultation with the Conference President, to arrange to reconvene the Conference for three weeks, preferably early in 1986.

Sugar. The International Sugar Agreement, 1984, the text of which was established by the United Nations Sugar Conference in 1984,[96] entered into force provisionally on 1 January 1985 and definitively on 4 April 1985, when the proper instruments of adherence had been deposited on behalf of Governments holding 50 per cent of the votes of the exporting countries and 50 per cent of the votes of the importing countries.

During the year, the International Sugar Council of the International Sugar Organization, the body responsible for administering the Agreement and supervising its operation, three times extended the time-limit for the deposit of instruments of ratification, acceptance or approval: on 21 January, it was extended until 30 June; on 23 May, until 31 December; and on 21 November, until 31 December 1986.

Tropical timber. The International Tropical Timber Agreement, 1983, adopted in 1983[97] and opened for signature in January 1984,[96] entered into force provisionally on 1 April 1985 when instruments of ratification, acceptance and provisional application were deposited by the required number of producing and consuming countries.

On 24 June, at its first session, the International Tropical Timber Council, the body responsible for administering the Agreement and supervising its operation, decided that the condition of accession for non-signatory Governments would be that they accept all the obligations of the Agreement. It further decided that the time-limit for the deposit of instruments of accession should be the date of the opening of the Council's second session.

Minerals and metals

Iron ore. The Fourth Preparatory Meeting on Iron Ore (Geneva, 21-25 October 1985)[98] considered international measures and statistical issues with regard to iron ore, and discussed follow-up action to be recommended. As requested in 1984,[99] the UNCTAD secretariat prepared a report on alternative forms of co-operation and dialogue between exporting and importing countries.[100] The report discussed possible areas of co-operation and institutional options for advancing co-operation and dialogue. Institutional options included: further _ad hoc_ meetings within UNCTAD; regular (perhaps annual) meetings within UNCTAD without establishing a standing body; a standing consultative intergovernmental body as part of the UNCTAD machinery; an autonomous body; or a specialized body on minerals and metals in general as part of the UNCTAD machinery. The report stated that productive specialized intergovernmental consideration of iron ore would depend on the attitudes of the principal Governments concerned and their determination to co-operate.

The secretariat also prepared statistical tables on iron ore[101] and, pursuant to a 1984 request,[99] a note on possibilities for improvements in the quality and coverage of such statistics.[102] Both reports were considered by an expert group on statistical issues (23 and 24 October), which reported to the Preparatory Meeting.

On 25 October, the Meeting recommended that TDB convene an intergovernmental group of experts on iron ore to meet in 1986 and 1987 to review market developments and report thereon to the Fifth Preparatory Meeting. Participation in the group would be open to all UNCTAD member States and to relevant international organizations.

Nickel. Following a request from Australia and Canada on behalf of a number of UNCTAD member States that participated in a 1984 Intergovernmental Exploratory Meeting on Nickel (Geneva, 22-24 October), co-hosted by those two countries, a Preparatory Meeting on Nickel (Geneva, 10-18 April 1985)[103] considered further a proposal to establish an intergovernmental nickel discussion group, an international statistical system for nickel, secretariat arrangements, a draft agreement for establishment of such a group and draft rules of procedure.

In agreed conclusions adopted on 18 April, the consensus of the Preparatory Meeting was that: there was scope for improving intergovernmental co-operation on nickel, particularly by improving information on the nickel economy and by providing a forum for discussions; it would be appropriate to seek the agreement of Governments to participate in a negotiating conference aimed at establishing an autonomous international nickel study group; draft terms of reference and draft rules of procedure for such a group, annexed to the Meeting's report,[103] were a suitable basis for negotiating the final terms and rules to be agreed by the proposed negotiating conference; TDB should request the UNCTAD Secretary-General to convene for two weeks a negotiating conference on the establishment of such a group, if possible after the International Lead and Zinc Study Group session in October 1985; the conference should consider the form of the group's secretariat, the nature of the statistics and system for data collection, analysis and dissemination, as well as its inaugural meeting.

The United Nations Conference on Nickel, 1985 (Geneva, 28 October–7 November), discussed the establishment of the study group. By a 7 November resolution,[104] it adopted the terms of reference for an International Nickel Study Group, except those relating to their coming into effect, and recommended the draft rules of procedure, except those concerning finance and the secretariat, for adoption by the Group. The United Nations Secretary-General was requested to reconvene the Conference, preferably from 28 April to 2 May 1986, to: finalize work on the terms of reference and the draft rules of procedure; consider, with the participation of industry advisers, a work programme on statistics for the Group; and confirm arrangements, prepare an agenda and decide on dates for an inaugural meeting of the Group. The International Lead and Zinc Study Group was invited to indicate its willingness to establish a joint secretariat with a Nickel Study Group.

Tungsten. At its seventeenth session (Geneva, 11-15 November 1985),[105] the Committee on

Tungsten reviewed discussions and proposals on stabilizing the tungsten market with a view to enabling producing and consuming countries to agree on market stabilization measures and the convening of a negotiating conference.

A sessional working group established by the Committee in 1984[99] also held meetings at which it reviewed the current market situation and outlook and examined statistics provided by the UNCTAD secretariat. A secretariat note,[106] with a statistical compendium, reviewed recent developments in the tungsten market and examined the short-term outlook. Another[107] examined structural and technological change in the tungsten industry with reference to scrap recycling in Western Europe.

The producers/exporting countries proposed to the Committee that the secretariat's next customary survey of the market situation should, in particular: refer to the effect of varying currency-exchange rates on each country's tungsten production and consumption; review the world economy and its effect on tungsten production and consumption; update reports on pricing indicators and on trade in intermediate products; assess trade in stocks held by producers, consumers, traders and Governments; and study the markets for other related primary mineral commodities compared to the tungsten market. The Committee decided to discuss the question of stabilization of the tungsten market at its next (1986) session.

Consumer protection

In accordance with a 1984 decision,[108] the General Assembly, in April 1985, at its resumed thirty-ninth session, considered a draft resolution deferred from its regular 1984 session, containing guidelines for consumer protection.

On an oral proposal by its President to adopt the 1984 text, the Assembly, on 9 April 1985, adopted, without vote, **resolution 39/248**, to which were annexed the guidelines.

Consumer protection

The General Assembly,

Recalling Economic and Social Council resolution 1981/62 of 23 July 1981, in which the Council requested the Secretary-General to continue consultations on consumer protection with a view to elaborating a set of general guidelines for consumer protection, taking particularly into account the needs of the developing countries,

Recalling further General Assembly resolution 38/147 of 19 December 1983,

Taking note of Economic and Social Council resolution 1984/63 of 26 July 1984,

1. *Decides* to adopt the guidelines for consumer protection annexed to the present resolution;

2. *Requests* the Secretary-General to disseminate the guidelines to Governments and other interested parties;

3. *Requests* all organizations of the United Nations system that elaborate guidelines and related documents on specific areas relevant to consumer protection to distribute them to the appropriate bodies of individual States.

ANNEX
Guidelines for consumer protection

I. Objectives

1. Taking into account the interests and needs of consumers in all countries, particularly those in developing countries; recognizing that consumers often face imbalances in economic terms, educational levels, and bargaining power; and bearing in mind that consumers should have the right of access to non-hazardous products, as well as the importance of promoting just, equitable and sustainable economic and social development, these guidelines for consumer protection have the following objectives:

(*a*) To assist countries in achieving or maintaining adequate protection for their population as consumers;

(*b*) To facilitate production and distribution patterns responsive to the needs and desires of consumers;

(*c*) To encourage high levels of ethical conduct for those engaged in the production and distribution of goods and services to consumers;

(*d*) To assist countries in curbing abusive business practices by all enterprises at the national and international levels which adversely affect consumers;

(*e*) To facilitate the development of independent consumer groups;

(*f*) To further international co-operation in the field of consumer protection;

(*g*) To encourage the development of market conditions which provide consumers with greater choice at lower prices.

II. General principles

2. Governments should develop, strengthen or maintain a strong consumer protection policy, taking into account the guidelines set out below. In so doing, each Government must set its own priorities for the protection of consumers in accordance with the economic and social circumstances of the country, and the needs of its population, and bearing in mind the costs and benefits of proposed measures.

3. The legitimate needs which the guidelines are intended to meet are the following:

(*a*) The protection of consumers from hazards to their health and safety;

(*b*) The promotion and protection of the economic interests of consumers;

(*c*) Access of consumers to adequate information to enable them to make informed choices according to individual wishes and needs;

(*d*) Consumer education;

(*e*) Availability of effective consumer redress;

(*f*) Freedom to form consumer and other relevant groups or organizations and the opportunity of such organizations to present their views in decision-making processes affecting them.

4. Governments should provide or maintain adequate infrastructure to develop, implement and monitor consumer protection policies. Special care should be taken to ensure that measures for consumer protection

are implemented for the benefit of all sectors of the population, particularly the rural population.

5. All enterprises should obey the relevant laws and regulations of the countries in which they do business. They should also conform to the appropriate provisions of international standards for consumer protection to which the competent authorities of the country in question have agreed. (Hereinafter references to international standards in the guidelines should be viewed in the context of this paragraph.)

6. The potential positive role of universities and public and private enterprises in research should be considered when developing consumer protection policies.

III. Guidelines

7. The following guidelines should apply both to home-produced goods and services and to imports.

8. In applying any procedures or regulations for consumer protection, due regard should be given to ensuring that they do not become barriers to international trade and that they are consistent with international trade obligations.

A. *Physical safety*

9. Governments should adopt or encourage the adoption of appropriate measures, including legal systems, safety regulations, national or international standards, voluntary standards and the maintenance of safety records to ensure that products are safe for either intended or normally foreseeable use.

10. Appropriate policies should ensure that goods produced by manufacturers are safe for either intended or normally foreseeable use. Those responsible for bringing goods to the market, in particular suppliers, exporters, importers, retailers and the like (hereinafter referred to as "distributors"), should ensure that while in their care these goods are not rendered unsafe through improper handling or storage and that while in their care they do not become hazardous through improper handling or storage. Consumers should be instructed in the proper use of goods and should be informed of the risks involved in intended or normally foreseeable use. Vital safety information should be conveyed to consumers by internationally understandable symbols wherever possible.

11. Appropriate policies should ensure that if manufacturers or distributors become aware of unforeseen hazards after products are placed on the market, they should notify the relevant authorities and, as appropriate, the public without delay. Governments should also consider ways of ensuring that consumers are properly informed of such hazards.

12. Governments should, where appropriate, adopt policies under which, if a product is found to be seriously defective and/or to constitute a substantial and severe hazard even when properly used, manufacturers and/or distributors should recall it and replace or modify it, or substitute another product for it; if it is not possible to do this within a reasonable period of time, the consumer should be adequately compensated.

B. *Promotion and protection of consumers' economic interests*

13. Government policies should seek to enable consumers to obtain optimum benefit from their economic resources. They should also seek to achieve the goals of satisfactory production and performance standards, adequate distribution methods, fair business practices, informative marketing and effective protection against practices which could adversely affect the economic interests of consumers and the exercise of choice in the market-place.

14. Governments should intensify their efforts to prevent practices which are damaging to the economic interests of consumers through ensuring that manufacturers, distributors and others involved in the provision of goods and services adhere to established laws and mandatory standards. Consumer organizations should be encouraged to monitor adverse practices, such as the adulteration of foods, false or misleading claims in marketing and service frauds.

15. Governments should develop, strengthen or maintain, as the case may be, measures relating to the control of restrictive and other abusive business practices which may be harmful to consumers, including means for the enforcement of such measures. In this connection, Governments should be guided by their commitment to the Set of Multilaterally Agreed Equitable Principles and Rules for the Control of Restrictive Business Practices adopted by the General Assembly in resolution 35/63 of 5 December 1980.

16. Governments should adopt or maintain policies that make clear the responsibility of the producer to ensure that goods meet reasonable demands of durability, utility and reliability, and are suited to the purpose for which they are intended, and that the seller should see that these requirements are met. Similar policies should apply to the provision of services.

17. Governments should encourage fair and effective competition in order to provide consumers with the greatest range of choice among products and services at the lowest cost.

18. Governments should, where appropriate, see to it that manufacturers and/or retailers ensure adequate availability of reliable after-sales service and spare parts.

19. Consumers should be protected from such contractual abuses as one-sided standard contracts, exclusion of essential rights in contracts, and unconscionable conditions of credit by sellers.

20. Promotional marketing and sales practices should be guided by the principle of fair treatment of consumers and should meet legal requirements. This requires the provision of the information necessary to enable consumers to take informed and independent decisions, as well as measures to ensure that the information provided is accurate.

21. Governments should encourage all concerned to participate in the free flow of accurate information on all aspects of consumer products.

22. Governments should, within their own national context, encourage the formulation and implementation by business, in co-operation with consumer organizations, of codes of marketing and other business practices to ensure adequate consumer protection. Voluntary agreements may also be established jointly by business, consumer organizations and other interested parties. These codes should receive adequate publicity.

23. Governments should regularly review legislation pertaining to weights and measures and assess the adequacy of the machinery for its enforcement.

C. *Standards for the safety and quality of consumer goods and services*

24. Governments should, as appropriate, formulate or promote the elaboration and implementation of standards, voluntary and other, at the national and inter-

national levels for the safety and quality of goods and services and give them appropriate publicity. National standards and regulations for product safety and quality should be reviewed from time to time, in order to ensure that they conform, where possible, to generally accepted international standards.

25.   Where a standard lower than the generally accepted international standard is being applied because of local economic conditions, every effort should be made to raise that standard as soon as possible.

26.   Governments should encourage and ensure the availability of facilities to test and certify the safety, quality and performance of essential consumer goods and services.

D.   *Distribution facilities for essential
consumer goods and services*

27.   Governments should, where appropriate, consider:

(*a*)   Adopting or maintaining policies to ensure the efficient distribution of goods and services to consumers; where appropriate, specific policies should be considered to ensure the distribution of essential goods and services where this distribution is endangered, as could be the case particularly in rural areas. Such policies could include assistance for the creation of adequate storage and retail facilities in rural centres, incentives for consumer self-help and better control of the conditions under which essential goods and services are provided in rural areas;

(*b*)   Encouraging the establishment of consumer co-operatives and related trading activities, as well as information about them, especially in rural areas.

E.   *Measures enabling consumers to obtain redress*

28.   Governments should establish or maintain legal and/or administrative measures to enable consumers or, as appropriate, relevant organizations to obtain redress through formal or informal procedures that are expeditious, fair, inexpensive and accessible. Such procedures should take particular account of the needs of low-income consumers.

29.   Governments should encourage all enterprises to resolve consumer disputes in a fair, expeditious and informal manner, and to establish voluntary mechanisms, including advisory services and informal complaints procedures, which can provide assistance to consumers.

30.   Information on available redress and other dispute-resolving procedures should be made available to consumers.

F.   *Education and information programmes*

31.   Governments should develop or encourage the development of general consumer education and information programmes, bearing in mind the cultural traditions of the people concerned. The aim of such programmes should be to enable people to act as discriminating consumers, capable of making an informed choice of goods and services, and conscious of their rights and responsibilities. In developing such programmes, special attention should be given to the needs of disadvantaged consumers, in both rural and urban areas, including low-income consumers and those with low or non-existent literacy levels.

32.   Consumer education should, where appropriate, become an integral part of the basic curriculum of the educational system, preferably as a component of existing subjects.

33.   Consumer education and information programmes should cover such important aspects of consumer protection as the following:

(*a*)   Health, nutrition, prevention of food-borne diseases and food adulteration;

(*b*)   Product hazards;

(*c*)   Product labelling;

(*d*)   Relevant legislation, how to obtain redress, and agencies and organizations for consumer protection;

(*e*)   Information on weights and measures, prices, quality, credit conditions and availability of basic necessities; and

(*f*)   As appropriate, pollution and environment.

34.   Governments should encourage consumer organizations and other interested groups, including the media, to undertake education and information programmes, particularly for the benefit of low-income consumer groups in rural and urban areas.

35.   Business should, where appropriate, undertake or participate in factual and relevant consumer education and information programmes.

36.   Bearing in mind the need to reach rural consumers and illiterate consumers, Governments should, as appropriate, develop or encourage the development of consumer information programmes in the mass media.

37.   Governments should organize or encourage training programmes for educators, mass media professionals and consumer advisers, to enable them to participate in carrying out consumer information and education programmes.

G.   *Measures relating to specific areas*

38.   In advancing consumer interests, particularly in developing countries, Governments should, where appropriate, give priority to areas of essential concern for the health of the consumer, such as food, water and pharmaceuticals. Policies should be adopted or maintained for product quality control, adequate and secure distribution facilities, standardized international labelling and information, as well as education and research programmes in these areas. Government guidelines in regard to specific areas should be developed in the context of the provisions of this document.

39.   *Food.* When formulating national policies and plans with regard to food, Governments should take into account the need of all consumers for food security and should support and, as far as possible, adopt standards from the Food and Agriculture Organization of the United Nations and the World Health Organization Codex Alimentarius or, in their absence, other generally accepted international food standards. Governments should maintain, develop or improve food safety measures, including, *inter alia*, safety criteria, food standards and dietary requirements and effective monitoring, inspection and evaluation mechanisms.

40.   *Water.* Governments should, within the goals and targets set for the International Drinking Water Supply and Sanitation Decade, formulate, maintain or strengthen national policies to improve the supply, distribution and quality of water for drinking. Due regard should be paid to the choice of appropriate levels of service, quality and technology, the need for education programmes and the importance of community participation.

41.   *Pharmaceuticals.* Governments should develop or maintain adequate standards, provisions and ap-

propriate regulatory systems for ensuring the quality and appropriate use of pharmaceuticals through integrated national drug policies which could address, *inter alia*, procurement, distribution, production, licensing arrangements, registration systems and the availability of reliable information on pharmaceuticals. In so doing, Governments should take special account of the work and recommendations of the World Health Organization on pharmaceuticals. For relevant products, the use of that organization's Certification Scheme on the Quality of Pharmaceutical Products Moving in International Commerce and other international information systems on pharmaceuticals should be encouraged. Measures should also be taken, as appropriate, to promote the use of international non-proprietary names (INNs) for drugs, drawing on the work done by the World Health Organization.

42. In addition to the priority areas indicated above, Governments should adopt appropriate measures in other areas, such as pesticides and chemicals, in regard, where relevant, to their use, production and storage, taking into account such relevant health and environmental information as Governments may require producers to provide and include in the labelling of products.

IV. International co-operation

43. Governments should, especially in a regional or subregional context:

(a) Develop, review, maintain or strengthen, as appropriate, mechanisms for the exchange of information on national policies and measures in the field of consumer protection;

(b) Co-operate or encourage co-operation in the implementation of consumer protection policies to achieve greater results within existing resources. Examples of such co-operation could be collaboration in the setting up or joint use of testing facilities, common testing procedures, exchange of consumer information and education programmes, joint training programmes and joint elaboration of regulations;

(c) Co-operate to improve the conditions under which essential goods are offered to consumers, giving due regard to both price and quality. Such co-operation could include joint procurement of essential goods, exchange of information on different procurement possibilities and agreements on regional product specifications.

44. Governments should develop or strengthen information links regarding products which have been banned, withdrawn or severely restricted in order to enable other importing countries to protect themselves adequately against the harmful effects of such products.

45. Governments should work to ensure that the quality of products, and information relating to such products, does not vary from country to country in a way that would have detrimental effects on consumers.

46. Governments should work to ensure that policies and measures for consumer protection are implemented with due regard to their not becoming barriers to international trade, and that they are consistent with international trade obligations.

General Assembly resolution 39/248

9 April 1985   Meeting 106   Adopted without vote

Oral proposal by President to adopt draft referred to resumed session in 1985 by Assembly decision 39/444 of 18 December 1984; agenda item 12.

REFERENCES

[1]*Trade and Development Report, 1985* (UNCTAD/TDR/5), Sales No. E.85.II.D.16. [2]*World Economic Survey 1985* (E/1985/54), Sales No. E.85.II.C.1. [3]YUN 1982, p. 1598. [4]E/1985/29. [5]YUN 1983, p. 543. [6]YUN 1984, p. 529. [7]A/40/15, vol. II (dec. 320(XXXI)). [8]A/C.2/40/L.114. [9]A/C.2/40/L.128. [10]YUN 1984, p. 530. [11]YUN 1983, p. 544. [12]TD/B/1037 & Add.1-3. [13]TD/B/1039 (Part I) & Corr.1. [14]*Ibid.* (Part II) & Corr.1. [15]A/40/15, vol. I (dec. 310(XXX)). [16]A/C.2/40/L.8. [17]YUN 1980, p. 627. [18]YUN 1981, p. 542. [19]YUN 1982, p. 727. [20]YUN 1983, p. 546. [21]YUN 1984, p. 530. [22]*Ibid.*, p. 531, GA dec. 39/432, 18 Dec. 1984. [23]YUN 1983, p. 545. [24]YUN 1984, p. 531. [25]A/40/15, vol. I (dec. 309(XXX)). [26]TD/B/1066. [27]TD/B/1052. [28]TD/B/C.5/96 & Corr.1. [29]TD/B/C.5/95. [30]YUN 1984, p. 532. [31]*Ibid.*, p. 1289. [32]TD/B/C.5/106. [33]TD/B/C.5/102. [34]YUN 1982, p. 729. [35]TD/B/C.5/WG(X)/2. [36]TD/B/C.5/WG(X)/3. [37]TD/B/1083. [38]TD/B/C.7/68. [39]YUN 1984, p. 533. [40]TD/B/1063 & Corr.1 & Add.1 & Add.1/Corr.1. [41]TD/B/1061. [42]YUN 1969, p. 345. [43]A/40/15, vol. II (dec. 321(XXXI)). [44]YUN 1968, p. 370. [45]YUN 1972, p. 273. [46]YUN 1976, p. 400. [47]A/40/15, vol. II (dec. 322(XXXI)). [48]YUN 1983, p. 548. [49]ITC/AG(XIX)/100 & Add.1. [50]YUN 1984, p. 534. [51]YUN 1983, p. 550. [52]ITC/AG(XVIII)/98 & Add.1. [53]A/40/15, vol. I (dec. 305(XXX)). [54]YUN 1984, p. 535. [55]YUN 1980, p. 626. [56]TD/B/1054. [57]YUN 1983, p. 551. [58]TD/B/RBP/29. [59]YUN 1980, p. 630, GA res. 35/63, 5 Dec. 1980. [60]TD/RBP/CONF.2/8 & Corr.1. [61]TD/RBP/CONF.2/4 & Corr.1,2. [62]TD/RBP/CONF.2/3 & Add.1-5. [63]A/C.2/40/12. [64]TD/B/C.1/265. [65]YUN 1984, p. 537. [66]YUN 1979, p. 561. [67]YUN 1983, p. 553. [68]TD/B/1041. [69]TD/B/C.1/252. [70]TD/B/C.1/253 & Corr.1. [71]TD/B/1041 (dec. 20(S-II)). [72]TD/B/1057. [73]TD/B/C.1/270. [74]TD/B/1057 (dec. 21(S-III)). [75]TD/B/1085. [76]TD/B/C.1/274 & Corr.1. [77]TD/B/1085 (res. 22(XI)). [78]*Ibid.* (dec. 23(XI)). [79]YUN 1976, p. 394. [80]TD/B/1085 (agreed conclusion 24(XI)). [81]A/C.2/40/L.81. [82]YUN 1980, p. 621. [83]*Multilateral Treaties Deposited with the Secretary-General: Status as at 31 December 1985* (ST/LEG/SER.E/4), Sales No. E.86.V.3. [84]A/40/717. [85]A/C.5/40/79. [86]YUN 1983, p. 555. [87]TD/B/C.1/276. [88]YUN 1976, p. 409. [89]YUN 1980, p. 622. [90]YUN 1984, p. 538. [91]TD/COCOA.7/12. [92]YUN 1979, p. 586. [93]TD/RUBBER.2/4. [94]TD/RUBBER.2/3. [95]TD/RUBBER.2/8. [96]YUN 1984, p. 539. [97]YUN 1983, p. 556. [98]TD/B/IPC/IRON ORE/22. [99]YUN 1984, p. 540. [100]TD/B/IPC/IRON ORE/19. [101]TD/B/IPC/IRON ORE/21. [102]TD/B/IPC/IRON ORE/20. [103]TD/B/1051. [104]TD/NICKEL/6 & Add.1. [105]TD/B/C.1/280. [106]TD/B/C.1/TUNGSTEN/58 & Add.1. [107]TD/B/C.1/TUNGSTEN/57. [108]YUN 1984, p. 541, GA dec. 39/444, 18 Dec. 1984.

OTHER PUBLICATIONS

Handbook of State Trading Organizations of Developing Countries, 1985 (UNCTAD/ECDC/95/Rev.1), Sales No. A/E/F/S.85.II.D.7. *Trade in Manufactures and Semi-Manufactures of Developing Countries: 1980-1981 Review* (TD/B/C.2/221), Sales No. E.85.II.D.8. *Manual on Trading with the Socialist Countries of Eastern Europe* (UNCTAD/ST/TSC/1), Sales No. E.85.II.D.10. *Collusive Tendering* (TD/B/RBP/12/Rev.2), Sales No. E.85.II.D.11. *Handbook of International Trade and Development Statistics, 1985 Supplement* (TD/STAT/13), Sales No. E/F.85.II.D.12. *Services and the Development Process*

(TD/B/1008/Rev.1), Sales No. E.85.II.D.13. *Trade and Co-operation between the Socialist Countries of Eastern Europe and the Developing Countries in the Field of Food and Agriculture* (TD/B/1033/Rev.1), Sales No. E.85.II.D.14. *Operation and Effects of the Generalized System of Preferences* (TD/B/C.5/100), Sales No. E.85.II.D.15. *Export Processing Free Zones in Developing Countries: Implications for Trade and Industrialization Policies* (TD/B/C.2/211/Rev.1), Sales No. E.85.II.D.17. *Trade and Development: An UNCTAD Review*, No. 6, 1985 (UNCTAD/OSG/316), Sales No. E.85.II.D.20. *Yearbook of International Commodity Statistics, 1985* (TD/B/C.1/STAT/2 & Corr.1), Sales No. E.85.II.D.24. *Marketing Management in East-West Trade* (TRADE/INF.6), Sales No. E.85.II.E.33.

Finance

During 1985, monetary and financial issues, particularly the debt problems of developing countries, received considerable attention in the United Nations bodies that discussed economic and development matters. The March session of TDB addressed the debt and development problems of poorer developing countries, particularly LDCs, while its September session discussed debt and development problems of developing countries in general. The interdependence of problems of trade, development finance and the international monetary system were considered at both sessions.

The Committee on Invisibles and Financing related to Trade, meeting in a two-part session, devoted the second part, in February/March, to international monetary issues in general, and the debt and development finance problems of developing countries in particular, while the first part of the session (earlier in February) focused on questions of insurance.

In June, at its fourteenth special session, TDB requested the UNCTAD Secretary-General to convene in 1986 an intergovernmental group of experts to continue to analyse the need for a new facility for the compensatory financing of export earnings shortfalls.

In December, the *Ad Hoc* Group of Experts on International Co-operation in Tax Matters reviewed the experience of countries in the bilateral application of the United Nations Model Double Taxation Convention between Developed and Developing Countries.

Financial policy

The Committee for Development Planning, in the report on its November 1984 and April 1985 meetings,[1] noted that the volatility of exchange rates in the international monetary and financial system as currently structured had generated uncertainty and disruption, particularly for the poorest countries which were least able to protect themselves against it. Prolonged exchange-rate misalignments had also impeded the orderly adjustment of international imbalances. CDP supported moves towards greater co-ordination of the macro-economic policies of the key currency countries as long as it was aimed at maintaining high levels of growth and employment. However, the world-wide implications of those countries' economic policies required that such co-ordination should also be a matter for discussions at international bodies. More effective IMF surveillance of industrial countries' policies had long been an important aspiration and the limited effectiveness of previous consultation and surveillance procedures suggested that new IMF arrangements would have to be more forceful. Efforts to manage and improve the supply of international liquidity should also be taken within the framework of the IMF mandate and, in the mean time, its role as a source of liquidity should continue to be reviewed. The aim of the provision of liquidity and of policy conditions should be to pace and structure adjustments so as to minimize the cost in terms of growth, employment and poverty.

The *Trade and Development Report, 1985*[2] stated that disparities in demand expansion and the misalignment of exchange rates resulting from the monetary and fiscal policies of the major developed countries had created an increasingly untenable situation for the world economy at large. Disparities in interest and exchange rates, and in rates of growth of demand and output, could not be resolved through market processes alone or by unilateral policy adjustments. However, unless government policies changed in order to remove the disparities, markets were bound to bring about certain corrections in their own way and at their own pace, with adverse repercussions. Adjustments through that route were likely to involve further recession and increased debt-servicing difficulties.

In conclusions and recommendations for possible action on key issues, the *World Economic Survey 1985*[3] said that a gradual reduction of the United States budget deficit would be an important step towards removing uncertainties in the world economy. However, since a reduction could begin at a time when the United States economy was slowing down and before other industrial economies had started to gather momentum, a substantial deceleration in the growth of the world economy could occur. That situation might be avoided by relaxing cautious fiscal stances in developed countries in a position to do so.

Debt problems of developing countries

Debt and development finance was considered by CDP[1] to be a major and immediate challenge to the world community. The Committee recommended establishing a consultative process among debtors and creditors within the context of broader efforts to construct a more orderly long-term basis for providing liquidity and development finance. Multiyear rescheduling of debt repayment, which had been adopted for a few countries, should be broadened and include debt from official sources, with such relief measures being co-ordinated with other policies such as aid and other financial flows. The Committee urged a renewed effort, led by the multilateral banks, to restore levels of external finance and called for reinforcement of the stabilization and financing roles of IMF and the World Bank by providing them with expanded resources.

Debt, development and the world economy was a major focus of the *Trade and Development Report, 1985*,[2] which traced the origins and evolution of the debt crisis, examined the influence exerted by debt on the development process and discussed prospects for the future. Efforts by developing countries to tackle external deficits resulting from various shocks, particularly from the drying-up of financial flows, had involved inordinately large sacrifices, which had only partly been reflected in improved debt positions and had endangered development potential. Indeed, the main casualty of adjustment measures appeared to have been investment and price stability. Problems of debt, growth and development had to be dealt with through a broad strategy which could not be worked out without the full participation of both developed and developing countries or outside a framework which gave due weight to development objectives.

In preparation for the comprehensive review of the debt and development problems of poorer developing countries, particularly LDCs, to be undertaken by TDB in March 1985, those issues were discussed during the second part of the eleventh session (Geneva, 25 February–8 March 1985) of the Committee on Invisibles and Financing related to Trade.[4] The Committee had before it an UNCTAD secretariat report on official development assistance (ODA) and related debt service, examining the scope for further debt relief in favour of LDCs and other poorer developing countries.[5] Despite low debt-service indicators, the report noted, many of those countries had encountered severe difficulties in managing their external accounts. Given the gloomy prospects for export growth and for the volume of gross financial flows from all sources, the capacity of many of those countries to adjust and deal with the projected rise in debt-service payments was likely to deteriorate further. A strong case existed for donors to realign debt-service obligations of those countries to their evolving debt-servicing capacity and to take other measures to strengthen the process of adjustment.

On 8 March, the Committee adopted agreed conclusions in which it noted that many developing countries had adopted adjustment policies, often at great economic and social cost, and had reduced their current-account deficits. In many countries the anticipated rise in debt-service payments could exert further pressure on their debt-service capacity and development prospects. A satisfactory resolution of debt problems related to ODA facing a number of developing countries required measures such as encouraging long-term financial flows and improved access to foreign markets, a process that would be facilitated by lower interest rates in developed countries and by intensified policies supportive of long-term growth and development by developing countries. The Committee noted the efforts by most developed market-economy countries to implement a 1978 TDB resolution on debt[6] and urged States to implement commitments undertaken in that resolution; a variety of measures could be taken by developed donor countries, such as cancelling debts, converting loans into grants and paying debt services in local currency. The Board was invited at its next session (see below) to examine the Committee's conclusions.

TDB action. In accordance with a 1984 decision,[7] TDB at its March 1985 session reviewed the implementation of its 1978 resolution on the debt and development problems of poorer developing countries, particularly LDCs,[6] to be taken into account during preparations for the 1985 midterm review of the implementation of the Substantial New Programme of Action for the 1980s for LDCs (SNPA) (see p. 434). On 29 March, the Board decided to annex to its report a draft resolution on the subject submitted by the Group of 77 developing countries, by which TDB would have recognized that many poorer developing countries, particularly LDCs, dependent on ODA to finance their economic development, faced serious debt-servicing and development problems and that their capacity to deal with debt-service payments had been under continuing pressure. It would have agreed that developed donor countries should adopt financial measures to lighten the burden of bilateral ODA debt, including the writing-off of debt for LDCs and countries in Africa affected by the unprecedented drought. The Board would have been invited to review the implementation of those recommendations in 1986.

During the mid-term global review of the implementation of SNPA, conclusions and recommendations were made by UNCTAD's Intergovernmental Group on LDCs regarding the debt problems of those countries. Those findings were endorsed by the General Assembly when it adopted **resolution 40/205**, to which they were annexed.

Using information in the *Trade and Development Report, 1985* as a basis for its discussions, TDB considered the debt and development problems of developing countries at its September 1985 session. In a summary of the debate, which was annexed to the TDB report,[8] the Board's President said that certain positive trends in world development, such as renewed economic growth, reduced inflation in developed countries, lower interest rates, and resumed growth in world trade, were contributing to a certain easing of the debt situation. However, the sacrifices being made by developing countries under heavy debt burdens were extremely onerous. In many debtor developing countries, debt service was absorbing a significant part of export earnings and gross national product, their social and economic development had suffered a serious set-back, and reduced rates of investment had weakened the capacity for growth and debt service in the future. The framework for debt rescheduling required further attention to ensure that debt servicing was tailored to repayment capacity and development needs, and that adjustment programmes were underpinned by the availability of adequate net inflows of funds. Further consideration should be given to proposals concerning the servicing of ODA and commercial debt, entailing a substantial lengthening of maturities and reduction of interest rates.

GENERAL ASSEMBLY ACTION

In November, a draft resolution[9] on the external debt crisis and development was submitted to the General Assembly's Second Committee by Yugoslavia on behalf of the Group of 77. Thereby, the Assembly would have reaffirmed that the development of developing countries was an essential priority for all countries, but was being negatively affected by the external debt crisis. It would have urged creditor developed countries and debtor developing countries, as well as international financial institutions, to find a mutually agreed solution to the debt problem of developing countries, to be sought with the following guidelines: equity and symmetry between developed and developing countries in distributing the costs of economic adjustment; lower and stable interest rates, stretching out of payments, grace and consolidated periods; improved and stable access to markets; standstill and rollback of protectionism; reversing the trend towards disruptive market practices, discrimination and managed trade; stabilization of commodity markets with fair and remunerative prices; reversing the net outflow of financial resources from developing to developed countries; reinitiation of the financial flow of resources for development; limiting debt-service payments to a percentage of export earnings compatible with development needs; easing the conditionality applied by IMF and avoidance of cross-conditionality; and special treatment for the poorer

and least developed countries in solving their external debt problems. Creditor developed countries and multilateral financial institutions would have been called on to adopt measures to solve Africa's indebtedness, including action on terms and conditions of the existing debt and the provision of additional resources on concessional terms. The Secretary-General would have been requested to take initiatives towards fulfilling the draft's objectives and to report in 1986 on the evolution of the process.

By a draft resolution on debt and related issues,[10] submitted in December to the Second Committee by Luxembourg on behalf of EEC, the Assembly would have urged further strengthening of international economic co-operation aimed at resolving debt problems and ensuring non-inflationary, sustained world economic growth. It would have stressed the need for convergent economic policies, particularly among major industrialized countries. Debtor countries would have been called on to continue their adjustment efforts. The Assembly would also have called for further action to strengthen the open and multilateral trading system, reverse protectionist trends, improve the functioning of the international monetary system and seek greater stability in exchange markets. The need to improve the stability and predictability of earnings from commodities and primary products would have been stressed, as well as the importance of ensuring adequate national and international resource flows to developing countries, and, in that context, the crucial role of IMF and the World Bank. The Assembly would have called for full implementation of TDB resolutions of 1978[6] and 1980[11] on the debt problems of developing countries and invited multilateral assistance institutions to take into account in their lending programmes for LDCs their overall debt-service burden. It would also have commended the growing spirit of dialogue and co-operation reflected in recent international economic meetings and statements, particularly through the initiatives of IMF and the World Bank to consider debt problems in a broader context.

On 17 December, the Assembly adopted **decision 40/445** by which it decided to reconvene the Second Committee for one week in 1986 to consider ways in which international co-operation in the interrelated areas of money, finance, debt, resource flows, trade and development could be promoted effectively, and to deal with unfinished business in those areas, including the two aforementioned draft texts.

Development finance

In the report on its November 1984 and April 1985 session,[1] CDP stated that in 1983, the last year for which complete information was available, financial flows to developing countries from all sources reached $110.3 billion, down from $138.4 billion in 1981. Concessional flows represented $35.9 billion, down from $39.3 billion in 1981, and non-concessional flows $74.4 billion, down from $99.1 billion. ODA declined by $3.4 billion. Bank lending declined from $52.5 billion to $34 billion in 1983 and preliminary estimates showed that new commercial bank lending to developing countries declined further to $14 billion in 1984; foreign direct investment declined from $17.2 billion in 1981 to $7.8 billion in 1983; and net export credits declined from $13 billion in 1981 to $7.6 billion in 1983. In the light of the uncertainties surrounding the supply of those three main sources of non-concessional flows, the slow-down and virtual stagnation of ODA flows, the major form of external assistance to the low-income countries, were most disturbing.

Based on an overview of the sources of financial flows to developing countries, there was a strong likelihood that those flows would in future be lower in real terms and would grow more slowly. Such lower levels of financial assistance would lead to lower rates of growth and economic advance. CDP urged a renewed effort, led by the multilateral banks, to restore levels of external finance and called for reinforcement of the stabilization and financing roles of IMF and the World Bank by providing them with expanded resources.

The *World Economic Survey 1985*[3] stated that investment in the least developed and other low-income countries remained depressed and their international reserve position was precarious. A larger inflow of bilateral and multilateral ODA, as well as debt relief, was required in the short term to ease some of the most pressing constraints on growth.

The effect of lower levels of development finance on the long-term development prospects of developing countries was discussed in a report of the Secretary-General on the overall socio-economic perspective of the world economy to the year 2000[12] (see p. 415). Access to external resources was confirmed as an essential requirement for the accelerated development of developing countries in the conclusions[13] of the Committee on the Review and Appraisal of the Implementation of the International Development Strategy for the Third United Nations Development Decade (see p. 418).

At the second part of its eleventh session,[4] the Committee on Invisibles and Financing related to Trade had before it an UNCTAD secretariat report which examined the role of foreign direct investment (FDI) in development finance,[14] especially the possibility of its substituting for other forms of financial flows. The report reviewed international proposals for converting existing external debt into FDI and for a multilateral investment in-surance scheme, and explored other international policy options. It found that, whereas FDI had been viewed as a proxy for risk capital, the pure equity component of FDI was small and had shrunk in the past several years. It raised the question of whether other investment instruments might be developed that would allow payments by debtor countries to be more closely tailored to their capacity to pay. Another report, on selected policy issues connected with ODA,[15] reviewed major trends and prospects in ODA, focused on evolving aid requirements and addressed the questions of aid effectiveness, distribution and co-ordination. The report concluded that the recent ODA performance of developed donor countries had been disquieting and that aid prospects for the remainder of the 1980s were bleak. It identified areas where scope existed for policy action by both donors and recipients to enhance the provision and use of aid.

On 8 March, the Committee adopted agreed conclusions, taking note of the serious economic difficulties facing many developing countries heavily dependent on ODA for financing their economic development, and underscoring the importance of an expanded and sustained flow of ODA in supporting orderly adjustment and growth. Serious concern was expressed that net ODA to developing countries during 1981-1983 had declined in real terms. The Committee noted with satisfaction the efforts by donor countries that had maintained their ODA performance above the international target established in the International Development Strategy and was encouraged by the progress made by a number of others to reach the target by 1990; the remaining donors were urged to redouble their efforts to fulfil their commitments. The Committee expressed disappointment that ODA flows to LDCs would not, as foreseen in SNPA,[16] have doubled by 1985 and noted that further attention would be paid to the performance of donors at the mid-term review (see p. 434). The Committee underlined the importance of multilateral development finance institutions and recalled that their funding at an adequate level was essential to provide a sound basis for continuing significant growth in their lending. It stressed that its review and monitoring role could be strengthened by developed donor countries' providing full and transparent information on all aspects of UNCTAD resolution 164(VI).[17]

GENERAL ASSEMBLY ACTION

The 1985 session of the General Assembly took no action on a draft decision[18] referred to it in 1984[19] by which it would have requested the Secretary-General to undertake consultations with Governments on an international conference on money and finance for development and to report thereon.

A draft resolution[20] on the subject was introduced in the Second Committee in November 1985 by Yugoslavia on behalf of the Group of 77. By that resolution, the Assembly would have requested the Secretary-General to undertake consultations on the terms of reference, format and time frame of such a conference, with a view to convening an intergovernmental committee to commence preparations by April 1986. He would also have been called on to make available the documentation for the preparatory body and to submit a report on the preparatory process to the Economic and Social Council and subsequently to the Assembly in 1986.

On 17 December, the Assembly adopted **decision 40/445** by which it decided to reconvene the Second Committee immediately prior to the first regular session of the Economic and Social Council of 1986 to deal with unfinished business on various draft texts, including that on an international conference on money and finance for development.

Mobilization of savings

On 28 May 1985, the Economic and Social Council adopted without vote **decision 1985/126** on mobilization of personal savings, by which it requested the Secretary-General to prepare and circulate, before the end of June, a brief report on the Third International Symposium on the Mobilization of Personal Savings in Developing Countries (Yaoundé, Cameroon, 10-14 December 1984). The decision, originally proposed in the First (Economic) Committee by France, also on behalf of Cameroon, Jamaica, Malaysia, Pakistan and Sweden,[21] was resubmitted in revised form by a Committee Vice-Chairman[22] following informal consultations; it was approved without vote on 21 May, and the six-nation text was withdrawn.

In accordance with the Council's request, an informal paper was circulated which contained summaries of the most important points made in the Symposium debate, and conclusions and recommendations concerning: interest rates and mobilization of savings; improving the efficiency of the institutional and the non-institutional sectors; strengthening the link between those sectors; and continuation of the Integrated Programme of International Co-operation for the Mobilization of Personal Savings in Developing Countries, undertaken by the United Nations Department of International Economic and Social Affairs to integrate efforts to promote the mobilization of savings and channel them to investors, and to encourage at the national level the mobilization of each country's financial resources for financing development.

The informal paper was included as Part One of the final report of the Symposium;[23] Part Two contained selected papers presented to the Symposium.

Trade-related finance

Export earnings

In accordance with UNCTAD resolution 157(VI),[24] the fourteenth special session of TDB (Geneva, 10-15 and 27 June) considered the report of an expert group on the compensatory financing of export earnings shortfalls, which had met in 1984.[25]

On 27 June,[26] the Board noted with concern the instability of export earnings from commodities of the developing countries. It also noted that a large number of countries were convinced of the need for an additional compensatory financing facility, while others considered that Governments needed further information to facilitate continuing intergovernmental discussion of issues raised in the expert group's report, including the need for an additional complementary facility. The Board invited UNCTAD members, its secretariat, the United Nations regional commissions and competent international organizations to comment on the report, including any case-studies. The UNCTAD Secretary-General was requested to convene an intergovernmental group of experts in early 1986 to continue to analyse the need for a new facility, to undertake further work on the rules and modalities of any additional complementary facility, to complete its work by June 1986 and to report to a two-week special session of the Board. The special session would decide on follow-up action, including the possible convening of a negotiating conference on an additional complementary facility.

Insurance

The first part of the eleventh session of the UNCTAD Committee on Invisibles and Financing related to Trade (Geneva, 18-22 February) was devoted exclusively to questions of insurance.

On 22 February, the Committee adopted a resolution[27] by which it considered that a secretariat study[28] on establishing life insurance tax policy in developing countries provided valuable guidance on the establishment of such policies, invited Governments of those countries to bring the study to the attention of their tax and insurance authorities, and asked the secretariat to continue to study measures that developing countries could adopt to improve the investment performance of life insurers.

By another 22 February resolution,[29] on motor insurance in developing countries, the Committee considered that two secretariat studies— one on compensation of victims of motor accidents, with reference to alternative legal systems for developing countries,[30] the other on reforming the legal systems governing motor accident victims' compensation in developing countries[31]—provided valuable guidance in instituting reforms in those countries' systems of compensating victims of motor vehicle accidents. It endorsed the conclusion of the first-mentioned study that the choice of legal system for compensating accident victims was the responsibility of each State and recommended that developing countries make use of the measures suggested therein to compensate victims without endangering the solvency of insurance companies. Developing countries were urged to compile statistics so as to be able to assess objectively their compensation system and analyse the desirability and feasibility of reforms.

By a further 22 February resolution,[32] on risk management in developing countries, the Committee recommended undertaking a study on the applicability of modern risk management techniques, including the prevention, treatment and financing of losses, to commercial and industrial enterprises in developing countries, and the important role that insurance could play in that area.

On the same date, the Committee adopted a resolution[33] on reinsurance and local retention in developing countries, by which it considered that two secretariat studies—on insurance in developing countries, reviewing developments in 1982-1983,[34] and on the impact of captive insurance companies on the insurance markets of developing countries[35]—provided valuable information on contemporary concerns related to providing international reinsurance cover. It urged developing countries to increase local retention and exert maximum efforts to satisfy the insurance requirements of domestic enterprises, including those of local affiliates of foreign-owned corporations, and not become mere vehicles for exporting premiums abroad through unwarranted reinsurance, but not overlooking the possible advantages of using international reinsurance markets. Developing countries should continue to promote regional and interregional co-operation in insurance and reinsurance as a means of increasing their local retention. The Committee requested a study on all the criteria for assessing the security and credibility of reinsurers, seeking the opinion of representatives of the various interests involved and other experts. The secretariat was also asked to continue its studies on the activities of foreign insurance and reinsurance companies, including captive companies, in the developing countries.

In another 22 February resolution,[36] on insurance for domestic projects in developing countries, the Committee invited countries involved in projects in developing countries to broaden their co-operation in various forms of insurance by ex-tending their assistance and technical support to the efforts of developing countries so that the involvement of local markets in the insurance of such projects could be encouraged, taking into account the need to ensure adequate security.

Taxation

The *Ad Hoc* Group of Experts on International Co-operation in Tax Matters held its third meeting at Geneva from 9 to 20 December 1985.[37] In accordance with proposals made at its second meeting in 1983[38] and approved by the Economic and Social Council in 1984,[39] the *Ad Hoc* Group reviewed the experience of countries in the bilateral application of the United Nations Model Double Taxation Convention between Developed and Developing Countries, adopted by a predecessor Group in 1979.[40] The Group's review was based on replies to a questionnaire sent to Member States which asked whether the Model Convention had stimulated negotiations on bilateral tax treaties between developed and developing countries, to what extent it had influenced how such treaties were negotiated, and how useful it was in negotiating them and whether it could be made more useful.

The Group noted that the Model Convention had stimulated the negotiation of many bilateral double taxation treaties during the seven-year period ending on 31 December 1983; 24 respondent countries indicated that they had carried on negotiations for some 250 treaties, of which some 100 had been concluded within the period and almost 100 were in operation. Of the 250, a small number related to treaties between developing countries. Replies also indicated that the Convention had had a substantial influence on the way bilateral treaties were negotiated; all but one of the respondent countries had used the Convention (or the guidelines that had preceded it) to varying degrees. The Group noted that, in general, respondent countries had found it "moderately useful", "useful" or "very useful", and had suggested various ways in which it could be made more useful.

The *Ad Hoc* Group approved a list of topics connected with monitoring the impact of the Convention for possible consideration at its next meeting, and also discussed the possibility of providing for tax administrations a compendium of domestic measures taken by Governments to combat tax evasion.

REFERENCES

[1]E/1985/29. [2]*Trade and Development Report, 1985* (UNCTAD/TDR/5), Sales No. E.85.II.D.16. [3]*World Economic Survey 1985* (E/1985/54), Sales No. E.85.II.C.1. [4]TD/B/1045. [5]TD/B/C.3/195. [6]YUN 1978, p. 429. [7]YUN 1984, p. 543. [8]A/40/15, vol. II. [9]A/C.2/40/L.52. [10]A/C.2/40/L.129.

[11]YUN 1980, p. 616. [12]A/40/519. [13]A/40/48. [14]TD/B/C.3/196. [15]TD/B/C.3/198. [16]YUN 1981, p. 406. [17]YUN 1983, p. 564. [18]A/C.2/40/L.7. [19]YUN 1984, p. 545, GA dec. 39/438, 18 Dec. 1984. [20]A/C.2/40/L.30. [21]E/1985/C.1/L.2. [22]E/1985/C.1/L.4. [23]*Savings for Development. Report of the Third International Symposium on the Mobilization of Personal Savings in Developing Countries* (ST/ESA/171), Sales No. E.85.II.A.17. [24]YUN 1983, p. 566. [25]YUN 1984, p. 545. [26]A/40/15, vol. I (dec. 317(S-XIV)). [27]TD/B/1044 (res. 25(XI)). [28]TD/B/C.3/193. [29]TD/B/1044 (res. 26(XI)). [30]TD/B/C.3/190. [31]TD/B/C.3/191. [32]TD/B/1044 (res. 27(XI)). [33]*Ibid.* (res. 28(XI)). [34]TD/B/C.3/189. [35]TD/B/C.3/192. [36]TD/B/1044 (res. 29(XI)). [37]*International Co-operation in Tax Matters. Report of the* Ad Hoc *Group of Experts on International Co-operation in Tax Matters on the Work of Its Third Meeting* (ST/ESA/185), Sales No. E.87.XVI.1. [38]YUN 1983, p. 567. [39]YUN 1984, p. 546, ESC dec. 1984/114, 16 May 1984. [40]YUN 1980, p. 531.

OTHER PUBLICATIONS

Multilateral Development Finance Institutions of Developing Countries and the Promotion of Economic Co-operation and Integration (TD/B/C.7/64), Sales No. E.85.II.D.1. *The International Monetary System and Financial Markets: Recent Developments and the Policy Challenge* (TD/B/C.3/194/Rev.1), Sales No. E.85.II.D.5. *Financial Solidarity for Development: 1985 Review* (TD/B/C.3/208-TD/B/C.7/76), Sales No. E.85.II.D.22. *The Activities of UNCTAD's Special Programme on Insurance* (UNCTAD/INS/99), Sales No. E.85.II.D.23. *Supplement No. 43 to International Tax Agreements*, vol. IX, Sales No. E.85.XVI.1; *Supplement No. 44*, Sales No. E.85.XVI.2.

Programme and finances of UNCTAD

The UNCTAD Working Party on the Medium-term Plan and the Programme Budget held two sessions in 1985. In April, it discussed the UNCTAD section of the proposed United Nations programme budget for 1986-1987, and in October reviewed UNCTAD's technical assistance activities.

The General Assembly called for the commencement of preparations for the seventh session of UNCTAD, to be held in 1987, and confirmed the appointment of Kenneth K. S. Dadzie as UNCTAD Secretary-General beginning on 1 January 1986.

UNCTAD programme

The Trade and Development Board—the executive body of UNCTAD—held three sessions in 1985, all at Geneva. Its thirtieth session was held from 18 to 29 March and on 2 May; its fourteenth special session, from 10 to 15 and on 27 June to consider compensatory financing of export earnings shortfalls (see p. 579); and its thirty-first session from 16 to 27 September.

The Board adopted four resolutions and 18 decisions during 1985. A resolution adopted in March dealt with technical and operational assistance provided by the Advisory Service on Transfer of Technology (see p. 717). Three resolutions adopted in September dealt with action related to the particular needs and problems of land-locked developing countries (see p. 451), the technological transformation of developing countries in the pharmaceutical sector (see p. 717), and the transfer and development of technology, with reference to issues in individual sectors of critical importance to developing countries (see p. 717).

GENERAL ASSEMBLY ACTION

The Board's 1985 report[1] was considered by the General Assembly in November and December. The Economic and Social Council had, without vote, taken note of the first part of the report,[2] on its thirtieth session, on 25 July by **decision 1985/171**, an action recommended by the Council's First Committee, on an oral proposal by its Chairman.

On 17 December, on the recommendation of the Second Committee, the Assembly adopted **resolution 40/189**, without vote.

Report of the Trade and Development Board
The General Assembly,

Recalling its resolution 1995(XIX) of 30 December 1964, as amended, on the establishment of the United Nations Conference on Trade and Development as an organ of the General Assembly, and its resolutions 3201(S-VI) and 3202(S-VI) of 1 May 1974, containing the Declaration and the Programme of Action on the Establishment of a New International Economic Order, 3281(XXIX) of 12 December 1974, containing the Charter of Economic Rights and Duties of States, 3362(S-VII) of 16 September 1975 on development and international economic co-operation and 35/56 of 5 December 1980, the annex to which contains the International Development Strategy for the Third United Nations Development Decade,

Mindful of the forthcoming seventh session of the United Nations Conference on Trade and Development, to take place in 1987, which constitutes a major opportunity for progress in key issues in the field of international trade and related areas of international economic co-operation for development,

Noting that the *Trade and Development Report, 1985* has made a constructive contribution to the examination by the Trade and Development Board, at its thirty-first session, of the world economic situation and its future prospects,

1. *Takes note* of the report of the Trade and Development Board on the work of its thirtieth, fourteenth special and thirty-first sessions;

2. *Requests* the United Nations Conference on Trade and Development to continue and intensify its important contribution and the role it has been playing in the revitalization and strengthening of international trade and related areas of international economic co-operation for development;

3. *Calls upon* all Governments and the relevant international organizations to commence intensive

and thorough preparations for the seventh session of the United Nations Conference on Trade and Development.

General Assembly resolution 40/189

17 December 1985   Meeting 119   Adopted without vote

Approved by Second Committee (A/40/989/Add.3) without vote, 9 December (meeting 49); draft by Yugoslavia, for Group of 77 (A/C.2/40/L.84), orally amended by Vice-Chairman based on informal consultations; agenda item 84 *(c)*.
Meeting numbers. GA 40th session: 2nd Committee 31, 36, 41, 45-49; plenary 119.

On 17 December, the Assembly adopted five other resolutions on various aspects of the UNCTAD programme not covered in this chapter; they dealt with: specific action related to the particular needs and problems of land-locked developing countries (**resolution 40/183**); an international code of conduct on the transfer of technology (**40/184**); the United Nations Conference on Conditions for Registration of Ships (**40/187**); the reverse transfer of technology (**40/191**); and implementation of SNPA (**40/205**).

Programme policy decisions

At its ninth session, the TDB Working Party on the Medium-term Plan and the Programme Budget (Geneva, 15-24 April 1985)[3] reviewed the UNCTAD section of the proposed United Nations programme budget for 1986-1987 and discussed programme evaluation and steps taken to effect economies in the 1984-1985 budget. It also addressed the question of the duration and frequency of its sessions.

On 19 April, the Working Party adopted agreed conclusions by which it: noted that adjustments were needed in the UNCTAD section of the 1986-1987 programme budget to take full account of recent decisions and resolutions, as well as of subsequent decisions during implementation of the budget; welcomed the establishment of a Programme Co-ordination and Evaluation Unit within the UNCTAD secretariat and invited the UNCTAD Secretary-General to keep the Working Party informed of the Unit's work, of economies necessary to implement decisions taken by intergovernmental bodies and conferences, particularly by UNCTAD VI in 1983, and of the outcome of secretariat review processes under way; recommended to TDB that its main committees, particularly the Committees on Manufactures, on Commodities and on Economic Co-operation among Developing Countries, give increased attention to reviewing their work programmes and implementing their decisions, in accordance with a 1981 TDB resolution;[4] invited the UNCTAD Secretary-General to consider ways to strengthen the Special Programme for Least Developed, Land-locked and Island Developing Countries and how to meet additional requirements placed on the Manufactures Division as a result of a 1985 TDB decision on services (see p. 557); and recommended that a further session of the Working Party be scheduled later in 1985.

Annexed to the Working Party's report was a position paper on the review of the UNCTAD section of the 1986-1987 budget, submitted on behalf of the Group D members (centrally planned economies) of the Working Party.

At its tenth session (Geneva, 14-18 October),[5] the Working Party focused on UNCTAD's technical assistance activities and their financing (see below), and again considered programme evaluation and redeployment of resources.

On 18 October, the Working Party adopted agreed conclusions by which it noted with concern the implications of the continuing decline in resources for technical co-operation, particularly from UNDP, and invited the UNCTAD Secretary-General: periodically to indicate to Governments possible areas of technical assistance activities, expertise required and financing options; to intensify efforts to find additional extrabudgetary resources for such activities and include information in that regard in the next annual report; to review, and involve Governments in updating, the UNCTAD roster of candidates for technical co-operation assignments, ensuring that it was the main source for recruiting experts; and to keep the Working Party informed on the internal evaluation of the secretariat. It decided to consider programme evaluation at a future session, reiterated its recommendation that main committees review their work programmes and implement their decisions, and reiterated its interest in being informed of economies and redeployment in the secretariat.

Other related action. At its twenty-fifth session (New York, 29 April–1 June),[6] the Committee for Programme and Co-ordination (CPC) requested that greater efforts be made to improve the presentation of UNCTAD's proposed programme budget. In the light of its recommendations on the triennial review of the manufactures programme (see p. 598), CPC expressed the view that UNCTAD, to avoid duplication, should strengthen its efforts to co-ordinate its activities with those of other agencies. It welcomed the establishment of the Evaluation Unit, hoped for close collaboration between it and the United Nations Office for Programme Planning and Co-ordination and recommended that two outputs under the international monetary issues programme be combined. With regard to manufactures and semi-manufactures, CPC recommended that highest priority be given to implementation and improvement of GSP and of special and differential treatment for developing countries, cautioned against disproportionate growth in advisory services compared to other areas, and recommended that UNCTAD strengthen co-ordination with other organizations, especially UNDP, the United Nations Industrial Development Organization and the International Labour Organisation.

CPC recommended that the General Assembly approve, with the suggested changes, the UNCTAD section (section 15) of the proposed programme budget (see ADMINISTRATIVE AND BUDGETARY QUESTIONS, Chapter I).

Technical co-operation

Total project expenditure incurred by UNCTAD in 1985 for technical co-operation activities amounted to some $7.2 million, a decrease of $2.1 million in comparison with 1984. Allocations from UNDP totalling $5.8 million were still the main source of funds, but had fallen from $7.2 million in 1984. In 1985, the total number of projects implemented was 107, compared to 117 in 1984. Activities remained predominantly intercountry-oriented. By region, compared with 1984, expenditures for the Americas, Europe, the Arab States and interregional activities registered an increase in 1985, whereas those for Africa and Asia declined. Among the regions, however, Africa continued to receive the largest share, with 42.2 per cent of total UNCTAD expenditures.

The main sectors in which UNCTAD provided assistance were: maritime and multimodal transport; economic co-operation among developing countries; assistance to the least developed, land-locked and island developing countries; money, finance and development; manufactures and semi-manufactures; trade in commodities; transfer of technology; insurance and reinsurance; trade among countries having different economic and social systems; and trade facilitation.

In addition to these activities, ITC continued to provide technical assistance for trade promotion (see p. 561).

The UNCTAD secretariat's annual report[7] on technical co-operation activities, prepared for the twelfth (October 1986) session of the Working Party on the Medium-term Plan and the Programme Budget, reviewed UNCTAD's activities by region and by programme area, discussed their financing, provided information on evaluations of 1985-1986 technical co-operation activities and noted co-operation between UNCTAD and its partners in the United Nations development system.

Organizational questions

Conferences and meetings

UNCTAD VII

By a 27 September decision,[8] the Trade and Development Board took note with interest of an offer by the Government of Cuba, originally made in 1981,[9] to host the seventh (1987) session of the United Nations Conference on Trade and Development, but postponed a decision on the question to early 1986. It decided to request the Board's President to hold consultations and to report to the Board at its March 1986 session in order to enable it to recommend to the General Assembly the place, date and duration of the seventh session.

By **resolution 40/189**, the Assembly called on Governments and international organizations to commence intensive and thorough preparations for UNCTAD VII.

Calendar of UNCTAD meetings

On 29 March,[10] TDB approved a calendar of meetings for the remainder of 1985 and for 1986 and a tentative schedule for 1987. On 27 September,[11] it approved revisions of those calendars.

An Interim Committee, established in 1984[12] to seek agreement on holding a ministerial session of TDB, held meetings and several rounds of consultations at the end of 1984 and in early 1985. On 29 March,[13] following an oral report by the Chairman of the Committee, the Board decided to continue the Committee with the mandate to seek agreement on issues where full consensus had not yet emerged. The Committee was to report to the Board at its May or June session with a view to taking a decision to hold the ministerial session later in 1985 and to initiating preparations, with which the UNCTAD Secretary-General was to be fully associated at all stages.

On 27 June, at its fourteenth special session, the Board accepted the understanding that the Committee had completed its work; it had not been able to reach agreement on the matters entrusted to it.

Scheduling of TDB meetings

By a 22 January letter,[14] the President of TDB informed the President of the Economic and Social Council that, although the Board had been informed of the Council's 1984 decision[15] authorizing consultations between them on scheduling Board sessions, the Board had not considered the matter further. However, the subject had been included in the agenda for its March 1985 session. That session's report could be submitted to the General Assembly through the Council's July 1985 session, while the report on the Board's September session could be submitted directly to the Assembly.

By **decision 1985/106** of 8 February 1985—proposed by the Council President on behalf of the Bureau of the Council and adopted without vote—the Council decided: to invite TDB to pursue its efforts to find a flexible and practical approach to resolving the issue; to consider the report of the Board's March session at its own July session; and to request the Secretary-General, without prejudice to future consideration of current arrangements, to transmit the Board's reports on its fourteenth special (June) and thirty-first (September) sessions directly to the Assembly.

On 29 March,[16] TDB, noting the Council's invitation to pursue efforts to resolve the issue, established an informal 19-member working group to consider all aspects of scheduling the Board's regular sessions, which was to report to the Board at its September 1985 session.

In its September report,[17] the working group stated that it had been proposed that the Board should hold one regular session a year in two parts on a September-to-September cycle: a one-week first part in September of one year and a three-week second part in March/April of the following year. The Board would report to the Assembly on both parts; any matter of particular importance occurring during the first part would be sent to the Assembly that same year in the form of an extract. Some regional groups had indicated that they had not had sufficient time to study the proposal. On 25 September,[18] TDB decided that the working group should continue to consider the subject for report at its March 1986 session.

Servicing of meetings

On 29 March,[19] TDB, having heard oral reports by the UNCTAD secretariat in response to a 1984 Board resolution[20] on meetings scheduling and document preparation, agreed to revert to the matter at its September 1985 session, and requested the UNCTAD Secretary-General to conduct a further monitoring exercise on meetings servicing requests during a major United Nations conference organized under UNCTAD auspices, to hold consultations on the results before the September session and to report to the Board.

A secretariat report on the monitoring exercise[21] concluded that interpretation resources provided for the meetings monitored were sufficient to cover all but very occasional requests; the established servicing structure could generally cope with needs. It was suggested that TDB might wish to enjoin the regional groups, which were provided with interpretation services only on an "as available" basis, to make most effective use of those services when they were available. On 25 September, the Board took note of the report.

Appointment of the UNCTAD Secretary-General

At the resumed 1984 session of the General Assembly on 16 September 1985, following a statement by the Assembly President on the United Nations Secretary-General's continuing consultations, begun in 1984,[20] regarding the appointment of the Secretary-General of UNCTAD, the Assembly adopted **decision 39/324 B** without vote.

Confirmation of the appointment of the Secretary-General of the United Nations Conference on Trade and Development

At its 108th plenary meeting, on 16 September 1985, the General Assembly:

(a) Took note of the statement by which the President of the Assembly indicated that the Secretary-General was continuing his consultations in regard to an appointment to the post of the Secretary-General of the United Nations Conference on Trade and Development and hoped to be in a position to appoint the Secretary-General of the Conference at the fortieth session of the Assembly, and that, in the interim, the senior Deputy Secretary-General of the Conference would continue to act as Officer-in-Charge of the Conference;

(b) Decided to include in the draft agenda of its fortieth session the item entitled "Confirmation of the appointment of the Secretary-General of the United Nations Conference on Trade and Development".

General Assembly decision 39/324 B

Adopted without vote

Oral proposal by President; agenda item 17 *(i)*.

In a November note to the Assembly,[22] the Secretary-General stated that he had completed his consultations with regional groups. He proposed to appoint Kenneth K. S. Dadzie of Ghana as Secretary-General of UNCTAD. On 21 November, the Assembly adopted **decision 40/308** without vote.

Confirmation of the appointment of the Secretary-General of the United Nations Conference on Trade and Development

At its 87th plenary meeting, on 21 November 1985, the General Assembly, on the proposal of the Secretary-General, confirmed the appointment of Mr. Kenneth K. S. Dadzie as Secretary-General of the United Nations Conference on Trade and Development for a term of office of three years beginning on 1 January 1986.

General Assembly decision 40/308

Adopted without vote

Oral proposal by President; agenda item 17 *(k)*.

REFERENCES

[1]A/40/15, vols. I & II. [2]A/40/15, vol. I. [3]TD/B/1053. [4]YUN 1981, p. 535. [5]TD/B/1079. [6]A/40/38. [7]TD/B/WP/47 & Corr.1 & Add.1 & Add.1/Corr.1 & Add.2. [8]A/40/15, vol. II (dec. 323(XXXI)). [9]YUN 1981, p. 537. [10]A/40/15, vol. I (dec. 315(XXX)). [11]A/40/15, vol. II (dec. 324(XXXI)). [12]YUN 1984, p. 548. [13]A/40/15, vol. I (dec. 312(XXX)). [14]E/1985/50. [15]YUN 1984, p. 549, ESC dec. 1984/161, 25 July 1984. [16]A/40/15, vol. I (dec. 314(XXX)). [17]TD/B/1075. [18]A/40/15, vol. II (dec. 318(XXXI)). [19]A/40/15, vol. I (dec. 313(XXX)). [20]YUN 1984, p. 549. [21]TD/B/1071. [22]A/40/901.

Chapter V

Transport and tourism

The United Nations Conference on Trade and Development (UNCTAD) and its subsidiaries continued in 1985 to deal with problems of transport, particularly maritime transport. The UNCTAD secretariat provided training assistance, advisers and consultants.

The second and third parts of the United Nations Conference on Conditions for Registration of Ships (Geneva, 28 January–15 February and 8-19 July) considered an international agreement. The General Assembly in April (resolution 39/213 B) decided to convene the third part in July, and in December (resolution 40/187) it decided on a reconvening in 1986.

UNCTAD's Working Group on International Shipping Legislation (eleventh session, Geneva, 14-22 October) took up the lack of international uniformity in the area of maritime liens and mortgages and the inadequacy in the means of their enforcement. The Working Group recommended that the UNCTAD Trade and Development Board convene, jointly with the International Maritime Organization (IMO), an expert group on the subject.

The *Ad Hoc* Intergovernmental Group to Consider Means of Combating All Aspects of Maritime Fraud, including Piracy, held its second session (Geneva, 23 October–1 November). The Director of the UNCTAD Shipping Division stressed the seriousness and persistence of maritime fraud.

During 1985, seven States became parties to the 1974 Convention on a Code of Conduct for Liner Conferences, making a total of 66 States parties. The Code was aimed at opening international shipping trade, organized in a system of liner conferences, to more countries, particularly developing ones.

The Group of Rapporteurs and the Group of Experts on Explosives, two subsidiary bodies of the Committee of Experts on the Transport of Dangerous Goods, met at Geneva from 5 to 16 August and from 16 to 20 September, respectively. The Economic and Social Council, in resolution 1985/9, recommended that, because of increasing concern about the transport of dangerous substances, especially hazardous wastes, the 1984 recommendations of the Committee should be taken into account. The new and amended recommendations served as a basis for the formulation of regulations by Member States and international organizations. Following consideration of a proposal by the Secretary-General to enlarge the Committee's membership, broadening also geographical representation in it, the Council requested the Secretary-General to propose ways of encouraging developing countries' participation in the Committee's work.

Taking note of a report on progress made in implementing the 1980 Manila Declaration on World Tourism and the 1982 Acapulco Document, the General Assembly, by resolution 40/172, invited States, when formulating their travel policies and strategies, to consider the new approach suggested by the World Tourism Organization, in which tourism was seen in the wider context of travel, making a positive contribution to economic development.

Topics related to this chapter. Regional economic and social activities: Africa—Transport and Communications Decade in Africa; Africa-Europe link through the Strait of Gibraltar; Asia and the Pacific—transport and communications.

Transport

Maritime transport

The total volume of international seaborne trade in 1985 was estimated at 3.33 billion tons, the UNCTAD secretariat stated in its *Review of Marine Transport, 1985*,[1] prepared in accordance with the work programme of the Committee on Shipping.[2] The size of the world merchant fleet continued to decline, to 664.8 million deadweight tons (dwt) at mid-1985, 9.7 million dwt or 1.4 per cent less than the previous year. Since the peak of 1982, a decrease of 28.7 million dwt or 4.1 per cent had been recorded.

Four types of vessel—oil tankers, bulk and combined carriers, general cargo and unitized ships—constituted in 1985, as in previous years, the main part of the world fleet. They constituted 637.3 million dwt, representing 94.6 per cent of the world fleet, compared with 94.3 per cent in 1984.

Ownership remained concentrated in the developed market-economy and open-registry countries, with a combined tonnage amounting at mid-1985 to 73.1 per cent of the total world merchant fleet. The share of developing countries increased to 17.1 per cent in 1985, while the socialist countries of Eastern Europe and Asia owned 8.8 per cent; their share of tonnage had remained fairly constant at the level of 1970.

The participation of developing countries in the world merchant fleet continued to be considerably lower than their share of international seaborne trade.

In 1985, they generated 37 per cent of world cargo moving in international seaborne trade (exports and imports combined), while developed market-economy countries, either directly or indirectly through open-registry tonnage, generated 56 per cent.

Supply/demand disequilibrium remained one of the most serious problems in the world shipping industry, although in 1985 the surplus decreased slightly as compared with 1984, partly as a result of higher levels of demolition. Tonnage reported to be sold for scrapping during the year amounted to 41.7 million dwt, which was 43.3 per cent more than in 1984. Nevertheless, surplus tonnage as at 1 July 1985 was still estimated at 161.8 million dwt or 24.3 per cent.

The proportion of freight costs to cost, insurance, freight import values for developing countries continued to be approximately twice as high as that for developed market-economy countries (9.8 per cent against 5.1 per cent). Almost all freight rate indices (except that for vessels engaged in liner shipping and medium-size crude carriers) showed a decline in 1985.

Shipping

UN Conference on registration of ships

The second and third parts of the United Nations Conference on Conditions for Registration of Ships were held at Geneva from 28 January to 15 February 1985[3] and from 8 to 19 July,[4] respectively (for participating States and officers, see APPENDIX III). The Conference, convened pursuant to a 1982 General Assembly resolution,[5] considered an international agreement concerning the conditions under which vessels should be accepted on national shipping registers. The first part of the Conference had been held in 1984.[6]

Resumed conference (second part)

On 15 February 1985, at the close of the second part, the Conference decided to resume in July for a two-week period and requested the Secretary-General to seek the General Assembly's approval. The Secretary-General brought that request to the Assembly's attention by a note of 21 March.[7]

GENERAL ASSEMBLY ACTION (April)

On 12 April, the General Assembly adopted without vote **resolution 39/213 B**.

The General Assembly,

Recalling its resolutions 37/209 of 20 December 1982 and 39/213 A of 18 December 1984,

Recognizing that substantial progress has been achieved at the resumed session, from 28 January to 15 February 1985, of the United Nations Conference on Conditions for Registration of Ships,

Recognizing that there is a need for a resumption of the Conference for a further period of two weeks in order to enable it to complete its work,

1. *Takes note* of the note by the Secretary-General of 21 March 1985;

2. *Endorses* the resolution of the United Nations Conference on Conditions for Registration of Ships adopted on 15 February 1985;

3. *Decides* to convene a resumed session of the Conference to be held at Geneva for a period of two weeks in July 1985;

4. *Requests* the Secretary-General of the United Nations Conference on Trade and Development to make all the necessary arrangements for holding the resumed session of the United Nations Conference on Conditions for Registration of Ships;

5. *Requests* the Secretary-General of the United Nations Conference on Trade and Development to report to the General Assembly at its fortieth session.

General Assembly resolution 39/213 B

12 April 1985   Meeting 107   Adopted without vote

Draft by Egypt, for Group of 77 (A/39/L.46); agenda item 80 *(c)*.
Financial implications. 5th Committee, A/39/886; S-G, A/C.5/39/101.
Meeting numbers. GA 39th session: 5th Committee 57; plenary 107.

Resumed conference (third part)

At the conclusion of the third part on 19 July, the Conference approved a composite text of the proposed agreement as elaborated and amended.[8] As a result of negotiations in the Contact Group of the President and in the First Committee, the following articles were agreed on: article 2 on manning of vessels, with one reservation; article 3 on the role of flag States in the management of shipowning companies and vessels, with a few reservations on paragraphs 1 and 3; and article 4 on ownership of vessels, with some reservations on paragraphs 1 and 2. The articles on maritime administration, management and ownership were transmitted to the Drafting Committee.

The Conference adopted on the same date a resolution[9] requesting the General Assembly at its 1985 session to authorize, within its budgetary appropriation for 1986-1987, the resumption of the Conference for three weeks in early 1986 in order to finalize its work; it also requested the UNCTAD Secretary-General to make all the necessary arrangements for the resumed session at Geneva.

GENERAL ASSEMBLY ACTION (December)

On 17 December 1985, on the recommendation of the Second (Economic and Financial) Committee, the Assembly adopted without vote **resolution 40/187**.

United Nations Conference on Conditions for Registration of Ships

The General Assembly,

Recalling its resolutions 37/209 of 20 December 1982, 39/213 A of 18 December 1984 and 39/213 B of 12 April 1985,

Recognizing the very substantial progress achieved by the United Nations Conference on Conditions for Registration of Ships during the third part of its session held from 8 to 19 July 1985, in particular with respect to the crucial issues before the Conference,

Recognizing that there is a need to resume once again the Conference, this time for a period of three weeks, in order to enable it to complete its work,

1. *Endorses* resolution 3 of 19 July 1985 of the United Nations Conference on Conditions for Registration of Ships;

2. *Decides* to reconvene the Conference for the fourth part of its session at Geneva for a period of three weeks from 20 January to 7 February 1986;

3. *Requests* the Secretary-General of the United Nations Conference on Trade and Development to make all the necessary arrangements for holding the fourth part of the session of the United Nations Conference on Conditions for Registration of Ships;

4. *Also requests* the Secretary-General of the United Nations Conference on Trade and Development to report on the outcome of the United Nations Conference on Conditions for Registration of Ships to the General Assembly at its forty-first session.

General Assembly resolution 40/187

17 December 1985   Meeting 119   Adopted without vote

Approved by Second Committee (A/40/989/Add.3) without vote, 5 December (meeting 48); draft by Chairman (A/C.2/40/L.77), based on informal consultations; agenda item 84 *(c)*.

Financial implications. 5th Committee, A/40/1052; S-G, A/C.2/40/L.98, A/C.5/40/85.

Meeting numbers. GA 40th session: 2nd Committee 48; 5th Committee 61; plenary 119.

In the Fifth (Administrative and Budgetary) Committee, the Chairman said that, on the basis of the oral recommendations of the Advisory Committee on Administrative and Budgetary Questions, adoption of the draft would give rise to conference-servicing requirements of $334,200; additional appropriations that might be required would be considered in the context of a consolidated statement.

Following approval of the draft in the Second Committee, the United States expressed the hope that the consolidated statement would indicate that the servicing costs could be covered from within existing resources, a position endorsed by the United Kingdom.

International shipping legislation

The Working Group on International Shipping Legislation (eleventh session, Geneva, 14-22 October 1985),[10] took up the subject of maritime liens and mortgages. Referring to an August report[11] prepared by the UNCTAD secretariat, the Director of the UNCTAD Shipping Division stated that investigations had established that commercial, political and legal considerations were involved in financing ships, and that registered mortgages were the principal means for securing that financing. However, there was concern at the lack of international uniformity in the area of maritime liens and mortgages and the inadequacy in the means of their enforcement. The report set out a possible methodology

of future work on maritime liens, mortgages and arrest of ships. It suggested that a joint UNCTAD/IMO approach would be the most practical and constructive, and the issues were so technical that a group of experts might be the best mechanism. The Working Group might therefore wish to consider establishing such a group.

On 22 October, the Working Group adopted a draft resolution submitted by the Chairman, by which it recommended that the Trade and Development Board (TDB) take steps to provide for the convening, jointly with IMO, of an intergovernmental group of experts which might consider a review of maritime liens and mortgages conventions and related enforcement procedures, such as arrest; preparation of model laws or guidelines; and the feasibility of an international registry of maritime liens and mortgages. The UNCTAD and IMO secretariats were requested to prepare the necessary studies and documentation for the group.

Convention on a code of conduct for liner conferences

As at 31 December 1985, the Convention on a Code of Conduct for Liner Conferences,[12] which entered into force in 1983,[13] had 66 States parties.[14] Seven States—Denmark, Finland, France, Norway, Saudi Arabia, Sweden and the United Kingdom—became parties during 1985.

Technical assistance and training

During 1985,[1] the UNCTAD secretariat executed 50 technical assistance projects financed by the United Nations Development Programme (UNDP), recipient countries and funds-in-trust (as against 44 the previous year). The projects were mainly concerned with providing advisers and consultants, training (fellowships and group training), and to a lesser degree equipment procurement; 18 projects were initiated and 10 were completed. Eighty-five experts were engaged in the projects and 3,200 fellows/course participants followed training activities. The total budget for UNDP-financed projects was $2.2 million, as against $2 million in 1984.

The secretariat developed and organized training in shipping, ports and multimodal transport and began a programme in maritime legislation. It continued to train senior, middle and junior management in those areas as a high priority, with special attention to the elaboration of complementary training packages, either developed centrally through the Improving Port Performance (IPP) project or through centralized and decentralized development (TRAINMAR).

Under IPP, financed by the Swedish International Development Authority (SIDA), the secretariat provided materials for a training course on the management of general cargo operations and prepared a training programme on equipment management and maintenance. A training programme, in the form of materials for a seminar on container terminal development policy, also financed by SIDA, was completed; the seminar was designed for policy makers, such as senior civil servants and port managers; the materials consisted of six video programmes supported by case-studies and exercises.

In 1985, the TRAINMAR programme expanded its role in maritime training; its activities included the establishment of four training centres, the development of three courses and the exchange of pedagogical materials.

Maritime fraud

The *Ad Hoc* Intergovernmental Group to Consider Means of Combating All Aspects of Maritime Fraud, including Piracy (second session, Geneva, 23 October–1 November 1985),[15] considered five UNCTAD secretariat reports on: ship-related information and information needed to combat maritime fraud;[16] shipping agents;[17] the feasibility of a bank super-service;[18] the feasibility of improving the administrative and legal procedures of prosecuting authorities in cases of maritime fraud;[19] and the status of the work of non-governmental organizations (NGOs) to combat maritime fraud.[20]

Speaking before the Group, the Director of the UNCTAD Shipping Division stressed the seriousness and persistence of maritime fraud, pointing out that one estimate had placed the losses to the shipping industry in excess of $13 billion a year, with developing countries the most frequent victims. He commended the idea of creating an international ship information register as the best means of reducing the opportunities for fraud resulting from ignorance and misinformation. He suggested it might be useful to formulate uniform minimum standards regarding financial and professional qualifications for shipping agents and other intermediaries. He noted the proposals of NGOs concerning precautions which might be taken in the use of bills of lading, but urged their replacement by sea waybills as the most effective means of combating documentary fraud. In addition to those preventive measures, he invited the Group to consider the desirability of an international agreement to combat maritime fraud.

On 1 November, the Group adopted a resolution submitted by its Chairman, requesting TDB to instruct the UNCTAD secretariat to complete its study on preventing documentary fraud, including the possibility of replacing bills of lading with sea waybills; to make a comparative study of the different minimum standards applied by professional associations of shipping agents, national and international, and to prepare a draft set of standards; to elaborate proposals for improving the dissemination of international information relevant to combating maritime fraud; and to contact bankers'

associations and submit to the Committee on Shipping a list of those which had accepted the creation of a bank super-service. The Group also requested the Committee to examine ways to increase co-operation in investigating and prosecuting maritime fraud, and called on UNCTAD to continue developing a training programme and educational package on measures to combat maritime fraud.

Transport of dangerous goods

In 1985, work continued on harmonizing codes and regulations relating to the transport of hazardous substances such as liquefied gases, radioactive and toxic materials and explosives. The Committee of Experts on the Transport of Dangerous Goods, which did not meet in 1985, published the fourth revised edition of its recommendations.[21] New and amended recommendations had been approved by the Committee in 1984.[22]

In April 1985, the Secretary-General submitted a report to the Economic and Social Council[23] describing the work of the Committee and its subsidiary bodies during 1983-1984.

The Committee's Group of Rapporteurs and Group of Experts on Explosives met at Geneva from 5 to 16 August 1985 (thirty-third session) and from 16 to 20 September (twenty-fifth session), respectively. The Group of Rapporteurs considered such matters as the definition of divisions of classes as pertaining to volatile substances, a revised hazard precedence table, temperature control, test criteria and transport in tanks of organic peroxides, gas cylinders and environmentally hazardous substances.[24] The Group of Experts took up, among other things, revision of the official designations of transport for explosive materials and objects and the establishment of a glossary.[25]

In a May 1985 note[26] to the Council, the Secretary-General reiterated a proposal to enlarge the Committee by, *inter alia*, converting observers into full members, and to widen its decision-making base through broader geographical representation. The Committee, at its 1980, 1982 and 1984 sessions, had expressed the view that a wider decision-making base was desirable. The Council, in 1983, had requested the Secretary-General to examine the implications of enlarging the membership and widening the Committee's decision-making base.[27] Acting on a 22 May recommendation by its First (Economic) Committee, the Council took note of the Secretary-General's note in **decision 1985/123** of 28 May.

ECONOMIC AND SOCIAL COUNCIL ACTION

Also on 28 May, on the recommendation of its First Committee, the Council adopted without vote **resolution 1985/9**.

Work of the Committee of Experts on the Transport of Dangerous Goods

The Economic and Social Council,

Recalling its resolutions 468 G (XV) of 15 April 1953, 645 G (XXIII) of 26 April 1957, 994(XXXVI) of 16 December 1963, 1110(XL) of 7 March 1966, 1488(XLVIII) of 22 May 1970, 1744(LIV) of 4 May 1973, 1973(LIX) and 1974(LIX) of 30 July 1975, 2050(LXII) of 5 May 1977, 1979/42 of 11 May 1979, 1981/3 of 4 May 1981 and 1983/7 of 26 May 1983,

Noting the ever-increasing volume of dangerous goods in world-wide commerce and the rapid expansion of technology and innovation,

Bearing in mind the constant need to meet the growing concern for the protection of life and property through the safe transport of dangerous goods, while at the same time facilitating trade,

Aware that in order to achieve internationally harmonized laws, complete reliance is placed on the work of the Committee of Experts on the Transport of Dangerous Goods by the specialized agencies and other international organizations and by interested Member States which are committed to taking the recommendations of the Committee as a basis for the formulation of their requirements and regulations,

1. *Takes note* of the report of the Secretary-General on the work of the Committee of Experts on the Transport of Dangerous Goods in the biennium 1983-1984 and of the new and amended recommendations approved by the Committee for inclusion in its existing recommendations;

2. *Requests* the Secretary-General:

   (a) To incorporate in the existing recommendations of the Committee of Experts on the Transport of Dangerous Goods all of the new and amended recommendations approved by the Committee at its thirteenth session;

   (b) To publish the new and amended recommendations in all the official languages of the United Nations, in the most cost-effective manner, before the end of 1985 at the latest;

   (c) To circulate the new and amended recommendations immediately after their publication to the Governments of Member States, the specialized agencies, the International Atomic Energy Agency and the other international organizations concerned;

3. *Invites* all Governments, the specialized agencies, the International Atomic Energy Agency and the other international organizations concerned to transmit to the Secretary-General their views on the Committee's work, together with any comments they may wish to make on the amended recommendations;

4. *Invites* all interested Governments and the international organizations concerned, when developing appropriate codes and regulations, to take full account of the recommendations of the Committee of Experts on the Transport of Dangerous Goods;

5. *Recommends* that, in view of the increasing concern being expressed in many international and regional bodies about environmental considerations in respect of the transport of dangerous substances, in particular hazardous wastes, transport requirements concerning the protection of the environment should take into account, *inter alia*, the recommendations of the Committee of Experts;

6. *Also requests* the Secretary-General to make available, within existing resources, the staff necessary for the adequate servicing of the Committee of Experts, recalling that the request made by the Council in this regard in resolution 1983/7 has not yet been implemented;

7. *Further requests* the Secretary-General to prepare a comprehensive report, as requested by the Council in resolution 1983/7, for submission to the Council at its second regular session of 1986, on the participation of Member States, particularly developing countries, in the Committee of Experts on the Transport of Dangerous Goods, taking into account, *inter alia*, the desirability of appointing observers as full members in view of their active participation in its work over a continuous period and, at the same time, of widening the decision-making base of the Committee through broader geographical representation, and to propose ways and means of encouraging the participation of developing countries in the future work of the Committee.

Economic and Social Council resolution 1985/9

28 May 1985   Meeting 22   Adopted without vote

Approved by First Committee (E/1985/91) without vote, 22 May (meeting 9); draft by Vice-Chairman (E/1985/C.1/L.5), based on informal consultations on draft by Committee of Experts on Transport of Dangerous Goods (E/1985/21 & Corr.1); agenda item 12.

Stating its position after adoption of the text, the United States said the Committee's recommendations served as a basis for the formulation of requirements and regulations by Member States, specialized agencies and international organizations. It expressed support for broadening the geographical distribution of the Committee membership, as did the Federal Republic of Germany, the USSR and the United Kingdom. The United States noted, however, that the five seats allocated to developing countries remained vacant, and it hoped that the report called for in paragraph 7 would address all the reasons behind their non-participation and would provide a basis to encourage their participation. Participation in the Committee should be at an informed and technical level, the United Kingdom added. Through enlarging the membership, especially through participation of developing countries, more substantial and informed input could be provided, the Federal Republic of Germany believed. The United States insisted that the staff necessary for adequate servicing of the Committee should be made available within existing resources. The Federal Republic of Germany and the United Kingdom also hoped that the Secretariat would frame its proposals in such a way as to keep them within existing resources; the USSR understood that there were no financial implications as no such document had been presented. Argentina considered the transport of dangerous goods to be an issue of far-reaching importance and felt that the thinking of developing countries should be brought to bear on it; the report envisaged in paragraph 7 should take into account the full range of opinions.

REFERENCES

[1]*Review of Maritime Transport, 1985* (TD/B/C.4/299 & Corr.1), Sales No. E.86.II.D.3. [2]TD/B/301. [3]TD/RS/CONF/15 & Add.1 & Add.1/Corr.1. [4]TD/RS/CONF/19. [5]YUN 1982, p. 748, GA res. 37/209, 20 Dec. 1982. [6]YUN 1984, p. 551. [7]A/39/867. [8]TD/RS/CONF/19/Add.1 & Add.1/Corr.1. [9]TD/RS/CONF/18. [10]TD/B/C.4/295. [11]TD/B/C.4/ISL/52 & Corr.1. [12]YUN 1974, p. 460. [13]YUN 1983, p. 572. [14]*Multilateral Treaties Deposited with the Secretary-General: Status as at 31 December 1985* (ST/LEG/SER.E/4), Sales No. E.86.V.3. [15]TD/B/C.4/296. [16]TD/B/C.4/AC.4/5 & Corr.1. [17]TD/B/C.4/AC.4/6. [18]TD/B/C.4/AC.4/7. [19]TD/B/C.4/AC.4/8. [20]TD/B/C.4/AC.4/9. [21]*Recommendations on the Transport of Dangerous Goods* (ST/SG/AC.10/1/Rev.4), Sales No. E.85.VIII.3. [22]YUN 1984, p. 554. [23]E/1985/21 & Corr.1. [24]ST/SG/AC.10/C.2/21. [25]ST/SG/AC.10/C.1/14 & Add.1. [26]E/1985/37. [27]YUN 1983, p. 575, ESC res. 1983/7, 26 May 1983.

OTHER PUBLICATIONS

Catalogue of Studies in the Field of Transport, 1985, Sales No. E.85.II.A.10. *European Agreement Concerning the International Carriage of Dangerous Goods by Road (ADR) and Protocol of Signature*, vols. I-III (ECE/TRANS/60), Sales No. E.85.VIII.1. *Recommendations on the Transport of Dangerous Goods: Tests and Criteria* (ST/SG/AC.10/11), Sales No. E.85.VIII.2.

Tourism

As requested by the General Assembly in 1983,[1] the Secretary-General of the World Tourism Organization (WTO) reported[2] on progress made in implementing the Manila Declaration on World Tourism, adopted in 1980 by the World Tourism Conference,[3] and the Acapulco Document, adopted by the World Tourism Meeting at Acapulco, Mexico, in 1982.[4]

The holiday market was a new market which had existed in its current form for 35 years at most, and holidays were a vested right only of employees in the industrialized countries, totalling 1 billion people at most, the report stated. For the 3.6 billion people living in the developing countries or in the depressed areas of other countries, the holiday market was still tenuous and insubstantial. To develop that potential market, States should stimulate it by all appropriate means, focusing not exclusively on holiday travel but on movements of persons of all kinds, be it for reasons of business, trade, religion, health or family. The development of movements of persons and travel must be accompanied by development in other production sectors with which there existed an interdependence, and communications networks, travel routes and travel enterprises must be set up. WTO was expanding its aims to ensure that its work was not confined solely to holidays but embraced travel as a whole.

The responses of United Nations bodies and other international or regional intergovernmental organizations and NGOs dealing with tourism to WTO invitations for co-operation had been highly grati-

fying, the report said; WTO had a working and co-operation arrangement with the Economic Commission for Africa and was negotiating a similar arrangement with the Economic and Social Commission for Asia and the Pacific. Negotiation and co-operation agreements or working arrangements had been concluded with the United Nations, UNDP and a number of other United Nations organizations. By giving the movements of persons, travel and tourism the priority they deserved, they could become a consistent motive force in economic development.

The Economic and Social Council took note of the report in **decision 1985/198** of 26 July.

GENERAL ASSEMBLY ACTION

On 17 December, on the recommendation of the Second Committee, the General Assembly adopted without vote **resolution 40/172**.

World Tourism Organization

The General Assembly,

Recalling its resolutions 32/156 and 32/157 of 19 December 1977, 33/122 of 19 December 1978, 34/134 of 14 December 1979, 36/41 of 19 November 1981 and 38/146 of 19 December 1983,

1. *Takes note* of the report of the Secretary-General of the World Tourism Organization on the progress made in implementing the Manila Declaration and the Acapulco Document on World Tourism, and recognizes that the new approach of the World Tourism Organization, in which tourism is seen in the wider context of travel, can make a positive contribution to economic development;

2. *Invites* States to take that approach into account when formulating their travel policies and strategies, in accordance with their development plans;

3. *Requests* the United Nations Development Programme and other bodies of the United Nations system with an interest in this area to co-operate with the World Tourism Organization in accordance with the Manila Declaration and the Acapulco Document on World Tourism;

4. *Requests* the Secretary-General of the World Tourism Organization to submit to the General Assembly at its forty-second session, through the Economic and Social Council, a report on the progress made in implementing the present resolution and the relevant resolutions of the World Tourism Organization, particularly on the contribution of world tourism to regional development and the preservation of and respect for the cultural heritage of developing countries.

General Assembly resolution 40/172

17 December 1985   Meeting 119   Adopted without vote

Approved by Second Committee (A/40/1009/Add.1) without vote, 25 November (meeting 43); draft by Vice-Chairman (A/C.2/40/L.47), based on informal consultations on draft by Mexico, Morocco, Nepal, Philippines, Spain and Tunisia (A/C.2/40/L.27); agenda item 12.
Meeting numbers. GA 40th session: 2nd Committee 29, 43; plenary 119.

REFERENCES

[1]YUN 1983, p. 577, GA res. 38/146, 19 Dec. 1983. [2]A/40/363-E/1985/97. [3]YUN 1981, p. 573. [4]YUN 1983, p. 577.

Chapter VI

Industrial development

The United Nations Industrial Development Organization (UNIDO), established by the General Assembly in 1966[1] to promote the industrialization of developing countries, was converted into a United Nations specialized agency in 1985, after its Constitution entered into force on 21 June.

In August, the UNIDO General Conference, meeting at Vienna, Austria, as the principal legislative organ of the new agency, approved a draft relationship agreement with the United Nations, as prepared by the Economic and Social Council, and named Domingo L. Siazon, Jr., as UNIDO Director-General.

In December, the Assembly adopted the relationship agreement (resolution 40/180) and endorsed various administrative and financial aspects of the agreement (decision 40/463); it also appropriated a $24 million loan to the new agency to meet the expenses for 1986 (resolution 40/253 A).

As decided by the Assembly in 1979—that the status of UNIDO would change at the end of the year in which the General Conference met in a new capacity—UNIDO ceased to to exist as an Assembly organ as at 31 December 1985, prepared to assume its functions fully as a specialized agency beginning on 1 January 1986.

The Industrial Development Board—the principal advisory body of UNIDO—met at Vienna in two different capacities during the year: first as an organ of the Assembly (nineteenth session, May) and later as that of a specialized agency (first session, August, November, December). In May, it adopted a conclusion on the Industrial Development Decade for Africa (see Chapter VIII of this section) as well as 17 other conclusions dealing with, among other things, assistance to the Namibian people (see TRUSTEESHIP AND DECOLONIZATION, Chapter III) and the South African national liberation movements (see POLITICAL AND SECURITY QUESTIONS, Chapter V), and integration of women in development (see Chapter XIX of this section).

In its new capacity, the Board adopted five decisions in August and 33 more in November and December dealing with organizational, financial, administrative and legal matters.

Topics related to this chapter. Africa: aid programmes and inter-agency co-operation. Regional economic and social activities: implementation of the programme for the Industrial Development Decade for Africa. Energy: energy resources in industry. Science and technology: technology transfer. Environment: environment and industry. Women: women in development.

REFERENCE
[1]YUN 1966, p. 302, GA res. 2152(XXI), 17 Nov. 1966.

Conversion of UNIDO to a specialized agency

During 1985, UNIDO was converted in several stages into a specialized agency of the United Nations.[1]

A recommendation that the conversion take place was adopted by the Second General Conference of UNIDO in 1975 as part of the Lima Declaration and Plan of Action on Industrial Development and Co-operation.[2] Following a 1977 Assembly decision,[3] the United Nations Conference on the Establishment of UNIDO as a Specialized Agency adopted in 1979 a UNIDO Constitution, opening it for signature on 8 April 1979.[4] Subsequently, the Assembly approved transitional arrangements in 1979,[5] and recommended, in 1982,[6] the process of consultations among States to determine the date of the Constitution's entry into force.

Those consultations were concluded on 10 June 1985 in New York; the Constitution entered into force, in accordance with its article 25, on 21 June, when 80 States which had deposited instruments of ratification, acceptance or approval agreed on its entry and so notified the Secretary-General as depositary.

As at 31 December 1985, 140 States had signed the UNIDO Constitution as a specialized agency; 138 had ratified, accepted, approved or acceded to it.[7]

The following States had adhered to the Constitution (italics indicate 1985 action):

Afghanistan, Algeria, *Angola*, Argentina, Australia, Austria, Bangladesh, Barbados, Belgium, Benin, Bhutan, Bolivia, *Botswana*, Brazil, *Bulgaria*, Burkina Faso, Burundi, *Byelorussian SSR*, Cameroon, Canada, Cape Verde, Central African Republic, Chile, China, Colombia, *Comoros*, Congo, Cuba, Cyprus, *Czechoslovakia*, Democratic People's Republic of Korea, Democratic Yemen, Denmark, Dominica, Dominican Republic, Ecuador, Egypt, Equatorial Guinea,

Ethiopia, Fiji, Finland, France, Gabon, *German Democratic Republic*, Germany, Federal Republic of, Ghana, Greece, Guatemala, Guinea, Guinea-Bissau, Guyana, Haiti, Honduras, Hungary, India, Indonesia, *Iran*, Iraq, Ireland, Israel, *Italy*, Ivory Coast, Jamaica, Japan, Jordan, Kenya, Kuwait, Lao People's Democratic Republic, Lebanon, Lesotho, Libyan Arab Jamahiriya, Luxembourg, Madagascar, Malawi, Malaysia, Mali, Malta, Mauritania, Mauritius, Mexico, *Mongolia*, *Morocco*, Mozambique, Nepal, Netherlands, *New Zealand*, Nicaragua, Niger, Nigeria, Norway, Oman, Pakistan, Panama, Paraguay, Peru, Philippines, *Poland*, Portugal, *Qatar*, Republic of Korea, Romania, Rwanda, *Saint Christopher and Nevis*, Saint Lucia, *Sao Tome and Principe*, *Saudi Arabia*, Senegal, Seychelles, Sierra Leone, Somalia, Spain, Sri Lanka, Sudan, Suriname, Swaziland, Sweden, Switzerland, Syrian Arab Republic, Thailand, Togo, Trinidad and Tobago, Tunisia, Turkey, Uganda, *Ukrainian SSR*, *USSR*, United Arab Emirates, United Kingdom, United Republic of Tanzania, United States, Uruguay, Venezuela, Viet Nam, Yemen, Yugoslavia, Zaire, Zambia, *Zimbabwe*.

Seven States had signed but not formally adhered to the Constitution as at 31 December (italics indicate 1985 action): Antigua and Barbuda, Chad, Costa Rica, Djibouti, El Salvador, Liberia, *Papua New Guinea*.

Communications. In May and June, the Secretary-General received communications from Bulgaria,[8] the Byelorussian SSR,[9] the German Democratic Republic,[10] Mongolia,[11] the Ukrainian SSR[12] and the USSR,[13] on their ratification or acceptance of the UNIDO Constitution and on what they expected of the new agency.

UN/UNIDO Agreement

In 1985, UNIDO's Industrial Development Board and the General Conference held their first sessions—comprising several segments starting in August—in their new capacity as principal organs of a newly-emerging specialized agency.

The 53-member Board (first session, Vienna, 13-17 August (part one),[14] 4-15 November (part two),[15] and 10 and 11 December (resumed part two)[16]) established a committee, on 17 August, to negotiate with a corresponding body of the Economic and Social Council (see below) a relationship agreement between the United Nations and UNIDO; it also recommended that the UNIDO General Conference authorize the provisional application of the agreement.

The new UNIDO General Conference (first session, Vienna, 12-17 August (part one) and 9-13 December (part two))—open to all UNIDO members—authorized the provisional application of the draft agreement and affirmed the conclusions of the 1983 formal meeting on the conversion of UNIDO,[17] particularly concerning the programme of work, financial questions, and

secretariat structure and staffing of the new UNIDO. It also took note of a draft relationship agreement between the United Nations Development Programme (UNDP) and UNIDO, prepared by the secretariat, and requested the UNIDO Director-General to establish a final text with the UNDP Administrator.

The Secretary-General transmitted three notes concerning the United Nations/UNIDO relationship agreement to the Economic and Social Council's Committee on Negotiations with Intergovernmental Agencies (New York, 14 and 18-20 November).[18] By one, he forwarded the text and an analysis of the draft agreement.[19] By another,[20] he transmitted a 10 September letter from the Director-General of the World Intellectual Property Organization (WIPO), in which the latter declared that WIPO was not bound by those provisions in the draft agreement attempting to entrust tasks to UNIDO that affected other specialized agencies. By a third note,[21] he transmitted a request by the UNIDO Director-General that the Council Committee consider the agreement as approved by the UNIDO Committee on the Negotiation of a Relationship Agreement with the United Nations, and the texts of two Board decisions relating to the agreement.

ECONOMIC AND SOCIAL COUNCIL ACTION

In 1985, the Economic and Social Council acted twice on the relationship agreement, authorizing its subsidiary body in July to negotiate with a UNIDO counterpart, and approving the draft text in December.

On 26 July, the Council adopted **resolution 1985/74** without vote.

Arrangements for the negotiation of an agreement between the United Nations and the United Nations Industrial Development Organization

The Economic and Social Council,

Recalling General Assembly resolution 34/96 of 13 December 1979, in which the Assembly requested the Council to arrange for the negotiation with the United Nations Industrial Development Organization of an agreement to constitute it as a specialized agency in accordance with Articles 57 and 63 of the Charter of the United Nations,

Recalling also Council decision 1983/105 of 4 February 1983, in which it authorized the President of the Council to appoint from among the States members of the Council, in consultation with the Chairmen of the regional groups, the members of the Committee on Negotiations with Intergovernmental Agencies,

1. *Takes note* of the appointment by the President of the Economic and Social Council of the members of the Committee on Negotiations with Intergovernmental Agencies;

2. *Authorizes* the Committee on Negotiations with Intergovernmental Agencies to meet at an appropriate time to negotiate with the United Nations Industrial Development Organization a relationship agreement between

the United Nations and the United Nations Industrial Development Organization;

3. *Requests* the Secretary-General to transmit directly to the Committee on Negotiations with Intergovernmental Agencies relevant proposals regarding the relationship agreement;

4. *Requests* the President of the Council, in consultation with the members of the Bureau, to convene, if necessary, a resumed session of the Economic and Social Council to consider the outcome of the work of the Committee with a view to taking appropriate action;

5. *Invites* the Committee on Conferences to make appropriate arrangements, within existing resources, for the meetings of the Committee on Negotiations with Intergovernmental Agencies.

Economic and Social Council resolution 1985/74

26 July 1985   Meeting 52   Adopted without vote

Draft by President (E/1985/L.59); agenda item 12.

At its resumed second regular session of 1985, on 12 December, the Council adopted **resolution 1985/81** without vote.

Agreement between the United Nations and the United Nations Industrial Development Organization

The Economic and Social Council,

Recalling paragraph 11 of General Assembly resolution 34/96 of 13 December 1979, as well as Council decision 1983/105 of 4 February 1983 and resolution 1985/74 of 26 July 1985,

Having considered the text of the draft agreement negotiated by its Committee on Negotiations with Intergovernmental Agencies and the Industrial Development Board Committee on the Negotiation of a Relationship Agreement with the United Nations for the purpose of bringing the United Nations Industrial Development Organization into relationship with the United Nations in accordance with Article 57 and paragraph 1 of Article 63 of the Charter of the United Nations,

Aware that the text of the draft agreement was approved by the Industrial Development Board on 10 December 1985,

1. *Approves* the Agreement between the United Nations and the United Nations Industrial Development Organization, the text of which is set forth in the annex to the present resolution;

2. *Recommends* to the General Assembly that it approve the Agreement at the earliest opportunity;

3. *Decides*, in accordance with paragraph 11 of General Assembly resolution 34/96 and article 21, paragraph *(b)*, of the Agreement, that the Agreement shall apply provisionally pending its entry into force upon the approval of the General Assembly and of the General Conference of the United Nations Industrial Development Organization.

[For the text of the annex, see annex to Assembly resolution 40/180 below]

Economic and Social Council resolution 1985/81

12 December 1985   Meeting 53   Adopted without vote

Draft by President (E/1985/L.60); agenda item 12.

GENERAL ASSEMBLY ACTION

On 17 December, on the recommendation of the Second (Economic and Financial) Committee, the General Assembly adopted **resolution 40/180** without vote.

Agreement between the United Nations and the United Nations Industrial Development Organization

The General Assembly,

Recalling paragraph 11 of its resolution 34/96 of 13 December 1979,

Having considered Economic and Social Council resolution 1985/81 of 12 December 1985, and the draft agreement annexed thereto, intended to bring the United Nations Industrial Development Organization into relationship with the United Nations in accordance with Articles 57 and 63 of the Charter of the United Nations,

Approves the Agreement between the United Nations and the United Nations Industrial Development Organization set forth in the annex to the present resolution.

ANNEX
Agreement between the United Nations and the United Nations Industrial Development Organization

Preamble

In consideration of the provisions of Article 57 of the Charter of the United Nations and of article 18 of the Constitution of the United Nations Industrial Development Organization, the United Nations and the United Nations Industrial Development Organization agree as follows:

Article 1
Recognition

The United Nations recognizes the United Nations Industrial Development Organization (hereinafter called the "Organization") as a specialized agency within the United Nations system as defined in its Constitution and as being responsible for taking appropriate action in accordance with its Constitution, as well as with any treaties and agreements administered by it.

Article 2
Co-ordination and co-operation

In its relations with the United Nations, its organs and the agencies of the United Nations system, the Organization recognizes the co-ordinating role, as well as the comprehensive responsibilities in promoting economic and social development, of the General Assembly and the Economic and Social Council under the Charter of the United Nations. The Organization, in exercise of its central co-ordinating role in the field of industrial development, recognizes the need for effective co-ordination and co-operation with the United Nations, its organs and the agencies within the United Nations system. Accordingly, the Organization agrees to co-operate with the United Nations in whatever measure may be necessary to effect the required co-ordination of policies and activities. The Organization agrees further to participate in the work of any United Nations bodies which have been established or may be established for the purpose of facilitating such co-operation and co-ordination, in particular through membership in the Administrative Committee on Co-ordination.

Article 3
Reciprocal representation

(a) Representatives of the United Nations shall be invited to attend the sessions of all the bodies of the Organiza-

tion and all such other meetings convened by the Organization, and to participate, without the right to vote, in the deliberations of such bodies and at such meetings. Written statements presented by the United Nations shall be distributed by the Organization to its members.

(b) Representatives of the Organization shall be invited to attend meetings and to participate, without the right to vote and in accordance with the relevant rules of procedure, in the deliberations of the Economic and Social Council, its commissions and committees, of the Main Committees and other organs of the General Assembly, of the Governing Council of the United Nations Development Programme, and of the conferences and meetings of the United Nations, with respect to items of the agenda relating to industrial development matters within the scope of the activities of the Organization and other matters of mutual interest. Written statements presented by the Organization shall be distributed by the Secretariat of the United Nations to the members of the above-mentioned bodies, in accordance with the relevant rules of procedure.

(c) Representatives of the Organization shall be invited, for purposes of consultation, to attend meetings of the General Assembly when matters as defined in paragraph *(b)* above are under discussion.

Article 4
Proposal of agenda items

(a) After such preliminary consultation as may be necessary, the United Nations may propose items for consideration by the Organization. The Organization shall arrange for the inclusion of such items in the provisional agenda of its General Conference, Industrial Development Board, Programme and Budget Committee, or any other subsidiary body, as appropriate.

(b) After such preliminary consultation as may be necessary, the Organization may propose items for consideration by the United Nations. The United Nations shall arrange for the inclusion of such items in the provisional agenda of the Economic and Social Council or, as appropriate and in accordance with the relevant rules of procedure, of other organs or bodies of the United Nations.

Article 5
Recommendations of the United Nations

(a) Having regard to the obligation of the United Nations to promote the objectives set forth in Article 55 of the Charter of the United Nations and the function and power of the Economic and Social Council, under Article 62 of the Charter, to make or initiate studies and reports with respect to international economic, social, cultural, educational, health and related matters and to make recommendations concerning these matters to the specialized agencies concerned, and having regard also to the responsibility of the United Nations, under Articles 58 and 63 of the Charter, to make recommendations for the co-ordination of the policies and activities of such specialized agencies, the Organization agrees to arrange for the submission, as soon as possible, to the appropriate organ of the Organization, of all formal recommendations which the United Nations may make to it.

(b) The Organization agrees to enter into consultation with the United Nations upon request with respect to such recommendations, and in due course to report to the United Nations on the action taken by the Organization or by its members to give effect to such recommendations, or on the other results of their consideration.

Article 6
Annual report of the Organization, information and documents

(a) The Organization shall submit to the United Nations an annual report on its activities.

(b) Subject to such arrangements as may be necessary for the safeguarding of confidential material, full and prompt exchange of appropriate information and documents shall be made between the United Nations and the Organization.

Article 7
Statistical services

(a) The United Nations and the Organization agree to strive for the maximum co-operation, the elimination of all undesirable duplication between them and the most efficient use of their technical personnel in their respective collection, analysis, publication and dissemination of statistical information. They agree to combine their efforts to secure the greatest possible usefulness and utilization of statistical information and to minimize the burden placed upon Governments and other organizations from which such information may be collected.

(b) The Organization recognizes the United Nations as the central agency for the collection, analysis, publication, standardization and improvement of statistics serving the general purposes of international organizations.

(c) The United Nations recognizes the Organization as an appropriate agency for the collection, analysis, publication, standardization and improvement of statistics within its sphere, without prejudice to the right of the United Nations, its organs and other agencies within the United Nations system to concern themselves with such statistics in so far as they may be essential for their own purposes or for the improvement of statistics throughout the world.

(d) The United Nations shall, in consultation with the Organization and other agencies within the United Nations system, develop administrative instruments and procedures through which effective statistical co-operation may be secured between the United Nations, the Organization and other agencies within the United Nations system brought into relationship with it.

(e) It is recognized as desirable that the collection of statistical information should not be duplicated by the United Nations or any of the agencies within the United Nations system whenever it is practicable for any of them to utilize information or materials which another may have available.

(f) In order to collect statistical information for general use, it is agreed that data supplied to the Organization for incorporation in its basic statistical series or special reports should, so far as is practicable, be made available to the United Nations on request.

(g) It is agreed that data supplied to the United Nations for incorporation in its basic statistical series or special reports should, so far as is practicable and appropriate, be made available to the Organization upon request.

Article 8
Assistance to the United Nations

The Organization shall, in accordance with the Charter of the United Nations and the Constitution of the Organization, as well as any treaties and agreements administered by it, co-operate with the United Nations by furnishing to it such information, special reports and studies, and by rendering such assistance to it, as the United Nations may request.

Article 9
Technical assistance
The United Nations and the Organization undertake to work together in the provision of technical assistance in the field of industrial development. In particular, they undertake to avoid undesirable duplication of activities and services and agree to take such measures as may be required to achieve effective co-ordination within the framework of existing co-ordinating machinery in the field of technical assistance, taking into account the respective roles and responsibilities of the United Nations and the Organization under their constitutive instruments, as well as those of other organizations participating in technical assistance activities. To this end, the Organization recognizes the overall responsibilities of the resident co-ordinators for operational activities for development, as formulated in the relevant General Assembly resolutions, and agrees to give consideration to the common use of available services as far as is practicable. The United Nations will make available to the Organization its administrative services in this field for use as requested.

Article 10
Transfer of technology
The Organization agrees to co-operate within the field of its competence with the United Nations and its organs, particularly the United Nations Conference on Trade and Development and the United Nations Development Programme, as well as the agencies within the United Nations system, in promoting and facilitating the transfer of technology to and among developing countries in such a manner as to assist the Organization in attaining the objectives set forth in the Constitution.

Article 11
Trust, Non-Self-Governing and other Territories
The Organization agrees to co-operate within the field of its competence with the United Nations in giving effect to the principles and obligations set forth in Chapters XI, XII and XIII of the Charter of the United Nations and other internationally recognized principles and obligations regarding colonial countries and peoples, with regard to matters affecting the well-being and development of the peoples of the Trust, Non-Self-Governing and other Territories.

Article 12
International Court of Justice
(a) The Organization agrees to furnish any information which may be requested by the International Court of Justice in pursuance of Article 34 of the Statute of the Court.

(b) The General Assembly of the United Nations authorizes the Organization to request advisory opinions of the International Court of Justice on legal questions arising within the scope of the Organization's activities other than questions concerning the mutual relationships between the Organization and the United Nations or other agencies within the United Nations system.

(c) Such requests may be addressed to the International Court of Justice by the General Conference or by the Industrial Development Board of the Organization.

(d) When requesting the International Court of Justice to give an advisory opinion, the Organization shall inform the Economic and Social Council of the request.

Article 13
Relations with other agencies within the United Nations system
The Organization shall inform the Economic and Social Council of matters of inter-agency concern within its competence, and of any formal agreement on such matters to be concluded between the Organization and another agency within the United Nations system.

Article 14
Administrative co-operation
(a) The United Nations and the Organization recognize the desirability of co-operation in administrative matters of mutual interest.

(b) Accordingly, the United Nations and the Organization undertake to consult together, and with other agencies concerned within the United Nations system, from time to time concerning these matters, particularly the most efficient and harmonized use of facilities, staff and services and appropriate methods of avoiding the establishment and operation of competitive or overlapping facilities and services with a view to securing as much uniformity in these matters as possible.

(c) The consultations referred to in this article shall be utilized to establish the most equitable manner in which any special services or assistance furnished, on request, by the Organization to the United Nations or by the United Nations to the Organization shall be financed.

(d) The consultations referred to in this article shall also explore the possibility of continuing or establishing common facilities or services in specific areas, including the possibility of one organization providing such facilities or services to one or several other organizations, and establish the most equitable manner in which such facilities or services shall be financed.

Article 15
Regional and branch offices
Any regional or branch offices which the Organization may establish shall closely co-operate with the regional or branch offices which the United Nations has established or may establish, in particular the offices of the regional commissions and of the resident co-ordinators.

Article 16
Personnel arrangements
(a) The United Nations and the Organization agree to develop, in the interests of uniform standards of international employment and to the extent feasible, common personnel standards, methods and arrangements designed to avoid unjustified differences in terms and conditions of employment, to avoid competition in recruitment of personnel, and to facilitate any mutually desirable and beneficial interchange of personnel. For this purpose the Organization agrees to accept the Statute of the International Civil Service Commission.

(b) The United Nations and the Organization agree:

(i) To consult together from time to time concerning matters of mutual interest relating to the terms and conditions of employment of the officers and staff, with a view to securing as much uniformity in these matters as may be feasible;

(ii) To co-operate in the interchange of personnel when desirable, on a temporary or a permanent basis, making due provision for the retention of seniority and pension rights;

(iii) That the Organization shall participate in the United Nations Joint Staff Pension Fund in accordance with the Regulations of the Fund and shall accept the jurisdiction of the United Nations Administrative Tribunal in matters involving applications alleging non-observance of these Regulations;

(iv) To co-operate with the agencies in the United Nations system in the establishment and operation of suitable machinery for the settlement of disputes arising in connection with the employment of personnel and related matters.

(c) The United Nations and the Organization agree to co-operate fully in ensuring that, to the extent possible, all members of the staff of the United Nations who were assigned to the United Nations Industrial Development Organization when it was a United Nations organ should be offered appointments by the Organization that preserve their acquired rights and contractual status.

(d) The terms and conditions under which any facilities or services of the Organization or the United Nations in connection with the matters referred to in this article are to be extended to the other shall, where necessary, be the subject of complementary agreements concluded for this purpose.

Article 17
Budgetary and financial matters

(a) The Organization recognizes the desirability of establishing close budgetary and financial relationships with the United Nations in order that the administrative operations of the United Nations and the agencies within the United Nations system shall be carried out in the most efficient and economical manner possible, and that the maximum measure of co-ordination and uniformity with respect to these operations shall be secured.

(b) The Organization agrees to accept the Statute of the Joint Inspection Unit.

(c) The Organization agrees to conform, as far as may be practicable and appropriate, to standard practices and forms recommended by the United Nations.

(d) Financial and budgetary arrangements entered into between the United Nations and the Organization shall be approved in accordance with their respective constitutive instruments.

(e) In the preparation of the budget of the Organization, the Director-General of the Organization shall consult with the Secretary-General of the United Nations with a view to achieving, in so far as is practicable, uniformity in presentation of the budgets of the United Nations and of the agencies within the United Nations system for the purposes of providing a basis for comparison of the several budgets.

(f) The Organization agrees to transmit its proposed budgets to the United Nations not later than when the said budgets are transmitted to its members so as to enable the General Assembly of the United Nations to examine them and make recommendations, in accordance with paragraph 3 of Article 17 of the Charter of the United Nations.

(g) Representatives of the Organization shall be entitled to participate, without vote, in the deliberations of the General Assembly or any committee thereof established by it, at all times when the budget of the

Organization or general administrative or financial questions concerning the Organization are under consideration.

Article 18
United Nations laissez-passer

Officials of the Organization shall be entitled, in accordance with such special arrangements as may be concluded between the Secretary-General of the United Nations and the Director-General of the Organization, to use the laissez-passer of the United Nations.

Article 19
Implementation of the Agreement

The Secretary-General of the United Nations and the Director-General of the Organization may enter into such supplementary arrangements for the implementation of this Agreement as may be found desirable.

Article 20
Amendment and revision

This Agreement may be amended or revised by agreement between the United Nations and the Organization and any such amendment or revision agreed upon between the Economic and Social Council of the United Nations and the Industrial Development Board of the Organization shall come into force on approval by the General Assembly of the United Nations and the General Conference of the Organization.

Article 21
Entry into force

(a) This Agreement shall enter into force on its approval by the General Assembly of the United Nations and the General Conference of the Organization.

(b) Without prejudice to the provision of paragraph (a) of this article, the present Agreement shall be applied provisionally when it has been approved by the Economic and Social Council upon authorization of the General Assembly and by the Industrial Development Board of the Organization upon authorization of the General Conference of the Organization.

General Assembly resolution 40/180

17 December 1985   Meeting 119   Adopted without vote

Approved by Second Committee (A/40/1009/Add.2) without vote, 13 December (meeting 51); draft orally proposed by Chairman; agenda item 12.
Meeting numbers. GA 40th session: 2nd Committee 36, 39, 48-51; plenary 119.

Budgetary aspects of the conversion. In a November 1985 report to the Assembly,[22] the Secretary-General reviewed the transitional measures contemplated by the Assembly in 1979[5] for the UNIDO conversion and their financial implications to the United Nations budget, including the arrangements for the provision of conference and joint services at the Vienna International Centre where a number of United Nations and related offices were located (see ADMINISTRATIVE AND BUDGETARY QUESTIONS, Chapter IV). He concluded that the conversion would result in a reduction of $68,850,300 in the 1986-1987 United Nations budget. At the same time, he proposed a $24 million loan to UNIDO, recalling that the Assembly in 1979[5] had authorized him, in consultation with the Advisory Committee on Administrative and Budgetary Questions (ACABQ), to lend to the new agency, until it received sufficient contributions or advances from its members, an amount not exceeding one half of the appropriations for UNIDO (as an Assembly organ) for the last calendar year of its existence, to meet its initial operations expenses for the calendar year following that in which its General Conference was first convened, and to take the necessary budgetary measures.

Having studied the Secretary-General's report, ACABQ[23] informed the Assembly in December that it supported his proposed loan; in addition, its recommendations based on analysis of the Secretary-General's proposals on conference services and new posts would result in increasing by $2,361,800 the overall net reduction proposed by him in the United Nations budget.

On 18 December, the Assembly took two decisions on the recommendation of the Fifth (Administrative and Budgetary) Committee. In one, it approved administrative and financial aspects of the draft Agreement between the United Nations and UNIDO (**decision 40/463**). In the other, it approved the loan (**resolution 40/253 A**), following a 10 December recommendation to that effect by the Fifth Committee—by a recorded vote of 103 to 9 (Bulgaria, Byelorussian SSR, Czechoslovakia, German Democratic Republic, Hungary, Mongolia, Ukrainian SSR, USSR, United States) (see also ADMINISTRATIVE AND BUDGETARY QUESTIONS, Chapter I).

Austria felt the loan should be seen in the context of the United Nations financial emergency. While agreeing to the loan, Japan questioned whether a loan of that magnitude was justified. The United States declared it unacceptable that countries would be assessed twice for the loan, as United Nations Member States and again as UNIDO members. The United Kingdom asserted that the loan should be repaid in full by the end of 1987.

REFERENCES

[1]IDB.2/10. [2]YUN 1975, p. 473. [3]YUN 1977, p. 501, GA res. 32/167, 19 Dec. 1977. [4]YUN 1979, p. 618. [5]*Ibid.*, p. 622, GA res. 34/96, 13 Dec. 1979. [6]YUN 1982, p. 760, GA res. 37/213, 20 Dec. 1982. [7]*Multilateral Treaties Deposited with the Secretary-General: Status as at 31 December 1985* (ST/LEG/SER.E/4), Sales No. E.86.V.3. [8]A/40/366-E/1985/123. [9]A/40/384-E/1985/127. [10]A/40/340-E/1985/118. [11]A/40/534-E/1985/159. [12]A/40/374-E/1985/126. [13]A/40/347-E/1985/121. [14]UNIDO/IDB.1/6 & Corr.1. [15]UNIDO/GC.1/7 & Corr.1. [16]UNIDO/GC.1/7/Add.1 & Add.1/Corr.3. [17]YUN 1983, p. 583. [18]E/1985/161. [19]E/C.1/1985/2 & Add.1,2. [20]E/C.1/1985/3. [21]E/C.1/1985/1. [22]A/C.5/40/48. [23]A/40/7/Add.14.

Programme and finances of UNIDO

Programme policy

In its continuing effort to promote the industrial development of developing countries, UNIDO activities in 1985 included training programmes and fellowships, research and studies, statistics collection and holding Consultations on a number of industries, taking into account the International Development Strategy for the Third United Nations Development Decade (the 1980s)[1] and related Assembly decisions and recommendations. In 1985, 126 project evaluation reports were prepared; combined with tripartite reviews—conducted by UNIDO, UNDP and the recipient Government—they provided grounds on which to evaluate the experience gained and facilitate management decisions on projects.

At its nineteenth session (Vienna, 13-31 May),[2] the Industrial Development Board recalled a 1984 General Assembly agreement[3] on the need for UNIDO to have adequate resources for full implementation of its mandates, and observed that the proposed programme budget for 1986-1987 needed to be readjusted, taking into account the priorities established at the Fourth General Conference of UNIDO[4] (see below) and previously. It reaffirmed the following priority areas for UNIDO activities: energy-related and other industrial technology, industrial production, human resources development, special measures for least developed countries (LDCs), the System of Consultations, the Industrial Development Decade for Africa (IDDA) (the 1980s), and industrial co-operation among developing countries. It requested the relevant organs to consider including as priority areas rural development, industrial restructuring and redeployment, and integration of women in industrial development.

In other action, the Board emphasized the need to strengthen and improve the Senior Industrial Development Field Adviser (SIDFA) programme, recommended that UNIDO after its conversion consider evaluating the programme so as to enhance the accruing benefits, and invited the UNDP Governing Council to finance the maximum number of SIDFA posts in 1986-1987. It also adopted the report of its Permanent Committee on the work of its 1984 session,[5] which dealt with the proposed programme of work for 1986-1987, the SIDFA programme, co-ordination, evaluation, and control and limitation of documentation.

Under another Board conclusion, preliminary work began on topics for possible future Consultations in 1988-1989 (see also p. 603). Among the industries considered were food processing, building material, capital goods, fertilizer, small- and medium-scale enterprises, electronics, wood and wood products, pesticides, and offshore industry. In that context, a UNIDO expert group meeting was convened (Vienna, 17 and 18 December) with the Development Centre of the Organisation for Economic Co-operation and Development on the mobilization and allocation of domestic financial resources in developing countries.

The 27-member Programme and Budget Committee—a subsidiary organ of UNIDO as a specialized agency—held its first session at Vienna from 30 September to 11 October and on 9 December.

On 25 July, by **decision 1985/169**, the Economic and Social Council took note of the report of the Industrial Development Board on its nineteenth session.[2]

GENERAL ASSEMBLY ACTION

In 1985, the General Assembly took note of the Secretary-General's note on the implementation of the IDDA programme (**decision 40/435**) (see Chapter VIII of this section). Other related Assembly action which had bearing on UNIDO activities included: implementation of the Substantial New Programme of Action for the 1980s for LDCs (**resolution 40/205**); the critical economic situation in Africa (**40/40**); development of the energy resources of developing countries (**40/208**); co-ordination in the United Nations system (**40/177**); operational activities for development (**40/211**); and administrative and budgetary co-ordination of the United Nations with the specialized agencies and the International Atomic Energy Agency (**40/250**).

Co-ordination in the UN system

As in previous years, UNIDO maintained programme co-ordination with other United Nations organizations and specialized agencies.

In April 1985, the Secretary-General submitted to the Committee for Programme and Co-ordination (CPC) (twenty-fifth session, New York, 29 April–1 June), at its 1984 request,[6] a report on the co-ordination and rationalization of UNIDO activities,[7] in which he concluded that current mechanisms available to UNIDO appeared adequate in avoiding duplication of work and promoting co-operation, both internally and with others in the United Nations system, in programme planning and implementation.

Reviewing the report, CPC[8] regretted that the document had failed to present the views of the Office for Programme Planning and Co-ordination on the topic, recommended rationalizing UNIDO's external relations activities so as to release resources for higher priority activities, and suggested better co-ordination of UNIDO activities with those of the United Nations Conference on Trade and Development (UNCTAD) relating to the transfer of technology. It also recommended that a cross-organizational programme analysis of all industrial development activities in the United Nations system should be undertaken at an appropriate time.

Follow-up to the Fourth General Conference of UNIDO

In March 1985, the UNIDO Executive Director reported to the Industrial Development Board on activities undertaken in 1984/85[9] as follow-up to the Fourth General Conference, held in 1984.[4] The activities focused on human resources development, strengthening of scientific and technological capacities in developing countries, energy and industrialization, domestic industrial processing of raw materials, industrial policies and measures for rural development and self-sufficiency in food supplies, UNIDO's co-ordinating role in the United Nations system on industrial development, assistance to Lebanon for reconstructing its industrial sector, and mobilization of financial resources for industrial development.

Field projects in human resources development in industry included training, and particular attention was given to the needs of African countries within the IDDA programme. In scientific and technological development, two expert meetings were held at Vienna, as pilot activities, on the protein enrichment of cassava (11-13 March) and on the manufacture of improved wood-burning stoves (18-20 March); a roster was being prepared of high-level scientists and technologists in micro-electronics, biotechnology and energy for an international referral system. Assistance in the energy sector was provided for the development of integrated national plans, a programme in Africa, investment promotion in the energy capital goods sector, and the repair and maintenance of those goods. Processing of domestic raw materials was emphasized in agrobased industries, and efforts were made to reduce developing countries' dependency on imported raw materials, for example, by creating opportunities for industries to be interlinked or by introducing mobile facilities to generate industrial skills in rural areas.

The UNIDO secretariat reviewed information regarding industrial development activities in other organizations and agencies of the United Nations system. It continued to participate in meetings of the Inter-Agency Working Group on Assistance to Lebanon; a proposal for creating a feasibility study unit within the Lebanese Ministry of Industry and Petroleum had been elaborated and was being considered for UNDP financing.

In another follow-up report[10] to the Conference, the Executive Director discussed the preliminary findings of UNIDO studies on the social aspects of industrialization, based on a set of North-South socio-economic indicators, reviewed the developing countries' experience, examined the situation in African LDCs, assessed the interaction of industrialization and social development, and presented some hypotheses concerning the role of social development and infrastructure in determining the ability of developing countries to respond positively to external shocks and uncertainty.

Taking note of the reports, the Industrial Development Board, on 31 May, expressed concern at the insufficient rate of growth in the share of developing countries in world industrial production, and requested the Executive Director to continue implementing the Conference decisions and the 1984 General Assembly resolution[11] on world industrial restructuring and redeployment. The Board also suggested that international financial organizations consider allocating an adequate share of their resources to industrial development, invited the Assembly to continue consideration of a draft resolution on mobilization of financial resources (see p. 606), and reiterated a request for assistance to Lebanon for reconstruction of its industrial sector.

No action was taken on a proposal made by the Executive Director in 1981[12] to establish an international bank for industrial development.

Financial questions

UN Industrial Development Fund

In a March 1985 report to the Industrial Development Board,[13] the Executive Director stated that total pledges to the United Nations Industrial Development Fund (UNIDF), since it became operational in 1978, amounted to $91.6 million.

Pledged contributions for 1985 totalled $15.8 million, of which $14.9 million was collected during the year. The number of projects approved was 171 in 1985, valued at $14.5 million. Total expenditures stood at $12.3 million. Pledges for 1986 and

1987 were estimated at $15 million and $16 million, respectively.

Projects amounting to $12.65 million (excluding programme support costs) were approved as follows:[14] Africa, including African Arab States, $2.78 million (22 per cent); the Americas, $1.83 million (14.4 per cent); Arab States, excluding African Arab States, $300,000 (2.4 per cent); Asia and the Pacific, $1.21 million (9.5 per cent); and global and interregional, $6.54 million (51.7 per cent). To ensure the maximum impact of the Fund's limited resources, emphasis continued to be placed on innovative projects of a pilot nature which would have a global, interregional or subregional impact.

On 31 May, the Industrial Development Board[2] took note of the Executive Director's report, approved the proposed programme for 1986 and plan for 1986-1987, except for the proposal to earmark a small component within the Fund's general-purpose segment for disaster relief assistance, and agreed to continue to delegate authority to the Executive Director to approve projects for financing in 1986 and 1987. The Board called on all countries, particularly the developed ones, to contribute so as to enable the Fund to reach the desirable annual funding level of $50 million, as endorsed by the General Assembly in 1977.[15]

The Assembly, in **resolution 40/238**, accepted the report of the Board of Auditors on the Fund for 1984.[16]

CONTRIBUTIONS TO THE UN INDUSTRIAL DEVELOPMENT FUND, 1985 AND 1986

(as at 31 December 1985; in US dollar equivalent)

Country	1985 payment	1986 pledge	Country	1985 payment	1986 pledge
Afghanistan	—	1,500	Fiji	1,083	1,019
Algeria	80,000	—	France	894,737	1,568,627
Argentina	90,900	—	German Democratic Republic	102,577	528,000
Australia	111,261	137,931	Germany, Federal Republic of	2,231,421	2,800,000
Austria	611,224	790,960	Greece	36,000	36,000
Bangladesh	(5,355)	2,420	Guatemala	5,000	10,000
Barbados	2,000	—	Guinea	108,600	—
Belgium	470,588	470,588	Haiti	10,000	—
Bhutan	1,200	1,450	Honduras	1,000	—
Bolivia	—	1,000	Hungary	110,994	134,021
Botswana	5,535	—	India	1,000,000	1,000,000
Brazil	30,000	15,000	Indonesia	50,000	50,000
Bulgaria	203,046	100,000	Iran	—	115,808
Burma	1,000	—	Iraq	161,290	—
Cameroon	6,132	—	Italy	2,274,053	2,332,362
Chile	10,000	10,000	Ivory Coast	70,991	—
China	723,088	379,718	Japan	1,117,842	155,948
Colombia	4,275	5,700	Kenya	7,808	14,110
Congo	10,655	—	Kuwait	75,000	75,000
Costa Rica	7,584	—	Lao People's Democratic Republic	1,500	1,500
Cuba	22,436	22,060	Lebanon	2,000	—
Cyprus	2,093	1,786	Luxembourg	4,394	7,392
Czechoslovakia	162,999	173,913	Madagascar	6,134	1,661
Democratic People's Republic			Malawi	1,955	2,222
of Korea	—	20,921	Malaysia	20,000	20,000
Democratic Yemen	4,000	4,400	Malta	1,167	—
Dominica	1,000	1,852	Mauritius	—	680
Ecuador	1,360	6,500	Mexico	10,497	15,000
Egypt	93,972	—	Mongolia	1,939	2,124
Ethiopia	1,111	1,111	Morocco	5,358	—

Country	1985 payment	1986 pledge	Country	1985 payment	1986 pledge
Mozambique	4,186	—	Syrian Arab Republic	5,372	—
Nepal	700	700	Thailand	20,129	20,129
Netherlands	344,084	—	Togo	1,053	—
Niger	975	—	Trinidad and Tobago	5,025	13,400
Oman	—	12,000	Tunisia	20,241	23,845
Pakistan	72,327	71,340	Turkey	207,972	317,857
Panama	2,000	2,000	Uganda	25	3,000
Papua New Guinea	—	13,131	USSR	628,141	647,668
Philippines	7,808	10,000	United Kingdom	259,902	370,920
Poland	135,338	136,426	United Republic of Tanzania	1,194	1,194
Portugal	23,131	15,000	Venezuela	20,963	11,467
Qatar	30,000	—	Viet Nam	834	—
Republic of Korea	30,000	28,000	Yemen	7,000	—
Rwanda	4,000	4,000	Yugoslavia	132,354	147,157
Saudi Arabia	1,000,000	1,000,000	Zaire	—	3,000
Senegal	887	2,000	Zambia	14,648	—
Sierra Leone	2,828	—	Zimbabwe	7,915	—
Spain	72,812	—			
Sri Lanka	3,061	—	Subtotal	14,692,418	14,187,056
Swaziland	—	1,533			
Sweden	297,229	—	*Non-governmental organizations*	215,022	—
Switzerland	362,840	311,005	Total	14,907,440	14,187,056

SOURCE: A/41/5/Add.9 for 1985; A/CONF.132/2 for 1986.

NOTE: Since UNIDO was to be converted into a specialized agency on 1 January 1986, it would no longer be included in the annual United Nations Pledging Conference for Development Activities.

Budgetary resources of UNIDO

The UNDP indicative planning figure continued in 1985 to be the largest source from which UNIDO technical co-operation activities were financed. Other sources of financing included the UNDP Special Industrial Services programme and UNIDF.

Activities other than technical co-operation projects were financed from appropriations from the United Nations regular budget for UNIDO.

In March, the UNIDO Executive Director submitted two programme budget and financial reports to the Industrial Development Board. One contained the proposed 1986-1987 programme budget of UNIDO,[17] as prepared by the Secretary-General, taking into account the imminent conversion of UNIDO into a specialized agency. In the other,[18] the Executive Director proposed tentative allocations for 1986-1987 of the UNIDO regular programme of technical co-operation, based on indications that the appropriation would be $6,610,600.

In April, revised programme budget estimates were submitted by the Secretary-General to the General Assembly.[19]

REFERENCES

[1]YUN 1980, p. 503, GA res. 35/36, annex, 5 Dec. 1980. [2]A/40/16. [3]YUN 1984, p. 562, GA res. 39/232, 18 Dec. 1984. [4]*Ibid.*, p. 558. [5]*Ibid.*, p. 564. [6]*Ibid.*, p. 567. [7]E/AC.51/1985/11. [8]A/40/38. [9]ID/B/337. [10]ID/B/338 & Corr.1. [11]YUN 1984, p. 577, GA res. 39/235, 18 Dec. 1984. [12]YUN 1981, p. 591. [13]ID/B/333 & Corr.1. [14]IDB.2/10. [15]YUN 1977, p. 502, GA res. 32/166, 19 Dec. 1977. [16]A/40/5/Add.9. [17]ID/B/336. [18]ID/B/335. [19]A/C.5/40/1.

Industrial development activities

Technical co-operation

The UNIDO technical co-operation programme totalled $94.5 million in 1985, compared to $87.2 million in 1984, according to a report of the Secretary-General to the UNDP Governing Council;[1] 1,694 projects were implemented or under implementation. Activities were funded from UNDP main programmes (65 per cent) and UNDP-administered trust funds (2 per cent), from UNIDF and other trust funds (23 per cent) and from the regular programme budget (10 per cent). The increased delivery of technical co-operation projects in 1985 resulted mainly from a higher level of implementation in UNDP-financed projects and from a higher rate of projects financed under the UNIDO regular programme which included an additional $5 million for IDDA.

Approved were 666 new projects with a total value of $72.5 million, compared to 633 valued at $73.5 million in 1984. The total value of new project approvals for LDCs was $16.5 million, compared to $20.4 million in 1984. The main areas of implementation continued to be chemical, engineering, agricultural and metallurgical industries, as well as industrial infrastructure. The focus of technical co-operation according to the Executive Director[2] continued to shift towards a higher degree of specialization, including sophisticated technology, as reflected in an increased use of short-term specialized international experts and split missions in UNIDO projects.

Africa, including African Arab States, accounted for 39 per cent of project delivery; Asia and the Pacific, 32 per cent; Arab States, excluding African Arab States, 3 per cent; the Americas, 12 per cent; Europe, 3 per cent; and global and interregional projects, 9 per cent. Of 1,628 newly appointed experts, 31 per cent came from developing countries. A total of 2,815 placement arrangements were made for 1,725 fellowship and study-tour candidates; 26 per cent of those placements were made in developing countries, thus contributing to technical co-operation among developing countries (TCDC).

Chemical industries accounted for $24.5 million of technical co-operation activities; engineering industries, $13.9 million; agro-industries, $9.9 million; institutional infrastructure, $9.8 million; industrial planning, $7.3 million; metallurgical industries, $7.2 million; training, $5.8 million; feasibility studies, $5.3 million; and factory establishment, $3.9 million. Some $6.9 million was allotted to other related activities.

By project component, personnel accounted for $44.3 million (46.9 per cent); equipment, $22.6 million (23.9 per cent); fellowships and training, $13.5 million (14.3 per cent); sub-contracts, $11.8 million (12.5 per cent); and miscellaneous, $2.3 million (2.4 per cent).

UNIDO assistance to African countries concentrated on long-range industrial plans and strategies, industry performance, institutional infrastructure, and the development and transfer of technologies; special IDDA projects were integrated closely with regular technical co-operation activities for enhanced effect. In the Americas, Governments saw in industrial planning techniques a way of responding to basic social needs through improved technologies and increased local production; particular attention was paid to modernizing the food-processing, textile, clothing, building materials and construction industries, as well as the energy and transportation sectors, and to developing the capital goods sector aimed at technological improvement. Differing levels of development characterized African Arab and West Asian Arab States due to the effect of prices of mineral oil and its derivative products on the development of oil-exporting and oil-importing countries; major trends in the region included assistance in the preparation and evaluation of feasibility studies, the strengthening of specialized engineering institutions and the introduction of integrated repair, maintenance and inventory control programmes. In Asia and the Pacific, requests increased for advisory services to meet the needs of small- and medium-scale industries which, by using advanced technologies, had good prospects for becoming suppliers to large industries within and outside the respective country. In the Pacific

UNIDO TECHNICAL CO-OPERATION AND SUPPORT EXPENDITURES BY PROGRAMME COMPONENT, 1985

(as at 31 December 1985; in thousands of US dollars)

Programme component	Technical co-operation	Support
Policy-making organs	—	2,229
Executive direction and management*	175	1,705
Policy co-ordination		
Economic co-operation among developing countries	304	443
Field reports monitoring	214	447
Inter-agency programme co-ordination	—	382
Least developed countries	(38)	580
Negotiations	149	1,873
New York Liaison Office	—	312
Non-governmental organizations	7	369
Programme development and evaluation	582	2,260
Programme formulation and direction	76	1,874
Subtotal	1,294	8,540
Industrial operations		
Agro-industries	9,918	1,096
Chemical industries	24,470	1,578
Engineering industries	13,931	901
Factory establishment and management	3,905	734
Feasibility studies	5,307	673
Industrial planning	7,290	784
Institutional infrastructure	9,845	1,112
Investment co-operative programme	2,933	1,285
Metallurgical industries	7,188	727
Programme formulation and direction	482	975
Project personnel recruitment†	—	1,388
Purchase and contract	—	1,141
Training	5,825	1,086
Subtotal	91,094	13,480
Industrial studies		
Development and transfer of technology	784	1,005
Global and conceptual studies	10	1,111
Industrial and Technological Information Bank	—	317
Industrial information	73	496
Programme formulation and direction	232	1,049
Regional and country studies	541	1,583
Sectoral studies	54	1,335
Technological advisory services	25	256
Subtotal	1,719	7,152
Conference services, public information and external relations	146	—
Conference service	—	6,383
Governments and intergovernmental organizations relations	—	333
IDB secretariat	—	277
Programme formulation and direction	—	233
Public information	—	422
Subtotal	146	7,648
Administrative and common services		
Financial service	—	2,134
General services	—	1,574
Legal service	—	196
Personnel service	—	2,117
Programme direction‡	—	2,503
Subtotal	—	8,524
Unspecified	40	—
Total	94,468	49,278

SOURCE: IDB.2/10.

*Including UNIDO representation at Geneva.

†Including Technical Assistance Recruitment Service at Geneva and in New York.

‡Including electronic data processing.

subregion, a programme was initiated with a view to consolidating and optimizing the effectiveness of technical co-operation; assistance was requested in identifying and using local energy resources. The developing countries of Europe, which generally possessed the know-how for industrial progress, requested assistance in specific areas of sophisticated technology and computer application. Issues receiving special attention included the strengthening of institutional infrastructure and industrial energy conservation.

Under the regular programme, UNIDO activities amounted to $4.2 million. The regular programme continued to supplement other resources for industrial manpower development through individual fellowships, group training and the establishment and strengthening of training facilities in developing countries. Other regular programme components included regional advisory services and consultations with Governments. The UNIDO Executive Director provided the Industrial Development Board in March 1985[3] with information on UNIDO technical assistance activities during 1982-1984, by country, projects approved and delivered, and the number of expert assignments filled.

On 31 May,[4] noting with concern that the real value of resources for the UNIDO regular programme of technical co-operation had been declining steadily since 1980, the Board recommended to the General Assembly that the real value be maintained, and approved the tentative allocations for 1986-1987.

CPC consideration. In April 1985, the Secretary-General submitted to CPC at its request a triennial review[5] of the implementation of its 1980 recommendations[6] on United Nations activities in manufactures, carried out primarily by UNCTAD and UNIDO. The Secretary-General had submitted to CPC in 1984[7] a comprehensive evaluation of the UNDP-financed UNIDO activities in that sector.

After reviewing the progress achieved and difficulties encountered, the Secretary-General suggested, for improved programme implementation, that UNCTAD continue seeking funds for expanded use of the generalized system of preferences and for the control of restrictive business practices. In addition to the need for both UNCTAD and UNIDO to develop adequate systems of receiving and benefiting from feedback from Governments, industrialists and experts, he suggested, among other things, that the UNIDO Evaluation Unit might expand its activities to cover research, policy analysis and negotiations and follow-up, and that the UNIDO secretariat might ensure circulation of consultation recommendations among all its headquarters and field staff for optimal results.

CPC, at its April-June session,[8] stated that the report should have relied less on information from the organizational units concerned and more on an independent assessment, that both UNCTAD and UNIDO should develop procedures for collecting the end-users' opinions for evaluation activities, and that special care should be taken to avoid duplication between the two bodies. CPC deplored the tendency it saw in the review to give priority to the implementation of substantive recommendations in preference to those of a programming, planning or co-ordination nature, and stressed the importance of giving equal treatment to all its recommendations. On 29 May, CPC recommended that the General Assembly approve the proposed regular programme of technical co-operation for 1986-1987.

Training of personnel

In 1985, expenditures for fellowships and training components in technical co-operation projects implemented by UNIDO totalled $13.5 million, compared to $11.7 million in 1984. Of that total, $8.3 million was spent on fellowships and study tours and $5.2 million on group training activities and meetings. A total of 229 projects were completed or being implemented.

The number of individual training programmes (fellowships) initiated in 1985 for managerial and technical personnel of industrial projects in developing countries was 35 per cent higher than in 1984 (1,725 compared to 1,278); placement arrangements by host countries were 30 per cent higher (2,815 compared to 2,166). Of those placements, 727 or 25.8 per cent were arranged in developing countries; 315 (18.2 per cent) of the trainees came from LDCs and 207 (12 per cent) were female.

Following up on the recommendations of the Fourth (1984) General Conference of UNIDO,[9] emphasis was placed on accelerating human resource development for industrialization. A training programme in management of human resource development for industry was held in the USSR and a workshop on the role of women in industry was organized in Argentina. A national training scheme, begun in Mozambique with 90 participants, featured a TCDC arrangement, in which Brazil provided consultants and trainers in Mozambique and made training facilities available to Mozambicans in Brazil.

Training activities geared to small- and medium-scale industries included a seminar on financing, organized in Gabon with the Central African Customs and Economic Union (Cameroon, Central African Republic, Chad, Congo, Equatorial Guinea, Gabon); its recommendations for a subregional programme were endorsed in December by the heads of State and Government of the six countries. A mobile team of trainers visited the Comoros, Madagascar and Mauritius, training managers of such enterprises in overall management techniques. A group training programme in policy and consultancy activities in small-scale industries was held in Italy for the Palestinian people, in co-operation with the International Centre for Advanced Technical and Vocational Training. In the Niger, the training needs of 40 industrial enterprises were surveyed; some 150 participants took part in subsequent training programmes on industrial management.

Training programmes in the food industry included courses on modern packaging techniques in Italy and Morocco, maintenance of refrigerators and deep-freezer equipment in Egypt, France and Ireland, and food-processing topics in China, the German Democratic Republic, Romania, the USSR and Yugoslavia. UNIDO evaluated the training capabilities of the Food Technology Institute in Senegal in the drying and freezing of fish.

Within the framework of IDDA, a seminar was held in the Ivory Coast on training of trainers for financial institutions, and a regional project for the establishment of training facilities in the design and production of agricultural machinery and implements was completed covering Cameroon, the Sudan and the United Republic of Tanzania. An in-plant group training programme on agricultural machinery also took place in China.

Training materials were developed for instructors of seminars on industrial maintenance and the design of a modular approach for courses in maintenance.

The fourteenth issue of the *UNIDO Guide to Training Opportunities for Industrial Development* and the *UNIDO Industrial Training Offer Programme for 1986* were published.

Strengthening the SIDFA programme

Senior Industrial Development Field Advisers continued to assist in 1985 in programming and implementing technical co-operation projects.

On 31 May, the Industrial Development Board[4] underlined the need to strengthen the SIDFA programme; stressed that it be maintained at its current level of 30 posts; and reaffirmed that it should continue to take into account the special needs of LDCs. It also endorsed the 1984 recommendations of the Permanent Committee in regard to SIDFAs;[10] invited the UNDP Governing Council to finance the maximum number of SIDFA posts in 1986-1987; and recommended that UNIDO after its conversion consider evaluating, and enhancing the benefits of, the programme.

On 29 June,[11] the UNDP Governing Council requested the Administrator to make a policy review of the future of the SIDFA programme. UNDP and UNIDO subsequently agreed on a joint review by two senior consultants of the effectiveness of current arrangements and of ways to respond more effectively through the SIDFA programme to the industrialization requirements of developing countries.

The number of Junior Professional Officers (JPOs), who assisted SIDFAs in co-ordinating and monitoring UNIDO activities, increased to 75 during 1985, compared with 65 in 1984. JPO training courses, attended by 30 JPOs and donor country representatives, were held in April and November. As in 1984, the programme was supported by Belgium, Denmark, Finland, the Federal Republic of Germany, Italy, Japan, the Netherlands, Norway, Sweden and Switzerland.

Special Industrial Services

The Special Industrial Services (SIS) programme enabled UNIDO to meet urgent requests for assistance from developing countries by providing them with short-term, high-level advisory services, under UNDP financing.

A shortage of resources and inflationary factors limited the programme's scope in 1985. Expenditures during the year totalled $2.7 million, covering 263 projects related mainly to chemical industries, agro-industries, and metallurgical and engineering industries.

At the end of 1985, a UNDP mission evaluated the SIS programme—using questionnaires, a review of randomly selected projects, and a field visit by a consultant to five countries—to provide the UNDP Governing Council with a basis on which to decide in 1986 on the continuation and allocation of SIS funds for 1987-1991.

Industrial co-operation

System of Consultations

The Industrial Development Board examined a number of reports in 1985 as it continued the process of appraisal, begun in 1984,[12] of the System of Consultations, a mechanism for identifying possible areas for technical co-operation.

The President of the Board's 1984 session reported[13] that an open-ended informal working group—meeting on 27 November 1984 and 22 January, 8 February and 16 April 1985—considered the current functioning and future prospects of the System, as well as the Consultations' preparation, implementation and follow-up, and recognized the System's continuing validity in promoting the industrialization of developing countries. It proposed a number of improvements in the operational aspects of the System, among them government involvement at all stages of Consultations, an increase in the number of outside experts and consultants from developing countries, and an emphasis in documents on concrete problems and specific solutions.

The UNIDO secretariat submitted a compilation of the views of member States[14] presented during the Board's 1984 session, along with 18 written communications subsequently received on achievements and possible improvements to the System. Many States recognized the System as a useful framework within which specific sectoral problems of industrialization could be examined, leading to concrete results.

In his annual report,[2] the Executive Director stated that an extensive examination had generated greater understanding among member States of the System's limitations and potentialities, and that recommendations from previous Consultations had been re-examined with a view to improving implementation and follow-up.

The Executive Director, in a report on the benefits of the System,[15] listed among them the identification of problems associated with industrialization in developing countries, the monitoring of trends in world industry, and the promotion of international industrial co-operation. He concluded that the System's success could not be divorced from the world-wide industrial climate and the closely associated policy, economic and financial perspectives, and that the benefits derived from the System depended on the participants and on the use they made of it. In addition to the importance of problem identification and project implementation at the regional level, he considered it desirable to organize the Consultations on a two-tier approach—a global consultation of professionals, followed by the Board's consideration at the intergovernmental level—to meet the views often expressed in the Board in favour of a greater involvement of industry without government interference.

The Executive Director also provided information,[16] requested by the Board in 1984, in respect of the sectors proposed for inclusion in the programme of Consultations for 1986-1987 and 1988-1989, and suggested that the Board decide on the inclusion of pesticides in the programme.

Three Consultations were held in 1985: the First Consultation on the Building Materials Industry (Greece, March), organized jointly with the United Nations Centre for Human Settlements; the Second Consultation on the Capital Goods Industry with Special Emphasis on Energy-related Technology and Equipment (Sweden, June); and the Third Consultation on the Petrochemical Industry (Austria, December).

On 31 May,[4] the Board took note of the report by the 1984 President. It decided that Consultations should be held in 1986-1987 on the fisheries industry, industrial manpower training, agricultural machinery (interregional consultation), non-ferrous metals, iron and steel, and pharmaceuticals.

Also in May, CPC[8] considered the Secretary-General's report on United Nations activities in manufactures (see p. 602), in which he suggested that a procedure might be established in the UNIDO secretariat for obtaining regular feedback from the System's users with a view to enhancing the effectiveness of Consultations.

Co-operation among developing countries

In 1985, UNIDO activities to promote economic and technical co-operation among developing countries focused on: organizing solidarity ministerial meetings and round-table ministerial and high-level meetings as well as workshops and training programmes; and identifying new forms and institutional machinery for industrial co-operation, such as multinational production enterprises and enterprise-to-enterprise co-operation.

At a solidarity ministerial meeting (Bujumbura, Burundi, 12-15 March), participants from developing countries and five international organizations and financial institutions agreed on co-operation on most of the 22 projects examined covering agro-industries, chemical and pharmaceutical industries and industrial promotion. Representatives of 18 developing countries considered 109 co-operation projects at a round-table ministerial meeting on co-operation among developing countries in the food-processing industries (Novi Sad, Yugoslavia, 7-11 May) and discussed a practical approach to South-South co-operation for mutual benefits. A high-level intergovernmental meeting on co-operation among developing countries in agro-industry development (Brasilia, Brazil, 18-22 November), attended by representatives of 18 developing countries, resulted in bilateral and multilateral agreements on projects and joint ventures among the participating countries, such as a feasibility study by Argentina, Brazil, Paraguay and Uruguay on the establishment of a co-operative system for the production, processing and marketing of milk and milk products.

The UNIDO programme for the promotion of joint industrial programmes and projects continued to organize study tours and exchanges of experience in industrial free-zones, food research institutes, small-scale cement technologies, solar energy, and light industries. Missions were sent to Nigeria, the United Republic of Tanzania, Zambia and Zimbabwe to promote a joint UNIDO/Economic Commission for Africa programme for co-operation among African countries in industrial manpower development.

A technical and economic co-operation programme between China and Nicaragua on mini-plants for the production of basic nitrogen fertilizers was initiated in 1985 for implementation in 1986. An agreement was concluded in December between UNIDO and the National

Institute of Industrial Technology of Argentina on establishing a working arrangement for a systematic programme of action to promote TCDC in specific areas of industrial technology.

Expert group meetings were held on enterprise-to-enterprise co-operation within the Latin American plastics industry (Buenos Aires, Argentina, 4-6 November), the establishment of multinational production enterprises in developing countries (Vienna, 25-28 November) and the preparation of guidelines for the establishment of mini-plants on iron and steel with special emphasis on Africa (Vienna, 2-5 December).

On 31 May,[4] the Industrial Development Board welcomed the call by the Fourth General Conference for strengthening economic co-operation among developing countries,[17] and agreed that adequate resources should be provided to UNIDO to that end.

International trade aspects

In April 1985, the UNIDO secretariat submitted to the Board a report,[18] prepared in co-ordination with the UNCTAD secretariat, on trade and trade-related aspects of industrial collaboration arrangements at the enterprise level. Based on the conclusions of the *Ad Hoc* UNCTAD/UNIDO Group of Experts, which had examined the topic in 1979[19] and 1981,[20] the report provided a general descriptive overview of the main trends, the characteristics, modalities and factors influencing the development of collaboration arrangements. It stated that Governments might consider new modes of co-ordination at the macro-economic level, for example through framework agreements, with a view to creating a climate of trust at an intergovernmental level, further laying down conditions for safeguarding the mutual interests of the partners, and facilitating industrial adjustments in the productive systems of the partners. Industrial collaboration, still in its early phase of development, would benefit from flexible, forward-looking, balanced and stable frameworks at the intergovernmental level, the report concluded.

Industrial development of LDCs

Against the background of declining growth rates in the industrial sector of LDCs, UNIDO continued in 1985 to support industrial development projects, giving special attention to rehabilitating factories and increasing industrial efficiency.

Total funding for technical assistance to LDCs reached $17.6 million in 1985—an increase of $3.6 million or 25.8 per cent over that in 1984.

In Nepal, assistance was provided for the manufacturing of ayurvedic drugs from medicinal plants; in Cape Verde, a laboratory was established to improve the quality of pharmaceutical products; and in Lesotho, engineering services were provided for manufacturing agricultural equipment.

The UNCTAD Intergovernmental Group on LDCs (sixth session, Geneva, 30 September–12 October) carried out a mid-term global review of the progress in implementing the Substantial New Programme of Action (SNPA) for the 1980s for LDCs (see p. 434). As part of SNPA monitoring, UNIDO completed industrial development reviews for Bangladesh, Mali, the Sudan and the United Republic of Tanzania; and as part of its advisory services, it organized two investment promotion meetings—one at Khartoum, Sudan (4-8 March), for East African countries, and the other at Libreville, Gabon (5-8 December), for Central African countries.

On 31 May,[4] the Industrial Development Board expressed concern at the deteriorating socio-economic situation of LDCs, including African countries affected additionally by drought and desertification, and underlined the need for urgent attention and large-scale support by the international community. The Board requested UNIDO to accelerate SNPA implementation in the field of industrialization, and reiterated its call for a strengthening of the LDC section within UNIDO.

On 17 December, the General Assembly stressed that LDCs should continue to give priority in their industrial development to agro-industry and industries based on local raw materials, favour the development of national productive enterprises, and improve the incentives for entrepreneurship and support for local initiatives according to national policies (**resolution 40/205**). It called on donor countries, among other things, to combine technical and management training with financial assistance and to assist in developing local sources of raw materials to make local industry less vulnerable to balance-of-payments problems.

Redeployment of industrial production to developing countries

The Executive Director, in an April 1985 report[21] to the Industrial Development Board, reviewed the concepts and issues relating to industrial restructuring and redeployment in the light of the Fourth General Conference of UNIDO and the latest UNIDO studies on the topic. He observed that developing countries were under pressure to align their industrial structures with an unclear, unpredictable international restructuring pattern and were confronted with several internal dilemmas, such as the problem of reconciling the need for drastic austerity measures in the economy with the need for adjusting the structure of the manufacturing sector. The creation of a dynamic industry presupposed that both Governments and companies had a long-term vision of development prospects and a built-in capability to respond to changing parameters and to seize opportunities. Restructuring and redeployment had to be seen in the context of the efforts by each developing country to pursue industrial development in accordance with its national objectives. In supporting those endeavours—through its programmes of technical assistance, investment promotion, Consultations and others—the UNIDO secretariat intended to direct its studies to identify and help interpret the pertinent trends and issues as a service to policy-makers.

On 31 May,[4] the Industrial Development Board stressed again the importance of redeploying industry from industrialized to developing countries on the principle of dynamic comparative advantage and in accordance with the national policies and priorities of member States.

Industrial financing

In 1985, UNIDO, and its Investment Cooperative Programme in particular, maintained close links with national, regional and international financing and promotion institutions, while providing advisory services on sources and terms of industrial financing.

GENERAL ASSEMBLY ACTION

The General Assembly, which in 1984[22] had referred to its 1985 session consideration of a draft resolution on mobilization of financial resources for industrial development, decided, on 17 December 1985, to defer consideration of the draft until its 1986 session (**decision 40/434**).

The draft originated in the Fourth General Conference of UNIDO in 1984, where no consensus agreement had been reached. It was subsequently forwarded to the Secretary-General with a request that the Assembly consider it in 1984.[23] By the draft, the Conference, in agreed provisions, would have recommended that consideration be given to providing adequate financial support for the developing countries to meet their industrialization needs and that developed countries promote increased investment in the developing countries.

Investment promotion

The network of UNIDO Investment Promotion Services helped facilitate the flow of external financial, technological and managerial resources to developing countries. In addition to the Services currently operating in Cologne, New York, Paris, Tokyo, Vienna, Warsaw and Zurich, UNIDO signed an agreement with Italy in August 1985 to establish a Service at Milan, and pursued discussions on opening a Service at Seoul, Republic of Korea. During the year, the Zurich and Paris Services were extended for five and three years respectively, and an agreement was also signed to extend the Vienna Service until 31 January 1987.

In 1985, the Services launched 93 industrial projects in developing countries for a total investment value of some $628 million (as against 47 projects valued at $165 million in 1984); nine projects totalled $491 million, while the remaining projects averaged between $1 million and $2 million each.

Forty-nine country presentation meetings on investment opportunities were organized for Antigua and Barbuda, Argentina, the Bahamas, Burma, Cameroon, China, Colombia, the Congo, Cuba, Dominica, Ecuador, Grenada, India, Mexico, Panama, Sri Lanka, Saint Christopher and Nevis, Saint Lucia, Saint Vincent and the Grenadines, the Sudan, Tunisia, the United Republic of Tanzania and Zimbabwe.

Five investment promotion meetings (investors' forums), with some 460 potential partners from their countries participating, were held in the Sudan (Khartoum, 4-8 March), Colombia (Cali, 28-31 October), Ecuador (Quito, 18-21 November), China (Xiamen, 25-29 November) and Gabon (Libreville, 5-8 December). Some 300 industrial investment projects were presented at the Khartoum meeting for Djibouti, Egypt, Somalia, the Sudan, Uganda and Yemen, and resulted in 45 letters of intent. At Cali, the Investment Forum on Agro-Industry and Fishery considered 200 projects. The Investors' Forum for Ecuador considered 60 project proposals and concluded with at least 10 letters of intent. At Xiamen, discussion of 84 project proposals resulted in the signing of 50 letters of intent and conclusion of eight contractual joint venture agreements. The Industrial Forum for Central Africa at Libreville considered 141 projects from Burundi, Cameroon, the Central African Republic, Chad, the Congo, Equatorial Guinea, Gabon, and Sao Tome and Principe and concluded with 20 letters of intent.

Industrial management

In 1985, expenditures for technical co-operation activities in factory establishment and management totalled $3.9 million, with 93 per cent coming from UNDP; increased disbursement was noted in subcontracting and equipment components, mainly in computers and energy. Fifty projects were implemented or under implementation during the year.

In response to the continued need for improved management skills, a greater number of seminars—including one each on energy-related matters, industrial consultancy and general management—were carried out, and efforts continued to involve universities in support activities to industry.

Interest continued to grow in using microcomputers as a management tool for improved industrial productivity. In Cuba, the assistance of four experts was provided to introduce computer-aided management tools, including production and quality-control programmes, in a pharmaceutical plant; the project was expected to serve as a case-study for similar problems elsewhere. Based on the model of a Barbados project completed early in 1985, increased activities were expected in the Caribbean region to improve management through computer support.

A regional network for industrial consultancy was being prepared for Asia, and envisaged for Africa. In Egypt, short-term consultancy services focused on the manufacture of electric motors, dry batteries and chemicals, particularly pesticides. In Pakistan, *ad hoc* consultancy services were provided in finance, marketing, chemicals and mechanical engineering. Under a number of projects aimed at improving efficiency of public sector and other industries, assistance was provided to government ministries in Ethiopia, Malawi, Somalia and the Sudan. In China, a consultancy seminar was held with the help of a UNIDF special-purpose contribution provided by Spain. A seminar, organized jointly by UNIDO and UNDP for the Democratic People's Republic of Korea, dealt with project formulation and management. A large-scale project was begun in India to strengthen a cement research institute and improve the productivity and technological level of cement industry units.

In Europe, a regional co-operation project in energy conservation was launched in July; the first round of discussion on conservation in the most energy-intensive industries of the participating countries was held in Romania (Bucharest, 14-18 October), Czechoslovakia (Pilsen, 10-15 November; Prague, 18-22 November), Hungary (Budapest, 25-30 November) and Yugoslavia (Novi Sad, 9-13 December). Projects in the Philippines, the Republic of Korea and Sri Lanka concentrated on strengthening institutions for energy management and conservation; services included energy auditing of industrial enterprises, organization of seminars and workshops and preparation of manuals on energy conservation. Under a UNIDF special-purpose contribution provided by Australia, 11 specialists from nine Asian countries and 16 Australian experts took part in a regional energy management course at Melbourne in October.

Industrial planning

Industrial planning expenditures in 1985 amounted to $7.3 million, with about 80 per cent coming from UNDP. Of that amount, Africa accounted for 63 per cent, the Americas 21 per cent,

and Asia and the Pacific 12 per cent. Ninety-one projects were implemented or being implemented.

Owing to economic crisis and debt burden, a large number of developing countries were paying increased attention to medium- and long-term industrial planning. Planning activities included: an assessment of industrial development at sectoral and subsectoral levels; the identification of subsectors with development potential and comparative advantage; formulation of medium- and long-range master plans; restructuring; formulation of policies and policy measures; strengthening of technical and institutional capabilities for planning; and promotion of multinational and regional co-operation.

UNIDO assisted a number of countries in policy formulation. In Cameroon, it assisted in promoting an integrated strategy on optimum use of the country's agricultural potential and natural resources (wood, petroleum, aluminium and iron ores), with a view to contributing to the sixth 5-year plan (1986-1991). Under an inter-agency agreement with the United Nations Department of Technical Co-operation for Development, UNIDO assisted Afghanistan in implementing its annual industrial plans and in formulating its new 5-year plan. A project was completed in 1985 in assisting the Malaysian Industrial Development Authority in preparing an industrial master plan for 1986-1995. UNIDO assisted in preparing the industrial portion of the 1987-1991 national economic development plan of Honduras, and contributed to Venezuela's policy formulation through the recruitment of national and international experts.

In an innovative project that became operational in 1985, the International Institute of Applied Systems Analysis (Laxenburg, Austria), contracted by UNIDO, provided India with the know-how for developing a nation-wide environmental monitoring system; in an additional case-study, industrial pollution was to be investigated.

Developing countries receiving UNIDO assistance in 1985 in establishing or strengthening industrial planning institutions included Sierra Leone, where an industrial development department was set up within the Ministry of Trade and Industry. In Algeria, assistance was given to the Institut supérieur de gestion et de planification in the regulation and management of the industrial public sector. In Ghana, a new planning structure was being considered for the Ministry of Science and Technology.

Within the IDDA framework, national workshops on industrial strategy were held in Uganda (Jinja, 25-30 March), Mauritania (Nouakchott, 21-25 April), Benin (Cotonou, 24-29 June), Burkina Faso (Ouagadougou, 14-18 October), the Niger (Niamey, 26 October–2 November) and Sierra Leone (Freetown, 3-6

December). Further assistance at the subregional level included the strengthening of the industrial planning systems of the Economic Community of West African States (ECOWAS), the Economic Community of the Great Lakes Countries and the Preferential Trade Area for Eastern and Southern African States.

Industrial studies

As in the past, UNIDO continued to carry out global and conceptual, regional and country, sectoral and statistical studies, with a view to assisting in policy-making and in providing the framework for its technical assistance programme.

It prepared short-term forecasts providing industrial policy-makers with a coherent picture of global industrial development on the basis of anticipated levels of demand, changes in technology and competitiveness, and price trends. The UNIDO economic model system, expanded to include a wide range of recent information sources, was used to estimate the level of economic activity in 150 individual countries and to spell out implications for development potential in various industrial sectors, with the expectation that placing national estimates in a global context would contribute to consistent policy-making. A Trade Impact Analysis Model, completed in 1985, described the impact of changed bilateral export structure on production and imports and analysed the potential for intensifying South-South trade. In addition, studies were completed on the mineral trade potential of African LDCs, African external debt problems, and the interaction between agriculture and industry in the development process. The quarterly journal *Industry and Development* continued to be issued and *Industry and Development: Global Report 1985* was published.

Studies at the regional and country levels focused on economic analyses and data on national and international industrial structures, resources, industrialization prospects and policy options. Research support was given to the Preferential Trade Area for Eastern and Southern African States and to the Southern African Development Co-ordination Conference. Studies were prepared on prospects for co-operation in the textile industry in the Association of South-East Asian Nations, trends in the automotive industry and their implications for Latin America, and prospects and new measures for small-scale industry development in Asia and the Pacific. A review of industrial policy pursued in East Asia was initiated.

Among sectoral studies issued or completed were a typology (first phase) of the fisheries industrial systems of 64 developing countries, world trade of oilseeds and related products, and prospects for petrochemical industries in developing countries; a study of regional co-operation among developing countries in the production of tanning chemicals was started. Research continued on: a decision-making model for the production of pharmaceuticals by organic chemical synthesis; opportunities for mini-fertilizer plants; current conditions of the iron and steel industry in developing countries; and energy use and conservation in selected industrial sectors.

The development of industrial statistics continued to be emphasized, with efforts to enhance international comparability and consistency, data collection for African countries, and data dissemination. Statistical activities financed under the regular budget were complemented by the collection of field statistics funded by a grant from the Ministry of International Trade and Industry of Japan.

Industrial technology

The thrust of the technology programme remained twofold: to assist developing countries in the selection, acquisition and development of technology, and to strengthen their technological capabilities to respond better to changes in the world technological scene (see also Chapter XII of this section). Activities dealt with policies, technological advances, selection and acquisition, and technology for rural and small industries.

In 1985, a regional micro-electronics network was established for Latin America and the Caribbean. An international roster of scientists and technologists in micro-electronics, genetic engineering, biotechnology and renewable energy was completed. The tenth meeting of heads of technology transfer registries (Cairo, Egypt, 8-13 December) reviewed trends in technology transfer flows and contractual arrangements, and the development of a computerized registry information system.

In a March report[24] to the Industrial Development Board, the UNIDO Executive Director analysed the 1984 secretariat activities in technology development and transfer—including the role of the Industrial and Technological Information Bank (see below)—against the general background of industrial technology for the 1980s.

On 31 May,[4] the Board took note of the report, and requested the Executive Director to present a report on the development and transfer of technology to the next session of the relevant UNIDO organs.

Industrial and Technological Information Bank

During 1985, increased interaction with information sources and users and the use of networking for faster information flow marked the activities of the Industrial and Technological Information Bank (INTIB).

An advisory group of INTIB users, meeting at Vienna (23-27 September), made the first review since 1978 of the work of INTIB, and noted with satisfaction the result of a survey among users in developing countries that INTIB was among the first 10 information services found useful. At the same time, the group emphasized the need for expansion and reorientation of activities and for a medium-term programme for INTIB to keep up with developments in information technology.

The importance of the links between INTIB and external data bases in the region served by the Economic and Social Commission for Asia and the Pacific (ESCAP) was discussed at an ESCAP/FAO/UNIDO Regional Consultation on Computerized Fertilizer Information Handling (Bangkok, Thailand, 18-22 November). A project was implemented, within the framework of IDDA, to provide 10 African countries (Algeria, Cameroon, Egypt, Ivory Coast, Kenya, Nigeria, Senegal, United Republic of Tanzania, Tunisia, Zambia) with access to external sources of information through INTIB and to promote the exchange of industrial information among themselves.

As in previous years, INTIB's Industrial Inquiry Service received about 1,300 inquiries from industrial enterprises, information centres, international organizations, research and development institutions, engineering and consulting firms, government officials, universities, development banks and others. They dealt with chemicals and pharmaceuticals, agro-industries, food processing, capital goods, fabricated metal products, nonmetallic minerals, textile and leather goods, pulp and paper and others. The preparation of technological information profiles for mini-cement and mini-lime plants was intiated.

Work continued on a consolidated edition of the *Industrial Development Abstracts* data base, which contained more than 15,000 entries. Four volumes of the *Abstracts* were issued in 1985.

REFERENCES

[1]DP/1986/48/Add.2. [2]IDB.2/10. [3]ID/B/340/Add.1. [4]A/40/16. [5]E/AC.51/1985/10. [6]YUN 1980, p. 992. [7]YUN 1984, p. 570. [8]A/40/38. [9]YUN 1984, p. 572. [10]*Ibid.*, p. 573. [11]E/1985/32 (dec. 85/41). [12]YUN 1984, p. 574. [13]ID/B/349. [14]ID/B/346. [15]ID/B/341. [16]ID/B/334. [17]YUN 1984, p. 575. [18]ID/B/348. [19]YUN 1979, p. 588. [20]YUN 1981, p. 590. [21]ID/B/339. [22]YUN 1984, p. 579, GA dec. 39/447, 18 Dec. 1984. [23]*Ibid.*, p. 578. [24]ID/B/342.

Development of specific industries

During 1985, many of UNIDO's technical co-operation activities related to specific industrial sectors or industries. The major sectors were agro-industries, and chemical, engineering, and metallurgical and mineral industries.

Agro-industries

Technical co-operation expenditures under the heading agro-industries amounted to $9.9 million in 1985, with some 45 per cent financed from UNDP resources. Of the total, Africa accounted for 23 per cent; the Americas, 30; the Arab States (excluding those in Africa), 4; Asia and the Pacific, 35; Europe, 2; and interregional/global, 6. A total of 172 projects were implemented or being implemented, 14 of them greater than $1 million in value, 53 greater than $150,000 and 105 below $150,000.

Projects covered the subsectors in wood products and wood processing, textile production and garment making, food processing and packaging, leather and leather products, and rubber products.

Clothing and textile industry

Technical assistance in developing the textile and garment production industry continued to be provided in Bangladesh, Egypt, Sri Lanka and the Syrian Arab Republic. At the plant level, assistance continued to be provided in India and the Republic of Korea; projects were completed in Bangladesh, Egypt, Montserrat and Viet Nam. In the United Republic of Tanzania, a three-month training programme in garment manufacture was held for women from the Pan African Congress of Azania.

Preparatory missions to formulate large-scale textile projects were carried out to establish a garment technology centre in China, to strengthen the College of Textile Technology in Bangladesh, and to assist the Indian Jute Industrial Research Associations. Under a project financed by the Voluntary Fund for the United Nations Decade for Women, assistance was given to the Kurasimi Women Tailoring Society in the United Republic of Tanzania in selecting and ordering garment manufacturing equipment.

Fisheries industry

Arrangements were completed with FAO in 1985 to sponsor the first Consultation on the fisheries industry to be held at Gdansk, Poland, in 1987. Organization was begun of a regional preparatory meeting on the fisheries industry in Latin America, to be hosted by Peru and co-sponsored by the Latin American Fishery Development Organization. Preparations also began for a regional meeting for Africa, to be held at Dakar, Senegal, in 1986.

Food industry

During 1985, UNIDO concentrated on implementing the recommendations[1] of the Second (1984) Consultation on the Food-Processing Industry with Special Emphasis on Vegetable Oils and Fats,[2] relating to an integrated approach to food processing and the role of co-operatives and small- and medium-scale enterprises in the food-processing industry. A study was undertaken on measures to stimulate co-operation among co-operatives and food-processing industries, in which context a project was initiated among the counterparts in Bulgaria and in selected African countries.

In Peru, UNIDO continued to co-operate with the United Nations Fund for Drug Abuse Control in developing the food industry in support of drug plantation eradication efforts. Installation was completed in Bangladesh of a $3.8 million rice bran oil-extraction plant with a 40 tons/day capacity, financed by the United Nations Capital Development Fund and UNIDF. Consultancy or expert services were provided for the construction, test runs and performance guarantee operations of the Grand Harbour Grain Terminal in Malta, and to the Centre de recherche agro-alimentaire at Lubumbashi, Zaire, where economic evaluations were carried out for various food industries. Among other projects under implementation were those dealing with an industrial bakery in Mozambique, a soya milk–processing plant in El Salvador, demonstration plants for the processing of cassava, onions and tomatoes in the Niger and for cassava processing in Sierra Leone, and processing of sugar-cane by-products in Cuba. UNIDO also analysed the potential of vegetable protein production in developing countries for human consumption, and examined, in co-operation with the General Agreement on Tariffs and Trade and UNCTAD, the impact of tariff and non-tariff barriers on the development of the vegetable oils and fats industry.

Leather industry

As a follow-up to the recommendations[1] made in 1984 by the Third Consultation on the Leather and Leather Products Industry,[3] a model study was prepared in Africa for the manufacture of footwear components, subsequently examined by the UNIDO Leather and Leather Products Industry Panel (eighth session, Vienna, 20-22 November), and was to constitute the background material for an African regional consultation in 1986. Several other regional studies, begun during the year on regional co-operation in tanning chemicals and footwear auxiliaries, were also expected to be presented to expert group meetings envisaged in the African, Asian and Latin American regions.

Technical co-operation in leather and leather products continued in Brazil, China, Costa Rica, India, Kenya, Pakistan, the Philippines and the United Republic of Tanzania. A quality control laboratory project in Kenya and a tannery effluent treatment project in Brazil entered the second phase of implementation. Preparatory missions were conducted in Burma, Indonesia and Madagascar to formulate large-scale leather products development projects.

Packaging industry

Major projects in Brazil, Cuba, Jamaica and Turkey provided technical assistance in the manufacture and conversion of packaging materials, and in analysis of package performance with regard to contents, markets and distribution systems. Projects were concluded in Jamaica, on infrastructure improvement, and in Mali, on fruit-juice packaging. Under a project sponsored by UNIDO and the Arab Industrial Development Organization for establishing an Arab regional packaging centre, seminars and training courses took place at Dubai (United Arab Emirates), Casablanca (Morocco) and Tunis (Tunisia), and a study tour was organized for participants from Arab countries to a packaging exhibition, advanced packaging industries and research centres in Scandinavia. In addition, UNIDO organized a seminar-cum-study tour of packaging managers from Arab countries to Argentina and Brazil.

Wood-using industry

Following up on the 1983 recommendations of the First Consultation on the Wood and Wood Products Industry,[4] activities focused on preparation of training manuals, development of an international strength grouping system for tropical and other timber from developing countries, and promotion of education and training in wood technology and wood-using construction. A second training workshop on production management in public sector mechanical wood-processing industries was held in Yugoslavia, and a training course on the use of coconut wood in construction was held in the Philippines for 16 participants from nine developing countries. Studies on timber bridge construction, computer-aided design and promotion needs in timber construction were submitted as background documents to an expert group meeting on the use of timber in construction (Vienna, 2-6 December).

Among the 1985 projects, prefabricated wooden bridges were built in Dominica and Ecuador and several bridge projects were begun in Bhutan, Bolivia, Chile, Honduras, Nicaragua and Peru. A congress of furniture manufacturers' federations was established in Latin America. In Asia, a preparatory mission initiated assistance to Viet Nam in the production of textile loom shuttles, while assistance continued to a pilot furniture plant in the Lao People's Democratic Republic.

Chemical industries

In 1985, technical co-operation expenditures for chemical industries amounted to $24.5 million, with about 53 per cent financed from UNDP resources. Of that amount, Africa accounted for 47.5 per cent; the Americas, 6; Arab States (excluding those in

Africa), 1; Asia and the Pacific, 36; Europe, 4; and interregional/global, 5.5. A total of 347 projects were implemented or under implementation, 32 of them greater than $1 million in value, 105 less than that but greater than $150,000, and 210 less than $150,000.

Activities concentrated on five broad subsectors: building materials and construction industries; petrochemical industries; fertilizers, pesticides and organic chemicals industries; pharmaceutical industries; and basic chemicals, environment, and pulp and paper.

UNIDO participated in organizing the First World Congress on Non-Metallic Minerals (Belgrade, Yugoslavia, 15-19 April). A techno-economic study was completed in the Syrian Arab Republic on establishing a plant for the production of alkyd resins, polyvinyl acetate dispersion paints and adhesives, with up to 50 per cent of domestic raw material. In China, a dyestuffs research and demonstration project continued; two experts were dispatched to examine technology available for recycling plastic waste. A pilot plant for the production of liquid natural rubber became operational in the Ivory Coast.

Research and demonstration programmes received support in developing alternative energy sources, such as those based on coal and agricultural residues. Emphasis was placed on the development of biofuels technology, including ethanol production from lignocellulosic materials in Brazil, India and Romania, and on thermochemical conversion technologies for the production of solid and gaseous fuels from wood waste and agricultural residues in Ethiopia, Paraguay, the Philippines, Somalia, the Sudan, Uruguay and Zimbabwe.

In the Philippines, a project on sucro-based chemicals was approaching a successful conclusion. In the area of basic chemicals, UNIDO activities promoting the manufacture of salt in developing countries expanded further. Activities in the pulp and paper sector concentrated on the use of non-wood fibre material; a technical workshop and a seminar were held at Bangkok on the utilization of waste paper in pulp and paper-making and on comparative pulping processes. Environment-related activities included transfer of low and non-waste technology to developing countries, recycling of waste materials, industrial water development, monitoring and abatement of industrial pollution, management of hazardous wastes and materials, and the elaboration of industrial safety procedures.

Building materials industry

Activities in the building materials and construction industries focused on accelerating the industrial use of non-metallic mineral resources for manufacturing low-cost building materials for housing, as well as their use in the glass, ceramics and chemical industries.

The promotion of brickmaking continued to be significant, especially in Africa; experience gained in soil stabilization during a brick-industry project, completed in the Niger in 1985, was to be applied also in field activities, initiated in late 1985, in Chad, Madagascar and the United Republic of Tanzania. A project on the development of low-cost building materials in Indonesia resulted in several model production units, which were currently demonstrating the production of clay roofing tiles and related products.

A project to assist the marble and stone industry in Ethiopia was completed in 1985; three marble factories in Addis Ababa were rehabilitated and production restarted. Assistance was provided for the modernization of the lime and gypsum industries in Cuba and for the strengthening of a cement development centre in China.

The First Consultation on the Building Materials Industry (Athens, Greece, 26-30 March),[5] sponsored by UNIDO and the United Nations Centre for Human Settlements, brought together 181 participants—of whom 25 per cent were from industry and 57 per cent from specialized government and non-governmental agencies—to discuss measures for increased production of building materials in developing countries. The Consultation recommended that UNIDO should help developing countries to improve their planning systems for the building materials industry; provide up-to-date information on the technological options for building material production; promote research in domestic raw-material resources and their suitability for the production of building materials; and strengthen training in appraisal of offers, selection of technologies and negotiating skills. It further recommended that international and national banking institutions give priority to the building materials sector commensurate with its importance and that developing countries establish a framework of regulations based on those existing in national, regional or international organizations.

Fertilizer industry

The UNIDO programme in the fertilizer and pesticides sector promoted the use of indigenous materials, such as fertilizer production from low-grade phosphate rock in India and bentonite as a soil conditioner in Ethiopia.

Activities carried out in implementation of the 1984 recommendations of the Fourth Consultation on the Fertilizer Industry[6] included preparation of guidelines for fertilizer project management and capital cost control, and the approval of a project for pre-feasibility studies on establishing mini-fertilizer plants in four African countries. An examination began of successful joint venture arrangements between developing countries in the fertilizer sector, with the aim of identifying the requirements related to markets, raw materials, production, technology options and skilled and managerial expertise.

Petrochemical industry

During 1985, UNIDO activities in the petrochemical sector focused on the development of polymer industries—plastics, synthetic fibres and rubbers. The use of plastics in agriculture and water management was encouraged in an effort to assist developing countries to become self-sufficient in food production; a regional project was established to assist African countries in that regard and a workshop on plastics in agriculture was held in Egypt. Projects on major petrochemical complex optimization continued in Egypt and India. Solutions were sought to problems of plant management and operation, energy and raw material utilization, and environment and quality control. Special attention was given to the further development of national plastics centres in Bangladesh and India.

An International Conference on Man-made Fibres (Beijing, 18-22 November), attended by 320 participants from 22 countries, provided China with an opportunity to demonstrate to developing country participants the outcome of its joint efforts with UNIDO and UNDP in establishing a synthetic fibre research centre. Annual training courses—on plastics technology, mould making and synthetic fibres—were held at Vienna in co-operation with the Government of Austria.

The Third Consultation on the Petrochemical Industry (Vienna, 2-6 December) adopted conclusions and recommendations emphasizing the importance of continued efforts to update the UNIDO petrochemical data base and the need for a detailed analysis of the current status and future prospects of polymer industries in developing countries with emphasis on the application of plastics in agriculture.

Pesticides industry

In the pesticides sector, activities included the strengthening of facilities for toxicological evaluation in the Republic of Korea, research and development in new pesticides in China, the formulation of pesticides in India, and the establishment of facilities for the manufacture of intermediate ingredients in Egypt and of solid formulation in Cuba.

Pharmaceutical industry

UNIDO activities to increase pharmaceutical production in developing countries focused on the use of indigenous medicinal plants and petrochemical by-products, the adaptation of technology for local production, production of biologicals to enhance preventive measures and the strengthening of national research and development efforts.

Projects for the industrial utilization of medicinal and aromatic plants continued in Afghanistan, Mali, Nepal, Thailand and Turkey, while a similar project was completed in Cameroon. In Nepal, implementation began of a second UNDP-financed project for the commercial processing of essential oils and herbal preparations; similar pilot plants had been installed in Burkina Faso, Rwanda and the United Republic of Tanzania. A project was initiated in Madagascar for the processing of herbal medicines and preparatory assistance was given to Viet Nam for local medicine production. In Cuba, a multi-purpose plant for the bulk production of essential synthetic drugs was inaugurated in March. Similar projects of an exploratory nature were initiated in Zimbabwe, the Arab region and Morocco.

In Guinea, a pilot plant was being established under IDDA auspices for the production of oral rehydration salts and intravenous fluids, and projects for the local production of those salts in several African countries were under preparation.

The *Ad Hoc* Panel of Experts on Contractual Arrangements in the Pharmaceutical Industry (third meeting, Vienna, 22-24 April) finalized documents on contractual arrangements relating to the production of bulk drugs and intermediates, licensing arrangements relating to the formulation of pharmaceutical dosage forms, and the transfer of technology. The Panel also considered outlines for further documentation related to the establishment of turnkey plants and arrangements for technical assistance in the formulation of pharmaceuticals. The Advisory Panel on Preventive Medicine (third meeting, Bilthoven, Netherlands, 6 and 7 June) advised UNIDO on its programme on the industrial production of biologicals and discussed a model programme for vaccine production in developing countries. Within the framework of IDDA, a pilot demonstration plant for vaccine production for Africa was established at Garoua, Cameroon. Projects on human plasma fractions and sterile enzyme preparations from animal sources were begun in Mongolia. Preparations were being made for the third Consultation on the pharmaceutical industry to be held in 1987.

The directory of sources of supply for pharmaceuticals, chemicals and their intermediates was expanded from an initial list of 26 essential bulk drugs to 100 included in the World Health Organization model list of essential drugs.

Engineering industries

In 1985, technical co-operation expenditures in engineering industries amounted to $13.9 million, of which some 90 per cent was financed by UNDP. Africa accounted for 19 per cent; the Americas, 9; Arab States (excluding those in Africa), 4; Asia and the Pacific, 63; Europe, 4; and interregional/global,

1. A total of 183 projects were implemented or under implementation, of which 29 were greater than $1 million in value, 63 greater than $150,000 but less than $1 million, and 91 less than $150,000.

Activities focused on industrial technology and production, energy-related technology, and development of human resources. The main subsectors receiving assistance were agricultural machinery and implements, electronic and electrical machinery and products, computer equipment, metalworking and machine tools, land-based or water-borne transport equipment, and energy-related equipment.

Agricultural machinery

Activities related to agricultural machinery included two expert group meetings—one on guidelines for the import, assembly and manufacture of agricultural machinery and training (Vienna, 9-12 September) and the other on integrated training programmes in agricultural machinery industries (Rosario, Argentina, 9-14 December). Efforts were made to upgrade physical facilities, technical skills and the work programme in agricultural machinery production, and UNIDO assisted Bangladesh, China, Hungary, India and Poland in strengthening their research and design capabilities. A UNDP-financed project provided assistance to the China Agricultural Machinery Testing Centre.

Within the IDDA programme framework, assistance was given to integrate agricultural machinery with the engineering and capital goods sector, promote rehabilitation and upgrading of multi-purpose plants, develop an engineering design and adaptation capability, apply research and development to manufacturing, develop subregional and regional programme networks, and promote economic and technical co-operation among developing countries.

Haiti, Lesotho, Senegal and Togo received assistance in agricultural machinery production. A project continued in India on the development of microprocessor-based agro- and dairy instruments. In Viet Nam, large-scale projects were being implemented to rehabilitate sugar mills, including local manufacture of spare parts, and to establish a maintenance and repair centre for rice mills.

Preparations were made, in co-operation with FAO, for the third Consultation on the agricultural machinery industry in 1986.

Electronic and electrical machinery

Technical assistance in electronic and electrical machinery concentrated on design and development, testing and quality control, maintenance and repair and extension service to industry. Assistance was given to, among other things: the establishment of an instrument design and development centre and an electronics service and training centre in India, an electrical research facility in Iraq, and a maintenance and repair centre in Viet Nam; expansion of dry batteries production in Egypt; and increasing the efficiency of a radio factory in Rwanda. Other 1985 projects included the manufacture of quality-controlled consumer electronic products in China.

Computer equipment

In Bulgaria, development continued of programmable industrial robots, simple robots for training and software tools for industrial control. Progress was made in a project on the development and application of microcomputer systems in China, and in the design of a process control microcomputer system to improve the efficiency of the Sichuan Medical Factory and control the quality of tetracycline produced there. Assistance was given to establishing a pilot plant in integrated circuits production in the Democratic People's Republic of Korea.

Metalworking and machine tools

A significant part of the activities carried out in 1985 in the metalworking and machine tools sector involved the batch production of simple metal products with emphasis on rural industrialization. Assistance continued to be provided to small-scale local industries in Cameroon and Madagascar in maintenance and repair services, and progress was achieved in Mali in the manufacture of manual water pumps. A project to develop tool and die production in Trinidad and Tobago was extended for a year, training continued in Tunisia in mould fabrication for the production of plastic articles, and prototypes of incremental encoders were developed to meet a request from Bulgaria for a new measuring technique for machine-tool motions and positions that would save raw materials.

A project began in India to develop microprecision engineering techniques. A large-scale project to develop numerically controlled machine tools became operational in the Democratic People's Republic of Korea, and 28 of its nationals received training in the German Democratic Republic and Poland. Facilities were improved at the National Institute of Design at Ahmedabad, India, where a programme was started for training fellows from Bangladesh, Indonesia, Pakistan, the Philippines and Sri Lanka. A UNIDF-financed project on the establishment of a pump repair section within an existing mechanical workshop and foundry was completed at Mogadiscio, Somalia; a project on maintenance and repair at Conakry, Guinea, was upgraded; and a training centre for the maintenance and repair of bio-medical equipment was established in Hungary.

Transport equipment

Among technical assistance provided in transport engineering and maintenance, the preparatory assistance phase was initiated for a testing and service centre for the automotive ancillary and allied industries in Indonesia. A number of large-scale projects in India dealt with automotive emission control, a fatigue-testing laboratory and data acquisition on road loads. In Hong Kong, a project to control motor vehicle emissions made progress. Expertise and test equipment were provided to the Pakistan Automobile Corporation to assist local manufacturers in producing automobile parts formerly imported. A network of motor vehicle service stations was established in Bhutan.

UNIDO initiated technical discussions with the Union of African Railways and the Railway Union of Arab States as well as with the Association of Engineering Companies in Spain, Belgium and Norway with a view to developing co-operative programmes. ECOWAS received assistance in railway wagons and equipment manufacturing.

UNIDO activities with respect to water-borne transport included: advising Governments on development programmes for their shipbuilding industries; giving technical and managerial advice to shipyards and port authorities; developing new technologies in ship and boat production; and undertaking techno-economic studies or evaluation of existing maritime facilities and of prospects for their rehabilitation or expansion.

A regional expert group meeting in Mauritius (Curepipe, 9-14 December) made recommendations regarding the development of small-scale boat building and repair in East African countries. An interregional project on marine technology for shipbuilding and offshore technology was initiated by UNIDO and Norway.

Within the framework of the United Nations Transport and Communications Decade in Africa (1978-1988), UNIDO activities emphasized promotion of African industry in transport and communication equipment, upgrading and rehabilitation of existing industries, production of spare parts, maintenance and repair, training and regional co-operation.

Energy-related equipment

Energy-related activities covered energy production equipment, process engineering, energy conservation and hardware improvement for efficient utilization of non-conventional sources of energy. Assistance was given to Chile in applying new computer techniques and strategies to the national electric power system, to Egypt in establishing an industrial energy conservation centre, and to India in developing internal combustion engines using methanol as fuel. A study tour by representatives of the University of Madagascar aimed at obtaining current information on the use of renewable energy sources. In Jordan, progress continued on the design, development and testing of solar water heaters for industrial application. A project in the Asia and Pacific region provided training in the manufacture and use of solar collectors.

Metallurgical and mineral industries

In 1985, technical co-operation expenditures in the metallurgical industries sector amounted to $7.2 million, with some 78 per cent financed from UNDP resources. Of that amount, Africa accounted for 27 per cent; the Americas, 25; Arab States (excluding those in Africa), 2; Asia and the Pacific, 40.5; and Europe, 5.5. A total of 153 projects were implemented or under implementation, 13 of them greater than $1 million in value, 47 less than that but greater than $150,000, and 93 less than $150,000.

Activities continued in extractive, process and physical metallurgy covering the production of light and heavy non-ferrous metals (aluminium, titanium, copper), the iron and steel industry (conventional routes and direct reduction of iron ores), ferrous and non-ferrous foundries and other metal transformation and forming processes (rolling, forging, heat treatment, extruding, welding), and the strengthening and establishment of laboratories, institutes or centres for metallurgical research and development.

Emphasis was given to the planning, establishment or expansion and improved operations of metallurgical plants. The first expert group meeting on computerized maintenance systems in metallurgy was held in Czechoslovakia (Prague, 28 January–1 February). Metallurgical investigations and testing to establish the characteristics of raw materials were being implemented in Chile, China, Cuba, India, Iran, Jamaica, Mozambique, Sri Lanka and Viet Nam.

UNIDO continued to promote the transfer of sophisticated technology, such as the production of de-ironed refractory-grade bauxite in Greece, the bacterial leaching of copper ores in Chile and Peru, the production of super purity aluminium in India, the production of special alloy steels and processing of silica raw materials in Pakistan, the manufacture of magnetic materials for the electronic industry in Viet Nam, surface finishing and anti-corrosion treatment of metals in the Republic of Korea, testing of alternative raw materials for aluminium production in Iran, and the introduction of special heat treatment techniques in China. A project on dynamic testing of coal-mining machines was elaborated in the Republic of Korea.

Iron and steel industry

During 1985, preparations were made for the fourth Consultation on the iron and steel industry to be held in 1986. Studies were completed on the crisis in the iron and steel industry and its impact on developing countries, and on the possibilities of integrated development of the industry with other economic sectors in Latin America and in eastern and southern Africa. An *ad hoc* expert group (Vienna, 16-18 October) considered the question of integrated development between the iron and steel and capital goods sectors.

Follow-up actions to the 1982 recommendations of the Third Consultation[7] focused on mini-steel plant technology, personnel training and financing infrastructure. In a survey on mini-steel technology, data collected for 74 such plants in various developing and developed countries were analysed; an expert group met (Vienna, 2-5 December) to prepare guidelines for the establishment of mini-plants with special emphasis on Africa.

The establishment of a mini-steel plant in Mongolia with annual production capacity of 100,000 tons was recommended, following a techno-economic evaluation project. Assistance was given to the General Pipe Company in the Libyan Arab Jamahiriya to improve the operation of three steel pipe and tube plants. Scrap collection/processing projects were under implementation in Angola and Mozambique, and the first such plant commissioned in Angola during 1985 provided raw material for the local steelmaking industry.

Technical advisory missions covered, among others, Bolivia, Mongolia, Trinidad and Tobago, Viet Nam and Zambia.

Non-ferrous metals

Preparations continued for the first Consultation on the non-ferrous metals industry to be held in 1987. Within the global perspective based on an analysis of the 1983-1984 survey of the industry, an expert group meeting on the industry's restructuring (Vienna, 18-21 March) was held with the participation of the United Nations Centre on Transnational Corporations and UNCTAD.

Among the projects for developing the light and heavy non-ferrous metals industries, focusing on bauxite/alumina/aluminium, a pilot plant for bauxite processing inaugurated in Jamaica became the first in a developing country for full-range testing of the Bayer alumina production process.

An interim report was completed on the possible utilization of aluminiferous ores (alunites) as raw materials for aluminium production in Iran. Other aluminium production projects were carried out in Hungary, India and Mozambique. A series of tests were conducted on Greek diasporic bauxites with a view to developing a commercial process for reducing iron content and obtaining a better-refined bauxite.

Foundries

Special attention was accorded to strengthening the foundry industry sector, particularly the im-provement of foundry operations and overall plant performance. A workshop and demonstration of appropriate technologies and equipment for the metallurgical and metal processing industries for African countries, organized by UNIDO and the Polish Chamber of Foreign Trade, was held at Katowice from 25 to 29 August. A foundry performance im-provement programme was conducted for the National Engineering Corporation in the United Republic of Tanzania. In Nicaragua, an assessment was made of the state of the art of the foundry industry, and training started in improved foundry operations. Assistance to modernize the Foundry and Mechanical Workshop in Somalia involved expertise provided by Egypt.

Other industrial categories

Capital goods industry with emphasis on energy-related technology

The Second Consultation on the Capital Goods Industry with Special Emphasis on Energy-related Technology and Equipment (Stockholm, Sweden, 10-14 June 1985), attended by 147 participants, considered such key issues as the obstacles faced by developing countries in entering the sector, strategies for integrated manufacture, and the development of the electric power equipment sector and technology unpackaging. The Consultation urged UNIDO to continue promoting the development of the sector in developing countries through, among other things, the testing and the dissemination of methodologies for production planning and technological project screening. It also asked UNIDO to promote activities for the development of small hydropower plants in view of the importance of rural electrification and potential uses of electric power in agriculture.

Preparatory activities for the Consultation included the Second Regional Expert Group Meeting on Capital Goods in Latin America (Santiago, Chile, 4-6 March).

REFERENCES

[1]ID/B/347. [2]YUN 1984, p. 584. [3]*Ibid.*, p. 585. [4]YUN 1983, p. 600. [5]ID/335. [6]YUN 1984, p. 587. [7]YUN 1982, p. 783.

PUBLICATIONS

Industry and Development: Global Report 1985 (ID/333), Sales No. E.85.II.B.1. *Industry and Development*, No. 12 (ID/SER.M/12), Sales No. E.84.II.B.4; No. 13 (ID/SER.M/13), Sales No. E.84.II.B.5; No. 14 (ID/SER.M/14), Sales No. E.85.II.B.3; No. 15 (ID/SER.M/15), Sales No. E.85.II.B.7; No. 16 (ID/SER.M/16), Sales No. E.85.II.B.10. *Regional Industrial Co-operation: Experiences and Perspectives of ASEAN and the Andean Pact* (ID/309), Sales No. E.85.II.B.5. *Input-Output Tables for Developing Countries*, vol. 2 (ID/325/Add.1), Sales No. E.85.II.B.6. *Industry in the 1980s: Structural Change and Interdependence* (ID/331), Sales No. E.85.II.B.8. *International Comparative Advantage in Manufacturing: Changing Profiles of Resources and Trade* (ID/334), Sales No. E.85.II.B.9. *Case Study on the Leather and Leather Products (Except Footwear) Industry: Trade Implications for Developing Countries* (TD/B/C.2/210/Rev.1), Sales No. E.85.II.D.19. *International Trade in the Petrochemical Sector: Implications for Developing Countries* (TD/B/C.2/209/Rev.1), Sales No. E.85.II.D.21.

Chapter VII

Transnational corporations

Transnational corporations (TNCs) continued to play a key role in the world economy, shaping international trade, foreign direct investment and international transfer of financial resources. Questions such as the regulation of their activities and their impact on the economies of host countries, especially developing ones, were ongoing considerations before the international community.

The Commission on Transnational Corporations held its eleventh session in New York from 10 to 19 April 1985 and decided, owing to a divergence of views, to postpone until 1986 its consideration of the question of meeting biennially instead of annually. As in previous years, a special session of the Commission was reconvened (New York, 17-21 June), and examined the outstanding issues in the draft code of conduct on TNCs. The Commission's Intergovernmental Working Group of Experts (third session, New York, 11-22 March) discussed international standards of accounting and reporting.

The United Nations Centre on TNCs conducted extensive research, continued to develop a comprehensive information system, and carried out technical co-operation projects focusing on low-income countries. It continued to monitor, and acted as the secretariat for public hearings on, the activities of TNCs in South Africa and Namibia (see p. 149).

In July, the Economic and Social Council took note of the Commission's report on its 1985 regular session (decision 1985/194) and approved the provisional agenda and documentation for the 1986 session (decision 1985/192).

Topics related to this chapter. Africa: transnational corporations. Development policy and international economic co-operation: International Development Strategy for the Third United Nations Development Decade. International trade: trade policy; restrictive business practices. Human rights: human rights violations—Africa.

Draft code of conduct

The task of formulating a code of conduct on TNCs, first considered in 1975,[1] continued in 1985. At its April session,[2] the Commission on TNCs urged that every effort be made to conclude negotiations on the code, and requested the Secretary-General to prepare a study on the outstanding issues, to be circulated to Governments prior to the reconvened special session. The study[3] was issued in May.

At its June special session,[4] reconvened pursuant to a 1984 General Assembly decision,[5] the Commission examined the main outstanding issues, which included the question of international law/obligations, permanent sovereignty, renegotiation of contracts, nationalization and compensation, fair and equitable treatment, national treatment, choice of law and means of dispute settlement, non-interference in internal affairs, non-collaboration by TNCs with South Africa, conflict of jurisdiction, and the transfer by TNCs of payments related to their investments. All delegations expressed willingness to consider the outstanding issues anew and in a flexible way. Many felt that the 1983 Chairmen's proposals[6] constituted the most appropriate basis for negotiations. During five formal and a number of informal meetings, various suggestions were made towards a compromise solution aimed at narrowing the differences. The Commission recommended the reconvening of the special session in 1986 to agree on an overall solution to the outstanding issues and to complete the code of conduct. It also suggested that the expert advisers who had attended the 1985 session be invited to the 1986 reconvened session.

The expert advisers attending the 1985 session (see APPENDIX III) submitted a statement[7] making suggestions for the resolution of the key outstanding issues. The USSR expert did not participate in formulating the text while the United States expert had reservations on it.

By **decision 1985/193** of 26 July, the Economic and Social Council decided to reconvene the Commission's special session from 20 to 31 January 1986 and to invite the expert advisers to participate, and requested the Secretary-General to revise his report on outstanding issues,[3] taking into account the suggestions made during the discussions.

Definition of TNC

The problem of defining TNCs continued to be examined by the Commission in 1985, as it had been every year since its first session 10 years previously, and a January 1985 report[8] by the

Centre's secretariat provided background information on the topic. The question had usually been deferred pending the outcome of negotiations on a code of conduct (see above), in which definition was a major issue. An important point of disagreement related to the nature of the ownership of the enterprise. The key issue was whether the code was applicable to State-owned or public enterprises as well as enterprises of private or mixed ownership. The report summarized the evolution of that definition over the years, outlining a progressive narrowing of differences.

At the Commission's April session,[2] delegations reiterated their previously stated views. Some stressed that the code should be a truly universal instrument that applied to all entities with TNCs, and called for flexibility to resolve the outstanding issues. Others emphasized the importance of finding an acceptable solution to the problems of the definition of TNCs and the scope of application of the code in their close interrelationships with other outstanding issues.

At the Commission's June session, the Chairman orally reported on consultations held in February, April and June, which produced a text to which there was no objection, although some expressed a preference for another text not specifying, as the first did, the point of private, public or mixed ownership. It was agreed that the final solution of this issue would depend on the satisfactory settlement of other outstanding issues.

Bilateral, regional and international arrangements relating to TNCs

The Centre on TNCs continued in 1985 to collect, monitor and analyse developments regarding international, regional and bilateral arrangements relating to TNCs. It was preparing technical papers on bilateral investment agreements, the key elements of international and regional arrangements having a bearing on TNC activities, and the experience gained in implementing the Declaration on International Investment and Multinational Enterprises of the Organisation for Economic Co-operation and Development.

In accordance with a 1984 Commission request,[9] the Centre submitted to the Commission's April session a report on developments under international arrangements and agreements on TNC-related matters.[10] The report examined the main developments under five international instruments, dealing with guidelines for TNCs, social policy, control of restrictive business practices, transfer of technology, and marketing of breast-milk substitutes. The report concluded that even if those instruments were of a voluntary nature, their adoption had generated impetus for their observance. Much activity was taking place, especially at the national level, to make those

instruments more effective, and TNCs themselves had felt the need to apply them. Such instruments had also provided a useful framework for international co-operation, and various international efforts were under way to establish additional standards on aspects of TNC activities.

The Commission requested the Centre to take into account, in its future work on the topic, the views expressed at its April 1985 session.[2]

REFERENCES

[1]YUN 1975, p. 484. [2]E/1985/28. [3]E/C.10/1985/S/2. [4]E/1985/109. [5]YUN 1984, p. 593, GA dec. 39/443, 18 Dec. 1984. [6]YUN 1983, p. 605. [7]E/C.10/1986/S/2. [8]E/C.10/1985/16. [9]YUN 1984, p. 594. [10]E/C.10/1985/6.

Standards of accounting and reporting

The Intergovernmental Working Group of Experts on International Standards of Accounting and Reporting, established by the Economic and Social Council in 1982,[1] held its third session in New York from 11 to 22 March 1985.[2] Before it were five studies prepared by the Centre on TNCs on the following topics: review of important current developments in accounting and reporting by TNCs;[3] legislative backing and enforcement, prudence and reserve accounting;[4] accounting and reporting for transactions denominated in foreign currencies;[5] accounting and reporting for research and development activities;[6] and ways of developing education, research and practical training in accounting and reporting in Member States.[7]

The Group's Chairman pointed out that in the dynamic business environment in which TNCs operated, opportunities for developing international accounting and reporting continued to arise, while there was a need to deal with new accounting and reporting issues. In the situation created by the recent global recession, international co-operation was needed to promote economic development in the public and private sectors, where accounting and reporting had an important role to play. To improve the availability of information disclosed by TNCs operating in developing countries, it was important to identify accounting and reporting standards applicable to TNCs. International harmonization was needed, but it did not imply uniformity of accounting standards and practices.

The Group considered legislative backing and enforcement to ensure compliance with standards promulgated by organizations, particularly the accountancy profession. It recalled the importance of each country having an effective legal means of implementing generally accepted standards, but felt that different mechanisms would be appropriate in different countries in view of the diversity of national legal systems and traditions.

Dealing with accounting and reporting for transactions denominated in foreign currencies, the Group agreed that there was a need for disclosure of information on methods of accounting, methods used in translating financial statements, and methods of accounting for unsettled balances. It identified additional items, recommending that they be considered for disclosure.

Considering accounting and reporting for research and development activities, the Group agreed on criteria relating to identification of cost elements, criteria to capitalize costs, and necessary disclosures. On ways of developing education, research and training in Member States, the Group pointed to the growing demand for accountants in developing countries, noted that efforts to increase their number were being restrained by the limited resources available for education programmes, and called for increased development assistance in that respect.

In April, the Commission took note of the Group's report and agreed that it would, after three years, review the Group's mandate, terms of reference and achievements, including the advisability of its continuation.[8]

ECONOMIC AND SOCIAL COUNCIL ACTION

On 26 July, on the recommendation of its First (Economic) Committee, the Economic and Social Council adopted **resolution 1985/71** without vote.

Intergovernmental Working Group of Experts on International Standards of Accounting and Reporting

The Economic and Social Council,

Recalling its resolutions 1979/44 of 11 May 1979 and 1982/67 of 27 October 1982,

Having considered the report of the Intergovernmental Working Group of Experts on International Standards of Accounting and Reporting on its third session,

Acting upon the recommendation of the Group at its third session concerning its future work,

1. *Decides* that the Intergovernmental Working Group of Experts on International Standards of Accounting and Reporting should continue to meet on the basis of its existing mandate;

2. *Agrees* that the results of the work of the Group should be brought to the attention of Governments, standard-setting bodies, the accountancy profession, transnational corporations and other interested parties through United Nations publications.

Economic and Social Council resolution 1985/71

26 July 1985   Meeting 52   Adopted without vote

Approved by First Committee (E/1985/146) without vote, 24 July (meeting 28); draft by Commission on TNCs (E/1985/28); agenda item 9.

REFERENCES

[1]YUN 1982, p. 788, ESC res. 1982/67, 27 Oct. 1982. [2]E/C.10/1985/12 & Corr.1. [3]E/C.10/AC.3/1985/2. [4]E/C.10/

AC.3/1985/3. [5]E/C.10/AC.3/1985/4. [6]E/C.10/AC.3/1985/5. [7]E/C.10/AC.3/1985/6. [8]E/1985/28.

Centre on TNCs

In 1985, the United Nations Centre on TNCs, the principal Secretariat unit for TNC-related matters, carried out research (see p. 621), continued to develop an information system (see p. 619), and conducted and sponsored technical co-operation activities (see p. 622). It assisted the Commission in formulating a code of conduct on TNCs (see p. 616), by preparing reports and by organizing intergovernmental meetings on the code (Baghdad, Iraq, and Buenos Aires, Argentina, November; and Bangkok, Thailand, December). It prepared studies for the Intergovernmental Working Group of Experts on International Standards of Accounting and Reporting (see above), and continued to monitor arrangements relating to TNCs (see p. 617).

As requested by the Committee for Programme and Co-ordination (CPC) in 1983, the Secretary-General submitted to it in March 1985 a report[1] on the triennial review of implementation of its 1979 recommendations[2] on the programme on TNCs. CPC[3] took note of the report's conclusion that the Centre had implemented all recommendations in the areas of programme formulation and the review process, policy analysis (research), the comprehensive information system, the code of conduct for TNCs and advisory services. It endorsed two of the report's proposals for further improvement, namely, that the Centre should intensify its efforts to utilize experience gained in its advisory and training projects as input into the design and orientation of other projects and should improve the feedback system for assessing the impact of the advisory services. CPC could not reach consensus on the other proposals.

In April,[4] the Commission on TNCs considered the Centre's activities since mid-1984, took note of the Secretary-General's report on them,[5] and requested him to report similarly in 1986. It took note of his intention to submit in 1986 a report on the Centre's utilization of resources during 1984-1985.

ECONOMIC AND SOCIAL COUNCIL ACTION

In July 1985, the Economic and Social Council, acting on the recommendation of its First Committee, adopted **decision 1985/195** by roll-call vote.

Work of the United Nations Centre on Transnational Corporations

At its 52nd plenary meeting, on 26 July 1985, the Council, bearing in mind General Assembly decision 39/443 of 18 December 1984, taking note of the proposals contained in draft resolutions E/1985/C.1/L.14 and E/1985/C.1/L.15, bearing in mind that those draft resolutions related to some important outstanding issues of the negotiations on the code of conduct on transnational corporations, and recognizing the importance of an early and successful completion of the code of conduct in a spirit of co-operation and understanding, decided that the issues raised in those draft resolutions should be considered after the reconvened special session of the Commission on Transnational Corporations in January 1986 at an appropriate occasion.

Economic and Social Council decision 1985/195

33-7 (roll-call vote)

Approved by First Committee (E/1985/146) by roll-call vote (29-7), 24 July (meeting 28); draft by Egypt, for Group of 77 (E/1985/C.1/L.20); agenda item 9.

Roll-call vote in Council as follows:

In favour: Algeria, Argentina, Bangladesh, Brazil, Bulgaria, China, Colombia, Ecuador, German Democratic Republic, Guinea, Haiti, India, Indonesia, Malaysia, Mexico, Morocco, Nigeria, Poland, Romania, Rwanda, Saudi Arabia, Senegal, Somalia, Sri Lanka, Suriname, Thailand, Turkey, Uganda, USSR, Venezuela, Yugoslavia, Zaire, Zimbabwe.

Against: Canada, Finland, Iceland, Japan, New Zealand, Sweden, United States.

In the First Committee, Luxembourg, on behalf of the member States of the European Economic Community (EEC), proposed an amendment to the draft decision, by which the Council, bearing in mind that State-owned enterprises from all groups of countries currently conducted transnational operations in many countries, and recognizing the importance of the completion of the code of conduct, would have decided that the above issues should be taken into account by the Centre in carrying out its work. The Committee, by a roll-call vote of 29 to 13, with 1 abstention, decided not to take action on the proposed amendment.

Earlier, Luxembourg, on behalf of EEC, had introduced in the Committee a draft resolution[6] by which the Council would have requested the Centre on TNCs to take into account in carrying out its work the fact that State-owned enterprises from all groups of countries currently conducted significant operations in many developing countries and that ownership should not be a determining criterion in defining the Centre's areas of activity. A United States draft with a similar thrust[7] added a provision that country of origin should also not be a determining criterion.

Speaking in the Council, Egypt said it had proposed the decision to safeguard the ongoing negotiations on the code of conduct, leaving outstanding issues to be discussed after the January 1986 session of the Commission on TNCs.

The United States said it would vote against the text, mainly because it ensured that the mandate of the Centre would continue to be unbalanced and unfair and that the Centre would lack clear approval to include in its work programme State-owned transnational enterprises from both market and centrally planned economies.

Luxembourg said the EEC members would be unable to participate in the voting; the draft merely delayed any decision on the issue. Spain (which did not participate in the voting) endorsed that statement, and Canada said it would vote against for the reasons explained by Luxembourg.

Speaking for the Eastern European socialist countries and Mongolia, Bulgaria said they had voted in favour in accordance with their general policy in favour of a code of conduct for TNCs.

Information system

During 1985, the Centre's comprehensive information system continued to acquire, process and disseminate information on TNCs and to respond to requests for information from Governments, organizations and others. The system focused on six areas: national laws and regulations related to TNCs; contracts and agreements between TNCs and host country entities; trends in TNC activities; TNC activities in various sectors; individual corporations; and sources of data and information.

The system continued to supply statistical data on flows and stocks of foreign direct investment obtained from intergovernmental organizations and Governments. It collected information on individual corporations (the subject on which the greatest number of requests were received) and began to collect data on the largest corporations in the service sectors. It continued to update its collection of contracts and agreements between TNCs and host country entities. A project was undertaken in 1985 to create a systematic index to the provisions of the Centre's growing collection of petroleum agreements.

The Centre assisted several developing countries in establishing and managing national information systems. It developed its roster of experts, entering the personal histories of more than 1,200 into its data base. It replied to 1,370 requests for information requiring some research, 570 of which were from developing countries. A total of 733 requests came from non-governmental organizations—trade unions, business organizations, academic institutions, public interest groups and the media. In addition, 1,700 short-answer requests were received.

In April,[4] the Commission on TNCs took note of a February progress report on the information system[8] and requested another report in 1986.

Joint units with regional commissions

Joint units established between the Centre on TNCs and the United Nations regional commissions in Africa, Asia and the Pacific, Europe, Latin America and the Caribbean, and Western Asia continued to operate in 1985.[9] Each unit's work programme was tailored to the needs of the region and complemented the work of the Centre; it included research on the economic, social and institutional issues of TNCs, information dissemination, and training and advisory services. During 1985, the work programmes of the units and of the Centre were further integrated.

The joint unit of the Centre and the Economic Commission for Africa undertook studies on activities of TNCs in the region, with emphasis on agricultural food and non-food commodities and mineral commodities. Research also concentrated on the flow of capital and other resources through the activities of transnational banks; a study on the role of those banks and financial institutions in Africa's development was completed, and case-studies on the role of TNCs in the banking sector in Nigeria and Liberia were undertaken. Studies were under way on joint ventures, on hotels and tourism, on the social and cultural impact of TNCs, and on the possibility of establishing African-owned multinational enterprises. A policy paper on TNC activities in the production and marketing of Africa's primary commodities and a progress report on the draft code of conduct on TNCs were submitted to the eighth Conference of African Ministers of Trade (Brazzaville, Congo, October), which expressed support for the code and appealed for its early adoption. A regional workshop was held for English-speaking African countries on the role of TNCs in Africa's mining industry (Manzini, Swaziland, July). Advisory and fact-finding missions were undertaken to Burundi, Cameroon, the Congo, the Ivory Coast, Togo and Zambia on the transfer of technology by TNCs in selected economic sectors.

The joint unit with the Economic Commission for Europe focused its research on two ongoing projects: an interregional project on transnational banks, and the role of developed country–based public development finance corporations and TNCs in enhancing private direct investment in developing countries. The unit assisted the Centre by providing information on technical expertise available in the region and of use to developing countries, and aided it in its technical assistance and advisory projects related to specific industries.

The joint unit with the Economic Commission for Latin America and the Caribbean focused on studies designed to enhance the negotiating capacity of the region's countries in their dealings with TNCs. It completed studies on the behaviour of TNCs in the context of the crisis affecting Latin America; on TNCs and Latin America's foreign trade; on computer services and information processing in development; on the behaviour of TNCs and State-owned corporations in the development of mining; on the bargaining capacity of countries in the area of commodities; and on the impact of TNCs in the economies of Argentina and Ecuador.

The unit advised one Government on renegotiating its debt to transnational banks and on company planning methods. In co-operation with Argentina and the Centre, it organized an expert group meeting on the code of conduct (Buenos Aires, November); it also took part in other regional meetings. Studies were under way on the impact of TNCs in the economies of Colombia and Paraguay; on transnational banks in Argentina and Uruguay; and on policies towards and negotiations with TNCs. Case-studies were begun on the comparative behaviour of TNCs, and on the changes in the balance between direct investment and loans in external financing. Work also began on setting up a data bank on the most significant variables relating to external capital, particularly that of TNCs.

The joint unit with the Economic and Social Commission for Asia and the Pacific (ESCAP) completed studies on export processing zones in selected Asian countries; on TNCs and the external financial flows of developing countries of the region; and on transnational trading corporations and State trading enterprises in India. Research was commenced on the views of host developing countries *vis-à-vis* TNCs based in those countries. Case-studies were under way for a project on technology acquisition through alternative arrangements with TNCs in selected countries of the region. With the Centre and the State Science and Technology Commission of China, the unit conducted a training workshop on regulating technology transfer through TNCs (Fuzhou, October). In co-operation with the Centre, it organized an expert group meeting on the code of conduct (Bangkok, December), followed by an *ad hoc* intergovernmental meeting on TNCs. It supported training workshops and advisory missions conducted by the Centre, participated in various meetings and conferences, and continued to establish focal points in several ESCAP member countries to provide direct, two-way communications between the unit and member countries.

The joint unit with the Economic and Social Commission for Western Asia prepared a report highlighting the widespread involvement of TNCs in Western Asia and its growing dependence on them. It produced an executive summary highlighting the main issues of the code relevant to Western Asian countries, and held, together with the Centre, a regional intergovernmental meeting on the code (Baghdad, November). Studies were in progress on the transfer of technology through TNCs and on external sovereign lending by transnational banks. Case-studies were under way on transnational banks in Oman and in the United Arab Emirates, and on the impact of TNC operations on development in the Gulf Co-operation Council region.

Research

The Centre's 1985 research activities comprised five broad areas: studies on the code of conduct and other international arrangements and agreements relating to TNCs; overall trends in TNC activities; strengthening of Governments' negotiating capacity in their relations with TNCs; political, social and cultural impact of TNCs; and specific issues and selected sectors.[10]

Research continued to concentrate on the activities of TNCs in South Africa and Namibia and in 1985 the Centre focused on the public hearings on TNC activities there (see p. 149) and acted as the secretariat for the hearings.

The Centre continued to analyse the impact of TNCs on the environment, publishing, with the United Nations Environment Programme (UNEP), a technical report on the subject. The Centre initiated a study on TNC environmental management policies and practices, and organized with UNEP an informal seminar (Geneva, December) to further international cooperation for the environmental management of industrial process safety and hazards.

The Centre published studies on international accounting and reporting issues,[11] on national legislation and regulations relating to TNCs,[12] on trends in foreign direct investment,[13] and on TNCs and international trade.[14] Two issues of the periodical *The CTC Reporter*[15] (circulation 10,000) were also published. Other studies and reports dealt with the draft code of conduct, the definition of TNCs, technology transfer, engineering and technical assistance consultancy contracts, and data services in Latin America and the Caribbean. An interregional project with some of the joint units was initiated, focusing on the role of transnational banks in the development process.

In April,[4] the Commission took note of a report on ongoing and future research.[10] Some delegations suggested that greater emphasis be attached to the positive effects of TNCs, and one stated that the free play of market forces should be a possibility examined when considering arrangements *vis-à-vis* TNCs. Others felt that inadequate attention had been given to the negative effects of TNCs, and that future research should examine TNC interference in the internal affairs of States and their adverse impact on host developing countries. Those delegations emphasized the importance of the study of the role of TNCs in the armaments industry and in the transfer of military technology. One delegation reiterated its opposition to such a study. Suggestions were made on possible future research topics. The Commission requested the Centre, in implementing its research programme, to take account of those views.

Transborder data flows

While the importance of transborder data flows was widely recognized, no organization except the Commission on TNCs was currently examining the role that TNCs played in that area, the Centre's Executive Director stated at the Commission's April session.[4] Many delegations requested the Centre to intensify its work on the subject, and suggested areas of further work. The Commission took note of a January 1985 report on that role (see below), agreed that work should continue along the same lines as in the past, taking into account the views expressed at the session, and agreed that a stronger link should be sought between the Centre's research on the topic and its technical assistance activities.

The Centre in 1985 continued its study of TNCs in trade and foreign direct investment in data services. Responding to a request by the Economic System for Latin America for a study on data services in Latin America and the Caribbean, the Centre prepared a report reviewing the status of the data-services industry in the region and the relevant policies pursued, focusing on the role of TNCs and discussing policy options available to countries interested in data services. The study was discussed at a workshop co-sponsored by Mexico in June, and the revised study was submitted to a Latin American Council meeting (Caracas, Venezuela, 27 November–8 December).[9]

A January 1985 report of the Centre[16] reviewed the principal developments relating to transborder data flows in a number of forums, presented a summary of a country case-study on transborder data flows and Poland,[17] and contained observations and suggestions on the Commission's future course of action on the subject.

TNCs and international economic relations

Research activities in 1985 also examined recent developments related to TNCs and international economic relations. The Centre submitted to the Commission two complementary reports on the topic, pursuant to a 1984 Commission request.

The first[18] examined capital flows to and from developing countries, focusing on the recent marked changes in the nature and magnitude of private sector inflows and outflows, particularly foreign direct investment. International lending by transnational banks, the report said, had increased rapidly during the 1970s and early 1980s, but had fallen abruptly in 1982, remaining thereafter at a comparatively low level. Flows of foreign direct investment by TNCs had also experienced a sharp reduction since their 1981 peak. These tendencies served to increase the debt of developing countries; in several cases, new inflows of private capital were insufficient to cover the various outflows relating to the stock of such capital. General trends in the volume and pattern of capital flows to developing countries since the mid-1970s indicated the debt-oriented nature of most flows, the high interest and related outflows to which they gave rise, and the consequent financing difficulties faced by the borrowing countries. Action suggested by the report included international efforts to ensure a global economic environment more favourable to developing countries; the early adoption of a code of conduct, minimizing the negative effects of foreign investment and giving TNCs assurance of a fair return on such investments; and new forms of co-operation between the public and private sectors in investment for development.

The second report[19] dealt with TNCs in international trade and foreign direct investment by TNCs, including capital inflows and outflows. It examined key aspects of the role of TNCs in international trade, with particular reference to policy issues relevant to developing countries. The report concluded by presenting two basic policy issues facing developing and developed countries alike. The first was the role played by TNCs in the continuing shifts of comparative advantage in world production and world trade, and the equally important role of the policy actions of host and home countries in trying to affect these shifts. The second was related to the problem of reverse net transfer of resources from developing countries observed since 1982-1983. While in the past developing countries had been capital importers (to finance the deficit in their balance of payments due to high goods and services imports), beginning in 1983 they had become capital exporters by running a surplus in the balance of trade and non-capital services. Their combined annual current deficit in 1984 and 1985 was estimated at $45 billion, while their net interest and payments and profit remittances were estimated at $54 billion in 1984 and $60 billion in 1985. The problem was ultimately a trade problem, and one in which action by TNCs was critical, due to their essential role in trade. While not necessarily part of the problem, TNCs were certainly part of any eventual solution.

In April,[4] the Commission requested the Secretary-General to prepare for its 1986 session a report on the existing situation with regard to statistics on foreign direct investment.

Technical co-operation

During 1985, the Centre saw a steady expansion of its technical co-operation activities. Many developing countries turned to the Centre for information and technical assistance in formulating their foreign investment and technology policies or in negotiating with TNCs. Programming missions were undertaken to Africa, Asia and the Pacific, as well as to the headquarters of regional and subregional organizations, resulting in various programmes being drawn up, to be executed mostly with funding from the United Nations Development Programme (UNDP).[9]

As part of its effort to support economic and technical co-operation among developing countries, the Centre continued to maintain close working relationships with over 20 subregional and regional centres and institutions. In 1985 numerous requests were received from those bodies for advisory, information and training services, and assistance was provided to member countries of the organizations in collaboration with their respective secretariats.

The Centre completed or initiated 113 advisory and information projects, 57 of which were in the natural resources sector and 22 in a number of industries in the manufacturing and service sectors. Of the total, 70 were in Africa, 35 in Asia and the Pacific, 6 in Latin America and the Caribbean and 2 in Western Asia.

Particular attention was given to low-income countries. Programming missions assisted them in identifying projects and in strengthening the professional expertise of officials in dealing with TNCs. During 1985, 61 advisory, information and training projects in low-income countries were executed or initiated.

The Centre organized 19 training projects, made up of training workshops/seminars, round tables and study tours, for some 500 government officials, executives of State enterprises, and private sector managers of various developing countries. Nine projects were held in Asia and the Pacific, five in Latin America, three in Africa, and one each in Western Asia and Europe.

Support to management institutes and higher learning institutions continued, with a view to sharpening the professional skills of public officials and private sector managers in TNC-related matters. Assistance to institutions in Asia and the Pacific included a training seminar for lecturers and instructors. Support to management and public administration institutes in selected African countries focused on a round-table meeting for their directors/principals. The meeting reviewed a multidisciplinary curriculum for a training programme on TNCs in Africa, and discussed the Centre's support in implementing the programme in various institutes.

In response to 1984 Commission requests, the Centre submitted two reports to the April 1985 Commission session. One evaluated the Centre's technical co-operation activities,[20] while the other examined measures adopted by developing countries in the previous 20 years to strengthen their negotiating capacity in dealing with TNCs, and suggested further international action to enhance their capabilities in that respect.[21]

In April,[4] the Commission reaffirmed the importance it attached to the Centre's technical co-operation programme.

Financing

The Centre's technical co-operation programme continued to be financed primarily by extrabudgetary resources from the Centre's Trust Fund and allocations from UNDP.[9] Total extrabudgetary resources amounted to $2,570,639. Contributions to the Trust Fund were made in 1985 by China ($20,000), Finland ($38,628), the Netherlands ($60,015), Norway ($163,604), the Republic of Korea ($10,172), Sweden ($190,006), Switzerland ($97,314) and Zambia ($2,451). The Fund's opening balance amounted to $921,260, and interest income to $120,000; resources made available by UNDP amounted to $947,189.

Total expenditures amounted to $1,384,915 in 1985, of which the UNDP share was 68.3 per cent, up from 66.3 per cent in 1984. Of this amount, advisory projects took $534,459, while workshops and other training activities took $850,456.

REFERENCES

[1]E/AC.51/1985/5. [2]YUN 1979, p. 625. [3]A/40/38. [4]E/1985/28. [5]E/C.10/1985/4. [6]E/1985/C.1/L.14. [7]E/1985/C.1/L.15. [8]E/C.10/1985/11. [9]E/C.10/1986/4. [10]E/C.10/1985/10. [11]*International Accounting and Reporting Issues: 1985 Review* (ST/CTC/85), Sales No. E.85.II.A.13. [12]*National Legislation and Regulations Relating to Transnational Corporations* (ST/CTC/53), Sales No. E.85.II.A.14. [13]*Trends and Issues in Foreign Direct Investment and Related Flows* (ST/CTC/59), Sales No. E.85.II.A.15. [14]*Transnational Corporations and International Trade: Selected Issues* (ST/CTC/52), Sales No. E.85.II.A.4. [15]*The CTC Reporter*, Nos. 19 and 20. [16]E/C.10/1985/13. [17]*Transborder Data Flows and Poland: Polish Case Study* (ST/CTC/50), Sales No. E.84.II.A.8. [18]E/C.10/1985/2. [19]E/C.10/1985/3. [20]E/C.10/1985/14/Add.1. [21]E/C.10/1985/15.

OTHER PUBLICATIONS

Environmental Aspects of the Activities of Transnational Corporations, (ST/CTC/55), Sales No. E.85.II.A.11; *Activities of Transnational Corporations in South Africa and Namibia and the Responsibilities of Home Countries with Respect to Their Operations in This Area* (ST/CTC/84), Sales No. E.85.II.A.16.

Chapter VIII

Regional economic and social activities

The regional commissions of the United Nations continued to work to increase regional economic and social co-operation during 1985.

Four of the five commissions held their regular intergovernmental sessions: the Economic and Social Commission for Asia and the Pacific (ESCAP) at Bangkok, Thailand (19-29 March); the Economic Commission for Europe (ECE)' at Geneva (16-27 April); the Economic Commission for Western Asia (which changed its name in 1985 to the Economic and Social Commission for Western Asia (ESCWA)) at Baghdad, Iraq (20-25 April); and the Economic Commission for Africa (ECA) at Addis Ababa, Ethiopia (25-29 April). The Economic Commission for Latin America and the Caribbean (ECLAC) did not meet in regular session.

Among issues of concern to the regional commissions considered by the General Assembly in 1985 were: a Preferential Trade Area for Eastern and Southern African States (resolution 40/186), the particular problems facing Zaire with regard to transport, transit and access to foreign markets (40/190), co-operation between the United Nations and the Southern African Development Co-ordination Conference (SADCC) (40/195), and questions relating to the proposed programme budget for the biennium 1986-1987 (sections V, VI and VIII of resolution 40/252).

The Assembly, in **resolution 40/105**, invited incorporation of the interests of women in the work programmes of the regional commissions (see AD-MINISTRATIVE AND BUDGETARY QUESTIONS, Chapter III).

The Economic and Social Council, in July, took action in support of the Industrial Development Decade for Africa (resolution 1985/61), the African Institute for Economic Development and Planning (1985/62), the Substantial New Programme of Action (SNPA) for the 1980s for the Least Developed Countries (LDCs) in the African LDCs during the second half of the decade (1985/63), the Transport and Communications Decade in Africa (1985/65), women and development in Africa (1985/67) and the Europe-Africa permanent link through the Strait of Gibraltar (1985/70). The Council, in addition, decided to include Portuguese among the official working languages of ECA (resolution 1985/68), amended the terms of reference of ESCAP (1985/60) in the light of Brunei Darussalam and Tuvalu becoming members, and

sought to strengthen the directorships of Multinational Programming and Operational Centres (MULPOCs) (1985/66).

The Council took note of summaries of the annual surveys of current economic and social conditions in each region, prepared by commission secretariats, during its discussion of the world economic situation in July (decision 1985/182).

Topics related to this chapter. Development policy and international economic co-operation: economic and social trends and policy. Operational activities for development. Economic assistance, disasters and emergency relief. Food. Environment. United Nations officials: personnel management—status of women in the Secretariat.

Regional co-operation

The executive secretaries of the five regional commissions met at Addis Ababa on 25 and 26 February and at Geneva on 12 July under the chairmanship of the Director-General for Development and International Economic Co-operation. They reviewed the regional economic situation in the context of the global situation, problems facing LDCs, and interregional and multilateral co-operation. The February meeting examined initiatives to promote technical and economic co-operation among the developing countries of the different regions, as called for by the Council in 1983[1] and the General Assembly in 1984,[2] to identify new proposals to strengthen their co-operation and to establish appropriate consultation and co-ordination mechanisms for carrying out activities. Project proposals to promote interregional technical and economic co-operation in a number of areas were identified and a regional commission was designated to take the lead role in co-ordinating activities for each proposal.

Project outlines prepared by the lead commissions were circulated to other commissions for comment and further examined during the July meeting of the executive secretaries. Draft documents were to be further considered by them in 1986. Funding was to be dealt with when the documents were finalized.

In reports on regional co-operation of June 1985[3] and June 1986[4] to the Economic and Social Council, covering the periods from mid-year to mid-year for 1984/85 and 1985/86, respectively, the Secretary-General described the work of the regional commissions and the meetings of the executive secretaries and drew attention to issues and decisions of the commissions calling for Council action or attention.

On 26 July, the Council adopted without vote **decision 1985/191**, taking note of several reports it had considered in connection with the question of regional co-operation, including the Secretary-General's June 1985 report.

Pursuant to a 1982 General Assembly resolution,[5] the Secretary-General reported[6] to the Committee for Programme and Co-ordination (CPC) in April on progress made in the decentralization of United Nations activities. He stated that, while consultations between regional commissions and global entities continued to take place on the distribution of responsibilities, no specific activities and corresponding resources had been identified for redeployment from global entities to the regional commissions in the programme budget proposals for the 1986-1987 biennium. However, a higher than average growth had been proposed for the commissions, which had been given priority consideration and reinforcement with respect to current programme budget proposals.

REFERENCES

[1]YUN 1983, p. 418, ESC res. 1983/66, 29 July 1983. [2]YUN 1984, p. 402, GA res. 39/216, 18 Dec. 1984. [3]E/1985/106. [4]E/1986/98. [5]YUN 1982, p. 828, GA res. 37/214, 20 Dec. 1982. [6]E/AC.51/1985/13.

Africa

A good 1985 rainy season broke the intensity of the 1983-1985 drought, but that did not mean Africa's economic crisis was over, the ECA Executive Secretary stated in his biennial report for 1984-1985.[1] While the food situation improved significantly, the prices of export commodities, including minerals, fell sharply, government expenditures declined due to shortfalls in foreign exchange earnings as well as to adjustments proposed by the International Monetary Fund (IMF) and the World Bank or undertaken independently of their advice, unemployment increased, official development assistance (ODA) remained stagnant, capital inflows decreased, and external indebtedness rose under unfavourable borrowing terms and a decrease in repayment capacity.

ECA activities. The major activities of the Economic Commission for Africa were aimed at achieving the goals of the 1980 Lagos Plan of Action for the Implementation of the Monrovia Strategy for the Economic Development of Africa.[2] The twentieth session of the Commission (eleventh meeting of its Conference of Ministers) was held from 25 to 29 April at Addis Ababa.[3] The Conference, whose main theme was the African economic and social crisis, adopted 31 resolutions on 29 April, on such matters as industrial development, women and development, the African Institute for Economic Development and Planning, measures to implement an action plan for LDCs, social welfare policies and transport and communications.

The Conference, after a mid-term review of progress in implementing the Lagos Plan, adopted a series of recommendations[4] for accelerating attainment of its goals, covering all major socio-economic sectors, and it asked[5] that they be transmitted to the twenty-first ordinary session of the Assembly of Heads of State and Government of the Organization of African Unity (OAU) (Addis Ababa, 18-20 July). The recommendations constituted a programme for the structural adjustment of the African economies devastated by drought, desertification and natural calamities. While Africa had the primary responsibility for dealing with the crisis, its magnitude called for international assistance. The recommendations covered food and agriculture, industry, natural and human resources, science and technology, transport and communications, trade and finance, economic and technical co-operation, environment and development, LDCs, energy, women and development, development planning, statistics and population. It also outlined a special programme of action for improving the food situation and for rehabilitating agriculture in Africa, and proposed a common platform for action through strengthened or newly created international negotiation and consultation measures and institutions. The Conference of Ministers also adopted the Second Special Memorandum on international action for relaunching the initiative for long-term development and economic growth in Africa[6] (see below), for presentation to the Economic and Social Council, and approved a memorandum submitted to it by the Conference of Ministers of African Least Developed Countries in April on the mid-term global review of the implementation of SNPA in Africa, for presentation to the high-level meeting of the United Nations Conference on Trade and Development (UNCTAD) Intergovernmental Group on LDCs (see p. 434).

The recommendations were considered by the OAU Assembly, which adopted a priority programme for economic recovery to be implemented during 1986-1990.

Economic and social trends

Regional output, which in 1983 had grown imperceptibly, stagnated in 1984, according to a summary[7] of the survey of economic and social conditions in Africa, 1983-1984, which disclosed that apart from central Africa, where gross domestic product (GDP) increased by 2.8 per cent in 1983 and 4.3 per cent in 1984, there was a recession across the continent. The area most affected was western Africa, where output had declined since 1980. Oil-exporting countries recorded a decline in output, although non-members of the Organization of Petroleum Exporting Countries (OPEC), such as Angola, Cameroon, the Congo and Egypt, generally recorded good performances. Among OPEC members, Nigeria was the most seriously hurt by an oil glut; its export revenues were reduced by half during 1980-1983. In contrast, Algeria maintained growth by diversifying its hydrocarbon sector, particularly through the expansion of gas production and exports, and streamlining its industrial sector. Ghana and Uganda achieved growth following currency adjustments.

The African drought was reflected in a 2.6 per cent drop in gross agricultural output during 1983, the downturn reaching 6.6 per cent in western Africa. Lack of rain affected nearly 182 million people in 27 countries, a vast area from the Sahel to eastern and southern Africa. Industrialization stalled, with the average growth of manufacturing output in developing Africa being only 1.5 per cent for 1980-1984. The only subregion with continuous growth was northern Africa, increasing 5.2 per cent in 1984 and averaging 4.5 per cent between 1980 and 1984.

The Economic and Social Council, on 25 July, took note of the summary report, among others, when it adopted **decision 1985/182**.

Overall prospects were uncertain for 1985. Food shortages were expected to remain a major problem in 21 countries. In the event of further drought, growth would probably fall to 1 per cent.

The ECA Conference approved a resolution[8] expressing its gratitude to the countries, organizations and individuals that had provided generous aid to crisis-affected African countries and appealing for continued aid. The General Assembly, in **resolution 40/100**, noted the critical economic and social situation in Africa and called for full implementation of its 1984 Declaration on the Critical Economic Situation in Africa.[9] (See also Chapter III of this section.)

Activities in 1985

Development policy and regional economic co-operation

The ECA Conference of Ministers in April 1985 adopted a Second Special Memorandum,[6] dealing with international action for relaunching the initiative for long-term development and economic growth in Africa (the first was adopted in 1984[10]). About 70 per cent of Africa's population was currently either destitute or below the poverty line, with per capita annual incomes equivalent to less than

$59 and $115 at 1972 prices respectively, the Memorandum said. Approximately half of the labour force was unemployed or underemployed; close to 60 per cent of the population lived in slums or squatter settlements; the availability of water remained a critical problem; child mortality in sub-Saharan Africa was almost double the average of that in other developing countries; and the number of malnourished people was estimated to have increased from 80 million in the early 1970s to more than 100 million in 1984.

At the root of Africa's crisis were the internal structural imbalances of African economies and their excessive outward orientation and overt dependence—a legacy of their colonial past. Post-independence development policies had not brought about significant change in the lopsided production structure, heavily dominated by export-oriented agriculture, a small industrial base, and a mining sector which was dependent on external finance, technology and management and whose output was predominantly exported.

It was beyond the capacity of African Governments to tackle the crisis unaided. International assistance must be directed to supporting Africa's efforts to attack the root causes of the socio-economic crisis and underdevelopment. The ECA Conference reaffirmed its commitment to both the philosophy and objectives of the Lagos Plan of Action, spelling out the long-term measures required for the restructuring of African economies. The Conference outlined international support measures needed in such priority areas as population; food and agricultural, industrial and infrastructural development; trade and finance; natural resources; combating drought and desertification; science and technology; and human resources.

On 29 April, the Conference adopted[11] the Second Special Memorandum, asking that it be transmitted, along with the decisions of the OAU Assembly, to the Economic and Social Council for consideration and action in support of the proposals. It appealed to the international community to support the priority areas outlined, and appealed to African member States to intensify their efforts to attack the root causes of the crisis by implementing the measures proposed.

On the same date, it adopted a resolution[12] on the subregional, regional and interregional economic and technical co-operation needed to deal with the crisis in Africa, including drought and desertification. It urged ECA member States to co-operate within their respective regional institutions as well as with their subregions, with the assistance of MULPOCs, in tackling the crisis. It called on States to rededicate themselves to implementing each sector of the Lagos Plan of Action.

ECA continued diverse technical co-operation activities in 1985, utilizing United Nations, multilateral and bilateral funds. United Nations funds provided support to 10 regional advisers and to MULPOCs' advisory services, in the areas of economic co-operation, statistics, social and manpower development, energy, public administration and finance, transport and communications, research and administration. United Nations Development Programme (UNDP) funds also supported MULPOCs and financed projects in statistics, industry, national accounts, transport and communications, and integration of women in development. United Nations Fund for Population Activities (UNFPA) funds supported population activities. Funds made available by the Voluntary Fund for the United Nations Decade for Women and the United Nations Trust Fund for African Development, and direct grants from Governments, supplied training, supported projects and provided experts for a wide variety of programmes.

Implementation of the 1980 Lagos Plan of Action

A report[13] on progress in implementing the 1980 Lagos Plan of Action[2] was submitted to the Economic and Social Council by the ECA secretariat in April 1985. It covered activities—studies, reports, programmes, advisory services, conferences, workshops, seminars—undertaken in various sectors to implement the Plan, the five main pillars of which were: promotion of national self-sufficiency; acceleration of intra-African economic integration; democratization of the development process; eradication of mass poverty and mass unemployment; and equitable distribution of benefits of development and economic growth.

Also submitted was a report[14] on implementation of the Final Act of Lagos, an integral part of the Plan of Action, under which African States committed themselves to set up an African economic community by the year 2000. The report stressed that African countries must realize that as long as they were strongly attached to pre-independence political, economic, social and cultural relations and as long as socio-economic policy was still oriented to the outside world, intra-African co-operation would be extremely difficult to bring about. It was necessary for States to rededicate themselves to sectoral co-operation under the Plan of Action. It was suggested that technical and political preparations be made in phases between 1986 and 1997, through a comprehensive programme of studies and meetings at various levels, for the establishment of the African economic community.

ECA, in addition, presented to the Council an appraisal[15] of economic performance in Africa for 1980-1985, in the light of the International Development Strategy for the Third United Nations Development Decade (the 1980s)[16] (see Chapter I of this section) as well as the Lagos Plan of Action. It reported that the African region had fallen far behind the Strategy's objective of a 7 per cent annual increase in GDP; at 1980 prices, GDP had decreased by 1.3 per cent in 1981, increased by that amount in 1982, stagnated in 1983 and declined by 0.1 per cent in 1984.

After reviewing the progress made in implementing the Plan of Action and the Final Act of Lagos, the ECA Conference adopted recommendations[4] to accelerate achievement of the Plan's objectives, and asked[5] that they be transmitted to OAU (see p. 802).

UN Trust Fund for African Development

In 1985, according to ECA,[17] the United Nations Trust Fund for African Development made available $100,585 for projects in industry, agriculture, natural resources, public administration, trade, economic co-operation and socio-economic research and planning.

Several States and intergovernmental organizations pledged about $2 million at the fifth biennial pledging conference for the Fund, held during the April meeting of the ECA Conference.[1] The Conference[18] urged States to deposit any unpaid pledges and appealed for generous contributions to the Fund.

Development planning

. Action was taken by the ECA Conference on three organizations concerned with development and planning—the Pan-African Documentation and Information System (PADIS), the African Centre of Meteorological Applications for Development (ACMAD), and the African Institute for Economic Development and Planning (IDEP).

The exchange of data among member States and their development institutions was promoted through PADIS, whose central co-ordination office was located at Addis Ababa. The PADIS data base on economic and social development literature in Africa currently contained more than 5,000 references.

Other PADIS activities included: publication at regular intervals of DEVINDEX-Africa, an index of literature on African development; publication at regular intervals of the Referral Information System where data bases in support of technical co-operation among developing countries (TCDC) contained personnel skills, research projects, development institutions and training programmes; training personnel of African documentation centres; and assisting member States in establishing national documentation centres.

The Regional Technical Committee for PADIS, set up in 1984,[19] at its first meeting (Addis Ababa, 26-28 March 1985)[20] discussed and made recommendations on the establishment of a regional co-operative information system and of a data-transmission network, increased assistance to member States and African institutions, the choice of computer technologies for PADIS, and financial implications of and capacity to execute the PADIS programme.

On the Technical Committee's recommendation, the ECA Conference adopted a resolution[21] empowering the ECA Executive Secretary to negotiate with development aid agencies for financial assistance to PADIS, with member States on their participation in the technical and financial aspects of PADIS, and with technical bodies on the feasibility of establishing a pan-African data-transmission network. The Executive Secretary was asked to set up a team of technical advisers to help implement the project.

In another action,[22] the Conference decided to establish ACMAD to improve the understanding of atmospheric and climatic processes in the continent, collect, analyse and disseminate meteorological and hydrological data as an early warning system, and train scientists and technicians in applying meteorology to development. It appealed to the United Nations Sudano-Sahelian Office (UNSO) and UNDP to provide financial support to ACMAD. Recommendations on the composition of its governing body were made at the third meeting of the Joint Intergovernmental Regional Committee on Human Settlements and Environment (Addis Ababa, 22-26 July); the directors of national meteorological services at the Second Technical Conference on the Management of Meteorological Services in Africa (Bujumbura, Burundi, 13-18 November)[23] of the World Meteorological Organization (WMO) set up an *ad hoc* committee to work with ECA on the preparatory phase.

The Conference also adopted a resolution[24] urging the Executive Secretary to mobilize extrabudgetary resources for IDEP through technical assistance programmes, asked countries to pay their arrears and make voluntary contributions, and recommended that UNDP continue its financial support.

ECONOMIC AND SOCIAL COUNCIL ACTION

On 26 July, on the recommendation of its First (Economic) Committee, the Economic and Social Council adopted by vote **resolution 1985/62**.

African Institute for Economic Development and Planning

The Economic and Social Council,

Recalling resolutions 285(XII) of 28 February 1975, 350(XIV) of 27 March 1979, 399(XV) of 12 April 1980 and, particularly, 433(XVII) of 30 April 1982 of the Conference of Ministers of the Economic Commission for Africa, on the African Institute for Economic Development and Planning,

Recalling also Conference of Ministers resolution 526(XIX) of 26 May 1984, in which the Conference expressed concern about the deepening economic and social crisis in Africa and its grave implications for the peoples and economies of the continent, and considering the role and contribution that the Institute can play in alleviating and managing the present economic crisis,

Considering that at its twenty-seventh meeting, held at Addis Ababa on 9 and 10 January 1985, the Governing Council of the Institute requested the Conference of Ministers of the Commission, at its eleventh meeting, to prepare and adopt a resolution urging Member States, the United Nations Development Programme and the General Assembly to assist in the future funding of the African Institute for Economic Development and Planning,

Noting that the Institute should expand its teaching and research activities in line with the objectives of the Lagos Plan of Action for the Implementation of the Monrovia Strategy for the Economic Development of Africa and that the major obstacle to its doing so is the inadequacy of financial resources,

Conscious that there is a need to consolidate and strengthen the financial position of the Institute in the medium term,

1. *Recommends* that the United Nations Development Programme should continue its financial support to the African Institute for Economic Development and Planning in view of the fact that it can serve as a resource institution assisting the Secretary-General and the Programme in their intensified efforts to help Africa alleviate its economic and social crisis;

2. *Recommends* to the General Assembly the incorporation of four posts for core professional staff for the African Institute for Economic Development and Planning into the United Nations regular budget as a contribution to the long-term financing of the Institute, in the same spirit as it has done for other regional institutions in Africa, such as the Multinational Programming and Operational Centres, and, outside Africa, in the region of the Economic Commission for Latin America and the Caribbean.

Economic and Social Council resolution 1985/62

26 July 1985   Meeting 52   28-5-12

Approved by First Committee (E/1985/145) by roll-call vote (28-5-12), 23 July (meeting 27); draft by ECA (E/1985/106), orally amended by Secretary following informal consultations; agenda item 8.
Financial implications. S-G, E/1985/C.1/L.11/Rev.1.

Before the vote in both the First Committee and the Council, a separate vote was taken on paragraph 2—at the request of the United Kingdom in the First Committee, where it was adopted by a roll-call vote of 27 to 7, with 10 abstentions, and in the Council by 28 votes to 7, with 8 abstentions.

Explaining its opposition, the United States said the resolution involved totally unjustified financial implications for the regular budget. Luxembourg said the European Economic Community (EEC) member countries had also been unable to support the text: ECA's practice of submitting draft resolutions with financial implications to the Council was not acceptable; moreover, they had been submitted without adequate explanation, and the information provided had come too late for referral to Governments.

Least developed countries

The Intergovernmental Committee of Experts of African Least Developed Countries held its fourth meeting at Addis Ababa (11-13 April)[25] and the Conference of Ministers of African LDCs its fifth (23 and 24 April).[26]

The Intergovernmental Committee considered four major topics focusing on African LDCs; their economic and social situation; the implementation of SNPA; pricing policies; and ECA activities in 1983 and 1984. It recommended to the Conference of Ministers a resolution on measures to ensure the accelerated implementation of SNPA in African LDCs during the second half of the 1980s, which the Conference adopted[27] and which was the basis for **resolution 1985/63** adopted by the Economic and Social Council in July.

The fifth meeting reviewed economic and social conditions in the African LDCs in 1981-1984, implementation of SNPA for those years, the impact on LDCs of industrial capacity underutilization, and ECA activities in 1984, its work programme in 1985 and the special operational work programme in favour of LDCs for 1986-1987. It submitted to the ECA Conference of Ministers a memorandum on the mid-term global review of the implementation of SNPA in Africa, for presentation to the high-level meeting of the UNCTAD Intergovernmental Group on LDCs in September/October (see p. 434).

ECONOMIC AND SOCIAL COUNCIL ACTION

On 26 July, on the recommendation of its First Committee, the Economic and Social Council adopted without vote **resolution 1985/63**.

Measures to ensure the effective and accelerated implementation of the Substantial New Programme of Action in the African least developed countries during the second half of the 1980s

The Economic and Social Council,

Recalling General Assembly resolutions 37/224 of 20 December 1982, 38/195 of 20 December 1983 and 39/174 of 17 December 1984 on the implementation of the Substantial New Programme of Action for the 1980s for the Least Developed Countries,

Recalling also resolution 397(XV) of 12 April 1980 of the Conference of Ministers of the Economic Commission for Africa, by which the Conference of Ministers entrusted the Conference of Ministers of African Least Developed Countries with the responsibility for ensuring the co-ordination of efforts, establishing priorities, monitoring and evaluating progress under the Comprehensive New Programme of Action for the Least Developed Countries in African least developed countries, and Conference of Ministers resolution 503(XIX) of 26 May 1984 on measures for the effective implemen-

tation of the Substantial New Programme of Action in African least developed countries,

Deeply concerned about the continued serious deterioration in the economic and social conditions of the African least developed countries, exacerbated by the severe drought which has spread across the African region, creating enormous imbalances in food supply and consequently widespread famine in many countries,

Recognizing that there is therefore a need to assist the African least developed countries to effect the necessary structural changes and that they will need increased aid from donors in order to achieve this objective,

Noting with satisfaction the results of the Conference on the Emergency Situation in Africa, convened at Geneva on 11 and 12 March 1985 by the Secretary-General, which was aimed at mobilizing the international community to provide the necessary financial and technical assistance in favour of African countries, especially the least developed among them,

Expressing deep concern and disappointment at the painfully slow pace in the implementation of the Substantial New Programme of Action in the least developed countries, twenty-six of which are located in Africa, since its adoption in September 1981, and at the negative results of the negotiations on the resolution concerning the implementation of the Substantial New Programme of Action at the sixth session of the United Nations Conference on Trade and Development, held at Belgrade from 6 June to 2 July 1983,

Recognizing that primary responsibility for their development rests with the least developed countries themselves,

Noting the tremendous efforts made by the African least developed countries in the organization of their respective country review meetings, especially in devising strategies and policies aimed at ensuring the successful implementation of their national development plans and public investment programmes and projects,

1. *Strongly urges* the African least developed countries to prepare themselves adequately, with the assistance of the Economic Commission for Africa, for the mid-term global review of the implementation of the Substantial New Programme of Action for the 1980s for the Least Developed Countries, to be carried out in September/October 1985, in order to make practical proposals for the readjustment of the Substantial New Programme of Action, as appropriate, to take into consideration their special circumstances and expedite its implementation during the second half of the 1980s;

2. *Urges* all countries, multilateral financing institutions, United Nations organizations and other concerned intergovernmental, non-governmental and international organizations to be represented at a high level at the meeting on the mid-term global review and to take appropriate measures to put the Substantial New Programme of Action into its proper perspective in order to ensure its effective implementation during the second half of the 1980s;

3. *Urges* the African least developed countries to intensify their efforts towards increased agricultural production, especially of food, as a means of reducing their ever-increasing dependence on external sources for food, and calls upon the international community to provide the necessary technical and financial assistance for agricultural and rural development in the African least developed countries;

4. *Urges:*

(*a*) The developed countries to reaffirm the commitments they undertook under the International Development Strategy for the Third United Nations Development Decade with respect to the target of 0.7 per cent of gross national product as official development assistance and to the achievement of that goal by 1985, and in any case not later than in the second half of the Decade;

(*b*) Donor countries, within the overall context of the Substantial New Programme of Action for the 1980s for the Least Developed Countries, as adopted, and of progress towards the 0.7 per cent target, to attain 0.15 per cent of their gross national product as official development assistance or to double their official development assistance to the least developed countries by 1985 or as soon as possible thereafter;

5. *Calls upon* the General Assembly to consider increasing the human and financial resources at the disposal of the programme for the African least developed countries of the Economic Commission for Africa so that those countries can be given more effective assistance.

Economic and Social Council resolution 1985/63

26 July 1985   Meeting 52   Adopted without vote

Approved by First Committee (E/1985/145) without vote, 23 July (meeting 27); draft by ECA (E/1985/106), orally amended by Secretary following informal consultations; agenda item 8.

The United States said that, although it had not voted against the text, it had previously reserved its position on the ODA target as well as on SNPA, and did not hold itself committed to reaching those targets. The Federal Republic of Germany and the United Kingdom said they were prepared to accept the target, but not the time scales envisaged. The Federal Republic of Germany added that acceptance of paragraph 4 could not prejudge the outcome of the forthcoming negotiations on the mid-term review of SNPA.

International trade and finance

The Conference of African Ministers of Trade (eighth session, Brazzaville, Congo, 28-31 October)[28] considered and made recommendations on recent developments in Africa's international trade relations, domestic and intra-African trade expansion, trade promotion and market research, activities of transnational corporations (TNCs) in Africa and establishment of an African Monetary Fund. It adopted three resolutions, by one of which it decided to convene a preparatory meeting of African experts prior to any future round of multilateral trade negotiations to harmonize the African position, asking the meeting to accord priority to agricultural products, special trade preferences and trade in services. By another, it expressed appreciation of joint ECA International Trade Centre activities for the establishment of trade data banks and a regional trade information system based on use of PADIS, and invited support for those activities. By the third, it expressed support for and urged expeditious con-

clusion of negotiations for a code of conduct on TNCs.

The ECA Conference in April adopted a resolution[29] on the role of trade and finance in alleviating Africa's social and economic crisis. It recommended that African countries develop effective distribution channels in domestic trade and finance and perhaps set up national units to monitor external debt and advise Governments on debt management. It urged them, through subregional and regional institutions, to launch a "Buy African goods" campaign; decided to establish a Conference of African Ministers of Finance to meet at least every two years to assess the impact of the international situation on African economies, assess Africa's external debts, suggest ways to increase resource flows, promote information exchange and devise strategies to strengthen Africa's position in financial negotiations; and appealed to developed countries and lending institutions to increase resource flows to Africa on more concessional terms.

The secretariat concentrated on three main areas: trade and finance information, trade promotion, and advisory services and training. It gave attention to helping African countries diversify their structural and geographical export and import patterns. Studies were completed of domestic trade structure, mechanisms and distribution channels in the Niger, Senegal and Sierra Leone.

Proposed financing

In a report[30] on progress in setting up an African Monetary Fund, submitted to the sixth meeting of the Technical Preparatory Committee of the Whole (Arusha, United Republic of Tanzania, 15-22 April), ECA stated that its advantages could not be over-emphasized. It would provide African countries with access to an autonomous African monetary system, the possibility of having a common unit of accounting, new sources of additional credit tranche and capital resources, exchange-rate surveillance, technical support programmes, balance-of-payment support, an African monitoring policy and an African-oriented adjustment programme.

A feasibility study on the Fund was adopted at the second meeting of ECA's Intergovernmental Group of Experts from Ministries of Finance and Central Banks on the establishment of an African Monetary Fund (Addis Ababa, 11-15 April).[31] It had been commissioned by the Group in 1982[32] and prepared in collaboration with the secretariats of four African organizations.

Preferential Trade Area for Eastern and Southern African States

GENERAL ASSEMBLY ACTION

On 17 December, on the recommendation of the Second (Economic and Financial) Committee, the

General Assembly adopted without vote **resolution 40/186**. The draft had been deferred from its 1984 session.[33]

Preferential Trade Area for Eastern and Southern African States

The General Assembly,

Recalling its resolutions 3362(S-VII) of 16 September 1975 on development and international economic co-operation and 36/180 of 17 December 1981, in which the international community was invited to apply special measures for the social and economic development of Africa in the 1980s,

Recalling also its resolution 37/139 of 17 December 1982, in which it, *inter alia*, called upon donor Governments and organs, organizations and bodies of the United Nations system to provide substantial resources for promoting the accelerated development of African countries and the effective implementation of the Lagos Plan of Action for the Implementation of the Monrovia Strategy for the Economic Development of Africa, and the Final Act of Lagos,

Appreciating in this regard the establishment of the Preferential Trade Area for Eastern and Southern African States in December 1981,

Noting the progress made in the reduction of tariffs among member States to stimulate growth and development in the area, in the launching of clearance and payments arrangements and in the measures taken to intensify co-operation among member States in the agricultural, industrial, educational, cultural and other sectors, with a view to creating an economic community of the eastern and southern African States by the year 1992,

1. *Invites* donor Governments to provide substantial financial and technical assistance to the Preferential Trade Area for Eastern and Southern African States to accelerate its development into an economic community;

2. *Invites also* the United Nations Development Programme to continue to make resources available to the Preferential Trade Area from its regional indicative planning figures on an urgent basis;

3. *Calls upon* international financial institutions, particularly the World Bank, the International Development Association, the International Fund for Agricultural Development and the African Development Bank, to provide immediate assistance to the Preferential Trade Area;

4. *Invites* the organs, organizations and bodies of the United Nations system to take into account in their work programmes co-operation with the Preferential Trade Area;

5. *Requests* the Secretary-General to report to the General Assembly at its forty-first session on the implementation of the present resolution.

General Assembly resolution 40/186

17 December 1985   Meeting 119   Adopted without vote

Approved by Second Committee (A/40/989/Add.3) without vote, 5 December (meeting 48); 12-nation draft (A/C.2/40/L.9), orally amended by Vice-Chairman based on informal consultations; agenda item 84 *(c)*.

Sponsors: Burundi, Djibouti, Ethiopia, Kenya, Lesotho, Malawi, Rwanda, Somalia, Swaziland, Uganda, Zambia, Zimbabwe.

External debt

The view was unanimously expressed in the ECA Conference of Ministers that Africa's indebtedness was a serious burden, weighing heavily on the debtor countries' scant resources. ECA reports were prepared on the management of Africa's external debt[34] and on its balance-of-payments problems.[35] The first report outlined specific measures—emergency, medium- and long-term—to deal with Africa's debt crisis. It proposed that Africa call for an international conference on its external indebtedness at which lenders should agree on ways to deal with the debt crisis. It also proposed that a Conference of African Ministers of Finance be constituted as a subsidiary organ of the ECA Conference of Ministers to deal with the crisis and to suggest better policies for resource mobilization and use (see also p. 630). Countries should establish a national committee of external debt management to determine debt policy and external resources use and propose measures to avoid future crises.

The second report stressed that the balance-of-payments problem was basically a structural one, requiring domestically initiated growth and fundamental structural change. There must be a shift in emphasis from the production of a narrow range of primary commodities for export to the use of domestic energies to bring about domestic growth. Available resources must be invested in basic industries that would make for an integrated economy and create internal demand. Africa's physical and service infrastructure—transport, banking, insurance, shipping and other ancillary services—must be reoriented to enhance domestic growth. Full use must be made of regional co-operative arrangements, and intra-African trade and development plans must be drawn up with that end in view.

The second report was introduced at a Round Table of Governors of African Central Banks and Senior Officials of International Finance Institutions (Addis Ababa, 4-7 February),[36] which discussed and made recommendations on the balance-of-payments and foreign exchange problems of African countries.

Transport and communications

Transport and Communications Decade in Africa (1978-1988)

The Secretary-General submitted in June 1985 his annual report[37] to the General Assembly and the Economic and Social Council on the Transport and Communications Decade in Africa, proclaimed by the Assembly in 1977.[38] He stated that the report did not include the final results of the first phase of the Decade (1980-1983) because some projects had not been completed and serious information-gathering problems had been encountered.

With respect to the second phase (1984-1988), projects in the transport sector had been classified as follows: maintenance and rehabilitation; training and technical assistance; inter-State links; regional and subregional; and national priority projects. Communications projects were classified somewhat differently, as follows: maintenance and rehabilitation; training; technical assistance; regional, subregional and national, with subregional impact; and other national projects. Reliable data had been obtained (for all or part of their projects) from 28 countries (for transport) and 21 countries (for communications). The data related to 149 projects in transport (out of 581) and to 104 projects in communications (out of 472). The estimated cost of the 149 transport projects, after revision, was $4,472 million; of the 104 communications projects, $543.06 million. Results of the second phase one year after its launching were satisfactory, the Secretary-General said, at least as far as national projects were concerned, although there were indications that the remainder of the programme would be more difficult to finance.

In a further report[39] to the Assembly on the Decade, in October, the Secretary-General stated that 91 air transport projects were also envisaged, at a cost of $974.08 million; 84 railway projects at $3,362 million; and 134 postal projects, $528 million.

ECA issued a report[40] in April on the need for the rehabilitation and reconstruction of African transport and communications infrastructure, and the ECA Conference of Ministers that month adopted a resolution[41] on the Decade. The Conference asked the Secretary-General for resources to organize both the Fifth Conference of African Ministers of Transport, Communications and Planning in 1986 and co-financing meetings for regional projects and projects for land-locked countries. It asked the ECA Executive Secretary to organize at least two co-financing meetings a year to the end of the Decade, and appealed for donor country and financial institution participation in three technical consultative meetings on air transport, railways and postal services scheduled for May, September and November 1985, for financial support for second-phase projects and for transport and communications experts to strengthen the Decade Co-ordination Unit.

JIU report. The Joint Inspection Unit (JIU) presented a report[42] in September analysing the conception of the Decade and the validity of the approach adopted, as well as the results of its first phase, and presented a number of recommendations; in transmitting the report to the Assembly, the Secretary-General[43] commented on each recommendation. The JIU Inspector felt that a different approach could be considered, i.e. focusing the Decade more on increasing global awareness of African needs, clearly defined, rather than on financing a heterogeneous collection of individual

projects and concentrating ECA's role on identifying and executing regional and subregional projects rather than national ones.

Commenting favourably in general on JIU's 10 recommendations, the Secretary-General agreed that the ECA secretariat should assist African Governments in presenting their projects in a format acceptable to financial institutions (recommendation 2), and felt that either of two alternative proposed solutions to the problem of financing regional and subregional projects could be appropriate: either the establishment of an autonomous authority to mobilize finances and implement projects, or, more flexibly, a committee on which States affected by a regional project would be represented (1). ECA should identify by special studies fundamental inter-State projects and facilitate negotiations towards taking follow-up decisions, ensure that projects conformed to Decade objectives, organize fund-raising activities, support and assist African subregional organizations and seek a juridical framework for financing and implementing inter-State projects (5). He suggested that the Conference consider in 1988, rather than in 1986, a suggested medium- and long-term plan to be drawn up defining the role of the Conference of Ministers of Transport and Communications in fund-raising, monitoring, evaluation, etc., and activities to be undertaken by various actors after the end of the Decade (3). JIU recommended (4) a two-year period of reflection and analysis at the end of the Decade to prepare the plan as well as studies called for in recommendation 6 on problems of evaluating the Decade programme, a work programme for an end-of-Decade evaluation and a study of the efficiency of the Decade secretariat; the latter recommendation also suggested that a monitoring and evaluation unit be established at ECA to carry out the activities suggested by JIU, and Governments be assisted in setting up their own evaluation machinery. The Secretary-General said the setting of an institutional framework for co-operation in transport and communications by the regional commissions (recommendation 7) would be discussed by the executive secretaries. He supported arranging in-depth consultations between the ECA and Decade secretariats (8), noted that vacancies in the relevant divisions and units concerned with the Decade had been filled or were under recruitment and early action would be taken to return posts temporarily redeployed (9), and was in general agreement that procedures and central services of ECA provided to the Decade secretariat should be improved (10).

ECONOMIC AND SOCIAL COUNCIL ACTION

On 26 July, on the recommendation of its First Committee, the Economic and Social Council, by

decision 1985/191, took note of the Secretary-General's June report[37] on the Decade, among others, and adopted by vote **resolution 1985/65**.

Transport and Communications Decade in Africa
The Economic and Social Council,
Recalling its resolution 2097(LXIII) of 29 July 1977 and General Assembly resolution 32/160 of 19 December 1977, by which the Assembly proclaimed the Transport and Communications Decade in Africa during the years 1978-1988,
Recalling also resolution 464(XVIII) of 2 May 1983 of the Conference of Ministers of the Economic Commission for Africa, by which the Conference of Ministers requested the Executive Secretary of the Commission to ensure that the programme for the second phase of the Decade would, *inter alia*, promote harmonization and co-ordination of the various modes of transport and communications, and resolution 487(XIX) of 26 May 1984, by which the Conference of Ministers endorsed the programme for the second phase,
Referring to Council resolution 1984/68 of 27 July 1984 and General Assembly resolutions 38/150 of 19 December 1983 and 39/230 of 18 December 1984,
Noting that financial resources have been allocated by the General Assembly for the activities envisaged in its resolutions 38/150 and 39/230, including the studies on the harmonization and co-ordination of the various modes of transport and communications,
1. *Expresses its appreciation* to the Administrator of the United Nations Development Programme for his continuing support of the Transport and Communications Decade in Africa through the financing of the Decade Co-ordination Unit and requests him to continue to provide funds to the Economic Commission for Africa during the next programming cycle to enable it to complete the task of monitoring the implementation of the programme for the Decade and to evaluate the results of the whole programme for the Decade;
2. *Welcomes* the role played by the Inter-Agency Co-ordinating Committee under the Economic Commission for Africa as lead agency in co-ordinating activities and its contribution to realizing the objectives of the Decade;
3. *Requests* the Secretary-General to provide adequate financial resources to the Economic Commission for Africa to enable it to organize the Fifth Conference of African Ministers of Transport, Communications and Planning in 1986;
4. *Requests* the Executive Secretary of the Commission:
   (a) To organize, in collaboration with other United Nations bodies and African intergovernmental organizations, a co-financing meeting each year until the end of the Decade, for the purpose of submitting specific regional projects and transport corridor projects to appropriate donor countries and financial institutions;
   (b) To intensify efforts to contact as many donor countries and financial institutions as possible to promote the programme for the Decade;
5. *Also requests* the Secretary-General to make available to the Commission sufficient financial resources to enable it to organize co-financing meetings for specific regional projects and projects located in corridors affording access to the sea for land-locked countries;

6. *Reiterates* the appeals previously made to donor countries and international financial institutions to give increased financial support to the programme for the second phase of the Decade and to accord particular attention to the financing of the regional projects and projects related to the maintenance and rehabilitation of infrastructures, training and technical assistance, and projects in corridors affording access to the sea for land-locked countries.

Economic and Social Council resolution 1985/65

| 26 July 1985 | Meeting 52 | 27-1-16 |

Approved by First Committee (E/1985/145) by roll-call vote (27-1-16), 23 July (meeting 27); draft by ECA (E/1985/106), amended by Secretary following informal consultations; agenda item 8.
Financial implications. S-G, E/1985/C.1/L.9/Rev.1.

The Secretary-General estimated the resolution's additional budget requirements for 1986-1987 at $140,000.

Both the Committee and the Council voted separately, at the request of the Federal Republic of Germany, on paragraphs 3 to 5 of the resolution, adopting them together, respectively, by a roll-call vote of 27 to 4, with 13 abstentions, and by 26 votes to 7, with 10 abstentions.

Luxembourg stated that the EEC members had been unable to support the draft resolution, whose financial implications had been submitted without adequate explanation. The United States said those implications were substantial and totally unjustified.

Egypt said that if all countries favoured the long-term development of Africa, it saw no reason why some delegations should object to contributing to the Decade.

GENERAL ASSEMBLY ACTION

On 17 December, on the recommendation of the Second Committee, the Assembly took note, by **decision 40/435**, of several documents, including the JIU report and the comments of the Secretary-General thereon, as well as the Secretary-General's June and October reports on the Decade.

Satellite communications and remote sensing

The Inter-Agency Co-ordinating Committee for the establishment of a regional African satellite communications system reached an agreement on the terms of reference and organization of a feasibility study on such system. It secured $600,000 from UNDP, obtained a promise of seed money from the United Nations Educational, Scientific and Cultural Organization (UNESCO), and sought further financing from the African Development Bank (ADB) and EEC.

The ECA secretariat sent a mission to the headquarters of the African Remote Sensing Council (ARSC) in Bamako, Mali, in September to assess the problems of the Council's secretariat. It found the Council's activities nearly paralysed due mainly to lack of resources. ECA assisted by hosting the sixth meeting of the ARSC Conference of Plenipotentiaries in November.

Strait of Gibraltar (Europe-Africa link)

In an interim report transmitted to the Economic and Social Council in June,[44] the executive secretaries of ECA and ECE stated that Morocco and Spain were continuing their technical studies of a Europe-Africa permanent link through the Strait of Gibraltar. Three options—a tunnel, a floating bridge, a fixed-support bridge—and a combination of those options were being examined. The report noted the importance of legal studies, especially of shipping in the Strait and the legal provisions governing the operation of the structure; given the magnitude of the problems of liability, establishment of an international guarantee fund probably should be considered. The executive secretaries were of the view that the mandate given by the Council[45] should be extended, and possibly expanded, and the material means made available for that purpose.

The Economic and Social Council took note of the interim report, among others, on 26 July in **decision 1985/191**.

ECONOMIC AND SOCIAL COUNCIL ACTION

On 26 July, on the recommendation of its First Committee, the Economic and Social Council adopted without vote **resolution 1985/70**.

Europe-Africa permanent link through the Strait of Gibraltar

The Economic and Social Council,

Recalling its resolutions 1982/57 of 30 July 1982, 1983/62 of 29 July 1983 and 1984/75 of 27 July 1984, concerning the Europe-Africa permanent link through the Strait of Gibraltar,

Referring to the conclusions contained in the interim reports prepared by the Executive Secretaries of the Economic Commission for Africa and the Economic Commission for Europe pursuant to those resolutions and bearing in mind the discussion on this question in the First (Economic) Committee of the Economic and Social Council at its second regular session of 1985,

1. *Takes note* of the development of studies and work on the Europe-Africa permanent link through the Strait of Gibraltar and the efforts made by Morocco and Spain as co-sponsors of the project, in consultation and co-operation with the Governments of the countries concerned and the international organizations and research institutes of the western Mediterranean region;

2. *Invites* the Governments of Morocco and Spain to continue to furnish information to Governments, international organizations, research institutes and universities in the Mediterranean area and other regions, as well as to the Economic Commission for Europe and the Economic Commission for Africa, to continue consultations and co-operation with them and to make con-

certed efforts with a view to the elaboration of the project;

3. *Requests* Governments, international organizations and research institutes to continue to co-operate with the Governments of Morocco and Spain and with the Economic Commission for Europe and the Economic Commission for Africa in developing studies and work on the project;

4. *Requests* the Secretary-General to explore the possibility of using extrabudgetary funds to provide the competent commissions with the necessary resources to carry out economic studies on the development of transport in the Mediterranean region in relation to the Europe-Africa permanent link through the Strait of Gibraltar;

5. *Requests* the Executive Secretaries of the Economic Commission for Africa and the Economic Commission for Europe to submit an interim report on the development of project studies to the Economic and Social Council at its second regular session of 1987.

Economic and Social Council resolution 1985/70

26 July 1985   Meeting 52   Adopted without vote

Approved by First Committee (E/1985/145/Add.1) without vote, 24 July (meeting 28); 5-nation draft (E/1985/C.1/L.10/Rev.1); agenda item 8.
Sponsors: Lebanon, Morocco, Somalia, Spain, Zaire.
Financial implications. S-G, E/1985/C.1/L.18.

Transport and trade of Zaire

GENERAL ASSEMBLY ACTION

On 17 December, on the recommendation of the Second Committee, the General Assembly adopted without vote **resolution 40/190**.

Particular problems facing Zaire with regard to transport, transit and access to foreign markets

The General Assembly,

Referring to its resolution 32/160 of 19 December 1977, in which it recalled Economic and Social Council resolution 2097(LXIII) of 29 July 1977 and proclaimed the period 1978-1988 the Transport and Communications Decade in Africa,

Referring also to its resolutions 34/193 of 19 December 1979, 35/59 of 5 December 1980, 36/139 of 16 December 1981, 37/205 of 20 December 1982 and 38/143 of 19 December 1983 on particular problems facing Zaire with regard to transport, transit and access to foreign markets, and approving the organization in 1985 of a second round-table meeting with donor countries and financing institutions for Zaire's projects in these three fields,

Recalling resolution 110(V) of 3 June 1979, of the United Nations Conference on Trade and Development,

Recalling also Economic and Social Council decision 249(LXIII) of 25 July 1977 and resolution 1981/68 of 24 July 1981, as well as resolution 293(XIII) of 26 February 1977 adopted by the Conference of Ministers of the Economic Commission for Africa,

Bearing in mind the report of the Secretary-General on the outcome of the first round-table meeting on the financing of the transport projects of Zaire, held at Kinshasa on 28 and 29 June 1983,

1. *Requests* the Secretary-General to take the necessary steps to ensure that the programme submitted to the first round-table meeting on the financing of the transport projects of Zaire, held in 1983, as updated,

is again submitted to donors and financial institutions before the forty-first session of the General Assembly, through a second round-table meeting or any other appropriate mechanism;

2. *Also requests* the Secretary-General to submit to the General Assembly at its forty-first session a report on the implementation of the present resolution.

General Assembly resolution 40/190

17 December 1985   Meeting 119   Adopted without vote

Approved by Second Committee (A/40/989/Add.3) without vote, 11 December (meeting 50); draft by Vice-Chairman (A/C.2/40/L.117), based on informal consultations on draft by Argentina, Benin, Burundi, Cape Verde, Central African Republic, Chad, Ecuador, Equatorial Guinea, Gabon, Guinea, Guinea-Bissau, Madagascar, Mauritania, Morocco, Niger, Peru, Rwanda, Senegal, Uganda, Zaire and Zambia (A/C.2/40/L.49); agenda item 84 (c).

Meeting numbers. GA 40th session: 2nd Committee 41, 50; plenary 119.

Industrial development in Africa

Implementation of the programme for the Industrial Development Decade for Africa

Activities in support of the Industrial Development Decade for Africa (IDDA) (1980-1990), proclaimed by the General Assembly in 1980,[46] continued in 1985.

A fourth progress report[47] on IDDA, prepared in response to a 1984 Assembly request[48] by the Executive Director of the United Nations Industrial Development Organization (UNIDO), in co-operation with the ECA Executive Secretary, was considered by the UNIDO Industrial Development Board (IDB) in May 1985 and later submitted by the Secretary-General[49] to the Assembly through the Economic and Social Council. The report described co-operation between ECA, OAU and UNIDO during 1984 in respect of IDDA and was prepared by the secretariats of the three organizations, summarizing their activities in accordance with the priorities established within the framework of the Lagos Plan of Action.[2] An executive summary[50] of the report was prepared by ECA.

On 31 May,[51] IDB took note of the progress report, expressed concern at the deteriorating economic situation in Africa, urged Governments, particularly those of developed countries, and organizations to increase their support of IDDA, and called on UNIDO to intensify its efforts to implement the programme for the Decade.

The ECA Conference of Ministers, in April,[52] called on member States to adjust their IDDA programmes, allocate needed resources and take the necessary measures to implement industrial priority projects. It urged States and intergovernmental organizations to endorse subregional integrated industrial promotion programmes, welcomed the Assembly's decision to increase from $1 million to $5 million the annual allocation from the United Nations regular budget to UNIDO for the Decade, and called on the Assembly to consider allocating $700,000 annually to enable ECA and MULPOCs to conduct negotiations on implementing multinational projects.

An African regional workshop of experts was held (Addis Ababa, 11-13 December) to promote fuller participation of private businesses and parastatals in the implementation of IDDA.

IDDA activities. ECA continued to gear activities in the industrial development sector to support for IDDA. According to the 1984-1985 report[1] of the Executive Secretary, activities were organized around four subprogrammes. One was concerned with general policy and institutional matters, reflecting the secretariat's concern with deficiencies in member States' capacity to formulate and promote industrial programmes. The others related to basic, agro- and forest-based, and small-scale industries.

The ECA secretariat provided consultancy services, particularly to the African Regional Centre for Engineering Design and Manufacturing. Small-scale industry development services were provided to countries in West and Central Africa. In the agro- and forest-based industries, a *Compendium on Composite Flours* was published in English and French, and the secretariat took part in a Seminar on Composite Flours (Lagos, Nigeria, June). Advisory services were provided to the Congo and Zaire on how best to transfer and adapt cassava processing technology from the Ivory Coast. Advisory services were also provided to MULPOCs' member States in the forest industries subsector and, in April/May, to Djibouti, Madagascar and the Comoros in support of work on chemicals and fertilizers. The Eastern and Southern African MULPOC project on traditional medicines was under way; its objectives included the production of essential drugs using local materials and plants.

In the engineering industries, the secretariat undertook field work in the Gambia, Ghana and Sierra Leone during November and December to determine industrial capacities and potentials. Assistance was provided to Burundi and Rwanda to determine ways of upgrading existing foundry, forging, heat treatment and metal forming machine shops, tool rooms and metal coating shops and, in addition, to Kenya, Mauritius, Uganda, the United Republic of Tanzania, Zambia and Zimbabwe to determine needs for the manufacture of spare parts for mining, ore refining, iron and steel, engineering and agricultural and transport equipment.

Technical assistance was provided in collaboration with the West Africa MULPOC to the Mano River Union and the Economic Community of West African States (ECOWAS) in identifying metallurgical projects within the IDDA framework; a study on alternative technologies for sponge iron production was prepared and an evaluation of potential iron and steel projects in Preferential Trade Area countries was conducted.

On 26 July, on the recommendation of its First Committee, the Economic and Social Council adopted without vote **resolution 1985/61**.

Industrial Development Decade for Africa

The Economic and Social Council,

Recalling resolution 491(XIX) of 26 May 1984 of the Conference of Ministers of the Economic Commission for Africa on the implementation of the programme for the Industrial Development Decade for Africa,

Recalling also General Assembly resolution 39/233 of 18 December 1984, in which the Assembly endorsed the appeal made by the Seventh Conference of African Ministers of Industry, held at Addis Ababa from 26 to 28 March 1984, for the allocation of at least $5 million, on a permanent annual basis, from the regular budget of the United Nations to enable the United Nations Industrial Development Organization to assist the African countries and the intergovernmental organizations concerned in the implementation of the programme for the Industrial Development Decade for Africa,

Welcoming the declaration on the critical economic situation in Africa made by the Assembly of Heads of State and Government of the Organization of African Unity at its twentieth ordinary session, held at Addis Ababa from 12 to 15 November 1984, in which it endorsed the programme for the Decade and the recommendations of the Seventh Conference of African Ministers of Industry, in particular resolution 1(VII) on the implementation of the programme for the Decade,

Conscious of the need to alleviate the effects of the current economic crisis in Africa, particularly in the priority industries which support the rehabilitation and revitalization of the food and agricultural sector,

Recalling resolution 2(VIII) of March 1985 of the Lusaka-based Multinational Programming and Operational Centre and similar resolutions of other such centres on the role that the centres have to play in the effective and speedy implementation of the Decade at the subregional level, particularly with respect to multinational projects,

1. *Recognizes,* and expresses appreciation for, measures taken or under way in Member States, intergovernmental organizations and the secretariats of the Organization of African Unity, the Economic Commission for Africa and the United Nations Industrial Development Organization to implement the programme for and the activities of the Industrial Development Decade for Africa, and urges all concerned to continue and intensify their efforts;

2. *Takes note* of the decision of the General Assembly to increase to an annual minimum of $5 million the allocation from the regular budget of the United Nations to the United Nations Industrial Development Organization for the Decade;

3. *Calls upon* the General Assembly to consider the allocation to the Economic Commission for Africa of $700,000, to be absorbed from the $5 million already approved—in Assembly resolution 39/233—in the regular budget for the biennium 1986-1987, to enable the Commission and the Multinational Programming and Operational Centres to conduct consultations and negotiations on ways of implementing multinational projects, including investment promotion;

4. *Requests* the secretariats of the Organization of African Unity, the Economic Commission for Africa and the United Nations Industrial Development Organization to continue providing their services to enable member States to implement the programme for the Decade effectively.

Economic and Social Council resolution 1985/61

26 July 1985   Meeting 52   Adopted without vote

Approved by First Committee (E/1985/145) without vote, 23 July (meeting 27); draft by ECA (E/1985/106), orally amended by Secretary following informal consultations; agenda item 8.

The Council on 25 July, by **decision 1985/170**, adopted on the recommendation of the First Committee, took note of the fourth progress report of the UNIDO Executive Director and the ECA Executive Secretary on IDDA.

In a related action, the ECA Conference on 29 April adopted a resolution[53] urging countries to ratify the agreement establishing the African Industrial Development Fund, appealing for contributions and requesting ADB to consider the most economical ways of managing the Fund.

Natural resources and energy

During 1985, the ECA programme in mineral resources provided technical and administrative assistance to member States, the Eastern and Southern African Mineral Resources Development Centre at Dodoma, United Republic of Tanzania, and the Central African Mineral Resources Development Centre at Brazzaville.

The Second Regional Conference on the Development and Utilization of Mineral Resources in Africa (Lusaka, Zambia, 12 and 13 March)[54] discussed the latest developments in intra-African mineral trade, development financing, small-scale mining and technical issues covering mineral commodities, and adopted the Lusaka Programme of Action for the Development and Utilization of Mineral Resources in Africa,[55] which outlined measures to tackle the constraints affecting performance in the mineral sector.

The ECA Conference of Ministers in April adopted a resolution[56] endorsing and urging implementation of the recommendations of the Second Regional Conference and urging member States to implement those of the Lusaka Programme of Action. It called on the Economic Community of Central African States, ECOWAS, SADCC and other subregional organs to promote multicountry co-operation in mineral resources development. It asked that the third regional conference be convened in 1987.

Surveys of copper, bauxite, alumina, aluminium, gold, cassiterite and associated minerals as well as building and fertilizer raw materials were conducted in Cameroon, the Central African Republic, Equatorial Guinea, Ghana, Guinea, Mauritania and the Niger.

The data base of records on geological, technical and economic aspects of mineral industries was increased from 5,000 to 7,500 references.

Marine and water resources

The ECA secretariat undertook an advisory mission to Somalia in October/November on the development of human and material resources for exploiting sea resources. It organized the African intergovernmental meeting of experts on aspects of exploration and exploitation of sea-bed resources in the context of the United Nations Convention on the Law of the Sea (Addis Ababa, 11-14 November). It carried out a study[57] on African capabilities for the exploration, exploitation and development of marine resources.

Advisory missions to Burkina Faso, Ghana, Guinea, the Ivory Coast, Mali, the Niger and Somalia assisted in the assessment, development and management of their water resources. Studies were carried out on the African crisis and water development, preservation and utilization,[58] and on progress in the implementation of the Mar del Plata Plan of Action[59] in Africa (1978-1984).[60]

Energy

The exploration, exploitation and optimum use of hydrocarbons and coal was studied by missions to Botswana, Chad, the Congo, Malawi, Mozambique, Nigeria, Swaziland, Zambia and Zimbabwe. Advisory services on integrated energy policies were rendered to Burundi, Liberia, the Niger, Rwanda and Sierra Leone. A report[61] on the possibility of developing ocean energy resources of East African coastal States was submitted to the ECA Conference of Ministers in April.

The Conference adopted a resolution[62] requesting the Executive Director of the United Nations Centre on Transnational Corporations, with the ECA Executive Secretary, to study the role of TNCs in the petroleum industry in Africa. Special reference was to be given to price fluctuations *vis-à-vis* the producer countries and the cost to African countries of oil and oil products.

Food and agriculture

About 150 million people in Africa were currently suffering from malnutrition and hunger, the Secretary-General stated in a June report[63] prepared in response to a 1984 General Assembly request,[64] in spite of the continent's immense potential to increase production several-fold.

Africa had undergone a drastic decline in food production in 1983-1984, and the food situation had continued to deteriorate. In 1984-1985, 21 African countries experienced exceptional food shortages: cereal production was 14 per cent lower than the 1983 output which had been affected by drought, and 23 per cent below the 1981-1982 average. The total import requirement was estimated at 10.2 million tons. Besides food deliveries, critical needs included seeds, fertilizers, chemicals, water, veterinary medicine, livestock feed and destocking operations compatible with pasture carrying-capacity. Provision of trucks, spare parts and maintenance facilities was extremely important for relief operations. The report also examined trends in agricultural production and trade, causes of the long-term agricultural decline, proposals for recovery, and the production of selected food crops, by subregion.

In a July note[65] to the Economic and Social Council, the Secretary-General expressed regret that, because of demands on the Secretariat as a result of the emergency situation in Africa, there had been a delay in elaborating plans for a proposed international year for the mobilization of financial and technological resources to increase food production in Africa, as the Assembly had requested in 1983.[66]

In his June report[67] on regional co-operation (see p. 624), the Secretary-General stated that the ECA Conference of Ministers had recognized the critical food situation as originating in the unwillingness of African Governments to accept that agriculture was the major engine for economic development and to allocate resources accordingly. Policies in many African countries still bore the signs of the colonial legacy. Many countries still followed urban-biased development, with rural-urban terms of trade skewed against the food and agriculture sector. The situation had been aggravated by drought, pests, desertification and natural disasters and by external factors, including prolonged world economic recession, lack of market access, worsening terms of trade and increased interest rates.

The ECA Conference in April adopted a resolution[68] calling on African Governments to design and implement self-sustaining agricultural development policies and to increase domestic investment in agriculture, with emphasis on research, technology, incentive packages geared to smallholder producers, irrigation, and manpower training, and calling for assistance from financial institutions and donors. It also adopted a resolution[69] urging donor countries to accelerate the second replenishment process for the International Fund for Agricultural Development, which was evolving a special programme for Africa.

ECA and the Food and Agriculture Organization of the United Nations (FAO) organized an expert consultation (Arusha, 12-14 November) to identify specific food marketing–related activities which could be improved through TCDC and between African countries and discuss establishment of a regional institution for such TCDC activities.

The ECA secretariat prepared a report on planning issues for the development of subsistence farming, discussing deficiencies in planning machineries and ways to remedy the situation, which was presented at the seventh round table of the African Association for Public Administration and Management (Accra, Ghana, 2-7 December). It also prepared a summary report[70] on the African food and agriculture crisis—prospects and proposals for 1985 and 1986.

Science and technology

The implementation in the African region of the 1979 Vienna Programme of Action on Science and Technology for Development[71] was reviewed at the seventh session of the Intergovernmental Committee on Science and Technology for Development (New York, 28 May-7 June). The ECA secretariat hosted the fifth ECA/UNESCO joint meeting (Addis Ababa, 8 and 9 July) to review their collaborative activities, and organized the fourth meeting of the Intergovernmental Committee of Experts for Science and Technology Development (Addis Ababa, 18-22 November),[72] which asked ECA to explore establishment of a conference of African ministers responsible for science and technology to harmonize policies.

An advisory mission to Madagascar in July studied the national infrastructure and recommended the establishment of a national science and technology commission.

An ECA Conference of Ministers April resolution[73] urged EEC to provide African countries, through the African Institute for Higher Technical Training and Research, with assistance for industrial manpower development.

A Rural Technology Demonstration Centre was established in 1985 at Dakar, Senegal, by ECA and India. The Centre would provide training and facilitate replication and popularization of appropriate rural technologies, with the help of local entrepreneurs.

Human resources and social development

The fourth Conference of African Ministers of Social Affairs (Addis Ababa, 25 and 26 March),[74] organized by ECA and OAU, agreed to establish an African Rehabilitation Institute for Disabled Persons.

An expert consultation on the role of rural co-operatives in Africa was organized by the secretariat, in collaboration with FAO, UNIDO, the International Labour Organisation (ILO) and the International Co-operative Alliance (Addis Ababa, 7-11 October).

The secretariat prepared reports on the crisis of unemployment and human resources management in Africa[75] and human resources management in Africa—an agenda for action.[76] Recom-

mendations contained in the reports, as well as the report of the second Conference of Ministers Responsible for Human Resources Planning, Development and Utilization (Addis Ababa, 9 and 10 October 1984),[77] were endorsed by the ECA Conference of Ministers.[78]

ECA participated in the Seventh United Nations Congress on the Prevention of Crime and the Treatment of Offenders (Milan, Italy, 26 August-6 September), which adopted a resolution[79] requesting the creation of an African Regional Institute for the Prevention of Crime and the Treatment of Offenders.

The second Conference of Vice-Chancellors, Rectors and Presidents of Institutions of Higher Learning in Africa (Mbabane, Swaziland, 18-22 February),[80] adopted the Mbabane Programme of Action on means of strengthening those institutions' contribution to Africa's socio-economic development. It included recommendations on the revision of education content and research, greater research of development-related topics, general improvement of the education system, improved training for teachers and research workers, and tapping private sources of funds to supplement public funding for education. The ECA Conference of Ministers in April adopted a resolution[81] urging African institutions of higher learning to implement the Mbabane Programme and African Governments to assist in its implementation.

Population

Representatives at an ECA/Regional Institute for Population Studies (RIPS) regional training workshop on demographic estimates and projections (Accra, 15-29 July) shared experiences in the use of national population projections in planning and received training in the use of the United Nations computer programme in preparing the projections. The workshop also dealt with subnational and sectoral projections.

The secretariat provided technical support to RIPS in the organization of a seminar on internal migration and regional African development (Accra, 2-8 August) and organized the first advisory meeting of the Population Information Network for Africa (POPIN-Africa) (Addis Ababa, December).

Population information activities under POPIN-Africa included the publication of the *African Population Newsletter*; *POPINDEX Africa*, a population abstract journal; and *POPIN-Africa Briefs*, a newsletter of the Network.

The ECA Conference of Ministers in April[82] urged African Governments to continue their support of the African demographic training institutes, urged the member countries of the Institut de formation et de recherche démographiques at

Yaoundé, Cameroon, to pay the arrears on their contributions and members of RIPS to pay their contributions, and appealed to UNFPA to restore its funding of the institutes at least to 1983 levels and to continue such funding beyond 1987.

Environment

The ECA Conference of Ministers considered a report[83] recommending long-term measures for drought and desertification control in Africa, including the drawing up of a national control plan and national co-ordination and evaluation machinery, the promotion of public participation, vegetation and water resources conservation and protection of common ecosystems, the use of alternative sources of energy to ease deforestation, and manpower and institutional development.

The third meeting of the Joint Intergovernmental Regional Committee on Human Settlements and Environment (Addis Ababa, 22-26 July)[84] reviewed progress on environmental matters, including long-term measures to combat drought and desertification; the implementation of an ECA/United Nations Environment Programme (UNEP) project on incorporating environmental components into the training programmes of ECA-sponsored institutions; the establishment or improvement of national standards for the protection of the African environment; national environmental legislation and ECA/OAU technical projects on implementing treaties on the environment; and an ECA/WMO feasibility study on establishing an African Centre of Meteorological Applications for Development (see p. 627).

With regard to environmental education and training, the secretariat visited in 1985 various African institutions to assist in the development of a core curriculum. An ECA/UNEP/ADB training workshop was subsequently held (Abidjan, Ivory Coast, 18-23 November) at which lecturers from ECA-sponsored institutions adapted the core curriculum to the training of bankers, development planners, social workers, aerial survey technicians and design engineers.

An African Environmental Conference organized by UNEP (Cairo, Egypt, 16-18 December)[85] recommended a joint ECA/ UNEP/OAU permanent secretariat to implement the Conference's Cairo Programme for African Co-operation in Environment and Development (see Chapter XVI of this section).

The General Assembly in **resolution 40/198 B** endorsed a UNEP Governing Council decision to add the United Republic of Tanzania to the list of countries to be assisted by UNSO in their efforts to combat desertification.

Human settlements

The Joint Intergovernmental Regional Committee on Human Settlements and Environment, at its July meeting, in addition to considering drought and desertification (see above), received country reports from member States on human settlements projects aimed at improving housing for low-income groups and the ongoing preparations for the International Year of Shelter for the Homeless (1987), human settlements policies, land problems in urban areas and housing programmes for the masses, development of decentralized systems of building materials production, and indicators for revised building codes and regulations.

The Committee declared[84] that seven main areas of action with respect to land for low-income housing called for national measures: the constitution of public land reserves; tax policy; credit policy; involvement of the private sector in housing construction; security of tenure for squatters; government intervention in land prices; and increasing government involvement in land development. International action could include the establishment of a data bank, pooling of information and experience, training of manpower and implementation of pilot projects.

Women in development in Africa

ECA focused on the promotion of training opportunities for the participation of women in development activities. Seminars on women and decision-making in the media (Addis Ababa, 11-14 February) and on improving the data base, statistics and indicators for women and development in Africa (Harare, Zimbabwe, 29 April-7 May) were held and two subregional seminars, one for women managers and one on management and development planning for women, were organized at Arusha, in June and September, respectively.

To encourage technical co-operation among women, ECA organized an interregional workshop on women's textile and garment co-operatives (Bamako, 13 October-2 November).

Two training workshops on women in entrepreneurship were held in Kenya (15 April-21 June and 14 October-20 December) for English-speaking Africans and another two in the Ivory Coast (25 February-3 May and 20 May-26 July) for those from French-speaking countries.

The ECA Conference of Ministers, in April, considered the report[86] of the 1984 Regional Intergovernmental Preparatory Meeting[87] for the 1985 World Conference to Review and Appraise the Achievements of the United Nations Decade for Women: Equality, Development and Peace/Third Regional Conference on the Integration of Women in Development (see Chapter XIX of this section). The sixth meeting of the Africa Regional Co-ordinating Committee on the Integration of Women in Development (Addis Ababa, 15-17 April)[88] adopted the report of the Third Regional Conference and asked Governments and institutions to begin applying the Arusha Forward-looking Strategies for the Advancement of African Women beyond the Decade for Women, as contained in that report. It also requested States to sign the 1979 Convention on the Elimination of All Forms of Discrimination against Women,[89] asked for sustained assistance for national integration machinery, and called on African Governments to include women in their delegations to international and regional meetings. It also asked those Governments to allow a satisfactory number of high-level representatives to attend the 1985 World Conference and urged African women to take a united stand to ensure that the interests of the continent were safeguarded. These and other provisions were also included in two resolutions[90] of the ECA Conference of Ministers.

ECONOMIC AND SOCIAL COUNCIL ACTION

On 26 July, on the recommendation of its First Committee, the Economic and Social Council adopted without vote **resolution 1985/67**.

Women and development in Africa

The Economic and Social Council,

Recalling resolution 28 of the World Conference of the United Nations Decade for Women: Equality, Development and Peace, on the Convention on the Elimination of All Forms of Discrimination against Women,

Bearing in mind resolution 512(XIX) of 26 May 1984 of the Conference of Ministers of the Economic Commission for Africa on the mobilization of human and financial resources for the women's programme of the Commission beyond the end of the United Nations Decade for Women,

Bearing in mind also that women subjected to the policies of *apartheid* and women in illegally occupied Namibia are still victims of all forms of injustice, violent oppression and atrocities perpetrated by the racist régime of South Africa, and that the status of women in the frontline States has been seriously affected by the aggression and destabilizing policies of South Africa,

1. *Requests* Governments and international organizations to sustain their assistance for national machineries concerned with the integration of women in development to enable them to formulate and execute national programmes for women's development, taking into account, in particular, the Arusha Forward-looking Strategies for the Advancement of African Women beyond the United Nations Decade for Women;

2. *Urgently requests* States which have not yet done so to sign the Convention on the Elimination of All Forms of Discrimination against Women and States which have signed it to ratify it and do everything possible to ensure its application;

3. *Requests* the Secretary-General and the Executive Secretary of the Economic Commission for Africa to spare no effort to procure regular budget posts and appropriations for the African Training and Research Centre for Women and the Multinational Programming and Operational Centres, through the redeployment of vacant posts and in the context of the proposed programme budget for the biennium 1986-1987, in order to ensure the continuity of the United Nations regional and subregional women's programmes.

Economic and Social Council resolution 1985/67

26 July 1985   Meeting 52   Adopted without vote

Approved by First Committee (E/1985/145/Add.1) without vote, 24 July (meeting 28); draft by ECA (E/1985/106), orally amended by Secretary following informal consultations and by Zimbabwe; agenda item 8.

Statistics

The fourth meeting of directors of centres participating in the Statistical Training Programme for Africa (STPA) (Addis Ababa, 4-8 November)[91] made recommendations on an evaluation of STPA and future work programmes; the impact of training guide syllabuses at STPA and other training centres and statistical offices; the co-operative development of teaching programmes; special assistance to Portuguese-speaking African countries in statistical training; and technical and financial assistance and dissemination of information on training activities.

Other meetings included a seminar on the development of a statistical data base (30 September–4 October) and a Working Group on the Development of Civil Registration Systems and Vital Statistics Collection in Africa (21-26 October), both at Addis Ababa.

Programme, organizational and administrative questions

ECA work programme and sessions

Portuguese as a working language

ECONOMIC AND SOCIAL COUNCIL ACTION

On 26 July, on the recommendation of its First Committee, the Economic and Social Council adopted by vote **resolution 1985/68**.

Inclusion of Portuguese among the official working languages of the Economic Commission for Africa

The Economic and Social Council,

Considering the number of States members of the Economic Commission for Africa and the growing numbers of people in those countries that use Portuguese as an official working language,

Noting that basic economic, social and cultural development in any country depends on the transmission of technical and scientific information through the medium of language,

Recognizing that, at various summit meetings in Africa, the question of the Portuguese language has been discussed and has been of concern to the heads of State and Government of five countries that officially use Portuguese,

Realizing that, because of language difficulties, the people of those countries do not derive maximum benefit from the technical assistance, professional training, seminars and other activities that might facilitate their integration into the social and economic programmes being carried out at the subregional and regional levels,

1. *Decides* that Portuguese should be introduced gradually as an official working language of the Economic Commission for Africa;

2. *Requests* the General Assembly to make the necessary arrangements to this effect.

Economic and Social Council resolution 1985/68

26 July 1985   Meeting 52   30-12-5

Approved by First Committee (E/1985/145/Add.1) by roll-call vote (28-11-5), 24 July (meeting 28); draft by ECA (E/1985/106), orally amended by Secretary following informal consultations; agenda item 8.
Financial implications. S-G, E/1985/C.1/L.12/Rev.1.

Luxembourg, on behalf of the EEC member countries, stated that since Portuguese was not an official United Nations language, its introduction into ECA would be an unfortunate precedent. Moreover, further charges on the United Nations regular budget should be avoided, in view of the current financial situation.

Sweden, speaking also on behalf of Finland and Iceland, said they had abstained because resources were limited and they were not convinced that the proposal could be regarded as a priority matter. The United States opposed the text on the grounds of its financial implications and the prospects of much greater costs in the future.

The Secretary-General, in a September report,[92] noting the Council's decision, said it would be proposed to the General Assembly, to commence in 1986. Translations of some documents, but no interpretation to and from Portuguese, would be provided to ECA meetings. Additional requirements for 1986-1987 were estimated at $167,400.

The Advisory Committee on Administrative and Budgetary Questions (ACABQ) pointed out in October[93] that the term "official working language" was new and the question arose as to precisely what services would be required for Portuguese. It believed that the definition of the term should be referred back to ECA and the Council for clarification and, pending Assembly consideration, no action be taken with regard to the resources requested.

GENERAL ASSEMBLY ACTION

On 18 December, on the recommendation of the Fifth (Administrative and Budgetary) Committee, the General Assembly adopted without vote **section VIII of resolution 40/252**.

**Inclusion of Portuguese among the official
and/or working languages
of the Economic Commission for Africa**

[*The General Assembly . . .*]

Having considered the report of the Secretary-General on the inclusion of Portuguese among the official and/or working languages of the Economic Commission for Africa and the related report of the Advisory Committee on Administrative and Budgetary Questions,

1. *Decides* to take no action with regard to the resources requested for the inclusion of Portuguese among the "official working languages" of the Economic Commission for Africa;

2. *Further decides* to refer the question of the meaning of the expression "official working language" to the Economic Commission for Africa and the Economic and Social Council for clarification in time for consideration by the General Assembly at its forty-first session;

. . .

General Assembly resolution 40/252, section VIII

18 December 1985   Meeting 122   Adopted without vote

Approved by Fifth Committee (A/40/1069) without objection, 2 December (meeting 52); oral proposal by Chairman; agenda item 116.

Work programme

The ECA Conference of Ministers in April endorsed[94] ECA's proposals for its work programme and priorities for 1986-1987 and urged support for them in CPC, specifically to ensure that adequate resources were made available to ECA, particularly in the priority sectors of food and agriculture, drought and desertification, water development, transport and communications and industrial development.

Sessions

On 8 February, the Economic and Social Council adopted **decision 1985/109**, by which it decided that the twentieth session of ECA and eleventh meeting of the ECA Conference of Ministers, to be held in April, should be held at Addis Ababa. This action was orally proposed by the Council President on behalf of the Bureau, following informal consultations, and was approved without vote.

On 15 March,[95] the United Republic of Tanzania offered to host the meetings at Arusha; the Council accepted that offer on 22 March by **decision 1985/112**, but, on 8 April,[96] the Council President advised that the offer had been withdrawn owing to unforeseen events, and that the meetings would be held at Addis Ababa instead.

Cameroon, in a 22 July letter,[97] annexed a statement it had made to an informal meeting of the Council's First Committee on 19 July, inviting ECA to hold in April 1986 its twenty-first session and the Conference of Ministers' twelfth meeting at Yaoundé, declaring that it would pay the additional required expenditure of $250,100 estimated by the Secretary-General.[98] The Council adopted **decision 1985/189** on 26 July, accepting Cameroon's offer, on the recommendation of the First Committee.

Expansion and maintenance of ECA conference facilities and buildings

Responding to a 1984 General Assembly resolution,[99] the Secretary-General submitted in November 1985 a progress report[100] on the construction of ECA conference facilities at Addis Ababa. He stated that it had been decided to hold a competition in 1986 for the design of new construction (one large, one medium and four small conference rooms) and that the completion date for them was approximately five years after General Assembly approval, i.e. December 1989. Construction was to start in the fourth quarter of 1987. Through 31 December 1985, expenditures for the project were estimated at $270,000; the balance of the appropriation for the 1984-1985 biennium ($2,850,000) would be carried over into the 1986-1987 biennium. No new appropriation was, therefore, being requested, since estimated expenditures for 1986-1987 for a quantity surveyor, architectural competition and architect/engineers' fees, construction and other expenses were $2,800,000.

The Secretary-General also submitted[101] proposals for limited remodelling and repair of the main conference room in Africa Hall in 1986-1987. The estimated cost was $3,074,500. ACABQ[102] believed that the remodelling proposal should be evaluated in the context of the overall construction project and pending the outcome of the design competition. Also it should be deferred in the light of 13 other priority maintenance projects scheduled for 1986-1987. In the same report, the Secretary-General submitted details of the 13 major maintenance projects, part of a 10-year building maintenance programme for ECA. The projects were estimated to cost $1,225,900, reduced by $138,500 previously allocated, plus $115,000 to establish maintenance shops; ACABQ recommended an additional appropriation of $1,202,400 for those purposes.

The Fifth Committee, in approving the 1986-1987 budget estimates under section 32 (construction, alteration, improvement and major maintenance of premises) on 27 November by a recorded vote of 85 to 2, with 15 abstentions, approved an additional appropriation of $1,202,400 for the biennium.

GENERAL ASSEMBLY ACTION

On 18 December, on the recommendation of the Fifth Committee, the General Assembly adopted without vote **section VI of resolution 40/252**.

Building management, maintenance and alterations at the Headquarters of the Economic Commission for Africa

[_The General Assembly_ . . .]

Requests the Secretary-General to report to the General Assembly on the implementation of the building maintenance projects at the headquarters of the Economic Commission for Africa, in the context of his annual progress reports on the construction of conference facilities at Addis Ababa;

. . .

General Assembly resolution 40/252, section VI

18 December 1985   Meeting 122   Adopted without vote

Approved by Fifth Committee (A/40/1069) without objection, 27 November (meeting 49); oral proposal by Chairman; agenda item 116.
Meeting numbers. GA 40th session: 5th Committee 48, 49; plenary 122.

ECA-sponsored institutions

The Fifth Conference of Chief Executives of ECA-sponsored Regional and Subregional Institutions (Addis Ababa, 10 and 11 January)[103] called on institutions to contribute to the Buffer Fund for the publication of the bulletin of ECA-sponsored institutions, decided that the second such bulletin, _The Institutions at Work_, should come out during the April meeting of the ECA Conference of Ministers, and also decided that the chief executives should send to ECA their comments on proposals for a group insurance scheme for the institutions.

A consolidated biennial report[104] on the activities of ECA-sponsored institutions for 1984-1985 was submitted to the Conference of Ministers. The report covered more than 30 African intergovernmental institutions which, individually, African Governments had found too costly to operate on their own. The institutions were active in such areas as manpower development, management training, trade and transport, natural resources and industrial development, and financial and monetary affairs.

The _Ad Hoc_ Committee on ECA- and OAU-sponsored institutions, established in 1983 by the ECA Conference of Ministers to evaluate and make proposals regarding those institutions, submitted its final report[105] in April. The report contained recommendations on harmonization and merger of the institutions; it stressed that African countries should pay their contributions to the institutions to which they belonged or cease to be members.

The Conference approved[106] a number of the _Ad Hoc_ Committee's recommendations, among them: to ascertain from the Governments belonging to and those hosting the sponsored institutions whether they were still interested in them and the extent to which they would support them financially; the institutions should explore ways to increase revenues and reduce costs. The Conference of Ministers also adopted a resolution[107] urging member States to give high priority to improving their institutions for public administration, management development and public financial management and requesting the ECA Executive Secretary to provide increased assistance to States in those fields.

Multinational Programming and Operational Centres

On 26 July, on the recommendation of its First Committee, the Economic and Social Council adopted by vote **resolution 1985/66**. Similar provisions had been included in a Conference of Ministers resolution[108] of 29 April.

Appointment of directors of Multinational Programming and Operational Centres

The Economic and Social Council,

Taking note of the fact that most of the Multinational Programming and Operational Centres of the Economic Commission for Africa are currently headed by interim rather than by titular directors,

Conscious of the importance of the economic role of the Multinational Programming and Operational Centres for subregional co-operation and integration and of the need for them to be appropriately staffed at the highest level, having regard to the sensitive nature of their responsibilities,

Aware of the need to procure the services of persons possessing the highest standards of efficiency, competence and integrity and to observe United Nations rules concerning the equitable geographical distribution of posts among the Member States,

1. *Requests* the Secretary-General to take all the necessary steps to ensure that the posts of directors of the Multinational Programming and Operational Centres are expeditiously filled;

2. *Further requests* the Secretary-General to ensure that the directors of the Multinational Programming and Operational Centres are, whenever appropriate, nationals of the States members of the centres, in accordance with the practice followed in the Economic Commission for Africa.

Economic and Social Council resolution 1985/66

26 July 1985   Meeting 52   34-1-9

Approved by First Committee (E/1985/145) by roll-call vote (34-1-9), 23 July (meeting 27); draft by ECA (E/1985/106), orally amended by Secretary following informal consultations; agenda item 8.

Both the First Committee and the Council voted separately on paragraph 2 (in the Committee at the request of Luxembourg), which was adopted in Committee by a roll-call vote of 31 to 10, with 3 abstentions, and in the Council by 33 votes to 10, with 3 abstentions.

Luxembourg declared that although EEC member States favoured strengthening MULPOCs, they were unable to vote in favour since paragraph 2 specified particular nationalities for particular posts, which ran counter to the United Nations principle of universality. The United States said it was not the function of the Council to instruct the Secretary-General to hire individuals of particular nationalities.

Co-operation between the United Nations and SADCC

Pursuant to a 1984 General Assembly resolution,[109] the Secretary-General presented in September 1985 a request[110] on co-operation between the United Nations and the Southern African Development Co-ordination Conference. The sixth SADCC Conference (Mbabane, 31 January and 1 February) focused on food and agriculture, but working groups were also established to review co-operation in energy, transport and communications, manpower, and industry and mining. In addition to the nine SADCC member States (Angola, Botswana, Lesotho, Malawi, Mozambique, Swaziland, United Republic of Tanzania, Zambia, Zimbabwe), the Conference was attended by representatives of 23 other Governments and 18 international organizations.

The sixth SADCC Summit of heads of State (Arusha, 9 August) welcomed an initiative by the Nordic countries to broaden their involvement with SADCC.

GENERAL ASSEMBLY ACTION

On 17 December, on the recommendation of the Second Committee, the General Assembly adopted without vote **resolution 40/195**.

Co-operation between the United Nations and the Southern African Development Co-ordination Conference

The General Assembly,

Recalling its resolutions 37/248 of 21 December 1982, 38/160 of 19 December 1983 and 39/215 of 18 December 1984, by which it, *inter alia*, requested the Secretary-General to promote co-operation between the organs, organizations and bodies of the United Nations system and the Southern African Development Co-ordination Conference and urged intensification of contacts in order to accelerate the achievement of the objectives of the Lusaka Declaration of 1 April 1980, by which the Conference was established,

Having considered the report of the Secretary-General on co-operation between the United Nations and the Southern African Development Co-ordination Conference,

Noting the significant progress made by the Conference in formulating concrete development programmes, and that most of these are at the implementation stage,

Recognizing that successful implementation of these programmes can be achieved only if the Conference has adequate resources at its disposal,

Deeply concerned about the deteriorating economic and security situation in southern Africa and the particularly difficult environment for regional co-operation caused by acts of destabilization by South Africa,

Convinced that increased self-reliance by States members of the Conference would contribute to the struggle against the *apartheid* policies of South Africa,

Welcoming the progress made by some organs, organizations and bodies of the United Nations system in formulating and executing co-operation programmes with the Conference,

1. *Takes note* of the report of the Secretary-General on co-operation between the United Nations and the Southern African Development Co-ordination Con-

ference, which describes the progress made in the implementation of the relevant resolutions of the General Assembly;

2. *Commends* the Member States and organs, organizations and bodies of the United Nations system that have established contacts with and extended concrete assistance to the Conference;

3. *Appeals* to the international community to increase substantially its financial and material support to the Conference;

4. *Also appeals* to the specialized agencies and other organs and organizations of the United Nations system to co-operate fully in the development programmes of the Conference;

5. *Requests* the Secretary-General, in consultation with the Executive Secretary of the Conference, to continue and intensify contacts aimed at promoting and harmonizing co-operation between the United Nations and the Conference;

6. *Also requests* the Secretary-General to report to the General Assembly at its forty-second session on the implementation of the present resolution.

General Assembly resolution 40/195

17 December 1985   Meeting 119   Adopted without vote

Approved by Second Committee (A/40/989/Add.5) without vote, 4 December (meeting 47); 17-nation draft (A/C.2/40/L.40); agenda item 84 *(e)*.

Sponsors: Angola, Botswana, Canada, Comoros, Denmark, Finland, Kenya, Lesotho, Malawi, Mozambique, Netherlands, Norway, Swaziland, Sweden, United Republic of Tanzania, Zambia, Zimbabwe.

Meeting numbers. GA 40th session: 2nd Committee 36, 47; plenary 119.

The Assembly in **resolution 40/64 I** appealed to States, organizations and institutions to give more assistance to the front-line States and SADCC to increase their economic strength and independence from South Africa.

REFERENCES

[1]E/ECA/CM.12/3. [2]YUN 1980, p. 548. [3]E/1985/36. [4]E/ECA/CM.11/80/Rev.1. [5]E/1985/36 (res. 556(XX)). [6]E/ECA/CM.11/77/Rev.1. [7]E/1985/81. [8]E/1985/36 (res. 558(XX)). [9]YUN 1984, p. 470, GA res. 39/29, annex, 3 Dec. 1984. [10]Ibid., p. 603. [11]E/1985/36 (res. 555(XX)). [12]Ibid. (res. 549(XX)). [13]E/ECA/CM.11/74. [14]E/ECA/CM.11/70. [15]E/ECA/CM.11/14 & Corr.1. [16]YUN 1980, p. 503, GA res. 35/56, annex, 5 Dec. 1980. [17]E/1986/33. [18]E/1985/36 (res. 539(XX)). [19]YUN 1984, p. 605. [20]E/ECA/CM.11/51; E/ECA/CM.11/51/Summary. [21]E/1985/36 (res. 534(XX)). [22]Ibid. (res. 540(XX)). [23]E/ECA/CM.12/14 & Add.1; E/ECA/CM.12/14/Summary. [24]E/1985/36 (res. 537(XX)). [25]E/ECA/CM.11/49. [26]E/ECA/CM.11/78. [27]E/1985/36 (res. 538(XX)). [28]E/ECA/CM.12/8. [29]E/1985/36 (res. 541(XX)). [30]E/ECA/CM.11/23. [31]E/ECA/CM.11/76. [32]YUN 1982, p. 804. [33]YUN 1984, p. 606, GA dec. 39/433, 18 Dec. 1984. [34]E/ECA/CM.11/65. [35]E/ECA/CM.11/8 & Corr.1. [36]E/ECA/CM.11/48 & Corr.1. [37]A/40/409-E/1985/107. [38]YUN 1977, p. 603, GA res. 32/160, 19 Dec. 1977. [39]A/40/735. [40]E/ECA/CM.11/31. [41]E/1985/36 (res. 544(XX)). [42]A/40/633. [43]A/40/633/Add.1. [44]E/1985/108. [45]YUN 1984, p. 609, ESC res. 1984/75, 27 July 1984. [46]YUN 1980, p. 662, GA res. 35/66 B, 5 Dec. 1980. [47]ID/B/330. [48]YUN 1984, p. 612, GA res. 39/233, 18 Dec. 1984. [49]A/40/420-E/1985/111 & Corr.1. [50]E/ECA/CM.11/7/Summary. [51]A/40/16 (conclusion 1985/3). [52]E/1985/36 (res. 532(XX)). [53]Ibid. (res. 531(XX)). [54]E/ECA/CM.11/52. [55]E/ECA/CM.11/41. [56]E/1985/36 (res. 542(XX)). [57]E/ECA/CM.11/18. [58]E/ECA/CM.11/30. [59]YUN 1977, p. 555. [60]E/ECA/CM.11/9 & Corr.1. [61]E/ECA/CM.11/24. [62]E/1985/36 (res. 560(XX)). [63]A/40/329-E/1985/80. [64]YUN 1984, p. 615, GA res. 39/165, 17 Dec. 1984. [65]E/1985/113. [66]YUN 1983, p. 623, GA res. 38/198, 20 Dec. 1983. [67]E/1985/106. [68]E/1985/36 (res. 548(XX)). [69]Ibid. (res. 559(XX)). [70]E/ECA/CM.11/29. [71]YUN 1979, p. 636. [72]E/ECA/CM.12/4. [73]E/1985/36 (res. 547(XX)). [74]E/ECA/CM.11/46. [75]E/ECA/CM.11/33. [76]E/ECA/CM.11/40. [77]E/ECA/CM.11/10; E/ECA/CM.11/10/Summary. [78]E/1985/36 (res. 545(XX)). [79]A/CONF.121/22/Rev.1 (res. 4). [80]E/ECA/CM.11/47. [81]E/1985/36 (res. 546(XX)). [82]Ibid. (res. 533(XX)). [83]E/ECA/CM.11/38 & Add.1. [84]E/ECA/CM.12/9; E/ECA/CM.12/9/Summary. [85]E/ECA/CM.12/27. [86]E/ECA/CM.11/13 & Corr.1. [87]YUN 1984, p. 618. [88]E/ECA/CM.11/50. [89]YUN 1979, p. 895, GA res. 34/180, annex, 18 Dec. 1979. [90]E/1985/36 (res. 535(XX) & 536(XX)). [91]E/ECA/PSD.4/20. [92]A/C.5/40/13 & Corr.1 & Add.1,2. [93]A/40/7/Add.5. [94]E/1985/36 (res. 554(XX)). [95]E/1985/59. [96]E/1985/64. [97]E/1985/155. [98]E/1985/C.1/L.8. [99]YUN 1984, p. 620, GA res. 39/236, sect. III, 18 Dec. 1984. [100]A/C.5/40/31/Rev.1. [101]E/C.5/40/361. [102]A/40/7/Add.11. [103]E/ECA/CM.11/22. [104]E/ECA/CM.12/25 & Add.1. [105]E/ECA/CM.11/17 & Add.1. [106]E/1985/36 (res. 550(XX)). [107]Ibid. (res. 551(XX)). [108]Ibid. (res. 552(XX)). [109]YUN 1984, p. 621, GA res. 39/215, 18 Dec. 1984. [110]A/40/579 & Corr.1.

PUBLICATION

Sub-Saharan Africa: *Towards Oblivion or Reconstruction?*, Journal of Development Planning, No. 15, 1985 (ST/ESA/162), Sales No. E.85.II.A.6.

Asia and the Pacific

The Economic and Social Commission for Asia and the Pacific held its forty-first session at Bangkok, Thailand, from 19 to 29 March. In its annual reports for the periods 28 April 1984–29 March 1985[1] and 30 March 1985–2 May 1986,[2] it appraised the implementation of the International Development Strategy for the Third United Nations Development Decade[3] (the 1980s) and the Substantial New Programme of Action for the 1980s for the Least Developed Countries.[4] Consideration was given to the implementation of the Tokyo Programme on Technology for Development in Asia and the Pacific—a 1984 Commission resolution adopting the ESCAP Plan of Action on Technology for Development[5]—and to the programmes for the Transport and Communications Decade for Asia and the Pacific (1985-1994),[6] which was formally launched in January at the Meeting of Ministers Responsible for Transport and Communications.

The Commission also considered sectoral issues in various ESCAP fields of activity, endorsed the 1986-1987 draft programme of work and priorities, reviewed the functioning of regional institutions and special projects, and endorsed proposals by the Executive Secretary relating to improvement of the functions of the legislative committees.

ESCAP committees discussed food and agriculture and rural development; transnational corporations; industry, technology and human settlements; the environment; international trade; natural resources and energy; population; shipping, ports and inland waterways; transport, communication and tourism; and statistics. An Asian and Pacific Ministerial Conference on Social Welfare and Social Development was held in October in lieu of the fourth session of the Committee on Social Development, originally scheduled for 1984.

Brunei Darussalam and Tuvalu were admitted as full members of ESCAP, which consisted of 38 member and six associate member nations.

The mid-year to mid-year work of the regional commissions, including ESCAP, was summarized in a June report[7] of the Secretary-General. The report also reflected the main issues discussed at the meetings of the commissions' executive secretaries at Addis Ababa on 25 and 26 February (see p. 624), and transmitted to the Economic and Social Council issues for its attention or decisions calling for its action.

Economic and social trends

The annual *Economic and Social Survey of Asia and the Pacific 1985*[8] stated that economic growth in the developing economies of Asia and the Pacific was generally less robust in 1985 than in 1984, though the region's performance remained stronger than that of other regions. The slow-down was most marked in export-oriented economies hit by protectionism, slipping demand for manufactures and extremely low prices for primary commodities. The island economies of the Pacific, LDCs and several others dependent on commodity markets were severely affected. Some growth was achieved in the region's LDCs but there was no increase in the net inflow of resources from abroad. Progress in reducing unemployment, alleviating poverty and eradicating illiteracy continued to be slow. Generating stronger stimuli for self-sustaining growth remained an important concern. Initiatives to foster healthier international financial conditions and a more stable exchange rate were taken in late 1985, expected to bring about increased inflows of capital at lower interest rates.

The Commission considered the issues related to the integration of population factors into overall socio-economic development. It particularly noted the need for integrated development plans which would slow population growth, use natural resources efficiently, protect the environment and promote economic development. It urged the ESCAP secretariat to study the relationship between population, resources, environment and development with a view to developing practical measures which countries could adopt.

The Economic and Social Council on 25 July, by **decision 1985/182**, took note of, among other documents, a summary[9] of the *Economic and Social Survey of Asia and the Pacific 1984*.[10]

Activities in 1985

Development policy and regional economic co-operation

The Commission, reviewing the implementation of the International Development Strategy, highlighted the issues of international trade, external flows, technology and population. Noting disturbing trends such as high real interest rates and other terms of credit, ESCAP felt that there was considerable scope for expanded trade flows and economic co-operation among countries of the region. It stressed the need to raise their technological capacity, especially in the least developed, land-locked and island countries. It decided that in future reviews of the Strategy, the focus should be on international trade, money and finance, food and agriculture, industrialization and energy.

Development planning activities included a regional seminar on an interlinked country model system (Bangkok, November). The seminar suggested improvements in national models, and discussed technical procedures for operating a model system using trade flows as linkage. An Expert Group on Development Issues and Policies met at Bangkok in October. Two workshops on how LDCs could mobilize domestic savings were conducted (Dhaka, Bangladesh, April; Kathmandu, Nepal, December).

The Asian and Pacific Development Centre expanded its activities to include East Asia and the Pacific island States; previously it had concentrated its efforts in South and South-East Asia.

Publication began of the *Development Planning Newsletter*, which was to be issued every four months.

Implementation of SNPA for LDCs

The Commission took note of the report[11] of the High-level Meeting prior to the Mid-term Global Review of the Implementation of SNPA (Bangkok, 28-31 January), directed towards accelerated implementation of SNPA in the second half of the decade. It expressed concern about the lack of progress and urged speedy implementation. On 29 March, it adopted a resolution[12] requesting developed and developing countries, United Nations organizations and bodies, and funding agencies to provide increased financial and technical assistance to the region's LDCs so they might implement their SNPA-related plans and programmes.

Mekong River basin development

The twenty-first session of the Interim Committee for Co-ordination of Investigations of the Lower Mekong Basin, originally scheduled for January at Hanoi, Viet Nam, was held instead at Vientiane, Lao People's Democratic Republic, from 29 July to 3 August. According to the Committee's annual report for 1985,[13] transmitted to ESCAP in March,[14] the work programme for 1985 comprised 111 projects under six programme sectors—hydrology and meteorology, basin planning, land and water resources development, navigation improvement, agriculture and fisheries, and power, industry and minerals—requiring an initial investment of about $307 million. All were geared to promoting food production, generating hydroelectric power and improving navigation.

Technical co-operation activities

During 1985, the Secretary-General reported[15] to the UNDP Governing Council, ESCAP had responded to 44 requests for technical and advisory services from 20 countries by means of 37 missions under the United Nations regular programme of technical co-operation. The majority of the requests were from LDCs and island developing countries.

The ESCAP Pacific Operations Centre at Port Vila, Vanuatu, provided short-term advisory services to developing island countries under the United Nations Development Advisory Team for the South Pacific and UNDP.

The Commission reaffirmed the catalytic role that ESCAP could play in supporting technical and economic co-operation among its members and associate members. In that connection, it adopted a resolution[16] on 29 March asking the Executive Secretary to give high priority to activities that supported technical and economic co-operation among developing countries (TCDC/ECDC), and requesting developing and associate member countries to strengthen their national focal points for such co-operation for better planning and co-ordination and to provide information on their needs and capabilities; it also invited contributions to the supplementary fund for TCDC.

An intergovernmental meeting of national focal points (Bangkok, 5-10 November)[17] recommended a revised methodology for the organization of regional intergovernmental TCDC consultations, preparation of basic guidelines for planning of TCDC activities, measures to strengthen the capacity of TCDC/ECDC focal points, and formulation of TCDC activities in 1986-1987 in agro- and allied industries.

International trade

The fourth Asia-Pacific International Trade Fair (Beijing, 15-30 November)[18]—the first in 13 years—promoted trade expansion, economic co-operation and development of industry and technology. Some 1,200 commercial and industrial firms from 20 ESCAP member and six non-member countries participated; about 800,000 visitors from throughout China and 10,000 foreign visitors attended. With UNDP support, ESCAP organized during the Fair a seminar on investment and trade-creating joint ventures and another on transfer of technology.

A regional seminar on import management was held in Beijing, with study tours to Guangzhou and Shenzhen, in April, organized by ESCAP, ITC and the Helsinki School of Economics, Finland.

A regional seminar on the establishment of market information services on jute and jute products (Bangladesh, April) and the third session of the Regional Consultative Group on Silk (Kuala Trengganu, Malaysia, July) reviewed developments in their respective industries.

A meeting of senior trade information officials on the Regional Trade Information Network (Bangkok, September) discussed strengthening trade information services and making them more user-oriented.

Transport and communications

The Meeting of Ministers Responsible for Transport and Communications (Bangkok, 23-25 January)[19] considered and made recommendations on roads and road transport, railways, shipping, ports and inland waterways, air transport and telecommunications. To help accelerate the development of transport and communication infrastructure in LDCs, the Meeting stressed the need for more flexibility by donor countries and agencies in applying strict economic viability criteria to projects. To its report the Meeting annexed extracts from the report of the Intergovernmental Meeting of Senior Highway Officials (Bangkok, 16-22 January) detailing the region's road transport problems and offering recommendations.

The ninth session of the Committee on Shipping, and Transport and Communications (Transport, Communications and Tourism Wing) (Bangkok, 10-16 December)[20] considered major issues in general transport planning, railway, road and air cargo transport, containerization, containerization in relation to inland transport, facilitation of international transport, telecommunications, postal services and tourism.

A note by the secretariat[21] examined the components of a development strategy for regional railways. It annexed railway project profiles of the Regional Action Programme for the Transport and Communications Decade for Asia and the Pacific (1985-1994).

Seminars, workshops and study tours were conducted on containerization (Lahore, Pakistan, April), excessive rail and wheel wear and derailments (Kuala Lumpur, Malaysia, September), railway track maintenance and toll roads (Austria and France, September/October), and road accidents and railway electrification (Bangkok, November).

Transport and Communications Decade for Asia and the Pacific (1985-1994)

The Commission noted the work of its secretariat towards the implementation of the Transport and Communications Decade for Asia and the Pacific, 1985-1994, in compliance with 1984 General Assembly[22] and Economic and Social Council[23] resolutions. The preparatory phase of the Decade's work culminated in January 1985 with a series of intergovernmental meetings on highways, railways and shipping, ports and inland waterways. The Commission noted that ECWA had, as requested by the Assembly,[22] taken steps to participate. The Commission urged the secretariat to assign priorities for action.

On 25 January,[19] the Meeting of Ministers Responsible for Transport and Communications issued a Declaration, the adoption of which was known as "The Launching of the Transport and Communications Decade for Asia and the Pacific, 1985-1994". The Declaration recommended that the Decade's programmes be carried out so as to achieve a framework for decision-making in the transport and communication sectors, an integrated multisectoral and intermodal approach in medium- and long-term planning, improvement in the efficiency of existing transport and communication systems, facilitation of international traffic and communications, energy conservation, enhancement of technology, development of human resources and expertise, and safe and secure international traffic. It reaffirmed the Committee on Shipping, and Transport and Communications' primary role in reviewing progress of the Decade, and resolved that a conference of ministers responsible for transport and communications would be held from time to time to evaluate progress and provide policy guidance for the programmes.

The ESCAP secretariat[24] listed 22 "thrust areas" comprising the strategy for the Decade—nine having high, seven regular and six low priority levels—and 47 project proposals by thrust area for regional action.

Shipping, ports and inland waterways

The eighth session of the Committee on Shipping, and Transport and Communications (Shipping, Ports and Inland Waterways Wing) (Bangkok, 8-14 January)[25] considered developments, issues and activities in such areas as manpower development, maritime policy and institutions, merchant marines and shipping services, ports and port management, inland water transport and waterways, and shippers' organizations and co-operation.

A Meeting of Experts on Inland Water Transport (Bangkok, 20-22 November)[26] discussed the role of inland waterways in the development of the economies of ESCAP member countries. It recommended the establishment of a regional inland water transport centre in Bangladesh for an initial period of five years (1987-1991) to implement a set of priority projects based mainly on the report of a programming mission which had visited nine countries of the region from February to April, had identified more than 160 inland water transport issues and problems and had recommended 71 projects to deal with them.

Industrial development

The ninth session of the Committee on Industry, Technology, Human Settlements and the Environment (Bangkok, 10-16 September)[27] recommended, among other things, that the secretariat expand pilot project activities on energy management and energy audit training for small- and medium-scale industries to a larger number of member countries. It also urged UNDP to give high funding priority to a proposed programme for investment promotion in the region.

Three training workshops were organized dealing with energy audit and energy conservation in small-scale industry (Kathmandu, September/October; Jinan, China, October; and Bangkok, November).

Transnational corporations

The *Ad Hoc* Intergovernmental Meeting on Transnational Corporations (Bangkok, 19-23 December)[28] considered the status of negotiations and outstanding issues on the draft code of conduct on TNCs (see p. 616) and regional co-operation on TNC matters. The Meeting endorsed recommendations of the United Nations Centre on TNCs/ESCAP Expert Group Meeting on the code of conduct (Bangkok, 17 and 18 December), which underlined the need for an early conclusion of the negotiations.

Natural resources and energy

The Committee on Natural Resources, at its twelfth session (Bangkok, 29 October–4 November):[29] noted a growing interest among ESCAP countries in exploring, evaluating and developing their hydrocarbon resources; recommended that the secretariat identify the metals and minerals on which exploration activities could be concentrated in the light of projected demand; strongly supported activity on geology for urban planning; urged the recruitment of experts in various fields relevant to the needs of LDCs; emphasized that conventional energy sources would continue to be major sources of energy supply for development; and endorsed the regional remote sensing programme and a request to UNDP to provide support to the programme from 1987 to 1991.

Workshops, symposia and training courses were listed in a report[30] of the Regional Mineral Resources Development Centre, including: a workshop on the environmental impact of mineral development in the humid tropics (Manila, Philippines, 15-18 February); a workshop on geochemistry in mineral exploration (Bandung, 8-13 April); a workshop on applied geophysics related to ground-water exploration (Bandung and Jogjakarta, Indonesia, 7-28 May); a workshop on Kuroko-type mineralization (Tsukuba/Odate, Japan, 1-11 September); a workshop on drilling, sampling and borehole logging (Wuxi, China, 5-16 November); a post-graduate geology training course (India, 15 November 1985–15 October 1986); and a symposium on mineral deposit modelling (Manila, 5-14 December). In addition, five round-table talks on uranium exploration were held (Jakarta, Indonesia, 7-14 July; Kuala Lumpur/Ipoh, 1-10 August; Seoul, Republic of Korea, 23 August–6 September; Dhaka, 20-27 October; Colombo, Sri Lanka, 1-6 December).

Water resources. An inter-agency mission on the establishment of a regional network for training in water resources development was carried out by ESCAP and ILO from 21 July to 9 August, visiting Malaysia, Pakistan, the Philippines, the Republic of Korea and Sri Lanka. All the participating institutes welcomed the proposal to establish the network.

The Inter-agency Task Force on Water for Asia and the Pacific held its fourteenth, fifteenth and sixteenth sessions (Bangkok; January, July and November); it discussed two projects—the accelerated local manufacture of hand pumps for rural water supply and the proposed regional training network.

A Meeting on the Establishment of a Cyclone Council for the South Pacific (Port Vila, February) recommended that a tropical cyclone committee be established as a working group of WMO within the framework of its Tropical Cyclone Programme. An expert group meeting on the improvement of disaster prevention systems based on risk analysis of natural disasters related to typhoons and heavy rainfall was held (Bangkok, July), and a seminar/study tour on the efficient use of in-vestments in the development of water management was conducted (Tashkent, USSR, September).

To effect global co-ordination in water resources development, ESCAP participated in the sixth session of the Intersecretariat Group for Water (New York, October) of the Administrative Committee on Co-ordination, attended by United Nations agencies involved with water.

Energy resources. The Commission, while commending the work of the secretariat on new and renewable energy sources, particularly solar photovoltaic power-generation, biomass and biogas, solar, wind and small hydropower, expressed the view that conventional sources of energy, such as oil, coal and natural gas, would continue to play an important role in economic and social development in the foreseeable future. It emphasized the importance of a balanced mix of diverse energy resources, both conventional and alternative. The Commission also took note of a regional expert group meeting (Bangkok, January) for the United Nations Conference for the Promotion of International Co-operation in the Peaceful Uses of Nuclear Energy (see p. 684); the meeting identified constraints in the uses of nuclear isotope techniques in food and agriculture, health and medicine, hydrology, geophysics and industry, as well as in the wider use of nuclear power, and suggested regional measures to help overcome them.

A number of other meetings were held at Bangkok, including: a regional expert seminar on solar photovoltaic technology (June); a training course on renewable energy planning (August); an expert group meeting on natural gas production and use (September); and an ESCAP/Asian Institute of Technology training course on solar hot-water systems (December).

Three major regional co-operative programmes were financed by extrabudgetary resources: the Regional Energy Development Programme and the Pacific Energy Development Programme, both funded by UNDP, and the Regional Network on Biomass, Solar and Wind Energy, funded by Japan and Australia. The secretariat reported on the implementation of the Pacific Energy Development Programme during 1985[31] and on the activities of the second phase of the Regional Energy Development Programme (1984-1986).[32]

Food and agriculture

The sixth session of the Committee on Agricultural Development (Bangkok, 1-7 October)[33] endorsed the recommendations of an expert group meeting (Bangkok, 7-9 May) on the development of fertilizer use in the ESCAP region. It emphasized that the ESCAP/FAO/UNIDO Fertilizer Advisory, Development and Information Network for Asia and the Pacific should foster regional co-operation in fertilizer production, procurement, marketing, distribution and use. The Committee also considered such matters as agricultural development planning, the responsibility system in agriculture in China, farm broadcasting, the agro-climatic drought early warning programme, fisheries and aquaculture, use of agricultural residues as an energy source, promotion of non-farm employment and income among rural workers, and the role of women in agriculture.

A March progress report[34] on co-operation between FAO and ESCAP in food and agricultural activities was submitted by the Secretary-General to the April/May session of CPC. In its report[35] to the Assembly, CPC expressed satisfaction with the progress made in the past two years in furthering co-operation; it encouraged FAO and ESCAP to continue their efforts and report to it if they encountered any difficulties.

The Governing Board of the Regional Coordination Centre for Research and Development of Coarse Grains, Pulses, Roots and Tuber Crops in the Humid Tropics of Asia and the Pacific held its third session at Denpasar, Indonesia, from 22 to 25 January.[36] The Board reviewed studies conducted by the Centre in 1984 of those crops in East Asia; of soybean production in Indonesia; of the potential of cassava; and of socio-economic constraints to increased production of food legumes and coarse grains. In a report[37] on the Centre's 1985 activities, the Board stated that the Centre's efforts that year focused mainly on soybean and maize in South-East Asia and selected grain legumes in South Asia.

Science and technology

On 29 March, the Commission adopted a resolution[38] calling on members and associate members to improve their national institutes for science and technology and consider making them available to other members, and urging developed members and the United Nations system to give priority to developing members' efforts to enhance their technological capabilities. It asked the Executive Secretary to facilitate the exchange of experience among members.

By another resolution,[39] it adopted the statute of the Asian and Pacific Centre for Transfer of Technology, changing the name of the Regional Centre for Technology Transfer inaugurated in 1977. The statute laid down the Centre's objectives, functions and organization, as well as the composition and functions of the Governing Board and Technical Advisory Committee of Experts; it also stipulated the resources required for the Centre's functioning. The Centre was located in Bangalore, India, and its major objectives were to assist ESCAP members and associate members by strengthening their capabilities to develop, transfer, adapt and apply technology, to improve the terms of transfer of technology and identify and promote the development and transfer of technologies relevant to the region. With UNDP funding, the Centre began implementing three programmes: facilitating technology transfer through information services, promoting transfer and utilization of selected technologies, and strengthening technology policies and planning infrastructure. The Technical Advisory Committee held its first session at Bangalore in September.

In September, the Committee on Industry, Technology, Human Settlements and the Environment[27] (see p. 647) emphasized that, in addition to projects on solar photovoltaic power systems, research, development and demonstration, the Tokyo Programme on Technology for Development in Asia and the Pacific[5] should be extended to cover such areas as biotechnology and genetic engineering, metallurgy, new industrial materials and laser technology. It endorsed a proposal to convene the first session of the Technical Advisory Group on Industry and Technology in 1986.

Expert group meetings on the technological dimensions of human resources development and on the Technology Atlas for Asia and the Pacific were convened in Bangkok in October.

Social and cultural development

The Third Asian and Pacific Ministerial Conference on Social Welfare and Social Development (Bangkok, 9-15 October)[40] reviewed the regional socio-economic situation, considered the social effects of development and examined planning, resources and administration needs in socio-economic development; it also adopted recommendations addressing those issues for action at the national, regional and international levels.

The Commission called for full implementation of the Programme of Action[41] for the Second Half of the United Nations Decade for Women (1976-1985). It noted that the deliberations of a 1984 Regional Intergovernmental Preparatory Meeting for the 1985 World Conference to appraise the Decade's achievements (see Chapter XIX of this section) and the ESCAP/South Pacific Commission Subregional Pacific Meeting on Women (Rarotonga, Cook Islands, March) could provide valuable inputs to the World Conference. With respect to International Youth Year (1985) in the region, the Commission reiterated its support for the secretariat's youth development activities and its efforts to promote youth participation in national development (see Chapter XX of this section).

Workshops on prevention and rehabilitation schemes for young women in prostitution and related occupations (Bangkok, June) and on the role of youth organizations in the prevention of crime among youth (Tokyo, July) were held in 1985.

Population

The growth rate of the 2.7 billion people who lived in the ESCAP region fell from about 2.5 per cent annually in the late 1960s to about 1.7 per cent in 1984, ESCAP reported.[42] In the 1950s, 16 per cent of the region's children died before their first birthday; currently the figure was about 8 per cent (compared with about 1 per cent in the developed countries). The decline in fertility was attributed to investments in disease control, health facilities, education and family planning programmes.

Population issues and activities in the ESCAP region were considered by the Committee on Population at its fourth session (Bangkok, 13-19 August).[43] The Committee recalled the target of a minimum of 55 years of life expectancy at birth by the end of the 1980s, set by the Asia-Pacific Call for Action on Population and Development in 1982.[44] It conducted a number of training courses in 1985, most of them concerned with the use of microcomputers for demographic information-handling and data analysis.

Environment

A Declaration and Framework for Action Plans for the Management of the Asian Environment, 1985, was adopted by a Ministerial-level Conference on the Environment in Asia (Bangkok, 11 and 12 February).[45] The Framework was intended to provide general guidance for developing environmental programmes; it directed attention to the management of terrestrial ecosystems, protection of the marine environment, environmental health and natural and cultural heritages, planning and management of the urban environment, human settlements, promotion of environmental awareness, institutional and legislative structures, and recommendations for implementation.

The Commission expressed concern that vast tracts of land in the ESCAP region were afflicted or threatened by desertification. It agreed that the 1977 United Nations Plan of Action to Combat Desertification[46] was a good basis for initiating action, urging countries to assign priorities to control programmes and projects and establish national committees. The secretariat submitted a report[47] on the regional and country status of desertification, stating that what stood out most was the inability thus far to mobilize the funds to implement the Plan of Action.

The Committee on Industry, Technology, Human Settlements and the Environment in September[27] asked the secretariat to support efforts to implement the Framework, stating that integration of environmental considerations into the development process and the sectoral activities of ESCAP were of the utmost importance. Environmental impact analysis should be promoted and desertification control measures should receive high priority, including convening of an intergovernmental meeting on a proposed regional network of training and research centres for desertification control. The Committee urged extrabudgetary support for the Asian Forum of Environmental Journalists, established at the Regional Media Conference on Environment and Development (New Delhi, India, February) to promote regional environmental awareness.

Typhoons

The Typhoon Committee (eighteenth session, Beijing, 8-14 October)[48] reported that members had made considerable progress in typhoon forecasting and warning services, especially with the operation of the Geostationary Meteorological Satellite by Japan and the establishment of additional radar and upgrading of telecommunication facilities.

The Committee endorsed the concept for regional co-operation among Committee members proposed by an expert meeting in planning regional co-operation for the typhoon area (Tokyo, August).

Human settlements

The Commission expressed satisfaction that, pursuant to a 1983 General Assembly resolution,[49] 21 countries of the ESCAP region had established national focal points for the International Year of Shelter for the Homeless (1987) (see p. 827) and identified 30 projects for the Year in nine countries.

The Committee on Industry, Technology, Human Settlements and the Environment[27] emphasized the importance of national action to solve the shelter problem through new ways and means and stressed the need to give shelter higher priority in economic development plans. It recommended that member countries examine a 1984 proposal[50] for a financial and advisory institution for human settlements in the region (see p. 823). It also recommended that special assistance be given to LDCs in pursuance of the objectives of the International Year, for whose programme countries were urged to provide generous support, and SNPA. The secretariat was urged to help countries adopt suitable standards for low-income shelter. The Committee endorsed a proposal to establish a network of local authorities for the management of human settlements. There was also a need for a regional network to promote information-sharing and a need for increased community participation in planning and development.

Statistics

The sixth session of the Committee on Statistics (Bangkok, 19-25 November)[51] reviewed statistical activities in the region and discussed the development of overall national statistical capabilities, including the National Household Survey Capability Programme and statistical training, the development of economic and social statistics, and publication policy for regional statistics.

The Statistical Institute for Asia and the Pacific reported[52] that it had conducted training programmes in general statistics, automatic data processing, indicators for economic and social development, and economic censuses, as well as given courses for training trainers, awarded fellowships to test statistical software packages and helped organize an expert group meeting on developing statistics of household economic activities (Bangkok, 23-28 September).

Programme, organizational and administrative questions

Amendment of terms of reference

On 29 March, noting that Brunei Darussalam and Tuvalu had become members of ESCAP, the Commission approved a draft resolution for action by the Economic and Social Council to amend those paragraphs of the Commission's terms of reference which listed full and associate members.

ECONOMIC AND SOCIAL COUNCIL ACTION

On 26 July, on the recommendation of its First Committee, the Economic and Social Council adopted without vote **resolution 1985/60**.

Amendment of the terms of reference of the Economic and Social Commission for Asia and the Pacific: membership of Brunei Darussalam and Tuvalu
The Economic and Social Council,
Noting that Brunei Darussalam and Tuvalu have become members of the Economic and Social Commission for Asia and the Pacific in accordance with paragraph 3 of the terms of reference of the Commission,
Decides to amend paragraphs 3 and 4 of the terms of reference of the Economic and Social Commission for Asia and the Pacific accordingly.

Economic and Social Council resolution 1985/60

26 July 1985   Meeting 52   Adopted without vote

Approved by First Committee (E/1985/145) without vote, 23 July (meeting 27); draft by ESCAP (E/1985/106); agenda item 8.

Activities in the Pacific

The Commission welcomed the establishment on 1 July 1984 of the ESCAP Pacific Operations Centre at Port Vila, combining the ESCAP Pacific Liaison Office, located in Nauru, and the United Nations Development Advisory Team for the Pacific, located in Fiji. The Centre focused on providing advisory services through staff advisers or consultants, facilitating training and maintaining liaison with island Governments. The Commission requested[53] the ESCAP Executive Secretary

to take steps, within the United Nations programme planning and budgeting cycle, to incorporate a new subprogramme on "Special measures in favour of island developing countries" within the programme on development issues and policies, to assist Pacific island countries to make better use of the services of multilateral organizations by identifying the avenues of assistance, and to ensure that the Centre was in a position to assist those countries in drafting project proposals for presenting to those organizations.

During 1985, it was noted[54] that the Centre undertook 40 of ESCAP's 109 advisory missions, provided consultancy services, offered training activities, and disseminated information and reports to Pacific island countries and territories.

Work programme for 1986-1987

In considering the draft programme of work and priorities for 1986-1987, the Commission stressed that primary responsibility for programming should be at the regional level, where problems were better understood, so that revisions could be avoided and resources used more effectively. In that context, the Commission urged that the sectoral legislative committees and the Advisory Committee of Permanent Representatives and Other Representatives Designated by Members of the Commission (ACPR) play a larger role in formulating the work programme. It reaffirmed the importance of priority-setting at the programme-element level. It decided that the activities addressed to specific problems of LDCs and the developing land-locked and island countries should be given special priority. The Commission endorsed, with some changes, the work programme and priorities for 1986-1987;[55] included was a new programme on marine resources.

Recognizing the uncertainties surrounding the current international economic situation and the declining global resources available for development, the Commission adopted a resolution[16] on mobilization of resources for TCDC/ECDC, by which it requested the Economic and Social Council to recommend to the General Assembly that it should continue to provide appropriate resources to enable the Commission to utilize fully its potential.

JIU reports

In May,[56] the Secretary-General transmitted to the General Assembly and Economic and Social Council a report by the Joint Inspection Unit on ESCAP, the first such report in 15 years.[57] The new report discussed ESCAP's mandate, its structure, functions and work as a regional multidisciplinary centre for social and economic development, its technical co-operation activities, and issues common to all regional commissions.

It also presented recommendations, on which the Secretary-General commented:[58] ESCAP members should ensure that programmes conformed to Commission criteria, that they were commensurate with expected resources and overprogramming discouraged, and that meetings were reduced to a manageable number; and they should consider establishing a programme preparation and review committee to formalize some of ACPR's functions and make viability a decisive criterion for regulating institutions (recommendations 1 and 3). The Secretary-General agreed with recommendation 1 but observed that, since over-programming was linked to the provision of extrabudgetary contributions, the size of such contributions should be estimated more realistically when formulating the programme budget. In principle, he accepted the establishment of the new committee, but since it would have budgetary implications the matter should be further examined.

Addressing recommendation 2, that the secretariat should analyse the impact of meetings and improve the quality of documents, the Secretary-General felt a comparative analysis of the impact of all ESCAP activities should be made to determine their importance and for rationalizing and improving its work as a whole. The Executive Secretary should examine the feasibility of combining the Programme Co-ordination and Monitoring Office and the Technical Co-operation Division (recommendation 4) and ensure that the contributions of donor Governments were in keeping with and promoted Commission criteria (6). The Secretary-General felt that the units' approaches and type of personnel were so different that amalgamation would not improve performance, but agreed with the recommendation on contributions and took note of recommendation 5, that he should review the grade level of the deputy executive secretaries of the regional commissions.

On 26 July, the Economic and Social Council adopted **decision 1985/191** by which it took note of, among other things, the JIU report and the Secretary-General's comments. By the same decision, it took note of a 1984 JIU report[5] on the contribution of the United Nations system to conservation and management of cultural and natural heritage in Asia and the Pacific, and comments of the Secretary-General thereon.

Improving the functions of the legislative committees

The Commission conducted its 1985 session under a new structure of the plenary session and two Committees of the Whole, in which the functions of the former Technical Drafting Committee and the Informal Working Group on Draft Resolutions had been subsumed under those of the two Committees. The Commission considered proposals by the Executive Secretary dealing with such complex questions as the functions of the legislative committees, the documentation provided to them, scrutiny of the work programme, issue-oriented agendas and the possible establishment of a programme co-ordination committee. The Commission, while endorsing the proposals pertaining to the improved functioning of the legislative committees, decided that the question of the establishment of a programme co-ordination committee should be examined further by the Executive Secretary and ACPR.

UN accommodation at Bangkok

The Secretary-General, in response to a 1984 General Assembly resolution,[59] submitted in October 1985 a progress report[60] on the expansion of the conference facilities of ESCAP. He stated that a supplementary agreement to the 1954 Headquarters Agreement between the United Nations and Thailand had been signed on 26 January 1985 in Bangkok. It provided that the United Nations would have the right to occupy and use an expanded headquarters site for as long as it remained at Bangkok and would own the building constructed thereon. Construction was expected to begin in 1986 and the new facilities were expected to be in full operation by early 1989. An appropriation of $18,313,100 was requested for the 1986-1987 biennium under section 32 (Construction, alterations, improvements and major maintenance of premises) of the programme budget; the amount was approved by ACABQ.[61]

GENERAL ASSEMBLY ACTION

On 18 December, on the recommendation of the Fifth Committee, the General Assembly adopted without vote **section V** of **resolution 40/252.**

United Nations accommodation at Bangkok
[The General Assembly . . .]

Takes note of the report of the Secretary-General on the United Nations accommodation at Bangkok;

. . .

General Assembly resolution 40/252, section V

18 December 1985   Meeting 122   Adopted without vote

Approved by Fifth Committee (A/40/1069) without objection, 27 November (meeting 49); oral proposal by Chairman; agenda item 116.
Financial implications. ACABQ, A/40/7/Add.11; S-G, A/C.5/40/29.
Meeting numbers. GA 40th session: 5th Committee 48, 49; plenary 122.

On 27 November, the Fifth Committee approved, by a recorded vote of 85 to 2, with 15 abstentions, the requested additional appropriation of $18,313,100. The United States said it voted against the appropriation because the expansion of the ESCAP conference facilities was not currently justified. The USSR said it had abstained because the estimates were too high. The United Kingdom voted against and Canada abstained, saying they opposed the ESCAP project. France abstained, believing that construction work should not receive priority at the current time.

REFERENCES

[1]E/1985/33. [2]E/1986/32. [3]YUN 1980, p. 503, GA res. 35/56, annex, 5 Dec. 1980. [4]YUN 1981, p. 406. [5]YUN 1984, p. 626. [6]*Ibid.*, p. 623. [7]E/1985/106. [8]*Economic and Social Survey of Asia and the Pacific 1985* (ST/ESCAP/405), Sales No. E.86.II.F.1 (summary, E/1986/64). [9]E/1985/66. [10]YUN 1984, p. 622. [11]E/ESCAP/464 & Corr.1. [12]E/1985/33 (res. 242(XLI)). [13]MKG/85001. [14]E/ESCAP/527. [15]DP/1986/48/Add.2. [16]E/1985/33 (res. 245(XLI)). [17]E/ESCAP/513. [18]E/ESCAP/505. [19]E/ESCAP/429. [20]E/ESCAP/473 & Corr.1. [21]E/ESCAP/430. [22]YUN 1984, p. 624, GA res. 39/227, 18 Dec. 1984. [23]*Ibid.*, p. 623, ESC res. 1984/78, 27 July 1984. [24]E/ESCAP/480. [25]E/ESCAP/425 & Corr.1. [26]E/ESCAP/501. [27]E/ESCAP/471. [28]E/ESCAP/503. [29]E/ESCAP/472. [30]E/ESCAP/518. [31]E/ESCAP/524. [32]E/ESCAP/523. [33]E/ESCAP/489. [34]E/AC.51/1985/4. [35]A/40/38 & Corr.1 & Add.1. [36]E/ESCAP/454/Add.1. [37]E/ESCAP/519. [38]E/1985/33 (res. 241(XLI)). [39]*Ibid.* (res. 243(XLI)). [40]E/ESCAP/491 & Corr.1. [41]YUN 1980, p. 890. [42]E/ESCAP/484. [43]E/ESCAP/483. [44]YUN 1982, p. 847. [45]E/ESCAP/417 & Corr.1. [46]YUN 1977, p. 509. [47]E/ESCAP/421. [48]E/ESCAP/530. [49]YUN 1983, p. 795, GA res. 38/168, 19 Dec. 1984. [50]YUN 1984, p. 627. [51]E/ESCAP/495. [52]E/ESCAP/520. [53]E/1985/33 (res. 244(XLI)). [54]E/ESCAP/516 & Corr.1. [55]E/ESCAP/443 & Corr.1. [56]A/40/295-E/1985/72. [57]YUN 1970, p. 436. [58]A/40/295/Add.1-E/1985/72/Add.1. [59]YUN 1984, p. 628, GA res. 39/236, sect. XI, 18 Dec. 1984. [60]A/C.5/40/29. [60]A/40/7/Add.11.

OTHER PUBLICATIONS

Transport and Communications Bulletin for Asia and the Pacific, No. 56 (ST/ESCAP/SER.E/56), Sales No. E.85.II.F.6. *Industry and Technology Development News—Asia and the Pacific, 1985*, No. 15 (ST/ESCAP/301), Sales No. E.85.II.F.10. *Statistical Indicators for Asia and the Pacific*, vol. XV: No. 1, March 1985 (ST/ESCAP/337), Sales No. E.85.II.F.11; No. 2, June 1985 (ST/ESCAP/350), Sales No. E.85.II.F.17; No. 3, September 1985 (ST/ESCAP/377), Sales No. E.85.II.F.20; No. 4, December 1985 (ST/ESCAP/403), Sales No. E.86.II.F.7. *Water as a Factor in Energy Resources Development*, Water Resources Series, No. 60 (ST/ESCAP/SER.F/60), Sales No. E.85.II.F.7. *Launching of the Transport and Communications Decade for Asia and the Pacific, 1985-1994*, Transport and Communications Bulletin for Asia and the Pacific, No. 57 (ST/ESCAP/SER.E/57), Sales No. E.85.II.F.9. *Proceedings of the Tenth Session of the Committee on Natural Resources*, Water Resources Series No. 59 (ST/ESCAP/SER.F/59), Sales No. E.85.II.F.14. *Small Industry Bulletin for Asia and the Pacific*, No. 20 (ST/ESCAP/SER.M/38), Sales No. E/F.85.II.F.22. *Quarterly Bulletin of Statistics for Asia and the Pacific*, vol. XV: No. 1, March 1985 (ST/ESCAP/385), Sales No. E.86.II.F.2; No. 2, June 1985 (ST/ESCAP/411), Sales No. E.86.II.F.8; No. 3, September 1985 (ST/ESCAP/426), Sales No. E.86.II.F.11; No. 4, December 1985 (ST/ESCAP/436), Sales No. E.86.II.F.14. *Economic Bulletin for Asia and the Pacific*, vol. XXXVI: No. 1, June 1985 (ST/ESCAP/404), Sales No. E.86.II.F.9; No. 2, December 1985 (ST/ESCAP/430), Sales No. E.86.II.F.16. *Statistical Yearbook for Asia and the Pacific 1985* (ST/ESCAP/427), Sales No. E/F.86.II.F.24. *Foreign Trade Statistics of Asia and the Pacific, 1981-1985* (ST/ESCAP/543), Sales No. E.87.II.F.11.

Europe

The Economic Commission for Europe held its fortieth session at Geneva from 16 to 27 April 1985. In its annual reports covering the periods 15 April 1984–27 April 1985[1] and 28 April 1985–27 April 1986,[2] it reviewed the economic situation in Europe, its activities and those of its subsidiary bodies, and set out future work programmes. On 27 April, it adopted a resolution and 14 decisions pertaining to various aspects of its work.

By the resolution,[3] ECE called on member Governments to continue to take full advantage of its potential as an instrument for dialogue and for strengthening economic relations and multilateral co-operation in the region. It considered that full respect for the principles guiding relations set out in the Final Act of the 1975 Helsinki Conference on Security and Co-operation in Europe (CSCE)[4] and in the Concluding Document of the Madrid meeting of representatives of the participating States of CSCE (11 November 1980–9 September 1983) was an essential basis for the development of economic co-operation among them. It called on ECE members to contribute to the work of other economic organs of the United Nations system which aimed at stimulating international trade and recovery of the world economy.

A summary of the work of ECE for the year preceding April 1985 and of the other regional commissions was contained in a June 1985 report[5] of the Secretary-General which also discussed the February meetings of the executive secretaries of the commissions (see p. 684).

Economic trends

The annual growth rate of total output in the ECE region declined from more than 4 per cent in 1984 to about 2.5 per cent in 1985. The drop, according to a summary[6] of the *Economic Survey of Europe in 1985-1986*, reflected a slow-down in the United States and to a lesser extent in the centrally planned economies; in Western Europe, the growth rate was little changed.

Recovery in output growth in ECE market economies faltered in the first half of 1985. In Western Europe, GDP in the four largest economies fell in the first quarter, mainly because of the harsh winter which depressed output in the construction industry (particularly in France and the Federal Republic of Germany). After a modest recovery in the second quarter, Western European output strengthened in the second half of the year; Western European growth for the year as a whole was about 2.25 per cent. In the United States, GNP growth was sluggish in the first half of 1985 (at around 2.3 per cent), but then picked up, partly as a result of financial incentives to boost automobile sales.

Inflation rates continued to fall in 1985. The anti-inflationary stance of monetary and fiscal policies in most countries was reinforced by the continued fall in world commodity prices. In Western Europe, those favourable influences were amplified by the appreciation of exchange rates against the dollar. Consumer prices fell from an average year-on-year increase of 5.5 per cent in Western Europe in the second quarter of 1985 to about 4.5 per cent in the last quarter. In southern Europe, inflation rates continued higher than in the region's other market economies. In the United States, inflation remained about 3.5 per cent.

Employment rose in the market economies, though less than half a percentage point, and was concentrated in North America. In Western Europe, the average increase was about 0.6 per cent, compared with 2 per cent in the United States. By mid-1985, the number of persons unemployed in the market economies (excluding southern Europe) was about 22.5 million, about 57 per cent of them in Western Europe. In southern Europe, unemployment rates were very high (more than 20 per cent in Spain and Turkey) and generally worsened during the year.

In six countries of Eastern Europe and the USSR, the acceleration in the overall pace of economic growth, which had begun in 1982-1983, did not continue in 1985. Net material product (NMP)—national income originating in sectors of the material sphere—grew by 4.1 per cent in 1983, easing to 3.8 per cent in 1984 and to an estimated 3.2 per cent in 1985. In the USSR, where stagnating agricultural output had pulled down the NMP-produced growth rate to 3.2 per cent in 1984 from 4.2 per cent in 1983, the level of agricultural production was unchanged in 1985; however, industrial production continued to expand at about the same rate as in 1984 (by 3.9 per cent, compared with 4.1 per cent). Throughout the area in 1985, supply and demand factors shaped economic developments. On the supply side, an unusually harsh winter had a considerable impact, with coal and electricity production adversely affected in most Eastern European countries and the USSR. All countries except Czechoslovakia and the German Democratic Republic experienced energy shortages, which affected output in other sectors, particularly industry. In addition, a prolonged drought which had lasted for several years in Bulgaria, Hungary and Romania affected agricultural output and exports.

On the demand side, the slow-down in world trade and, in particular, in demand from the developed market economies, combined with increasing competition from both developed and developing countries, depressed the exports of most Eastern European countries and the USSR.

The growth of world trade slowed to less than 4 per cent in 1985, after an increase of about 8 per cent in 1984. Among the developed market economies, exports increased 5 to 6 per cent in Western Europe and Japan but remained virtually unchanged in the United States. Imports into North America continued to grow substantially faster than exports. Exports from the European centrally planned economies fell for the first time since 1960, while imports accelerated at a rate of more than 5 per cent.

East-West trade developed unevenly. Western exports to Eastern Europe picked up, but the pace of exports to the USSR slackened. By contrast, there was a fall in Western imports from Eastern Europe and in particular from the USSR.

The Economic and Social Council, by **decision 1985/182** of 25 July, took note of a summary[7] of the *Economic Survey of Europe in 1984-1985*,[8] among other documents.

Activities in 1985

Regional economic co-operation

The twenty-first session of the Senior Economic Advisers to ECE Governments (Geneva, 18-22 February) gave a central place to work on preparation of an overall economic perspective (OEP) to the year 2000. *Ad hoc* working groups examined in depth selected key problems, with the participation of national experts and rapporteurs appointed by Governments. In October the Bureau prepared an interim version of the core document.

ECE in April adopted a decision[9] welcoming the decisions taken by the Senior Advisers with respect to OEP and expressing the hope that they would focus, in their information exchange and joint consideration of economic trends and prospects in the region, on the long-term implications of national economic policies. It stressed the significance to OEP of the Seminar on the Interrelationships between Structural Changes and Investment Policies (Kiev, Ukrainian SSR, 23-27 September), the findings of which were to form the basis for a chapter in OEP.

Co-operation among Mediterranean countries

ECE requested[10] the Executive Secretary to continue his co-operation with the secretariats of ECWA and ECA and with non-ECE Mediterranean countries on subjects within the competence of ECE of common interest to those countries. It requested its subsidiary bodies to continue their efforts to identify areas of interest for economic co-operation in the Mediterranean.

The Executive Secretaries of ECE and ECA in June submitted an interim report[11] on a proposed Europe-Africa permanent link through the Strait of Gibraltar. The Economic and Social Council took note of the report on 26 July by **decision 1985/191**. The Council, by **resolution 1985/70**, invited Morocco and Spain to continue consultations and asked the Secretary-General to explore the possibility of using extrabudgetary funds to provide the two commissions with resources to carry out related economic studies.

International trade

The thirty-fourth session of the Committee on the Development of Trade (Geneva, 2-6 December 1985)[12] adopted its programme of work for 1986-1990. Its work during the year had been directed especially towards encouraging trade and co-operation between countries of the region, particularly those with different economic and social systems, and aiding them in their trade promotion and marketing efforts. A special meeting of experts on industrial co-operation (Geneva, 8-10 July), under the Committee's auspices, identified major areas for future co-operation and proposals for further developing East-West industrial development. Two sessions each of the Working Party on Facilitation of International Trade Procedures (Geneva, 7 and 8 March; 19 and 20 September) and the Group of Experts on International Contract Practices in Industry (Geneva, 15-17 July; 9-11 December) furthered the Committee's work.

ECE in April[13] called on its member Governments to increase their efforts to expand trade and economic co-operation in the region, taking into account the provisions of the Final Act of CSCE and of the Madrid Concluding Document (see p. 653).

Transport

Among the developments in transport during 1985 were the opening for signature in September of the European Agreement on Main International Railway Lines (concluded at Geneva on 31 May); work on the Trans-European North-South Motorway; the entry into force on 15 October of the 1982 International Convention on the Harmonization of Frontier Controls of Goods;[14] the completion of the revised "E-road network"; and work on amending the 1957 European Agreement concerning the International Carriage of Dangerous Goods by Road.[15]

The Commission noted[10] the decisions of the 1984 meeting on transport development in the Mediterranean[16] and considered that they could contribute to a better understanding of the transport situation in the region. It requested the Inland Transport Committee and the Executive Secretary to study the definition of the status of the transport centres established at that meeting, with a view to recommending that the Economic and Social Council grant them United Nations status.

The forty-sixth session of the Inland Transport Committee (Geneva, 28 January–1 February)[17] considered the application of international transport agreements, transport development trends, the forecasting of international traffic, international transport infrastructure investments, the development of a European railway network, facilitation of the international transport of goods by road, inland navigation questions, urban transport, transport statistics, international harmonization of technical requirements for the construction of motor vehicles, facilitating the movement of disabled and elderly persons, customs questions and the transport of dangerous goods and of perishable foodstuffs. The Committee recommended preliminary technical and operating requirements for thin-walled vehicles used for the international carriage of perishable foodstuffs under high-temperature conditions.

The secretariat reproduced[18] a note submitted to the Committee by the Chairman of the Group of Experts on Track Costs, outlining some studies on the attribution of road track costs.

Groups of experts met on construction of vehicles (March, June and October), customs questions affecting transport (March, July and October), the transport of dangerous goods (May and October), the transport of dangerous goods by rail (March and September/October), the standardization of rules of the road and signs and signals in inland navigation (May and September), combined transport (June), road traffic safety (June and October), the standardization of technical requirements for vessels and of ships' papers (August), transport statistics (September), the transport of perishable foodstuffs (September/October), transport economics (October) and transport trends and policy (November).

Industry

The eighteenth session of the Chemical Industry Committee (Geneva, 2-4 October)[19] reviewed projects in the chemical industry and endorsed the report of the twelfth session of the Group of Experts on the Periodic Survey of the Chemical Industry (Geneva, 30 September and 1 October) which recommended, among other things, continuation of the Committee's statistical activities. The Committee agreed on a list of possible topics for future studies or seminars: automation and robotics; application of lasers and radiation; the effects of chemical production on environment and health; trends in energy requirements; standardization of packaging and labelling; the importance of the fertilizer sector; possibilities of chemical technology transfer; chemical household products; and East-West trade in chemical products. It adopted its programme of work for 1986-1990. A Seminar on Trends and Development in the Fertilizer Industry was held at Istanbul, Turkey, in May.

ECE approved[20] the work programme and meeting calendar of the Working Party on Engineering Industries and Automation, and decided to consider in 1986 a possible change in the status of the Working Party to that of a principal subsidiary body. The Working Party (fifth session, Geneva, 27 February–1 March) decided to study the role of engineering industries in national, regional and global economies. A Seminar on the Development and Use of Powder Metallurgy in Engineering Industries was held at Minsk, Byelorussian SSR, from 25 to 29 March.

The Steel Committee (fifty-third session, 23-25 October)[21] considered trends in the steel market and its prospects, structural changes in the international steel trade, and steel statistics, and adopted a work programme for 1986-1990. The Committee convened a Seminar on Steel Tubes and Their Raw-Material Quality Requirements (Helsinki, 13-17 May). A study tour of changes in production capacities and processes took place in the USSR (2-8 June). The Committee endorsed the report of the Working Party on Steel Statistics (fourteenth session, 21 and 22 October) and included in its programme of work a project on the revision of the steel statistical system.

Energy resources

In April, ECE decided[22] to convene the fifth session of the Senior Advisers to ECE Governments on Energy from 23 to 27 September. In their report,[23] the Senior Advisers reviewed activities since their fourth session in 1981[24] and heard statements on the energy situation in the ECE region by various countries. The Executive Secretary declared that issues giving rise to concern included energy efficiency, unsatisfactory levels of oil dependence for most countries, uncertainty about world energy prices and the absence of new and renewable energy sources from national energy programmes.

The Coal Committee (eighty-first session, 7-10 October)[25] considered the coal situation and its prospects in the ECE region, world coal trade up to the year 2000 and the activities of the Working Party on Coal Trade (twenty-sixth session, 1-3 July) as well as the activities of the groups of experts on productivity and management problems in the coal industry (June), on the utilization and preparation of solid fuels (June), on coal statistics (July) and on open-cast mines (Gyongyos, Hungary, 8-11 October 1984).

The Committee on Electric Power (forty-third session, 14-18 January)[26] reviewed the electric power situation, its medium- and long-term prospects, regional energy problems, such as problems of improving efficiency of electric power transmission systems and environmental problems, and statistics and standardization. A Seminar on High Voltage Direct Current Techniques was held at Stockholm, Sweden, from 6 to 8 May. Groups of experts met at Geneva on problems of planning and operating large power systems (April) and on the relationship between electricity and the environment (November), and at Istanbul on electric power stations (September/October).

The Committee on Gas (thirty-first session, 21-25 January)[27] discussed general energy problems, the gas situation and markets in the region, developments, prospects and statistics. Preparations were discussed for the symposium on the liquefied petroleum gas situation in the ECE region during 1985-2000 (Madrid, Spain, 23-25 October). Groups of experts met on gas statistics and forecasting problems (June), the use and distribution of gas (May), the transport and storage of gas (May) and natural gas resources (October).

Water

The Committee on Water Problems (seventeenth session, 25-29 November)[28] entrusted the Group of Experts on Aspects of Water Quality and Quantity (which had met in May) with elaboration of a second revision of draft principles on co-operation in transboundary waters, and entrusted government rapporteurs with preparing a second revision of draft principles on ground-water management. ECE recognized[29] the significance of strengthening co-operation among member countries in water pollution control matters. A Seminar on the Rational Use of Water in Industrial Processes (Paris, 21-25 October) highlighted the use of water-saving techniques such as recycling and dry processes and adopted recommendations to ECE Governments.

A declaration on co-operation among the Danube States in relation to problems of water management in the River Danube, particularly the protection of its waters against pollution, adopted by the Conference of Danube States (Bucharest, Romania, 10-13 December) was later transmitted by Romania to the Secretary-General.[30] The Danube States declared that they would act to reduce and prevent pollution of the river, especially by dangerous and radioactive substances, would systematically monitor effluents discharged into it, would monitor the water at sampling stations where the river crossed borders and would exchange information.

Agriculture and timber

The Committee on Agricultural Problems (thirty-sixth session, 11-15 March)[31] reviewed agricultural developments, including developments in trade, in the region in 1984. The Committee also discussed the annual market reviews for the major agricultural commodities in Europe—grains, livestock and meat, milk and dairy products, and eggs.

The Commission in April[32] drew the Committee's attention to such important topics as agrarian structure and farm rationalization, agricultural mechanization, technological and economic issues of land use, soil quality and fertility, fertilizers, pollution problems and efficient energy use, and rational use of water resources.

Groups of experts met at Geneva on standardization of dry and dried produce (April), of poultry meat (July), of cut flowers (September), of perishable produce (October), and of seed potatoes (November); and at Warsaw, Poland, in May on co-ordination of standardization of fresh fruit and vegetables. A symposium on optimizing animal production from high-roughage rations was held at Geneva from 21 to 25 January.

The Timber Committee (forty-third session, 14-18 October)[33] conducted an analysis of the forest products market situation, noting the strong competition in Europe, with a resultant weakening tendency in prices for some forest products. It drew up tables of estimates for 1985 and 1986 of domestic requirements, production, imports and exports of sawn softwood and softwood logs, sawn hardwood and hardwood logs (temperate-zone and tropical), particle board, plywood, fibreboard and pulpwood. Seminars were held on occupational health and rehabilitation of forest workers (Kuopio, Finland, 3-7 June), on the technology and mechanization of logging operations in mountainous regions and related environmental problems (Krasnodar, USSR, 5-7 September), and, jointly with FAO, on the practical application of remote sensing in forestry (Jönköping, Sweden, 28-31 May).

Science and technology

The Senior Advisers to ECE Governments on Science and Technology (thirteenth session, 16-20 September)[34] considered current developments in science and technology policies, including changes in overall policies, a review of bilateral agreements, national policies aimed at increasing the effectiveness of research and development activities, and policy issues associated with the introduction of electronics in some industries. The Senior Advisers requested the secretariat to undertake a consultation with users on the structure and content of the *Manual of Licensing Procedures in Member Countries of the United Nations Economic Commission for Europe*, and held a Symposium on the Importance of Biotechnology for Future Economic Development (Szeged, Hungary, 3-7 June).

Environment

ECE, in April 1985,[35] appealed to all contracting parties to the 1979 Convention on Long-range Transboundary Air Pollution[36] to sign the Protocol on the Financing of the Co-operative Programme on Monitoring and Evaluation of the Long-range Transmission of Air Pollutants in Europe[37] as soon as possible, and the Protocol on the Reduction of Sulphur Emissions or Their Transboundary Fluxes, to be opened for signature during the third session of the Convention's Executive Body (Helsinki, Finland, 8-12 July) (see Chapter XVI of this section). The Commission also appealed to Governments to implement a decision of the Executive Body on reducing total annual national emissions of nitrogen oxides, and called on them to consider providing sufficient unleaded petrol of appropriate quality for introducing low-emission technologies in motor vehicles.

The Executive Body established a Working Group on Nitrogen Oxides to prepare the necessary substantiation for measures aimed at reducing nitrogen oxide emissions. It also launched programmes aimed at determining the effects of the emissions on materials, including historic and cultural monuments, assessing and monitoring the acidification of rivers and lakes, and assessing air pollution effects on forests.

The Senior Advisers to ECE Governments on Environmental Problems were invited by the Commission[38] to continue their work on implementing the 1979 Declaration on Low- and Non-Waste Technology and Reutilization and Recycling of Wastes,[36] on protection of flora, fauna and their habitats, and on environmental impact assessment. The Advisers (thirteenth session, 5-8 March)[39] had agreed on an outline for the elaboration of a long-term regional strategy for environmental protection and rational use of natural resources. They also endorsed the recommendations of a Seminar on Low-Waste Technology (Tashkent, USSR, 15-19 October 1984).

The Working Party on Low- and Non-Waste Technology and Reutilization and Recycling of Wastes (fifth session, 9-11 January) added 13 new contributions to the *Compendium on Low- and Non-Waste Technology*, bringing to 127 the number of descriptions of environmentally sound manufacturing technologies. The Group of Experts on Environmental Impact Assessment held its third session from 16 to 18 January.

Human settlements

The Committee on Housing, Building and Planning (forty-sixth session, 9-13 September)[40] reviewed human settlements trends and policies in the region, integrated settlements policies and strategies, urban regional planning, housing and building policies and statistics, and considered its possible contributions to the International Year of Shelter for the Homeless (1987).

Projects discussed by the Working Party on Building (sixteenth session, 26-29 March) included environmental problems arising from construction, building technology, energy conservation, promotion of trade in building and building products, the ECE *Compendium of Model Provisions for Building Regulations*, approval and control rules, renovation and modernization, and building pathology and prevention of disorders.

Participants in a Seminar on Modern Building Technologies (Warsaw, 7-11 October) exchanged information and studied technological developments in the building materials and construction industries.

The Working Party on Housing (thirteenth session, 22-25 October) discussed long-term perspectives for regional human settlements development, and considered housing financing, forecasting and programming, and methodologies for evaluating the quality and use value of dwellings.

The Group of Experts on Human Settlements Problems in Southern Europe (Sarajevo, Yugoslavia, 5-8 November) discussed macroeconomic aspects of tourism and their impact on town planning and housing policies.

A Seminar on Financing of Housing (Copenhagen, Denmark, 10-14 June) adopted recommendations on raising and allocating funds for housing investment, on housing subsidy systems and on new trends in the financing of housing investments.

Statistics

The Conference of European Statisticians (thirty-third session, 17-21 June)[41] continued work on the development and harmonization of statistical concepts, classifications and nomenclatures in the region. It devoted particular attention to international comparisons of main economic aggregates, to environment statistics and to the use of computers in statistical offices, and discussed the problems of publication, dissemination and interpretation of data.

ECE invited[42] the Conference to continue to offer members methodological assistance to overcome problems in providing official statistics and continue work towards harmonizing statistical nomenclatures and standards.

The joint FAO/ECE Study Group on Food and Agricultural Statistics in Europe (sixteenth session, Geneva, 15-18 July) amended the existing guidelines and recommendations regarding statistics on area, yield, production and utilization of crops and on livestock numbers and products in ECE member countries.

The first joint ECE/International Research and Training Institute for the Advancement of Women Meeting on Statistics and Indicators on the Role and Situation of Women (Geneva, 11-14 March) stressed the importance of associating both producers and users in the development of new types of statistics on women.

A series of meetings were held on specific aspects of environment statistics to finalize ECE standard international classifications of water use and quality (Geneva, 14-17 January), fauna and flora (24-26 September), solid wastes (25 and 26 November) and environmental indicators (17-29 November), as well as a meeting on frameworks for environment statistics (2-6 December). A Seminar on Methodological Questions relating to Farm Book-keeping Data was held at Voorburg, Netherlands, from 21 to 25 October.

Standardization

The Group of Experts on Standardization Policies (twelfth session, Geneva, 21-23 January;[43] thirteenth, Piestany, Czechoslovakia, 28 October–1 November[44]) continued its review of an ECE Standardization List of sectors in which ECE Governments felt that a lack of mutual recognition of certain international classifications and tests raised barriers to trade and co-operation.

In April, ECE approved[45] the work programme on standardization and related areas proposed by the Group, and decided to convene the Ninth Meeting of Government Officials Responsible for Standardization Policies in 1986.

Programme of work

The Commission requested its Executive Secretary in April[46] to collaborate with UNFPA in implementing recommendations of the Regional Meeting on Population and the 1984 International Conference on Population[47] and in periodically convening a regional meeting of experts on population. It also requested[48] him, taking into account the results of the 1985 World Conference to Review and Appraise the Achievements of the United Nations Decade for Women (see Chapter XIX of this section), to continue assessing developments concerning the economic role of women in the region in conjunction with other research activities.

The Commission[49] approved a new format for work programmes of its principal subsidiary bodies and instructed them, in drafting those programmes, to proceed with an eye to securing better results, efficiency, rational utilization of resources and the removal of overlaps. It decided to select for detailed consideration at annual sessions activities in one major area, from the viewpoint of concentration, integration and co-ordination.

A report[50] by the Executive Secretary on the integration of the Commission's work programme contained recommendations concerning management training, telematics, standardization, processing of agricultural products, hazardous wastes, land-use planning, international financing for road infrastructure networks, a special micro-circuit ("smart") card for international transport of goods by road, woodpulp, paper and paperboard, and financing of intra-regional trade.

REFERENCES

[1]E/1985/34. [2]E/1986/31. [3]E/1985/34 (res. 1(40)). [4]YUN 1975, p. 100. [5]E/1985/106. [6]E/1986/81. [7]E/1985/101. [8]YUN 1984, p. 629. [9]E/1985/34 (dec. N(40)). [10]*Ibid.* (dec. H(40)). [11]E/1985/108. [12]ECE/TRADE/153. [13]E/1985/34 (dec. D(40)). [14]YUN 1982, p. 853. [15]YUN 1957, p. 378. [16]YUN 1984, p. 630. [17]ECE/TRANS/61. [18]ECE/TRANS/61/Add.1. [19]ECE/CHEM/57. [20]E/1985/34 (dec. K(40)). [21]ECE/STEEL/51. [22]E/1985/34 (dec. F(40)). [23]ECE/ENERGY/11. [24]YUN 1981, p. 654. [25]ECE/COAL/88. [26]ECE/EP/61. [27]ECE/GAS/77. [28]ECE/WATER/42. [29]E/1985/34 (dec. L(40)). [30]A/41/392 & Corr.1. [31]ECE/AGRI/81. [32]E/1985/34 (dec. B(40)). [33]ECE/TIM/28. [34]ECE/SC.TECH/29. [35]E/1984/34 (dec. E(40)). [36]YUN 1979, p. 710. [37]YUN 1984, p. 632. [38]E/1985/34 (dec. M(40)). [39]ECE/ENV/45. [40]ECE/HBP/58. [41]ECE/CES/26. [42]E/1985/34 (dec. C(40)). [43]STAND/GE.1/25. [44]STAND/GE.1/27. [45]E/1985/34 (dec. I(40)). [46]*Ibid.* (dec. G(40)). [47]YUN 1984, p. 714. [48]E/1985/34 (dec. J(40)). [49]*Ibid.* (dec. A(40)). [50]E/ECE/1070.

PUBLICATIONS

Economic Survey of Europe in 1984-1985, Sales No. E.85.II.E.1. *Building Regulations in ECE Countries: Second Report* (ECE/HBP/52 and Corr.1), Sales No. E.85.II.E.14. *Pilot and Demonstration Projects for Energy Savings in Human Settlements* (ECE/HBP/46), Sales No. E.85.II.E.15. *Relationship between Housing and the National Economy,* synthesis report on a seminar held in Prague (Czechoslovakia), 10-14 May 1982 (ECE/HBP/56), Sales No. E.85.II.E.16. *Air Pollution across Boundaries* (ECE/EB.AIR/5), Sales No. E.85.II.E.17. *International Comparison of Gross Domestic Product in Europe, 1980,* Statistical Standards and Studies, No. 37, Sales No. E.85.II.E.18. *The Economic Role of Women in the ECE Region: Developments 1975/1985* (E/ECE/1100), Sales No. E.85.II.E.20. *Working Environment in the Construction Industry: National Policies and Legislation in ECE Countries* (ECE/HBP/59), Sales No. E.85.II.E.27. *Correspondence Table between the International Standard Industrial Classification of All Economic Activities of the United Nations (ISIC) and the Classification of Branches of the National Economy of the Council for Mutual Economic Assistance (CBNE),* Statistical Standards and Studies, No. 38, Sales No. E/R.85.II.E.29. *Human Settlements Situation in the ECE Region around 1980* (ECE/HBP/60), Sales No. E.85.II.E.30. *The Forest Resources of the ECE Region (Europe, the USSR, North America)* (ECE/TIM/27), Sales No. E.85.II.E.31. *Marketing Management in East-West Trade,* a digest of materials presented to the Sixth Seminar on East-West Trade Promotion, Marketing and Business Contacts (Geneva, 25-27 March 1985) (TRADE/INF.6), Sales No. E.85.II.E.33. *Recent Trends in Flexible Manufacturing* (ECE/ENG.AUT/22), Sales No. E.85.II.E.35. *UN/ECE Standard for Poultry Meat and Explanatory Brochure* (ECE/AGRI/86), Sales No. E.85.II.E.41. *Annual Review of Engineering Industries and Automation, 1983-1984,* vols. I & II (ECE/ENG.AUT/19), Sales No. E.85.II.E.43. *1985 Annual Bulletin of Housing and Building Statistics for Europe,* vol. XXIX, Sales No. E/F/R.86.II.E.2. *Annual Bulletin of Electric Energy Statistics for Europe, 1985,* vol. XXXI, Sales No. E/F/R.86.II.E.3. *Annual Bulletin of Steel Statistics for Europe, 1985,* vol. XIII, Sales No. E/F/R.86.II.E.4. *Annual Bulletin of Gas Statistics for Europe,*

1985, vol. XXXI, Sales No. E/F/R.86.II.E.5. *Annual Bulletin of Transport Statistics for Europe, 1985,* vol. XXXVII, Sales No. E/F/R.86.II.E.6. *Annual Bulletin of Coal Statistics for Europe, 1985,* vol. XX, Sales No. E/F/R.86.II.E.7. *Statistics of World Trade in Steel, 1985,* Sales No. E/F/R.86.II.E.9. *Statistics of Road Traffic Accidents in Europe, 1985,* vol. XXXII, Sales No. E/F/R.86.II.E.11. *Prices of Agricultural Products and Selected Inputs in Europe and North America 1984/85* (ECE/AGRI/88), Sales No. E.86.II.E.13. *Agricultural Review for Europe, No. 28, 1984 and 1985:* vol. I—*General Review* (ECE/AGRI/89, vol. I), Sales No. E.86.II.E.14; vol. II—*Agricultural Trade* (ECE/AGRI/89, vol. II), Sales No. E.86.II.E.15; vol. III—*The Grain Market* (ECE/AGRI/89, vol. III), Sales No. E.86.II.E.16; vol. IV—*The Livestock and Meat Market* (ECE/AGRI/89, vol. IV), Sales No. E.86.II.E.17; vol. V—*The Milk and Dairy Products Market* (ECE/AGRI/89, vol. V), Sales No. E.86.II.E.18. *The Steel Market in 1985* (ECE/STEEL/53), Sales No. E.86.II.E.24. *Annual Bulletin of Trade in Chemical Products, 1985,* vol. XII, Sales No. E/F/R.86.II.E.27. *Annual Bulletin of General Energy Statistics for Europe, 1985,* vol. XVIII, Sales No. E/F/R.87.II.E.9. *Bulletin of Statistics on World Trade in Engineering Products, 1985,* Sales No. E/F/R.87.II.E.10. *Annual Review of the Chemical Industry, 1985* (ECE/CHEM/63), Sales No. E.87.II.E.15. *Market Trends for Selected Chemical Products 1960-1985 and Prospects to 1989,* vol. I (ECE/CHEM/64, vol. I), Sales No. E.87.II.E.26; vol. II (ECE/CHEM/64, vol. II), Sales No. E.87.II.E.27.

Latin America and the Caribbean

The Economic Commission for Latin America and the Caribbean did not hold a formal session during 1985, in accordance with its biennial calendar of meetings. On 26 July, the Economic and Social Council decided, by decision 1985/188, that ECLAC's next (twenty-first) session should be held at Mexico City in 1986.

The ECLAC Committee of the Whole (eighteenth session, Buenos Aires, Argentina, 21-23 August 1985) examined aspects of long-term social and economic development policies that could provide guidelines to meet the current crisis in the region and the transformations which the international economy had made necessary. Resolutions were adopted on the implications of and prospects for Latin American external debt on the economic problems peculiar to Caribbean island developing countries and on a change of name of the Latin American Institute for Economic and Social Planning to the Latin American and Caribbean Institute for Economic and Social Planning.

The Committee of High-Level Government Experts (CEGAN) (tenth session, Buenos Aires, 19 and 20 August)[1] considered regional socio-economic development policies. It adopted by consensus a position paper on the options open to Latin America and the Caribbean to meet the current crisis and the long-term economic and social development policies which could apply in the light of the changes in the international economy. It also adopted two resolutions: one affirmed that the international community had a responsibility to support the development and structural adjustment efforts of the Caribbean countries, whose development assistance needs were urgent, and supported the World Bank's efforts to reconsider the issue of graduation, by which some Caribbean countries, by virtue of their per capita income levels, were being graduated out of eligibility for concessionary financial resources; the other asked the Executive Secretary to prepare for the 1986 sessions of CEGAN and ECLAC a study on the implications of the Latin American and Caribbean external debt for their economies and the likely prospects.

A meeting of experts (Santiago, Chile, 29 April–3 May)[2] analysed the nature, depth and scope of the crisis in Latin America, as well as ways of making adjustment and stabilization consistent with reactivation of the economies and medium- and long-term options of Latin American countries in the face of technological changes in the international economy. Some 100 experts from Latin America and other regions attended.

A summary of the activities from mid-1984 to mid-1985 of the ECLAC Committee of the Whole and of auxiliary bodies and special committees, as well as an account of the February meetings of the executive secretaries of the regional commissions (see p. 684) and a listing of issues calling for action by the Economic and Social Council, were given by the Secretary-General in a June 1985 report.[3]

Economic trends

The year 1984 had witnessed an interruption of the sharp downward trend that the rate of growth in the economic activity of Latin America had been showing since 1979, according to the *Economic Survey of Latin America and the Caribbean, 1984*.[4] The Economic and Social Council took note of a summary of the *Survey*,[5] among other documents, in its **decision 1985/182** of 25 July 1985. The rate of inflation rose in half the Latin American economies and, in the region as a whole, reached a new all-time high. The simple average rate of increase of consumer prices rose from 66 per cent in 1983 to 164 per cent in 1984 and the rate weighted by population jumped in the same period from 130 to 185 per cent.

In 1985, according to an advance summary of the 1985 *Economic Survey*,[6] feeble growth in economic activity, concentrated in only a few countries, the generalization and accentuation of inflation (with, however, progress in Argentina, Bolivia and Peru where inflation had reached extraordinarily high levels), and the deterioration of the external sector were the main features of economic evolution in Latin America.

Preliminary figures indicated that GDP increased by 2.7 per cent, compared with 3.2 per cent the year before, permitting an increase in the per capita product of barely 0.4 per cent, a level almost 9 per cent below 1980, about equal to 1977. Further, the economic expansion was due to the activity in a few countries; if Brazil (which grew by 8.2 per cent) was excluded, overall output stagnated, while the per capita product fell 2 per cent. The per capita product went down in 12 of the 20 economies for which data were available.

Inflation continued to increase and became more widespread. The simple average rate of consumer price increases rose to 440 per cent in 1985, while the population-weighted rate rose to 275 per cent. Consumer prices grew by less than 10 per cent in only five of the 22 countries for which data were available, while rising rapidly in many economies where inflation traditionally had been low.

Because of the loss of dynamism in world trade, whose volume grew by less than 3 per cent compared to 9 per cent in 1984, and marked declines in the international prices of basic commodities, the value of Latin American exports dropped by nearly 5 per cent. The terms of trade fell somewhat more than 3 per cent—a total deterioration of more than 17 per cent in the five-year period 1981-1985.

As a result of the decline in exports, the merchandise trade surplus went down in 1985, despite a 1 per cent reduction in imports. After having increased more than fourfold between 1982 and 1984 to a record level of $38.7 billion, the surplus dropped to $34.9 billion in 1985. The current account deficit, which had fallen spectacularly from $41 billion in 1982 to $1 billion in 1984, rose to $3.9 billion in 1985. Since there was simultaneously a drop in the net inflow of capital, the balance of payments closed with a surplus of about $700 million, after having registered more than a $9 billion surplus the year before.

Latin America's external debt was estimated at $368 billion at the end of 1985, having increased by a little more than 2 per cent. While there was a slight reduction in the external indebtedness of Brazil and Venezuela, and that of Mexico increased only slightly, the indebtedness of Bolivia, Colombia, El Salvador, Guatemala, Haiti, Honduras, Nicaragua and Paraguay grew rapidly. Interest rates declined on the main international financial markets, with Latin American interest payments going down by about 4 per cent.

A publication, *Panorama Económico de América Latina*, issued for the first time in October 1985, described the basic economic characteristics of the main countries of the region during the first half of the year.

Activities in 1985

The 1985 activities of ECLAC were detailed in its biennial report[7] covering the period 7 April 1984 to 25 April 1986.

Development policy and regional economic co-operation

Uruguay transmitted to the Secretary-General, in a letter of 18 March,[8] the Final Communiqué of the Third Ministerial Meeting of the Consultation and Follow-up Machinery of the Cartagena Consensus (Santo Domingo, Dominican Republic, 7 and 8 February 1985). The meeting was attended by the ministers responsible for the financial affairs of the countries signatories to the 1984 Cartagena Consensus[9] on the economic and social situation of Latin America—Argentina, Bolivia, Brazil, Chile, Colombia, the Dominican Republic, Ecuador, Mexico, Peru, Uruguay and Venezuela.

The Communiqué stated that in recent months some Latin American countries had concluded with the international financial community programmes for restructuring their external debts and that the terms in those restructurings must be extended to countries which were currently renegotiating their debts. Nevertheless, those debt restructurings merely postponed the problem, since negotiations with commercial banks provided no opportunity to take up questions such as the joint responsibility of debtors and creditors, balanced adjustment, the implications for the debtor countries and the evolution of international trade and finance, which would make a permanent solution to the debt problem possible. There could be no stable solution to the problem unless the debtor and creditor countries agreed on a political framework for those questions as a whole and engaged in a political dialogue. The ministers decided to present their position to meetings of IMF and the World Bank–IMF Development Committee in April.

The Fifth Conference of Ministers and Heads of Planning of Latin America and the Caribbean (Mexico City, 15-17 April) examined the external crisis and revival programmes in future economic and social policies. In addition, a working party considered centralization and decentralization in the public-sector decision-making process, employment, income and social programmes in the second half of the 1980s.

The Technical Committee of the Latin American Institute for Economic and Social Planning (ILPES) held its sixth meeting during the Conference (16 April). The meeting approved bringing up to date the new institutional project (1984-1986), originally adopted in 1983, and gave its support to a policy of decentralization; the new institutional project restructured ILPES's relations with member Governments, inaugurated a dif-

ferent level of activities and established a new system of intergovernmental financial support linked with UNDP backing. The meeting also adopted a name change for ILPES to include the Caribbean countries in its title, although retaining the acronym ILPES; the change was subsequently ratified by the ECLAC Committee of the Whole (see p. 659). The Joint ECLAC/ILPES Planning Unit for the Caribbean was set up and began operating at Port of Spain, Trinidad, in September.

During 1985, ILPES carried out training, research and advisory programmes. Advisory services for planning bodies were provided to Argentina, Belize, Brazil, Colombia, Costa Rica, Chile, the Dominican Republic, Ecuador, Guatemala, Guyana, Honduras, Paraguay, Peru and Uruguay, covering such areas as economic policy, municipal and regional planning, and information systems. Training activities were highlighted by the twenty-sixth international course on development, planning and public policies (Santiago, 24 June–6 December); the third course-seminar on foreign trade policies (Asunción, Paraguay, 10-28 June); the third course-workshop on current problems and development strategy options (Mexico City, 9 September–29 November); the inter-American course-workshop in construction of indexes of foreign trade (Santiago, 2 September–31 October); and seminars on national economic management issues in the Caribbean (Barbados, 11-15 February), current problems and challenges in Latin American education (Santiago, third week of March), and the environmental dimension in development planning (Buenos Aires, 17-19 June). Research was conducted in various countries in planning, economic and social policies and regional development.

Caribbean area

The Caribbean Development and Co-operation Committee (CDCC) (ninth session, Port of Spain: technical stage, 29-31 May; ministerial stage, 3 and 4 June)[10] considered technical co-operation among Caribbean countries, agriculture, social development, transport and communications, international trade and financial issues, energy and natural resources, and population questions. It adopted resolutions setting out a programme of support for small island developing countries,[11] preparing future CDCC areas of action[12] and establishing a CDCC committee for review, co-ordination and evaluation of its work.[13]

International trade and finance

With regard to international trade and financing, efforts were made to form closer relations with economic actors in both the public and private sectors through the Second Meeting of Officials Responsible for External Trade in Latin America

(Rio de Janeiro, Brazil, 28-30 January) and the Meeting of Entrepreneurs of the Member Countries of the Latin American Integration Association on Trade and Financing (Montevideo, Uruguay, 26-28 August), at which subjects relating to international and regional co-operation and integration of Latin America were discussed and analysed.

Technical co-operation

The Secretary-General transmitted to the Economic and Social Council in October 1985[14] the second volume of a two-part report by JIU on United Nations technical co-operation. Volume II covered the Caribbean; the first part, volume I, on Central America,[15] had been conveyed in 1984. The Council, without vote on 26 July, took note of volume I and the comments of the Secretary-General thereon; they were among several documents of which the Council took note in **decision 1985/191**.

Volume II covered 22 island countries plus Guyana and Suriname. Most were small with limited resources, had serious soil erosion problems, were net importers of food, were highly dependent on traditional cash crops and light industrial products, and had exports subject to price fluctuations in international markets.

Serious attempts had been made to establish institutions and joint programmes and activities in areas of mutual interest; these institutions provided a basic framework and mechanisms for channelling assistance, but their influence in many countries was weak and they were often unable to respond to national needs.

Among recommendations were: (1) the United Nations development system and Governments should give more attention to the institution-building process; (2) basic agreements on creating human resources pools should be initiated, with training as one of the highest priorities in projects where the need was identified; and (4) Governments should place more emphasis on employing young professionals emerging from universities and regional institutes. UNDP and DTCD should ensure through project agreements with Governments that trainees were given the opportunity to use their newly acquired skills (3), should adopt more projects on a regional basis, especially for problems common to all, such as soil erosion and conservation (6), and, to ensure objectivity, should use independent teams of experts to evaluate projects (10). UNDP should review methods used in determining indicative planning figures, and take into consideration unemployment and other socio-economic factors (9). Long-term projects should be well-monitored with regard to preparation of counterparts for future take-over (7); projects concerned with energy, exploration in hydrocarbons and hydroelectric plants should be approached

with extreme caution as to costs, debt servicing and priority (8); and optimum and long-term use should be taken into account in all equipment purchases (5).

Commenting on the report, the Secretary-General observed[16] that the United Nations supported recommendations 1, 2, 3, 5, 7 and 8. The validity of regional projects for smaller countries was recognized (recommendation 6) but there was also a need for flexibility within such projects to cater to specific needs of individual countries which might be at a different level of development. Recommendations 2, 3 and 4 called for actions which were already being undertaken by regional institutions, with UNDP and DTCD's help, and recommendation 9 would be brought to UNDP's attention, which had already taken steps to increase availability to Governments of independent advice in project evaluation and assessment as proposed in recommendation 10.

Transport

During 1985, a meeting was held by ECLAC on the bicycle as a suitable transport technology for Latin America (Santiago, 12 August).

Other meetings included a Meeting of High-Level Government Experts on Maritime Transport, organized by the secretariat of the Latin American Economic System (SELA) (Caracas, Venezuela, 25 February–1 March), an *Ad Hoc* Expert Meeting on Maritime Transport (Caracas, 16-22 June), and a Second Meeting of the Operational Regional Co-operation Network between Maritime Authorities (Lima, Peru, 2-6 September). Seminars on customs transit were held at Bogotá, Colombia, and at Caracas, and a seminar on transport in the southern region, at Coyhaique, Chile, all in April.

ECLAC maintained close collaboration with the Statistical Office of DIESA for the development of a Uniform System of Maritime Transport Statistics.

Industrial development

ECLAC continued to support co-operative efforts among producers of capital goods. Also, some research was initiated on industrial restructuring and new strategies for industrialization. The second meeting of the working party on industrial reorganization (Bogotá, September) considered the reorganization of the Latin American automotive sector.

The Second Meeting of Experts on Capital Goods Industries in Latin America and the Caribbean (4-6 March) and the Fourth Meeting of Latin American Entrepreneurs on Capital Goods (20-22 May) were held at Santiago.

The first issue of a periodic report on industrialization and technological developments, disseminating information on the industrial reorganization and industrialization process in Latin America, was published in December 1985, setting out a number of short studies of both a global and a sectoral nature.

Natural resources, energy and environment

ECLAC carried out various activities during the year relating to the development of water resources, to ocean resources and to new and renewable sources of energy.

It convened a meeting of experts from Latin America and the Caribbean (Santiago, 15-18 April) as part of the preparations for the 1986 United Nations Conference for the Promotion of International Co-operation in the Peaceful Uses of Nuclear Energy (see p. 695).

The first meeting of industrial mining entrepreneurs of Latin America (9-11 September) and the first regular General Assembly of the Latin American Mining Agency (12 and 13 September) were convened at Buenos Aires.

A Regional Seminar on the Environmental Dimension in Development Planning (Buenos Aires, 17-19 June) discussed crisis, planning and the environment; the environmental dimension in global, sectoral and regional planning; science, technology and the environment; natural resources and environmental impact evaluations; public and legal institutions; and horizontal co-operation and the environment.

Food and agriculture

An ECLAC/FAO workshop on agricultural policy and rural development (Santiago, 26-30 August) considered the role of the State in technological change and production growth, ways in which peasants and labourers were brought into new production structures, changes in social composition as a result of the expansion of agriculture, and the social impact of those changes.

Two ECLAC/FAO workshops were held on the analysis and design of economic policy in the agro-food sector. The first (Lima, 6-9 August) examined the formulation of economic policy for the sector and the main features and problems of the food systems of the Andean countries. It also analysed the processes of primary production, agro-industrial processing, and food distribution and consumption, towards formulating food security strategies. The second workshop (Port of Spain, 16-18 December) focused on the food systems and policies of the English-speaking Caribbean countries. Another workshop (Mexico City, 4-8 March) was held on problems and programmes for increasing the production of peasant farming in Latin America and two seminars were held on changes in the agriculture of Latin America, Spain and Portugal (Lisbon, Portugal, 3-6 June) and on

food security in Latin America (Santiago, 28 and 29 November).

Science and technology

A Regional Microelectronics Network for Latin America and the Caribbean was established by a UNIDO/ECLAC/SELA meeting (Caracas, 3-7 June). Its objective was to strengthen technological capabilities in microelectronics through information exchange, establishment of national design centres, regional co-operation, joint manufacture of semiconductors, the application of microelectronics in certain industries, and training.

The Fifth Latin American Seminar on Food Sciences and Technology was held at Viña del Mar, Chile, from 13 to 16 October.

Social and cultural development

ECLAC continued to give priority to activities related to the International Youth Year (1985) (IYY) (see Chapter XX of this section) and to research on women's participation in development and the social structures of society (see Chapter XIX).

The second Latin American and Caribbean regional meeting for IYY (Montevideo, 26-29 August)[17] considered youth in a time of change and crisis and approved policies to complement a regional IYY plan of action.[18]

Seminars were held: on problems and prospects of the university and on the co-operative movement (Montevideo, August and November), on alternatives in social concertation (São Paulo, Brazil, April), on regional social changes (Quito, Ecuador, November), on primary education in areas of rapid urbanization (Santiago, December), to draw up a comparative analysis of the situation of Latin American youth and on policies and strategies for the participation of youth in Latin America (Buenos Aires, June and August), on youth policies in Andean countries (Bogotá, September), on youth and the future of Chile (Santiago, November), and on the role of women in the use of new and renewable sources of energy (Santo Domingo, February), statistical analysis of women on the labour market using household surveys (Montevideo, June), and young women in Latin America (Madrid, Spain, November).

Population

A Demography Unit was established by ECLAC and the Latin American Demographic Centre (CELADE) at Port of Spain in January 1985 to broaden CELADE's sphere of action within the population field in the English-speaking Caribbean.

Activities relating to demographic statistics and population trends, population and development, education and training, and documentation and data processing continued to be carried out by CELADE.[19]

Statistics

In 1985, ECLAC's Division of Statistics and Quantitative Analysis continued activities under three subprogrammes—a regional framework of statistical information, studies in methods and quantitative analysis, and statistical development and regional statistical co-operation—publishing documents, holding seminars, meetings and conferences, and providing technical assistance.

Seminars on basic statistics for social and economic planning (Mar del Plata, Argentina, March) and information systems for employment (Santiago, August) were organized.

Programme, organizational and administrative questions

Venue of the 1986 session

The Economic and Social Council, in **decision 1985/188**, adopted by 34 votes to 8, with 4 abstentions, on 26 July, decided that the twenty-first session of ECLAC should be held at Mexico City in early 1986 rather than at ECLAC headquarters in Santiago. The decision had been orally proposed by Ecuador in the First Committee, which approved it on 23 July by 32 votes to 8, with 5 abstentions.

The Secretary-General estimated that the change of venue would result in additional expenses totalling $108,800.[20]

The United States objected to the decision, not only because it considered that there was a discrepancy between the amount needed and that requested in the programme budget for meeting at the established headquarters, but also because the decision did not adhere to the principle, enunciated by the Assembly in 1976,[21] that a host country should be responsible for the additional costs of a meeting away from commission headquarters; Mexico's proposed contribution did not cover all additional costs, it said. Luxembourg said the EEC members could not support the decision as it conflicted with the Assembly's 1976 resolution, a view shared by Canada. Expressing concern about the Organization's financial situation, Japan said sessions should in principle be held at ECLAC headquarters.

Rules of procedure on venue

In **decision 1985/190** of 26 July, the Council requested ECLAC to analyse rule 2 of its rules of procedure at its 1986 session, taking into account the Assembly's 1976 resolution[21] containing general principles for meetings of United Na-

tions bodies away from their headquarters, and report thereon to the Council at its second regular session, in July 1986. Rule 2[22] stated that ECLAC's recommendation regarding the place of meeting for its sessions should be taken with due consideration for the principle that the countries of Latin America be chosen in rotation. The text was orally proposed in the First Committee by Mexico, on 23 July, and adopted without vote the next day.

1984 resolution on El Salvador

By a letter of 11 January[23] to the President of the Economic and Social Council, El Salvador asked the Council to take note of and possibly endorse a 1984 resolution[24] of the ECLAC Committee of the Whole adopted in response to the emergency situation in that country. The second paragraph of the resolution had recommended that, although El Salvador was not officially on the list of LDCs approved by the General Assembly in 1971,[25] it be accorded to the maximum extent possible, until the situation returned to normal, a treatment equivalent to that given to LDCs.

The Council noted, in **decision 1985/110** adopted without vote on 8 February—orally proposed by the President on behalf of the Bureau following informal consultations—that the Committee of the Whole had adopted the resolution concerning assistance to El Salvador without signifying any agreement by the Council with paragraph 2 regarding the treatment of countries as LDCs. It emphasized that as a general practice the existing procedures for the inclusion of countries in the list should be followed by all bodies of the United Nations system.

REFERENCES

[1]LC/G.1364. [2]LC/G.1351. [3]E/1985/106. [4]YUN 1984, p. 634. [5]E/1985/98. [6]LC/G.1413. [7]E/1986/34. [8]A/40/184-E/1985/61. [9]YUN 1984, p. 389. [10]LC/G.1361. [11]*Ibid.* (res. 18(IX)). [12]*Ibid.* (res. 20(IX)). [13]*Ibid.* (res. 19(IX)). [14]E/1985/3/Add.2. [15]YUN 1984, p. 636. [16]E/1985/3/Add.3. [17]LC/G.1362. [18]YUN 1983, p. 651. [19]LC/G.1396. [20]E/1985/C.1/L.8. [21]YUN 1976, p. 908, GA res. 31/140, 17 Dec. 1976. [22]E/CN.12/850. [23]E/1985/15. [24]YUN 1984, p. 638. [25]YUN 1971, p. 235, GA res. 2768(XXVI), 18 Nov. 1971.

PUBLICATIONS

Notes on Integration, Welfare and Project Evaluation, Sales No. E.85.III.F.16. *Economic Policy, Social Organization and Regional Development* (E/CEPAL/ILPES/G.13), Sales No. E.85.III.F.35. *Planning a System of Regions* (E/CEPAL/ILPES/G.5), Sales No. E.85.III.F.65. *Market Structure, Firm Size and Brazilian Exports* (LC/G.1335), Sales No. E.85.II.G.7. *Trade Relations between Brazil and the United States* (LC/G.1357), Sales No. E.85.II.G.15. *The Water Resources of Latin America and the Caribbean and Their Utilization* (LC/G.1358), Sales No. E.85.II.G.16. *Statistical Yearbook for Latin America and the Caribbean, 1985* (LC/G.1420 & Corr.1,2), E/S.86.II.G.1. *Economic Survey of Latin America and the Caribbean, 1985* (LC/G.1466), Sales No. E.87.II.G.2.

Western Asia

The Economic Commission for Western Asia, which held its twelfth session, at the ministerial level, at Baghdad, Iraq, on 24 and 25 April,[1] considered progress made in the implementation of its work programme, follow-up action at the regional level on United Nations world conferences, co-operation among developing countries and regional organizations, and issues and problems facing the countries of the region. The chief issues discussed were food security and agricultural development, technology and its ramifications, and the role of joint ventures in promoting economic co-operation.

The Commission endorsed its work programme and priorities for 1986-1987 and recommendations thereon by its Technical Committee;[2] asked the Executive Secretary, in his report to the 1986 session, to give details on the implementation of changes in the programme, amounts allocated and spent, elements scheduled and carried out, and problems encountered, with proposed solutions;[3] asked him to expedite the filling of vacancies in the ECWA secretariat;[4] called on him to include all available data on the occupied Palestinian territories in all Commission studies and statistical abstracts, and include studies in the work programme for 1986-1987 on economic and social conditions in those territories, including studies on population, the Israeli settlement policy and the industrial sector;[5] and asked for revision of a 1983 study[6] of the economic and social situation of the Palestinian Arab people, with the assistance of a sub-committee it had set up earlier to help with the text, whose work was to be completed by August 1985 for approval by an intergovernmental meeting of the Commission by the end of October[7] (see also p. 344).

Other resolutions concerned science and technology, technical co-operation activities, and transport and communications (see under subject headings below).

The Commission's Technical Committee, its only subsidiary body, held its third session at Baghdad from 20 to 23 April.[8] It discussed ECWA's work programme and priorities for 1986-1987, and recommended to it resolutions on that programme, on the economic and social conditions of the Palestinian Arab people under occupation, on the Transport and Communications Decade for Asia and the Pacific (1985-1994) proclaimed in 1984,[9] which included Western Asia, and on the name change of the Commission (see below). Attention centred on the priority programmes of social development, new and renewable sources of energy, science and technology, and statistics.

A summary of the Commission's activities from mid-1984 to mid-1985 and an account of the February meetings of the executive secretaries of the regional commissions (see p. 684), as well as issues and resolutions calling for action by the Economic and Social Council, were transmitted by the Secretary-General in a June 1985 report.[10]

ECONOMIC AND SOCIAL COUNCIL ACTION

On 26 July, on the recommendation of its First Committee, the Economic and Social Council adopted, without vote, **resolution 1985/69.**

Amendment of the terms of reference of the Economic Commission for Western Asia: change of name of the Commission

The Economic and Social Council,

Recalling its resolution 1818(LV) of 9 August 1973, by which it established the Economic Commission for Western Asia and laid down its terms of reference,

Recalling paragraph 1 *(f)* of those terms of reference,

Aware of the extreme importance of social development in the context of the overall development of the economies of Member States, and with the aim of achieving congruence between the subject-matter of the major activities undertaken by the Commission in the economic and social domains and its designation,

Recalling resolution 133(XII) of 24 April 1985 of the Economic Commission for Western Asia on the designation of the Commission,

1. *Decides* to change the name of the Economic Commission for Western Asia to "Economic and Social Commission for Western Asia";

2. *Also decides* to amend the terms of reference of the Commission as contained in Council resolution 1818(LV) to reflect the new name.

Economic and Social Council resolution 1985/69

26 July 1985   Meeting 52   Adopted without vote

Approved by First Committee (E/1985/145/Add.1) without vote, 24 July (meeting 28); draft by ECWA (E/1985/106); agenda item 8.

Economic and social trends

Two major factors—the decline of the United States dollar since February 1985 and the continued decline of oil prices which had begun in 1983—had a negative impact on the nations of Western Asia during 1985. Since oil payments were made primarily in dollars, the declining value of the dollar further reduced the purchasing power of the already shrinking oil revenues of Western Asia oil exporters, according to the *Survey of Economic and Social Developments in the ESCWA Region.*[11] The Economic and Social Council took note on 25 July in **decision 1985/182** of a summary[12] of the *Survey,* among other documents. The summary was updated in 1986.[13]

Another negative effect of the decline in the dollar's value on the countries of Western Asia was that the value of their international reserves and foreign assets fell in terms of other currencies. Kuwait, Saudi Arabia, and the United Arab Emirates were the most affected.

Since the late 1970s and early 1980s, Western Asia members of OPEC had suffered from a double squeeze, the growth of non-oil energy supplies and the expansion of production of non-OPEC oil producers. Moreover, market economies' demand for oil declined in 1985 to 45.6 million barrels per day, from 46.1 million barrels in 1984, and ESCWA countries' share in world oil production fell to 15.76 per cent from the 1984 level of 17.39 per cent.

With the slow-down in world economic growth and trade, protectionism among developed countries increased in 1985. In particular, Western Asia was affected by EEC's imposition of a tariff on Saudi Arabia's petrochemical products. Together with other Gulf countries, Saudi Arabia had invested billions of dollars in the petrochemical industry in an effort to diversify its economy and exports. At the same time, other major exports such as textiles and clothes continued to suffer from restrictions on their access to the markets of developed countries.

Activities in 1985

Development policy and regional economic co-operation

The Commission held various meetings and undertook a number of activities intensifying its co-operation with specialized agencies and other organs, such as the United Nations Centre for Science and Technology for Development (UNCSTD), the Voluntary Fund for the United Nations Decade for Women (subsequently to become the United Nations Development Fund for Women (UNIFEM)), FAO, the United Nations Centre for Human Settlements, UNDP, UNEP, UNFPA and UNIDO, examples of which are given below.

Current issues in economic co-operation and integration in Western Asia, in the context of progress made in implementing the International Development Strategy for the Third United Nations Development Decade (the 1980s)[14] (see Chapter I of this section), were considered in a January report[15] to the Commission. Among the issues were subregional co-operation, joint ventures, trade promotion and economic co-operation agreements, private sector involvement, institutional developments, resource transfers and labour movements.

A report on the role of joint ventures in promoting economic co-operation and integration in Western Asia was submitted in March.[16] The report examined the implications of the differences between inter-Arab and developing-country multinational joint ventures, some achievements of the inter-Arab ventures, their benefits and costs, policy issues, and new areas for joint ventures.

Technical co-operation

The Commission continued to undertake technical co-operation activities in the region during 1985,

providing short-term advisory services and monitoring and backstopping technical assistance projects. In a report to UNDP,[17] the Secretary-General noted that, within the framework of its regular programme of regional advisory services, ECWA rendered assistance to member States in development planning, electronics and information processing, human resources development, industrial project identification, formulation and appraisal, household surveys, transport and communications, and new and renewable sources of energy.

Under UNFPA-funded regional advisory services, assistance was provided to two countries in demography and to four countries in population statistics. Advice was provided to three countries through UNIDO-sponsored regional advisory services in industrial and mechanical engineering.

Other activities included the development of statistical services in Yemen, assistance to the Arab Planning Institute in Kuwait, and UNIFEM-funded work related to the role of women in national development.

On 25 April,[18] ECWA requested the Executive Secretary to increase the elements of the technical co-operation and assistance programme in accordance with members' needs, to specify in that programme advisory services to be provided and the projects to be financed from extrabudgetary resources, and to submit an outline of the main features of the next programme.

International trade and finance

A report on recent developments in international trade and payments in the countries of Western Asia[19] and a mid-term (1980-1984) review and analysis of progress in achieving objectives of the International Development Strategy on regional monetary and financial issues and developments[20] were submitted to the Commission. In addition, a review of fiscal and monetary issues and developments in the region, 1984, was issued in July 1985.[21] In December,[22] a consultant's report on the implications of external debt problems for the debtor and creditor countries of Western Asia was presented to the Commission.

Transport and communications

The Commission's activities concentrated on the development of integrated transport and formulation of a regional transport strategy in Western Asia. Reports and studies were published on transport harmonization and standardization, on inter- and intraregional land transport links, on the development of bulk shipping fleets, and on the Transport and Communications Decade for Asia and the Pacific.

On 24 April,[23] the Commission invited member States and urged international and regional organizations, particularly Arab organizations and funds, to contribute to the implementation of the Decade's programme of action.

Recommendations to facilitate border crossings, including the simplification and standardization of transport documents and the improvement of administrative measures and terminal facilities, were submitted to the Commission in February[24] with a secretarial suggestion that draft procedures on a draft convention on the subject might be prepared.

The first issue of the ESCWA *Transport Bulletin* was published in December.

Industrial development

Industrial pollution control in Western Asia—in particular, the environmental stresses of industrialization, waste control practices, environmentally sound technology, institutional organization for pollution control, regulatory policy and enforcement, incentives for abatement of industrial wastes and recommendations for an action programme—was examined in a Commission report.[25]

Other reports covered regional industrial trends, the iron and steel industry and automotive industries. A framework for a master plan was completed in the area of oil refining, petrochemicals and fertilizers, outlining the technological capabilities in engineering and design of countries in the region.

An *Ad Hoc* Expert Group Meeting on Capital Goods Industries (Amman, Jordan, 27 and 28 November) reviewed pre-feasibility and pre-investment studies on telephone exchanges and instruments, electric power turbines and generators, transformers, telephone and power cables, equipment for chemical industries, construction, agricultural machinery and automotive manufacturing.

Transnational corporations

A regional intergovernmental meeting of the countries of Western Asia on the United Nations draft code of conduct on TNCs (Baghdad, 18 and 19 November) reviewed the status of the negotiations on the code and examined outstanding issues (see Chapter VII of this section).

Reports were completed on the scope of activities of TNCs in Western Asia, highlighting the region's growing dependence on the international market for its petrochemicals and other manufactures, and on the operations of TNCs in the industrial sector in Bahrain.

Environment, natural resources and energy

A report was issued on the environmental consequences of urbanization in Western Asia, highlighting the status and trends of urbanization,

major environmental problems, environmental services in metropolitan centres, a proposed institutional structure for urban environmental management and a plan for environmental monitoring.

A survey of recent activities in water resources development in the region was completed in 1985.

Work on formulating energy planning methodologies for Jordan, Kuwait and the Syrian Arab Republic was completed, and an Expert Group Meeting on Integrated Energy Planning met at Amman from 30 November to 3 December.

A technical meeting for participating institutions in the regional New and Renewable Sources of Energy Information Network (Baghdad, 2 and 3 September)[26] examined the current use and supply of information and the role and obligations of the participants and secretariat, and suggested terms of reference for national focal points.

A joint ESCWA/FAO/UNEP mission identified a desertification control project in Yemen.

Food and agriculture

An expert consultation on agrarian systems and the socio-economic implications of fragmented holdings in the Near East was convened by the joint ESCWA/FAO Agriculture Division in December. An expert group meeting on critical factors in wheat production and distribution was also organized by the Commission and FAO in December.

A training workshop on the use of computers for analysis of agricultural and rural development projects was held in November at ESCWA headquarters, in co-operation with FAO and the National Institute for Planning of Iraq.

Science and technology

The Commission co-operated with UNCSTD in promoting subregional and regional co-operation for the strengthening of national scientific and technological capabilities.

The *Ad Hoc* Expert Group Meeting on the Mid-Decade Review of the Implementation of the 1979 Vienna Programme of Action on Science and Technology for Development[27] (Baghdad, 17-20 February) submitted a report[28] to the Commission, which, on 25 April,[29] requested the Executive Secretary to review the implementation of the Programme for 1986-1987 and up to the end of the decade.

Social development

UNIFEM supported technical assistance projects on women and development through research, seminars, training and studies.

The Commission convened a workshop (Baghdad, 25 June–2 July), in co-operation with the Federation of Arab Women, to acquaint delegations with the procedures and issues of the 1985 World Conference to Review and Appraise the Achievements of the United Nations Decade for Women (1976-1985) (see Chapter XIX of this section).

Formulation of an Arab strategy for social development was the focus of a United Nations/League of Arab States sectoral meeting (Amman, 19-21 August) and a Symposium on Contemporary Problems of the Arab Gulf Societies (Baghdad, November).

Thirteen publications were produced by the Commission in its series on Arab women in development, covering such subjects as national planning, mass media and community self-help activities.

Population

Implementing its population programme, the Commission co-operated closely with UNFPA, which financed subprogrammes on demographic data collection and analysis, population and development policy, and population education and information.

An expert group meeting was held with the Arab Planning Institute (Kuwait, 25-28 November), which discussed characteristics, prospects and employment and migration policies of the Arab labour force.

A report[30] on the status of statistics dealing with international migration in the region was submitted by the ECWA Statistics Division in March. It included proposals designed to establish statistical methods better suited to the region, to standardize its statistical concepts, definitions and classification methods, and to enhance co-operation between the countries of the region in statistics.

A technical paper on population projections for nationals in Bahrain, Kuwait, Qatar and the United Arab Emirates, 1980-2005, was published. Issues of the *Population Bulletin of ESCWA* were published in Arabic and English in June and December, respectively.

Human settlements

Human settlements country studies on Democratic Yemen, Iraq and Jordan were completed in 1985. The studies analytically reviewed human settlements issues relating to population, housing, the construction industry, infrastructure services, environment, financial resources for housing development and human settlements policies, intended to serve as a basis for the preparation of settlement policies and strategies. A study on the Syrian Arab Republic was initiated.

In addition, a preliminary study for the establishment of a brick-making plant in Democratic Yemen and a report on the feasibility of a brick factory in Yemen were completed.

Urban environmental management in Alexandria, Egypt, and Amman was assessed by the Commission and UNEP, which also financed a training workshop on the integrated planning of human settlements, sanitation and waste management.

Statistics

Various statistical projects were supported by UNDP, mainly in connection with national household surveys to provide information required for development planning, policies and programmes, and the development of statistical services.

The first meeting of the heads of central statistical organizations in the ESCWA region (Baghdad, 3-5 December) considered the ESCWA statistical programme for 1986-1987; endorsed a draft agreement between the secretariats of ESCWA and the League of Arab States containing projects on statistics; called for more financial support and participation in the National Household Survey Capability Programme; called on ESCWA members to participate in the fifth phase of the International Comparison Programme, having examined a study on the methodology of real income comparison in States of the region; and reviewed agricultural, environmental, income distribution, migration and national accounts statistics.

The eighth issue of *Statistical Abstract of the Region of the Economic and Social Commission for Western Asia* was published, covering 1974 to 1983 and presenting data on population, social statistics, national accounts, agriculture, forestry and fisheries, transport, communications and tourism.

REFERENCES

[1]E/1985/35. [2]*Ibid.* (res. 134(XII)). [3]*Ibid.* (res. 135(XII)). [4]*Ibid.* (res. 140(XII)). [5]*Ibid.* (res. 139(XII)). [6]YUN 1983, p. 653. [7]E/1985/35 (res. 141(XII)). [8]E/ECWA/XII/4/Rev.1. [9]YUN 1984, p. 624, GA res. 39/227, 18 Dec. 1984. [10]E/1985/106. [11]E/ESCWA/DPD/86/1/Rev.1. [12]E/1985/77. [13]E/1986/69. [14]YUN 1980, p. 503, GA res. 35/56, annex, 5 Dec. 1980. [15]E/ECWA/XII/5/Add.3. [16]E/ECWA/XII/9. [17]DP/1986/48/Add.2. [18]E/1985/35 (res. 137(XII)). [19]E/ECWA/XII/5/Add.2. [20]E/ECWA/XII/5/Add.9. [21]E/ECWA/DPD/85/9. [22]E/ESCWA/DPD/85/12. [23]E/1985/35 (res. 138(XII)). [24]E/ECWA/XII/5/Add.10. [25]E/ECWA/XII/5/Add.5. [26]E/ESCWA/13/4/Add.10. [27]YUN 1979, p. 636. [28]E/ECWA/XII/5/Add.6. [29]E/1985/35 (res. 136(XII)). [30]E/ECWA/XII/5/Add.8.

Chapter IX

Natural resources and cartography

The United Nations Revolving Fund for Natural Resources Exploration, administered by the United Nations Development Programme (UNDP), continued to assist developing countries during 1985. For the third consecutive year, however, the Fund's expenditures declined, and its financial situation was rapidly reaching a critical stage, according to the UNDP Administrator. The Economic and Social Council, in resolution 1985/51, recognized the urgent need for increased financial support.

The Committee on Natural Resources held its ninth session in New York from 8 to 17 April. Acting on the Committee's recommendations, the Council adopted resolutions on mineral resources (1985/48), small-scale mining (1985/47), electronic data processing in mineral exploration (1985/50), permanent sovereignty over natural resources (1985/52), co-ordinating United Nations natural resources programmes (1985/53), water resources development (1985/49 A and B) and rationalizing the Committee's work (1985/54). The Council also adopted resolutions on improving secretariat support for the Committee (1985/55) and on marine affairs (1985/75).

In December, the General Assembly adopted resolution 40/171 on drinking water supply and sanitation services.

The Third United Nations Regional Cartographic Conference for the Americas was held in New York from 19 February to 1 March.

Topics related to this chapter. Law of the sea: sea-bed mining code. Middle East: occupied territories—permanent sovereignty over national resources. Development policy and international economic co-operation: special economic areas—least developed countries. Operational activities for development. Regional economic and social activities. Energy resources—general aspects. Environment: environmental activities—ecosystems.

General aspects of natural resources

Exploration

**UN Revolving Fund
for Natural Resources Exploration**

Activities

The United Nations Revolving Fund for Natural Resources Exploration (UNRFNRE), a financing source for developing countries in natural resources exploration and development, continued its activities during 1985, its eleventh year of operation. Its 1985 activities were summarized in a March 1986 report of the UNDP Administrator.[1]

The overriding priority of the Fund in 1985 was to seek increased donor support in view of a financial situation rapidly becoming critical. Virtually all the Fund's financial resources available for new programming had been allocated, emphasizing the need for new and higher levels of contributions. Consequently, the Fund had tried to make itself better known among Member States, but the results had been limited.

The Fund intensified its efforts to promote investment. It collaborated with Argentina in a call for international tenders to include feasibility work and development/exploitation options on the Huemules gold discovery. Ecuador and a small international mining group agreed to promote investment interest in the San Bartolomé silver deposit discovered by the Fund; however, with the continued depressed price of silver, the economic viability of exploiting that resource remained uncertain.

A kaolin-exploration drilling programme in Benin resulted in the Fund's discovery of a second mineral deposit; it was hoped that the discovery would lead to investment in domestic industrial facilities.

In a continuing exploration programme in Haiti, the Fund and the Government took a new approach to interest mining groups in a gold vein system discovered in the Faille B area near Cap Haitien. At the Fund's suggestion, the Government began discussions with the international mining sector for further evaluation and exploration of its gold properties; the aim was to interest the private sector in a take-over of activities, eliminating the gap between the reporting of a successful Fund project and investment follow-up. Meanwhile, the Fund continued its work in Haiti to define the mineralization.

In 1985, the Fund reached major co-financing arrangements for the first time with bilateral donors in consultation with host Governments: with the United States Agency for International Development for a geothermal exploration project in Saint Lucia, and with France on a feasibility study as follow-up to an offshore phosphate discovery near Pointe Noire in the

Congo, parallel to a financing arrangement. In a third co-financing arrangement, Belgium assisted in the financing of beneficiation tests on a bulk-silver sample from the San Bartolomé, Ecuador, discovery.

The Fund's co-financing initiatives for specific projects with donor Governments were important particularly in the short term, allowing the Fund to extend its limited resources to more countries. Without co-financing, it would have been impossible to consider relatively more expensive projects, particularly for geothermal exploration.

The UNDP Governing Council, on 28 June,[2] approved projects for gold exploration in Rwanda and geothermal exploration drilling at Las Planillas, Jalisco State, Mexico. The Council noted the approval by the Administrator of supplementary short-term funding for mineral exploration in the Migori area of Kenya, and his successful efforts to obtain co-financing for the project in Saint Lucia. The Council also endorsed the appointment of Shigeaki Tomita as the new UNRFNRE Director.

Subsequent to the Council's June meeting, the Administrator approved allocations for geothermal exploration in the Qualibou Caldera, Saint Lucia, as well as for exploration for precious and base metals in Honduras and the Ivory Coast.

Approving the 1986 budget, the Council, on 29 June,[3] appropriated $1,486,600 for the Fund.

Contributions and expenditures

UNRFNRE project expenditures declined for the third consecutive year, from $3.6 million in 1984[4] to $2.6 million in 1985. To finance seven projects at a value of $18.2 million, the Fund allocated all of its cumulative financial resources ($12.7 million) available for programming in 1985; an additional allocation of $2.2 million was requested from the UNDP Governing Council. In addition, the Fund obtained for the first time substantial third-party co-financing of projects, amounting to $3.3 million. Government contributions in 1985 totalled $4.4 million.

In his March 1985 annual report on the Fund,[5] the UNDP Administrator stated that the degree to which UNRFNRE could carry out its mandate rested on voluntary and eventual replenishment contributions, supplemented by co-financing; in the long run, however, success would be achieved only through sustained core programme financing.

The UNDP Governing Council in June[2] noted with concern the depletion of Fund resources and renewed its appeal to Member States to contribute to the Fund in order for it to fulfil its mandate.

CONTRIBUTIONS TO UNRFNRE, 1985 AND 1986

(as at 31 December 1985; in US dollar equivalent)

Country	1985 payment	1986 pledge
Bangladesh	1,256	1,210
Benin	—	500
Burundi	—	877
Chile	5,000	5,000
Indonesia	10,000	10,000
Japan	4,000,000	—
Norway	381,194	397,351
Rwanda	—	500
Saint Lucia	—	5,000
Zaire	—	500
Total	4,397,450	420,938

SOURCE: A/41/5/Add.1.

UNRFNRE PROJECT EXPENDITURES, 1985

(as at 31 December 1985; in thousands of US dollars)

Country	Amount
Argentina	85
Benin	270
Brazil	5
Burkina Faso	(66)
Burundi	5
Chile	28
China	28
Congo	80
Cyprus	(1)
Dominican Republic	14
Ecuador	32
Ethiopia	3
Ghana	5
Guatemala	23
Guyana	6
Haiti	505
Honduras	93
India	2
Ivory Coast	33
Kenya	78
Liberia	(19)
Mali	(63)
Mexico	36
Peru	699
Philippines	18
Portugal	2
Rwanda	27
Saint Lucia	113
Samoa	4
Sierra Leone	477
Sri Lanka	18
Suriname	5
Turkey	11
United Republic of Tanzania	(3)
Vanuatu	2
Zambia	14
Zimbabwe	4
Total	2,573

SOURCE: DP/1986/11/Add.6.

ECONOMIC AND SOCIAL COUNCIL ACTION

On 25 July 1985, on the recommendation of its First (Economic) Committee, the Economic and Social Council adopted without vote **resolution 1985/51.**

United Nations Revolving Fund for Natural Resources Exploration

The Economic and Social Council,

Recalling General Assembly resolution 3167(XXVIII) of 17 December 1973 and Economic and Social Council resolution 1762(LIV) of 18 May 1973, concerning the establishment of the United Nations Revolving Fund for Natural Resources Exploration,

1. *Takes note* of the report of the Administrator of the United Nations Development Programme on the United Nations Revolving Fund for Natural Resources Exploration and requests the Administrator to provide, in his next report, detailed information on deposits discovered;

2. *Welcomes* the efforts of the Fund to promote pre-investment follow-up to its successful mineral discoveries, in close co-operation with the recipient Governments;

3. *Also welcomes* the new activities of the Fund in geothermal exploration;

4. *Recognizes* the urgent requirement to increase financial support to the Fund by means of voluntary contributions;

5. *Welcomes* the efforts made by the Fund to seek co-financing partners as a means of expanding its immediate funding capacity to meet the demands for projects.

Economic and Social Council resolution 1985/51

25 July 1985	Meeting 52	Adopted without vote

Approved by First Committee (E/1985/148) without vote, 15 July (meeting 21); draft by Committee on Natural Resources (E/1985/27); agenda item 11.

Electronic data processing in natural resources exploration and development

A report on electronic data processing in mineral exploration, development and production was submitted by the Secretary-General in March 1985[6] to the Committee on Natural Resources, in response to a 1983 Economic and Social Council resolution.[7]

The report, a follow-up to one submitted in 1983 on new exploration techniques,[8] reflected the conclusions of a group convened by the Secretary-General in 1984.[9] It stated that electronic data processing methods had made valuable contributions to mineral exploration, development and operation, but warned against applying computers to tasks that were better done manually. As the use of electronic methods in developing countries varied widely, some countries having little or no experience, the support required for activities needed to be correctly identified. Areas yielding demonstrable economic returns were production reporting, maintenance scheduling, spare parts inventory control, process control and mine planning, and data-intensive activities such as financial analysis, geological modelling and ore reserve estimation had been established areas for many years. Applications to other areas might not be uneconomic, but their viability had to be established.

The development of computer applications should depend on the satisfaction of several conditions: the prospect of real benefit from introduction of the computer; user understanding of the application; availability of suitable software and hardware; and adequate training of operators and users. It was recommended that, where possible, emphasis be placed on providing training programmes in developing countries for executives, professionals and data preparation staff.

The United Nations should continue to expand the application of computer techniques in its technical co-operation projects and should develop guidelines for hardware and software application in those projects; its Department of Technical Co-operation for Development (DTCD) planned to increase substantially its activities in that area.

ECONOMIC AND SOCIAL COUNCIL ACTION

On 25 July 1985, on the recommendation of its First Committee, the Economic and Social Council adopted without vote **resolution 1985/50**.

Application of microcomputer technology in the development of water, energy and mineral resources

The Economic and Social Council,

Recognizing the rapid growth and the development potential of computer technology, in particular the advent of inexpensive and reliable microcomputers and the need of developing countries for information on hardware, software and training materials,

Bearing in mind the advantages that developing countries could derive from a wider application of such techniques in the implementation of natural resources development policy,

Taking note of the report of the Secretary-General on the application of computer technology in mineral exploration and development and of the information provided on the current activities of the Department of Technical Co-operation for Development of the United Nations Secretariat in this field,

Taking note also of the progress made in the application of computer technology for the assessment and development of energy and water resources in the developing countries through various technical co-operation activities,

Mindful of the importance of the transfer of technology, in particular appropriate new technology, that will strengthen the capabilities of developing countries,

1. *Requests* the Secretary-General to continue activities related to the application of microcomputer technology in the assessment, development and planning of natural resources—water, energy and mineral resources—in such areas as the development and dissemination of appropriate software technology;

2. *Also requests* the Secretary-General to report to the Committee on Natural Resources at its tenth and subsequent sessions on the progress made in the application of the technology referred to in paragraph 1 above.

Economic and Social Council resolution 1985/50

25 July 1985	Meeting 52	Adopted without vote

Approved by First Committee (E/1985/148) without vote, 15 July (meeting 21); draft by Committee on Natural Resources (E/1985/27); agenda item 11.

Permanent sovereignty over natural resources

The Secretary-General, in response to a 1983 Economic and Social Council request,[10] the latest in a series since 1977,[11] submitted to the Committee on Natural Resources in February 1985 a report[12] on the exercise of control by developing countries over their natural resources. The report reviewed such issues as strengthening of national capabilities to finance and manage exploration, exploitation and processing of natural resources; investment promotion; possibilities for economic and technical co-operation; and issues related to the conservation of natural resources and environment protection. It also dealt with new developments regarding arbitration and renegotiation as they related to the principles of permanent sovereignty, and briefly summarized DTCD technical co-operation activities in the natural resources field.

The report saw an acute need for specific technical co-operation activities related to natural resources in developing countries. In the past, attention had focused on the development by Governments and international companies of export-oriented large-scale projects; the current situation, however, warranted a measure of reorientation to domestic efforts, small-scale mining and mineral production for national or regional consumption. Institutional arrangements in developing countries for mineral sector development might also be reviewed; such arrangements included the organization of respective ministries, geological and mining agencies, State mineral enterprises and financing arrangements.

Another issue was how to find and agree on a neutral body to recommend mining and petroleum law experts with experience in developing countries, who could act as arbitrator when the parties themselves could not agree on either institutional international arbitration bodies or on a third arbitrator. DTCD maintained a computerized roster of experts, a service available to Governments at their request.

From experience with rehabilitation of rundown mines, it was evident that many could be rehabilitated relatively easily, given a more favourable economic environment, efficient project management and financial support. Governments might wish to examine closed mines and mines in decline, with United Nations technical co-operation, to determine their rehabilitation potential; it might also be useful for them to review all mineral development opportunities and examine strategies for investment follow-up.

The Commission on Transnational Corporations (TNCs) took up at a special session in June (see p. 616) the principal outstanding issues, including respect for national sovereignty, in a draft code of conduct on TNCs. It was proposed that a provision in the code declare that TNCs respect the right of each State to exercise permanent sovereignty over its natural resources and wealth.

ECONOMIC AND SOCIAL COUNCIL ACTION

On 25 July, on the recommendation of its First Committee, the Economic and Social Council, without vote, adopted **resolution 1985/52**.

Permanent sovereignty over natural resources
The Economic and Social Council,
Recognizing the problems caused by the present international economic situation to most countries, in particular the developing countries,
Noting the importance for all countries, in particular the developing countries, to maximize the benefits from the exploration for, and the exploitation and processing of, their natural resources in order to strengthen their economic development,
Having taken note of the report of the Secretary-General on permanent sovereignty over natural resources and of the comments made thereon by the Committee on Natural Resources at its ninth session,
Taking into account the work done in other forums of the United Nations system regarding permanent sovereignty over natural resources,
1. *Requests* the Committee on Natural Resources to continue, at its tenth session, its consideration of the item entitled "Permanent sovereignty over natural resources", including:
(*a*) Strengthening of national capabilities to explore for, exploit and process natural resources for the national benefit;
(*b*) National experience of different countries in developing natural resources;
(*c*) Impact of the international economic situation on the exploitation of natural resources, particularly in the developing countries;
(*d*) Promotion of investments in natural resources to meet basic priorities in the developing countries, taking into account, *inter alia*, the perspectives of national and world markets;
(*e*) Creation of new industries in developing countries, based on an integrated transformation and industrialization of their natural resources;
(*f*) Technical and technological developments related to natural resources in developing countries;
(*g*) Conservation of natural resources;
(*h*) Environment and natural resources;
2. *Requests* the Secretary-General to prepare a report on the question of permanent sovereignty over natural resources, taking into account the matters referred to in paragraph 1 above and the comments made by the Committee at its ninth session;
3. *Reaffirms*, in this context, the importance of the ongoing work of the Commission on Transnational Corporations on a code of conduct on transnational corporations, as it relates to natural resources.

Economic and Social Council resolution 1985/52

25 July 1985　　　　　Meeting 52　　　　　Adopted without vote

Approved by First Committee (E/1985/148) without vote, 15 July (meeting 21); draft by Committee on Natural Resources (E/1985/27); agenda item 11.

The General Assembly, in **resolution 40/56**, requested Member States, as well as organizations of the United Nations system, to ensure that the permanent sovereignty of colonial Territories over their natural resources was fully respected and safeguarded.

Committee on Natural Resources

The Committee on Natural Resources held its ninth session in New York from 8 to 17 April 1985.[13] It discussed mineral, energy, and water resources; new techniques, including remote sensing, for exploring natural resources; activities and financing of UNRFNRE; permanent sovereignty over natural resources; utilization of subsurface space; co-ordination of United Nations natural resources programmes; and the provisional agenda for its tenth (1987) session. The Committee recommended to the Economic and Social Council for adoption eight draft resolutions and one draft decision. By another decision, it recommended that the Council transmit to the General Assembly a draft resolution on the International Drinking Water Supply and Sanitation Decade (see p. 680); three other decisions were brought to the Council's attention.

On 25 July, on the recommendation of its First Committee, the Economic and Social Council adopted without vote **resolution 1985/54**.

Rationalization of the work of the Committee on Natural Resources

The Economic and Social Council,

Reiterating the need to increase the efficiency and effectiveness of the work of the Committee on Natural Resources,

Reiterating that a timely distribution of documents is essential to an improvement of the efficiency of the work of the Committee,

Reiterating that the Committee could make recommendations on appropriate priorities and programme emphasis to the Economic and Social Council and through the Council to Governments and other bodies, such as the United Nations Development Programme,

Reaffirming the terms of reference of the Committee set out in Council resolution 1535(XLIX) of 27 July 1970,

Recalling its resolution 1982/50 of 28 July 1982 on the revitalization of the Council and the views expressed on that subject by the Committee at its eighth session,

1. *Reiterates* that the documents for each session of the Committee on Natural Resources should be distributed in the appropriate languages at least six weeks before the commencement of the session;

2. *Requests* the Secretary-General to report on the programme activities of the United Nations system, in particular of the appropriate divisions of the Department of International Economic and Social Affairs and the Department of Technical Co-operation for Development of the United Nations Secretariat, in the field of natural resources, particularly with regard to mineral resources, energy and water; this information will assist the Committee in fulfilling its analytical and advisory role in the field of natural resources, outlined in its terms of reference;

3. *Decides* that, as an experiment, the Committee shall give priority at each of its sessions, on a cyclical basis, to the examination of one of the main subjects of natural resources set out in paragraph 4 *(a)* of Council resolution 1535(XLIX); in this connection, with due respect for the concept of the sovereignty of every State, attention shall also be paid to the other main subjects, as well as to other subjects within the terms of reference of the Committee;

4. *Also decides* that the Committee, at its tenth session, shall give priority consideration to the subject of water resources;

5. *Requests* the Secretary-General, in consultation with the appropriate organizations of the United Nations system, to pay special attention to the priority subject of water resources in preparing the documents for the tenth session of the Committee.

Economic and Social Council resolution 1985/54

25 July 1985   Meeting 52   Adopted without vote

Approved by First Committee (E/1985/148) without vote, 15 July (meeting 21); draft by Committee on Natural Resources (E/1985/27); agenda item 11.

On the same date, on the recommendation of its First Committee, the Council adopted without vote **resolution 1985/55**.

Improvement of secretariat servicing and substantive support services for the Committee on Natural Resources

The Economic and Social Council,

Taking into account the concerns expressed at the ninth session of the Committee on Natural Resources and at the second regular session of 1985 of the Economic and Social Council regarding the need to improve secretariat servicing and substantive support services for future sessions of the Committee on Natural Resources,

Recalling the recommendation made by the Committee for Programme and Co-ordination at its twenty-fifth session concerning the early issuance of the Secretary-General's bulletin and the sections of the organizational manual for the relevant United Nations offices and departments in the economic and social field,

1. *Requests* the Secretary-General to make the necessary arrangements, within existing resources and existing secretariat machinery, to assign secretariat responsibility which would ensure, on an ongoing basis, adequate and timely preparations, including documentation, for future sessions of the Committee on Natural Resources;

2. *Also requests* the Secretary-General to report to the Economic and Social Council at its organizational session for 1986 on the action taken in this regard.

Economic and Social Council resolution 1985/55

25 July 1985   Meeting 52   Adopted without vote

Approved by First Committee (E/1985/148) without vote, 15 July (meeting 21); 7-nation draft (E/1985/C.1/L.7); agenda item 11.
Sponsors: Argentina, Canada, India, Netherlands, Norway, Pakistan, United States.

Also on 25 July, the Council, by **decision 1985/166**, took note of the report of the Committee on Natural Resources on its 1985 session and approved the provisional agenda and documentation for its 1987 session. The decision originated in the Committee on Natural Resources.

Co-ordination of UN activities

The Secretary-General, pursuant to a 1983 Economic and Social Council request,[14] submitted to the Committee on Natural Resources in March 1985 a report[15] on programme co-ordination, describing co-ordination arrangements as well as inter-agency co-operation in water resources development (see p. 679). A report on mineral resources had been submitted to the Committee in 1983.[16]

ECONOMIC AND SOCIAL COUNCIL ACTION

On 25 July 1985, on the recommendation of its First Committee, the Economic and Social Council adopted without vote **resolution 1985/53.**

Co-ordination of programmes within the United Nations system in the field of natural resources
The Economic and Social Council,

Recalling its resolution 1535(XLIX) of 27 July 1970, by which it decided to establish the Committee on Natural Resources and set out its terms of reference, specifically charging the Committee to maintain liaison between the activities in the field of natural resources of the regional commissions, the specialized agencies, the International Atomic Energy Agency and other bodies doing relevant work, with a view to ensuring the utmost efficiency and co-operation,

Mindful of the vital contribution made by bilateral and multilateral technical co-operation programmes in enhancing national capabilities in developing countries effectively to explore for, manage and develop their natural resources,

Concerned that the Committee should effectively advise the Council in order to ensure maximum co-ordination, and thus the effectiveness and economy of the activities of the United Nations,

Recognizing that co-ordination of technical assistance activities within the United Nations system has significant potential for increasing the efficiency and expanding the results of United Nations and other resource development activities within existing funding constraints,

Observing that available information on United Nations and related activities in natural resources co-operation should be taken into consideration by the Committee in preparing its recommendations,

Having considered the report of the Secretary-General on co-ordination and co-operation in water resources development,

1. *Takes note* of the report of the Secretary-General on co-ordination and co-operation in water resources development and requests the Secretary-General to update that report for the tenth session of the Committee on Natural Resources;

2. *Requests* the Secretary-General to submit to the Committee at its eleventh session a report based, *inter alia*, on information made available by Governments, documenting United Nations and related activities in mineral resources directed at:

(a) Strengthening national institutions in developing countries for the conduct of exploration, development and planning activities;

(b) Conducting surveys and studies to assist in the identification of mineral resources and the encouragement of their development;

(c) Enhancing national technical capabilities through the transfer and application of necessary technology for the development of basic resource information, and for the exploration for, assessment and development of natural resources, including the training of both technical and managerial personnel;

3. *Requests* the Committee on Natural Resources, at its eleventh session, on the basis of the report requested in paragraph 2 above, to make recommendations to the Economic and Social Council on ways to ensure and improve co-operation and the overall efficiency of all the aforementioned activities;

4. *Invites* Governments to take that report into account in their activities directed at co-operation in mineral resources.

Economic and Social Council resolution 1985/53

25 July 1985   Meeting 52   Adopted without vote

Approved by First Committee (E/1985/148) without vote, 15 July (meeting 21); draft by Committee on Natural Resources (E/1985/27); agenda item 11.

Other aspects

Utilization of subsurface space

In response to a 1983 Economic and Social Council resolution,[17] the Secretary-General submitted in February 1985 to the Committee on Natural Resources a report on the development and utilization of subsurface space.[18] The report dealt with steps to strengthen support mechanisms relating to the use of subsurface space as well as progress made in the development and use of such space in various countries. It included a summary of activities by various United Nations organizations in that sector and recommendations concerning steps to bring the potential uses of subsurface space more effectively to the attention of developing countries.

Only limited resources had been made available to strengthen support mechanisms, the report concluded. Since the use of subsurface space could make a significant impact on development activity in developing countries, Governments might wish to consider ways of placing greater emphasis on it. Subsurface space offered opportunities for improving transport facilities, food storage and public utilities, for storage of water, oil, gas and certain wastes, and for alleviating space problems in crowded urban areas. It was important that experience in utilizing subsurface space was shared with and among developing countries, and that the availability of qualified national professionals was increased. Basic issues in the use and development of such space needed to be identified, and the establishment of criteria for underground structures could be given greater priority.

To create awareness of the uses of subsurface space, the report recommended that the United Nations provide expert advisory services to developing countries and that information on subsurface space be identified with a view to preparing a publication for use by Member States.

The Committee took note of the report on 16 April.[19]

REFERENCES

[1]DP/1986/51. [2]E/1985/32 (dec. 85/25). [3]*Ibid.* (dec. 85/36). [4]YUN 1984, p. 646. [5]DP/1985/46 & Add.1. [6]E/C.7/1985/7. [7]YUN 1983, p. 659, ESC res. 1983/54, 28 July 1983. [8]*Ibid.*, p. 658. [9]YUN 1984, p. 647. [10]YUN 1983, p. 660, ESC res. 1983/56, 28 July 1983. [11]YUN 1977, p. 568, ESC res. 2120(LXIII), 4 Aug. 1977. [12]E/C.7/1985/8. [13]E/1985/27. [14]YUN 1983, p. 664, ESC res. 1983/59, 28 July 1983. [15]E/C.7/1985/10. [16]YUN 1983, p. 664. [17]*Ibid.*, p. 660, ESC res. 1983/58, 28 July 1983. [18]E/C.7/1985/9. [19]E/1985/27 (dec. 9/4).

PUBLICATION

Unconsolidated Mineral Deposits in the Exclusive Economic Zone: A Resource Search Methodology and Its Application to the West African Coastal Zone (ST/ESA/137), Sales No. E.85.II.A.3.

Mineral resources

Technical co-operation

During 1985, DTCD, in addition to UNRFNRE, continued to provide developing countries with assistance in mineral exploration, institution building and strengthening, project design, mineral sector planning, mine development and rehabilitation, mining legislation and contract negotiations, advanced technology transfer, the application of computer techniques in mineral exploration, and training.

A total of 61 technical assistance projects were operational in 43 countries, with expenditures of $12.5 million. The projects were described in an addendum to a report of the Secretary-General on United Nations technical co-operation activities.[1]

Fifteen projects were concerned mainly with strengthening government institutions (universities, geological survey departments, State corporations), central laboratories and pilot plants. They included training for mineral exploration in Ethiopia, training support to the Geological Survey of India, strengthening of the Mozambique Ministry of Mineral Resources and similar endeavours in Bhutan, China, the Dominican Republic, Gabon, Guinea, Guyana, Nicaragua, Pakistan, Somalia and Turkey.

Large-scale mineral exploration programmes continued in Burkina Faso, Burundi, Haiti, Rwanda and the United Republic of Tanzania.

Work was carried forward in Mali evaluating newly-discovered gold deposits. Operational assistance to the Ghana State Gold Mining Corporation continued, together with rehabilitation of its mines.

A geophysical survey of Malawi was launched in 1985, aimed at improving knowledge of its geological structure and mineral potential. Exploration for tin in the Andaman Sea (Thailand) continued, utilizing offshore shallow seismic techniques and drilling. Interest was evident in non-metallic minerals—potash in China, lignite in Greece and gemstones in Pakistan.

A major regional programme—involving remote sensing, airborne geophysical surveying and training of geoscientists—continued in Democratic Yemen and Yemen. A major regional mineral exploration project was concluded in Egypt/Sudan.

Training—fellowships, lecturing, on-the-job instruction, seminars and technology transfer—was a major component of most projects. More than 100 missions were undertaken by DTCD inter-regional and technical advisers to assist in mining legislation, contract negotiations and mineral sector planning, electronic data processing, mining engineering, geology, geochemistry and geophysics.

Exploitation and processing

The Secretary-General, responding to a 1983 Economic and Social Council decision,[2] submitted in March 1985 to the Committee on Natural Resources a report[3] on trends and salient issues in the development of mineral resources. The recent growth of the world economy had not led to substantial price increases for most minerals and metals, he stated; the prices of several of them in real terms were at or near record low levels, and nearly all mineral and metal producing companies had responded by reducing production or closing mines, at least temporarily. The low prices affected the economies of producing countries, most of which were developing countries. Long-term developments, such as increased recycling and substitution, decline in rates of growth of consumption and reluctance in many countries to reduce production also resulted in pressure on prices. Marketing and investment problems had increased with the nationalization and breakup of the vertical integration of many international mining companies, and the use of long-term contracts to provide collateral for long-term financing and a reliable market had declined.

Counter-trade in the form of barter, counter-purchase, buy-back, compensation agreements, bilateral co-operation agreements or switch-trading was increasingly used by developing countries to develop new projects and secure markets in a situation characterized by overcapacity and a decline in demand for mineral raw materials.

New mining projects, in both developed and developing countries, were likely to be based on the development of small, high-grade deposits of high-value minerals produced in a relatively short time with low capital budgets so as to minimize interest cost. For most developing countries with established mines, the immediate outlook appeared to require increased mining efficiency and reduced costs, if mining was to continue without adverse economic consequences.

A report on prospects for the development of non-metallic mineral raw materials, with special reference to bentonite, mica, magnesite, feldspar, fluorspar and baryte, was presented by the Secretary-General to the Committee in February 1985,[4] in response to a 1983 Economic and Social Council resolution.[5]

Prospects for production in developing countries of those raw materials depended not only on their availability and quality but on the size of the market, the legislative framework, location of deposits and transportation costs, the report concluded. Measures should be taken to accelerate their exploration and development; to begin with, increased attention could be paid to those minerals during general mapping programmes of a country. As many developing countries did not have the means to prepare an inventory of resources, the Committee might wish to recommend that surveys be undertaken to enable them to prepare such inventories with DTCD assistance.

The Committee, on 17 April,[6] took note of the February report.[4]

ECONOMIC AND SOCIAL COUNCIL ACTION

On 25 July, on the recommendation of its First Committee, the Economic and Social Council adopted without vote **resolution 1985/48**.

Mineral resources

The Economic and Social Council,

Recalling General Assembly resolutions 3201(S-VI) and 3202(S-VI) of 1 May 1974, containing the Declaration and the Programme of Action on the Establishment of a New International Economic Order, 3281(XXIX) of 12 December 1974, containing the Charter of Economic Rights and Duties of States, and 3362(S-VII) of 16 September 1975 on development and international economic co-operation,

Recalling the guidelines for action in the development of natural resources adopted by the Committee on Natural Resources at its second session,

Taking note of the report of the Secretary-General on trends and salient issues in the development of mineral resources,

Recognizing the difficult situation of raw material exporting countries and the negative implications of that situation, particularly for the developing countries,

1. *Requests* the Committee on Natural Resources to consider at its tenth session the question of short-term and long-term trends and salient issues in the field of mineral resources;

2. *Also requests* the Committee to consider ways of increasing the efficiency of the mining sector, *inter alia*, by expanding the exploitation and processing of co-products and by-products.

Economic and Social Council resolution 1985/48

25 July 1985   Meeting 52   Adopted without vote

Approved by First Committee (E/1985/148) without vote, 15 July (meeting 21); draft by Committee on Natural Resources (E/1985/27); agenda item 11.

Small-scale mining

ECONOMIC AND SOCIAL COUNCIL ACTION

On 25 July, on the recommendation of its First Committee, the Economic and Social Council adopted without vote **resolution 1985/47**.

Small-scale mining

The Economic and Social Council,

Recalling its resolution 1535(XLIX) of 27 July 1970 setting out the terms of reference of the Committee on Natural Resources, in particular paragraph 4 (g) thereof,

Recognizing the effective contribution of small-scale mining and quarrying to the economic and social development of some countries, in particular as a source of employment and regional development,

Taking note of the fact that in some developing countries much mining is accomplished by small-scale operations, and that many of these operations face special problems, including lack of mechanized equipment, absence of expertise in the exploration for and operation of small mines, legal frameworks that, in some countries, differ from those of large-scale mining, and different marketing circumstances,

Taking note also of the fact that developing countries might benefit from an exchange of information on all aspects of exploration for, assessment of, development and operation of small mines and that continued studies on the problems of infrastructure, equipment and exploitation constitute an important step in finding an optimal scale for mining,

Taking into account the discussions in the Committee on Natural Resources at its last three sessions on fertilizer raw materials and non-metallic mineral resources,

1. *Recommends* that the Committee on Natural Resources, at its eleventh session, should consider small-scale mining in the context of its deliberations on mineral resources;

2. *Requests* the Secretary-General to take small-scale mining into account when preparing reports for the eleventh session of the Committee; those reports should include an overview of small-scale mining and an evaluation of experience gained through technical co-operation projects;

3. *Also requests* the Secretary-General to examine whether there exist small-scale mining operations that could serve as demonstration projects for training and for developing new approaches to small-scale mining, in accordance with national development plans and priorities, and to report thereon to the Committee on Natural Resources at its eleventh session;

4. *Urges* Governments to submit to the Secretary-General at an early date information and reports on small-scale mining in their countries.

Economic and Social Council resolution 1985/47

25 July 1985   Meeting 52   Adopted without vote

Approved by First Committee (E/1985/148) without vote, 15 July (meeting 21); draft by Committee on Natural Resources (E/1985/27); agenda item 11.

Evaluation

In March 1985,[7] the Secretary-General submitted to the Committee for Programme and Co-ordination (CPC) a triennial review of the implementation of CPC's 1982 recommendations on the United Nations mineral resources programme.[8] The report was based on the responses to questionnaires of nine United Nations entities involved in mineral resources development: the Department of International Economic and Social Affairs, DTCD, three regional commissions, the United Nations Centre on Transnational Corporations, the United Nations Conference on Trade and Development (UNCTAD), UNDP and UNRFNRE. Its major recommendations concerned the organization of in-depth evaluations and formulation of recommendations, co-ordination at the intergovernmental and organizational levels, assessment of technical advisory services, modalities for post-exploration assistance, improving project implementation and programme planning and design, and expanding and monitoring the distribution of documents.

Owing to time constraints, CPC decided on 25 May 1985[9] to defer consideration of the Secretary-General's report to its 1986 session.

REFERENCES

[1]DP/1986/48/Add.1. [2]YUN 1983, p. 661, ESC dec. 1983/176, 28 July 1983. [3]E/C.7/1985/2. [4]E/C.7/1985/3. [5]YUN 1983, p. 663, ESC res. 1983/52, 28 July 1983. [6]E/1985/27 (dec. 9/2). [7]E/AC.51/1985/9. [8]YUN 1982, p. 880. [9]A/40/38.

Water and marine resources

Water resources development

Implementation of the 1977 Mar del Plata Action Plan

In response to a 1979 General Assembly resolution,[1] the Secretary-General submitted to the Committee on Natural Resources in April 1985 a report[2] on progress in implementing the Mar del Plata Action Plan for the development of water resources, adopted by the 1977 United Nations Water Conference at Mar del Plata, Argentina.[3] The report was prepared on the basis of information from 91 Governments, and dealt with, among other subjects, policy, planning, legislation and institutional arrangements; development of shared water resources; assessment of water resources; and flood-loss management.

Three quarters of the developing countries and two thirds of the industrialized countries responding had formulated national policy statements for water resources. A very high proportion of countries had legislation regulating the ownership, use and protection of both surface and ground waters.

Most developing countries (73 per cent) had established central co-ordinating mechanisms or national bodies for water interests. The highest percentage of them reporting those mechanisms was in Latin America and the Caribbean (87 per cent); the lowest in Western Asia (50 per cent). A large proportion of industrialized countries (61 per cent) also indicated that they had set up national co-ordinating mechanisms.

Since the 1977 Water Conference, a number of significant agreements had been concluded on shared water resources: in Africa, a 1977 agreement to establish an organization for the development of the Kagera Basin, a 1978 convention relating to the River Gambia, and a 1980 convention creating the Niger Basin Authority; in Latin America, a 1977 treaty on co-operation in utilizing the natural resources and the development of the Mirin Lagoon Basin, the 1978 treaty for Amazonian co-operation and development, and a 1979 agreement for harmonizing separate binational hydro-development projects on the Paraná River.

Far from a strengthening of water resources assessment, as called for by the 1977 Conference, activities in that sector had been barely maintained, if not actually reduced, because of scarcity of capital and lack of manpower and equipment. That was particularly the case in drought-stricken Africa, where national agencies had great difficulties maintaining even minimum ability to supply basic information.

Many countries suffering from floods had established policy and institutional arrangements to deal with them, but weakness persisted in regard to their adequacy and reliability. Of 66 developing countries, 33 indicated that floods were a major characteristic of their hydrological régime. Flood forecasting and warning systems appeared to be adequate in 25 per cent of developing countries, compared to 83 per cent in developed countries; flood plain zoning and flood risk mapping appeared to be adequate in 19 per cent of the former, compared to 63 per cent of the latter. Catchment areas for flood prevention were deemed adequate by 39 per cent of developing countries, compared to 61 per cent of developed countries; the differences with regard to dikes, retention reservoirs and river channel improvement were about the same. Shortage of financial resources and lack of equipment were reported to be the most serious constraints in efforts to mitigate losses from floods.

Other subjects covered in the report were drinking water supply and sanitation (see p. 680); water resources for agriculture; education and training (see p. 679); public information and participation; research and development; and technical co-operation among developing countries (TCDC).

In another report to the Committee, on United Nations co-ordination in water resources development (see p. 679), the Secretary-General also described inter-agency co-operation in specific areas of the Action Plan, such as water resources assessment, management, policy, legislation and administration; development of ground-water resources; mitigation of flood and drought losses; water use; education and training; hydropower and inland transport; TCDC; and technical co-operation activities.

ECONOMIC AND SOCIAL COUNCIL ACTION

On 25 July, on the recommendation of its First Committee, the Economic and Social Council adopted without vote **resolution 1985/49 A**.

Progress in the implementation of the Mar del Plata Action Plan

The Economic and Social Council,

Recalling General Assembly resolution 34/191 of 18 December 1979, in which the Assembly requested the Committee on Natural Resources, at its regular biennial sessions during the 1980s, to review the progress made by Governments in the implementation of the Mar del Plata Action Plan,

Recalling also Council resolutions 1979/67, 1979/68 and 1979/70 of 3 August 1979, 1981/80 and 1981/81 of 24 July 1981 and 1983/57 of 28 July 1983, concerning the implementation of the Mar del Plata Action Plan,

Recalling further its resolution 1984/73 of 27 July 1984,

1. *Takes note* of the reports of the Secretary-General on the progress achieved and prospects in the implementation by Governments of the Mar del Plata Action Plan, and on education and training in the field of water resources in developing countries;

2. *Reaffirms* the importance of the implementation of the recommendations contained in the Mar del Plata Action Plan;

3. *Expresses once again its concern* that, notwithstanding the progress achieved with regard to some aspects of the Mar del Plata Action Plan, far greater efforts need to be made, particularly in the African region in view of the present drought;

4. *Urges* Governments to intensify their efforts to develop their water resources, to assign high priority thereto, and to formulate or revise, as appropriate, national policies for the development and rational and environmentally sound utilization of water resources, in the context of their overall development plans, and to translate those policies into specific plans and programmes;

5. *Also urges* Governments to take steps, in the framework of national water plans and policies, to implement the recommendations contained in the Mar del Plata Action Plan concerning the assessment of water resources, for which increased efforts are urgently needed in many parts of the world;

6. *Requests* the Economic Commission for Africa to undertake a thorough review of the situation with regard to the development of water resources in the drought-stricken countries of the region, with a view to formulating short-term, medium-term and long-term frameworks for action at the national and international levels, and to report thereon to the Committee on Natural Resources at its tenth session;

7. *Invites* the international conference on hydrology which is to be convened by the World Meteorological Organization and the United Nations Educational, Scientific and Cultural Organization at Geneva in March 1987 to formulate recommendations and develop programmes designed to assist Governments in the acceleration of their efforts to attain the objectives established by the United Nations Water Conference in the area of water resource assessment;

8. *Urges* Governments to develop public information programmes designed to make planners and decision makers aware of the role of water resources in socio-economic development, and to enhance the participation of the populations concerned in the resolution of major issues related to water;

9. *Also urges* Governments to continue their efforts to formulate or revise their water legislation, in the context of national social and economic objectives, placing emphasis on the conservation of surface and ground water and the protection of water quality;

10. *Calls upon* Governments to investigate, formulate and apply measures for the development of irrigated agriculture which incorporate lower-cost solutions and accelerated returns, including the greater involvement of local populations and institutions, phased investments in a complementary mix of small and large schemes and extensive training programmes, and to draw heavily on a transfer of experience on a regional and, where appropriate, interregional scale;

11. *Appeals* to Governments to strengthen mechanisms for co-ordination among national, regional and local agencies dealing with water resources in order to improve the formulation and implementation of policies and the effective planning, development, management and utilization of water resources;

12. *Draws attention* to the risk of degradation of water and soil resources as a result of increased intensification of land use for agriculture, and stresses the need for associated conservation measures to ensure sustained production and the protection of natural resources and the environment;

13. *Reiterates* the importance of carrying out the recommendations contained in the Mar del Plata Action Plan with regard to the assessment of manpower and training needs, and of strengthening, as needed, educational and training programmes and facilities;

14. *Takes note* of the activities of the organizations of the United Nations system for the development of integrated and comprehensive approaches and programmes concerning education and training, and requests the Secretary-General, in consultation with the Administrative Committee on Co-ordination, to continue his efforts in this regard;

15. *Requests* Governments and the United Nations organizations concerned, other support agencies and

non-governmental organizations to intensify their technical and financial co-operation with developing countries, in particular the least developed countries and the drought-stricken countries of Africa, with a view to improving the assessment, development, utilization and management of water resources.

Economic and Social Council resolution 1985/49 A

25 July 1985   Meeting 52   Adopted without vote

Approved by First Committee (E/1985/148) without vote, 15 July (meeting 21); draft by Committee on Natural Resources (E/1985/27); agenda item 11.

Proposed high-level meeting

ECONOMIC AND SOCIAL COUNCIL ACTION

On 25 July, on the recommendation of its First Committee, the Economic and Social Council adopted without vote **resolution 1985/49 B**.

High-level meeting of experts on the implementation of the Mar del Plata Action Plan

The Economic and Social Council,

Mindful of the fact that 1987 represents the tenth anniversary of the adoption of the Mar del Plata Action Plan,

Bearing in mind that some specialized agencies will organize technical meetings in 1987 geared to the discussion of water-related issues stemming from the Mar del Plata Action Plan,

1. *Takes note with appreciation* of the proposal made by the Government of Argentina to sponsor a high-level meeting of experts to propose possible solutions in a number of key problem areas to facilitate the implementation of the Mar del Plata Action Plan, and requests the Secretary-General to provide the necessary assistance in the preparations for and the organization of the meeting, within existing budgetary resources;

2. *Invites* the regional commissions and the specialized agencies to co-operate with the Secretary-General in preparing for the meeting;

3. *Requests* the Secretary-General to inform the Committee on Natural Resources at its tenth session of the results of the high-level meeting.

Economic and Social Council resolution 1985/49 B

25 July 1985   Meeting 52   Adopted without vote

Approved by First Committee (E/1985/148) without vote, 15 July (meeting 21); draft by Committee on Natural Resources (E/1985/27); agenda item 11.

Education and training

Pursuant to a 1981 Economic and Social Council request,[4] the Secretary-General presented to the Committee on Natural Resources in February 1985 a report[5] on water resources education and training in developing countries. The report gave an account of the activities of three regional commissions—ECA, ESCAP and ECWA—and other international organizations regarding the establishment of regional networks for training in water resources development. ILO, for instance, was training managers, supervisors, technicians and workers on drinking water supply, while FAO organized workshops and seminars on irrigation, provided support to the International Institute for

Advanced Mediterranean Agronomic Studies (Italy), and initiated a programme for improved land and water management in Africa. UNESCO was publishing teaching guides for training technicians, sponsored an international network of postgraduate courses in hydrology, engineering and management, and assisted Governments in organizing training courses on water resources assessment and development. Training courses on related general and specialized subjects were organized also by IAEA, UNEP, WHO and WMO. A training component was also included in the World Bank's lending programme in water resources; through the Economic Development Institute, the Bank also conducted regional training courses.

In addition, the report described the efforts of the United Nations system to develop integrated programmes for education and training in water resources, including manpower surveys, on-the-job training, and a review of education and training materials.

The Economic and Social Council, in **resolution 1985/49 A**, took note of the activities related to water resources development, and requested the Secretary-General to continue his efforts, in consultation with the Administrative Committee on Co-ordination (ACC).

Inter-agency co-ordination

In a March 1985 report[6] to the Committee on Natural Resources submitted in accordance with a 1983 Economic and Social Council resolution,[7] the Secretary-General described inter-agency co-ordination in water resources development. The main inter-agency mechanism for such co-ordination at the global level was the ACC Intersecretariat Group for Water Resources, which held its annual meeting from 21 to 25 October 1985. The Group continued to monitor the progress achieved and to promote co-operation among United Nations organizations in implementation of the Mar del Plata Action Plan.

At the regional level, ECE, ESCAP and ECLAC had mechanisms for intersecretariat consultations which dealt with all aspects of the Action Plan. Annual consultations between the regional commissions and Headquarters units were held to ensure complementarity of programmes and avoid duplication. In addition to the formal global and regional mechanisms, there were numerous agreements between two or three United Nations organizations on specific aspects of water resources development and utilization.

Water resources management, policy, legislation and administration, including shared water resources and environmental aspects, involved most United Nations organizations, either from an overall point of view, as in the case of DTCD, or with regard to the sectoral aspects of water resources development, such as drinking water supply and sanitation or water for agriculture, as, for example, in the case of WHO and FAO.

The existing network of co-ordination mechanisms provided a range of possibilities for effective co-operation, the report concluded. The global and regional intersecretariat mechanisms played an important role in identifying areas where further efforts were needed, while implementation of co-operative approaches was often facilitated by formal or informal agreements between the organizations concerned.

The report considered it essential for those organizations to participate in the various inter-agency meetings; in particular, the role assigned to the regional commissions in implementing the Action Plan made it necessary for them to participate actively in the Intersecretariat Group meetings and to consult regularly with Headquarters units.

The Intersecretariat Group was initiating a review designed to bring about a better integration of approaches to water resources management, policy, legislation and administration, and particularly to the development of shared water resources. Especially needed was greater interaction among United Nations organizations in the development of both short- and long-term programmes for water resources development in Africa.

Co-ordination and co-operation were particularly important in relation to field projects, which involved both executing and funding agencies; interdisciplinary aspects had to be taken into account at the early stages of project formulation. The guidelines for joint action, agreed upon by the Intersecretariat Group, were a useful tool in ensuring that projects were executed as effectively and efficiently as possible.

By **resolution 1985/53**, the Economic and Social Council took note of the Secretary-General's report and requested him to update it for the 1987 session of the Committee on Natural Resources.

International Drinking Water Supply and Sanitation Decade

The basic principle underlying the International Drinking Water Supply and Sanitation Decade (1981-1990) was that access to safe drinking water and sanitation facilities was a human right. The effects of contaminated drinking water and poor sanitation had been well documented; it was estimated that some 15 million children under the age of five died each year in developing countries, mainly because of water-borne diseases. The same diseases exacted a heavy toll of mortality and morbidity among adults.

The Secretary-General, pursuant to the 1980 General Assembly resolution proclaiming the Decade,[8] submitted in March 1985 a report on progress made towards its goals.[9] The number of countries with plans for the Decade had grown from 9 in 1981 to 59 in 1983, and an additional 31 reported that they were preparing such plans. Some Governments strengthened institutional arrangements for Decade planning, management and co-ordination, but only limited progress was made. Shortages of trained manpower continued to be a major problem.

Proportions of national budgets allocated to drinking water supply and sanitation remained relatively stable, in the range of 1 to 6 per cent. However, some countries—Djibouti, Ethiopia, Lesotho, Malawi, Uganda, Zambia—reported proportions exceeding 10 per cent. Governments were becoming more aware of the importance of using least-cost technologies; costs might be cut by installing simpler technologies, reducing water losses in piped systems and using locally supplied or manufactured materials. New types of easily maintained water supply handpumps were being installed in rural Ghana, India, the Ivory Coast, Kenya and the United Republic of Tanzania. India and several countries in East Africa were also installing thousands of improved latrines.

Despite such progress, most of the enormous task of providing water supply and sanitation services lay ahead, the Secretary-General concluded. It was estimated that some 1.2 billion people needed safe drinking water and that some 1.9 billion did not have adequate sanitation. The Secretary-General offered recommendations to the Committee on Natural Resources for possible government and United Nations action. The United Nations might wish, for example, to focus resources on the poorest countries; give special attention to the long-term needs of African countries south of the Sahara; continue to support UNDP resident representatives as focal points for the Decade; and continue efforts to increase external assistance.

On 28 June,[10] the UNDP Governing Council approved an allocation of $319,200 for information and communication support for the Decade in 1986.

On 25 July 1985, the Economic and Social Council adopted **decision 1985/168**, taking note of the Secretary-General's report, and **decision 1985/167**, transmitting a draft resolution on the Decade, which originated in the Committee on Natural Resources, to the General Assembly (see below).

In the Council's First Committee, the Netherlands introduced and then withdrew a draft resolution,[11] by which the Council would have welcomed the Secretary-General's recommendations and conclusions, and recommended that the Assembly take into account proposals to enhance the effectiveness of activities at the country level, i.e., that Governments ensure that safe drinking water supply and sanitation systems were brought to the poorest urban and rural populations and were properly maintained; ensure that equitable cost-recovery policies were implemented; organize consultative meetings or other co-ordinating processes with major donor agencies; and review plans and develop mechanisms to increase collaboration with non-governmental organizations (NGOs) in planning and implementing Decade activities.

After adoption of decision 1985/167, the Netherlands stated its regret that the Council had been unable to hold a substantive discussion on its text; it hoped that the Assembly would be able to adopt a resolution that took the expressions of support for the Netherlands proposals fully into account and did justice to efforts made to strengthen implementation of the goals of the Decade.

GENERAL ASSEMBLY ACTION

On 17 December, on the recommendation of the Second (Economic and Financial) Committee, the General Assembly adopted without vote **resolution 40/171**.

International Drinking Water Supply and Sanitation Decade

The General Assembly,

Recalling its resolution 32/158 of 19 December 1977, in which it approved the Mar del Plata Action Plan adopted by the United Nations Water Conference,

Recalling also its resolution 35/18 of 10 November 1980, by which it proclaimed the period 1981-1990 as the International Drinking Water Supply and Sanitation Decade,

Recalling further Economic and Social Council resolution 1983/57 of 28 July 1983, in which the Council urged Governments of developing countries to adopt national targets for drinking water supply and sanitation services, commensurate with resource availability, absorptive capacity and ability, and to formulate action plans and programmes for reaching the targets set,

Mindful of the fact that significant progress towards meeting the objectives of the Decade by 1990 will require a much greater sense of urgency and priority on the part of Governments and the continued support of the international community,

1. *Welcomes* the recommendations and conclusions contained in the report of the Secretary-General on progress in the attainment of the goals of the International Drinking Water Supply and Sanitation Decade;

2. *Encourages* Governments to seek to implement the recommendations for action contained in the report, in particular:

(*a*) To strengthen national capabilities for policy formulation and for the preparation, implementation and monitoring of water supply and sanitation programmes and projects;

(*b*) To prepare and implement national strategies to meet and develop both present and longer-term needs for skilled human resources;

(*c*) To intensify efforts to improve the mobilization and utilization of national financial resources;

(*d*) To increase the attention devoted to health education and community participation and to the need for close operational linkages between health and water supply agencies;

(*e*) To formulate and implement strategies that will enhance the participation of women in the planning, operation and assessment of water and sanitation programmes and projects;

3. *Calls upon* organs, organizations and bodies of the United Nations system, as well as other multilateral, bilateral and non-governmental organizations, to continue and, where possible, increase their assistance to Governments in support of national plans and programmes for the Decade as well as in support of efforts to implement the above-mentioned recommendations for action;

4. *Urges* the international community to take note of the need to enhance co-ordination of technical co-operation activities at the global and national levels and, in this regard, supports the role of the resident representatives of the United Nations Development Programme as focal points for the Decade at the country level;

5. *Takes note* of the need to focus efforts and resources on the least developed countries where requirements for drinking water and sanitation are the greatest, and of the need to give special consideration to the countries of sub-Saharan Africa;

6. *Requests* the Secretary-General, at the end of the Decade, in 1990, to prepare a report on the progress achieved during the Decade, providing a detailed comparative analysis based as much as possible on quantitative data, as well as recommendations for future and follow-up action that may be required, for submission to the General Assembly at its forty-fifth session.

General Assembly resolution 40/171

17 December 1985   Meeting 119   Adopted without vote

Approved by Second Committee (A/40/1009/Add.1) without vote, 25 November (meeting 43); draft transmitted by Economic and Social Council decision 1985/167 (A/C.2/40/L.5); agenda item 12.

In the Committee, the Netherlands expressed disappointment at the rather limited willingness to consider some amendments to the draft resolution which had been submitted in the Economic and Social Council; the Netherlands intended to resubmit those amendments to the next session of the Committee on Natural Resources.

Marine resources

Following up on a 1984 report,[12] the Secretary-General transmitted to CPC in February 1985 a joint report by the International Maritime Organization (IMO) and UNCTAD[13] outlining consultations between the two organizations on future arrangements for co-operation in marine affairs. They reported having reached agreement on a method of dealing with maritime liens and mortgages which would avoid duplication of work and facilitate co-operation; the agreement was appended to the report. In addition, their secretariats were considering arrangements for assisting developing countries in maritime transport and for involving the regional commissions in those arrangements.

Taking note of the information provided,[14] CPC recommended that IMO and UNCTAD should continue to strengthen co-ordination and co-operation to avoid overlapping and duplication of work.

The Secretary-General, in response to a 1983 Economic and Social Council resolution,[15] submitted in June 1985 a report[16] on economic and technical trends and developments in marine affairs, covering the development of marine resources (living, mineral and energy) and of economic infrastructure (marine industries and technologies, communications, transport and offshore structures); marine research; protection of the marine environment; support activities and services (meteorology, safety and labour); and regional trends. The first phase of a conference on economic, scientific and technical co-operation in the Indian Ocean in marine affairs was held (Colombo, Sri Lanka, 15-20 July 1985); the second phase was scheduled for 1987.

ECONOMIC AND SOCIAL COUNCIL ACTION

On 26 July 1985, on the recommendation of its Third (Programme and Co-ordination) Committee, the Economic and Social Council adopted **resolution 1985/75** by vote.

Economic and technical aspects of marine affairs

The Economic and Social Council,

Recalling its resolutions 1980/68 of 25 July 1980 on co-operation in the uses of the sea and coastal area development and 1983/48 of 28 July 1983 on marine affairs, in response to which the Secretary-General has submitted to the Council, at its second regular session of 1985, a report on economic and technical trends and developments in marine affairs,

Convinced that the resources of the ocean represent an important existing and potential contribution to the development process,

Noting that an increasing number of Member States, especially developing countries, have embarked on activities designed to make full, rational use of the resources of the ocean, in particular in their exclusive economic zones,

Noting also that, in accordance with the programme on economic and technical aspects of marine affairs contained in chapter 25 of the medium-term plan for the period 1984-1989, the Secretary-General has directed his efforts specifically towards assisting Member States in developing and managing ocean resources in their exclusive economic zones,

1. *Endorses* the efforts of the Secretary-General to make the programme on economic and technical aspects of marine affairs responsive to the growing needs of Member States;

2. *Takes note* of the report of the Secretary-General on economic and technical trends and developments in marine affairs;

3. *Requests* the Secretary-General to pursue, in close co-operation with all the competent organizations of the United Nations system, activities relating to the economic and technical aspects of marine affairs, and to report on new developments in this area to the

Economic and Social Council at its second regular session of 1989;

4. *Further requests* the Secretary-General, within the mandate and terms of reference of the United Nations regarding the economic and technical aspects of marine affairs, to submit to the Council at its second regular session of 1987 a report identifying specific and practical needs and problems encountered by countries, in particular developing countries, in the management of their exclusive economic zones and the development of resources therein, as well as the types of activities and approaches to their implementation required for countries, with the support of the United Nations, to respond most effectively to those needs and problems, and to transmit to the General Assembly at its forty-second session the conclusions and recommendations of the Council.

Economic and Social Council resolution 1985/75

26 July 1985   Meeting 52   43-0-4

Approved by Third Committee (E/1985/141) without vote, 19 July (meeting 20); 14-nation draft (E/1985/C.3/L.5), orally revised; agenda item 19.

Sponsors: Algeria, Botswana, Canada, Colombia, France, Ghana, Liberia, Madagascar, Morocco, Netherlands, Sri Lanka, United Republic of Tanzania, Yugoslavia, Zimbabwe.

The Council, by 13 votes to 9, with 16 abstentions, rejected an amendment[17] to paragraph 4 by the USSR, by which the words "in accordance with the provisions of the United Nations Convention on the Law of the Sea" would have been inserted after "in the management of their exclusive economic zones and the development of resources therein". The USSR explained that the purpose of the amendment was to ensure that, in preparing the requested report, the Secretary-General would be guided by the Convention's provisions; the addition was in keeping with previous Council resolutions. In the Committee, the USSR expressed regret that the sponsors insisted on immediate action on the draft, thus preventing some Council members from participating in the formulation of the text and its adoption by consensus.

Speaking on behalf of the sponsors, Madagascar stated that the Convention had been ratified by only about 20 States and no one could say when it would enter into force; the sponsors had sought to request that technical assistance be provided to developing countries without delay to help them introduce the dimension of the resources of the sea into their development. Finland, which abstained on the text, declared that the amendment did not create any difficulty for it from the standpoint of substance. Colombia associated itself with Finland's position.

Living marine resources

Public concern about the threatened status of many marine mammals had provided the impetus for positive action, the UNEP Executive Director declared in his annual report for 1985.[18] Under a joint FAO/UNEP Global Plan of Action for the Conservation, Management and Utilization of

Marine Mammals, endorsed by the FAO Committee on Fisheries in 1983 and by the UNEP Governing Council in 1984,[12] nine projects were approved by UNEP during 1985; they covered seals, dolphins and sea-cows, as well as public awareness activities. Two consultative meetings on the Plan of Action were held in 1985 (Geneva, 7 and 8 March; Gland, Switzerland, 28-30 October); the United Nations agencies, intergovernmental organizations and NGOs participating in the meetings agreed to co-ordinate their activities to implement the Plan.

REFERENCES

[1]YUN 1979, p. 684, GA res. 34/191, 18 Dec. 1979. [2]E/C.7/1985/5. [3]YUN 1977, p. 555. [4]YUN 1981, p. 681, ESC res. 1981/80, 24 July 1981. [5]E/C.7/1985/6. [6]E/C.7/1985/10. [7]YUN 1983, p. 664, ESC res. 1983/59, 28 July 1983. [8]YUN 1980, p. 712, GA res. 35/18, 10 Nov. 1980. [9]A/40/108-E/1985/49. [10]E/1985/32 (dec. 85/8). [11]E/1985/C.1/L.6. [12]YUN 1984, p. 650. [13]E/AC.51/1985/3 & Add.1. [14]A/40/38. [15]YUN 1983, p. 669, ESC res. 1983/48, 28 July 1983. [16]E/1985/79. [17]E/1985/L.54. [18]UNEP/GC.14/2.

PUBLICATIONS

Proceedings of the Tenth Session of the Committee on Natural Resources, Water Resources Series No. 59 (ST/ESCAP/SER.F/59), Sales No. E.85.II.F.14. *Water as a Factor in Energy Resources Development,* Water Resources Series No. 60 (ST/ESCAP/SER.F/60), Sales No. E.85.II.F.7. *Consolidated Catalogue of Publications on Water Resources in Print from 1971 to 1985* (ST/ESA/182), Sales No. E/F/S.87.II.A.7.

Cartography

Third UN Regional Cartographic Conference for the Americas

The Third United Nations Regional Cartographic Conference for the Americas was held in New York from 19 February to 1 March 1985. It was attended by 126 representatives or observers from 45 countries, the Economic Commission for Latin America and the Caribbean, three specialized agencies, six intergovernmental and international scientific organizations and the Palestine Liberation Organization (for participating States and officers, see APPENDIX III). The Secretary-General submitted his report on the Conference to the Economic and Social Council in April.[1]

The Conference reviewed the latest technology and its relationship to policy, economy and development in the following areas: cartographic data acquisition, manipulation and depiction, and policies and management of national mapping and charting programmes. Four technical committees were established to consider those questions. The Conference also considered matters of technical assistance and transfer of technology in cartography, and the suitability and feasibility of holding United Nations interregional cartographic conferences.

The Conference adopted 19 resolutions. It recognized, in particular, the importance of the regional cartographic conference, the general desire to increase its effectiveness, and the need to involve countries of the region in preparing its agenda. The Conference noted the increasing importance of systematic management and presentation of geographic information and the role of the United Nations Secretariat in that matter. It recognized further potential applications of satellite remote sensing and digital mapping technologies, as well as of land information systems, and a need for extended financial, advisory and training assistance in those areas. The establishment or strengthening of capabilities of national authorities dealing with hydrographic and nautical charting and geographical names was recommended. Slow progress in the production of revised sheets of the International Map of the World on the Millionth Scale was noted; it was recommended that a United Nations study on the question be undertaken. In addition, the Conference recommended that every effort be made by Member States to expedite the revision of national map coverages. It recognized the urgent need to generate thematic mapping and recommended that training be organized to inform high-level personnel of possibilities of mapping for planning and management.

On 28 May, the Economic and Social Council, in **decision 1985/124,** approved the Conference's recommendation to convene a fourth regional conference for the Americas in 1989 and requested the Secretary-General to take measures, where appropriate, to implement its other recommendations. In **decision 1985/125,** also of 28 May, the Council took note of the Secretary-General's report on the Conference.

The Secretary-General, in an addendum to his report,[2] estimated that, should the Council decide to convene a fourth conference, servicing costs would total $270,800.

Both decisions were approved by the Council's First Committee on 22 May. In Committee, the draft that became **decision 1985/124** was orally amended by the USSR to the effect that implementation of the Conference recommendations would take fully into account the views expressed in the Council.

REFERENCES

[1]E/1985/38. [2]E/1985/38/Add.1.

PUBLICATIONS

Third United Nations Regional Cartographic Conference for the Americas, vol. I: Report of the Conference (E/CONF.77/3), Sales No. E.85.I.14. *World Cartography,* vol. XVIII (ST/ESA/SER.L/18), Sales No. E.85.I.23.

Chapter X

Energy resources

During 1985, a number of United Nations bodies continued to focus attention on the energy problems of developing countries, whose ability to carry out energy programmes was hampered by financial constraint as well as by the complexities of energy planning, by rapidly changing technology and by environmental factors.

The United Nations Development Programme (UNDP) and the World Bank co-operated in energy development projects and an assessment of energy options. Since 1981, the UNDP Energy Account had allocated $20.3 million to about 50 energy projects; $1.9 million had been earmarked by the end of 1985 for new projects. The United Nations University (UNU) carried out research on specific energy problems and designed energy-related training programmes and curricula. Activities encouraging the transfer of energy technology to developing countries, the dissemination of technical know-how and the training of skilled manpower were continued by the United Nations Conference on Trade and Development (UNCTAD) and the Secretariat's Department of Technical Co-operation for Development (DTCD). The General Assembly, in resolution 40/184, noted progress in negotiations for an international code of conduct on the transfer of technology, although there were still important problems outstanding (see Chapter XII of this section).

By resolution 40/208, the Assembly called on Member States, in co-operation with the United Nations system, to examine ways to support developing countries' efforts to develop their energy resources, and requested the Secretary-General to continue to undertake studies and analyses of trends in energy exploration and development.

After considering the report of the International Atomic Energy Agency (IAEA), the Assembly adopted resolution 40/8, affirming its confidence in IAEA's role in applying nuclear energy for peaceful purposes and urging States to co-operate in carrying out its work, which included the promotion of nuclear safety. The Assembly noted that the Preparatory Committee for the United Nations Conference for the Promotion of International Co-operation in the Peaceful Uses of Nuclear Energy had decided that the Conference should be held at Geneva in March/April 1987, rather than in 1986 (resolution 40/95).

Topics related to this chapter. Disarmament: nuclear weapons. Peaceful uses of outer space. Regional economic and social activities: energy resources—Africa; Asia and the Pacific; Europe; Latin America; Western Asia. Statistics: energy statistics.

General aspects

The Secretary-General submitted to the Committee on Natural Resources in March 1985 a report[1] dealing with trends and salient issues in the development of energy resources. He stated that since the early 1980s energy prices and interest rates had tended to dampen investment in energy development. Prices had been generally weak, as demand fell. Energy consumption in the market economy area, after peaking in 1979 at 87.2 million barrels of oil per day equivalent, had declined steadily until 1983, when it reached a level of 80.3 million barrels. From 1979 to 1984, long-term interest rates averaged about 11 per cent, compared to an average of about 8 per cent over the preceding five years. The rise of nearly 40 per cent in rates had had a deleterious effect on investment and on energy resource development.

In market economy countries, coal development had been slowed by excess production capacity. The slow rate of growth in coal demand meant that their coal reserves could last at least another 225 years. In the centrally planned economies, lignite development had become very important. From a developmental viewpoint, a great deal would depend on the exploitation of the solid fuel resources of the USSR, particularly lignite deposits in the Kazakhstan region and the deposits of solid fuels in Siberia.

Nuclear power capacity had been found to exceed estimated market-economy electricity demand, resulting in cancellation of orders and a stretch-out of construction schedules. About one third of world-wide nuclear power capacity currently existed in the United States, but there had been no new orders for reactors in that country since 1978; moreover, 75 reactors had been cancelled since that year, including 28 already under construction. Sweden had chosen to phase out nuclear power by 2010, while moratoria existed in several other western European countries. On the other hand, nuclear power capacity in the centrally planned economies had grown rapidly (see p. 693).

Some issues that arose during energy resource development, such as domestic energy pricing policy, rural electrification and most environmental constraints, were amenable to national solutions. Others—technology transfer and augmenting the flow of external capital to developing countries—called for an international approach. A problem which had recently become more acute in market economy countries was excess production capacity in the "downstream" phase (crude oil distillation and subsequent cracking processes) of petroleum production. The problem had become of greater interest with the opening of large new refining facilities in the developing world, a situation that might stimulate protectionist sentiments. Over the period 1984-1986, three new refineries were to come on stream in Saudi Arabia and one in the Libyan Arab Jamahiriya. Later, other developing countries were expected to join the ranks of those exporting petroleum products.

Certain possibilities of resolving the issues were discerned. At the national level, renewed attention needed to be given to energy pricing so as to provide incentives to resource development. For countries developing their energy resources with the aid of foreign direct investment, policies that generated detailed national geologic data and a legal structure that defined foreign participation in resource development were advantageous. All countries could usefully pursue policies of energy conservation, and joint development of shared energy resources should not be overlooked. Finally, bilateral and multilateral assistance to developing countries in energy resource development needed to be expanded.

Energy resources development

Reports of the Secretary-General. The Secretary-General presented reports to the General Assembly in August[2] and September[3] on the development of energy resources in developing countries.

Pursuant to Assembly resolutions of 1982,[4] 1983[5] and 1984,[6] the August report discussed prospects for the development of energy resources, constraints on their development, and the role of different national and international policies. Energy sources were considered in terms of their estimated availability. For example, with regard to oil and natural gas deposits, of the 600 sedimentary basins thought to represent the prospective areas for hydrocarbons in the world, excluding deep offshore basins, 160 had been fairly intensively explored and were currently producing oil and gas, 240 had been partially explored and were not producing, and 200 remained essentially unexplored. Of the total prospective area, 47 per cent was located in developing countries. Further, it was estimated that in developing countries not members of the Organization of Petroleum Exporting Countries (OPEC),

more than 40 per cent of the prospective area was located in 55 countries where only initial or fragmentary exploration had taken place.

Of the estimated 2,670 billion barrels of ultimately recoverable oil resources of the world, 1,583 billion barrels, or 59 per cent, were located in developing countries, and of the 672 billion barrels of proved recoverable resources of the world, 78 per cent were located in those countries.

Total commercial energy consumption was expected to increase from 16.8 million barrels of oil per day equivalent in 1980 to 53 million in the year 2000, at an average annual rate of 5.9 per cent. To bring about production increases, it had been projected that an average annual investment of $92 billion (1982 values) was required. Of that sum, $78 billion would have to be invested by domestic enterprises and $14 billion by foreign companies. It was believed that foreign energy companies would be able to arrange the required financing of $14 billion annually and that domestic enterprises could mobilize $51 billion annually, leaving an annual shortfall of $27 billion. But that figure should be used only as a crude indication of the magnitude of the financing gap.

Significantly larger financial resources needed to be mobilized by developing countries for energy development. One very important instrument was price policy. In countries where domestic energy prices could be raised, the higher prices could be used to generate surpluses for investment. However, raising energy prices had political and social implications; in those cases, the increases could perhaps be done through a series of systematic adjustments over a period of time. Credit policy could be deployed not so much for increasing as for channelling capital. Institutions could be established within the credit framework of the country in order to finance small energy projects, as had been done in Mexico and Brazil, where institutions had been established to provide credit and technical assistance to small-scale mining.

Given the limitations of some of the existing multilateral financial institutions, new arrangements could be explored. The establishment of an energy affiliate of the World Bank had been suggested—a legal entity separate from the World Bank but linked administratively to it, with an initial capitalization of $10 billion to $15 billion.

Developing countries, meanwhile, faced other constraints which reduced their capacity to implement energy programmes. Energy planning and management were complex because the resource base was uncertain, the technology was often new, rapidly changing and risky to adopt, investments were highly discontinuous and costly with long gestation periods, energy demand was difficult to project, and environmental considerations needed to be incorporated into the programmes.

The September report[3] responded to a 1984 Assembly resolution[6] asking for a report on developing countries' efforts to develop energy resources, which included in 1985 a symposium on financing petroleum exploration and development in developing countries (Athens, Greece, 22-26 April). The report said that active discussion of an energy affiliate of the World Bank seemed to have waned and that there had been little progress in achieving a consensus on the need for new institutional arrangements to channel financial resources to the developing countries for energy resource development. The symposium had been attended by 180 participants from 63 countries and 15 United Nations bodies and international organizations. Among the subjects taken up were oil consumption and potential, exploration strategies, cost of exploration and production, financing requirements and methods, exploration and development agreements, financial and technical assistance, and co-operation among developing countries.

UNDP action. The energy sector assessment programme, introduced by UNDP and the World Bank in 1980, had assisted 70 developing countries faced with high fuel costs and heavy debt-service requirements to develop their energy options, the UNDP Administrator stated in his 1985 report on project results.[7] With substantial support from donor countries, the programme had helped decision-makers to frame coherent overviews of the energy sector, focus on key policy and investment decisions, and establish priorities. All scheduled assessments were expected to be completed at the end of 1986. Field work had been concluded in 61 of the 70 countries receiving assistance, and 50 final reports had been issued; slightly more than half the countries covered were in sub-Saharan Africa. The assessments had had substantial impact in three major areas: energy policy and strategy, institutional improvements, and key energy issues.

Significant policy changes had been promoted by choices identified through energy assessments. Examples included: the rationalization of petroleum and electricity prices in Sri Lanka; the creation of a more orderly financing mechanism for petroleum imports in the Sudan; the reduction of import duties on coal to encourage fuel-oil substitution in Kenya; major increases in the price of kerosene to remove cross-subsidies in Indonesia; and the lowering of disproportionately high gasoline taxation in Thailand to forestall an uneconomic shift to diesel in the transport sector. The assessments had also aided Governments to reorient energy-sector strategies by identifying new investment options, such as the greater use of geothermal energy in Saint Lucia and natural gas in the Syrian Arab Republic.

Institutional, managerial, training and staffing arrangements in several countries had been strengthened in the light of energy assessment recommendations. Better co-ordinated decision-making had been achieved through more coherent energy planning. In Indonesia, an interministerial energy commission had been established, while in Malawi an energy planning unit had been organized. In Burundi and Rwanda, emphasis had been laid on individual subsectoral strategies as a basis for overall sectoral planning, and Thailand's energy assessment report had been featured as a background document at an energy planning conference in October 1985.

In many countries, critical problems, such as the low efficiency of energy-producing and -consuming facilities, had been identified and measures taken to resolve them. High economic returns and foreign exchange savings were possible through conservation measures and modest investment in the rehabilitation and maintenance of existing facilities. That was particularly true of electric power generation, where the benefits that accrued from reduced power system losses far outweighed the required investments. In Bangladesh, for example, a $50 million investment in six projects to promote energy efficiency was expected to yield economic benefits of $36 million a year.

The UNDP/World Bank Energy Sector Management Assistance Programme (ESMAP), initiated in 1983,[8] helped developing and donor countries to implement recommendations contained in individual energy assessment reports. ESMAP had established itself as a follow-up vehicle for accelerating the preparation and implementation of priority technical assistance and investment projects. By 1985, 54 such projects in 27 developing countries had been evaluated or were under preparation, the total cost of which was expected to be about $500 million; $250 million in financing had either been committed or was being reviewed by multilateral and bilateral agencies. ESMAP had already aided Sri Lanka to define steps for achieving more efficient and reliable electric power generation; Uganda to begin a feasibility study for an integrated fuelwood/forestry project; Mauritius to develop a comprehensive, least-cost energy programme based on surplus bagasse; and the Sudan to prepare an action plan for solar water-heating technology. Assistance was also provided to the least developed countries (LDCs) in preparing energy-related documentation and proposals for their UNDP-sponsored round-table consultations and for World Bank–supported consultative group meetings.

The UNDP Energy Account, established in 1980,[9] continued to play a catalytic role in attracting the participation of bilateral and multilateral partners in energy activities in developing countries. The Administrator reported[10] that the Djibouti geothermal exploration and development project, initiated by the Energy Account with a $1 million contribution, resulted in the mobilization of an additional $15.5 million from the World Bank, the African Development Bank, the OPEC Fund for International Development, and Italy. A small-scale hydropower project in the Dominican Republic, also started up by the Energy Account with $65,000, had led to the mobilization of $435,000 from a donor institution and the equivalent of $2 million from local resources.

The total resources made available by donors to the Energy Account since 1981, including estimated income for 1986 and future years, amounted to $22.2 million, the UNDP Administrator reported in an April 1986 overview report of Energy Account activities.[11] Of the total available resources, $20.3 million had been allocated to about 50 energy projects by the end of 1985, and the balance of $1.9 million earmarked to new projects to be undertaken shortly. Activities covered such areas as energy assessment and planning, energy management and conservation, development of specific sources of new and renewable energies, training and information flows.

The UNDP Governing Council, in a 29 June decision,[12] authorized the Administrator to continue the Energy Account as long as it received adequate donor support, and called on Governments in a position to do so to increase their contributions. It noted the progress achieved in assisting the countries of the South Pacific through the Regional Energy Development Programme, including financing of the services of energy planners from the Energy Account, and requested the Administrator to continue supporting the priority energy requirements of the Pacific and other regions. The Council also requested him to report in 1986 on the results of activities financed by the Energy Account, particularly the extent to which it helped to mobilize additional funds to implement the 1981 Nairobi Programme of Action for the Development and Utilization of New and Renewable Sources of Energy (see p. 691).

UNDP ENERGY ACCOUNT PROJECT EXPENDITURES, 1985

(in thousands of US dollars)

Country/region	Amount
Barbados	75
Colombia	225
Djibouti	209
Honduras	(2)
Jamaica	13
Morocco	38
Niger	28
Solomon Islands	42
Tonga	30
Viet Nam	95
Zambia	143
Subtotal	896
Latin America and the Caribbean	82
Global and interregional	3,353
Subtotal	3,435
Total	4,331

SOURCE: DP/1986/11Add.6

CONTRIBUTIONS TO THE UNDP ENERGY ACCOUNT, 1985 AND 1986

(as at 31 December 1985; in US dollar equivalent)

Source	1985 payment	1986 pledge
Austria	—	56,497
Belgium	—	75,000
Colombia	125,300	—
Denmark	90,909	109,890
European Economic Community	—	270,193
Iceland	40,000	—
Italy	—	420,000
Netherlands	455,329	187,500
Norway	117,500	—
OPEC Fund	—	1,449,613*
Sweden	63,694	—
Switzerland	456,621	478,469
Other income	420,805	—
Total	1,770,158	3,047,162

*Represented the balance due against signed project documents. There remained a balance of $3,525,112 from the OPEC Fund's pledge of $6 million to the Energy Account.

SOURCE: DP/1986/54.

UNU activities. The need for affordable, appropriate sources of energy was addressed by the Council of the United Nations University[13] within its programme area on energy systems and policy. The first phase of an energy planning and management project concentrated research on specific problems in developing countries and on developing curricula and training programmes in energy planning and modelling. Work was carried out by institutions in Argentina, Brazil, Chile (with the support of a Canadian institute), France, India and European centres sponsored by the European Economic Community (EEC). A workshop was held at the UNU centre in Tokyo in April 1985 to present the results of the first phase, which stressed the need for management of demand rather than optimization of energy production.

The Integrated Rural Energy Systems Association undertook a series of small-scale projects to promote the development and testing of new energy technologies and monitoring systems and a handbook on integrated rural energy systems. A solar water-purification technique, a wind desalination unit, fuel briquettes made from agricultural waste, and fuelwood-efficient stoves were being developed or tested.

The UNU Energy Research Group, which was assisted by the International Development Research Centre in Canada, ended its work in 1985. Of the papers commissioned by the Group, 103 had been completed and would be used as input to a synthesis report of the Group. As at December 1985, 11 fellows and one special fellow had completed training and 27 fellows were in training. The Abstracts of Selected Solar Energy Technology network published its monthly journal *ASSET* in 1985.

On 17 December, on the recommendation of the Second (Economic and Financial) Committee, the General Assembly adopted without vote **resolution 40/208**.

Development of the energy resources of developing countries

The General Assembly,

Recalling the Declaration and the Programme of Action on the Establishment of a New International Economic Order contained in its resolutions 3201(S-VI) and 3202(S-VI) of 1 May 1974, the Charter of Economic Rights and Duties of States, contained in its resolution 3281(XXIX) of 12 December 1974, its resolution 3362(S-VII) of 16 September 1975 on development and international economic co-operation, and the International Development Strategy for the Third United Nations Development Decade contained in the annex to its resolution 35/56 of 5 December 1980,

Recalling also its resolutions 37/251 of 21 December 1982, 38/151 of 19 December 1983 and 39/176 of 17 December 1984 on the development of the energy resources of developing countries,

Reaffirming the importance of the development of the energy resources of developing countries and the need for measures by the international community to assist and support the efforts of the developing countries, in particular the energy-deficient among them, for developing their energy resources, in order to meet their needs through co-operation, assistance and investment in the field of conventional and of new and renewable sources of energy, consistent with their national plans and priorities,

1. _Reaffirms_ its resolutions 38/151 and 39/176 and calls for the effective implementation of all their provisions;

2. _Takes note_ of the reports of the Secretary-General on the development of the energy resources of developing countries;

3. _Welcomes_ the convening of symposia and other similar undertakings called for in resolutions 38/151 and 39/176 and calls upon interested Member States, in co-operation with the appropriate organs, organizations and bodies of the United Nations system, to continue to explore ways and means to support the efforts of developing countries in the exploration and development of their energy resources;

4. _Requests_ the Secretary-General to continue to undertake appropriate studies and analyses of trends in energy exploration and development, taking into account the activities of relevant organizations of the United Nations system in this field, including the results of the joint United Nations Development Programme/World Bank energy sector assessment programme and the suggestions resulting from the symposia held, as called for in resolutions 38/151 and 39/176, and to report to the General Assembly at its forty-first session, through the Economic and Social Council at its second regular session of 1986.

General Assembly resolution 40/208

17 December 1985   Meeting 119   Adopted without vote

Approved by Second Committee (A/40/989/Add.13) without vote, 4 December (meeting 47); draft by Vice-Chairman (A/C.2/40/L.100), based on informal consultations on draft by Yugoslavia, for Group of 77 (A/C.2/40/L.80); agenda item 84 (o).

Meeting numbers. GA 40th session: 2nd Committee 45, 47; plenary 119.

The Assembly, in **resolution 40/205**, endorsed the conclusion that the natural resources and energy targets of the Substantial New Programme of Action for the 1980s for LDCs[14] remained valid, although they had not yet been achieved (see Chapter I of this section). The energy deficit experienced by most LDCs often led to their balances of payments being heavily mortgaged, as well as to destructive environmental consequences. Most LDCs lacked the means to assess and plan their energy resources in a sufficiently comprehensive manner, thus impeding their rational exploitation. LDCs were called on to include energy conservation measures in their energy development plans and to assess the consumption pattern of energy sources, including fuelwood, and its impact on the environment. Donor countries were asked to assist LDCs in planning and implementing those measures and to support steps to ensure energy supply and conservation, particularly through the development of renewable sources of energy and reforestation.

Technology transfer

The Secretary-General, in his March report on trends and salient issues in the development of energy resources,[1] stated that the acceleration of technology transfer from developed to developing countries was a perennial United Nations concern. Energy resource development offered many well-developed channels for the transfer of know-how. In current practice, contracts governing large energy projects to be designed and constructed by foreign firms contained detailed provisions relating to the training of local nationals in the operation of the facilities constructed. A number of such projects, in fact, were joint ventures between developed and developing countries that provided for joint financing, management, and interest in the disposition of the products produced. Scientific co-operation among developing countries had also evolved over the past decade or so, and offered the prospect of even wider dissemination of technical knowledge.

As for policy prescription, there was no cut-and-dried solution to the technology transfer question. Guidelines had been laid down at a 1982 meeting of governmental experts on technology transfer in energy,[15] convened by UNCTAD.

A Meeting of Governmental Experts on Co-operative Exchange of Skills among Developing Countries (Geneva, 6-15 February 1985) considered ways of systematically promoting such exchange of skills as an instrument for promoting economic co-operation and general development. Reaffirming the important role of technical co-operation among developing countries, it recommended that the UNCTAD Secretary-General undertake an in-depth study on a broad geographical basis on the role of technical co-operation and exchange of skills, assessing their current contribution in the technological transformation of developing countries and proposing measures for the transfer of technology.

The sixth session of the United Nations Conference on an International Code of Conduct on the Transfer of Technology was convened at Geneva in May/June (see Chapter XII of this section). In December, the General Assembly adopted **resolution 40/184** inviting consultations to identify solutions to outstanding issues in the code.

UNCTAD activities. Three reports on energy technology issues in developing countries were prepared by the UNCTAD secretariat during 1985 as follow-up to the recommendations of the 1982 Meeting of Governmental Experts on the Transfer, Application and Development of Technology in the Energy Sector[15] and in response to a 1983 General Assembly request.[5]

One report[16] discussed biomass-ethanol technology in relation to developing countries, new developments in that market, and the role of the public sector; in addition, it presented case-studies of biomass programmes in Brazil and the United States. It concluded that for a country where feedstock costs were relatively low, where there was an excess of food production and where a technology chosen was not too capital-intensive, it was likely that the production of ethanol would have a positive influence on the balance of payments. The technology itself was in a tremendous state of flux. Research and development efforts were resulting in advanced biomass-to-ethanol conversion technologies with much higher overall efficiencies, although they were more capital-intensive and automated than conventional processes and not necessarily best suited to developing countries. Thus, the advanced-technology ethanol plants would probably remain in the highly industrialized countries in the foreseeable future.

Power alcohol programmes in Kenya and Zimbabwe were reviewed in another report.[17] The historical background, feedstock, technical aspects, economics and investment strategy were considered in each case. Based on the experience of the two countries, it was concluded that alcohol fuel production could be attractive in certain situations but that decisions to proceed were highly case-specific. Strategies called for to enhance the technology's viability included: further research and development, based on constraints commonly encountered in developing countries, to increase feedstock yields and plant efficiency and reduce energy and chemical requirements; the establishment of "honest brokers" to evaluate the technical choices available and advise countries of their

technological capabilities; the development of cohesive government energy policies; and the provision of untied multilateral or bilateral finance.

Technology "unpackaging" (disaggregation of an investment project with a view to undertaking some activities using domestic enterprises) in the Republic of Korea was considered in a report on that country's experience in the power-plant sector—the development of the sector, procurement and indigenization policy, and the domestic technological capacity for plant engineering and manufacture of plant equipment.[18] Concluding that the country's policy in that sector had been successful, the report observed that the policy had been devised as part of the country's much broader industrial development strategy, and that the institutional arrangements created by the Government for policy formulation and implementation had brought together in a co-operative effort the main agents on both the demand and the supply side of power projects.

The conclusions of a 1983 meeting[19] of the Expert Group on Energy Co-operation among Economic Co-operation and Integration Organizations were approved by the Working Party on Trade Expansion and Regional Economic Integration among Developing Countries (third session, Geneva, 28 January–1 February). The Working Party requested that the Expert Group's report[20] be issued and circulated to all economic co-operation and integration groupings, specialized energy organizations and research institutions for their comments.

DTCD activities. Energy-related technical co-operation provided by the Department of Technical Co-operation for Development was concentrated in three main areas: conventional energy, electric power, and new and renewable energy. During 1985, 142 energy projects were under execution, with $18.1 million expended against $24.7 million budgeted for the sector, according to a 1986 report of the Secretary-General[21] to the UNDP Governing Council.

Despite a decline in the price of imported energy, interest in the production and management of domestic energy supplies continued to be strong in developing countries. A user-friendly microcomputer software package was developed by DTCD for energy planners. Called ENERPLAN, the software assisted in national energy planning by preparing national energy balances, simulating various energy supply and demand scenarios, and preparing hypothetical energy balances on the basis of selected parameters. Draft versions of the programme were tested in Thailand and Costa Rica.

Coal and oil projects continued. In Romania, assistance was given in enhanced oil recovery, reservoir engineering and simulation techniques to further a Black Sea drilling programme. Similar assistance was provided to China and India.

Development of new and renewable sources also continued. Geothermal energy projects were carried out in 10 countries and work in solar, wind and biogas energy, as well as in energy conservation and rural energy supply, in 12 countries. A programme to survey small hydropower sources progressed, with 11 countries identified for coverage in 1986 and 1987; the survey was to be followed by a second phase, during which feasibility and design studies would be implemented in 12 countries. DTCD also provided development assistance to the Energy Secretariat of the Southern African Development Coordination Conference. In Pakistan, feasibility studies were planned in a project to harness sophisticated technology to resources development.

Electricity supply projects focused on the introduction of computerized utility management, application of new technologies in thermal power-plant fuel cycles and use of computerized training simulators. A thermal power-plant operator training centre continued in China. A training simulator in India facilitated the study of the management of high-voltage electric power systems. A data base for the planning of the Egyptian electricity supply system was strengthened through provision of a computer centre. Two interregional studies on the use of solid fuels for power generation went ahead, one examining energy sources and the other the handling and disposal of ash. DTCD also helped to establish centres to test power-plant components in Bhutan and Iran.

ECONOMIC AND SOCIAL COUNCIL ACTION

The Economic and Social Council, in **resolution 1985/50**, noted the progress made in applying computer technology to the assessment and development of energy resources in developing countries through various technical co-operation activities. It requested the Secretary-General to continue activities related to its application.

Energy resources in industry

In recognition of energy's important role in industrialization, the United Nations Industrial Development Organization (UNIDO) had since 1980 steadily increased its energy-related technical assistance projects. In 1985, according to its annual report,[22] 113 energy projects (compared to 90 in 1984) were being implemented, with an expenditure of some $10.5 million ($8.4 million in 1984). Technical co-operation projects in the Asian and Pacific region accounted for about 45 per cent of energy-related expenditures in 1985, followed by Africa with some 25 per cent.

Priority areas were: development of locally available energy resources; improved industrial energy efficiency; local manufacturing of energy equipment; and small hydropower for rural electrification. (See also p. 615.)

The first European regional co-operation project in industrial energy conservation was formulated at a regional technical meeting (Vienna, Austria, 1-4 July) and initiated in October. The project demonstrated the role of UNIDO in improving the exchange of information on increased energy use in manufacturing, on enhancing energy efficiency through good housekeeping practices and on improved energy utilization in industrial processes. Seven European countries—Bulgaria, Czechoslovakia, Hungary, Poland, Portugal, Romania and Yugoslavia—participated, with additional input from other European countries provided through a sub-contract with the Economic Commission for Europe (ECE).

As follow-up to the recommendations of the Second Consultation on the Capital Goods Industry, with Special Emphasis on Energy-related Technology and Equipment (Stockholm, Sweden, 10-14 June), a project was started on developing standardized small hydropower plants from design stage to manufacture. The project's main objectives were to elaborate engineering parameters for standardized hydropower plants with different capacities and to prepare a study of the local or regional manufacturing of small hydropower plants or equipment. Its general aim was the increased use of hydraulic resources for decentralized electricity generation to facilitate rural industrial development.

An information survey was completed in 1985 on the current and future African energy situation. It identified priority areas for more detailed studies towards strengthening UNIDO's technical co-operation programme on energy and industrialization within the framework of the Industrial Development Decade for Africa (the 1980s) (see p. 635). It also was expected to provide guidance to African Governments in establishing their long-term energy-industry development policies and to initiate co-operative programmes with other international, regional and national organizations.

Energy-related topics were also the subject of discussions with the Food and Agriculture Organization of the United Nations, the International Labour Organisation, the United Nations Environment Programme (UNEP), the Economic Commission for Africa (ECA) and ECE. A memorandum of understanding was signed with the Latin American Energy Organization on co-operation on energy-related matters, supplementing aspects of already established co-operation in small hydropower.

REFERENCES

[1]E/C.7/1985/4. [2]A/40/511 & Corr.1. [3]A/40/637. [4]YUN 1982, p. 890, GA res. 37/251, 21 Dec. 1982. [5]YUN 1983, p. 676, GA res. 38/151, 19 Dec. 1983. [6]YUN 1984, p. 656, GA res. 39/176, 17 Dec. 1984. [7]DP/1986/11/Add.2 (Part II). [8]YUN 1983, p. 675. [9]YUN 1980, p. 586. [10]DP/1986/11/Add.1. [11]DP/1986/54. [12]E/1985/32 (dec. 85/31). [13]A/41/31. [14]YUN 1981, p. 406. [15]YUN 1982, p. 891. [16]UNCTAD/TT/64. [17]UNCTAD/TT/61. [18]UNCTAD/TT/60. [19]YUN 1983, p. 674. [20]UNCTAD/ST/ECDC/26. [21]DP/1986/48/Add.1. [22]IDB.2/10 & Corr.1.

New and renewable energy sources

Implementation of the 1981 Nairobi Programme of Action

The Secretary-General, in response to a 1984 General Assembly resolution,[1] submitted in August 1985, a report[2] on the implementation of the 1981 Nairobi Programme of Action for the Development and Utilization of New and Renewable Sources of Energy.[3] He pointed out that the Programme of Action placed great emphasis on resource mobilization for the development of new and renewable energy sources. Various ways to mobilize financial resources had been considered by the Committee on the Development and Utilization of New and Renewable Sources of Energy in 1983.[4] In line with its recommendations, the process of convening a World Bank consultative group and UNDP round-table meetings was continued and a number of such national consultative meetings were held. A global consultative meeting (New York, 13-15 March) was convened by the Director-General for Development and International Economic Co-operation. Donor countries and organizations, several developing countries, United Nations bodies and other intergovernmental organizations expressed support for the implementation of a number of projects. Many national focal points had been designated by Governments to provide information about new and renewable sources of energy. A computerized data base on activities, projects and programmes was being developed within the Unit on New and Renewable Sources of Energy of the United Nations Secretariat.

The development of new and renewable energy sources was considered by the Secretary-General in two other reports. In a March report,[5] prepared for the Committee on Natural Resources, the Secretary-General discussed the trends and salient issues in the development of energy resources, including new and renewable sources. Those sources had been affected by the adverse resource developmental climate. Specific projects had been completed, but the further elaboration of energy technologies in their infancies had been deferred, often indefinitely. Schemes had been developed, for example, to enhance the overall management of forest resources; fuelwood plantations had been planned and thought given to the efficient distribution of fuelwood; improved kilns for charcoal preparation had been designed; and several new cooking-stove designs had been advanced, some claiming improvements of 30 per cent in efficiency. Most of those developments had not attained full fruition because of the absence of a training infrastructure and the lack of financial resources.

The expansion of use of two new energy sources—oil shale and tar sands—had been similarly held back. Both materials offered developing countries the possibility of local production of liquid fuels, the most critical aspect of those countries' energy situation. However, in the past three years, the competitive position of synthetic crude-oil production had eroded markedly, and the few still active projects were being supported by substantial government subsidies. Finally, while work on several new and renewable energy sources in the conceptual or early pilot-plant stage had not stopped, the effort devoted to them had been cut.

Pursuant to a 1984 Assembly resolution,[6] the Secretary-General, in an August report,[7] surveyed the prospects for the development in developing countries of hydropower, traditional energy sources such as fuelwood and organic residues, biomass energy, oil shale and tar sands, and geothermal, solar, wind, and ocean energy.

A number of papers were prepared by UNCTAD during 1985 on the transfer, application and development of energy technology (see p. 689).

ACC action. In its annual overview report for 1984/85,[8] the Administrative Committee on Coordination (ACC) noted that the Inter-Agency Group on New and Renewable Sources of Energy, established in 1983[4] to increase United Nations responsiveness to the Nairobi Programme of Action,[3] considered at its fourth session (New York, 11 and 12 March 1985),[9] progress in implementing the 1984 recommendations[10] of the Committee on the Development and Utilization of New and Renewable Sources of Energy. It reviewed the implementation of the Nairobi Programme of Action, information collected on activities, resource mobilization and the co-ordination of activities.

The Group took up the Committee's request for a report by the Secretary-General on proposals made by ACC in 1982[11] for carrying out the Nairobi Programme. It agreed to make an inventory of activities corresponding to such projects and to prepare a co-ordinated package on the basis of planned activities in need of funding for submission to the Committee.

The Group noted the progress so far in the collection of information, and agreed on measures to be taken in the preparation of the Secretary-General's report on monitoring the Nairobi Programme's implementation. It reviewed the progress in convening consultative meetings on resource mobilization and agreed to co-operate with ECA in preparations for a regional consultative meeting. Considering the Committee's request for an assessment of the Group's performance and achievements, it was agreed that a draft would be circulated to participants for comments.

The Group also provided a forum for the preparation and co-ordination of project packages submitted recently to two regional and two global consultative meetings on projects in new and renewable sources of energy.

In October,[12] ACC's Consultative Committee on Substantive Questions (Programme Matters) took note of the Group's report.[9]

UNDP activities. The UNDP Administrator described in an April 1985 report[13] a number of projects related to new and renewable energy sources. With the World Bank and other institutions, UNDP supported a programme to develop and promote investment in biomass gasifiers. The project monitored 11 power gasifier installations in countries such as Brazil, Burundi, Kenya, Mali and the Philippines; it also co-operated with EEC on projects in the South Pacific. In two or three years, at the end of the programme, it was expected that it would have contributed to newly emerging heat gasifier technology and to improvement in the operation of the increasing number of gasifier systems.

A project on promotion and strengthening of energy information networks was attempting to create an awareness in developing countries of existing sources of information about the economic and technical status of new and renewable energy sources, and stimulate use of the information. The concept was being developed in the following areas: gasifiers, fuelwood and stoves, windpumping and rural energy technology.

Small-scale hydropower benefited from the support of many bilateral and multilateral donors. However, the experience of many UNDP- and World Bank–supported projects in that area showed that their implementation could be more efficient. A prerequisite was for officials to be aware of recent technical developments. With that in mind, UNDP, DTCD and UNIDO organized a workshop (Klaekken, Norway, 10-18 June) for developing countries' representatives on available electro-mechanical equipment, how to conduct small-scale hydropower feasibility assessments and the problems of the construction cycle.

On 29 June, the UNDP Governing Council adopted a decision on energy development programmes (see p. 687).

Five hundred experts from throughout the world attended the Third International Conference on Heavy Crude and Tar Sands, organized by UNDP and the United Nations Institute for Training and Research (UNITAR) (Long Beach, California, United States, 22-31 July) and reported by the Executive Director of UNITAR.[14] Among the subjects considered were: new geological aspects for heavy crude and tar sands; experience with new exploration and assessment methods; new knowledge on resources; new chemical and geochemical research and results; biotechnology and microbiology research and results in heavy crude exploration and production; drilling and production of heavy crude on land; offshore drilling and production of heavy crude; and refining of heavy crude.

The UNITAR/UNDP Centre on Small Energy Resources—a clearing-house for the development of small energy resources which serves as a bridge for improved collaboration between donor Governments, the private sector and developing countries—established in 1984 at Rome, Italy, became operational in 1985. In April, a meeting of energy experts from governmental bodies and the private sector agreed on the Centre's terms of reference and its planned activities.

UNU activities. UNU provided research support for renewable energy research networks, according to the report of the UNU Council covering its 1985 activities.[15] For example, biogas digesters had been built in Guyana, modelled on the Chinese biogas system at the Xinbu commune. A video tape of the Chinese model, which had been used to demonstrate the advantages of biogas systems to rural Guyanese, was made available to other developing countries in local languages. UNU also continued to assist biofuel research at the Guangzhou Institute of Energy Conversion in China, which included: disposal of soluble industrial organic waste-water using continuous up-flow digesters; biogas systems for a new energy village; new anaerobic digestion techniques; the ecology of micro-organisms involved in anaerobic digestion; gasification technology for solid biomass; and monofuel biogas internal-combustion engines for electric power generation.

UNIDO activities. In the area of biofuels, UNIDO gave support to research and demonstration programmes for the development of alternative sources of energy.[16] Examples of such assistance included a biofuel demonstration programme in Ethiopia on the utilization of agricultural residues and a project in Zimbabwe on the development of technologies for the use of agricultural and food-processing residues as fuels and of efficient charcoal-making techniques in order to reduce deforestation.

UNEP action. UNEP continued to collect, study and disseminate information on the environmental impact of all energy sources, and to support energy conservation development and environmentally appropriate sources of energy in developing countries.

According to the 1985 annual report of the Executive Director,[17] a field demonstration project on the planting and efficient use of fuelwood in Kenya's rural areas was concluded in August. Local people were taught how to produce fuel-efficient stoves and plant fast-growing trees, resulting in the substantial lowering of the fuelwood consumption of some 15,000 Kenyans. Work continued on similar projects in Brazil and Bolivia.

In co-operation with a Finnish film company, UNEP produced three films on the main areas of its energy programme—environmental impacts of energy sources, harnessing new and renewable energy sources, and energy conservation.

The Executive Director was requested by the UNEP Governing Council on 23 May[18] to sharpen the focus of the energy programme in 1986-1987, giving high priority to: the environmental impacts of the production and use of renewable sources of energy, particularly biomass energy; support for studies on the environmental aspects of new energy technologies, especially the exploitation of oil shales and tar sands and coal liquefaction and gasification; and training in energy management and conservation for developing countries.

GENERAL ASSEMBLY ACTION

On 17 December, on the recommendation of the Second Committee, the General Assembly adopted, without vote, **decision 40/444**, by which it took note of the Secretary-General's report on new and renewable energy sources[2] and decided that the Committee on the Development and Utilization of New and Renewable Sources of Energy should hold its third session from 21 April to 2 May 1986.

The Second Committee had approved the draft,[19] submitted by a Vice-Chairman, without vote on 5 December.

REFERENCES

[1]YUN 1984, p. 662, GA res. 39/173, 17 Dec. 1984. [2]A/40/548. [3]YUN 1981, p. 689. [4]YUN 1983, p. 681. [5]E/C.7/1985/4. [6]YUN 1984, p. 656, GA res. 39/176, 17 Dec. 1984. [7]A/40/511 & Corr.1. [8]E/1985/57. [9]ACC/1985/PG/7. [10]YUN 1984, p. 660. [11]YUN 1982, p. 894. [12]ACC/1985/20. [13]DP/1985/52. [14]A/41/14. [15]A/41/31. [16]IDB.2/10 & Corr.1. [17]UNEP/GC.14/2. [18]A/40/25 (dec. 13/17). [19]A/C.2/40/L.99.

Nuclear energy

Nuclear power had expanded impressively in the 1980s, the Secretary-General stated in a March report[1] on trends and salient issues in the development of energy resources. Between 1980 and 1983, the number of nuclear power reactors in operation had grown from 202 to 246 in developed market economies, 9 to 16 in developing countries, and 42 to 55 in centrally planned economies. In 12 countries (10 developed market economies and two centrally planned economies), nuclear-generated electricity constituted more than 10 per cent of electricity produced in 1982; in six of these, nuclear power represented more than 25 per cent of all power generated.

When current prospects were considered, however, the nuclear power picture appeared less bright. The number of reactors under construction had fallen each year since 1980 in the developed market economies, and since 1981 in the developing countries; only in the centrally planned economies had construction steadily increased. Reactors under construction had declined between 1980 and 1983 from 179 to 130 in developed market economies, from 22 to 20 in developing countries and from 230 to 209 world-wide; however, their numbers had increased from 29 to 59 in centrally planned economies.

United Nations technical work relating to nuclear energy continued to be dealt with mainly by IAEA. (For information on IAEA activities in 1985, see PART II, Chapter I.)

IAEA report

The IAEA report for 1984 was transmitted to the General Assembly by the Secretary-General in September 1985.[2]

Presenting the report in the Assembly on 31 October, the IAEA Director General said that, during 1984, total nuclear power capacity world-wide had increased by 17 per cent, the largest annual increase since large-scale introduction of nuclear power began in the early 1970s. Nuclear power currently accounted for some 13 per cent of the world's electricity and by the year 2000 it was expected to generate about 20 to 25 per cent. He felt that in a world where economic development and growth were resuming and where fossil fuels posed environmental problems in the form of acid rain and carbon dioxide, nuclear power would be viewed increasingly as an indispensable option. New types of more efficient nuclear fuel and longer operation cycles were making nuclear power more attractive economically. In most places, nuclear power had a clear economic edge over coal. Standardized plant design, streamlined regulatory procedures and rigid management controls were ways to keep costs down.

Nevertheless, financing nuclear plants had become a major constraint because of the high initial capital investment required. Total capital cost, including interest during construction, was about $1.5 billion to $2 billion for a plant in the 600-700 megawatt (MW) range. The use of small and medium-sized reactors would bring nuclear power within the reach of a larger number of developing countries. Some 23 designs for plants with an electrical output below 600 MW were available.

With regard to nuclear safety, the Director General said that the world had accumulated experience of some 3,600 reactor years without a fatal radiation accident in a commercial nuclear plant. Accidents and incidents occurred, but better maintenance and operation had reduced their number and limited their consequences. The IAEA safety programme had been expanded in the past few years through an incident reporting system, radiation protection advisory teams and an International Nuclear Safety Advisory Group, established in 1985.

Experts were convinced that no scientific or technological breakthroughs were needed for safe disposal of high-level nuclear waste. However, fears about nuclear waste were behind much of the opposition to nuclear power. The construction of storage installations for high-level waste and the dissemination of more factual information about the waste issue could be expected to influence public opinion favourably. Pursuant to the 1975 Convention on the Prevention of Marine Pollution by Dumping of Wastes and Other Matter, IAEA had revised the definition of high-level wastes unsuitable for sea disposal. At a September meeting of the contracting parties to the Convention, the majority had agreed to a suspension of dumping at sea of radioactive wastes until further studies had been made.

In a 19 September letter to the Secretary-General,[3] Papua New Guinea transmitted a 6 August communiqué of the South Pacific Forum (Rarotonga, Cook Islands, 5 and 6 August). The Forum had reaffirmed its opposition to the dumping of radioactive waste in the region's oceans. Forum members hoped for the early conclusion of the convention and protocols being negotiated under the auspices of the South Pacific Regional Environment Programme which would preclude such dumping.

GENERAL ASSEMBLY ACTION

On 8 November, the General Assembly adopted, without vote, **resolution 40/8**.

Report of the International Atomic Energy Agency

The General Assembly,

Having received the report of the International Atomic Energy Agency to the General Assembly for the year 1984,

Taking note of the statement of the Director General of the International Atomic Energy Agency of 31 October 1985, which provides additional information on the main development of the Agency's activities during 1985,

Recognizing the importance of the work of the Agency to promote further the application of nuclear energy for peaceful purposes, as envisaged in its Statute,

Also recognizing the special needs of the developing countries for technical assistance by the Agency in order to enlarge the contribution of nuclear energy and its applications to their economic development,

Conscious of the importance of the work of the Agency in the implementation of the safeguards provisions of the Treaty on the Non-Proliferation of Nuclear Weapons and other international treaties, conventions and agreements designed to achieve similar objectives, as well as ensuring, as far as it is able, that the assistance provided by the Agency or at its request or under its supervision or control is not used in such a way as to further any military purposes, as stated in article II of its Statute,

Recognizing the importance of the work of the Agency on nuclear power, nuclear safety, radioactive waste management, radiological protection and, in particular, of its work directed towards assisting developing countries in planning for the introduction of nuclear power in accordance with their needs,

Noting that the General Conference of the International Atomic Energy Agency at its twenty-ninth regular session approved the reappointment by the Board of Governors of the Agency of Mr. Hans Blix as Director General of the Agency for a further term of four years, commencing on 1 December 1985,

Bearing in mind resolutions GC(XXIX)/RES/442, GC(XXIX)/RES/443 and GC(XXIX)/RES/444, adopted on 27 September 1985 by the General Conference of the Agency at its twenty-ninth regular session,

1. *Takes note* of the report of the International Atomic Energy Agency;

2. *Affirms* its confidence in the role of the International Atomic Energy Agency in the application of nuclear energy for peaceful purposes;

3. *Urges* all States to strive for effective and harmonious international co-operation in carrying out the work of the International Atomic Energy Agency, pursuant to its Statute, in promoting the use of nuclear energy and the application of nuclear science and technology for peaceful purposes; in strengthening technical assistance and co-operation for developing countries; and in ensuring the effectiveness and efficiency of the Agency's safeguards system;

4. *Requests* the Secretary-General to transmit to the Director General of the International Atomic Energy Agency the records of the fortieth session of the General Assembly relating to the Agency's activities.

General Assembly resolution 40/8

8 November 1985   Meeting 69   Adopted without vote

3-nation draft (A/40/L.8); agenda item 14.
Sponsors: Indonesia, Poland, Sweden.
Meeting numbers. GA 40th session: plenary 56, 68, 69.

Several other resolutions were adopted by the Assembly in 1985 on the related subjects of nuclear disarmament and nuclear power sources (see POLITICAL AND SECURITY QUESTIONS, Chapters I and II).

Preparations for the Conference on nuclear energy

Preparatory Committee activities. Established by the General Assembly in 1980,[4] the Preparatory Committee for the United Nations

Conference for the Promotion of International Co-operation in the Peaceful Uses of Nuclear Energy convened its sixth session at Vienna from 21 October to 1 November 1985.[5] The Committee had before it the reports of four of the five regional expert group meetings held during 1985 as part of the preparations for the Conference—Asian and Pacific region (Bangkok, Thailand, 14-17 January);[6] Latin American and Caribbean region (Santiago, Chile, 15-18 April);[7] Western Asian region (Baghdad, Iraq, 13-16 May);[8] and African region (Addis Ababa, Ethiopia, 1-4 July).[9] (The fifth regional meeting, for Europe, the United States and Canada, was held at Vienna from 4 to 6 November,[10] following the Committee's session.) The Committee, which had previously agreed that the Conference should meet in 1986,[11] reconsidered the matter and decided that it should be held from 23 March to 10 April 1987 at Geneva, unless Yugoslavia offered Belgrade as the venue for the same dates. It further decided that its seventh session should be held at Vienna from 10 to 21 November 1986, and approved a provisional agenda.

The Committee established an inter-sessional intergovernmental Working Group to decide on its programme of work, to assess the current situation regarding international co-operation in the peaceful uses of nuclear energy and formulate options for the enhancement of such co-operation, and to develop an outline of the Conference's final document(s). It was to meet in 1986.

An oral report was submitted to the Committee on the work of its informal contact group which had been considering the establishment of a meeting of a group of internationally eminent experts. The contact group had failed to agree on a mandate for the meeting of experts owing to two areas of contention—whether or not to include a reference to non-proliferation of nuclear weapons and how such a reference might be formulated; and whether or not the group should discuss problems concerning the financing of the capital-intensive investments required by the nuclear industry. The Committee concluded that it should not be convened.

The Committee decided that the Conference should have 25 Vice-Presidents, recommended that the Assembly take a decision on the provision of summary records for the Conference, requested that IAEA and United Nations organizations submit to the Committee revised or updated texts of input documents, and took note of a list of non-governmental organizations which had expressed their interest in being invited.

Communications. In 1985, the Secretary-General received communications relating to the promotion of international co-operation in the peaceful uses of nuclear energy.

On 18 November[12] and 4 December,[13] the USSR transmitted statements by the General Secretary of the Central Committee of the Communist Party of the USSR. At a 13 November meeting with a delegation of Nobel Prize winners, he had stated that the mastery of nuclear fusion was a promising area of international co-operation, that the building of a fusion reactor was believed to be technically feasible in the comparatively near future, and that its achievement would make it possible to solve one of the world's most acute problems—energy. In a report presented to a 27 November session of the Supreme Soviet, he had pointed out that scientists from different countries had begun work on the Tokamak fusion reactor, which opened up the opportunity for a radical solution of the energy problem—the creation before the end of the century of an inexhaustible source of thermonuclear energy.

On 5 November, Angola forwarded the Final Political Declaration adopted by the Conference of Foreign Ministers of Non-Aligned Countries (Luanda, 4-7 September).[14] The Ministers stressed the importance of international co-operation among the non-aligned and other developing countries in the peaceful uses of nuclear energy; expressed concern about obstacles which the developed countries placed in the way of transfer of peaceful nuclear technologies; reiterated that non-proliferation should not be made a pretext for preventing States from developing peaceful nuclear technology; and expressed satisfaction at the progress in preparations for the Conference.

GENERAL ASSEMBLY ACTION

On 12 December, the General Assembly adopted **resolution 40/95** without vote.

United Nations Conference for the Promotion of International Co-operation in the Peaceful Uses of Nuclear Energy

The General Assembly,

Reaffirming the principles and provisions of its resolution 32/50 of 8 December 1977,

Recalling its subsequent resolutions 33/4 of 2 November 1978, 34/63 of 29 November 1979, 35/112 of 5 December 1980, 36/78 of 9 December 1981, 37/167 of 17 December 1982, 38/60 of 14 December 1983 and 39/74 of 13 December 1984,

Noting that the Preparatory Committee for the United Nations Conference for the Promotion of International Co-operation in the Peaceful Uses of Nuclear Energy at its sixth session decided to establish a Working Group to carry out formal/official inter-sessional intergovernmental work under the guidance of the Chairman of the Committee, participation being open to members of the Preparatory Committee and to other interested Member States, and that the Working Group will conclude its deliberations in time to submit its report to the

Preparatory Committee for consideration at its seventh session to be held at Vienna from 10 to 21 November 1986,

Noting further that the Preparatory Committee, upon reconsideration of the dates of the Conference on practical considerations and on the understanding that this did not constitute a reopening of the question of timing in any substantive sense, decided that the Conference should be held at Geneva from 23 March to 10 April 1987,

1. *Approves* the conclusions and decisions contained in the report of the Preparatory Committee for the United Nations Conference for the Promotion of International Co-operation in the Peaceful Uses of Nuclear Energy on its sixth session, including the dates for the seventh session of the Preparatory Committee, from 10 to 21 November 1986, and the new dates of the Conference, from 23 March to 10 April 1987;

2. *Expresses its appreciation* for the efforts of the Chairman of the Preparatory Committee and the Secretary-General of the Conference in pursuance of paragraph 3 of General Assembly resolution 39/74;

3. *Notes with satisfaction* the progress made in the preparations for the Conference and requests the Secretary-General of the Conference to continue with the preparations;

4. *Invites* the International Atomic Energy Agency, the specialized agencies and other relevant organizations of the United Nations system to contribute further to the preparations of the Conference by revising and updating, as necessary and appropriate, their input documents for the Conference, bearing in mind paragraph 7 of General Assembly resolution 39/74 and in the light of the comments by the members of the Preparatory Committee at its sixth session;

5. *Invites* all States to co-operate actively in the preparations for the Conference and to make available at the earliest the information requested in paragraph 9 of General Assembly resolution 36/78 and in the broad questionnaire circulated by the Secretary-General of the Conference in March 1984;

6. *Decides* to include in the provisional agenda of its forty-first session the item entitled "United Nations Conference for the Promotion of International Co-operation in the Peaceful Uses of Nuclear Energy".

General Assembly resolution 40/95

12 December 1985   Meeting 114   Adopted without vote

3-nation draft (A/40/L.35); agenda item 37.
Sponsors: Bulgaria, Italy, Yugoslavia.
Financial implications. 5th Committee, A/40/1031; S-G, A/C.5/40/86.
Meeting numbers. GA 40th session: 5th Committee 59, 60; plenary 114.

REFERENCES

[1]E/C.7/1985/4. [2]A/40/576 & Corr.1. [3]A/40/672-S/17488. [4]YUN 1980, p. 164, GA res. 35/112, 5 Dec. 1980. [5]A/40/47. [6]A/CONF.108/PC/14. [7]A/CONF.108/PC/15. [8]A/CONF.108/PC/16. [9]A/CONF.108/PC/17. [10]A/CONF.108/PC/18 & Corr.1,2 & Corr.2/Add.1. [11]YUN 1984, p. 665. [12]A/40/900. [13]A/40/987-S/17670. [14]A/40/854-S/17610 & Corr.1.

PUBLICATION

1985 Energy Statistics Yearbook (ST/ESA/STAT/SER.J/29), Sales No. E/F.86.XVII.13.

Chapter XI

Food

The World Food Programme (WFP)—a joint undertaking of the United Nations and the Food and Agriculture Organization of the United Nations (FAO), each of which celebrated its fortieth anniversary in 1985 (see also pp. 403 and 1287)—continued during the year to provide food aid to developing countries in support of development projects and to meet emergency needs. It received from 90 donors pledges of cash and commodities worth $1 billion for 1985-1986—the highest amount ever—while contributions to the International Emergency Food Reserve also reached a record level, of over 800,000 metric tons. During the year, WFP supervised 361 projects in 90 countries and delivered emergency food aid to about 11 million people. The Committee on Food Aid Policies and Programmes, WFP's governing body, held two sessions and approved projects at a total cost of some $526 million.

The World Food Council (WFC)—the highest-level international body dealing with food problems—meeting in Paris from 10 to 13 June, reviewed the global food and development situation and focused on Africa's food crisis.

In December, the General Assembly affirmed that food represented an essential element of the world's economic, social and political development process (resolution 40/181) and established a $1.4 billion target for 1987-1988 voluntary contributions to WFP (40/176).

Topics related to this chapter. Economic assistance, disasters and emergency relief. Regional economic and social activities: Africa—food and agriculture. Health and human resources: health and nutrition. Human rights: right to food. Women: women in rural areas. Children: nutrition. Refugees and displaced persons: assistance.

Food problems

The attention of the international community remained focused in 1985 on the continuing economic and food crisis in Africa and on the limited progress in other developing regions in tackling the silent and growing crisis of chronic hunger and malnutrition, a crisis exacerbated by global economic difficulties which weakened the efforts of those countries.

Despite growing food imports and food aid, 21 countries in Africa had exceptional food shortages and an estimated 150 million people suffered from malnutrition and hunger, the Secretary-General stated in a June 1985 report[1] on the critical situation of food and agriculture in Africa in 1984-1985—submitted in response to a 1984 General Assembly request[2] and taken note of by the Economic and Social Council on 26 July 1985 (**decision 1985/197**). While drought and other natural disasters aggravated food problems, the main long-term cause rested with the inability of African countries to reach a "take-off" stage for sustained economic and social development and with policies that denied agriculture its priority role in the development process. Proposals for recovery and rehabilitation included the establishment of an early warning system in drought-prone countries and of emergency seed stocks, provision of appropriate seeds and draught animals, supply of fertilizers and chemicals, assistance to livestock owners, and improvement of food transportation, storage and distribution.

The Committee on Food Aid Policies and Programmes, in a June 1985 report,[3] stated that food aid should be integrated into the national development plans of recipient countries to support humanitarian objectives and to provide an incentive for increased production. Since the 1974 World Food Conference,[4] progressively increasing resources had enabled WFP to raise its annual commitments for development projects by more than six times, and about 80 per cent of all cereal food aid was currently destined to low-income, food-deficit countries. However, the minimum annual food aid target, established by the Conference, of 10 million tons of grain had not been met despite considerable stocks in major food-exporting countries, while the ability of low-income countries to import food on commercial terms had decreased.

The WFC Executive Director submitted several reports during the year on food problems in the world.

In a March note reviewing the 1984 world food situation,[5] he found that although all regions produced more food that year, the gain was offset by population growth; some 70 countries produced even less per caput in 1984 than during 1974-1976, and a rise in the value of the United States dollar in 1983-1984 exacerbated an already severe debt problem for many developing countries, reducing their ability to import food.

In another report,[6] the Executive Director recommended for WFC action a phased approach to eliminating hunger and malnutrition, consisting of preventing a recurrence of famine, reducing infant deaths from malnutrition, reversing the trend of increasing world hunger in the coming few years, and adopting development strategies for reducing chronic hunger and malnutrition in the 1990s. In addition, it was suggested that WFC might recommend improved monitoring of both the means for and progress in achieving the phased approach.

In a third report,[7] he analysed external economic constraints on meeting food objectives and the need for expanding world trade.

As regards the effectiveness of aid in support of food strategies,[8] he examined four issues affecting the quality of such aid to Africa: the domestic policy environment, donors' policies, the international economic environment, and the particular place of food aid in Africa as the principal famine-emergency resource. He also suggested improving the quality of aid through flexible and realistic national food policy implementation, greater selectivity of aid on the part of recipients, and enhanced co-ordination of recipient-donor efforts.

Assessing the status of food plans and strategies in Africa,[9] the Executive Director observed that those countries, struck by one of the worst economic crises in their history and preoccupied with emergency relief, had suffered a set-back in implementing national food strategies. He recommended, among other things, establishing an analytical monitoring framework for use by all concerned, giving priority to food production, stepping up emergency assistance to speed recovery from the current crisis and conserve resources for long-term development programmes, building up human resources and infrastructure for food strategy implementation, and providing adequate external support.

WFC activities. The 36-member WFC held its eleventh ministerial session in Paris from 10 to 13 June 1985[10] and reviewed the global food and development situation. It expressed concern over the growing crisis, exacerbated by global economic difficulties, of chronic hunger and malnutrition in developing regions, and directed particular attention to measures for protecting the fragile food and nutrition level of low-income groups and for reducing hunger during the remainder of the century. WFC concluded that increased external assistance, while indispensable, could not substitute for a more equitable international economic, trade and financial environment with provisions to reduce trade protectionism, resolve the developing countries' debt problems, and improve international monetary stability.

As regards Africa, where millions of people including growing numbers of refugees remained threatened by famine, WFC—which had sponsored a workshop on accelerated food strategies implementation in Africa (Abidjan, Ivory Coast, 25-27 February)[11]—reaffirmed that emergency relief should be accompanied by rehabilitation and long-term development efforts. It called, among other things, for a common monitoring system for a more systematic follow-up of food strategy implementation and hunger reduction, and agreed to continue promoting food strategy development and implementation, including international mobilization of resources. The Council suggested that a major food and economic recovery programme for Africa should: establish priorities; co-ordinate investments; apply improved technology; integrate emergency and development assistance; provide incentives for producers; promote more balanced food-crop and export-crop policies; support small-scale irrigation; deal with rural poverty; upgrade technical and managerial skills affecting food production and nutrition; strengthen African institutions and administration, including restructuring the role of parastatals and strengthening the managerial capacity to design and implement projects and programmes; give increased attention to population issues; and provide for careful planning and programming to reform Africa's pricing and marketing policies to increase food production.

WFC declared that the effectiveness of external assistance in support of food strategies could be enhanced when used to supplement national policies for increased domestic food production and poverty alleviation. It recommended that development food aid be programmed on a multiyear basis, with a system to assess its impact on national priorities, and supported the strengthening of related co-ordination mechanisms of the United Nations.

On improving access to food by the under-nourished, WFC urged Governments to make the elimination of hunger and malnutrition a central objective in national development, and recommended action to prevent famine, reduce infant mortality, and limit and reduce hunger. The Council also reviewed the international financial and trade situation as it affected developing countries' capacities for resolving their food problems. It urged all countries to adjust their manufacture and agriculture sectors, and to refrain from creating obstacles to agricultural imports, especially from developing countries. It also recommended that adjustment programmes for resolving debt problems be phased to take account of developing countries' food and social needs on a long-term basis; that the Committee on Trade in Agriculture of the General Agreement on Tariffs and Trade be encouraged to accelerate work towards more effective rules and disciplines for trade and domestic farm policies; and that the

WFC Executive Director report to it in 1986 on the origins of, and possible solutions to, current conflicts in international food trade.

ECONOMIC AND SOCIAL COUNCIL ACTION

On 26 July, the Economic and Social Council decided to transmit to the General Assembly for its consideration a draft resolution on food and agricultural problems (**decision 1985/196**). The text was transmitted in a September note by the Secretariat.[12]

GENERAL ASSEMBLY ACTION

On 17 December, the General Assembly, on the recommendation of the Second (Economic and Financial) Committee, adopted **resolution 40/181** without vote.

Food and agricultural problems

The General Assembly,

Recalling the Declaration and the Programme of Action on the Establishment of a New International Economic Order, contained in its resolutions 3201(S-VI) and 3202(S-VI) of 1 May 1974, the Charter of Economic Rights and Duties of States, contained in its resolution 3281(XXIX) of 12 December 1974, resolution 3362(S-VII) of 16 September 1975 on development and international economic co-operation, and the International Development Strategy for the Third United Nations Development Decade, contained in the annex to its resolution 35/56 of 5 December 1980,

Reaffirming the Universal Declaration on the Eradication of Hunger and Malnutrition adopted by the World Food Conference and the Programme of Action adopted by the World Conference on Agrarian Reform and Rural Development,[13]

Stressing the imperative need to keep food and agricultural issues at the centre of global attention,

Stressing also the urgent need for the international community in its development efforts to take determined action towards the elimination of, *inter alia*, poverty, hunger and malnutrition, and infant mortality,

Reaffirming the Declaration on the Critical Economic Situation in Africa, adopted by the General Assembly on 3 December 1984,

Reaffirming that food and agricultural problems in developing countries should be considered in a comprehensive manner in their different dimensions and in their immediate, short-term and long-term perspectives,

Affirming the urgent need for sustained international support for the efforts of the African countries towards rehabilitation and long-term development of their food and agriculture,

Reaffirming that the right to food is a universal human right which should be guaranteed to all people and, in that context, believing in the general principle that food should not be used as an instrument of political pressure,

Reaffirming also that the maintenance of peace and security and the strengthening of international co-operation in food and agriculture are important for improved economic conditions and enhanced food security,

1. *Reaffirms* its resolutions 38/158 of 19 December 1983 and 39/166 of 17 December 1984, and Economic and Social Council resolution 1984/54 of 25 July 1984,

as well as all other relevant resolutions concerning food and agriculture, and calls for their immediate and effective implementation;

2. *Welcomes* the conclusions and recommendations, as adopted, contained in the report of the World Food Council on the work of its eleventh ministerial session, held in Paris from 10 to 13 June 1985;

3. *Welcomes also* the conclusions and recommendations contained in the tenth annual report of the Committee on Food Aid Policies and Programmes of the World Food Programme and in the report of the Committee on its nineteenth session;

4. *Affirms* that food represents an essential element of the world's economic, social and political development process and should therefore be treated with the highest priority by all Governments in their rededication to the principles and purposes of the Charter of the United Nations in this fortieth anniversary year of the United Nations and to the commitment of the World Food Conference to eliminate hunger and malnutrition;

5. *Reaffirms* that urgent action should be taken to increase food production, which is one of the most important elements in meeting the food needs of the developing countries; that, in this regard, sustained efforts at the national, regional and international levels should be pursued; and that the national food strategies, plans and programmes of developing countries should play a central role in the process of establishing priorities, in co-ordinating national and international funding and in the application of technology and human resources development, in order to promote food production and increase the national self-reliance of the developing countries;

6. *Welcomes* the positive efforts of developing countries for the development of their food and agricultural production, and calls upon the international community to provide effective support to those efforts;

7. *Emphasizes* the need for priority attention at the national, subregional, regional and international levels to the timely delivery of food to those requiring assistance, especially in African countries, and the need to assist recipient countries in developing and strengthening their logistic, transportation and administrative capacities, as well as internal distribution systems, and that emergency food aid programmes should, whenever possible, procure supplies within the region;

8. *Appeals* to the international community to provide, as a matter of extreme urgency, the logistic agricultural inputs, and fulfil the unmet aid needs of the drought- and famine-affected African countries;

9. *Notes with deep concern* the substantial decline in international market prices for agricultural commodities over the last five years, which, coupled with deteriorating terms of trade for commodity exporting countries, have had particularly serious effects on developing countries, and in this context calls for appropriate measures to overcome foreign exchange constraints, including measures to diversify and increase export earnings, and for continuous efforts for the conclusion of commodity agreements and arrangements, as appropriate, particularly within the framework of the Integrated Programme for Commodities, and agrees that efforts should continue in order to improve the effectiveness of appropriate export earning stabilization schemes and to seek agreement on more effective co-operation in

international commodity policy, notably through the early entry into force of the Agreement Establishing the Common Fund for Commodities;[(14)]

10. *Emphasizes* that the success of efforts of developing countries to solve their food and agricultural problems requires, as a major element, economic growth, which is severely constrained by, *inter alia*, the burden of external debt; and that, in accordance with recommendations of the World Food Council at its eleventh ministerial session, adjustment programmes for resolution of debt problems should take into account the food and social needs of the developing countries on a sustained and long-term basis;

11. *Stresses* the need to continue and to intensify the support for programmes and policies for increasing food and agricultural production and raising nutritional standards in developing countries, particularly in Africa and the least developed countries, and in this context urges the international community, particularly the developed countries, to take determined action, in support of the efforts of developing countries, to increase the flow of resources, particularly the concessional flow by, *inter alia*, increasing their contributions to multilateral agencies;

12. *Calls upon* the parties concerned urgently to achieve the conclusion of the negotiations on the second replenishment of the International Fund for Agricultural Development in the light of the broad agreement achieved at the seventh meeting of the consultation on the replenishment;

13. *Urges* developed countries to provide the International Development Association with the necessary financial resources, including, *inter alia*, supplementary financing, to enable it to cover any shortfall and to increase its assistance to developing countries, particularly in the development of food and agriculture;

14. *Recommends* that the International Wheat Council should continue to explore the possibilities of raising the minimum overall commitment under the Food Aid Convention to 10 million tons;

15. *Recommends* that the Committee on Trade in Agriculture of the General Agreement on Tariffs and Trade should continue, within its mandate, to accelerate to the greatest extent possible progress towards more operationally effective rules and disciplines for trade in agriculture, bearing in mind the concerns of all developing countries, including wider and more predictable access to markets;

16. *Urges* all countries to demonstrate the requisite political will by refraining from creating obstacles to agricultural imports, especially those from developing countries, and all exporting countries, particularly developed countries, to endeavour to limit export subsidies and analogous practices which might hinder trade, especially that of developing countries;

17. *Notes with satisfaction* paragraph 2 *(e)* of Trade and Development Board resolution 286(XXVIII) of 6 April 1984, in which the Board decided that, in the annual review of the problems of protectionism and structural adjustment, attention should be given to strengthening the participation of developing countries in agro-industrial production and trade and, in this regard, paragraph *(g)* of Board decision 310(XXX) of 29 March 1985, in which the Board recommended that, in preparing the documentation for the annual review to be carried out at the thirty-second session of the Board, the secretariat of the United Nations Conference on Trade

and Development should give particular attention to this question and special attention to the difficulties of the African and the least developed countries;

18. *Recognizes* the important contribution and potential of women in the development of the food and agricultural sectors and the need adequately to reward their contribution to those sectors, and urges Governments to ensure and enhance women's participation in the formulation and implementation of national food and agricultural policies, plans and projects;

19. *Recognizes* the importance of implementing famine prevention measures and, in this regard, welcomes the increased activity and proposed strengthening of the Global Information and Early Warning System in Food and Agriculture of the Food and Agriculture Organization of the United Nations, and emphasizes the importance of establishing and improving national and regional early warning systems;

20. *Appreciates* the measures taken by the World Food Programme to ensure speedy and timely delivery of food aid as well as the development of an information system for the dissemination on a regular basis of all relevant information on food aid to facilitate planning and operational co-ordination;

21. *Urges* the donor community to provide the necessary financial support for the effective implementation of the programmes of action adopted by the FAO World Conference on Fisheries Management and Development;[(15)]

22. *Urges* the World Food Council, within the context of its mandate, to mobilize and sustain greater efforts in the struggle to overcome hunger, to continue to review and report on major problems and policy issues, and to continue to serve as a co-ordinating mechanism in the field of food and other related policy matters within the United Nations system and, in this connection, notes that the Council, in its report to the General Assembly, addressed the question of strengthening its effectiveness and other related issues, and expresses the hope that necessary action, as appropriate, will be taken in that regard;

23. *Stresses* the need to strengthen subregional, regional and interregional co-operation for the promotion of food security and the development of agriculture in developing countries and, in this context, calls upon the relevant entities of the United Nations system to accord priority support to economic and technical co-operation among developing countries in food and agriculture.

General Assembly resolution 40/181

17 December 1985   Meeting 119   Adopted without vote

Approved by Second Committee (A/40/1009/Add.2) without vote, 13 December (meeting 51); draft by Vice-Chairman (A/C.2/40/L.130), based on informal consultations on draft transmitted by Economic and Social Council decision 1985/196 (A/C.2/40/L.4); agenda item 12.
Meeting numbers. GA 40th session: 2nd Committee 36, 39, 48-51; plenary 119.

The draft proposed by the Economic and Social Council had contained less detailed formulation of paragraphs 9 to 11, by which the Assembly would have: called for the conclusion of agreements and arrangements within the framework of the Integrated Programme for Commodities, and for the entry into force of the Agreement Establishing the Common Fund for Commodities; expressed concern that external debts and measures under adjustment policies affected the capacity of most developing countries to tackle their food problems; and noted with concern stagnation in commitments of external resources for the agricultural sector and the overall hardening of terms, and urged donors to increase contributions to multilateral agencies and concessional flows to developing countries.

In explanation of position, Canada said that export earning stabilization schemes based on balance-of-payments requirements were appropriate, while those that sought to compensate for shortfalls in export earnings from individual commodities were not. It continued to question the need for an additional financing facility, and hoped that greater emphasis would be given in the future to humanitarian aspects and to improving agricultural production and distribution. Australia also questioned the appropriateness of commodity-specific schemes. The Federal Republic of Germany, also on behalf of Belgium and the United Kingdom, said that the narrow interpretation in paragraph 9 of "international market prices" in terms of United States dollars disregarded the fact that, because well over 75 per cent of key agricultural commodities were traded on European markets, their prices were denominated in a European national currency.

The United States, referring to paragraph 8, said it was the responsibility of each Government to ensure that its people were not denied food; that except in the case of total embargoes, its grain was available to all purchasers; and that it had the right to decide how its resources should be used. Egypt considered it appropriate for the text to refer to the substantial decline in international market prices and the need for economic growth; it regretted that amendments were submitted to paragraphs 9 to 11 after the issues had been discussed.

In other 1985 action, the Assembly dealt with food and agriculture and rural development (**resolution 40/205**), negotiations on the replenishment of the International Fund for Agricultural Development (**40/211**), and donors' response to the emergency food situation in Africa (**40/20**). The Economic and Social Council dealt with an international year for the mobilization of financial and technological resources to increase food and agricultural production in Africa (**decision 1985/199**).

REFERENCES
[1]A/40/329-E/1985/80. [2]YUN 1984, p. 615, GA res. 39/165, 17 Dec. 1984. [3]E/1985/110. [4]YUN 1974, p. 488. [5]WFC/1985/7. [6]WFC/1985/4. [7]WFC/1985/5. [8]WFC/1985/3. [9]WFC/1985/2. [10]A/40/19. [11]WFC/1985/2/Add.1. [12]A/C.2/40/L.4. [13]YUN 1979, p. 500. [14]*Agreement Establishing the Common Fund for Commodities*, Sales No. E.81.II.D.8. [15]YUN 1984, p. 672.

Food aid

World Food Programme

In 1985, WFP continued to provide developing countries with food aid for development purposes and emergency relief.

CFA activities

At its nineteenth session, held at Rome, Italy, from 20 to 31 May 1985,[1] the Committee on Food Aid Policies and Programmes (CFA)—the WFP governing body—conducted its tenth annual review of food aid policies and programmes, focusing on co-ordination of food aid operations in beneficiary countries. It emphasized that food aid must be integrated into the development process and co-ordinated with financial and technical assistance, and that the recipient Governments should bring food aid within their national development plans and establish appropriate management units to co-ordinate all food aid operations. CFA also recommended that developing countries improve the assessment of their food aid needs and establish national early warning systems to detect impending emergency situations.

The Committee approved 18 projects at a total cost of some $300 million, in addition to four budget increases for approved projects, making a combined total of approximately $344 million (equivalent to 1 million tons of food).

At its twentieth session at Rome from 30 September to 10 October,[2] CFA urged WFP to increase its activity in support of development so as to attack the root causes of hunger and to reduce the need for emergency relief in the future. Recognizing the increasing food aid needs of the developing countries, it proposed for 1987-1988 a target—later endorsed by the General Assembly (see p. 703)—of $1.4 billion, comprising 3.25 million tons of food at current prices and $405 million in cash.

The Committee approved 20 projects at a total cost of $226 million and six budget increases for approved projects. The combined value amounted to approximately $255 million, equivalent to about 700,000 tons of food. In addition, the Committee was informed that between 1 January and 30 June 1985, the Executive Director had approved five projects of up to $1.5 million each in food value, at a total cost to WFP of $7.3 million.

WFP activities

In 1985, WFP committed 1.8 million tons of food worth $642 million to development projects, mainly in low-income, food-deficit countries; provided emergency support worth $225 million to 11 million people; supervised the implementation of 361 projects worth $3.64 billion in some 90 countries; and carried out 29 evaluation missions.

Intensifying its emergency response to the African food crisis, WFP's Africa Task Force secretariat co-ordinated information and logistics, and helped deliver an unprecedented total of 5.8 million tons of food aid to 20 sub-Saharan countries affected by drought and civil strife. While commitments for emergency aid totalled some 336,000 tons of food, costing $129 million, WFP shipped 647,000 tons of its own food for both emergency and development operations in sub-Saharan Africa, in addition to 313,000 tons on behalf of bilateral donors. Of $873 million of total WFP resources committed for both development and emergencies in 1985, $321 million, or about 37 per cent, was for that subregion.

The special FAO/WFP task force, set up in April 1983[3] to monitor the agricultural and food supply situation in Africa, continued its work. The initial phase of the WFP management information system became operational in 1985, and a computerized system—containing food aid and related logistics information for African countries receiving emergency food aid—was created and installed in April.

Agreements were reached during the year between WFP and the United Nations Development Programme on their relations in the field and between WFP and the Office of the United Nations High Commissioner for Refugees on more effective handling of food aid for refugees. The United Nations/FAO Joint Task Force on WFP Relationship Problems began its work in January.

Development assistance

In 1985, WFP committed $642 million of resources, representing 1.8 million tons of food, to development projects. Of the total, $550 million (86 per cent) was approved in the form of 55 new projects; of these, 38 projects (valued at $526 million) were approved by CFA and 17 projects (valued at $24 million) by the Executive Director under his delegated authority. Eighty-five per cent of the food went to low-income, food-deficit countries; in value terms, the share of commitments for the poorest countries was 79 per cent. Asia and the Pacific continued to receive the largest share of commitments ($237 million or 37 per cent of the total), followed by Africa south of the Sahara

($192 million or 30 per cent), North Africa and the Near East ($151 million or 23 per cent) and Latin America and the Caribbean ($62 million or 10 per cent).

In 1985, $499 million went to agricultural and rural development projects, focusing on rehabilitation of agricultural land through irrigation, flood control and soil conservation, and on forestry. Other projects included agricultural reforms, such as price stabilization programmes in Mali and Mauritania, to which $15 million was committed. Commitments to human resources development amounted to $144 million, of which $107 million went for nutritional support for vulnerable groups, including primary school children.

Emergency operations

During 1985, WFP committed $225 million to provide 733,000 tons of food—including $186 million worth of food drawn from the International Emergency Food Reserve (IEFR)—to 55 emergency operations in 32 countries, as well as $5.2 million to provide cash subsidies for six operations which had been approved the previous year. Over 11 million people were targeted beneficiaries of WFP emergency food aid approved in 1985.

Of the year's total emergency assistance, 56 per cent (in dollar terms) went for 34 operations in sub-Saharan Africa, 36 per cent for 12 operations in Asia, 4 per cent for 6 operations in Latin America and the Caribbean and 4 per cent for 3 operations in North Africa and the Near East. Seventy per cent of the total tonnage—511,445 tons worth $145 million—was channelled to some 4.7 million refugees, returnees and persons displaced by internal strife. WFP co-ordinated the bilateral and multilateral food aid distribution to refugees in Pakistan and Somalia and the displaced persons along the Thai-Kampuchean border (see also Chapter XXI of this section).

WFP arranged for the international transport of over 2 million tons of food to 84 countries, using 1,822 vessels; its direct management of large truck fleets in Chad, Ethiopia and the Sudan enabled it to reach more people in remote areas. Considerable attention was given to speedier delivery of emergency supplies; for instance, within 24 hours of the 13-14 November eruption of the Nevado del Ruiz volcano, which buried the town of Armero, Colombia, under mud and debris, WFP delivered to the disaster site food airlifted by helicopter from Bogotá by the national authorities.

WFP resources

Total net WFP commitments in 1985, for development projects, emergency operations and administrative costs, were $868 million. Its total expenditure was $814 million.

Pledges and contributions

During 1985, total WFP resources reached $1,316 million, including $1,003 million in pledges by 90 donors to regular resources, $211 million to IEFR channelled through WFP, and $76 million contributed under the 1980 Food Aid Convention.[4] The $1,003 million pledged for 1985-1986 represented 74 per cent of the $1,350 million target set at the eleventh (1984) pledging conference.[5]

For the fourth time since inception, IEFR's target of 500,000 tons of cereals was exceeded in 1985; by year's end, announced contributions exceeded 825,000 tons of food (766,541 tons in cereals), valued at $227 million. Of the total 1985 contributions, 90 per cent were channelled multilaterally through WFP. Twenty-nine donors, including seven developing countries, contributed to IEFR in 1985.

ECONOMIC AND SOCIAL COUNCIL ACTION

On 26 July 1985, the Economic and Social Council, on the recommendation of its First (Economic) Committee, adopted **resolution 1985/73** without vote.

Pledging target for contributions to the World Food Programme for the biennium 1987-1988

The Economic and Social Council,

Noting that the Committee on Food Aid Policies and Programmes, at its nineteenth session, held from 20 to 31 May 1985, postponed consideration of the pledging target for contributions to the World Food Programme for the biennium 1987-1988 to its twentieth session, to be held from 30 September to 11 October 1985,

Taking into account the fact that the pledging target will serve as a guiding figure for donor countries at the pledging conference for contributions to the World Food Programme for the biennium 1987-1988, to be convened early in 1986,

Recommends the General Assembly to consider at its fortieth session the pledging target for contributions to the World Food Programme for the biennium 1987-1988.

Economic and Social Council resolution 1985/73

26 July 1985   Meeting 52   Adopted without vote

Approved by First Committee (E/1985/147) without vote, 25 July (meeting 30); draft by Vice-Chairman (E/1985/C.1/L.19), based on informal consultations; agenda item 10.

GENERAL ASSEMBLY ACTION

On 17 December 1985, the General Assembly, on the recommendation of the Second Committee, adopted **resolution 40/176** without vote.

Target for World Food Programme pledges for the period 1987-1988

The General Assembly,

Recalling the provisions of its resolution 2095(XX) of 20 December 1965 to the effect that the World Food Programme is to be reviewed before each pledging conference,

Recalling also the provisions of paragraph 4 of its resolution 38/176 of 19 December 1983 that, subject to the review mentioned above, the next pledging conference should be convened at the latest early in 1986, at which time Governments and appropriate donor organizations should be invited to pledge contributions for the biennium 1987-1988, with a view to reaching such a target as may be then recommended by the General Assembly and the Conference of the Food and Agriculture Organization of the United Nations,

Noting that the review of the Programme was undertaken by the Committee on Food Aid Policies and Programmes of the World Food Programme at its twentieth session,

Having considered the recommendations of the Committee on Food Aid Policies and Programmes,

Recognizing the value of multilateral food aid as implemented by the World Food Programme since its inception and the necessity for continuing its action both as a form of capital investment and for meeting emergency food needs,

1. *Establishes* for the two years 1987 and 1988 a target for voluntary contributions to the World Food Programme of $1.4 billion, comprising 3.25 million tons of food at current prices and $405 million in cash, and expresses the hope that such resources will be augmented by substantial additional contributions from other sources in recognition of the prospective volume of sound project requests and the capacity of the Programme to operate at a higher level;

2. *Urges* States Members of the United Nations and members and associate members of the Food and Agriculture Organization of the United Nations and appropriate donor organizations to make every effort to ensure the full attainment of the target;

3. *Requests* the Secretary-General, in co-operation with the Director-General of the Food and Agriculture Organization of the United Nations, to convene a pledging conference for this purpose at United Nations Headquarters early in 1986;

4. *Decides* that, subject to the review provided for in its resolution 2095(XX), the next pledging conference at which Governments and appropriate donor organizations should be invited to pledge contributions for the biennium 1989-1990, with a view to reaching such a target as may be then recommended by the General Assembly and the Conference of the Food and Agriculture Organization of the United Nations, should be convened, at the latest, early in 1988.

General Assembly resolution 40/176

17 December 1985   Meeting 119   Adopted without vote

Approved by Second Committee (A/40/1009/Add.2) without vote, 5 December (meeting 48); draft by Vice-Chairman (A/C.2/40/L.97), based on informal consultations; agenda item 12.

Meeting numbers. GA 40th session: 2nd Committee 36, 39, 48; plenary 119.

In explanation of position, the United Kingdom, cautioning against setting excessively high targets for food aid, said it was important to assess accurately the relative cost of food aid in the context of total assistance, and to ensure that the developing countries did not become overly dependent on such aid.

REFERENCES
[1]WFP/CFA:19/22. [2]WFP/CFA:20/20. [3]YUN 1983, p. 696. [4]YUN 1980, p. 691. [5]YUN 1984, p. 675.

FOOD AID FOR DEVELOPMENT
(Projects approved in 1985 by CFA)

Country	Field of activity	Amount (in US dollars)	Country	Field of activity	Amount (in US dollars)
Angola	Reconstruction of southern Angola	3,431,500	India *(cont.)*	Irrigation and command area development, Karnataka	12,301,000
Bangladesh	National works programme for water works and rural roads	72,706,000		Food assistance for labour working on the Indira Gandhi canal	13,873,000
Bhutan	Food assistance to education development	7,232,000	Jordan	Development of the highland agricultural regions	17,485,000
Burundi	Multi-purpose rural development	2,777,500	Mali	Food security, price stabilization and restructuring of cereal marketing	12,642,000
Cameroon	Assistance under the fifth and sixth development plans	22,967,000	Mauritania	School feeding	2,306,000
China	Improved land use of the Loess Plateau, Shanxi province	8,870,000	Morocco	Development of northern provinces	17,714,000
	Rural water supplies, Liaoning and Shanxi provinces	15,191,610		Feeding in primary schools	24,243,000
	Erosion control, Liaoning province	16,007,000	Mozambique	Agricultural and social development in the tea industry	25,108,000
	Development of coastal aquaculture, Bohai Bay	18,938,000	Niger	Assistance to school canteen programme	6,473,000
	Land protection and wood production through forestry development, Shandong and Sichuan provinces	13,645,000	Pakistan	Mangla watershed management, Kashmir	2,466,000
Colombia	Development of rural indigenous communities	4,743,000	Peru	Development of agricultural and regional infrastructure in depressed areas	16,525,000
Democratic Yemen	Multisectoral project for agricultural, social and rural community development	12,885,000	Rwanda	Improvement and maintenance of roads and mineral prospecting	2,558,000
Egypt	Development of the Sinai	7,711,000	Somalia	Feeding of vulnerable groups	19,286,000
	Settlement on newly developed lands	20,658,000	Syrian Arab Republic	Assistance to land settlement, fruit-tree planting and crop intensification activities	21,512,000
El Salvador	Assistance to displaced persons	3,906,000	Togo	Multi-purpose rural development	5,007,000
Equatorial Guinea	School feeding programme	8,422,410	Uganda	Education integrated into rural development	17,043,000
Gambia	Rural primary school feeding	9,892,600	Viet Nam	Development of water resources, Binh Tri Thien and Nghe Tinh provinces	13,995,000
Guatemala	Nutrition education and supplementary feeding of vulnerable groups and primary school children	14,568,000		Protection of agricultural areas by the afforestation of dunes and hills, Nghe Tinh, Binh Tri Thien and Quang Nam-Danang provinces	13,585,000
Honduras	Production of basic food crops by organized small farmers	4,904,000			
India	Employment through forestry activities, Rajasthan	12,173,800	Total		525,751,420

SOURCE: WFP/CFA:19/22, WFP/CFA:20/20.

EMERGENCY ALLOCATIONS APPROVED IN 1985

Country	Nature of emergency	Amount (in US dollars) IEFR	WFP	Country	Nature of emergency	Amount (in US dollars) IEFR	WFP
Algeria	Drought	380,700	113,400	Pakistan	Refugees	17,162,000	3,864,700
Angola	Displaced persons	1,046,000	—		Refugees	19,499,000	—
Bangladesh	Typhoon	546,000	—		Refugees	1,595,000	1,595,000
Botswana	Drought	130,000	342,100		Refugees	215,600	554,400
	Drought	413,000	—		Refugees	29,825,000	—
Burkina Faso	Drought	1,163,200	—	Philippines	Refugees	711,100	5,000
Cameroon	Drought	168,500	—	Rwanda	Refugees/returnees	974,400	57,600
Chad	Drought	12,036,400	2,821,500		Refugees	712,000	—
Colombia	Eruption	442,900	—	Senegal	Drought	1,031,700	—
El Salvador	Displaced persons	4,163,000	—	Sierra Leone	Returnees	134,500	—
Ethiopia	Drought	8,613,000	—	Somalia	Refugees	4,872,000	1,811,800
	Refugees	1,687,400	43,600		Refugees	10,989,000	4,348,400
Gambia	Drought	452,000	30,300		Refugees	5,280,000	1,400,000
Honduras	Refugees	1,331,500	166,500		Refugees	5,520,000	1,845,000
	Refugees	1,434,000	—	Sudan	Refugees	6,809,400	—
Indonesia	Refugees	—	315,000		Refugees	5,131,000	2,851,900
	Refugees	398,000	—		Drought	6,125,000	2,068,300
	Refugees	243,000	—		Drought	360,000	5,490,000
Lebanon	Displaced persons	4,855,700	1,819,200	Syrian Arab Republic	Drought	960,000	—
Mali	Drought	3,616,500	—	Uganda	Drought	14,400	1,286,500
Mauritania	Drought	2,430,000	599,300	United Republic of Tanzania	Drought	1,211,000	—
	Drought	674,900	206,800	Viet Nam	Typhoon	—	4,600,000
Mexico	Refugees	450,000	—		Typhoon	1,175,000	—
	Earthquake	2,105,500	—	Zaire	Refugees	347,300	972,000
Mozambique	Drought	—	242,400		Refugees	1,736,000	—
	Drought	3,929,200	—	Zambia	Refugees	191,700	—
Niger	Drought	9,022,000	—				
	Drought	1,014,000	—	Total		185,638,200	39,534,000
	Returnees	309,700	83,300				

SOURCE: WFP/CFA:21/9.

CONTRIBUTIONS UNDER THE INTERNATIONAL EMERGENCY FOOD RESERVE
(as at 31 December 1985)

Contributor	Contribution	Quantity (in metric tons)	Estimated value (including costs for transportation) (in US dollars)	Contributor	Contribution	Quantity (in metric tons)	Estimated value (including costs for transportation) (in US dollars)
Multilateral				Norway (cont.)	Grain	9,900	2,343,015
Austria	Grain	5,000	944,671	Spain	Grain	6,500	1,456,000
Belgium	Grain	5,000	2,000,000	Sweden	Grain	35,000	7,782,000
Canada	$Can 29,500,000	67,385	22,050,246		Vegetable oil	2,500	3,875,000
Denmark	DKr 21,500,000	8,131	1,827,118	Switzerland	SwF 250,000	—	93,116
	Grain	20,000	5,300,000		$US 41,000	—	41,000
EEC	Grain	40,000	8,720,500		Grain	27,497	2,877,472
	Vegetable oil	2,000	2,137,560		Dried skimmed milk	375	578,850
	Sugar	500	281,000		Corn soya milk	216	844,842
Egypt	Rice	50	22,350	Togo	CFAF 200,000	1	500
Finland	Fmk 15,000,000	1,727	2,654,100	United Kingdom	Grain	20,000	4,507,000
France	Grain	23,000	4,698,500	United States	Various commodities	291,508	95,461,040
Germany, Federal Republic of	$US 3,435,550	11,650	3,435,550	Subtotal		742,803	207,594,981
	$US 256,429	1,193	256,429				
	DM 8,500,000	9,058	3,178,703	Bilateral			
	Grain	20,000	4,020,000	Australia	Grain	50,000	11,200,000
Greece	$US 100,000	258	100,000	Burma	Rice	500	127,500
Iceland	$US 8,700	24	8,700	Denmark	Grain	5,000	1,045,000
India	Grain	100,000	16,500,000	France	Grain	4,000	1,048,000
Italy	Lit 500 million	—	260,417	Japan	$US 2,000,000	8,464	2,000,000
	Lit 10 billion	21,992	4,926,108	Spain	Grain	3,500	784,000
Japan	$US 1,500,000	2,000	1,500,000	Sri Lanka	Tea	20	48,000
Lesotho	$US 4,000	11	4,000	Sweden	Grain	10,000	2,240,000
Malta	$US 970	3	970	Switzerland	Dried whole milk	42	200,000
Mauritius	Mau Rs 11,500	4	833	United States	Vegetable oil	800	784,000
Netherlands	Grain	8,250	1,765,950	Subtotal		82,326	19,476,500
New Zealand	Grain	472	105,820				
Norway	$US 20,000	—	20,000	Total		825,129	227,071,481
	Edible fat	1,598	1,015,621				

SOURCE: WFP/CFA:21/9.

CONTRIBUTIONS UNDER THE FOOD AID CONVENTION MADE AVAILABLE TO WFP
(as at 31 December 1985; in US dollars)

CONTRIBUTOR	CROP YEAR 1985/86 Commodity (metric tons)	Value	CASH	CROP YEAR 1986/87 Commodity (metric tons)	Value	CASH
Food Aid Convention net						
Ireland	4,024	643,840	241,440	4,000	604,000	240,000
Norway	30,000	4,800,000	1,800,000	30,000	4,530,000	1,800,000
Subtotal	34,024	5,443,840	2,041,440	34,000	5,134,000	2,040,000
Convention through regular programme						
Australia	200,000	22,620,689	8,275,862	108,109	10,719,797	—
Belgium	—	—	—	13,000	1,963,000	780,000
EEC	70,000	7,335,720	4,200,000	102,876	13,901,426	4,706,577
Finland	20,000	3,200,000	1,200,000	25,000	4,129,681	1,500,000
Germany, Federal Republic of	15,000	2,400,000	900,000	15,000	2,265,000	900,000
Netherlands	16,750	3,571,429	1,005,000	21,750	5,737,685	1,305,000
Sweden	40,000	8,156,862	2,400,000	40,000	9,066,965	2,400,000
United Kingdom	50,000	8,000,000	3,000,000	50,000	7,550,000	3,000,000
Subtotal	411,750	55,284,700	20,980,862	375,735	55,333,554	14,591,577
Convention through IEFR*						
Australia	—	—	—	34,983	5,310,962	2,960,000
Belgium	—	—	—	4,000	520,000	800,000
EEC	40,000	6,400,000	2,360,000	57,124	8,404,913	2,780,000
Germany, Federal Republic of	20,000	3,200,000	1,180,000	44,000	6,824,000	2,620,000

CONTRIBUTOR	CROP YEAR 1985/86			CROP YEAR 1986/87		
	Commodity (metric tons)	Value	CASH	Commodity (metric tons)	Value	CASH
Convention through IEFR (cont.)						
Netherlands	8,250	1,320,000	487,000	8,841	1,680,000	728,155
Switzerland	10,000	1,600,000	590,000	27,442	2,555,612	1,350,000
United Kingdom	5,000	800,000	295,000	5,000	800,000	300,000
Subtotal	83,250	13,320,000	4,912,000	181,390	26,095,487	11,538,155
Total	529,024	74,048,540	27,934,302	591,125	86,563,041	28,169,732

*Under IEFR, donor countries cover all transportation costs.

SOURCE: WFP/CFA:21/4/Add.1, WFP/CFA:25/P/4/Add.1.

ANNOUNCED PLEDGES TO THE WORLD FOOD PROGRAMME, 1985-1986

(as at 31 December 1985; in US dollar equivalent)

Contributor	Commodities	Cash and services	Total	Contributor	Commodities	Cash and services	Total
Afghanistan	—	3,000	3,000	Malawi	—	5,000	5,000
Algeria	—	132,250	132,250	Malaysia	16,461	8,036	24,497
Argentina	305,529	—	305,529	Malta	—	2,600	2,600
Australia	56,275,862	28,137,930	84,413,792	Mauritania	—	4,085	4,085
Austria	6,075,000	675,000	6,750,000	Mauritius	—	1,488	1,488
Bangladesh	990,000	—	990,000	Mexico	—	100,000	100,000
Barbados	—	6,955	6,955	Morocco	—	15,645	15,645
Belgium	3,277,157	2,100,014	5,377,171	Nepal	—	7,500	7,500
Bhutan	—	1,500	1,500	Netherlands	42,252,021	14,406,132	56,658,153
Bolivia	—	10,000	10,000	New Zealand	306,513	141,093	447,606
Burkina Faso	—	1,075	1,075	Nicaragua	—	13,571	13,571
Canada	172,463,767	34,352,325	206,816,092	Nigeria	—	250,000	250,000
Chile	—	20,000	20,000	Norway	21,763,123	10,146,532	31,909,655
China	—	1,000,000	1,000,000	Pakistan	750,000	—	750,000
Colombia	500,000	11,000	511,000	Panama	—	1,000	1,000
Cuba	1,000,000	—	1,000,000	Philippines	—	46,666	46,666
Cyprus	—	3,425	3,425	Republic of Korea	—	100,000	100,000
Democratic Yemen	—	12,650	12,650	Rwanda	—	1,500	1,500
Denmark	22,983,486	10,967,846	33,951,332	Sao Tome and Principe	—	750	750
Djibouti	—	2,000	2,000	Saudi Arabia	27,500,000	27,500,000	55,000,000
EEC	79,392,622	16,511,750	95,904,372	Seychelles	—	100	100
Egypt	400,000	—	400,000	Sierra Leone	—	471	471
Equatorial Guinea	—	1,000	1,000	Somalia	—	204	204
Fiji	—	1,712	1,712	Spain	—	377,779	377,779
Finland	17,166,422	5,661,322	22,827,744	Sri Lanka	109,328	—	109,328
France	—	2,105,263	2,105,263	Sudan	10,000	—	10,000
Germany, Federal Republic of	26,013,471	11,019,526	37,032,997	Swaziland	—	1,000	1,000
Greece	250,000	—	250,000	Sweden	29,899,217	11,628,757	41,527,974
Guatemala	—	11,111	11,111	Switzerland	2,851,675	1,013,097	3,864,772
Guinea	—	2,000	2,000	Syrian Arab Republic	—	128,205	128,205
Haiti	—	10,000	10,000	Thailand	35,000	—	35,000
Honduras	—	7,500	7,500	Togo	—	1,044	1,044
Hungary	440,000	—	440,000	Tonga	—	2,000	2,000
Iceland	—	27,600	27,600	Tunisia	—	60,500	60,500
India	1,760,000	—	1,760,000	Turkey	216,000	—	216,000
Iran	—	40,000	40,000	Uganda	—	5,000	5,000
Ireland	2,157,055	984,930	3,141,985	United Kingdom	16,250,000	9,328,805	25,578,805
Israel	10,000	—	10,000	United Republic of Tanzania	—	13,253	13,253
Italy	5,830,904	2,915,451	8,746,355	United States	188,000,000	62,000,000	250,000,000
Jamaica	—	10,000	10,000	Venezuela	—	26,667	26,667
Japan	14,000,000	7,000,000	21,000,000	Viet Nam	—	12,000	12,000
Jordan	—	75,000	75,000	Yemen	—	10,000	10,000
Kuwait	—	250,000	250,000	Zaire	—	2,000	2,000
Lao People's Democratic Republic	—	1,000	1,000	Zambia	—	517	517
Lesotho	—	10,000	10,000	Total	741,250,613	261,455,293	1,002,705,906
Luxembourg	—	10,161	10,161				

SOURCE: WFP/CFA:21/4/Add.1.

Chapter XII

Science and technology

Restructuring international scientific and technological relations continued to occupy an important place on the agenda of many United Nations bodies throughout 1985. Working in accordance with guidelines set by the 1979 Vienna Programme of Action, they directed their efforts at enhancing the scientific and technological capacities of developing countries by trying to mobilize financial resources, improve institutional arrangements and balance the international flows of technology.

As a halfway point of the decade, 1985 was a logical choice for carrying out a comprehensive analysis of progress made over the previous five years in implementing the Vienna Programme. The results of the mid-decade review prompted the Intergovernmental Committee on Science and Technology for Development, the main directing and policy-making body, to express disappointment with the progress achieved and to urge the international community to provide additional resources and co-operation for implementing the Programme. The Intergovernmental Committee, which held its seventh session in May/June 1985, also focused on the issue of information systems for science and technology for development, concluding that setting up and strengthening national systems should form the major activity in developing a global information network. The Committee's resolutions and decisions were endorsed by the General Assembly (resolution 40/193).

Effective policy and planning advice to the Intergovernmental Committee on all the issues under consideration was provided by the Advisory Committee on Science and Technology for Development, which held its fifth session in February. Two of the Advisory Committee's panels of experts met in 1985 for an in-depth examination of questions relating to information systems and mobilizing financial resources for scientific and technological development in developing countries. Both the Intergovernmental and Advisory Committees continued to receive substantive secretariat support from the Centre for Science and Technology for Development which prepared studies on information systems, maintained regular contacts with national focal points and worked to develop further the Advance Technology Alert System. With regard to inter-agency co-ordination, it assisted the Task Force on Science and Technology for Development of the Administrative Committee on Co-ordination (ACC). The Task Force held its sixth session in January focusing specifically on the financing aspects of joint activities and the criteria for building endogenous capacities in developing countries.

For the United Nations Financing System for Science and Technology for Development (UNFSSTD), 1985 proved a difficult year, with the continued uncertainty of its long-term financing and institutional arrangements hindering mobilization of resources through normal pledging procedures, which yielded less than $150,000. After reviewing proposals by an open-ended intergovernmental working group, the Intergovernmental Committee reaffirmed in June the importance of such arrangements and appealed to all Member States to pledge the maximum resources to UNFSSTD. Proposals on improving the System's financial situation were made in October by the Secretary-General. The Assembly (resolution 40/194) requested him to report on the results of an April 1986 pledging conference, together with his views on the future of the System, including its orderly termination, should pledges fall short of the average level achieved by the System over the previous three years.

Promoting a more balanced flow of technology between developed and developing countries remained a high priority for several bodies, particularly the United Nations Conference on Trade and Development (UNCTAD). After the United Nations Conference on an International Code of Conduct on the Transfer of Technology made some progress at its sixth session in May/June, the Assembly invited the UNCTAD Secretary-General to report in 1986 on possible solutions to issues outstanding in the draft code of conduct (resolution 40/184). Regarding the reverse transfer of technology or brain drain, the Assembly called for further studies of the problem at various levels (resolution 40/191).

Topics related to this chapter. Disarmament: peaceful uses of science and technology. Development policy and international economic co-operation: scientific-technological co-operation. Operational activities for development: technical co-operation among developing countries. Industrial development: industrial technology. Regional economic and social activities: Africa—science and technology; Asia and the Pacific—science and technology; Europe—science and technology. Human rights: human rights and science and technology. Women: science and technology and women.

Implementation of the Vienna Programme of Action

In-depth examination of pre-selected substantive subjects was a major United Nations activity in 1985, aimed at implementing the 1979 Vienna Programme of Action on Science and Technology for Development.[1] Following a 1984 decision of the Intergovernmental Committee on Science and Technology for Development,[2] the question of information systems for science and technology for development was the subject of a comprehensive analysis in a number of reports and discussions at the Committee's 1985 session. Another important aspect of its activities during the year was evaluation of the progress achieved over the previous five years in implementing the Vienna Programme.

Mid-decade review

In 1985, the United Nations launched a major effort to evaluate progress made in implementing the Vienna Programme of Action. The assessment was made in the form of a mid-decade review, as provided for by the Programme's 1981 operational plan[3] and the medium-term plan for 1984-1989 adopted in 1982.[4]

Reports by the Secretary-General. Serving as a basis for the Intergovernmental Committee's mid-decade review were three reports by the Secretary-General, which examined activities of the United Nations system and progress at the regional level, and also provided an overall assessment of the implementation process.

In his overall assessment,[5] the Secretary-General reviewed the main trends relating to the Vienna Programme's objectives over the previous five years, indicated the progress or lack of it in different areas, analysed constraints to the implementation process and identified opportunities for initiating specific steps in the near future. He concluded that the situation called for mobilizing science and technology for development, and exploring strategic options for implementing the Programme. The Secretary-General recommended a number of ways to build scientific and technological capabilities of developing countries, in part through measures allowing them to take advantage of the international market, adopting a deliberate policy to manage technological options, establishing depositories of scientific and technological policies and plans, and expanding

international co-operation. Enhancing societal capabilities for innovation was another dimension involved in the design of scientific and technological strategies. Noting a lack of scientific and technological infrastructure and human resources in many developing countries, the Secretary-General said intensive efforts were needed to mobilize support from international governmental and non-governmental organizations in resolving the situation, particularly in the least developed countries. His other suggestions concerned assessment and choice of technologies and resource allocation.

In the light of the conclusions of the mid-decade review, the Secretary-General proposed that the Intergovernmental Committee consider at its 1985 session conducting a more comprehensive review at the end of the decade, in 1989, instead of annual and biennial reviews. He suggested that the Committee should outline a broad framework for that review to identify relevant data and to enable analytical contributions from national focal points, United Nations entities and a variety of other concerned organizations.

The report analysing the progress in implementing the Vienna Programme at the regional level[6] contained a brief description of each region's salient features and a review of its accomplishments, generally within the framework of the 1981 operational plan's eight programme areas. In his conclusions, the Secretary-General noted that the contributions of the countries of each region for the respective regional review had further stimulated national interests in identifying the major gaps in science and technology endeavours related to the Programme's objectives and in seeking alternative solutions.

An overview of the activities undertaken by the organizations of the United Nations system in the context of the Vienna Programme was the focus of the Secretary-General's third report.[7] It covered achievements at programme level, assessed perspectives regarding the role of the United Nations system in implementing the Programme and highlighted major changes in policies and institutional arrangements introduced over the reporting period. The report also contained a section describing the role of respective organizations in implementing the Programme. In his conclusions, the Secretary-General pointed to a growing need in developing countries for assistance from external sources and particularly from the United Nations system. He said that the system's future efforts in implementing the Vienna Programme would be determined on the basis of national needs for assistance in the context of special areas of interest of each organization.

The information provided in the above reports was supplemented by the Director-General for

Development and International Economic Co-operation (DIEC), who reported[8] on activities of the ACC Task Force and the Centre for Science and Technology for Development (see below), not covered by the Secretary-General.

Advisory Committee consideration. The mid-decade review of the implementation of the Vienna Programme was high on the agenda of the February session of the Advisory Committee on Science and Technology for Development.[9] The Committee's main contribution to the review was a discussion of the global context for the application of science and technology to development, which was based on the results of the 1984 *ad hoc* panel on long-term perspectives.[10] While noting a number of changes in various fields since the adoption of the Vienna Programme, the Advisory Committee found it difficult to evaluate individual responses by countries or groups of countries to the Programme, a problem further compounded by the lack of data on changes at the national level in developing countries. A consensus was reached that both the Advisory and Intergovernmental Committees should pay greater attention to the fuller dissemination of the results of their deliberations in order to promote further the emerging consciousness among scientific communities of the need to apply science and technology to development.

Intergovernmental Committee action. Taking note of the Secretary-General's three reports on the mid-decade review, the Intergovernmental Committee, on 7 June,[11] said it was disappointed with the progress made in implementing the Vienna Programme and was concerned about the adverse world economic situation that imposed constraints on the development of endogenous scientific and technological capabilities of developing countries. It urged the international community to provide the additional resources and co-operation required and recommended that developing countries should be further supported in attaining the critical mass of scientific and technological human resources. The Intergovernmental Committee requested the Advisory Committee to continue to report on the impact of the emerging trends in science and technology on developing countries and the way of assimilating these technologies in their development process. With regard to the reports of the Centre on United Nations activities in implementing the Programme, the Committee decided that the Centre should give special attention to the substantive themes and other programme areas it had specified in 1981.[12] It also decided to undertake in 1989 a comprehensive review of the Programme's implementation.

GENERAL ASSEMBLY ACTION

The General Assembly, in **resolution 40/193**, noted the Intergovernmental Committee's actions and, in **resolution 40/178**, stressed the willingness of Member States to strengthen the United Nations system as a framework for dialogue and joint efforts in solving scientific-technological problems, especially those confronting the developing countries.

Information systems for science and technology

Following a 1984 decision,[2] the Intergovernmental Committee focused on information systems for science and technology for development as a substantive theme for in-depth consideration in 1985. The ACC Task Force on Science and Technology for Development took up the matter at its sixth session (Geneva, 29-31 January),[13] when it examined the results of a meeting of the Advisory Committee's *Ad Hoc* Panel of Experts on Information Systems for Science and Technology for Development (Rome, Italy, 21-25 January)[14] and proposals of the Centre regarding a long-term plan for a global information network. The Task Force agreed that the gradual establishment of a global information network should begin with a source referral function and that the International Referral System for sources of environmental information (INFOTERRA) of the United Nations Environment Programme (UNEP) (see Chapter XVI of this section) was best suited to carry it out. A detailed study, however, was necessary to assess the feasibility of transforming INFOTERRA into the referral system of a global information network.

Reports of the Secretary-General. Three documents by the Secretary-General, prepared in co-operation with the Centre for Science and Technology for Development, served as the basis for consideration by the Intergovernmental Committee.

In a report reviewing the nature of information systems as related to the needs of developing countries,[15] the Secretary-General stressed the crucial role of scientific and technological information in the development process but pointed out that the existing facilities for collecting, storing and disseminating such information were inadequate in most developing countries. It was essential to develop the basic institutional infrastructure, combining the development of primary information sources, such as books, periodicals and technical documentation, with the growth of institutional capabilities and with mechanisms to supply information to various user groups. In view of resource constraints, the Secretary-General recommended that the introduction of computerized information systems and telecommunications should be introduced in a phased manner and that a flexible mix of modern and traditional techniques should be adopted. He also emphasized that the development of national information systems in developing countries would require greater international co-operation.

Analysis of another aspect of the substantive theme was provided by the Secretary-General in a study on the long-term plan of action for the establishment of the global information network.[16] The report assessed the results of various studies of the problem during the previous two years and the opinions from individuals and institutions involved in scientific and technological information activities. It outlined the general approach to creating a global network and to formulating criteria for developing it at the national and international levels. In his conclusions, the Secretary-General recommended that the initial stage of establishing the network should include the following basic elements: strengthening international assistance to developing countries in setting up their own national information systems and networks, especially through UNESCO's Intergovernmental Programme for Co-operation in the Field of Scientific and Technological Information; assigning to UNEP's INFOTERRA the functions of the science and technology global source referral network to be established under the auspices of the United Nations; enhancement of inter-agency co-ordination between the Advisory Committee for the Co-ordination of Information Systems (ACCIS) and the ACC Task Force on Science and Technology for Development; and formulation of pioneer projects to provide developing countries with basic primary information sources through voluntary contributions.

Following a 1983 request of the Intergovernmental Committee,[17] the Secretary-General also submitted a review of the existing and planned scientific and technological information systems and services of various United Nations entities.[18]

Activities of UNU. Questions related to scientific and technological information constituted part of a major programme area of the United Nations University (UNU).[19] Its activities were aimed at strengthening the capacity and monitoring the development of information and communication technologies in developing countries and devising new modes for sharing knowledge. In 1984-1985, UNU had co-operated in organizing special training courses and regional training colleges in Colombia and Sri Lanka and at the International Centre for Theoretical Physics (Trieste, Italy), and launched a training programme jointly with Trinity College (Dublin, Ireland). In Malaysia, a joint project focused on the applications of microprocessor and microcomputer technology in agriculture and educational local area networks. By the end of 1985, the Communication Centre of Scientific Knowledge, established in 1984 under UNU auspices, had produced for distribution in India 50 manuals in various local languages on food, water, environment, housing, rural energy, health and social co-operation. UNU was also a co-sponsor of a regional workshop for communicating scientific knowledge useful for underprivileged groups at the Indian Institute of Technology at Madras.

Advisory Committee consideration. After discussing, at its February session,[9] the ways available to the international community to create a global information network, the Advisory Committee arrived at the following conclusions: adequate national efforts represented the essential base upon which any network might be built; there was an urgent need for a minimum of primary information in each developing country to sustain scientific and technological activities; at the international level, a global referral service should be developed enabling national systems to locate relevant information sources; and such an international referral system should provide for linkages among existing systems and services, while avoiding duplication. The Committee also recommended that a series of projects should be initiated to furnish the universities, scientific and technological institutions and the national libraries of the less developed countries with important scientific journals through voluntary contributions. In addition, it proposed initiating a permanent programme to assist the formulation of national scientific and technological information policies, with the creation and improvement of corresponding instruments and institutions.

Intergovernmental Committee action. The Intergovernmental Committee, on 7 June,[20] decided that developing countries should be encouraged to seek international assistance, particularly that of United Nations entities, to strengthen their own national information systems and that strong national capabilities were indispensable for the development of a global information network. The Committee requested the entities and other organizations to support the developing countries in setting up those systems. It further requested the ACC Task Force in co-operation with ACCIS to study the feasibility of extending INFOTERRA to all sciences and technologies and asked the Secretary-General to elicit information from Governments regarding their requirements from a global network and their most urgent technical assistance and training needs. He was also to seek information on Governments' possible contributions towards organizing the network by allowing access to their national systems, their offers of facilities for training specialized personnel from developing countries and their provision to those countries of technical and other kinds of support. In addition, the Committee requested the Secretary-General to disseminate to Governments and other users the Advisory Committee's 1985 directory of United Nations data bases and information systems; urged the regional commissions to enhance their efforts to set up regional information systems; and asked the Centre for science and technology to report biennially on the implementation of the Intergovernmental Committee's recommendations. Developing countries were invited to formulate projects aimed at providing them with basic primary information sources, such as journals and magazines.

In **resolution 40/193**, the General Assembly noted the Intergovernmental Committee's conclusion that setting up and strengthening national information systems should form the major activity in developing a global information network.

REFERENCES

[1]YUN 1979, p. 636. [2]YUN 1984, p. 690. [3]YUN 1981, p. 734. [4]YUN 1982, p. 1430, GA res. 37/234, 21 Dec. 1982. [5]A/CN.11/61. [6]A/CN.11/62. [7]A/CN.11/63. [8]A/CN.11/58. [9]A/CN.11/59. [10]YUN 1984, p. 681. [11]A/40/37 (res. 4(VII)). [12]YUN 1981, pp. 744-749. [13]ACC/1985/2. [14]*Scientific and Technological Information for Development* (proceedings of the *Ad Hoc* Panel of Experts on Information Systems for Science and Technology for Development), Sales No. E.85.II.A.7. [15]A/CN.11/55. [16]A/CN.11/56. [17]YUN 1983, p. 707. [18]A/CN.11/57. [19]A/41/31. [20]A/40/37 (res. 1(VII)).

OTHER PUBLICATIONS

The Capital Goods Sector in Developing Countries: Technology Issues and Policy Options (UNCTAD/TT/78), Sales No. E.85.II.D.4. *ATAS Bulletin*, No. 1, *Tissue Culture Technology and Development* (ST/STD/ATAS/1) (issued without sales number); No. 2, *Microelectronics-Based Automation Technologies and Developing Countries* (ST/STD/ATAS/2), Sales No. E.85.II.A.8; No. 3, *New Information Technologies and Development* (ST/STD/ATAS/3), Sales No. E.85.II.A.18.

Financing

UN Financing System

In its fourth year of operation since January 1982,[1] the United Nations Financing System for Science and Technology for Development continued, despite diminishing finances, to assist developing countries in strengthening their scientific and technological capacities. By October 1985, it had financed 103 projects and served as a forum for the exchange of experience, with inputs totalling about $60 million. Since mobilization of resources through normal pledging procedures had been hindered by uncertainty of the System's long-term financial and institutional arrangements, co-operative arrangements with Governments and non-governmental and private organizations had assumed critical importance, according to a report on UNFSSTD operations in 1985,[2] prepared by the Administrator of UNDP in consultation with the DIEC Director-General.

Operational activities

In allocating funds for its operational activities UNFSSTD was guided by priorities in science and technology as expressed by developing countries. Thus, of the total of $55.5 million approved by the System in 1985, most of the resources went to the two programme areas dealing with the linkage of research and development activities to the productive sphere (36 per cent) and strengthening of scientific

and technological infrastructure (26 per cent). In the research/production sphere, a UNFSSTD-sponsored project in Jordan resulted in a breakthrough in low-cost housing techniques; in China, international assistance was channelled for new technologies in the food industry; and in Jamaica, a project was brought to completion with the inauguration in June of facilities for bauxite testing and processing. Projects dealing with infrastructure included establishing a Centre for Earth Sciences and Geological Cartography in Tunisia and expansion of the Asian Institute of Technology which provided post-graduate and continuing education for countries in the region.

In the programme area covering science and technology policies and plans for development, UNFSSTD-supported projects were completed in the Caribbean and Guinea, while a new project was begun in Ethiopia to assist in planning and institution-strengthening in the aftermath of natural disasters. With regard to human resources development, projects on science teaching took place in Swaziland and Zambia and three projects were completed in Latin America dealing with training in artisanal coastal fishery (Haiti), post-graduate studies in the chemistry of natural products (Paraguay) and master programmes in sciences (Peru). The preparatory stage of a UNFSSTD-supported Technological Information Pilot System (TIPS) project continued during 1985, focusing on the nature and structure of the national focal points designed to distribute technical information among TIPS users.

Despite a slow-down in the flow of project requests, over 1,000 official requests had been received from developing countries by the end of 1985, with the majority of new submissions generated by country and subregional programming exercises being carried out in Africa. Since the number of requests far exceeded available resources, the project portfolio was extensively revised to select the most promising projects endorsed by requesting Governments, appraised through UNFSSTD established channels and further strengthened by technical inputs of UNDP, the concerned United Nations entities and independent experts. In the absence of substantial replenishment of the Financing System's core resources, trust fund operations had become a significant funding source, with three major funds launched in 1985 amounting to $7.8 million.

The lack of core resources also had an impact on follow-up activities. Efforts to secure funding by bilateral or multilateral agencies, particularly the UNDP indicative planning figures (IPFs), brought only limited success: co-financing arrangements with IPFs included a project to establish a metallurgical research and development institute in Nigeria and a small-scale remote sensing and satellite photo-interpretation training centre in Ethiopia. In Latin America and the Caribbean, 17 countries took part in implementing the second phase of the Regional

Non-Destructive Testing Network, with more than 1,500 operators trained and certified during the year. UNFSSTD was also involved in events aimed at promoting international exchange in science and technology. In April, a national remote sensing centre in China hosted an international seminar on the development and application of remote sensing, organized in co-operation with the Department of Technical Co-operation for Development and the State Scientific and Technological Commission of China. The System was invited by UNCTAD to sponsor an inter-agency project related to pharmaceutical supplies (see p. 717). A seminar on institutional linkages between research and productive sectors (São Paulo, Brazil, November) was sponsored by UNFSSTD and the São Paulo government as part of the latter's two-year technical co-operation programme.

Continuing in 1985 its evaluation programme to ensure project quality, UNFSSTD had projects in India, Jamaica, Somalia and Tunisia reviewed by outside experts.

Financial situation

Following a 1984 General Assembly decision,[3] an informal open-ended intergovernmental working group reviewed the long-term financial and institutional arrangements for the Financing System and outlined its proposals at the June session of the Intergovernmental Committee.[4] The group Chairman noted that there had been a broad consensus on the uncertain immediate outlook for additional resources and on the usefulness of UNFSSTD under current arrangements; agreement on its continuation, however, was dependent on its potential to attract additional resources. The suggestions presented by the Chairman on his own behalf included: continuing the current arrangements for mobilizing resources during a further two-year period beginning in 1986; additional efforts by the Secretary-General to mobilize adequate funding for those arrangements; establishing a relationship between core and non-core resources; reviewing the arrangements between UNDP and UNFSSTD in order to enlarge support to the System during the proposed extended period; consultations by the Secretary-General with interested Governments with a view to convening a consultative meeting on science and technology in 1986; and strengthening the working relations between the UNFSSTD secretariat and the Centre for science and technology. The Intergovernmental Committee was to provide guidelines on the proposals and assess their implementation in its annual review of the System's operations.

The Committee, on 7 June,[5] reaffirmed the importance of establishing the long-term financial and institutional arrangements for UNFSSTD and appealed to all Member States to participate and to pledge the maximum possible to the System at the November 1985 United Nations Pledging Conference for Development Activities (see p. 463). The Com-

mittee requested the Secretary-General to consult with Member States on broadening the System's financial base and to submit his recommendations to the General Assembly not later than October. In other action of the same date,[6] the Committee urged Governments to bring about as early as possible the long-term arrangements.

Reporting on his consultations, the Secretary-General, in October,[7] proposed to make UNFSSTD more secure through closer linkage with UNDP. As envisaged by the Secretary-General, it would have two types of operational resources (core and non-core) and a separate administrative account; its institutional structure would consist of the Intergovernmental Committee for overall policy guidance and the UNDP Governing Council for operational activities; it would have closer working arrangements with UNDP units; and its operations would focus on project appraisal, funding, implementation and evaluation. The Secretary-General recommended that the Assembly implement his suggestions in 1986 for three years, to be reviewed at the end of that period, and urged Governments to indicate their willingness to contribute during the current Assembly session and at the November Pledging Conference. The Secretary-General stressed that all core and non-core resources received through September were fully committed and that other resources were insufficient to maintain normal operations beyond 1985. He emphasized that if no funds were forthcoming in 1986 or earlier, Governments would have to decide on terminating UNFSSTD.

Those recommendations were considered informally during the Assembly session, when a general consensus was reached regarding the need for adjustments to existing arrangements.

UNDP Governing Council action. In June 1985, the UNDP Governing Council considered a report[8] of the UNDP Administrator describing the operations of UNFSSTD from March 1984 to March 1985. The report outlined new project development initiatives and co-operative arrangements with Governments and NGOs, including the emergence of trust funds as an important source of new project funding. The status of intergovernmental negotiations on the long-term institutional and financial arrangements for UNFSSTD was also summarized.

On 28 June,[9] the Council approved two projects to be funded by UNFSSTD. It called on the Administrator to assist the Secretary-General to carry out the responsibilities entrusted to him by the Intergovernmental Committee with regard to technology transfer (see p. 718) and requested him to keep Council members informed on relevant developments.

GENERAL ASSEMBLY ACTION

On 17 December, on the recommendation of the Second (Economic and Financial) Committee, the

General Assembly adopted **resolution 40/194** without vote.

United Nations Financing System for Science and Technology for Development

The General Assembly,

Taking note with interest of the report of the Secretary-General on the United Nations Financing System for Science and Technology for Development and on the financial and institutional structure of the System for the next three years, as called for under resolution 6(VII) of 7 June 1985 of the Intergovernmental Committee on Science and Technology for Development,

Regretting that the current resource outlook of the Financing System does not at this time permit the full implementation of the long-term financial and institutional arrangements set out in General Assembly resolution 37/244 of 21 December 1982,

Expressing its appreciation for the contribution which the Financing System has made, despite its meagre financial base, to enhancing science and technology capabilities in developing countries as called for in the Vienna Programme of Action on Science and Technology for Development and in General Assembly resolution 34/218 of 19 December 1979,

Emphasizing the importance of continuing the operational activities of the Financing System,

1. *Requests* the Secretary-General to review the recommendations contained in his report on the United Nations Financing System for Science and Technology for Development in the light of comments made by Governments during the fortieth session of the General Assembly, to hold informal consultations with Governments early in 1986 to arrive at final proposals and to transmit the resulting proposals to Governments by 1 March 1986;

2. *Also requests* the Secretary-General to convene by 30 April 1986 a Pledging Conference for the United Nations Financing System for Science and Technology for Development to enable Governments to pledge resources for 1986 and to give indications of intent to provide other resources for 1986 and the following years;

3. *Further requests* the Secretary-General to take all steps necessary to bring about a successful outcome of the pledging conference;

4. *Decides* that, to maintain a viable level of operations, the total resources made available to the Financing System in 1986 should be sufficient to permit a level of operations not less than the average level achieved by the System over the past three years,* and which would result in a reasonable balance between core and non-core resources;

5. *Decides further* that, should the amounts realized for 1986 fall below this level, the Secretary-General should report on the results of the pledging conference, together with his views on the future of the Financing System, including its orderly termination, to the Intergovernmental Committee on Science and Technology for Development at its eighth session;

6. *Requests* the Administrator of the United Nations Development Programme to bring this matter to the attention of the Governing Council of the Programme at its thirty-third session with a view to seeking authorization to carry out possible new responsibilities that may be assigned to the Programme with regard to the Financing System, including the provision of such administrative support for specific functions and/or posts as may be required;

7. *Urges* Governments to make every effort to provide the maximum support possible for the financing and operations of the Financing System.

---

*Approximately $10 million.

General Assembly resolution 40/194

17 December 1985   Meeting 119   Adopted without vote

Approved by Second Committee (A/40/989/Add.4) without vote, 13 December (meeting 51); draft by Vice-Chairman (A/C.2/40/L.126), based on informal consultations; agenda item 84 (d).

Meeting numbers. GA 40th session: 2nd Committee 30, 51; plenary 119.

Other aspects of science and technology financing

Mobilizing financial resources for science and technology was also taken up by the Advisory Committee at its February session.[10] The Committee proposed convening a panel to develop recommendations for enhancing the process.

An *ad hoc* panel of specialists on mobilizing financial resources for scientific and technological development in developing countries was held at Islamabad, Pakistan, from 4 to 10 November.[11] Noting that there was no real alternative to domestic efforts at resource mobilization, the panel emphasized the need for political commitment at the highest level and creation of a central government entity to deal with science and technology. It submitted that the very condition of acute underdevelopment and poverty required modest but critical investment, stressed the importance of technical education and post-education and called for integrating science and technology into the framework of other national policies and plans. Upon examining the effectiveness of various resource-generating techniques, the panel presented a list of policy instruments which could be used by developing countries in line with their specific needs. It concluded, however, that mobilization *per se* would be of no avail unless the efficiency and management of scientific and technological institutions improved.

Contributions and expenditures

Uncertainty regarding the long-term financial and institutional arrangements for the Financing System again hindered the mobilization of resources through normal pledging procedures, with less than $150,000 pledged in that manner during 1985.

CONTRIBUTIONS TO THE UN FINANCING SYSTEM FOR SCIENCE AND TECHNOLOGY FOR DEVELOPMENT, 1985 AND 1986

(as at 31 December 1985; in US dollar equivalent)

Country	1985 payment	1986 pledge
Bangladesh	—	2,600
Bhutan	3,020	1,730
Cameroon	—	5,222
Cuba	30,613	—
Cyprus	500	500
Democratic Yemen	2,000	—
Fiji	1,000	926
Honduras	2,000	2,000
Indonesia	12,000	15,000
Kenya	—	49,080

Country	1985 payment	1986 pledge
Lao People's Democratic Republic	–	1,000
Lesotho	1,575	766
Madagascar	3,205	3,205
Malawi	–	1,637
Mauritius	1,896	–
Mexico	150,000	–
Mongolia	264	289
Panama	2,000	2,000
Philippines	1,000	5,000
Republic of Korea	60,000	30,000
Senegal	–	2,000
Sierra Leone	(857)	–
Togo	213	–
Zaire	–	1,000
Zambia	23,605	–
Zimbabwe	4,349	–
Total	298,383	123,955

SOURCE: A/41/5/Add.1.

EXPENDITURES OF THE UN FINANCING SYSTEM FOR SCIENCE AND
TECHNOLOGY FOR DEVELOPMENT BY COUNTRY OR AREA, 1985

(as at 31 December 1985; in thousands of US dollars)

Country/area	Amount
Bangladesh	806
Bolivia	28
Botswana	1
Brazil	112
Burundi	21
Cape Verde	2
China	894
Costa Rica	584
Cuba	1
Djibouti	(1)
Ethiopia	4
Gambia	12
Guinea	63
Guinea-Bissau	13
Haiti	8
Honduras	14
Indonesia	987
Ivory Coast	7
Jamaica	30
Jordan	(5)
Lesotho	39
Madagascar	244
Malawi	2
Maldives	12
Mauritius	6
Mexico	2
Mongolia	68
Mozambique	2
Nepal	190
Nigeria	34
Pakistan	(9)
Paraguay	29
Philippines	16
Senegal	152
Seychelles	12
Sierra Leone	20
Somalia	45
Sri Lanka	65
Sudan	13
Swaziland	106
Thailand	18
United Republic of Tanzania	(6)
Uruguay	(7)
Zambia	214
Other	(11)
Subtotal	4,837
Regional Africa	74
Regional Arab States	27
Regional Asia and the Pacific	131
Regional Latin America and the Caribbean	559
Global and interregional	834
Subtotal	1,625
Total	6,462

NOTE: Figures in parentheses are negative amounts representing adjustments
from previous expenditures.
SOURCE: DP/1986/11/Add.6.

REFERENCES

[1]YUN 1982, p. 937. [2]A/CN.11/73. [3]YUN 1984, p. 686, GA
dec. 39/428, 17 Dec. 1984. [4]A/40/37. [5]*Ibid.* (res. 6(VII)). [6]*Ibid.*
(res. 4(VII)). [7]A/C.2/40/4. [8]DP/1985/49. [9]E/1985/32 (dec.
85/28). [10]A/CN.11/59. [11]A/CN.11/AC.1/VI/3.

Institutional arrangements

National focal points

The Centre for science and technology continued
its efforts to establish and maintain an up-to-date
registry of national focal points for science and
technology for development. As requested by the
Intergovernmental Committee in 1982,[1] the
Secretary-General presented a list of national focal
points updated as at February 1985[2] and including
additional information provided by Member States
since March 1983, when the initial registry had been
compiled.[3] The registry listed the 159 Member
States of the United Nations and five non-member
States maintaining permanent observer missions
at Headquarters (Democratic People's Republic of
Korea, Holy See, Monaco, Republic of Korea,
Switzerland). In 17 cases, the designation of the national
focal point had been made temporarily and in three
cases the Centre was awaiting information. In the
interim, the registry listed the permanent mission
of each country to the United Nations or, in its absence,
the Ministry of Foreign Affairs.

Intergovernmental Committee

Strengthening effectiveness of work methods

The question of enhancing the role and effectiveness of the Intergovernmental Committee was
a major topic at its May/June 1985 session.[4] On
7 June,[5] the Committee adopted guidelines for
selecting substantive themes, which in its view should:
be closely related to the programme areas of the
Vienna Programme's operational plan; address policy
issues related to strengthening endogenous scientific and technological capacities in developing countries; promote those countries' collective self-reliance;
cut across several sectors of science and technology;
and be of relevance to developed and developing
countries and to the activities of concerned United
Nations entities. The Committee selected two substantive themes for consideration at its 1987 session:
the application of science and technology to the study,
prevention, monitoring and combating of drought
and other natural disasters; and the impact of new
and emerging areas of science and technology on
the development of developing countries. The Advisory

Committee was requested to prepare for the in-depth study of those themes and to comment on the guidelines for theme selection.

In other action of the same date,[6] the Intergovernmental Committee invited a more active participation in it and a more effective contribution to its work and urged a further strengthening and development of substantive themes. Affirming its commitment to comply with a 1984 General Assembly resolution[7] by which the Assembly had identified science and technology for development for biennial consideration by the Second Committee in odd-numbered years, the Committee decided that the biennial cycle of its own meetings should begin in 1987. It further decided that at each session the Chairman for the following session should be elected, that appropriate country groups should nominate the other members of the Bureau, and that the Chairman should be elected for calendar years, should assist in preparations for each session and for contacts with the Advisory Committee, and should be responsible for reporting the session's results to the Economic and Social Council and the Assembly.

ECONOMIC AND SOCIAL COUNCIL ACTION

The Intergovernmental Committee's report on its seventh (1985) session (New York, 28 May–7 June)[4] was submitted to the Economic and Social Council, which took note of it on 25 July by **decision 1985/175.**

GENERAL ASSEMBLY ACTION

On 17 December, the General Assembly, on the recommendation of the Second Committee, adopted **resolution 40/193** without vote.

Report of the Intergovernmental Committee on Science and Technology for Development

The General Assembly,

Recalling the Vienna Programme of Action on Science and Technology for Development and General Assembly resolution 34/218 of 19 December 1979,

Noting that the Intergovernmental Committee on Science and Technology for Development, at its seventh session, considered as a substantive theme the question of information systems for science and technology for development, and noting the conclusion, in Committee resolution 1(VII) of 7 June 1985, that the setting up and strengthening of national information systems and networks should form the major activity in the process of development of a global information network,

Noting further the mid-decade review of the implementation of the Vienna Programme of Action conducted by the Committee and its decision, in its resolution 4(VII) of 7 June 1985, to undertake a comprehensive review in 1989,

1. *Takes note* of the report of the Intergovernmental Committee on Science and Technology for Development on its seventh session;

2. *Endorses* the resolutions and decisions contained therein.

General Assembly resolution 40/193

17 December 1985   Meeting 119   Adopted without vote

Approved by Second Committee (A/40/989/Add.4) without vote, 11 November (meeting 30); draft by Chairman (A/C.2/40/L.19), based on informal consultations and orally revised; agenda item 84 *(d)*.

Advisory Committee

The Advisory Committee on Science and Technology for Development, established to provide policy and planning advice for the deliberations of the Intergovernmental Committee, held its fifth session in New York from 4 to 13 February 1985,[8] focusing on the two substantive themes selected by the Intergovernmental Committee for consideration in 1985: a mid-decade review of the Vienna Programme, and information systems for science and technology for development (see above, under respective headings). The Advisory Committee also reviewed its work in the medium term, considering the guidelines for a November 1985 panel on mobilization of financial resources (see p. 713) and a panel on science, technology and self-sufficiency in food, scheduled for January 1986. Looking to the medium-term future, the Committee outlined several broad themes related to the Vienna Programme to serve as the basis for its work programme: generation and support of the scientific and technological community in developing countries; the innovation process in developing countries; multilateral co-operation; science and technology and long-term ecological crises; and problems of rapidly growing urban areas. In addition, the Committee identified other areas of interest requiring further investigation and proposed a tentative schedule for panel meetings on the new topics.

On 7 June,[9] the Intergovernmental Committee took note of the Advisory Committee's report and expressed appreciation to Austria, Canada, Italy, Japan, Swaziland, the USSR and the United States for their co-operation in holding panels and workshops in 1984 and 1985. In implementing its work programme, the Advisory Committee was requested to take into account the substantive themes chosen by the Intergovernmental Committee and to use the guidelines for selecting those themes in planning future activities. The Intergovernmental Committee recommended that the General Assembly authorize the Advisory Committee to constitute a maximum of four *ad hoc* panels of specialists in 1986 and 1987, with no more than two one-week panel meetings held each year. Certain aspects of the Advisory Committee's work were covered by other Intergovernmental Committee resolutions of the same date (see pp. 714 and 716).

Centre for science and technology

Serving as the secretariat for the Intergovernmental Committee, the Advisory Committee and the ACC Task Force on Science and Technology for Development, the Centre for Science and Technology for Development continued throughout 1985 to provide support for the implementation of the 1979 Vienna Programme of Action. Since the Centre had no mandate for undertaking operational projects, its efforts had been mainly directed towards promoting in-depth analysis of the issues pertaining to the Programme and catalysing action for fulfilling its objectives.

A major focus in 1985 was on scientific and technological information systems for development. The Centre prepared background documents for the January *ad hoc* panel of experts in Rome (see p. 709), carried out a number of studies leading to the final report on the establishment of the global network of scientific and technological information, prepared a survey on the existing and planned information services in the United Nations system (see p. 710), and organized an interregional seminar on the role of information in accelerating scientific and technological progress in developing countries (Moscow, 24 September–5 October). It also organized a preparatory workshop in New York (13 and 14 August) and an *ad hoc* panel of specialists in Islamabad (4-10 November) on mobilization of financial resources, and a preparatory workshop on science, technology and food security (Cairo, Egypt, 21-25 October).

The Centre maintained its regular interaction with the national focal points (see p. 714), Governments and regional organizations and published its newsletter *UPDATE*, covering the work of the Intergovernmental and Advisory Committees and other organizations. In a continued effort to alert developing countries to the positive and negative implications of new technologies, it worked to develop further the Advance Technology Alert System (ATAS), launched in 1984,[10] putting out the *ATAS Bulletin*, each issue of which focused on a specific area of new technology.

An assessment of the Centre's activities for the previous five years was presented in a report by the Secretary-General on the mid-decade review of the implementation of the Vienna Programme.[11]

The Intergovernmental Committee, on 7 June,[12] decided that the Centre's regular reports on the activities of the United Nations system in implementing the Vienna Programme should give special attention to the subjects related to the substantive themes and to other programme areas. It also requested the Centre's Executive Director to submit to the Committee at its 1986 session a proposal for a working methodology for a 1989

end-of-decade review (see also p. 709). Also on the same date,[13] The Committee took note of the Centre's efforts in implementing the ATAS programme, publishing the proceedings of the *ad hoc* panels and seminars convened by the Advisory Committee and organizing follow-up activities to the recommendations of the Intergovernmental and Advisory Committees. Expressing thanks to all Governments and organizations which provided support for those efforts, the Intergovernmental Committee encouraged the Centre to accord higher priority to them during 1986 and 1987 and reiterated its request to all national and international potential donors to support the growth of the Centre's activities.

Co-ordination in the UN system

Established by ACC to promote closer co-operation among United Nations bodies in implementing the Vienna Programme, the Task Force on Science and Technology for Development held its sixth session at Geneva from 29 to 31 January 1985.[14] After discussing follow-up and implementation of joint activities, the Task Force agreed that financing remained the principal problem, requiring greater commitment from United Nations organizations and agencies, and suggested thematic joint programming meetings to be held by the lead agencies to implement individual projects. The Task Force also drafted a decision for adoption by ACC (see below) and proposed that the Intergovernmental Committee request United Nations agencies to include joint activities in their 1986-1987 programme budgets. With regard to criteria for building endogenous capacities in developing countries, the Task Force decided to set up an open-ended working group under the chairmanship of the International Labour Organisation (ILO) to formulate terms of reference for policy-oriented studies and inter-agency missions to developing countries at their request. After examining a mid-decade review on implementing the Vienna Programme, the Task Force agreed to issue a list of documents on the subject published by United Nations organizations. Other items on the session's agenda concerned information systems for science and technology (see p. 709), proposed themes for consideration at the Intergovernmental Committee's 1986 session, follow-up to the Advisory Committee's *ad hoc* panels, and co-operation with the Organization of the Islamic Conference.

Acting on the Task Force's conclusions, ACC decided, in April,[15] that preparation of programme budget proposals for 1986-1987 provided an opportunity for submitting to respective governing bodies proposed allocations to joint activities, and requested executive heads of the lead agencies to explore ways of mobilizing extrabudgetary resources.

On 7 June,[16] the Intergovernmental Committee called for enhancing the effectiveness of the Task Force's inter-agency co-ordination mechanisms in co-operation with ACCIS. Also that day,[12] the Committee recommended that the cross-organizational programme analysis on the activities of the United Nations system, planned by the Committee for Programme and Co-ordination for 1987, should examine measures for ensuring compatibility between the medium-term plans of United Nations entities.

REFERENCES

[1]YUN 1982, p. 936. [2]A/CN.11/INF/7. [3]YUN 1983, p. 712. [4]A/40/37. [5]*Ibid.* (res. 2(VII)). [6]*Ibid.* (res. 3(VII)). [7]YUN 1984, p. 986, GA res. 39/217, 18 Dec. 1984. [8]A/CN.11/59. [9]A/40/37 (dec. 2(VII)). [10]YUN 1984, p. 682. [11]A/CN.11/63. [12]A/40/37 (res. 4(VII)). [13]*Ibid.* (dec. 1(VII)). [14]ACC/1985/2. [15]ACC/1985/DEC/1-13 (dec. 1985/13). [16]A/40/37 (res. 1(VII)).

Technology transfer

Questions of choice, acquisition and transfer of technology continued to be in the focus of attention of several United Nations bodies during 1985, particularly UNCTAD and the United Nations Industrial Development Organization (UNIDO).

UNCTAD activities. A major emphasis in the work of UNCTAD's Trade and Development Board in 1985 was follow-up to decisions adopted at the 1984 sessions of the Committee on Transfer of Technology.[1] With regard to technical and operational assistance provided by the Advisory Service on Transfer of Technology, the Board, on 29 March,[2] noted the progress made by the Service in responding to developing countries' requirements and requested the UNCTAD Secretary-General to continue providing information on its work, including data for a 1986 review by the Committee on Transfer of Technology. The Board requested the Service to give priority to requests of developing countries in formulating and implementing related plans; utilizing technologies in the public domain; formulating strategies for the technological development of sectors important to individual developing countries; preparing training programmes and operational tools; establishing efficient co-operative arrangements among developing countries; and improving their access to United Nations–funded research and development. The Board urged that the Service be provided with sufficient resources.

Concerning new and emerging technologies, the Board, also on 29 March,[3] underscored their major implications for world trade and develop-ment and for the technological transformation of developing countries. Taking note of the UNCTAD secretariat's preliminary work on the economic, commercial and developmental aspects of those technologies, the Board requested the UNCTAD Secretary-General to prepare a study of those issues, particularly examining their impact on the export performance of developing countries. He was also requested to ensure the integrated study of those issues within the secretariat and to submit his report to the Committee on Transfer of Technology at its 1986 session.

In other March actions,[4] the Board took note of the Committee's report on its 1984 regular session,[1] and authorized its Chairman to continue informal consultations on issues in individual sectors of critical importance to developing countries. The latter question was again addressed by the Board on 27 September,[5] when it requested the UNCTAD Secretary-General to convene before the 1986 session of the Committee an intergovernmental expert group on the transfer, application and development of technology in the energy sector, with particular attention to new and renewable sources of energy (see Chapter X of this section). He was invited to seek extrabudgetary resources to offset the cost of participation by experts from the least developed countries, and also requested to expedite work on the transfer, application and development of technology in the food sector and to report the results to the Committee in 1986. The Committee was requested to convene the remaining meetings of governmental experts, as had been decided by UNCTAD in 1983.[6]

Also on 27 September,[7] the Board invited the UNCTAD Secretary-General to report to the Committee on Transfer of Technology in 1986 on development aspects of the work in pharmaceuticals by the World Health Organization (WHO). It also invited UNFSSTD to give priority to the joint inter-agency project on formulation of strategies for facilitating pharmaceutical supplies to developing countries and requested the UNCTAD Secretary-General to report in 1986 to the Committee on Transfer of Technology on the results of a WHO-sponsored conference at Nairobi, Kenya (see PART II, Chapter V) and on UNCTAD activities in the pharmaceutical sector.

During 1985, UNCTAD published a number of case-studies which examined aspects of the transfer of technology: implications of technology transfer by small and medium-sized metalworking enterprises in Argentina and Brazil;[8] establishment of an information and documentation system on the transfer of technology in Ethiopia;[9] international transfer of technology by Japan's small and medium enterprises in developing countries;[10] policy and institutional issues of transfer of technology in Nepal;[11] and implementation of laws and regulations on transfer of technology in Nigeria.[12]

Conscious of the importance of effective mechanisms for the transfer of technology, the Intergovernmental Committee, on 7 June,[13] requested the Secretary-General to contact Member States informally on ways of tackling issues left unresolved by the 1979 United Nations Conference on Science and Technology for Development,[14] possibly at a special session of the Intergovernmental Committee; he was to report on the outcome in 1986.

UNIDO activities. The thrust of UNIDO's work in technology transfer and acquisition during 1985, as described in its annual report,[15] continued to be strengthening negotiating capabilities of developing countries. As part of that effort, UNIDO provided advisory services on request; conducted technical workshops in Greece, Mali and Nigeria; held a technical workshop in Poland on contract negotiation and project preparation for African countries; prepared guidelines for guarantees and warranties; and consolidated training material for strengthening negotiating capabilities in African countries. Much of the work continued to be channelled through the Technological Information Exchange System (TIES). Data on some 800 contracts were added during the year to the information contributed under TIES and maintained by the UNIDO secretariat. The Tenth Meeting of Heads of Technology Transfer Registries (Cairo, December) reviewed trends in technology transfer flows and contractual arrangements, and assessed the development of the computerized registry information system as an important element of TIES.

On 31 May,[16] the Industrial Development Board requested the UNIDO Executive Director to present a report on the development and transfer of technology, including the Industrial and Technological Information Bank, to the next session of the competent organs of UNIDO, and reaffirmed the relevant resolutions of the 1984 Fourth General Conference of UNIDO[17] and the previous conclusions of the Board on the subject.

Draft code of conduct

Following a 1983 decision of the General Assembly,[18] the sixth session of the United Nations Conference on an International Code of Conduct on the Transfer of Technology, initially convened under UNCTAD auspices in 1978,[19] was held at Geneva from 13 May to 5 June 1985. The Conference continued working on the draft code—comprising a preamble and nine chapters—by initially establishing two working groups to examine, respectively, issues outstanding in chapter 4, on restrictive practices, and chapter 9, on applicable law and settlement of disputes. A third working group, established at a later stage, dealt with a number of issues still outstanding in chapters 1 (scope of application), 5 (obligations) and 8 (international institutional machinery).

Describing the status of the negotiations at the conclusion of the sixth session, the UNCTAD secretariat noted[20] that most of the unresolved issues fell under a broad category of provisions concerning the regulation of transfer of technology transactions and the conduct of parties to them. Regarding chapter 4, the Conference succeeded in drawing up a list of 14 restrictive practices to be avoided; three of them, however, needed further elaboration. In addition, despite substantial progress made in formulating an introductory section setting forth the characteristics of the practices to be avoided, the relevant circumstances and the applicability of the chapter to transactions between affiliated enterprises, certain differences had persisted among regional groups. The text of chapter 9 had not been formally drafted; while there appeared to be a broad consensus on the formulation of the provisions on conciliation and arbitration, differences remained in the approaches proposed by regional groups with respect to the choice of law.

The provisions of the code falling under another broad category, related to action by Governments, had all been agreed upon, except for two subparagraphs in chapter 8 concerning the nature of the institutional machinery and the nature, mandate and timing of the review conference.

In view of the fact that the sixth session was unable to complete the negotiations on an international code of conduct, the Conference, on 5 June, requested the General Assembly to consider the possibility of reconvening the negotiations. The UNCTAD Secretary-General was requested to transmit to the Assembly the draft code and the appropriate documentation.

GENERAL ASSEMBLY ACTION

On 17 December, on the recommendation of the Second Committee, the General Assembly adopted **resolution 40/184** without vote.

International code of conduct on the transfer of technology

The General Assembly,

Recalling its resolution 38/153 of 19 December 1983,

Taking note of the decision adopted on 5 June 1985 by the United Nations Conference on an International Code of Conduct on the Transfer of Technology, at its sixth session, in which it requested the General Assembly to take the measures necessary for further action, including the possible reconvening of negotiations on an international code of conduct on the transfer of technology,

1. *Notes* that progress has been made in the negotiations on an international code of conduct on the transfer of technology but that there are still important problems outstanding;

2. *Further notes* that at the sixth session of the United Nations Conference on an International Code of Conduct on the Transfer of Technology, progress was made in identifying common ground, as well as divergences, in respect of the issues outstanding in chapter 4 of the draft code, on restrictive practices, and in chapter 9, on applicable law and settlement of disputes;

3. *Believes* that further work, continuing the genuine efforts made by all parties concerned, is required in the search for possible solutions to the outstanding issues in order to complete successfully the negotiations on a code of conduct;

4. *Invites* the Secretary-General of the United Nations Conference on Trade and Development and the President of the United Nations Conference on an International Code of Conduct on the Transfer of Technology to consult, as appropriate, with regional groups and Governments, taking into account the need for balanced geographical representation, with a view to identifying appropriate solutions to the issues outstanding in the code of conduct;

5. *Further invites* the Secretary-General of the United Nations Conference on Trade and Development to report to the General Assembly at its forty-first session on the progress made in the consultations referred to in paragraph 4 above and decides to take, at that session, further action on the negotiations on an international code of conduct on the transfer of technology.

General Assembly resolution 40/184

17 December 1985   Meeting 119   Adopted without vote

Approved by Second Committee (A/40/989/Add.3) without vote, 3 December (meeting 46); draft by Chairman (A/C.2/40/L.79), based on informal consultations; agenda item 84 *(c)*.
Meeting numbers. GA 40th session: 2nd Committee 31, 36, 41, 45, 46; plenary 119.

REFERENCES

[1]YUN 1984, p. 691. [2]A/40/15, vol. I (res. 308(XXX)). [3]*Ibid.* (dec. 307(XXX)). [4]A/40/15, vol. I. [5]A/40/15, vol. II (res. 326(XXXI)). [6]YUN 1983, p. 717. [7]A/40/15, vol. II (res. 325(XXXI)). [8]UNCTAD/TT/69. [9]UNCTAD/TT/77. [10]UNCTAD/TT/68.   [11]UNCTAD/TT/80. [12]UNCTAD/TT/74. [13]A/40/37 (res. 5(VII)). [14]YUN 1979, p. 633. [15]IDB.2/10. [16]A/40/16 (conclusion 1985/6). [17]YUN 1984, p. 558. [18]YUN 1983, p. 718, GA res. 38/153, 19 Dec. 1983. [19]YUN 1978, p. 503. [20]TD/CODE TOT/49.

PUBLICATION

Fertilizer Supplies for Developing Countries: Issues in the Transfer and Development of Technology (UNCTAD/TT/45/Rev.1), Sales No. E.85.II.D.2.

Brain drain

In 1985, UNCTAD and the General Assembly continued to search for solutions to the problem of the outflow of skilled personnel from developing countries, known as the reverse transfer of technology or brain drain.

UNCTAD activities. Pursuant to a 1984 General Assembly resolution,[1] the Third Meeting of Governmental Experts on the Reverse Transfer of Technology was held at Geneva from 26 August to 4 September 1985. The Meeting examined studies prepared by the UNCTAD secretariat on policy approaches and measures; a preliminary outline of a set of guidelines; and elements for a questionnaire on quantitative and qualitative information on the reverse transfer of technology.

In its conclusions and recommendations, included in the Trade and Development Board's report on its September session,[2] the Meeting stressed that, reinforced by the current adverse economic situation, outflows of skilled manpower had increased and taken new forms, undermining developing countries' efforts to accelerate their development processes and prompting implications of global concern. Although measures had been adopted to mitigate the adverse effects of the brain drain, concerted international action was needed to complement national efforts. The Meeting concluded that a foundation had been established for moving to a universal approach and that improvement of policy implementation and information dissemination was closely linked to establishing guidelines for an integrated action programme. It recommended that the documentation submitted to the Meeting and its report[3] be circulated to all UNCTAD member States, intergovernmental and non-governmental organizations and United Nations entities. The UNCTAD Secretary-General was requested to convene, not later than the first quarter of 1987, the next expert meeting to consider an action programme on the reverse transfer of technology. Regretting the absence of receiving developed countries from the three meetings, the Third Meeting urged those countries to participate fully and asked United Nations entities to co-operate with UNCTAD in its work.

Inter-agency group meeting. The Inter-Agency Group on Reverse Transfer of Technology, established in 1984[4] to enhance the effectiveness of the United Nations system in responding to the needs of the countries concerned, met on 24 and 25 June 1985 at Geneva. The meeting, held under the chairmanship of UNCTAD, was convened in pursuance of a 1984 Assembly request.[1] The Group's report[5] summarized information provided by ILO, UNCTAD, UNDP, UNIDO and the United Nations Centre on Transnational Corporations on their activities related to the brain drain. In its concluding remarks, the Group noted that joint projects launched by ILO with the Intergovernmental Committee for Migration were a good example of United Nations action to achieve better results. The Group emphasized that its meetings played a catalytic role in the co-ordination of efforts and stressed that its 1984 conclusions[4] constituted a constructive framework for co-operation.

GENERAL ASSEMBLY ACTION

On 17 December, the General Assembly, on the recommendation of the Second Committee, adopted **resolution 40/191** by recorded vote.

Reverse transfer of technology

The General Assembly,

Recalling its resolutions 3201(S-VI) and 3202(S-VI) of 1 May 1974, 3281(XXIX) of 12 December 1974, 3362(S-VII) of 16 September 1975, 35/56 of 5 December 1980 and the resolutions on the reverse transfer of technology,

Continuing to believe that since the outflow of skilled personnel from developing countries seriously hampers their development, there is an urgent need to formulate national and international policies to avoid the "brain drain" and to obviate its adverse effects,

Convinced that the search for durable solutions to the problem of the reverse transfer of technology requires the full participation of all parties concerned,

1. *Takes note* of the report of the Inter-Agency Group on Reverse Transfer of Technology, covering meetings held at Geneva on 24 and 25 June 1985;

2. *Takes note also* of the outcome of the Third Meeting of Governmental Experts on the Reverse Transfer of Technology, held at Geneva from 26 August to 4 September 1985;

3. *Requests* the Secretary-General of the United Nations Conference on Trade and Development to convene a meeting of governmental experts to review the current situation with respect to all aspects of the international migration of skilled personnel from developing countries; the governmental experts should focus, in their study, on the nature, scale and effect of such flows, taking into account the concerns of all parties, with a view to proposing to the Conference and, as appropriate, other international organizations, further work that they may carry out to mitigate adverse consequences of this phenomenon, especially as it affects the developing countries, also taking into account, as appropriate, the work done thus far by governmental expert groups, and any other relevant material;

4. *Also requests* the Secretary-General of the United Nations Conference on Trade and Development to prepare studies providing:

(a) A review of the existing situation with respect to the international migration of skilled personnel from developing countries based on the most recently available and generally acceptable statistics;

(b) A comprehensive bibliography of current literature in this field;

5. *Recommends* that the Secretary-General of the United Nations Conference on Trade and Development should invite all interested organs and bodies of the United Nations system and other appropriate international organizations to participate in the preparation of the studies and in the work of the meeting of governmental experts;

6. *Requests* the Secretary-General of the United Nations Conference on Trade and Development to report on the outcome of the meeting of governmental experts to the General Assembly at its forty-second session, through the Trade and Development Board;

7. *Requests* the Secretary-General to convene further meetings of the Inter-Agency Group on Reverse Transfer of Technology and to report on the results of those meetings to the General Assembly at its forty-second session.

General Assembly resolution 40/191

17 December 1985   Meeting 119   152-1 (recorded vote)

Approved by Second Committee (A/40/989/Add.3) by recorded vote (127-1), 11 December (meeting 50); draft by Yugoslavia, for Group of 77 (A/C.2/40/L.31/Rev.1 & Rev.1/Corr.1); agenda item 84 (c).
Meeting numbers. GA 40th session: 2nd Committee 31, 36, 41, 45, 46, 48-50; plenary 119.

Recorded vote in Assembly as follows:

In favour: Afghanistan, Algeria, Angola, Antigua and Barbuda, Argentina, Australia, Austria, Bahamas, Bahrain, Bangladesh, Barbados, Belgium, Benin, Bhutan, Bolivia, Botswana, Brazil, Brunei Darussalam, Bulgaria, Burkina Faso, Burma, Burundi, Byelorussian SSR, Cameroon, Canada, Cape Verde, Central African Republic, Chad, Chile, China, Colombia, Comoros, Congo, Costa Rica, Cuba, Cyprus, Czechoslovakia, Democratic Kampuchea, Democratic Yemen, Denmark, Djibouti, Dominica, Dominican Republic, Ecuador, Egypt, El Salvador, Equatorial Guinea, Ethiopia, Fiji, Finland, France, Gabon, Gambia, German Democratic Republic, Germany, Federal Republic of, Ghana, Greece, Grenada, Guatemala, Guinea, Guinea-Bissau, Guyana, Haiti, Honduras, Hungary, Iceland, India, Indonesia, Iran, Iraq, Ireland, Italy, Ivory Coast, Jamaica, Japan, Jordan, Kenya, Kuwait, Lao People's Democratic Republic, Lebanon, Lesotho, Liberia, Libyan Arab Jamahiriya, Luxembourg, Madagascar, Malawi, Malaysia, Maldives, Mali, Malta, Mauritania, Mauritius, Mexico, Mongolia, Morocco, Mozambique, Nepal, Netherlands, New Zealand, Nicaragua, Niger, Nigeria, Norway, Oman, Pakistan, Panama, Papua New Guinea, Paraguay, Peru, Philippines, Poland, Portugal, Qatar, Romania, Rwanda, Saint Christopher and Nevis, Saint Lucia, Saint Vincent and the Grenadines, Samoa, Sao Tome and Principe, Saudi Arabia, Senegal, Sierra Leone, Singapore, Somalia, Spain, Sri Lanka, Sudan, Suriname, Swaziland, Sweden, Syrian Arab Republic, Thailand, Togo, Trinidad and Tobago, Tunisia, Turkey, Uganda, Ukrainian SSR, USSR, United Arab Emirates, United Kingdom, United Republic of Tanzania, Uruguay, Vanuatu, Venezuela, Viet Nam, Yemen, Yugoslavia, Zaire, Zambia, Zimbabwe.

Against: United States.

Speaking in the Second Committee on behalf of the Eastern European countries and Mongolia, Bulgaria said that the approved text should in no way restrict the existing mandate of UNCTAD on matters relating to the reverse transfer of technology. Canada welcomed the fact that the Committee had been able to approve a revised text in a spirit of compromise. The United Kingdom said it voted in favour without prejudice to the position it had taken on previous resolutions on the subject. Yugoslavia, for the Group of 77 developing countries, regretted that paragraph 4 (a) had caused difficulties for some delegations, since it felt that the reference to generally acceptable statistics did not change the work methods of the UNCTAD secretariat.

REFERENCES

(1)YUN 1984, p. 694, GA res. 39/211, 18 Dec. 1984. (2)A/40/15, vol. II. (3)TD/B/1073. (4)YUN 1984, p. 694. (5)A/40/798.

Chapter XIII

Social and cultural development

Poverty and underdevelopment remained major obstacles to social progress in 1985. Statistics of total output showed the grip of recession on different country groups and the uneven recovery towards mid-decade, which was strong in North America but hardly felt in much of Western Europe, parts of Asia, many countries in Latin America and the Caribbean, and most of Africa.

In a context of persistent underdevelopment and growing insecurity, the world social situation continued to be marked by violence, economic and other imbalances and contradictions, the emergence of new problems due to shifting economic, social and national interests, and the increasing use of adjustment or austerity measures.

The Commission for Social Development held its twenty-ninth session at Vienna, Austria, from 18 to 27 February 1985. Following its recommendations, the Economic and Social Council adopted resolutions on the family (1985/29), an inter-regional consultation on developmental social welfare policies (1985/26), the co-operative movement (1985/22), welfare of migrant workers and their families (1985/24) and timely distribution of documents (1985/20). The Council also adopted resolutions on the social aspects of development (1985/31), implementation of the 1969 Declaration on Social Progress and Development (1985/34) and the progress of the Commission's work (1985/36).

Both the Council and the General Assembly dealt with the world social situation—in resolutions 1985/21 and 40/100, respectively—and with national experience in achieving social and economic changes—1985/32 and 40/23.

In addition, the Assembly adopted a resolution on improving the United Nations role in social development (40/98) and the Council dealt with social welfare policies for African migrant workers (resolution 1985/64).

The Seventh United Nations Congress on the Prevention of Crime and the Treatment of Offenders was held at Milan, Italy, from 26 August to 6 September. It adopted the Milan Plan of Action on crime prevention and criminal justice and Guiding Principles for crime prevention in the context of development, as well as four other major international instruments and 26 resolutions.

The Assembly expressed its appreciation to Italy for hosting the Congress (40/37). It approved the Milan Plan and recommended the Guiding Prin-

ciples for action (40/32). It adopted Standard Minimum Rules for the Administration of Juvenile Justice (40/33) and a Declaration of Basic Principles of Justice for Victims of Crime and Abuse of Power (40/34). Also on the recommendation of the Congress, it adopted two resolutions on the development of standards for the prevention of juvenile delinquency (40/35) and on domestic violence (40/36).

Efforts continued by the United Nations Educational, Scientific and Cultural Organization (UNESCO) to promote the return or restitution of cultural property to the countries of origin. The Assembly, by resolution 40/19, welcomed the steady increase in the number of States parties to the 1970 UNESCO Convention on the Means of Prohibiting and Preventing the Illicit Import, Export and Transfer of Ownership of Cultural Property.

Topics related to this chapter. Development policy and international economic co-operation—economic and social trends and policy; rural development; special economic areas. Health and human resources: disabled persons; the role of qualified national personnel in development. Human rights: popular participation; right to development; rights of migrant workers. Women: women and development. Children, youth and aging: child welfare.

Social development and welfare

World social situation

The *1985 Report on the World Social Situation*,[1] submitted in accordance with guidelines set forth in 1982 General Assembly[2] and 1983 Economic and Social Council[3] resolutions, was the eleventh in the series issued by the United Nations since 1952. It sought to reflect the complex and changing relations between the economic and social, national and international facets of development, while providing an intersectoral analysis of trends and treatment of issues and policies, bearing in mind different social and cultural traditions. The *Report*, which appeared at a time when the United Nations was celebrating the fortieth anniversary of its founding, noted that social conditions had changed profoundly since 1945 by technology and decolonization, to take two prominent influences, but stubbornly resisted change in other areas as testified to by violent conflict and mass poverty.

The *Report* was divided into two parts. The first considered major obstacles to social progress, such as underdevelopment and the difficulties of international economic co-operation, conflicts and militarism, and violence to groups and individuals. The second part took up the forces of change, including education, technology, information and communication, employment, urbanization and changes in values, and the role of the State.

Poverty and underdevelopment remained major obstacles to social progress, and stark inequalities among countries diminished opportunities for co-operation. A feature of the preceding few years had been the simultaneous adjustment to external imbalances by a large number of countries by cutting the imports which would have been the others' exports; that added to surplus world export capacity and unemployment while domestic needs in many parts of the world went unmet. The tragedy of famine at a time of ample food supplies in global markets pointed to another long-standing imbalance. Another symptom was a widespread tendency to cut what were considered to be dispensable social expenditures. It had become more difficult to keep in perspective the importance of a balance between social investment and long-term economic health and development.

In connection with the *Report*, the Secretary-General presented in January 1985 an analysis[4] of the co-ordination between the United Nations and its specialized agencies in the collection of social statistics and the preparation of reports on social issues, also requested by the Assembly in 1982.[2] The report identified three types of reports on social issues produced by the United Nations—recurrent analytical reports, world-wide or regional in coverage; reports on the implementation of strategies and plans of action; and *ad hoc* reports on specific issues. Primary responsibilities for the international collection, compilation and dissemination of social statistics were basically decentralized by subject-matter in the international statistical services. Offices engaged in collecting data included the statistical services of the United Nations Secretariat, ILO, FAO, UNESCO and WHO. The Commission for Social Development took note of the report on 27 February 1985.[5]

The United Nations University organized during 1985 a number of symposia and workshops and prepared research papers on human and social development.[6]

ECONOMIC AND SOCIAL COUNCIL ACTION

On 29 May 1985, on the recommendation of its Second (Social) Committee, the Economic and Social Council adopted **resolution 1985/21** without vote.

World social situation

The Economic and Social Council,

Recalling General Assembly resolution 37/54 of 3 December 1982,

Having considered the report of the Commission for Social Development on its twenty-ninth session,

1. *Endorses* the conclusions reached by the Commission for Social Development on the world social situation and on the 1985 report on the world social situation, annexed to the present resolution;

2. *Transmits* those conclusions to the General Assembly for its consideration.

ANNEX
Conclusions of the Commission for Social Development

I. World social situation

1. The Commission notes that recent years have seen a worsening of the social situation in many parts of the world, particularly in Africa, as a result of the disruptive consequences of the global economic crisis. Achievements registered in certain regions and countries or in specific areas of social development do not alter the fact that this deterioration affects the developing countries in particular. Long-lasting problems that have an important bearing on the situation remain unsolved. Additionally, new problems have appeared, both in developing and in industrial countries, and much remains to be done to achieve the various objectives adopted by the international community. Some countries appear to remain untouched by the general deterioration.

2. The Commission reaffirms that the ultimate aim of development is the constant improvement of the well-being of the entire population on the basis of its full participation in the process of development and a fair distribution of the benefits therefrom.

3. Four decades after the victory over fascism and nazism and the founding of the United Nations, pressing social problems continue to exist.

4. It is necessary to achieve the rapid and complete elimination of the obstacles to the economic and social progress of peoples. Colonialism, neo-colonialism, racism, racial discrimination, *apartheid*, aggression, occupation and foreign domination and all other forms of inequality and exploitation of peoples constitute major obstacles to the economic and social progress of developing countries and peoples. It is indeed regrettable that even after the four decades that have elapsed since the founding of the United Nations, progress in the eradication of *apartheid* in South Africa remains slow and unsatisfactory.

5. The existing inequities and imbalances in international economic relations are widening the gap between developed and developing countries, thereby constituting a major obstacle to the development of the developing countries and adversely affecting international relations and the promotion of world peace and security. The arms race and the aggravation of international tension continue to contribute to the deterioration of the world social situation. Disarmament would release resources that could be used for the development of developing countries and could contribute to the well-being and prosperity of all.

6. It is necessary to have a reduction of social and economic disparities and the adoption of measures to ensure the effective participation of all people in the preparation and execution of national policies for economic and social development, based on equal opportunities for all and a full enjoyment of human rights.

7. The adverse social situation reflects the lack of implementation of the Declaration on Social Progress and Development, other relevant United Nations charters and declarations in the social and economic fields, and the objectives and overall development goals adopted and reaffirmed in the International Development Strategy for the Third United Nations Development Decade.

8. Certain social and economic changes have occurred that have had broad and negative repercussions on the elements constituting the social sphere. There is a need to adapt governmental policies to the new and urgent needs that have arisen.

9. Greater attention needs to be accorded to a unified approach to development, as well as to the pursuance of international economic policies in areas of trade, and monetary and fiscal policies consistent with the overall objectives of growth and development. The interdependence that exists between economic development and social development is much more apparent in developing countries facing a crushing debt burden, which at present is having a devastating impact on the social conditions of vulnerable groups. The worsening of the social situation has a serious impact in particular areas and countries, notably on employment and income distribution. Even though additional measures are required for social progress, economic development is an essential prerequisite. It has been stressed that social change and development can exert a positive influence in extricating societies from their economic difficulties. The establishment of the new international economic order has become of great importance for social progress.

10. A more rational use of various available resources should be made by Governments, communities, local authorities and voluntary organizations to deal with the worsening social situation, paying greater attention to the most essential and deserving aspects of social development.

11. The 1985 report on the world social situation and the discussion on the report in the Commission clearly indicate that existing approaches to socio-economic development have not always been able to solve the problems of mass poverty and underdevelopment. Alternative development methods are needed, involving, in particular, more effective participation by the people. Hopeful prospects for future progress towards social amelioration are emerging in developed countries. Technological marvels have appeared on the scene in those countries and been socially assimilated by them at a remarkable rate. The potential exists for applying existing and future technologies to the enhancement of social and productive life in the developing countries.

12. The social situation should be monitored in depth on a regular basis, paying special attention to the manner of implementation of the Declaration on Social Progress and Development and the International Development Strategy for the Third United Nations Development Decade.

II. 1985 report on the world social situation

13. The Commission, conscious of its responsibility for the serious consideration and discussion of the issues before it, expresses its concern at the considerable delay in the circulation of the documents, including the 1985 report on the world social situation, and urges the Secretary-General to ensure that the documents and the report to be considered by the Commission are distributed as prescribed under the rules of procedure of the functional commissions of the Economic and Social Council.

14. The Commission is of the view that the report on the world social situation will better serve the purpose of analysis of the world social situation and trends if it is prepared at four-yearly intervals, as this provides a reasonable time-span for measuring change.

15. For the sessions held in the intervening years, the Commission should have before it a draft framework of the forthcoming report on the world social situation, to allow it to make suggestions in regard to the preparation of the report, and an updated report on the main issues and trends of international concern that have emerged since the last report on the world social situation was prepared.

16. The next report on the world social situation should envisage an overview of trends, within the framework of overall development, and of the impact of continuing imbalances in the world economy and international economic crises that particularly affect developing countries. The report should provide an intersectoral analysis of trends, issues and policies in the national, regional and international contexts. It should cover ways of overcoming obstacles to social progress, the relationship between peace and development, the need for disarmament and major international social and economic concerns, in line with the priorities indicated by the General Assembly and the Economic and Social Council.

17. The next report should also include a more thorough analysis of the impact of new and emerging technologies on socio-economic conditions, particularly in developing countries. It should analyse the progress that has been made in the international diffusion of appropriate technology and application of technology in improving social conditions in developing countries.

Economic and Social Council resolution 1985/21

| 29 May 1985 | Meeting 23 | Adopted without vote |

Approved by Second Committee (E/1985/96 & Corr.1) without vote, 17 May (meeting 8); draft by Commission for Social Development (E/1985/24 & Corr.1); agenda item 17.

In **resolution 1985/20**, the Council requested the Secretary-General to ensure that future reports on the world social situation were distributed no later than 12 weeks before the commencement of the Commission session.

GENERAL ASSEMBLY ACTION

On 13 December, on the recommendation of the Third (Social, Humanitarian and Cultural) Committee, the General Assembly adopted **resolution 40/100** by recorded vote.

World social situation

The General Assembly,

Recalling its resolutions 34/152 of 17 December 1979 and 37/54 of 3 December 1982 on the world social situation,

Recalling also its resolutions 3201(S-VI) and 3202(S-VI) of 1 May 1974, containing the Declaration and the Programme of Action on the Establishment of a New

International Economic Order, 3281(XXIX) of 12 December 1974, containing the Charter of Economic Rights and Duties of States, 3362(S-VII) of 16 September 1975 on development and international economic co-operation, 35/56 of 5 December 1980, the annex to which contains the International Development Strategy for the Third United Nations Development Decade, and 36/194 of 17 December 1981, in which it endorsed the Substantial New Programme of Action for the 1980s for the Least Developed Countries,

Recalling further its resolution 39/29 of 3 December 1984 on the critical economic situation in Africa,

Bearing in mind its resolutions 40/14 of 18 November 1985 on the International Youth Year: Participation, Development, Peace and 40/17 of 18 November 1985 on channels of communication between the United Nations and youth and youth organizations,

Recognizing that social progress and development are founded on respect for the dignity and value of the human person,

Bearing in mind that the ultimate aim of development is the constant improvement of the well-being of the entire population on the basis of its full participation in the process of development and the fair distribution of the benefits therefrom, and that the pace of development in the developing countries as a whole should be accelerated substantially in order to enable them to achieve this goal,

Mindful that the existing inequalities and imbalances in the international economic system are widening the gap between developed and developing countries and thereby constitute a major obstacle to the development of the developing countries and adversely affect international relations and the promotion of world peace and security,

Conscious that each country has the sovereign right freely to adopt the economic and social system that it deems the most appropriate and that each Government has a primary role in ensuring the social progress and well-being of its people,

Reaffirming that economic growth must go hand in hand with qualitative and structural changes, the reduction of social and economic disparities and the adoption of measures to ensure the effective participation of all peoples in the preparation and execution of their national policies for economic and social development,

Convinced of the urgent necessity rapidly to eradicate colonialism, neo-colonialism, racism and all forms of racial discrimination, *apartheid*, terrorism in all its forms, aggression, foreign occupation and alien domination and all forms of inequality, exploitation and subjugation of peoples, which constitute major obstacles to economic and social progress as well as to the promotion of world peace and security,

Reaffirming the existence of the interrelationship of peace, disarmament and development and therefore the imperative need to halt the arms race, thereby releasing valuable resources that could be used for the development of the developing countries and could contribute to the well-being and prosperity of all,

Reaffirming also that the primary responsibility for their development rests with the developing countries themselves and that the commitment from other countries to support these efforts is of vital importance for achievement of this aim,

Having considered the *1985 Report on the World Social Situation,*

1. *Takes note* of the *1985 Report on the World Social Situation;*

2. *Takes note also* of the conclusions of the Commission for Social Development at its twenty-ninth session;

3. *Notes with deep concern* the continuing deterioration of the economic and social situation of the world, in particular in the developing countries, whose position has been further worsened by sharp fluctuations in exchange rates, high real rates of interest, the severe fall in commodity prices, serious deterioration in the terms of trade of developing countries, increased protectionist pressures, the reverse transfer of resources from developing countries, crushing debt burdens, the restrictive adjustment process demanded by financial and development institutions, the decline in official development assistance in real terms and the severe inadequacy of resources experienced by multilateral development and financial institutions;

4. *Notes further with deep concern* that the economic and social situation in Africa continues to be critical and that it has been exacerbated by the world recession and by famine, drought and desertification;

5. *Calls* for full implementation of General Assembly resolution 39/29 on the critical economic situation in Africa;

6. *Notes with great concern* the slow progress in the implementation of the Declaration on Social Progress and Development[7] and in the attainment of the objectives and overall development goals adopted and reaffirmed in the International Development Strategy for the Third United Nations Development Decade;[8]

7. *Reaffirms* that the social aspects and goals of development are an integral part of overall development and that it is the sovereign right of each country freely to determine and implement appropriate policies for social development within the framework of its development plans and priorities;

8. *Emphasizes* the importance, for the achievement of social progress, of the establishment of the new international economic order;

9. *Reaffirms* the urgent need to implement the socio-economic development objectives contained in the Declaration on Social Progress and Development and the International Development Strategy for the Third United Nations Development Decade, as well as the need to implement the socio-economic objectives of the Substantial New Programme of Action for the 1980s for the Least Developed Countries;

10. *Emphasizes again* that the rapid socio-economic progress of developing countries requires substantially enhanced multilateral and bilateral financial support and advanced technological assistance to national development efforts, rendered within the framework of the development plans of developing countries;

11. *Calls upon* all Member States to promote economic development and social progress by the formulation and implementation of an interrelated set of policy measures to achieve the goals and objectives established within the framework of national plans and priorities in the fields of employment, education, health, nutrition, housing facilities, crime prevention, the well-being of children, equal opportunities for the disabled and the aged, full participation of youth in the development process and full integration and participation of women in development;

12. *Calls upon* the relevant organs, organizations and bodies of the United Nations system to mobilize the necessary resources to undertake measures aimed at improving social conditions and achieving the main objectives set forth in the Declaration on Social Progress and Development, the International Development Strategy for the Third United Nations Development Decade and the Substantial New Programme of Action for the 1980s for the Least Developed Countries;

13. *Also calls upon* Member States to make all efforts to promote the accelerated and complete elimination of such fundamental elements hindering economic and social progress and development as colonialism, neocolonialism, racism and all forms of racial discrimination, *apartheid*, terrorism in all its forms, aggression, foreign occupation, alien domination and all forms of inequality and exploitation of peoples, and also to undertake effective measures to lessen international tensions and to halt the arms race and redistribute released resources in order to promote social and economic development;

14. *Requests* the Secretary-General to continue monitoring the world social situation in depth on a regular basis and to submit the next full report on the world social situation to the General Assembly in 1989, for consideration at its forty-fourth session, through the Economic and Social Council;

15. *Also requests* the Secretary-General, in preparing the next report on the world social situation, to take into account the observations made by Member States on the 1985 report as well as the conclusions of the Commission for Social Development contained in the report on its twenty-ninth session;

16. *Further requests* the Secretary-General to make the necessary arrangements for wide dissemination of the reports on the world social situation;

17. *Invites* the organs, organizations and bodies of the United Nations system to co-operate fully with the Secretary-General in the preparation of future reports by making available all relevant information pertaining to their respective areas of competence;

18. *Decides* to include in the provisional agenda of its forty-fourth session the item entitled "World social situation".

General Assembly resolution 40/100

13 December 1985   Meeting 116   127-1-24 (recorded vote)

Approved by Third Committee (A/40/963) by vote (120-1-23), 27 November (meeting 56); draft by Yugoslavia, for Group of 77 (A/C.3/40/L.12/Rev.1), orally revised; agenda item 90.

Meeting numbers. GA 40th session: 3rd Committee 16-23, 30, 37, 55, 56; plenary 116.

Recorded vote in Assembly as follows:

In favour: Afghanistan, Albania, Algeria, Angola, Antigua and Barbuda, Argentina, Bahamas, Bahrain, Bangladesh, Barbados, Belize, Benin, Bhutan, Bolivia, Botswana, Brazil, Brunei Darussalam, Bulgaria, Burkina Faso, Burma, Burundi, Byelorussian SSR, Cameroon, Cape Verde, Central African Republic, Chad, Chile, China, Colombia, Comoros, Congo, Cuba, Cyprus, Czechoslovakia, Democratic Kampuchea, Democratic Yemen, Djibouti, Dominican Republic, Ecuador, Egypt, El Salvador, Equatorial Guinea, Ethiopia, Fiji, Gabon, Gambia, German Democratic Republic, Ghana, Guatemala, Guinea, Guinea-Bissau, Guyana, Haiti, Honduras, Hungary, India, Indonesia, Iran, Iraq, Ivory Coast, Jamaica, Jordan, Kenya, Kuwait, Lao People's Democratic Republic, Lebanon, Lesotho, Liberia, Libyan Arab Jamahiriya, Madagascar, Malaysia, Maldives, Mali, Malta, Mauritania, Mauritius, Mexico, Mongolia, Morocco, Mozambique, Nepal, Nicaragua, Niger, Nigeria, Oman, Pakistan, Panama, Papua New Guinea, Peru, Philippines, Poland, Qatar, Romania, Rwanda, Saint Christopher and Nevis, Saint Lucia, Samoa, Sao Tome and Principe, Saudi Arabia, Senegal, Sierra Leone, Singapore, Somalia, Sri Lanka, Sudan, Suriname, Swaziland, Syrian Arab Republic, Thailand, Togo, Trinidad and Tobago, Tunisia, Turkey, Uganda, Ukrainian SSR, USSR, United Arab Emirates, United Republic of Tanzania, Uruguay, Vanuatu, Venezuela, Viet Nam, Yemen, Yugoslavia, Zaire, Zambia, Zimbabwe.

Against: United States.

Abstaining: Australia, Austria, Belgium, Canada, Denmark, Finland, France, Germany, Federal Republic of, Greece, Grenada, Iceland, Ireland, Israel, Italy, Japan, Luxembourg, Malawi, Netherlands, New Zealand, Norway, Portugal, Spain, Sweden, United Kingdom.

Yugoslavia, on behalf of the sponsors, declared that the wording of the draft resolution had been revised to achieve consensus. However, since there had been a request for a vote, the original paragraph 3 should replace the revision, which had expressed concern at the economic crisis and decline that developing countries had had to face as a result of deep global recession.

The United States opposed the text because it contained a formulation on economic issues outside the competence of the Third Committee and presented too negative a view of the economic and social situation. It had serious difficulties in particular with the economic language in paragraphs 3, 8 and 10 and the seventh preambular paragraph, and considered that paragraph 13 and the tenth and eleventh preambular paragraphs contained political elements inappropriate in a Third Committee draft.

Speaking for the Nordic countries, Finland regretted the lack of normal pre-consultations on the text, elements of which, it felt, fell within the mandate of other Main Committees; Luxembourg expressed a similar view, on behalf of the States members of the European Economic Community, Portugal and Spain. Japan did not agree with the wording of some paragraphs, particularly paragraph 3. Australia believed that the language of paragraph 3 would have been more appropriate in the Second (Economic and Financial) Committee. Austria regretted the inclusion of the original paragraph 3. Canada felt that paragraphs 3 and 4 contained an inexact description of the world situation.

Social aspects of development

The Economic and Social Council and/or the General Assembly adopted resolutions on the social aspects of development, social progress and development, implementation of the 1969 Declaration on Social Progress and Development,[7] national experience in achieving social progress and impact of development on the family. The Secretary-General reported on social aspects of rural development.

ECONOMIC AND SOCIAL COUNCIL ACTION

On 29 May 1985, on the recommendation of its Second Committee, the Economic and Social Council adopted **resolution 1985/31** without vote.

Social aspects of development

The Economic and Social Council,

Mindful of the resolve enshrined in the Charter of the United Nations to promote social progress and better standards of life in larger freedom and for these ends to employ international machinery for the promotion of the economic and social advancement of all peoples,

Bearing in mind the relevant provisions of the International Covenant on Economic, Social and Cultural Rights,

Recalling the Declaration on Social Progress and Development,

Recalling also the Declaration and the Programme of Action on the Establishment of a New International Economic Order and the Charter of Economic Rights and Duties of States,

Aware that the attainment of the goals of the International Development Strategy for the Third United Nations Development Decade calls for a concerted effort to promote genuine social development,

Convinced that men and women can achieve complete fulfilment of their aspirations only within a just social and political order and that it is consequently of cardinal importance to accelerate social and economic progress and the respect of human rights and fundamental freedoms everywhere, thus contributing to international peace and security,

Persuaded that social development can be promoted by friendly relations and co-operation among States with different social, economic or political systems, as well as by effective arms reduction and disarmament measures,

Aware that mounting economic problems in various parts of the world, unprecedented in the history of the United Nations, negatively affect and diminish the status of social development policies,

1. *Recognizes* the significance of social aspects of development and the constant need to elaborate their national and international dimensions;

2. *Calls upon* all Governments and all institutions, both national and international, to intensify their organizational, intellectual and financial efforts with a view to promoting the social aspects of development;

3. *Decides* to include the question of the social aspects of development in the provisional agenda for the thirtieth session of the Commission for Social Development.

Economic and Social Council resolution 1985/31

| 29 May 1985 | Meeting 23 | Adopted without vote |

Approved by Second Committee (E/1985/96 & Corr.1) without vote, 21 May (meeting 11); 6-nation draft (E/1985/C.2/L.2), orally revised; agenda item 17.

Sponsors: Bulgaria, German Democratic Republic, Mongolia, Poland, Togo, Ukrainian SSR.

Social progress and development

On 13 December 1985, following a recommendation of the Third Committee, the General Assembly adopted without vote **resolution 40/98**.

Improvement of the role of the United Nations in the field of social development

The General Assembly,

Recalling the Declaration on Social Progress and Development based on the Charter of the United Nations and solemnly proclaimed on 11 December 1969,

Recalling also its resolutions 3201(S-VI) and 3202(S-VI) of 1 May 1974, containing the Declaration and the Programme of Action on the Establishment of a New International Economic Order, 33/48 of 14 December 1978 on world social development and 35/56 of 5

December 1980, the annex to which contains the International Development Strategy for the Third United Nations Development Decade,

Bearing in mind the Nairobi Forward-looking Strategies for the Advancement of Women, adopted by the World Conference to Review and Appraise the Achievements of the United Nations Decade for Women: Equality, Development and Peace, and the need for the implementation thereof,

Recalling resolution 40/14 of 18 November 1985 on the International Youth Year: Participation, Development, Peace, adopted by the General Assembly acting as the United Nations World Conference for the International Youth Year,

Recalling also its resolution 39/25 of 23 November 1984 on the question of aging,

Referring to its resolution 39/26 of 23 November 1984 on the United Nations Decade of Disabled Persons,

Recalling its resolution 32/197 of 20 December 1977 in which it, *inter alia*, requested the United Nations Secretariat to prepare, on a regular basis, global economic and social surveys and projections,

Taking into account its resolutions 34/152 of 17 December 1979 and 37/54 of 3 December 1982 on the world social situation,

Having regard to Economic and Social Council resolutions 10(II) of 21 June 1946 establishing a permanent Social Commission, 830 J (XXXII) of 2 August 1961 on the strengthening of the work of the United Nations in the social field and 1139(XLI) of 29 July 1966 in which it adopted the present mandate and present designation of the Commission for Social Development,

Taking note of Economic and Social Council resolution 1985/36 of 29 May 1985 entitled "Progress of work of the Commission for Social Development",

Taking into account the discussion of the Economic and Social Council, during its first regular session of 1985, on the work of the Commission,

Having considered the *1985 Report on the World Social Situation,*

Noting with concern that, although recovery and growth are under way in some States, the recession that has afflicted the world economy in recent years has had a deep negative impact on the economies of many countries,

1. *Notes with concern* that the ideals of the Declaration on Social Progress and Development have not been implemented nor have the objectives and overall development goals adopted and reaffirmed in the International Development Strategy for the Third United Nations Development Decade been achieved yet;

2. *Reaffirms* that the socio-economic aspects and goals of development are an integral part of the overall development process;

3. *Reaffirms also* the urgency of taking effective measures aimed at further promoting social progress and development;

4. *Emphasizes* the importance of making analyses of, and exchanging information on, the fundamental problems of socio-economic development in order to formulate and implement policy measures in the fields of employment, education, health, nutrition, housing facilities, crime prevention, the well-being of children, equal opportunities for the disabled and the aged, full participation of youth in the development process and the full integration and participation of women in development;

5. *Calls upon* the relevant organs, organizations and bodies of the United Nations system to undertake measures aimed at improving social conditions and achieving the main objectives set forth in the Declaration on Social Progress and Development and in the International Development Strategy for the Third United Nations Development Decade;

6. *Notes* the role of the Commission for Social Development in the field of social development and humanitarian affairs;

7. *Invites* the Economic and Social Council to consider, at its first regular session of 1986, existing ways and means of improving the work of the Commission.

General Assembly resolution 40/98

13 December 1985   Meeting 116   Adopted without vote

Approved by Third Committee (A/40/963) without vote, 11 November (meeting 37); 2-nation draft (A/C.3/40/L.13/Rev.1), orally revised; agenda item 90.
Sponsors: Poland, Ukrainian SSR.
Meeting numbers. GA 40th session: 3rd Committee 16-23, 30, 37; plenary 116.

The General Assembly, by adopting **resolution 40/205**, endorsed conclusions and recommendations on human resources and social development made during the mid-term global review of the implementation of the Substantial New Programme of Action for the 1980s for the Least Developed Countries (LDCs).

In **resolution 40/212**, the Assembly invited Governments to observe annually on 5 December an International Volunteer Day for Economic and Social Development.

Implementation of the 1969 Declaration

On 29 May 1985, on the recommendation of its Second Committee, the Economic and Social Council adopted without vote **resolution 1985/34**.

Implementation of the Declaration on Social Progress and Development

The Economic and Social Council

Recommends to the General Assembly the adoption of the following draft resolution:

"*The General Assembly,*

"*Recalling* the Declaration on Social Progress and Development, based on the Charter of the United Nations and solemnly proclaimed on 11 December 1969,

"*Recalling also* its resolutions 2543(XXIV) of 11 December 1969 and 34/59 of 29 November 1979 on the implementation of the Declaration,

"*Recalling further* its resolutions 3201(S-VI) and 3202(S-VI) of 1 May 1974, containing the Declaration and the Programme of Action on the Establishment of a New International Economic Order, 35/56 of 5 December 1980, the annex to which contains the International Development Strategy for the Third United Nations Development Decade, 33/48 of 14 December 1978 on world social development, and 34/152 of 17 December 1979 and 37/54 of 3 December 1982 on the world social situation,

"*Convinced* that international peace and security, on the one hand, and social progress and economic development, on the other, are closely interdependent and influence each other,

"*Bearing in mind* that the ultimate aim of development is the constant improvement of the social situation of entire populations and ensuring their full participation in the process of development and the fair distribution of the benefits therefrom,

"*Reaffirming* that social progress and development shall be founded on respect for the dignity and value of the human person and shall ensure the promotion of human rights and social justice,

"*Aware* of the fact that, fifteen years after the adoption and proclamation of the Declaration on Social Progress and Development, its main objectives, embodied also in the International Development Strategy for the Third United Nations Development Decade, *inter alia*, elimination of unemployment, hunger, malnutrition and poverty, eradication of illiteracy, assurance of the right to universal access to culture, provision of health protection of the entire population, provision of free, universal education at the primary level, and promotion of human rights and social justice, have not yet been universally realized,

"*Recalling* that the peoples of the United Nations expressed in the United Nations Charter their determination to save future generations from the scourge of war and to promote social progress and better standards of life in larger freedom,

"*Fully conscious* of the urgent need of intensifying the efforts by the international community and relevant organs, organizations and bodies of the United Nations system to achieve the objectives set forth in the Declaration on Social Progress and Development and in the International Development Strategy for the Third United Nations Development Decade,

"1. *Reaffirms* the lasting validity and importance of the principles and objectives proclaimed in the Declaration on Social Progress and Development;

"2. *Urges* all States and relevant organs, organizations and bodies of the United Nations system to take the Declaration resolutely into consideration and in their policies, plans, programmes and the implementation machinery increasingly to take into consideration, as far as they are concerned, the principles, objectives, means and methods of the Declaration;

"3. *Urges* all Governments to take into account the provisions of the Declaration in their bilateral and multilateral relations in the field of development;

"4. *Recommends* that international organizations and agencies concerned with development should consider the Declaration as an important international document in the formulation of strategies and programmes designed to achieve social progress and development, and that it may be taken into consideration in the drafting of instruments that the United Nations may undertake in the field of social progress and development;

"5. *Requests* the Secretary-General to prepare a substantive report on possible ways and means of increasing the contribution of the relevant organs, organizations and bodies of the United Nations system, as far as they are concerned, to achieving the full realization of the principles and objectives contained in the Declaration and to submit it, through the Commission for Social Development and the Economic and Social Council, to the General Assembly at its forty-second session;

"6. *Further requests* the Secretary-General to continue to inform the General Assembly, in a summary form in annexes to the reports on the world social situation, of the measures adopted by Governments—not included in other reports provided on a regular basis—and by the international organizations concerned for the realization of the provisions of the Declaration and for the implementation of the present resolution."

Economic and Social Council resolution 1985/34

29 May 1985   Meeting 23   Adopted without vote

Approved by Second Committee (E/1985/96 & Corr.1) without vote, 24 May (meeting 15); 6-nation draft (E/1985/C.2/L.3/Rev.1); agenda item 17.
Sponsors: Argentina, Byelorussian SSR, Mongolia, Poland, Ukrainian SSR, Viet Nam.

The Commission for Social Development, in its conclusions endorsed by the Economic and Social Council in **resolution 1985/21**, asserted that the adverse social situation reflected the lack of implementation of the 1969 Declaration[7] and other United Nations declarations on social and economic matters, and of the goals of the 1980 International Development Strategy for the Third United Nations Development Decade.[8]

GENERAL ASSEMBLY ACTION

In **resolution 40/98**, the General Assembly noted with concern that the ideals of the Declaration had not been implemented nor had the objectives of the Strategy been achieved, and called on United Nations bodies to improve social conditions and achieve the main objectives set forth in those instruments.

National experience in achieving social progress

The Secretary-General, in response to a 1983 General Assembly request,[9] submitted a report on national experience in achieving far-reaching social and economic changes for social progress,[10] based on 11 replies as at 30 April 1985 to a note verbale sent by him to Member States. Austria, Denmark, the Federal Republic of Germany and Poland provided information on recent changes in social policies; the Byelorussian SSR, Greece, Iraq, Mongolia, the Syrian Arab Republic, the Ukrainian SSR and the USSR gave information on the overall objectives of national development efforts.

ECONOMIC AND SOCIAL COUNCIL ACTION

On 29 May 1985, on the recommendation of its Second Committee, the Economic and Social Council adopted **resolution 1985/32** by recorded vote.

National experience in achieving far-reaching social and economic changes for the purpose of social progress

The Economic and Social Council,

Guided by the desire to promote a higher standard of life, full employment and conditions for economic and social progress and development,

Bearing in mind the Declaration on Social Progress and Development,

Mindful of the provisions of the Declaration and the Programme of Action on the Establishment of a New International Economic Order, as well as the Charter of Economic Rights and Duties of States,

Noting its resolutions 1581 A (L) of 21 May 1971, 1667(LII) of 1 June 1972 and 1746(LIV) of 16 May 1973 concerning the importance of fundamental structural socio-economic changes for the strengthening of national independence and the achievement of the ultimate goals of social progress,

Recalling General Assembly resolutions 3273(XXIX) of 10 December 1974, 31/38 of 30 November 1976, 36/19 of 9 November 1981 and 38/25 of 22 November 1983, in which the Assembly reaffirmed the importance for every State to exercise its inalienable right to carry out fundamental social and economic changes for the purpose of social progress and the necessity of studying national experience in this field,

Desirous of securing a speedy and complete removal of all obstacles to the economic and social progress of peoples,

Convinced that peaceful coexistence and co-operation among States create favourable international conditions for the socio-economic development of all countries, in particular developing countries,

Considering that the exchange of national experience in achieving far-reaching social and economic changes for the purpose of social progress would contribute to the implementation of the International Development Strategy for the Third United Nations Development Decade,

Reaffirming the sovereign and inalienable right of all peoples freely to determine their political status and freely to pursue their economic, social and cultural development,

1. *Takes note* of the report of the Secretary-General on national experience in achieving far-reaching social and economic changes for the purpose of social progress;

2. *Calls upon* all States to give special attention in their national development plans and programmes to the social aspects of development with a view to increasing the well-being of the population on the basis of its full participation in the process of development and a fair distribution of the benefits therefrom;

3. *Requests* the Secretary-General to make arrangements for holding the interregional seminar called for in paragraph 3 of General Assembly resolution 38/25 within the resources already requested for sectoral and regional advisory services;

4. *Invites* all States to submit to the Secretary-General national reports on their experience in carrying out far-reaching social and economic changes for the purpose of social progress;

5. *Further requests* the Secretary-General to prepare, in consultation with all States, a further report on national experience in achieving far-reaching social and economic changes for the purpose of social progress, taking into account the provisions of General Assembly resolutions 36/19 and 38/25, and to submit it to the Assembly at its forty-second session through the Commission for Social Development and the Economic and Social Council;

6. *Requests* the Commission for Social Development to consider at its thirtieth session the question of national experience in achieving far-reaching social and economic changes for the purpose of social progress.

Economic and Social Council resolution 1985/32

29 May 1985   Meeting 23   46-1-3 (roll-call vote)

Approved by Second Committee (E/1985/96 & Corr.1) by vote (46-1-3), 21 May (meeting 11); 7-nation draft (E/1985/C.2/L.4), orally revised; agenda item 17.
Sponsors: Congo, Cuba, Mongolia, Nicaragua, Poland, Ukrainian SSR, Viet Nam.

Roll-call vote in Council as follows:

In favour: Algeria, Argentina, Bangladesh, Botswana, Brazil, Bulgaria, China, Colombia, Congo, Costa Rica, Djibouti, Ecuador, Finland, France, German Democratic Republic, Guyana, Iceland, India, Indonesia, Japan, Lebanon, Luxembourg, Malaysia,

Mexico, Morocco, Netherlands, New Zealand, Nigeria, Papua New Guinea, Poland, Romania, Rwanda, Saudi Arabia, Senegal, Sierra Leone, Somalia, Spain, Sri Lanka, Sweden, Thailand, Turkey, USSR, Venezuela, Yugoslavia, Zaire, Zimbabwe.
Against: United States.
Abstaining: Canada, Germany, Federal Republic of, United Kingdom.

In the opinion of the United States, the inter-regional seminar and additional report requested were wasteful of scarce resources; the reports prepared on the subject for the past several years had proved to be of no practical value. The United Kingdom also had reservations with regard to the report requested.

GENERAL ASSEMBLY ACTION

On 29 November 1985, on the recommendation of the Third Committee, the General Assembly adopted **resolution 40/23** by recorded vote.

National experience in achieving far-reaching social and economic changes for the purpose of social progress

The General Assembly,

Guided by the desire to promote a higher standard of life, full employment and conditions for economic and social progress and development,

Bearing in mind the Declaration on Social Progress and Development,

Mindful of the provisions of the Declaration and the Programme of Action on the Establishment of a New International Economic Order, as well as the Charter of Economic Rights and Duties of States,

Noting Economic and Social Council resolutions 1581 A (L) of 21 May 1971, 1667(LII) of 1 June 1972 and 1746(LIV) of 16 May 1973 concerning the importance of fundamental structural socio-economic changes for the strengthening of national independence and the achievement of the ultimate goals of social progress,

Recalling its resolutions 3273(XXIX) of 10 December 1974, 31/38 of 30 November 1976, 36/19 of 9 November 1981 and 38/25 of 22 November 1983, in which it reaffirmed the importance for every State to exercise its inalienable right to carry out fundamental social and economic changes for the purpose of social progress and the necessity of studying national experience in this field,

Desirous of securing a speedy and complete removal of all obstacles to the economic and social progress of peoples, especially colonialism, neo-colonialism, racism, racial discrimination, *apartheid*, military, political and economic intervention and pressure, foreign aggression and occupation or alien domination, as well as all forms of inequality and exploitation of peoples,

Convinced that peaceful coexistence and co-operation among States, as well as effective measures in the field of disarmament, create favourable international conditions for the socio-economic development of all countries, in particular developing countries,

Considering that the exchange of national experience in achieving far-reaching social and economic changes for the purpose of social progress would contribute to the implementation of the International Development Strategy for the Third United Nations Development Decade,

Reaffirming the sovereign and inalienable right of all peoples freely to determine their political status and freely to pursue their economic, social and cultural development,

1. *Takes note* of the report of the Secretary-General on national experience in achieving far-reaching social and economic changes for the purpose of social progress;

2. *Calls upon* all States to give special attention in their national development plans and programmes to the social aspects of development with a view to increasing the well-being of the population on the basis of its full participation in the process of development and a fair distribution of the benefits therefrom;

3. *Requests* the Secretary-General to proceed with the implementation of Economic and Social Council resolution 1985/32 of 29 May 1985, paying special attention to paragraphs 3 and 5 thereof;

4. *Further requests* the Secretary-General to make arrangements for holding in 1986 the interregional seminar called for in paragraph 3 of General Assembly resolution 38/25, within the resources allotted to the programme for sectoral and regional advisory services;

5. *Decides* to include in the provisional agenda of its forty-second session the item entitled "National experience in achieving far-reaching social and economic changes for the purpose of social progress".

General Assembly resolution 40/23

29 November 1985   Meeting 96   133-1-11 (recorded vote)

Approved by Third Committee (A/40/879) by recorded vote (120-1-15), 11 November (meeting 37); 15-nation draft (A/C.3/40/L.16); agenda item 91.

Sponsors: Afghanistan, Angola, Benin, Burkina Faso, Byelorussian SSR, Cuba, Ethiopia, Hungary, Lao People's Democratic Republic, Madagascar, Mongolia, Mozambique, Nicaragua, Poland, Viet Nam.

Meeting numbers. GA 40th session: 3rd Committee 16-23, 30, 37; plenary 96.

Recorded vote in Assembly as follows:

In favour: Afghanistan, Albania, Algeria, Angola, Argentina, Austria, Bahamas, Bahrain, Bangladesh, Barbados, Benin, Bhutan, Bolivia, Botswana, Brazil, Brunei Darussalam, Bulgaria, Burkina Faso, Burma, Burundi, Byelorussian SSR, Cameroon, Cape Verde, Central African Republic, Chad, Chile, China, Comoros, Congo, Cuba, Cyprus, Czechoslovakia, Democratic Kampuchea, Democratic Yemen, Denmark, Djibouti, Dominican Republic, Ecuador, Egypt, El Salvador, Equatorial Guinea, Ethiopia, Fiji, Finland, France, Gabon, German Democratic Republic, Ghana, Greece, Grenada, Guatemala, Guinea, Guinea-Bissau, Guyana, Honduras, Hungary, Iceland, India, Indonesia, Iran, Iraq, Ireland, Ivory Coast, Jamaica, Japan, Jordan, Kenya, Kuwait, Lao People's Democratic Republic, Lebanon, Lesotho, Liberia, Libyan Arab Jamahiriya, Madagascar, Malaysia, Maldives, Mali, Malta, Mauritania, Mauritius, Mexico, Mongolia, Morocco, Mozambique, Nepal, Nicaragua, Niger, Nigeria, Norway, Oman, Pakistan, Panama, Papua New Guinea, Peru, Philippines, Poland, Portugal, Qatar, Romania, Rwanda, Saint Lucia, Samoa, Sao Tome and Principe, Saudi Arabia, Senegal, Seychelles, Sierra Leone, Somalia, Spain, Sri Lanka, Sudan, Suriname, Swaziland, Sweden, Syrian Arab Republic, Thailand, Togo, Trinidad and Tobago, Tunisia, Turkey, Uganda, Ukrainian SSR, USSR, United Arab Emirates, United Republic of Tanzania, Uruguay, Venezuela, Viet Nam, Yemen, Yugoslavia, Zaire, Zambia, Zimbabwe.

Against: United States.

Abstaining: Australia, Belgium, Canada, Germany, Federal Republic of, Israel, Italy, Luxembourg, Malawi, Netherlands, New Zealand, United Kingdom.

The United States said the item was superfluous and illustrated the tendency to ask for reports on various questions, which then spawned resolutions asking for still more reports; yet the reports had been unenlightening over the years and implementation of the current resolution would merely further divert limited resources into unproductive activities.

Chile would have preferred the sixth preambular paragraph to refer also to terrorism in all its forms.

Impact of development on the family

In response to a 1983 Economic and Social Council resolution,[11] the Secretary-General submitted in January 1985 a report on the impact of development on the institution of the family.[12] He stated that changes brought about by development often had mixed results. Development improved health, sanitation and nutrition, diminished morbidity and mortality, and increased income, standards of living, levels of education, employment, housing and transportation. It also was seen as impoverishing families, creating inequalities between men and women, and pushing innovations with no consideration for the effects on family life.

A number of trends concerning family structure were associated with the development process, the Secretary-General observed. Families were becoming smaller, with a decline in birth rates, while divorce rates and frequency of remarriage and single-parent families were increasing. There also was a greater trend towards perceiving familial arrangements, especially among the poor, as rational strategies for coping with adversity.

The needs of families should be taken into account to a greater extent by those responsible for development activities, the report concluded. In view of the limited data available, a better understanding of how families were affected by development should be sought. The tendency of additional services to replace familial functions was an area requiring greater study. National policies should address wider structural deficiencies and give more attention to bringing about positive changes in families' environments, as well as to preventing negative effects, such as child labour.

ECONOMIC AND SOCIAL COUNCIL ACTION

On 29 May 1985, on the recommendation of its Second Committee, the Economic and Social Council adopted without vote **resolution 1985/29**.

The family

The Economic and Social Council,

Recalling its resolution 1983/23 of 26 May 1983 on the role of the family in the development process,

Taking note with satisfaction of the report of the Secretary-General on the impact of development on the institution of the family, and of its conclusions,

Emphasizing the need for the greatest importance to be given to the family as basic unit of society and natural environment for the growth and well-being of all its members,

Affirming the importance of national policies which meet the needs of families and enable them to perform their essential role,

Recognizing that consideration of the needs of families is made more necessary by the special constraints which families are experiencing in social situations that are often difficult, and that it has also become more complex as a result of the growing diversity that can be observed in the forms of the institution of the family,

1. *Renews* its invitation to Member States to expand their efforts at the national and community levels to consider, examine, identify and evaluate the needs of families and the ways in which those needs may be more effectively met;

2. *Appeals* to future United Nations meetings on developmental social welfare policies and programmes to include in their deliberations the question of development and families, paying particular attention to the support of the family unit as a framework in which and through which social welfare policies and programmes can provide more effective support to family members;

3. *Invites* the various regional meetings at ministerial level scheduled to take place in 1985 and 1986 to consider also the question of development and families, so that each region's concerns may be fully represented;

4. *Requests* the Secretary-General to obtain information, to be supplied by countries and relevant international organizations, on policies and programmes concerning families, and to promote the improvement of the scope, availability and comparability of statistics and indicators relating to families;

5. *Requests* the Secretary-General to ensure consistency between the policies and concepts contained in United Nations programmes and plans of action having a bearing on the family, in co-operation with the Commission on the Status of Women, the Population Commission and other relevant bodies;

6. *Also requests* the Secretary-General to study the data available in the reports and action plans developed in the course of recent United Nations activities such as the World Assembly on Aging, the International Year of Disabled Persons, the International Year of the Child and the United Nations Decade for Women: Equality, Development and Peace, taking into account the need to strengthen policies for the welfare of the entire society;

7. *Further requests* the Secretary-General to study further the impact of development on the family as an institution and to submit a progress report to the Council at its first regular session of 1987, through the Commission for Social Development at its thirtieth session, on developments concerning national family policies and programmes;

8. *Invites* the General Assembly to consider the possibility of including in the provisional agenda of its forty-first session an item entitled "Families in the development process", with a view to considering a possible request to the Secretary-General to initiate a process of development of global awareness of the issues involved, directed towards Governments, intergovernmental and non-governmental organizations and public opinion.

Economic and Social Council resolution 1985/29

29 May 1985   Meeting 23   Adopted without vote

Approved by Second Committee (E/1985/96 & Corr.1) without vote, 17 May (meeting 8); draft by Commission for Social Development (E/1985/24 & Corr.1); agenda item 17.

Social aspects of rural development

In accordance with a 1983 Economic and Social Council resolution,[13] the Secretary-General submitted in January 1985 a report on the social aspects of rural development,[14] which the Council took note of in **decision 1985/135** on 29 May, on the President's oral proposal. The Secretary-General stated that despite set-backs, frustrations and changes in developmental directions, the record of developing countries in rural development in past decades had been quite good.

Notwithstanding the general progress, a certain amount of waste and missed opportunities had been associated with many rural development programmes. An incoherent multiplicity of projects reflecting the carry-over remnants of past approaches, unco-ordinated donor initiatives and *ad hoc* pressures posed by domestic interest groups had probably achieved less than if there had been an overall sound, focused policy. Further, owing to budgetary constraints, many projects in recent years had collapsed once foreign assistance had been withdrawn, or had remained inadequately supplied, as frequently was the case in rural health centres, or insufficiently maintained, as was true of many rural roads.

An increasing number of countries had begun to adopt far-reaching reform measures in agricultural pricing, subsidies and parastatal policies, which appeared to favour production over welfare objectives. Those measures had also been endorsed by several multilateral and bilateral agencies, and had been promoted by them sometimes as part of their lending and assistance programmes.

If unaccompanied by developmental programmes and projects, however, price incentive policies might end up primarily benefiting farmers in a position to take advantage of them, namely, commercial farmers in relatively developed, fertile areas. To reach emergent farmers, it would be necessary to continue programmes ranging from extension services and infrastructure development to the testing of commercial plant hybrids for rainfed areas, improving erosion controls and so forth. To achieve growth in most rural areas, however, and to ensure greater social equity in opportunities and work, more would be needed than pricing policy reforms.

Evaluation of UN social development activities

On 29 May 1985, in **resolution 1985/36** on the progress of work of the Commission for Social Development, the Economic and Social Council requested the Committee for Programme and Coordination (CPC) to review the current evaluation timetable and study the possibility of evaluating in depth the effectiveness, relevance and impact of United Nations social development activities.

On 6 December,[15] in a follow-up to the resolution, a note by the Secretariat recalled that in 1984 CPC had established a timetable for in-depth evaluation of programmes between 1986 and 1992.[16] It had been stressed that if the need arose, CPC might alter the topics or the order in which they were to be considered. In the light of that, CPC might wish to consider replacing one of the existing topics in the timetable by social development or adding social development to the list, for review in 1994.

Social welfare

Social welfare policies and programmes

Regional and interregional activities

Three regional intergovernmental meetings on developmental social welfare policies and programmes were held during 1985: the Fourth Conference of African Ministers of Social Affairs (Addis Ababa, Ethiopia, 18-26 March); the Third Asian and Pacific Ministerial Conference on Social Welfare and Development (Bangkok, Thailand, 9-15 October); and the Pan-Arab Regional Conference on Social Welfare Policies (Tunis, Tunisia, 12-15 October).

The United Nations and the League of Arab States held a sectoral meeting on social development (Amman, Jordan, 19-21 August 1985),[17] in response to a 1983 General Assembly resolution.[18] A range of items were discussed, including: the volume and level of technical assistance provided for social development by the United Nations in the Arab region; a review and assessment of past efforts; assistance to youth; United Nations participation in the October 1985 Tunis Conference (see above); Arab projects on population, education, development, the communications media, illiteracy, technical education and correctional institutions; and establishment of an Arab Centre for Research and Training in Social Development. The meeting emphasized the usefulness of United Nations–League endeavours in social development research, training, exchange of information and publications, technical assistance and meetings.

Interregional consultation

The Secretary-General, in accordance with a 1983 Economic and Social Council resolution,[19] presented in January 1985 a report[20] reviewing Secretariat activities in social development, with particular reference to the convening of an interregional consultation on developmental social welfare policies and programmes. The Secretary-General concluded that there was much support for such a consultation to review developments and set targets for the year 2000 and beyond.

ECONOMIC AND SOCIAL COUNCIL ACTION

On 29 May 1985, following the recommendation of its Second Committee, the Economic and Social Council adopted without vote **resolution 1985/26**.

Interregional consultation on developmental social welfare policies and programmes

The Economic and Social Council,

Recalling its resolution 1983/22 of 26 May 1983, concerning the taking of steps to convene an interregional consultation on developmental social welfare policies and programmes, within existing budgetary resources,

Recalling also its resolutions 1979/18 of 9 May 1979 and 1981/20 of 6 May 1981 on the strengthening of developmental social welfare policies and programmes,

Noting that government policy affects the well-being of all citizens and thus requires continuous interaction between its social, economic and other elements,

Aware of the serious consequences of the world-wide economic recession for the welfare of peoples and for the funding and delivery of social services which are even more essential now than in periods of economic growth,

Convinced that there is a need to reassess social welfare policy in the light of past experience and present issues, in order to arrive at effective strategies for the future,

Taking note of the efforts made to relate the concerns expressed in Council resolution 1983/22 to the preparations for the Fourth Conference of African Ministers of Social Affairs, held at Addis Ababa from 18 to 26 March 1985, the Third Asian and Pacific Ministerial Conference on Social Welfare and Social Development, to be held at Bangkok from 9 to 15 October 1985, the Pan-Arab Regional Conference on Social Welfare Policies, to be held in September 1985, and looking forward to similar conferences in Europe, Latin America and the Caribbean,

Taking note of the report of the Secretary-General concerning steps taken with a view to convening an interregional consultation on developmental social welfare policies and programmes and the necessity of the active involvement of regional intergovernmental organizations in this effort,

1. *Requests* the Secretary-General to proceed with the organization of the interregional consultation on developmental social welfare policies and programmes to be held, within existing budgetary resources, at Vienna, at an appropriate policy-making level, in the autumn of 1987 when regional preparations will be completed, and to which all States would be invited, with the objective of appraising present policies and programmes and developing themes and setting goals in the social field for the year 2000, taking into account the Declaration on Social Progress and Development;

2. *Also requests* the Secretary-General to assist in the conduct of regional intergovernmental meetings, which would consider, *inter alia*, issues relating to the interregional consultation;

3. *Further requests* the Secretary-General to submit, on the basis of consultations with Governments, to the Commission for Social Development at its thirtieth session for final comments, an annotated draft agenda for the interregional consultation, with relevant documentation to the extent possible.

Economic and Social Council resolution 1985/26

29 May 1985   Meeting 23   Adopted without vote

Approved by Second Committee (E/1985/96 & Corr.1) without vote, 17 May (meeting 8); draft by Commission for Social Development (E/1985/24 & Corr.1); agenda item 17.

In **resolution 1985/64**, the Council urged all Member States, particularly LDCs, to prepare for and be adequately represented at the interregional consultation.

Social integration policies

Pursuant to a 1983 Economic and Social Council resolution,[21] the Secretary-General submitted in January 1985 to the Commission for Social Development a report on recent trends in strategies for the social integration of less-advantaged population groups in developing countries.[22] Such groups generally included the poor and landless, migrant workers, disadvantaged youth, aged persons, the disabled, racial and ethnic minorities and persons discriminated against by gender. A major obstacle to a solution of the problem of the disadvantaged was their exclusion from policy- and decision-making. Analysis indicated a need for comprehensive and integrated policy approaches. Measures to establish a more positive environment and support attempts by the disadvantaged to improve their own situation included: strengthening legal codes to ensure the rights and freedoms of the disadvantaged; establishing a legal and administrative basis for affirmative action; strengthening Governments' role in advancing social integration; accelerating social and economic changes for the elimination of disparities between social groups; improving social planning and the co-ordination of activities of governmental and non-governmental groups; and providing material and legal support to facilitate participation by the disadvantaged in policy- and decision-making.

The Commission on 27 February 1985[23] took note of the report.

Co-operatives

The Secretary-General, in response to a 1983 Economic and Social Council resolution,[24] submitted in January 1985 a report on national experience in promoting the co-operative movement,[25] which was based, in part, on information from 22 Member States and, in addition, on a review of recent publications. It discussed the role of co-operatives in social and economic development and in improving the welfare of their members; the participation of all people in co-operatives; the interrelationship between agrarian reform and agricultural co-operatives; strengthening movement-to-movement activities among co-operatives; the role of co-operatives in improving the production, marketing and consumption of food; training and educational programmes to promote the effectiveness of co-operatives; difficulties faced by countries in establishing co-operatives; and the role of Governments in promoting them.

The report concluded that Member States might wish to renew their commitment to promoting co-operatives in a manner consistent with preserving their autonomy and democratic character; to encourage rural co-operatives to become more directly involved in the production of food for domestic consumption; to support efforts to strengthen the movement-to-movement concept among co-operatives as an important step in promoting co-operative development; to promote the development of urban co-operatives in such areas as industrial production, credit, housing and social services; to explore ways to strengthen the involvement of women, young people, disabled persons and the aging in co-operative and self-help organizations; to promote co-operative activities among the poorest elements of society; and to encourage programmes to improve the management of co-operatives through training and educational programmes.

ECONOMIC AND SOCIAL COUNCIL ACTION

On 29 May 1985, on the recommendation of its Second Committee, the Economic and Social Council adopted without vote **resolution 1985/22**.

National experience in promoting the co-operative movement

The Economic and Social Council,

Recalling General Assembly resolutions 2459(XXIII) of 20 December 1968, 3273(XXIX) of 10 December 1974, 31/37 of 30 November 1976, 33/47 of 14 December 1978 and 36/18 of 9 November 1981, and Council resolution 1983/15 of 26 May 1983,

Desiring to promote the implementation of the International Development Strategy for the Third United Nations Development Decade,

Bearing in mind the importance of the establishment and growth of co-operatives as an instrument for the full economic, social and cultural development of all members of society,

Reaffirming the important role played by co-operatives in the socio-economic development of developing countries,

Recognizing the necessity of training and educational programmes at various levels for the growth, diversification and professionalization of the management of co-operatives,

Convinced that the exchange among countries of national experience relating to the co-operative movement plays an essential role in strengthening co-operatives for the benefit of their members and in overcoming difficulties in the development of various co-operatives,

Convinced of the important role that co-operatives in the various sectors of the economy can play in improving the production, marketing and consumption of food, with particular reference to special population groups,

1. *Takes note* of the report of the Secretary-General on national experience in promoting the co-operative movement;

2. *Invites* the regional commissions and specialized agencies concerned to make further efforts to promote the co-operative movement as an effective instrument for the improvement of the well-being of all people, and special population groups in particular;

3. *Invites* the Secretary-General to include pertinent information and data on the co-operative movement in developing and developed countries in relevant periodic United Nations publications;

4. *Requests* the Secretary-General to prepare, with particular attention to developing countries, in consultation with Member States, relevant organizations of the United Nations system and non-governmental organizations, and drawing on the work already under way

elsewhere in the United Nations system, a comprehensive report on national experience in promoting the co-operative movement, paying special attention, *inter alia*, to the following aspects of the question:

(a) The role of co-operatives in overall social and economic development, particularly in rural areas;

(b) The role of agricultural, savings, handicraft and other types of co-operative organizations in the production, marketing and consumption of food and related goods and services;

(c) The role of co-operative and co-operative-type organizations in promoting development in urban areas;

(d) The participation of all people, including women, youth, disabled persons and the aging, in co-operatives;

(e) The participation of peasants, including landless peasants, in co-operatives;

(f) The role and extent of government support in promoting co-operatives;

(g) Training and educational programmes to promote the effectiveness of co-operatives and make them more responsive to the needs of their members;

(h) Difficulties faced by countries in the establishment and development of co-operatives and their experience in overcoming them;

(i) Progress made in strengthening "movement-to-movement" activities;

(j) Progress made in promoting membership in and the growth of co-operatives;

5. *Further requests* the Secretary-General to submit that report, through the Commission for Social Development and the Economic and Social Council, to the General Assembly at its forty-second session for consideration under the item entitled "National experience in achieving far-reaching social and economic changes for the purpose of social progress".

Economic and Social Council resolution 1985/22

29 May 1985   Meeting 23   Adopted without vote

Approved by Second Committee (E/1985/96 & Corr.1) without vote, 17 May (meeting 8); draft by Commission for Social Development (E/1985/24 & Corr.1); agenda item 17.

Situation of workers

Income distribution

As requested by the Economic and Social Council in 1983,[26] the Secretary-General submitted to the Commission for Social Development in January 1985[27] a report on the conclusions of an income distribution project, including those relating to the adverse effects of the world economic crisis on income in developing countries. He said developing countries had taken a broad approach to social equity, in which equitable income distribution was a consideration, but often not a precisely formulated objective. The eradication of poverty remained a central social issue. Government efforts typically focused on such measures as extending essential services to the whole population, improving facilities in less endowed areas, removing specific barriers to the social mobility and welfare of disadvantaged groups, and promoting mechanisms for participation in society.

Among the most important factors determining income distribution were: type of economic system; land and capital ownership; technology; sectoral, regional and employment structures; education; and social stratification. Governments wishing to bring about lasting change in income distribution had to consider the impact of their policy measures on those factors.

The Commission for Social Development took note of the report on 27 February.[28]

Employment and workers' rights

Communications. On 28 May 1985,[29] Czechoslovakia, also on behalf of Bulgaria, the Byelorussian SSR, the German Democratic Republic, Hungary, Mongolia, Poland, the Ukrainian SSR and the USSR, transmitted to the Secretary-General their declaration on the situation in the International Labour Organisation (ILO). The declaration, which had been conveyed earlier to the ILO Director-General, charged that the basic concept and structure of ILO had remained unchanged since 1919; that ILO had virtually ignored the admission of socialist and developing countries to its membership and, in effect, served the interests of only one socio-political system, that of capitalism; and that while some useful activities on social and labour problems had been carried out, a radical change was needed in the organization's work.

On 3 July,[30] Costa Rica transmitted a document which had been before the ILO Governing Body (May/June session, Geneva) and which responded to issues raised by the socialist countries, concerning ILO activities relating to employment, disarmament, alleged ILO interference in countries' internal affairs, supervision of international labour standards by ILO machinery, alleged ILO resistance to East-West trade union co-operation, lack of East-West co-operation, assistance to employers' organizations in developing countries, technical co-operation projects, ILO structure and staffing, filling of elective posts and seat distribution in ILO bodies, and efficient use of budgetary resources.

On 9 July,[31] Australia, Belgium, Canada, Denmark, France, the Federal Republic of Germany, Ireland, Italy, Luxembourg, the Netherlands, New Zealand, Norway, Portugal, Sweden, the United Kingdom and the United States requested that the ILO document be circulated as an official document of the General Assembly and the Economic and Social Council in order for all delegations to be adequately informed.

Welfare of migrant workers

In accordance with a 1983 Economic and Social Council resolution,[32] the Secretary-General submitted to the 1985 session of the Commission for Social Development a report on the social situation of migrant workers and their families.[33]

Current adverse economic conditions were contributing to a global increase in irregular migration and, consequently, were making migrants more vulnerable to exploitation, discrimination and abuse, the Secretary-General observed. In many parts of the world, hostility was growing towards migrants, who had to live in permanent insecurity, uncertain about their own and their children's future. A dramatic increase in foreign labour in oil-producing Middle Eastern countries, which had promoted contract or project-tied migration, also had serious implications. In that type of situation, virtually every aspect of the migrant workers' lives was controlled by the employer: they were forbidden to form unions and usually were housed in work camps situated away from population centres; the incidence of work-related deaths and injuries was high.

Greater efforts were needed to improve the situation of children of migrants, particularly with respect to education, vocational training and employment. Those issues should be fully taken into account in policies and programmes aiming to resolve problems caused by migration.

Progress had been made in drafting an international convention on the protection of the rights of migrant workers and their families (see Chapter XVIII of this section). However, if the convention was to contribute significantly to improving their position, it should include explicit provisions with regard to family reunion, housing, education of children, health care and preservation of national and cultural identity.

The General Assembly adopted **resolution 40/130** on measures to improve the situation and ensure the human rights of migrant workers.

ECONOMIC AND SOCIAL COUNCIL ACTION

On 29 May, on the recommendation of its Second Committee, the Economic and Social Council adopted without vote **resolution 1985/24**.

Welfare of migrant workers and their families

The Economic and Social Council,

Recalling its resolutions 1979/12 of 9 May 1979, 1981/21 of 6 May 1981 and 1983/16 of 26 May 1983,

Having taken note with appreciation of the report of the Secretary-General on the social situation of migrant workers and their families,

Concerned by the fact that the changing conditions of international migration resulting from current economic trends adversely affect the situation of migrants, whether they remain abroad under increasingly difficult conditions or return to their country of origin,

Aware of the new needs and problems emerging as a result of the changing migration patterns of migrant workers and their families,

Noting with concern the inadequacy or lack of programmes and social services to help migrant workers to adapt themselves to the language, culture and customs of the host country, and to settle down in decent material conditions and send for their families,

Recalling that the family is the natural and fundamental group unit of society and is entitled to protection by society and the State and that, in that context, the families of migrant workers are entitled to the same protection as the migrant workers themselves,

Noting with appreciation the progress made by the Working Group on the Drafting of an International Convention on the Protection of the Rights of All Migrant Workers and Their Families, established in accordance with General Assembly resolution 34/172 of 17 December 1979,

Recognizing the need for further efforts at the national, bilateral, regional and international levels to improve the social situation of migrant workers and their families,

1. *Invites* Member States to establish and/or expand programmes and services designed to improve the welfare of migrant workers and their families and to meet the new needs and problems emerging as a result of the changing circumstances of the international migration of labour;

2. *Emphasizes* that such programmes should give major attention to the protection of families of migrant workers and to a substantial improvement in the conditions for genuine integration of members of migrants' families, particularly women, children and youth, into the host society; special care should be paid to the education of children, so that they maintain and develop the knowledge of their maternal language and their cultural heritage;

3. *Invites* Member States, both countries of origin and host countries, to facilitate the reintegration of migrant workers and their families in the case of their return to their country of origin; the participation of the host country in that process is not to be regarded as a moral obligation only, but rather as a way of assisting those who actively contributed to building up the economy of the host country;

4. *Affirms* the need for the Governments of the Member States concerned to enact or strictly apply legislation to prevent or punish discriminatory or xenophobic activities against migrants, to enable the migrant workers to enjoy the benefits of association within the law;

5. *Requests* the Secretary-General, in co-operation with intergovernmental organizations, specialized agencies and organs of the United Nations system, to prepare a document incorporating guidelines for establishing social services for migrant workers and their families;

6. *Also requests* the Secretary-General to encourage operational activities within available resources, and to consider the implementation of measures based on studies already conducted by the United Nations and other international organizations concerned to benefit migrant workers and their families;

7. *Invites* the intergovernmental and non-governmental organizations concerned to continue and strengthen their efforts in this field, in co-operation with the United Nations;

8. *Further requests* the Secretary-General to report to the Commission for Social Development, at its thirtieth session, on the progress made in strengthening programmes designed to improve the social situation of migrant workers and their families and in meeting the needs and problems emerging as a result of the changing conditions of international migration.

Economic and Social Council resolution 1985/24

29 May 1985   Meeting 23   Adopted without vote

Approved by Second Committee (E/1985/96 & Corr.1) without vote, 17 May (meeting 8); draft by Commission for Social Development (E/1985/24 & Corr.1); agenda item 17.

African migrant workers

ECONOMIC AND SOCIAL COUNCIL ACTION

On 26 July 1985, on the recommendation of its First (Economic) Committee, the Economic and Social Council adopted without vote **resolution 1985/64**.

Developmental social welfare policies and programmes on the situation of African migrant workers

The Economic and Social Council,

Aware of the serious consequences of the critical African socio-economic situation for the living conditions of the peoples in Africa, and for the funding and delivery of social services, which are even more essential now than in previous periods of economic development,

Reaffirming the essential role of social welfare in overall development and in dealing with pressing issues arising notably from food shortages, problems relating to refugees and displaced persons, the breakup of families, lack of adequate health and educational facilities, unemployment and underemployment, urbanization, and high rates of population growth,

Having considered the issue of African migrant workers and the impact it has on the socio-economic development of the sending and receiving countries,

Noting that, since 1979, work has been under way on an international convention on the protection of the rights of all migrant workers and their families,

1. *Urges* all Member States, particularly the least developed countries, to prepare for and be adequately represented at the Interregional Consultation on Developmental Social Welfare Policies and Programmes, to be held in 1987;

2. *Requests* the Executive Secretary of the Economic Commission for Africa to prepare a report on the issues identified in Council resolution 1983/22 of 26 May 1983, with special emphasis on those issues of particular concern for or relevance to Africa, and to ensure that the substance of that report is taken into full consideration in the agenda and documentation of the Interregional Consultation;

3. *Further requests* the Executive Secretary of the Economic Commission for Africa to make the necessary arrangements for an in-depth study of the situation of African migrant workers in both receiving and sending countries, in order to elicit appropriate action and measures to promote the welfare and protection of the rights of the migrant workers and their families, as well as appropriate policies for their social integration;

4. *Recommends* the General Assembly to approve the technical and financial implications of the involvement of the Economic Commission for Africa in both activities, as submitted in section 13 of the proposed programme budget for the biennium 1986-1987.

Economic and Social Council resolution 1985/64
26 July 1985   Meeting 52   Adopted without vote

Approved by First Committee (E/1985/145) without vote, 23 July (meeting 27); draft
by ECA (E/1985/106), orally amended following informal consultations; agenda
item 8.

Institutional machinery

UN Research Institute for Social Development

In 1985, the United Nations Research Institute for Social Development (UNRISD) continued research on food systems, popular participation, improving development data and social conditions of refugees.[34] Food security research had been conducted in 10 countries in Africa, Asia and Latin America. The failure of conventional national and international food policies to prevent recurrent food crises in Africa showed the need for a comprehensive food systems approach in analysing the root causes of hunger and famine. Moreover, research indicated that many proposed solutions to food security problems, such as decreased protectionism, rapid economic growth, increased aid, transnational investments and improved technology, might have a contrary impact, unless applied as part of carefully developed strategies.

Popular participation research examined social movements among rural workers, peasants, marginal urban populations, ethnic groups and industrial workers, and studied how such movements emerged, evolved and interacted with political parties, non-governmental organizations, élites and the State.

New approaches to the collection and analysis of development data and the testing of their practical applicability and utility were pursued. Social and economic developments were researched jointly, and a country development profile, based on 19 selected indicators, was proposed. Reports were issued on a workshop on local monitoring and analysis (Geneva, 8-10 July) and on a pilot project on local monitoring at Kerala, India.

Research on the social conditions of refugees, which had focused mainly on Africa and to a lesser extent on Asia, was expanded to include Latin America. Case-studies in the three continents helped Governments and international agencies to understand the social systems of refugee communities and reach target populations more efficiently. For example, in collaboration with El Colegio de México, a study was undertaken on the integration of Guatemalan refugees in south-east Mexico and the response of the Mexican population and authorities.

Income in 1985 amounted to $2,261,520, consisting of $791,613 in government contributions to UNRISD general funds, $1,340,250 special-purpose contributions to project trust funds, $113,227 interest and $16,430 of miscellaneous income. Expenditures totalled $1,241,205.

On 27 February,[35] the Commission for Social Development took note of the report of the Board of UNRISD on UNRISD activities during 1983[36] and 1984.[37]

Commission for Social Development

In the report on its February 1985 session,[38] the Commission for Social Development recommended to the Economic and Social Council the adoption of 10 resolutions and two decisions. Seven other decisions adopted by the Commission were brought to the Council's attention.

The resolutions covered the timely distribution of documents (see p. 737), the world social situation (see p. 722), national experience in promoting the co-operative movement (see p. 733), youth in the contemporary world (see Chapter XX of this section), welfare of migrant workers (see p. 734), the International Development Strategy for the Third United Nations Development Decade (see p. 420), an interregional consultation on developmental social welfare policies (see p. 731), efforts to secure the human rights of youth (see Chapter XX of this section), implementation of the International Plan of Action on Aging (see Chapter XX of this section) and the family (see p. 730).

ECONOMIC AND SOCIAL COUNCIL ACTION

On 29 May 1985, on the recommendation of its Second Committee, the Economic and Social Council adopted without vote **resolution 1985/36**.

Progress of work of the Commission for Social Development

The Economic and Social Council,

Recalling the terms of reference of the Commission for Social Development set forth in Economic and Social Council resolutions 10(II) of 21 June 1946, 830 J (XXXII) of 2 August 1961 and 1139(XLI) of 29 July 1966,

Reaffirming the central role of the Commission for Social Development within the United Nations in considering matters relating to social development,

Reaffirming that, within the United Nations system, the Centre for Social Development and Humanitarian Affairs of the Department of International Economic and Social Affairs of the United Nations Secretariat has a major role to play in matters relevant to social development,

Recognizing the importance for the Commission for Social Development of exchanges of information on activities with other functional commissions of the Economic and Social Council with mandates in the social development sector, in particular the Commission on the Status of Women and the Population Commission,

Concerned that the Commission should have available to it sufficient information on social development activities within the United Nations system to enable it to make an appropriate contribution towards the fulfilment of overall development objectives, and to provide appropriate direction to the Centre for Social Development and Humanitarian Affairs with respect to its work in the field of social development,

Recalling General Assembly resolutions 36/228 A and B of 18 December 1981, in which guidelines were laid down by which organizations in the United Nations system were to create mechanisms for the evaluation of their work, and in which the Secretary-General was requested to strengthen the United Nations evaluation system through a series of five separate actions, including self-evaluation,

Recognizing that programmes in the field of social development are formulated within the framework of the medium-term plan, and of the biennial budgets established in accordance with that plan,

1. *Requests* the Secretary-General to make available to the Commission for Social Development at future sessions such details as may be available of the proposed programme of work for the forthcoming biennium so as to allow the Commission to make recommendations on matters pertaining to the social sector to the appropriate intergovernmental bodies;

2. *Encourages* the Secretary-General to make available to the Economic and Social Council information on areas of complementarity among the work programmes of the Commission for Social Development, the Commission on the Status of Women, the Population Commission and other relevant bodies, and to optimize the flow of information on social development within the United Nations system;

3. *Recommends* that the Centre for Social Development and Humanitarian Affairs, in preparing its overview reports for the Commission for Social Development, should draw on information relating to the activities of the specialized agencies in the social development field and such other information as it considers appropriate;

4. *Requests* the Committee for Programme and Coordination to review the current evaluation timetable and to study the possibility of conducting an in-depth evaluation of the effectiveness, relevance and impact of United Nations social development activities, with a view to submitting it to the Commission for Social Development.

Economic and Social Council resolution 1985/36

29 May 1985   Meeting 23   Adopted without vote

Approved by Second Committee (E/1985/96 & Corr.1) without vote, 24 May (meeting 15); 5-nation draft (E/1985/C.2/L.6/Rev.1); agenda item 17.
Sponsors: Canada, Denmark, France, Italy, United States.

GENERAL ASSEMBLY ACTION

The General Assembly, in **resolution 40/98**, noted the Commission's role in social development and humanitarian affairs and invited the Council at its first regular 1986 session to consider ways of improving the Commission's work.

Report of the Commission

On 27 February 1985, the Commission for Social Development adopted the report on its twenty-ninth session.[38]

On 29 May, on the oral proposal of its President, the Economic and Social Council took note of the report in **decision 1985/136**.

Timely distribution of documents

ECONOMIC AND SOCIAL COUNCIL ACTION

On 29 May, on the recommendation of its Second Committee, the Economic and Social Council adopted without vote **resolution 1985/20**.

Ensuring the timely distribution of conference documents

The Economic and Social Council,

Noting with regret that the majority of the documents for the twenty-ninth session of the Commission for Social Development, one of which was the comprehensive 1985 report on the world social situation, did not reach the Commission until the first meeting of the session,

Conscious of the Commission's responsibility for maintaining the quality of its deliberations and decisions,

Considering that adequate information on the contents of the documents relating to the items of the agenda of the Commission constitutes a prerequisite therefor,

Considering that representatives should be accorded sufficient time to study the documents adequately and to orient themselves further if required,

Recalling the rules of procedure of the functional commissions of the Economic and Social Council, in rule 6, paragraph 1, of which it is stated that the Secretary-General shall communicate, not less than six weeks before the opening of the session, the provisional agenda and transmit the basic documents related to each item appearing therein,

1. *Requests* the Secretary-General to ensure, as a matter of priority and urgency, that from now on the distribution of the documents concerned will correspond strictly to the rules of procedure;

2. *Further requests* the Secretary-General to ensure that future reports on the world social situation are distributed no later than twelve weeks before the commencement of the session of the Commission.

Economic and Social Council resolution 1985/20

29 May 1985   Meeting 23   Adopted without vote

Approved by Second Committee (E/1985/8 & Corr.1) without vote, 17 May (meeting 8); draft by Commission for Social Development (E/1985/24 & Corr.1); agenda item 17.

Agenda and documentation for the 1987 Commission session

By **decision 1985/133** of 29 May 1985, adopted on the recommendation of its Second Committee, the Economic and Social Council approved the provisional agenda and documentation for the thirtieth (1987) session of the Commission for Social Development. The decision was based on a draft submitted by the Commission.

Trust funds

As at 31 December 1985, the Trust Fund for Social Development which financed training and research activities totalled $104,242; during 1984-1985, its income had amounted to $20,221 and its expenditures to $23,221. The Trust Fund for European Social Development totalled $2,220, having received $1,780 and spent $28,250 during the biennium.

REFERENCES

[1]*1985 Report on the World Social Situation* (ST/ESA/165), Sales No. E.85.IV.2. [2]YUN 1982, p. 959, GA res. 37/54, 3 Dec. 1982. [3]YUN 1983, p. 723, ESC res. 1983/8, 26 May 1983. [4]E/CN.5/1985/3. [5]E/1985/24 & Corr.1 (dec. IV). [6]A/41/31. [7]YUN 1969, p. 433, GA res. 2542(XXIV), 11 Dec. 1969. [8]YUN 1980, p. 503, GA res. 35/56, annex, 5 Dec. 1980. [9]YUN 1983, p. 722, GA res. 38/25, 22 Nov. 1983. [10]A/40/65-E/1985/7 & Add.1. [11]YUN 1983, p. 733, ESC res. 1983/23, 26 May 1983. [12]E/1985/9 & Corr.1. [13]YUN 1983, p. 732, ESC res. 1983/10, 26 May 1983. [14]E/1985/8. [15]E/AC.51/1986/2. [16]YUN 1984, p. 972. [17]A/40/481/Add.1. [18]YUN 1983, p. 394, GA res. 38/6, 28 Oct. 1983. [19]*Ibid.*, p. 728, ESC res. 1983/22, 26 May 1983. [20]E/CN.5/1985/7 & Add.1. [21]YUN 1983, p. 729, ESC res. 1983/13, 26 May 1983. [22]E/CN.5/1985/6. [23]E/1985/24 & Corr.1 (dec. VIII). [24]YUN 1983, p. 734, ESC res. 1983/15, 26 May 1983. [25]A/40/78-E/1985/10. [26]YUN 1983, p. 725, ESC res. 1983/11, 26 May 1983. [27]E/CN.5/1985/5. [28]E/1985/24 & Corr.1 (dec. VII). [29]A/40/342-E/1985/119. [30]A/40/458-E/1985/135. [31]A/40/489-E/1985/143. [32]YUN 1983, p. 822, ESC res. 1983/16, 26 May 1983. [33]E/CN.5/1985/8. [34]E/CN.5/1987/10. [35]E/1985/24 & Corr.1 (dec. III). [36]YUN 1983, p. 735. [37]YUN 1984, p. 698. [38]E/1985/24 & Corr.1.

OTHER PUBLICATIONS

Administration of Social Welfare: A Survey of National Organizational Arrangements (ST/ESA/147), Sales No. E.85.IV.1. *Living Conditions in Developing Countries in the Mid-1980s* (ST/ESA/165/Add.1), Sales No. E.85.IV.3.

Crime prevention

Seventh UN Congress

The Seventh United Nations Congress on the Prevention of Crime and the Treatment of Offenders was held at Milan, Italy, from 26 August to 6 September 1985.[1] Its theme was crime prevention for freedom, justice, peace and development. The Congress was attended by 124 States and observers from 14 United Nations organs and offices, 10 intergovernmental organizations, 59 non-governmental organizations (NGOs) and two national liberation movements (for participating States and officers, see APPENDIX III).

Five major topics were considered: new dimensions of criminality and crime prevention in the context of development (topic 1); criminal justice processes and perspectives in a changing world (topic 2); victims of crime (topic 3); youth, crime and justice (topic 4); and United Nations standards in criminal justice (topic 5).

Prior to the Congress, an interregional preparatory meeting of experts on topic 1 took place at New Delhi, India, from 22 to 26 April 1985; it called on Governments to give high priority to the integration of crime prevention and criminal justice policies in national development planning. Preparatory meetings on the other four topics had been held in 1984.[2]

Leticia R. Shahani (Philippines), Assistant Secretary-General for Social Development and Humanitarian Affairs of the United Nations Secretariat, was named Secretary-General of the Seventh Congress.

The Congress adopted by consensus the Milan Plan of Action on crime prevention and criminal justice (see below), Guiding Principles for Crime Prevention and Criminal Justice in the Context of Development and a New International Economic Order (see p. 742) and four other major international instruments; 26 resolutions on a broad range of crime-related issues; and a decision approving the report of the Credentials Committee.

Decisions of the Congress

Milan Plan of Action

The Milan Plan of Action recommended that Governments accord high priority to crime prevention and criminal justice; co-operate bilaterally and multilaterally to strengthen crime prevention measures and the criminal justice process; eradicate racial discrimination, particularly *apartheid;* and develop public participation in preventing and combating crime. It further recommended that the United Nations and Member States give particular attention in research to possible inter-relationships between criminality and such aspects of development as population, urbanization, industrialization, housing, migration and employment opportunities. Additional study of crime in relation to human rights and fundamental freedoms was needed. The Plan also recommended that priority be given to combating terrorism and controlling illicit drug traffic and organized crime, while the United Nations would reinforce its technical co-operation activities, particularly in the areas of training, planning, exchange of information and reappraisal of legal systems.

The Plan called for continued attention to the improvement of criminal justice systems; for the strengthening of regional and interregional United Nations institutes for crime prevention; and for continued NGO involvement in the work of the United Nations on crime prevention and criminal justice. The Secretary-General was requested to review that work, together with the Committee on Crime Prevention and Control, in order to establish priorities.

Other Congress action

Recommended by the Congress for adoption by the General Assembly were two major instruments—United Nations Standard Minimum Rules for the Administration of Juvenile Justice (see p. 746) and Declaration of Basic Principles of Justice for Victims of Crime and Abuse of Power (see p. 742)—and two resolutions—on the development of standards for the prevention of juvenile delinquency (see p. 756) and on domestic violence (see p. 745). In addition, the Congress adopted a Model Agreement on the Transfer of Foreign Prisoners and recommendations on the treatment of foreign prisoners, and Basic Principles on the Independence of the Judiciary (see p. 757).

The Congress called on Member States to combat organized crime more effectively by introducing new offences directed at novel and sophisticated forms of criminal activity; providing for the forfeiture of illegally acquired assets; facilitating the obtaining of evidence abroad for use in national courts; modernizing national extradition laws and developing bilateral extradition treaties; conducting campaigns against drug abuse; strengthening law enforcement authorities; establishing national crime commissions; and reviewing laws related to taxation, the abuse of bank secrecy and gaming houses, and the transfer of funds for or the proceeds of organized crime across national boundaries (resolution 1).

On illicit drug trafficking and drug abuse control, the Congress recommended that a new international instrument provide for effective penalties, establish all drug trafficking offences as extraditable offences, establish a system of control of precursor substances and chemicals used in the manufacture of illicit drugs, establish jurisdictional issues regarding drug trafficking on the high seas, introduce the investigative technique of controlled delivery in cases involving major drug violators, and develop measures to counter drug smuggling through international postal systems; and invited Member States to take full advantage of the facility offered by the United Nations Fund for Drug Abuse Control to pool resources and thus achieve greater impact (resolutions 2 and 3).

The Congress requested the early establishment of an African Regional Institute for the Prevention of Crime and the Treatment of Offenders (resolution 4).

In other resolutions, the Congress proposed measures to enhance technical co-operation in the field of crime prevention and criminal justice (resolution 5); called for fair treatment of women by the criminal justice system (resolution 6); recommended that Member States avoid political, social, racial, religious, cultural, sexual or other kind of discrimination in the selection of prosecutors (resolution 7); and recommended the development of guidelines for the training of criminal justice personnel (resolution 8) and of crime and criminal justice information and statistical systems (resolution 9).

The Congress also welcomed the approval in 1984 by the Economic and Social Council[3] of procedures for implementing effectively the Standard Minimum Rules for the Treatment of Prisoners (resolution 10); condemned extra-legal, arbitrary and summary executions and requested the Secretary-General to submit a review of documents on the prevention, investigation and elimination of such executions (resolution 11); and invited States retaining the death penalty to implement the safeguards guaranteeing the rights of those facing the death penalty, approved by the Economic and Social Council in 1984[4] (resolution 15).

With respect to youth and crime, the Congress called on Member States to eliminate conditions such as illiteracy, unemployment, racial and national discrimination and other forms of social inequality (resolution 19); adopted principles, guidelines and priorities relating to research on youth crime (resolution 20); and recommended that the Committee on Crime Prevention and Control develop standard minimum rules for the protection of juveniles deprived of their liberty (resolution 21).

The Congress further urged States to facilitate the application of law enforcement measures against terrorists and to strengthen co-operation in the areas of extradition and mutual legal assistance (resolution 23).

In seven other resolutions, the Congress considered the transfer of criminal proceedings (resolution 12) and of supervision of foreign offenders (resolution 13); the 1979 Code of Conduct for Law Enforcement Officials[5] (resolution 14); the role of lawyers (resolution 18); alternatives to imprisonment and social integration of offenders (resolution 16); the human rights of prisoners (resolution 17); and crime prevention in the context of development (resolution 22).

The Congress expressed its thanks to the people and Government of Italy for their hospitality (resolution 24).

Reports of the Secretary-General. In July 1985, the Secretary-General presented to the Seventh Congress a report[6] on implementation by States of the recommendations of the Sixth Congress in 1980,[7] in pursuance of a 1982 Economic and Social Council resolution.[8] The Secretary-General declared that the Caracas Declaration, unanimously adopted by the Sixth Congress, represented a major step towards international co-operation in the struggle against crime. In implementing the Declaration, the United Nations Secretariat had undertaken research, with special attention to new types of criminality in the context of socio-economic changes, focusing on the linkages between crime and urbanization, industrialization, unemployment and rural-urban migration. The aim was to improve the identification of socio-economic factors accompanying high and low crime rates, thus assisting Member States to develop crime prevention policies. National and international action on each of the 19 resolutions adopted by the 1980 Congress also was reported.

In October 1985, the Secretary-General, responding to a 1984 General Assembly resolution,[9] submitted a report[10] on the implementation of the conclusions of the Seventh Congress. He stated that the Congress had significantly enlarged the scope of United Nations activities in crime prevention and criminal justice by adding new mandates and amplifying the modalities of ongoing work. The Milan Plan of Action contained the elements of a worldwide programme for crime prevention and criminal justice, including the allocation of adequate resources, action-oriented research, and technical assistance to developing countries. The new Guiding Principles for crime prevention (see p. 742) would promote effective, coherent policies and allow adjustments to particular socio-economic and cultural circumstances. The Secretary-General summarized the major resolutions and instruments adopted by the Congress and made recommendations for the initial phase of their implementation.

GENERAL ASSEMBLY ACTION

On 29 November 1985, on the recommendation of the Third Committee, the General Assembly adopted without vote **resolution 40/37**.

Expression of appreciation to the Government and people of Italy on the occasion of the Seventh United Nations Congress on the Prevention of Crime and the Treatment of Offenders

The General Assembly,

Taking into account the significance and the results of the Seventh United Nations Congress on the Prevention of Crime and the Treatment of Offenders, held at Milan, Italy, from 26 August to 6 September 1985,

Expresses its deep appreciation to the Government and people of Italy for acting as host to the Seventh United Nations Congress on the Prevention of Crime and the Treatment of Offenders.

General Assembly resolution 40/37

29 November 1985   Meeting 96   Adopted without vote

Approved by Third Committee (A/40/881) without vote, 11 November (meeting 37); 9-nation draft (A/C.3/40/L.25); agenda item 98.
Sponsors: Australia, Canada, Czechoslovakia, Finland, Indonesia, Philippines, Senegal, Venezuela, Zaire.
Meeting numbers. GA 40th session: 3rd Committee 30, 37; plenary 96.

Also on 29 November, following the recommendation of the Third Committee, the Assembly adopted without vote **resolution 40/32**.

Seventh United Nations Congress on the Prevention of Crime and the Treatment of Offenders

The General Assembly,

Recalling its resolution 35/171 of 15 December 1980, in which it endorsed the Caracas Declaration, annexed to that resolution, and urged implementation of the conclusions relating to the new perspectives for international co-operation in crime prevention in the context of development adopted by the Sixth United Nations Congress on the Prevention of Crime and the Treatment of Offenders,

Recalling also its resolution 36/21 of 9 November 1981, in which the Seventh United Nations Congress on the Prevention of Crime and the Treatment of Offenders was invited to consider current and emerging trends in crime prevention and criminal justice, with a view to defining new guiding principles for the future course of crime prevention and criminal justice in the context of development needs, the goals of the International Development Strategy for the Third United Nations Development Decade and the Declaration and the Programme of Action on the Establishment of a New International Economic Order, taking into account the political, economic, social and cultural circumstances and traditions of each country and the need for crime prevention and criminal justice systems to be consonant with the principles of social justice,

Recalling further its resolution 39/112 of 14 December 1984, in which the Secretary-General was requested to ensure that the substantive and organizational work of the Seventh Congress was fully adequate for its successful outcome,

Emphasizing the responsibility assumed by the United Nations in crime prevention under General Assembly resolution 415(V) of 1 December 1950, which was affirmed by the Economic and Social Council in its resolutions 731 F (XXVIII) of 30 July 1959 and 830 D (XXXII) of 2 August 1961, and in the promotion and strengthening of international co-operation in this field in accordance with Assembly resolutions 3021(XXVII) of 18 December 1972, 32/59 and 32/60 of 8 December 1977, 35/171 of 15 December 1980 and 36/21 of 9 November 1981,

Bearing in mind the theme of the Seventh Congress, "Crime prevention for freedom, justice, peace and development", and the importance of preserving peace as a condition for development and international co-operation,

Welcoming the fact that the Congress, in accordance with General Assembly resolution 39/112, paid particular attention to the question of illicit drug trafficking,

Alarmed by the growth and seriousness of crime in many parts of the world, including conventional and non-conventional criminality, which have a negative impact on development and the quality of life,

Considering that crime, particularly in its new forms and dimensions, seriously impairs the development process of many countries, as well as their international relations,

Noting that the function of the criminal justice system is to contribute to the protection of the basic values and norms of society,

Aware of the importance of enhancing the efficiency and effectiveness of criminal justice systems,

Noting that to limit effectively the harm caused by modern economic and unconventional crime, policy measures should be based on an integrated approach, the main emphasis being placed on the reduction of opportunities to commit crime and on the strengthening of norms and attitudes against it,

Aware of the importance of crime prevention and criminal justice, which embraces policies, processes and institutions aimed at controlling criminality and ensuring equal and fair treatment for all those involved in the criminal justice process,

Mindful that the incorporation of crime prevention and criminal justice policies in the planning process can help to ensure a better life for people throughout the world, promote the equality of rights and social security, enhance the effectiveness of crime prevention, especially in such spheres as urbanization, industrialization, education, health, population growth and migration, housing and social welfare, and substantially reduce the social costs directly and indirectly related to crime and crime control by ensuring social justice, respect for human dignity, freedom, equality and security,

Convinced that due attention should be paid to crime prevention and criminal justice and the related processes, including the fate of victims of crime, the role of youth in contemporary society and the application of United Nations standards and norms,

Determined to improve regional, interregional and international co-operation and co-ordination to achieve further progress in this area, including effective and full implementation of the resolutions of the Seventh Congress,

Having considered the report of the Seventh United Nations Congress on the Prevention of Crime and the Treatment of Offenders, the report of the Secretary-General on the implementation of the recommendations of the Sixth United Nations Congress on the Prevention of Crime and the Treatment of Offenders, and the report of the Secretary-General on the implementation of the conclusions of the Seventh United Nations Congress on the Prevention of Crime and the Treatment of Offenders, all submitted in pursuance of General Assembly resolution 39/112,

1. *Expresses its satisfaction* with the report of the Seventh United Nations Congress on the Prevention of Crime and the Treatment of Offenders and with the preparatory work carried out by the Committee on Crime Prevention and Control, as the preparatory body for the Congress, at its seventh and eighth sessions and by the regional and interregional preparatory meetings convened in co-operation with the regional commissions, interregional and regional crime prevention institutes and interested Governments;

2. *Takes note* of the report of the Secretary-General on the implementation of the recommendations of the Sixth United Nations Congress on the Prevention of Crime and the Treatment of Offenders and of his report on the conclusions of the Seventh Congress;

3. *Approves* the Milan Plan of Action, adopted by consensus by the Seventh Congress, as a useful and effective means of strengthening international co-operation in the field of crime prevention and criminal justice;

4. *Recommends* the Guiding Principles for Crime Prevention and Criminal Justice in the Context of Development and a New International Economic Order for national, regional and international action, as appropriate, taking into account the political, economic, social and cultural circumstances and traditions of each country on the basis of the principles of the sovereign equality of States and of non-interference in their internal affairs;

5. *Endorses* the other resolutions adopted unanimously by the Seventh Congress;

6. *Invites* Governments to be guided by the Milan Plan of Action in the formulation of appropriate legislation and policy directives and to make continuous efforts to implement the principles contained in the Caracas Declaration and other relevant resolutions and recommendations adopted by the Sixth Congress, in accordance with the economic, social, cultural and political circumstances of each country;

7. *Also invites* Member States to monitor systematically the steps being taken to ensure coordination of efforts in the planning and execution of effective and humane measures to reduce the social costs of crime and its negative effects on the development process, as well as to explore new avenues for international co-operation in this field;

8. *Invites* the Committee on Crime Prevention and Control to review, at its ninth session, the Milan Plan of Action, the resolutions and recommendations adopted unanimously by the Seventh Congress and their implications for the programmes of the United Nations system and to make specific recommendations on the implementation thereof in its report to the Economic and Social Council at its first regular session of 1986;

9. *Requests* the Economic and Social Council to examine, at its first regular session of 1986, the report of the Committee on Crime Prevention and Control and the recommendations of the Seventh Congress for further implementation of the Milan Plan of Action in order to provide, within the United Nations system, overall policy guidance on crime prevention and criminal justice, and to undertake periodically the review, monitoring and appraisal of the Milan Plan of Action;

10. *Urges* the United Nations system, including the regional and interregional institutes in the field of crime prevention and the treatment of offenders and the relevant non-governmental organizations having consultative status with the Economic and Social Council to become actively involved in the implementation of the recommendations of the Seventh Congress;

11. *Also urges* the Department of Technical Co-operation for Development of the Secretariat and the United Nations Development Programme to give their full support to projects of technical assistance, in particular to developing countries, in the field of crime prevention and criminal justice and to encourage technical co-operation among developing countries;

12. *Requests* the Secretary-General to make every effort to translate into action, as appropriate, the relevant recommendations and policies stemming from the Milan Plan of Action and the Guiding Principles for Crime Prevention and Criminal Justice in the Context of Development and a New International Economic Order and to ensure that the other resolutions and recommendations adopted unanimously by the Seventh Congress are followed up adequately;

13. *Also requests* the Secretary-General, in his report to the Committee on Crime Prevention and Control, to initiate a review, as a matter of urgency, of the functioning and programme of work of the United Nations in the field of crime prevention and criminal justice, including the United Nations regional and interregional institutes, paying special attention to improving the co-ordination of relevant activities within the United Nations in all related areas in order to establish priorities and ensure the continuing relevance and responsiveness of the United Nations to emerging needs, and to submit the final report to the Economic and Social Council at its first regular session of 1987;

14. *Further requests* the Secretary-General to circulate the report of the Seventh Congress to Member States and intergovernmental organizations in order to ensure

that it is disseminated as widely as possible, and to strengthen information activities in this field;

15. *Requests* the Secretary-General to submit to the General Assembly, at its forty-first session, a report on the measures taken to implement the present resolution;

16. *Decides* to include in the provisional agenda of its forty-first session the item entitled "Crime prevention and criminal justice".

General Assembly resolution 40/32

29 November 1985   Meeting 96   Adopted without vote

Approved by Third Committee (A/40/881) without vote, 11 November (meeting 37); 21-nation draft (A/C.3/40/L.24), orally revised; agenda item 98.

Sponsors: Argentina, Australia, Bolivia, Canada, Colombia, Costa Rica, Finland, France, Greece, Indonesia, Italy, Morocco, Lebanon, Netherlands, New Zealand, Rwanda, Senegal, Spain, Uruguay, Venezuela, Yugoslavia.

Meeting numbers. GA 40th session: 3rd Committee 16-23, 30, 37; plenary 96.

In related action, the Assembly in **resolution 40/146** took note of the Seventh Congress recommendations regarding treatment of prisoners, the Code of Conduct for Law Enforcement Officials and the rights of those facing the death penalty; called on Member States to implement them; and requested the Secretary-General to report on their implementation to the Committee on Crime Prevention and Control.

Provisional rules of procedure

By a May 1985 note[11] to the Economic and Social Council, the Secretary-General stated that the Council might wish to consider changes in the provisional rules of procedure for United Nations crime congresses.

On 29 May, on the recommendation of its Second Committee, the Council adopted without vote **decision 1985/134**, approving the amendments adopted in 1980 by the Sixth Congress to rule 6 (raising the number of officers constituting the General Committee to 28) and rule 44, paragraph 1 (reducing the number of committee Vice-Chairmen to one), of the 1979 provisional rules of procedure,[12] as revised in 1980.[13] The Council decided to defer until a later date consideration of other amendments proposed by the Committee on Crime Prevention and Control in 1984.[14] It also decided that, at the 1985 Congress, the rules of procedure should be modified to take into account the appointment of the Secretary-General of the Congress.

Questions related to criminal justice

Crime prevention and development

The Seventh Congress on crime, by resolution 22, reaffirmed that crime prevention must be examined in the context of socio-economic and political systems, social and cultural values, and social change. It also reaffirmed the need for increased efforts of the international community and Member States, in the context of a proposed new international economic order (see p. 420), for

crime prevention, achievement of human rights and development of nations; deplored the increase and gravity of crime; called on Member States to take measures to eliminate conditions of life that degrade human dignity, including unemployment, poverty, illiteracy, racial discrimination, *apartheid* and social injustice; recommended that States promote the people's broadest participation in political, social and other measures to prevent crime; reiterated that the international community must accord priority to the search for crime prevention solutions; and requested that the Eighth United Nations Congress on crime examine new dimensions of criminality in the context of development, on the basis of information provided by Member States.

The Congress also adopted Guiding Principles for Crime Prevention and Criminal Justice in the Context of Development and a New International Economic Order, which addressed itself to many issues, including various types of crime and their impact on development, planning for crime prevention and criminal justice, the role of criminal justice systems and prerequisites for international action in crime control. New approaches to meet new problems more effectively were recommended, while the potential of traditional forms of social control were simultaneously recognized. The Guiding Principles, in addition, stressed the need to protect human rights, reduce social marginality and injustice, and encourage cooperation among States through the United Nations.

The General Assembly, in **resolution 40/32**, recommended the Guiding Principles for national, regional and international action, and requested the Secretary-General to translate them into action.

Declaration of principles for victims of crime and abuse of power

GENERAL ASSEMBLY ACTION

The General Assembly, on the recommendation of the Third Committee, adopted without vote **resolution 40/34** on 29 November 1985.

Declaration of Basic Principles of Justice for Victims of Crime and Abuse of Power

The General Assembly,

Recalling that the Sixth United Nations Congress on the Prevention of Crime and the Treatment of Offenders recommended that the United Nations should continue its present work on the development of guidelines and standards regarding abuse of economic and political power,

Cognizant that millions of people throughout the world suffer harm as a result of crime and the abuse of power and that the rights of these victims have not been adequately recognized,

Recognizing that the victims of crime and the victims of abuse of power, and also frequently their families, witnesses and others who aid them, are unjustly subjected to loss, damage or injury and that they may, in addition, suffer hardship when assisting in the prosecution of offenders,

1. *Affirms* the necessity of adopting national and international measures in order to secure the universal and effective recognition of, and respect for, the rights of victims of crime and of abuse of power;

2. *Stresses* the need to promote progress by all States in their efforts to that end, without prejudice to the rights of suspects or offenders;

3. *Adopts* the Declaration of Basic Principles of Justice for Victims of Crime and Abuse of Power, annexed to the present resolution, which is designed to assist Governments and the international community in their efforts to secure justice and assistance for victims of crime and victims of abuse of power;

4. *Calls upon* Member States to take the necessary steps to give effect to the provisions contained in the Declaration and, in order to curtail victimization as referred to hereinafter, endeavour:

(*a*) To implement social, health, including mental health, educational, economic and specific crime prevention policies to reduce victimization and encourage assistance to victims in distress;

(*b*) To promote community efforts and public participation in crime prevention;

(*c*) To review periodically their existing legislation and practices in order to ensure responsiveness to changing circumstances, and to enact and enforce legislation proscribing acts that violate internationally recognized norms relating to human rights, corporate conduct and other abuses of power;

(*d*) To establish and strengthen the means of detecting, prosecuting and sentencing those guilty of crimes;

(*e*) To promote disclosure of relevant information to expose official and corporate conduct to public scrutiny, and other ways of increasing responsiveness to public concerns;

(*f*) To promote the observance of codes of conduct and ethical norms, in particular international standards, by public servants, including law enforcement, correctional, medical, social service and military personnel, as well as the staff of economic enterprises;

(*g*) To prohibit practices and procedures conducive to abuse, such as secret places of detention and incommunicado detention;

(*h*) To co-operate with other States, through mutual judicial and administrative assistance, in such matters as the detection and pursuit of offenders, their extradition and the seizure of their assets, to be used for restitution to the victims;

5. *Recommends* that, at the international and regional levels, all appropriate measures should be taken:

(*a*) To promote training activities designed to foster adherence to United Nations standards and norms and to curtail possible abuses;

(*b*) To sponsor collaborative action-research on ways in which victimization can be reduced and victims aided, and to promote information exchanges on the most effective means of so doing;

(*c*) To render direct aid to requesting Governments designed to help them curtail victimization and alleviate the plight of victims;

(*d*) To develop ways and means of providing recourse for victims where national channels may be insufficient;

6. *Requests* the Secretary-General to invite Member States to report periodically to the General Assembly on the implementation of the Declaration, as well as on measures taken by them to this effect;

7. *Also requests* the Secretary-General to make use of the opportunities, which all relevant bodies and organizations within the United Nations system offer, to assist Member States, whenever necessary, in improving ways and means of protecting victims both at the national level and through international co-operation;

8. *Further requests* the Secretary-General to promote the objectives of the Declaration, in particular by ensuring its widest possible dissemination;

9. *Urges* the specialized agencies and other entities and bodies of the United Nations system, other relevant intergovernmental and non-governmental organizations and the public to co-operate in the implementation of the provisions of the Declaration.

ANNEX
Declaration of Basic Principles of Justice for Victims of Crime and Abuse of Power

A. *Victims of crime*

1. "Victims" means persons who, individually or collectively, have suffered harm, including physical or mental injury, emotional suffering, economic loss or substantial impairment of their fundamental rights, through acts or omissions that are in violation of criminal laws operative within Member States, including those laws proscribing criminal abuse of power.

2. A person may be considered a victim, under this Declaration, regardless of whether the perpetrator is identified, apprehended, prosecuted or convicted and regardless of the familial relationship between the perpetrator and the victim. The term "victim" also includes, where appropriate, the immediate family or dependants of the direct victim and persons who have suffered harm in intervening to assist victims in distress or to prevent victimization.

3. The provisions contained herein shall be applicable to all, without distinction of any kind, such as race, colour, sex, age, language, religion, nationality, political or other opinion, cultural beliefs or practices, property, birth or family status, ethnic or social origin, and disability.

Access to justice and fair treatment

4. Victims should be treated with compassion and respect for their dignity. They are entitled to access to the mechanisms of justice and to prompt redress, as provided for by national legislation, for the harm that they have suffered.

5. Judicial and administrative mechanisms should be established and strengthened where necessary to enable victims to obtain redress through formal or informal procedures that are expeditious, fair, inexpensive and accessible. Victims should be informed of their rights in seeking redress through such mechanisms.

6. The responsiveness of judicial and administrative processes to the needs of victims should be facilitated by:

(*a*) Informing victims of their role and the scope, timing and progress of the proceedings and of the disposition of their cases, especially where serious crimes are involved and where they have requested such information;

(b) Allowing the views and concerns of victims to be presented and considered at appropriate stages of the proceedings where their personal interests are affected, without prejudice to the accused and consistent with the relevant national criminal justice system;

(c) Providing proper assistance to victims throughout the legal process;

(d) Taking measures to minimize inconvenience to victims, protect their privacy, when necessary, and ensure their safety, as well as that of their families and witnesses on their behalf, from intimidation and retaliation;

(e) Avoiding unnecessary delay in the disposition of cases and the execution of orders or decrees granting awards to victims.

7. Informal mechanisms for the resolution of disputes, including mediation, arbitration and customary justice or indigenous practices, should be utilized where appropriate to facilitate conciliation and redress for victims.

Restitution

8. Offenders or third parties responsible for their behaviour should, where appropriate, make fair restitution to victims, their families or dependants. Such restitution should include the return of property or payment for the harm or loss suffered, reimbursement of expenses incurred as a result of the victimization, the provision of services and the restoration of rights.

9. Governments should review their practices, regulations and laws to consider restitution as an available sentencing option in criminal cases, in addition to other criminal sanctions.

10. In cases of substantial harm to the environment, restitution, if ordered, should include, as far as possible, restoration of the environment, reconstruction of the infrastructure, replacement of community facilities and reimbursement of the expenses of relocation, whenever such harm results in the dislocation of a community.

11. Where public officials or other agents acting in an official or quasi-official capacity have violated national criminal laws, the victims should receive restitution from the State whose officials or agents were responsible for the harm inflicted. In cases where the Government under whose authority the victimizing act or omission occurred is no longer in existence, the State or Government successor in title should provide restitution to the victims.

Compensation

12. When compensation is not fully available from the offender or other sources, States should endeavour to provide financial compensation to:

(a) Victims who have sustained significant bodily injury or impairment of physical or mental health as a result of serious crimes;

(b) The family, in particular dependants of persons who have died or become physically or mentally incapacitated as a result of such victimization.

13. The establishment, strengthening and expansion of national funds for compensation to victims should be encouraged. Where appropriate, other funds may also be established for this purpose, including in those cases where the State of which the victim is a national is not in a position to compensate the victim for the harm.

Assistance

14. Victims should receive the necessary material, medical, psychological and social assistance through governmental, voluntary, community-based and indigenous means.

15. Victims should be informed of the availability of health and social services and other relevant assistance and be readily afforded access to them.

16. Police, justice, health, social service and other personnel concerned should receive training to sensitize them to the needs of victims, and guidelines to ensure proper and prompt aid.

17. In providing services and assistance to victims, attention should be given to those who have special needs because of the nature of the harm inflicted or because of factors such as those mentioned in paragraph 3 above.

B. *Victims of abuse of power*

18. "Victims" means persons who, individually or collectively, have suffered harm, including physical or mental injury, emotional suffering, economic loss or substantial impairment of their fundamental rights, through acts or omissions that do not yet constitute violations of national criminal laws but of internationally recognized norms relating to human rights.

19. States should consider incorporating into the national law norms proscribing abuses of power and providing remedies to victims of such abuses. In particular, such remedies should include restitution and/or compensation, and necessary material, medical, psychological and social assistance and support.

20. States should consider negotiating multilateral international treaties relating to victims, as defined in paragraph 18.

21. States should periodically review existing legislation and practices to ensure their responsiveness to changing circumstances, should enact and enforce, if necessary, legislation proscribing acts that constitute serious abuses of political or economic power, as well as promoting policies and mechanisms for the prevention of such acts, and should develop and make readily available appropriate rights and remedies for victims of such acts.

General Assembly resolution 40/34

29 November 1985   Meeting 96   Adopted without vote

Approved by Third Committee (A/40/881) without vote, 11 November (meeting 37); draft by Seventh Congress on crime (A/C.3/40/L.21); agenda item 98.
Meeting numbers. GA 40th session: 3rd Committee 16-23, 30, 37; plenary 96.

Domestic violence

Report of the Secretary-General. In May 1985, the Secretary-General submitted to the Seventh Congress a report[15] on the situation of women as crime victims, as requested by the Economic and Social Council in 1984.[16] The report analysed the factors contributing to the persistent, worldwide victimization of women through crime, in various old and newly emerging forms, as well as crime-related abuses of power, and discussed policy implications and presented action alternatives aimed at ameliorating female victimization and the treatment of female victims by criminal justice systems. In that respect, the report concluded, the international community could take concrete steps by providing policy models, devising new programmes, training personnel, encouraging research, collecting data, exchanging information and making technical assistance available.

On 29 November 1985, on the recommendation of the Third Committee, the General Assembly adopted without vote **resolution 40/36**.

Domestic violence

The General Assembly,

Recalling Economic and Social Council resolution 1984/14 of 24 May 1984 on violence in the family,

Recalling also resolution 9 adopted by the Sixth United Nations Congress on the Prevention of Crime and the Treatment of Offenders, in which the Congress called for the fair treatment of women by the criminal justice system,

Bearing in mind the recommendations made on the subject of domestic violence by the World Conference to Review and Appraise the Achievements of the United Nations Decade for Women: Equality, Development and Peace,

Having regard to the Declaration of the Rights of the Child, in particular principle 9 concerning the protection of the child against exploitation, neglect and cruelty, and the Convention on the Elimination of All Forms of Discrimination against Women,

Mindful of the important role of the family in ensuring the proper development of the young and their integration into the mainstream of society, and in preventing delinquency,

Mindful further of the social aspects of domestic violence and of the great importance of emphasizing and developing appropriate methods of conflict resolution between the parties involved,

Recognizing that abuse and battery in the family are critical problems that have serious physical and psychological effects on individual family members, especially the young, and jeopardize the health and survival of the family unit,

Recognizing further the adverse effects of exposure to domestic violence, especially at an early stage of human development, and the incalculable harm thereof,

Convinced that the problem of domestic violence is a multifaceted one which should be examined from the perspective of crime prevention and criminal justice in the context of socio-economic circumstances,

Convinced also of the necessity to improve the situation of the victims of domestic violence,

Concerned that the abuse of alcohol, narcotic drugs and psychotropic substances may be an exacerbating factor in domestic violence and that the effects thereof should be further examined,

1. *Takes note with appreciation* of the report of the Secretary-General on the situation of women as victims of crime;

2. *Invites* Member States concerned to take specific action urgently in order to prevent domestic violence and to render the appropriate assistance to the victims thereof;

3. *Requests* the Secretary-General to intensify research on domestic violence from a criminological perspective to formulate distinct action-oriented strategies that could serve as a basis for policy formulation and to report thereon to the Eighth United Nations Congress on the Prevention of Crime and the Treatment of Offenders;

4. *Requests* the Economic and Social Council to invite the Committee on Crime Prevention and Control to examine the problem of domestic violence;

5. *Urges* all relevant United Nations bodies, agencies and institutes to collaborate with the Secretary-General in ensuring a concerted and sustained effort to combat this problem;

6. *Invites* the Eighth United Nations Congress on the Prevention of Crime and the Treatment of Offenders to consider the problem of domestic violence under a separate agenda item dealing with domestic violence;

7. *Invites* Member States to adopt specific measures with a view to making the criminal and civil justice system more sensitive in its response to domestic violence, including the following:

   (*a*) To introduce, if not already in existence, civil and criminal legislation in order to deal with particular problems of domestic violence, and to enact and enforce such laws in order to protect battered family members and punish the offender and to offer alternative ways of treatment for offenders, according to the type of violence;

   (*b*) To respect, in all instances of the criminal proceeding, starting with the police investigation, the special and sometimes delicate position of the victim, in particular in the manner in which the victim is treated;

   (*c*) To initiate preventive measures, such as providing support and counselling to families, in order to improve their ability to create a non-violent environment, emphasizing principles of education, equality of rights and equality of responsibilities between women and men, their partnership and the peaceful resolution of conflicts;

   (*d*) To inform the public, as necessary, through all available channels, about serious acts of violence perpetrated against children, in order to create public awareness of this problem;

   (*e*) To deliver appropriate, specialized assistance to victims of domestic violence, as an integral part of social policy;

   (*f*) To provide, as a temporary solution, shelters and other facilities and services for the safety of victims of domestic violence;

   (*g*) To provide specialized training and units for those who deal in some capacity with victims of domestic violence;

   (*h*) To initiate or intensify research and collect data on the background, extent and types of domestic violence;

   (*i*) To make legal remedies to domestic violence more accessible and, in view of the criminogenic effects of the phenomenon, in particular on young victims, to give due consideration to the interests of society by maintaining a balance between intervention and the protection of privacy;

   (*j*) To ensure that social welfare and health administration systems are engaged more intensely in providing assistance to victims of familial violence and abuses, and to make all efforts to co-ordinate social welfare and criminal justice measures.

General Assembly resolution 40/36
29 November 1985   Meeting 96   Adopted without vote

Approved by Third Committee (A/40/881) without vote, 11 November (meeting 37);
draft by Seventh Congress on crime (A/C.3/40/L.23); agenda item 98.
Meeting numbers. GA 40th session: 3rd Committee 16-23, 30, 37; plenary 96.

Juvenile delinquents

Minimum rules for administration of juvenile justice

The Secretary-General, in response to a resolution adopted in 1980 by the Sixth United Nations Congress on crime,[17] submitted in April 1985 a report[18] to the Seventh Congress on progress in the formulation of standard minimum rules for the administration of juvenile justice, finalized at a 1984 interregional preparatory meeting at Beijing, China.[2]

GENERAL ASSEMBLY ACTION

On 29 November 1985, on the recommendation of the Third Committee, the General Assembly adopted without vote **resolution 40/33.**

United Nations Standard Minimum Rules for the Administration of Juvenile Justice (The Beijing Rules)

The General Assembly,

Bearing in mind the Universal Declaration of Human Rights, the International Covenant on Civil and Political Rights and the International Covenant on Economic, Social and Cultural Rights, as well as other international human rights instruments pertaining to the rights of young persons,

Also bearing in mind that 1985 was designated the International Youth Year: Participation, Development, Peace and that the international community has placed importance on the protection and promotion of the rights of the young, as witnessed by the significance attached to the Declaration of the Rights of the Child,

Recalling resolution 4 adopted by the Sixth United Nations Congress on the Prevention of Crime and the Treatment of Offenders, which called for the development of standard minimum rules for the administration of juvenile justice and the care of juveniles which could serve as a model for Member States,

Recalling also Economic and Social Council decision 1984/153 of 25 May 1984, by which the draft rules were forwarded to the Seventh United Nations Congress on the Prevention of Crime and the Treatment of Offenders, held at Milan, Italy, from 26 August to 6 September 1985, through the Interregional Preparatory Meeting held at Beijing from 14 to 18 May 1984,

Recognizing that the young, owing to their early stage of human development, require particular care and assistance with regard to physical, mental and social development, and require legal protection in conditions of peace, freedom, dignity and security,

Considering that existing national legislation, policies and practices may well require review and amendment in view of the standards contained in the rules,

Considering further that, although such standards may seem difficult to achieve at present, in view of existing social, economic, cultural, political and legal conditions, they are nevertheless intended to be attainable as a policy minimum,

1. *Notes with appreciation* the work carried out by the Committee on Crime Prevention and Control, the Secretary-General, the United Nations Asia and Far East Institute for the Prevention of Crime and the Treatment of Offenders and other United Nations institutes in the development of the United Nations Standard Minimum Rules for the Administration of Juvenile Justice;

2. *Takes note with appreciation* of the report of the Secretary-General on the draft United Nations Standard Minimum Rules for the Administration of Juvenile Justice;

3. *Commends* the Interregional Preparatory Meeting held at Beijing for having finalized the text of the rules submitted to the Seventh United Nations Congress on the Prevention of Crime and the Treatment of Offenders for consideration and final action;

4. *Adopts* the United Nations Standard Minimum Rules for the Administration of Juvenile Justice recommended by the Seventh Congress, contained in the annex to the present resolution, and approves the recommendation of the Seventh Congress that the Rules should be known as "the Beijing Rules";

5. *Invites* Member States to adapt, wherever this is necessary, their national legislation, policies and practices, particularly in training juvenile justice personnel, to the Beijing Rules and to bring the Rules to the attention of relevant authorities and the public in general;

6. *Calls upon* the Committee on Crime Prevention and Control to formulate measures for the effective implementation of the Beijing Rules, with the assistance of the United Nations institutes on the prevention of crime and the treatment of offenders;

7. *Invites* Member States to inform the Secretary-General on the implementation of the Beijing Rules and to report regularly to the Committee on Crime Prevention and Control on the results achieved;

8. *Requests* Member States and the Secretary-General to undertake research and to develop a data base with respect to effective policies and practices in the administration of juvenile justice;

9. *Requests* the Secretary-General and invites Member States to ensure the widest possible dissemination of the text of the Beijing Rules in all of the official languages of the United Nations, including the intensification of information activities in the field of juvenile justice;

10. *Requests* the Secretary-General to develop pilot projects on the implementation of the Beijing Rules;

11. *Requests* the Secretary-General and Member States to provide the necessary resources to ensure the successful implementation of the Beijing Rules, in particular in the areas of recruitment, training and exchange of personnel, research and evaluation, and the development of new alternatives to institutionalization;

12. *Requests* the Eighth United Nations Congress on the Prevention of Crime and the Treatment of Offenders to review the progress made in the implementation of the Beijing Rules and of the recommendations contained in the present resolution, under a separate agenda item on juvenile justice;

13. *Urges* all relevant bodies of the United Nations system, in particular the regional commissions and specialized agencies, the United Nations institutes for the prevention of crime and the treatment of offenders, other intergovernmental organizations and non-

governmental organizations to collaborate with the Secretariat and to take the necessary measures to ensure a concerted and sustained effort, within their respective fields of technical competence, to implement the principles contained in the Beijing Rules.

ANNEX
United Nations Standard Minimum Rules for the Administration of Juvenile Justice (The Beijing Rules)

Part one. General principles

1. *Fundamental perspectives*

1.1 Member States shall seek, in conformity with their respective general interests, to further the well-being of the juvenile and her or his family.

1.2 Member States shall endeavour to develop conditions that will ensure for the juvenile a meaningful life in the community, which, during that period in life when she or he is most susceptible to deviant behaviour, will foster a process of personal development and education that is as free from crime and delinquency as possible.

1.3 Sufficient attention shall be given to positive measures that involve the full mobilization of all possible resources, including the family, volunteers and other community groups, as well as schools and other community institutions, for the purpose of promoting the well-being of the juvenile, with a view to reducing the need for intervention under the law, and of effectively, fairly and humanely dealing with the juvenile in conflict with the law.

1.4 Juvenile justice shall be conceived as an integral part of the national development process of each country, within a comprehensive framework of social justice for all juveniles, thus, at the same time, contributing to the protection of the young and the maintenance of a peaceful order in society.

1.5 These Rules shall be implemented in the context of economic, social and cultural conditions prevailing in each Member State.

1.6 Juvenile justice services shall be systematically developed and co-ordinated with a view to improving and sustaining the competence of personnel involved in the services, including their methods, approaches and attitudes.

Commentary

These broad fundamental perspectives refer to comprehensive social policy in general and aim at promoting juvenile welfare to the greatest possible extent, which will minimize the necessity of intervention by the juvenile justice system, and in turn, will reduce the harm that may be caused by any intervention. Such care measures for the young, before the onset of delinquency, are basic policy requisites designed to obviate the need for the application of the Rules.

Rules 1.1 to 1.3 point to the important role that a constructive social policy for juveniles will play, *inter alia*, in the prevention of juvenile crime and delinquency. Rule 1.4 defines juvenile justice as an integral part of social justice for juveniles, while rule 1.6 refers to the necessity of constantly improving juvenile justice, without falling behind the development of progressive social policy for juveniles in general and bearing in mind the need for consistent improvement of staff services.

Rule 1.5 seeks to take account of existing conditions in Member States which would cause the manner of implementation of particular rules necessarily to be different from the manner adopted in other States.

2. *Scope of the Rules and definitions used*

2.1 The following Standard Minimum Rules shall be applied to juvenile offenders impartially, without distinction of any kind, for example as to race, colour, sex, language, religion, political or other opinions, national or social origin, property, birth or other status.

2.2 For purposes of these Rules, the following definitions shall be applied by Member States in a manner which is compatible with their respective legal systems and concepts:

 (a) A *juvenile* is a child or young person who, under the respective legal systems, may be dealt with for an offence in a manner which is different from an adult;

 (b) An *offence* is any behaviour (act or omission) that is punishable by law under the respective legal systems;

 (c) A *juvenile offender* is a child or young person who is alleged to have committed or who has been found to have committed an offence.

2.3 Efforts shall be made to establish, in each national jurisdiction, a set of laws, rules and provisions specifically applicable to juvenile offenders and institutions and bodies entrusted with the functions of the administration of juvenile justice and designed:

 (a) To meet the varying needs of juvenile offenders, while protecting their basic rights;

 (b) To meet the needs of society;

 (c) To implement the following rules thoroughly and fairly.

Commentary

The Standard Minimum Rules are deliberately formulated so as to be applicable within different legal systems and, at the same time, to set some minimum standards for the handling of juvenile offenders under any definition of a juvenile and under any system of dealing with juvenile offenders. The Rules are always to be applied impartially and without distinction of any kind.

Rule 2.1 therefore stresses the importance of the Rules always being applied impartially and without distinction of any kind. The rule follows the formulation of principle 2 of the Declaration of the Rights of the Child.

Rule 2.2 defines "juvenile" and "offence" as the components of the notion of the "juvenile offender", who is the main subject of these Standard Minimum Rules (see, however, also rules 3 and 4). It should be noted that age limits will depend on, and are explicitly made dependent on, each respective legal system, thus fully respecting the economic, social, political, cultural and legal systems of Member States. This makes for a wide variety of ages coming under the definition of "juvenile", ranging from 7 years to 18 years or above. Such a variety seems inevitable in view of the different national legal systems and does not diminish the impact of these Standard Minimum Rules.

Rule 2.3 is addressed to the necessity of specific national legislation for the optimal implementation of these Standard Minimum Rules, both legally and practically.

3. *Extension of the Rules*

3.1 The relevant provisions of the Rules shall be applied not only to juvenile offenders but also to juveniles who may be proceeded against for any specific behaviour that would not be punishable if committed by an adult.

3.2 Efforts shall be made to extend the principles embodied in the Rules to all juveniles who are dealt with in welfare and care proceedings.

3.3 Efforts shall also be made to extend the principles embodied in the Rules to young adult offenders.

Commentary

Rule 3 extends the protection afforded by the Standard Minimum Rules for the Administration of Juvenile Justice to cover:

(*a*) The so-called "status offences" prescribed in various national legal systems where the range of behaviour considered to be an offence is wider for juveniles than it is for adults (for example, truancy, school and family disobedience, public drunkenness, etc.) (rule 3.1);

(*b*) Juvenile welfare and care proceedings (rule 3.2);

(*c*) Proceedings dealing with young adult offenders, depending of course on each given age limit (rule 3.3).

The extension of the Rules to cover these three areas seems to be justified. Rule 3.1 provides minimum guarantees in those fields, and rule 3.2 is considered a desirable step in the direction of more fair, equitable and humane justice for all juveniles in conflict with the law.

4. *Age of criminal responsibility*

4.1 In those legal systems recognizing the concept of the age of criminal responsibility for juveniles, the beginning of that age shall not be fixed at too low an age level, bearing in mind the facts of emotional, mental and intellectual maturity.

Commentary

The minimum age of criminal responsibility differs widely owing to history and culture. The modern approach would be to consider whether a child can live up to the moral and psychological components of criminal responsibility; that is, whether a child, by virtue of her or his individual discernment and understanding, can be held responsible for essentially anti-social behaviour. If the age of criminal responsibility is fixed too low or if there is no lower age limit at all, the notion of responsibility would become meaningless. In general, there is a close relationship between the notion of responsibility for delinquent or criminal behaviour and other social rights and responsibilities (such as marital status, civil majority, etc.).

Efforts should therefore be made to agree on a reasonable lowest age limit that is applicable internationally.

5. *Aims of juvenile justice*

5.1 The juvenile justice system shall emphasize the well-being of the juvenile and shall ensure that any reaction to juvenile offenders shall always be in proportion to the circumstances of both the offenders and the offence.

Commentary

Rule 5 refers to two of the most important objectives of juvenile justice. The first objective is the promotion of the well-being of the juvenile. This is the main focus of those legal systems in which juvenile offenders are dealt with by family courts or administrative authorities, but the well-being of the juvenile should also be emphasized in legal systems that follow the criminal court model, thus contributing to the avoidance of merely punitive sanctions. (See also rule 14.)

The second objective is "the principle of proportionality". This principle is well-known as an instrument for curbing punitive sanctions, mostly expressed in terms of just desert in relation to the gravity of the offence. The response to young offenders should be based on the consideration not only of the gravity of the offence but also of personal circumstances. The individual circumstances of the offender (for example social status, family situation, the harm caused by the offence or other factors affecting personal circumstances) should influence the proportionality of the reaction (for example by having regard to the offender's endeavour to indemnify the victim or to her or his willingness to turn to a wholesome and useful life).

By the same token, reactions aiming to ensure the welfare of the young offender may go beyond necessity and therefore infringe upon the fundamental rights of the young individual, as has been observed in some juvenile justice systems. Here, too, the proportionality of the reaction to the circumstances of both the offender and the offence, including the victim, should be safeguarded.

In essence, rule 5 calls for no less and no more than a fair reaction in any given case of juvenile delinquency and crime. The issues combined in the rule may help to stimulate development in both regards: new and innovative types of reactions are as desirable as precautions against any undue widening of the net of formal social control over juveniles.

6. *Scope of discretion*

6.1 In view of the varying special needs of juveniles as well as the variety of measures available, appropriate scope for discretion shall be allowed at all stages of proceedings and at the different levels of juvenile justice administration, including investigation, prosecution, adjudication and the follow-up of dispositions.

6.2 Efforts shall be made, however, to ensure sufficient accountability at all stages and levels in the exercise of any such discretion.

6.3 Those who exercise discretion shall be specially qualified or trained to exercise it judiciously and in accordance with their functions and mandates.

Commentary

Rules 6.1, 6.2 and 6.3 combine several important features of effective, fair and humane juvenile justice administration: the need to permit the exercise of discretionary power at all significant levels of processing so that those who make determinations can take the actions deemed to be most appropriate in each individual case; and the need to provide checks and balances in order to curb any abuses of discretionary power and to safeguard the rights of the young offender. Accountability and professionalism are instruments best apt to curb broad discretion. Thus, professional qualifications and expert training are emphasized here as a valuable means of ensuring the judicious exercise of discretion in matters of juvenile offenders. (See also rules 1.6 and 2.2.) The formulation of specific guidelines on the exercise of discretion and the provision of systems of review, appeal and the like in order to permit scrutiny of decisions and accountability are emphasized in this context. Such mechanisms are not specified here, as they do not easily lend themselves to incorporation into international standard minimum rules, which cannot possibly cover all differences in justice systems.

7. *Rights of juveniles*

7.1 Basic procedural safeguards such as the presumption of innocence, the right to be notified of the charges, the right to remain silent, the right to counsel, the right to the presence of a parent or guardian, the right to confront and cross-examine witnesses and the right to appeal to a higher authority shall be guaranteed at all stages of proceedings.

Commentary

Rule 7.1 emphasizes some important points that represent essential elements for a fair and just trial and that are internationally recognized in existing human rights instruments. (See also rule 14.) The presumption of innocence, for instance, is also to be found in article 11 of the Universal Declaration of Human Rights and in article 14, paragraph 2, of the International Covenant on Civil and Political Rights.

Rules 14 *seq.* of these Standard Minimum Rules specify issues that are important for proceedings in juvenile cases, in particular, while rule 7.1 affirms the most basic procedural safeguards in a general way.

8. *Protection of privacy*

8.1 The juvenile's right to privacy shall be respected at all stages in order to avoid harm being caused to her or him by undue publicity or by the process of labelling.

8.2 In principle, no information that may lead to the identification of a juvenile offender shall be published.

Commentary

Rule 8 stresses the importance of the protection of the juvenile's right to privacy. Young persons are particularly susceptible to stigmatization. Criminological research into labelling processes has provided evidence of the detrimental effects (of different kinds) resulting from the permanent identification of young persons as "delinquent" or "criminal".

Rule 8 also stresses the importance of protecting the juvenile from the adverse effects that may result from the publication in the mass media of information about the case (for example the names of young offenders, alleged or convicted). The interest of the individual should be protected and upheld, at least in principle. (The general contents of rule 8 are further specified in rule 21.)

9. *Saving clause*

9.1 Nothing in these Rules shall be interpreted as precluding the application of the Standard Minimum Rules for the Treatment of Prisoners adopted by the United Nations and other human rights instruments and standards recognized by the international community that relate to the care and protection of the young.

Commentary

Rule 9 is meant to avoid any misunderstanding in interpreting and implementing the present Rules in conformity with principles contained in relevant existing or emerging international human rights instruments and standards—such as the Universal Declaration of Human Rights; the International Covenant on Economic, Social and Cultural Rights and the International Covenant on Civil and Political Rights; and the Declaration of the Rights of the Child and the draft convention on the rights of the child. It should be understood that the application of the present Rules is without prejudice to any such international instruments which may contain provisions of wider application. (See also rule 27.)

Part two. Investigation and prosecution

10. *Initial contact*

10.1 Upon the apprehension of a juvenile, her or his parents or guardian shall be immediately notified of such apprehension, and, where such immediate notification is not possible, the parents or guardian shall be notified within the shortest possible time thereafter.

10.2 A judge or other competent official or body shall, without delay, consider the issue of release.

10.3 Contacts between the law enforcement agencies and a juvenile offender shall be managed in such a way as to respect the legal status of the juvenile, promote the well-being of the juvenile and avoid harm to her or him, with due regard to the circumstances of the case.

Commentary

Rule 10.1 is in principle contained in rule 92 of the Standard Minimum Rules for the Treatment of Prisoners.

The question of release (rule 10.2) shall be considered without delay by a judge or other competent official. The latter refers to any person or institution in the broadest sense of the term, including community boards or police authorities having power to release an arrested person. (See also the International Covenant on Civil and Political Rights, article 9, paragraph 3.)

Rule 10.3 deals with some fundamental aspects of the procedures and behaviour on the part of the police and other law enforcement officials in cases of juvenile crime. To "avoid harm" admittedly is flexible wording and covers many features of possible interaction (for example the use of harsh language, physical violence or exposure to the environment). Involvement in juvenile justice processes in itself can be "harmful" to juveniles; the term "avoid harm" should be broadly interpreted, therefore, as doing the least harm possible to the juvenile in the first instance, as well as any additional or undue harm. This is especially important in the initial contact with law enforcement agencies, which might profoundly influence the juvenile's attitude towards the State and society. Moreover, the success of any further intervention is largely dependent on such initial contacts. Compassion and kind firmness are important in these situations.

11. *Diversion*

11.1 Consideration shall be given, wherever appropriate, to dealing with juvenile offenders without resorting to formal trial by the competent authority, referred to in rule 14.1 below.

11.2 The police, the prosecution or other agencies dealing with juvenile cases shall be empowered to dispose of such cases, at their discretion, without recourse to formal hearings, in accordance with the criteria laid down for that purpose in the respective legal system and also in accordance with the principles contained in these Rules.

11.3   Any diversion involving referral to appropriate community or other services shall require the consent of the juvenile, or her or his parents or guardian, provided that such decision to refer a case shall be subject to review by a competent authority, upon application.

11.4   In order to facilitate the discretionary disposition of juvenile cases, efforts shall be made to provide for community programmes, such as temporary supervision and guidance, restitution, and compensation of victims.

Commentary

Diversion, involving removal from criminal justice processing and, frequently, redirection to community support services, is commonly practised on a formal and informal basis in many legal systems. This practice serves to hinder the negative effects of subsequent proceedings in juvenile justice administration (for example the stigma of conviction and sentence). In many cases, non-intervention would be the best response. Thus, diversion at the outset and without referral to alternative (social) services may be the optimal response. This is especially the case where the offence is of a non-serious nature and where the family, the school or other informal social control institutions have already reacted, or are likely to react, in an appropriate and constructive manner.

As stated in rule 11.2, diversion may be used at any point of decision-making—by the police, the prosecution or other agencies such as the courts, tribunals, boards or councils. It may be exercised by one authority or several or all authorities, according to the rules and policies of the respective systems and in line with the present Rules. It need not necessarily be limited to petty cases, thus rendering diversion an important instrument.

Rule 11.3 stresses the important requirement of securing the consent of the young offender (or the parent or guardian) to the recommended diversionary measure(s). (Diversion to community service without such consent would contradict the Abolition of Forced Labour Convention.) However, this consent should not be left unchallengeable, since it might sometimes be given out of sheer desperation on the part of the juvenile. The rule underlines that care should be taken to minimize the potential for coercion and intimidation at all levels in the diversion process. Juveniles should not feel pressured (for example in order to avoid court appearance) or be pressured into consenting to diversion programmes. Thus, it is advocated that provision should be made for an objective appraisal of the appropriateness of dispositions involving young offenders by a "competent authority upon application". (The "competent authority" may be different from that referred to in rule 14.)

Rule 11.4 recommends the provision of viable alternatives to juvenile justice processing in the form of community-based diversion. Programmes that involve settlement by victim restitution and those that seek to avoid future conflict with the law through temporary supervision and guidance are especially commended. The merits of individual cases would make diversion appropriate, even when more serious offences have been committed (for example first offence, the act having been committed under peer pressure, etc.).

12. *Specialization within the police*

12.1   In order to best fulfil their functions, police officers who frequently or exclusively deal with juveniles or who are primarily engaged in the prevention of juvenile crime shall be specially instructed and trained. In large cities, special police units should be established for that purpose.

Commentary

Rule 12 draws attention to the need for specialized training for all law enforcement officials who are involved in the administration of juvenile justice. As police are the first point of contact with the juvenile justice system, it is most important that they act in an informed and appropriate manner.

While the relationship between urbanization and crime is clearly complex, an increase in juvenile crime has been associated with the growth of large cities, particularly with rapid and unplanned growth. Specialized police units would therefore be indispensable, not only in the interest of implementing specific principles contained in the present instrument (such as rule 1.6) but more generally for improving the prevention and control of juvenile crime and the handling of juvenile offenders.

13. *Detention pending trial*

13.1   Detention pending trial shall be used only as a measure of last resort and for the shortest possible period of time.

13.2   Whenever possible, detention pending trial shall be replaced by alternative measures, such as close supervision, intensive care or placement with a family or in an educational setting or home.

13.3   Juveniles under detention pending trial shall be entitled to all rights and guarantees of the Standard Minimum Rules for the Treatment of Prisoners adopted by the United Nations.

13.4   Juveniles under detention pending trial shall be kept separate from adults and shall be detained in a separate institution or in a separate part of an institution also holding adults.

13.5   While in custody, juveniles shall receive care, protection and all necessary individual assistance—social, educational, vocational, psychological, medical and physical—that they may require in view of their age, sex and personality.

Commentary

The danger to juveniles of "criminal contamination" while in detention pending trial must not be underestimated. It is therefore important to stress the need for alternative measures. By doing so, rule 13.1 encourages the devising of new and innovative measures to avoid such detention in the interest of the well-being of the juvenile.

Juveniles under detention pending trial are entitled to all the rights and guarantees of the Standard Minimum Rules for the Treatment of Prisoners as well as the International Covenant on Civil and Political Rights, especially article 9 and article 10, paragraphs 2 *(b)* and 3.

Rule 13.4 does not prevent States from taking other measures against the negative influences of adult offenders which are at least as effective as the measures mentioned in the rule.

Different forms of assistance that may become necessary have been enumerated to draw attention to the broad range of particular needs of young detainees to be addressed (for example females or males, drug addicts, alcoholics, mentally ill juveniles, young persons suffering from the trauma, for example, of arrest, etc.).

Varying physical and psychological characteristics of young detainees may warrant classification measures by which some are kept separate while in detention pending trial, thus contributing to the avoidance of victimization and rendering more appropriate assistance.

The Sixth United Nations Congress on the Prevention of Crime and the Treatment of Offenders, in its resolution 4 on juvenile justice standards, specified that the Rules, *inter alia*, should reflect the basic principle that pre-trial detention should be used only as a last resort, that no minors should be held in a facility where they are vulnerable to the negative influences of adult detainees and that account should always be taken of the needs particular to their stage of development.

Part three. *Adjudication and disposition*

14. *Competent authority to adjudicate*

14.1 Where the case of a juvenile offender has not been diverted (under rule 11), she or he shall be dealt with by the competent authority (court, tribunal, board, council, etc.) according to the principles of a fair and just trial.

14.2 The proceedings shall be conducive to the best interests of the juvenile and shall be conducted in an atmosphere of understanding, which shall allow the juvenile to participate therein and to express herself or himself freely.

Commentary

It is difficult to formulate a definition of the competent body or person that would universally describe an adjudicating authority. "Competent authority" is meant to include those who preside over courts or tribunals (composed of a single judge or of several members), including professional and lay magistrates as well as administrative boards (for example the Scottish and Scandinavian systems) or other more informal community and conflict resolution agencies of an adjudicatory nature.

The procedure for dealing with juvenile offenders shall in any case follow the minimum standards that are applied almost universally for any criminal defendant under the procedure known as "due process of law". In accordance with due process, a "fair and just trial" includes such basic safeguards as the presumption of innocence, the presentation and examination of witnesses, the common legal defences, the right to remain silent, the right to have the last word in a hearing, the right to appeal, etc. (See also rule 7.1.)

15. *Legal counsel, parents and guardians*

15.1 Throughout the proceedings the juvenile shall have the right to be represented by a legal adviser or to apply for free legal aid where there is provision for such aid in the country.

15.2 The parents or the guardian shall be entitled to participate in the proceedings and may be required by the competent authority to attend them in the interest of the juvenile. They may, however, be denied participation by the competent authority if there are reasons to assume that such exclusion is necessary in the interest of the juvenile.

Commentary

Rule 15.1 uses terminology similar to that found in rule 93 of the Standard Minimum Rules for the Treatment of Prisoners. Whereas legal counsel and free legal aid are needed to assure the juvenile legal assistance, the right of the parents or guardian to participate as stated in rule 15.2 should be viewed as general psychological and emotional assistance to the juvenile—a function extending throughout the procedure.

The competent authority's search for an adequate disposition of the case may profit, in particular, from the co-operation of the legal representatives of the juvenile (or, for that matter, some other personal assistant who the juvenile can and does really trust). Such concern can be thwarted if the presence of parents or guardians at the hearings plays a negative role, for instance, if they display a hostile attitude towards the juvenile; hence, the possibility of their exclusion must be provided for.

16. *Social inquiry reports*

16.1 In all cases except those involving minor offences, before the competent authority renders a final disposition prior to sentencing, the background and circumstances in which the juvenile is living or the conditions under which the offence has been committed shall be properly investigated so as to facilitate judicious adjudication of the case by the competent authority.

Commentary

Social inquiry reports (social reports or pre-sentence reports) are an indispensable aid in most legal proceedings involving juveniles. The competent authority should be informed of relevant facts about the juvenile, such as social and family background, school career, educational experiences, etc. For this purpose, some jurisdictions use special social services or personnel attached to the court or board. Other personnel, including probation officers, may serve the same function. The rule therefore requires that adequate social services should be available to deliver social inquiry reports of a qualified nature.

17. *Guiding principles in adjudication and disposition*

17.1 The disposition of the competent authority shall be guided by the following principles:

(*a*) The reaction taken shall always be in proportion not only to the circumstances and the gravity of the offence but also to the circumstances and the needs of the juvenile as well as to the needs of the society;

(*b*) Restrictions on the personal liberty of the juvenile shall be imposed only after careful consideration and shall be limited to the possible minimum;

(*c*) Deprivation of personal liberty shall not be imposed unless the juvenile is adjudicated of a serious act involving violence against another person or of persistence in committing other serious offences and unless there is no other appropriate response;

(*d*) The well-being of the juvenile shall be the guiding factor in the consideration of her or his case.

17.2 Capital punishment shall not be imposed for any crime committed by juveniles.

17.3 Juveniles shall not be subject to corporal punishment.

17.4 The competent authority shall have the power to discontinue the proceedings at any time.

Commentary

The main difficulty in formulating guidelines for the adjudication of young persons stems from the fact that there are unresolved conflicts of a philosophical nature, such as the following:

(a) Rehabilitation versus just desert;

(b) Assistance versus repression and punishment;

(c) Reaction according to the singular merits of an individual case versus reaction according to the protection of society in general;

(d) General deterrence versus individual incapacitation.

The conflict between these approaches is more pronounced in juvenile cases than in adult cases. With the variety of causes and reactions characterizing juvenile cases, these alternatives become intricately interwoven.

It is not the function of the Standard Minimum Rules for the Administration of Juvenile Justice to prescribe which approach is to be followed but rather to identify one that is most closely in consonance with internationally accepted principles. Therefore the essential elements as laid down in rule 17.1, in particular in subparagraphs (a) and (c), are mainly to be understood as practical guidelines that should ensure a common starting point; if heeded by the concerned authorities (see also rule 5), they could contribute considerably to ensuring that the fundamental rights of juvenile offenders are protected, especially the fundamental rights of personal development and education.

Rule 17.1 (b) implies that strictly punitive approaches are not appropriate. Whereas in adult cases, and possibly also in cases of severe offences by juveniles, just desert and retributive sanctions might be considered to have some merit, in juvenile cases such considerations should always be outweighed by the interest of safeguarding the well-being and the future of the young person.

In line with resolution 8 of the Sixth United Nations Congress, rule 17.1 (b) encourages the use of alternatives to institutionalization to the maximum extent possible, bearing in mind the need to respond to the specific requirements of the young. Thus, full use should be made of the range of existing alternative sanctions and new alternative sanctions should be developed, bearing the public safety in mind. Probation should be granted to the greatest possible extent via suspended sentences, conditional sentences, board orders and other dispositions.

Rule 17.1 (c) corresponds to one of the guiding principles in resolution 4 of the Sixth Congress which aims at avoiding incarceration in the case of juveniles unless there is no other appropriate response that will protect the public safety.

The provision prohibiting capital punishment in rule 17.2 is in accordance with article 6, paragraph 5, of the International Covenant on Civil and Political Rights.

The provision against corporal punishment is in line with article 7 of the International Covenant on Civil and Political Rights and the Declaration on the Protection of All Persons from Being Subjected to Torture and Other Cruel, Inhuman or Degrading Treatment or Punishment, as well as the Convention against Torture and Other Cruel, Inhuman or Degrading Treatment or Punishment and the draft convention on the rights of the child.

The power to discontinue the proceedings at any time (rule 17.4) is a characteristic inherent in the handling of juvenile offenders as opposed to adults. At any time, circumstances may become known to the competent authority which would make a complete cessation of the intervention appear to be the best disposition of the case.

18. *Various disposition measures*

18.1 A large variety of disposition measures shall be made available to the competent authority, allowing for flexibility so as to avoid institutionalization to the greatest extent possible. Such measures, some of which may be combined, include:

(a) Care, guidance and supervision orders;

(b) Probation;

(c) Community service orders;

(d) Financial penalties, compensation and restitution;

(e) Intermediate treatment and other treatment orders;

(f) Orders to participate in group counselling and similar activities;

(g) Orders concerning foster care, living communities or other educational settings;

(h) Other relevant orders.

18.2 No juvenile shall be removed from parental supervision, whether partly or entirely, unless the circumstances of her or his case make this necessary.

Commentary

Rule 18.1 attempts to enumerate some of the important reactions and sanctions that have been practised and proved successful thus far, in different legal systems. On the whole they represent promising options that deserve replication and further development. The rule does not enumerate staffing requirements because of possible shortages of adequate staff in some regions; in those regions measures requiring less staff may be tried or developed.

The examples given in rule 18.1 have in common, above all, a reliance on and an appeal to the community for the effective implementation of alternative dispositions. Community-based correction is a traditional measure that has taken on many aspects. On that basis, relevant authorities should be encouraged to offer community-based services.

Rule 18.2 points to the importance of the family which, according to article 10, paragraph 1, of the International Covenant on Economic, Social and Cultural Rights, is "the natural and fundamental group unit of society". Within the family, the parents have not only the right but also the responsibility to care for and supervise their children. Rule 18.2, therefore, requires that the separation of children from their parents is a measure of last resort. It may be resorted to only when the facts of the case clearly warrant this grave step (for example child abuse).

19. *Least possible use of institutionalization*

19.1 The placement of a juvenile in an institution shall always be a disposition of last resort and for the minimum necessary period.

Commentary

Progressive criminology advocates the use of non-institutional over institutional treatment. Little or no difference has been found in terms of the success of institutionalization as compared to non-institutionalization. The many adverse influences on an individual that seem unavoidable within any institutional setting evidently cannot be outbalanced by treatment efforts. This is especially the case for juveniles, who are vulnerable to negative influences. Moreover, the negative effects, not only of loss of liberty but also of separation from the usual social environment, are certainly more acute for juveniles than for adults because of their early stage of development.

Rule 19 aims at restricting institutionalization in two regards: in quantity ("last resort") and in time ("minimum necessary period"). Rule 19 reflects one of the basic guiding principles of resolution 4 of the Sixth United Nations Congress: a juvenile offender should not be incarcerated unless there is no other appropriate response. The rule, therefore, makes the appeal that if a juvenile must be institutionalized, the loss of liberty should be restricted to the least possible degree, with special institutional arrangements for confinement and bearing in mind the differences in kinds of offenders, offences and institutions. In fact, priority should be given to "open" over "closed" institutions. Furthermore, any facility should be of a correctional or educational rather than of a prison type.

20. *Avoidance of unnecessary delay*

20.1 Each case shall from the outset be handled expeditiously, without any unnecessary delay.

Commentary

The speedy conduct of formal procedures in juvenile cases is a paramount concern. Otherwise whatever good may be achieved by the procedure and the disposition is at risk. As time passes, the juvenile will find it increasingly difficult, if not impossible, to relate the procedure and disposition to the offence, both intellectually and psychologically.

21. *Records*

21.1 Records of juvenile offenders shall be kept strictly confidential and closed to third parties. Access to such records shall be limited to persons directly concerned with the disposition of the case at hand or other duly authorized persons.

21.2 Records of juvenile offenders shall not be used in adult proceedings in subsequent cases involving the same offender.

Commentary

The rule attempts to achieve a balance between conflicting interests connected with records or files: those of the police, prosecution and other authorities in improving control versus the interests of the juvenile offender. (See also rule 8.) "Other duly authorized persons" would generally include, among others, researchers.

22. *Need for professionalism and training*

22.1 Professional education, in-service training, refresher courses and other appropriate modes of instruction shall be utilized to establish and maintain the necessary professional competence of all personnel dealing with juvenile cases.

22.2 Juvenile justice personnel shall reflect the diversity of juveniles who come into contact with the juvenile justice system. Efforts shall be made to ensure the fair representation of women and minorities in juvenile justice agencies.

Commentary

The authorities competent for disposition may be persons with very different backgrounds (magistrates in the United Kingdom of Great Britain and Northern Ireland and in regions influenced by the common law system; legally trained judges in countries using Roman law and in regions influenced by them; and elsewhere elected or appointed laymen or jurists, members of community-based boards etc.). For all these authorities, a minimum training in law, sociology, psychology, criminology and behavioural sciences would be required. This is considered as important as the organizational specialization and independence of the competent authority.

For social workers and probation officers, it might not be feasible to require professional specialization as a prerequisite for taking over any function dealing with juvenile offenders. Thus, professional on-the-job instruction would be minimum qualifications.

Professional qualifications are an essential element in ensuring the impartial and effective administration of juvenile justice. Accordingly, it is necessary to improve the recruitment, advancement and professional training of personnel and to provide them with the necessary means to enable them to properly fulfil their functions.

All political, social, sexual, racial, religious, cultural or any other kind of discrimination in the selection, appointment and advancement of juvenile justice personnel should be avoided in order to achieve impartiality in the administration of juvenile justice. This was recommended by the Sixth Congress. Furthermore, the Sixth Congress called on Member States to ensure the fair and equal treatment of women as criminal justice personnel and recommended that special measures should be taken to recruit, train and facilitate the advancement of female personnel in juvenile justice administration.

Part four. Non-institutional treatment

23. *Effective implementation of disposition*

23.1 Appropriate provisions shall be made for the implementation of orders of the competent authority, as referred to in rule 14.1 above, by that authority itself or by some other authority as circumstances may require.

23.2 Such provisions shall include the power to modify the orders as the competent authority may deem necessary from time to time, provided that such modification shall be determined in accordance with the principles contained in these Rules.

Commentary

Disposition in juvenile cases, more so than in adult cases, tends to influence the offender's life for a long period of time. Thus, it is important that the competent authority or an independent body (parole board, probation office, youth welfare institutions or others) with qualifications equal to those of the competent authority that originally disposed of the case should monitor the implementation of the disposition. In some countries, a *juge de l'exécution des peines* has been installed for this purpose.

The composition, powers and functions of the authority must be flexible; they are described in general terms in rule 23 in order to ensure wide acceptability.

24. *Provision of needed assistance*

24.1 Efforts shall be made to provide juveniles, at all stages of the proceedings, with necessary assistance such as lodging, education or vocational training, employment or any other assistance, helpful and practical, in order to facilitate the rehabilitative process.

Commentary

The promotion of the well-being of the juvenile is of paramount consideration. Thus, rule 24 emphasizes the importance of providing requisite facilities, services and other necessary assistance as may further the best interests of the juvenile throughout the rehabilitative process.

25. *Mobilization of volunteers and other community services*

25.1 Volunteers, voluntary organizations, local institutions and other community resources shall be called upon to contribute effectively to the rehabilitation of the juvenile in a community setting and, as far as possible, within the family unit.

Commentary

This rule reflects the need for a rehabilitative orientation of all work with juvenile offenders. Co-operation with the community is indispensable if the directives of the competent authority are to be carried out effectively. Volunteers and voluntary services, in particular, have proved to be valuable resources but are at present underutilized. In some instances, the co-operation of ex-offenders (including ex-addicts) can be of considerable assistance.

Rule 25 emanates from the principles laid down in rules 1.1 to 1.6 and follows the relevant provisions of the International Covenant on Civil and Political Rights.

Part five. Institutional treatment

26. *Objectives of institutional treatment*

26.1 The objective of training and treatment of juveniles placed in institutions is to provide care, protection, education and vocational skills, with a view to assisting them to assume socially constructive and productive roles in society.

26.2 Juveniles in institutions shall receive care, protection and all necessary assistance—social, educational, vocational, psychological, medical and physical—that they may require because of their age, sex and personality and in the interest of their wholesome development.

26.3 Juveniles in institutions shall be kept separate from adults and shall be detained in a separate institution or in a separate part of an institution also holding adults.

26.4 Young female offenders placed in an institution deserve special attention as to their personal needs and problems. They shall by no means receive less care, protection, assistance, treatment and training than young male offenders. Their fair treatment shall be ensured.

26.5 In the interest and well-being of the institutionalized juvenile, the parents or guardians shall have a right of access.

26.6 Inter-ministerial and inter-departmental co-operation shall be fostered for the purpose of providing adequate academic or, as appropriate, vocational training to institutionalized juveniles, with a view to ensuring that they do not leave the institution at an educational disadvantage.

Commentary

The objectives of institutional treatment as stipulated in rules 26.1 and 26.2 would be acceptable to any system and culture. However, they have not yet been attained everywhere, and much more has to be done in this respect.

Medical and psychological assistance, in particular, are extremely important for institutionalized drug addicts, violent and mentally ill young persons.

The avoidance of negative influences through adult offenders and the safeguarding of the well-being of juveniles in an institutional setting, as stipulated in rule 26.3, are in line with one of the basic guiding principles of the Rules, as set out by the Sixth Congress in its resolution 4. The rule does not prevent States from taking other measures against the negative influences of adult offenders, which are at least as effective as the measures mentioned in the rule. (See also rule 13.4.)

Rule 26.4 addresses the fact that female offenders normally receive less attention than their male counterparts, as pointed out by the Sixth Congress. In particular, resolution 9 of the Sixth Congress calls for the fair treatment of female offenders at every stage of criminal justice processes and for special attention to their particular problems and needs while in custody. Moreover, this rule should also be considered in the light of the Caracas Declaration of the Sixth Congress, which, *inter alia*, calls for equal treatment in criminal justice administration, and against the background of the Declaration on the Elimination of Discrimination against Women and the Convention on the Elimination of All Forms of Discrimination against Women.

The right of access (rule 26.5) follows from the provisions of rules 7.1, 10.1, 15.2 and 18.2. Inter-ministerial and inter-departmental co-operation (rule 26.6) are of particular importance in the interest of generally enhancing the quality of institutional treatment and training.

27. *Application of the Standard Minimum Rules for the Treatment of Prisoners adopted by the United Nations*

27.1 The Standard Minimum Rules for the Treatment of Prisoners and related recommendations shall be applicable as far as relevant to the treatment of juvenile offenders in institutions, including those in detention pending adjudication.

27.2 Efforts shall be made to implement the relevant principles laid down in the Standard Minimum Rules for the Treatment of Prisoners to the largest possible extent so as to meet the varying needs of juveniles specific to their age, sex and personality.

Commentary

The Standard Minimum Rules for the Treatment of Prisoners were among the first instruments of this kind to be promulgated by the United Nations. It is generally agreed that they have had a world-wide impact. Although there are still countries where implementation is more an aspiration than a fact, those Standard

Minimum Rules continue to be an important influence in the humane and equitable administration of correctional institutions.

Some essential protections covering juvenile offenders in institutions are contained in the Standard Minimum Rules for the Treatment of Prisoners (accommodation, architecture, bedding, clothing, complaints and requests, contact with the outside world, food, medical care, religious service, separation of ages, staffing, work, etc.) as are provisions concerning punishment and discipline, and restraint for dangerous offenders. It would not be appropriate to modify those Standard Minimum Rules according to the particular characteristics of institutions for juvenile offenders within the scope of the Standard Minimum Rules for the Administration of Juvenile Justice.

Rule 27 focuses on the necessary requirements for juveniles in institutions (rule 27.1) as well as on the varying needs specific to their age, sex and personality (rule 27.2). Thus, the objectives and content of the rule interrelate to the relevant provisions of the Standard Minimum Rules for the Treatment of Prisoners.

28. *Frequent and early recourse to conditional release*

28.1 Conditional release from an institution shall be used by the appropriate authority to the greatest possible extent, and shall be granted at the earliest possible time.

28.2 Juveniles released conditionally from an institution shall be assisted and supervised by an appropriate authority and shall receive full support by the community.

Commentary

The power to order conditional release may rest with the competent authority, as mentioned in rule 14.1, or with some other authority. In view of this, it is adequate to refer here to the "appropriate" rather than to the "competent" authority.

Circumstances permitting, conditional release shall be preferred to serving a full sentence. Upon evidence of satisfactory progress towards rehabilitation, even offenders who had been deemed dangerous at the time of their institutionalization can be conditionally released whenever feasible. Like probation, such release may be conditional on the satisfactory fulfilment of the requirements specified by the relevant authorities for a period of time established in the decision, for example relating to "good behaviour" of the offender, attendance in community programmes, residence in half-way houses, etc.

In the case of offenders conditionally released from an institution, assistance and supervision by a probation or other officer (particularly where probation has not yet been adopted) should be provided and community support should be encouraged.

29. *Semi-institutional arrangements*

29.1 Efforts shall be made to provide semi-institutional arrangements, such as half-way houses, educational homes, day-time training centres and other such appropriate arrangements that may assist juveniles in their proper reintegration into society.

Commentary

The importance of care following a period of institutionalization should not be underestimated. This rule emphasizes the necessity of forming a net of semi-institutional arrangements.

This rule also emphasizes the need for a diverse range of facilities and services designed to meet the different needs of young offenders re-entering the community and to provide guidance and structural support as an important step towards successful reintegration into society.

Part six. Research, planning, policy formulation and evaluation

30. *Research as a basis for planning, policy formulation and evaluation*

30.1 Efforts shall be made to organize and promote necessary research as a basis for effective planning and policy formulation.

30.2 Efforts shall be made to review and appraise periodically the trends, problems and causes of juvenile delinquency and crime as well as the varying particular needs of juveniles in custody.

30.3 Efforts shall be made to establish a regular evaluative research mechanism built into the system of juvenile justice administration and to collect and analyse relevant data and information for appropriate assessment and future improvement and reform of the administration.

30.4 The delivery of services in juvenile justice administration shall be systematically planned and implemented as an integral part of national development efforts.

Commentary

The utilization of research as a basis for an informed juvenile justice policy is widely acknowledged as an important mechanism for keeping practices abreast of advances in knowledge and the continuing development and improvement of the juvenile justice system. The mutual feedback between research and policy is especially important in juvenile justice. With rapid and often drastic changes in the life-styles of the young and in the forms and dimensions of juvenile crime, the societal and justice responses to juvenile crime and delinquency quickly become outmoded and inadequate.

Rule 30 thus establishes standards for integrating research into the process of policy formulation and application in juvenile justice administration. The rule draws particular attention to the need for regular review and evaluation of existing programmes and measures and for planning within the broader context of overall development objectives.

A constant appraisal of the needs of juveniles, as well as the trends and problems of delinquency, is a prerequisite for improving the methods of formulating appropriate policies and establishing adequate interventions, at both formal and informal levels. In this context, research by independent persons and bodies should be facilitated by responsible agencies, and it may be valuable to obtain and to take into account the views of juveniles themselves, not only those who come into contact with the system.

The process of planning must particularly emphasize a more effective and equitable system for the delivery of necessary services. Towards that end, there should be a comprehensive and regular assessment of the wide-ranging, particular needs and problems of juveniles and an identification of clear-cut priorities. In that connection, there should also be a co-ordination in the use of existing resources, including alternatives and community support that would be suitable in setting up specific procedures designed to implement and monitor established programmes.

General Assembly resolution 40/33

29 November 1985   Meeting 96   Adopted without vote

Approved by Third Committee (A/40/881) without vote, 11 November (meeting 37); draft by Seventh Congress on crime (A/C.3/40/L.20); agenda item 98.
Meeting numbers. GA 40th session: 3rd Committee 16-23, 30, 37; plenary 96.

Prevention of juvenile delinquency

Key problems, priorities and major issues relating to youth crime and juvenile justice were highlighted in an April 1985 working paper prepared by the United Nations Secretariat for the Seventh Congress.[19] The paper discussed models of juvenile justice; the Beijing Rules (see above); youth in the context of juvenile justice administration; perspectives on youth crime and juvenile justice; dimensions and characteristics of youth criminality; marginalization, victimization and changing socio-economic factors in youth crime; the prevention of youth crime; and regional, international and inter-agency co-operation for the prevention of youth crime.

GENERAL ASSEMBLY ACTION

On 29 November 1985, the General Assembly, on the recommendation of the Third Committee, adopted without vote **resolution 40/35**.

Development of standards for the prevention of juvenile delinquency

The General Assembly,

Recalling resolution 4 adopted by the Sixth United Nations Congress on the Prevention of Crime and the Treatment of Offenders, held at Caracas from 25 August to 5 September 1980, in which the Congress called for the elaboration of a set of standard minimum rules for the administration of juvenile justice and for the care of juveniles,

Noting that the United Nations Standard Minimum Rules for the Administration of Juvenile Justice (the Beijing Rules) recommended by the Seventh United Nations Congress on the Prevention of Crime and the Treatment of Offenders, held at Milan, Italy, from 26 August to 6 September 1985, are limited to the administration of juvenile justice and the assurance of legal guarantees in respect of young persons in conflict with the law,

Mindful of the need to develop national, regional and international strategies for the prevention of delinquency among the young,

Recognizing that the prevention of juvenile delinquency includes measures for the protection of juveniles who are abandoned, neglected, abused and in marginal circumstances and, in general, those who are at social risk,

Recognizing further the existence of a large number of young persons who are not in conflict with the law but who are at social risk,

Acknowledging that one of the basic aims of the prevention of juvenile delinquency is the provision of requisite assistance and a range of opportunities to meet the varying needs of the young, especially those who are most likely to commit crime or to be exposed to crime, and to serve as a supportive framework to safeguard their proper development,

1. *Takes note with appreciation* of the work undertaken by the United Nations regional institutes for the prevention of crime and the treatment of offenders and the regional commissions in the field of crime prevention;

2. *Also takes note with appreciation* of the working paper prepared by the Secretariat on youth, crime and justice;

3. *Endorses* the recommendations contained in the report of the Interregional Preparatory Meeting for the Seventh United Nations Congress on the Prevention of Crime and the Treatment of Offenders, held at Beijing from 14 to 18 May 1984;

4. *Requests* the Secretary-General and Member States to take the necessary steps to establish joint programmes in the field of juvenile justice and the prevention of juvenile delinquency with the United Nations Social Defence Research Institute, the United Nations regional institutes for the prevention of crime and the treatment of offenders, the Arab Security Studies and Training Centre at Riyadh and other national and regional institutes, and with the assistance of regional commissions and national correspondents, which would include the following activities:

(a) To study the situation of juveniles at social risk and to examine the relevant policies and practices of prevention within the context of socio-economic development;

(b) To intensify efforts in training, research and advisory services for the prevention of juvenile delinquency;

5. *Invites* Member States to adopt distinct measures and systems appropriate to the interest of juveniles at social risk;

6. *Calls upon* the Economic and Social Council to request the Committee on Crime Prevention and Control, with the assistance of the United Nations institutes for the prevention of crime and the treatment of offenders, the regional commissions and the specialized agencies, to develop standards for the prevention of juvenile delinquency which would assist Member States in formulating and implementing specialized programmes and policies, emphasizing assistance and care and the active involvement of the community, and to report to the Eighth United Nations Congress on the Prevention of Crime and the Treatment of Offenders on the progress achieved in the development of the proposed standards, for review and final action;

7. *Requests* that the prevention of delinquency among the young should be considered regularly by the Committee on Crime Prevention and Control and that it should be considered by the Eighth United Nations Congress on the Prevention of Crime and the Treatment of Offenders, under a separate agenda item;

8. *Urges* all relevant bodies within the United Nations system to collaborate with the Secretary-General in taking appropriate measures to ensure the implementation of the present resolution.

General Assembly resolution 40/35

29 November 1985   Meeting 96   Adopted without vote

Approved by Third Committee (A/40/881) without vote, 11 November (meeting 37); draft by Seventh Congress on crime (A/C.3/40/L.22); agenda item 98.
Meeting numbers. GA 40th session: 3rd Committee 16-23, 30, 37; plenary 96.

UN standards and norms in criminal justice

The Seventh Congress unanimously adopted Basic Principles on the Independence of the Judiciary, a Model Agreement on the Transfer of Foreign Prisoners and recommendations on the treatment of foreign prisoners.

In **resolution 40/146**, the General Assembly requested the Economic and Social Council, through the Committee on Crime Prevention and Control, to give special attention to ways of implementing existing human rights standards in the administration of justice, and to pay due attention to new developments in that area. It invited the United Nations system and intergovernmental and non-governmental organizations to continue to co-operate with the Secretary-General in those endeavours by providing assistance and by submitting proposals for action to the Committee on crime.

Basic Principles on the Independence of the Judiciary

The Basic Principles on the Independence of the Judiciary stated, *inter alia*, that the judiciary's independence would be guaranteed by the State, that the judiciary would decide matters impartially and that it would have jurisdiction over all judicial issues. The Congress recommended the Basic Principles for national, regional and interregional implementation; urged United Nations bodies and intergovernmental and non-governmental organizations to become involved in their implementation; called on the Committee on crime to consider, as a priority matter, their effective implementation; and requested the Secretary-General to ensure their widest possible dissemination.

In **resolution 40/146**, the Assembly welcomed the Basic Principles, invited Governments to respect them, and encouraged the Sub-Commission on Prevention of Discrimination and Protection of Minorities of the Commission on Human Rights to take them into account in its consideration of the independence of the judiciary, jurors, assessors and lawyers.

Model Agreement on foreign prisoner transfer

The Model Agreement on the Transfer of Foreign Prisoners provided a set of principles for the social resettlement of offenders and transfer of prisoners, stipulating that such transfer should be effected on the basis of mutual respect for national sovereignty and jurisdiction, the agreement of both the sentencing and the administering State and the consent of the prisoner. The Secretary-General was requested to assist Member States, at their request, in developing transfer agreements and to report regularly thereon to the Committee on crime.

The General Assembly, in **resolution 40/146**, took note of the Model Agreement and invited Member States to take it into account in establishing or revising treaty relations.

UN Trust Fund for Social Defence

In 1985, the United Nations Trust Fund for Social Defence supplied $549,975 to the United Nations Social Defence Research Institute at Rome, Italy. The Fund was established pursuant to a 1965 resolution of the Economic and Social Council to strengthen United Nations work in social defence.[20] Contributions to the Fund in 1985 totalled $520,175, from the following 12 countries: Canada ($14,753), France ($16,842), Greece ($7,035), Italy ($374,424), Japan ($36,892), Nigeria ($10,531), Norway ($17,355), Sweden ($24,952), Switzerland ($11,732), Thailand ($974), Tunisia ($4,000) and Yugoslavia ($685).

REFERENCES

[1]*Seventh United Nations Congress on the Prevention of Crime and the Treatment of Offenders, Milan, 26 August –6 September 1985* (A/CONF.121/22/Rev.1), Sales No. E.86.IV.1. [2]YUN 1984, p. 699. [3]YUN 1984, p. 705, ESC res. 1984/47, 25 May 1984. [4]*Ibid.*, p. 709, ESC res. 1984/50, 25 May 1984. [5]YUN 1979, p. 779, GA res. 34/169, annex, 17 Dec. 1979. [6]A/40/482 & Corr.1,2. [7]YUN 1980, p. 780. [8]YUN 1982, p. 965, ESC res. 1982/29, 4 May 1982. [9]YUN 1984, p. 700, GA res. 39/112, 14 Dec. 1984. [10]A/40/751. [11]E/1985/L.23. [12]YUN 1979, p. 774, ESC dec. 1979/25, 9 May 1979. [13]YUN 1980, p. 786, ESC dec. 1980/105, 6 Feb. 1980. [14]YUN 1984, p. 701, ESC dec. 1984/152, 25 May 1984. [15]A/CONF.121/16. [16]YUN 1984, p. 709, ESC res. 1984/49, 25 May 1984. [17]YUN 1980, p. 781. [18]A/CONF.121/14 & Corr.1. [19]A/CONF.121/7. [20]YUN 1965, p. 409, ESC res. 1086 B (XXXIX), 30 July 1965.

Cultural development

Restitution of cultural property

The Secretary-General, in response to a 1983 General Assembly request,[1] submitted a report in June 1985[2] on the return or restitution of cultural property to the countries of origin, annexed to which was a report by the Director-General of the United Nations Educational, Scientific and Cultural Organization (UNESCO). UNESCO efforts in that regard had been particularly devoted to implementing the recommendations of the 1983 session[3] of the Intergovernmental Committee for Promoting the Return of Cultural Property to Its Countries of Origin or Its Restitution in Case of Illicit Appropriation.

At its fourth session (Athens and Delphi, Greece, 2-5 April 1985), the Intergovernmental Committee considered ways and means of more effectively promoting bilateral negotiations for the return or restitution of cultural property. It reiterated recommendations made at previous sessions with respect to measures against illicit traffic in cultural property and again stressed the importance of inventories of movable cultural property. The Committee recommended that its fifth session be organized in Paris, in 1987.

GENERAL ASSEMBLY ACTION

On 21 November 1985, the General Assembly adopted **resolution 40/19** by recorded vote.

Return or restitution of cultural property to the countries of origin

The General Assembly,

Recalling its resolutions 3026 A (XXVII) of 18 December 1972, 3148(XXVIII) of 14 December 1973, 3187(XXVIII) of 18 December 1973, 3391(XXX) of 19 November 1975, 31/40 of 30 November 1976, 32/18 of 11 November 1977, 33/50 of 14 December 1978, 34/64 of 29 November 1979, 35/127 and 35/128 of 11 December 1980, 36/64 of 27 November 1981 and 38/34 of 25 November 1983,

Recalling also the Convention on the Means of Prohibiting and Preventing the Illicit Import, Export and Transfer of Ownership of Cultural Property, adopted on 14 November 1970 by the General Conference of the United Nations Educational, Scientific and Cultural Organization,

Taking note with satisfaction of the report of the Secretary-General submitted in co-operation with the Director-General of the United Nations Educational, Scientific and Cultural Organization,

Noting with satisfaction that following its appeal other Member States have become parties to the Convention on the Means of Prohibiting and Preventing the Illicit Import, Export and Transfer of Ownership of Cultural Property,

Aware of the importance attached by the countries of origin to the return of cultural property which is of fundamental spiritual and cultural value to them, so that they may constitute collections representative of their cultural heritage,

Noting with satisfaction that some countries have taken positive steps towards the return or restitution of museum pieces, archives and *objets d'art* to their countries of origin,

Reaffirming the importance of inventories as an essential tool for the understanding and protection of cultural property and for the identification of dispersed heritage and as a contribution to the advancement of scientific and artistic knowledge and intercultural communication,

Deeply concerned at the clandestine excavations and the illicit traffic in cultural property that continue to impoverish the cultural heritage of all peoples,

Supporting the solemn appeal made on 7 June 1978 by the Director-General of the United Nations Educational, Scientific and Cultural Organization for the return of irreplaceable cultural heritage to those who created it,

1. *Commends* the United Nations Educational, Scientific and Cultural Organization and the Intergovernmental Committee for Promoting the Return of Cultural Property to its Countries of Origin or its Restitution in Case of Illicit Appropriation on the work they have accomplished, in particular through the promotion of bilateral negotiations, for the return or restitution of cultural property, the preparation of inventories of movable cultural property, the reduction of illicit traffic in cultural property and the dissemination of information to the public;

2. *Reaffirms* that the restitution to a country of its *objets d'art*, monuments, museum pieces, archives, manuscripts, documents and any other cultural or artistic treasures contributes to the strengthening of international co-operation and to the preservation and flowering of universal cultural values through fruitful co-operation between developed and developing countries;

3. *Recommends* that Member States adopt or strengthen the necessary protective legislation with regard to their own heritage and that of other peoples;

4. *Invites* Member States to continue drawing up, in co-operation with the United Nations Educational, Scientific and Cultural Organization, systematic inventories of cultural property existing in their territory and of their cultural property abroad;

5. *Also invites* Member States engaged in seeking the recovery of cultural and artistic treasures from the seabed, in accordance with international law, to facilitate by mutually acceptable conditions the participation of States having a historical and cultural link with those treasures;

6. *Appeals* to Member States to co-operate closely with the Intergovernmental Committee for Promoting the Return of Cultural Property to its Countries of Origin or its Restitution in Case of Illicit Appropriation and to conclude bilateral agreements for this purpose;

7. *Also appeals* to Member States to encourage the mass information media and educational and cultural institutions to strive to arouse a greater and more general awareness with regard to the return or restitution of cultural property to its country of origin;

8. *Endorses* the opinion expressed at the World Conference on Cultural Policies, held at Mexico City from 26 July to 6 August 1982, that the return of cultural property to its country of origin should be accompanied by the training of key personnel and technicians and the provision of the necessary facilities for the satisfactory conservation and presentation of the property restored;

9. *Welcomes* the steady increase in the number of States parties to the Convention on the Means of Prohibiting and Preventing the Illicit Import, Export and Transfer of Ownership of Cultural Property;

10. *Invites once again* those Member States that have not yet done so to sign and ratify the Convention;

11. *Requests* the Secretary-General, in co-operation with the Director-General of the United Nations Educational, Scientific and Cultural Organization, to submit to the General Assembly at its forty-second session a report on the implementation of the present resolution;

12. *Decides* to include in the provisional agenda of its forty-second session the item entitled "Return or restitution of cultural property to the countries of origin".

General Assembly resolution 40/19

21 November 1985   Meeting 87   123-0-15 (recorded vote)

18-nation draft (A/40/L.18 & Add.1); agenda item 20.

Sponsors: Benin, Burundi, Central African Republic, Chad, Congo, Cuba, Ecuador, Egypt, Gabon, Greece, Guinea, Mali, Morocco, Oman, Peru, Rwanda, Senegal, Zaire.

Although it shared the objectives of the co-sponsors, the Federal Republic of Germany believed that UNESCO was the appropriate body to deal with the matter. The United Kingdom could not accept the principle that cultural property which over the years had been acquired freely and legitimately should be returned to other countries, but it condemned illicit trafficking in such property.

The Byelorussian SSR felt that the United Nations should encourage UNESCO's efforts to promote bilateral negotiations for the return of cultural property and also to draft measures prohibiting the illegal export or trade in art objects. Iraq felt that no real progress had been made and no genuine response elicited on the return of cultural property to its original owners; it hoped that the United Nations would take effective action. Nepal pointed out that illicit traffickers had been plundering its cultural property for years, and called for appropriate steps by UNESCO and the International Council of Museums to curb them. Supporting the principle underlying the text, the Syrian Arab Republic reserved its right to recover its cultural property plundered by Israeli authorities and taken from its territory during foreign occupation and during the period of the British Mandate.

Proposed World Decade for Cultural Development

The UNESCO Director-General was preparing, in consultation with other organizations of the United Nations system, a plan of action for a World Decade for Cultural Development,[4] which he had proposed[5] should be proclaimed in 1986. The plan was to take into account proposals received as well as the results of discussions at the 1985 sessions of the ACC Consultative Committee on Substantive Questions (Programme Matters). The Committee considered at its second regular session in October[6] the UNESCO draft plan, an analysis of the main features of the plan, suggestions on the role of participants, a proposal for a co-ordinating machinery and a possible timetable. Noting that the Decade would begin in 1988, the Committee felt that, at the current stage, organizations should continue to communicate their views on the plan individually to UNESCO.

On 8 November 1985, the UNESCO General Conference adopted a resolution on the Decade, approving the major proposals set forth in the draft plan; emphasized that the active participation of UNESCO member States, the United Nations system, and international governmental and non-governmental organizations was important for the Decade's success; and invited member States to contribute to its objectives and the Director-General to take the necessary steps for its proclamation to be submitted to the General Assembly.

Centenary of the Berne Convention

By a letter of 20 December 1985 to the Secretary-General,[7] the Director-General of the World Intellectual Property Organization (WIPO) transmitted a resolution adopted on 1 October by the Conference of WIPO and the Assembly of the International Union for the Protection of Literary and Artistic Works (Berne Union), noting that 9 September 1986 would be the one hundredth anniversary of the adoption of the Berne Convention for the Protection of Literary and Artistic Works, inviting all States to consider adhering to the Convention and requesting that the resolution be brought to the attention of the Economic and Social Council in 1986 for the adoption of an appropriate recommendation.

REFERENCES

[1]YUN 1983, p. 741, GA res. 38/34, 25 Nov. 1983. [2]A/40/344. [3]YUN 1983, p. 740. [4]E/1985/57. [5]YUN 1984, p. 713. [6]ACC/1985/20. [7]E/1986/11.

Chapter XIV

Population

In 1985, the United Nations system continued its efforts to meet the needs of countries and the international community for population information, research, policy analysis and technical assistance. The United Nations Fund for Population Activities (UNFPA)—the largest internationally funded source of assistance to population programmes in developing countries—was at the forefront of technical co-operation in this field, with the Governing Council of the United Nations Development Programme (UNDP) acting as the Fund's governing body. The major portion of UNFPA funds, which came mainly from voluntary governmental contributions, were allocated to family planning projects.

During the year, the Population Commission—the functional commission of the Economic and Social Council which advises it on population matters—reviewed recommendations adopted at the 1984 International Conference on Population and their implications for the activities of the United Nations system. It also examined its work programme for 1986-1987 and the progress of work on the 1984-1985 programme.

The Secretary-General, in his 1985 report on the work of the Organization (see p. 4), pointing out that in the last 40 years the population of the world had more than doubled and that in the next 15 years it was expected to increase by one third, said that some of the strains and stresses in the world community would certainly stem from the pressure on institutions and resources resulting from this population explosion.

Acting on the recommendation of its First (Economic) Committee, the Economic and Social Council, in May, adopted several resolutions proposed to it by the Population Commission, including one on the implications of the recommendations of the International Conference on Population (1985/4), and others on the United Nations work programme in the population field (1985/5), on population structure (1985/3) and on the status and role of women and population (1985/6) (see Chapter XIX of this section).

The General Assembly, in December, expressed its concern about the shortfall of resources of UNFPA and the impact on its ability to carry out its planned programmes, urging all countries to continue and increase their support to the Fund (resolution 40/211).

The third annual (1985) United Nations Population Award went to the International Planned Parenthood Federation, an international non-governmental organization (NGO), for its outstanding contribution to the awareness of population questions and to their solutions.

Topics related to this chapter. Regional economic and social activities: population—Africa; Asia and the Pacific; Latin America and the Caribbean; Western Asia. Statistics: population and housing censuses.

Follow-up to the 1984 Conference on Population

Population Commission consideration. The 1984 International Conference on Population[1] adopted the Mexico City Declaration on Population and Development and a series of recommendations for the further implementation of the 1974 World Population Plan of Action.[2] The General Assembly in 1984[3] had asked the Population Commission to review those recommendations and their implications for the activities of the United Nations system.

The Secretary-General, in a January 1985 report[4] to the Commission, reviewed the implications of the recommendations for the work programme on population of the Secretariat's Department of International Economic and Social Affairs (DIESA) and Department of Technical Co-operation for Development (DTCD). The report identified the substantive results of the Conference having major significance for the activities of the two Departments, examined the programmatic implications of major population themes for their medium-term plans of work, and described the institutional implications for the United Nations of a number of recommendations currently under consideration.

The Population Commission, at its twenty-third session (New York, 19-28 February 1985),[5] highlighted certain themes in its discussion of the Conference's recommendations, such as the continuing seriousness of population problems in general and, in particular, of high population growth rates, the interrelationships between population and development, the role and status of women, human rights, the rights of individuals and couples to decide freely the number of their children, national sovereignty, the need to improve standards of living and reduce morbidity and mortality, and the independent role of population policies and family planning programmes in the achievement of national population goals. The continuing importance of peace, security, disarmament and cooperation and the implications of demographic change for population distribution and structure also received attention.

The Commission noted the extensive range of topics proposed for the attention of the DIESA Population Division following the recommendations of the Conference. To the extent possible, the major themes that had emerged would be integrated into the entire range of population variables rather than treated as separate topics. In the field of urbanization and internal migration, the Commission was informed that emphasis would be placed on the study of urban structures and various forms of territorial mobility. Regarding international migration, it stressed the need to study separately the consequences of different types of migration flows as, for example, the effect of migration on fertility. The Commission also took note with satisfaction of the attention given to the preparation and dissemination of estimates and projections, and it endorsed plans to make them more readily accessible and more broadly useful to planners and policy-makers. Increased emphasis would be given to research on management and evaluation of population policies. Work planned in the area of factors affecting reproduction would be broadened to focus on such factors as contraceptive use and marriage and fertility patterns by age.

In regard to DTCD's work programme as affected by the Conference, reference was made to the need for action-oriented training related to programmes and policies for demographers, planners and programme managers, for strengthening institutional mechanisms such as population units to integrate population and development in national planning, for strengthening demographic data analysis and activities to monitor population change through population censuses, civil registration and sample surveys, for strengthening programmes of an interdisciplinary nature in population and development and for strengthening technical co-operation activities among developing countries. It recognized that the main thrust of the programme carried by DTCD was to help developing countries achieve national self-sufficiency in all areas related to population training, demographic analysis and population policy development and planning. The Commission also took note of DTCD's readiness to accommodate the activities that it might recommend as a result of the Conference, although it was pointed out that resources currently available were insufficient to meet these growing needs.

During the year, population activities were also undertaken by various bodies of the United Nations system, including the regional commissions, UNFPA and specialized agencies, as well as by NGOs.

ACC activities. The Administrative Committee on Co-ordination (ACC) Task Force on the International Conference on Population met in New York from 13 to 15 February 1985 to discuss the implications of and follow-up actions to the recommendations of the Conference for different units, bodies and organizations of the United Nations system. Its report[6] was submitted to the Population Commission to facilitate its consideration of the subject.

At its first 1985 regular session (Geneva, 26-29 March),[7] ACC's Consultative Committee on Substantive Questions (Operational Activities) took note of the report and decided that additional meetings of the Task Force would not be necessary, although, if required, further inter-agency consultations could be arranged.

UNFPA activities. The UNFPA Executive Director, in an April 1985 report[8] to the UNDP Governing Council, said that, with a view to enhancing the effectiveness of its assistance, as well as to reflect the changes of emphasis implied in the Conference's recommendations, UNFPA would strengthen its programmes dealing with family planning, information, education and communication, women's activities, and population and development. In addition to giving greater attention to newly emerging concerns about population distribution, youth and aging, the Fund would continue its support for both data collection and analysis and research and training.

In a June addendum,[9] the Executive Director informed the Governing Council that the Director-General for Development and International Economic Co-operation had appointed a Steering Committee comprising the Under-Secretaries-General of DIESA and of DTCD, and himself, to initiate and supervise the preparation of a report, called for in a 1984 Assembly resolution,[3] on further steps taken to implement the Conference recommendations, in particular recommendation 83 on strengthening UNFPA to ensure more effective delivery of population assistance.

The UNDP Governing Council on 29 June[10] requested the UNFPA Executive Director to continue concentrating UNFPA's assistance in its core areas and give increased emphasis to strengthening its activities at the national level, and to circulate to all Council members the forthcoming report on Conference recommendations for implementing the World Population Plan of Action.

ECONOMIC AND SOCIAL COUNCIL ACTION

On 28 May 1985, on the recommendation of its First Committee, the Economic and Social Council adopted **resolution 1985/4** without vote.

Implications of the recommendations of the International Conference on Population

The Economic and Social Council,

Recalling General Assembly resolution 39/228 of 18 December 1984,

Having examined at its first regular session of 1985 the implications of the recommendations for the further implementation of the World Population Plan of Action made by the International Conference on Population, in order to provide overall policy guidelines within the United Nations system on population questions,

Recognizing the important role of international co-operation in the implementation of the recommendations,

Having considered the recommendations on the role of international co-operation, in particular recommendation 83, in which the Conference referred to the leading role of the United Nations Fund for Population Activities in population matters and urged that the Fund should be strengthened further, so as to ensure the more effective delivery of population assistance, taking into account the growing need in this field,

Having also considered recommendation 88 on the review and appraisal of the World Population Plan of Action and the monitoring of population trends and policies and of multilateral population programmes of the United Nations system,

1. *Reaffirms* the role of the Population Commission as the principal intergovernmental body to arrange for studies and advise the Council on:

(a) The size and structure of populations and the changes therein;

(b) The interplay of demographic factors and economic and social factors;

(c) Policies designed to influence the size and structure of populations and the changes therein;

(d) Any other demographic questions on which either the principal or the subsidiary organs of the United Nations or the specialized agencies may seek advice;

2. *Welcomes* the information provided by the representative of the Secretary-General on the plans for carrying out the task entrusted to him in paragraph 13 of General Assembly resolution 39/228;

3. *Requests* the Secretary-General, in carrying out this task, to take into account the views expressed by the Population Commission on the need for:

(a) Assessing the performance, achievements and effectiveness of the work of the United Nations system relating to research on demographic developments, formulation of population policies and provision of financial support and technical assistance for population activities;

(b) Consistency in policy guidelines of different organizations within the United Nations system, taking into account the distinctive role of each body;

(c) Improved communication, co-operation and co-ordination in population matters between the different organizations;

(d) Delivering population assistance to countries which request it, with efficiency and effectiveness;

4. *Invites* the Secretary-General, in carrying out this task, to avail himself of the advice of members of the Population Commission, the Governing Council of the United Nations Development Programme, the specialized agencies and, as appropriate, related non-governmental organizations and experts in population and other relevant matters;

5. *Recommends*, in view of the growing commitment of the developing countries, increased efforts by the international community to mobilize resources, as called for in recommendations 79 and 82 of the International Conference on Population, for meeting the increasing need of the developing countries for assistance for population activities;

6. *Requests* the Secretary-General to submit to the Economic and Social Council, through the Population Commission and, as appropriate, the Governing Council of the United Nations Development Programme, reports on the substantive and technical aspects of the monitoring of population trends and policies, and of multilateral population assistance, and an overview of population activities within the United Nations system;

7. *Invites* the Population Commission, at its twenty-fourth session, to review those reports and to transmit its views thereon to the Economic and Social Council at its first regular session of 1987.

Economic and Social Council resolution 1985/4

28 May 1985   Meeting 22   Adopted without vote

Approved by First Committee (E/1985/89) without vote, 17 May (meeting 6); draft by Population Commission (E/1985/25); agenda item 10.

In a related action, the Council, by **decision 1985/119**, decided to invite the governing bodies of the appropriate organs, organizations and bodies of the United Nations system to take the necessary and appropriate measures for the effective implementation of the report of the International Conference on Population, containing the recommendations of the Conference, within their respective spheres of competence and mandates.

The text was sponsored in the First Committee by Bangladesh,[11] which also orally revised it; it was approved without vote in both the Committee and the Council on 17 and 28 May, respectively.

REFERENCES

[1]YUN 1984, p. 714. [2]YUN 1974, p. 522. [3]YUN 1984, p. 717, GA res. 39/228, 18 Dec. 1984. [4]E/CN.9/1985/2. [5]E/1985/25. [6]ACC/1985/PG/3. [7]ACC/1985/3. [8]DP/1985/37. [9]DP/1985/37/Add.1. [10]E/1985/32 (dec. 85/19). [11]E/1985/C.1/L.3.

UN Fund for Population Activities

UNFPA activities

In 1985—the year designated by the General Assembly as International Youth Year—UNFPA focused on reaching young people, particularly through the funding of information, education and communication programmes in developing countries. In-school and out-of-school programmes designed to create an awareness of responsible parenthood and the consequences of population trends and growth helped forge an understanding of those subjects among young people, said the

Executive Director in his annual report for 1985.[1] He pointed out that between 1985 and the year 2000, the world's youth population—between the ages of 15 and 24—was projected to increase from 940 million to 1.06 billion.

UNFPA also concentrated its efforts on priority programme areas outlined in 1981[2] by the UNDP Governing Council—family planning; communication and education; population dynamics; basic data collection; formulation and evaluation of population policies; multisectoral activities; special programmes; and implementation of policies. In response to a large number of requests for assistance, attention was given to planning for future years. Evaluation of activities receiving UNFPA support was given a greater role in Fund programming, as were activities such as human resource development that would help in countries' eventual self-sufficient population and development policies.

Total UNFPA income in 1985 was $142.9 million compared with $138.4 million in 1984. Project allocations, which amounted to $141.4 million, are broken down in the tables below by major function and executing agency as well as geographically. Expenditures were $148.9 million, including $91.4 million for country programmes, $32.8 million for intercountry programmes, $4.6 million for the budgets of UNFPA Deputy Representatives and Senior Advisers on Population, $7.5 million for overhead payments, and $12.7 million for the administrative budget.

At year's end, UNFPA was assisting 2,667 projects—2,067 country, 285 regional, 141 interregional and 174 global. In 1985, 64 projects were completed, bringing the cumulative total to 2,257.

UNFPA assistance for maternal and child health and family planning (MCH/FP) programmes, which amounted to $72.5 million, or over half the total allocations, emphasized extension of service delivery to both rural and marginal urban areas. It also focused on projects to enhance accessibility and quality of services through personnel development and training at the country level, preparation of training materials and methodologies, management and evaluation, and contraceptive and family planning research. Particular attention was given to improving management of integrated MCH/FP programmes. Workshops brought together staff of technical agencies and UNFPA to study the development and execution of UNFPA-supported programmes.

Funds for population education and communication totalled $20.3 million, or 14.4 per cent of programme allocations. Information, education and communication activities were one of the key areas for UNFPA's encouragement of innovation in the population assistance field. Projects in 1985 included a television programme for Mexican

teenagers, use of itinerant theatre and dance groups in remote villages and various population modules for primary and secondary schools. These types of activities were more effective in conjunction with MCH/FP services.

Assistance to population dynamics projects totalled $15.9 million. As data pools had increased over the past 15 years, the need for population dynamics activities also increased. UNFPA funds assisted countries with population research, demographic training, institution-building and dissemination and utilization of research findings on specific population trends.

Activities in basic data collection totalled $11.5 million, providing support for 116 population censuses, 64 demographic and population surveys, 54 civil registration and vital statistics systems and 25 related demographic projects. Assistance continued to emphasize technical assistance, training and the provision of supplies and equipment.

Support for formulating and evaluating population policies and programmes totalled $9.6 million and included assistance for the creation of national population units and for the organization of seminars, study tours and other activities preparatory to the formulation of national population policy, as well as for country studies on population and development strategies and the management and co-ordination of population activities.

Assistance for special programme interests, which totalled $1.7 million, included issues of women in population and development, youth and aging. UNFPA participated and provided financial support for the participation of 36 women from 33 developing countries in the World Conference to Review and Appraise the Achievements of the United Nations Decade for Women (Nairobi, Kenya, July 1985) (see Chapter XIX of this section). Thirty projects with a budget close to $2 million were approved to improve the status of women. Within the Fund, a Special Unit for Women and Youth was established by the Executive Director. Most UNFPA-supported youth projects dealt with population and family life education in both the formal and informal educational sectors. In co-operation with the Economic Commission for Europe, the Fund also supported studies on the economic and social consequences of aging and other studies, seminars and workshops in this field.

Policy implementation accounted for $600,000. As an example of UNFPA's work in that area, the Fund sponsored an expert group meeting on population and development planning in which 11 country experts and 12 international experts participated. The recommendations of the meeting (New York, January 1985) would assist UNFPA in drawing up guidelines for more effective project formulation and implementation.

UNFPA ALLOCATIONS BY MAJOR FUNCTION, 1985

	Amount (in millions of US dollars)	Percentage of total programme
Family planning	72.5	51.3
Communication and education	20.3	14.4
Population dynamics analysis	15.9	11.2
Basic data collection	11.5	8.2
Formulation and evaluation of population policies	9.6	6.8
Multisector activities	9.3	6.5
Special programmes	1.7	1.2
Implementation of policies	0.6	0.4
Total*	141.4	100.0

*Excludes allocations of $5.1 million for Deputy Representatives and Senior Advisers on Population.

SOURCE: DP/1986/32 (Part I).

UNFPA ALLOCATIONS BY EXECUTING AGENCY, 1985

	Amount (in millions of US dollars)	Percentage of total programme
Governments (directly executed)	33.2	23.5
UNFPA	20.3	14.4
WHO	28.8	20.3
United Nations	17.3	12.2
Non-governmental organizations	14.4	10.2
Regional commissions	7.7	5.4
UNESCO	7.4	5.2
ILO	7.2	5.1
UNICEF	2.3	1.6
FAO	2.2	1.6
UNDP	0.6	0.5
Total	141.4	100.0

SOURCE: DP/1986/32 (Part I).

UNFPA PROJECT ALLOCATIONS, 1985
(in US dollars)

COUNTRY, TERRITORY AND REGIONAL PROJECTS	ALLOCATION
Africa south of the Sahara	
Angola*	274,293
Benin*	559,330
Botswana	372,712
Burkina Faso*	1,292,259
Burundi*	893,532
Cameroon	304,573
Cape Verde	102,182
Central African Republic*	226,800
Chad*	179,408
Comoros*	214,341
Congo	399,390
Equatorial Guinea*	197,742
Ethiopia*	521,691
Gabon	80,466
Gambia*	352,594
Ghana*	413,920
Guinea*	713,191
Guinea-Bissau	147,281
Ivory Coast	503,200
Kenya*	551,424
Lesotho*	529,590
Liberia*	479,466
Madagascar*	270,726
Malawi*	744,130
Mali*	791,480
Mauritania*	777,050
Mauritius	205,421
Mozambique*	1,063,146
Niger*	570,782
Nigeria	1,369,341
Rwanda*	681,283
Sao Tome and Principe*	234,391
Senegal*	691,817
Seychelles	66,471
Sierra Leone*	742,812
Swaziland	611,259
Togo	356,139
Uganda*	331,232
United Republic of Tanzania*	1,376,034
Zaire*	326,131
Zambia*	951,167
Zimbabwe*	822,018
Regional	5,795,286
Subtotal	28,087,501

COUNTRY, TERRITORY AND REGIONAL PROJECTS	ALLOCATION
Asia and the Pacific	
Afghanistan*	484,408
Bangladesh*	3,312,455
Bhutan*	188,770
Burma*	96,246
China*	13,045,739
Cook Islands	39,258
Democratic People's Republic of Korea	25,227
Fiji	645,039
Hong Kong	28,648
India*	12,654,569
Indonesia*	4,147,798
Iran	168,423
Kiribati	76,139
Lao People's Democratic Republic*	794,027
Malaysia	1,455,040
Maldives*	351,739
Mongolia	665,947
Nepal*	2,563,860
Pakistan*	2,153,696
Papua New Guinea	182,456
Philippines	2,430,155
Republic of Korea	453,315
Samoa*	269,722
Singapore	13,408
Solomon Islands*	54,613
Sri Lanka*	913,087
Thailand	1,813,485
Tonga	119,054
Trust Territory of the Pacific Islands	295,919
Tuvalu	39,245
Vanuatu	155,433
Viet Nam*	4,941,703
Regional	6,159,202
Subtotal	60,737,825
Latin America and the Caribbean	
Antigua and Barbuda	23,150
Argentina	55,981
Bahamas	25,530
Barbados	27,415
Belize	49,613

COUNTRY, TERRITORY AND REGIONAL PROJECTS	ALLOCATION
Bermuda	5,720
Bolivia	510,466
Brazil	2,032,465
British Virgin Islands	7,925
Chile	11,426
Colombia	489,567
Costa Rica	233,867
Cuba	1,032,579
Dominica*	63,935
Dominican Republic	736,446
Ecuador	555,367
El Salvador	541,916
Grenada	44,850
Guatemala	599,897
Guyana	42,875
Haiti*	1,007,288
Honduras	806,451
Jamaica	345,180
Mexico	3,020,553
Montserrat	13,172
Nicaragua	959,257
Panama	409,804
Paraguay	499,598
Peru	569,832
Saint Christopher and Nevis	52,974
Saint Lucia	113,935
Saint Vincent and the Grenadines	66,794
Suriname	32,000
Trinidad and Tobago	137,624
Turks and Caicos Islands	4,310
Uruguay	195,022
Venezuela	223,666
Regional	3,477,342
Subtotal	19,025,792
Middle East and the Mediterranean	
Algeria	68,120
Bahrain	141,569
Democratic Yemen*	1,005,667
Djibouti	67,650
Egypt*	996,804
Iraq	51,539
Jordan	680,780
Morocco	1,647,695
Somalia*	747,040

COUNTRY, TERRITORY AND REGIONAL PROJECTS	ALLOCATION	COUNTRY, TERRITORY AND REGIONAL PROJECTS	ALLOCATION	COUNTRY, TERRITORY AND REGIONAL PROJECTS	ALLOCATION
Middle East and the Mediterranean (cont.)		*Europe*		Regional	529,866
		Albania	153,097	Subtotal	1,940,272
Sudan*	1,480,399	Bulgaria	539,183		
Syrian Arab Republic	766,037	Greece	113,973	*INTERREGIONAL AND GLOBAL PROJECTS*	
Tunisia	715,881	Hungary	311,613		
Turkey	552,650	Poland	38,906	Interregional	16,097,229
Yemen*	1,224,512	Portugal	109,554	Global	3,302,027
Regional	2,013,444	Romania	6,394		
		Yugoslavia	137,686	Subtotal	19,399,256
Subtotal	12,159,787			Total	141,350,433

*Classified as a priority country for UNFPA assistance.
SOURCE: DP/1986/34 (Parts I & II).

Country and intercountry programmes

In 1985, UNFPA continued to address the needs of the countries given priority status for UNFPA assistance (see table above), of which 30 were in Africa, 15 in Asia and the Pacific, 2 in Latin America and the Caribbean, and 5 in the Middle East and the Mediterranean. Of the year's total UNFPA project allocations of $141.4 million, those for regional, interregional and country activities amounted to $103.9 million, or 86.3 per cent of the total.

Intercountry programmes (regional, interregional and global), which totalled $37.3 million in 1985, represented 26.4 per cent of total allocations. Activities included technical assistance and backstopping, training, research, and information exchange through clearing-houses and population information networks.

On 29 June,[3] the UNDP Governing Council reiterated its goal of devoting up to two thirds of country programme assistance to the priority countries. It approved UNFPA assistance to large-scale country programmes for Bangladesh, Brazil, Cuba, Ghana, India, Indonesia, the Ivory Coast, Nicaragua, Sierra Leone and Uganda. The Council asked the Executive Director to strengthen efforts to improve project implementation as well as Governments' capacity to implement their population programmes and report in 1987 on implementation experience relating to allocations and expenditures with different executing agencies. It also asked for a progress report on the regional and interregional demographic training and research centres.

Family planning research

The UNFPA Executive Director submitted to the UNDP Governing Council in March 1985 a problem-oriented analysis[4] of UNFPA's experience in the family planning area. The report stated that, in view of the large number of women entering the reproductive years, the demand for family planning, both as a health and a fertility-limiting measure, would increase considerably. It had been estimated that, in order to reach the level of contraceptive prevalence required to attain a total fertility rate of 3.3 children per woman by the year 2000, an investment of $5.6 billion would be needed. The report analysed various situational and organizational variables relevant to implementing family planning activities and considered the issue of adequacy of contraceptives, outlining insights considered useful to countries, to UNFPA and to other donors in designing and implementing family planning programmes.

Another March report[5] examined the use of incentives and disincentives (i.e. rewards or penalties tied to some kind of fertility behaviour) in family planning programmes. Incentives might be paid to acceptors (those who accept rewards), motivators (who attempt to pursuade others) or service providers; disincentives were aimed almost exclusively at individuals or couples. The report noted their use in a number of countries, examined the types used and their target groups, their effects on the quality of services, and their relationship to free and informed choice. The Executive Director stressed that, in assessing the complex ethical and human rights issues raised, it was vital to take into account the socio-cultural context within which they operated—value systems, community consensus, individual and national perceptions, and the overall programme for socio-economic development.

On 29 June,[3] the Governing Council took note of the March reports and requested the UNFPA Executive Director to continue improving the design, management, monitoring and evaluation of family planning programmes and projects. The Council also asked him to encourage and support research on the effects of incentive and disincentive schemes on the quality of services offered and on the individual's free and informed choice.

As requested by the UNDP Governing Council in 1984,[6] the Executive Director submitted to it in March 1985 a report[7] on the results of the recommendations of the Policy and Co-ordination Committee of the Special Programme of Research, Development and Research Training in Human Reproduction of the World Health Organization, together with a recommendation for the level of UNFPA funding for 1986-1989.

The Council on 29 June,[3] approved the allocation by UNFPA of an additional $500,000 to the Special Programme for 1985, raising the total for that year to $2.5 million, and decided that allocations to that Programme should be increased if possible to $2.75 million for 1986, $3 million for 1987, $3.25 million for 1988, and $3.5 million for 1989. It also noted greater co-ordination of international efforts in contraceptive research.

Work programmes

The income assumptions in the UNFPA work plan for 1986-1989,[8] prepared by the Executive Director, were based on Government contributions for 1985 at the exchange rate as at January 1985 and on increases of 5.5, 6, 6.5 and 7 per cent, respectively, for the years 1986-1989, and on some expected increases in interest earnings. After deductions for operational costs and additions to the operational reserve, programmable resources were expected to total $505.4 million for the four years of the work plan: $116.3 million for 1986, $122 million for 1987, $129.2 million for 1988 and $137.9 million for 1989. Intercountry activities for that period would account for 26.7 per cent ($135 million) of total programmable resources, and country activities for 73.3 per cent ($370.4 million). The report also updated information in a 1982 report on the review and reassessment of the UNFPA programme for 1982-1985, concerning the resource situation, overall resource use, distribution of new programmable resources between country and intercountry activities and allocations to country activities. It also contained information on implementation of plans in a 1984 review, and reassessment and revisions required for 1985.

On 29 June,[3] the UNDP Governing Council approved the update and the work plan, and gave approval authority—on the understanding that the Executive Director would limit approval of projects to available resources—for net additional amounts of $40.3 million for 1986, $39.7 million for 1987, $39.1 million for 1988 and $38.6 million for 1989.

With regard to a report[9] of the Executive Director on the status of financial implementation of Council-approved UNFPA programmes and projects, the Council noted the proportional distribution of allocations between country and intercountry activities achieved in 1984, reaffirmed the existing target of up to 25 per cent of programmable resources for intercountry activities, and requested that a report

clarifying the definition of intercountry activities and reviewing the possibility of revising the definition and the target be presented in 1986.

Programme planning and evaluation

During 1985, seven independent, in-depth evaluations were undertaken of UNFPA-assisted programmes and projects in Haiti, Honduras, Mozambique, Nepal, Pakistan, Paraguay and the Sudan, the results of which were presented to the UNDP Governing Council in the report of the UNFPA Executive Director for 1985.[1]

In another report[10] to the Council, on UNFPA evaluation activities, the Executive Director analysed, compared and reviewed the results of evaluations regarding basic data collection, population and development, MCH/FP, population education and communication, and the role and status of women. It also provided information on the evaluation activities of UNFPA during 1984-1985 and discussed plans for activities in that area.

On 29 June,[3] the Governing Council noted the Fund's intention to address the need for further developing and strengthening the system of monitoring and evaluation and for the feedback of the results into its policies and programmes.

Financial and administrative questions

Budget for 1986-1987

On 1 January 1985, UNFPA's balance was $17,499,884. During the year, the Fund received income of $142,945,106 and had expenditures of $148,889,281, which resulted in an excess of expenditure over income of $5,994,175. The Fund's balance as at 31 December was $7,555,709; unspent allocations totalled $18,035,576.

In May[11] the UNFPA Executive Director submitted to the UNDP Governing Council the budget estimates for administrative and programme support services for the 1986-1987 biennium. On 29 June,[12] the Council took note of the Fund's report, as well as of the report[13] of the Advisory Committee on Administrative and Budgetary Questions (ACABQ) which, commenting on the estimates, suggested reducing travel and communications costs. In the same report, ACABQ also commented on a report[14] dealing with the financial implications for support services of a job classification exercise and another[15] on the inclusion of UNFPA Deputy Representatives and other field and headquarters posts into the regular manning table and on UNFPA basic manpower requirements (see p. 768). The Governing Council approved net appropriations for the biennium in the amount of $36,643,669 to finance administrative and programme support services, and asked the Executive Director to keep support services costs to a minimum. It also asked him, when presenting the financial and budgetary situation of UNFPA, to follow the guidelines used by UNDP.

Contributions

During 1985, 86 countries and Territories paid a total of $122.1 million in voluntary contributions to UNFPA (see table below), compared with $122.5 million from 81 countries and Territories in 1984.[16] This figure, together with additions and adjustments to pledges for prior years, exchange-rate and currency revaluation adjustments, interest, donations and other miscellaneous income, gave a total 1985 income of $142.9 million. Pledges for 1986 and future years from 78 countries and Territories totalled $92.1 million as at 31 December 1985 (see table below), compared with $109.8 million from 76 countries and Territories at the end of the previous year.

On 29 June 1985,[3] the UNDP Governing Council urged all countries that were able to do so to increase their contributions in 1986 and future years, and to make their contribution payments as early as possible. It authorized the Executive Director to request a special session of the Governing Council should developments in regard to the Fund's resource situation and the necessity for reprogramming of available resources warrant it.

CONTRIBUTIONS TO UNFPA, 1985 AND 1986
(as at 31 December 1985; in US dollar equivalent)

Country or Territory	1985 payment	1986 pledge	Country or Territory	1985 payment	1986 pledge
Afghanistan	—	2,000	Lesotho	—	1,073
Albania	1,429	1,571	Luxembourg	—	6,863
Anguilla	500	—	Madagascar	—	5,000
Australia	909,563	775,862	Malawi	725	819
Austria	93,000	120,000	Maldives	871	871
Bahamas	4,000	—	Malta	389	—
Bangladesh	15,950	17,256	Mauritius	5,237	—
Barbados	3,000	—	Mexico	2,208	2,120
Belgium	380,527	392,157	Mongolia	449	491
Benin	—	500	Montserrat	738	—
Bhutan	3,800	2,100	Morocco	4,000	—
Bolivia	—	5,000	Mozambique	985	985
Botswana	811	—	Nepal	3,750	3,750
Brazil	—	10,000	Netherlands	9,619,902	14,285,714
British Virgin Islands	2,700	—	New Zealand	184,100	—
Bulgaria	30,000	30,000	Norway	10,893,455	13,814,570
Burma	6,002	6,002	Oman	—	10,000
Burundi	16,393	877	Pakistan	341,526	325,000
Cameroon	—	5,222	Panama	2,250	1,500
Canada	7,632,704	8,152,174	Papua New Guinea	2,000	1,515
Chile	5,000	5,000	Paraguay	—	15,000
China	550,000	500,000	Philippines	138,794	71,784
Colombia	25,714	40,000	Poland	14,467	13,643
Comoros	—	2,611	Portugal	—	20,000
Cook Islands	2,400	800	Qatar	30,000	—
Cyprus	750	750	Republic of Korea	41,000	38,267
Democratic People's Republic of Korea	—	8,368	Rwanda	1,000	1,000
Democratic Yemen	—	2,420	Saint Christopher and Nevis	850	—
Denmark	4,967,229	6,043,956	Saint Lucia	1,500	—
Djibouti	8,000	—	Saint Vincent and the Grenadines	500	—
Dominica	1,000	—	Sao Tome and Principe	675	—
Ecuador	—	22,000	Saudi Arabia	30,000	30,000
Egypt	228,921	228,921	Senegal	—	5,000
El Salvador	5,000	—	Seychelles	500	—
Fiji	3,724	1,852	Solomon Islands	500	—
Finland	1,545,651	2,752,294	Somalia	203	269
France	231,579	287,582	Spain	91,693	116,129
Germany, Federal Republic of	13,171,434	15,080,000	Sri Lanka	17,500	10,000
Greece	5,000	5,000	Sudan	38,776	—
Grenada	500	—	Sweden	6,323,864	16,993,464*
Guatemala	1,852	—	Switzerland	2,173,913	2,631,579
Honduras	10,000	10,000	Syrian Arab Republic	5,500	—
Hungary	11,749	13,402	Thailand	48,772	48,400
Iceland	2,600	2,600	Tunisia	21,714	21,764
India	337,553	421,941	Turkey	10,000	10,000
Indonesia	150,000	150,000	United Kingdom	5,977,057	6,676,558
Italy	1,966,292	1,749,271	United States	36,000,000	—
Ivory Coast	11,254	—	Viet Nam	1,000	1,500
Japan	17,716,000	—	Yemen	—	2,850
Jordan	22,099	22,000	Yugoslavia	2,040	1,856
Kenya	—	2,761	Zaire	—	1,000
Kuwait	25,000	25,000	Zimbabwe	1,863	1,818
Lao People's Democratic Republic	1,000	500	**Total**	**122,143,946**	**92,071,902**

*Includes pledge of $8,496,732 made in 1985 for 1987.

SOURCE: A/41/5/Add.7.

Accounts for 1984

Following the audit of the UNFPA financial statements for the year ended 31 December 1984, the Board of Auditors[17] observed that expenditures for project delivery had in some cases exceeded allotments or were incurred without them, while in some projects allotments remained unutilized. It recommended again that control of project allocations and expenditures be strengthened and that the year-end rephasing-of-allocations exercise be monitored more closely. The Board recommended that measures be taken to speed up clearance procedures for financial reports for clearing up discrepancies between the annual field office status-of-allotments reports and the amounts recorded in the year-end financial report produced by headquarters. Noting uncollected pledges of $807,083 pertaining to 1982 and earlier years, the Board reiterated that write-off action should be initiated when appropriate. The Board considered that UNFPA could enhance the effectiveness of its support to conferences, meetings and workshops of NGOs by participating more actively in the evaluation of their final outcome and impact.

The UNFPA Executive Director said the Administration would take measures to comply with the Board's recommendations and comments on budgetary control. He pointed out that uncollected pledges pertaining to 1982 and earlier years represented less than 0.0001 per cent of total pledges for those years; he added that UNFPA would continue to take the necessary measures for the collection and audit adjustment of unpaid pledges.

By **resolution 40/238** of 18 December 1985, the General Assembly accepted the UNFPA financial report and audited financial statements and the audit opinion of the Board of Auditors. It requested that remedial action be taken as required.

Audited accounts, 1983

On 29 June 1985,[12] the UNDP Governing Council took note of the audited accounts of the participating and executing agencies relating to funds allocated to them by UNFPA as at the end of 1983.[18]

In a report,[19] requested in 1984,[20] on the reaction of those agencies and the Panel of External Auditors to views expressed on the importance of receiving narrative audit reports, it was noted that none of the agencies objected to the external auditors' providing narrative audit reports which disclosed audit results sufficiently wide in scope to cover areas the Council had identified in previous decisions, including the audit of the effectiveness of financial management.

The Council requested the UNFPA Executive Director to reiterate to agencies the importance it attached to long-form narrative reports, and to continue his efforts to obtain them.

Staffing

Pursuant to a June 1984 request,[21] the Executive Director submitted to the UNDP Governing Council in April 1985 a report[15] on the inclusion of UNFPA Deputy Representatives and Senior Advisers on Population in the regular staffing table. The report, after reviewing briefly UNFPA's current position and future prospects, outlined considerations requiring the fuller integration of field and headquarters staff into a combined staffing table financed by the regular administrative and programme support services budget. The report also outlined the Executive Director's views as to UNFPA's basic manpower requirements for future years, focusing primarily on two bienniums—1986-1987 and 1988-1989.

ACABQ[13] concluded that justifications submitted in the Executive Director's report were insufficient to warrant the proposed integration of the project-funded headquarters and field posts in the numbers and grade levels proposed. However, it recommended that the Governing Council should accept the proposed integration of 33 Deputy Representative and Senior Adviser project-funded posts into the regular staffing table, and that the Executive Director should ensure that the Council was kept aware of all new project-funded posts established in the future.

On 29 June,[12] the Council requested the Executive Director to present to it for approval at its 1986 session draft guidelines for what should be regarded as project-related personnel expenditures (budgeted as project costs) and what should be regarded as administration-related personnel expenditures (budgeted as administrative costs). It also decided to establish in the regular administrative and programme support services budget for 1986-1987 33 Deputy Representative and Senior Adviser posts, nine international programme officer posts and 10 Professional posts at headquarters. Project-funded Professional and General Service posts at headquarters were to be abolished after the contracts of current incumbents had expired, as well as currently vacant General Service posts. A report on implementation was requested for 1986.

A note[14] on job classification results and their financial implications indicated that the results of the classification of the UNFPA General Service staff into the new seven-level structure would be implemented effective 1 January 1985, and those for the Professional category a year later. For the General Service, $52,500 would be needed to cover salary increases in 1985; $400,000 would be required annually for 1986-1987 for the Professionals. ACABQ did not interpose any objection to the results of the classification exercise, but felt that the Council might wish to consider correcting UNFPA's grading structure, given the continuing decline in lower-level posts.

The Governing Council, on 29 June,[12] authorized the Executive Director to implement the results of the job classification exercise and the new salary scale for General Service staff of UNFPA when the Secretary-General implemented them for United Nations General Service; he was to implement the reclassification results for Professional posts effective 1 January 1986.

The Council also asked the Executive Director to prepare for 1986 a comprehensive report on personnel management, with recommendations, including a study of the link between the work-load and personnel structure in UNFPA, priorities to be set in order to strengthen specific areas, career development, feasibility of redeployment of posts and personnel rotation between the field and headquarters, and recruitment policies.

REFERENCES

[1]DP/1986/32 (Parts I & II). [2]YUN 1981, p. 782. [3]E/1985/32 (dec. 85/19). [4]DP/1985/31. [5]DP/1985/32. [6]YUN 1984, p. 722. [7]DP/1985/34. [8]DP/1985/35. [9]DP/1985/36. [10]DP/1986/37. [11]DP/1985/39 & Corr.1. [12]E/1985/32 (dec. 85/20). [13]DP/1985/40. [14]DP/1985/39/Add.1. [15]DP/1985/38 & Corr.1,2. [16]YUN 1984, p. 723. [17]A/40/5/Add.7. [18]DP/1985/41. [19]DP/1985/42. [20]YUN 1984, p. 724. [21]*Ibid.*, p. 725.

Other population activities

Population Commission

The Population Commission held its twenty-third session in New York from 19 to 28 February 1985,[1] discussing the implications of the recommendations of the 1984 International Conference on Population,[2] the action to be taken by the United Nations to implement those recommendations, population trends and policies, the programme of work in population for 1986-1987 and implementation of the programme budget for 1984-1985. Issues it discussed included world demographic analysis, demographic projections, population policies, population and development, monitoring, review and appraisal of population trends, factors affecting patterns of reproduction, dissemination of population information, technical co-operation and demographic statistics.

ECONOMIC AND SOCIAL COUNCIL ACTION

On 28 May, the Economic and Social Council took note of the report of the Population Commission on its twenty-third session (**decision 1985/121**). It also approved the provisional agenda and documentation for the twenty-fourth (1986) session of the Commission (**decision 1985/118**). The first decision was orally proposed by the Council President; the second had been proposed by the Population Commission and was approved on 17 May by the Council's First Committee. Both texts were adopted without vote.

Population work programme

In a December 1984 report[3] to the Population Commission, the Secretary-General described the progress achieved by DIESA and DTCD in implementing their programmes of work in the field of population during 1984.[4] He also transmitted notes[5] on the population programmes of work of the two Departments for the biennium 1986-1987.

ECONOMIC AND SOCIAL COUNCIL ACTION

On 28 May, the Economic and Social Council adopted, without vote, **resolution 1985/5**, as recommended by the First Committee.

Work programme in the field of population

The Economic and Social Council,

Recalling General Assembly resolutions 3344(XXIX) and 3345(XXIX) of 17 December 1974, concerning the recommendations of the World Population Conference and the further implementation of the World Population Plan of Action,

Recalling also Council resolution 1981/28 of 6 May 1981 on the strengthening of actions concerned with the fulfilment of the World Population Plan of Action,

Stressing the supportive role of the work programme of the United Nations system in the field of population in the attainment of the goals and objectives of the International Development Strategy for the Third United Nations Development Decade and the pursuit of goals of economic co-operation,

Having reviewed the preamble, the section on peace, security and population, and the sections containing the recommendations for action and for the further implementation of the World Population Plan of Action adopted by the International Conference on Population, at which it was reaffirmed that the principles and objectives of the World Population Plan of Action remained fully valid and which placed emphasis on a number of issues in the field of population that will continue to be included in the work programme, as appropriate,

Bearing in mind the Mexico City Declaration on Population and Development,

Reaffirming the role of the Population Commission in advising the Council on population questions,

Taking note of the report of the Population Commission on its twenty-third session and the views expressed therein on the progress of work and on the work programme in the field of population,

1. *Takes note with satisfaction* of the progress made in the implementation of the programme of work for the biennium 1984-1985 and the medium-term plan for the period 1984-1989;

2. *Requests* the Secretary-General:

(*a*) To continue vigorously the work of monitoring world population trends and policies and the work necessary for the review and appraisal of the World Population Plan of Action;

(*b*) To strengthen and draw together the work on interrelationships between the role and status of women and population, following the guidelines of the recommendations of the International Conference on Population;

(c) To continue the work programme in mortality analysis, with special emphasis on age patterns, sex differentials and the relationship of mortality to other demographic and non-demographic processes;

(d) To continue the work programme in the areas of urbanization and internal and international migration, with special emphasis on the role of urban structures and their relationship to the development process; on the variety of population mobility; and on the demographic consequences of international migration for both sending and receiving countries;

(e) To continue the work programme in fertility and family planning, with special emphasis on the assessment of the impact of the family planning programme, key factors affecting fertility such as contraceptive use and marriage patterns, and adolescent fertility;

(f) To continue to prepare estimates of the size of population and demographic indicators, such as fertility, mortality and migration trends, and to prepare projections for all countries and areas of the world, by age and sex and by urban, rural and city population, including changes in population structures, families and households;

(g) To continue work in the area of population policies, with special emphasis on the Sixth Population Policy Inquiry among Governments, the population policy data bank, and research on the formulation, implementation and evaluation of all aspects of population policies;

(h) To continue research in the area of socio-economic development and population with emphasis on the demographic consequences of major development projects; the socio-economic consequences of the aging of populations; successful experiences in the integration of demographic factors into development planning; and improving the analysis of interactions between population, resources, environment and development;

(i) To continue the development of the international Population Information Network (POPIN);

(j) To continue technical co-operation activities in the field of population, fully utilizing the available interdisciplinary capacity of the United Nations, in three main fields:

(i) Training in demography and population matters, emphasizing in particular an interdisciplinary approach;

(ii) Evaluation and analysis of basic population and demographic data, using computer programmes for demographic analysis;

(iii) Population policy and development planning, in particular through the strengthening of appropriate national institutional mechanisms;

(k) To continue to undertake analysis and evaluation of experience gained in implementing technical co-operation activities in the field of population and to continue publishing the results thereof;

3. *Re-emphasizes* the importance of maintaining the effectiveness and efficiency of the global population programme and of continuing to strengthen co-ordination and collaboration among the Department of International Economic and Social Affairs, the Department of Technical Co-operation for Development, the regional commissions, the United Nations Fund for Population Activities and organizations of the United Nations

system in the planning and execution of their population programmes, as well as the need for organizations of the United Nations system to strengthen collaboration and co-ordination with other appropriate intergovernmental and national organizations.

Economic and Social Council resolution 1985/5

28 May 1985   Meeting 22   Adopted without vote

Approved by First Committee (E/1985/89) without vote, 17 May (meeting 6); draft by Population Commission (E/1985/25); agenda item 10.

Population structure

The Population Commission in February proposed for the Economic and Social Council's adoption a draft resolution on population structure.

In a report[6] on the world population situation (see below), the Secretary-General noted views expressed by Governments that changing population age structure was having a negative impact on some economies. The large proportion of youth among some populations affected education and employment, increasing numbers of women in the reproductive ages could contribute to higher population growth rates, and the aging of the population was of concern to both developing and developed countries.

ECONOMIC AND SOCIAL COUNCIL ACTION

The Economic and Social Council, on 28 May, adopted **resolution 1985/3**, without vote, as recommended by the First Committee.

Population structure

The Economic and Social Council,

Recalling the recommendations of the World Population Conference, in particular those contained in the World Population Plan of Action, especially paragraphs 63, 64 and 66 thereof, where emphasis is laid on the need to take fully into account the implications of changing proportions of youth, working-age groups and the aged, which affect a growing number of developed and developing countries,

Recalling also the recommendations of the International Conference on Population, in particular recommendations 57 and 58, in which the Conference called for an intensification of efforts in the execution of specific programmes related to youth and requested that further efforts should be made to analyse the issue of aging, particularly its implications for overall development,

Noting the findings of the studies undertaken in preparation for the World Assembly on Aging,

Affirming the need to implement the Specific Programme of Measures and Activities to be undertaken prior to and during the International Youth Year: Participation, Development, Peace,

Affirming also the need to implement the International Plan of Action on Aging,

Bearing in mind the deliberations of the Population Commission at its twenty-third session on the implications of the recommendations of the International Conference on Population,

Taking note of General Assembly resolution 39/228 of 18 December 1984, by which the Assembly reaffirmed the need to pay attention to specific problems of population structure,

1. *Urges* all Governments, when formulating their social and economic policies, plans and programmes, to take fully into account the existing and anticipated demographic structures of their populations, paying particular attention to their relation to the following:

(a) The number of students and the need for teachers and schools, in connection with ongoing and future technological change;

(b) The changing organization and role of the family, particularly families made up of young people;

(c) The formation of new household and housing needs;

(d) The changing patterns of consumption and savings;

(e) The needs of youth for productive employment opportunities;

(f) The needs of the elderly for social and economic security, and their potential contribution to development;

2. *Requests* the Secretary-General, in supporting the activities of Governments in these efforts, to consider fully the relevant aspects of changing age structures and in this respect:

(a) To continue the work of assessing current and future population structures in both developed and developing countries, paying particular attention to the increase in the proportions of youth and the aged in those populations;

(b) To continue and strengthen efforts to study the implications of changing population structure for social and economic development, for family and household structure, and for social services, medical care and other related fields;

(c) To continue and strengthen efforts to monitor and analyse policies to address specific requirements arising from changing population structure, especially for youth and the aged;

(d) To report to the Population Commission, on a timely basis, the findings of studies on these issues, as well as estimates and projections on the youth and the aged populations, and to make that information available to Governments, non-governmental organizations and others concerned.

Economic and Social Council resolution 1985/3

28 May 1985   Meeting 22   Adopted without vote

Approved by First Committee (E/1985/89) without vote, 17 May (meeting 6); draft by Population Commission (E/1985/25); agenda item 10.

World population situation

In March 1985, the Secretary-General submitted to the General Assembly, through the Economic and Social Council, a summary and the conclusions of his biennial report on the world population situation,[6] even though the previous such report had been submitted in 1984[7] for consideration in connection with preparations for the International Conference on Population. The report surveyed trends in population growth, structure, fertility, mortality, distribution, internal and international migration, and the social and economic implications of demographic trends. It also included a summary of the views expressed by Governments at the 1984 Conference, relating to: national sovereignty, human rights, cultural values and peace; population and the status of women; mortality and morbidity; population growth and fertility; population structure; migration and population distribution; population and development; and international co-operation.

The report estimated that, by the year 2000, the world's population would be close to 6.1 billion, of which nearly 80 per cent would be residing in developing countries, compared to 4.5 billion in 1980. The current rate of global population growth was estimated at 1.65 per cent per year, down from 2 per cent during the 1960s. Declines of growth rates occurred in both developed and developing countries. Among the developing regions, in which the annual growth rate declined as a group from 2.5 per cent during 1970-1975 to 2 per cent during 1980-1985—although if China were excluded (whose growth rate dropped from 2.4 to 1.2 per cent per year during the same period), the decline for that group would be less significant (from 2.5 to 2.4 per cent per year)—Africa showed a still-rising growth rate of over 3 per cent during 1980-1985, and Western Asia, 2.9 per cent, with no sign of significant changes. Other South Asian regions and Latin America had respective growth rates of 2.1 and 2.4 per cent during the period, and had been declining over the past decade.

By **decision 1985/120**, the Economic and Social Council, on 28 May, on an oral proposal by its President, took note of the Secretary-General's report.[6]

UN Population Award

By a 5 December 1985 letter to the Secretary-General,[8] Bangladesh, as Chairman of the Committee for the United Nations Population Award, transmitted a note on the Award for 1985.

The Committee had received 21 nominations. Meeting on 25 and 26 February, the Committee had selected the International Planned Parenthood Federation (IPPF) as laureate for the 1985 Award. Established in 1952 with headquarters in London, IPPF was described as the largest international NGO working directly in the promotion of voluntary family planning services throughout the world, operating in 121 countries. The 1985 Award—a diploma, a gold medal and $25,000— was presented by the Secretary-General at a ceremony on 7 June at United Nations Headquarters.

By the end of 1984, the Trust Fund for the United Nations Population Award, administered by the Executive Director of UNFPA, amounted to $455,867; expenditures in 1984 totalled $55,074. Early in 1985, India contributed $50,000.

REFERENCES

[1]E/1985/25. [2]YUN 1984, p. 714. [3]E/CN.9/1985/3 & Add.1. [4]YUN 1984, p. 728. [5]E/CN.9/1985/4 & Add.1. [6]A/40/190-E/1985/20. [7]YUN 1984, p. 729. [8]A/C.2/40/13.

PUBLICATIONS

World Population Trends, Population and Development Interrelations and Population Policies, 1983 Monitoring Report, vol. II (ST/ESA/SER.A/93/Add.1), Sales No. E.85.XIII.2. *Consequences of Mortality Trends and Differentials* (ST/ESA/SER.A/95), Sales No. E.85.XIII.3. *Determinants of Mortality Change and Differentials in Developing Countries* (ST/ESA/SER.A/94), Sales No. E.85.XIII.4. *Women's Employment and Fertility: A Comparative Analysis of World Fertility Survey Results for 38 Developing Countries* (ST/ESA/SER.A/96), Sales No. E.85.XIII.5. *Population Bulletin of the United Nations,* No. 18, *1985* (ST/ESA/SER.N/18), Sales No. E.85.XIII.6. *Socio-Economic Differentials in Child Mortality in Developing Countries* (ST/ESA/SER.A/97), Sales No. E.85.XIII.7. *Demographic Yearbook 1985* (ST/ESA/STAT/SER.R/15), Sales No. E/F.86.XIII.1.

Chapter XV

Health and human resources

Health risks increased during 1985 as more chemicals were released, used or dumped into the environment. Demand grew for action to counter the threats to health by chemical, biological and physical environmental agents. The United Nations Environment Programme and the World Health Organization, particularly in developing countries, identified potentially harmful agents and promoted the enactment of control measures.

The majority of the population in many developing countries continued to be afflicted by chronic dietary energy deficiency; the United Nations University (UNU) sponsored research into the nature of the problem. During the year, UNU had 78 ongoing projects and subprojects under nine programme areas: peace and conflict resolution; global economy; energy systems and policy; resource policy and management; food-energy nexus; food, nutrition, biotechnology and poverty; human and social development; regional perspectives; and science, technology and the information society.

Measures were undertaken by the United Nations system to implement the World Programme of Action concerning Disabled Persons within the framework of the United Nations Decade of Disabled Persons (1983-1992). In May, the Economic and Social Council requested the Secretary-General to continue to support and monitor implementation of the Programme of Action, and to include the United Nations Trust Fund for the International Year of Disabled Persons among the programmes for which funds were pledged at the annual United Nations Pledging Conference for Development Activities (resolution 1985/35). The Fund was renamed by the General Assembly, in November, as the Voluntary Fund for the United Nations Decade of Disabled Persons; the Assembly also invited States to give high priority to projects for the prevention of disabilities, rehabilitation and equal opportunities for disabled persons (resolution 40/31).

In December, the Assembly requested the Secretary-General to take into account the need for an integrated, multidisciplinary approach to human resources development in developing countries, particularly the training of qualified national personnel (40/213), and decided to grant the United Nations Institute for Training and Research (UNITAR) an amount of $600,000, corresponding to the unspent balance of a grant authorized in 1984 (decision 40/451). The need for a decision on UNITAR's long-term financing and future was stressed in another December resolution (40/214).

The Economic and Social Council requested the University for Peace in Costa Rica, which had held its first course in 1984, to report to the Secretary-General on its development, activities and future plans, including post-graduate programmes (1985/2).

Topics related to this chapter. Operational activities: technical co-operation through UNDP—staff-related matters. Food: food problems; food aid. Science and technology: brain drain. Environment: environmental activities. Human rights: human rights of disabled persons.

Health

Human and environmental health

During 1985, health-related environmental activities were conducted by the United Nations Environment Programme (UNEP), the World Health Organization (WHO) and the Food and Agriculture Organization of the United Nations (FAO).

A healthy environment was one of the main prerequisites for human health as well as for environmental protection, the UNEP Executive Director stated in his 1985 annual report.[1] That understanding was the basis for close co-operation between UNEP and WHO on projects related to the chemical, biological and physical safety of man and of the environment.

Two concurrent trends were noticeable with regard to environmental health. The first was the increasing risk as more and more chemicals were released, used or dumped, many of them being mutagens or highly toxic, affecting humans, animals and other biological species. Apart from the damage they caused in terms of suffering and the death of individual victims, they could also lead to the extinction of whole species. The second trend was a growing demand for positive action to counter the threats of chemical, biological and physical environmental agents.

UNEP played a central role, particularly in developing countries, in identifying potentially harmful agents, promoting the enactment and enforcement of improved control measures on their use and movement, and providing advice and technical materials to improve environmental health (see p. 801).

WHO, in co-operation with the World Federation of Associations of Clinical Toxicology Centres and Poison Control Centres, prepared to assist developing countries in establishing facilities for medical emergencies arising from acute chemical intoxication. It also prepared chemical safety data sheets for the chemicals used in those countries, summarizing information *inter alia* on the physical, chemical and toxicological properties of those substances; on first aid, environment protection measures, and explosion and fire hazards; and on safety, storage and transport precautions, and spillage and disposal procedures.

The UNEP Global Environmental Monitoring System (see p. 800), in co-operation with WHO, monitored urban air, water quality and food contamination. Under a UNEP/WHO Human Exposure Assessment Locations programme, health-related monitoring continued (see p. 803).

The assessment of air, water and land pollution sources on the basis of WHO guidelines was promoted through national workshops—for example, at Buenos Aires, Argentina (July), and Jilin, China (September); through regional courses, as in Kuwait (September); and through co-operative activities for intercountry training, such as those of the Pan American Center for Human Ecology and Health. As a result of those workshops, national experts drew up pollution source inventories in a number of countries.

An International Code of Conduct on the Distribution and Use of Pesticides was approved by the FAO Conference in November. The Code's basic objectives were to identify potential health and environmental hazards in the distribution and use of pesticides, and to define responsibilities and set voluntary standards for the regulation, distribution and use of pesticides. Pesticide poisoning was estimated to kill more than 10,000 persons a year world-wide and cause serious illness in about 400,000 others.

Health and nutrition

In 1985, UNU (see p. 785) conducted work on food, nutrition, biotechnology and poverty.[2] Policy-oriented activities aimed at helping developing countries increase and improve food supplies, increase knowledge of human nutrition and simultaneously reduce poverty through employment and improvement of income levels. The work on biotechnology was to help ensure that the developing world would benefit from major advances.

Chronic dietary energy deficiency continued to affect the majority of the population in many developing countries. Definitive information on the benefits of increasing caloric intake and additional studies on chronic energy deficiency in individual societies were urgently needed. The Sub-Committee on Nutrition of the Administrative Committee on Coordination (ACC) shared the costs of a workshop (Washington, D. C., 28 October–1 November) organized by UNU to evaluate research results and formulate guidelines for further research.

Studies were completed in villages in Egypt and Indonesia on the functional consequences of iron deficiency.

As part of the start-up activities of a regional food and nutrition project for Africa, UNU sponsored a workshop on need-based information service in appropriate food science and technology for Africa (Lagos, Nigeria, 3-8 June). Participants from 16 African nations met with information, documentation and library science experts to identify food science and technology information needs in Africa.

UNU and the United Nations Children's Fund (UNICEF) jointly supported studies by social scientists in 14 developing countries on the impact of nutrition and primary health care on the health knowledge and health-seeking behaviour of families. WHO was strongly supportive of the research.

Activities in 1985 of the International Network of Food Data Systems, set up by UNU to facilitate world-wide access, retrieval, interchange and harmonization of food composition data, included the preparation of guidelines for methodological improvement and quality control and for classification and nomenclature of foods, and plans for the computer storage and retrieval of regional data.

Scientists from developed and developing countries carried out research on nitrogen fixation in the root system of rice, using advanced techniques such as recombinant deoxyribonucleic acid (DNA) and tissue culture. Seven research projects had been started in China, Malaysia, Nigeria, Sri Lanka, Thailand, Viet Nam and the Korean peninsula, jointly with FAO and the International Atomic Energy Agency and with institutes in Canada, France, Japan, the Netherlands, the USSR and the United States.

In co-operation with Venezuela, UNU was examining possibilities for establishing a biotechnology programme in Latin America and the Caribbean which would lead to the setting up of a UNU research and training centre at Caracas. The University began work on vaccines and diagnostics to combat brucellosis in animals and humans, a disease most prevalent in the Latin America region.

The University was attempting to establish one or more networks for biotechnology research in Africa. Together with the International Foundation for Science, of Stockholm, Sweden, it organized a workshop on possible areas of research (Douala, Cameroon, 10-20 October), attended by more than

30 African scientists. UNU also sponsored a meeting for policy-makers (Helsinki, Finland, 12-16 August) on educational, social, legal, ethical, industrial and environmental issues affecting the implementation of biotechnology in developing countries.

During 1985, four issues of the *Food and Nutrition Bulletin* were published with a total of 46 articles; the special September issue was devoted to household-level food production. UNU supported a *Directory of Anthropologists and Sociologists Concerned with Food and Nutrition*, compiled by the International Commission on Anthropology and Food of the International Union of Anthropology and Ethnographic Sciences, and co-published with Oxford University Press *Nutrition and Development*, a collection of nine papers prepared following a 1980 meeting of the International Food Policy Research Institute.

ACC activities

In its annual overview report for 1984/85,[3] ACC discussed the work of its Sub-Committee on Nutrition in carrying out inter-agency work. The Sub-Committee had previously identified three areas for priority action by the United Nations system which had been endorsed by ACC in 1984:[4] improving country-level support for nutrition activities; control of vitamin-A and iodine deficiencies; and increased attention to Africa's food and nutrition problems.

Much of the Sub-Committee's eleventh session (Nairobi, Kenya, 11-15 February 1985)[5] was devoted to discussing co-ordinated support of nutrition activities in Kenya; should those efforts prove successful, attempts would be made to introduce the approach in other countries.

ACC endorsed the Sub-Committee's proposal for a 10-year programme to prevent and control vitamin-A deficiency, xerophthalmia and nutritional blindness. The proposal described the prevalence and severity of the problem, national prevention and control programmes and activities that could be included in the programme. The work had been outlined in detail by WHO which the Sub-Committee had designated as lead-agency; other organizations were requested to prepare similar outlines.

At its second regular 1985 session in October,[6] ACC endorsed a report on the prevention and control of endemic goitre, endemic cretinism and other iodine deficiency disorders;[7] assigned high priority to the control and prevention of iodine deficiency disorders; and urged United Nations organizations to collaborate with the Sub-Committee in preparing a 10-year plan of action, also with WHO as lead agency. The Sub-Committee strongly favoured formation of a consultative group on iodine deficiency disease.

Discussing the famine crisis in Africa and the role of nutritionists in its alleviation, the Sub-Committee decided that its Advisory Group on Nutrition was to prepare a work plan and make recommendations. The Consultative Committee on Substantive Questions (Programme Matters) (CCSQ(PROG)) of ACC, at its April 1985 session, expressed appreciation for the initiative, trusting that the Sub-Committee would bear in mind the desirability of not extending its mandate beyond its technical scope, particularly with regard to the African crisis.

Disabled persons

Implementation of the Programme of Action

A number of measures were undertaken in 1985 by the United Nations system[8] to implement the 1982 World Programme of Action concerning Disabled Persons[9] and the United Nations Decade of Disabled Persons (1983-1992), also proclaimed in 1982.[10]

The International Initiative against Avoidable Disablement (IMPACT), established in 1983 in collaboration with the United Nations Development Programme (UNDP), UNICEF, WHO and the United Nations Centre for Social Development and Humanitarian Affairs (CSDHA) to support the Decade, continued to promote disability prevention and effective rehabilitation at the national and regional levels through low-cost techniques.

Advisory services on disability policies and programmes were provided during 1984-1985 by the United Nations Department of Technical Co-operation for Development (DTCD), in co-operation with CSDHA, to 14 countries: Angola, Bahrain, China, Djibouti, Guinea, Jamaica, Jordan, Kuwait, Libyan Arab Jamahiriya, Madagascar, Malta, Morocco, Peru, Philippines. DTCD was also establishing a National Orthopaedic and Rehabilitation Centre at Nouakchott, Mauritania.

In 1985, the Office of the United Nations High Commissioner for Refugees supported 26 projects for 5,719 disabled refugees in Africa, Asia, Europe and Latin America. It also provided severely disabled refugees with specialized medical treatment abroad and resettlement. The United Nations Relief and Works Agency for Palestine Refugees in the Near East continued to provide disabled Palestinian refugee children with basic education, training and home-based services, and ran a training centre for visually disabled persons in the Gaza Strip.

Following a severe volcanic eruption in Colombia in November, the United Nations Disaster Relief Co-ordinator provided artificial limbs for about 100 persons.

The 1983 Vocational Rehabilitation and Employment (Disabled Persons) Convention[11] of the International Labour Organisation (ILO) became operative on 20 June 1985. During 1985, ILO provided nearly 50 developing countries with expert and consultant assistance, advisory services, fellowships and equipment, with special attention to alleviating the shortage of national vocational rehabilitation personnel.

Attention was given by the United Nations Educational, Scientific and Cultural Organization (UNESCO) to improving methods for integrating disabled children and youth into normal education structures and incorporating disability concerns into teacher training programmes. During 1984-1985, more than 60 countries benefited from UNESCO's special education activities.

Childhood disability prevention and rehabilitation were included in the activities of UNICEF. Disability prevention and community-based rehabilitation were promoted in a number of major primary health care programmes of WHO.

The 1985 FAO Conference requested that disability prevention and services be expanded in rural areas. CSDHA, entrusted with helping implement the World Programme of Action,[10] published four issues of the *Disabled Persons Bulletin* in English, French and Spanish.

In several countries, national committees established for the 1981 International Year of Disabled Persons (IYDP) continued to promote activities in support of the Decade; in others, the work had been transferred to the private sector. Disability-related activities had been assumed by governmental bodies in a number of other States.

The World Programme of Action encouraged Member States to make use of the technical expertise and promotional capabilities of non-governmental organizations (NGOs). A group of NGOs based at Vienna, Austria, established in December 1985 the Vienna Non-Governmental Organization Committee on Disabled Persons to assist the United Nations in publicizing the Decade.

Disabled Peoples' International reported that its Second World Congress (Nassau, Bahamas, 19-22 September), organized with the financial support of the Voluntary Fund for the United Nations Decade of Disabled Persons, directed attention to the Decade and to the issue of human rights and disabled persons. Other 1985 activities of Disabled Peoples' International included a European regional conference of disabled persons, organized in co-operation with the Swedish National Society for Associations of the Disabled (Gothenburg, 3 and 4 June), and a leadership development seminar, for the southern Africa subregion, organized in co-operation with the National Council of Disabled Persons of Zimbabwe (Bulawayo, 29 June-6 July).

Among other NGOs, the World Medical Association gave wide publicity to the Decade. The World Veterans Federation adopted at its eighteenth General Assembly (Rotterdam, Netherlands, 18-22 November) a resolution on the basic rights of disabled persons. The League of Red Cross and Red Crescent Societies identified roles that its members could play in implementing the World Programme of Action. The International Federation of Disabled Workers and Civilian Handicapped requested member organizations to support the Decade. A project by the World Blind Union, setting forth action plans for visually disabled persons in Africa, Asia and Latin America, was presented in May to Governments and organizations around the world.

Two NGO umbrella bodies, the Council of World Organizations Interested in the Handicapped and Disabled Peoples' International, participated regularly in inter-agency meetings on the Decade (see below).

Inter-agency co-operation. Inter-agency co-operation in the disability field continued to be carried out in response to specific programme and project needs. The third inter-agency meeting on the United Nations Decade of Disabled Persons (Vienna, 11-13 March 1985)[12] discussed position papers by United Nations organs and NGOs on implementation of the World Programme of Action; the procedure for monitoring the Programme's implementation; the terms of reference, cost and time-frame of inter-organizational task forces; and the activities of the United Nations Trust Fund for IYDP (see p. 779), IMPACT (see above), the Trust Fund for Victims of Torture (see Chapter XVIII of this section) and the Trust Fund for Handicapped Refugees. It was recommended that a fourth inter-agency meeting be held for three days in March 1986.

In its 1984/85 overview report,[3] ACC noted that CCSQ(PROG) had approved the convening of the March 1986 inter-agency meeting, and that there had been close co-operation within the ACC framework regarding implementation of the Programme and the Decade.

The second regional inter-agency consultation on the Decade by the Economic and Social Commission for Asia and the Pacific (Bangkok, Thailand, August) reconstituted itself as the nucleus of an Asia-Pacific inter-organizational task force on disability issues.

Reports of the Secretary-General. In response to a 1984 General Assembly resolution,[13] the Secretary-General submitted in October 1985 a report on the implementation of the World Programme of Action and the Decade.[14] As at 9 August, 44 Governments had replied to a request for information on national committees which had continued to function beyond the 1981 IYDP or which had been established for the Decade. Twenty Governments had established IYDP committees, which were continuing to co-ordinate activities on behalf of the disabled. The report also reviewed measures undertaken by the United Nations system, such as the setting of guidelines for priority actions, dissemination of information, and the employment of disabled persons within the system.

The Commission for Social Development, at its February 1985 session,[15] considered a November 1984 progress report by the Secretary-General on national experience in implementing the Programme of Action.[16] Due to lack of consensus, the Commission did not take action on a draft resolution by which the Economic and Social Council would have expressed concern about the lack of publicity given to the Decade, and requested the Secretary-General to use the United Nations Trust Fund for IYDP to meet growing requests for technical co-operation and to continue to support and monitor the Programme of Action as a major activity of the disability programme of CSDHA.

ECONOMIC AND SOCIAL COUNCIL ACTION

On 29 May 1985, on the recommendation of its Second (Social) Committee, the Economic and Social Council adopted without vote **resolution 1985/35**.

United Nations Decade of Disabled Persons

The Economic and Social Council,

Taking into consideration General Assembly resolutions 37/52 of 3 December 1982, by which the Assembly adopted the World Programme of Action concerning Disabled Persons, and 37/53 of 3 December 1982 on the implementation of the World Programme of Action, in which the Assembly proclaimed the period 1983-1992 United Nations Decade of Disabled Persons,

Also taking into consideration Council resolution 1983/19 of 26 May 1983, in which the Council, *inter alia*, requested the Secretary-General to monitor and support the implementation of the World Programme of Action by enlisting extrabudgetary resources,

Further taking into consideration General Assembly resolution 39/26 of 23 November 1984, in which the Assembly reiterated the need for an effective implementation of the World Programme of Action,

Taking note with appreciation of the reports of the Secretary-General on national experience in implementing the World Programme of Action concerning Disabled Persons and related activities of the United Nations and other international organizations and on the implementation of the World Programme of Action,

Concerned with the necessity of keeping alive the momentum generated by the International Year of Disabled Persons and of observing the United Nations Decade of Disabled Persons and using it, in particular, as a time frame for the implementation of the World Programme of Action,

Noting that the Centre for Social Development and Humanitarian Affairs of the Department of International Economic and Social Affairs of the United Nations Secretariat has been designated, in paragraph 156 of the World Programme of Action concerning Disabled Persons, as the focal point within the United Nations system for co-ordinating and monitoring the implementation

of the World Programme of Action, including its review and appraisal,

Recalling that in paragraph 195 of the World Programme of Action it is stated that the United Nations system should carry out a critical periodic evaluation of progress made in implementing the World Programme of Action and to that end should select appropriate indicators for evaluation in consultation with Member States, and that the Commission for Social Development should play an important role in this respect,

1. *Appeals* to Member States, organizations of the United Nations system and non-governmental organizations to help make the United Nations Decade of Disabled Persons more widely known as a time frame for the implementation of the World Programme of Action concerning Disabled Persons and to continue to take action to implement the objectives of the World Programme of Action;

2. *Requests* the Secretary-General to pursue his efforts, with a view to ensuring optimal utilization of resources in order to give appropriate publicity to the objectives of the United Nations Decade of Disabled Persons proclaimed by the General Assembly as a long-term plan of action for the implementation of the World Programme of Action concerning Disabled Persons;

3. *Requests* the Secretary-General to continue to support, monitor and evaluate the implementation of the World Programme of Action, including its periodic revisions, as a major activity of the programme on disabled persons of the Centre for Social Development and Humanitarian Affairs, and to continue to organize on a regular basis, at least once a year, the inter-agency meetings on the United Nations Decade of Disabled Persons for co-operation and harmonization of action by the United Nations system in this field;

4. *Also requests* the Secretary-General to enlist and utilize the resources of the United Nations Trust Fund for the International Year of Disabled Persons to meet growing requests for assistance, advisory services and technical co-operation programmes submitted by developing countries and organizations of disabled persons for the implementation of the World Programme of Action;

5. *Also requests* the Secretary-General, in order to facilitate contributions by Governments, to include the United Nations Trust Fund for the International Year of Disabled Persons, on an annual basis, among the programmes for which funds are pledged at the United Nations Pledging Conference for Development Activities;

6. *Further requests* the Secretary-General to continue to keep the Commission for Social Development informed of progress made in the monitoring and evaluation of the implementation of the World Programme of Action.

Economic and Social Council resolution 1985/35

29 May 1985   Meeting 23   Adopted without vote

Approved by Second Committee (E/1985/96 & Corr.1) without vote, 24 May (meeting 15); 6-nation draft (E/1985/C.2/L.5/Rev.1), orally revised; agenda item 17.
Sponsors: Belgium, Canada, Costa Rica, Finland, Italy, Morocco.

GENERAL ASSEMBLY ACTION

On 29 November 1985, the General Assembly, on the recommendation of the Third (Social, Humanitarian and Cultural) Committee, adopted without vote **resolution 40/31**.

**Implementation of the World Programme of Action
concerning Disabled Persons and
United Nations Decade of Disabled Persons**

The General Assembly,

Recalling its resolutions 37/52 of 3 December 1982, by which it adopted the World Programme of Action concerning Disabled Persons, 37/53 of 3 December 1982, by which, *inter alia,* it proclaimed the period 1983-1992 the United Nations Decade of Disabled Persons, 38/28 of 22 November 1983, in which it recognized the United Nations Trust Fund for the International Year of Disabled Persons as an important instrument for the implementation of the World Programme of Action concerning Disabled Persons and the desirability of the continuation of the Trust Fund throughout the Decade, and 39/26 of 23 November 1984, by which it adopted further specific measures for implementation of the World Programme of Action,

Taking note of Economic and Social Council resolution 1985/35 of 29 May 1985, in which, *inter alia,* the Secretary-General was requested, in order to facilitate contributions by Governments, to include, on an annual basis, the United Nations Trust Fund for the International Year of Disabled Persons among the programmes for which funds are pledged at the United Nations Pledging Conference for Development Activities,

Noting with satisfaction the concrete measures already carried out by the Governments of Member States, the bodies and organizations of the United Nations system and non-governmental organizations to implement the objectives of the World Programme of Action within the framework of the United Nations Decade of Disabled Persons,

Noting with appreciation the steps taken by the United Nations system and by non-governmental organizations concerned to establish a monitoring procedure and prepare a consolidated questionnaire to monitor the implementation of the World Programme of Action,

Noting with concern that, in spite of a number of contributions made by Governments between 1981 and 1985 and constant appeals by the General Assembly and other United Nations organs to contribute to the financing of activities for the disabled, progress towards the improvement of the situation of the disabled in the developing countries has been slow,

Noting with serious concern the alarming situation of disabled persons in developing countries and the critical economic situation in a number of countries, in particular in Africa and Latin America and the least developed countries,

Mindful that, since developing countries are experiencing difficulties in mobilizing resources, international co-operation should be encouraged to assist national efforts in implementing the World Programme of Action and the United Nations Decade of Disabled Persons,

Taking note of the report of the Secretary-General on the implementation of the World Programme of Action concerning Disabled Persons and the United Nations Decade of Disabled Persons,

Expressing its appreciation to Member States and organizations, in particular to the twenty-five States that have donated $1.6 million over the past few years,

Expressing its appreciation of the useful role played by the United Nations Trust Fund for the International Year of Disabled Persons in implementing the World Programme of Action,

1. *Urges* all Member States and other donors to consider further generous contributions to the United Nations Trust Fund for the International Year of Disabled Persons;

2. *Expresses its appreciation* to Member States that have established national committees or similar bodies to co-ordinate activities in the field of disability and encourages all Member States to do so;

3. *Invites* Member States to reinforce national committees as focal points for the United Nations Decade of Disabled Persons, to stimulate activities at the national level, to mobilize public opinion on behalf of the Decade, to participate in the implementation of disability projects with regard to the International Year of Disabled Persons and to assist in monitoring and evaluating the implementation of the World Programme of Action concerning Disabled Persons;

4. *Encourages* Member States to translate the World Programme of Action into national languages;

5. *Invites* Member States, in close collaboration with the national committees and non-governmental organizations concerned, to submit their replies to the questionnaire for the first round of monitoring and implementing the World Programme of Action to the Secretary-General as soon as possible for inclusion in his report on the evaluation of progress at mid-Decade, to be submitted to the General Assembly at its forty-second session;

6. *Urges* the Secretary-General to comply with paragraphs 157 and 158 of the World Programme of Action;

7. *Invites* all States to give high priority to consideration of projects concerning the prevention of disabilities, rehabilitation and the equalization of the opportunities of disabled persons within the framework of bilateral assistance;

8. *Reiterates* the need to give greater publicity to the United Nations Decade of Disabled Persons and calls upon Member States, national committees and non-governmental organizations to assist in publicizing the Decade by all appropriate means;

9. *Takes note* of the measures taken by the bodies and organizations of the United Nations system to promote equal employment opportunities for disabled persons and urges them to continue their efforts in this field;

10. *Endorses,* in particular, the terms of reference proposed in the report of the Secretary-General for the United Nations Trust Fund for the International Year of Disabled Persons, henceforth to be called the Voluntary Fund for the United Nations Decade of Disabled Persons;

11. *Requests* the Secretary-General to continue to administer donated funds, using them for projects under the present structure of the Trust Fund, and in addition to make new provisions in order to offer a selection of projects to donor countries which might be willing to finance a particular programme under the "Special Purpose Contributions";

12. *Reaffirms* that the resources of the Trust Fund should be used to support catalytic and innovative activities in order to implement further the objectives of the World Programme of Action within the framework of the United Nations Decade of Disabled Persons, with priority given, as appropriate, to programmes and projects of the least developed countries;

13. *Requests* all bodies and organizations of the United Nations system administering assistance projects

to take into account the concerns of disabled persons in their projects for the rehabilitation of the disabled and their integration into society, as well as to include disabled persons in their overall planning objectives;

14. *Requests* the Secretary-General to report to the General Assembly at its forty-first session on the implementation of the present resolution;

15. *Further requests* the Secretary-General to include in the report requested in paragraph 14 above information on preparations for the meeting of experts to evaluate progress at the mid-Decade, as provided for in paragraph 16 of resolution 37/53 and paragraph 13 of resolution 39/26, as well as information on the establishment of inter-organizational task forces, as recommended by the Advisory Committee for the International Year of Disabled Persons at its third and fourth sessions and by the General Assembly in paragraph 17 of its resolution 36/77 in order to provide support services for the exchange of technical information and transfer of technological know-how and other activities in the fields of prevention, rehabilitation and equalization of opportunities in developing countries;

16. *Decides* to include in the provisional agenda of its forty-first session the item entitled "Implementation of the World Programme of Action concerning Disabled Persons and United Nations Decade of Disabled Persons".

General Assembly resolution 40/31

29 November 1985   Meeting 96   Adopted without vote

Approved by Third Committee (A/40/880) without vote, 11 November (meeting 37); 35-nation draft (A/C.3/40/L.18), orally revised; agenda item 97.

Sponsors: Austria, Bangladesh, Belgium, Botswana, Burkina Faso, Canada, Central African Republic, Chile, China, Colombia, Costa Rica, Egypt, Gambia, Germany, Federal Republic of, Guinea, Jordan, Kenya, Libyan Arab Jamahiriya, Morocco, Nigeria, Oman, Pakistan, Paraguay, Peru, Philippines, Romania, Senegal, Somalia, Sudan, Swaziland, United States, Uruguay, Venezuela, Yugoslavia, Zaire.

Meeting numbers. GA 40th session: 3rd Committee 16-23, 30, 37; plenary 96.

UN employment of disabled persons

The March 1985 inter-agency meeting on the United Nations Decade of Disabled Persons (see p. 776) stated that persons with disabilities should have the same rights as any other citizens in being considered for posts for which they were qualified, and that the United Nations should declare employment opportunities open to all qualified applicants, regardless of sex, religion, ethnic origin or disability. The quota system was not an appropriate method of increasing work opportunities for disabled persons, the meeting stated; it was considered divisive and discriminatory by disabled persons themselves and by many concerned organizations. Medical and personnel departments should be instructed to ensure that disabled persons were given full opportunity to compete for available posts. External recruitment drives should ensure that disabled applicants were informed of job opportunities and encouraged to compete on equal terms with non-disabled persons.

CCSQ(PROG), at its first regular session of 1985 in April,[17] endorsed in general the principles and recommendations elaborated at the meeting and referred them to the Consultative Committee on Administrative Questions (Personnel Matters) (CCAQ(PER)) for consideration of their administrative implications.

In his October 1985 report[14] on implementation of the World Programme of Action (see p. 776), the Secretary-General stated that there were employment opportunities for disabled persons at the United Nations and recruitment had included such persons, including consultants, for a variety of functions. The United Nations Office of Personnel Services (OPS) continued to support the work of CCAQ(PER) in connection with the drafting of a policy statement on employment of disabled persons in United Nations organizations; specific recommendations to improve employment opportunities of disabled persons at all levels had been formulated in 1983, and further action in pursuit of policy objectives related to such opportunities in the Secretariat was being undertaken by OPS in consultation with staff representatives.

In **resolution 40/31**, the General Assembly noted the measures taken by United Nations organizations to promote equal employment opportunities for disabled persons and urged them to continue their efforts.

Trust funds

Voluntary Fund for the Decade

The United Nations Trust Fund for IYDP, renamed in November 1985 Voluntary Fund for the United Nations Decade of Disabled Persons, continued to support activities to implement the World Programme of Action and to realize the Programme's objectives of equalization of opportunities for disabled persons, prevention of disabilities and rehabilitation. Fund-supported activities included promotional activities; support to organizations of or concerned with disabled persons; data collection and applied research; training; and information. Between January 1980 and June 1985, the Fund disbursed more than $1.1 million for 51 projects, the majority of them (61 per cent) in developing regions, with Africa accounting for approximately one fourth of resources disbursed. While the priority in the allocation of Fund resources continued to be for catalytic and innovative activities, requests for Fund resources increasingly related to national capability-building efforts as an essential means to further implementation of the Programme of Action.

Since resources available were considerably less than those required to meet requests for assistance, contributions having substantially diminished since IYDP, the Fund sought to establish co-financing agreements for disability-related projects of developing countries with bilateral development assistance agencies, non-governmental funding entities and the private sector.

In 1985, the Trust Fund had a total income of $175,100 and expenditures of $313,042. Contributions to the Fund were made by Austria ($6,713), France ($10,526), Greece ($5,000), Oman ($5,000) and Zambia ($435).[18]

At the third inter-agency meeting on the Decade in March (see p. 776), attention was called to the problem of replenishing the Fund. The meeting concluded that organizations and bodies should present to future inter-agency meetings a detailed account of their Fund projects, and interested NGOs should use their good offices to approach Governments on behalf of the Fund.[12]

The Economic and Social Council, in **resolution 1985/35**, requested the Secretary-General to utilize the Fund's resources to meet growing requests by developing countries and organizations of disabled persons for assistance, advisory services and technical co-operation programmes, and to include the Fund among the programmes for which funds were pledged at the United Nations Pledging Conference for Development Activities.

The Fund participated for the first time in the November 1985 Pledging Conference (see p. 463), at which it received pledges from six Governments totalling $52,861.

In his October report on implementation of the World Programme of Action,[14] the Secretary-General stated that the Fund had been an important component of efforts to maintain the momentum generated by IYDP and its continuation would be essential for successful implementation of the Programme. The Decade having been proclaimed on the understanding that no additional resources from the United Nations would be required, extrabudgetary resources would be necessary.

Taking into account the views expressed at the 1984 General Assembly session and in the light of the Fund's operational experience, the Secretary-General elaborated further the terms of reference for its continuation. The Fund's resources should be used to finance consultative and advisory services concerning the design and development of long-term national disability policies and programmes; technical co-operation activities and promoting the exchange of information, transfer of technology and know-how in the areas of prevention, rehabilitation and equalization of opportunities; the development of human resources and training activities; inter-agency collaboration at the national, regional and international levels; and data collection, research and analysis. The Fund's resources should be used mainly within two priority areas: to support catalytic and innovative projects of special importance and activities in new and emerging areas concerning disabled persons. In order to reflect the Fund's future scope of activities, the Secretary-General proposed to rename it United Nations Fund on Disability.

As part of the monitoring activities concerning implementation of the World Programme of Action at the mid-point of the Decade, in 1987, preparations were under way to convene a meeting of experts, as recommended by the Assembly in 1984,[13] the Secretary-General stated in his conclusions.

By **resolution 40/31**, the Assembly endorsed the terms of reference proposed by the Secretary-General for the Fund, which it renamed the Voluntary Fund for the United Nations Decade of Disabled Persons. It urged Member States and other donors to contribute generously, and requested the Secretary-General to continue to administer funds, for projects under the current Fund structure, and, in addition, to make new provisions to offer a selection of projects to donor countries willing to finance a particular programme under Special Purpose Contributions. The Assembly reaffirmed that the Fund should be used to support catalytic and innovative activities, with priority given to programmes of the least developed countries.

Trust Fund for Norway's Contribution to the International Year

In 1985, the income of the Trust Fund for Norway's Contribution to the International Year of Disabled Persons was $113,432, while expenditures totalled $68,005.

REFERENCES

[1]UNEP/GC.14/2. [2]A/41/31. [3]E/1985/57. [4]YUN 1984, p. 735. [5]ACC/1985/PG/5 & Add.1. [6]ACC/1985/DEC/16-29 (dec. 1985/29). [7]ACC/1985/OC/CRP.5. [8]A/41/605 & Corr.1. [9]YUN 1982, p. 981, GA res. 37/52, 3 Dec. 1982. [10]*Ibid.*, p. 983, GA res. 37/53, 3 Dec. 1982. [11]YUN 1983, p. 1221. [12]ACC/1985/PG/8. [13]YUN 1984, p. 733, GA res. 39/26, 23 Nov. 1984. [14]A/40/728 & Corr.1. [15]E/1985/24. [16]YUN 1984, p. 734. [17]ACC/1985/4. [18]A/41/5, vol. 1.

Human resources

Human resources development

In June 1985, the Governing Council of UNDP considered an April note by the UNDP Administrator,[1] in which he proposed to convene an international workshop of eminent experts to advise him on human resources development, its role in the development process, factors affecting it, new approaches and technical co-operation, which might be followed by regional and subregional workshops or round-table meetings.

The Council, in a decision of 28 June,[2] welcomed the proposal for a series of workshops and appealed to Governments to support them.

In another April note,[3] the Administrator proposed establishing a UNDP human resources facility to supply skilled manpower to developing countries through short-term missions. The Council, on 29 June,[4] authorized him to establish for a trial period of two years, beginning on 1 July 1985, a UNDP focal point or clearing-house to channel highly qualified advisers to developing countries; the focal point would collaborate with the United Nations system, NGOs and other interested organizations in making expertise available. The Council urged United Nations agencies and other parties on 28 June[5] to improve their recruitment policies and procedures with respect to UNDP project personnel (see p. 484).

The Secretary-General, responding to a 1984 General Assembly resolution,[6] submitted a report in September 1985, with a later addendum,[7] on the role of qualified national personnel in the social and economic development of developing countries. To his request for information on the matter, he had received replies from 20 countries and four United Nations organizations and specialized agencies.

In an 18 November statement before the Assembly's Second (Economic and Financial) Committee, the UNDP Administrator pointed out that, although the human factor in development had not always been given the attention it deserved, there seemed to be agreement that the economic performance of many developing countries did not always match the expectations created by capital inflows. Experience had shown the importance of creating the human and infrastructural capacities needed for capital to be utilized effectively; accordingly, action had been taken to meet developing countries' needs for specialized knowledge and skills. A Round Table on the Human Dimensions of Development had been convened (Istanbul, Turkey, 1-4 September), and Japan had agreed to co-sponsor with UNDP a global human resources workshop at Tokyo in 1986.

GENERAL ASSEMBLY ACTION

On 17 December 1985, on the recommendation of the Second Committee, the General Assembly adopted without vote **resolution 40/213**.

Role of qualified national personnel in the social and economic development of developing countries
The General Assembly,
Referring to its resolutions 33/135 of 19 December 1978, 35/80 of 5 December 1980, 37/228 of 20 December 1982 and 39/219 of 18 December 1984 on the role of qualified national personnel in the social and economic development of developing countries,
Recalling its resolutions 3201(S-VI) and 3202(S-VI) of 1 May 1974, containing the Declaration and the Programme of Action on the Establishment of a New International Economic Order, and 3281(XXIX) of 12 December 1974, containing the Charter of Economic Rights and Duties of States,

Desiring to promote full implementation of the provisions of the International Development Strategy for the Third United Nations Development Decade concerning the important role of qualified national personnel in the achievement of the development goals of the developing countries,
Reaffirming the crucial role of human resources in the socio-economic development process of developing countries,
Taking into account the increasing importance of United Nations activities in the field of human resources development as they are envisaged in future years,
Recognizing that the training of qualified national personnel is an important and integral part of human resources development,
1. *Takes note* of the report of the Secretary-General on the role of qualified national personnel in the social and economic development of developing countries;
2. *Reaffirms* the importance of implementing the provisions of its resolution 37/228;
3. *Requests* the Secretary-General to continue to monitor the further implementation of its resolution 39/219;
4. *Further requests* the Secretary-General to take into account the need for an integrated and multidisciplinary approach to all aspects of human resources development, in particular the training of qualified national personnel, in the programmes of work of the United Nations and the organizations of its system;
5. *Invites* the Secretary-General to continue his consultations with the Governments of Member States, in accordance with paragraph 2 of resolution 39/219, on the role of qualified national personnel in the social and economic development of developing countries, and to submit a progress report, through the Governing Council of the United Nations Development Programme and the Economic and Social Council, to the General Assembly at its forty-second session.

General Assembly resolution 40/213

17 December 1985   Meeting 120   Adopted without vote

Approved by Second Committee (A/40/1041) without vote, 9 December (meeting 49); draft by Vice-Chairman (A/C.2/40/L.108), based on informal consultations on draft by Afghanistan, Algeria, Angola, Bangladesh, Benin, Bulgaria, Burkina Faso, Cape Verde, Congo, Cuba, Democratic Yemen, Ethiopia, German Democratic Republic, Guinea-Bissau, Guyana, Lao People's Democratic Republic, Madagascar, Mali, Mongolia, Nicaragua, Syrian Arab Republic, Ukrainian SSR, Viet Nam and Zambia (A/C.2/40/L.90); agenda item 85 *(e)*.

Meeting numbers. GA 40th session: 2nd Committee 35-42, 44, 46, 49; plenary 120.

By adopting **resolution 40/205**, the Assembly endorsed conclusions and recommendations on human resources made during the mid-term global review of the implementation of the Substantial New Programme of Action for the 1980s for the Least Developed Countries.

UN Institute for Training and Research

Activities of UNITAR

The 1985 activities of the United Nations Institute for Training and Research, an autonomous organization within the United Nations system, were described by its Executive Director in a report to the General Assembly covering the period from 1 July 1984 to 30 June 1986.[8]

UNITAR's training programme included training courses in multilateral diplomacy and international co-operation for diplomats, government and United Nations officials, and workshops on the structure, retrieval and use of United Nations documentation, international legal instruments, and international negotiation. Its training programme for economic and social development emphasized training in development management; modernization of public administration, in particular in least developed countries; management of public enterprises; and finance management. Activities included an international symposium on the modernization of public administration training in African countries (Berlin, 15-26 July) and an international workshop on participation of women in rural development (Bacu, USSR, 20 October–2 November).

Under UNITAR's research programme, financed mainly through special purpose grants, the UNITAR/UNDP Information Centre for Heavy Crude and Tar Sands continued to develop its activities and organized the Third International Conference on Heavy Crude and Tar Sands (Long Beach, California, United States, 22-31 July) (see p. 692). The UNITAR/UNDP Centre on Small Energy Resources, established in 1984 at Rome, Italy, as a clearing-house and bridge between donors and developing countries, became operational in 1985. Preparations were launched in May for a conference on the future of Latin America, to be held at Caracas, Venezuela, in 1986.

The Secretary-General reported in October 1985 to the Assembly[9] that the UNITAR Board of Trustees (New York, 9-11 September) considered a consultant's report outlining three possible options for UNITAR's future: the closing down of the Institute; its transformation into a perspective studies and analysis unit attached to the Office of the Secretary-General; and its restructuring with alternative institutional arrangements. The Board agreed that closing down UNITAR was undesirable and that attaching it to the Secretary-General's Office would be tantamount to shutting it down. The suggestion for restructuring came closest to the Board's own view of a future direction for UNITAR.

The Director-General for Development and International Economic Co-operation, in an 8 November statement before the Assembly's Second Committee, supported the Secretary-General's opinion that the option most likely to result in UNITAR's rejuvenation would involve a concentration of research activities on United Nations policy issues; such research would complement the work of the Secretariat and reflect the interests of Member States. In future, the Institute's training activities would be more closely related to its research programmes, while continuing to focus on enhancing the knowledge of diplomats and national officials in multilateral co-operation. The Secretary-General was not proposing any change in the institutional position of UNITAR, although closer co-operation with UNU should be explored.

Finances of UNITAR

Income and expenditures in 1985

In 1985, UNITAR's General Fund income—mainly from government contributions and a $600,000 United Nations subvention—totalled $2,510,721 and expenditures $2,407,365. The income of the Special Purpose Grants Fund was $2,077,618 and expenditures $1,991,630.[10]

CONTRIBUTIONS TO THE UNITAR GENERAL FUND, 1985
(as at 31 December 1985; in US dollar equivalent)

Country	Amount
Algeria	10,000
Argentina	20,000
Austria	21,730
Bahamas	1,000
Barbados	250
Burundi	2,500
Cameroon	32,098
Canada	65,694
Chile	5,000
Denmark	37,583
Egypt	6,000
Finland	77,255
France	37,765
Germany, Federal Republic of	171,245
Greece	5,000
Guinea	1,000
Indonesia	10,000
Iran	10,000
Ireland	11,127
Israel	4,000
Italy	57,984
Ivory Coast	28,568
Jamaica	2,000
Japan	100,000
Kuwait	20,000
Libyan Arab Jamahiriya	50,000
Luxembourg	1,478
Malawi	930
Malta	545
Netherlands	43,453
New Zealand	4,253
Nigeria	12,111
Norway	108,950
Oman	10,000
Pakistan	10,000
Philippines	1,000
Qatar	10,000
Republic of Korea	10,000
Saudi Arabia	50,000
Spain	23,542
Sweden	101,336
Switzerland	60,845
United Republic of Tanzania	3,582
Venezuela	17,200
Yemen	1,400
Yugoslavia	5,000
Total	1,263,424

SOURCE: A/41/5/Add.4.

Accounts for 1984

In June 1985, the United Nations Board of Auditors submitted to the General Assembly the financial statements of UNITAR for 1984.[11]

In its September 1985 report on audited financial statements,[12] the Advisory Committee on Administrative and Budgetary Questions commented on the Board's remarks.

The Assembly in December, by **resolution 40/238**, accepted the 1984 financial report and statements.

Financing for 1986

The Secretary-General, in an October 1985 report,[9] recalled that the General Assembly in 1984[13] had decided to grant UNITAR up to $1.5 million, on an exceptional basis, to supplement its General Fund in 1985; the UNITAR Board of Trustees eventually had decided to reduce the UNITAR budget so as to use as little as possible of that grant. If anticipated 1985 contributions materialized, only about $750,000 of the grant would have been used; however, a significant portion of the contributions remained to be paid. Considering the uncertainty about the level of contributions, the Secretary-General recommended that the unused portion of the grant be made available to UNITAR in 1986.

The Assembly noted with regret in **resolution 40/214** that the 1985 United Nations Pledging Conference for Development Activities had been unable to provide UNITAR with the resources required to maintain the Institute during 1986; as at 30 June 1986, pledges totalled $1,273,497.

GENERAL ASSEMBLY ACTION

In December, the Assembly adopted **decision 40/451** by recorded vote.

United Nations Institute for Training and Research

At its 120th plenary meeting, on 17 December 1985, the General Assembly, on the recommendation of the Second Committee, having considered the report of the Secretary-General, decided to grant the United Nations Institute for Training and Research, in order to supplement the funds raised through voluntary contributions for its 1986 budget, an amount corresponding to the unspent balance of the grant of $1.5 million authorized for the Institute in resolution 39/177 of 17 December 1984.

General Assembly decision 40/451

122-15-13 (recorded vote)

Approved by Second Committee (A/40/1042) by recorded vote (91-15-12), 13 December (meeting 51); 2-nation draft (A/C.2/40/L.125); agenda item 86.

Sponsors: Egypt, Pakistan.

Financial implications. 5th Committee, A/40/1056; S-G, A/C.2/40/L.101, A/C.5/40/94.

Meeting numbers. GA 40th session: 2nd Committee 29, 45, 47, 51; 5th Committee 65; plenary 120.

Recorded vote in Assembly as follows:

In favour: Afghanistan, Algeria, Angola, Antigua and Barbuda, Argentina, Bahamas, Bahrain, Bangladesh, Barbados, Belize, Benin, Bhutan, Bolivia, Botswana, Brunei Darussalam, Burkina Faso, Burma, Burundi, Cameroon, Canada, Cape Verde, Central African Republic, Chad, Chile, China, Colombia, Comoros, Congo, Costa Rica, Cuba, Cyprus, Democratic Kampuchea, Democratic Yemen, Denmark, Djibouti, Dominica, Dominican Republic, Ecuador, Egypt, El Salvador, Equatorial Guinea, Ethiopia, Fiji, Finland, Gabon, Gambia, Ghana, Guatemala, Guinea, Guinea-Bissau, Haiti, Honduras, Iceland, Indonesia, Iran, Iraq, Ireland, Ivory Coast, Jamaica, Jordan, Kenya, Kuwait, Lao People's Democratic Republic,

Lesotho, Liberia, Libyan Arab Jamahiriya, Madagascar, Malawi, Malaysia, Maldives, Mali, Malta, Mauritania, Mauritius, Mexico, Morocco, Mozambique, Nepal, Nicaragua, Niger, Nigeria, Norway, Oman, Pakistan, Panama, Papua New Guinea, Paraguay, Peru, Philippines, Qatar, Rwanda, Saint Vincent and the Grenadines, Samoa, Sao Tome and Principe, Saudi Arabia, Senegal, Sierra Leone, Singapore, Somalia, Sri Lanka, Sudan, Suriname, Swaziland, Sweden, Syrian Arab Republic, Thailand, Togo, Trinidad and Tobago, Tunisia, Turkey, Uganda, United Arab Emirates, United Republic of Tanzania, Uruguay, Vanuatu, Venezuela, Viet Nam, Yemen, Yugoslavia, Zaire, Zambia, Zimbabwe.

Against: Australia, Belgium, Bulgaria, Byelorussian SSR, Czechoslovakia, France, German Democratic Republic, Hungary, Luxembourg, New Zealand, Poland, Ukrainian SSR, USSR, United Kingdom, United States.

Abstaining: Austria, Brazil, Germany, Federal Republic of, Greece, Grenada, Israel, Italy, Japan, Mongolia, Netherlands, Portugal, Romania, Spain.

Australia and the United Kingdom stated that organizations funded voluntarily should not receive funds from the regular United Nations budget. Bulgaria, speaking also on behalf of the Byelorussian SSR, Czechoslovakia, the German Democratic Republic, Hungary, Mongolia, Poland, the Ukrainian SSR and the USSR, said they objected to granting UNITAR funds from the general budget.

Brazil abstained, having also abstained on paragraph 5 of the 1984 resolution by which the Assembly had decided to grant UNITAR $1.5 million.[13] Japan believed that the Institute should operate with voluntary contributions, the Federal Republic of Germany noted that the UNITAR statute required voluntary funding, and Italy felt that Governments should contribute to UNITAR more generously on a voluntary basis.

Argentina voted for the draft decision in view of the exceptional circumstances described in resolution 40/214 on long-term financing and future of UNITAR. Canada and Sweden voted in favour as part of a package with resolution 40/214 and to ensure adequate funds in 1986. Denmark supported the decision despite its concern about the use of regular-budget funds to cover the cost of UNITAR activities.

The Assembly's Fifth (Administrative and Budgetary) Committee decided by a recorded vote of 63 to 15, with 11 abstentions, to inform the Assembly that, should it adopt the draft decision, an additional appropriation of $600,000 would be required as a grant to UNITAR under the 1986-1987 programme budget. The United States declared that it would reduce its voluntary UNITAR contribution by an amount equal to its share of the regular-budget cost of the proposed grant. The USSR also opposed charging to the regular budget activities that should be financed from voluntary contributions.

Long-term financing

Discussing the financial situation of UNITAR, the Secretary-General declared in his October 1985 report on the Institute,[9] requested by the General Assembly in 1984[13] since it had not been able to agree on long-term financial arrangements, that he was exploring ways of reducing UNITAR's operational and administrative costs;

in recent years, the latter had increased disproportionately to the costs of programme activities. The
Secretary-General and UNITAR's Executive Director were examining ways in which the United Nations might take further responsibility for the Institute's financial and administrative functions,
and ways of cutting the cost of the functioning of
the Board of Trustees. Meanwhile, the Secretary-
General had not proposed any further financing
of the Institute's activities in the proposed programme budget for 1986-1987. The Executive
Director would include $100,000 in the UNITAR
budget as the first instalment towards the reimbursement to the regular budget for the advance
of $886,000 approved by the Assembly in 1983.(14)

GENERAL ASSEMBLY ACTION

On 17 December 1985, on the recommendation
of the Second Committee, the General Assembly
adopted without vote **resolution 40/214.**

**Long-term financing and future of the United
Nations Institute for Training and Research**
The General Assembly,

Recalling its resolution 39/177 of 17 December 1984,
in which it requested the Secretary-General to prepare
a comprehensive study on the United Nations Institute
for Training and Research, its activities in training and
research, its funding and its future role, keeping in mind
related activities within the United Nations system and
the relevant provisions of the statute of the Institute, in
order to determine the most effective manner of
discharging those functions, and to submit his report
together with the comments of the Board of Trustees
of the United Nations Institute for Training and
Research thereon, to the General Assembly at its fortieth session,

Recalling also its resolutions 37/142 of 17 December
1982 and 38/177 of 19 December 1983, in which it called
upon the Secretary-General to submit a report on long-
term financing arrangements for the Institute which
would place its financing on a more predictable, assured
and continuous basis,

Having considered the report of the Secretary-General
and the statement made on 8 November 1985 by the
Director-General for Development and International
Economic Co-operation,

Noting with regret that, so far, no agreement has been
reached on the future role and, in particular, the long-
term funding of the Institute,

Noting also with regret that the 1985 United Nations
Pledging Conference for Development Activities was
unable to provide the General Fund of the United Nations Institute for Training and Research with the level
of resources required to maintain the Institute as a viable
entity during 1986,

Acknowledging with regret that voluntary contributions
to the Institute have so far been insufficient to guarantee
the level of resources needed to maintain it as a viable
entity, and that it has not been possible to reach agreement on any of the three options for long-term financing arrangements for the Institute recommended by the
Board of Trustees, namely, the setting up of a reserve

fund, the adoption of a replenishment system or the
establishment of an endowment fund,

1. *Takes note with appreciation* of the report of the
Secretary-General;

2. *Reaffirms* the continuing relevance of the mandate
entrusted to the United Nations Institute for Training
and Research, namely, to enhance the effectiveness of
the United Nations, and takes note of the view of the
Secretary-General that this mandate continues to be
essential to the functioning of the Organization today;

3. *Takes note* of the administrative, staffing and
organizational arrangements outlined in the report of
the Secretary-General on the future work of the Institute;

4. *Stresses* the need to take a final decision on the
long-term financing and future of the Institute at the
latest at the forty-first session of the General Assembly
and, to this end, requests the Secretary-General to
prepare comprehensive specific plans for the future of
the Institute based on two options contained in his
report:

(a) To close down the Institute, including the
possibility of re-allocating the functions of the Institute
to other agencies and bodies throughout the United Nations system where those functions could be undertaken
in an efficient and cost-effective manner;

(b) To restructure the Institute, including the
possibility of transferring to the Institute appropriate
ongoing and planned training and research functions
of other agencies and bodies throughout the United Nations system;

such plans should include a detailed assessment of the
financial implications of the two options, including a
blueprint for a specific scheme for the long-term and
stable funding of the Institute, which could be tried on
an experimental basis;

5. *Requests* the Secretary-General to keep in mind,
while preparing the plans requested in paragraph 4
above, the need for specific suggestions for the improvement of administrative arrangements to ensure cost-
effectiveness;

6. *Also requests* the Secretary-General to consult, as
appropriate, with all States and the Board of Trustees
of the United Nations Institute for Training and
Research before finalizing the plans, which should be
submitted to the General Assembly not later than 1
September 1986;

7. *Urges* all States that have not yet contributed to
the United Nations Institute for Training and Research
to do so, and calls upon all countries, especially those
donor countries that are not contributing at a level commensurate with their capacity, to increase their voluntary contributions in order to meet the needs of the Institute.

General Assembly resolution 40/214

17 December 1985   Meeting 120   Adopted without vote

Approved by Second Committee (A/40/1042) without vote, 13 December (meeting
51); draft by Vice-Chairman (A/C.2/40/L.124), based on informal consultations
on drafts by Egypt, India, Ivory Coast, Mali and Pakistan (A/C.2/40/L.87) and
by Canada and Denmark (A/C.2/40/L.88); agenda item 86.
Meeting numbers. GA 40th session: 2nd Committee 29, 45, 47, 51; plenary 120.

Stating its position, Algeria said emphasis
should be placed on restructuring UNITAR and on
long-term funding to ensure its future. Cameroon
was confident that the Secretary-General would

submit an analysis removing any obstacles to providing UNITAR with the means to fulfil its mandate. Liberia reaffirmed its commitment to UNITAR. France felt that the option to close UNITAR should not be considered until all possible remedies were explored, a view supported by Pakistan. The United States said it had become increasingly concerned about the quality of UNITAR's work, particularly its research; in any case, it should be funded by voluntary contributions. New Zealand hoped a final decision on UNITAR's future could be reached in 1986.

UN University

Activities of the University

The United Nations University,[15] an autonomous academic institution within the United Nations system, continued in 1985 under the medium-term perspective (1982-1987)[16] to respond to the problems of peace and progress at three levels: the material quality of life; distribution of resources; and the long-term structures of society and the processes of change. The UNU programme had an overarching goal of better understanding of the dynamics of development, as it encompassed welfare and survival, as well as an improved material standard of living. It aimed to help develop conceptual and practical tools to enable people, institutions and States to participate in development.

In 1985, UNU had 78 ongoing projects and subprojects under the five themes and nine programme areas of the medium-term perspective.[16] Five projects and subprojects on energy research, urban development, new social thought, migration and Arab alternative futures were completed. Dissemination of results in the form of publications and other media, such as video, was expanded. There was also an increase in the number of trainees and the forms of training offered.

Cross-cultural, policy-oriented research was carried out on administrative issues in crime prevention and control. Eight comparative case-studies for the project were completed in 1985 in Colombia, Costa Rica, Japan, Kenya, Nigeria, Poland, Singapore and Thailand; the final reports were discussed at a concluding project meeting hosted in August 1985 by the United Nations Social Defence Research Institute at Rome, and a summary of the discussions was submitted to the Seventh United Nations Congress on the Prevention of Crime and the Treatment of Offenders (see p. 738).

Considerable progress was made in setting up the University's own research and training centres, with the start of activities in Finland of the World Institute for Development Economics Research (WIDER), following the appointment of its governing Board and first Director. At a Board meeting (Helsinki, 29-31 May), the 1985-1986 WIDER work programme was approved, with three themes under which research would be clustered: hunger and poverty—the poorest billion; money, finance and trade—reforms for world development; and development and technological transformation—the management of change. Preparatory work to establish an Institute for Natural Resources in Africa and a research and training centre in Japan also moved forward.

The Special Committee on Africa completed its work with a symposium (Nairobi, 12-15 November) on science and technology in Africa in relation to development; a significant outcome of the Committee's efforts was the emergence of a core of African intellectuals, functioning as a group dealing with the African crisis from an African perspective.

The University sponsored or co-sponsored a number of other symposia, workshops and meetings, including a workshop on energy planning and management (Tokyo, 3 April); a meeting, jointly with the International Development Research Centre of Canada, on energy research and technology assessment (Manizales, Colombia, 26-30 August); a workshop on the uses of multipurpose trees in agro-forestry systems, co-sponsored by the International Union of Forest Research Organizations and the German Agency of Technical Co-operation (Turrialba, Costa Rica, 24-28 June); and a workshop on tropical home garden agro-forestry systems (Bandung, Indonesia, 2-8 December).

Other workshops discussed Arab progressive movements (Nyon, Switzerland, 20-22 March); the political economy of fiscal policy (Kyoto, Japan, 17-19 April); the global impact of human migration (Colombo, Sri Lanka, 28-30 May); the ecological impact of pioneer settlements in unpopulated or sparsely populated regions (Kuala Lumpur, Malaysia, 16-20 September); self-reliance in science and technology for national development (Beijing, China, 5-8 October); and cinema as a factor of unity and diversity in the Arab world (Cairo, Egypt, 6 and 7 November).

Meetings were held on the educational and cultural problems of a multi-ethnic society (Mexico City, September) and on Asian perspectives—the State, people and culture (Penang, Malaysia, 23-27 October).

The University participated in a meeting, organized by the International Centre for Ethnic Studies, on ethnic minorities in Buddhist societies (Bangkok, 25-28 June), and was represented at the Conference of the Association of Development Research and Training Institutes of Asia and the Pacific (Bangkok, June) and the Conference of the

Association of Asian Social Science Research Councils (Bali, Indonesia, September).

The University organized a seminar on the climatic and biological effects of nuclear war (Tokyo, 4-9 February). It co-sponsored with several universities a seminar on international organizations (Hakone, Japan, 8-15 September), and, with the Japan Society of Information and Communication Research, a forum on communication for development (Tokyo, 14 and 15 November).

A series of seminars and meetings were held on social movements in Latin America: emerging democracy at the local level (Mexico City, 12-15 March); the political system and emerging democracy in the federal states of Mexico (Mexico City, 16-23 May); and social movements in Mexico (Mexico City, 13 and 14 May) and in South America (Lima, Peru, 29-31 May).

The University continued to expand collaboration with other institutions, organizations and groups involved in activities of international concern. Institutions associated with UNU numbered 39. The number of Fellows, including three Special Fellows, in training was 125 as at 31 December 1985; 72 Fellows and 10 Special Fellows completed training during the year. New forms of training were being developed as research results were presented.

The University published 40 scholarly publications during the year. The name of the UNU newsletter was changed from *Newsletter* to *Work in Progress*.

Plans went ahead for the construction of UNU's permanent headquarters building in Tokyo. Discussions concerning the site which had been allocated were held with the Japanese Ministry of Education and the Tokyo Metropolitan Government.

The General Assembly, in **resolution 40/109**, invited UNU and other academic and research institutions to undertake programmes encouraging understanding, tolerance and respect in relation to freedom of religion.

Activities of the Council

The UNU Council met twice during 1985, holding its twenty-fifth session at Mexico City from 8 to 12 July, and its twenty-sixth session in Tokyo from 9 to 13 December.[15]

In July, the UNU Rector presented an oral report on progress since the Council's December 1984 session, together with information on UNU's activities in Africa and his thoughts on the second medium-term perspective. The Rector also presented reports on networking and fund-raising. The Council took note of progress reports by WIDER and on the proposed Institute for Natural Resources in Africa, the permanent headquarters building and the proposed research and training

centre in Japan. It adopted a draft provisional statute on training through fellowships; expressed its intent to continue the UNU association with *Development Forum* for two years; and designated two new associated institutions—Universidade de São Paulo (Brazil) and University of Nairobi (Kenya).

In December 1985, the Council concentrated on the proposed programme and budget for 1986-1987, its report for 1985, a paper on dissemination and co-operation with UNITAR.

The Economic and Social Council, by **decision 1985/165** of 19 July 1985, took note of the UNU Council's report on work in 1984.[17]

Finances of the University

Total UNU income in the 1984-1985 biennium was $53.4 million, while expenditures totalled $34.5 million. The University's financial statements for the biennium were expanded to include the WIDER Trust Fund.

CONTRIBUTIONS TO UNU, 1985 AND 1986
(as at 31 December 1985; in US dollar equivalent)

COUNTRY	1985 payment	1986 pledge
Endowment Fund		
China	50,000	—
Germany, Federal Republic of	318,424	—
Japan	2,000,000	—
Nigeria	37,036	—
Saudi Arabia	930,000	—
Trinidad and Tobago	20,730	—
Zambia	7,353	—
Subtotal	3,363,543	—
General Operating Fund		
Austria	71,454	—
Greece	40,000	—
Norway	109,069	—
Sri Lanka	5,000	16,666
Tunisia	6,044	—
Subtotal	231,567	16,666
WIDER Trust Fund—Endowment Fund		
Finland	5,002,712	14,000,000
WIDER Trust Fund—Operating Fund		
Finland	1,428,329	1,100,917
Total	10,026,151	15,117,583

SOURCE: A/41/5, vol. III.

University for Peace

In a letter to the Secretary-General,[18] Costa Rica requested that the Economic and Social Council include a supplementary item on the University for Peace in the provisional agenda of its first regular session of 1985. Annexed to the letter were an explanatory memorandum and a draft resolution. The memorandum stated that the University had held its first course in 1984, attended by 25 students from different countries; various other activities also took place, including seminars in all continents on matters related to education for peace.

The University was a specialized international institution for post-graduate studies, research and dissemination of knowledge specifically aimed at training for peace. Its establishment, proposed by Costa Rica in 1978,[19] was approved by the General Assembly in 1980.[20]

ECONOMIC AND SOCIAL COUNCIL ACTION

On 24 May 1985, the Economic and Social Council adopted without vote **resolution 1985/2**.

University for Peace

The Economic and Social Council,

Recalling General Assembly resolution 34/111 of 14 December 1979, by which the Assembly approved the idea of establishing a University for Peace,

Also recalling General Assembly resolution 35/55 of 5 December 1980, by which the Assembly approved the establishment of the University for Peace,

Aware of the positive response of the international community to the establishment of that institution,

Considering that it is important to follow up the development of the University for Peace in its initial stage,

Recognizing the important work carried out by the University for Peace during the first stage of its institutional life,

1. *Decides* to request the University for Peace to sub-mit a report to the Secretary-General on the various aspects of its development, its existing activities and its future plans, including programmes of post-graduate studies;

2. *Requests* the Secretary-General to transmit to the Economic and Social Council at its first regular session of 1986 the report submitted by the University for Peace in pursuance of paragraph 1 above;

3. *Decides* to consider this question at its first regular session of 1986.

Economic and Social Council resolution 1985/2

24 May 1985   Meeting 21   Adopted without vote

28-nation draft (E/1985/L.25); agenda item 9.

Sponsors: Algeria, Argentina, Australia, Bahamas, Bolivia, Chile, China, Colombia, Costa Rica, Dominican Republic, Ecuador, El Salvador, Finland, Greece, Guatemala, Honduras, Morocco, Nicaragua, Nigeria, Pakistan, Panama, Philippines, Senegal, Sri Lanka, Thailand, Togo, Uruguay, Venezuela.

Meeting numbers. ESC 14, 21.

REFERENCES

[1]DP/1985/22. [2]E/1985/32 & Corr.1 (dec. 85/5). [3]DP/1985/14. [4]E/1985/32 & Corr.1 (dec. 85/13). [5]*Ibid.* (dec. 85/10). [6]YUN 1984, p. 736, GA res. 39/219, 18 Dec. 1984. [7]A/40/549 & Add.1. [8]A/41/14. [9]A/40/788. [10]A/41/5/Add.4. [11]A/40/5/Add.4. [12]A/40/635. [13]YUN 1984, p. 739, GA res. 39/177, 17 Dec. 1984. [14]YUN 1983, p. 763, GA res. 38/177, 19 Dec. 1983. [15]A/41/31. [16]YUN 1981, p. 811. [17]E/1985/55. [18]E/1985/14. [19]YUN 1978, p. 792. [20]YUN 1980, p. 1006, GA res. 34/55, 5 Dec. 1980.

Chapter XVI

Environment

Signs of a global environmental crisis—
desertification, acid rain, depletion of the ozone
layer, destruction of tropical forests—formed the
background to the 1985 work of the United Nations Environment Programme (UNEP), which
continued to co-ordinate efforts by the United Nations system to protect the Earth's environment.

The effects of that crisis were apparent in 1985.
Desertification and drought in the Sudano-
Sahelian region of Africa created critical food shortages in 21 countries and placed over 30 million
people at risk. Destruction of forests continued
unabated. The buildup of so-called greenhouse
gases in the atmosphere pointed to major climatic
changes. Risks of significant ozone layer depletion
were confirmed and environmental conditions in
many cities became worse.

But the year also brought positive signs. The
Vienna Convention for the Protection of the
Ozone Layer was adopted in March and a protocol to the 1979 Convention on Long-Range
Transboundary Air Pollution to reduce sulphur
emissions by 30 per cent was concluded. The
United Nations Sudano-Sahelian Office continued
to combat desertification, and allocated $12 million
for projects in the region. The first African
Ministerial Conference on the Environment
brought together African policy-makers to discuss
common problems and the first Global Meeting
on Environment and Development saw representatives of 109 non-governmental organizations examine sustainable development strategies.

The UNEP Governing Council approved further
measures to combat desertification and urged intensified efforts in that regard. By resolution
40/198 A, the General Assembly called for increased
assistance to affected countries in their desertification
control programmes and urged those countries to
accord priority to long-term strategies against the
problem, and, by resolution 40/198 B, also
underscored the urgency of implementing the Plan
of Action to Combat Desertification in the Sudano-
Sahelian region. By resolution 40/175, the Assembly
recommended that the international community
continue to assist drought-stricken countries and
to provide all forms of support.

UNEP continued its action to protect the marine
environment, to conserve wildlife and protected
areas, to monitor various aspects of the environment (climate, global resources, transport of
pollutants), and to promote the development of en-

vironmental law and the establishment of national
conservation strategies. The Global Resource Information Data Base became fully operational and
preparation of an Environmental Perspective to the
Year 2000 and Beyond progressed. Other activities
included management of tropical forests and soil
resources, protection against harmful products and
pollutants, research on genetic resources, and linkages
between environment and development, energy, industry, human settlements and education.

By resolution 40/200, the Assembly endorsed the
UNEP Council's 1985 decisions and dealt with
various international environmental co-operation
questions. By resolution 40/197, it requested the
Secretary-General to continue his efforts with the
countries responsible for planting mines and the
affected developing countries to ensure the removal
of material remnants of war.

Sixty-three new projects were approved by the
Environment Fund in 1985; 62 were closed. The
Fund disbursed $23.53 million for programme ac-
tivities; government contributions totalled $28.26
million.

Comprehensive information covering all aspects
of UNEP 1985 activities was given in the UNEP Executive Director's annual report.[1]

Topics related to this chapter. Africa: co-
operation with the Organization of African Unity.
Asia: Iran-Iraq armed conflict. Middle East:
Mediterranean–Dead Sea canal project. Economic
assistance, disasters and emergency relief: drought-
stricken areas of Africa. Regional economic and
social activities: environment. Natural resources:
water resources. Energy resources: nuclear energy.
Health and human resources: health. Human settlements. Human rights: other human rights
questions.

REFERENCE

[1]UNEP/GC.14/2.

Programme and finances of UNEP

At its thirteenth session, held at UNEP headquarters, Nairobi, Kenya, from 14 to 24 May 1985,
the UNEP Governing Council adopted decisions on
environmental and administrative matters which
were contained in its report on the ses-

sion.[1] That report was taken note of by the Economic and Social Council on 25 July 1985 when it adopted **decision 1985/172**.

Programme policy

On 23 May,[2] the Council noted the UNEP Executive Director's reports[3] on the implementation of its 1984 policy decisions and noted the 1984 resolutions adopted by the General Assembly and the Economic and Social Council calling for action by UNEP. The Council also addressed itself to new initiatives: various conferences organized or supported by UNEP (see p. 796); the initiation of the UNEP Global Resource Information Data Base (GRID) (see p. 801); the Executive Director's suggestions on UNEP activities for International Youth Year (1985) (see p. 976); and his proposals on the UNEP role *vis-à-vis* the 1985 Conference to review the achievements of the United Nations Decade for Women (see p. 937). In addition, the Council agreed to decide in 1987 on the method by which to consider the proposed system-wide medium-term environment programme for 1990-1995. The Council also took action regarding the UNEP clearing-house mechanism (see p. 795).

Also on 23 May,[4] the Council requested the Executive Director, in presenting to the Council in 1987 the UNEP programme budget for 1988-1989, to provide a statement of the programme strategy for each area of activity, indicating the main goals and the rationale for UNEP involvement. The statement was to indicate the relationship of the area of activity to at least one of the following criteria—that it addressed an environmental issue: essential to understand a major environmental problem or to stimulate action to solve it; global in nature; likely to cause serious damage to health or environment; important to the environment of developing countries; and occurring at the regional or subregional level or in many locations.

GENERAL ASSEMBLY ACTION

On 17 December, the General Assembly, on the recommendation of the Second (Economic and Financial) Committee, adopted **resolution 40/200** by recorded vote.

International co-operation in the field of the environment

The General Assembly,

Recognizing the international dimension of environmental problems, the role of environmental factors in the broader economic and social context, and the importance of taking environmental considerations fully into account in the implementation of the International Development Strategy for the Third United Nations Development Decade,

Having considered the report of the Governing Council of the United Nations Environment Programme on the work of its thirteenth session,

Having considered also the report of the Executive Director of the United Nations Environment Programme on international conventions and protocols in the field of the environment,

Noting with deep concern that the harmful consequences of the drought and desertification seriously affecting many countries, in particular African countries, are exacerbated by the continued erosion of the resource base for the development of those countries,

Reaffirming the importance of the interrelationships between resources, environment, people and development, and the need to take those interrelationships into account in development policies and strategies,

Stressing the importance of an international exchange of experience and knowledge concerning the protection of the environment,

Noting the activity of the United Nations Environment Programme on the subject "The arms race and the environment", in accordance with its programme of work as adopted by the General Assembly, the Economic and Social Council and the Governing Council of the United Nations Environment Programme,

Mindful of the sovereign rights of States over their natural resources, including their forests,

Noting also the activities of the United Nations and other international organizations, as well as the international initiatives being taken that are directed towards the important objective of rational management, protection and rehabilitation of the world's forests,

Recalling its resolution 38/161 of 19 December 1983 on the process of preparation of the Environmental Perspective to the Year 2000 and Beyond,

1. *Takes note* of the report of the Governing Council of the United Nations Environment Programme on the work of its thirteenth session and endorses the decisions contained therein, as adopted;

2. *Welcomes* the decision of the Governing Council to change to a biennial cycle of sessions on an experimental basis and in this regard takes note of the establishment of the open-ended Committee of Permanent Representatives to facilitate this process;

3. *Invites* the Governing Council, when reviewing the experiment with the organization of a biennial work programme, to consider changes that may in consequence be necessary in the functioning of the Council, including the term of membership;

4. *Welcomes* section III of decision 13/1 of 23 May 1985, and decision 13/10 of 24 May 1985 by which the Governing Council initiated steps towards the preparation of the system-wide medium-term environment programme for the period 1990-1995 and invited the Administrative Committee on Co-ordination to review and further develop the methodology in the light of the experience gained in the system-wide medium-term environment programme for the period 1984-1989;

5. *Takes note* of the work done by the Special Commission on the Environmental Perspective to the Year 2000 and Beyond, which has adopted the name World Commission on Environment and Development, and by the Intergovernmental Inter-sessional Preparatory Committee on the Environmental Perspective to the Year 2000 and Beyond in the preparation of their reports, and recalls the relationship between the Commission and the Committee, as set out in General Assembly resolution 38/161;

6. *Takes note* of the progress on international conventions and protocols in the field of the environment

during 1985, including the adoption of the Vienna Convention for the Protection of the Ozone Layer and of an international protocol to the 1979 Convention on Long-range Transboundary Air Pollution, on sulphur emissions and fluxes, and the organization of the first meeting of the Conference of the Parties to the Convention on the Conservation of Migratory Species of Wild Animals;

7. *Considers* that measures to deal with the erosion of the natural resource base in countries affected by drought and desertification should have as one of their major aims the sustainable exploitation and increased productivity of that natural resource base;

8. *Welcomes* the importance attached by the Governing Council to regional approaches and programmes relating to international co-operation in the field of the environment, and in this context stresses the relevance of specific regional planning identified by the regions themselves;

9. *Notes with appreciation* the convening of the first African Ministerial Conference on the Environment at Cairo from 16 to 18 December 1985;

10. *Calls upon* the Executive Director of the United Nations Environment Programme to co-ordinate further the activities of the Programme with those of other organizations of the United Nations system, to co-operate appropriately with the organizers of the international initiatives on the future of the forests, and to report thereon to the Governing Council;

11. *Reaffirms* the need to strengthen the co-ordinating role of the United Nations Environment Programme and the need for additional resources to assist developing countries in dealing with serious environmental problems, and urges the Executive Director of the Programme, in consultation with Governments and the international organizations concerned, to accelerate and intensify his efforts in that field;

12. *Expresses its appreciation* to the Governments that continue to contribute to the Fund of the United Nations Environment Programme, particularly those that have increased their contributions, and urges those Governments that have not yet paid their pledged contributions to the Fund for 1985 or made pledges for 1986 to do so in the near future.

General Assembly resolution 40/200

17 December 1985   Meeting 119   149-0-6 (recorded vote)

Approved by Second Committee (A/40/989/Add.6) by recorded vote (126-0-7), 11 December (meeting 50); 16-nation draft (A/C.2/40/L.37/Rev.1), orally revised after informal consultations; agenda item 84 *(f)*.

Sponsors: Argentina, Australia, Canada, Congo, Denmark, Finland, Gambia, Iceland, India, Indonesia, Kenya, Nepal, Netherlands, Norway, Senegal, Sweden.

Meeting numbers. GA 40th session: 2nd Committee 22, 30, 34, 36, 43, 47, 50; plenary 119.

Recorded vote in Assembly as follows:

In favour: Afghanistan, Algeria, Angola, Antigua and Barbuda, Argentina, Australia, Austria, Bahamas, Bahrain, Bangladesh, Barbados, Belgium, Belize, Benin, Bhutan, Bolivia, Botswana, Brazil, Brunei Darussalam, Bulgaria, Burkina Faso, Burma, Burundi, Byelorussian SSR, Cameroon, Canada, Cape Verde, Central African Republic, Chad, Chile, China, Colombia, Comoros, Congo, Costa Rica, Cuba, Cyprus, Czechoslovakia, Democratic Kampuchea, Democratic Yemen, Denmark, Djibouti, Dominica, Dominican Republic, Ecuador, Egypt, El Salvador, Equatorial Guinea, Ethiopia, Fiji, Finland, Gabon, Gambia, German Democratic Republic, Ghana, Greece, Grenada, Guatemala, Guinea, Guinea-Bissau, Guyana, Haiti, Honduras, Hungary, Iceland, India, Indonesia, Iran, Iraq, Ireland, Italy, Ivory Coast, Jamaica, Japan, Jordan, Kenya, Kuwait, Lao People's Democratic Republic, Lebanon, Lesotho, Liberia, Libyan Arab Jamahiriya, Luxembourg, Madagascar, Malawi, Malaysia, Maldives, Mali, Malta, Mauritania, Mauritius, Mexico, Mongolia, Morocco, Mozambique, Nepal, Netherlands, New Zealand, Nicaragua, Niger, Nigeria, Norway, Oman, Pakistan, Panama, Papua New Guinea, Paraguay, Peru, Philippines, Poland, Qatar, Romania, Rwanda, Saint

Christopher and Nevis, Saint Lucia, Saint Vincent and the Grenadines, Samoa, Sao Tome and Principe, Saudi Arabia, Senegal, Sierra Leone, Singapore, Somalia, Spain, Sri Lanka, Sudan, Suriname, Swaziland, Sweden, Syrian Arab Republic, Thailand, Togo, Trinidad and Tobago, Tunisia, Turkey, Uganda, Ukrainian SSR, USSR, United Arab Emirates, United Republic of Tanzania, Uruguay, Vanuatu, Venezuela, Viet Nam, Yemen, Yugoslavia, Zaire, Zambia, Zimbabwe.

Against: None.

Abstaining: France, Germany, Federal Republic of, Israel, Portugal, United Kingdom, United States.

In the Second Committee, the USSR submitted two amendments[5] to the original draft resolution; they were later withdrawn in the light of their incorporation into the approved text.

France, which requested separate recorded votes on the seventh preambular paragraph—relating to UNEP activity on the arms race and the environment—and on the draft as a whole, said UNEP had no mandate with regard to the arms race; it was improper, in a text designed to endorse all UNEP's activities, to single out one element on which there had never been consensus.

The Committee approved the paragraph by 102 to 7, with 18 abstentions; the Assembly similarly adopted it by 123 to 8, with 17 abstentions.

Opposing the paragraph in the Committee, the United States said that the arms race was not an important item for UNEP to consider, since it could not do anything useful about it; inclusion of that paragraph was an effort to inject extraneous political elements into the text—a view shared by the Federal Republic of Germany, Israel and the United Kingdom, which believed that disarmament should be discussed elsewhere in the Assembly.

China, Japan and Spain, which abstained on the paragraph, gave similar explanations.

Bulgaria, speaking also on behalf of the Byelorussian SSR, Czechoslovakia, the German Democratic Republic, Hungary, Mongolia, Poland, the Ukrainian SSR and the USSR, said that the threat the arms race posed to nature and human life was a grim reality, and the work of UNEP on the subject should be intensified in accordance with its mandate and the Assembly's resolutions; it was understood that the Special Commission on the Environmental Perspective would follow its mandate as contained in a 1983 Assembly resolution,[6] and that reports on disarmament would be made to the UNEP Council or the Intergovernmental Inter-sessional Preparatory Committee. Peru said that the arms race was a significant aspect of the historical responsibility of States for the preservation of the environment, and a broad approach was needed which embraced the maintenance of international peace and security, the establishment of a new international economic order and détente. Norway, speaking on behalf of the draft's sponsors, stressed that it was the first text on the environment to contain, for the sake of precision, a blanket endorsement of all UNEP Governing Council decisions. Canada agreed with the reasons which had made a consensus impossible on the seventh preambular paragraph.

State of the environment

Monitoring the state of the environment continued throughout the year. Reports to the Governing Council examined emerging environmental issues (see p. 792), and chemical accidents that occurred in 1984 and early 1985,[7] including the serious 1984 accident at Bhopal, India, which resulted in more than 1,400 deaths from a leakage of methyl isocyanate from a pesticide plant. Guidelines for national state-of-the-environment reports were published and distributed to Governments (see p. 792). UNEP also began preparing the first of a series of periodic environmental data reports, in collaboration with three bodies dealing with the environment—the Monitoring Assessment and Research Centre, University of London; the World Resources Institute, Washington, D.C.; and the London-based International Institute for Environment and Development. Efforts also concentrated on support to the initial phase of GRID (see p. 801); a project on computerization of data of selected environmental subjects within GRID was helping to ensure quality control of data related to the physical environment, pollution and natural resources. The data were to be used to prepare environmental assessments by the Global Environmental Monitoring System (GEMS) (see p. 800) and for the periodic review of key environmental indicators.

1985 report

Population and the environment and the environmental aspects of emerging agricultural technologies were the 1985 themes examined in the Executive Director's annual report on the state of the environment,[8] as requested in 1984 by the UNEP Council.[9]

The report stated that there was no simple correlation between population and environment. Some patterns of development had improved environmental conditions, while others had degraded them irreversibly. The capacity of a number of developing countries to manage their environment was under severe stress because of rapid population growth, mass poverty, environmental degradation and slow development. Population policies could have only limited success when poverty remained widespread, environmental conditions deteriorated and natural resource availability was low; environmental programmes did not have the intended impact when population continued to grow rapidly.

The world had the natural resources, technology and expertise to provide for a decent quality of life for the projected high levels of global population, but co-ordinated action on population, resources, environment and development was urgently needed. Population and environment policies were coming to respond to the needs of social and economic development, and their interface had become clearer. Basic education, improvement in the status of women, public works to improve infrastructure and natural resource availability, land reform, provision of drinking-water supply and sanitation, and spatially balanced industrial, agricultural and settlements development were areas needing urgent attention. Countries experiencing environmental stress and high population densities needed to pursue their population, environment and development goals. Their efforts had to be supported by greater international economic co-operation and development assistance.

On the environmental aspects of emerging agricultural technologies, the report pointed out that abundant and cheap sources of fossil-fuel energy during the previous 30 to 50 years had enabled farmers to enjoy extraordinary output growth, mostly in developed countries. But this technical revolution was not wholly beneficial and, pushed to the extreme, was detrimental to the environment. Moreover, it did not suit the needs of hundreds of millions of poor third-world farmers, and the wisdom of pursuing this agricultural technology in the future would be called into question in view of the world energy situation.

In many parts of the world the environmental costs of agricultural technologies were high, but there was no commonly accepted measure of these costs, due to the difficulty of identifying and quantifying all the impacts of damage to land, water and ecosystems.

Long-term solutions leading to environmentally sound agricultural development included technologies generating lower environmental costs than those currently used. Such technologies had to suit local conditions and be acceptable to farmers. They included integrated pest management, minimum tillage, and the development of new types of seeds tolerant of salt or disease, or capable of enhancing biological nitrogen fixation or increasing the efficiency of photosynthesis.

On 24 May,[10] the Governing Council endorsed the report's recommendations. The Executive Director was requested to bring them to the attention of Governments and United Nations and other organizations. He was also requested to provide assistance, experimentally, to six countries (two from Africa, two from Asia and two from Latin America) in implementing agricultural policies selected from among those listed in the report, in co-operation with the Food and Agriculture Organization of the United Nations (FAO) and other United Nations bodies and the Governments concerned. Various United Nations bodies were also invited to consider the recommendations and support their implementation.

Follow-up on the 1984 report

Referring to the 1984 state-of-the-environment report,[11] whose topic was environment in the dialogue between and among developed and developing countries, the Governing Council on 24 May[12] urged Governments to continue addressing the major environmental issues to which they had agreed in the 1984-1989 system-wide medium-term environment programme.[13] The Council endorsed the Executive Director's recommendations—annexed to the decision—identifying some prerequisites for the success of dialogue on such issues. It felt that no new institutional arrangement was required to deal with the subject of the 1984 report, and that action should arise within current international or intergovernmental treatment of the individual issues. It requested the Executive Director to monitor concerns of Governments on those issues and to report on the progress made.

Future reports

On 24 May,[14] the Governing Council expressed the hope that future state-of-the-environment reports would increasingly become basic documents for the Council's deliberations, especially when based on GRID statistical data, and decided that future reports should examine, in alternate years, the economic and social aspects of the environment, and environmental data and assessment. It also decided that the topic for the 1986 report would be health and the environment, and that the 1987 report should attempt, as the first world state-of-the-environment report, to present a comprehensive survey also utilizing the data and results available through GEMS.

Emerging environmental issues

An updated list of emerging environmental issues[15] was submitted to the 1985 Governing Council session by the Executive Director. The list, which was to be updated annually in line with the Council's 1984 request,[16] included data on possible climatic change brought about by the increasing concentration of carbon dioxide and other so-called greenhouse gases in the atmosphere (see p. 804); land and soil loss caused by urban and industrial development; environmental risks resulting from the increasing production and use of chemicals (see p. 802); municipal solid wastes in developing countries; aquaculture; and the effects of military activity (see p. 817).

On 24 May,[17] the Council requested the report's wider circulation, and decided that the 1987 state-of-the-environment report should examine municipal solid waste in developing countries and aquaculture.

National reports

On 23 May,[18] the Governing Council requested the Executive Director to assist developing countries in preparing their national state-of-the-environment reports, which should include information on the implementation of previous decisions and the results in terms of environmental improvement. It also requested him to assist Governments in preparing, by the Council's 1987 session, examples of those reports for three countries from Africa, three from Asia and the Pacific and three from Latin America, each representing different eco-zones.

Following that decision, guidelines for preparing the reports were distributed to Governments in 1985. Their purpose was to avoid existing wide variations in the presentation of data and trends, which made comparisons between countries extremely difficult. To facilitate understanding, the guidelines suggested that the reports should be produced regularly, and be organized on a sectoral rather than on an ecosystem basis. Thirteen forms were also designed, to collect the basic information needed, taking into account the state of environmental information in developing countries.

Environmental Perspective

The UNEP Council addressed again in 1985 the preparation of an Environmental Perspective to the Year 2000 and Beyond, to be submitted to the General Assembly in 1987. To assist in preparing the Perspective, the Council had established in 1983[19] an open-ended Intergovernmental Intersessional Preparatory Committee and a Special Commission, an action endorsed by the Assembly.[6] In February 1985, the Executive Director reported[20] that the Commission, which had adopted the name World Commission on Environment and Development, had set up a secretariat in Geneva, and a work plan which envisaged seven regular meetings between March 1985 and the end of 1986.

The Preparatory Committee had held its first session in Nairobi in May 1984, and, in conformity with its approved mandate,[6] had produced a document, annexed to the Executive Director's report,[20] giving the expectations of the Council for consideration by the Commission, which was transmitted to the Commission in October 1984. Discussions between Committee and Commission representatives were held in May and November 1984 and March 1985.

At its second[21] and third sessions (Nairobi, 22 and 23 May, 2 and 3 December 1985), the Committee examined the Commission's work and discussed the Perspective's preparation.

The Governing Council, on 24 May,[22] stated that the Environmental Perspective should promote international co-operation and national efforts to pursue environmentally sound development, and invited Governments to contribute to that end. The Council invited the Commission to make known to the Committee its preliminary conclusions, and hoped that the Commission's report would be available to the Committee at an early stage.

Regional activities

Major regional initiatives in 1985 included the organization of the first African Ministerial Conference on the Environment, the hosting of the Workshop on Youth for the Environment, and information activities (see below).

UNEP also continued providing support to staff of its regional offices, including regional advisers; individual experts from developing countries wishing to participate in environment-related meetings, symposia, workshops and seminars; the Environment Co-ordinating Units in the United Nations regional commissions, with the exception of the Economic Commission for Europe (ECE); and a few small technical co-operation projects.

Africa

Ministerial Conference

Suggested by the Governing Council in 1983,[23] the first African Ministerial Conference on the Environment (Cairo, Egypt, 16-18 December), attended by 41 delegations from African countries, reviewed national priorities, identified common problems calling for regional action, and adopted the Cairo Programme for African Co-operation. The Programme included a decision to select 150 villages (three per country) and 30 semi-arid stock-raising zones (one in each of 30 countries) to help them to become self-sufficient in food and energy within five years. Another action was to institutionalize the Conference, which would meet every two years. To improve technical and scientific co-operation, the Conference established eight regional networks on environmental monitoring, climatology, soils and fertilizers, water resources, energy, genetic resources, science and technology, and education and training.

On 23 May,[24] the Council had approved the Executive Director's proposal to convene the Conference.

Workshop on Youth for the Environment

To encourage the interest of youth in environmental issues, UNEP hosted an African Workshop on Youth for the Environment (Nairobi, 25 and 26 November). Attended by youth leaders from 24 International Youth Year African national co-ordinating committees and from many non-governmental organizations, the Workshop drew up recommendations for youth action on the environment, and stressed the need to involve young women and women's groups in this action.

Latin America and the Caribbean

In spite of the current economic and financial crisis, Governments of Latin America and the Caribbean were requested to redouble their efforts in applying environmental policies. That request was made by the Fourth Intergovernmental Regional Meeting on the Environment in Latin America and the Caribbean (Cancún, Mexico, 18-20 April),[25] attended by 12 countries of the region and 10 international organizations. The Meeting also urged Governments to consolidate national institutional and legal provisions on the environment, and to use natural resources as a priority to generate long-term development. It further considered environmental trends and prospects for the year 2000, regional seas programmes, the Environmental Training Network for Latin America and the Caribbean (see below), other regional programmes of common interest and innovative means of financing.

On 24 May 1985,[26] the Governing Council endorsed a number of the Meeting's calls. The Council called on Governments of the region and UNEP to include in future meetings an item aimed at strengthening dialogue on the relationship between economic and social issues and the application of environmental policies. Those Governments were invited to conduct quantitative and social cost-benefit environmental studies as a basis for guiding national policies, and to prepare state-of-the-environment reports. The Executive Director was requested to support programmes of common interest and to assess their progress, communicating his views to the Governments. He was also to conduct an inventory of the resources of regional and international organizations and bilateral sources to support regional environmental programmes. In addition, he was to draw up a roster of experts to support regional and subregional projects that had already been allocated priority.

Considering the Latin American and Caribbean Environmental Training Network,[27] the Council on 23 May endorsed the Meeting's decision by urging the region's Governments to adopt formally the Network's programme adopted by the Meeting,[25] and requested the Executive Director to assist them in preparing proposals for financing and operating the Network in 1986-1987. Governments were urged to furnish details of the contributions they could commit for courses, seminars, research and publications within the framework of the regional strategy adopted for the Network. The Executive Director was requested to prepare, based on government contributions, a regional co-operation project, and to convene at the end of 1985 a meeting of Network focal points to approve the regional project and establish machinery to operate the Network programme.

That meeting (Caracas, Venezuela, 2-6 December) identified measures for the Network's continued operation, including Governments' contributions in cash, fellowships and personnel, as well as funding for courses, workshops and seminars.

Regional information activities

Regional information activities highlighted environmental issues. Inter Press Service disseminated 100 environmental news features in Spanish in Latin America and the Caribbean. Co-operation with the Press Foundation of Asia led to the placement of many items which were reported to have been well received by the targeted media. In the Arab region, UNEP and the Egyptian daily *Al-Ahram* co-operated to produce a special supplement on the environment for *Al-Ahram*'s *Youth, Science and Future* magazine, which was distributed to 20,000 subscribers. Throughout the year, UNEP continued to support the Africa Press Service, and this led to the production of three environmental features per month in English and Kiswahili. With a world-wide distribution network of 400 specialists, Earthscan, the media unit of the UNEP-supported International Institute for Environment and Development, continued its feature service in English, French and Spanish; press cuttings showed that considerable placement was achieved.

Co-ordination

United Nations co-ordination

Co-ordination of environmental activities continued to be monitored by the Administrative Committee on Co-ordination (ACC). In its report to the 1985 session of the UNEP Governing Council,[28] ACC welcomed the start of negotiations by UNEP and other United Nations bodies on drawing up the second (1986-1987) programme budget of the system-wide medium-term environment programme (1984-1989), and expressed support to United Nations organizations in concentrating their environmental programmes on sustainable development. ACC also considered that the subject of interrelationships between people, resources, environment and development (see also p. 430) deserved support from all United Nations bodies. On the Plan of Action to Combat Deser-

tification (see p. 807), ACC noted the seven pledges to finance its implementation, and emphasized the need for additional contributions.

At its October 1985 session, ACC approved its 1986 report to the UNEP Council[29] and decided to consider co-operation in environmental matters at its April 1986 session.[30]

On 24 May,[31] the Governing Council expressed appreciation for ACC's continued co-operation with UNEP and for the co-operation shown by the United Nations system in developing the methodology for preparing the system-wide medium-term environment programme for 1984-1989, and invited ACC to develop the methodology as the first step towards preparing the 1990-1995 programme.

Regarding that programme, the Council on 23 May[2] noted that in the United Nations system the medium-term plan cycles had been aligned, and that consequently the consideration and approval by the relevant intergovernmental forums of such plans for 1990-1995, including the United Nations medium-term plan, would in accordance with past practice take place in 1988. It agreed to decide in 1987 on the method by which the proposed system-wide medium-term environment programme for 1990-1995 would be considered.

In December, in **resolution 40/200**, the General Assembly invited ACC to develop the methodology in the light of the experience gained in the 1984-1989 programme, and called on the UNEP Executive Director to co-ordinate further UNEP activities with those of other United Nations organizations, and to report to the Governing Council.

During 1985, 90 UNEP Fund projects were being implemented in co-ordination with other United Nations organizations, including FAO (19 projects), UNESCO (18), WHO (12), WMO (8), UNSO (6) and UNCHS (5). Out of a total expenditure of $23.53 million for Fund programme activities in 1985, $6.6 million (28 per cent) was implemented by co-operating agencies.

Cross-organizational programme analysis

Cross-organizational programme analyses were carried out regularly in the United Nations system to assess current activities of United Nations organizations in a given sector as a basis for improved co-ordination. In March 1985,[32] the UNEP Executive Director recalled that in 1984 the ACC Consultative Committee on Substantive Questions (Programme Matters) had indicated that environment would be the most appropriate subject for the 1987 analysis, as preparations for the 1990-1995 system-wide medium-term environment programme would then be well under way, as would work on the Environmental Perspective (see p. 792). The Committee for Programme and

Co-ordination (CPC) had confirmed in 1984 that the analysis should be reviewed by the competent intergovernmental body. There would be no session of the Governing Council in 1986, the Executive Director recalled, and its 1987 session would probably overlap with the CPC session expected to be considering the subject.

In May 1985, a paper[33] prepared by the United Nations and UNEP secretariats was forwarded to the UNEP Council. The paper outlined the background to the analyses, and suggested some issues relating to the environment analysis which required resolution.

Meeting in April and May 1985, CPC decided to consider the cross-organizational programme analysis on the environment at its 1988 session,[34] and the President of the Economic and Social Council was so informed on 16 May.[35] On 24 May, he received a telegram from the President of the UNEP Governing Council,[36] stating that the UNEP Council considered that in preparing the 1990-1995 system-wide environment programme during 1987, for adoption by the Governing Council in 1988, UNEP and the United Nations system would benefit from consideration of the analysis. Accordingly, the Council would appreciate its preparation for consideration by CPC in 1987.

Meanwhile, the Governing Council on 24 May[37] welcomed CPC's decision to consider the analysis. Noting the joint paper,[33] it requested United Nations bodies to assist the secretariat in preparing a description of mandates guiding the United Nations environment-related work; suggested that including activities in the system-wide medium-term environment programme constituted a working definition of the scope of environmental activities in the United Nations system, for the purposes of the analysis; endorsed the suggestion that that programme should be used in formulating the structure of the analysis; and requested the Designated Officials for Environmental Matters to participate in its preparation.

Joint meetings with UNCHS

In 1985, the UNEP Council again considered the subject of meetings between UNEP and the United Nations Centre for Human Settlements (UNCHS). A report[38] on the seventh joint meeting, held in November 1984, was submitted to the Council by the UNEP Executive Director. On 23 May,[39] noting an 8 May resolution of the Commission on Human Settlements (see p. 833), the Council concurred with that resolution and adopted a text with identical provisions.

On 17 December, by **resolution 40/199**, the General Assembly, acting on a suggestion submitted by the respective Executive Directors, decided to discontinue those meetings.

Co-ordination with and among Governments

In view of its 1983 decision[40] not to hold a session in 1986, the UNEP Council on 23 May[41] laid down guidelines for providing information to Governments between the 1985 and 1987 sessions. It recommended that three annual reports be continued: that on the state of the environment, and those of the Executive Director and ACC. The Council specified various subjects to be examined in those documents.

Desiring to institute a more formal and regular system of consultation among Governments and between Governments and the Executive Director, particularly in view of the fact that there would be no session in 1986, the Council, also on 23 May,[42] established an open-ended Committee of Permanent Representatives and/or Government-designated officials, which was to meet quarterly and whenever deemed necessary with the Executive Director to make recommendations to the Council.

UNEP clearing-house mechanism

Established by the Governing Council in 1982,[43] the clearing-house was meant to expand UNEP's ability to assist developing countries in specific environmental problems, while maintaining its co-ordinating rather than operational role. UNEP's role was usually limited to project formulation, monitoring and evaluation; financing and implementation were negotiated with willing donors. During 1985, four long-term programmes designed in 1983-1984 through the clearing-house mechanism commenced: in Botswana (management of soil and water resources), Indonesia (environmental management of the Jakarta-Puncak corridor region), Jordan (range rehabilitation demonstration project in the low rainfall zone) and Peru (environmental management of the upper Selva region).

In 1985, the programme received support from Argentina, the Federal Republic of Germany, the Netherlands, Norway, Sweden, the United Kingdom, the United States and the European Economic Community (EEC). Two additional country programmes were formulated for Papua New Guinea and Tunisia. In addition, three multi-country programmes received financing, and short-term advisory services were provided to: Bangladesh (designing a pilot industrial waste-water treatment plant); Burundi (national parks management and assessing the pollution of Lake Tanganyika); Rwanda (organizing a national environment seminar); the Syrian Arab Republic (air pollution assessment); and Togo (preparing an environment code). A project for the management of Andean ecosystems in Peru was also initiated during the year.

On 23 May,[2] the Council expressed its appreciation to Governments and institutions which had supported the clearing-house, called on donor countries and aid institutions to increase their support for projects presented through it, and called on developing countries to make wider use of the clearing-house, particularly in technical co-operation among them.

Relations with NGOs

Close co-operation with environmentally concerned non-governmental organizations (NGOs) was again given high priority in 1985, principally through the Nairobi-based Environmental Liaison Centre (ELC), co-ordinator of a network of over 6,000 such NGOs. ELC continued to disseminate information on UNEP and played a leading role in promoting NGO activities on World Environment Day (5 June).

With financial and other assistance from UNEP, ELC organized a Global Meeting on Environment and Development for NGOs (Nairobi, 4-8 February), the first of its kind in that it brought together environmental and non-environmental NGOs. Attended by 140 participants representing 109 NGOs from 48 countries, as well as 83 guests and observers, the Meeting dealt with rural and urban economy, northern development and North-South relations. It adopted 119 action proposals and recommendations[44] on sustainable development, environment action and NGO co-operation and effectiveness. The Meeting established a common strategy among NGOs to work for sustainable development and called on UNEP to support the strategy and its extension to other NGOs around the world.

Activities in Asia and the Pacific included UNEP's collaboration with the Asian Mass Communication Research and Information Centre in a research project on the use of traditional media for environmental communication. UNEP also cooperated with Wildlife Fund Thailand on the Buddhist perception of nature. Other initiatives included the production of reports on pesticide poisoning in Asia and the Pacific and on the lessons of the 1984 Bhopal accident, in collaboration with the International Organization of Consumers Unions; the organization of several workshops for journalists, in co-operation with the Press Foundation of Asia and the Sukothai Thammathirat Open University of Thailand; and the co-ordination of tree-planting projects in India, New Caledonia, Sri Lanka and Thailand, with financial support from the National Federation of UNESCO Associations in Japan.

In Kenya, assistance was provided to promotional activities and seminars of the Greenbelt Movement, the tree-planting NGO organized by the National Council of Women.

UNEP continued its close partnership with the major international environmental NGOs. Thus,

during 1985, the International Union for the Conservation of Nature and Natural Resources was carrying out 15 activities with UNEP support, the Scientific Committee on Problems on the Environment had six and the International Institute for Environment and Development had three.

Underlining the unique role that NGOs could play at all levels, the Governing Council on 23 May[45] urged the Executive Director to improve mechanisms by which UNEP, in consultation with Governments, utilized the capacities of NGOs. He was also urged to help develop the ability of NGOs, especially those in developing countries, to become more effective partners in development with Governments, international agencies and development institutions, and to report on progress in these matters in 1987.

UNEP Fund

During 1985, expenditures of the UNEP Fund on programme and programme reserve activities totalled $23.53 million, broken down as follows: environmental awareness, $3.94 million; Earthwatch, $3.5 million; oceans, $3.02 million; terrestrial ecosystems, $2.61 million; health and human settlements, $2.5 million; desertification, $2.37 million; environment and development, $2.27 million; water, $1.4 million; regional and technical co-operation, $1.38 million; Fund programme reserve, $0.43 million; arms race and the environment, $0.11 million.

In 1985, 63 new projects were approved, compared with 48 in 1984; 62 projects were closed. At the end of the year, 295 projects were still open. Geographical distribution of Fund expenditures was as follows: global, $15,179,952; regional, $6,313,823; and interregional, $2,038,135.

Contributions

On 23 May,[46] the Governing Council expressed appreciation to Governments that had increased their pledges to the Environment Fund, appealed to those that had not done so to pledge their 1985 contribution, and urged Governments to contribute at the beginning of a year and to support Fund programme activities in which they were particularly interested by making counterpart contributions to individual projects. The Executive Director was requested to seek increased contributions to implement projects at the agreed expenditure level.

Making similar appeals to Governments, the General Assembly in **resolution 40/200** reaffirmed the need for additional resources to deal with developing countries' environmental problems.

CONTRIBUTIONS TO THE UNEP FUND, 1985

(as at 31 December 1985)

Country	Amount (in US dollars)	Country	Amount (in US dollars)	Country	Amount (in US dollars)
Algeria	11,000	Greece	10,000	Philippines	8,919
Argentina	70,000	Hungary	21,539	Poland	20,464
Australia	320,310	Iceland	4,500	Portugal	3,000
Austria	300,000	India	104,004	Qatar	10,000
Bahamas	500	Indonesia	12,000	Saudi Arabia	500,000
Bangladesh	5,224	Ireland	19,622	Seychelles	100
Barbados	1,000	Italy	279,883	Singapore	1,000
Botswana	561	Japan	4,000,000	Somalia	269
Brazil	20,000	Jordan	10,000	Spain	269,986
Bulgaria	10,152	Kenya	45,000	Sri Lanka	3,000
Byelorussian SSR	14,338	Kuwait	200,000	Swaziland	441
Cameroon	11,680	Lao People's Democratic Republic	2,027	Sweden	1,824,753
Canada	848,900	Luxembourg	5,200	Switzerland	376,045
Chile	5,000	Malawi	2,857	Thailand	10,000
China	64,925	Malaysia	15,000	Trinidad and Tobago	5,000
Colombia	35,243	Malta	1,361	Tunisia	15,180
Costa Rica	103	Mauritius	1,000	Turkey	6,000
Cyprus	2,000	Mexico	21,169	Uganda	2,000
Czechoslovakia	25,316	Mongolia	791	Ukrainian SSR	36,995
Democratic Yemen	2,000	Morocco	10,277	USSR	3,030,868
Denmark	358,887	Nepal	1,000	United Kingdom	1,063,125
Egypt	24,340	Netherlands	481,105	United States	9,865,433
Finland	600,000	New Zealand	55,755	Venezuela	57,333
France	751,222	Norway	736,937	Yugoslavia	22,414
Gabon	6,000	Oman	15,000	Zambia	6,522
German Democratic Republic	118,936	Pakistan	5,000	Zimbabwe	4,017
Germany, Federal Republic of	1,418,216	Panama	4,000		
Ghana	9,570	Papua New Guinea	13,000	Total	28,256,314

Accounts for 1984-1985

As at 31 December 1985, total income of the Fund for 1984-1985 amounted to $61,448,423 and the total expenditure to $60,713,714, leaving an excess of income over expenditure of $734,709.

Comments and recommendations on the accounts of the UNEP Fund were made by the Board of Auditors.[47]

Programme budgets

1984-1985

In February 1985,[48] the Executive Director reported on the implementation of the approved programme and programme support costs budget for 1984-1985, and indicated the revisions it required. He recalled the Governing Council's request to keep those costs within 33 per cent of the estimated contributions for any given year. To do so in 1985, costs would have to be reduced to $9.9 million, but such a reduction was not possible. Projected 1985 requirements amounted to $12.3 million, but the Executive Director would try to limit expenditure to $11.5 million. It was essential for the Council to accept a situation, deplored by him, of having the costs in question possibly consuming 40 per cent of contributions, making it impossible to have a meaningful programme implementation. Such a situation would occur if most Governments continued to hold stationary or reduce their contributions to the Fund. He recommended the approval of a revised, lower ap-

propriation of $22,811,000 for 1984-1985—a recommendation shared by the Advisory Committee on Administrative and Budgetary Questions (ACABQ).[49]

On 23 May,[50] the Governing Council approved the revised appropriation and requested the Executive Director to reduce the proportion of the costs as soon as possible.

1986-1987

On 23 May,[51] the Governing Council approved the proposed programme budget for 1986-1987 and the activities contained therein. On the same day,[46] it approved an appropriation of $60 million for Fund programme activities and $2 million for Fund programme reserve activities for 1986-1987, and set out the apportionment for them. The Executive Director was requested to adjust the financial reserve of the Fund in 1986 to 7.5 per cent of the total programme approved by the Council for 1986-1987.

Also on the same date,[50] the Council approved the appropriation of $26,207,700 for the programme and programme support costs budget for 1986-1987—an amount recommended by ACABQ.[52]

Resources available to the Fund in 1986 were estimated at $53.07 million. Based on this, an expenditure of $32.35 million was planned in 1986, broken down as follows: programme and programme support costs, $11 million, plus Fund programme activities and reserve activities, $28.35 million, less underspending of $7 million. The balance of $20.72 million was to be carried forward to 1987.

The Executive Director allocated $45.2 million for Fund programme activities in 1986-1987: $27.85 million for 1986 and $17.35 million for 1987. He also allocated $1 million for reserve activities covering both years.

1988-1989

On 23 May,[46] the Governing Council authorized the Executive Director to enter into forward commitments of up to $16 million for Fund programme activities in 1988-1989, and requested him to draw up a programme for Fund activities and reserve activities in 1988-1989 which would result in an estimated level of project expenditures of approximately $50 million.

Also on that day,[50] the Council requested him to identify more clearly the real administrative costs of UNEP and to present them in the 1988-1989 budget.

The Executive Director stated that he did not expect to incur a high level of commitments for 1988-1989 activities during 1986-1987, although some forward commitments would be necessary. Only $10,000 commitments for those years had been incurred by 31 March 1986.

Trust funds

Three new technical assistance funds were established after the 1984 session of the Governing Council: to provide short-term experts to developing countries, and for a pilot project on environmental management and protection of Andean ecosystems, both financed by the Federal Republic of Germany; and to promote technical co-operation and assistance in industrial, environmental and raw material management, financed by the Swedish International Development Authority.[53] In the same period, one other trust fund, the Interim Special Account for the Establishment of the Special Commission on the Environmental Perspective to the Year 2000 and Beyond, was closed. This brought the number of trust funds administered by UNEP to 15.

On 23 May,[54] the Council expressed appreciation to Governments that had pledged to increase their contributions to the various funds, and urged Governments to pay promptly, at the beginning of a calendar year, and to support Fund programme activities in which they were particularly interested by making counterpart contributions to individual projects. The Council approved the extension of six trust funds established under the rules of the Environment Fund and approved, on a contingency basis, the establishment of a Regional Seas Trust Fund for the Eastern African

Region. It also took note of the establishment of the three technical assistance funds mentioned above.

(For the Trust Fund for the Convention on the Conservation of Migratory Species of Wild Animals, see p. 813.)

Additional sources of funding

In accordance with a 1982 Governing Council request,[43] the Executive Director continued to seek resources additional to those provided by contributions to the Environment Fund. Additional pledges totalling $956,822 were secured as counterpart contributions for 12 projects in 1985 and a further $81,932 for three projects in 1986. Twelve Governments contributed $779,926 for 1985, while the European Atomic Energy Community, EEC, several industrial corporations and NGOs contributed a total of $176,896.

Concerned at the decline in the Environment Fund's real resources, the Council on 23 May[55] urged States to contribute or to increase their contributions. The Executive Director was requested to seek additional funds for specific activities; to initiate cost-effective mechanisms to utilize national currencies and contributions in kind; to intensify co-operation between UNEP and the United Nations Development Programme (UNDP); to secure support to supplement secretariat staff by direct recruitment under agreements with Governments; to consult with United Nations Headquarters on the possibility of issuing conservation stamps to finance environmental activities; to encourage the establishment of national environmental committees; and to explore other possibilities.

Other administrative and organizational questions

UNEP public information

Information activities and special events helped to increase environmental awareness during 1985. On the tenth anniversary of GEMS (see p. 800) and the launching of GRID (see p. 801), a visit to UNEP by astronaut George B. Nelson and cosmonaut Anatoly Nicolaevich Berezovoy attracted major media attention. Press coverage of the visit of Pope John Paul II to the United Nations Office at Nairobi (18 August) was augmented by the distribution of speeches for the occasion to church leaders. World Environment Day (5 June) was observed in more than 70 countries and received global media attention.

An Information Advisory Committee of independent information experts to advise on promoting environmental awareness held its first meeting at Geneva in November. Under the first

UNEP Journalist Attachment Programme, representatives of major newspapers were invited for three weeks in May to observe UNEP's functioning and the Governing Council's session. Liaison with the Nairobi-based media was reinforced with regular monthly briefings and some 100 news releases, features and background papers.

Six issues of *UNEP News*, in English, French and Spanish, were produced. A new publications series aimed at the general public was launched. The initial titles were: *Environment—A Dialogue among Nations*, *Environmental Refugees* and *Radiation, Risks, Doses and Effects*. Other publications included five technical papers, a series of eight thematic fact sheets (in four languages) and six associated posters (in three languages). In Thailand, Dr. Seuss's children's book *The Lorax* was released in Thai and distributed free of charge to all school libraries on World Environment Day.

The non-convertible-currency-funded publications and information programmes with China and the USSR continued. The UNEP/China project published four issues of the Chinese-language quarterly *World Environment* (circulation 25,000), provided information support to a UNEP/FAO/China seminar on pest control, and started preparing the Chinese version of *The Lorax*. Various publications were printed under the UNEP/USSR project. Its audio-visual component selected Soviet entries for the global environmental film/video catalogue, and started work on a biosphere reserve slide show.

The audio-visual services produced three radio programmes on behalf of all English-language radio stations in Africa; dubbed into Spanish the film *Pills and Pesticides*; translated into Arabic, French and Spanish the slide show *Harvest of Dust*; and prepared a photographic display on women in the environment.

The UNEP-sponsored Television Trust for the Environment (TVE) produced, in co-operation with Thailand and the United Press International Television Network, a five-minute news item and a 25-minute film feature for World Environment Day. TVE also produced a film on desertification control in China.

(For regional information activities, see p. 794.)

Reform of the information service

As part of the ongoing reform of the UNEP information programme, the Executive Director reported[32] that target audiences had been identified and objectives set. Information needs of developing countries had been analysed, as had been the opportunities for use of non-traditional media in those countries. Staff and financial resources for the information programme had been reviewed, and an organizational structure drawn up. A 1985 information programme had been defined and *UNEP News* issued every two months.

On 23 May,[56] the Governing Council urged the Executive Director to continue streamlining information activities, and requested him to provide Governments, through the Committee of Permanent Representatives, with information on the use of funds for such activities.

Future Council sessions

Biennial cycle of sessions

In 1983, the UNEP Governing Council had decided, experimentally, to hold no session in 1986 and decide in 1987 on the periodicity of its sessions.[40] In **resolution 40/200**, the General Assembly welcomed that decision and invited the Council, when reviewing the experiment with the organization of a biennial work programme, to consider changes that might be necessary in the Council's functioning, including the term of membership.

1987 session

On 24 May,[1] the Governing Council decided to hold its 1987 session at Nairobi, in April-June, at dates to be relayed to Governments after consultations. It also approved a provisional agenda for the session.

REFERENCES

[1]A/40/25. [2]*Ibid.* (dec. 13/1). [3]UNEP/GC.13/2 & Corr.1,2; UNEP/GC.13/3 & Corr.1,2 & Add.1-6 & Add.6/Corr.1 & Add.7. [4]A/40/25 (dec. 13/15). [5]A/C.2/40/L.93 & Corr.1 & L.94. [6]YUN 1983, p. 771, GA res. 38/161, 19 Dec. 1983. [7]UNEP/GC.13/4/Add.2. [8]UNEP/GC.13/4. [9]YUN 1984, p. 743. [10]A/40/25 (dec. 13/9 A). [11]YUN 1984, p. 744. [12]A/40/25 (dec. 13/9 C). [13]YUN 1982, p. 1005. [14]A/40/25 (dec. 13/9 D). [15]UNEP/GC.13/4/Add.1 & Add.1/Corr.1. [16]YUN 1984, p. 743. [17]A/40/25 (dec. 13/9 B). [18]*Ibid.* (dec. 13/23). [19]YUN 1983, p. 771. [20]UNEP/GC.13/3/Add.2. [21]UNEP/GC/IIPC.2/2. [22]A/40/25 (dec. 13/4 A & B). [23]YUN 1983, p. 773. [24]A/40/25 (dec. 13/6). [25]UNEP/IG.57/8. [26]A/40/25 (dec. 13/32). [27]*Ibid.* (dec. 13/21). [28]UNEP/GC.13/5. [29]ACC/1985/DEC/16-29 (dec. 1985/19). [30]*Ibid.* (dec. 1985/20). [31]A/40/25 (dec. 13/10). [32]UNEP/GC.13/3 & Corr.1,2. [33]UNEP/GC.13/3/Add.6 & Add.6/Corr.1. [34]A/40/38. [35]E/1985/86. [36]E/1985/120. [37]A/40/25 (dec. 13/11). [38]UNEP/GC.13/6. [39]A/40/25 (dec. 13/12). [40]YUN 1983, p. 769. [41]A/40/25 (dec. 13/3). [42]*Ibid.* (dec. 13/2). [43]YUN 1982, p. 999. [44]UNEP/GC.13/3/Add.4. [45]A/40/25 (dec. 13/13). [46]*Ibid.* (dec. 13/36). [47]A/41/5/Add.6. [48]UNEP/GC.13/11. [49]UNEP/GC.13/L.4. [50]A/40/25 (dec. 13/35). [51]*Ibid.* (dec. 13/14). [52]UNEP/GC.13/L.5. [53]UNEP/GC.13/14 & Add.1. [54]A/40/25 (dec. 13/34). [55]*Ibid.* (dec. 13/33). [56]*Ibid.* (dec. 13/22).

Environmental activities

Environmental monitoring

Environmental monitoring continued to be one of UNEP's main tasks throughout 1985. Its global environment assessment programme, Earthwatch, was conceived as a co-ordinated global system of national facilities and services to study the interaction between man and the environment and determine the status of selected natural resources. Earthwatch had four functions: evaluation and forecasting, monitoring, research, and information exchange.

Since 1974, some 50 projects had been completed within Earthwatch; 20 were ongoing, for a total projected cost of $36 million, half provided by UNEP and half by co-operating agencies. The corner-stone of the programme was the Global Environmental Monitoring System (GEMS), with nearly 150 countries participating in one or more of its six monitoring networks which dealt with renewable resources; climate; health; long-range transboundary pollution; integrated monitoring; and the Global Resource Information Data Base (GRID).

The Environmental Law and Machinery Unit continued to promote the development of environmental law by collating and disseminating data, supporting the enforcement of international agreements, promoting new agreements and assisting States to enforce environmental law. In 1985, three years after the Governing Council had approved[1] the 1981 Montevideo (Uruguay) programme for the development and periodic review of environmental law,[2] the priority tasks of the programme had been accomplished, with the adoption in 1985 of the global Convention on protecting the ozone layer (see p. 804) and two sets of international guidelines, prepared by a series of *ad hoc* working groups of governmental experts on the basis of drafts prepared by UNEP.

On 24 May, the Governing Council addressed various issues concerning environmental law:[3] protecting the ozone layer (see p. 804), protecting the marine environment (see p. 815), management of hazardous wastes (see p. 803), harmful products (see p. 801), environmental impact assessment (see below), offshore mining (see p. 816), international conventions (see below), and the Convention on conservation of migratory animals (see p. 813).

Environmental impact assessment

Taking note of progress made in developing guidelines for environmental impact assessment by the Working Group of Experts on Environmental Law (first session, Washington, D.C., 26-29 June 1984),[4] the Council, on 24 May 1985, requested the Executive Director to provide for additional sessions to complete the guidelines for submission to the Council in 1987.[3]

International conventions

The Vienna Convention for the Protection of the Ozone Layer was adopted in March (see p. 804) and a protocol to the 1979 Convention on Long-Range Transboundary Air Pollution[5] on the

reduction of sulphur emissions or their transboundary fluxes by at least 30 per cent was concluded at Helsinki, Finland, on 8 July 1985. As at 31 December 1985, 21 States had signed the protocol, drawn up within the framework of ECE, while one (Canada) had ratified it.[6]

In 1985 UNEP continued its work relating to various aspects of other international conventions relating to the environment. Revised and updated versions of the *Register of International Treaties and Other Agreements in the Field of the Environment,* the *Directory of Principal Governmental Bodies Dealing with the Environment* and the survey of *Environmental Law in the United Nations Environment Programme* were prepared and distributed for use by Governments. In addition, all guidelines and principles on environmental law adopted under UNEP auspices since 1972 were reissued as a documentation series in all official languages. A report[7] on progress with regard to environment co-operation by States concerning shared natural resources, prepared on behalf of the Governing Council for the General Assembly in response to a 1982 request,[8] indicated that the 1978 principles relating to such resources[9] had found wide international acceptance. The report summarized the comments of 46 Governments and 11 international organizations on the question.

Information on developments regarding international conventions and protocols on the environment was submitted to the Council by the Executive Director.[10] His report listed new conventions and gave changes in the status of existing ones.

By **decision 40/441** of 17 December, the General Assembly took note of a Secetariat note drawing attention to the Executive Director's report.

Environment information networks

INFOTERRA

The International Referral System for sources of environmental information (INFOTERRA), UNEP's global information system linking national and international institutions and experts, expanded its activities in 1985. The number of Government-designated INFOTERRA national focal points reached 126, of which 103 were in developing countries. The number of queries reached 10,600, an increase over the 9,100 in 1984; over half were from developing countries. In 1985, over 60 per cent of all queries processed by INFOTERRA national focal points received direct answers. INFOTERRA also provided information and referral services to every user who contacted it. About 70 per cent of all users contacted were satisfied or very satisfied with the information they received.

Work continued to identify leading institutions in environmental subject areas and to engage them to act as INFOTERRA special sectoral sources for the provision of information. Four additional institutions were contracted to search their data bases to produce bibliographic references, abstracts and documentation in answer to queries from users, bringing the total to nine.

A training course on basic INFOTERRA operations was held (Nairobi, October) for 20 new national focal points, and three national seminars were organized by Bulgaria, China and the Ukrainian SSR, with UNEP assistance. The INFOTERRA Advisory Committee held its second meeting (Sochi, USSR, April) and discussed the system's development.

The seventh edition of the INFOTERRA *International Directory of Sources* was published in January in English, French, Russian and Spanish. It listed 5,213 information sources on nearly 1,000 environmental topics. Promotional material and the bi-monthly *INFOTERRA Bulletin* were produced and distributed to all national focal points.

Global Resource Information Data Base

The Global Resource Information Data Base (GRID) was established in 1985 within GEMS to provide an analytical basis for continuous geographically referenced assessment statements on key global environmental issues. Designed as a data management service for the United Nations system, it enabled environmental data to be transformed into information useful to decision makers. It integrated data on the basis of geographical location—an effective common denominator in environmental planning and management—making them available for national and international users. The GRID processor facility in Geneva was opened in September. By year's end, the tasks of compiling global resource data sets and developing demonstration data sets and models to test the applicability of national geographic-information-system technology was well under way.

On 23 May 1985,[11] the Governing Council welcomed the establishment of GRID, expressed appreciation to Governments that had supported it, invited others to do so, and invited developing countries to consider how best they could use GRID for their environmental and developmental objectives. The Executive Director was requested to report in 1987 on progress in its development.

Integrated monitoring

During 1985, a methodology for integrated monitoring, developed by UNEP in conjunction with WMO and UNESCO, was being tested in a pilot project in comparable North and South American temperate forests. Preliminary results, based on a year's data collection at each project site (Torres del Paine National Park, Chile, and Olympic National Park, Washington, United States), confirmed that both locations were suitable for baseline data

collection and examination of pollutant fluxes between and accumulations within environmental compartments. Consideration was given to how this study might be linked to similar work carried out in Council for Mutual Economic Assistance (CMEA) countries in order to provide the basis for a new GEMS global network.

National conservation strategies

On 23 May,[12] the Governing Council requested the Executive Director to encourage Governments that had not done so to prepare national conservation strategies, and to recommend to the December African environmental conference (see p. 793) that it consider such strategies with a view to evolving a common approach.

Protection against harmful products and pollutants

Activities regarding pollution assessment continued throughout 1985. With UNEP/GEMS support, the Monitoring and Assessment Research Centre (MARC) of the University of London continued to assess environmental pollution. It produced reports on pathways analysis and exposure commitment assessments of environmental pollutants, in consultation with UNEP's International Register of Potentially Toxic Chemicals (see below); a report on polyaromatic hydrocarbons, aluminium and zinc was published in 1985. MARC also prepared reviews of biological monitoring techniques, evaluating the usefulness of the whole spectrum of living organisms as integrators of exposure and indicators of the effects of environmental pollutants. In association with WHO and with UNEP support, MARC produced a report on historical monitoring which reviewed for the first time global concentrations of metal, organic and radioactive pollutants in both living and non-living materials, over time, using retrospective data.

UNEP and the Scientific Committee on Problems of the Environment continued to collect and analyse information on elements cycling in the environment through their joint Carbon Unit in the Federal Republic of Germany and the Sulphur Unit in the USSR. A project on the transport of carbonaceous compounds from the land to the sea by the major world rivers was under way, and the Carbon Unit published the third part of its report on transport of carbon and minerals in major world rivers. A workshop (Tianjin, China, 13-17 May) discussed the use of modelling and remote sensing to improve understanding of the carbon cycle.

Action to promote environmental health continued. In 1985 UNEP reviewed eight demonstration projects in bilharzia control, established in collaboration with the Egyptian Academy of Scientific Research and Technology and the Theodor Bilharz Research Institute in Cairo.

Under the UNEP-supported International Programme on Chemical Safety (IPCS), new priority chemicals were evaluated, on the basis of which environmental health criteria documents were published to provide national and international institutions with information on dangerous chemicals and with data on their effects on man and the environment. Two training courses organized under IPCS involved 39 participants from developing countries. One on environmental toxicology and ecotoxicology, held in the United Kingdom, dealt with safe disposal of chemicals; the other on preventive toxicology, held in the USSR, upgraded knowledge of agrochemicals to improve the formulation of national standards and exposure limits and the development of measures for hazard control.

In co-operation with FAO and the USSR Commission for UNEP (UNEPCOM), a training course was organized in the USSR on food contamination control with special reference to mycotoxins, involving 16 participants from developing countries.

In collaboration with the International Agency for Research on Cancer, UNEP published a manual on environmental carcinogens which included recommended analytical methods. In co-operation with ECE, UNEP evaluated airborne sulphur pollution and transboundary air pollution, and published two reports assessing air pollution effects on the environment.

In the area of management of agricultural chemicals and residues, the fourth International Meeting on Perception and Management of Pests and Pesticides (Chiang Mai, Thailand, 5-14 January) reviewed ongoing studies on the perceptions of pest managers and farmers; updated national profiles on pesticide production and distribution and pest management practices in developing countries; made recommendations on education and training; and reviewed information on the international flow of pesticides.

A meeting sponsored by UNEP, FAO and China (Guangzhou, China, 16-22 June), attended by 48 participants, aimed at enhancing developing country capabilities for biological control of agricultural pests.

With UNEP support, a training course to create self-reliance in ecological pest management in the tropics was held at the Regional Centre for Training in Plant Protection at Yaoundé, Cameroon (November/December). Its aim was to enable four selected African countries to design programmes for integrated crop pest and livestock vector management, in order to minimize the negative effects of indiscriminate pesticide use. The course was attended by 25 participants.

The second session of the *Ad Hoc* Working Group of Experts for the Exchange of Information on Potentially Harmful Chemicals (in particular Pesticides) in International Trade was held at Rome, Italy, in January/February. The Group reviewed the provisional notification scheme for banned and severely restricted chemicals;[13] approved standard notification forms annexed to the scheme; and revised the draft guidelines for the exchange of information on potentially harmful chemicals in international trade. Sixty-one Governments were participating in the notification scheme.

On 24 May,[3] the Governing Council noted with appreciation an offer by the United Kingdom to host the third session of the *Ad Hoc* Working Group in early 1987. The Executive Director was requested to convene the session before that of the Governing Council in order to complete the draft guidelines. He was also requested to facilitate, through IPCS and in co-operation with the organizations concerned, the provision of technical assistance and training to developing countries to establish and improve national institutions dealing with the issue.

International Register of Potentially Toxic Chemicals

The potential threat posed by the increasing production, trade and use of chemicals became a major issue in 1985 as a result of chemical-related accidents such as the ones at Bhopal, India, and at the Fly River estuary, Papua New Guinea, where 2,700 sixty-litre barrels of sodium cyanide spilled in 1984. UNEP's International Register of Potentially Toxic Chemicals (IRPTC) became more involved in providing information, assistance and advice on chemical safety and hazard control. IRPTC expanded in 1985 its global information exchange network involving national institutions, international organizations, NGOs and industry. Training in the establishment and operation of national chemical information systems, in particular in developing countries, became a regular part of its work. With other international bodies, IRPTC organized training courses and seminars on the optimal use of data for the protection of health and the environment. In partnership with other parts of the United Nations, IRPTC maintained a global data base on prohibitions and restrictive regulatory measures imposed on chemicals by Governments.

The Query-Response Service continued to receive queries on chemicals at an increasing rate. Over 330 came in during 1985 (43 per cent from developing countries), most (44 per cent) on agrochemicals.

The IRPTC Legal File, containing data on regulatory measures and recommendations for hazard control on 400 chemicals, covering 12 countries and six international organizations, was expanded in 1985 to contain occupational exposure limits for 1,258 chemicals from 20 countries. The File was accessible on-line, world-wide, from the Environmental Chemicals Data and Information Network of the Commission of the European Communities as a result of an agreement between UNEP and the Commission.

IRPTC updated its loose-leaf manual on toxic chemicals and continued to develop its data profiles of 500 chemicals of international significance stored in its data bank.

Two issues of the *IRPTC Bulletin* were published in English, French, Russian and Spanish and distributed to 9,200 recipients. The *Bulletin* contained information on activities by UNEP and other organizations on chemicals; the results of risk assessments of chemicals; and chemicals which were the subject of controls or restrictive measures. With USSR co-operation, publication continued of the series *Scientific Reviews of Soviet Literature on Toxicity and Hazards of Chemicals*, which comprised 94 publications. The English edition of *Principles of Pesticide Toxicology* was published.

An international expert consultation on toxicometric methodology, held jointly with IPCS (Moscow, November), reviewed a draft document on recommendations and methods of toxicometry, providing basic information on the experiences of CMEA countries in safety-testing of chemicals, and made proposals for its finalization and use.

Close working links were maintained with the new national chemical information systems established in Colombia, the Gambia, Malaysia, Sri Lanka and the United Republic of Tanzania during 1984 under UNEP's clearing-house mechanism (see p. 795). Plans were developed for a second phase, involving six more developing countries.

In response to a 1984 Governing Council request,[14] IRPTC continued to send to Governments, international organizations, NGOs and industry a report on environmentally dangerous chemical substances and processes of global significance. A revision of the report based on government and other comments was begun.

Responding to another Council request,[13] IRPTC continued to assist in implementing the provisional notification scheme for banned and severely restricted chemicals (see p. 802). By the end of 1985, Governments had started issuing notifications of control action for specific chemicals for dissemination to others through IRPTC.

During 1985, IRPTC continued to collaborate with IPCS, OECD, CMEA, the Commission of the European Communities, ILO and other United Nations bodies.

On 23 May,[15] the Governing Council, noting that IRPTC had achieved specific successes, recognized that the current international information exchange systems on chemicals for the protection of human health and the environment, in which IRPTC played an important role, were failing to keep abreast of the growing requirements placed on them. The Council felt that it was urgent to raise the effectiveness of IRPTC by increasing the number of chemicals it covered, intensifying information exchange, providing access to additional organizations, institutions and bodies, and expanding training programmes. The Council urged Governments, international organizations and industry to provide information for inclusion in the IRPTC files, and called on the Executive Director to continue giving high priority to IRPTC's work and to increase its financial resources from non-convertible currency contributions to the Environment Fund.

Managing hazardous wastes

On 24 May,[3] the Governing Council requested the Executive Director to convene a third session of the *Ad Hoc* Working Group of Experts on the Environmentally Sound Management of Hazardous Wastes, to enable it to complete guidelines and principles on that subject for the Council's consideration in 1987. The Group had held its first two sessions in 1984.[16]

The Working Group met at Cairo (4-9 December), and adopted the Cairo Guidelines and Principles for the Environmentally Sound Management of Hazardous Wastes,[17] together with several recommendations addressed to Governments and the UNEP Executive Director.

Health-related monitoring

In the area of health-related monitoring, work continued under the UNEP/WHO Human Exposure Assessment Locations (HEALs) programme, expected to lead to major advances in assessing pollution-exposure risk to various sectors of the population in industrialized and developing countries. During 1985, final discussions were held with participating countries (Japan, Sweden, United States and Yugoslavia) on implementing the first stage of the programme. In the next two stages, HEALs was to be extended to advanced developing countries and then to less developed countries.

At the end of 1985 GEMS had, in co-operation with WHO, three operational networks monitoring urban air, water and food contamination. On urban air, 50 countries (27 developing) were participating, with some 175 monitoring sites in 75 cities. Regarding water, 250,000 data points had been returned from 448 stations in 59 countries or territories. Concerning food contamination, 26 joint FAO/WHO monitoring centres and institutions were operational. In addition, the health-related monitoring programme had resulted in initiating or strengthening national monitoring in 25 developing countries.

Monitoring long-range transport of pollutants

The first phase of a project begun in 1984 with ECE[13] to assess the effects of acidifying deposition on forests in ECE countries and to recommend guidelines for a unified methodology for sampling, analysis and assessment of damage to forests from air pollution continued in 1985. A planned second phase was to monitor damage to forests by applying methodology developed in the first phase.

Ecosystems

Atmosphere

Protection of the ozone layer

Seven years of efforts by the international community culminated in the adoption of the Vienna Convention for the Protection of the Ozone Layer on 22 March by a conference of plenipotentiaries (Vienna, 18-22 March). Sponsored by UNEP with the support of the Austrian Government, the conference was attended by 43 States (including 14 developing countries) and seven international organizations. As at 31 December 1985,[6] the Convention had been signed by 25 States and EEC. It was to enter into force after 20 States had ratified or accepted it.

The conference was preceded by a meeting of the *Ad Hoc* Working Group of Legal and Technical Experts for the Elaboration of a Global Framework Convention for the Protection of the Ozone Layer (Geneva, 21-25 January) and by an informal negotiation meeting. In view of the urgent need for a protocol on the control of chlorofluorocarbons, UNEP convened two *ad hoc* steering committee meetings (London, 17 and 18 September, and Brussels, 16 December) to arrange for a 1986 workshop as a basis for elaborating such a protocol.

Justification for the Convention was based largely on the continuing process of assessment of ozone layer modification and its impact carried out through the UNEP Co-ordinating Committee on the Ozone Layer. A December 1985 assessment report, prepared by the United States National Aeronautics and Space Administration based on work by several bodies, including UNEP and WMO, contained more refined data on the atmosphere than ever before, and confirmed the risk of significant ozone depletion should chlorine-containing chemicals, particularly chlorofluorocarbons, be emitted to the atmosphere at a higher rate than was currently happening. Also stressed was the possibility of climate change occurring as a result of increasing levels of tropospheric ozone as well as of the so-called greenhouse gas properties of ozone-modifying substances.

To promote awareness of the ozone layer issue in developing countries, a seminar for developing country scientists on global environmental problems was held at UNEP headquarters in November, with participants from Argentina, Brazil, China, Egypt, India, Kenya, Malaysia and Nigeria.

On 24 May,[3] the Governing Council urged States which had not signed and ratified the Vienna Convention to do so and requested the Executive Director to convene a working group on a protocol on chlorofluorocarbons, authorizing him, pending the Convention's entry into force, to convene a diplomatic conference to adopt such a protocol. The Council urged States and regional economic integration organizations, pending the protocol's entry into force, to control their emissions of chlorofluorocarbons and urged interested parties to sponsor a workshop on the subject under UNEP auspices, and to set up a steering committee to prepare for it. The Council also set out the committee's terms of reference.

Climate-related monitoring

At the end of 1985, the WMO/UNEP Background Air Pollution Monitoring Network involved 95 participating countries, 65 of which had operational stations and 55 were regularly reporting data on the state of the atmosphere. During 1985, five other stations became operational. Emphasis continued to be on improving the quantity and density of data, replacing outmoded instruments by modern ones, and improving quality assurance procedures.

The World Glacier Inventory was completed in 1985 and responsibility for its continuation passed to the UNEP-supported World Glacier Monitoring Service. A selection of key reference glaciers in various regions was being made by the Service, which would also provide annual data on the mass balance changes of the glaciers. These data would contribute to understanding global climatic changes and variability, and provide an indication of water availability from glaciers in areas where they occurred.

Climate impact studies

In 1985 the World Climate Impact Studies programme (WCIP)—the UNEP-led element of the World Climate Programme (WCP) of WMO, which had resulted from the 1979 World Climate Conference[18]—focused on reducing the risks of adverse climatic impact on food systems and agriculture, developing methodologies for climate impact assessment, and analysing greenhouse-gas-induced climate changes. Mounting scientific evidence indicated that the earth's atmosphere was gradually warming, because of excessive amounts of gases (mainly the by-products of the burning of fossil fuels) which trapped heat in the atmosphere, much as glass traps heat in a greenhouse (leading to the term "greenhouse effect").

The highlight of WCIP was the second joint UNEP/WMO/International Council of Scientific Unions assessment of the role of carbon dioxide and other greenhouse gases in climate variations and their associated impacts. The assessment was carried out at a conference (Villach, Austria, 7-15 October), attended by scientists from 29 countries, which stated that, in the first half of the next century, a rise of global mean temperature could occur that would be greater than any in history. The increase in global mean equilibrium surface temperature due to increases in carbon dioxide and other greenhouse gases was likely to be in the range of 1.5-4.5° C. Further, the expected global mean temperature due to a doubling of carbon dioxide was about the same magnitude as the change of global temperature from the last glacial period to the current interglacial one. A global warming of 1.5 to 4.5° C would lead to an estimated sea-level rise of between 20 and 165 centimetres. A future change of climate of such an order could have profound effects on global ecosystems. The conference drew attention to the linkages between climate change and other major environmental issues such as acidic deposition and threats to the Earth's ozone shield, and noted that actions to limit one environmental threat could have repercussions on other environmental areas. The conference called on scientists and policy-makers to explore jointly alternative policies.

Various WCIP projects were concluded during 1985. Under the project on integrated approaches to climate impact assessment, a two-volume *Assessment of Climate Impacts on Agriculture* was finalized for publication in 1986. Under the project on improving the science of climate impact studies, a publication, *Climate Impact Assessment*, was issued and distributed free to developing countries. Under a joint UNEP/UNRISD/Centre for Regional, Ecological and Science Studies in Development Alternatives project, on reducing the vulnerability of food systems to climate in north-east India, the *Perception Study of Food Vulnerability to Climatic Variability in the Region* was published in October.

WCIP's Scientific Advisory Committee held its fourth meeting (Vienna, 4-8 February) to review implementation of WCIP and recommend future activities. Among these were: following up on the Villach conference's recommendations; encouraging development of national climate programmes, including impact studies; and urging national participation in WCP.

UNEP and the United States National Centre for Atmospheric Research held a workshop (Lugano, Switzerland, 11-15 November) on El Niño and Southern Oscillation (ENSO) events, thought to be associated with climatic anomalies, including drought, in many parts of the world. The workshop considered impacts on socio-economic systems, agriculture, fisheries and ecology attributed to ENSO in 10 world regions.

During 1985, UNEP-supported experts began investigating the impact of climatic variations on agriculture in the humid tropics of South America. Three countries were involved in the investigation, carried out by the Inter-Agency Group on Agricultural Biometeorology. Interim results were discussed at an expert group meeting (Lima, Peru, November).

Noting the progress in implementing WCP, particularly WCIP, the Governing Council on 23 May[19] invited the Executive Director, in co-operation with WMO, to support WCP by encouraging the development of national climate programmes in countries where none existed, and by facilitating closer co-operation among such programmes and between them and WCP.

Terrestrial ecosystems

Desertification and drought control

In Africa, famine, malnutrition and deaths arising from drought and desertification remained for most of 1985 the most visible sign of a broader crisis. At its peak, in 1984-1985, chronic malnutrition was affecting 150 million people with over 30 million at risk, of whom about 10 million were displaced. Towards the end of 1985, in most of the 21 seriously affected countries, the food supply seemed to move back to normal, after average to above-average crop harvests. There was also an increased awareness by Governments of the desertification threat and the need for long-term solutions. But poverty and lack of resources remained acute.

In a June 1985 preliminary report on the stricken countries,[20] submitted to the General Assembly pursuant to its 1984 request,[21] the Secretary-General stated that 74 countries throughout the world had a substantial portion of their territories affected. Most of the 37 least developed countries (see p. 433) were stricken by drought and desertification, and were in a state of extreme deprivation. Many other countries were also affected, including some industrialized ones.

The current African drought had persisted, with certain variations, for the past 17 years. Despite its length, there was no evidence of a long-term change in the African climate. Computer simulations indicated that the current drought, although the worst in the century, was within a normal range of variability. The disturbing conclusion was that drought was a recurrent phenomenon that the affected countries, especially in Africa, must learn to live with.

The combination of drought and desertification had had disastrous consequences, the report said. In 1983-1984, more than 150 million Africans were facing extreme hunger, malnutrition and shortages of potable water. The Secretary-General stressed that, in concert with the heads of concerned United Nations organizations, he was reviewing all aspects of the problem, and would present more specific recommendations on future action in accordance with any further decision of the Economic and Social Council and the Assembly.

Africa's Priority Programme for Economic Recovery 1986-1990, adopted by the Assembly of Heads of State and Government of the Organization of African Unity (Addis Ababa, Ethiopia, 18-20 July),[22] recommended national strategies, such as drought and desertification control plans; action areas, such as vegetation conservation, water resources, firewood substitution and protecting common ecosystems; and co-operation at all levels.

In its final resolution, the second Ministerial Conference for a joint policy to combat desertification (Dakar, Senegal, 1-9 November)[23] defined 29 major projects for finalization and funding, listed measures for international co-operation, and decided to hold such a conference every two years.

ECONOMIC AND SOCIAL COUNCIL ACTION

On 25 July 1985, the Economic and Social Council, by **decision 1985/176**, requested the Secretary-General to submit the final report as soon as possible to the Assembly, taking into account views expressed by delegations during the Council's July 1985 session. By **decision 1985/102** of 8 February 1985, the Council had decided to consider countries stricken by desertification and drought at the same time as international co-operation on the environment.

GENERAL ASSEMBLY ACTION

On 17 December, the General Assembly adopted two resolutions concerning desertification and drought, both recommended by the Second Committee. It adopted **resolution 40/175** without vote.

Countries stricken by desertification and drought

The General Assembly,

Recalling its resolution 39/208 of 17 December 1984 and Economic and Social Council decision 1985/176 of 25 July 1985, as well as its Declaration on the Critical Economic Situation in Africa, annexed to its resolution 39/29 of 3 December 1984,

Noting Africa's Priority Programme for Economic Recovery 1986-1990, adopted by the Assembly of Heads of State and Government of the Organization of African Unity at its twenty-first ordinary session, held at Addis Ababa from 18 to 20 July 1985,

Congratulating the Government of Senegal for having taken the initiative of convening the Ministerial Conference for a joint policy to combat desertification in the countries of the Permanent Inter-State Committee on Drought Control in the Sahel and the Economic Community of West African States, in the Maghreb countries and in Egypt and the Sudan, which met at Dakar, for the first time from 18 to 27 July 1984,[24] and for the second time from 1 to 9 November 1985,

Congratulating the Government of Egypt for having invited the first African Environmental Conference, organized by the United Nations Environment Programme in consultation with the Economic Commission for Africa and the Organization of African Unity, to be held at Cairo in December 1985,

Congratulating also the Government of France for having taken the initiative of convening an international conference on tree and forest, to be held in Paris in February 1986,

Noting the positive action taken by the United Nations Sudano-Sahelian Office, as part of a joint effort by the United Nations Development Programme and the United Nations Environment Programme to help twenty-two African countries, on behalf of the United Nations Environment Programme, implement the Plan of Action to Combat Desertification,

Taking note of decision 12/10 of 28 May 1984 on desertification, adopted by the Governing Council of the United Nations Environment Programme,[25]

Welcoming the establishment by six east African countries—Djibouti, Ethiopia, Kenya, Somalia, the Sudan and Uganda—of an Intergovernmental Authority for Drought and Development for the purpose of combating the effects of drought in those countries,

Deeply concerned by the tragic consequences of the acceleration of desertification, combined with persistent drought—the most serious recorded this century—which have resulted in a substantial drop in the agricultural output of many developing countries and have contributed particularly to a worsening of the current economic crisis in Africa,

Noting with great anxiety that desertification and drought continue to spread and intensify in developing countries, particularly in Africa,

Aware that the problems of desertification and drought are increasingly assuming a structural and endemic character and that real and permanent solutions must be found in increased global efforts based on concerted action by the stricken countries and the international community,

Bearing in mind that the majority of the countries affected by desertification and drought are low-income countries and, for the most part, belong to the group of the least developed countries, particularly those in Africa,

Aware that the prime responsibility in the struggle against desertification and the effects of drought rests with the countries concerned and that such action is an essential component of their development,

Recognizing, however, that given the scope and the intensity of desertification and drought, particularly in the least developed countries, the attainment of the objectives of programmes to combat these scourges requires financial and human resources beyond the means of the affected countries,

Considering the interdependence between developed countries and those affected by desertification and drought, and the negative impact of those phenomena on the economies of the countries concerned,

Emphasizing the fundamental importance of all forms of South-South co-operation in executing programmes to combat desertification and drought,

Taking note of the preliminary report of the Secretary-General on the countries stricken by desertification and drought,

1. *Welcomes* the results of the Ministerial Conference for a joint policy to combat desertification in the countries of the Permanent Inter-State Committee on Drought Control in the Sahel and the Economic Community of West African States, in the Maghreb countries and in Egypt and the Sudan, and takes note with satisfaction of the final resolution adopted by the Conference in 1984 and that adopted in 1985;

2. *Takes note with satisfaction* of the establishment by the Organization of African Unity of the Special Emergency Assistance Fund for Drought and Famine in Africa;

3. *Recommends* that high priority should be given in the development plans and programmes of the affected countries themselves to the problem of desertification and to problems resulting from drought;

4. *Recognizes* that particular attention should be given to countries stricken by desertification and drought and that special efforts should be made by the international community, particularly the developed countries, in support of action taken individually or collectively by the affected countries;

5. *Recommends* that the international community, above all the developed countries, should continue to provide coherent short-term, medium-term and long-term assistance to those countries in order to support the rehabilitation process effectively—in particular through intensive reafforestation—and the renewal of growth of agricultural production in the countries stricken by desertification and drought, particularly in Africa;

6. *Recommends* that, within the framework of bilateral and multilateral development aid programmes, the fight against desertification and drought should be granted priority in view of the extent of those problems;

7. *Appeals* to all members of the international community, including organs and agencies of the United Nations system, regional and subregional financial institutions, and non-governmental organizations, to continue to provide full support, in all forms—including financial, technical or any other form of assistance—to the development efforts of countries stricken by desertification and drought;

8. *Takes note with satisfaction* of the generosity with which the international community has responded to the assistance needs resulting from the emergency in Africa, particularly as regards food aid, transport and medical assistance;

9. *Requests* the appropriate organs and agencies of the United Nations to provide the Secretary-General, for transmission to the stricken countries, with all relevant studies carried out in their respective spheres of competence, in particular with respect to food and agricultural production, development of water resources,

industrialization and raw materials, including the studies carried out by the United Nations Conference on Trade and Development on the impact of desertification and drought on the foreign trade of the stricken countries,[26] including similarly, the studies to determine the interaction between forest zones and arid regions and their influence on the acceleration of desertification, particularly in Africa;

10. *Requests* the Secretary-General to take all necessary steps to ensure that his final report on the implementation of resolution 39/208, which is to be submitted to the General Assembly through the Economic and Social Council at its second regular session of 1986, contains proposals for specific action to be undertaken, as indicated in the present resolution.

General Assembly resolution 40/175

17 December 1985   Meeting 119   Adopted without vote

Approved by Second Committee (A/40/1009/Add.1) without vote, 3 December (meeting 46); draft by Vice-Chairman (A/C.2/40/L.76), based on informal consultations on draft by Algeria, Angola, Argentina, Austria, Bangladesh, Benin, Burkina Faso, Burundi, Cape Verde, Central African Republic, Chad, Chile, China, Comoros, Congo, Djibouti, Egypt, Ethiopia, France, Gambia, Germany, Federal Republic of Guinea, Guinea-Bissau, India, Indonesia, Italy, Ivory Coast, Jamaica, Kenya, Lesotho, Liberia, Luxembourg, Madagascar, Mali, Mauritania, Mexico, Mozambique, Netherlands, Niger, Nigeria, Pakistan, Romania, Rwanda, Senegal, Togo, Trinidad and Tobago, Tunisia, United Kingdom, United States, Yugoslavia, Zaire and Zambia (A/C.2/40/L.33); agenda item 12.
Meeting numbers. GA 40th session: 2nd Committee 22, 23, 29, 30, 34, 36, 39, 42, 43, 46; plenary 119.

The General Assembly adopted **resolution 40/209** without vote.

Desertification and drought

The General Assembly,

Aware of the importance of problems relating to desertification and drought for a large number of countries,

Bearing in mind that such problems are discussed under a number of agenda items in the Second Committee,

1. *Emphasizes* the importance of existing mandates under its resolutions relating to desertification and drought;

2. *Requests* the Secretary-General to ensure that all problems relating to desertification and drought will be considered in future years under one sub-item, to be entitled "Desertification and drought", under the item entitled "Development and international economic co-operation" and will be dealt with in odd years, in accordance with the biennial programme of work of the Second Committee.

General Assembly resolution 40/209

17 December 1985   Meeting 119   Adopted without vote

Approved by Second Committee (A/40/989/Add.14) without vote, 25 November (meeting 43); draft by Vice-Chairman (A/C.2/40/L.65), based on informal consultations on draft by Finland (A/C.2/40/L.39); agenda item 84.
Meeting numbers. GA 40th session: 2nd Committee 31, 38, 41, 43; plenary 119.

Implementation of the Plan of Action to Combat Desertification

Throughout 1985, several bodies took part in the effort to combat desertification. The first African Ministerial Conference on the Environment (see p. 793) took action to implement several programmes on desertification, including a regional co-operation programme among the most-affected countries, strengthening of the North Saharan green belt project, efforts to combat desert advance in the South Saharan zone and the Gum Belt (Sudan) and greater co-operation in research.

The fifth session of the Consultative Group for Desertification Control (Geneva, 18-24 July) was attended by seven United Nations co-sponsor agencies, 14 core members, 21 invited countries and other organizations. Fourteen anti-desertification project proposals were presented to the Group, which expressed interest in six of them, costed at $20.82 million; consultations between donors and recipients followed. The Group also made recommendations on resource mobilization for implementing the 1977 Plan of Action to Combat Desertification.[27]

An expert meeting (Nairobi, 11-14 March) reviewed progress concerning the Desertification Assessment and Mapping Methodology and Data Base being developed by FAO and UNEP. The meeting discussed methodologies for monitoring and mapping desertification and the preparation of a World Atlas of Thematic Maps on Desertification called for in the Plan of Action.

UNEP began work on a Desertification Information System, to organize and code the thousands of documents in the library of UNEP's Desertification Control Programme Activity Centre (DC/PAC), as well as country and project files, for entry into a microcomputer. The work entailed creating several data bases to respond to world-wide requests for information.

In 1985, three television documentaries on desertification were produced. *The Crowded Desert*, on India's Thar Desert, and a six-part series *Seeds of Hope*, on land degradation in Ethiopia, were produced by UNEP and Central Independent Television (United Kingdom). *Trees for Tomorrow* showed a DC/PAC tree-planting project in southern India (see below). DC/PAC also participated in Australian and Japanese television documentaries, and organized trips for journalists to areas in Kenya undergoing desertification. One issue of the *Desertification Control Bulletin* and a report on *Research and Training for Desertification Control: the United Nations Effort* were published. A directory of world-wide institutions concerned with desertification, containing more than 500 entries, was prepared for publication in 1986. The two-volume *Desertification Control in Africa: Actions (I)* and *Directory of Institutions (II)* was updated and reprinted.

UNEP assisted the Tunisian Government to formulate a national plan against desertification and to integrate it in its national development plan. In Tunisia UNEP also initiated a pilot project to map desertification, study indigenous plants for use in sand-dune fixation, and carry out desertification control training courses. A UNEP/UNEP-COM project on integrated agricultural development as a means to combat desertification continued in Democratic Yemen. A project involving tree planting, the training of schoolchildren and farmers in afforestation and the setting up of nurseries was launched in southern India, in support of the NGO Millions of Trees Club. In addition, UNEP decided to develop an approach for a project in the Sudano-Sahelian region for ACC consideration.

In a UNEP-sponsored training course held in the United Republic of Tanzania, five scientists from the Institute of Desert Research, China, organized seminars on desertification control. A UNEP-sponsored training course on afforestation and sand-dune fixation in dry zones was held in Moscow and Ashkabad, USSR, for 20 specialists from 16 developing countries.

In response to a 1983 General Assembly request,[28] the Secretary-General submitted in September 1985 a report[29] summarizing the substantive views of 46 Member States, some of which had been received in 1982[30] and 1983,[31] on financing the Plan of Action, particularly the establishment of an international financial corporation to fund non-commercial initiatives. The majority of countries did not support the proposed modalities, and while half of them supported the setting up of the financial corporation, few were willing to finance it. There seemed to be no general support for additional financing. The Secretary-General suggested that the Consultative Group for Desertification Control be asked to consider innovative approaches for the Plan's financing.

UNEP Council action. On 23 May,[32] the Governing Council urged Governments, United Nations bodies, research institutions and other organizations to intensify their efforts to combat desertification and expressed appreciation for the emergency assistance offered to countries facing famine. It called on affected countries to prepare national plans, and on donor countries to assist affected countries to curb desertification. Noting the role played by NGOs in many of the most successful anti-desertification efforts, the Council called on Governments and international organizations to utilize NGOs to a greater degree. It invited the Executive Director to consult the principal international organizations funding desertification control activities to ascertain how UNEP could best assist them, and to recommend to the Council in 1987 measures that could enhance co-operation between UNEP and those institutions. The Council approved measures to enhance the work of the Inter-Agency Working Group on Desertification, requested the Executive Director to consider including the States members of the Southern African Development Coordination Conference (SADCC) in the list of countries eligible to receive assistance through the United Nations Sudano-Sahelian Office (see below), and urged him to seek alternative sources of funding to assist SADCC countries in particular.

GENERAL ASSEMBLY ACTION

On 17 December, the General Assembly, on the recommendation of the Second Committee, adopted **resolution 40/198 A** without vote.

Implementation and financing of the Plan of Action

The General Assembly,

Recalling its resolution 32/172 of 19 December 1977, by which it approved the Plan of Action to Combat Desertification,

Recalling also its resolutions 33/89 of 15 December 1978, 34/184 of 18 December 1979, 36/191 of 17 December 1981, 37/220 of 20 December 1982 and 38/163 of 19 December 1983, dealing with the implementation and financing of the Plan of Action to Combat Desertification,

Recalling further the Declaration on the Critical Economic Situation in Africa, adopted by the General Assembly in its resolution 39/29 of 3 December 1984,

Noting with dismay and grave concern the continuing spread and intensification of desertification in developing countries, especially in Africa, and the grave human suffering, economic losses and social disruption caused by this phenomenon,

Having considered the report of the Governing Council of the United Nations Environment Programme on the work of its thirteenth session and decision 13/30 A of 23 May 1985 of the Governing Council on the implementation of the Plan of Action to Combat Desertification,

Having also considered the report of the Secretary-General on financing the Plan of Action to Combat Desertification,

1. *Takes note* of decision 13/30 A of the Governing Council of the United Nations Environment Programme;

2. *Shares* the concern of the Governing Council over the slow implementation of the Plan of Action to Combat Desertification;

3. *Urges* Governments, organizations of the United Nations system and other intergovernmental bodies to intensify their efforts in combating desertification and to accord the highest priority to actions recommended in the Plan of Action and decision 13/30 A of the Governing Council;

4. *Notes* the significant role that non-governmental organizations are playing in the anti-desertification efforts, and calls upon Governments and organizations of the United Nations system and other intergovernmental bodies to explore all opportunities of involving them more in this effort;

5. *Urges* the international community to increase its assistance to the countries concerned with a view to the implementation of their national and regional programmes aimed at desertification control;

6. *Endorses* the Governing Council's invitation to the Executive Director of the United Nations Environment Programme to consult with the principal international organizations which are funding desertification control activities in order to ascertain how the Programme can facilitate funding activities, and to recommend measures to enhance co-operation in this field;

7. *Urges* Governments of countries affected by desertification to accord sustained priority to medium-term and long-term strategies and programmes for combating desertification and to ensure that these are smoothly integrated with their national development plans and regional co-operative programmes to curb the spread of environmental degradation;

8. *Notes* the measures approved by the Governing Council of the United Nations Environment Programme in its decision 13/30 A to enhance the work of the Inter-Agency Working Group on Desertification and calls upon all members of the Working Group to intensify their joint efforts for the effective implementation of the Plan of Action;

9. *Requests* the Governing Council of the United Nations Environment Programme to report to the General Assembly at its forty-second session, through the Economic and Social Council, on the progress made in the implementation of the Plan of Action;

10. *Takes note* of the report of the Secretary-General on financing the Plan of Action to Combat Desertification;

11. *Notes* the dearth of reactions and replies on the measures for providing additional resources needed for financing the Plan of Action recommended in the three reports[35] prepared by high-level financial experts convened by the Executive Director in accordance with General Assembly resolution 32/172;

12. *Considers* that the expert studies deserve further consideration and requests the Executive Director of the United Nations Environment Programme to take due account of them under his responsibility with respect to the implementation of the Plan of Action, as well as within the framework of the mandate of the Consultative Group on Desertification Control;

13. *Requests* the Secretary-General to report to the General Assembly at its forty-second session, through the Economic and Social Council, on the implementation of the present resolution.

General Assembly resolution 40/198 A

17 December 1985   Meeting 119   Adopted without vote

Approved by Second Committee (A/40/989/Add.6) without vote (parts A & B together), 25 November (meeting 43); draft by Vice-Chairman (A/C.2/40/L.66), based on informal consultations on draft by Burkina Faso, Cape Verde, Chad, Comoros, Ecuador, France, Gambia, Guinea, Guinea-Bissau, Italy, Kenya, Liberia, Mali, Mauritania, Netherlands, Niger, Panama, Senegal and United Republic of Tanzania (A/C.2/40/L.35); agenda item 84 (f).

Meeting numbers. GA 40th session: 2nd Committee 22, 30, 34, 36, 43; plenary 119.

Implementation of the Plan of Action in the Sudano-Sahelian region

In 1985 the drought continued to be particularly acute in the Sudano-Sahelian region, and most international aid was emergency assistance. The United Nations Sudano-Sahelian Office (UNSO), a joint UNDP/UNEP venture, working on UNEP's behalf to implement the Plan of Action to Combat Desertification in the Sudano-Sahelian region, co-operated closely in this endeavour, especially with the Office of Emergency Operations for Africa (see Chapter III of this section).

UNSO raised almost $13 million in new pledges to the United Nations Trust Fund for Sudano-Sahelian Activities in 1985 (not including UNEP and UNDP contributions). It allocated over $12 million for projects against desertification, mainly for reforestation, energy-related activities, range and water resources management, soil protection and sand-dune fixation, planning, research and information exchange.

Major forestry initiatives were carried out in Ethiopia. UNSO expanded a reforestation programme involving 3,000 hectares in the Debre Birhan area, with a contribution from the Danish International Development Agency (DANIDA), and undertook a joint mission with the Finnish International Development Agency (FINNIDA) for a project in Dese which would expand the total planted area to 7,500 hectares. UNSO also received a commitment from FINNIDA for forestry management in Somalia. In Mauritania, UNSO obtained a contribution from DANIDA for institutional support to the Department for the Protection of Nature. In the Niger, Norway pledged to finance the expansion of green-belt plantations around Niamey. A project for family woodlots in Burkina Faso continued.

To reduce the demand for fuelwood, UNSO continued working on alternative energy sources. In Somalia, a wind energy project started with DANIDA financing. In Cape Verde, where wind turbines had been installed with DANIDA financing, UNSO investigated a wider use of wind energy. A project in Senegal to develop the use of peat as household fuel and a programme in the Gambia on improved wood-burning stoves were started with DANIDA contributions.

To combat moving sand dunes, UNSO was carrying out dune fixation using vegetation. In 1985, three projects were under way in Somalia and one in Senegal. In Cape Verde, soil protection began with a contribution from the Norwegian Agency for International Development.

In range management, a project to establish a centre for the ecological monitoring of pastoral ecosystems in Senegal started with a DANIDA contribution. In the Gambia, range-land development and protection began with a contribution from the Arab Gulf Programme for United Nations Development Organizations. In Mali, the integrated development of the Niger River flood plains progressed.

With their inclusion in the list of countries eligible for UNSO assistance, planning missions went to Ghana and Togo to assist them in initiating desertification strategies. UNSO also supported seminars on desertification in Benin, Burkina Faso and Senegal, assisted the second Ministerial Conference on desertification (see p. 806), and sponsored a symposium on drought and desertification (Washington, D.C., October).

Responding to a June 1985 UNDP Governing Council request,[34] the UNDP Administrator[35] described 1985 UNSO activities to implement the medium- and long-term recovery and rehabilitation programme in the Sudano-Sahelian region (see

p. 537). These activities were aimed at mitigating the effects of drought, helping countries to become self-sufficient in food production, enhancing socio-economic development and arresting desertification. Under the road programme, construction was under way in Burkina Faso, Cape Verde, the Gambia, the Niger and Senegal. National activities included reforestation and road construction in Burkina Faso, airport runways construction in Cape Verde, water resources management in the Gambia and reforestation in Niger. Regional and international activities included support to the Institut du Sahel and assistance in establishing (January 1986) the Intergovernmental Authority for Drought and Development, comprising Djibouti, Ethiopia, Kenya, Somalia, the Sudan and Uganda. UNSO continued to assist the members of the Permanent Inter-State Committee on Drought Control in the Sahel (CILSS) (Burkina Faso, Cape Verde, Chad, Gambia, Mali, Mauritania, Niger, Senegal). Funds mobilized by UNSO amounted to $87.8 million at the end of 1985.

Activities carried out in 1984 to implement the Plan of Action in the Sudano-Sahelian region were described in a February 1985 report of the UNEP Executive Director.[36]

By **decision 40/441** of 17 December, the General Assembly took note of a Secretariat note drawing attention to the Executive Director's report.

On 23 May,[37] the UNEP Governing Council welcomed UNSO's steps to implement the Plan of Action in 21 countries of the Sudano-Sahelian and neighbouring regions. It urged the UNEP and UNDP executive heads to consolidate the UNSO achievements and to intensify efforts to mobilize resources for combating desertification. It also included the United Republic of Tanzania in the list of countries authorized to receive assistance through UNSO (with that inclusion, the list stood at 22).

On 28 June,[38] the UNDP Governing Council urged Governments, United Nations bodies and other organizations to intensify their assistance to the countries of the region, and urged Governments of the affected areas to intensify their co-ordination efforts in combating desertification. It also endorsed the UNEP Governing Council's action regarding the United Republic of Tanzania. On the same day,[34] the UNDP Council expressed gratitude to those contributing to the implementation of the Sudano-Sahelian recovery programme, appealed to donors to strengthen their support for UNSO, and requested it to continue co-operating with CILSS and its members. The UNDP Administrator was requested to continue reporting annually on the implementation of the recovery programme.

GENERAL ASSEMBLY ACTION

On 17 December, the General Assembly, on the recommendation of the Second Committee, adopted **resolution 40/198 B** without vote.

Implementation in the Sudano-Sahelian region of the Plan of Action

The General Assembly,

Recalling its resolutions 36/190 of 17 December 1981, 37/216 of 20 December 1982, 38/164 of 19 December 1983, and 39/168 of 17 December 1984,

Noting decision 13/30 B of 23 May 1985 of the Governing Council of the United Nations Environment Programme on the implementation in the Sudano-Sahelian region of the Plan of Action to Combat Desertification,

Noting also Economic and Social Council resolutions 1984/65 of 26 July 1984 on the implementation in the Sudano-Sahelian region of the Plan of Action to Combat Desertification, and 1984/72 of 27 July 1984 on environment and development in Africa,

Considering the report of the Executive Director of the United Nations Environment Programme on the implementation in the Sudano-Sahelian region of the Plan of Action to Combat Desertification,

Considering also the report of the Secretary-General on the critical situation of food and agriculture in Africa, 1984-1985,[39]

1. *Takes note* of the report of the Executive Director of the United Nations Environment Programme on the implementation in the Sudano-Sahelian region of the Plan of Action to Combat Desertification;

2. *Notes with concern:*

(a) The damage wrought by drought on the countries of Africa south of the Sahara;

(b) That insufficient financial resources continue to be a serious constraint in combating desertification;

(c) That the struggle against desertification requires financial and human resources beyond the means of the affected countries;

3. *Notes with satisfaction* the progress that the United Nations Sudano-Sahelian Office has made in the face of these obstacles in assisting, on behalf of the United Nations Environment Programme, the Governments of the countries of the region in combating desertification, under a joint venture between the United Nations Environment Programme and the United Nations Development Programme;

4. *Endorses* the decision of the Governing Council of the United Nations Environment Programme to add the United Republic of Tanzania to the list of countries to be assisted by the United Nations Sudano-Sahelian Office in their efforts to implement the Plan of Action to Combat Desertification, contained in Council decision 13/30 B;

5. *Commends* the Executive Director of the United Nations Environment Programme and the Administrator of the United Nations Development Programme for the effective and co-ordinated manner in which they have continued to develop the joint venture through the United Nations Sudano-Sahelian Office;

6. *Recommends* the Governing Council of the United Nations Environment Programme and the Governing Council of the United Nations Development Programme to continue and increase their support for the United Nations Sudano-Sahelian Office in order to enable it to respond more adequately to the pressing needs of the countries of the Sudano-Sahelian and adjacent regions;

7. *Expresses its gratitude* to the Governments, specialized agencies, other intergovernmental organizations and all organizations that have contributed to the implementation in the Sudano-Sahelian region of the Plan of Action to Combat Desertification;

8. *Draws the attention* of the international community to the need to increase the efforts to implement the Plan of Action in the Sudano-Sahelian region and urges it to contribute to this implementation through appropriate means, including the United Nations Trust Fund for Sudano-Sahelian Activities, as well as to respond favourably to requests for assistance from the Governments of the countries of the region;

9. *Recommends* the Governing Council of the United Nations Environment Programme to make the necessary arrangements, in conformity with General Assembly resolution 39/217 of 18 December 1984, for submitting to the Assembly, through the Economic and Social Council, a report on the implementation in the Sudano-Sahelian region of the Plan of Action to Combat Desertification.

General Assembly resolution 40/198 B

17 December 1985   Meeting 119   Adopted without vote

(For other procedural details, see p. 809).

Soil management

In many parts of the world the soil was being over-used, and mismanagement was robbing it of its wealth, the UNEP Executive Director stated in his annual report.[40] Examples of the results of this abuse were the growing of steppe in the monocultures of different regions in Canada and the United States, soil erosion in Armenia and Kasachstan and the salinization of soils of Sudanese peanut plantations as a result of irrigation. Signs of a looming world-wide ecological catastrophe were clearly recognizable. The UNEP 1982 World Soils Policy[41] addressed the issue of sustainable agriculture, and in 1985 UNEP sought to obtain financial support for the Policy's Plan of Action.[42] But in spite of many positive comments, few Governments were ready to support Plan-related projects through in-kind contributions, and this had prevented the Plan from becoming operational.

Land management techniques were the subject of a training course (Georgia, USSR, September) for 22 participants, mainly from the Andean region, under a joint Bulgaria/UNEP/UNEPCOM project on land/soil management in mountain ecosystems. In October, as part of the UNEP/UNEPCOM project on the impact of agricultural management on the environment, a workshop on ecological management of irrigated farming in arid and semi-arid zones was held in the southern provinces of the USSR for 20 participants from developing countries.

On 23 May,[43] the UNEP Governing Council urged Governments to establish national soil policies. Governments and international organizations were urged to intensify efforts to combat soil degradation and to co-operate with UNEP in implementing the World Soils Policy Plan of Action.

The Executive Director was invited to continue his efforts to secure commitments from Governments and international bodies to the Plan's implementation, and to assist Governments in formulating national soils policies.

Lithosphere

In May 1985, under the UNEP/UNESCO/USSR project on geology and the environment, the first session of the International Scientific Council on Geology and Environment Problems was held at Yalta, USSR. It was attended by 29 scientists, who elaborated draft international guidelines on geology and land-use planning, and drew up the curriculum for a 1986 training course to be held in the USSR.

Forest ecosystems

Tropical forests

Despite efforts by the international community to reverse the destruction of tropical forests, no significant changes in the downward trend were perceived. But those efforts continued, and during 1985 several major events in which UNEP played a role took place. In April, the International Tropical Timber Agreement came into force provisionally (see p. 570); it included environmental considerations for the conservation of the resource base of the commodity. The ninth World Forestry Congress was held in Mexico; FAO declared 1985 the International Year of the Forest; the President of France decided to convene in 1986 a high-level political conference on the protection of forests in Europe and the African region north of the equator; and in November several Governments and international organizations met at The Hague, Netherlands, to analyse the financial implications and mechanisms of the Tropical Forests Action Plan, originally proposed at an expert meeting held in Nairobi in 1980.[44] (For reforestation projects in the Sudano-Sahelian region, see p. 810.)

Addressing the General Assembly's Second Committee,[45] the UNEP Executive Director warned that the world had 20 years, or even less, to turn from a course of irrevocable destruction. He called for a high-level non-technical conference on the future of tropical forests. Such a conference could tackle two difficult international problems: the reconciliation of the non-contested national sovereignty on forests with the legitimate concerns of the world as a whole; and the frank analysis of why, when the technical means to conserve forests existed and the need to use them was so widely acknowledged, nothing much was being done. He also suggested that the Assembly consider proclaiming 1990 as United Nations Year of the Tropical Forest.

During 1985, under the UNEP/UNESCO pilot project on research and training in tropical forest areas, a regional training course on computer-based quantitative methods for environmental biologists was held at Singapore; a training workshop on agroforestry in the humid tropical zones of West and Central Africa was held in Makokou, Gabon; and a training course on entomological research in tropical forest ecosystems was held in Abidjan and Tai, Ivory Coast. Fellowships were provided to specialists from India, the Ivory Coast, Malaysia, Sri Lanka and Viet Nam. With funds from the National Federation of UNESCO Associations in Japan, reforestation/afforestation projects started in Sri Lanka, Thailand and New Caledonia. Under a joint UNEP/FAO project on appropriate management of forest genetic resources, case-studies on conservation of these resources were carried out in Cameroon, Malaysia and Peru.

In **resolution 40/200**, the Assembly called on the Executive Director to co-ordinate further UNEP activities with those of other United Nations bodies, to co-operate with the organizers of international initiatives on the future of the forests, and to report to the Governing Council.

Mountain ecosystems

An integrated pilot project on the environmental management and protection of Andean ecosystems started in 1985. Financed by a trust fund of the Federal Republic of Germany, it aimed at improving the Andean farmers' living conditions in a demonstration area close to the city of Cajamarca, Peru.

Conservation of wildlife and protected areas

Protecting endangered species, managing national parks and creating national conservation strategies continued to be major concerns. UNEP continued to exercise its co-ordinating role in implementing the 1980 World Conservation Strategy[44] by providing secretariat services to the Ecosystem Conservation Group (ECG), comprising UNEP, FAO, UNESCO, the International Union for Conservation of Nature and Natural Resources (IUCN) and the World Wildlife Fund (WWF). Priority was given to preparing national conservation strategies and their integration in national development planning. One of the countries selected by ECG for assistance was Uganda, where UNEP, in co-operation with the Government and IUCN, was supporting the development of a national conservation strategy. Several United Nations bodies, donor agencies and NGOs were participating in that project. In 1985 UNEP also co-operated with Nepal, IUCN and the United States Agency for International Development (USAID) in formulating a national conservation strategy for that country.

UNEP continued to assist Governments in improving the management of wildlife and protected areas by reviewing the existing protected area coverage of habitats and species and their management, to ensure that critical habitats were protected and other measures taken to maintain the entire range of biological diversity. Towards this end, three expert group meetings were held in 1985 under a joint UNEP/IUCN project: in the Indo-Malayan realm (Corbett National Park, India, February); the Antarctica realm (Bonn, Federal Republic of Germany, May); and the Afro-tropical realm (Kasungu National Park, Malawi, June).

The third South Pacific National Parks and Reserves Conference (Apia, Samoa, June/July), convened by the South Pacific Regional Environment Programme, IUCN, UNEP and WWF, was attended by participants from 15 South Pacific island nations, Australia, New Zealand, the United States and various international organizations. Conference outputs included an action strategy for protected areas in the region, technical papers and a training workshop for field managers from 11 countries.

The conservation of endangered animal species focused on elephants, rhinoceroses, primates, cats and polar bears, whose status was reviewed in five UNEP/IUCN workshops which produced action plans. The improvement in managing the vicuña, a South American animal related to the llama, was examined in a workshop (Arica, Chile, March) attended by over 40 participants from all countries of South America where vicuña existed and Ecuador, which was planning to reintroduce it.

Plans to reintroduce the Przewalski horse into its native habitat in Central Asia were further developed. That horse, the original wild horse from which domesticated varieties derived, had ceased to exist in the wild in the late 1960s, but a number of zoological gardens had successfully bred it. At a UNEP-supported expert consultation (Moscow, May), the directors of zoological gardens holding Przewalski horses agreed to provide animals for reintroduction. The experts' recommendations and an action plan were distributed to the Governments concerned.

The proceedings of the first (1983) International Biosphere Reserve Congress,[46] containing an overview of the state of the world's biosphere reserves and future perspectives, were published and distributed to Governments and international organizations. Based on the Congress's recommendations, an Action Plan was elaborated. A Biosphere Reserve Scientific Advisory Panel was established and met in September 1985 at Cancún.

On 23 May,[47] the UNEP Council urged States to set up or improve biosphere reserves and take part in the development of the world network of biosphere reserves, and invited the Executive Director to support and assist the implementation of the 1984 Biosphere Reserves Action Plan.[48]

UNEP continued to support international measures to conserve wild animals and plants and their habitats, such as the 1973 Convention on International Trade in Endangered Species of Wild Fauna and Flora (CITES). The CITES secretariat (Lausanne, Switzerland), provided by UNEP, brought stricter control to international trade in threatened wildlife and wildlife products by stipulating that government permits be required for such trade. At the fifth meeting of the Conference of the Parties to the CITES Convention (Buenos Aires, Argentina, April/May), attended by 450 participants, 22 resolutions were adopted, including some on control of ivory trade and plant species.

In collaboration with IUCN, UNESCO and the International Waterfowl Research Bureau, UNEP continued to support the Convention on Wetlands of International Importance Especially as Waterfowl Habitat. The Convention Task Force met at The Hague in May and adopted conclusions on the Convention's implementation, subsequently conveyed to all contracting parties.

Convention on the conservation of migratory animals

As requested in 1984 by the Governing Council,[49] UNEP provided secretariat services for the Convention on the Conservation of Migratory Species of Wild Animals, and organized the first meeting of the Conference of the Parties to the Convention (Bonn, 21-26 October).

On 24 May,[3] the Council appealed to Governments and international organizations concerned to participate in the meeting and called on States not parties to the Convention to consider early adherence to it.

The meeting, attended by scientific experts and conservation officials from 63 countries and 33 organizations, revised the appendices to the Convention, established a Standing Committee and Scientific Council to supervise its implementation, and adopted financial rules and the first triennial budget of the secretariat. It gave impetus to transfrontier co-operation in protecting migratory species and adopted procedures for regional agreements under the Convention. It also requested the UNEP Executive Director, with the approval of the Governing Council, to seek the Secretary-General's consent to establish a trust fund for the Convention, initially for three years. The Executive Director subsequently reported[40] that he had secured that consent and, as there was to be no 1986 Council session, he would establish the fund on an interim basis.

Genetic resources

With UNEP and FAO support, the International Board for Plant Genetic Resources continued to stimulate activities for the exploration and collection of crop plant genetic resources. In 1985 it undertook the collection of crop germplasm in Madagascar, Sri Lanka and Uganda to complement earlier collections. The material collected was deposited in various gene banks, including those of the global network housing the World Base Collection co-ordinated by the Board.

The FAO International Undertaking on Plant Genetic Resources was discussed at the first meeting of the FAO Commission on Plant Genetic Resources (Rome, March) in which UNEP participated, with the aim of improving the conservation and management of such resources. During 1985 FAO, with UNEP support, started pilot projects in Cameroon, Malaysia and Peru, to develop and test methodologies for *in situ* conservation of forest genetic resources within existing nature reserves and protected areas, and to produce management plans for different categories of protected areas where aspects of genetic resources conservation would be incorporated.

Other activities aimed to create data banks and conservation schemes for animal genetic resources in developing countries. Under a joint FAO/UNEP project, field work on conserving the Kenana breed of cattle in the Sudan started; co-operation with research centres in Ethiopia, the Gambia and Kenya on trypanotolerant breeds of cattle continued; plans for conservation schemes for Sahiwal breeds in Pakistan were prepared; studies on the collection and shipment of semen continued; and activities towards the establishment of regional data banks in developing regions were discussed at an expert consultation meeting.

Research activities of the UNEP-supported regional Microbiological Resources Centres in Brazil, Egypt, Guatemala, Kenya, Senegal and Thailand dealt with the environmental application of microbial resources in increasing legume protein production, soil fertility through biological nitrogen fixation, upgrading of coffee processing by-products, bio-conversion of cassava surplus and by-products into power alcohol, and the degradation of persistent, key environmental pollutants. Each Centre also organized training activities and provided fellowships for applied research.

UNEP continued to support the World Data Centre for Micro-organisms (Brisbane, Australia), established to promote access to information on culture collections and to produce specialized inventories of microbial genetic resources of environmental and economic value. It also organized the third design meeting of the International Microbial Strain Data Network Working Group (Helsinki, August), in association with the Seventh International Conference on Global Impacts of Applied Microbiology.

Photosynthesis and bioproductivity

In 1985, work continued on the UNEP-supported project on primary productivity and photosynthesis in natural ecosystems of the tropics in relation to environmental variables, established in 1983 in co-operation with the University of London. The project secured the support of regional centres in Brazil, China, Kenya, Mexico and Thailand, which applied new technologies to determine the photosynthesis potential of major ecosystems of the tropics.

The interim results of regional studies undertaken in India, Kenya, Venezuela and Yugoslavia were presented to an expert group on photosynthesis in relation to bioproductivity which met in March at UNEP headquarters. The meeting, attended by scientists from 10 countries, considered future research priorities, particularly in developing countries.

In co-operation with Tycooly Publishers, UNEP issued a comprehensive work on *Photosynthesis in Relation to Plant Production in Terrestrial Environments* and, in co-operation with Pergamon Press, Oxford, published a second, updated edition of *Techniques in Photosynthesis and Bioproductivity*.

Freshwater ecosystems

In 1985, UNEP concentrated on the preparation of a comprehensive water programme, management of international water systems, environmental training on water management and support for the International Drinking Water Supply and Sanitation Decade (1981-1990), proclaimed by the General Assembly in 1980[50] (see p. 680).

As part of the programme on the environmental management of the common river system of the Zambezi,[51] the preparation of a plan for the sound management of that river system by the countries concerned—the Zambezi Action Plan (ZACPLAN)—started in 1985. In February, representatives of UNEP, FAO, UNESCO, WHO, WMO and IAEA attended an inter-agency consultative meeting at Geneva to discuss the programme's development. In April, with UNEP support, the first meeting of a working group of government experts on the Zambezi river system was held at Nairobi, attended by Botswana, Malawi, Mozambique, the United Republic of Tanzania, Zambia and Zimbabwe. Based on reports from those countries, UNEP prepared drafts of a diagnostic study on the state of the ecology and the environmental management of the river system and of ZACPLAN.

UNEP initiated a project on effluent monitoring and pollution control in the Lake Victoria basin, aimed at enabling the Lake Basin Development Authority to monitor water quality and other environmental conditions.

As a member of the International Scientific Council of the International Training Centre for Water Resources Management (CEFIGRE), UNEP attended its eighth session (Sophia Antipolis, France, April), which stressed the need to integrate environmental considerations in CEFIGRE training courses. During 1985, UNEP supported three such courses: on water pollution control, with 25 participants mainly from Africa (Sophia Antipolis, June); on water resources management to assist the basin countries in the preparation of ZACPLAN, with 15 participants from six Zambezi countries (Harare, Zimbabwe, October); and on rural water supply and sanitation, with 20 participants mainly from Asia (Bangkok, Thailand, November/December).

UNEP supported a training workshop on the chemistry of natural waters, organized by UNEP-COM (Kishinev, USSR, October) and attended by 15 professionals from developing countries. An Interregional Seminar on Assessment and Evaluation of Multiple Objective Water Resources Projects (Budapest, October), organized by the Secretariat's Department of Technical Co-operation for Development and supported by UNEP and Hungary, was attended by 55 professionals from 25 countries and seven international organizations. The second meeting of the Working Group on Large-Scale Water Development Projects (Athens, Greece, December) provided UNEP with suggestions on how to prepare guidelines on environmentally sound management of water resources, to be used for training. A study on *Large-Scale Water Transfers: Emerging Environmental and Social Experiences*, prepared by the Working Group, was published and distributed to member States and professionals.

UNEP continued to support the objectives of the International Drinking Water Supply and Sanitation Decade. Two projects started in 1984 in co-operation with WHO progressed satisfactorily. Under the first (on drinking-water quality control), three pilot sites in Indonesia, Peru amd Zambia were selected for surveillance activities, and programmes for the sites were developed. Two international workshops on hygienic criteria of drinking-water quality (Tashkent and Kiev, May) were attended by 28 professionals from 22 developing countries. Under the second project (on health hazards of waste-water use), a joint UNEP/WHO/UNDP/World Bank review meeting on evaluating the health hazards of waste-water and excreta use (Engelberg, Switzerland, July) developed a model showing health risks associated with re-use and prepared a statement on health aspects of such use in agri- and aquaculture.

On 23 May,[52] the UNEP Governing Council requested the Executive Director to accord high priority to training in the areas of water, and to support for studies and action-oriented activities dealing with domestic waste-water management and environmental problems related to water supply.

Marine ecosystems

Protecting the marine environment

UNEP continued during 1985 to assess marine pollution problems. Much of that work was carried out through its regional seas programme (see below).

The Joint Group of Experts on the Scientific Aspects of Marine Pollution was the main inter-agency mechanism to review marine pollution problems. Through it, work continued on evaluating the hazards of harmful substances carried by ships. Reviews were completed on arsenic, selenium and mercury as marine pollutants, to be published by WHO. Similar reviews on organosilicons and carcinogenic substances were under way.

Methodologies for assessing land-sea boundary flux of pollutants were formulated by the working group concerned, and work was in progress on a report on air-sea interchange of pollutants as modified by atmospheric contaminants. A methodology and guidelines for impact assessment of pollutants from land-based sources on the marine environment were elaborated. The scientific rationale for an integrated global ocean monitoring programme was examined, and preparations started on a global assessment of the state of the marine environment.

Work on developing reference methods for marine pollution studies continued, with the co-operation of several agencies, and 16 reference method documents were issued. To ensure global comparability of marine pollution data, a number of standards, certified reference materials and intercomparison samples were prepared. Using these reference methods, intercalibration exercises on a regional, interregional and global basis were conducted for three of the major classes of pollutants. Publication of specialized directories and bibliographies continued in co-operation with FAO and other bodies.

In late 1985, UNEP completed the move of its Oceans and Coastal Areas Programme Activity Centre from Geneva to Nairobi.

The third meeting of the *Ad Hoc* Working Group of Experts on the Protection of the Marine Environment against Pollution from Land-based Sources (Montreal, Canada, 11-19 April), attended by experts from 32 countries and six international organizations, finalized the Montreal Guidelines on that subject.[53] The Governing Council, on 24 May,[3] encouraged States and international organizations to take the Guidelines into account when developing agreements, and requested the Executive Director to distribute them to those concerned.

On 23 May,[54] the Council urged the Executive Director to continue to contribute to the global debate on the environmental implications of disposing radioactive and other hazardous wastes at sea, and urged him to strengthen interregional exchange of information and experience and to contribute to protecting the global marine environment. Noting progress made in adopting action plans and regional agreements to protect that environment, the Council called on him to complete the preparatory phase leading to the adoption of regional seas action plans and conventions where they had yet to be adopted, and to continue to assist States to implement those already adopted.

Shared natural resources and offshore mining

A December 1984 report of the Executive Director,[7] submitted in response to a 1982 General Assembly request,[8] described progress made in environmental co-operation concerning natural resources shared by two or more States, and in the use made of the conclusions of the 1981 study of the legal aspects concerning the environment related to offshore mining and drilling within the limits of national jurisdiction.[55]

On 24 May,[3] the Governing Council called on Governments to make use of the 1979 principles on natural resources shared by two or more States,[56] and the conclusions of the 1981 study, as guidelines in formulating conventions.

By **decision 40/441** of 17 December, the General Assembly took note of a Secretariat note drawing attention to the Executive Director's report.

Regional seas programme

Since May 1985, UNEP's regional seas programme had been pursuing activities in 10 regions involving more than 120 coastal States, more than 30 global and regional organizations, and a network of some 250 national institutions. By year's end, action plans had been adopted in nine regions and regional conventions signed in seven; preparations for adopting a convention for the South Pacific region were at an advanced stage. UNEP continued to provide overall co-ordination for the programme and to serve as the secretariat for four action plans and three conventions.

Activities included:

Mediterranean. The Fourth Ordinary Meeting of the Contracting Parties to the Barcelona Convention (Genoa, Italy, September), attended by delegations from 16 Mediterranean States and from EEC, adopted a Declaration on the Second Mediterranean Decade, by which the parties reaffirmed their commitment to protecting the Mediterranean through the Mediterranean Action Plan. They also agreed on 10 priority targets to be achieved during the Decade, to adopt measures to ensure that the quality of bathing waters conformed with the proposed WHO/UNEP environmental quality

criteria on faecal coliforms, and accepted the FAO/UNEP recommendations on mercury in seafood.

Kuwait region. UNEP co-ordinated the implementation of IAEA assistance to projects of the Regional Organization for the Protection of the Marine Environment, and advised on environmental matters. The organization's Council held its fourth meeting (Kuwait, April) and approved four new projects.

Caribbean. The fifth ratification of the 1983 Convention for the Protection and Development of the Marine Environment of the Wider Caribbean Region and its Protocol concerning Co-operation in Combating Oil Spills[46] was received in 1985. The Third Intergovernmental Meeting on the Action Plan for the Caribbean Environment Programme (Cancún, April) approved eight projects.

West and Central Africa. The parties to the Convention for Co-operation in the Protection and Development of the Marine and Coastal Environment of the West and Central African Region had their first meeting (Abidjan, Ivory Coast, April), in which they decided to establish at Abidjan a regional co-ordination unit for the Convention and set priorities for project implementation. Highest priority was given to ongoing projects on contingency planning for pollution emergencies and marine pollution research and monitoring, in co-operation with FAO, IAEA, IMO, IOC, UNESCO and WHO.

East Africa. A Conference of Plenipotentiaries (Nairobi, June) adopted a Regional Convention for the Protection, Management and Development of the Marine and Coastal Environment, an Action Plan, a Protocol concerning Protected Areas and Wild Fauna and Flora, and a Protocol concerning Co-operation in Combating Marine Pollution in Cases of Emergency. The Protocols and the Convention were signed by France, Madagascar, Seychelles and Somalia.

East Asian seas. The fourth meeting of the Co-ordinating Body on the Seas of East Asia (Manila, Philippines, April) decided to continue all seven ongoing projects, financed by the East Asian Seas Trust Fund and by UNEP.

Red Sea and Gulf of Aden. In May, Saudi Arabia became the fourth State to ratify the 1982 Regional Convention for the Conservation of the Red Sea and Gulf of Aden Environment and the Protocol concerning Regional Co-operation in Combating Pollution by Oil and Other Harmful Substances in Cases of Emergency.[57] The Convention and attached Protocol entered into force in July 1985.

South Pacific. UNEP continued its support to the South Pacific Regional Environment Programme. An expert meeting (November) discussed a draft convention on protecting the region's natural resources and environment and two protocols. A seminar (Suva, Fiji, October) was held to facilitate negotiations on those instruments.

South-east Pacific. The Second Intergovernmental Meeting on the Action Plan for the Protection of the Marine Environment and Coastal Areas of the South-east Pacific (Galápagos, Ecuador, August) approved support to the programme for research on and monitoring of marine pollution from domestic, agricultural, mining and industrial sources. The programme, involving 15 institutions from all five participating States, was largely supported by UNEP.

South Asian seas. Work on four of the five national reports on environmental problems in the region was completed; the reports would be used for drafting a regional action plan. A report on the management and conservation of renewable marine resources in the region was produced jointly with IUCN.

Environmental aspects of political, economic and other issues

Arms race and the environment

Alarmed by the possible environmental dangers stemming from arms research, production and stockpiling—ranging from risk of accidents to a post-war nuclear winter—UNEP continued to collaborate with the Stockholm International Peace Research Institute (SIPRI) in publishing and distributing scientific literature on the subject. A 1985 book, *Explosive Remnants of War: Mitigating the Environmental Effects,* examined the problem of unexploded mines and munitions, especially acute in developing countries, where most wars had been fought since 1945.

UNEP and SIPRI jointly organized the second meeting of the Advisory Group on the Arms Race and the Environment (Geneva, September 1985), which examined ongoing projects and made recommendations for action, and a symposium on global resources and international conflict (Stockholm, Sweden, October).

The climatic consequences of a nuclear war— the so-called nuclear winter—were again considered by the General Assembly in 1985 (see p. 39).

Material remnants of war

In response to a 1984 General Assembly request,[58] the Secretary-General submitted in September 1985 a report on the problem of remnants of war.[59] He had been asked to collect information on expertise and available equipment, so as to evaluate the needs of developing countries affected and assist them in detecting and clearing war remnants. Countries responsible for such remnants had been requested to intensify bilateral consultations to solve the problem.

By 13 August 1985, 13 States had replied to his request for information: Belgium, Burkina Faso, Burundi, Chile, Finland, Mexico, Netherlands, Pakistan, Poland, Qatar, Saint Vincent and the Grenadines, South Africa, Tuvalu.

Of those, one said that the matter was not within UNEP's competence; one suggested that bilateral negotiations between the countries concerned should be encouraged; another stated that measures should be taken to alleviate the problem, and responsibility placed on the countries that had planted the instruments of war. One country did not have current problems, but was concerned about future difficulties resulting from the Gulf war and would appreciate assistance in that regard; one was prepared to consider providing experts to developing countries to remove remnants of war. One country had no remnants as outlined by the Assembly in 1984; another, never having had any instrument of war in its territory, was not in a position to provide information. One did not have equipment or expertise within government agencies. Several countries had no comments.

The Secretary-General concluded that, since most Member States had not provided information on available equipment and expertise, or on bilateral negotiations undertaken to solve the problem, he was unable to evaluate the needs of the developing countries affected so as to assist them in detecting and clearing war remnants.

GENERAL ASSEMBLY ACTION

On 17 December, on the recommendation of the Second Committee, the General Assembly adopted **resolution 40/197** by recorded vote.

Remnants of war

The General Assembly,

Recalling its resolutions 3435(XXX) of 9 December 1975, 35/71 of 5 December 1980, 36/188 of 17 December 1981, 37/215 of 20 December 1982, 38/162 of 19 December 1983 and 39/167 of 17 December 1984 concerning the problem of remnants of war,

Recalling also decisions 80(IV) of 9 April 1976, 101(V) of 25 May 1977, 9/5 of 25 May 1981 and 10/8 of 28 May 1982 of the Governing Council of the United Nations Environment Programme,

Recalling further resolution 32 adopted by the Fifth Conference of Heads of State or Government of Non-Aligned Countries, held at Colombo from 16 to 19 August 1976, and resolution 26/11-P adopted by the Eleventh Islamic Conference of Foreign Ministers, held at Islamabad from 17 to 22 May 1980,

Convinced that the responsibility for the removal of the remnants of war should be borne by the countries that planted them,

Recognizing that the presence of the material remnants of war, including mines, in the territories of developing countries seriously impedes their development efforts and causes loss of life and property,

1. *Takes note* of the report of the Secretary-General on the problem of remnants of war;

2. *Requests* the Secretary-General, in co-operation with the Executive Director of the United Nations Environment Programme, to continue his efforts with the countries responsible for planting the mines and the affected developing countries in order to ensure the implementation of the relevant resolutions;

3. *Requests* the Secretary-General to submit to the General Assembly at its forty-second session a detailed and comprehensive report on the implementation of the present resolution.

General Assembly resolution 40/197

17 December 1985   Meeting 119   132-0-23 (recorded vote)

Approved by Second Committee (A/40/989/Add.6) by recorded vote (104-0-22), 11 November (meeting 30); 43-nation draft (A/C.2/40/L.16), orally amended by Argentina; agenda item 84 *(f)*.

In the Second Committee, Italy requested the recorded vote. In explanation of vote, the United Kingdom, speaking also on behalf of the Federal Republic of Germany and Italy, said they had abstained because of reservations also expressed on a similar draft in 1984,[60] the problem being a matter for bilateral negotiations, and the obligations referred to in the draft had no basis in international law. The United States, while not unsympathetic to the problems caused by war remnants, also thought that their removal could be best dealt with bilaterally. Sweden reiterated the reasons it gave in 1984, and stated that practical results could best be achieved by setting aside the issue of international responsibility and compensation.

The USSR expressed its support for the demands of developing countries suffering from material remnants of what it said were imperialist and colonialist wars. India felt that the text applied only to actions resulting from such wars. Iran said that it understood that the removal of remnants of war applied only to those developed countries which had planted them. Chad said it had supported the text even if skeptical about the intentions of its principal sponsor, the Libyan Arab Jamahiriya, which it said was stockpiling a vast quantity of weapons on Chadian territory—a charge denied by the Jamahiriya. Morocco said that the draft sought to promote international co-operation in solving a problem with complex legal implications.

Environmental aspects of *apartheid*

In South Africa black miners faced harsh working conditions: in some gold mines temperatures were often 50° C (120° F), working shifts lasted 10 hours and the noise produced by drilling and blasting operations was intolerably high. Occupational diseases such as infections of the lung were widespread. Accident rates were very high. Most black miners were compelled to live in barrack-style hostels, overcrowded and with minimal facilities, each holding as many as 8,000. The unfavourable environmental conditions of workers had serious adverse social, medical and psychological effects on them and their families. High incidence of tuberculosis also affected the black population at large, due to the general poverty of blacks, the insanitary conditions in which they were obliged to live, especially in the black townships, widespread malnutrition and the inadequacy of the health care available to almost all of them, especially those living in the so-called homelands.

This information was contained in a report of the Executive Director on the environmental impacts of *apartheid*.[61] It concluded that the agenda for future action in improving the environmental working conditions for blacks was very long. An effective trade union for them could have immense possibilities for bettering the conditions of millions of black workers and their dependants.

On 23 May,[62] the UNEP Council reaffirmed its solidarity with the victims of *apartheid* and its condemnation of that system, and requested the Executive Director to continue monitoring the environmental impacts of *apartheid* in South Africa and to report on the issue in 1987.

Mediterranean-Dead Sea canal project

On 23 May,[63] the Governing Council stated its position concerning the question of Israel's decision to build a canal linking the Mediterranean Sea to the Dead Sea (see p. 351).

Environment and development

Convinced of the close link between development and the environment, UNEP continued providing guidance on including environmental considerations in development decision-making.

A UNEP project carried out within the framework of the ACC Consultative Committee on Substantive Questions (Programme Matters)[64] dealt with the deforestation of the Himalayan foothills. The project's ongoing and past work was assessed at a meeting (New Delhi, 29 April–1 May) convened by UNEP and India, attended by experts from Bhutan, India and Nepal.

Jointly with Australia, the Commonwealth Secretariat and the East-West Centre, UNEP launched a programme to apply economic analysis to dryland degradation and rehabilitation. Aimed at preparing technical guidelines, the programme was based on analyses of case-studies from

Australia and developing countries in Africa, Asia and Latin America.

IUCN and UNEP continued an experiment to integrate conservation objectives into four major development projects in Costa Rica, Fiji, Pakistan and Zimbabwe.

UNEP held consultations with the Syrian Arab Republic's Planning Office on integrating environmental considerations into development planning, and began collaboration with Cyprus to improve its environmental impact assessment.

A report on integrated area development in the humid tropics, prepared by UNEP, the Organization of American States and Peru, contained an environmental assessment of the Central Selva of Peru, and recommendations for environmentally sound development from which a regional environmental management plan was expected to evolve.

ECLAC and UNEP prepared reports on the integration of environmental considerations into Latin American development planning processes. They also co-operated with Argentina in convening a regional seminar on the subject (Buenos Aires, June).

Under UNEP–World Bank auspices, the third expert group meeting on environmental accounting and its use in development policy and planning (Paris, 29 September–2 October) formulated guidelines on presenting environmental issues in national economic analyses. The sixth meeting of the Committee of International Development Institutions on the Environment (Washington, D.C., June) reviewed progress made in implementing the Declaration of Environmental Policies and Procedures relating to Economic Development.

On 24 May,[65] the Governing Council requested the Executive Director to continue reviewing, in co-operation with the Declaration's signatories, progress achieved in response to the Declaration, and called on the signatories to accord special consideration to major environmental problems within developing countries' development needs.

Among the Executive Director's recommendations on the environment in the dialogue between and among developed and developing countries, annexed to the Council's decision on his 1984 state-of-the-environment report (see p. 792), were a number of environmental issues suggested for such consultations.

GENERAL ASSEMBLY ACTION

During the mid-term global review of the implementation of the Substantial New Programme of Action for the 1980s for the Least Developed Countries (LDCs), several conclusions and recommendations were made by UNCTAD's Intergovernmental Group on LDCs regarding environmental

considerations in those countries (see p. 433). Those findings were endorsed by the General Assembly when it adopted **resolution 40/205**.

Environment and energy

Throughout 1985, UNEP continued to pursue a number of activities aimed at reducing the impact on the environment of the production of energy (see p. 692).

Environment and industry

UNEP's catalytic action in the crucial area of the environment and industry included organizing meetings and disseminating technical information. The first meeting of the UNEP Environmental Consultative Committee on the Iron and Steel Industry (Geneva, 28 and 29 March) discussed environmental control for the industry and the retrofitting of pollution abatement facilities for older plants, newly developed environmental technology, solid waste disposal, and the development of legal and regulatory measures. A UNEP-supported African regional meeting (Abidjan, 23-26 July) called on industry in the developed countries to assist African countries to solve their industry-related environment problems. A conference on industry and the environment (Ankara, 24 and 25 October), organized by UNEP and the Environmental Problems Foundation of Turkey and attended by some 180 participants, examined industrial pollution, the "polluter pays" principle, foreign investment and the environment, and Government/industry consultations in choosing environmental management strategies. An International Symposium on Clean Technologies, organized by UNEP and the Federal Republic of Germany (Karlsruhe, 7-18 October), was attended by some 60 participants (mainly from developing countries) and included presentations on clean technologies and field visits to industrial plants.

UNEP continued to disseminate information on the impact of industry and transportation on the environment. It published 17 issues in the various language versions of the quarterly *Industry and Environment*, each focusing on a specific industrial topic. Seven other specialized publications were issued during the year. At UNEP's request, the International Petroleum Industry Environmental Conservation Association prepared a draft technical review on environmental management of petroleum refineries and terminals, which was widely circulated.

Environment and human settlements

With environmental conditions in many urban areas deteriorating, UNEP continued to work to combat this situation with various United Nations agencies, especially UNCHS, including support for the International Year of Shelter for the Homeless (1987) (see p. 827).

Having completed environmental guidelines for human settlements planning, UNEP and UNCHS launched a project to apply the guidelines in four cities in Africa, Asia and Latin America, aimed at establishing institutional mechanisms by which environmental considerations would be routinely included in human settlements management. Under a joint UNEP/WHO project on environmental criteria for housing and urban planning, guidelines for improving indoor air quality were completed, and a kit was produced to guide communities in controlling insects and rodents. Assistance was provided to the Kenyan Government in a project to rehabilitate the Lamu town sea wall, affected by coastal erosion.

In collaboration with UNEPCOM and ESCWA, UNEP organized a training course (Moscow and Tbilisi, USSR, November) for 18 technicians from Arab-speaking countries on environmental aspects of human settlements planning and waste management.

Environmental education and training

The main activities under the UNEP/UNESCO International Environmental Education Programme (IEEP) included preparing environmental education materials, and pilot projects on integrating environmental education into general education and into university, technical, vocational and adult education.

A UNEP-sponsored regional seminar on university and the environment in Latin America and the Caribbean (Bogotá, Colombia, October) adopted an action plan to incorporate the environmental dimension into university education in the region. In December this action was duplicated for the Arab States under an IEEP project in Qatar. Pursuant to these seminars and the first African Ministerial Conference on the Environment (see p. 793), regional programmes of action in environmental education and training, developed with UNEP assistance, were adopted by Governments in the African, Asia and the Pacific, Latin American and Arab regions.

Under UNEP auspices, experts met in Bangkok in November to develop and adopt an action programme for environmental education and training.

In the area of training, Strategem-1, a computer-based resource management game, was designed by the International Network of Resource Information Centres, with UNEP funds. Its purpose was to help people to understand the concept of sustainable development. The players assumed the role of ministers in a hypothetical country and had to manage its resources over 50 years. Success depended on the players' ability to balance sectors such as energy, agriculture, industry, environmental protection and foreign exchange, while developing human resources and improving living standards. The game was played at workshops in Nairobi and Budapest, used in a training course for USAID programme managers, and adopted in some 20 teaching and research centres around the world.

A UNEP/IUCN International Training Workshop on Youth and the Environment (Moscow, September), attended by youth leaders from most African countries, developed a conservation agenda for environmental activities in the region and a draft manual for training youth leaders.

A UNEP/ECA workshop aimed at introducing environmental components into the training programme of 11 ECA-sponsored institutions (Abidjan, November) provided training to 20 participants and produced a core curriculum in environmental training for those institutions. Twenty trainers received training under a UNEP/ILO project to incorporate environmental components in the training activities of ILO-sponsored institutions; by the end of 1985, 100 management trainers had been trained and training manuals had been produced under a UNEP/ILO project to introduce environmental components in ILO management development programmes. The ninth international graduate course on resource management and environmental impact assessment in developing countries (Dresden, October 1985–July 1986), organized by UNEP, UNESCO and the German Democratic Republic, had involved 125 participants from 40 developing countries by the end of 1985.

On 23 May, the Governing Council adopted three decisions on education and training. By the first[66] it requested the Executive Director to consider convening in 1987 an international meeting on environmental education and training, in co-operation with UNESCO and the USSR, to appraise the achievements in this area in the preceding decade and to make proposals for the future.

By the second,[67] the Council requested the Executive Director, in co-operation with international organizations, to accord priority in 1986-1987 to training in Africa on: water management, with particular reference to rural areas; domestic waste-water management and recycling of waste water for agriculture; energy management, with emphasis on efficiency of energy utilization; and soil conservation. The Executive Director was also requested to accelerate the establishment of subregional African centres of excellence for environmental education and training, and to take into account the recommendations of the African environmental conference (see p. 793) in formulating other 1986-1987 activities for Africa.

The third decision[68] dealt with the Latin American and Caribbean Environmental Training Network (see p. 793).

(see p. 793)

REFERENCES

[1]YUN 1982, p. 1030. [2]YUN 1981, p. 839. [3]A/40/25 (dec. 13/18). [4]UNEP/WG.107/3. [5]YUN 1979, p. 710. [6]*Multilateral Treaties Deposited with the Secretary-General; Status as at 31 December 1985* (ST/LEG/SER.E/4), Sales No. E.86.V.3). [7]UNEP/GC.13/9/Add.1. [8]YUN 1982, p. 1003, GA res. 37/217, 20 Dec. 1982. [9]YUN 1978, p. 537. [10]UNEP/GC.13/10. [11]A/40/25 (dec. 13/1). [12]*Ibid.* (dec. 13/29). [13]YUN 1984, p. 750. [14]*Ibid.*, pp. 751 & 754. [15]A/40/25 (dec. 13/31). [16]YUN 1984, p. 755. [17]UNEP/WG.122/3. [18]YUN 1979, p. 1312. [19]A/40/20 (dec. 13/24). [20]A/40/392-E/1985/117. [21]YUN 1984, p. 757, GA res. 39/208, 17 Dec. 1984. [22]A/40/666. [23]A/C.2/40/10. [24]YUN 1984, p. 508. [25]*Ibid.*, pp. 756 & 759. [26]TD/B/1082. [27]YUN 1977, p. 509. [28]YUN 1983, p. 776, GA res. 38/163, 19 Dec. 1983. [29]A/40/644. [30]YUN 1982, p. 1017. [31]YUN 1983, p. 776. [32]A/40/25 (dec. 13/30 A). [33]YUN 1978, p. 541; YUN 1980, p. 727; YUN 1981, p. 827. [34]E/1985/32 (dec. 85/30). [35]DP/1986/82. [36]UNEP/GC.13/7/Add.1. [37]A/40/25 (dec. 13/30 B). [38]E/1985/32 (dec. 85/29). [39]A/40/329-E/1985/80. [40]UNEP/GC.14/2. [41]YUN 1982, p. 1021. [42]YUN 1984, p. 763. [43]A/40/25 (dec. 13/27). [44]YUN 1980, p. 717. [45]A/C.2/40/SR.14. [46]YUN 1983, p. 784. [47]A/40/25 (dec. 13/28). [48]YUN 1984, p. 764. [49]*Ibid.*, p. 770. [50]YUN 1980, p. 712, GA res. 35/18, 10 Nov. 1980. [51]YUN 1984, p. 649. [52]A/40/25 (dec. 13/26). [53]UNEP/GC.13/9/Add.3. [54]A/40/25 (dec. 13/25). [55]YUN 1981, p. 832. [56]YUN 1979, p. 692. [57]YUN 1982, p. 1022. [58]YUN 1984, p. 767, GA res. 39/167, 17 Dec. 1984. [59]A/40/650. [60]YUN 1984, p. 768. [61]UNEP/GC.13/3/Add.1. [62]A/40/25 (dec. 13/7). [63]*Ibid.* (dec. 13/8). [64]E/1985/57. [65]A/40/25 (dec. 13/16). [66]*Ibid.* (dec. 13/19). [67]*Ibid.* (dec. 13/20). [68]*Ibid.* (dec. 13/21).

OTHER PUBLICATION

Treatment and Disposal Methods for Waste Chemicals (IRPTC No. 5), Sales No. E.85.III.D.2.

Chapter XVII

Human settlements

In a world where 1 billion people lacked adequate shelter, the United Nations Centre for Human Settlements (UNCHS), known also as Habitat, continued in 1985 to assist developing countries in all aspects of their human settlements activities by providing technical co-operation, research and development (including training) and information dissemination.

As lead agency in the United Nations system for co-ordinating activities for the 1987 International Year of Shelter for the Homeless (IYSH), UNCHS continued to play a key role in its preparations. Those preparations were considered by the General Assembly and the Commission on Human Settlements. The Assembly, in resolution 40/203, requested countries that had not done so to formulate national plans of action for IYSH and to designate IYSH projects for the improvement of human settlements, and appealed for financial contributions to the programme for the Year. The Commission, which held its eighth session at Kingston, Jamaica (29 April–10 May), approved various measures with regard to IYSH, adopted 24 resolutions and two decisions, and accepted Turkey's invitation to hold its 1986 session at Istanbul. Four resolutions requiring action by the Assembly pertained to IYSH, the Commission's biennial cycle of sessions, a housing programme for the Palestinian population in the occupied Palestinian territories (see p. 326), and the tenth anniversary of Habitat: United Nations Conference on Human Settlements.

By resolution 40/202 A, the General Assembly called on all Governments to accord priority in their development programmes to human settlements activities, urged the international community to consider more flexible strategies in lending for human settlements programmes, and decided to designate the first Monday of October of every year as World Habitat Day. It also welcomed the Commission's decision to adopt a biennial cycle for its sessions (resolution 40/202 B), and requested the Secretary-General to ensure UNCHS participation in the work of the Administrative Committee on Co-ordination and its machinery (resolution 40/202 C).

Topics related to this chapter. Middle East: territories occupied by Israel—living conditions of the Palestinians; settlements policy; Mediterranean–Dead Sea canal project. Development and international economic and social policy: International Development Strategy. Economic assistance, disasters and emergency relief: disaster preparedness and prevention. Regional economic and social activities: Asia and the Pacific—human settlements; Africa—human settlements. Refugees.

Programme and finances of UNCHS

Programme policy

The report of the Commission on Human Settlements on its 1985 session[1] was considered by both the Economic and Social Council and the General Assembly. On 25 July, the Council took note of the report by **decision 1985/173**.

GENERAL ASSEMBLY ACTION

On 17 December 1985, on the recommendation of the Second (Economic and Financial) Committee, the General Assembly adopted **resolution 40/202 A** without vote.

Report of the Commission on Human Settlements

The General Assembly,

Recalling its resolutions 3201(S-VI) and 3202(S-VI) of 1 May 1974, containing the Declaration and the Programme of Action on the Establishment of a New International Economic Order, 3281(XXIX) of 12 December 1974, containing the Charter of Economic Rights and Duties of States, and 3362(S-VII) of 16 September 1975 on development and international economic co-operation,

Recalling also its resolutions 32/162 of 19 December 1977 on institutional arrangements for international co-operation in the field of human settlements and 34/116 of 14 December 1979 on the strengthening of human settlements activities,

Conscious of the very substantial gap between the resources available through voluntary contributions to the United Nations Centre for Human Settlements (Habitat) and the needs of developing countries requesting assistance from the Centre,

Having considered the report of the Commission on Human Settlements on the work of its eighth session,

1. *Takes note* of the report of the Commission on Human Settlements on the work of its eighth session;

2. *Takes note with appreciation* of the progress which the Commission and its secretariat, the United Nations Centre for Human Settlements (Habitat), have continued to make in providing guidance and assistance to

Governments in their efforts to provide adequate shelter and services to their people, particularly the poor and disadvantaged;

3. *Calls upon* all Governments to accord the requisite priority in their development and development assistance programmes to human settlements activities as a proved means of promoting economic and social development, as well as to the fair distribution of the benefits of such development to all segments of the population;

4. *Takes note* of Commission on Human Settlements resolution 8/12 of 8 May 1985 and, in that context, urges the international community, including multilateral institutions and agencies, to consider, as appropriate, more flexible strategies in lending for human settlements projects and programmes;

5. *Commends* those Governments and others that have made voluntary financial contributions to the United Nations Habitat and Human Settlements Foundation, particularly those that have done so on a regular basis, and appeals to those that have not contributed to do so at the earliest opportunity;

6. *Decides*, in accordance with Commission on Human Settlements resolution 8/4 of 8 May 1985, to designate the first Monday of October of every year as "World Habitat Day".

General Assembly resolution 40/202 A

17 December 1985   Meeting 119   Adopted without vote

Approved by Second Committee (A/40/989/Add.7) without vote (parts A, B and C together), 25 November (meeting 43); draft by Vice-Chairman (A/C.2/40/L.43), based on informal consultations on drafts by Colombia, Gambia, India, Jamaica, Kenya, Lesotho, Netherlands, Panama, Philippines, Sri Lanka and Zambia (A/C.2/40/L.24) and by Gambia, Jamaica, Kenya, Netherlands and Sri Lanka (A/C.2/40/L.25); agenda item 84 *(g)*.

Meeting numbers. GA 40th session: 2nd Committee 22, 24, 29, 30, 43; plenary 119.

Explaining its position, the USSR said that a World Habitat Day was unjustified, since such measures often turned into expensive official ceremonies which diverted limited resources away from the principal United Nations activities. The United Kingdom was concerned by the proliferation of special days, and understood that participation in the Day would be voluntary and that the Secretary-General would be responsible for all connected expenses. Norway, speaking on behalf of the Nordic countries, noted that 30 days of the year were given to celebrating various causes, and said that it would be advisable to avoid multiplying such celebrations because such a practice might run counter to the desired goal. Canada associated itself with Norway's comments.

Human settlements planning and management

The UNCHS Executive Director submitted to the 1985 Commission session a report on planning and management of human settlements, with emphasis on small and intermediate towns and local growth points.[2] The report was prepared in response to a 1983 decision,[3] by which the Commission had designated the subject as a special theme for discussion in 1985.

Focusing on recommendations for national action relating to small and intermediate centres, the report said that such centres had potential for helping developing countries meet their goals for social and economic improvements. Two functions of the centres were identified: to provide social and technical services to the majority of the population; and (applicable only to certain centres) to contribute to the national strategy for economic diversification and growth. International organizations could help strengthen these centres in developing countries, especially in local resource development and training of urban planners and managers.

On 8 May,[4] the Commission endorsed the report and urged Governments to recognize the locational implications of economic development and trends, to promote the interests of small and intermediate settlements, and to recognize that comprehensive planning and management of intermediate settlements was required, since it could contribute to regional economic expansion and to employment. Governments were also urged to integrate local government into local development programmes and to encourage collaboration between all economic sectors, since no one sector had the resources necessary to achieve its development goals alone. Aid agencies were urged to give attention, in their programmes for small and intermediate settlements, to support for low-income groups in the form of improved housing and living facilities. The Commission requested countries, in their projects and strategies for IYSH (see p. 827), to expand the role of small and intermediate settlements to meet the Year's objectives, and requested the Executive Director to give special attention to those settlements in future UNCHS work programmes.

On 10 May,[5] the Commission invited the Executive Director to form a working group of secretariat and Commission members to develop guidelines for eliciting more substantive discussions on special themes, and requested that the guidelines be applied experimentally, beginning at the 1986 Commission session.

Proposed financial and advisory institution for Asia and the Pacific

Further progress was made in 1985 towards setting up a financial and advisory institution for human settlements in Asia and the Pacific, an idea first considered by the Commission in 1981.[6] On 8 May,[7] the Commission requested the UNCHS Executive Director to circulate the proposal on the modalities for setting up the institution, submitted by a working group in 1984,[8] to the countries of the region and other interested countries and institutions, to consult with them and to report to the Commission in 1986.

Financing

Concern over the financial resources available for human settlements activities was expressed by the Commission on Human Settlements several times in 1985. On 8 May,[9] it called on the international community, particularly multilateral financial institutions, to be more flexible in lending for human settlements projects and to develop more creative financing strategies, particularly regarding secondary mortgage financing, urging them to utilize existing regional and national financial institutions to channel resources for housing and human settlements development. It also urged multilateral and bilateral agencies to restructure their technical assistance, in order to give more emphasis to providing infrastructure, equipment and training.

Other Commission actions of the same date, on various aspects of human settlements financing, dealt with mobilizing resources for the United Nations Habitat and Human Settlements Foundation (see below) and IYSH (see p. 827); payment of extrabudgetary resources for timely completion of UNCHS's 1986-1987 work programme and the 1984-1989 medium-term plan (see p. 827); and a proposed financial and advisory institution for human settlements in Asia and the Pacific (see p. 823).

GENERAL ASSEMBLY ACTION

The General Assembly, in **resolution 40/202 A**, urged the international community, including multilateral institutions and agencies, to consider more flexible strategies in lending for human settlements projects and programmes.

In **resolution 40/203**, it again appealed to Governments that had not announced a voluntary contribution to IYSH, especially those of developed countries, as well as to international financial institutions and other organizations, to provide financial and other support to the programme for the Year.

Extrabudgetary resources

The UNCHS Executive Director, in a February 1985 report,[10] described the use of extrabudgetary resources by the Centre during 1984-1985. These resources came from four sources: the United Nations Habitat and Human Settlements Foundation (see below); programme support income from the execution of projects financed by the United Nations Development Programme (UNDP) and trust funds ($3,672,000); a subvention from the World Food Programme (WFP) ($194,000); and programme support from the Fund of the United Nations Environment Programme (UNEP) ($66,800), for a total of $3,932,800.

During 1984-1985, UNCHS expected project delivery amounting to $27,183,000, broken down as projects financed by UNDP ($22,400,000), the UNEP Fund ($83,000) and other sources ($4,700,000). Projects financed by other sources were funded under various arrangements: trust-fund agreements under which technical co-operation projects were financed by recipient Governments or through agreements with donor agencies such as the World Bank; funding from various Governments for specific training programmes; contributions from Governments, agencies and foundations for specific projects; and associate-expert arrangements, with Governments providing experts at their cost. In 1984, 33 associate experts (from Austria, Belgium, Denmark, France, Italy, the Netherlands, Norway, Sweden and Switzerland) were working on technical co-operation projects; a similar number was expected in 1985.

UNCHS expected to earn $3,672,000 from the projects, to be used to support them; a similar income was expected in 1986-1987.

UN Habitat and Human Settlements Foundation

The declining real resources of the United Nations Habitat and Human Settlements Foundation, impeding the launching of new programmes and projects and preventing the implementation of approved ones, was addressed by the Commission on Human Settlements in 1985. On 8 May,[11] it requested the UNCHS Executive Director to seek additional financing through counterpart contributions and trust and special funds, and to intensify co-operation with UNDP, thereby ensuring more financing from it. The Commission recommended that he make an inventory of potential resources available from multilateral organizations and bilateral financial sources, and create an information system relating to them. He was also authorized to offer alternatives to Governments, such as additional contributions, so that they used national currency and inputs in kind in executing priority projects. Governments were urged to strengthen international co-operative machinery in which use was made of such currency and inputs, to try to gear it to human settlements projects, to promote the allocation of financial resources to those projects, and to try to ensure that their technical co-operation projects for developing countries included human settlements components. States, particularly developed ones, were requested to increase and deliver promptly their voluntary contributions to the Foundation.

On the same day,[12] the Commission decided that, in addition to the United Nations Pledging Conference for Development Activities (see p. 463), there would be a pledging meeting for voluntary contributions to the Foundation on the second day in plenary of all future Commission sessions.

Also on 8 May,[13] the Commission commended the Executive Director for his good financial management in utilizing the Foundation's limited resources. It approved the proposed allocation of funds for programme implementation, programme support, projects and reserve purposes for 1986-1987,[14] and the proposed utilization of resources for IYSH-related activities (see below).

GENERAL ASSEMBLY ACTION

In **resolution 40/202 A**, the General Assembly commended Governments and others that had contributed to the Foundation, particularly those that had done so regularly, and appealed to those that had not contributed to do so at the earliest opportunity.

Accounts

The audited financial statements of the Habitat and Human Settlements Foundation[15] showed a combined excess of expenditure over income for 1984-1985 amounting to $1,127,718. However, a saving from liquidation of previous financial period unliquidated obligations of $491,310 was realized as at 31 December 1985. The Foundation had a combined unencumbered fund balance of $8,529,340 available for existing and future commitments. The combined total income of $8,016,470 included contributions to the Foundation and IYSH. Expenditures for 1984-1985 totalled $7,829,813; of that amount, $3,422,962 related to programme and programme support activities and $4,406,851 to project activities of the Foundation and IYSH.

During 1984-1985, pledges by Governments for the Foundation and IYSH amounted to $6,487,220; collections and adjustments of $5,705,639 were made, of which $879,438 was for the previous period and $5,000 against future years' pledges. Current and previous years' pledged contributions in respect of the Foundation and IYSH in the amount of $1,211,950 and $796,076, respectively, remained unpaid as at 31 December 1985; unpaid pledged contributions for future years amounted to $379,220 and $717,640 respectively.

Contributions

In 1985, nearly $3 million in contributions for the Foundation was received from 35 countries; pledges for future years amounted to $387,220.

CONTRIBUTIONS TO THE UN HABITAT AND
HUMAN SETTLEMENTS FOUNDATION

(as at 31 December 1985; in US dollar equivalent)

Country	1985 payment	Pledges for future years
Bangladesh	5,000	—
Barbados	976	—
Belgium	103,899	—
Botswana	5,777	—
Cameroon	3,703	—
Canada	302,400	158,534
Chile	5,000	—
Colombia	9,000	—
Cyprus	130	—
Denmark	216,844	—
Egypt	15,392	—
Finland	123,609	—
France	65,989	—
Gabon	12,000	—
Germany, Federal Republic of	25,723	—
Ghana	3,000	—
India	144,512	—
Indonesia	20,000	—
Jamaica	15,000	10,000
Japan	997,323	—
Jordan	3,000	—
Kenya	(20)	—
Kuwait	15,000	—
Lesotho	(3,000)	3,000
Malawi	807	—
Netherlands	459,329	—
Norway	131,748	—
Pakistan	5,000	—
Republic of Korea	20,000	—
Sri Lanka	4,000	—
Swaziland	2,916	—
Sweden	179,445	215,686
Trinidad and Tobago	1,000	—
Tunisia	15,973	—
Turkey	5,858	—
Venezuela	40,134	—
Zaire	(1,000)	—
Zimbabwe	12,150	—
Total	**2,967,617**	**387,220**

SOURCE: A/41/5/Add.8.

REFERENCES

[1]A/40/8 & Corr.1. [2]HS/C/8/3 & Add.1-5. [3]YUN 1983, p. 800. [4]A/40/8 & Corr.1 (res. 8/23). [5]*Ibid.* (res. 8/24). [6]YUN 1981, p. 856. [7]A/40/8 (res. 8/5). [8]YUN 1984, p. 780. [9]A/40/8 (res. 8/12). [10]HS/C/8/7. [11]A/40/8 (res. 8/16). [12]*Ibid.* (res. 8/8). [13]*Ibid.* (dec. 8/25). [14]HS/C/8/6 & Corr.1. [15]A/41/5/Add.8.

Human settlements activities

UNCHS (Habitat)

Activities of UNCHS

The 1984-1985 work programme of UNCHS was based on eight subprogrammes: policies and strategies, settlements planning, shelter and community services, the indigenous construction sector, low-cost infrastructure, land, mobilization of finance, and institutions and management.[1]

Under the first subprogramme, in 1985 the most important UNCHS undertaking was the preparation of the *Global Report on Human Set-*

tlements, which reviewed the conditions of settlements throughout the world and outlined priority actions for Governments. In addition to this general reference work, policy statements were produced on women in human settlements and on youth in human settlements. UNCHS also prepared its regular biennial report on financial assistance to and among developing countries, and a theme paper on the role of small and intermediate centres in national development (see p. 823). Research continued on resource allocation for human settlements investment in national plans.

As part of settlements planning, a report was prepared on regional planning guidelines, based on case-studies in developing countries. In the area of environmental planning, a training course was held in Moscow in conjunction with UNEP and the Economic and Social Commission for Western Asia. Preparations were made for the test application in four cities of developing countries of environmental guidelines developed by UNCHS and UNEP. Work continued on the review of planning methods supported by microcomputers.

The execution of demonstration projects on the upgrading of slums and squatter settlements was a high priority under shelter and community services. In 1985, a demonstration project was in progress at Colombo, Sri Lanka, and for 1986-1987 a new project had been identified at Bangkok, Thailand. Community participation training with the support of the Danish International Development Agency was carried out in Bolivia, Sri Lanka and Zambia, and training materials were widely distributed. The Centre also carried out activities for IYSH (see p. 827).

Regarding the indigenous construction sector, UNCHS produced documentation on building codes, and began establishing a network of agencies involved in building-technology research. Various publications were in hand on building materials technologies and on expanded production of those materials through small-scale processes. Attention was also given to increasing the efficiency of the private construction sector—particularly its informal element.

Concerning low-cost infrastructure, publications were issued on energy-efficient building design and on efficient energy use in producing building materials. Extensive work was in hand on replacing conventional energy sources by new and renewable sources in the operation of human settlements. With regard to sanitation, a design manual for shallow small-bore sewerage systems was being prepared, drawing on experience in Brazil and Pakistan. On transportation, a publication was prepared on simple non-motorized vehicles for developing countries and work started on a publication about simple motorized vehicles.

These studies were undertaken in collaboration with the International Labour Organisation.

With regard to land, a report on land-assembly methods was completed. Under the subprogramme on mobilization of finance, a publication on informal-sector activities in low-income settlements and an audio-visual presentation on financial institutions were produced.

As part of the subprogramme on institutions and management, the training activities of UNCHS throughout 1984-1985 were very successful. The Centre achieved a 100 per cent performance for the 142 programmed outputs and was able to carry out other activities as well. Nine courses and workshops were held, and 187 fellowships were awarded. In addition, the Centre conducted a system-wide exercise to promote co-operation in human settlements training. UNCHS also organized a global meeting of aid agencies, scheduled for June 1986, to agree on human settlements training support in developing countries, based on guidelines given by the Commission on Human Settlements to member Governments. In the area of management, a report was issued on national institutional arrangements for human settlements and work began on a study of such arrangements for large cities, as an input to the May 1986 Conference on Population and the Urban Future (Barcelona, Spain), co-sponsored by UNCHS and the United Nations Fund for Population Activities.

UNCHS information activities included the production of a variety of monographs, information documents, posters, and audio-visual presentations. Three issues of *Habitat News* were published in 1985, including an index of the newsletter (1979-1983) and special inserts on the 1985 Conference to review the achievements of the United Nations Decade for Women (see p. 937).

UNCHS continued its pioneering work in the application of microcomputers to the planning and management of human settlements. It developed the Urban Data Management Software (UDMS), a package designed as a training and demonstration tool to show the potential for microcomputer-based data management in the work of urban and regional planning agencies. UDMS was installed in a number of developed and developing countries.

A second package, the Housing Finance Software (HFS), was developed to assist small housing-development and loan agencies in financial management and reporting. Following a successful installation in Seychelles, UNCHS started worldwide distribution of HFS. By the end of 1985, the software had been provided to 12 governmental, parastatal and non-profit housing-development and loan institutions.

New efforts were made to investigate available software relevant to human settlement planning and management. A network of users was initiated through the publication of a directory, which at the end of 1985 included over 300 entries.

Work continued on a number of information systems projects. A comprehensive directory of organizations working in human settlements was under way, produced in co-operation with an information centre of the Federal Republic of Germany. A trilingual thesaurus on human settlements neared completion. Two other publications were produced with the assistance of the Swedish Institute of Building Documentation. HABIRES, the data base on ongoing research projects, was also nearing completion. In September 1985, a two-week training course on the handling of human settlements documentation was held at UNCHS headquarters at Nairobi, Kenya, in collaboration with the French Government. It was attended by 10 documentalists and librarians from French- and English-speaking Africa.

The demand for technical advisory services increased significantly. Resources available fell far short of demand, even though these services were limited to only a few specific subjects and were provided for a maximum of four weeks per country. Of particular interest were the advisory services related to microcomputer applications to human settlements planning and management: 25 missions were carried out, resulting in 19 formal mission reports and 13 draft project documents prepared for Governments.

Technical co-operation

During 1985,[2] the Centre had under execution 151 technical co-operation projects in 77 countries—51 in least developed countries (LDCs). Of the total, 88 were financed by UNDP, representing approximately 70 per cent of the funds budgeted for technical co-operation during the year by UNCHS.

A total of 16 projects were also supplemented by trust-fund arrangements. The United Nations Habitat and Human Settlements Foundation funded 43 small-scale projects, designed to provide assistance in preparing project documents for submission to UNDP, donor Governments and donor agencies.

Regular programme funds were used for special advisory services and training, with emphasis on supporting human settlements activities in LDCs. In 1985, 51 missions were fielded. Some of the special advisory missions resulted in project documents for funds-in-trust financing. Special advisory missions were provided in data management, building materials and low-cost construction technologies, human settlements finance and the rehabilitation of existing housing stock.

Resources were provided under UNDP sectoral support to UNCHS for identifying national and technical co-operation needs in human settlements and for formulating project documents and proposals for financing by UNDP and other sources.

UNCHS continued its co-operation with other agencies. The WFP/UNCHS co-ordinator assisted in appraisal and project development missions. Collaboration with the Office of the United Nations High Commissioner for Refugees (UNHCR) continued through the assistance of a UNHCR/UNCHS human settlements officer in project development in refugee settlements.

In addition, UNCHS had, in response to requests from developing countries, prepared 99 projects which were awaiting funding for implementation in 58 countries.[3] The overall budget for these projects was $66,709,686, with a first-year budget of $17,141,122. Each had been formulated in close co-operation with the Governments concerned and with UNDP.

Programme and budget for 1986-1987

On 8 May,[4] the Commission on Human Settlements urged Governments to ensure that extrabudgetary resources were made available to UNCHS for timely completion of its 1986-1987 work programme and the 1984-1989 medium-term plan, and approved the outputs and activities proposed in the draft work programme for 1986-1987. It requested the UNCHS Executive Director, in implementing the programme, to accord a relatively higher priority to: land policies and practices; development of a local construction industry and appropriate technology; low-cost infrastructure, with special emphasis on sanitation; planning and management of a rational settlements pattern, with appropriate emphasis on small and intermediate centres; and development of alternative financial modules or systems that could reduce dependence on government budgetary allocations or borrowing.

Co-operation with NGOs

On 8 May,[5] the Commission recognized the contribution which non-governmental organizations (NGOs) such as the Habitat International Council could make to the promotion of human settlements development and expressed satisfaction with the efforts made to ensure co-operation between UNCHS and NGOs. It requested the UNCHS Executive Director to continue and extend his co-operation with NGOs, in particular in four areas: development and implementation of the UNCHS work programme; technical co-operation; training, and the collection and dissemination of information; and IYSH, including implementation of the information policy for it.

International Year of Shelter for the Homeless (1987)

During 1985, UNCHS continued preparing for the International Year of Shelter for the Homeless, having been designated by the General Assembly in 1982 as the lead agency for co-ordinating the programmes and activities for the Year.[6] It sponsored the holding of three IYSH subregional meetings: for southern African countries (Lusaka, Zambia, 25-29 March); for South Pacific countries (Lae, Papua New Guinea, 14-21 June); and for Asian countries (New Delhi, India, 10-14 December).

The Centre continued to produce and distribute IYSH information material, such as technical reports, posters and brochures. It started a series of monographs on human settlements projects and put out three issues of *IYSH Bulletin*, a new periodical highlighting national activities.

In a January 1985 report to the Commission on Human Settlements,[7] the Executive Director of UNCHS described its preparatory activities since the 1984 Commission session, and presented a set of future actions, pointing out that action had been taken on all activities approved by the Commission for 1984-1985.

As of 31 January 1985, pledges of voluntary contributions for the Year's programme totalling $2.3 million had been made by 25 developing and four developed countries. However, an additional $2 million was required to avoid curtailment of activities.

A total of 115 IYSH national focal points had been designated in 92 developing and 23 developed countries. India, Kenya, Mexico, the Netherlands, Nigeria, the Syrian Arab Republic, Uganda and the United Arab Emirates had established national organizational structures to support an IYSH national action programme; India and the Netherlands had held national meetings to develop a national programme.

An IYSH trust fund had been established by a group of NGOs in the Netherlands and the United Kingdom to support domestic and international activities. The United Kingdom group had also been designated as the national focal point.

A total of 135 IYSH projects had been identified in 60 countries. Various bilateral and multilateral agencies intended to designate IYSH projects.

In 1984, the Administrative Committee on Co-ordination's Consultative Committee on Substantive Questions (Programme Matters) (CCSQ (Prog)) had agreed that United Nations agencies and the regional commissions would provide UNCHS with information relating to their IYSH activities.[8] As of 31 January 1985, eight bodies had responded.[7]

Responding to a 1984 Commission request, the Executive Director submitted in January 1985 a report[9] outlining a long-term information strategy for IYSH to guide the United Nations system, Member States and interest groups, based on three main components: shelter policy, technical support and awareness.

In a March 1985 report,[10] the Executive Director examined the geographical and substantive coverage of IYSH projects, noting that while

there were a number addressing issues in shelter and services, there were few in the more critical areas of policy, legislative and institutional change. Few projects addressed problems of land, finance, building materials, transportation, training, employment and information. There were a number of schemes in water supply and sanitation, but not on a scale that would service large communities of low-income people. Important issues like solid-waste disposal and maintenance of infrastructure and services had not figured in any project. In addition, a number of Governments had not designated projects for the Year, while other Governments and agencies had not submitted complete information on their projects.

With few exceptions, most projects, though relevant, were not on a scale to convince policy makers of their potential for wider application. It would have been of greater value if projects contained replicability and affordability features with clear policy and programme implications.

Geographically, although there was fair representation from all parts of the world, there was scope for better coverage. Large parts of Africa, Asia and the Pacific, Latin America and the Middle East did not figure in the projects list. There were almost none in the United States, or in Western or Eastern Europe. While the main focus of IYSH was the developing world, it was expected that developed countries would not only support IYSH programmes in developing countries but also highlight the problem of homelessness in their own countries and the ways in which it was being addressed.

Action by the Commission on Human Settlements. The Commission, on 10 May,[11] endorsed the Executive Director's reports and recommended to the General Assembly the adoption of a draft resolution on the Year. That text formed the basis of **resolution 40/203** (see below).

Earlier, on 8 May,[12] the Commission expressed appreciation to Governments that had made contributions to IYSH, appealed to those that had not announced a voluntary contribution and to financial institutions and other organizations to provide financial and other support, and decided to have special pledging provision at its 1986 and 1987 sessions.

Other resolutions adopted in conjunction with IYSH dealt with human settlements in territories occupied by Israel, women and human settlements, Latin America and the Caribbean, and human settlements and peace (see under relevant subject headings in this chapter).

The Commission also decided to hold a special session devoted to follow-up to IYSH, a decision endorsed by the Assembly in **resolution 40/202 B**.

Report of the Secretary-General. A July 1985 report of the Secretary-General[13] summed up progress made up to June 1985 in preparing for IYSH. The report, submitted pursuant to a 1984 Assembly request,[14] noted that there was optimism in relation to the Year's immediate objectives, although there was concern about improving the shelter and neighbourhood of all poor within a specified time-frame. Considerable optimism stemmed from the resilience of the urban and rural poor who, everywhere, had displayed remarkable enterprise to cope with shelter problems. Their self-help spirit, manifested in a variety of projects being carried out with little or no outside assistance, was a beacon of hope in an otherwise difficult situation in most developing countries. The role of Governments as facilitators of these remarkable initiatives of ordinary people was increasingly recognized.

But the report noted areas of concern. Shelter and settlement issues were too frequently perceived by development ministries and aid agencies as peripheral to the development process, whereas for most countries they represented a major development opportunity in terms of capital formation, employment generation and socio-political stability. Many intergovernmental agencies had not sufficiently seized the opportunity provided by IYSH to demonstrate in their activities the indispensable role of shelter and decent living conditions for the achievement of objectives in areas such as health, environment, alleviation of poverty and the like. The paucity of contributions from developed nations was a source of deep concern.

ACC consideration. UNCHS submitted a progress report on preparations for IYSH to the 1985 first regular session of CCSQ (Prog) (Geneva, 1-4 April),[15] which endorsed further co-operative action.

GENERAL ASSEMBLY ACTION

On 17 December 1985, on the recommendation of the Second Committee, the General Assembly adopted without vote **resolution 40/203**.

International Year of Shelter for the Homeless
The General Assembly,

Recalling its resolutions 37/221 of 20 December 1982, 38/168 of 19 December 1983 and 39/171 of 17 December 1984 on the International Year of Shelter for the Homeless,

Noting with satisfaction that more than one hundred and fifteen countries have designated official national focal points for the International Year of Shelter for the Homeless, that many countries have already launched intensive national programmes for the Year and reported thereon to the Commission on Human Settlements at its eighth session, and that more than one hundred and sixty projects for the Year are under way in sixty-five countries,

Expressing its appreciation to the twenty-nine developing countries and five developed countries that have already made or pledged voluntary contributions to the International Year of Shelter for the Homeless,

Recognizing that an estimated one quarter of the world's population does not have adequate shelter and lives in extremely unhealthy and unsanitary conditions and that the programme for the International Year of Shelter for the Homeless provides a necessary and unique opportunity for countries to review their prospects and priorities for shelter and settlements and to develop, before or during 1987, new national policies and strategies for improving shelter for, and the neighbourhoods of, the poor and disadvantaged by the year 2000,

Noting that most of the voluntary contributions pledged to date have been pledged by developing countries and that further voluntary contributions are now needed in order to carry out effectively the overall plans endorsed by the General Assembly for activities to be undertaken before and during the International Year of Shelter for the Homeless,

1. *Requests* those countries that have not yet established official national focal points for the International Year of Shelter for the Homeless to do so in the near future, along the lines specified in the annex to General Assembly resolution 38/168;

2. *Also requests* those countries that have not yet formulated national programmes and plans of action for the International Year of Shelter for the Homeless to do so and periodically to provide information on them to the United Nations Centre for Human Settlements (Habitat) so that all national focal points can be regularly informed of the activities, progress and achievements of the Year in countries around the world;

3. *Further requests* those countries and international organizations that have not yet done so to designate projects for the International Year of Shelter for the Homeless aimed at improving access to land, financing, building materials, training and employment, giving special attention to legal and institutional measures, and to send a project information sheet on each project to the United Nations Centre for Human Settlements (Habitat);

4. *Requests* all countries in their periodic reports on their national programmes and projects for the Year, especially in reports to the Commission on Human Settlements at its ninth session, to give special attention to their plans for developing and implementing new national policies and strategies for improving shelter for, and the neighbourhoods of, the poor and disadvantaged by the year 2000;

5. *Appeals once again* to all Governments that have not yet announced a voluntary contribution, especially those of developed countries, as well as to international financial institutions and intergovernmental and non-governmental organizations, to provide effective financial and other support to the programme for the International Year of Shelter for the Homeless;

6. *Requests* the Secretary-General to submit a report to the Economic and Social Council at its second regular session of 1986 on progress achieved in the implementation of the approved programme of measures and activities to be undertaken before and during the International Year of Shelter for the Homeless;

7. *Invites* the Economic and Social Council to include a special account of its deliberations on the subject in its report to the General Assembly at its forty-first session;

8. *Decides*, in view of the fact that 1987 is the International Year of Shelter for the Homeless, to devote special attention to the Year at its forty-first session.

General Assembly resolution 40/203

17 December 1985   Meeting 119   Adopted without vote

Approved by Second Committee (A/40/989/Add.8) without vote, 25 November (meeting 43); draft by Vice-Chairman (A/C.2/40/L.34), based on informal consultations on draft by Bangladesh, Botswana, Burundi, Canada, Costa Rica, Cyprus, Ecuador, Egypt, Fiji, Gambia, Greece, India, Indonesia, Jamaica, Jordan, Kenya, Lesotho, Liberia, Malawi, Maldives, Morocco, Netherlands, Pakistan, Panama, Papua New Guinea, Philippines, Romania, Rwanda, Seychelles, Sri Lanka, Sudan, Swaziland, Thailand, Tunisia, Turkey, Uganda, United States, Venezuela, Yugoslavia and Zambia (A/C.2/40/L.29); agenda item 84 *(h)*.
Meeting numbers. GA 40th session: 2nd Committee 29, 43; plenary 119.

Explaining its position, the USSR said that, in implementing the resolution, the criteria set forth by the Economic and Social Council in 1980[16] should be respected. This meant that the IYSH programme should be financed voluntarily, that the Commission on Human Settlements should consider celebrating IYSH within the limits of its resources, and that the participation of UNCHS should not entail expenditures exceeding those available from the United Nations regular budget.

In **resolution 40/202 B**, the Assembly endorsed a Commission decision (see p. 833) to hold a special session of shorter duration in 1988 devoted exclusively to ensuring effective follow-up to IYSH.

Political, economic and social issues

Assistance to Africa

Assistance to victims of apartheid

Responding to a 1984 request by the Commission on Human Settlements,[17] the UNCHS Executive Director outlined in a January 1985 report[18] the assistance provided by UNCHS to victims of *apartheid* and colonialism in Africa. Aid was provided through 16 projects under way in Botswana, Lesotho, Mozambique, Swaziland, the United Republic of Tanzania and Zimbabwe, with a total budget of $2,883,556 in 1984. Various other projects had been prepared and would be implemented as soon as funds became available.

On 8 May 1985,[19] the Commission condemned South Africa for its inhuman repression there and its illegal occupation of Namibia, as well as for its aggression and destabilization against front-line and other neighbouring States, and for its continuous forced removal of the African population from their homes. It commended the Organization of African Unity and others for their support of the struggle against *apartheid* and colonialism in southern Africa. In commending the Executive Director for efforts made in implementing its 1984 resolution[17] on assistance to victims of *apartheid*, it requested him to intensify those efforts, to continue providing additional aid to countries in which human settlements had been disrupted by the South African régime, and to report in 1986 on progress made.

Assistance to displaced Namibians

On 8 May 1985,[20] the Commission made similar requests to the Executive Director with regard to assistance to Namibian refugee settlements. It also condemned any unilateral action by racist South Africa leading towards an internal settlement outside the terms of Security Council resolution 435(1978)[21] and declared the establishment of the so-called interim Government as null and void.

A number of recommendations to facilitate implementation of the United Nations plan for Namibian independence were made by the Commission to the United Nations Council for Namibia on 10 May.[22] The Council should follow up the implementation of the Commission's 8 May resolution.[20] In the event that Namibia did not achieve independence before the 1986 Commission session, the Council should include that session in its 1986 work programme, with a view to assessing the implementation of the 8 May resolution and to making recommendations for 1987. The policy options for the various sectors of an independent Namibian society that were researched by the United Nations Institute for Namibia should be disseminated at Commission meetings, at which other member States might have an opportunity to make suggestions, thereby contributing to more refined planning and future implementation of those policy options. The Council should therefore include a representative of the Institute in its delegations to Commission meetings.

Human settlements in territories occupied by Israel

Matters relating to human settlements in Israeli-occupied territories were again considered by the Commission in 1985 which examined a January study,[23] submitted by the UNCHS Executive Director in response to a 1984 Commission request,[17] on the possibility, on the occasion of IYSH, of a housing programme for Palestinians in the occupied territories.

The study, pointing out that it had not been possible to locate up-to-date comprehensive studies on the housing situation of Palestinians, drew broad conclusions on the situation, and stated that additional information would be necessary to determine the nature and magnitude of a housing programme. It concluded that preparation of such a programme would require a team of experts to visit the territories to obtain first-hand information and carry out studies.

On 8 May,[24] the Commission, noting that the information in the study was incomplete and inaccurate, requested the Executive Director to prepare anew the study, in co-ordination with the Palestine Liberation Organization (PLO) and concerned United Nations agencies, and to submit it in 1986.

On 10 May,[25] the Commission recommended a draft resolution on the housing programme to the General Assembly. By that text, the Assembly would have requested the Secretary-General to convene an international seminar leading to a comprehensive general housing programme for the Palestinian population in the occupied Palestinian territories, with the co-operation of specialized agencies and UNCHS and the participation of PLO. That text was examined by the Assembly when it considered and adopted **resolution 40/201** on the living conditions of Palestinians in the occupied territories.

Women and human settlements

Noting the participation of UNCHS in the July 1985 Conference to review the achievements of the United Nations Decade for Women (see p. 937), the Commission on Human Settlements on 8 May 1985[26] invited Governments to remain attentive to the concerns expressed by women regarding housing and urban development, and invited countries to co-operate to ensure better satisfaction of women's needs in housing, especially in developing countries. It requested the Executive Director to continue to give an appropriate place, in examining human settlements questions, to the impact of the evolution of women's tasks in society, and proposed that UNCHS consider sponsoring a seminar, as part of IYSH, to define the role of women in the conception, utilization and maintenance of human settlements.

Human settlements and peace

After considering its contribution to the International Year of Peace (1986) (see p. 122), the Commission on Human Settlements on 8 May 1985[27] stressed the importance of that contribution in implementing the objectives of the Year and stated that it recognized the close interdependence between the Year's objectives and those of IYSH. It requested the UNCHS Executive Director to submit to the 1986 General Assembly session a report on the Commission's contribution to the strengthening of peace and the implementation of the objectives of the International Year of Peace.

REFERENCES

[1]HS/C/9/2. [2]DP/1986/48/Add.2. [3]HS/C/8/INF.7. [4]A/40/8 (res. 8/15). [5]*Ibid.* (res. 8/22). [6]YUN 1982, p. 1043, GA res. 37/221, 20 Dec. 1982. [7]HS/C/8/4. [8]YUN 1984, p. 777. [9]HS/C/8/4/Add.1. [10]HS/C/8/4/Add.2. [11]A/40/8 (res. 8/2). [12]*Ibid.* (res. 8/8). [13]A/40/406 & Corr.1. [14]YUN 1984, p. 777, GA res. 39/171, 17 Dec. 1984. [15]ACC/1985/4. [16]YUN 1980, p. 1029, ESC res. 1980/67, 25 July 1980. [17]YUN 1984, p. 780. [18]HS/C/8/2. [19]A/40/8 (res. 8/18). [20]*Ibid.* (res. 8/6). [21]YUN 1978, p. 915, SC res. 435(1978), 29 Sep. 1978. [22]A/AC.131/192. [23]HS/C/8/2/Add.1/Rev.1. [24]A/40/8 (res. 8/9). [25]*Ibid.* (res. 8/3). [26]*Ibid.* (res. 8/19). [27]*Ibid.* (res. 8/11).

Organizational questions

Co-ordination in the UN system

Throughout 1985,[1] UNCHS continued collaborating with other United Nations bodies.

UNDP remained the main funding source for UNCHS field projects. At the end of 1985, UNDP financing constituted 70 per cent of the UNCHS technical co-operation projects budget, as compared with 72 per cent at the end of 1984. UNDP also continued to provide modest resources to UNCHS under its sectoral support programme for the identification of national technical co-operation needs in human settlements and for formulating project documents and proposals for financing by UNDP and other sources.

UNCHS and the United Nations Industrial Development Organization co-sponsored the first Global Consultation on the Building Materials Industry (Athens, Greece, 25-30 March), attended by over 170 participants from 72 countries and 15 international organizations (see p. 611).

Co-operation with the United Nations Educational, Scientific and Cultural Organization (UNESCO) continued in developing a microcomputer programme for storing bibliographic data to facilitate the exchange of scientific and technical information among developing countries. In November, updated software was installed at UNCHS headquarters by UNESCO experts.

UNCHS and UNHCR continued to collaborate in refugee assistance, among other things through the UNCHS/UNHCR human settlements officer in the Special Support Unit in UNHCR at Geneva. UNCHS was designated executing agency for a refugee settlements project in Kyaka II county in Uganda, aimed at establishing a rural settlement for 25,000 refugees. Another joint project was assisting a Philippines refugee processing centre in the Bataan peninsula.

Collaboration continued with the Office of the United Nations Disaster Relief Co-ordinator (UNDRO) in planning and managing human settlements in earthquake-prone areas. During 1985, the two agencies also continued co-operating with the UNEP Regional Activity Centre, within the context of the priority actions programme of the Mediterranean Action Plan, with regard to land-use planning and management in seismic zones.

The question of UNCHS participating in the work of the Administrative Committee on Co-ordination (ACC) was again considered by both the Commission on Human Settlements and the General Assembly.

On 8 May 1985,[2] the Commission noted that UNCHS, although participating in the subsidiary machinery of ACC, was not an ACC member and had not been able to support adequately the Commission's central co-ordinating role. The Commission reconfirmed that only full membership would enable UNCHS to discharge its mandate properly—to ensure harmonization of human settlements programmes and to assist the Commission in co-ordinating activities in the United Nations system. The Secretary-General was requested to take account of these views in reporting to the Assembly on co-ordination of human settlements programmes.

In his October report,[3] requested by the Assembly in 1984,[4] on his efforts to ensure the participation of UNCHS, the Secretary-General stated that UNCHS had been kept informed of matters to be considered in ACC and its subsidiary bodies, and had participated in all meetings of the three main subsidiaries. The Centre's Executive Director had been invited to participate in all 1984 and 1985 ACC meetings when he had indicated in advance that the items of those meetings were of interest to the Centre. Noting the Commission's comments, the Secretary-General agreed that the effectiveness of UNCHS should be enhanced to assist the Commission in discharging its central co-ordinating role and mentioned the channels for co-ordination used in the past few years, adding that he would continue to review ways by which they could be made more effective. Regarding UNCHS participation in the work of ACC and its subsidiaries, the Secretary-General felt that the current arrangements should continue, while recognizing the need to keep them under careful review.

The co-ordinating role of UNCHS was also taken up by the Commission when it considered a 1984 cross-organizational programme analysis of human settlements activities (see p. 833).

GENERAL ASSEMBLY ACTION

On 17 December, the General Assembly, on the recommendation of the Second Committee, adopted **resolution 40/202 C** without vote.

Co-ordination of human settlements programmes within the United Nations system

The General Assembly,

Having considered the report of the Secretary-General concerning the co-ordination of human settlements programmes within the United Nations system,

Taking note of the view on co-ordination expressed in Commission on Human Settlements resolution 8/13 of 8 May 1985,

Requests the Secretary-General to ensure effective participation of the United Nations Centre for Human Settlements (Habitat) in the work of the Administrative Committee on Co-ordination and its subsidiary machinery relevant to its mandate, as contained in General Assembly resolution 32/162 of 19 December 1977, taking into account Assembly resolutions 32/197 of 20 December 1977, 35/77 C of 5 December 1980 and

37/223 C of 20 December 1982, and to keep the matter under review for consideration by the Economic and Social Council at its second regular session in 1987 on the implementation of the present resolution, taking into consideration the follow-up of the cross-organizational programme analysis in human settlements by the Committee on Programme and Co-ordination.

General Assembly resolution 40/202 C

17 December 1985   Meeting 119   Adopted without vote

(For other procedural details, refer to p. 823.)

Regional co-ordination

After reviewing the draft work programmes in human settlements for 1986-1987 of the regional commissions,[5] on 8 May 1985 the Commission on Human Settlements[6] urged those commissions to co-operate closely with UNCHS in implementing their work programmes. It requested the Executive Director, when submitting the commissions' work programmes for 1988-1989, to supply a synoptic chart showing the relationship between the subprogramme elements of the Centre and the commissions' programmes, and recommended that he continue co-ordinating those programmes and take their relevant work into account in developing and implementing the UNCHS work programme.

Latin America and the Caribbean

Two 8 May 1985 actions by the Commission on Human Settlements were aimed at strengthening the co-ordination of human settlements activities in Latin America and the Caribbean. By the first,[7] the Commission commended the UNCHS Executive Director for having reached an agreement with the Economic Commission for Latin America and the Caribbean (ECLAC) on establishing a joint human settlements unit. It requested him to continue supporting the activities undertaken in the region, to give more support to the Centre's linkage offices there, particularly to its Information Office for Central America and the Caribbean, whose efficiency was a priority for participating countries, and to consider opening other information offices in the region.

By the second action,[8] the Commission noted that the Latin American Organization for Housing and Development of Human Settlements and the Permanent Committee of Housing and Development for Central America and Panama had as objectives to assist in improving housing conditions of low-income groups of the region, and invited them to collaborate with the Commission in executing IYSH programmes. It requested the Executive Director to take into account the Latin American organization as an important organism which could mobilize the political support of its member countries, to consider the Committee as a permanent subregional institution and to establish links for mutual support in technical co-operation programmes in Central America. It also appealed to the Executive Director to consider giving additional support to ECLAC in order to increase its regional activities in conjunction with the two organizations, especially in information dissemination and participation.

Cross-organizational programme analysis

At its 1985 session, the Commission on Human Settlements took up the Secretary-General's 1984 cross-organizational programme analysis and the assessment and recommendations thereon of the Committee for Programme and Co-ordination.[9] On 8 May,[10] the Commission stated that what should be included in the human settlements activities of the United Nations system could most appropriately be defined by listing areas of action along the lines made in the recommendations adopted in 1976 by Habitat: United Nations Conference on Human Settlements.[11] It noted that a statistical summing-up of the activities of United Nations bodies within their different areas of action did not give the guidance needed for co-ordination of work and setting of priorities, and underlined that much of the co-ordination work could best be carried out through agency-to-agency contact, based on information taking into account the nature of the work of each agency. The Commission further underlined that priorities for action should take due account of activities covered outside the United Nations system, and requested the UNCHS Executive Director, in preparation for the 1990-1995 medium-term plan, to carry out a comprehensive study of activities and priorities of the system, indicating possible areas for co-ordination, and to submit his findings to the Commission in 1987.

In **resolution 40/202 C**, the General Assembly, in asking the Secretary-General to ensure UNCHS participation in the work of ACC, said that follow-up of the cross-organizational programme analysis should be taken into consideration.

Joint meetings with UNEP

As requested by the Commission on Human Settlements in 1984,[12] the UNCHS Executive Director in February 1985 submitted his report[13] on the implications of discontinuing joint UNCHS/UNEP meetings. He suggested their abolition, coupled with reinforced institutional measures for co-operation between the two bodies. He felt that this was the most practical and cost-effective option, under which both the Commission and the UNEP Governing Council would take up the matter of co-operation separately, based on a common progress report prepared by the respective Executive Directors.

On 8 May 1985,[14] the Commission included co-operation between the two in its future agenda

and recommended to the UNEP Governing Council that it do likewise, requesting it to agree that the item be discussed by each governing body based on the common report. The Commission felt that joint meetings would then no longer be necessary.

The UNEP Governing Council, on 23 May,[15] concurred with the Commission and requested the UNEP Executive Director to consult with his UNCHS counterpart to recommend to the General Assembly that the meetings be discontinued (see also p. 795).

The Assembly decided to discontinue the annual meetings in adopting **resolution 40/199**.

Commission on Human Settlements

Biennial cycle of sessions

Further to a 1984 Commission resolution on the question of a biennial cycle for Commission sessions,[12] the UNCHS Executive Director suggested in a January 1985 report[16] that the Commission hold biennial sessions meeting only in odd-numbered years, with no substitute meetings in even years, thereby complying with the latest requests of the General Assembly[4] and the Economic and Social Council.[17] Since Commission members were currently elected for three-year terms on a rotating system by which one third of the membership changed each year, it was suggested that the term length be changed to four years, with half the members changing every two years, thus allowing each member to participate in two Commission sessions.

On 10 May 1985,[18] the Commission decided that, experimentally, sessions would be held only during odd-numbered years as of 1987, and that it would hold a shorter special session in 1988 devoted to follow-up to IYSH. The Executive Director was requested to propose its agenda and duration to the Commission in 1987, and in 1989 to report on low-cost alternatives to inter-sessional consultations with Governments after 1989. The Commission recommended to the Assembly that it change the term of office of Commission members from three to four years, beginning in 1986.

GENERAL ASSEMBLY ACTION

On 17 December 1985, on the recommendation of the Second Committee, the General Assembly adopted **resolution 40/202 B** without vote.

Biennial cycle of sessions of the Commission on Human Settlements

The General Assembly,

Recalling its resolution 32/162 of 19 December 1977, by which it provided for the establishment of the Commission on Human Settlements and specified the duration of the term of office of members of the Commission,

Recalling also its decision 38/429 of 19 December 1983 on the rationalization of the work of the Second Committee and its resolution 39/170 B of 17 December 1984, in which it required the Commission on Human Settlements to consider adopting a biennial cycle of sessions,

Taking note with satisfaction of Commission on Human Settlements resolution 8/1 of 10 May 1985 on a biennial cycle of sessions for the Commission,

Having considered the recommendation of the Commission that the duration of the term of office of its members should be changed from three to four years in recognition of the change to a biennial cycle of sessions,

1. *Welcomes* the decision of the Commission on Human Settlements contained in its resolution 8/1 that, beginning in 1987, its sessions will, on an experimental basis, be held only in odd-numbered years;

2. *Endorses* the decision of the Commission on Human Settlements contained in its resolution 8/1 to hold a special session of shorter duration in 1988 devoted exclusively to ensuring effective follow-up to the International Year of Shelter for the Homeless which, pursuant to General Assembly resolution 37/221 of 20 December 1982, will be observed in 1987;

3. *Decides* that, beginning with the terms of office commencing on 1 January 1987, membership in the Commission on Human Settlements will be for a term of four years instead of three.

General Assembly resolution 40/202 B

17 December 1985   Meeting 119   Adopted without vote

(For other procedural details, refer to p. 823.)

Themes for future sessions

Themes for future Commission sessions were again considered by the Commission in 1985. On 10 May,[19] it decided to discuss the small-scale production of building materials at its 1986 session, in addition to considering the role of community participation in human settlements work. It also decided that there would be no special theme apart from discussion of IYSH at its 1987 session, and decided to consider including in its 1989 session a theme on the roles, responsibilities and capabilities of different levels and organizations in governmental and non-governmental sectors, and opportunities for co-operation among them.

Earlier, on 8 May,[20] the Commission recommended that the UNCHS Executive Director, in preparing 1986 documentation, take into consideration: the importance of community solutions recognized in several developing countries as implementable using available resources; the need to emphasize social, political and economic factors in solutions to housing and human settlements problems; the importance of promoting knowledge and taking advantage of appropriate technologies to be used by the beneficiaries in their own regions and of adapting the solutions already achieved by old civilizations as the expression of their cultural development; and the need to intensify the study and utilization of non-conventional financing mechanisms that had shown positive results.

REFERENCES

[1]HS/C/9/2. [2]A/40/8 (res. 8/13). [3]A/40/689. [4]YUN 1984, p. 781, GA res. 39/170 B, 17 Dec. 1984. [5]HS/C/8/CRP.2. [6]A/40/8 (res. 8/21). [7]*Ibid.* (res. 8/7). [8]*Ibid.* (res. 8/10). [9]YUN 1984, p. 782. [10]A/40/8 (res. 8/17). [11]YUN 1976, p. 443. [12]YUN 1984, p. 783. [13]HS/C/8/8/Add.2. [14]A/40/8 (res. 8/14). [15]A/40/25 (dec. 13/12). [16]HS/C/8/8/Add.1. [17]YUN 1984, p. 772, ESC res. 1984/57 A, 26 July 1984. [18]A/40/8 (res. 8/1). [19]*Ibid.* (dec. 8/26). [20]*Ibid.* (res. 8/20).

Chapter XVIII

Human rights

In 1985, the United Nations continued its efforts to foster human rights and fundamental freedoms world-wide. The drafting of an international convention on the protection of the rights of all migrant workers and their families continued, as did work on a draft Body of Principles for the Protection of All Persons under Any Form of Detention and Imprisonment. Elaboration of a convention on the rights of the child moved forward, as did work on a draft body of principles, guidelines and guarantees for the protection of persons detained on grounds of mental ill-health or suffering from mental disorder.

A United Nations Voluntary Fund for Indigenous Populations was established. The General Assembly also adopted a Declaration on the Human Rights of Individuals Who are not Nationals of the Country in which They Live.

Under the United Nations programme established for the purpose, experts provided advisory services to several countries in the implementation of international human rights instruments, adherence to which continued to be encouraged. The Secretary-General deplored that many States had not ratified important international conventions, nor brought their laws or institutions into conformity with the international standards proclaimed by the United Nations (see p. 10).

Protection of detained persons was again a substantive part of the United Nations work in the human rights field. The Convention against Torture and Other Cruel, Inhuman or Degrading Treatment or Punishment, adopted in 1984, was opened for signature in New York on 4 February 1985; by the end of the year, 41 States had signed it. The Working Group on Enforced or Involuntary Disappearances continued to investigate cases of disappearances in several countries.

Among economic, social and cultural rights, the rights to food and development received particular attention. The Working Group of Governmental Experts on the Implementation of the International Covenant on Economic, Social and Cultural Rights—renamed the Committee on Economic, Social and Cultural Rights—was reorganized to make its work more effective.

Situations involving alleged violations of human rights on a large scale in several countries were again examined. The Secretary-General appealed to all States to support, strengthen and take part in the procedures established to examine such violations. Persecutions for political, religious or racial reasons

continued, the Secretary-General stated, and minorities and indigenous populations were often inadequately protected; there were also instances in which, in his view, the co-operation of Governments with the United Nations and its organs left much to be desired.

Actions on these and other human rights issues taken by the Commission on Human Rights at its forty-first session, held at Geneva from 4 February to 15 March, were embodied in 54 resolutions and 14 decisions; those by its Sub-Commission on Prevention of Discrimination and Protection of Minorities at its thirty-eighth session, held also at Geneva, from 5 to 30 August, numbered 36 resolutions and 12 decisions.

Topics related to this chapter. Asia and the Pacific: Kampuchea situation; Afghanistan situation. Mediterranean: Cyprus question. Middle East: territories occupied by Israel. Social and cultural development: crime prevention. Women. Namibia. Other colonial Territories.

Discrimination

Racial discrimination

Second Decade to Combat Racism and Racial Discrimination (1983-1993)

Implementation of the Programme for the Decade

In 1985, United Nations efforts to implement the Programme of Action for the Second Decade to Combat Racism and Racial Discrimination were carried out in accordance with the plan of activities for 1985-1989.[1] Pursuant to a 1984 resolution,[2] the Secretary-General submitted to the Economic and Social Council in April 1985 his annual report,[3] and later an October addendum, summarizing activities undertaken or contemplated by Governments, United Nations bodies, specialized agencies and other international and regional organizations, as well as non-governmental organizations (NGOs), to achieve the objectives of the Decade. In September,[4] the Secretary-General reported to the Assembly on measures taken to implement the 1984 resolution.

Human Rights Commission action. On 26 February 1985,[5] the Commission on Human

Rights commended all States that had ratified or acceded to the international instruments relevant to the Decade and appealed to others to do the same. It urged co-operation from all States and international organizations in implementing the plan of activities for 1985-1989, requested the Secretary-General to provide annual progress reports, and decided to consider each year a selected topic within the plan. It chose "International assistance to peoples and movements struggling against colonialism, racism, racial discrimination and *apartheid*" as the topic for 1987 and recommended to the Economic and Social Council that an international seminar on that subject be organized in Africa in 1986.

CERD consideration. Questions related to improved public awareness of Second Decade objectives were discussed at the March 1985 session of the Committee on the Elimination of Racial Discrimination (CERD) (see p. 839), which emphasized that there should be the greatest possible dissemination of information on its work during the Decade and supported the idea of organizing a seminar on the implementation of the International Convention on the Elimination of All Forms of Racial Discrimination during a part of one of its regular sessions, to be held preferably in an African country.

ECONOMIC AND SOCIAL COUNCIL ACTION

The Economic and Social Council decided, on 30 May 1985, by **decision 1985/141**, to organize in 1986, in Africa, an international seminar on international assistance and support to peoples and movements struggling against colonialism, racism, racial discrimination and *apartheid*.

The text, which was proposed by the Commission on Human Rights, was approved by the Second (Social) Committee on 24 May by 52 votes to 1, the same voting pattern by which the Council adopted it by roll-call vote. The United States cast the dissenting vote, based, it said, solely on the excessive financial implications of the seminar, not only because additional costs were entailed since it would be held away from the United Nations Centre for Human Rights headquarters at Geneva— on which point the United Kingdom also expressed reservations—but also that travel costs would be diverted from the Centre's limited advisory services budget. Japan also felt the funds could be put to more effective use, and expressed doubts as to the appropriateness of the subject of the seminar.

On 29 May, the Council adopted **resolution 1985/19** without vote.

Implementation of the Programme of Action for the Second Decade to Combat Racism and Racial Discrimination

The Economic and Social Council,

Welcoming the consensus support for the Second Decade to Combat Racism and Racial Discrimination demonstrated by the General Assembly in its resolutions 38/14 of 22 November 1983 and 39/16 of 23 November 1984,

Mindful of the responsibilities conferred by the General Assembly upon the Council for co-ordinating and evaluating the activities undertaken in implementation of the Programme of Action for the Second Decade,

Recalling the guidance provided to the Secretary-General by the General Assembly in its resolution 39/16,

Having considered the report of the Secretary-General on the implementation of the Programme of Action for the Second Decade,

1. *Takes note* of the report of the Secretary-General on the implementation of the Programme of Action for the Second Decade to Combat Racism and Racial Discrimination;

2. *Welcomes* the initiatives being taken to co-ordinate the full range of programmes under implementation by the United Nations system as they relate to the objectives of the Second Decade to Combat Racism and Racial Discrimination;

3. *Also welcomes* the additional project, introduced during the thirty-ninth session of the General Assembly, to organize a media round-table in Europe in 1985 concerning international legal issues relating to *apartheid*, racism and racial discrimination, and requests the Secretary-General to proceed with the implementation of that project;

4. *Invites* all Governments to take or continue to take all the necessary measures to combat all forms of racism and racial discrimination and to support the work of the Decade by making contributions to the Trust Fund for the Programme for the Decade for Action to Combat Racism and Racial Discrimination;

5. *Invites* all Governments, United Nations bodies, the specialized agencies and other intergovernmental organizations, as well as interested non-governmental organizations in consultative status with the Economic and Social Council, to participate in the implementation of the plan of activities for the period 1985-1989 by intensifying and expanding their efforts to ensure the rapid elimination of *apartheid* and all forms of racism and racial discrimination and to co-operate fully with the Council in its co-ordinating role of the activities related to the Second Decade;

6. *Requests* the Secretary-General to submit annual reports on the implementation of the Programme of Action for the Second Decade, taking into account the relevant resolutions and recommendations of the United Nations, including the Programme for the first Decade annexed to General Assembly resolution 3057(XXVIII) of 2 November 1973.

Economic and Social Council resolution 1985/19

29 May 1985   Meeting 23   Adopted without vote

Draft by Mozambique, for African Group (E/1985/L.26); agenda item 2.
Meeting numbers. ESC 10-14, 16, 23.

Study by the Special Rapporteur. As requested by the Economic and Social Council in 1984,[6] Special Rapporteur Asbjorn Eide (Norway) submitted to the Sub-Commission in July 1985 the first part of a study[7] on the achievements made and obstacles encountered during the first Decade for Action to Combat Racism and Racial Discrimination (1973-1983), containing a descriptive summary of the Decade's goals and policy measures recommended, of activities undertaken to achieve the Decade's objectives, and of obstacles encountered. The second part of the study evaluating those objectives and measures was to be submitted in 1986.

Study by the Secretary-General. Pursuant to a 1984 request by the General Assembly,[2] the Secretary-General submitted in October 1985 a preliminary report[8] summarizing results of a study on the effects of racial discrimination in education, training and employment as it affected the children of minorities, particularly those of migrant workers (for further information on migrant workers, see p. 848). The study analysed the relevant international standards, discussed efforts to combat racial discrimination as it affected the children of minorities and indicated approaches to bringing social practice in line with recognized legal norms. A section was devoted to the situation of children in South Africa. However, in order to finalize the study for submission to the Assembly's 1986 session, the Secretary-General sought authorization from the Assembly to solicit relevant information from Member States, NGOs, specialized agencies and regional intergovernmental organizations for inclusion in the final study.

GENERAL ASSEMBLY ACTION

On 29 November 1985, acting on the recommendation of the Third (Social, Humanitarian and Cultural) Committee, the General Assembly adopted **resolution 40/22**, without vote.

Second Decade to Combat Racism and Racial Discrimination

The General Assembly,

Reaffirming its objective contained in the Charter of the United Nations to achieve international co-operation in solving international problems of an economic, social, cultural or humanitarian character, and in promoting and encouraging respect for human rights and fundamental freedoms for all without distinction as to race, sex, language or religion,

Reaffirming its firm determination and its commitment to eradicate totally and unconditionally racism in all its forms, racial discrimination and *apartheid,*

Recalling the Universal Declaration of Human Rights, the International Convention on the Elimination of All Forms of Racial Discrimination, the International Convention on the Suppression and Punishment of the Crime of *Apartheid* and the Convention against Discrimination in Education adopted by the United Nations Educational, Scientific and Cultural Organization on 14 December 1960,

Recalling also its resolution 3057(XXVIII) of 2 November 1973, on the first Decade for Action to Combat Racism and Racial Discrimination, and its resolution 38/14 of 22 November 1983, on the Second Decade to Combat Racism and Racial Discrimination,

Recalling further the two World Conferences to Combat Racism and Racial Discrimination, held at Geneva in 1978 and 1983, respectively,

Taking note once again of the *Report of the Second World Conference to Combat Racism and Racial Discrimination,*

Convinced that the Second World Conference represented a positive contribution by the international community towards attaining the objectives of the Decade, through its adoption of a Declaration and an operational Programme of Action for the Second Decade to Combat Racism and Racial Discrimination,

Noting with concern that, despite the efforts of the international community, the principal objectives of the first Decade for Action to Combat Racism and Racial Discrimination were not attained and that millions of human beings continue to this day to be the victims of varied forms of racism, racial discrimination and *apartheid,*

Recalling its resolution 39/16 of 23 November 1984,

Emphasizing the necessity of attaining the objectives of the Second Decade to Combat Racism and Racial Discrimination,

Convinced of the need to take more effective and sustained international measures for the elimination of all forms of racism and racial discrimination and the total eradication of *apartheid* in South Africa,

1. *Resolves once again* that all forms of racism and racial discrimination, particularly in their institutionalized form, such as *apartheid,* or resulting from official doctrines of racial superiority or exclusivity, are among the most serious violations of human rights in the contemporary world and must be combated by all available means;

2. *Appeals* to the international community, in general, and the United Nations, in particular, to continue to give the highest priority to programmes for combating racism, racial discrimination and *apartheid,* and to intensify its own efforts, during the Second Decade to Combat Racism and Racial Discrimination, to provide assistance and relief to the victims of racism and all forms of racial discrimination and *apartheid,* especially in South Africa and Namibia and in occupied territories and territories under alien domination;

3. *Appeals* to all Governments and to international and non-governmental organizations to increase and intensify their activities to combat racism, racial discrimination and *apartheid* and to provide relief and assistance to the victims of these evils;

4. *Appeals* to all Governments, organizations and individuals in a position to do so to contribute generously to the Trust Fund for the Programme for the Decade for Action to Combat Racism and Racial Discrimination so as to enable the Secretary-General to implement the various programme elements outlined in his report on the plan of activities for 1985-1989;

5. *Takes note with appreciation* of the reports of the Secretary-General containing information on the activities of Governments, specialized agencies, regional intergovernmental organizations and non-governmental organizations, as well as United Nations organs, to give effect to the Programme of Action for the Second Decade to Combat Racism and Racial Discrimination;

6. *Acknowledges* the progress made in preparing the study on the effects of racial discrimination in the field of education, training and employment as it affects the children of minorities, in particular those of migrant workers, authorizes the Secretary-General to solicit relevant information and views from Governments, specialized agencies, regional intergovernmental

organizations and non-governmental organizations in consultative status with the Economic and Social Council and requests him to submit the final study to the General Assembly at its forty-first session;

7. *Congratulates* the Secretary-General on the organization of the Round Table on International Legal Issues relating to *Apartheid*, Racism and Racial Discrimination, held at The Hague from 4 to 6 September 1985;

8. *Expresses its satisfaction* at the convening of the Seminar on Community Relations Commissions and Their Functions, held at Geneva from 9 to 20 September 1985, and invites the Secretary-General to disseminate the report of the Seminar widely;

9. *Reiterates its invitation* to the Secretary-General to proceed with the implementation of the activities outlined in his report on the plan of activities for 1985-1989 and to submit to the General Assembly at its forty-first session the study on the role of private group action to combat racism and racial discrimination and to the Assembly at its forty-third session the global compilation of national legislation against racial discrimination;

10. *Requests* the Secretary-General to prepare and issue as soon as possible a collection of model legislation for the guidance of Governments in the enactment of further legislation against racial discrimination;

11. *Invites* the Secretary-General to organize in New York in 1987 a training course for legislative draftsmen with the aim of focusing on the preparation of national legislation against racism and racial discrimination;

12. *Invites* the United Nations Educational, Scientific and Cultural Organization to expedite the preparation of teaching materials and teaching aids to promote teaching, training and educational activities on human rights and against racism and racial discrimination, with particular emphasis on activities at the primary and secondary levels of education;

13. *Requests* the Sub-Commission on Prevention of Discrimination and Protection of Minorities of the Commission on Human Rights to consider the possible need for updating the study on racial discrimination;

14. *Authorizes* the Secretary-General to organize in 1988 a global consultation on racial discrimination involving representatives of the United Nations system, regional intergovernmental organizations and interested non-governmental organizations in consultative status with the Economic and Social Council, to focus on the co-ordination of international activities to combat racism and racial discrimination;

15. *Welcomes* Economic and Social Council decision 1985/141 of 30 May 1985, by which the Council authorized the organization in 1986 in Africa of a seminar on international assistance and support to peoples and movements struggling against colonialism, racism, racial discrimination and *apartheid*, and requests that the report thereon be made available to the General Assembly at its forty-first session;

16. *Invites* the Secretary-General to report to the General Assembly at its forty-first session on the implementation of the present resolution;

17. *Requests* the Economic and Social Council, during the period of the Second Decade, to submit an annual report to the General Assembly, containing, *inter alia:*

(a) An enumeration of the activities undertaken or contemplated to achieve the objectives of the Second Decade, including the activities of Governments, United Nations bodies, the specialized agencies and other inter-

national and regional organizations, as well as non-governmental organizations;

(b) A review and appraisal of those activities;

(c) Its suggestions and recommendations;

18. *Decides* that the item entitled "Implementation of the Programme of Action for the Second Decade to Combat Racism and Racial Discrimination" should be on its agenda throughout the Second Decade and should be considered as a matter of the highest priority at its forty-first session.

General Assembly resolution 40/22

29 November 1985   Meeting 96   Adopted without vote

Approved by Third Committee (A/40/861) without vote, 4 November (meeting 30); draft by Nigeria, for African Groups (A/C.3/40/L.7); agenda item 88.
Financial implications. 5th Committee, A/40/953; S-G, A/C.3/40/L.10, A/C.5/40/42.
Meeting numbers. GA 40th session: 3rd Committee 3-15, 30, 31; 5th Committee 48; plenary 96.

Israel said if the text had been put to a vote, it would have voted against it because of the abuses which the Decade had generated, most notably the Assembly resolution[9] equating zionism with racism. The United States recalled that for the same reason it had not taken part in the activities of either Decade, and expressed concern about the financial implications of holding the seminar mentioned in paragraph 15 away from Headquarters. Canada said allocating funds from the advisory services programme to organize a seminar in Africa was inappropriate.

The United Kingdom said it had reservations with regard to paragraph 1; "combated by all available means" was to be interpreted in accordance with the Charter and could not include armed struggle—a view also held by France and the Federal Republic of Germany. Japan reserved its position with regard to the report of the seminar mentioned in paragraph 8, since the report was not yet available. France observed that its position in opposition to the Declaration adopted by the Second World Conference to Combat Racism and Racial Discrimination had not changed. It also felt the wording in paragraph 2 referring to "occupied territories and territories under alien domination" to be ambiguous and inappropriate. Iraq and the Syrian Arab Republic said they understood the expression to mean the occupied Arab territories. The Netherlands held that the reference in paragraph 2 did not imply that racism and racial discrimination were inevitably practised in occupied territories.

The Federal Republic of Germany would have preferred not to see any reference to situations other than that of South Africa, and did not believe that the status of migrant workers, mentioned in paragraph 6, was in itself a criterion for racial discrimination.

Other activities. In the framework of activities for the Decade, a Seminar on Community Relations Commissions and Their Functions was held at Geneva from 9 to 20 September;[10] it was financed from resources under the advisory services programme on human rights (see p. 893).

Convention on the Elimination of Racial Discrimination

Accessions and ratifications

As at 31 December 1985, there were 124 parties to the International Convention on the Elimination of All Forms of Racial Discrimination, adopted by the General Assembly in 1965[11] and in force since 1969.[12]

The same number of parties was given in the Secretary-General's annual report to the Assembly on the status of the Convention,[13] which listed States that had signed, ratified or acceded to the Convention as at 1 September 1985.

GENERAL ASSEMBLY ACTION

On 29 November, acting on the recommendation of the Third Committee, the General Assembly adopted **resolution 40/26**, without vote.

Status of the International Convention on the Elimination of All Forms of Racial Discrimination

The General Assembly,

Recalling its resolutions 3057(XXVIII) of 2 November 1973, 3135(XXVIII) of 14 December 1973, 3225(XXIX) of 6 November 1974, 3381(XXX) of 10 November 1975, 31/79 of 13 December 1976, 32/11 of 7 November 1977, 33/101 of 16 December 1978, 34/26 of 15 November 1979, 35/38 of 25 November 1980, 36/11 of 28 October 1981, 37/45 of 3 December 1982, 38/18 of 22 November 1983 and 39/20 of 23 November 1984,

Expressing its satisfaction with the entry into force, on 3 December 1982, of the competence of the Committee on the Elimination of Racial Discrimination, under article 14 of the International Convention on the Elimination of All Forms of Racial Discrimination, to accept and to examine communications from persons or groups of persons, and with the fact that since that date more States parties have made the declaration provided for in that article,

1. *Takes note* of the report of the Secretary-General on the status of the International Convention on the Elimination of All Forms of Racial Discrimination;

2. *Expresses its satisfaction* at the number of States that have ratified the Convention or acceded thereto;

3. *Reaffirms once again its conviction* that ratification of or accession to the Convention on a universal basis and implementation of its provisions are necessary for the realization of the objectives of the Second Decade to Combat Racism and Racial Discrimination;

4. *Requests* those States that have not yet become parties to the Convention to ratify it or accede thereto;

5. *Calls upon* States parties to the Convention to consider the possibility of making the declaration provided for in article 14 of the Convention;

6. *Requests* the Secretary-General to continue to submit to the General Assembly annual reports concerning the status of the Convention, in accordance with Assembly resolution 2106 A (XX) of 21 December 1965.

General Assembly resolution 40/26

29 November 1985   Meeting 96   Adopted without vote

Approved by Third Committee (A/40/914) without vote, 4 November (meeting 30); 23-nation draft (A/C.3/40/L.4), amended by 14 nations (A/C.3/40/L.8); agenda item 94 *(b)*.

Sponsors of draft: Algeria, Argentina, Australia, Bahamas, Barbados, Belgium, Bulgaria, Burkina Faso, Cuba, Cyprus, Egypt, Germany, Federal Republic of, Hungary, India, Morocco, New Zealand, Nicaragua, Pakistan, Portugal, Rwanda, Spain, Venezuela, Yugoslavia.

Sponsors of amendments: Colombia, Costa Rica, Denmark, Ecuador, Finland, France, Iceland, Italy, Netherlands, Norway, Peru, Senegal, Sweden, Uruguay.

Meeting numbers. GA 40th session: 3rd Committee 3-15, 30; plenary 96.

Prior to approving the draft resolution as a whole, the Third Committee adopted, by a recorded vote of 79 to 1, with 41 abstentions, amendments sponsored by 14 nations. The amendments added the second preambular paragraph and paragraph 5.

Implementation of the Convention

CERD activities. Devoting most of its work to an examination of reports by States parties to the Convention on measures taken to implement its provisions, the Committee on the Elimination of Racial Discrimination, set up under article 8 of the Convention, held two sessions in 1985: the thirty-first in New York from 4 to 22 March; and the thirty-second at Geneva from 5 to 23 August. After considering reports submitted by 37 States under article 9 of the Convention, the Committee provided, in its annual report to the General Assembly,[14] a summary of its members' views on each country report and of statements made by the States parties concerned. The report also described action taken to resolve the problem of delays and non-submission of reports.

In conformity with article 15 of the Convention, CERD considered petitions and reports, and other information relating to Trust and Non-Self-Governing Territories transmitted by the Trusteeship Council (see TRUSTEESHIP AND DECOLONIZATION, Chapter II) and by the Special Committee on the Situation with regard to the Implementation of the Declaration on the Granting of Independence to Colonial Countries and Peoples. CERD examined reports related to African Territories, including Namibia, Atlantic Ocean and Caribbean Territories, including Gibraltar, and Pacific and Indian Ocean Territories, stating with regret that it had not been provided with information relevant to its task under article 15 in the submissions on Anguilla and on Pacific and Indian Ocean Territories.

With regard to article 3 of the Convention, condemning racial segregation and *apartheid*, CERD, on 20 August,[15] strongly condemned the racist régime of South Africa for the crimes perpetrated under the *apartheid* system and appealed to States parties to implement Security Council resolution 569(1985) of 26 July 1985, which was consistent with the aims of the Convention. In a separate decision (General Recommendation VII)[16] relating to article 4, concerning measures to eradicate incitement to and acts of racial discrimination, the Committee recommended that States parties whose legislation did not satisfy the provisions of the article take steps to fulfil its requirements. It requested that States parties provide fuller information on this matter in their periodic reports, including decisions by national tribunals and other State institutions.

At its August session, CERD also continued considering, under article 14 of the Convention, communications from individuals or groups of individuals claiming violation of their rights under the Convention by a State party recognizing CERD competence to receive and consider such communications. As in the previous year, 11 of the 124 States parties—Costa Rica, Ecuador, France, Iceland, Italy, the Netherlands, Norway, Peru, Senegal, Sweden and Uruguay—had declared such recognition. By the end of the August 1985 session, work under the article had not reached the reporting stage.

Communications. In connection with the observance, on 21 March, of the International Day for the Elimination of Racial Discrimination, 20 Member States (one of them on behalf of the 10 members of the European Community (EC), one non-member State, two specialized agencies and eight NGOs sent messages to the Special Committee against *Apartheid*[17] (see POLITICAL AND SECURITY QUESTIONS, Chapter V). By letters of 10 January[18] and 2 December 1985,[19] respectively, Israel drew attention to what it called extreme examples of anti-Semitic outbursts in United Nations forums during November and December 1984 and protested against what it called racial and religious incitements by Bahrain during deliberations in the General Assembly's Third Committee (for further details, see p. 263).

GENERAL ASSEMBLY ACTION

On 29 November, the General Assembly, acting on the recommendation of the Third Committee, adopted **resolution 40/28**, by recorded vote.

Report of the Committee on the Elimination of Racial Discrimination

The General Assembly,

Recalling its resolutions 39/21 of 23 November 1984 on the report of the Committee on the Elimination of Racial Discrimination and 40/26 of 29 November 1985 on the status of the International Convention on the Elimination of All Forms of Racial Discrimination, as well as its other relevant resolutions on the implementation of the Programme of Action for the Second Decade to Combat Racism and Racial Discrimination,

Having considered the report of the Committee on the Elimination of Racial Discrimination on the work of its thirty-first and thirty-second sessions, submitted under article 9, paragraph 2, of the Convention,

Emphasizing the need for Member States to intensify, at the national and international levels, the struggle against acts or practices of racial discrimination and the vestiges or manifestations of racist ideologies wherever they exist,

Bearing in mind that the Convention is being implemented in different economic, social and cultural conditions prevailing in individual States parties,

Mindful of the obligation of all States parties to comply fully with the provisions of the Convention,

Aware of the importance of the contribution of the Committee to the implementation of the Programme of Action for the Second Decade to Combat Racism and Racial Discrimination and to the elimination of all forms of discrimination based on race, colour, descent or national or ethnic origin,

Taking note of the decisions adopted and recommendations made by the Committee at its thirty-first and thirty-second sessions,

1. *Takes note* of the report of the Committee on the Elimination of Racial Discrimination on its thirty-first and thirty-second sessions;

2. *Also takes note* of the part of the report relating to Trust and Non-Self-Governing Territories and other Territories to which General Assembly resolution 1514(XV) of 14 December 1960 applies;

3. *Draws the attention* of the relevant United Nations bodies to the opinion and recommendations of the Committee relating to the Territories mentioned in paragraph 2 above, calls upon those bodies to ensure that the Committee is supplied with all relevant information on the Territories and urges all administering Powers to co-operate with those bodies by providing all the necessary information in order to enable the Committee to discharge fully its responsibilities under article 15 of the International Convention on the Elimination of All Forms of Racial Discrimination;

4. *Considers* that the Committee should not take into consideration information on Territories to which General Assembly resolution 1514(XV) applies unless such information is communicated by the competent United Nations bodies in conformity with article 15 of the Convention;

5. *Strongly condemns* the policy of *apartheid* in South Africa and Namibia as a crime against humanity and urges all Member States to adopt effective political, economic and other measures in conformity with the relevant resolutions of the General Assembly, the Security Council and other United Nations bodies, in order to support the legitimate struggle of the oppressed peoples of South Africa and Namibia for their national liberation and human dignity and to secure the elimination of the racist *apartheid* system;

6. *Commends* the Committee for its continuous endeavours towards the elimination of all forms of discrimination based on race, colour, descent or national or ethnic origin, in particular the elimination of *apartheid* in South Africa and Namibia, and welcomes the decision on *apartheid* adopted by the Committee at its thirty-second session;

7. *Notes with appreciation* the Committee's continued participation in the activities within the framework of the Programme of Action for the Second Decade to Combat Racism and Racial Discrimination;

8. *Welcomes* the efforts of the Committee aimed at the elimination of all forms of discrimination against national or ethnic minorities, persons belonging to such minorities and indigenous populations, wherever such discrimination exists, and the attainment of the full enjoyment of their human rights through the implementation of the principles and provisions of the Convention;

9. *Welcomes further* the efforts of the Committee aimed at the elimination of all forms of discrimination against migrant workers and their families, the promotion of their rights on a non-discriminatory basis and the achievement of their full equality, including the freedom to maintain their cultural characteristics;

10. *Calls upon* Member States to adopt effective legislative, socio-economic and other necessary measures in order to ensure the prevention or elimination of discrimination based on race, colour, descent or national or ethnic origin;

11. *Further calls upon* the States parties to the Convention to protect fully, by the adoption of the relevant legislative and other measures, in conformity with the Convention, the rights of national or ethnic minorities and persons belonging to such minorities, as well as the rights of indigenous populations;

12. *Commends* the States parties to the Convention on measures taken to ensure, within their jurisdiction, the availability of appropriate recourse procedures for the victims of racial discrimination;

13. *Reiterates its invitation* to the States parties to the Convention to provide the Committee, in accordance with its general guidelines, with information on the implementation of the provisions of the Convention, including information on the demographic composition of their populations and on their relations with the racist régime of South Africa;

14. *Appeals* to the States parties to take fully into consideration their obligation under the Convention to submit their reports in due time;

15. *Commends* the Committee for its efforts towards a further universalization and a more consistent implementation of the Convention and welcomes its General Recommendation VII relating to the implementation of article 4 of the Convention;

16. *Requests* the Secretary-General to take the necessary steps to ensure wider publicity of the work of the Committee, which would facilitate its task to implement effectively its functions under the Convention, and to inform the General Assembly at its forty-first session of the action taken in that regard.

General Assembly resolution 40/28

29 November 1985   Meeting 96   136-1-9 (recorded vote)

Approved by Third Committee (A/40/914) by recorded vote (129-1-8), 19 November (meeting 46); 12-nation draft (A/C.3/40/L.14/Rev.1); agenda item 94 *(a)*.
Sponsors: Angola, Bangladesh, Cape Verde, China, Cuba, Guinea-Bissau, Madagascar, Nigeria, Yemen, Yugoslavia, Zambia, Zimbabwe.
Meeting numbers. GA 40th session: 3rd Committee 3-15, 37, 46; plenary 96.

Recorded vote in Assembly as follows:

In favour: Afghanistan, Albania, Algeria, Angola, Argentina, Australia, Austria, Bahamas, Bahrain, Bangladesh, Barbados, Benin, Bhutan, Bolivia, Botswana, Brazil, Brunei Darussalam, Bulgaria, Burkina Faso, Burma, Burundi, Byelorussian SSR, Cameroon, Canada, Cape Verde, Central African Republic, Chad, Chile, China, Colombia, Comoros, Congo, Cuba, Cyprus, Czechoslovakia, Democratic Kampuchea, Democratic Yemen, Denmark, Djibouti, Dominican Republic, Ecuador, Egypt, El Salvador, Equatorial Guinea, Ethiopia, Fiji, Finland, Gabon, German Democratic Republic, Ghana, Greece, Guatemala, Guinea, Guinea-Bissau, Guyana, Honduras, Hungary, Iceland, India, Indonesia, Iran, Iraq, Ireland, Ivory Coast, Jamaica, Japan, Jordan, Kenya, Kuwait, Lao People's Democratic Republic, Lebanon, Lesotho, Liberia, Libyan Arab Jamahiriya, Madagascar, Malawi, Malaysia, Maldives, Mali, Malta, Mauritania, Mauritius, Mexico, Mongolia, Morocco, Mozambique, Nepal, New Zealand, Nicaragua, Niger, Nigeria, Norway, Oman, Pakistan, Panama, Papua New Guinea, Peru, Philippines, Poland, Qatar, Romania, Rwanda, Saint Lucia, Samoa, Sao Tome and Principe, Saudi Arabia, Senegal, Seychelles, Sierra Leone, Singapore, Somalia, Spain, Sri Lanka, Sudan, Suriname, Swaziland,[a] Sweden, Syrian Arab Republic, Thailand, Togo, Trinidad and Tobago, Tunisia, Turkey, Uganda, Ukrainian SSR, USSR, United Arab Emirates, United Republic of Tanzania, Uruguay, Venezuela, Viet Nam, Yemen, Yugoslavia, Zaire, Zambia, Zimbabwe.
Against: United States.

Abstaining: Belgium, France, Germany, Federal Republic of, Grenada, Italy, Luxembourg, Netherlands, Portugal, United Kingdom.
[a]Later advised the Secretariat it had intended to abstain.

Before adopting the text as a whole, the Assembly voted separately on paragraphs 4 and 5 and on the phrase "including information on the demographic composition of their populations and on their relations with the racist régime of South Africa" in paragraph 13. The paragraphs were retained by recorded votes of, respectively, 93 to 9, with 32 abstentions, and 122 to 1, with 22 abstentions; the phrase was retained by 122 votes to none, with 23 abstentions.

The Third Committee had also voted on the same paragraphs and phrase, retaining them by recorded votes of, respectively: 82 to 9, with 36 abstentions; 116 to 1, with 21 abstentions; and 110 to none, with 24 abstentions.

The United States said it voted against the text because paragraph 5 contained a reference to *apartheid* as a crime against humanity, as well as other divisive elements not directly relevant to the CERD report. Japan understood that the term "crime against humanity" had no legal implications.

Luxembourg, on behalf of the 10 States members of EC, voiced reservations on paragraph 4, which it described as being political in nature and introducing irrelevant and controversial elements, as well as on paragraphs 5 and 13, on the same grounds as in 1984.[20] The conviction that it was not for the Third Committee to direct CERD's work also motivated France to cast a negative vote, and Senegal to abstain, in the vote on paragraph 4. The United Kingdom said the paragraph failed to take account of the reporting obligations of States parties which were also administering Powers; in addition, it said it had difficulties with paragraph 6, and felt the text contained decisions and opinions that exceeded the Committee's terms of reference. Canada and Portugal were concerned, respectively, about the undue politicization of the CERD report and the Convention, while Belgium regretted that the text had not been worded in such a way as to enable its adoption by consensus.

Denmark, explaining the Nordic countries' abstention in the separate votes, said the wording of paragraphs 2 to 4 failed to focus on racial discrimination as the Committee's main purpose and called on it to take action beyond the scope of its mandate, a view shared by Austria. Australia abstained in the vote on paragraphs 4 and 5, citing lack of balance and certain legal difficulties. China said it accepted paragraph 4 on the understanding that it reaffirmed the relevant articles of the Convention and did not relate to or affect the positions of Governments in regard to certain specific questions. Noting that the Convention did not mention "national or ethnic minorities" or "indigenous populations", India understood that the rights referred to in paragraphs 8 and 11 were to be interpreted strictly within the meaning of article 1. Morocco abstained in the vote on paragraph 4, which it felt presented legal difficulties in relation to paragraph 14. Turkey considered that parts of the CERD report did not reflect the true historical context of certain questions.

Explaining its vote in favour of paragraph 4, Algeria said it had been intended to prevent any deviations from article 15 of the Convention, according to which CERD was to receive information on Territories from United Nations bodies and in no case from administering Powers or States parties; it was not an attempt to modify the provisions of the Convention or CERD's mandate.

Measures against nazism and fascism

Human Rights Commission action. On 13 March 1985,[21] the Commission on Human Rights condemned all totalitarian or other ideologies and practices, including Nazi, Fascist and neo-Fascist, based on racial or ethnic exclusiveness or intolerance, hatred, terror, or systematic denial of human rights and fundamental freedoms. Noting, in particular, the totalitarian nature of racist régimes, it urged States to draw attention to threats to democratic institutions by such ideologies and practices and called for measures against them. It requested the Secretary-General to submit to its 1986 session a report on the implementation of the Assembly's December 1984 resolution[22] on the subject.

Report of the Secretary-General and communications. In response to a 1984 Assembly request,[22] the Secretary-General submitted, in April 1985, a report, with later addenda,[23] summarizing comments from 24 States, three specialized agencies, one intergovernmental organization and 19 NGOs on ongoing and planned measures to eradicate nazism, fascism and related ideologies and practices.

By a letter of 17 June,[24] Israel protested against Palestine Liberation Organization (PLO) leader Yasser Arafat's public praise, in April 1985 in Indonesia, of two Palestinians who, Israel charged, had been Nazi collaborators. On 6 November,[25] Israel accused the Syrian Arab Republic of sheltering a Nazi war criminal (see p. 314).

GENERAL ASSEMBLY ACTION

On 13 December 1985, on the recommendation of the Third Committee, the General Assembly adopted **resolution 40/148**, by recorded vote.

**Measures to be taken against Nazi, Fascist and
neo-Fascist activities and all other forms
of totalitarian ideologies and practices
based on racial intolerance, hatred and terror**
The General Assembly,
Recalling that the United Nations emerged from the struggle against nazism, fascism, aggression and foreign occupation, and that the peoples expressed their resolve

in the Charter of the United Nations to save future generations from the scourge of war,

Reaffirming the purposes and principles laid down in the Charter, which are aimed at maintaining international peace and security, developing friendly relations among nations based on respect for the principle of equal rights and the self-determination of peoples and achieving international co-operation in promoting and encouraging respect for human rights and fundamental freedoms for all,

Recalling that 8 and 9 May 1985 marked the days of the fortieth anniversary of victory over nazism and fascism in the Second World War and of that struggle against them,

Bearing in mind the suffering, destruction and death of millions of victims of aggression, foreign occupation, nazism and fascism,

Recalling also the close relationship between all totalitarian ideologies and practices based on racial or ethnic exclusiveness or intolerance, hatred and terror and the systematic denial of human rights and fundamental freedoms,

Firmly convinced that the best bulwark against nazism and racial discrimination is the establishment and maintenance of democratic institutions, that the existence of genuine political, social and economic democracy is an effective vaccine and an equally effective antidote against the formation or development of Nazi movements and that a political system which is based on freedom and effective participation by the people in the conduct of public affairs and under which economic and social conditions are such as to ensure a decent standard of living for the population makes it impossible for fascism, nazism or other ideologies based on racism and racial discrimination, hatred and terror to succeed,

Emphasizing that all totalitarian or other ideologies and practices, including Nazi, Fascist and neo-Fascist ones, based on racial or ethnic exclusiveness or intolerance, hatred, terror or systematic denial of human rights and fundamental freedoms, or which have such consequences, may jeopardize world peace and constitute obstacles to friendly relations between States and to the realization of human rights, fundamental freedoms and social progress in the world,

Acknowledging with satisfaction the fact that many States have established systems based on the inherent dignity and the equal and inalienable rights of all human beings, which are the basis of a democratic society and the best bulwark against totalitarian ideologies and practices, and have set up legal regulations which are suited to prevent the activities of Nazi, Fascist and neo-Fascist groups and organizations,

Noting that, nevertheless, in the contemporary world there continue to exist various forms of totalitarian ideologies and practices which entail contempt for the individual or denial of the intrinsic dignity and equality of all human beings, of equality of opportunity in civil, political, economic, social and cultural spheres, and of social justice,

Deeply alarmed at the existence of groups and organizations which propagate totalitarian ideologies and practices, including Nazi, Fascist and neo-Fascist ones, which violate human rights and fundamental freedoms, in particular the rights to self-determination, to life, liberty and security of person and to freedom from discrimination, and which thereby constitute a threat to the purposes and principles laid down in the Charter of the United Nations,

Conscious of the need to counter the spread of totalitarian ideologies and practices based on the systematic denial of human rights and fundamental freedoms, racial intolerance, hatred and terror,

Stressing that totalitarian régimes based on racial or ethnic exclusiveness or intolerance, hatred or terror or the systematic denial of human rights and fundamental freedoms seek to ensure their domination and their economic and social privileges at the expense of other peoples or racial or ethnic groups, which they oppress and exploit,

Reaffirming that the prosecution and punishment of war crimes and crimes against peace and humanity, as laid down in General Assembly resolutions 3(I) of 13 February 1946 and 95(I) of 11 December 1946, constitute a universal commitment for all States,

Mindful of the principles of international co-operation in the detection, arrest, extradition and punishment of persons guilty of war crimes and crimes against humanity, set forth in General Assembly resolution 3074(XXVIII) of 3 December 1973,

Recalling its resolutions 2331(XXII) of 18 December 1967, 2438(XXIII) of 19 December 1968, 2545(XXIV) of 11 December 1969, 2713(XXV) of 15 December 1970, 2839(XXVI) of 18 December 1971, 34/24 of 15 November 1979, 35/200 of 15 December 1980, 36/162 of 16 December 1981, 37/179 of 17 December 1982, 38/99 of 16 December 1983 and 39/114 of 14 December 1984,

Recalling further the Declaration on Social Progress and Development, the United Nations Declaration on the Elimination of All Forms of Racial Discrimination, the Declaration on the Granting of Independence to Colonial Countries and Peoples and the Declaration on the Elimination of All Forms of Intolerance and of Discrimination Based on Religion or Belief,

Underlining the importance of the Universal Declaration of Human Rights, the International Covenants on Human Rights, the International Convention on the Elimination of All Forms of Racial Discrimination, the Convention on the Prevention and Punishment of the Crime of Genocide, the Convention on the Non-Applicability of Statutory Limitations to War Crimes and Crimes against Humanity, the International Convention on the Suppression and Punishment of the Crime of *Apartheid* and other relevant international instruments,

Reaffirming that the ideologies and practices described above are incompatible with the purposes and principles of the Charter of the United Nations and the above-mentioned international instruments,

Mindful that the fortieth anniversary of the end of the Second World War served to mobilize efforts of the world community in its struggle against those ideologies and practices,

Viewing with deep concern that the proponents of Fascist ideologies have, in a number of countries, intensified their activities and are increasingly co-ordinating them on an international scale,

Expressing its concern that Fascist and Nazi and other totalitarian ideologies and practices are inherited, *inter alia*, by repressive racist régimes practising gross and flagrant violations of human rights and the systematic denial of human rights and fundamental freedoms,

1. *Again condemns* all totalitarian or other ideologies and practices, including Nazi, Fascist and neo-Fascist ideologies, based on racial or ethnic exclusiveness or intolerance, hatred and terror, which deprive people of basic human rights and fundamental freedoms and of equality of opportunity, and expresses its determination to combat those ideologies and practices;

2. *Urges* all States to draw attention to the threat to democratic institutions by the above-mentioned ideologies and practices and to consider taking measures, in accordance with their national constitutional systems and with the provisions of the Universal Declaration of Human Rights and the International Covenants on Human Rights, to prohibit or otherwise deter activities by groups or organizations or whoever is practising those ideologies;

3. *Invites* Member States to adopt, in accordance with their national constitutional systems and with the provisions of the Universal Declaration of Human Rights and the International Covenants on Human Rights, as a matter of high priority, measures declaring punishable by law any dissemination of ideas based on racial superiority or hatred and of war propaganda, including Nazi, Fascist and neo-Fascist ideologies;

4. *Calls upon* all States, in accordance with the basic principles of international law, to refrain from practices aimed at the violation of basic human rights and which constitute a threat to peace and international security;

5. *Welcomes* the fact that on 8 May 1985 the Economic and Social Council held a solemn commemorative ceremony, in the light of General Assembly resolution 39/114, the purpose of which was to underline the continuing relevance of the Charter of the United Nations, the importance of international co-operation towards peace, security and development and the promotion of human rights and fundamental freedoms and in particular the fundamental right to life, liberty and security of person;

6. *Gives expression to the respect* felt by today's generation for the victims of and the struggle of peoples against nazism and fascism in the Second World War and for the establishing of the United Nations in order to save mankind from the scourge of war and to reaffirm faith in fundamental human rights and in the dignity and worth of the human person;

7. *Appeals* to all States that have not yet done so to become parties to the International Covenants on Human Rights, the Convention on the Prevention and Punishment of the Crime of Genocide, the International Convention on the Elimination of All Forms of Racial Discrimination, the Convention on the Non-Applicability of Statutory Limitations to War Crimes and Crimes against Humanity and the International Convention on the Suppression and Punishment of the Crime of *Apartheid;*

8. *Reiterates its request* to the appropriate specialized agencies, as well as other intergovernmental organizations and international non-governmental organizations, to initiate or intensify measures against the ideologies and practices described in paragraph 1 above;

9. *Requests* the Secretary-General to ensure that the Department of Public Information of the Secretariat pays due attention to the dissemination of information exposing the ideologies and practices described in paragraph 1 above;

10. *Invites* all States and international organizations to submit to the Secretary-General their comments and information on the implementation of the present resolution;

11. *Requests* the Secretary-General to submit a report, through the Economic and Social Council, to the General Assembly at its forty-first session in the light of the discussion that will take place in the Commission on Human Rights and on the basis of comments provided by States and international organizations.

General Assembly resolution 40/148

13 December 1985   Meeting 116   121-2-27 (recorded vote)

Approved by Third Committee (A/40/1007) by recorded vote (96-2-24), 6 December (meeting 71); 14-nation draft (A/C.3/40/L.85), orally revised; agenda item 12.
Sponsors: Afghanistan, Angola, Bulgaria, Byelorussian SSR, Cuba, Czechoslovakia, German Democratic Republic, Hungary, Lao People's Democratic Republic, Mongolia, Nicaragua, Poland, Ukrainian SSR, Viet Nam.
Meeting numbers. GA 40th session: 3rd Committee 55, 61, 63, 64, 66-68, 71; plenary 116.

Recorded vote in Assembly as follows:

In favour: Afghanistan, Algeria, Angola, Argentina, Austria, Bahrain, Bangladesh, Benin, Bhutan, Bolivia, Botswana, Brazil, Brunei Darussalam, Bulgaria, Burkina Faso, Burma, Burundi, Byelorussian SSR, Cameroon, Cape Verde, Central African Republic, Chad, Chile, China, Colombia, Comoros, Congo, Costa Rica, Cuba, Cyprus, Czechoslovakia, Democratic Yemen, Djibouti, Dominican Republic, Ecuador, Egypt, El Salvador, Equatorial Guinea, Ethiopia, Fiji, Finland, Gabon, Gambia, German Democratic Republic, Ghana, Guatemala, Guinea, Guinea-Bissau, Guyana, Haiti, Honduras, Hungary, India, Indonesia, Iran, Iraq, Ivory Coast, Jordan, Kenya, Kuwait, Lao People's Democratic Republic, Lebanon, Lesotho, Liberia, Libyan Arab Jamahiriya, Madagascar, Malawi, Malaysia, Maldives, Mali, Malta, Mauritania, Mauritius, Mexico, Mongolia, Morocco, Mozambique, Nepal, Nicaragua, Niger, Nigeria, Pakistan, Panama, Peru, Philippines, Poland, Qatar, Romania, Rwanda, Saint Lucia, Saint Vincent and the Grenadines, Sao Tome and Principe, Saudi Arabia, Senegal, Sierra Leone, Somalia, Sri Lanka, Sudan, Suriname, Swaziland, Sweden, Syrian Arab Republic, Thailand, Togo, Trinidad and Tobago, Tunisia, Turkey, Uganda, Ukrainian SSR, USSR, United Arab Emirates, United Republic of Tanzania, Uruguay, Vanuatu, Venezuela, Viet Nam, Yemen, Yugoslavia, Zaire, Zambia, Zimbabwe.
Against: Israel, United States.
Abstaining: Antigua and Barbuda, Australia, Bahamas, Belgium, Belize, Canada, Denmark, France, Germany, Federal Republic of, Greece, Grenada, Iceland, Ireland, Italy, Japan, Luxembourg, Netherlands, New Zealand, Norway, Oman, Papua New Guinea, Paraguay, Portugal, Saint Christopher and Nevis, Samoa, Spain, United Kingdom.

The Netherlands and the United Kingdom submitted amendments[26] to the text, some of which the sponsors took into account in their oral revisions. The amendments were withdrawn; however the United Kingdom requested a recorded vote. The Netherlands said the text failed to strike a balance between the various elements and was unacceptable in the current state, a view shared by United Kingdom, which noted that a resolution of that type was valid only if it represented the unanimous opinion of all States.

Prior to voting on the text as a whole, the Assembly added the words "and social progress in the world" in the seventh preambular paragraph by a recorded vote of 106 to 19, with 13 abstentions.

Fortieth anniversary of the victory over nazism and fascism

Communications. The fortieth anniversary of the victory over nazism and fascism was the subject of a number of communications to the Secretary-General. By a letter of 5 February 1985,[27] a group of Eastern European countries—Bulgaria, the Byelorussian SSR, Czechoslovakia, the German Democratic Republic, Hungary, Poland, the Ukrainian SSR and the USSR—and the Lao People's Democratic Republic, Mongolia and Viet Nam requested the Economic and Social Council, at its 1985 organizational session, to devise ways to hold a solemn celebration, on 8 and 9 May 1985, of the anniversary. In connection with the anniversary, Czechoslovakia transmitted, on 17 May,[28] a joint statement by the same Eastern European countries, as well as Cuba and Viet Nam, at the Council's May/June 1985 session. The German Democratic Republic, on 20 March,[29] provided information on activities it was undertaking to observe the anniversary of the end of Nazi rule, whose commemoration was also the subject of an 8 May message from the President of Madagascar, transmitted 13 May.[30]

Human Rights Commission action. On 13 March 1985,[31] the Commission on Human Rights paid a tribute to the people whose efforts and sufferings had led to the end of the Second World War and the establishment of the United Nations, and considered that celebration of that anniversary should serve the promotion of human rights and fundamental freedoms. On 6 February,[32] it had requested the Economic and Social Council, in considering its 1985 work programme, to take into account the fact that 8 and 9 May represented the fortieth anniversary of the end of the Second World War.

Action by CERD. Recalling that the Assembly in 1984[22] had considered that the occasion of the fortieth anniversary of the victory over nazism and fascism should serve to mobilize efforts in the struggle against Nazi, Fascist, neo-Fascist and other totalitarian ideologies and practices, CERD on 22 March 1985[33] expressed appreciation of the victory, paid tribute to the memory of those who fought against and were the victims of nazism and fascism, condemned racism, racial discrimination and *apartheid*, and reminded the States parties to the International Convention on the Elimination of All Forms of Racial Discrimination of their obligation to adopt measures during the Second Decade to Combat Racism and Racial Discrimination aimed at ending such ideologies.

ECONOMIC AND SOCIAL COUNCIL ACTION

On 8 February, in adopting its work programme for 1985 and 1986 (see p. 1055), the Council decided to hold on 8 or 9 May a solemn commemorative ceremony in the light of the Assembly's 1984 resolution,[22] bearing in mind the continuing relevance of the Charter, in particular its emphasis on the importance of international co-operation towards peace, security and development, fundamental human rights and the dignity of the human person, and fundamental freedoms for all without distinction as to race, sex, language or religion.

The text, which became a provision of **decision 1985/101**, was based on a draft decision[34] submitted by the Council President on behalf of the Bureau, with changes agreed upon during further informal consultations, based on information on consultations on two different drafts: one submitted by Bulgaria, the Byelorussian SSR, Czechoslovakia, the German Democratic Republic, Hungary, the Lao People's Democratic Republic, Mongolia, Poland, the Ukrainian SSR, the USSR and Viet Nam;[35] the other by Belgium, Canada, France, the Federal Republic of Germany, Italy, Luxembourg, the Netherlands, Norway, the United Kingdom and the United States.[36]

On 30 May, on the recommendation of its Second Committee, the Council adopted **resolution 1985/44**, without vote.

Solemn commemorative ceremony in the light of General Assembly resolution 39/114

The Economic and Social Council,

Taking note of General Assembly resolution 39/114 of 14 December 1984, in which the Assembly declared that 8 and 9 May 1985 would be the days of the fortieth anniversary of victory over nazism and fascism in the Second World War and of that struggle against them,

Taking note also of Commission on Human Rights resolutions 1985/31 of 13 March 1985, entitled "Measures to be taken against all totalitarian or other ideologies and practices, including Nazi, Fascist and neo-Fascist, based on racial or ethnic exclusiveness or intolerance, hatred, terror, systematic denial of human rights and fundamental freedoms, or which have such consequences", and 1985/32 of 13 March 1985, entitled "Fortieth anniversary of the end of the Second World War",

Paying a tribute of respect to the peoples whose great efforts and sufferings led to the end of the Second World War and to the establishment of the United Nations forty years ago,

Recalling that the United Nations Organization embodies the resolve of peoples to save succeeding generations from the scourge of war and to reaffirm faith in fundamental human rights and in the dignity and worth of the human person,

Noting that on 8 May 1985 the Economic and Social Council held a solemn commemorative ceremony in the light of General Assembly resolution 39/114, bearing in mind the continuing relevance of the Charter of the United Nations, in particular its emphasis on the importance of international co-operation towards peace, security and development, fundamental human rights and the dignity of the human person, and fundamental freedoms for all without distinction as to race, sex, language or religion,

1. *Takes note*, with appreciation, of the report of the Secretary-General and decides to transmit it to the General Assembly;

2. *Acknowledges with satisfaction* that many States have taken measures for the solemn commemoration of this anniversary and of the founding of the United Nations;

3. *Considers* that the solemn commemoration by the Council of this anniversary should serve the promotion of human rights and fundamental freedoms, in particular the fundamental right to life, liberty and security of person.

Economic and Social Council resolution 1985/44

30 May 1985   Meeting 25   Adopted without vote

Approved by Second Committee (E/1985/95 & Corr.1) without vote, 24 May (meeting 15); draft based on consultations on draft by Afghanistan, Bulgaria, Byelorussian SSR, Cuba, Czechoslovakia, German Democratic Republic, Hungary, Mongolia, Poland, Ukrainian SSR, USSR and Viet Nam (E/1985/C.2/L.11/Rev.1) and amendments by Netherlands and United Kingdom (E/1985/C.2/L.14); agenda item 16.

Other aspects of discrimination

Religious freedom

Communication. On 22 August,[37] Morocco transmitted a statement made by King Hassan II introducing Pope John Paul II, who addressed a rally on 19 August at Casablanca on interfaith dialogue and understanding.

Human Rights Commission action. Pursuant to a 1984 General Assembly request,[38] the Commission on Human Rights continued in 1985 to consider measures to implement the 1981 Declaration on the Elimination of All Forms of Intolerance and of Discrimination Based on Religion or Belief.[39] On 14 March,[40] the Commission urged States to provide adequate constitutional and legal guarantees for freedom of thought, conscience, religion and belief, and examine the possibility of establishing national institutions to promote tolerance of religion and the training of their public officials to ensure that they did not in their duties discriminate against persons professing other religions or beliefs. The United Nations University and other academic and research institutions were invited to undertake programmes on the encouragement of respect in matters relating to freedom of religion, and the Secretary-General was asked to prepare a compendium of national legislation and regulations on freedom of religion or belief and report in 1986 on measures to implement this resolution.

With regard to a 1984 Seminar on the Encouragement of Understanding, Tolerance and Respect in Matters relating to Freedom of Religion or Belief,[41] the Commission took note of its report,[42] which was subsequently transmitted by the Secretary-General to the Assembly. Participants from 24 States and observers from 16 countries, as well as representatives of several United Nations bodies, inter- and non-governmental organizations and liberation movements attended.

Emphasizing the importance of tolerance for religion or other belief and the role world religions could play in promoting such attitudes, the Seminar stressed the fundamental and universal character of the right to freedom of thought, conscience, religion or belief, expressed concern over violations of that right and called for action at all levels to ensure respect for it. The Seminar urged that high priority be given to implementing United Nations instruments for the protection of freedom of religion and belief and pointed to the need for an international convention on the matter. It recommended that States provide adequate constitutional and legal guarantees for that freedom and examine the possibility of establishing national institutions for promoting tolerance. Education should play a significant role in attaining that goal, particularly through promotional programmes in educational and cultural institutions and the training of public officials and teachers in the spirit of tolerance.

The Seminar urged increased interfaith dialogue and improved dissemination of information, and called for launching an action programme for translating the Declaration into the greatest possible number of national and local languages and for issuing a multilanguage publication containing the various international standards relating to freedom of religion. Viewing studies on the major religions and beliefs as important for combating intolerance, the Seminar suggested examining the links between discrimination on grounds of religion or belief and discrimination on grounds of race or origin. It recommended that Governments utilize the advisory services of the Centre for Human Rights for drafting legislation on establishing institutions in this field, and that NGOs develop proposals on issues of tolerance, religion or belief.

Sub-Commission action. On 27 August 1985,[43] the Sub-Commission decided to postpone consideration of the item to its 1986 session. By a resolution[44] adopted on 29 August 1985 by 11 votes to 1, with 3 abstentions, it requested the Human Rights Commission to urge Albania to provide constitutional and legal measures to ensure freedom of religion or belief, proscribe discrimination on ground of religion or belief, and provide safeguards and remedies against such discrimination.

GENERAL ASSEMBLY ACTION

On 13 December, acting without vote on the recommendation of the Third Committee, the General Assembly adopted **resolution 40/109**.

Elimination of all forms of religious intolerance

The General Assembly,

Conscious of the need to promote universal respect for, and observance of, human rights and fundamental freedoms for all without distinction as to race, sex, language or religion,

Reaffirming its resolution 36/55 of 25 November 1981, in which it proclaimed the Declaration on the Elimination of All Forms of Intolerance and of Discrimination Based on Religion or Belief,

Recalling subsequent resolutions, in which the Assembly requested the Commission on Human Rights to consider what measures might be necessary to implement the Declaration,

Recalling also Economic and Social Council resolution 1984/39 of 24 May 1984, in which the Council authorized the Sub-Commission on Prevention of Discrimination and Protection of Minorities to entrust its Special Rapporteur with the preparation of a study, in accordance with the terms of Sub-Commission resolution 1983/31 of 6 September 1983, on the current dimensions of the problems of intolerance and of discrimination on the grounds of religion or belief,

Taking note of the progress report thereon submitted by the Special Rapporteur to the Sub-Commission at its thirty-eighth session,

Concerned that the Special Rapporteur has not yet received sufficiently relevant or detailed information to discharge her tasks effectively,

Recalling the Seminar on the Encouragement of Understanding, Tolerance and Respect in Matters relating to Freedom of Religion or Belief, held at Geneva from 3 to 14 December 1984,

Recognizing that it is desirable to enhance the promotional and public information activities of the United Nations in matters relating to freedom of religion or belief and that both Governments and non-governmental organizations have an important role to play in this domain,

Aware that intolerance and discrimination based on religion or belief continue to exist in many parts of the world,

Believing that further efforts are, therefore, required to promote and protect the right to freedom of thought, conscience, religion or belief,

1. *Reaffirms* that freedom of thought, conscience, religion and belief is a right guaranteed to all without discrimination;

2. *Urges* States, therefore, in accordance with their respective constitutional systems, to provide, where they have not already done so, adequate constitutional and legal guarantees of freedom of thought, conscience, religion and belief;

3. *Endorses* the request of the Commission on Human Rights to the Secretary-General, contained in its resolution 1985/51 of 14 March 1985, to prepare a compendium of the national legislation and regulations of States on the question of freedom of religion or belief, with particular regard to the measures taken to combat intolerance or discrimination in this field;

4. *Encourages* Governments, specialized agencies, intergovernmental organizations and non-governmental organizations to supply the Special Rapporteur of the Sub-Commission on Prevention of Discrimination and Protection of Minorities, as requested, with information relevant to the study she is preparing on the current dimensions of the problems of intolerance and of discrimination on the grounds of religion or belief, so as to enable her to submit the final report to the Sub-Commission as soon as possible;

5. *Takes note with appreciation* of the report of the Seminar on the Encouragement of Understanding, Tolerance and Respect in Matters relating to Freedom of Religion or Belief;

6. *Urges* all States to take all appropriate measures to combat intolerance and to encourage understanding,

tolerance and respect in matters relating to freedom of religion or belief and, in this context, to examine where necessary the supervision and training of their civil servants, educators and other public officials to ensure that, in the course of their official duties, they respect different religions and beliefs and do not discriminate against persons professing other religions or beliefs;

7. *Invites* the United Nations University and other academic and research institutions to undertake programmes and studies on the encouragement of understanding, tolerance and respect in matters relating to freedom of religion or belief;

8. *Invites* the Secretary-General to continue to give high priority to the dissemination of the text of the Declaration on the Elimination of All Forms of Intolerance and of Discrimination Based on Religion or Belief, in all official languages of the United Nations, and to take all appropriate measures to make the text available for use by United Nations information centres, as well as by other interested bodies;

9. *Requests* the Secretary-General in this context to invite interested non-governmental organizations to consider what further role they could envisage playing regarding the dissemination of the Declaration in national and local languages;

10. *Requests* the Commission on Human Rights to continue its consideration of measures to implement the Declaration and to report, through the Economic and Social Council, to the General Assembly at its forty-first session;

11. *Decides* to include in the provisional agenda of its forty-first session the item entitled "Elimination of all forms of religious intolerance" and to consider the report of the Commission on Human Rights under that item.

General Assembly resolution 40/109

13 December 1985   Meeting 116   Adopted without vote

Approved by Third Committee (A/40/968) without vote, 2 December (meeting 60); 26-nation draft (A/C.3/40/L.61), orally revised; agenda item 101.
Sponsors: Australia, Austria, Belgium, Canada, Costa Rica, Dominican Republic, Fiji, Finland, France, Gambia, Honduras, Ireland, Italy, Ivory Coast, Japan, Morocco, Netherlands, New Zealand, Norway, Rwanda, Samoa, Senegal, Suriname, Sweden, Uganda, United States.
Meeting numbers. GA 40th session: 3rd Committee 46-48, 50-53, 58, 60; plenary 116.

Indigenous populations

Human Rights Commission action. On 11 March,[45] the Commission on Human Rights, having considered the 1984 activities of the Sub-Commission's Working Group on Indigenous Populations,[46] urged it to intensify its efforts in developing international standards on human rights of indigenous populations. On the same date,[47] it recommended to the Economic and Social Council the issuance, in a consolidated form of the full report of Special Rapporteur José R. Martínez Cobo (Ecuador) on the problem of discrimination against indigenous populations, which had been presented to the Sub-Commission in 1983.[48]

ECONOMIC AND SOCIAL COUNCIL ACTION

On 30 May 1985, the Council adopted without vote **decision 1985/137**—as recommended by the Human Rights Commission and approved by the

Council's Second Committee on 24 May—requesting the Secretary-General to issue the Special Rapporteur's 1983 report in a consolidated form and to disseminate it to Governments, agencies, organizations and institutions. The Council decided that the conclusions and recommendations of the report should be printed, with an introduction by the Secretary-General.

Working Group activities. The Working Group on Indigenous Populations continued to review, at its fourth session (Geneva, 29 July–2 August and 23 August),[49] developments pertaining to the promotion and protection of rights and freedoms of indigenous populations. It considered the preliminary version of seven draft principles—dealing with the right to enjoy universally recognized fundamental rights, to be equal to all other human beings, to life, to religious freedom, to education, to preserve cultural identity, and to promote intercultural information and education—for inclusion in a future declaration on those rights. At future sessions, emphasis was to be placed on the Group's standard-setting activities.

Sub-Commission action. The Sub-Commission, on 29 August 1985,[50] requested the Working Group to focus in 1986 on drafting specific proposals for the content and scope of the seven rights and principles under consideration and on gathering information on other rights and principles. It asked the Secretary-General to assist the Working Group in discharging its duties and ensure adequate dissemination of all relevant material.

On the same date,[51] the Sub-Commission proposed to its parent Commission a draft resolution for adoption by the Council recommending that the Group meet for up to eight working days before the annual sessions of the Sub-Commission.

UN Voluntary Fund for Indigenous Populations

Human Rights Commission action. On 11 March 1985,[52] the Commission on Human Rights proposed to the Economic and Social Council a draft resolution recommending the establishment by the General Assembly of a voluntary fund to provide financial assistance to representatives of indigenous communities and organizations to participate in the Working Group.

ECONOMIC AND SOCIAL COUNCIL ACTION

By **resolution 1985/38**, adopted without vote on 30 May 1985, the Council, following approval without vote of the Commission's text by its Second Committee on 24 May, recommended that the Assembly adopt the proposed text, which it attached to its resolution.

United Nations Voluntary Fund for Indigenous Populations

The Economic and Social Council,

Recalling its resolution 1982/34 of 7 May 1982, authorizing the establishment annually of a working group on indigenous populations,

Recommends the following draft resolution to the General Assembly for adoption:

[For text, see General Assembly resolution 40/131 below.]

GENERAL ASSEMBLY ACTION

On 13 December, on the recommendation of the Third Committee, the General Assembly adopted **resolution 40/131**, without vote.

United Nations Voluntary Fund for Indigenous Populations

The General Assembly,

Taking note of Economic and Social Council resolution 1982/34 of 7 May 1982, by which the Council authorized the Sub-Commission on Prevention of Discrimination and Protection of Minorities to establish annually a working group on indigenous populations,

Taking note of Commission on Human Rights resolution 1984/32 of 12 March 1984,

Convinced that the establishment of a voluntary trust fund for indigenous populations would constitute a significant development for the future promotion and protection of the human rights of indigenous populations,

Decides to establish a voluntary trust fund in accordance with the following criteria:

(*a*) The name of the fund shall be the United Nations Voluntary Fund for Indigenous Populations;

(*b*) The purpose of the Fund shall be to assist representatives of indigenous communities and organizations to participate in the deliberations of the Working Group on Indigenous Populations by providing them with financial assistance, funded by means of voluntary contributions from Governments, non-governmental organizations and other private or public entities;

(*c*) The only type of activity to be supported by the Fund is that described in subparagraph (*b*) above;

(*d*) The only beneficiaries of assistance from the Fund shall be representatives of indigenous peoples' organizations and communities:

(i) Who are so considered by the Board of Trustees of the United Nations Voluntary Fund for Indigenous Populations described in subparagraph (*e*) below;

(ii) Who would not, in the opinion of the Board, be able to attend the sessions of the Working Group without the assistance provided by the Fund;

(iii) Who would be able to contribute to a deeper knowledge on the part of the Working Group of the problems affecting indigenous populations and who would secure a broad geographical representation;

(*e*) The Fund shall be administered in accordance with the Financial Regulations and Rules of the United Nations and other relevant provisions set forth in the annex to the note by the Secretary-General, with the advice of a Board of Trustees composed of five persons with relevant experience on issues affecting indigenous populations, who will serve in their personal capacity;

the members of the Board of Trustees shall be appointed by the Secretary-General for a three-year term renewable in consultation with the current Chairman of the Sub-Commission; at least one member of the Board shall be a representative of a widely recognized organization of indigenous people.

General Assembly resolution 40/131

13 December 1985   Meeting 116   Adopted without vote

Approved by Third Committee (A/40/1007) without vote, 6 December (meeting 70); draft recommended by Economic and Social Council resolution 1985/38 (A/C.3/40/L.32); agenda item 12.
Meeting numbers. GA 40th session: 3rd Committee 54, 61-64, 69, 70; plenary 116.

In **resolution 40/28**, the Assembly welcomed CERD's efforts to eliminate discrimination against persons belonging to indigenous populations and to attain full enjoyment of their human rights.

Migrant workers

Communication. By a letter of 20 August 1985,[53] Egypt's Minister for Foreign Affairs protested what he described as wide-ranging acts of mass expulsion of Egyptian nationals working in the Libyan Arab Jamahiriya. On 23 August,[54] the latter rejected the charges. The reduction of foreign workers, it said, had been gradual, the result of a three-year-old decision, and was not directed against any State. (See also p. 259.)

Draft convention

In March 1985, the Commission on Human Rights considered the progress made by the Working Group on the Drafting of an International Convention on the Protection of the Rights of All Migrant Workers and Their Families, as described in the Group's 1984 reports.[55] The Working Group convened twice in 1985, in June and in September/October. The General Assembly decided in December that the Working Group should continue drafting the convention at an inter-sessional meeting in 1986.

The welfare of migrant workers was also dealt with by the Secretary-General in a report to the Commission for Social Development (see p. 734); following its consideration, the Economic and Social Council adopted **resolution 1985/24**.

Human Rights Commission action. On 14 March 1985,[56] the Commission on Human Rights commended the Working Group for concluding, in first reading, the drafting of the preamble and articles which would serve as the basis for second reading of the draft convention on the rights of migrant workers. It invited all Member States to continue co-operating with the Group and reiterated its hope for a speedy conclusion of the convention.

Working Group activities. The open-ended Working Group on the Drafting of an International Convention on the Protection of the Rights of All Migrant Workers and Their Families, established by the General Assembly in 1979,[57] held its fifth inter-sessional meeting in New York from 3 to 14 June 1985,[58] and its sixth session from 23 September to 4 October.[59]

In June, the Group adopted in second reading the preamble of the draft convention and began consideration of part I, relating to the scope of and definitions in the convention, adopting a paragraph defining the term "migrant worker". At its September/October session, the Group continued consideration of part I, adopting, in second reading, three articles on the convention's applicability and on terms defining various categories of migrant workers.

GENERAL ASSEMBLY ACTION

On 13 December, acting on the recommendation of the Third Committee, the General Assembly adopted **resolution 40/130**, without vote.

Measures to improve the situation and ensure the human rights and dignity of all migrant workers
The General Assembly,

Reaffirming once more the permanent validity of the principles and standards embodied in the basic instruments regarding the international protection of human rights, in particular in the Universal Declaration of Human Rights, the International Covenants on Human Rights, the International Convention on the Elimination of All Forms of Racial Discrimination and the Convention on the Elimination of All Forms of Discrimination against Women,

Bearing in mind the principles and standards established within the framework of the International Labour Organisation and the United Nations Educational, Scientific and Cultural Organization, and the importance of the task carried out in connection with migrant workers and their families in other specialized agencies and in various organs of the United Nations,

Reiterating that, in spite of the existence of an already established body of principles and standards, there is a need to make further efforts to improve the situation and ensure the human rights and dignity of all migrant workers and their families,

Recalling its resolution 34/172 of 17 December 1979, by which it decided to establish a working group open to all Member States to elaborate an international convention on the protection of the rights of all migrant workers and their families,

Recalling also its resolutions 35/198 of 15 December 1980, 36/160 of 16 December 1981, 37/170 of 17 December 1982, 38/86 of 16 December 1983 and 39/102 of 14 December 1984, by which it renewed the mandate of the Working Group on the Drafting of an International Convention on the Protection of the Rights of All Migrant Workers and Their Families and requested it to continue its work,

Having examined the progress made by the Working Group during its fifth inter-sessional meeting, held from 3 to 14 June 1985, as well as the report of the Working Group during the current session of the General Assembly, during which the Group continued with the second reading of the draft convention,

1. *Takes note with satisfaction* of the reports of the Working Group on the Drafting of an International Convention on the Protection of the Rights of All Migrant Workers and Their Families and, in particular, of the progress made by the Working Group on the drafting, in second reading, of the draft convention;

2. *Decides* that, in order to enable it to complete its task as soon as possible, the Working Group shall again hold an inter-sessional meeting of two weeks' duration in New York, immediately after the first regular session of 1986 of the Economic and Social Council;

3. *Invites* the Secretary-General to transmit to Governments the reports of the Working Group so as to enable the members of the Group to continue the drafting, in second reading, of the draft convention during the inter-sessional meeting to be held in the spring of 1986, as well as to transmit the results obtained at that meeting to the General Assembly for consideration during its forty-first session;

4. *Also invites* the Secretary-General to transmit the above-mentioned documents to the competent organs of the United Nations and to international organizations concerned, for their information, so as to enable them to continue their co-operation with the Working Group;

5. *Decides* that the Working Group shall meet during the forty-first session of the General Assembly, preferably at the beginning of the session, to continue the second reading of the draft international convention on the protection of the rights of all migrant workers and their families.

General Assembly resolution 40/130

13 December 1985   Meeting 116   Adopted without vote

Approved by Third Committee (A/40/1007) without vote, 2 December (meeting 60); 25-nation draft (A/C.3/40/L.70); agenda item 12.
Sponsors: Algeria, Argentina, Benin, Cameroon, Colombia, Ecuador, Egypt, Finland, France, Greece, Italy, Mali, Mexico, Morocco, Nicaragua, Norway, Pakistan, Portugal, Rwanda, Senegal, Spain, Sweden, Tunisia, Turkey, Yugoslavia.
Financial implications. 5th Committee, A/40/1035; S-G, A/C.3/40/L.74, A/C.5/40/78.
Meeting numbers. GA 40th session: 3rd Committee 54, 57, 59-61, 63, 64, 66; 5th Committee 59, 70; plenary 116.

The United States said it supported the principle of drafting a convention, but felt that such a task should be the responsibility of the International Labour Organisation (ILO). The United Kingdom expressed reservations as to the usefulness of the work of the Working Group.

By **resolution 40/28**, the Assembly welcomed CERD's efforts to eliminate discrimination against migrant workers and their families, to promote their rights and to achieve their full equality, including the freedom to maintain their cultural characteristics.

Protection of minorities

Activities related to protection of minorities continued to focus in 1985 on the elaboration of a draft declaration on the rights of persons belonging to national, ethnic, religious and linguistic minorities. As in previous years, the Commission on Human Rights set up an informal open-ended working group which held meetings on 20 February and 5 March. The preambular part of the draft declaration, on much of which preliminary agreement had been reached, was annexed to the Working Group's report.[60] Noting that a definition of the term "minority" was essential, a task on which the Sub-Commission was working, the group decided to postpone work on the draft to its next session. It was agreed that the Commission should urge the Sub-Commission to submit proposals on the definition of the term by that time and that the Secretariat should be requested to compile proposals and comments by Governments and organizations on the articles of the revised draft.

On 14 March,[61] the Commission urged its Sub-Commission to give highest priority to consideration of proposals for the definition of "minority" and to submit them to the Commission's 1986 session, when it would set up another working group to continue elaboration of the declaration.

After considering a study[62] and a proposed definition of the term "minority" by one of its members, Jules Deschênes (Canada), the Sub-Commission decided on 28 August[63] to transmit it to the Commission, together with the records of the Sub-Commission's discussion.

In **resolution 40/28**, the General Assembly welcomed CERD's efforts to eliminate all forms of discrimination against national or ethnic minorities, among others, and called on States parties to the 1965 Convention against racial discrimination[11] to adopt legislative and other measures, in conformity with the Convention, to protect fully their rights.

Draft declaration on the human rights of non-citizens

Pursuant to a 1984 Assembly resolution,[64] the Secretary-General, in January 1985, requested all Member States to submit comments on a draft declaration on the human rights of individuals not citizens of the country in which they lived; the text had been elaborated since 1980 by a sessional working group established for that purpose. Replies from nine Governments were included in a report[65] of 18 September and later addenda.

In a bid to finalize the draft declaration, an open-ended Working Group that met during the Assembly's 1985 session held 11 meetings between 7 October and 3 December. After completing the second reading of the operative part, the Group adopted the draft declaration as a whole by consensus and annexed it to its report[66] to the Assembly's Third Committee.

GENERAL ASSEMBLY ACTION

Acting without vote on the recommendation of the Third Committee, the General Assembly adopted **resolution 40/144** on 13 December 1985.

Declaration on the human rights of individuals who are not nationals of the country in which they live

The General Assembly,

Having considered the question of the human rights of individuals who are not nationals of the country in which they live,

Decides to adopt the Declaration on the Human Rights of Individuals Who are not Nationals of the Country in which They Live, which is annexed to the present resolution.

ANNEX
Declaration on the Human Rights of Individuals Who are not Nationals of the Country in which They Live

The General Assembly,

Considering that the Charter of the United Nations encourages universal respect for and observance of the human rights and fundamental freedoms of all human beings, without distinction as to race, sex, language or religion,

Considering that the Universal Declaration of Human Rights proclaims that all human beings are born free and equal in dignity and rights and that everyone is entitled to all the rights and freedoms set forth in that Declaration, without distinction of any kind, such as race, colour, sex, language, religion, political or other opinion, national or social origin, property, birth or other status,

Considering that the Universal Declaration of Human Rights proclaims further that everyone has the right to recognition everywhere as a person before the law, that all are equal before the law and entitled without any discrimination to equal protection of the law, and that all are entitled to equal protection against any discrimination in violation of that Declaration and against any incitement to such discrimination,

Being aware that the States parties to the International Covenants on Human Rights undertake to guarantee that the rights enunciated in these Covenants will be exercised without discrimination of any kind as to race, colour, sex, language, religion, political or other opinion, national or social origin, property, birth or other status,

Conscious that, with improving communications and the development of peaceful and friendly relations among countries, individuals increasingly live in countries of which they are not nationals,

Reaffirming the purposes and principles of the Charter of the United Nations,

Recognizing that the protection of human rights and fundamental freedoms provided for in international instruments should also be ensured for individuals who are not nationals of the country in which they live,

Proclaims this Declaration:

Article 1

For the purposes of this Declaration, the term "alien" shall apply, with due regard to qualifications made in subsequent articles, to any individual who is not a national of the State in which he or she is present.

Article 2

1. Nothing in this Declaration shall be interpreted as legitimizing the illegal entry into and presence in a State of any alien, nor shall any provision be interpreted

as restricting the right of any State to promulgate laws and regulations concerning the entry of aliens and the terms and conditions of their stay or to establish differences between nationals and aliens. However, such laws and regulations shall not be incompatible with the international legal obligations of that State, including those in the field of human rights.

2. This Declaration shall not prejudice the enjoyment of the rights accorded by domestic law and of the rights which under international law a State is obliged to accord to aliens, even where this Declaration does not recognize such rights or recognizes them to a lesser extent.

Article 3

Every State shall make public its national legislation or regulations affecting aliens.

Article 4

Aliens shall observe the laws of the State in which they reside or are present and regard with respect the customs and traditions of the people of that State.

Article 5

1. Aliens shall enjoy, in accordance with domestic law and subject to the relevant international obligations of the State in which they are present, in particular the following rights:

(a) The right to life and security of person; no alien shall be subjected to arbitrary arrest or detention; no alien shall be deprived of his or her liberty except on such grounds and in accordance with such procedures as are established by law;

(b) The right to protection against arbitrary or unlawful interference with privacy, family, home or correspondence;

(c) The right to be equal before the courts, tribunals and all other organs and authorities administering justice and, when necessary, to free assistance of an interpreter in criminal proceedings and, when prescribed by law, other proceedings;

(d) The right to choose a spouse, to marry, to found a family;

(e) The right to freedom of thought, opinion, conscience and religion; the right to manifest their religion or beliefs, subject only to such limitations as are prescribed by law and are necessary to protect public safety, order, health or morals or the fundamental rights and freedoms of others;

(f) The right to retain their own language, culture and tradition;

(g) The right to transfer abroad earnings, savings or other personal monetary assets, subject to domestic currency regulations.

2. Subject to such restrictions as are prescribed by law and which are necessary in a democratic society to protect national security, public safety, public order, public health or morals or the rights and freedoms of others, and which are consistent with the other rights recognized in the relevant international instruments and those set forth in this Declaration, aliens shall enjoy the following rights:

(a) The right to leave the country;

(b) The right to freedom of expression;

(c) The right to peaceful assembly;

(d) The right to own property alone as well as in association with others, subject to domestic law.

3. Subject to the provisions referred to in paragraph 2, aliens lawfully in the territory of a State shall enjoy the right to liberty of movement and freedom to choose their residence within the borders of the State.

4. Subject to national legislation and due authorization, the spouse and minor or dependent children of an alien lawfully residing in the territory of a State shall be admitted to accompany, join and stay with the alien.

Article 6

No alien shall be subjected to torture or to cruel, inhuman or degrading treatment or punishment and, in particular, no alien shall be subjected without his or her free consent to medical or scientific experimentation.

Article 7

An alien lawfully in the territory of a State may be expelled therefrom only in pursuance of a decision reached in accordance with law and shall, except where compelling reasons of national security otherwise require, be allowed to submit the reasons why he or she should not be expelled and to have the case reviewed by, and be represented for the purpose before, the competent authority or a person or persons specially designated by the competent authority. Individual or collective expulsion of such aliens on grounds of race, colour, religion, culture, descent or national or ethnic origin is prohibited.

Article 8

1. Aliens lawfully residing in the territory of a State shall also enjoy, in accordance with the national laws, the following rights, subject to their obligations under article 4:

(a) The right to safe and healthy working conditions, to fair wages and equal remuneration for work of equal value without distinction of any kind, in particular, women being guaranteed conditions of work not inferior to those enjoyed by men, with equal pay for equal work;

(b) The right to join trade unions and other organizations or associations of their choice and to participate in their activities. No restrictions may be placed on the exercise of this right other than those prescribed by law and which are necessary, in a democratic society, in the interests of national security or public order or for the protection of the rights and freedoms of others;

(c) The right to health protection, medical care, social security, social services, education, rest and leisure, provided that they fulfil the requirements under the relevant regulations for participation and that undue strain is not placed on the resources of the State.

2. With a view to protecting the rights of aliens carrying on lawful paid activities in the country in which they are present, such rights may be specified by the Governments concerned in multilateral or bilateral conventions.

Article 9

No alien shall be arbitrarily deprived of his or her lawfully acquired assets.

Article 10

Any alien shall be free at any time to communicate with the consulate or diplomatic mission of the State of which he or she is a national or, in the absence thereof, with the consulate or diplomatic mission of any other State entrusted with the protection of the interests of the State of which he or she is a national in the State where he or she resides.

General Assembly resolution 40/144
13 December 1985   Meeting 116   Adopted without vote

Approved by Third Committee (A/40/1007) without vote, 6 December (meeting 71);
draft by Morocco (A/C.3/40/L.80), orally revised; agenda item 12.
Meeting numbers. GA 40th session: 3rd Committee 69, 71; plenary 116.

Algeria and India felt that not enough time had been given to study the Declaration. Algeria reserved its position with respect to provisions it thought might be incompatible with the convention on the rights of migrant workers currently being drafted. Yugoslavia felt that the wording of Article 5, paragraph 1, implied that domestic law was subordinate to the international instruments to which a State adhered. Mexico did not believe that the provisions of article 8, guaranteeing rights to aliens lawfully residing in a State, were consistent with those of the Universal Declaration of Human Rights[67] and the International Covenant on Economic, Social and Cultural Rights,[68] which stipulated that those rights should be granted to everyone without restriction. India said it would apply the provisions of the Declaration in accordance with its position with respect to the two International Covenants on Human Rights and its national legislation. Cuba reserved its position with respect to the provisions of the resolution.

Malaysia maintained reservations in view of the complexities of the matter, which it said needed further extensive study by Malaysian local authorities. Denmark observed that national legislation might contain provisions under which the enjoyment of certain rights were subject to authorization by national authorities; this understanding pertained in particular to article 5, paragraphs 2 (c) and 4. It pointed out that article 1, read in conjunction with the other articles, did not clearly specify which aliens were covered by the individual articles. Cameroon reserved its position on paragraph 2 of article 2, and on articles 5 and 8, until the appropriate authorities could ascertain whether they were in keeping with its legislation.

REFERENCES

[1]YUN, 1984, p. 785. [2]*Ibid.,* p. 787, GA res. 39/16, 23 Nov. 1984. [3]E/1985/16 & Add.1. [4]A/40/416. [5]E/1985/22 (res. 1985/11). [6]YUN 1984, p. 788, ESC res. 1984/24, 24 May 1984. [7]E/CN.4/Sub.2/1985/7. [8]A/40/694 & Add.1. [9]YUN 1975, p. 599, GA res. 3379(XXX), 10 Nov. 1975. [10]ST/HR/SER.A/17. [11]YUN 1965, p. 440, GA res. 2106 A (XX), annex, 21 Dec. 1965. [12]YUN 1969, p. 488. [13]A/40/607. [14]A/40/18. [15]*Ibid.* (dec. 1(XXXII)). [16]*Ibid.* (dec. 2(XXXII)). [17]A/AC.115/L.620. [18]A/40/77. [19]A/40/966-S/17665. [20]YUN 1984, p. 792. [21]E/1985/22 (res. 1985/31). [22]YUN 1984, p. 793, GA res. 39/114, 14 Dec. 1984. [23]A/40/232-E/1985/40 & Add.1-3. [24]A/40/398-S/17292. [25]A/C.3/40/9. [26]A/C.3/40/L.89. [27]A/39/862-E/1985/51. [28]A/40/320-E/1985/82. [29]A/40/201. [30]A/40/308. [31]E/1985/22 (res. 1985/32). [32]*Ibid.* (dec. 1985/102). [33]A/40/18 (dec. 1(XXXI)). [34]E/1985/L.19. [35]E/1985/L.16 & Corr.1. [36]E/1985/L.17. [37]A/40/570. [38]YUN 1984, p. 795, GA res. 39/131, 14 Dec. 1984. [39]YUN 1981, p. 881, GA res. 36/55, 25 Nov. 1981. [40]E/1985/22 (res. 1985/51). [41]YUN 1984, p. 795. [42]A/40/361. [43]E/CN.4/1986/5 (dec. 1985/106). [44]*Ibid.* [45]E/1985/22 (res. 1985/21). [46]YUN 1984, p. 796. [47]E/1985/22 (dec. 1985/103). [48]YUN 1983, p. 821. [49]E/CN.4/Sub.2/1985/22 & Add.1. [50]E/CN.4/1986/5 (res. 1985/22). [51]*Ibid.* (res. 1985/25). [52]E/1985/22 (res. 1985/29). [53]A/40/569. [54]A/40/578. [55]YUN 1984, p. 797. [56]E/1985/22 (res. 1985/52). [57]YUN 1979, p. 875, GA res. 34/172, 17 Dec. 1979. [58]A/C.3/40/1. [59]A/C.3/40/6. [60]E/CN.4/1985/65. [61]E/1985/22 (res. 1985/53). [62]E/CN.4/Sub.2/1985/31 & Corr.1. [63]E/CN.4/1986/5 (res. 1985/6). [64]YUN 1984, p. 799, GA res. 39/103, 14 Dec. 1984. [65]A/40/638 & Add.1-4. [66]A/C.3/40/12. [67]YUN 1948-49, p. 535, GA res. 217 A (III), 10 Dec. 1948. [68]YUN 1966, p. 419, GA res. 2200 A (XXI), annex, 16 Dec. 1966.

Civil and political rights

In a September 1985 report[1] on international conditions and human rights (see p. 882), the Secretary-General reviewed the situation with regard to civil and political rights. The right to life in particular was affected by intensified armed conflicts in many parts of the world and by the threat resulting from the existence and proliferation of nuclear weapons. Other practices involving denial of the right to life included summary and arbitrary executions and disappearances. During the two-year review period, there had also been an alarming number of reported cases of torture and other cruel, inhuman or degrading treatment in various parts of the world, and there were allegations of grave and persistent violations of the rights of detained persons in many countries, such as arrests and detentions on vague charges or without grounds, imprisonment of individuals on account of the non-violent exercise of their fundamental rights, detention without trial, extraterritorial abduction and forced repatriation, detention incommunicado, unfair trial procedures, abuse of executive and preventive detention, and death during detention. Other major human rights problems, such as violations of trade union rights and related civil liberties and the persistence of different forms of forced labour, were consistently referred to in reports by ILO.

While those problems provided serious cause for concern, the Secretary-General felt that the overall picture of the past two years also reflected a number of positive and highly encouraging developments, most notably the return to democratic forms of government by a number of countries and the continuation of efforts in other States to achieve a more democratic order and to reconcile in a constructive manner the sometimes conflicting interests of differing population groups within national borders. The return to democracy had in many instances been accompanied by a spirit of national renewal and a major effort to secure justice both for victims and perpetrators of human rights violations.

At the international level, the Secretary-General said, the establishment of various procedures for monitoring human rights problems was a tribute to the increasing recognition by States of the importance of identifying, exposing and seeking to remedy major violations at the earliest possible moment. In addition, States were increasingly prepared to co-operate in applying those procedures.

Covenant on Civil and Political Rights and Optional Protocol

Accessions and ratifications

As at 31 December 1985, the International Covenant on Civil and Political Rights and the Optional Protocol thereto, adopted by the General Assembly in 1966[2] and in force since 1976,[3] had been ratified or acceded to by 80 and 35 States, respectively, after San Marino's accession in October 1985. San Marino and Spain were the two States which acceded to the Optional Protocol in 1985. Spain made the declaration under article 41 of the Covenant recognizing the competence of the Human Rights Committee to receive and consider communications that a State party claimed that another was not fulfilling its obligations under the Covenant.

In his report to the Assembly on the International Covenants on Human Rights,[4] the Secretary-General provided information on the status of the Covenant and the Protocol as at 1 September 1985 (see p. 891).

Implementation

ECONOMIC AND SOCIAL COUNCIL ACTION

Pursuant to an interim arrangement of the Human Rights Committee under which the Committee was to transmit regularly to the Council the texts of the general comments adopted by the Committee and transmit its full annual report directly to the Assembly later in the year, the Secretary General, by a note of 11 March,[5] transmitted the Committee's general comments on Covenant articles 1 and 14 and article 6 adopted, respectively, at the Committee's March/April and October/November 1984 sessions.[6] The Economic and Social Council, by **decision 1985/105** of 8 February, had agreed to the interim arrangement and, without prejudice to further Council consideration of the current arrangements, authorized the Secretary-General to transmit the Committee's annual report directly to the Assembly. On 24 May, by **decision 1985/117**, the Council requested the Secretary-General to transmit the report (see below) directly to the 1985 regular session. The Council also took note of the Secretary-General's March note. The text of the decision had been orally proposed by the Council President, on behalf of the Bureau, following information consultations.

Human Rights Commission action. The Commission on Human Rights, on 14 March,[7] expressed appreciation for the Human Rights Committee's continued striving for uniform standards in implementing the Covenant and the Optional Protocol and invited States to become parties to them and to consider making the declaration under article 41. Emphasizing the importance of strict compliance with those instruments, it stressed the obligation of a State party availing itself of the Covenant's right of derogation immediately to inform the other States parties of its reasons for doing so. The Commission hoped that representation by experts for presentation of reports would become universal and encouraged Governments to give the Covenant and Protocol the widest possible publicity. It requested a report in 1986 on the status of these instruments, as well as on the Council's work on implementing the International Covenant on Economic, Social and Cultural Rights,[8] and asked the Secretary-General to consider ways of assisting States parties to prepare their reports.

Human Rights Committee activities. The Human Rights Committee, established under article 28 of the Covenant, held three sessions in 1985: the twenty-fourth in New York from 25 March to 12 April; the twenty-fifth and twenty-sixth at Geneva from 8 to 26 July and from 21 October to 8 November.

The Committee considered reports and additional information submitted by nine States—Afghanistan, the Dominican Republic, Finland, Luxembourg, New Zealand (Cook Islands), Spain, Sweden, the Ukrainian SSR and the United Kingdom—under article 40 of the Covenant. The Committee also concluded consideration of adopted views on six communications from individuals claiming that their rights under the Covenant had been violated and that they had exhausted all available domestic remedies. The cases concerned Finland (1), Madagascar (2), Suriname (1) and Uruguay (2). The Committee decided that eight other such communications from individuals were inadmissible.

On 25 July, the Committee unanimously adopted its ninth annual report[9] to the Assembly.

GENERAL ASSEMBLY ACTION

Taking note, in **resolution 40/115** (see p. 891), of the Human Rights Committee's report, the General Assembly expressed satisfaction with the Committee's performance, asked the Secretary-General to give the Committee's work more publicity, and voiced appreciation to those States parties to the Covenant that had submitted their reports, while urging others to do the same, including those that had been requested to provide additional information, and urging all those that had not become parties to the Covenant to do so. It further invited the States parties to consider making the declaration under article 41. It noted with satisfaction that the majority of parties to the Covenant had been represented by experts for the presentation of their reports. The Assembly emphasized the importance of the strictest compliance with the Covenant and the Protocol, requested the Secretary-General to submit in 1986 a report on the status of those instruments and encouraged all Governments to publish them in as many languages as possible and ensure for them widest possible publicity.

State of siege or emergency

ECONOMIC AND SOCIAL COUNCIL ACTION

In 1984, the Sub-Commission had requested[10] that it be authorized to appoint a special rapporteur to prepare an explanatory paper on the best way of drawing up and annually updating a list of countries that proclaimed or terminated a state of emergency. An annual report by the Sub-Commission on compliance with national and international rules governing the legality of the introduction of a state of siege or emergency was to contain that information (the right of derogation from provisions of the Covenant in a state of emergency was provided for in article 4).

The Commission on Human Rights recommended a draft resolution to the Economic and Social Council in response to the Sub-Committee's request. The Council, on the recommendation of its Second Committee, adopted it on 30 May, as **resolution 1985/37**, without vote. The Commission had approved the text on 11 March[11] by 28 votes to none, with 9 abstentions.

The administration of justice and the human rights of detainees

The Economic and Social Council

1. *Authorizes* the Sub-Commission on Prevention of Discrimination and Protection of Minorities to appoint a special rapporteur to carry out the work referred to in paragraph 1 of Sub-Commission resolution 1983/30 of 6 September 1983 and Commission on Human Rights resolution 1983/18 of 22 February 1983 and decision 1984/104 of 6 March 1984 on an annual basis;

2. *Requests* the Secretary-General to give the special rapporteur all the assistance he may require in his work;

3. *Requests* the special rapporteur to submit his first annual report to the Sub-Commission at its thirty-ninth session.

Economic and Social Council resolution 1985/37

30 May 1985   Meeting 25   Adopted without vote

Approved by Second Committee (E/1985/95 & Corr.1) without vote, 24 May (meeting 15); draft by Commission on Human Rights (E/1985/22); agenda item 16.

Sub-Commission action. By a 30 August 1985 resolution,[12] the Sub-Commission expressed ap-

preciation to Special Rapporteur Leandro Despouy (Argentina) for an explanatory paper on the topic that he had presented at the current session. It requested him to draw up a list of countries that had proclaimed or terminated a state of emergency and present his first annual report to the Sub-Commission in 1986.

Chile

In March, the Commission on Human Rights urgently called on Chilean authorities to end the régime of exception and especially the practice of declaring states of emergency, under which serious violations of human rights were committed (see p. 913).

Paraguay

Following a 1984 request by the Sub-Commission,[10] the Secretary-General submitted to it in July 1985 a note[13] containing information on new developments in the question of ending the state of siege in Paraguay. In response to his request of 28 May for relevant information, Paraguay had explained on 20 June that the state of siege was applied only in the area of the capital, that a declaration of an amnesty was pointless because there were no political prisoners in the country, and that the Commission on Human Rights had been informed at its recent sessions of the work on modernizing Paraguayan penal legislation. An additional inquiry had established, the Secretary-General said, that Paraguay was not a State party to the American Convention on Human Rights and was under no obligation to inform the Commission pursuant to that Convention of any derogations from it.

The Sub-Commission, on 29 August,[14] considered with appreciation the spirit of co-operation of the Paraguayan authorities, inviting them to persevere in their efforts. While satisfied by recent releases of political prisoners, the Sub-Commission insisted that exiled or banished persons be allowed to return. It requested the Commission once more to recommend that Paraguay ratify the International Covenant on Civil and Political Rights, and asked the Secretary-General to report to it in 1986 on new developments.

Self-determination of peoples

Six resolutions adopted by the Commission on Human Rights in 1985 reaffirmed the right to self-determination for: Palestinians,[15] Kampucheans,[16] Afghans,[17] the people of Western Sahara,[18] Namibians[19] and South Africans.[20]

The Commission's actions and debate on the right of people to self-determination, as well as action taken by the Economic and Social Council in 1985, were summarized by the Secretary-General in a report[21] to the General Assembly on the universal realization of that right. The report also contained a summary of responses from nine Governments, eight specialized agencies and three NGO's to the Assembly's 1984 request[22] for information on their assistance to colonial Territories and peoples.

Following the pattern of previous years, the Assembly adopted in 1985 two resolutions on the right to self-determination—a right it repeatedly reaffirmed for individual Non-Self-Governing Territories (see TRUSTEESHIP AND DECOLONIZATION, Chapter IV). The Assembly also reaffirmed, in **resolution 40/158**, the legitimacy of the struggle of peoples under colonial domination, foreign occupation or racist régimes and their inalienable right to self-determination and independence.

GENERAL ASSEMBLY ACTION

On 29 November 1985, acting on the recommendation of the Third Committee, the General Assembly adopted two resolutions concerning the right of people to self-determination. **Resolution 40/24** was adopted without vote.

Universal realization of the right of peoples to self-determination

The General Assembly,

Reaffirming the importance, for the effective guarantee and observance of human rights, of the universal realization of the right of peoples to self-determination enshrined in the Charter of the United Nations and embodied in the International Covenants on Human Rights, as well as in the Declaration on the Granting of Independence to Colonial Countries and Peoples contained in General Assembly resolution 1514(XV) of 14 December 1960,

Welcoming the progressive exercise of the right to self-determination by peoples under colonial, foreign or alien occupation and their emergence into sovereign statehood and independence,

Deeply concerned at the continuation of acts or threats of foreign military intervention and occupation that are threatening to suppress, or have already suppressed, the right to self-determination of an increasing number of sovereign peoples and nations,

Expressing grave concern that, as a consequence of the persistence of such actions, millions of people have been and are being uprooted from their homes as refugees and displaced persons, and emphasizing the urgent need for concerted international action to alleviate their condition,

Recalling the relevant resolutions regarding the violation of the right of peoples to self-determination and other human rights as a result of foreign military intervention, aggression and occupation, adopted by the Commission on Human Rights at its thirty-sixth, thirty-seventh, thirty-eighth, thirty-ninth, fortieth and forty-first sessions,

Reiterating its resolutions 35/35 B of 14 November 1980, 36/10 of 28 October 1981, 37/42 of 3 December 1982, 38/16 of 22 November 1983 and 39/18 of 23 November 1984,

Taking note of the report of the Secretary-General,

1. *Reaffirms* that the universal realization of the right of all peoples, including those under colonial, foreign and alien domination, to self-determination is a fundamental condition for the effective guarantee and observance of human rights and for the preservation and promotion of such rights;

2. *Declares its firm opposition* to acts of foreign military intervention, aggression and occupation, since these have resulted in the suppression of the right of peoples to self-determination and other human rights in certain parts of the world;

3. *Calls upon* those States responsible to cease immediately their military intervention and occupation of foreign countries and territories and all acts of repression, discrimination, exploitation and maltreatment, particularly the brutal and inhuman methods reportedly employed for the execution of these acts against the peoples concerned;

4. *Deplores* the plight of the millions of refugees and displaced persons who have been uprooted by the aforementioned acts and reaffirms their right to return to their homes voluntarily in safety and honour;

5. *Requests* the Commission on Human Rights to continue to give special attention to the violation of human rights, especially the right to self-determination, resulting from foreign military intervention, aggression or occupation;

6. *Requests* the Secretary-General to report on this issue to the General Assembly at its forty-first session under the item entitled "Importance of the universal realization of the right of peoples to self-determination and of the speedy granting of independence to colonial countries and peoples for the effective guarantee and observance of human rights".

General Assembly resolution 40/24

29 November 1985   Meeting 96   Adopted without vote

Approved by Third Committee (A/40/863) without vote, 4 November (meeting 30); 21-nation draft (A/C.3/40/L.5); agenda item 93.
Sponsors: Brunei Darussalam, Chile, Comoros, Costa Rica, Djibouti, Ecuador, Jordan, Kuwait, Malaysia, Morocco, Oman, Pakistan, Papua New Guinea, Philippines, Qatar, Samoa, Saudi Arabia, Singapore, Somalia, Sudan, Thailand.
Meeting numbers. GA 40th session: 3rd Committee 3-15, 25, 30, 31; plenary 96.

India said its non-opposition was without prejudice to its position on the International Covenants and relevant Human Rights Commission resolutions.

The second text, **resolution 40/25**, was adopted by recorded vote.

Importance of the universal realization of the right of peoples to self-determination and of the speedy granting of independence to colonial countries and peoples for the effective guarantee and observance of human rights

The General Assembly,

Reaffirming its faith in the importance of the implementation of the Declaration on the Granting of Independence to Colonial Countries and Peoples contained in its resolution 1514(XV) of 14 December 1960,

Reaffirming the importance of the universal realization of the right of peoples to self-determination, national sovereignty and territorial integrity and of the speedy granting of independence to colonial countries and peoples as imperatives for the full enjoyment of all human rights,

Reaffirming the obligation of all Member States to comply with the principles of the Charter of the United Nations and the resolutions of the United Nations regarding the exercise of the right to self-determination by peoples under colonial and foreign domination,

Recalling its resolution 2649(XXV) of 30 November 1970 and all resolutions on this question,

Recalling also its resolution 1514(XV) and all resolutions concerning the implementation of the Declaration on the Granting of Independence to Colonial Countries and Peoples,

Recalling further its resolutions 3103(XXVIII) of 12 December 1973, 3314(XXIX) of 14 December 1974 and 38/137 of 19 December 1983, as well as Security Council resolutions 405(1977) of 14 April 1977, 419(1977) of 24 November 1977, 496(1981) of 15 December 1981 and 507(1982) of 28 May 1982, in which the United Nations condemned the recruiting and the use of mercenaries, in particular against developing countries and national liberation movements,

Recalling further its resolutions on the question of Namibia, in particular resolution ES-8/2 of 14 September 1981, and Security Council resolutions 532(1983) of 31 May 1983, 539(1983) of 28 October 1983 and 566(1985) of 19 June 1985,

Recalling the Paris Declaration on Namibia and the Programme of Action on Namibia, adopted by the International Conference in Support of the Struggle of the Namibian People for Independence,

Bearing in mind the outcome of the International Conference on the Alliance between South Africa and Israel, held at Vienna from 11 to 13 July 1983,

Welcoming the holding at Tunis from 7 to 9 August 1984 of the Conference of Arab Solidarity with the Struggle for Liberation in Southern Africa,

Recalling resolutions CM/Res.1002(XLII) on South Africa and CM/Res.1003(XLII) on Namibia adopted by the Council of Ministers of the Organization of African Unity at its forty-second ordinary session, held at Addis Ababa from 10 to 17 July 1985,

Reaffirming that the system of *apartheid* imposed on the South African people constitutes a violation of the fundamental rights of that people, a crime against humanity and a constant threat to international peace and security,

Gravely concerned at the continuation of the illegal occupation of Namibia by South Africa and the continued violations of the human rights of the people in the Territory and of the other peoples still under colonial domination and alien subjugation,

Expressing its profound indignation at and its preoccupation with the brutal repression that followed the imposition of the so-called "new constitution" and the state of emergency by the *apartheid* régime of South Africa in defiance of world public opinion,

Reaffirming its resolution 39/2 of 28 September 1984 and recalling Security Council resolution 554(1984) of 17 August 1984, which rejected the so-called "new constitution" as null and void, and Council resolution 569(1985) of 14 August 1985,

Deeply concerned at the continued terrorist acts of aggression committed by the Pretoria régime against independent African States in the region,

Deeply indignant at the continued occupation of part of the territory of Angola by the troops of the racist régime of South Africa and the persistent, hostile and unprovoked acts of aggression and sustained armed invasions carried out by that régime in violation of the sovereignty, airspace and territorial integrity of Angola, in particular the armed invasion of Angola on 28 September 1985,

Recalling Security Council resolutions 527(1982) of 15 December 1982 and 535(1983) of 29 June 1983 on Lesotho, and Council resolutions 568(1985) of 21 June 1985 and 572(1985) of 30 September 1985 on Botswana,

Reaffirming the national unity and territorial integrity of the Comoros,

Recalling the Political Declaration adopted by the First Conference of Heads of State and Government of the Organization of African Unity and the League of Arab States, held at Cairo from 7 to 9 March 1977,

Recalling further its relevant resolutions on the question of Palestine, in particular resolutions 3236(XXIX) and 3237(XXIX) of 22 November 1974, 36/120 of 10 December 1981, ES-7/6 of 19 August 1982, 37/86 of 10 December 1982, 38/58 of 13 December 1983 and 39/49 D of 11 December 1984,

Recalling the Geneva Declaration on Palestine and the Programme of Action for the Achievement of Palestinian Rights, adopted by the International Conference on the Question of Palestine,

Considering that the denial of the inalienable rights of the Palestinian people to self-determination, sovereignty, independence and return to Palestine and the repeated acts of aggression by Israel against the people of the region constitute a serious threat to international peace and security,

Deeply shocked and alarmed at the deplorable consequences of the Israeli invasion of Lebanon and recalling all the relevant resolutions of the Security Council, in particular resolutions 508(1982) of 5 June 1982, 509(1982) of 6 June 1982, 520(1982) of 17 September 1982 and 521(1982) of 19 September 1982,

1. *Calls upon* all States to implement fully and faithfully all the resolutions of the United Nations regarding the exercise of the right to self-determination and independence by peoples under colonial and foreign domination;

2. *Reaffirms* the legitimacy of the struggle of peoples for their independence, territorial integrity, national unity and liberation from colonial domination, *apartheid* and foreign occupation by all available means, including armed struggle;

3. *Reaffirms* the inalienable right of the Namibian people, the Palestinian people and all peoples under foreign and colonial domination to self-determination, national independence, territorial integrity, national unity and sovereignty without foreign interference;

4. *Strongly condemns* those Governments that do not recognize the right to self-determination and independence of all peoples still under colonial domination and alien subjugation, notably the peoples of Africa and the Palestinian people;

5. *Calls* for the full and immediate implementation of the declarations and programmes of action on Namibia and on Palestine adopted by the international conferences on those questions;

6. *Reaffirms* its vigorous condemnation of the continued illegal occupation of Namibia by South Africa;

7. *Condemns* the racist régime of South Africa for its installation of a so-called "interim administration" at Windhoek and declares that action to be illegal, null and void;

8. *Further condemns* the policy of "bantustanization" and reiterates its support for the oppressed people of South Africa in its just and legitimate struggle against the racist minority régime of Pretoria;

9. *Reaffirms* its rejection of the so-called "new constitution" as null and void and reiterates that peace in South Africa can only be guaranteed by the establishment of majority rule through the full and free exercise

of adult suffrage by all the people in a united and un-divided South Africa;

10. *Strongly condemns* the wanton killing of peaceful and defenceless demonstrators and workers on strike, as well as the arbitrary arrests of the leaders and activists of the United Democratic Front, National Forum, trade unions and other mass organizations, and demands their immediate and unconditional release, in particular that of Nelson Mandela and Zephania Mothopeng;

11. *Strongly condemns* South Africa for the imposition of the state of emergency under its repugnant Internal Security Act and calls for the immediate lifting of the state of emergency, as well as the repeal of the Internal Security Act;

12. *Condemns* South Africa for its increasing oppres-sion of the Namibian people, for the massive militariza-tion of Namibia and for its armed attacks launched against the States in the region in order to destabilize them politically and to sabotage and destroy their economies;

13. *Strongly condemns* the establishment and use of armed terrorist groups by South Africa with a view to pitting them against the national liberation movements and destabilizing the legitimate Governments of southern Africa;

14. *Strongly condemns* the repeated acts of aggression and the continued occupation of parts of southern Angola and demands the immediate and unconditional withdrawal of the South African troops from Angolan territory;

15. *Strongly condemns* the persistent, hostile and un-provoked acts of aggression and sustained armed inva-sions carried out by the racist régime of South Africa in violation of the sovereignty, airspace and territorial integrity of Angola, in particular the armed invasion of Angola on 28 September 1985;

16. *Strongly reaffirms* its solidarity with the indepen-dent African countries and national liberation movements that are victims of murderous acts of ag-gression and destabilization by the racist régime of Pretoria, and calls upon the international community to render increased assistance and support to those coun-tries in order to enable them to strengthen their defence capacity, defend their sovereignty and territorial integrity and peacefully rebuild and develop;

17. *Reaffirms* that the practice of using mercenaries against sovereign States and national liberation movements constitutes a criminal act and calls upon the Governments of all countries to enact legislation declar-ing the recruitment, financing and training of mercenaries in their territories and the transit of mercenaries through their territories to be punishable offences, and prohibiting their nationals from serving as mercenaries, and to report on such legislation to the Secretary-General;

18. *Strongly condemns* the continued violations of the human rights of the peoples still under colonial domina-tion and alien subjugation, the continuation of the il-legal occupation of Namibia, South Africa's attempts to dismember its Territory, the perpetuation of the racist minority régime in southern Africa and the denial to the Palestinian people of their inalienable national rights;

19. *Further strongly condemns* the racist régime of Pretoria for its acts of destabilization, armed aggression and economic blockade against Lesotho and strongly urges the international community to extend maximum assistance to Lesotho to enable it to fulfil its interna-tional humanitarian obligations towards refugees and to use its influence on the racist régime so that it would desist from its terrorist acts against Lesotho;

20. *Strongly condemns* the unprovoked and unwar-ranted military attack on the capital of Botswana and demands that the racist régime pay full and adequate compensation to Botswana for the loss of life and damage to property;

21. *Denounces* the collusion between Israel and South Africa and expresses support for the Declaration of the International Conference on the Alliance between South Africa and Israel;

22. *Strongly condemns* the policy of those Western States, Israel and other States whose political, economic, military, nuclear, strategic, cultural and sports relations with the racist minority régime of South Africa en-courage that régime to persist in its suppression of the aspirations of peoples to self-determination and in-dependence;

23. *Again demands* the immediate application of the mandatory arms embargo against South Africa, imposed under Security Council resolution 418(1977) of 4 November 1977, by all countries and more particularly by those countries that maintain military and nuclear co-operation with the racist Pretoria régime and con-tinue to supply it with related *matériel;*

24. *Calls* for the full implementation of the provi-sions of the Paris Declaration on Sanctions against South Africa and the Special Declaration on Namibia adopted by the International Conference on Sanctions against South Africa, held under the auspices of the United Na-tions and the Organization of African Unity;

25. *Demands once again* the immediate implementa-tion of its resolution ES-8/2 on the question of Namibia;

26. *Reaffirms* all relevant resolutions adopted by the Organization of African Unity and the United Nations on the question of Western Sahara, including General Assembly resolution 39/40 of 5 December 1984, and calls upon the current Chairman of the Organization of African Unity and the Secretary-General of the United Nations to continue their efforts to find a just and lasting solution to this matter;

27. *Urges* all States, the specialized agencies, com-petent organizations of the United Nations system and other international organizations to extend their sup-port to the Namibian people through its sole and legitimate representative, the South West Africa Peo-ple's Organization, in its struggle to gain its right to self-determination and independence in accordance with the Charter of the United Nations;

28. *Notes* the contacts between the Government of the Comoros and the Government of France in the search for a just solution to the problem of the integra-tion of the Comorian island of Mayotte into the Com-oros, in accordance with the resolutions of the Organiza-tion of African Unity and the United Nations on the question;

29. *Calls* for a substantial increase in all forms of assistance given by all States, United Nations organs, the specialized agencies and non-governmental organiza-tions to the victims of racism, racial discrimination and *apartheid* through their national liberation movements recognized by the Organization of African Unity;

30. *Demands* the immediate release of women and children detained in Namibia and South Africa;

31. *Strongly condemns* the constant and deliberate violations of the fundamental rights of the Palestinian people, as well as the expansionist activities of Israel in the Middle East, which constitute an obstacle to the achievement of self-determination and independence by the Palestinian people and a threat to peace and stability in the region;

32. *Demands* the immediate and unconditional release of all persons detained or imprisoned as a result of their struggle for self-determination and independence, full respect for their fundamental individual rights and compliance with article 5 of the Universal Declaration of Human Rights, under which no one shall be subjected to torture or to cruel, inhuman or degrading treatment;

33. *Urges* all States, the specialized agencies, competent organizations of the United Nations system and other international organizations to extend their support to the Palestinian people through its sole and legitimate representative, the Palestine Liberation Organization, in its struggle to regain its right to self-determination and independence in accordance with the Charter;

34. *Expresses its appreciation* for the material and other forms of assistance that peoples under colonial rule continue to receive from Governments, organizations of the United Nations system and intergovernmental organizations, and calls for a substantial increase in this assistance;

35. *Urges* all States, the specialized agencies and other competent organizations of the United Nations system to do their utmost to ensure the full implementation of the Declaration on the Granting of Independence to Colonial Countries and Peoples and to intensify their efforts to support peoples under colonial, foreign and racist domination in their just struggle for self-determination and independence;

36. *Requests* the Secretary-General to give maximum publicity to the Declaration on the Granting of Independence to Colonial Countries and Peoples and to give the widest possible publicity to the struggle of oppressed peoples for the achievement of their self-determination and national independence and to report periodically to the General Assembly on his activities in this regard;

37. *Decides* to consider this item again at its forty-first session on the basis of the reports that Governments, organizations of the United Nations system and intergovernmental and non-governmental organizations have been requested to submit concerning the strengthening of assistance to colonial territories and peoples.

General Assembly resolution 40/25

29 November 1985   Meeting 96   118-17-9 (recorded vote)

Approved by Third Committee (A/40/863) by recorded vote (105-17-9), 4 November (meeting 30); draft by Nigeria for African Group except Morocco (A/C.3/40/L.9), orally revised; agenda item 93.

Meeting numbers. GA 40th session: 3rd Committee 3-15, 25, 30, 31; plenary 96.

Recorded vote in Assembly as follows:

In favour: Afghanistan, Albania, Algeria, Angola, Argentina, Bahamas, Bahrain, Bangladesh, Barbados, Benin, Bhutan, Bolivia, Botswana, Brazil, Brunei Darussalam, Bulgaria, Burkina Faso, Burma, Burundi, Byelorussian SSR, Cameroon, Cape Verde, Central African Republic, Chad, China, Comoros, Congo, Cuba, Cyprus, Czechoslovakia, Democratic Kampuchea, Democratic Yemen, Djibouti, Dominican Republic, Ecuador, Egypt, Equatorial Guinea, Ethiopia, Fiji, Gabon, German Democratic Republic, Ghana, Grenada, Guinea, Guinea-Bissau, Guyana, Hungary, India, Indonesia, Iran, Iraq, Ivory Coast, Jamaica, Jordan,

Kenya, Kuwait, Lao People's Democratic Republic, Lebanon, Lesotho, Liberia, Libyan Arab Jamahiriya, Madagascar, Malawi, Malaysia, Maldives, Mali, Malta, Mauritania, Mauritius, Mexico, Mongolia, Morocco, Mozambique, Nicaragua, Niger, Nigeria, Oman, Pakistan, Panama, Papua New Guinea, Peru, Philippines, Poland, Qatar, Romania, Rwanda, Saint Lucia, Samoa, Sao Tome and Principe, Saudi Arabia, Senegal, Seychelles, Sierra Leone, Singapore, Somalia, Sri Lanka, Sudan, Suriname, Swaziland, Syrian Arab Republic, Thailand, Togo, Trinidad and Tobago, Tunisia, Turkey, Uganda, Ukrainian SSR, USSR, United Arab Emirates, United Republic of Tanzania, Uruguay, Venezuela, Viet Nam, Yemen, Yugoslavia, Zaire, Zambia, Zimbabwe.

Against: Australia, Belgium, Canada, Denmark, Finland, France, Germany, Federal Republic of, Iceland, Israel, Italy, Luxembourg, Netherlands, New Zealand, Norway, Sweden, United Kingdom, United States.

Abstaining: Austria, El Salvador, Greece, Guatemala, Honduras, Ireland, Japan, Portugal, Spain.

Before adopting the text as a whole, the Assembly voted on paragraph 26, retaining it by a recorded vote of 84 to 5, with 39 abstentions. Prior to that, the Third Committee had retained the paragraph by a recorded vote of 74 to 4, with 39 abstentions.

Speaking on behalf of the 10 EC members, Luxembourg said they could not support the text, submitted without consultation with various groups, because it lacked balance in several respects and neglected to mention the situations in Afghanistan and Kampuchea. The Ten, as well as Spain, could not accept the assertion that maintaining relations with a State was tantamount to approving its policies. Israel said the text, singling it out for attack, bore no relation to reality, reflected the prejudices of certain delegations and the diktats of the automatic majority at the United Nations, and failed to mention and condemn the links between the Arab States and South Africa. It also protested the description of PLO as the sole and legitimate representative of the Palestinian people. Uruguay said it was up to the Palestinians to choose their representatives once they could freely exercise their right to self-determination. Australia said it opposed the text because of long-standing objections to a number of elements; both Australia and Spain had reservations about reaffirming resolutions of the Organization of African Unity (OAU) of which they were not members. The United Arab Emirates said its affirmative vote was based on its support of a 1975 Assembly resolution,[23] because it felt that the link between racism and zionism must be stressed. Turkey said it was opposed to singling out Member States and groups of countries for criticism and condemnation.

Although agreeing with many elements of the text, Austria, Portugal, Spain and Uruguay said they could not support all of it, particularly the reference to armed struggle in paragraph 2. Botswana reserved its position on the paragraphs pertaining to economic sanctions, noting that while supportive of them in principle it had not the capacity to participate in them, but did not wish to serve as an excuse for the failure of others to impose sanctions. Honduras felt that the text represented a confusion of ideas and subjects already dealt with by the Assembly in specific resolutions.

Malaysia said it abstained in the vote on paragraph 26 in keeping with its vote on the 1984 Assembly resolution[24] on the question of Western Sahara. Morocco voted in favour to act in unison with the African Group, but opposed the reference to that resolution. Zaire said it voted against paragraph 26 because of its firm conviction that the problem of Western Sahara could be solved only through a referendum. Swaziland had reservations concerning the twelfth preambular paragraph and paragraphs 23, 24 and 26 on sanctions. While supporting the overall text, Argentina and Burma said they had reservations with regard to the wording of some provisions. Portugal objected to the wording of the eighth, ninth and twenty-third preambular paragraphs, and operative paragraphs 2, 5, 21, 22, 24 and 31. It recalled reservations it had expressed at international conferences on Namibia and Palestine, and had not participated in the conferences mentioned in paragraphs 21 and 24. Ecuador also could not support paragraphs referring to conferences in which it had not taken part. Mexico said paragraph 5 referred to a Palestinian programme of action on which it had reservations; moreover, paragraph 21 mentioned a Declaration in whose drafting it had not participated.

Afghanistan

On 13 March 1985,[17] the Commission on Human Rights, by a roll-call vote of 31 to 7, with 5 abstentions, reaffirmed its profound concern that the people of Afghanistan continued to be denied their right to self-determination, to determine their own form of government, and to choose their economic, political and social system free from outside intervention, subversion, coercion or constraint. It called for a political settlement based on immediate foreign troop withdrawal from Afghanistan, full respect for the country's independence, sovereignty, territorial integrity and non-aligned status, and strict observance of the principle of non-intervention and non-interference. Affirming the right of the Afghan refugees to return to their homes, the Commission urged a settlement enabling the Afghan people to determine their destiny free from outside interference. It requested the Secretary-General to continue to search for a political solution, urged all concerned to continue to co-operate with him, and appealed for humanitarian relief assistance to alleviate, in co-ordination with the Office of the United Nations High Commissioner for Refugees (UNHCR), the hardships of Afghan refugees.

(See also p. 905 and, for details of the situation in Afghanistan, see p. 232.)

Kampuchea

Reiterating its condemnation of persistent human rights violations in Kampuchea, particularly the repeated attacks by the occupying forces against civilians along the Thai-Kampuchean border, the Commission on Human Rights reaffirmed, by a resolution adopted by a roll-call vote of 28 to 8, with 5 abstentions, on 27 February 1985,[16] that the continued illegal occupation of Kampuchea by foreign forces deprived Kampucheans of their right to self-determination and constituted the primary human rights violation in that country. The Commission emphasized that the withdrawal of forces, restoration of Kampuchea's independence, sovereignty and territorial integrity, recognition of the Kampucheans' right to self-determination and a commitment by all States to non-interference were essential components for a solution to the Kampuchea problem. It reaffirmed its call for a cessation of hostilities and for an immediate withdrawal of foreign forces, to enable Kampucheans to exercise their fundamental human rights free from foreign interference and to determine their future through free and fair elections under United Nations supervision, and make possible the return of all refugees and efforts towards a political solution within the framework of the 1981 Declaration on Kampuchea.[25] The Commission asked the Secretary-General to intensify efforts towards a political settlement and restoration of human rights in Kampuchea and requested the *Ad Hoc* Committee of the International Conference on Kampuchea (see p. 225) to continue its work.

ECONOMIC AND SOCIAL COUNCIL ACTION

Acting on the recommendation of its Second Committee, the Economic and Social Council adopted **decision 1985/155**, by roll-call vote.

Right of peoples to self-determination and its application to peoples under colonial or alien domination or foreign occupation

At its 25th plenary meeting, on 30 May 1985, the Council fully endorsed Commission on Human Rights resolution 1985/12 of 27 February 1985, by which the Commission, *inter alia*, reaffirmed that the continuing illegal occupation of Kampuchea by foreign forces deprived the people of Kampuchea of the exercise of their right to self-determination and constituted the primary violation of human rights in Kampuchea at present. The Council reaffirmed its decisions 1981/154 of 8 May 1981, 1982/143 of 7 May 1982, 1983/155 of 27 May 1983 and 1984/148 of 24 May 1984 and reiterated its call for the withdrawal of all foreign forces from Kampuchea in order to allow the people of Kampuchea to exercise their fundamental freedoms and human rights, including the right to self-determination as contained in the Declaration on Kampuchea adopted by the International Conference on Kampuchea on 17 July 1981 and in General Assembly resolutions 34/22 of 14 November 1979, 35/6 of 22 October 1980, 36/5 of 21 October 1981, 37/6 of 28 October 1982, 38/3 of 27 October 1983 and 39/5 of 30 October 1984.

The Council expressed its grave concern at the increasing activities of the foreign forces in Kampuchea, particularly at the severity and the scope of the attacks on Kampuchean civilian encampments along the

Thai-Kampuchean border since November 1984, resulting in serious loss of life and property of Kampucheans and forcing more than 230,000 Kampuchean civilians to flee into Thailand.

The Council took note of the statements made by the Secretary-General on 27 December 1984 and 13 March 1985 expressing serious concern about the escalation of fighting along the Thai-Kampuchean border and his appeal to all concerned to avoid endangering thousands of Kampuchean civilian lives and adding to the misery and deprivation which already afflict these most unfortunate people. The Council noted with appreciation the visit undertaken by the Secretary-General to the South-East Asian region in January-February 1985 in an effort to bring about a peaceful solution to the Kampuchean problem.

The Council requested the Secretary-General to report to the Council any further violations of humanitarian principles perpetrated against Kampuchean civilian refugees by the foreign occupying troops along the border, and also requested him to continue to monitor closely the developments in Kampuchea and to intensify efforts, including the use of his good offices, to bring about a comprehensive political settlement of the Kampuchean problem and the restoration of fundamental human rights in Kampuchea.

The Council took note of the communiqués issued by the *Ad Hoc* Committee of the International Conference on Kampuchea on 17 January 1985 and 15 February 1985. The Council noted with appreciation the ongoing efforts of the Committee and requested that the Committee should continue its work, pending the reconvening of the Conference.

Economic and Social Council decision 1985/155

38-5-7 (roll-call vote)

Approved by Second Committee (E/1985/95 & Corr.1) by roll-call vote (37-5-7), 24 May (meeting 15); 34-nation draft (E/1985/C.2/L.8); agenda item 16.

Sponsors: Bangladesh, Belgium, Brunei Darussalam, Canada, Costa Rica, Fiji, Germany, Federal Republic of, Honduras, Iceland, Italy, Japan, Liberia, Luxembourg, Malaysia, Morocco, Nepal, Netherlands, New Zealand, Oman, Pakistan, Papua New Guinea, Philippines, Saint Lucia, Samoa, Senegal, Singapore, Somalia, Spain, Swaziland, Thailand, Turkey, United Kingdom, Uruguay, Zaire.

Recorded vote in Council as follows:

In favour: Argentina, Bangladesh, Botswana, Brazil, Canada, China, Colombia, Costa Rica, Djibouti, Ecuador, France, Germany, Federal Republic of, Haiti, Iceland, Indonesia, Japan, Luxembourg, Malaysia, Morocco, Netherlands, New Zealand, Nigeria, Papua New Guinea, Rwanda, Saudi Arabia, Senegal, Somalia, Spain, Sri Lanka, Sweden, Thailand, Turkey, United Kingdom, United States, Venezuela, Yugoslavia, Zaire, Zimbabwe.*

Against: Bulgaria, German Democratic Republic, India, Poland, USSR.

Abstaining: Algeria, Congo, Finland, Lebanon, Mexico, Suriname, Uganda.

*Subsequently said its vote should have been recorded as an abstention.

Viet Nam said the text, while reflecting political manoeuvres aimed at subjecting Kampucheans to the Pol Pot régime, distorted the actual human rights situation in Kampuchea, failed to take account of the different views of the parties and constituted interference in the affairs of a sovereign State. Sharing the view that it represented unacceptable interference in Kampuchea's affairs, the Lao People's Democratic Republic felt that, instead of protecting rights, the text would violate the United Nations Charter and international human rights instruments, and reduce the chances for a settlement in South-East Asia.

The USSR, speaking also on behalf of Bulgaria, the German Democratic Republic and Poland, said

they opposed attempts to use United Nations bodies to buttress the Pol Pot criminals, and pointed out that instead of condemning an undeclared war being waged by mercenaries against Kampuchea, the decision sought to return the Kampucheans to the era of that genocidal régime.

Democratic Kampuchea said that the only objective of the current struggle of the Kampucheans and the Coalition Government of Democratic Kampuchea was the total withdrawal of Vietnamese forces from Kampuchea.

Sweden said that, although it had voted in favour, it did not subscribe to every formulation in the Commission's February resolution. Withdrawal of all foreign forces, the restoration of sovereignty and the right of the Kampucheans to self-determination must be the basis for any just settlement.

(For details on the Kampuchea situation, see p. 221).

Palestinians

The Commission on Human Rights, by a resolution[15] adopted on 26 February 1985 by a roll-call vote of 29 to 7, with 7 abstentions, condemned the continued occupation of the Palestinian and other Arab territories by Israel and its aggression and practices against the Palestinians, and demanded Israel's immediate, unconditional and total withdrawal. The Commission reaffirmed the right of the Palestinian people to self-determination, to an independent and sovereign State, and to return to their homes and property. It recognized their right to regain their rights by all means in accordance with the Charter, and reaffirmed that their future could be decided only with their participation, through their legitimate and sole representative, PLO.

The Commission rejected all partial agreements and separate treaties in so far as they violated Palestinian rights and contradicted the principles of a just and comprehensive Middle East solution, as well as the "autonomy" plan under the 1978 Camp David accords,[26] declaring them invalid. Reaffirming its support for the 1983 Geneva Declaration on Palestine[27] and for the idea of an international peace conference on the Middle East under United Nations auspices, the Commission regretted the negative attitude of Israel and the United States towards such a conference. States, United Nations bodies and other international organizations were urged to support the Palestinians, through PLO, in the struggle to restore their rights.

(For other resolutions dealing with human rights violations in the occupied Arab territories, see p. 925; see also p. 326.)

South Africa and Namibia

On 26 February 1985, the Commission on Human Rights adopted, by a roll-call vote of 32 to 4, with 7 abstentions, a resolution[20] calling on States to take steps to enable the dependent peoples of South Africa and Namibia to exercise fully and without further delay their right to self-determination and independence. It reaffirmed the right of Namibians to freedom and independence in a united Namibia, as well as the legitimacy of their struggle and that of the oppressed people of South Africa by all means, including armed struggle. It urged States to assist them and called for immediate implementation of the 1983 Paris Declaration and Programme of Action on Namibia.[28] Rejecting the so-called "new constitution" as null and void and stressing that majority rule through full and free adult suffrage was the only guarantee of peace, the Commission demanded full respect for the human rights of all people detained or imprisoned in South Africa because of their struggle for independence, and demanded their immediate release.

It reaffirmed that continued colonialism in all forms and manifestations was incompatible with the Charter, the 1948 Universal Declaration of Human Rights[29] and the 1960 Declaration on the Granting of Independence to Colonial Countries and Peoples.[30] The Commission condemned South Africa's illegal occupation of Namibia, its attempts to dismember the Territory, its repression, torture and killing of workers, schoolchildren and other opponents of *apartheid*, its policy of bantustanization and its acts of aggression and destabilization against front-line and other neighbouring States. It also condemned collaboration with South Africa, calling on Western and other countries to sever relations with the régime, and the continuing activities of foreign economic and other interests impeding the implementation of the 1960 Declaration. It declared the illegal occupation of Namibia to be an act of aggression and demanded the withdrawal of South Africa's occupation forces from Angola. Reaffirming that using mercenaries against national liberation movements and States was a criminal act and that mercenaries were criminals, the Commission called on Governments to enact legislation declaring their recruitment, financing, training and transit to be punishable offences, to prohibit their nationals from serving as mercenaries, and to report on such legislation to the Secretary-General.

Pursuant to a similar provision of a 1984 Commission resolution[31] on self-determination as it applied to South Africa and Namibia, seven Governments provided the information requested, which the Secretary-General summarized in a report[32] submitted to the Commission in 1985.

(For details on a draft convention against mercenaries, see p. 1165.)

In a related resolution[33] of 26 February, the Commission reaffirmed the inalienable right of the oppressed people of South Africa and Namibia to self-determination and independence (see p. 903); in another,[34] it reiterated that that right could be legally exercised by the Namibian people only in accordance with conditions determined by the Security Council in 1978[35] (see p. 899).

Noting with deep regret the announcement on 18 April 1985 of the installation by South Africa of an "interim Government" in Namibia, the Sub-Commission, by a resolution[36] adopted on 27 August by 18 votes to none, with 2 abstentions, reaffirmed the rights of the Namibians to self-determination and independence in a united Namibia with complete territorial integrity, and the importance of urgent implementation of the 1978 Security Council resolution[37] approving the United Nations plan for the independence of Namibia. The Sub-Commission demanded that all Namibian political prisoners be immediately and unconditionally released and that all captured freedom fighters be accorded prisoner-of-war status. It called on United Nations Members to take measures against South Africa under Chapter VII of the Charter in order to isolate it, and requested the Commission Chairman to convey to the Secretary-General and the Presidents of the General Assembly and the Economic and Social Council the Sub-Commission members' deep concern at the continuing failure to bring about Namibia's independence and at South Africa's latest efforts to impose an "internal settlement".

(For details on the situation in Namibia, see p. 1090.)

Western Sahara

On 26 February 1985,[18] by a roll-call vote of 30 to none, with 12 abstentions, the Commission on Human Rights reaffirmed that the question of Western Sahara was one of decolonization to be completed through the exercise of the people's right to self-determination, and that a political solution lay in the implementation of the 1983 OAU resolution quoted in an Assembly resolution.[38] The Commission requested the parties to the conflict to negotiate directly towards bringing about a cease-fire and creating conditions for a referendum for self-determination, welcomed OAU and United Nations efforts to promote a just solution and decided to consider the question again in 1986. (See also p. 1137.)

Rights of detained persons

Treatment of prisoners and detainees

Report of the Secretary-General. In connection with the Sub-Commission's annual review of developments in the administration of justice and the human rights of detainees, the Secretary-General in May 1985 submitted a report, with later addenda,[39] summarizing information from 13 Governments, three specialized agencies and two intergovernmental organizations. In July, he presented a synopsis of material from NGOs.[40]

Activities of the Working Group on Detention. A five-member sessional Working Group on Detention, set up by the Sub-Commission, met between 12 and 22 August.[41]

The Group recommended to the Sub-Commission a draft declaration on unacknowledged detention (see p. 865) and decided to transmit the question of administrative detention without charge or trial to the Sub-Commission for consideration. After examining the subject of use of force by law enforcement officials and military personnel, the Working Group suggested that the Sub-Commission consider proposing, through the Secretary-General, that the Seventh United Nations Congress on the Prevention of Crime and the Treatment of Offenders study ways to promote international technical co-operation in restraints on the use of force by those persons (see p. 866).

GENERAL ASSEMBLY ACTION

On 13 December, on the recommendation of the Third Committee, the General Assembly adopted **resolution 40/146**, without vote.

Human rights in the administration of justice
The General Assembly,

Convinced of the need for further co-ordinated and concerted action in promoting respect for human rights in the administration of justice,

Guided by the principles embodied in articles 3, 5, 9, 10 and 11 of the Universal Declaration of Human Rights, as well as the relevant provisions of the International Covenant on Civil and Political Rights, in particular article 6, which explicitly states that no one shall be arbitrarily deprived of his life,

Bearing in mind its resolutions 2858(XXVI) of 20 December 1971 and 3144(XXVIII) of 14 December 1973 on human rights in the administration of justice,

Recalling Economic and Social Council resolutions 1984/47 and 1984/50 of 25 May 1984, in which, _inter alia,_ the Council approved the procedures for the effective implementation of the Standard Minimum Rules for the Treatment of Prisoners and the safeguards guaranteeing protection of the rights of those facing the death penalty,

Bearing in mind also the provisions of the Convention against Torture and Other Cruel, Inhuman or Degrading Treatment or Punishment,

Considering the work in progress with regard to the draft Body of Principles for the Protection of All Persons under Any Form of Detention or Imprisonment,

Recalling its resolution 39/118 of 14 December 1984, in which, _inter alia,_ it requested the Seventh United Nations Congress on the Prevention of Crime and the Treatment of Offenders to give urgent attention to the matter of devising ways and means to ensure more effective application of existing standards and to report thereon to the General Assembly at its fortieth session,

Acknowledging the important work accomplished by the Seventh Congress, in particular in relation to the formulation and application of United Nations standards and norms in the administration of justice under item 7 of its agenda,

1. _Deplores_ the continued use of cruel, inhuman or degrading treatment or punishment, prohibited under international law, and strongly condemns the practice of summary or arbitrary executions;

2. _Welcomes_ the Basic Principles on the Independence of the Judiciary, adopted unanimously by the Seventh United Nations Congress on the Prevention of Crime and the Treatment of Offenders, and invites Governments to respect them and to take them into account within the framework of their national legislation and practice;

3. _Encourages_ the Sub-Commission on Prevention of Discrimination and Protection of Minorities of the Commission on Human Rights, in giving further consideration to the question of the independence and impartiality of the judiciary, jurors and assessors and the independence of lawyers, which is currently on its agenda, to take into account the Basic Principles adopted by the Seventh Congress in making final recommendations at its thirty-ninth session;

4. _Takes note with appreciation_ of the Model Agreement on the Transfer of Foreign Prisoners and recommendations on the treatment of foreign prisoners, also adopted unanimously by the Seventh Congress, and invites Member States to take the Model Agreement into account in establishing treaty relations with other Member States or in revising existing treaty relations;

5. _Also takes note with appreciation_ of the recommendations made by the Seventh Congress with a view to ensuring more effective application of existing standards, in particular the Standard Minimum Rules for the Treatment of Prisoners, the Code of Conduct for Law Enforcement Officials and safeguards guaranteeing the rights of those facing the death penalty;

6. _Calls upon_ Member States to spare no effort in providing for adequate mechanisms, procedures and resources so as to ensure the implementation of these recommendations, both in law and in practice;

7. _Requests_ the Secretary-General to assist Member States, at their request, in implementing these recommendations and to report thereon to the Committee on Crime Prevention and Control;

8. _Requests_ the Economic and Social Council, through the Committee on Crime Prevention and Control, to give special attention to effective ways and means of implementing existing standards, to pay due attention to new developments in this area and to keep these matters under constant review;

9. _Invites_ the specialized agencies and other organizations of the United Nations system, as well as intergovernmental and non-governmental organizations concerned, to continue to co-operate with the Secretary-General in these endeavours by providing assistance, as may be appropriate, and by submitting proposals for relevant action to the Committee on Crime Prevention and Control;

10. _Decides_ to consider at its forty-first session the question of human rights in the administration of justice.

General Assembly resolution 40/146

13 December 1985   Meeting 116   Adopted without vote

Approved by Third Committee (A/40/1007) without vote, 6 December (meeting 71); 17-nation draft (A/C.3/40/L.82); agenda item 12.

Sponsors: Argentina, Australia, Austria, Bolivia, Canada, Colombia, Costa Rica, Denmark, Finland, Gambia, Iceland, Netherlands, Norway, Samoa, Spain, Sweden, Uruguay.
Meeting numbers. GA 40th session: 3rd Committee 69, 71; plenary 116.

Draft principles for the protection of detainees

In 1985, a Working Group open to all members of the General Assembly's Sixth (Legal) Committee continued work on a draft Body of Principles for the Protection of All Persons under Any Form of Detention and Imprisonment. The draft originated from a text adopted by the Sub-Commission in 1978,[42] which had since undergone revisions by a succession of working groups: of the Third Committee in 1980;[43] and of the Sixth Committee in 1981,[44] 1982,[45] 1983[46] and 1984.[47]

The 1985 Working Group, established pursuant to a 1984 Assembly decision,[48] met in New York between 26 September and 22 November. It concluded the first reading of principles 29 to 35, which covered: the right to a request or complaint regarding treatment; inquiry into the death or disappearance of a detainee or prisoner; the right to compensation; presumption of innocence; prompt appearance before a judicial authority; entitlement to trial or release; and opportunity to obtain provisional release. The approved provisional texts of all the articles were annexed to the Group's report.[49]

On 11 December, the General Assembly adopted **decision 40/420**, on the recommendation of the Sixth Committee, taking note with appreciation of the Working Group's report. The Assembly decided that an open-ended working group of the Sixth Committee would be established at the 1986 session with a view to expediting the finalization of the draft Body of Principles; it requested the Secretary-General to circulate to Member States the report of the 1985 Working Group.

The Assembly acted without vote, as had the Sixth Committee,[50] which approved the text on 27 November, as proposed by Sweden.[51]

Protection of juvenile prisoners

On 29 August 1985,[52] the Sub-Commission requested the Secretary-General to invite Governments, United Nations organs and agencies, intergovernmental organizations, the International Committee of the Red Cross (ICRC) and NGOs to submit information on the incarceration of persons under the age of 18 with adult prisoners, and to solicit their views on ways of preventing that practice for a report in 1987. States were encouraged to maintain records on children placed in adult penal facilities.

Torture and cruel treatment

Human Rights Commission action. On 13 March 1985,[53] the Commission on Human Rights decided, by a roll-call vote of 30 to none, with 12 abstentions, to appoint for one year a special rapporteur who, working with discretion, would examine questions relevant to torture—seeking information from Governments, specialized agencies and inter- and non-governmental organizations—and report in 1986 on the occurrence and extent of its practice, together with his conclusions and recommendations. The Secretary-General was asked to assist the rapporteur and to appeal to all Governments to do likewise. Pursuant to the Commission's request, its Chairman appointed on 12 May Peter H. Kooijmans (Netherlands) as Special Rapporteur.

The Commission's decision was approved by the Economic and Social Council on 30 May by **decision 1985/144**. The Council acted without vote, on the recommendation of its Second Committee, which similarly approved on 24 May the text as proposed by the Commission.

Status of the Convention against torture

Following its adoption by the General Assembly in December 1984,[54] the Convention against Torture and Other Cruel, Inhuman or Degrading Treatment or Punishment was opened for signature in New York on 4 February 1985.

Human Rights Commission action. By an 11 March 1985 resolution,[55] the Commission on Human Rights invited all States to become parties to the Convention as a matter of priority. It asked its Sub-Commission to include the Convention in its list[56] of international human rights instruments to which it sought to find ways of encouraging adherence. It also requested the Secretary-General to submit to the Assembly in 1985 and the Commission in 1986 a report on its status.

Report of the Secretary-General. As requested by the Commission, the Secretary-General reported to the Assembly that 33 States had signed the Convention as at 1 September.[57] By 31 December 1985, eight more States had signed, bringing the total to 41.

GENERAL ASSEMBLY ACTION

The item "Torture and other cruel, inhuman or degrading treatment or punishment" was placed on the agenda of the General Assembly's 1985 session at the request of the Netherlands.[58]

On 13 December, on the recommendation of the Third Committee, the Assembly adopted **resolution 40/128**, without vote.

Status of the Convention against Torture and Other Cruel, Inhuman or Degrading Treatment or Punishment

The General Assembly,

Recalling article 5 of the Universal Declaration of Human Rights and article 7 of the International Covenant on Civil and Political Rights, both of which provide that no one shall be subjected to torture or to cruel, inhuman or degrading treatment or punishment,

Recalling also the Declaration on the Protection of All Persons from Being Subjected to Torture and Other Cruel, Inhuman or Degrading Treatment or Punishment, adopted by the General Assembly in its resolution 3452(XXX) of 9 December 1975,

Recalling further its resolution 39/46 of 10 December 1984, by which it adopted and opened for signature, ratification and accession the Convention against Torture and Other Cruel, Inhuman or Degrading Treatment or Punishment and called upon all Governments to consider signing and ratifying the Convention as a matter of priority,

Mindful of the relevance, for the eradication of torture and other cruel, inhuman or degrading treatment or punishment, of the Code of Conduct for Law Enforcement Officials and of the Principles of Medical Ethics,

Convinced of the desirability of early finalization and subsequent adoption of the draft Body of Principles for the Protection of All Persons under Any Form of Detention or Imprisonment,

Seriously concerned about the alarming number of reported cases of torture and other cruel, inhuman or degrading treatment or punishment taking place in various parts of the world,

Determined to promote the full implementation of the prohibition, under international and national law, of the practice of torture and other cruel, inhuman or degrading treatment or punishment,

Welcoming the decision of the Commission on Human Rights, in its resolution 1985/33 of 13 March 1985, to appoint a special rapporteur to examine questions relevant to torture,

1. *Takes note with appreciation* of the report of the Secretary-General on the status of the Convention against Torture and Other Cruel, Inhuman or Degrading Treatment or Punishment;

2. *Expresses its satisfaction* at the number of States that have signed the Convention since it was opened for signature, ratification and accession on 4 February 1985;

3. *Requests* all States that have not yet done so to sign and to ratify the Convention as a matter of priority;

4. *Invites* all States, upon ratification of or accession to the Convention, to consider the possibility of making the declarations provided for in articles 21 and 22 of the Convention;

5. *Requests* the Secretary-General to submit to the Commission on Human Rights at its forty-second session and to the General Assembly at its forty-first session a report on the status of the Convention against Torture and Other Cruel, Inhuman or Degrading Treatment or Punishment;

6. *Decides* to consider the report of the Secretary-General provided for in paragraph 5 above at its forty-first session under the item entitled "Torture and other cruel, inhuman or degrading treatment or punishment".

General Assembly resolution 40/128

13 December 1985   Meeting 116   Adopted without vote

Approved by Third Committee (A/40/982) without vote, 2 December (meeting 60); 34-nation draft (A/C.3/40/L.71); agenda item 144.

Sponsors: Argentina, Australia, Austria, Belgium, Bolivia, Canada, Colombia, Costa Rica, Cyprus, Denmark, Dominican Republic, Ecuador, Finland, France, Gambia, Greece, Iceland, Italy, Luxembourg, Netherlands, New Zealand, Nicaragua, Norway, Panama, Peru, Portugal, Samoa, Senegal, Singapore, Spain, Sweden, United Kingdom, Uruguay, Venezuela.

Meeting numbers. GA 40th session: 3rd Committee 46-48, 50-52, 58, 60; plenary 116.

Fund for victims of torture

On 11 March 1985,[59] the Commission on Human Rights asked the Secretary-General to transmit its appeal to Governments, organizations and individuals to contribute to the United Nations Voluntary Fund for Victims of Torture, established in 1981.[60] It also asked him to assist the Fund's Board of Trustees to publicize the Fund's humanitarian work and to keep the Commission annually informed of the Fund's operations.

The Secretary-General stated in his annual report[61] on the status of the Fund that the Board, which had held its fourth session in April, had recommended to him approval of 36 grants totalling $817,400 for 30 projects in 16 countries located in four continents. The projects were mainly for therapy and rehabilitation of victims of torture and were usually carried out by humanitarian organizations, often related to churches or religious bodies. In some cases, UNHCR served as an implementing channel. As examples of Fund-supported programmes, the Board Chairman, in an annex outlining the Board's activities during the three years of Fund operations, mentioned projects in Argentina, Guinea and Uruguay, which often involved psychological help to children and families of victims and medical assistance. The Fund also financed training courses and teaching seminars.

The Fund's balance at the end of the year was $1,458,876.

GENERAL ASSEMBLY ACTION

On 13 December, on the recommendation of the Third Committee, the General Assembly adopted **resolution 40/127**, without vote.

United Nations Voluntary Fund for Victims of Torture

The General Assembly,

Recalling article 5 of the Universal Declaration of Human Rights, which states that no one shall be subjected to torture or to cruel, inhuman or degrading treatment or punishment,

Again recalling the Declaration on the Protection of All Persons from Being Subjected to Torture and Other Cruel, Inhuman or Degrading Treatment or Punishment,

Recalling also its resolution 39/46 of 10 December 1984, by which it adopted and opened for signature, ratification and accession the Convention against Torture and Other Cruel, Inhuman or Degrading Treatment or Punishment,

Recalling further its resolution 36/151 of 16 December 1981, in which it noted with deep concern that acts of torture took place in various countries, recognized the need to provide assistance to the victims of torture in a purely humanitarian spirit and established the United Nations Voluntary Fund for Victims of Torture,

Convinced that the struggle to eliminate torture includes the provision of assistance in a humanitarian spirit to the victims and members of their families,

Taking note of the report of the Secretary-General,

1. *Expresses its gratitude and appreciation* to those Governments, organizations and individuals that have

already contributed to the United Nations Voluntary Fund for Victims of Torture;

2. *Calls upon* all Governments, organizations and individuals in a position to do so to respond favourably to requests for initial as well as further contributions to the Fund;

3. *Expresses its appreciation* to the Board of Trustees of the Fund for the work it has carried out;

4. *Expresses its appreciation* to the Secretary-General for the support given to the Board of Trustees of the Fund;

5. *Requests* the Secretary-General to make use of all existing possibilities, including the preparation, production and dissemination of information materials, to assist the Board of Trustees of the Fund in its efforts to make the Fund and its humanitarian work better known and in its appeal for contributions.

General Assembly resolution 40/127

13 December 1985   Meeting 116   Adopted without vote

Approved by Third Committee (A/40/982) without vote, 2 December (meeting 60); 20-nation draft (A/C.3/40/L.57); agenda item 144.
Sponsors: Australia, Belgium, Bolivia, Canada, Costa Rica, Cyprus, Denmark, Finland, France, Germany, Federal Republic of, Greece, Iceland, Ireland, Kenya, Mexico, Netherlands, Norway, Spain, Sweden, United States.
Meeting numbers. GA 40th session: 3rd Committee 46, 58, 60; plenary 116.

Detention on grounds of mental illness

The sessional working group set up by the Sub-Commission in 1984[62] to examine further the draft body of guidelines, principles and guarantees for the protection of persons detained on grounds of mental ill-health or suffering from mental disorder was reconvened in four meetings between 15 and 26 August 1985.[63] The group heard comments by four NGOs and began its second preliminary reading of the draft body of guidelines.

The group agreed to retain as they stood the introductory comments; it also retained article 2 as it stood and amended articles 1 and 3 (on application of the guidelines) and articles 4, 6 and 7 (on fundamental freedoms as basic rights of the patient). It decided to reconsider at a later stage paragraph 2 of article 5 (to the effect that difficulties of adaptation to certain moral, social, cultural or political values or religious beliefs should not be a determining factor in diagnosing mental illness).

GENERAL ASSEMBLY ACTION

On 13 December, on the recommendation of the Third Committee, the General Assembly adopted **resolution 40/110**, without vote.

Implications of scientific and technological developments for human rights

The General Assembly,

Recalling its resolution 33/53 of 14 December 1978, in which it requested the Commission on Human Rights to urge the Sub-Commission on Prevention of Discrimination and Protection of Minorities to undertake, as a matter of priority, a study of the question of the protection of those detained on the grounds of mental ill-health, with a view to formulating guidelines,

Recalling also its resolution 39/132 of 14 December 1984, in which it urged the Commission on Human Rights and

the Sub-Commission to expedite their consideration of this question, so that the Commission could submit its views and recommendations, including a draft body of guidelines, principles and guarantees, to the General Assembly at its forty-first session, through the Economic and Social Council,

Recalling further Economic and Social Council resolution 1984/33 and decision 1984/142 of 24 May 1984,

Noting with concern that the Commission on Human Rights will not be in a position to submit its views and recommendations to the General Assembly at its forty-first session through the Economic and Social Council because the Sub-Commission has still not concluded its consideration of the draft body of guidelines, principles and guarantees,

Reaffirming its conviction that detention of persons in mental institutions on account of their political views or on other non-medical grounds is a violation of their human rights,

Again urges the Commission on Human Rights and, through it, the Sub-Commission on Prevention of Discrimination and Protection of Minorities to expedite their consideration of the draft body of guidelines, principles and guarantees, so that the Commission can submit its views and recommendations, including a draft body of guidelines, principles and guarantees, to the General Assembly at its forty-second session, through the Economic and Social Council.

General Assembly resolution 40/110

13 December 1985   Meeting 116   Adopted without vote

Approved by Third Committee (A/40/969) without vote, 2 December (meeting 60); 15-nation draft (A/C.3/40/L.62); agenda item 102.
Sponsors: Bolivia, Colombia, Costa Rica, Fiji, Honduras, Italy, Ivory Coast, Jamaica, Morocco, Netherlands, Norway, Samoa, Singapore, Sweden, United Kingdom.
Meeting numbers. GA 40th session: 3rd Committee 48, 53, 58, 60; plenary 116.

Draft declaration against unacknowledged detention

By a resolution of 29 August 1985,[64] adopted by 14 votes to 1, the Sub-Commission approved a one-paragraph draft declaration against unacknowledged detention of persons, prepared by its Working Group on Detention[41] (see p. 862), and recommended it to the Commission on Human Rights for adoption. The draft declaration stated that Governments were to disclose the identity, location and condition of all persons detained by members of their police, military or security authorities, or others acting with their knowledge, together with the cause of such detention, and seek to locate all other persons who had disappeared. In countries where legislation to that effect did not exist, steps were to be taken to enact such legislation as soon as possible.

The Working Group was asked to consider possible further provisions relating to the draft.

Detention without charge or trial

On 11 March 1985,[65] the Commission requested the Sub-Commission to analyse available information about the practice of administrative detention without charge or trial and to make recommendations regarding its use. The Sub-Commission, on 29

August,[66] requested Louis Joinet (France) to prepare before its 1986 session a paper suggesting procedures by which the Sub-Commission might carry out that responsibility.

Use of force by law officials

In June 1985, the Secretary-General presented to the Sub-Commission a report[67] on restraints in the use of force by law enforcement officials and military personnel, supplementary to a 1984 report.[68] The 1985 report contained information submitted by Kuwait, Madagascar, Morocco, the Netherlands, Norway and Pakistan, the United Nations Centre for Social Development and Humanitarian Affairs, the International Criminal Police Organization (INTERPOL) and an NGO.

Following a proposal by its Working Group on Detention,[41] the Sub-Commission, on 29 August,[69] decided to submit to the Seventh United Nations Congress on the Prevention of Crime and the Treatment of Offenders (see p. 738), through the Secretary-General, a proposal that the Congress study ways to promote international technical co-operation in the area of restraints on the use of force by law enforcement officials and military personnel. It also asked the Secretary-General to inform it of the results of the Congress in this matter, a subject it would consider in 1986.

Capital punishment

In April 1985, the Secretary-General submitted to the Economic and Social Council his third quinquennial report[70] on the use of and trends in capital punishment, and on legal changes, initiatives and results of research compiled since 1979. Based on information received from 48 countries, mostly non-retentionist, the report contained information on practices and statutory rules governing the right of a person sentenced to death to petition for pardon, commutation or reprieve, and noted newly adopted safeguards for those facing the death penalty.

The information provided suggested that there had been few significant changes between 1979 and 1983, in comparison with the previous reporting period, 1974-1978. However, the decisions of three countries to abolish capital punishment (totally in two States and for ordinary crimes in the third) and an apparent decrease in the number of capital sentences and executions made it possible to conclude that the movement towards abolition had progressed somewhat. Significant initiatives had been taken in 1984 by the adoption by the Economic and Social Council of safeguards[71] for those facing the death penalty and an Assembly resolution[72] endorsing the Council's action.

ECONOMIC AND SOCIAL COUNCIL ACTION

On 29 May, on the recommendation of its Second Committee, the Economic and Social Council adopted **resolution 1985/33**, without vote.

Capital punishment

The Economic and Social Council,

Recalling its resolutions 1745(LIV) of 16 May 1973, 1930(LVIII) of 6 May 1975 and 1984/50 of 25 May 1984,

Recalling also General Assembly resolutions 2857(XXVI) of 20 December 1971, 32/61 of 8 December 1977 and 39/118 of 14 December 1984,

Having examined the third quinquennial report of the Secretary-General on capital punishment,

Concerned at the fact that only 48 Governments responded to the questionnaire addressed to them for the preparation by the Secretary-General of the third quinquennial report,

1. *Invites* Member States to provide the Secretary-General with the information required for preparation of the fourth quinquennial report on capital punishment in 1990;

2. *Takes note* of the fact that in the period under review in the report of the Secretary-General some countries have abolished capital punishment, others have adopted a policy of reducing the number of capital offences or have reported not imposing death sentences on offenders, while others have retained capital punishment;

3. *Requests* the Committee on Crime Prevention and Control to keep the question of capital punishment under constant review;

4. *Requests* the Secretary-General, in preparing the fourth quinquennial report, to draw on all available data, including current criminological research, and to invite the comments of specialized agencies and intergovernmental and non-governmental organizations on this question.

Economic and Social Council resolution 1985/33

29 May 1985	Meeting 23	Adopted without vote

Approved by Second Committee (E/1985/96 & Corr.1) without vote, 21 May (meeting 11); 10-nation draft (E/1985/C.2/L.7), orally revised; agenda item 17.

Sponsors: Austria, Colombia, Costa Rica, Germany, Federal Republic of, Italy, Netherlands, Nicaragua, Portugal, Sweden, Uruguay.

In a statement of position after the vote, Saudi Arabia said the abolition of capital punishment not only ran counter to the Islamic Shariah, which permitted retaliation in kind in cases of premeditated murder, but also violated the Universal Declaration of Human Rights,[29] which guaranteed freedom of religion, and the principle of national sovereignty.

Proposed second optional protocol to the Covenant on Civil and Political Rights

The idea of a second optional protocol to the International Covenant on Civil and Political Rights, aimed at the abolition of the death penalty, originated in the General Assembly in 1980.[73] Pursuant to a 1982 Assembly request,[74] the Commission on Human Rights, in 1984,[75] invited its Sub-Commission to consider elaborating a second protocol. On a recommendation of 14 March 1985[76] of the Commission, the Economic and Social Council, by **resolution 1985/41**, entrusted a Special Rapporteur, Marc Bossuyt (Belgium), with analysing the proposal. Also on 14 March,[77] the Commission decided to consider the issue further at its 1987 session.

ECONOMIC AND SOCIAL COUNCIL ACTION

On 30 May 1985, on the recommendation of its Second Committee, the Economic and Social Council adopted **resolution 1985/41**, without vote.

Elaboration of a second optional protocol to the International Covenant on Civil and Political Rights aiming at the abolition of the death penalty

The Economic and Social Council,

Noting resolution 1984/7 of 28 August 1984 of the Sub-Commission on Prevention of Discrimination and Protection of Minorities and Commission on Human Rights resolution 1985/46 of 14 March 1985 concerning the idea of elaborating a draft of a second optional protocol to the International Covenant on Civil and Political Rights aiming at the abolition of the death penalty,

1. *Authorizes* the Sub-Commission on Prevention of Discrimination and Protection of Minorities to entrust Mr. M. Bossuyt, as Special Rapporteur, with the task of preparing an analysis concerning the proposal to elaborate a second optional protocol to the International Covenant on Civil and Political Rights aiming at the abolition of the death penalty;

2. *Requests* the Special Rapporteur to take into account the documents considered and the views expressed in the General Assembly, the Commission on Human Rights and the Sub-Commission in favour of or against the idea of elaborating such a protocol;

3. *Invites* the Special Rapporteur to present, on the basis of his analysis, recommendations for further consideration by the Sub-Commission at its thirty-ninth session;

4. *Requests* the Secretary-General to provide the Special Rapporteur with all necessary assistance for the completion of his task.

Economic and Social Council resolution 1985/41

30 May 1985	Meeting 25	Adopted without vote

Approved by Second Committee (E/1985/95 & Corr.1) without vote, 24 May (meeting 15); draft by Commission on Human Rights (E/1985/22); agenda item 16.

Saudi Arabia said it had joined in the consensus although it had voted against the 1984 Assembly resolution[78] on the subject. It did, however, maintain the right not to abolish the death penalty, as such an action would run counter to Islamic law.

Extra-legal executions

In conformity with a 1984 Economic and Social Council request,[79] Special Rapporteur S. Amos Wako (Kenya) submitted to the Commission on Human Rights in February 1985 a report[80] on summary or arbitrary executions. He updated the information contained in two previous reports submitted in 1983[81] and 1984,[82] reporting on the activities he had undertaken since then, including examination of situations in which such executions allegedly had taken place. He also presented information on his visit to Suriname in July 1984 to examine the alleged occurrence of the summary execution of 15 persons in December 1982, the official measures taken to determine the facts, and the safeguards adopted or envisaged to enhance the protection of the right to life.

The Special Rapporteur had received appeals from various sources making allegations of imminent or threatened summary executions, indicating that the practice was still widespread. He reported that 15 Governments had not replied to his inquiries concerning allegations of executions in their countries, and strongly appealed to them to respond without delay. He recommended that the Commission continue to monitor extra-legal executions and consider ways by which all such cases could be brought to its attention. His review of national legislation made it clear, he said, that a number of exceptions had been made in regard to safeguards to the right to life. Some Governments had resorted to harsh penalties to cope with rampant crime. Lack of respect for the right to life was evident in groups other than Governments or quasi-governmental agencies, and numerous executions had occurred as countermeasures by Governments responding to killing by non-governmental groups; the Commission should give urgent attention to the responsibility of such groups. In addition, Governments should be urged to set up training programmes for law enforcement officials. He hoped that the trend towards impartial investigation, prosecution and punishment of those involved in extra-legal executions would continue.

ECONOMIC AND SOCIAL COUNCIL ACTION

On 30 May, on the recommendation of its Second Committee, the Economic and Social Council adopted **resolution 1985/40**, without vote. The Commission on Human Rights had recommended the text on 13 March.[83]

Summary or arbitrary executions

The Economic and Social Council,

Recalling the Universal Declaration of Human Rights, which guarantees the right to life, liberty and security of person,

Having regard to the provisions of the International Covenant on Civil and Political Rights, in which it is stated that every human being has the inherent right to life, that this right shall be protected by law and that no one shall be arbitrarily deprived of his life,

Recalling General Assembly resolution 34/175 of 17 December 1979, in which the Assembly reaffirmed that mass and flagrant violations of human rights were of special concern to the United Nations and urged the

Commission on Human Rights to take timely and effective action in existing and future cases of mass and flagrant violations of human rights,

Mindful of General Assembly resolutions 36/33 of 9 November 1981, 37/182 of 17 December 1982, 38/96 of 16 December 1983 and 39/110 of 14 December 1984,

Taking note of resolution 1982/13 of 7 September 1982 of the Sub-Commission on Prevention of Discrimination and Protection of Minorities, in which the Sub-Commission recommended that effective measures should be adopted to prevent the occurrence of summary or arbitrary executions,

Taking note also of the work done by the Committee on Crime Prevention and Control in the area of summary and arbitrary executions, including the elaboration of minimum legal guarantees and safeguards to prevent recourse to such extra-legal executions, to be considered by the Seventh United Nations Congress on the Prevention of Crime and the Treatment of Offenders in 1985,

Deeply alarmed at the occurrence on a large scale of summary or arbitrary executions, including extra-legal executions,

1. *Strongly deplores*, once again, the large number of summary or arbitrary executions, including extra-legal executions, which continue to take place in various parts of the world;

2. *Appeals urgently* to Governments, United Nations bodies, the specialized agencies, regional intergovernmental organizations and non-governmental organizations to take effective action to combat and eliminate summary or arbitrary executions, including extra-legal executions;

3. *Takes note with appreciation* of the report of Mr. S. Amos Wako, Special Rapporteur;

4. *Decides* to continue the mandate of the Special Rapporteur, Mr. S. Amos Wako, for another year, in order to enable him to submit further conclusions and recommendations to the Commission on Human Rights;

5. *Requests* the Special Rapporteur in carrying out his mandate to continue to examine situations of summary or arbitrary executions;

6. *Also requests* the Special Rapporteur in carrying out his mandate to respond effectively to information that comes before him, in particular when a summary or arbitrary execution is imminent or threatened;

7. *Considers* that the Special Rapporteur in carrying out his mandate should continue to seek and receive information from Governments, United Nations bodies, specialized agencies, regional intergovernmental organizations and non-governmental organizations in consultative status with the Economic and Social Council and to take due account of official declarations and government information which come to his attention;

8. *Requests* the Secretary-General to continue to provide all necessary assistance to the Special Rapporteur so that he may carry out his mandate effectively;

9. *Urges* all Governments and all others concerned to co-operate with and assist the Special Rapporteur;

10. *Requests* the Commission on Human Rights to consider the question of summary or arbitrary executions as a matter of high priority at its forty-second session under the item entitled "Question of the violation of human rights and fundamental freedoms in any part of the world, with particular reference to colonial and other dependent countries and territories".

Economic and Social Council resolution 1985/40

30 May 1985   Meeting 25   Adopted without vote

Approved by Second Committee (E/1985/95 & Corr.1) without vote, 24 May (meeting 15); draft by Commission on Human Rights (E/1985/22); agenda item 16.

GENERAL ASSEMBLY ACTION

On 13 December, on the recommendation of the Third Committee, the General Assembly adopted **resolution 40/143**, without vote.

Summary or arbitrary executions

The General Assembly,

Recalling the provisions of the Universal Declaration of Human Rights, which states that every human being has the right to life, liberty and security of person,

Having regard to the provisions of the International Covenant on Civil and Political Rights, which states that every human being has the inherent right to life, that this right shall be protected by law and that no one shall be arbitrarily deprived of his life,

Recalling also its resolution 34/175 of 17 December 1979, in which it reaffirmed that mass and flagrant violations of human rights are of special concern to the United Nations and urged the Commission on Human Rights to take timely and effective action in existing and future cases of mass and flagrant violations of human rights,

Recalling further its resolution 36/22 of 9 November 1981, in which it condemned the practice of summary or arbitrary executions, and its resolutions 37/182 of 17 December 1982, 38/96 of 16 December 1983 and 39/110 of 14 December 1984,

Deeply alarmed at the continued occurrence on a large scale of summary or arbitrary executions, including extra-legal executions,

Recalling resolution 1982/13 of 7 September 1982 of the Sub-Commission on Prevention of Discrimination and Protection of Minorities, in which the Sub-Commission recommended that effective measures should be adopted to prevent the occurrence of summary or arbitrary executions,

Welcoming Economic and Social Council resolution 1984/50 of 25 May 1984, and the safeguards guaranteeing protection of the rights of those facing the death penalty annexed thereto, which resolution was endorsed by the Seventh United Nations Congress on the Prevention of Crime and the Treatment of Offenders in its resolution 15, as well as the ongoing work on summary or arbitrary executions within the Committee on Crime Prevention and Control,

Convinced of the need for appropriate action to combat and eventually eliminate the practice of summary or arbitrary executions, which represents a flagrant violation of the most fundamental human right, the right to life,

1. *Strongly condemns* the large number of summary or arbitrary executions, including extra-legal executions, which continue to take place in various parts of the world;

2. *Demands* that the practice of summary or arbitrary executions be brought to an end;

3. *Welcomes* Economic and Social Council resolution 1982/35 of 7 May 1982, in which the Council decided to appoint for one year a special rapporteur to examine the questions related to summary or arbitrary executions;

4. *Also welcomes* Economic and Social Council resolution 1985/40 of 30 May 1985, in which the Council decided to continue the mandate of the Special Rapporteur, Mr. S. A. Wako, for a further year and requested the Commission on Human Rights to consider the question of summary or arbitrary executions as a matter of high priority at its forty-second session;

5. *Urges* all Governments and all others concerned to co-operate with and assist the Special Rapporteur of the Commission on Human Rights in the implementation of his mandate;

6. *Requests* the Special Rapporteur, in carrying out his mandate, to respond effectively to information that comes before him, in particular when a summary or arbitrary execution is imminent or threatened, or when such an execution has recently occurred;

7. *Also requests* the Special Rapporteur to consider, in his next report, possible measures to be taken by the appropriate authorities when a death occurs in custody, including adequate autopsy;

8. *Considers* that the Special Rapporteur, in carrying out his mandate, should continue to seek and receive information from Governments, United Nations bodies, specialized agencies, regional intergovernmental organizations and non-governmental organizations in consultative status with the Economic and Social Council;

9. *Requests* the Secretary-General to provide all necessary assistance to the Special Rapporteur so that he may effectively carry out his mandate;

10. *Again requests* the Secretary-General to continue to use his best endeavours in cases where the minimum standard of legal safeguards provided for in articles 6, 14 and 15 of the International Covenant on Civil and Political Rights appear not to be respected;

11. *Requests* the Commission on Human Rights at its forty-second session, on the basis of the report of the Special Rapporteur to be prepared in conformity with Economic and Social Council resolutions 1982/35, 1983/36, 1984/35 and 1985/40, to make recommendations concerning appropriate action to combat and eventually eliminate the abhorrent practice of summary or arbitrary executions.

General Assembly resolution 40/143

13 December 1985   Meeting 116   Adopted without vote

Approved by Third Committee (A/40/1007) without vote, 6 December (meeting 71); 27-nation draft (A/C.3/40/L.77), orally revised; agenda item 12.
Sponsors: Argentina, Austria, Belgium, Canada, Costa Rica, Cyprus, Denmark, Dominican Republic, Ecuador, Finland, France, Gambia, Greece, Iceland, Ivory Coast, Japan, Kenya, Luxembourg, Morocco, Netherlands, Norway, Portugal, Senegal, Spain, Sweden, United Kingdom, Zambia.
Meeting numbers. GA 40th session: 3rd Committee 54, 60, 62-65, 69, 71; plenary 116.

Other action. The Seventh United Nations Congress on the Prevention of Crime and the Treatment of Offenders (Milan, Italy, 26 August–6 September) (see p. 738), by a consensus resolution,[84] condemned extra-legal, arbitrary and summary executions, and called on Governments to investigate such acts, punish those found guilty and take measures to prevent such executions; it requested the Secretary-General to submit an analytical review of documents on the prevention, investigation and elimination of such executions

for consideration by the Committee on Crime Prevention and Control.

Persons detained by Israel

On 11 March, the Commission on Human Rights adopted, by a roll-call vote of 32 to 1, with 9 abstentions, a resolution[85] strongly condemning Israel for ill-treatment and torture of Palestinian detainees. It urged Israel to release immediately all civilians arbitrarily detained since the beginning of the armed conflict in Lebanon, as well as those rearrested and detained again at Al-Ansar camp in southern Lebanon, in violation of a 1983 agreement on prisoner exchange,[86] and to release the 125 prisoners transferred from that camp to Atlit prison. It urged Israel to co-operate with ICRC and allow it to visit all detainees in the detention centres under its control, to recognize prisoner-of-war status for all combatants captured during the conflict and treat them accordingly, and to ensure protection for Palestinian civilians, including released detainees, in the areas under its occupation. The Commission called on all parties to the conflict to inform ICRC of persons who were missing or who disappeared following the Israeli invasion of Lebanon, and requested the Secretary-General to make all information on that matter available. (See also p. 334.)

Disappearance of persons

Human Rights Commission action. On 11 March 1985,[87] the Commission on Human Rights decided to extend the mandate of the Working Group on Enforced or Involuntary Disappearances for another year and to study in 1986 the possibility of extending it for two years. The Group was requested to submit at the 1986 session a report with conclusions and recommendations, discharging its mandate with discretion so as to protect persons providing information or to limit the dissemination of information provided by Governments and observing United Nations standards and practices in dealing with communications. The Group was also requested to present to the Commission all necessary information.

The Commission requested the Secretary-General to appeal to Governments to co-operate with the Group, to invite countries with numerous cases of disappearance to envisage the establishment of a national body to investigate and answer requests for information on them, and to ensure that the Group received all necessary assistance and resources. The Commission encouraged Governments to consider with special attention any wish expressed by the Group to visit their country.

Working Group activities. In an addendum[88] to its 1984 report,[89] the five-member Working Group on Enforced or Involuntary Disappearances reported in February 1985 on developments since its last session in December 1984. The addendum contained additional communications from Governments as well as information on cases of enforced or involuntary disappearances transmitted during January 1985; such cases had been reported in Bolivia, Colombia, Cyprus, El Salvador, Ethiopia, Guatemala, Honduras, Iran, Morocco, Nicaragua, Peru, the Philippines and Uganda.

The Working Group, established in 1980,[90] held three sessions in 1985:[91] its sixteenth (Buenos Aires, Argentina, 5-14 June), seventeenth (Geneva, 9-13 September) and eighteenth (Geneva, 4-13 December).

In 1985, the Working Group received some 4,500 reports on enforced or involuntary disappearances and after examination transmitted some 2,200 of the newly reported cases to the Governments concerned. Under its urgent action procedure, the Group transmitted 322 cases to Governments in 1985. Replies included in the report were from Colombia, Peru and the Philippines.

The Group also retransmitted summaries of all cases unclarified to date to Governments that had either never replied to the Group's transmittals or which had asked to be informed of the status of outstanding cases. The Group further informed Governments whenever a case was clarified by new information. It invited all Governments to which it had transmitted reports on disappearances to send representatives to its sessions, and maintained correspondence with relatives of missing persons, their associations and various NGOs which submitted information. It gave particular attention to reports of harassment, threats and assassination of relatives of missing persons and conveyed its feeling of deep preoccupation to the Governments concerned, stressing their responsibility to prevent such acts.

Two members of the Working Group visited Peru from 17 to 22 June and provided the Commission with an analysis of the situation of disappearances in the country.

To enhance the effectiveness of its activities, the Group decided to add to or slightly modify some of its procedures: to retransmit to Governments that had never replied to the Group's communications the summaries of all outstanding cases in conjunction with an invitation to attend the Group's three annual sessions; to inform Governments of clarifications provided by non-governmental sources whenever they appeared to be reliable, and no longer to ask them for confirmation or disproval of such information; to communicate relevant information to the Commission's special rapporteurs dealing with country situations, summary or arbitrary executions and torture; to revise the statistical presentation of outstanding cases in its report; and to renew its efforts to have NGOs and family associations submitting reports present cases in a detailed and well-documented manner.

ECONOMIC AND SOCIAL COUNCIL ACTION

By **decision 1985/142** of 30 May 1985, the Economic and Social Council approved the Commission's decision to extend the Working Group's mandate for another year, as well as its request to the Secretary-General to ensure that it received the necessary staff and resources required to work effectively and expeditiously. The Council acted without vote, following similar approval by its Second Committee on 24 May of a text proposed by the Commission.

GENERAL ASSEMBLY ACTION

On 13 December, on the recommendation of the Third Committee, the General Assembly adopted **resolution 40/147**, without vote.

Question of enforced or involuntary disappearances
    The General Assembly,
    Recalling its resolution 33/173 of 20 December 1978 concerning disappeared persons, and its resolution 39/111 of 14 December 1984 on the question of enforced or involuntary disappearances,
    Deeply concerned about the persistence, in certain cases, of the practice of enforced or involuntary disappearances,
    Expressing its profound emotion at the anguish and sorrow of the families concerned, who should know the fate of their relatives,
    Convinced of the importance of implementing the provisions of its resolution 33/173 and of the other United Nations resolutions on the question of enforced or involuntary disappearances, with a view to finding solutions for cases of disappearances and helping to eliminate such practices,
    Bearing in mind Commission on Human Rights resolution 1985/20 of 11 March 1985, in which the Commission decided to extend for one year the term of the mandate of the Working Group on Enforced or Involuntary Disappearances, and Economic and Social Council decision 1985/142 of 30 May 1985, in which the Council approved the Commission's decision,
    1. *Expresses its appreciation* to the Working Group on Enforced or Involuntary Disappearances for its humanitarian work and to those Governments that have co-operated with it;
    2. *Welcomes* the decision of the Commission on Human Rights to extend for one year the term of the mandate of the Working Group, as well as to study at its forty-second session the possibility of extending to two years the term of the mandate of the Working Group;
    3. *Also welcomes* the provisions made by the Commission on Human Rights in its resolution 1985/20 to enable the Working Group to fulfil its mandate with even greater efficiency;
    4. *Appeals* to all Governments to provide the Working Group and the Commission on Human Rights with the full co-operation warranted by their strictly humanitarian objectives and their working methods based on discretion;
    5. *Encourages* the Governments concerned to consider with special attention the wish of the Working Group, when such a wish is expressed, to visit their countries,

thus enabling the Group to fulfil its mandate even more effectively;

6. *Calls upon* the Commission on Human Rights to continue to study this question as a matter of priority and to take any step it may deem necessary to the pursuit of the task of the Working Group when it considers the report to be submitted by the Group to the Commission at its forty-second session;

7. *Renews its request* to the Secretary-General to continue to provide the Working Group with all necessary assistance.

General Assembly resolution 40/147

13 December 1985   Meeting 116   Adopted without vote

Approved by Third Committee (A/40/1007) without vote, 6 December (meeting 71); 21-nation draft (A/C.3/40/L.84); agenda item 12.

Sponsors: Argentina, Austria, Bolivia, Canada, Colombia, Costa Rica, France, Gambia, Germany, Federal Republic of, Greece, Italy, Luxembourg, Mexico, Morocco, Netherlands, Portugal, Rwanda, Senegal, Spain, Sweden, United Kingdom.

Meeting numbers. GA 40th session: 3rd Committee 54, 60, 62-64, 66, 69, 71; plenary 116.

Other aspects of civil and political rights

Slavery

Human Rights Commission action. By an 11 March 1985 resolution,[92] the Commission on Human Rights invited States to sign or ratify as soon as possible the 1949 Convention for the Suppression of the Traffic in Persons and of the Exploitation of the Prostitution of Others.[93] It requested the Secretary-General to invite States parties to that Convention, and to the 1926 Slavery Convention and the 1956 Supplementary Convention on the Abolition of Slavery, the Slave Trade, and Institutions and Practices Similar to Slavery,[94] to report regularly on their compliance with those instruments. It requested him also to transmit to the Governments concerned, and to the United Nations bodies and agencies mentioned by the Working Group on Slavery in its recommendations, statements by NGOs containing specific allegations of slavery-like practices, together with the relevant parts of the Working Group's report. It invited States, United Nations organs and agencies, intergovernmental and nongovernmental organizations and INTERPOL to continue to supply information to the Working Group.

The Commission requested its Sub-Commission to consider undertaking studies on alleged slavery-like practices against women and children and ways they could be assisted and rehabilitated and on debt bondage. It recommended that the struggle against procuring be intensified at the national level and that international measures be adopted to dismantle the networks feeding prostitution and to repatriate and assist the victims. It further recommended that the mass media, including those of the United Nations system, more widely publicize the evils of slavery and that Governments avail themselves of the advisory services programme for its elimination. The United Nations Children's Fund (UNICEF), ILO, the Food and Agriculture Organization of the United Nations (FAO) and the United Nations Educational, Scientific and Cultural Organization (UNESCO) were requested to give particular attention in their technical assistance programmes to situations where poverty was leading to or perpetuating such practices.

On 18 December 1985, by **decision 40/461**, the General Assembly decided to include in the provisional agenda of its 1986 session an item on the celebration of the one-hundred-and-fiftieth anniversary of the emancipation of slaves in the British Empire.

Activities of the Working Group. The Sub-Commission's Working Group on Slavery, at its eleventh session (Geneva, 29 July–2 August 1985),[95] reviewed and made recommendations on developments in slavery and the slave trade, including questions relating to Mauritania (see below), the exploitation of child labour (see p. 930), the traffic in persons and the exploitation of prostitution of others, and slavery-like practices of *apartheid* and colonialism. It also discussed debt bondage.

The Group recommended: that Governments ratify the Convention for the Suppression of the Traffic in Persons and of the Exploitation of the Prostitution of Others; that UNICEF commit itself to eradicating the sexual exploitation of children and that it be designated as the lead agency for research and education in that area; that Governments be encouraged to establish national policies to protect children from such exploitation; that strong measures be taken to ensure a social status for women equal to that of men and that the mass media publicize their fundamental equality; that special attention be devoted to the problem of child prostitution; and that a World Day for the Abolition of Slavery in All its Forms be proclaimed.

It recommended that the Human Rights Commission Chairman be authorized to pressure South Africa to obtain the release of political prisoners and to engage in a dialogue with black-majority leaders (see p. 899).

Slavery-like practices in Mauritania

Human Rights Commission action. By an 11 March 1985 resolution,[96] the Commission on Human Rights expressed appreciation to Mauritania for inviting a Sub-Commission mission to visit and for its exemplary co-operation. Expressing appreciation to Marc Bossuyt (Belgium) for the report on his 1984 mission,[97] the Commission decided to transmit it to Mauritania, inviting it to inform the Sub-Commission of any action it felt able to take thereon, and to various United Nations agencies, regional and subregional organizations and United Nations Development Programme (UNDP) donors, inviting them to consider what assistance they could give to Mauritania to help eradicate the consequences of slavery, in accordance with Mauritanian development objectives. The expert was requested to prepare a follow-up report on the basis of the replies received, and submit an interim report to the Sub-Commission in 1985 and a final report in 1986.

ECONOMIC AND SOCIAL COUNCIL ACTION

On the recommendation of its Second Committee, the Economic and Social Council, by **decision 1985/143** of 30 May 1985, approved the Commission's request to the expert to prepare a follow-up report—based on replies received and taking into account the views expressed by the Sub-Commission at its 1984 session and by the Commission at its 1985 session, in particular with respect to assistance which could be provided to Mauritania—and submit an interim report to the Sub-Commission in 1985 and a final report in 1986. The Council acted without vote, following similar action by the Committee on 24 May, approving a text proposed by the Commission.

Interim report by the expert. The Sub-Commission's expert presented to the Sub-Commission in July an interim report,[98] giving a synopsis of the replies he had received and the views expressed by the Sub-Commission and the Commission, in particular with respect to assistance that could be provided to Mauritania. At the time of preparation of the report, no reply had been received from Mauritania. UNDP and four specialized agencies had replied, as well as the Economic Commission for Africa. Those replies, he stated, already gave indications as to what kind of assistance could be given; efforts needed to be made by the United Nations, in co-operation with Mauritania, to promote co-ordination and stimulate interest. In the expert's opinion, the Sub-Commission should consider proposing that a co-ordinating role be vested in the Secretary-General or a person designated by him.

Working Group on Slavery. At its July/August session,[95] the Working Group on Slavery recommended that: Mauritania, as well as international organizations, donor countries and other recipients of the expert's report, be invited to respond early to it; consideration be given to the method of co-ordinating the various assistance programmes to Mauritania; the opinion of anti-slavery organizations be taken into consideration in planning development projects and they be assured of independence of action; and consideration be given to the proposals for Mauritania's development put forward by the Anti-Slavery Society, which formed part of the Working Group's report.

At the Group's session, the representative of the Anti-Slavery Society said the full rehabilitation and reinsertion of former slaves would call for thorough social reforms and a restructuring of Mauritanian society. The social problems facing Mauritania were particularly difficult and had to be tackled in the context of a critical situation of near-famine and consequent massive population drift. Mauritania needed international assistance on a large scale if it was to survive.

Sub-Commission action. Following consideration of the expert's interim report, the Sub-Commission, on 29 August,[99] expressed appreciation to him, to Mauritania for its continued co operation, and to the bodies that had informed the Sub-Commission of the assistance they could provide to Mauritania. It requested the Secretary-General to renew the invitation to those that had not yet replied and to UNDP donor States. It expressed the hope that UNDP and other organs and agencies would consider undertaking an additional specific effort to help Mauritania eliminate the consequences of slavery, and invited the Commission on Human Rights to consider ways to ensure co-ordination of such assistance. The Sub-Commission looked forward to information from Mauritania on action it felt able to take on the expert's recommendations.

Freedom of movement

On 11 March 1985,[100] the Commission on Human Rights welcomed the progress made by Special Rapporteur Chama L. C. Mubanga-Chipoya (Zambia) in his study on everyone's right to leave any country, including one's own, and to return to one's country. It appealed to Governments to respond to his questionnaire, and requested the Sub-Commission to consider his next report as a matter of priority, with a view to submitting a draft declaration as soon as possible.

Following consideration of a progress report,[101] the Sub-Commission, on 30 August,[102] requested the Special Rapporteur to continue his work and present to it in 1986 a final report and a preliminary draft declaration and, in 1987, a final draft of a declaration and a report on the right to employment, on the right to return to one's own country, and on the phenomenon of the "brain drain", i.e. the outflow of trained personnel from developing countries. The Sub-Commission called on Governments, international and non-governmental organizations to respond expeditiously to the Special Rapporteur's questionnaire, requesting the Secretary-General to remind them to do so.

Freedom of speech

On 11 March 1985,[103] the Commission on Human Rights expressed concern at the extensive occurrence, in many parts of the world, of detention of persons who exercised their right to freedom of opinion and expression. The Commission called on States to allow full realization of that right, and appealed to them to ensure respect and support for the rights of those who exercised that right and to release those who had been detained solely for doing so. It affirmed that further national and international measures might be required to ensure respect for that right.

Conscientious objectors

As requested by the Economic and Social Council in 1984,[104] the Secretary-General submitted to the 1985 session of the Commission on Human Rights a report[105] containing comments and observations from States, United Nations bodies and NGOs on the question of conscientious objection to military service. As at 14 February, information had been received from eight countries—Australia, Austria, Cyprus, Czechoslovakia, the Federal Republic of Germany, the Netherlands, Sweden and the United Kingdom—two United Nations organs and nine NGOs.

The Commission decided on 14 March[106] to adjourn until its 1987 session the debate on a draft resolution on the question submitted by Austria, Costa Rica, France, the Netherlands, Spain and the United Kingdom.

Amnesty

In 1985, Special Rapporteur Louis Joinet (France) submitted to the Sub-Commission his study[107] on amnesty laws and their role in the safeguarding and promotion of human rights, taking into account the specific characteristics of various legal systems. The report had been requested in 1984[108] following consideration of an interim report. The Special Rapporteur set out the practices followed by States concerning amnesties and compared them, with a view to deducing rules or constants which might serve as guidelines for authorities proposing to initiate an amnesty, as well as for jurists responsible for drafting legislation—a frame of reference which, he stated, might also be of use to various specialized international supervisory bodies to enable them better to assess the impact of an amnesty law. He concluded that the amnesty process could be effective only if coupled with certain measures: in the short term, the repeal of emergency laws as a corollary of amnesty; in the medium term, the holding of elections; and in the long term, implementation of economic, social and political measures attacking the root causes of conflict or dissension.

The Sub-Commission, on 30 August,[109] expressed appreciation to the Special Rapporteur and recommended that the Commission on Human Rights propose to the Economic and Social Council that the study be published and disseminated as widely as possible in all official United Nations languages.

Independence of the judicial system

A final report on a study of the independence and impartiality of the judiciary, jurors and assessors and the independence of lawyers was submitted to the Sub-Commission in July 1985[110] by Special Rapporteur L. M. Singhvi (India). It included a draft declaration on the independence of justice prepared by the Rapporteur; draft principles on the independence of the legal profession formulated at a May 1982 meeting at Noto, Sicily (Italy), of a Committee of Experts organized by the International Association of Penal Law and the International Commission of Jurists; and a Universal Declaration on the Independence of Justice adopted at the June 1983 World Conference on the Independence of Justice at Montreal, Canada. His research confirmed those principles, the Rapporteur stated, and he suggested that the United Nations adopt a declaration or a convention on the independence of justice and that specific studies investigate violations of the independence of justice. He saw a need for a representative world organization, as a clearinghouse for information, to protect and promote the independence of judges, jurors, assessors and lawyers and to provide education and research.

The Sub-Commission, on 27 August,[111] postponed consideration of the study to its 1986 session, asking the Secretary-General to circulate the study to Sub-Commission members before December 1985 and invite them to submit written comments on it, which the Special Rapporteur would take into account when presenting his report in 1986.

REFERENCES

[1]A/40/677. [2]YUN 1966, p. 423, GA res. 2200 A (XXI), annex, 16 Dec. 1966. [3]YUN 1976, p. 609. [4]A/40/605. [5]E/1985/56. [6]YUN 1984, p. 801. [7]E/1985/22 (res. 1985/45). [8]YUN 1966, p. 419, GA res. 2200 A (XXI), annex, 16 Dec. 1966. [9]A/40/40. [10]YUN 1984, p. 802. [11]E/1985/22 (res. 1985/23). [12]E/CN.4/1986/5 (res. 1985/32). [13]E/CN.4/Sub.2/1985/41. [14]E/CN.4/1986/5 (res. 1985/13). [15]E/1985/22 (res. 1985/4). [16]*Ibid.* (res. 1985/12). [17]*Ibid.* (res. 1985/3). [18]*Ibid.* (res. 1985/5). [19]*Ibid.* (res. 1985/7). [20]*Ibid.* (res. 1985/6). [21]A/40/465 & Add.1,2. [22]YUN 1984, p. 803, GA res. 39/17, 23 Nov. 1984. [23]YUN 1975, p. 599, GA res. 3379(XXX), 10 Nov. 1975. [24]YUN 1984, p. 1067, GA res. 39/40, 5 Dec. 1984. [25]YUN 1981, p. 242. [26]YUN 1978, p. 327. [27]YUN 1983, p. 274. [28]*Ibid.*, p. 1045. [29]YUN 1948-49, p. 535, GA res. 217 A (III), 10 Dec. 1948. [30]YUN 1960, p. 49, GA res. 1514(XV), 14 Dec. 1960. [31]YUN 1984, p. 810. [32]E/CN.4/1985/13. [33]E/1985/22 (res. 1985/9). [34]*Ibid.* (res. 1985/7). [35]YUN 1978, pp. 915 & 916, SC res. 435(1978) & 439(1978), 29 Sep. & 13 Nov. 1978. [36]E/CN.4/1986/5 (res. 1985/4). [37]YUN 1978, p. 915, SC res. 435(1978), 29 Sep. 1978. [38]YUN 1983, p. 1087, GA res. 38/40, 7 Dec. 1983. [39]E/CN.4/Sub.2/1985/12 & Add.1-3. [40]E/CN.4/Sub.2/1985/13. [41]E/CN.4/Sub.2/1985/17. [42]YUN 1978, p. 698. [43]YUN 1980, p. 842. [44]YUN 1981, p. 900. [45]YUN 1982, p. 1079. [46]YUN 1983, p. 838.

(47)YUN 1984, p. 811. (48)*Ibid.*, p. 812, GA dec. 39/418, 13 Dec. 1984. (49)A/C.6/40/L.18. (50)A/40/981. (51)A/C.6/40/L.22. (52)E/CN.4/1986/5 (res. 1985/19). (53)E/1985/22 (res. 1985/33). (54)YUN 1984, p. 813, GA res. 39/46, 10 Dec. 1984. (55)E/1985/22 (res. 1985/18). (56)YUN 1979, p. 854. (57)A/40/604. (58)A/40/191. (59)E/1985/22 (res. 1985/19). (60)YUN 1981, p. 906, GA res. 36/151, 16 Dec. 1981. (61)A/40/876. (62)YUN 1984, p. 820. (63)E/CN.4/Sub.2/1985/20. (64)E/CN.4/1986/5 (res. 1985/26). (65)E/1985/22 (res. 1985/16). (66)E/CN.4/1986/5 (dec. 1985/110). (67)E/CN.4/Sub.2/1985/14. (68)YUN 1984, p. 831. (69)E/CN.4/1986/5 (dec. 1985/108). (70)E/1985/43. (71)YUN 1984, p. 709, ESC res. 1984/50, 25 May 1984. (72)*Ibid.*, p. 707, GA res. 39/118, 14 Dec. 1984. (73)YUN 1980, p. 789, GA dec. 35/437, 15 Dec. 1980. (74)YUN 1982, p. 1078, GA res. 37/192, 18 Dec. 1982. (75)YUN 1984, p. 821. (76)E/1985/22 (res. 1985/46). (77)*Ibid.* (dec. 1985/109). (78)YUN 1984, p. 822, GA res. 39/137, 14 Dec. 1984. (79)*Ibid.*, p. 823, ESC res. 1984/35, 24 May 1984. (80)E/CN.4/1985/17. (81)YUN 1983, p. 843. (82)YUN 1984, p. 823. (83)E/1985/22 (res. 1985/37). (84)A/CONF.121/22/Rev.1 (res. 11). (85)E/1985/22 (res. 1985/15). (86)YUN 1983, p. 279. (87)E/1985/22 (res. 1985/20). (88)E/CN.4/1985/15/Add.1. (89)YUN 1984, p. 826. (90)YUN 1980, p. 843. (91)E/CN.4/1986/18 & Add.1. (92)E/1985/22 (res. 1985/25). (93)YUN 1948-49, p. 613, GA res. 317(IV), annex, 2 Dec. 1949. (94)YUN 1956, p. 228. (95)E/CN.4/Sub.2/1985/25. (96)E/1985/22 (res. 1985/24). (97)YUN 1984, p. 828. (98)E/CN.4/Sub.2/1985/26. (99)E/CN.4/1986/5 (res. 1985/11). (100)E/1985/22 (res. 1985/22). (101)E/CN.4/Sub.2/1985/9. (102)E/CN.4/1986/5 (res. 1985/29). (103)E/1985/22 (res. 1985/17). (104)YUN 1984, p. 829, ESC res. 1984/27, 24 May 1984. (105)E/CN.4/1985/25 & Add.1-4. (106)E/1985/22 (dec. 1985/114). (107)E/CN.4/Sub.2/1985/16/Rev.1. (108)YUN 1984, p. 825. (109)E/CN.4/1986/5 (res. 1985/33). (110)E/CN.4/Sub.2/1985/18 & Add.1-4, Add.5/Rev.1 & Add.6. (111)E/CN.4/1986/5 (dec. 1985/107).

Economic, social and cultural rights

In a September 1985 report[1] on international conditions and human rights (see p. 882), the Secretary-General stated, with regard to economic, social and cultural rights, that the poorest and most vulnerable countries and groups were the hardest hit and the situation continued to give cause for concern. The impact of current international conditions on those rights could best be illustrated by reviewing the situation with respect to the right to food and the right to work. With regard to the former, the World Food Council had in its most recent report characterized the situation as deplorable, referring specifically to the millions of people in Africa threatened by famine, 15 million child deaths annually world-wide from malnutrition and disease and the growing numbers of chronically undernourished.

The widespread non-realization of the right to work had been emphasized in a report, transmitted in April[2] (see p. 877), by the Committee of Experts on the Application of Conventions and Recommendations of the International Labour Organisation on progress in achieving observance of the 1966 International Covenant on Economic, Social and Cultural Rights.[3] The Committee noted that serious problems of unemployment and underemployment in many parts of the world had continued to increase;

such problems tended to be particularly acute in rural areas and less developed regions, and among certain population groups, such as young people, women, older workers or handicapped persons. The Committee recalled that those problems were not only dependent on national policies but were substantially influenced by international economic relations. At the same time that official development assistance to developing countries declined, debt repayment requirements exacerbated economic and social conditions, making it even more difficult for many Governments to ensure full realization of economic, social and cultural rights.

Human Rights Commission action. By a 14 March resolution,[4] adopted by a roll-call vote of 29 to 6, with 5 abstentions, the Commission on Human Rights appealed to States to pursue policies directed towards implementing civil, political, economic, social and cultural rights, and called on them to co-operate in creating conditions conducive to the enjoyment of all human rights. It urged its Sub-Commission to pursue the study on the right to food and invited the Directors-General of ILO, FAO, UNESCO and the World Health Organization (WHO) to submit in 1986 a report on the state of implementation of the rights to work, food, education and health, respectively, so that the Commission could undertake a global assessment of progress and problems in implementing those rights. The Sub-Commission was also requested to examine and update for the Commission's 1987 session the conclusions and recommendations in the 1974 study on *The Realization of Economic, Social and Cultural Rights: Problems, Policies, Progress.*[5]

GENERAL ASSEMBLY ACTION

On 13 December 1985, on the recommendation of the Third Committee, the General Assembly adopted **resolution 40/114**, by recorded vote.

Indivisibility and interdependence of economic, social, cultural, civil and political rights

The General Assembly,

Mindful of the obligations of States under the Charter of the United Nations to promote social progress and better standards of life in larger freedom and universal respect for, and observance of, human rights and fundamental freedoms for all without distinction as to race, sex, language or religion,

Recalling the Universal Declaration of Human Rights, as well as the International Covenant on Economic, Social and Cultural Rights and the International Covenant on Civil and Political Rights,

Acknowledging that the International Covenant on Economic, Social and Cultural Rights and the International Covenant on Civil and Political Rights have created new standards and obligations to which States should conform,

Recalling that 1986 marks the twentieth anniversary of the adoption of the International Covenants on Human Rights,

Also recalling the Declaration on Social Progress and Development, based on the Charter of the United Nations and solemnly proclaimed on 11 December 1969,

Taking note of the *1985 Report on the World Social Situation*,

Reaffirming the provisions of its resolution 32/130 of 16 December 1977 that all human rights and fundamental freedoms are indivisible and interdependent and that the promotion and protection of one category of rights can never exempt or excuse States from the promotion and protection of the other rights,

Convinced that the full realization of civil and political rights is inseparably linked with the enjoyment of economic, social and cultural rights,

Convinced also that the achievement of lasting progress in the implementation of human rights is dependent upon sound and effective national and international policies of economic, social and political development,

Desirous of removing all obstacles to the full realization of human rights, in particular colonialism, neo-colonialism, racism, racial discrimination in all its forms, *apartheid*, foreign intervention, occupation, aggression, discrimination and domination,

Recognizing the fundamental rights of every people to exercise full sovereignty over its natural wealth and resources,

Recognizing also that the realization of the right to development could help to promote the enjoyment of economic, social and cultural rights,

Reaffirming that there is a close relationship between disarmament and development, that progress in the field of disarmament could considerably promote progress in the field of development and that resources released through disarmament measures would contribute to the economic and social development and well-being of all peoples, in particular those of the developing countries,

Recalling Commission on Human Rights resolution 1985/42 of 14 March 1985, in which the Commission stated that the promotion and implementation of economic, social and cultural rights and the obstacles to their realization have not received sufficient attention within the framework of United Nations organs,

Requesting the Secretary-General to enhance his efforts under the programme of advisory services to States in the implementation of the International Covenants on Human Rights,

1. *Recognizes* that equal attention should be given to the implementation, promotion and protection of economic, social and cultural rights and civil and political rights;

2. *Appeals* to all States, on the occasion of the twentieth anniversary of the adoption of the International Covenants on Human Rights, to pursue policies directed to the full implementation of the rights contained therein;

3. *Requests* the Commission on Human Rights to continue its consideration of the realization of economic, social and cultural rights and to submit to the General Assembly at its forty-second session, through the Economic and Social Council, its views and recommendations on these human rights;

4. *Welcomes* the decision of the Economic and Social Council, in its resolution 1985/17 of 28 May 1985, to establish the Committee on Economic, Social and Cultural Rights, which will be entrusted from 1987 on with the important task of overseeing the implementation of the International Covenant on Economic, Social and Cultural Rights;

5. *Encourages* Governments to give careful consideration to nominations for membership of the Committee on Economic, Social and Cultural Rights in due recognition of the status of Committee members as experts with recognized competence in the field of human rights, serving in their personal capacity;

6. *Urges* the Secretary-General to take determined steps, within existing resources, to give publicity to the Committee on Economic, Social and Cultural Rights and to ensure that it receives full administrative support in order to enable it to commence its functions effectively;

7. *Decides* to convene, on 16 December 1986, during its forty-first session, a commemorative plenary meeting of the General Assembly devoted to the twentieth anniversary of the adoption of the International Covenants on Human Rights;

8. *Decides also* to discuss at its forty-first session, under the item entitled "International Covenants on Human Rights", the question of the indivisibility and interdependence of economic, social, cultural, civil and political rights.

General Assembly resolution 40/114

13 December 1985   Meeting 116   134-1-19 (recorded vote)

Approved by Third Committee (A/40/983) by recorded vote (119-1-18), 2 December (meeting 60); 8-nation draft (A/C.3/40/L.55), orally amended by Pakistan; agenda item 104.

Sponsors: Bulgaria, Byelorussian SSR, Gambia, German Democratic Republic, Hungary, Mongolia, Nicaragua, Syrian Arab Republic.

Meeting numbers. GA 40th session: 3rd Committee 46-48, 50-53, 58, 60; plenary 116.

Recorded vote in Assembly as follows:

In favour: Afghanistan, Algeria, Angola, Antigua and Barbuda, Argentina, Australia, Bahamas, Bahrain, Bangladesh, Barbados, Belize, Benin, Bhutan, Bolivia, Botswana, Brazil, Brunei Darussalam, Bulgaria, Burkina Faso, Burma, Burundi, Byelorussian SSR, Cameroon, Cape Verde, Central African Republic, Chad, Chile, China, Colombia, Comoros, Congo, Costa Rica, Cuba, Cyprus, Czechoslovakia, Democratic Kampuchea, Democratic Yemen, Djibouti, Dominica, Dominican Republic, Ecuador, Egypt, El Salvador, Equatorial Guinea, Ethiopia, Fiji, Gabon, Gambia, German Democratic Republic, Ghana, Greece, Guatemala, Guinea, Guinea-Bissau, Guyana, Haiti, Honduras, Hungary, India, Indonesia, Iran, Iraq, Ireland, Ivory Coast, Jamaica, Jordan, Kenya, Kuwait, Lao People's Democratic Republic, Lebanon, Lesotho, Liberia, Libyan Arab Jamahiriya, Madagascar, Malaysia, Maldives, Mali, Malta, Mauritania, Mauritius, Mexico, Mongolia, Morocco, Mozambique, Nepal, Netherlands, New Zealand, Nicaragua, Niger, Nigeria, Oman, Pakistan, Panama, Papua New Guinea, Paraguay, Peru, Philippines, Poland, Qatar, Romania, Rwanda, Saint Lucia, Samoa, Sao Tome and Principe, Saudi Arabia, Senegal, Sierra Leone, Singapore, Somalia, Spain, Sri Lanka, Sudan, Suriname, Swaziland, Syrian Arab Republic, Thailand, Togo, Trinidad and Tobago, Tunisia, Turkey, Uganda, Ukrainian SSR, USSR, United Arab Emirates, United Republic of Tanzania, Uruguay, Vanuatu, Venezuela, Viet Nam, Yemen, Yugoslavia, Zaire, Zambia, Zimbabwe.

Against: United States.

Abstaining: Austria, Belgium, Canada, Denmark, Finland, France, Germany, Federal Republic of, Grenada, Iceland, Israel, Italy, Japan, Luxembourg, Malawi, Norway, Portugal, Saint Christopher and Nevis, Sweden, United Kingdom.

Separate recorded votes were taken on the eighth, tenth and eleventh preambular paragraphs in both the Assembly and the Third Committee. The eighth paragraph was adopted by 125 votes to 7, with 20 abstentions; its approval in the Committee was by 107 votes to 8, with 18 abstentions. The Assembly vote on the tenth paragraph was 130 to 1, with 23 abstentions; the Committee had approved it by 113 to 1, with 21 abstentions. The vote on the eleventh paragraph was 130 to 7, with 17 abstentions in the Assembly and 113 to 7, with 16 abstentions, in Committee.

A Moroccan oral proposal to reverse the order in which the Covenants were listed in the second and third preambular paragraphs was not accepted.

The United States regarded the text as an attempt by a small group to pursue its political ends and said the text aimed at redefining and reinterpreting the concept of human rights set forth in the principal international instruments; it was unable to support the attempt to place the controversial concept of the indivisibility, inseparability or interdependence of various categories of rights as a permanent item on the Committee's agenda.

The Federal Republic of Germany said the ambitious title of the text did not have much to do with its content; the term "interdependence" was incorrect since there was only a straightforward relationship between different kinds of rights. Moreover, the wording in the eleventh preambular paragraph did not correspond to the terms used in the International Covenant on Economic, Social and Cultural Rights—a point also noted by Ireland, Italy, Japan, the Netherlands and the United Kingdom—and the thirteenth preambular paragraph addressed questions that were within the exclusive competence of other Main Committees.

Similarly, Italy and the United Kingdom could not accept the assertion that all human rights were interdependent; although they agreed that a relationship between both sets of rights existed, they could not accept that the exercise of civil and political rights should be made dependent on the realization of economic, social and cultural rights. Costa Rica held a similar view.

Ireland could not accept that the realization of one category of rights should be subordinated to the other; it had serious reservations regarding the agenda item under which the initiative had been taken and on certain paragraphs based on the same notion. Australia added that it should not be suggested that the realization of economic rights took priority over or constituted a pre-condition for the exercise of civil and political rights. Australia and the Netherlands interpreted the eighth preambular paragraph as meaning that the realization of both categories of rights was mutually reinforcing.

Japan also had difficulty in accepting the concept of indivisibility and interdependence of both categories of rights; it felt that the necessary weight should be given to the essential difference between the rights set forth in the Covenants, and the progressive realization of one category of rights should not delay enjoyment of the other.

Austria felt that the term interdependence was not sufficiently clear; both sets of rights should receive equal attention and be implemented equally. Instead of referring to the interdependence of both categories of rights, Uruguay remarked, it would have been better to speak of the indivisibility of those rights and the links between them.

The United Kingdom also could not accept the implication that the principal obstacles to the realization of human rights had been set forth in the tenth preambular paragraph, since, in order for that provision to be comprehensive, totalitarian ideologies should also be added, a view shared by the Federal Republic of Germany. The United Kingdom also did not accept that the non-self-governing status of certain Territories in itself deprived their inhabitants of the full enjoyment of their human rights if they were free to exercise their right to self-determination. It also had difficulties accepting the twelfth and thirteenth preambular paragraphs.

New Zealand said it would have preferred the eighth preambular paragraph to have been worded so as to be clearly in accordance with the central proposition in operative paragraph 1.

Egypt had reservations concerning the expression "within existing resources" in paragraph 6.

Australia and Japan had difficulty with the concept of the right to development; Australia said the right was not recognized in the Covenant and therefore could not be considered as being inherent in its implementation.

Canada stated it had difficulties in accepting the inclusion in the preamble of references to the world social situation, disarmament and the right to development, which were not relevant to the question under consideration.

Covenant on Economic, Social and Cultural Rights

As at 31 December 1985, the International Covenant on Economic, Social and Cultural Rights, adopted by the General Assembly in 1966[3] and in force since 1976,[6] had been ratified or acceded to by 85 States. Greece and San Marino became parties to it during 1985.

The Secretary-General reported on the status of ratifications or accessions to the Covenant as at 1 September,[7] as well as on other questions related to its implementation (see p. 891).

Implementation of the Covenant

The Secretary-General, in a February note,[8] reported on the status of the submission of reports by States parties to the Covenant.

The Sessional Working Group of Governmental Experts on the Implementation of the Covenant met for its seventh session in New York from 22 April to 9 May 1985.[9] The Group was set up in 1978[10] and restructured in 1982[11] to comprise 15 States parties to the Covenant (see APPENDIX III). The Group examined 13 reports from 11 States parties on their implementation of specific provisions of the Covenant. On each report, the Group heard statements by, and put questions to, the State representatives concerned. Under a programme established by the Council in 1976,[12] reports required under the Covenant were to be submitted in three biennial cycles or stages, each stage covering a related group of articles of the Covenant.

For the first stage (due 1 September 1977), the Group examined a report from Iraq,[13] concerning rights covered by articles 6 to 9 (the right to work and to favourable conditions of work, the rights of trade unionists, the right to social security). At their request, consideration of first-stage reports from the Democratic People's Republic of Korea[14] and Mexico[15] was deferred. Second-stage reports (due 1 September 1983) examined came from Australia,[16] Bulgaria,[17] the German Democratic Republic,[18] Madagascar,[19] Romania[20] and the United Kingdom;[21] one from Colombia[22] was deferred at its request.

The Group examined an initial report (due 1 September 1979) from Portugal[23] on rights covered by articles 10 to 12 (protection of the family, mothers and children, an adequate living standard, and physical and mental health). Consideration of a report from Hungary[24] was deferred at its request.

Also examined were reports (due 1 September 1981) on implementation of articles 13 to 15 (education, including compulsory education, and participation in cultural life) from France,[25] Guyana,[26] Iraq,[27] Nicaragua[28] and Portugal.[29]

In addition, the Group considered an April 1985 note[2] by the Secretary-General transmitting the seventh report of the Committee of Experts on the Application of Conventions and Recommendations of ILO (see p. 874). The report detailed progress in observing the provisions of articles 6 to 9 of the Covenant, within the scope of ILO's activities, by 28 respondent States.

The Group suggested to the Economic and Social Council that it might wish to remind States parties of their obligation to submit reports and urge them to cover the entire cycle of initial reports before submitting second periodic reports; the Group should be instructed not to consider second periodic reports if that condition was not met. The Secretary-General should be requested to revise the guidelines for preparation of reports in accordance with the Group's suggestions; in the mean time, States parties should comply with the existing guidelines. Reports should be balanced, go beyond a mere transcription of legislative and administrative measures or a reproduction of statistical data; they should be limited to a reasonable length and contain a brief introduction with general information on the country and basic data on economic, social and constitutional conditions.

Reports scheduled for consideration by the Group should be made available at least six weeks before the opening of the Group's session. Each State party should send an expert on the subjects covered in its report. If necessary, additional information should be supplied within one year.

The Group recommended that the Council request the agencies to provide their views on implementation of the Covenant within their special fields of competence. It drew attention to the fact that its meetings were public and States parties, United Nations Members and agencies could participate. It urged the Council to ensure continued press coverage of its proceedings.

The Group expressed serious concern about non-submission and delays in the submission of reports; the Council might wish to consider requesting States parties to inform it of difficulties in preparing and submitting their reports. It emphasized the need for the Secretary-General to devise and implement a programme of advisory services and technical assistance on report submission. The Group recommended to the Council that, under the second and subsequent cycles, reports be submitted every three years to allow more time for their preparation.

ECONOMIC AND SOCIAL COUNCIL ACTION

Taking note of the Working Group's recommendation, the Economic and Social Council decided on 28 May, by **decision 1985/132**, to prolong by one year the periodicity of reporting under the second and subsequent cycles of the reporting procedure, while maintaining the current biennial reporting for the first cycle under article 16 of the Covenant.

The text[30] was proposed by Australia, Bulgaria, Canada, Colombia, Costa Rica, Denmark, the German Democratic Republic, the Federal Republic of Germany, Guinea, Italy, Morocco, the Netherlands, Senegal, Spain, Uruguay and Venezuela, and adopted without vote.

GENERAL ASSEMBLY ACTION

Commending, by **resolution 40/115**, the States parties to the Covenant that had submitted their reports under article 16, and urging those that had not to do so as soon as possible, the Assembly noted with satisfaction that an increasing number of parties had been represented by experts for the presentation of their reports, and hoped they would arrange such representation in the future. It again urged States to become parties to the Covenant, emphasized the importance of strict compliance with their obligations thereunder, recommended that they continually review any reservation they might have made in respect of its provisions, welcomed the Council's decision to establish the Committee on Economic, Social and Cultural Rights (see below) to oversee implementation, and encouraged Governments to publish the text of the Covenant in as many languages as possible and distribute and make it known as widely as possible (see also p. 891).

Composition, organization and administrative arrangements of the Working Group

Taking into account the fact that it had not been possible to achieve full attendance of all its members, the Sessional Working Group discussed several options for improving its composition, organization and administrative arrangements.

The Commission on Human Rights, on 14 March,[31] had stated that it looked forward to the Secretary-General's report to the Council on that subject and welcomed the Council's 1984 decision[32] to undertake its triennial review of the composition, organization and administrative arrangements early in 1985 to allow time for a full discussion.

The Secretary-General submitted his report[33] to the Council in March, providing a comparative analysis of the composition, organizational structure and administrative arrangements of the Sessional Working Group and those of other bodies carrying out similar functions under existing international human rights instruments, including those bodies' composition, elections and membership, members' qualifications, number, duration and timing of sessions, and annual reports.

ECONOMIC AND SOCIAL COUNCIL ACTION

On 28 May 1985, the Economic and Social Council adopted **resolution 1985/17** by recorded vote, renaming the Sessional Working Group the Committee on Economic, Social and Cultural Rights, increasing its membership from 15 to 18, and setting out rules for its elections, periodicity of meetings and reporting procedures; its venue would alternate between New York and Geneva.

Review of the composition, organization and administrative arrangements of the Sessional Working Group of Governmental Experts on the Implementation of the InternationalCovenant on Economic, Social and Cultural Rights

The Economic and Social Council,

Recalling its resolution 1988(LX) of 11 May 1976, by which it noted the important responsibilities placed upon the Economic and Social Council by the International Covenant on Economic, Social and Cultural Rights, in particular those resulting from articles 21 and 22 of the Covenant, and expressed its readiness to fulfil those responsibilities,

Recalling its decision 1978/10 of 3 May 1978, by which it decided to establish a Sessional Working Group on the Implementation of the International Covenant on Economic, Social and Cultural Rights, for the purpose of assisting the Council in the consideration of reports submitted by States parties to the Covenant in accordance with Council resolution 1988(LX), and determined the composition of the Working Group,

Recalling also its resolution 1979/43 of 11 May 1979, by which it approved the methods of work of the Working Group, and its decision 1981/158 of 8 May 1981, by which it incorporated certain changes in, and modified the methods of work of, the Working Group,

Recalling further its resolution 1982/33 of 6 May 1982, by which it modified the composition, organization and administrative arrangements of the Sessional Working Group of Governmental Experts and decided to review the composition, organization and administrative arrangements of the Group at its first regular session of 1985,

Having considered the report of the Secretary-General on the composition, organization and administrative arrangements of the Sessional Working Group of Governmental Experts on the Implementation of the International Covenant on Economic, Social and Cultural Rights and other bodies established in accordance with existing international instruments in the field of human rights,

Having considered the report of the Sessional Working Group of Governmental Experts on the Implementation of the International Covenant on Economic, Social and Cultural Rights,

Decides that:

(*a*) The Working Group established by Economic and Social Council decision 1978/10 and modified by Council decision 1981/158 and resolution 1982/33 shall be renamed "Committee on Economic, Social and Cultural Rights" (hereinafter referred to as "the Committee");

(*b*) The Committee shall have eighteen members who shall be experts with recognized competence in the field of human rights, serving in their personal capacity, due consideration being given to equitable geographical distribution and to the representation of different forms of social and legal systems; to this end, fifteen seats will be equally distributed among the regional groups, while the additional three seats will be allocated in accordance with the increase in the total number of States parties per regional group;

(*c*) The members of the Committee shall be elected by the Council by secret ballot from a list of persons nominated by States parties to the International Covenant on Economic, Social and Cultural Rights under the following conditions:

(i) The members of the Committee shall be elected for a term of four years and shall be eligible for re-election at the end of their term, if renominated;

(ii) One half of the membership of the Committee shall be renewed every second year, bearing in mind the need to maintain the equitable geographical distribution mentioned in subparagraph (*b*) above;

(iii) The first elections shall take place during the Council's first regular session of 1986; immediately after the first elections, the President of the Council shall choose by lot the names of nine members whose term shall expire at the end of two years;

(iv) The terms of office of members elected to the Committee shall begin on 1 January following their election and expire on 31 December following the election of members that are to succeed them as members of the Committee;

(v) Subsequent elections shall take place every second year during the first regular session of the Council;

(vi) At least four months before the date of each election to the Committee the Secretary-General shall address a written invitation to the States parties to the Covenant to submit their nominations for membership of the Committee within three months; the Secretary-General shall prepare a list of the persons thus nominated, with an indication of the States parties which have nominated them, and shall submit it to the Council no later than one month before the date of each election;

(d) The Committee shall meet annually for a period of up to three weeks, taking into account the number of reports to be examined by the Committee, with the venue alternating between Geneva and New York;

(e) The members of the Committee shall receive travel and subsistence expenses from United Nations resources;

(f) The Committee shall submit to the Council a report on its activities, including a summary of its consideration of the reports submitted by States parties to the Covenant, and shall make suggestions and recommendations of a general nature on the basis of its consideration of those reports and of the reports submitted by the specialized agencies, in order to assist the Council to fulfil, in particular, its responsibilities under articles 21 and 22 of the Covenant;

(g) The Secretary-General shall provide the Committee with summary records of its proceedings, which shall be made available to the Council at the same time as the report of the Committee; the Secretary-General shall further provide the Committee with the necessary staff and facilities for the effective performance of its functions, bearing in mind the need to give adequate publicity to its work;

(h) The procedures and methods of work established by Council resolution 1979/43 and the other resolutions and decisions referred to in the preamble to the present resolution shall remain in force in so far as they are not superseded or modified by the present resolution;

(i) The Council shall review the composition, organization and administrative arrangements of the Committee at its first regular session of 1990, and subsequently every five years, taking into account the principle of equitable geographical distribution of its membership.

Economic and Social Council resolution 1985/17

28 May 1985   Meeting 22   43-1-4 (recorded vote)

24-nation draft (E/1985/L.29), orally revised; agenda item 3.
Sponsors: Australia, Bolivia, Bulgaria, Colombia, Costa Rica, Denmark, France, Gambia, German Democratic Republic, Germany, Federal Republic of, Guinea, Italy, Luxembourg, Mongolia, Morocco, Netherlands, Nicaragua, Norway, Senegal, Sierra Leone, Spain, Sweden, Uruguay, Venezuela.
Financial implications. S-G, E/1985/L.31.
Meeting numbers. ESC 21, 22.

Recorded vote in Council as follows:

In favour: Algeria, Argentina, Botswana, Bulgaria, Canada, Colombia, Congo, Costa Rica, Djibouti, Ecuador, Finland, France, German Democratic Republic, Germany, Federal Republic of, Guinea, Iceland, India, Lebanon, Luxembourg, Mexico, Morocco, Netherlands, New Zealand, Nigeria, Papua New Guinea, Poland, Romania, Rwanda, Saudi Arabia, Senegal, Sierra Leone, Somalia, Spain, Sri Lanka, Suriname, Sweden, Turkey, Uganda, USSR, United Kingdom, Venezuela, Yugoslavia, Zaire.
Against: United States.
Abstaining: Bangladesh, Brazil, Japan, Malaysia.

The United States, which had asked for the vote, said that although it understood that some adjustments might be desirable, it was not convinced that the conversion of the Sessional Working Group into a Committee of experts was the most appropriate manner for the Council to fulfil its responsibility under the Covenant; at the time of extreme budgetary austerity, the related expenses were not justified.

The United Kingdom believed that the proposed changes would enhance the application of the Covenant and the attitude of States towards it; efforts should be made to cover the new expense by redeployment.

The USSR supported the text, saying it ensured the participation of experts from all States and might even effect savings in the Committee's expenses.

By **decision 1985/161** of 28 May, the Economic and Social Council approved the provisional agenda for 1986 of the Sessional Working Group. By **decision 1985/162** of the same date, the Council decided on the membership of the Bureau for 1986 of the Working Group (see APPENDIX III). Both decisions had been recommended to the Council by the Working Group and both were adopted by the Council without vote.

GENERAL ASSEMBLY ACTION

On 18 December, on the recommendation of the Fifth (Administrative and Budgetary) Committee, the General Assembly adopted **section VII of resolution 40/252**, without vote.

Venue of the meeting of the Committee on Economic, Social and Cultural Rights in 1988

[*The General Assembly* . . .]

Invites the Economic and Social Council to reconsider its decision to allow the Committee on Economic, Social and Cultural Rights to meet in New York in 1988;

. . .

General Assembly resolution 40/252, section VII

18 December 1985   Meeting 122   Adopted without vote

Approved by Fifth Committee (A/40/1069) without objection, 2 December (meeting 52); oral proposal by Chairman, based on recommendation of Committee on Conferences (A/C.5/40/13/Add.2); agenda item 116.
Financial implications. S-G, A/C.5/40/13 & Corr.1 & Add.1; ACABQ, A/40/7/Add.5.

Right to development

Human Rights Commission action. By a 14 March 1985 resolution,[34] adopted by a roll-call vote of 25 to 10, with 6 abstentions, the Commission on Human Rights reiterated that the right to development was an inalienable human right and that equality of opportunities for development was a prerogative both of nations and of individuals. The Commission decided to transmit to the General Assembly the part of its report and summary records that dealt with that right. It decided to convene its Working Group of Governmental Experts on the Right to Development for three weeks in January 1986 to study ways to promote that right, so that the Group could submit its proposals to the Commission.

By a May 1985 note,[35] the Secretary-General transmitted to the Economic and Social Council and the General Assembly the Commission's resolution and a draft declaration on the right to development, which had been annexed to a letter[36] of 7 March from Yugoslavia to the Commission Chairman.

ECONOMIC AND SOCIAL COUNCIL ACTION

In May, on the recommendation of its Second Committee, the Economic and Social Council adopted **decision 1985/149**, by roll-call vote.

The right to development

At its 25th plenary meeting, on 30 May 1985, the Council, noting Commission on Human Rights resolution 1985/43 of 14 March 1985, approved the Commission's decision to transmit to the General Assembly, through the Council, the report of the Working Group of Governmental Experts on the Right to Development, the part of the report of the Commission on Human Rights dealing with the right to development, the summary records of the Commission's discussion on the question during its forty-first session and any other relevant documents, so as to enable the Assembly to adopt a declaration on the right to development. The Council further approved the Commission's decision to convene the Working Group for three weeks in January 1986 to study the measures necessary to promote the right to development and its request to the Secretary-General to provide all necessary assistance to the Working Group.

Economic and Social Council decision 1985/149

37-9-6 (roll-call vote)

Approved by Second Committee (E/1985/95 & Corr.1) by recorded vote (34-9-7), 24 May (meeting 15); draft by Commission on Human Rights (E/1985/22); agenda item 16.

Roll-call vote in Council as follows:

In favour: Algeria, Argentina, Bangladesh, Botswana, Brazil, Bulgaria, China, Colombia, Congo, Costa Rica, Djibouti, Ecuador, German Democratic Republic, Guinea, Haiti, India, Indonesia, Lebanon, Malaysia, Mexico, Morocco, Nigeria, Papua New Guinea, Poland, Romania, Rwanda, Saudi Arabia, Sierra Leone, Sri Lanka, Suriname, Thailand, Uganda, USSR, Venezuela, Yugoslavia, Zaire, Zimbabwe.

Against: Canada, Finland, Germany, Federal Republic of, Iceland, Japan, New Zealand, Sweden, United Kingdom, United States.

Abstaining: France, Luxembourg, Netherlands, Somalia, Spain, Turkey.

Speaking after the vote, the Netherlands said the text gave effect to a Commission resolution which had constituted a regrettable break with the consensus approach followed theretofore by the Commission on the question. Human rights could not be unilaterally proclaimed; they required universality, which formed the corner-stone of international law. Consensus was essential, the Federal Republic of Germany said, if the right to development was to become recognized as a universal right. Japan agreed that an important instrument such as a declaration on the right to development required wide consultations and had no value unless it was adopted by consensus. This view was shared by the United Kingdom.

The Netherlands and Japan found unacceptable the decision to convene the Working Group for three weeks in January 1986, because, they said, that would prejudge the outcome of the General Assembly debate.

Japan and Sweden, the latter speaking also on behalf of Finland and Iceland, said they considered it premature to refer the matter to the Assembly; it was unacceptable to schedule a meeting to discuss measures of implementation even before

the right to development had been defined and a declaration adopted.

The Federal Republic of Germany held a similar view; the concept of a right to development was relatively new both in national and international law and practice, and extreme care must be taken to arrive at a precise definition of its nature and scope. The Working Group had not even arrived at tentative recommendations, it added. To convene the Working Group to study the implementation of a right before an accepted definition existed was not only illogical but also appeared to contradict the Group's mandate.

France was opposed to giving the Assembly the task of drafting the basic principles.

The United Kingdom said it voted against the text mainly for procedural reasons; a wider measure of agreement should have been achieved before it was referred to the Assembly. It was illogical to reconvene the Working Group if the Commission was now transmitting its work to the Assembly; it was not even clear that there was a mandate for reconvening the Group since it had been originally established to do work different from that which the decision would require it to complete.

New Zealand also considered it premature and prejudicial to forward the Working Group's documentation to the Assembly at the current stage.

GENERAL ASSEMBLY ACTION

By **decision 40/425** adopted on 13 December, on the recommendation of the Third Committee,[37] the General Assembly, having considered the question of a draft declaration on the right to development, decided to transmit the draft and all relevant documents, including an amendment by Pakistan,[38] to its 1986 session, with a view to considering the question then.

The decision, approved by the Committee on 29 November without vote, was orally proposed by Yugoslavia on behalf of a group of sponsors that had also submitted a draft resolution[39] by which the Assembly would have adopted a declaration on the right to development: Bangladesh, Brazil, Bulgaria, Colombia, Cyprus, Ethiopia, German Democratic Republic, Guyana, Nigeria, Peru, United Republic of Tanzania, Yugoslavia. An amendment to the draft declaration, proposed by France and the Netherlands,[40] would incorporate article 1, paragraph 2, of the International Covenant on Civil and Political Rights[41] into a provision stating that the right to development implied full realization of the right to self-determination, which included the inalienable right to sovereignty over natural wealth and resources.

Pakistan's amendment would add a new article 4 stating that the achievement of the right to development required concerted international and national efforts to eliminate economic deprivation, hunger and disease in all parts of the world without discrimination, and identifying the objectives of international co-operation in that respect.

Introducing the draft resolution for the sponsors, Yugoslavia said the original draft declaration[35] transmitted to the Council and Assembly had been slightly revised to meet the concerns of a number of delegations; the sponsors were working to achieve consensus. Subsequently, in the absence of that consensus, Yugoslavia and the sponsors proposed the decision to defer consideration of the draft.

Among the documents to be forwarded to the Assembly's 1986 session in accordance with the decision was a draft declaration[42] on the right to development submitted to the Third Committee by India, on behalf of the experts from the non-aligned countries of the Working Group of Governmental Experts of the Commission on Human Rights.

Also on the Third Committee's recommendation, the Assembly adopted, without vote, **decision 40/427** on 13 December, by which it considered that the meeting of that Working Group scheduled for January 1986 should be postponed, so that the Commission at its 1986 session could provide guidance to the Group in the light of the Assembly's current discussions and decisions. The Committee approved the text, orally proposed by its Chairman, without vote on 6 December.

In **resolution 40/124**, the Assembly expressed concern at the current situation with regard to the achievement of the objectives and goals for establishing a new international economic order and the adverse effects of that situation on the full realization of human rights, in particular the right to development, which, the Assembly reaffirmed, was an inalienable human right. The Assembly again requested the Commission to take the necessary measures to promote that right, and welcomed its decision concerning the future work of the Working Group. It also requested the Secretary-General to submit in 1986 information on the Group's progress.

Right to food

In a progress report to the Sub-Commission,[43] Special Rapporteur Asbjorn Eide (Norway), entrusted by the Economic and Social Council in 1983[44] with the preparation of a study on the right to adequate food as a human right, stated that he had found it desirable to postpone completion of the study until 1986 because of certain ongoing activities at the international level—food-related conferences, committee meetings, studies, workshops—the outcome of which should be reported in the final study. A draft of the study's first five chapters had been submitted in 1984.[45]

At the intergovernmental level, the Special Rapporteur reported, the Director-General of FAO, at the request of the Committee on World Food Security, had prepared a draft text on a World Food Security Compact which addressed several issues of significance for the current study. The Compact (later adopted by the FAO Conference in November 1985) sought the achievement of everyone's fundamental right to be free from hunger and to make food security an integral objective of economic and social plans. According to the Compact, action should be aimed at attaining desirable levels of food production, increasing stability of food supply, and ensuring access to food supplies for those in need. Food should not be used to exert political pressure. Governments should give overriding priority to food security and reaffirm their commitment to strengthen global food security. The Compact, he said, was not cast in binding legal terms, but rather was intended as a set of moral and political commitments.

The Special Rapporteur concluded that interest in the right to food had substantially increased.

The Sub-Commission decided on 22 August[46] to invite the Special Rapporteur to present his study to the 1986 session.

In a 14 March resolution[4] on the realization of economic, social and cultural rights, the Commission on Human Rights had urged the Sub-Commission to pursue the study on the right to food as a priority matter and submit it to the Commission as soon as possible. It invited the Director-General of FAO to submit to it in 1986 a concise report on the state of implementation of the right to food.

Popular participation and human rights

Human Rights Commission action. Taking note of a final study[47] by the Secretary-General on popular participation in its various forms as an important factor in development and in the full realization of all human rights, the Commission on Human Rights requested on 14 March[48] that the study be submitted to the General Assembly and circulated to Member States, United Nations organs and agencies and NGOs for comments. The Secretary-General was requested to submit to the Commission a report containing those comments.

In his study, requested in 1983,[49] the Secretary-General described the evolution of the concept of popular participation and examined the relationships between participation and development and participation and human rights. He also analysed the question of recognizing popular participation as a right in national and international legislation. Although seldom explicitly guaranteed as a right in national legislation, there seemed to be a growing trend towards its recognition as a right in one or more areas of economic, social and political life, he stated, for example with regard to trade union rights, enterprise councils and membership of co-operatives. In international legal instruments, he said, the right to popular participation did not appear to be expressly established as such; on the other hand, a number of international texts of varying legal nature contained elements of it, some of which went so far as to enunciate a global right to participation.

The Secretary-General reported to the Assembly on the topic in August,[50] pursuant to an Assembly request of 1983,[51] reviewing progress made since then in the consideration of the question by the Commission on Human Rights and the Economic and Social Council.

GENERAL ASSEMBLY ACTION

On 13 December 1985, on the recommendation of the Third Committee, the General Assembly adopted **resolution 40/99**, without vote.

Popular participation in its various forms as an important factor in development and in the full realization of all human rights
The General Assembly,

Recalling its resolutions 34/152 of 17 December 1979, 37/55 of 3 December 1982 and 38/24 of 22 November 1983,

Taking note of Economic and Social Council resolution 1983/31 of 27 May 1983 and decision 1984/131 of 24 May 1984, as well as of Commission on Human Rights resolution 1985/44 of 14 March 1985,

Reaffirming that popular participation in all sectors of public life, including the participation of workers in management and workers' self-management where they exist, constitutes an important factor in socio-economic development and in the full realization of all human rights and the dignity of the human person,

1. *Takes note* of the study by the Secretary-General;

2. *Invites* Governments, the concerned specialized agencies and other organizations of the United Nations system and the relevant non-governmental organizations to transmit to the Secretary-General their comments on the study;

3. *Requests* the Commission on Human Rights to continue to consider at its forty-second and, if desired by the Commission, at its forty-third, forty-fourth and forty-fifth sessions, the question of popular participation in its various forms as an important factor in the full realization of all human rights, and to inform the General Assembly at its forty-fourth session, through the Economic and Social Council, of the results of that consideration;

4. *Decides* to continue the consideration of this question at its forty-fourth session, in the context of the item relating to the world social situation, under the sub-item entitled "Popular participation in its various forms as an important factor in development and in the full realization of all human rights".

General Assembly resolution 40/99

13 December 1985   Meeting 116   Adopted without vote

Approved by Third Committee (A/40/963) without vote, 11 November (meeting 37); 16-nation draft (A/C.3/40/L.19), orally revised; agenda item 90 (b).

Sponsors: Algeria, Bangladesh, China, Cuba, Cyprus, India, Iraq, Libyan Arab Jamahiriya, Madagascar, Mexico, Poland, Romania, Sri Lanka, Syrian Arab Republic, Yemen, Yugoslavia.
Meeting numbers. GA 40th session: 3rd Committee 16-23, 30, 37; plenary 116.

In **resolution 40/124**, the Assembly reaffirmed that, in order to facilitate the full enjoyment of all rights and complete personal dignity, it was necessary to promote the rights to education, work, health and proper nourishment through the adoption of measures at the national level, including those that provided for workers' participation in management.

REFERENCES

[1]A/40/677. [2]E/1985/63. [3]YUN 1966, p. 419, GA res. 2200 A (XXI), annex, 16 Dec. 1966. [4]E./1985/22 (res. 1985/42). [5]YUN 1974, p. 679. [6]YUN 1976, p. 609. [7]A/40/605. [8]E/1985/52. [9]E/1985/18. [10]YUN 1978, p. 727, ESC res. 1978/10, 3 May 1978. [11]YUN 1982, p. 1090, ESC res. 1982/33, 6 May 1982. [12]YUN 1976, p. 615, ESC res. 1988(LX), 11 May 1976. [13]E/1984/6/Add.3,8. [14]E/1984/6/Add.7. [15]E/1984/6/Add.2,10. [16]E/1984/7/Add.22. [17]E/1984/7/Add.18. [18]E/1984/7/Add.3,23. [19]E/1984/7/Add.19. [20]E/1984/7/Add.17. [21]E/1984/7/Add.20. [22]E/1984/7/Add.21. [23]E/1980/6/Add.35/Rev.1. [24]E/1980/6/Add.37. [25]E/1982/3/Add.30 & Corr.1. [26]E/1982/3/Add.32. [27]E/1982/3/Add.26. [28]E/1982/3/Add.31 & Corr.1. [29]E/1982/3/Add.27/Rev.1. [30]E/1985/L.30. [31]E/1985/22 (res. 1985/45). [32]YUN 1984, p. 833, ESC res. 1984/9, 24 May 1984. [33]E/1985/17. [34]E/1985/22 (res. 1985/43). [35]A/40/277-E/1985/70. [36]E/CN.4/1985/62. [37]A/40/970. [38]A/C.3/40/L.60. [39]A/C.3/40/L.53. [40]A/C.3/40/L.63. [41]YUN 1966, p. 423, GA res. 2200 A (XXI), annex, 16 Dec. 1966. [42]A/C.3/40/11. [43]E/CN.4/Sub.2/1985/23. [44]YUN 1983, p. 857, ESC dec. 1983/140, 27 May 1983. [45]YUN 1984, p. 837. [46]E/CN.4/1986/5 (dec. 1985/105). [47]E/CN.4/1985/10 & Add.1,2. [48]E/1985/22 (res. 1985/44). [49]YUN 1983, p. 730, ESC res. 1983/31, 27 May 1983. [50]A/40/513 & Corr.1. [51]YUN 1983, p. 730, GA res. 38/24, 22 Nov. 1983.

Advancement of human rights

Report of the Secretary-General. In September 1985,[1] the Secretary-General presented to the General Assembly an overview of current international conditions and human rights, based on information from four Governments—Cuba, Nigeria, Panama, Qatar—seven United Nations bodies and agencies and an intergovernmental organization. The report was a follow-up to two previous reports, submitted in 1981[2] and 1983.[3] Despite a number of positive developments since then, the Secretary-General stated, the picture was far from encouraging, the overall situation being characterized by continuing large-scale breaches of civil and political as well as economic, social and cultural rights. In spite of the problems and obstacles encountered, the United Nations was attempting to respond to them through different mechanisms and procedures, and international co-operation in that regard was intensifying. However, those efforts could not succeed unless matched by corresponding national efforts; the effort of the international community must therefore be geared to improving national conditions in every domain.

The information received provided cause for cautious optimism, the Secretary-General said. Perhaps the most significant development was a heightening awareness of human rights issues by Governments and international organizations, which also manifested itself in further ratifications of international human rights conventions. There was also continued progress in the drafting of conventions on the rights of the child and of migrant workers and other instruments dealing with the rights of aliens, the right to development, abolition of the death penalty and the protection of detainees. The increasing number of situations under consideration by the Commission on Human Rights in recent years attested not only to the severity of human rights violations around the world, but also to an increased willingness by Member States to focus on specific situations with a view to terminating violations. There was also growing emphasis on the advisory services programme, to help Governments strengthen their laws and institutions.

Some respondents, he reported, felt that certain issues, such as the safeguarding of peace and the promotion of development, should be further examined from their human rights perspective. The right to life, the right to development, the need to curb the arms race, and human rights violations resulting from aggression, occupation, exploitation and foreign intervention were mentioned; an unjust international economic order having adverse consequences for human rights, racial discrimination, particularly *apartheid*, and discrimination against women were cited as issues that should retain the international community's attention.

GENERAL ASSEMBLY ACTION

On 13 December 1985, on the recommendation of the Third Committee, the General Assembly adopted **resolution 40/124** by recorded vote.

Alternative approaches and ways and means within the United Nations system for improving the effective enjoyment of human rights and fundamental freedoms

The General Assembly,

Recalling that in the Charter of the United Nations the peoples of the United Nations declared their determination to reaffirm faith in fundamental human rights, in the dignity and worth of the human person and in the equal rights of men and women and of nations large and small and to employ international machinery for the promotion of the economic and social advancement of all peoples,

Recalling also the purposes and principles of the Charter to achieve international co-operation in solving international problems of an economic, social, cultural or humanitarian character, and in promoting and encouraging respect for human rights and for fundamental freedoms for all without distinction as to race, sex, language or religion,

Emphasizing the significance and validity of the Universal Declaration of Human Rights and of the International Covenants on Human Rights in promoting respect for and observance of human rights and fundamental freedoms,

Recalling its resolution 32/130 of 16 December 1977, in which it decided that the approach to the future work within the United Nations system with respect to human rights questions should take into account the concepts set forth in that resolution,

Recalling also its resolutions 34/46 of 23 November 1979, 35/174 of 15 December 1980, 36/133 of 14 December 1981, 38/124 of 16 December 1983 and 39/145 of 14 December 1984,

Taking into account Commission on Human Rights resolution 1985/43 of 14 March 1985,

Underlining the fact that the right to development is an inalienable human right,

Recognizing that the human being is the main subject of development and that everyone has the right to participate in, as well as to benefit from, the development process,

Reiterating once again that the establishment of the new international economic order is an essential element for the effective promotion and the full enjoyment of human rights and fundamental freedoms for all,

Reiterating also its profound conviction that all human rights and fundamental freedoms are indivisible and interdependent and that equal attention and urgent consideration should be given to the implementation, promotion and protection of both civil and political and economic, social and cultural rights,

Reaffirming the importance of furthering the activities of the existing organs of the United Nations system in the field of human rights in conformity with the principles of the Charter,

Underlining the need for the creation of conditions at the national and international levels for the promotion and full protection of the human rights of individuals and peoples,

Recognizing that international peace and security are essential elements for the full realization of human rights, including the right to development,

Considering that the resources that would be released by disarmament could contribute significantly to the development of all States, in particular the developing countries,

Recognizing that co-operation among all nations on the basis of respect for the independence, sovereignty and territorial integrity of each State, including the right of each people to choose freely its own socio-economic and political system and to exercise full sovereignty over its wealth and natural resources, subject to the principles referred to in article 1, paragraph 2, and article 25 of the International Covenant on Economic, Social and Cultural Rights, is essential for the promotion of peace and development,

Convinced that the primary aim of such international co-operation must be the achievement by each human being of a life of freedom and dignity and freedom from want,

Acknowledging the progress so far achieved by the international community in the promotion and protection of human rights and fundamental freedoms,

Concerned, however, at the occurrence of violations of human rights in the world,

Reaffirming that nothing in the Universal Declaration of Human Rights or in the International Covenants on Human Rights may be interpreted as implying for any State, group or person the right to engage in any activity or perform any act aimed at the destruction of any of the rights and freedoms set forth therein,

Affirming that the ultimate aim of development is the constant improvement of the well-being of the entire population, on the basis of its full participation in the process of development and a fair distribution of the benefits therefrom,

Emphasizing that Governments have the duty to ensure respect for all human rights and fundamental freedoms,

Taking note of the work done by the Working Group of Governmental Experts on the Right to Development, as reflected in its reports to the Commission on Human Rights,

1. *Reiterates its request* that the Commission on Human Rights continue its current work on the overall analysis with a view to further promoting and improving human rights and fundamental freedoms, including the question of the Commission's programme and working methods, and on the overall analysis of the alternative approaches and ways and means for improving the effective enjoyment of human rights and fundamental freedoms, in accordance with the provisions and concepts of General Assembly resolution 32/130 and other relevant texts;

2. *Affirms* that a primary aim of international co-operation in the field of human rights is a life of freedom, dignity and peace for all peoples and for each human being, that all human rights and fundamental freedoms are indivisible and interrelated and that the promotion and protection of one category of rights should never exempt or excuse States from the promotion and protection of the others;

3. *Affirms its profound conviction* that equal attention and urgent consideration should be given to the implementation, promotion and protection of both civil and political and economic, social and cultural rights;

4. *Reaffirms* that it is of paramount importance for the promotion of human rights and fundamental freedoms that Member States should undertake specific obligations through accession to, or ratification of, international instruments in this field and, consequently, that the standard-setting work within the United Nations system in the field of human rights and the universal acceptance and implementation of the relevant international instruments should be encouraged;

5. *Reiterates once again* that the international community should accord, or continue to accord, priority to the search for solutions to mass and flagrant violations of human rights of peoples and individuals affected by situations such as those mentioned in paragraph 1 (*e*) of General Assembly resolution 32/130, paying due attention also to other situations of violations of human rights;

6. *Reaffirms* its responsibility for achieving international co-operation in promoting and encouraging respect for human rights and fundamental freedoms for all, and expresses its concern at serious violations of human rights, in particular mass and flagrant violations of these rights, wherever they occur;

7. *Expresses concern* at the present situation with regard to the achievement of the objectives and goals for establishing the new international economic order and its adverse effects on the full realization of human rights, in particular the right to development;

8. *Reaffirms* that the right to development is an inalienable human right;

9. *Reaffirms also* that international peace and security are essential elements in achieving the full realization of the right to development;

10. *Recognizes* that all human rights and fundamental freedoms are indivisible and interdependent;

11. *Considers* it necessary that all Member States promote international co-operation on the basis of respect for the independence, sovereignty and territorial integrity of each State, including the right of each people to choose freely its own socio-economic and political system and to exercise full sovereignty over its wealth and natural resources, subject to the principles referred to in article 1, paragraph 2, and article 25 of the International Covenant on Economic, Social and Cultural Rights, with a view to resolving international problems of an economic, social and humanitarian character;

12. *Expresses concern* at the disparity existing between the established norms and principles and the actual situation of all human rights and fundamental freedoms in the world;

13. *Urges* all States to co-operate with the Commission on Human Rights in the promotion and protection of human rights and fundamental freedoms;

14. *Reiterates* the need to create, at the national and international levels, conditions for the full promotion and protection of the human rights of individuals and peoples;

15. *Reaffirms once again* that, in order to facilitate the full enjoyment of all rights and complete personal dignity, it is necessary to promote the rights to education, work, health and proper nourishment through the adoption of measures at the national level, including those that provide for workers' participation in management, as well as the adoption of measures at the international level, including the establishment of the new international economic order;

16. *Again requests* the Commission on Human Rights to take the necessary measures to promote the right to development, and welcomes the decision of the Commission, in its resolution 1985/43, concerning the future work of the Working Group of Governmental Experts on the Right to Development;

17. *Requests* the Secretary-General to transmit to the General Assembly at its forty-first session a report containing information on the progress made by the Working Group in the accomplishment of its tasks;

18. *Decides* to include in the provisional agenda of its forty-first session the item entitled "Alternative approaches and ways and means within the United Nations system for improving the effective enjoyment of human rights and fundamental freedoms".

General Assembly resolution 40/124

13 December 1985   Meeting 116   130-1-22 (recorded vote)

Approved by Third Committee (A/40/970) by recorded vote (116-1-21), 27 November (meeting 56); 22-nation draft (A/C.3/40/L.40); agenda item 107.

Sponsors: Algeria, Angola, Argentina, Bangladesh, Benin, Bolivia, Colombia, Cuba, Cyprus, Democratic Yemen, Ethiopia, India, Libyan Arab Jamahiriya, Madagascar, Mexico, Mozambique, Nicaragua, Panama, Romania, Syrian Arab Republic, Viet Nam, Yugoslavia.

Meeting numbers. GA 40th session: 3rd Committee 33, 35, 36, 56, 57; plenary 116.

Recorded vote in Assembly as follows:

In favour: Afghanistan, Algeria, Angola, Antigua and Barbuda, Argentina, Bahamas, Bahrain, Bangladesh, Barbados, Benin, Bhutan, Bolivia, Botswana, Brazil, Brunei Darussalam, Bulgaria, Burkina Faso, Burma, Burundi, Byelorussian SSR, Cameroon, Cape Verde, Central African Republic, Chad, Chile, China, Colombia, Comoros, Congo, Costa Rica, Cuba, Cyprus, Czechoslovakia, Democratic Kampuchea, Democratic Yemen, Djibouti, Dominican Republic, Ecuador, Egypt, El Salvador, Equatorial Guinea, Ethiopia, Fiji, Gabon, German Democratic Republic, Ghana, Grenada, Guatemala, Guinea, Guinea-Bissau, Guyana, Haiti, Honduras, Hungary, India, Indonesia, Iran, Iraq, Ivory Coast, Jamaica, Jordan, Kenya, Kuwait, Lao People's Democratic Republic, Lebanon, Lesotho, Liberia, Libyan Arab Jamahiriya, Madagascar, Malaysia, Maldives, Mali, Malta, Mauritania, Mauritius, Mexico, Mongolia, Morocco, Mozambique, Nepal, New Zealand, Nicaragua, Niger, Nigeria, Oman, Pakistan, Panama, Papua New Guinea, Paraguay, Peru, Philippines, Poland, Qatar, Romania, Rwanda, Saint Christopher and Nevis, Saint Lucia, Saint Vincent and the Grenadines, Samoa, Sao Tome and Principe, Saudi Arabia, Senegal, Sierra Leone, Singapore, Solomon Islands, Somalia, Sri Lanka, Sudan, Suriname, Swaziland, Syrian Arab Republic, Thailand, Togo, Trinidad and Tobago, Tunisia, Turkey, Uganda, Ukrainian SSR, USSR, United Arab Emirates, United Republic of Tanzania, Uruguay, Vanuatu, Venezuela, Viet Nam, Yemen, Yugoslavia, Zaire, Zambia, Zimbabwe.

Against: United States.

Abstaining: Australia, Austria, Belgium, Canada, Denmark, Finland, France, Germany, Federal Republic of, Greece, Iceland, Ireland, Israel, Italy, Japan, Luxembourg, Malawi, Netherlands, Norway, Portugal, Spain, Sweden, United Kingdom.

After a procedural debate, the Committee decided by 90 votes to 19, with 13 abstentions, to take immediate action on the text. Any decision on the draft resolution, said Senegal, depended on the decision on the 12-nation draft resolution which contained the draft declaration on the right to development (see p. 879); the main priority was adoption of the latter. That view was supported by Pakistan.

Canada and Italy felt that the two drafts should have been considered together. Greece said delegations had been led to believe they would be. Austria, Canada and the Federal Republic of Germany said it was illogical to take a decision on a text with references to the right to development before the conclusion of negotiations on the draft declaration. No decision on the text should have been taken until the draft declaration had been considered, according to Australia, Brazil, France, the Federal Republic of Germany, Italy, Japan and the United Kingdom. The Netherlands stated that it would not be able to join a consensus on the text before the draft declaration had been considered.

Cuba, Mauritania and Yugoslavia, on the other hand, believed that the two should not be linked. The Syrian Arab Republic saw no reason to wait for adoption of the declaration before acting on the resolution.

The Federal Republic of Germany said the eleventh preambular paragraph did not adequately reflect the different proposals made to strengthen and further develop existing organs to ensure protection of human rights. The text contained vague concepts concerning the international framework for the promotion of human rights, particularly in the ninth and thirteenth to fifteenth preambular paragraphs and paragraphs 2, 7, 9, 15 and 16. The notion should not be given, the Federal Republic said, that putting into effect such concepts as a new

international economic order was a pre-condition for the guarantee of human rights, a view that Finland also expressed on behalf of the Nordic countries. Issues concerning international peace and security and disarmament and development should be dealt with in more competent forums, the Federal Republic added.

Australia had reservations concerning the seventh to ninth, fifteenth and sixteenth preambular paragraphs, which it said might prejudge results of negotiations aimed at defining the right to development. Italy also felt that those negotiations might be prejudged by the reference to the Commission's decisions. Japan had difficulties in particular with paragraph 8, referring to the right to development. Spain said it believed that the references in paragraphs 16 and 17 to the Working Group of Governmental Experts on the Right to Development and the task entrusted to it by the Commission on Human Rights were in contradiction with each other.

Ireland said the text did not focus clearly on the nature of human rights and gave undue attention to factors which impaired its balance. It was not sufficient to discuss approaches; the text must also deal with ways to improve enjoyment of human rights and the role of the United Nations in respect of human rights violations.

National institutions for human rights protection

In July 1985, the Secretary-General submitted a report[4] on national institutions for the protection and promotion of human rights, as requested by the General Assembly in 1984.[5] The Assembly had also encouraged all Member States to take steps to establish or strengthen such national institutions. In the light of information received, the Secretary-General was to prepare for publication, as a handbook for the use of Governments, a consolidated report on the various types and models of national and local institutions for promoting and protecting human rights.

As at 15 June, information had been received from Barbados, Cyprus and France. Periodic reports under various international human rights instruments would be taken into account in preparing the report, the Secretary-General stated, as would information from inter- and non-governmental organizations and specialized agencies, especially ILO and UNESCO.

The report annexed the table of contents of the first study on national institutions.

GENERAL ASSEMBLY ACTION

On 13 December, on the recommendation of the Third Committee, the General Assembly adopted **resolution 40/123**, without vote.

National institutions for the protection and promotion of human rights

The General Assembly,

Recalling its resolutions 32/123 of 16 December 1977, 33/46 of 14 December 1978, 34/49 of 23 November 1979, 36/134 of 14 December 1981, 38/123 of 16 December 1983 and 39/144 of 14 December 1984,

Mindful of the guidelines on the structure and functioning of national and local institutions for the promotion and protection of human rights, endorsed by the General Assembly in its resolution 33/46,

Emphasizing the importance of the Universal Declaration of Human Rights, the International Covenants on Human Rights and other international human rights instruments for promoting respect for and observance of human rights and fundamental freedoms,

Conscious of the significant role that institutions at the national level can play in protecting and promoting human rights and fundamental freedoms and in developing and enhancing public awareness and observance of those rights and freedoms,

Welcoming the organization at Geneva, under the auspices of the United Nations, of a seminar on the experience of different countries in the implementation of international standards on human rights, held from 20 June to 1 July 1983, and a seminar on community relations commissions and their functions, held from 9 to 20 September 1985,

1. *Takes note* of the report of the Secretary-General;
2. *Emphasizes* the importance of developing, in accordance with national legislation, effective national institutions for the protection and promotion of human rights, and of maintaining their independence and integrity;
3. *Encourages* all Member States to take appropriate steps for the establishment or, where they already exist, the strengthening of national institutions for the protection and promotion of human rights;
4. *Draws attention* to the constructive role that national non-governmental organizations can play in the work of such national institutions;
5. *Encourages* all Member States to take appropriate steps to promote the exchange of information and experience concerning the establishment of such national institutions;
6. *Requests* the Secretary-General to give due attention to the role of national institutions and non-governmental organizations concerned with the protection and promotion of human rights and to provide all necessary assistance to Member States, upon their request, in the implementation of paragraphs 3 and 5 above, according high priority to the needs of developing countries;
7. *Also requests* the Secretary-General to continue to provide and, as appropriate, to enhance assistance in the field of human rights to Governments, at their request, within the framework of the programme of advisory services in the field of human rights;
8. *Welcomes and encourages* the efforts of the Secretary-General to prepare and submit to the General Assembly, through the Commission on Human Rights and the Economic and Social Council, a consolidated report, for eventual publication as a United Nations handbook, on national institutions for the use of Governments, in-cluding information on the various types and models of national and local institutions for the protection and promotion of human rights, taking into account differing social and legal systems;

9. *Requests* the Secretary-General to report to the General Assembly at its forty-first session on the implementation of the present resolution.

General Assembly resolution 40/123

13 December 1985   Meeting 116   Adopted without vote

Approved by Third Committee (A/40/970) without vote, 27 November (meeting 56); 7-nation draft (A/C.3/40/L.39); agenda item 107.

Sponsors: Australia, India, Iraq, New Zealand, Nigeria, Norway, Sri Lanka.

Meeting numbers. GA 40th session: 3rd Committee 33, 35, 36, 56; plenary 116.

UN machinery

Human Rights Commission action. On 14 March 1985,[6] the Commission on Human Rights decided to consider in 1986 the possible establishment of an open-ended working group to continue the overall analysis of alternative ways and means within the United Nations system for improving the effective enjoyment of human rights and fundamental freedoms, and of further promoting those rights and freedoms, including the question of the Commission's programme and methods of work.

Commission on Human Rights

Organization of work of the 1986 session

Taking into account its heavy work schedule and that of its sessional working groups, the Commission on 14 March 1985[7] decided to recommend that the Economic and Social Council authorize 20 fully serviced additional meetings, including summary records, for the Commission's 1986 session, whose Chairman was to make every effort to organize the work within the normal allotted time.

ECONOMIC AND SOCIAL COUNCIL ACTION

On the Commission's and the Second Committee's recommendation, the Council, by **decision 1985/151** of 30 May 1985, approved without vote by all three bodies, authorized, if possible within existing financial resources, the requested 20 additional meetings and summary records. It also took note of the Commission's decision to request the Chairman of the 1986 session to make every effort to ensure that additional meetings were utilized only if absolutely necessary.

Report of the Commission

On 30 May 1985, by **decision 1985/154**, the Economic and Social Council took note without vote of the report[8] of the Commission on Human Rights on its forty-first session (Geneva, 4 February–15 March 1985). The Council's Second Committee had approved the text, recommended by the Commission, on 24 May.

Sub-Commission on Prevention of Discrimination and Protection of Minorities

Review of the work of the Sub-Commission

Human Rights Commission action. On 11 March 1985,[9] the Commission on Human Rights noted that its Sub-Commission in 1984 had reviewed and made suggestions for improving its work;[10] it endorsed the desirability of better continuity in that work and requested the Secretary-General, after consultation with Member States, to report to the Commission in 1986 on existing election procedures which could provide for such continuity so that the Commission could decide on the matter. The Commission stressed that it was important that States nominate as members and alternates experts not subject to government instructions. It recommended that the Sub-Commission propose a new study only when a previously authorized study was in the final stage of completion; it also requested the Sub-Commission to give priority to topics on which standards were being prepared and give due consideration to recommendations for the printing and distribution of studies, taking into account the long-term plan for studies for 1985-1989 and the availability of financial resources. The Sub-Commission was invited to seek the widest possible agreement on draft resolutions proposed for adoption, bearing in mind that they should reflect thorough discussion and be consistent with the Sub-Commission's role as a body of independent experts; it was also requested to complete the review of its work and submit in 1986 recommendations for its further rationalization.

Working Group activities. The sessional Working Group on the Review of the Work of the Sub-Commission, which first met in 1984,[11] held four meetings between 7 and 20 August 1985. Summarizing its observations and comments, especially regarding points taken up by the Commission in its March resolution, the Working Group recommended in its report[12] to the Sub-Commission that the review be continued by the Sub-Commission as a whole.

Sub-Commission action. By a 29 August 1985 resolution,[13] adopted by 18 votes to 1, the Sub-Commission recommended to the Commission that, in order to ensure greater continuity of its membership, half of its members be elected every two years, which would require that the term of membership be increased to four years. In order to enable a maximum of three sessional working groups to meet concurrently, additional services for three 3-hour meetings should be authorized. Consideration should be given to changing the name of the Sub-Commission to Sub-Commission of Experts on Human Rights, and ways should be explored to ensure the quality of the studies of special rapporteurs

and provide them with more resources. The Sub-Commission decided that the Working Group should discontinue its work so that further discussion by all Sub-Commission members would be reflected in the summary records.

On 28 August,[14] the Sub-Commission requested the Secretary-General to inform the Committee on Conferences of its view that the summary records of the Sub-Commission could not be further abbreviated, and asked him to continue to provide them in the existing format.

Future work of the Sub-Commission

On 30 August 1985,[15] the Sub-Commission decided that the following items would be considered on a biennial basis, starting in 1986: the new international economic order and the promotion of human rights; elimination of all forms of intolerance and discrimination based on religion or belief; and international peace and security as an essential condition for the enjoyment of human rights, above all the right to life. The items on human rights and disability, human rights and scientific and technological developments, and encouragement of universal acceptance of human rights instruments would also be considered biennially, starting in 1987.

Report of the Sub-Commission for 1985

By **decision 1985/153** of 30 May, the Economic and Social Council approved a 14 March decision[16] of the Commission on Human Rights to invite the Sub-Commission to be present, through the Chairman or a designated member, at the consideration of its 1985 report by the Commission in 1986. The Council's Second Committee had approved the decision on 24 May.

In a 29 August 1985 resolution[13] on review of its work (see above), the Sub-Commission requested the Secretary-General to inform it in 1986 of the Commission's consideration of its 1985 report.

Inter-sessional meetings of the Bureau

By a 29 August resolution,[17] adopted by 7 votes to 4, with 8 abstentions, the Sub-Commission requested authorization for the Bureau elected at each of its sessions to hold two inter-sessional meetings per year, so that it could review developments and ensure timely collection of information needed for bringing to the Commission's attention any situation which it believed revealed a consistent pattern of human rights violations (see p. 898).

Public information activities

In a February 1985 report to the Commission on Human Rights,[18] the Secretary-General gave an overview of public information activities in the human rights field by the United Nations Department of Public Information (DPI) and United Nations information centres, as well as by Governments and NGOs.

By a resolution of 14 March,[(19)] the Commission requested Governments to facilitate publicity on United Nations human rights activities, with particular reference to the work of the Commission and expert bodies, and to accord priority to the dissemination of the Universal Declaration of Human Rights and the International Covenants on Human Rights.

The Commission requested the Secretary-General to issue by the end of 1986 a personalized version of the Universal Declaration of Human Rights in the six official United Nations languages, and afterwards to produce personalized versions in national and local languages. It requested him to build up the reference works on human rights in each information centre and requested United Nations agencies to send reference material to the Centre for Human Rights for distribution. It also asked the Secretary-General to make greater use of audiovisual techniques and computer technology to collect relevant, already prepared material, prepare a basic human rights teaching booklet in the six official languages, and examine how the United Nations system might assist in the dissemination of human rights material. The Commission asked the regional commissions to assist in dissemination and investigate ways of promoting co-operation within the regions to that end. Governments, United Nations agencies and NGOs were requested to submit further comments and proposals for enhancing United Nations promotional activities, and the Secretary-General was to report to it in 1986 on implementation of the resolution, including a status report on the availability of the principal international human rights instruments in official and other languages, the amount in stock and a summary of the activities of the information centres related to human rights.

GENERAL ASSEMBLY ACTION

On 13 December 1985, on the recommendation of the Third Committee, the General Assembly adopted **resolution 40/125**, without vote.

Development of public information activities in the field of human rights

The General Assembly,

Reaffirming that activities to improve public knowledge in the field of human rights are necessary to the fulfilment of the purposes of the United Nations set out in Article 1, paragraph 3, of the Charter of the United Nations,

Recalling its resolutions on the status of the International Covenants on Human Rights, including resolution 39/136 of 14 December 1984,

Taking into account the relevant General Assembly resolutions concerning the further promotion of human rights, including resolution 39/144 of 14 December 1984 relating to the activities of national institutions in the field of human rights,

Welcoming Commission on Human Rights resolution 1985/49 of 14 March 1985 on the development of public information activities in the field of human rights,

Recognizing the fundamental importance of national and regional public information activities in the field of human rights and the catalytic effect that initiatives of the United Nations can have on these activities,

Reaffirming that programmes of teaching, education and information in the field of human rights are central to the achievement of lasting respect for human rights and fundamental freedoms,

Noting the importance of making available United Nations materials on human rights in national and local languages, including in simplified form, and of making more effective use of the mass media and of new technologies in order to reach a wider audience, especially the less-educated and those in isolated areas,

Believing that the promotional activities of the United Nations system in the field of human rights should be enhanced and strengthened,

1. *Requests* all Member States to take appropriate steps, by all available means, including the mass media, to give publicity to the activities of the United Nations in the field of human rights and to accord priority to the dissemination, in their respective national and local languages, of the Universal Declaration of Human Rights, the International Covenants on Human Rights and other international conventions;

2. *Calls upon* all relevant bodies of the United Nations system, including the specialized agencies and the regional commissions, to assist further in the dissemination of United Nations material on human rights;

3. *Welcomes* the efforts of the Secretary-General to issue a personalized version of the Universal Declaration of Human Rights in the six official languages of the United Nations, having in mind the desirability of completing this task in 1986, and also welcomes the preparation of a list of basic reference works on human rights for use by United Nations information centres and other interested bodies;

4. *Takes note with satisfaction* of the request of the Commission on Human Rights to the Secretary-General, in its resolution 1985/49, to collect relevant material, including that prepared by specialized agencies, regional bodies, groups, non-governmental organizations and individuals, with a view to preparing a basic teaching booklet on human rights in the six official languages of the United Nations;

5. *Recommends* that all Member States consider including, in their educational curricula, material relevant to a comprehensive understanding of human rights issues;

6. *Urges* the Commission on Human Rights to give special attention at its forty-second session to the development of public information activities in the field of human rights and to submit to the General Assembly at its forty-first session, through the Economic and Social Council, its views and recommendations on further action;

7. *Decides* to continue its consideration of this question at its forty-first session under the item entitled

"Alternative approaches and ways and means within the United Nations system for improving the effective enjoyment of human rights and fundamental freedoms".

General Assembly resolution 40/125

13 December 1985   Meeting 116   Adopted without vote

Approved by Third Committee (A/40/970) without vote, 29 November (meeting 57); 23-nation draft (A/C.3/40/L.46); agenda item 107.
Sponsors: Argentina, Australia, Barbados, Bolivia, Canada, Colombia, Costa Rica, Cyprus, Ecuador, El Salvador, Finland, Gambia, India, Ireland, Mexico, Morocco, Netherlands, New Zealand, Norway, Peru, Samoa, United Kingdom, Yugoslavia.
Meeting numbers. GA 40th session: 3rd Committee 33, 36, 56, 57; plenary 116.

Regional arrangements

Taking note of the Secretary-General's 1984 report[20] to the General Assembly on regional arrangements for the promotion and protection of human rights, the Commission on Human Rights, on 14 March 1985,[21] invited States members of the Economic and Social Commission for Asia and the Pacific (ESCAP) to submit comments on the 1982 Seminar on National, Local and Regional Arrangements for the Promotion and Protection of Human Rights in the Asian Region,[22] in particular on the conclusions and recommendations concerning development of regional arrangements in Asia and the Pacific. ESCAP, the other regional commissions and intergovernmental bodies dealing with human rights were also invited to submit their comments, to be incorporated in an interim report by the Secretary-General to the Commission in 1986.

The Commission requested the Secretary-General, in co-operation with ESCAP and Governments of the region, to consider establishing a regional depository centre for human rights materials.

International human rights instruments

In a June 1985 note to the Sub-Commission,[23] the Secretary-General reported on the status of several international human rights instruments, including the 1966 International Covenants on Human Rights,[24] the 1965 International Convention on the Elimination of All Forms of Racial Discrimination,[25] the 1973 International Convention on the Suppression and Punishment of the Crime of *Apartheid*,[26] and the 1979 Convention on the Elimination of All Forms of Discrimination against Women.[27]

The Secretary-General transmitted in a note[28] to the Sub-Commission the replies of five Governments, as of 1 May, to his invitation, issued in accordance with a 1984 Sub-Commission request,[29] to provide information on circumstances which had prevented them from adhering to human rights instruments.

By a 27 August 1985 resolution,[30] adopted by 15 votes to 1, with 4 abstentions, the Sub-Commission decided to include the 1984 Convention against Torture and Other Cruel, Inhuman or Degrading Treatment or Punishment[31] in the list of human rights instruments whose universal acceptance was to be encouraged. It requested the Secretary-General to renew the invitation for submission of information, to examine further the idea of offering legal training to local staff or providing experts to assist in the drafting of legislation and regulations, with a view to enabling States to ratify or accede to those instruments, to keep under review the idea of designating regional advisers on international human rights standards, to continue informal consultations with government representatives on prospects for ratification, and to update the table of country-by-country developments in connection with ratification or accession. The Sub-Commission decided, until further review of its mandate, to suspend the work of the Working Group on the Encouragement of Universal Acceptance of Human Rights Instruments and asked its Chairman to appoint a member to report in 1987 on information received.

By a note verbale of 10 December,[32] the Syrian Arab Republic transmitted to the Secretary-General a statement of its Ministry of Foreign Affairs on the occasion of the thirty-seventh anniversary of the Universal Declaration of Human Rights, relating the Declaration to its constitution and stressing the need for the international community to continue to combat continuing violations of human rights.

Reporting obligations of States parties

Report of the Secretary-General. In September 1985,[33] the Secretary-General presented to the General Assembly a report on reporting obligations of States parties to United Nations conventions on human rights. Reporting obligations were contained in six such instruments, including the two International Covenants,[24] the Conventions against racial discrimination[25] and against *apartheid*,[26] and the Convention on eliminating discrimination against women.[27] (The sixth, the Convention against torture,[31] was not yet in force.) States parties undertook to submit initial and periodic reports to an international supervisory body responsible for monitoring implementation of each Convention. The periodicity of reporting after the entry into force varied from one instrument to the other. As at 1 June 1985, the system of reporting under the conventions comprised 138 States which were parties to at least one of those instruments; overdue reports totalled 384. Approximately half of the outstanding reports were overdue from a group of 27 States parties which seemed to encounter difficulties in submitting them, the Secretary-General stated; another characteristic common to that group was that most of them were parties either to four or to all five conventions.

An addendum to the report contained a compilation of general guidelines on the form and content of the various reports to be submitted under the five conventions in force.

On 13 December 1985, on the recommendation of the Third Committee, the General Assembly adopted **resolution 40/116**, without vote.

Reporting obligations of States parties to United Nations conventions on human rights

The General Assembly,

Recalling its resolution 37/44 of 3 December 1982, in which it noted with concern the critical situation with regard to overdue reports under the International Convention on the Elimination of All Forms of Racial Discrimination and affirmed the necessity of considering that situation within the overall framework of all reporting obligations of States parties to United Nations conventions on human rights,

Recalling also its resolution 38/117 of 16 December 1983, in which it noted that many delays were also occurring in the submission of reports under the International Covenant on Economic, Social and Cultural Rights, as indicated by the Secretary-General in his first report on the overall situation with regard to reporting obligations,

Recalling further its resolution 39/138 of 14 December 1984, in which the General Assembly, having considered the report of the meeting of the Chairmen of the supervisory bodies entrusted with the consideration of reports submitted under United Nations conventions on human rights and of the Commission on Human Rights, held at Geneva on 16 and 17 August 1984, expressed its concern about the problems experienced by those bodies in the functioning of the reporting procedures and its conviction of the need to improve the existing reporting system in order to resolve the problems experienced both by those bodies and by the States parties to the various conventions on human rights,

Having considered the report of the Secretary-General containing updated information as at 1 June 1985 on the general situation of the submission of reports of States parties to United Nations conventions on human rights and a compilation of the general guidelines elaborated by the various human rights bodies under the human rights instruments containing reporting obligations,

Noting with deep concern that the number of reports overdue from States parties to at least one of the conventions on human rights has increased seriously and may even increase further unless appropriate steps are taken to ascertain better the root causes of the situation and to devise appropriate types of action that can progressively remove the difficulties being experienced,

Recalling, in this respect, Commission on Human Rights resolution 1985/26 of 11 March 1985 concerning the programme of advisory services in the field of human rights, and also resolution 1985/45 of 14 March 1985, in which the Commission, having considered the status of the International Covenants on Human Rights, requested the Secretary-General to consider ways and means of making advice and assistance available to States parties to these instruments in the preparation of their reports,

Recognizing once again and with deeper concern the burden that several coexisting reporting systems place upon Member States that are parties to various conventions, which in future may become more acute in relation to the ratification of other conventions,

Reiterating the importance it attaches to the fulfilment of obligations under international conventions on human rights, including reporting obligations,

1. *Takes note with appreciation* of the very comprehensive second report of the Secretary-General on reporting obligations of States parties to United Nations conventions on human rights, which contains:

(a) Updated information on the general situation of the submission of reports of States parties to the five conventions currently in force;

(b) Consideration of and suggestions on the question of consolidating the guidelines of the supervisory bodies entrusted with the consideration of the reports of States parties on the implementation of the conventions;

(c) A list of articles dealing with related rights under the various conventions and a compilation of the current guidelines;

2. *Expresses its deep concern* about the alarming number of reports overdue from many States parties to the international conventions on human rights, which negatively affects the reporting systems of those conventions, in particular the International Convention on the Elimination of All Forms of Racial Discrimination and the International Covenant on Economic, Social and Cultural Rights;

3. *Expresses particular concern* that some States that are parties to four or to five conventions seem to have serious difficulties in submitting their reports, as indicated by the repeated reminders addressed to them by the Secretary-General at the request of the competent supervisory bodies;

4. *Takes note with interest* of Economic and Social Council decision 1985/132 of 28 May 1985, by which, while maintaining the first six-year cycle of the reporting procedures on the implementation of the International Covenant on Economic, Social and Cultural Rights, the Council decided to establish a nine-year period for the subsequent cycles, and considers this decision a first step towards the necessary lightening of the heavy burden of reporting obligations placed upon the States parties to that Covenant;

5. *Supports* the request addressed to the Secretary-General by the Commission on Human Rights, in its resolution 1985/45, concerning the provision of practical assistance to States, under the programme of advisory services in the field of human rights, in the preparation of their reports under United Nations conventions;

6. *Commends* the United Nations Institute for Training and Research for having organized in the Caribbean region, at the suggestion of the Centre for Human Rights and with its close co-operation, a training course on the preparation and submission of reports under international conventions on human rights, and expresses the hope that other courses of that type may be organized in Africa and Asia;

7. *Believes* that new timely steps are needed in order to ascertain better the most relevant causes of the present situation regarding the non-submission of reports and to devise feasible types of action intended to remove the difficulties being encountered;

8. *Requests* the Secretary-General, to this end, to send a note verbale to all States parties to the five United

Nations conventions on human rights having at 1 February 1986 more than two reports overdue, inviting them to indicate, if they so wish, the reasons for their difficulties in complying with the reporting obligations with regard to the conventions under which their reports are overdue and their interest, if any, in technical advice and assistance with a view to better fulfilling their reporting obligations;

9. *Invites* the supervisory bodies entrusted with the consideration of reports submitted under all conventions currently in force to give particular attention, during the usual consideration of the action taken by the General Assembly on their annual reports, to the report of the Secretary-General and to the present resolution;

10. *Recommends* to the States parties to the International Convention on the Elimination of All Forms of Racial Discrimination that, at their next meeting, they consider suggesting to the Committee on the Elimination of Racial Discrimination the adoption, as a general rule, of the practice already being followed by the Committee of considering two successive reports in one single text;

11. *Requests* the Secretary-General to submit to the General Assembly at its forty-first session a report containing updated information on the general situation with regard to overdue reports, an assessment of the operational and financial implications of increasing training activities in this field and the results of the request addressed to him in paragraph 8 above;

12. *Decides* to consider at its forty-first session the convening, in 1987, of another meeting of the Chairmen of the supervisory bodies, including the Committee on the Elimination of Discrimination against Women and, if already established, the committee against torture, in order to consider jointly the report of the Secretary-General requested in paragraph 11 above;

13. *Fully concurs* with the considerations and suggestions of the Secretary-General on the question of consolidating the guidelines of the supervisory bodies entrusted with the consideration of reports of the States parties on the implementation of the conventions on human rights;

14. *Takes note with appreciation* of the compilation of the general guidelines elaborated by the various supervisory bodies and of the list of articles dealing with related rights under the five conventions, both of which are very helpful for States parties in the preparation of their reports;

15. *Decides* to include in the provisional agenda of its forty-first session a separate item entitled "Reporting obligations of States parties to the United Nations conventions on human rights".

General Assembly resolution 40/116

13 December 1985   Meeting 116   Adopted without vote

Approved by Third Committee (A/40/983) without vote, 2 December (meeting 60); 11-nation draft (A/C.3/40/L.73), orally revised; agenda item 104 *(c)*.
Sponsors: Austria, Belgium, Canada, Costa Rica, Finland, Germany, Federal Republic of, Italy, Morocco, Nicaragua, Suriname, Venezuela.
Meeting numbers. GA 40th session: 3rd Committee 46-48, 50, 52, 53, 58, 60; plenary 116.

International Covenants on Human Rights

Human Rights Commission action. On 14 March 1985,[34] the Commission on Human Rights reaffirmed the importance of the 1966 International Covenants on Human Rights[24] in

promoting universal respect for and observance of human rights and fundamental freedoms. It invited States to become parties to the Covenants and to consider acceding to the Optional Protocol to the International Covenant on Civil and Political Rights, emphasizing the importance of strict compliance with the obligations under those instruments. The Commission noted with satisfaction the number of parties that had been represented by experts for the presentation of their reports. It urged the Secretary-General to give more publicity to the work of the supervisory committees and improve administrative and related arrangements to enable them to carry out their functions effectively. It encouraged all Governments to publish and distribute the texts of the Covenants in as many languages as possible. The Commission requested the Secretary-General to consider ways to assist States parties in preparing their reports, including fellowships, regional training courses and other possibilities under the programme of advisory services. It also requested him to report in 1986 on the status of the Covenants. (See also p. 853.)

Report of the Secretary-General. In September 1985,[35] the Secretary-General reported to the General Assembly on the status of ratifications and accessions to the two Covenants and on questions related to their implementation. As at 1 September 1985, the International Covenant on Economic, Social and Cultural Rights had been ratified or acceded to by 84 States, while those adhering to the International Covenant on Civil and Political Rights numbered 80. In addition, nine States had signed the former, 10 the latter, and seven had signed the Optional Protocol to the latter Covenant. Eighteen States had made the declaration provided for in article 41 of the International Covenant on Civil and Political Rights, recognizing the competence of the Human Rights Committee established under article 28 to receive and consider communications to the effect that a State party claimed that another State party was not fulfilling its obligations under the Covenant. (See also pp. 853 and 876.)

GENERAL ASSEMBLY ACTION

On 13 December 1985, the General Assembly adopted **resolution 40/115**, without vote, as recommended by the Third Committee.

International Covenants on Human Rights

The General Assembly,

Recalling its resolutions 33/51 of 14 December 1978, 34/45 of 23 November 1979, 35/132 of 11 December 1980, 36/58 of 25 November 1981, 37/191 of 18 December 1982, 38/116 and 38/117 of 16 December 1983, and 39/136 and 39/138 of 14 December 1984,

Taking note of the report of the Secretary-General on the status of the International Covenant on Economic,

Social and Cultural Rights, the International Covenant on Civil and Political Rights and the Optional Protocol to the International Covenant on Civil and Political Rights,

Noting with appreciation that, following its appeal, more Member States have acceded to the International Covenants on Human Rights,

Recognizing the important role of the Human Rights Committee in the implementation of the International Covenant on Civil and Political Rights and the Optional Protocol thereto,

Taking into account the useful work of the Sessional Working Group of Governmental Experts on the Implementation of the International Covenant on Economic, Social and Cultural Rights,

Bearing in mind the important responsibilities of the Economic and Social Council in relation to the International Covenants on Human Rights,

Calling attention to the twentieth anniversary, in 1986, of the adoption of the International Covenant on Economic, Social and Cultural Rights and the International Covenant on Civil and Political Rights,

1. *Takes note with appreciation* of the report of the Human Rights Committee on its twenty-third, twenty-fourth and twenty-fifth sessions, and expresses its satisfaction with the serious and constructive manner in which the Committee is continuing to perform its functions;

2. *Expresses its appreciation* to those States parties to the International Covenant on Civil and Political Rights that have submitted their reports to the Human Rights Committee under article 40 of the Covenant and urges States parties that have not yet done so to submit their reports as speedily as possible;

3. *Urges* those States parties to the International Covenant on Civil and Political Rights that have been requested by the Human Rights Committee to provide additional information to comply with that request;

4. *Commends* those States parties to the International Covenant on Economic, Social and Cultural Rights that have submitted their reports under article 16 of the Covenant and urges States that have not yet done so to submit their reports as soon as possible;

5. *Notes with satisfaction* that the majority of States parties to the International Covenant on Civil and Political Rights, and an increasing number of States parties to the International Covenant on Economic, Social and Cultural Rights, have been represented by experts for the presentation of their reports, thereby assisting the Human Rights Committee and the Economic and Social Council in their work, and hopes that all States parties to both Covenants will arrange such representation in the future;

6. *Again urges* all States that have not yet done so to become parties to the International Covenant on Economic, Social and Cultural Rights and the International Covenant on Civil and Political Rights, as well as to consider acceding to the Optional Protocol to the International Covenant on Civil and Political Rights;

7. *Invites* the States parties to the International Covenant on Civil and Political Rights to consider making the declaration provided for in article 41 of the Covenant;

8. *Emphasizes* the importance of the strictest compliance by States parties with their obligations under the International Covenant on Economic, Social and Cultural Rights and the International Covenant on Civil

and Political Rights and, where applicable, the Optional Protocol to the International Covenant on Civil and Political Rights;

9. *Stresses* the importance of avoiding the erosion of human rights by derogation and underlines the necessity of strict observance of the agreed conditions and procedures for derogation;

10. *Recommends* to States parties that they continually review whether any reservation made in respect of the provisions of the International Covenants on Human Rights should be upheld;

11. *Urges* States parties to continue to pay active attention to the protection and promotion of civil and political rights, as well as economic, social and cultural rights;

12. *Welcomes* the decision of the Economic and Social Council, in its resolution 1985/17 of 28 May 1985, to establish the Committee on Economic, Social and Cultural Rights, which will be entrusted from 1987 on with the important task of overseeing the implementation of the International Covenant on Economic, Social and Cultural Rights;

13. *Requests* the Secretary-General to keep the Human Rights Committee informed of the relevant activities of the General Assembly, the Economic and Social Council, the Commission on Human Rights, the Sub-Commission on Prevention of Discrimination and Protection of Minorities, the Committee on the Elimination of Racial Discrimination and the Committee on the Elimination of Discrimination against Women, and also to transmit the annual reports of the Human Rights Committee to those bodies;

14. *Also requests* the Secretary-General to submit to the General Assembly at its forty-first session a report on the status of the International Covenant on Economic, Social and Cultural Rights, the International Covenant on Civil and Political Rights and the Optional Protocol to the International Covenant on Civil and Political Rights;

15. *Again urges* the Secretary-General, taking into account the suggestions of the Human Rights Committee, to take determined steps within existing resources to give more publicity to the work of the Committee and, similarly, to the work of the Economic and Social Council and to improve administrative and related arrangements to enable them to carry out their respective functions effectively under the International Covenants on Human Rights;

16. *Welcomes* the progress already made towards the publication of the official public records of the Human Rights Committee in bound volumes and looks forward to receiving in the near future the volumes covering the first two sessions;

17. *Encourages* all Governments to publish the texts of the International Covenant on Economic, Social and Cultural Rights, the International Covenant on Civil and Political Rights and the Optional Protocol to the International Covenant on Civil and Political Rights in as many languages as possible and to distribute them and make them known as widely as possible in their territories;

18. *Requests* the Secretary-General to ensure that the Centre for Human Rights of the Secretariat effectively assists the Human Rights Committee and the Economic and Social Council in the implementation of their respective functions under the International Covenants on Human Rights.

General Assembly resolution 40/115

13 December 1985   Meeting 116   Adopted without vote

Approved by Third Committee (A/40/983) without vote, 2 December (meeting 60); 18-nation draft (A/C.3/40/L.56), orally revised; agenda item 104.

Sponsors: Australia, Bulgaria, Canada, Costa Rica, Cyprus, Denmark, Ecuador, Finland, France, Iceland, Italy, Netherlands, Nicaragua, Norway, Peru, Spain, Sweden, United Kingdom.

Meeting numbers. GA 40th session: 3rd Committee 46-48, 50-53, 58, 60; plenary 116.

Advisory services

In 1985, under the United Nations programme of advisory services in human rights, established in 1955,[36] experts provided advisory services in the implementation of international human rights instruments, particularly the International Covenants. As reported[37] by the Secretary-General to the Commission on Human Rights, such assistance was provided during the year to Bolivia, Equatorial Guinea, Haiti and Uganda (see below). The programme also included training courses, seminars and fellowships. In 1985, recommendations were made for the award of 33 individual fellowships to candidates from 30 countries. Under the programme, a Seminar on Ways to Eliminate the Exploitation of Child Labour in All Parts of the World was held in co-operation with ILO (see p. 930); a Seminar on Community Relations Commissions and Their Functions (Geneva, 9-20 September),[38] held in the framework of activities to implement the Second Decade to Combat Racism and Racial Discrimination, was financed by resources allocated from the programme.

Reports of the Secretary-General. In January 1985,[39] the Secretary-General reported on progress made in providing expert assistance to Governments in the human rights field. He informed the Commission on Human Rights that he had maintained contacts with the Governments of Bolivia, Equatorial Guinea and Haiti, and activities would be followed up in 1985 in the light of the Commission's deliberations on the three reports for those countries.

Various suggestions for a long-term programme of action had been made, including: the development of promotional, public information, regional and field activities; the promotion of ratifications of the International Covenants on Human Rights; the utilization of commemorative activities; the development of practical training; the development of model legislation; technical assistance for the strengthening of legal institutions; and the development of programmes within the Centre for Human Rights.

In his report, the Secretary-General reiterated recommendations for the provision of advisory services and technical assistance made at a meeting in August 1984[40] of the chairmen of the Human Rights Commission and the supervisory bodies of human rights instruments.

In another January 1985 report,[41] the Secretary-General gave a synopsis of 1984 decisions and recommendations of United Nations bodies affecting the advisory services programme. He also gave a brief overview of seminars and training courses held or planned under the programme. He stated that he would continue to provide human rights fellowships in 1985 within available resources.

Human Rights Commission action. On 11 March 1985,[42] the Commission on Human Rights encouraged the Secretary-General to enhance his efforts to provide advisory services assistance to States in the implementation of international human rights instruments, particularly the Covenants, and requested him to examine ways to facilitate the flow of bilateral human rights assistance to States which had indicated a need—giving consideration in such cases to the organization of information and/or training courses for government personnel—and to consider the possibility of using voluntary contributions to implement projects under the programme. In cases in which assistance was being considered at a Government's request, the Secretary-General was invited to report to the Commission in 1986 on progress in implementing the programme and to continue considering suggestions for long- and short-term programmes of action.

On the same date, the Commission also adopted individual decisions on advisory services and technical assistance to Bolivia, Equatorial Guinea, Haiti and Uganda (see below).

Follow-up action. Pursuant to the Commission's resolution, the Secretary-General brought to the attention of all Governments and UNDP resident representatives the Commission's call for due consideration to be given, when awarding fellowships, to officials whose responsibilities related to the implementation of international human rights conventions.

Practical assistance to States was given in that regard by the United Nations Institute for Training and Research (UNITAR) which, in co-operation with the Centre for Human Rights, arranged in 1985 a pilot training course (Barbados, June), the first in a series of three to focus on the training of persons whose tasks related to human rights conventions. The second and third courses were to be held in 1986 in Africa and Asia.

Also following the Commission's recommendation, the Secretary-General offered to organize in Bolivia, Equatorial Guinea, Haiti and Uganda similar information and/or training courses. He transmitted projects presented by Bolivia and Uganda to other Governments and international organizations for consideration of any technical assistance they could offer.

Bolivia

Report of the Secretary-General. In accordance with a 1984 Economic and Social Council request,[43] the Secretary-General reported[44] to the

Commission on Human Rights in February 1985 on assistance to Bolivia and on implementation of the recommendations made in 1984 by Special Envoy Héctor Gros Espiell (Uruguay).[45] Contacts between government representatives and the Centre for Human Rights were continuing on the possibilities for providing assistance in disseminating human rights instruments in local languages, the development of teaching about human rights and the organization of a training course for law enforcement and prison officials. The Centre also expressed its readiness to offer two fellowships for the promotion of human rights. Letters had been sent in November 1984 to ILO, UNESCO and WHO drawing specific projects to their attention and asking for their comments.

When faced with such cases, the Secretary-General concluded, the most practical form of action which could be speedily organized by the United Nations, in co-operation with the Government concerned, would be training and/or information courses for civil servants, judges, law enforcement and prison officials, teachers and NGO representatives.

Annexed to the Secretary-General's report were replies from the Netherlands and seven United Nations bodies and organizations containing information on assistance they had provided to Bolivia in this field.

Human Rights Commission action. On 13 March 1985,[46] the Commission urged the Secretary-General to implement the projects mentioned in his report and invited Governments and international organizations to consider assisting projects to introduce the teaching of human rights as a subject at all education levels, to create a chair of human rights in the various higher-education centres, to increase human rights fellowships, to reform the national prison system and train specialized personnel, to look into the matter of enforced or involuntary disappearances, and to improve basic economic and health conditions and conditions of extreme poverty. The Commission again invited all Member States, United Nations organizations and NGOs to support Bolivia in its efforts to strengthen the enjoyment of human rights, and requested the Centre to maintain contacts with the agencies responsible for the various assistance programmes to Bolivia.

The Secretary-General initiated contacts with Bolivia, expressing the Centre's readiness to organize a training course for relevant government personnel, inviting the Government to nominate candidates for fellowships and offering teaching assistance and help in reproducing and disseminating international human rights instruments in local languages.

Equatorial Guinea

Appointed in accordance with a 1984 Economic and Social Council request,[47] an expert, Fernando Volio Jiménez (Costa Rica), undertook a mission to Equatorial Guinea from 13 to 20 November 1984. His report,[48] transmitted to the Commission on Human Rights in January 1985, contained recommendations to improve the human rights situation there which, he stated, had already changed significantly in accordance with the Government-approved plan of action he had suggested following a 1980 visit.[49] The positive results achieved so far would make it possible to continue to work towards the full restoration of human rights. He strongly recommended that relations between the Government and the United Nations be maintained with a view to implementing fully the plan of action and adopting other measures suited to the situation.

Recommending a number of administrative and constitutional changes, including a review of and amendments to the "Fundamental Law of Equatorial Guinea", the expert noted that United Nations co-operation was especially needed for the drafting of legislation, the training of legal and administrative staff and lawyers, the improvement of mass media and obtaining equipment to reopen a newspaper, and the identification of economic and social priorities. To work out better co-ordination between the Government and the Centre for Human Rights in implementing the plan of action, he suggested the establishment of a group of United Nations specialists or co-operation experts.

Commending the expert for his report and noting the improvement in the observance of human rights in Equatorial Guinea evident from it, the Commission on Human Rights, on 11 March 1985,[50] recommended to the Economic and Social Council adoption of a resolution on the subject.

ECONOMIC AND SOCIAL COUNCIL ACTION

On 30 May, acting on the recommendation of its Second Committee, the Economic and Social Council adopted **resolution 1985/39**, without vote.

Situation in Equatorial Guinea

The Economic and Social Council,

Recalling its resolutions 1982/36 of 7 May 1982, 1983/35 of 27 May 1983 and 1984/36 of 24 May 1984,

Bearing in mind Commission on Human Rights resolution 1985/30 of 11 March 1985,

Considering that the conclusions and recommendations of the expert appointed by the Secretary-General pursuant to Council resolution 1984/36 concerning his recent mission to Equatorial Guinea indicate that more needs to be done by the United Nations and the Government of Equatorial Guinea to implement and make better use of the plan of action proposed by the United Nations and accepted by the Government of Equatorial Guinea,

1. *Requests* the Government of Equatorial Guinea to consider the possibility of continuing to implement the plan of action, taking particular account of the expert's new proposals, especially those concerning amendments to the Fundamental Law of that country;

2. *Further requests* the Government of Equatorial Guinea to take steps to facilitate the repatriation of all refugees and exiles, including the adoption of measures enabling all citizens of Equatorial Guinea to participate fully in the country's political, economic, social and cultural affairs, thus helping to relieve the shortage of specialized personnel mentioned in the report of the expert;

3. *Appeals* to the Government of Equatorial Guinea to accede to the International Covenant on Economic, Social and Cultural Rights, the International Covenant on Civil and Political Rights and the Optional Protocol to the International Covenant on Civil and Political Rights, among other international instruments concerning human rights and fundamental freedoms;

4. *Requests* the Secretary-General, in accordance with the report of the expert, to hold discussions with the Government of Equatorial Guinea with a view to carrying out the expert's recommendations regarding assistance to that country, so that the plan of action can be fully implemented in the interests of the full and effective observance of human rights and fundamental freedoms;

5. *Further requests* the Secretary-General to appoint an expert to co-operate with the Government of Equatorial Guinea in the full implementation of the plan of action proposed by the United Nations and accepted by that Government;

6. *Requests* the Commission on Human Rights to consider this matter further at its forty-second session.

Economic and Social Council resolution 1985/39

30 May 1985   Meeting 25   Adopted without vote

Approved by Second Committee (E/1985/95 & Corr.1) without vote, 24 May (meeting 15); draft by Commission on Human Rights (E/1985/22); agenda item 16.

Follow-up action. As the expert had recommended, a series of meetings were held in New York from 21 to 25 October between him and the President of Equatorial Guinea, its Minister for Foreign Affairs and Co-operation and high officials of his Ministry. In addition, the expert met with representatives of UNDP and a number of countries providing assistance.

In his discussions with the country's representatives, the expert examined an April request from Equatorial Guinea to the Secretary-General that two legal experts be sent to Malabo to assist in drafting certain basic legal texts. On his suggestion, two Costa Rican legal experts—Fernando Cruz and Oscar Fernández—were named for the drafting of a penal code and a code of criminal procedure, and later a civil code, commercial code and code of civil procedure. The experts left in late December for Equatorial Guinea, the Secretary-General reported.[51]

Other items discussed during the talks in New York included: the possibility of sending other specialists to the country in 1986 and 1987 to help the Government draft other provisions of the Constitution in matters pertaining to the protection of human rights; the training of staff for the judiciary and, in general, for legal assistance to citizens; and the promotion of women and training in government administration.

Haiti

In accordance with a 1984 Economic and Social Council decision,[52] the Secretary-General reported to the Commission on Human Rights in January 1985[53] on human rights assistance to Haiti. To explore further with the Government ways of facilitating the realization of full enjoyment of human rights, he had called on Jonas K. D. Foli (Ghana) to make contact with the Haitian authorities and the National Human Rights Commission, a national NGO, to ascertain what assistance the United Nations could provide. The expert met with the Commission during his visit to Haiti in October 1984 to discuss the establishment of a documentation centre or library for the Commission, the award of fellowships in human rights, and the organization and promotion of seminars. It was decided that all the points raised during the meetings with the Commission would be embodied in a recommendation made by the Commission to the Government which, it was hoped, would send concrete proposals to the United Nations. At the date of the completion of the report, no such proposals had been received. Meanwhile, the United Nations Centre for Human Rights had ensured the dispatch to the National Commission of a number of human rights documents as a nucleus for a prospective documentation centre.

In conformity with an 11 March recommendation[42] by the Commission on Human Rights, the Secretary-General reported,[54] a formal proposal was made to the Government on 5 July regarding the organization of a national training course designed specifically for officials directly involved in human rights protection.

Uganda

On 11 March 1985,[55] the Commission on Human Rights requested the Secretary-General to continue his contacts with Uganda and to identify external sources of human rights–related assistance on which it might draw. It invited States, United Nations bodies and agencies, and humanitarian and non-governmental organizations to assist Uganda in its efforts to guarantee human rights, and commended those which had been providing such assistance. The Secretary-General was requested to report in 1986 on progress made in helping Uganda in this area.

The Secretary-General reported[56] that in July he had informed the Ugandan Government that the Centre for Human Rights had offered two fellowships and, in September, he had asked for assistance and support to Uganda from States and the above-mentioned organizations. As at 10

December, positive replies had been received from
ILO, FAO, UNESCO, WHO, UNCTAD, UNIDO and
an NGO.

Technical assistance to strengthen legal institutions

In July 1985, the Secretary-General submitted
to the Sub-Commission a report[57] on technical
assistance for the strengthening of legal institutions, in accordance with a 1984 Sub-
Commission resolution.[58] He had invited
Governments receiving aid from UNDP to indicate their needs with regard to establishing or
strengthening law faculties, developing law
libraries, training judges, drafting legal texts,
publishing official law journals, and collecting
and classifying legal material. As at 9 August
1985, replies had been received from six States
which indicated their need for assistance (Argentina, Chad, Cyprus, Dominica, Ethiopia, Peru)
and from two States (Australia, Norway) and
four specialized agencies which provided
assistance.

Responsibility to promote and protect human rights

Because it had not been possible to convene—
as had been decided in 1984[59]—an open-ended
working group to draft a declaration on the right
and responsibility of individuals, groups and
organs of society to promote and protect universally recognized human rights and fundamental
freedoms, the Commission on Human Rights
decided in 1985 that the group should be convened for one week before its 1986 session, taking into account reports and documentation
from the Sub-Commission arising from its work
on draft principles on the subject. The Commission's decision[60] was taken by 30 votes to none,
with 11 abstentions, on 14 March, and it proposed a draft to that effect for adoption by the
Economic and Social Council.

In June 1985, Special Rapporteur Erica-Irene
A. Daes (Greece) submitted to the Sub-
Commission a resolution containing a draft body
of principles,[61] in accordance with her 1984
mandate.[62] Expressing appreciation for the
Special Rapporteur's efforts, the Sub-
Commission decided, by a 30 August resolution[63] adopted by 15 votes to 1, with 1 abstention, to refer the draft to the Commission for further consideration by its working group.

ECONOMIC AND SOCIAL COUNCIL ACTION

In May 1985, on the recommendation of its Second Committee, the Economic and Social Council adopted **decision 1985/152**, without vote.

Question of the violation of human rights and fundamental freedoms in any part of the world, with particular reference to colonial and other dependent countries and territories

At its 25th plenary meeting, on 30 May 1985, the
Council approved the decision taken by the Commission on Human Rights, in its decision 1985/112 of 14
March 1985, that the working group established under
Commission decision 1984/116 of 16 March 1984 to draft
a declaration on the right and responsibility of individuals, groups and organs of society to promote and
protect universally recognized human rights and fundamental freedoms, would be convened at the forty-
second session of the Commission, meeting for one week
prior to the session.

Economic and Social Council decision 1985/152

Adopted without vote

Approved by Second Committee (E/1985/95 & Corr.1) without vote, 24 May (meeting
15); draft by Commission on Human Rights (E/1985/22); agenda item 16.

Proposed establishment of a new international humanitarian order

In October 1985,[64] the Secretary-General
reported to the General Assembly, in accordance
with its 1983 request,[65] on the proposed
establishment of a new international humanitarian
order. The proposal had been advanced by Jordan in 1981.[66]

The Secretary-General's report was based on
views and comments from 34 States and took account of the views offered in various consultations
undertaken by the Secretary-General, including
those with United Nations departments and
organizations and other international organizations, in particular the Independent Commission
on International Humanitarian Issues established
in 1983.

The most acute humanitarian issues identified,
the Secretary-General observed, were hunger,
health and environmental conditions, unemployment, illiteracy, the situation of women and
children, genocide, summary executions, torture,
disappearances, slavery, armed conflicts, gross
human rights violations, weapons that caused unnecessary suffering, disrespect for basic human
rights standards, humanitarian law, refugees,
migrant workers and non-citizens, natural and
man-made disasters and disaster relief, mass exoduses, population questions, vulnerable groups
whose survival was threatened, racial and religious
intolerance, and the drug problem.

The term "humanitarian", the Secretary-
General said, could be used to describe a specific
body of law, created around the turn of the century to ameliorate conditions in armed conflicts,
or that developed since 1864 under the aegis of
ICRC, such as the 1949 Geneva Conventions. At
times it denoted an approach emphasizing protection of and assistance to the individual, as opposed
to politically influenced considerations; at other

times, the term reflected a broader sentiment, to relieve human suffering and help realize human needs. A conceptual understanding of the humanitarian international order must encompass all those aspects and include the internationally established norms on human rights.

In practical terms, humanitarian emergencies arose in situations of natural or man-made disasters, armed conflicts, internal disturbances and refugee outflows. A normative and institutional framework to deal with those areas existed, but certain issues required further standards, a continuing task of the international community, as was implementation of existing norms.

The basic issue was whether emphasis was to be given to a broad, future-based approach or to the immediate solution of concrete and practical problems. Whatever approach was adopted by the Assembly, he felt that priority should be given to existing humanitarian emergencies, effective implementation of internationally recognized standards, universal ratification of relevant instruments, education, training and dissemination of information to create greater awareness of those standards, and the setting of standards addressing current problems.

Since an extensive body of international norms already existed, the Secretary-General said, perhaps a distillation of humanitarian principles might be the subject of a publication. A universal declaration on a new international humanitarian order would perforce draw on the existing human rights instruments; it was open to discussion whether principles could be drawn up in a new declaration that would extend much further. An attempt to "renegotiate" existing principles might weaken them; an incremental approach involving the addition of standards dealing with pressing new problems might, however, avoid such risks. The tasks of consolidation, systematization, codification and progressive development might for the time being be left to be resolved through evolving practice and to the endeavours of scholars, he concluded.

GENERAL ASSEMBLY ACTION

On 13 December 1985, acting on the recommendation of the Third Committee, the General Assembly adopted **resolution 40/126**, without vote.

New international humanitarian order
The General Assembly,
Recalling its resolutions 36/136 of 14 December 1981, 37/201 of 18 December 1982 and 38/125 of 16 December 1983,
Taking note of the report of the Secretary-General,
Welcoming the views and comments of Governments regarding the proposal to promote a new international

humanitarian order contained in the report of the Secretary-General,
Reiterating that the work of the Independent Commission on International Humanitarian Issues, established outside the framework of the United Nations, could be useful for further study of the proposal,
1. *Expresses its appreciation* to the Secretary-General for his report;
2. *Takes note* of the activities of the Independent Commission on International Humanitarian Issues, as described in the report of the Secretary-General, and looks forward to the outcome of its efforts and its final report;
3. *Invites* Governments that have not yet done so to communicate to the Secretary-General their views regarding the proposal to promote a new international humanitarian order;
4. *Requests* the Secretary-General, in the light of further views received, to submit to the General Assembly at its forty-first session an addendum to his report, including a survey of specific humanitarian issues;
5. *Decides* to review at its forty-first session the question of a new international humanitarian order.

General Assembly resolution 40/126

13 December 1985   Meeting 116   Adopted without vote

Approved by Third Committee (A/40/1006) without vote, 6 December (meeting 69); 26-nation draft (A/C.3/40/L.88); agenda item 108.
Sponsors: Australia, Austria, Bangladesh, Canada, Costa Rica, Djibouti, Egypt, Greece, Iraq, Italy, Japan, Jordan, Lebanon, Mauritania, Morocco, Oman, Pakistan, Qatar, Romania, Senegal, Somalia, Sri Lanka, Tunisia, United Republic of Tanzania, Yemen, Yugoslavia.

REFERENCES

[1]A/40/677. [2]YUN 1981, p. 926. [3]YUN 1983, p. 858. [4]A/40/469. [5]YUN 1984, p. 841, GA res. 39/144, 14 Dec. 1984. [6]E/1985/22 (dec. 1985/110). [7]*Ibid.* (dec. 1985/111). [8]E/1985/22. [9]*Ibid.* (res. 1985/28). [10]YUN 1984, p. 843. [11]*Ibid.*, p. 842. [12]E/CN.4/Sub.2/1985/2. [13]E/CN.4/1986/5 (res. 1985/24). [14]*Ibid.* (res. 1985/8). [15]*Ibid.* (res. 1985/34). [16]E/1985/22 (dec. 1985/113). [17]E/CN.4/1986/5 (res. 1985/15). [18]E/CN.4/1985/16. [19]E/1985/22 (res. 1985/49). [20]YUN 1984, p. 849. [21]E/1985/22 (res. 1985/48). [22]YUN 1982, p. 1106. [23]E/CN.4/Sub.2/1985/3. [24]YUN 1966, pp. 419 & 423, GA res. 2200 A (XXI), annex, 16 Dec. 1966. [25]YUN 1965, p. 440, GA res. 2106 A (XX), annex, 21 Dec. 1965. [26]YUN 1973, p. 103, GA res. 3068(XXVII), annex, 30 Nov. 1973. [27]YUN 1979, p. 895, GA res. 34/180, annex, 18 Dec. 1979. [28]E/CN.4/Sub.2/1985/27. [29]YUN 1984, p. 844. [30]E/CN.4/1986/5 (res. 1985/5). [31]YUN 1984, p. 813, GA res. 39/46, annex, 10 Dec. 1984. [32]A/C.3/40/15. [33]A/40/600 & Add.1. [34]E/1985/22 (res. 1985/45). [35]A/40/605. [36]YUN 1955, p. 164, GA res. 926(X), 14 Dec. 1955. [37]E/CN.4/1986/34 & Add.1-6. [38]ST/HR/SER.A/17. [39]E/CN.4/1985/30. [40]YUN 1984, p. 845. [41]E/CN.4/1985/36. [42]E/1985/22 (res. 1985/26). [43]YUN 1984, p. 847, ESC res. 1984/32, 24 May 1984. [44]E/CN.4/1985/31. [45]YUN 1984, p. 847. [46]E/1985/22 (res. 1985/34). [47]YUN 1984, p. 848, ESC res. 1984/36, 24 May 1984. [48]E/CN.4/1985/9 & Add.1. [49]YUN 1981, p. 938. [50]E/1985/22 (res. 1985/30). [51]E/CN.4/1986/34/Add.2. [52]YUN 1984, p. 875, ESC dec. 1984/143, 24 May 1984. [53]E/CN.4/1985/32. [54]E/CN.4/1986/34/Add.3. [55]E/1985/22 (res. 1985/27). [56]E/CN.4/1986/34/Add.4. [57]E/CN.4/Sub.2/1985/24 & Add.1,2. [58]YUN 1984, p. 848. [59]*Ibid.*, p. 849. [60]E/1985/22 (dec. 1985/112). [61]E/CN.4/Sub.2/1985/30 & Add.1. [62]YUN 1984, p. 849, ESC res. 1984/38, 24 May 1984. [63]E/CN.4/1986/5 (res. 1985/30). [64]A/40/348 & Add.1,2. [65]YUN 1983, p. 870, GA res. 38/125, 16 Dec. 1983. [66]YUN 1981, p. 968.

Human rights violations

Situations involving alleged violations of human rights on a large scale in several countries were again examined in 1985 by the General Assembly, the Economic and Social Council and the Commission on Human Rights, as well as by special bodies and officials appointed to examine some of those situations.

In addition, situations of alleged human rights violations involving the self-determination of peoples (see above, under "Civil and political rights") were discussed with regard to Afghanistan, Kampuchea, South Africa and Namibia, Western Sahara and the Palestinian people.

Under a procedure established by the Council in 1970[1] to deal with communications alleging denial or violation of human rights, the Commission held closed meetings in 1985 to study confidential documents, observations thereon submitted by Governments and a confidential report by a working group set up in 1984[2] to examine the material.

The Economic and Social Council, by **decision 1985/138**, adopted without vote on 30 May 1985, approved a 5 March decision[3] of the Commission to set up a similar five-member working group to meet for one week prior to its 1986 session to examine particular situations that might be referred to it by the Sub-Commission at its 1985 session under its procedure for dealing with confidential documents, and those of which the Commission was seized. The decision was approved by the Council's Second Committee on 24 May, also without vote.

The Council decided that material relating to Argentina dealt with by the Commission under the same procedure should cease to be confidential (see p. 912); a similar decision was taken with regard to material relating to Uruguay (see p. 924).

The Sub-Commission, by a resolution[4] adopted on 29 August by 7 votes to 4, with 8 abstentions, requested the Commission's and the Council's authorization for the Bureau it elected at each of its sessions to hold two inter-sessional meetings per year, to enable it to review developments and ensure timely collection of needed information, so that it could bring to the Commission's attention any situation which revealed a consistent pattern of human rights violations in any country and assist the Commission in carrying out its responsibilities under a 1979 General Assembly resolution[5] to take timely and effective action in cases of mass and flagrant violations.

The General Assembly, in **resolution 40/124**, reiterated that the international community should continue to accord priority to the search for solutions to mass and flagrant violations of human rights of peoples and individuals, paying due attention also to other situations of human rights violations. It reaffirmed its responsibility for achieving international co-operation in promoting and encouraging respect for human rights and fundamental freedoms for all and expressed its concern in particular at mass and flagrant violations, wherever they occurred.

Africa

South Africa and Namibia

Working Group reports. The six-member *Ad Hoc* Working Group of Experts on southern Africa, established in 1967[6] by the Commission on Human Rights, submitted in January 1985 its annual report[7] to the Commission. It observed that the preceding year had witnessed persistent massive repression of protests and demonstrations, a growing number of arrests of political prisoners and detentions without trial, allegations of torture in both South Africa and Namibia, continuation of the policy of forced removals of populations and harassment of activists.

Following up on a report[8] submitted to the Commission in 1983 and the corresponding Commission decision,[9] the *Ad Hoc* Working Group submitted in January 1985 a report[10] on the effects of *apartheid* on the non-white population, in particular on black women and children, in South Africa and Namibia. The Group examined the extent to which acts of *apartheid* might be likened to those designated as acts of genocide. Its conclusion was that the practical implementation of *apartheid* resulted in certain criminal consequences which coincided with acts prohibited under article II of the 1948 Convention on the Prevention and Punishment of the Crime of Genocide,[11] which characterized as genocide such acts as killing members of a group, causing bodily or mental harm to them, or imposing measures intended to prevent births within the group or transferring the group's children. The policy of *apartheid*, viewed as a whole and over the long term, would ultimately produce consequences identical to those prohibited under another provision of article II (i.e. deliberately inflicting on the group conditions of life calculated to bring about its physical destruction in whole or in part).

The Working Group requested the Commission to authorize it to continue its investigations so as to complete its information, taking into account the way in which the South African régime implemented its *apartheid* policy, henceforth considered as a kind of genocide. The Commission might also wish to authorize the Group to study in which areas of life the racially oppressed peoples in South Africa felt the effects of genocide and how far those consequences had gone, and examine the question of international penal responsibility of States, groups and individuals. The Group requested the Commission to call on the General Assembly to seek an advisory opinion from the International Court of Justice on the extent to which *apartheid* as a policy entailed criminal effects bordering on genocide. The Group suggested that the Commission might wish to take steps to revise the 1948 Convention and to arrive at an up-to-date definition of the crime of genocide. It also recommended that the Commission invite the Assembly to request the International Law Commission rapidly to conclude preparation of the draft code of offences against the peace and security of mankind (see p. 1163).

Human Rights Commission action. By a roll-call vote of 41 to 1, with 1 abstention, taken on 26 February 1985,[12] the Commission on Human Rights adopted the Working Group's conclusions and recommendations. It also took note of the Group's studies and findings[10] concerning the relationship between *apartheid* and genocide and requested the Group to continue investigating the matter. The Commission reaffirmed its rejection as null and void of the so-called constitutional arrangements in South Africa, as they served to perpetuate *apartheid* and other forms of racial discrimination and continued to exclude the black majority from participating in the country's political, social, economic and cultural life and to deny the black population their full citizenship rights.

The Commission denounced the policy of "bantustanization", the forced removals of the black population and the policy of denationalization, and expressed profound indignation at, particularly, the intimidation and suppression of opponents of *apartheid*, the indiscriminate arrest and torture of political activists, the extreme use of violence in dealing with legitimate protests, the killing and ill-treatment of detainees, the discriminatory and inferior quality of black education, and the continued adverse effects of *apartheid*, especially on women and children. It condemned South Africa for its military pressures on front-line States and for its support and encouragement to bandits who sought to destabilize those and other neighbouring States.

The Commission demanded that South Africa end *apartheid* and other gross human rights violations, called for the unconditional release of all political prisoners, and called on South Africa to respect international standards on trade union rights. It renewed the mandate of the Working Group to continue to study violations of human rights in South Africa and Namibia, and requested it to continue to bring to the Commission Chair-

man's attention particularly serious violations. It requested the Working Group, in co-operation with the Special Committee against *Apartheid*, to continue to investigate ill-treatment and deaths of detainees and authorized the Group Chairman to participate in events connected with action against *apartheid* organized under that Committee's auspices. It renewed its request to South Africa to allow the Working Group to make on-the-spot investigations of treatment and living conditions in prisons of South Africa and Namibia. It requested the Working Group to report to the Commission in 1987, with a progress report in 1986, and asked the Secretary-General to assist the Group.

Also on 26 February,[13] the Commission adopted, by a roll-call vote of 39 to none, with 4 abstentions, the conclusions and recommendations concerning Namibia in the report[7] of the *Ad Hoc* Working Group. It reaffirmed the right of the Namibian people to self-determination and independence under conditions determined by the Security Council in 1978.[14] The Commission strongly condemned South Africa for the military buildup in Namibia, the recruitment and training of Namibians for tribal armies, the use of mercenaries, torture and brutality against the population and captured freedom fighters, and the military conscription of Namibians. Condemning South Africa for its continued attempts to circumvent the United Nations plan for the independence of Namibia, the Commission demanded that it co-operate to bring about Namibia's independence. The Commission decided that the *Ad Hoc* Working Group should continue to study the policies and practices violating human rights in Namibia, to study ways in which the Commission might effectively contribute to eliminating *apartheid* there, to inquire about persons suspected of having committed the crime of *apartheid* or other serious violations of human rights in Namibia, and to bring particularly serious violations to the Commission's attention.

ECONOMIC AND SOCIAL COUNCIL ACTION

In May 1985, on the recommendation of its Second Committee, the Economic and Social Council adopted **decision 1985/140**, by roll-call vote.

Situation of human rights in South Africa

At its 25th plenary meeting, on 30 May 1985, the Council, noting Commission on Human Rights resolution 1985/8 of 26 February 1985, approved the Commission's decision to renew the mandate of the *Ad Hoc* Working Group of Experts on southern Africa. The Council also approved the authorization given by the Commission to the Chairman of the *Ad Hoc* Working Group to participate in conferences, symposia, seminars or other events connected with action against *apartheid* organized under the auspices of the Special Committee against *Apartheid*.

Economic and Social Council decision 1985/140

30 May 1985   Meeting 25   52-1 (roll-call vote)

Approved by Second Committee (E/1985/95 & Corr.1) by vote (51-1), 24 May (meeting 15); draft by Commission on Human Rights (E/1985/22); agenda item 16.
Financial implications: S-G, A/C.5/40/13 & Corr.1.

Roll-call vote in Council as follows:

In favour: Algeria, Argentina, Bangladesh, Botswana, Brazil, Bulgaria, Canada, China, Colombia, Congo, Costa Rica, Djibouti, Ecuador, Finland, France, German Democratic Republic, Germany, Federal Republic of, Guinea, Haiti, Iceland, India, Indonesia, Japan, Lebanon, Luxembourg, Malaysia, Mexico, Morocco, Netherlands, New Zealand, Nigeria, Papua New Guinea, Poland, Romania, Rwanda, Saudi Arabia, Senegal, Sierra Leone, Somalia, Spain, Sri Lanka, Suriname, Sweden, Thailand, Turkey, Uganda, USSR, United Kingdom, Venezuela, Yugoslavia, Zaire, Zimbabwe.

Against: United States.

While it shared the international community's revulsion at the abhorrent system of *apartheid*, the United States said, it voted against the text because of its position on the underlying Commission on Human Rights resolution[12] and because of its concern about the excessive financial implications of more than $1 million.

Follow-up action by the Working Group. The *Ad Hoc* Working Group of Experts on southern Africa met on 14 June 1985 at Geneva for an emergency meeting, the first since its establishment. The Group examined a number of recent incidents involving human rights violations in South Africa and discussed various possibilities for further action. It concluded that the events, because of their seriousness and cruelty, should be investigated thoroughly within its mandate, and expressed the expectation that the international community would take bold and decisive measures to eliminate *apartheid*.

The special report[15] of the meeting was transmitted on 18 July to the Presidents of the General Assembly and the Security Council and to the Secretary-General, as well as to the South African Government. In October,[16] the Secretary-General drew the Assembly's attention to that report as well as the Group's earlier report.[7]

In a progress report[17] to be submitted to the Commission in 1986, the Working Group said that, in August 1985, it became highly concerned at the avalanche of reported cases of serious violations, particularly in the wake of the declaration of the state of emergency in South Africa. Since the cases revealed, in the Working Group's view, a flagrant contempt for the right to life, it decided, in consultation with the Special Rapporteur on summary or arbitrary executions, to send a joint mission to Lusaka, Zambia, to determine the extent of the alleged violations. The Chairman of the Group and the Special Rapporteur visited Lusaka from 13 to 19 November, gathering evidence from 19 witnesses, covering violations of the right to life, effects of the implementation of the constitutional reforms and harsher bantustan policy, torture, victimization, harassment, destruction of property, detention and ill-treatment.

Sub-Commission action. The Sub-Commission's Working Group on Slavery, at its August 1985 session[18] (see p. 871), also dealt with *apartheid* and colonialism, practices it considered to be similar to slavery. The Working Group recommended that the Chairman of the Commission on Human Rights be authorized to bring pressure on the South African Government to order the unconditional release from gaol of Nelson Mandela, leader of the African National Congress, and Zephania Mothopeng, leader of the Pan Africanist Congress of Azania, as well as other political prisoners, and to engage in a meaningful dialogue with the black majority leaders.

On 30 August,[19] the Sub-Commission reaffirmed that *apartheid* was an international crime and that the *apartheid* régime was illegitimate and contrary to the Universal Declaration of Human Rights.[20] It strongly condemned South Africa for acts of terrorism against the black majority and against the front-line and other neighbouring States, as well as for its refusal to implement the United Nations plan for Namibia's independence. It demanded the lifting of the state of emergency, the cessation of all acts of brutality by South African police and military forces, and the immediate release of all political prisoners, and called on the international community to continue its efforts towards total isolation of South Africa.

On 8 August,[21] the Sub-Commission authorized its Chairman to send an urgent communication to the Commission Chairman requesting him to cable South Africa urging that Messrs. Mandela and Mothopeng, in particular, be released and be allowed to come to Geneva to participate in the current Sub-Commission session.

On 29 August,[22] the Sub-Commission decided to observe at the beginning of its future annual sessions a minute of silence in honour of the victims of the *apartheid* system.

1973 Convention against apartheid

As at 31 December 1985, there were 82 parties to the International Convention on the Suppression and Punishment of the Crime of *Apartheid*, which was adopted by the General Assembly in 1973[23] and entered into force in 1976.[24] In 1985, Argentina ratified, and Bangladesh and Iran acceded to, the Convention.

In his annual report[25] to the General Assembly on the status of the Convention, the Secretary-General annexed a list of the 35 States that had signed, 29 that had ratified and 52 that had acceded to it and the date thereof, as of 1 September.

Activities of the Group of Three. The Group of Three—established under article IX of the Convention to consider reports by States parties on measures taken to implement the Convention and in 1985 composed of Mexico, Senegal and the Ukrainian SSR—held its eighth session at Geneva from 28 January to 1 February.[26]

The Group examined an initial report from Algeria, a second periodic report from Madagascar, a third from Yugoslavia, and fourth reports from Bulgaria, the Byelorussian SSR, Cuba, the Ukrainian SSR and the USSR. The Group also continued to examine the question of whether actions of transnational corporations (TNCs) operating in South Africa came under the definition of the crime of *apartheid* and whether legal action could be taken under the Convention. The Group noted that several United Nations organs and States parties had repeatedly drawn the attention of the international community to the close interconnection between TNC activities in South Africa and that country's persistence in pursuing its policy of *apartheid*. The Group was of the view that effective international action to eradicate *apartheid* had been hampered by TNCs and reiterated that article III of the Convention, pertaining to international criminal responsibility, could apply. The Group felt that further examination of the matter was needed and that views of States parties on TNCs' responsibility for the continued existence of *apartheid* would be very useful.

The Group noted with concern that less than half of the States parties had submitted a report and it urged in particular those which had not submitted their initial report to do so as soon as possible. When preparing their reports, States parties should take into account the general guidelines and provide more information on legislative, judicial and administrative measures to suppress *apartheid* and to prosecute persons responsible for acts of *apartheid*, on difficulties encountered in taking such measures, on teaching and education measures for fuller implementation of the Convention, and on implementation of article XI on the extradition of such persons; they should also identify individuals, organizations, institutions and representatives of States deemed responsible for crimes enumerated in article II, and those against whom legal proceedings had been undertaken. It again drew attention to the desirability of disseminating more information about the Convention, its implementation and the work of the Group.

The Group appealed again to States parties to strengthen their international co-operation to implement fully United Nations decisions on *apartheid*. It recommended that the fortieth anniversary of the victory over fascism and nazism and of the founding of the United Nations be celebrated by mobilizing international efforts to eliminate *apartheid*. It noted that *apartheid* was a form of genocide and as such fell under the 1968 Convention on the Non-Applicability of Statutory Limitations to War Crimes and Crimes against Humanity;[27] it recommended to the Commission that such interdependence be reflected in its resolutions as well as the fact that adherence to the Convention against *apartheid* was an indication of the implementation of the Convention on genocide.

The Group once again drew attention to the importance of assistance to the national liberation movements in southern Africa. It recommended that States parties be invited to express their views on the responsibility of TNCs for the continued existence of *apartheid*, and that the parties, specialized agencies and NGOs be invited to provide information on the types of the crime of *apartheid* committed by TNCs in South Africa.

Human Rights Commission action. By a 26 February 1985 resolution,[28] adopted by a roll-call vote of 32 to 1, with 10 abstentions, the Commission on Human Rights took note with appreciation of the Group of Three's conclusions and recommendations. The Commission urged States to adhere to the *apartheid* Convention without delay, especially those which had jurisdiction over TNCs operating in South Africa and Namibia, and also to ratify the genocide Convention.

The Commission urged States parties to the Convention against *apartheid* to take full account of the guidelines laid down by the Group of Three in 1978 for the submission of reports, and reiterated its recommendation that they be represented when their country's report was considered by the Group. It requested the Secretary-General once more to invite States parties to express their views on the extent and responsibility of TNCs for the continued existence of *apartheid*. The Group was requested to continue examining legal actions that could be taken against TNCs whose operations came under the crime of *apartheid*, and to report to the Commission in 1986.

The Commission called on States parties to strengthen national and international co-operation in order to implement fully United Nations decisions concerning the prevention, suppression and punishment of the crime of *apartheid*, drew their attention to the desirability of disseminating further information on the Convention, its implementation and the work of the Group, and noted the importance of their measures in teaching and education for fuller implementation of the Convention. The Group was to meet for up to five days before the Commission's 1986 session. The Secretary-General was asked to give it the necessary assistance.

GENERAL ASSEMBLY ACTION

On 29 November 1985, on the recommendation of the Third Committee, the General Assembly adopted **resolution 40/27**, by recorded vote.

**Status of the International Convention on the
Suppression and Punishment of the Crime of *Apartheid***

The General Assembly,

Recalling its resolution 3068(XXVIII) of 30 November
1973, by which it adopted and opened for signature and
ratification the International Convention on the Suppression and Punishment of the Crime of *Apartheid*, and its
subsequent resolutions on the status of the Convention,

Reaffirming its conviction that *apartheid* constitutes a total
negation of the purposes and principles of the Charter
of the United Nations, a gross violation of human rights
and a crime against humanity, seriously threatening international peace and security,

Taking note of the finding of the Group of Three of the
Commission on Human Rights, established in accordance with article IX of the Convention, that the crime
of *apartheid* is a form of the crime of genocide,

Strongly condemning South Africa's continued policy of
apartheid and its continued illegal occupation of Namibia,
as well as its recent acts of aggression against Angola and
other African States,

Alarmed by the aggravation of the situation in South
Africa, in particular the further escalation of ruthless
repression by the Fascist-like *apartheid* régime, including
the use of the armed forces against the opposing people
and the imposition of virtual martial-law conditions intended to facilitate the brutal oppression of the black
population,

Condemning the continued collaboration of certain
States and transnational corporations with the racist
régime of South Africa in the political, economic,
military and other fields as an encouragement to the
intensification of its odious policy of *apartheid*,

Firmly convinced that the legitimate struggle of the oppressed peoples in southern Africa against *apartheid*,
racism and colonialism and for the effective exercise of
their inalienable right to self-determination and independence demands more than ever all necessary support by the international community and, in particular,
further action by the Security Council in accordance
with Chapter VII of the Charter of the United Nations,

Underlining that ratification of or accession to the Convention on a universal basis and the implementation of
its provisions without delay are necessary for its effectiveness, and therefore will contribute to the eradication of the crime of *apartheid*,

1. *Takes note* of the report of the Secretary-General
on the status of the International Convention on the
Suppression and Punishment of the Crime of *Apartheid;*

2. *Commends* those States parties to the Convention
that have submitted their reports under article VII
thereof;

3. *Appeals once again* to those States that have not yet
done so to ratify or to accede to the Convention without
further delay, in particular those States that have jurisdiction over transnational corporations operating in South
Africa and Namibia and without whose co-operation
such operations cannot be halted;

4. *Takes note with appreciation* of the report of the
Group of Three of the Commission on Human Rights,
established in accordance with article IX of the Convention, and, in particular, of the conclusions and
recommendations contained in that report;

5. *Draws the attention* of all States to the opinion expressed by the Group of Three in its report that article

III of the Convention could apply to the actions of
transnational corporations operating in South Africa;

6. *Requests* the Commission on Human Rights to intensify, in co-operation with the Special Committee
against *Apartheid*, its efforts to compile periodically the
progressive list of individuals, organizations, institutions
and representatives of States deemed responsible for
crimes enumerated in article II of the Convention, as
well as those against whom or which legal proceedings
have been undertaken;

7. *Requests* the Secretary-General to circulate the above-
mentioned list to all States parties to the Convention and
all Member States and to bring such facts to the attention of the public by all means of mass communication;

8. *Requests* the Secretary-General to invite the States
parties to the Convention, the specialized agencies and
non-governmental organizations to provide the Commission on Human Rights with relevant information concerning the forms of the crime of *apartheid*, as described
in article II of the Convention, committed by transnational corporations operating in South Africa;

9. *Appeals* to all States, United Nations organs, the
specialized agencies and international and national non-
governmental organizations to step up their activities in
enhancing public awareness by denouncing the crimes
committed by the racist régime of South Africa;

10. *Requests* the Secretary-General to intensify his efforts, through appropriate channels, to disseminate information on the Convention and its implementation
with a view to promoting further ratification of or accession to the Convention;

11. *Requests* the Secretary-General to include in his
next annual report under General Assembly resolution
3380(XXX) of 10 November 1975 a special section concerning the implementation of the Convention.

General Assembly resolution 40/27

29 November 1985   Meeting 96   120-1-24 (recorded vote)

Approved by Third Committee (A/40/914) by recorded vote (111-1-23), 4 November
(meeting 30); 19-nation draft (A/C.3/40/L.6); agenda item 94 *(c)*.

Sponsors: Afghanistan, Algeria, Angola, Bulgaria, Burkina Faso, Cuba, Czecho-
slovakia, Ethiopia, German Democratic Republic, Hungary, Lao People's
Democratic Republic, Madagascar, Mongolia, Nicaragua, Nigeria, Syrian Arab
Republic, Ukrainian SSR, Viet Nam, Zambia.

Meeting numbers. GA 40th session: 3rd Committee 3-15, 30, 31; plenary 96.

Recorded vote in Assembly as follows:

In favour: Afghanistan, Albania, Algeria, Angola, Argentina, Bahamas, Bahrain,
Bangladesh, Barbados, Benin, Bhutan, Bolivia, Botswana, Brazil, Brunei
Darussalam, Bulgaria, Burkina Faso, Burma, Burundi, Byelorussian SSR, Cam-
eroon, Cape Verde, Central African Republic, Chad, Chile, China, Comoros,
Congo, Cuba, Cyprus, Czechoslovakia, Democratic Kampuchea, Democratic
Yemen, Djibouti, Dominican Republic, Ecuador, Egypt, El Salvador, Equatorial
Guinea, Ethiopia, Fiji, Gabon, German Democratic Republic, Ghana, Guatemala,
Guinea, Guinea-Bissau, Guyana, Honduras, Hungary, India, Indonesia, Iran, Iraq,
Ivory Coast, Jamaica, Jordan, Kenya, Kuwait, Lao People's Democratic Republic,
Lebanon, Lesotho, Liberia, Libyan Arab Jamahiriya, Madagascar, Malaysia,
Maldives, Mali, Malta, Mauritania, Mauritius, Mexico, Mongolia, Morocco,
Mozambique, Nepal, Nicaragua, Niger, Nigeria, Oman, Pakistan, Panama, Papua
New Guinea, Peru, Philippines, Poland, Qatar, Romania, Rwanda, Saint Lucia,
Samoa, Sao Tome and Principe, Saudi Arabia, Senegal, Seychelles, Sierra Leone,
Singapore, Somalia, Sri Lanka, Sudan, Suriname, Syrian Arab Republic, Thailand,
Togo, Trinidad and Tobago, Tunisia, Turkey, Uganda, Ukrainian SSR, USSR,
United Arab Emirates, United Republic of Tanzania, Uruguay, Venezuela, Viet
Nam, Yemen, Yugoslavia, Zaire, Zambia, Zimbabwe.

Against: United States.

Abstaining: Australia, Austria, Belgium, Canada, Denmark, Finland, France,
Germany, Federal Republic of, Greece, Iceland, Ireland, Israel, Italy, Japan, Lux-
embourg, Malawi, Netherlands, New Zealand, Norway, Portugal, Spain,
Swaziland, Sweden, United Kingdom.

Before adopting the text as a whole, the
Assembly adopted paragraphs 5 and 8 by recorded

votes of 118 to 11, with 14 abstentions, and 119 to 11, with 12 abstentions, respectively; the Committee had done the same, by recorded votes of 104 to 11, with 16 abstentions, and 107 to 11, with 12 abstentions. The third preambular paragraph was adopted by the Assembly by a recorded vote of 114 to 9, with 16 abstentions, having been approved by the Committee by a recorded vote of 108 to 10, with 15 abstentions.

Luxembourg, speaking on behalf of the 10 member States of the European Economic Community (EEC), as well as Spain and Portugal, said they considered that the Convention had made no real contribution to eliminating *apartheid* and, although they supported its ultimate objective, they had serious reservations on the envisaged methods, which posed legal problems with reference to the fundamental characteristics of the crime of *apartheid*, the territorial application rules and the international jurisdictional competence of States. Turkey also said the text raised legal problems for it, but had voted in favour because it firmly opposed *apartheid*.

The Ten had difficulty accepting paragraphs 5 and 8, since they deemed it inadmissible that treaties should have a legal effect on third States and that restrictions of competence should be imposed on them without their consent. They considered that the Group of Three was not competent to formulate the conclusions in question and that genocide had been clearly defined by the 1948 Convention. A text like the resolution, without the force of a treaty, by which the Assembly would extend the field of application of the Convention, had no basis in law.

On behalf of the Nordic delegations, Sweden said that, not being parties to the Convention, they had abstained, though not to reflect any positions taken regarding the substance of the resolution, which carried unclear but potentially far-reaching international legal implications. Japan felt certain provisions of the Convention itself contained legally ambiguous concepts and definitions. The Convention also raised legal and constitutional problems for Australia and Austria. Australia also had difficulties with the paragraphs voted on, in particular paragraph 5; it rejected any implications that article II of the Convention applied to TNCs. Not being a party to the Convention, it did not wish to be involved in any request to the Secretary-General in the terms set out in paragraph 8, which presupposed the applicability of the Convention to TNCs, a proposition it could not endorse.

Foreign support of South Africa

Human Rights Commission action. By a resolution of 26 February,[29] adopted by a roll-call vote of 31 to 5, with 7 abstentions, the Commission reaffirmed the right of the oppressed peoples of South Africa and Namibia to self-determination, independence and enjoyment of their natural resources, to dispose of those resources for their greater well-being and to obtain just reparation for the exploitation, depletion, loss or depreciation of those resources, including reparation for the exploitation and abuse of their human resources. The Commission vigorously condemned the increased assistance to South Africa by major Western countries and Israel, particularly in the military field, and demanded that assistance, which it was convinced was a hostile action against the people of South Africa, Namibia and the neighbouring States, be immediately terminated. Condemning the continuing nuclear collaboration of certain Western States, Israel and others with South Africa, the Commission urged them to stop supplying it with nuclear equipment and technology. It strongly condemned the activities of all foreign economic interests exploiting Namibia's resources and demanded that TNCs refrain from new investment or activities in Namibia, withdraw from it and end their co-operation with the South African administration. The Commission called on all Governments to take legislative, administrative or other measures to stop their nationals and corporations under their jurisdiction from trade, manufacturing and investment activities in South Africa and Namibia, to end technological assistance or collaboration in the manufacture of arms and military supplies there and to cease nuclear collaboration with South Africa.

The Commission rejected all policies that encouraged the régime to intensify its repression of South Africans and Namibians and to escalate its aggression against neighbouring States. It welcomed the General Assembly's request that the Security Council consider mandatory sanctions against South Africa, in particular regarding collaboration in arms manufacture, in military supplies and in the nuclear field, loans (including International Monetary Fund (IMF) and World Bank loans), investments, trade, petroleum and its products and other strategic goods, and called for mobilizing international public opinion in favour of sanctions.

The Commission appealed to States, specialized agencies and NGOs to co-operate with the liberation movements of southern Africa. Strongly condemning South Africa for its persistent aggression against Angola, the Commission called on it to withdraw its troops from there and demanded that it cease destabilizing the political institutions of neighbouring States.

The Commission, reaffirming that the updating of the report containing the list of banks, TNCs and other organizations assisting the régime was of the greatest importance for the fight against *apartheid*, welcomed the Assembly's 1984 invitation[30] to the Special Rapporteur to continue to update the list. It attached special importance to the widest dissemination of the updated report as a United Nations publication, called on Governments to give it wide publicity, and requested the Secretary-General to assist the Special Rapporteur, in particular in establishing direct contacts with the Centre on TNCs and the Centre against *Apartheid*, in expanding the annotation of selected cases and in continuing the computerization of future lists.

Report of the Special Rapporteur. Special Rapporteur Ahmed Mohamed Khalifa (Egypt) presented to the Sub-Commission in 1985 an updated report[31] on the adverse consequences for the enjoyment of human rights of political, military, economic and other assistance to South Africa, with addenda containing an updated list of banks, insurance companies, firms and other organizations assisting South Africa, directly or indirectly and through assistance to Namibia, and the names which were to be deleted from that list.

Sub-Commission action. By a 27 August resolution,[32] adopted by 19 votes to none, with 3 abstentions, the Sub-Commission welcomed issuance of the Special Rapporteur's report as a United Nations publication and invited him to continue to update the list of organizations assisting South Africa, using all available material from United Nations organs and agencies, Member States, inter- and non-governmental organizations and other sources in order to indicate the volume and nature of that assistance. In doing so, the Sub-Commission invited him to intensify direct contacts with the Centre on TNCs and the Centre against *Apartheid*.

The Sub-Commission recommended to the Commission that it adopt a text along the lines of its own resolution and that, in addition, it call on Governments to co-operate with the Special Rapporteur to make the report even more accurate and informative, and disseminate the report and give it the widest possible publicity.

Report of the Secretary-General. In a September 1985 report[33] on international conditions and human rights, the Secretary-General stated that the deteriorating situation in South Africa and Namibia, as described by the *Ad Hoc* Working Group of Experts on southern Africa (see p. 898), exacerbated by the declaration of a state of emergency, was nevertheless accompanied by increasing compliance with United Nations resolutions calling for a cessation of all foreign investment there; the campaign to encourage investors to divest themselves of shares in corporations trading in South Africa had gained considerable momentum during the past two years.

Trade union rights

Report of the *Ad Hoc* Working Group of Experts. The *Ad Hoc* Working Group of Experts on southern Africa continued in 1985 to study the situation relating to allegations of infringements of trade union rights. Its findings, included in its report,[7] were submitted to the Council separately in April.[34]

The Working Group expressed the opinion that developments concerning the right to work and freedom of association, including the situation of trade unions formed by black workers, could not but be seen in the context of political developments in South Africa, in the face of which black workers had had to organize themselves better and black trade unions found themselves in the vanguard of black emancipation. However, the growth in both stature and size of worker organizations had been an uphill and often bitter struggle; the sharp increase in black trade union membership had been met with a determination by the régime to impose controls and limit the extent to which unions might participate in broader issues and, in particular, the extent to which they could play a part in mobilizing political resistance. Where unions and workers had challenged or ignored the establishment and where their actions had gone beyond the narrow sphere to which the Government wished to confine them, State repression had set in, directed at the growing strength and organization of black workers. Police intervention in strikes had become a regular feature; unions which had most clearly aligned themselves with political resistance had been the principal targets.

ECONOMIC AND SOCIAL COUNCIL ACTION

On 30 May, on the recommendation of its Second Committee, the Economic and Social Council adopted **resolution 1985/43**, without vote.

Report of the *Ad Hoc* Working Group of Experts of the Commission on Human Rights on allegations of infringements of trade union rights in the Republic of South Africa

The Economic and Social Council,

Recalling its resolution 1984/42 of 24 May 1984,

Having examined the extract from the progress report of the *Ad Hoc* Working Group of Experts on southern Africa,

Noting with grave concern that police and State interference in industrial disputes and repression against the independent black trade union movement have intensified,

Noting further with indignation the severe repression against trade unionists in the so-called "homelands",

1. *Takes note* of the extract from the progress report of the *Ad Hoc* Working Group of Experts on southern Africa;

2. *Deplores* the repression by the Government of South Africa against the growing independent black trade union movement;

3. *Demands once again* the cessation of persecution of trade unionists and repression of the independent black trade union movement by the Government of South Africa;

4. *Calls once again* for the immediate recognition of the unimpeded exercise of freedom of association and

trade union rights by the entire population of South Africa, without discrimination of any kind;

5. *Demands* the immediate release of all trade unionists imprisoned for exercising their legitimate trade union rights and the lifting of the orders banning trade unionists and trade union organizations;

6. *Requests* the *Ad Hoc* Working Group of Experts to continue to study the situation and to report thereon to the Commission on Human Rights and the Council;

7. *Also requests* the *Ad Hoc* Working Group of Experts, in the discharge of its mandate, to consult with the International Labour Organisation and the Special Committee against *Apartheid*, as well as with international and African trade union confederations;

8. *Decides* to consider at its first regular session of 1986 the question of allegations of infringements of trade union rights in South Africa as a sub-item of the item entitled "Human rights questions".

Economic and Social Council resolution 1985/43

30 May 1985   Meeting 25   Adopted without vote

Approved by Second Committee (E/1985/95 & Corr.1) without vote, 24 May (meeting 15); 30-nation draft (E/1985/C.2/L.10), orally revised; agenda item 16.

Sponsors: Algeria, Australia, Bangladesh, Botswana, China, Congo, Costa Rica, Cyprus, Djibouti, Egypt, Finland, Guinea, Haiti, India, Mali, Morocco, Nigeria, Pakistan, Rwanda, Saudi Arabia, Senegal, Sierra Leone, Somalia, Sudan, Turkey, Uganda, Yugoslavia, Zaire, Zambia, Zimbabwe.

Asia and the Pacific

Afghanistan

Report of the Special Rapporteur (February). As requested by the Economic and Social Council in 1984,[35] the Chairman of the Commission on Human Rights had appointed in October a Special Rapporteur, Felix Ermacora (Austria), to examine the human rights situation in Afghanistan and formulate proposals for the full protection of human rights before, during and after the withdrawal of all foreign forces. The Rapporteur presented a report to the Commission in February 1985.[36]

Unable to obtain the Government's permission to visit the country, he had gone to Pakistan in December 1984 to interview a number of Afghan refugees and to visit four refugee camps and four hospitals set aside for Afghan wounded. With a view to obtaining clarification of information concerning allegations of serious human rights violations, the Special Rapporteur, by a letter of 4 January 1985, drew the Afghan Government's attention to his need for co-operation.

Because of the enormous bulk of data, he based his report on a cross-section of personal-experience cases illustrating the situation, in addition to documentation on the subject by individuals and humanitarian organizations with direct knowledge and experience.

Concluding, the Special Rapporteur stated that the current régime installed in December 1979, like its immediate predecessors, was not elected by the people and therefore unrepresentative. It had instituted a series of reforms, not only applying

them with severity but requesting and accepting that foreign armed forces join in their imposition, at a pace apparently unacceptable to the population at large. Although both Afghanistan and the USSR were parties to the 1949 Geneva Conventions, the parties to the conflict did not co-operate with ICRC or did so only selectively. By the same token, the opposition movements would seem not to have been able to ensure full application of international norms by their fighting forces. Practices had taken place violating common article 3 of the 1949 Conventions: the use of anti-personnel mines and so-called toy-bombs; the victimization of the civilian population, particularly women and children; and the non-acceptance of members of the Afghan opposition forces as prisoners of war.

As a result, many lives had been lost, many people were incarcerated in conditions far removed from respect for their rights, and many had been tortured or had disappeared; some 4 million Afghans had fled the country and sought refuge abroad, particularly in Pakistan, Iran and India. Also negatively affected were the population's economic and social rights.

The Special Rapporteur was of the view that, as a first step, the Government ought to make every effort to re-establish a national consensus, an indispensable requirement for which was the withdrawal of all foreign forces and the elimination of foreign influence. There must be an immediate application of the norms of human rights and humanitarian law by all parties involved. A fundamental law or constitution should be promulgated in line with the Universal Declaration of Human Rights and the International Covenant on Civil and Political Rights, and the rule of law in the country must be re-established consistent with those standards. Dialogue with and support by the international community would be vital in that process.

The Special Rapporteur recommended that the Government fully respect its obligations under the international human rights instruments to which it was a party; torture of opponents, which he said was commonplace, should be halted. The party in power and the various opposition movements should establish a representative assembly aimed at the constitution of a *Loya Jirgah* (Grand Assembly) or its equivalent, to initiate the normalization process.

An independent international humanitarian organization such as ICRC should be entrusted with ensuring respect for humanitarian principles and allowed access to prisons, places of detention, refugee camps or other such places, and to airfields, or alternatively the parties should be invited to nominate organizations worthy of their confidence so as to form mixed commissions for that purpose. Government and opposition forces should be reminded of their duty to apply fully the rules of international law without discrimination. All forces engaged in the conflict should be recognized as combatants under international humanitarian law. The rights of the refugees to return to their homes should be respected and a general amnesty formally proclaimed for everyone. The Government should co-operate fully with the United Nations, in particular in clarifying the fate of missing persons, and do everything possible to help restore and uphold human rights.

Commission and Sub-Commission action. In a 13 March resolution[37] adopted by a roll-call vote of 26 to 8, with 8 abstentions, the Commission expressed concern and distress at the grave and massive human rights violations as reflected in the Special Rapporteur's report. It called on the parties to the conflict to apply fully the principles and rules of international humanitarian law and to facilitate operations of international humanitarian organizations to alleviate the suffering of Afghans. It urged Afghanistan to end violations of human rights, particularly military repression against the civilian population. Deciding to extend the mandate of the Special Rapporteur and to have him report to the Assembly in 1985 and the Commission in 1986, the Commission urged the Afghan authorities to co-operate with him and requested the Secretary-General to give him all necessary assistance. (See also p. 859.)

On 30 August,[38] the Sub-Commission requested the Commission to ask the Special Rapporteur to look in particular into the fate of women and children as a consequence of the conflict in Afghanistan, and to ask all concerned in the conflict and United Nations agencies to collaborate fully with him.

ECONOMIC AND SOCIAL COUNCIL ACTION

In May, on the recommendation of its Second Committee, the Economic and Social Council adopted **decision 1985/147**, by roll-call vote.

Question of human rights and fundamental freedoms in Afghanistan

At its 25th plenary meeting, on 30 May 1985, the Council, noting Commission on Human Rights resolution 1985/38 of 13 March 1985, approved the Commission's decision to extend for one year the mandate of the Special Rapporteur on the question of human rights and fundamental freedoms in Afghanistan and to request him to report to the General Assembly at its fortieth session and to the Commission at its forty-second session on the situation of human rights in that country, including the human and material losses resulting from bombardments of the civilian population. The Council further approved the Commission's request to the Secretary-General to give all necessary assistance to the Special Rapporteur.

Economic and Social Council decision 1985/147

38-5-8 (roll-call vote)

Approved by Second Committee (E/1985/95 & Corr.1) by vote (38-5-7), 24 May (meeting 15); draft by Commission on Human Rights (E/1985/22); agenda item 16.

Roll-call vote in Council as follows:

In favour: Argentina, Bangladesh, Botswana, Brazil, Canada, China, Colombia, Costa Rica, Djibouti, France, Germany, Federal Republic of, Guinea, Haiti, Iceland, Japan, Lebanon, Luxembourg, Malaysia, Mexico, Morocco, Netherlands, New Zealand, Nigeria, Papua New Guinea, Rwanda, Saudi Arabia, Senegal, Sierra Leone, Somalia, Spain, Sri Lanka, Suriname, Sweden, Thailand, Turkey, United Kingdom, United States, Venezuela.

Against: Bulgaria, German Democratic Republic, India, Poland, USSR.

Abstaining: Algeria, Congo, Ecuador, Finland, Uganda, Yugoslavia, Zaire, Zimbabwe.

The USSR, speaking also on behalf of Bulgaria, the German Democratic Republic and Poland, said the decision endorsed an unlawful campaign of slander against Afghanistan and in effect approved a "report" which distorted the truth, an exercise that violated the basic principles of integrity and sought to divert attention from crimes committed by mercenaries and to justify extension of an undeclared war against Afghanistan. The USSR called for an immediate termination of the Special Rapporteur's mandate.

Afghanistan said there was not the slightest justification for the investigation of human rights conditions in Afghanistan. It asserted that the document was biased, contained outright lies, insulted its people, portrayed steps towards eradication of many evil relationships in Afghan society as violations of human rights, and ignored its measures to ensure the universal enjoyment of many human rights and freedoms, including its accession to and decision to implement numerous major international human rights instruments.

Communications. On 20 May,[39] Afghanistan transmitted a statement of its Ministry of Foreign Affairs of the same date, saying that no human rights violations took place in the country which warranted any investigation and reporting; the decision to appoint a Special Rapporteur had been imposed on the Commission in violation of the rules of procedure and established practice, and in disregard of Article 2, paragraph 7, of the Charter, proscribing United Nations intervention in the internal affairs of a State. The appointment as Rapporteur of one whom it called an infamous personality revealed, Afghanistan said, the true intentions of the forces behind that decision. Lastly, the report fabricated and distorted facts.

Referring to that letter, Austria, on 14 June,[40] reiterated its view that the position of the Special Rapporteur was based on his designation by the Commission Chairman, the report was compiled in his personal capacity and nothing in the report could in any way be imputed to the Austrian Government. Any doubts voiced with respect to his commitment to the cause of human rights, however, were completely inappropriate.

On 5 December,[41] Afghanistan transmitted to the Secretary-General a message of the President of the Revolutionary Council of Afghanistan on the occasion of the thirty-seventh anniversary of the Universal Declaration of Human Rights,[20] stating that Afghanistan attached great importance to the Declaration and the reputable instruments in that field. Respect for democracy, national freedom, humanism, progress, social justice, religion, family, property and other human rights comprised the fundamental principles of its democratic revolution. Constructive steps, such as expanding State leadership organs to include representatives to reflect diverse strata and different groups in society, and measures for possible principled amnesty, reconciliation and nation-wide peace, were under way. If intervention and terrorism had not been imposed on its people, its achievement in promoting and protecting human rights would have been far greater, the President said.

Report by the Special Rapporteur (November). Pursuant to the Commission's March request (see above), the Special Rapporteur submitted to the General Assembly in November an interim report[42] providing information related to respect for human rights in Afghanistan, on casualties resulting from bombardments of the civilian population and on the relevant constitutional and international legal framework in regard to human rights.

In his conclusions—which, he stated, reflected his personal views on the overall human rights situation in Afghanistan and dealt with a sample of personal experiences of persons who claimed to have been victims of the bombardments—the Special Rapporteur stated that the conflict continued to engender human rights violations on a large scale. He listed such practices as the use of anti-personnel mines, so-called toy-bombs and heavy weapons; indiscriminate mass killings of civilians, particularly women and children; discrimination against persons not adhering to the People's Democratic Party; and the non-acceptance of members of the Afghan opposition movements as prisoners of war. The rights of the refugees and displaced persons to education, to work and to health were affected, as were basic rights embodied in the International Covenant on Economic, Social and Cultural Rights, in particular outside Kabul and other cities.

Reiterating the recommendations made in his earlier report to the Commission (see above), the Special Rapporteur also suggested that the parties to the conflict consider establishing neutral zones under international supervision to shield the civilian population. He felt it might be advisable for Afghanistan to commit itself to a policy of non-alignment or permanent neutrality.

On 13 December, acting on the recommendation of the Third Committee, the General Assembly adopted **resolution 40/137**, by recorded vote.

Question of human rights and fundamental freedoms in Afghanistan

The General Assembly,

Guided by the principles embodied in the Charter of the United Nations, the Universal Declaration of Human Rights, the International Covenants on Human Rights and the humanitarian rules set out in the Geneva Conventions of 12 August 1949,

Aware of its responsibility to promote and encourage respect for human rights and fundamental freedoms for all and resolved to remain vigilant with regard to violations of human rights wherever they occur,

Emphasizing the obligation of all Governments to respect and protect human rights and to fulfil the responsibilities they have assumed under various international instruments,

Recalling Commission on Human Rights resolution 1984/55 of 15 March 1984, in which the Commission expressed its concern and anxiety at the continuing presence of foreign forces in Afghanistan, as well as Economic and Social Council resolution 1984/37 of 24 May 1984, in which the Council requested the Chairman of the Commission on Human Rights to appoint a special rapporteur to examine the situation of human rights in Afghanistan,

Taking note of Commission on Human Rights resolution 1985/38 of 13 March 1985, in which the Commission expressed its profound concern at the grave and massive human rights violations in Afghanistan and urged the authorities in that country to put a stop to those violations, in particular the military repression being conducted against the civilian population of Afghanistan,

Recalling Economic and Social Council decision 1985/147 of 30 May 1985, by which the Council approved the decision of the Commission on Human Rights to extend the mandate of the Special Rapporteur and to request him to report to the General Assembly at its fortieth session and to the Commission at its forty-second session on the situation of human rights in Afghanistan, including the human and material losses resulting from the bombardments of the civilian population,

Taking note of resolution 1985/35 of 30 August 1985 of the Sub-Commission on Prevention of Discrimination and Protection of Minorities, in which the Sub-Commission requested the Commission on Human Rights to ask the Special Rapporteur to look, in particular, into the fate of women and children as a consequence of the conflict in Afghanistan,

Having carefully examined the interim report of the Special Rapporteur on the question of human rights in Afghanistan, which reveals continuing grave and massive violations of fundamental human rights in that country,

Recognizing that a situation of armed conflict continues to exist in Afghanistan, leaving large numbers of victims without protection or assistance,

Deploring the continuing refusal of the Afghan authorities to co-operate with the Special Rapporteur,

1. *Commends* the Special Rapporteur for his report on the question of human rights in Afghanistan;

2. *Expresses its profound concern* that, as revealed in the findings of the Special Rapporteur, disregard for human rights is more widespread, the conflict continues to engender human rights violations on a large scale and, as a result, not only the lives of individuals but the existence of whole groups of persons and tribes are endangered;

3. *Expresses its deep concern* that the Afghan authorities, with heavy support from foreign troops, are acting with great severity against their opponents and suspected opponents without any respect for the international human rights obligations which they have assumed;

4. *Also expresses its deep concern* at the severe consequences for the civilian population of indiscriminate bombardments and military operations aimed primarily at the villages and the agricultural structure;

5. *Shares the conviction* of the Special Rapporteur that the prolongation of the conflict increases the seriousness of the gross and systematic violations of human rights already existing in the country;

6. *Expresses its profound distress and alarm*, in particular, at the widespread violations of the right to life, liberty and security of person, including the commonplace practice of torture and summary executions of the opponents of the régime, as well as at increasing evidence of a policy of religious intolerance;

7. *Notes with great concern* that such widespread violations of human rights, that have already caused millions of people to flee their homes and country, are still giving rise to large flows of refugees and displaced persons;

8. *Calls upon* the parties to the conflict to apply fully the principles and rules of international humanitarian law and to admit international humanitarian organizations, in particular the International Committee of the Red Cross, and to facilitate their operations for the alleviation of the suffering of the people in Afghanistan;

9. *Urges* the authorities in Afghanistan to co-operate with the Commission on Human Rights and its Special Rapporteur, in particular by allowing him to visit Afghanistan;

10. *Requests* the Secretary-General to give all necessary assistance to the Special Rapporteur;

11. *Decides* to keep under consideration, during its forty-first session, the question of human rights and fundamental freedoms in Afghanistan, in order to examine this question anew in the light of additional elements provided by the Commission on Human Rights and the Economic and Social Council.

General Assembly resolution 40/137

13 December 1985   Meeting 116   80-22-40 (recorded vote)

Approved by Third Committee (A/40/1007) by recorded vote (75-23-33), 6 December (meeting 70); 21-nation draft (A/C.3/40/L.48/Rev.1); agenda item 12.

Sponsors: Antigua and Barbuda, Belgium, Canada, Costa Rica, Denmark, France, Germany, Federal Republic of, Greece, Ireland, Italy, Japan, Luxembourg, Netherlands, Norway, Portugal, Saint Lucia, Samoa, Singapore, Spain, Sweden, United Kingdom.

Meeting numbers. GA 40th session: 3rd Committee 54, 56, 59-67, 69-71; plenary 116.

Recorded vote in Assembly as follows:

In favour: Albania, Antigua and Barbuda, Argentina, Australia, Austria, Bangladesh, Barbados, Belgium, Belize, Botswana, Brazil, Brunei Darussalam, Canada, Chad, Chile, China, Colombia, Comoros, Costa Rica, Democratic Kampuchea, Denmark, Djibouti, Dominican Republic, Egypt, El Salvador, Equatorial Guinea, Fiji, France, Gabon, Gambia, Germany, Federal Republic of, Greece, Grenada, Honduras, Iceland, Ireland, Israel, Italy, Ivory Coast, Jamaica, Japan, Jordan, Kenya, Lesotho, Luxembourg, Malaysia, Mexico, Morocco, Netherlands,

New Zealand, Niger, Norway, Oman, Pakistan, Panama, Papua New Guinea, Paraguay, Peru, Philippines, Portugal, Rwanda, Saint Christopher and Nevis, Saint Lucia, Saint Vincent and the Grenadines, Samoa, Saudi Arabia, Senegal, Sierra Leone, Singapore, Somalia, Spain, Sudan, Sweden, Thailand, Togo, Turkey, United Kingdom, United States, Uruguay, Venezuela.

Against: Afghanistan, Angola, Benin, Bulgaria, Byelorussian SSR, Czechoslovakia, Democratic Yemen, Ethiopia, German Democratic Republic, Hungary, India, Lao People's Democratic Republic, Libyan Arab Jamahiriya, Mongolia, Nicaragua, Poland, Romania, Syrian Arab Republic, Ukrainian SSR, USSR, Viet Nam.

Abstaining: Algeria, Bahamas, Bahrain, Bhutan, Burkina Faso, Burma, Burundi, Cameroon, Cape Verde, Central African Republic, Congo, Cyprus, Ecuador, Finland, Ghana, Guinea-Bissau, Iraq, Kuwait, Lebanon, Liberia, Madagascar, Malawi, Maldives, Mali, Malta, Mauritania, Mauritius, Nepal, Nigeria, Sri Lanka, Suriname, Swaziland, Trinidad and Tobago, Tunisia, Uganda, United Republic of Tanzania, Yugoslavia, Zaire, Zambia, Zimbabwe.

Before approval of the text in the Third Committee, a procedural debate took place on a motion by the Syrian Arab Republic that debate on the draft, as well as on a draft pertaining to human rights in Iran (see p. 910), should be adjourned. By a recorded vote of 60 to 37, with 16 abstentions, the Committee overruled a ruling by the Chairman that the Syrian proposal was admissible, a ruling that had been challenged by France.

In explanation of vote, Afghanistan said that it had been selectively and unfairly singled out for examination of its human rights conditions. It felt that the discussion of the matter in the Commission on Human Rights violated the rules of procedure and that the Special Rapporteur, selected in contravention of an established practice, did not have the necessary moral authority to prepare an impartial report. The report was entirely based on unsubstantiated allegations, Afghanistan said, and contained language that was false, divorced from human rights issues, politically motivated, interventionist and unacceptable. It rejected the resolution and declared it would not attach any validity to it or regard itself bound by its terms. Mongolia, sharing Afghanistan's view regarding the appointment of the Special Rapporteur and his identity and in agreement that the text represented interference in the internal affairs of a sovereign State, said the resolution also obstructed the Afghan people's right to self-determination and to choose a social system. The Libyan Arab Jamahiriya observed that while the situation in Afghanistan concerned the right of the Afghan people to select the political system of their choice, some were exploiting the question of human rights to exert political pressure.

Expressing hope for normalization of the situation, Bolivia said that, for reasons of State, it would not take part in the voting. Iran expressed disappointment with the human rights machinery of the United Nations; dissociating itself from the draft, it felt that it unfairly reduced the situation in Afghanistan to an issue of human rights violations and undermined the original issue of principle. Zaire believed that investigations and studies should be carried out in respect of all Members of the United Nations, as flagrant and repeated violations of human rights werc noted even in the seemingly most democratic countries.

China concurred with the Special Rapporteur's conclusions, stressing, as did Ecuador and Pakistan, that violations of human rights in Afghanistan resulted from foreign military intervention and were a threat to the Afghan people's fundamental rights and freedoms, particularly the right to self-determination. Uruguay shared the deep concern raised by the conclusions of the Special Rapporteur. Madagascar considered it unacceptable that Governments should use human rights questions to interfere in other States' internal affairs.

Iran

Report of the Special Representative (February). As requested by the Commission on Human Rights in 1984,[43] the Chairman designated, in October of that year, Andrés Aguilar (Venezuela) as Special Representative of the Commission to study the human rights situation in Iran. In his preliminary report submitted to the Commission in February 1985,[44] the Special Representative said he had addressed a letter and cable to Iran seeking its co-operation in carrying out his mandate, and hoped that the Government would respond positively. He had received four documents from its Permanent Mission in Geneva dealing mainly with what the documents described as terrorist activities in Iran, and, from various sources, communications and documents containing information on alleged human rights violations. Owing to the lack of direct contact with Iranian authorities, he had not been in a position to evaluate those allegations, but noted with concern their number and gravity, in particular those related to the rights to life, to liberty and security of persons, to a fair trial, and to freedom from arbitrary arrest, freedom from torture, and freedom of thought, conscience and religion.

The Special Representative pointed out that Iran, being a party to the International Covenants on Human Rights, was legally bound by their provisions. He appealed to Iran to co-operate in good faith with him and the Commission and to open a dialogue, so that he could submit a more complete report.

Human Rights Commission action. By a 13 March 1985 resolution,[45] adopted by a roll-call vote of 21 to 5, with 15 abstentions, the Commission on Human Rights endorsed the Special Representative's general observations. The Commission expressed deep concern at the number and gravity of alleged human rights violations in Iran and urged Iran to ensure to all individuals within its territory and subject to its jurisdiction the rights recognized in the International Covenant on Civil and Political Rights.

The Commission extended the mandate of the Special Representative for another year, requesting him to present to the Assembly in 1985 an interim report on the human rights situation in Iran, including the situation of minority groups such as the Baha'is, and to submit a final report to the Commission in 1986. It urged Iran to co-operate with the Special Representative and requested the Secretary-General to give him all necessary assistance.

ECONOMIC AND SOCIAL COUNCIL ACTION

In May, acting on the recommendation of its Second Committee, the Economic and Social Council adopted **decision 1985/148**, by roll-call vote.

Situation of human rights in the Islamic Republic of Iran

At its 25th plenary meeting, on 30 May 1985, the Council, noting Commission on Human Rights resolution 1985/39 of 13 March 1985, approved the Commission's decision to extend for one year the mandate of the Special Representative on the situation of human rights in the Islamic Republic of Iran, as set out in Commission resolution 1984/54 of 14 March 1984, and its request to the Special Representative to submit an interim report to the General Assembly at its fortieth session on the human rights situation in that country, including the situation of minority groups such as the Baha'is, and a final report to the Commission at its forty-second session. The Council further approved the Commission's request to the Secretary-General to give all necessary assistance to the Special Representative of the Commission.

Economic and Social Council decision 1985/148

23-2-20 (roll-call vote)

Approved by Second Committee (E/1985/95 & Corr.1) by vote (24-2-20), 24 May (meeting 15); draft by Commission on Human Rights (E/1985/22); agenda item 16.

Roll-call vote in Council as follows:

In favour: Bulgaria, Canada, Colombia, Congo, Costa Rica, Finland, France, Germany, Federal Republic of, Iceland, Japan, Luxembourg, Mexico, Morocco,[a] Netherlands, New Zealand, Rwanda, Spain, Suriname, Sweden, Uganda, USSR, United Kingdom, United States.

Against: Algeria, Bangladesh.

Abstaining: Argentina, Botswana, Brazil, China, Ecuador, German Democratic Republic, Haiti, India, Malaysia, Nigeria, Poland, Senegal, Sierra Leone, Sri Lanka, Thailand, Turkey, Venezuela, Yugoslavia, Zaire, Zimbabwe.

[a]Subsequently said its vote should have been recorded as an abstention.

Sub-Commission action. By a resolution adopted on 29 August by 10 votes to 3, with 4 abstentions,[46] the Sub-Commission expressed alarm at the continuing reports of gross violations of human rights and fundamental freedoms in Iran and at the evidence of persecution of the Baha'i religious minority and of political, ethnic and national minorities such as the Kurds. It endorsed the general observations in the Special Representative's preliminary report and expressed the hope that the initial contacts of the Iranian Government with him would develop into co-operation. The Sub-Commission asked the Secretary-General to bring to the attention of the Commission and the Special Representative the allegations and information received by the Sub-Commission concerning grave human rights violations in Iran, and to inform it of action taken by the General Assembly, the Economic and Social Council and the Commission in response to the Special Representative's reports and other information.

Report of the Special Representative (November). In an interim report of November 1985,[47] the Special Representative informed the General Assembly of action taken in accordance with his mandate, his exchange of communications with Iran and his consultations with government representatives. He stated that his attention had been drawn to information published by the Foreign Ministry concerning alleged terrorist acts by opposition groups against Iranian officials, security agents and civilians. Although he believed the Government had the right to take measures it deemed appropriate to protect its agents and the population in general, the examination of such activity was beyond his mandate. Although Iran had been involved for several years in an armed conflict that had inflicted heavy losses on its army, civilian population and economic resources, it continued to be bound by the international human rights instruments to which it was a party, he said.

The Special Representative noted with appreciation that the Government had taken a positive step towards co-operation by providing him with a "Report on the performance of the Islamic Republic of Iran in 1985" (which he annexed to his report); nevertheless, he noted that while the report described some of Iran's legal provisions relative to human rights, it failed to provide information on the way they were applied in practice. No reply had been given to specific questions he had asked concerning summary and arbitrary executions and the death of persons due to ill-treatment. His 29 August letter referring, *inter alia*, to allegations of torture and religious persecution had also remained without reply. Further, the information available to him appeared to contradict the situation described in the Government's report, in particular with regard to the use of torture, arrests without any given reason, prolonged detention without trial, and denial of visits to prisoners by lawyers and family members. He was, therefore, obliged to conclude that those allegations could not be dismissed as groundless unless proved to be so on the basis of detailed information which the Government was in the best position to collect and provide. He believed that a continued monitoring of the human rights situation in Iran was called for and reiterated his appeal to the Government to continue the dialogue with him and the Commission.

Communication. On 4 December,[48] Iran transmitted a statement to the Secretary-General

concerning the recent proceedings in the Assembly's Third Committee where, it charged, certain countries, with political intentions, exploited the United Nations machinery for the protection of human rights. The Special Representative's report was based on presumptions, Iran said; his line of questioning as well as his conclusions showed that he was also affected by the misinformation campaign of the imperialist media. Iran stated that information in the report had been supplied by terrorist groups and that the allegations of torture and arbitrary and summary executions, all supplied by one of them, were baseless. In commenting on the issue of political prisoners, Iran continued, which had already been dealt with conclusively by a team of experts representing the Secretary-General (see p. 244), the Special Representative had gone beyond his mandate. His claim that Iran's report merely enumerated constitutional provisions concerning human rights was wrong, Iran continued; it contained specific regulations and the legal framework governing Iran's criminal justice system, as well as safeguards for implementation of those rules, including remedies in cases of their violation. Iran said it was regrettable that the Representative was unable to use fully the opportunity for a constructive and meaningful dialogue initiated by Iran, and that he insisted on a visit to the country; for one unfamiliar with Iran's legal framework, a visit would only entail a superficial examination of the subject. A more constructive approach by him and the relevant international bodies could bring a more useful and constructive dialogue and ensure continuing progress.

GENERAL ASSEMBLY ACTION

On 13 December 1985, acting on the recommendation of the Third Committee, the General Assembly adopted **resolution 40/141**, by recorded vote.

Situation of human rights in the Islamic Republic of Iran

The General Assembly,

Guided by the principles embodied in the Charter of the United Nations, the Universal Declaration of Human Rights and the International Covenants on Human Rights,

Reaffirming that all Member States have an obligation to promote and protect human rights and fundamental freedoms and to fulfil the obligations they have undertaken under the various international instruments in this field,

Recalling Commission on Human Rights resolutions 1982/27 of 11 March 1982 and 1983/34 of 8 March 1983,

Bearing in mind Commission on Human Rights resolution 1984/54 of 14 March 1984, in which the Commission expressed deep concern at the continuing serious violations of human rights and fundamental freedoms in the Islamic Republic of Iran and requested its Chairman to appoint a special representative to make a thorough study of the situation of human rights in that country,

Taking note, in particular, of Commission on Human Rights resolution 1985/39 of 13 March 1985, by which the Commission decided to extend the mandate of its Special Representative for one year and requested him to present an interim report to the General Assembly at its fortieth session on the situation of human rights in the Islamic Republic of Iran, including the situation of minority groups such as the Baha'is, and a final report to the Commission at its forty-second session,

Mindful of resolution 1985/17 of 29 August 1985 of the Sub-Commission on Prevention of Discrimination and Protection of Minorities, in which the Sub-Commission expressed its alarm at the continuing reports of gross violations of human rights and fundamental freedoms in the Islamic Republic of Iran,

Regretting that the Government of the Islamic Republic of Iran has still not extended its full co-operation to the Commission on Human Rights and its Special Representative, in particular by not allowing the Special Representative to visit the country,

Taking into account the specific and detailed allegations of grave and extensive violations of human rights to which the Special Representative refers in his interim report on the situation of human rights in the Islamic Republic of Iran and to which the Government of that country has not responded,

Endorsing the conclusion of the Special Representative that continued monitoring of the human rights situation in the Islamic Republic of Iran is called for,

1. *Takes note with appreciation* of the interim report of the Special Representative of the Commission on Human Rights on the situation of human rights in the Islamic Republic of Iran and of the general observations contained therein;

2. *Expresses its deep concern* over the specific and detailed allegations of violations of human rights in the Islamic Republic of Iran to which the Special Representative refers in his interim report, and, in particular, those related to the right to life, such as summary and arbitrary executions, the right to freedom from torture or cruel, inhuman or degrading treatment or punishment, the right to liberty and security of person and to freedom from arbitrary arrest or detention, the right to a fair trial, the right to freedom of thought, conscience and religion and to freedom of expression, and the right of religious minorities to profess and practise their own religion;

3. *Endorses* the conclusion of the Special Representative that, on the basis of the information available to him, specific and detailed allegations concerning grave violations of human rights cannot be dismissed, and urgently appeals to the Government of the Islamic Republic of Iran to respond satisfactorily to these allegations;

4. *Urges* the Government of the Islamic Republic of Iran, as a State party to the International Covenant on Civil and Political Rights, to respect and to ensure to all individuals within its territory and subject to its jurisdiction the rights recognized in that Covenant;

5. *Requests* the Commission on Human Rights to study carefully the final report of the Special Representative, as well as other information pertaining to the situation of human rights in the Islamic Republic of Iran, and to consider further steps for securing effective respect for human rights and fundamental freedoms for all in that country;

6. *Urges* the Government of the Islamic Republic of Iran to extend its full co-operation to the Special Representative of the Commission on Human Rights, and, in particular, to permit him to visit that country;

7. *Requests* the Secretary-General to give all necessary assistance to the Special Representative;

8. *Decides* to continue its examination of the situation of human rights in the Islamic Republic of Iran, including the situation of minority groups such as the Baha'is, during its forty-first session in order to examine this situation anew in the light of additional elements provided by the Commission on Human Rights and the Economic and Social Council.

General Assembly resolution 40/141

13 December 1985   Meeting 116   53-30-45 (recorded vote)

Approved by Third Committee (A/40/1007) by recorded vote (53-22-41), 6 December (meeting 71); 12-nation draft (A/C.3/40/L.75); agenda item 12.
Sponsors: Antigua and Barbuda, Australia, Belgium, Canada, Costa Rica, France, Luxembourg, Netherlands, Norway, Saint Lucia, Samoa, United Kingdom.
Meeting numbers. GA 40th session: 3rd Committee 54-56, 60-71; plenary 116.

Recorded vote in Assembly as follows:

In favour: Antigua and Barbuda, Argentina, Australia, Austria, Barbados, Belgium, Belize, Botswana, Canada, Chile, Colombia, Costa Rica, Denmark, Dominican Republic, El Salvador, Equatorial Guinea, Fiji, Finland, France, Germany, Federal Republic of, Greece, Grenada, Honduras, Iceland, Iraq, Ireland, Israel, Italy, Jamaica, Jordan, Kenya, Lesotho, Luxembourg, Mauritius, Mexico, Netherlands, New Zealand, Norway, Panama, Paraguay, Peru, Portugal, Rwanda, Saint Christopher and Nevis, Saint Vincent and the Grenadines, Samoa, Spain, Sweden, Togo, Uganda, United Kingdom, United States, Venezuela.
Against: Albania, Algeria, Angola, Bahrain, Bangladesh, Benin, Brunei Darussalam, Comoros, Cuba, Democratic Yemen, Indonesia, Iran, Kuwait, Libyan Arab Jamahiriya, Malaysia, Nicaragua, Niger, Pakistan, Poland, Qatar, Romania, Saudi Arabia, Sierra Leone, Somalia, Sudan, Syrian Arab Republic, Turkey, United Arab Emirates, United Republic of Tanzania, Yemen.
Abstaining: Bahamas, Bhutan, Brazil, Burkina Faso, Burma, Burundi, Cameroon, Cape Verde, Central African Republic, Chad, Congo, Cyprus, Ecuador, Egypt, Ethiopia, Gabon, Ghana, Guinea-Bissau, India, Ivory Coast, Japan, Lebanon, Liberia, Malawi, Maldives, Mali, Malta, Mauritania, Nepal, Nigeria, Oman, Papua New Guinea, Philippines, Senegal, Singapore, Sri Lanka, Suriname, Swaziland, Thailand, Trinidad and Tobago, Tunisia, Yugoslavia, Zaire, Zambia, Zimbabwe.

The draft resolution was the subject of two procedural motions in the Third Committee: one was linked with the voting on the resolution on human rights in Afghanistan (see p. 907); the other was a motion by Pakistan, seconded by the Libyan Arab Jamahiriya, that no action be taken on the text. Pakistan's motion was rejected by a recorded vote of 55 to 28, with 29 abstentions. The Netherlands opposed the motion on the grounds that it constituted an abuse of the rules of procedure and was aimed solely at preventing the Committee from discharging its responsibilities.

Iran considered it neither constructive nor useful to vote on the text which, it said, basically represented the position of the terrorists who were behind all the allegations made against it; the text's adoption would close the door against any future co-operation between Iran and the Committee. In addition, the text referred explicitly to the Baha'is, whose historic links with zionism were well known, Iran said.

The Libyan Arab Jamahiriya said it felt that the text was a plot by the Western countries to present the Iranian revolution in a bad light; the interim report was biased and inaccurate since it was not based on objective testimony and disregarded Iran's response. The Baha'is, it added, were not a religious sect but a dissident group that had always co-operated with imperialism and zionism and whose aim was to create disturbance in Iran and other countries.

Pakistan considered the text to be excessive and coloured by a negative and stereotyped view of the political changes in Iran. There was no reason to continue monitoring the human rights situation there. The text was not objective and the interim report drew primarily on 13 witnesses whose testimony remained unsubstantiated; it even referred to incidents between 1980 and 1983, which would not reflect the current situation. The statement that Iran had still not extended its full co-operation was inaccurate; the report on Iran's performance in 1985 replied satisfactorily to the questions raised by the Special Representative, who had drawn no conclusion which could validate the allegations of violations.

Zaire remarked that the Assembly could not confine itself to taking decisions on situations in only certain countries, while flagrant and repeated human rights violations in others were not considered.

In Colombia's opinion, the report of the Special Representative required the international community to appeal to Iran to end the violations described; a revolution in no way justified the perpetration of such violations. Iraq said the text should have contained a reference to oppressed minorities in Iran, such as the Turkmens, the Kurds and the Baluchis.

Ecuador observed that where there were separate votes in particular cases where it considered that there had been selectivity on human rights issues, it would abstain. Bolivia declared it would not take part in the voting for reasons of State; it declared its support, however, for the right to freedom of religion, including freedom for the Baha'i faith in Iran.

Kampuchea

The Commission on Human Rights and the Economic and Social Council both affirmed that continued occupation by foreign forces constituted primary human rights violations in Kampuchea (see p. 859).

Pakistan

The Sub-Commission, by a resolution[49] adopted on 29 August 1985 by 10 votes to 2, with 6 abstentions, expressed grave concern at the promulgation by Pakistan of Ordinance XX of 28 April 1984 which, the Sub-Commission stated, violated the rights to liberty and security of persons, to freedom from arbitrary arrest or detention, to freedom of thought, expression, conscience

and religion and to an effective legal remedy, as well as the right of religious minorities to practise their own religion. It also expressed grave concern that persons charged with and arrested for violations of that ordinance had reportedly been subjected to punishments and confiscation of personal property, and that affected groups had been subjected to discrimination in employment and education and to the defacement of their religious property. Alerting the Commission on Human Rights of the situation in Pakistan as a situation with great potential to cause a mass exodus, especially of members of the Ahmadi community, the Sub-Commission requested the Commission to call on Pakistan to repeal Ordinance XX and restore the human rights and fundamental freedoms of all persons under its jurisdiction.

Europe and the Mediterranean area

Albania

By a resolution of 29 August 1985,[50] the Sub-Commission dealt with religious freedom in Albania (see p. 846).

Cyprus

On 13 March 1985,[51] the Commission on Human Rights postponed debate on the question of human rights in Cyprus until its 1986 session, on the understanding that action required by previous Commission resolutions on the subject remained operative, including the request for a report on their implementation.

Effective 28 April 1985, the Secretary-General appointed Paul Wurth (Switzerland) to succeed the late Claude Pilloud as the ICRC representative on the three-member Committee on Missing Persons in Cyprus. The other members were selected by each of the two Cypriot communities.

Latin America

Argentina

On 30 May 1985, the Economic and Social Council decided, in view of a 1984 decision of the Commission on Human Rights to terminate the study of the situation with respect to human rights in Argentina and in view of the full restoration of human rights in that country, that material relating to Argentina, which had been before the Commission under a procedure established by the Council in 1970[1] for dealing confidentially with communications alleging violations of human rights, should cease to be confidential. **Decision 1985/156** was adopted without vote, following similar approval by the Second Committee on 24 May of a text[52] proposed by Argentina, Brazil, Colombia, Costa Rica, Ecuador, Mexico and Venezuela.

Chile

Human Rights Commission action. Following examination of a 1984 report[53] by Special Rapporteur Rajsoomer Lallah (Mauritius) on the situation of human rights in Chile, the Commission on Human Rights, by a resolution[54] adopted on 14 March 1985 by a roll-call vote of 32 to 1, with 8 abstentions, again expressed dismay at the suppression in Chile of the traditional democratic legal order and its institutions and their replacement by a Constitution which did not reflect the people's will, freely expressed, and whose provisions considerably reduced the exercise of human rights through institutionalization and consolidation of states of emergency and extension of the jurisdiction of military tribunals. The Commission expressed indignation at the increase in serious and systematic human rights violations as described by the Special Rapporteur, in particular at the violent suppression of popular protest in the face of the authorities' refusal to restore the democratic order, leading to mass arrests and large numbers of dead and injured. It denounced again the fact that the repressive and arbitrary activities of the police and security agencies, in particular of the National Information Agency, had gone unpunished.

The Commission expressed profound concern about the ineffectiveness of *habeas corpus* or *amparo* and of legal protection, owing to the fact that the judiciary did not exercise its powers of investigation, monitoring and supervision and functioned under severe restrictions undermining its independence. It again urged the Chilean authorities to restore and respect human rights in accordance with their obligations under international instruments and re-establish legality, democratic institutions and effective exercise of civil and political rights and freedoms, in particular: to end the régime of exception, especially the practice of declaring states of emergency; to investigate without delay the fate of disappeared persons, inform and assist their families and punish those responsible; to end intimidation and persecution, arbitrary arrests and imprisonment in secret places, and halt torture and other inhuman treatment; to respect the right of Chileans to live in and freely enter and leave the country, and cease assignment to forced residence and forced exile; and to restore full labour rights and economic, social and cultural rights, in particular the rights of the indigenous populations to their land and cultural identity.

The Commission again exhorted the Chilean authorities to co-operate with the Special Rapporteur—whose mandate it extended for another year—and to submit their comments to the Commission in 1986.

ECONOMIC AND SOCIAL COUNCIL ACTION

On 30 May 1985, by **decision 1985/150**, the Economic and Social Council, noting the Commission's March resolution, approved without vote the decision to renew the Special Rapporteur's mandate for one year. The Council requested him to report on the human rights situation in Chile to the Assembly's 1985 session and to the Commission's 1986 session. That portion of the decision had been proposed by the Commission. Adding a phrase proposed by Mexico and approved in the Council's Second Committee, the Council also requested the Secretary-General to ensure the necessary financial resources and sufficient staff to implement the Commission's resolution. The Council acted on the recommendation of its Second Committee, which approved the decision on 24 May, also without vote.

The United States said that, although the Commission's resolution did not accurately describe the situation in Chile, it did not oppose extending the Special Rapporteur's mandate. It did oppose consideration of Chile under a separate agenda item of the Commission, rather than on the same basis as other cases debated. Ecuador said the selective criterion which singled out a few countries for criticism of what was passed over in silence where others were concerned was counter-productive. The United Kingdom observed that despite some States' reservations they had not stood in the way of consensus adoption—a significant departure from past practice that would improve the credibility and authority of the special rapporteurs.

The Netherlands said it was its understanding that the Rapporteur's field missions were primarily to hear witnesses; travel and subsistence expenses for such witnesses to visit New York was regrettably absent from the financial implications in the Commission's report.

Sub-Commission action. On 30 August 1985,[55] the Sub-Commission urged the Chilean authorities to end all measures of repression such as intimidation, persecution, assignment to forced residence, torture and cruel, inhuman or degrading treatment, and called on them to identify those responsible for all repressive measures, in particular disappearances, torture and mistreatment, and punish the guilty. It called on those authorities to respect and restore economic, social and cultural rights, in particular those of indigenous populations, including the right to their land, to preserve their cultural identity and to improve their economic and social status. It recommended that the Commission urgently appeal to the Chilean authorities to respect and promote human rights and end the "states of exception" under which serious violations were committed.

Report of the Special Rapporteur. In September 1985,[56] the Secretary-General transmitted to the General Assembly a preliminary report by Fernando Volio Jiménez (Costa Rica), who had been appointed as Special Rapporteur on the situation of human rights in Chile at the end of January following the resignation of Rajsoomer Lallah. The report took into consideration the more important official texts adopted during 1985, as well as information from national and international governmental and nongovernmental organizations, and from representatives of the Chilean Government. The Special Rapporteur had also met on several occasions with Chilean citizens inside and outside the country. Information based on purely subjective assessments or not sufficiently verified had not been taken into account, he stressed. The situation in Chile was assessed in terms of the norms contained in international treaties ratified by Chile, as well as other universally applicable norms of international human rights law.

Between January and June 1985, the Special Rapporteur stated, he had studied disturbing accounts of occurrences which would constitute serious violations of fundamental freedoms, including abduction and murder. The situation was aggravated by widely spreading terrorist activities which clearly hindered the creation of a climate propitious to restoring democracy.

The absence of normal political activity prevented political parties from functioning; without a democratic legal and political structure, he stated, the risk of further deterioration of the human rights situation increased. The lifting of the state of siege on 17 June marked a positive change, he added, although a state of emergency was declared on the same day.

The problem of exiles had a most adverse effect on the human rights situation and national reconciliation. The Government was gradually reducing the number of people allegedly barred from entering the country (some 4,200), but its current measures were not sufficient to resolve the problem satisfactorily. Administrative banishment or assignment to forced residence was being imposed without the benefit of due process. He also believed that the problems afflicting Chile's indigenous minorities deserved closer examination.

The judiciary appeared to lack the independence necessary to exercise its authority. The judicial and executive branches should make a joint effort, he said, to expedite the resolution of outstanding cases, in particular serious violations he had mentioned in a memorandum of 24 July to the Government.

The official recognition as of 16 July of the Special Rapporteur's mandate and the cooperation extended to him was also a constructive step forward, although he had not obtained permission to visit the country.

The restructuring of the *carabineros*, the armed forces responsible for maintaining law and order, he said, begun following a judicial decision in a case of abduction and murder, should be carried out thoroughly and urgently. Also, the practice of torture must be eliminated. New official mechanisms must be set up to move towards a lasting solution to the problem of exiles and the Government should recognize and publicize the currently unofficial list of persons allegedly barred from entering the country; administrative banishment or restricted residence measures should be transformed into jurisdictional measures. Court proceedings should be speeded up as an immediate task to improve the human rights situation, and the country's legal order should be reformed to guarantee the maximum effectiveness of recourses for the protection of public freedoms such as *amparo* (which included *habeas corpus*).

Terrorism had to be tackled urgently; the new anti-terrorist laws in force would achieve their objective provided that they were used reasonably and abuses were prevented. Citizens, especially those involved in community and religious activities and human rights, must be given increased protection.

The Special Rapporteur recommended that the process of drafting, approving and implementing constitutional laws relating to the structure of the political process be speeded up, within a shorter time-frame than that established, and that the Government promote the broadest possible participation of interested political circles in restoring representative democracy.

GENERAL ASSEMBLY ACTION

On 13 December 1985, acting on the recommendation of the Third Committee, the General Assembly adopted **resolution 40/145**, by recorded vote.

Situation of human rights and fundamental freedoms in Chile

The General Assembly,

Aware of its responsibility to promote and encourage respect for human rights and fundamental freedoms for all, and determined to remain vigilant with regard to violations of human rights wherever they occur,

Noting the obligation of the Chilean authorities to respect and protect human rights in accordance with the international instruments to which Chile is a party,

Bearing in mind that the concern of the international community at the situation of human rights in Chile was expressed by the General Assembly in its resolutions 3219(XXIX) of 6 November 1974, 3448(XXX) of 9 December 1975, 31/124 of 16 December 1976, 32/118 of 16 December 1977, 33/175 of 20 December 1978, 34/179 of 17 December 1979, 35/188 of 15 December 1980, 36/157 of 16 December 1981, 37/183 of 17 December 1982, 38/102 of 16 December 1983 and 39/121 of 14 December 1984, as well as in its resolution 33/173 of 20 December 1978 on disappeared persons,

Recalling the relevant resolutions of the Commission on Human Rights, in particular resolution 1985/47 of 14 March 1985, in which the Commission decided, *inter alia*, to extend the mandate of the Special Rapporteur for a year and to consider the question as a matter of high priority in view of the increase in serious violations of human rights in Chile,

Considering that the Special Rapporteur proposes to submit to the Commission on Human Rights at its forty-second session a final report on the situation of human rights in Chile,

Considering also the public and notorious nature of many of the deeds which constitute serious and systematic violations of human rights and fundamental freedoms in Chile,

Deploring once again the fact that the repeated appeals of the General Assembly, the Commission on Human Rights and other international organs to re-establish human rights and fundamental freedoms have been ignored by the Chilean authorities,

Considering further, inter alia, the recent reports, resolutions and conclusions of the Human Rights Committee, the Sub-Commission on Prevention of Discrimination and Protection of Minorities and the International Labour Organisation, as well as the Chilean Human Rights Committee and the Vicaría de la Solidaridad of the Catholic Church in Chile,

Recognizing the importance of the fact that the Chilean authorities have announced their intention to permit the entry into Chile of the Special Rapporteur, in the exercise of his mandate, to investigate the situation of human rights in that country,

1. *Takes note* of the preliminary report of the Special Rapporteur on the situation of human rights in Chile, submitted in accordance with Commission on Human Rights resolution 1985/47;

2. *Once again expresses its dismay* at the suppression in Chile of the traditional democratic legal order and its institutions and their replacement by a constitution which does not reflect the freely expressed will of the people and whose provisions considerably restrict the enjoyment and exercise of human rights and fundamental freedoms through the institutionalization and consolidation of states of emergency and the extension of the jurisdiction of the military tribunals, all of which amounts to an integrated system negating civil and political rights and freedoms;

3. *Expresses its indignation* at the persistence of serious and systematic violations of human rights in Chile, in particular the suppression of social protests which has caused a considerable number of deaths and injuries and mass and individual arrests, at the intimidation of national human rights organizations, at the frequent reports of torture and ill-treatment, and at the treacherous crimes in which the police forces are judicially implicated;

4. *Reiterates its alarm* at the fact that, in general, the arbitrary or improper actions of the State police and security agencies continue to go unpunished;

5. *Reiterates its concern* at the ineffectiveness of the remedies of *habeas corpus* or of *amparo* and of protection, owing to the fact that the judiciary, notwithstanding some positive actions in this field, does not always exercise its powers of investigation, monitoring and supervision in this respect, and performs its functions under severe restrictions which undermine its independence;

6. *Once again calls urgently upon* the Chilean authorities to restore and respect human rights in accordance with the obligations they have assumed under various international instruments, so as to re-establish the principle of legality, democratic institutions and the effective enjoyment and exercise of human rights and fundamental freedoms, and, in particular:

(a) To put an end not only to the state of seige, as was done in June 1985, but also to the régime of exception and especially the practice of declaring "constitutional states of emergency" under which serious and continuing violations of human rights are committed;

(b) To investigate and clarify without delay the fate of persons who were arrested for political reasons and later disappeared, to assist and inform their families of the results of such investigation and to bring to trial and punish those responsible for their disappearance;

(c) To respect the right to life and the right to physical and moral integrity by putting an end to the practice of torture and other cruel, inhuman or degrading treatment or punishment and to put an immediate end to intimidation and persecution as well as to kidnappings, arbitrary or abusive detention and imprisonment in secret places;

(d) To respect the right of nationals to live in and freely enter and leave their country, without arbitrary restrictions or conditions, and to cease the practice of *relegación* (assignment to forced residence) and forced exile;

(e) To restore the full enjoyment and exercise of labour rights, including the right to organize trade unions, the right to collective bargaining and the right to strike, to put an end to the suppression of the activities of trade union leaders and their organizations and to comply with the provisions of the international agreements of the International Labour Organisation to which Chile has subscribed;

(f) To respect and, where necessary, restore economic, social and cultural rights, in particular the rights intended to preserve the cultural identity and improve the economic and social status of the indigenous populations, including the right to their land;

7. *Concludes*, on the basis of the preliminary report of the Special Rapporteur and of other data at its disposal, that it is necessary to continue to monitor the human rights situation in Chile;

8. *Expresses its conviction* that an unrestricted, *in situ* investigation of the human rights situation in Chile requires that the Special Rapporteur, in fulfilment of his mandate, should have access to all the information and data which could be provided by those persons and bodies that are interested in the situation of human rights in Chile;

9. *Requests* the Chilean authorities to co-operate more fully with the Special Rapporteur and to submit their comments on his report to the Commission on Human Rights at its forty-second session;

10. *Invites* the Commission on Human Rights, at its forty-second session, to proceed to an in-depth consideration of the report of the Special Rapporteur and, taking account of all the relevant information at its disposal, to adopt the most appropriate measures for the effective restoration of human rights and fundamental freedoms in Chile, including the extension of the mandate of the Special Rapporteur, and requests the Com-

mission to report to the General Assembly at its forty-first session, through the Economic and Social Council.

General Assembly resolution 40/145

13 December 1985   Meeting 116   88-11-47 (recorded vote)

Approved by Third Committee (A/40/1007) by recorded vote (82-9-38), 6 December (meeting 71); 15-nation draft (A/C.3/40/L.81); agenda item 12.

Sponsors: Algeria, Australia, Cuba, Denmark, France, Greece, Italy, Luxembourg, Mexico, Netherlands, Norway, Portugal, Spain, Sweden, Yugoslavia.

Meeting numbers. GA 40th session: 3rd Committee 54-56, 60-67, 70, 71; plenary 116.

Recorded vote in Assembly as follows:

In favour: Afghanistan, Albania, Algeria, Angola, Antigua and Barbuda, Argentina, Australia, Austria, Bahrain, Barbados, Belgium, Benin, Botswana, Bulgaria, Burkina Faso, Burundi, Byelorussian SSR, Canada, Cape Verde, Congo, Costa Rica, Cuba, Cyprus, Czechoslovakia, Democratic Yemen, Denmark, Dominican Republic, Ethiopia, Finland, France, Gambia, German Democratic Republic, Germany, Federal Republic of, Ghana, Greece, Guinea, Guinea-Bissau, Guyana, Hungary, Iceland, India, Ireland, Italy, Jamaica, Kenya, Kuwait, Lao People's Democratic Republic, Lesotho, Libyan Arab Jamahiriya, Luxembourg, Maldives, Mali, Mauritania, Mauritius, Mexico, Mongolia, Mozambique, Netherlands, New Zealand, Nicaragua, Norway, Poland, Portugal, Qatar, Romania, Rwanda, Samoa, Sao Tome and Principe, Senegal, Sierra Leone, Spain, Sri Lanka, Sweden, Togo, Tunisia, Uganda, Ukrainian SSR, USSR, United Arab Emirates, United Kingdom, United Republic of Tanzania, Uruguay, Vanuatu, Venezuela, Viet Nam, Yugoslavia, Zambia, Zimbabwe.

Against: Bangladesh, Chile, El Salvador, Guatemala, Indonesia, Lebanon, Morocco, Pakistan, Paraguay, Thailand, United States.

Abstaining: Bahamas, Belize, Bhutan, Brazil, Brunei Darussalam, Burma, Cameroon, Central African Republic, Chad, China, Colombia, Democratic Kampuchea, Ecuador, Egypt, Equatorial Guinea, Fiji, Gabon, Grenada, Honduras, Israel, Ivory Coast, Japan, Jordan, Liberia, Malawi, Malaysia, Nepal, Niger, Nigeria, Oman, Panama, Papua New Guinea, Peru, Philippines, Saint Christopher and Nevis, Saint Lucia, Saint Vincent and the Grenadines, Saudi Arabia, Singapore, Somalia, Sudan, Suriname, Swaziland, Trinidad and Tobago, Turkey, Yemen, Zaire.

Chile characterized the text as illegal, unjust, discriminatory and inconsistent and as exceeding the United Nations competence; Chile had given clear evidence of its co-operation and its attachment to the international instruments to which it was party. Far from seriously dealing with human rights, the text was a libel with a political intent; it interfered in aspects within the country's exclusive competence and disregarded the real situation in the country. In addition, the Assembly was dealing selectively with human rights violations, which occurred in various regions of the world.

The selective treatment of human rights violations was criticized by Zaire. Any selectivity, whereby a few countries were criticized for violations while others were passed over in silence, weakened the system, said Ecuador; it advocated that the United Nations should consolidate its mechanisms for dealing with human rights and should present an annual report on the observance of those rights in each Member State. Madagascar considered it unacceptable that certain States should use human rights questions to interfere in other States' internal affairs.

Costa Rica and the United States would have preferred it if the text had explicitly praised the constructive preliminary report and recognized the positive changes in the human rights situation in Chile, whose Government had for the first time expressed willingness to consider the Special Rapporteur's recommendations. The United States said it hoped Chile would adopt and promptly im-

plement those recommendations Costa Rica said it was rather strange that the eighth preambular paragraph made no mention of the report of the Inter-American Commission on Human Rights and of the Organization of American States, and believed that paragraph 6 was designed to provoke the Chilean Government and might lead it to deny co-operation to the Special Rapporteur.

Bolivia hoped that the human rights situation in the country would return to normal; for reasons of State, it declared, it would not take part in the vote on the text.

Visit to Chile by the Special Rapporteur. In exercise of his mandate, the Special Rapporteur visited Chile from 8 to 19 December 1985, interviewing a large number of senior officials of the Government and judiciary, senior representatives of the Catholic Church, representatives of numerous human rights, social and trade union organizations and private individuals to obtain first-hand information on reports of human rights violations. The report on his mission was to be submitted to the 1986 session of the Commission on Human Rights.

El Salvador

Report of the Special Representative (February). Special Representative José Antonio Pastor Ridruejo, in fulfilment of his mandate extended by the Commission on Human Rights in 1984,[57] submitted a report to the Commission in February 1985.[58] Summing up his overview, he observed that the considerable gap between the Government's intentions to improve the situation and its ability to achieve results had narrowed.

The Special Representative again recommended that both sides—the Salvadorian regular army and the guerrilla forces—immediately terminate attacks on the lives of non-combatants. He further recommended that the Government and the left-wing opposition continue their dialogue initiated at La Palma in October 1984 to ensure peace in the country; until that was achieved, both sides should scrupulously comply with the 1949 Geneva Conventions and the 1977 Additional Protocols.[59]

In addition, he recommended to the authorities the following measures: repeal of all legislative and other measures incompatible with international human rights instruments binding on El Salvador; strengthening of government control over the members and units of the armed forces and security bodies, and over all armed individuals and organizations; adoption of measures to prevent, investigate and punish human rights violations rapidly and effectively, including the dismissal of those committing such violations; intensification of mass campaigns to promote respect for human rights; and broadening of administrative and social reforms, including agrarian reform.

Human Rights Commission action. The Commission on Human Rights, by a resolution[60] adopted on 13 March 1985 by a roll-call vote of 39 to none, with 3 abstentions, expressed deep concern that, despite the sharp drop in political assassinations, detentions and disappearances, many human rights violations continued and the number of attacks on life and the economic structure was still a cause for concern.

The Commission welcomed the release and exchange of prisoners of war and the recent Christmas and New Year's truce, appealed to States to support those measures and to co-operate fully with humanitarian organizations dedicated to alleviating the suffering of the civilians, and recommended that, until peace was achieved, the Government and the guerrilla forces should humanize the conflict by complying with the Geneva Conventions and Additional Protocols.

The Commission recognized the right of the Salvadorian people freely to determine their future without outside interference and through a genuine democratic process free from intimidation and terror. It welcomed the invitation to a dialogue made by the President of El Salvador during the General Assembly's 1984 session, as well as the favourable reply to that invitation by the Frente Democrático Revolucionario–Frente Farabundo Martí para la Liberación Nacional. It urged the parties to continue a serious dialogue with a view to achieving a negotiated solution that would end the armed conflict and help institutionalize and strengthen the democratic system.

Deeply deploring the lack of perceptible change in the judicial system, the Commission again urged the authorities to speed up the reform process with a view to punishing those responsible for the serious violations still being committed. It called on them to amend legislation or measures incompatible with international human rights instruments. In addition, it recommended the intensification of economic and social reforms, including agrarian reform.

Extending the Special Representative's mandate for another year, the Commission requested him to report to it on further developments in 1986, after reporting to the Assembly in 1985. It renewed its appeal to the Government and other parties to continue to co-operate with the Special Representative and requested the necessary assistance from the Secretary-General.

ECONOMIC AND SOCIAL COUNCIL ACTION

On 30 May, by **decision 1985/145**, adopted, without vote, on the recommendation of its Second Committee, the Economic and Social Council approved the Commission's decision to extend the Special Representative's mandate for another year and asked him to submit his report on further developments in the situation of human rights in El Salvador to the Assembly in 1985 and the Commission in 1986. The Council also approved the Commission's request to the Secretary-General to assist the Special Representative.

The Second Committee had approved the text, proposed by the Commission, on 24 May without vote.

Sub-Commission action. By a resolution[61] adopted on 29 August 1985 by 16 votes to 3, with 1 abstention, the Sub-Commission expressed deep concern that, although the number of human rights violations in El Salvador had decreased, the Government continued to commit serious violations as a result, primarily, of its non-observance of the 1949 Geneva Conventions. The Sub-Commission recognized that there existed in El Salvador an armed conflict not of an international character where article 3 common to the Geneva Conventions and Additional Protocol II applied, and ratified the point stated by the Special Representative that, according to the 1949 Conventions, as long as the so-called masses did not participate directly in combat, although they might sympathize with insurgents, they preserved their civilian character and must not be subjected to military attacks and forced displacement by government forces.

The Sub-Commission recommended that the Special Representative inform the Commission on whether both parties accepted their obligation to respect the 1949 Conventions, and how well they were doing so, especially concerning the protection of war prisoners, military hospitals, wounded persons, medical personnel and civilians. It regretted that the hostilities on both sides had resulted in numerous civilian victims and material damage. It welcomed the fact that the parties had agreed in their first round of talks to create a Joint Commission to develop mechanisms to integrate all sectors of national life in the search for peace, study measures to humanize the conflict and consider all aspects that could lead to peace in the shortest time possible. The Sub-Commission requested the Commission to reiterate its appeal to the Government and the Frente Maribundo Martí para la Liberación Nacional–Frente Democrático Revolucionario for an immediate resumption of talks and implementation of their agreements to achieve a negotiated, comprehensive political settlement that would guarantee all Salvadorians full respect of their human rights. It urged all States to refrain from intervening in the country's internal situation and to encourage a just and lasting settlement, instead of supplying arms and military assistance. It requested a report on the Special Representative's investigation.

Report of the Special Representative (November). In November 1985, the Secretary-

General transmitted to the General Assembly an interim report by the Special Representative on the human rights situation in El Salvador.[62] The Representative had visited the country from 8 to 18 September. During his visit, he had interviews with the country's President and a number of high-ranking government officials, representatives of the church and NGOs.

After giving an overview of the situation in the country as it affected human rights, he concluded that the situation described in previous reports had not changed significantly with regard to economic, social and cultural rights; one symptom of that situation was the growing labour unrest. He noted with concern the effects which the attacks by the military forces and in particular systematic attacks by the guerrilla forces on the country's economic infrastructure had had on those rights.

He was convinced that, during 1985, political murders of civilians had continued, some victims having been abducted and subsequently having disappeared, on occasion perpetrated by extreme right-wing paramilitary organizations, some of which were presumably connected with or tolerated by lower-ranking agents of the State.

The Special Representative also had found indications that severe psychological pressure, equivalent to cruel, inhuman or degrading treatment, had been exerted in extrajudicial interrogations of some political prisoners, although he did not believe that this represented a deliberate policy.

Taking note of the attempts to reform the legal system and the organization of the judiciary, and of the difficulties involved, the Special Representative continued to consider that judicial procedures for investigating and punishing acts of collaboration with the armed opposition were excessively slow and did not always respect the law.

He noted with concern that violations committed in military operations by the Salvadorian army continued, resulting in civilian death and injuries and property damage, although civilian victims appeared to be fewer than in the year before. The most significant result of the Government's policy with regard to respect for human rights in 1985 could be seen in the armed forces' combat behaviour.

With regard to non-combat-related violations by the guerrilla forces, the Special Representative observed a disturbing increase in murders, as well as in abductions of civilians, and their combat actions had caused unjustified deaths and injuries among civilians and damage to property.

The Special Representative again recommended that all interested parties immediately terminate attacks on the lives of non-combatants, in both combat and non-combat situations. He continued to believe that civil peace was a vital prerequisite for the respect of the right to life, as well as other

civil and political rights, and for gradual improvement of the enjoyment of economic, social and cultural rights. He again strongly recommended that the Government and the left-wing opposition forces end violence and war and endeavour to ensure peace through a sincere and open dialogue; until a negotiated peace was achieved, both had the obligation to respect the 1949 Geneva Conventions and the 1977 Additional Protocols to which El Salvador was a party.

He recommended that the legislative, executive and judicial authorities in El Salvador repeal all legislative and other measures incompatible with international human rights instruments; strengthen government control over the armed forces, security bodies and armed individuals and organizations, including in particular the so-called "death squads"; increase monitoring of investigations carried out in the security bodies to eliminate torture or other cruel treatment; adopt measures to investigate and punish violations in the swiftest, most exemplary and most effective manner, including the dismissal of officials and officers who committed such violations; intensify, particularly among the armed forces and security bodies, mass campaigns to promote respect for human rights; and broaden administrative and social reforms, including judicial and agrarian reform.

GENERAL ASSEMBLY ACTION

On 13 December 1985, acting on the recommendation of the Third Committee, the General Assembly adopted **resolution 40/139**, by recorded vote.

Situation of human rights and fundamental freedoms in El Salvador

The General Assembly,

Guided by the principles of the Charter of the United Nations, the Universal Declaration of Human Rights, the International Covenant on Civil and Political Rights and the humanitarian rules set out in the Geneva Conventions of 12 August 1949 and Additional Protocols I and II thereto,

Aware that the Governments of all Member States have an obligation to promote and protect human rights and fundamental freedoms and to carry out the responsibilities they have undertaken under various international human rights instruments,

Recalling that, in its resolutions 35/192 of 15 December 1980, 36/155 of 16 December 1981, 37/185 of 17 December 1982, 38/101 of 16 December 1983 and 39/119 of 14 December 1984, it expressed deep concern at the situation of human rights in El Salvador,

Bearing in mind Commission on Human Rights resolutions 32(XXXVII) of 11 March 1981, in which the Commission decided to appoint a special representative on the situation of human rights in El Salvador, 1982/28 of 11 March 1982, 1983/29 of 8 March 1983, 1984/52 of 14 March 1984 and 1985/35 of 13 March 1985, whereby the Commission extended the mandate of the Special Representative for another year and requested him to report, *inter alia*, to the General Assembly,

Noting that the Special Representative of the Commission on Human Rights points out in his interim report that, in the process of the democratic normalization of the country, the question of respect for human rights is an important part of the current policy of the Republic of El Salvador, but that nevertheless a situation of generalized warlike violence continues to exist, that the number of attacks on life and the economic structure remains a cause for concern, and that the number of political prisoners and abductions has increased,

Deeply concerned that in El Salvador, in addition to the continuing armed conflict, the scarcely initiated dialogue between the Government and the Frente Farabundo Martí para la Liberación Nacional–Frente Democrático Revolucionario has been interrupted,

Considering that, while the armed conflict of a non-international character continues, the Government and the insurgent forces are obliged to apply the minimum standards of protection of human rights and of humanitarian treatment set out in article 3 common to the Geneva Conventions of 12 August 1949, as well as Additional Protocol II thereto, to which the Republic of El Salvador is party,

Aware that a political solution to the Salvadorian conflict may be thwarted if external forces, rather than assisting the resumption of the dialogue, contribute in any way to the intensification or prolongation of the war,

Recognizing the value of dialogue as the best way to achieve genuine national reconciliation and the importance of the fact that different sectors of the country favour an overall negotiated political solution which would put an end to the suffering of the Salvadorian people and stem the tide of refugees and internally displaced persons,

1. *Commends* the Special Representative of the Commission on Human Rights for his interim report on the situation of human rights in El Salvador;

2. *Recognizes with interest* and emphasizes that it is important that the Special Representative should have indicated in his interim report that the Government of El Salvador is continuing its policy of attempting to improve the situation of human rights;

3. *Expresses, nevertheless, its deep concern* at the fact that serious and numerous violations of human rights continue to take place in El Salvador owing above all to non-fulfilment of the humanitarian rules of war and therefore requests the Government of El Salvador and the insurgent forces to adopt measures conducive to the humanization of the conflict by observing scrupulously the Geneva Conventions of 1949 and the Additional Protocols thereto, and also recommends that the Special Representative should, for the duration of the armed conflict, continue to observe and to inform the General Assembly and the Commission on Human Rights of the extent to which the contending parties are respecting those rules, particularly as regards humanitarian treatment and respect for the civilian population, prisoners of war, those wounded in combat, health personnel and military hospitals of either party;

4. *Reaffirms once again* the right of the Salvadorian people freely to determine their political, economic and social future without interference from outside, through a genuine democratic process, in which all sectors of the population participate freely and effectively;

5. *Requests* all States to refrain from intervening in the internal situation in El Salvador and, instead of helping in any way to prolong and intensify the war, to encourage the continuation of the dialogue until a just and lasting peace is achieved;

6. *Deeply regrets* the interruption of the dialogue initiated in October 1984 between the Government of El Salvador and the Frente Farabundo Martí para la Liberación Nacional–Frente Democrático Revolucionario and therefore calls upon these parties to renew their talks so that by means of sincere, generous and open dialogue they may achieve a negotiated comprehensive political solution which will put an end to the armed conflict and contribute to the institutionalization and strengthening of the democratic system based on the full exercise by all Salvadorians of their civil and political rights and their economic, social and cultural rights;

7. *Calls upon* the Government and the opposition forces, as agreed at the meeting held at La Palma on 15 October 1984, to establish as soon as possible appropriate mechanisms to study the plans and proposals submitted by both parties and to include all sectors of national life in the search for peace;

8. *Views with concern* that, as a consequence of the prolonged armed conflict, the number of refugees and internally displaced persons, who already constitute a considerable part of the Salvadorian population, continues to increase and requests all States to collaborate in the reception of the refugees and to support the autonomous organizations responsible for looking after internally displaced persons in El Salvador;

9. *Again reiterates its appeal* to the Government of El Salvador and to the opposition forces to co-operate fully with the humanitarian organizations dedicated to alleviating the suffering of the civilian population, wherever these organizations operate in the country, and to permit the International Committee of the Red Cross to continue to evacuate those wounded and maimed by war to where they can receive the medical attention they need;

10. *Deeply deplores* the fact that the capacity of the judicial system in El Salvador to investigate, prosecute and punish violations of human rights continues to be patently unsatisfactory and therefore urges the competent authorities to continue and strengthen the process of reform of the Salvadorian judicial system, in order to punish speedily and effectively those responsible for the serious human rights violations which have been committed and are still being committed in that country;

11. *Recommends* the continuation and broadening of the reforms necessary in El Salvador, including effective application of agrarian reform, for the solution of the economic and social problems which are the basic cause of the internal conflict in that country;

12. *Calls upon* the competent authorities in El Salvador to introduce changes in the laws and other measures that are incompatible with the provisions contained in the international instruments binding on the Government of El Salvador in respect of human rights;

13. *Renews its appeal* to the Government of El Salvador, as well as to other parties concerned, to continue to co-operate with the Special Representative of the Commission on Human Rights;

14. *Decides* to keep under consideration, during its forty-first session, the situation of human rights and fundamental freedoms in El Salvador, in order to examine

this situation anew in the light of additional elements provided by the Commission on Human Rights and the Economic and Social Council, in the hope that there will be improvement.

General Assembly resolution 40/139

13 December 1985   Meeting 116   100-2-42 (recorded vote)

Approved by Third Committee (A/40/1007) by recorded vote (92-3-38), 6 December (meeting 71); 13-nation draft (A/C.3/40/L.54), orally revised; agenda item 12.
Sponsors: Algeria, Costa Rica, Denmark, France, Greece, Mexico, Morocco, Netherlands, Norway, Spain, Sweden, Venezuela, Yugoslavia.
Meeting numbers. GA 40th session: 3rd Committee 54-56, 60-71; plenary 116.

Recorded vote in Assembly as follows:

In favour: Afghanistan, Albania, Algeria, Angola, Antigua and Barbuda, Argentina, Australia, Austria, Bahrain, Barbados, Belgium, Benin, Botswana, Brazil, Bulgaria, Burkina Faso, Byelorussian SSR, Canada, Cape Verde, Colombia, Congo, Costa Rica, Cuba, Cyprus, Czechoslovakia, Democratic Yemen, Denmark, Dominican Republic, Egypt, Ethiopia, Finland, France, Gabon,[a] Gambia, German Democratic Republic, Germany, Federal Republic of, Ghana, Greece, Guinea, Guinea-Bissau, Guyana, Hungary, Iceland, India, Iraq, Ireland, Italy, Jamaica, Japan, Kenya, Kuwait, Lao People's Democratic Republic, Lesotho, Libyan Arab Jamahiriya, Luxembourg, Mali, Mauritania, Mauritius, Mexico, Mongolia, Morocco, Mozambique, Netherlands, New Zealand, Nicaragua, Nigeria, Norway, Panama, Papua New Guinea, Peru, Poland, Portugal, Qatar, Rwanda, Samoa, Sao Tome and Principe, Saudi Arabia, Senegal, Seychelles, Sierra Leone, Spain, Sudan, Swaziland, Sweden, Syrian Arab Republic, Togo, Tunisia, Uganda, Ukrainian SSR, USSR, United Arab Emirates, United Kingdom, United Republic of Tanzania, Uruguay, Vanuatu, Venezuela, Viet Nam, Yugoslavia, Zambia, Zimbabwe.

Against: Chile, Guatemala.

Abstaining: Bahamas, Belize, Bhutan, Brunei Darussalam, Burma, Burundi, Cameroon, Central African Republic, Chad, China, Ecuador, Equatorial Guinea, Fiji, Grenada, Honduras, Indonesia, Israel, Ivory Coast, Jordan, Lebanon, Liberia, Malawi, Malaysia, Maldives, Nepal, Niger, Oman, Pakistan, Philippines, Romania, Saint Lucia, Saint Vincent and the Grenadines, Singapore, Somalia, Sri Lanka, Suriname, Thailand, Trinidad and Tobago, Turkey, United States, Yemen, Zaire.

[a]Later advised the Secretariat it had intended to abstain.

The Third Committee originally approved the text by a recorded vote of 92 to 4, with 40 abstentions; however, on a motion by the United States that the resolution be reconsidered—a motion approved by a recorded vote of 59 to 22, with 17 abstentions, the required two-thirds majority—a second vote was taken.

Although agreeing that the text contained significant positive features, El Salvador none the less believed that it fell short of recognizing a whole series of government achievements and failed to indicate unambiguously those currently responsible for the majority of human rights violations. The text was repetitive in its references to the armed conflict, but while extremist groups without popular support were trying to impose violence, the Government had a constitutional obligation to maintain national security and public order and to enable State institutions to function. Although El Salvador recognized the need and urgency of the reforms mentioned in the text, it could not accept interference in matters within its domestic jurisdiction.

Countries' use of human rights questions for such interference was the reason given by Madagascar for its non-participation. Iran said that it was not able to take part in any action with regard to the text, disappointed as it was with the human rights machinery of the United Nations, but its condemnation of the crimes committed

against the oppressed people of El Salvador still held—and in Chile and Guatemala as well.

While the text recognized the progress made by El Salvador, the United States said, the text had significant defects: it did not take note of the Government's efforts, made in good faith and under the most difficult conditions, to ensure the primacy of law; unlike the Commission's resolution it did not recognize the legitimacy of the Salvadorian Government; it did not devote adequate attention to the brutal violations by the insurgents to which it seemed to give the same moral and legal status as the democratically elected Government, even though they had refused to participate in four free and fair elections; and it implied that the Special Representative's mandate should continue, whereas the progress made could justify allowing it to expire.

Ecuador—which, along with Zaire, said it abstained when it considered there had been selectivity on human rights violations—noted the progress regarding human rights in El Salvador and appealed for their full observance, while Zambia expressed great concern about the widespread violations.

Bolivia, not taking part in the voting for reasons of State, hoped that the human rights situation in the country would return to normal.

Guatemala

Report of the Special Rapporteur (February). In February 1985, Special Rapporteur Viscount Colville of Culross (United Kingdom) submitted a report[63] on the human rights situation in Guatemala, as had been requested by the Commission on Human Rights in 1984.[64] He updated information contained in two reports[65] submitted during 1984, including new material derived from a visit to the country from 20 to 26 January 1985, and also dealt with the situation of Guatemalan refugees in Belize, Honduras and Mexico.

The Special Rapporteur recommended that the process of a return to a democratically elected Government, begun in 1984, should be given every support; the new Constitution should be drawn up so as to guarantee the rights contained in the two International Covenants on Human Rights and ensure that positions of power would be in civilian hands. Independence for the judiciary should be established and violence and disappearances should be prevented; an improvement in the climate of violence was urgently needed if a wider range of political parties was to be persuaded to participate in the next elections. Technical assistance and training was needed to enable judges and court officials to restore credibility to the judicial system. The Guatemalan Assembly should be encouraged to set up an autonomous body to watch over the human rights situation and insist on the investigation and correction of violations; and refugees in the surrounding countries, particularly in Mexico, should be supplied with full information about the situation in Guatemala, to enable them freely to decide whether they wished to return. The development programme and trade union activity should be encouraged, standards of living for migrant workers should be raised, distribution of land title should continue, and technical assistance should be provided to enable rural people to rise above subsistence levels.

Human Rights Commission action. The Commission on Human Rights, by a 13 March 1985 resolution[66] adopted by a roll-call vote of 32 to none, with 10 abstentions, again expressed deep concern at continuing serious and systematic human rights violations in Guatemala, particularly acts of violence against non-combatants, disappearances, killings, torture and extrajudicial executions, and at measures restricting the freedoms of rural and indigenous populations, notably their displacement and relocation in development centres and forced participation in civilian patrols organized and controlled by the armed forces.

The Commission urged the Government to ensure that its authorities and agencies, including security forces, respected human rights, and urged all other parties to do likewise; all were appealed to to ensure application of the norms of international humanitarian law applicable in armed conflicts of a non-international character. It urged Guatemala to establish the independence of the judiciary and enable it to uphold the rule of law, including the right of *habeas corpus*, and to prosecute and speedily punish those found responsible for violations. It appealed to the Government to allow an independent and impartial body into the country to investigate alleged violations, and to allow international humanitarian organizations to assist in investigating the fate of disappeared persons, to visit detainees and assist civilians in areas of conflict. Welcoming the dialogue between the Government and the Mutual Support Group of the families of the disappeared, and the establishment of a commission to investigate and clarify the fate of disappeared persons, the Commission on Human Rights urged that commission to act expediently and called particularly on the police and army to co-operate with the commission. It asked Guatemala to publish a list of cases which fell within the jurisdiction of special tribunals, indicating their outcome.

The Commission requested all States to refrain from intervening in the country's internal situation, appealed to the Government to adhere to its new timetable for the return to democracy and to ensure conditions which would allow full participa-

tion of all in the political process, and appealed to all parties to the conflict to create a climate free from intimidation and terror. Extending the mandate of the Special Rapporteur for another year, it requested him to submit an interim report to the General Assembly in 1985 and a final report to the Commission in 1986; the report, with recommendations, should take into account information from all reliable sources and should assess in particular allegations of politically motivated killings, disappearances, torture, extrajudicial executions and confinement in clandestine prisons. The Government and other parties concerned were invited to co-operate fully with the Rapporteur.

ECONOMIC AND SOCIAL COUNCIL ACTION

On 30 May, the Economic and Social Council approved a text proposed by the Commission on Human Rights to extend the Special Rapporteur's mandate. **Decision 1985/146** was adopted without vote by the Council, having been similarly approved by its Second Committee on 24 May.

The Council thereby approved the Commission's decision to extend for another year the mandate of the Special Rapporteur on the situation of human rights in Guatemala, to enable him to continue his thorough study of the human rights situation in that country. The Council also approved the Commission's request to the Rapporteur, in preparing his report, to continue to take into account information from all reliable sources, to assess in particular allegations of politically motivated killings, disappearances, acts of torture, extrajudicial executions and confinement in clandestine prisons, to draw conclusions from his findings and to make further recommendations designed to help bring about improvements in the situation of human rights in Guatemala. Further, it approved the Commission's request to the Special Rapporteur to submit an interim report to the General Assembly in 1985 and a final report to the Commission in 1986, and approved the request to the Secretary-General to give him all necessary assistance.

Sub-Commission action. Deep concern at massive and systematic human rights violations in Guatemala and at restrictions on the freedom of the indigenous rural population was expressed by the Sub-Commission in a resolution[67] adopted on 30 August by 11 votes to 1, with 6 abstentions. The Sub-Commission again urged the Government to ensure full respect for human rights by its authorities, agencies and forces, to punish those responsible for violations, and to clarify the fate of disappeared persons. It also called on the Government to halt harassment and persecution of members and leaders of the Mutual Support Group and to respond to their demands.

Noting with satisfaction that the Government had invited certain international human rights organizations to visit the country to assess the situation, the Sub-Commission expected that Guatemala would take their reports into due account and would allow international humanitarian organizations, in particular ICRC, to aid the civilians in the areas of conflict and investigate the fate of the disappeared. It called on the parties concerned to ensure the application of international law.

The Sub-Commission expressed its conviction that solutions would be greatly facilitated by allowing the people freely to determine their future without foreign interference. It expressed concern at the climate of intimidation and terror in the country, which it considered to be an impediment to the free participation of all political forces, social sectors and citizens in the presidential election process beginning November 1985, to which it had been invited, as well as at the insufficient conditions for the effective participation in the political processes of the indigenous, rural and peasant populations. The Sub-Commission noted the promulgation of a new Constitution by the National Constitutent Assembly, of electoral and constitutional laws and of the final timetable for elections to a constitutional Government which was to take office on 14 January 1986. It urged again all Governments to abstain from intervening in the internal situation, in particular from providing arms and military assistance as long as grave violations of human rights continued to occur. In preparing his reports, the Rapporteur was urged to take due account of the situation of the indigenous population, as well as testimonies submitted to the Sub-Commission.

Report of the Special Rapporteur (November). In November 1985, the Special Rapporteur presented to the General Assembly an interim report[68] on the human rights situation in Guatemala. After discussing some questions of methodology, in response to criticism by an opposition group as well as from the country's Human Rights Commission, and giving an account of his use of sources of information additional to his own research, the report dealt with: the role of the police and the judiciary in solving cases of human rights violations; internal and non-governmental organizations concerned with human rights; particular allegations of violations; disappearances; clandestine prisons and civil patrols; development areas or "poles" and model villages; other projects concerning social and economic rights; and Guatemalan refugees in Mexico. It omitted any detailed discussion of the platform of the various political parties competing in the election. The Special Rapporteur stressed that he had received every possible facility and co-operation from the Government and everyone else in the execution of his mandate.

The Special Rapporteur pointed out that the situation in Guatemala was complex and continuously changing. He concluded that there was agreement that violence and disappearances were still a serious problem in 1985; the police had demonstrated considerable success in detecting such crimes but not in relation to many of the cases that excited much international condemnation. There was impatience and frustration over the delay in publishing the results of investigations into disappearances. The criminal justice system was not equipped to bring to trial many persons accused of the most controversial offences; under those circumstances, it was no wonder that people felt free to resort to violence.

The Government had denied allegations that security forces were involved in violence, other than in their military activities against the guerrillas; some allegations were almost certainly untrue, the Rapporteur said, but in other cases the denunciations did not appear to correspond to the facts. The human rights situation continued to give cause for serious concern.

Noting that the existing Government might not wish to make policy decisions that could fetter the incoming administration, the Special Rapporteur recommended that the international community consider providing technical assistance and advice to the judiciary and police to enable them more effectively to bring to justice and trial those responsible for serious crimes. Efforts should be made to clear up serious unsolved crimes and a new attempt made to gain the co-operation of the public. Consideration should be given to methods whereby bodies concerned with human rights might safely operate inside Guatemala and to an invitation to ICRC to establish a presence there. He suggested that UNHCR send to the Government the names of the refugees in Mexico, Honduras and Belize, for comparison with the list of disappearances, and that the results of the Tripartite Commission's investigation into disappearances be published. The new Government should reconsider the policy regarding of the civil patrols in the light of criticism that such an obligation placed on civilians constituted in itself a violation of the right to freedom of association.

The Special Rapporteur also recommended that recognition be made of the various projects in process to improve the standards of living, health, nutrition and education for the poorest sectors of the population.

GENERAL ASSEMBLY ACTION

On 13 December, on the recommendation of the Third Committee, the General Assembly adopted **resolution 40/140**, by recorded vote.

Situation of human rights and fundamental freedoms in Guatemala

The General Assembly,

Reiterating that the Governments of all Member States have an obligation to promote and protect human rights and fundamental freedoms,

Recalling its resolutions 37/184 of 17 December 1982, 38/100 of 16 December 1983 and 39/120 of 14 December 1984,

Recalling also Commission on Human Rights resolution 1984/53 of 14 March 1984, and taking note of Commission resolution 1985/36 of 13 March 1985, in which it expressed its deep concern at the continuing serious and systematic violations of human rights in Guatemala and at restrictive measures that limit the freedoms of the rural and indigenous populations,

Mindful of resolution 1985/28 of 30 August 1985 of the Sub-Commission on Prevention of Discrimination and Protection of Minorities,

Welcoming the general elections held on 3 November 1985 for President, Vice-President and representatives to the national Congress and of municipalities, with the participation of various political parties,

Noting with satisfaction the set of provisions to safeguard human rights and fundamental freedoms contained in the new Constitution, which, when fully complied with by the new Government and all others concerned, could lead to a significant improvement in the situation of human rights in Guatemala,

Alarmed at the continuation of politically motivated violence, particularly killings and kidnappings, as well as enforced and involuntary disappearances and the lack of effective measures by the authorities in investigating such practices,

Recognizing that the internal armed conflict of a non-international character which continues to exist in Guatemala stems from economic, social and political factors of a structural nature,

Expressing its concern at the widespread suffering caused by disregard for the principles of international humanitarian law applicable to that conflict,

Welcoming the co-operation of the Government of Guatemala with the Special Rapporteur of the Commission on Human Rights as well as the invitation by the Government to several international human rights organizations to assess the situation of human rights and fundamental freedoms,

1. *Welcomes* the efforts of the Special Rapporteur of the Commission on Human Rights to fulfil his mandate and takes note of his interim report on the situation of human rights in Guatemala, submitted in accordance with Commission resolution 1985/36;

2. *Expresses the hope* that the recent elections will be the first step in a process leading to complete and effective enjoyment of human rights by the people of Guatemala;

3. *Notes with satisfaction* that a new Government and Congress are to take office on 14 January 1986, following a second round in the presidential elections on 8 December 1985, and that a new Constitution, which provides, *inter alia*, for the establishment of a national commission on human rights as well as a commissioner for human rights, is to take effect on the same date in January 1986;

4. *Reiterates its deep concern* at the continuing grave and widespread violations of human rights in Guatemala, particularly the violence against non-combatants, the widespread repression, killings, including extrajudicial executions, the practice of torture, disappearances and secret detention, as well as at practices such as the displacement of rural and indigenous populations, their confinement in development centres and their forced participation in civilian patrols organized and controlled by the armed forces;

5. *Strongly urges* the Government of Guatemala to take all measures necessary to halt violations of human rights and fundamental freedoms, particularly enforced and involuntary disappearances, as well as to take effective measures, within the framework of the Constitution, to ensure that all its authorities and agencies, civilian as well as military, fully respect the human rights and fundamental freedoms of all Guatemalans, such as trade unionists, catechists and the predominantly indigenous rural and peasant population;

6. *Again requests* the Government of Guatemala to investigate and clarify the fate of those who have disappeared and whose whereabouts continue to be unknown, and to include within the framework of such an investigation the publication of the full details of the report of the Tripartite Commission;

7. *Further urges* the Government of Guatemala to establish the necessary conditions to ensure the independence of the judicial system and to enable the judiciary to uphold the rule of law, including the right of *habeas corpus*, and to prosecute and punish speedily and effectively those who are responsible for violations of human rights, including members of the military and security forces;

8. *Calls upon* the Government of Guatemala to allow independent and impartial bodies to function in the country to monitor and investigate alleged human rights violations, as well as to respect and protect human rights defenders such as the Mutual Support Group;

9. *Calls upon* the Government of Guatemala to guarantee to the rural and indigenous population the freedom to choose their place of residence and freedom from forced participation in civilian patrols;

10. *Calls upon* all parties to the conflict to apply fully the principles and rules of international humanitarian law and reiterates its appeal to the Government of Guatemala to admit the International Committee of the Red Cross to the country, and subsequently to facilitate its operations for the alleviation of the suffering of the Guatemalan people;

11. *Calls upon* all Governments to refrain from intervening in any way in the internal situation in Guatemala, which could intensify the internal armed conflict and increase violations of human rights;

12. *Deeply deplores* the continuing gross violations of human rights arising from that conflict, which are largely due to the failure of the military and security forces to conduct their activities with the necessary respect for protecting the human rights of all Guatemalans;

13. *Invites* the Government of Guatemala and other parties concerned to continue co-operating with the Special Rapporteur of the Commission on Human Rights;

14. *Invites* the Commission on Human Rights to study carefully the report of its Special Rapporteur, as well as other information pertaining to the human rights situation in Guatemala, and to consider further steps

for securing effective respect for human rights and fundamental freedoms for all in that country including, if so requested by the Government of Guatemala, the provision of appropriate technical assistance under the programme of advisory services in the field of human rights;

15. *Decides* to continue its examination of the situation of human rights and fundamental freedoms in Guatemala at its forty-first session.

General Assembly resolution 40/140

13 December 1985   Meeting 116   91-8-47 (recorded vote)

Approved by Third Committee (A/40/1007) by recorded vote (85-6-40), 6 December (meeting 71); 10-nation draft (A/C.3/40/L.59/Rev.2); agenda item 12.

Sponsors: Austria, Canada, Denmark, France, Greece, Ireland, Netherlands, Norway, Spain, Sweden.

Meeting numbers. GA 40th session: 3rd Committee 54-56, 58, 60-71; plenary 116.

Recorded vote in Assembly as follows:

In favour: Albania, Algeria, Angola, Antigua and Barbuda, Argentina, Australia, Austria, Bahrain, Barbados, Belgium, Benin, Botswana, Brazil, Bulgaria, Burkina Faso, Byelorussian SSR, Canada, Cape Verde, Colombia, Congo, Costa Rica, Cuba, Cyprus, Czechoslovakia, Democratic Yemen, Denmark, Dominican Republic, Ethiopia, Finland, France, Gambia, German Democratic Republic, Germany, Federal Republic of, Ghana, Greece, Guinea-Bissau, Guyana, Hungary, Iceland, India, Iraq, Ireland, Italy, Jamaica, Japan, Kenya, Kuwait, Lao People's Democratic Republic, Lesotho, Libyan Arab Jamahiriya, Luxembourg, Mali, Mauritania, Mauritius, Mexico, Mongolia, Mozambique, Netherlands, New Zealand, Nicaragua, Nigeria, Norway, Papua New Guinea, Poland, Portugal, Qatar, Rwanda, Samoa, Sao Tome and Principe, Saudi Arabia, Senegal, Sierra Leone, Spain, Swaziland, Sweden, Syrian Arab Republic, Togo, Tunisia, Uganda, Ukrainian SSR, USSR, United Arab Emirates, United Kingdom, United Republic of Tanzania, Uruguay, Vanuatu, Venezuela, Viet Nam, Yugoslavia, Zambia, Zimbabwe.

Against: Bangladesh, Chile, El Salvador, Guatemala, Indonesia, Morocco, Pakistan, Paraguay.

Abstaining: Bahamas, Belize, Bhutan, Brunei Darussalam, Burma, Burundi, Cameroon, Central African Republic, Chad, China, Democratic Kampuchea, Ecuador, Egypt, Equatorial Guinea, Fiji, Gabon, Grenada, Honduras, Israel, Ivory Coast, Jordan, Lebanon, Liberia, Malawi, Malaysia, Maldives, Nepal, Niger, Oman, Panama, Peru, Philippines, Romania, Saint Christopher and Nevis, Saint Lucia, Saint Vincent and the Grenadines, Singapore, Somalia, Sri Lanka, Sudan, Suriname, Thailand, Trinidad and Tobago, Turkey, United States, Yemen, Zaire.

The adopted text incorporated some elements of amendments[69] submitted by Colombia, Costa Rica and Venezuela, which were then withdrawn.

Guatemala said that, although the Special Rapporteur had underscored the co-operation and support of the Government, the sponsors of the resolution, combining arrogance with paternalism, had submitted a selective, partial and discriminatory text that reflected neither the real situation in the country nor the changes and progress taking place. In the fifth preambular paragraph, they showed some reticence in recognizing that free and fair elections had been held in an electoral process which would culminate on 14 January 1986 with the installation of a new civilian Government. The ninth preambular paragraph spoke of principles of international humanitarian law applicable to the conflict in the country, whereas in fact what was involved were clandestine groups who perpetrated murders, kidnappings and destruction of property and public buildings; the Government had the duty to ensure the safety of property and persons and to maintain public order. Paragraph 4 compounded the false assertions: no outside observer had ever noted the many and serious violations in question. The text failed to mention the common will of the

Government and the Guatemalan people to establish a pluralist and representative democracy and to favour national reconciliation and economic development.

The United States said that, although it had not voted against the text, the resolution was unbalanced, referring to gross human rights violations arising from the conflict. Since the Government had begun to co-operate with the Commission on Human Rights, the situation had become quite comparable to that of other Latin American countries whose situation was not being examined. The text made no mention of the responsibility of the rebels or extremist groups for the violence in the country. The Special Rapporteur's conclusions contained no evidence of restrictions on the freedom of movement in the rural development centres, forced participation in civilian patrols or the existence of secret detention centres; the rebels, not the Government, were responsible for the displacement of the rural population.

Welcoming the elections as a strengthening of democratic institutions, Ecuador appealed to Guatemala fully to observe human rights. Bolivia, for reasons of State, did not take part in the voting. Venezuela said the improvement of the situation in Guatemala would occur when freedom, democracy and stability were instituted; it hoped that the new Government would further that process because, as the Special Rapporteur had pointed out, the situation still left much to be desired and the Government appeared not to have controlled certain forces.

Costa Rica said United Nations bodies had introduced political considerations into human rights resolutions that did little to promote a serious and objective analysis of the situation. They had also acted selectively in the case of Guatemala, as in the cases of El Salvador and Chile, by closing their eyes to what was going on in other States. Zaire held a similar position.

Paraguay

The situation in Paraguay, which had been under a state of siege for 30 years, was again the subject of a Sub-Commission resolution[70] (see p. 854).

Uruguay

At a closed meeting on 8 March 1985, the Commission on Human Rights decided[71] to discontinue consideration of the human rights situation in Uruguay under the confidential procedure established by the Economic and Social Council in 1970[1] to deal with communications alleging denial or violations of human rights, and, taking account of a request by the Uruguayan Government that the material before the Commission should no longer be restricted, recommended a draft decision for adoption by the Council to that effect.

ECONOMIC AND SOCIAL COUNCIL ACTION

Noting the Commission's decision, the Economic and Social Council, by **decision 1985/139** adopted without vote on 30 May, encouraged the Government of Uruguay to persist in its endeavours fully to restore respect for human rights and fundamental freedoms throughout the country, and decided, as Uruguay had requested, that the material relating to Uruguay which had been before the Commission under the Council's procedure for dealing with confidential communications alleging human rights violations should no longer be restricted. The Council's action followed approval of the decision without vote on 24 May by its Second Committee.

Middle East

Lebanon

Human Rights Commission action. By a resolution[72] on the situation in southern Lebanon, adopted on 13 March by a roll-call vote of 24 to 1, with 16 abstentions, the Commission on Human Rights strongly condemned Israel for its human rights violations—assassinations, mass arrests of civilians, abductions, demolition of houses, desecration of places of worship and other inhuman acts—and called on it to end such practices immediately and release the persons detained and abducted. Demanding Israel's immediate and total withdrawal from southern Lebanon, the Commission called on Governments to end economic, political and military aid to Israel, which encouraged that country to persevere with its policy of aggression, expansion and colonial settlements. The Secretary-General was requested to monitor implementation of the resolution and submit to the Assembly a report on the results of his efforts.

ECONOMIC AND SOCIAL COUNCIL ACTION

In May, on the recommendation of its Second Committee, the Economic and Social Council adopted **decision 1985/157**, by roll-call vote.

Situation in southern Lebanon

At its 25th plenary meeting, on 30 May 1985, the Council, noting Commission on Human Rights resolution 1985/41 of 13 March 1985, endorsed the request of the Commission to the Secretary-General to monitor the implementation of that resolution and to submit to the General Assembly at its fortieth session a report on the results of his efforts in that regard.

Economic and Social Council decision 1985/157

29-1-18 (roll-call vote)

Approved by Second Committee (E/1985/95 & Corr.1) by roll-call vote (30-1-19), 24 May (meeting 15); 5-nation draft (E/1985/C.2/L.12); agenda item 16.
Sponsors: Lebanon, Morocco, Saudi Arabia, Syrian Arab Republic, Tunisia.

Roll-call vote in Council as follows:

In favour: Algeria, Bangladesh, Botswana, Brazil, Bulgaria, China, Congo, Djibouti, Ecuador, German Democratic Republic, Guinea, India, Indonesia, Lebanon, Malaysia, Morocco, Nigeria, Poland, Romania, Rwanda, Saudi Arabia, Senegal, Sri Lanka, Suriname, Turkey, Uganda, USSR, Yugoslavia, Zimbabwe.
Against: United States.

Abstaining: Argentina, Canada, Colombia, Costa Rica, Finland, France, Germany, Federal Republic of, Iceland, Japan, Luxembourg, Mexico, Netherlands, New Zealand, Spain, Sweden, United Kingdom, Venezuela, Zaire.

Israel said the Commission's resolution had not reflected the real situation in Lebanon; rival factions were engaged in fratricidal massacres in Beirut, yet the decision related to southern Lebanon, the only part of the country where peace reigned.

The United States could not accept the dual standard the decision implied; it focused on events in one part of Lebanon in an inaccurate and inflammatory way and was totally irrelevant to the tragic reality of violence and destruction in many other parts.

In Venezuela's view, the decision contained inappropriate language. Argentina and Costa Rica did not agree with the wording of the decision, nor with that of the Commission's resolution. Ecuador said that resolution lacked objectivity in failing to refer to Israeli troop withdrawals from Lebanon; it voted in favour solely because of its position of principle concerning the inadmissibility of occupying territory by force.

(See also p. 295.)

Territories occupied by Israel

In 1985, the question of human rights violations in the territories occupied by Israel as a result of the 1967 hostilities in the Middle East was again considered by the Commission on Human Rights. This was in addition to the consideration of political and other aspects by the General Assembly, its Special Committee to Investigate Israeli Practices Affecting the Human Rights of the Population of the Occupied Territories and other bodies (see p. 326).

Human Rights Commission action. By a 19 February 1985 resolution,[73] adopted by a roll-call vote of 28 to 5, with 8 abstentions, the Commission on Human Rights reaffirmed that occupation itself was a fundamental violation of the human rights of the civilian population of the Palestinian and other occupied Arab territories. It denounced Israel's continued refusal to allow the Special Committee on Israeli practices access to the territories, and reiterated the Committee's alarm at Israel's policy based on the so-called "homeland" doctrine envisaging a monoreligious (Jewish) State that would include territories occupied by Israel since 1967—a policy which, as affirmed by the Committee, not only denied the population its right to self-determination but was also the source of systematic human rights violations.

The Commission confirmed that Israel's continuous grave breaches of the 1949 (fourth) Geneva Convention relative to the Protection of Civilian Persons in Time of War and the 1977 Additional Protocols[59] were war crimes and an affront to humanity. It firmly rejected and reiterated its condemnation of Israel's decision to annex Jerusalem and change the physical character, demographic composition, institutional structure or status of the occupied territories, including the Holy City—measures which the Commission considered null and void. It strongly condemned Israel's attempts to subject the West Bank and the Gaza Strip to Israeli laws, as well as the terrorist actions against Palestinian inhabitants by what it called Jewish gangs.

The Commission strongly condemned Israeli policies and practices, administrative and legislative measures to promote and expand the establishment and expansion of settler colonies, as well as the following practices: the annexation of parts of the territories, including Jerusalem; the continuing establishment and expansion of Israeli settlements on Arab lands, and the transfer of an alien population there; the arming of settlers to commit acts of violence and to strike at Moslem and Christian religious and holy places; the evacuation, deportation, expulsion, displacement and transfer of Arab inhabitants and the denial of their right to return; the confiscation and expropriation of Arab property; the destruction and demolition of Arab houses; mass arrests, collective punishments, administrative detention and ill-treatment of the Arab population, as well as torture and inhuman prison conditions; the pillaging of archaeological and cultural property; interference with religious freedoms and practices, as well as with family rights and customs; the systematic repression of cultural and educational institutions, closing them or restricting and impeding their academic activities; the expropriation and exploitation of the inhabitants' natural wealth, water and other resources; the dismantling of municipal services; dismissing elected mayors and municipal councils; and preventing the flow of Arab aid funds to the territories.

The Commission called on Israel: to take immediate steps for the return of the displaced inhabitants to their homes and property; to arrange for the immediate return of the municipal chiefs to their municipalities; and to release all Arabs detained or imprisoned as a result of their struggle for the territories' self-determination and liberation and, pending their release, to accord them the protection envisaged under international instruments concerning the treatment of prisoners of war. The Commission condemned Israel for its continued detention of Ziyad Abu Eain, calling for his release and the release of others detained at Al-Ansar camp, which must be closed under a November 1983 agreement.

The Commission again called on States, in particular the parties to the fourth Geneva Convention, and international organizations not to recognize any changes carried out by Israel in the territories, including Jerusalem, and avoid action or aid that might be used by Israel in its annexation and colonization policies. It urged Israel to refrain from practices violating human rights in the territories; requested the Assembly to recommend the adoption of measures under Chapter VII of the Charter; and requested the Secretary-General to give the Commission's resolution wide publicity and to report to the Commission in 1986, also bringing to its attention all United Nations reports on the situation appearing until then.

By another resolution[74] adopted on the same day by a roll-call vote of 33 to 1, with 7 abstentions, the Commission, expressing deep concern at the consequences of Israel's systematic refusal to apply the fourth Geneva Convention to the occupied territories, including Jerusalem, reaffirmed its applicability, condemned Israel for its failure to acknowledge its applicability, and urged all States parties to ensure compliance with its provisions in all Arab territories. The Commission called on Israel to respect its obligations under the Charter and other international instruments; repeated the request in the above-mentioned resolution for release of all Arabs detained for fighting for self-determination and liberation, pending which to accord them prisoner-of-war status; and demanded that Israel cease all acts of torture and ill-treatment of Arab prisoners. The Commission requested the Secretary-General to report in 1986 on progress in implementing this resolution after bringing it to the attention of Governments, United Nations organs and agencies, and intergovernmental, humanitarian and non-governmental organizations.

By a third resolution[75] adopted on 19 February, by a roll-call vote of 30 to 1, with 10 abstentions, the Commission condemned Israel for its failure to comply with United Nations resolutions on the Syrian Golan Heights. It called on Israel to rescind its 1981 decision[76] to impose its laws, jurisdiction and administration on the territory which, the Commission said, resulted in its effective annexation and which it had declared null and void; it reaffirmed its request to United Nations Members not to recognize any such measures. The Commission strongly deplored the negative vote and pro-Israeli position of a Security Council permanent member which had prevented the Council from adopting measures against Israel under Chapter VII of the Charter. It deplored the inhuman treatment, terror and practices contrary to human rights that Israel continued to apply against Syrian citizens in the Golan Heights by reason of their refusing Israeli nationality, and called for an end to such practices. The Commission emphasized that Israel must allow the evacuees from among the Golan population to return and recover their property and residences, and firmly emphasized the necessity of total and unconditional Israeli withdrawal from all Palestinian and Syrian territories. (See also p. 313.)

Sub-Commission action. The Sub-Commission, by a resolution[77] adopted on 29 August by a roll-call vote of 10 to 1, with 6 abstentions, strongly reaffirmed that the perpetuation of Israeli occupation of the Palestinian and other Arab territories, including Jerusalem, could only be a source of increasing violations of the human rights of the population and of increasing tension. It reiterated that the inalienable rights of the Palestinians included their right to self-determination, to return to their homes and property, and to establish a sovereign State of Palestine. It reaffirmed that their future could only be decided with their full participation and through PLO. It affirmed its support for the Geneva Declaration on Palestine adopted in 1983 by the International Conference on the Question of Palestine[78] and welcomed the call for an international peace conference on the Middle East under United Nations auspices and with the participation of all parties. It affirmed that Palestinian and other freedom fighters detained by Israel were entitled to the status of prisoners of war and that the Palestinian and other civilians arbitrarily detained by Israel should be released immediately. It strongly reaffirmed that the fourth Geneva Convention was fully applicable to the occupied territories, and expressed deep concern at the consequences of Israel's refusal to apply the Convention. The Secretary-General was requested to supply the Sub-Commission in 1986 with a list of latest reports, studies, documents, statistics and United Nations decisions on the occupied territories, including Lebanon. The Sub-Commission also recommended to the Commission adoption of a resolution strongly condemning Israeli policies and terrorist actions against the inhabitants of the territories, and calling on it to withdraw in order to restore the Palestinians' national rights.

Mass exoduses

Welcoming the steps taken by the United Nations to examine the problem of massive outflows of refugees and displaced persons, the Commission on Human Rights, by a 13 March resolution,[79] invited Governments and international organizations to intensify their co-operation and assistance in world-wide efforts to address the problem. It welcomed the designation by the Secretary-General of special representatives on humanitarian issues, reiterating its request to him that he follow closely developments on the issue, and encouraged his efforts to establish an early warning system to anticipate and react more adequately and speedily to cases requiring humanitarian assistance, as mentioned in his 1984 report[80] on the work of the Organization. The Commission asked its Sub-Commission to keep in mind the need to consider the relationship between human rights violations and mass exoduses and to make recommendations. It recommended that special rapporteurs and special representatives studying human rights violations pay attention to the problems resulting in mass exoduses.

On 13 December, on the recommendation of the Third Committee, the General Assembly adopted **resolution 40/149**, without vote.

Human rights and mass exoduses

The General Assembly,

Mindful of its general humanitarian mandate under the Charter of the United Nations to promote and encourage respect for human rights and fundamental freedoms,

Deeply disturbed by the continuing scale and magnitude of exoduses of refugees and displacements of population in many regions of the world and by the suffering of millions of refugees and displaced persons,

Conscious of the fact that human rights violations are among the multiple and complex factors causing mass exoduses of refugees, as indicated in the study of the Special Rapporteur of the Commission on Human Rights on this subject,

Considering the efforts which have been made to address this subject within the United Nations, in particular by the Commission on Human Rights,

Aware of the recommendations concerning mass exoduses made by the Commission on Human Rights to its Sub-Commission on Prevention of Discrimination and Protection of Minorities and to the special rapporteurs for their study of the violations of human rights in any part of the world,

Deeply preoccupied by the increasingly heavy burden being imposed upon the international community as a whole, particularly upon developing countries with limited resources of their own, by these sudden mass exoduses and displacements of population,

Stressing the need to improve international co-operation aimed at the prevention of new massive flows of refugees in parallel with the provision of adequate solutions to actual refugee situations,

Taking note of the report of the Group of Governmental Experts on International Co-operation to Avert New Flows of Refugees,

Taking note once again of the report of the Secretary-General on human rights and mass exoduses,

Recalling its resolutions 35/196 of 15 December 1980, 37/186 of 17 December 1982, 38/103 of 16 December 1983 and 39/117 of 14 December 1984 and Commission on Human Rights resolutions 30(XXXVI) of 11 March 1980, 29(XXXVII) of 11 March 1981, 1982/32 of 11 March 1982, 1983/35 of 8 March 1983 and 1985/40 of 13 March 1985,

1. *Welcomes* the steps taken so far by the United Nations to examine the problem of massive outflows of refugees and displaced persons in all its aspects, including its root causes;

2. *Invites* Governments and international organizations to intensify their co-operation and assistance in world-wide efforts to address the serious problem of mass exoduses of refugees and displaced persons;

3. *Welcomes* the special interest which the Secretary-General has taken in this question, and reiterates its

request to him to follow closely developments in the field of human rights and mass exoduses;

4.   *Encourages* the Secretary-General in his efforts to enable the United Nations to anticipate and react more adequately and speedily to cases requiring humanitarian assistance, as mentioned in the report of the Secretary-General on the work of the Organization submitted to the General Assembly at its thirty-ninth session;

5.   *Invites* the Commission on Human Rights to keep the question of human rights and mass exoduses under review with the objective of making appropriate recommendations concerning the further measures to be taken in this field;

6.   *Decides* to review the question of human rights and mass exoduses at its forty-first session.

General Assembly resolution 40/149

13 December 1985   Meeting 116   Adopted without vote

Approved by Third Committee (A/40/1007) without vote, 6 December (meeting 71); 11-nation draft (A/C.3/40/L.86), orally revised; agenda item 12.
Sponsors: Australia, Bangladesh, Canada, Colombia, Costa Rica, Germany, Federal Republic of, Japan, Jordan, Pakistan, Rwanda, Sudan.
Meeting numbers. GA 40th session: 3rd Committee 61-63, 65-67, 69, 71; plenary 116.

By **resolution 40/166**, the General Assembly, having examined a report of the Group of Governmental Experts on International Co-operation to Avert New Flows of Refugees, extended the Group's mandate in order that it might conclude its comprehensive review of the problem.

Genocide

Report of the Special Rapporteur. Special Rapporteur Ben Charles George Whitaker (United Kingdom) appointed in 1983[81] to prepare a study on the question of the prevention and punishment of the crime of genocide, presented to the Sub-Commission in July 1985 a report[82] revising and updating his preliminary report submitted in 1984.[83]

In response to a questionnaire sent by him in 1984 to obtain information for his report, 24 States had replied as at 20 May 1985; in addition, five specialized agencies, one intergovernmental regional organization and 16 NGOs had submitted information.

After a historical survey and a brief outline of the concept of genocide, the report discussed future options for preventing it, among them an early warning system, possibly through an international body. The report also analysed the 1948 Convention on the Prevention and Punishment of the Crime of Genocide[11] and reproduced the 1968 Convention on the Non-Applicability of Statutory Limitations to War Crimes and Crimes against Humanity[27] and the 1984 Convention against Torture and Other Cruel, Inhuman or Degrading Treatment or Punishment.[84]

Sub-Commission action. By a resolution[85] adopted on 29 August 1985 by 14 votes to 1, with 4 abstentions, the Sub-Commission took note of the updated and revised study. It recommended that the United Nations renew its efforts to make universal the ratification of the 1948 Convention on genocide.

GENERAL ASSEMBLY ACTION

On 13 December, acting on the recommendation of the Third Committee, the General Assembly adopted **resolution 40/142**, without vote.

Status of the Convention on the Prevention and Punishment of the Crime of Genocide
The General Assembly,

Recalling its resolution 260 A (III) of 9 December 1948, by which it approved and proposed for signature and ratification or accession the Convention on the Prevention and Punishment of the Crime of Genocide,

Mindful of the fact that the year 1986 marks the thirty-fifth anniversary of the entry into force of the Convention,

Reaffirming its conviction that genocide is a crime under international law, contrary to the spirit and aims of the United Nations,

Expressing its conviction that implementation of the provisions of the Convention by all States is necessary for the prevention and punishment of the crime of genocide,

Bearing in mind that the fortieth anniversary of the victory over nazism and fascism in the Second World War is being commemorated in 1985,

1.   *Once again strongly condemns* the crime of genocide;

2.   *Reaffirms* the necessity of international co-operation in order to liberate mankind from such an odious scourge;

3.   *Takes note with appreciation* of the fact that many States have ratified the Convention on the Prevention and Punishment of the Crime of Genocide or have acceded thereto;

4.   *Urges* those States that have not yet become parties to the Convention to ratify it or accede thereto without further delay;

5.   *Invites* the Secretary-General to submit to the General Assembly at its forty-first session a report on the status of the Convention;

6.   *Requests* the Commission on Human Rights to consider at its forty-second session the question of promoting the full implementation of the Convention and to submit its observations and proposals thereon, through the Economic and Social Council, to the General Assembly at its forty-first session.

General Assembly resolution 40/142

13 December 1985   Meeting 116   Adopted without vote

Approved by Third Committee (A/40/1007) without vote, 6 December (meeting 71); 3-nation draft (A/C.3/40/L.76); agenda item 12.
Sponsors: Byelorussian SSR, Mongolia, Poland.
Meeting numbers. GA 40th session: 3rd Committee 61, 64, 69, 71; plenary 116.

As at 31 December 1985, 96 States were parties to the Convention; there were no new accessions or ratifications during the year.

REFERENCES
[1]YUN 1970, p. 530, ESC res. 1503(XLVIII), 27 May 1970. [2]YUN 1984, p. 852, ESC dec. 1984/154, 24 May 1984. [3]E/1985/22 (dec. 1985/106). [4]E/CN.4/1986/5 (res. 1985/15). [5]YUN 1979, p. 832, GA res. 34/175, 17 Dec. 1979. [6]YUN 1967, p. 509. [7]E/CN.4/1985/8. [8]YUN 1983, p. 155. [9]*Ibid.*, p. 156. [10]E/CN.4/1985/14. [11]YUN 1948-49, p. 959, GA res. 260 A (III), annex, 9 Dec. 1948. [12]E/1985/22 (res. 1985/8). [13]*Ibid.* (res. 1985/7). [14]YUN 1978, pp. 915 & 916, SC res. 435(1978) & 439(1978), 29 Sep. & 13 Nov. 1978.

[15]E/CN.4/1986/3. [16]A/C.3/40/7. [17]E/CN.4/1986/9. [18]E/CN.4/Sub.2/1985/25. [19]E/CN.4/1986/5 (res. 1985/36). [20]YUN 1948-49, p. 535, GA res. 217 A (III), 10 Dec. 1948. [21]E/CN.4/1986/5 (dec. 1985/103). [22]*Ibid.* (dec. 1985/109). [23]YUN 1973, p. 103, GA res. 3068(XXVIII), annex, 30 Nov. 1973. [24]YUN 1976, p. 575. [25]A/40/606. [26]E/CN.4/1985/27. [27]YUN 1968, p. 609, GA res. 2391(XXIII), annex, 26 Nov. 1968. [28]E/1985/22 (res. 1985/10). [29]*Ibid.* (res. 1985/9). [30]YUN 1984, p. 857, GA res. 39/15, 23 Nov. 1984. [31]E/CN.4/Sub.2/1985/8 & Add.1,2. [32]E/CN.4/1986/5 (res. 1985/3). [33]A/40/677. [34]E/1985/41. [35]YUN 1984, p. 807, ESC res. 1984/37, 24 May 1984. [36]E/CN.4/1985/21. [37]E/1985/22 (res. 1985/38). [38]E/CN.4/1986/5 (res. 1985/35). [39]E/1985/87. [40]E/1985/125. [41]A/C.3/40/14. [42]A/40/843. [43]YUN 1984, p. 860. [44]E/CN.4/1985/20. [45]E/1985/22 (res. 1985/39). [46]E/CN.4/1986/5 (res. 1985/17). [47]A/40/874. [48]A/C.3/40/13. [49]E/CN.4/1986/5 (res. 1985/21). [50]*Ibid.* (res. 1985/20). [51]E/1985/22 (dec. 1985/108). [52]E/1985/C.2/L.9. [53]YUN 1984, p. 864. [54]E/1985/22 (res. 1985/47). [55]E/CN.4/1986/5 (res. 1985/27). [56]A/40/647. [57]YUN 1984, p. 866. [58]E/CN.4/1985/18. [59]YUN 1977, p. 706. [60]E/1985/22 (res. 1985/35). [61]E/CN.4/1986/5 (res. 1985/18). [62]A/40/818. [63]E/CN.4/1985/19. [64]YUN 1984, p. 872. [65]*Ibid.*, pp. 871 & 873. [66]E/1985/22 (res. 1985/36). [67]E/CN.4/1986/5 (res. 1985/28). [68]A/40/865. [69]A/C.3/40/L.87. [70]E/CN.4/1986/5 (res. 1985/13). [71]E/1985/22 (dec. 1985/107). [72]*Ibid.* (res. 1985/41). [73]*Ibid.* (res. 1985/1 A). [74]*Ibid.* (res. 1985/1 B). [75]*Ibid.* (res. 1985/2). [76]YUN 1981, p. 308. [77]E/CN.4/1986/5 (res. 1985/16). [78]YUN 1983, p. 274. [79]E/1985/22 (res. 1985/40). [80]YUN 1984, p. 8. [81]YUN 1983, p. 899. [82]E/CN.4/Sub.2/1985/6 & Corr.1. [83]YUN 1984, p. 878. [84]*Ibid.*, p. 813, GA res. 39/46, annex, 10 Dec. 1984. [85]E/CN.4/1986/5 (res. 1985/9).

Other human rights questions

Rights of the child

Draft convention

Working group activities. As authorized by the Economic and Social Council in 1984,[1] an open-ended working group to continue drafting a convention on the rights of the child met between 28 January and 1 February and on 8 March 1985.

The group adopted articles 12 *bis*, 14, 15, 16 and 17, concerning, respectively: health care for children; the right to an adequate standard of living; the right to education; directing education to the development of the child's personality, talents and abilities; and the right to recreation and leisure and to participate in cultural life. There was a preliminary discussion of article 18 concerning children's employment. The text of these articles, together with those previously adopted, were annexed to the Group's report.[2] Also annexed were proposed draft articles and amendments which the group could not discuss for lack of time.

Human Rights Commission action. On 14 March,[3] the Commission on Human Rights decided to continue in 1986 its work on a draft convention with a view to completing it. The Commission requested the Economic and Social Council to authorize a one-week session of an open-ended working group prior to the Commission's 1986 session, and proposed the text of a draft resolution to that effect.

ECONOMIC AND SOCIAL COUNCIL ACTION

On 30 May 1985, acting on the recommendation of its Second Committee, the Economic and Social Council adopted **resolution 1985/42**, without vote.

Question of a convention on the rights of the child

The Economic and Social Council,

Recalling General Assembly resolution 39/135 of 14 December 1984, by which the Assembly requested the Commission on Human Rights to give the highest priority to and to make every effort at its forty-first session to complete the draft convention on the rights of the child and to submit it, through the Economic and Social Council, to the General Assembly at its fortieth session,

Considering that it was not found possible to complete the work on the draft convention during the forty-first session of the Commission on Human Rights,

Taking note of Commission on Human Rights resolution 1985/50 of 14 March 1985,

1. *Authorizes* a meeting of an open-ended working group for a period of one week prior to the forty-second session of the Commission on Human Rights, with a view to completing the work on the draft convention on the rights of the child at that session;

2. *Requests* the Secretary-General to extend all facilities to the working group for its meeting prior to and during the forty-second session of the Commission to enable it to fulfil its task successfully, and notes the usefulness of providing the working group, in advance of its session, with such working documents as a compilation of all amendments and new proposals, and relevant provisions of other international instruments.

Economic and Social Council resolution 1985/42

30 May 1985	Meeting 25	Adopted without vote

Approved by Second Committee (E/1985/95 & Corr.1) without vote, 24 May (meeting 15); draft by Commission on Human Rights (E/1985/22); agenda item 16.

GENERAL ASSEMBLY ACTION

Poland submitted to the Third Committee in October a document[4] on the status of the elaboration of the draft convention on the rights of the child. The initiator of the proposal for such a convention in 1978,[5] Poland outlined progress in its elaboration, and transmitted the text approved by the Commission's working group; it included modified proposals on the remaining articles, meant to offer, Poland said, a constructive stimulus towards completion of the work.

On 13 December, on the recommendation of the Third Committee, the General Assembly adopted **resolution 40/113**, without vote.

Question of a convention on the rights of the child

The General Assembly,

Recalling its resolutions 33/166 of 20 December 1978, 34/4 of 18 October 1979, 35/131 of 11 December 1980,

36/57 of 25 November 1981, 37/190 of 18 December 1982, 38/114 of 16 December 1983 and 39/135 of 14 December 1984,

Recalling also Commission on Human Rights resolutions 20(XXXIV) of 8 March 1978, 19(XXXV) of 14 March 1979, 36(XXXVI) of 12 March 1980, 26(XXXVII) of 10 March 1981, 1982/39 of 11 March 1982, 1983/52 of 10 March 1983, 1984/24 of 8 March 1984 and 1985/50 of 14 March 1985, as well as Economic and Social Council resolutions 1978/18 of 5 May 1978, 1978/40 of 1 August 1978, 1982/37 of 7 May 1982, 1983/39 of 27 May 1983, 1984/25 of 24 May 1984 and 1985/42 of 30 May 1985 and Council decisions 1980/138 of 2 May 1980 and 1981/144 of 8 May 1981,

Reaffirming, on the fortieth anniversary of the United Nations, that children's rights require special protection and call for continuous improvement of the situation of children all over the world, as well as their development and education in conditions of peace and security,

Profoundly concerned that the situation of children in many parts of the world remains critical as a result of unsatisfactory social conditions, natural disasters, armed conflicts, exploitation, hunger and disability, and convinced that urgent and effective national and international action is called for,

Mindful of the important role of the United Nations Children's Fund and the United Nations in promoting the well-being of children and their development,

Convinced that an international convention on the rights of the child would make a positive contribution to ensuring the protection of children's rights and their well-being,

Welcoming the growing interest in the elaboration of an international convention on the rights of the child displayed by a great number of Member States representing all geographical regions and socio-political systems, as well as by governmental and non-governmental international organizations,

Noting with appreciation that further progress was made during the forty-first session of the Commission on Human Rights in the elaboration of a draft convention on the rights of the child,

Noting the document entitled "Status of elaboration of a draft convention on the rights of the child", submitted by Poland,

1. *Welcomes* Economic and Social Council resolution 1985/42, in which the Council authorized a meeting of an open-ended working group of the Commission on Human Rights for a period of one week prior to the forty-second session of the Commission with a view to completing the work on a draft convention on the rights of the child;

2. *Requests* the Commission on Human Rights to give the highest priority to, and to make every effort at its forty-second session to complete, the draft convention and to submit it, through the Economic and Social Council, to the General Assembly at its forty-first session;

3. *Invites* all Member States to offer their active contribution to the completion of the draft convention on the rights of the child at the forty-second session of the Commission on Human Rights;

4. *Requests* the Secretary-General to provide all necessary assistance to the working group in order to ensure its smooth and efficient work in the fulfilment of its important task;

5. *Decides* to include in the provisional agenda of its forty-first session the item entitled "Question of a convention on the rights of the child".

General Assembly resolution 40/113

13 December 1985   Meeting 116   Adopted without vote

Approved by Third Committee (A/40/971) without vote, 2 December (meeting 60); 51-nation draft (A/C.3/40/L.51); agenda item 103.

Sponsors: Afghanistan, Algeria, Argentina, Australia, Austria, Bahamas, Bangladesh, Bolivia, Bulgaria, Byelorussian SSR, Canada, China, Colombia, Congo, Costa Rica, Cuba, Cyprus, Czechoslovakia, Denmark, Egypt, Finland, German Democratic Republic, Greece, Guinea, Hungary, Iceland, Indonesia, Italy, Ivory Coast, Jordan, Madagascar, Mexico, Mongolia, Morocco, Nigeria, Norway, Peru, Philippines, Poland, Rwanda, Senegal, Spain, Sri Lanka, Sweden, Syrian Arab Republic, Ukrainian SSR, USSR, Venezuela, Viet Nam, Yugoslavia, Zaire.

Meeting numbers. GA 40th session: 3rd Committee 46-48, 50-53, 60; plenary 116.

Sale of children and child labour

The Working Group on Slavery of the Sub-Commission on Prevention of Discrimination and Protection of Minorities at its July/August 1985 session (see p. 871), also considered the issue of the sale of children for prostitution, begging or hard labour, and the exploitation of child labour. To combat those problems, it recommended in its report[6] that in all societies appropriate employment legislation be adopted, education be made available at the place of work, a legal minimum wage for children be introduced, and all United Nations agencies, development banks and intergovernmental bodies involved in development projects ensure that no children under 14 years of age were employed.

The Sub-Commission, on 29 August,[7] recommended to the Commission adoption of a draft resolution designed to help protect children from exploitation and abusive labour, including sexual exploitation.

Under the programme of advisory services in human rights (see p. 893), the Secretary-General organized, in co-operation with ILO, a Seminar on Ways to Eliminate the Exploitation of Child Labour in All Parts of the World (Geneva, 28 October–8 November). The holding of such a seminar had been requested by the Economic and Social Council in 1984,[8] on a recommendation by the Commission on Human Rights which took up a recommendation of its Special Rapporteur on the subject.

Youth and human rights

On 11 March 1985, the Commission on Human Rights adopted two resolutions related to youth and their enjoyment of human rights. By the first,[9] it reaffirmed the role of youth in promoting full enjoyment of human rights, and appealed to Governments to consider measures to ensure that young people had equal opportunities to participate in the economic, social, cultural, civil and political life of society, as well as in promoting human rights, international peace, co-operation, understanding, tolerance and friendship among nations. It requested the Sub-Commission to pay due attention to the role of youth in the human rights field, particularly in achieving the objectives of International Youth Year (1985) (see p. 978), and requested the Secretary-General, in consultation with specialized agencies, to give special emphasis in 1985 to educational material and programmes for youth as key elements in the United Nations activities for the promotion of human rights.

By the second resolution,[10] the Commission called on States, governmental and non-governmental organizations, and United Nations organs and agencies to devote constant attention to the exercise and use by young people of all human rights, including the right to education and vocational training and the right to work, with a view to ensuring full employment and solving the problem of unemployment among them. The Commission called for legislative, administrative and other action by States for the exercise by youth of all human rights, to create conditions for their active participation in their country's economic and social development. It requested the Secretary-General, in his report reviewing measures and activities for the Year, to give attention to implementation of all its aspects.

On 29 August,[11] the Sub-Commission requested Dumitru Mazilu (Romania) to prepare a report on human rights and youth, analysing efforts for securing the enjoyment by youth particularly of the right to life, education and work. It requested the Secretary-General to provide the necessary assistance and decided to deal with the question at its 1986 session.

The Economic and Social Council, by **resolution 1985/27**, called on all States, governmental and non-governmental organizations and interested United Nations bodies and agencies to continue to give priority to formulating and implementing measures to secure the exercise by youth of the rights to life, education and work in conditions of peace.

By **resolution 40/15**, the General Assembly asked the Commission for Social Development, when examining youth issues, and national co-ordination and policy- and programme-implementing organs to give adequate attention and priority to the enjoyment by youth of human rights, particularly the right to education and to work.

Human rights of disabled persons

In June 1985, Special Rapporteur Leandro Despouy (Argentina) submitted a preliminary report[12] on human rights and disability, in accordance with a 1984 Sub-Commission mandate.[13] As at 15 June 1985, he had received, in response to requests for information on discrimination against disabled persons and on care and abuses, replies from 20 Member States, 12 United Nations bodies and agencies, one intergovernmental organization and five NGOs.

After discussing various definitions of disability that would have to be taken into account, the Special Rapporteur briefly described the objectives of the study and causes of disability, human rights violations and discrimination against disabled persons, economic, social and cultural rights in relation to disability, and problems related to disabled persons' rights in the context of the International Covenants on Human Rights.

He stated that discrimination to which disabled persons were subjected not only violated their human rights but in most cases also aggravated their disability. The United Nations must pay particular attention to human rights violations causing disability, such as military conflicts, torture, cruel and inhuman treatment and others. Penalties, whether based on internal law or religion, disabling an individual should be regarded as contrary to international law. In addition to control mechanisms that needed to be implemented, the best way to mitigate the effects of the current situation was to ensure the participation of disabled persons in all fields of social life.

The Special Rapporteur recommended that the rights of the disabled and the obligations of Governments and of the national and international community towards them should be specified. When reporting on implementation of the international human rights instruments, Governments should also provide information on respect for disabled persons' rights, on progress in their education, vocational training and rehabilitation and on their integration. The Committee on the Elimination of Racial Discrimination also should examine discrimination against disabled persons, within the framework of *apartheid* in particular.

The Sub-Commission, on 29 August 1985,[14] requested the Special Rapporteur to continue his work and submit a progress report in 1987. The Secretary-General was requested to provide him with all possible assistance.

Human rights of the individual and international law

Work continued in 1985 on a study of the status of the individual and contemporary international law, mandated by the Commission on Human Rights in 1981 and authorized by the Economic and Social Council the same year.[15]

Because she had recently received additional important replies and documentation which she felt should be taken into account in preparing the final report, Special Rapporteur Erica-Irene A. Daes (Greece) asked to be allowed to submit the report in 1986. By a resolution[16] of 30 August, the Sub-Commission expressed appreciation to her for the work thus far, and requested her to continue working on the study with a view to submitting a final report in 1986. The Secretary-General was requested to give her the assistance needed.

Human rights and science and technology

On 11 March 1985,[17] the Commission on Human Rights requested the Sub-Commission to reconsider the studies it had suggested in 1984,[18] one on current dimensions and problems arising from unlawful human experimentation, and another on the implications for human rights of recent advances in computer and microcomputer technology, with a view to integrating them in the work already being undertaken in the Commission and Sub-Commission under the agenda item on human rights and scientific and technological developments.

The Secretary-General transmitted to the General Assembly in 1985 the additional replies[19] he had received—from the Dominican Republic, Guyana, Solomon Islands and Venezuela, as well as four specialized agencies—in response to a 1980 request,[20] and subsequent reminders, for information on implementation of the 1975 Declaration on the Use of Scientific and Technological Progress in the Interests of Peace and for the Benefit of Mankind.[21]

GENERAL ASSEMBLY ACTION

On 13 December 1985, acting on the recommendation of the Third Committee, the General Assembly adopted **resolution 40/112**, by recorded vote.

Human rights and scientific and technological developments

The General Assembly,

Noting that scientific and technological progress is one of the important factors in the development of human society,

Recalling that the year 1985 marks the tenth anniversary of the Declaration on the Use of Scientific and Technological Progress in the Interests of Peace and for the Benefit of Mankind, adopted by the General Assembly in its resolution 3384(XXX) of 10 November 1975,

Considering that implementation of the Declaration will contribute to the strengthening of international peace and the security of peoples and to their economic and social development, as well as to international co-operation in the field of human rights,

Bearing in mind the relevant provisions of the Declaration on Social Progress and Development,

Seriously concerned that the results of scientific and technological progress could be used for the arms race to the detriment of international peace and security and social progress, human rights and fundamental freedoms and the dignity of the human person,

Convinced that in the era of modern scientific and technological progress the resources of mankind and the activities of scientists should be used for the peaceful economic, social and cultural development of countries and for improvement of the living standards of all people,

Recognizing that the establishment of the new international economic order calls in particular for an important contribution to be made by science and technology to economic and social progress,

Bearing in mind that the exchange and transfer of scientific and technological knowledge is one of the important ways to accelerate the social and economic development of the developing countries,

Taking note with satisfaction of the report of the Secretary-General on human rights and scientific and technological developments,

1.   *Stresses* the importance of the implementation by all States of the provisions and principles contained in the Declaration on the Use of Scientific and Technological Progress in the Interests of Peace and for the Benefit of Mankind in order to promote human rights and fundamental freedoms;

2.   *Calls upon* all States to make every effort to use the achievements of science and technology in order to promote peaceful social, economic and cultural development and progress;

3.   *Requests* the specialized agencies and other organizations of the United Nations system to take into account in their programmes and activities the provisions of the Declaration;

4.   *Invites* those Member States, specialized agencies and other organizations of the United Nations system that have not yet done so to submit their information pursuant to General Assembly resolution 35/130 A of 11 December 1980;

5.   *Requests* the Commission on Human Rights to continue to give special attention, in its consideration of the item entitled "Human rights and scientific and technological developments", to the question of the implementation of the provisions of the Declaration;

6.   *Invites* the Commission on Human Rights to take appropriate measures to assist the Sub-Commission on Prevention of Discrimination and Protection of Minorities in preparing the study requested by the Commission in its resolutions 1982/4 of 19 February 1982 and 1984/29 of 12 March 1984;

7.   *Decides* to include in the provisional agenda of its forty-first session the item entitled "Human rights and scientific and technological developments".

General Assembly resolution 40/112

13 December 1985   Meeting 116   131-0-22 (recorded vote)

Approved by Third Committee (A/40/969) by recorded vote (113-0-23), 2 December (meeting 60); 35-nation draft (A/C.3/40/L.69); agenda item 102.

Sponsors: Afghanistan, Algeria, Angola, Argentina, Bangladesh, Benin, Bolivia, Bulgaria, Burkina Faso, Byelorussian SSR, Cameroon, Cuba, Cyprus, Czechoslovakia, Democratic Yemen, Dominican Republic, German Democratic Republic, Guinea-Bissau, Hungary, Ivory Coast, Lao People's Democratic Republic, Madagascar, Mali, Mauritania, Mongolia, Morocco, Mozambique, Nepal, Nicaragua, Poland, Romania, Sierra Leone, Syrian Arab Republic, Viet Nam, Zambia.

Meeting numbers. GA 40th session: 3rd Committee 47, 48, 50-53, 58, 60; plenary 116.

Recorded vote in Assembly as follows:

In favour: Afghanistan, Algeria, Angola, Antigua and Barbuda, Argentina, Bahamas, Bahrain, Bangladesh, Barbados, Belize, Benin, Bhutan, Bolivia, Botswana, Brazil, Brunei Darussalam, Bulgaria, Burkina Faso, Burma, Burundi, Byelorussian SSR, Cameroon, Cape Verde, Central African Republic, Chad, Chile, China, Colombia, Comoros, Congo, Costa Rica, Cuba, Cyprus, Czechoslovakia, Democratic Kampuchea, Democratic Yemen, Djibouti, Dominica, Dominican Republic, Ecuador, Egypt, El Salvador, Equatorial Guinea, Ethiopia, Fiji, Gabon, Gambia, German Democratic Republic, Ghana, Greece, Guatemala, Guinea, Guinea-Bissau, Guyana, Haiti, Honduras, Hungary, India, Indonesia, Iran, Iraq, Ivory Coast, Jamaica, Jordan, Kenya, Kuwait, Lao People's Democratic Republic, Lebanon, Lesotho, Liberia, Libyan Arab Jamahiriya, Madagascar, Malawi, Malaysia, Maldives, Mali, Malta, Mauritania, Mauritius, Mexico, Mongolia, Morocco, Mozambique, Nepal, Nicaragua, Niger, Nigeria, Oman, Pakistan, Panama, Papua New Guinea, Paraguay, Peru, Philippines, Poland, Qatar, Romania, Rwanda, Saint Christopher and Nevis, Saint Lucia,

Samoa, Sao Tome and Principe, Saudi Arabia, Senegal, Sierra Leone, Singapore, Somalia, Sri Lanka, Sudan, Suriname, Swaziland, Syrian Arab Republic, Thailand, Togo, Trinidad and Tobago, Tunisia, Turkey, Uganda, Ukrainian SSR, USSR, United Arab Emirates, United Republic of Tanzania, Uruguay, Vanuatu, Venezuela, Viet Nam, Yemen, Yugoslavia, Zaire, Zambia, Zimbabwe.

Against: None.

Abstaining: Australia, Austria, Belgium, Canada, Denmark, Finland, France, Germany, Federal Republic of, Iceland, Ireland, Israel, Italy, Japan, Luxembourg, Netherlands, New Zealand, Norway, Portugal, Spain, Sweden, United Kingdom, United States.

With regard to paragraph 6, the United Kingdom remarked that it concerned a study against which it had voted in 1984 in the Commission on Human Rights. Japan voiced reservations on the same paragraph, saying it had abstained on the 1982[22] and 1984[18] Commission resolutions mentioned.

Hazardous technologies

Stating that inadequate information and the absence of uniform protection and safety measures with regard to the potential dangers of hazardous technologies resulted in a grave threat to the right to health and to life, and noting with concern industrial accidents involving very large loss of lives, particularly in developing countries where potentially harmful and hazardous products banned or restricted in other countries continued to be used, the Sub-Commission, on 28 August 1985,[23] requested that all TNCs and enterprises disclose the information at their disposal regarding the hazards to human lives of their processes, products and technologies to Governments, employees, consumers and the general public. It requested the Secretary-General to communicate its resolution to all Governments so that they could obtain relevant information from enterprises under their jurisdiction for transmittal to the Secretary-General, who would then pass it on to the Sub-Commission in 1987.

Computerized personal files

In June 1985, Special Rapporteur Louis Joinet (France) submitted to the Sub-Commission revised draft guidelines for the regulation of computerized personal data files. They were annexed to a report[24] analysing comments from States and international organizations on provisional draft guidelines, which had been transmitted to them in accordance with a 1984 Sub-Commission request.[25]

From those comments, he said, a consensus emerged on the desirability of encouraging the formulation of guidelines, both for States wishing to adopt domestic legislation and for international organizations and agencies in respect of the status of their own personal data files. Suggestions he deemed worthy of particular attention included the following.

There should be a balance in any legislation between the protection of privacy, the principle of free movement of ideas and opinions, and the authorities' need for information to carry out their tasks. Specific characteristics of different legal systems should be taken into account, as should cultural differences. The possibility of supplementing the general principle by "sectoral" rules should be left open. In the case of personnel files, it was proposed that ILO draw up guidelines. In order to supervise observance of the principles, a specialized and independent body should be set up.

Comments were also made concerning proposed amendments to different principles, the application of the principles and the power to make exceptions.

The question of files kept by international organizations had been discussed at the March 1985 session of the Consultative Committee on Administrative Questions (CCAQ).[26] The guidelines submitted to the agencies concerning those files were considered, in general, acceptable; opinions were divided, however, on the advisability of a supervisory body. The outcome of CCAQ's discussions was that it should be left to the governing bodies of each organization to decide how they were to be applied. In its reply to the Special Rapporteur, ILO, however, favoured a specific supervisory body, at least in respect of internal personnel files, the matter being left open with regard to external files (for example, UNHCR files on refugees, the United Nations Centre for Human Rights files on disappearances). In some replies, it was suggested that the supervisory body should report periodically to the Commission on Human Rights.

The Sub-Commission on 29 August[27] requested the Secretary-General to continue to obtain Governments' comments and suggestions on the revised draft guidelines, and to assist the Special Rapporteur to submit his final report in 1987.

Human rights and peace

Sub-Commission action. In June 1985, the Secretary-General submitted to the Sub-Commission the guide,[28] requested in 1984,[29] to conventions, resolutions and reports of the United Nations concerning the adverse consequences of the arms race, particularly the nuclear-arms race, for the realization of human rights, and a progress report[30] on the relationship between human rights violations and international peace.

By a resolution[31] adopted on 27 August 1985 by 19 votes to none, with 3 abstentions, the Sub-Commission requested the Secretary-General to provide it in 1987 with a report on the interrelationship between human rights and international peace in all its aspects and dimensions, including the adverse impact of escalating military expenditure, particularly of nuclear-weapon States, on the international social and economic situation and the right to development. In particular, the report was to examine the adverse consequences of the extension and dissemination of nuclear arms in non-nuclear regions for international peace and security, the social and economic development of the countries of the region, and the enjoyment of human rights. The Sub-Commission recommended that the Commission include in its

1987 agenda an item on the adverse consequences of the arms race, especially the dissemination of nuclear arms in non-nuclear regions, for international peace and security and for the protection of human rights.

By another resolution[32] adopted on the same day by 16 votes to 5, with 1 abstention, the Sub-Commission recognized that maintenance of international peace and security was an essential condition for the enjoyment of the entire range of economic, social, cultural, civil and political rights, above all the right to life, and that violation of basic rights might threaten international peace and security. It stressed the importance of its contribution to the strengthening of international peace and security and the achievement of the objectives of the International Year of Peace (1986) (see p. 122). It requested the Secretary-General, in the light of comments of Member States, United Nations organizations and NGOs, to report in 1986 on that contribution, and decided to continue considering the contribution as a sub-item of the agenda item on international peace and security as an essential condition for the enjoyment of human rights, above all the right to life.

GENERAL ASSEMBLY ACTION

On 13 December, the General Assembly, acting on the recommendation of the Third Committee, adopted **resolution 40/111**, by recorded vote.

Human rights and use of scientific and technological developments

The General Assembly,

Reaffirming the determination of the peoples of the United Nations to save succeeding generations from the scourge of war, to reaffirm faith in the dignity and worth of the human person, to maintain international peace and security and to develop friendly relations among peoples and international co-operation in promoting and encouraging universal respect for human rights and fundamental freedoms,

Recalling the relevant provisions of the Universal Declaration of Human Rights, the International Covenant on Economic, Social and Cultural Rights and the International Covenant on Civil and Political Rights,

Recalling also the Charter of Economic Rights and Duties of States and the Declaration and the Programme of Action on the Establishment of a New International Economic Order,

Recalling further the Declaration on the Strengthening of International Security, the Declaration on the Use of Scientific and Technological Progress in the Interests of Peace and for the Benefit of Mankind, the Declaration on the Preparation of Societies for Life in Peace, the Declaration on the Prevention of Nuclear Catastrophe and the Declaration on the Right of Peoples to Peace, as well as General Assembly resolutions 36/92 I of 9 December 1981, on the non-use of nuclear weapons and prevention of nuclear war, and 37/100 C of 13 December 1982 and 38/73 G of 15 December 1983, on a convention on the prohibition of the use of nuclear weapons,

Bearing in mind that, in its resolution 38/75 of 15 December 1983, the General Assembly resolutely, unconditionally and for all time condemned nuclear war as being contrary to human conscience and reason, as the most monstrous crime against peoples and as a violation of the foremost human right—the right to life,

Recalling its appeal for the conclusion of an international convention on the prohibition of the use of nuclear weapons with the participation of all the nuclear-weapon States,

Recalling with appreciation Commission on Human Rights resolutions 1982/7 of 19 February 1982, 1983/43 of 9 March 1983 and 1984/28 of 12 March 1984,

Reaffirming the inherent right to life,

Profoundly concerned that international peace and security continue to be threatened by the arms race in all its aspects, particularly the nuclear arms race, as well as by violations of the principles of the Charter of the United Nations regarding the sovereignty and territorial integrity of States and the self-determination of peoples,

Aware that all the horrors of past wars and all other calamities that have befallen people would pale in comparison with what is inherent in the use of nuclear weapons capable of destroying civilization on Earth,

Noting the pressing need for urgent measures towards general and complete disarmament, particularly nuclear disarmament, for the sake of life on Earth,

Bearing in mind that, in accordance with the International Covenant on Civil and Political Rights, any propaganda for war shall be prohibited by law,

Recalling the historic responsibility of the Governments of all countries of the world to remove the threat of war from the lives of people, to preserve civilization and to ensure that everyone enjoys his inherent right to life,

Recognizing that the fortieth anniversary of the United Nations—established at the conclusion of the Second World War, which had brought untold sorrow to mankind—should serve to promote the right to life,

Convinced that for no people in the world today is there a more important question than that of the preservation of peace and of ensuring the cardinal right of every human being, namely, the right to life,

1. _Reaffirms_ that all peoples and all individuals have an inherent right to life and that the safeguarding of this cardinal right is an essential condition for the enjoyment of the entire range of economic, social and cultural, as well as civil and political, rights;

2. _Stresses once again_ the urgent need for the international community to make every effort to strengthen peace, remove the growing threat of war, particularly nuclear war, halt the arms race and achieve general and complete disarmament under effective international control and prevent violations of the principles of the Charter of the United Nations regarding the sovereignty and territorial integrity of States and the self-determination of peoples, thus contributing to ensuring the right to life;

3. _Stresses further_ the foremost importance of the implementation of practical measures of disarmament for releasing substantial additional resources, which should be utilized for social and economic development, particularly for the benefit of the developing countries;

4. _Calls upon_ all States to do their utmost to assist in ensuring the right to life through the adoption of appropriate measures at both the national and the international level;

5. _Calls upon_ all States, appropriate organs of the United Nations, specialized agencies and intergovern-

mental and non-governmental organizations concerned to take the necessary measures to ensure that the results of scientific and technological progress are used exclusively in the interests of international peace, for the benefit of mankind and for promoting and encouraging universal respect for human rights and fundamental freedoms;

6. *Again calls upon* all States that have not yet done so to take effective measures with a view to prohibiting any propaganda for war, in particular the formulation, propounding and dissemination of propaganda for doctrines and concepts aimed at unleashing nuclear war;

7. *Looks forward* to further efforts by the Commission on Human Rights with a view to ensuring the inherent right of all peoples and all individuals to life;

8. *Decides* to consider this question at its forty-first session under the item entitled "Human rights and scientific and technological developments".

General Assembly resolution 40/111

13 December 1985   Meeting 116   127-9-16 (recorded vote)

Approved by Third Committee (A/40/969) by recorded vote (109-6-19), 2 December (meeting 60); 27-nation draft (A/C.3/40/L.65); agenda item 102.

Sponsors: Afghanistan, Angola, Benin, Bulgaria, Byelorussian SSR, Cuba, Czechoslovakia, Democratic Yemen, Ethiopia, German Democratic Republic, Guinea-Bissau, Hungary, India, Lao People's Democratic Republic, Libyan Arab Jamahiriya, Mali, Mongolia, Mozambique, Nicaragua, Nigeria, Poland, Romania, Syrian Arab Republic, Ukrainian SSR, USSR, Viet Nam, Zambia.

Meeting numbers. GA 40th session: 3rd Committee 47, 48, 50-53, 58, 60; plenary 116.

Recorded vote in Assembly as follows:

In favour: Afghanistan, Algeria, Angola, Antigua and Barbuda, Argentina, Bahamas, Bahrain, Bangladesh, Barbados, Belize, Benin, Bhutan, Bolivia, Botswana, Brazil, Brunei Darussalam, Bulgaria, Burkina Faso, Burma, Burundi, Byelorussian SSR, Cameroon, Cape Verde, Central African Republic, Chad, China, Colombia, Comoros, Congo, Costa Rica, Cuba, Cyprus, Czechoslovakia, Democratic Kampuchea, Democratic Yemen, Djibouti, Dominican Republic, Ecuador, Egypt, El Salvador, Equatorial Guinea, Ethiopia, Fiji, Gabon, German Democratic Republic, Ghana, Greece, Guatemala, Guinea, Guinea-Bissau, Guyana, Haiti, Honduras, Hungary, India, Indonesia, Iran, Iraq, Ivory Coast, Jamaica, Jordan, Kenya, Kuwait, Lao People's Democratic Republic, Lebanon, Lesotho, Liberia, Libyan Arab Jamahiriya, Madagascar, Malawi, Malaysia, Maldives, Mali, Malta, Mauritania, Mauritius, Mexico, Mongolia, Morocco, Mozambique, Nepal, Nicaragua, Niger, Nigeria, Oman, Pakistan, Panama, Papua New Guinea, Paraguay, Peru, Philippines, Poland, Qatar, Romania, Rwanda, Saint Christopher and Nevis, Saint Lucia, Samoa, Sao Tome and Principe, Saudi Arabia, Senegal, Sierra Leone, Singapore, Somalia, Sri Lanka, Sudan, Suriname, Swaziland, Syrian Arab Republic, Thailand, Togo, Trinidad and Tobago, Tunisia, Uganda, Ukrainian SSR, USSR, United Arab Emirates, United Republic of Tanzania, Uruguay, Vanuatu, Venezuela, Viet Nam, Yemen, Yugoslavia, Zaire, Zambia, Zimbabwe.

Against: Belgium, Canada, France, Germany, Federal Republic of, Italy, Netherlands, Portugal, United Kingdom, United States.

Abstaining: Australia, Austria, Chile, Denmark, Dominica, Finland, Iceland, Ireland, Israel, Japan, Luxembourg, New Zealand, Norway, Spain, Sweden, Turkey.

The Netherlands said the text went beyond the agenda item under which it had been submitted and beyond the Third Committee's competence, a view shared by Canada, France, Japan and the United Kingdom. Japan added that the text had nothing to do with the question of human rights under the current agenda item. Canada and France considered certain formulations in the preamble unacceptable. The United Kingdom found the text similar to previously adopted resolutions which it had opposed. Canada added that, in paragraph 1, the right to life was attributed not only to individuals but also to peoples; to dilute the most fundamental individual right in that manner was unacceptable. Paragraphs 3 and 6 dealt with questions of disarmament which were being examined in other United Nations bodies.

Speaking for the Nordic countries, Norway said that, although they supported all proposals which could help to stop the arms race, they were of the opinion that those topics should be dealt with by the competent bodies. They had reservations on paragraph 6 similar to those they had on article 20 of the 1966 International Covenant on Civil and Political Rights[33] on the same subject. They also had reservations on the fourth preambular paragraph which referred to Assembly resolutions they had not been able to support.

Non-interference in States' internal affairs

On 13 December 1985, by **decision 40/426**, the General Assembly, acting on the recommendation of the Third Committee, decided without vote to defer until its 1986 session consideration of a draft resolution on the inadmissibility of exploitation or distortion of human rights issues for interference in the internal affairs of States, as well as amendments to the text. The draft resolution[34] was sponsored by Angola, Czechoslovakia, Ethiopia, the Lao People's Democratic Republic, the Syrian Arab Republic, the Ukrainian SSR and Viet Nam. The text would have had the Assembly reaffirm the duty of and call on States to refrain from the activities referred to in its title, invite Governments to communicate their views on measures to prevent such activities, and ask for a report in 1986. It would also have condemned campaigns and propaganda by South Africa and Israel to prolong their occupation and oppression and interfere in neighbouring States' internal affairs. Extensive amendments to it were proposed by Pakistan,[35] intended, it said, to broaden the scope of the draft and accentuate the priority to be accorded to mass and flagrant violations of human rights.

The proposal to postpone, orally introduced by the Ukrainian SSR, was approved by the Third Committee on 6 December without vote.

REFERENCES

[1]YUN 1984, p. 880, ESC res. 1984/25, 24 May 1984. [2]E/CN.4/1985/64. [3]E/1985/22 (res. 1985/50). [4]A/C.3/40/3 & Corr.1. [5]YUN 1978, p. 723. [6]E/CN.4/Sub.2/1985/25. [7]E/CN.4/1986/5 (res. 1985/23). [8]YUN 1984, p. 881, ESC res. 1984/28, 24 May 1984. [9]E/1985/22 (res. 1985/13). [10]*Ibid.* (res. 1985/14). [11]E/CN.4/1986/5 (res. 1985/12). [12]E/CN.4/Sub.2/1985/32. [13]YUN 1984, p. 882. [14]E/CN.4/1986/5 (res. 1985/10). [15]YUN 1981, p. 976, ESC dec. 1981/142, 5 May 1981. [16]E/CN.4/1986/5 (res. 1985/31). [17]E/1985/22 (dec. 1985/104). [18]YUN 1984, p. 883. [19]A/40/493 & Add.1,2. [20]YUN 1980, p. 878, GA res. 35/130 A, 11 Dec. 1980. [21]YUN 1975, p. 631, GA res. 3384(XXX), 10 Nov. 1975. [22]YUN 1982, p. 1139. [23]E/CN.4/1986/5 (res. 1985/7). [24]E/CN.4/Sub.2/1985/21. [25]YUN 1984, p. 887. [26]ACC/1985/6. [27]E/CN.4/1986/5 (res. 1985/14). [28]E/CN.4/Sub.2/1985/10. [29]YUN 1984, p. 885. [30]E/CN.4/Sub.2/1985/11. [31]E/CN.4/1986/5 (res. 1985/2). [32]*Ibid.* (res. 1985/1). [33]YUN 1966, p. 423, GA res. 2200 A (XXI), annex, 16 Dec. 1966. [34]A/C.3/40/L.83/Rev.1. [35]A/C.3/40/L.90.

Chapter XIX

Women

In July 1985, the end of the United Nations Decade for Women (1976-1985) was marked by a World Conference at Nairobi, Kenya. Following a review of the activities of the previous 10 years in implementing the World Plan of Action and the Programme of Action for the Second Half of the Women's Decade, the deliberations of the Conference culminated in the adoption of the Nairobi Forward-looking Strategies for the Advancement of Women—a set of measures to overcome the obstacles to the Decade's goals and objectives of equality, development and peace during the remainder of the century. In December, the General Assembly endorsed the Forward-looking Strategies and affirmed that their implementation should result in eliminating inequality between women and men and in integrating women into the development process (resolution 40/108). The Assembly also expressed its appreciation to the Government and people of Kenya for hosting the World Conference (40/107).

The Commission on the Status of Women held its third session as the preparatory body for the Conference (Vienna, 4-13 March), made recommendations on preparations and considered the rules of procedure and other organizational aspects of the Conference. Pursuant to a decision by the Assembly at its resumed session in April (decision 39/459), the Commission met again in New York from 19 April to 7 May to complete its work. In May, the Economic and Social Council authorized its Bureau to assist delegations to resolve outstanding issues relating to the Conference's rules of procedure (1985/158) and, on 20 June, transmitted to the Conference its recommendations on two outstanding rules (1985/164).

A major document before the Conference was the *World Survey on the Role of Women in Development*, which gave an overview of the interrelations between key developmental issues concerning the role of women in relation to agriculture, industry, money and finance, science and technology, trade, energy, and self-reliance and the integration of women in development. Having taken note of the *Survey*, the Assembly requested the Secretary-General to update it on a regular basis, with the first update to be submitted to the Assembly in 1989 (resolution 40/204). With regard to women in rural areas, the Assembly requested the Secretary-General to prepare a comprehensive report on their current status and perspectives for improving their situation and submit

it to its 1989 session (40/106). A report by the Secretary-General reviewing the situation of women and development in the medium-term plans of United Nations organizations was submitted to the Economic and Social Council in May 1985. The Council requested the Secretary-General to formulate a system-wide medium-term plan on women and development, taking into account the recommendations of the Nairobi Conference, and requested the Committee for Programme and Co-ordination (CPC) to undertake in 1989 a cross-organizational programme analysis (COPA) of activities and resources for the advancement of women (resolution 1985/46).

In 1985, the United Nations Development Fund for Women, formerly the Voluntary Fund for the United Nations Decade for Women, became a separate entity in autonomous association with the United Nations Development Programme (UNDP). It continued to assist grass-roots initiatives, particularly those of women's and community groups at local levels and, by December 1985, had funded 473 projects valued at more than $30 million. Governments were urged by the Assembly to increase their contributions to the Fund (resolution 40/104).

The International Research and Training Institute for the Advancement of Women (INSTRAW) continued to undertake research and establish training programmes for the integration and mobilization of women in development. Its Board of Trustees held its fifth session at Havana, Cuba, from 28 January to 1 February. In May, the Economic and Social Council appealed to Governments and other potential donors to contribute to the INSTRAW Trust Fund in view of the increasing importance of research and training for women's participation in the development process (resolution 1985/45). The General Assembly reiterated in November the call for contributions and requested INSTRAW to strengthen its research and training activities, especially those in statistics, indicators and data relevant to women, and to emphasize innovative methodological approaches related to women and development in its programmes (resolution 40/38). In April, the Assembly endorsed INSTRAW's statute, as approved by the Economic and Social Council in 1984 (resolution 39/249).

The Committee on the Elimination of Discrimination against Women (CEDAW), at its fourth session (Vienna, 21 January–1 February), considered initial reports of five States parties on their implementation of the Convention. The Economic and Social Council in May (resolution 1985/18) and the General Assembly in December (resolution 40/39) emphasized the importance of the strictest compliance by States parties with their obligations under the Convention and urged them to submit their initial reports in accordance with the Convention.

In May, the Economic and Social Council urged all Governments participating in the 1985 World Conference on Women to incorporate into the Forward-looking Strategies aspects of the 1984 Mexico City Declaration on Population and Development and those recommendations of the 1984 World Population Plan of Action relating to the status and role of women in the context of population (resolution 1985/6).

In other action in December, the General Assembly: appealed to Governments, international organizations and non-governmental organizations (NGOs) to recognize the importance of the role of women in society—as mothers, as participants in economic development and in public life (resolution 40/101); pledged its determination to encourage participation of women in the economic, social, cultural, civil and political affairs of society and in the endeavour to promote international peace and co-operation (40/102); and invited the Economic and Social Council to consider the question of the suppression of traffic in persons and of the exploitation of the prostitution of others (40/103).

Topics related to this chapter. Operational activities for development: inter-agency co-operation. Regional economic and social activities: Africa—women in development in Africa. Food: food problems. Social and cultural development: domestic violence. Human settlements: women and human settlements. United Nations officials: status of women in the Secretariat; women's programme officers posts at regional commissions.

Conference on the Decade for Women

The World Conference to Review and Appraise the Achievements of the United Nations Decade for Women: Equality, Development and Peace, was held at Nairobi, Kenya, from 15 to 26 July. The Conference assessed progress made towards improving the situation of women during the Decade (1976-1985) which was proclaimed by the General Assembly in 1975—International Women's Year.[1] The Conference was preceded on 13 and 14 July by consultations, open to all Conference participants,

on procedural and organizational matters, while activities in preparation for the Conference were organized earlier in 1985 throughout the United Nations system (see below).

Convened 10 years after the International Women's Year, the Nairobi meeting was the third international conference on the status of women sponsored by the United Nations. The first, the World Conference of the International Women's Year, met at Mexico City in 1975;[2] the second, the World Conference of the United Nations Decade for Women, was held at mid-Decade in 1980 at Copenhagen, Denmark.[3]

The Conference was attended by representatives of 157 States, as well as by representatives of the Secretariat, regional commissions, other United Nations organs and programmes and eight specialized agencies. Also represented were 17 intergovernmental organizations and a large number of NGOs. Four national liberation movements attended as or were represented by observers: the African National Congress of South Africa, the Palestine Liberation Organization, the Pan-Africanist Congress of Azania and the South West Africa People's Organization. The United Nations Council for Namibia and the Special Committee against *Apartheid* were also represented.

At its first meeting, on 15 July, the Conference elected as its President Margaret Kenyatta (Kenya), and, at its second meeting, elected a Rapporteur-General and 30 Vice-Presidents. (For Conference participants and officers, see APPENDIX III.)

Addressing the Conference's inaugural ceremony, the United Nations Secretary-General said that the positive trends of the Decade were encouraging. However, efforts to ensure equality of women's rights with those of men must not flag. He was confident that the international community would respond to the challenges of the promotion of peace, the fostering of economic and social development and the universal observance of human rights, but stressed that, without the full partnership of women and men, goals would remain elusive.

The ceremony was also addressed by the President of Kenya, who stated that the success of the Conference would depend crucially on the will of Governments to implement its recommendations, but the onus remained on women to unite and take full advantage of the opportunities created.

On 26 July, the Conference adopted by consensus the Nairobi Forward-looking Strategies for the Advancement of Women. Following adoption of the Strategies, statements in explanation of vote on paragraphs or expressing reservations were made or submitted by Albania, Argentina, Australia, Belgium, Canada, Chile, Denmark, Ecuador, Finland, France, the Federal Republic of Germany, the Holy See, Ireland, Israel, Japan, Luxembourg (on behalf of the European Community, Portugal and Spain), Malaysia, the Netherlands, Norway, Portugal, Spain, Sweden, Switzerland, the United Kingdom, the United States and Uruguay.

The Strategies comprised 372 paragraphs organized into five chapters. The introduction described the historical background of the Conference and analysed economic, social and political factors and trends expected to have a bearing on the advancement of women over the next 15 years. It stated that the measures proposed were designed for immediate action, with monitoring and evaluation every five years. Each country would have the option to set its own priorities, based on its own development policics and resource capacities. The mode of implementation would vary according to each country's political process and administrative capabilities.

The next three chapters approached the themes of the Decade—equality, development and peace—in terms of obstacles encountered in efforts to reach those objectives, basic strategies for overcoming the obstacles, and steps to be taken at the national level to put the strategies into effect. Measures for implementing the basic strategies for equality at the national level were recommended in the following areas: constitutional and legal steps; equality in social participation; and equality in political participation and decision-making. Specific measures with regard to development were recommended in the fields of: employment; health; education; food, water and agriculture; industry; trade and commercial services; science and technology; communications; housing, settlement, community development and transport; energy; environment; and social services. The chapter on strategies for peace made particular reference to women and children under *apartheid*, Palestinian women and children, and women in areas affected by armed conflicts, foreign intervention and threats to peace. National measures with regard to peace were recommended under the headings of women's participation in efforts for peace and education for peace.

The fourth chapter, which dealt with areas of special concern, addressed: the situation of women in areas affected by drought; urban poor women; elderly women; young women; abused women; destitute women; women victims of trafficking and involuntary prostitution; women deprived of traditional means of livelihood; women as sole supporters of families; physically and mentally disabled women; women in detention and subject to penal law; refugee and displaced women and children; migrant women; and minority and indigenous women.

The final chapter recommended measures of international and regional co-operation to advance the status of women in such areas as monitoring the implementation of the Forward-looking Strategies; technical co-operation, training and advisory services; institutional co-ordination; research and policy analysis; participation of women in activities at the international and regional levels and in decision-making; and information dissemination.

In other action, the Conference adopted a resolution expressing its gratitude to the host country and deciding that the Conference's final documents would be known as "The Nairobi Forward-looking Strategies for the Advancement of Women".

On 26 July, the Conference decided that the texts of 85 draft resolutions—and a draft declaration on which it had not taken any action owing to lack of time—would be reproduced in an annex to its report[4] and brought to the attention of the General Assembly for consideration and action as appropriate.

The role of women in development was the subject of the majority of the resolutions: women and development priorities; future perspectives and equal opportunities; principles and priorities of women in development (2); Governments' responsibilities for the advancement of women; contribution to food security (2); women and industrialization; women, population and development; participation in restructuring international economic relations; women and new technologies; implementation and evaluation of the Decade's objectives; a programme to the year 2000; integration in development projects; strengthening women's machineries at all levels to ensure implementation of the Forward-looking Strategies; and establishment and support of national and regional bodies for women's development.

Several drafts dealt with women's contribution to peace: the role of women in preparing societies for life in peace; women and peace; increased participation in United Nations activities in peace, disarmament and arms limitation; contribution to realizing the right of people to peace; women's role in promoting peace and international co-operation for the removal of obstacles to peace and social progress; and disarmament, development and women.

Others considered the situation of women in areas of conflict: assistance to refugees from Afghanistan; women and children living in armed conflict zones; assistance to Sahrawi women; obstacles preventing women from realizing the aims of the Decade due to the Iraq-Iran conflict; obstacles preventing Syrian women in the occupied Golan Heights from realizing the aims of the Decade; Chadian women and children living in armed conflict areas; Palestinian women and children; global concerns for peace and the plight of women; Namibia; refugee and displaced women (2); *apartheid*; and front-line States.

A number of resolutions addressed questions of health: health and well-being (2); the health and well-being of women in the South Pacific; immunization; maternal mortality; collaboration with NGOs in health; improvement of the condition of physically and mentally disabled women; and improvement of the condition of those who have a person with a disability in their family.

The social advancement of women was dealt with in resolutions concerning: the right to education; women's role in society; education, training and job promotion; the family code; educational perspectives for the year 2000; improving conditions of work and life; international human rights; and improved conditions and opportunities. Environmental concerns were the focus of three resolutions: women and the environment; women and water; and drought and desertification in Africa.

Other resolutions concerned: assistance from NGOs to women and children, particularly in drought-stricken countries; elimination of discrimination; the Convention on the Elimination of All Forms of Discrimination against Women; the fortieth anniversary of the end of the Second World War; promotion of breast-feeding; women in island developing countries; the effects of the external debt of developing countries on women; commercial publicity harmful to dignity; classification in census documents; women and shelter; unemployment; genetic technology; sexual violence against women and children; domestic violence against women; Latin American and Caribbean women and the critical situation; a reporting system on the advancement of women; establishing a system of data and information networks; women and aging; participation of men in reaching the Decade's objectives; migrant women; indigenous women; improving the situation of women in rural areas; technical assistance for women in rural and marginal urban areas; international kidnapping of children; a world conference on women in the year 2000; strengthening the Commission on the Status of Women; the United Nations Development Fund for Women; INSTRAW; the International Centre for Public Enterprises in Developing Countries; and women in the United Nations; and strengthening co-ordination and implementation of activities for advancement within the United Nations system.

By the draft declaration on which no action was taken, the World Conference would have declared that the objectives of the Decade remained valid and would have called on States to implement them with a view to eradicating all forms of discrimination against women. States and international organizations would have been urged to adopt special measures to overcome developing countries' economic and social problems and the United Nations system would have been urged to give greater attention to developing countries, especially the least developed countries (LDCs), and mobilize resources to assist them in dealing with the crisis and its ramifications. The Conference would have appealed to States to channel relief and rehabilitation assistance to drought-affected African countries and called on States to continue integrating women fully in development processes, reaffirming that strengthening international peace, security and co-operation were the most important prerequisites for ensuring socio-economic progress and equal rights for women. The Conference would have declared that only the total eradication of *apartheid* could lead to a just and lasting solution of the explosive situation in South Africa. It would have strongly condemned Israel for oppression and repression of the Palestinians and called on the international community to ensure their inalienable rights. Governments would have been urged to implement the Forward-looking Strategies, the United Nations system would have been called on to draw up programmes to implement them and the Secretary-General would have been asked to submit proposals to implement them. The Conference would have recommended that the 1985 General Assembly declare that the period to the year 2000 be dedicated to women for the advancement of the goals of equality, development and peace.

Basic documents submitted to the Conference included the report[5] of the Secretary-General on the review and appraisal of progress achieved and obstacles encountered at that level in the realization of the goals and objectives of the Decade. In addition to outlining key issues and constraints at the national level in improving the situation of women, the report summarized replies from 107 Governments to a United Nations questionnaire on general trends in equality, development and peace, the first part of which dealt with national development plans and policies, national machinery and programmes, legislation, political participation, international co-operation and strengthening international peace, and technical co-operation; the second part analysed development in sectoral areas.

Other documents included the *World Survey on the Role of Women in Development*[6] (see below, under "Women and development"), the Secretary-General's reports on the situation of women and children living in the occupied Arab territories and other occupied territories[7] (see below, under "Palestinian women"), on a review and appraisal of the situation of women and children living under racist minority régimes[8] (see below, under "Women under *apartheid*"), on a review and appraisal of progress achieved and obstacles encountered at the regional and international levels by the United Nations system in attaining the goals and objectives of the Decade for Women[9] (see below, under "Women in the UN Secretariat"), on recommendations of regional intergovernmental preparatory meetings,[10] on the activities and programmes of the United Nations High Commissioner for Refugees (UNHCR) on behalf of refugee women[11] (see below, under "Refugee women"), on NGO participation in the Decade,[12] as well as a report[13] of CEDAW on the achievements of and obstacles encountered by States parties in implementing the Convention on the Elimination of All Forms of Discrimination against Women[14] (see below, under "Convention on Discrimination against Women").

GENERAL ASSEMBLY ACTION

On 13 December, on the recommendation of the Third (Social, Humanitarian and Cultural) Committee, the General Assembly adopted **resolution 40/108** without vote.

Implementation of the Nairobi Forward-looking Strategies for the Advancement of Women

The General Assembly,

Recalling its resolution 3520(XXX) of 15 December 1975, in which it proclaimed the period from 1976 to 1985 the United Nations Decade for Women: Equality, Development and Peace,

Bearing in mind the Convention on the Elimination of All Forms of Discrimination against Women, which was adopted on 18 December 1979 and which came into force on 3 September 1981,

Recalling also the principles and objectives set forth in the Declaration of Mexico on the Equality of Women and their Contribution to Development and Peace, 1975, the World Plan of Action for the Implementation of the Objectives of the International Women's Year and the Programme of Action for the Second Half of the United Nations Decade for Women,

Bearing in mind also its resolutions 3201(S-VI) and 3202(S-VI) of 1 May 1974, containing the Declaration and Programme of Action on the Establishment of a New International Economic Order, 3281(XXIX) of 12 December 1974, containing the Charter of Economic Rights and Duties of States, 3362(S-VII) of 16 September 1975 on development and international economic co-operation and 2542(XXIV) of 11 December 1969 proclaiming the Declaration on Social Progress and Development,

Bearing in mind further the consensus achieved in the text of the International Development Strategy for the Third United Nations Development Decade, contained in the annex to its resolution 35/56 of 5 December 1980, in particular regarding the implementation of the objectives of the United Nations Decade for Women within the framework of the Strategy,

Recalling also its resolution 37/63 of 3 December 1982, by which it proclaimed the Declaration on the Participation of Women in Promoting International Peace and Co-operation,

Recalling further its resolution 39/29 of 3 December 1984 on the critical economic situation in Africa,

Recalling its resolution 35/136 of 11 December 1980, in which it decided to convene in 1985, at the conclusion of the Decade, a World Conference to Review and Appraise the Achievements of the United Nations Decade for Women,

Conscious of the considerable and constructive contribution made by the Commission on the Status of Women acting as preparatory body for the Conference, the specialized agencies, the regional commissions and other organizations of the United Nations system, Member States and non-governmental organizations in the preparations for the Conference,

Aware of the continued contribution made by the Non-Governmental Organizations Forum to the advancement of women,

Convinced that the full integration of women in all aspects of political, economic and social life, at the international, regional and national levels, is essential if the obstacles to the achievement of the goals and objectives of the Decade are to be overcome,

Having considered the report of the World Conference to Review and Appraise the Achievements of the United Nations Decade for Women: Equality, Development and Peace,

Convinced that the Conference, by adopting the Nairobi Forward-looking Strategies for the Advancement of Women, has made an important and positive contribution to the attainment of the objectives of the Decade and provided a policy framework for advancing the status of women to the year 2000,

Further convinced that the Conference has made an important and constructive contribution by appraising the progress achieved and obstacles encountered in the implementation of the objectives of the Decade and by preparing and adopting strategies to advance the status of women for the next fifteen years,

Stressing that during the period 1986-2000 the primary responsibility for implementing the Forward-looking Strategies rests with individual countries, as they are intended to serve as guidelines for a process of continuous adaptation to diverse and changing situations at speeds and in modes determined by overall national priorities, within which the integration of women in development should rank high,

Reaffirming that the realization of equal rights for women at all levels and in all areas of life will contribute to the achievement of a just and lasting peace, to social progress and to respect for human rights and fundamental freedoms, and that the integration of women in the mainstream of the development process requires not only commitment at the national, regional and international levels, but also continuing financial and technical support, and also requires the establishment of the new international economic order,

Considering that the Forward-looking Strategies should immediately be translated into concrete action by Governments, as determined by overall national priorities, by organizations of the United Nations system, specialized agencies and intergovernmental and non-governmental organizations, including women's organizations,

Persuaded of the importance of taking measures to ensure system-wide co-ordination within the United Nations in order to develop a comprehensive and integrated approach to the issues which are crucial to the advancement of women,

1. *Takes note with satisfaction* of the report of the World Conference to Review and Appraise the Achievement of the United Nations Decade for Women: Equality, Development and Peace;

2. *Endorses* the Nairobi Forward-looking Strategies for the Advancement of Women;

3. *Affirms* that the implementation of the Forward-looking Strategies should result in the elimination of all forms of inequality between women and men and in the complete integration of women into the development process and that that should guarantee broad participation by women in efforts to strengthen peace and security in the world;

4. *Declares* that the objectives of the United Nations Decade for Women: Equality, Development and Peace, with the subtheme "Employment, Health and Education", remain valid;

5. *Calls upon* Governments to allocate adequate resources and to take effective appropriate measures to implement the Forward-looking Strategies as a matter of high priority, including the establishment or reinforcement, as appropriate, of national machineries to promote the advancement of women, and to monitor the implementation of these strategies with a view to ensuring the full integration of women in the political, economic, social and cultural life of their countries;

6. *Calls upon* all Governments of Member States to appoint women to decision-making positions, bearing in mind their contribution to national development;

7. *Invites* Governments, when preparing and evaluating national plans and programmes of action, to incorporate measurable targets for overcoming obstacles to the advancement of women and to include measures for the involvement of women in development, both as agents and beneficiaries, on an equal basis with men, and to review the impact of development policies and programmes on women;

8. *Invites* governmental, intergovernmental and non-governmental organizations to give high priority to the implementation of the Forward-looking Strategies and, in particular, to ensure that sectoral policies and programmes for development include strategies to promote the participation of women as agents and beneficiaries on an equal basis with men;

9. *Urges* all Governments to contribute to the strengthening of institutional co-ordination in their regions and subregions in order to establish collaborative arrangements and to develop approaches for the implementation of the Forward-looking Strategies at those levels;

10. *Urges* all organizations of the United Nations system, including the regional commissions and all specialized agencies, to take the necessary measures to ensure a concerted and sustained effort for the implementation of the provisions of the Forward-looking Strategies with a view to achieving a substantial improvement in the status of women by the year 2000 and to ensure that all projects and programmes take into account the need for the complete integration of women and women's concerns;

11. *Requests* the Secretary-General and the specialized agencies and bodies of the United Nations system to establish, where they do not already exist, focal points on women's issues in all sectors of the work of the organizations of the United Nations system;

12. *Urges* the Administrative Committee on Co-ordination to review periodically the system-wide implementation of the Forward-looking Strategies and to hold regular inter-agency meetings on women within the framework of the Administrative Committee on Co-ordination;

13. *Emphasizes* the central role of the Commission on the Status of Women in matters related to the advancement of the status of women and calls upon it to promote the implementation of the Forward-looking Strategies to the year 2000 based on the goals of the United Nations Decade for Women: Equality, Development and Peace, and the subtheme "Employment, Health and Education", and urges all organizations of the United Nations system to co-operate with the Commission in this task;

14. *Requests* the Secretary-General to ensure that the Commission on the Status of Women receives the support services it requires to fulfil its central role effectively;

15. *Also requests* the Secretary-General to invite Governments, organizations of the United Nations system, including regional commissions and specialized agencies, intergovernmental and non-governmental organizations to report periodically through the Commission on the Status of Women to the Economic and Social Council on the activities undertaken at all levels to implement the Forward-looking Strategies;

16. *Further requests* the Secretary-General, in preparing the note on the integrated reporting system for periodic review and appraisal of progress in the advancement of women for submission to the Commission on the Status of Women at its thirty-first session, as called for in Economic and Social Council decision 1984/123 of 24 May 1984, to include proposals for a reporting system to facilitate the monitoring of the implementation of the Forward-looking Strategies as set out in paragraph 15 above, taking into account the experience gained during the Decade, the views of Governments and the need not to duplicate existing reporting obligations, bearing in mind the need to carry out periodical in-depth sectoral reviews of progress achieved and obstacles encountered in implementing the Forward-looking Strategies to the year 2000;

17. *Recommends* that the Secretary-General prepare and submit to the Commission on the Status of Women at its thirty-first session, bearing in mind the remarks and concrete recommendations made during the debate at the fortieth session, in particular the proposals about increasing the number of members and the frequency of meetings of the Commission, a report on alternative measures to strengthen the Commission in the discharge of its functions following the United Nations Decade for Women, and also recommends that the recommendations of the Commission on the matter be reported to the General Assembly at its forty-first session through the Economic and Social Council;

18. *Reaffirms* the role of the Centre for Social Development and Humanitarian Affairs of the Department of International Economic and Social Affairs of the Secretariat, in particular the Branch for the Advancement of Women, as the substantive secretariat of the Commission and as a focal point for matters on women, and requests the Secretariat to collect and disseminate information on system-wide activities related to the implementation of the Forward-looking Strategies;

19. *Takes note with satisfaction* of the appointment of the Co-ordinator for the Improvement of the Status of Women in the Secretariat of the United Nations, in

accordance with General Assembly resolution 39/245 of 18 December 1984, and, in this context, of the fact that the Secretary-General should continue to plan and implement positive actions and programmes to improve the status of women in the Secretariat and to monitor the progress achieved;

20. *Calls upon* the Secretary-General and the heads of the specialized agencies and other United Nations bodies to establish new five-year targets at each level for the percentage of women in Professional and decision-making positions, in accordance with the criteria established by the General Assembly, in particular that of equitable geographical distribution, in order that a definite upward trend in the application of Assembly resolution 33/143 of 20 December 1978 be registered in the number of Professional and decision-making positions held by women by 1990 and to set additional targets every five years;

21. *Welcomes* Economic and Social Council resolution 1985/46 of 31 May 1985 regarding women and development and, noting the particular importance of paragraph 4 of that resolution, recommends that immediate measures be taken to ensure that future medium-term plans of the United Nations and the specialized agencies should contain intersectoral presentations of the various programmes dealing with issues of concern to women and that revisions of current plans should be considered in the light of the results of the World Conference to Review and Appraise the Achievements of the United Nations Decade for Women: Equality, Development and Peace;

22. *Requests* the Secretary-General to take into account the requirements of the Forward-looking Strategies in preparing the programme budget and programme of work for the biennium 1988-1989;

23. *Urges* all financial institutions and all international regional and subregional organizations, institutions, development banks and general funding agencies to ensure that their policies and programmes promote the full participation of women as agents and beneficiaries in the development process;

24. *Invites* the Secretary-General to circulate the report of the Conference among Member States, all organizations of the United Nations system and specialized agencies, intergovernmental and non-governmental organizations in order to ensure that the Forward-looking Strategies are publicized and disseminated as widely as possible, and encourages Governments to translate the Strategies into their national languages;

25. *Requests* the Secretary-General and the heads of all organizations within the United Nations system and of the specialized agencies to continue to give high priority in their public information programmes to disseminating information concerning women and, in particular, the Forward-looking Strategies and, in the light of the recommendations contained in the Strategies, further requests the Secretary-General to provide in the regular budget for the continuation of the existing weekly radio programmes on women, with adequate provision for distributing them in different languages;

26. *Also requests* the Secretary-General to report to the General Assembly at its forty-first session on measures taken to implement the present resolution;

27. *Decides* to consider these questions further at its forty-first session under an item entitled "Forward-

looking strategies for the advancement of women to the year 2000".

General Assembly resolution 40/108

13 December 1985   Meeting 116   Adopted without vote

Approved by Third Committee (A/40/1008) without vote, 29 November (meeting 57); draft by Yugoslavia, for Group of 77 (A/C.3/40/L.47/Rev.1), orally amended by Australia; agenda item 92 *(b)*.
Financial implications. 5th Committee, A/40/1036; S-G, A/C.3/40/L.58, A/C.5/40/66.
Meeting numbers. GA 40th session: 3rd Committee 24-34, 46, 48, 55-57; 5th Committee 59; plenary 116.

Australia's amendment expanded the last phrase in paragraph 25, which had previously requested the Secretary-General "to continue the United Nations weekly radio programmes on women". The paragraph was then adopted separately in the Third Committee by 134 votes to 2, with 2 abstentions.

Also on 13 December, on the recommendation of the Third Committee, the Assembly adopted **resolution 40/107** without vote.

Expression of appreciation to the Government and people of Kenya on the occasion of the World Conference to Review and Appraise the Achievements of the United Nations Decade for Women: Equality, Development and Peace

The General Assembly,

Taking into account the significance and the results of the World Conference to Review and Appraise the Achievements of the United Nations Decade for Women: Equality, Development and Peace, held at Nairobi from 15 to 26 July 1985,

Expresses its deep appreciation to the Government and people of Kenya for acting as host to the World Conference to Review and Appraise the Achievements of the United Nations Decade for Women: Equality, Development and Peace.

General Assembly resolution 40/107

13 December 1985   Meeting 116   Adopted without vote

Approved by Third Committee (A/40/1008) unanimously, 27 November (meeting 56); 32-nation draft (A/C.3/40/L.29); agenda item 92 *(b)*.
Sponsors: Argentina, Australia, Benin, Burundi, Cameroon, Canada, Chile, China, Costa Rica, Czechoslovakia, Denmark, Djibouti, Egypt, Guinea, Indonesia, Jordan, Mexico, Nepal, Pakistan, Philippines, Rwanda, Senegal, Suriname, Swaziland, Thailand, Trinidad and Tobago, Uganda, United Republic of Tanzania, Yugoslavia, Zaire, Zambia, Zimbabwe.
Meeting numbers. GA 40th session: 3rd Committee 24-34, 46, 48, 55, 56; plenary 116.

Preparations for the Conference

The Commission on the Status of Women, as the preparatory body for the 1985 World Conference, met in Vienna from 4 to 13 March 1985 for its third session and in New York from 29 April to 7 May in a resumed session.[15]

The Commission recommended to the Economic and Social Council that the report[13] of CEDAW on the achievements of and obstacles encountered by States parties in implementing the 1979 Convention[14] be submitted to the Conference and that the Committee's Chairperson be invited to introduce that report.

It was also recommended that the Council authorize the Secretary-General to accept special contributions to assist representatives of LDCs, Trust

Territories, land-locked countries and developing countries in the Caribbean to participate in the Conference. With regard to documentation, the Commission recommended that the Secretary-General's report[16] on participation of NGOs in the Decade be submitted to the Conference as a basic document and that a report[17] on women and *apartheid* in South Africa and Namibia, originally submitted to an African regional preparatory meeting, be submitted as a background document.

In other action, the Commission referred a note[18] by the Secretary-General—containing the draft provisional rules of procedure of the World Conference and three of his recommendations[19] on outstanding questions on organizational aspects and other activities related to the Conference—to the Economic and Social Council. It agreed that he would submit to the Conference, through the Council, a proposal[20] by the Group of 77 developing countries for the reformulation of the forward-looking strategies on which there was no consensus, with an explanatory note.

The Commission had before it for review the report of the Secretary-General on the forward-looking strategies and other of his reports which were subsequently submitted to the Conference. Following a General Assembly decision (see below), the Commission resumed its session on 19 April to consider the Conference's rules of procedure and organizational and other questions related to the Conference.

GENERAL ASSEMBLY ACTION

On 12 April 1985, during its resumed thirty-ninth session, the General Assembly adopted **decision 39/459** without vote.

Preparations for the World Conference to Review and Appraise the Achievements of the United Nations Decade for Women: Equality, Development and Peace

At its 107th plenary meeting, on 12 April 1985, the General Assembly:

(*a*) Reaffirmed the need to ensure a successful outcome for the World Conference to Review and Appraise the Achievements of the United Nations Decade for Women: Equality, Development and Peace, to be held at Nairobi from 15 to 26 July 1985 in accordance with General Assembly resolutions 35/136 of 11 December 1980 and 39/129 of 14 December 1984;

(*b*) Decided to request the Commission on the Status of Women acting as the preparatory body for the Conference to resume its third session in New York for a period of no more than seven days starting from 29 April 1985, in order to complete successfully its preparatory work for the Conference;

(*c*) Decided to request the Economic and Social Council to consider, with priority, during its first regular session of 1985, the results of the deliberations of the preparatory body.

General Assembly decision 39/459

Adopted without vote

Draft by Egypt (A/39/L.47); agenda item 93 *(b)*.

ECONOMIC AND SOCIAL COUNCIL ACTION

Following consideration of the report of the Commission on the Status of Women acting as Preparatory Body for the Conference,[15] the Economic and Social Council adopted **decision 1985/158** without vote.

Preparations for the World Conference to Review and Appraise the Achievements of the United Nations Decade for Women: Equality, Development and Peace

At its 26th plenary meeting, on 31 May 1985, the Council, having examined the reports of the Commission on the Status of Women acting as the Preparatory Body for the World Conference to Review and Appraise the Achievements of the United Nations Decade for Women: Equality, Development and Peace on its third and resumed third sessions,

(*a*) Took note of the reports and expressed its appreciation for the work done by the Preparatory Body;

(*b*) Endorsed the recommendation contained in paragraph 1 of the report on the third session and recommendations I and II contained in paragraph 1 of the report on the resumed third session;

(*c*) Decided to invite Mrs. Rosario Manalo, Chairperson of the Commission on the Status of Women acting as the Preparatory Body for the World Conference to Review and Appraise the Achievements of the United Nations Decade for Women: Equality, Development and Peace at its third and resumed third sessions, to hold informal consultations in New York, prior to the Conference, with a view to facilitating, as far as possible, the deliberations at the Conference regarding the forward-looking strategies of implementation for the advancement of women and concrete measures to overcome obstacles to the achievement of the goals and objectives of the United Nations Decade for Women: Equality, Development, Peace, for the period 1986 to the year 2000, and to make available the results of those consultations to the Conference, as appropriate;

(*d*) Authorized its Bureau to continue making every effort, through informal consultations, to assist delegations in resolving outstanding issues relating to the provisional rules of procedure for the Conference and to submit the results to the Council at a resumption of its first regular session of 1985, on 20 June 1985.

Economic and Social Council decision 1985/158

Adopted without vote

Draft orally proposed by Vice-President based on informal consultations; agenda item 5.

On 20 June the Council adopted without vote **decision 1985/164**, by which it decided to transmit to the World Conference its recommendations concerning rules 6 and 15 of the provisional rules of procedure. By rule 6, the Conference would elect a President, one Vice-President for Co-ordination, 29 other Vice-Presidents, a Rapporteur-General and a Presiding Officer for each of the main committees. By rule 15, the Conference, at its first meeting, would elect its officers and constitute its subsidiary organs, adopt its rules of procedure and agenda, and decide on the organization of its work. Recommendations resulting from pre-Conference consultations would, in principle, be acted on without further discussion.

ACC action. An inter-agency meeting on preparations for the Conference (Vienna, 15 March)[21] recommended that the Consultative Committee on Substantive Questions (Programme Matters) (CCSQ(PROG)) of the Administrative Committee on Co-ordination (ACC) approve the holding of an inter-agency meeting immediately after the February/March 1986 session of the Commission on the Status of Women. The meeting should consider the Conference's recommendations and discuss future inter-agency co-operation as follow-up action to the Conference. The meeting also agreed that it would be worth while to hold informal consultations among representatives of the various parts of the United Nations system during the Conference to enhance co-ordination.

CCSQ(PROG) considered the meeting's report at a session held at Geneva from 1 to 4 April.[22] It endorsed the meeting's recommendations and agreed that a further such meeting should be held after the Conference to discuss inter-agency co-ordination. It was suggested that use be made of existing inter-agency mechanisms which were already considering the issue of women under their sectoral concerns, such as the Task Force on Rural Development with regard to rural women.

UNEP action. In his introductory report[23] to the thirteenth session of the Governing Council of the United Nations Environment Programme (UNEP) (Nairobi, Kenya, 14-24 May 1985),[24] the UNEP Executive Director stated that UNEP's contribution to the 1985 World Conference on women would take into account views expressed by the Governing Council on the role women should play in stimulating environmental protection. He would be addressing the Conference on that role. Several events would be organized by UNEP during the Conference.

In a 23 May decision,[25] the Governing Council, considering that a major burden of the environmental crisis in most developing countries fell on women and that an improvement in their status would bring added emphasis to the environmental cause, endorsed the Executive Director's proposals concerning UNEP's role in the Conference.

Conference follow-up

CCSQ(PROG), at a meeting held in New York (10-16 October 1985),[26] heard an oral report by the Assistant Secretary-General for Social Development and Humanitarian Affairs outlining the results of the World Conference. CCSQ(PROG) decided to consider at a subsequent session the im-

plementation of the Conference's decisions based on decisions taken by the General Assembly at its 1985 session. It decided to approve the convening of an inter-agency meeting in March 1986 at Vienna, immediately after the session of the Commission on the Status of Women, to consider the follow-up activities to the Conference and discuss the system-wide medium-term plan for women and development.

In **resolution 40/164 A**, the Assembly urged the Department of Public Information to disseminate in its programmes and information activities the positive results of the Conference.

REFERENCES

[1]YUN 1975, p. 666, GA res. 3520(XXX), 15 Dec. 1975. [2]*Ibid.*, p. 645. [3]YUN 1980, p. 886. [4]*Report of the World Conference to Review and Appraise the Achievements of the United Nations Decade for Women: Equality, Development and Peace* (A/CONF.116/28/Rev.1), Sales No. E.85.IV.10. [5]A/CONF.116/5 & Add.1-14 & Add.1-14/Corr.1 & Add.4/Corr.2, Add.5/Corr.2, Add.11/Corr.2 & Add.12/Corr.2. [6]*World Survey on the Role of Women in Development* (A/CONF.116/4/Rev.1) (ST/ESA/180), Sales No. E.86.IV.3. [7]A/CONF.116/6. [8]A/CONF.116/7. [9]A/CONF.116/8 & Corr.1. [10]A/CONF.116/9 & Corr.1. [11]A/CONF.116/11. [12]A/CONF.116/14. [13]A/CONF.116/13. [14]YUN 1979, p. 895, GA res. 34/180, annex, 18 Dec. 1979. [15]A/CONF.116/PC/25 & Add.1 & Add.1/Corr.1, Add.2 & Add.2/Corr.1, Add.3. [16]A/CONF.116/PC/23. [17]E/ECA/RCIWD/OAU/7. [18]A/CONF.116/PC/11. [19]A/CONF.116/PC/24 & Corr.1. [20]A/CONF.116/PC/21. [21]ACC/1985/PG/9. [22]ACC/1985/4. [23]UNEP/GC.13/3. [24]A/40/25. [25]A/40/25 (dec. 13/1). [26]ACC/1985/20.

PUBLICATION

Activities for the Advancement of Women: Equality, Development and Peace (E/1983/7) (ST/ESA/174), Sales No. E.85.IV.11.

Women and development

The 1985 World Conference on the Decade for Women took note of the *World Survey on the Role of Women in Development.*[1] In accordance with a 1984 General Assembly resolution,[2] the *Survey* in its final form was also submitted to the 1985 Assembly session.

The *Survey* comprised eight parts, starting with an overview assessing the role of women in economic development, the benefits accruing to women from development and the effects on them of economic trends. A main generalization emerging from the *Survey* was that women's contribution to national production activities had increased steadily since 1950 and was projected to increase further to the year 2000. Their contribution to economic development was underestimated in national and international statistics. In agriculture, active women were sometimes counted as inactive and in industry were involved more often than men in the informal economy, so that neither their work nor their production was fully recorded.

Women were disproportionately active in services because employment in that area responded to supply pressures more than in other sectors of the economy and because household skills could be transferred to services sectors more readily than to industry.

The second main generalization was that women benefited on average less than men from their contribution to national production. In industry, women still belonged largely to the secondary labour force, taking jobs for which men were unavailable or which men were unwilling to take, resulting in lower average hourly wages. In addition, women were protected by social legislation less than men, even in countries with such legislation, and fixed and generally long working hours made it difficult for women's productive and domestic activities to be compatible. In agriculture, men tended to take higher paying jobs requiring technical skills, while women were generally confined to lower-paid manual labour. Also, in the sectors of services, science and technology, financial institutions, insurance, real estate and business, positions held by women and the benefits accruing to them were lower than men's. Women seldom held decision-making positions in any of those sectors or in the institutions that determined national policies affecting them.

The next six parts dealt with women's roles in agriculture, industrial development, money and finance, science and technology, trade, and the development, use and conservation of energy resources. Finally, the concept of self-reliance and the integration of women into development was discussed.

Pursuant to the 1984 Assembly resolution[2] on the *World Survey*, the Secretary-General submitted to the 1985 session a note[3] summarizing comments made on the *Survey* at the World Conference. It had been widely felt among delegations that the three goals of the Decade—equality, development and peace—were strongly interrelated and that the integration of women into development would have been greatly accelerated by favourable international economic and political relations. Although there was a broad consensus that during the Decade, and partly as a result of it, there had been much progress, it was felt that much remained to be done to take advantage of women's potential.

By a 3 June letter,[4] India forwarded to the Secretary-General the report of the Ministerial Conference of Non-Aligned and Other Developing Countries on the Role of Women in Development (New Delhi, 10 and 11 April 1985) and requested that it be circulated to the General Assembly.

GENERAL ASSEMBLY ACTION

On 17 December, on the recommendation of the Second (Economic and Financial) Committee, the General Assembly adopted without vote **resolution 40/204**.

Effective mobilization and integration of women in development

The General Assembly,

Taking note with appreciation of the world survey on the role of women in development,

Recognizing that although the survey was submitted to the World Conference to Review and Appraise the Achievements of the United Nations Decade for Women: Equality, Development and Peace, it has yet to receive the detailed attention it deserves,

Noting with satisfaction the adoption by the Conference of the Nairobi Forward-looking Strategies for the Advancement of Women, which constitute an important and positive contribution to the attainment of the objectives of the Decade and provide a policy framework for the advancement of women to the year 2000,

1. *Invites* the Commission on the Status of Women at its thirty-first session to make specific action-oriented recommendations based on the world survey on the role of women in development as a part of the overall implementation of and follow-up to the Nairobi Forward-looking Strategies for the Advancement of Women, which should be for action at the national and international levels, including co-operation among developing countries, within an economic context, and should address sectoral and cross-sectoral problems identified in the survey, and requests that the report of the Commission be made available, through the Economic and Social Council at its second regular session of 1986, to the General Assembly at its forty-second session under the sub-item entitled "Effective mobilization and integration of women in economic development";

2. *Requests* the Secretary-General to take those recommendations into account when formulating the system-wide medium-term plan for women and development and to invite the specialized agencies and other organizations of the United Nations system, in particular the United Nations Industrial Development Organization, the International Labour Organisation, the Food and Agriculture Organization of the United Nations and the International Training and Research Institute for the Advancement of Women, to take into account the implications of the world survey when preparing their contributions to that plan;

3. *Also requests* the Secretary-General to update the survey on the role of women in development on a regular basis, focusing on selected emerging development issues that have an impact on the role of women in the economy at the local, national, regional and international levels;

4. *Decides* that the first update of the survey should be submitted to the General Assembly at its forty-fourth session, in 1989;

5. *Invites* the Commission on the Status of Women at its thirty-first session to make a recommendation on future updates of the survey after 1989, bearing in mind the need for effective co-ordination with the follow-up activities of the World Conference to Review and Appraise the Achievements of the United Nations Decade for Women: Equality, Development and Peace;

6. *Also invites* the Commission on the Status of Women to suggest terms of reference for the first update of the survey, which should contain improved data and information on the role of women in development, including, *inter alia*, their role in the informal sector of the economy;

7. *Urges* the specialized agencies and other organizations of the United Nations system to contribute to the preparation of the first update of the survey;

8. *Requests* the Secretary-General to submit to the General Assembly, at its forty-second session, a progress report on the preparation of the first regular update of the survey, including preliminary views on its scope and content, so that the Commission on the Status of Women, at its thirty-second session, can take that report into account, together with the comments on the subject made by delegations in the General Assembly;

9. *Also requests* the Secretary-General to utilize the input provided by the Commission on the Status of Women at its thirty-second session and by the Economic and Social Council in 1988 for the preparation of the first update of the survey.

General Assembly resolution 40/204

17 December 1985   Meeting 119   Adopted without vote

Approved by Second Committee (A/40/989/Add.9) without vote, 25 November (meeting 43); draft by Vice-Chairman (A/C.2/40/L.71), based on informal consultations on draft by Algeria, Australia, Bangladesh, Canada, Congo, Denmark, Finland, France, Gambia, Iceland, Jamaica, Kenya, Morocco, Netherlands, Niger, Norway, Pakistan, Poland, Sweden (A/C.2/40/L.23/Rev.1); agenda item 84 *(i)*.
Financial implications. SG, A/C.2/40/L.42.
Meeting numbers. GA 40th session: 2nd Committee 24, 43; plenary 119.

By **decision 40/442** of 17 December 1985, the General Assembly took note of the Secretary-General's note[3] on the *World Survey*. The decision was adopted without vote, as it had been in the Second Committee on 25 November, on an oral proposal by the Chairman.

During the mid-term global review of the implementation of the Substantial New Programme of Action for the 1980s for the Least Developed Countries, several conclusions and recommendations were made by the Intergovernmental Group on LDCs of the United Nations Conference on Trade and Development (UNCTAD) regarding the position of women in those countries (see p. 434). Those findings were endorsed by the General Assembly when it adopted **resolution 40/205**.

UNIDO action. At its May 1985 session, the Industrial Development Board (IDB) of the United Nations Industrial Development Organization (UNIDO) (see Chapter VI of this section), adopted a conclusion on the integration of women in industrial development.[5] The Board thereby stressed the need for further progress in designing training programmes to increase the managerial competence of women in industry and the need to encourage national and regional training institutions to conduct such programmes. It also stressed the need for guidelines to ensure that the integration of women would be considered in designing, implementing and evaluating technical co-operation activities and in the studies programme, and requested a secretariat report on action in that regard. The Board stressed the need for intensified efforts to recruit more women to Professional posts, particularly at the policy, planning and decision-making level, and the impor-

tance of the Focal Point for the Integration of Women in Industrial Development within the Office of the Director, Division of Policy Coordination, as a means of collecting, analysing and disseminating information on women's participation in different industrial sectors, both within and outside UNIDO. It noted with satisfaction the introduction in the proposed 1986-1987 budget of a programme element on integrating women in industrial development and expressed the hope that adequate staff and other resources would be made available.

During the second part of its first regular session (Vienna, 9-13 December 1985), the UNIDO General Conference adopted a decision[6] on the integration of women in industrial development. It took note of the Economic and Social Council recommendations on women and development (see below) and of the results of the World Conference as reflected in the Nairobi Forward-looking Strategies, which contained sections on industry and science and technology. It considered that, in implementing UNIDO's programme and budget for 1986-1987, account should be taken of the results of the World Conference as related to industrialization. The General Conference reaffirmed the content of its (1984) Fourth General Conference resolution[7] and IDB's 1985 conclusion on the subject, stressed UNIDO's essential role in both rural and urban areas in implementing the Nairobi Strategies as related to industrialization, and emphasized the importance of the UNIDO Focal Point in implementing the Strategies. The UNIDO Director-General was urged to ensure that: UNIDO pre-investment study programmes paid greater attention to the social, cultural and economic costs and benefits that investment projects had on the role of women in national economies; industrial research and study activities included socio-economic and human resource factors and paid greater attention to training, research and data collection; and headquarters and field staff were fully aware of and took into account the important role of women in industrial development. He was requested to implement United Nations decisions regarding employment of women in the United Nations system at all levels in the Professional categories.

UNDP action. By a March 1985 note,[8] the UNDP Administrator submitted a summary report of the interorganizational assessment of women's participation in development to the UNDP Governing Council (New York, 3-29 June 1985). The study, co-ordinated and prepared by UNDP, involved all United Nations organizations with a significant interest in promoting women's participation.

The report discussed the methodology of the assessment and went on to give the key findings and recommendations of country case-studies in

Democratic Yemen, Haiti, Indonesia and Rwanda. It then addressed the quantitative framework of the assessment and its implications. Finally, the Administrator recommended that the Governing Council endorse a series of recommendations for action by Governments, United Nations organizations and NGOs.

In a report[9] to the Governing Council on women in development, prepared in response to a 1982 Council decision,[10] the Administrator stated that the apparent downward trend in women's participation in UNDP-supported projects in 1980 was reversed in 1981, and the level of participation in 1982 and 1983 remained well above that of earlier years. Women's participation increased in such key sectors as development planning, agriculture, health, employment, and social conditions and equity.

The report also contained information on the response by field offices to *ad hoc* programming assistance to further women's participation in development. It concluded that, with the possible exception of the African region, that type of assistance was not in high demand. Instead, continuation of a standing concern for women's participation in all aspects of project design and planning was needed, as well as increased staff training. Those points were also among the recommendations in the report on interorganizational assessment.

By a 28 June decision,[11] the Governing Council, having considered the Administrator's reports, urged Governments to give more priority to using special programming assistance offered by the United Nations development system. That system, Governments and NGOs were strongly urged to implement the recommendations in the Administrator's report on the interorganizational assessment. The Administrator was requested to develop, for presentation to the Council in 1986, an internal strategy to strengthen UNDP's capacity to deal with women's issues in development. Calling on the experience of the United Nations Development Fund for Women, verifiable objectives and a time-frame for implementation would be established. Special attention should also be given to improved staff training, monitoring existing guidelines, instructions and procedures for including the subject in programming missions and strengthening the focal point in UNDP headquarters for co-ordinating women's programmes.

By a 29 June decision[12] on the integration of issues relevant to women into promotional and operational activities for technical co-operation among developing countries (TCDC), the Governing Council invited United Nations agencies and organizations to include reference to women in all promotional activities for TCDC and to elaborate and disseminate guidelines on incorporating issues relevant to advancement of women into TCDC programmes and projects. Developing countries were invited to elaborate proposals for such projects benefiting women. The Council reiterated the importance of networking and strengthening linkages between focal points for TCDC and women's organizations and professional organizations having experience with women's and development issues. It requested the Administrator to strengthen co-operation with organizations, such as INSTRAW, which were active in the area of women and development.

Women in rural areas

In response to a 1984 General Assembly resolution,[13] the Secretary-General submitted to the 1985 Assembly a note[14] compiling observations and comments made at the 1985 World Conference on a report of the 1984 Interregional Seminar on National Experience relating to the Improvement of the Situation of Women in Rural Areas.[15] Several delegations had described the situation of rural women in their countries, reported on progress made during the Decade and outlined strategies and policies adopted to continue the advancement of rural women. Main obstacles cited were the lack of systematic and reliable information on rural women, particularly on the quantity and type of women's production, which could eventually lead to incorporating women's concerns in national and sectoral planning. Above all, emphasis was placed on the need to increase rural women's productivity in economic activities: agriculture, handicrafts and small-scale industrial production. Delegations proposed several policies to that end, of which training was among the most often mentioned.

Other requirements were granting women access to the resources and factors of production, selecting and providing appropriate technology to women farmers, and credit. Social development also had to be strengthened: emphasis was placed on maternal and child health care, family planning, literacy and adult education.

To spread awareness of the needs and priorities of rural women among planners and decision-makers and increase the effectiveness of self-help initiatives, many delegations acknowledged the need to strengthen women's national machineries, voluntary associations, co-operatives and the like.

GENERAL ASSEMBLY ACTION

On 13 December, on the recommendation of the Third Committee, the General Assembly adopted **resolution 40/106** without vote.

National experience relating to the improvement of the situation of women in rural areas

The General Assembly,

Referring to the Nairobi Forward-looking Strategies for the Advancement of Women, adopted by the World Conference to Review and Appraise the Achievements of the United Nations Decade for Women: Equality, Development and Peace,

Recalling its resolutions 34/14 of 9 November 1979, 37/59 of 3 December 1982 and 39/126 of 14 December 1984, concerning the improvement of the situation of women in rural areas,

Reaffirming the importance attached in the Programme of Action for the Second Half of the United Nations Decade for Women and in the Convention on the Elimination of All Forms of Discrimination against Women to the need to improve the status of women and ensure their full participation, both as agents and as beneficiaries, in the development process,

Recognizing the urgent need to take additional appropriate measures aimed at further improving the situation of women in rural areas,

Convinced that the eradication of *apartheid*, all forms of racial discrimination, colonialism, neo-colonialism, aggression, foreign occupation and domination is essential to the further improvement of the situation of rural women,

Considering that the strengthening of international peace and co-operation is one of the factors contributing to the further improvement of the situation of rural women,

1. *Takes note* of the report of the Interregional Seminar on National Experience Relating to the Improvement of the Situation of Women in Rural Areas, held at Vienna from 17 to 28 September 1984, as well as the compilation of observations and comments made by Member States;

2. *Calls upon* Governments to elaborate and implement, as a part of national development strategies, special comprehensive programmes for improving the situation of women in rural areas and to establish monitoring and evaluating mechanisms, involving women themselves, for these programmes;

3. *Requests* the organizations and funds concerned within the United Nations system to pay greater attention to the needs of rural women and to assist Member States, especially the developing countries, in the implementation of their national policies and programmes aimed at the advancement of rural women;

4. *Requests* the Secretary-General to prepare, in consultation with the Member States, a comprehensive report on the present status and perspectives for the improvement of the situation of rural women, paying special attention, *inter alia*, to:

(a) Participation of rural women in socio-economic and political life;

(b) Questions of the exercise by rural women of their rights;

(c) Role of agricultural co-operatives in the improvement of the situation of women;

(d) Agrarian reform, particularly in favour of rural women, with a view to improving their situation;

(e) Elimination of illiteracy among rural women and upgrading of their educational level;

(f) Assistance to rural women in the improvement of their situation;

5. *Also requests* the Secretary-General to submit the report to the General Assembly at its forty-fourth session through the Economic and Social Council.

General Assembly resolution 40/106

13 December 1985   Meeting 116   Adopted without vote

Approved by Third Committee (A/40/1008, draft resolution VI) without vote, 27 November (meeting 56); 18-nation draft (A/C.3/40/L.34); agenda item 92.

Sponsors: Afghanistan, Bangladesh, Benin, Burkina Faso, Cameroon, Cuba, German Democratic Republic, Guinea, Ivory Coast, Lao People's Democratic Republic, Madagascar, Mongolia, Morocco, Nepal, Nicaragua, Nigeria, Rwanda, Viet Nam.

Meeting numbers. GA 40th session: 3rd Committee 24-34, 46, 48, 55, 56; plenary 116.

France and the United States said that they would join in the consensus, although they had reservations about the fifth and sixth preambular paragraphs which omitted mention of other factors—for example, the denial of basic civil and political rights—or introduced notions which were in no way connected to rural women.

Co-ordination

In 1984, when approving its basic programme of work, the Economic and Social Council decided to review in 1985, on a cross-organizational basis, the question of women and development. In accordance with that decision, the Secretary-General submitted to the Economic and Social Council in April a report[16] reviewing selected major issues in the medium-term plans of the organizations of the United Nations system in that area.

The report outlined the common policies of the system, how well it addressed the pertinent issues relating to women and how those policies could be better translated into programmes. It also attempted to see whether existing plans, taken together, constituted a coherent whole in their approaches to the problems. It was noted that the report's conclusions were somewhat tentative, since the July World Conference might call for changes in emphasis which could have important implications.

The report stated that the Council might wish to recommend priorities and approaches to be reflected in the system's planning documents for 1984-1989, particularly in relation to women's access to productive resources, income and employment, to participation in the decision-making process, and to the development of statistics and indicators. It could also recommend increased emphasis on the problems of poor urban women. Other recommendations might propose: that inter-agency consultations be held to formulate programmes within a system-wide framework; that CPC consider undertaking a COPA on the subject in 1988; that the medium-term plan of the United Nations, and those of the specialized agencies, should contain intersectoral presentations of the various programmes dealing with the issue; that ACC carry out joint thematic reviews on rural women and social indicators where inter-agency mechanisms were already in place, in order to define proposals for action to be incorporated into work programmes and operational policy statements; that linkage between programme and technical co-operation activities be explicitly identified in the planning and programming process; and that, where women constituted a significant proportion of the intended beneficiaries, it should be clearly indicated when formulating strategies and broad programme statements.

ECONOMIC AND SOCIAL COUNCIL ACTION.

On 31 May, the Economic and Social Council adopted **resolution 1985/46** without vote.

Women and development

The Economic and Social Council,

Recalling its resolutions 1982/50 of 28 July 1982 and 1983/78 of 29 July 1983, as well as its decision 1984/101 of 10 February 1984, by which it decided to review the question of women and development at its first regular session of 1985,

Having considered the report of the Secretary-General reviewing the issue of women and development in the medium-term plans of the organizations of the United Nations system,

Confirming the importance of the objectives of the United Nations Decade for Women: Equality, Development and Peace,

Convinced of the importance of integrating women fully into all aspects of the development process both as agents and as beneficiaries,

Recognizing the need for greater coherence and efficiency of the policies and programmes related to women and development of the organizations of the United Nations system,

Bearing in mind its resolution 1984/12 of 24 May 1984, pursuant to which the Commission on the Status of Women, at its thirty-first session, will review the ways in which the needs and concerns of women can be integrated into all planning and programme activities of the United Nations system,

1. *Welcomes* the report of the Secretary-General reviewing the issue of women and development in the medium-term plans of the organizations of the United Nations system, and the recommendations contained therein, as a first step towards a coherent approach by the organizations of the United Nations system to policies and programmes related to women and development;

2. *Urges* all United Nations bodies, including the regional commissions, and the specialized agencies which have not yet done so, to develop and implement comprehensive policies for women and development and to incorporate them into their medium-term plans, statements of objectives, programmes and other major policy statements;

3. *Requests* the Secretary-General, in his capacity as Chairman of the Administrative Committee on Co-ordination, to take the initiative in formulating a system-wide medium-term plan for women and development, taking into account the priorities recommended by the Council, the recommendations of the World Conference to Review and Appraise the Achievements of the United Nations Decade for Women: Equality, Development and

Peace, to be held at Nairobi from 15 to 26 July 1985, and the relevant decisions of the respective governing bodies of the organizations of the United Nations system, to be submitted, through the Commission on the Status of Women at its thirty-first session, to the Committee for Programme and Co-ordination at its twenty-sixth session and to the Council at its second regular session of 1986;

4. *Recommends* that future medium-term plans of the United Nations and the specialized agencies should contain intersectoral presentations of the various programmes dealing with issues of concern to women and that revisions of current plans should be considered in the light of the results of the Nairobi Conference;

5. *Also recommends* that in formulating programmes and projects it should explicitly be indicated where women constitute a significant proportion of the intended beneficiaries;

6. *Invites* the Commission on the Status of Women, beginning in 1986, to review regularly the priorities and strategies for the advancement of women of the organizations of the United Nations system and to report biennially to the Council on progress made system-wide in their implementation;

7. *Requests* the Committee for Programme and Co-ordination to undertake in 1989 a cross-organizational programme analysis in order to review systematically the activities for and resources allocated to the advancement of women, and requests the Secretary-General to submit the proposed general framework and approach of that cross-organizational programme analysis for comment to the Commission on the Status of Women at its thirty-second session;

8. *Decides* to transmit the report of the Secretary-General to the World Conference to Review and Appraise the Achievements of the United Nations Decade for Women: Equality, Development and Peace for its consideration in formulating forward-looking strategies for the advancement of women at the international and regional levels;

9. *Requests* the Secretary-General to report to the Council at its regular sessions of 1986 on the implementation of the present resolution.

Economic and Social Council resolution 1985/46

31 May 1985   Meeting 26   Adopted without vote

10-nation draft (E/1985/L.33), orally revised; agenda item 5.
Sponsors: Australia, Bangladesh, Canada, Colombia, Costa Rica, India, Japan, Morocco, Netherlands, United States.
Meeting numbers. ESC 25, 26.

UN Development Fund for Women

In accordance with a 1984 General Assembly resolution,[17] the Voluntary Fund for the United Nations Decade for Women, renamed the United Nations Development Fund for Women (UNIFEM), was transferred from the United Nations Secretariat to autonomous association with UNDP on 1 July 1985.

In an October 1985 report[18] to the General Assembly, the Secretary-General gave information on the implementation of the 1984 resolution on arrangements for the management of the Fund, outlined project-cycle activities and mentioned

Fund activities in connection with the 1985 World Conference. The report stated that contributions from Governments and non-governmental sources had risen gradually since 1980 to reach a high point of $3.4 million in 1984. However, expenditures were also on the increase. During 1985, programming and/or evaluation missions were sent to 30 countries, as a result of which 16 project proposals were scheduled for implementation in 1986 and future years, according to a report[19] on the Fund by the UNDP Administrator. Projects ranged from the training of rural trainers to village bakeries, poultry-raising and horticulture. A total of 144 project proposals were received and approval of 36 projects totalling $2.7 million was recommended by the Fund's Consultative Committee. By the end of 1985, UNIFEM had provided assistance to all regions of the world through 473 projects with a total value of $30.4 million.

In 1985, UNIFEM received contributions and pledges from 54 Member States. The $3.5 million in pledges towards the Fund's general resources in 1985 represented an increase of 35 per cent over 1984 pledges, exclusive of contributions earmarked for specific projects. A further $122,451 was received from individuals, NGOs and national committees on the Fund. Also, one donor provided $89,000 for two projects in the African region and $50,000 for donor round-table activities.

At the 1985 Pledging Conference for Development Activities held in November (see Chapter II of this section), 38 countries pledged $3 million to UNIFEM for 1986. Although four traditional major donors were unable to announce their pledges at the Conference, the 1986 total was expected to reach $4 million—more than a 14 per cent increase over 1985.

The Fund maintained a balance between income and expenditures during the year, with an estimated total project expenditure of $4.3 million, representing an increase over the $3.2 million recorded for 1984.

UNDP activities. In a May 1985 report[20] to the UNDP Governing Council on UNIFEM, the Administrator gave an overview of its mandate and activities, and noted that, in view of the full agenda of the General Assembly's Advisory Committee on Administrative and Budgetary Questions (ACABQ), the biennial budget for the Fund's administrative costs would be submitted to the Assembly's 1985 session in September (see below). The Administrator, therefore, sought authorization to act on any ACABQ recommendations before the Council's 1986 session.

By a 29 June decision,[21] the Council welcomed the Administrator's arrangements to accept responsibility for UNIFEM as of 1 July 1985 and requested him to prepare the Fund's 1986-1987 budget estimates for review by ACABQ; the Council would consider the budget proposals, as well as staffing matters, at its 1986 organizational session. It authorized the Administrator to maintain the current level of staffing and budgetary expenditures, pending Council approval of the 1986-1987 budget, and requested him to report to the Council annually on the establishment of administrative arrangements relating to the Fund's association with UNDP.

ACABQ consideration. The UNDP Administrator's budget estimates[22] for UNIFEM for 1986-1987 were reviewed by ACABQ later in the year.[23]

As at 31 August 1985, from the inception of the Fund, contributions amounted to $25.4 million, including $24 million in pledges from States and $1.4 million from non-governmental sources. As at 31 October 1985, the level of unpaid pledges was $1.2 million and some $400,000 in income had not been taken into account in connection with the Fund's financial transfer from the United Nations to UNDP. ACABQ had no objection to the Administrator's staffing requirements of 13 posts, an increase of two over the 1984-1985 biennium. It was informed that the Fund was developing a knowledge-bank pilot project; it felt that before further implementation, the impact of the project on the Fund, its costs and potential users should be carefully weighed.

CONTRIBUTIONS AND PLEDGES TO THE VOLUNTARY FUND
FOR THE UNITED NATIONS DECADE FOR WOMEN
(as at 30 June 1985; in US dollar equivalent)

Country	1985 payment	Pledge for future years
Algeria	10,000	10,000
Australia	89,859	78,574
Austria	21,000	21,000
Belgium	65,574	85,106
Botswana	3,521	—
Burundi	—	971
Cameroon	—	2,755
Canada	14,599	729,927
Chile	5,000	—
China	30,000	30,000
Colombia	2,000	2,000
Cuba	5,097	—
Cyprus	300	500
Democratic Yemen	1,760	1,940
Denmark	100,000	150,000
Egypt	2,000	2,000
Finland	154,512	186,916
France	26,316	44,444
Germany, Federal Republic of	31,852	43,972
Greece	3,500	3,500
Guinea	1,000	—
Guyana	1,000	1,448
Honduras	1,000	1,000
Iceland	6,000	—
India	20,000	20,000
Indonesia	3,000	5,000
Ireland	20,230	40,770
Italy	184,211	225,080
Jamaica	235	—
Japan	300,000	—
Lao People's Democratic Republic	1,500	1,500
Lesotho	—	944
Maldives	1,000	—
Mauritius	—	211
Mexico	1,466	577
Netherlands	130,435	230,769
New Zealand	12,698	—
Nigeria	24,352	—
Norway	790,960	1,052,632
Oman	10,000	—

Country	1985 payment	Pledge for future years
Pakistan	8,772	7,622
Philippines	1,000	1,000
Qatar	5,000	—
Republic of Korea	2,000	1,867
Rwanda	—	500
Sao Tome and Principe	444	535
Senegal	1,500	1,500
Seychelles	272	—
Spain	17,647	—
Sweden	111,111	164,609
Thailand	—	3,000
Trinidad and Tobago	—	672
Turkey	5,000	5,000
Uganda	2,146	403
United Kingdom	125,000	74,963
United States	500,000	239,000
Yugoslavia	4,000	4,000
Zaire	—	500
Zambia	2,451	—
Zimbabwe	—	3,030
Total	2,862,320	3,481,737

SOURCE: A/40/727 for 1985; A/CONF.132/2 for 1986.

GENERAL ASSEMBLY ACTION

On 13 December, on the recommendation of the Third Committee, the Assembly adopted **resolution 40/104** without vote.

United Nations Development Fund for Women

The General Assembly,

Recalling its resolution 39/125 of 14 December 1984, in which it decided, *inter alia*, that the activities of the Voluntary Fund for the United Nations Decade for Women should be continued through establishment of a separate and identifiable entity in autonomous association with the United Nations Development Programme,

Taking note of decision 85/33 of 29 June 1985 of the Governing Council of the United Nations Development Programme, as well as decision 85/7 of 28 June 1985, in which the Governing Council requested the Administrator of the United Nations Development Programme to develop an internal implementation strategy to strengthen the capacity of the Programme to deal with issues of women in development which, calling on the experience of the Fund, would establish verifiable objectives and a time-frame for implementation,

Recognizing the Fund's dual priorities, to serve as a catalyst with the goal of ensuring the appropriate involvement of women in mainstream development activities, as often as possible at pre-investment stages, and to support activities directly benefiting women in line with national and regional priorities,

Considering the innovative and experimental activities of the Fund directed towards strengthening both governmental and non-governmental institutional capacities to ensure access for women to development co-operation resources and their full participation at all levels in the development process,

Stressing that general questions of development and access of women to development resources have, as a common objective, the creation of conditions which will improve the quality of life for all,

Aware of the broad range of linkages of the Fund with Governments, national women's groups, non-governmental organizations and women's research in-

stitutes, besides its close co-operation with United Nations development agencies, including the regional commissions,

Reaffirming that the World Conference to Review and Appraise the Achievements of the United Nations Decade for Women: Equality, Development and Peace, in adopting the Nairobi Forward-looking Strategies for the Advancement of Women, underlined the necessity of strengthening the role of women in national and international development programmes,

Taking note of the reports of the Consultative Committee on the Fund on its seventeenth and eighteenth sessions,

Taking note also of the report of the Secretary-General,

1. *Expresses its satisfaction* that the establishment of the United Nations Development Fund for Women, in autonomous association with the United Nations Development Programme, was effected on the agreed target date of 1 July 1985, in accordance with the arrangements set out in General Assembly resolution 39/125;

2. *Approves* the name United Nations Development Fund for Women, with the acronym UNIFEM, as the new name for the Fund, as proposed by the Consultative Committee on the Fund at its seventeenth session, held from 25 to 29 March 1985, in accordance with paragraph 4 of resolution 39/125 and as reflected in the annex to that resolution;

3. *Notes with satisfaction* the steps that are being undertaken to implement resolution 39/125, as well as the commitment expressed by the Administrator of the United Nations Development Programme to ensure the appropriate involvement of women in mainstream development activities;

4. *Stresses* the need for close and continuous working relationships between the Fund, the United Nations Development Programme and those bodies, organs and organizations of the United Nations system and other agencies concerned with women's issues and development co-operation;

5. *Expresses its appreciation* for the contributions to the Fund made by Governments, intergovernmental and non-governmental organizations and individuals, which have a vital role to play in maintaining and increasing the financial viability of the Fund and the effectiveness of its work;

6. *Urges* Governments to continue and, where possible, to increase their contributions to the Fund, and calls upon those Governments that have not yet done so to consider contributing to the Fund, in order to enable the Fund to give greater support to deserving requests received for technical assistance;

7. *Requests* the Consultative Committee on the Fund to continue to monitor the process of implementing the new arrangements for the management of the Fund, as set out in the annex to resolution 39/125;

8. *Requests* the Administrator of the United Nations Development Programme to submit to the Governing Council of the Programme an annual report on the operations, management and budget of the Fund, taking into account the advice of the Consultative Committee on the Fund;

9. *Also requests* the Administrator of the United Nations Development Programme to submit to the General Assembly at its forty-first session, through the Secretary-General, a report on the activities of the Fund, in accordance with resolution 39/125.

General Assembly resolution 40/104

13 December 1985　　　　Meeting 116　　　　Adopted without vote

Approved by Third Committee (A/40/1008) without vote, 21 November (meeting 48); 32-nation draft (A/C.3/40/L.37); agenda item 92 *(c)*.
Sponsors: Australia, Bolivia, Botswana, Cameroon, Canada, Colombia, Comoros, Costa Rica, Ethiopia, Gambia, German Democratic Republic, Guyana, Honduras, India, Ivory Coast, Jamaica, Japan, Kenya, Lesotho, Mali, Morocco, Netherlands, Nigeria, Norway, Philippines, Rwanda, Senegal, Swaziland, Sweden, Uganda, United Kingdom, Zaire.
Meeting numbers. GA 40th session: 3rd Committee 24-34, 46, 48; plenary 116.

In **resolution 40/29**, the Assembly requested the Secretary-General, in implementing the programme on aging, to pay special attention to the question of elderly women, and invited UNIFEM to give due consideration to projects aimed at benefiting elderly women.

By **decision 40/470**, the Assembly suspended its fortieth session on 18 December 1985 and decided to resume it at a date to be announced to consider a number of agenda items, among which was the appointment of members of the Consultative Committee on UNIFEM.

REFERENCES

[1]*World Survey on the Role of Women in Development* (A/CONF.116/4/Rev.1) (ST/ESA/180), Sales No. E.86.IV.3. [2]YUN 1984, p. 910, GA res. 39/172, 17 Dec. 1984. [3]A/40/703 & Corr.1. [4]A/40/365. [5]A/40/16 (conclusion 1985/15). [6]GC.1/INF.6 (GC.1/Dec.29). [7]YUN 1984, p. 908. [8]DP/1985/10. [9]DP/1985/55. [10]YUN 1982, p. 1156. [11]E/1985/32 (dec. 85/7). [12]*Ibid.* (dec. 85/27). [13]YUN 1984, p. 910, GA res. 39/126, 14 Dec. 1984. [14]A/40/239/Add.1. [15]YUN 1984, p. 910. [16]E/1985/45. [17]YUN 1984, p. 893, GA res. 39/125, 14 Dec. 1984. [18]A/40/727 & Corr.1. [19]DP/1986/55. [20]DP/1985/68. [21]E/1985/32 (dec. 85/33). [22]DP/1986/6 & Corr.1. [23]DP/1986/71.

PUBLICATION

United Nations Development Fund for Women (ST/ESA/159), Sales No. E.85.IV.6.

Status of women

Research and Training Institute for the Advancement of Women

The fifth session of the Board of Trustees of the International Research and Training Institute for the Advancement of Women was held at Havana, Cuba, from 28 January to 1 February 1985.[1] In addition to reviewing the Institute's activities during 1984,[2] the Board discussed INSTRAW's participation in the 1985 World Conference (see above), progress in establishing a network of focal points and correspondents active in the field of women and development, the Institute's proposed medium-term plan for 1986-1992, and proposed fund-raising activities.

The Board adopted a series of decisions to be brought to the attention of the Economic and Social Council. With regard to the priority programme on women and international economic relations, the Board looked forward to: the reproduction of studies on the subject; publication of a consolidated report on the studies; the widest possible dissemination of the consolidated report in different languages; and the participation of Board members and IN-STRAW focal points and correspondents in that endeavour. The Board recommended that the results of INSTRAW activities continue to be disseminated as widely as possible and that its public information programme be given priority. It recommended the use of a new logo for the Institute, to be selected in a competition, with the United Nations emblem on all INSTRAW publications.

The Board decided that the balance of the IN-STRAW Trust Fund appropriations approved for the 1984-1985 biennium should be released in 1985, including the remainder of the posts approved but not authorized; it requested the Institute's Director to recruit the necessary staff, particularly local staff. The Board requested that the classification of Professional and local-level posts be re-evaluated to reflect changes in functions and that particular attention be given to upgrading the posts of Chief of Research and Training and Administrative Officer. The Director was requested to review and implement the results after approval by the United Nations Department of Administration and Management.

Recommending that the Institute promote its activities at both the Nairobi Conference and the concurrent NGO forum, the Board endorsed the proposed activities for INSTRAW's participation in the Conference.

The Board decided also to endorse activities proposed for establishing a network of focal points and correspondents, encouraged the Director to intensify related activities, endorsed the focal points already designated for co-operation with the Institute, and expressed its desire to organize a meeting of designated focal points as soon as possible.

The Board endorsed the Institute's medium-term plan (1986-1992) and recommended that activities emphasize network-building, methodological approaches related to women and development, training, and the information, documentation and communication programme, including the establishment of data banks. It further recommended that the medium-term plan reflect the outcome of the World Conference with regard to research, training and information.

The Board decided that every effort should be made to seek additional contributions to the Institute, endorsed the Director's proposals on fund-raising activities, and requested the Economic and Social Council to appeal for contributions.

In other action, the Board authorized the Director to evaluate each request for new activities in the light of the work programme and financial situation. It agreed in principle that Arabic should be one of its official languages but felt that it was not currently possible and requested a report on the proposal for its 1986 session.

ECONOMIC AND SOCIAL COUNCIL ACTION

On 31 May, the Economic and Social Council adopted **resolution 1985/45** without vote.

International Research and Training Institute for the Advancement of Women

The Economic and Social Council,

Recalling its decision 1984/124 of 24 May 1984 on the Statute of the International Research and Training Institute for the Advancement of Women,

Further recalling General Assembly resolutions 39/122 of 14 December 1984 and 39/249 of 9 April 1985,

Having considered the report of the Board of Trustees of the International Research and Training Institute for the Advancement of Women on its fifth session,

1. *Expresses its satisfaction* for the significant achievements in the programme of work of the International Research and Training Institute for the Advancement of Women;

2. *Takes note* of the decisions of the Board of Trustees contained in the report on its fifth session;

3. *Notes* the decision of the Board of Trustees by which it requested the Economic and Social Council to make an appeal for contributions from Governments and other potential donors;

4. *Appeals* to Governments and other potential donors to contribute to the Trust Fund established for the International Research and Training Institute for the Advancement of Women in view of the increasing importance of research and training for full participation of women in the development process at all levels.

Economic and Social Council resolution 1985/45

31 May 1985	Meeting 26	Adopted without vote

25-nation draft (E/1985/L.32); agenda item 5.

Sponsors: Algeria, Argentina, Bangladesh, Chile, China, Colombia, Congo, Costa Rica, Cuba, Cyprus, Dominican Republic, Ecuador, Egypt, Greece, Indonesia, Mexico, Morocco, Nigeria, Spain, Sri Lanka, Sudan, Uruguay, Venezuela, Yugoslavia, Zaire.

Meeting numbers. ESC 25, 26.

INSTRAW programme activities

In response to a 1984 General Assembly resolution,[3] the Secretary-General transmitted to the Assembly in October 1985 a report[4] prepared by INSTRAW on its programme activities. The report outlined the general methodological framework of the Institute's work in research, training and information, documentation and communication, and its method of implementation.

The report also presented information on IN-STRAW's work programme in 1984-1985. The Institute had worked closely with the United Nations Statistical Office to improve statistics, indicators and data on the situation of women. In co-operation with the Economic Commission for Europe, it held an expert meeting on statistics and indicators on the role and situation of women (Geneva, 11-14 March), attended by participants from 18 countries and a number of United Nations bodies and other inter-

national organizations. In collaboration with the Economic Commission for Africa and the Statistical Office, a subregional seminar met to discuss improved statistics and indicators for women in development (Harare, Zimbabwe, 29 April–7 May), attended by 45 participants from 15 countries. A subregional seminar on statistical analysis of the situation of women in the labour market through household surveys, organized with the Economic Commission for Latin America and the Caribbean (Montevideo, Uruguay, 3-6 June), was attended by 25 participants from 10 countries. As part of a joint, long-term project on households, gender and age, INSTRAW and the United Nations University met in February at Santo Domingo, Dominican Republic, to review four studies. A workshop on social indicators for Dominican women was held by the Dominican Republic's National Office of Statistics and INSTRAW (Santo Domingo, 6-10 May).

The report also contained information about the Institute's work on women and international economic relations, implementation of policies of individual and collective self-reliance, water supply and sanitation, industrial development, new and renewable sources of energy, food systems, training and fellowships, and documentation and communication.

The Institute's work programme was financed entirely by voluntary contributions. Assets as at 30 June 1985 amounted to $2,509,519, while resources available were $2,302,368.

CONTRIBUTIONS TO INSTRAW, 1985 AND 1986

(as at 31 December 1985; in US dollar equivalent)

Country	1985 payment	1986 pledge
Argentina	10,000	5,000
Austria	7,000	7,000
Brazil	3,000	—
Cameroon	—	1,305
China	10,000	10,000
Cyprus	500	500
Denmark	50,000	—
Egypt	—	1,000
France	52,632	66,876
Greece	2,500	2,500
Guinea-Bissau	106	—
India	3,870	—
Indonesia	—	5,000
Jamaica	184	—
Madagascar	—	401
Malta	100	—
Mexico	5,758	5,758
Nigeria	—	5,000
Norway	272,691	331,126
Pakistan	4,229	42,222
Philippines	1,000	1,000
Senegal	—	2,000
Spain	27,207	35,204
Thailand	3,000	—
Trinidad and Tobago	1,000	672
Tunisia	—	3,871
Turkey	4,996	5,000
Yugoslavia	1,224	1,034
Zaire	—	500
Total	460,997	532,969

SOURCE: Interim United Nations financial statements for the 12-month period of the biennium 1984-1985 ended 31 December 1985: schedules of individual trust funds.

GENERAL ASSEMBLY ACTION

On 29 November 1985, on the recommendation of the Third Committee, the Assembly adopted **resolution 40/38** without vote.

International Research and Training Institute for the Advancement of Women

The General Assembly,

Recalling its resolutions 37/56 of 3 December 1982, 38/104 of 16 December 1983 and 39/122 of 14 December 1984, as well as Economic and Social Council resolution 1985/45 of 31 May 1985,

Taking note with satisfaction of the report of the International Research and Training Institute for the Advancement of Women on its activities,

Taking note with interest of the Institute's mode of operation, through the use of networks, in carrying out its functions at the international, regional and national levels,

Recognizing the importance of research, training and information activities for the increased participation of women in the development process at all levels,

Recognizing also the importance of research, training and information activities for the implementation of the Nairobi Forward-looking Strategies for the Advancement of Women,

1. *Requests* the International Research and Training Institute for the Advancement of Women to strengthen its activities in research and training for the formulation of policy analysis, planning and programming relevant to the increased participation of women in development, especially its activities in statistics, indicators and data relevant to women, in particular in the developing countries, at the national and regional levels;

2. *Also requests* the Institute to give particular emphasis in its programme of activities to innovative methodological approaches related to women and development in research, training and information programmes;

3. *Calls upon* competent institutions and organizations within and outside the United Nations system to continue their collaboration with the Institute by strengthening the network of co-operative arrangements related to programmes concerning women and development;

4. *Invites* States, intergovernmental and non-governmental organizations to contribute to the United Nations Trust Fund for the International Research and Training Institute for the Advancement of Women, in view of the long-term projection for the work of the Institute;

5. *Requests* the Secretary-General to submit to the General Assembly at its forty-second session a report on the activities of the Institute;

6. *Decides* to include in the provisional agenda of its forty-second session the item entitled "International Research and Training Institute for the Advancement of Women".

General Assembly resolution 40/38

29 November 1985   Meeting 96   Adopted without vote

Approved by Third Committee (A/40/926) without vote, 21 November (meeting 49); 52-nation draft (A/C.3/40/L.30); agenda item 99.
Sponsors: Algeria, Angola, Argentina, Austria, Bahamas, Bangladesh, Barbados, Bolivia, Bulgaria, Burkina Faso, Cameroon, Central African Republic, Chile, China, Colombia, Comoros, Congo, Costa Rica, Cuba, Cyprus, Denmark, Dominican Republic, Ecuador, Equatorial Guinea, Fiji, France, Greece, Guatemala, Guinea-

Bissau, India, Indonesia, Jamaica, Japan, Mali, Mexico, Morocco, Nicaragua, Nigeria, Norway, Pakistan, Peru, Philippines, Senegal, Spain, Sri Lanka, Sudan, Swaziland, Trinidad and Tobago, Uruguay, Venezuela, Yugoslavia, Zaire.
Meeting numbers. GA 40th session: 3rd Committee 24-34, 49; plenary 96.

INSTRAW statute

At its resumed thirty-ninth session, which took place from 9 to 12 April 1985, the General Assembly took up the question of the statute of INSTRAW which had been approved by the Economic and Social Council in 1984.[5]

On 9 April, the Assembly, on the recommendation of the Fifth (Administrative and Budgetary) Committee, adopted **resolution 39/249** without vote.

Statute of the International Research and Training Institute for the Advancement of Women

The General Assembly,

Having considered the statute of the International Research and Training Institute for the Advancement of Women, which was approved by the Economic and Social Council in its decision 1984/124 of 24 May 1984, and the related report of the Advisory Committee on Administrative and Budgetary Questions,

1. *Concurs* with the observations of the Advisory Committee on Administrative and Budgetary Questions;

2. *Endorses* the statute of the International Research and Training Institute for the Advancement of Women.

General Assembly resolution 39/249

9 April 1985   Meeting 106   Adopted without vote

Approved by Fifth Committee (A/39/613) without objection, 24 October 1984 (meeting 16); draft orally proposed by Chairman; agenda items 12 and 92.

Women and society

On 13 December, the General Assembly, on the recommendation of the Third Committee, adopted **resolution 40/101** without vote.

The role of women in society

The General Assembly,

Reaffirming the objectives of the United Nations Decade for Women: Equality, Development and Peace, as well as the importance of the Declaration of Mexico on the Equality of Women and their Contribution to Development and Peace, 1975, the World Plan of Action for the Implementation of the Objectives of the International Women's Year and the Programme of Action for the Second Half of the United Nations Decade for Women,

Welcoming the results of the World Conference to Review and Appraise the Achievements of the United Nations Decade for Women: Equality, Development and Peace, held at Nairobi from 15 to 26 July 1985, in particular the adoption of the Nairobi Forward-looking Strategies for the Advancement of Women,

Noting that just and lasting peace and social progress, as well as the establishment of a new international economic order, require the active participation of women in promoting international peace and co-operation and in the process of development,

Bearing in mind that economic inequality, colonialism, racism, racial discrimination, *apartheid*, foreign intervention, occupation, alien domination and terrorism in all its forms, acts of aggression and interference in the internal affairs of others and violations of human rights and fundamental freedoms constitute an impediment to the achievement of real and genuine equality and to the integration of women in society,

Convinced of the necessity to secure for all women full realization of the rights embodied in the Convention on the Elimination of All Forms of Discrimination against Women, in the International Covenants on Human Rights and in other relevant instruments in this field,

Recognizing that the achievement of equal and full participation of women in all spheres of activities constitutes an inseparable part of the political, economic, social and cultural development of all countries,

Aware that efforts to promote the status of women in all its aspects and their complete integration in society go beyond the problem of legal equality and that deeper structural transformations of society and changes in present-day economic relations, as well as elimination of traditional prejudices through education and dissemination of information, are required so as to create conditions for women to develop fully their intellectual and physical capacities and to participate actively in the decision-making process in political, economic, social and cultural development,

Mindful of the necessity to enlarge the possibilities for both men and women to combine parental duties and household work with paid employment and social activities,

Aware that the role of women in childbearing should not be the cause of inequality and discrimination, and that child rearing demands shared responsibilities among women, men and society as a whole,

Deeply appreciating the increasing participation of women in political, economic, social and cultural life and their contribution thereto,

1. *Appeals* to all Governments, international organizations and non-governmental organizations to recognize in their activities the importance of all inter-related aspects of the role of women in society—as mothers, as participants in economic development and as participants in public life—without underestimating any one of them;

2. *Calls upon* all Governments to encourage such social and economic development that would secure the participation of women in all spheres of work, equal pay for work of equal value and equal opportunities for education and for professional and vocational training, taking into consideration the necessity of combining all aspects of the role of women in society;

3. *Appeals* to Governments, international organizations and non-governmental organizations to promote conditions that would enable women to participate as equal partners with men in public and political life, in the decision-making process at all levels and in the management of different spheres of life in society;

4. *Calls upon* Governments to recognize the special status and social importance of motherhood and to take, in the context of their specific abilities and conditions, all necessary measures to promote its protection, including maternity leave with pay, and to provide security for their jobs as long as necessary, so as to allow women, if they so wish, to fulfil their role as mothers without prejudice to their professional and public activities;

5. *Appeals* to Governments to promote the establishment of appropriate facilities for child-care and education of children as a means of combining parenthood with economic, political, social, cultural and other ac-

tivities and thus to provide assistance to women in integrating fully into their societies;

6. *Decides* to consider the question of the role of women in society at its forty-first session under an item entitled "Forward-looking strategies for the advancement of women to the year 2000".

General Assembly resolution 40/101

13 December 1985   Meeting 116   Adopted without vote

Approved by Third Committee (A/40/1008) without vote, 19 November (meeting 46); 9-nation draft (A/C.3/40/L.28/Rev.1), orally amended by Pakistan and Colombia; agenda item 92.
Sponsors: Argentina, Bulgaria, Burkina Faso, Cuba, German Democratic Republic, Mongolia, Nigeria, Viet Nam, Zambia.
Meeting numbers. GA 40th session: 3rd Committee 24-34, 46; plenary 116.

Women and peace

On 13 December 1985, on the recommendation of the Third Committee, the General Assembly adopted **resolution 40/102** without vote.

Participation of women in promoting international peace and co-operation

The General Assembly,

Confirming the noble goal enshrined in the Charter of the United Nations to maintain peace and security in the world and the determination of the States Members of the United Nations expressed therein to save present and succeeding generations from the scourge of war,

Recalling that the World Conference to Review and Appraise the Achievements of the United Nations Decade for Women: Equality, Development and Peace, held at Nairobi from 15 to 26 July 1985, in adopting the Nairobi Forward-looking Strategies for the Advancement of Women, underlined the importance of the participation of women in promoting international peace and co-operation,

Convinced that the International Year of Peace, proclaimed for the year 1986 by the General Assembly in its resolution 40/3 of 24 October 1985, could give new impulses for safeguarding international peace and security,

Reaffirming its resolution 37/63 of 3 December 1982, by which it proclaimed the Declaration on the Participation of Women in Promoting International Peace and Co-operation,

Recalling its resolution 39/124 of 14 December 1984, in which it requested the Commission on the Status of Women to consider what measures might be necessary in order to implement the Declaration,

Wishing to encourage the active participation of women in promoting international peace and security and co-operation,

Convinced that increased efforts are required to eliminate still existing forms of discrimination against women in every field of human endeavour,

Conscious of the need to implement the provisions of the Declaration,

1. *Pledges its determination* to encourage the full participation of women in the economic, social, cultural, civil and political affairs of society and in the endeavour to promote international peace and co-operation;

2. *Appeals* to all Governments to take the necessary measures for putting into practice the principles and provisions of the Declaration on the Participation of Women in Promoting International Peace and Co-operation;

3. *Invites* all Governments to give wide publicity to the Declaration and its implementation;

4. *Requests* the Secretary-General to continue to take adequate steps to ensure that publicity is given to the Declaration;

5. *Invites* the United Nations Educational, Scientific and Cultural Organization, the World Health Organization and other appropriate bodies within the United Nations system to consider adequate measures to implement the Declaration;

6. *Requests* the Commission on the Status of Women to consider measures which may be necessary to implement the Declaration in the context of the Nairobi Forward-looking Strategies for the Advancement of Women for the period up to the year 2000;

7. *Decides* to consider the further implementation of the Declaration at its forty-first session, as a sub-item of an item entitled "Forward-looking strategies for the advancement of women to the year 2000".

General Assembly resolution 40/102

13 December 1985   Meeting 116   Adopted without vote

Approved by Third Committee (A/40/1008) without vote, 21 November (meeting 48); 21-nation draft (A/C.3/40/L.33); agenda item 92.
Sponsors: Afghanistan, Angola, Bulgaria, Congo, Cuba, Czechoslovakia, Democratic Yemen, Ethiopia, Gambia, German Democratic Republic, Hungary, Iraq, Lao People's Democratic Republic, Madagascar, Mali, Mongolia, Nicaragua, Nigeria, Poland, Ukrainian SSR, Viet Nam.
Meeting numbers. GA 40th session: 3rd Committee 24-34, 46, 48; plenary 116.

Women under *apartheid*

In its annual report to the General Assembly,[6] the Special Committee against *Apartheid* (see also p. 127) stated that it had organized, in co-operation with the United Republic of Tanzania and the Organization of African Unity (OAU), an International Conference on Women and Children under *Apartheid* (Arusha, United Republic of Tanzania, 7-10 May). A mission of the Special Committee to Angola, Zambia and the United Republic of Tanzania, from 3 to 16 April, preceded the Conference, consulting with Governments and liberation movements and visiting refugee camps. The mission's report was the main document before the Conference.

The Conference was convened to publicize the plight of women and children under *apartheid*, promote moral and material assistance to them in their struggle for liberation and contribute to the July World Conference on the Decade for Women (see above). By a 15 May letter,[7] the Acting Chairman of the Special Committee transmitted, for forwarding to the World Conference, the text of the Declaration adopted by the World Conference on 9 May.

The Conference considered the plight of women and children in South Africa and Namibia and their struggle for national liberation, measures to promote international assistance to them and action to demonstrate solidarity with them in their legitimate struggle. The Conference reiterated that *apartheid* was a crime against humanity and an intolerable affront to the conscience of mankind,

commended the peoples of South Africa and Namibia on their heroic resistance, and condemned the massacres, killings and other atrocities against the oppressed people of South Africa, as well as forced removals which had driven millions of people, mostly women and children, off their ancestral lands and deprived them of their South African nationality. The Conference condemned the Pretoria régime for subjecting women and children to oppression and humiliation, for separating families, and for killing, imprisoning, restricting and torturing women and children for opposing *apartheid*. The Conference also: condemned the manipulation of "family planning" by the South African Government; was appalled that the majority of refugees in neighbouring countries consisted of women and children fleeing the *apartheid* system; urged countries to grant asylum, food, shelter, medical care, legal protection and guarantee of fundamental human rights, counselling, education, training and employment to women and children from southern Africa; and stressed that the 1985 World Conference should focus on women in South Africa and Namibia in the light of the Decade's themes.

In addition, the Conference called for intensified support for the women and children of South Africa and Namibia and in front-line States, in particular: wide dissemination of information on the situation of women and children in South Africa; national campaigns for the unconditional release of political prisoners there; regional and national meetings on the plight of women and children under *apartheid*; increased contributions to funds supporting the oppressed people of South Africa; financial assistance to women in the national liberation movements to enable them to attend major international conferences and seminars and undertake speaking tours; and activities of the southern African liberation movements recognized by OAU.

The Conference encouraged the Special Committee and the International Committee of Solidarity with the Struggle of Women of South Africa and Namibia to redouble their efforts to promote publicity and assistance, and appealed to Governments and organizations to lend them full co-operation.

By a 26 February 1985 resolution,[8] the Commission on Human Rights expressed its indignation at the continued violations of human rights in South Africa, particularly the continued adverse effects on women and children of the policies of *apartheid*.

In accordance with a 1981 General Assembly resolution,[9] the Special Committee against *Apartheid* observed 9 August as the International Day of Solidarity with the Struggle of Women of South Africa and Namibia.

In July, the World Conference had before it a report[10] of the Secretary-General on the situation of women and children living under racist minority régimes. The report appraised the political, social and economic aspects of women living under *apartheid*, gave accounts of recent activities to promote awareness of their plight and contained information on assistance provided by United Nations organizations, specialized agencies and NGOs.

By **resolution 40/25** of 29 November 1985, the General Assembly demanded the immediate release of women and children detained in Namibia and South Africa.

Women and population

As a follow-up to the 1984 Conference on Population,[11] whose Declaration emphasized the positive influence on family life and size of improving the status of women, the Economic and Social Council, on the recommendation of its First (Economic) Committee, adopted **resolution 1985/6**, without vote, on 28 May 1985.

Status and role of women and population

The Economic and Social Council,

Considering that the World Conference to Review and Appraise the Achievements of the United Nations Decade for Women: Equality, Development and Peace is scheduled to be held at Nairobi from 15 to 26 July 1985,

Recalling that the International Conference on Population, in its recommendations for the further implementation of the World Population Plan of Action, identified the role and status of women as an area of priority action in the field of population,

Recalling also that the Mexico City Declaration on Population and Development emphasized the fact that the improvement of the status of women and the enhancement of their role were important goals in themselves and that the achievement of those goals would influence family life and size in a positive way,

Recalling further General Assembly resolution 39/228 of 18 December 1984, in which the Assembly, *inter alia*, reaffirmed the importance attached to the formulation and implementation of concrete policies which would enhance the status and role of women in the area of population policies and programmes,

1. *Urges* all Governments participating in the World Conference to Review and Appraise the Achievements of the United Nations Decade for Women: Equality, Development and Peace, to incorporate fully into the forward-looking strategies for the advancement of women for the period up to the year 2000 those aspects of the Mexico City Declaration on Population and Development and the recommendations for the further implementation of the World Population Plan of Action which relate to the status and role of women in the context of population;

2. *Requests* the Secretary-General, in the framework of the ongoing monitoring, review and appraisal of progress made towards the implementation of the recommendations of the World Population Plan of Action, to focus periodically on those recommendations which

make special reference to the relation between the role and status of women and population, and to report thereon to the Economic and Social Council, through the Population Commission.

Economic and Social Council resolution 1985/6

28 May 1985   Meeting 22   Adopted without vote

Approved by First Committee (E/1985/89) without vote, 17 May (meeting 6); draft by Population Commission (E/1985/25); agenda item 10.

Prevention of prostitution

In March, the Secretary-General submitted a report[12] to the Economic and Social Council on implementation of a 1983 Council resolution[13] on suppression of traffic in persons and of the exploitation of the prostitution of others. The replies of seven Governments to a note verbale from the Secretary-General had been transmitted to the Working Group on Slavery of the Sub-Commission on Prevention of Discrimination and Protection of Minorities in 1984 and replies from a further eight Governments were considered by the Working Group at its 1985 session (Geneva, 29 July–2 August). Replies from regional commissions, specialized agencies, other United Nations organizations and an NGO to another note verbale had also been transmitted to the Working Group.

At its 1984 session, the Working Group had recommended that the 1983 Council resolution be made widely known to Member States and that they be urged to implement a national policy against violating the fundamental rights of women and children. It had also recommended that they be urged to implement social and legal measures to ensure reinsertion into society of victims of prostitution, and supported the adoption of international measures aimed at dismantling the networks that fed prostitution and repatriating and assisting their victims.

The Working Group's report was considered by the Sub-Commission in 1984,[14] which had recommended to the Commission on Human Rights that it be requested to undertake a study on slavery-like practices against women and children. It had also recommended that the struggle against procurement be intensified at the national level and reiterated the Working Group's recommendations regarding dismantling of prostitution networks and the repatriation and reinsertion into society of prostitution's victims.

In accordance with the 1983 Council resolution, United Nations agencies and organs and NGOs were invited to co-operate with the Centre for Human Rights in preparing two studies: one on the sale of children and the other on the legal and social problems of sexual minorities, including male prostitution. Action was also being taken to reproduce as a United Nations publication a 1983 report[15] on the suppression of traffic in persons and exploitation of the prostitution of others.

In an 11 March 1985 resolution,[16] the Commission on Human Rights invited States to sign or ratify the 1949 Convention for the Suppression of the Traffic in Persons and of the Exploitation of the Prostitution of Others;[17] it also recommended that the struggle against procuring be intensified, that the networks of prostitution be dismantled and that States adopt measures to ensure victims' orderly and effective reinsertion into society.

The Working Group on Slavery, at its eleventh session (Geneva, 29 July–2 August 1985),[18] recommended that all Governments ratify and implement the 1949 Convention and that strong measures be taken to ensure that women reached a social status equal to that of men and that the mass media publicize their fundamental equality.

(See also p. 872.)

GENERAL ASSEMBLY ACTION

On 13 December, on the recommendation of the Third Committee, the General Assembly adopted **resolution 40/103** without vote.

Prevention of prostitution

The General Assembly,

Having considered the report of the Special Rapporteur on the subject of the suppression of the traffic in persons and of the exploitation of the prostitution of others, prepared in pursuance of Economic and Social Council resolution 1982/20 of 4 May 1982,

Recalling its resolution 38/107 of 16 December 1983 and Economic and Social Council resolution 1983/30 of 26 May 1983, as well as the report of the World Conference to Review and Appraise the Achievements of the United Nations Decade for Women: Equality, Development and Peace,

Considering that the suppression of the traffic in persons and of the exploitation of the prostitution of others requires a threefold concerted effort, involving prevention, punishment of all forms of procuring and solidarity in order to facilitate the social rehabilitation of the victims,

1. *Congratulates* the Economic and Social Commission for Asia and the Pacific, the United Nations Educational, Scientific and Cultural Organization and the World Tourism Organization for the action they have begun to take in implementation of Economic and Social Council resolution 1983/30;

2. *Invites once again* the Economic and Social Council to consider the whole question of the suppression of the traffic in persons and of the exploitation of the prostitution of others at its first regular session of 1986 in connection with the agenda item on human rights, together with the reports requested by the Council in its resolution 1983/30;

3. *Invites* the Working Group on Slavery of the Sub-Commission on Prevention of Discrimination and Protection of Minorities to transmit its report to the Commission on the Status of Women at its next session;

4. *Requests* the Secretary-General to expedite the issuance as a United Nations document of the report on the suppression of the traffic in persons and of the exploitation of the prostitution of others prepared in pursuance of Economic and Social Council resolution 1982/20.

General Assembly resolution 40/103

13 December 1985   Meeting 116   Adopted without vote

Approved by Third Committee (A/40/1008) without vote, 21 November (meeting 48); 9-nation draft (A/C.3/40/L.36); agenda item 92 *(d)*.

Sponsors: Central African Republic, France, Germany, Federal Republic of, Honduras, Italy, Lebanon, Rwanda, Senegal, Spain.

Meeting numbers. GA 40th session: 3rd Committee 24-34, 46, 48; plenary 116.

Palestinian women

In response to a 1984 recommendation[19] of the Commission on the Status of Women acting as the Preparatory Body for the World Conference, which was approved by the Economic and Social Council in 1984,[20] the Secretary-General submitted to the Conference a report on the situation of women and children living in the occupied Arab territories and other occupied territories.[21]

The report described the effects of Israeli settlements, which had forced transfers of the indigenous Arab population from the West Bank and Gaza, and gave examples of oppressive practices such as arrest, detention, demolition of houses, imposition of curfews and other measures applied to the Palestinian population. The report also gave information on employment and working conditions, housing, education and health, and listed assistance activities being carried out by the United Nations and the specialized agencies in the political, social, economic and humanitarian spheres.

By a letter[22] of 19 March 1985 to the Secretary-General, Israel submitted a rebuttal to the Secretary-General's report. Israel's paper on Arab women and children under Israeli administration took issue with what it called the more blatant inaccuracies, mistakes and misrepresentations in the Secretary-General's report and presented the members of the Conference's Preparatory Body with supplementary material which it said might assist them in determining whether to approve the report. The paper contained information and statistics on population, legal matters, economic and social development, employment, education and health.

Refugee women

The Secretary-General submitted to the World Conference a report on the activities and programmes of the Office of the United Nations High Commissioner for Refugees (UNHCR) on behalf of refugee women.[23] The report stated that most large-scale influxes of refugees were composed largely of women and children. UNHCR tried to ensure that refugee women had equal access with men to benefits that accelerated social integration and contributed to their physical, psychological and material well-being. One of the most important problems of refugee women was the violation of their physical safety; experience had shown that a UNHCR presence in border areas and refugee camps could have a deterrent effect. The report provided information on assistance given by UNHCR to refugee women and children in the areas of health, education and employment.

The High Commissioner believed that work should continue in the following areas: securing accession of further States to the 1951 Convention relating to the Status of Refugees[24] and its 1967 Protocol,[25] which applied to all refugees, regardless of sex; ensuring that international refugee instruments provided protection to refugee women, despite social, economic or cultural constraints governing the condition of women; ensuring liberal practices by States regarding the granting of asylum, the determination of refugee status and the treatment of refugees and asylum-seekers; ensuring the physical safety of refugees, particularly women; increasing awareness of the importance of the needs of refugee women and pressing for increased funding of programmes to meet those needs; promoting self-sufficiency among refugee women by offering literacy, adult education, vocational and formal education programmes and developing their ability to participate in productive activities and income-generating projects; increasing their participation in health education and mental health programmes, supportive ethnic and communal structures and community organization activities; providing for the special needs of refugee women who were heads of families and of handicapped and disabled refugee women.

By **resolution 40/118**, the General Assembly commended the High Commissioner's programmes for refugee and displaced women, especially those undertaken to secure their protection and to help them to become self-sufficient through educational, vocational and income-generating projects.

Women in the UN Secretariat

Pursuant to the recommendations of the 1983 session[26] of the Commission on the Status of Women that were endorsed by a 1983 Economic and Social Council decision[27] and General Assembly resolution,[28] a report[29] of the Secretary-General on progress achieved and obstacles encountered with regard to the employment and advancement of women within the United Nations system during the United Nations Decade for Women was submitted to the World Conference. The information was based on replies to a questionnaire sent to the organizations of the system and reflected the situation that prevailed from 1976 to 1983. Data received were tabulated for 31 December 1975, the beginning of the Decade, 31 December 1979, the mid-point, and 31 December 1983, towards the end of the Decade. It was noted that incompleteness of responses limited the analysis and the conclusions that could be reached.

The report concluded that efforts made during the Decade had produced some positive results, such as a higher overall percentage of women employed in the secretariats of most organizations. For the most part, however, the increase had been slight or negligible at the higher levels. The executive heads of some organizations had indicated a serious commitment to equality of female and male staff. In some cases, institutional measures, such as appointing a coordinator, designating a focal point or establishing a panel or board, had been taken. As the Decade drew to a close, it appeared that earlier initiatives either had not been sustained or had not been very effective; most targets had not been met. It appeared that bolder strategies were required.

By **resolution 40/258 B**, the General Assembly welcomed the Secretary-General's efforts to improve the status of women in the Secretariat, requested him to increase the number of women in geographical posts to achieve an overall participation rate of 30 per cent by 1990, and to report in 1986 on progress. The Assembly reiterated its request to Member States to nominate more women candidates in the Professional category.

By **resolution 40/105**, the Assembly invited the regional commissions to propose measures for incorporating women's concerns in their work programmes for 1988-1989. The Secretary-General was requested to report on their proposals, to take into account the regional commissions' role in promoting the advancement of women when formulating the system-wide medium-term plan for women and development and when implementing the Forward-looking Strategies, and to report in 1986 on progress made in implementing its 1984 resolution[30] on senior women's programme officers posts at the regional commissions.

REFERENCES

[1]E/1985/44. [2]YUN 1984, p. 900. [3]YUN 1984, p. 901, GA res. 39/122, 14 Dec. 1984. [4]A/40/707. [5]YUN 1984, p. 902. ESC dec. 1984/124, 24 May 1984. [6]A/40/22-S/17562. [7]A/40/319-S/17197. [8]E/1985/22 (res. 1985/8). [9]YUN 1981, p. 199, GA res. 36/172 K, 17 Dec. 1981. [10]A/CONF.116/7. [11]YUN 1984, p. 715. [12]E/1985/46. [13]YUN 1983, p. 918, ESC res. 1983/30, 26 May 1983. [14]YUN 1984, p. 829. [15]YUN 1983, p. 917. [16]E/1985/22 (res. 1985/25). [17]YUN 1948-49, p. 613, GA res. 317(IV), annex, 2 Dec. 1949. [18]E/CN.4/Sub.2/1985/25. [19]YUN 1984, p. 890. [20]YUN 1984, p. 891, ESC dec. 1984/125, 24 May 1984. [21]A/CONF.116/6. [22]A/40/188-E/1985/60. [23]A/CONF.116/11. [24]YUN 1951, p. 520. [25]YUN 1967, p. 769. [26]YUN 1983, p. 908. [27]*Ibid.*, ESC dec. 1983/132, 26 May 1983. [28]*Ibid.*, p. 909, GA res. 38/108, 16 Dec. 1983. [29]A/CONF.116/8 & Corr.1. [30]YUN 1984, p. 1171, GA res. 39/127, 14 Dec. 1984.

Convention on Discrimination against Women

The Committee on the Elimination of Discrimination against Women, established in 1982[1] under the Convention on the Elimination of All Forms of Discrimination against Women, adopted in 1979,[2] held its fourth session at Vienna from 21 January to 1 February 1985.[3]

The Committee had before it six initial reports of States parties on legislative, judicial, administrative and other measures they had adopted to give effect to the Convention, which had entered into force in 1981.[4] The Committee considered the reports of Austria, Bulgaria, Canada, Panama and Yugoslavia; it was unable to discuss El Salvador's report due to the absence of that country's representative.

CEDAW recommended to the Economic and Social Council that adequate funds and staff be made available to provide services for its effective functioning and that the standard of travel accorded to members be commensurate with that provided to comparable committees of experts.

The Committee also discussed its contribution to the 1985 World Conference, and agreed to use as a basis for its report a compendium of information based on national reports on the achievements and obstacles experienced in implementing the Convention. It agreed to recommend to the Economic and Social Council that its report should be placed on the Conference's agenda and that the Council should invite the CEDAW Chairperson to present the report, and decided to request the Secretary-General to facilitate the Chairperson's attendance. CEDAW decided that its 1986 session would be held in New York and its 1987 session at Vienna.

In its report to the World Conference,[5] CEDAW noted that, although 52 States parties should have submitted their initial reports by the end of December 1984, only 26 of them had been received. It appealed to States parties to present their reports in due time. Based on information provided in the reports of 18 States parties and during Committee sessions, the report discussed: general measures to guarantee equality of women and men and prohibit discrimination on the ground of sex; measures to provide equal rights for women in political and public life; equal rights in education and employment; equal access to health care services, including family planning and services for pregnant women; legal equality in areas of economic and social life; measures to ensure application of the Convention to women in rural areas; equality of women and men before the law; and rights pertaining to marriage and family relations.

ECONOMIC AND SOCIAL COUNCIL ACTION

On 28 May 1985, the Economic and Social Council adopted **resolution 1985/18** without vote.

Convention on the Elimination of All Forms of Discrimination against Women

Recalling General Assembly resolution 34/180 of 18 December 1979, by which the Assembly adopted the Convention on the Elimination of All Forms of Discrimination against Women annexed thereto,

Recalling also General Assembly resolutions 35/140 of 11 December 1980, 36/131 of 14 December 1981, 37/64 of 3 December 1982, 38/109 of 16 December 1983 and 39/130 of 14 December 1984, and Economic and Social Council resolutions 1983/1 of 17 May 1983, 1984/8 of 22 May 1984 and 1984/10 of 24 May 1984,

Having considered the report of the Committee on the Elimination of Discrimination against Women on its fourth session, notably the recommendation concerning the submitting of the report of the Committee on the achievements of and obstacles experienced by States parties in the implementation of the Convention,

1. *Urges* all States that have not yet ratified or acceded to the Convention on the Elimination of All Forms of Discrimination against Women to do so as soon as possible, taking into account the World Conference to Review and Appraise the Achievements of the United Nations Decade for Women: Equality, Development and Peace to be held at Nairobi from 15 to 26 July 1985;

2. *Takes note* of the report of the Committee on the Elimination of Discrimination against Women on its fourth session;

3. *Emphasizes* the importance of the strictest compliance by States parties with their obligations under the Convention on the Elimination of All Forms of Discrimination against Women;

4. *Urges* States parties to make all possible efforts to submit their initial implementation reports in accordance with article 18 of the Convention and requests the Committee in organizing its work to ensure that the reports of States parties are adequately reviewed within the quadrennial cycle envisaged;

5. *Requests* the Secretary-General to ensure that the report of the Committee on the achievements of and obstacles experienced by States parties in the implementation of the Convention is considered in connection with the relevant agenda item at the World Conference to Review and Appraise the Achievements of the United Nations Decade for Women: Equality, Development and Peace;

6. *Also requests* the Secretary-General to make all efforts to ensure adequate servicing for the effective functioning of the Committee on the Elimination of Discrimination against Women as a treaty body of the United Nations;

7. *Takes note once again* of the deliberations of the Committee at its third session concerning the inclusion in the agenda of a future session of an item on ways and means of implementing article 21 of the Convention, which provides that the Committee may make suggestions and general recommendations based on the examination of reports;

8. *Requests* the Secretary-General to transmit the report of the Committee on the Elimination of Discrimination against Women to the General Assembly at its fortieth

session, as well as to the Commission on the Status of Women, for information.

Economic and Social Council resolution 1985/18

28 May 1985   Meeting 22   Adopted without vote

13-nation draft (E/1985/L.28), orally revised; agenda item 4.
Sponsors: Australia, Bulgaria, Canada, China, Costa Rica, Ecuador, German Democratic Republic, Greece, Iceland, Mexico, Portugal, Rwanda, Sweden.
Meeting numbers. ESC 20, 22.

GENERAL ASSEMBLY ACTION

On 29 November 1985, on the recommendation of the Third Committee, the General Assembly adopted **resolution 40/39** without vote.

Convention on the Elimination of All Forms of Discrimination against Women

The General Assembly,

Bearing in mind that one of the purposes of the United Nations, as stated in Articles 1 and 55 of the Charter, is to promote universal respect for human rights and fundamental freedoms for all without distinction of any kind, including distinction as to sex,

Reaffirming that women and men should participate equally in social, economic and political development, should contribute equally to such development and should share equally in improved conditions of life,

Recalling its resolution 34/180 of 18 December 1979, by which it adopted the Convention on the Elimination of All Forms of Discrimination against Women,

Recalling also its resolutions 35/140 of 11 December 1980, 36/131 of 14 December 1981, 37/64 of 3 December 1982, 38/109 of 16 December 1983 and 39/130 of 14 December 1984,

Taking note of the report of the Secretary-General on the status of the Convention,

Having considered the report of the Committee on the Elimination of Discrimination against Women on the work of its fourth session,

1. *Notes with appreciation* the increasing number of Member States that have ratified or acceded to the Convention on the Elimination of All Forms of Discrimination against Women;

2. *Urges* all States that have not yet ratified or acceded to the Convention to do so as soon as possible, taking into account the World Conference to Review and Appraise the Achievements of the United Nations Decade for Women: Equality, Development and Peace, held at Nairobi from 15 to 26 July 1985;

3. *Requests* the Secretary-General to submit annually to the General Assembly a report on the status of the Convention;

4. *Takes note* of the report of the Committee on the Elimination of Discrimination against Women on the work of its fourth session;

5. *Emphasizes* the importance of the strictest compliance by States parties with their obligations under the Convention;

6. *Urges* States parties to make all possible efforts to submit their initial implementation reports in accordance with article 18 of the Convention and the guidelines of the Committee, and requests the Committee, in organizing its work, to ensure that the reports of States parties are adequately reviewed within the quadrennial cycle envisaged in the Convention;

7. *Requests* the Secretary-General to make all efforts to ensure adequate servicing for the effective functioning of the Committee as a treaty body of the United Nations;

8. *Takes note once again* of the discussion in the Committee, at its third session, concerning the inclusion in the agenda of a future session of an item on ways and means of implementing article 21 of the Convention, which provides that the Committee may make suggestions and general recommendations based on the examination of reports;

9. *Requests* the Secretary-General to transmit the report of the Committee on the Elimination of Discrimination against Women to the Commission on the Status of Women, for information.

General Assembly resolution 40/39

29 November 1985   Meeting 96   Adopted without vote

Approved by Third Committee (A/40/927) without vote, 21 November (meeting 49); 40-nation draft (A/C.3/40/L.35); agenda item 100.
Sponsors: Australia, Austria, Bulgaria, Canada, China, Colombia, Comoros, Costa Rica, Cuba, Denmark, Ecuador, Egypt, Ethiopia, Finland, France, German Democratic Republic, Greece, Hungary, Iceland, Indonesia, Jamaica, Japan, Liberia, Mexico, Nepal, Nigeria, Norway, Peru, Philippines, Poland, Portugal, Rwanda, Spain, Sri Lanka, Swaziland, Sweden, Thailand, Uruguay, Viet Nam, Yugoslavia.
Meeting numbers. GA 40th session: 3rd Committee 24-34, 49; plenary 96.

Ratifications, accessions and signatures

As at 31 December 1985, the Convention on the Elimination of All Forms of Discrimination against Women had received 93 signatures and 84 ratifications or accessions. During the year, it was signed by Mali and Trinidad and Tobago and ratified or acceded to by Argentina, Belgium, Cyprus, the Federal Republic of Germany, Guinea-Bissau, Iceland, Ireland, Italy, Japan, Mali, New Zealand, Nigeria, Saint Christopher and Nevis, Senegal, Thailand, Tunisia, Turkey, Uganda, the United Republic of Tanzania, and Zambia.

In September 1985, the Secretary-General submitted to the General Assembly his annual report on the status of the Convention,[6] containing information on signatures, ratifications or accessions to the Convention as at 23 August 1985 and the texts of reservations, declarations and objections made between 9 July 1984 and 23 August 1985.

By **resolution 40/39**, the Assembly noted with appreciation the increasing number of Member States that had ratified or acceded to the Convention, urged others to do so as soon as possible, and requested the Secretary-General to submit annually a report on the Convention's status.

REFERENCES
(1)YUN 1982, p. 1149. (2)YUN 1979, p. 895, GA res. 34/180, annex, 18 Dec. 1979. (3)A/40/45. (4)YUN 1981, p. 994. (5)A/CONF.116/13. (6)A/40/623.

Chapter XX

Children, youth and aging persons

With 15 million children under the age of five dying each year, reducing infant and child mortality rates remained an imperative for the United Nations in 1985. Some 1.4 billion children, mainly in the developing countries of Africa, Asia, Latin America and the Mediterranean area, were provided with life's basic necessities by the Organization during the year, primarily through the United Nations Children's Fund (UNICEF). Through two UNICEF programmes alone (immunization and oral rehydration), more than a million children who would not otherwise have survived were alive at year's end. The General Assembly urged intensified efforts to attain the objectives relating to children in the International Development Strategy for the Third United Nations Development Decade (the 1980s). It also took action aimed at having the draft Declaration relating to the protection of children, especially regarding fostering, adopted in 1986.

The commemoration of International Youth Year (IYY) was the highlight of 1985 youth activities during which the United Nations World Conference for IYY—a series of Assembly meetings—adopted guidelines representing a global strategy for future work concerning youth.

The first review of the 1982 International Plan of Action on Aging took place in 1985. After the review had identified priorities for action, the Assembly and the Economic and Social Council urged that priority attention be given to the question of aging and that the United Nations Trust Fund for Aging be strengthened.

Topics related to this chapter. Human rights: rights of the child; youth and human rights; human rights of aging persons. Women: women and children under *apartheid*. Refugees. Social and cultural development: crime prevention.

Children

Assistance for children in 118 countries—in Africa, Asia, Latin America and the Mediterranean area—was provided by UNICEF during 1985 with the help of other United Nations bodies, and covered such areas as health services, social welfare, nutrition, education, water supply and sanitation, and emergency relief. UNICEF continued to support a variety of low-cost programmes aimed at improving children's health

and reducing child mortality and morbidity. Of grave concern was the situation of children and their families in many African countries, particularly in the sub-Saharan region.

The General Assembly, in resolution 40/210, urged that UNICEF's fortieth anniversary in 1986 be observed by intensified efforts towards attaining the goals of the International Development Strategy for the Third United Nations Development Decade (the 1980s),[1] which stressed children's immunization against major diseases by 1990 and which aimed at reducing the infant mortality rate to under 50 per 1,000 live births in all countries by the year 2000.

The Assembly, in decision 40/422, requested the Sixth (Legal) Committee to consult informally in 1986 with a view to adopting the draft Declaration on Social and Legal Principles relating to the Protection and Welfare of Children, with Special Reference to Foster Placement and Adoption, Nationally and Internationally.

UN Children's Fund

In 1985, UNICEF co-operated in programmes in 118 countries, with a child population under 16 years of age of approximately 1.4 billion. Total expenditure amounted to $390 million; $279 million of this was for programmes, or an average expenditure of 20 cents per child. Support was given to health services in 110 countries, social welfare services in 104, nutrition and non-formal education in 100, water supply and sanitation in 93, formal education in 92, and emergency relief in 30. Of the total programme expenditure, 30 per cent was spent for health, 21 per cent for water supply and sanitation, 13 per cent for emergency relief, 7 per cent for formal education, 6 per cent for nutrition, 5 per cent for social welfare services and 4 per cent for non-formal education.

The UNICEF Executive Board held its regular 1985 session in New York from 15 to 26 April. It also met on 11 and 14 June to elect officers for the period 1 August 1985 to 31 July 1986. The Board's report,[2] taken note of by the Economic and Social Council in **decision 1985/186**, was considered by the Council in connection with operational activities for development (see Chapter II of this section). The Programme Committee met from 19 to 22 April 1985 and the Committee on Administration and Finance from 23 to 25 April.

The dominant concerns throughout the Board's deliberations were the severity of the situation of children and families in many African countries, the need to strengthen UNICEF actions there and the need to accelerate the implementation of child survival and development actions.

Programme policy decisions

At its 1985 session,[2] the Executive Board reviewed UNICEF's performance in 1984, endorsed an emergency assistance programme for several African countries, approved initiatives to accelerate child survival and development actions, particularly towards achieving by 1990 universal immunization of children against their six major communicable diseases (diphtheria, pertussis, tetanus, measles, poliomyelitis, tuberculosis). It also adopted a comprehensive policy framework for UNICEF programmes concerning women, acted to improve the Board's administration and role and approved UNICEF revised budget estimates for 1984-1985 as well as 1986-1987 estimates.

The Board approved general resource commitments totalling $303 million and "noted" projects in the amount of $223.2 million for financing through specific-purpose contributions. It also endorsed the UNICEF emergency programme in Africa.

As a result of the Board's action, UNICEF would be assisting projects in 117 countries: 43 in Africa, 26 in the Americas, 37 in Asia and 11 in the Middle East and northern Africa.

On the recommendation of the Programme Committee, the Board approved for follow-up the conclusions of the twenty-fifth session (Geneva, 28-30 January 1985) of the UNICEF/WHO Joint Committee on Health Policy and endorsed its support for actions towards the 1990 goal of universal immunization.

A working group, established by the Board in 1984 to examine the Board's future work and procedures and ways of improving the use of the secretariat's limited resources in preparing for Board sessions, made recommendations calling for, among other things, preparation and submission to the Board of UNICEF-assisted country programmes with longer programming cycles, bearing in mind the need to maintain and strengthen mid-term reviews and corrections of UNICEF country programmes. The Board renewed the Group's mandate and approved its recommendations.

Medium-term plan for 1984-1988

In April 1985,[2] the Executive Board approved the UNICEF 1984-1988 medium-term plan.[3] The Board stressed the importance of ensuring that child survival and development actions were integrated with other UNICEF efforts and implemented within the primary health care framework and basic services strategy. It also supported efforts in all developing countries to protect mothers and children through structural adjustment measures.

In approving the medium-term plan, the Board authorized new programme recommendations totalling $190 million to be presented at its 1986 session. It also approved the financial objectives contained in the medium-term plan, projecting that UNICEF income would increase from $390 million in 1985 to $470 million in 1988, while annual expenditure would increase from $372 million to $448 million.

Policy review: women's concerns

A policy review paper on UNICEF's response to women's concerns[4] was considered by the Board at its 1985 session. The role of women in the current world situation and the relationship between the health and well-being of women and children were underscored. New guidelines were developed for including women as integral parts of programming. Support was expressed for extending UNICEF policy beyond the mother/child relationship to include the economic role of women. Increased emphasis was placed on income-generation, exploring potential markets and providing access to technical expertise and management skills and the availability of easier channels and terms of credit for productive activities by disadvantaged women. A positive aspect of the year's experience was the strengthening of the linkage, conceptually and operationally, between health, nutrition, literacy, training, credit and economic activity in women's programmes.

The Board, which supported the paper's recommendations, noted, among other things, that an improvement in the general conditions of women was essential to the implementation of strategies for child survival and development. It also agreed that women-centred activities should be development-oriented rather than welfare-based and made integral to all UNICEF-assisted projects and programmes and executed in the context of each country's national development.

Maurice Pate Memorial Award

The UNICEF Board approved at its April session the Executive Director's recommendation that for 1985 the annual Maurice Pate Memorial Award, established to commemorate the first Executive Director of UNICEF, be awarded to the National Institute of Public Co-operation and Child Development of India.[5] The Institute, recognized for its work in developing services for children, training, research and advocacy, planned to use the $25,000 award to strengthen its services, especially with regard to child survival and development.

Information and external relations

During 1985, UNICEF external relations activities centred on continuing with national and international partners the social mobilization effort and spreading the child survival and development message aimed at improving the well-being of children even in difficult economic times.

The aims of UNICEF advocacy were significantly enhanced world-wide through publications, audio-visual productions, exhibitions and extensive coverage of child-related concerns in the electronic and print media. These channels of exchange were multiplied through an enlarging network of allies in the cause of children, namely UNICEF goodwill ambassadors, national committees, government communication systems, and an increasing number of non-governmental organizations (NGOs), such as women's and youth organizations, religious and cultural groups, professional and business forums, school systems, service clubs and voluntary agencies.

UNICEF and the NGO Committee for UNICEF hosted (New York, 25 October 1985) a People's Forum on universal child immunization by 1990 (UCI-1990) in celebration of the United Nations fortieth anniversary. The Forum brought together heads of State, prime ministers, foreign ministers, celebrities and over 800 NGO representatives who signed a Declaration of Commitment to UCI-1990. In April, the Executive Board recommended that the NGO Committee be encouraged to organize a broader-based Forum with the participation of national committees for UNICEF and the Board in association with its 1986 regular session, bearing in mind themes appropriate for UNICEF's fortieth anniversary.

UNICEF fortieth anniversary

In April, the Board discussed preparations for the fortieth anniversary of UNICEF, to be commemorated in 1986, and decided that its theme would be "Children first".

GENERAL ASSEMBLY ACTION

On 17 December, the General Assembly, on the recommendation of the Second (Economic and Financial) Committee, adopted **resolution 40/210** without vote.

Fortieth anniversary of the United Nations Children's Fund

The General Assembly,

Recalling that, by its resolution 57(I) of 11 December 1946, it established the United Nations Children's Fund as a manifestation of the responsibility of nations and society for children as the most vital resource of the future world, and noting that the year 1986 represents the fortieth anniversary of this expression of commitment to children,

Reaffirming the principles and guidelines for programme activities established by the Executive Board of the United Nations Children's Fund in its efforts to bring about a major world-wide improvement in child survival and child development, taking special advantage of new developments in primary health care techniques and in communications,

Acutely aware that the effect of the adverse global economic situation is more severe on vulnerable groups, such as children, particularly in developing countries, and therefore makes the need for the efforts of the United Nations Children's Fund all the more critical,

Noting that the fortieth anniversary of the United Nations Children's Fund presents a unique opportunity for advancing the above-mentioned principles, which have the potential for a virtual revolution in child survival,

Aware that many developing countries have recently embarked upon major child survival and development efforts and noting with appreciation in this regard the positive response of many world leaders to the commendable initiative taken by the Secretary-General on the occasion of the fortieth anniversary of the United Nations, regarding the renewed potential for achieving the goal of universal child immunization by 1990, which is an important part of the primary health care strategy,

Welcoming the continued co-operation between the United Nations Children's Fund and the World Health Organization in achieving their common objective, particularly as it relates to the goal of universal child immunization by 1990,

1. *Urges* that the fortieth anniversary of the United Nations Children's Fund be observed by intensifying the ongoing efforts towards attaining the objectives relating to children envisaged in the International Development Strategy for the Third United Nations Development Decade and notes the important role of the child survival and child development strategy in meeting those objectives;

2. *Notes* that "Children first" has been adopted by the Executive Board of the United Nations Children's Fund as the umbrella theme for the observance of the fortieth anniversary of the Fund;

3. *Calls upon* the United Nations Children's Fund, with the participation of Governments, the organizations of the United Nations system, non-governmental organizations and individuals, to commemorate the fortieth anniversary of the Fund by reaffirming, through commitment and action, the responsibility of the international community for the survival and development of children;

4. *Requests* the United Nations Children's Fund, with the guidance of its Executive Board, to continue to develop and promote appropriate means by which Governments, the United Nations and other international organizations, as well as individuals, may express this commitment, particularly during the period of the fortieth anniversary;

5. *Appeals* to all Governments to increase their support, assistance and contributions during the period of the fortieth anniversary and subsequently, so that the United Nations Children's Fund may be able to strengthen its co-operation with developing countries and respond to the urgent needs of children;

6. *Requests* all countries to observe the fortieth anniversary of the United Nations Children's Fund in a befitting manner, through governmental and non-governmental participation.

General Assembly resolution 40/210

17 December 1985   Meeting 120   Adopted without vote

Approved by Second Committee (A/40/1041) without vote, 11 December (meeting 50); draft by Vice-Chairman (A/C.2/40/L.110), based on informal consultations on draft by Bangladesh, Chile, China, Colombia, Ethiopia, Finland, Gambia, Japan, Lebanon, Poland, Romania, Senegal and Tunisia (A/C.2/40/L.96); agenda item 85.

Meeting numbers. GA 40th session: 2nd Committee 35-42, 44, 46-50; plenary 120.

UNICEF programmes by region

In 1985, programme expenditures for Africa increased by 35 per cent over 1984; for the Americas, by 27 per cent; by 6 per cent for east Asia and Pakistan; by 2 per cent for south central Asia; and by 31 per cent for the Middle East and north Africa. For the third successive year, there were no expenditures for Europe.

The tables on the following pages show expenditures and commitments for 1985 and commitments and "notings" (for projects awaiting funding) approved by the Executive Board in April.

1985 UNICEF EXPENDITURE AND MULTIYEAR COMMITMENTS
(as at 31 December 1985; in US dollars)

	Expenditure	Approved new commitment		Expenditure	Approved new commitment
Africa			**Americas** (cont.)		
Angola	4,126,633	—	Dominica	21,249	—
Benin	991,705	—	Dominican Republic	447,263	—
Botswana	182,369	—	Ecuador	491,069	—
Burkina Faso	3,250,851	—	El Salvador	210,458	852,000
Burundi	2,700,360	—	Guatemala	687,793	—
Cameroon	432,848	2,747,000	Guyana	96,921	—
Cape Verde	104,975	—	Haiti	1,603,122	—
Central African Republic	855,431	—	Honduras	586,013	—
Chad	3,367,361	6,210,000	Jamaica	107,779	—
Comoros	72,287	—	Mexico	1,093,099	2,479,452
Congo	124,665	—	Nicaragua	1,860,132	—
Djibouti	1,020,765	206,000	Panama	30,573	147,000
Equatorial Guinea	166,044	—	Paraguay	279,989	989,000
Ethiopia	20,359,116	—	Peru	1,578,870	—
Gambia	429,787	—	Saint Lucia	58,904	—
Ghana	1,879,665	8,574,000	Suriname	19,534	—
Guinea	905,894	1,861,000	Regional projects	2,207,231	—
Guinea-Bissau	688,972	—			
Ivory Coast	739,343	1,998,000	Subtotal	19,410,984	4,921,452
Kenya	1,330,260	6,366,000			
Lesotho	423,233	—	**East Asia and Pakistan**		
Liberia	451,357	—	Bangladesh	12,626,080	—
Madagascar	1,048,676	5,082,000	Burma	8,701,813	—
Malawi	1,003,844	—	China	6,657,676	—
Mali	3,346,617	—	Indonesia	7,562,267	44,408,000
Mauritania	1,581,333	—	Kampuchea	4,201,339	2,020,000
Mauritius	71,659	—	Kampuchean relief	(50,862)	—
Mozambique	4,203,991	13,370,000	Lao People's Democratic Republic	1,312,329	—
Niger	3,304,239	5,198,000	Malaysia	270,127	—
Nigeria	6,246,819	—	Pacific islands	431,258	—
Rwanda	1,001,932	—	Pakistan	7,925,311	—
Sao Tome and Principe	19,521	—	Papua New Guinea	51,228	—
Senegal	1,843,384	—	Philippines	3,331,935	—
Seychelles	59,040	—	Republic of Korea	558,565	—
Sierra Leone	502,146	4,456,000	Thailand	4,676,634	—
Somalia	3,002,574	—	Viet Nam	5,432,199	—
Swaziland	172,978	—	Regional projects	140,747	—
Togo	426,583	—			
Uganda	7,549,540	10,305,000	Subtotal	63,828,646	46,428,000
United Republic of Tanzania	9,150,874	—			
Zaire	2,367,572	—	**South central Asia**		
Zambia	471,167	—	Afghanistan	1,777,023	—
Zimbabwe	1,274,235	—	Bhutan	909,370	—
Regional projects	1,861,333	—	India	31,884,642	140,437,000
			Maldives	308,761	—
Subtotal	95,113,978	66,373,000	Mongolia	3,527	—
			Nepal	4,857,050	—
Americas			Sri Lanka	3,145,940	—
Antigua and Barbuda	24,195	—			
Argentina	497,615	—	Subtotal	42,886,313	140,437,000
Belize	485,656	—			
Bolivia	3,272,463	—	**Middle East and north Africa**		
Brazil	1,144,224	—	Algeria	180,681	135,000
Chile	188,250	206,000	Bahrain	106,933	—
Colombia	2,200,938	—	Democratic Yemen	694,636	3,550,000
Costa Rica	114,127	248,000	Egypt	5,286,254	—
Cuba	103,517	—			

Middle East and north Africa (cont.)	Expenditure	Approved new commitment	Middle East and north Africa (cont.)	Expenditure	Approved new commitment
Iran	74	—	Yemen	1,250,185	1,590,000
Jordan	230,299	—	Palestinian children and mothers	957,270	—
Lebanon	5,443,063	—	Regional projects	44,928	—
Lebanon rehabilitation	1,008,055	—			
Morocco	1,190,474	—	Subtotal	26,039,207	5,575,000
Oman	516,189	300,000			
Sudan	7,618,931	—	Interregional	—	39,345,526
Syrian Arab Republic	515,285	—			
Tunisia	663,279	—	Savings (cancellation)	—	(26,556)
Turkey	332,671	—	Total	247,279,128	303,053,422

NOTE: Expenditures are financed from general resources, supplementary funds and funds-in-trust from the United Nations system for the year ended 31 December 1985. New commitments are as approved by the Executive Board at its 1985 session, and include only general resources, and not supplementary funds.

SOURCES: A/41/5/Add.2, E/1985/31.

COMMITMENTS AND "NOTINGS" APPROVED BY THE EXECUTIVE BOARD
IN 1985 FOR INTERREGIONAL PROJECTS
(in US dollars)

	Period	Commitments	
		General resources	Supplementary funds
Interregional programme for essential drugs	1985-1987	—	23,000,000*
Training of communicators for the child survival and development revolution	1985-1987	—	2,996,000
Interregional fund for programme preparation, promotion and evaluation	1986-1987	18,000,000	—
Global infant mortality reduction reserve	1985-1987	18,000,000	—
Maurice Pate Memorial Award	1985	25,000	—
Emergency Reserve Fund (replenishment)	1985	3,263,000†	—
Commitment to cover over-expenditure	—	57,526	—
Total		39,345,526	25,996,000

*Comprising $3 million for programmatic elements and $20 million capital fund (revolving).

†The Fund is automatically replenished at the start of each calendar year by an amount corresponding to the disbursements authorized by the Executive Director during the previous year.

SOURCE: E/1985/31.

Africa

Concern for the critical situation of children and their families as a result of the situation in many African countries continued to be the focus of UNICEF emergency assistance in 1985 (see Chapter III of this section). Total programme expenditure in Africa increased from $78 million in 1984 to $102 million in 1985, representing some 38 per cent of UNICEF's total global programme expenditure. As a result of increased needs, UNICEF's field capacity was strengthened by upgrading 14 offices to full UNICEF country offices, with a staff increase of some 40 per cent in eastern and southern Africa and almost 50 per cent in western and central Africa. This expansion was accompanied by improvements in the effectiveness of country programmes in linking emergency relief with long-term development action, furthering child survival and development (CSD) and relating programme activities to regional situation analyses.

There were six major crises in 1985 in the eastern and southern Africa region:[6] mounting external debt, food shortages, drought, civil strife, continued rapid population growth and instability caused by *apartheid*. UNICEF allocated a total of $28 million for emergencies, in addition to $59 million for regular programmes. The emergency situation led to a rethinking of strategy for the survival and development of children in the region through community-based integrated primary health care (PHC) linked with household food security programmes and accelerated immunization.

Steady gains were made during the year to achieve UCI-1990. UNICEF supported courses on planning and management, maintenance and repair of cold-chain equipment (refrigerators, cold boxes, transport), and communication and evaluation techniques. Mass media communication support systems were being developed, community health worker coverage was expanded and immunization activities were integrated into maternal and child health (MCH) programmes. Gains were also made in oral rehydration therapy (ORT)—a method of preventing dehydration caused by diarrhoea, a major cause of child mortality—in producing oral rehydration salts (ORS), in the control of diarrhoeal diseases through national programmes and in breastfeeding and family planning programmes. The UNICEF health commitment averaged $22 million for all countries in eastern and southern Africa: 52 per cent, or $11.4 million, for MCH/PHC activities; 19 per cent, or $4.3 million, for the expanded programme of immunization; and 29 per cent, or $6.4 million, for other health activities such as general health manpower training and essential drugs.

An increase in food supply allowed the scaling down of emergency feeding and nutrition programmes, while regional support to developing food and nutrition information systems continued. In response to the reduction of surplus food stocks as a result of limitations on available goods, UNICEF made essential goods available to the economy in exchange for surplus food.

The analysis of UNICEF's response to women revealed a shift away from welfare towards economically oriented programmes favouring employment and income generation, food production, support to women farmers and strengthening women's development through group organization, education and an increased capacity to ensure the well-being of children and families.

UNICEF also delivered large quantities of vaccines, drugs and ORS to camps and drought-stricken areas and continued its support in health, nutrition and emergency water supply sectors. Relief camp programmes were supported for returning refugees and UNICEF assistance was significant in the development of emergency preparedness recognition capacities to prevent, or at least forecast, famine. In April 1985, UNICEF supported a seminar at Nairobi, Kenya, on abandoned and abused children and their rights as persons.

In western and central Africa,[7] despite the diminished threat of drought and massive grain supplies from abroad, malnutrition and hunger remained the fate of large numbers of people; consequently, the development of food self-sufficiency continued to be a priority. Since nutritional problems of children were correlated with the educational and economic level of mothers, nutrition and growth surveillance programmes included a strong educational component. Support for food production for both consumption and sale became the focus of UNICEF action, leading to a special concern for the African woman, and UNICEF assisted in disseminating improved agricultural techniques. Following the July 1985 World Conference to review and appraise the United Nations Decade for Women, regional women founded an International Committee for Development Projects for African Women, with headquarters at Abidjan, Ivory Coast, opening a new area of co-operation. UNICEF also supported instruction for mothers and schoolchildren through various strategies, while assistance to pre-school education continued to be a regional priority.

The combination of strained economic circumstances and weakened populations moved Governments further towards developing PHC structures. With UNICEF assistance, maternal growth charts were distributed through MCH centres and increased support was provided for control of diarrhoeal diseases. All the region's countries supported the goal of UCI-1990, enabling UNICEF to support governmental efforts for CSD and PHC.

UNICEF co-operation in various programmes—rural water supply, hygiene and latrine construction and sanitation education—led to the establishment of village committees responsible for water supplies. It also trained national personnel and assisted in developing technical team work.

The drought, which peaked in 1984-1985, required UNICEF to seek special funding and to develop a long-term approach for further development beyond the emergency situation. Assistance was provided to Governments with resettlement programmes by enabling people to produce their own food on sites chosen for their adequate water supply.

In Angola, where the emergency problem stemmed from an internal conflict, most international aid, including supplementary and emergency water supplies, truck transportation and maintenance, and food distribution centre supervision, was channelled through UNICEF.

The year 1985 saw a marked development and extension of linkages with institutional partners. Advocacy for children was increasingly directed towards international financial institutions whose decisions affected those of national policy-makers.

Americas and the Caribbean

In 1985, UNICEF continued its basic services programmes in Latin America and the Caribbean,[8] a region suffering from serious restrictions imposed by the servicing of heavy external debts, internal adjustment policies, and the moderate expansion of the world economy.

During the year, UNICEF advocacy for CSD actions and its readiness to provide timely technical and financial support helped to strengthen the political commitment of several Governments to meet the basic needs of children, especially in health services. UNICEF was able in that region to mobilize public and private institutions to endorse and support basic actions for the survival and development of deprived children. Its offices intensified high-level advocacy, broadened contacts with government decision-makers and worked to identify programme alternatives for the development of innovative and low-cost activities. In co-ordination with UNICEF and the Pan American Health Organization/World Health Organization (PAHO/WHO), Central American Governments prepared a five-year national plan for CSD.

Efforts continued for the accelerated implementation of the expanded programme of immunization and a co-ordinated regional plan was proposed. An inter-agency committee was created to guarantee co-ordination of technical and financial support to participating agencies.

UNICEF supported other initiatives, including a nutrition surveillance project, installation of an

ORS plant in Cuba, which aimed at self-sufficiency in the production and distribution of packets to other countries, and an effective programme of co-operation with PAHO/WHO at the regional level and in several countries to implement acute respiratory infection programmes through training and publications.

UNICEF gave priority to revising early child development programmes emphasizing an integrated view of the child, which included a regional workshop in Colombia. A Latin American seminar on child education, held in Brazil, provided an opportunity to collaborate with Spanish- and Portuguese-speaking countries of Africa.

A seminar, jointly sponsored by the Colombian Government, the Catholic Church, NGOs and UNICEF, discussed problems of children and adolescents in difficult situations and analysed alternative strategies, programmes and community experiences being developed for them. UNICEF also supported community-based preventive programmes for street children in several countries through intensive staff training and communication activities.

All regional offices were involved in providing special technical and financial support to mobilize the greatest number of governmental and private agencies to adopt and implement effective short- and medium-term actions benefiting poor women.

UNICEF co-operated with several Governments in developing urban basic services programmes to improve conditions for children, adolescents and women living in slum areas.

Co-operation with religious organizations and the mobilization of NGOs was strengthened and accelerated. Social communication used the media to promote CSD and UCI-1990 and study tours were arranged for members of national committees from Europe and North America.

Asia

In the east Asia and Pakistan region,[9] progress was made in implementing CSD actions, improving PHC and basic service structures and actions, accelerating the immunization process and mobilizing Governments' commitment to, and support for, UCI-1990. Significant improvements in the promotion of ORT were registered: the production of oral rehydration salts increased in Bangladesh and Thailand, an experimental production programme was started in Viet Nam, and there were both local production and imported supplies in Burma.

Family spacing activities were undertaken within the context of MCH programmes, as in the case of the preparations for Bangladesh's third population project of the World Bank where UNICEF supported a more balanced approach to family planning practices, with priority given to tetanus toxoid immunization of women, safe delivery, use of ORS and the training of 30,000 traditional birth attendants. UNICEF assisted in efforts to provide food supplementation by distributing kits including seeds and tools in Kampuchea and in designing a project in Fiji to correct the dietary imbalance created by imported foods. Other country programmes included support to women's farm groups and small-scale family production as well as a larger-scale home gardening project. Advocacy in favour of upgrading women's education and literacy was important and UNICEF encouraged the use of newly acquired knowledge through income-generating groups. Support was also provided for upgrading the training of village health workers, community members, government officials and field workers. Substantial quantities of essential drugs, supplies and equipment were also distributed.

Malnutrition continued to be a serious problem, but the WHO/UNICEF joint nutrition support programme helped to strengthen the nutrition unit in the Burmese Department of Health. In Bangladesh, efforts centred on training over 11,000 nutrition workers, and the control of iodine deficiency diseases was advanced through strategies which supported legislation on iodating salt and the provision of iodated injections. There was also an increase in the number of wells drilled and hand-pumps installed, village volunteers were trained, and technical personnel were financed to assist a gravity-flow project at the state/division level in Burma.

On education, the regional office convened a meeting between UNICEF and UNESCO staff to assess educational interventions. It also supported research on curriculum objectives and contents, provided assistance to schools and introduced CSD concerns in primary education in several countries. In addition, UNICEF supported women's activities in the areas of female education, income generation and the advocacy of equal rights, as well as the upgrading of slums and squatter settlements through the introduction of PHC and basic social services.

UNICEF staff conducted seminars, evaluations, programme reviews and situation analyses in several areas and countries of the region. An assessment of the situation of children in especially difficult circumstances resulted in an interregional consultation at Bangkok, Thailand, and support to local and international NGOs involved in child care.

In external relations, UNICEF involvement included co-operation with the media and NGOs, the provision of technical back-up services for print and audio-visual productions, and the establishment of a new office in Singapore for the Greeting Card Operation. The regional office co-operated with many United Nations organizations and bilateral co-operation agencies and participated in a number of inter-agency task forces.

In south central Asia,[10] UNICEF activities focused on enhancing co-operation with and among NGOs and the media, the re-orientation of education, the delivery of basic services, the preventive dimensions of PHC and improved infant feeding practices beginning with maternal nutrition and including home management of childhood diarrhoea. Immunization activities included developing mobile immunization teams, initiating cold-chain equipment in regional hospitals, training community members and teachers and developing media campaigns. UNICEF also assisted in providing at least one perennial source of potable water in 80 per cent of all villages in the region. It continued the control of iodine deficiency disorders through the production and dissemination of information materials, support for a UNICEF/WHO inter-country workshop, the organization of study visits and advocacy with public health officials. Monitoring of programmes was refined to facilitate evaluation and cost-effectiveness, and improvements involved the expanded use of computers. In addition, UNICEF expanded its use of communication for programme purposes and for wider public information through a broad variety of media, including electronic formats and person-to-person forums.

North Africa and Eastern Mediterranean

With UCI-1990 as a priority, UNICEF further developed its position in the Middle East and north Africa[11] by practical approaches to social mobilization, accomplished through joint efforts with WHO and the involvement of the media as well as religious leaders and the army.

Given the diversity of the region, the regional office developed a matrix to consolidate country-specific information from the situation analysis and to guide strategy development in an effort to reduce infant mortality below 50 per 1,000 live births in the region by 1990. Further, the office responded to the need for a demand-oriented health services strategy by reinforcing support for information, education and communication (social mobilization), with attention paid to country specifics in practical campaign planning focusing on sustainability.

Joint CSD programmes were initiated with bilateral agencies, Canada, Italy, the United States Agency for International Development, the Arab Gulf Programme for United Nations Development Organizations and the UNESCO regional office for Arab States. A comprehensive programme on breast-feeding, weaning and growth monitoring was established with the International Baby Food Action Network, and UNICEF participated in an inter-country WHO/Eastern Mediterranean regional office workshop for expanded programme of immunization (EPI) managers to set annual coverage targets for UCI-1990 and discuss strategies using an EPI planning and programming check-list developed by the regional office. Country programmes supported management of dehydration with ORT, and many promoted breast-feeding, proper weaning practices and personal hygiene. Water supply and sanitation programmes helped promote community receptivity to other CSD interventions. Progress was achieved towards more realistic identification of programmatic possibilities within countries to initiate, develop and support appropriate programmes for women, especially female literacy.

Communication and social marketing gained momentum and a training manual was developed describing the role of communication in effecting social change. A health and communication materials project relating to CSD was finalized, with materials distributed to UNICEF offices for health educational programmes and to promote the use of mass communication.

In the Sudan, UNICEF was involved in emergency operations through staffing, emergency allocations and activities in health care, nutrition surveillance, supplementary feeding, vitamin-A distribution and water supply. In south Lebanon, in addition to ongoing rehabilitation and construction, UNICEF met emergency water and sanitation needs and expedited the procurement of relief supplies for displaced persons (see p. 548).

UNICEF programmes by sector

In 1985, UNICEF programmes concentrated on bringing about a virtual revolution in CSD through growth monitoring, oral rehydration, breast-feeding, immunization, feeding, family spacing and female literacy.

The programmes aimed at: reducing infant and young child mortality; improving child development through PHC; clean water; sanitation; limitation of severe malnutrition; universal and primary education; abolition of widespread illiteracy; improving the situation of women, an essential condition to ensure CSD; and enhancing family and community capacities to prevent childhood disability and help disabled children.

As in the previous seven years, child health accounted for the largest segment of UNICEF expenditure. The table below gives details of UNICEF expenditures and commitments by sector.

1985 UNICEF EXPENDITURE AND COMMITMENTS,
BY MAIN FIELD OF CO-OPERATION

(in thousands of US dollars)

	1985 expenditure	Approved commitments
Child survival*	–	61,820
Child health	82,328	29,403
Water supply and sanitation	58,526	45,937
Child nutrition	16,642	11,803
Social welfare services for children	14,458	65,662
Formal education	20,887	25,579
Non-formal education	11,497	12,427
Emergency relief	35,441	–
General	38,798	58,128
Programme support services	66,354	–
Total	344,931	299,759

*Child survival refers specifically to growth monitoring, oral rehydration, breast-feeding, immunization, feeding, family spacing and female literacy.

SOURCE: A/41/5/Add.2 & Add.2/Corr.1.

Primary health care

During 1985, UNICEF continued to expand community-based activities to promote primary health care, a highest priority towards the goal of CSD, spending $82.3 million in that sector. Its assistance reached 110 countries (42 in Africa, 23 in the Americas, 32 in Asia and 13 in the Middle East and north Africa) and included grants for training, orientation and refresher courses for 154,000 health workers, technical assistance and equipment for 201,100 health centres, especially in rural areas, and medicines and vaccines against tuberculosis, diphtheria, tetanus, typhoid, measles, poliomyelitis and other diseases.

Health and nutrition of infants and young children were given the highest priority by UNICEF throughout the year. Efforts were guided by the PHC strategy. With UNICEF's assistance, national health systems increasingly put the PHC concept into practice, relying on community-based health workers' services and drawing on successful experiences in immunization and ORT—the most cost-effective means of treating and preventing diarrhoeal dehydration in infants and young children. Global supply and use of packaged ORS rose sharply in 1985. Total production world-wide increased from 173 million packets to 250 million, two thirds of which were made in some 40 developing countries in Africa, the Middle East, Asia and Latin America with UNICEF/WHO assistance.

Somalia and Morocco provided examples of the shift from conventional medical care to PHC. Pakistan, Papua New Guinea, the Philippines and, to a lesser extent, Nepal decentralized their health programmes to make them community-based. Inter-sectoral approaches to PHC progressed in Kenya, Malawi, Sierra Leone, Uganda and Zambia. National immunization campaigns in Burkina Faso, Colombia and Turkey led to greater emphasis on allied PHC elements in support of CSD and revitalized the existing PHC structures or established new ones. Community participation expanded through committees in Cameroon, the Gambia and Zambia, and community volunteer movements were a significant element of the health sector in India, Indonesia, the Philippines and Sri Lanka. As part of this trend, government ministries other than health, NGOs, and professional and religious groups in a number of countries became increasingly involved in PHC development.

There were major health problems of relevance to CSD. Since acute respiratory infection (ARI) was next only to diarrhoeal disease as a cause of child deaths in developing countries, UNICEF supported ARI control programmes in Argentina, Brazil, Colombia, the Gambia, Nepal, Paraguay and Viet Nam. Malaria continued to be a major public health problem in Africa and was showing resurgence in south and South-East Asia, posing a threat to 2 billion people, with resistance to chloroquine spreading rapidly. Treatment of cases, prophylaxis during pregnancy and control of mosquito breeding grounds were among the strategies applied. Other programmes included efforts to control diarrhoeal diseases in over 75 countries, and implementation of preventive programmes which encouraged breast-feeding, safe drinking-water, hygiene and sanitation, clean preparation and storage of food, and health and nutrition education for parents.

World-wide efforts towards UCI-1990 against six childhood killer diseases (measles, poliomyelitis, diphtheria, pertussis, tetanus and tuberculosis) gathered momentum during 1985. Over 60 countries made national commitments to this effort, leading to national mobilization for immunization. UNICEF spent some $20 million on immunization in 1985 and provided about $13 million worth of vaccines.

During 1985, growth monitoring was used in conjunction with education and selective feeding, PHC, community organization and women's self-help programmes. Although few countries reached national scale, progress was impressive: Indonesia and Thailand expanded their programmes to cover over half of their children; Brazil expected to reach universal coverage by 1990; Colombia provided a growth chart to every child being immunized; and China prepared for a national growth monitoring plan. In India, some 30 million growth charts were distributed and over 6 million children were monitored regularly. Ninety or more per cent of children in Botswana, the Gambia, Maldives and Seychelles had their growth periodically checked. A consultation on growth monitoring (New York, April) suggested a step-up in global and national advocacy, sharing of information, expanding the activity in selected countries, study-and-action projects to enhance programme efficiency, and institutional support at regional and country levels.

UNICEF/WHO co-operation on essential drugs continued and some 80 countries had initiated national essential-drugs programmes, including the development of their own lists as a means of rationalizing the use of drugs within health services. UNICEF, with financial help from the Danish International Development Agency, supplied essential drugs to the United Republic of Tanzania worth $18 million, and supported programmes in Burkina Faso, Ethiopia, Guinea-Bissau, Mozambique and Somalia through a $15-million contribution from Italy. In addition to providing increased supplies of essential drugs worth some $35 million in 1985, UNICEF and WHO assisted Governments with their essential-drug policies.

Child welfare in urban areas

In 1985, UNICEF continued expanding support to community-based activities in the urban areas of developing countries[12] with emphasis on PHC and CSD actions, including water supply and sanitation and immunization.

Urban PHC projects in many cities, for example in Addis Ababa, Ethiopia, and Kabul, Afghanistan, made great progress in universal child immunization, and several, including Bangkok, Thailand, and Colombo, Sri Lanka, achieved universal immunization. In many urban basic services programmes, low-cost water supply and sanitation projects were developed in connection with diarrhoea management, since the incidence of this disease was particularly widespread in poor and congested urban settlements.

Childhood malnutrition remained a serious urban problem because of low income in a cash economy, early discontinuation of breast-feeding by working mothers, diarrhoea resulting from poor health and insanitary conditions, and the direct consequences of economic recession bearing even more heavily on the urban than the rural poor. Despite the limited space available in many cities for kitchen gardens, efforts were made to encourage urban gardening. Other measures to reduce malnutrition included immunization against measles, control of malaria, continuance of breast-feeding, birth-spacing to reduce the incidence of low birth-weight babies, supplementary food for pregnant mothers and for timely weaning, routine deworming, safe water, improved sanitation, health education and income-generating activities for women.

The presence of street children and working children in the world, a result of poverty, natural and man-made disasters and the urbanizing process, was on the increase. In Brazil, contact was maintained with some 300 community groups working directly with those children. That experience became the basis for new projects carried out in four departments of Colombia, five states of Mexico, and the two principal cities of Ecuador. Local projects were also started in Argentina and the Dominican Republic. The lessons of these countries were shared with African countries (Ethiopia, Kenya, Mozambique, Somalia) as well as with the Philippines and Thailand, resulting in new situation analyses of children's needs.

UNICEF learned that efforts to establish community-based services for the urban poor had to be complemented by assisting the rural poor through agriculture and agro-based industry so that they had fewer reasons to migrate to larger cities.

Education

UNICEF's activities in education programmes (both formal and non-formal) in 1985 reached 112 countries—42 in Africa, 29 in Asia, 28 in the Americas and 13 in the Middle East and North Africa—with a total expenditure of $32.4 million, an increase of $1.9 million over 1984. Programmes included: providing stipends for training teachers; equipping primary schools, teacher-training institutions and vocational training centres with teaching aids; and assisting countries to prepare textbooks locally by funding printing units, bookbinding and paper.

Illiteracy remained heavy in south Asia and sub-Saharan Africa. In west Asia and north Africa, primary education was expanding, but adults, particularly women, remained mostly illiterate. In east Asia, where primary enrolment was close to universal, not all children completed the cycle. In Latin America, many continued to be denied educational opportunities. UNICEF's activities, often carried out in co-operation with UNESCO, the World Bank, bilateral agencies and NGOs, were directed to qualitative improvement and efficiency in primary education, literacy and non-formal education for women and youth, supportive educational elements in other basic services and the care and education of young and pre-school children. Its support of non-formal learning for children, youth and adults, especially girls and women, continued as a strong component of basic education, with efforts to make education relevant and to reach the unserved poor. Priority attention was given to the development of three- to six-year-old children. Pre-school centres served as locations for contact, interchange and delivery of services such as immunization, growth monitoring, early detection of disability, women's literacy, economic activity, small-scale food production, sanitation activity and community education.

A joint UNICEF/UNESCO programme—the universal primary education and literacy project—funded by special contributions and initiated in 1983 to achieve education for all by the end of the century[13] was operating in Bangladesh, Bolivia, Ethiopia, Nepal, Nicaragua and Peru. The projects complemented ongoing activities to expand primary education and literacy courses for women and girls; redesign school programmes for disadvantaged groups; improve instructional materials and teachers' skills; and incorporate knowledge and activities that enhanced the health and well-being of children and their families.

Other programmes to educate parents using home-based learning methods and materials were also tried out among some disadvantaged groups and, in the Philippines, an innovative non-formal project for pre-schools among the Badjao community was started in the isolated south-westerly islands. Appropriate curricula for rural community-based programmes in Kenya, Mexico and the United Republic of Tanzania were under preparation. Projects geared to the special needs of refugee children were expanded in Lebanon, Mexico, Mozambique, Pakistan, the Sudan and Thailand.

At the April session of the Executive Board,[2] UNICEF was urged to give priority to improving the situation of women and children in Africa. Also emphasized was the importance of women's literacy and education as a means of improving their social and economic positions and of supporting child survival and development.

Nutrition

In 1985, UNICEF co-operated in nutrition programmes in 100 countries—37 in Africa, 29 in Asia, 24 in the Americas and 10 in the Middle East and north Africa—with a total expenditure of $16.6 million. Its activities included expanding nutrition programmes in 35,700 villages, equipping nutrition centres and demonstration areas, community and school orchards and gardens, and fish and poultry hatcheries, providing stipends to train 164,600 village-level nutrition workers, and delivering some 13,470 metric tons of donated foods for distribution through nutrition and emergency feeding programmes.

The five-year UNICEF/WHO joint nutrition support programme (JNSP), set up in 1982[14] and financed by Italy, supported 16 country projects: eight in Africa (Angola, Ethiopia, Mali, Mozambique, Niger, Somalia, Sudan, United Republic of Tanzania), five in the Americas (Haiti, Nicaragua, Peru, eastern Carribean—for Dominica and Saint Vincent and the Grenadines) and three in Asia (Burma, Nepal, Pakistan), aimed at combining dietary and non-dietary measures within the broad context of PHC to reduce child mortality and morbidity and improve child development and maternal nutrition. There were encouraging signs during the year regarding the sustainability of JNSP projects and approach. For

example, Burma and Nepal planned to absorb project staff salaries once JNSP resources were no longer available; in the United Republic of Tanzania, JNSP developed a community-based system to monitor children's nutritional status and provide nutritional supplementation to the malnourished; in Bolivia, it achieved success in salt iodization for human consumption and injection of iodized oil for goitre control; in Haiti, it widened the knowledge of ORT among the population; and, in Nicaragua, it mobilized political support and achieved multisectoral co-ordination.

In April, at the UNICEF Board session,[2] JNSP objectives were endorsed and the view was expressed that increased attention should be given to maternal nutrition, especially for pregnant and lactating women, since it would reduce the rate of infant deaths and complications often caused by low birth weight. The importance of the role of women as agricultural producers also was stressed and UNICEF was urged to provide them with technical resources to improve domestic food production, particularly through more direct support for strengthening household food surveys.

Water supply and sanitation

UNICEF continued in 1985 to co-operate in supplying safe water and improving sanitation in 93 countries: 36 in Africa, 21 in the Americas, 25 in Asia and 11 in the Middle East and north Africa. It completed over 92,500 water supply systems benefiting some 16.8 million persons and completed nearly 307,200 excreta disposal installations benefiting 6 million people.

UNICEF support for water supply and sanitation programmes recorded an increase in the number of hand-pumps installed, wells dug, deep tube-wells drilled, spring protections with simple gravity-feed schemes and sanitation projects completed. Beneficiaries increased by 11 per cent over 1984, with the cost of delivery being reduced considerably resulting in a 30 per cent productivity increase. In most countries, water supply projects supported by UNICEF were, in varying degrees, linked with sanitation and health education. A major breakthrough came first in the south and South-East Asian countries, followed by many African countries, led by Nigeria. Even countries with severe and persistent internal strife, such as Angola and Mozambique, were able to include strong health and education elements in their programmes.

In 1985, UNICEF became the first recipient of the Crystal Drop Award by the International Water Resources Association for excellence in bringing water resources to good use by human populations.

At the Board's April session, it was stressed that water supply and sanitation services remained a high priority in many areas and needed to be included in CSD activities, and that UNICEF assistance should focus on sanitation, hygiene and health education as well as on the provision of drilling rigs and pumps. Regarding the African crisis, the need for increased inputs for water supply and sanitation, in addition to what was provided through emergency assistance, in order to ensure positive long-term results was stressed. The importance of strengthening the role of women in water and sanitation projects was also emphasized.

UNICEF finances

Total 1985 income was almost $375 million (including $48 million for emergencies, mostly for that in Africa), compared with $332 million in 1984. Income growth came mainly from more favourable exchange rates and increases in contributions for the Africa emergency. Income from Governments accounted for 74 per cent of the total and contributions from private and other sources for 26 per cent. General resources income was $249 million, an increase over 1984 but $21 million below the planned figure for 1985.

Total expenditure in 1985 was $390 million, compared with $345 million in 1984. General resources expenditure totalled $272 million. The imbalance of $23 million between general resources income and expenditure was absorbed by movements in non-cash assets, while general resources cash balances remained stable.

The Executive Board, in April,(2) endorsed the recommendations of the Advisory Committee on Administrative and Budgetary Questions (ACABQ)(15) regarding supplementary budget requests, whereby amounts needed were to be limited to the effects of fluctuations in exchange rates, inflation or other unforeseen developments or to cover the financial implications of specific decisions of the legislative body for which no financial provision had been made. Supplementary appropriations were not to be requested in the middle of the biennium to expand existing activities or to start new ones.

Financial plan for 1985-1988

The UNICEF financial plan for 1985-1988, set out in the 1984-1988 medium-term work plan,(3) projected an income of $390 million for 1985, and $420 million, $445 million and $470 million for the following three years. Projected expenditures for the same period were $372 million, $402 million, $425 million and $448 million, respectively.

In April,(2) the Executive Board approved the medium-term plan as a framework of projections, including the preparation of up to $190 million in programme commitments from general resources to be submitted to the Board in 1986. That amount was subject to the availability of resources and to the condition that the plan's estimates of income and expenditure would continue to be valid. As requested by the Board in 1983,(16) a revised format of UNICEF budget estimates had been submitted and approved in 1984.(17) In 1985,(2) the Board recognized that the format was an improvement, but decided that it should be further improved in line with ACABQ's recommendations.(15)

Contributions

Contributions to UNICEF received in or pledged for 1985 totalled $332,492,552, after a deduction of $7,838,448 in adjustments to prior years' income (see table below).

CONTRIBUTIONS TO UNICEF
(INCLUDING GENERAL RESOURCES AND SUPPLEMENTARY FUNDS)
(as at 31 December 1985; in US dollar equivalent)

	Received in or pledged for 1985		*Pledged for 1986*
Country or organization	*Governmental*	*Non-governmental*	*Governmental*
Afghanistan	30,000	—	30,000
Algeria	142,000	944	162,833
Angola	5,000	—	—
Antigua and Barbuda	300	—	—
Argentina	38,507	30,901	162,300
Australia	5,906,594	1,135,418	1,778,500
Austria	1,170,295	187,094	1,026,316
Bahamas	3,000	—	—
Bahrain	12,500	4,790	7,500
Bangladesh	8,321	1,502	9,029
Barbados	4,250	—	3,000
Belgium	1,068,442	992,167	1,276,596
Belize	—	—	4,942
Benin	7,500	—	1,500
Bhutan	4,170	—	4,790
Bolivia	—	321	1,000
Botswana	2,467	—	3,793
Brazil	44,611	13,597	100,000
British Virgin Islands	150	315	—
Bulgaria	60,914	—	60,000
Burkina Faso	1,222	14	2,204
Burma	181,710	—	—
Burundi	—	—	971
Byelorussian SSR	69,530	—	79,225
Cameroon	74,074	—	41,322
Canada	15,304,635	10,135,468	10,583,942
Chile	70,000	2,570	70,000
China	400,000	62	450,000
Colombia	456,816	20,385	455,785
Congo	14,619	—	—
Costa Rica	30,000	—	4,369
Cuba	116,545	—	58,140
Cyprus	—	76,838	500
Czechoslovakia	82,576	—	94,162

Country or organization	Received in or pledged for 1985 Governmental	Received in or pledged for 1985 Non-governmental	Pledged for 1986 Governmental	Country or organization	Received in or pledged for 1985 Governmental	Received in or pledged for 1985 Non-governmental	Pledged for 1986 Governmental
Democratic People's Republic of Korea	—	—	21,186	Panama	25,000	—	25,000
Democratic Yemen	7,040	—	7,740	Peru	120,000	—	—
Denmark	7,721,768	79,925	7,198,688	Philippines	262,302	10,147	215,432
Djibouti	1,000	—	1,000	Poland	61,593	—	71,963
Dominica	—	—	741	Portugal	—	47,809	15,000
Ecuador	25,407	1,800	25,407	Qatar	200,000	—	—
Egypt	82,202	329	82,204	Republic of Korea	147,000	39,204	137,200
El Salvador	19,858	20,619	9,480	Romania	13,043	—	11,848
Ethiopia	—	1,349	49,275	Rwanda	4,285	—	4,000
Fiji	2,000	—	1,869	Saint Lucia	—	—	2,576
Finland	7,383,618	961,308	11,400,000	Saint Vincent and the Grenadines	750	—	—
France	3,688,631	9,440,142	4,827,586	San Marino	3,082	2,538	4,003
German Democratic Republic	412,903	6,061	127,273	Saudi Arabia	1,000,000	117,047	1,000,000
Germany, Federal Republic of	6,087,159	6,340,437	7,045,455	Senegal	6,000	—	6,000
Ghana	—	—	998	Sierra Leone	10,214	—	12,118
Greece	187,239	199,120	150,000	Singapore	—	5,162	—
Guatemala	19,930	—	13,537	Spain	435,650	1,057,574	730,613
Guyana	3,253	—	3,140	Sri Lanka	13,361	922	15,000
Haiti	—	45	—	Sudan	25,000	—	10,357
Holy See	1,000	—	1,000	Suriname	2,500	—	2,825
Honduras	21,143	—	20,000	Swaziland	2,490	—	2,790
Hong Kong	14,587	—	14,418	Sweden	27,412,646	227,537	30,178,326
Hungary	21,539	12,466	35,383	Switzerland	9,501,160	2,356,620	6,842,105
Iceland	8,006	—	12,107	Syrian Arab Republic	64,103	769	—
India	1,797,197	80	2,144,000	Thailand	154,669	3,571	251,546
Indonesia	300,000	807	300,000	Togo	—	—	1,305
Iran	50,000	—	—	Tonga	854	—	—
Iraq	—	653	—	Trinidad and Tobago	—	260,000	6,944
Ireland	380,000	441,521	540,541	Tunisia	36,309	—	53,248
Israel	50,000	—	50,000	Turkey	68,814	—	60,210
Italy	34,077,420	622,113	21,221,865	Uganda	3,359	—	806
Ivory Coast	64,375	400	20,290	Ukrainian SSR	139,061	—	158,451
Jamaica	3,114	12,500	—	USSR	750,927	—	855,634
Japan	18,938,561	7,674,206	16,000,000	United Arab Emirates	984,932	108,757	—
Jordan	26,824	—	—	United Kingdom	9,825,119	1,643,868	9,723,310
Kenya	15,951	2,802	22,128	United Republic of Tanzania	21,146	16,928	14,160
Kuwait	200,000	84	200,000	United States	70,838,255	10,980,283	51,430,000
Lao People's Democratic Republic	5,000	—	5,000	Uruguay	—	—	45,000
Lebanon	59,933	—	5,155	Venezuela	114,667	—	114,667
Lesotho	2,500	—	1,502	Viet Nam	6,000	—	7,000
Liechtenstein	2,000	—	—	Yemen	12,910	—	20,327
Luxembourg	16,667	13,115	62,961	Yugoslavia	305,972	65,588	250,000
Madagascar	5,609	—	5,609	Zaire	—	—	2,000
Malawi	5,944	—	2,809	Zambia	7,759	5,745	5,302
Malaysia	102,204	—	85,980	Zimbabwe	18,634	6	18,182
Maldives	3,000	—	2,996				
Mali	1,000	—	—	Subtotal	260,925,716	59,590,312	220,512,935
Malta	4,084	—	5,107				
Mauritania	—	—	7,163	*Intergovernmental agencies*			
Mauritius	3,109	—	3,745				
Mexico	102,420	44,300	23,810	AGFUND	5,282,500	14,326	—
Monaco	3,410	—	5,506	EEC	14,114,030	—	—
Mongolia	3,598	—	4,500	OPEC Fund	250,000	—	—
Nepal	6,837	76	5,978				
Netherlands	8,317,839	4,089,639	8,546,154	Subtotal	19,646,530	14,326	—
New Zealand	830,717	18,390	—				
Nicaragua	—	—	714	*United Nations system*	—	154,116	—
Nigeria	308,292	—	714				
Norway	21,405,003	5,513	21,317,358	Adjustments to prior years' income	(4,664,193)	(3,174,255)	—
Oman	50,000	—	50,000				
Pakistan	164,511	48,051	45,610	Total	275,908,053	56,584,499	220,512,935

SOURCES: A/41/5/Add.2, A/CONF.132/2.

Accounts

1983

In April 1985,[2] the Executive Board reviewed the comments of the Board of Auditors and of ACABQ on the 1983 UNICEF financial report and the financial report of the Greeting Card Opera- tion (GCO) for the 1982/83 season,[18] as well as the comments made and action taken by the Executive Director in response to those observations.[19]

The Board acted on the recommendation of its Committee on Administration and Finance, which met in New York from 23 to 25 April.[20]

1984

In June 1985, the United Nations Board of Auditors submitted to the General Assembly the financial statements of UNICEF, including GCO, for 1984.[21] In its September 1985 report on audited financial statements,[22] ACABQ commented on the Board's remarks.

The UNICEF Executive Board considered the 1984 financial report and statements in April 1985[2] and in December, the General Assembly—in **resolution 40/238**—accepted them and requested that the required remedial action be taken.

Organizational questions

Greeting Card Operation

For the fourth successive year, a downward trend was registered in sales of greeting cards. During the 1984 GCO season (1 May 1984–30 April 1985), 111.2 million cards were sold[23] compared with some 113 million the previous season. Except for North America, all regions showed increases: an additional 2.7 million cards were sold in Europe; 1 million in Asia; 0.3 million in Central and South America; 0.2 million each in Africa and the eastern Mediterranean; and 0.1 million in the south-west Pacific. Sales generated $48.5 million in gross revenues for all GCO products (cards, $39,184,000; calendars, $3,010,000; stationery, $1,769,000; educational material, $1,653,000; other products, $2,853,000), or $0.4 million higher than the previous year, yielding a net operational income of $10.1 million to UNICEF general resources, $4.7 million lower than in 1983, mainly because of a weaker operational performance due to higher production and marketing costs ($1.7 million) and exchange rate losses and other adjustments outside GCO operational control ($3 million).

The UNICEF Executive Board in April 1985[2] approved the work plan for the 1985 GCO season (1 May 1985–30 April 1986) recommended by the Executive Director,[24] in which planned card production ranged from 117 million to 137 million, expenditure from $28.9 million to $31.9 million and corresponding revenue projections from $15.8 million to $20.8 million. The Executive Director was asked to report in 1986 on the problem of sales stagnation and measures to change that trend.

Headquarters arrangements

In 1984,[25] the Executive Board had decided to lease space from the United Nations Development Corporation (UNDC) for UNICEF headquarters in a new building, to be available for occupancy in late 1986 or early 1987. Plans for the building (UNDC-III) on East 44th Street in New York City—to be known as UNICEF House—were discussed at the Board's April 1985 session,[2] at which many delegations reaffirmed their concern that UNICEF House should be modest reflecting UNICEF's mandate to serve children and women in need. It was suggested that donor countries should contribute furnishings to reduce the organization's financial burden. The secretariat was requested to prepare a proposal regarding the financing of necessary furnishings.

Following ACABQ's[15] comments that using a $4-million credit facility offered by UNDC was not the best solution, the Board approved an allocation of $2 million in the 1986-1987 budget instead of the $630,000 set aside as amortization payment. In November,[26] the Executive Director recommended, as the best alternative for financing the $5,977,500 one-time installation costs associated with the move, to accept a UNDC abatement proposal which for the first year of the lease (1 January–31 December 1987) would reduce UNICEF base rental payments by $4,581,250. That amount excluded a maximum $2 per square foot base rent contingency provided for under the lease which might be imposed by UNDC, depending on the final development and construction costs of the building. To offset the loss of rental income resulting from the rent abatement, UNDC had proposed a revised rental schedule covering the initial 15-year lease period (1987-2001) which would, except for the first year, increase UNICEF base rent by a fixed amount of $3.87 per square foot. However, ACABQ was not in favour of that proposal. In view of the need for budgetary restraint, particularly with respect to administrative expenses, ACABQ felt that the only way to deal with the one-time costs was by meeting them as they arose instead of deferring them to future years, thereby incurring additional costs.[27] It therefore recommended that the Executive Director be authorized to allocate up to $1 million, to the extent possible from within existing resources, in addition to the $2 million already appropriated. Any additional needs could be reported to the Board in 1987 in the revised 1986-1987 estimates.

Inter-agency co-operation

During 1985, UNICEF co-operation with other agencies of the United Nations system was strengthened. It participated in the UNDP resident representatives' meeting at Copenhagen, Denmark, where activities and programme areas of the two organizations were stressed, and in activities of the International Drinking Water Supply and Sanitation Decade (1981-1990). In addition, UNICEF chaired a task force on hand-pumps testing and co-chaired one on women and water with the International Research and Training Institute for the Advancement of Women.

The Joint Consultative Group on Policy—comprising UNICEF, UNDP, UNFPA and WFP—met regularly during the year. Responding to the

African emergency, UNICEF co-operated with the Office for Emergency Operations in Africa and WFP. It also continued its dialogue with the World Bank, IMF and other organizations on the human dimension of adjustment policies.

Collaboration between UNICEF and WHO was reinforced during the year. The two organizations worked closely to ensure complementary interaction between UNICEF advocacy of child survival and development in the broader context of primary health care and the WHO objective of Health for All by the Year 2000. Working agreements were reached between the regional directors of the two organizations for Africa and the Middle East/eastern Mediterranean regions. Co-operation with UNESCO continued on education, health education, nutrition, education for child survival, appropriate technology, water and sanitation, with special emphasis on female education, improving external and internal efficiency and education for child survival and development. UNICEF also collaborated with ILO in analysing the situation of working children and factors affecting the well-being of children and women.

Draft Declaration on adoption and foster placement

The question of a draft Declaration on adoption and foster placement of children was again taken up by the General Assembly in 1985.

In October, the Netherlands, the Philippines, Sweden and Venezuela addressed a letter[28] to the Secretary-General stating that, on the Netherlands initiative, consultations had been held in New York from 16 to 27 September between Member States representing different legal systems concerning the draft Declaration on Social and Legal Principles relating to the Protection and Welfare of Children, with Special Reference to Foster Placement and Adoption, Nationally and Internationally. In 1984,[29] the Assembly had appealed to States to hold the consultations. In a report annexed to the October letter, the Chairman of the consultations stated that he was able to submit a revised draft Declaration offering a good prospect for consensus.

The draft Declaration had originally been prepared by a group of experts in response to a 1975 Economic and Social Council resolution,[30] and was submitted to the Council in 1979.[31]

GENERAL ASSEMBLY ACTION

On 11 December 1985, the General Assembly, acting on the Sixth Committee's recommendation, adopted **decision 40/422** by which it decided that the Committee would hold informal consultations at the beginning of the 1986 Assembly session to consider the remaining questions with a view to adopting the draft Declaration at that time.

REFERENCES
[1]YUN 1980, p. 503, GA res. 35/56, annex, 5 Dec. 1980. [2]E/1985/31. [3]E/ICEF/1985/3 & Corr.1. [4]E/ICEF/1985/L.1. [5]E/ICEF/1985/P/L.27. [6]E/ICEF/1986/5. [7]E/ICEF/1986/6. [8]E/ICEF/1986/7. [9]E/ICEF/1986/8 & Corr.1. [10]E/ICEF/1986/9. [11]E/ICEF/1986/10 & Corr.1. [12]E/ICEF/1986/2 & Corr.1. [13]YUN 1983, p. 932. [14]YUN 1982, p. 1171. [15]E/ICEF/1985/AB/L.2 & Corr.1. [16]YUN 1983, p. 934. [17]YUN 1984, p. 922. [18]*Ibid.*, p. 924. [19]E/ICEF/1985/AB/L.3. [20]E/ICEF/1985/AB/L.8. [21]A/40/5/Add.2. [22]A/40/635. [23]E/ICEF/1986/AB/L.5. [24]E/ICEF/1985/AB/L.6 & Corr.1. [25]YUN 1984, p. 925. [26]E/ICEF/1986/L.1. [27]E/ICEF/1986/AB/L.3. [28]A/40/244. [29]YUN 1984, p. 925, GA res. 39/89, 13 Dec. 1984. [30]YUN 1975, p. 684, ESC res. 1925(LVIII), 6 May 1975. [31]YUN 1979, p. 765.

PUBLICATION
Socio-Economic Differentials in Child Mortality in Developing Countries (ST/ESA/SER.A/97), Sales No. E.85.XIII.7.

Youth

After six years of planning, 1985 was commemorated by the United Nations system as International Youth Year (IYY) to bring about awareness of the situation of young people between the ages of 15 and 24. The culmination of the Year came with a series of meetings of the General Assembly, designated as the United Nations World Conference for IYY, which adopted guidelines for follow-up concerning youth beyond the Year. Because of the guidelines' importance towards developing national youth policies, the Economic and Social Council, in resolution 1985/23, and the Assembly, in resolution 40/14, called for their implementation by Governments and organizations at all levels. In resolution 40/16, the Assembly called on States to increase work opportunities for young people and, in resolution 40/17, it invited the Secretary-General further to improve communication between the United Nations and youth and youth organizations. In resolution 40/15, it made a further call for the implementation of its previous resolutions on human rights relating to youth, particularly regarding education and work, as did the Council, which also stressed the right to life, in adopting resolution 1985/27.

Youth in the 1980s

The situation of youth in the 1980s was examined by the Secretary-General in a January 1985 report[1] to the General Assembly. The report, transmitted through the Economic and Social Council at its 1983 request,[2] provided an overview of the global situation of youth near the mid-point of the decade. With the world's youth population—estimated at 922 million and constituting 19.4 per cent of the total population—projected to exceed 1 billion towards the end of the decade, the Secretary-General outlined, from a regional and sectoral perspective, the major problems confronting young people in regard to development, the family, the world of work and culture. Although the situation of youth varied from country to country and from one region to another, that should not prevent their problems being considered within a global perspective, through which many problems affecting youth at the national level could be better appreciated and remedial action taken. The Secretary-General recommended that Governments continue their efforts to develop integrated youth policies and that the momentum generated by IYY be maintained.

The report was considered at the February 1985 session of the Commission for Social Development,[3] which agreed that IYY provided an opportunity for increasing global awareness of youth problems.

ECONOMIC AND SOCIAL ACTION

On 29 May 1985, the Economic and Social Council, on the recommendation of its Second (Social) Committee, adopted **resolution 1985/23** without vote.

Youth in the contemporary world

The Economic and Social Council,

Noting with great interest the importance attached by the General Assembly and other United Nations bodies to the concerns of youth,

Recalling its resolutions 1979/16 of 9 May 1979, 1981/16 of 6 May 1981 and 1983/14 of 26 May 1983 on youth in the contemporary world, and General Assembly resolution 39/22 of 23 November 1984 on the International Youth Year: Participation, Development, Peace,

Noting with satisfaction that the Declaration on the Promotion among Youth of the Ideals of Peace, Mutual Respect and Understanding between Peoples, continues to provide a useful basis and incentive for further action in the field of youth, at the national, regional and international levels,

Convinced that the preservation and strengthening of international peace and security are prerequisites for a secure and happy future for the youth of all countries,

Recognizing the importance of integrating young people into the overall life of society and of taking fully into account their special needs when formulating national plans and programmes,

Reaffirming the necessity of intensifying and consolidating the efforts of the United Nations so as to give effect to a co-ordinated and practical approach to the youth programmes of all the United Nations agencies involved, as well as strengthening co-operation with non-governmental youth organizations or organizations dealing directly with youth,

1. *Takes note* of the report of the Secretary-General on the situation of youth in the 1980s;

2. *Requests* the Secretary-General to ensure appropriate publicity for that report in the context of the activities undertaken for the observance of the International Youth Year: Participation, Development, Peace;

3. *Decides* that the Commission for Social Development should consider at its thirtieth session ways and means by which it could more effectively deal with youth issues within the appropriate guidelines to be prepared by the Advisory Committee for the International Youth Year and approved by the General Assembly on the occasion of the observance of the International Youth Year;

4. *Decides* to include the theme "Youth in the contemporary world" in the provisional agenda for the thirtieth session of the Commission under the appropriate item and that the Commission should consider a preliminary report of the Secretary-General on the appraisal of the results of the International Youth Year.

Economic and Social Council resolution 1985/23

29 May 1985   Meeting 23   Adopted without vote

Approved by Second Committee (E/1985/96 & Corr.1) without vote, 17 May (meeting 8); draft by Commission for Social Development (E/1985/24 & Corr.1); agenda item 17.

Activities of the UN system

The Secretary-General, in an April 1985 report to the Economic and Social Council,[4] described action by the United Nations system and other organizations to facilitate co-ordination and information in the field of youth. The report, prepared in accordance with a 1984 Council resolution,[5] was based on information received from those bodies on progress achieved and activities undertaken in the context of IYY.

With preparations for IYY intensifying and improving the co-ordination of efforts concerning youth, networks were organized to streamline co-operation and communication. It was necessary to follow up and enlarge upon the experience gained, the Secretary-General said. In addition, the co-ordination of efforts at the national level should be continued during implementation of the guidelines for further planning and suitable follow-up in regard to youth (see p. 978). The Secretary-General stressed that national co-ordinating mechanisms should be encouraged to increase further the involvement of young people in their activities, and he urged that channels of communication between the United Nations and youth and their organizations be strengthened (see p. 980).

Recommendations for youth involvement in environmental issues were made at an African Workshop on Youth for the Environment (Nairobi, 25 and 26 November), organized by the United Nations Environment Programme (see p. 793).

ECONOMIC AND SOCIAL COUNCIL ACTION

On 29 May, the Economic and Social Council, on the recommendation of its Second Committee, adopted **resolution 1985/30** without vote.

Co-ordination and information
in the field of youth

The Economic and Social Council,

Recalling its resolutions 1979/27 of 9 May 1979, 1980/25 of 2 May 1980, 1981/25 of 6 May 1981, 1982/28 of 4 May 1982, 1983/26 of 26 May 1983 and 1984/44 of 21 May 1984, on co-ordination and information in the field of youth,

Recalling also General Assembly resolutions 34/151 of 17 December 1979, 36/28 of 13 November 1981, 37/48 of 3 December 1982, 38/22 of 22 November 1983 and 39/22 of 23 November 1984 on the International Youth Year: Participation, Development, Peace,

Considering that the process of preparation and observance of the International Youth Year, on the basis of the Specific Programme of Measures and Activities to be undertaken prior to and during the International Youth Year, of the recommendations made by the Advisory Committee for the International Youth Year and endorsed by the General Assembly, and of the relevant recommendations of the five regional meetings devoted to the International Youth Year held in 1983, has contributed to intensifying and improving the co-ordination of the activities of the United Nations and specialized agencies relating to youth,

Convinced of the importance of giving widespread publicity to the activities of the United Nations in the field of youth, especially in the context of the observance of the International Youth Year,

Taking note of the report of the Secretary-General on co-ordination and information in the field of youth,

1. *Endorses* the conclusions contained in the report of the Secretary-General on co-ordination and information in the field of youth;

2. *Invites again* all United Nations bodies, specialized agencies, regional commissions and other intergovernmental organizations, as well as non-governmental organizations concerned, to consider at their regular meetings appropriate ways and means for the improvement of co-ordination and information in the field of youth in the context of the observance of the International Youth Year and of the follow-up of future programmes devoted to youth;

3. *Requests* the Secretary-General to take all necessary measures for the successful organization of the appropriate number of plenary meetings at the fortieth session of the General Assembly, in 1985, designated as the United Nations Conference for the International Youth Year, in accordance with paragraph 2 of General Assembly resolution 39/22;

4. *Decides* to consider at its first regular session of 1986, on the basis of a report of the Secretary-General, the achievements in co-ordination and information in the field of youth.

Economic and Social Council resolution 1985/30

29 May 1985   Meeting 23   Adopted without vote

Approved by Second Committee (E/1985/96 & Corr.1) without vote, 17 May (meeting 8); 46-nation draft (E/1985/C.2/L.1); agenda item 17.

Sponsors: Argentina, Bangladesh, Botswana, Chile, China, Colombia, Congo, Costa Rica, Djibouti, Ecuador, Egypt, France, Gambia, Germany, Federal Republic of, Greece, Guinea, Guyana, Haiti, India, Indonesia, Italy, Jamaica, Japan, Malaysia, Malta, Mexico, Morocco, Mozambique, Netherlands, Nigeria, Pakistan, Philippines, Romania, Rwanda, Senegal, Sierra Leone, Somalia, Spain, Sri Lanka, Sudan, Suriname, Turkey, United States, Venezuela, Yugoslavia, Zaire.

International Youth Year

International Youth Year, with its theme of participation, development and peace, was observed by the United Nations in 1985.

Marking the twentieth anniversary of the Declaration on the Promotion among Youth of the Ideals of Peace, Mutual Respect and Understanding between Peoples,[6] IYY was commemorated by the General Assembly at six plenary meetings held between 13 and 18 November—designated as the United Nations World Conference for IYY.

The Assembly had proclaimed 1985 as IYY in 1979 and at the same time set up an intergovernmental Advisory Committee for the Year.[7]

The Committee's report on its fourth session (Vienna, Austria, 25 March–3 April 1985) was submitted to the Assembly by the Secretary-General.[8] As decided by the Assembly in 1984,[9] the Committee prepared a set of guidelines for further planning and suitable follow-up in the field of youth by Governments, the United Nations system and other organizations, especially youth organizations, so as to encourage action in keeping with IYY objectives, and in particular: to enhance awareness of the situation of youth and to increase recognition of youth rights and aspirations on the part of decision-makers and the general public; to promote youth policies as an integral part of social and economic development; to enhance the participation of youth and youth organizations in society, particularly in promoting and achieving development and peace; and to promote among youth the ideals of peace, mutual respect and understanding among people.

In an October 1985 report[10] requested by the Advisory Committee,[11] the Secretary-General informed the Assembly that 158 national co-ordinating committees or other similar structures had been formed, making IYY unique among international events. Considerable interest had been created in the general situation of youth, and the young themselves were involved in preparing for and observing the Year. The report pointed out that general commitment of the cause of youth came from the manifold activities of NGOs at all levels, which had contributed significantly to the outcome of IYY. In addition, the co-ordinated efforts of various intergovernmental organizations and the United Nations system, including its regional commissions, had made a major contribution. Achievements were accomplished by maximizing the use of existing resources.

While there was little doubt about the successful outcome of IYY—whose preparations had been under way since 1980—the Secretary-General stressed that its success was not permanent. There was a need to consolidate what had been achieved and to build further on it, and the guidelines for further planning recommended by the Advisory

Committee provided the general parameters within which youth policies, plans or activities could operate in accordance with each country's priorities. The guidelines envisaged continuing the Trust Fund for IYY after 1985, as a part of the larger attempt to increase technical co-operation activities commensurate with the needs of youth in the developing countries and particularly those in the least developed countries. Therefore, the Secretary-General recommended that the Fund be renamed the United Nations Youth Fund to deal with activities beyond the Year.

The Administrative Committee on Co-ordination, in its annual overview report for 1984/85,[12] recommended strengthening IYY inter-agency co-operation in four main areas: public information; support to national co-ordinating committees; inter-agency co-ordination at the regional level; and the future of inter-agency co-ordination at the global level. It also agreed that publicity be continued and that *Channels*, the IYY secretariat's monthly publication, be more widely distributed through each agency's local, national and regional channels.

In communications to the Secretary-General, the following countries reported on activities relating to IYY. Democratic Yemen (30 May): a statement delivered to its youth on the occasion of IYY.[13] Morocco (22 August): a statement by King Hassan II and an address delivered by Pope John Paul II at Casablanca on 19 August.[14] Romania (11 September): the joint statement of the World Conference of National Committees for IYY, Bucharest, 3-6 September.[15] Spain (18 October): the Barcelona Statement adopted by the World Congress on Youth held under UNESCO auspices, 8-15 July.[16] Ivory Coast (22 October): a message to its youth on the occasion of the formal opening of IYY.[17] Ecuador (5 November)[18] and Poland (13 November):[19] their respective messages in connection with the United Nations World Conference for IYY. USSR: (18 June) its reply to a questionnaire on the Specific Programme of Measures and Activities to be undertaken prior to and during IYY;[20] (9 May) the measures carried out to stimulate Soviet youth participation in politics, socio-economics and culture;[21] (12 August) the appeal of the XII World Festival of Youth and Students (Moscow, 27 July–3 August) to youth and students of the world;[22] and (8 October) the results of the Festival.[23] Jamaica (23 May): the Kingston Declaration of Principles adopted by the International Youth Conference, 6-9 April.[24] Uruguay (1 October): the report of the second Latin American and Caribbean Regional Meeting for IYY, Montevideo, 26-29 August.[25] Hungary (23 October): the report of the European Meeting on Co-operation in the Field of Youth Policies,

Budapest, 26-30 September.[26] German Democratic Republic (14 November): a report on IYY activities.[27]

GENERAL ASSEMBLY ACTION

On 18 November, the General Assembly, acting on the recommendation of the Third (Social, Humanitarian and Cultural) Committee, adopted **resolution 40/14** without vote.

International Youth Year: Participation, Development, Peace

The General Assembly, acting as United Nations World Conference for the International Youth Year,

Recognizing the profound importance of the direct participation of youth in shaping the future of mankind and the valuable contribution that youth can make in all sectors of society, as well as its willingness to express its ideas concerning the building of a better and more just world in which it can attain the objectives of the International Youth Year: Participation, Development, Peace,

Considering it necessary to disseminate among youth the ideals of peace, respect for human rights and fundamental freedoms, human solidarity and dedication to the objectives of progress and development,

Convinced that youth should be encouraged to contribute its energies, enthusiasm and creative abilities to the task of nation-building, the observance of the principles of the Charter of the United Nations, the realization of the right to self-determination and national independence, the respect for sovereignty and non-interference in the internal affairs of each State, the economic, social and cultural advancement of peoples, the implementation of a new international economic order and the promotion of international co-operation and understanding to achieve the objectives of the International Youth Year: Participation, Development, Peace,

Recognizing the important role of United Nations bodies, the specialized agencies and the regional commissions in promoting international co-operation in the field of youth and recognizing that they should continue to give more attention to the role of young people in the world of today, to their ideas and initiatives and to their demands for the world of tomorrow,

Convinced that the preparation for and observance in 1985 of the International Youth Year with the motto "Participation, Development, Peace" have offered a useful and significant opportunity for drawing attention to the situation and the specific needs and aspirations of youth, for increasing co-operation at all levels in dealing with youth issues, for undertaking concerted action programmes in favour of youth and for improving the participation of young people in the study, decision-making processes and resolution of major national, regional and international problems,

Bearing in mind that the International Youth Year has served to mobilize efforts at the local, national, regional and international levels in order to promote the best educational, professional and living conditions for young people, to ensure their active participation in the overall development of society and to encourage their participation in the preparation of new national and local policies and programmes in accordance with the experience, conditions and priorities of each country,

Conscious that the International Youth Year has contributed to strengthening the rights, the ability and the willingness of young people to participate in all activities relevant to them and to promote their own interests,

Commending the organizers of international youth conferences and festivals and other specific activities devoted to the International Youth Year for the results of those events inspired by the motto of the International Youth Year, "Participation, Development, Peace",

Noting with satisfaction the outcome of the World Congress on Youth, held at Barcelona, Spain, from 8 to 15 July 1985 under the auspices of the United Nations Educational, Scientific and Cultural Organization,

Mindful that national committees or other mechanisms to facilitate the planning, implementation and coordination of the activities related to the preparation for and observance of the International Youth Year have been established in a majority of States,

Convinced that the timely and significant impetus generated by the activities of the International Youth Year should be maintained and reinforced with appropriate follow-up action at all levels,

Expressing its appreciation to the Advisory Committee for the International Youth Year and to the United Nations Secretariat for their important contribution to the whole process of preparation and observance of the International Youth Year,

Having considered the report of the Advisory Committee for the International Youth Year on its fourth session, held at Vienna from 25 March to 3 April 1985,

Having considered also the report of the Secretary-General on the implementation of the guidelines and additional guidelines for the improvement of channels of communication between the United Nations and youth and youth organizations,

1. *Endorses* the guidelines for further planning and suitable follow-up in the field of youth as contained in the report of the Advisory Committee for the International Youth Year on its fourth session;

2. *Requests* the Secretary-General to transmit the guidelines for further planning and suitable follow-up in the field of youth to all States, United Nations bodies, the specialized agencies and regional commissions, as well as to other international organizations concerned;

3. *Calls upon* all States, all United Nations bodies, the specialized agencies, regional commissions and intergovernmental and non-governmental organizations concerned, in particular youth organizations, to exert all possible efforts for the implementation of the guidelines for further planning and suitable follow-up in the field of youth, in accordance with their experience, conditions and priorities;

4. *Urges* all States to make every effort to consolidate and build further on the results of the International Youth Year;

5. *Considers* that, as the case may be, the continuing of national committees and other appropriate co-ordination measures at the national level devoted to the International Youth Year could be usefully considered, and notes with satisfaction the intention of national committees in many countries to ensure a proper follow-up, including adequate funding and the integration of the results of the Year into future activities and policies in order to continue to pursue the objectives of the International Youth Year: Participation, Development, Peace;

6. *Requests* the appropriate United Nations bodies and the specialized agencies to consider taking up in their programmes every year one or more specific youth-related projects to be elaborated in close co-operation with non-governmental youth organizations on such themes as communication, housing, culture, youth employment and education;

7. *Recommends* that the Secretary-General keep under review the youth element in the programmes of appropriate United Nations bodies and the specialized agencies;

8. *Requests* the Commission for Social Development to examine, on a regular basis, specific youth issues, in keeping with the objectives of the International Youth Year: Participation, Development, Peace;

9. *Stresses again* the importance of the active and direct participation of youth and youth organizations in the activities organized at the local, national, regional and international levels in the field of youth;

10. *Emphasizes* the importance of improving the active use of the channels of communication between the United Nations system and youth organizations, at both the national and international levels;

11. *Invites* Governments again to consider the regular inclusion of youth representatives in their national delegations to the General Assembly and other relevant United Nations meetings;

12. *Decides* to include in the provisional agenda of its forty-first session an item entitled "Policies and programmes involving young people: Participation, Development, Peace" and to evaluate, in this framework, the results of the International Youth Year on the basis of a report of the Secretary-General.

General Assembly resolution 40/14

18 November 1985   Meeting 80   Adopted without vote

Approved by Third Committee (A/40/855) without vote; 4 November (meeting 30); 97-nation draft (A/C.3/40/L.3); agenda item 89.

Sponsors: Angola, Argentina, Austria, Bahamas, Bangladesh, Barbados, Benin, Botswana, Brazil, Brunei Darussalam, Burkina Faso, Cameroon, Canada, Cape Verde, Central African Republic, Chile, China, Colombia, Comoros, Congo, Costa Rica, Cuba, Cyprus, Djibouti, Dominican Republic, Ecuador, Ethiopia, Finland, France, Gambia, Ghana, Greece, Guatemala, Guinea, Guinea-Bissau, Haiti, Honduras, India, Indonesia, Iran, Iraq, Italy, Ivory Coast, Jamaica, Jordan, Kenya, Kuwait, Lebanon, Lesotho, Liberia, Libyan Arab Jamahiriya, Madagascar, Malaysia, Mali, Malta, Mexico, Morocco, Mozambique, Nepal, Netherlands, Niger, Nigeria, Norway, Oman, Pakistan, Peru, Philippines, Qatar, Romania, Rwanda, Saint Christopher and Nevis, Saint Lucia, Sao Tome and Principe, Senegal, Sierra Leone, Singapore, Somalia, Spain, Sri Lanka, Sudan, Suriname, Swaziland, Syrian Arab Republic, Thailand, Togo, Trinidad and Tobago, Turkey, United Arab Emirates, United Republic of Tanzania, United States, Uruguay, Venezuela, Viet Nam, Yemen, Yugoslavia, Zaire, Zambia.

Meeting numbers. GA 40th session: 3rd Committee 16-23, 30; plenary 75-80.

On 16 December, the Assembly, in **resolution 40/164 A**, urged the Department of Public Information of the Secretariat to ensure the dissemination of information on the guidelines.

Strengthening communication between youth and the United Nations

Channels of communication between the United Nations and youth had been operating for a number of years. To improve these channels further, the General Assembly in 1984[28] had requested the Secretary-General to report on implementation of 1977[29] and 1981[30] guidelines on the topic.

Responding in October 1985,[31] the Secretary-General described developments in implementing the guidelines. Preparations for IYY had resulted in increased communication between the United Nations and youth and youth organizations. Many Governments had included information on the United Nations system in the educational curricula of schools and universities; young people often obtained their first knowledge of the United Nations from these programmes. In that way, educational systems had served as primary, if perhaps unrecognized, channels of communication. Several Governments had also established programmes to facilitate the participation of youth delegates in intergovernmental meetings dealing with youth issues. Such delegates were present at several regional meetings devoted to IYY, at sessions of the Advisory Committee and at General Assembly meetings. In addition, United Nations bodies and NGOs had found innovative ways of mobilizing efforts at all levels in carrying out specific youth programmes. Consideration needed to be given to finding ways to maintain the strong commitment to improving channels of communication and to strengthening co-operation in regard to youth. The dissemination and promotion of the guidelines, prepared by the Advisory Committee for further planning and suitable follow-up concerning youth (see p. 978), required a strengthening of communication channels which, to be more effective, should focus on information dealing with peace and international co-operation, development, employment, environment, and culture and leisure.

Therefore, the Secretary-General suggested the following measures to strengthen those channels: NGOs concerned with youth activities, particularly those at national and regional levels, should apply for consultative status with the Economic and Social Council; involving the family as an information channel should be encouraged; the role of educational institutions in channelling information should be strengthened; use of film and video should be increased; and the translation of information on youth into more languages should be encouraged.

In reply to a questionnaire by the Secretary-General on improving the channels of communication in question, the USSR (17 June) gave its suggestions.[32]

GENERAL ASSEMBLY ACTION

On 18 November, the General Assembly, on the recommendation of the Third Committee, adopted **resolution 40/17** without vote.

Channels of communication between the United Nations and youth and youth organizations

The General Assembly,

Recalling its resolutions 32/135 of 16 December 1977 and 36/17 of 9 November 1981, in which it adopted guidelines for the improvement of the channels of communication between the United Nations and youth and youth organizations, and also recalling its resolution 39/24 of 23 November 1984,

Bearing in mind the importance of the existence of effective channels of communication between the United Nations and youth and youth organizations as a necessary instrument for the information of young people and their participation in the work of the United Nations and the specialized agencies at the national, regional and international levels, and also for informing the United Nations of the problems facing youth with a view to finding solutions to such problems,

Taking note with appreciation of the reports of the Secretary-General on the implementation of the guidelines and additional guidelines for the improvement of channels of communication between the United Nations and youth and youth organizations and on the situation of youth in the 1980s,

Taking note of the report of the Advisory Committee for the International Youth Year on its fourth session, held at Vienna from 25 March to 3 April 1985,

Taking note further of the outcome of the youth conferences and meetings held during 1985 in observance of the International Youth Year: Participation, Development, Peace,

Convinced that the effective and proper functioning of the channels of communication between the United Nations and youth and youth organizations forms a basic prerequisite for the active involvement of young people in the work of the United Nations,

Convinced further that the participation of youth representatives from Member States in international conferences and meetings dealing with youth-related issues can enhance and strengthen the channels of communication through the discussion of such issues, with a view to finding solutions to problems confronting youth in the contemporary world,

1. *Calls upon* Member States, United Nations bodies, the specialized agencies and other governmental and intergovernmental organizations to implement fully the guidelines relating to the channels of communication adopted by the General Assembly in its resolutions 32/135 and 36/17, not only in general terms but also by concrete measures reflecting the issues of importance to young people;

2. *Invites* the Secretary-General to continue his efforts to make use of, further improve and, if possible, extend the existing channels of communication between the United Nations and youth and youth organizations;

3. *Calls upon* national youth mechanisms that have been set up by youth and youth organizations at the national, regional and interregional levels to continue to act as channels of communication between the United Nations and youth and youth organizations, and, where such mechanisms do not exist, recommends that national co-ordinating committees of the International Youth Year should continue to act as channels of communication;

4. *Takes note* of the recommendations on the channels of communication between the United Nations and youth and youth organizations, as contained in the report of the Secretary-General;

5. *Decides* to consider at its forty-first session the item entitled "Policies and programmes relating to youth", on the basis of a report of the Secretary-General.

General Assembly resolution 40/17

18 November 1985   Meeting 80   Adopted without vote

Approved by Third Committee (A/40/856) without vote, 4 November (meeting 30); 35-nation draft (A/C.3/40/L.17); agenda item 95.

Sponsors: Algeria, Austria, Benin, Bolivia, Botswana, Colombia, Costa Rica, Denmark, Djibouti, Dominican Republic, Ecuador, Egypt, Finland, Germany, Federal Republic of, Greece, Guinea, Ivory Coast, Jordan, Kenya, Lebanon, Mali, Morocco, Norway, Panama, Peru, Philippines, Rwanda, Senegal, Somalia, Spain, Sudan, Sweden, Togo, Uruguay, Zaire.

Meeting numbers. GA 40th session: 3rd Committee 16-23, 30; plenary 75-80.

Integrating youth in development and society

During consideration of the situation of youth in the 1980s (see p. 976) by the Commission for Social Development in February 1985,[3] several representatives referred to the serious consequences of the international economic situation for youth, particularly with regard to unemployment, and expressed the view that special efforts should be directed to diminishing its harmful effects. The need to develop job opportunities in rural areas and the necessity of establishing a closer conjunction between education, training and employment were also stressed. The formulation of national youth policies that were capable of an integrated solution of youth problems was also underlined.

On 15 October,[33] Canada forwarded to the Secretary-General the resolutions adopted at the seventy-fourth Inter-Parliamentary Conference (Ottawa, 2-5 September), among which was one on the full exercise of the right of youth to education, vocational training, work and social security.

ECONOMIC AND SOCIAL COUNCIL ACTION

On 29 May 1985, the Economic and Social Council, on the recommendation of its Second Committee, adopted **resolution 1985/27** without vote.

Efforts and measures for securing the implementation and enjoyment by youth of human rights, particularly the rights to life, education and work

The Economic and Social Council,

Drawing attention to the exceptional importance of all forms of assistance in the large-scale integration of young people into the social and economic development of their respective countries on the basis of ensuring the economic, social, cultural, political and civil rights of youth, in particular the rights to life, education and work, in conditions of peace,

Convinced that it is necessary to ensure full enjoyment by youth of the rights stipulated in the Universal Declaration of Human Rights, in the International Covenant on Economic, Social and Cultural Rights and in the International Covenant on Civil and Political Rights, with special regard for the rights to life, education and work, in conditions of peace,

Recalling General Assembly resolutions 36/29 of 13 November 1981, 37/49 of 3 December 1982 and 38/23 of 22 November 1983, and Economic and Social Council resolutions 1979/16 of 9 May 1979, 1981/16 of 6 May 1981 and 1983/17 of 26 May 1983, in which, *inter alia*, the need to adopt appropriate measures for securing the implementation and the enjoyment by youth of human rights, particularly the rights to life, education and work, is recognized,

Considering that the fortieth anniversary of the victory in the Second World War occurs in 1985 and should serve to mobilize efforts and measures for the implementation and enjoyment by youth of the rights to life, education and work,

Convinced that youth can make a valuable contribution to efforts to create a new international economic order,

Recognizing that in many countries the majority of young people, under the prevailing conditions of social and economic crisis, are facing serious problems in the exercise of their rights, particularly the rights to life, education and work,

Aware of the fact that insufficient education and the unemployment of young people limits their ability to participate in the development process and, in this regard, emphasizing the importance of the secondary and higher education of young people, and their access to appropriate technical, vocational guidance and training programmes,

1. *Calls upon* all States, all governmental and non-governmental organizations, interested United Nations bodies and specialized agencies to continue to give priority to the formulation and implementation of effective measures for securing the exercise by youth of the rights to life, education and work, in conditions of peace;

2. *Notes with concern* that there are at present a rapidly growing number of unemployed young people in the world, many of whom have never had work, and that with the growth of unemployment it is becoming increasingly difficult to ensure the basic social and economic rights of youth, especially the rights to life, education and work;

3. *Requests* the Secretary-General to take into account the views expressed in the Commission for Social Development concerning ways and means of realizing the rights of youth, in particular the rights to life, education and work, and also the provisions of the present resolution, in the preparation of documentation for the forthcoming session of the Advisory Committee for the International Youth Year: Participation, Development, Peace;

4. *Requests* the Commission for Social Development to consider at its thirtieth session the progress achieved in connection with the participation of young people in the development of their respective countries and in the realization and exercise of their rights to life, education and work, in conditions of peace.

Economic and Social Council resolution 1985/27

29 May 1985   Meeting 23   Adopted without vote

Approved by Second Committee (E/1985/96 & Corr.1) without vote, 17 May (meeting 8); draft by Commission for Social Development (E/1985/24 & Corr.1); agenda item 17.

GENERAL ASSEMBLY ACTION

On 18 November, the General Assembly adopted two resolutions dealing with youth, both on the recommendation of the Third Committee.

The Assembly adopted **resolution 40/15** without vote.

Efforts and measures for securing the implementation and the enjoyment by youth of human rights, particularly the right to education and to work

The General Assembly,

Recalling its resolutions 36/29 of 13 November 1981, 37/49 of 3 December 1982, 38/23 of 22 November 1983 and 39/23 of 23 November 1984, in which it, *inter alia,* recognized the need to adopt appropriate measures for securing the implementation and the enjoyment by youth of human rights, particularly the right to education and to work,

Recalling also its resolution 34/151 of 17 December 1979, by which it decided to designate 1985 as International Youth Year: Participation, Development, Peace,

Convinced that it is necessary to ensure full enjoyment by youth of the rights stipulated in the Universal Declaration of Human Rights, the International Covenant on Economic, Social and Cultural Rights and the International Covenant on Civil and Political Rights, with special regard to the right to education and to work,

Aware of the fact that insufficient education and the unemployment of young people limit their ability to participate in the development process, and, in this regard, emphasizing the importance of secondary and higher education for young people, as well as access for them to appropriate technical and vocational guidance and training programmes,

Expressing its serious interest in consolidating and building further on the results of the International Youth Year in order to contribute, *inter alia,* to the increasing participation of young people in the socio-economic life of their country,

1. *Calls upon* all States, all governmental and non-governmental organizations and the interested bodies of the United Nations and the specialized agencies to pay continuous attention, in further planning and suitable follow-up in the field of youth, to the implementation of General Assembly resolutions 36/29, 37/49, 38/23 and 39/23 relating to efforts and measures aimed at the promotion of human rights and their enjoyment by youth, particularly the right to education and vocational training and to work, with a view to resolving the problem of unemployment among youth;

2. *Requests* the Commission for Social Development, in examining specific youth issues, to pay adequate attention to the enjoyment by youth of human rights, particularly the right to education and to work;

3. *Invites* national organs of co-ordination or organs implementing policies and programmes in the field of youth to give appropriate priority in the activities to be undertaken after the International Youth Year: Participation, Development, Peace to the implementation and the enjoyment by youth of human rights, particularly the right to education and to work.

General Assembly resolution 40/15

18 November 1985   Meeting 80   Adopted without vote

Approved by Third Committee (A/40/855) without vote, 4 November (meeting 30); 18-nation draft (A/C.3/40/L.11); agenda item 89.

Sponsors: Afghanistan, Algeria, Angola, Bulgaria, Byelorussian SSR, Cuba, Czechoslovakia, Democratic Yemen, German Democratic Republic, Guinea-Bissau, Lao People's Democratic Republic, Mongolia, Mozambique, Nicaragua, Nigeria, Syrian Arab Republic, Viet Nam, Zambia.

Meeting numbers. GA 40th session: 3rd Committee 16-23, 30; plenary 75-80.

The Assembly adopted **resolution 40/16** without vote.

Opportunities for youth

The General Assembly,

Mindful of the need to secure the employment of youth, which is a concern of global character,

Seriously concerned about the widespread lack of satisfactory integration of young people into the workplace in many countries,

Aware that the solid educational and vocational background of young people is of paramount importance in their aspirations to enter professional life,

Noting that many young people, having finished compulsory or primary education, do not enter any institution of higher education or vocational training, or, after beginning such education or training, are unable to complete it, and find it increasingly difficult to be suitably employed,

Seriously concerned that in a number of developing countries, particularly in the least developed ones, a substantial part of the school-age population has a limited possibility of receiving any kind of education, especially among the poor in both rural and urban areas,

Bearing in mind that in many developing countries the widespread lack of opportunity to receive appropriate education and training thus remains a serious impediment to the participation of youth in the development of their societies and to the attainment of the goals set out in the International Development Strategy for the Third United Nations Development Decade,

Recognizing that greater awareness should be brought about by Governments and in the economic sectors in order to accord the highest priority to the elimination of youth unemployment where it exists,

Further recognizing that industrialization should duly take into account the requirements of the promotion of employment, especially for youth,

Taking note of the intention of the Government of Austria to organize and act as host to an international symposium of experts on the questions referred to below, to be held at Vienna in the spring of 1987,

Recalling the results and achievements of the International Youth Year: Participation, Development, Peace, in particular the guidelines for further planning and suitable follow-up in the field of youth,

1. *Calls upon* Member States to lend increased attention to programmes to combat illiteracy and to young people who, after having finished compulsory or primary education, do not enter institutions of higher education or vocational training, or who, after beginning such education or training, are unable to complete it;

2. *Invites* Member States to consider steps to enable more young people to begin and complete higher education or vocational training;

3. *Urges* Member States to dedicate, whenever possible, more resources, through increased technical co-operation activities, to narrowing the gap between demand for and supply of educational and training opportunities at all levels in developing countries, particularly in the least developed ones, and thus to contribute to the achievement of greater equality of employment opportunities for young people in those countries;

4. *Calls upon* Member States to promote a better awareness of the need to preserve, whenever possible,

and to increase work opportunities for young people of both sexes, with particular emphasis on equal opportunities for girls and young women;

5. *Recommends* to Member States that they should promote initiatives whereby new demands, fields or types of occupation are explored, including the fields of protection of the environment, agro-industries and other natural resource-based industries, new technologies as well as "alternative employment opportunities";

6. *Invites* Member States to examine more closely the consequences that the introduction of new technologies in developed and developing countries alike may have with regard to the number of work opportunities, especially for young people, and to find ways to offset any possible adverse consequences, ensuring that such technologies are only introduced in a socially compatible manner;

7. *Requests* the Secretary-General to include in his report on the implementation of the long-term plan of action on youth, to be submitted to the General Assembly at its forty-second session, a detailed analysis of the results of the symposium to be held at Vienna.

General Assembly resolution 40/16

18 November 1985   Meeting 80   Adopted without vote

Approved by Third Committee (A/40/855) without vote, 4 November (meeting 30); 25-nation draft (A/C.3/40/L.15), orally revised; agenda item 89.

Sponsors: Argentina, Austria, Bangladesh, Canada, Egypt, Finland, France, Gambia, Germany, Federal Republic of, Guatemala, Guinea-Bissau, Indonesia, Italy, Japan, Malaysia, Mali, Philippines, Rwanda, Senegal, Singapore, Somalia, Spain, Swaziland, Zaire, Zambia.

Meeting numbers. GA 40th session: 3rd Committee 16-23, 30; plenary 75-80.

REFERENCES

[1]A/40/64-E/1985/5. [2]YUN 1983, p. 939, ESC res. 1983/14, 26 May 1983. [3]E/1985/24 & Corr.1. [4]E/1985/42. [5]YUN 1984, p. 927, ESC res. 1984/44, 25 May 1984. [6]YUN 1965, p. 480, GA res. 2037(XX), 7 Dec. 1965. [7]YUN 1979, p. 983, GA res. 34/151, 17 Dec. 1979. [8]A/40/256. [9]YUN 1984, p. 930, GA res. 39/22, 23 Nov. 1984. [10]A/40/701. [11]YUN 1984, p. 929. [12]E/1985/57. [13]A/40/359. [14]A/40/570. [15]A/40/626. [16]A/40/768. [17]A/40/791. [18]A/40/864. [19]A/C.3/40/10. [20]A/40/390. [21]A/40/298-E/1985/74. [22]A/40/546. [23]A/C.3/40/4. [24]A/40/336. [25]A/40/706. [26]A/40/790. [27]A/40/897. [28]YUN 1984, p. 928, GA res. 39/24, 23 Nov. 1984. [29]YUN 1977, p. 801, GA res. 32/135, annex, 16 Dec. 1977. [30]YUN 1981, p. 1018, GA res. 36/17, annex, 9 Nov. 1981. [31]A/40/631. [32]A/40/389. [33]A/40/837.

PUBLICATIONS

Statistical Indicators on Youth (ST/ESA/STAT/SER.Y/1), Sales No. E/F.85.XVII.12. *National Youth Policies in Developing Countries* (ST/ESA/166), Sales No. E.85.IV.7. *Youth: Identifying Measures for Strengthening Channels of Communication between the United Nations and Youth and Youth Organizations* (ST/ESA/167), Sales No. E.85.IV.9. *Assessment of the Impact of Measures and Activities Accomplished during the International Youth Year: Participation, Development, Peace (1985)* (ST/ESA/200), Sales No. E.87.IV.5.

Aging persons

The question of the aging—persons aged 60 and over—continued to be discussed during 1985 in the context of implementing the Vienna International Plan of Action on Aging adopted by the 1982 World

Assembly on Aging[1] and endorsed by the General Assembly in the same year.[2] The Plan's primary aim was to assist States to deal with the needs of the elderly. The Commission for Social Development, which had been entrusted with the implementation review every four years, undertook its first review in 1985, taking into account a study on the world aging situation estimating that by the year 2025 over 70 per cent of persons aged 60 years and above would live in less developed regions. The Commission identified priorities for action, such as creating national committees on aging, co-ordinated planning, and strengthening of information exchange, training, research and education programmes.

The Economic and Social Council (in resolution 1985/28) and the Assembly (in resolutions 40/29 and 40/30) requested Governments and organizations to promote the Plan of Action, and called for increased contributions to the United Nations Trust Fund for Aging. The Assembly also requested the Secretary-General, in implementing the programme on aging, to pay special attention to the question of elderly women and to respond favourably to a request by the African Regional Conference on Aging (Dakar, Senegal, December 1984) for assistance in establishing an African gerontological society.

Study on the world aging situation. In a study prepared by the United Nations Department of International Economic and Social Affairs (DIESA),[3] it was estimated that, by the year 2025, only 25 per cent of the world's population would be in the 0-14 age group and nearly 14 per cent in the 60-plus group, compared with 1980 when the figures were 35 and 8.5 per cent respectively. The number of persons 60 years of age and above was projected to jump from some 375 million in 1980 to more than 1 billion in 2025, with over 70 per cent living in less developed regions. The study, which brought together data from an abundance of literature stimulated by the 1982 World Assembly, focused on demographic concepts and developmental and humanitarian issues.

Implementation of the Plan of Action

As entrusted by the Assembly in 1982,[2] the Commission for Social Development undertook in February 1985[4] the first review and appraisal of the implementation of the International Plan of Action on Aging. The Commission had before it a report[5] by the Secretary-General, who stated that, in general, the first review indicated that efforts to implement the Plan had succeeded in improving world-wide understanding of the economic, social and cultural implications for the processes of development of the aging of the population, as well as of the related humanitarian and developmental issues.

The Secretary-General suggested further action to ensure the Plan's implementation. He urged Governments to establish a focal point for aging within the national office responsible for population in order to promote national co-ordination of aging questions among agencies dealing with developmental and humanitarian issues, including health, housing and the environment, consumer protection, social welfare, income security and employment and education. In addition, to respond to the need expressed by Governments in every region, it was essential that resources be strengthened for promoting policies on aging through information exchange, data collection and analysis, training and education and research. Taking into consideration the disparity between the current resources of the United Nations Trust Fund for Aging and the number of requests for assistance, it was essential that its resources be strengthened to meet the rapidly increasing needs of the aging in the developing countries, particularly in the least developed. In view of its expertise, the involvement of the United Nations Fund for Population Activities (UNFPA) on aging questions should be strengthened to provide resources for technical co-operation activities, and the Centre for Social Development and Humanitarian Affairs (CSDHA) of DIESA should continue its role as the United Nations focal point in promoting the Plan's implementation.

ECONOMIC AND SOCIAL COUNCIL ACTION

On 29 May, the Economic and Social Council, acting on the recommendation of its Second Committee, adopted **resolution 1985/28** without vote.

First review and appraisal of the implementation of the International Plan of Action on Aging

The Economic and Social Council,

Recalling General Assembly resolution 37/51 of 3 December 1982, in which the Assembly endorsed the International Plan of Action on Aging adopted by the World Assembly on Aging, and requested the Economic and Social Council, through the Commission for Social Development, to review the implementation of the Plan of Action every four years, beginning in 1985,

Mindful of the International Plan of Action on Aging, in which, *inter alia*, it is pointed out that various problems of older people can find their real solution under conditions of peace,

Reaffirming General Assembly resolution 39/25 of 23 November 1984, in which the Assembly recognized the increasing awareness of issues related to aging in many countries and of the need to provide national authorities, at their request, with technical and financial assistance in their efforts to implement policies and programmes,

Noting with appreciation the efforts made by Member States and intergovernmental and non-governmental organizations to implement the principles and recommendations contained in the International Plan of Action on Aging and described in the report of the Secretary-General on the first review and appraisal of the implementation of the Plan of Action,

Recalling General Assembly resolution 39/228 of 18 December 1984, in which the Assembly endorsed the report of the International Conference on Population, containing the recommendations for the further implementation of the World Population Plan of Action, in recommendation 58 of which Governments were urged to reaffirm their commitment to the implementation of the International Plan of Action on Aging,

Recalling also the reaffirmation in General Assembly resolution 39/228 of the need to pay attention to specific problems of population structures,

Reaffirming further General Assembly resolution 39/25, in which the Secretary-General was urged to include advisory services to developing countries that requested them in technical co-operation programmes,

Recalling further that the General Assembly, in resolution 37/51, requested the Secretary-General to continue to use the United Nations Trust Fund for the World Assembly on Aging to meet the rapidly increasing needs of the aging in the developing countries, in particular in the least developed ones,

Convinced that the Trust Fund has a unique contribution to make and a catalytic role to play in the technical co-operation field to implement the goals and recommendations of the International Plan of Action on Aging and to promote innovative and experimental activities in the field of aging,

Stressing the need for close and continuous working relationships between the Trust Fund and those bodies, organs and organizations of the United Nations system concerned with the question of aging, and the need for the Centre for Social Development and Humanitarian Affairs of the Department of International Economic and Social Affairs of the United Nations Secretariat to continue its role as the focal point for promoting the implementation of the International Plan of Action on Aging,

Expressing its appreciation to those Governments and non-governmental organizations which, through their contributions, have upheld the vital role of the Trust Fund,

Noting with concern the disparity between the current resources of the Trust Fund and the large number of requests for assistance, and the fact that the Trust Fund has not been able to consider all the deserving requests for technical assistance received owing to the minimal contributions received during the last two years,

Noting with appreciation the continuing support of the United Nations Fund for Population Activities for population assistance in the field of aging,

1. *Takes note with appreciation* of the report of the Secretary-General on the first review and appraisal of the implementation of the International Plan of Action on Aging;

2. *Urges* Governments and intergovernmental and non-governmental organizations to continue to strengthen their efforts to implement the principles and objectives of the International Plan of Action on Aging;

3. *Invites* Governments to strengthen or establish mechanisms, when necessary, to facilitate the co-ordinated planning and implementation of activities in the field of aging and, where appropriate, to establish a focal point for aging within the national office responsible for population activities;

4.   *Requests* the Secretary-General to continue his efforts to ensure a well co-ordinated system-wide response for the implementation of the Plan of Action at the national, regional and international levels;

5.   *Urges* Governments and governmental and non-governmental organizations, as well as the specialized agencies, to exchange information and experience concerning the adoption of measures to meet the needs of the elderly, including those who contributed to the victory which ended the Second World War;

6.   *Affirms* the role of the Centre for Social Development and Humanitarian Affairs of the Department of International Economic and Social Affairs of the United Nations Secretariat as a focal point for the exchange of such experience between the organizations of the United Nations system;

7.   *Reaffirms* the importance of the provisions of the International Plan of Action on Aging regarding the necessity of halting the arms race and rechannelling the resources spent for military purposes to the needs of economic and social development, particularly for the improvement of the social status of the elderly;

8.   *Urges* the Secretary-General to take the necessary steps to ensure that advisory and other services to developing countries that request them are provided to the extent feasible in technical co-operation programmes and/or through the resources of the Trust Fund for Aging;

9.   *Urges* the United Nations Fund for Population Activities, as a leading organization in international population assistance, to sustain its financial support for technical co-operation activities in respect of aging, particularly in view of the importance given to that issue by the International Conference on Population in its recommendations for the further implementation of the World Population Plan of Action;

10.   *Requests* the Secretary-General to take concrete measures on an urgent basis to promote the financial viability and effectiveness of the Trust Fund;

11.   *Urges* Governments and non-governmental organizations to continue and, where possible, to increase their contributions to the Trust Fund, and calls upon Governments and non-governmental organizations that have not yet done so to consider contributing to the Trust Fund;

12.   *Requests* the Secretary-General, in order to facilitate contributions by Governments, to include the Trust Fund, on an annual basis, among the programmes for which funds are pledged at the United Nations Pledging Conference for Development Activities;

13.   *Further requests* the Secretary-General to report to the General Assembly at its forty-first session on the implementation of the present resolution, in particular on the measures and steps he has taken to further develop the Trust Fund.

Economic and Social Council resolution 1985/28

29 May 1985   Meeting 23   Adopted without vote

Approved by Second Committee (E/1985/96 & Corr.1) without vote, 17 May (meeting 8); draft by Commission for Social Development (E/1985/24 & Corr.1); agenda item 17.

In an October 1985 report[6] to the General Assembly on implementing the International Plan of Action on Aging as assessed in the first review and appraisal, the Secretary-General, as requested in 1984,[7] transmitted his findings. He said that the review showed, at the national level, that progress had been made since 1982 but that opportunities remained limited for the Plan's implementation because of the world economic situation, which had been marked by slow economic growth, inflation, growing unemployment, curbs on government spending for social programmes and, in many developing countries, heightened poverty and hunger spurred by economic decline and population growth. Responding to a questionnaire, 72 countries had indicated that their national committees were facilitating the planning, implementation and co-ordination of activities recommended in the Plan, and that such activities included convening national conferences, improving delivery systems for the elderly and developing their income security systems.

At the international and regional levels, the information exchange network on aging had been strengthened and included some 60 organizations representing all world regions. Concerning the exchange of information and experience, the Secretary-General referred to an interregional seminar (Kiev, Ukrainian SSR, 6-22 September 1985)[8] to promote the Plan's implementation which, in addition to United Nations agencies and NGOs, was attended by developing countries. Regarding research and training, reference was made to the study on the world aging situation,[3] analysing aging trends, summarizing information on the conditions and needs of the aging in diverse regions, and presenting national policies developed to respond to the developmental and humanitarian implications of the aging of populations. The increased coverage and circulation of the quarterly *Bulletin on Aging* reflected the growing volume of United Nations information exchange activities on aging. In addition, the annual *Periodical on Aging*, published by the United Nations, provided scholarly information to policy-makers, planners, human service practitioners and researchers.

The Trust Fund for Aging continued to support technical co-operation projects for the formulation and implementation of programmes on aging. During 1985, six projects—at the national, regional and international levels—were financed on various subjects: needs-assessment surveys, policy elaboration, research, formal and informal training, and seminars to exchange knowledge and experience on questions pertaining to the aging. Particular attention was given to technical co-operation among developing countries as well as to communication and dissemination of information. The Secretary-General reported that, despite his appeals and promotional efforts, voluntary contributions during 1984-1985 had failed to reach a level comparable to that of 1982-1983. In view of the number of projects pending approval, he intended to continue to promote the Fund as an essential instrument for realizing the goals of the Plan of Action. To that end, the Trust Fund had been included in the November 1985 United Nations Pledging Conference for Development Activities (see p. 463), as requested by the Economic and Social Council in resolution 1985/28. Contributions in 1985 totalled $19,830, including $8,000 in pledges. The balance available as at 31 December 1985 was $467,856.

Co-operation within the United Nations system and with other intergovernmental organizations continued. Specialized agencies having had a substantive concern with aging issues included ILO, FAO, UNESCO and WHO; several were designated to execute projects supported by the Trust Fund and also played a major role in the first review and appraisal of the implementation of the Plan of Action. Regional commissions were similarly instrumental in eliciting national interest in the Fund and in encouraging national responses to the review. Co-operation between CSDHA and UNFPA had remained strong since the 1982 World Assembly on Aging.

As for NGOs, the Secretary-General remarked that they had continued to be active in promoting related United Nations work. They were ensuring that aging was considered in the context of United Nations international events, such as the World Conference to Review and Appraise the Achievements of the United Nations Decade for Women (see p. 936), the Seventh United Nations Congress on the Prevention of Crime and the Treatment of Offenders (see p. 738) and International Youth Year (see p. 978). The NGO Committee in New York, for example, conducted an all-day conference on elderly women to promote awareness of the issues related to older women to be considered at the World Conference. The NGO Committee in Vienna worked closely with the IYY secretariat to promote intergenerational activities designed to maintain and strengthen the interdependence of youth and the aging.

GENERAL ASSEMBLY ACTION

On 29 November, the General Assembly, on the recommendation of the Third Committee, adopted two resolutions on aging persons.

The Assembly adopted **resolution 40/29** without vote.

Question of aging

The General Assembly,

Reaffirming its resolution 39/25 of 23 November 1984, in which it recognized the increasing awareness in many countries of issues related to aging and of the need to provide national authorities, at their request,

with technical and financial assistance in their efforts to implement policies and programmes,

Endorsing Economic and Social Council resolution 1985/28 of 29 May 1985, in which Governments and intergovernmental and non-governmental organizations were urged to continue to strengthen their efforts to implement the principles and objectives of the International Plan of Action on Aging and in which the Secretary-General was requested to include, on an annual basis, the United Nations Trust Fund for Aging among the programmes for which funds are pledged at the United Nations Pledging Conference for Development Activities,

Emphasizing the importance of regional meetings to consider the implementation of the recommendations of the Plan of Action, as demonstrated by the African Regional Conference on Aging, held at Dakar in December 1984,

Emphasizing also the positive results of the convening of seminars and meetings to exchange information, knowledge and experience on the question of aging, particularly among developing countries,

Recognizing that the dramatic increase in the numbers and proportion of older adults has serious socio-economic implications and is resulting in an increasing need for research and training at all levels,

Recalling the recommendations of the International Conference on Population, which paid particular attention to the urgent and emerging issues of aging,

Appreciating the efforts of the Director-General for Development and International Economic Co-operation to establish a steering committee and a working group to follow up the implementation of General Assembly resolution 39/228 of 18 December 1984 on the International Conference on Population,

Appreciating the attention given to the question of elderly women by the World Conference to Review and Appraise the Achievements of the United Nations Decade for Women: Equality, Development and Peace and the inclusion of this issue in the Nairobi Forward-looking Strategies for the Advancement of Women,

Stressing the importance of the activities of the United Nations Trust Fund for Aging to assist countries, at their request, in formulating and implementing policies and programmes on aging,

Noting with concern the discrepancies between the resources of the Trust Fund and the number of requests received for assistance,

1. *Takes note with appreciation* of the report of the Secretary-General on the question of aging;

2. *Calls upon* Governments to ensure that the question of aging is incorporated into their national development plans in accordance with the culture and traditions of their countries;

3. *Encourages* Governments to consider convening regional and subregional meetings on the applicability of the recommendations of the International Plan of Action on Aging to their particular needs and conditions;

4. *Requests* the Secretary-General to continue to promote the exchange of information and experience in order to stimulate progress on the question of aging, to encourage the adoption of measures to respond to the economic and social implications of aging and to meet the needs of older persons;

5. *Requests* the Secretary-General to ensure that due consideration is given to the question of aging in the work of the steering committee and the working group to follow up the implementation of General Assembly resolution 39/228 on the International Conference on Population;

6. *Requests* the Secretary-General, in implementing the programme on aging, to pay special attention to the question of elderly women;

7. *Invites* the United Nations Development Fund for Women to give due consideration to projects aimed at benefiting elderly women;

8. *Requests* the Secretary-General to respond favourably to the request of the African Regional Conference on Aging for assistance in establishing an African gerontological society;

9. *Urges* the Secretary-General to take immediate and urgent steps to promote the United Nations Trust Fund for Aging so that it may effectively continue to provide assistance to developing countries, at their request;

10. *Urges* the Secretary-General to include in technical co-operation programmes, to the extent feasible under the funding of those programmes, advisory services to developing countries that request them;

11. *Invites* Governments and non-governmental organizations to continue and, where possible, to increase their contributions to the United Nations Trust Fund for Aging, and calls upon Governments and non-governmental organizations that have not yet done so to consider contributing to the Trust Fund;

12. *Invites* the United Nations Fund for Population Activities to consider co-operating with the United Nations Trust Fund for Aging in providing assistance for projects received by the Trust Fund that fall within its mandate;

13. *Requests* the Secretary-General to submit to the General Assembly at its forty-first session a progress report on the implementation of the recommendations contained in the present resolution;

14. *Decides* to include in the provisional agenda of its forty-first session the item entitled "Question of aging".

General Assembly resolution 40/29

29 November 1985   Meeting 96   Adopted without vote

Approved by Third Committee (A/40/928) without vote, 11 November (meeting 37); 19-nation draft (A/C.3/40/L.27); agenda item 96.
Sponsors: Austria, Bangladesh, Cyprus, Dominican Republic, Egypt, Gambia, Germany, Federal Republic of, Greece, Guatemala, Guinea, Indonesia, Jordan, Malta, Morocco, Philippines, Romania, Senegal, Sudan, Thailand.
Meeting numbers. GA 40th session: 3rd Committee 16-23, 37; plenary 96.

The Assembly adopted **resolution 40/30** without vote.

Implementation of the International Plan of Action on Aging

The General Assembly,

Recalling its resolution 33/52 of 14 December 1978, by which it decided to organize a World Assembly on Aging in 1982 as a forum to launch an international programme of action aimed at guaranteeing economic and social security to older persons, as well as opportunities for them to contribute to national development,

Recalling further its resolution 37/51 of 3 December 1982, by which it endorsed the International Plan of Action on Aging adopted by consensus by the World Assembly on Aging,

Reaffirming the part of the preamble of the Plan of Action that solemnly recognizes that the quality of life is no less important than longevity and that the aging should therefore, as far as possible, be enabled to enjoy in their own families and communities a life of fulfilment, health, security and contentment and be appreciated as an integral part of society,

Well aware that the formulation and implementation of policies on aging are the sovereign right and responsibility of each State, and recognizing that the promotion of the activities, safety and well-being of the elderly should be an essential part of an integrated and concerted development effort,

Concerned that the report of the Secretary-General on the first review and appraisal of the implementation of the Plan of Action shows that, in 1985, 55.4 per cent of the global population of the elderly is living in developing regions and that, according to projections, by the year 2025 more than 70 per cent of all persons sixty years of age and over will live in developing countries, which are least prepared to meet the economic and social consequences of this drastic shift in population structure,

Convinced that the elderly must be considered an important and necessary element in the development process at all levels within a given society,

Convinced also that increasing longevity is an achievement of mankind and a sign of progress, and that the aged are an asset and not a liability to society because of the invaluable contribution they can make by virtue of their accumulated wealth of knowledge and experience,

Mindful that 1985 is the first year in which the General Assembly has had the opportunity to review the progress made in implementing the Plan of Action, adopted in 1982,

Noting with concern that contributions pledged to the United Nations Trust Fund for Aging decreased to $39,110 in the twelve-month period ending in December 1984, despite the repeated appeals of the Secretary-General to increase contributions,

Noting also with concern that the expenditures of the Trust Fund are expected to decrease from $450,000 in the biennium 1984-1985 to $150,000 in the next biennium,

Alarmed that the proposed programme budget for the biennium 1986-1987 shows a projected cut of 30 per cent in the funds to be allocated from the regular budget to the Aging Unit of the Centre for Social Development and Humanitarian Affairs,

Deeply preoccupied with the fact that the Aging Unit lacks the structural organization, autonomy, funds and necessary manpower to carry out effectively its mandate of implementing the Plan of Action,

1. *Requests* the Secretary-General to invite Member States, the specialized agencies and other organizations concerned within the United Nations system to comment on ways and means of implementing the International Plan of Action on Aging and, in particular, on the desirability and viability of elaborating a United Nations programme for the implementation of the Plan of Action, and to prepare a report on the basis of these comments for submission to the Economic and Social Council at its first regular session of 1986;

2. *Further requests* the Secretary-General to include in that report a full analysis of the programmatic and financial aspects of activities undertaken by all organs, bodies and organizations of the United Nations system under the Plan of Action since its inception;

3. *Invites* interested non-governmental organizations in consultative status with the Economic and Social Council to provide, through the Secretary-General, information and documentation that will facilitate this work;

4. *Requests* the Economic and Social Council to consider the report at its first regular session of 1986 and to submit appropriate recommendations to the General Assembly at its forty-first session;

5. *Decides* to consider at its forty-first session the recommendations of the Economic and Social Council as a matter of high priority.

General Assembly resolution 40/30

29 November 1985   Meeting 96   Adopted without vote

Approved by Third Committee (A/40/928) without vote, 19 November (meeting 46); draft by Canada, France, Greece, and Yugoslavia for Group of 77 (A/C.3/40/L.26/Rev.1), orally revised; agenda item 96.
Meeting numbers. GA 40th session: 3rd Committee 16-23, 37, 46, 53; plenary 96.

REFERENCES

[1]YUN 1982, p. 1184. [2]*Ibid.*, p. 1186, GA res. 37/51, 3 Dec. 1982. [3]*The World Aging Situation: Strategies and Policies* (ST/ESA/150), Sales No. E.85.IV.5. [4]E/1985/24 & Corr.1. [5]E/1985/6 & Corr.1. [6]A/40/714. [7]YUN 1984, p. 933, GA res. 39/25, 23 Nov. 1984. [8]*Report of the Interregional Seminar to Promote the Implementation of the International Plan of Action on Aging (Vienna)* (ST/ESA/181), Sales No. E.86.IV.5.

Chapter XXI

Refugees and displaced persons

In the thick of the major emergency in Africa and the persistence of difficult situations in many other parts of the world, the Office of the United Nations High Commissioner for Refugees (UNHCR) continued to seek long-term solutions and provide care and maintenance to refugees throughout 1985. Wherever feasible, relief efforts were complemented by self-sufficiency activities. Regarding international protection, some encouraging developments in respect of improved standards of treatment of refugees were offset by mounting concern over the movements of refugees across continents and over the grant of asylum. Violations of physical safety continued to cause grave concern. The need to identify new responses to problems posed by the exodus of asylum-seekers fleeing situations of generalized violence rather than individual persecution also became apparent. The Secretary-General stressed that international efforts for the relief of refugees and their voluntary return or resettlement represented one of the most practical expressions of international solidarity (see p. 11).

The African emergency, in which UNHCR confronted a situation of mass exodus in the midst of severe drought and famine, absorbed much of the Office's energies, particularly in the Central African Republic, Ethiopia, Somalia and the Sudan.

While the emergency represented a serious setback to hopes expressed at the Second (1984) International Conference on Assistance to Refugees in Africa (ICARA II), UNHCR continued to link the issues of refugee aid and development by encouraging programmes in Africa similar to a UNHCR–World Bank pilot project in Pakistan. With a growing number of Afghan refugees, Pakistan remained the country hosting the largest single refugee population, estimated at 2.7 million. Approximately 1.8 million Afghan refugees were also in Iran. In South-East Asia, resettlement in third countries remained the main durable solution for refugees in camps, though an increasing number of Indo-Chinese long-stayers awaiting resettlement caused concern. Under the Orderly Departure Programme, 100,000 Indo-Chinese had by year's end been reunited with family members abroad. UNHCR also continued helping some 112,000 refugees in Central America and Mexico. Voluntary repatriation programmes were carried out for Lao refugees from Thailand, Ugandan refugees from the Sudan and Zaire, and Argentine refugees from other countries in Latin America.

As before, assistance to Palestine refugees was provided by the United Nations Relief and Works Agency for Palestine Refugees in the Near East (see p. 353).

The Executive Committee of the UNHCR Programme held in 1985 its resumed thirty-fifth session (Geneva, 24 January), at which it considered a number of administrative and financial items deferred from 1984, and its thirty-sixth session (Geneva, 7-18 October). The Committee described international protection as a pillar of UNHCR work and urged Governments to co-operate in providing protection to refugees, a subject again taken up by its Sub-Committee on international protection.

In December, the General Assembly called on States to promote durable solutions and to contribute generously to the High Commissioner's humanitarian programmes (resolution 40/118). It also urged the international community to maintain the momentum created by ICARA II (40/117), and called for emergency assistance to returnees and displaced persons in Chad (40/136), displaced persons in Ethiopia (40/133) and refugees in Somalia (40/132) and in the Sudan (40/135). The Assembly also called for humanitarian assistance to refugees in Djibouti (40/134) as well as aid to student refugees in southern Africa (40/138).

The Assembly further requested the Group of Governmental Experts on International Co-operation to Avert New Flows of Refugees to conclude its review of the problem (resolution 40/166).

The 1985 Nansen Medal—named for Fridtjof Nansen, first League of Nations High Commissioner for Refugees—went to Cardinal Paulo Evaristo Arns, Archbishop of São Paulo, Brazil, for his efforts to assist refugees and address the root causes of their problems.

Poul Hartling, High Commissioner for Refugees since 1978, relinquished that post at the end of 1985. Thanking him for his dedication (resolution 40/119), the Assembly elected Jean-Pierre Hocké (Switzerland) for a three-year term beginning on 1 January 1986 (decision 40/310).

Topics related to this chapter. Middle East: Palestine refugees. Economic assistance, disasters and emergency relief. Human rights: human rights of non-citizens; mass exoduses. Women. Children.

Programme and finances of UNHCR

Programme policy

Executive Committee action. At its October 1985 session, the Executive Committee of the UNHCR Programme[1] expressed deep concern at the seriousness of the emergency in Africa. It was also concerned at the continuing severity of refugee situations in other parts of the world, particularly in Asia and Central America, and called for further efforts to meet needs in those areas and tackle the root causes. It also welcomed the increase of budgetary resources allocated to durable solutions and urged the pursuit of such solutions, particularly voluntary repatriation.

Commending the secretariat for a report[2] on action taken on its decisions, the Committee requested similar reports in the future.

The Committee took note of progress made in promoting development projects to assist refugees, and urged the High Commissioner to continue that work in co-operation with United Nations bodies and non-governmental organizations (NGOs). It encouraged UNHCR to promote resettlement when neither voluntary repatriation nor local integration was feasible and appealed to Governments to facilitate the admission of refugees by a flexible application of selection criteria in providing resettlement opportunities. It noted the need for continued support for the Disembarkation Resettlement Offers and Rescue at Sea Resettlement Offers schemes and commended UNHCR's continuing efforts to promote the Orderly Departure Programme from Viet Nam (see p. 1008).

Regarding refugee and displaced women, the Committee welcomed the recommendations of the July World Conference to Review and Appraise the Achievements of the United Nations Decade for Women (see Chapter XIX of this section).

In meeting refugee needs, UNHCR continued co-operating with other United Nations organizations, in particular with the World Food Programme (WFP) in providing some 490,000 metric tonnes of emergency food aid in 1985, with the World Bank and the International Labour Organisation in promoting self-reliance and income-generating or employment opportunities, and with the United Nations Children's Fund (UNICEF) in supplying primary health care, water supplies and basic sanitation. It also co-operated with the Organization of African Unity (OAU), the Intergovernmental Committee for Migration, the League of Arab States, the Organization of the Islamic Conference, the European Parliament and the Council of Europe, as well as liberation movements and NGOs.

Following consideration of the 1985 report of the High Commissioner,[3] the General Assembly, on the recommendation of the Third (Social, Humanitarian and Cultural) Committee, adopted on 13 December **resolution 40/118** without vote.

Report of the United Nations High Commissioner for Refugees

The General Assembly,

Having considered the report of the United Nations High Commissioner for Refugees on the activities of his Office, as well as the report of the Executive Committee of the Programme of the High Commissioner on the work of its thirty-sixth session, and having heard the statement made by the High Commissioner on 11 November 1985,

Recalling its resolution 39/140 of 14 December 1984,

Reaffirming the purely humanitarian and non-political character of the activities of the Office of the High Commissioner,

Deeply concerned that refugees and displaced persons of concern to the High Commissioner continue to face distressingly serious problems in all parts of the world,

Particularly concerned that in various regions the safety and welfare of refugees and asylum-seekers continue to be seriously jeopardized on account of military or armed attacks, acts of piracy and other forms of brutality,

Stressing the fundamental importance of the High Commissioner's function to provide international protection and the need for States to co-operate with the High Commissioner in the exercise of this essential function, particularly in view of the continued and persistent violations of the basic rights of refugees and asylum-seekers,

Emphasizing that voluntary repatriation or return remains the most desirable solution to the problems of refugees and displaced persons of concern to the High Commissioner,

Emphasizing also the importance for the international community to continue to provide assistance and resettlement opportunities for those refugees for whom no other durable solution may be in sight, particularly in regions where countries of first refuge continue generously to receive refugees arriving by land or by sea,

Commending States that, despite severe economic and developmental problems of their own, continue to admit large numbers of refugees and displaced persons into their territories,

Noting with deep appreciation the valuable support extended by many Governments to the High Commissioner in the performance of his humanitarian tasks,

Deeply concerned about the shortage of funds faced by the High Commissioner and its consequences for his ability to fulfil his mandate,

Noting with satisfaction the efforts of the High Commissioner, in the field of international protection, to address the special problems of refugee and displaced women and children resulting from their vulnerable position, which in many cases exposes them to a variety of difficult situations affecting their physical and legal protection as well as their psychological and material well-being,

Noting with satisfaction and encouraging the continuing and increasing co-operation between the Office of the High Commissioner and other bodies of the United Nations system, as well as intergovernmental and non-governmental organizations,

Desirous of ensuring the speedy implementation of the recommendations and pledges made at the Second International Conference on Assistance to Refugees in Africa, held at Geneva from 9 to 11 July 1984,

1. *Commends* the United Nations High Commissioner for Refugees and his staff for the dedicated and efficient manner in which they discharge their responsibilities;

2. *Strongly reaffirms* the fundamental nature of the High Commissioner's function to provide international protection and the need for Governments to continue to co-operate fully with his Office in order to facilitate the effective exercise of this function, in particular by acceding to and implementing the relevant international and regional refugee instruments and by scrupulously observing the principles of asylum and *non-refoulement;*

3. *Condemns* all violations of the rights and safety of refugees and asylum-seekers, in particular those perpetrated by military or armed attacks against refugee camps and settlements and other forms of brutality and by the failure to rescue asylum-seekers in distress at sea;

4. *Welcomes* the fact that arrangements introduced by the High Commissioner have increased significantly the rescue of asylum-seekers in distress at sea and that preventive measures have resulted in a decline in the number of refugee boats attacked by pirates;

5. *Urges* all States, in co-operation with the Office of the High Commissioner and other competent international bodies, to take all measures necessary to ensure the safety of refugees and asylum-seekers;

6. *Also urges* all States to support the High Commissioner in his efforts to achieve durable solutions to the problem of refugees and displaced persons of concern to his Office, primarily through voluntary repatriation or return, including assistance to returnees, as appropriate, or, wherever appropriate, through integration into countries of asylum or resettlement in third countries;

7. *Endorses* the conclusions on voluntary repatriation adopted by the Executive Committee of the Programme of the High Commissioner at its thirty-sixth session and urges States to extend their full co-operation to the High Commissioner to that effect;

8. *Expresses its warm appreciation* for the work done by the High Commissioner to put into practice the concept of development-oriented assistance to refugees and returnees, as initiated at the Second International Conference on Assistance to Refugees in Africa, and urges him to continue that process, wherever appropriate, in co-operation with the World Bank, the United Nations Development Programme and other organizations, and, further, urges Governments to support these efforts;

9. *Commends* the High Commissioner's programmes for refugee and displaced women, especially those undertaken to secure their protection and to help them to become self-sufficient through educational, vocational and income-generating projects;

10. *Expresses deep appreciation* for the valuable material and humanitarian response of receiving countries, in particular those developing countries that, despite limited resources, continue to admit, on a permanent or temporary basis, large numbers of refugees and asylum-seekers, and, reaffirming the principle of international solidarity and burden-sharing, urges the international community to assist receiving countries in order to enable them to cope with the additional burden created by the presence of those refugees and asylum-seekers;

11. *Commends* all States that facilitate the attainment of durable solutions and contribute generously to the High Commissioner's programmes;

12. *Expresses deep appreciation* for the valuable co-operation between the Office of the High Commissioner and intergovernmental and non-governmental agencies;

13. *Calls upon* all States to promote durable solutions and to contribute generously to the High Commissioner's humanitarian programmes in order to assist refugees, returnees and displaced persons of concern to the High Commissioner in a spirit of international solidarity and burden-sharing.

General Assembly resolution 40/118

13 December 1985   Meeting 116   Adopted without vote

Approved by Third Committee (A/40/934) without vote, 21 November (meeting 49); 38-nation draft (A/C.3/40/L.43), orally revised; agenda item 105 *(a).*
Sponsors: Argentina, Australia, Austria, Bangladesh, Belgium, Bolivia, Canada, Costa Rica, Cyprus, Denmark, Djibouti, Dominican Republic, Egypt, Finland, France, Gambia, Germany, Federal Republic of, Greece, Honduras, Iceland, Italy, Japan, Lesotho, Morocco, Netherlands, New Zealand, Nicaragua, Norway, Pakistan, Philippines, Portugal, Senegal, Sierra Leone, Spain, Sudan, Sweden, Thailand, Zaire.
Meeting numbers. GA 40th session: 3rd Committee 37-41, 49; plenary 116.

Financial and administrative questions

UNHCR voluntary funds expenditure in 1985 amounted to $459 million as compared with $445 million in 1984. Of that total, some $282 million was spent on General Programmes and $177 million on Special Programmes and other trust funds.

Total income for 1985 was $435.4 million.

Expressing appreciation for the 1985 contributions, the UNHCR Executive Committee[1] voiced concern at the critical funding situation affecting the 1985 and future General Programmes and urged Governments to announce increased contributions for 1986.

Contributions

Contributions from government sources totalled over $322.8 million in 1985. In addition, intergovernmental organizations provided $53.5 million, and NGOs and private sources made donations valued at $16.5 million.

Appeals by the Commissioner for contributions to Special Programmes[4] continued in response to specific needs, such as: the African emergency; returnees to Ethiopia, Kampuchea, the Lao People's Democratic Republic and Uganda; the Refugee Education Account; the South-East Asia Anti-Piracy Programme; and the Orderly Departure Programme from Viet Nam.

At its October session,[1] the Executive Committee approved a target of $320.4 million (not including $10 million for the Emergency Fund) for 1986 General Programmes, urging donors, especially Governments, to recognize their primary importance and to make higher contributions.

Government contributions were announced at a 15 November 1985 meeting of the *Ad Hoc* Committee of the General Assembly for the Announcement of Voluntary Contributions to the 1986 Programme of UNHCR.[5]

CONTRIBUTIONS PAID OR PLEDGED TO UNHCR ASSISTANCE PROGRAMMES, 1985
(as at 31 December 1985; in US dollar equivalent)

State or Territory	1985 payment or pledge	State or Territory	1985 payment or pledge	State or Territory	1985 payment or pledge
Algeria	50,000	Kuwait	249,103	Thailand	15,000
Argentina	19,235	Lao People's Democratic Republic	6,000	Trinidad and Tobago	2,073
Australia	5,854,137	Liechtenstein	12,230	Tunisia	23,033
Austria	458,240	Luxembourg	115,579	Turkey	17,399
Bahamas	4,500	Madagascar	801	United Kingdom	18,278,980
Bangladesh	4,975	Malaysia	20,000	United Republic of Tanzania	2,254
Barbados	2,250	Maldives	500	United States	123,957,115
Belgium	3,178,402	Mali	13,055	Uruguay	1,998
Bermuda	10,000	Malta	948	Venezuela	20,000
Botswana	976	Mauritius	3,000	Viet Nam	950
Brunei Darussalam	10,000	Mexico	60,000	Yugoslavia	19,211
Cameroon	22,988	Monaco	1,025	Zambia	1,709
Canada	12,324,824	Netherlands	9,775,859	Zimbabwe	16,770
Chile	20,000	New Zealand	211,405		
China	441,131	Nicaragua	1,000	Subtotal	322,830,715
Colombia	13,500	Norway	12,350,537		
Costa Rica	5,000	Oman	6,000	*Intergovernmental*	
Cyprus	3,409	Pakistan	3,145	European Economic Community	52,881,351
Denmark	14,280,794	Panama	500	OPEC Fund	334,000
Djibouti	3,000	Papua New Guinea	999	United Nations African	
Egypt	9,740	Philippines	4,622	Emergency Fund	97,400
El Salvador	2,000	Portugal	100,000	UNICEF	10,375
Finland	2,669,729	Qatar	35,000	United Nations Trust Fund for	
France	5,591,457	Republic of Korea	10,000	Population Activities	28,648
Germany, Federal Republic of	30,198,441	Rwanda	4,816	United Nations Trust Fund for	
Greece	77,878	Saudi Arabia	4,115,033	Southern Africans	165,000
Holy See	52,500	Senegal	3,000	United Nations Voluntary Fund	
Iceland	30,200	Sierra Leone	566	for Victims of Torture	10,000
Indonesia	4,000	Somalia	598		
Ireland	506,674	Spain	1,175,192	Subtotal	53,526,774
Israel	40,000	Sudan	5,000		
Italy	5,875,821	Swaziland	1,036	*Private sources*	16,463,798
Ivory Coast	3,691	Sweden	13,200,535		
Japan	47,021,317	Switzerland	10,196,330	Total	392,821,287

SOURCE: A/41/5/Add.5.

Accounts of voluntary funds for 1984

The audited financial statements on the voluntary funds administered by UNHCR for the year ended 31 December 1984 showed a total expenditure of $444.8 million and total income of $388.9 million.[6]

In a September 1985 report,[7] the Advisory Committee on Administrative and Budgetary Questions (ACABQ) commented on the Board of Auditors' report.[6]

In October,[1] the UNHCR Executive Committee took note of the accounts and reports and, noting the further efforts to improve financial planning and control, stressed the importance of pursuing and strengthening them.

In December, the General Assembly, in **resolution 40/238**, accepted the Board's financial report and audit opinions, concurred with ACABQ's observations and requested the High Commissioner to take the required remedial action.

UN High Commissioner for Refugees

With Poul Hartling, a national of Denmark, United Nations High Commissioner for Refugees since 1 January 1978, due to relinquish his duties on 31 December 1985, the General Assembly in December by **decision 40/310** elected Jean-Pierre Hocké, from Switzerland, to that position for three years, beginning 1 January 1986. The Assembly took that action on the Secretary-General's proposal.[8]

GENERAL ASSEMBLY ACTION

On 13 December, on the recommendation of the Third Committee, the General Assembly adopted **resolution 40/119** without vote.

Expression of appreciation to the United Nations High Commissioner for Refugees

The General Assembly,

Noting with deep regret that the United Nations High Commissioner for Refugees will shortly be relinquishing his duties,

Recognizing the significant progress achieved under his guidance in promoting humanitarian solutions to the problems of refugees and displaced persons in various parts of the world,

Considering his unrelenting efforts to alleviate human suffering through the special humanitarian tasks entrusted to him in addition to the original functions of his Office,

1. *Expresses its sincere appreciation and thanks* to Mr. Poul Hartling for the effective and dedicated manner in which he has performed his functions as United Nations High Commissioner for Refugees;

2. *Extends its good wishes* to him for success in his future undertakings.

General Assembly resolution 40/119

13 December 1985   Meeting 116   Adopted without vote

Approved by Third Committee (A/40/934) without vote, 21 November (meeting 49); 18-nation draft (A/C.3/40/L.44); agenda item 105.
Sponsors: China, Colombia, Costa Rica, Denmark, Djibouti, Egypt, France, Gabon, Germany, Federal Republic of, Indonesia, Mexico, Pakistan, Philippines, Rwanda, Sudan, Thailand, United States, Zaire.
Meeting numbers. GA 40th session: 3rd Committee 37-41, 49; plenary 116.

REFERENCES

[1]A/40/12/Add.1. [2]A/AC.96/665. [3]A/40/12. [4]A/AC.96/659 & Corr.1. [5]A/AC.228/SR.1. [6]A/40/5/Add.5. [7]A/40/635. [8]A/40/1014.

Activities for refugees

Assistance

During 1985, General Programmes expenditure totalled $282 million ($346 million in 1984).[1] This amount included $5.9 million obligated from the Emergency Fund which was used mostly in Africa— $3 million went to finance assistance to refugees and persons of concern to UNHCR in the Sudan, while $2 million was spent on relief assistance to returnees in Ethiopia. An amount of $100,000 was also utilized to assist displaced persons in Lebanon. UNHCR continued to improve its emergency preparedness and response capabilities.

The provision of intermediate assistance to refugees in the form of care and maintenance (food, shelter, water, health services and sanitation, education, counselling) accounted for some 53 per cent of total General Programmes expenditure, down from 59 per cent in 1984.

The largest single care and maintenance programme was the assistance programme for Afghan refugees in Pakistan, for which $46.5 million was obligated under the 1985 General Programme. Over $10.5 million of this amount was devoted to income-generating and self-sufficiency measures. An amount of $34.4 million was obligated for Indo-Chinese refugees in East and South-East Asia, of which $20.9 million was for care and maintenance in Thailand pending identification of a more durable solution. In Somalia, $10.6 million was allocated for Ethiopian refugees; in Central America, $15.5 million was obligated for care and maintenance because local integration in Costa Rica, Honduras, Mexico and Nicaragua remained relatively slow.

Self-sufficiency activities were intensified in Costa Rica, Djibouti, Kenya, Pakistan and the Sudan, which were supported by some 80 community counselling service projects in 47 countries.

Elementary education continued to be provided in local government schools or in specially established settlement schools. UNHCR had over 113 world-wide programmes in post-primary, vocational/technical and academic education. In addition, $10.6 million was spent to enable 16,000 refugee students to study at the secondary and tertiary levels—24 per cent of them took technical training courses, 67 per cent attended secondary academic schools and 9 per cent were enrolled in universities.

Promoting durable solutions remained the primary objective of UNHCR. Renewed efforts were made to achieve voluntary repatriation, local integration in the country of first asylum, or resettlement to a third country when other options were not feasible. Almost 42 per cent of General Programmes resources were used to finance the implementation of durable solutions, notably local integration in Africa, Central America and China, while UNHCR succeeded in phasing out its assistance to relatively self-reliant rural settlements in the United Republic of Tanzania, Zaire and Zambia. The year 1985 witnessed major voluntary repatriation operations in Africa, Asia, Latin America and Western Europe as a result of concerted approaches to such repatriation. Successful initiatives and actions regarding the continuing linkage between refugee aid and development were undertaken with the World Bank and the United Nations Development Programme (UNDP).

Approximately 107,600 refugees were resettled in third countries, including 25,000 Vietnamese who were helped through the Orderly Departure Programme to reunite with their families abroad. Resettlement remained the principal durable solution for Indo-Chinese refugees—some 59,000 were resettled in 1985.

UNHCR strengthened its efforts to ensure that handicapped refugees benefited from medical facilities and services in their respective countries of asylum. The needs of over 5,700 were met at a cost of $775,000 obligated under General Programmes in 1985. In addition, some 51 severely handicapped refugees who could not be rehabilitated locally were referred to medical centres abroad at a cost of $100,000 obligated under Special Programmes, while some 270 others were resettled in Europe, North America and Australia.

While implementing durable solutions continued in various parts of the world, expenditure in Africa under UNHCR voluntary funds reached some $225.8 million, of which $97 million was obligated under General Programmes and $128.8 million under Special Programmes.

In October,[2] the UNHCR Executive Committee noted with concern that the basic rights of refugees continued to be disregarded and that, in particular, they were being exposed to violent acts, arbitrary detention and *refoulement*. It welcomed the fact that provision of resettlement places had made it possible for the Rescue at Sea Resettlement Offers scheme to commence on a trial basis as from May 1985. It requested shipowners to inform shipmasters in the South China Sea of their responsibility to rescue asylum-seekers in distress. It expressed concern at both the serious emergency in Africa and the severity of the refugee situations in Central America and South-East and South-West Asia, and called for further efforts to meet needs in those areas. The Committee commended Governments that provided emergency resettlement places at short notice and urged others to provide such places. It also commended UNHCR's continuing efforts to promote the Orderly Departure Programme from Viet Nam.

To facilitate planning and rapid action, UNHCR continued to issue basic data on countries receiving large numbers of refugees; profiles on Ethiopia, Pakistan and the Sudan were completed in 1985.

A plan of operations for the Sudan was prepared. A guide to in-kind contributions was also drawn up. The UNHCR *Handbook for Emergencies*, published in English, French and Spanish, was distributed widely, as well as a large number of health, field and nutritional kits. The magazine *Refugees*, providing up-to-date information on world-wide refugee problems, was published monthly in English, French and Spanish, and special editions were also issued in Arabic, German and Italian.

During the year, UNHCR released two documentary films—"Fugitives in Africa" and "Casualties of Conflict"—and co-produced a series of films with television networks and film companies. Films, photographs, slide shows, maps and various printed materials were also provided to media, Governments, intergovernmental organizations and voluntary agencies for educational and fund-raising purposes. It also organized in March an itinerant media seminar in South-East Asia for journalists from the international media, and in September UNHCR initiated an emergency management training programme.

UNHCR EXPENDITURE IN 1985 BY COUNTRY OR AREA*

(in thousands of US dollars)

Country or area	Local settlement	Resettlement	Voluntary repatriation	Relief† and other assistance	Total
AFRICA					
Algeria	3,265.8	—	—	6.5	3,272.3
Angola	4,771.5	—	15.4	88.8	4,875.7
Botswana	977.6	11.4	3.5	87.5	1,080.0
Burundi	614.8	0.5	10.0	50.9	676.2
Cameroon	1,586.8	0.6	—	· 1.0	1,588.4
Central African Republic	431.8	1.6	—	2,499.1	2,932.5
Djibouti	2,509.3	1.7	5.2	90.2	2,606.4
Egypt	1,566.2	168.0	—	67.0	1,801.2
Ethiopia	13,751.6	194.8	4,556.3	2,370.0	20,872.7
Kenya	1,920.4	15.4	2.9	628.0	2,566.7
Lesotho	538.7	6.0	—	46.6	591.3
Mozambique	268.8	8.0	2.0	110.0	388.8
Nigeria	756.8	—	—	—	756.8
Rwanda	4,683.1	5.8	378.1	30.7	5,097.7
Senegal	616.1	139.8	—	10.4	766.3
Somalia	17,785.3	0.8	5.3	23,050.8	40,842.2
Sudan	14,725.9	121.2	150.0	86,713.7	101,710.8
Swaziland	844.5	8.1	—	49.9	902.5
Uganda	1,113.5	1.1	2,450.6	75.0	3,640.2
United Republic of Tanzania	3,402.3	5.0	5.0	257.5	3,669.8
Zaire	9,633.0	27.5	454.1	83.8	10,198.4
Zambia	1,292.0	19.0	120.4	542.3	1,973.7
Zimbabwe	203.4	1.5	—	1,008.0	1,212.9
Other	2,463.2	16.9	46.2	422.4	2,948.7
Follow-up on recommendations of Pan African Conference on Refugees	—	—	—	162.8	162.8
Subtotal	89,722.4	754.7	8,205.0	118,452.9	217,135.0
AMERICAS					
Argentina	974.6	52.3	281.5	622.5	1,930.9
Costa Rica	1,760.9	16.2	85.0	5,528.9	7,391.0
Honduras	2,964.6	3.3	210.0	7,843.5	11,021.4
Mexico	6,884.3	26.4	532.6	4,232.7	11,676.0
Nicaragua	916.6	9.5	166.6	268.6	1,361.3

Country or area	Local settlement	Resettlement	Voluntary repatriation	Relief and other assistance	Total
AMERICAS (cont.)					
Peru	106.6	4.0	—	22.5	133.1
Other Central America and the Caribbean	867.1	36.2	189.4	277.4	1,370.1
Other north-western South America	305.5	—	104.3	119.7	529.5
Other southern Latin America	548.4	226.0	50.0	213.0	1,037.4
North America	—	73.2	73.7	157.7	304.6
Subtotal	15,328.6	447.1	1,693.1	19,286.5	36,755.3
EAST AND SOUTH ASIA AND OCEANIA					
Australia	—	1.8	4.6	—	6.4
China	3,600.0	70.5	—	18.8	3,689.3
Hong Kong	—	709.0	—	3,303.6	4,012.6
Indonesia	—	2,096.8	0.7	1,749.5	3,847.0
Lao People's Democratic Republic	—	1.6	855.8	—	857.4
Malaysia	1,048.3	781.8	0.3	4,002.0	5,832.4
Philippines	—	6,775.5	—	1,534.4	8,309.9
Thailand	246.1	1,580.7	161.1	25,327.8	27,315.7
Viet Nam	1,086.0	1,878.2	—	—	2,964.2
Other	299.9	429.2	—	9,393.6	10,122.7
Subtotal	6,280.3	14,325.1	1,022.5	45,329.7	66,957.6
EUROPE					
Austria	241.1	51.6	19.2	50.2	362.1
Belgium	79.3	0.2	59.1	36.2	174.8
France	269.4	52.8	354.3	38.4	714.9
Germany, Federal Republic of	242.4	0.2	10.1	1,463.2	1,715.9
Greece	679.3	221.1	—	541.0	1,441.4
Italy	458.5	1,120.9	59.1	868.3	2,506.8
Portugal	261.2	—	—	76.3	337.5
Spain	129.5	26.0	625.0	42.4	822.9
Turkey	56.0	544.8	—	16.0	616.8
United Kingdom	23.4	—	13.2	148.8	185.4
Yugoslavia	80.6	223.1	2.0	1,532.4	1,838.1
Other	163.1	81.9	99.5	265.3	609.8
Subtotal	2,683.8	2,322.6	1,241.5	5,078.5	11,326.4
MIDDLE EAST AND SOUTH-WEST ASIA					
Cyprus	5,435.5	15.3	—	499.1	5,949.9
Iran	9,088.3	26.4	—	2,760.0	11,874.7
Lebanon	63.9	8.1	—	115.0	187.0
Pakistan	10,694.9	287.6	—	55,474.2	66,456.7
Western Asia	229.3	114.4	3.1	232.4	579.2
Subtotal	25,511.9	451.8	3.1	59,080.7	85,047.5
GLOBAL AND REGIONAL	1,068.0	583.7	229.8	1,697.2	3,578.7
Total	140,595.0	18,885.0	12,395.0	248,925.5	420,800.5

*Not including expenditure for programme support and administration.
†Including donations in kind, such as food.
SOURCE: A/41/12.

Africa

In the first months of 1985, large numbers of persons continued to cross borders to seek help, particularly in the Horn of Africa, imposing an additional burden on neighbouring Governments at a time when the effects of the drought on their own nationals were already severe. Throughout the year, UNHCR established emergency programmes in Ethiopia, Somalia and the Sudan, and for limited periods in the Central African Republic and Djibouti. Relief was provided to large numbers in desperate need of food, water and medical care. By year's end, the overall situation had improved in many areas but the emergency was not over.

Beneficiaries included not only persons of direct concern to UNHCR but also those who had left their country solely because of the drought. At the height of the food shortages, some nationals physically close to refugee reception centres also temporarily availed themselves of UNHCR emergency assistance. Such extensions of aid proved necessary because of difficulties in making clear distinctions in the prevailing circumstances and also as there were no other funding or implementing arrangements.

In October,[2] the UNHCR Executive Committee, deeply concerned at the seriousness of the emergency in Africa, where drought and famine affecting refugees and local populations had caused great hardship and loss of life, commended the High Commissioner for his efforts to alleviate the problem, and thanked the donors to the UNHCR African emergency programmes. It regretted that the emergency had represented a severe set-back for durable solutions in Africa, including those submitted at ICARA II, and urged that their importance not be overlooked.

UNHCR co-operated with the Office for Emergency Operations in Africa (see p. 496), which was established in 1984,[3] and, as a member of the United Nations Africa Emergency Task Force, it also played an important role in the United Nations system's co-ordination of relief assistance.

Despite better harvests in 1985, the severe and even increasing economic difficulties facing many asylum countries continued to hinder efforts to promote self-sufficiency through rural settlement and agriculture or employment opportunities and income generation. In addition, developments in southern Africa created new and potentially grave problems. Thus, although substantial progress was made in stabilizing several critical emergency situations, progress in achieving durable solutions fell short of expectations in many countries. At the same time, the impact of spontaneously settled refugees on national infrastructures tended to increase, necessitating new approaches in the wider context of the development of areas affected by the presence of refugees.

Yet progress was recorded in several areas: Chadians repatriated voluntarily from the Central African Republic; political developments in Uganda allowed a return of Ugandan refugees from neighbouring countries; many Ethiopians, who had entered the Sudan in late 1984 and early 1985, returned home spontaneously; and assistance to settlements in the United Republic of Tanzania and upper Zaire was phased out as their inhabitants became self-supporting.

In 1985, UNHCR voluntary fund expenditure in Africa amounted to some $225.8 million, of which $97 million was obligated under General Programmes and $128.8 million under Special Programmes.

The General Assembly, in **resolution 40/20** on co-operation between the United Nations and OAU, urged Governments and organizations, as well as NGOs, to help African countries of asylum cope with the heavy burden imposed on their limited resources and weak infrastructures by large numbers of refugees, and it invited them to contribute generously to implementing the Declaration and Programme of Action of ICARA II. The Assembly also adopted resolutions on ICARA II; returnees and displaced persons in Chad; refugees in Djibouti, Ethiopia, Somalia and the Sudan; and South African student refugees (see below).

In his September 1985 report to the Security Council on refugee safety in Botswana and assistance to South African refugees in that country[4] (see p. 189), the Secretary-General transmitted the report of a mission which had visited Botswana (27 July–2 August). The mission stressed that the country's geographic location resulted in a continuous refugee influx and that, in spite of a military attack on its capital, Gaborone, by South Africa on 14 June, Botswana was determined to keep its doors open to South African refugees. The mission recommended that the international community enhance assistance to Botswana in ensuring the safety, protection and welfare of refugees; it also pointed out that it was the right of asylum countries to be secure from attack or coercion by refugee-producing countries.

Follow-up to the Second International Conference on Assistance to Refugees in Africa

Pursuant to recommendations in the Declaration and Programme of Action adopted at the Second International Conference on Assistance to Refugees in Africa in 1984,[5] UNHCR reviewed the continuing refugee/returnee needs in Africa in terms of both normal programming and ICARA II projects. To prepare for and to follow up on the Conference, close collaboration took place between UNDP and UNHCR. They jointly funded development projects embracing all the population in an area west of the White Nile which had been severely affected by a heavy influx of refugees. Their collaboration was also extended to include Somalia and served as a timely precedent which was being pursued in other countries.

While additional needs were met in 1985, when UNHCR assistance in Africa reached an all-time high, the assistance provided to refugees and returnees was of necessity more for emergency relief than rehabilitation. UNDP continued monitoring development programmes for countries affected by their presence.

In July,[6] the OAU Assembly of Heads of State and Government adopted a declaration and a resolution on the economic situation in Africa, and a resolution on its special emergency assistance fund for drought and famine in Africa. The OAU Council of Ministers, also in July,[6] appealed to the international community to increase its contribution to UNHCR, to enable it to deal better with recent influxes of refugees and returnees and to intensify programmes leading to durable solutions. It also appealed to donor countries to contribute urgently to ICARA II projects aimed at facilitating assistance to refugees and returnees. It further appealed to OAU member States to co-operate among themselves and with UNHCR to improve the living and working conditions of refugees and promote voluntary repatriation. The OAU Secretary-General was requested to report on the question in 1986.

On 9 July 1985, the High Commissioner orally informed the Economic and Social Council's Third (Programme and Co-ordination) Committee of the grave crisis caused by the drought in Africa that affected certain UNHCR refugee programmes there. He also reported, on behalf of the Secretary-General, on humanitarian assistance provided to refugees in Somalia and to displaced persons in Ethiopia, the situation of refugees in the Sudan, and assistance to student refugees in southern Africa. On 25 July, the Council, by **decision 1985/185**, took note of the report.

The Secretary-General, in a July 1985 report on assistance to refugees in Africa[7] submitted in response to a 1984 General Assembly request,[8] stated that, since ICARA II, Africa had been confronted with a crisis of dramatic magnitude and that persistent economic difficulties and emergency situations involving massive population movements had overshadowed the Conference, as international attention concentrated on endeavours to avert a human and economic catastrophe. It was imperative to undertake rehabilitation and medium-term development actions as soon as possible, even though in the crises of famine and drought the alleviation of immediate needs might appear a more urgent requirement. The Secretary-General remarked that the attention given by OAU member States to the root causes of refugee situations, the funding of refugee-related developmental projects, and the consultations and co-operation undertaken by all concerned were a pledge and a guarantee that efforts to implement the ICARA II Programme of Action would continue.

GENERAL ASSEMBLY ACTION

On 13 December, on the recommendation of the Third Committee, the General Assembly adopted without vote **resolution 40/117**.

Second International Conference on Assistance to Refugees in Africa

The General Assembly,

Recalling its resolutions 37/197 of 18 December 1982, 38/120 of 16 December 1983 and 39/139 of 14 December 1984 relating to the Second International Conference on Assistance to Refugees in Africa,

Having considered the report of the Secretary-General on assistance to refugees in Africa,

Mindful that the fundamental purpose of the Declaration and Programme of Action adopted by the Second International Conference on Assistance to Refugees in Africa, held at Geneva from 9 to 11 July 1984, was to launch collective action by the international community aimed at achieving lasting solutions,

Gravely concerned at the persistent and serious problem of large numbers of refugees on the African continent,

Aware of the heavy burden borne by African countries of asylum on account of the presence of these refugees and its consequences for their economic and social development, and of the heavy sacrifices made by them, despite their limited resources,

Deeply concerned that the refugee situation has been severely affected by the critical economic situation in Africa, as well as by drought and other natural disasters,

Recognizing that the efforts of the countries of asylum require the concerted support of the international community to meet the needs for emergency relief and for medium- and long-term development aid,

Taking note of the declarations and resolutions adopted by the Assembly of Heads of State and Government of the Organization of African Unity at its twenty-first ordinary session, held at Addis Ababa from 18 to 20 July 1985, and of the resolutions adopted by the Council of Ministers of the Organization of African Unity at its forty-second ordinary session, held at Addis Ababa from 10 to 17 July 1985, in particular resolution CM/Res.989(XLII) on the situation of refugees in Africa,

Emphasizing the collective responsibility of sharing the urgent and overwhelming burden of the problem of African refugees through effective mobilization of additional resources to meet the urgent and long-term needs of the refugees and to strengthen the capacity of countries of asylum to provide adequately for the refugees while they remain in those countries, as well as to assist the countries of origin in rehabilitating voluntary returnees,

Reiterating the vital importance of the complementarity between refugee aid and development assistance,

Desirous of ensuring the speedy implementation of the recommendations and pledges made at the Second International Conference on Assistance to Refugees in Africa,

1. *Expresses its deep appreciation* to African host countries, which are the biggest donors, for their generous contribution and continuous efforts to alleviate the plight of refugees in spite of their critical economic situation;

2. *Reiterates its appreciation* to all donor countries, the organizations and specialized agencies of the United Nations system, regional organizations and intergovernmental and non-governmental organizations for their initial support and response to the projects submitted to the Second International Conference on Assistance to Refugees in Africa;

3. *Urges* the international community to maintain the momentum created by the Conference and to translate into reality the projects submitted as well as the principles of the Declaration and Programme of Action adopted by the Conference;

4. *Emphasizes* the vital importance of the complementarity of refugee aid and development assistance and of achieving durable solutions to the problems of refugees in Africa and the necessity of providing assistance for the strengthening of the social and

economic infrastructures of African countries receiving refugees and returnees;

5. *Requests* the United Nations High Commissioner for Refugees to continue to keep the situation of refugees in Africa under constant review so as to ensure that adequate assistance is available for care and maintenance and for bringing about durable solutions;

6. *Requests* the United Nations Development Programme to increase its efforts to mobilize additional resources for refugee-related development projects and, in general, to promote and co-ordinate with the host countries and the donor community the integration of refugee-related activities into national development planning;

7. *Calls upon* all Member States and organizations of the United Nations system concerned, as well as relevant regional, intergovernmental and non-governmental organizations, to lend their support to the speedy implementation of the recommendations and pledges made at the Conference;

8. *Requests* the Secretary-General, in accordance with the Declaration and Programme of Action, to monitor, in consultation and close co-operation with the Organization of African Unity, the United Nations High Commissioner for Refugees and the United Nations Development Programme, the follow-up to the Conference;

9. *Also requests* the Secretary-General to report to the General Assembly at its forty-first session, through the Economic and Social Council, on the implementation of the present resolution.

General Assembly resolution 40/117

13 December 1985   Meeting 116   Adopted without vote

Approved by Third Committee (A/40/934) without vote, 21 November (meeting 49); draft by Costa Rica, and Mauritius for African Group (A/C.3/40/L.42); agenda item 105 *(b)*.

Meeting numbers. GA 40th session: 3rd Committee 37-41, 49; plenary 116.

The Assembly, in **resolution 40/118**, thanked the High Commissioner for putting into practice the concept of development-oriented assistance to refugees and returnees, as initiated at ICARA II, urged him to continue that process in co-operation with the World Bank, UNDP and other organizations, and urged Governments to support those efforts.

Chad

Pursuant to a 1984 General Assembly request,[9] the Office of the United Nations Disaster Relief Co-ordinator (UNDRO) on 26 November 1985 reported orally to the Assembly's Third Committee on emergency assistance to returnees and displaced persons in Chad. The drought there had affected nearly one third of its population. Some 500,000 people, in search of food, had settled in an area where crops were non-existent and water supplies were used to the maximum. The largest concentration of displaced persons, about 50,000, centred on the capital, and another 30,000 were grouped at the Ati camp in Batha, one of the most severely affected prefectures. That camp and others had been helped by specific programmes executed by UNICEF, the League of Red Cross Societies and other NGOs. Following the Chadian Government's

pacification efforts—on 13 November, it had issued a general amnesty in favour of refugees and persons in exile abroad—there had been a significant movement of spontaneous returnees from the Central African Republic, and food had been distributed to them by local authorities in co-operation with NGOs and UNDRO. In view of the increasing number of returnees and displaced persons—185,000 displaced persons had been resettled by year's end—the Chadian Government requested the Secretary-General to initiate a programme of assistance.

GENERAL ASSEMBLY ACTION

On 13 December, on the recommendation of the Third Committee, the General Assembly adopted **resolution 40/136** without vote.

Emergency assistance to returnees and displaced persons in Chad

The General Assembly,

Recalling its resolution 39/106 of 14 December 1984,

Taking note of the report made by the United Nations Disaster Relief Co-ordinator on 26 November 1985 on the situation of returnees in Chad,

Deeply concerned by the persistence of the drought, which is compounding the already precarious food and health situation in Chad,

Conscious that the large number of voluntary returnees and displaced persons as a result of the war and the drought in Chad poses a serious problem of integrating them into society,

Considering that, in addition to being a land-locked country and one of the least developed countries, Chad is placed in a particularly difficult situation by reason of the war and the drought,

Bearing in mind the many appeals made by the Government of Chad, in particular that made on 9 October 1985 to the General Assembly, and by humanitarian organizations regarding the gravity of the food and health situation in Chad,

Recalling the urgent appeal made by the General Assembly during its thirty-ninth session for international emergency assistance to the voluntary returnees and displaced persons in Chad afflicted by natural disasters,

1. *Endorses* the appeals made by the Government of Chad and by humanitarian organizations concerning emergency assistance to the voluntary returnees and displaced persons in Chad;

2. *Reiterates its appeal* to all States and intergovernmental and non-governmental organizations to support by generous contributions the efforts being made by the Government of Chad to assist and resettle the voluntary returnees and displaced persons;

3. *Takes note with satisfaction* of the action undertaken by the various bodies of the United Nations system and the specialized agencies with a view to mobilizing emergency humanitarian assistance to the voluntary returnees and displaced persons in Chad;

4. *Again requests* the United Nations High Commissioner for Refugees and the United Nations Disaster Relief Co-ordinator to mobilize emergency humanitarian assistance to the voluntary returnees and displaced persons in Chad;

5. *Requests* the Secretary-General, in co-operation with the United Nations Disaster Relief Co-ordinator and the United Nations High Commissioner for Refugees, to report to the General Assembly at its forty-first session on the implementation of the present resolution.

General Assembly resolution 40/136

13 December 1985   Meeting 116   Adopted without vote

Approved by Third Committee (A/40/1007) without vote, 6 December (meeting 70); 36-nation draft (A/C.3/40/L.78); agenda item 12.

Sponsors: Algeria, Burkina Faso, Cameroon, Cape Verde, Central African Republic, Chad, Chile, China, Comoros, Congo, Djibouti, Egypt, France, Gabon, Gambia, Germany, Federal Republic of, Greece, Guinea, Haiti, Indonesia, Italy, Ivory Coast, Japan, Madagascar, Mali, Netherlands, Niger, Nigeria, Pakistan, Rwanda, Senegal, Somalia, Sudan, Thailand, Togo, Zaire.

Meeting numbers. GA 40th session: 3rd Committee 69, 70; plenary 116.

In **resolution 40/218**, the Assembly requested the Secretary-General to continue monitoring, with the agencies concerned, the humanitarian needs, particularly food and health, of the people of Chad displaced by war and drought. It also requested him to mobilize special humanitarian assistance for persons who had suffered as a result of the war and drought and for the resettlement of displaced persons.

Djibouti

In pursuance of a 1984 Assembly request,[10] the High Commissioner submitted a report in August 1985 on humanitarian assistance to refugees in Djibouti.[11] He stated that the limited water supply, which had been further diminished by drought, had hindered the planning of local integration for rural refugees and, as resettlement placement had not kept pace with demand, voluntary repatriation had remained the most viable of the standard durable solutions promoted by UNHCR. At the end of 1985, there were still approximately 17,000 refugees in Djibouti, mostly Ethiopians. Between 1982 and 1985, some 33,000 refugees had repatriated voluntarily to Ethiopia, either under UNHCR auspices or spontaneously. An estimated 10,000 drought victims at Aseyla, who entered the country in 1985, also returned home spontaneously after a few months. UNHCR continued during the year to provide assistance to the remaining refugees, consisting mainly of food distribution, improvements in the supply and storage of potable water and the upgrading of sanitary conditions.

GENERAL ASSEMBLY ACTION

On 13 December, on the recommendation of the Third Committee, the General Assembly adopted without vote **resolution 40/134**.

Humanitarian assistance to refugees in Djibouti

The General Assembly,

Recalling its resolutions 35/182 of 15 December 1980, 36/156 of 16 December 1981, 37/176 of 17 December 1982, 38/89 of 16 December 1983 and 39/107 of 14 December 1984 on humanitarian assistance to refugees in Djibouti,

Having heard the statement made on 11 November 1985 by the United Nations High Commissioner for Refugees,

Having considered with satisfaction the reports of the United Nations High Commissioner for Refugees on humanitarian assistance to refugees in Djibouti,

Appreciating the determined and sustained efforts made by the Government of Djibouti, despite its modest economic resources and limited means, to cope with the pressing needs of the refugees,

Aware of the social and economic burden placed on the Government and people of Djibouti as a result of the presence of refugees and of the consequent impact on the development and infrastructure of the country,

Deeply concerned about the continuing plight of the refugees and displaced persons in the country, which has been aggravated by the devastating effects of the prolonged drought,

Noting with appreciation the steps taken by the Government of Djibouti, in close co-operation with the High Commissioner, to implement adequate, appropriate and lasting solutions in respect of the refugees in Djibouti,

Also noting with appreciation the concern and unremitting efforts of the Office of the United Nations High Commissioner for Refugees, the United Nations Development Programme, the United Nations Children's Fund, the World Health Organization, the World Food Programme, the Food and Agriculture Organization of the United Nations, the intergovernmental and non-governmental organizations and the voluntary agencies which have worked closely with the Government of Djibouti in the relief and rehabilitation programme for the refugees in that country,

1. *Takes note with appreciation* of the reports of the United Nations High Commissioner for Refugees on humanitarian assistance to refugees in Djibouti and appreciates his efforts to keep their situation under constant review;

2. *Welcomes* the steps taken by the Government of Djibouti, in close co-operation with the High Commissioner, to implement adequate, appropriate and lasting solutions in respect of the refugees in Djibouti;

3. *Requests* the High Commissioner to mobilize the necessary resources to implement lasting solutions in respect of the refugees in Djibouti;

4. *Urges* the High Commissioner to continue to take the necessary measures to ensure that adequate, appropriate and lasting solutions are implemented to assist the refugees in Djibouti, in co-operation with Member States, intergovernmental and non-governmental organizations and the voluntary agencies concerned, with a view to mobilizing the necessary assistance to enable the Government of Djibouti to cope effectively with the refugee problem, which has been particularly aggravated by the debilitating effects of the prolonged drought;

5. *Appreciates* the assistance provided thus far by Member States, the specialized agencies, intergovernmental and non-governmental organizations and voluntary agencies to the relief and rehabilitation programmes for the refugees and displaced persons in Djibouti;

6. *Calls upon* all Member States, the organizations of the United Nations system, the specialized agencies, intergovernmental and non-governmental organizations

and voluntary agencies to continue to support the efforts constantly being made by the Government of Djibouti to cope with the current needs of the refugees and the other victims of drought in that country;

7. *Requests* the High Commissioner, in close co-operation with the Secretary-General, to report to the General Assembly at its forty-first session on the implementation of the present resolution.

General Assembly resolution 40/134

13 December 1985   Meeting 116   Adopted without vote

Approved by Third Committee (A/40/1007) without vote, 6 December (meeting 70); 89-nation draft (A/C.3/40/L.67); agenda item 12.
Sponsors: Algeria, Argentina, Austria, Bahrain, Bangladesh, Benin, Botswana, Brunei Darussalam, Burkina Faso, Burundi, Cameroon, Cape Verde, Central African Republic, Chad, China, Comoros, Congo, Costa Rica, Cuba, Democratic Yemen, Djibouti, Dominican Republic, Egypt, Equatorial Guinea, Ethiopia, France, Gabon, Gambia, Germany, Federal Republic of, Ghana, Greece, Guinea, Guinea-Bissau, Haiti, Honduras, India, Indonesia, Iran, Iraq, Italy, Ivory Coast, Jamaica, Japan, Jordan, Kenya, Kuwait, Lebanon, Lesotho, Liberia, Libyan Arab Jamahiriya, Madagascar, Malawi, Mali, Mauritania, Mauritius, Morocco, Nepal, Netherlands, Niger, Nigeria, Oman, Pakistan, Panama, Philippines, Qatar, Rwanda, Saudi Arabia, Senegal, Sierra Leone, Singapore, Somalia, Sri Lanka, Sudan, Swaziland, Syrian Arab Republic, Thailand, Togo, Trinidad and Tobago, Tunisia, Turkey, Uganda, United Arab Emirates, United Republic of Tanzania, United States, Yemen, Yugoslavia, Zaire, Zambia, Zimbabwe.
Meeting numbers. GA 40th session: 3rd Committee 69, 70; plenary 116.

Ethiopia

In an August 1985 report to the Assembly on assistance to displaced persons in Ethiopia,[12] submitted in pursuance of a 1984 request,[13] the Secretary-General noted that voluntary repatriation of Ethiopian refugees from Djibouti continued during the year under the 1983 tripartite agreement between Djibouti, Ethiopia and UNHCR.[14] At its third meeting (Djibouti, 21 November 1984), the Tripartite Commission decided that the formal large-scale repatriation programme would end on 31 December 1984, and that refugees who wished to return to Ethiopia after that date would be processed on a case-by-case basis. By December 1984, 32,859 persons had been registered as repatriates from Djibouti. Due to the drought in the area, some rehabilitation assistance programmes to repatriates, which had been temporarily suspended in 1984, were resumed in 1985.

On 4 April 1985, the United Nations High Commissioner issued an appeal to the international community for $23.5 million to implement a programme to assist returnees in the Hararghe province. The programme was aimed at expanding or establishing rural settlements and improving the quality and quantity of potable water for about 100,000 agriculturalists among the returnee population. In addition, 100,000 pastoralists were to be assisted to re-establish their herds and watering points were to be developed to provide adequate water for animal survival. The Relief and Rehabilitation Commission, the World University Service of Canada, the Lutheran World Federation and the Ethiopian Water Works Construction Authority were responsible for the programme's implementation, in co-operation with UNDP, FAO and IFAD in order to avoid duplication and to ensure complementarity with longer-term developmental activities.

The influx of Sudanese refugees to the Illubabor region of western Ethiopia continued. The Government of Ethiopia estimated that the refugee population in that region totalled 180,000 persons. UNHCR assistance was limited to refugees who had been registered in the Itang camp and to whom UNHCR had unlimited access. The latter population, which increased from 59,100 at the end of 1984 to 85,000 by December 1985, was assisted with food, health care, basic household utensils and water, as well as through a pilot rural settlement scheme. Refugees received counselling and education aimed at identifying durable solutions.

GENERAL ASSEMBLY ACTION

On 13 December, on the recommendation of the Third Committee, the General Assembly adopted **resolution 40/133** without vote.

Assistance to displaced persons in Ethiopia
The General Assembly,
Recalling its resolutions 35/91 of 5 December 1980, 36/161 of 16 December 1981, 37/175 of 17 December 1982, 38/91 of 16 December 1983 and 39/105 of 14 December 1984, as well as Economic and Social Council resolutions 1980/54 of 24 July 1980 and 1982/2 of 27 April 1982,
Recalling also the report of the Secretary-General prepared pursuant to Economic and Social Council resolution 1980/8 of 28 April 1980,
Taking note of the report of the Secretary-General on assistance to displaced persons in Ethiopia,
Having considered the report of the United Nations High Commissioner for Refugees,
Recognizing the increasing number of voluntary returnees and refugees in Ethiopia,
Deeply concerned at the plight of displaced persons and voluntary returnees in the country, which has been aggravated by the devastating effect of the prolonged drought,
Aware of the heavy burden placed on the Government of Ethiopia in caring for displaced persons and victims of natural disasters, as well as for returnees and refugees,
1. *Commends* the efforts made so far by various organs of the United Nations and the specialized agencies in mobilizing humanitarian assistance to assist the efforts of the Government of Ethiopia;
2. *Appeals* to Member States and to international organizations and voluntary agencies to render maximum material, financial and technical assistance to the Government of Ethiopia in its efforts to provide relief and rehabilitation to displaced persons, voluntary returnees and refugees in Ethiopia;
3. *Requests* the United Nations High Commissioner for Refugees to intensify his efforts in mobilizing humanitarian assistance for the relief, rehabilitation and resettlement of voluntary returnees, refugees and displaced persons in Ethiopia;
4. *Requests* the Secretary-General, in co-operation with the High Commissioner, to apprise the Economic

and Social Council, at its second regular session of 1986, of the implementation of the present resolution and to report thereon to the General Assembly at its forty-first session.

General Assembly resolution 40/133

13 December 1985   Meeting 116   Adopted without vote

Approved by Third Committee (A/40/1007) without vote, 6 December (meeting 70); 73-nation draft (A/C.3/40/L.66); agenda item 12.

Sponsors: Afghanistan, Algeria, Angola, Argentina, Austria, Bangladesh, Benin, Botswana, Bulgaria, Burkina Faso, Cameroon, Cape Verde, Central African Republic, China, Colombia, Comoros, Congo, Cuba, Cyprus, Democratic Yemen, Djibouti, Dominican Republic, Egypt, Equatorial Guinea, Ethiopia, Gambia, German Democratic Republic, Ghana, Greece, Guinea, Guinea-Bissau, Hungary, India, Iran, Italy, Ivory Coast, Japan, Jordan, Kenya, Lao People's Democratic Republic, Lesotho, Liberia, Madagascar, Malawi, Mali, Mauritania, Mongolia, Morocco, Mozambique, Netherlands, Nicaragua, Niger, Nigeria, Pakistan, Philippines, Rwanda, Senegal, Sierra Leone, Sri Lanka, Swaziland, Syrian Arab Republic, Togo, Trinidad and Tobago, Uganda, Ukrainian SSR, USSR, Vanuatu, Viet Nam, Yemen, Yugoslavia, Zaire, Zambia, Zimbabwe.

Meeting numbers. GA 40th session: 3rd Committee 69, 70; plenary 116.

Somalia

Pursuant to a 1984 Assembly request,[15] the High Commissioner appraised the refugee situation in Somalia in an August 1985 report.[16] According to government estimates, in 1985 there were 807,000 refugees in the regions of Hiran, Gedo, the north-west and Lower Shebelle, of whom some 700,000 had arrived from the Ogaden region of Ethiopia following events in the Horn of Africa in 1977-1978 and 107,000 had come in 1984-1985. Emergency relief assistance was provided to them (approximately 77 per cent were women and children) during the year and seven new centres were established. Assistance requirements for refugees in 1985 and the estimated needs for 1986 were $97.3 million and $99.7 million respectively.

Due to the scarcity of natural resources, progress towards durable solutions was limited and the majority of the refugees required relief assistance. Basic food supplies were provided mainly by WFP, which co-ordinated bilateral and multilateral donations. On several occasions since 1983, the Government of Somalia had reaffirmed its policy that voluntary repatriation was considered the most desirable solution, but that local settlement would be permitted for those wishing to remain. The voluntary repatriation of 642 persons from Somalia to Ethiopia took place in late 1985.

Discussions took place to elaborate a local refugee settlement project in Furjano in the Lower Shebelle region. In other regions, small agricultural and income-generating projects aimed at encouraging partial self-sufficiency for some refugees. Assistance was also provided to improve and expand existing farms near refugee camps by maintaining and upgrading the existing irrigation and draining facilities, and some 14,300 refugee farmers were being trained in farming methods, in the maintenance of irrigation systems and pumps, as well as in marketing.

GENERAL ASSEMBLY ACTION

On 13 December, on the recommendation of the Third Committee, the General Assembly adopted without vote **resolution 40/132.**

Assistance to refugees in Somalia

The General Assembly,

Recalling its resolutions 35/180 of 15 December 1980, 36/153 of 16 December 1981, 37/174 of 17 December 1982, 38/88 of 16 December 1983 and 39/104 of 14 December 1984 on the question of assistance to refugees in Somalia,

Having considered the report of the United Nations High Commissioner for Refugees on assistance to refugees in Somalia, in particular section IV of that report,

Taking note of the report of the Secretary-General on assistance to refugees in Africa,

Deeply concerned that the refugee problem in Somalia has not yet been resolved,

Aware of the additional burden imposed by the new influx of refugees and the consequent urgent need for additional international assistance,

Aware of continuing and serious shortfalls in the provision of food assistance, which have resulted in dangerous ration restrictions, epidemics related to malnutrition, other shortages and extreme hardship in refugee camps in Somalia,

Recognizing from the recommendations contained in the report of the High Commissioner that there remains an urgent need for increased assistance in the provision of food, water and medicines, in the areas of transport and logistics, shelter and domestic items, construction, the strengthening of health and educational facilities, and the expansion of the number of self-help schemes and small-scale farming and settlement projects necessary for the promotion of self-reliance among the refugees,

Aware of the continued consequences of the social and economic burden placed on the Government and people of Somalia as a result of the continued presence of refugees and new refugee flows and the consequent impact on national development and the infrastructure of the country,

1.   *Takes note* of the report of the United Nations High Commissioner for Refugees;

2.   *Expresses its appreciation* to the Secretary-General and the High Commissioner for their continued efforts to mobilize international assistance on behalf of the refugees in Somalia;

3.   *Takes note with satisfaction* of the assistance rendered to refugees in Somalia by various Member States, the Office of the United Nations High Commissioner for Refugees, the World Food Programme, the United Nations Children's Fund and other concerned intergovernmental and non-governmental organizations;

4.   *Appeals* to Member States, international organizations and voluntary agencies to render maximum and timely material, financial and technical assistance to the Government of Somalia in its efforts to provide all necessary assistance to the refugees;

5. *Appeals* to the donor community to give urgent and favourable consideration to the development-related refugee projects submitted by the Government of Somalia to the Second International Conference on Assistance to Refugees in Africa, held at Geneva from 9 to 11 July 1984, and to fulfil the pledges undertaken at or after that Conference;

6. *Requests* the High Commissioner, in consultation with the Secretary-General, to apprise the Economic and Social Council, at its second regular session of 1986, of the refugee situation in Somalia;

7. *Also requests* the High Commissioner, in consultation with the Secretary-General, to submit to the General Assembly at its forty-first session a report on the progress achieved in the implementation of the present resolution.

General Assembly resolution 40/132

13 December 1985   Meeting 116   Adopted without vote

Approved by Third Committee (A/40/1007) without vote, 6 December (meeting 70); 69-nation draft (A/C.3/40/L.64); agenda item 12.
Sponsors: Algeria, Argentina, Bahrain, Bangladesh, Barbados, Botswana, Brunei Darussalam, Cameroon, Central African Republic, Chad, Chile, China, Comoros, Cyprus, Democratic Kampuchea, Democratic Yemen, Djibouti, Egypt, Gambia, Germany, Federal Republic of, Greece, Guinea, Indonesia, Iran, Iraq, Italy, Ivory Coast, Jamaica, Japan, Jordan, Kenya, Kuwait, Lebanon, Liberia, Libyan Arab Jamahiriya, Madagascar, Malaysia, Mali, Mauritania, Morocco, Netherlands, Niger, Nigeria, Oman, Pakistan, Philippines, Qatar, Rwanda, Saudi Arabia, Senegal, Sierra Leone, Singapore, Somalia, Spain, Sri Lanka, Sudan, Swaziland, Syrian Arab Republic, Thailand, Togo, Trinidad and Tobago, Tunisia, Turkey, United Arab Emirates, United States, Yemen, Yugoslavia, Zaire, Zambia.
Meeting numbers. GA 40th session: 3rd Committee 69, 70; plenary 116.

Sudan

The Secretary-General, in a September 1985 report[17] submitted in response to a 1984 General Assembly request,[18] stated that the refugee population in the Sudan had risen significantly. According to government statistics, the Sudan was at the end of 1985 hosting over 1 million refugees and displaced persons: approximately 790,000 were from Ethiopia, 250,000 from Uganda, 120,000 from Chad and 5,000 from Zaire. Of that number, 635,000 persons—446,000 Ethiopians, 124,000 Ugandans and 65,000 Chadians—were assisted in settlements and reception centres under UNHCR programmes. The remaining refugees were spontaneously settled among the local population and generally received no direct assistance from the international community.

The large-scale influx of refugees from Ethiopia, which had begun in 1984, continued in 1985, reaching a total of 338,000 new arrivals by April 1985. Some 231,000 new arrivals were recorded in reception centres during 1985. Arrivals were partially offset by the spontaneous return to Ethiopia of 55,000 persons at the beginning of the 1985 planting season (April/May). UNHCR also assisted over 130,000 Ethiopian refugees who had arrived in the Sudan before 1984.

There were some 90,000 Ugandan refugees in 30 settlements on the west bank of the Nile and 33,000 in 17 settlements on the east bank in the Equatoria region; many others were spontaneously settled and did not receive direct assistance. Some

3,800 Ugandan refugees voluntarily repatriated with UNHCR assistance during 1985. Organized repatriation was suspended in August owing to the unsettled political situation in Uganda, though several thousand Ugandans, mostly spontaneously settled, were known to have returned to Uganda during the latter part of 1985.

Towards the end of 1985, some 75,000 Chadian refugees were assisted by UNHCR in three reception centres in the Darfur region. Many Chadians were also assisted in food distribution centres established for Sudanese drought victims in Darfur, just as some Sudanese initially benefited from assistance in the reception centres. With the departure of Sudanese from those centres and the dispersal of some Chadians, the number of refugees assisted by UNHCR was estimated at 62,000.

Regular assistance activities in eastern Sudan were virtually suspended during 1985 as attention focused on meeting the urgent needs of new arrivals and providing emergency food and other relief aid to the established refugees affected by the drought.

UNHCR's 1985 programme of assistance to refugees and displaced persons in the Sudan totalled over $90.3 million—$16.3 million in local settlement and over $74 million in other programmes, including $2 million for emergency procurement and shipment of relief items for new arrivals in eastern Sudan, $4 million for assistance to refugees from Chad, Ethiopia and Uganda and $64.5 million for assistance to persons of concern to UNHCR in the Sudan.

GENERAL ASSEMBLY ACTION

Acting on the recommendation of the Third Committee, the General Assembly on 13 December adopted without vote **resolution 40/135**.

Situation of refugees in the Sudan

The General Assembly,

Recalling its resolutions 35/181 of 15 December 1980, 36/158 of 16 December 1981, 37/173 of 17 December 1982, 38/90 of 16 December 1983 and 39/108 of 14 December 1984 on the situation of refugees in the Sudan,

Having considered the reports of the United Nations High Commissioner for Refugees on the situation of refugees in the Sudan,

Appreciating the measures which the Government of the Sudan is taking in order to provide shelter, food, education, and health and other humanitarian services to the growing number of refugees in the Sudan,

Recognizing the heavy burden placed on the Government of the Sudan and the sacrifices it is making in caring for the refugees and the need for substantially increased international assistance to enable it to continue its efforts to provide assistance to the refugees,

Expressing its appreciation for the assistance rendered to the Sudan by Member States and intergovernmental and non-governmental organizations in support of the refugee programme,

Recognizing the need to view refugee-related development projects within local and national development plans,

1. *Takes note* of the report of the United Nations High Commissioner for Refugees on the implementation of resolution 39/108;

2. *Commends* the measures that the Government of the Sudan is taking to provide material and humanitarian assistance to refugees in spite of the drought and the serious economic situation it faces;

3. *Expresses its appreciation* to the Secretary-General, the High Commissioner, donor countries and intergovernmental and non-governmental organizations for their efforts to assist the refugees in the Sudan;

4. *Expresses grave concern* at the shrinking resources available for refugee programmes in the Sudan and the serious consequences of this situation on the country's ability to continue to act as host and provide assistance to the increasing numbers of refugees;

5. *Requests* the Secretary-General, in view of the massive and increasing presence of the refugees, shrinking financial resources, drought and the serious economic situation in the country, to send, in co-operation and co-ordination with the High Commissioner and relevant specialized agencies, a high-level inter-agency mission to assess the needs and the magnitude of assistance required by the programmes for refugees in the Sudan, as well as the impact of the refugees on the economy and vital public services, with a view to preparing a comprehensive programme of assistance to be submitted to the international community;

6. *Also requests* the Secretary-General to mobilize the necessary financial and material assistance for the full implementation of the projects submitted by the Government of the Sudan to the Second International Conference on Assistance to Refugees in Africa, held at Geneva from 9 to 11 July 1984;

7. *Appeals* to Member States, the appropriate organs, organizations and bodies of the United Nations, intergovernmental and non-governmental organizations and the international financial institutions to provide the Government of the Sudan with the necessary resources for the implementation of development assistance projects in regions affected by the presence of refugees;

8. *Requests* the High Commissioner to continue co-ordination with the appropriate specialized agencies in order to consolidate and ensure the continuation of essential services to the refugees in their settlements;

9. *Requests* the Secretary-General to report to the General Assembly at its forty-first session, through the Economic and Social Council, on the implementation of the present resolution.

General Assembly resolution 40/135

13 December 1985   Meeting 116   Adopted without vote

Approved by Third Committee (A/40/1007) without vote, 6 December (meeting 70); 81-nation draft (A/C.3/40/L.72/Rev.1); agenda item 12.
Sponsors: Algeria, Argentina, Bahrain, Bangladesh, Botswana, Brunei Darussalam, Burkina Faso, Cameroon, Canada, Cape Verde, Central African Republic, Chad, Chile, China, Comoros, Cyprus, Democratic Yemen, Djibouti, Egypt, Equatorial Guinea, France, Gambia, Germany, Federal Republic of, Ghana, Greece, Guinea, Guyana, India, Indonesia, Iran, Iraq, Italy, Ivory Coast, Jamaica, Japan, Jordan, Kenya, Kuwait, Lebanon, Lesotho, Liberia, Libyan Arab Jamahiriya, Madagascar, Malawi, Malaysia, Mali, Mauritania, Mauritius, Morocco, Nepal, Netherlands, Niger, Nigeria, Oman, Pakistan, Philippines, Qatar, Romania, Rwanda, Saudi Arabia, Senegal, Sierra Leone, Singapore, Somalia, Sri Lanka, Sudan, Swaziland, Syrian Arab Republic, Thailand, Togo, Trinidad and Tobago, Tunisia, Turkey, United Arab Emirates, United Kingdom, United States, Yemen, Yugoslavia, Zaire, Zambia, Zimbabwe.
Meeting numbers. GA 40th session: 3rd Committee 69, 70; plenary 116.

Other countries

Algeria. The refugee population in Algeria remained unchanged at some 2,000, comprising elderly people of European origin and refugees from Latin America, Africa and the Middle East. UNHCR continued its multi-purpose assistance to some 165,000 people identified by the Algerian Government as Sahrawi refugees living in 24 camps in the Tindouf area.

Angola. The refugee total in Angola was estimated at 92,200 in 1985—70,000 Namibians, 13,200 Zairians and 9,000 South Africans. The UNHCR programme for Namibians remained one of care and maintenance pending return to their homeland. Emphasis was given to self-sufficiency projects for Zairian refugees. Assistance to South African refugees continued to be directed mainly at developing agricultural production at the Malange farm.

Benin. The number of refugees in Benin, mainly Chadians, increased steadily from 846 at the beginning of the year to over 3,600 in December. UNHCR assistance consisted mainly of food, clothing and shelter. Some skilled refugees were helped to establish small-scale income-generating projects. Educational aid was also provided.

Botswana. There were 5,500 refugees in Botswana at year's end, the majority being Zimbabweans receiving assistance in the Dukwe settlement. However, the continuing drought affected progress towards self-sufficiency.

Burundi. Of 256,000 refugees in Burundi, some 60,000 received help from UNHCR in the form of education, counselling and services in the settlement areas.

Cameroon. Cameroon estimated that, at the end of 1985, there were over 30,000 refugees in its northern provinces, of whom 5,200 received assistance from UNHCR in the Ridania camp near Poli. A multi-purpose assistance programme was put into effect to meet essential requirements and to promote self-sufficiency.

Central African Republic. As a result of a return to Chad, refugees in the Central African Republic, estimated at 47,000 in March 1985, dropped to some 30,000 at the end of the year. UNHCR met the immediate needs of rural refugees in providing food and medical care, and establishing reception facilities in new settlement sites.

Kenya. Of approximately 8,800 refugees in Kenya in 1985, whose background was mainly urban, 4,150 had come from Uganda, 1,900 from Ethiopia, 1,950 from Rwanda and 800 from other countries. The care and maintenance of needy refugees continued in parallel with the pursuit of durable solutions through repatriation, local integration and income generation. Over 600 Ugandans, who had registered with UNHCR, repatriated voluntarily during the year.

Lesotho. Lesotho estimated that its refugee population, mostly South Africans, remained stable at some 11,500, with new arrivals counterbalancing departures, of which 200 received assistance from UNHCR.

Morocco. The assistance provided in Morocco to a small number of cases was in the form of integration of elderly Europeans, supplementary aid to people of diverse origin (Africa, Middle East) and scholarships to African refugee students.

Mozambique. At the end of 1985, there were approximately 700 refugees in Mozambique, the majority South Africans; some 470 were directly assisted by UNHCR.

Nigeria. There were some 5,000 refugees, including 4,000 Chadians, living in Nigeria in 1985. UNHCR provided aid for small-scale income-generating projects. Educational assistance reflected opportunities made available by the authorities to both refugees residing in Nigeria and others, mainly Namibians, who came to the country to study.

Rwanda. The majority of the 31,000 Ugandan refugees who had been assisted in camps located in the north of Rwanda had repatriated by the end of 1985. Some 19,000 refugees from Burundi remained, but individually required only occasional assistance.

Senegal. The number of refugees in Senegal remained stable at 5,500, of whom 5,000 were from Guinea-Bissau engaged in an agricultural scheme on the outskirts of M'Bour. Educational assistance remained a major aspect for UNHCR in view of educational placement opportunities offered to refugee students, especially at higher secondary and university levels.

Swaziland. During 1985, the number of refugees in Swaziland increased by some 2,000 and reached a total of 10,500, which included 6,900 South Africans and 3,450 Mozambicans. While South African refugees were mainly self-sufficient, relief assistance was provided to the Mozambicans.

Tunisia. UNHCR assisted a small number of cases in Tunisia—local integration of elderly Europeans, supplementary aid to people of diverse origin (Africa, Middle East) and scholarships to African refugee students.

Uganda. The political strife which characterized 1985 was accompanied by uncertainty and population movements within and outside Uganda. The refugee population was estimated at 151,000 persons, of whom 119,400 (118,000 from Rwanda and 1,400 from Zaire) lived in eight rural settlements in the south-west. Over 31,000 others from Zaire, who had arrived in Uganda during the 1960s, had settled spontaneously in western Uganda and no longer required UNHCR assistance.

UNHCR also assisted Ugandan refugees returning from the Sudan and Zaire under a 1984 special programme to rehabilitate returnees in the West Nile province; by mid-1985, 31,000 persons had benefited from that programme, which provided for their immediate needs.

United Republic of Tanzania. The refugee population in 1985 was estimated at 207,000, including largely self-sufficient refugees from Burundi who represented 80 per cent of the refugee population. In addition, there were some 20,000 refugees from Rwanda and 16,000 from Zaire. UNHCR programmes concentrated on establishing large and economically viable rural settlements and strengthening the infrastructure.

Zaire. Refugees in Zaire reached an estimated 317,000 in 1985. Approximately 263,000 were from Angola, 30,000 from Uganda and 24,000 from other countries. The Ugandan population in upper Zaire decreased due to voluntary repatriation, and a self-sufficiency programme was implemented for those who remained. A multi-purpose assistance programme to cover basic needs of over 60,000 Angolan refugees in Shaba was initiated. The Government of Zaire co-operated in the final phase of UNHCR's activities in lower Zaire.

Zambia. There was a significant influx of refugees into Zambia in 1985, mainly from Mozambique and Angola. By year's end, the refugee population was estimated at 104,000—75 per cent from Angola and the remainder mainly from Mozambique, Namibia, South Africa and Zaire. In addition to direct assistance to settlements, assistance was also provided to spontaneously settled refugees.

Zimbabwe. The number of Mozambican refugees and displaced persons increased to some 62,500 by the end of 1985. Of that number, approximately 24,000 were assisted in camps, while others were spontaneously dispersed among the local population. There were also in Zimbabwe 250 urban refugees, mainly South Africans.

Southern African student refugees

Pursuant to a 1984 General Assembly request,[19] the High Commissioner submitted a report[20] on assistance to student refugees in southern Africa—Botswana, Lesotho, Swaziland, Zambia and Zimbabwe—from 1 July 1984 to 30 June 1985.

During that time, 138 refugees from South Africa and 7 from Namibia arrived in Botswana, bringing the totals to 266 and 103, respectively; 83 South African and 32 Namibian refugee students were attending secondary schools, vocational training institutions and university, and 70 South African and 8 Namibian students were assisted to pursue their studies abroad, mainly in other African countries.

An estimated 11,500 refugees were still in Lesotho, the majority South Africans. Of the 348 registered with UNHCR, some 260 received assistance. During the first quarter of 1985, there was an influx of some 130 refugees from South Africa; 85 per cent of them were affiliated with liberation movements and were relocated to the United Republic of Tanzania, which also accommodated 282 school-age South Africans for educational purposes.

Among the 8,000 refugees in Swaziland, 85 per cent were South Africans. Of the 217 South African and Namibian refugee students who were attending educational institutions in the country, 167 were sponsored by UNHCR. Seven South African students were granted scholarships to study abroad. UNHCR assisted an additional 97 South Africans to travel from Swaziland to the United Republic of Tanzania for education.

In Zambia, an estimated 7,000 Namibians—mostly young women and school-age children—received educational assistance, food, clothing and medicines from UNHCR.

In Zimbabwe, which registered 440 South African refugees, UNHCR assistance concentrated on formal education and developing vocational and technical skills.

In the period under review, the High Commissioner reported that projects being financed by UNHCR or in co-operation with it amounted to $4,401,900—Botswana was allocated $1,270,700, Lesotho $491,000, Swaziland $663,000 and Zambia $1,977,200.

UNHCR also covered the expenses of students studying outside their countries of asylum. A total of $962,433 went to scholarships awarded to 386 Namibians and 2 South Africans for studies at west African educational institutions, and $197,465 to cover travel for education purposes. In addition, the Otto Beneke Foundation, a voluntary agency of the Federal Republic of Germany, sponsored 516 refugee students—266 Namibians and 250 South Africans—and was preparing a vocational training programme for some 260 beneficiaries, with special consideration to be given to Namibian and South African refugees.

GENERAL ASSEMBLY ACTION

On 13 December, on the recommendation of the Third Committee, the General Assembly adopted without vote **resolution 40/138**.

Assistance to student refugees in southern Africa
The General Assembly,

Recalling its resolution 39/109 of 14 December 1984, in which it, *inter alia*, requested the Secretary-General, in co-operation with the United Nations High Commissioner for Refugees, to continue to organize and implement an effective programme of educational and other appropriate assistance for student refugees from Namibia and South Africa who have been granted asylum in Botswana, Lesotho, Swaziland and Zambia,

Having considered the report of the High Commissioner on the assistance programme to student refugees from South Africa and Namibia,

Noting with appreciation that some of the projects recommended in the report on assistance to student refugees in southern Africa have been successfully completed,

Noting with concern that the discriminatory and repressive policies which continue to be applied in South Africa and Namibia cause a continued and increasing influx of student refugees into Botswana, Lesotho, Swaziland and Zambia,

Conscious of the burden placed on the limited financial, material and administrative resources of the host countries by the increasing number of student refugees,

Appreciating the efforts of the host countries to deal with their student refugee populations, with the assistance of the international community,

1. *Takes note with satisfaction* of the report of the United Nations High Commissioner for Refugees;

2. *Expresses its appreciation* to the Governments of Botswana, Lesotho, Swaziland and Zambia for granting asylum and making educational and other facilities available to the student refugees, in spite of the pressure which the continuing influx of those refugees exerts on facilities in their countries;

3. *Also expresses its appreciation* to the Governments of Botswana, Lesotho, Swaziland and Zambia for the co-operation which they have extended to the High Commissioner on matters concerning the welfare of these refugees;

4. *Notes with appreciation* the financial and material support provided for the student refugees by Member States, the Office of the United Nations High Commissioner for Refugees, other bodies of the United Nations system and intergovernmental and non-governmental organizations;

5. *Requests* the High Commissioner, in co-operation with the Secretary-General, to continue to organize and implement an effective programme of educational and other appropriate assistance for student refugees from Namibia and South Africa who have been granted asylum in Botswana, Lesotho, Swaziland and Zambia;

6. *Urges* all Member States and intergovernmental and non-governmental organizations to continue contributing generously to the assistance programme for student refugees, through financial support of the regular programmes of the High Commissioner and of the projects and programmes, including unfunded projects, which were submitted to the Second International Conference on Assistance to Refugees in Africa, held at Geneva from 9 to 11 July 1984;

7. *Also urges* all Member States and all intergovernmental and non-governmental organizations to assist the countries of asylum materially and otherwise to enable them to continue to discharge their humanitarian obligations towards refugees;

8. *Appeals* to the Office of the United Nations High Commissioner for Refugees, the United Nations Development Programme and all other competent United Nations bodies, as well as other international and non-governmental organizations, to continue providing humanitarian and development assistance so as to facilitate and expedite the settlement of student refugees from South Africa who have been granted asylum in Botswana, Lesotho, Swaziland and Zambia;

9. *Calls upon* agencies and programmes of the United Nations system to continue co-operating with

the Secretary-General and the High Commissioner in the implementation of humanitarian programmes of assistance for the student refugees in southern Africa;

10. *Requests* the High Commissioner, in co-operation with the Secretary-General, to continue to keep the matter under review, to apprise the Economic and Social Council, at its second regular session of 1986, of the current status of the programmes and to report to the General Assembly at its forty-first session on the implementation of the present resolution.

General Assembly resolution 40/138

13 December 1985   Meeting 116   Adopted without vote

Approved by Third Committee (A/40/1007) without vote, 6 December (meeting 71); 45-nation draft (A/C.3/40/L.79); agenda item 12.

Sponsors: Algeria, Angola, Bahamas, Botswana, Burkina Faso, Burundi, Cameroon, China, Comoros, Congo, Djibouti, Egypt, Ethiopia, Gambia, Ghana, Guinea, Guinea-Bissau, Indonesia, Ivory Coast, Kenya, Lesotho, Liberia, Madagascar, Malawi, Mali, Morocco, Mozambique, Nigeria, Philippines, Rwanda, Senegal, Sierra Leone, Singapore, Somalia, Sudan, Suriname, Swaziland, Togo, Trinidad and Tobago, Uganda, United Republic of Tanzania, Yugoslavia, Zaire, Zambia, Zimbabwe.

Meeting numbers. GA 40th session: 3rd Committee 69, 71; plenary 116.

In related action, the Assembly in **resolution 40/97 E** requested UNHCR to expand its assistance for the basic needs of Namibian refugees.

The Americas and Europe

UNHCR obligations in the Americas and Europe totalled $52.2 million in 1985, of which $48.5 million was under General Programmes and $3.7 million under Special Programmes.[1]

The Americas

In 1985, the overall refugee population in Latin America—which exceeded 300,000—remained relatively unchanged, with a slight increase in numbers registered in Costa Rica and Honduras being compensated for by the repatriation of refugees from Argentina and Uruguay. UNHCR's activities concentrated in Central America and Mexico, where 112,000 refugees were being assisted.

In Costa Rica, 19,411 refugees were assisted in 1985. The local integration of Salvadorian and Nicaraguan refugees of urban background was relatively successful, but integration of 5,300 Nicaraguans of rural background remained in its early stages, and by the end of the year 4,000 were still receiving assistance.

In Honduras, 20,700 Salvadorian and 530 Guatemalan refugees continued to receive assistance in camps. Some 5,300 Nicaraguan Ladino refugees also received assistance in two Honduran villages while the search for a suitable resettlement area in the region continued. Approximately 13,300 Nicaraguan refugees of Indian origin became partially self-sufficient in Mosquitia.

In Mexico, 18,500 Guatemalan refugees in the Campeche and Quitana Roo states were achiev-ing self-sufficiency on land provided by the Mexican Government, while in the Chiapas state 21,000 persons were still being assisted pending a more durable solution.

In October,[2] the UNHCR Executive Committee expressed concern at the difficult refugee situation in Central America and called for further efforts to meet refugee needs there.

Europe

Refugees and asylum-seekers arriving in Western Europe, particularly through irregular channels, continued to be of increasing concern to those Governments. To identify problems and propose practical solutions, UNHCR held consultations on the subject (Geneva, 28-31 May 1985). An informal meeting was also organized by Sweden (Stockholm, 25 and 26 November 1985).

Those seeking asylum in European countries in 1985 increased from 103,500 persons to an estimated 165,000. The countries receiving the most asylum-seekers continued to be the Federal Republic of Germany, with over 73,000 persons, followed by France, Sweden and Switzerland. Italy and Turkey granted transit facilities to asylum-seekers.

East and South Asia and Oceania

The number of Indo-Chinese refugees in camps and centres in asylum countries in East and South Asia and Oceania stood at 159,665 at the end of 1985, of whom 34,143 were boat people. Among first-asylum countries, Thailand continued to host the largest number—93,257 Lao, 31,761 Kampucheans and 5,395 Vietnamese. Other countries and territories providing temporary asylum to significant numbers included Hong Kong, Indonesia, Japan, Macau, Malaysia, the Philippines, the Republic of Korea and Singapore. In addition, two refugee processing centres, at Bataan (Philippines) and Galang (Indonesia), provided temporary accommodation to some 11,600 Indo-Chinese refugees who had already been accepted for resettlement by third countries. There were also an estimated 20,000 refugees benefiting from UNHCR assistance in Viet Nam.

Resettlement in third countries remained the most viable solution for the majority. However, Kampucheans and Lao who returned to their home countries from Thailand, through organized or spontaneous repatriation, benefited from UNHCR assistance to facilitate their reintegration.

Following the arrival in Papua New Guinea of some 10,500 refugees from the province of Irian Jaya (Indonesia), UNHCR, at the request of Papua New Guinea, launched an aid programme at border sites, pending a durable solution.

During 1985, $61.6 million was obligated for assistance in East and South Asia and Oceania under General Programmes and $9.7 million under Special Programmes. Of that amount, $39.9 million was spent to aid Indo-Chinese refugees in the region.

The High Commissioner told the Executive Committee in October[2] that he was heartened by the United Kingdom's decision to make a new effort to relieve the burden of Hong Kong which had, proportionately, one of the biggest case-loads of Indo-Chinese refugees. He was also pleased that other major resettlement countries had decided to maintain or only marginally reduce their South-East Asian refugee quotas. He was encouraged by the steady pace of the Orderly Departure Programme from Viet Nam and by the number of lives saved by Thailand's implementation of the Anti-Piracy Programme. Thanking Governments participating in the Rescue at Sea Resettlement Offers scheme, he expressed concern for Kampuchean refugees in camps in Thailand or Viet Nam for whom a durable solution seemed remote.

The Committee[2] expressed concern about the continuing severity of refugee situations in South-East Asia, reiterated the need for durable solutions and called on Governments that were not doing so to participate in the resettlement effort and to allow the admission of refugees who did not have links to a third country.

In his October report on Kampuchea,[21] the Secretary-General stated that, during the previous six years, substantial humanitarian assistance had been channelled to Kampucheans. Those who had sought refuge along the Thai-Kampuchean border and at Khao-I-Dang (the UNHCR holding centre in Thailand) remained dependent on aid. As of 1 October 1985, there were 21,000 Kampuchean refugees in Thailand, compared with 175,000 in 1980. With the co-operation of donor Governments, resettlement countries and the host country, nearly 200,000 refugees had been resettled from Thailand since 1975 and another 6,500, accepted for resettlement, were awaiting departure for third countries. Because of an upsurge of hostilities along the Thai-Kampuchean border, the year had again been very difficult for the Kampuchean refugees on the borders and for the United Nations Border Relief Operation. Nearly all refugees were moved and given temporary refuge inside Thailand.

The donors to the programme of humanitarian assistance for the Kampuchean people met four times during 1985 (20 February, 2 May, 11 September and 25 November) to announce pledges and contributions and consider the latest developments in the region.

During the year, the Secretary-General continued to receive communications on incidents near the common border of Democratic Kampuchea and Thailand that also dealt with the refugee problem on that border (see p. 221).

In **resolution 40/7**, the General Assembly appealed to the international community to continue emergency assistance to Kampuchean refugees still in need, especially along the Thai-Kampuchean border and in holding centres.

UNHCR role in South-East Asia

The report of the Joint Inspection Unit (JIU) on the UNHCR role in South-East Asia (1979-1983)[22] was transmitted to the General Assembly in February 1985 by the Secretary-General. It reviewed the operations, achievements and difficulties of UNHCR in fulfilling its mandate in that region.

Focusing on Indo-Chinese refugees falling under UNHCR mandate, the report mentioned that close to 1 million Indo-Chinese refugees had found a permanent home in resettlement countries, mostly in Western Europe and North America, representing the largest intercontinental movement of refugees in the history of UNHCR. Since 1979, UNHCR had channelled some $700 million in emergency and multi-purpose relief assistance to refugees in South-East Asia; in addition, it had attracted other sources of local and external refugee relief assistance, in particular from the NGO community, which had proved to be crucial to it in discharging its responsibilities in the region. Despite the High Commissioner's impressive results in stimulating the necessary political and financial support for solving the crisis, not all difficulties had been overcome. While some of those difficulties were of a political nature, most of them resulted from a weak UNHCR field establishment, which required significant strengthening.

The report recommended, among other things, that UNHCR field offices in South-East Asia should be adequately equipped to perform their responsibilities regarding international protection, programming and co-ordination of assistance activities, administration and financial management, and public information. It also recommended that the High Commissioner and the UNHCR Executive Committee should examine the feasibility of convening a humanitarian regional meeting of all parties concerned by the Indo-Chinese refugee problem with the objective of working out measures aimed at a permanent solution. In addition, it recommended that UNHCR should establish a formal working agreement with the Committee for Co-ordination of Services to Displaced Persons in Thailand (CCSDPT) which would spell out the respective responsibilities and tasks of both parties concerning refugees under UNHCR protection in that country.

In his comments on the JIU recommendations,[23] the Secretary-General said that field offices in South-East Asia were adequately staffed in proportion to the refugee situation; they had a pool of experienced administrative and financial officers and the local administrative staff were generally highly qualified. Referring to the convening of a regional conference, he felt that, given the nature of the refugee problem in South-East Asia, it would have to encompass political as well as humanitarian considerations; such a conference should therefore be convened by other United Nations organs. As for CCSDPT, the Secretary-General pointed out that it was a forum for NGOs in Thailand rather than an operational organization. Besides, CCSDPT—which had had a formal agreement with UNHCR since 1980—had not sought to be recognized as an international organization.

Middle East and South-West Asia

During 1985, $56.7 million was obligated to assist refugees in the Middle East and South-West Asia under General Programmes and $30.2 million under Special Programmes.

Afghans in Pakistan, estimated at 2.7 million in 1985, continued to represent the world's largest concentration of refugees. UNHCR assistance programmes, for which $67.6 million was obligated, were geared towards self-help and self-reliance, including projects to provide training and employment. The three-year UNHCR–World Bank project, to provide employment and income for refugees and the local population, improved, and by the end of 1985 the target for the second year had been achieved, especially in regard to its refugee labour component. Some refugees who arrived in Pakistan during the year were assisted in the Mianwali district of the Punjab, which hosted 110,000 refugees.

Afghan refugees in Iran continued to number approximately 1.8 million, 50 per cent of whom resided in Khorasan and Sistan-Baluchistan provinces. In 1985, $9.1 million was obligated to finance programmes implemented by the Council for Afghan Refugees.

In **resolution 40/12**, the General Assembly again appealed for humanitarian assistance for Afghan refugees.

Despite the precarious situation in Lebanon (see p. 295), the UNHCR regional office in Beirut continued to assist some 2,900 refugees in that country, and emergency assistance totalling $100,000 was also provided to 20,500 families who had been uprooted from their homes as a result of continuing strife.

In Yemen, UNHCR provided basic assistance to 1,800 refugees of Eritrean origin living on the Red Sea coast.

In Cyprus, UNHCR continued to co-ordinate aid to persons displaced as a result of the 1974 events (see p. 257).

The question of Palestine refugees was addressed by the Assembly in **resolutions 40/165 A-K**.

Refugee protection

During 1985, it became obvious that only concerted international action could create conditions in which it would be possible to find solutions to refugee problems while, at the same time, facilitating the High Commissioner's task of providing international protection. Thus, the refugee situations of the 1980s were affecting countries world-wide, as evidenced by growing transcontinental movements of refugees and asylum-seekers. The relevance of those considerations was particularly apparent in Europe where increased numbers of refugees arrived. Their problems and those of European States were the subject of consultations in May and November 1985 (see p. 1007).

In the Middle East and Asia, there were no major developments. In general, countries in those regions offered only temporary asylum to refugees and asylum-seekers, either on condition that they be resettled in third countries or until such time as a voluntary return to the country of origin could be envisaged. In both instances, the majority had to remain in refugee camps during the intervening period. A different situation prevailed in Africa, where more liberal asylum practices were followed by most countries. In the American hemisphere, Central American refugees were a source of concern during the year, since the majority of them lived in camps often located close to their country of origin, thereby constituting a potential for the conflict to spill over frontiers. A similar situation existed also in some African and Asian countries.

The physical protection of refugees continued to be of great concern to UNHCR. Military attacks on refugee camps and settlements occurred in southern Africa, Lebanon, Central America and South-East Asia. Refugees were also vulnerable to other violence, both within and outside their camps and settlements. A UNHCR/Thai Government Anti-Piracy Programme continued in 1985 to deal with piracy attacks against asylum-seekers in the South China Sea.

UNHCR continued to provide refugees and asylum-seekers with various measures of protection, against a growing trend among countries to be restrictive in granting asylum. The principle of *non-refoulement*—whereby refugees and asylum-seekers would not forcibly be returned to countries where they faced persecution or other danger—was respected almost universally. There was, however, a growing trend to put such persons in detention as part of a policy of deterrence. Similarly, some countries progressively introduced legal and other restrictions, rendering it more difficult for refugees to obtain employment or otherwise enjoy economic rights.

There was a growing recognition among countries of the importance of appropriate documentation. At the request of several Governments,

UNHCR printed thousands of refugee identity cards. It also contributed to the cost of producing such cards locally in other countries. In addition, UNHCR provided Governments with over 9,300 convention travel documents and offered help where difficulties were encountered in obtaining or renewing travel documents and visas.

In 1985, UNHCR intensified its activities in the promotion, advancement and dissemination of refugee-law principles, in co-operation with the Asian-African Legal Consultative Committee, the Council of Europe, the League of Arab States, the Organization of African Unity, the Organization of American States and the Organization of the Islamic Conference. In addition, UNHCR organized with the International Institute of Humanitarian Law at San Remo, Italy, seminars and meetings on refugee law; it also collaborated with the International Institute of Human Rights at Strasbourg, France, and the Regional Centre for Third World Studies at Bogotá, Colombia.

A seminar on the international protection of refugees in east and southern Africa—attended by Botswana, Lesotho, Malawi, Mozambique, Swaziland, the United Republic of Tanzania, Zambia and Zimbabwe, and OAU, UNHCR and UNDP representatives—was held at Addis Ababa, Ethiopia, from 28 January to 1 February 1985.

In October,[2] the UNHCR Executive Committee, recognizing that UNHCR's international protection function had become increasingly difficult due to the growing complexity of current refugee problems, reiterated that that function could be carried out effectively only with full government support, particularly through durable solutions. It welcomed the fact that many States, including those confronted with economic and developmental difficulties, continued to grant asylum to large numbers of refugees. At the same time, it noted with concern the growing phenomenon of refugees and asylum-seekers who, having found protection in one country, moved irregularly to another country, and hoped that that problem could be mitigated through global solutions. That issue was considered by the Sub-Committee of the Whole on International Protection at its tenth session (Geneva, 30 September, 1 and 4 October 1985). Since the Executive Committee could not reach a consensus on how to deal with the problem, it requested the High Commissioner to continue consultations with a view to reaching agreement on the matter. In addition to the question of irregular movements of asylum-seekers and refugees, the Committee adopted other conclusions, prepared by the Sub-Committee, on refugee women and international protection (see below); military attacks on refugee camps and settlements in southern Africa and elsewhere; problems relating to the rescue of asylum-seekers in distress at sea; and voluntary repatriation.

Refugee women and international protection

Since refugee women and young girls currently constituted most of the world's refugee population, an understanding of their special problems and social condition was necessary to enable the international community to provide them with equal and adequate protection. Although refugee men and women often found themselves in similar difficult situations, the physical safety and integrity of refugee women were in many instances threatened or violated.

In response to the special needs of refugee women, UNHCR had developed programmes which included income-generating and self-sufficiency projects. As far as the violation of their physical integrity and safety was concerned, measures needed to be taken to strengthen UNHCR presence in border areas and on flight routes, as well as in areas where women were exposed to such dangers.

The UNHCR Executive Committee adopted several conclusions. Among them, it welcomed the round table on refugee women (Geneva, April 1985) and the recommendations regarding the situation of refugee and displaced women adopted in July by the World Conference to Review and Appraise the Achievements of the United Nations Decade for Women (see Chapter XIX of this section). It also stressed the need for a better understanding of the special needs and problems of refugee women in the international protection field and for gathering data concerning refugee women and girls in order to identify and implement appropriate mechanisms to ensure their effective protection. The Executive Committee requested the High Commissioner to report to it on the needs of refugee women and on existing and proposed programmes for their benefit.

In **resolution 40/118**, the General Assembly reaffirmed the fundamental nature of the High Commissioner's function to protect refugees and the need for Governments to continue to co-operate with his Office, particularly by observing the principles of asylum and *non-refoulement*.

International instruments

As at 31 December 1985, the 1951 Convention relating to the Status of Refugees[24] and its 1967 Protocol[25] had been ratified or acceded to by 95 and 94 States, respectively. There was no accession to those instruments during 1985.[26]

Other intergovernmental legal instruments of benefit to refugees included the 1969 OAU Convention governing the Specific Aspects of Refugee Problems in Africa, the 1957 Agreement relating to Refugee Seamen and its 1973 Protocol, the 1959 European Agreement on the Abolition of Visas for Refugees, the 1980 European Agreement on Transfer of Responsibility for Refugees, and the 1969 American Convention on Human Rights, Pact of San José, Costa Rica.

As at 31 December 1985, there were 35 States parties to the 1954 Convention relating to the Status of Stateless Persons[27] and 14 States parties to the 1961 Convention on the Reduction of Statelessness.[28]

The General Assembly by **resolution 40/144** adopted a Declaration on the human rights of individuals not nationals of the country where they live, and in **resolution 40/118** stressed the need for Governments to accede to and implement international and regional refugee instruments.

REFERENCES

[1]A/41/12. [2]A/40/12/Add.1. [3]YUN 1984, p. 468. [4]S/17453. [5]YUN 1984, p. 943. [6]A/40/666. [7]A/40/425. [8]YUN 1984, p. 944, GA. res. 39/139, 14 Dec. 1984. [9]*Ibid.*, p. 945, GA res. 39/106, 14 Dec. 1984. [10]*Ibid.*, p. 946, GA res. 39/107, 14 Dec. 1984. [11]A/40/588. [12]A/40/587. [13]YUN 1984, p. 947, GA res. 39/105, 14 Dec. 1984. [14]YUN 1983, p. 957. [15]YUN 1984, p. 948, GA res. 39/104, 14 Dec. 1984. [16]A/40/586. [17]A/40/589. [18]YUN 1984, p. 949, GA res. 39/108, 14 Dec. 1984. [19]*Ibid.*, p. 950, GA res. 39/109, 14 Dec. 1984. [20]A/40/590. [21]A/40/759. [22]A/40/135. [23]A/40/135/Add.1. [24]YUN 1951, p. 520. [25]YUN 1967, p. 769. [26]*Multilateral Treaties Deposited with the Secretary-General: Status as at 31 December 1985* (ST/LEG/SER.E/4), Sales No. E.86.V.3. [27]YUN 1954, p. 416. [28]YUN 1961, p. 533.

OTHER PUBLICATION
Environmental Refugees, Sales No. E.85.III.D.1.

International co-operation to avert new refugee flows

In 1985, the Group of Governmental Experts on International Co-operation to Avert New Flows of Refugees, established by the General Assembly in 1981[1] to review the problem and develop recommendations, held its fifth and sixth sessions (New York, 25 March–4 April and 3-14 June).[2] The Group's work covered, among other things, the circumstances causing new massive flows of refugees and international co-operation to avert them. In view of its complex task, the Group requested that its mandate be renewed for two further 2-week sessions during 1986, preferably in March and April. The Group's composition was to remain unchanged, unless nominating Governments chose to replace their experts.

GENERAL ASSEMBLY ACTION

On the recommendation of the Special Political Committee, the General Assembly, on 16 December 1985, adopted **resolution 40/166** without vote.

International co-operation to avert new flows of refugees

The General Assembly,

Reaffirming its resolutions 36/148 of 16 December 1981, 37/121 of 16 December 1982, 38/84 of 15 December 1983

and 39/100 of 14 December 1984 on international co-operation to avert new flows of refugees,

Having examined the report of the Group of Governmental Experts on International Co-operation to Avert New Flows of Refugees,

Considering the urgency, magnitude and complexity of the task before the Group of Governmental Experts,

Welcoming the fact that experts coming from least developed countries were enabled to participate in the 1984 and 1985 sessions of the Group,

Recognizing the necessity of having all the experts participate in the future sessions of the Group,

1.   *Welcomes* the report of the Group of Governmental Experts on International Co-operation to Avert New Flows of Refugees, including its recommendations, as a further constructive step in the fulfilment of its mandate;

2.   *Reaffirms and extends* the mandate of the Group of Governmental Experts as defined in General Assembly resolutions 36/148 and 37/121;

3.   *Calls upon* the Secretary-General, without prejudice to the rule contained in resolution 36/148, to continue to assist, as far as possible and by way of exception, the experts coming from least developed countries, appointed by the Secretary-General, to participate fully in the work of the Group of Governmental Experts so that it may fulfil its mandate;

4.   *Calls upon* the Group of Governmental Experts to work expeditiously on the fulfilment of its mandate in two sessions of two weeks' duration each during 1986 and to conclude its comprehensive review of the problem in all its aspects;

5.   *Requests* the Group of Governmental Experts to submit its report in time for consideration by the General Assembly at its forty-first session;

6.   *Decides* to include in the provisional agenda of its forty-first session the item entitled "International co-operation to avert new flows of refugees".

General Assembly resolution 40/166

16 December 1985   Meeting 118   Adopted without vote

Approved by Special Political Committee (A/40/808) without vote, 15 October (meeting 10); 37-nation draft (A/SPC/40/L.6); agenda item 80.

Sponsors: Australia, Austria, Bangladesh, Brunei Darussalam, Cameroon, Canada, Chad, Comoros, Costa Rica, Denmark, Djibouti, Egypt, Germany, Federal Republic of, Honduras, Iceland, Indonesia, Ireland, Italy, Japan, Jordan, Lesotho, Luxembourg, Malaysia, Mali, Norway, Pakistan, Philippines, Rwanda, Samoa, Senegal, Sierra Leone, Singapore, Somalia, Spain, Sudan, Thailand, Togo.

Financial implications. 5th Committee, A/40/956; S-G, A/C.5/40/28, A/SPC/40/L.7.

Meeting numbers. GA 40th session: 5th Committee 49; SPC 8-10; plenary 118.

In other action, the Assembly, in **resolution 40/24**, deplored the plight of millions of refugees and displaced persons uprooted by military intervention and other acts, and reaffirmed their right to return to their homes voluntarily in safety and honour. In **resolution 40/149**, it invited the Commission on Human Rights to keep human rights and mass exoduses under review with the objective of making recommendations concerning further measures to be taken.

REFERENCES

[1]YUN 1981, p. 1053, GA res. 36/148, 16 Dec. 1981. [2]A/40/385.

Chapter XXII

Drugs of abuse

In 1985, the abuse of drugs in many parts of the world remained at a high level and in some countries was escalating. The steady deterioration in recent years had moved the international community to launch unprecedented and comprehensive counter-attacks against abuse, illicit cultivation, manufacture and trafficking.

The Secretary-General, in his 1985 report on the work of the Organization (see p. 10), stated that the plague of drug abuse and illicit trafficking, fuelled by the immense profits which they generated, had reached an emergency stage. He said that the first global conference on the subject, which he had proposed, should serve to raise the level of world-wide awareness of the escalating problems of drug abuse and result in a programme of action at the international, regional and national levels.

In December, the General Assembly approved the programme of action for 1986, the fifth year of the United Nations basic five-year programme of the International Drug Abuse Control Strategy (resolution 40/129). As recommended by the Secretary-General, it decided to convene at Vienna, Austria, in 1987, at the ministerial level, an International Conference on Drug Abuse and Illicit Trafficking (40/122). As the Economic and Social Council had done in February (decision 1985/104), the Assembly requested that the Commission on Narcotic Drugs prepare a draft convention against illicit traffic in narcotic drugs (resolution 40/120), and recommended subjects for action at a 1986 interregional meeting at Vienna of heads of national law enforcement agencies, as part of the international campaign against traffic in drugs (40/121).

The Economic and Social Council, in May, recommended the promotion of preventive education and community participation against drug abuse (resolution 1985/14), and urged Governments to restrict production to meeting mainly their domestic requirements (1985/16). The Council called for measures against the diversion in international commerce of specific precursors, chemicals and solvents used in the illicit manufacture of narcotic drugs and psychotropic substances (1985/12), urged steps to reduce the risk of illicit traffic in commercial carriers (1985/13) and asked Governments to furnish information to the International Narcotics Control Board (INCB) on the countries of origin of imports and the countries of destination of exports of psychotropic substances (1985/15). It requested the Secretary-General to convene regular meetings of

the heads of the national drug control and law enforcement agencies in Africa to establish more effective mechanisms for co-operation (1985/11).

The Commission on Narcotic Drugs, which held its thirty-first session at Vienna from 11 to 20 February, considered matters pertaining to the aims and implementation of drug treaties and recommended seven draft resolutions and four decisions for adoption by the Economic and Social Council on the control of narcotic drugs and psychotropic substances. The Commission also reviewed action on international drug control at the international level, i.e. the activities of the specialized agencies and international organs and organizations, initiated preparation of a draft convention against illicit traffic in narcotic drugs and psychotropic substances, discussed implementation of the International Drug Control Strategy and its financing, and reviewed the situation and trends in drug abuse and illicit traffic.

In July, the Council decided that the Commission should hold a special session in 1986 to consider scheduling of substances under the provisions of the 1971 Convention on Psychotropic Substances and to review INCB's report (resolution 1985/79).

INCB met twice during the year at Vienna—13-24 May (thirty-seventh session) and 8-25 October (thirty-eighth session)—continuing its evaluation and overall supervision of governmental implementation of drug control treaties. It reviewed annual estimates of licit narcotic drug requirements submitted by Governments limiting the manufacture and trade in narcotic drugs to medical and scientific purposes, and monitored the licit movement of psychotropic substances.

The Narcotics Laboratory Section of the United Nations Secretariat's Division of Narcotic Drugs, whose functions included assistance to national narcotics laboratories in techniques for the identification and analysis of seized drugs, in 1985 trained 16 national scientists from 11 countries at Vienna.

The United Nations Fund for Drug Abuse Control (UNFDAC) continued to assist Governments, at their request, in the financing of projects aimed at reducing the illicit supply of and demand for drugs—for example, projects to replace illicit opium poppy cultivation, treat and rehabilitate drug addicts, strengthen control measures and organize information and education programmes. UNFDAC, which depended entirely on voluntary contributions, assisted 50 projects in 25 countries during the year.

On the initiative of the Secretary-General, the question of increasing the system-wide effort in drug abuse control was included in the agenda of the Administrative Committee on Co-ordination (ACC) at its second regular session on 28 and 29 October.

To enhance co-ordination and help provide a United Nations system-wide response to the drug abuse phenomenon, two in a series of *ad hoc* inter-agency meetings on co-ordination in matters of international drug abuse control were held in 1985: one at Vienna on 21 and 22 February; the other at Rome, Italy, from 11 to 13 September.

Topics related to this chapter. Social and cultural development: crime prevention.

Drug abuse and international control

INCB report for 1985. The International Narcotics Control Board, in its 1985 annual report,[1] stated that the abuse of a variety of drugs—cannabis, cocaine, opiates, psychotropic substances and other dependence-producing drugs—remained at a high level in most parts of the world. Health hazards were being aggravated by the simultaneous consumption of two or more drugs, frequently in combination with alcohol, by the emergence of new and even more potent drugs of abuse, and by the use of ever more dangerous means of drug-taking. Wherever illicit cultivation, production and trafficking occurred, abuse by the local population almost inevitably ensued. The Board observed that abuse by young people gravely imperilled the future of countries, and that very few countries were unaffected by drug abuse.

The Board stressed that responsibility for implementing the international drug control system established by treaties rested above all on national authorities, since they alone were able to control the movement of substances within their respective jurisdictions. INCB's role, in co-operation with parties and non-parties, was to help countries achieve the aims of the treaties. In analysing the drug control situation world-wide, the Board benefited from information obtained from Governments, United Nations organs, specialized agencies and other international organizations, notably the International Criminal Police Organization (Interpol). While reviewing the situation in respect of all countries, INCB said it gave special attention to countries in which problems of drug abuse, illicit trafficking and uncontrolled or illicit production were most acute, and to countries where developments were of particular interest to the international community.

It pointed out that the adoption of more collective and vigorous countermeasures on the basis of strengthened political will by Governments had nevertheless resulted in progress during the year.

That applied to, *inter alia:* joint enforcement operations, including the eradication of illicit cultivation; and the imposition of tighter controls on chemicals and solvents for illicit manufacture, notably of heroin and cocaine. The Board welcomed proposals to facilitate extradition and to strengthen legislation to ensure the seizure of traffickers' illicitly acquired assets. It also welcomed the growing involvement of public and community leaders in preventing and reducing drug abuse, as well as new initiatives adopted to fight all aspects of drug abuse. Drawing attention to the so-called "designer drugs"—analogues of controlled substances—its President said that international action might be necessary to prevent the emergence of a fashion involving clandestine manufacture and abuse of those substances.

INCB stressed the need for the broadest possible international co-operation and co-ordination in the realm of anti-drug action. It was essential that resources be provided to national, bilateral and multilateral drug control programmes. The Board also hoped that the trend, which became more pronounced in 1985, towards providing greater resources to support the drug control programmes of developing countries would continue.

INCB report for 1984. At its February 1985 session,[2] the Commission on Narcotic Drugs considered the INCB 1984 annual report[3] and a related note by the Secretary-General.[4] Introducing the report, the INCB President presented a broad assessment of the problems of drug control, touching on the legal trade in drugs as well as the non-medical use of, and illicit traffic in, drugs. He said that Governments had launched unparalleled and innovative countermeasures, which INCB welcomed. Controls over psychotropic substances were beginning to function more effectively. Data provided by both parties and non-parties to the 1971 Convention on Psychotropic Substances[5] had led to the detection of attempts at large-scale diversion. The President drew attention to the INCB recommendations that Governments ensure that penalties for drug trafficking were sufficiently strict. He reminded Governments that the 1961 Single Convention on Narcotic Drugs,[6] as amended by the 1972 Protocol,[7] could in certain circumstances serve in lieu of an extradition treaty.

On 28 May 1985, the Economic and Social Council, by **decision 1985/129**, took note of the INCB report for 1984,[3] which had been issued in summary form in February.[8]

JIU report. By an April note,[9] the Secretary-General submitted to the Assembly his comments and those of the executive heads of organizations within the United Nations system on the 1984 report of the Joint Inspection Unit (JIU) on drug abuse control activities in the United Nations system.[3] He accepted JIU recommendations to propose in ACC positive concerted actions that could be taken on drug abuse control, to continue inter-agency co-ordination meetings at a higher level of participation, and that drug abuse control projects in developing countries should have specific conditions which would require Governments to enforce their purpose and goals (recommendations 1, 3 and 5). He accepted in principle recommendation 4 that the Under-Secretary-General for Political and General Assembly Affairs attend the inter-agency meetings and those of the Commission on Narcotic Drugs, and had conveyed recommendation 2—that specialized agencies develop drug control programmes to be regularly reported on and reviewed by ACC—to the agencies.

In May,[10] the Committee for Programme and Co-ordination (CPC) considered the report of JIU and the comments of the Secretary-General thereon. It recommended that recommendations 1 and 3 be implemented by the Secretary-General and that the Assembly ask the agencies to develop drug control programmes as envisaged in recommendation 2. Recommendations 4 and 5 were not acceptable to CPC.

In-depth evaluation of the drug control programme

Report of the Secretary-General. The Secretary-General submitted to CPC in April 1985 an in-depth evaluation of the drug control programme[11] for the period 1978-1983—with an addendum to include action by the Secretary-General in 1984-1985 to improve co-ordination of drug control activities in the United Nations system—reviewing the activities of the three United Nations entities which had jurisdiction in the field of drug abuse control: the Division of Narcotic Drugs, the secretariat of INCB and UNFDAC. The report also reviewed four UNFDAC-financed field projects (two each in Turkey and Thailand) and assessed co-ordination efforts in drug-related activities of the United Nations system to curb the problem of drug abuse.

The Secretary-General reported that the three drug control units had in general been effective. He made the following recommendations: (1) the harmonization of the 1961 and 1971 Conventions should continue to be reviewed periodically for implementation; (2) the role and work programme of the United Nations Narcotics Laboratory (see p. 1016) should be reviewed, and an expert study made to determine whether some of its functions should be decentralized to national or regional laboratories; (3) an effort should be made through protocols to make it possible to trace, freeze and seize assets acquired illegally and to extradite drug criminals; (4) increased emphasis should be given to demand reduction; (5) the Division of Narcotic Drugs should be given additional technical capacity;

(6) the possibility of the drug units sharing common services and facilities should be looked into; (7) the Assembly might appeal for increased unearmarked contributions to UNFDAC; (8) a small technical committee should be set up to advise the Executive Director of UNFDAC on projects and priorities; (9) UNFDAC should assist countries facing the illicit drug problem, under conditions that would require Governments to enforce the goals of the projects; and (10) drug control secretariats should eliminate duplication of efforts, ensure teamwork and improve co-ordination.

CPC consideration. In May,[10] CPC took note of the Secretary-General's report. It considered that the alarming global dimension of the drug abuse problem and the need for optimum utilization of the limited resources available to curb it required effective co-ordination of all efforts. It welcomed the assignment in May 1984 to the Under-Secretary-General for Political and General Assembly Affairs of responsibility for overall co-ordination of all United Nations drug control–related activities; it recommended that he undertake further corrective measures outlined by the Secretary-General, such as clearly spelling out the division of responsibilities among the units. The Committee recommended that recommendations 1 and 3 be considered by the Commission on Narcotic Drugs, accepted recommendations 2, 4, 5, 9 and 10, and agreed in principle with recommendation 6.

Implementation of the International Drug Abuse Control Strategy

In January,[12] the Secretary-General submitted to the Commission on Narcotic Drugs a note reviewing the implementation of the 1981 International Drug Abuse Control Strategy[13] and the five-year programme of action (1982-1986). The note covered implementation of the programme for the third year (1984) and set out the proposed programmes for 1985 and 1986, noting activities that might be undertaken under the regular United Nations budget, and those suggested for extrabudgetary financing.

The Secretary-General also submitted to the Assembly in October, in response to a 1979 Assembly resolution,[14] a report[15] on international co-operation in drug abuse control. He gave details of activities carried out in 1985 by the Office of the Under-Secretary-General for Political and General Assembly Affairs, the Division of Narcotic Drugs, INCB, UNFDAC, the Centre for Social Development and Humanitarian Affairs, the United Nations Social Defence Research Institute, the United Nations Development Programme (UNDP), the United Nations Industrial Development Organization, the World Food Programme, the International Labour Organisation, the Food and Agriculture Organization of the United Nations, the United Nations Educational, Scientific and Cultural Organization, the

International Civil Aviation Organization and the World Health Organization (WHO). The report provided an overview of related developments and plans.

A second October report,[16] submitted pursuant to a 1983 Assembly request,[17] gave an overview of the drug control activities being carried out by the organizations and programmes within the United Nations system.

In a further October note to the Assembly, on strategy and policies for drug control,[18] the Secretary-General submitted a possible programme of action for 1986, the fifth year of the United Nations basic five-year programme of action.

One project of the fourth year of the five-year programme, adopted along with the International Drug Abuse Control Strategy by the Assembly in 1981,[19] was the convening of an Expert Group on the Reduction of Excessive Stocks of Licit Opiate Raw Materials (Vienna, 23-27 September 1985)[20] (see p. 1019). Two other expert groups on drug control strategy and policies also met in 1985: the Expert Group on Cocaine and Heroin Analysis and Recommended Methods of Testing (Wiesbaden, Federal Republic of Germany, 21-25 October)[21] and the Expert Group on Countermeasures to Drug Smuggling by Air and Sea (Vienna, 9-13 December).[22]

Activities of the Commission on Narcotic Drugs. The Commission, which had been constituted as the task force envisaged in the Assembly's 1981 resolution,[19] adopting the International Drug Abuse Control Strategy and the five-year programme of action, to review, monitor and co-ordinate their implementation, met in February 1985,[2] when it considered the Secretary-General's January report. It adopted a resolution[23] on international drug abuse control strategy and future priority, by which, noting that the basic five-year programme of action would be completed in 1986, it recommended that future such programmes be formulated within the framework of the United Nations medium-term plans and biennial budgets. To that end, it asked the Secretary-General to present to it at future sessions a comprehensive document containing a co-ordinated overview of the budget's international drug control programmes and comparing the current programme and costs with the proposed ones. He was also asked to adjust the proposed 1986-1987 budget to take account of Commission proposals at the current session. The Commission recommended that the text of its resolution be submitted to the General Assembly for consideration.

GENERAL ASSEMBLY ACTION

On 13 December, on the recommendation of the Third (Social, Humanitarian and Cultural) Committee, the General Assembly adopted **resolution 40/129** without vote.

Strategy and policies for drug control

The General Assembly,

Recalling its resolution 32/124 of 16 December 1977, in which it requested the Commission on Narcotic Drugs to study the possibility of launching a meaningful programme of international drug abuse control strategy and policies,

Recalling also its resolution 36/168 of 16 December 1981, by which it adopted the International Drug Abuse Control Strategy and the basic five-year programme of action proposed by the Commission on Narcotic Drugs in its resolution 1(XXIX) of 11 February 1981, as well as its resolution 38/98 of 16 December 1983, in which it decided that, beginning with its eighth special session, the Commission on Narcotic Drugs, meeting in plenary during its sessions and in the presence of all interested observers, would constitute the task force envisaged in General Assembly resolution 36/168 to review, monitor and co-ordinate the implementation of the International Drug Abuse Control Strategy and the basic five-year programme of action,

Taking note of resolution 2(XXXI) of 20 February 1985 of the Commission on Narcotic Drugs and Economic and Social Council decision 1985/130 of 28 May 1985,

Approves the programme of action for 1986, the fifth year of the United Nations basic five-year programme of the International Drug Abuse Control Strategy, reviewed by the Commission on Narcotic Drugs at its thirty-first session.

General Assembly resolution 40/129

13 December 1985   Meeting 116   Adopted without vote

Approved by Third Committee (A/40/1007) without vote, 27 November (meeting 56); 7-nation draft (A/C.3/40/L.50); agenda item 12.
Sponsors: Bahamas, Bolivia, Costa Rica, Malaysia, Morocco, Senegal, Sweden.
Meeting numbers. GA 40th session: 3rd Committee 54-56; plenary 116.

UN Fund for Drug Abuse Control

During 1985, the United Nations Fund for Drug Abuse Control continued to provide assistance to countries in need, by implementing projects designed as elements of individual country programmes and supporting agency-executed projects designed for the common benefit of various countries. The total UNFDAC budget for 1985 amounted to $18.7 million ($4.4 million greater than for 1984), providing assistance for 50 projects in 25 countries. According to a November 1985 interim report on the Fund,[24] major efforts under the technical co-operation programmes were directed to countries where large-scale programmes had been developed, particularly Bolivia, Burma, Colombia, Pakistan, Peru, Thailand and Turkey. Agreements were initiated or renewed for activities in Afghanistan, China, Colombia, Ecuador, Jamaica, Pakistan, Peru, Sri Lanka and Turkey. UNFDAC supported 19 headquarters activities which consisted mainly of research, dissemination of information, organization of meetings and seminars, and training.

CONTRIBUTIONS TO UNFDAC, 1985 AND FUTURE YEARS
(as at 31 December 1985; in US dollar equivalent)

Country or Territory	1985 payment	Pledge for future years
Argentina	12,000	12,000
Australia	181,904	137,931
Austria	69,126	84,746
Bahamas	2,000	—
Barbados	500	—
Belgium	32,424	18,137
Brazil	5,000	—
Cameroon	—	2,611
Canada	242,103	—
Chile	5,000	4,000
China	—	20,000
Cyprus	—	1,000
Denmark	13,091	16,484
Ecuador	—	2,500
Egypt	993	2,000
Finland	39,994	—
France	157,132	196,078
Germany, Federal Republic of	750,813	1,680,000
Greece	2,000	5,000
Hong Kong	12,858	—
Iceland	2,000	2,000
India	10,000	15,000
Indonesia	2,000	2,000
Iran	—	2,000
Ireland	5,000	—
Israel	—	5,000
Italy*	5,927,863	34,024,205
Ivory Coast	1,036	—
Japan	809,241	—
Kenya	3,730	3,386
Madagascar	—	2,000
Malawi	335	—
Malaysia	17,000	8,500
Malta	193	—
Mexico	—	280
New Zealand	20,680	—
Norway	1,493,894	1,660,927
Pakistan	1,238	611
Panama	6,175	2,470
Philippines	—	2,000
Portugal	—	10,000
Republic of Korea	2,000	2,000
Saudi Arabia	50,000	770,000
Senegal	—	5,000
South Africa	4,758	—
Spain	35,387	64,516
Suriname	—	2,825
Sweden	442,600	—
Switzerland	47,519	95,694
Thailand	—	5,000
Turkey	15,510	17,500
United Kingdom	704,972	5,934,719
United States	2,000,000	4,520,000
Venezuela	5,000	3,763
Yugoslavia	12,000	6,000
Zaire	—	500
Total	13,147,069	49,350,383

SOURCE: Accounts for the 12-month period of the biennium 1984-1985 ended 31 December 1985—Schedules of individual trust funds.
*In 1983, Italy pledged $40,880,530 to be used over a five-year period for agreed projects.

In December, the General Assembly, by **resolution 40/121**, acknowledged the vital role played by UNFDAC and called on Member States to contribute or to continue contributing to it. By **resolution 40/122**, the Assembly instructed that the issue of strengthening United Nations co-ordination in drug abuse control activities by increasing support for UNFDAC should be included in the comprehensive multidisciplinary outline of future activities to be adopted by a 1987 conference on drug abuse and illicit trafficking.

The Seventh United Nations Congress on the Prevention of Crime and the Treatment of Offenders (Milan, Italy, August/September 1985) invited States to use UNFDAC to pool resources for greater impact through improved co-ordination and unified programming, and urged new and increased contributions.[25]

UN Narcotics Laboratory

In 1985, the Narcotics Laboratory Section of the United Nations Division of Narcotic Drugs assisted national narcotics laboratories through the selection and procurement of basic equipment, reference books and standard texts, and made available reference samples of drugs under international control. It also provided information on the collection and analysis of seized samples of traditional drugs such as heroin, cocaine and cannabis. The Secretary-General's 1984 report[26] on the scientific research and work of the Section was discussed by the Commission on Narcotic Drugs in February 1985,[2] along with a manual prepared for use by national authorities on the establishment and operational needs of narcotics laboratories.

Proposed International Conference on Drug Abuse and Illicit Trafficking (1987)

The Secretary-General, in a speech to the Economic and Social Council on 24 May 1985, said that drug abuse presented as destructive a threat to current and future generations as the plagues which swept many parts of the world in earlier centuries. Unless controlled, its effect would be more insidious and devastating. He believed the moment had arrived for the international community to expand its efforts in a global undertaking to meet that peril. Accordingly, he proposed that a world conference be convened at the ministerial level in 1987 to deal with all aspects of drug abuse. Specifically, he said, the conference should be multidisciplinary in nature and focus on the following key areas: the promotion of education and community participation in prevention and reduction of the demand for illicit drugs; crop substitution and other methods of reducing supply; improved methods to limit the use of narcotics to medical and scientific purposes; forfeiture of illegally acquired proceeds and the extradition of persons arrested for drug-related crimes; strengthening of resources of law enforcement authorities; and treatment and rehabilitation of drug addicts.

In October, ACC decided[27] to consider, in its programme of work for 1986, preparations for the proposed world conference. Its *Ad Hoc* Inter-Agency Meeting on Co-ordination in Matters of International Drug Abuse Control (Rome, 11-13

September)[28] had outlined the genesis of the Secretary-General's proposal, and expressed the hope that the conference would elicit an increase in the human and financial resources allocated by Member States at the national and intergovernmental organization levels to cope more effectively with the drug abuse phenomenon.

An October note by the Secretary-General,[29] which annexed his speech to the Council, elaborated on the purposes, objectives, preparations for and organization of the proposed conference.

On 5 November 1985,[30] Angola forwarded to the Secretary-General the Declarations adopted by the Conference of Foreign Ministers of Non-Aligned Countries (Luanda, 4-7 September). In the Final Economic Declaration, the Ministers expressed their support for the proposed conference and urged prompt agreement on technical and economic co-operation programmes to assist countries most affected by drug abuse, illicit production and trafficking.

The Bahamas, on 28 October,[31] transmitted a communiqué adopted by heads of Governments of Commonwealth States (Nassau, 16-22 October), in which they welcomed the Secretary-General's proposal.

ECONOMIC AND SOCIAL COUNCIL ACTION

On an oral proposal of its President, the Economic and Social Council, on 28 May 1985, by **decision 1985/131** adopted without vote, took note of the statement made by the Secretary-General on 24 May on the question of narcotic drugs.

GENERAL ASSEMBLY ACTION

On 13 December, on the recommendation of the Third Committee, the General Assembly adopted **resolution 40/122**, without vote.

International Conference on Drug Abuse and Illicit Trafficking

The General Assembly,

Conscious of the common concern that exists among nations of the world regarding the awesome and vicious effects of drug abuse and illicit trafficking, which threaten the stability of nations and the well-being of mankind and which therefore constitute a grave threat to the security and development of many countries,

Aware of the dangers posed for producer, consumer and transit countries alike by the illegal cultivation, production and manufacture of and demand for drugs and by their illicit traffic,

Recalling its resolutions 39/141, 39/142 and 39/143 of 14 December 1984 and relevant resolutions and decisions of the Economic and Social Council and the Commission on Narcotic Drugs in the international campaign against traffic in and abuse of narcotic drugs and psychotropic substances,

Mindful of relevant regional and other initiatives, such as the Declaration of Principle to Combat the Abuse of Narcotic Drugs adopted by the Association of South-

East Asian Nations on 26 June 1976, the Quito Declaration against Traffic in Narcotic Drugs of 11 August 1984, the New York Declaration against Drug Trafficking and the Illicit Use of Drugs of 1 October 1984, the report entitled "Options for individual and collective action to intensify the fight against drug abuse" issued at the Bonn Summit held from 2 to 4 May 1985, the joint statement on the international problem of drug abuse and drug trafficking issued on 9 July 1985 by the Ministers for Foreign Affairs of the States members of the Association of South-East Asian Nations, the Lima Declaration of 29 July 1985, the concern expressed at the Conference of Foreign Ministers of Non-Aligned Countries held at Luanda from 4 to 7 September 1985, and the communiqué adopted at the meeting of heads of Governments of Commonwealth States, held at Nassau from 16 to 22 October 1985, as well as the First Ladies' Conferences on Drug Abuse held in Washington in April 1985 and in New York in October 1985,

Recognizing the importance of adherence to existing international legal instruments, including the Single Convention on Narcotic Drugs of 1961, as amended by the 1972 Protocol Amending the Single Convention on Narcotic Drugs of 1961, and the Convention on Psychotropic Substances of 1971, and the need to encourage Member States that have not yet done so to ratify these instruments and the need for States that have already ratified to implement fully their obligations under these instruments,

Noting the relevant provisions of the International Drug Abuse Control Strategy adopted by the General Assembly at its thirty-sixth session,

Mindful of the special responsibilities of the United Nations and the international community to seek viable solutions to the growing scourge of drug abuse and illicit trafficking,

Noting the work of the Commission on Narcotic Drugs towards the preparation of a draft convention against illicit traffic in narcotic drugs and psychotropic substances,

Noting with appreciation the statement made by the Secretary-General before the Economic and Social Council on 24 May 1985, referred to in Council decision 1985/131 of 28 May 1985, which drew attention to the gravity, magnitude and complexities of the international drug problem and in response proposed a world-wide conference at the ministerial level in 1987 to consider all aspects of the problem,

Recognizing that the interregional meeting of heads of national drug law enforcement agencies, to be convened at Vienna in 1986, could make a significant contribution to the deliberations of the conference at the ministerial level proposed by the Secretary-General,

Taking into account the various reviews of the activities of the United Nations agencies in the narcotics field that have already been undertaken and noting with satisfaction the Secretary-General's designation of the Under-Secretary-General for Political and General Assembly Affairs as the overall co-ordinator of all United Nations activities related to drug control,

Having considered the note by the Secretary-General on a proposed United Nations conference on drug abuse control,

1.   *Strongly urges* all States to summon the utmost political will to combat drug abuse and illicit trafficking by generating increased political, cultural and social awareness;

2. *Calls upon* the United Nations, the specialized agencies and other organizations of the United Nations system to give the highest attention and priority possible to international measures to combat illicit production of, trafficking in and demand for drugs;

3. *Also calls upon* all States that have not already done so to become parties to the Single Convention on Narcotic Drugs of 1961 and the 1972 Protocol Amending the Single Convention on Narcotic Drugs of 1961 and to the Convention on Psychotropic Substances of 1971, and, in the mean time, to make serious efforts to comply with the provisions of these instruments;

4. *Decides* to convene, in 1987, an International Conference on Drug Abuse and Illicit Trafficking at the ministerial level at the Vienna International Centre as an expression of the political will of nations to combat the drug menace, with the mandate to generate universal action to combat the drug problem in all its forms at the national, regional and international levels and to adopt a comprehensive multidisciplinary outline of future activities which focuses on concrete and substantive issues directly relevant to the problems of drug abuse and illicit trafficking, *inter alia:*

(a) To consider whether existing mechanisms, whereby experiences, methodologies and other information in law enforcement, preventive education, treatment and rehabilitation, research and development of manpower relating to the prevention and control of drug abuse can be exchanged, should be improved or, if necessary, complemented by new mechanisms;

(b) To intensify concerted efforts by governmental, intergovernmental and non-governmental organizations to combat all forms of drug abuse, illicit trafficking and related criminal activities leading to the further development of national strategies that could be a basis for international action;

(c) To create heightened national and international awareness and sensitivity concerning the pernicious effects of the abuse of narcotic drugs and psychotropic substances, paying due attention to the demand dimension of the drug problem and to the role of the mass media, non-governmental organizations and other channels of dissemination of information about all aspects of the drug problem, especially in the prevention of drug abuse;

(d) To achieve as much harmonization as possible and to reinforce national legislation, bilateral treaties, regional arrangements and other international legal instruments, especially as they relate to enforcement and penalties against those involved in all aspects of illicit trafficking, including forfeiture of illegally acquired assets and extradition, and to develop co-operation in dealing with drug abusers, including their treatment and rehabilitation;

(e) To make further progress towards eradicating the sources of raw materials for illicit drugs through a comprehensive programme of integrated rural development, the development of alternative means of livelihood and retraining, law enforcement and, where appropriate, crop substitution;

(f) To control more effectively the production, distribution and consumption of narcotic drugs and psychotropic substances with a view to limiting their use exclusively to medical and scientific purposes, in accordance with existing conventions, and, in this connection, to underline the central role of the International Narcotics Control Board;

(g) To strengthen the United Nations co-ordination of drug abuse control activities by, *inter alia*, increasing support for the United Nations Fund for Drug Abuse Control and to reinforce regional and other co-operation between Member States;

(h) To support strongly current high-priority initiatives and programmes of the United Nations, including the elaboration of a convention against illicit traffic in narcotic drugs and psychotropic substances which considers, in particular, those aspects of the problem not envisaged in existing international instruments;

5. *Requests* the Secretary-General to facilitate co-ordination and interaction between Member States and the specialized agencies and other organizations of the United Nations system and, in this regard, to appoint the Secretary-General of the International Conference on Drug Abuse and Illicit Trafficking at the earliest possible time;

6. *Requests* the Economic and Social Council, at its organizational session for 1986, to invite the Commission on Narcotic Drugs to act as the preparatory body for the Conference, which shall be open to the participation of all States, and, for this purpose, to extend by one week the ninth special session of the Commission at Vienna in February 1986 in order to consider the agenda and the organizational arrangements for the Conference and, further, to submit its report on these matters to the Council at its first regular session of 1986;

7. *Reaffirms* the central role of the specialized expert input of the Commission on Narcotic Drugs and calls upon all United Nations bodies to co-operate fully with the Commission and with the Secretary-General of the Conference in order to ensure effective preparations for the Conference;

8. *Requests* the Secretary-General, without prejudice to ongoing initiatives, programmes and work of the United Nations in the field of drugs, to cover as much as possible of the cost of holding the Conference through absorption within the regular budget for the biennium 1986-1987 and to facilitate consideration of the financial implications of the present resolution through established procedures, and further requests the Secretary-General to submit progress reports on the financial arrangements and implementation of the present resolution, through the Commission on Narcotic Drugs, to the Economic and Social Council at its first regular session of 1986;

9. *Further requests* the Secretary-General to report to the General Assembly at its forty-first session on the implementation of the present resolution.

General Assembly resolution 40/122

13 December 1985   Meeting 116   Adopted without vote

Approved by Third Committee (A/40/984) without vote, 3 December (meeting 61); 43-nation draft (A/C.3/40/L.49), orally revised; agenda item 106.

Sponsors: Australia, Austria, Bahamas, Bangladesh, Barbados, Bolivia, Brunei Darussalam, Canada, China, Colombia, Democratic Kampuchea, Ecuador, Egypt, Fiji, Finland, France, Germany, Federal Republic of, Indonesia, Ivory Coast, Jamaica, Madagascar, Malawi, Malaysia, Mali, New Zealand, Nigeria, Norway, Pakistan, Philippines, Samoa, Senegal, Singapore, Somalia, Sri Lanka, Sudan, Sweden, Thailand, Turkey, United Kingdom, United States, Vanuatu, Venezuela, Zaire.

Financial implications. ACABQ, A/40/7/Add.17; 5th Committee, A/40/1040; S-G, A/C.3/40/L.68, A/C.5/40/80.

Meeting numbers. GA 40th session: 3rd Committee 42-45, 55, 56, 60, 61; 5th Committee 61; plenary 116.

In **resolution 40/121**, the Assembly expressed its appreciation to the Secretary-General for his proposal to convene an International Conference. In **resolution 40/120**, it requested him to submit to the Conference a report on progress made towards completing a new convention against drug trafficking.

Preventive education

ECONOMIC AND SOCIAL COUNCIL ACTION

On 28 May, on the recommendation of its Second (Social) Committee, the Economic and Social Council adopted **resolution 1985/14** without vote.

Promotion of preventive education and community participation against drug abuse

The Economic and Social Council,

Recalling article 38, paragraph 3, of the Single Convention on Narcotic Drugs, 1961, the Single Convention on Narcotic Drugs, 1961, as amended by the 1972 Protocol, and article 20, paragraph 3, of the 1971 Convention on Psychotropic Substances,

Recalling also its resolution 1981/9 of 6 May 1981,

Noting with concern the alarming spread of drug abuse in most parts of the world and its detrimental effects on all societies and individuals, particularly young people,

Recognizing that the elimination of the illicit supply of and demand for drugs is the ultimate objective of the community of nations,

Mindful that, given the present state of knowledge in the treatment of drug addiction, a permanent cure is not always an attainable objective,

Aware of the urgent need to protect future generations from the scourge of drug abuse,

Conscious of the impact that informed public opinion will have in increasing the effectiveness of the fight against drug abuse,

Recognizing that information aimed solely at emphasizing the dangers of drug abuse is often of limited effectiveness in discouraging drug misuse,

1. *Urges* the Governments of countries facing problems of drug abuse, as part of a comprehensive strategy, to give priority to programmes which aim to create in the young a deep respect for their own health, fitness and well-being and, taking into account cultural and social factors, to provide appropriate information and judicious advice for all sectors of their communities with regard to drug abuse, its effects and the ways in which members of those communities can respond;

2. *Invites* Governments to enlist, as an ongoing strategy, the participation of intergovernmental and non-governmental organizations, youth groups, teachers and parents in carrying out preventive activities;

3. *Requests* Governments to share their experience in this field, through bilateral arrangements, the Division of Narcotic Drugs of the United Nations Secretariat, the World Health Organization, other specialized agencies, and intergovernmental and non-governmental organizations;

4. *Requests* the Secretary-General to transmit the present resolution to the Governments of Member States, the specialized agencies, and intergovernmental and non-governmental organizations for their consideration and appropriate action.

Economic and Social Council resolution 1985/14

28 May 1985   Meeting 22   Adopted without vote

Approved by Second Committee (E/1985/83) without vote, 15 May (meeting 4); draft by Commission on Narcotic Drugs (E/1985/23); agenda item 18.

Supply and demand

Narcotic raw materials for licit use

At its February session, the Commission on Narcotic Drugs[2] reported that INCB had requested Governments concerned to provide, pursuant to a 1984 Economic and Social Council resolution,[32] information on measures taken or contemplated to implement a series of Council resolutions to promote a lasting balance between supply and demand. INCB prepared a special report[33] in which it summarized the current situation and trends in the demand and supply of opiates for medical and scientific needs, as well as international efforts aimed at ensuring a proper balance. The report also contained statements by Governments on measures they had taken or contemplated taking to implement the Council resolutions on the subject. According to the report, global production and demand of opiates had remained in balance since 1980. The problem of abnormally high accumulated stocks of both opium and poppy straw was accentuated by the fact that, since 1974, demand for opiates had levelled out—at approximately 190 tonnes of morphine equivalent per year.

An Expert Group on the Reduction of Excessive Stocks of Licit Opiate Raw Materials (Vienna, 23-27 September)[20] concluded that conversion of excess stock of such materials by refining it, or destroying medically useful excess opium stocks, were not currently desirable solutions, that the possibility might be explored of making available through WHO the unsatisfied medical needs for codeine in developing countries, and that the World Bank, UNDP and UNFDAC might consider extending technical assistance to India to assess agro-economic issues relating to opiate raw-material stock and production.

ECONOMIC AND SOCIAL COUNCIL ACTION

On 28 May, on the recommendation of its Second Committee, the Economic and Social Council adopted **resolution 1985/16** by vote.

Supply of and demand for opiates for medical and scientific needs

The Economic and Social Council,

Recalling its resolutions 1979/8 of 9 May 1979, 1980/20 of 30 April 1980, 1981/6 of 6 May 1981, 1982/12 of 30 April 1982, 1983/3 of 24 May 1983 and 1984/21 of 24 May 1984, as well as Commission on Narcotic Drugs resolution 1(XXIX) of 11 February 1981 entitled "Strategy and policies for drug control",

Having considered the report of the International Narcotics Control Board for 1984 on the demand and supply of opiates for medical and scientific needs,

Noting with concern the increasing production of opiate raw materials in excess of domestic need and for export in some non-traditional supplier countries, as brought out in that report,

Noting also with concern that the traditional supplier countries continue to hold large accumulated stocks of opiate raw materials which constitute heavy financial and other burdens for them,

Bearing in mind the urgent need to liquidate the accumulated stocks held by the traditional supplier countries with a view to achieving a lasting world-wide balance between demand and supply of opiates for medical and scientific purposes,

Taking note of the position set out in paragraph 58 of the report of the International Narcotics Control Board,

Noting with appreciation the consultations held and the steps taken by the International Narcotics Control Board to facilitate the implementation of Economic and Social Council resolution 1984/21,

1. *Urges* the Governments of those countries that have not already done so to take urgent and effective steps to implement Council resolution 1984/21;

2. *Urges* the Governments of importing countries to take urgent and effective steps to support the traditional supplier countries and to give to those countries all the practical assistance they can, in order to avoid the proliferation of sources of production of opiate raw materials for export;

3. *Urges* the Governments of producing and manufacturing countries which have recently set up additional capacities for export to take urgent and effective measures to restrict their production programmes to meeting mainly their domestic requirements;

4. *Requests* the International Narcotics Control Board to further pursue the implementation of the above-mentioned resolutions with the Governments of those countries which have not yet implemented them, and to devise such other measures as may be deemed appropriate with a view to promoting and monitoring the urgent implementation of those resolutions;

5. *Requests* the Secretary-General to continue his efforts towards the expeditious implementation of project A-1, on the reduction of excessive stocks of licit opiate raw materials, under the programme of action for the biennium 1984-1985 of the Basic Five-Year Programme of Action of the International Drug Control Strategy;

6. *Requests* the International Narcotics Control Board to assist, in consultation with the producing and consuming countries and the concerned United Nations bodies, in the implementation of project A-1;

7. *Requests* the Secretary-General to transmit the present resolution to all Governments for their consideration and implementation.

Economic and Social Council resolution 1985/16

28 May 1985   Meeting 22   35-0-15

Approved by Second Committee (E/1985/83) by vote (26-0-13), 15 May (meeting 4); draft by Commission on Narcotic Drugs (E/1985/23); agenda item 18.

Illicit traffic

INCB reported[1] that the Commission on Narcotic Drugs, at its February 1985 session,[2] noted that increasingly clear links existed in many parts of the world between drug trafficking, the illegal traffic in firearms, subversion, international terrorism and other criminal activities. On the recommendation of its Sub-Commission on Illicit Drug Traffic and Related Matters in the Near and Middle East (see p. 1025), the Commission asked to receive information on such links through the annual reporting system.

INCB observed that traffickers attempted to hide their profits by "laundering" (concealing or disguising the nature, source, disposition, movement or ownership) them through legitimate enterprises—a process which undermined the economic and social order, spread violence and corruption, and jeopardized the very political stability and security of some countries. INCB further pointed to the emergence and abuse of new and hazardous drugs, such as "designer drugs"—analogues of controlled substances which, slightly altered, did not fall within the legal controls. They could be more potent than the parent substances and entailed a substantial threat to health and even life.

The Commission, in February,[2] initiated preparation of a draft convention on illicit traffic in narcotic drugs and psychotropic substances (see p. 1023).

Two subsidiary bodies of the Commission—the Sub-Commission on Illicit Drug Traffic and Related Matters in the Near and Middle East and the Operational Heads of National Narcotics Law Enforcement Agencies (HONLEA), Far East Region (see p. 1022)—continued to serve as co-ordination mechanisms for drug law enforcement at the regional level. They were among the co-ordination mechanisms noted in an October report[34] of the Secretary-General on the international campaign against traffic in drugs, prepared in response to a 1984 Assembly request.[35] Measures to alleviate the special problems of transit States were also addressed, as was the possibility of convening a world ministerial-level conference on drug abuse (see p. 1016). Three interregional seminars were mentioned, as approved by UNDP for 1986, on replacement of opium-poppy cultivation.

GENERAL ASSEMBLY ACTION

On the recommendation of the Third Committee, the Assembly, on 13 December, adopted **resolution 40/121** without vote.

International campaign against traffic in drugs

The General Assembly,

Recalling its resolutions 35/195 of 15 December 1980, 36/168 of 16 December 1981, 37/168 of 17 December 1982, 37/198 of 18 December 1982 and 38/98 and 38/122 of 16 December 1983, as well as its resolutions 36/132 of 14 December 1981, 38/93 of 16 December 1983, 39/141 and 39/143 of 14 December 1984 and other relevant provisions,

Recalling also its resolution 39/142 of 14 December 1984, by which it adopted the Declaration on the Control of Drug Trafficking and Drug Abuse, which describes drug trafficking and drug abuse as an international criminal activity whose total elimination demands urgent attention and maximum priority,

Taking note of the reiterated concern expressed by the Secretary-General in his report on the work of the Organization, in which he recognizes that the drug problem can no longer be regarded as a merely social, and largely domestic, concern and proposes that an effective range of strategies be developed to meet the challenge,

Taking note once again of the provisions of the Quito Declaration against Traffic in Narcotic Drugs of 11 August 1984, the New York Declaration against Drug Trafficking and the Illicit Use of Drugs of 1 October 1984, in which drug trafficking is considered to be a crime against humanity, and the Lima Declaration of 29 July 1985, which draws attention to the need for integrated, effective and urgent regional and international action supported by the resources necessary for successfully overcoming the problem,

Commending the work of the Commission on Narcotic Drugs and the International Narcotics Control Board, as well as the positive action of the United Nations Fund for Drug Abuse Control in allocating funds to integrated rural development programmes, including substitution of illegal crops in the most severely affected areas, and their efforts to achieve greater law enforcement,

Considering that, despite the efforts made, the situation continues to deteriorate and the international community is confronted with transnational criminal organizations whose activities, including terrorist practices, constitute a threat to the well-being of peoples, the stability of democratic institutions and the sovereignty of States,

Acknowledging once more that the eradication of this scourge calls for integrated action which will simultaneously tackle the problems of reduction and control of illicit demand, production, distribution and marketing, and that action designed to eliminate illicit drug cultivation and trafficking should be accompanied, when necessary, by economic and social development programmes, including crop substitution, in the affected areas,

Endorsing the statement made by the Secretary-General before the Economic and Social Council on 24 May 1985, referred to in Council decision 1985/131 of 28 May 1985, on the need for a new United Nations offensive against drug trafficking and drug abuse, and his proposal to convene a world conference at the ministerial level in 1987,

Aware of the decision of the Secretary-General to convene an interregional meeting of heads of national drug law enforcement agencies in 1986, in accordance with paragraph 10 of General Assembly resolution 39/143,

Conscious of the contribution that this interregional meeting could make to bilateral and multilateral efforts, including proposals that might be taken into account in the preparation of a draft convention against illicit traffic in narcotic drugs and at the International Conference on Drug Abuse and Illicit Trafficking to be held in 1987,

Acknowledging the important role that Member States and relevant bodies of the United Nations system must play in order to ensure that the interregional meeting produces significant results in the continuing fight against illicit drug trafficking and drug abuse,

Acknowledging once more that law enforcement officials represent an important line of defence against organized crime, the illegal arms trade and other forms of criminal activity associated with illicit traffic in drugs that threaten the stability and security of many States,

Reiterating the importance of ratifying or acceding to international treaties on the control of narcotic drugs and psychotropic substances,

1. *Takes note* of the reports of the Secretary-General;

2. *Reaffirms* that maximum priority must be given to the fight against the illicit production of, demand for and traffic in drugs and related international criminal activities, such as the illegal arms trade and terrorist practices, which also have an adverse effect not only on the well-being of peoples but also on the stability of institutions, as well as posing a threat to the sovereignty of States;

3. *Acknowledges* the work of bodies of the United Nations system, in particular the drug-control bodies, in assisting efforts and initiatives designed to increase international co-operation, and recommends that this work be intensified;

4. *Encourages* Member States and the relevant bodies of the United Nations system to provide technical assistance to the developing countries most affected by the illicit production of, traffic in and use of drugs and psychotropic substances, in order to combat the problem;

5. *Expresses* its appreciation to the Secretary-General for his proposal to convene in 1987, at the ministerial level, an International Conference on Drug Abuse and Illicit Trafficking to deal with all aspects of drug abuse;

6. *Takes note with satisfaction* of the decision of the Secretary-General to hold an interregional meeting of heads of national drug law enforcement agencies at Vienna from 28 July to 1 August 1986, in accordance with paragraph 10 of General Assembly resolution 39/143;

7. *Recommends* to the Commission on Narcotic Drugs that it advise the interregional meeting to examine in depth the most important aspects of the problem, especially those that would enhance ongoing bilateral and multilateral efforts, in particular the preparation of a draft convention against illicit traffic in narcotic drugs and psychotropic substances and the proposed International Conference on Drug Abuse and Illicit Trafficking, to be convened by the Secretary-General at the ministerial level, and to recommend action on, *inter alia:*

(a) Extradition;

(b) Mechanisms that would enhance interregional co-ordination and co-operation on a permanent basis;

(c) Modalities of ensuring rapid and secure means of communication between law enforcement agencies at the national, regional and international levels;

(d) Techniques of controlled delivery;

(e) Measures to reduce the vulnerability of States affected by the transit of illicit drugs;

8. *Encourages* Member States to be represented at the interregional meeting by officials at the decision-making level of national organizations concerned with the suppression of illicit traffic in drugs and psychotropic substances;

9. *Invites* the competent bodies within the United Nations system, as well as the International Criminal Police Organization and the Customs Co-operation Council, to provide technical expertise and to participate actively in the interregional meeting;

10. *Requests* the Secretary-General to submit to the General Assembly at its forty-first session an interim report

containing the recommendations of the interregional meeting of heads of national drug law enforcement agencies and to submit a final report to the Economic and Social Council, through the Commission on Narcotic Drugs at its next session;

11. *Reiterates its request* to the Secretary-General to continue to make the necessary arrangements for holding, within the framework of advisory services, interregional seminars on the experience gained within the United Nations system in integrated rural development programmes that include the substitution of illegal crops in affected areas, particularly in the Andean region;

12. *Acknowledges* the vital role played by the United Nations Fund for Drug Abuse Control and calls upon Member States to contribute or to continue contributing to the Fund;

13. *Calls upon* the specialized agencies and all relevant bodies of the United Nations system actively to implement the present resolution and requests the Secretary-General to report thereon to the General Assembly at its forty-first session;

14. *Decides* to include in the provisional agenda of its forty-first session the item entitled "International campaign against traffic in drugs".

General Assembly resolution 40/121

13 December 1985   Meeting 116   Adopted without vote

Approved by Third Committee (A/40/984) without vote, 27 November (meeting 56); 17-nation draft (A/C.3/40/L.52), orally revised; agenda item 106.
Sponsors: Argentina, Bahamas, Bolivia, Chile, Colombia, Costa Rica, Dominican Republic, Ecuador, Guatemala, Ivory Coast, Malaysia, Morocco, Peru, Senegal, Thailand, Uruguay, Venezuela.
Meeting numbers. GA 40th session: 3rd Committee 42-45, 55, 56; plenary 116.

Drug law enforcement

The Commission on Narcotic Drugs reported[2] that HONLEA, at its eleventh meeting (Bangkok, Thailand, 26-30 November 1984),[36] had considered the serious drug trafficking situation within the Far East region. Not only were illicit opiates being illegally exported to other regions, but there had been a growing influx of illicit opiates and cannabis resin from parts of the Near and Middle East, and of psychotropic substances from Europe. Trafficking routes and methods had become increasingly complex and sophisticated, and a spread of multiple drug abuse, especially among young people, had been registered. The HONLEA Chairman drew the Commission's attention to desirable countermeasures, and stressed that the main thrust of its work was to increase the capacity of drug law enforcement agencies to render effective and practical mutual judicial and other assistance. As proposed by HONLEA, the Commission, on 13 February,[37] decided that the Secretary-General should be asked to invite Vanuatu to future HONLEA meetings.

At its twelfth meeting (Colombo, Sri Lanka, 4-8 November),[38] HONLEA made recommendations and suggestions relating to the interregional meeting of heads of national drug law enforcement agencies to be convened at Vienna in 1986; they concerned the level of representation and suggested topics for consideration. It also asked for more information concerning designer drugs, and discussed elements for inclusion in the convention on illicit drug traffic.

The Seventh United Nations Congress on the Prevention of Crime and the Treatment of Offenders (Milan, August/September 1985) adopted three resolutions on action against drug abuse.

In one resolution,[39] it invited States to strengthen instruments and legislation against illicit drug trafficking and maximize co-operation, urged ratification of the relevant instruments, and recommended that a new instrument on the subject address extradition, effective penalties, control of chemicals and precursors used in illicit manufacture, controlled delivery, traffic on the high seas, smuggling through the mails, and control in free-trade zones and ports.

In another resolution,[40] it called on States to modernize criminal laws and procedures, including those relating to extradition, the forfeiture of illegally acquired assets and obtaining of evidence abroad, to conduct national campaigns, to strengthen law enforcement, to establish investigative institutions and to review laws for their adequacy to fight organized crime. It recommended that the Commission on Narcotic Drugs be urged to continue to disseminate information on treatment, rehabilitation and educational programmes to deal with drug abuse. (For the third resolution, see p. 1016.)

In its 1985 report,[1] INCB endorsed a recommendation of the Congress concerning effective penalties and recommended that it, as well as provisions to facilitate the exercise of criminal jurisdiction on board foreign vessels passing through territorial seas or on the high seas, be embodied in the new convention on illicit trafficking.

ECONOMIC AND SOCIAL COUNCIL ACTION

On 28 May, on the recommendation of its Second Committee, the Economic and Social Council adopted two resolutions on drug law enforcement. It adopted **resolution 1985/12** without vote.

Measures against the diversion in international commerce of specific precursors, chemicals and solvents used in the illicit manufacture of narcotic drugs and psychotropic substances

The Economic and Social Council,

Recalling that the Single Convention on Narcotic Drugs, 1961, and the 1971 Convention on Psychotropic Substances oblige Parties thereto to endeavour, to the best of their abilities, to apply such measures of supervision as may be practicable to substances which do not fall within the provisions of the conventions, but which may nevertheless be used for the illicit manufacture of substances falling within those provisions,

Aware that such substances include precursors, chemicals and solvents, the ready availability of which has led to an increase in the clandestine production of narcotic drugs and psychotropic substances in many parts of the world,

Noting that particular vigilance is desired in the case of ephedrine, ephedrol, phenyl-2-propanone, ergotamine, anthranilic acid, piperidine, ethyl ether and acetic anhydride, which are frequently used for the illicit manufacture of amphetamine, methamphetamine (+)-Lysergide (LSD), methaqualone and phencyclidine, as well as cocaine and heroin,

Bearing in mind paragraphs 40 to 42 of the report of the International Narcotics Control Board for 1984, in which is emphasized the need to take urgent measures, at both national and international levels, to monitor the movement of such substances in the international trade, with a view to preventing their availability for the illicit manufacture of drugs,

1. *Invites* Governments, particularly of those countries in which illicit drug manufacture is known to take place, and which have not already done so, to introduce, consistent with domestic laws, a licensing or monitoring system for the supply and import of such precursors, chemicals and solvents used in the manufacture of narcotic drugs and psychotropic substances, or to prohibit the import of those substances where there is no licit need for them;

2. *Also invites* the Governments of countries in which such substances are manufactured, the Governments of countries which import them, and the Governments of countries in which illicit drugs are manufactured, to monitor international trade in those substances and to co-operate closely and exchange information promptly with regard to abnormal shipments which give rise to suspicion; to inform their law enforcement services of the existence of such information exchange programmes; and to keep the International Narcotics Control Board notified accordingly;

3. *Recommends* that Governments should seize any such substances, as well as any equipment used in, or intended for use in, any of the offences referred to in article 36 of the Single Convention on Narcotic Drugs, 1961, and article 22 of the 1971 Convention on Psychotropic Substances;

4. *Invites* all Governments to supply to the Board and to concerned Governments, on a voluntary basis, such information as can be obtained on ephedrine, ephedrol, phenyl-2-propanone, ergotamine, anthranilic acid, piperidine, ethyl ether and acetic anhydride which may be useful for the detection and prevention of diversion;

5. *Decides* to include this question in the provisional agenda for the next regular session of the Commission on Narcotic Drugs;

6. *Requests* the Secretary-General to transmit the text of the present resolution to all Governments, for consideration and action as appropriate.

Economic and Social Council resolution 1985/12

28 May 1985   Meeting 22   Adopted without vote

Approved by Second Committee (E/1985/83) without vote, 15 May (meeting 4); draft by Commission on Narcotic Drugs (E/1985/23); agenda item 18.

The Council also adopted **resolution 1985/13** without vote.

The need to reduce the risk of illicit traffic in narcotic drugs and psychotropic substances carried by commercial carriers

The Economic and Social Council,

Bearing in mind that a high proportion of illicit narcotic drugs and psychotropic substances has been seized in connection with commercial carrier operations,

Convinced that commercial carriers have a responsibility to take an active role in improving employee integrity and the security of their operations in order to minimize the risk of illicit trafficking by their own employees or by those using the carriers' services,

Noting that physical safeguards at international ports and airports contribute significantly to the security efforts of the commercial carriers using those facilities,

Recognizing that various measures could be taken by Governments with a view to encouraging greater security at international ports and airports and to facilitating the detection and seizure of illicit drugs,

1. *Requests* Governments which have not yet done so to initiate or expand training programmes for their law enforcement agencies in order to promote intensified and more effective searches, better analysis of potential risks, and greater overall security within and around their international ports and airports;

2. *Urges* Governments which have not yet done so to develop ways of improving their security operations, together with officials of the commercial carriers which use their international ports and airports and to encourage those carriers to discharge their responsibility to improve employee integrity and the security of their operations;

3. *Also urges* Governments which have not yet done so to improve the capabilities of authorities at international ports and airports with a view to controlling access to cargo and commercial carriers;

4. *Requests* Governments to improve means of communication among themselves in order to permit the most rapid possible exchange of information concerning illicit traffic in narcotic drugs and psychotropic substances by commercial carriers;

5. *Invites* the United Nations Fund for Drug Abuse Control, the Division of Narcotic Drugs of the United Nations Secretariat, the Customs Co-operation Council, the International Criminal Police Organization and Governments to consider supporting the training of enforcement personnel in improved techniques of search and security, advising commercial carriers as well as authorities at international ports and airports on ways of improving employee integrity and the security of their operations, and implementing programmes to ensure that those security improvements are being carried out;

6. *Requests* the Secretary-General to transmit the text of the present resolution to all Governments for appropriate action.

Economic and Social Council resolution 1985/13

28 May 1985   Meeting 22   Adopted without vote

Approved by Second Committee (E/1985/83) without vote, 15 May (meeting 4); draft by Commission on Narcotic Drugs (E/1985/23); agenda item 18.

Draft convention against illicit traffic

In response to a 1984 General Assembly resolution[41] and Economic and Social Council decision 1985/104 (see below), the Commission on Narcotic Drugs initiated preparation in February 1985 of a draft convention against the illicit traffic in narcotic drugs, using a draft convention annexed to the Assembly's resolution as a working paper.

Following discussion of the matter, the Commission adopted on 20 February a resolution[42] in which it requested the Secretary-General to seek from United Nations Member States and States parties to the conventions on narcotic drugs comments and proposals on the elements they would like to have incorporated in the draft convention, to compile and consolidate them, and report back to the States by 1 November 1985. The Commission was to consider that report at a special session in 1986.

In an October 1985 report[43] to the Assembly on the international campaign against traffic in drugs, the Secretary-General said that on 15 March he had transmitted to Members and States parties the relevant documents with a request for their comments by 1 July. In September, he forwarded to the Commission a consolidated report (addenda through February 1986)[44] based on a compilation of replies received from Governments and relevant studies.

The Milan Plan of Action, adopted by the Seventh United Nations Congress on the Prevention of Crime and the Treatment of Offenders,[45] stated that, as an essential element of an effective plan of action, it was imperative to launch a major effort to control and eradicate illicit drug traffic and abuse, and organized crime, which disrupted and destabilized societies.

In their October communiqué[31] (see p. 1017), the heads of Government of Commonwealth States expressed deep concern at the rising incidence of drug abuse and illicit drug trafficking, recognized that it called for a wide range of responses, and expressed the hope that action would be expedited on the proposed new convention.

The Conference of Foreign Ministers of Non-Aligned Countries in September, in the Final Economic Declaration[30] (see p. 1017), expressed concern that continued abuse and illicit trafficking would endanger and undermine the development of nations, and called for the early conclusion of a convention against traffic in narcotic drugs and psychotropic substances and related activities.

ECONOMIC AND SOCIAL COUNCIL ACTION

In February 1985, the Economic and Social Council adopted **decision 1985/104** without vote.

Draft convention against the illicit traffic in narcotic drugs

At its 5th plenary meeting, on 8 February 1985, the Council, pursuant to General Assembly resolution 39/141 of 14 December 1984, decided:

(a) To request the Commission on Narcotic Drugs, at its thirty-first session, to initiate, as a matter of priority, the preparation of a draft convention against illicit traffic in narcotic drugs which considers the various aspects of the problem as a whole, in particular those not envisaged in existing international instruments, and, to that end, to transmit to the Commission as a working paper

the draft convention annexed to Assembly resolution 39/141;

(b) To request the Commission to report to the Council, if possible at its first regular session of 1985, on the results achieved in this respect.

Economic and Social Council decision 1985/104

Adopted without vote

Draft by President, for Bureau (E/1985/L.18), based on informal consultations; agenda item 2.
Meeting numbers. ESC 1, 5.

GENERAL ASSEMBLY ACTION

On 13 December, the General Assembly, acting on the recommendation of the Third Committee, adopted **resolution 40/120**, without vote.

Preparation of a draft convention against illicit traffic in narcotic drugs and psychotropic substances

The General Assembly,

Recalling its resolutions 33/168 of 20 December 1978, 35/195 of 15 December 1980, 36/132 of 14 December 1981, 36/168 of 16 December 1981, 37/168 of 17 December 1982, 37/198 of 18 December 1982, 38/93 and 38/122 of 16 December 1983, 39/141 and 39/143 of 14 December 1984 and other relevant provisions,

Recalling also the Declaration on the Control of Drug Trafficking and Drug Abuse of 14 December 1984, in which it is stated, *inter alia,* that the eradication of trafficking in narcotic drugs is the collective responsibility of all States and that States shall utilize the legal instruments against the illicit production of and demand for, abuse of and illicit traffic in drugs and adopt additional measures to counter new manifestations of this crime,

Bearing in mind the Quito Declaration against Traffic in Narcotic Drugs of 11 August 1984, the New York Declaration against Drug Trafficking and the Illicit Use of Drugs of 1 October 1984 and the Lima Declaration of 29 July 1985, in which profound alarm was expressed at the seriousness of the problem,

Noting the report entitled "Options for individual and collective action to intensify the fight against drug abuse" that emerged from the Bonn Summit held from 2 to 4 May 1985,

Noting also the joint statement on the international problem of drug abuse and drug trafficking issued on 9 July 1985 by the Ministers for Foreign Affairs of the States members of the Association of South-East Asian Nations, which praised the ongoing efforts of the international community in preparing the draft of a new convention against illicit traffic in narcotic drugs and psychotropic substances,

Taking into account the fact that, at the Conference of Foreign Ministers of Non-Aligned Countries held at Luanda from 4 to 7 September 1985, the Ministers expressed deep concern over the growing problem of drug abuse and illicit trafficking in narcotic drugs and renewed their support for the efforts being undertaken by the international community to combat it,

Taking into account also the paragraphs on drug abuse and illicit trafficking in drugs in the communiqué adopted at the meeting of heads of Governments of Commonwealth States held at Nassau from 16 to 22 October 1985, in which the hope was expressed that action would be expedited on the related proposed new convention,

Recalling with appreciation the thorough consideration given to drug abuse and trafficking issues by the Seventh United Nations Congress on the Prevention of Crime and the Treatment of Offenders, in particular its resolution 2, in which the Congress recommended that the preparation of a new international instrument against illicit drug traffic should be considered as an absolute priority, and the Milan Plan of Action, especially paragraph 5 *(g)* thereof,

Deeply concerned by the constant upward trend in illicit traffic and drug abuse verified and reported by an increasing number of Member States, which poses serious dangers for individual human rights and for the economic, cultural and political structures of society,

Reaffirming its conviction that the magnitude and complexity reached in illicit drug trafficking and its grave consequences emphasize the urgent need to carry out the mandate given by the General Assembly, in its resolution 39/141, to the Commission on Narcotic Drugs, through the Economic and Social Council, to initiate, as a matter of priority, the preparation of a draft convention against illicit traffic in narcotic drugs which considers the various aspects of the problem as a whole, in particular those not envisaged in existing international instruments,

Welcoming the statement made by the Secretary-General before the Economic and Social Council on 24 May 1985, in which he proposed the convening in 1987 of a world conference at the ministerial level to deal with all aspects of drug abuse, and his note on drug abuse control of 22 October 1985,

Recognizing the valuable contribution made by existing international legal instruments in their specialized areas, including the Single Convention on Narcotic Drugs of 1961, as amended by the 1972 Protocol Amending the Single Convention on Narcotic Drugs of 1961, and the Convention on Psychotropic Substances of 1971,

Expressing deep satisfaction with Commission on Narcotic Drugs resolution 1(XXXI) of 20 February 1985, approved by the Economic and Social Council in its decision 1985/130 of 28 May 1985,

1. *Expresses its appreciation* to Member States for their response to the request made by the Secretary-General in accordance with paragraph 1 of Commission on Narcotic Drugs resolution 1(XXXI) and urges those Member States that have not yet done so to comply with the request forthwith;

2. *Commends* the Secretary-General for his effective response to the request set forth in paragraphs 1 and 2 of Commission on Narcotic Drugs resolution 1(XXXI) and for the preparation of his comprehensive report, which will contribute to the preparation of a draft convention against illicit traffic in narcotic drugs and psychotropic substances, as mandated by the General Assembly in its resolution 39/141;

3. *Requests* the Economic and Social Council, in accordance with General Assembly resolution 39/141 and resolution 1(XXXI) of the Commission on Narcotic Drugs, to instruct the Commission to decide, following consideration at its ninth special session of the report of the Secretary-General, on the elements that could be included in the convention and to request the Secretary-General to prepare a draft on the basis of those elements, and to submit a progress report, including completed elements of the draft, to the Commission for consideration at its thirty-second session;

4. *Requests* the Secretary-General to submit to the International Conference on Drug Abuse and Illicit Trafficking, to be held in 1987, a report on progress made towards completing a new convention against drug trafficking;

5. *Emphasizes* the importance of resolution 2 adopted by the Seventh United Nations Congress on the Prevention of Crime and the Treatment of Offenders, approved by the General Assembly in its resolution 40/32 of 29 November 1985, in which the Congress recommended that absolute priority should be accorded to the preparation of a new international instrument against illicit drug traffic, as well as the importance of paragraph 5 *(g)* of the Milan Plan of Action;

6. *Recommends* that the new convention should take into account the interests of all countries in order that it may be an effective, operative instrument in the struggle against illicit drug trafficking;

7. *Requests* the Commission on Narcotic Drugs to report to the Economic and Social Council at its first regular session of 1986 on the results achieved in this respect during its ninth special session;

8. *Urges once again* all States that have not yet done so to adhere to and ratify the Single Convention on Narcotic Drugs of 1961, the 1972 Protocol Amending the Single Convention on Narcotic Drugs of 1961 and the Convention on Psychotropic Substances of 1971;

9. *Requests* the Secretary-General to report to the General Assembly at its forty-first session on the implementation of the present resolution.

General Assembly resolution 40/120

13 December 1985   Meeting 116   Adopted without vote

Approved by Third Committee (A/40/984) without vote, 27 November (meeting 56); 45-nation draft (A/C.3/40/L.45), orally revised; agenda item 106.

Sponsors: Australia, Bolivia, Brazil, Brunei Darussalam, Cameroon, Canada, Chile, China, Colombia, Costa Rica, Cyprus, Dominican Republic, Ecuador, Egypt, El Salvador, Equatorial Guinea, Finland, Greece, Guatemala, Guinea, Guyana, Honduras, India, Indonesia, Ivory Coast, Jamaica, Malaysia, Mexico, Morocco, Nicaragua, Nigeria, Panama, Philippines, Rwanda, Senegal, Saint Lucia, Spain, Suriname, Thailand, Turkey, United Kingdom, United States, Uruguay, Venezuela, Zaire.

Meeting numbers. GA 40th session: 3rd Committee 42-45, 55, 56; plenary 116.

Near East and Middle East

The Sub-Commission on Illicit Drug Traffic and Related Matters in the Near and Middle East held its nineteenth session at Vienna on 7 February 1985.[46] It noted that there was great difficulty in identifying, with precision, sources of supply of illicit raw materials and recommended that the Secretary-General be requested to make arrangements to assist concerned Governments to identify with accuracy such sources of illicit supply. It also recommended to the Commission on Narcotic Drugs the adoption of a decision on links between the illicit drug traffic, the illegal traffic in firearms, subversion, international terrorism and organized crime.

On 13 February,[47] the Commission decided that more information on such links was needed. It considered that Governments and reporting authorities should be asked to address this issue in the annual reports questionnaires on the working of international treaties (see p. 1029) and when reporting on drug seizures. Summaries of this information should be submitted regularly to the Commission with a view to developing more co-ordinated countermeasures. Also on the Sub-Commission's recommendation, the Commission, on the same date,[48] noting the difficulty of identifying with precision sources of supply of illicit narcotic raw materials, requested the Secretary-General to assist Governments to identify such sources in order to assist them, with international community support if necessary, to eradicate illicit supply.

At its twentieth session (Teheran, Iran, 11-18 September),[49] the Sub-Commission adopted two recommendations: in one, it decided on measures for more accurate identification of illicit sources of production and cultivation of opium, and asked the Commission to endorse those measures and ensure finances to put them into effect; in the other, it recommended that the Commission encourage a more carefully balanced policy of contributions to and expenditures by UNFDAC to maintain equilibrium between different drug-related activities and also between different regions and illicit drugs and drug types.

INCB reported[1] that in 1985 the large quantities of opium and heroin seized in the Near and Middle East indicated the existence not only of extensive areas of illicit poppy cultivation but also of a substantial heroin manufacturing capacity. Cannabis and its resin were also seized frequently and in large amounts. Opium traditionally had been abused in the region, but the abuse of easily available, locally manufactured heroin was escalating. If an effective attack was to be mounted against illicit production, a systematic survey was needed of areas in which illicit poppy cultivation was believed to be taking place. Countries in the region which were not already doing so ought to conduct periodic epidemiological surveys to determine the actual extent of abuse, since those surveys were prerequisites for the formulation of demand-reduction programmes. The Board stressed that it was crucial for Governments to place special emphasis on intra- and interregional efforts to identify major traffickers and seize their assets, and to curtail the availability of acetic anhydride for heroin manufacture.

Africa

According to INCB,[1] evidence of spreading drug abuse in Africa was mounting. The region was attracting larger numbers of drug traffickers, who took advantage of inadequate control arrangements in many countries; it was a source of cannabis, abused locally and trafficked abroad. In recent years some countries, particularly Nigeria, had been used as transit points for heroin, trafficked mainly from the Middle East and South Asia and destined for Western Europe and North

America. Heroin abuse had begun to appear in some countries. Traffickers were trying to establish Africa as a major illicit market for psychotropic substances and as a transit point for traffic in such substances. Trafficking had begun to include cocaine as well. Those trends signalled a deteriorating situation which required urgent attention, the Board said.

ECONOMIC AND SOCIAL COUNCIL ACTION

On 28 May, on the recommendation of its Second Committee, the Economic and Social Council adopted **resolution 1985/11** without vote.

Co-operation for the control of illicit drug trafficking and drug abuse in the African region
The Economic and Social Council,

Recalling General Assembly resolutions 37/198 of 18 December 1982 and 38/98 and 38/122 of 16 December 1983,

Recalling, in particular, General Assembly resolution 39/142 of 14 December 1984, entitled "Declaration on the Control of Drug Trafficking and Drug Abuse",

Recalling also Economic and Social Council resolution 1845(LVI) of 15 May 1974 on co-operation for drug law enforcement in the Far East region and Commission on Narcotic Drugs resolution 6(XXX) of 16 February 1983 on the need for activities in the African countries,

Recognizing the urgent need to establish co-ordination mechanisms for similar drug law enforcement co-operation in the African region,

Bearing in mind General Assembly resolution 39/143 of 14 December 1984, in which the Assembly requested the Secretary-General to ensure that a meeting of heads of national drug law enforcement agencies would be convened in 1986,

1. *Requests* the Secretary-General to convene regular meetings of the operational heads of the national drug control and law enforcement agencies of States in the African region to study questions related to illicit drug traffic in the region and to establish more effective mechanisms for co-operation and mutual assistance in the suppression of illicit drug traffic within, from and into the region;

2. *Recommends* that the United Nations Fund for Drug Abuse Control should consider providing the financial support for those regional meetings, including the travel expenses and subsistence of one participant from each State in the region if, in the absence of such support, the Government concerned would not be represented;

3. *Decides* that the first regional meeting will be held at the headquarters of the Economic Commission for Africa, following consultations with the Executive Secretary of the Commission to determine an appropriate date in 1987;

4. *Requests* the Secretary-General to invite observers from the International Criminal Police Organization, the Customs Co-operation Council and other competent international and intergovernmental organizations to participate in the regional meetings at their own expense;

5. *Also requests* the Secretary-General, at his discretion, to invite observers from States which request

observer status and which are actively involved in countering the illicit drug traffic in the region to participate as observers in the meetings, on the understanding that any expenses incurred by their attendance shall be borne by the States concerned;

6. *Invites* the International Narcotics Control Board to participate as an observer in the regional meetings;

7. *Further requests* the Secretary-General to report on the regional meetings to the Commission on Narcotic Drugs.

Economic and Social Council resolution 1985/11

28 May 1985   Meeting 22   Adopted without vote

Approved by Second Committee (E/1985/83) without vote, 15 May (meeting 4); draft by Commission on Narcotic Drugs (E/1985/23); agenda item 18.

The Americas

In its 1985 report,[1] INCB observed that the abuse and illicit trafficking of drugs was a matter of growing concern to Canada. Cannabis and its derivatives—the most commonly abused drugs—continued to be widely available in the country. Other available drugs included cocaine, heroin and various opiates and benzodiazepines which had been diverted from licit supplies. The clandestine manufacture of LSD and methamphetamine continued to concern authorities. To contain drug abuse and counter trafficking, the Canadian Government was taking strong measures.

Mexico had restated its firm commitment to the eradication of all illicit cultivation on its territory. INCB indicated that, during the first half of 1985, the Mexican authorities had destroyed approximately 4,500 hectares of poppy crops, double the area of the previous year. In the case of cannabis, the most abused drug, the area eradicated during the same period decreased from 1,456 hectares in 1984 to 896 in 1985.

According to INCB, the illicit consumption of drugs in the United States remained a serious public health problem. Most of the cannabis—the most widely abused drug—and all the heroin abused in the country originated abroad. The cocaine originated and was processed mainly in Latin America, although some clandestine cocaine-conversion laboratories were also discovered in the United States, where synthetic narcotics were also manufactured. The United States placed great emphasis on education and prevention. In April 1985, the President's wife, Nancy Reagan, sponsored a First Ladies' Conference on Drug Abuse, attended by the wives of 18 heads of State, to discuss the prevention of drug abuse by youth. A second such conference met in New York in October. Enforcement efforts focused on traditional and financial investigations aimed at immobilizing drug trafficking syndicates, seizures, raids and destruction of laboratories. Investigations were facilitated by the exchange of financial records and data between the United States and other countries.

In the Caribbean and Central and South America, the destabilizing and otherwise negative effects of illicit drug production and trafficking became ever more evident, reported INCB. Highly organized trafficking syndicates and their operations were often linked to the smuggling of weapons and the spreading of violence and terrorism. Drug abuse was growing rapidly throughout the region. Encouraging signs in the fight against it were the degree of commitment at the highest levels of government in several countries, and the intensified counter-offensives which were being pursued nationally, regionally and interregionally. In addition to existing bilateral agreements, the foreign ministers of the Andean countries had agreed to develop a multilateral agreement against drug trafficking, to be named after Colombian Minister of Justice Rodrigo Lara Bonilla, assassinated in 1984.

Effective action in some countries gave rise to hope that progress was being made in the region as a whole. Although the area cultivated with coca bush appeared to be expanding, manual destruction was taking place and action pursued to identify safer and more effective methods which would allow for eradication on a wider scale. Moreover, countries were undertaking joint intelligence and enforcement operations and concluding extradition agreements. Substantial eradication of cannabis occurred in some countries; however, the increase in cultivation in others confirmed that the traffickers were actively seeking new sources of supply.

Rapidly escalating domestic abuse, particularly of cocaine and coca paste, sometimes mixed with cannabis, continued to threaten the well-being of the populations of many countries. Treatment and rehabilitation programmes were being carried out in several countries and special emphasis placed on campaigns directed at high-risk groups, particularly young people. The difficult issue of essential chemicals and solvents used in the illicit manufacture of cocaine was still unresolved. Despite legislation to place those substances under control, their availability close to the coca leaf–growing areas posed a threat which could be neutralized only with stricter controls in both exporting and importing countries.

Asia

INCB reported that in 1985[1] some countries in East and South-East Asia continued to be major producers and suppliers of opiates and cannabis which, in addition to being abused locally, were channelled by traffickers to other regions. Abuse of heroin was widespread, particularly among youth, and the abuse of other drugs was increasing. During 1985, an expansion of eradication activities was recorded, which was attributed to both the political will of the Governments and the use of more precise crop-location methods. The chemicals needed for heroin manufacture continued to be available. Some countries were enforcing measures to prevent their diversion; in others, traffickers were taking advantage of the absence of effective control. Bilateral, regional and interregional action against drug-related activities was developed and expanded during the year, receiving attention at the highest levels of government, as evidenced by the emphasis placed on that question at a ministerial meeting of the Association of South-East Asian Nations in July 1985.

In South Asia, India had become a transit country for traffic in heroin and cannabis, originating mainly in parts of the Near and Middle East. Opium was illicitly trafficked, mainly internally. India's reservations under the 1961 Convention permitted cannabis to be used for non-medical purposes until 1989. Although the import, manufacture and sale of methaqualone had been prohibited since January 1984, accumulated stocks posed a risk of diversion. There was an imminent danger that heroin abuse would escalate, as it had in neighbouring countries. To curb trafficking, comprehensive narcotics legislation was enacted during 1985, enhancing penalties for drug offences and providing for improved controls and intensified investigations, and an Indian-Pakistani joint commission considered measures to curb narcotics smuggling along the common border.

INCB observed that Sri Lanka was a transit point for opiates and cannabis resin which had led to growing abuse within the country. In response, the Government had taken measures in 1984 that were among the most severe in the region.

China's accession on 23 August 1985 to the 1971 Convention represented the attainment of virtual universality in the international control system. In February, it joined with UNFDAC and WHO in a three-year project for the prevention of drug dependence in China.

A conference of heads of the Australian states in April mounted a national campaign agains drug abuse and advocated steps to strengthen drug control. Effective enforcement severely restricted availability of supplies for abusers in New Zealand, and authorities were using sophisticated equipment to detect cannabis cultivation, which was increasing.

The twelfth meeting of HONLEA, in November 1985,[38] agreed on the importance of Governments' establishing a concerted national policy to counter the smuggling of illicit drugs through the mail.

Europe

Though general drug abuse did not constitute a serious public health problem in Eastern Europe, due to their geographical position some countries continued to be used for transit trafficking of illicit narcotics, usually from east to west, according to INCB.[1] To deal with the problem, control measures and co-operation with source countries and countries of destination were strengthened. In 1985, in pursuance of its continuing dialogues with countries of Eastern Europe, INCB sent a mission to Czechoslovakia, the German Democratic Republic, Hungary and Poland.

A variety of drugs continued to be available and abused in Western Europe, and trafficking operated throughout. In 1985, a larger number of countries experienced growing consumption of cocaine. While heroin abuse appeared to have declined in a few countries, there was an escalation of heroin abuse in the United Kingdom. Throughout the region, cannabis continued to be the drug most widely abused, although certain psychotropic substances and amphetamines were the drugs of choice of some abusers. There was a growing tendency to use several drugs together, frequently in combination with alcohol.

Most of the abused drugs came from abroad. Substantial cannabis supplies originated in Lebanon and Morocco, with Africa south of the Sahara emerging as a significant source. Cocaine supplies were trafficked from South America. An estimated 80 per cent of the opiates originated in the Near and Middle East and South Asia, and 20 per cent in South-East Asia. Abused psychotropic substances originated mainly within the region. Data revealed substantial availability of heroin, although the amounts seized during the first half of 1985 appeared to represent a decrease over 1984. Availability of and trafficking in cocaine had increased sharply in recent years.

In 1984, for the second consecutive year, more than a tonne of cocaine was seized; seizures reported to Interpol during the first half of 1985 totalled nearly half a tonne, attesting to a high level of enforcement activity. The health-threatening situation arising from abuse and trafficking received attention at the highest levels, not only of many Governments but also of the Council of Europe and the Pompidou Group (Belgium, Denmark, France, Federal Republic of Germany, Greece, Ireland, Italy, Luxembourg, Netherlands, Norway, Spain, Sweden, Turkey, United Kingdom). In several countries, laws were strengthened and comprehensive drug control plans, including treatment and prevention programmes, were devised and carried out.

Conventions

As at the end of 1985,[50] States parties to the Single Convention on Narcotic Drugs, 1961, numbered 115. The number of parties to the Convention as amended by the Protocol of 25 March 1972 was 76, with Greece and Venezuela ratifying it in 1985, and the States parties to the 1971 Convention on Psychotropic Substances rose to 81, with the accession of Afghanistan, Bolivia and China.

The Commission on Narcotic Drugs discussed a note of the Secretary-General[51] on progress in the ongoing revision of the questionnaire completed by States parties when fulfilling the annual reports requirement of these conventions. On 12 February,[52] the Commission requested that draft sections of the three revised parts of the questionnaire be circulated to Governments for their comments. It also decided to review the questionnaire further at its 1987 session.

The Commission also reported that WHO had established new guidelines for the review of dependence-producing psychoactive substances eligible for international control. WHO expected to review non-controlled barbiturates and non-sedative hypnotics in 1986, and opioid agonists and antagonists in 1987.

On 13 December, the General Assembly, by **resolutions 40/120** and **40/122**, urged States to adhere to and ratify the international drug treaties, and, in the mean time, endeavour to comply with their provisions.

1971 Convention on Psychotropic Substances

INCB, in its 1985 report,[1] stressed the importance of achieving world-wide adherence to the 1971 Convention at the earliest possible time. According to the report, some 150 States and regions—both parties and non-parties—had provided data on psychotropic substances during the year.

The Commission on Narcotic Drugs, in February 1985, considered two WHO notifications[53]—with comments from Governments and a substance-by-substance summary reviewing amphetamine-like drugs for scheduling, as the Economic and Social Council had requested in 1984[54]—recommending that 2,5-dimethoxy-4-bromoamphetamine (known as DOB) and 3,4-methylenedioxyamphetamine (referred to as MDA) be placed under international control by inclusion in Schedule I—one of four categories of international control under the 1971 Convention. By unanimous votes the Commission decided[55] to include both DOB and MDA in Schedule I.

The Council, by **resolution 1985/79**, decided that the Commission was also to consider scheduling of substances under the Convention's provisions at its special session in 1986.

ECONOMIC AND SOCIAL COUNCIL ACTION

On 28 May, on the recommendation of its Second Committee, the Economic and Social Council adopted **resolution 1985/15** without vote.

Improvement of the control of international trade in psychotropic substances listed in Schedules III and IV of the 1971 Convention on Psychotropic Substances

The Economic and Social Council,

Having considered the report of the International Narcotics Control Board for 1984, especially that part concerned with trade in psychotropic substances,

Recognizing with concern that the 1971 Convention on Psychotropic Substances does not require import and export authorizations for international trade in substances listed in Schedules III and IV, thus facilitating the diversion of some of those substances into illicit channels,

Concerned that this lack of a treaty requirement makes it difficult for the competent authorities of both exporting and importing countries to prevent shipments of substances prohibited under article 13 of the Convention,

Bearing in mind that the International Narcotics Control Board needs relevant information in order to monitor effectively the international trade in substances listed in Schedules III and IV,

1. *Requests* all Governments, to the extent possible, voluntarily to extend the system of import and export authorizations provided for in article 12, paragraph 1, of the 1971 Convention on Psychotropic Substances to cover international trade in substances listed in Schedule III;

2. *Also requests* all Governments to establish, in any event, mechanisms for monitoring exports of substances listed in Schedules III and IV in order that importing countries may be alerted, in advance, of shipments that may be a cause of concern;

3. *Further requests* all Governments, to the extent possible, voluntarily to furnish information to the International Narcotics Control Board on the countries of origin of imports and the countries of destination of exports of substances listed in Schedules III and IV;

4. *Requests* all Governments which have decided to prohibit the import of substances listed in Schedules III and IV of the 1971 Convention on Psychotropic Substances to notify the Secretary-General of this decision, in accordance with article 13, paragraph 1, of the Convention;

5. *Requests* the Secretary-General to transmit the present resolution to all Governments for their consideration and implementation.

Economic and Social Council resolution 1985/15

28 May 1985   Meeting 22   Adopted without vote

Approved by Second Committee (E/1985/83) without vote, 15 May (meeting 4); draft by Commission on Narcotic Drugs (E/1985/23); agenda item 18.

Organizational questions

Commission on Narcotic Drugs

The Commission on Narcotic Drugs held its thirty-first session at Vienna from 11 to 20 February 1985. On the first day, it adopted by consensus a revised agenda which included, as requested by the General Assembly,[41] an item to initiate the preparation of a draft convention against the illicit traffic in narcotic drugs (see p. 1023).

ECONOMIC AND SOCIAL COUNCIL ACTION

Acting on the recommendation of its Third (Programme and Co-ordination) Committee, the Economic and Social Council on 26 July 1985 adopted without vote **resolution 1985/79**. The text had been deferred from the Council's May session (where it had been considered by the Second Committee) in accordance with a Council decision of 7 May to consider recommendations relating to the calendar of conferences and meetings for 1986-1987 at its July session.

Ninth special session of the Commission on Narcotic Drugs

The Economic and Social Council,

Recalling its resolution 2001(LX) of 12 May 1976,

Recognizing that the social and human problems created by drug abuse continue to increase,

Aware of the probable need for the Commission on Narcotic Drugs to examine the urgent question of scheduling a number of substances under the provisions of the 1971 Convention on Psychotropic Substances, following receipt of recommendations to that effect from the World Health Organization,

Decides that the Commission on Narcotic Drugs shall hold a special session of five days' duration in 1986 at a time when it will not overlap with other meetings, and within existing United Nations resources, to consider scheduling of substances under the provisions of the 1971 Convention on Psychotropic Substances, follow-up action to General Assembly resolutions 39/141 and 39/143 of 14 December 1984, the review of the report of the International Narcotics Control Board for 1985, and other urgent matters.

Economic and Social Council resolution 1985/79

26 July 1985　　　　　Meeting 52　　　　　Adopted without vote

Approved by Third Committee (E/1985/144) without vote, 19 July (meeting 20); draft by Commission on Narcotic Drugs (E/1985/23); agenda item 23.

In related action on 28 May, the Council, by **decision 1985/128**, approved the provisional agenda and documentation for the thirty-second (1987) session of the Commission; it also took note of the report of the Commission on its thirty-first (1985) session[2] (**decision 1985/130**). The Council also approved on 26 July the provisional agenda and documentation for the ninth special (1986) session of the Commission (**decision 1985/201**).

International Narcotics Control Board

In 1985, INCB held two sessions at Vienna—the thirty-seventh from 13 to 24 May, and the thirty-eighth from 8 to 25 October.

Co-ordination in the UN system

The *Ad Hoc* Inter-Agency Meeting on Co-ordination in Matters of International Drug Abuse Control[28] (see p. 1016) examined recent developments relating to co-ordination of drug abuse control activities in the United Nations system. The view was expressed that all specialized agencies and entities concerned should be allowed to participate in the preparation of a global strategy, and that there was a need to integrate in a common approach all elements concerning drug abuse and to establish an inter-agency clearing-house to help gather and distribute information at the country and subregional levels. The participants expressed their support of the Secretary-General's proposal for a world drug conference and the readiness of their organizations to co-operate in special activities of a supportive nature, including publications, subject to approval by the General Assembly and their governing bodies.

REFERENCES

[1]*Report of the International Narcotics Control Board for 1985* (E/INCB/1985/1), Sales No. E.85.XI.1. [2]E/1985/23. [3]YUN 1984, p. 955. [4]E/CN.7/1985/20. [5]YUN 1971, p. 380. [6]YUN 1961, p. 382. [7]YUN 1972, p. 397. [8]E/1985/47. [9]A/40/260. [10]A/40/38. [11]E/AC.51/1985/8 & Corr.1 & Add.1. [12]E/CN.7/1985/17 & Corr.1. [13]YUN 1981, p. 1057. [14]YUN 1979, p. 933, GA res. 34/177, 17 Dec. 1979. [15]A/40/771. [16]A/40/772. [17]YUN 1983, p. 970, GA res. 38/93, 16 Dec. 1983. [18]A/40/773. [19]YUN 1981, p. 1058, GA res. 36/168, 16 Dec. 1981. [20]E/CN.7/1986/11/Add.1. [21]E/CN.7/1986/11/Add.2. [22]E/CN.7/1986/11/Add.3. [23]E/1985/23 (res. 2(XXXI)). [24]E/CN.7/1986/10. [25]A/CONF.121/22/Rev.1 (res. 3). [26]YUN 1984, p. 957. [27]ACC/1985/DEC/16-29 (dec. 1985/17). [28]ACC/1985/PG/15. [29]A/C.3/40/8. [30]A/40/854-S/17610 & Corr.1. [31]A/40/817. [32]YUN 1984, p. 958, ESC res. 1984/21, 24 May 1984. [33]*Report of the International Narcotics Control Board for 1985—Demand and Supply of Opiates for Medical and Scientific Needs* (E/INCB/1985/1/Supp.), Sales No. E.85.XI.7. [34]A/40/778. [35]YUN 1984, p. 960, GA res. 39/143, 14 Dec. 1984. [36]E/CN.7/1985/9. [37]E/1985/23 (dec. 6(XXXI)). [38]MNAR/1985/2. [39]A/CONF.121/22/Rev.1 (res. 2). [40]*Ibid.* (res. 1). [41]YUN 1984, p. 961, GA res. 39/141, 14 Dec. 1984. [42]E/1985/23 (res. 1(XXXI)). [43]A/40/777. [44]E/CN.7/1986/2 & Add.1-3. [45]A/CONF.121/22/Rev.1. [46]E/CN.7/1985/7. [47]E/1985/23 (dec. 5(XXXI)). [48]*Ibid.* (dec. 4(XXXI)). [49]MNAR/1985/1. [50]*Multilateral Treaties Deposited with the Secretary-General: Status as at 31 December 1985* (ST/LEG/SER.E/4), Sales No. E.86.V.3. [51]E/CN.7/1985/13. [52]E/1985/23 (dec. 3(XXXI)). [53]E/CN.7/1985/15 & Add.1,2. [54]YUN 1984, p. 965, ESC res. 1984/23, 24 May 1984. [55]E/1985/23 (dec. 1(XXXI) & 2(XXXI)).

OTHER PUBLICATIONS

Bulletin on Narcotics, vol. XXXVII, Nos. 1-4 (quarterly). *Estimated World Requirements of Narcotic Drugs in 1985* and Supplements Nos. 1-12 (E/INCB/1984/2 & Supp.1-12), Sales No. E/F/S.84.XI.5 & Supp.1-12. *Extradition for Drug-related Offences* (ST/NAR/5), Sales No. E.85.XI.6. *Statistics on Narcotic Drugs for 1985 Furnished by Governments in accordance with the International Treaties and Maximum Levels of Opium Stock* (E/INCB/1986/3), Sales No. E/F/S.86.XI.3.

Chapter XXIII

Statistics

In 1985, the United Nations Statistical Commission met to review developments in economic, social and demographic statistics that had taken place since its previous session in 1983. Among issues discussed were ways of improving the dissemination of international statistics and the integration of social, demographic and related statistics. The Sub-Committee on Statistical Activities of the Administrative Committee on Co-ordination (ACC) met in June and discussed decisions and recommendations of the Statistical Commission that had implications for its work. In September, the Commission's Working Group on International Statistical Programmes and Co-ordination reviewed the provisional agenda for the Commission's 1987 session and suggested documentation and special topics to be considered by the Commission.

In May, the Economic and Social Council, acting on the Commission's recommendations, adopted resolution 1985/7 on international economic classifications, and resolution 1985/8 on the 1990 World Population and Housing Census Programme.

By resolution 40/179, adopted in December, the General Assembly requested the Secretary-General to prepare a report on patterns of consumption and related socio-economic indicators for consideration by the Statistical Commission in 1987.

UN statistical bodies

Statistical Commission

The Statistical Commission held its twenty-third session in New York from 25 February to 6 March 1985.[1] It recommended to the Economic and Social Council the adoption of two draft resolutions, one on international economic classifications and the other on the 1990 World Population and Housing Census Programme, as well as a draft decision on the report on its 1985 session and provisional agenda and documentation for its 1987 session (see below). The Council's attention was also drawn to other decisions and recommendations of the Commission.

Working Group on Statistical Programmes and Co-ordination

The Statistical Commission in February/March examined the 1983 report[2] of its Working Group on International Statistical Programmes and Co-ordination. It endorsed the Group's views on the co-ordination of international statistical data col-

lection aimed at reducing the reporting burden on countries and welcomed the inventory of statistical data collection activities sent to all national statistical offices at the Working Group's request. It urged that additional reviews be undertaken to investigate new possibilities for further reducing unnecessary duplication of requests to countries for data.

The Working Group met at Geneva from 2 to 4 September 1985[3] to review the agenda and documentation for the twenty-fourth (1987) session of the Statistical Commission. The Group also discussed the results of a review of alternative approaches to the problem of assessing the effectiveness of technical co-operation in statistics, considered special problems in the statistically least developed of the developing countries (see below, under "Technical co-operation") and reviewed and revised a list of special topics to be taken up by the Commission during its next several sessions.

On 28 May 1985, by **decision 1985/122**, adopted without vote, the Economic and Social Council took note of the Statistical Commission's report and approved the provisional agenda and documentation for its twenty-fourth (1987) session. The text had been proposed by the Statistical Commission; it was approved without vote by the Council's First (Economic) Committee on 21 May.

ACC Sub-Committee

The ACC Sub-Committee on Statistical Activities (nineteenth session, Madrid, Spain, 24-28 June),[4] discussed co-ordination aspects of statistical work being planned or carried out by organizations of the United Nations system and matters raised at the Statistical Commission's 1985 session. Other issues included: international economic classifications; the National Household Survey Capability Programme (NHSCP); the Living Standards Measurement Study (LSMS); technical co-operation in statistics; special problems of the statistically least developed countries; local area statistics; social statistics; service statistics; the Statistical Computing Project; tourism and migration statistics; trade and transport statistics; price statistics, including the International Comparison Project (ICP); revision of the System of National Accounts (SNA); energy and environment statistics; and the International Classification of Diseases.

The Sub-Committee recommended that an invitation to hold its twentieth session at the headquarters of the International Labour Organisation (ILO) at Geneva in April 1986 be accepted.

Economic statistics

Energy, environment and mineral resources statistics

Following consideration of the Secretary-General's 1984 report on standards, methods and classifications of energy statistics and the environment statistics programme,[5] the Statistical Commission requested the United Nations Statistical Office to continue its work programme on collecting and compiling energy statistics, to pursue its efforts in the methodological field, particularly in regard to new and renewable sources of energy, and to explore the development of energy statistics in value terms. The Commission requested that the Statistical Office's environment statistics work programme focus on: promoting the application of the *Framework for the Development of Environment Statistics*,[6] published in 1984; preparing a technical manual for compiling statistics on human settlements and natural resources; developing an international programme of collection and dissemination of environment statistics; and providing technical co-operation support. The Statistical Office was urged to continue co-ordinating international activities on environment statistics, and the Secretary-General was requested to submit progress reports on energy and environment statistics to the Commission's 1987 session.

Having taken steps to enlarge its coverage of minerals and to change its methods and form of reporting on production of some minerals, in response to the 1983 recommendations of the Group of Experts on the Standardization of Definitions and Terminology for Statistics on Mineral Resources Production and Consumption,[7] discussed in a 1984 report[8] of the Secretary-General, the Commission strongly supported the recommendations and decided that work in that field should go forward provided that specialized resources were made available.

National accounts and balances

Following consideration of the Secretary-General's 1984 report[9] on progress made in revising the System of National Accounts, the Statistical Commission: endorsed the work programme for the SNA review proposed by the Secretariat and requested it to provide annual reports on its implementation; welcomed the co-ordinating role of the Inter-Secretariat Working Group on National Accounts, regarding it as an excellent example of co-operation between international organizations; emphasized the need to maintain a small common group of experts in all the specialized expert groups on SNA revision to ensure continuity and co-ordination; recommended that special attention be paid to difficulties faced by developing countries as a consequence of the weakness of the basic information they used, that basic data be evaluated, that handbooks on sources and methods of compiling national accounts be prepared, and that technical assistance and training be provided; and reiterated the importance of maintaining continuity in data series by avoiding major changes in definitions and classifications of SNA.

With regard to a 1984 report[9] on the System of Statistical Balances of the National Economy (MPS) by the Council for Mutual Economic Assistance, the Commission took note of progress achieved in developing MPS, urged continued elaboration of the system, and agreed to consider the improved version of MPS at its 1987 session.

The Commission also endorsed a 1984 report[9] of the Secretary-General on links between SNA and MPS and agreed that work in that area should continue. It decided that priority should be given to revising the 1979 publication entitled *Comparisons of the System of National Accounts and the System of Balances of the National Economy, Part One: Conceptual Relationships*,[10] and requested the Secretary-General to submit to the Commission in 1987 a report on progress achieved in linking the two systems.

Price statistics

After considering a 1984 report of the Secretary-General on the International Comparison Project and the International Price Statistics Programme (IPSP), the Commission endorsed plans for phase V of ICP and noted that the question of quality of data and further methodological improvements would also receive attention. It emphasized the need for the Statistical Office to play a strong co-ordinating role in ICP, asked the Secretary-General to submit to it in 1987 a progress report on phase V and continue efforts to obtain extrabudgetary resources to support ICP, and reaffirmed its 1983 decision[11] to assign low priority to other work on IPSP.

In June,[4] the ACC Sub-Committee on Statistical Activities expressed concern that the absence of funding for ICP put at risk the high investment in the project already made by international organizations.

International economic classifications

Following consideration of the Secretary-General's 1984 report[9] on harmonization of international economic classifications, the Statistical Commission endorsed continuation of the work of the Statistical Office on the subject and asked the Secretary-General for a progress report in 1987. It also asked that a draft of the complete revised International Standard Industrial Classification of All Economic Activities and of the complete Central Production Classification (previously known as the Combined Trade/Production Goods Classification) be submitted in 1987. It approved the second draft of a third revision of the Standard International Trade Classification (SITC), subject to editorial corrections and amendments to take into account some suggestions made during the session. It recommended that, if States were unable to adopt the full detailed classification for certain commodities, they adopt the special coding procedures described in the Secretary-General's report.

Other recommendations were incorporated in a draft resolution recommended to the Economic and Social Council for adoption.

ECONOMIC AND SOCIAL COUNCIL ACTION

On 28 May 1985, the Economic and Social Council, acting on the recommendation of its First Committee, adopted **resolution 1985/7**, without vote.

International economic classifications

The Economic and Social Council,

Recalling its resolution 229 B (XI) of 12 July 1950,

Considering:

(*a*) The marked improvement in the international comparability of external trade statistics which has resulted since 1976 from the implementation by Governments and international agencies of the Standard International Trade Classification (SITC), Revision 2,

(*b*) The action taken by the Customs Co-operation Council to maintain the correspondence of the Customs Co-operation Council Nomenclature (CCCN) with SITC Revision 2,

(*c*) The action taken by the Customs Co-operation Council to revise the CCCN and group the headings thereof under a detailed Harmonized Commodity Description and Coding System (HS),

(*d*) The proposed revision of SITC Revision 2, as described in the report of the Secretary-General on the harmonization of international economic classifications, to be known as the Standard International Trade Classification, Revision 3,

1. *Recommends* that Member States should report internationally data on external trade statistics according to the Standard International Trade Classification, Revision 3, as far and as soon as possible, it being understood that Member States may not wish to make the change until they would in any case be reviewing their customs nomenclature;

2. *Requests* the Secretary-General:

(*a*) To publish SITC Revision 3, together with commodity indexes and correlation codes between SITC Revision 3, the Harmonized Commodity Description and Coding System and the Customs Co-operation Council Nomenclature and between SITC Revision 3 and the *Classification by Broad Economic Categories*;

(*b*) To continue and complete, as a matter of priority, the development of the convertibility indexes between

SITC Revision 2 and the Standard Foreign Trade Classification used for external trade by States members of the Council for Mutual Economic Assistance, and to establish similar convertibility indexes in respect of SITC Revision 3 and the Standard Foreign Trade Classification;

(*c*) To arrange that, beginning not later than with data for the full year 1988, the publication of SITC data by United Nations bodies should be, as far as possible, in the form of SITC Revision 3.

Economic and Social Council resolution 1985/7

28 May 1985   Meeting 22   Adopted without vote

Approved by First Committee (E/1985/90) without vote, 21 May (meeting 8); draft by Statistical Commission (E/1985/26); agenda item 11.

Social and demographic statistics

Social indicators

Following consideration of 1984 reports[9] by the Secretary-General on the future direction of work on social indicators and on progress in the development of such indicators and the integration of social, demographic and related statistics, the Statistical Commission requested that work on the indicators should continue. It agreed that the work of the Statistical Office on the subject should give highest priority to methodologies and to compiling statistics, indicators and data bases on special population groups such as women, children, youth, the elderly and disabled persons. The Commission expressed support for the work of the Statistical Office and the ACC Sub-Committee on Statistical Activities on co-ordination of international work on social statistics and indicators. It requested that a planned handbook on social indicators be prepared to provide countries with technical information, suitable for training activities, on approaches to developing and using social indicators and on data sources for indicators, and emphasized the need for international co-ordination in preparing the handbook. It was agreed that the United Nations should give priority to promoting and facilitating exchanges of experience in resolving problems related to developing social statistics and indicators. The Commission commended ILO on its plans to revise the International Standard Classification of Occupations (ISCO) and requested it to take a variety of uses of ISCO into account in preparing the revision, including statistics on special groups and the development of social statistics and indicators in developing countries in a variety of social and economic fields, as well as the need for technical guidance in developing detailed national classifications of occupations. The Commission concluded that international requests to countries for indicators for international use should be limited to the minimum essential information that could be provided on a comparable basis and was not already available, and that national sources of internationally published indicators should be carefully identified in publications.

Population and housing censuses

The Statistical Commission commended national, regional and international efforts in successfully implementing the 1980 World Population and Housing Census Programme, strongly endorsed the 1990 Programme to be carried out between 1985 and 1994, and approved a proposed work programme pertaining to the 1990 census decade. It requested the Secretariat to submit to it in 1987 draft supplementary recommendations on population and housing censuses and to work closely with the regional commissions, specialized agencies and donors to prepare technical documentation and training to ensure adequate planning and successful implementation of the 1990 Programme.

The Commission recommended to the Economic and Social Council adoption of a resolution it drafted on the 1990 Programme. On 28 May 1985, the Council, acting on the recommendation of its First Committee, adopted **resolution 1985/8**, without vote.

1990 World Population and Housing Census Programme

The Economic and Social Council,

Having examined the report of the Statistical Commission on its twenty-third session,

Recalling its resolution 1947(LVIII) of 7 May 1975, in which it endorsed the development of the 1980 World Population and Housing Census Programme and recommended that States Members of the United Nations should take into account international recommendations relating to population and housing censuses when undertaking national censuses during the period 1975-1984, as well as its earlier resolutions endorsing previous decennial programmes,

Noting with satisfaction the unprecedented efforts made by States Members of the United Nations, in all regions, to carry out population and housing censuses as part of the 1980 World Population and Housing Census Programme and also the activities of the Secretary-General in support of national efforts in this regard,

Further recalling the importance placed on population censuses in the World Population Plan of Action adopted by the World Population Conference held in 1974 and reaffirmed by the International Conference on Population held in 1984,

Takes note, in particular, of recommendation 65 adopted by the International Conference on Population, by which all countries were required to participate in the 1990 World Population and Housing Census Programme in order to assist, *inter alia*, in the evaluation of population and development trends at all levels,

Convinced that periodic population and housing censuses, since they provide comparable information for a country as a whole and for each administrative area therein, are one of the primary sources of data needed for effective development planning, monitoring of population trends and policies and the sound administration of national and local activities aimed at fostering the improvement of living standards,

Stressing that population and housing censuses should provide valuable statistics and indicators for assessing the situation of various special population groups, such as women, children, youth, the elderly, refugees and the homeless, and changes therein,

Recognizing that population and housing censuses place heavy demands on the statistical and administrative resources of countries, and that careful preparatory work is essential for maximizing the usefulness and efficiency of census activities,

Further recognizing that census methodology is constantly advancing and that an exchange of national experience and know-how will significantly contribute to the quality and timeliness of census results and the efficiency and effectiveness of census operations,

1. *Recommends* that States Members of the United Nations should undertake to carry out population and housing censuses during the period 1985-1994, taking into account international and regional recommendations relating to population and housing censuses and giving particular attention to the timely publication of census results so that the censuses meet national data requirements;

2. *Requests* the States Members of the United Nations, in carrying out population and housing censuses, to continue to provide basic census results to the United Nations and other appropriate intergovernmental organizations to assist in the study of global and regional issues;

3. *Requests* the Secretary-General to proceed with the development of a 1990 World Population and Housing Census Programme, to be carried out during the period 1985-1994, and to make all necessary preparations with a view to assisting interested Member States to plan and carry out improved censuses during this period.

Economic and Social Council resolution 1985/8

28 May 1985   Meeting 22   Adopted without vote

Approved by First Committee (E/1985/90) without vote, 21 May (meeting 8); draft by Statistical Commission (E/1985/26); agenda item 11.

National Household Survey Capability Programme

Having considered the 1984 report[12] of the Secretary-General on the National Household Survey Capability Programme, the Statistical Commission emphasized the importance of mobilizing resources for implementing country projects, urged donor agencies and participating developing countries to accord high priority to NHSCP in their technical co-operation activities in statistics, and recommended continued coordination within the United Nations system, and with other multilateral and bilateral agencies, in carrying out the Programme. It emphasized the importance of and the need for further work in technical studies and documentation, and requested the Secretary-General to submit a progress report on NHSCP in 1987.

The ACC Sub-Committee on Statistical Activities[4] recognized that mobilization of additional resources for NHSCP was of central concern, since many country projects were delayed for lack of external assistance and, in a few cases, the sums required were small. The creation of a modest central fund could overcome such difficulties, it stated. While acknowledging that urgent priority survey activities should not be sacrificed, the Sub-Committee concurred with the Commission's recommendation that donor agencies make use of NHSCP rather than fund *ad hoc* surveys to meet country data needs.

Living Standards Measurement Study

Following consideration of a 1984 World Bank report[12] on its Living Standards Measurement Study, and an oral statement at its 1985 session by a World Bank representative on the same subject, the Statistical Commission noted the progress on and the technical and methodological innovations that were part of LSMS, requested that efforts be made to ensure co-ordination among LSMS, NHSCP and national statistical services on technical and operational matters, and requested a report in 1987 on the results of the prototype surveys and on plans for further work.

Patterns of consumption

On 17 December 1985, on the recommendation of the Second (Economic and Financial) Committee, the General Assembly adopted **resolution 40/179**, without vote.

Patterns of consumption: qualitative aspects of development

The General Assembly,

Bearing in mind the provisions of the Charter of the United Nations, in particular Article 55, and the provisions of articles 22 to 26 of the Universal Declaration of Human Rights, as well as the International Covenant on Economic, Social, and Cultural Rights,

Recalling General Assembly resolution 3345(XXIX) of 17 December 1974 and Economic and Social Council resolution 1981/51 of 22 July 1981 on the interrelationships between population, resources, environment and development, as well as the discussion of the reports of the Secretary-General on the question,

Taking note of the report of the Secretary-General on the overall socio-economic perspective of the world economy to the year 2000,

Convinced of the necessity to preserve in the long term the balance between resources, population, environment and development, taking into account the advances made in science and technology and the progress accomplished in the transfer of technological innovations to developing countries,

Recalling further, as stated in paragraph 8 of the International Development Strategy for the Third United Nations Development Decade, that the development process must promote human dignity, economic growth, productive employment and social equity and that the ultimate aim of development is the constant improvement of the well-being of the entire population on the basis of its full participation in the process of development and a fair distribution of the benefits therefrom, within the framework of the development plans and national priorities of each country,

Reaffirming, in accordance with the goals and objectives of the International Development Strategy for the Third United Nations Development Decade, in particular paragraph 42 thereof, that the international community will provide technical and financial support to achieve immediate and long-term social and economic objectives in the context of an overall substantial increase in resources for development, paying due respect to the cultural identities of nations and peoples,

Considering that, in order to satisfy the fundamental socio-economic needs, it is important to promote, in accordance with national economic plans and priorities, the production of goods and services necessary for the improvement of the human condition,

Noting that the United Nations has undertaken to establish consolidated inventories of data on the environment, natural resources, existing infrastructures and population, including the structure and socio-economic needs of population groups,

Recalling also that the Statistical Commission, the United Nations Research Institute for Social Development and other bodies in the United Nations system have undertaken studies of socio-economic indicators,

Aware of the need for methods to measure with greater accuracy the level of satisfaction of socio-economic needs in the developing countries, in order to facilitate the search for better ways of improving living standards,

1. *Reaffirms* the common goal pursued by the international community of realizing, through national efforts and international co-operation, and in accordance with the organization and resources of each country, the enjoyment of the economic, social and cultural rights indispensable for the development of the human condition as well as for the well-being of individuals and their families, especially in regard to food, clothing, housing, education, health care and necessary social services;

2. *Considers* that an accurate assessment of the advances in living standards requires a reliable measuring instrument consisting of a set of indicators related to living conditions, employment and the circumstances underlying them, and the improvement of basic national statistical programmes and capabilities related to food, clothing, housing, education, health care and necessary social services;

3. *Notes* the importance of identifying, for national use, indicative patterns of consumption that adequately meet fundamental socio-economic needs and are tailored to local and national requirements, particularly in developing countries, taking into account national experience, plans and strategies;

4. *Encourages*, in this regard, countries to undertake efforts to collect, tabulate and regularly publish accurate and updated data on consumption and living standards for different population groups, bearing in mind the need for more international attention to be given to the qualitative aspects of development;

5. *Requests* the Secretary-General to continue to implement General Assembly resolution 3345(XXIX) in order to assist all States, particularly developing countries, and the organs of the United Nations in their efforts to advance knowledge on the interrelated issues of resources, population, environment and development;

6. *Further requests* the Secretary-General to prepare a report on patterns of consumption and related socio-economic indicators, based on the views of all interested States and on information about the work done so far

by relevant bodies in the United Nations system, in particular the United Nations Research Institute for Social Development, and to submit the report to the Statistical Commission at its twenty-fourth session for consideration, and requests the Economic and Social Council to report thereon to the General Assembly at its forty-second session.

General Assembly resolution 40/179

17 December 1985   Meeting 119   Adopted without vote

Approved by Second Committee (A/40/1009/Add.2) without vote, 11 December (meeting 50); draft by Vice-Chairman (A/C.2/40/L.122), orally revised, based on informal consultations on draft by Equatorial Guinea, Mauritania, Morocco, Peru and Zaire (A/C.2/40/L.44); agenda item 12.

Meeting numbers. GA 40th session: 2nd Committee 39, 50; plenary 119.

Other statistical activities

Technical co-operation

During 1985, the United Nations Department of Technical Co-operation for Development (DTCD), in co-operation with the Statistical Office, provided technical co-operation to developing countries in statistical organization, national accounts and demographic and social statistics, including population censuses, surveys, civil registration and statistical data processing. The Secretary-General reported[13] that, during the year, there were 180 statistics and data processing projects involving expenditures of $17.7 million, an increase of about 43 per cent over 1984.

Training was a central component of the technical co-operation programme. The on-the-job statistical training programme, under way since 1983, enabled junior statisticians and programmers from developing countries to work in the statistical offices of other developing countries and to benefit from their expertise. In 1985, the project involved 14 trainees from 10 countries, working in seven host countries.

Following consideration of the Secretary-General's 1984 report[12] on technical co-operation in statistics rendered by the United Nations system and other agencies, the Statistical Commission requested the Secretary-General to submit to its 1987 session a report on technical co-operation in statistics, including contributions from the system, other international organizations and countries, taking into account suggestions made at its 1985 session. It also requested that a report assessing the effectiveness of technical co-operation in statistics be submitted to it in 1987, and requested the Secretary-General to examine the possibility of discussions in another forum, comprising more developing countries and donors, which might assist the Commission with a supplementary detailed review of technical co-operation in statistics.

In June 1985,[4] the ACC Sub-Committee on Statistical Activities discussed assessment of the effectiveness of technical co-operation in statistics. Background notes prepared by the Statistical Office reviewed some alternative approaches to the problem and specific case-studies of assessment of effectiveness, and proposed an approach that was thought to be feasible within the resources and time available to the Statistical Office. The Sub-Committee suggested that some version of the more limited project assessment suggested by the Statistical Office should be recommended, together with an account of various agency experiences. The Sub-Committee agreed that the document to be submitted to the 1987 Statistical Commission session, in addition to presenting an assessment on a partial projects approach, should contain a detailed proposal and work plan with budgetary requirements for a more in-depth assessment based on a few selected countries.

In September 1985, the Working Group on International Statistical Programmes and Co-ordination[3] also considered the question of assessment of the effectiveness of technical co-operation, agreed that a country approach rather than a project approach was appropriate and that the Statistical Office should pursue the country approach by developing a plan and start to carry it out within available resources, with progress being reported to the Statistical Commission's 1987 session. The Working Group also recommended that the Statistical Office identify or develop appropriate global indicators of national statistical capability and use them to assess the change in capability on a global scale over a recent period of time. The results should be included in the report to the Commission, along with relevant experiences of international or national agencies in assessment, an outline of plans and projected costs for the complete country approach and a timetable for reporting on the matter to the Commission.

Special problems in the statistically least developed countries

Following consideration of a 1984 report[12] by the Secretary-General on the special problems of the statistically least developed countries, the Statistical Commission expressed its strong support for continuing work on identifying the special statistical problems of those countries and endorsed the convening of an expert group to study them further and seek a solution.

After discussing the issue at its June meeting,[4] the ACC Sub-Committee on Statistical Activities expressed support for assembling the accumulated knowledge of statistical advisers in international organizations, along with that of country representatives, for a study of a few selected countries to identify problems. The focus of the report to be presented to the Commission in 1987 should be on generic problems rather than on problems related to specific subject areas. Possible types of countries to be considered for the study included very small countries, many of which were island countries, least developed countries, and countries not having the minimal set of series or a good survey system.

At its September 1985 meeting,[3] the Working Group on International Statistical Programmes and Co-ordination decided that the report to be presented in 1987 on special problems in the statistically least developed countries should incorporate a review of problems and policy conclusions based on an investigation of several such countries, and a review based on accumulated knowledge of statistical advisers of a number of organizations. The Working Group agreed that initial material for the first-mentioned review would be prepared by a consultant based on visits to two or three selected countries.

The Working Group stated that the question of defining statistically least developed countries should not be addressed in the report but that countries should be selected from the following categories: countries identified by the General Assembly as least developed countries (see p. 433); small island developing countries; and land-locked and other developing countries with special problems in statistics.

Publication policy

Following consideration of a 1984 report[12] by the Secretary-General on meeting user needs for and improving the dissemination of international statistics, and another[12] on aspects of the publication policies of statistical agencies, the Statistical Commission urged further cost-effective efforts to improve the content of statistical publications and the dissemination of comparable international statistics in a timely and efficient manner. The Statistical Office was requested to continue to develop closer contacts with users and producers of statistics to improve the quality and dissemination of international statistics, and the Secretary-General was requested to submit to the Commission in 1987 a progress report on action taken in response to the Commission's comments.

REFERENCES

[1]E/1985/26. [2]YUN 1983, p. 982. [3]E/CN.3/1987/21. [4]ACC/1985/15. [5]YUN 1984, p. 967. [6]*A Framework for the Development of Environment Statistics* (ST/ESA/STAT/SER.M/78), Sales No. E.84.XVII.12. [7]YUN 1983, p. 979. [8]YUN 1984, p. 967. [9]*Ibid.*, p. 968. [10]*Comparisons of the System of National Accounts and the System of Balances of the National Economy, Part One: Conceptual Relationships* (ST/ESA/STAT/SER.F, Part I), Sales No. E.77.XVII.6. [11]YUN 1983, p. 980. [12]YUN 1984, p. 969. [13]DP/1986/48/Add.1.

PUBLICATIONS

National Accounts Statistics: Compendium of Income Distribution Statistics, Series M, No. 79 (ST/ESA/STAT/SER.M/79), Sales No. E.85.XVII.6. *Consolidated Statistics of All International Arrivals and Departures, A Technical Report*, Series F, No. 36 (ST/ESA/STAT/SER.F/36), Sales No. E.85.XVII.8. *Statistical Indicators on Youth* (ST/ESA/STAT/SER.Y/1), Sales No. E/F.85.XVII.12. *World Statistics in Brief*, Ninth Edition (ST/ESA/STAT/SER.V/9), Sales No. E.85.XVII.13. *1985 International Trade Statistics Yearbook*, Volume I (ST/ESA/STAT/SER.G/34); Volume II (ST/ESA/STAT/SER.G/34/Add.1), Sales No. E/F.87.XVII.3, Vols. I & II. *Statistical Pocketbook—World Statistics in Brief*, Tenth Edition (ST/ESA/STAT/SER.V/10), Sales No. E.86.XVII.8. *World Comparisons of Purchasing Power and Real Product for 1980*, Part One (ST/ESA/STAT/SER.F/42 (Part I)), Sales No. E.86.XVII.9; Part Two (ST/ESA/STAT/SER.F/42 (Part II)), Sales No. E.86.XVII.10. *Handbook of National Accounting, Accounting for Production: Sources and Methods* (ST/ESA/STAT/SER.F/39), Sales No. E.86.XVII.11. *Standard International Trade Classification, Revision 3*, Series M, No. 34/Rev.3 (ST/ESA/STAT/SER.M/34/Rev.3), Sales No. E.86.XVII.12. *Energy Statistics Yearbook* (ST/ESA/STAT/SER.J/29), Sales No. E/F.86.XVII.13. *National Accounts Statistics: Study of Input-Output Tables, 1970-80* (ST/ESA/STAT/SER.X/7), Sales No. E.86.XVII.15. *Manual for the Development of Criminal Justice Statistics*, Studies in Methods, Series F, No. 43 (ST/ESA/STAT/SER.F/43), Sales No. 86.XVII.16. *National Data Sources and Programmes for Implementing the United Nations Recommendations on Statistics of International Migration*, Studies in Methods, Series F, No. 37 (ST/ESA/STAT/SER.F/37), Sales No. E.86.XVII.22. *Concept and Methods for Integrating Social and Economic Statistics on Health, Education and Housing* (ST/ESA/STAT/SER.F/40), Sales No. E.86.XVII.23. *Classification by Broad Economic Categories* (ST/ESA/STAT/SER.M/53/Rev.2), Sales No. E.86.XVII.24. *Construction Statistics Yearbook 1985* (ST/ESA/STAT/SER.U/14), Sales No. E.87.XVII.2. *1984-1985 International Sea-borne Trade Statistics Yearbook* (ST/ESA/STAT/SER.D/84-85), Sales No. E.87.XVII.7. *Industrial Statistics Yearbook 1985*, Volume I, *General Industrial Statistics* (ST/ESA/STAT/SER.P/24 (Vol. I)), Sales No. E.87.XVII.8; Volume II, *Commodity Production Statistics 1976-1985* (ST/ESA/STAT/SER.P/24 (Vol. II)), Sales No. E.87.XVII.9. *National Accounts Statistics: Main Aggregates and Detailed Tables, 1985* (ST/ESA/STAT/SER.X/9 & Corr.1), Sales No. E.87.XVII.10. *National Accounts Statistics: Analysis of Main Aggregates, 1985* (ST/ESA/STAT/SER.M/10), Sales No. E.87.XVII.11. *Bulletin of Statistics on World Trade in Engineering Products*, Sales No. E.86.II.E.10.

Chapter XXIV

Institutional arrangements

In 1985, the Administrative Committee on Co-ordination (ACC) and the Committee for Programme and Co-ordination (CPC) continued to seek greater harmonization of programmes within the United Nations system and a higher level of co-ordination and co-operation in their implementation. With the same end in view, the Economic and Social Council recommended measures for the effective functioning of the Joint Meetings of those two Committees, called for the improvement of programming and co-ordination instruments and, in this connection, endorsed CPC recommendations on cross-organizational programme analyses (COPAs). In December, the Assembly called for recommendations from the Secretary-General to enhance co-ordination.

A report by the Joint Inspection Unit (JIU) on the subject of reporting to the Council, and the Secretary-General's comments on it, were examined by CPC, which called for implementation of measures suggested by the Secretary-General.

Co-operation between the United Nations and the Agency for Cultural and Technical Co-operation, an intergovernmental organization, was pursued, as was co-operation with non-governmental organizations (NGOs). Other organizational and institutional arrangements included adoption by the Council of its work programme for 1985-1986, and approval by the Assembly of the biennial programme of work for 1986-1987 of the Second (Economic and Financial) Committee.

In December, the Assembly approved an Agreement between the United Nations and the United Nations Industrial Development Organization (UNIDO), whereby the United Nations would recognize UNIDO as a specialized agency within the United Nations system upon the Agreement's entry into force (see p. 591).

Topics related to this chapter. Industrial development: conversion of UNIDO to a specialized agency; co-ordination in the UN system. Regional economic and social activities: strengthening of regional commissions. United Nations programmes: programme planning; administrative and budgetary co-ordination.

Co-ordination in the UN system

Following the regular consideration by United Nations bodies of matters pertaining to co-operation and co-ordination in the United Nations system, the General Assembly, in December 1985, requested the Secretary-General to report with recommendations on ways to enhance future co-ordination.

GENERAL ASSEMBLY ACTION

Acting on the recommendation of the Second Committee, the General Assembly on 17 December adopted without vote **resolution 40/177**.

Co-ordination in the United Nations and the United Nations system

The General Assembly,

Recalling relevant parts of Articles 15, 17, 57, 58, 63 and 64 of the Charter of the United Nations,

Reaffirming its resolution 32/197 of 20 December 1977, by which it, *inter alia*, endorsed the conclusions and recommendations, as amended, of the *Ad Hoc* Committee on the Restructuring of the Economic and Social Sectors of the United Nations System, among which were guidelines and directives on inter-agency co-ordination,

Reaffirming further Economic and Social Council resolution 1985/77 of 26 July 1985,

Taking note of the references which were made to the importance of co-ordination in statements during the fortieth anniversary session of the United Nations,

Convinced of the pressing need for effective co-ordination and co-operation within the framework of the United Nations system, at both the intergovernmental and intersecretariat levels, to ensure coherent, efficient and responsive implementation of programmes in the future,

Bearing in mind problems that have arisen in co-ordination,

Considering that it is important to take steps to improve further the effectiveness of the United Nations system,

1. *Stresses* the need for effective and improved co-ordination in the United Nations system as laid down in the Charter of the United Nations and the agreements between the United Nations and the specialized agencies, and calls upon all concerned to observe more vigorously their responsibilities in this regard;

2. *Requests* the Secretary-General, after consultation with the executive heads of the specialized agencies, to re-examine critically and constructively all aspects of the question of co-ordination in the United Nations and the United Nations system; to submit to the General Assembly at its forty-second session, through the Committee for Programme and Co-ordination and the Economic and Social Council, a comprehensive report setting out his considered views on current mechanisms and procedures, and his specific recommendations aimed at enhancing co-ordination in the future, as envisaged in the Charter of the United Nations and the agreements between the United Nations and the specialized agencies and in accordance with the relevant resolutions; to report orally to the

Economic and Social Council at its second regular session of 1986 and to submit a progress report to the Assembly early in its forty-first session.

General Assembly resolution 40/177

17 December 1985   Meeting 119   Adopted without vote

Approved by Second Committee (A/40/1009/Add.2) without vote, 5 December (meeting 49); draft by Vice-Chairman (A/C.2/40/L.109), based on informal consultations on draft by Bangladesh, Belgium, China, Denmark, France, Germany, Federal Republic of, Italy, Liberia, Netherlands, Pakistan, Trinidad and Tobago, Uganda, United Kingdom and Yugoslavia (A/C.2/40/L.41); agenda item 12.
Meeting numbers. GA 40th session: 2nd Committee 36, 39, 48, 49; plenary 119.

ACC activities

In 1985, ACC and its subsidiary machinery dealt with a number of programme, operational and administrative policy issues with implications for the United Nations system. Among these were questions relating to development and international economic co-operation (see p. 411), including policy responses to the continuing slow-down of world economic activity and a co-ordinated approach to the social aspects of the development process. ACC examined the underlying causes of the critical economic situation in Africa with a view to integrating immediate relief efforts and longer-term activities (see p. 499). It discussed co-ordination of system-wide observances of the fortieth anniversary of the United Nations (see p. 403), and past, current and future COPAs (see p. 1044). Its Consultative Committee on Substantive Questions (Programme Matters) (CCSQ (PROG)) considered further approaches to and mechanisms for joint planning.

ACC sought to strengthen further the co-ordination of information systems (see ADMINISTRATIVE AND BUDGETARY QUESTIONS, Chapter IV), and the Inter-Agency Group on New and Renewable Sources of Energy reviewed co-operation and co-ordination in implementing the 1981 Nairobi Programme of Action for the Development and Utilization of New and Renewable Sources of Energy (see p. 691). ACC endorsed a 10-year programme of support to countries in the prevention and control of vitamin-A deficiency and related disorders, and set in motion preparations for a similar plan for the prevention of iodine deficiency (see p. 775). It considered co-ordination of preparatory work for international conferences (on crime prevention, women, disarmament and development, drug abuse), years (of youth, peace, shelter for the homeless) and decades (of disabled persons, and for cultural development).

ACC's Consultative Committee on Substantive Questions (Operational Activities) (CCSQ(OPS)) undertook a preliminary examination of major issues relating to the links between emergency relief, rehabilitation and longer-term development activities in the context of the current crisis in Africa (see p. 500). It continued to simplify and harmonize aid modalities, especially as regards project monitoring and evaluation, and discussed the various opportunities open to United Nations organizations for interaction with bilateral aid agencies and conditions for effective fellowship programmes.

ACC continued to review management and institutional policy issues to promote their harmonization, improve efficiency and achieve economies. In the area of personnel and general administration (see ADMINISTRATIVE AND BUDGETARY QUESTIONS, Chapter III), ACC set out its position on: the determination of the margin between net remuneration in the United Nations common system and that of the comparator civil service, the operation of the post adjustment system, and the determination of the level of pensionable remuneration and pension benefits. The two components of its Consultative Committee on Administrative Questions (CCAQ) reviewed a number of conditions of service, including allowances and benefits, field conditions, leave, health insurance, daily subsistence allowances, education grants, staff-management relations, and financial and budgetary questions in five areas: programmes and budgets; accounting and financial reporting; staff salaries and allowances; cash management; and general financial systems (see ADMINISTRATIVE AND BUDGETARY QUESTIONS, Chapter I).

Also during the year, ACC prepared and approved its comments on a JIU report on the United Nations development system's support to implementation of the 1978 Buenos Aires Plan of Action for Promoting and Implementing Technical Co-operation among Developing Countries (see p. 490) and decided that the JIU reflections on reform of the United Nations should be the subject of ACC comments (see ADMINISTRATIVE AND BUDGETARY QUESTIONS, Chapter II).

ACC described the foregoing activities in its annual overview reports for 1984/85[1] and 1985/86.[2] It adopted 29 decisions in 1985—13 at its first regular session (Geneva, 22 and 23 April),[3] two at a special session (Geneva, 4 July)[4] and 14 at its second regular session (New York, 28 and 29 October)[5]—relating to the topics mentioned above and matters concerning ACC machinery.

The principal subsidiary bodies of ACC met during the year as follows:

Organizational Committee (New York, 11 and 12 February, 17-21 and 30 October, and 25 October (special meeting); Geneva, 10-12 April and 1 July); CCAQ (Personnel and General Administrative Questions) (sixty-second session, London, 4-21 March; sixty-third session, New York, 27 June–17 July); CCAQ (Financial and Budgetary Questions) (sixty-second session, Geneva, 11-15 March; sixty-third session, New York, 9-13 September); CCSQ(OPS) (first regular session, Geneva, 26-29 March; second regular session,

New York, 7-9 October); CCSQ(PROG) (first regular session, Geneva, 1-4 April; second regular session, New York, 10-16 October).

ACC bodies on specific subjects met as follows:

Advisory Committee for the Co-ordination of Information Systems, special and third sessions, Geneva, 14 and 15 January, 23 and 24 September; panel of specialists on information systems for science and technology for development, Rome, 21-25 January; Task Force on Science and Technology for Development, sixth session, Geneva, 29-31 January; inter-agency meetings on COPAs, of the activities of the United Nations system in the area of economic and social research and policy analysis, and on economic and technical co-operation among developing countries, New York, 4 and 5 February and 6-8 February, respectively; fourth, fifth and sixth inter-agency consultations on the follow-up of the Substantial New Programme of Action for the 1980s for the Least Developed Countries, Geneva, 11 and 12 February, 29 April, and 29 and 30 July, respectively; Sub-Committee on Nutrition and its Advisory Group, eleventh session, Nairobi, Kenya, 11-15 February; *Ad Hoc* Task Force on the International Conference on Population, fourth session, New York, 13-15 February; Task Force on Rural Development, thirteenth session, New York, 6-8 March; Inter-Agency Group on New and Renewable Sources of Energy, fourth session, New York, 11 and 12 March; third inter-agency meeting on the United Nations Decade of Disabled Persons, Vienna, Austria, 11-13 March; third inter-agency meeting on preparations for the World Conference to Review and Appraise the Achievements of the United Nations Decade for Women, Vienna, 15 March; fourth *ad hoc* inter-agency consultation on International Youth Year, Vienna, 21 and 22 March; Joint United Nations Information Committee, twelfth session, Rome, Italy, 15-19 April; Sub-Committee on Statistical Activities, nineteenth session, Madrid, Spain, 24-28 June; *ad hoc* inter-agency meeting on co-ordination in matters of international drug abuse control, Rome, 11-13 September; inter-agency meeting on outer space activities, Paris, 30 September–2 October; Intersecretariat Group for Water Resources, sixth session, New York, 21-25 October; meeting of senior fellowship officers, Geneva, 4-7 November.

Report for 1984/85

Owing to constraints of time, CPC[6] on 25 May decided, on the proposal of its Bureau, to transmit without discussion the ACC annual overview report for 1984/85[1] to the Economic and Social Council at its second (July) regular session.

By section VII of **resolution 1985/76**, the Council took note of that report and requested ACC to continue to improve its annual overview report, which should contain an analytical review of its activities, the status of co-ordination efforts among United Nations organizations and recommendations for further co-operation and co-ordination among them.

CPC activities

In 1985, CPC met in New York for its organizational meeting on 1 April and for its twenty-fifth session from 29 April to 1 June.[6]

Most of the session was devoted to a section-by-section consideration of the programme aspects of the proposed programme budget for the 1986-1987 biennium, including its foreword and introduction (see ADMINISTRATIVE AND BUDGETARY QUESTIONS, Chapter I). CPC took note of initiatives to improve the process of programme budgeting and the programme budget document for future bienniums. It considered the Secretary-General's related reports on: experience gained in providing statements of programme budget implications to the 1984 General Assembly; the harmonization of food and agricultural programmes between the Food and Agriculture Organization of the United Nations and the Economic and Social Commission for Asia and the Pacific; aspects of co-ordination and rationalization of UNIDO activities (see p. 598); and the further implementation of a 1982 Assembly resolution[7] on decentralization of responsibilities from global to regional entities (see p. 625). It deferred consideration of a report on recurrent United Nations publications (see ADMINISTRATIVE AND BUDGETARY QUESTIONS, Chapter IV).

In addition to taking decisions on the role of the COPA as a tool for its work, CPC examined four reports on past, current and future COPAs (see p. 1044). It acted on triennial review reports on implementation of its recommendations on the programmes on transnational corporations (TNCs), mineral resources and manufactures (see pp. 618, 677 and 602, respectively). CPC also examined an in-depth evaluation report of the drug control programme, together with a JIU report on drug abuse control activities in the United Nations system (see p. 1013).

Other JIU reports considered or deferred to 1986 dealt with reporting to the Economic and Social Council, publications policy and practice in the United Nations system, the evaluation system of the United Nations Development Programme (UNDP), and UNDP field offices. (See p. 1228.)

Also discussed were an ACC report on co-ordination of United Nations information systems (see ADMINISTRATIVE AND BUDGETARY QUESTIONS, Chapter IV), and the provisional agenda for the 1985 Joint Meetings of ACC and CPC (see p. 1044).

ECONOMIC AND SOCIAL COUNCIL ACTION

Acting on the recommendation of its Third (Programme and Co-ordination) Committee, the Economic and Social Council adopted without vote **resolution 1985/76** on 26 July.

Report of the Committee for Programme and Co-ordination on the work of its twenty-fifth session

The Economic and Social Council,

Having considered the report of the Committee for Programme and Co-ordination on the work of its twenty-fifth session,

I

1. *Takes note with appreciation* of the report of the Committee for Programme and Co-ordination on the work of its twenty-fifth session and endorses the conclusions and recommendations contained therein;

2. *Re-emphasizes* the importance of the programming and co-ordination functions carried out by the Committee in accordance with its mandate and in the context of a continuing need for greater efficiency and effectiveness in the United Nations system;

3. *Recalls* that the Committee for Programme and Co-ordination is the main subsidiary organ of the Economic and Social Council and the General Assembly for planning, programming and co-ordination;

4. *Requests* the Secretary-General, in accordance with Chapters IX and X of the Charter of the United Nations and the relevant resolutions of the Economic and Social Council and the General Assembly, to secure the follow-up and implementation by the organizations of the United Nations system of the conclusions and recommendations of the Committee for Programme and Co-ordination, once approved by the Council and/or the Assembly;

5. *Welcomes* the decision of the Committee to include in the provisional agenda for its twenty-sixth session an item on the improvement of its work and the duration of its sessions, and invites it to take into account the views expressed at its twenty-fifth session and at the second regular session of 1985 of the Economic and Social Council;

II
Instruments for programming and co-ordination

1. *Reiterates* that the effectiveness of the instruments at the disposal of the Committee for Programme and Co-ordination to fulfil its functions, notably cross-organizational programme analyses, in-depth evaluations and triennial reviews of the implementation of its recommendations thereon, programme-budget mechanisms and medium-term plans, should continue to be improved;

2. *Re-emphasizes* the need to strengthen the links between the recommendations derived from cross-organizational programme analyses and evaluation exercises, on the one hand, and the preparation of programme budgets and medium-term plans, on the other hand;

3. *Requests* the Secretary-General, when presenting documents such as cross-organizational programme analyses and evaluations to the Committee for Programme and Co-ordination, to ensure that they are concise and include objective and critical assessments of the activities and organizational arrangements under review, and of the relationships between activities and mandates;

III
Proposed programme budget for the biennium 1986-1987

1. *Takes note with satisfaction* of the improvements in the format of the proposed programme budget and of the improvements towards the timeliness of its submission to the Committee for Programme and Co-ordination and requests the Secretary-General to take steps to ensure further improvement;

2. *Reaffirms* the importance of monitoring and evaluation in the programme planning and budgeting cycle and urges the Secretary-General to refine further the methods employed in those exercises;

3. *Reiterates* that the medium-term plan constitutes the principal policy directive of the United Nations and should continue to serve as the framework for the formulation of the biennial budget;

4. *Recognizes* that the Secretary-General should keep the issue of decentralization under review and report to the Committee as required on the better distribution of responsibilities between global and regional entities;

IV
Cross-organizational programme analyses

1. *Endorses* the conclusions and recommendations of the Committee for Programme and Co-ordination concerning the importance, objectives, methodology, style, presentation and follow-up of cross-organizational programme analyses and future areas for such analyses;

2. *Stresses* the importance of the effective implementation of the recommendations made by the Committee on the cross-organizational programme analysis of the activities of the United Nations system in the area of economic and technical co-operation among developing countries;

3. *Requests* the Secretary-General to take fully into account the recommendations of the Committee for the preparation of the cross-organizational programme analysis of economic and social research and policy analysis;

4. *Suggests* that the Committee for Programme and Co-ordination, in the context of its discussion on the cross-organizational programme analysis of economic and social research and policy analysis, should consider the report of the Secretary-General on recurrent publications of the United Nations with a view to identifying duplication and undue overlaps;

V
Cross-organizational review of selected major sectors in the medium-term plans of the organizations of the United Nations system

Decides to choose at its organizational session for 1986 a topic for the next cross-organizational review of the medium-term plans of the organizations of the United Nations system, to be considered at the second regular session of 1987 of the Council;

VI
Report of the Joint Inspection Unit on reporting to the Economic and Social Council

1. *Takes note* of the conclusions and recommendations of the Committee for Programme and Co-ordination on the report of the Joint Inspection Unit on reporting to the Economic and Social Council;

2. *Endorses* the recommendation of the Committee that the Secretary-General should submit to it at its

twenty-sixth session a report describing the existing expert bodies within the United Nations system;

3. *Considers* that the Secretary-General, taking into account the views expressed in the Committee for Programme and Co-ordination and the Economic and Social Council, should continue his efforts to bring about improvements, as suggested in his further comments on the report of the Joint Inspection Unit, and should keep the Council informed;

VII
Reports of the Administrative Committee on Co-ordination

1. *Takes note* of the annual overview report of the Administrative Committee on Co-ordination for 1984/85;

2. *Requests* the Administrative Committee on Co-ordination, in the light of the debate at the second regular session of 1985 of the Economic and Social Council, to continue to improve its annual overview report, which should contain an analytical review of the activities of the Committee, the status of co-ordination efforts among the organizations of the United Nations system and recommendations for further co-operation and co-ordination among them;

3. *Takes note* of the Register of Development Activities proposed by the Administrative Committee on Co-ordination in response to Council resolution 1982/71 of 10 November 1982 and General Assembly resolution 37/226 of 20 December 1982 and urges its early implementation;

4. *Invites* the Administrative Committee on Co-ordination to proceed with the technical design for the establishment and operation of the Register and to submit a detailed progress report to the Committee for Programme and Co-ordination at its twenty-sixth session, including, *inter alia*, information on cost, funding, assessment of utility to Member States and agency participation; with regard to the funding, the cost to be borne by the United Nations should be limited to the resources appropriated in the regular budget in connection with paragraph 23 of General Assembly resolution 37/226.

Economic and Social Council resolution 1985/76

26 July 1985   Meeting 52   Adopted without vote

Approved by Third Committee (E/1985/141) without vote, 19 July (meeting 20); draft by Chairman (E/1985/C.3/L.8), based on informal consultations and orally revised; agenda item 19.

Following adoption of the resolution, the United States said it had joined in the consensus on the text, but had several reservations concerning the CPC report, in particular the chapter on TNCs.

Work programme and organization

In drawing up its 1986 provisional agenda for review by the Economic and Social Council and the General Assembly, CPC[6] included an item on the improvement of its work, particularly in relation to its review of future programme budgets and medium-term plans.

By section II of **resolution 1985/76**, the Council reiterated its call for continued improvement of such CPC programming and co-ordination instruments as COPAs, in-depth evaluations and triennial reviews of the implementation of its rec-

ommendations thereon, programme-budget mechanisms and medium-term plans. It re-emphasized the need to strengthen the links between the recommendations derived from COPAs and evaluations, on the one hand, and the preparation of programme budgets and medium-term plans on the other. It asked the Secretary-General to ensure that COPAs and evaluations were concise, as well as objective and critical in their assessments of the activities and organizational arrangements under review, and of the relationships between activities and mandates.

In **resolution 40/240** on programme planning, the Assembly endorsed the decision of CPC to include in its 1986 provisional agenda an item on the improvement of its work, *inter alia*, with a view to its consideration of future programme budgets and medium-term plans, as well as to enhance the instruments of co-ordination. The Assembly considered that decision a step towards enhancing CPC's effectiveness as the main subsidiary organ of the Council and the Assembly for planning, programming and co-ordination.

Joint Meetings of CPC and ACC

As it had decided in 1984,[8] the Economic and Social Council reviewed, at its February 1985 organizational session, the functioning of the Joint Meetings of CPC and ACC. Doubt was expressed regarding the effectiveness of the Meetings as currently organized. The United States said it was impossible to give the necessary attention to questions under consideration; therefore, the Meetings should be dispensed with and the resources thus released made available to the Office for Emergency Operations in Africa. The Netherlands suggested limiting the agenda and streamlining the decision-making process. The dialogue between the executive heads of the specialized agencies should be made more specific and practical, France suggested, possibly by relating the preparation of documentation and the scheduling of meetings to the choice of the issues considered; a Council Vice-President could be put in charge of helping CPC and the Council to consider those issues. Indonesia felt that ACC should consider improvements suggested by the Council itself and that CPC should also help to improve the Meetings.

ECONOMIC AND SOCIAL COUNCIL ACTION

Following its review of the functioning of the Joint Meetings, the Economic and Social Council adopted **decision 1985/107** without vote.

Review of the functioning of the Joint Meetings of the Committee for Programme and Co-ordination and the Administrative Committee on Co-ordination

At its 5th plenary meeting, on 8 February 1985, the Council, reiterating its resolution 1984/61 B of 26 July 1984, recommended that the Joint Meetings of the Committee for Programme and Co-ordination and the Administrative Committee on Co-ordination for 1985 should focus on the effectiveness and co-ordination of relief efforts in Africa by United Nations organs and specialized agencies.

Economic and Social Council decision 1985/107

Adopted without vote

Draft by President, for Council Bureau (E/1985/L.18), based on informal consultations; agenda item 2.
Meeting numbers. ESC 2, 5.

CPC action. On 31 May, CPC[6] considered the proposed agenda for the 1985 Joint Meetings. While some members questioned the usefulness of the Meetings, others felt that focusing discussion on the agenda items and relevant background papers would improve dialogue. CPC approved the agenda and requested the Secretary-General to take all possible measures to improve the work of the Joint Meetings substantially and thus provide guidance for the activities of the United Nations system.

Activities of the Joint Meetings. CPC and ACC held the twentieth in their series of Joint Meetings at Geneva on 2 and 3 July 1985.[9] In accordance with the Council's decision (see above), the Joint Meetings held a wide-ranging debate on the question of the effectiveness and co-ordination of United Nations organs and specialized agencies in relief efforts in Africa, with an ACC background paper as a basis for the debate. Also discussed were economic and technical co-operation among developing countries (see p. 427) and the agenda for the 1986 Joint Meetings.

In his statement, the CPC Chairman referred to the highly complex mechanism into which the United Nations had grown and the expansion of its activities to all spheres of international life, economic and social in particular; such a development had increased the need for ensuring system-wide co-ordination of activities so as to minimize, if not eliminate, duplication of work and waste of resources. CPC and ACC had gained importance, he said, and the Joint Meetings had proved their usefulness: they provided a unique opportunity for the exchange of views between Governments and executive heads of the specialized agencies, aimed at increasing the efficient use of available capacities and resources; they had also given Governments an opportunity to gain a better knowledge of the difficulties and problems facing ACC members.

The Joint Meetings concluded that, while some progress had been made in the preparations for and in the conduct of the current Meetings, there remained room for improvement. Statements could be shorter and more focused, and inputs to the Meetings should provide more critical assessments and be more action-oriented.

Acting on the recommendation of its Third Committee, the Economic and Social Council on 26 July adopted **resolution 1985/77** without vote.

Joint Meetings of the Committee for Programme and Co-ordination and the Administrative Committee on Co-ordination
The Economic and Social Council,
Recalling Articles 57, 58, 63 and 64 of the Charter of the United Nations,
Recalling also its resolutions 2008(LX) of 14 May 1976 and 1984/61 B of 26 July 1984,
Recalling further General Assembly resolution 32/197 of 20 December 1977, in particular paragraphs 2 and 3 thereof,
Having considered the report of the Chairmen of the Committee for Programme and Co-ordination and the Administrative Committee on Co-ordination on the twentieth series of Joint Meetings of the two Committees,

1. *Takes note* of the efforts made in the preparations for and in the conduct of the twentieth series of Joint Meetings of the Committee for Programme and Co-ordination and the Administrative Committee on Co-ordination and stresses the need for improvement in the functioning of the Meetings;

2. *Takes note also* of the report of the Chairmen of the Committee for Programme and Co-ordination and the Administrative Committee on Co-ordination on the Joint Meetings of the two Committees, which includes the conclusions reached and the views expressed on the effectiveness and co-ordination of United Nations organs and specialized agencies in relief efforts in Africa and on economic and technical co-operation among developing countries;

3. *Stresses* the need for more vigorous observance of the responsibilities laid down in the Charter of the United Nations and the agreements between the United Nations and the specialized agencies, bearing in mind problems which have arisen in co-ordination and the pressing need for effective co-ordination among all the organizations of the United Nations system, including co-ordination between the United Nations and the specialized agencies;

4. *Urges* the development of an open and constructive dialogue in the Joint Meetings in order to reach concrete solutions to problems of interorganizational co-ordination; to that effect, requests that the background paper for the Meetings should be submitted sufficiently in advance to allow careful study; and also requests that that document should highlight the problems faced by organizations in the field of interorganizational co-ordination and difficulties of implementation and should be action-oriented;

5. *Recommends* that normally only one item should be chosen to serve as a focus for discussion at the Joint Meetings; the item chosen should be sufficiently precise and of such a nature as to allow a concrete discussion among members, centred on the issues identified in the background paper;

6. *Calls upon* Member States and members of the Administrative Committee on Co-ordination to be represented at a high level in order to maximize the usefulness of the Joint Meetings;

7. *Suggests* that problems of co-ordination should be more systematically taken into account in the work of the governing bodies of the organizations of the United Nations system in view of the discussion in the Committee for Programme and Co-ordination and at the Joint Meetings.

Economic and Social Council resolution 1985/77

26 July 1985   Meeting 52   Adopted without vote

Approved by Third Committee (E/1985/141) without vote, 19 July (meeting 20); draft by Chairman (E/1985/C.3/L.9), based on informal consultations; agenda item 19.

Cross-organizational programme analyses

In 1985, in addition to considering reports on previous COPAs in marine affairs and human settlements (see pp. 681 and 834, respectively), ACC and its subsidiaries discussed the preparation of COPAs in the areas of economic and social research and policy analysis, science and technology for development, and the environment (see p. 794), for submission to CPC in 1986, 1987 and 1988, respectively.

CPC[6] examined a COPA of economic and technical co-operation among developing countries, incorporating a cross-organizational review (CORE) of medium-term plans on the same subject (see p. 426). It also examined a report of the Secretary-General[10]—submitted in response to its 1984 request[11]—on the scope and general approach of the COPA of economic and social research and policy analysis, currently in preparation. It undertook a review of the concept, structure and future development of the COPA as a tool for its work, and offered a series of conclusions and recommendations that it considered should be taken into account when preparing the COPA which was the subject of the Secretary-General's report and future COPAs (see p. 1228).

CPC concluded that the COPA should be responsive to the needs of Governments and of the United Nations system, its subject well chosen and its scope clearly defined. It should be carefully documented and the system-wide activities in the programme area critically assessed. To fulfil its main objective of facilitating the programme planning process from the standpoint of co-operation and co-ordination, the COPA should identify duplication, overlaps and gaps in activities. The programme area to be analysed should be of high priority to Member States and one requiring improved co-operation and co-ordination within the system. The methodology should be precise but flexible enough to accommodate the circumstances particular to the subject. The report should be short and specific and should contain a set of clearly outlined conclusions to enable CPC to formulate meaningful recommendations. A follow-up of such recommendations should be ensured, with CPC being regularly informed of the practical results.

CPC requested a report in 1986 on the results of past COPAs. It decided to consider a COPA of ac-

tivities in science and technology for development in 1987, with its scope and general approach to be considered in 1986, and one in the area of the environment in 1988. To assist it in selecting future topics, CPC recommended that the Secretary-General, in consultation with ACC, propose more than one topic.

By section IV of **resolution 1985/76**, the Economic and Social Council endorsed the CPC conclusions and recommendations, and requested the Secretary-General to take them fully into account when preparing the COPA of economic and social research and policy analysis.

Medium-term plans

In January 1985, ACC circulated to organizations the second draft of a CORE of the issue of women and development in the medium-term plans of the organizations of the United Nations system. Revisions were incorporated in the draft before its submission to the Economic and Social Council (see p. 948).

By section V of **resolution 1985/76**, the Council decided that, at its 1986 organizational session, it would choose a topic for the next CORE, to be considered at its 1987 second regular session.

Written communications on ILO

On 28 May,[12] Czechoslovakia transmitted to the Secretary-General a declaration by Bulgaria, the Byelorussian SSR, Czechoslovakia, the German Democratic Republic, Hungary, Mongolia, Poland, the Ukrainian SSR and the USSR on the situation in the International Labour Organisation (ILO). The declaration criticized various aspects of the activities, budget and structure of ILO, including its role in world labour and disarmament problems, the functioning of machinery to supervise international labour standards, alleged resistance to East-West trade union co-operation, membership of ILO bodies, and geographical distribution of staff.

The ILO Director-General addressed those criticisms in an ILO document. Circulation of that document to the General Assembly and the Economic and Social Council was requested on 3 July[13] by Costa Rica and on 9 July[14] by Australia, Belgium, Canada, Denmark, France, the Federal Republic of Germany, Ireland, Italy, Luxembourg, the Netherlands, New Zealand, Norway, Portugal, Sweden, the United Kingdom and the United States.

REFERENCES

[1]E/1985/57. [2]E/1986/13. [3]ACC/1985/DEC/1-13. [4]ACC/1985/DEC/14-15. [5]ACC/1985/DEC/16-29. [6]A/40/38 & Corr.1 & Add.1. [7]YUN 1982, p. 828, GA res. 37/214, 20 Dec. 1982. [8]YUN 1984, p. 975, ESC res. 1984/1, 10 Feb. 1984. [9]E/1985/112. [10]E/AC.51/1985/6. [11]YUN 1984, p. 976. [12]A/40/342-E/1985/119. [13]A/40/458-E/1985/135. [14]A/40/489-E/1985/143.

Economic and Social Council

Reporting procedures

Pursuant to a 1984 Economic and Social Council resolution,[1] CPC on 20 May 1985 considered in depth a 1984 JIU study[2] on reporting to the Council, together with the preliminary comments of the Secretary-General. CPC also considered the Secretary-General's further comments,[3] submitted in May 1985 in response to the same resolution.

As the Secretary-General had observed in his preliminary comments, the JIU study presented a comprehensive critique of the structure and functioning of United Nations intergovernmental bodies and Secretariat support services. It sought, through the example of the Council, to examine the broader question of the role of, and relationship between, the Secretariat and intergovernmental organs in the economic and social field.

In his further comments, the Secretary-General stated that he shared the JIU view that there were a number of technical problems relating to Secretariat support services whose solution was possible despite the difficult political context within which they existed; he was therefore ready, whenever feasible and appropriate, to introduce changes and improvements suggested by JIU to enable the Secretariat to respond more effectively to the needs of intergovernmental bodies (the Council and its subsidiary bodies).

The Secretary-General observed, with regard to documentation for consideration by economic and social bodies: first, many documents tended to be more descriptive than analytical, key policy issues were not always precisely identified and policy recommendations were often lacking; second, there was a tendency to rely on established views within the Secretariat, due in part to the complexity of issues dealt with and to the sensitivities relating to some of them; and third, requests for additional documentation were sometimes used as a substitute for compromise, concession and agreement, and many were repetitive although no new developments justified such requests. To improve the situation, it was necessary for the Secretariat to reorient its approaches to the preparation of reports and for Member States to exercise restraint in their requests for documentation, in particular annual or recurrent reports.

The Secretary-General concurred with JIU's call (recommendation 2) for documentation that was concise and analytical and listed precisely stated recommendations. He agreed (recommendation 3) that, to improve the Council's function of defining policies, the form of the general debate and the formulation of its conclusion needed to be

reconsidered, and made specific proposals to that end. The format of the *World Economic Survey* was under review and changes in its structure and content were expected beginning in 1986. Consultations among the system's secretariats on the preparation of other general economic and social analyses and surveys was to be strengthened so as to harmonize definitions of statistics, take account of interactions between economic, social and other issues, and avoid overlapping and duplication. As to the recommended revision of the operations of the Committee for Development Planning (CDP) (recommendation 4), the Secretary-General would continue providing all necessary support to CDP, including consultants' services as required; CDP had indicated readiness to continue its informal consultation with the Council begun in 1984.

Stating that the Council should again review its objectives and functioning in relation to its responsibilities for system-wide co-ordination, the Secretary-General commented on specific reports and mechanisms designed to support the exercise of those responsibilities. Among these was the ACC annual overview report, concerning which the Secretary-General concurred with JIU that it should be more analytical in its treatment of the main issues confronting the system and the intersecretariat co-ordination machinery. He agreed that COREs presented directly to the Council, and COPAs presented to CPC, should be improved; he felt, however, that the core of the issue was not documentation as such but the prevailing approaches to inter-agency co-ordination. As to the ineffectiveness of the CPC/ACC Joint Meetings noted by JIU, the Secretary-General pointed to the 1984 Council recommendations[4] for improvement. He would continue to assist CPC to enhance its functioning; however, for the reasons set out in his preliminary comments,[2] he did not agree with the recommendations that intergovernmental bodies use outside experts to examine the problems of co-ordinating system-wide programmes and activities, for which CPC would draw up a list of subjects earmarked for COPAs and another of approved experts, and provide the funds required (recommendation 5), and that CPC be given the means necessary for that task (recommendation 6).

The Secretary-General said he would carefully consider the proposal (recommendation 7) that programme planning documents should include an examination of the draft medium-term plan, draft programme budgets, programme performance reports, studies on operational activities, evaluation reports, and COPAs, subject to the constraints of the calendar of meetings. He would ensure speedy distribution of planning, programming and evaluation documents (recommendation 8). As to a calendar being drawn up to allow documents to be considered in good time (recommendation 9), he said the timing of meetings was often dictated by considerations other than those of programme planning so that in some cases documents could not be examined until after they had been considered centrally (by CPC, the Advisory Committee on Administrative and Budgetary Questions (ACABQ), the Council and the Assembly). Concerning the recommendation (10) that the regulations and rules governing programme planning be given wide circulation, he noted that this had already been done and would draw the attention of subsidiary bodies to their importance.

Commenting on the remaining proposals (recommendations 11-13), the Secretary-General said he would continue, as necessary, to engage outside expertise for the development of programming and evaluation tools, agreed that it would be useful to develop a set format to highlight recommendations in evaluation reports and that recommendations of decision-making bodies on reports should be structured to indicate whether or not they had been approved or approved with reservations, and felt it useful to define procedures concerning decision-making on recommendations as a means of ensuring that recommendations were treated as requested when transmitted from one intergovernmental body to another.

Having taken note of the JIU report and comments thereon, CPC recommended that the Secretary-General continue improvements as suggested in his further comments and keep the Council informed. It asked him to submit to it in 1986 a report describing existing expert bodies established by the Assembly outside the structure of the Secretariat to provide independent evaluation and advice. On 26 July, the Council, by section VI of **resolution 1985/76**, took similar action in taking note of CPC's conclusions and recommendations on the JIU report. On the same date, it took note of the JIU report and the Secretary-General's comments, by **decision 1985/198**.

Co-operation with other organizations

Non-governmental organizations

The Committee on Non-Governmental Organizations met three times in 1985: in New York from 11 to 22 March[5] and on 8 May;[6] and at Geneva on 4 July.[7]

At its March meetings, following its review of applications from NGOs for consultative status with the Economic and Social Council or for a reclassification of their status, the Committee recommended one NGO for category I consultative status, 26 for category II and 13 for the Roster. It decided to reclassify one organization from category II to category I and seven from the Roster

to category II, and withdraw the consultative status of the International Police Association.

Four applications for consultative status and three requests for reclassification were not approved; 20 applications were deferred to 1987 and three requests were not considered; and six requests for reclassification were deferred to 1987. The Committee also deferred to 1987 consideration of the quadrennial reports submitted by 45 NGOs in categories I and II on their United Nations–related activities during 1980-1984.[8]

In addition to approving its 1987 provisional agenda and recommending it for Council approval, the Committee also discussed matters relating to a review and rationalization of its future activities. In this connection, its attention was drawn to a statement of principles and concerns adopted by the Board of the Conference of Non-Governmental Organizations in Consultative Status with the Economic and Social Council (Geneva, 11 and 12 October 1984).[9]

In May and July, the Committee heard requests from NGOs with consultative status to address the Council or its committees in connection with items on the Council's agenda at its first and second regular 1985 sessions. The Council received statements from three NGOs[10] concerning specific areas of its work.

ECONOMIC AND SOCIAL COUNCIL ACTION

Acting on the recommendation of the Committee on NGOs, the Economic and Social Council decided on 9 May to hear during its current session the NGOs listed in the Committee's May report.[6] On 10 May, it adopted two decisions concerning the consultative status of NGOs.

The first, **decision 1985/113**, was adopted without vote.

Applications for consultative status and requests for reclassification received from non-governmental organizations

At its 11th plenary meeting, on 10 May 1985, the Council:

(*a*) Took note of the report of the Committee on Non-Governmental Organizations;

(*b*) Decided to grant the following non-governmental organizations consultative status:

Category I

Greek Orthodox Archdiocesan Council of North and South America

Category II

American Mideast Educational and Training Services, Inc.

Anglican Consultative Council

Arab Women Solidarity Association

Association of African Women for Research and Development

Christian Children's Fund, Incorporated

Covenant House

European Federation of Conference Towns

General Arab Women Federation
General Conference of the Seventh Day Adventists
Housewives in Dialogue
Human Rights Advocates, Inc.
Indigenous World Association
Institute of Cultural Affairs (International)
Institute of Social Studies Trust
Inter African Union of Lawyers
International Association of Women in Radio and
  Television
Inter-University European Institute on Social Welfare
Islamic African Relief Agency
Italian Centre of Solidarity
Latin American Federation of Associations of Relatives
  of Disappeared Detainees
Liberal International (World Liberal Union)
National Aboriginal and Islander Legal Services
  Secretariat
Save the Children Fund (United Kingdom)
Unión Iberoamericana de Colegios y Agrupaciones de
  Abogados
Women's Missionary Society of the African Methodist
  Episcopal Church
World Vision International

Roster

Asian Non-Governmental Organizations Coalition for
  Agrarian Reform and Rural Development
Dayemi Complex, Dhaka
Hunger Project, The
International Assets Valuation Standard Committee
International Association for Driving Instruction and
  Traffic Education
International Emergency Action
International Federation for the Protection of the Rights
  of Ethnic, Religious, Linguistic and Other Minorities
International Movement for the Apostolate of Children
International New Towns Association
International Society for General Semantics
PACE—United Kingdom
Parliamentary Association for Euro-Arab Co-operation
SUNSAT Energy Council

(c) Decided to reclassify one organization from category II to category I consultative status and seven others from the Roster to category II consultative status, as follows:

Category I

Zonta International

Category II

International Association of Judges
International Committee on the Management of
  Population Programmes
International Social Science Council
Population Council, The
Union of International Technical Associations
World Association for Element Building and
  Prefabrication
World Federation of UNESCO Clubs and Associations

Economic and Social Council decision 1985/113

Adopted without vote

Draft by Committee on NGOs (E/1985/19), orally revised by President; agenda item 8.
Meeting numbers. ESC 9-11.

The Council President's oral revision added subparagraph *(a)*.

The second decision, **decision 1985/114**, was also adopted without vote.

Withdrawal of consultative status

At its 11th plenary meeting, on 10 May 1985, the Council decided to withdraw consultative status from the International Police Association.

Economic and Social Council decision 1985/114

Adopted without vote

Draft by Committee on NGOs (E/1985/19); agenda item 8.

As a result of the foregoing decisions and other additions to the Roster, the number of NGOs in consultative status with the Council rose to 758 during 1985.[11] They were divided into three groups: category I—organizations representative of major population segments in a large number of countries, involved with the economic and social life of the areas they represented; category II—international organizations having special competence in a few of the Council's areas of activity; and organizations on the Roster—considered able to make occasional and useful contributions to the Council's work.

NGOs in consultative status with the Economic and Social Council
(as at 31 December 1985)

Category I

Greek Orthodox Archdiocesan Council of North and South America
International Alliance of Women—Equal Rights, Equal Responsibilities
International Association of French-Speaking Parliamentarians
International Chamber of Commerce
International Confederation of Free Trade Unions
International Co-operative Alliance
International Council of Voluntary Agencies (ICVA)
International Council of Women
International Council on Social Welfare
International Federation of Agricultural Producers
International Federation of Business and Professional Women
International Organization for Standardization (IOS)
International Organization of Consumers' Unions (IOCU)
International Organizations of Employers
International Planned Parenthood Federation
International Social Security Association (ISSA)
International Union of Local Authorities (IULA)
International Youth and Student Movement for the United Nations
Inter-Parliamentary Union
League of Red Cross Societies
Muslim World League
Organization of African Trade Union Unity (OATUU)

Society for International Development (SID)
Soroptomist International
United Towns Organization
Women's International Democratic Federation
World Assembly of Youth (WAY)
World Confederation of Labour
World Federation of Democratic Youth (WFDY)
World Federation of Trade Unions (WFTU)
World Federation of United Nations Associations (WFUNA)
World Muslim Congress
World Veterans Federation
Zonta International

Category II

Academy of Criminal Justice Sciences (ACJS)
African Association of Education for Development (AFASED)
African Institute of Private International Law
Afro-Asian Peoples' Solidarity Organization (AAPSO)
AFS International/Intercultural Programs, Inc.
Agudas Israel World Organization
Airport Associations Co-ordinating Council (AACC)
All-India Women's Conference
All Pakistan Women's Association
American Mideast Educational and Training Services, Inc.
Amnesty International
Anglican Consultative Council
Anti-*Apartheid* Movement, The
Anti-Slavery Society for the Protection of Human Rights, The
Arab Lawyers Union
Arab Women Solidarity Association
Asociación Interamericana Presupuesto Público
Associated Country Women of the World
Association for Childhood Education International
Association for the Study of the World Refugee Problem
Association of African Women for Research and Development
Bahá'í International Community
Balkan-ji-Bari International (formerly Children's Own Garden International)
Baptist World Alliance
CARE (Cooperative for American Relief Everywhere, Inc.)
Caritas Internationalis (International Confederation of Catholic Charities)
Carnegie Endowment for International Peace
Catholic Relief Services—United States Catholic Conference, Inc.
Chamber of Commerce of the United States of America
Christian Children's Fund, Incorporated
Christian Democratic International (formerly Christian Democratic World Union)
Christian Peace Conference
Church World Service, Inc.
Commission of the Churches on International Affairs of the World Council of Churches
Commonwealth Human Ecology Council (CHEC)
Consultative Council of Jewish Organizations
Co-ordinating Board of Jewish Organizations (CBJO)
Co-ordinating Committee for International Voluntary Service
Council of European and Japanese National Shipowners' Associations, The (CENSA)
Council of European Churches (CEC)
Covenant House
Democratic Youth Community of Europe
Disabled Peoples' International
Eastern Regional Organization for Public Administration (EROPA)
Environment Liaison Centre
European Association of National Productivity Centres
European Federation of Conference Towns
European Insurance Committee
European League for Economic Co-operation
European Organization for Quality Control (EOQC)
Experiment in International Living, The
Federation for the Respect of Man and Humanity
Federation of Arab Scientific Research Councils
Federation of Associations of Former International Civil Servants (FAFICS)

Foundation for the Peoples of the South Pacific, Inc., The
Four Directions Council
Friends World Committee for Consultation
General Arab Women Federation
General Conference of the Seventh Day Adventists
Geneva Informal Meeting of International Youth Non-Governmental Organizations (GIM)
Greenpeace International (formerly Stichting Greenpeace Council)
Housewives in Dialogue
Howard League for Penal Reform
Human Rights Advocates, Inc.
Human Rights Internet (HRI)
Ibero-American Institute of Aeronautic and Space Law and Commercial Aviation
Indigenous World Association
Institute for Policy Studies—Transnational
Institute of Cultural Affairs (International)
Institute of Electrical and Electronic Engineers, Inc.
Institute of Social Studies Trust
Inter African Union of Lawyers
Inter-American Federation of Touring and Automobile Clubs (FITAC)
Inter-American Planning Society
Inter-American Press Association
Inter-American Statistical Institute
International Abolitionist Federation
International Air Transport Association
International Association against Painful Experiments on Animals
International Association for Religious Freedom (IARF)
International Association for Social Progress
International Association for the Protection of Industrial Property
International Association for Water Law (IAWL)
International Association of Democratic Lawyers
International Association of Educators for World Peace
International Association of Judges (formerly International Union of Judges)
International Association of Juvenile and Family Court Magistrates
International Association of Penal Law
International Association of Ports and Harbours (IAPH)
International Association of Schools of Social Work
International Association of Women in Radio and Television
International Astronautical Federation
International Automobile Federation (FIA)
International Bar Association
International Cargo Handling Co-ordination Association
International Catholic Child Bureau
International Catholic Migration Commission
International Catholic Union of the Press
International Centre for Industry and the Environment (ICIE)
International Centre for Local Credit
International Centre of Social Gerontology
International Chamber of Shipping
International Christian Union of Business Executives (UNIAPAC)
International Civil Airports Association
International College of Surgeons
International Commission of Jurists
International Commission on Irrigation and Drainage
International Committee for European Security and Co-operation
International Committee of the Red Cross
International Committee on the Management of Population Programmes
International Co-operation for Development and Solidarity (formerly International Co-operation for Socio-Economic Development (CIDSE))
International Co-ordinating Committee of Financial Analysts' Associations
International Council for Adult Education (ICAE)
International Council for Building Research, Studies and Documentation
International Council of Environmental Law
International Council of Jewish Women
International Council of Monuments and Sites (ICOMOS)
International Council of Scientific Unions
International Council of Societies of Industrial Design (ICSID)
International Council on Alcohol and Addictions

International Council on Jewish Social and Welfare Services
International Defence and Aid Fund for Southern Africa
International Driving Tests Committee (IDTC)
International Electrotechnical Commission
International Federation for Home Economics (IFHE)
International Federation for Housing and Planning
International Federation of Associations of the Elderly
International Federation of Beekeepers' Associations
International Federation of Disabled Workers and Civilian Handicapped
International Federation of Human Rights
International Federation of Journalists
International Federation of Landscape Architects
International Federation of Resistance Movements
International Federation of Senior Police Officers
International Federation of Settlements and Neighbourhood Centres
International Federation of Social Workers
International Federation of the Little Brothers of the Poor
International Federation of University Women
International Federation of Women in Legal Careers
International Federation of Women Lawyers
International Federation on Aging
International Fellowship of Reconciliation
International Hotel Association
International Indian Treaty Council
International Institute for Vital Registration and Statistics (IIVRS)
International Institute of Administrative Sciences
International Institute of Humanitarian Law
International Islamic Federation of Student Organizations
International Law Association
International League for Human Rights
International League of Societies for Persons with Mental Handicap
International Movement ATD Fourth World
International Movement for Fraternal Union among Races and Peoples (UFER)
International Organization for the Elimination of All Forms of Racial Discrimination (EAFORD)
International Organization of Journalists
International Organization of Supreme Audit Institutions (INTOSAI)
International Petroleum Industry Environmental Conservation Association (IPIECA)
International Prisoners Aid Association
International Road Federation
International Road Transport Union
International Rural Housing Association
International Savings Banks Institute
International Senior Citizens Association, Inc., The
International Social Science Council
International Social Service
International Society for Criminology
International Society for Research on Aggression (ISRA)
International Society of Social Defence
International Statistical Institute
International Touring Alliance
International Union for Child Welfare
International Union for Conservation of Nature and Natural Resources
International Union for Inland Navigation
International Union for the Scientific Study of Population
International Union of Architects
International Union of Building Societies and Savings Associations
International Union of Family Organizations
International Union of Latin Notariat
International Union of Lawyers
International Union of Producers and Distributors of Electrical Energy
International Union of Public Transport
International Union of Students
International Union of Young Christian Democrats (IUYCD)
International Young Christian Workers
Inter-University European Institute on Social Welfare
Inuit Circumpolar Conference
Islamic African Relief Agency
Italian Centre of Solidarity
Jaycees International
Latin American Association of Development Organizations

Latin American Association of Finance Development Institutions (ALIDE)
Latin American Council of Catholic Women
Latin American Federation of Associations of Relatives of Disappeared Detainees
Latin American Iron and Steel Institute
Law Association for Asia and the Western Pacific (LAWASIA)
Liberal International (World Liberal Union)
Lions International—The International Association of Lions Clubs
Lutheran World Federation
Mutual Assistance of the Latin American Government Oil Companies (ARPEL)
National Aboriginal and Islander Legal Services Secretariat
OISCA—International (Organization for Industrial, Spiritual and Cultural Advancement—International)
Organization for International Economic Relations (IER)
OXFAM
Pan-African Institute for Development
Pan-African Women's Organization
Pan-American Federation of Engineering Societies (UPADI)
Pan-Pacific and South-East Asia Women's Association
Parliamentarians for World Order
Pax Christi, International Catholic Peace Movement
Pax Romana
   (International Catholic Movement for Intellectual and Cultural Affairs)
   (International Movement of Catholic Students)
Permanent International Association of Road Congresses (PIARC)
Population Council, The
Prison Fellowship International (PFI)
Rädda Barnen International (Save the Children Federation)
Rehabilitation International
St. Joan's International Alliance
Salvation Army, The
Save the Children Federation
Save the Children Fund (United Kingdom)
Socialist International
Socialist International Women (SIW)
Société internationale de prophylaxie criminelle
Society for Comparative Legislation
Studies and Expansion Society—International Scientific Association (SEC)
Third World Foundation
Unión Iberoamericana de Colegios y Agrupaciones de Abogados
Union of Arab Jurists
Union of International Associations
Union of International Fairs
Union of International Technical Associations
United Kingdom Standing Conference on World Development (formerly United Kingdom Standing Conference on the Second United Nations Development Decade)
Universal Federation of Travel Agents Associations
Vienna Institute for Development
War Resisters International
Women's International League for Peace and Freedom
Women's International Zionist Organization
Women's Missionary Society of the African Methodist Episcopal Church
World Alliance of Young Men's Christian Associations
World Association for Element Building and Prefabrication
World Association of Former United Nations Internes and Fellows
World Association of Girl Guides and Girl Scouts
World Association of World Federalists
World Blind Union (includes the former International Federation of the Blind and the World Council for the Welfare of the Blind)
World Confederation of Organizations of the Teaching Profession
World Conference on Religion and Peace
World Council of Credit Unions, Inc. (WCOCU)
World Council of Indigenous Peoples (WCIP)
World Energy Conference
World Federation for Mental Health
World Federation of Development Financing Institutions
World Federation of Methodist Women (WFMW)
World Federation of the Deaf

World Federation of UNESCO Clubs and Associations
World Jewish Congress
World Leisure and Recreation Association
World Movement of Mothers
World Organization of the Scout Movement (World Scout Bureau)
World Peace Through Law Centre
World Population Society
World Society for the Protection of Animals
World Student Christian Federation
World Trade Centers Association
World Union of Catholic Women's Organizations
World University Service
Worldview International Foundation
World Vision International
World Women's Christian Temperance Union
World Young Women's Christian Association

Roster

Organizations included by action
of the Economic and Social Council

African Medical and Research Foundation
Altrusa International, Inc.
American Association of Engineering Societies, Inc.
American Foreign Insurance Association
American Foreign Law Association, Inc.
American Society for Engineering Education (ASEE)
Asian Cultural Forum on Development (ACFOD)
Asian Development Center (ADC)
Asian Non-Governmental Organizations Coalition for Agrarian
  Reform and Rural Development
Asian Pacific Youth Forum, The (APYF)
Asian Youth Council
Association for World Education
Association of Geoscientists for International Development
Battelle Memorial Institute
Brahma Kumaris World Spiritual University
Bureau international de la récupération
Canadian Comprehensive Auditing Foundation (CCAF)
Caribbean Conservation Association
Catholic International Union for Social Service
Center for Inter-American Relations
Commission to Study the Organization of Peace
Committee for Economic Development
Committee for European Construction Equipment (CECE)
Confederation of Asian Chambers of Commerce
Congress of Racial Equality (CORE)
Continental Africa Chamber of Commerce (CACC)
Council of European National Youth Committees (CENYC)
Council on Religion and International Affairs (CRIA)
Data for Development (DFD)
Dayemi Complex, Dhaka
Defense for Children International Movement
Economic Research Committee of the Gas Industry (COMETEC-GAZ)
Electoral Reform Society of Great Britain and Ireland
Environmental Coalition for North America (ENCONA)
European Alliance of Press Agencies
European Association of Refrigeration Enterprises (AEEF)
European Confederation of Woodworking Industries
European Container Manufacturers' Committee
European Federation for the Welfare of the Elderly (EURAG)
European Liquefied Petroleum Gas Association
European Mediterranean Commission on Water Planning
European Union of Women
Ex-Volunteers International
Federation of European Manufacturers of Friction Materials
Federation of National Committees in the International Christian Youth
  Exchange
Foster Parents Plan International (PLAN)
Foundation for the Establishment of an International Criminal
  Court, The
Friedrich Ebert Foundation

Gray Panthers
Habitat International Council
Help the Aged
Hunger Project, The
Indian Council of South America (CISA)
Indian Law Resource Centre
Institute of International Containers Lessors
Institute of International Education, Inc. (IIE)
International Advertising Association (IAA)
International Assets Valuation Standards Committee
International Association against Noise
International Association for Bridge and Structural Engineering
International Association for Community Development
International Association for Driving Instruction and Traffic Education
International Association for Housing Science
International Association for Hydrogen Energy
International Association for Research into Income and Wealth
International Association for Rural Development
International Association for the Child's Right to Play
International Association for the Defence of Religious Liberty
International Association for the Exchange of Students of Technical
  Experience
International Association for the Promotion of Democracy under God
  (Pro Deo)
International Association of Airport and Seaport Police
International Association of Chiefs of Police
International Association of Gerontology
International Association of the Soap and Detergent Industry
International Association of University Presidents
International Board of Co-operation for the Developing Countries
  (EMCO)
International Bureau of Motor-cycle Manufacturers
International Center for Dynamics of Development
International Centre of Sociological, Penal and Penitentiary Research
  and Studies
International Committee against *Apartheid*, Racism and Colonialism
  in Southern Africa
International Committee of Outer Space Onomastics (ICOSO)
International Committee on Public Relations in Rehabilitation (ICPRR)
International Confederation of Associations of Experts and Consultants
International Confederation of Ex-Prisoners of War
International Container Bureau
International Council for Commercial Arbitration
International Council for Game and Wildlife Conservation
International Council of Psychologists
International Emergency Action
International Federation for Documentation
International Federation for the Protection of the Rights of Ethnic,
  Religious, Linguistic and Other Minorities
International Federation of Chemical Energy and General Workers'
  Unions
International Federation of Free Journalists
International Federation of Freight Forwarders Associations
International Federation of International Furniture Removers
International Federation of Operational Research Societies
International Federation of Pedestrians
International Federation of Rural Adult Catholic Movements
International Federation of Surveyors
International Fiscal Association
International Halfway House Association (IHHA)
International Human Rights Internship Program
International Hydatidological Association
International Inner Wheel
International Institute for Research and Advice on Mental Deficiency
  (IAMER)
International Institute of Public Finance
International Institute of Rural Reconstruction (IIRR)
International Iron and Steel Institute
International Juridical Organization (IJO)
International League for the Rights and Liberation of Peoples
International League of Surveillance Societies, The
International Movement for the Apostolate of Children
International Narcotic Enforcement Officers Association, Inc. (INEOA)
International New Towns Association

International Olive Oil Federation (formerly International Olive Growers Federation)
International Organization of Experts (ORDINEX)
International Organization of Psychophysiology (IOP)
International Peace Academy
International Peace Bureau (includes the former International Confederation for Disarmament and Peace)
International Permanent Bureau of Automobile Manufacturers
International Press Institute (IPI)
International Prevention of Road Accidents
International Progress Organization (IPO)
International Public Policy Institute
International Public Relations Association (IPRA)
International Real Estate Federation
International Research Center for Environmental Structures—Pio Manzú (formerly The Pio Mansú International Research Centre for Environmental Structures)
International Research Institute for Immigration and Emigration Politics
International Schools Association
International Shipping Federation (ISF)
International Society for General Semantics
International Society for Prosthetics and Orthotics
International Solar Energy Society
International Textile Manufacturers Federation
International Union of Marine Insurance
International Union of Police Federations
International Union of Social Democratic Teachers
International Union of Tenants
International Women's Anthropology Conference, Inc. (IWAC)
International Working Group for the Construction of Sports and Leisure Facilities
Islamic Chamber of Commerce, Industry and Commodity Exchange (ICCICE)
La Leche League International, Inc. (LLLI)
Latin American Confederation of Tourist Organizations (COTAL)
Latin American Official Workers' Confederation (CLATE)
Liberation
Minority Rights Group
Movement against Racism and for Friendship among Peoples
Movement for a Better World
National Indian Youth Council, The
National Organization for Women (NOW)
National Parks and Conservation Association
Open Door International (for the Economic Emancipation of the Woman Worker)
Overseas Education Fund of the League of Women Voters
PACE—United Kingdom
Pan American Development Foundation
Parliamentary Association for Euro-Arab Co-operation
Permanent International Association of Navigation Congresses
Planetary Citizens
Procedural Aspects of International Law Institute (formerly known as Procedural Aspects of International Law Institute—International Human Rights Law Group)
Program for the Introduction and Adaptation of Contraceptive Technology (PIACT)
Quota International Incorporated
Regional Studies Association (RSA)
Romani Union
Rotary International
SERVAS International
Society for Social Responsibility in Science
Soka Gakkai International
SOS-Kinderdorf International
SUNSAT Energy Council
Survival International Ltd.
Transfigoroute International
Union of Technical Assistance for Motor Vehicle and Road Traffic (UNATAC)
United Nations of Yoga (UNY)
United Schools International
United Way International
Universal Esperanto Association

Water Supply Improvement Association
World Alliance of Reformed Churches
World Association for Christian Communication
World Confederation for Physical Therapy
World Development Movement
World Environment and Resources Council (WERC)
World Federation of Christian Life Communities
World Federation of Health Agencies for the Advancement of Voluntary Surgical Contraception
World Mining Congress
World Union for Progressive Judaism
Young Lawyers' International Association (AIJA)

Organizations included by action of the Secretary-General

Agri-Energy Roundtable, Inc.
American Association for the Advancement of Science
Asian Environmental Society
Association for the Advancement of Agricultural Sciences in Africa
Center for Research on the New International Economic Order, The
Center of Concern
Committee for International Co-operation in National Research in Demography (CICRED)
Council for Development of Economic and Social Research in Africa, The (CODESRIA)
Fauna Preservation Society, The
Foresta Institute for Ocean and Mountain Studies
Friends of the Earth (FOE)
Institut de la vie
International Advisory Committee on Population and Law
International Association on Water Pollution Research (IAWPR)
International Educational Development, Inc.
International Institute for Environment and Development
International Ocean Institute
International Society for Community Development
International Studies Association
International Union of Anthropological and Ethnological Sciences
International Women's Tribune Centre
National Audubon Society
Natural Resources Defence Council, Inc.
Population Crisis Committee
Population Institute
Sierra Club
Third World Movement against the Exploitation of Women
Trilateral Commission, The
World Education
World Society for Ekistics
World Society of Victimology

Organizations included because of consultative status with other United Nations bodies or specialized agencies

Organization	In consultative status with
African Adult Education Association	UNESCO
African Bureau of Educational Sciences	UNESCO
African Centre for Monetary Studies	UNCTAD
Arab Federation for Engineering Industries	UNCTAD
Arab Federation of Chemical Fertilizer Producers	UNIDO
Arab Iron and Steel Union (AISU)	UNIDO
Asian Mass Communication and Research Centre	UNESCO
Association of African Universities	UNESCO
Association of Arab Universities	UNESCO
Association of European Jute Industries	UNCTAD
Association of Partially and Wholly French-Language Universities	UNESCO
Association of West European Builders, The (AWES)	IMO

Organization	In consultative status with
Baltic and International Maritime Conference, The	IMO, UNCTAD
B'nai B'rith International Council	UNESCO
Catholic International Education Office	UNESCO
Centre Europe—Tiers Monde (CETIM)	UNCTAD
Centre for Latin American Monetary Studies	UNCTAD
Club de Dakar	FAO, UNIDO
Committee on Space Research (COSPAR)	ITU
Confederation of International Trading Houses Associations	UNCTAD
Co-ordination Committee for the Textile Industries in the European Economic Communities (COMI-TEXTILE)	UNCTAD
Council for International Organizations of Medical Sciences (CIOMS)	UNESCO, WHO
Engineering Committee on Oceanic Resources (ECOR)	IMO
European Academy of Arts, Sciences and Humanities	UNESCO
European Association for Animal Production	FAO
European Broadcasting Union	ITU, UNESCO
European Computer Manufacturers Association (ECMA)	ITU
European Confederation of Agriculture	FAO, IAEA, ILO, UNESCO
European Council of Chemical Manufacturers' Federations	IMO, UNCTAD
European Federation of National Associations of Engineers	UNESCO, UNIDO
European Federation of National Maintenance Societies	UNIDO
European Tea Committee	FAO
European Tugowners Association (ETA)	IMO
European Union of Public Relations	UNIDO
Federación Latinoamericana de Periodistas	UNESCO
Federation of Afro-Asian Insurers and Reinsurers	UNCTAD
Federation of European Chemical Societies	UNIDO
Federation of Western European Rope and Twine Industries	UNCTAD
General Union of Chambers of Commerce, Industry and Agriculture for Arab Countries	UNCTAD
Institute of Air Transport	ICAO
Institute of International Law	ICAO
Institute on Man and Science	UNESCO
Inter-American Association of Broadcasters	ITU, UNESCO
International Academy of Pathology	WHO
International Aeronautical Federation	ICAO
International Agency for the Prevention of Blindness (Vision International)	WHO
International Amateur Radio Union	ITU
International Association for Cereal Chemistry (ICC)	FAO, UNIDO
International Association for Educational Assessment	UNESCO
International Association for Mass Communication Research	UNESCO
International Association for Suicide Prevention	WHO
International Association for the Study of the Liver	WHO
International Association of Agricultural Economists	UNCTAD

Organization	In consultative status with
International Association of Agricultural Librarians and Documentalists	FAO
International Association of Art (IAA)	UNESCO
International Association of Cancer Registries	WHO
International Association of Classification Societies	IMO
International Association of Conference Interpreters	ILO, UNESCO
International Association of Crafts and Small and Medium-sized Enterprises	UNIDO
International Association of Drilling Contractors (IADC)	IMO
International Association of Dry Cargo Shipowners	UNCTAD
International Association of Fish Meal Manufacturers	FAO
International Association of Horticultural Producers	FAO
International Association of Lighthouse Authorities	IMO, ITU
International Association of Literary Critics	UNESCO
International Association of Logopedics and Phoniatrics	UNESCO, WHO
International Association of Medical Laboratory Technologists (IAMLT)	WHO
International Association of Mutual Insurance Companies	UNCTAD
International Association of Students in Economics and Management	ILO, UNESCO
International Association of the Third Age Universities	ILO
International Association of Universities	UNESCO
International Association of University Professors and Lecturers	UNESCO
International Baccalaureate Office	UNESCO
International Board on Books for Young People	UNESCO
International Bureau of Social Tourism	ILO, UNESCO
International Centre of Films for Children and Young People	UNESCO
International Cocoa Trades Federation	UNCTAD
International Commission on Illumination	ICAO, ILO
International Commission on Occupational Health (formerly Permanent Commission and International Association on Occupational Health)	ILO, WHO
International Commission on Radiological Protection (ICRP)	WHO
International Committee for Plastics in Agriculture	UNIDO
International Committee for Standardization in Haematology	WHO
International Committee of Catholic Nurses	ILO, WHO
International Confederation of European Beet Growers	UNCTAD
International Confederation of Midwives	ILO, WHO
International Conference of Historians of the Labour Movement	UNESCO
International Copyright Society	UNESCO
International Council for Distance Education	UNESCO
International Council for Philosophy and Humanistic Studies	UNESCO
International Council of Aircraft Owner and Pilot Associations	ICAO

Organization	In consultative status with	Organization	In consultative status with
International Council of Marine Industry Associations (ICOMIA)	IMO	International Federation of Translators	UNESCO
International Council of Nurses	ILO, UNESCO, WHO	International Federation of Travel Journalists and Writers	UNESCO
International Council of Sport and Physical Education	UNESCO	International Fertilizer Industry Association	FAO, IMO, UNCTAD, UNIDO
International Council on Archives	UNESCO	International Food Policy Research Institute	FAO, UNCTAD
International Council on Education for Teaching	UNESCO	International Foundation for Development Alternatives	FAO, UNCTAD, UNIDO
International Cystic Fibrosis (Mucoviscidosis) Association	WHO	International Gas Union	ITU
International Dairy Federation	FAO	International Hospital Federation (IHF)	WHO
International Dental Federation	WHO	International Humanist and Ethical Union	UNESCO
International Diabetes Federation	WHO	International Institute for Audio-Visual Communication and Cultural Development (MEDIACULT)	UNESCO
International Epidemiological Association	WHO	International Institute for Peace	UNESCO
International Ergonomics Association	ILO, WHO	International League against Rheumatism	WHO
International Falcon Movement	UNESCO	International Leprosy Association	WHO
International Federation for Information Processing	ITU, UNESCO, WHO	International Maritime Pilots' Association	IMO
International Federation for Medical and Biological Engineering	WHO	International Music Council	ILO, UNESCO
International Federation for Parent Education	UNESCO	International Organization against Trachoma	WHO
International Federation of Air Line Pilots Associations	ICAO, WMO	International Paediatric Association	WHO
International Federation of Automatic Control	UNIDO	International Peace Research Association	UNCTAD, UNESCO
International Federation of Catholic Universities	UNESCO	International PEN	UNESCO
International Federation of Clinical Chemistry	WHO	International Pharmaceutical Federation	WHO
International Federation of Educative Communities	UNESCO	International Phosphate Industry Organization	FAO, IMO, UNCTAD, UNIDO
International Federation of Film Archives	UNESCO	International Political Science Association	UNESCO
International Federation of Gynecology and Obstetrics	WHO	International Press Telecommunications Council	ITU
International Federation of Health Records Organizations	WHO	International Publishers Association	UNESCO
International Federation of Library Associations and Institutions (IFLA)	UNESCO	International Radiation Protection Association	WHO
International Federation of Margarine Associations	FAO	International Round Table for the Advancement of Counselling (IRTAC)	ILO, UNESCO
International Federation of Medical Student Associations	WHO	International Scientific Film Association	UNESCO
International Federation of Multiple Sclerosis Societies	WHO	International Secretariat of Catholic Technologists, Agriculturists and Economists	ILO
International Federation of Musicians	UNESCO	International Shipowners' Association	IMO, UNCTAD
International Federation of Newspaper Publishers	UNESCO	International Society and Federation of Cardiology	WHO
International Federation of Organizations of School Correspondence and Exchanges	UNESCO	International Society for Burn Injuries	WHO
		International Society for Human and Animal Mycology	WHO
International Federation of Pharmaceutical Manufacturers Associations	UNCTAD, UNIDO, WHO	International Society for Photogrammetry and Remote Sensing	UNESCO
		International Society of Citriculture	FAO
International Federation of Physical Medicine and Rehabilitation	WHO	International Society of City and Regional Planners	UNESCO
		International Society of Endocrinology	WHO
International Federation of Plantation, Agricultural and Allied Workers	FAO	International Society of Haematology	WHO
		International Society of Radiographers and Radiological Technicians	WHO
International Federation of Popular Travel Organizations	UNESCO	International Society of Soil Science	FAO, UNESCO, WMO
International Federation of Purchasing and Materials Management (IFPMM)	UNCTAD	International Sociological Association	UNESCO, WHO
		International Time Bureau	ITU
International Federation of Surgical Colleges	WHO	International Transport Workers' Federation	ICAO
International Federation of the Periodical Press	UNESCO	International Union against Tuberculosis	ILO, WHO

Organization	In consultative status with
International Union for Health Education	UNESCO, WHO
International Union of Aviation Insurers	ICAO
International Union of Biological Sciences	WHO
International Union of Forestry Research Organizations (IUFRO)	FAO
International Union of Geodesy and Geophysics	ICAO
International Union of Independent Laboratories	UNIDO
International Union of Microbiological Societies	WHO
International Union of Nutritional Sciences	FAO, WHO
International Union of Pure and Applied Chemistry	FAO, WHO
International Union of School and University Health and Medicine	UNESCO, WHO
International Union of Socialist Youth	ILO, UNESCO
International Water Supply Association	WHO
International Young Catholic Students	UNESCO
International Youth Hostel Federation	UNESCO
Inter-Union Commission on Frequency Allocations for Radio, Astronomy and Space Science	ITU
Latin American Federation of Pharmaceutical Industries	UNIDO
Latin American Industrialists Association	UNIDO
Latin American Social Science Council	UNESCO
Liaison Office of the Rubber Industries of the European Economic Community	UNCTAD
Licensing Executives Society International	UNCTAD, UNIDO
Medical Women's International Association	WHO
Medicus Mundi Internationalis (International Organization for Co-operation in Health Care)	WHO
Miners' International Federation	UNCTAD
Oil Companies' International Marine Forum (OCIMF)	IMO
Oil Industry International Exploration and Production	UNESCO
Organization for Flora Neotropica	UNESCO
Pacific Science Association	UNESCO, WMO
Pan American Standards Commission	UNESCO
Société internationale de télécommunications aéronautiques (SITA)	ITU
Society of Chemical Industry	UNIDO
Sri Aurobindo Society	UNESCO
Standing Conference of Rectors and Vice-Chancellors of the European Universities	UNESCO
Trade Unions International of Agricultural, Forestry and Plantation Workers	FAO
UNDA—Catholic International Association for Radio and Television	UNESCO
Union of Industries of the European Community (UNICE)	UNCTAD, UNIDO
United Seamen's Service, Inc.	ILO
United States Trademark Association, The	UNCTAD
World Assembly of Small and Medium Enterprises	UNIDO
World Association for Educational Research	UNESCO

Organization	In consultative status with
World Association for the School as an Instrument of Peace	UNESCO
World Association of Industrial and Technological Research Organizations	UNIDO
World Association of Societies of (Anatomic and Clinical) Pathology	WHO
World Confederation of Teachers	UNESCO
World Crafts Council	UNESCO
World Education Fellowship, The	UNESCO
World Federation for Medical Education	WHO
World Federation of Agricultural Workers	FAO
World Federation of Associations of Clinical Toxicology Centres and Poison Control Centres	WHO
World Federation of Engineering Organizations	UNESCO, UNIDO
World Federation of Foreign-Language Teachers' Associations	UNESCO
World Federation of Neurosurgical Societies	WHO
World Federation of Nuclear Medicine and Biology	WHO
World Federation of Occupational Therapists	WHO
World Federation of Public Health Associations	WHO
World Federation of Scientific Workers	UNESCO
World Federation of Societies of Anaesthesiologists	WHO
World Federation of Teachers' Unions	UNESCO
World Federation of Workers in Food, Tobacco and Hotel Industries	FAO
World Future Studies Federation	UNESCO
World Medical Association	ILO
World Movement of Christian Workers	ILO, UNESCO
World Organization for Early Childhood Education	UNESCO
World Organization of Former Students of Catholic Teaching	UNESCO
World ORT Union	ILO
World Packaging Organization	UNIDO
World Peace Council	UNCTAD, UNESCO
World Poultry Science Association	FAO
World Psychiatric Association	WHO
World Veterinary Association	FAO, WHO

Agenda for the 1987 session

ECONOMIC AND SOCIAL COUNCIL ACTION

Acting without vote in May, on a recommendation of the Committee on NGOs, the Economic and Social Council adopted **decision 1985/115**.

Provisional agenda and documentation for the session of the Committee on Non-Governmental Organizations to be held in 1987

At its 11th plenary meeting, on 10 May 1985, the Council approved the provisional agenda and documentation set out below for the session of the Committee on Non-Governmental Organizations to be held in 1987.

1. Election of officers
2. Adoption of the agenda and other organizational matters
3. Applications for consultative status and requests for reclassification received from non-governmental organizations

Documentation
        New applications for consultative status
        Requests for reclassification
        Deferred applications for consultative status
            and deferred requests for reclassification
4. Review of quadrennial reports submitted by non-
    governmental organizations in categories I and II
    consultative status with the Economic and Social Council
    Documentation
        Quadrennial reports on the activities of non-
            governmental organizations in categories I
            and II consultative status with the Economic
            and Social Council
5. Review of future activities
6. Provisional agenda and documentation for the ses-
    sion of the Committee to be held in 1989
7. Adoption of the report of the Committee

Economic and Social Council decision 1985/115

Adopted without vote

Draft by Committee on NGOs (E/1985/19); agenda item 8.

Intergovernmental organizations

Agency for Cultural and Technical Co-operation

GENERAL ASSEMBLY ACTION

Acting, without vote, on the recommendation of the Second Committee, the General Assembly adopted **resolution 40/174** on 17 December 1985, requesting an update of a 1983 report[12] of the Secretary-General.

Co-operation between the United Nations and the Agency for Cultural and Technical Co-operation

The General Assembly,

Recalling its resolution 33/18 of 10 November 1978, by which it accorded observer status to the Agency for Cultural and Technical Co-operation,

Recalling also its resolution 36/174 of 17 December 1981, in which it recognized the necessity of strengthening co-operation between the United Nations and the Agency for Cultural and Technical Co-operation, and its resolution 37/132 of 17 December 1982,

1. *Requests* the Secretary-General, in collaboration with the Secretary-General of the Agency for Cultural and Technical Co-operation, to update his report on co-operation between the United Nations and the Agency for Cultural and Technical Co-operation;

2. *Also requests* the Secretary-General to submit the updated report to the General Assembly at its forty-first session, through the Economic and Social Council at its second regular session of 1986.

General Assembly resolution 40/174

17 December 1985   Meeting 119   Adopted without vote

Approved by Second Committee (A/40/1009/Add.1) without vote, 25 November (meeting 43); 14-nation draft (A/C.2/40/L.36); agenda item 12.
Sponsors: Belgium, Benin, Canada, Comoros, France, Gabon, Lao People's Democratic Republic, Lebanon, Luxembourg, Rwanda, Senegal, Tunisia, Viet Nam, Zaire.
Meeting numbers. GA 40th session: 2nd Committee 34, 43; plenary 119.

Other organizational matters

Work programme for 1985-1986

At its 1985 organizational session (New York, 5-8 February and 22 March), the Economic and Social Council considered its draft basic programme of work for 1985-1986, submitted by the Secretary-General,[13] as well as a draft provisional agenda for its first and second regular 1985 sessions and other decisions proposed by its President on behalf of the Bureau of the Council[14] and items and reports for inclusion in its programme of work for 1986.[15]

Following consideration of these documents, the Council adopted **decision 1985/101**, without vote, on 8 February. Before its adoption, the 1985 basic work programme had been orally revised; among the revisions, a subparagraph was included by which the Council would hold, on 8 or 9 May 1985, a solemn commemorative ceremony in observance of the fortieth anniversary of victory over nazism and fascism in the Second World War, in the light of a 1984 General Assembly resolution[16] (see p. 845).

By other provisions of section I of the decision, the Council approved the basic programme and provisional agenda for its 1985 first and second regular sessions and allocated items to its sessional committees and plenary meetings. It decided to consider at its first regular session any recommendations of the Commission on Transnational Corporations concerning the report of the *Ad Hoc* Committee on the Preparations for the Public Hearings on the Activities of Transnational Corporations in South Africa and Namibia. It decided to give priority consideration at its 1985 second regular session to the immediate and longer-term aspects of the critical economic situation in Africa, to consider interregional co-operation to promote and support economic and technical co-operation among developing countries, and to review in depth the report of the UNIDO Industrial Development Board and that of the World Food Council.

In addition, the Council decided: to consider in 1985 the Secretary-General's reports on the work of the Office of the United Nations Disaster Relief Co-ordinator and on implementation of the medium- and long-term recovery and rehabilitation programme in the Sudano-Sahelian region, and thereafter to consider those reports biennially in even-numbered years, and similarly that of the Council of the United Nations University as from 1986; to review at its 1986 organizational session the periodicity of annual reports submitted by the Secretariat to the General Assembly through the Council; to request the Secretary-General, in his reports to the Assembly through the Council, to draw attention to matters requiring Council action, in particular co-ordination questions; and to direct its subsidiary bodies to act on relevant 1984 Assembly resolutions and decisions.

Except for recommendations directly addressed to it, the Council decided not to consider proposals on the reports of the Governing Council of the

United Nations Environment Programme, the Commission on Human Settlements and the Intergovernmental Committee on Science and Technology for Development; the same applied to those parts of the UNDP Governing Council report dealing with the United Nations Capital Development Fund, United Nations technical co-operation activities and the United Nations Volunteers programme.

By section II of the decision, the Council took note of a list of questions for inclusion in its 1986 work programme.

The Council held its first regular session in New York from 7 to 31 May and on 20 June, its second regular session at Geneva from 3 to 26 July, and its resumed second regular session in New York on 12 December. The First (Economic) and Second (Social) Committees and the Sessional Working Group of Governmental Experts on the Implementation of the International Covenant on Economic, Social and Cultural Rights met during the first session; and the First and Third (Programme and Co-ordination) Committees met during the second session.

Agenda of 1985 sessions

On 5 February 1985, the Economic and Social Council adopted the provisional agenda for its organizational session, which contained six items together with background information on each;[17] a Secretariat note added information on a changed venue for the 1985 session of the Economic Commission for Africa (ECA),[18] which was the subject of a separate decision (**decision 1985/109**). At the opening of its first regular session on 7 May, the Council adopted the provisional agenda for that session—listing the same 20 items approved on 8 February by **decision 1985/101**—as annotated,[19] together with the proposed plan for the organization and schedule of its work,[20] as revised. The schedule of work was further revised on 14 May.[21]

By **decision 1985/163**, adopted without vote on 31 May, the Council approved the draft provisional agenda for its second regular session—which contained the same 23 items approved by **decision 1985/101** and an additional item on elections—together with a suggested organization of work.[22] The agenda[23] as adopted on 3 July at the opening of the session was based on an annotated provisional agenda.[24]

Calendar of meetings

On 19 July, the Council's Third Committee approved the provisional calendar of conferences and meetings for 1986 and 1987,[25] as orally revised, with the exception of four entries on the 1986 calendar which were to be taken up directly in plenary meeting. Those entries concerned a reconvened special session of the Commission on

TNCs and sessions of bodies of ECA and the Economic Commission for Latin America and the Caribbean; they were subsequently approved by the Council in the light of the recommendations of the First Committee.

On 26 July, acting on the recommendation of its Third Committee, the Council adopted without vote **decision 1985/202** approving the calendar of conferences and meetings, as orally corrected, annexed to the Committee's report.[26]

Limitation of documentation

In May 1985,[27] the Secretariat reported on the state of preparedness of documentation for the first regular session of the Economic and Social Council, and in June[28] for its second regular session. The reports were submitted pursuant to 1979 Council resolutions[29] on the limitation of documentation and its circulation in all working languages six weeks in advance of Council sessions and those of its subsidiary bodies.

The reports noted that, to allow adequate time for clearances and editing, documents for the first session should have been submitted by 19 February and circulated by 26 March, and, for the second, by 17 April and circulated by 22 May. A table on the status of documentation annexed to each report showed the documents that failed to make the circulation dates; explanations for the delay were to be provided by the responsible offices.

In July, the Council took action on the question of summary records for its sessional committees and subsidiary bodies (see below).

ECONOMIC AND SOCIAL COUNCIL ACTION

Acting without vote on the recommendation of its Third Committee, the Economic and Social Council adopted **decision 1985/200**.

Summary records of sessional committees and subsidiary bodies of the Economic and Social Council

At its 52nd plenary meeting, on 26 July 1985, the Council, recalling its resolutions 1979/69 of 2 August 1979 and 1981/83 of 24 July 1981 and its decision 1983/184 of 29 July 1983, decided to maintain, for a further period of two years, from 1986, the discontinuance of summary records for its sessional committees (First (Economic) Committee, Second (Social) Committee and Third (Programme and Co-ordination) Committee) and for the following subsidiary bodies:

Commission for Social Development;
Commission on the Status of Women;
Commission on Narcotic Drugs;
Economic Commission for Europe;
Economic and Social Commission for Asia and the Pacific;
Economic Commission for Latin America and the Caribbean;
Economic Commission for Africa;
Committee on Non-Governmental Organizations;

Committee on Natural Resources;
Committee for Programme and Co-ordination;
Commission on Transnational Corporations.

Economic and Social Council decision 1985/200

Adopted without vote

Approved by Third Committee (E/1985/144) without vote, 18 July (meeting 18); draft orally proposed by Chairman, based on Secretariat note (E/1985/L.40); agenda item 23.

Financial implications
of resolutions and decisions

In July,[30] the Secretary-General submitted a summary of estimates of programme budget implications of resolutions and decisions adopted by the Economic and Social Council in 1985. The estimated costs for 1984-1985, 1986-1987 and 1988-1989, excluding conference-servicing costs, totalled $2,167,700. This figure was subject to change in the light of a review by the Assembly to determine how much of the costs might be absorbed within appropriations.

By **decision 1985/205** of 26 July, the Council took note of the Secretary-General's report.

As later approved by the General Assembly, on the recommendation of the Fifth (Administrative and Budgetary) Committee, a net addition of $214,300 was made to the 1986-1987 budget to cover several 1985 Council actions having financial implications. This amount had been approved by the Fifth Committee on 2 December 1985 by a recorded vote of 88 to 1, with 4 abstentions, based on a recommendation of ACABQ.[31] In examining the Secretary-General's report revising his initial submission for the budget as a whole,[32] ACABQ recommended that no action be taken on an amount requested ($167,400) to introduce Portuguese among the official working languages of ECA, pending clarification by the Council and ECA and consideration of the matter by the Assembly in 1986 (see Chapter VIII of this section).

The financial implications of Council resolutions and decisions requiring urgent action and supplementary needs for meetings in 1985 were to be covered by additional appropriations to be sought by the Secretary-General within the framework of the final performance report on the 1984-1985 programme budget, under the terms of a 1983 Assembly resolution[33] on unforeseen and extraordinary expenses; those arising from other Council resolutions and decisions were dealt with separately by the Fifth Committee when it considered the financial implications of Assembly resolutions on the same topics. Conference-servicing costs were also dealt with separately (see ADMINISTRATIVE AND BUDGETARY QUESTIONS, Chapter IV).

Report for 1985

The work of the Economic and Social Council at its organizational session and two regular ses-

sions in 1985 was summarized in its annual report to the General Assembly.[34] Parts of the report were considered by the plenary Assembly, others by the Second, Third (Social, Humanitarian and Cultural), Fourth, Fifth and Sixth (Legal) Committees.

In December, the Assembly adopted without vote four decisions by which it took note of the chapters of the report, as follows: on 11 December, chapter I, following consideration of the related Sixth Committee report[35] (**decision 40/423**); on 17 December, chapters I, II, III (sections E to G, J and K), IV, VI, VIII and IX (sects. A, B, D and G to K), following consideration of the relevant Second Committee report[36] (**decision 40/431**); and on 18 December, chapters I, II, III (sects. F and H), VI (sect. E), VIII and IX (sects. A and B) (**decision 40/458**), considered in plenary meetings, and chapters I, IV (sects. D, G and J), V (sect. A), VI (sects. C, D and F), VII, VIII and IX (sects. J and L), as recommended by the Fifth Committee[37] (**decision 40/462**).

REFERENCES

[1]YUN 1984, p. 979, ESC res. 1984/62, 26 July 1984. [2]*Ibid.,* p. 978. [3]A/40/284-E/1985/71. [4]YUN 1984, p. 975, ESC res. 1984/61 B, 26 July 1984. [5]E/1985/19 & Corr.1. [6]E/1985/73. [7]E/1985/132. [8]E/C.2/1985/2 & Add.1,2. [9]E/C.2/1985/NGO/1. [10]E/1985/NGO/1-3. [11]E/1985/INF/7. [12]YUN 1983, p. 1002. [13]E/1985/1. [14]E/1985/L.19. [15]E/1985/1/Add.1. [16]YUN 1984, p. 793, GA res. 39/114, 14 Dec. 1984. [17]E/1985/2. [18]E/1985/L.13. [19]E/1985/30 & Corr.1. [20]E/1985/L.22. [21]E/1985/L.24/Rev.1. [22]E/1985/L.34. [23]E/1985/134. [24]E/1985/100. [25]E/1985/L.35 & Corr.1. [26]E/1985/144. [27]E/1985/L.20/Rev.1. [28]E/1985/L.36. [29]YUN 1979, pp. 1217 & 1218, ESC res. 1979/1 & 1979/69, 9 Feb. & 2 Aug. 1979. [30]E/1985/158. [31]A/40/7/Add.5. [32]A/C.5/40/13 & Corr.1 & Add.1. [33]YUN 1983, p. 1153, GA res. 38/237, 20 Dec. 1983. [34]A/40/3/Rev.1. [35]A/40/997. [36]A/40/1009. [37]A/40/1068.

PUBLICATIONS

Index to Proceedings of the Economic and Social Council, Organizational Session, First Regular Session, Second Regular Session—1985 (ST/LIB/SER.B/E.62), Sales No. E.86.I.13. *Resolutions and Decisions of the Economic and Social Council, 1985:* organizational session (New York, 5-8 February and 22 March); first regular session (New York, 7-31 May and 20 June); second regular session (Geneva, 3-26 July); resumed second regular session (New York, 12 December), E/1985/85 & Add.1,2.

Other institutional arrangements

In 1985, the General Assembly for the first time considered and approved a biennial programme of work for the Second Committee, beginning with the biennium 1986-1987, to improve complementarity between the work of the Assembly and that of the Economic and Social Council.

Work programme of the Second Committee

In 1985, a draft biennial programme of work for 1986-1987 for the General Assembly's Second Committee[1] was before that Committee for consideration and approval. Submitted pursuant to a 1984 Assembly resolution requesting that such a submission be made each year,[2] the proposed work programme took into account the draft resolutions that had been approved or were pending action by the Second Committee during 1985.

The Committee Secretary, in addition to making several oral revisions to the draft to take account of decisions approved by the Committee, noted that later revisions would be made to take account also of any Committee action at the Assembly's resumed session in 1986. As to reports not envisaged in the draft programmes of either the Committee or the Economic and Social Council but requested in a draft proposal, the Secretariat would systematically inform Committee members of such cases to allow them to make an exception if they so desired. It would follow the same procedure with regard to proposals formulated by committees of the Assembly and the Council. Before a decision was taken on a draft resolution requesting a report, the Secretariat would also indicate whether that report could be completed in time for the session concerned.

GENERAL ASSEMBLY ACTION

Acting without vote on the recommendation of the Second Committee,[3] the General Assembly on 17 December 1985 adopted **decision 40/436**. By that decision, the Assembly approved the Committee's biennial programme of work, annexed to the decision, subject to Second Committee decisions to be adopted at the Assembly's resumed session in 1986 on unfinished work under agenda item 84, entitled "Development and international economic co-operation". The text had been orally proposed by the Second Committee Chairman, as orally amended by Bangladesh to include mention of resumed session decisions.

Also, in section II of **resolution 40/243,** the Assembly urged intergovernmental bodies reporting to the Second Committee that had not yet adjusted their meeting cycles to conform to that Committee's biennial programme of work to do so as soon as possible.

REFERENCES

(1)A/C.2/40/L.123. (2)YUN 1984, p. 986, GA res. 39/217, 18 Dec. 1984. (3)A/40/1009/Add.2.

Trusteeship and decolonization

General questions relating to colonial countries

In 1985, the General Assembly's Special Committee on the Situation with regard to the Implementation of the Declaration on the Granting of Independence to Colonial Countries and Peoples (Committee on colonial countries) observed the twenty-fifth anniversary of the Assembly's adoption of the Declaration in 1960 by holding an extraordinary plenary session in Tunisia in May, preceded by two regional seminars. The Assembly itself held a special commemorative meeting in October.

In the year which also marked the fortieth anniversary of the founding of the United Nations—whose membership grew from 51 to 159 during that period—the Secretary-General stated in his annual report on the work of the Organization that the international community witnessed for the first time in history a world of independent sovereign States and a virtually universal world body. He told the Committee on colonial countries that the emergence, since the Declaration was adopted, of more than 80 million people from a dependent to a sovereign status was a historic achievement, in which the United Nations had played a central role.

In addition to the general question of decolonization, the Committee on colonial countries examined situations in the following individual Territories: Trust Territory of the Pacific Islands (see next chapter); Namibia (see Chapter III of this section); American Samoa, Anguilla, Bermuda, British Virgin Islands, Cayman Islands, East Timor, Falkland Islands (Malvinas), Gibraltar, Guam, Montserrat, Pitcairn Islands, St. Helena, Tokelau, Turks and Caicos Islands, United States Virgin Islands, Western Sahara (see Chapter IV of this section).

In July, the Economic and Social Council reaffirmed the need for assistance by the United Nations system to the peoples of the colonial Territories and their national liberation movements (resolution 1985/59).

In December, the General Assembly, acting on recommendations by the Committee on colonial countries, again called on Member States to assist peoples under colonial rule in their struggle towards self-determination and independence (resolution 40/56), called on all States to terminate any investment in Namibia or loans to South Africa (40/52), requested the United Nations system to withhold from South Africa any form of co-operation and assistance (40/53) and condemned all military activities and arrangements by colonial Powers in Territories under their administration that were detrimental to the rights and interests of the colonial peoples concerned (decision 40/415). The Assembly also requested the Committee to continue to seek suitable means for the immediate and full implementation of the Declaration (40/57), and called for wider dissemination of information on decolonization (40/58). As regards Non-Self-Governing Territories (NSGTs), the Assembly requested the administering Powers to transmit information as prescribed in the United Nations Charter as well as information on political and constitutional developments in the Territories concerned (resolution 40/51). States were again invited to make offers of study and training facilities to the inhabitants of those Territories (40/55).

Topics related to this chapter. Africa: South Africa and *apartheid*. Namibia. Other colonial Territories.

The 1960 Declaration on colonial countries

In 1985, the international community observed the twenty-fifth anniversary of the adoption by the General Assembly of the 1960 Declaration on the Granting of Independence to Colonial Countries and Peoples.[1]

The right of peoples to self-determination was reaffirmed in a number of communications in 1985, including a note verbale of 11 March from Yemen[2] transmitting the final communiqué and resolutions adopted at the Fifteenth Islamic Conference of Foreign Ministers (Sanaa, 18-22 December 1984), and a 1 May letter from Indonesia[3] forwarding the Declaration of the Commemorative Meeting in Observance of the Thirtieth Anniversary of the Asian-African Conference (Bandung, 24 and 25 April 1985).

Committee on colonial countries

The Committee on colonial countries, in addition to holding an extraordinary plenary session in Tunisia from 13 to 17 May (see below), met at United Nations Headquarters on 21 February and from 1 to 15 August.[4]

Its Sub-Committee on Petitions, Information and Assistance held 21 meetings as well as a number of informal meetings, between 25 February and 2 August; the Sub-Committee on Small Territories held 20 meetings and additional unofficial meetings, between 20 March and 25 June. Based on their recommendations, the Committee took action on the implementation of the Declaration by international organizations, on foreign interests and military bases impeding implementation of the Declaration in NSGTs, on dissemination of information on decolonization and on reports on the Territories supplied by their administering Powers and by visiting missions of the Committee (see Chapter IV of this section).

By a letter dated 9 January 1985 addressed to the President of the General Assembly,[5] Australia stated that the Committee's work had been reduced considerably because of the success of the decolonization process and, given its other commitments within the United Nations system, it had decided to withdraw from the Committee membership (see APPENDIX III).

Twenty-fifth anniversary (1985)

Action by the Committee on colonial countries. In 1985, the Committee on colonial countries observed the twenty-fifth anniversary of the adoption of the 1960 General Assembly Declaration on the Granting of Independence to Colonial Countries and Peoples[1] by holding two regional seminars and an extraordinary plenary session away from Headquarters, in accordance with the programme of activities adopted by the Assembly in 1984.[6]

The seminar for the Asia/Pacific region (Port Moresby, Papua New Guinea, 4-7 March)[7] focused on the implementation of the Declaration with respect to the remaining Territories with which the Committee was concerned and the dissemination of information on decolonization. It was attended by the following Committee members: Chile, Cuba, Czechoslovakia, Fiji, Sweden, the Syrian Arab Republic, Tunisia, the USSR, the United Republic of Tanzania and Yugoslavia. The seminar for the Latin American region (Havana, Cuba, 8-10 April)[8] examined activities that might be impeding the implementation of the Declaration, such as those of foreign economic and other interests, and military activities and arrangements by colonial Powers in Territories under their administration. Committee members attending the seminar were Afghanistan, Bulgaria, China, the Congo, Cuba, India, Indonesia, the Ivory Coast, Sweden, Trinidad and Tobago, Tunisia and Venezuela. Other participants in the seminars included some 35 representatives of non-governmental and intergovernmental organizations.

The Committee, at its extraordinary plenary session at Tunis, Tunisia (13-17 May), held a general debate, discussed and adopted a consensus decision on the question of Namibia, and adopted the conclusions and recommendations of the two regional seminars.

On 15 August, the Committee recommended to the Assembly the adoption of a resolution on the twenty-fifth anniversary of the Declaration.

Related activities. In pursuance of a 1984 Assembly request,[9] the United Nations Department of Public Information (DPI) undertook a wide range of activities, including organizing a media encounter at Tunis on 10 and 11 May, preceding the extraordinary session, and a journalists' encounter at United Nations Headquarters on 30 August.

In response to a 1984 Assembly resolution,[6] arrangements were made by the United Nations Postal Administration for the slogan cancellation, "Decolonization, Freedom, Independence," marking the twenty-fifth anniversary of the Declaration, to be put into effect from 15 October 1985 until 14 January 1986.

Communications. A number of messages were received by the Chairman of the Committee on colonial countries, or by the Secretary-General, on the occasion of the twenty-fifth anniversary.

The Chairman received messages from Afghanistan, India, New Zealand, Sweden and Viet Nam.[10] Poland[11] transmitted to the Committee the text of a 5 July statement delivered by the group of Eastern European countries in the Economic and Social Council.

In an October note with a later addendum,[12] the Secretary-General transmitted to the Assembly messages received from China, Democratic Kampuchea, the German Democratic Republic, Mongolia, Nicaragua, Tunisia, Turkey, the USSR and Yugoslavia, and from the Organization of the Islamic Conference. A message was also received from the General Secretary of the Central Committee of the Communist Party of the USSR[13] to participants in the Assembly's commemorative meeting in October (see below). Canada transmitted the text of a resolution, adopted by the seventy-fourth Inter-Parliamentary Conference (Ottawa, 2-7 September),[14] on the contribution of parliaments towards terminating and consolidating the work of decolonization started 40 years earlier by the United Nations.

The Conference of Foreign Ministers of Non-Aligned Countries (Luanda, Angola, 4-7 September)[15] recalled the role the non-aligned movement had played in the struggle against colonialism; noted that most of the newly independent countries in recent decades had opted to join the movement; and demanded the immediate implementation of the Declaration and other relevant United Nations resolutions in the cases of the Falkland Islands (Malvinas), Micronesia, Namibia, New Caledonia, Puerto Rico, and other Territories.

GENERAL ASSEMBLY ACTION

On 16 October, the General Assembly held a special meeting to mark the twenty-fifth anniversary of the adoption of the Declaration. Statements were made at the meeting by the Assembly President, the Secretary-General, the Chairman of the Committee on colonial countries, the Chairman of the Special Committee against *Apartheid*, the Acting President of the United Nations Council for Namibia and the chairmen of the regional groups of Member States at the United Nations.

The Assembly President said the Committee's role as a focal point of the international community in support of the peoples under colonial rule had facilitated the emergence of independent States. The Secretary-General stated that, since the adoption of the Declaration in 1960, some 59 former colonial Territories with more than 80 million inhabitants had attained independence and joined the United Nations as sovereign Member States; the Organization had benefited from the principle of universality, from which flowed much of the authority for collective action. The Chairman of the Committee on colonial countries added that some 3 million people remained under colonial rule, over one third of whom lived in Namibia under repression. The Chairman of the Special Committee against *Apartheid* said the Namibia situation was a classic colonial problem, and attempts to portray it in any other context should be repudiated. The Acting President of the Council for Namibia, asserting that the adoption of the Declaration was a historic step in the development of international law with regard to self-determination, called for rededication of energy to completing the unfinished task, focusing on Namibia.

On 2 December 1985, the General Assembly adopted by recorded vote **resolution 40/56**, proposed by the Committee on colonial countries.

Twenty-fifth anniversary of the Declaration on the Granting of Independence to Colonial Countries and Peoples

The General Assembly,

Recalling the Declaration on the Granting of Independence to Colonial Countries and Peoples, contained in its resolution 1514(XV) of 14 December 1960,

Having held, in the year of the fortieth anniversary of the United Nations, a special plenary meeting in observance of the twenty-fifth anniversary of the Declaration on the Granting of Independence to Colonial Countries and Peoples,

Recalling the provisions of the Charter of the United Nations, in which the peoples of the world proclaimed their determination to reaffirm faith in fundamental human rights, in the dignity and worth of the human person and in the equal rights of men and women and of nations large and small and to promote social progress and better standards of life in larger freedom,

Recalling also the relevant provisions of the Declaration on Principles of International Law concerning Friendly Relations and Co-operation among States in accordance with the Charter of the United Nations,

Recalling its resolutions 2621(XXV) of 12 October 1970, containing the programme of action for the full implementation of the Declaration on the Granting of Independence to Colonial Countries and Peoples, and 35/118 of 11 December 1980, the annex to which contains the Plan of Action for the Full Implementation of the Declaration,

Considering that the process of national liberation is irresistible and irreversible, and recalling that the Declaration solemnly proclaimed the necessity speedily and unconditionally to put an end to colonialism in all its forms and manifestations,

Recognizing the significant and commendable role played by the United Nations, since its very inception, in the field of decolonization and noting the emergence, during this period, of about one hundred States into sovereign existence,

Noting with satisfaction, in particular, that during the past twenty-five years a large number of former colonial Territories have achieved independence, mainly through the courageous liberation struggle carried out by the peoples of those countries, led by their national liberation movements, and that many former Trust and Non-Self-Governing Territories have exercised their right to self-determination and independence in accordance with the Declaration,

Noting also with satisfaction the important contribution made by the Special Committee on the Situation with regard to the Implementation of the Declaration on the Granting of Independence to Colonial Countries and Peoples in furthering the aims and objectives of the Declaration with a view to the liberation of peoples from colonial rule,

Noting further with satisfaction the active and important role being played by former colonial Territories, as States Members of the United Nations and members of the other organizations of the United Nations system in the realization of the purposes and principles of the Charter, the preservation of international peace and security, decolonization and the promotion of human progress, as well as the profound impact thereof on contemporary international relations,

Conscious of the fact that the Declaration has played an important role in assisting the peoples under colonial rule and will continue to serve as an inspiration in their efforts to achieve self-determination and independence in accordance with the Charter and in mobilizing world public opinion for the complete elimination of colonialism in all its forms and manifestations,

Deeply concerned at the fact that, twenty-five years after the adoption of the Declaration, colonialism in the world has not yet been totally eradicated, particularly in Namibia,

Strongly condemning the continuing illegal occupation of Namibia and the colonial oppression of its people by the racist régime of Pretoria, which completely disregards the inalienable right of the people of Namibia to self-determination and independence,

Reaffirming that all peoples have the right to self-determination and independence and that the subjection of peoples to colonial domination constitutes a denial of fundamental human rights and is a serious impediment to the maintenance of international peace and security and the development of peaceful relations among nations,

Increasingly aware of the importance of economic, social and cultural development and self-reliance of colonial countries and peoples for the attainment and consolidation of genuine independence,

Convinced that the total eradication of racial discrimination, *apartheid* and violations of the basic human rights of the peoples in the remaining colonial Territories, particularly in Namibia, will be achieved peacefully and most expeditiously by the faithful and complete implementation of the Declaration,

Determined to take effective measures leading to the complete and unconditional elimination of colonialism in all its forms and manifestations without further delay,

1. *Reaffirms* the inalienable right of all peoples under colonial rule to self-determination and independence in accordance with the Declaration on the Granting of Independence to Colonial Countries and Peoples, contained in General Assembly resolution 1514(XV);

2. *Declares* that the continuation of colonialism in all its forms and manifestations, including racism and *apartheid*, is incompatible with the Charter of the United Nations, the Declaration and the principles of international law;

3. *Expresses its conviction* that the twenty-fifth anniversary of the Declaration should provide an opportunity for Member States to rededicate themselves to the principles and objectives enunciated in that document and for concerted efforts to be made to remove the last vestiges of colonialism in all regions of the world;

4. *Strongly condemns* South Africa's continued illegal occupation of Namibia, its defiance of United Nations resolutions, its brutal repression of the Namibian people, its aggressive activities and acts of destabilization against neighbouring independent African States and its policies of *apartheid*, as well as its acquisition of nuclear-weapon capability, which constitute a threat to international peace and security;

5. *Calls upon* Member States, in particular colonial Powers, to take effective steps with a view to the complete, unconditional and speedy eradication of colonialism in all its forms and manifestations and to the faithful and strict observance of the relevant provisions of the Charter, the Declaration on the Granting of Independence to Colonial Countries and Peoples and the Universal Declaration of Human Rights, as well as other relevant resolutions and decisions of the General Assembly and those of the Security Council;

6. *Urges* Member States to do their utmost to promote, in the United Nations and the specialized agencies and other organizations of the United Nations system, effective measures for the full and speedy implementation of the Declaration in all colonial Territories to which the Declaration applies;

7. *Calls upon* Member States to render, as a matter of urgency, all moral and material assistance to the peoples under colonial rule in their struggle to exercise their right to self-determination and independence, in accordance with the Charter and the Declaration;

8. *Urges* the administering Powers and other Member States to ensure that the activities of foreign economic and other interests in colonial Territories do not run counter to the interests of the inhabitants of those Territories and do not impede the implementation of the Declaration;

9. *Requests* Member States to take legislative, administrative or other measures in respect of their nationals and the bodies corporate under their jurisdiction that illegally own and operate enterprises, including transnational corporations, in the international Territory of Namibia in order to put an end to such operations;

10. *Urges* Member States to discontinue all economic, financial, trade and other relations with the racist minority régime of South Africa in respect of Namibia and to refrain from entering into any relations with South Africa which may lend legitimacy or support to its continued illegal occupation of that Territory;

11. *Requests* Member States, as well as the organizations of the United Nations system, to ensure that the permanent sovereignty of the colonial Territories over their natural resources is fully respected and safeguarded;

12. *Reaffirms* that all administering Powers are obliged, under the Charter and in accordance with the Declaration, to create economic, social and other conditions in the Territories under their administration which will enable those Territories to achieve genuine independence and economic self-reliance;

13. *Requests* the administering Powers concerned to adopt the necessary measures to discourage or prevent any systematic influx of immigrants and settlers into the Territories under their administration which might disrupt the demographic composition of those Territories and prevent the genuine exercise of the right to self-determination and independence by their peoples, and to avoid any forced displacement, complete or partial, of the population of colonial Territories;

14. *Further requests* the administering Powers to preserve the cultural identity, as well as the national unity, of the Territories under their administration and to encourage the full development of the indigenous culture, with a view to facilitating the unfettered exercise of the right to self-determination and independence by the peoples of those Territories;

15. *Reaffirms its strong conviction* that the presence of all kinds of military bases and installations in colonial Territories could constitute a major obstacle to the implementation of the Declaration and that it is the responsibility of the administering Powers concerned to ensure that the existence of such bases and installations does

not hinder the peoples of the Territories from exercising their right to self-determination and independence in conformity with the purposes and principles of the Charter and the Declaration;

16. *Calls upon* the administering Powers concerned to continue to take all necessary measures not to involve those Territories in any offensive acts or interference against other States and to comply fully with the purposes and principles of the Charter, the Declaration and the resolutions and decisions of the United Nations relating to military activities and arrangements by colonial Powers in the Territories under their administration;

17. *Requests* Member States, in particular the administering Powers, to adopt appropriate measures to prevent the recruitment, financing, training and transit of mercenaries in their territories for use against the national liberation movements struggling for freedom and independence from the yoke of colonialism, racism and *apartheid;*

18. *Considers* it incumbent upon the United Nations to continue to play an active role in the process of decolonization and to intensify its efforts for the widest possible dissemination of information on decolonization, with a view to the further mobilization of international public opinion in support of complete decolonization;

19. *Urges* Member States to ensure the full and speedy implementation of the Declaration contained in General Assembly resolution 1514(XV) and other relevant resolutions of the United Nations;

20. *Invites* the Security Council to continue to give special attention to the situation in and around Namibia and to consider imposing mandatory sanctions against South Africa under Chapter VII of the Charter;

21. *Requests* the specialized agencies and other organizations of the United Nations system to render, or continue to render, within their respective spheres of competence, all possible moral and material assistance to the peoples of the colonial Territories and to their national liberation movements, to take measures to withhold from the *apartheid* régime of South Africa any form of collaboration or assistance in the financial, economic and technical fields and to discontinue all support to that régime until the people of Namibia have exercised their right to self-determination and independence in a united Namibia and until *apartheid* has been eradicated and a non-racial, united and democratic State based on the will of all South African people has been established in accordance with the relevant resolutions and decisions of the General Assembly and the Security Council;

22. *Invites* non-governmental organizations having a special interest in the field of decolonization to intensify their activities in co-operation with the United Nations;

23. *Requests* the Special Committee on the Situation with regard to the Implementation of the Declaration on the Granting of Independence to Colonial Countries and Peoples to continue to examine the full compliance of all States with resolution 1514(XV) and other relevant resolutions on the question of decolonization, to seek the most suitable ways for the speedy and total application of the Declaration to all Territories to which it applies and to propose to the General Assembly specific measures for the complete implementation of the Declaration in the remaining colonial Territories;

24. *Invites* all States to co-operate fully with the Special Committee in the complete fulfilment of its mandate.

General Assembly resolution 40/56

2 December 1985   Meeting 99   139-0-13 (recorded vote)

Draft by Committee on colonial countries (A/40/23); agenda item 18.
Meeting numbers. GA 40th session: plenary 36, 96, 97, 99.

Recorded vote in Assembly as follows:

In favour: Afghanistan, Albania, Algeria, Angola, Antigua and Barbuda, Argentina, Australia, Austria, Bahamas, Bahrain, Bangladesh, Barbados, Benin, Bhutan, Bolivia, Botswana, Brazil, Brunei Darussalam, Bulgaria, Burkina Faso, Burma, Burundi, Byelorussian SSR, Cameroon, Cape Verde, Central African Republic, Chad, Chile, China, Colombia, Comoros, Congo, Costa Rica, Cuba, Cyprus, Czechoslovakia, Democratic Kampuchea, Democratic Yemen, Denmark, Djibouti, Dominican Republic, Ecuador, Egypt, El Salvador, Equatorial Guinea, Ethiopia, Fiji, Finland, Gabon, Gambia, German Democratic Republic, Ghana, Greece, Guatemala, Guinea, Guinea-Bissau, Guyana, Haiti, Honduras, Hungary, Iceland, India, Indonesia, Iran, Iraq, Ireland, Ivory Coast, Jamaica, Jordan, Kenya, Kuwait, Lao People's Democratic Republic, Lebanon, Lesotho, Liberia, Libyan Arab Jamahiriya, Madagascar, Malaysia, Maldives, Mali, Malta, Mauritania, Mauritius, Mexico, Mongolia, Morocco, Mozambique, Nepal, New Zealand, Nicaragua, Niger, Nigeria, Norway, Oman, Pakistan, Panama, Papua New Guinea, Peru, Philippines, Poland, Qatar, Romania, Rwanda, Saint Lucia, Samoa, Sao Tome and Principe, Saudi Arabia, Senegal, Seychelles, Sierra Leone, Singapore, Solomon Islands, Somalia, Spain, Sri Lanka, Sudan, Suriname, Swaziland, Sweden, Syrian Arab Republic, Thailand, Togo, Trinidad and Tobago, Tunisia, Turkey, Uganda, Ukrainian SSR, USSR, United Arab Emirates, United Republic of Tanzania, Uruguay, Vanuatu, Venezuela, Viet Nam, Yemen, Yugoslavia, Zaire, Zambia, Zimbabwe.

Against: None.

Abstaining: Belgium, Canada, France, Germany, Federal Republic of, Israel, Italy, Japan, Luxembourg, Malawi, Netherlands, Portugal, United Kingdom, United States.

In explanation of vote, the Netherlands, the United Kingdom and the United States asserted that the resolution clung to an outdated presumption that imperialism and colonial domination remained the predominant reality. The United Kingdom considered the resolution as being used to trumpet tendentious propositions about colonialism, and the United States saw it as serving the interests of those who sought to feed old resentments. The Netherlands and the United Kingdom viewed the text as almost equating colonialism with racial discrimination and human rights violations. Along with the Netherlands, which felt that the resolution was grating in its comments on the role played by the colonial Powers, the United States believed that the international community and the peoples of the Territories themselves deserved a large share of the credit for their achievements.

The Netherlands said the text suggested that independence was the only possible outcome of the exercise of the right to self-determination and that the situation in South Africa was colonial in nature. For the United Kingdom, the resolution also deflected attention from other, more pressing, matters, such as the military occupation of a small non-aligned country or the application of self-determination to Namibia. In the view of the United States, some provisions encouraged politicization of the United Nations specialized agencies, asserted principles of sovereignty over resources in Territories contrary to internationally accepted principles and called for action in southern Africa under the Charter contrary to United States policy.

Australia, Austria, Canada, Finland (on behalf of the five Nordic countries) and Portugal had reservations about certain elements. Japan expressed reservations on paragraphs 20 and 21. Italy felt that the commemorative character of the text would have been better served by avoiding some elements, such as those in paragraphs 10, 19, 20 and 21.

In related action, the Assembly, by **resolution 40/164 A**, drew attention to the conclusions and recommendations adopted by the Committee on colonial countries at its Tunis session and to the need for intensified public-information dissemination activities.

Implementation of the Declaration

GENERAL ASSEMBLY ACTION

On 2 December 1985, the General Assembly again called for the implementation of its 1960 Declaration when it adopted by recorded vote **resolution 40/57**.

Implementation of the Declaration on the Granting of Independence to Colonial Countries and Peoples

The General Assembly,

Having examined the report of the Special Committee on the Situation with regard to the Implementation of the Declaration on the Granting of Independence to Colonial Countries and Peoples,

Recalling its resolutions 1514(XV) of 14 December 1960, containing the Declaration on the Granting of Independence to Colonial Countries and Peoples, 2621(XXV) of 12 October 1970, containing the programme of action for the full implementation of the Declaration, and 35/118 of 11 December 1980, the annex to which contains the Plan of Action for the Full Implementation of the Declaration,

Recalling all its previous resolutions concerning the implementation of the Declaration, in particular resolution 39/91 of 14 December 1984, as well as the relevant resolutions of the Security Council,

Having adopted resolution 40/56 of 2 December 1985 on the twenty-fifth anniversary of the Declaration on the Granting of Independence to Colonial Countries and Peoples,

Reiterating its conviction that the total eradication of racial discrimination, *apartheid* and violations of the basic human rights of the peoples of colonial Territories will be achieved most expeditiously by the faithful and complete implementation of the Declaration, particularly in Namibia, and by the speediest possible complete elimination of the presence of the illegal occupying régime therefrom,

Recalling the consensus on Namibia, adopted by the Special Committee at its extraordinary session held at Tunis from 13 to 17 May 1985 and the relevant provisions of the Declaration and Programme of Action contained in the Final Document adopted by the United Nations Council for Namibia at its extraordinary plenary meetings held at Vienna from 3 to 7 June 1985,

Condemning the continued colonialist and racist repression of millions of Africans, particularly in Namibia, by the Government of South Africa through its persistent, illegal occupation of the international Territory and its intransigent attitude towards all efforts being made to bring about an internationally acceptable solution to the situation obtaining in the Territory,

Deeply conscious of the urgent need to take all necessary measures to eliminate forthwith the last vestiges of colonialism, particularly in respect of Namibia where desperate attempts by South Africa to perpetuate its illegal occupation have brought untold suffering and bloodshed to the people,

Strongly condemning the policies of those States which, in defiance of the relevant resolutions of the United Nations, have continued to collaborate with the Government of South Africa in its domination of the people of Namibia,

Conscious that the success of the national liberation struggle and the resultant international situation have provided the international community with a unique opportunity to make a decisive contribution towards the total elimination of colonialism in all its forms and manifestations in Africa,

Noting with satisfaction the work accomplished by the Special Committee with a view to securing the effective and complete implementation of the Declaration and the other relevant resolutions of the United Nations,

Noting also with satisfaction the co-operation and active participation of the administering Powers concerned in the relevant work of the Special Committee, as well as the continued readiness of the Governments concerned to receive United Nations visiting missions in the Territories under their administration,

Keenly aware of the pressing need of the newly independent and emerging States for assistance from the United Nations and its system of organizations in the economic, social and other fields,

1. *Reaffirms* its resolution 1514(XV) and all other resolutions on decolonization and calls upon the administering Powers, in accordance with those resolutions, to take all necessary steps to enable the dependent peoples of the Territories concerned to exercise fully and without further delay their inalienable right to self-determination and independence;

2. *Affirms once again* that the continuation of colonialism in all its forms and manifestations—including racism, *apartheid*, those activities of foreign economic and other interests contrary to the Charter of the United Nations and the Declaration on the Granting of Independence to Colonial Countries and Peoples, as well as the violations of the right to self-determination and basic human rights of the peoples of colonial Territories and continuous policies and practices to suppress legitimate national liberation movements—is incompatible with the Charter, the Universal Declaration of Human Rights and the Declaration on the Granting of Independence to Colonial Countries and Peoples and poses a serious threat to international peace and security;

3. *Reaffirms its determination* to take all necessary steps with a view to the complete and speedy eradication of colonialism and to the faithful and strict observance by all States of the relevant provisions of the Charter, the Declaration on the Granting of Independence to Colonial Countries and Peoples and the guiding principles of the Universal Declaration of Human Rights;

4. *Affirms once again* its recognition of the legitimacy of the struggle of the peoples under colonial and alien

domination to exercise their right to self-determination and independence by all the necessary means at their disposal;

5. *Approves* the report of the Special Committee on the Situation with regard to the Implementation of the Declaration on the Granting of Independence to Colonial Countries and Peoples covering its work during 1985, including the programme of work envisaged for 1986;

6. *Calls upon* all States, in particular the administering Powers, as well as the specialized agencies and other organizations of the United Nations system within their respective spheres of competence, to give effect to the recommendations contained in the report of the Special Committee for the speedy implementation of the Declaration contained in General Assembly resolution 1514(XV) and other relevant resolutions of the United Nations;

7. *Condemns* the continuing activities of foreign economic and other interests which are impeding the implementation of the Declaration with respect to the colonial Territories, particularly Namibia;

8. *Strongly condemns* all collaboration, particularly in the nuclear and military fields, with the Government of South Africa and calls upon the States concerned to cease forthwith all such collaboration;

9. *Requests* all States, directly and through their action in the specialized agencies and other organizations of the United Nations system, to withhold assistance of any kind from the Government of South Africa until the inalienable right of the people of Namibia to self-determination and independence within a united and integrated Namibia, including Walvis Bay, has been restored, and to refrain from taking any action which might imply recognition of the legitimacy of the illegal occupation of Namibia by that régime;

10. *Calls upon* the colonial Powers to withdraw immediately and unconditionally their military bases and installations from colonial Territories, to refrain from establishing new ones and not to involve those Territories in any offensive acts or interference against other States;

11. *Urges* all States, directly and through their action in the specialized agencies and other organizations of the United Nations system, to provide all moral and material assistance to the oppressed people of Namibia and, in respect of the other Territories, requests the administering Powers, in consultation with the Governments of the Territories under their administration, to take steps to enlist and make effective use of all possible assistance, on both a bilateral and a multilateral basis, in the strengthening of the economies of those Territories;

12. *Requests* the Special Committee to continue to seek suitable means for the immediate and full implementation of General Assembly resolution 1514(XV) in all Territories that have not yet attained independence and, in particular:

(*a*) To formulate specific proposals for the elimination of the remaining manifestations of colonialism and to report thereon to the General Assembly at its forty-first session;

(*b*) To make concrete suggestions which could assist the Security Council in considering appropriate measures under the Charter with regard to developments in colonial Territories that are likely to threaten international peace and security;

(*c*) To continue to examine the compliance of Member States with resolution 1514(XV) and other relevant resolutions on decolonization, particularly those relating to Namibia;

(*d*) To continue to pay special attention to the small Territories, in particular through the dispatch of visiting missions to those Territories whenever the Special Committee deems it appropriate, and to recommend to the General Assembly the most suitable steps to be taken to enable the populations of those Territories to exercise their right to self-determination and independence;

(*e*) To take all necessary steps to enlist world-wide support among Governments, as well as national and international organizations having a special interest in decolonization, for the achievement of the objectives of the Declaration and the implementation of the relevant resolutions of the United Nations, particularly as concerns the oppressed people of Namibia;

13. *Calls upon* the administering Powers to continue to co-operate with the Special Committee in the discharge of its mandate and, in particular, to permit the access of visiting missions to the Territories to secure first-hand information and ascertain the wishes and aspirations of their inhabitants;

14. *Requests* the Secretary-General and the specialized agencies and other organizations of the United Nations system to provide or continue to provide to the newly independent and emerging States all possible assistance in the economic, social and other fields;

15. *Requests* the Secretary-General to provide the Special Committee with the facilities and services required for the implementation of the present resolution, as well as of the various resolutions and decisions on decolonization adopted by the General Assembly and the Special Committee.

General Assembly resolution 40/57

2 December 1985   Meeting 99   141-3-7 (recorded vote)

23-nation draft (A/40/L.21 & Add.1); agenda item 18.
Sponsors: Afghanistan, Algeria, Byelorussian SSR, Congo, Cuba, Cyprus, Czechoslovakia, Ethiopia, India, Lao People's Democratic Republic, Madagascar, Mongolia, Nicaragua, Papua New Guinea, Sierra Leone, Syrian Arab Republic, Trinidad and Tobago, Tunisia, Ukrainian SSR, United Republic of Tanzania, Venezuela, Viet Nam, Yugoslavia.
Financial implications. 5th Committee, A/40/955; S-G, A/C.5/40/64.
Meeting numbers. GA 40th session: 5th Committee 50; plenary 36, 96, 97, 99.
Recorded vote in Assembly as follows:

In favour: Afghanistan, Albania, Algeria, Angola, Antigua and Barbuda, Argentina, Australia, Austria, Bahamas, Bahrain, Bangladesh, Barbados, Benin, Bhutan, Bolivia, Botswana, Brazil, Brunei Darussalam, Bulgaria, Burkina Faso, Burma, Burundi, Byelorussian SSR, Cameroon, Cape Verde, Central African Republic, Chad, Chile, China, Colombia, Comoros, Congo, Costa Rica, Cuba, Cyprus, Czechoslovakia, Democratic Kampuchea, Democratic Yemen, Denmark, Djibouti, Ecuador, Egypt, El Salvador, Equatorial Guinea, Ethiopia, Fiji, Finland, Gabon, Gambia, German Democratic Republic, Ghana, Greece, Guatemala, Guinea, Guinea-Bissau, Guyana, Haiti, Honduras, Hungary, Iceland, India, Indonesia, Iran, Iraq, Ireland, Ivory Coast, Jamaica, Japan, Jordan, Kenya, Kuwait, Lao People's Democratic Republic, Lebanon, Lesotho, Liberia, Libyan Arab Jamahiriya, Madagascar, Malaysia, Maldives, Mali, Malta, Mauritania, Mauritius, Mexico, Mongolia, Morocco, Mozambique, Nepal, Netherlands, New Zealand, Nicaragua, Niger, Nigeria, Norway, Oman, Pakistan, Panama, Papua New Guinea, Peru, Philippines, Poland, Portugal, Qatar, Romania, Rwanda, Saint Lucia, Samoa, Sao Tome and Principe, Saudi Arabia, Senegal, Seychelles, Sierra Leone, Singapore, Solomon Islands, Somalia, Spain, Sri Lanka, Sudan, Suriname, Swaziland, Sweden, Syrian Arab Republic, Thailand, Togo, Trinidad and Tobago, Tunisia, Turkey, Uganda, Ukrainian SSR, USSR, United Arab Emirates, United Republic of Tanzania, Uruguay, Vanuatu, Venezuela, Viet Nam, Yemen, Yugoslavia, Zaire, Zambia, Zimbabwe.
Against: Israel, United Kingdom, United States.
Abstaining: Belgium, Canada, France, Germany, Federal Republic of, Italy, Luxembourg, Malawi.

In explanation of vote, Israel and the United States expressed their opposition to singling out countries for selective condemnation; such reference was made in the reports endorsed in the text. The United Kingdom said the language of the text was disobliging, ungenerous and took scant account of the real needs and wishes of dependent peoples. Owing to the inclusion of what it considered to be unnecessarily repetitive and excessively polemical phraseology, Canada could not support the resolution.

Reservations on paragraph 2 were expressed by Australia, which did not believe the existence of NSGTs constituted a threat to international peace and security, and by New Zealand, which declared that the reference to violations of the right to self-determination and basic human rights of the peoples of colonial Territories did not apply to Tokelau, the one remaining NSGT for which New Zealand still had responsibility. Australia, Austria, Finland (on behalf of the five Nordic countries), Japan, the Netherlands and New Zealand expressed reservations on paragraph 4, saying that the United Nations should encourage only peaceful settlement of disputes. Reservations on paragraph 10 were expressed by Ireland, Japan and the Netherlands. Turkey found the draft lacking in balance, as did the Nordic countries, which added that the text should have been restricted to those activities detrimental to the rights of the peoples of NSGTs. Japan also had reservations on paragraphs 5, 6 and 7, and the Netherlands on paragraphs 2, 7 and 8.

In 1985, the Assembly also adopted resolutions on the universal realization of the right of peoples to self-determination (**resolution 40/24**), and on the importance of the universal realization of that right and of the speedy granting of independence for the effective guarantee and observance of human rights (**40/25**). In addition, the Assembly declared the use of force in attempts to prevent the implementation of the Declaration as incompatible with the idea of international co-operation for disarmament (**40/152 I**), and urged Member States to take effective measures for the speedy completion of the implementation of the Declaration (**40/158**).

Implementation by international organizations

Report of the Secretary-General. By a May report with a later addendum,[16] the Secretary-General transmitted to the General Assembly summaries of information submitted by 14 specialized agencies and institutions associated with the United Nations, in response to several 1984 Assembly requests—on action taken in implementation of the Declaration[17] and on action taken or envisaged with regard to Namibia.[18]

Those providing information were: International Labour Organisation; the Food and Agriculture Organization of the United Nations; the United Nations Educational, Scientific and Cultural Organization (UNESCO); the World Health Organization; the World Bank; the International Civil Aviation Organization; the Universal Postal Union; the World Intellectual Property Organization; the Office of the United Nations High Commissioner for Refugees; the United Nations Conference on Trade and Development; and the United Nations Development Programme (UNDP). The International Atomic Energy Agency responded, as did the International Monetary Fund (IMF) and the World Food Programme.

Report of the President of the Economic and Social Council. In a June report,[19] the Economic and Social Council President reviewed his continuing consultations with the Chairman of the Committee on colonial countries concerning the implementation of the Declaration by the United Nations system. They noted that, according to the Secretary-General's report,[16] an increasing number of organizations had extended or formulated programmes of assistance from within their own budgetary resources, in addition to intensifying their collaboration with UNDP as an executing agency. They considered it imperative, however, that efforts be intensified to provide moral and material assistance to the oppressed peoples of Namibia and South Africa.

ECONOMIC AND SOCIAL COUNCIL ACTION

On 26 July, the Economic and Social Council adopted by roll-call vote **resolution 1985/59**, as recommended by its Third (Programme and Co-ordination) Committee.

Implementation of the Declaration on the Granting of Independence to Colonial Countries and Peoples by the specialized agencies and the international institutions associated with the United Nations

The Economic and Social Council,

Bearing in mind that 1985 marks the fortieth anniversary of the founding of the United Nations, as well as the twenty-fifth anniversary of the adoption of the Declaration on the Granting of Independence to Colonial Countries and Peoples,

Having examined the report of the Secretary-General and the report of the President of the Economic and Social Council concerning the question of the implementation of the Declaration on the Granting of Independence to Colonial Countries and Peoples by the specialized agencies and the international institutions associated with the United Nations,

Having heard the statements of the Chairman of the Special Committee on the Situation with regard to the Implementation of the Declaration on the Granting of Independence to Colonial Countries and Peoples and the representative of the Chairman of the Special Committee against *Apartheid*,

Recalling General Assembly resolution 1514(XV) of 14 December 1960, containing the Declaration on the Granting of Independence to Colonial Countries and

Peoples, and all other resolutions adopted by United Nations bodies on this subject, including in particular Assembly resolution 39/43 of 5 December 1984 and Council resolution 1984/55 of 25 July 1984,

Deeply concerned that the objectives of the Charter of the United Nations and the Declaration have not been fully achieved as regards the peoples under colonial and alien domination, particularly those struggling in Namibia and South Africa under the repressive rule of the racist régime of Pretoria,

Reaffirming the responsibility of the specialized agencies and other organizations within the United Nations system to take all effective measures, within their respective spheres of competence, to assist in the full and speedy implementation of the Declaration on the Granting of Independence to Colonial Countries and Peoples and other relevant resolutions of United Nations bodies,

Noting with deep concern that South Africa presents a serious and continuing threat to international peace and security owing to its practice of *apartheid*, its illegal occupation of Namibia and its acts of aggression and destabilization against the front-line and neighbouring States,

Recalling Security Council resolution 566(1985) of 19 June 1985, in which the Council, *inter alia*, condemned the racist régime of South Africa for its installation of a so-called interim Government in Namibia and declared that action to be illegal and null and void,

Reaffirming that the denial of full political and civil rights to the majority of the population of South Africa is the result of the continuation of a colonial situation in that country,

Deeply conscious of the continuing critical need of the people of Namibia and their national liberation movement, the South West Africa People's Organization, for concrete assistance from the specialized agencies and the international institutions associated with the United Nations in their struggle for liberation from the illegal occupation of their country by the racist minority régime of South Africa,

Appreciating that progress has been maintained through the continuing efforts of the United Nations High Commissioner for Refugees in the extension of assistance to refugees from southern Africa,

Deeply concerned that the action taken thus far by the organizations and agencies concerned in the provision of assistance generally to the people of Namibia is still far from adequate to meet their urgent and growing needs,

Gravely concerned at the continued collaboration of the International Monetary Fund with the Government of South Africa, in disregard of relevant General Assembly resolutions,

Noting with satisfaction the continuing efforts of the United Nations Development Programme in the extension of assistance to the national liberation movements concerned, and commending the initiative taken by that organization in establishing channels for closer, periodic contacts and consultations between the specialized agencies and United Nations institutions and the Organization of African Unity and the national liberation movements in the formulation of assistance programmes,

Bearing in mind the document on Namibia adopted by the Special Committee on the Situation with regard to the Implementation of the Declaration on the Granting of Independence to Colonial Countries and Peoples at its extraordinary session, held at Tunis from 13 to 17 May 1985, and the Declaration and the Programme of Action adopted at Vienna on 7 June 1985 by the United Nations Council for Namibia at its extraordinary plenary meetings,

1. *Takes note* of the report of the President of the Economic and Social Council and endorses the observations and suggestions contained therein;

2. *Reaffirms* that the recognition by the General Assembly, the Security Council and other United Nations organs of the legitimacy of the struggle of colonial peoples to exercise their right to self-determination and independence entails, as a corollary, the extension by the United Nations system of organizations of all the necessary moral and material assistance to the peoples of Namibia and South Africa and their national liberation movements;

3. *Expresses its appreciation* to those specialized agencies and organizations within the United Nations system which have continued to co-operate in varying degrees with the United Nations and the Organization of African Unity in the implementation of the Declaration on the Granting of Independence to Colonial Countries and Peoples and other relevant resolutions of United Nations bodies, and urges all the specialized agencies and other organizations within the United Nations system, in particular the World Bank and the International Finance Corporation and the International Monetary Fund, to contribute to the full and speedy implementation of the relevant provisions of those resolutions;

4. *Requests* the specialized agencies and other organizations within the United Nations system, in the light of the intensification of the liberation struggle in Namibia, to do everything possible as a matter of urgency to render increased assistance to the people of Namibia, in consultation with the Organization of African Unity and the United Nations Council for Namibia, in particular in connection with the Nationhood Programme for Namibia;

5. *Requests* the specialized agencies and other organizations within the United Nations system, in view of the deteriorating situation in South Africa and the acts of aggression and destabilization by the *apartheid* régime against States in the region, to increase their assistance to the front-line and neighbouring States and to the liberation movements in South Africa;

6. *Also requests* the specialized agencies and other organizations within the United Nations system to continue to take, in accordance with the relevant resolutions of the General Assembly and the Security Council, all necessary measures to withhold any financial, economic, technical or other assistance from the Government of South Africa until that Government restores to the people of Namibia their inalienable right to self-determination and independence, and to refrain from taking any action which might imply recognition of, or support for, the illegal occupation of Namibia by that régime;

7. *Further requests* the specialized agencies and other organizations within the United Nations system, in accordance with the relevant resolutions of the General Assembly and the Security Council on the *apartheid* policy of the Government of South Africa, to intensify their support for the oppressed people of South Africa and to take such measures as will totally isolate the

apartheid régime and mobilize world public opinion against *apartheid*;

8. *Condemns* the persistent non-compliance of the Government of South Africa with United Nations resolutions and decisions, in particular Security Council resolution 435(1978) of 29 September 1978 containing the United Nations plan for the independence of Namibia, and declares illegal and null and void its installation on 17 June 1985 of a so-called interim Government at Windhoek;

9. *Deeply deplores* the persistent collaboration of the International Monetary Fund with the Government of South Africa, in disregard of repeated General Assembly resolutions to the contrary, and urgently calls upon the Fund to put an end to such collaboration;

10. *Recommends* that a separate item on assistance to national liberation movements recognized by the Organization of African Unity should be included in the agenda of future high-level meetings of the General Secretariat of the Organization of African Unity and the secretariats of the United Nations and other organizations within the United Nations system, with a view to strengthening further the existing measures for co-ordination of action to ensure the best use of available resources for assistance to the peoples of the colonial Territories;

11. *Notes with satisfaction* the inclusion of Namibia, represented by the United Nations Council for Namibia, in the membership of various agencies and organizations within the United Nations system and urges those which have not yet granted full membership to the United Nations Council for Namibia to do so without delay;

12. *Notes with satisfaction also* the arrangements made by several specialized agencies and United Nations institutions which enable representatives of the national liberation movements recognized by the Organization of African Unity to participate fully as observers in proceedings relating to matters concerning their respective countries, and calls upon those international institutions which have not yet done so to follow that example and make the necessary arrangements without delay, including arrangements to defray the costs of the participation of those representatives;

13. *Recommends* that all States should intensify their efforts in the specialized agencies and other organizations within the United Nations system of which they are members to ensure the full and effective implementation of the Declaration on the Granting of Independence to Colonial Countries and Peoples and other relevant resolutions of United Nations bodies;

14. *Urges* those specialized agencies and organizations within the United Nations system which have not already done so to include in the agenda of the regular meetings of their governing bodies a separate item on the progress made and action to be taken by those organizations in their implementation of the Declaration on the Granting of Independence to Colonial Countries and Peoples and other relevant resolutions of United Nations bodies;

15. *Also urges* the executive heads of the specialized agencies and other organizations within the United Nations system to formulate, with the active co-operation of the Organization of African Unity, and to submit, as a matter of priority, to their governing and legislative organs concrete proposals for the full implementation of the relevant United Nations decisions;

16. *Draws the attention* of the Special Committee on the Situation with regard to the Implementation of the Declaration on the Granting of Independence to Colonial Countries and Peoples to the present resolution and to the discussions on the subject at the second regular session of 1985 of the Economic and Social Council;

17. *Requests* the President of the Economic and Social Council to continue consultations on these matters with the Chairman of the Special Committee on the Situation with regard to the Implementation of the Declaration on the Granting of Independence to Colonial Countries and Peoples and the Chairman of the Special Committee against *Apartheid* and to report thereon to the Council;

18. *Requests* the Secretary-General to follow the implementation of the present resolution and to report thereon to the Council at its second regular session of 1986;

19. *Decides* to keep these questions under continuous review.

Economic and Social Council resolution 1985/59

| 26 July 1985 | Meeting 52 | 39-1-9 (roll-call vote) |

Approved by Third Committee (E/1985/138) by vote (36-1-8), 12 July (meeting 10); 17-nation draft (E/1985/C.3/L.1/Rev.1); agenda item 21.

Sponsors: Algeria, Bangladesh, China, Ethiopia, Ghana, Haiti, India, Indonesia, Lebanon, Malaysia, Nigeria, Sierra Leone, Somalia, Sri Lanka, Syrian Arab Republic, Thailand, Yugoslavia.

Roll-call vote in Council as follows:

In favour: Algeria, Argentina, Bangladesh, Botswana, Brazil, Bulgaria, China, Colombia, Congo, Costa Rica, Ecuador, Finland, German Democratic Republic, Guinea, Iceland, India, Indonesia, Lebanon, Malaysia, Mexico, Morocco, Nigeria, Poland, Romania, Rwanda, Saudi Arabia, Senegal, Sierra Leone, Somalia, Sri Lanka, Suriname, Sweden, Thailand, Turkey, Uganda, USSR, Yugoslavia, Zaire, Zimbabwe.

Against: United States.

Abstaining: Canada, France, Germany, Federal Republic of, Japan, Luxembourg, Netherlands, New Zealand, Spain, United Kingdom.

Before the draft was approved by the Third Committee, separate votes were taken on the seventh (36 in favour to 2 against, with 7 abstentions) and thirteenth (roll-call vote of 32-2-11) preambular paragraphs, and on operative paragraphs 3 (36-2-7), 6 (36-2-7), 7 (36-2-7) and 9 (roll-call vote of 32 to 3, with 10 abstentions). The USSR had suggested, and subsequently withdrew, a proposal to insert a new fifth preambular paragraph expressing the conviction that colonialism prevented the development of international economic co-operation, hindered the development of dependent peoples and militated against the United Nations ideal of universal peace.

The Council—taking separate votes on paragraphs at the request of the United Kingdom, and roll-call votes on the thirteenth preambular paragraph and on the text as a whole at the request of Zimbabwe—adopted the seventh preambular paragraph by 31 to 2, with 8 abstentions; the thirteenth preambular paragraph by 31 to 2 (the United Kingdom, the United States), with 12 abstentions; operative paragraph 3 by 31 to 2, with 8 abstentions; paragraph 6 by 33 to 2, with 9 abstentions; paragraph 7 by 36 to 2, with 8 abstentions; paragraph 9 by 35 to 3, with 11 abstentions; and the text as a whole by 39 to 1, with 9 abstentions.

Luxembourg, on behalf of the Western European countries members of the Council, said that, rather than isolating South Africa, means of communication should be maintained to persuade it to reject *apartheid*; moreover, the independence of IMF should be respected, and the reference to the World Bank was unjustified. Spain said the terms used in the text, and the reference to IMF and the Bank, made it abstain. Canada and the United States did not believe the text represented the best way of eliminating *apartheid*. Bulgaria, on behalf of the Eastern European countries members of the Council, said the text would have had greater impact if it had condemned and called for an end to assistance by Western countries to Pretoria.

Action by the Committee on colonial countries. The Committee on colonial countries continued in August 1985[(4)] to consider the role of the specialized agencies and other United Nations bodies in implementing the 1960 Declaration. It endorsed the conclusions and recommendations of its Sub-Committee on Petitions, Information and Assistance which, among other things, took note of information from the World Bank that it had made no loans to South Africa since 1966 and that all links with regard to previous loans had ended. The Committee also drafted a resolution which it recommended the Assembly adopt.

GENERAL ASSEMBLY ACTION

On 2 December, the General Assembly adopted, by recorded vote, **resolution 40/53**, drafted by the Committee on colonial countries and recommended by the Fourth Committee.

Implementation of the Declaration on the Granting of Independence to Colonial Countries and Peoples by the specialized agencies and the international institutions associated with the United Nations

The General Assembly,

Having considered the item entitled "Implementation of the Declaration on the Granting of Independence to Colonial Countries and Peoples by the specialized agencies and the international institutions associated with the United Nations",

Recalling the Declaration on the Granting of Independence to Colonial Countries and Peoples, contained in its resolution 1514(XV) of 14 December 1960, and the Plan of Action for the Full Implementation of the Declaration, contained in the annex to its resolution 35/118 of 11 December 1980, as well as all other relevant resolutions adopted by the General Assembly on this subject, including in particular resolution 39/43 of 5 December 1984,

Having examined the reports submitted on the item by the Secretary-General, the Economic and Social Council and the Special Committee on the Situation with regard to the Implementation of the Declaration on the Granting of Independence to Colonial Countries and Peoples,

Recalling also its resolutions ES-8/2 of 14 September 1981 and 39/50 of 12 December 1984 on the question of Namibia,

Taking into account the relevant provisions of the Paris Declaration on Namibia and the Programme of Action on Namibia, adopted at the International Conference in Support of the Struggle of the Namibian People for Independence, and the Declaration and Programme of Action contained in the Final Document adopted by the United Nations Council for Namibia at its extraordinary plenary meetings held at Vienna from 3 to 7 June 1985,

Bearing in mind the relevant provisions of the Political Declaration adopted by the Seventh Conference of Heads of State or Government of Non-Aligned Countries, held at New Delhi from 7 to 12 March 1983, the Final Document of the Extraordinary Ministerial Meeting of the Co-ordinating Bureau of Non-Aligned Countries on the question of Namibia, held at New Delhi from 19 to 21 April 1985, and other documents of the Co-ordinating Bureau,

Aware that the struggle of the people of Namibia for self-determination and independence is in its crucial stage and has sharply intensified as a consequence of the stepped-up aggression of the illegal colonialist régime of Pretoria against the people of the Territory and the increased general support rendered to that régime by certain Western countries, and the so-called policy of constructive engagement, coupled with efforts to deprive the Namibian people of their hard-won victories in the liberation struggle, and that it is therefore incumbent upon the entire international community decisively to intensify concerted action in support of the people of Namibia and their sole and authentic representative, the South West Africa People's Organization, for the attainment of their goal,

Concerned that the policy of "constructive engagement" with the *apartheid* régime of South Africa, linked with the economic and military collaboration maintained by some Western countries and Israel with Pretoria, has only encouraged and strengthened the racist régime in its continued illegal occupation and massive militarization and exploitation of Namibia in violation of the relevant resolutions and decisions of the United Nations,

Gravely concerned at the continued imperialist and neo-colonialist support for South Africa's oppressive and aggressive policies in Namibia and with respect to independent States in southern Africa, in particular the front-line States, as exemplified by the discussions and resolutions of the Security Council,

Conscious of the worsening of the situation in southern Africa because of South Africa's racist policies of oppression, aggression and occupation, which constitute a clear threat to world peace and security,

Deeply conscious of the continuing critical need of the Namibian people and their national liberation movement, the South West Africa People's Organization, and of the peoples of other colonial Territories for concrete assistance from the specialized agencies and other organizations of the United Nations system in their struggle for liberation from colonial rule and in their efforts to achieve and consolidate their national independence,

Deeply concerned that, although there has been progress in the extension of assistance to refugees from Namibia, the action taken hitherto by the organizations concerned in providing assistance to the people of the Territory through their national liberation movement, the South West Africa People's Organization, still remains inadequate to meet the urgent and growing needs of the Namibian people,

Reaffirming the responsibility of the specialized agencies and other organizations of the United Nations system to take all the necessary measures, within their respective spheres of competence, to ensure the full and speedy implementation of the Declaration on the Granting of Independence to Colonial Countries and Peoples and other relevant resolutions of the United Nations, particularly those relating to the provision of moral and material assistance, on a priority basis, to the peoples of the colonial Territories and their national liberation movements,

Expressing its firm belief that closer contacts and consultations between the specialized agencies and other organizations of the United Nations system on the one hand and the Organization of African Unity and the South West Africa People's Organization on the other will help those agencies and organizations to overcome procedural and other difficulties which have impeded or delayed the implementation of some assistance programmes,

Recalling its resolution 39/50 C of 12 December 1984 requesting all specialized agencies and other organizations and conferences of the United Nations system to grant full membership to the United Nations Council for Namibia as the legal Administering Authority for Namibia,

Expressing its appreciation to the General Secretariat of the Organization of African Unity for the continued co-operation and assistance it has extended to the specialized agencies and other organizations of the United Nations system in connection with the implementation of the relevant resolutions of the United Nations,

Expressing its appreciation also to the Governments of the front-line States for the steadfast support extended to the people of Namibia and their national liberation movement, the South West Africa People's Organization, in their just and legitimate struggle for the attainment of freedom and independence, despite increased armed attacks by the forces of the racist régime of South Africa, and aware of the particular needs of those Governments for assistance in that connection,

Commending the continued substantial contribution of the United Nations Educational, Scientific and Cultural Organization to the implementation of the Declaration on the Granting of Independence to Colonial Countries and Peoples and the effective support it provides to the liberation movements in educating the populations of colonial Territories concerning self-determination and independence,

Noting the support given by the specialized agencies and other organizations of the United Nations system to the implementation of the Nationhood Programme for Namibia, in accordance with General Assembly resolution 32/9 A of 4 November 1977,

Deploring the continued links with and assistance rendered to South Africa by certain specialized agencies in the financial, economic, technical and other fields in contravention of the relevant resolutions of the United Nations, thus enhancing neo-colonialist practices in the system of international relations,

Gravely concerned at the continued collaboration between the International Monetary Fund and the Government of South Africa in disregard of relevant General Assembly resolutions, in particular resolution 37/2 of 21 October 1982,

Mindful of the imperative need to keep under continuous review the activities of the specialized agencies and other organizations of the United Nations system in the implementation of the various United Nations decisions relating to decolonization,

Bearing in mind the importance of the activities of non-governmental organizations aimed at putting an end to the assistance which is still being rendered to South Africa by some specialized agencies, and taking into account the consultations held by the Special Committee with non-governmental organizations and the relevant conclusions and recommendations on the seminars held by the Special Committee with non-governmental organizations at Port Moresby from 4 to 7 March 1985 and at Havana from 8 to 10 April 1985,

1. *Approves* the chapter of the report of the Special Committee on the Situation with regard to the Implementation of the Declaration on the Granting of Independence to Colonial Countries and Peoples relating to the question;

2. *Reaffirms* that the specialized agencies and other organizations and institutions of the United Nations system should continue to be guided by the relevant resolutions of the United Nations in their efforts to contribute, within their spheres of competence, to the full and speedy implementation of the Declaration on the Granting of Independence to Colonial Countries and Peoples, contained in General Assembly resolution 1514(XV);

3. *Reaffirms also* that the recognition by the General Assembly, the Security Council and other United Nations organs of the legitimacy of the struggle of colonial peoples to exercise their right to self-determination and independence entails, as a corollary, the extension by the specialized agencies and other organizations of the United Nations system of all the necessary moral and material assistance to those peoples and their national liberation movements;

4. *Expresses its appreciation* to those specialized agencies and other organizations of the United Nations system which have continued to co-operate in varying degrees with the United Nations and the Organization of African Unity in the implementation of General Assembly resolution 1514(XV) and other relevant resolutions of the United Nations, and urges all the specialized agencies and other organizations of the United Nations system to accelerate the full and speedy implementation of the relevant provisions of those resolutions;

5. *Expresses its concern* that the assistance extended thus far by certain specialized agencies and other organizations of the United Nations system to the colonial peoples, particularly the people of Namibia and their national liberation movement, the South West Africa People's Organization, is far from adequate in relation to the actual needs of the peoples concerned;

6. *Requests* all specialized agencies and other organizations and bodies of the United Nations system, in accordance with the relevant resolutions of the General Assembly and the Security Council, to take all necessary measures to withhold from the racist régime of South Africa any form of co-operation and assistance in the financial, economic, technical and other fields and to discontinue all support to that régime until the people of Namibia have exercised fully their inalienable right to self-determination, freedom and national independence in a united Namibia and until the inhuman system of *apartheid* has been totally eradicated;

7. *Reiterates its conviction* that the specialized agencies and other organizations and bodies of the United Nations system should refrain from taking any action which might imply recognition of, or support for, the legitimacy of the domination of the Territory of Namibia by the racist régime of South Africa;

8. *Regrets* that the World Bank and also the International Monetary Fund continue to maintain links with the racist régime of Pretoria, as exemplified by the continued participation of South Africa in the work of both agencies, and expresses the view that the two agencies should put an end to all links with the racist régime;

9. *Strongly condemns* the persistent collaboration between the International Monetary Fund and South Africa in disregard of repeated resolutions to the contrary by the General Assembly, and calls upon the International Monetary Fund to put an end to such collaboration and not to grant any new loans to the racist régime of South Africa;

10. *Urges once again* the executive heads of the World Bank and the International Monetary Fund to draw the particular attention of their governing bodies to the present resolution with a view to formulating specific programmes beneficial to the peoples of the colonial Territories, particularly Namibia;

11. *Requests* the specialized agencies and other organizations of the United Nations system to render or continue to render, as a matter of urgency, all possible moral and material assistance to the colonial peoples struggling for liberation from colonial rule, bearing in mind that such assistance should not only meet their immediate needs but also create conditions for development after they have exercised their right to self-determination and independence;

12. *Requests once again* the specialized agencies and other organizations of the United Nations system to continue to provide all moral and material assistance to the newly independent and emerging States so as to enable them to achieve genuine economic independence;

13. *Reiterates its recommendation* that the specialized agencies and other organizations of the United Nations system should initiate or broaden contacts and co-operation with the colonial peoples and their national liberation movements directly or, where appropriate, through the Organization of African Unity, and review, and introduce greater flexibility in, their procedures with respect to the formulation and preparation of assistance programmes and projects so as to be able to extend the necessary assistance without delay to help the colonial peoples and their national liberation movements in their struggle to exercise their inalienable right to self-determination and independence in accordance with General Assembly resolution 1514(XV);

14. *Recommends* that a separate item on assistance to national liberation movements recognized by the Organization of African Unity should be included in the agenda of future high-level meetings between the General Secretariat of the Organization of African Unity and the secretariats of the United Nations and other organizations of the United Nations system with a view to strengthening further the existing measures of co-ordination of action to ensure the best use of available resources for assistance to the peoples of the colonial Territories;

15. *Urges* the specialized agencies and other organizations of the United Nations system that have not already done so to include in the agenda of the regular meetings of their governing bodies a separate item on the progress they have made in the implementation of General Assembly resolution 1514(XV) and the other relevant resolutions of the United Nations;

16. *Urges* the specialized agencies and other organizations and institutions of the United Nations system to extend, as a matter of priority, substantial material assistance to the Governments of the front-line States in order to enable them to support more effectively the struggle of the people of Namibia for freedom and independence and to resist the violation of their territorial integrity by the armed forces of the racist régime of South Africa directly or, as in Angola and Mozambique, through puppet traitor groups in the service of Pretoria;

17. *Notes with satisfaction* the arrangements made by several specialized agencies and other organizations of the United Nations system which enable representatives of the national liberation movements recognized by the Organization of African Unity to participate fully as observers in the proceedings relating to matters concerning their respective countries, and calls upon those agencies and organizations that have not yet done so to follow this example and to make the necessary arrangements without delay;

18. *Urges* the specialized agencies and other organizations and institutions of the United Nations system to assist in accelerating progress in all sectors of the national life of colonial Territories, particularly in the development of their economies;

19. *Requests* the specialized agencies to abide by Security Council resolution 566(1985) of 19 June 1985, in which the Council condemned the racist régime of South Africa for its installation of a so-called interim Government in Namibia and declared that action to be illegal and null and void;

20. *Recommends* that all Governments should intensify their efforts in the specialized agencies and other organizations of the United Nations system of which they are members to ensure the full and effective implementation of General Assembly resolution 1514(XV) and other relevant resolutions of the United Nations and, in that connection, should accord priority to the question of providing assistance on an emergency basis to the peoples of the colonial Territories and their national liberation movements;

21. *Reiterates its proposal,* under article III of the Agreement between the United Nations and the International Monetary Fund, for the urgent inclusion in the agenda of the Board of Governors of the Fund of an item dealing with the relationship between the Fund and South Africa, and further reiterates its proposal that, in pursuance of article II of the Agreement, the relevant organs of the United Nations should participate in any meeting of the Board of Governors called by the Fund for the purpose of discussing the item, and urges the Fund to discuss its relationship with South Africa at its annual meeting, in compliance with the above-mentioned Agreement, and to report to the Secretary-General of the United Nations on the action taken;

22. *Draws the attention* of the specialized agencies and other organizations of the United Nations system to the Plan of Action for the Full Implementation of the Declaration on the Granting of Independence to Colonial Countries and Peoples, contained in the annex to

General Assembly resolution 35/118, in particular to those provisions calling upon the agencies and organizations to render all possible moral and material assistance to the peoples of the colonial Territories and to their national liberation movements;

23. *Urges* the executive heads of the specialized agencies and other organizations of the United Nations system, having regard to the provisions of paragraphs 13 and 22 above, to formulate, with the active co-operation of the Organization of African Unity where appropriate, and to submit, as a matter of priority, to their governing and legislative organs concrete proposals for the full implementation of the relevant United Nations decisions, in particular specific programmes of assistance to the peoples of the colonial Territories and their national liberation movements;

24. *Requests* the Secretary-General to continue to assist the specialized agencies and other organizations of the United Nations system in working out appropriate measures for implementing the relevant resolutions of the United Nations and to prepare for submission to the relevant bodies, with the assistance of those agencies and organizations, a report on the action taken in implementation of the relevant resolutions, including the present resolution, since the circulation of his previous report;

25. *Requests* the Economic and Social Council to continue to consider, in consultation with the Special Committee on the Situation with regard to the Implementation of the Declaration on the Granting of Independence to Colonial Countries and Peoples, appropriate measures for co-ordination of the policies and activities of the specialized agencies and other organizations of the United Nations system in implementing the relevant resolutions of the General Assembly;

26. *Requests* the specialized agencies to report periodically to the Secretary-General of the United Nations on their implementation of the present resolution;

27. *Requests* the Special Committee to continue to examine this question and to report thereon to the General Assembly at its forty-first session.

General Assembly resolution 40/53

2 December 1985   Meeting 99   126-3-22 (recorded vote)

Approved by Fourth Committee (A/40/885) by recorded vote (119-3-25), 8 November (meeting 20); draft by Committee on colonial countries (A/40/23); agenda items 12 and 111.
Meeting numbers. GA 40th session: 4th Committee 11, 12, 15-20; plenary 99.

Recorded vote in Assembly as follows:

In favour: Afghanistan, Albania, Algeria, Angola, Antigua and Barbuda, Argentina, Bahamas, Bahrain, Bangladesh, Barbados, Benin, Bhutan, Bolivia, Botswana, Brazil, Brunei Darussalam, Bulgaria, Burkina Faso, Burma, Burundi, Byelorussian SSR, Cameroon, Cape Verde, Central African Republic, Chad, Chile, China, Colombia, Comoros, Congo, Costa Rica, Cuba, Cyprus, Czechoslovakia, Democratic Kampuchea, Democratic Yemen, Djibouti, Dominican Republic, Ecuador, Egypt, Equatorial Guinea, Ethiopia, Gabon, Gambia, German Democratic Republic, Ghana, Greece, Grenada, Guatemala, Guinea, Guinea-Bissau, Guyana, Haiti, Honduras, Hungary, India, Indonesia, Iran, Iraq, Jamaica, Jordan, Kenya, Kuwait, Lao People's Democratic Republic, Lebanon, Lesotho, Liberia, Libyan Arab Jamahiriya, Madagascar, Malaysia, Maldives, Mali, Malta, Mauritania, Mauritius, Mexico, Mongolia, Morocco, Mozambique, Nepal, Nicaragua, Niger, Nigeria, Oman, Pakistan, Panama, Papua New Guinea, Peru, Philippines, Poland, Qatar, Romania, Rwanda, Saint Lucia, Samoa, Sao Tome and Principe, Saudi Arabia, Senegal, Seychelles, Sierra Leone, Singapore, Solomon Islands, Somalia, Sri Lanka, Sudan, Suriname, Swaziland, Syrian Arab Republic, Thailand, Togo, Trinidad and Tobago, Tunisia, Turkey, Uganda, Ukrainian SSR, USSR, United Arab Emirates, Uruguay, Vanuatu, Venezuela, Viet Nam, Yemen, Yugoslavia, Zaire, Zambia, Zimbabwe.

Against: Israel, United Kingdom, United States.

Abstaining: Australia, Austria, Belgium, Canada, Denmark, Fiji, Finland, France, Germany, Federal Republic of, Iceland, Ireland, Italy, Ivory Coast, Japan, Luxembourg, Malawi, Netherlands, New Zealand, Norway, Portugal, Spain, Sweden.

In the Assembly's Fourth Committee, an amendment[20] proposed by Israel to delete the words "and Israel" from the eighth preambular paragraph was rejected by a recorded vote of 77 to 40, with 26 abstentions.

In explanation of vote on the amendment, objections to the arbitrary or selective condemnation of certain countries were voiced by Australia, Canada, Chile, Colombia, Greece, Honduras, Japan, the Netherlands, Singapore, the United Kingdom and the United States. Saying that the selective condemnation of Israel had originated from an ally of the USSR, the United States referred to a 1984 report on operational activities of the United Nations system,[21] according to which 91 per cent of the total contributions by Member States to the regular budgets of the agencies and organizations of the United Nations system was paid by the Western countries, 8 per cent by the developing countries and 1 per cent by the USSR and the Eastern European countries; it was easy to deduce from those figures which States wished to politicize the activities of the specialized agencies, the United States said. Voting against the amendment, Iran asserted that Israel's collaboration with South Africa constituted a virtual alliance which threatened international peace and security. Oman, Saudi Arabia and the United Arab Emirates voted in like manner.

On the text as a whole, serious reservations or objections were expressed by Australia, Canada, France, Sweden (for the five Nordic countries) and the United Kingdom to the draft's disregard of the autonomy, impartiality and universality of the specialized agencies. The Netherlands objected to the criticism levelled against institutions in the twentieth and twenty-first preambular paragraphs and in paragraphs 8 and 9, asserting that such an attempt at politicization struck at the agencies' foundation and diverted them from their main task of assisting member countries in their economic development, a view shared by the United Kingdom. Japan additionally objected to paragraph 6. Ireland also objected to the criticism of IMF and the World Bank, and Italy added that imposing outside restrictions on IMF activities would be detrimental to the economies of all the countries which enjoyed its assistance.

Sweden, speaking for the five Nordic countries, said it deplored the sweeping or inaccurate statements and the inclusion of paragraphs irrelevant to the substance of the resolution. The Netherlands viewed the text as an incoherent, sprawling mass of words. The United Kingdom felt that the resolution—a free-floating contentious text irrelevant to the role of the specialized agencies—exemplified how far the Committee had become detached from reality; the text focused in highly political terms on South Africa and Namibia, and made no reference to other Territories.

Greece and Uruguay, despite certain reservations, voted in favour because the draft recognized the role played by the specialized agencies in promoting decolonization. Honduras regretted the controversial wording. Chile, a member of the Committee on colonial countries, and Colombia, in solidarity with all colonial peoples, supported the text. Sierra Leone said the text was based on specific reports and had resulted from extensive negotiations.

In other 1985 action, the Assembly urged the specialized agencies and other organizations of the United Nations system within their respective spheres of competence: to contribute to the speedy implementation of the Declaration and to provide assistance to the newly emerging States (**resolution 40/57**); and to disseminate information on decolonization (**40/58**).

Foreign interests impeding implementation of the Declaration

The Committee on colonial countries and the General Assembly reaffirmed in 1985 their concern that the activities of foreign economic, financial and other interests operating in colonial Territories, particularly in southern Africa, obstructed the political independence of indigenous populations.

The Committee drafted a resolution on the activities of foreign interests which it recommended for adoption by the Assembly.

GENERAL ASSEMBLY ACTION

On 2 December, acting on the recommendation of the Fourth Committee, the General Assembly adopted **resolution 40/52**, by recorded vote.

Activities of foreign economic and other interests which are impeding the implementation of the Declaration on the Granting of Independence to Colonial Countries and Peoples in Namibia and in all other Territories under colonial domination and efforts to eliminate colonialism, *apartheid* and racial discrimination in southern Africa

The General Assembly,

Having considered the item entitled "Activities of foreign economic and other interests which are impeding the implementation of the Declaration on the Granting of Independence to Colonial Countries and Peoples in Namibia and in all other Territories under colonial domination and efforts to eliminate colonialism, *apartheid* and racial discrimination in southern Africa",

Having examined the chapter of the report of the Special Committee on the Situation with regard to the Implementation of the Declaration on the Granting of Independence to Colonial Countries and Peoples relating to the item,

Taking into consideration the relevant chapters of the report of the United Nations Council for Namibia,

Recalling its resolutions 1514(XV) of 14 December 1960, containing the Declaration on the Granting of Independence to Colonial Countries and Peoples, 2621(XXV) of 12 October 1970, containing the programme of action for the full implementation of the Declaration,

and 35/118 of 11 December 1980, the annex to which contains the Plan of Action for the Full Implementation of the Declaration, as well as all other resolutions of the United Nations relating to the item,

Reaffirming the solemn obligation of the administering Powers under the Charter of the United Nations to promote the political, economic, social and educational advancement of the inhabitants of the Territories under their administration and to protect the human and natural resources of those Territories against abuses,

Reaffirming that any economic or other activity which impedes the implementation of the Declaration on the Granting of Independence to Colonial Countries and Peoples and obstructs efforts aimed at the elimination of colonialism, *apartheid* and racial discrimination in southern Africa and other colonial Territories is in direct violation of the rights of the inhabitants and of the principles of the Charter and all relevant resolutions of the United Nations,

Reaffirming that the natural resources of all Territories under colonial and racist domination are the heritage of the peoples of those Territories and that the exploitation and depletion of those resources by foreign economic interests, in particular in Namibia, in association with the occupying régime of South Africa, constitute a direct violation of the rights of the peoples and of the principles of the Charter and all relevant resolutions of the United Nations,

Recalling the relevant provisions of the consensus on Namibia adopted by the Special Committee on the Situation with regard to the Implementation of the Declaration on the Granting of Independence to Colonial Countries and Peoples at its extraordinary session held at Tunis from 13 to 17 May 1985,

Bearing in mind the relevant provisions of the Economic Declaration and other documents of the Seventh Conference of Heads of State or Government of Non-Aligned Countries, held at New Delhi from 7 to 12 March 1983, and of the Final Document of the Extraordinary Ministerial Meeting of the Co-ordinating Bureau of Non-Aligned Countries on the question of Namibia, held at New Delhi from 19 to 21 April 1985,

Taking into account the relevant provisions of the Declaration and Programme of Action contained in the Final Document adopted by the United Nations Council for Namibia at its extraordinary plenary meetings held at Vienna from 3 to 7 June 1985,

Noting with profound concern that the colonial Powers and certain States, through their activities in the colonial Territories, have continued to disregard United Nations decisions relating to the item and that they have failed to implement, in particular, the relevant provisions of General Assembly resolutions 2621(XXV) of 12 October 1970 and 39/42 of 5 December 1984, by which the Assembly called upon the colonial Powers and those Governments that had not yet done so to take legislative, administrative or other measures in respect of their nationals and the bodies corporate under their jurisdiction that own and operate enterprises in colonial Territories, particularly in Africa, which are detrimental to the interests of the inhabitants of those Territories, in order to put an end to such enterprises and to prevent new investments that run counter to the interests of the inhabitants of those Territories,

Condemning the intensified activities of those foreign economic, financial and other interests which continue to exploit the natural and human resources of the colonial Territories and to accumulate and repatriate huge profits to the detriment of the interests of the inhabitants, particularly in the case of Namibia, thereby impeding the realization by the peoples of the Territories of their legitimate aspirations for self-determination and independence,

Strongly condemning the support which the racist minority régime of South Africa continues to receive from those foreign economic, financial and other interests which are collaborating with the régime in the exploitation of the natural and human resources of the international Territory of Namibia, in the further entrenchment of its illegal racist domination over the Territory and in the strengthening of its system of *apartheid*,

Strongly condemning the investment of foreign capital in the production of uranium and the collaboration by certain Western and other countries with the racist minority régime of South Africa in the nuclear field which, by providing that régime with nuclear equipment and technology, enables it to develop nuclear and military capabilities and to become a nuclear Power, thereby promoting South Africa's continued illegal occupation of Namibia,

Reaffirming that the natural resources of Namibia, including its marine resources, are the inviolable and incontestable heritage of the Namibian people and that the exploitation of those resources by foreign economic interests under the protection of the illegal colonial administration, in violation of the Charter, of the relevant resolutions of the General Assembly and the Security Council and of Decree No. 1 for the Protection of the Natural Resources of Namibia, enacted by the United Nations Council for Namibia on 27 September 1974, and in disregard of the advisory opinion of the International Court of Justice of 21 June 1971, is illegal, contributes to the maintenance of the illegal occupation régime and is a grave threat to the integrity and prosperity of an independent Namibia,

Concerned about the conditions in other colonial Territories, including certain Territories in the Caribbean and the Pacific Ocean regions, where foreign economic, financial and other interests continue to deprive the indigenous populations of their rights over the wealth of their countries, and where the inhabitants of those Territories continue to suffer from a loss of land ownership as a result of the failure of the administering Powers concerned to restrict the sale of land to foreigners, despite the repeated appeals of the General Assembly,

Conscious of the continuing need to mobilize world public opinion against the involvement of foreign economic, financial and other interests in the exploitation of natural and human resources, which impedes the independence of colonial Territories and the elimination of racism, particularly in southern Africa, and emphasizing the importance of action by local authorities, trade unions, religious bodies, academic institutions, mass media, solidarity movements and other non-governmental organizations, as well as individuals, in exercising pressure on transnational corporations to refrain from any investment or activity in the Territory of Namibia, in encouraging a policy of systematic divestment of any financial or other interest in corporations doing business with South Africa and in counteracting all forms of collaboration with the occupation régime in Namibia,

1. *Reaffirms* the inalienable right of the peoples of dependent Territories to self-determination and in-

dependence and to the enjoyment of the natural resources of their Territories, as well as their right to dispose of those resources in their best interests;

2. *Reiterates* that any administering or occupying Power that deprives the colonial peoples of the exercise of their legitimate rights over their natural resources or subordinates the rights and interests of those peoples to foreign economic and financial interests violates the solemn obligations it has assumed under the Charter of the United Nations;

3. *Reaffirms* that, by their depletive exploitation of natural resources, the continued accumulation and repatriation of huge profits and the use of those profits for the enrichment of foreign settlers and the perpetuation of colonial domination and racial discrimination in the Territories, the activities of foreign economic, financial and other interests operating at present in the colonial Territories, particularly in southern Africa, constitute a major obstacle to political independence and racial equality, as well as to the enjoyment of the natural resources of those Territories by the indigenous inhabitants;

4. *Condemns* the activities of foreign economic and other interests in the colonial Territories impeding the implementation of the Declaration on the Granting of Independence to Colonial Countries and Peoples, contained in General Assembly resolution 1514(XV), and the efforts to eliminate colonialism, *apartheid* and racial discrimination;

5. *Condemns* the policies of Governments that continue to support or collaborate with those foreign economic and other interests engaged in exploiting the natural and human resources of the Territories, including, in particular, illegally exploiting Namibia's marine resources, violating the political, economic and social rights and interests of the indigenous peoples and thus obstructing the full and speedy implementation of the Declaration in respect of those Territories;

6. *Strongly condemns* the collusion of the Governments of certain Western and other countries with the racist minority régime of South Africa in the nuclear field, and calls upon those and all other Governments to refrain from supplying that régime, directly or indirectly, with installations that might enable it to produce uranium, plutonium and other nuclear materials, reactors or military equipment;

7. *Requests* the Special Committee on the Situation with regard to the Implementation of the Declaration on the Granting of Independence to Colonial Countries and Peoples to continue to monitor closely the situation in the remaining colonial Territories so as to ensure that all economic activities in those Territories are aimed at strengthening and diversifying their economies in the interests of the indigenous peoples, at promoting the economic and financial viability of those Territories and at speeding their accession to independence, and, in that connection, requests the administering Powers concerned to ensure that the peoples of the Territories under their administration are not exploited for political, military and other purposes detrimental to their interests;

8. *Strongly condemns* those Western and all other countries, as well as the transnational corporations, which continue their investments in, and supply of armaments and oil and nuclear technology to, the racist régime of South Africa, thus buttressing it and aggravating the threat to world peace;

9. *Calls upon* all States, in particular certain Western States, to take urgent, effective measures to terminate all collaboration with the racist régime of South Africa in the political, diplomatic, economic, trade, military and nuclear fields and to refrain from entering into other relations with that régime in violation of the relevant resolutions of the United Nations and of the Organization of African Unity;

10. *Calls once again upon* all Governments that have not yet done so to take legislative, administrative or other measures in respect of their nationals and the bodies corporate under their jurisdiction that own and operate enterprises in colonial Territories, particularly in Africa, which are detrimental to the interests of the inhabitants of those Territories, in order to put an end to such enterprises and to prevent new investments that run counter to the interests of the inhabitants of those Territories;

11. *Calls upon* all States to terminate, or cause to have terminated, any investments in Namibia or loans to the racist minority régime of South Africa and to refrain from any agreements or measures to promote trade or other economic relations with that régime;

12. *Requests* all States that have not yet done so to take effective measures to end the supply of funds and other forms of assistance, including military supplies and equipment, to the racist minority régime of South Africa, which uses such assistance to repress the people of Namibia and their national liberation movement;

13. *Strongly condemns* South Africa for its continued exploitation and plundering of the natural resources of Namibia, leading to the rapid depletion of such resources, in complete disregard of the legitimate interests of the Namibian people, for the creation in the Territory of an economic structure dependent essentially upon its mineral resources and for its illegal extension of the territorial sea and its proclamation of an economic zone off the coast of Namibia;

14. *Declares* that all activities of foreign economic interests in Namibia are illegal under international law and that consequently South Africa and all the foreign economic interests operating in Namibia are liable to pay damages to the future lawful Government of an independent Namibia;

15. *Calls upon* those oil-producing and oil-exporting countries that have not yet done so to take effective measures against the oil companies concerned so as to terminate the supply of crude oil and petroleum products to the racist régime of South Africa;

16. *Reiterates* that the exploitation and plundering of the marine and other natural resources of Namibia by South African and other foreign economic interests, including the activities of those transnational corporations which are engaged in the exploitation and export of the Territory's uranium ores and other resources, in violation of the relevant resolutions of the General Assembly and the Security Council and of Decree No. 1 for the Protection of the Natural Resources of Namibia, are illegal, contribute to the maintenance of the illegal occupation régime and are a grave threat to the integrity and prosperity of an independent Namibia;

17. *Condemns* the plunder of Namibian uranium, and calls upon the Governments of all States, particularly those whose nationals and corporations are involved in the mining or enrichment of, or traffic in, Namibian uranium, to take all appropriate measures in compliance with the provisions of Decree No. 1 for the Protection of the Natural Resources of Namibia, including the practice of requiring negative certificates of origin, to prohibit and prevent State-owned and other corporations, together with their subsidiaries, from dealing in Namibian uranium and from engaging in uranium prospecting activities in Namibia;

18. *Requests* the Governments of the Federal Republic of Germany, the Netherlands and the United Kingdom of Great Britain and Northern Ireland, which operate the Urenco uranium enrichment plant, to have Namibian uranium specifically excluded from the Treaty of Almelo, which regulates the activities of Urenco;

19. *Requests* all States to take legislative, administrative and other measures, as appropriate, in order effectively to isolate South Africa politically, economically, militarily and culturally, in accordance with General Assembly resolutions ES-8/2 of 14 September 1981, 36/121 B of 10 December 1981, 37/233 A of 20 December 1982, 38/36 A of 1 December 1983 and 39/50 A of 12 December 1984;

20. *Calls once again upon* all States to discontinue all economic, financial and trade relations with the racist minority régime of South Africa concerning Namibia and to refrain from entering into any relations with South Africa, purporting to act on behalf of or concerning Namibia, which may lend support to its continued illegal occupation of that Territory;

21. *Invites* all Governments and organizations of the United Nations system, having regard to the relevant provisions of the Declaration on the Establishment of a New International Economic Order, contained in General Assembly resolution 3201(S-VI) of 1 May 1974, and of the Charter of Economic Rights and Duties of States, contained in Assembly resolution 3281(XXIX) of 12 December 1974, to ensure, in particular, that the permanent sovereignty of the colonial Territories over their natural resources is fully respected and safeguarded;

22. *Urges* the administering Powers concerned to take effective measures to safeguard and guarantee the inalienable right of the peoples of the colonial Territories to their natural resources and to establish and maintain control over their future development, and requests the administering Powers to take all necessary steps to protect the property rights of the peoples of those Territories;

23. *Calls upon* the administering Powers concerned to abolish all discriminatory and unjust wage systems and working conditions prevailing in the Territories under their administration and to apply in each Territory a uniform system of wages to all the inhabitants without any discrimination;

24. *Requests* the Secretary-General to undertake, through the Department of Public Information of the Secretariat, a sustained and broad campaign with a view to informing world public opinion of the facts concerning the pillaging of natural resources in colonial Territories and the exploitation of their indigenous populations by foreign monopolies and, in respect of Namibia, the support they render to the racist minority régime of South Africa;

25. *Appeals* to mass media, trade unions and other non-governmental organizations, as well as individuals, to co-ordinate and intensify their efforts to mobilize international public opinion against the policy of the *apartheid* régime of South Africa and to work for the en-

forcement of economic and other sanctions against that régime and for encouraging a policy of systematic divestment in corporations doing business in South Africa;

26. *Requests* the Special Committee on the Situation with regard to the Implementation of the Declaration on the Granting of Independence to Colonial Countries and Peoples to continue to examine this question and to report thereon to the General Assembly at its forty-first session.

General Assembly resolution 40/52

2 December 1985   Meeting 99   125-9-16 (recorded vote)

Approved by Fourth Committee (A/40/883) by recorded vote (98-9-15), 29 October (meeting 10); draft by Committee on colonial countries (A/40/23); agenda item 110.
Meeting numbers. GA 40th session: 4th Committee 2-10; plenary 99.

Recorded vote in Assembly as follows:

In favour: Afghanistan, Albania, Algeria, Angola, Antigua and Barbuda, Argentina, Australia, Bahamas, Bahrain, Bangladesh, Barbados, Benin, Bhutan, Bolivia, Botswana,[a] Brazil, Brunei Darussalam, Bulgaria, Burkina Faso, Burma, Burundi, Byelorussian SSR, Cameroon, Cape Verde, Central African Republic, Chad, Chile, China, Colombia, Comoros, Congo, Costa Rica, Cuba, Cyprus, Czechoslovakia, Democratic Kampuchea, Democratic Yemen, Djibouti, Dominican Republic, Ecuador, Egypt, Equatorial Guinea, Ethiopia, Fiji, Gabon, Gambia, German Democratic Republic, Ghana, Guatemala, Guinea, Guinea-Bissau, Guyana, Haiti, Honduras, Hungary, India, Indonesia, Iran, Iraq, Jamaica, Jordan, Kenya, Kuwait, Lao People's Democratic Republic, Lebanon, Liberia, Libyan Arab Jamahiriya, Madagascar, Malaysia, Maldives, Mali, Malta, Mauritania, Mauritius, Mexico, Mongolia, Morocco, Mozambique, Nepal, New Zealand, Nicaragua, Niger, Nigeria, Oman, Pakistan, Panama, Papua New Guinea, Peru, Philippines, Poland, Qatar, Romania, Rwanda, Saint Lucia, Samoa, Sao Tome and Principe, Saudi Arabia, Senegal, Seychelles, Sierra Leone, Singapore, Solomon Islands, Somalia, Sri Lanka, Sudan, Suriname, Syrian Arab Republic, Thailand, Togo, Trinidad and Tobago, Tunisia, Turkey, Uganda, Ukrainian SSR, USSR, United Arab Emirates, Uruguay, Vanuatu, Venezuela, Viet Nam, Yemen, Yugoslavia, Zaire, Zambia, Zimbabwe.

Against: Belgium, France, Germany, Federal Republic of, Italy, Luxembourg, Netherlands, Portugal, United Kingdom, United States.

Abstaining: Austria, Canada, Denmark, Finland, Greece, Iceland, Ireland, Israel, Ivory Coast, Japan, Lesotho, Malawi, Norway, Spain, Swaziland, Sweden.

[a]Later advised the Secretariat that it had intended to abstain.

Speaking in explanation of vote in the Fourth Committee, a number of countries felt that the draft made an erroneous assumption and a sweeping condemnation that all foreign economic interests were detrimental to the decolonization process.

Portugal deplored the way the topic had been handled for political aims by some. The United Kingdom saw contradictions between the wholesale condemnation of foreign economic involvement in NSGTs and the frequent calls made in other resolutions asking administering Powers to accelerate and expand economic development in dependent Territories; it also asserted that the isolation of South Africa advocated in paragraphs 19 and 20 would prejudice prospects for a negotiated settlement, while causing widespread economic damage. Belgium said the text was unbalanced; it avoided any reference to the satisfactory evolution of many Territories and censured foreign investments as being prejudicial to the interests of the population. Similarly, the Netherlands, objecting to paragraph 3, found it amazing that year after year certain speakers tried to depict the situation in NSGTs as one of unmitigated colonial extortionism when, with the exception of South Africa's illegal occupation of Namibia, Secretariat reports left no doubt that the administering Powers continued to promote the in-

terests of the inhabitants.

The Federal Republic of Germany considered foreign investment to be an asset to newly independent States in their efforts to build up economic systems of their own, as did Italy, which believed that NGSTs needed substantial inputs of capital and technology for their economic and social development. France also felt that foreign economic activities could contribute to development.

Denmark, on behalf of the five Nordic countries, and Turkey said the text should have distinguished between various kinds of foreign economic activities. The Nordic countries also had reservations of principle regarding a number of paragraphs which, it felt, failed to take into account Charter provisions concerning the division of competence between the General Assembly and the Security Council. Ireland, while supporting the part of the draft related to foreign economic interests in Namibia, said the text failed to address the complex range of issues confronting the remaining small NSGTs, for which carefully promoted economic development remained an important factor in the independence process. Japan asserted that foreign economic interests could make beneficial contributions to Territories, especially in technology transfer, managerial skills and job opportunities; it considered the new paragraphs added to this year's text to be particularly unfortunate. Canada also felt that transnational corporations could have a beneficial impact on development and technology transfer; it could not support the contention in paragraph 14 that all foreign economic activities in Namibia were illegal under international law.

As a land-locked country, Swaziland had difficulty supporting paragraph 15, as it did not spell out any compensatory alternative for supplying petroleum products to States dependent on South Africa; it could not implement measures to isolate South Africa called for in paragraph 19 without hurting its own fragile economy.

Several countries which voted in favour of the text had reservations about certain aspects. Chile did not support the concept that all foreign economic interests obstructed the Declaration's implementation. Fiji asserted that, if properly regulated, such interests could contribute to development and higher living standards. Australia said that in many NSGTs constructive foreign investment had played a role in economic development and progress towards self-determination; it had misgivings about the paragraphs on southern Africa, particularly Namibia. New Zealand rejected the indiscriminate criticism of administering Powers, and declared that no element in the text had any relevance to New Zealand's administration of Tokelau.

Objections to the naming of countries for criticism, particularly in paragraph 18, were voiced by Chile,

Colombia, France, the Federal Republic of Germany, Japan, the Netherlands and Portugal. Italy added that the draft was more extreme than in the past and unfriendly to some Member States.

Afghanistan, Cuba, Czechoslovakia, Democratic Yemen, the Lao People's Democratic Republic and the Syrian Arab Republic, on the other hand, said the text should have condemned Israel and the United States by name. Agreeing that the text should have named all the States co-operating with South Africa, Mongolia felt it also should have included an appeal to the Security Council to impose comprehensive sanctions against the régime, and the USSR added that it should have contained stronger wording against colonialism and neo-colonialism. Bulgaria and the USSR deplored the rejection of the consensus reached in the Committee on colonial countries. The Libyan Arab Jamahiriya stated that, on account of the weakness of the resolutions adopted in the past, the situation in Namibia had not improved over the past 39 years.

Military activities in colonial countries

Action by the Committee on colonial countries. Pursuant to a 1984 General Assembly request,[22] the Committee on colonial countries continued to discuss in 1985 military activities and bases in colonial Territories, approving a decision on the topic on 7 August and recommending a draft decision to the Assembly for adoption.

GENERAL ASSEMBLY ACTION

In December, the Assembly adopted **decision 40/415**, by recorded vote.

Military activities and arrangements by colonial Powers in Territories under their administration which might be impeding the implementation of the Declaration on the Granting of Independence to Colonial Countries and Peoples
At its 99th plenary meeting, on 2 December 1985, the General Assembly, on the recommendation of the Fourth Committee, adopted the following text:
"1. The General Assembly, having examined the chapter of the report of the Special Committee on the Situation with regard to the Implementation of the Declaration on the Granting of Independence to Colonial Countries and Peoples relating to an item on the Special Committee's agenda entitled 'Military activities and arrangements by colonial Powers in Territories under their administration which might be impeding the implementation of the Declaration on the Granting of Independence to Colonial Countries and Peoples', and recalling its decision 39/412 of 5 December 1984 on this subject, deplores the fact that the colonial Powers concerned have taken no steps to implement the request that the Assembly has repeatedly addressed to them, most recently in paragraph 10 of its resolution 39/91 of 14 December 1984, to withdraw immediately and unconditionally their military bases and installations from colonial Territories and to refrain from establishing new ones.

"2. The General Assembly, in recalling its resolution 1514(XV) of 14 December 1960 and all other United Nations resolutions and decisions relating to military bases and installations in colonial and Non-Self-Governing Territories, reaffirms its strong conviction that the presence of military bases and installations in the colonial and Non-Self-Governing Territories could constitute a major obstacle to the implementation of the Declaration on the Granting of Independence to Colonial Countries and Peoples and that it is the responsibility of the administering Powers to ensure that the existence of such bases and installations does not hinder the populations of the Territories from exercising their right to self-determination and independence in conformity with the purposes and principles of the Charter of the United Nations and the Declaration. Furthermore, aware of the presence of military bases and installations of the administering Powers concerned and other countries in those Territories, the Assembly urges the administering Powers concerned to continue to take all necessary measures not to involve those Territories in any offensive acts or interference against other States and to comply fully with the purposes and principles of the Charter, the Declaration and the resolutions and decisions of the United Nations relating to military activities and arrangements by colonial Powers in Territories under their administration.

"3. The General Assembly reiterates its condemnation of all military activities and arrangements by colonial Powers in Territories under their administration that are detrimental to the rights and interests of the colonial peoples concerned, especially their right to self-determination and independence. The Assembly once again calls upon the colonial Powers concerned to terminate such activities and eliminate such military bases in compliance with the relevant resolutions of the Assembly, in particular with paragraph 9 of the Plan of Action for the Full Implementation of the Declaration on the Granting of Independence to Colonial Countries and Peoples, contained in the annex to Assembly resolution 35/118 of 11 December 1980.

"4. The General Assembly declares that the colonial Territories and areas adjacent thereto should not be used for nuclear testing, dumping of nuclear wastes or deployment of nuclear and other weapons of mass destruction.

"5. The General Assembly notes with serious concern that, in southern Africa in general and in and around Namibia in particular, a critical situation continues to prevail as a result of South Africa's continued illegal occupation of the Territory and its inhuman repression of the people of South Africa. The racist régime has resorted to desperate measures in order to suppress by force the legitimate aspirations of those peoples and, in its escalating war against them and their national liberation movements, struggling for freedom, justice and independence, the régime has repeatedly committed acts of armed aggression against the neighbouring independent African States, particularly Angola and Botswana, which have caused extensive loss of human lives and destruction of the economic infrastructure.

"6. The General Assembly strongly condemns South Africa for its ever-increasing and large-scale military build-up in Namibia, particularly its massive military offensive launched recently in northern Namibia, its introduction of compulsory military service for Namibians, its forced recruitment and training of Namibians for tribal armies, its use of mercenaries to reinforce its illegal occupation of the Territory and to participate in its attacks against independent African States and its illegal use of Namibian territory for acts of aggression against those States. The Assembly calls upon all States to take effective measures to prevent the recruitment, training and transit of mercenaries for service in Namibia. It condemns the continued military, nuclear and intelligence collaboration between South Africa and certain countries, which constitutes a violation of the arms embargo imposed against South Africa by the Security Council in its resolution 418(1977) of 4 November 1977, and which poses a threat to international peace and security. The Assembly urges that the Security Council consider, as a matter of urgency, the report of the Committee established under its resolution 421(1977) of 9 December 1977 and that it should adopt further measures to widen the scope of resolution 418(1977) in order to make it more effective and comprehensive. The Assembly also calls for the scrupulous observance of Security Council resolution 558(1984) of 13 December 1984 enjoining Member States to refrain from importing armaments from South Africa. The Assembly is particularly mindful in that regard of the relevant resolutions of the Organization of African Unity, the Final Document of the Extraordinary Ministerial Meeting of the Co-ordinating Bureau of Non-Aligned Countries on the question of Namibia, held at New Delhi from 19 to 21 April 1985, the Final Document adopted by the United Nations Council for Namibia at its extraordinary plenary meetings held at Vienna from 3 to 7 June 1985, and Security Council resolutions 567(1985) of 20 June 1985 and 568(1985) of 21 June 1985.

"7. The General Assembly demands the urgent dismantling of all military bases in the international Territory of Namibia and calls for the immediate cessation of the war of oppression waged by the racist minority régime against the people of Namibia and their national liberation movement, the South West Africa People's Organization, their sole and authentic representative. Reaffirming the legitimacy of the struggle of the people of Namibia to achieve their freedom and independence, the Assembly appeals to all States to render sustained and increased moral and political support, as well as financial, military and other material assistance, to the South West Africa People's Organization to enable it to intensify its struggle for the liberation of Namibia.

"8. The General Assembly considers that the acquisition of nuclear-weapons capability by the racist régime of South Africa, with its infamous record of violence and aggression, constitutes a further effort on its part to terrorize and intimidate independent States in the region into submission while also posing a threat to all mankind. The continuing assistance rendered to the South African régime by certain Western and other countries in the military and nuclear fields belies their stated opposition to the racist practice of the South African régime and makes them willing partners of its hegemonistic and criminal policies. The Assembly condemns the continued nuclear co-operation by certain Western and other countries with South Africa. It calls upon the States concerned to end all such co-operation and, in particular, to halt the supply to South Africa of equipment, technology, nuclear materials and related training, which increases its nuclear capability.

"9. The General Assembly, noting that the militarization of Namibia has led to the forced conscription of Namibians, to a greatly intensified flow of refugees and to a tragic disorganization of the family life of the Na-

mibian people, strongly condemns the forcible and wholesale displacement of Namibians from their homes for military and political purposes and the introduction of compulsory military service for Namibians and declares that all measures by the illegal occupation régime to enforce military conscription in Namibia are null and void. In this connection, the Assembly urges all Governments, the specialized agencies and other intergovernmental organizations to provide increased material assistance to the thousands of refugees who have been forced by the *apartheid* régime's oppressive policies in Namibia and South Africa to flee into the neighbouring States.

"10. The General Assembly, in recalling its resolution ES-8/2 of 14 September 1981, by which it strongly urged States to cease forthwith, individually and collectively, all dealings with South Africa in order totally to isolate it politically, economically, militarily and culturally, strongly condemns the continuing collaboration of certain countries with the racist régime in the political, economic, military and nuclear fields. It calls for the termination forthwith of all such collaboration as it undermines international solidarity against the *apartheid* régime and helps to perpetuate that régime's illegal occupation of Namibia.

"11. The General Assembly deprecates the continued alienation of land in colonial Territories for military installations. While it has been argued that the servicing of such installations creates employment, nevertheless, the large-scale utilization of local economic and manpower resources for this purpose diverts resources that could be more beneficially utilized in promoting the economic development of the Territories concerned and is thus contrary to the interests of their populations.

"12. The General Assembly requests the Secretary-General to continue, through the Department of Public Information of the Secretariat, an intensified campaign of publicity with a view to informing world public opinion of the facts concerning the military activities and arrangements in colonial Territories that are impeding the implementation of the Declaration on the Granting of Independence to Colonial Countries and Peoples, contained in Assembly resolution 1514(XV).

"13. The General Assembly requests the Special Committee to continue its consideration of the item and to report thereon to the Assembly at its forty-first session."

General Assembly decision 40/415

125-10-15 (recorded vote)

Approved by Fourth Committee (A/40/883) by recorded vote (95-11-14), 29 October (meeting 10); draft by Committee on colonial countries (A/40/23); agenda item 110.

Meeting numbers. GA 40th session: 4th Committee 2-11; plenary 99.

Recorded vote in Assembly as follows:

In favour: Afghanistan, Albania, Algeria, Angola, Antigua and Barbuda, Argentina, Bahamas, Bahrain, Bangladesh, Barbados, Benin, Bhutan, Bolivia, Botswana,[a] Brazil, Brunei Darussalam, Bulgaria, Burkina Faso, Burma, Burundi, Byelorussian SSR, Cameroon, Cape Verde, Central African Republic, Chad, China, Colombia, Comoros, Congo, Costa Rica, Cuba, Cyprus, Czechoslovakia, Democratic Kampuchea, Democratic Yemen, Djibouti, Dominican Republic, Ecuador, Egypt, Equatorial Guinea, Ethiopia, Fiji, Gabon, Gambia, German Democratic Republic, Ghana, Grenada, Guatemala, Guinea, Guinea-Bissau, Guyana, Haiti, Hungary, India, Indonesia, Iran, Iraq, Ivory Coast, Jamaica, Jordan, Kenya, Kuwait, Lao People's Democratic Republic, Lebanon, Lesotho, Liberia, Libyan Arab Jamahiriya, Madagascar, Malaysia, Maldives, Mali, Malta, Mauritania, Mauritius, Mexico, Mongolia, Morocco, Mozambique, Nepal, Nicaragua, Niger, Nigeria, Oman, Pakistan, Panama, Papua New Guinea, Peru, Philippines, Poland, Qatar, Romania, Rwanda, Saint Lucia, Samoa, Sao Tome and Principe, Saudi Arabia, Senegal, Seychelles, Sierra Leone, Singapore, Solomon Islands, Somalia, Sri Lanka, Sudan, Suriname, Swaziland, Syrian Arab Republic, Thailand, Togo, Trinidad and Tobago, Tunisia, Turkey, Uganda, Ukrainian SSR, USSR, United

Arab Emirates, Uruguay, Vanuatu, Venezuela, Viet Nam, Yemen, Yugoslavia, Zaire, Zambia, Zimbabwe.

Against: Belgium, Canada, France, Germany, Federal Republic of, Italy, Japan, Luxembourg, Portugal, United Kingdom, United States.

Abstaining: Australia, Austria, Denmark, Finland, Greece, Honduras, Iceland, Ireland, Israel, Malawi, Netherlands,[b] New Zealand, Norway, Spain, Sweden.

[a]Later advised the Secretariat that it had intended to abstain.
[b]Later advised the Secretariat that it had intended to vote against.

In explanation of vote, a number of countries expressed concern over the procedural irregularity of voting on a draft dealing with a subject that was not among the agenda items allocated to the Fourth Committee. These States included Australia, Canada, the Federal Republic of Germany, Luxembourg (also on behalf of the European Community member States), New Zealand, Portugal and the United Kingdom. In addition, Canada saw in the text misleading and exaggerated language and unsubstantiated criticisms of individual countries. The United Kingdom felt the decision served only to keep alive the outdated mythology of colonialism by those who were implacably hostile to Western interests. Australia had difficulties with the substance of the text, as did New Zealand, which did not accept the implication that military activities or the presence of military bases in colonial Territories necessarily impeded the decolonization process. Denmark, speaking for the five Nordic countries, had reservations regarding United Nations endorsement of the use of armed struggle and the call for military assistance.

Although voting in favour, Fiji said it was for the inhabitants of the Territories themselves to decide if their right to self-determination was being affected by foreign military installations. Turkey, expressing reservations on references to Western countries and disapproval of express mention of countries when responsibility could not be imputed with certainty, stated that paragraphs 2, 3 and 11 could have been drafted in a more balanced way.

For Viet Nam, the use of the words "could" and "might" in the text cast doubt on the obvious realities—that foreign military installations and activities impeded the implementation of the Declaration—and should have been deleted, along with the words "to continue" in paragraph 2. Afghanistan, Czechoslovakia, the Lao People's Democratic Republic and the Syrian Arab Republic said Israel and the United States should have been mentioned and condemned by name. Mongolia also felt that the text should have made specific reference to Israel, the United States and other Western countries whose military co-operation, particularly in the nuclear field, helped South Africa pursue its genocidal policy; it also believed that those NSGTs being used as beachheads of imperialism should have been specified by name.

Information dissemination

The Committee on colonial countries considered, on 16 May and 9 August, dissemination of information on decolonization, approving in August the recommendations made by its Sub-Committee on Petitions, Information and Assistance, including recommendations concerning Namibia (see Chapter III of this section).

The Sub-Committee suggested that the Committee encourage NGOs to continue assisting colonial peoples and their national liberation movements and making efforts to counteract the hostile campaign being waged by South Africa and its Western and other allies to depict national liberation movements as terrorist organizations. It also recommended that its Chairman discuss with the presiding officers of the Special Committee against *Apartheid* and the Council for Namibia the holding of periodic consultations in order to co-ordinate the activities of the three bodies.

Other recommendations included: continuing information dissemination by the United Nations Department of Political Affairs, Trusteeship and Decolonization and by DPI; making the international community aware that United Nations recognition of the legitimacy of the liberation struggle by the people of southern Africa entailed extending moral and material support to them and their national liberation movements; updating and ensuring greater distribution of studies and monographs on decolonization; underlining in DPI activities the high priority the United Nations gave to eradicating colonialism; strengthening co-operation with the pool of non-aligned press agencies; providing feedback reports from United Nations information centres; and requesting DPI to obtain wider coverage by the mass media, particularly in Western Europe and the Americas, which received limited coverage. The Special Committee should appeal to the mass media to regard it as their task to contribute to eliminating the remaining vestiges of colonialism and to render support to colonial peoples. Both Departments were called on to increase their speaking engagements at North American universities on the subject of decolonization, with particular emphasis on Namibia.

Information dissemination efforts during the year included a series of United Nations activities—in co-operation with DPI, assisted by the information centres—in observance of the Week of Solidarity with the Peoples of Namibia and All Other Colonial Territories, as well as those in South Africa, Fighting for Freedom, Independence and Human Rights (May). The Committee, the Special Committee against *Apartheid* and the Council for Namibia postponed a joint meeting in observance of the Week and Africa Liberation Day, in the light of a series of conferences and meetings being held during 1985 within their respective mandates.

The Committee's continuing co-operation with NGOs included representation by its Chairman at a meeting with NGOs, organized by DPI at United Nations Headquarters (February); media encounters, also organized by DPI (May, August); and NGO participation at the Committee's regional seminars (see also p. 1060).

On 2 December, the General Assembly adopted **resolution 40/58** by recorded vote.

Dissemination of information on decolonization

The General Assembly,

Having examined the chapters of the report of the Special Committee on the Situation with regard to the Implementation of the Declaration on the Granting of Independence to Colonial Countries and Peoples relating to the dissemination of information on decolonization and publicity for the work of the United Nations in the field of decolonization,

Recalling its resolution 1514(XV) of 14 December 1960, containing the Declaration on the Granting of Independence to Colonial Countries and Peoples, and all other resolutions and decisions of the United Nations concerning the dissemination of information on decolonization, in particular General Assembly resolution 39/92 of 14 December 1984,

Reiterating the importance of publicity as an instrument for furthering the aims and purposes of the Declaration and mindful of the continuing pressing need to take all possible steps to acquaint world public opinion with all aspects of the problems of decolonization, with a view to assisting effectively the peoples of the colonial Territories to achieve self-determination, freedom and independence,

Aware of the increasingly important role being played in the widespread dissemination of relevant information by a number of non-governmental organizations having a special interest in decolonization, and noting with satisfaction the intensified efforts of the Special Committee in enlisting the support of those organizations in that regard,

1. *Approves* the chapters of the report of the Special Committee on the Situation with regard to the Implementation of the Declaration on the Granting of Independence to Colonial Countries and Peoples relating to the dissemination of information on decolonization and publicity for the work of the United Nations in the field of decolonization;

2. *Considers* it incumbent upon the United Nations to continue to play an active role in the process of self-determination and independence and to intensify its efforts for the widest possible dissemination of information on decolonization, with a view to the further mobilization of international public opinion in support of complete decolonization;

3. *Requests* the Secretary-General, having regard to the suggestions of the Special Committee, to continue to take concrete measures through all the media at his disposal, including publications, radio and television, to give widespread and continuous publicity to the work of the United Nations in the field of decolonization, and, *inter alia*:

(a) To continue, in consultation with the Special Committee, to collect, prepare and disseminate basic material, studies and articles relating to the problems of decolonization and, in particular, to continue to publish the periodical *Objective: Justice* and other publications, special articles and studies, including the *Decolonization* series, and to select from them appropriate material for wider dissemination by means of reprints in various languages;

(b) To seek the full co-operation of the administering Powers concerned in the discharge of the tasks referred to above;

(c) To intensify the activities of all United Nations information centres;

(d) To maintain a close working relationship with the Organization of African Unity by holding periodic consultations and by systematically exchanging relevant information with that organization;

(e) To enlist, with the close co-operation of United Nations information centres, the support of non-governmental organizations having a special interest in decolonization in the dissemination of the relevant information;

(f) To ensure the availability of the necessary facilities and services to that end;

(g) To report to the Special Committee on the measures taken in implementation of the present resolution;

4. *Requests* all States, in particular the administering Powers, the specialized agencies and other organizations of the United Nations system and non-governmental organizations having a special interest in decolonization to undertake or intensify, in co-operation with the Secretary-General and within their respective spheres of competence, the large-scale dissemination of the information referred to in paragraph 2 above;

5. *Requests* the Special Committee to follow the implementation of the present resolution and report thereon to the General Assembly at its forty-first session.

General Assembly resolution 40/58

2 December 1985   Meeting 99   142-3-6 (recorded vote)

23-nation draft (A/40/L.22 & Add.1); agenda item 18.

Sponsors: Afghanistan, Algeria, Congo, Cuba, Cyprus, Czechoslovakia, Ethiopia, German Democratic Republic, India, Lao People's Democratic Republic, Madagascar, Mongolia, Nicaragua, Papua New Guinea, Romania, Sierra Leone, Syrian Arab Republic, Trinidad and Tobago, Tunisia, United Republic of Tanzania, Venezuela, Viet Nam, Yugoslavia.

Financial implications. 5th Committee, A/40/955; S-G, A/C.5/40/64.

Meeting numbers. GA 40th session: 5th Committee 50; plenary 36, 96, 97, 99.

Recorded vote in Assembly as follows:

In favour: Afghanistan, Albania, Algeria, Angola, Antigua and Barbuda, Argentina, Australia, Austria, Bahamas, Bahrain, Bangladesh, Barbados, Benin, Bhutan, Bolivia, Botswana, Brazil, Brunei Darussalam, Bulgaria, Burkina Faso, Burma, Burundi, Byelorussian SSR, Cameroon, Canada, Cape Verde, Central African Republic, Chad, Chile, China, Colombia, Comoros, Congo, Costa Rica, Cuba, Cyprus, Czechoslovakia, Democratic Kampuchea, Democratic Yemen, Denmark, Djibouti, Ecuador, Egypt, El Salvador, Equatorial Guinea, Ethiopia, Fiji, Finland, Gabon, Gambia, German Democratic Republic, Ghana, Greece, Guatemala, Guinea, Guinea-Bissau, Guyana, Haiti, Honduras, Hungary, Iceland, India, Indonesia, Iran, Iraq, Ireland, Ivory Coast, Jamaica, Japan, Jordan, Kenya, Kuwait, Lao People's Democratic Republic, Lebanon, Lesotho, Liberia, Libyan Arab Jamahiriya, Madagascar, Malawi, Malaysia, Maldives, Mali, Malta, Mauritania, Mauritius, Mexico, Mongolia, Morocco, Mozambique, Nepal, New Zealand, Nicaragua, Niger, Nigeria, Norway, Oman, Pakistan, Panama, Papua New Guinea, Peru, Philippines, Poland, Portugal, Qatar, Romania, Rwanda, Saint Lucia, Samoa, Sao Tome and Principe, Saudi Arabia, Senegal, Seychelles, Sierra Leone, Singapore, Solomon Islands, Somalia, Spain, Sri Lanka, Sudan, Suriname, Swaziland, Sweden, Syrian Arab Republic, Thailand, Togo, Trinidad and Tobago, Tunisia, Turkey, Uganda, Ukrainian SSR, USSR, United Arab Emirates, United Republic of Tanzania, Uruguay, Vanuatu, Venezuela, Viet Nam, Yemen, Yugoslavia, Zaire, Zambia, Zimbabwe.

Against: Israel, United Kingdom, United States.

Abstaining: Belgium, France, Germany, Federal Republic of, Italy, Luxembourg, Netherlands.

In explanation of vote, Israel objected to having been singled out in a discriminatory way, adding that, if such action was justified, the Committee on colonial countries should have published a list of at least 50 Member States from all political and regional groupings that maintained links with South Africa. The United Kingdom asserted that information work in the decolonization area should diminish rather than intensify as the era of decolonization drew to a close. Italy, objecting to unjustified criticism of countries or to references to questions not within the Committee mandate, saw as inappropriate any request to DPI which might result in unfriendly activities towards Member States. In a similar vein, the Netherlands said the Committee recommendations sought to use the Organization's resources for a campaign of unwarranted and selective criticism of one particular group of countries.

Japan expressed reservations on paragraph 1, as did Finland (for the five Nordic countries), which did not approve all the specific parts of the Committee's chapter on information dissemination.

Puerto Rico

The Committee on colonial countries, reviewing the list of Territories to which the 1960 Declaration applied, considered a separate item based on its 24 August 1984 decision[23] concerning Puerto Rico.

At meetings held between 12 and 14 August, the Committee heard the representatives of 26 organizations, mainly from Puerto Rico. By a resolution of 14 August, adopted by 11 votes to 1, with 10 abstentions, the Committee reaffirmed the inalienable right of the people of Puerto Rico to self-determination and the applicability of the principles of the 1960 Declaration to Puerto Rico, expressed the hope that its people might exercise that right without hindrance and requested the Rapporteur to report to the Committee on the implementation of its resolutions on Puerto Rico. The resolution was transmitted to the United States.

Two reports on the topic were submitted by the Committee's Rapporteur: in August,[24] dealing with an exchange of communications involving Cuba, the United States, the Committee Chairman and the Rapporteur; and in December,[25] a study on recent developments in Puerto Rico, United Nations actions and the views of the parties concerned on the question of Puerto Rico's political status.

In the Final Political Declaration adopted by the Conference of Foreign Ministers of Non-Aligned Countries, and forwarded to the Secretary-General by Angola,[15] the Ministers noted with interest the Committee's 14 August resolution and reaffirmed their support for the inalienable right of the people of Puerto Rico to self-determination and independence in accordance with the 1960 Declaration.

New Caledonia

By a letter of 21 June,[26] Papua New Guinea informed the Secretary-General that the Foreign Ministers of Solomon Islands, Vanuatu and Papua New Guinea met at Vila, Vanuatu, on 3 June to obtain information from the Front de libération nationale kanak et socialiste (FLNKS) on the Territory's development since the November 1984 Territorial Assembly elections. The four participants refuted the credibility and genuineness of France's efforts to bring independence for New Caledonia, condemned the French military buildup in New Caledonia, and agreed on reinscribing the Territory on the United Nations list of NSGTs.

The sixteenth South Pacific Forum (Rarotonga, Cook Islands, 5 and 6 August), in a 6 August communiqué,[27] reaffirmed its support for New Caledonia's early transition to independence, urged the French Government to undertake electoral reforms prior to the act of self-determination scheduled to take place before the end of 1987, and agreed to seek information from the United Nations on the applicability to New Caledonia of the United Nations Charter and the 1960 Declaration, without accepting reinscription at that juncture of New Caledonia on the United Nations NSGTs list.

The Committee agreed on 9 August to continue consideration, in 1986, of the question of the list of Territories to which the Declaration applied.

The September Conference of Foreign Ministers of Non-Aligned Countries [17] expressed their support for self-determination and the early transition to an independent New Caledonia in accordance with the rights and aspirations of the indigenous people, and in a manner which guaranteed the rights and interests of all its inhabitants, and commended the administering Power and the people of New Caledonia for their stated desire for a speedy and peaceful solution.

On 2 October, Papua New Guinea[28] transmitted to the Committee Chairman information on New Caledonia describing its historical and political evolution and focusing on the situation of the indigenous Melanesian Kanaks. A FLNKS communiqué on elections held in the Territory on 29 September 1985 was annexed.

REFERENCES

[1]YUN 1960, p. 49, GA res. 1514(XV), 14 Dec. 1960. [2]A/40/173-S/17033. [3]A/40/276-S/17138. [4]A/40/23. [5]A/40/92. [6]YUN 1984, p. 994, GA res. 39/93, annex, 14 Dec. 1984. [7]A/AC.109/821. [8]A/AC.109/822 & Add.1. [9]YUN 1984, p. 356, GA res. 39/98 A, 14 Dec. 1984. [10]A/AC.109/828. [11]A/AC.109/846. [12]A/40/757 & Add.1. [13]S/17571. [14]A/40/837. [15]A/40/854-S/17610 & Corr.1. [16]A/40/318 & Add.1. [17]YUN 1984, p. 1004, GA res. 39/43, 5 Dec. 1984. [18]*Ibid.*, pp. 1033, 1042 & 1058, GA res. 39/50 A, C & E, 12 Dec. 1984. [19]E/1985/114. [20]A/C.4/40/L.13. [21]YUN 1984, p. 426. [22]*Ibid.* p. 1012, GA dec. 39/412, 5 Dec. 1984. [23]YUN 1984, p. 1017. [24]A/AC.109/L.1571. [25]A/AC.109/L.1572 & Corr.1,2. [26]S/17316 & Corr.1. [27]A/40/672-S/17488. [28]A/AC.109/847.

Other general questions concerning NSGTs

Scholarships

In a report to the General Assembly covering 1 October 1984 to 30 September 1985,[1] the Secretary-General stated that the following 33 States had offered to make scholarships available to persons from NSGTs for academic and vocational studies: Austria, Brazil, Bulgaria, Cyprus, Czechoslovakia, Egypt, the German Democratic Republic, the Federal Republic of Germany, Ghana, Greece, Hungary, India, Iran, Israel, Italy, the Libyan Arab Jamahiriya, Malawi, Malta, Mexico, Pakistan, the Philippines, Poland, Romania, Sri Lanka, the Sudan, the Syrian Arab Republic, Tunisia, Turkey, Uganda, the USSR, the United Arab Emirates, the United States and Yugoslavia. Information about these offers was included in the twenty-fourth edition of the handbook *Study Abroad (1983/84, 1984/85, 1985/86)*, published by UNESCO.

During the period covered, 82 students, mostly not inhabitants of NSGTs, requested information and application forms from the Secretariat. Namibian students were referred to the Office of the United Nations Commissioner for Namibia. Some applicants contacted the offering States directly, or were requested to do so in the case of study opportunities in Ghana, Poland, the USSR and the United States.

Several offering States informed the Secretary-General of developments in their facilities: Austria had awarded scholarships in 1984 to two inhabitants of Namibia; Czechoslovakia offered 20 scholarships annually for inhabitants of NSGTs; the Federal Republic of Germany sponsored three students from Namibia, seven post-graduate students and 334 stipendiaries in practical and vocational training; 30 Namibian students completed a four-year course in Malta's trade schools, with another 12 students starting a two-year nursing course; and 154 students from NSGTs studied in the Byelorussian SSR, the Ukrainian SSR and the USSR. For the 1985/86 academic year, Poland would grant three scholarships; the Sudan, a university scholarship; and Turkey, a scholarship to a Namibian student.

GENERAL ASSEMBLY ACTION

On 2 December, the General Assembly, on the recommendation of the Fourth Committee, adopted **resolution 40/55**, without vote.

Offers by Member States of study and training facilities for inhabitants of Non-Self-Governing Territories

The General Assembly,

Recalling its resolution 39/45 of 5 December 1984,

Having considered the report of the Secretary-General on offers by Member States of study and training facilities for inhabitants of Non-Self-Governing Territories, prepared pursuant to General Assembly resolution 845(IX) of 22 November 1954,

Considering that more scholarships should be made available to the inhabitants of Non-Self-Governing Territories in all parts of the world and that steps should be taken to encourage applications from students in those Territories,

1. *Takes note* of the report of the Secretary-General;

2. *Expresses its appreciation* to those Member States that have made scholarships available to the inhabitants of Non-Self-Governing Territories;

3. *Invites* all States to make or continue to make generous offers of study and training facilities to the inhabitants of those Territories that have not yet attained self-government or independence and, wherever possible, to provide travel funds to prospective students;

4. *Urges* the administering Powers to take effective measures to ensure the widespread and continuous dissemination in the Territories under their administration of information relating to offers of study and training facilities made by States and to provide all the necessary facilities to enable students to avail themselves of such offers;

5. *Requests* the Secretary-General to report to the General Assembly at its forty-first session on the implementation of the present resolution;

6. *Draws the attention* of the Special Committee on the Situation with regard to the Implementation of the Declaration on the Granting of Independence to Colonial Countries and Peoples to the present resolution.

General Assembly resolution 40/55

2 December 1985   Meeting 99   Adopted without vote

Approved by Fourth Committee (A/40/887) without vote, 8 November (meeting 20); 40-nation draft (A/C.4/40/L.6); agenda item 113.

Sponsors: Algeria, Angola, Australia, Bangladesh, Bulgaria, Burkina Faso, Colombia, Cuba, Cyprus, Czechoslovakia, Egypt, Fiji, Guinea, Guinea-Bissau, Guyana, India, Jamaica, Japan, Kenya, Madagascar, Mali, New Zealand, Nicaragua, Nigeria, Pakistan, Papua New Guinea, Philippines, Samoa, Sierra Leone, Syrian Arab Republic, Togo, Trinidad and Tobago, Tunisia, Turkey, United Republic of Tanzania, United States, Venezuela, Yugoslavia, Zambia, Zimbabwe.

Meeting numbers. GA 40th session: 4th Committee 11, 12, 15-20; plenary 99.

Information to the United Nations

States responsible for the administration of Territories which had not attained full self-government continued to transmit regularly to the Secretary-General information on the Territories' economic, social and educational conditions under the terms of Article 73 *e* in Chapter XI of the United Nations Charter and in accordance with several General Assembly resolutions. In the most recent such resolution, in 1984,[2] the Assembly requested the fullest possible information on political and constitutional developments. In a September 1985 report,[3] the Secretary-General stated that he had received information with respect to the following NSGTs:

New Zealand: Tokelau

United Kingdom: Anguilla, Bermuda, British Virgin Islands, Cayman Islands, Falkland Islands (Malvinas), Gibraltar, Montserrat, Pitcairn, St. Helena, Turks and Caicos Islands

United States: American Samoa, Guam, United States Virgin Islands

On 25 February 1985,[4] Portugal informed the Secretary-General that it had nothing to add to the information provided in a 1979 note[5] which stated that conditions in East Timor had prevented it from assuming its responsibilities for the Territory's administration. (See also Chapter IV of this section.)

With respect to Western Sahara, the Secretary-General noted in his report that Spain had informed him in 1976[6] that, with the termination of its presence in the Territory, it considered itself exempt from any international responsibility in connection with the Territory's administration. (See also Chapter IV of this section.)

GENERAL ASSEMBLY ACTION

On 2 December, the General Assembly, on the recommendation of the Fourth Committee, adopted by recorded vote **resolution 40/51**, drafted by the Committee on colonial countries.

Information from Non-Self-Governing Territories transmitted under Article 73 *e* of the Charter of the United Nations

The General Assembly,

Having examined the chapter of the report of the Special Committee on the Situation with regard to the Implementation of the Declaration on the Granting of Independence to Colonial Countries and Peoples relating to the information from Non-Self-Governing Territories transmitted under Article 73 *e* of the Charter of the United Nations and the action taken by the Committee in respect of that information,

Having also examined the report of the Secretary-General on the question,

Recalling its resolution 1970(XVIII) of 16 December 1963, in which it requested the Special Committee to study the information transmitted to the Secretary-General in accordance with Article 73 *e* of the Charter and to take such information fully into account in examining the situation with regard to the implementation of the Declaration on the Granting of Independence to Colonial Countries and Peoples, contained in General Assembly resolution 1514(XV) of 14 December 1960,

Recalling also its resolution 39/41 of 5 December 1984, in which it requested the Special Committee to continue to discharge the functions entrusted to it under resolution 1970(XVIII),

1. *Approves* the chapter of the report of the Special Committee on the Situation with regard to the Implementation of the Declaration on the Granting of Independence to Colonial Countries and Peoples relating to the information from Non-Self-Governing Territories transmitted under Article 73 *e* of the Charter of the United Nations;

2. *Reaffirms* that, in the absence of a decision by the General Assembly itself that a Non-Self-Governing Territory has attained a full measure of self-government in terms of Chapter XI of the Charter, the administering Power concerned should continue to transmit information under Article 73 *e* of the Charter with respect to that Territory;

3. *Requests* the administering Powers concerned to transmit, or continue to transmit, to the Secretary-General the information prescribed in Article 73 *e* of the Charter, as well as the fullest possible information on political and constitutional developments in the Territories concerned, within a maximum period of six months following the expiration of the administrative year in those Territories;

4. *Requests* the Special Committee to continue to discharge the functions entrusted to it under General Assembly resolution 1970(XVIII), in accordance with established procedures, and to report thereon to the Assembly at its forty-first session.

General Assembly resolution 40/51

2 December 1985   Meeting 99   149-0-3 (recorded vote)

Approved by Fourth Committee (A/40/884) by recorded vote (131-0-3), 8 November (meeting 20); draft by Committee on colonial countries (A/40/23); agenda item 109.
Meeting numbers. GA 40th session: 4th Committee 11, 12, 15-20; plenary 99.

Recorded vote in Assembly as follows:

In favour: Afghanistan, Albania, Algeria, Angola, Antigua and Barbuda, Argentina, Australia, Austria, Bahamas, Bahrain, Bangladesh, Barbados, Belgium, Benin, Bhutan, Bolivia, Botswana, Brazil, Brunei Darussalam, Bulgaria, Burkina Faso, Burma, Burundi, Byelorussian SSR, Cameroon, Canada, Cape Verde, Central African Republic, Chad, Chile, China, Colombia, Comoros, Congo, Costa Rica, Cuba, Cyprus, Czechoslovakia, Democratic Kampuchea, Democratic Yemen, Denmark, Djibouti, Dominican Republic, Ecuador, Egypt, Equatorial Guinea, Ethiopia, Fiji, Finland, Gabon, Gambia, German Democratic Republic, Germany, Federal Republic of, Ghana, Greece, Grenada, Guatemala, Guinea, Guinea-Bissau, Guyana, Haiti, Honduras, Hungary, Iceland, India, Indonesia, Iran, Iraq, Ireland, Israel, Italy, Ivory Coast, Jamaica, Japan, Jordan, Kenya, Kuwait, Lao People's Democratic Republic, Lebanon, Lesotho, Liberia, Libyan Arab Jamahiriya, Luxembourg, Madagascar, Malawi, Malaysia, Maldives, Mali, Malta, Mauritania, Mauritius, Mexico, Mongolia, Morocco, Mozambique, Nepal, Netherlands, New Zealand, Nicaragua, Niger, Nigeria, Norway, Oman, Pakistan, Panama, Papua New Guinea, Paraguay, Peru, Philippines, Poland, Portugal, Qatar, Romania, Rwanda, Saint Lucia, Samoa, Sao Tome and Principe, Saudi Arabia, Senegal, Seychelles, Sierra Leone, Singapore, Solomon Islands, Somalia, Spain, Sri Lanka, Sudan, Suriname, Swaziland, Sweden, Syrian Arab Republic, Thailand, Togo, Trinidad and Tobago, Tunisia, Turkey, Uganda, Ukrainian SSR, USSR, United Arab Emirates, Uruguay, Vanuatu, Venezuela, Viet Nam, Yemen, Yugoslavia, Zaire, Zambia, Zimbabwe.

Against: None.

Abstaining: France, United Kingdom, United States.

In explanation of vote, the United Kingdom said the draft implied that it was for the Assembly to decide when an NSGT had attained a full measure of self-government, whereas such decisions should be left to the administering Power and the local Government.

Visiting missions

In August, the Committee on colonial countries adopted a resolution on the question of sending visiting missions to Territories,[7] stressing the need to dispatch periodic missions to facilitate full implementation of the 1960 Declaration,[8] calling on the administering Powers concerned to continue to co-operate with the United Nations by permitting access to Territories under their administration, and requesting its Chairman to continue consultations with those Powers regarding such missions.

In **resolution 40/57** of 2 December (see above), the General Assembly called on the administering Powers to continue to co-operate with the Committee and, in particular, to permit visiting missions to secure first-hand information and ascertain the wishes and aspirations of their inhabitants.

The Assembly also dealt with the topic in individual resolutions on Territories (see Chapter IV of this section).

REFERENCES

(1)A/40/718. (2)YUN 1984, p. 1018, GA res. 39/41, 5 Dec. 1984. (3)A/40/629. (4)A/40/159. (5)YUN 1979, p. 1117. (6)YUN 1976, p. 738. (7)A/40/23 (A/AC.109/838). (8)YUN 1960, p. 49, GA res. 1514(XV), 14 Dec. 1960.

Chapter II

International Trusteeship System

On behalf of the Security Council, the Trusteeship Council continued during 1985 to supervise the one Trust Territory remaining under the International Trusteeship System—the Trust Territory of the Pacific Islands, a strategic territory administered by the United States.

The Trusteeship Council considered the Administering Authority's annual report, heard 15 petitioners, and examined five written petitions and three communications regarding the Territory.

The Council held its fifty-second session at United Nations Headquarters from 13 May to 11 July 1985; of its five members (China, France, USSR, United Kingdom, United States), China did not participate.

Trust Territory of the Pacific Islands

Conditions in the Territory

The Trust Territory of the Pacific Islands, designated as a strategic area and administered by the United States in accordance with the Trusteeship Agreement approved by the Security Council in 1947,[1] comprised three archipelagos of more than 2,100 islands and atolls (about 100 of which were inhabited) scattered over some 7.8 million square kilometres of the western Pacific Ocean, north of the Equator. The Territory, collectively known as Micronesia, had an estimated population of 155,900 in 1984.

There were four constitutional Governments within the Territory—the Federated States of Micronesia, the Marshall Islands, the Northern Mariana Islands and Palau. As a result of referendums, each had its popularly elected legislature and executive head.

Trusteeship Council action. The Trusteeship Council at its 1985 session adopted its report[2] to the Security Council after considering the annual report for the year ending 30 September 1984 by the United States as the Administering Authority for the Trust Territory.[3] It also had before it a working paper prepared by the Secretariat[4] outlining the conditions in the Trust Territory.

The Trusteeship Council's report, covering the period 19 July 1984 to 11 July 1985, contained conclusions and recommendations—prepared by its Drafting Committee (France and the United

Kingdom)[5] on the basis of the Council's discussions and adopted by 3 votes to 1—on questions relating to the Territory's political, economic, social and educational advancement.

In explanation of its negative vote, the USSR asserted that the Micronesian people had not been given an opportunity to exercise their right to self-determination and independence because of their complete economic and political dependence on the Administering Authority; the conclusions served to reaffirm the political and military interests of the United States and justify its policy aimed at annexing Micronesia. France said it was for the people of the Territory to determine their political future, and for the Council to monitor and advise. The United Kingdom said the report reflected the views expressed by the freely elected representatives of the Micronesian people.

Action by the Committee on colonial countries. The General Assembly's Special Committee on the Situation with regard to the Implementation of the Declaration on the Granting of Independence to Colonial Countries and Peoples (Committee on colonial countries)[6] considered the Trust Territory on 1 and 7 August and adopted conclusions and recommendations made by its Sub-Committee on Small Territories. In its consideration of the question, the Committee had before it a Secretariat working paper on conditions in the Territory.[7]

The Committee recommended the adoption of a draft resolution, by which the Assembly, among other things, would call on the Administering Authority to ensure its representation at Committee meetings on the item and not to impede the Territory's unity or the rights of its people in accordance with the 1960 Declaration on the Granting of Independence to Colonial Countries and Peoples.[8] The Assembly would reaffirm its conviction that the presence of military bases and installations in the Territory could constitute an obstacle to implementing the Declaration, recognize that it was ultimately for the people of the Territory to decide their political destiny, and note with regret the lack of co-operation between the Committee and the Trusteeship Council (see p. 1089).

General Assembly consideration. Consideration of the topic was referred to the General Assembly's Fourth Committee. On 8 November, its Chairman suggested, based on consultations with the Chairman of the Committee on colonial countries and with concerned delegations, that no action be taken on the draft resolution. That suggestion was adopted without objection.[9] (See also p. 1088.)

Self-determination and independence

Trusteeship Council action. The Trusteeship Council[2] reaffirmed the right of the Micronesian people to self-determination, including the right to independence, and reiterated that free association was an option compatible with the Trusteeship Agreement, provided that the population concerned had freely accepted it.

The Council noted the calls for termination of that Agreement made by the representatives of the territorial Governments at its 1985 session. It reiterated that it was for the Administering Authority to initiate in due course procedures leading to the termination of the Agreement, and noted that "fixed-term commitments" as regards defence arrangements and economic assistance following the Agreement's termination were not incompatible with self-government.

The Council noted the United States view that, according to the terms of the Palau compact, the approval requirements remained incomplete due to perceived incompatibilities between the compact and Palau's Constitution; it reiterated the view that the United States and Palau might seek a mutually acceptable solution to bring the compact into effect.

Action by the Committee on colonial countries. The Committee on colonial countries[6] reaffirmed the right of the people of the Territory to self-determination and independence in conformity with the United Nations Charter and the 1960 Declaration,[8] and reiterated that the Administering Authority was responsible for ensuring that the existence of military bases and installations did not hinder the people from exercising that right. The Committee recalled its previous appeals to the Authority that the people of Micronesia be given the fullest opportunity to inform and educate themselves about the options open to them in the exercise of their right to self-determination and independence, and expressed the view that such programmes should be extended and reinforced. The Committee recognized that it was ultimately for the Micronesians to decide their political destiny and called on the Administering Authority not to take any action which might impede the unity of the Territory or the rights of the people, in accordance with the Declaration, until those rights were implemented.

Communication. In a 6 August communiqué[10] of the Sixteenth South Pacific Forum (Rarotonga, Cook Islands, 5 and 6 August), heads of Government members of the Forum noted that the peoples of the Federated States of Micronesia, the Republic of the Marshall Islands and the Commonwealth of the Northern Mariana Islands had exercised their right to self-determination in free and fair plebiscites observed by the United Nations; they looked forward to early approval of the termination of the Trusteeship Agreement over those territories, as well as over Palau, by the United States.

Politics and government

Trusteeship Council action. The Trusteeship Council[2] took note of the view of the Administering Authority that the status of free association as defined in the compacts would involve a considerable degree of autonomy, notably in the area of foreign affairs. It noted that international contacts by the territorial Governments continued to expand, with the approval and encouragement of the Administering Authority, and that activities had been organized in Palau in connection with International Youth Year (1985).

Action by the Committee on colonial countries. The Committee on colonial countries[6] noted that the responsibility for administrative matters throughout the Trust Territory was exercised by local authorities but regretted that the High Commissioner of the Territory still maintained the power to suspend certain legislation. The Committee took note of the intention of the Administering Authority to seek speedy termination of the Trusteeship Agreement and recalled that the Authority was duty-bound to transfer all power to the people of the Territory in accordance with the Charter and the 1960 Declaration.[8]

Economic conditions

Trusteeship Council action. The Trusteeship Council[2] noted that economic planning had become the prerogative of the Territory's four constitutional Governments, requested the Administering Authority to encourage establishment of an economic development office for the whole Territory, and welcomed the intergovernmental consultations begun on the initiative of various entities on issues of common interest.

As regards public finance, the Council noted that the Administering Authority had granted for fiscal year 1983/84 a total of $114 million for the Federated States of Micronesia, the Marshall Islands and Palau, in addition to federal categorical grants of some $35 million. It noted with satisfaction that all functions of programme management and financial administration were performed by each Government with the technical assistance of the Administering Authority.

Concerning international trade, the Council believed in the importance of promoting investment, particularly originating from Japan and the United States, and requested the Administering Authority to encourage visits to the Territory by representatives of chambers of commerce and other professional associations with a view to attracting foreign capital.

The Council noted with satisfaction that the Administering Authority recognized the primary importance of agriculture for internal consumption and for export and that it granted aid for studies on forestry and livestock production. Stressing the importance of marine resources development, the Council requested the Administering Authority to protect the Territory's fisheries interests and noted with satisfaction the establishment of the National Fisheries Corporation for fisheries development in each of the Federated States of Micronesia.

Recalling that the creation and maintenance of a communications infrastructure was crucial in development because of the distances separating the archipelagos, the Council urged efforts in that area and called for the improvement of the port infrastructure to promote trade with foreign countries. It noted that marked progress had been made in developing small-scale industries and handicrafts, encouraged the Administering Authority to continue assisting in local industry development, and considered it necessary to encourage the training of a specialized labour force to develop the construction industry.

The Council recalled that the growth of tourism must be based on careful planning so that it was in harmony with the economic progress of the Territory and in keeping with local traditions.

The Council was pleased to note that the land leased in the Northern Mariana Islands for contingency military purposes would, for the time being, be put to productive use by the local people. It also noted that the United States had no plans for establishing military bases on any part of the Trust Territory.

Action by the Committee on colonial countries. The Committee on colonial countries[6] noted that the Territory was still economically and financially dependent on the Administering Authority and that the structural imbalance in the economy appeared not to have been reduced. It believed that the Administering Authority should increase its economic assistance to the Trust Territory in order to enable its people to achieve maximum economic independence and to reduce the structural imbalance in the economy.

The Committee urged the Authority to continue safeguarding and guaranteeing, in co-operation with the local authorities, the right of the people of Micronesia to own and to dispose freely of the natural resources and to establish and maintain control of their future development. It added that the rights of the people over the 200-mile exclusive maritime zone should be respected and that they should receive all benefits deriving from it.

Social conditions

The Trusteeship Council[2] noted the view of the Administering Authority that continued co-operation between it and the territorial Governments in the health field might be feasible in the immediate post-Trusteeship period, if the parties concerned deemed it desirable. It took note of the construction or renovation of health-care facilities in the Territory and urged the Administering Authority to look favourably to the request by the Marshall Islands Government for $700,000 for the improvement of the outer island's dispensary system. The Council expressed concern at the incidence of leprosy in the Territory.

Noting with satisfaction that the Trust Territory Office of Health Services received a family planning grant from the United States and that the United Nations Development Programme and the World Health Organization collaborated in family planning activities, the Council hoped that such support would continue and recommended that assistance be concentrated on the training of experts.

The Council also noted the situation as regards community development, youth issues, housing and the labour force.

Education

The Trusteeship Council[2] noted that, despite significant progress in the past five years in student academic achievement, the overall standard was still lower than that in schools in the United States. At the same time, the Council noted with satisfaction that the United States Congress had authorized funding for the continuation of the Territorial Teacher-Training Assistance Programme for a further five-year period; that an increasing number of Trust Territory students pursued post-secondary education in the United States and elsewhere; and that the Governments of the Federated States of Micronesia, the Marshall Islands and Palau were determined to support "a unified College of Micronesia system", by combining a number of liberal arts, vocational and occupational post-secondary colleges in the three entities.

Claims

The Trusteeship Council[2] noted with concern that the problem of unpaid war claims remained to be settled and that it continued to be a matter of some aggravation in the Trust Territory, particularly in the Northern Mariana Islands. It was pleased with the indication from the Administering Authority that consideration was being given to settling the matter definitively.

Radioactive waste management

The Trusteeship Council[2] was pleased that the Administering Authority, as a signatory to the 1975 Convention on the Prevention of Marine

Pollution by Dumping of Wastes and Other Matter (the London Convention), had no plans for dumping nuclear waste anywhere near the Trust Territory. The Council hoped that the Authority would deal severely with any country that had given evidence of having such plans.

By a letter of 18 March 1985,[11] Japan informed the Secretary-General that it had no intention of disposing of low-level radioactive wastes in the Pacific Ocean in disregard of the concern expressed by the communities of the region.

Compensation for nuclear testing

The Trusteeship Council[2] considered as a major achievement the amicable out-of-court settlement in respect of the clean-up of Bikini, noting that, according to the Administering Authority, the people of Bikini would receive an annual income of over $16,000 per family during the first 15 years of the compact and thereafter would have a trust fund of $65.5 million to address the needs of future generations. The Council further noted that the people of Enewetak would have an average family income of over $11,000 and a trust fund of $13.46 million, and that similar arrangements would be made for the people of Rongelap and Utirik.

The Council noted the reluctance of the Administering Authority to finance a further independent radiological survey of the northern Marshall Islands on the grounds that it had satisfied itself that, with the exception of Bikini, none of the other atolls were seriously affected. While accepting that explanation, the Council asked the Administering Authority to continue monitoring the situation and to respond sympathetically to requests from the Marshall Islands Government for future assistance in radiation matters, particularly as regards medical assistance.

Visiting mission

TRUSTEESHIP COUNCIL ACTION

The Trusteeship Council[2]—by **resolution 2179(LII)**, adopted without objection on 7 June—decided to dispatch in July a periodic visiting mission to the Trust Territory of the Pacific Islands. The Council had last dispatched such a mission in 1982.[12] The USSR did not object to the text's adoption on the understanding that the mission would be a periodic mission similar to those previously dispatched to ascertain the situation in the Trust Territory, and that it would not have any additional terms of reference beyond the regular mandate of such missions.

Terms of reference of the United Nations Visiting Mission to the Trust Territory of the Pacific Islands, 1985

The Trusteeship Council,

Having decided to dispatch a periodic visiting mission to the Trust Territory of the Pacific Islands in 1985,

Having decided that the Visiting Mission should be composed of members of the Council wishing to participate, except the Administering Authority, which will provide an escort officer,

Having decided that the Visiting Mission should visit the Trust Territory in July 1985,

1. *Directs* the Visiting Mission to investigate and report as fully as possible on the steps taken in the Trust Territory of the Pacific Islands towards the realization of the objectives set forth in Article 76*b* of the Charter of the United Nations and to pay special attention to the question of the future of the Territory, in the light of the relevant Articles of the Charter and the Trusteeship Agreement;

2. *Directs* the Visiting Mission to give attention, as may be appropriate in the light of discussion in the Trusteeship Council and of resolutions adopted by it, to issues raised in connection with the annual reports on the administration of the Territory, in the petitions received by the Council concerning the Territory, in the reports of the previous periodic visiting missions to the Territory, in the reports of the visiting missions that have observed plebiscites in the Territory and in the observations of the Administering Authority on those reports;

3. *Directs* the Visiting Mission to receive petitions, without prejudice to its action in accordance with the rules of procedure of the Council, and to investigate on the spot such of the petitions as, in its opinion, warrant special investigation;

4. *Requests* the Visiting Mission to submit to the Council as soon as practicable a report on its visit to the Trust Territory of the Pacific Islands containing its findings, with such observations, conclusions and recommendations as it may wish to make;

5. *Requests* the Secretary-General to provide the necessary staff and facilities to assist the Visiting Mission in the performance of its functions.

Trusteeship Council resolution 2179(LII)

7 June 1985   Meeting 1597   Adopted without objection

Draft by France and United Kingdom (T/L.1246); agenda item 6.

Report of the Visiting Mission. The Council's 1985 Visiting Mission,[13] composed of one representative each from France and the United Kingdom, began its visit to the Trust Territory at Majuro, Marshall Islands, on 16 July and ended it at Koror, Palau, on 3 August.

In its conclusions and recommendations, the Mission recommended that the Trusteeship Agreement be terminated as soon as possible. It noted that, except for the State of Pohnpei (formerly Ponape) and for one opposition party and some individuals elsewhere, there was general support for the compact of free association negotiated with the Administering Authority; it hoped that all parties involved would strive to resolve the difficulties—including the constitutional problem in Palau—that were impeding the early implementation of the compact. It took note of what it called hypothetical anxiety expressed everywhere about a possible negative decision by the Security Council and especially about a negative vote by a permanent member of the Council on a draft resolution recommending termination of the Trusteeship Agreement.

Among other observations, the Mission reported that it was impressed by the standard and flexibility of the judicial system instituted by the Administering Authority. It noted many improvements made since 1982 in infrastructure, such as roads and airports; considered that local inhabitants themselves could contribute more to maintaining existing facilities; and considered unjustified most of the demands made for increased financial help from the United States, which, in the Mission's view, had already made available large sums of money. It added that it was not possible during the visit to investigate fully some of the issues raised, including the development of the outer islands, unemployment and reduction of bureaucracy.

Hearings

Trusteeship Council consideration. Between 15 and 28 May 1985, the Trusteeship Council[2] heard 15 petitioners on various issues concerning the conditions in, and the future status of, the Trust Territory. The petitioners were: Jonathan M. Weisgall, Counsel for the people of Bikini; Douglas Faulkner; Susan Quass, United Methodist Church; Senator Ataji Balos, Kwajalein representative in the Marshall Islands Nitijela (Parliament); Glenn H. Alcalay, National Committee for Radiation Victims; Leslie Tewid, on behalf of the Airai State Governor, the Airai State Council and Airai State (one of the 16 states of Palau); Father William Wood, Focus on Micronesia Coalition; Susanne R. Roff, Minority Rights Group (New York), Inc.; Jovita Nabors, a citizen of the Northern Mariana Islands; Robert R. Solenberger; Roger Clark, International League for Human Rights; Senator Ismael John and David R. Anderson, for the people of Enewetak; and Jose R. Cruz and Pedrus T. Silbanus, Old People's Square Level and Justice Organization of Ponape and Kosrae.

General Assembly consideration. On 30 and 31 October, the General Assembly's Fourth Committee heard statements by Glenn H. Alcalay; Senator Jeton Anjain, Marshall Islands; Glenn Petersen; Department of Sociology and Anthropology, Bernard M. Baruch College, New York; J. Roman Bedor, a citizen of Palau; Susan Quass; Susanne R. Roff; and Jose R. Cruz.

In the Fourth Committee, France, the United Kingdom and the United States said it was beyond the competence of the Committee to hear petitioners on the question of the Trust Territory, which was expressly reserved, under Article 83 of the Charter, to the Security Council and the Trusteeship Council. (See also p. 1084.)

Petitions, communications and observations

The Trusteeship Council[2] on 23 May took decisions on three written communications—from Seth Chaiklin, Jonathan M. Weisgall, and the House of Representatives, Fourth Northern Marianas Commonwealth Legislature—and five written petitions—from Ossie Cruse, Chairman, Pacific Region of the World Council of Indigenous Peoples; Erhart Aten, Governor of Truk, Federated State of Micronesia; the Congress of the Federated States of Micronesia; and the Association of Pacific Island Legislatures (two petitions).

REFERENCES

[1]YUN 1946-47, p. 398. [2]S/17334 & Corr.1. [3]S/17105 (T/1871). [4]T/L.1244. [5]T/L.1245. [6]A/40/23. [7]A/AC.109/827 & Corr.1. [8]YUN 1960, p. 49, GA res. 1514(XV), 14 Dec. 1960. [9]A/40/906. [10]A/40/672-S/17488. [11]T/1870. [12]YUN 1982, p. 1286. [13]T/1878.

Other aspects of the International Trusteeship System

Fellowships and scholarships

Under a scholarship programme launched by the General Assembly in 1952,[1] 11 Member States had in past years made scholarships available for students from Trust Territories: Czechoslovakia, Hungary, Indonesia, Italy, Mexico, Pakistan, Philippines, Poland, Tunisia, USSR, Yugoslavia. In a report to the Trusteeship Council covering the period from 18 May 1984 to 20 May 1985,[2] the Secretary-General stated that he had asked for up-to-date information, receiving a reply from one offering State, the USSR, which said that currently no inhabitant from the Trust Territory of the Pacific Islands was studying in the USSR.

In the Council, the USSR said the statements made by Micronesians showed that there was a dearth of highly trained workers and specialists in the Territory. It was unfortunate that the report did not describe the offers of stipends and fellowships or indicate how Micronesians could take advantage of them; since none of the USSR's offers had been accepted, it was clear that information was not reaching the Micronesians.

The High Commissioner of the Trust Territory informed the Council that all offers of training were immediately transmitted to the Governments of the four Micronesian entities for their choice and decision. The Micronesian representatives stated that information on study opportunities was received directly by them or through the Office of the High Commissioner; States offering study/training opportunities included Japan, the Netherlands and Papua New Guinea.

On 23 May, the Council took note of the report without objection.[3]

Information dissemination

A report of the Secretary-General covering the period 1 May 1984 to 30 April 1985[4] described the distribution by the United Nations Department of Public Information (DPI) of United Nations documents, official records and information materials throughout the Trust Territory. Relevant publications on the activities of the Committee on colonial countries were also distributed. An information officer from the United Nations Information Centre in Tokyo was scheduled to make another visit to the Territory later in 1985 to assess the needs of all interested users of United Nations materials.

The USSR said the Administering Authority had not provided detailed information on the dissemination of information and the Trusteeship Council should urge the Authority and DPI to improve the means of dissemination in the Territory.

On 23 May, the Council,[3] without objection, took note of the Secretary-General's report.

Trusteeship Council

The Trusteeship Council held its fifty-second session in New York from 13 May to 11 July 1985. Following the adoption of its agenda on 13 May,[5] it held 15 meetings between 13 and 28 May; it adopted, on 7 June, the report of its Drafting Committee containing the Council's conclusions and recommendations, and its report to the Security Council on 11 July.[3]

The United States transmitted two letters to the Secretary-General. On 13 September,[6] it requested the convening of a special session of the Trusteeship Council on 15 October to consider recent developments in and affecting the future of the Trust Territory and, in particular, the question of self-determination, along with the report of the 1985 Visiting Mission. On 18 November,[7] it withdrew that request.

Co-operation with the
Committee on colonial countries

At its 1985 annual session, the Trusteeship Council[3] again considered together the question of self-government or independence by the Trust Territory and co-operation with the Committee on colonial countries.

During the debate, the USSR stated that the Administering Authority stubbornly ignored the 1960 Declaration on the Granting of Independence to Colonial Countries and Peoples[8] and did not provide information on its implementation. There was nothing in Article 83 of the Charter to prevent the General Assembly or any other United Nations organ from following the situation in the Territory.

France, the United Kingdom and the United States said that Article 83, paragraph 1, of the Charter made it clear that all functions of the United Nations relating to strategic areas would be exercised by the Security Council. As far as co-operation with the Committee on colonial countries was concerned, the same distinction applied, since the sole remaining Trust Territory was a strategic one.

Co-operation with CERD and the
Decade against racial discrimination

In 1985, the Trusteeship Council[3] considered together the question of co-operation with the Committee on the Elimination of Racial Discrimination (CERD) and the Decade for Action to Combat Racism and Racial Discrimination.

During the discussion, the USSR said that the position taken by the Council's Western members had prevented the Council from co-operating with CERD or participating in activities relating to the Decade; the Council should co-operate with CERD by providing it with all relevant material, including petitioners' statements. The USSR added that the most obvious instance of discrimination was the prolonged nuclear testing programme which had polluted the environment and irreparably harmed the health of the people.

The United Kingdom, joined by the United States, said that under Article 83 of the Charter, the Trusteeship Council reported only to the Security Council; there was no obligation for a major organ to co-operate with a committee. The United Kingdom recalled that in 1984 one of the Micronesian representatives had stated unequivocally that racial discrimination did not exist in the Territory; nothing that the Council heard in 1985 could be remotely equated with racial discrimination. Similarly, France noted the absence of information from any Micronesian source showing any trace of racial discrimination.

The United States said that racial discrimination was unknown in Micronesia, as confirmed by the representatives of the Federated States of Micronesia. The settlement of nuclear claims by the United States on terms favourable to those affected showed that there had been no anti-Micronesian discrimination in that area as charged. As to the Decade, the United States did not consider that the item appropriately belonged on the Council's agenda.

On 28 May, the Council[3] took note, without objection, of the statements made.

REFERENCES

[1]YUN 1951, p. 788, GA res. 557(VI), 18 Jan. 1952. [2]T/1874. [3]S/17334 & Corr.1. [4]T/1873. [5]T/1872. [6]T/1877. [7]T/1879. [8]YUN 1960, p. 49, GA res. 1514(XV), 14 Dec. 1960.

Chapter III

Namibia

In 1985, the United Nations continued its efforts to bring about the independence of Namibia, the largest Territory remaining under colonial rule. The United Nations Council for Namibia, the legal Administering Authority for Namibia until independence, held extraordinary plenary meetings at Vienna in June, which culminated in the adoption of a Declaration stating that South Africa's illegal occupation of Namibia constituted a threat to international peace and security, and of a Programme of Action urging the Security Council to act decisively to implement its resolutions on Namibia.

The Security Council considered the Namibian question at various times during the year. In May, after consultations, the Council President issued a statement on behalf of the members condemning a decision by South Africa to establish a so-called interim government in Namibia and declaring that any unilateral measures taken by the illegal administration there were null and void. In June, the Council adopted resolution 566(1985), condemning South Africa for its continued illegal occupation of Namibia, for its installation of an interim government in Windhoek which it declared to be illegal, null and void, and for its obstruction of the implementation of the United Nations plan for Namibian independence. It reiterated that Council resolution 435(1978) embodied the only internationally accepted basis for settling the Namibian problem and urged Member States to consider taking voluntary measures against South Africa, which could include the suspension of new investments, re-examination of maritime and aerial relations, prohibition of the sale of krugerrands and restrictions on sports and cultural relations.

In November, South Africa transmitted a request to the Secretary-General to select a system of proportional representation as a framework for elections leading to Namibian independence; the Secretary-General confirmed agreement on the proportional representation system. Later, a draft resolution, which would have provided for comprehensive mandatory sanctions against South Africa, was not adopted because of the negative vote of two permanent members of the Council.

Six resolutions were adopted by the General Assembly on the problem of Namibia in December. By resolution 40/97 A, the Assembly decided that the Council for Namibia should proceed to establish its administration in Namibia in 1986; reaffirmed that the independence of Namibia could be achieved only with the direct participation of the South West Africa People's Organization; and condemned South Africa for the imposition of an interim government and for its military buildup in Namibia. It also demanded the release of all Namibian political prisoners, and urged the Security Council to adopt comprehensive mandatory sanctions against South Africa.

The Assembly, in resolution 40/97 B, rejected manœuvres to divert attention from the central issue, the decolonization of Namibia, and called on the Western permanent members of the Security Council to support enforcement measures against South Africa. In resolution 40/97 C, the Assembly decided on the work programme of the Council for Namibia, and, in resolution 40/97 D, requested the Council to increase dissemination of information on Namibia.

Further, it decided, by resolution 40/97 E, to allocate $1.5 million from the regular 1986 United Nations budget to the United Nations Fund for Namibia, and by resolution 40/97 F, to hold a special session on Namibia in 1986.

The Council for Namibia, which in 1974 had enacted a decree aimed at protecting Namibia's natural resources, decided in 1985 to undertake legal action in the domestic courts of States and other appropriate bodies against corporations or individuals exploiting, transporting, processing or purchasing those resources.

The Secretary-General submitted three reports on the question of Namibia during the year. He found that South Africa had not changed its position linking the withdrawal of Cuban troops from Angola to the implementation of the United Nations plan for Namibian independence. He declared that no progress had been made in the carrying out of resolution 435(1978), which had endorsed the plan.

Assistance to Namibians outside their country continued to be provided by the United Nations, primarily through the Fund for Namibia. In 1985, the Fund spent $7 million; voluntary contributions by States to the Fund totalled $4.5 million. Funding was also provided from the regular United Nations budget, the United Nations Development Programme and specialized agencies. The Fund operated three main programmes—the Nationhood Programme for Namibia, the United

Nations Institute for Namibia, and educational, social and relief assistance. The Nationhood Programme and Institute functioned in relation to the future attainment of independence. The assistance programme dealt with the immediate needs of Namibians in connection with their struggle for independence.

Topics related to this chapter. Africa: South Africa and *apartheid*; Angola–South Africa armed incidents and South African occupation of Angola. Human rights: human rights violations—South Africa and Namibia. Refugees and displaced persons: Africa. General questions relating to colonial countries.

Namibia question

Activities of the UN Council for Namibia. During 1985, the United Nations Council for Namibia continued to act as the legal Administering Authority for Namibia until independence, the function assigned to it by the General Assembly in 1967.[1] To that end, the Assembly endowed the Council with the power to promulgate laws and decrees, as might be necessary for the administration of the Territory and for the protection of the interests of the Namibian people. In its report to the Assembly on the period from 1 September 1984 to 31 August 1985,[2] the Council gave its assessment of the situation in Namibia, an account of its activities as Administering Authority and its recommendations for Assembly action. Later 1985 activities were described in its 1986 report.[3]

The Council participated in the work of the Security Council on the Namibian question and in that of other United Nations bodies whenever they dealt with the question and related matters. In particular, the Council took part in meetings of the Special Committee on the Situation with regard to the Implementation of the Declaration on the Granting of Independence to Colonial Countries and Peoples (Committee on colonial countries) and the Special Committee against *Apartheid*. Similarly, the Council continued to invite those bodies to its own meetings and events. In addition, the Council continued to co-operate with the Organization of African Unity (OAU) and the Movement of Non-Aligned Countries by taking part in their meetings and contributing to their declarations and resolutions on Namibia.

In accordance with a 1984 Assembly resolution,[4] the Council continued to consult with the South West Africa People's Organization (SWAPO) in formulating and implementing its programme of work, while SWAPO participated in the work of the Council, its Steering Committee and other subsidiary bodies. It also continued to consider questions relating to the accession of Namibia to international conventions, covenants and agreements.

Also in response to that resolution, by which the Council had been requested to hold plenary meetings in Western Europe during 1985 and to recommend appropriate action to the Assembly in the light of South Africa's refusal to co-operate in implementing the 1978 United Nations plan for Namibia's independence,[5] meetings were held at Vienna from 3 to 7 June 1985.

On 11 June,[6] the Council transmitted to the Secretary-General the Final Document of the Vienna meetings, containing a Declaration and Programme of Action. During the meetings, particular attention was given to unilateral actions by South Africa to press ahead with the installation of a so-called interim government in Namibia. It drew attention to the fact that South Africa's action had been condemned by the Extraordinary Ministerial Meeting of the Co-ordinating Bureau of Non-Aligned Countries on Namibia (New Delhi, India, 19-21 April) and by the President of the Security Council on 3 May. The Council condemned and rejected South Africa's decision to install an interim government and stated categorically that the 1978 Security Council resolution[5] remained the only basis for a peaceful settlement.

In the Declaration, the Council reaffirmed the right of the Namibian people to self-determination, freedom and national independence; declared once again that South Africa's illegal occupation of Namibia constituted an act of aggression and was a threat to international and regional peace and security; condemned the South African régime for its ruthless repression of the Namibian people, its policy and practice of *apartheid* and other gross violations of human rights perpetrated against the Namibian people; and reaffirmed its support for SWAPO and its conviction that the armed liberation struggle of the Namibian people was an important factor in their efforts to achieve independence. In addition, the Council rejected and condemned persistent attempts by the United States and South Africa to link Namibian independence with irrelevant issues, such as the withdrawal of Cuban forces from Angola; and reiterated that there were only two parties to the Namibian conflict—the people of Namibia and South Africa—and that the Namibian question was a decolonization issue to be resolved in accordance with the 1960 Declaration on the Granting of Independence to Colonial Countries and Peoples.[7]

Under the Programme of Action, the Council, among other things, urged the Security Council to act decisively to implement its resolutions 385(1976),[8] 435(1978)[5] and 539(1983)[9] by taking action against South Africa's manoeuvres and schemes to bypass or undermine the United Nations plan for Namibian independence, and resolved to promote the imposition of mandatory sanctions against South Africa by the Security Council, in order to ensure its compliance with the plan. It said it would continue to carry out high-level consultations with SWAPO, and urged non-governmental organizations (NGOs), particularly trade unions, to campaign in their countries for comprehensive sanctions against South Africa. The Council invited the United Nations and Member States to take cognizance of the fact that 1985 marked the fortieth year of United Nations consideration of the Namibian question and urged that the Namibian cause be highlighted in the context of the observance of the twenty-fifth anniversary of the Declaration on the Granting of Independence to Colonial Countries and Peoples.[7]

As part of its efforts to protect Namibia's interests, the Council had adopted in 1974[10] Decree No. 1 for the Protection of the Natural Resources of Namibia and embarked on a series of activities to implement it. During 1985, culminating several years of preparation, the Council decided to take legal action in the domestic courts of States against corporations or individuals involved in the exploitation, transport, processing or purchase of Namibia's natural resources, with such legal action to commence in the Netherlands. In its Vienna Programme of Action, the Council stated that it would promote actively the implementation of the Decree through legal action in the domestic courts of States and through political action and consultations intended to put an end to the plunder of Namibia's natural resources.

Another Council function was the dissemination of information on the Namibian question and the mobilization of international public opinion in support of the Namibian people's struggle for independence. The Council held a number of symposia and seminars during 1985, including a Seminar on the Intensification of International Action for the Immediate Independence of Namibia (Brazzaville, Congo, 25-29 March). The Seminar's participants called on States, particularly the Western countries, to stop transnational corporations (TNCs) from plundering Namibian resources, and urged Governments and academic institutions to afford Namibians the opportunity to acquire the skills and experience necessary for the development of an independent Namibia.

A Symposium on the Strengthening of International Solidarity with the Heroic Struggle of the Namibian People, Led by Their Sole and Authentic Representative, SWAPO (Sofia, Bulgaria, 22-26 April), examined the situation in Namibia resulting from the continued illegal occupation by South Africa. It urged the convening of a Security Council meeting to impose comprehensive, mandatory sanctions against South Africa and increased political, diplomatic, military, material and moral support for SWAPO to ensure the earliest possible achievement of independence.

A Symposium on the Immediate Independence of Namibia—a Common Responsibility (Singapore, 6-10 May) declared that more up-to-date information on the Namibian situation should be distributed to people in Asia in languages familiar to the majority and in such a way as to be readily understood by those with little knowledge of the issue.

The Seminar on the Intransigence of the South African Régime with regard to Namibia: Strategies for Hastening the Independence of Namibia (Georgetown, Guyana, 29 July–2 August) recommended that the United Nations assume its full responsibility for Namibia and counter attempts by South Africa, the Federal Republic of Germany, the United Kingdom and the United States to bypass the United Nations.

The Conference on the Intensification of International Action for the Independence of Namibia (New York, 11-13 September)[11] brought together parliamentarians/legislators, scholars, prominent personalities, representatives of NGOs and support groups, and members of the mass media from throughout the world. It adopted a Plan for the Intensification of International Action for the Independence of Namibia, in which it called on Governments to grant formal accreditation to SWAPO, and demanded the immediate release of political prisoners held by South Africa and the granting of prisoner-of-war status to Namibian freedom fighters. It also made a series of recommendations with regard to Namibia's natural resources and called for action by NGOs to disseminate accurate information on Namibia.

On 25 May, the Council held its annual meeting to observe Africa Liberation Day and the twenty-second anniversary of OAU. The Council also commemorated Namibia Day on 26 August and, pursuant to a 1976 General Assembly resolution,[12] the Week of Solidarity with the People of Namibia and Their Liberation Movement, SWAPO. In observance of the Week of Solidarity (28 October–1 November),[13] two special meetings of the Council were held on 28 October; messages of solidarity were received from a number of heads of State or Government, Foreign Ministers, United Nations permanent representatives and various organizations.

The Council represented Namibia throughout the year at meetings of United Nations specialized agencies and other entities. In addition, it undertook the Nationhood Programme (see p. 1130), channelled assistance to the Territory through the

United Nations Fund for Namibia (see p. 1127) and formulated policies for the United Nations Institute for Namibia (see p. 1131).

Missions. In accordance with a 1984 General Assembly resolution,[4] the Council sent missions of consultation in 1985 to Africa, Asia, and Western Europe,[2] covering the following: Saudi Arabia (16-18 March); the Congo, Angola and SWAPO (31 March–5 April); Indonesia and Brunei Darussalam (18 May); and Finland, Sweden, Denmark and Norway (20-30 May). The purpose of the missions was to promote implementation of United Nations resolutions on Namibia and mobilize greater international support for its speedy independence. A high-level Council delegation held consultations with SWAPO leaders (Luanda, Angola, 1 and 2 September)[3] and emphasized that the Council's objectives were the same as those of SWAPO; the mission also visited the SWAPO Health and Education Centre at Kwanza Sul, Angola, from 9 to 11 September.[14]

The missions urged the Governments visited, pending imposition by the Security Council of comprehensive mandatory sanctions against South Africa, to apply sanctions unilaterally and collectively so as to comply with the boycott of South Africa called for by the General Assembly in 1981.[15]

In Saudi Arabia, the Government observed that there were strong similarities between the struggles for self-determination and independence waged by the peoples of Namibia and Palestine. It stated that the wide-ranging collaboration in the economic, political, military and nuclear fields between South Africa and Israel was a source of concern to the international community. It assured the mission that it would continue to contribute generously to the United Nations Fund for Namibia.

In the Congo, both the mission and the Government condemned continuing attempts by South Africa to set up puppet political institutions and impose an "internal settlement" in Namibia, defying United Nations decisions. In that context, they rejected the puppet Multi-Party Conference (MPC) as the latest political stratagem devised by South Africa to impose a neo-colonial settlement in Namibia.

In Angola, the Government stated that the burden of the struggle for the liberation of Namibia had been left entirely to the front-line States and to Angola in particular. As a result, more Angolans had lost their lives and more property had been destroyed than during their own struggle for liberation. While in Angola, the mission reviewed developments with SWAPO, whose President proposed that the Council for Namibia take more initiative in disseminating information and mobilizing international public opinion in support of the Namibian cause, particularly in the United

States. He suggested that a mission be sent to consult with United States government officials.

The Indonesian Government and the mission stressed that the United Nations plan for Namibian independence, adopted by the Security Council in 1978,[5] remained unimplemented because of the so-called policy of linkage expounded by South Africa and the United States. The two parties rejected the linkage between Namibian independence and extraneous issues such as the presence of Cuban troops in Angola. They emphasized that the international community should impose comprehensive mandatory sanctions against South Africa.

Brunei Darussalam condemned the illegal occupation of Namibia by South Africa, and reaffirmed Namibia's legitimate right to struggle for self-determination by all means under SWAPO leadership.

In Finland, the mission outlined specific areas of increased assistance required by the Fund for Namibia. The Finnish Government declared that it was critical to get a consensus in the Security Council for a new United Nations initiative to expedite Namibia's independence, and stressed the importance of creating conditions in which the Council could adopt stronger measures.

The Swedish Government emphasized that foreign exploitation of Namibia's natural resources should be halted, and referred to a 1979 Swedish law extended in 1985 which prohibited further Swedish investment in South Africa and Namibia. Sweden had also declared that imports of uranium from Namibia were unacceptable.

Denmark underlined the importance of isolating the *apartheid* régime, and stated that it considered the policy of *apartheid* a threat to international peace and therefore supported binding sanctions by the Security Council.

The mission to Norway expressed concern regarding Norwegian involvement in the sale and transport of oil to South Africa. The Government replied that its policy was not to sell Norwegian oil to South Africa. Regarding its involvement in the transport of oil, the Government had taken limited unilateral measures, with all shipping companies transporting oil to South Africa being required to register with the Ministry of Foreign Affairs. The Government had also proposed a survey of the shipping companies to evaluate their activities with South Africa. Norway stated that Namibia was a priority area for assistance and promised an increase in its assistance to various projects.

Communications. During 1985, communications on different aspects of the situation in Namibia were addressed by a number of countries and organizations to the Secretary-General and the President of the Security Council.

In a 15 April letter,[16] South Africa transmitted a statement to the Security Council, reaffirming its commitment to the peaceful resolution of regional problems. South Africa trusted that its decision to complete the disengagement process in southern Angola would enhance prospects for peace, and in particular, be conducive to the withdrawal of Cubans from Angola. Such a development would open the way to the peaceful solution of the region's problems, including the question of Namibian independence.

Many countries declared that they considered to be null and void an announcement by South Africa that it intended to set up an interim government in Namibia. Among them were China (22 April),[17] Cuba (22 April) ,[18] the United Kingdom (22 April),[19] the United States (22 April),[20] France (23 April),[21] Egypt (24 April),[22] the USSR (30 April),[23] the Syrian Arab Republic (6 May),[24] Algeria (7 May),[25] Uruguay (13 May),[26] the Sudan (17 May),[27] Japan (20 May),[28] Mongolia (10 June),[29] Venezuela (13 June),[30] Democratic Kampuchea (17 June),[31] the United Republic of Tanzania (19 June),[32] Spain (20 June),[33] Brazil (20 June[34] and 21 June[35]), Yugoslavia (28 June),[36] Cyprus (5 July),[37] and the Ukrainian SSR (17 September).[38]

Similar views of the South African announcement were expressed by the Council for Namibia (5 June);[39] the Seventy-fourth Inter-Parliamentary Conference (Ottawa, Canada, 2-7 September) (15 October);[40] the heads of Government of Commonwealth States (Nassau, Bahamas, 16-22 October) (28 October),[41] and the thirtieth Plenary Assembly of the World Federation of United Nations Associations (Geneva, 30 September–5 October) (14 November).[42]

On 1 May,[43] Indonesia forwarded the Declaration of the Commemorative Meeting in Observance of the Thirtieth Anniversary of the Asian-African Conference (Bandung, 24 and 25 April), reiterating solidarity with the struggle of the Namibian people to achieve independence and condemning the South African decision to install a puppet administration in Namibia.

On 2 May,[44] Italy, on behalf of the 10 States members of the European Community (EC), transmitted a declaration on southern Africa adopted by the Ministers for Foreign Affairs of the Ten at the fifty-seventh Ministerial Meeting on European Political Co-operation (Luxembourg, 29 April), declaring null and void the setting up of an interim government in Namibia by South Africa.

Madagascar conveyed on 18 September[45] the text of a resolution adopted by the OAU Council of Ministers (forty-second session, Addis Ababa, Ethiopia, 10-17 July) which declared South Africa's installation of an interim government in Namibia to be illegal, null and void.

On 19 April[46] and 8 May,[47] India forwarded, respectively, a statement adopted at the inaugural session of the Extraordinary Ministerial Meeting of the Co-ordinating Bureau of Non-Aligned Countries on Namibia (New Delhi, 19-21 April) and the text of the Meeting's final document, condemning South Africa's decision to install a so-called internal administration in Namibia.

Argentina, on 10 June,[48] transmitted the text of a 24 May communiqué by its Ministry of Foreign Affairs and Public Worship, stating that the proposal to grant so-called autonomy to the Territory appeared to be another attempt to halt Namibian independence. It reiterated that the question was one of colonialism, and rejected the attempt to transform it into a matter of East-West confrontation.

The issue of Namibia's natural resources was addressed by the USSR in a 19 August note verbale[49] in which it condemned the continued plundering of those resources by TNCs of Western countries. It regarded their illegal exploitation as a violation of the United Nations Charter and of decisions of United Nations bodies. The USSR supported the General Assembly's appeal to the Security Council for the immediate imposition of mandatory sanctions against South Africa in accordance with the Charter.

Yemen annexed to a 15 October letter[50] the communiqué of the co-ordination meeting of the Ministers for Foreign Affairs of the Organization of the Islamic Conference (New York, 9 October); the Ministers reaffirmed their support of the Namibian people for independence, declared the continuing illegal occupation of Namibia by South Africa to be an act of aggression, and rejected any linkage between Namibian independence and the withdrawal of Cuban troops from Angola.

By a letter of 22 October,[51] Burkina Faso stated that its delegation to the 1985 session of the General Assembly would not participate in ceremonies commemorating the United Nations fortieth anniversary inasmuch as SWAPO and the Palestine Liberation Organization were excluded from them owing to the absence of an invitation to their respective leaders, Sam Nujoma and Yasser Arafat, to take part.

A resolution on the responsibilities of the Pan African News Agency (PANA) and the African press in the struggle against *apartheid*, adopted by the Conference of African Ministers of Information (first extraordinary session, Cairo, 23-25 November), was transmitted by Egypt on 4 December.[52] The resolution urged African information media and PANA to include as priority objectives the sensitization of African and international public opinion to the struggle of the peoples of South Africa and Namibia for freedom.

Reports of the Secretary-General. In June 1985,[53] the Secretary-General submitted to the Security Council a report containing an account of developments since his 1983 report[54] on the implementation of Council resolutions 435(1978)[5] and 439(1978)[55] on Namibia. He stated that there had been no change in South Africa's position regarding the withdrawal of Cuban troops from Angola as a pre-condition for the implementation of resolution 435(1978). Consequently, it was not possible to finalize arrangements to implement the United Nations plan for Namibia. Difficulties had been compounded by South Africa's recent decision to establish an interim government in Namibia. He thought it important that South Africa reconsider the implications of its decision and desist. He urged that South Africa and others in a position to help make a renewed effort to expedite implementation of resolution 435(1978).

Pursuant to a 19 June Security Council resolution (see p. 1097), the Secretary-General submitted a report in September[56] in which he reiterated that no progress had been made in implementing resolution 435(1978) and appealed once again to South Africa to proceed forthwith with its implementation, declaring that continuation of the current impasse did not serve the interest of any party.

In response to two 1984 General Assembly resolutions, one on the situation in Namibia[57] and the other[58] on implementing Council resolution 435(1978), the Secretary-General, in another September report,[59] conveyed to the Assembly replies received from 14 Governments on action taken by them to implement those resolutions.

Action by the Committee on colonial countries. A Secretariat working paper,[60] covering developments in Namibia from May 1984 to April 1985, was submitted to the Special Committee on the Situation with regard to the Implementation of the Declaration on the Granting of Independence to Colonial Countries and Peoples. The report considered the illegal occupation of the Territory by South Africa, efforts to achieve a peaceful settlement, the Namibian economy, and social and educational conditions. It stated that South Africa had escalated its suppression of resistance to the occupation, which was characterized by ruthless political repression, racial discrimination and *apartheid*, gross violations of human rights and economic exploitation. Peace efforts continued by the Security Council, the General Assembly, the Council for Namibia, regional and other intergovernmental bodies and groups. In terms of economic ties, Namibia was almost totally dependent on South Africa. The basic structure of the Namibian economy was typically colonial, almost exclusively tailored to the needs and demands of foreign capital. Virtually the entire output of the economy's primary sectors—mining, farming and fishing—was exported. Discriminatory laws continued to govern health services, education, housing and all other aspects of daily life.

The Committee on colonial countries (Tunis, Tunisia, 13-17 May) adopted by consensus a decision[61] in which it reaffirmed the right of the Namibian people to independence; reiterated that Namibia's accession to independence must be with its territorial integrity intact, including Walvis Bay, the Penguin Islands and other offshore islands; rejected attempts by the United States and South Africa to link Namibian independence with extraneous issues; demanded that South Africa release all Namibian political prisoners; condemned South Africa for its ever-increasing military buildup in Namibia; deplored the continuing collaboration of certain Western and other countries with South Africa; paid tribute to the front-line and other African States for their commitment to Namibian independence; called on the International Monetary Fund to end co-operation with the *apartheid* régime; and requested the Secretary-General to intensify his efforts to mobilize world public opinion against South Africa's Namibian policy.

The text of the decision was transmitted to the Security Council on 10 June[62] by the Chairman of the Committee. The Chairman drew the Council's attention to those paragraphs which reaffirmed that resolution 435(1978) remained the only basis for a peaceful settlement of the Namibian question; called for scrupulous observance of Council resolution 558(1984),[63] enjoining Member States to refrain from importing armaments from South Africa; and recommended that the Council impose forthwith mandatory sanctions against South Africa.

In a 7 August decision,[64] the Committee demanded the dismantling of all military bases in Namibia and cessation of the war against the Namibian people; condemned South Africa for its military buildup in Namibia, its introduction of compulsory military service for Namibians and its use of mercenaries to reinforce its illegal occupation; and urged Governments, specialized agencies and other intergovernmental organizations to increase material assistance to refugees forced to flee from Namibia and South Africa into neighbouring States.

Action by the Commission on Human Rights. The Commission on Human Rights, in a 26 February resolution on the situation in southern Africa,[65] reaffirmed the right of the Namibian people to self-determination, freedom and independence; condemned the continued violations of the human rights of peoples under colonial domination; and declared that the illegal occupation of Namibia by South Africa continued to constitute an act of aggression against the Namibian people.

Also on 26 February,[66] the Commission condemned South Africa for the military buildup in Namibia, the training of Namibians for tribal armies, the use of mercenaries to suppress the Namibian people, and the torture and other forms of brutality meted out to Namibians and captured SWAPO freedom fighters. In a further 26 February resolution,[67] the Commission renewed its request to the Government of South Africa to allow the *Ad Hoc* Working Group of Experts to make on-the-spot investigations of living conditions in South African and Namibian prisons and of the treatment of prisoners. (See also p. 860.)

ECONOMIC AND SOCIAL COUNCIL ACTION

The Economic and Social Council, in **resolution 1985/59**, requested United Nations organizations to withhold assistance to South Africa until it restored self-determination and independence to the Namibian people, and to refrain from any action which might imply recognition of, or support for, the occupation of Namibia. It condemned South Africa's non-compliance with United Nations resolutions and decisions, particularly Security Council resolution 435(1978), and declared illegal, null and void its installation of an interim government in Namibia.

SECURITY COUNCIL ACTION (May/June)

On 3 May 1985, following consultations, the Security Council President issued a statement,[68] on behalf of the members of the Council, as follows:

"Members of the Security Council have learned with indignation and grave concern of the decision taken in Pretoria to establish a so-called interim government in illegally occupied Namibia.

"This manœuvre is contrary to the expressed will of the international community and in defiance of United Nations resolutions and decisions, in particular Security Council resolutions 435(1978) and 439(1978), which declare that any unilateral measures taken by the illegal administration in Namibia in contravention of relevant Council resolutions are null and void.

"The latest action by the illegal occupation régime in Namibia is in disregard of the demands of the Namibian people for self-determination and genuine independence and of the will of the international community. It further complicates the efforts to proceed expeditiously with implementation of resolution 435(1978), which remains the only acceptable basis for a peaceful and internationally recognized settlement of the Namibian question. This once again calls into question South Africa's commitment to the implementation of resolution 435(1978).

"Members of the Council condemn and reject any unilateral action by South Africa leading towards an internal settlement outside resolution 435(1978) as unacceptable, and declare the establishment of the so-called interim government in Namibia to be null and void. They also declare that any further measures taken in pursuance of this action will be without effect. They call upon all States Members of the United Nations and the international community at large to repudiate this action and to refrain from according any recognition to it.

"Members of the Council call upon South Africa to rescind the action taken by it and to co-operate in and facilitate the implementation of the United Nations plan contained in resolution 435(1978), as called for in Council resolution 539(1983).

"Members of the Council reaffirm that the United Nations has primary and direct responsibility over Namibia. It is the intention of the Security Council, in fulfilment of that responsibility, to remain seized of the situation in and relating to Namibia, with a view to ensuring full compliance by South Africa in the expeditious and unconditional implementation of Council resolution 435(1978)."

South Africa responded to the statement in a letter of 4 May,[69] which enclosed a 4 May statement by the South African Foreign Minister, a draft *aide-mémoire*, and an 18 April statement to the South African Parliament by P. W. Botha, President of South Africa. The Foreign Minister said that South Africa considered the Council President's statement to be ill-founded and without effect; however, it reserved the right to withdraw unilaterally from the Territory at any time that it might so wish. In the *aide-mémoire*, South Africa declared that it remained committed to the implementation of the international settlement plan for Namibia, provided agreement could be reached on Cuban withdrawal from Angola. The South African Government was aware of its responsibilities in Namibia, which derived from its position that its presence in the Territory was legal and that there was no legally binding decision to the contrary of the International Court of Justice or of the United Nations taken in accordance with the Charter. The South African President told Parliament that MPC had requested the establishment of an internal government, that MPC had never claimed to be the sole representative of the Namibian people and that it was willing to discuss the future of Namibia with other political parties, including SWAPO. South Africa considered that the implementation of the MPC proposals could contribute to Namibian reconciliation and welfare and eventually independence.

The Security Council took up the Namibian question at 12 meetings between 10 and 19 June. It convened in response to requests of 23 May by India,[70] on behalf of the Movement of Non-Aligned Countries, and by Mozambique,[71] on behalf of the Group of African States.

Afghanistan, Algeria, Angola, Argentina, Bangladesh, Barbados, Bhutan, Bolivia, Botswana, Brazil, Bulgaria, Cameroon, Canada, the Congo, Cuba, Cyprus, Czechoslovakia, Democratic Yemen, Ethiopia, the German Democratic Republic, the Federal Republic of Germany, Ghana, Guatemala, Guyana, Haiti, Hungary, Indonesia, Iran, Jamaica, Japan, Kenya, Kuwait, the Lao People's Democratic Republic, Lesotho, Liberia, the Libyan Arab Jamahiriya, Malaysia, Malta, Mexico, Mongolia, Morocco, Mozambique, Nicaragua, Nigeria, Pakistan, Panama, Poland, Seychelles, South Africa, Sri Lanka, the Sudan, the Syrian Arab Republic, Turkey, Uganda, the United Arab Emirates, the United Republic of Tanzania, Viet Nam, Yugoslavia, Zambia and Zimbabwe were invited, at their request, to participate without vote in the Council's discussion.

Certain individuals were also invited to address the Council, under rule 39ᵃ of its provisional rules of procedure. At the request of Burkino Faso, Egypt and Madagascar, Sam Nujoma,[72] SWAPO President, Mfanafuthi J. Makatini,[73] representative of the African National Congress of South Africa (ANC), Gora Ebrahim,[74] representative of the Pan Africanist Congress of Azania (PAC), and Neo Mnumzana,[75] Deputy Chief Representative of ANC, were invited. At the request of the Sudan,[76] on behalf of the Arab Group, Clovis Maksoud, Permanent Observer of the League of Arab States, was invited.

Also under rule 39, the Council invited representatives of certain other United Nations bodies to participate: the Acting President of the Council for Namibia, the Chairman of the Special Committee against *Apartheid* and the Chairman of the Committee on colonial countries.

On 19 June, the Security Council adopted resolution 566(1985).

The Security Council,

Having considered the reports of the Secretary-General,

Having heard the statement by the Acting President of the United Nations Council for Namibia,

Having considered the statement by Mr. Sam Nujoma, President of the South West Africa People's Organization,

Commending the South West Africa People's Organization for its preparedness to co-operate fully with the Secretary-General of the United Nations and his Special Representative, including its expressed readiness to sign and observe a cease-fire agreement with South Africa, in the implementation of the United Nations plan for the independence of Namibia as embodied in Security Council resolution 435(1978),

Recalling General Assembly resolutions 1514(XV) of 14 December 1960 and 2145(XXI) of 27 October 1966,

Recalling and reaffirming its resolutions 269(1969), 276(1970), 301(1971), 385(1976), 431(1978), 432(1978), 435(1978), 439(1978), 532(1983) and 539(1983),

Recalling the statement by the President of the Security Council of 3 May 1985, on behalf of the Council, which, *inter alia*, declared the establishment of the so-called interim government in Namibia to be null and void,

Gravely concerned at the tension and instability created by the hostile policies of the *apartheid* régime throughout southern Africa and the mounting threat to the security of the region and its wider implications for international peace and security resulting from that régime's continued utilization of Namibia as a springboard for military attacks against and destabilization of African States in the region,

Reaffirming the legal responsibility of the United Nations over Namibia and the primary responsibility of the Security Council for ensuring the implementation of its resolutions, in particular resolutions 385(1976) and 435(1978) which contain the United Nations plan for the independence of Namibia,

Noting that 1985 marks the fortieth anniversary of the founding of the United Nations, as well as the twenty-fifth anniversary of the adoption of the Declaration on the Granting of Independence to Colonial Countries and Peoples, and expressing grave concern that the question of Namibia has been with the Organization since its inception and still remains unresolved,

Welcoming the emerging and intensified world-wide campaign of people from all spheres of life against the racist régime of South Africa in a concerted effort to bring about an end to the illegal occupation of Namibia and to *apartheid*;

1. *Condemns* South Africa for its continued illegal occupation of Namibia in flagrant defiance of resolutions of the General Assembly and decisions of the Security Council;

2. *Reaffirms* the legitimacy of the struggle of the Namibian people against the illegal occupation of the racist régime of South Africa and calls upon all States to increase their moral and material assistance to the Namibian people;

3. *Further condemns* the racist régime of South Africa for its installation of a so-called interim government in Windhoek and declares that this action, taken even while the Security Council has been in session, constitutes a direct affront to the Council and a clear defiance of its resolutions, particularly resolutions 435(1978) and 439(1978);

4. *Declares* that action to be illegal and null and void and states that no recognition will be accorded to it either by the United Nations or any Member State or to any representative or organ established in pursuance thereof;

5. *Demands* that the racist régime of South Africa immediately rescind the aforementioned illegal and unilateral action;

6. *Further condemns* South Africa for its obstruction of the implementation of Security Council resolution 435(1978) by insisting on conditions contrary to the provisions of the United Nations plan for the independence of Namibia;

7. *Rejects once again* South Africa's insistence on linking the independence of Namibia to irrelevant and

---

ᵃRule 39 of the Council's provisional rules of procedure states: "The Security Council may invite members of the Secretariat or other persons, whom it considers competent for the purpose, to supply it with information or to give other assistance in examining matters within its competence."

extraneous issues as incompatible with resolution 435(1978), other decisions of the Security Council and the resolutions of the General Assembly on Namibia, including resolution 1514(XV);

8. *Declares once again* that the independence of Namibia cannot be held hostage to the resolution of issues that are alien to resolution 435(1978);

9. *Reiterates* that resolution 435(1978), embodying the United Nations plan for the independence of Namibia, is the only internationally accepted basis for a peaceful settlement of the Namibian problem and demands its immediate and unconditional implementation;

10. *Affirms* that the consultations undertaken by the Secretary-General pursuant to paragraph 5 of resolution 532(1983) have confirmed that all the outstanding issues relevant to resolution 435(1978) have been resolved, except for the choice of the electoral system;

11. *Decides* to mandate the Secretary-General to resume immediate contact with South Africa with a view to obtaining its choice of the electoral system to be used for the election, under United Nations supervision and control, for the Constituent Assembly, in terms of resolution 435(1978), in order to pave the way for the adoption by the Security Council of the enabling resolution for the implementation of the United Nations plan for the independence of Namibia;

12. *Demands* that South Africa co-operate fully with the Security Council and the Secretary-General in the implementation of the present resolution;

13. *Strongly warns* South Africa that failure to do so would compel the Security Council to meet forthwith to consider the adoption of appropriate measures under the Charter, including Chapter VII, as additional pressure to ensure South Africa's compliance with the above-mentioned resolutions;

14. *Urges* States Members of the United Nations that have not done so to consider in the mean time taking appropriate voluntary measures against South Africa, which could include the following:

(a) Suspension of new investments and application of disincentives to that end;

(b) Re-examination of maritime and aerial relations with South Africa;

(c) Prohibition of the sale of krugerrands and all other coins minted in South Africa;

(d) Restrictions on sports and cultural relations;

15. *Requests* the Secretary-General to report on the implementation of the present resolution not later than the first week of September 1985;

16. *Decides* to remain seized of the matter and to meet immediately upon receipt of the Secretary-General's report for the purpose of reviewing progress in the implementation of resolution 435(1978) and, in the event of continued obstruction by South Africa, to invoke paragraph 13 of the present resolution.

Security Council resolution 566(1985)

19 June 1985   Meeting 2595   13-0-2

6-nation draft (S/17284/Rev.2).
Sponsors: Burkina Faso, Egypt, India, Madagascar, Peru, Trinidad and Tobago.
Meeting numbers. SC 2583-2590, 2592-2595
Vote in Council as follows:
    In favour: Australia, Burkina Faso, China, Denmark, Egypt, France, India, Madagascar, Peru, Thailand, Trinidad and Tobago, Ukrainian SSR, USSR.
    Against: None.
    Abstaining: United Kingdom, United States.

Explaining its abstention, the United Kingdom stated that it could not support any suggestion that armed struggle was to be preferred to negotiations, nor did it think that the Council should tie the hands of Member States or prejudge the outcome of future meetings. The United States said that there were a number of elements in the draft on which it was not in agreement, its central concern being that mandatory sanctions were likely to retard, rather than advance, Namibian independence.

Australia believed that only mandatory economic sanctions could really be effective and remained ready to support their imposition against South Africa in response to its *apartheid* policies. Noting that the international community was becoming increasingly irritated by South Africa's intransigence on Namibia, France asserted that, if there was no significant movement within 18 months, it would undertake unilateral economic measures against South Africa. The USSR felt that the resolution did not provide for effective measures that could compel South Africa to implement the Council's resolutions on Namibian independence and that South Africa would be brought to see reason only by the adoption of sanctions under Chapter VII of the United Nations Charter.

Speaking in the debate, India pointed out that the Council was meeting to consider the Namibian situation after a lapse of almost two years, a sad commentary on the lack of progress towards implementation of the United Nations plan for Namibia's independence. It was characteristic that South Africa should defy international public opinion and the Security Council and continue with plans to install a puppet administration in Namibia. If South Africa persisted in its intransigence, there could be no option but to impose mandatory sanctions.

The Acting President of the Council for Namibia urged the Security Council to act decisively to ensure South Africa's co-operation with resolution 435(1978), without modification or pre-conditions.

South Africa said it would be unrealistic to consider the question of Namibia outside the regional context, and countries in the region should abide by certain ground rules. No State should make its territory available to those wishing to promote violence against other States and no foreign forces should be permitted to intervene in the region; once a country allowed the USSR and its surrogates to establish a presence within its borders, it was difficult to get rid of them. The problems of Angola and Namibia were inextricably linked; however, the Namibian people could not wait indefinitely for the withdrawal of Cuban forces from Angola. If a firm agreement could be reached in that regard, South Africa would carry out its undertaking to implement the international settlement plan. The proposed arrangement for the internal administration of Namibia should be seen as an interim mechanism, pending agreement on the Territory's independence.

Angola stated that in order to break the deadlock on the Namibian problem, it had put forward a programme for reducing the number of Cuban troops on its territory. Features of that programme included the withdrawal of South African forces from Angola, a declaration by South Africa committing it to implement resolution 435(1978), a cease-fire agreement between South Africa and SWAPO, and the signing, under Security Council auspices, of an international agreement between Angola, South Africa, Cuba and SWAPO, defining each party's obligations to assure Namibian independence and the guarantees necessary to preserve Angolan security and territorial integrity. However, South Africa's attitude continued to be very hostile, an attitude made possible by the support of certain Western Powers which should be held responsible for the situation in southern Africa. Since January 1985, South Africa had been planning an operation aimed at destroying the Malongo oil complex in Angola's Cabinda province (see p. 181). Following the sabotage attempt, there had been increased reconnaissance flights by the South African air force over Angola.

Cuba maintained that the presence of Cuban forces in Angola was not connected with Namibia, that those forces had gone to Angola at the request of its Government to oppose an invasion by the South African army and other acts of aggression. Conditions for bringing about peace were Namibian independence, the end of aid to the counter-revolutionary bands of União Nacional para a Independência Total de Angola (UNITA) and an international guarantee that agreements would be respected.

The insistence on linkage by the United States and South Africa could only be interpreted as an undeclared repudiation of Security Council resolution 435(1978) and of the United Nations plan for Namibian independence, Zambia said. Czechoslovakia, Kuwait, the Libyan Arab Jamahiriya, Poland, the Syrian Arab Republic and Uganda agreed. Malaysia said that there had never been any justification for raising the linkage issue, that it was simply an exercise in raw power. The United States said there was a wide area of international consensus on Namibia. Foremost among the points of agreement was the need to bring the Territory to independence under resolution 435 (1978), a goal to which the United States remained dedicated. It had made its view of South Africa's announced intention to establish an "interim government" absolutely clear—any purported transfer of power to bodies established in Namibia

would be null and void; such institutions would have no standing. It was for the Namibian people to choose their own leaders in free and fair elections under United Nations supervision and control. A settlement could be within grasp, given sufficient will by the parties most concerned. Prior to the Security Council's previous meetings on Namibia, only one barrier had remained—South Africa's insistence on the withdrawal of Cuban troops from Angola—and by late summer of 1984 Cuban troop withdrawal was being discussed within the context of resolution 435(1978). Having been involved for several months in discussions with the two parties aimed at narrowing the gap between their positions, the United States remained convinced that the gap could be bridged, and would continue its efforts to bring the parties together.

A large number of countries called for the implementation of resolution 435(1978) as the only basis for the settlement of the Namibian problem. Among them were Afghanistan, Australia, Bangladesh, Barbados, Bolivia, Botswana, Brazil, Canada, the Congo, Cyprus, Democratic Yemen, Denmark, Egypt, Ethiopia, France, the Federal Republic of Germany, Haiti, Hungary, Japan, Kenya, Kuwait, the Lao People's Democratic Republic, Lesotho, Liberia, Madagascar, Malta, Morocco, Mozambique, Nicaragua, Panama, Peru, Seychelles, Sri Lanka, the Sudan, Thailand, Turkey, the Ukrainian SSR, the United Arab Emirates, Viet Nam and Zambia.

Upholding resolution 435(1978) as the basis for securing Namibian independence at the earliest possible date, the United Kingdom emphasized that the Security Council should not act in a way which jeopardized the plan or which could entail further delay. It had been suggested by some that further efforts at negotiation should be given up; that would be a tragic error.

The United Republic of Tanzania urged the Council to ensure that implementation of the United Nations plan for Namibia commenced.

Algeria warned that South Africa was preparing, commensurate with its intransigence, to impose a so-called internal solution on Namibia and ignore its decolonization. In the view of Australia, Bulgaria, Democratic Yemen, Egypt, the Federal Republic of Germany, Hungary, India, Indonesia, Mongolia, Mozambique, Pakistan, Panama, Poland, Thailand, the United Arab Emirates, the United Kingdom and Zimbabwe, South Africa's attempts to put together the political coalition of MPC and install an "interim government" in Namibia constituted a violation of resolution 435(1978) and were null and void.

Nigeria held that no amount of subterfuge could disguise the fact that Namibia was a classic case of decolonization; Nigeria was amazed at the latitude given South Africa to continue to determine the fate of a Territory over which it ceased to have legal responsibility almost 19 years previously, when the General Assembly had terminated South Africa's mandate over Namibia and assumed direct responsibility for the Territory.[77] In Ghana's opinion, action in respect of Namibia should be based on the understanding that South Africa's presence was illegal and an impediment to Namibian freedom. It urged the Council to set in train the plan contained in resolution 435(1978) and to agree on selective economic sanctions.

Nothing short of mandatory sanctions would force South Africa to comply with resolution 435(1978), Pakistan contended. Others favouring sanctions included Afghanistan, Argentina, Bulgaria, Czechoslovakia, Democratic Yemen, Ethiopia, the German Democratic Republic, Indonesia, Jamaica, Kenya, the Libyan Arab Jamahiriya, Madagascar, Malaysia, Mexico, the Sudan, the Syrian Arab Republic, the Ukrainian SSR, the United Arab Emirates and Viet Nam.

Burkina Faso appealed for an end to opposition to binding sanctions. The Council's debate would be significant only if it forged ahead, something it had failed to do in the past. Burkina Faso made its appeal not only to speed Namibia's achievement of independence, but above all so that the Universal Declaration of Human Rights[78] would no longer be scorned and so that democrats, patriots and revolutionaries would no longer languish in South African gaols.

If South Africa continued in its intransigence, there was no option but to impose comprehensive mandatory sanctions, said Yugoslavia.

The events of the previous two years, China stated, had further proved that South Africa was solely responsible for the failure to implement the relevant Security Council resolutions. The Council should promptly take the following actions: demand that South Africa stop its engineering of the "interim government" and implement resolution 435(1978); demand that all Council members, especially the permanent members, make genuine efforts to implement Council resolutions; entrust the Secretary-General with urging South Africa to enter into negotiations with SWAPO; call on all countries to exert greater pressure on South Africa through arms and oil embargoes; and appeal for greater assistance to SWAPO and the front-line States.

The Chairman of the Special Committee against *Apartheid* asserted that the time had come to repudiate all attempts to negotiate Namibian independence outside the context of the United Nations, to establish a time-frame for independence, to apply mandatory sanctions against South Africa, and to declare that linkage had no validity. The Chairman of the Committee on colonial countries called for the immediate implementation of resolution 435(1978), without modification, qualification or pre-conditions, the imposing of economic sanctions on South Africa and the extension of assistance to the Namibian people.

A number of countries, including Angola, Bulgaria, China, Cuba, Ethiopia, Ghana, Indonesia, the Lao People's Democratic Republic, Nicaragua, the Syrian Arab Republic, Trinidad and Tobago, the United Republic of Tanzania, Zambia and Zimbabwe, criticized the policy of constructive engagement—quiet diplomacy—which had been advanced as an alternative to sanctions.

Efforts of the Western contact group (Canada, France, Federal Republic of Germany, United Kingdom, United States) to negotiate South Africa's compliance with the independence plan had reached an impasse, according to Nigeria. Canada admitted that the contact group had not succeeded, any more than others had, in bringing independence to Namibia, but said it should not disband because it still had a role to play.

Cameroon said that current events in Namibia posed a grave threat to international peace and security. That threat was a direct consequence of the use of force within Namibia and against neighbouring States and of the continuing pillage of Namibia's natural resources. The risk of local conflicts becoming generalized threatened the very survival of mankind in the nuclear age—an aspect which was particularly relevant, given South Africa's exploitation of Namibian uranium in pursuing its nuclear programme.

Bangladesh reiterated the call to all States, as contained in Decree No. 1,[10] to take legislative action to prevent the exploitation, processing, transporting and marketing of Namibian resources. Jamaica stressed that foreign economic interests, including some of the world's largest corporations from South Africa, Western Europe and North America, which had been lured to Namibia by the unusually high profits made available by South Africa's extension to the Territory of the *apartheid* system, were still actively exploiting Namibia's resources; those activities were a violation of Decree No. 1. Morocco demanded an end to the systematic plundering of Namibian resources in violation of the Decree.

Japan declared that Decree No. 1 had been brought to the attention of all relevant organizations and corporate executives in Japan. It did not maintain diplomatic relations with South Africa or engage in military or nuclear co-operation of any kind with South Africa, prohibited direct investments there, had called on Japanese foreign-exchange banks and their branches abroad to refrain from extending loans to South Africa and had taken measures to enforce restrictions on cultural, educational and sports contacts with it, in accordance with United Nations resolutions.

Years had passed without the implementation of resolution 435(1978) because of resources such as uranium, cobalt, manganese, platinum and other strategic metals which were being plundered in Namibia by United States companies, Iran said.

The USSR maintained that it would be naïve to assume that South Africa alone had been able to sabotage, for many decades, the process of decolonization in Namibia. South Africa could not continue that policy a single day if it did not receive support from its Western protectors, primarily the United States. It was the United States that continued to link Namibian independence with the withdrawal of the Cuban internationalists from Angola. Linkage was a plot to obstruct implementation of resolution 435(1978) and to hamper Angola's sovereign rights, including the right to self-defence. In its attempt to concoct from puppet parties a so-called interim government, South Africa was trying to hold up for decades the granting of independence to Namibia. The USSR supported the immediate adoption of effective measures against South Africa, including sanctions under Chapter VII of the Charter.

An attack on Gaborone, the capital of Botswana, by South African commandos (see p. 189) was condemned by Barbados, Botswana, China, the Congo, Guyana, Lesotho, Madagascar, Thailand, the United Arab Emirates, the United Kingdom, the United States and Zimbabwe.

SWAPO's representative urged the Security Council to act decisively to secure the implementation of resolutions 385(1976) and 435(1978), and to impose comprehensive sanctions under Chapter VII. Moreover, there was an imperative need for the nations of the world to increase their diplomatic, political, material, financial, humanitarian and military assistance to the struggle of the Namibian people. The United Nations system should continue existing assistance programmes which were currently of direct benefit to Namibians, including the United Nations Institute for Namibia, the Namibia Vocational Training School, the Nationhood Programme for Namibia and various scholarship programmes.

The Permanent Observer of the League of Arab States said South Africa's contempt for Security Council resolutions could not be restrained except by the imposition of credible sanctions under Chapter VII.

The representative of ANC said that the need to decolonize Namibia was as imperative as the need to eradicate *apartheid*, that it was time to implement without further delay resolution 435(1978), and that the most effective means to bring about compliance was to impose comprehensive sanctions. The representative of PAC said that if Western and other countries were sincere in their opposition to *apartheid*, they would act immediately to impose mandatory economic sanctions against South Africa.

SECURITY COUNCIL CONSIDERATION (November)

In letters of 11 November, India,[79] pursuant to a decision taken at the Conference of Foreign Ministers of Non-Aligned Countries (Luanda, 4-7 September), and Mauritius,[80] on behalf of the African Group, requested an urgent meeting of the Security Council to resume consideration of the Namibian situation.

South Africa transmitted[81] to the Secretary-General a 12 November letter from its Minister for Foreign Affairs stating that, on 6 November, the Government of National Unity in Windhoek had called on South Africa to select a system of proportional representation as a framework for elections leading to Namibian independence. South Africa had no objection to the request. Agreement would have to be reached on how the system would be implemented in practice. A 12 November statement by the Cabinet of the Transitional Government of National Unity was enclosed, declaring that the Security Council had hampered Namibian independence by dismissing that Government as "null and void", that it remained dissatisfied with the United Nations on the issue of impartiality and did not accept its designation of SWAPO as the sole representative of the Namibian people. It requested that representatives of the parties making up the Government of National Unity be permitted to address the Council when it again considered the question of Namibia.

In his 26 November reply to South Africa, the Secretary-General[82] confirmed that, following recent consultations, agreement had been reached on the system of proportional representation for the elections envisaged in resolution 435(1978). He proposed that the earliest possible date be established for a cease-fire and implementation of the resolution.

The Security Council considered the Namibian situation at five meetings between 13 and 15 November.

Meeting numbers. SC 2624-2626, 2628, 2629.

Cameroon, Canada, Cuba, Czechoslovakia, the German Democratic Republic, the Federal Republic of Germany, Ghana, Iran, the Libyan Arab Jamahiriya, Mauritius, Senegal, South Africa, the Syrian Arab Republic, Tunisia and Zambia, at their request, were invited to participate in the discussion without the right to vote.

At the request of Burkina Faso, Egypt and Madagascar,[83] Andimba Toivo ja Toivo, Secretary-General of SWAPO, was invited to participate in the discussion under rule 39[b] of the provisional rules of procedure.

[b]See footnote a on p. 1097.

Also invited to participate under rule 39, at their request, were the Acting President of the United Nations Council for Namibia, the Chairman of the Committee on colonial countries and the Chairman of the Special Committee against *Apartheid*.

A draft resolution,[84] later revised,[85] was submitted by Burkina Faso, Egypt, India, Madagascar, Peru and Trinidad and Tobago.

By the revised draft, the Council would have determined that South Africa's refusal to comply with Council and General Assembly resolutions on Namibia constituted a threat to international peace and security, that its illegal occupation of Namibia constituted a breach of international peace, and that the repeated armed attacks perpetrated from Namibia by South Africa against independent States in southern Africa constituted acts of aggression.

The Council would have condemned South Africa for its illegal occupation of Namibia and its refusal to comply with Council and Assembly resolutions; reaffirmed the legitimacy of the Namibians' struggle against illegal occupation; demanded that South Africa dismantle the interim government installed at Windhoek on 17 June 1985; declared that Namibian independence could not be held hostage to extraneous issues such as linkage and that South Africa's refusal to co-operate with the Security Council and the Secretary-General violated the United Nations Charter; and decided, under Chapter VII of the Charter, to impose mandatory selective sanctions against South Africa.

Accordingly, under Article 41, the Council would have adopted enforcement measures, including: oil and arms embargoes; prohibition of new investments in South Africa and Namibia; prohibition of new government and bank loans and credit guarantees; termination of export credit guarantees for exports to South Africa and Namibia; prohibition of importation or enrichment of uranium from Namibia and South Africa; prohibition of supply of technology, equipment and licences for nuclear plants in South Africa, including exchange of nuclear information with it; prohibition of visits to and from South Africa and Namibia by military, security, intelligence and other defence personnel; prohibition of the sale and export of computers capable of being used by the South African army, police and security forces; cessation of funding for trade missions or for participating in exhibitions and trade fairs in South Africa and Namibia; termination of double taxation agreements with South Africa; and prohibition of the sale of krugerrands and other coins minted in South Africa or Namibia.

Further, the Council would have called on States and United Nations specialized agencies to assist in the resolution's implementation; urged States

not Members of the United Nations to act in accordance with the resolution; established a Security Council committee to monitor its implementation; called on States and specialized agencies to report to the Secretary-General and on him to report to the Council on its implementation; and decided to remain seized of the matter.

On 15 November, the draft resolution received 12 votes in favour to 2 against (United Kingdom, United States), with 1 abstention (France), and was not adopted, owing to the negative vote of a permanent member of the Council.

The United Kingdom stated before the vote that it opposed the draft because it would have been counter-productive and would have pre-empted the strategy which it had agreed with its Commonwealth partners; it had made clear its readiness to vote for non-mandatory economic measures. A less than unanimous Council could only afford comfort to South Africa. The United States said it would vote against the draft because it would impose mandatory sanctions. Supporting mandatory sanctions would have negated the United States good offices in seeking a negotiated solution.

Explaining its abstention, France said it was concerned with achieving realism and effectiveness, but the draft did not meet those criteria. Its wording did not seem the most appropriate for enabling progress to be made towards solving the Namibian question. However, on its own initiative and within the European Economic Community (EEC), France would continue to exert increased pressure on South Africa.

Peru asserted that the non-aligned countries trusted that the growing awareness of the justice of Namibia's case would soon overcome disagreements and bring about the end of the illegal occupation. Australia supported mandatory sanctions to cause South Africa to accept its international obligations. It wished the Council had achieved unanimity and sent an unambiguous signal to South Africa.

During the debate, South Africa said it regretted that the Council once again had to devote its time to the question of Namibia. The world was full of threats to international peace which should be the subject of Council debate. By comparison with other parts of the world, Namibia was relatively peaceful. The violence which did exist had been initiated by SWAPO, supported and encouraged by the United Nations. Unlike the situation in most African countries, there was a multiplicity of political expression in Namibia. On 12 November 1985, the Government of National Unity in Windhoek had announced its choice of electoral system as proportional representation, a decision to which South Africa had no objection; however, agreement would have to be reached on how the system would work in practice. Although other obstacles to implementation of the settlement plan had been removed, a great deal of work remained on the question of the withdrawal of Cubans from Angola. If the United Nations wished to play a role in the future of Namibia, it would have to demonstrate that it would be able to carry out its functions impartially.

India recalled that during the past 40 years decolonization had swept across Africa and Asia but that Namibia remained a subject nation. South Africa had scornfully defied Council and Assembly resolutions, including those it had itself accepted. It had invoked one pretext after another—firstly the question of United Nations impartiality; then the composition of the United Nations Transition Assistance Group; then the electoral system; and currently the linkage between Cuban troops in Angola and Namibian independence. It was in the context of the establishment in Namibia of an illegal interim administration that resolution 566(1985) had been adopted, warning South Africa that if it did not co-operate the Council would be compelled to consider acting under Chapter VII. India, along with the Non-Aligned Movement, believed that mandatory sanctions would make South Africa pay heed and could bring about peaceful change in southern Africa, with justice for the majority of the people in that unhappy region.

The United Kingdom said that resolution 435(1978) remained the only internationally accepted basis for a settlement and that South Africa must be persuaded there was no future in clinging to the Territory. The United Kingdom welcomed South Africa's decision on the electoral system it preferred, but was disappointed at its uncompromising reiteration of reasons for not implementing a plan that was now complete. Commonwealth heads of Government had agreed in October to adopt a number of economic measures against South Africa and to review progress after six months. The best way of conveying to South Africa a unanimous message of persuasion and pressure would be the adoption by the Council of a resolution consistent with the Commonwealth accord.

Canada expressed the view that the Council had to remind South Africa that its previous commitments to Namibian independence must be honoured. That would best be done by a strong resolution reinforcing measures already recommended. The Federal Republic of Germany supported the United Kingdom's appeal to attach more importance to a common position of the international community than to short-lived voting successes.

A number of countries, including China, Peru, Senegal and Zambia, said South Africa had made clear that it had no intention of withdrawing from Namibia.

The imposition of sanctions was supported by Burkina Faso, Cameroon, China, Cuba, Egypt, the German Democratic Republic, Ghana, the Libyan Arab Jamahiriya, Madagascar, Mauritius, Peru, Senegal, the Syrian Arab Republic, Thailand, Trinidad and Tobago, Tunisia, the Ukrainian SSR, the USSR and Zambia. Egypt felt that the Security Council must use all the means available to ensure that South Africa would implement its resolutions; at stake were the lives of the people of Namibia, struggling for their independence against a racist occupier, and the security and stability of the whole of Africa.

Denmark said the Council should continue to step up the pressure on South Africa to implement resolution 435(1978). That pressure, however, should be brought to bear in unanimity, since it had been shown that a divided Council could not influence South Africa.

Australia had already introduced a number of voluntary measures against South Africa in line with its conviction that the international community had an obligation to demonstrate its opposition to South African policies in a clear and concrete manner. Ghana said South Africa had used all forms of subterfuge in the past to defer action and would not hesitate to indulge in them a few more times. Iran asked for the imposition of comprehensive mandatory sanctions instead of selective sanctions.

It was time to take resolute measures and have the Council adopt sanctions against South Africa which would compel it to liberate Namibia and refrain from attempts to establish its neo-colonialist hegemony throughout southern Africa, according to the USSR.

Suggestions that sanctions would hurt the black people of South Africa or that sanctions had not worked well in the past were rejected by India and Zambia. Cameroon said that if anyone was swayed by the argument that sanctions would hurt the blacks, let them listen to the story of those seeking freedom.

The Chairman of the Special Committee against *Apartheid* said the prevailing situation inside South Africa itself required sanctions. The argument regarding the non-effectiveness of sanctions was no longer relevant. Those that still postulated such arguments did so only in their selfish interests.

The time was overdue for the Council to impose comprehensive economic sanctions on South Africa, the Chairman of the Committee on colonial countries stated. Repeated attempts to bring about an independent Namibia by the exercise of reason, through negotiations, had been ignored and ridiculed by South Africa, as demonstrated by its repeated acts of aggression. The Committee's position was founded on its conviction that the United Nations was in duty bound to do everything possible to terminate South Africa's illegal occupation of Namibia.

Any approach to the Namibian problem must take account of certain developments in southern Africa during the past five months, the Acting President of the Council for Namibia declared. The grudging reforms offered to black people showed that South Africa still believed in white superiority. South Africa's occupation of southern Angola to give a boost to UNITA showed its intention to keep southern African States uncertain and afraid and to weaken them through acts of destabilization. Within Namibia, South Africa's efforts to eliminate SWAPO had intensified, as part of a design to crush resistance. Decisiveness had not been the most outstanding characteristic of the Security Council in relation to Namibia. Each passing time-frame had added to the urgent need for firm action by the Council. The Council must, through mandatory sanctions, galvanize the international community to put pressure on the South African régime.

The Secretary-General of SWAPO stated that South Africa's cynicism and delaying tactics had no limit. There had been no change in its position regarding the implementation of resolution 435(1978). As long as South Africa and the United States Administration remained intransigent, there would be no progress. Effective and binding sanctions should be the decision of the hour.

The Security Council, on 20 September in **resolution 571(1985)**, on 7 October in **resolution 574(1985)** and on 6 December in **resolution 577(1985)**, condemned South Africa for its utilization of Namibia as a springboard for perpetrating armed invasions and destabilization of Angola, as well as sustaining its occupation of part of that country.

GENERAL ASSEMBLY ACTION

Six 1985 General Assembly resolutions (40/97 A-F) dealt with Namibia; two of these (40/97 A and B) concerned the situation there.

On 13 December, the Assembly adopted **resolution 40/97 A** by recorded vote.

Situation in Namibia resulting from the illegal occupation of the Territory by South Africa
The General Assembly,

Recalling its resolution 2145(XXI) of 27 October 1966, by which it decided to terminate the Mandate of South Africa over Namibia and to place the Territory under the direct responsibility of the United Nations,

Recalling, in particular, its resolution 2248(S-V) of 19 May 1967, by which it established the United Nations Council for Namibia as the legal Administering Authority for Namibia until independence,

Recalling further its resolution 1514(XV) of 14 December 1960, containing the Declaration on the Granting of Independence to Colonial Countries and Peoples,

Having examined the report of the United Nations Council for Namibia,

Having examined also the relevant chapters of the report of the Special Committee on the Situation with regard

to the Implementation of the Declaration on the Granting of Independence to Colonial Countries and Peoples,

Recalling further other resolutions and decisions declaring the illegality of the continued occupation of Namibia by South Africa, in particular Security Council resolution 284(1970) of 29 July 1970 and the advisory opinion of the International Court of Justice of 21 June 1971,

Bearing in mind that 1986 will mark the twentieth anniversary of the termination of the Mandate of South Africa over Namibia by the General Assembly on 27 October 1966, and expressing its grave concern that, in the period of time that has elapsed, South Africa has continued its illegal occupation of Namibia in defiance of resolutions and decisions of the General Assembly,

Recalling also its resolutions 3111(XXVIII) of 12 December 1973 and 31/146 and 31/152 of 20 December 1976, by which it, *inter alia*, recognized the South West Africa People's Organization as the sole and authentic representative of the Namibian people and granted observer status to it,

Recalling further its resolutions ES-8/2 of 14 September 1981 and 36/121 B of 10 December 1981, by which it called upon States to cease forthwith, individually and collectively, all dealings with South Africa in order totally to isolate it politically, economically, militarily and culturally,

Taking note of Security Council resolution 566(1985) of 19 June 1985, by which the Council condemned the racist régime of South Africa for its installation of a so-called interim government and declared such action to be illegal, null and void,

Noting also the Final Document of the Extraordinary Ministerial Meeting of the Co-ordinating Bureau of Non-Aligned Countries on the question of Namibia, held at New Delhi from 19 to 21 April 1985, the consensus on Namibia adopted by the Special Committee on the Situation with regard to the Implementation of the Declaration on the Granting of Independence to Colonial Countries and Peoples at its extraordinary session held at Tunis from 13 to 17 May 1985, the Final Document adopted by the United Nations Council for Namibia at its extraordinary plenary meetings held at Vienna from 3 to 7 June 1985, the resolution on Namibia adopted by the Organization of African Unity Co-ordinating Committee for the Liberation of Africa at its forty-fourth session, held at Arusha, United Republic of Tanzania, from 4 to 6 July 1985, and by the Council of Ministers of the Organization of African Unity at its forty-second ordinary session, held at Addis Ababa from 10 to 17 July 1985, and the Final Political Declaration adopted by the Conference of Foreign Ministers of Non-Aligned Countries, held at Luanda from 4 to 7 September 1985,

Strongly reiterating that the continuing illegal and colonial occupation of Namibia by South Africa, in defiance of repeated General Assembly and Security Council resolutions, constitutes an act of aggression against the Namibian people and a challenge to the authority of the United Nations, which has direct responsibility for Namibia until independence,

Stressing the solemn responsibility of the international community to take all possible measures in support of the Namibian people in their liberation struggle under the leadership of the South West Africa People's Organization,

Noting that 1985 marks the twenty-fifth anniversary of the creation of the South West Africa People's Organization,

Reaffirming its full support for the armed struggle of the Namibian people, under the leadership of the South West Africa People's Organization, to achieve self-determination, freedom and national independence in a united Namibia, and recognizing that 1986 will mark the twentieth anniversary of the launching of the armed struggle by the South West Africa People's Organization against South Africa's colonial occupation,

Indignant at South Africa's persistent refusal to comply with resolutions of the Security Council, in particular resolutions 385(1976) of 30 January 1976, 435(1978) of 29 September 1978, 439(1978) of 13 November 1978, 532(1983) of 31 May 1983, 539(1983) of 28 October 1983 and 566(1985) of 19 June 1985, and at its manœuvres aimed at perpetuating its illegal occupation of Namibia and its brutal exploitation of the Namibian people, ·

Deploring South Africa's continued intransigence and insistence on irrelevant and unacceptable pre-conditions to the independence of Namibia, its attempts to bypass the United Nations and its designs aimed at perpetuating its illegal occupation of the Territory through the establishment of puppet political institutions,

Deeply concerned at South Africa's increasing militarization of Namibia, the forced conscription of Namibians, the creation of tribal armies and the use of mercenaries for the repression of the Namibian people and for carrying out aggression against neighbouring States,

Strongly condemning the racist régime of South Africa for developing a nuclear capability for military and aggressive purposes,

Expressing its grave concern at the continued occupation of parts of southern Angola by South African troops, which has been facilitated by support extended to the racist régime and to subversive elements within Angola by certain Western States,

Expressing its strong condemnation of South Africa's use of Namibian territory as a springboard for its continuing acts of aggression against independent African States, particularly Angola and Botswana, which have caused extensive loss of human life and destruction of economic infrastructures,

Reaffirming that the resources of Namibia are the inviolable heritage of the Namibian people and that the exploitation of those resources by foreign economic interests under the protection of the illegal colonial régime of South Africa, in violation of the Charter of the United Nations, of the relevant resolutions of the General Assembly and the Security Council, of Decree No. 1 for the Protection of the Natural Resources of Namibia, enacted by the United Nations Council for Namibia on 27 September 1974, and in disregard of the advisory opinion of the International Court of Justice of 21 June 1971, is illegal and encourages the occupation régime to be even more intransigent and defiant,

Taking note of the decision of the United Nations Council for Namibia of 2 May 1985 to initiate legal proceedings in the domestic courts of States against corporations or individuals involved in the exploitation, transport, processing or purchase of Namibia's natural resources, as part of its efforts to give effect to Decree No. 1 for the Protection of the Natural Resources of Namibia,

Deeply deploring the continued collaboration between certain States and South Africa in the political, military, economic and nuclear fields, in disregard of the relevant resolutions of the General Assembly and the Security Council,

Deeply concerned at the continued assistance rendered to the racist Pretoria régime by certain international organizations and institutions, in disregard of the relevant resolutions of the General Assembly,

Indignant at the continuing arbitrary imprisonment and detention of leaders, members and supporters of the South West Africa People's Organization, the killing, torture and murder of innocent Namibians and other inhuman measures by the illegal occupation régime designed to intimidate the Namibian people and to destroy their determination to fulfil their legitimate aspirations for self-determination, freedom and national independence in a united Namibia,

Noting with grave concern that the Security Council has been prevented, on account of the vetoes cast by one or more of its Western permanent members, from taking effective action against South Africa in the discharge of its responsibilities under Chapter VII of the Charter,

Commending the efforts of the United Nations Council for Namibia in the discharge of the responsibilities entrusted to it under the relevant resolutions of the General Assembly as the legal Administering Authority for Namibia until independence,

1. *Approves* the report of the United Nations Council for Namibia;

2. *Takes special note* of the Final Document containing the Declaration and Programme of Action, adopted by the United Nations Council for Namibia at its extraordinary plenary meetings held at Vienna from 3 to 7 June 1985;

3. *Takes note* of the important debate on the question of Namibia, held in the Security Council from 10 to 19 June 1985;

4. *Further takes note* of Security Council resolution 566(1985) by which the Council, *inter alia*, condemned South Africa for its installation of a so-called interim government in Namibia and further condemned that régime for its obstruction of the implementation of Council resolution 435(1978) by insisting on conditions contrary to the provisions of the United Nations plan for the independence of Namibia as embodied in that resolution;

5. *Reaffirms* the inalienable right of the people of Namibia to self-determination, freedom and national independence in a united Namibia, in accordance with the Charter of the United Nations and as recognized in General Assembly resolutions 1514(XV) and 2145(XXI) and in subsequent resolutions of the Assembly relating to Namibia, as well as the legitimacy of their struggle by all the means at their disposal, including armed struggle, against the illegal occupation of their territory by South Africa;

6. *Strongly condemns* the South African régime for its continued illegal occupation of Namibia in defiance of the resolutions of the United Nations relating to Namibia;

7. *Declares* that South Africa's illegal occupation of Namibia constitutes an act of aggression against the Namibian people in terms of the Definition of Aggression contained in General Assembly resolution 3314(XXIX) of 14 December 1974, and supports the armed struggle

of the Namibian people, under the leadership of the South West Africa People's Organization, to repel South Africa's aggression and to achieve self-determination, freedom and national independence in a united Namibia;

8. *Reiterates* that, in accordance with its resolution 2145(XXI), Namibia is the direct responsibility of the United Nations until genuine self-determination and national independence are achieved in the Territory and, for this purpose, reaffirms the mandate given to the United Nations Council for Namibia as the legal Administering Authority for Namibia until independence under resolution 2248(S-V) and subsequent resolutions of the General Assembly;

9. *Reaffirms* its decision that the United Nations Council for Namibia, in accordance with the mandate conferred upon it by General Assembly resolution 2248(S-V), should proceed to establish its administration in Namibia in 1986;

10. *Reaffirms* that the South West Africa People's Organization, the national liberation movement of Namibia, is the sole and authentic representative of the Namibian people;

11. *Further reaffirms* that the genuine independence of Namibia can be achieved only with the direct and full participation of the South West Africa People's Organization in all efforts to implement the resolutions of the United Nations relating to Namibia;

12. *Reaffirms* that Security Council resolution 435(1978) remains the only acceptable basis for a peaceful settlement of the Namibian question, and calls once again for its immediate and unconditional implementation;

13. *Expresses its dismay* at the failure to date of the Security Council to discharge effectively its responsibilities for the maintenance of peace and security in southern Africa, owing to the opposition of its Western permanent members;

14. *Urges* the Security Council to act decisively in fulfilment of the direct responsibility of the United Nations over Namibia and to take, without further delay, appropriate action to ensure that the United Nations plan, as embodied in Council resolution 435(1978), is not undermined or modified in any way and that it is fully respected and implemented;

15. *Reiterates its conviction* that South Africa's continued illegal occupation of Namibia, its defiance of United Nations resolutions, its brutal repression of the Namibian people, its acts of destabilization and aggression against independent African States and its policies of *apartheid* constitute a threat to international peace and security;

16. *Declares* that comprehensive mandatory sanctions under Chapter VII of the Charter of the United Nations are the most effective measures to ensure South Africa's compliance with the resolutions and decisions of the United Nations;

17. *Strongly condemns* South Africa for the imposition of the so-called interim government in Namibia on 17 June 1985, declares this measure null and void, and affirms that this new manoeuvre clearly shows once again that Pretoria does not have the slightest intention of respecting the United Nations plan, as embodied in Security Council resolution 435(1978), and is seeking, quite to the contrary, to consolidate its illegal hold over the Territory by creating puppet political institutions to serve its own interests;

18. *Denounces* all fraudulent constitutional and political schemes by which the illegal racist régime of South Africa attempts to perpetuate its colonial domination of Namibia, and, in particular, calls upon the international community to continue to refrain from according any recognition or extending any co-operation to any régime imposed by the illegal South African administration upon the Namibian people in violation of Security Council resolutions 385(1976), 435(1978), 439(1978), 532(1983), 539(1983) and 566(1985) and of other relevant resolutions of the General Assembly and the Council;

19. *Reaffirms* that all such manoeuvres are fraudulent and null and void and that they must be rejected categorically by all States as called for in the relevant resolutions of the General Assembly and the Security Council;

20. *Declares* that all so-called laws and proclamations issued by the illegal occupation régime in Namibia are illegal, null and void;

21. *Strongly urges* the Security Council to act decisively against any dilatory manoeuvres and fraudulent schemes of the illegal occupation régime aimed at frustrating the legitimate struggle of the Namibian people, under the leadership of the South West Africa People's Organization, for self-determination and national liberation;

22. *Reiterates* that there are only two parties to the conflict in Namibia, namely, the people of Namibia, led by their sole and authentic representative, the South West Africa People's Organization, on the one hand, and the illegal occupation régime of South Africa, on the other;

23. *Further reiterates* that Member States must exert all efforts to counter any manoeuvres aimed at circumventing the United Nations and undermining its primary responsibility for the decolonization of Namibia;

24. *Welcomes and endorses* the universal and categorical rejection of the "linkage" advanced by South Africa between the independence of Namibia and irrelevant and extraneous issues, such as the presence of Cuban forces in Angola, and emphasizes unequivocally that such "linkage", in addition to delaying the decolonization process in Namibia, constitutes an interference in the internal affairs of Angola;

25. *Welcomes and endorses* the world-wide and justified condemnation of the policy of constructive engagement with South Africa as one which, in addition to encouraging South Africa's intransigence and thereby delaying Namibia's independence, has been discredited and made bankrupt by the very actions of the Pretoria régime both within South Africa and in the southern African region as a whole;

26. *Expresses its appreciation* to the front-line States and the South West Africa People's Organization for their statesmanlike and constructive attitude in the efforts aimed at implementing Security Council resolution 435(1978);

27. *Reaffirms its conviction* that the solidarity and support of the front-line States for the Namibian cause continues to be a factor of paramount importance in the efforts to bring genuine independence to the Territory;

28. *Strongly urges* the international community to increase, as a matter of urgency, financial, material, military and political support to the front-line States so as to enable them to resolve their own economic

difficulties, which are largely a consequence of Pretoria's policies of aggression and subversion, and to defend themselves better against South Africa's persistent attempts to destabilize them;

29. *Requests* Member States urgently to extend all necessary assistance to Angola and other front-line States, in order to enable them to strengthen their defence capacity against South Africa's acts of aggression;

30. *Commends* the South West Africa People's Organization for its continued intensification of the struggle on all fronts, including the armed struggle, and for its commitment to embrace all Namibian patriots in an effort to strengthen further national unity so as to ensure the territorial integrity and sovereignty of a united Namibia, and welcomes the consolidation of unity in action by the patriotic forces in Namibia under the leadership of the South West Africa People's Organization, during the critical phase of their struggle for national and social liberation;

31. *Reaffirms* its solidarity with, and support for, the South West Africa People's Organization, the sole and authentic representative of the Namibian people, and pays tribute to that organization for the sacrifices it has made in the field of battle and also for the spirit of statesmanship, co-operation and far-sightedness it has displayed in the political and diplomatic arena despite the most extreme provocations on the part of the racist Pretoria régime;

32. *Calls upon* Member States and the specialized agencies and other organizations of the United Nations system to render sustained and increased support, as well as material, financial, military and other assistance, to the South West Africa People's Organization so as to enable it to intensify its struggle for the liberation of Namibia;

33. *Urges* all Governments and the specialized agencies and other intergovernmental organizations to provide increased material assistance to the thousands of Namibian refugees who have been forced by the *apartheid* régime's oppressive policies to flee Namibia, especially into the neighbouring front-line States;

34. *Solemnly reaffirms* that Namibia's accession to independence must be with its territorial integrity intact, including Walvis Bay and the offshore islands, and reiterates that, in accordance with the resolutions of the United Nations, in particular Security Council resolution 432(1978) of 27 July 1978 and General Assembly resolutions S-9/2 of 3 May 1978 and 35/227 A of 6 March 1981, any attempt by South Africa to annex them is, therefore, illegal, null and void;

35. *Calls upon* the Security Council to declare categorically that Walvis Bay is an integral part of Namibia and that the question should not be left as a matter for negotiation between an independent Namibia and South Africa;

36. *Strongly condemns* South Africa for obstructing the implementation of United Nations resolutions, in particular Security Council resolutions 385(1976), 435(1978), 439(1978), 532(1983), 539(1983) and 566(1985), and for its manœuvres, in contravention of those resolutions, designed to consolidate its colonial and neo-colonial interests at the expense of the legitimate aspirations of the Namibian people for genuine self-determination, freedom and national independence in a united Namibia;

37. *Strongly condemns* the continuing collaboration between South Africa and certain Western countries in the political, economic, diplomatic and financial fields, and expresses its conviction that such collaboration helps to prolong South Africa's domination and control over the people and Territory of Namibia;

38. *Deplores*, in this context, the establishment and operation by racist South Africa of the so-called Namibia Information Offices in France, the Federal Republic of Germany, the United Kingdom of Great Britain and Northern Ireland and the United States of America, aimed at legitimizing its puppet institutions in Namibia, in particular the so-called interim government for which the racist régime has been condemned by the Security Council and the international community, and demands their immediate closure;

39. *Notes with appreciation* the recent measures taken by some States, parliamentarians, institutions and non-governmental organizations in order to exert pressure on the racist régime of South Africa and calls upon them to redouble and intensify their efforts to force the racist régime to comply with the resolutions and decisions of the United Nations relating to Namibia and South Africa;

40. *Calls once again upon* all Governments, especially those which have close links with South Africa, to support, in co-operation with the United Nations Council for Namibia, the actions of the United Nations to defend the national rights of the Namibian people until independence and to isolate the racist régime of South Africa;

41. *Strongly condemns* South Africa for its military buildup in Namibia, its introduction of compulsory military service for Namibians, its proclamation of a so-called security zone in Namibia, its recruitment and training of Namibians for tribal armies, its use of mercenaries to suppress the Namibian people and to carry out its military attacks against independent African States, its threats and acts of subversion and aggression against those States and the forcible displacement of Namibians from their homes;

42. *Strongly condemns* South Africa for its imposition of military conscription of all Namibian males between seventeen and fifty-five years of age into the occupying colonial army, in yet further sinister attempts to suppress the national liberation struggle of the Namibian people and to force Namibians to kill one another, and declares that all measures taken by racist South Africa by which the illegal occupation régime attempts to enforce military conscription in Namibia are illegal, null and void;

43. *Strongly condemns* the racist régime of South Africa for its utilization of the international Territory of Namibia as a springboard for perpetrating armed invasions, subversion, destabilization and aggression against neighbouring African States;

44. *Strongly condemns* South Africa, in particular for its persistent acts of aggression and subversion against Angola, including the continued occupation of parts of Angolan territory in gross violation of its sovereignty and territorial integrity, and calls upon South Africa to cease all acts of aggression against Angola and withdraw immediately and unconditionally all its troops from that country;

45. *Expresses its grave concern* at the acquisition of nuclear-weapon capability by the racist régime of South

Africa and declares that such acquisition constitutes a threat to peace and security in Africa while posing a danger to all mankind;

46. *Condemns* and calls for an immediate end to the continuing military collaboration on the part of certain Western countries with the racist régime of South Africa, and expresses its conviction that such collaboration, in addition to strengthening the aggressive military machinery of the Pretoria régime, thereby constituting a hostile action against the people of Namibia and the front-line States, is also in violation of the arms embargo imposed against South Africa under Security Council resolution 418(1977) of 4 November 1977;

47. *Declares* that such collaboration encourages the Pretoria régime in its defiance of the international community and obstructs efforts to eliminate *apartheid* and bring South Africa's illegal occupation of Namibia to an end, and calls for the immediate cessation of such collaboration;

48. *Calls upon* all States to implement fully the arms embargo imposed against South Africa under Security Council resolution 418(1977);

49. *Calls upon* the Security Council to adopt the necessary measures to tighten the arms embargo imposed against South Africa under Council resolution 418(1977) and to ensure strict compliance with the embargo by all States;

50. *Further calls upon* the Security Council to implement, as a matter of urgency, the recommendations contained in the report of the Security Council Committee established in pursuance of resolution 421(1977);

51. *Calls upon* all States to comply with Security Council resolution 558(1984) of 13 December 1984 and to refrain from importing arms, ammunition of all types and military vehicles produced in South Africa;

52. *Condemns* all collaboration with the Pretoria régime in the nuclear field, and calls upon all States that do so to terminate such collaboration, including refraining from supplying the racist minority régime of South Africa, directly or indirectly, with installations, equipment or material that might enable it to produce uranium, plutonium or other nuclear materials or reactors;

53. *Reiterates its call* upon all States to take legislative and other appropriate measures to prevent the recruitment, training and transit of mercenaries for service in Namibia;

54. *Strongly condemns* the illegal occupation régime of South Africa for its massive repression of the people of Namibia and their liberation movement, the South West Africa People's Organization, in an attempt to intimidate and terrorize them into submission;

55. *Demands once again* that South Africa immediately release all Namibian political prisoners, including all those imprisoned or detained under the so-called internal security laws, martial law or any other arbitrary measures, whether such Namibians have been charged or tried or are being held without charge in Namibia or South Africa;

56. *Demands* that South Africa account for all "disappeared" Namibians and release any who are still alive, and declares that South Africa shall be liable to compensate the victims, their families and the future lawful Government of an independent Namibia for the losses sustained;

57. *Reaffirms* that the natural resources of Namibia, including its marine resources, are the inviolable heritage of the Namibian people, and expresses its deep concern at the depletion of these resources, particularly its uranium deposits, as a result of their plunder by South Africa and certain Western and other foreign economic interests, in violation of the pertinent resolutions of the General Assembly and of the Security Council, of Decree No. 1 for the Protection of the Natural Resources of Namibia and in disregard of the advisory opinion of the International Court of Justice of 21 June 1971;

58. *Endorses* the decision by the United Nations Council for Namibia at its extraordinary plenary meetings, held at Vienna from 3 to 7 June 1985, that it will, in the exercise of its rights under the United Nations Convention on the Law of the Sea, proclaim an exclusive economic zone for Namibia, the outer limit of which shall be 200 miles, and states that any action for the implementation of that decision should be taken in consultation with the South West Africa People's Organization, the representative of the people of Namibia;

59. *Declares* that all activities of foreign economic interests in Namibia are illegal under international law and that all the foreign economic interests operating in Namibia are liable to pay damages to the future lawful Government of an independent Namibia;

60. *Calls upon* the United Nations Council for Namibia, in pursuance of the relevant provisions of Decree No. 1 for the Protection of the Natural Resources of Namibia, to take the necessary steps to compile statistical information on the wealth illegally extracted from Namibia with a view to assessing the extent of compensation eventually due to an independent Namibia;

61. *Strongly condemns* the activities of all foreign economic interests operating in Namibia which are illegally exploiting the resources of the Territory, and demands that these interests comply with all the relevant resolutions and decisions of the United Nations by immediately refraining from any new investment or any other activity in Namibia, by withdrawing from the Territory and by putting an end to their co-operation with the illegal South African administration;

62. *Declares* that, by their incessant exploitation of the human and natural resources of the Territory and their continued accumulation and repatriation of huge profits, the foreign economic, financial and other interests operating in Namibia constitute a major obstacle to its independence;

63. *Requests once again* all Member States, particularly those States whose corporations are engaged in the exploitation of Namibian resources, to take all appropriate measures, including legislative and enforcement action, to ensure the full application of, and compliance by all corporations and individuals within their jurisdiction with, the provisions of Decree No. 1 for the Protection of the Natural Resources of Namibia;

64. *Calls upon* the Governments of all States, particularly those whose corporations are involved in the mining and processing of Namibian uranium, to take all appropriate measures in compliance with United Nations resolutions and decisions and Decree No. 1 for the Protection of the Natural Resources of Namibia, including the practice of requiring negative certificates of origin, to prohibit State-owned and other corporations, together with their subsidiaries, from dealing in Namibian uranium and from engaging in any uranium-prospecting activities in Namibia;

65. *Approves* of the decision of the United Nations Council for Namibia of 2 May 1985 to initiate legal proceedings in the domestic courts of States against corporations or individuals involved in the exploitation, transport, processing or purchase of Namibia's natural resources, as part of its efforts to give effect to Decree No. 1 for the Protection of the Natural Resources of Namibia;

66. *Requests* the Governments of the Federal Republic of Germany, the Netherlands and the United Kingdom of Great Britain and Northern Ireland, which operate the Urenco uranium-enrichment plant, to have Namibian uranium specifically excluded from the Treaty of Almelo, which regulates the activities of Urenco;

67. *Urges* the United Nations Council for Namibia, in its capacity as the legal Administering Authority for Namibia until independence, to consider the promulgation of additional legislation in order to protect and promote the interests of the people of Namibia and to implement effectively such legislation;

68. *Calls upon* all specialized agencies, in particular the International Monetary Fund, to terminate all collaboration with, and assistance to, the racist régime of South Africa, since such assistance serves to augment the military capability of the Pretoria régime, thus enabling it not only to continue the brutal repression in Namibia and South Africa itself, but also to commit aggression against independent neighbouring States;

69. *Reiterates its request* to all States, pending the imposition of comprehensive mandatory sanctions against South Africa, to take legislative, administrative and other measures individually and collectively, as appropriate, in order effectively to isolate South Africa politically, economically, militarily and culturally, in accordance with General Assembly resolutions ES-8/2 and 36/121 B, and its resolution 37/233 A of 20 December 1982;

70. *Requests* the United Nations Council for Namibia, in its implementation of paragraph 15 of General Assembly resolution ES-8/2 and of the relevant provisions of Assembly resolutions 36/121 B and 37/233 A, to continue to monitor the boycott of South Africa and to submit to the Assembly at its forty-first session a comprehensive report on all contacts between Member States and South Africa containing an analysis of the information received from Member States and other sources on the continuing political, economic, financial and other relations of States and their economic and other interest groups with South Africa and of measures taken by States to terminate all dealings with the racist régime of South Africa;

71. *Requests* all States to co-operate fully with the United Nations Council for Namibia in the fulfilment of its task concerning the implementation of General Assembly resolutions ES-8/2, 36/121 B and 37/233 A and to report to the Secretary-General by the forty-first session of the Assembly on the measures taken by them in the implementation of those resolutions;

72. *Declares* that the liberation struggle in Namibia is a conflict of an international character in terms of article 1, paragraph 4, of Additional Protocol I to the Geneva Conventions of 12 August 1949, and, in this regard, demands that the Conventions and Additional Protocol I be applied by South Africa, and in particular that all captured freedom fighters be accorded prisoner-of-war status as called for by the Geneva Convention relative to the Treatment of Prisoners of War and the Additional Protocol thereto;

73. *Declares* that South Africa's defiance of the United Nations, its illegal occupation of the international Territory of Namibia, its war of repression against the Namibian people, its persistent acts of aggression against independent African States, its policies of *apartheid* and its development of nuclear capability constitute a serious threat to international peace and security;

74. *Strongly urges* the Security Council, in view of the persistent refusal by the racist régime of South Africa to comply with the resolutions and decisions of the United Nations on the question of Namibia, particularly Security Council resolutions 385(1976), 435(1978), 539(1983) and 566(1985), and, in the light of the serious threat to international peace and security posed by South Africa, to impose comprehensive mandatory sanctions against that country as provided for in Chapter VII of the Charter of the United Nations;

75. *Requests* the Secretary-General to report to the General Assembly at its forty-first session on the implementation of the present resolution.

General Assembly resolution 40/97 A

13 December 1985   Meeting 115   131-0-23 (recorded vote)

Draft by Council for Namibia (A/40/24); agenda item 34.
Financial implications. 5th Committee, A/40/1039; S-G, A/C.5/40/87 & Corr.1.
Meeting numbers. GA 40th session: 5th Committee 60, 61; plenary 80-87, 115.

Recorded vote in Assembly as follows:

In favour: Afghanistan, Albania, Algeria, Angola, Antigua and Barbuda, Argentina, Bahamas, Bahrain, Bangladesh, Barbados, Belize, Benin, Bhutan, Bolivia, Botswana, Brazil, Brunei Darussalam, Bulgaria, Burkina Faso, Burma, Burundi, Byelorussian SSR, Cameroon, Cape Verde, Central African Republic, Chad, China, Colombia, Comoros, Congo, Costa Rica, Cuba, Cyprus, Czechoslovakia, Democratic Kampuchea, Democratic Yemen, Djibouti, Dominican Republic, Ecuador, Egypt, El Salvador, Equatorial Guinea, Ethiopia, Fiji, Gabon, Gambia, German Democratic Republic, Ghana, Grenada, Guatemala, Guinea, Guinea-Bissau, Guyana, Haiti, Honduras, Hungary, India, Indonesia, Iran, Iraq, Israel, Ivory Coast, Jamaica, Jordan, Kenya, Kuwait, Lao People's Democratic Republic, Lebanon, Lesotho, Liberia, Libyan Arab Jamahiriya, Madagascar, Malaysia, Maldives, Mali, Malta, Mauritania, Mauritius, Mexico, Mongolia, Morocco, Mozambique, Nepal, Nicaragua, Niger, Nigeria, Oman, Pakistan, Panama, Papua New Guinea, Peru, Philippines, Poland, Qatar, Romania, Rwanda, Saint Lucia, Saint Vincent and the Grenadines, Samoa, Sao Tome and Principe, Saudi Arabia, Senegal, Seychelles, Sierra Leone, Singapore, Solomon Islands, Somalia, Sri Lanka, Sudan, Suriname, Swaziland, Syrian Arab Republic, Thailand, Togo, Trinidad and Tobago, Tunisia, Turkey, Uganda, Ukrainian SSR, USSR, United Arab Emirates, United Republic of Tanzania, Uruguay, Vanuatu, Venezuela, Viet Nam, Yemen, Yugoslavia, Zaire, Zambia, Zimbabwe.

Against: None.

Abstaining: Australia, Austria, Belgium, Canada, Denmark, Finland, France, Germany, Federal Republic of, Greece, Iceland, Ireland, Italy, Japan, Luxembourg, Malawi, Netherlands, New Zealand, Norway, Portugal, Spain, Sweden, United Kingdom, United States.

Also on 13 December, the Assembly adopted **resolution 40/97 B** by recorded vote.

Implementation of Security Council resolution 435(1978)

The General Assembly,

Indignant at South Africa's persistent refusal to comply with Security Council resolutions 385(1976) of 30 January 1976, 431(1978) of 27 July 1978, 435(1978) of 29 September 1978, 439(1978) of 13 November 1978, 532(1983) of 31 May 1983, 539(1983) of 28 October 1983 and 566(1985) of 19 June 1985 and at its manœuvres aimed at gaining international recognition for illegitimate groups which it has installed in Namibia and which are subservient to Pretoria's interests, in order to maintain its policies of domination and exploitation of the people and natural resources of Namibia,

Reaffirming the imperative need to proceed, without further delay, with the implementation of Security

Council resolution 435(1978) which, together with Council resolution 385(1976), is the only basis for a peaceful settlement of the question of Namibia,

Reaffirming the inalienable right of the Namibian people to self-determination and independence, in accordance with the Declaration on the Granting of Independence to Colonial Countries and Peoples contained in General Assembly resolution 1514(XV) of 14 December 1960,

Strongly condemning racist South Africa for its continued illegal occupation of Namibia and its manœuvres aimed at obstructing the implementation of Security Council resolutions, in particular resolutions 385(1976) and 435(1978),

Strongly condemning racist South Africa for its continued denial to the Namibian people of the exercise of their inalienable right to self-determination and independence,

Recalling that the "linkage" insisted upon by South Africa of the independence of Namibia with totally irrelevant and extraneous issues, such as the presence of Cuban forces in Angola, has been rejected by the General Assembly and the Security Council and has been condemned world wide,

Reaffirming that the Cuban forces are in Angola by a sovereign act of the Government of Angola, in accordance with the provisions of the Charter of the United Nations, and that any attempts to link their presence in that country with Namibia's independence constitute a gross and unwarranted interference in the internal affairs of Angola,

Reaffirming that the only parties to the conflict in Namibia are, on the one hand, the Namibian people represented by the South West Africa People's Organization, their sole and authentic representative, and, on the other, the racist régime of South Africa, which illegally occupies the Territory,

Expressing its dismay at the fact that the Security Council has been prevented by its three Western permanent members from adopting effective measures against South Africa in the discharge of its responsibilities for the maintenance of international peace and security,

Recalling its call upon all States, in view of the threat to international peace and security posed by South Africa, to impose comprehensive mandatory sanctions against that country in accordance with the provisions of the Charter,

Commending the South West Africa People's Organization for its preparedness to co-operate fully with the Secretary-General of the United Nations and his Special Representative, including its expressed readiness to sign and observe a cease-fire agreement with South Africa, in the implementation of the United Nations plan for the independence of Namibia, as embodied in Security Council resolution 435(1978),

Condemning the racist régime of South Africa for its installation of a so-called interim government in Namibia, in violation of Security Council resolutions 435(1978) and 439(1978),

Expressing grave concern that, forty years after the founding of the United Nations, the question of Namibia, which has been with the Organization since its inception, still remains unresolved,

Expressing grave concern at the lack of progress in implementing Security Council resolution 435(1978), as indicated in the further reports of the Secretary-General

dated 29 December 1983, 6 June 1985 and 6 September 1985, concerning the implementation of Security Council resolutions 435(1978) and 439(1978),

Recalling Security Council resolution 566(1985) by which the Council, *inter alia*, demanded that South Africa co-operate fully with the Security Council and the Secretary-General in the implementation of that resolution and warned that failure to do so would compel the Council to meet forthwith to consider the adoption of appropriate measures under the Charter,

Recalling its request to the Security Council, in view of the persistent refusal by the racist régime of South Africa to comply with the resolutions and decisions of the United Nations on Namibia, particularly Security Council resolutions, and, in the light of the serious threat to international peace and security posed by South Africa, to impose comprehensive mandatory sanctions against that country as provided for in Chapter VII of the Charter, in fulfilment of its responsibilities under the Charter and in response to the overwhelming demand of the international community,

1. *Strongly condemns* South Africa for obstructing the implementation of Security Council resolutions 385(1976), 435(1978), 439(1978), 532(1983), 539(1983) and 566(1985) and for its manœuvres, in contravention of those resolutions, designed to consolidate its colonial and neo-colonial interests at the expense of the legitimate aspirations of the Namibian people for genuine self-determination, freedom and national independence in a united Namibia;

2. *Reaffirms* the direct responsibility of the United Nations for Namibia pending its achievement of genuine self-determination and national independence;

3. *Reiterates* that Security Council resolutions 385(1976) and 435(1978), relating to the United Nations plan for the independence of Namibia, constitute the only internationally accepted basis for a peaceful settlement of the Namibian problem, and demands their immediate and unconditional implementation;

4. *Condemns* the continuing attempts by racist South Africa to set up puppet political institutions and impose an "internal settlement" in Namibia, in defiance of resolutions and decisions of the United Nations, and, in this context, condemns and rejects the puppet "Multi-Party Conference" as the latest in a series of political stratagems through which Pretoria attempts to impose a neo-colonial settlement in Namibia;

5. *Strongly condemns* the racist régime for the installation of the so-called interim government in Namibia on 17 June 1985, declares this measure null and void, and calls upon the international community to continue to refrain from according any recognition or extending any co-operation to any régime imposed by the illegal South African administration upon the Namibian people, in violation of Security Council resolutions 385(1976), 435(1978), 439(1978), 532(1983) and 566(1985) and other relevant resolutions of the Council and the General Assembly;

6. *Demands* that the racist régime of South Africa immediately rescind the aforementioned illegal and unilateral action;

7. *Further demands* that South Africa urgently comply fully and unconditionally with the resolutions of the Security Council, in particular resolutions 385(1976) and 435(1978) and subsequent resolutions of the Council relating to Namibia;

8. *Emphasizes once again* that the only parties to the conflict in Namibia are, on the one hand, the Namibian people represented by the South West Africa People's Organization, their sole and authentic representative, and, on the other, the racist régime of South Africa, which illegally occupies the Territory;

9. *Rejects* all manœuvres aimed at diverting attention from the central issue of the decolonization of Namibia by introducing East-West confrontation to the detriment of the legitimate aspirations of the Namibian people to self-determination, freedom and national independence;

10. *Strongly condemns and rejects* the persistent attempts by South Africa to establish a "linkage" or "parallelism" between the independence of Namibia, in accordance with Security Council resolution 435(1978) and any extraneous and irrelevant issues, in particular the presence of Cuban forces in Angola, and emphasizes unequivocally that all such attempts are designed to delay further the independence of Namibia and that they constitute a gross and unwarranted interference in the internal affairs of Angola;

11. *Demands* that racist South Africa desist from its reprehensible position in order to allow Namibia to attain its long overdue independence;

12. *Calls upon* all States to condemn and reject any attempt to link the independence of Namibia with extraneous and irrelevant issues;

13. *Requests* the Security Council to exercise its authority with regard to the implementation of its resolutions 385(1976), 435(1978), 532(1983), 539(1983) and 566(1985), so as to bring about the independence of Namibia without further delay, and to act decisively against any dilatory manœuvres and fraudulent schemes of the South African administration in Namibia aimed at frustrating the legitimate struggle of the Namibian people for independence;

14. *Strongly condemns* the use of the veto by the two Western permanent members of the Security Council on 15 November 1985, as a result of which the Council was prevented from taking effective measures under Chapter VII of the Charter of the United Nations against South Africa, and appeals to them to desist from further misuse of the veto;

15. *Strongly urges* the Security Council, in view of the persistent refusal by the racist régime of South Africa to comply with the resolutions and decisions of the United Nations on the question of Namibia, particularly Security Council resolutions 385(1976), 435(1978), 539(1983) and 566(1985), and, in the light of the serious threat to international peace and security posed by South Africa, to impose comprehensive mandatory sanctions against that country as provided for in Chapter VII of the Charter of the United Nations;

16. *Calls upon* the Western permanent members of the Security Council to support the imposition of enforcement measures by it in order to ensure South Africa's compliance with the resolutions of the Council;

17. *Calls upon* all States, the specialized agencies and other organizations of the United Nations system, corporations, institutions, non-governmental organizations and individuals, pending the imposition by the Security Council of comprehensive mandatory sanctions against the racist régime of South Africa under Chapter VII of the Charter, to cease all co-operation with that régime in the political, economic, diplomatic, military, nuclear, cultural, sports and other fields;

18. *Requests* the Secretary-General to report to the General Assembly at its forty-first session on the implementation of the present resolution.

General Assembly resolution 40/97 B

13 December 1985   Meeting 115   130-0-25 (recorded vote)

Draft by Council for Namibia (A/40/24); agenda item 34.
Financial implications. 5th Committee, A/40/1039; S-G, A/C.5/40/87 & Corr.1.
Meeting numbers. GA 40th session: 5th Committee 60, 61; plenary 80-87, 115.

Recorded vote in Assembly as follows:

In favour: Afghanistan, Albania, Algeria, Angola, Antigua and Barbuda, Argentina, Bahamas, Bahrain, Bangladesh, Barbados, Belize, Benin, Bhutan, Bolivia, Botswana, Brazil, Brunei Darussalam, Bulgaria, Burkina Faso, Burma, Burundi, Byelorussian SSR, Cameroon, Cape Verde, Central African Republic, Chad, Chile, China, Colombia, Comoros, Congo, Costa Rica, Cuba, Cyprus, Czechoslovakia, Democratic Kampuchea, Democratic Yemen, Djibouti, Dominican Republic, Ecuador, Egypt, El Salvador, Equatorial Guinea, Ethiopia, Fiji, Gabon, Gambia, German Democratic Republic, Ghana, Grenada, Guatemala, Guinea, Guinea-Bissau, Guyana, Haiti, Honduras, Hungary, India, Indonesia, Iran, Iraq, Ivory Coast, Jamaica, Jordan, Kenya, Kuwait, Lao People's Democratic Republic, Lebanon, Lesotho, Liberia, Libyan Arab Jamahiriya, Madagascar, Malaysia, Maldives, Mali, Malta, Mauritania, Mauritius, Mexico, Mongolia, Morocco, Mozambique, Nepal, Nicaragua, Niger, Nigeria, Oman, Pakistan, Panama, Papua New Guinea, Peru, Philippines, Poland, Qatar, Romania, Rwanda, Saint Lucia, Saint Vincent and the Grenadines, Samoa, Sao Tome and Principe, Saudi Arabia, Senegal, Seychelles, Sierra Leone, Singapore, Somalia, Sri Lanka, Sudan, Suriname, Swaziland, Syrian Arab Republic, Thailand, Togo, Trinidad and Tobago, Tunisia, Turkey, Uganda, Ukrainian SSR, USSR, United Arab Emirates, United Republic of Tanzania, Uruguay, Vanuatu, Venezuela, Viet Nam, Yemen, Yugoslavia, Zaire, Zambia, Zimbabwe.

Against: None.

Abstaining: Australia, Austria, Belgium, Canada, Denmark, Finland, France, Germany, Federal Republic of, Greece, Iceland, Ireland, Israel, Italy, Japan, Luxembourg, Malawi, Netherlands, New Zealand, Norway, Portugal, Solomon Islands, Spain, Sweden, United Kingdom, United States.

In explanation of vote, Australia, Finland (for the Nordic countries), Ireland, Luxembourg (for the EC countries, Spain and Portugal) and the Netherlands noted that the drafts contained elements that caused them difficulties, stirred up controversies and side-tracked the Assembly into acrimonious exchanges. Therefore, they would be unable to vote for some of them.

Australia, Austria, Belgium, Luxembourg (for the EC countries, Spain and Portugal) and the Netherlands said they could not support armed struggle as a means of achieving Namibian independence and they were bound under the Charter to seek peaceful solutions to international disputes. They also felt it was inappropriate to characterize SWAPO as the sole, authentic representative of the Namibian people, thereby prejudging elections to be held under resolutions 385(1976) and 435(1978).

The United States emphasized that it was unfortunate that the drafts contained numerous instances of name-calling. It felt strongly that the direct, hostile and unjustified references to the United States were contrary to basic Assembly principles of civility, fairness and, above all, accuracy. Such language was detrimental to the goals of the United Nations. It opposed objectionable language which criticized it and another country for exercising the right to veto a draft resolution in the Security Council, which condemned the policy of constructive engagement, rejected linkage and singled out the United States for collaboration with South Africa. Many States throughout the world continued to co-operate with South Africa, especially in trade. The policies pursued by the United States had contributed to limited improvements in the lives of oppressed South Africans; it had no pre-conditions for agreement on Namibian independence and had asserted no theory of linkage.

Australia, Canada and the United Kingdom concurred with the United States view of name-calling and distortion of truth. Belize also rejected name-calling and placing blame.

Declining to cast aspersions on the actions of some countries because they differed from the majority approach, Belgium said it would vote against retention of the wording whose deletion had been requested by the United States (see below). Austria, Chile, Ireland and Turkey did not believe that the selective singling out of certain countries for criticism and condemnation would promote the Assembly's objectives.

The Federal Republic of Germany and the United States said that as members of the Western contact group they would abstain on the drafts. Canada stressed that its intention to abstain was purely procedural, due to its membership in the contact group. Although it had suspended its active participation in the contact group in December 1983, France would abstain, pending implementation of the United Nations plan for Namibia.

Honduras said that the drafts, like those in previous years, had positive elements and other elements on which it had reservations; nevertheless, it would vote in favour of them because it supported Namibian independence. Its favourable votes must not be construed as prejudicing the principle of the peaceful settlement of disputes. It did not believe that Namibia would be brought closer to independence by the selective accusation of certain Member States, and was certain the texts could be improved upon.

While voting for the draft resolutions, Togo said it would abstain in the separate votes on paragraphs in keeping with its position which refused selectively to condemn certain countries for co-operating with South Africa.

Botswana said it would vote for the drafts, even if it had to treat with anxious circumspection the paragraphs seeking the imposition of comprehensive mandatory sanctions against a South Africa to which it was closely linked economically.

Malta said it supported the draft resolutions, but that did not mean it was in accord with every provision; on such an important issue, more effort should have been made to search for drafts that would command universal support.

The draft resolutions and amendments to them required a two-thirds majority, since under Article 18 of the United Nations Charter they were considered an important question. Oral amendments

to four paragraphs in the draft that became resolution 40/97 A were proposed. In paragraph 24, a reference to linkage "advanced by the United States" was deleted (by recorded vote of 63 to 55, with 30 abstentions), as was mention of the United States in connection with the pursuit of the policy of constructive engagement in paragraph 25 (59-58-29). Mention of the United States and Israel in paragraph 37 was not retained (58-57-29), nor was a reference to Israel in paragraph 46 (79-47-25).

Oral amendments were also proposed to the text that became resolution 40/97 B. In the sixth preambular paragraph, retention of a reference to the United States was rejected (64-55-29). A paragraph which would have condemned the United States policy of constructive engagement was rejected (59-40-47). A reference to the United States Administration in paragraph 11 was omitted (54-63-29) and paragraph 14 was retained (81-30-34).

Earlier, on 20 September, the Assembly, having decided to consider the Namibian question directly in plenary meetings, decided that hearings of concerned organizations would be held in the Fourth Committee.

In November,[86] representatives of the World Peace Council at the United Nations, the Afro-Asian Peoples' Solidarity Organization, the American Committee on Africa, Episcopal Churchpeople for a Free Southern Africa, the National Lawyers Guild, the United States National Committee of the Lutheran World Federation and Professor A. W. Singham, Department of Political Science, Brooklyn College, New York, requested hearings. The Committee granted their requests and heard their statements on 12 November.

The Assembly took note on 18 November in **decision 40/409** of the Fourth Committee's report on the hearings.[87]

On 12 December, the Fifth (Administrative and Budgetary) Committee decided, by a recorded vote of 90 to 7, with 11 abstentions, to inform the Assembly that, should it adopt the Council for Namibia's recommendations,[2] an additional appropriation of $3,487,300 would be required under the proposed programme budget for the 1986-1987 biennium.

Related action was taken by the Assembly in **resolution 40/25**, by which it reaffirmed the Namibian people's right to self-determination and its condemnation of South Africa's continued illegal occupation of Namibia. It condemned South Africa for its installation of a so-called interim administration at Windhoek and declared it to be null and void, called for the immediate implementation of the declarations and programmes of action on Namibia adopted by international conferences, condemned South Africa for its increasing oppression of Namibians, for the militarization of Namibia and for its attacks on the States in the region, condemned the continued violations of the human rights of peoples under colonial domination, demanded the implementation of a 1981 resolution on Namibia,[15] and urged States and United Nations and other international organizations to support SWAPO.

In **resolution 40/57**, the Assembly requested States to withhold assistance from South Africa until the right of the Namibian people to self-determination had been restored, and, in **resolution 40/56**, condemned South Africa's brutal repression of the Namibian people and invited the Security Council to continue to give special attention to the Namibian situation. Also, it demanded, in **resolution 40/64 B**, that South Africa end its illegal occupation of Namibia. Further, in **resolution 40/53**, it requested United Nations specialized agencies and other bodies to withhold assistance from South Africa and to refrain from any action which might imply recognition of the legitimacy of South Africa's domination of Namibia. In **decision 40/415**, the Assembly noted that a critical situation continued to exist in southern Africa, particularly around Namibia, and condemned South Africa's increasing military buildup in Namibia.

Work programme of the UN Council for Namibia

On 13 December, the General Assembly adopted **resolution 40/97 C** by recorded vote.

Programme of work of the United Nations Council for Namibia

The General Assembly,

Having examined the report of the United Nations Council for Namibia,

Reaffirming that Namibia is the direct responsibility of the United Nations and that the Namibian people must be enabled to attain self-determination and independence in a united Namibia,

Recalling its resolution 2145(XXI) of 27 October 1966, by which it decided to terminate the Mandate of South Africa over Namibia and to place the Territory under the direct responsibility of the United Nations,

Recognizing that 1986 will mark the twentieth anniversary of the termination by the General Assembly of the Mandate of South Africa over Namibia and the assumption by the United Nations of direct responsibility for the Territory,

Recalling its resolution 2248(S-V) of 19 May 1967, by which it established the United Nations Council for Namibia as the legal Administering Authority for Namibia until independence,

Taking into consideration the Final Document containing the Declaration and Programme of Action, adopted by the United Nations Council for Namibia at its extraordinary plenary meetings held at Vienna from 3 to 7 June 1985,

Convinced of the need for continued consultations with the South West Africa People's Organization in the formulation and implementation of the programme of work of the United Nations Council for Namibia, as well as in any matter of interest to the Namibian people,

Deeply conscious of the urgent and continuing need to press for the termination of South Africa's illegal occupation of Namibia and to put an end to its repression of the Namibian people and its exploitation of the natural resources of the Territory,

1. *Approves* the report of the United Nations Council for Namibia, including the recommendations contained therein, and decides to make adequate financial provision for their implementation;

2. *Expresses its strong support* for the efforts of the United Nations Council for Namibia in the discharge of the responsibilities entrusted to it, both as the legal Administering Authority for Namibia and as a policy-making organ of the United Nations;

3. *Requests* all Member States to co-operate fully with the United Nations Council for Namibia in the discharge of the mandate entrusted to it under the provisions of General Assembly resolution 2248(S-V) and subsequent resolutions of the Assembly;

4. *Decides* that the United Nations Council for Namibia, in the discharge of its responsibilities as the legal Administering Authority for Namibia until independence, shall:

(a) Continue to mobilize international support in order to press for the speedy withdrawal of the illegal South African administration from Namibia in accordance with the resolutions of the United Nations relating to Namibia;

(b) Counter the policies of South Africa against the Namibian people and against the United Nations, as well as against the United Nations Council for Namibia as the legal Administering Authority for Namibia;

(c) Denounce and seek the rejection by all States of all kinds of schemes through which South Africa attempts to perpetuate its illegal presence in Namibia;

(d) Ensure non-recognition of any administration or entity installed at Windhoek not ensuing from free elections in Namibia conducted under the supervision and control of the United Nations, in accordance with the relevant resolutions of the Security Council, in particular resolutions 385(1976) of 30 January 1976, 435(1978) of 29 September 1978, 439(1978) of 13 November 1978, 532(1983) of 31 May 1983, 539(1983) of 28 October 1983 and 566(1985) of 19 June 1985;

(e) Undertake a concerted effort to counter the attempts to establish a "linkage" or "parallelism" between the independence of Namibia and extraneous issues such as the withdrawal of Cuban forces from Angola;

5. *Decides* that the United Nations Council for Namibia shall send missions of consultation to Governments in order to co-ordinate efforts for the implementation of resolutions of the United Nations on the question of Namibia and to mobilize support for the Namibian cause;

6. *Decides further* that the United Nations Council for Namibia shall represent Namibia in United Nations conferences and intergovernmental and non-governmental organizations, bodies and conferences to ensure that the rights and interests of Namibia shall be adequately protected;

7. *Decides* that Namibia, represented by the United Nations Council for Namibia, shall participate as a full member in all conferences and meetings organized by the United Nations to which all States or, in the case

of regional conferences and meetings, all African States, are invited;

8. *Requests* all committees and other subsidiary bodies of the General Assembly and of the Economic and Social Council to continue to invite the United Nations Council for Namibia to participate whenever the rights and interests of Namibians are discussed, and to consult closely with the Council before submitting any draft resolution which may involve the rights and interests of Namibians;

9. *Reiterates its request* to all specialized agencies and other organizations and institutions of the United Nations system to grant full membership to Namibia, represented by the United Nations Council for Namibia, so that the Council may participate as the legal Administering Authority for Namibia in the work of those agencies, organizations and institutions;

10. *Reiterates its request* to all specialized agencies and other organizations of the United Nations system that have not yet done so to grant a waiver of the assessment of Namibia during the period in which it is represented by the United Nations Council for Namibia;

11. *Again requests* all intergovernmental organizations, bodies and conferences to ensure that the rights and interests of Namibia are protected and to invite Namibia, represented by the United Nations Council for Namibia, to participate as a full member, whenever such rights and interests are involved;

12. *Requests* the United Nations Council for Namibia, in its capacity as the legal Administering Authority for Namibia, to accede to any international conventions, as it may deem appropriate in close consultation with the South West Africa People's Organization;

13. *Requests* the United Nations Council for Namibia to promote and secure the implementation of the Final Document adopted at its extraordinary plenary meetings held at Vienna;

14. *Takes note* of the call for action, appeals for action, conclusions and recommendations adopted by the regional symposia and seminars, the Final Document adopted at Vienna and the Plan adopted by the Conference on the Intensification of International Action for the Independence of Namibia, held in New York from 11 to 13 September 1985;

15. *Decides* that the United Nations Council for Namibia shall:

(a) Consult regularly with the leaders of the South West Africa People's Organization by inviting them to New York and by sending high-level missions to the headquarters of that organization, whenever necessary, in order to review the progress of the liberation struggle in Namibia;

(b) Review the progress of the liberation struggle in Namibia in its political, military and social aspects and prepare comprehensive and analytical periodic reports related thereto;

(c) Review the compliance of Member States with the relevant resolutions and decisions of the United Nations relating to Namibia and, taking into account the advisory opinion of the International Court of Justice of 21 June 1971, prepare annual reports on the subject with a view to recommending appropriate policies to the General Assembly, in order to counter the support which those States give the illegal South African administration in Namibia;

(d) Take all measures to ensure the full implementation of Decree No. 1 for the Protection of the Natural Resources of Namibia, enacted by the United Nations Council for Namibia on 27 September 1974;

(e) Consider the illegal activities of foreign economic interests, particularly the transnational corporations operating in Namibia, including the exploitation of and trade in Namibian uranium with a view to recommending appropriate policies to the General Assembly, in order to put an end to such activities;

(f) Undertake measures to ensure the closure of the so-called information offices created by the illegal South African occupation régime in certain Western countries for promoting its puppet institutions in Namibia, in violation of the resolutions and decisions of the United Nations on the question of Namibia;

(g) Notify the Governments of States whose corporations, whether public or private, operate in Namibia of the illegality of such operations and urge them to take measures to end such operations;

(h) Consider sending missions of consultation to Governments of States whose corporations have investments in Namibia in order to persuade them to take all possible measures to terminate such investments;

(i) Contact institutions and municipalities to encourage them to divest their investments in Namibia and South Africa;

(j) Contact specialized agencies and other international institutions associated with the United Nations, in particular the International Monetary Fund, with a view to protecting Namibia's interests;

(k) Continue to draw the attention of States, the specialized agencies and private corporations to Decree No. 1 for the Protection of the Natural Resources of Namibia, with a view to ensuring their compliance with the Decree;

(l) Organize international and regional activities, as required, in order to obtain relevant information on all aspects of the situation in and relating to Namibia, in particular the exploitation of the people and resources of Namibia by South African and foreign economic interests, and to expose such activities, with a view to intensifying active support for the Namibian cause;

(m) Prepare and publish reports on the political, economic, military, legal and social situation in and relating to Namibia;

(n) Secure the territorial integrity of Namibia as a unitary State, including Walvis Bay and the offshore islands of Namibia;

16. *Decides* to make adequate financial provision in the section of the programme budget of the United Nations relating to the United Nations Council for Namibia to finance the office of the South West Africa People's Organization in New York, in order to ensure appropriate representation of the people of Namibia at the United Nations through that organization;

17. *Decides* to continue to defray the expenses of representatives of the South West Africa People's Organization, whenever the United Nations Council for Namibia so decides;

18. *Requests* the United Nations Council for Namibia to continue to consult with the South West Africa People's Organization in the formulation and implementation of its programme of work, as well as on all matters of interest to the Namibian people;

19. *Requests* the United Nations Council for Namibia to facilitate the participation of the liberation movements recognized by the Organization of African Unity in meetings of the Council away from United Nations Headquarters, whenever such participation is deemed necessary;

20. *Decides* that an International Conference for the Immediate Independence of Namibia shall be held in Western Europe in 1986, preceding the special session of the General Assembly on the question of Namibia;

21. *Requests* the Secretary-General to organize the above-mentioned Conference in co-operation with the United Nations Council for Namibia and, in this connection, to appoint, in consultation with the Council, a Secretary-General of the Conference and provide other necessary staff and services for the Conference;

22. *Decides* that, in order to expedite training of the personnel required for an independent Namibia, qualified Namibians should be given opportunities to develop further their skills in the work of the United Nations Secretariat and the specialized agencies and other organizations of the United Nations system, and authorizes the United Nations Council for Namibia, in consultation with the South West Africa People's Organization, to take, on an urgent basis, necessary action towards that end;

23. *Requests* the Secretary-General, in consultation with the President of the United Nations Council for Namibia, to review the personnel requirements and the facilities of all units which service the Council, so that the Council may fully and effectively discharge all tasks and functions arising out of its mandate;

24. *Requests* the Secretary-General to provide the Office of the United Nations Commissioner for Namibia with the necessary resources in order for it to strengthen, under the guidance of the United Nations Council for Namibia, the assistance programmes and services for Namibians, the implementation of Decree No. 1 for the Protection of the Natural Resources of Namibia, the preparation of economic and legal studies and the existing activities of dissemination of information undertaken by the Office.

General Assembly resolution 40/97 C

13 December 1985   Meeting 115   147-0-6 (recorded vote)

Draft by Council for Namibia (A/40/24); agenda item 34.
Financial implications. 5th Committee, A/40/1039; S-G, A/C.5/40/87 & Corr.1.
Meeting numbers. GA 40th session: 5th Committee 60, 61; plenary 80-87, 115.

Recorded vote in Assembly as follows:

In favour: Afghanistan, Albania, Algeria, Angola, Antigua and Barbuda, Argentina, Australia, Austria, Bahamas, Bahrain, Bangladesh, Barbados, Belgium, Belize, Benin, Bhutan, Bolivia, Botswana, Brazil, Brunei Darussalam, Bulgaria, Burkina Faso, Burma, Burundi, Byelorussian SSR, Cameroon, Cape Verde, Central African Republic, Chad, Chile, China, Colombia, Comoros, Congo, Costa Rica, Cuba, Cyprus, Czechoslovakia, Democratic Kampuchea, Democratic Yemen, Denmark, Djibouti, Dominican Republic, Ecuador, Egypt, El Salvador, Equatorial Guinea, Ethiopia, Fiji, Finland, Gabon, German Democratic Republic, Ghana, Greece, Grenada, Guatemala, Guinea, Guinea-Bissau, Guyana, Haiti, Honduras, Hungary, Iceland, India, Indonesia, Iran, Iraq, Ireland, Italy, Ivory Coast, Jamaica, Japan, Jordan, Kenya, Kuwait, Lao People's Democratic Republic, Lebanon, Lesotho, Liberia, Libyan Arab Jamahiriya, Luxembourg, Madagascar, Malawi, Malaysia, Maldives, Mali, Malta, Mauritania, Mauritius, Mongolia, Morocco, Mozambique, Nepal, Netherlands, New Zealand, Nicaragua, Niger, Nigeria, Norway, Oman, Pakistan, Panama, Papua New Guinea, Peru, Philippines, Poland, Portugal, Qatar, Romania, Rwanda, Saint Lucia, Saint Vincent and the Grenadines, Samoa, Sao Tome and Principe, Saudi Arabia, Senegal, Seychelles, Sierra Leone, Singapore, Solomon Islands, Somalia, Spain, Sri Lanka, Sudan, Suriname, Swaziland, Sweden, Syrian Arab Republic, Thailand, Togo, Trinidad and Tobago, Tunisia, Turkey, Uganda, Ukrainian SSR, USSR, United Arab Emirates, United Republic of Tanzania, Uruguay, Vanuatu, Venezuela, Viet Nam, Yemen, Yugoslavia, Zaire, Zambia, Zimbabwe.

Against: None.
Abstaining: Canada, France, Germany, Federal Republic of, Israel, United Kingdom, United States.

Concern about the financial implications of the Council for Namibia's work programme was expressed by Australia, Canada, Finland (for the Nordic countries), Luxembourg (for the EC members, Spain and Portugal), the Netherlands, the United Kingdom and the United States. Australia believed that much remained to be done in scaling back the Council's expenditures and making its programmes more cost-effective. Finland regretted that a Council review of its functions and priorities was not sufficiently reflected in its 1986 work programme; money and manpower could be used in a more effective manner. Luxembourg held that more careful scrutiny of the Council's work programme would have made possible financial reductions without impairing its goals. The United Kingdom and the United States deplored proposals to hold both a special Assembly session and an international conference on Namibia at a time of United Nations budgetary restraint.

The Netherlands noted that the 1986 work programme provided for a number of seminars, an international conference in Western Europe, and a special session of the General Assembly on Namibia; since it seemed that those meetings would cover the same terrain, it was hard pressed to find a justification for the lavish expenditure on repetitive activities.

Ireland stated that it voted in favour of the resolution because it supported in general the efforts of the Council to end South Africa's illegal occupation of Namibia; however, it had reservations about the Council's powers in regard to certain issues and also some difficulties about certain Council recommendations.

Information dissemination

During 1985, the Council for Namibia continued to disseminate information to Governments, leading opinion makers, the media, political and academic institutions and NGOs in order to mobilize international public opinion on behalf of Namibian independence.[2] The Council worked with the United Nations Department of Public Information (DPI) and the Department of Conference Services to increase the dissemination of information on Namibia and on specific information projects for the general public.

The Council organized extensive publicity for its symposia, seminars and missions (see p. 1092). It distributed press releases in English and French to the press, delegations and NGOs at Headquarters and to United Nations information centres (UNICs) around the world, and provided material to the pool of non-aligned news agencies.

On the occasion of Namibia Day (26 August) and the Week of Solidarity with the People of Namibia and Their Liberation Movement, SWAPO (week of 27 October),[3] coverage was provided in press releases, radio and television, and a special photo exhibit was mounted at Headquarters. For both of those events, most UNICs issued press releases and background papers and organized activities, such as the screening of United Nations films, lectures and round-tables on the role of the United Nations in the liberation of Namibia, essay contests, exhibits of United Nations posters, press conferences and television interviews.

Pamphlets on political developments, social conditions, the military situation and foreign economic interests in Namibia were produced and distributed.

The question of Namibia was featured in several radio programmes, including *Perspective*, and the anti-*apartheid* programme series. A series of six programmes, *Namibia: Update*, was distributed in English, French and Spanish. Screenings of the films *Free Namibia* and *Namibia: A Trust Betrayed* were presented by UNICs. A 60-second television spot was produced in commemoration of Namibia Day in Arabic, English, French and Spanish.

The Council organized six journalists' encounters in advance of its symposia, seminars and extraordinary plenary meetings. The encounters took the form of discussions between a Council panel and journalists and broadcasters. They focused on the media's role in generating greater public awareness of the Namibian cause and promoting the implementation of United Nations resolutions on Namibia.

In consultation with SWAPO, the Council made financial contributions to a number of NGOs, including: to the African-American Committee on the United Nations, for its fifth annual conference to develop strategies for black church action for an independent Namibia; to Mouvement anti-*apartheid*, France, to launch a national campaign on Namibia; to the Namibia Association of Norway, in co-operation with other Nordic NGOs, for a political campaign supporting Namibia; to the Campaign against Racial Exploitation, Australia, for the convening of a conference on Namibia; to the Association of West European Parliamentarians for Action against *Apartheid* for organizing a seminar on Namibia, *apartheid* and sanctions against South Africa; to the United States Peace Council, New York, for its educational campaign against *apartheid* and the illegal occupation of Namibia; and to the Holland Committee on Southern Africa for an international conference and publication of background information on Namibia.

The Office of the United Nations Commissioner for Namibia also continued to provide information on the Namibian situation. It prepared the

Namibia Bulletin, a monthly review, and *Namibia in the News*, a weekly newsletter, and gave briefings to support and student groups and individuals. It also assisted the Council in publishing United Nations booklets and posters on Namibian subjects, distributing a comprehensive economic map of Namibia, acquiring non–United Nations materials on Namibia, and reproducing available films on Namibia.

In the Vienna Declaration and Programme of Action (see p. 1091), the Council recognized the relevance of its meetings in Western Europe to mobilizing public opinion for Namibian independence; emphasized the importance of the media in stimulating support for Namibia, particularly in the Western countries; and voiced its determination to keep the Namibian problem in the forefront of international attention. To that end, it would intensify its information programme.

In a decision of 16 May,[61] the Committee on colonial countries requested the Secretary-General, in view of the publicity campaign by South Africa to justify its illegal occupation of Namibia, to intensify his efforts to mobilize world public opinion against South Africa's Namibian policy, and in particular to increase the dissemination of information in all parts of the world about the Namibian people's liberation struggle.

GENERAL ASSEMBLY ACTION

On 13 December, the General Assembly adopted **resolution 40/97 D** by recorded vote.

Dissemination of information and mobilization of international public opinion in support of Namibia

The General Assembly,

Having examined the report of the United Nations Council for Namibia and the relevant chapters of the report of the Special Committee on the Situation with regard to the Implementation of the Declaration on the Granting of Independence to Colonial Countries and Peoples,

Recalling its resolution 1514(XV) of 14 December 1960, containing the Declaration on the Granting of Independence to Colonial Countries and Peoples,

Recalling its resolutions 2145(XXI) of 27 October 1966, 2248(S-V) of 19 May 1967 and 39/50 A to E of 12 December 1984, as well as all other resolutions of the General Assembly and the Security Council relating to Namibia,

Underlining the fact that, twenty years after the termination by the General Assembly of the Mandate of South Africa over Namibia and the assumption by the United Nations of direct responsibility for the Territory, the racist régime of South Africa continues illegally to occupy the Territory in violation of the relevant resolutions and decisions of the United Nations,

Underlining that 1986 will mark the twentieth anniversary of the launching of the armed struggle by the Namibian people under the leadership of the South West Africa People's Organization, the sole and authentic representative of the Namibian people,

Strongly condemning the racist régime of South Africa for its continued illegal occupation of the international Territory of Namibia twenty years after the termination by the General Assembly of the Mandate of South Africa over Namibia and the assumption of direct responsibility by the United Nations for Namibia,

Taking into consideration the Final Document containing the Declaration and Programme of Action, adopted by the United Nations Council for Namibia at its extraordinary plenary meetings held at Vienna from 3 to 7 June 1985,

Taking into consideration also the call for action, appeals for action, conclusions and recommendations adopted by the regional symposia and seminars and the Plan adopted by the Conference on the Intensification of International Action for the Independence of Namibia, held in New York from 11 to 13 September 1985,

Strongly condemning the continued assistance rendered by certain States to South Africa in the political, economic, diplomatic, military, nuclear, cultural, sports and other fields, and expressing its conviction that this assistance should be exposed by the United Nations Council for Namibia by all the means available to it, with a view to bringing an end to such assistance,

Stressing the urgent need to mobilize international public opinion on a continuous basis with a view to assisting effectively the people of Namibia in the achievement of self-determination, freedom and independence in a united Namibia and, in particular, to intensify the world-wide and continuous dissemination of information on the struggle for liberation being waged by the people of Namibia under the leadership of the South West Africa People's Organization, their sole and authentic representative,

Reiterating the importance of publicity as an instrument for furthering the mandate given by the General Assembly to the United Nations Council for Namibia, and mindful of the pressing need for the Department of Public Information of the Secretariat to intensify its efforts to acquaint world public opinion with all aspects of the question of Namibia, in accordance with policy guidelines formulated by the Council,

Recognizing the important role that non-governmental organizations are playing in the dissemination of information on Namibia and in the mobilization of international public opinion in support of the Namibian cause,

1. *Requests* the United Nations Council for Namibia, in pursuance of its international campaign in support of the struggle of the Namibian people for independence, to continue to consider ways and means of increasing the dissemination of information relating to Namibia and intensifying the international campaign for the imposition of comprehensive mandatory sanctions against South Africa under Chapter VII of the Charter of the United Nations;

2. *Requests* the Secretary-General to ensure that the Department of Public Information of the Secretariat, in all its activities of dissemination of information on the question of Namibia, follows the policy guidelines laid down by the United Nations Council for Namibia as the legal Administering Authority for Namibia;

3. *Requests* the Secretary-General to direct the Department of Public Information, in addition to its responsibilities relating to southern Africa, to assist, as a matter of priority, the United Nations Council for Namibia in the implementation of its programme of dissemination of information in order that the United Nations may intensify its efforts to generate publicity and disseminate information with a view to mobilizing public support for the independence of Namibia, particularly in the Western States;

4. *Decides* to intensify its international campaign in support of the cause of Namibia and denounce all acts of collaboration with the South African racists in the political, economic, diplomatic, military, nuclear, cultural, sports and other fields and, to this end, requests the United Nations Council for Namibia, in co-operation with the Department of Public Information, to include in its programme of dissemination of information for 1986 the following activities:

(*a*) Preparation and dissemination of publications on the political, economic, military and social consequences of the illegal occupation of Namibia by South Africa, as well as on legal matters, on the question of the territorial integrity of Namibia and on contacts between Member States and South Africa;

(*b*) Production and dissemination of radio programmes in the English, French, German and Spanish languages, designed to draw the attention of world public opinion to the current situation in and around Namibia;

(*c*) Production and dissemination of radio programmes in English and the local languages of Namibia, designed to counter the hostile propaganda of the racist régime of South Africa;

(*d*) Production of material for publicity through radio and television broadcasts;

(*e*) Placement of advertisements in newspapers and magazines;

(*f*) Production and dissemination of posters;

(*g*) Full utilization of the resources related to press releases, press conferences and press briefings in order to maintain a constant flow of information to the public on all aspects of the question of Namibia;

(*h*) Production and dissemination of a comprehensive economic map of Namibia;

(*i*) Production and dissemination of booklets on the activities of the Council, including two booklets on Namibia;

(*j*) Production and wide dissemination of an up-to-date booklet containing resolutions of the General Assembly and the Security Council relating to Namibia, together with relevant portions of Assembly resolutions on the activities of foreign economic interests in Namibia and on military activities in Namibia, relevant documents of the Movement of Non-Aligned Countries and the Organization of African Unity and decisions, declarations and communiqués of the front-line States on Namibia;

(*k*) Publicity for, and distribution of, an indexed reference book on transnational corporations which plunder the natural and human resources of Namibia, and on the profits extracted from the Territory;

(*l*) Production and wide dissemination, on a monthly basis, of a bulletin containing analytical and updated information intended to mobilize maximum support for the Namibian cause;

(*m*) Production and dissemination, on a weekly basis, of an information newsletter containing updated information on developments in and relating to Namibia, in support of the Namibian cause;

(*n*) Acquisition of books, pamphlets and other materials relating to Namibia for further dissemination;

(*o*) Organization of media encounters and press conferences on developments relating to Namibia;

(*p*) Preparation, in consultation with the South West Africa People's Organization, of a list of Namibian political prisoners;

5. *Requests* the United Nations Council for Namibia to continue to organize, in co-operation with the Department of Public Information, journalists' encounters prior to the activities of the Council during 1986, in order to mobilize further international public support for the just struggle of the Namibian people under the leadership of the South West Africa People's Organization, their sole and authentic representative;

6. *Requests* the United Nations Council for Namibia to assist the South West Africa People's Organization in the production, translation into all the official languages of the United Nations and distribution, of material related to Namibia;

7. *Requests* the United Nations Council for Namibia to organize, at the conclusion of the International Conference for the Immediate Independence of Namibia, to be held in Western Europe in 1986, a workshop for non-governmental organizations, parliamentarians, trade unionists, academics and media representatives concerned with the question of Namibia, at which the participants will consider their contribution to the implementation of the decisions of the Conference;

8. *Requests* the Secretary-General to allocate, in consultation with the United Nations Council for Namibia, sales numbers to publications on Namibia selected by the Council;

9. *Requests* the Secretary-General to provide the United Nations Council for Namibia with the work programme of the Department of Public Information for the year 1986 covering the activities of dissemination of information on Namibia, followed by periodic reports on the programme undertaken, including details of expenses incurred;

10. *Requests* the Secretary-General to group under a single heading in the section of the proposed programme budget of the United Nations for the biennium 1986-1987 relating to the Department of Public Information, all the activities of the Department relating to the dissemination of information on Namibia and to direct the Department to submit to the United Nations Council for Namibia a detailed report on the utilization of the allocated funds;

11. *Requests* the Secretary-General to direct the Department of Public Information to disseminate in 1986 the list of Namibian political prisoners, in order to intensify international pressure for their immediate and unconditional release;

12. *Requests* the Secretary-General to direct the Department of Public Information to give the widest possible publicity to, and disseminate information on, the activities undertaken in the context of the twentieth anniversary of the termination by the General Assembly of the Mandate of South Africa over Namibia and the assumption by the United Nations of direct responsibility for the Territory and the launching of the armed struggle by the South West Africa People's Organization, the sole and authentic representative of the Namibian people;

13. *Decides*, in the context of the twentieth anniversary of the launching of the armed struggle by the South West Africa People's Organization, the sole and authen-

tic representative of the Namibian people, the termination by the General Assembly of the Mandate of South Africa over Namibia and the assumption by the United Nations of direct responsibility for the Territory, to request the United Nations Council for Namibia:

(*a*) To organize, in close consultation with the South West Africa People's Organization and in co-operation with the Department of Public Information, exhibitions on the heroic struggle of the Namibian people for self-determination and genuine national independence;

(*b*) To undertake activities, in consultation with the South West Africa People's Organization and in co-operation with non-governmental organizations, to mark those anniversaries;

(*c*) To organize an international campaign to boycott Namibian and South African products, in co-operation with non-governmental organizations, as part of its efforts to implement Decree No. 1 for the Protection of the Natural Resources of Namibia;

14. *Requests* Member States to broadcast programmes on their national radio and television networks and to publish material in their official news media, informing their populations about the situation in and around Namibia and the obligation of Governments and peoples to assist in the struggle of Namibia for independence;

15. *Requests* the United Nations Council for Namibia, in co-operation with the Department of Public Information and the Department of Conference Services of the Secretariat, to continue to inform and provide information material to leading opinion makers, media leaders, academic institutions, trade unions, cultural organizations, support groups and other concerned persons and non-governmental organizations about the objectives and functions of the United Nations Council for Namibia and the struggle of the Namibian people under the leadership of the South West Africa People's Organization, and also to hold consultations with, and seek the co-operation of, those personalities and institutions by inviting them on special occasions to participate in the deliberations of the Council, and to continue to establish for this purpose a regular and expeditious pattern of distribution of information material to political parties, universities, libraries, churches, students, teachers, professional associations and others falling into the general categories enumerated above;

16. *Requests* all Member States to observe Namibia Day in a befitting manner by giving the widest possible publicity to and dissemination of information on Namibia, including the issuance of special postage stamps for the occasion;

17. *Requests* the Secretary-General to direct the United Nations Postal Administration to issue a special postage stamp on Namibia, before the end of 1986, in observance of the twentieth anniversary of the termination of the Mandate of South Africa over Namibia and the assumption by the United Nations of direct responsibility for the Territory;

18. *Calls upon* the United Nations Council for Namibia to enlist the support of non-governmental organizations in its efforts to mobilize international public opinion in support of the liberation struggle of the Namibian people, under the leadership of the South West Africa People's Organization, their sole and authentic representative;

19. *Requests* the United Nations Council for Namibia to prepare, update and continually disseminate lists of non-governmental organizations from all over the world, in particular those in the major Western countries, in order to ensure better co-operation and co-ordination among non-governmental organizations working in support of the Namibian cause and against *apartheid;*

20. *Requests* the United Nations Council for Namibia to co-operate closely with relevant intergovernmental organizations, in order to increase the awareness of the international community regarding the twentieth anniversary of the assumption by the United Nations of direct responsibility for Namibia and regarding the continued illegal occupation of that Territory by the racist régime of South Africa;

21. *Decides* to allocate the sum of $500,000 to be used by the United Nations Council for Namibia for its programme of co-operation with non-governmental organizations, including support to conferences in solidarity with Namibia arranged by those organizations, dissemination of conclusions of such conferences and support to such other activities as will promote the cause of the liberation struggle of the Namibian people, subject to decisions of the Council in each individual case taken in consultation with the South West Africa People's Organization.

General Assembly resolution 40/97 D

13 December 1985   Meeting 115   132-0-23 (recorded vote)

Draft by Council for Namibia (A/40/24); agenda item 34.
Financial implications. 5th Committee, A/40/1039; S-G, A/C.5/40/87 & Corr.1.
Meeting numbers. GA 40th session: 5th Committee 60, 61; plenary 80-87, 115.

Recorded vote in Assembly as follows:

In favour: Afghanistan, Albania, Algeria, Angola, Antigua and Barbuda, Argentina, Australia, Bahamas, Bahrain, Bangladesh, Barbados, Belize, Benin, Bhutan, Bolivia, Botswana, Brazil, Brunei Darussalam, Bulgaria, Burkina Faso, Burma, Burundi, Byelorussian SSR, Cameroon, Cape Verde, Central African Republic, Chad, Chile, China, Colombia, Comoros, Congo, Costa Rica, Cuba, Cyprus, Czechoslovakia, Democratic Kampuchea, Democratic Yemen, Djibouti, Dominican Republic, Ecuador, Egypt, El Salvador, Equatorial Guinea, Ethiopia, Fiji, Gabon, Gambia, German Democratic Republic, Ghana, Grenada, Guatemala, Guinea, Guinea-Bissau, Guyana, Haiti, Honduras, Hungary, India, Indonesia, Iran, Iraq, Ivory Coast, Jamaica, Jordan, Kenya, Kuwait, Lao People's Democratic Republic, Lebanon, Lesotho, Liberia, Libyan Arab Jamahiriya, Madagascar, Malaysia, Maldives, Mali, Malta, Mauritania, Mauritius, Mexico, Mongolia, Morocco, Mozambique, Nepal, Nicaragua, Niger, Nigeria, Oman, Pakistan, Panama, Papua New Guinea, Peru, Philippines, Poland, Qatar, Romania, Rwanda, Saint Lucia, Saint Vincent and the Grenadines, Samoa, Sao Tome and Principe, Saudi Arabia, Senegal, Seychelles, Sierra Leone, Singapore, Solomon Islands, Somalia, Sri Lanka, Sudan, Suriname, Swaziland, Syrian Arab Republic, Thailand, Togo, Trinidad and Tobago, Tunisia, Turkey, Uganda, Ukrainian SSR, USSR, United Arab Emirates, United Republic of Tanzania, Uruguay, Vanuatu, Venezuela, Viet Nam, Yemen, Yugoslavia, Zaire, Zambia, Zimbabwe.

Against: None.

Abstaining: Austria, Belgium, Canada, Denmark, Finland, France, Germany, Federal Republic of, Greece, Iceland, Ireland, Israel, Italy, Japan, Luxembourg, Malawi, Netherlands, New Zealand, Norway, Portugal, Spain, Sweden, United Kingdom, United States.

Belgium believed that the size of the information programme was questionable and said it could not support some of the ideas to be transmitted. Ireland said it was forced to abstain because of the implicit endorsement of the armed struggle in paragraphs 12 and 13. The Netherlands felt it was inappropriate to characterize SWAPO as the sole and authentic representative of the Namibian people, thereby prejudging the outcome of the elections to be held under United Nations auspices.

In **resolution 40/164 A**, the Assembly requested DPI to continue its follow-up programmes implementing the Paris Declaration on Namibia[88] and the Vienna Final Document. The Secretary-General was requested to ensure more coherent coverage of and better knowledge about the work of the Council for Namibia, to intensify his efforts to alert world public opinion against the illegal occupation of Namibia and to disseminate as widely as possible information relating to the struggle of the Namibian people.

UN Commissioner for Namibia

Activities of the Commissioner

The Office of the United Nations Commissioner for Namibia, through his offices at Headquarters, Gaborone (Botswana), Luanda (Angola) and Lusaka (Zambia), was involved in 1985 in the protection of Namibian interests principally by means of the travel documents programme and by attempts to implement Decree No. 1 for the Protection of Natural Resources of Namibia[10] (see p. 1124). From 1 September 1984 to 31 August 1985, the offices of the Commissioner issued 456 new travel documents in Africa, North America and Western Europe and renewed 1,346 others. The offices also collected and analysed information relating to Namibia, followed internal political, economic and legal developments in South Africa concerning Namibia, and provided assistance to Namibians through the United Nations Fund for Namibia (see p. 1127).

In response to a 1982 General Assembly resolution,[89] the Office published in 1985 a reference book on TNCs operating or investing in Namibia.[90] A document was prepared, in accordance with another 1982 resolution,[91] on economic planning in an independent Namibia; under that project, several studies were prepared by consultants and a meeting to review them was held in March, followed by an international seminar in July at Lusaka to complete the study, to be published in 1986. Pursuant to the same resolution,[91] a demographic study of the Namibian population was carried out, analysing its socio-economic characteristics and making growth projections; a revised version of the study was finalized.

The Luanda Office continued to serve as liaison between SWAPO's provisional headquarters there and the New York Office. It was also responsible for 28 Nationhood Programme projects and eight projects under the United Nations Fund for Namibia. It co-ordinated assistance to SWAPO with other agencies of the United Nations system, and in that context organized three inter-agency meetings to integrate assistance programmes in general and on three projects in particular: the Loudima Namibia Secondary Technical School which was under construction in the Congo; a food, nutrition and education project for the SWAPO Women's Council; and an agricultural development project in

SWAPO settlements. It inaugurated the United Nations Vocational Training Centre for Namibia at Cuacra, Angola, for 200 trainees; provided training to 13 Namibians in broadcast journalism and radio-programme production; and obtained scholarships in Portuguese language study from Brazil for 25 SWAPO officials.

The Office at Lusaka operated as a centre for political, administrative and informational activities. It provided assistance and counselling to Namibians in many areas, and also performed consular functions by acting as liaison between Zambian and resident diplomatic missions and Namibians and by issuing travel documents to more than 2,500 Namibians. It served as a contact point with a number of African Governments, helping to place and monitor Namibian trainees in government institutions.

The Gaborone Office kept track of political events in South Africa and Namibia, and provided the New York Office with detailed briefs on developments. It placed four students for diploma courses in agriculture at the Egerton College of Agriculture, Kenya, two students at the Botswana Institute of Administration and Commerce in accountancy and business studies, and one student at the Botswana National Health Institute in pharmacy. It also administered the secondment programme for students on attachment to the Botswana Government for practical training; the number of students increased from 19 in 1984 to 24 in 1985.

Appointment of the Commissioner

On the Secretary-General's recommendation,[92] the General Assembly, by **decision 40/317** adopted without vote on 17 December 1985, extended the appointment of Brajesh Chandra Mishra as United Nations Commissioner for Namibia for a one-year term beginning on 1 January 1986; he was first appointed in 1982.[93]

Political and military aspects

The political and military aspects of the Namibian situation continued to be monitored by the Council for Namibia in 1985. The Council's Standing Committee II submitted reports on the situation in August[94] and September.[95]

Namibia continued to be occupied by about 100,000 South African troops stationed at 85 to 90 bases. Political repression, racial discrimination, *apartheid*, other gross human rights violations and economic exploitation characterized the occupation. Numerous cases of disappearances, extrajudicial executions, torture of detainees under interrogation, and collective punishment of entire communities were reported.

In January 1985, South Africa staged a military exercise, code-named "operation iron fist", in northern Namibia. It was carried out by the South African army, backed by tanks and aircraft, 50 kilometres south of Ruacana on the Angolan-Namibian border. According to the Council, the South African military had described the exercise as based on a simulated strike into Angola and stated that its troops had enhanced their preparedness to conduct cross-border operations. The Council condemned the operation, declaring that it further confirmed South Africa's determination to persist with its policies of repression and terror against the Namibian people.

The SWAPO President told the Extraordinary Ministerial Meeting of the Co-ordinating Bureau of Non-Aligned Countries in April that South Africa had recently imposed martial law over the northern half of Namibia. Access to the area was prohibited without a police permit and a dusk-to-dawn curfew was in place.

Political rallies were held by Namibians on 17 June 1985 to protest South Africa's installation of an interim government and on 25 August to commemorate the nineteenth anniversary of the launching of SWAPO's armed struggle. A unit of South Africa's "special forces" was said to have been used extensively in Windhoek in June to break up the demonstrations.

Attacks by the People's Liberation Army of Namibia (PLAN) on South African troops and installations had increased, and the level of fighting remained high. PLAN combatants successfully attacked enemy convoys, communications equipment, special agents, military bases, road systems and water pipelines. The commanding officer of the South West Africa Territorial Force, created by South Africa, stated on 18 June that some 40,000 South African soldiers were tied down in the northern war sector. According to SWAPO, the number was deliberately understated.

During July, PLAN engaged South African troops on more than 36 occasions. Fighting took place around South African military bases at Oshakati and Eenhana. PLAN attacked the military base at Ruacana in November, causing serious damage.

The South African military acknowledged that during 1985 there had been 123 SWAPO attacks, compared to 96 in 1984. The South African Defence Minister declined to give figures on the number of South African soldiers killed in the Namibian war.

In the Vienna Declaration and Programme of Action,[2] the Council denounced the South African military buildup in Namibia, stated that the acquisition of a nuclear-weapons capability by South Africa had added another dangerous dimension to a grave situation, condemned South Africa's use of Namibia as a base for aggression against neighbouring States, called on States to adopt measures to prevent the recruitment of mercenaries for service in Namibia, and demanded the release of Namibian political prisoners.

The Committee on colonial countries, on 16 May,[61] denounced manoeuvres by South Africa to bring about a sham independence in Namibia through fraudulent political schemes, condemned South Africa for its military buildup in Namibia, its introduction of compulsory military service for Namibians and its forced recruitment of Namibians for tribal armies, and deplored the collaboration of certain Western and other countries with South Africa in the political, economic, military and nuclear fields. The Committee, on 7 August,[64] demanded the dismantling of South African military bases in Namibia and immediate cessation of its war of oppression against the Namibian people and declared that South African measures to enforce military conscription in Namibia were null and void.

The Commission on Human Rights, on 26 February,[66] condemned South Africa for the military buildup in Namibia, the recruitment and training of Namibians for tribal armies, the use of mercenaries to suppress the Namibian people, and the torture meted out to the population, particularly captured SWAPO fighters.

By **decision 40/415**, the General Assembly condemned South Africa for its ever-increasing military buildup in Namibia, demanded the immediate cessation of the war waged by South Africa against the people of Namibia and urged increased assistance to refugees who had been forced to flee to neighbouring States. The Assembly, in **resolution 40/53**, requested the specialized agencies to abide by Security Council **resolution 566(1985)**, in which the Council condemned South Africa for its installation of an interim government in Windhoek, declaring it null and void, stated that no recognition would be accorded to it by either the United Nations or any Member State, and demanded that South Africa rescind its illegal action.

The Assembly, in **resolution 40/97 A**, condemned South Africa for its various military actions in Namibia and for its conscription of Namibian males between 17 and 55 years of age, expressed concern at its acquisition of nuclear-weapon capability, called for an end to military collaboration by certain Western countries with South Africa, declared that such collaboration encouraged South Africa in its defiance of the international community, and reiterated its call on States to take measures to prevent the recruitment of mercenaries for Namibia.

Proposed special session of General Assembly

On 13 December, the General Assembly adopted **resolution 40/97 F** by recorded vote.

Special session of the General Assembly on the question of Namibia

The General Assembly,

Taking into consideration its resolution 1514(XV) of 14 December 1960, containing the Declaration on the Granting of Independence to Colonial Countries and Peoples,

Recalling its resolution 2145(XXI) of 27 October 1966, by which it decided to terminate the Mandate of South Africa over Namibia,

Recalling its resolution 2248(S-V) of 19 May 1967, by which it established the United Nations Council for Namibia as the legal Administering Authority for Namibia until independence,

Recalling Security Council resolutions relating to Namibia, particularly resolutions 385(1976) of 30 January 1976 and 435(1978) of 29 September 1978, as well as subsequent resolutions relating to Namibia,

Gravely concerned that, twenty years after the termination by the General Assembly of the Mandate of South Africa over Namibia and the assumption by the United Nations of direct responsibility for the Territory, the racist régime of South Africa continues illegally to occupy the Territory in violation of the relevant resolutions and decisions of the United Nations,

Indignant at the continued non-implementation of Security Council resolution 435(1978), owing to South Africa's intransigence,

Strongly condemning South Africa for its persistent and arrogant defiance of the resolutions and decisions of the United Nations,

Decides to hold a special session on the question of Namibia before its forty-first session, on a date to be determined by the Secretary-General in consultation with the United Nations Council for Namibia.

General Assembly resolution 40/97 F

13 December 1985   Meeting 115   148-0-6 (recorded vote)

Draft by Council for Namibia (A/40/24); agenda item 34.
Financial implications. 5th Committee, A/40/1039; S-G, A/C.5/40/87 & Corr.1.
Meeting numbers. GA 40th session: 5th Committee 60, 61; plenary 80-87, 115.

Recorded vote in Assembly as follows:

In favour: Afghanistan, Albania, Algeria, Angola, Antigua and Barbuda, Argentina, Australia, Austria, Bahamas, Bahrain, Bangladesh, Barbados, Belgium, Belize, Benin, Bhutan, Bolivia, Botswana, Brazil, Brunei Darussalam, Bulgaria, Burkina Faso, Burma, Burundi, Byelorussian SSR, Cameroon, Cape Verde, Central African Republic, Chad, Chile, China, Colombia, Comoros, Congo, Costa Rica, Cuba, Cyprus, Czechoslovakia, Democratic Kampuchea, Democratic Yemen, Denmark, Djibouti, Dominican Republic, Ecuador, Egypt, El Salvador, Equatorial Guinea, Ethiopia, Fiji, Finland, Gabon, German Democratic Republic, Ghana, Greece, Grenada, Guatemala, Guinea, Guinea-Bissau, Guyana, Haiti, Honduras, Hungary, Iceland, India, Indonesia, Iran, Iraq, Ireland, Israel, Italy, Ivory Coast, Jamaica, Japan, Jordan, Kenya, Kuwait, Lao People's Democratic Republic, Lebanon, Lesotho, Liberia, Libyan Arab Jamahiriya, Luxembourg, Madagascar, Malaysia, Maldives, Mali, Malta, Mauritania, Mauritius, Mexico, Mongolia, Morocco, Mozambique, Nepal, Netherlands, New Zealand, Nicaragua, Niger, Nigeria, Norway, Oman, Pakistan, Panama, Papua New Guinea, Peru, Philippines, Poland, Portugal, Qatar, Romania, Rwanda, Saint Lucia, Saint Vincent and the Grenadines, Samoa, Sao Tome and Principe, Saudi Arabia, Senegal, Seychelles, Sierra Leone, Singapore, Solomon Islands, Somalia, Spain, Sri Lanka, Sudan, Suriname, Swaziland, Sweden, Syrian Arab Republic, Thailand, Togo, Trinidad and Tobago, Tunisia, Turkey, Uganda, Ukrainian SSR, USSR, United Arab Emirates, United Republic of Tanzania, Uruguay, Vanuatu, Venezuela, Viet Nam, Yemen, Yugoslavia, Zaire, Zambia, Zimbabwe.

Against: None.

Abstaining: Canada, France, Germany, Federal Republic of, Malawi, United Kingdom, United States.

The United Kingdom stated that the same speeches would be given and the same resolutions adopted, almost word for word, at the special session as at the regular 1986 Assembly session and at an international conference on Namibia to be held in 1986. The special session, which would cost an estimated $769,600, was unnecessary.

The Netherlands was hard pressed to find a justification for a special session when it seemed safe to predict that it would go over terrain already covered. Ireland believed that a special session could perhaps be of assistance in advancing towards an independent Namibia in accordance with the United Nations plan.

REFERENCES

[1]YUN 1967, p. 709, GA res. 2248(S-V), 19 May 1967. [2]A/40/24. [3]A/41/24. [4]YUN 1984, p. 1042, GA res. 39/50 C, 12 Dec. 1984. [5]YUN 1978, p. 915, SC res. 435(1978), 29 Sep. 1978. [6]A/40/375-S/17262. [7]YUN 1960, p. 49, GA res. 1514(XV), 14 Dec. 1960. [8]YUN 1976, p. 782, SC res. 385(1976), 30 Jan. 1976. [9]YUN 1983, p. 1054, SC res. 539(1983), 28 Oct. 1983. [10]YUN 1974, p. 152. [11]A/AC.131/91. [12]YUN 1976, p. 789, GA res. 31/150, 20 Dec. 1976. [13]A/AC.131/229. [14]A/AC.131/223. [15]YUN 1981, p. 1153, GA res. ES-8/2, 14 Sep. 1981. [16]A/40/233-S/17101. [17]A/40/263-S/17124. [18]A/40/261. [19]S/17120. [20]S/17119. [21]S/17123. [22]A/40/266-S/17128. [23]A/40/279-S/17141. [24]A/40/289. [25]A/40/290-S/17159. [26]A/40/312-S/17190. [27]A/40/325-S/17205. [28]A/40/328-S/17207. [29]A/40/369-S/17253. [30]A/40/380-S/17272. [31]A/40/386-S/17281. [32]A/40/394-S/17287. [33]S/17288. [34]S/17298. [35]A/40/463. [36]A/40/426-S/17319. [37]A/40/461-S/17324. [38]A/40/654-S/17471. [39]A/40/360-S/17243. [40]A/40/837. [41]A/40/817. [42]A/40/895. [43]A/40/276-S/17138. [44]A/40/280-S/17145. [45]A/40/666. [46]S/17114. [47]A/40/307-S/17184 & Corr.1. [48]A/40/370. [49]A/40/563-S/17410. [50]A/40/758-S/17570. [51]A/40/787-S/17585. [52]A/40/980. [53]S/17242 & Corr.1. [54]YUN 1983, p. 1058. [55]YUN 1978, p. 916, SC res. 439(1978), 13 Nov. 1978. [56]S/17442. [57]YUN 1984, p. 1033, GA res. 39/50 A, 12 Dec. 1984. [58]*Ibid.*, p. 1038, GA res. 39/50 B, 12 Dec. 1984. [59]A/40/687 & Add.1. [60]A/AC.109/824. [61]A/40/23 (A/AC.109/830). [62]S/17249. [63]YUN 1984, p. 143, SC res. 558(1984), 13 Dec. 1984. [64]A/40/23 (A/AC.108/841). [65]E/1985/22 (res. 1985/6). [66]*Ibid.* (res. 1985/7). [67]*Ibid.* (1985/8). [68]S/17151. [69]S/17152. [70]S/17213. [71]S/17222. [72]S/17244. [73]S/17264. [74]S/17265. [75]S/17271. [76]S/17255. [77]YUN 1966, p. 605, GA res. 2145(XXI), 27 Oct. 1966. [78]YUN 1948-49, p. 535, GA res. 217 A (III), 10 Dec. 1948. [79]S/17618. [80]S/17619. [81]S/17627. [82]S/17658. [83]S/17624. [84]S/17631. [85]S/17633. [86]A/C.4/40/8 & Add.1-6. [87]A/40/882. [88]YUN 1983, p. 1045. [89]YUN 1982, p. 1307, GA res. 37/233 D, 20 Dec. 1982. [90]*Reference Book on Major Transnational Corporations Operating in Namibia*, Sales No. E.85.II.A.5. [91]YUN 1982, p. 1314, GA res. 37/233 E, 20 Dec. 1982. [92]A/40/1055. [93]YUN 1982, p. 1310, GA dec. 36/325, 29 Mar. 1982. [94]A/AC.131/179. [95]A/AC.131/186.

Economic and social conditions

Foreign investment

The basic structure of the Namibian economy was typically colonial, almost exclusively tailored to the needs and demands of foreign capital with virtually the entire output of the economy's primary sectors being exported, according to a Secretariat working paper submitted in May 1985[1] to the Committee on colonial countries. The three principal industries were mining, farming and fishing, which accounted for more than two thirds of the gross domestic product (GDP), generated more than 90 per cent of exports and engaged more than 80 per cent of all paid employment. In terms of economic ties, Namibia was almost totally dependent on South Africa; close to 90 per cent of its imports and exports came from/went to South Africa.

The plunder of Namibia's natural and human resources continued, with some of the world's largest corporations and financial institutions conducting their operations under licences from South Africa. Four principal TNCs operated in the mining sector: Consolidated Diamond Mines of South West Africa, Ltd. (CDM), a wholly-owned subsidiary of De Beers Consolidated Mines, Ltd.; the Tsumeb Corporation, Ltd. (TCL), which was controlled by Gold Fields of South Africa; the Newmont Mining Corporation of the United States; and Rössing Uranium, Ltd., in which the Rio Tinto Zinc Corporation, Ltd. (RTZ) of the United Kingdom owned the majority equity capital. Those four corporations accounted for about 95 per cent of the Territory's mineral production and exports and held about 80 per cent of its mineral assets.

A number of South African corporations controlled the fishing industry, and Canadian and British firms were involved in marketing another of the Territory's major exports, caracul pelts (a valuable sheep fleece). Other major South African companies included two parastatals: the Iron and Steel Corporation of South Africa, Ltd., and the Industrial Development Corporation of South Africa, Ltd. The operations of the South African corporations were interwoven in a network of intermediate companies, reciprocal shareholdings and overlapping directorates.

Among Western European corporations in the mining, banking and petroleum sectors were Barclays Bank International, Ltd., the British Petroleum Company, Consolidated Gold Fields, Ltd., and RTZ, all of the United Kingdom; Dresdner Bank of the Federal Republic of Germany; and Shell Transport and Trading Company, Ltd., of the Royal Dutch/Shell Group.

Other corporations with operations in the Territory included the Standard Oil Company of California and Texaco, Inc., the Mobil Oil Corporation and the Hudson Bay Company of Canada.

The major banks involved in the Territory were Barclays National Bank and the Standard Bank of South West Africa, both subsidiaries of banking groups operating from the United Kingdom. Bank operations were directed exclusively to the needs of expatriates and South African and other foreign economic interests, and were instrumental in integrating the financial and customs systems of Namibia and South Africa.

Namibia's commercial and manufacturing sectors were similarly dominated by South African and other foreign economic interests. South Africa's intention was to limit industrial opportunity in Namibia in order to perpetuate its dependence on South Africa. The manufacturing sector, comprising fewer than 300 enterprises, accounted for less than 5 per cent of GDP and employed 10 per cent of the work force. Meat canning, the supply of some specialized equipment to the mining industry and some local assembly of imported materials from South Africa were the main activities. South African chains such as Barlows and OK Bazaars were very active in the wholesale and retail trade.[2]

A report,[3] prepared by the Secretary-General in response to Economic and Social Council **resolution 1985/72** and submitted in August 1985 to the Commission on Transnational Corporations, presented an overview of the activities of TNCs in Namibia. It set out the international legal framework in which TNCs operated, summarized their main functions in the Namibian economy, and discussed the support provided by them to South Africa's occupation of Namibia. The report concluded that overall it was difficult to identify any significant positive contribution by TNCs to the development of the Namibian economy. The negative effects, however, were manifest: TNCs operated in violation of international law; they had devoted negligible attention to training and upgrading the skills of their Namibian employees; and few had reinvested any of their profits in the Territory.

The Commission on Human Rights, on 26 February,[4] condemned the continuing activities of foreign economic and other interests which were impeding the implementation of the Declaration on the Granting of Independence to Colonial Countries and Peoples[5] with respect to colonial Territories, particularly Namibia. On the same date,[6] the Commission called on Governments that had not done so to take measures in regard to their nationals and bodies corporate under their jurisdiction to stop their trading, manufacturing and investing activities in South Africa and Namibia.

On 16 May,[7] the Committee on colonial countries demanded that those States whose TNCs operated in Namibia comply with United Nations resolutions by ending the co-operation of such corporations with South Africa and ensuring the withdrawal of all investments from Namibia. The Committee declared that the activities of foreign economic interests in Namibia were illegal under international law and that such interests would be liable to pay damages to the future lawful Government of an independent Namibia. On 7 August,[8] the Committee reaffirmed the illegality of foreign economic interests in Namibia and the liability of those interests to damages.

GENERAL ASSEMBLY ACTION

The General Assembly also took action relating to the operations of TNCs in Namibia. By **resolution 40/56**, it requested Member States to take measures in respect of their nationals and bodies corporate under their jurisdiction that illegally operated enterprises, including TNCs, in Namibia in order to end such operations. It urged Member States to refrain from relations with South Africa which might lend legitimacy to its occupation of the Territory. In **resolution 40/57**, the Assembly condemned the activities of foreign economic and other interests which were impeding the implementation of the Declaration with respect to colonial Territories, particularly Namibia.

The Assembly declared, in **resolution 40/97 A**, that the activities of foreign economic interests in Namibia were illegal and liable to damages and that by their incessant exploitation of the resources of the Territory and repatriation of huge profits, they constituted a major obstacle to Namibian independence. It called on States, in **resolution 40/52**, to terminate investments in Namibia and loans to South Africa and to refrain from any agreements with that régime to promote trade.

Natural resources

Mining was by far the largest sector of the Namibian economy, accounting for about half of the country's GDP and about 85 per cent of its exports.[3]

Although considerably reduced through exploitation, Namibia continued to possess a wide range of minerals, including large quantities of diamonds, uranium, lead, tin, zinc and copper. Other minerals, including gold, silver, arsenic, cadmium and tantalite, were also available in significant quantities, and it was believed that there were deposits of coal, iron ore and platinum. A natural gas field off the Namibian coast was currently being tested to determine its size.

The most recent mining operation was the Rössing uranium mine controlled by RTZ. Mining rights to the vast uranium deposits at Rössing, approximately 120 miles west of Windhoek and near the coastal town of Swakopmund, were acquired by RTZ in the mid-1960s. The mine reached its planned annual output of 5,000 short tons of uranium oxide in 1979. In reaching that capacity, Rössing became the largest open-cast uranium mine in the world. The identity of Rössing's buyers remained a closely guarded secret. The United Kingdom was the only country which admitted to importing Namibian uranium.

Since 1978, diamond exports had accounted for more than 60 per cent of Namibia's export earnings. The exploitation of Namibia's diamonds was monopolized by CDM, which had been mining Namibia's gem diamond deposits—the most extensive in the world—since 1920. It controlled mining rights in a strip of land along the southern portion of the Namibian coast, 60 miles wide and running for 220 miles from the mouth of the Orange River (Namibia's southern border with South Africa) to a little north of the port of Lüderitz. The date of termination of the rights has been extended to 31 December 2010. In recent years, CDM had been prospecting for diamonds along the north bank of the Orange River and northwards along the Atlantic coast, as well as in mining areas south of Lüderitz. The prospect of undersea diamonds had awakened interest in a dozen little islands off the Namibian coast. The Penguin Islands were said to be sitting among at least 2 million carats of diamonds worth at least $200 million—and probably much more.

Namibia's base metals were of strategic importance to South Africa and a number of Western countries. Its zinc output, in particular, had been important to South Africa's strategy of stockpiling reserves of minerals not available locally. Similarly, the Territory's lead and tin production were vital to various South African industries. The largest producer of base metals in Namibia was TCL, which operated four mines and the Territory's only copper smelter and lead refinery. The TCL mines contained half of the world reserve of germanium, which was estimated at about 1,500 metric tons. TCL was the third or fourth largest producer of germanium oxide, which was used primarily by the electronics industry for various forms of conductors, micro-processing and laser technology and for several military applications.

The Namibian fishing industry included both inshore and deep-sea fishing. Six companies controlled the industry in Namibia and South Africa—Fedfood, Irvin and Johnson, Ovenstone Investments, Willem Barendsz, Kaap-Kunene and the Oceana Fishing Group. They controlled 11 of the 12 pelagic-fish factory licences, 91 per cent of the pelagic fishing quota, all three of the lobster export licences, almost all of the snoek processing trade and 75 per cent of the seal cull. The largest non–South African companies in the inshore fishing industry were Metal Box and Reed International, both of the United Kingdom. All the tins for the fish-canning process were supplied by Metal Box from its factory in South Africa. Only companies which held licences could build fish factories; the licensees were exclusively designated by South African authorities.

In accordance with a 1981 General Assembly resolution,[9] which decided that the Council for Namibia should take measures to ensure compliance with the provisions of its Decree No. 1 for the Protection of the Natural Resources of Namibia,[10] including consideration of legal proceedings in the domestic courts of States and other appropriate bodies, the Council referred the matter to its Standing Committee II. Pursuant to a 1982 Standing Committee recommendation,[11] the Commissioner for Namibia arranged for studies on the possibilities of instituting legal proceedings, to be prepared by lawyers from the countries where most of the foreign economic interests were based.

Studies by lawyers from Belgium, France, the Federal Republic of Germany, Japan, the Netherlands, the United Kingdom and the United States, and observations by the Commissioner, were considered by the Council's Steering Committee on 9 April and 2 May 1985.[12]

The Commissioner stated that if legal action was undertaken, it would further the purpose of Decree No. 1; if taken, it would be difficult to maintain the Decree in its current status and it would be necessary to re-define it. After studying the lawyers' reports, the Commissioner concluded that legal action might lead to positive results if undertaken in one or more of the following countries: Belgium, the Netherlands and the United States. In the studies, the lawyers sought precedents, pertaining to other situations of illegal occupation. While citing certain cases from the Second World War, they were unable to find any contemporary cases that were relevant. It appeared that the case of Namibia was *sui generis*.

The Steering Committee decided to institute legal proceedings in the domestic courts of States and other appropriate bodies against corporations and individuals who were violating Decree No. 1 and that legal proceedings should commence in the Netherlands. The Council considered the implementation of the Decree at its meetings at Vienna in June.[13] It decided to promote actively the Decree's implementation in the domestic courts of States and requested the Commissioner to take the necessary steps after consultations with the Council President. In addition, it called on the Federal Republic of Germany, the Netherlands and the United Kingdom, which operated the Urenco uranium enrichment plant at Almelo, Netherlands, to have Namibian uranium specifically excluded from the 1970 Treaty of Almelo, which regulated Urenco activities, on the grounds that it was illegally obtained. It also stated that the Council would, in the exercise of its rights under the United Nations Convention on the Law of the Sea,[14] proclaim an exclusive economic zone for Namibia of 200 miles.

On 29 October,[15] the Acting President of the Council for Namibia testified in Washington, D.C., before the Subcommittee on Africa of the United States House of Representatives Committee on Foreign Affairs in a hearing on Namibia, the exploitation of natural resources and United States policy. The Subcommittee was considering a bill entitled the Namibian Natural Resource Protection Act. The Acting President pointed out that some 33 United States corporations were operating in Namibia. The Council had drawn their attention to the illegal nature of their activities in the Territory and asked to meet with them. Their responses had either been negative or there had been no response. The Acting President said that the Council had decided to initiate legal proceedings in the domestic courts of the Netherlands because of its favourable legal environment; the Netherlands recognized the Council as the legal Administering Authority for the Territory and its authority to legislate on Namibia's behalf. The Council was prepared to consider legal action in other countries in the near future.

The Commission on Human Rights, on 26 February,[6] condemned foreign economic interests which were illegally exploiting Namibia's resources, and demanded that TNCs comply with relevant United Nations resolutions by refraining from any new investment or activities in Namibia, by withdrawing from the Territory and by putting an end to their co-operation with the illegal South African administration.

On 16 May,[7] the Committee on colonial countries reaffirmed that Namibia's natural resources were the incontestable heritage of the Namibian people. It noted the rapid depletion of those resources and condemned their illegal exploitation by South Africa and foreign economic interests in disregard of United Nations resolutions, in particular Decree No. 1. The Committee also condemned the exploitation of Namibian uranium by State-owned or State-controlled corporations, which constituted a violation by the Governments involved of binding Security Council resolutions. It requested the Federal Republic of Germany, the Netherlands and the United Kingdom to have Namibian uranium specifically excluded from the Treaty of Almelo.

The Committee, on the same date,[8] condemned South Africa for its continued plundering of Namibia's natural resources, leading to their rapid depletion, in complete disregard of the interests of the Namibian people, and for its illegal extension of the territorial sea and proclamation of an economic zone off the Namibian coast. It reiterated that the plundering of Namibian resources by South Africa and other foreign economic interests was illegal, and called on States to take measures, including the requiring of negative certificates of origin, to prevent State-owned and other corporations from dealing in Namibian uranium.

GENERAL ASSEMBLY ACTION

By **resolution 40/52**, the General Assembly condemned South Africa for its continued exploitation of Namibia's natural resources. It reiterated that the plundering of its marine and other resources, including uranium, was illegal, a contribution to the maintenance of the illegal occupation régime and a threat to the prosperity of an independent Namibia, and called on Governments to prevent State-owned and other corporations from dealing in Namibian uranium. It re-

quested the Federal Republic of Germany, the Netherlands and the United Kingdom to have Namibian uranium excluded from the Treaty of Almelo.

The Assembly, in **resolution 40/97 A**, reaffirmed that Namibian resources, including marine resources, were the heritage of the Namibian people, expressed deep concern at their depletion, and endorsed the decision of the Council for Namibia to proclaim an exclusive economic zone for Namibia. Calling on the Council to compile statistical information on the wealth extracted from Namibia to assess the compensation due to an independent Namibia, the Assembly demanded that foreign economic interests withdraw from the Territory and end their co-operation with the illegal South African administration. It again requested Member States to ensure the compliance of corporations and individuals with Decree No. 1, and approved the Council's decision to initiate legal proceedings in the domestic courts of States against those exploiting Namibian resources.

The Assembly, by **resolution 40/89 B**, demanded that South Africa and other foreign interests end immediately their exploration for and exploitation of uranium resources in Namibia, and by **resolution 40/64 A**, again called on the Security Council to impose a total ban on nuclear collaboration with South Africa, including embargoes on the imports of South African and Namibian uranium.

Social conditions and the exploitation of labour

The Council for Namibia maintained a constant review of social conditions in Namibia.[2] Its Standing Committee II prepared a report on those conditions,[16] pursuant to a 1984 General Assembly resolution.[17]

The South African régime continued to maintain its illegal presence in Namibia and to apply existing ruthless and repressive laws and proclamations as well as to promulgate new ones, in defiance of Assembly and Security Council resolutions.

Under the Security Districts Proclamation Act imposed by South Africa in March 1985, journalists, foreign visitors and church people who were not residents of six areas covered by the Act could not enter them without South African permits. The districts covered more than half of Namibia, from Windhoek to the northern border with Angola, Botswana and Zambia; more than three quarters of Namibia's population lived there. Shortly after the installation of the interim government in June 1985, South Africa extended several of its laws to the Territory. They included: the Intimidation Act, which dealt with boycotts; the Demonstrations in or near Court Building Prohibition Act, used to suppress protests at political trials; and the Protection of Information Act.

Repressive measures against the Namibian people had been intensified, according to the Council, with acts of cold-blooded killings, systematic torture, abductions, detentions without trial and disappearances of civilians having become widespread. There were no accurate statistics for the number of people who had "disappeared". Among the murder squads that were committing atrocities were the "Koevoet," the "Takkies" and the "Etango". Both the "Takkies" and the "Etango" were cultural organizations used politically to mobilize the masses against SWAPO.

On 17 June, members of the South African occupation army and police force attacked SWAPO supporters in Windhoek as they left a rally against the installation of the interim government. Other attacks on SWAPO political gatherings took place on 4 May, 25 August and 30 September.

Hundreds of Namibians were reported being held without charge or trial, many in a detention camp in the Mariental District south of Windhoek and others in prisons and open-air camps throughout the country. At least 18 camps were believed to exist, with many prisoners being confined in underground cells.

The *apartheid* system governed conditions of labour in Namibia, with the labour force being divided along racial lines in the types of jobs available, wages earned and the right to organize in trade unions. Black workers were subjected to the notorious contract labour system which, while exlpoiting them at very low wages, separated males from their families for long periods of time. About 110,000 Namibians, almost half of the black labour force not involved in subsistence agriculture, were migrant workers on short-term contracts. There was no protective labour legislation that had meaning for the majority of workers. Labour practices on white-owned farms were semi-feudal and prison labour was often employed.

Namibians generally did not have financial security in their old age. Where pensions did exist, they were paid on a discriminatory basis according to race. Migrant workers were excluded from pension schemes by the requirement of "continuous service".

Structural inequalities in the earning capacity of blacks and whites were great. In the urban areas, white per capita income was more than 20 times that of blacks and income disparity in rural areas was twice that of the urban areas. Moreover, if the disproportionate access of blacks and whites to public and social services was taken into account, the gap was much wider than the income disparities indicated.

A survey of job categories and wages paid by CDM revealed that the majority of Namibian workers fell into the "unskilled" category, with only a handful at the skilled level and none in middle management or above. Another survey found that fish factory workers were paid less than a third of the official minimum hourly rate. Yet, during the same period, some fishing companies reported that their profits had increased by up to 100 per cent.

In order to guarantee a supply of cheap black labour, severe restrictions were placed on a worker's ability to seek work, to live in a family setting and to organize. Obstacles to effective union organization were overwhelming. The registration of trade unions was required by law, but it was extremely difficult for black unions to register. The National Union of Namibian Workers, founded in 1978 and affiliated with SWAPO, had operated underground since 1980 when South Africa shut down its offices and froze its assets.

Education was compulsory for whites, but not for black or "coloured" children. White children enjoyed a modern and comprehensive educational system, while educational facilities for black children were non-existent in some areas and mediocre at best in others. There were differences in school facilities, classroom practices, teacher-training programmes, teachers' salaries, teacher-pupil ratios and the amount of money spent annually per pupil. South Africa had introduced soldiers as teachers into black classrooms, carrying their arms as a matter of policy. The purpose was not only to intimidate the children, but also to indoctrinate them with propaganda, portraying SWAPO as an insurgent organization against which a counter-insurgency force was necessary to maintain stability.

The health sector was similarly characterized by gross inequalities. Health services for blacks were either rudimentary or virtually non-existent, those available to whites comparable to that of the best of any country. According to available statistics, blacks suffered an infant mortality rate of 163 per 1,000 live births compared with 21 per 1,000 for whites. Life expectancy for blacks ranged from 42 to 52 years, for whites from 68 to 72 years.

Housing provided by the South African régime for black Namibians was poor and insufficient. Temporary and makeshift camps were a common feature of black townships. Sanitary facilities were practically non-existent. Investigations by the local press had revealed that Okahandja, north of Windhoek, contained some of the most appalling camps in the country. Two camps in particular housed about 1,000 persons each in 1983, with new hovels being added daily. Between 7 and 12 people lived in each hovel. One of the camps had four water taps for 150 dwelling units; the other camp had no fresh water. On white-owned farms, accommodation for labourers was at the discretion of the farmer. Many farmers provided little or no accommodation; workers constructed tiny tin shanties. Mining workers lived in rigidly controlled hostels and compounds.

Black women were the most oppressed group in Namibian society. Some were employed in the farming, fishing and packing industries, but most worked at menial jobs as office cleaners or domestic servants. As a rule, they were not allowed to work as contract labourers, and therefore were left behind to a fate of loneliness and destitution when their husbands and sons went away on contract. Reports of rape of black women were of increasing concern. Cases were concentrated in the north and generally involved the South African army.

REFERENCES

[1]A/AC.109/826. [2]A/41/24. [3]E/C.10/AC.4/1985/6. [4]E/1985/22 (res. 1985/6). [5]YUN 1960, p. 49, GA res. 1514(XV), 14 Dec. 1960. [6]E/1985/22 (res. 1985/9). [7]A/40/23 (A/AC.109/830). [8]*Ibid.* (A/AC.109/840). [9]YUN 1981, p. 1163, GA res. 36/121 C, 10 Dec. 1981. [10]YUN 1974, p. 152. [11]YUN 1982, p. 1311. [12]A/AC.131/194. [13]A/40/375-S/17262. [14]YUN 1982, p. 178. [15]A/AC.131/214. [16]A/AC.131/187. [17]YUN 1984, p. 1042, GA res. 39/50 C, 12 Dec. 1984.

PUBLICATION

Activities of Transnational Corporations in South Africa and Namibia and the Responsibilities of Home Countries with respect to Their Operations in This Area (ST/CTC/84), Sales No. E.85.II.A.16.

International assistance

The Council for Namibia, in its Vienna Declaration and Programme of Action, included in its 1985 annual report,[1] expressed appreciation to Governments, United Nations specialized agencies and other international organizations that had contributed to the United Nations Fund for Namibia. It urged them to provide increased assistance to the thousands of Namibian refugees who had been forced to flee to neighbouring front-line States, and called on Governments to increase moral and political support, as well as financial, military and other material assistance, to SWAPO and to the Namibian people through SWAPO. The Council appealed to NGOs for intensified support of the liberation struggle. Further, it urged the fullest possible co-operation by all with the Council to facilitate concrete programmes of assistance and to implement projects for the economic and social development of an independent Namibia.

By **resolution 40/57**, the General Assembly urged States, directly and through the United Nations system, to provide moral and material assistance to the Namibian people. In **decision 40/415**, it appealed to all States to increase moral and political support and financial, military and other material assistance to SWAPO.

The Economic and Social Council, in **resolution 1985/59**, requested United Nations organizations to render increased assistance to the Namibian people, in consultation with OAU and the Council for Namibia, particularly in connection with the Nationhood Programme for Namibia.

UN Fund for Namibia

Activities of the Fund

The United Nations Fund for Namibia was financed mainly through voluntary contributions. The Council for Namibia acted as trustee of the Fund, which was the principal vehicle through which the Council channelled assistance to the Territory. The Fund's activities were concentrated in three programmes—the Nationhood Programme (see p. 1130), the United Nations Institute for Namibia (see p. 1131), and educational, social and relief assistance.

The Nationhood Programme and the Institute were set up with particular reference to the future attainment of independence, the establishment of State machinery and the assumption of administrative responsibilities by Namibians. The assistance programme emphasized the immediate needs of Namibians in their struggle for independence; assistance was administered, to the extent possible, through individual projects and scholarships, and was financed by the Fund's General Account.

During the period from 1 July 1984 to 30 June 1985,[1] 54 new awards were made and 26 students completed their courses. As of 1 July 1985, 142 students in 11 countries were pursuing studies in a wide variety of fields.

The Fund also provided medical care, social assistance and relief aid. During the period under review, assistance was given to 37 Namibians requiring emergency medical treatment and other humanitarian assistance.

The sum of $100,000 was made available from the Fund for emergency assistance. In addition to each field office of the Commissioner's Office being provided with $5,000 from the emergency funds, $7,000 was used to finance two shipments of textbooks, clothing and other relief goods to Namibian refugee centres in Angola; $20,000 to strengthen agricultural activities in a refugee settlement in Zambia; $9,000 to assist SWAPO's office in New York; $10,000 to repatriate 30 Namibian political prisoners to Luanda; $25,000 for fuel to transport food supplies from Luanda to refugee settlements; $6,000 to provide allowances to 25 Namibian students in Brazil; and $5,000 for a training programme in fleet operations for two Namibians in the United Republic of Tanzania.

Subscriptions to various publications on Namibia and southern Africa, books and library materials were made available to Namibian refugee camps and SWAPO offices. Funds were provided to facilitate the attendance of 25 Namibians at 12 international seminars and conferences.

Fund expenditures in 1985 for the three programmes totalled $6,996,863, as follows: Nationhood Programme, $1,754,244; Institute, $4,067,172; and educational, social and relief assistance, $1,174,447.

GENERAL ASSEMBLY ACTION

On 13 December, the General Assembly adopted **resolution 40/97 E** by recorded vote.

United Nations Fund for Namibia

The General Assembly,

Having examined the parts of the report of the United Nations Council for Namibia relating to the United Nations Fund for Namibia,

Recalling its resolution 2679(XXV) of 9 December 1970, by which it established the United Nations Fund for Namibia,

Recalling also its resolution 3112(XXVIII) of 12 December 1973, by which it appointed the United Nations Council for Namibia trustee of the United Nations Fund for Namibia,

Recalling its resolution 31/153 of 20 December 1976, by which it decided to launch the Nationhood Programme for Namibia,

Recalling further its resolution 34/92 A of 12 December 1979, by which it approved the Charter of the United Nations Institute for Namibia, and its resolution 37/233 E of 20 December 1982, by which it approved amendments to that Charter,

1. *Takes note* of the relevant parts of the report of the United Nations Council for Namibia;

2. *Decides* that the United Nations Council for Namibia shall:

(a) Continue to formulate policies of assistance to Namibians and co-ordinate assistance for Namibia provided by the specialized agencies and other organizations and institutions of the United Nations system;

(b) Continue to act as trustee of the United Nations Fund for Namibia and, in this capacity, administer and manage the Fund;

(c) Continue to provide broad guidelines and formulate principles and policies for the United Nations Institute for Namibia;

(d) Continue to co-ordinate, plan and direct the Nationhood Programme for Namibia in consultation with the South West Africa People's Organization, with the aim of consolidating all measures of assistance by the specialized agencies and other organizations and institutions of the United Nations system into a comprehensive assistance programme;

(e) Continue to consult with the South West Africa People's Organization in the formulation and implementation of assistance programmes for Namibians;

(f) Report to the General Assembly at its forty-first session on the programmes and activities undertaken through the United Nations Fund for Namibia;

3. *Decides* that the United Nations Fund for Namibia, which comprises the General Account, the United Nations Institute for Namibia Account and the Nationhood Programme Account, shall be the primary source of assistance to Namibians;

4. *Expresses its appreciation* to all States, specialized agencies and other organizations of the United Nations system, governmental and non-governmental organizations and individuals that have made contributions to the United Nations Fund for Namibia to support the activities under the General Account, the activities of the United Nations Institute for Namibia and the Nationhood Programme for Namibia, and calls upon them to increase their assistance to Namibians through those channels;

5. *Requests* the Secretary-General and the President of the United Nations Council for Namibia to intensify appeals to Governments, intergovernmental and non-governmental organizations and individuals for more generous voluntary contributions to the General Account, the Nationhood Programme Account and the United Nations Institute for Namibia Account of the United Nations Fund for Namibia in view of the increased activities undertaken through the Fund and, in this connection, emphasizes the need for contributions in order to increase the number of scholarships awarded to Namibians under the United Nations Fund for Namibia;

6. *Invites* Governments to appeal once more to their national organizations and institutions for voluntary contributions to the United Nations Fund for Namibia;

7. *Decides* to allocate as a temporary measure to the United Nations Fund for Namibia the sum of $1.5 million from the regular budget of the United Nations for 1986;

8. *Requests* the Office of the United Nations Commissioner for Namibia, in order to mobilize additional resources, to formulate, in consultation with the South West Africa People's Organization, a programme of assistance to the Namibian people to be undertaken by means of projects co-financed by Governments and non-governmental organizations;

9. *Requests* the specialized agencies and other organizations and institutions of the United Nations system, in the light of the urgent need to strengthen the programme of assistance to the Namibian people, to make every effort to expedite the execution of Nationhood Programme for Namibia projects and other projects in favour of Namibians on the basis of procedures which will reflect the role of the United Nations Council for Namibia as the legal Administering Authority for Namibia;

10. *Expresses its appreciation* to those specialized agencies and other organizations and institutions of the United Nations system that have contributed to the Nationhood Programme for Namibia and calls upon them to continue their participation in the Programme by:

(a) Implementing projects approved by the United Nations Council for Namibia;

(b) Planning and initiating new project proposals in co-operation with, and at the request of, the Council;

(c) Allocating funds from their own financial resources for the implementation of the projects approved by the Council;

11. *Requests* the United Nations Council for Namibia to continue and intensify its programme of field attachments, enabling Namibians trained under various programmes to gain practical on-the-job experience in Governments and institutions in various countries, particularly in Africa;

12. *Appeals* to all Governments, specialized agencies and other organizations and institutions of the United

Nations system, non-governmental organizations and individuals to make generous contributions to the United Nations Fund for Namibia in order to support the field attachment programme and to meet the required needs;

13. *Expresses its appreciation* to the United Nations Development Programme for its contribution to the financing and administration of the Nationhood Programme for Namibia and the financing of the United Nations Institute for Namibia, and calls upon it to continue to allocate, at the request of the United Nations Council for Namibia, funds from the indicative planning figure for Namibia for the implementation of the projects within the Nationhood Programme and for the United Nations Institute for Namibia;

14. *Notes with appreciation* the decision by the Governing Council of the United Nations Development Programme to maintain at least at the same level, on an exceptional basis, the indicative planning figure for Namibia for the 1987-1991 programming cycle;

15. *Calls upon* the United Nations Development Programme to raise the indicative planning figure for Namibia;

16. *Expresses its appreciation* for the assistance provided by the United Nations Children's Fund, the Office of the United Nations High Commissioner for Refugees and the World Food Programme to Namibian refugees, and requests them to expand their assistance in order to provide for the basic needs of the refugees;

17. *Expresses its appreciation* to those specialized agencies and other organizations of the United Nations system which have waived agency support costs in respect of projects in favour of Namibians, financed from the United Nations Fund for Namibia and other sources, and urges those that have not yet done so to take appropriate steps in this regard;

18. *Decides* that Namibians shall continue to be eligible for assistance through the United Nations Educational and Training Programme for Southern Africa and the United Nations Trust Fund for South Africa;

19. *Commends* the progress made in the implementation of the pre-independence components of the Nationhood Programme for Namibia and requests the United Nations Council for Namibia to elaborate and consider policies and contingency plans regarding the transitional and post-independence phases of the Programme;

20. *Commends* the United Nations Institute for Namibia for the effectiveness of its training programmes for Namibians and its research activities on Namibia, which contribute substantially to the struggle for freedom of the Namibian people and to the establishment of an independent State of Namibia;

21. *Urges* the specialized agencies and other organizations and institutions of the United Nations system to co-operate closely with the United Nations Institute for Namibia in strengthening its programme of activities;

22. *Requests* the United Nations Council for Namibia, through the United Nations Institute for Namibia, to finalize, publish and disseminate at an early date a comprehensive reference book on Namibia covering all aspects of the question of Namibia as considered by the United Nations since its inception;

23. *Notes with appreciation* the completion by the United Nations Institute for Namibia, in co-operation with the South West Africa People's Organization, the Office of the United Nations Commissioner for Namibia and the United Nations Development Programme, of a comprehensive document on all aspects of economic planning in an independent Namibia, and commends the Secretary-General for providing substantive support through the Office of the Commissioner for the preparation of that document;

24. *Requests* the United Nations Council for Namibia, in consultation with the Office of the United Nations Commissioner for Namibia, to finalize and publish at an early date a demographic study of the Namibian population and a study of its educational needs;

25. *Requests* the Secretary-General to continue to provide the Office of the United Nations Commissioner for Namibia with the necessary resources for the performance of the responsibilities entrusted to it by the United Nations Council for Namibia as the co-ordinating authority for the implementation of the Nationhood Programme for Namibia, as well as other assistance programmes.

General Assembly resolution 40/97 E

13 December 1985   Meeting 115   148-0-6 (recorded vote)

Draft by Council for Namibia (A/40/24); agenda item 34.
Financial implications. 5th Committee, A/40/1039; S-G, A/C.5/40/87 & Corr.1.
Meeting numbers. GA 40th session: 5th Committee 60, 61; plenary 80-87, 115.

Recorded vote in Assembly as follows:

In favour: Afghanistan, Albania, Algeria, Angola, Antigua and Barbuda, Argentina, Australia, Austria, Bahamas, Bahrain, Bangladesh, Barbados, Belgium, Belize, Benin, Bhutan, Bolivia, Botswana, Brazil, Brunei Darussalam, Bulgaria, Burkina Faso, Burma, Burundi, Byelorussian SSR, Cameroon, Cape Verde, Central African Republic, Chad, Chile, China, Colombia, Comoros, Congo, Costa Rica, Cuba, Cyprus, Czechoslovakia, Democratic Kampuchea, Democratic Yemen, Denmark, Djibouti, Dominican Republic, Ecuador, Egypt, El Salvador, Equatorial Guinea, Ethiopia, Fiji, Finland, Gabon, Gambia, German Democratic Republic, Ghana, Greece, Grenada, Guatemala, Guinea, Guinea-Bissau, Haiti, Honduras, Hungary, Iceland, India, Indonesia, Iran, Iraq, Ireland, Italy, Ivory Coast, Jamaica, Japan, Jordan, Kenya, Kuwait, Lao People's Democratic Republic, Lebanon, Lesotho, Liberia, Libyan Arab Jamahiriya, Luxembourg, Madagascar, Malawi, Malaysia, Maldives, Mali, Malta, Mauritania, Mauritius, Mexico, Mongolia, Morocco, Mozambique, Nepal, Netherlands, New Zealand, Nicaragua, Niger, Nigeria, Norway, Oman, Pakistan, Panama, Papua New Guinea, Peru, Philippines, Poland, Portugal, Qatar, Romania, Rwanda, Saint Lucia, Saint Vincent and the Grenadines, Samoa, Sao Tome and Principe, Saudi Arabia, Senegal, Seychelles, Sierra Leone, Singapore, Solomon Islands, Somalia, Spain, Sri Lanka, Sudan, Suriname, Swaziland, Sweden, Syrian Arab Republic, Thailand, Togo, Trinidad and Tobago, Tunisia, Turkey, Uganda, Ukrainian SSR, USSR, United Arab Emirates, United Republic of Tanzania, Uruguay, Vanuatu, Venezuela, Viet Nam, Yemen, Yugoslavia, Zaire, Zambia, Zimbabwe.
Against: None.
Abstaining: Canada, France, Germany, Federal Republic of, Israel, United Kingdom, United States.

Ireland said that it would as usual vote in favour of the draft, believing that the Fund provided valuable assistance to Namibians who had suffered as a result of South Africa's illegal occupation of their land.

Financing of the Fund

In 1985, 38 States made a total contribution of $4,462,963 to the United Nations Fund for Namibia (see table). Other income included $1 million from the United Nations regular budget as authorized by the General Assembly in 1984.[2] The United Nations Development Programme (UNDP) also provided funding and had established an indicative planning figure for Namibia of $7,750,000 for 1982-1986.

Fund-raising missions were organized by the Council for Namibia to Western Europe, visiting Denmark, Finland, Norway and Sweden from 20 to 30 May and Austria, Belgium, EEC, France, the Federal Republic of Germany, Italy and the Netherlands from 7 to 14 June.[1] Received at a high political level in all the countries visited, the missions reminded the Governments of the pressing needs of the Namibian people, explained the purposes of the Fund and reviewed the priority projects for which contributions were being sought. The Governments recognized the need to prepare Namibia for independence and expressed their continuing support for the Council's assistance programmes.

The Committee on colonial countries, on 16 May,[3] urgently called on States and the specialized agencies and other United Nations organizations to continue supporting the Fund and all Council assistance programmes.

CONTRIBUTIONS TO THE UN FUND FOR NAMIBIA, 1985

(as at 31 December 1985)

Amount (in US dollar equivalent)

Country	General Account	Nationhood Programme	Institute for Namibia
Algeria	10,000	–	–
Argentina	10,000	–	–
Australia	57,183	–	–
Austria	16,700	–	–
Bahamas	1,000	–	–
Barbados	500	–	–
Brazil	5,000	10,000	20,000
Cameroon	1,250	–	–
Canada	–	–	145,211
China	30,000	–	–
Cyprus	(39)	(39)	500
Denmark	–	126,021	574,096
Egypt	3,667	–	4,024
Finland	60,600	446,163	297,442
France	36,316	–	84,737
Germany, Federal Republic of	–	–	58,720
Greece	4,500	–	5,500
India	1,000	1,000	2,000
Indonesia	4,000	–	–
Iran	4,400	–	–
Ireland	21,242	–	–
Italy	–	–	50,045
Japan	10,000	–	210,000
Kuwait	4,000	–	1,000
Mexico	5,000	–	–
Netherlands	43,860	–	116,959
New Zealand	5,260	–	–
Nigeria	27,000	30,000	23,000
Norway	300,000	229,077	268,456
Pakistan	2,495	–	–
Panama	1,000	–	–
Republic of Korea	–	–	3,000
Sweden	394,965	170,354	454,287
Trinidad and Tobago	1,493	–	–
Turkey	1,500	1,500	1,500
Venezuela	2,000	–	1,000
Yugoslavia	10,000	–	–
Zimbabwe	51,518	–	–
Total	1,127,410	1,014,076	2,321,477

SOURCE: Accounts for the 12 month period of the biennium 1984-1985 ended 31 December 1985 — schedules of individual trust funds.

Nationhood Programme

The projects of the Nationhood Programme, launched by the General Assembly in 1976 to help

Namibia prepare for independence,[4] fell into three categories: pre-independence projects; transitional projects; and post-independence projects. The Programme consisted of two major components—manpower training programmes and surveys and analyses of the Namibian economic and social sectors.

In designing the projects, careful consideration was given to the special conditions under which the Programme was being implemented; assistance to a country under colonial domination required a different approach from that of technical assistance to independent countries. Implementation was made difficult by the unavailability of reliable socio-economic data, and further complicated by the lack of access to the Territory due to the illegal South African occupation. The training aspects of the projects required special attention because of the scarcity of educational opportunities for Namibians under South African rule.

The Council reported[1] that, during 1984 and the first half of 1985, Namibians continued their training in a number of countries and several new training activities were initiated. Six students began pre-engineering studies; 36, training in mining and railways; eight, a course in labour administration; and four, training in management of water development. A second group of 100 students began training at the Vocational Training Centre in Angola, which opened in 1983,[5] and 36 undertook remedial training in Zambia in English language, mathematics, basic sciences and social education.

Also during the reporting period, five students completed training with the Electricity Supply Board of Ireland and 34 completed a remedial course in English, mathematics and basic sciences. In Zambia, 34 disabled persons completed vocational training, two students finished their training with the Central Statistics Office and 11 finished their training at the Kabwe Railway Centre. Two completed training with the Nigerian Railway Corporation.

The Economic and Social Council, in **resolution 1985/59**, requested United Nations organizations in the light of the intensification of the liberation struggle to increase assistance to the Namibian people, particularly in connection with the Nationhood Programme.

By **resolution 40/97 E**, the General Assembly decided that the Council should continue to direct the Nationhood Programme, and requested that United Nations organizations expedite the execution of its projects. Expressing appreciation to those organizations which had contributed to the Programme, it called on them to continue implementing projects approved by the Council, to plan new project proposals and to allocate funds for their implementation. The Assembly also expressed appreciation to UNDP for its contribution to the financing and administration of the Nationhood Programme, and called on it to continue to allocate funds to its projects. It commended the progress made in the implementation of the pre-independence components of the Programme, and requested the Council to elaborate transitional and post-independence policies and contingency plans.

UN Institute for Namibia

The United Nations Institute for Namibia trained middle-level skilled manpower for an independent Namibia and carried out applied research in the various sectors of the Namibian economy. Admission to the Institute was open to all persons of Namibian origin who met the requirements of its Senate, a 16-member administering body. The Institute was financed by the Council for Namibia, with further financial assistance provided by UNDP and the United Nations High Commissioner for Refugees; it operated on an average annual budget of $4 million.

During 1985, 250 new students were admitted—150 in the management and development studies programme, 30 in the teacher-training upgrading programme, 50 in the secretarial programme and 20 in the special programme for magistrates. The Institute's total enrolment was 550.

In January, the sixth group of students (numbering 33) graduated from the Institute with diplomas in management and development studies, bringing the total number of Institute graduates to 407. In addition, the first group of 20 students graduated from the teacher-training upgrading programme and another 16 received certificates in the magistrates' programme.

Research was directed to provide basic documentation for policy formulations by the future Government of an independent Namibia. A number of studies were completed; others were under way, among them, mineral development strategy options, state succession, administrative system, mass participation, trade and monetary policy options, and wage and income policy options. A handbook on Namibia covering various aspects of the question of Namibia was completed.

An Extension Unit of the Institute continued to expand its education programme for Namibians denied education by the South African régime. It served some 40,000 Namibian adults and youths in Zambia and Angola.

Other UN assistance

UN Educational and Training Programme. The Secretary-General, in a report covering the period from 1 October 1984 to 15 October 1985,[6] stated that the United Nations Educational and Training Programme for Southern Africa (see p. 200) had granted 100 new scholarships to Namibians and extended 45. The scholarships did not include awards financed by the United Nations Fund for Namibia.

UNDP activities. In 1985, UNDP provided assistance to SWAPO through three ongoing educational projects and a new health project, according to a report[7] by the UNDP Administrator. The educational projects included assistance to the Namibia Education Centres at Kwanza Sul, Angola, and Nyango, Zambia, and training for the promotion of women's role in development. A project aimed at strengthening health services was discontinued at the end of 1984 and was financially completed in early 1985. A new project, giving support to community health services, was approved in December 1985 for implementation by the UNDP Office for Projects Evaluation.

A formulation mission for a future project of assistance in agricultural development was undertaken in 1985 with the Food and Agriculture Organization of the United Nations (FAO) as the executing agency. The four projects and the mission accounted for $623,100 in UNDP inputs, representing 26 per cent of total expenditures for national liberation movements as a whole.

Agency assistance. United Nations specialized agencies and other organizations continued to provide assistance to colonial countries, including Namibia, according to a May 1985 report[8] by the Secretary-General. Supplementary information was provided in a 1986 report.[9]

Assistance was given by some agencies, including FAO and the International Labour Organisation, through the Nationhood Programme. The United Nations Educational, Scientific and Cultural Organization trained teachers and provided school materials and laboratory and sports equipment to the educational centres operated by SWAPO. It also paid the salaries of support staff at those centres. The Office of the United Nations High Commissioner for Refugees allocated $3 million in aid to Namibian refugees, covering basic needs, education, health, transport, self-help construction of housing, agriculture and technical support. The World Health Organization made funds available to SWAPO for medical supplies and, as an associate member State, to Namibia itself for health activities and training of health personnel.

REFERENCES

[1]A/40/24. [2]YUN 1984, p. 1057, GA res. 39/50 E, 12 Dec. 1984. [3]A/40/23 (A/AC.109/830). [4]YUN 1976, p. 791, GA res. 31/153, 20 Dec. 1976. [5]YUN 1983, p. 1080. [6]A/40/781. [7]DP/1986/21. [8]A/40/318 & Add.1. [9]A/41/407 & Add.1.

Chapter IV

Other colonial Territories

In 1985, the Special Committee on the Implementation of the Declaration on the Granting of Independence to Colonial Countries and Peoples (Committee on colonial countries) continued to consider the situation in East Timor and Western Sahara, as well as the dispute between Argentina and the United Kingdom over the Falkland Islands (Malvinas).

In September, the General Assembly deferred consideration of the East Timor question until 1986 (decision 40/402). In November, it requested Argentina and the United Kingdom to initiate negotiations for resolving peacefully and definitively the pending problems between them, including all aspects on the future of the Falkland Islands (Malvinas), in accordance with the Charter of the United Nations (resolution 40/21); it also requested the Secretary-General to continue his good offices mission.

Reaffirming that the Western Sahara question was a decolonization issue, the Assembly, in December, again requested Morocco and the Frente Popular para la Liberación de Saguia el-Hamra y de Río de Oro to hold direct negotiations for a cease-fire and a referendum for self-determination of the people of Western Sahara, under the auspices of the Organization of African Unity and the United Nations (resolution 40/50).

With regard to Gibraltar, the Assembly welcomed two events that took place on 5 February: the initiation between Spain and the United Kingdom of negotiations at Geneva; and the establishment of equality and reciprocity of rights for Spaniards in Gibraltar and Gibraltarians in Spain, together with the free movement of persons, vehicles and goods between Gibraltar and the neighbouring territory (decision 40/413).

In addition, the Assembly took action on the questions of: American Samoa (resolution 40/41), Guam (40/42) and the United States Virgin Islands (40/49), under United States administration; and Anguilla (40/48), Bermuda (40/43), the British Virgin Islands (40/44), the Cayman Islands (40/45), Montserrat (40/46), the Turks and Caicos Islands (40/47) and St. Helena (decision 40/414), under United Kingdom administration. The Assembly took note of the decision of the Committee on colonial countries to send a visiting mission to Tokelau in 1986, at the invitation of New Zealand, the administering Power, and of the people of the Territory (decision 40/411).

Topics related to this chapter. General questions relating to colonial countries.

Falkland Islands (Malvinas)

Communications. During 1985, the Secretary-General received a series of communications from Argentina and the United Kingdom on the Falkland Islands (Malvinas) situation.

Argentina, in a 2 January press release by the Ministry of Foreign Affairs and Worship,[1] stated that, according to international news reports, the United Kingdom had authorized an oil company to explore and prospect for oil in the Malvinas Islands. Argentina declared that it would not recognize any claim to the right to explore for or exploit minerals or hydrocarbons in the Islands, over which it claimed sovereignty. In a reply of 24 January,[2] the United Kingdom rejected Argentina's claim of sovereignty, asserted that it continued to be guided in its administration of the Islands by the obligations under Article 73 of the United Nations Charter, and that the Falkland Islands Government's granting of a licence on 19 July 1984 to Firstland Oil and Gas PLC exemplified the exercise by the people of the Falkland Islands of the right freely to dispose of their natural resources.

In a government statement of 18 February,[3] Argentina expressed concern at reports that the United Kingdom was planning to reform the Malvinas Islands Constitution; it added that, since the Islands' inhabitants were not differentiated from the occupying Power, nor were they originally based in the territory, the misapplication of the principle of self-determination would only serve to validate an unlawful occupation. The United Kingdom, in a 13 March response,[4] said its intention to promulgate a new Constitution for the Falkland Islands to replace the 1948 Constitution, for entry into force at the time of the general election in the autumn of 1985, was consistent with its international obligations under the Charter and the International Covenant on Civil and Political Rights.

Referring to the the January exchange of letters, Argentina, on 18 March,[5] asserted that the United Kingdom was obligated under Article 33 of the Charter to seek a peaceful settlement of the sovereignty dispute. On 16 May,[6] Argentina's Minister for Foreign Affairs and Worship declared that the opening by the United Kingdom of a strategic airport on the Malvinas Islands, allegedly to promote economic development, represented an escalation in the militarization of the territory; it also rejected as incompatible with the aims of the 1959 Antarctic Treaty the United Kingdom's use of a military and nuclear base, contiguous to the geographical area covered by that agreement, to pursue its objectives in Antarctica.

Responding to the May letter, the United Kingdom stated on 29 May[7] that the new airport had a dual civil and military role. Its construction was necessary to deter aggression and defend the Islands against attack, and the presence of its forces contributed to peace and security in the region. Further, the United Kingdom denied a number of allegations made by Argentina, among them, that there was any North Atlantic Treaty Organization dimension to its involvement in the area; that it had introduced nuclear weapons into the South Atlantic; that the Falkland Islands was within the application of the Antarctic Treaty or that its activities contravened the Treaty's purposes; or that the Charter obligation to the peaceful settlement of disputes required, irrespective of circumstances, recourse to negotiations.

On 31 May,[8] Argentina transmitted the text of a resolution, entitled "Concern at the establishment by the United Kingdom of military installations on the Falkland Islands (Malvinas)", adopted the previous day by the Permanent Council of the Organization of American States. In it, the Permanent Council again appealed to the parties to renew negotiations to solve the sovereignty dispute and other differences, and expressed concern that the establishment by the United Kingdom of military installations on the Islands heightened tension and impeded the resumption of negotiations.

On 8 July,[9] the United Kingdom transmitted a written statement made in its Parliament that day by the Parliamentary Under-Secretary at the Foreign and Commonwealth Office, in which he stated that the Government's policy was as follows: that the sovereignty question was not for discussion; that better relations with Argentina could only realistically be achieved by seeking agreement on practical issues; and that, as a step in that direction, it was lifting, with effect from midnight that day, the ban on imports from Argentina which had been in place since April 1982.

In a 10 July press communiqué,[10] Argentina's Minister for Foreign Affairs and Worship welcomed the United Kingdom's announced lifting of the ban on imports from Argentina; declared that the stable political conditions and mutual trust needed for trade relations required dealing with the central issue of sovereignty and eliminating the military threat and the so-called protection zone; invited the United Kingdom to initiate in the coming 60 days negotiations preceded by preparations either through the Secretary-General's good offices or through friendly Powers representing each nation's respective interests; and expressed Argentina's readiness formally to declare cessation of hostilities when the United Kingdom agreed to negotiate.

On 12 July,[11] the Secretary of State for Foreign and Commonwealth Affairs of the United Kingdom called Argentina's 10 July statement a disappointing response to the lifting of the ban on Argentine imports, adding that the latter's insistence on the sovereignty issue as a pre-condition for better bilateral relations was neither realistic nor constructive.

In a 29 July letter,[12] Argentina charged that on 25 July one of its naval aircraft on a maritime transit control flight was intercepted for 12 minutes by two United Kingdom Phantom aircraft within the 200-mile area of Argentina's jurisdiction and more than 15 miles from the outer limit of the exclusion zone unilaterally set up around the Malvinas by the United Kingdom. In a 2 August response,[13] the United Kingdom said that when an aircraft was detected eight miles beyond the Falkland Islands protection zone, two United Kingdom aircraft were dispatched for inspection. They identified it as an Argentine Electra but made no contact and did not harass it. The three aircraft were flying in international airspace and there was no justification for Argentina to describe this routine operation as blatantly provocative. The United Kingdom added that, as Argentina had not declared a formal cessation of hostilities and continued to purchase sophisticated weaponry, forces had to be maintained at the minimum level necessary to defend the Islands from attack.

Argentina's Minister for Foreign Affairs and Worship, in a 12 September press communiqué,[14] noted that the 60-day period within which Argentina had offered to resume negotiations had ended the previous day. He asserted that the blatant indifference shown by the United Kingdom demonstrated how little importance that country attached to United Nations decisions, and renewed his Government's invitation to embark on comprehensive negotiations on the question. He reiterated Argentina's pledge to safeguard the interests of the Islands' inhabitants, and added that there was thus no remaining justification for the United Kingdom's conduct other than the attempt to perpetuate an anachronistic and illegal colonial situation.

On 18 September,[15] Argentina issued a press release following a meeting—facilitated by the

Socialist International secretariat—in Paris that day between the President of Argentina and the leader of the Labour Party (opposition) in the United Kingdom Parliament. Among a number of issues discussed at the meeting, Argentina reported that both sides had expressed the desire that negotiations be initiated to explore the means of resolving the outstanding problems between the two countries, including all aspects of the future of the Falkland Islands (Malvinas), taking fully into account the interests of the inhabitants.

Reporting on a 6 October meeting at Madrid, Spain, between the President of Argentina and the leader of the British Liberal Party, Argentina[16] said the two sides agreed that the process of achieving a peaceful and negotiated solution to the dispute should include a formal cessation of hostilities and a lifting of the exclusion zone, the restoration of diplomatic and trade relations, and the resumption of negotiations on all issues concerning the future of the Malvinas Islands, including sovereignty.

Other communications. On 12 August,[17] Peru transmitted the text of the Lima Declaration, signed on 29 July by the heads of State of Argentina, Bolivia, Colombia, the Dominican Republic, Panama, Peru and Uruguay, and by the representatives of Brazil, Chile, Costa Rica, Cuba, Ecuador, El Salvador, Guatemala, Haiti, Honduras, Mexico, Nicaragua, Paraguay and Venezuela. Among other issues, the signatories supported Argentina's sovereignty over the Malvinas Islands and called for immediate resumption of negotiations in accordance with United Nations resolutions.

Canada transmitted in October[18] the text of a resolution on decolonization, adopted at the Seventy-fourth Inter-Parliamentary Conference (Ottawa, 2-7 September), in which the participants urged the two Governments concerned to resume negotiations aimed at a peaceful solution to the sovereignty dispute with regard to the Falkland Islands (Malvinas).

Angola transmitted on 5 November[19] the text of the Final Political Declaration adopted by the Conference of Foreign Ministers of Non-Aligned Countries (Luanda, 4-7 September), in which the Ministers reiterated their support for Argentina's right to have its sovereignty over the Malvinas Islands restituted through negotiation. Urging the United Kingdom to agree to the resumption of negotiations, they asserted that the massive British military and naval presence in the area adversely affected stability there, and that the establishment of military installations on dependent Territories impeded the application of the 1960 Declaration on the Granting of Independence to Colonial Countries and Peoples.[20]

Action by the Committee on colonial countries. The Committee on colonial countries considered the Falkland Islands (Malvinas) question on 5, 6 and 9 August, hearing statements by Argentina, the United Kingdom as the administering Power, the Counsellor of the Legislative Council of the Falkland Islands (Malvinas), two petitioners and Committee members.

On 9 August,[21] the Committee, among other things: expressed regret that the resumption of talks had not taken place due to the United Kingdom's refusal to deal with the sovereignty issue within the framework of comprehensive negotiations; urged the two parties to resume negotiations to solve the sovereignty question; reiterated its support for a renewed good offices mission by the Secretary-General based on 1982,[22] 1983[23] and 1984[24] Assembly resolutions; and decided to keep the question under review, subject to Assembly directives.

Report of the Secretary-General. In November 1985, the Secretary-General, in pursuance of a 1984 Assembly resolution,[24] submitted a report on the question,[25] based on exchanges of views with the two Governments concerned, including meetings with the President of Argentina and the Prime Minister of the United Kingdom as well as their Foreign Ministers. The Secretary-General reported that their positions remained basically unchanged and that it had not been possible to implement the 1984 Assembly resolution. While deploring the lack of progress towards normalizing the situation in the South Atlantic, the Secretary-General reiterated his readiness to assist in promoting a dialogue leading to a just and lasting settlement of the basic issue involved.

GENERAL ASSEMBLY ACTION

On 27 November 1985, the General Assembly adopted **resolution 40/21** by recorded vote.

Question of the Falkland Islands (Malvinas)
The General Assembly,
Having considered the question of the Falkland Islands (Malvinas) and having received the report of the Secretary-General,
Aware of the interest of the international community in the peaceful and definitive settlement by the Governments of Argentina and the United Kingdom of Great Britain and Northern Ireland of all their differences, in accordance with the Charter of the United Nations,
Taking note of the interest repeatedly expressed by both parties in normalizing their relations,
Convinced that such purpose would be facilitated by a global negotiation between both Governments that will allow them to rebuild mutual confidence on a solid basis and to resolve the pending problems, including all aspects on the future of the Falkland Islands (Malvinas),
1. *Requests* the Governments of Argentina and the United Kingdom of Great Britain and Northern Ireland to initiate negotiations with a view to finding the means

to resolve peacefully and definitively the pending problems between both countries, including all aspects on the future of the Falkland Islands (Malvinas), in accordance with the Charter of the United Nations;

2. *Requests* the Secretary-General to continue his renewed mission of good offices in order to assist the parties in complying with the request made in paragraph 1 above, and to take the necessary measures to that end;

3. *Requests* the Secretary-General to submit to the General Assembly at its forty-first session a report on the progress made in the implementation of the present resolution;

4. *Decides* to include in the provisional agenda of its forty-first session the item entitled "Question of the Falkland Islands (Malvinas)".

General Assembly resolution 40/21

27 November 1985   Meeting 95   107-4-41 (recorded vote)

13-nation draft (A/40/L.19 & Add.1); agenda item 23.
Sponsors: Algeria, Bolivia, Brazil, Colombia, Cuba, Dominican Republic, Ecuador, Ghana, India, Mexico, Panama, Uruguay, Yugoslavia.
Meeting numbers. GA 40th session: plenary 92, 93, 95.

Recorded vote in Assembly as follows:

In favour: Afghanistan, Albania, Algeria, Angola, Antigua and Barbuda, Argentina, Australia, Austria, Barbados, Benin, Bolivia, Botswana, Brazil, Bulgaria, Burkina Faso, Burundi, Byelorussian SSR, Canada, Cape Verde, Central African Republic, Chad, Chile, China, Colombia, Comoros, Congo, Costa Rica, Cuba, Cyprus, Czechoslovakia, Democratic Kampuchea, Democratic Yemen, Djibouti, Dominican Republic, Ecuador, El Salvador, Equatorial Guinea, Ethiopia, France, Gabon, Gambia, German Democratic Republic, Ghana, Greece, Guatemala, Guinea, Guinea-Bissau, Guyana, Haiti, Honduras, Hungary, India, Indonesia, Iran, Iraq, Italy, Ivory Coast, Japan, Kuwait, Lao People's Democratic Republic, Lesotho, Liberia, Libyan Arab Jamahiriya, Madagascar, Malaysia, Mali, Mauritania, Mauritius, Mexico, Mongolia, Nicaragua, Niger, Nigeria, Pakistan, Panama, Paraguay, Peru, Poland, Romania, Rwanda, Samoa, Senegal, Seychelles, Singapore, Somalia, Spain, Sudan, Suriname, Sweden, Syrian Arab Republic, Togo, Trinidad and Tobago, Tunisia, Turkey, Uganda, Ukrainian SSR, USSR, United Republic of Tanzania, United States, Uruguay, Venezuela, Viet Nam, Yemen, Yugoslavia, Zaire, Zambia, Zimbabwe.
Against: Belize, Oman, Solomon Islands, United Kingdom.
Abstaining: Bahamas, Bahrain, Bangladesh, Belgium, Bhutan, Brunei Darussalam, Burma, Cameroon, Denmark, Egypt, Fiji, Finland, Germany, Federal Republic of, Grenada, Iceland, Ireland, Israel, Jamaica, Jordan, Kenya, Lebanon, Luxembourg, Malawi, Maldives, Malta, Nepal, Netherlands, New Zealand, Norway, Papua New Guinea, Portugal, Qatar, Saint Christopher and Nevis, Saint Lucia, Saint Vincent and the Grenadines, Saudi Arabia, Sierra Leone, Sri Lanka, Swaziland, Thailand, United Arab Emirates.

The Assembly rejected, by recorded votes requested by Argentina, two amendments proposed by the United Kingdom.[26] By 60 votes to 38, with 43 abstentions, it rejected a proposal to insert a new second preambular paragraph, by which the Assembly would have reaffirmed the right of all peoples to self-determination and "by virtue of that right they freely determine their political status and freely pursue their economic, social and cultural development". Another proposal, to add the phrase "and the right thereunder of peoples to self-determination" at the end of paragraph 1, was rejected by 57 votes to 36, with 47 abstentions.

Argentina said it did not request inclusion in the draft resolution of references to the principle of territorial integrity or the 1960 Declaration on decolonization; voting in favour of the British amendments would be taking the side of one of the parties to the dispute, while voting against them would not exclude what was advocated in the

proposals. The United Kingdom, saying it voted for self-determination and against an unbalanced resolution, declared that it would continue to fulfil its obligations to the people of the Falkland Islands who were at the centre of the issue.

In explanation of vote, Portugal said that, despite the undeniable merits in the draft, particularly with respect to the opportunities afforded for negotiations, it was wary of any text that could be construed in a way that failed to deal adequately with the global aspects stemming from the principle of self-determination. Solomon Islands felt that the lack of reference to the people of the Falkland Islands weakened the good intent of the draft and it regarded elements of the fourth preambular paragraph as an attempt to impose something on the people of the Islands. Papua New Guinea said that another principal party not included in the negotiation process was the people of the Falkland Islands (Malvinas); it would have supported the text if it had included the principle of self-determination. The Federal Republic of Germany and Ireland, which had voted for the amendments because of the importance of self-determination, had abstained on the resolution to reflect their wish not to take a position on the merits of the dispute. Maldives believed that a question involving the future of a people should accommodate the interests of the people concerned.

Belize voted for the amendments to ensure protection of the rights of the people of the Falkland Islands to self-determination. Also supporting the amendments, Samoa believed that the right of self-determination could have been more explicit in the draft, and Fiji added that the call for negotiations should not be at the cost of the fundamental right of the Falkland Islanders to have a say in their own future. Welcoming the conciliatory nature of the draft resolution, Botswana also supported the amendments, saying that the Falkland Islanders were entitled to the right to self-determination.

For Barbados, the phrase "all aspects of the future of the Falkland Islands (Malvinas)" in paragraph 1 seemed to leave the door open for a discussion of both sovereignty and self-determination; however, noting Argentina's position on the non-applicability of self-determination to the case, the acceptance of the proposed amendments would somewhat protect the United Kingdom's position regarding self-determination.

A number of delegations, considering the draft resolution to be constructive, also felt the adoption of the amendments would have further strengthened the text and voted in favour of both the amendments and the draft resolution. Among them, the Sudan thought the amendments would have increased the effectiveness of the text, even though the principle was already contained therein. Malawi accepted the amendments if that helped the two parties to begin negotiating. Egypt said that its votes reflected its conviction of the need to resolve issues by peaceful means. Kuwait asserted that the right to self-determination should be used not to perpetuate colonialism but to enhance the process of decolonization. Lesotho said that, although the amendments touched on the substance of the matter to be negotiated by the parties, it would support them as they concerned principles which could not be ignored in any negotiations.

Many delegations expressed misgivings or opposition to the amendments for fear their incorporation would disrupt the delicate balance in a procedural text, aimed at facilitating the opening of a dialogue between the parties.

Algeria viewed the draft resolution as being confined to defining a procedural framework for negotiations. The Central African Republic and Haiti said the draft did not concern the substance of the problem, put no pre-conditions and did not prejudice the positions of the parties. Japan said the amendments would have altered the basic thrust of the text. For France, the text made it possible to take into account all the relevant positions; express mention of the right to self-determination would in the circumstances have opened up a debate on matters of substance and introduced a destabilizing element into the text. The Syrian Arab Republic said the singling out of the principle of self-determination in the amendments was prejudicial. Ethiopia, which considered the text to be sufficiently conciliatory, felt the amendments introduced one particular element and narrowed the focus of envisaged negotiations as indicated in the fourth preambular paragraph and paragraph 1. Turkey added that the principle of self-determination was far from being the only one relevant to the dispute. The Congo expected the discussions to deal with all aspects of the dispute. Italy, which also believed the dialogue should dwell on all elements of the dispute, said the amendments would introduce into the text an element of predetermination of the solution. Greece felt that the amendments would alter the balance, possibly to the benefit of one party to the conflict; it did not see the vote on the amendments as reflecting positions on the principle of self-determination. Similarly, the Libyan Arab Jamahiriya opposed the amendments, notwithstanding its commitment to that principle. Although the Netherlands thought the amendments would have introduced an element not conducive to the resumption of a dialogue, it abstained on the text as it also fell short of achieving that objective.

Austria, Barbados, Chile, Italy, Samoa, Somalia and Trinidad and Tobago understood the reference in the draft to the United Nations Charter to include all the principles and rights embodied in that document. In addition, Sweden expressed regret that a consensus text was not possible.

Austria, the Federal Republic of Germany and Italy welcomed the absence in the draft resolution of reference to controversial elements. The Federal Republic of Germany added that the omission of controversial references to other texts and of an express mention of the sovereignty controversy constituted an important step in the right direction.

Malaysia said the scope of negotiations should not be limited by the effects of the 1982 conflict, and negotiations should resume on the same basis as that followed by the parties before that conflict.

Asserting that Argentina had sovereignty over the Malvinas Islands, Albania said the principle of self-determination, therefore, did not apply to the case. In a similar vein, Mongolia deplored what it called the United Kingdom's policy of preserving by military force the colonial status of the Territory. Iran stated that the principle of self-determination applied to the indigenous population, not to foreigners who had chosen to settle in a land originally under Argentina's sovereignty.

Also on 27 November, the Assembly took note of the report of the Fourth Committee[27] on the question (**decision 40/410**). The following petitioners had requested hearings[28] and made statements before the Committee on 27 November: John E. Cheek and D. L. Clifton, members of the Falkland Islands Council; Susan Couttes de Maciello and Alexander Jacob Betts, natives of the Falkland Islands (Malvinas); and Raúl Milton McBurney, an Argentine citizen.

REFERENCES

[1]A/40/72. [2]A/40/97. [3]A/40/132. [4]A/40/177. [5]A/40/187. [6]A/40/317-S/17196. [7]A/40/345-S/17229. [8]A/40/349-S/17233. [9]A/40/468. [10]A/40/478. [11]A/40/496. [12]A/40/516-S/17370. [13]A/40/527-S/17378. [14]A/40/646. [15]A/40/662. [16]A/40/734. [17]A/40/544. [18]A/40/837. [19]A/40/854-S/17610 & Corr.1. [20]YUN 1960, p. 49, GA res. 1514(XV), 14 Dec. 1960. [21]A/40/23 (A/AC.109/842). [22]YUN 1982, p. 1347, GA res. 37/9, 4 Nov. 1982. [23]YUN 1983, p. 1085, GA res. 38/12, 16 Nov. 1983. [24]YUN 1984, p. 1064, GA res. 39/6, 1 Nov. 1984. [25]A/40/891. [26]A/40/L.20. [27]A/40/949. [28]A/C.4/40/7 & Add.1-3.

East Timor

Communications. On 25 February 1985,[1] Portugal informed the Secretary-General that it had nothing to add to the information it had provided in 1979,[2] as required by Article 73 (*e*) of the Charter of the United Nations.

On 23 October,[3] Sao Tome and Principe transmitted to the Secretary-General a 20 July statement by Kay Rala Xanana Gusmão, President of the Revolutionary Council of National Resistance (CRRN)—the highest politico-military body of the Frente Revolucionária de Timor Leste Independente (FRETILIN)—and Commander-in-Chief of East Timor National Liberation Armed Forces, declaring the availability of the FRETILIN leadership for consultations within the framework of the 1982 General Assembly resolution on the question of East Timor.[4] Under a peace plan, unanimously adopted by CRRN and attached to the statement, FRETILIN envisaged direct talks among Portugal, Indonesia and CRRN to explore the creation of a multinational peace-keeping force, organization of free and democratic consultations of the Maubere people, and the setting of a date for the transfer of sovereignty. No preconditions were set to initiate preliminary talks with the Government of Indonesia for exploring other avenues for a comprehensive settlement of the Timor problem.

Action by the Commission on Human Rights. On 5 March 1985, the Chairman of the Commission on Human Rights[5] announced, following discussions in closed session, that the situation in East Timor was no longer under consideration by the Commission under a 1970 Economic and Social Council resolution.[6]

Action by the Committee on colonial countries. The Committee on colonial countries[7] considered the East Timor question at four meetings between 1 and 8 August. It had before it a Secretariat working paper which detailed action taken at the United Nations and described the military and human rights situations and economic, social and cultural conditions in the Territory.[8] The Committee heard statements by Cape Verde, Guinea-Bissau, Indonesia, Mozambique, Portugal and Sao Tome and Principe. It also granted requests for hearings to, and heard statements by, representatives of three non-governmental organizations and a FRETILIN representative.

Indonesia had told the Committee in February that the colonial status of East Timor had been terminated with its integration into Indonesia on 17 July 1976, and that discussion of the Territory, therefore, violated the principle of non-interference in the internal affairs of a sovereign State.

On 8 August, the Committee decided to continue consideration of the question in 1986, subject to Assembly directives.

Report of the Secretary-General. In September, the Secretary-General submitted a progress report to the General Assembly on his efforts to improve the humanitarian situation in East Timor and to promote a comprehensive settlement of the problem.[9] He said that, since his last report to the Assembly in July 1984,[10] he or Under-Secretary-General Rafeeuddin Ahmed had held consultations with high-level officials of the

Governments concerned, as a result of which Indonesia and Portugal conducted six rounds of substantive talks between November 1984 and August 1985. The talks centred on the questions of repatriating former Portuguese civil servants as well as certain East Timorese expatriates residing in Portugal, religious freedom, protection and preservation of the cultural heritage of the East Timorese people, and economic and social conditions in East Timor.

The Secretary-General stated that the International Committee of the Red Cross (ICRC), the Indonesian Red Cross and the United Nations Children's Fund carried out programmes aimed at improving the humanitarian situation of, or providing relief assistance to, the people of East Timor. As a result of discussions between the Indonesian authorities and ICRC, the latter was authorized to conduct a survey to assess the medical and nutritional situation; from 28 May to 16 June 1985, 25 villages in nine sub-districts, encompassing a total population of 41,000 inhabitants, were visited. The findings indicated that, at the time of the survey, the nutritional status and medical conditions were generally satisfactory, but the attention of the Indonesian authorities was drawn to instances where food and medicine shortages might possibly arise in the immediate future.

GENERAL ASSEMBLY ACTION

On 20 September, the General Assembly adopted **decision 40/402** by which it decided to include the East Timor question in its provisional 1986 agenda. It took this action after the General Committee had recommended that consideration of the item be deferred.[11]

REFERENCES

[1]A/40/159. [2]YUN 1979, p. 1117. [3]S/17592. [4]YUN 1982, p. 1349, GA res. 37/30, 23 Nov. 1982. [5]E/1985/22. [6]YUN 1970, p. 517, ESC res. 1503(XLVIII), 27 May 1970. [7]A/40/23. [8]A/AC.109/836. [9]A/40/622. [10]YUN 1984, p. 1066. [11]A/40/250.

Western Sahara

Action by the Commission on Human Rights. By a resolution of 26 February 1985,[1] the Commission on Human Rights reaffirmed that the question of Western Sahara was one of decolonization which remained to be completed on the basis of the exercise by the people of Western Sahara of their inalienable right to self-determination and independence, and requested the parties to the conflict, Morocco and the Frente Popular para la Liberación de Saguia el-Hamra y de Río de Oro (POLISARIO Front), to bring about a cease-fire to create the necessary conditions for a referendum for self-determination, under the auspices of the Organization of African Unity (OAU) and the United Nations. It welcomed the efforts of OAU to promote a just and definitive solution to the Western Sahara question in accordance with OAU and United Nations resolutions. It further welcomed the United Nations determination to co-operate with OAU with a view to implementing OAU decisions on the question, particularly that quoted in a 1983 General Assembly resolution on the question.[2]

Action by the Committee on colonial countries. The Committee on colonial countries[3] considered the Western Sahara question at three meetings between 1 and 8 August, having before it a Secretariat working paper on developments in the Territory[4] and a document dated 2 August[5] transmitted to the Committee Chairman by Morocco. It heard statements by Afghanistan, Cuba and Iran, in addition to those by a representative of the POLISARIO Front and two other individuals. It decided to continue consideration of the question in 1986, subject to General Assembly directives.

Communications. By a 2 August letter,[5] Morocco transmitted to the Secretary-General the document which had also been transmitted to the Chairman of the Committee on colonial countries. Morocco said the item should be deleted from the Committee's agenda as the decolonization of Western Sahara had been achieved by peaceful means when the General Assembly, in 1975,[6] took note of the tripartite agreement (Mauritania, Morocco, Spain) of November 1975. Algeria, in opposition to that peaceful solution, resorted to the use of mercenaries or to intervention; Algeria's request for direct negotiations with the POLISARIO Front or the admission of the so-called Saharan Arab Democratic Republic to OAU prejudged the results of the future referendum and sought to render it inoperative. In view of the impasse in which OAU found itself, it was up to the United Nations to ensure the holding of a referendum on self-determination in the Territory and the peaceful settlement of the question.

On 5 November,[7] Angola transmitted to the Secretary-General the text of the Final Political Declaration, adopted by the Conference of Foreign Ministers of Non-Aligned Countries (Luanda, 4-7 September 1985), in which the Ministers reaffirmed that the problem was one of decolonization which could only be solved when the people of Western Sahara exercised their right to self-determination and independence. The Ministers urged Morocco and POLISARIO to hold direct negotiations with a view to reaching a cease-fire agreement, so as to create the conditions necessary for a referendum of self-determination, under the auspices of OAU and the United Nations, without any administrative or military constraints.

Report of the Secretary-General. In a September report,[8] submitted to the General Assembly in response to a 1984 resolution,[9] the Secretary-General reviewed a number of contacts he had made with the parties concerned since December 1984.

He reported, among other things, that the Acting Secretary-General of OAU had informed him, in August 1985, of the admission of the Saharan Arab Democratic Republic as an OAU member at the November 1984 session of the Assembly of Heads of State and Government and of Morocco's withdrawal from the organization. The Acting Secretary-General had also stated that no progress could be envisaged as long as the 1983 OAU resolution[2] remained unimplemented.

The Secretary-General stated that the question of Western Sahara remained a matter of decolonization in the context of relevant United Nations resolutions, and recalled that all the parties concerned had agreed on the need for a referendum to enable the people of the Territory to exercise their right to self-determination. He expressed concern that the unresolved situation continued to be a source of tension in the subregion, and reiterated his readiness to assist in the search for a peaceful solution.

GENERAL ASSEMBLY ACTION

On 2 December 1985, on the recommendation of the Fourth Committee, the General Assembly adopted **resolution 40/50** by recorded vote.

Question of Western Sahara

The General Assembly,

Having considered in depth the question of Western Sahara,

Recalling the inalienable right of all peoples to self-determination and independence, in accordance with the principles set forth in the Charter of the United Nations and in General Assembly resolution 1514(XV) of 14 December 1960 containing the Declaration on the Granting of Independence to Colonial Countries and Peoples,

Recalling its resolution 39/40 of 5 December 1984 on the question of Western Sahara,

Having examined the relevant chapter of the report of the Special Committee on the Situation with regard to the Implementation of the Declaration on the Granting of Independence to Colonial Countries and Peoples,

Taking note of the report of the Secretary-General on the question of Western Sahara,

Recalling resolution AHG/Res.104(XIX) on Western Sahara, adopted by the Assembly of Heads of State and Government of the Organization of African Unity at its nineteenth ordinary session, held at Addis Ababa from 6 to 12 June 1983,

1. *Reaffirms* that the question of Western Sahara is a question of decolonization which remains to be completed on the basis of the exercise by the people of Western Sahara of their inalienable right to self-determination and independence;

2. *Reaffirms also* that the solution of the question of Western Sahara lies in the implementation of resolution AHG/Res.104(XIX) of the Assembly of Heads of State

and Government of the Organization of African Unity, which establishes ways and means for a just and definitive political solution to the Western Sahara conflict;

3. *Again requests*, to that end, the two parties to the conflict, the Kingdom of Morocco and the Frente Popular para la Liberación de Saguia el-Hamra y de Río de Oro, to undertake direct negotiations, in the shortest possible time, with a view to bringing about a cease-fire to create the necessary conditions for a peaceful and fair referendum for self-determination of the people of Western Sahara, a referendum without any administrative or military constraints, under the auspices of the Organization of African Unity and the United Nations;

4. *Welcomes* the efforts of the current Chairman of the Assembly of Heads of State and Government of the Organization of African Unity and the Secretary-General of the United Nations to promote a just and definitive solution of the question of Western Sahara;

5. *Invites* the current Chairman of the Assembly of Heads of State and Government of the Organization of African Unity and the Secretary-General of the United Nations to exert every effort to persuade the two parties to the conflict, the Kingdom of Morocco and the Frente Popular para la Liberación de Saguia el-Hamra y de Río de Oro, to negotiate, in the shortest possible time and in conformity with resolution AHG/Res.104(XIX) and the present resolution, the terms of a cease-fire and the modalities for organizing the said referendum;

6. *Reaffirms* the determination of the United Nations to co-operate fully with the Organization of African Unity with a view to implementing the relevant decisions of that organization, in particular resolution AHG/Res.104(XIX);

7. *Requests* the Special Committee on the Situation with regard to the Implementation of the Declaration on the Granting of Independence to Colonial Countries and Peoples to continue to consider the situation in Western Sahara as a matter of priority and to report thereon to the General Assembly at its forty-first session;

8. *Invites* the Secretary-General of the Organization of African Unity to keep the Secretary-General of the United Nations informed of the progress achieved in the implementation of the decisions of the Organization of African Unity relating to Western Sahara;

9. *Invites* the Secretary-General to follow the situation in Western Sahara closely with a view to the implementation of the present resolution and to report thereon to the General Assembly at its forty-first session.

General Assembly resolution 40/50

2 December 1985   Meeting 99   96-7-39 (recorded vote)

Approved by Fourth Committee (A/40/906) by recorded vote (91-6-43), 12 November (meeting 21); 43-nation draft (A/C.4/40/L.2/Rev.1); agenda item 18.

Sponsors: Afghanistan, Algeria, Angola, Belize, Benin, Botswana, Burkina Faso, Burundi, Cape Verde, Congo, Cuba, Cyprus, Democratic Yemen, Ethiopia, Ghana, Guinea-Bissau, Guyana, India, Iran, Lao People's Democratic Republic, Lesotho, Liberia, Madagascar, Malawi, Mali, Mauritania, Mexico, Mozambique, Nicaragua, Panama, Papua New Guinea, Rwanda, Saint Lucia, Sao Tome and Principe, Senegal, Seychelles, Sierra Leone, Uganda, United Republic of Tanzania, Vanuatu, Viet Nam, Yugoslavia, Zambia, Zimbabwe.

Meeting numbers. GA 40th session: 4th Committee 11-21; plenary 36, 96, 97, 99.

Recorded vote in Assembly as follows:

In favour: Afghanistan, Albania, Algeria, Angola, Antigua and Barbuda, Argentina, Australia, Austria, Bahamas, Barbados, Belize, Benin, Bhutan, Bolivia, Botswana, Brazil, Bulgaria, Burkina Faso, Burundi, Byelorussian SSR, Cameroon, Cape Verde, Colombia, Congo, Costa Rica, Cuba, Cyprus, Czechoslovakia,

Democratic Yemen, Dominican Republic, Ecuador, Egypt, Ethiopia, Fiji, Finland, Gambia, German Democratic Republic, Ghana, Greece, Grenada, Guinea-Bissau, Guyana, Haiti, Honduras,[a] Hungary, India, Iran, Jamaica, Kenya, Lao People's Democratic Republic, Lesotho, Liberia, Madagascar, Malawi, Mali, Malta, Mauritania, Mauritius, Mexico, Mongolia, Mozambique, New Zealand, Nicaragua, Niger, Nigeria, Panama, Papua New Guinea, Peru, Poland, Rwanda, Saint Lucia, Saint Vincent and the Grenadines, Sao Tome and Principe, Senegal, Seychelles, Sierra Leone, Spain, Sudan, Suriname, Swaziland, Sweden, Syrian Arab Republic, Togo, Trinidad and Tobago, Tunisia, Uganda, Ukrainian SSR, USSR, United Republic of Tanzania, Uruguay, Vanuatu, Venezuela, Viet Nam, Yugoslavia, Zambia, Zimbabwe.

Against: Central African Republic, Equatorial Guinea, Gabon, Guatemala, Morocco, Philippines, Zaire.

Abstaining: Belgium, Brunei Darussalam, Burma, Canada, Chad, Chile, Denmark, El Salvador, France, Germany, Federal Republic of, Guinea, Iceland, Indonesia, Iraq, Ireland, Israel, Italy, Ivory Coast, Japan, Jordan, Luxembourg, Malaysia, Maldives, Nepal, Netherlands, Norway, Pakistan, Paraguay, Portugal, Samoa, Saudi Arabia, Singapore, Solomon Islands, Somalia, Sri Lanka, Thailand, Turkey, United Kingdom, United States.

[a]Later advised the Secretariat it had intended to abstain.

Following approval of the draft in the Fourth Committee, another draft on the question[10]— submitted by the Central African Republic, the Comoros, El Salvador, Equatorial Guinea, Gabon, Guatemala, Morocco, Paraguay and Zaire—was withdrawn. That action followed the Committee's rejection, by a recorded vote of 54 to 27, with 45 abstentions, of Morocco's proposal that the debate on amendments to the draft it had co-sponsored, submitted by Algeria, Burkina Faso, Madagascar and Mozambique, be adjourned.

In making that proposal, Morocco stated that the so-called amendments were, in reality, a new draft identical in content with the 43-nation adopted draft, and were aimed at destroying the operational character of the nine-nation text, cancelling out the Secretary-General's efforts by giving him an impossible mission, and at preventing a just solution to the question. Zaire and Equatorial Guinea supported the motion. Algeria, on the other hand, asserted that Morocco's motion denied sovereign States the right to free expression or to propose amendments. India said acceptance of the motion would alter the Assembly's established position on the terms and conditions for the decolonization of Western Sahara and deny the people of the Territory its legitimate rights and aspirations.

The nine-nation draft would have had the Assembly decide to organize a referendum, beginning in January 1986, to enable the authentic populations of Western Sahara to exercise their right to self-determination. The Secretary-General would have been requested to organize that referendum and, to that end, to undertake consultations with the parties concerned, in co-operation with the OAU Chairman and Secretary-General.

In their proposed amendments to the nine-nation draft, Algeria, Burkina Faso and Mozambique all suggested that references be made to the OAU resolution quoted in a 1983 General Assembly resolution,[2] to that Assembly resolution itself, and to a 1984 Assembly resolution on the question.[9] In addition, Mozambique[11] proposed including in the preamble a reference to the principle of equal rights and self-determination of peoples. Burkina Faso[12] proposed that the preamble also contain a reference to the 1960 Declaration on Granting Independence to Colonial Countries and Peoples.[13] Madagascar[14] proposed that the Assembly request the United Nations Secretary-General and the current OAU Chairman to organize the referendum, taking into account the OAU resolution. Algeria[15] proposed that the Secretary-General, the current OAU Chairman and the OAU Secretary-General hold consultations with Morocco and the POLISARIO Front—named as the parties concerned in OAU and General Assembly resolutions—to prevail on them to negotiate the conditions of a cease-fire with a view to holding the referendum.

The Secretariat had orally informed the Fourth Committee that, as the Secretary-General was currently not in a position to prepare estimates for the programme budget implications of the two drafts, he intended to incur expenditures as might be necessary under unforeseen and extraordinary expenses.

In explanation of vote, Morocco said that, by adopting virtually the same resolution as in 1984, the Committee had opted for ineffective and inapplicable action. Like OAU, it had reached an impasse. While ready to seek compromise and dialogue, Morocco would not surrender its principles and had exhausted all recourses available to it; Morocco formally declared, therefore, that it would no longer participate in any discussion or negotiation on the Territory in the Fourth Committee, the Committee on colonial countries or other meetings of the General Assembly, nor would it consider itself bound by any resolution adopted by the Assembly in its absence.

Algeria found it difficult to see how the people of Western Sahara might express their wishes freely when Morocco continued to refuse to negotiate with their representatives and had decided never to withdraw its troops or administrative authorities from the Territory. In taking such action, Morocco was denying the Saharan people's right to self-determination and independence. The nine-nation draft asked the Assembly to repudiate its consensus resolutions, to review the question as a non-colonial issue and to legitimize procedures that simply accepted a *fait accompli*.

Burundi supported the 43-nation draft, which conformed to OAU and General Assembly resolutions; it considered the nine-nation draft to be completely at odds with the OAU peace plan. Bolivia said that negotiations between Morocco and the representatives of the Saharan people were the only proper framework for peace initiatives in the region. New Zealand interpreted paragraph 5 as inviting the Secretary-General to co-operate in the search for a peaceful solution to the dispute, consistent with the Charter and the principle of self-determination. Austria supported the text for its call for a peaceful settlement through negotiations between all the parties concerned, as did Sweden for its explicit reference to the relevant resolutions.

China, not participating, hoped that the parties concerned would negotiate, with the assistance of the Secretary-General and OAU, and settle the dispute according to the wishes of the people of the Territory. Australia felt that the 43-nation draft deserved support for insisting on the principle of self-determination; however, it would not support any wording that could be construed as prejudging the outcome of a referendum. For Pakistan, the 43-nation draft seemed to predetermine some issues that were better handled through diplomacy, and the nine-nation draft was not sufficiently specific on certain points.

Austria, Finland and Sweden said they had hoped for a consensus text. Support for both drafts was expressed by Australia, Costa Rica, Finland, Pakistan, Spain, the Sudan and Turkey. Costa Rica saw in the two texts alternative proposals for achieving the same goal; it took note of Morocco's promise to respect the results of the January 1986 referendum. The United States, which felt the 43-nation draft was unlikely to advance a settlement of the problem, would have voted for the nine-nation text which represented an advance in Morocco's position; it considered that the positions presented in the two drafts were very close and hoped that the Assembly would see in 1986 a resolution supported jointly by Algeria and Morocco. The Sudan said the nine-nation text in its original form contained a number of positive aspects. France regretted that the parties to the dispute could not agree on a referendum organized without any constraints and under international control, as agreed on by the United Nations and OAU. Finland expressed regret over the non-implementation of 1981 and 1983 OAU resolutions on organizing a referendum. Spain stressed that a solution required the participation of all parties in negotiations, with the assistance of the Secretary-General and OAU.

In November, the Fourth Committee heard the following petitioners at their request:[16] Teresa K. Smith, Western Sahara Campaign for Human Rights and Humanitarian Relief, United States; Mansour Omar, POLISARIO Front; Mr. Fofange, Minority Rights Group; Breika Zerouali, spokesman for "the elected representatives of the communities and the parents of persons abducted and illegally held in Algerian territory"; Mr. Biadi-Llah, for the deputies of Saguia el-Horura; Ahmed Rachid, Secretary-General of the Mouvement des originaires du Sahara and representative of the Mouvement de Résistance des Hommes Bleus; Mohamed Ta-quiollah Maalainine, on behalf of the representatives of Río de Oro; and Biadillah Mohamed Cheikh, for the deputies of Saguia el-Hamra.

REFERENCES

[1]E/1985/22 (1985/5). [2]YUN 1983, p. 1087, GA res. 38/40, 7 Dec. 1983. [3]A/40/23. [4]A/AC.109/832. [5]A/40/529. [6]YUN 1975, p. 819, GA res. 3458 B (XXX), 10 Dec. 1975. [7]A/40/854. [8]A/40/692 & Corr.1. [9]YUN 1984, p. 1067, GA res. 39/40, 5 Dec. 1984. [10]A/C.4/40/L.4. [11]A/C.4/40/L.8. [12]A/C.4/40/L.9. [13]YUN 1960, p. 49, GA res. 1514(XV), 14 Dec. 1960. [14]A/C.4/40/L.10. [15]A/C.4/40/L.11. [16]A/C.4/40/4 & Add.1-7.

Other Territories

In December 1985, the General Assembly adopted resolutions or decisions on other Territories, most of which were based on drafts suggested by the Committee on colonial countries[1] charged with overseeing the implementation of the 1960 Declaration on the Granting of Independence to Colonial Countries and Peoples.[2] As in previous years, the Secretariat provided the Committee with working papers on the situation in the Territories under consideration. The Committee held three sessions during 1985: 21 February, New York; 13-17 May, Tunis, Tunisia; 1-15 August, New York.

In June, Papua New Guinea brought to the attention of the Secretary-General the situation of New Caledonia (see p. 1081).

American Samoa

GENERAL ASSEMBLY ACTION

On 2 December 1985, the General Assembly, on the recommendation of the Fourth Committee, adopted without vote **resolution 40/41**.

Question of American Samoa

The General Assembly,

Having considered the question of American Samoa,

Having examined the relevant chapters of the report of the Special Committee on the Situation with regard to the Implementation of the Declaration on the Granting of Independence to Colonial Countries and Peoples,

Recalling its resolution 1514(XV) of 14 December 1960, containing the Declaration on the Granting of Independence to Colonial Countries and Peoples, and all other resolutions and decisions of the United Nations relating to American Samoa, including in particular its resolution 39/31 of 5 December 1984,

Taking into account the statement of the representative of the administering Power relating to American Samoa,

Conscious of the need to promote progress towards the full implementation of the Declaration in respect of American Samoa,

Noting with appreciation the continued participation of the administering Power in the work of the Special Committee in regard to American Samoa, thereby enabling it to conduct a more informed and meaningful examination of the situation in the Territory,

Noting that the first five-year economic development plan for the Territory, implemented by the Development Planning Office of the Government of American Samoa, expired at the end of 1984,

Aware of the special circumstances of the geographical location and economic conditions of the Territory, and bearing in mind the necessity of diversifying and strengthening further its economy as a matter of priority in order to promote economic stability,

Recalling the dispatch in 1981 of a United Nations visiting mission to the Territory,

Mindful that United Nations visiting missions provide an effective means of ascertaining the situation in the small Territories, and expressing its satisfaction at the willingness of the administering Power to receive visiting missions in the Territories under its administration,

1. *Approves* the chapter of the report of the Special Committee on the Situation with regard to the Implementation of the Declaration on the Granting of Independence to Colonial Countries and Peoples relating to American Samoa;

2. *Reaffirms* the inalienable right of the people of American Samoa to self-determination and independence in conformity with the Declaration on the Granting of Independence to Colonial Countries and Peoples contained in General Assembly resolution 1514(XV);

3. *Reiterates* the view that such factors as territorial size, geographical location, size of population and limited natural resources should in no way delay the speedy exercise by the people of the Territory of their inalienable right to self-determination and independence in conformity with the Declaration, which fully applies to American Samoa;

4. *Calls upon* the Government of the United States of America, as the administering Power, to take all necessary steps, taking into account the rights, interests and wishes of the people of American Samoa as expressed freely in conditions leading to real self-determination, to expedite the process of decolonization of the Territory in accordance with the relevant provisions of the Charter of the United Nations and the Declaration, and reaffirms the importance of fostering an awareness among the people of American Samoa of the possibilities open to them in the exercise of their right to self-determination and independence;

5. *Takes note* of the elections held on 6 November 1984 and of the fact that the newly elected Governor has stated his intention to recommend legislation establishing clearly the powers and duties of the various government departments in order to avoid conflicts of authority and to ensure sufficient budgetary control;

6. *Reaffirms* the responsibility of the administering Power, under the Charter, to promote the economic and social development of American Samoa, and calls upon the administering Power to intensify its efforts to strengthen and diversify the economy of the Territory and to make it more viable in order to reduce its heavy economic and financial dependence on the United States and to create employment opportunities for the people of the Territory;

7. *Expresses the hope* that the development planning process initiated by the first five-year development plan will be continued, and urges the administering Power, in co-operation with the territorial Government, to strengthen and extend the responsibilities of the Development Planning Office;

8. *Urges* the administering Power to continue to facilitate close relations and co-operation between the peoples of the Territory and the neighbouring island communities and between the territorial Government and the regional institutions in order to enhance further the economic and social welfare of the people of American Samoa;

9. *Urges* the administering Power, in co-operation with the territorial Government, to safeguard the inalienable right of the people of American Samoa to the enjoyment of their natural resources by taking effective measures to ensure their right to own and dispose of those resources and to establish and maintain control of their future development with a view to creating conditions for a balanced and viable economy;

10. *Considers* that the possibility of sending a further visiting mission to American Samoa should be kept under review;

11. *Requests* the Special Committee to continue the examination of this question at its next session, including the possible dispatch of a further visiting mission to American Samoa, in consultation with the administering Power, taking into account, in particular, the wishes of the people of the Territory, and to report thereon to the General Assembly at its forty-first session.

General Assembly resolution 40/41

2 December 1985   Meeting 99   Adopted without vote

Approved by Fourth Committee (A/40/906) without objection, 8 November (meeting 20); draft by Committee on colonial countries (A/40/23); agenda item 18.
Meeting numbers. GA 40th session: 4th Committee 11-20; plenary 99.

Anguilla

GENERAL ASSEMBLY ACTION

On 2 December, the General Assembly, on the recommendation of the Fourth Committee, adopted **resolution 40/48** without vote.

Question of Anguilla

The General Assembly,

Having considered the question of Anguilla,

Having examined the relevant chapters of the report of the Special Committee on the Situation with regard to the Implementation of the Declaration on the Granting of Independence to Colonial Countries and Peoples,

Recalling its resolution 1514(XV) of 14 December 1960, containing the Declaration on the Granting of Independence to Colonial Countries and Peoples, and all other resolutions and decisions of the United Nations relating to Anguilla, including in particular its resolution 39/39 of 5 December 1984,

Noting the stated position of the administering Power that it will respect the wishes of the people of Anguilla in determining the future political status of the Territory,

Conscious of the need to ensure the full and speedy implementation of the Declaration in respect of the Territory,

Noting with appreciation the continued participation of the administering Power in the work of the Special Committee in regard to Anguilla, thereby enabling it to conduct a more informed and meaningful examination of the situation in the Territory with a view to accelerating the process of decolonization for the purpose of the full implementation of the Declaration,

Reaffirming the responsibility of the administering Power to promote the economic and social development of the Territory,

Noting that during the period under review the economy of Anguilla remained buoyant,

Noting that, as a result of a comprehensive review of the civil service and police force undertaken during 1984, salaries and allowances were increased,

Welcoming the contribution to the development of the Territory by the United Nations Development Programme, specialized agencies and other organizations of the United Nations system operating in Anguilla, and noting the separate illustrative indicative planning figure established for Anguilla by the Programme for the period 1982-1986,

Reiterating the view that the participation of Territories as associate members in organizations of the United Nations system is a part of the overall strategy of accelerating the decolonization process,

Aware of the special circumstances of the geographical location and economic conditions of Anguilla, and bearing in mind the necessity of diversifying and strengthening further its economy as a matter of priority in order to promote economic stability,

Recalling the dispatch in 1984 of a United Nations visiting mission to the Territory,

Mindful that United Nations visiting missions provide an effective means of ascertaining the situation in the small Territories, and expressing its satisfaction at the willingness of the administering Power to receive visiting missions in the Territories under its administration,

1. *Approves* the chapter of the report of the Special Committee on the Situation with regard to the Implementation of the Declaration on the Granting of Independence to Colonial Countries and Peoples relating to Anguilla;

2. *Reaffirms* the inalienable right of the people of Anguilla to self-determination and independence in conformity with the Declaration on the Granting of Independence to Colonial Countries and Peoples, contained in General Assembly resolution 1514(XV);

3. *Reiterates* the view that such factors as territorial size, geographical location, size of population and limited natural resources should in no way delay the speedy exercise by the people of the Territory of their inalienable right to self-determination and independence in conformity with the Declaration, which fully applies to Anguilla;

4. *Reiterates* that it is the responsibility of the United Kingdom of Great Britain and Northern Ireland, as the administering Power, to create such conditions in Anguilla as will enable its people to exercise freely and without interference, from a well-informed standpoint as to the available options, their inalienable right to self-determination and independence in accordance with resolution 1514(XV), as well as all other relevant resolutions of the General Assembly;

5. *Reaffirms* that it is ultimately for the people of Anguilla themselves to determine their future political status in accordance with the relevant provisions of the Charter of the United Nations and the Declaration, and, in that connection, reaffirms the importance of foster-

ing an awareness among the people of the Territory of the possibilities open to them in the exercise of their right to self-determination and independence;

6. *Calls upon* the administering Power to continue, in co-operation with the territorial Government, to strengthen the economy of Anguilla and to increase its assistance to programmes of diversification;

7. *Notes* that, although the Territory was no longer in need of a grant from the administering Power to balance its recurrent budget for 1984, the Government of the United Kingdom agreed to provide a special grant to clear the deficit accumulated between 1977 and 1983;

8. *Urges* the administering Power to take effective measures, in co-operation with the territorial Government, to safeguard, guarantee and ensure the rights of the people of Anguilla to own and dispose of their natural resources and to establish and maintain control over their future development;

9. *Urges* the administering Power to continue, in co-operation with the territorial Government, the assistance necessary for the increased employment of the local population in the civil service, particularly at senior levels;

10. *Reiterates its request* to the administering Power, in the light of the observations, conclusions and recommendations of the United Nations Visiting Mission to Anguilla, 1984, to continue to enlist the assistance of the specialized agencies and other organizations of the United Nations system, as well as other regional and international bodies, in the development and strengthening of the economy of Anguilla;

11. *Calls upon* the administering Power to continue to facilitate the participation of Anguilla in the Economic Commission for Latin America and the Caribbean and its subsidiary body, the Caribbean Development and Co-operation Committee, and in other organizations of the United Nations system, including the Caribbean Group for Co-operation in Economic Development;

12. *Considers* that the possibility of sending a further visiting mission to Anguilla at an appropriate time should be kept under review;

13. *Requests* the Special Committee to continue the examination of this question at its next session, including the possible dispatch of a further visiting mission to Anguilla at an appropriate time and in consultation with the administering Power, and to report thereon to the General Assembly at its forty-first session.

General Assembly resolution 40/48

2 December 1985   Meeting 99   Adopted without vote

Approved by Fourth Committee (A/40/906) without objection, 8 November (meeting 20); draft by Committee on colonial countries (A/40/23); agenda item 18.
Meeting numbers. GA 40th session: 4th Committee 11-20; plenary 99.

Bermuda

GENERAL ASSEMBLY ACTION

On the recommendation of the Fourth Committee, the General Assembly, on 2 December 1985, adopted **resolution 40/43** without vote.

Question of Bermuda

The General Assembly,

Having considered the question of Bermuda,

Having examined the relevant chapters of the report of the Special Committee on the Situation with regard to the Implementation of the Declaration on the Granting of Independence to Colonial Countries and Peoples,

Recalling its resolution 1514(XV) of 14 December 1960, containing the Declaration on the Granting of Independence to Colonial Countries and Peoples, and all other resolutions and decisions of the United Nations relating to Bermuda, including in particular its resolution 39/33 of 5 December 1984,

Noting the stated position of the administering Power that it will fully respect the wishes of the people of Bermuda in determining the future constitutional status of the Territory,

Conscious of the need to ensure the full and speedy implementation of the Declaration in respect of the Territory,

Welcoming the continued co-operation of the administering Power in the work of the Special Committee in regard to Bermuda, which contributes to informed consideration of conditions in the Territory with a view to accelerating the process of decolonization for the purpose of the full implementation of the Declaration,

Aware of the special circumstances of the geographical location and economic conditions of Bermuda, and bearing in mind the necessity of diversifying and strengthening further its economy as a matter of priority in order to promote economic stability,

Mindful that United Nations visiting missions provide an effective means of ascertaining the situation in the small Territories, and expressing its satisfaction at the willingness of the administering Power to receive visiting missions in the Territories under its administration,

1. *Approves* the chapter of the report of the Special Committee on the Situation with regard to the Implementation of the Declaration on the Granting of Independence to Colonial Countries and Peoples relating to Bermuda;

2. *Reaffirms* the inalienable right of the people of Bermuda to self-determination and independence in conformity with the Declaration on the Granting of Independence to Colonial Countries and Peoples, contained in General Assembly resolution 1514(XV);

3. *Reiterates* the view that such factors as territorial size, geographical location, size of population and limited natural resources should in no way delay the speedy exercise by the people of the Territory of their inalienable right to self-determination and independence in conformity with the Declaration, which fully applies to Bermuda;

4. *Urges* the United Kingdom of Great Britain and Northern Ireland, as the administering Power, taking into account the rights, interests and wishes of the people of Bermuda expressed freely in conditions leading to real self-determination, to continue to take all necessary steps to ensure the full and speedy implementation of resolution 1514(XV);

5. *Reiterates* that it is the obligation of the administering Power to create such conditions in Bermuda as will enable the people of that Territory to exercise freely and without interference their inalienable right to self-determination and independence in accordance with resolution 1514(XV), and, in that connection, reaffirms the importance of fostering an awareness among the people of Bermuda of the possibilities open to them in the exercise of that right;

6. *Reaffirms* that, in accordance with the relevant provisions of the Charter of the United Nations and the Declaration contained in resolution 1514(XV), it is ultimately for the people of Bermuda themselves to determine their own future political status;

7. *Reaffirms its strong conviction* that the presence of military bases and installations in Bermuda could constitute a major obstacle to the implementation of the Declaration and that it is the responsibility of the administering Power to ensure that the existence of such bases and installations does not hinder the population of the Territory from exercising its right to self-determination and independence in conformity with the purposes and principles of the Charter;

8. *Urges* the administering Power to continue to take all necessary measures not to involve the Territory in any offensive acts or interference directed against other States and to comply fully with the purposes and principles of the Charter, the Declaration and the resolutions and decisions of the General Assembly relating to military activities and arrangements by colonial Powers in Territories under their administration;

9. *Urges once again* the administering Power, in co-operation with the territorial Government, to continue to take all effective measures to guarantee the right of the people of Bermuda to own and dispose of their natural resources and to establish and maintain control over their future development with a view to creating conditions for a balanced and viable economy;

10. *Welcomes* the role being played in the Territory by the United Nations Development Programme, specifically in programmes of agriculture, forestry and fisheries, and urges the specialized agencies and all other organizations of the United Nations system to continue to pay special attention to the development needs of Bermuda;

11. *Urges* the administering Power to continue, in co-operation with the territorial Government, the assistance necessary for the employment of the local population in the civil service, particularly at senior levels;

12. *Emphasizes* the desirability of sending a visiting mission to the Territory at the earliest possible opportunity;

13. *Requests* the Special Committee to continue the examination of this question at its next session, including the possible dispatch of a visiting mission to Bermuda at an appropriate time and in consultation with the administering Power, and to report thereon to the General Assembly at its forty-first session.

General Assembly resolution 40/43

2 December 1985   Meeting 99   Adopted without vote

Approved by Fourth Committee (A/40/906) without objection, 8 November (meeting 20); draft by Committee on colonial countries (A/40/23); agenda item 18.
Meeting numbers. GA 40th session: 4th Committee 11-20; plenary 99.

British Virgin Islands

GENERAL ASSEMBLY ACTION

On 2 December 1985, the General Assembly, on the recommendation of the Fourth Committee, adopted **resolution 40/44** without vote.

Question of the British Virgin Islands
The General Assembly,

Having considered the question of the British Virgin Islands,

Having examined the relevant chapters of the report of the Special Committee on the Situation with regard to the Implementation of the Declaration on the Granting of Independence to Colonial Countries and Peoples,

Recalling its resolution 1514(XV) of 14 December 1960, containing the Declaration on the Granting of In-

dependence to Colonial Countries and Peoples, and all other resolutions and decisions of the United Nations relating to the British Virgin Islands, including in particular its resolution 39/34 of 5 December 1984,

Noting the stated position of the administering Power that it will fully respect the wishes of the people of the British Virgin Islands in determining the future political status of the Territory,

Conscious of the need to ensure the full and speedy implementation of the Declaration in respect of the Territory,

Noting with appreciation the continued active participation of the administering Power in the work of the Special Committee in regard to the British Virgin Islands, thereby enabling it to conduct a more informed and meaningful examination of the situation in the Territory with a view to accelerating the process of decolonization for the purpose of the full implementation of the Declaration,

Reaffirming the responsibility of the administering Power to promote the economic and social development of the Territory,

Noting with concern that during the period under review the international economic crisis caused tourism and its supportive services, the mainstay of the economy, to slow down, and taking note that construction activities increased and that the territorial Government, in its continued efforts to broaden the base of the economy, was re-examining its industrialization programme,

Aware of the special circumstances of the geographical location and economic conditions of the British Virgin Islands, and bearing in mind the necessity of diversifying and strengthening further its economy as a matter of priority in order to promote economic stability,

Welcoming the contribution to the development of the Territory by the United Nations Development Programme, the United Nations Fund for Population Activities, the United Nations Children's Fund, the United Nations Industrial Development Organization, specialized agencies and other organizations of the United Nations system operating in the Territory, and noting the continued participation of the Territory in the Caribbean Group for Co-operation in Economic Development, as well as in regional organizations, including in particular the Caribbean Development Bank,

Welcoming also the participation of the Territory as an associate member in the work of the United Nations Educational, Scientific and Cultural Organization, the Economic Commission for Latin America and the Caribbean and its subsidiary body, the Caribbean Development and Co-operation Committee, as well as in various other international and regional organizations,

Recalling the dispatch in 1976 of a United Nations visiting mission to the Territory,

Mindful that United Nations visiting missions provide an effective means of ascertaining the situation in the small Territories, and expressing its satisfaction at the willingness of the administering Power to receive visiting missions in the Territories under its administration,

1. *Approves* the chapter of the report of the Special Committee on the Situation with regard to the Implementation of the Declaration on the Granting of Independence to Colonial Countries and Peoples relating to the British Virgin Islands;

2. *Reaffirms* the inalienable right of the people of the British Virgin Islands to self-determination and inde-

pendence in conformity with the Declaration on the Granting of Independence to Colonial Countries and Peoples, contained in General Assembly resolution 1514(XV);

3. *Reiterates* the view that such factors as territorial size, geographical location, size of population and limited natural resources should in no way delay the speedy exercise by the people of the Territory of their inalienable right to self-determination and independence in conformity with the Declaration, which fully applies to the British Virgin Islands;

4. *Reiterates* that it is the responsibility of the United Kingdom of Great Britain and Northern Ireland, as the administering Power, to create such conditions in the British Virgin Islands as will enable the people of the Territory to exercise freely and without interference their inalienable right to self-determination and independence in accordance with resolution 1514(XV), as well as all other relevant resolutions of the General Assembly;

5. *Reaffirms* that it is ultimately for the people of the British Virgin Islands themselves to determine their future political status in accordance with the relevant provisions of the Charter of the United Nations and the Declaration, and, in that connection, reaffirms the importance of fostering an awareness among the people of the Territory of the possibilities open to them in the exercise of their right to self-determination;

6. *Notes* the continuing commitment of the territorial Government to the goal of economic diversification, particularly in the areas of agriculture, fisheries and small industries, and reiterates its call upon the administering Power, in co-operation with the territorial Government, to intensify its efforts in this regard;

7. *Urges* the administering Power, in co-operation with the territorial Government, to safeguard the inalienable right of the people of the British Virgin Islands to the enjoyment of their natural resources by taking effective measures to ensure their right to own and dispose of those resources and to establish and maintain control of their future development;

8. *Urges* the specialized agencies and other organizations of the United Nations system to intensify measures to accelerate progress in the social and economic life of the Territory;

9. *Reiterates* its call upon the administering Power to facilitate the further participation of the British Virgin Islands in various international and regional organizations and in other organizations of the United Nations system;

10. *Considers* that the possibility of sending a further visiting mission to the British Virgin Islands at an appropriate time should be kept under review;

11. *Requests* the Special Committee to continue the examination of this question at its next session, including the possible dispatch of a visiting mission to the British Virgin Islands at an appropriate time and in consultation with the administering Power, and to report thereon to the General Assembly at its forty-first session.

General Assembly resolution 40/44

2 December 1985   Meeting 99   Adopted without vote

Approved by Fourth Committee (A/40/906) without objection, 8 November (meeting 20); draft by Committee on colonial countries (A/40/23); agenda item 18.
Meeting numbers. GA 40th session: 4th Committee 11-20; plenary 99.

Cayman Islands

GENERAL ASSEMBLY ACTION

Acting on the recommendation of the Fourth Committee, the General Assembly adopted **resolution 40/45** without vote on 2 December 1985.

Question of the Cayman Islands

The General Assembly,

Having considered the question of the Cayman Islands,

Having examined the relevant chapters of the report of the Special Committee on the Situation with regard to the Implementation of the Declaration on the Granting of Independence to Colonial Countries and Peoples,

Recalling its resolution 1514(XV) of 14 December 1960, containing the Declaration on the Granting of Independence to Colonial Countries and Peoples, and all other resolutions and decisions of the United Nations relating to the Cayman Islands, including in particular its resolution 39/35 of 5 December 1984,

Noting the stated position of the administering Power that it will fully respect the wishes of the people of the Cayman Islands in determining the future political status of the Territory,

Conscious of the need to ensure the full and speedy implementation of the Declaration in respect of the Territory,

Noting that although the main sectors of the economy of the Cayman Islands, specifically tourism, international finance and real estate, continued to sustain some degree of growth during the period under review, they have been negatively affected by the world economic crisis,

Aware of the special circumstances of the geographical location and economic conditions of the Cayman Islands, and bearing in mind the necessity of diversifying and strengthening further its economy as a matter of priority in order to promote economic stability,

Noting with appreciation the continued contribution of the United Nations Development Programme to the development of the Territory,

Recalling the dispatch in 1977 of a United Nations visiting mission to the Territory,

Mindful that United Nations visiting missions provide an effective means of ascertaining the situation in the small Territories, and expressing its satisfaction at the willingness of the administering Power to receive visiting missions in the Territories under its administration,

1. *Approves* the chapter of the report of the Special Committee on the Situation with regard to the Implementation of the Declaration on the Granting of Independence to Colonial Countries and Peoples relating to the Cayman Islands;

2. *Reaffirms* the inalienable right of the people of the Cayman Islands to self-determination and independence in conformity with the Declaration on the Granting of Independence to Colonial Countries and Peoples, contained in General Assembly resolution 1514(XV);

3. *Reiterates* the view that such factors as territorial size, geographical location, size of population and limited natural resources should in no way delay the speedy exercise by the people of the Territory of their inalienable right to self-determination and independence in conformity with the Declaration, which fully applies to the Cayman Islands;

4. *Notes with appreciation* the participation of the United Kingdom of Great Britain and Northern Ireland, as the administering Power, in the work of the Special Committee in regard to the Cayman Islands, thereby enabling it to conduct a more informed and meaningful examination of the situation in the Territory, with a view to accelerating the process of decolonization for the purpose of the full implementation of the Declaration;

5. *Reiterates* that it is the responsibility of the administering Power to create such conditions in the Cayman Islands as will enable the people of the Territory to exercise freely and without interference their inalienable right to self-determination and independence in accordance with resolution 1514(XV), as well as all other relevant resolutions of the General Assembly;

6. *Reaffirms* that it is ultimately for the people of the Cayman Islands themselves to determine their future political status in accordance with the relevant provisions of the Charter of the United Nations and the Declaration, and, in that connection, reaffirms the importance of fostering an awareness among the people of the Territory of the possibilities open to them in the exercise of their right to self-determination and independence;

7. *Reaffirms* the responsibility of the administering Power to promote the economic and social development of the Territory, and urges it, in co-operation with the territorial Government, to render continuing support, to the fullest extent possible, to the development of programmes of economic diversification which will benefit the people of the Territory;

8. *Takes note* of the statement of the administering Power to the effect that, despite the poor quality of the soil in the Territory, a study conducted by the territorial Government in 1984 revealed some possibilities in the field of poultry, agricultural and pastoral farming;

9. *Urges* the administering Power, in co-operation with the territorial Government, to safeguard the inalienable right of the people of the Territory to the enjoyment of their natural resources by taking effective measures to ensure their right to own and dispose of those resources and to establish and maintain control of their future development;

10. *Calls upon* the specialized agencies and other organizations of the United Nations system, as well as regional institutions such as the Caribbean Development Bank, to continue to take all necessary measures to accelerate progress in the social and economic life of the Cayman Islands;

11. *Notes with appreciation* the continued contribution of the United Nations Development Programme to the development of the Territory;

12. *Considers* that the possibility of sending a further visiting mission to the Cayman Islands at an appropriate time should be kept under review;

13. *Requests* the Special Committee to continue the examination of this question at its next session, including the possible dispatch of a visiting mission to the Cayman Islands at an appropriate time and in consultation with the administering Power, and to report thereon to the General Assembly at its forty-first session.

General Assembly resolution 40/45

2 December 1985   Meeting 99   Adopted without vote

Approved by Fourth Committee (A/40/906) without objection, 8 November (meeting 20); draft by Committee on colonial countries (A/40/23); agenda item 18.
Meeting numbers. GA 40th session: 4th Committee 11-20; plenary 99.

Gibraltar

Communications. During 1985, the Secretary-General received a number of communications regarding an agreement reached by Spain and the United Kingdom at Brussels, Belgium, in November 1984,[3] on the way in which their respective Governments would apply the 1980 Lisbon Declaration on the question of Gibraltar.[4] On 5 February 1985, at Geneva, the two Governments initiated the negotiating process provided for in the Brussels agreement.

In a letter of 30 January 1985,[5] Spain stated that the current location of the Customs and Police Control Administration at La Línea de la Concepción should not be interpreted as Spain's recognition of United Kingdom sovereignty over spaces other than those expressly ceded under article 10 of the Treaty of Utrecht, and that nothing in the 1984 Brussels agreement should be invoked as Spain's recognition of the permanence or continuity in the future of the current status of Gibraltar. The United Kingdom responded on 6 February,[6] by reaffirming its position concerning the sovereignty of the United Kingdom over all parts of Gibraltar and its status.

By a 1 July letter,[7] Spain and the United Kingdom informed the Secretary-General that they had exchanged notes on 13 June as the former country acceded to the European Community (EC). Spain notified the United Kingdom that its accession to EC and the application of EC regulations to the territory of Gibraltar did not alter its position concerning Gibraltar and did not affect the bilateral negotiating process established under the 1984 Brussels agreement. The United Kingdom confirmed that it had placed on record that Spain's accession did not involve any alteration in the United Kingdom's position concerning Gibraltar and did not affect the bilateral negotiating process.

Action by the Committee on colonial countries. Taking into account the continuing discussions between the parties concerned, the Committee on colonial countries decided on 9 August to continue considering the item at its 1986 session, subject to any Assembly directives.

GENERAL ASSEMBLY ACTION

In December 1985, the General Assembly, acting on the recommendation of the Fourth Committee, adopted **decision 40/413** without vote.

Question of Gibraltar

At its 99th plenary meeting, on 2 December 1985, the General Assembly, on the recommendation of the Fourth Committee, adopted the following text as representing the consensus of the members of the Assembly:

"The General Assembly, noting that the Governments of Spain and of the United Kingdom of Great Britain and Northern Ireland agreed at Brussels on 27 November 1984 on a statement whereby they decided to apply, before 15 February 1985, the Lisbon Declaration of 10 April 1980 in all its parts; noting that this involved, simultaneously, the provision of equality and reciprocity of rights for Spaniards in Gibraltar and Gibraltarians in Spain, the establishment of the free movement of persons, vehicles and goods between Gibraltar and the neighbouring territory and the establishment of a negotiating process; and noting that, as regards this last point, the Brussels statement reads as follows:

" '(c) The establishment of a negotiating process aimed at overcoming all the differences between them over Gibraltar and at promoting co-operation on a mutually beneficial basis on economic, cultural, touristic, aviation, military and environment matters. Both sides accept that the issues of sovereignty will be discussed in that process. The British Government will fully maintain its commitment to honour the wishes of the people of Gibraltar as set out in the preamble of the 1969 Constitution';

welcomes the fact that on 5 February 1985 equality and reciprocity of rights were established for Spaniards in Gibraltar and Gibraltarians in Spain, together with the free movement of persons, vehicles and goods between Gibraltar and the neighbouring territory; also welcomes the fact that the two Governments initiated, at Geneva on 5 February 1985, the negotiating process provided for in the Brussels statement and foreseen in the consensus approved by the Assembly on 14 December 1973;[8] and urges both Governments to continue this process with the object of reaching a lasting solution to the problem of Gibraltar in the light of the relevant resolutions of the Assembly and in the spirit of the Charter of the United Nations."

General Assembly decision 40/413

Adopted without vote

Approved by Fourth Committee (A/40/906) without objection, 12 November (meeting 21); draft consensus (A/C.4/40/L.7); agenda item 18.
Meeting numbers. GA 40th session: 4th Committee 11-21; plenary 99.

Guam

GENERAL ASSEMBLY ACTION

Acting on the recommendation of the Fourth Committee, the General Assembly adopted **resolution 40/42** without vote on 2 December 1985.

Question of Guam

The General Assembly,

Having considered the question of Guam,

Having examined the relevant chapters of the report of the Special Committee on the Situation with regard to the Implementation of the Declaration on the Granting of Independence to Colonial Countries and Peoples,

Recalling its resolution 1514(XV) of 14 December 1960, containing the Declaration on the Granting of Independence to Colonial Countries and Peoples, and all other resolutions and decisions of the United Nations relating to Guam, including in particular its resolution 39/32 of 5 December 1984,

Having heard the statement of the representative of the administering Power relating to Guam,

Noting with appreciation the continued active participation of the administering Power in the work of the Special Committee in regard to Guam, thereby enabling it to conduct a more informed and meaningful examination of the situation in the Territory with a view to accelerating the process of decolonization towards the full and speedy implementation of the Declaration,

Recalling that a Guam Commission on Self-Determination was appointed in February 1984 to deal with the status question in a manner acceptable to the people of the Territory,

Taking note of the statement by the representative of the administering Power that the Department of Defense had authorized the release of some 2,000 hectares of land previously under its control,

Noting the great potential offered for diversifying and developing the economy of the Territory, for example, commercial fishing and agriculture,

Taking note of the steps taken by the territorial Government, with the support of the administering Power, to develop and promote the language and culture of the Chamorro people, who are the indigenous people of the Territory,

Aware of the special circumstances of the geographical location and economic conditions of Guam, and bearing in mind the necessity of diversifying and strengthening further its economy as a matter of priority in order to promote economic stability,

Recalling the dispatch in 1979 of a United Nations visiting mission to the Territory,

Mindful that United Nations visiting missions provide an effective means of ascertaining the situation in the small Territories, and expressing its satisfaction at the willingness of the administering Power to receive visiting missions in the Territories under its administration,

1. *Approves* the chapter of the report of the Special Committee on the Situation with regard to the Implementation of the Declaration on the Granting of Independence to Colonial Countries and Peoples relating to Guam;

2. *Reaffirms* the inalienable right of the people of Guam to self-determination and independence in conformity with the Declaration on the Granting of Independence to Colonial Countries and Peoples, contained in General Assembly resolution 1514(XV);

3. *Reaffirms its conviction* that such factors as territorial size, geographical location, size of population and limited natural resources should in no way delay the implementation of the Declaration, which fully applies to Guam;

4. *Reaffirms* the importance of fostering an awareness among the people of Guam of the possibilities open to them with regard to their right to self-determination, and calls upon the administering Power, in co-operation with the territorial Government, to expedite the process of decolonization strictly in accordance with the expressed wishes of the people of the Territory;

5. *Takes note* of the statement by the representative of the administering Power that the Guam Commission on Self-Determination, which was appointed in February 1984 to deal with the status question in a manner acceptable to the people of the Territory for submission to the Congress of the United States of America for approval, hopes to hold a local referendum before the end of 1985;

6. *Takes note* of the statement of the representative of the United States affirming that his Government respects the wish of the Guamanians to control their own destiny both politically and economically;

7. *Reaffirms its strong conviction* that the presence of military bases and installations in the Territory could

constitute a major obstacle to the implementation of the Declaration and that it is the responsibility of the administering Power to ensure that the existence of such bases and installations does not hinder the population of the Territory from exercising its right to self-determination and independence in conformity with the purposes and principles of the Charter of the United Nations;

8. *Urges* the administering Power to continue to take all necessary measures not to involve the Territory in any offensive acts or interference against any other States and to comply fully with the purposes and principles of the Charter, the Declaration and the resolutions and decisions of the General Assembly relating to military activities and arrangements by colonial Powers in Territories under their administration;

9. *Reaffirms* the responsibility of the administering Power, under the Charter, for the economic and social development of Guam, and, in this connection, calls upon the administering Power to take all necessary steps to strengthen and diversify the economy of the Territory, with a view to reducing the Territory's economic dependence on the administering Power;

10. *Reiterates* the view that one obstacle to economic development, particularly in the agricultural sector, stems from the fact that large tracts of land are held by the federal authorities, and calls upon the administering Power, in co-operation with the local authorities, to continue the transfer of land to the people of the Territory;

11. *Notes* that a settlement was reached in 1984 between representatives of former Guamanian landowners and the administering Power under which the former will receive $39.5 million in compensation for land taken over by the United States Government from 1944 to 1963, it being the right of individual claimants not to participate in this settlement and continue to press their own claims;

12. *Reiterates its call* upon the administering Power to support measures by the territorial Government aimed at removing constraints to growth in the areas of agriculture and commercial fishing and to ensure their development to the fullest extent;

13. *Urges* the administering Power, in co-operation with the territorial Government, to continue to take effective measures to safeguard and guarantee the right of the people of Guam to their natural resources and to establish and maintain control over their future development, and requests the administering Power to take all necessary steps to protect the property rights of the people of the Territory;

14. *Reaffirms* the importance of further efforts by the territorial Government, with the support of the administering Power, to develop and promote the language and culture of the Chamorro people, who are the indigenous people of the Territory;

15. *Considers* that the possibility of sending a further visiting mission to Guam at an appropriate time should be kept under review;

16. *Requests* the Special Committee to continue the examination of this question at its next session, including the possible dispatch of a further visiting mission to Guam at an appropriate time and in consultation with the administering Power, and to report thereon to the General Assembly at its forty-first session.

General Assembly resolution 40/42

2 December 1985   Meeting 99   Adopted without vote

Approved by Fourth Committee (A/40/906) without objection, 8 November (meeting 20); draft by Committee on colonial countries (A/40/23); agenda item 18.
Meeting numbers. GA 40th session: 4th Committee 11-20; plenary 99.

The Fourth Committee received requests for hearings from two organizations,[9] and heard a statement on 31 October by Ronald Franquez Teehan, Secretary of the Guam Landowners' Association.

Montserrat

GENERAL ASSEMBLY ACTION

On 2 December 1985, the General Assembly, on the recommendation of the Fourth Committee, adopted **resolution 40/46** without vote.

Question of Montserrat
The General Assembly,

Having considered the question of Montserrat,

Having examined the relevant chapters of the report of the Special Committee on the Situation with regard to the Implementation of the Declaration on the Granting of Independence to Colonial Countries and Peoples,

Recalling its resolution 1514(XV) of 14 December 1960, containing the Declaration on the Granting of Independence to Colonial Countries and Peoples, and all other resolutions and decisions of the United Nations relating to Montserrat, including in particular its resolution 39/36 of 5 December 1984,

Noting the stated position of the administering Power that it will respect the wishes of the people of Montserrat in determining the future political status of the Territory,

Noting the view of the Government of Montserrat that independence was inevitable and desirable and, in that connection, that the territorial Government would prepare programmes of political education by which to increase the people's awareness of the benefits of independence,

Noting with concern that during the period under review the international economic crisis continued to have an adverse effect on the territorial economy and resulted in zero growth in the gross domestic product and a reduction in the rate of growth of employment and incomes,

Welcoming the fact that an increasing number of people from the Territory are being employed in the civil service, particularly at the higher echelon, including the appointment of a national as Chief Medical Officer, and noting the recommendations for salary increases made by the Salaries Commission on public service salaries and conditions,

Welcoming also the contribution to the development of Montserrat by the United Nations Development Programme, the United Nations Children's Fund, specialized agencies and other organizations of the United Nations system operating in the Territory, and noting the continued participation of the Territory in the Caribbean Group for Co-operation in Economic Development, as well as in regional organizations such as the Caribbean Community and its associated institutions, including the Caribbean Development Bank,

Aware of the special circumstances of the geographical location and economic conditions of Montserrat, and bearing in mind the necessity of diversifying and strengthening further its economy as a matter of priority in order to promote economic stability,

Recalling the dispatch in 1975 and 1982 of United Nations visiting missions to the Territory,

Mindful that visiting missions provide an effective means of ascertaining the situation in the small Territories, and expressing its satisfaction at the willingness of the administering Power to receive visiting missions in the Territories under its administration,

1. *Approves* the chapter of the report of the Special Committee on the Situation with regard to the Implementation of the Declaration on the Granting of Independence to Colonial Countries and Peoples relating to Montserrat;

2. *Reaffirms* the inalienable right of the people of Montserrat to self-determination and independence in conformity with the Declaration on the Granting of Independence to Colonial Countries and Peoples, contained in General Assembly resolution 1514(XV);

3. *Reiterates* the view that such factors as territorial size, geographical location, size of population and limited natural resources should in no way delay the speedy exercise by the people of the Territory of their inalienable right to self-determination and independence in conformity with the Declaration, which fully applies to Montserrat;

4. *Notes with appreciation* the continued participation of the United Kingdom of Great Britain and Northern Ireland, as the administering Power, in the work of the Special Committee in regard to Montserrat, thereby enabling it to conduct a more informed and meaningful examination of the situation in the Territory with a view to accelerating the process of decolonization for the purpose of the full implementation of the Declaration;

5. *Reiterates* that it is the responsibility of the administering Power to create such conditions in Montserrat as will enable its people to exercise freely and without interference, from a well-informed standpoint as to the available options, their inalienable right to self-determination and independence in accordance with resolution 1514(XV), as well as all other relevant resolutions of the General Assembly;

6. *Reaffirms* that it is ultimately for the people of Montserrat themselves to determine their future political status in accordance with the relevant provisions of the Charter of the United Nations and the Declaration, and reiterates its call upon the administering Power, in co-operation with the territorial Government, to launch programmes to foster an awareness among the people of the Territory of the possibilities available to them in the exercise of their right to self-determination and independence;

7. *Reaffirms* the responsibility of the administering Power to promote the economic and social development of Montserrat and, in co-operation with the territorial Government, to continue to strengthen the economy and to increase its assistance to programmes of diversification in order to promote the economic and financial viability of the Territory;

8. *Urges* the administering Power to take the necessary measures in co-operation with the territorial Government to restore sustained and balanced growth to the economy of Montserrat and to intensify its assistance in the development of all sectors thereof, which will benefit the people of the Territory;

9. *Also urges* the administering Power, in co-operation with the territorial Government, to take effective measures to safeguard, guarantee and ensure the rights of the people of Montserrat to own and dispose of their natural resources and to establish and maintain control of their future development;

10. *Urges* the administering Power to continue, in co-operation with the territorial Government, the assistance necessary for the employment of the local population in the civil service, particularly at senior levels;

11. *Calls upon* the United Nations system of organizations, as well as donor Governments and regional organizations, to intensify their efforts to accelerate progress in the economic and social life of the Territory;

12. *Considers* that the possibility of sending a further visiting mission to Montserrat at an appropriate time should be kept under review;

13. *Requests* the Special Committee to continue the examination of this question at its next session, including the possible dispatch of a further visiting mission to Montserrat at an appropriate time and in consultation with the administering Power, and to report thereon to the General Assembly at its forty-first session.

General Assembly resolution 40/46

2 December 1985   Meeting 99   Adopted without vote

Approved by Fourth Committee (A/40/906) without objection, 8 November (meeting 20); draft by Committee on colonial countries (A/40/23); agenda item 18.
Meeting numbers. GA 40th session: 4th Committee 11-20; plenary 99.

Pitcairn

GENERAL ASSEMBLY ACTION

In December, the General Assembly, on the recommendation of the Fourth Committee, adopted **decision 40/412** without vote.

Question of Pitcairn

At its 99th plenary meeting, on 2 December 1985, the General Assembly, on the recommendation of the Fourth Committee, adopted the following text as representing the consensus of the members of the Assembly:

"The General Assembly, having examined the relevant chapters of the report of the Special Committee on the Situation with regard to the Implementation of the Declaration on the Granting of Independence to Colonial Countries and Peoples, takes note of the statement of the representative of the United Kingdom of Great Britain and Northern Ireland affirming that his Government's policy was one of respect for the very individual life-style that the people of Pitcairn had freely chosen and that the United Kingdom perceived its role as the administering Power as doing what it could to preserve, promote and protect it. The Assembly requests the Special Committee to continue to examine the question at its next session and to report thereon to the Assembly at its forty-first session."

General Assembly decision 40/412

Adopted without vote

Approved by Fourth Committee (A/40/906) without objection, 8 November (meeting 20); draft by Committee on colonial countries (A/40/23); agenda item 18.
Meeting numbers. GA 40th session: 4th Committee 11-20; plenary 99.

St. Helena

GENERAL ASSEMBLY ACTION

On the recommendation of the Fourth Committee, the General Assembly, in December, adopted **decision 40/414** by recorded vote.

Question of St. Helena

At its 99th plenary meeting, on 2 December 1985, the General Assembly, on the recommendation of the Fourth Committee, having examined the relevant chapters of the report of the Special Committee on the Situation with regard to the Implementation of the Declaration on the Granting of Independence to Colonial Countries and Peoples and having heard the statement of the representative of the United Kingdom of Great Britain and Northern Ireland, as the administering Power, reaffirmed the inalienable right of the people of St. Helena to self-determination and independence in conformity with the Declaration on the Granting of Independence to Colonial Countries and Peoples, contained in Assembly resolution 1514(XV) of 14 December 1960. The Assembly noted the commitment of the Government of the United Kingdom to respect the wishes of the people of the Territory in relation to their future political status and, in that regard, urged the administering Power, in consultation with the Legislative Council and other representatives of the people of St. Helena, to continue to take all necessary steps to ensure the speedy implementation of the Declaration in respect of this Territory and in that connection reaffirmed the importance of promoting an awareness among the people of St. Helena of the possibilities open to them in the exercise of their right to self-determination. The Assembly expressed the hope that the administering Power would continue to implement infrastructure and community development projects aimed at improving the general welfare of the community, and to encourage local initiative and enterprise, particularly in the areas of fisheries development, forestry, handicrafts and agriculture. The Assembly reaffirmed that continued development assistance from the administering Power, together with any assistance that the international community might be able to provide, constituted an important means of developing the economic potential of the Territory and of enhancing the capacity of its people to realize fully the goals set forth in the relevant provisions of the Charter of the United Nations. The Assembly noted with concern the presence of military facilities on the dependency of Ascension Island and, in that regard, recalled all United Nations resolutions and decisions concerning military bases and installations in colonial and Non-Self-Governing Territories. Noting the positive attitude of the administering Power with respect to the question of receiving United Nations visiting missions in the Territories under its administration, the Assembly considered that the possibility of dispatching such a mission to St. Helena at an appropriate time should be kept under review. The Assembly requested the Special Committee to continue to examine the question at its next session, including the possible dispatch of a visiting mission to St. Helena, at an appropriate time and in consultation with the administering Power, and to report thereon to the Assembly at its forty-first session.

General Assembly decision 40/414

121-2-31 (recorded vote)

Approved by Fourth Committee (A/40/906) by recorded vote (112-3-25), 8 November (meeting 20); draft by Committee on colonial countries (A/40/23); agenda item 18.
Meeting numbers. GA 40th session: 4th Committee 11-20; plenary 99.

Recorded vote in Assembly as follows:

In favour: Afghanistan, Albania, Algeria, Angola, Antigua and Barbuda, Argentina, Bahamas, Bahrain, Bangladesh, Barbados, Benin, Bolivia, Botswana, Brazil, Bulgaria, Burkina Faso, Burma, Burundi, Byelorussian SSR, Cameroon, Cape Verde, Central African Republic, Chad, China, Colombia, Comoros, Congo, Costa Rica, Cuba, Cyprus, Czechoslovakia, Democratic Kampuchea, Democratic Yemen, Djibouti, Dominican Republic, Ecuador, Egypt, El Salvador, Equatorial Guinea, Ethiopia, Gabon, Gambia, German Democratic Republic, Ghana, Grenada, Guinea, Guinea-Bissau, Guyana, Haiti, Hungary, India, Indonesia, Iran, Iraq, Ivory Coast, Jamaica, Jordan, Kenya, Kuwait, Lao People's Democratic Republic, Lebanon, Lesotho, Liberia, Libyan Arab Jamahiriya, Madagascar, Malawi, Malaysia, Maldives, Mali,

Malta, Mauritania, Mauritius, Mexico, Mongolia, Morocco, Mozambique, Nepal, Nicaragua, Niger, Nigeria, Oman, Pakistan, Panama, Papua New Guinea, Paraguay, Peru, Philippines, Poland, Qatar, Romania, Rwanda, Saint Lucia, Sao Tome and Principe, Saudi Arabia, Senegal, Seychelles, Sierra Leone, Singapore, Somalia, Sri Lanka, Sudan, Suriname, Syrian Arab Republic, Thailand, Togo, Trinidad and Tobago, Tunisia, Uganda, Ukrainian SSR, USSR, United Arab Emirates, United Republic of Tanzania, Uruguay, Vanuatu, Venezuela, Viet Nam, Yemen, Yugoslavia, Zaire, Zambia, Zimbabwe.

Against: United Kingdom, United States.

Abstaining: Australia, Austria, Belgium, Belize, Brunei Darussalam,[a] Canada, Denmark, Fiji, Finland, France, Germany, Federal Republic of, Greece, Guatemala, Honduras, Iceland, Ireland, Israel, Italy, Japan, Luxembourg, Netherlands, New Zealand, Norway, Portugal, Saint Vincent and the Grenadines, Samoa, Solomon Islands, Spain, Swaziland, Sweden, Turkey.

[a]Later advised the Secretariat it had intended to vote in favour.

The Fourth Committee's approval of the draft followed a decision—by a recorded vote, requested by the United Kingdom, of 77 to 27, with 27 abstentions—to retain the fifth sentence of the text referring to the presence of military facilities on the dependency of Ascension Island. The United Kingdom objected to the sentence as inappropriate and prejudiced, adding that the links between Ascension Island and St. Helena were only administrative, and that the Island had had only stationing facilities for transport aircraft since 1942; if those facilities were felt to be a threat to peace and security, that concern should be taken to the Security Council.

Tokelau

Action by the Committee on colonial countries. On 1 August, the Committee on colonial countries[(1)] accepted the invitation extended to it in April and in May 1985 by New Zealand, the administering Power of Tokelau, to send a visiting mission to the Territory in 1986 for the purpose of making a further firsthand assessment of the situation there and of ascertaining the wishes of the people of the Territory concerning their future status.

GENERAL ASSEMBLY ACTION

On the recommendation of the Fourth Committee, the General Assembly, in December, adopted **decision 40/411** without vote.

Question of Tokelau

At its 99th plenary meeting, on 2 December 1985, the General Assembly, on the recommendation of the Fourth Committee, adopted the following text as representing the consensus of the members of the Assembly:

"The General Assembly, having examined the relevant chapters of the report of the Special Committee on the Situation with regard to the Implementation of the Declaration on the Granting of Independence to Colonial Countries and Peoples and having heard the statement of the representative of New Zealand with regard to Tokelau, notes with appreciation the willingness of the administering Power to maintain its close co-operation with the United Nations in the exercise of its responsibility towards Tokelau. The Assembly reaffirms the inalienable right of the people of Tokelau to self-determination and independence in conformity with the Declaration on the Granting of Independence to Colonial Countries and Peoples, contained in Assembly resolution 1514(XV) of 14 December 1960, and reaffirms further that it is the responsibility of the administering Power to keep the people of Tokelau fully informed of that right. In this regard, the Assembly notes that the people of the Territory have expressed the view that, for the time being, they do not wish to review the nature of the existing relationship between Tokelau and New Zealand but that they desire to be given some latitude and some degree of autonomy in decision-making. The Assembly welcomes the assurances of the administering Power that it will continue to be guided solely by the wishes of the people of Tokelau as to the future status of the Territory and that it is committed to responding positively to the expressed desires of the people of Tokelau. The Assembly calls upon the administering Power to continue its programme of fostering awareness among the people of Tokelau of the possibilities open to them in the exercise of their right to self-determination and within the context of its efforts to ensure the preservation of the identity and cultural heritage of the people of Tokelau. The Assembly is of the opinion that the administering Power should continue to inform the people of Tokelau of the consideration of their Territory by the United Nations. The Assembly recognizes that the political and economic development of Tokelau is an important element in the process of self-determination. In this connection, the Assembly notes with satisfaction that the General *Fono* (Council) of Tokelau is assuming greater authority in local political, economic and financial affairs. The Assembly notes with satisfaction that the General *Fono* has established two additional committees to deal with health and agriculture. The Assembly notes further the continuing efforts of the administering Power to promote the economic development of the Territory and the measures it has taken to safeguard and guarantee the rights of the people of Tokelau to all their natural resources and the benefits derived therefrom. In this regard, the Assembly also notes that the Tokelau public service, with support from the administering Power, is currently investigating ways of improving Tokelau's copra growing and marketing schemes. In particular, the Assembly notes with satisfaction the measures being taken to lessen the Territory's isolation, namely, the upgrading of telecommunications facilities and the study to determine the feasibility of constructing landing strips for aircraft on each of the three atolls, and the efforts to facilitate regular air transport to the Territory. The Assembly is of the opinion that the administering Power should continue to expand its programme of budgetary support and development aid to the Territory. The Assembly notes with appreciation the continuing efforts of the administering Power to make improvements in the fields of public health, public works and education. The Assembly reiterates its expression of appreciation to the specialized agencies and other organizations of the United Nations system, as well as to the regional organizations, for their assistance to Tokelau and calls upon them to continue providing assistance to the Territory. Mindful that United Nations visiting missions provide an effective means of ascertaining the situation in the small Territories, the Assembly welcomes the invitation from the administering Power, New Zealand, and from the people of the Territory, to send a visiting mission during 1986 and takes note of the related decision of the Special Committee. The Assembly requests the Special Com-

mittee to continue to examine the question at its next session and to report thereon to the Assembly at its forty-first session."

General Assembly decision 40/411

Adopted without vote

Approved by Fourth Committee (A/40/906) without objection, 8 November (meeting 20); draft by Committee on colonial countries (A/40/23); agenda item 18.
Meeting numbers. GA 40th session: 4th Committee 11-20; plenary 99.

Turks and Caicos Islands

GENERAL ASSEMBLY ACTION

Acting on the recommendation of the Fourth Committee, the General Assembly adopted **resolution 40/47** without vote on 2 December 1985.

Question of the Turks and Caicos Islands
The General Assembly,

Having considered the question of the Turks and Caicos Islands,

Having examined the relevant chapters of the report of the Special Committee on the Situation with regard to the Implementation of the Declaration on the Granting of Independence to Colonial Countries and Peoples,

Recalling its resolution 1514(XV) of 14 December 1960, containing the Declaration on the Granting of Independence to Colonial Countries and Peoples, and all other resolutions and decisions of the United Nations relating to the Turks and Caicos Islands, including in particular its resolution 39/37 of 5 December 1984,

Noting the stated position of the administering Power that it will fully respect the wishes of the people of the Turks and Caicos Islands in determining the future constitutional status of the Territory, and bearing in mind the importance of fostering an awareness among the people of the Territory of the possibilities open to them,

Conscious of the need to ensure the full and speedy implementation of the Declaration in respect of the Territory,

Noting with appreciation the participation of the administering Power in the work of the Special Committee in regard to the Turks and Caicos Islands, thereby enabling it to conduct a more informed and meaningful examination of the situation in the Territory,

Aware of the special circumstances of the geographical location and economic conditions of the Turks and Caicos Islands, and bearing in mind the necessity of diversifying and strengthening further its economy as a matter of priority in order to promote economic stability and to develop a wider economic base for the Territory,

Noting the statement of the administering Power that an experimental farm has been set up on North Caicos to study agricultural techniques,

Welcoming the continuing contribution of the United Nations Development Programme to the development of the Territory,

Recalling the dispatch in 1980 of two United Nations visiting missions to the Territory,

Mindful that United Nations visiting missions provide an effective means of ascertaining the situation in the small Territories, and expressing its satisfaction at the willingness of the administering Power to receive visiting missions in the Territories under its administration,

1. *Approves* the chapter of the report of the Special Committee on the Situation with regard to the Implementation of the Declaration on the Granting of Indepen-

dence to Colonial Countries and Peoples relating to the Turks and Caicos Islands;

2. *Reaffirms* the inalienable right of the people of the Turks and Caicos Islands to self-determination and independence in conformity with the Declaration on the Granting of Independence to Colonial Countries and Peoples, contained in General Assembly resolution 1514(XV);

3. *Reiterates* the view that such factors as territorial size, geographical location, size of population and limited natural resources should in no way delay the speedy exercise by the people of the Territory of their inalienable right to self-determination and independence in conformity with the Declaration, which fully applies to the Turks and Caicos Islands;

4. *Reiterates* that it is the obligation of the United Kingdom of Great Britain and Northern Ireland, as the administering Power, to create such conditions in the Turks and Caicos Islands as will enable the people of the Territory to exercise freely and without interference their inalienable right to self-determination and independence in accordance with resolution 1514(XV), as well as other relevant resolutions of the General Assembly;

5. *Reaffirms* that it is the responsibility of the administering Power under the Charter of the United Nations to develop its dependent Territories economically and socially, and urges the administering Power, in consultation with the territorial Government, to take the necessary measures to promote the economic and social development of the Turks and Caicos Islands and, in particular, to intensify and expand its programme of assistance in order to accelerate the development of the economic and social infrastructure of the Territory;

6. *Emphasizes* that greater attention should be paid to diversification of the economy, which will benefit the people of the Territory;

7. *Recalls* that it is the responsibility of the administering Power, in accordance with the wishes of the people of the Turks and Caicos Islands, to safeguard, guarantee and ensure the inalienable right of the people to the enjoyment of their natural resources by taking effective measures to guarantee their right to own and dispose of those natural resources and to establish and maintain control of their future development;

8. *Takes note* of the statement of the administering Power to the effect that the military facility in the Turks and Caicos Islands was closed in 1984, that the territorial Government now has complete control over the disposition of the land vacated by the base and that the land is now being used for various activities which are beneficial to the economy and the people of the Territory;

9. *Urges* the specialized agencies and other organizations of the United Nations system, as well as such regional institutions as the Caribbean Development Bank, to continue to pay special attention to the development needs of the Turks and Caicos Islands;

10. *Requests* the administering Power, in consultation with the territorial Government, to continue to provide the assistance necessary for the training of qualified local personnel in the skills essential to the development of various sectors of the economy and the society of the Territory;

11. *Considers* that the possibility of sending a further visiting mission to the Turks and Caicos Islands at an appropriate time should be kept under review;

12. *Requests* the Special Committee to continue the examination of this question at its next session, including the possible dispatch of a further visiting mission to the Turks and Caicos Islands at an appropriate time and in consultation with the administering Power, and to report thereon to the General Assembly at its forty-first session.

General Assembly resolution 40/47

2 December 1985   Meeting 99   Adopted without vote

Approved by Fourth Committee (A/40/906) without objection, 8 November (meeting 20); draft by Committee on colonial countries (A/40/23); agenda item 18.
Meeting numbers. GA 40th session: 4th Committee 11-20; plenary 99.

United States Virgin Islands

GENERAL ASSEMBLY ACTION

On 2 December 1985, the General Assembly, acting on the recommendation of the Fourth Committee, adopted **resolution 40/49** without vote.

Question of the United States Virgin Islands
The General Assembly,

Having considered the question of the United States Virgin Islands,

Having examined the relevant chapters of the report of the Special Committee on the Situation with regard to the Implementation of the Declaration on the Granting of Independence to Colonial Countries and Peoples,

Recalling its resolution 1514(XV) of 14 December 1960, containing the Declaration on the Granting of Independence to Colonial Countries and Peoples, and all other resolutions and decisions of the United Nations relating to the United States Virgin Islands, including in particular its resolution 39/38 of 5 December 1984,

Noting with appreciation the continued active participation of the administering Power and the representative of the territorial Government in the work of the Special Committee in regard to the United States Virgin Islands, thereby enabling it to conduct a more informed and meaningful examination of the situation in the Territory with a view to accelerating the process of decolonization for the purpose of the full implementation of the Declaration,

Taking into account the statement of the representative of the administering Power that the Territory of the United States Virgin Islands enjoys a large measure of self-government through its elected representatives, namely, the Governor, members of the Legislature and the Territory's non-voting delegate to the United States House of Representatives, and noting the recent general elections in the Territory,

Noting with concern that the economy of the Territory was, as described by the Governor, "temporarily depressed", particularly in the tourist, construction and industrial sectors, as well as in the delivery of government services, and noting that the Territory's industrial development programme would suffer a setback as a result of the announced plan of Martin Marietta Alumina, Inc. for the closure of its aluminium plant in the Territory in 1985,

Welcoming the continued participation of the United States Virgin Islands, as an associated member, in the work of the Economic Commission for Latin America and the Caribbean and its subsidiary bodies, including the Caribbean Development and Co-operation Committee and noting the participation of a representative of the Territory as a member of the delegation of the administering Power at annual meetings of the Caribbean Group for Co-operation in Economic Development since 1982,

Noting with satisfaction the statement of the administering Power that it endorsed the policy that representatives of the Territory should participate in forums in which the Territory was the subject of discussion,

Aware of the special circumstances of the geographical location and economic conditions of the United States Virgin Islands, and bearing in mind the necessity of diversifying and strengthening further its economy as a matter of priority in order to promote economic stability,

Recalling the dispatch in 1977 of a United Nations visiting mission to the Territory,

Mindful that United Nations visiting missions provide an effective means of ascertaining the situation in the small Territories, and expressing its satisfaction at the willingness of the administering Power to receive visiting missions in the Territories under its administration,

1. *Approves* the chapter of the report of the Special Committee on the Situation with regard to the Implementation of the Declaration on the Granting of Independence to Colonial Countries and Peoples relating to the United States Virgin Islands;

2. *Reaffirms* the inalienable right of the people of the United States Virgin Islands to self-determination and independence in conformity with the Declaration on the Granting of Independence to Colonial Countries and Peoples, contained in General Assembly resolution 1514(XV);

3. *Reiterates* the view that such factors as territorial size, geographical location, size of population and limited natural resources should in no way delay the speedy exercise by the people of the Territory of their inalienable right to self-determination and independence in conformity with the Declaration, which fully applies to the United States Virgin Islands;

4. *Reiterates* that it is the responsibility of the administering Power to create such conditions in the United States Virgin Islands as will enable the people of the Territory to exercise freely and without interference their inalienable right to self-determination and independence in conformity with resolution 1514(XV), as well as all other relevant resolutions of the General Assembly;

5. *Reaffirms* that it is ultimately for the people of the United States Virgin Islands themselves to determine their future political status in accordance with the relevant provisions of the Charter of the United Nations and the Declaration, and, in that connection, reaffirms the importance of fostering an awareness among the people of the Territory of the possibilities open to them in the exercise of their right to self-determination;

6. *Notes* that the Select Committee, established by the Legislature of the United States Virgin Islands in 1983 to ascertain the views of the people of the Territory on their future status and to make recommendations in that regard, conducted public hearings from March to August 1984 and submitted its report to the Sixteenth Legislature in January 1985;

7. *Also notes* that the Legislature endorsed the report, which included, *inter alia*, a recommendation that a referendum on the status issue should be held on 4 November 1986, in conjunction with the next general election, for people of the United States Virgin Islands

to choose between a variety of status options including independence, statehood, free association, incorporated territory, *status quo* or a compact of federal relations;

8. *Further notes* that the Legislature decided to appoint a new committee to continue the process of public hearings in order to ensure that the people of the United States Virgin Islands were fully aware of the implications of the various status options by the time of the referendum;

9. *Urges* the administering Power, in co-operation with the territorial Government, to strengthen the economy of the Territory by taking additional measures of diversification in all fields and developing an adequate infrastructure with a view to reducing the economic dependence of the Territory on the administering Power;

10. *Reaffirms* the responsibility of the administering Power under the Charter to promote the economic and social development of the United States Virgin Islands;

11. *Urges* the administering Power, in co-operation with the Government of the United States Virgin Islands, to safeguard the inalienable right of the people of the Territory to the enjoyment of their natural resources by taking effective measures to guarantee their right to own and dispose of those resources and to establish and maintain control of their future development;

12. *Urges* the administering Power to seek in the Caribbean Group for Co-operation in Economic Development a status for the territorial Government similar to that of other dependent Territories within the Group;

13. *Calls upon* the administering Power to facilitate further the participation of the United States Virgin Islands in various regional intergovernmental bodies and organizations, particularly in their central organs, and in other organizations of the United Nations system;

14. *Urges* the administering Power to continue to take all necessary measures to comply fully with the purposes and principles of the Charter, the Declaration and the relevant resolutions and decisions of the General Assembly relating to military activities and arrangements by colonial Powers in Territories under their administration;

15. *Considers* that the possibility of sending a further visiting mission to the United States Virgin Islands at an appropriate time should be kept under review;

16. *Requests* the Special Committee to continue the examination of this question at its next session, including the possible dispatch of a further visiting mission to the United States Virgin Islands at an appropriate time and in consultation with the administering Power, and to report thereon to the General Assembly at its forty-first session.

General Assembly resolution 40/49

| 2 December 1985 | Meeting 99 | Adopted without vote |

Approved by Fourth Committee (A/40/906) without objection, 8 November (meeting 20); draft by Committee on colonial countries (A/40/23); agenda item 18.
Meeting numbers. GA 40th session: 4th Committee 11-20; plenary 99.

REFERENCES

(1)A/40/23. (2)YUN 1960, p. 49, GA res. 1514(XV), 14 Dec. 1960. (3)YUN 1984, p. 1075. (4)YUN 1980, p. 1082. (5)A/40/113. (6)A/40/121. (7)A/40/429. (8)YUN 1973, p. 699. (9)A/C.4/40/3 & Add.1.

Legal questions

International Court of Justice

In 1985, the International Court of Justice considered four contentious cases and a request for an advisory opinion.

The General Assembly and the Security Council held elections in December to fill a vacancy created by the resignation in August of a judge whose term would have expired in February 1988 (see APPENDIX III).

In addition, the Assembly took action concerning emoluments, pension scheme and conditions of service for the members of the Court (resolutions 40/257 A-C).

Topics related to this chapter. Americas: Nicaragua situation. United Nations officials: other United Nations officials.

Judicial work of the Court

In 1985, the Court or its Chamber—meeting at The Hague, Netherlands—delivered Judgments in two cases involving continental shelf delimitation (Tunisia/Libyan Arab Jamahiriya, Libyan Arab Jamahiriya/Malta), and continued consideration of those concerning responsibility for military and paramilitary activities in and against Nicaragua (Nicaragua v. United States) and a frontier dispute (Burkina Faso/Mali). In addition, it remained seized of a request for an advisory opinion concerning a judgement of the United Nations Administrative Tribunal.

The 1985 activities of the International Court of Justice (ICJ) were contained in two reports to the General Assembly, covering the periods 1 August 1984 to 31 July 1985[1] and 1 August 1985 to 31 July 1986.[2] By **decision 40/406** of 25 October 1985, the Assembly took note of the 1984/85 report.

Continental shelf delimitation between Tunisia and the Libyan Arab Jamahiriya

From 13 to 18 June 1985, the Court held six public sittings during which speeches were made on behalf of Tunisia and the Libyan Arab Jamahiriya, on Tunisia's 1984 Application[3] for revision and interpretation of the Court's Judgment of 24 February 1982[4] on the continental shelf delimitation between the parties.

On 10 December, the Court delivered at a public sitting a Judgment,[5] whose operative provisions read as follows:

> *The Court,*
> A. Unanimously,
> *Finds inadmissible* the request submitted by the Republic of Tunisia for revision, under Article 61 of the Statute of the Court, of the Judgment given by the Court on 24 February 1982;
> B. Unanimously,
> (1) *Finds admissible* the request submitted by the Republic of Tunisia for interpretation, under Article 60 of the Statute of the Court, of the Judgment of 24 February 1982 as far as it relates to the first sector of the delimitation contemplated by that Judgment;
> (2) *Declares*, by way of interpretation of the Judgment of 24 February 1982, that the meaning and scope of that part of the Judgment which relates to the first sector of the delimitation are to be understood according to paragraphs 32 to 39 of the present Judgment;
> (3) *Finds* that the submission of the Republic of Tunisia of 14 June 1985 relating to the first sector of the delimitation cannot be upheld;
> C. Unanimously,
> *Finds* that the request of the Republic of Tunisia for the correction of an error is without object and that the Court is therefore not called upon to give a decision thereon;
> D. Unanimously,
> (1) *Finds admissible* the request submitted by the Republic of Tunisia for interpretation, under Article 60 of the Statute of the Court, of the Judgment of 24 February 1982 as far as it relates to the "most westerly point of the Gulf of Gabes";
> (2) *Declares*, by way of interpretation of the Judgment of 24 February 1982:
> (a) That the reference in paragraph 124 of that Judgment to "approximately 34° 10′ 30″ north" is a general indication of the latitude of the point which appeared to the Court to be the most westerly point of the shoreline (low-water mark) of the Gulf of Gabes, it being left to the experts of the Parties to determine the precise co-ordinates of that point; that the latitude of 34° 10′ 30″ was therefore not intended to be itself binding on the Parties but was employed for the pur-

pose of clarifying what was decided with binding force in paragraph 133 C (3) of that Judgment;

(b) That the reference in paragraph 133 C (2) of that Judgment to "the most westerly point of the Tunisian coastline between Ras Kaboudia and Ras Ajdir, that is to say, the most westerly point on the shoreline (low-water mark) of the Gulf of Gabes", and the similar reference in paragraph 133 C (3) are to be understood as meaning the point on that shoreline which is furthest to the west on the low-water mark; and

(c) That it will be for the experts of the Parties, making use of all available cartographic documents and, if necessary, carrying out an *ad hoc* survey *in loco*, to determine the precise co-ordinates of that point, whether or not it lies within a channel or the mouth of a wadi, and regardless of whether or not such point might be regarded by the experts as marking a change in direction of the coastline;

(3) *Finds* that the submission of the Republic of Tunisia, "that the most westerly point on the Gulf of Gabes lies on latitude 34° 05′ 20″ N (Carthage)", cannot be upheld;

E.   Unanimously,

Finds that, with respect to the submission of the Republic of Tunisia of 14 June 1985, there is at the present time no cause for the Court to order an expert survey for the purpose of ascertaining the precise co-ordinates of the most westerly point of the Gulf of Gabes.

Separate opinions were appended to the Judgment by Judges Ruda, Oda and Schwebel, and by Judge *ad hoc* Bastid.

Continental shelf delimitation between the Libyan Arab Jamahiriya and Malta

In July 1982, the Libyan Arab Jamahiriya and Malta had instituted proceedings by joint notification to the Court of a Special Agreement in force since March 1982.[6] The Agreement requested the Court to indicate the principles and rules applicable to delimitation of the continental shelf between the parties and the practical method for their application.

The Court considered various aspects of the matter in 1983[7] and 1984,[3] and held public sittings between 4 and 24 February 1985. On 3 June, it delivered at a public sitting a Judgment,[8] whose operative part read as follows:

The Court,

By fourteen votes to three,

Finds that, with reference to the areas of continental shelf between the coasts of the Parties within the limits defined in the present Judgment, namely the meridian 13° 50′ E and the meridian 15° 10′ E:

A.   The principles and rules of international law applicable for the delimitation, to be effected by agreement in implementation of the present Judgment, of the areas of continental shelf appertaining to the Socialist People's Libyan Arab Jamahiriya and to the Republic of Malta respectively are as follows:

(1)   The delimitation is to be effected in accordance with equitable principles and taking account of all relevant circumstances, so as to arrive at an equitable result;

(2)   The area of continental shelf to be found to appertain to either Party not extending more than 200 miles from the coast of the Party concerned, no criterion for delimitation of shelf areas can be derived from the principle of natural prolongation in the physical sense.

B.   The circumstances and factors to be taken into account in achieving an equitable delimitation in the present case are the following:

(1)   The general configuration of the coasts of the Parties, their oppositeness, and their relationship to each other within the general geographical context;

(2)   The disparity in the lengths of the relevant coasts of the Parties and the distance between them;

(3)   The need to avoid in the delimitation any excessive disproportion between the extent of the continental shelf areas appertaining to the coastal State and the length of the relevant part of its coast, measured in the general direction of the coastlines.

C.   In consequence, an equitable result may be arrived at by drawing, as a first stage in the process, a median line every point of which is equidistant from the low-water mark of the relevant coast of Malta (excluding the islet of Filfla) and the low-water mark of the relevant coast of Libya, that initial line being then subject to adjustment in the light of the abovementioned circumstances and factors.

D.   The adjustment of the median line referred to in subparagraph C above is to be effected by transposing that line northwards through eighteen minutes of latitude (so that it intersects the meridian 15° 10′ E at approximately latitude 34° 30′ N) such transposed line then constituting the delimitation line between the areas of continental shelf appertaining to the Socialist People's Libyan Arab Jamahiriya and to the Republic of Malta respectively.

In favour: President Elias; Vice-President Sette Câmara; Judges Lachs, Morozov, Nagendra Singh, Ruda, Ago, El-Khani, Sir Robert Jennings, de Lacharrière, Mbaye, Bedjaoui; Judges *ad hoc* Valticos, Jiménez de Aréchaga.

Against: Judges Mosler, Oda and Schwebel.

Judge El-Khani appended a declaration to the Judgment. Vice-President Sette Câmara appended a separate opinion; Judges Ruda and Bedjaoui and Judge *ad hoc* Jiménez de Aréchaga appended a joint separate opinion; Judge Mbaye and Judge *ad hoc* Valticos each appended separate opinions. Judges Mosler, Oda and Schwebel appended dissenting opinions.

Military and paramilitary activities in and against Nicaragua

On 18 January 1985, the Agent of the United States informed the Court that, notwithstanding the Judgment of 26 November 1984,[9] the United States considered the Court to be without jurisdiction to entertain the dispute concerning responsibility for military and paramilitary activities in and against Nicaragua, that the Nicaraguan Application of 9 April 1984[10] instituting proceedings against it was inadmissible and that accordingly it intended not to participate in any further proceedings in connection with the case. On 22 January, the Agent of Nicaragua informed the Court's President that his Government maintained its Application and availed itself of the rights provided for in Article 53 of the Statute of the Court whenever one of the parties did not appear before the Court or failed to defend its case (see APPENDIX II).

By an Order of 22 January 1985,[11] the President fixed time-limits for the filing of pleadings on the merits. Nicaragua filed its Memorial (written pleading) within the prescribed time-limit (30 April); the United States did not file a Counter-Memorial within the time-limit (31 May), nor request extension of such time-limit.

From 12 to 20 September, the Court held nine public sittings during which arguments were presented on behalf of Nicaragua, and five witnesses called by that country gave evidence; the United States was not represented.

Frontier dispute
between Burkina Faso and Mali

On 14 March 1985, Burkina Faso and Mali—which had referred to the Court in 1983[7] their dispute over the delimitation of part of their land frontier—asked the Court to form a chamber of five members, of whom two would be judges *ad hoc* chosen by themselves in accordance with Article 31 of the Statute. By an Order of 3 April,[12] the Court constituted a five-member Chamber composed of Judges Lachs, Ruda and Bedjaoui and Judges *ad hoc* François Luchaire, appointed by Burkina Faso, and Georges Michel Abi-Saab, appointed by Mali.

On 29 April, the Chamber held its first public sitting, and the Court President, by an Order of 12 April,[13] fixed 3 October as the time-limit for the filing of Memorials by both parties. Each party having filed its Memorial within the time-limit, the Chamber President, by an Order of 3 October,[14] fixed 2 April 1986 as the time-limit for the filing of Counter-Memorials.

At the end of 1985, armed incidents were reported in the frontier regions of Burkina Faso and Mali (see p. 198).

Review of a judgement by
the UN Administrative Tribunal

In 1985, the Court remained seized of a request for an advisory opinion, received in 1984[9] from the General Assembly's Committee on Applications for Review of Administrative Tribunal Judgements, on Vladimir Victorovich Yakimetz v. Secretary-General, involving the staff member's request for further employment after the expiry of his contract with the United Nations.

In accordance with the time-limit, extended to 28 February 1985,[15] written statements were submitted by the Governments of Canada, Italy, the USSR and the United States, and by the Secretary-General, who also transmitted a statement on behalf of Mr. Yakimetz.

The Court President fixed 31 May as the time-limit within which States and the Organization having filed statements might submit written comments on the statements presented by others. Following a request by the applicant, to which the Secretary-General saw no objection, and by a decision of the President, the time-limit was extended to 1 July. Written comments were submitted by the United States and by the Secretary-General, who also transmitted Mr. Yakimetz's comments.

Organizational questions

Conditions of service

The Secretary-General submitted to the General Assembly in October 1985 a report on conditions of service and compensation for members of ICJ,[16] incorporating proposals he had made in 1983,[17] but on which Assembly action had been deferred.[18] Also incorporated in the report were the 1984 comments by the Advisory Committee on Administrative and Budgetary Questions (ACABQ).[19]

The Secretary-General's 1985 report consisted of two parts. In part I, he recommended increasing the annual remuneration of ICJ members (from the current level of $82,000 to $85,000), special allowances of the President and the Vice-President when acting as President (from $12,200 to $15,000 per year for the former, and from $76 to $94 daily, or a maximum of $9,400 annually, for the latter), pensions (17.1 per cent increase) and compensation of judges *ad hoc* (for each day of exercising the functions, equivalent of 1/365th of the annual remuneration received by a Court member).

Part II concerned conditions of service for those judges who maintained a *bona fide* primary residence at The Hague during their service. As regards children's education allowances, the Secretary-General suggested $4,500 maximum per child per school year for the actual cost of education, in addition to one related travel per year to The Hague if attending school outside the Netherlands. As to expenses incurred in relocating outside the Netherlands after completion of service, he suggested a lump-sum payment equivalent to 18 weeks of annual net base salary, when retiring after a minimum of five consecutive years of service, or the equivalent of 24 weeks, after nine years. He proposed that, in the event of death while in office, survivors should receive a lump-sum payment equivalent to one month of base salary per year of service, subject to a minimum of three months and a maximum of nine months. The Secretary-General estimated the financial implications of his proposals and related ACABQ recommendations at $375,000 for 1986-1987.

In its November 1985 report,[20] ACABQ stated that it had no objection to the Secretary-General's recommendations as regards annual remuneration, and concurred with those relating to increased special allowances for the President of the Court, compensations to judges *ad hoc*, and conditions of service of ICJ members, provided that the effective date of implementing the proposals was no earlier than 1 January 1986.

GENERAL ASSEMBLY ACTION

On 18 December 1985, the General Assembly, on the recommendation of the Fifth (Administrative and Budgetary) Committee, adopted **resolutions 40/257 A-C** by recorded vote.

A
Emoluments

The General Assembly,

Recalling its resolutions 31/204 of 22 December 1976 and 35/220 A of 17 December 1980, on the emoluments of the members of the International Court of Justice,

Having considered the report of the Secretary-General and the related report of the Advisory Committee on Administrative and Budgetary Questions,

1. *Decides* that, with effect from 1 January 1986, the annual salary of the members of the International Court of Justice shall be $82,000 with an interim cost-of-living supplement of $3,000;

2. *Decides* to continue the system of interim cost-of-living supplements introduced pursuant to General Assembly resolution 31/204, paragraph 2, subject to rebasing and modifying the index used for this purpose, in accordance with the suggestion made by the Secretary-General in paragraph 22 of his report;

3. *Decides* that, with effect from 1 January 1986, the *ad hoc* judges referred to in Article 31 of the Statute of the International Court of Justice shall receive for each day they exercise their functions, one three-hundred-and-sixty-fifth of the sum of the annual base salary and interim cost-of-living supplement payable at the time to a member of the Court;

4. *Decides further* that, with effect from 1 January 1986, the President's special allowance shall be $15,000 per year and that the special daily allowance paid to the Vice-President when acting as President shall be $94 per day, up to a maximum of $9,400 per year, and takes note of the statement contained in paragraph 4 of the report of the Advisory Committee on Administrative and Budgetary Questions that such a maximum shall be removed only in extraordinary circumstances.

B
Pension scheme

The General Assembly,

Recalling its resolutions 1562(XV) of 18 December 1960, 1925(XVIII) of 11 December 1963, 2367(XXII) of 19 December 1967, 2890 A (XXVI) of 22 December

1971, 3193 A (XXVIII) of 18 December 1973, 3537 A (XXX) of 17 December 1975 and 38/239 of 20 December 1983, on the pension scheme for the members of the International Court of Justice,

Having considered the report of the Secretary-General and the related report of the Advisory Committee on Administrative and Budgetary Questions,

Decides that, with effect from 1 January 1986, and notwithstanding any provision to the contrary contained in the Pension Scheme Regulations for members of the International Court of Justice, the annual value of all pensions in course of payment as at 31 December 1985, including the pensions of any members of the Court who retire on or before that date, shall be increased by 17.1 per cent.

C
Conditions of service

The General Assembly,

Recalling its resolutions 37/237, section XIV, of 21 December 1982, 38/234, section XVII, of 20 December 1983 and 39/236, section V, of 18 December 1984, on conditions of service and compensation for officials other than Secretariat officials,

Having considered the report of the Secretary-General and the related report of the Advisory Committee on Administrative and Budgetary Questions,

1. *Decides* that, with effect from 1 January 1986, the President and members of the Court who have taken up primary residence in The Hague shall be reimbursed, up to a ceiling of $4,500, for the actual cost of educating their children in respect of each child each year up to the award of the first recognized degree and that provision shall be made for one related travel per year in respect of each child from the place of scholastic attendance, when outside the Netherlands, to The Hague;

2. *Decides* that, with effect from 1 January 1986, those members of the Court who have taken up and maintained a *bona fide* primary residence at The Hague for at least five continuous years during service with the Court shall be eligible to receive a lump sum equivalent to eighteen weeks of annual net base salary upon completion of their appointment and resettlement outside the Netherlands and that those members of the Court who have taken up and maintained a *bona fide* primary residence at The Hague for nine continuous years or more during service with the Court shall receive the equivalent of twenty-four weeks of annual net base salary upon completion of service and relocation outside the Netherlands;

3. *Decides* that, with effect from 1 January 1986, in the event of the death of a member of the Court during his service, compensation shall be provided to the survivors in the form of a lump-sum payment equivalent to one month of base salary per year of service, subject to a minimum of three months and a maximum of nine months.

General Assembly resolutions 40/257 A to C

18 December 1985　　　Meeting 122　　　121-11-15 (recorded vote)

Approved by Fifth Committee (A/40/1069) by recorded vote (60-14-19), 14 December (meeting 65); 5-nation draft (A/C.5/40/L.9); agenda item 116.
Sponsors. Algeria, China, India, Nigeria, Trinidad and Tobago.
Financial implications. ACABQ, A/40/7/Add.3,10; S-G, A/C.5/40/3 & Add.1.

Recorded vote in Assembly as follows:

In favour: Afghanistan, Algeria, Angola, Antigua and Barbuda, Argentina, Bahamas, Bahrain, Bangladesh, Barbados, Belize, Benin, Bhutan, Bolivia,

Botswana, Brazil, Brunei Darussalam, Burkina Faso, Burma, Burundi, Cameroon, Cape Verde, Central African Republic, Chad, Chile, China, Colombia, Congo, Costa Rica, Cuba, Cyprus, Democratic Kampuchea, Democratic Yemen, Denmark, Djibouti, Dominican Republic, Ecuador, Egypt, El Salvador, Equatorial Guinea, Ethiopia, Finland, Gabon, Gambia, Ghana, Greece, Guatemala, Guinea, Guinea-Bissau, Guyana, Haiti, Honduras, Iceland, India, Indonesia, Iran, Iraq, Ireland, Israel, Ivory Coast, Jamaica, Jordan, Kenya, Kuwait, Lebanon, Lesotho, Liberia, Libyan Arab Jamahiriya, Madagascar, Malawi, Malaysia, Maldives, Mali, Malta, Mauritania, Mauritius, Mexico, Morocco, Mozambique, Nepal, Nicaragua, Niger, Nigeria, Norway, Oman, Pakistan, Panama, Papua New Guinea, Paraguay, Peru, Philippines, Poland, Qatar, Rwanda, Saint Vincent and the Grenadines, Sao Tome and Principe, Saudi Arabia, Senegal, Sierra Leone, Singapore, Somalia, Sri Lanka, Sudan, Suriname, Swaziland, Sweden, Syrian Arab Republic, Thailand, Togo, Trinidad and Tobago, Tunisia, Turkey, Uganda, United Arab Emirates, United Republic of Tanzania, Uruguay, Vanuatu, Venezuela, Yemen, Zaire, Zambia, Zimbabwe.

Against: Australia, Austria, Belgium, Canada, France, Germany, Federal Republic of, Japan, Luxembourg, Portugal, United Kingdom, United States.

Abstaining: Bulgaria, Byelorussian SSR, Czechoslovakia, Fiji, German Democratic Republic, Hungary, Italy, Netherlands, New Zealand, Romania, Solomon Islands, Spain, Ukrainian SSR, USSR, Yugoslavia.

The recorded vote in the Fifth Committee was requested by the United States, which explained its vote by stating that the information before the Committee did not justify the increase. Belgium agreed, adding that, although ICJ judges' salary had remained unchanged in dollar terms since January 1981, it had risen in Netherlands guilders by 41 per cent, while the cost of living at The Hague had risen by some 15.2 per cent. Australia could not support the draft in the current climate of budgetary restraint; similarly, Austria and the Federal Republic of Germany considered a monthly salary of $7,000 to be sufficient. Sharing those views, the United Kingdom

urged careful management of the limited resources of the United Nations. France added that it could support an increase in the Court's operating cost, but not the emoluments of the judges. New Zealand also pointed to the level of the proposed emoluments as its reason for abstaining in the vote.

REFERENCES

[1]A/40/4. [2]A/41/4. [3]YUN 1984, p. 1083. [4]YUN 1982, p. 1365. [5]*Application for Revision and Interpretation of the Judgment of 24 February 1982 in the Case concerning the Continental Shelf (Tunisia/Libyan Arab Jamahiriya), Judgment of 10 December 1985*, I.C.J. Sales No. 517. [6]YUN 1982, p. 1366. [7]YUN 1983, p. 1103. [8]*Case concerning the Continental Shelf (Libyan Arab Jamahiriya/Malta), Judgment of 3 June 1985*, I.C.J. Sales No. 513. [9]YUN 1984, p. 1085. [10]*Ibid.*, p. 1084. [11]*Case concerning Military and Paramilitary Activities in and against Nicaragua (Nicaragua v. United States of America), Order of 22 January 1985*, I.C.J. Sales No. 508. [12]*Case concerning the Frontier Dispute (Burkina Faso/Mali), Order of 3 April 1985*, I.C.J. Sales No. 511. [13]*Ibid., Order of 12 April 1985*, I.C.J. Sales No. 512. [14]*Ibid., Order of 3 October 1985*, I.C.J. Sales No. 516. [15]YUN 1984, p. 1086. [16]A/C.5/40/32. [17]YUN 1983, p. 1104. [18]YUN 1984, p. 1170, GA res. 39/236, sect. V, 18 Dec. 1984. [19]*Ibid.*, p. 1170. [20]A/40/7/Add.10.

OTHER PUBLICATIONS

International Court of Justice: Reports of Judgments, Advisory Opinions and Orders, Index 1985, I.C.J. Sales No. 519. *International Court of Justice Yearbook 1984-1985*, No. 39, I.C.J. Sales No. 515; *1985-1986*, No. 40, I.C.J. Sales No. 522. *Bibliography of the International Court of Justice*, No. 39, *1985*, I.C.J. Sales No. 528.

Chapter II

Legal aspects of international political relations

More international law affecting virtually all areas of human activity had been codified in the past 40 years than in all the previous ones of recorded history; much of it had been done under the auspices of the General Assembly, the Secretary-General stated in 1985 (see p. 4).

In keeping with that process aimed at promoting friendly relations among States, the Assembly decided in 1985 that work should continue on the legal codification of: non-use of force in international relations (resolution 40/70), offences against the peace and security of mankind (40/69), and an international convention against mercenary activities (40/74). In addition, it requested the Secretary-General to continue preparing a handbook on settling disputes between States peacefully (40/68), agreed to continue identifying and clarifying the elements of good-neighbourliness (decision 40/419), and recommended that work continue on draft articles on the non-navigational uses of international watercourses.

Deep concern over the world-wide escalation of terrorist acts was expressed by both the Security Council and the General Assembly. The Council condemned specific instances, including hijacking and hostage-taking (resolution 579(1985)), and was joined by the Assembly (40/61) in appealing to States that had not done so to become parties to existing international conventions on various aspects of the problem.

Topic related to this chapter. International peace and security.

Peaceful settlement of disputes between States

In December 1985, the General Assembly again requested the Special Committee on the Charter of the United Nations and on the Strengthening of the Role of the Organization to continue work on the peaceful settlement of disputes between States, and asked the Secretary-General to continue preparing a draft handbook on the topic for the Committee's consideration in 1986.

Special Committee consideration. The Special Committee, at its March 1985 session,[1] continued work on the peaceful settlement of disputes, as called for by the Assembly in 1984,[2] in addition to considering two other main items— proposals on rationalizing the existing procedures

of the United Nations (see p. 1177) and ways to maintain international peace and security.

An open-ended Working Group of the Committee held nine meetings on the question between 7 and 12 March, at seven of which it examined, paragraph by paragraph, a proposal—submitted in 1983[3] by Nigeria, the Philippines and Romania, and considered in 1984[4]—to create a United Nations permanent commission on good offices, mediation and conciliation for settling disputes and preventing conflicts among States. At two meetings (8 and 11 March), the Working Group examined a progress report by the Secretary-General[5] on a draft handbook on the peaceful settlement of disputes between States, which was being prepared at the Assembly's 1984 request.[2]

On the recommendation of the Sixth (Legal) Committee, the General Assembly, on 11 December, adopted **resolution 40/68** without vote.

Peaceful settlement of disputes between States
The General Assembly,

Having examined the item entitled "Peaceful settlement of disputes between States",

Recalling its resolution 37/10 of 15 November 1982, by which it approved the Manila Declaration on the Peaceful Settlement of International Disputes, annexed thereto,

Recalling also its resolutions 38/131 of 19 December 1983 and 39/79 of 13 December 1984,

Deeply concerned at the continuation of conflict situations and the emergence of new sources of disputes and tension in international life, and especially at the growing tendency to resort to force or the threat of force and to intervention in internal affairs, and at the escalation of the arms race, which gravely endanger the independence and security of States as well as international peace and security,

Taking into account the need to exert the utmost effort in order to settle any situations and disputes between States exclusively by peaceful means and to avoid any military actions and hostilities against other States, which can only make more difficult the solution of existing problems,

Considering that the question of the peaceful settlement of disputes should represent one of the central concerns for States and for the United Nations, and that efforts for strengthening the process of peaceful settlement of disputes should be continued,

Taking note of the working papers on the establishment of a commission on good offices, mediation and conciliation for the settlement of disputes and the prevention of conflicts among States, submitted by Nigeria, the Philippines and Romania,

Taking into account the elaboration by the Special Committee on the Charter of the United Nations and on the Strengthening of the Role of the Organization of the outline for the handbook on the peaceful settlement of disputes between States and the conclusions thereon,

1. *Again urges* all States to observe and promote in good faith the provisions of the Manila Declaration on the Peaceful Settlement of International Disputes in the settlement of their international disputes;

2. *Stresses* the need to continue efforts to strengthen the process of the peaceful settlement of disputes through progressive development and codification of international law and through enhancing the effectiveness of the United Nations in this field;

3. *Requests* the Special Committee on the Charter of the United Nations and on the Strengthening of the Role of the Organization, during its session in 1986, to continue its work on the question of the peaceful settlement of disputes between States and, in this context:

(a) To continue the consideration of the proposal contained in working papers submitted by Nigeria, the Philippines and Romania;

(b) To examine the report of the Secretary-General on the progress of work on the draft handbook on the peaceful settlement of disputes between States;

4. *Requests* the Secretary-General to continue the preparation of a draft handbook on the peaceful settlement of disputes between States, on the basis of the outline elaborated by the Special Committee and in the light of the views expressed in the course of the discussions in the Sixth Committee and in the Special Committee, and to report to the Special Committee at its session in 1986 on the progress of work, before submitting to it the draft handbook in its final form, with a view to its approval at a later stage;

5. *Decides* to include in the provisional agenda of its forty-first session the item entitled "Peaceful settlement of disputes between States".

General Assembly resolution 40/68

11 December 1985   Meeting 112   Adopted without vote

Approved by Sixth Committee (A/40/999) without vote, 2 December (meeting 50); 27-nation draft (A/C.6/40/L.21); agenda item 132.
Sponsors: Bolivia, Chile, Cyprus, Dominican Republic, Egypt, Ethiopia, Guinea, Guyana, Indonesia, Madagascar, Mali, Mexico, Morocco, Nigeria, Panama, Philippines, Romania, Rwanda, Senegal, Sudan, Suriname, Togo, Uganda, Uruguay, Yugoslavia, Zaire, Zambia.
Meeting numbers. GA 40th session: 6th Committee 37-43, 48, 50; plenary 112.

In related action, the Assembly appealed to States in conflict to settle their disputes by negotiations and other peaceful means (**resolution 40/9**), and urged them to seek such settlement through more effective use of means provided for in the United Nations Charter (**40/158**).

Good-neighbourliness between States

In response to a 1984 General Assembly request,[6] the Sixth Committee set up on 25 September 1985 an open-ended sub-committee to identify and clarify the elements of good-neighbourliness.

The Sub-Committee on Good-Neighbourliness,[7] under the chairmanship of a Sixth Committee Vice-Chairman, Roberto Herrera Cáceres (Honduras), held four meetings—on 1, 7, 15 and 19 November—focusing on how to proceed with its work.

Documents before the Sub-Committee included two by Romania—a 1983 working paper suggesting an outline for an international document,[8] and a 1985 proposed structure for discussing the topic. Also before it were a number of reports submitted by the Secretary-General in previous years and in 1985, containing the views and suggestions of Member States on the content of good-neighbourliness and ways to strengthen it; the 1985 report[9] contained the replies of 10 States as well as those of seven intergovernmental organizations related to the United Nations and three United Nations bodies in response to the Assembly's 1984 invitation.[6]

Discussions arose as to whether the Sub-Committee should identify the elements of good-neighbourliness first or focus on the general principles of international law underlying that concept, and whether or not the concept had legal contents. It commenced consideration of areas of co-operation, methods and means, rules of international law of particular relevance, and observance of the principles of international law. In the absence of conclusions, the Chairman noted that the discussion in 1985 had had only a searching and exploratory character.

GENERAL ASSEMBLY ACTION

In December, the General Assembly, on the recommendation of the Sixth Committee, adopted **decision 40/419** without vote.

Development and strengthening of good-neighbourliness between States

At its 112th plenary meeting, on 11 December 1985, the General Assembly, on the recommendation of the Sixth Committee, having considered the item entitled "Development and strengthening of good-neighbourliness between States", decided:

(a) To take note of the report of the Sub-Committee on Good-Neighbourliness, set up by the Sixth Committee during the fortieth session;

(b) To continue and complete, on the basis of its resolution 39/78 of 13 December 1984, the task of identifying and clarifying the elements of good-neighbourliness within the framework of a sub-committee of the Sixth Committee, at the forty-first session;

(c) To include in the provisional agenda of its forty-first session the item entitled "Development and strengthening of good-neighbourliness between States".

General Assembly decision 40/419

Adopted without vote

Approved by Sixth Committee (A/40/1011) without vote, 3 December (meeting 51); draft by Romania (A/C.6/40/L.29); agenda item 131.
Meeting numbers. GA 40th session: 6th Committee 3, 21, 49, 51; plenary 112.

In explanation of position, Belgium—on behalf of the 10 States members of the European Community (EC) and of Spain and Portugal—said that, while they had agreed to the text's adoption without vote in a spirit of compromise, some would have liked a separate vote on subparagraph *(b)*.

Non-use of force in international relations

In December 1985, the General Assembly again decided that the Special Committee on Enhancing the Effectiveness of the Principle of Non-Use of Force in International Relations should continue working towards drafting a world treaty on that principle.

Special Committee consideration. The Special Committee, established in 1977[10] to consider proposals with a view to drafting a world treaty on the non-use of force in international relations, met in New York from 28 January to 22 February 1985.[11]

As in previous years, the 35-member Committee had before it a draft world treaty on the non-use of force, submitted in 1976 by the USSR;[12] a 1979 working paper by Belgium, France, the Federal Republic of Germany, Italy and the United Kingdom;[13] a 1981 revised working paper from 10 non-aligned countries (Benin, Cyprus, Egypt, India, Iraq, Morocco, Nepal, Nicaragua, Senegal, Uganda);[14] and the view of the German Democratic Republic, submitted in response to a 1984 Assembly invitation[15] for comments on the drafting of a world treaty, which was subsequently forwarded to the Assembly in August.[16] Also before the Committee was an informal paper by its 1982 Chairman, grouping together the suggestions made at that time.[17]

Different positions again persisted with regard to the desirability of a world treaty; while the States in support of the proposal pointed out that concepts such as "force", "deterrence" and "superiority" should be replaced by ideas of non-use of force, confidence, equality and mutual understanding, opponents of the proposal held that there existed general instruments including the United Nations Charter which left no doubts as to the scope of the principle of non-use of force.

An open-ended Working Group, re-established by the Committee in 1985, held 17 meetings between 5 and 22 February, focusing on an examination of headings contained in the 1982 informal paper—namely, peaceful settlement of disputes; role of the United Nations; manifestations, scope and dimensions of the threat or use of force; legitimate use of force; consequences of the use or threat of force; and disarmament and confidence-building measures. The Working Group's Chairman summarized the work of the Group in 1985 as having succeeded in isolating some concepts on which there was promise of agreement, and its discussion as having been more organized and purposeful than in previous years, thus rising above the inhibiting pressure of lack of general agreement on the mandate of the Special Committee.

On 22 February, the Committee approved the Group's report as well as its own. Since the Committee had not completed its work, it generally recognized the desirability of further considering the question.

Communications. Under the agenda item, Iran, by a letter of 30 May to the Secretary-General,[18] denied its involvement, alleged by the United States, in the kidnapping of United States nationals in Lebanon. Cuba transmitted to the Secretary-General on 1 November[19] its note of protest of the previous day to the United States over what Cuba said was a violation of its airspace by an aircraft belonging to the United States Air Force.

GENERAL ASSEMBLY ACTION

On 11 December, the General Assembly, on the recommendation of the Sixth Committee, adopted **resolution 40/70** by recorded vote.

Report of the Special Committee on Enhancing the Effectiveness of the Principle of Non-Use of Force in International Relations

The General Assembly,

Recalling its resolution 31/9 of 8 November 1976, in which it invited Member States to examine further the draft World Treaty on the Non-Use of Force in International Relations as well as other proposals made during the consideration of the item,

Recalling also its resolution 32/150 of 19 December 1977, by which it established the Special Committee on Enhancing the Effectiveness of the Principle of Non-Use of Force in International Relations,

Recalling, in particular, its resolutions 33/96 of 16 December 1978, 34/13 of 9 November 1979, 35/50 of 4 December 1980, 36/31 of 13 November 1981, 37/105 of 16 December 1982, 38/133 of 19 December 1983 and 39/81 of 13 December 1984, in which it decided that the Special Committee should continue its work,

Taking note of the statements made by the Chairmen of the Special Committee at its sessions in 1983, 1984, and 1985, based on the informal working paper presented by the Chairman of the Special Committee at its session in 1982,

Having considered the report of the Special Committee on the work of the session it held in 1985,

Taking into account that the Special Committee has not completed the mandate entrusted to it,

Reaffirming the need for effectiveness in the universal application of the principle of non-use of force in international relations and for assistance by the United Nations in this endeavour,

Taking into account the suggestions of States made during the consideration of the report of the Special Committee on the preparation at the present stage of a declaration on the non-use of force in international relations,

1. *Takes note* of the report of the Special Committee on Enhancing the Effectiveness of the Principle of Non-Use of Force in International Relations;

2. *Decides* that the Special Committee shall continue its work with the goal of drafting a world treaty on the non-use of force in international relations and, at the earliest possible date, as an intermediate stage, a declaration on the non-use of force in international relations, as well as the peaceful settlement of disputes or such other recommendations as the Committee deems appropriate;

3. *Invites* the Special Committee, in drafting the declaration, to take into consideration the results of work done in the preparation of the working paper containing the main elements of the principle of non-use of force in international relations, as well as the suggestions submitted to it and the efforts undertaken at its previous sessions;

4. *Invites* Governments to communicate their comments or suggestions on the question considered by the Special Committee;

5. *Requests* the Special Committee to be mindful of the importance of reaching general agreement whenever it has significance for the outcome of its work;

6. *Decides* that the Special Committee shall accept the participation of observers of Member States, including participation in the meetings of its working group;

7. *Requests* the Special Committee to concentrate its work in the framework of its working group;

8. *Requests* the Secretary-General to provide the Special Committee with the necessary facilities and services;

9. *Invites* the Special Committee to submit a report on its work to the General Assembly at its forty-first session, containing, *inter alia*, the concrete results achieved through the discussion of the elements referred to in paragraph 3 above;

10. *Decides* to include in the provisional agenda of its forty-first session the item entitled "Report of the Special Committee on Enhancing the Effectiveness of the Principle of Non-Use of Force in International Relations".

General Assembly resolution 40/70

11 December 1985   Meeting 112   119-14-12 (recorded vote)

Approved by Sixth Committee (A/40/1001) by recorded vote (90-15-11), 2 December (meeting 50); 34-nation draft (A/C.6/40/L.14); agenda item 134.

Sponsors: Afghanistan, Angola, Benin, Bulgaria, Byelorussian SSR, Cameroon, Cuba, Cyprus, Czechoslovakia, Democratic Yemen, Ecuador, Egypt, Ethiopia, German Democratic Republic, Hungary, India, Iraq, Lao People's Democratic Republic, Lesotho, Libyan Arab Jamahiriya, Madagascar, Mali, Mongolia, Mozambique, Nicaragua, Poland, Romania, Syrian Arab Republic, Uganda, Ukrainian SSR, USSR, Venezuela, Viet Nam, Yemen.

Financial implications. 5th Committee, A/40/1015; S-G, A/C.5/40/72, A/C.6/40/L.25.

Meeting numbers. GA 40th session: 5th Committee 56; 6th Committee 8-12, 44, 50; plenary 112.

Recorded vote in Assembly as follows:

In favour: Afghanistan, Algeria, Angola, Antigua and Barbuda, Argentina, Bahrain, Bangladesh, Barbados, Benin, Bhutan, Bolivia, Brunei Darussalam, Bulgaria, Burkina Faso, Burma, Burundi, Byelorussian SSR, Cameroon, Cape Verde, Central African Republic, Chad, China, Colombia, Comoros, Congo, Costa Rica, Cuba, Cyprus, Czechoslovakia, Democratic Kampuchea, Democratic Yemen, Djibouti, Dominican Republic, Ecuador, Egypt, El Salvador, Equatorial Guinea, Ethiopia, Fiji, Finland, Gabon, German Democratic Republic, Ghana, Greece, Grenada, Guatemala, Guinea, Guinea-Bissau, Guyana, Haiti, Honduras, Hungary, India, Indonesia, Iran, Iraq, Jamaica, Jordan, Kenya, Kuwait, Lao People's Democratic Republic, Lebanon, Lesotho, Liberia, Libyan Arab Jamahiriya, Madagascar, Malawi, Malaysia, Maldives, Mali, Malta, Mauritania, Mauritius, Mexico, Mongolia, Morocco, Mozambique, Nepal, Nicaragua, Niger, Nigeria, Oman, Pakistan, Panama, Papua New Guinea, Paraguay, Peru, Philippines, Poland,

Qatar, Romania, Rwanda, Saint Lucia, Sao Tome and Principe, Saudi Arabia, Senegal, Sierra Leone, Singapore, Somalia, Sri Lanka, Sudan, Suriname, Swaziland, Syrian Arab Republic, Thailand, Togo, Trinidad and Tobago, Tunisia, Ukrainian SSR, USSR, United Arab Emirates, United Republic of Tanzania, Uruguay, Venezuela, Viet Nam, Yemen, Yugoslavia, Zaire, Zambia.

Against: Belgium, Canada, Denmark, France, Iceland, Israel, Italy, Japan, Luxembourg, Netherlands, Norway, Portugal, United Kingdom, United States.

Abstaining: Australia, Austria, Brazil, Chile, Germany, Federal Republic of, Ireland, Ivory Coast, New Zealand, Samoa, Spain, Sweden, Turkey.

Explaining its vote, Spain accepted the idea of drafting a declaration, provided that it was not a step towards a world treaty. Brazil stressed that the Special Committee should identify elements that could enhance the effectiveness of the principle of the non-use of force; thought should be given later to the final form in which to present the result of its work. Iran supported the draft, notwithstanding what it called the opportunistic manœuvre by Iraq in sponsoring the text to achieve political objectives.

Draft Code of Offences against peace and security

In December 1985, the General Assembly requested the International Law Commission (ILC) to continue work on the draft Code of Offences against the Peace and Security of Mankind—a topic on which ILC had resumed work in 1982[20] pursuant to a 1981 Assembly invitation.[21] Prepared by ILC in 1954[22] in response to a 1947 Assembly request,[23] the draft Code defined offences which were crimes under international law and for which the responsible individual was to be punished.

ILC consideration. The Commission, at its 1985 session,[24] considered the third report submitted by its Special Rapporteur on the topic, Doudou Thiam (Senegal),[25] containing a draft outline of the future Code, whose scope of application was limited, for the time being, to acts committed by individuals.

The proposed outline, contained in paragraph 43 of the ILC report,[24] consisted of two parts: the first would deal with the scope of the draft articles, the definition of an offence against the peace and security of mankind, and the general principles governing the subject; the second would deal specifically with acts constituting such an offence, including a review of the traditional division of such offences into crimes against peace, war crimes and crimes against humanity. The Special Rapporteur also proposed a number of draft articles, some with alternative texts, on the scope of the articles (article 1), persons covered by the articles (article 2), definition of an offence against the peace and security of mankind (article 3), and acts constituting such an offence (article 4). The proposed article 4 covered acts such as aggression, threats of aggression, intervention, terrorist acts, violation by the State authorities of a treaty designed to ensure international peace and security, and colonial domination.

The Commission, having discussed the proposed draft articles and other related possible offences such as mercenarism and economic aggression, referred the first three articles and part of the fourth to its Drafting Committee; however, the Committee was not able to consider them in 1985 due to lack of time. The Commission decided to resume consideration of the remaining parts of article 4 in 1986 and took note of the Special Rapporteur's intention to devote his 1986 report to war crimes and crimes against humanity and to consider the question of general principles as soon as possible. These actions were contained in paragraphs 99-101 of the 1985 ILC report.[24]

GENERAL ASSEMBLY ACTION

The Secretary-General submitted to the General Assembly in September 1985 a report with later addenda,[26] containing comments received from 13 Member States in response to a 1984 Assembly invitation[27] for views on the 1984 conclusions of ILC.[28]

On 11 December, the Assembly, on the recommendation of the Sixth Committee, adopted **resolution 40/69** by recorded vote.

Draft Code of Offences against the Peace and Security of Mankind

The General Assembly,

Mindful of Article 13, paragraph 1 *a*, of the Charter of the United Nations, which provides that the General Assembly shall initiate studies and make recommendations for the purpose of encouraging the progressive development of international law and its codification,

Recalling its resolution 177(II) of 21 November 1947, by which it directed the International Law Commission to prepare a draft code of offences against the peace and security of mankind,

Having considered the draft Code of Offences against the Peace and Security of Mankind prepared by the International Law Commission and submitted to the General Assembly in 1954,

Recalling its belief that the elaboration of a code of offences against the peace and security of mankind could contribute to strengthening international peace and security and thus to promoting and implementing the purposes and principles set forth in the Charter of the United Nations,

Recalling also its resolution 36/106 of 10 December 1981, in which it invited the International Law Commission to resume its work with a view to elaborating the draft Code and to examine it with the required priority in order to review it, taking into account the results achieved by the process of the progressive development of international law,

Bearing in mind that the International Law Commission should fulfil its task on the basis of early elaboration of draft articles thereof,

Having considered chapter II of the report of the International Law Commission on the work of its thirty-seventh session, in particular paragraph 43 of the report, containing the outline of the future Code proposed by the Special Rapporteur, and paragraphs 99, 100 and 101 of the report containing the conclusions of the Commission,

Taking note of the report of the Secretary-General on the subject,

Taking into account the views expressed during the debate on this item at the current session,

Recognizing the importance and urgency of the subject,

1. *Invites* the International Law Commission to continue its work on the elaboration of the draft Code of Offences against the Peace and Security of Mankind by elaborating an introduction as well as a list of the offences, taking into account the progress made at its thirty-seventh session, as well as the views expressed during the fortieth session of the General Assembly;

2. *Requests* the Secretary-General to seek the views of Member States and intergovernmental organizations regarding the outline of the future Code proposed by the Special Rapporteur and contained in paragraph 43 of the report of the International Law Commission, and the conclusions contained in paragraphs 99, 100 and 101 of the said report;

3. *Further requests* the Secretary-General to include the views received from Member States and intergovernmental organizations in accordance with paragraph 2 above in a report to be submitted to the General Assembly at its forty-first session with a view to adopting, at the appropriate time, the necessary decision thereon;

4. *Decides* to include in the provisional agenda of its forty-first session the item entitled "Draft Code of Offences against the Peace and Security of Mankind", to be considered in conjunction with the examination of the report of the International Law Commission.

General Assembly resolution 40/69

11 December 1985   Meeting 112   127-6-9 (recorded vote)

Approved by Sixth Committee (A/40/1000) by recorded vote (98-6-8), 2 December (meeting 50); 28-nation draft (A/C.6/40/L.15); agenda item 133.

Sponsors: Algeria, Angola, Benin, Bolivia, Congo, Cuba, Cyprus, Egypt, Equatorial Guinea, Gabon, German Democratic Republic, Kenya, Mali, Mongolia, Morocco, Philippines, Poland, Qatar, Rwanda, Senegal, Sierra Leone, Sudan, Thailand, Tunisia, Uganda, Viet Nam, Zaire, Zambia.

Meeting numbers. GA 40th session: 6th Committee 23-36, 44, 50; plenary 112.

Recorded vote in Assembly as follows:

In favour: Afghanistan, Algeria, Angola, Antigua and Barbuda, Argentina, Australia, Austria, Bahamas, Bahrain, Bangladesh, Benin, Bhutan, Bolivia, Brazil, Brunei Darussalam, Bulgaria, Burkina Faso, Burundi, Byelorussian SSR, Cameroon, Cape Verde, Central African Republic, Chad, China, Colombia, Comoros, Congo, Costa Rica, Cuba, Cyprus, Czechoslovakia, Democratic Kampuchea, Denmark, Djibouti, Dominican Republic, Ecuador, Egypt, El Salvador, Equatorial Guinea, Ethiopia, Fiji, Finland, Gabon, German Democratic Republic, Ghana, Greece, Guatemala, Guinea, Guinea-Bissau, Guyana, Haiti, Honduras, Hungary, Iceland, India, Indonesia, Iran, Iraq, Ireland, Ivory Coast, Jamaica, Jordan, Kenya, Kuwait, Lao People's Democratic Republic, Lebanon, Lesotho, Liberia, Libyan Arab Jamahiriya, Madagascar, Malawi, Malaysia, Maldives, Mali, Malta, Mauritania, Mauritius, Mexico, Mongolia, Morocco, Mozambique, Nepal, New Zealand, Nicaragua, Niger, Nigeria, Norway, Oman, Pakistan, Panama, Papua New Guinea, Paraguay, Peru, Philippines, Poland, Qatar, Romania, Rwanda, Saint Lucia, Samoa, Sao Tome and Principe, Saudi Arabia, Senegal, Sierra Leone, Singapore, Somalia, Sri Lanka, Sudan, Suriname, Swaziland, Sweden, Syrian Arab Republic, Thailand, Togo, Trinidad and Tobago, Tunisia, Ukrainian SSR, USSR, United Arab Emirates, United Republic of Tanzania, Uruguay, Venezuela, Viet Nam, Yemen, Yugoslavia, Zaire, Zambia.

Against: Chile, France, Germany, Federal Republic of, Israel, United Kingdom, United States.

Abstaining: Belgium, Canada, Italy, Japan, Luxembourg, Netherlands, Portugal, Spain, Turkey.

The recorded vote in the Committee was requested by Egypt. Several delegations, in explanation of vote, questioned the wisdom of paragraph 4, which kept the topic separate from the agenda item on the ILC report. Along with France and Israel, which voted negatively for that reason, the United Kingdom considered the approach tantamount to exerting political pressure on the Commission, and questioned the validity of identifying specific offences before elaborating general criteria. The United States called the approach irrational and counter-productive, as did Chile, which felt the Commission should be free from pressure when its work needed to be rationalized. Turkey also feared the approach's long-term adverse effect on the ILC work programme. The Federal Republic of Germany considered paragraphs 2 and 3 to be additional shortcomings; Italy and Spain also objected to consulting intergovernmental organizations, referred to in paragraph 2. Agreeing that the ILC report should be considered as a whole, Portugal added that the Commission should study the topic in greater depth in view of the considerable disagreement to which the issue still gave rise. While voting in favour, Australia, Ireland and Norway (speaking also on behalf of Denmark, Finland, Iceland and Sweden) shared the misgivings expressed over paragraph 4.

Draft convention against mercenaries

In 1985, the General Assembly requested the *Ad Hoc* Committee on the Drafting of an International Convention against the Recruitment, Use, Financing and Training of Mercenaries to try to complete its mandate and submit a draft convention in 1986.

Work of the Committee against mercenaries. The *Ad Hoc* Committee held its fifth session in New York from 8 April to 3 May 1985,[29] in pursuance of a 1984 Assembly decision.[30]

As in the past, the Committee re-established two Working Groups: Group A to deal with definition and the convention's scope, and Group B with all other issues relevant to the future convention. In addition to the documents considered at its previous sessions, the Committee had before it a 1984 document it had prepared as a consolidated negotiating basis of a convention;[31] a draft convention proposed earlier in 1985 by Cuba;[32] and a topical summary of the Sixth Committee's 1984 discussion on the question,[33] prepared at the Assembly's request.[30]

The 1985 report of the *Ad Hoc* Committee incorporated its Working Groups' reports, a report of their joint meeting on a draft article dealing with whether mercenary activities constituted a crime against the peace and security of mankind, and

a revised version of the negotiating document. Not having completed its mandate, the *Ad Hoc* Committee recommended that the Assembly invite it to continue work in 1986 with a view to drafting a convention at the earliest possible date.

The Committee, which had had one vacancy since its inception in 1980,[34] attained full membership in September 1985 with the appointment of Viet Nam as its thirty-fifth member (see APPENDIX III).

In the course of 1985, the Secretary-General received a number of communications with requests that they be circulated under the agenda item on mercenaries. These letters dealt with the situations in Afghanistan (see p. 232) and Central America (see p. 205).

GENERAL ASSEMBLY ACTION

On 11 December, the General Assembly, on the recommendation of the Sixth Committee, adopted **resolution 40/74** without vote.

Drafting of an international convention against the recruitment, use, financing and training of mercenaries

The General Assembly,

Bearing in mind the need for strict observance of the principles of sovereign equality, political independence, territorial integrity of States and self-determination of peoples, enshrined in the Charter of the United Nations and developed in the Declaration on Principles of International Law concerning Friendly Relations and Cooperation among States in accordance with the Charter of the United Nations,

Recalling its resolutions, particularly resolutions 2395(XXIII) of 29 November 1968, 2465(XXIII) of 20 December 1968, 2548(XXIV) of 11 December 1969, 2708(XXV) of 14 December 1970 and 3103(XXVIII) of 12 December 1973, and its resolution 1514(XV) of 14 December 1960, as well as Security Council resolutions 405(1977) of 14 April 1977, 419(1977) of 24 November 1977, 496(1981) of 15 December 1981 and 507(1982) of 28 May 1982, in which the United Nations denounced the practice of using mercenaries, in particular against developing countries and national liberation movements,

Recalling in particular its resolution 39/84 of 13 December 1984, by which it renewed the mandate of the *Ad Hoc* Committee on the Drafting of an International Convention against the Recruitment, Use, Financing and Training of Mercenaries,

Having considered the report of the *Ad Hoc* Committee on its fifth session,

Recognizing that the activities of mercenaries are contrary to fundamental principles of international law, such as non-interference in the internal affairs of States, territorial integrity and independence, and seriously impede the process of self-determination of peoples struggling against colonialism, racism and *apartheid* and all forms of foreign domination,

Bearing in mind the pernicious impact that the activities of mercenaries have on international peace and security,

Considering that the progressive development and codification of the rules of international law on mercenaries would contribute immensely to the implementation of the purposes and principles of the Charter,

Taking account of the fact that, although the *Ad Hoc* Committee has made some progress, it has not yet fulfilled its mandate,

Reaffirming the need for the elaboration, at the earliest possible date, of an international convention against the recruitment, use, financing and training of mercenaries,

1. *Takes note* of the report of the *Ad Hoc* Committee on the Drafting of an International Convention against the Recruitment, Use, Financing and Training of Mercenaries and the progress made by the *Ad Hoc* Committee, especially during its fifth session;

2. *Decides* to renew the mandate of the *Ad Hoc* Committee to enable it to continue its work on the drafting of an international convention against the recruitment, use, financing and training of mercenaries;

3. *Requests* the *Ad Hoc* Committee, in the fulfilment of its mandate, to use the draft articles contained in chapter V of its report, entitled "Consolidated negotiating basis of a convention against the recruitment, use, financing and training of mercenaries" as a basis for future negotiation on the text of the proposed international convention;

4. *Invites* the *Ad Hoc* Committee to take into account the suggestions and proposals of Member States submitted to the Secretary-General on the subject and the views and comments expressed at the current session of the General Assembly;

5. *Decides* that the *Ad Hoc* Committee shall accept the participation of observers of Member States, including participation in the meetings of its working groups;

6. *Requests* the Secretary-General to provide the *Ad Hoc* Committee with any assistance and facilities it may require for the performance of its work;

7. *Decides* that the *Ad Hoc* Committee shall hold its sixth session for four weeks, from 16 June to 11 July 1986;

8. *Requests* the *Ad Hoc* Committee to make every effort to complete its mandate at its sixth session and to submit a draft convention to the General Assembly at its forty-first session;

9. *Decides* to include in the provisional agenda of its forty-first session the item entitled "Report of the *Ad Hoc* Committee on the Drafting of an International Convention against the Recruitment, Use, Financing and Training of Mercenaries".

General Assembly resolution 40/74

11 December 1985   Meeting 112   Adopted without vote

Approved by Sixth Committee (A/40/979 & Corr.1) by consensus, 27 November (meeting 48); 41-nation draft (A/C.6/40/L.12/Rev.1); agenda item 137.

Sponsors: Algeria, Angola, Bangladesh, Barbados, Benin, Cameroon, Cuba, Egypt, Ethiopia, Fiji, German Democratic Republic, Ghana, Guyana, India, Iraq, Jamaica, Kenya, Lesotho, Libyan Arab Jamahiriya, Madagascar, Mali, Mexico, Mongolia, Morocco, Mozambique, Niger, Nigeria, Romania, Senegal, Suriname, Syrian Arab Republic, Togo, Trinidad and Tobago, Tunisia, Turkey, Uganda, Ukrainian SSR, Viet Nam, Yugoslavia, Zaire, Zambia.

Financial implications. 5th Committee, A/40/1016; S-G, A/C.5/40/75, A/C.6/40/L.23.

Meeting numbers. GA 40th session: 5th Committee 56; 6th Committee 13-17, 44, 48; plenary 112.

In explanation of position, Iran charged that one of the text's sponsors, Iraq, used mercenaries in its military operations against Iran, that many had

been captured, and that there had been recent negotiations, through mediation by the Sudan, on repatriating the Sudanese elements recruited by Iraq. Rejecting those allegations, Iraq said the Arabs participating in the war were doing so in order to defend Iraq from the aggression against its territorial integrity.

Denmark (speaking for the Nordic countries) and the United States asserted that the fifth preambular paragraph had far-reaching implications in that, while the crimes or offences of individuals acting on their own behalf were reprehensible, they could not be attributed to States or be regarded as violations of international law. Belgium (for the 10 EC members, Portugal and Spain) agreed, adding that the *Ad Hoc* Committee should work with the understanding that a convention, to be successful, had to be adopted by consensus.

In other 1985 resolutions, the Assembly called on States to take legislative or other appropriate measures to prevent the recruitment, training and transit of mercenaries in their territories for use against national liberation movements (**40/25, 40/56**) or in Namibia (**40/97 A**). It also called on Governments to enact legislation declaring mercenary activities to be punishable offences and prohibiting their nationals from serving as mercenaries, and to report on such legislation to the Secretary-General (**40/25**).

Prevention of terrorism

Both the Security Council and the General Assembly were deeply disturbed over the increases in acts of terrorism in 1985. The Council, specifically condemning several instances of hijacking and hostage-taking, was joined by the Assembly in urging closer international co-operation to prevent and eliminate the problem. The Assembly also called on all States to observe and implement the 1979 recommendations of the *Ad Hoc* Committee on International Terrorism.[35]

Acts of terrorism, which had spread to all parts of the globe, were exceptionally difficult to cope with since they involved desperate acts by desperate people willing to violate law regardless of the risk to their own lives, the Secretary-General said (see p. 10). The most tragic aspect of the problem was the increasing loss of innocent civilian lives, he said, adding that, with some of the necessary international legal instruments already in existence, the essential political conditions were lacking as well as the sense of solidarity and mutual confidence to make those instruments work (see p. 3).

Communications. In the course of 1985, the Secretary-General received a number of communications dealing with situations in Central America, the Mediterranean or the Middle East (see POLITICAL AND SECURITY QUESTIONS, Chapters VI, VIII and IX), with requests that they be circulated under the item on terrorism.

On 22 October,[36] the Syrian Arab Republic requested the President of the General Assembly to circulate under the item its letter of 1 May 1984,[37] listing alleged Israeli terrorist acts since 1937. On 6 November,[38] Israel submitted a record, prepared by its Ministry of Foreign Affairs, of the alleged campaign of terror conducted by the Palestine Liberation Organization (PLO) since its expulsion from Lebanon in 1982, charging that PLO, under Yasser Arafat's leadership since February 1969, had perpetrated some 8,000 acts of terror.

Reports of the Secretary-General. Pursuant to a 1983 Assembly request,[39] the Secretary-General submitted in August 1985 a report, with later addenda,[40] containing the views and other information regarding terrorism received from seven Member States, the International Civil Aviation Organization (ICAO), the Universal Postal Union and two other international organizations. Annexed to the report was information on the state, as at 5 August 1985, of signatures of, ratifications of or accessions to a number of international conventions relating to terrorism, including two adopted by the Assembly and for which the Secretary-General served as the depositary: the 1973 Convention on the Prevention and Punishment of Crimes against Internationally Protected Persons, including Diplomatic Agents,[41] and the 1979 International Convention against the Taking of Hostages.[42] As at 31 December 1985, those instruments had 66 (see p. 1172) and 29 parties, respectively.[43]

GENERAL ASSEMBLY ACTION

In 1985, four draft resolutions on the topic were submitted to the Sixth Committee—three by delegations, and one by the Sixth Committee Chairman, which the Committee eventually approved.

The three texts submitted by delegations differed from that by the Chairman in a number of respects.

A draft by Cuba[44]—subsequently revised and sponsored also by Angola, Bolivia, Burkina Faso, Colombia, the Congo, Equatorial Guinea, Nicaragua and Peru[45]—would have had the Assembly condemn all terrorism activities, including State terrorism, as a crime against mankind, and call on States to refrain from participating in terrorist acts in other States, or acquiescing in activities within their territory directed towards the commission of such acts.

A draft by Australia, Austria, Belgium, Canada, Denmark, Finland, the Federal Republic of Ger-

many, Italy, Japan, New Zealand, Norway, Portugal, Spain, Sweden, Turkey and the United Kingdom[46] would have had the Assembly: urge States not to permit alleged political motivation or circumstances to obstruct the application of all appropriate law enforcement measures provided for in the relevant conventions to persons committing acts of international terrorism covered by those instruments; further urge States to co-operate in preventing acts of terrorism and in apprehending, prosecuting or extraditing the perpetrators of such acts, and to take measures to prevent violent attacks against all forms of public transport; and encourage ICAO to continue promoting universal acceptance of and strict compliance with the international air security conventions. The draft was subsequently revised,[47] with the United States as an additional sponsor, to include a request to the International Maritime Organization (IMO) to study the problem of terrorism abroad or against ships with a view to making recommendations and to report to the Assembly in 1987.

A draft by Colombia[48] would have had the Assembly request all States to adopt special measures to strengthen co-operation, especially with regard to exchange of information on international criminal activities, extradition and assistance in legal matters.

On the recommendation of the Sixth Committee, the General Assembly, on 9 December, adopted **resolution 40/61** without vote.

Measures to prevent international terrorism which endangers or takes innocent human lives or jeopardizes fundamental freedoms and study of the underlying causes of those forms of terrorism and acts of violence which lie in misery, frustration, grievance and despair and which cause some people to sacrifice human lives, including their own, in an attempt to effect radical changes

The General Assembly,

Recalling its resolutions 3034(XXVII) of 18 December 1972, 31/102 of 15 December 1976, 32/147 of 16 December 1977, 34/145 of 17 December 1979, 36/109 of 10 December 1981 and 38/130 of 19 December 1983,

Recalling also the Declaration on Principles of International Law concerning Friendly Relations and Co-operation among States in accordance with the Charter of the United Nations, the Declaration on the Strengthening of International Security, the Definition of Aggression and relevant instruments on international humanitarian law applicable in armed conflict,

Further recalling the existing international conventions relating to various aspects of the problem of international terrorism, *inter alia*, the Convention on Offences and Certain Other Acts Committed on Board Aircraft, signed at Tokyo on 14 September 1963, the Convention for the Suppression of Unlawful Seizure of Aircraft, signed at The Hague on 16 December 1970, the Convention for the Suppression of Unlawful Acts against the Safety of Civil Aviation, signed at Montreal on 23 September 1971, the Convention on the Prevention and Punishment of Crimes against Internationally Protected Persons, including Diplomatic Agents, signed at New York on 14 December 1973, and the International Convention against the Taking of Hostages, adopted at New York on 17 December 1979,

Deeply concerned about the world-wide escalation of acts of terrorism in all its forms, which endanger or take innocent human lives, jeopardize fundamental freedoms and seriously impair the dignity of human beings,

Taking note of the deep concern and condemnation of all acts of international terrorism expressed by the Security Council and the Secretary-General,

Convinced of the importance of expanding and improving international co-operation among States, on a bilateral and multilateral basis, which will contribute to the elimination of acts of international terrorism and their underlying causes and to the prevention and elimination of this criminal scourge,

Reaffirming the principle of self-determination of peoples enshrined in the Charter of the United Nations,

Reaffirming also the inalienable right to self-determination and independence of all peoples under colonial and racist régimes and other forms of alien domination, and upholding the legitimacy of their struggle, in particular the struggle of national liberation movements, in accordance with the purposes and principles of the Charter and of the Declaration on Principles of International Law concerning Friendly Relations and Co-operation among States in accordance with the Charter of the United Nations,

Mindful of the necessity of maintaining and safeguarding the basic rights of the individual in accordance with the relevant international human rights instruments and generally accepted international standards,

Convinced of the importance of the observance by States of their obligations under the relevant international conventions to ensure that appropriate law enforcement measures are taken in connection with the offences addressed in those conventions,

Expressing its concern that in recent years terrorism has taken on forms that have an increasingly deleterious effect on international relations, which may jeopardize the very territorial integrity and security of States,

Taking note of the report of the Secretary-General,

1. *Unequivocally condemns*, as criminal, all acts, methods and practices of terrorism wherever and by whomever committed, including those which jeopardize friendly relations among States and their security;

2. *Deeply deplores* the loss of innocent human lives which results from such acts of terrorism;

3. *Also deplores* the pernicious impact of acts of international terrorism on relations of co-operation among States, including co-operation for development;

4. *Appeals* to all States that have not yet done so to consider becoming party to the existing international conventions relating to various aspects of international terrorism;

5. *Invites* all States to take all appropriate measures at the national level with a view to the speedy and final elimination of the problem of international terrorism, such as the harmonization of domestic legislation with existing international conventions, the fulfilment of assumed international obligations, and the prevention

of the preparation and organization in their respective territories of acts directed against other States;

6. *Calls upon* all States to fulfil their obligations under international law to refrain from organizing, instigating, assisting or participating in terrorist acts in other States, or acquiescing in activities within their territory directed towards the commission of such acts;

7. *Urges* all States not to allow any circumstances to obstruct the application of appropriate law enforcement measures provided for in the relevant conventions to which they are party to persons who commit acts of international terrorism covered by those conventions;

8. *Also urges* all States to co-operate with one another more closely, especially through the exchange of relevant information concerning the prevention and combating of terrorism, the apprehension and prosecution or extradition of the perpetrators of such acts, the conclusion of special treaties and/or the incorporation into appropriate bilateral treaties of special clauses, in particular regarding the extradition or prosecution of terrorists;

9. *Further urges* all States, unilaterally and in co-operation with other States, as well as relevant United Nations organs, to contribute to the progressive elimination of the causes underlying international terrorism and to pay special attention to all situations, including colonialism, racism and situations involving mass and flagrant violations of human rights and fundamental freedoms and those involving alien occupation, that may give rise to international terrorism and may endanger international peace and security;

10. *Calls upon* all States to observe and implement the recommendations of the *Ad Hoc* Committee on International Terrorism contained in its report to the General Assembly at its thirty-fourth session;

11. *Also calls upon* all States to take all appropriate measures, as recommended by the International Civil Aviation Organization and as set forth in relevant international conventions, to prevent terrorist attacks against civil aviation transport and other forms of public transport;

12. *Encourages* the International Civil Aviation Organization to continue its efforts aimed at promoting universal acceptance of and strict compliance with the international air security conventions;

13. *Requests* the International Maritime Organization to study the problem of terrorism aboard or against ships with a view to making recommendations on appropriate measures;

14. *Requests* the Secretary-General to follow up, as appropriate, the implementation of the present resolution and to submit a report to the General Assembly at its forty-second session;

15. *Decides* to include the item in the provisional agenda of its forty-second session.

General Assembly resolution 40/61

9 December 1985   Meeting 108   Adopted without vote

Approved by Sixth Committee (A/40/1003) by vote (118-1-2), 6 December (meeting 55); draft by Chairman (A/C.6/40/L.31), orally revised; agenda item 129.
Meeting numbers. GA 40th session: 6th Committee 18-22, 54, 55; plenary 108.

When the Sixth Committee Chairman introduced the draft, Cuba proposed oral amendments to delete from the third preambular paragraph reference to specific conventions, and to include in paragraph 1 reference to State terrorism. A proposal by Colombia—that the Committee take no decision on those proposed amendments—was adopted by 52 votes to 32, with 33 abstentions. Cuba's subsequent proposal that the Committee take no decision on the Chairman's text was rejected by 63 votes to 9, with 38 abstentions. A further proposal by Cuba—that separate votes be taken on the third preambular paragraph and paragraphs 1, 6, 8, 11 and 12 of the draft—was rejected by 54 votes to 27, with 38 abstentions. The Committee then approved the draft by 118 votes to 1, with 2 abstentions.

In explanation of its negative vote on the draft, Cuba stated that the draft had failed to take account of State terrorism as practised, it charged, by the United States, Israel and South Africa. Burkina Faso, also condemning State terrorism, abstained. Iran did not participate in the voting, asserting that while the text rightly recognized the legitimacy of the struggle for national liberation and the right of self-determination, it failed to condemn State terrorism.

Many delegations, voting affirmatively, explained why they supported the text even though considering it not entirely satisfactory.

The USSR was pleased that the text did not equate national liberation movements with international terrorism; it would have preferred an explicit condemnation of State terrorism, the elements of which, it believed, were included in paragraphs 1 and 6. Iraq voted in favour, on the understanding that paragraph 1 did not exclude State terrorism. Algeria and the Syrian Arab Republic regretted that the text did not contain an unequivocal condemnation of State terrorism. Mongolia added that State terrorism was being practised in southern Africa and against States of Central America, and Nicaragua claimed itself to be a victim.

Though not wholly satisfied with the text, the Libyan Arab Jamahiriya supported it for its unequivocal condemnation of international terrorism, together with the affirmation of the right of peoples to self-determination and of the legitimacy of the struggle of national liberation movements. Democratic Yemen added that the text recognized that international terrorism could not be considered in isolation from the practices of colonial and racist régimes. Algeria, however, felt that some formulations were obscure and could serve as a pretext for lumping acts of criminal terrorism together with those forming part of the legitimate struggle of national liberation movements; it added that the appeal in paragraph 9 should have invoked the appropriate provisions of the Charter, particularly Chapter VII. The United States, which considered the reaffirmation of the principle of self-determination in the seventh preambular paragraph to be excessive, understood that paragraph 9 did not lay down a pre-condition for other actions called for in the draft; with its reference to human rights, the text was not totally lacking in balance, however. Honduras would have liked a specific reference to the Universal Declaration of Human Rights[49] and to various forms of terrorism, including the kind practised by States against their own nationals; omission in paragraph 2 of an explicit reference to forms of terrorism which jeopardized fundamental freedoms and human rights reflected an inconsistency between the title and the substance of the text.

Many felt that the text, despite certain shortcomings, represented the common will of a vast majority of Member States or was a generally acceptable compromise solution; among them, Benin, Chile, Morocco, the Philippines, the Sudan, Sweden and Yemen. Egypt and Pakistan supported it as an act of solidarity with non-aligned and other developing countries which had worked in good faith to arrive at an acceptable text. Similarly, Japan voted in favour out of respect for the efforts at achieving a consensus. Belgium felt the text represented a generally balanced and realistic compromise, and welcomed the reference to the role of ICAO and IMO. The United Kingdom would have liked to see the text declare that no cause could ever justify international terrorism; it added that the draft had positive features, in particular the provisions contained in paragraphs 1, 4, 6 and 13. While many welcomed the draft's condemnation of all forms of terrorism, the Federal Republic of Germany felt the Committee was about to miss a historic opportunity to rally all Member States in a common approach to one of the most difficult and important problems of the day. For Mexico, the text did not touch on the effects of terrorism on inter-State relations.

France believed that the rule of *aut dedere aut judicare* referred to in paragraph 8 must be interpreted as implying respect for the principle of timely prosecution of the right of asylum. The USSR considered that paragraph to be important in combating the hijacking of ships and aircraft and attacks on diplomatic and consular missions. Mexico, however, doubted whether the principle of extradition could be effectively applied in the case of international terrorism.

In related action in 1985, the Assembly called on the Secretariat's Department of Public Information to disseminate information concerning United Nations decisions dealing with acts of terrorism in all its forms (**resolution 40/164 A**).

SECURITY COUNCIL ACTION

On three occasions in 1985, the Security Council specifically condemned acts of terrorism, including hijacking and hostage-taking.

It did so on 9 October, when the Council's President, on behalf of its members,[50] welcomed the news of the release of the passengers and the crew of the cruise ship *Achille Lauro* (see p. 291).

On 18 December, the Council held a meeting, requested two days earlier by the United States because of what it said was the serious situation caused by hostage-taking and abduction,[51] and adopted **resolution 579(1985)** unanimously.

The Security Council,

Deeply disturbed at the prevalence of incidents of hostage-taking and abduction, several of which are of protracted duration and have included loss of life,

Considering that the taking of hostages and abductions are offences of grave concern to the international community, having severe adverse consequences for the rights of the victims and for the promotion of friendly relations and co-operation among States,

Recalling the statement of 9 October 1985 by the President of the Security Council, resolutely condemning all acts of terrorism, including hostage-taking,

Recalling also resolution 40/61 of 9 December 1985 of the General Assembly,

Bearing in mind the International Convention against the Taking of Hostages, adopted on 17 December 1979, the Convention on the Prevention and Punishment of Crimes against Internationally Protected Persons, including Diplomatic Agents, adopted on 14 December 1973, the Convention for the Suppression of Unlawful Acts against the Safety of Civil Aviation, signed on 23 September 1971, the Convention for the Suppression of Unlawful Seizure of Aircraft, signed on 16 December 1970, and other relevant conventions,

1. *Condemns unequivocally* all acts of hostage-taking and abduction;

2. *Calls for* the immediate safe release of all hostages and abducted persons wherever and by whomever they are being held;

3. *Affirms* the obligation of all States in whose territory hostages or abducted persons are held urgently to take all appropriate measures to secure their safe release and to prevent the commission of acts of hostage-taking and abduction in the future;

4. *Appeals* to all States that have not yet done so to consider the possibility of becoming parties to the International Convention against the Taking of Hostages, the Convention on the Prevention and Punishment of Crimes against Internationally Protected Persons, including Diplomatic Agents, the Convention for the Suppression of Unlawful Acts against the Safety of Civil Aviation, the Convention for the Suppression of Unlawful Seizure of Aircraft and other relevant conventions;

5. *Urges* the further development of international co-operation among States in devising and adopting effective measures which are in accordance with the rules of international law to facilitate the prevention, prosecution and punishment of all acts of hostage-taking and abduction as manifestations of international terrorism.

Security Council resolution 579(1985)

18 December 1985　　　　Meeting 2637　　　　Adopted unanimously

8-nation draft (S/17686).

Sponsors: Australia, Denmark, Egypt, France, Peru, Trinidad and Tobago, United Kingdom, United States.

On 30 December, following terrorist attacks at the airports at Rome, Italy, and at Vienna, Austria, the President read out the following statement[52] on behalf of the Council members:

"The members of the Security Council strongly condemn the unjustifiable and criminal terrorist attacks at the Rome and Vienna airports which caused the taking of innocent human lives.

"They urge that those responsible for these deliberate and indiscriminate killings be brought to trial in accordance with due process of law.

"They call upon all concerned to exercise restraint and to refrain from taking any action inconsistent with their obligations under the Charter of the United Nations and other relevant rules of international law.

"They affirm the statement by the President of the Security Council of 9 October 1985, Security Council resolution 579(1985), and endorse the Secretary-General's statement of 27 December 1985, in which he noted General Assembly resolution 40/61 of 9 December 1985 and expressed the hope that it would be followed by determined efforts by all Governments and authorities concerned, in accordance with established principles of international law, in order that all acts, methods and practices of terrorism may be brought to an end."

Draft articles on non-navigational uses of international watercourses

In 1985, ILC[24] continued work on the law of the non-navigational uses of international watercourses, as recommended by the General Assembly in 1984.[53] It appointed Stephen C. McCaffrey (United States) as new Special Rapporteur on the topic, to fill the post vacated by Jens Evensen (Norway) upon his election to the International Court of Justice, and asked Mr. McCaffrey to prepare a preliminary report.

In that report[54]—the sixth on the topic, including those prepared by three predecessors—the new Special Rapporteur reviewed the Commission's work on the topic to date[55] and said he proposed to follow, for the time being, the general organizational structure provided by the outline proposed by his predecessor in elaborating further draft articles on the topic.[56] He also suggested that the Drafting Committee take up, in 1986, draft articles 1 to 9 (dealing with introductory articles, general principles, rights and duties of watercourse States) which had been referred to it in 1984, while the Commission might address issues of co-operation and management relating to international watercourse systems. Members of the Commission generally supported the Special Rapporteur's intention to build as much as possible on the progress already achieved. It was recognized that the Commission must endeavour, without delay, to reach acceptable solutions to the difficult and sensitive topic, in view of the urgency of fresh-water problems confronting mankind.

In its 1985 resolution (**40/75**) on the work of ILC, the Assembly recommended that, taking into account government comments, ILC should continue its work on the topic.

REFERENCES

[1]A/40/33 & Corr.1. [2]YUN 1984, p. 1087, GA res. 39/79, 13 Dec. 1984. [3]YUN 1983, p. 1106. [4]YUN 1984, p. 1087. [5]A/AC.182/L.42. [6]YUN 1984, p. 1088, GA res. 39/78, 13 Dec. 1984. [7]A/C.6/40/L.28 & Corr.1. [8]YUN 1983, p. 1107. [9]A/40/450 & Add.1,2. [10]YUN 1977, p. 118, GA res. 32/150, 19 Dec. 1977. [11]A/40/41. [12]YUN 1976, p. 105. [13]YUN 1979, p. 153. [14]YUN 1981, p. 1204. [15]YUN 1984, p. 1090, GA res. 39/81, 13 Dec. 1984. [16]A/40/452. [17]YUN 1982, p. 1374. [18]A/40/346. [19]A/C.6/40/8. [20]YUN 1982, p. 1375. [21]YUN 1981, p. 1214, GA res. 36/106, 10 Dec. 1981. [22]YUN 1954, p. 411. [23]YUN 1947-48, p. 215, GA res. 177(II), 21 Nov. 1947. [24]A/40/10. [25]A/CN.4/387. [26]A/40/451 & Add.1-3. [27]YUN 1984, p. 1091, GA res. 39/80, 13 Dec. 1984. [28]*Ibid.*, p. 1091. [29]A/40/43. [30]YUN 1984, p. 1093, GA res. 39/84, 13 Dec. 1984. [31]*Ibid.*, p. 1092. [32]A/AC.207/L.22. [33]A/AC.207/L.23. [34]YUN 1980, p. 1145, GA res. 35/48, 4 Dec. 1980. [35]YUN 1979, p. 1146. [36]A/C.6/40/5. [37]YUN 1984, p. 316. [38]A/C.6/40/9. [39]YUN 1983, p. 1113, GA res. 38/130, 19 Dec. 1983. [40]A/40/445 & Add.1,2. [41]YUN 1973, p. 775, GA res. 3166(XXVIII), annex, 14 Dec. 1973. [42]YUN 1979, p. 1144, GA res. 34/146, annex, 17 Dec. 1979. [43]*Multilateral Treaties Deposited with the Secretary-General: Status as at 31 December 1985* (ST/LEG/SER.E/4), Sales No. E.86.V.3. [44]A/C.6/40/L.2. [45]A/C.6/40/L.2/Rev.1. [46]A/C.6/40/L.3. [47]A/C.6/40/L.3/Rev.1. [48]A/C.6/40/L.4. [49]YUN 1948-49, p. 535, GA res. 217 A (III), 10 Dec. 1948. [50]S/17554. [51]S/17685. [52]S/17702. [53]YUN 1984, p. 1117, GA res. 39/85, 13 Dec. 1984. [54]A/CN.4/393. [55]YUN 1984, p. 1094. [56]YUN 1983, p. 1115.

Chapter III

States and international law

The United Nations remained concerned, throughout 1985, with protecting diplomats and consular missions, as it received reports of incidents threatening their security and safety. Urging States to ensure their security and condemning acts of violence, the General Assembly in December asked the Secretary-General to survey in 1986 the operation of the reporting procedures. (resolution 40/73).

The International Law Commission (see p. 1197) continued work with a view to elaborating legal instruments on the status of the diplomatic courier and the diplomatic bag not accompanied by courier, jurisdictional immunities of States and their property, international liability for injurious consequences arising from acts not prohibited by international law, and State responsibility for internationally wrongful acts.

Topics related to this chapter. International organizations and international law: host country relations. Other legal questions: International Law Commission.

Diplomatic relations

Protection of diplomats

As at 31 December 1985, the number of parties to the various international instruments relating to the protection of diplomats and diplomatic and consular relations[1] was as follows: 145 States were parties to the 1961 Vienna Convention on Diplomatic Relations,[2] with Thailand ratifying and Turkey acceding in 1985; 42 States were parties to the Optional Protocol concerning acquisition of nationality,[3] with Thailand ratifying in 1985; and 52 States were parties to the Optional Protocol concerning the compulsory settlement of disputes.[3]

With the Netherlands acceding to the three instruments in 1985, the 1963 Vienna Convention on Consular Relations[4] had 110 parties; 33 States were parties to the Optional Protocol concerning the acquisition of nationality;[5] and 40 States were parties to the Optional Protocol concerning the compulsory settlement of disputes.[5]

The 1973 Convention on the Prevention and Punishment of Crimes against Internationally Protected Persons, including Diplomatic Agents,[6] had 66 States parties, Italy having ratified and New Zealand, the Niger, Spain and Switzerland having acceded in 1985.

Report of the Secretary-General. Following a 1984 General Assembly request,[7] the Secretary-General submitted in August 1985 a report with later addenda,[8] containing information from States on serious violations of the protection, security and safety of diplomatic and consular missions and representatives, and on action taken to bring offenders to justice.

Austria reported a November 1984 fatal shooting, in Vienna, of the Assistant Director of the United Nations Centre for Social Development and Humanitarian Affairs. Belgium reported an April 1985 bombing attack on the North Atlantic Assembly headquarters in Brussels and the resulting damage to the residence of the Counsellor of the Italian Embassy; and the discovery in December 1984 of explosives placed at a building inhabited by the Consul General of Turkey and the Counsellor of the Embassy of Greece.

Canada provided information on a March 1985 incident at the Turkish Embassy in Ottawa, involving serious injury to Turkey's Ambassador, the fatal shooting of a Canadian security guard, and hostage-taking of the Embassy occupants; three individuals apprehended faced trial in 1986. It also reported on the ongoing criminal prosecution or investigation of those involved in two 1982 incidents—the April assassination attempt against a Turkish diplomat and the August assassination of another.

France informed of the charges of complicity in two 1982 cases of murder, of a member of the United States Embassy in January and of a member of the Embassy of Israel in April.

The Federal Republic of Germany rejected charges made by the USSR in connection with certain incidents in 1984.[9]

Israel reported two August 1985 incidents—an explosion near its Embassy in Bangkok, Thailand, and the fatal shooting, in Cairo, Egypt, of an Embassy staff member and serious injuries to his wife and a secretary, also reported by Egypt. Kuwait reported the arrest of the suspected perpetrators of a March 1985 fatal shooting of an Iraqi diplomat and his son.

Portugal listed cases occurring there between 1975 and 1983, and Spain provided information on a December 1983 fatal shooting of a Jordanian Embassy employee and wounding of another. Turkey reported several attacks against and injuries to its diplomats in Teheran, Iran, in March 1984; the incident at its Embassy in Ottawa in March 1985 (see above); and the assassination of a Jordanian diplomat in Ankara in July 1985. The United Kingdom reported that six individuals had been convicted in 1985 of the February 1984 kidnapping and murder of a senior official of the Indian High Commission.

The USSR charged a number of countries with failing to provide adequate security protection—Canada for restricting the number of Consulate security staff; Switzerland whose police had forcibly detained a diplomat at Berne in February 1985; Canada and the United States for provocation against Soviet citizens and diplomatic couriers, and for enacting measures affecting the international status of nationals working at the United Nations; and the United Kingdom for not preventing the forced entry and burglary of residences of Embassy officials in London, and instances when its Embassy and other institutions were fired on. Responding to the last charge, the United Kingdom said the only USSR complaint had been made after two small holes were discovered in the windows of Intourist Moscow; forensic evidence suggested they were made by an air-gun or catapult.

Incidents involving the permanent missions to the United Nations in New York were also reported (see also p. 1180). Ghana, Nicaragua and the United Republic of Tanzania reported vandalism against the missions' official cars; responding to the complaint by Ghana, the United States said the incident was found to be a random act of non-political vandalism. Nicaragua also alleged that its diplomats had been harassed and intimidated by United States government officials. The Philippines charged that a diplomat's son had been manhandled and beaten up by New York City transit policemen in October 1984.

Australia, Denmark, the Dominican Republic, Malawi, Rwanda, the Sudan and Venezuela informed the Secretary-General that they had no incidents to report. Views on measures to enhance the protection of diplomatic missions and representatives were transmitted by Australia, Austria, Canada, Colombia, Denmark, Ecuador, France, Poland, Portugal, Rwanda, the Sudan, the Ukrainian SSR, the USSR, the United Kingdom and Venezuela.

Communications. By a letter of 8 October to the Secretary-General,[10] the USSR demanded the immediate and unconditional release of its four officials kidnapped in Lebanon on 30 September, one of whom was reportedly killed on 2 October; it charged that Israel was responsible for inciting internal strife in Lebanon, of which the USSR citizens had become victims. Calling the charges groundless, Israel declared on 23 October[11] that the USSR should realize that its encouraging and legitimizing terrorist acts in Lebanon guaranteed it no immunity.

GENERAL ASSEMBLY ACTION

On the recommendation of the Sixth (Legal) Committee, the General Assembly, on 11 December 1985, adopted **resolution 40/73** without vote.

Consideration of effective measures to enhance the protection, security and safety of diplomatic and consular missions and representatives

The General Assembly,

Having considered the report of the Secretary-General,

Emphasizing the important role of diplomatic and consular missions and representatives, as well as of missions and representatives to international intergovernmental organizations and officials of such organizations, in the maintenance of international peace and the promotion of friendly relations among States and also the need for enhancing global understanding thereof,

Convinced that respect for the principles and rules of international law governing diplomatic and consular relations, in particular those aimed at ensuring the inviolability of diplomatic and consular missions and representatives, is a basic prerequisite for the normal conduct of relations among States and for the fulfilment of the purposes and principles of the Charter of the United Nations,

Deeply concerned about the continued large number of failures to respect the inviolability of diplomatic and consular missions and representatives, and about the serious threat presented by such violations to the maintenance of normal and peaceful international relations, which are necessary for co-operation among States,

Alarmed by the increase of acts of violence against diplomatic and consular representatives, as well as against representatives to international intergovernmental organizations and officials of such organizations, which endanger or take innocent lives and seriously impede the normal work of such representatives and officials,

Expressing its sympathy for the victims of illegal acts against diplomatic and consular representatives and missions, as well as against representatives and missions to international intergovernmental organizations and officials of such organizations,

Emphasizing the duty of States to take all appropriate steps, as required by international law:

(a) To protect the premises of diplomatic and consular missions, as well as of missions to international intergovernmental organizations,

(b) To prevent any attacks on diplomatic and consular representatives, as well as on representatives to international intergovernmental organizations and officials of such organizations,

(c) To apprehend the offenders and to bring them to justice,

Noting that, in spite of the call by the General Assembly at its previous sessions, not all States have yet become parties to the relevant conventions concerning the inviolability of diplomatic and consular missions and representatives,

Convinced that the reporting procedures established under General Assembly resolution 35/168 of 15 December 1980 and further elaborated in later Assembly resolutions are important steps in the efforts to enhance the protection, security and safety of diplomatic and consular missions and representatives,

Desiring to maintain and further strengthen those reporting procedures,

1. *Takes note* of the report of the Secretary-General;

2. *Strongly condemns* acts of violence against diplomatic and consular missions and representatives, as well as against missions and representatives to international intergovernmental organizations and officials of such organizations, and emphasizes that such acts cannot be justified;

3. *Emphasizes* the importance of enhanced awareness throughout the world of the necessity of ensuring the protection, security and safety of such missions, representatives and officials, as well as of the role of the United Nations in this regard;

4. *Urges* States to observe and to implement the principles and rules of international law governing diplomatic and consular relations and, in particular, to take all necessary measures in conformity with their international obligations to ensure effectively the protection, security and safety of all diplomatic and consular missions and representatives officially present in territory under their jurisdiction, including practicable measures to prohibit in their territories illegal activities of persons, groups and organizations that encourage, instigate, organize or engage in the perpetration of acts against the security and safety of such missions and representatives;

5. *Calls upon* States to take all necessary measures at the national and international levels to prevent any acts of violence against diplomatic and consular missions and representatives, as well as against missions and representatives to international intergovernmental organizations and officials of such organizations, and, in accordance with national law and international treaties, to prosecute or extradite those who perpetrate such acts;

6. *Recommends* that States should co-operate closely through, *inter alia*, contacts between the diplomatic and consular missions and the receiving State, with regard to practical measures designed to enhance the protection, security and safety of diplomatic and consular missions and representatives and with regard to exchange of information on the circumstances of all serious violations thereof;

7. *Calls upon* States that have not yet done so to consider becoming parties to the instruments relevant to the protection, security and safety of diplomatic and consular missions and representatives;

8. *Calls upon* States, in cases where a dispute arises in connection with a violation of the principles and rules of international law concerning the inviolability of diplomatic and consular missions and representatives, to make use of the means for peaceful settlement of disputes, including the good offices of the Secretary-General;

9. *Requests:*

(a) All States to report to the Secretary-General as promptly as possible serious violations of the protection,

security and safety of diplomatic and consular missions and representatives;

(b) The State in which the violation took place— and, to the extent applicable, the State where the alleged offender is present—to report as promptly as possible on measures taken to bring the offender to justice and eventually to communicate, in accordance with its laws, the final outcome of the proceedings against the offender, and on measures adopted with a view to preventing a repetition of such violations;

10. *Requests* the Secretary-General:

(a) To circulate to all States, upon receipt, the reports received by him pursuant to paragraph 9 above, unless the reporting State requests otherwise;

(b) When a serious violation has been reported pursuant to paragraph 9 (a) above, to draw the attention, when appropriate, of the States directly concerned to the reporting procedures provided for in paragraph 9 above;

11. *Requests* the Secretary-General to invite States to inform him of their views with respect to any measures needed to enhance the protection, security and safety of diplomatic and consular missions and representatives;

12. *Also requests* the Secretary-General to submit to the General Assembly at its forty-first session a report containing:

(a) Information on the state of ratification of, and accessions to, the instruments referred to in paragraph 7 above;

(b) The reports received and views expressed pursuant to paragraphs 9 and 11 above;

13. *Further requests* the Secretary-General to prepare and to circulate to all States, by 31 July 1986, a survey of the operation, since their establishment, of the reporting procedures provided for in paragraph 9 above, with a view, in particular, to the strengthening of those procedures;

14. *Invites* the Secretary-General to submit to the General Assembly at its forty-first session any views he may wish to express on the matters referred to in paragraphs 12 and 13 above;

15. *Decides* to include in the provisional agenda of its forty-first session the item entitled "Consideration of effective measures to enhance the protection, security and safety of diplomatic and consular missions and representatives: report of the Secretary-General".

General Assembly resolution 40/73

11 December 1985   Meeting 112   Adopted without vote

Approved by Sixth Committee (A/40/936) by consensus, 14 November (meeting 38); 19-nation draft (A/C.6/40/L.11); agenda item 136.

Sponsors: Argentina, Australia, Austria, Canada, Denmark, Ecuador, Finland, Germany, Federal Republic of, Iceland, Ivory Coast, Japan, Mongolia, Nigeria, Norway, Philippines, Sierra Leone, Sweden, Turkey, Uruguay.

Meeting numbers. GA 40th session: 6th Committee 6, 7, 37, 38; plenary 112.

Status of diplomatic bags and couriers

In response to a 1984 General Assembly request,[12] the International Law Commission (ILC), at its 1985 session,[13] continued preparing draft articles on the status of the diplomatic courier and the diplomatic bag not accompanied by diplomatic courier, with a view to elaborating a legal instrument on the topic.

Taking up the sixth report[14] of the Special Rapporteur, Alexander Yankov (Bulgaria)—containing a proposed revised version of draft articles 36, 39 and 42, and a new article 37 replacing former draft articles 37 and 38—ILC discussed those and other articles concerned with: inviolability of the diplomatic bag (article 36); exemption from customs inspection, customs duties and all dues and taxes (article 37); protective measures in circumstances preventing the delivery of the diplomatic bag (article 39); obligations of the transit State in case of *force majeure* or fortuitous event (article 40); nonrecognition of States or Governments or absence of diplomatic or consular relations (article 41); and the relation to other conventions and international agreements (article 42). It also discussed a newly proposed draft article 43 (declaration of optional exceptions in regard to designated types of couriers and bags) and revised draft article 23 (later adopted as article 18), and referred all the draft articles to its Drafting Committee.

On the Committee's recommendation, ILC provisionally adopted in 1985 draft articles on the courier's immunity from jurisdiction (article 18), duration of privileges and immunities (article 21), waiver of immunities (article 22), status of the captain of a ship or aircraft entrusted with the diplomatic bag (article 23), identification of the bag (article 24), its contents (article 25), its transmission by postal service or by any mode of transport (article 26) and facilities accorded to the bag (article 27). The Commission also deleted the brackets from paragraph 2 of article 12 (on the diplomatic courier declared *persona non grata* or not acceptable) and adopted a new commentary thereto.

The articles provisionally adopted in 1985, along with those previously adopted, were transmitted to the Assembly by the Secretary-General in September.[15]

REFERENCES

[1]*Multilateral Treaties Deposited with the Secretary-General: Status as at 31 December 1985* (ST/LEG/SER.E/4), Sales No. E.86.V.3. [2]YUN 1961, p. 512. [3]*Ibid.*, p. 516. [4]YUN 1963, p. 510. [5]*Ibid.*, p. 512. [6]YUN 1973, p. 775, GA res. 3166(XXVIII), annex, 14 Dec. 1973. [7]YUN 1984, p. 1096, GA res. 39/83, 13 Dec. 1984. [8]A/40/453 & Add.1-10. [9]YUN 1984, p. 1096. [10]A/C.6/40/3. [11]A/C.6/40/6. [12]YUN 1984, p. 1117, GA res. 39/85, 13 Dec. 1984. [13]A/40/10. [14]A/CN.4/390 & Corr.1. [15]A/40/447.

State immunities, liability and responsibility

In response to the Assembly's 1984 recommendation,[1] ILC, at its 1985 session,[2] continued work on three aspects of international law concerning States: jurisdictional immunities of States and their property, international liability for injurious consequences arising out of acts not prohibited by international law, and State responsibility for internationally wrongful acts.

In December, the Assembly recommended that, taking into account government comments, ILC should continue its work on those topics (**resolution 40/75**).

Draft articles on State immunities

In 1985, ILC continued preparing draft articles on the jurisdictional immunities of States and their property, basing its work on the sixth and seventh reports—submitted in 1984[3] and 1985,[4] respectively—by the Special Rapporteur, Sompong Sucharitkul (Thailand).

The Commission completed consideration of, and provisionally adopted on the recommendation of its Drafting Committee, articles 19 (ships in commercial service) and 20 (arbitration), which were the two remaining articles comprising part III (exceptions to State immunity) in the sixth report.

The seventh report introduced the last two parts (IV and V) of the proposed draft articles. Part IV, on State immunity in respect of property from attachment and execution, dealt with its scope (article 21), State immunity from attachment and execution (article 22), modalities and effect of consent to attachment and execution (article 23) and types of State property permanently immune from attachment and execution (article 24). Part V, on miscellaneous provisions, covered immunities of personal sovereigns and other heads of State (article 25), service of process and judgement in default of appearance (article 26), procedural privileges (article 27) and restriction and extension of immunities and privileges (article 28). Due to lack of time, the Commission decided to consider part V at its 1986 session, and, after considering draft articles 21 to 24, referred them to the Drafting Committee.

In the Commission discussion, it was generally understood that the substance of part IV was related to the conceptual approach, nature, extent and scope of jurisdictional immunity itself, and that the emphasis placed in the seventh report on the significance of consent was essential to that part. Differing views were expressed on how to balance, in part IV, the competing interests involving Governments and private entities operating in international trade, in view of the fact that Governments in developing countries often conducted such trade for development rather than profit-making purposes.

Draft articles on State liability

ILC, at its 1985 session, continued work on international liability for injurious consequences arising out of acts not prohibited by international law.

On the death of the Special Rapporteur on the topic, Robert Q. Quentin-Baxter (New Zealand), the Commission appointed Julio Barboza (Argentina) as successor and requested him to prepare a preliminary report indicating the status of the work to date and his future course of action. However, the Commission was not able to discuss that report[5] in 1985; it would do so in 1986 along with a new report which the Commission hoped the Special Rapporteur might wish to present.

Draft articles on State responsibility

In 1985, ILC continued preparing draft articles on State responsibility for internationally wrongful acts, taking up the sixth report[6] by the Special Rapporteur, Willem Riphagen (Netherlands), containing a revised version of the remaining 12 draft articles (articles 5 to 16) of part II (content,

forms and degrees of State responsibility) dealing with the legal consequences of international crimes, including aggression. The report also set out a possible content of part III on implementation of international responsibility and dispute settlement.

Following an exchange of views—in which the proposals made for part III were generally considered acceptable—the Commission referred draft articles 7 to 16 to the Drafting Committee, and adopted provisionally draft article 5 dealing with definitions and certain rights of an injured State.

REFERENCES

[1]YUN 1984, p. 1117, GA res. 39/85, 13 Dec. 1984. [2]A/40/10. [3]YUN 1984, p. 1098. [4]A/CN.4/388 & Corr.1. [5]A/CN.4/394. [6]A/CN.4/389 & Corr.1.

Chapter IV

International organizations and international law

In its continuing efforts to strengthen the role of the United Nations in maintaining international peace and security, the General Assembly, in 1985 as in previous years, requested the Special Committee on the Charter of the United Nations and on the Strengthening of the Role of the Organization to accord priority to that question (resolution 40/78). The Assembly once more deferred consideration of an item on the implementation of United Nations resolutions until its resumed fortieth session in 1986, and of draft standard rules of procedure for United Nations conferences until its forty-first session later that year.

The Assembly, having considered the annual report of the Committee on Relations with the Host Country, urged that country, the United States, to continue ensuring effectively the security of the diplomatic missions accredited to the United Nations and their personnel (40/77).

Topics related to this chapter. International peace and security. Legal aspects of international political relations.

Strengthening the role of the United Nations

In 1985, the Special Committee on the Charter of the United Nations and on the Strengthening of the Role of the Organization continued consideration of the maintenance of international peace and security, with a view to strengthening the United Nations role in that regard and promoting co-operation among States.

Report of the Secretary-General for 1984/85

On the fortieth anniversary of the founding of the United Nations, the Secretary-General, in his annual report to the General Assembly on the work of the Organization (see p. 3), noted that the United Nations had come under harsh criticism, partly because of the new complexity of the expanded membership and new voting patterns, but also because of instances where division and conflict had been highlighted at the expense of broad areas of agreement and common interest. Despite the tendency to make the United Nations a scapegoat for current problems and to blame it for lack of international authority and responsibility, the Organization remained the best place to avoid the worst and to strive for im-

provement. In view of the importance, in the nuclear age, of an effective collective system of international peace and security, the Secretary-General urged that Member States reaffirm Charter obligations and direct their collective will to strengthening the United Nations.

Among measures for rationalizing General Assembly procedures, the Secretary-General suggested that Member States intensify pre-session intergovernmental consultation, strive for consensus on major issues and avoid divisive rhetoric. The Security Council might try to overcome such shortcomings as lack of unanimity and collegial spirit, incapacity to approach some problems, and failure to command compliance with its decisions. The Organization's interests might also be better served by developing further the Secretary-General's capacity to serve as an objective third party.

Activities of the Special Committee

The 47-member Special Committee on the Charter of the United Nations and on the Strengthening of the Role of the Organization,[1] meeting in New York from 4 to 29 March 1985, continued consideration of the maintenance of international peace and security, in addition to peaceful settlement of disputes between States (see p. 1160) and the rationalization of United Nations procedures, as requested by the General Assembly in 1984.[2]

An open-ended Working Group of the Committee devoted 15 meetings between 13 and 25 March to discussion of a revised text[3] of the working paper—first submitted in 1984[4] by Belgium, the Federal Republic of Germany, Italy, Japan, New Zealand and Spain—on prevention and removal by the United Nations of situations which might lead to international friction or give rise to a dispute. Two Committee meetings were held on 25 March on rationalizing the existing procedures of the United Nations, on which France and the United Kingdom submitted a working paper.[5] There was no agreement in the Committee on the future treatment of the topic.

Other activities

Security Council consideration. At a ministerial-level meeting on 26 September 1985 (see also p. 392), commemorating the fortieth anniversary of the Organization, the Security Council exchanged views on "United Nations for a better world and the responsibility of the Security Council in maintaining international peace and security". Speaking on behalf of the Council members, the President stressed that a collegial approach within the Council was desirable in discharging its responsibility as the main instrument for international peace, recognized the contribution made by United Nations peace-keeping forces, and called on United Nations Members to abide by Council decisions. In pledging to continue examining the possibilities for further improvement, the Council took note of the suggestions made in that regard by the Secretary-General in his annual report on the work of the Organization (see above).

JIU report. In December, the Secretary-General transmitted to the General Assembly a report by the Joint Inspection Unit (JIU) entitled "Some reflections on reform of the United Nations".[6] The report analysed problems confronting the United Nations system, called for an examination of its *raison d'être* and suggested changes aimed at making it more responsive to international issues. It comprised six chapters: the notion and feasibility of reform, managerial or structural shortcomings, the nature and the role of the Organization, pursuit of the three main objectives (peace and security, negotiation of economic problems leading to complementarity among national economic strategies, and an integrated approach to economic and social development), the focus of reflections with a view to reform, and conclusions.

The Inspector believed that the structure of the current system rested on three fallacious notions—that peace could be maintained through an institution, that a sectoral and therefore non-integrated approach could develop the poor countries, and that negotiations among 159 States were possible without a prior definition of agreed negotiating structures. He felt that a great deal of misunderstanding existed on the possible role of a world organization and that the confusion in people's minds on the subject was itself a political phenomenon whose harmful effects could be mitigated by reflection and clarification. The seriousness and the urgency of the problems justified focusing the search in directions so far little explored, leading to the conception of a third-generation world organization, replete with its new structure and notions more in keeping with reality. While it was impossible, in his view, to modify the structures of a political United Nations in the current context, reform should aim at building up an "economic" United Nations alongside the political institution by devising and installing entirely new structures in the development area and in that of the system of negotiations at world level.

The Administrative Committee on Co-ordination, in October 1985, requested its Organizational Committee to prepare draft comments on the JIU report for its consideration in 1986.[7]

Communication. In September, Iraq transmitted to the Secretary-General a study by the Asian-African Legal Consultative Committee (see also p. 1200) on strengthening the United Nations role through rationalization of functional modalities with special reference to the General Assembly.[8] The study suggested, among other things, that the Assembly streamline agenda items, ensure better allocation and conduct of work among its Main Committees, and adopt fewer resolutions by avoiding confrontational material and focusing on substantive recommendations or on matters requiring action.

GENERAL ASSEMBLY ACTION

Two draft texts were presented to the General Assembly in 1985 on strengthening the United Nations role, with the Assembly adopting one proposed by 39 countries.

On 11 December, the Assembly, on the recommendation of the Sixth (Legal) Committee, adopted **resolution 40/78** without vote.

Report of the Special Committee on the Charter of the United Nations and on the Strengthening of the Role of the Organization
The General Assembly,
Reaffirming its support for the purposes and principles set forth in the Charter of the United Nations,
Recalling its resolutions 686(VII) of 5 December 1952, 992(X) of 21 November 1955, 2285(XXII) of 5 December 1967, 2552(XXIV) of 12 December 1969, 2697(XXV) of 11 December 1970, 2968(XXVII) of 14 December 1972 and 3349(XXIX) of 17 December 1974,
Recalling also its resolutions 2925(XXVII) of 27 November 1972, 3073(XXVIII) of 30 November 1973 and 3282(XXIX) of 12 December 1974 on the strengthening of the role of the United Nations,
Recalling especially its resolution 3499(XXX) of 15 December 1975, by which it established the Special Committee on the Charter of the United Nations and on the Strengthening of the Role of the Organization, and its resolutions 31/28 of 29 November 1976, 32/45 of 8 December 1977, 33/94 of 16 December 1978, 34/147 of 17 December 1979, 35/164 of 15 December 1980, 36/122 of 11 December 1981, 37/114 of 16 December 1982, 38/141 of 19 December 1983 and 39/88 of 13 December 1984,
Taking note of the reports of the Secretary-General on the work of the Organization submitted to the General Assembly at its thirty-seventh, thirty-ninth and fortieth sessions, as well as of the views and comments expressed on them by Member States,
Having considered the report of the Special Committee on the Charter of the United Nations and on the Strengthening of the Role of the Organization on the work of the session it held in 1985,
Taking into account the work accomplished on the working paper on the prevention and removal of threats to the peace and of situations which may lead to international friction or give rise to a dispute,
Taking into account the elaboration by the Special Committee of the outline for the handbook on the peaceful settlement of disputes between States and the conclusions thereon,

Noting the importance that pre-session consultations among the members of the Special Committee and other interested States may have in facilitating the fulfilment of its task,

Considering that the Special Committee has not yet fulfilled the mandate entrusted to it,

1. *Takes note* of the report of the Special Committee on the Charter of the United Nations and on the Strengthening of the Role of the Organization;

2. *Decides* that the Special Committee shall convene its next session from 7 April to 2 May 1986;

3. *Requests* the Special Committee at its session in 1986:

(a) To accord priority, by devoting more time, to the question of the maintenance of international peace and security in all its aspects in order to strengthen the role of the United Nations, in particular the Security Council, and to enable it to discharge fully its responsibilities under the Charter in this field; this necessitates the examination, *inter alia*, of the prevention and removal of threats to the peace and of situations which may lead to international friction or give rise to a dispute; the Special Committee will work on all questions with the aim of submitting its conclusions to the General Assembly, in accordance with paragraph 5 below, for the adoption of such recommendations as the Assembly deems appropriate; in doing so, the Special Committee should work expeditiously on the working paper on the prevention and removal of threats to the peace and of situations that may lead to international friction or give rise to a dispute, or any revision thereof, as well as other proposals which might be made on that question, with a view to completing its consideration thereof;

(b) To continue its work on the question of the peaceful settlement of disputes between States and, in this context:

(i) To continue consideration of the proposal contained in the working papers on the establishment of a commission on good offices, mediation and conciliation;

(ii) To examine the progress report of the Secretary-General on the elaboration of the draft handbook on the peaceful settlement of disputes between States;

4. *Requests* the Special Committee to keep the question of the rationalization of the procedures of the United Nations under active review;

5. *Also requests* the Special Committee to be mindful of the importance of reaching general agreement whenever that has significance for the outcome of its work;

6. *Urges* members of the Special Committee to participate fully in its work in fulfilment of the mandate entrusted to it;

7. *Decides* that the Special Committee shall accept the participation of observers of Member States, including in the meetings of its working groups;

8. *Invites* Governments to submit or to bring up to date, if they deem it necessary, their observations and proposals, in accordance with General Assembly resolution 3499(XXX);

9. *Requests* the Secretary-General to render all assistance to the Special Committee;

10. *Requests* the Secretary-General to continue the preparation of a draft handbook on the peaceful settlement of disputes between States, on the basis of the outline elaborated by the Special Committee and in the light of the views expressed in the course of the discussions in the Sixth Committee and in the Special Committee, and to report to the Special Committee at its session in 1986

on the progress of work, before submitting to it the draft handbook in its final form, with a view to its approval at a later stage;

11. *Requests* the Special Committee to submit a report on its work to the General Assembly at its forty-first session;

12. *Decides* to include in the provisional agenda of its forty-first session the item entitled "Report of the Special Committee on the Charter of the United Nations and on the Strengthening of the Role of the Organization".

General Assembly resolution 40/78

11 December 1985   Meeting 112   Adopted without vote

Approved by Sixth Committee (A/40/1013) without vote, 2 December (meeting 50); 39-nation draft (A/C.6/40/L.10), orally revised; agenda item 141.

Sponsors: Argentina, Australia, Barbados, Belgium, Bolivia, Brunei Darussalam, Chile, Cyprus, Egypt, Germany, Federal Republic of, Guyana, Indonesia, Italy, Ivory Coast, Japan, Kenya, Liberia, Malaysia, Mexico, Morocco, Nepal, New Zealand, Nigeria, Oman, Papua New Guinea, Paraguay, Philippines, Romania, Rwanda, Samoa, Senegal, Spain, Thailand, Trinidad and Tobago, Uruguay, Venezuela, Yugoslavia, Zaire, Zambia.

Financial implications. 5th Committee, A/40/1017; S-G, A/C.5/40/77, A/C.6/40/L.24.

Meeting numbers. GA 40th session: 5th Committee 56; 6th Committee 37-43, 48, 50; plenary 112.

A second draft on the topic—sponsored by Iran and the Libyan Arab Jamahiriya[9]—was not acted on, when the Committee adopted, by recorded vote of 46 to 36, with 29 abstentions, a proposal to that effect made by Belgium on behalf of the 10 members of the European Community. The two-nation draft would have had the Assembly request the Special Committee to consider, among other things, the possibility of eliminating what the sponsors felt were the adverse effects, on the maintenance of international peace and security, of the abuse of the unanimity rule by the Security Council permanent members.

In other 1985 action, the Assembly adopted **resolution 40/178** on strengthening the United Nations role in international economic, scientific-technological and social co-operation.

Publication of repertories of practice

Pursuant to a 1981 General Assembly request[10] that the Secretary-General give priority to updating the supplements to the *Repertoire of the Practice of the Security Council* and the *Repertory of Practice of United Nations Organs*, volume II of Supplement No. 4 to the *Repertory*, covering 1 September 1966 to 31 December 1969, was published in French[11] and Spanish,[12] while volume II of Supplement No. 5, covering 1 January 1970 to 31 December 1978, was issued in English.[13]

Implementation of UN resolutions

GENERAL ASSEMBLY ACTION

The General Assembly, on 16 September 1985, decided to include in the agenda of its fortieth session the item on implementation of United Nations resolutions (**decision 39/465**); however, no consideration was given to the question during the session, and the Assembly decided in December to resume its fortieth session, at a date to be announced, for the purpose of considering nine items and four sub-items, one of which was the implementation of United Nations resolutions (**decision 40/470**).

REFERENCES

[1]A/40/33 & Corr.1. [2]YUN 1984, p. 1101, GA res. 39/88 A, 13 Dec. 1984. [3]A/AC.182/L.38/Rev.1. [4]YUN 1984, p. 1100. [5]A/AC.182/L.43. [6]A/40/988 & Add.1. [7]ACC/1985/DEC/16-29 (dec. 1985/22). [8]A/40/726 & Corr.1. [9]A/C.6/40/L.13/Rev.1. [10]YUN 1981, p. 1240, GA res. 36/123, 11 Dec. 1981. [11]*Repertory of Practice of United Nations Organs, Supplement No. 4* (covering 1 September 1966 to 31 December 1969), vol. II: *Articles 55-111 of the Charter*, Sales No. F.82.V.7. [12]*Ibid.*, Sales No. S.82.V.7. [13]*Repertory of Practice of United Nations Organs, Supplement No. 5* (covering 1 January 1970 to 31 December 1978), vol. II: *Articles 23-54 of the Charter*, Sales No. E.85.V.8.

Host country relations

The 15-member Committee on Relations with the Host Country continued its work in 1985,[1] in response to a 1984 General Assembly request,[2] and at five meetings considered various aspects of relations between the Headquarters diplomatic community and the United States, the host country. Summaries of communications by Member States on the security of their missions were contained in the Committee's report to the Assembly.[1]

The USSR complained, in February, of what it called terrorist attempts against its Mission, one of which involved the placing of an explosive device on one of its vehicles; it referred, in June, to continuing acts of hooliganism and disruptive phone calls against the Mission staff. It also complained in February that the wife of a diplomat at the Mission had been arrested in a store on false charges. The United States responded to all the complaints.

In February and May, the Committee examined the new reporting procedure, under the host country's 1983 Foreign Missions Amendments Act, regarding motor vehicle insurance.[3] The United States Mission had announced on 15 February 1985 that due to a large number of cases where its citizens had been injured by diplomats with no insurance, the minimum liability insurance coverage requirements had been raised to $300,000. In the Committee, Bulgaria and the USSR considered the new requirements to be discriminatory against diplomats; Seychelles wrote to the Committee Chairman, listing the difficulties the one-person mission from a developing country had encountered in complying with the requirements. At the Committee's request, the compliance deadline was extended to 1 April. The host country's answers to queries from the diplomatic community were annexed to the Committee's report.

The Committee's meeting in September focused on travel restrictions, announced on 29 August by the host country, applicable to United Nations staff members nationals of Afghanistan, the Byelorussian SSR, Cuba, Iran, the Libyan Arab Jamahiriya, the Ukrainian SSR, the USSR and Viet Nam.

The new regulation, effective as of 15 September, required such staff members to make arrangements and obtain prior approval through the United States Foreign Missions Service Bureau for travel outside a 25-mile radius of Columbus Circle, New York City (or beyond the five boroughs of the City in the case of Libyans); the host country also reserved the right to review whether or not proposed travel was an official United Nations assignment. The Secretary-General informed the United States in September that the proposed measures were incompatible with the international obligations assumed by the host country under the United Nations Charter, the Agreement between the United Nations and the United States of America regarding the Headquarters of the United Nations[4] and the Convention on the Privileges and Immunities of the United Nations,[5] in that they discriminated against international civil servants on the basis of their nationality and constrained his exercise of responsibilities.

Other matters brought to the Committee's attention included Cuba's complaint against the United States use of United Nations premises for what it called a disgraceful political show concerning alleged human rights violations in Cuba,[6] and Iraq's complaint of damage inflicted on cars belonging to its diplomats.[7]

The United States, answering Cuba's complaint on 4 March,[8] said it had held a press conference on 25 February at which it introduced three Cuban former political prisoners, whose testimony Cuba did not refute.

The Committee also considered questions related to entry visas issued by the host country, exemption from taxes, the possibility of establishing a commissary at Headquarters for the diplomatic community, and responsibilities of permanent missions in resolving their financial indebtedness. The United States submitted to the Committee a memorandum on participation by persons enjoying diplomatic status in criminal proceedings.[9]

By recommendations approved on 29 November, the Committee, among other things, urged the host country to prevent and punish acts violating the security of missions and safety of their personnel, to seek with the Secretary-General a solution to travel restrictions imposed on Secretariat members of certain nationalities, and to review measures relating to diplomatic vehicles with a view to facilitating the needs of the diplomatic community.

GENERAL ASSEMBLY ACTION

On 11 December 1985, the General Assembly, on the recommendation of the Sixth Committee, adopted **resolution 40/77** without vote.

Report of the Committee on Relations with the Host Country

The General Assembly,

Having considered the report of the Committee on Relations with the Host Country,

Recalling Article 105 of the Charter of the United Nations and the Convention on the Privileges and Immunities of the United Nations,

Recalling further that the problems related to the privileges and immunities of all missions accredited to the United Nations, the security of the missions and the safety of their personnel are of great importance and concern to Member States, as well as the primary responsibility of the host country,

Noting with deep concern the continued acts violating the security and the safety of the personnel of those missions accredited to the United Nations,

Recognizing that effective measures should continue to be taken by the competent authorities of the host country, in particular to prevent any acts violating the security of missions and the safety of their personnel,

Having considered the concerns regarding recent legislation of the host country pertaining to the travel of certain members of the Secretariat,

Taking note of the positions of the Secretary-General of the United Nations and the host country with regard to the application by the host country of the above-mentioned legislation,

1. *Endorses* the recommendations of the Committee on Relations with the Host Country contained in paragraph 56 of its report;

2. *Strongly condemns* any terrorist and criminal acts violating the security of missions accredited to the United Nations and the safety of their personnel;

3. *Urges* the host country to continue to take all necessary measures to ensure effectively the protection, security and safety of the missions accredited to the United Nations and their personnel, including practicable measures to prohibit illegal activities of persons, groups and organizations that encourage, instigate, organize or engage in the perpetration of acts and activities against the security and safety of such missions and representatives;

4. *Reiterates* that adherence of all Member States to the Agreement between the United Nations and the United States of America regarding the Headquarters of the United Nations and to other relevant agreements is an indispensable condition for the normal functioning of the Organization and permanent missions in New York and underlines the necessity for avoiding any action not consistent with obligations in accordance with the Agreement and international law;

5. *Urges* the host country and the Secretary-General to seek a solution that is in accord with the Agreement with regard to the recent legislation adopted by the host country;

6. *Calls upon* countries, especially the host country, to build up public awareness by explaining, through all available means, the importance of the role played by the United Nations and all missions accredited to it in the strengthening of international peace and security;

7. *Requests* the Secretary-General to remain actively engaged in all aspects of the relations of the United Nations with the host country and to continue to stress the importance of effective measures to avoid acts of terrorism, violence and harassment against the missions and their personnel, as well as the need for any pertinent legislation adopted by the host country to be in accord with the Agreement and its other relevant obligations;

8. *Requests* the Committee on Relations with the Host Country to continue its work, in conformity with General Assembly resolution 2819(XXVI) of 15 December 1971;

9. *Decides* to include in the provisional agenda of its forty-first session the item entitled "Report of the Committee on Relations with the Host Country".

General Assembly resolution 40/77

11 December 1985   Meeting 112   Adopted without vote

Approved by Sixth Committee (A/40/1012) without vote, 5 December (meeting 53); draft by Cyprus (A/C.6/40/L.32); agenda item 140.
Meeting numbers. GA 40th session: 6th Committee 52, 53; plenary 112.

REFERENCES

[1]A/40/26. [2]YUN 1984, p. 1103, GA res. 39/87, 13 Dec. 1984. [3]*Ibid.*, p. 1103. [4]YUN 1947-48, p. 199, GA res. 169(II), 31 Oct. 1947. [5]YUN 1946-47, p. 100, GA res. 22 A (I), annex, 13 Feb. 1946. [6]A/40/152. [7]A/AC.154/260. [8]A/40/160. [9]A/AC.154/257.

Draft standard rules of procedure for conferences

The General Assembly, which had asked the Secretary-General in 1980[1] to propose draft standard rules of procedure for special conferences of the United Nations, had deferred consideration of the topic since his first report in 1981.[2]

A September 1985 report of the Secretary-General,[3] submitted in pursuance of a 1984 Assembly request,[4] contained comments and observations received as at 1 August from one Government, four specialized agencies and the International Atomic Energy Agency; annexed was the text of draft rules, and the addendum contained a consolidated index of all comments received to date.

On 11 December, the Assembly, on the recommendation of the Sixth Committee, deferred until its forty-first (1986) session consideration of the Secretary-General's 1985 report and requested a further report in 1986 (**decision 40/421**).

REFERENCES

[1]YUN 1980, p. 1225, GA res. 35/10 C, 3 Nov. 1980. [2]YUN 1981, p. 1370. [3]A/40/611 & Add.1. [4]YUN 1984, p. 1106, GA dec. 39/419, 13 Dec. 1984.

Chapter V

Treaties and agreements

In 1985, the General Assembly made recommendations for action by the United Nations Conference on the Law of Treaties between States and International Organizations or between International Organizations, to be held in 1986 (resolution 40/76).

As in previous years, several multilateral treaties, concluded under United Nations auspices, were deposited with the Secretary-General. Efforts continued to eliminate the backlog in publishing the United Nations *Treaty Series.*

Treaties involving international organizations

Pursuant to a 1984 General Assembly resolution,[1] preparations were made in 1985 for the United Nations Conference on the Law of Treaties between States and International Organizations or between International Organizations, scheduled to be held at Vienna, Austria, from 18 February to 21 March 1986. The Conference was to conclude a convention on the topic based on the draft articles adopted by the International Law Commission (ILC) in 1982.[2]

At informal consultations[3] held between 18 March and 1 May and between 8 and 12 July, participants discussed the organization and methods of work of the Conference along with major issues of substance, including final clauses and settlement of disputes. In addition to preparing the draft rules of procedure, they also recommended that the United Nations should take part in, as well as service, the Conference.

GENERAL ASSEMBLY ACTION

On 11 December 1985, the General Assembly, on the recommendation of the Sixth (Legal) Committee, adopted **resolution 40/76** without vote.

**Preparation for the United Nations Conference
on the Law of Treaties between States
and International Organizations
or between International Organizations**

The General Assembly,

Recalling its resolution 37/112 of 16 December 1982, by which it decided that an international convention should be concluded on the basis of the draft articles on the law of treaties between States and international organizations or between international organizations adopted by the International Law Commission at its thirty-fourth session,

Recalling also its resolution 39/86 of 13 December 1984, by which it decided that the United Nations Conference on the Law of Treaties between States and International Organizations or between International Organizations should be held at Vienna from 18 February to 21 March

1986, and referred to the Conference, as the basic proposal for its consideration, the draft articles on the law of treaties between States and international organizations or between international organizations adopted by the International Law Commission at its thirty-fourth session,

Recalling further its appeal, in paragraph 8 of resolution 39/86, to participants in the Conference to organize consultations, primarily on the organization and methods of work of the Conference, including rules of procedure, and on major issues of substance, including final clauses and settlement of disputes, prior to the convening of the Conference in order to facilitate a successful conclusion of its work through the promotion of general agreement,

Reiterating the importance of enhancing the process of codification and progressive development of international law at a universal level,

1. *Considers* that the informal consultations held pursuant to paragraph 8 of resolution 39/86 have proved to be useful in enabling thorough preparation for successful conduct of the United Nations Conference on the Law of Treaties between States and International Organizations or between International Organizations;

2. *Expresses its satisfaction* with the successful outcome of the work of the informal consultations conducted by the co-Chairmen;

3. *Decides* that, in addition to the organizations referred to in paragraph 2 *(e)* of resolution 39/86, the United Nations should participate in the Conference;

4. *Decides* to transmit to the Conference and to recommend that it adopt the draft rules of procedure for the Conference, worked out during the informal consultations and annexed to the present resolution as annex I, taking into account that those draft rules were drafted for the specific use of that Conference in view of its particular nature and the subject-matter to be considered by it;

5. *Decides further* to transmit to the Conference for its consideration and action, as appropriate, a list of draft articles of the basic proposal, for which substantive consideration is deemed necessary and which are annexed to the present resolution as annex II;

6. *Refers* to the Conference for its consideration the draft final clauses presented by the co-Chairmen on which an exchange of views was held and which are annexed to the present resolution as annex III.

ANNEX I
**United Nations Conference on the Law of Treaties
between States and International Organizations
or between International Organizations
(Vienna, 18 February–21 March 1986)**
Draft rules of procedure

I. Representation and credentials
Composition of delegations

Rule 1

The delegation of each State, Namibia, represented by the United Nations Council for Namibia, and each organization referred to in rule 60 participating in the Conference shall consist of a head of delegation and such other representatives, alternate representatives and advisers as may be required.

Alternates and advisers
Rule 2

The head of delegation may designate an alternate representative or an adviser to act as a representative.

Credentials, corresponding documents and notifications of delegations
Rule 3

1. The credentials of representatives of States, the corresponding documents of the organizations mentioned in rule 60 as well as appropriate notifications, containing the names and titles of the members of each delegation referred to in rule 1 authorizing them to participate in the Conference shall be submitted early to the Executive Secretary of the Conference, and if possible not later than 24 hours after the opening of the Conference. Any subsequent change in the composition of delegations shall also be submitted to the Executive Secretary.

2. The credentials of representatives of States shall be issued by the head of State or Government or by the minister for foreign affairs.

3. The corresponding documents of organizations referred to in rule 60 shall be submitted to the Executive Secretary of the Conference together with a statement on behalf of the organization confirming that such document is issued in accordance with the internal rules and practices of the organization concerned.

Credentials Committee
Rule 4

A Credentials Committee shall be appointed at the beginning of the Conference. It shall consist of nine members from among the representatives of participating States who shall be appointed by the Conference on the proposal of the President. It shall examine the credentials of representatives of States and report to the Conference without delay. The Credentials Committee shall also verify the corresponding documents submitted by representatives of the organizations referred to in rule 60 in accordance with rule 3 and report to the Conference on those documents.

Provisional participation in the Conference
Rule 5

Pending a decision of the Conference on their credentials, representatives of States shall be entitled to participate provisionally in the Conference. Representatives of the organizations referred to in rule 60 shall likewise be entitled to participate provisionally in the Conference pending its decision on whether the documents submitted by them are in conformity with the requirements provided in rule 3.

II. Officers
Elections
Rule 6

The Conference shall elect from among the representatives of participating States the following officers: a President and twenty-two Vice-Presidents, as well as the Chairman of the Committee of the Whole provided for in rule 47 and the Chairman of the Drafting Committee provided for in rule 48. These officers shall be elected on the basis of ensuring the representative character of the General Committee. The Conference may also elect such other officers as it deems necessary for the performance of its functions.

General powers of the President
Rule 7

1. In addition to exercising the powers conferred upon him elsewhere by these rules, the President shall preside at the plenary meetings of the Conference, declare the opening and closing of each meeting, direct the discussion, ensure observance of these rules, accord the right to speak, promote the achievement of general agreement, put questions to the vote and announce decisions reached by general agreement or taken by vote. The President shall rule on points of order and, subject to these rules, shall have complete control of the proceedings and over the maintenance of order thereat. The President may propose to the Conference the closure of the list of speakers, a limitation on the time to be allowed to speakers and on the number of times each representative may speak on a question, the adjournment or the closure of the debate and the suspension or the adjournment of a meeting.

2. The President, in the exercise of his functions, remains under the authority of the Conference.

Acting President
Rule 8

1. If the President finds it necessary to be absent from a meeting or any part thereof, he shall designate a Vice-President to take his place.

2. A Vice-President acting as President shall have the powers and duties of the President.

Replacement of the President
Rule 9

If the President is unable to perform his functions, a new President shall be elected.

The President shall not vote
Rule 10

The President, or a Vice-President acting as President, shall not vote in the Conference, but may designate another member of his delegation to vote in his place.

III. General Committee
Composition
Rule 11

There shall be a General Committee consisting of twenty-five members which shall comprise the President and Vice-Presidents of the Conference, the Chairman of the Committee of the Whole and the Chairman of the Drafting Committee. The President of the Conference, or in his absence one of the Vice-Presidents designated by him, shall serve as Chairman of the General Committee.

Substitute members
Rule 12

If the President or a Vice-President of the Conference is to be absent during a meeting of the General Committee, he may designate a member of his delegation to sit and vote in the Committee. In case of absence, the Chairman of the Committee of the Whole shall designate the Vice-Chairman of that Committee as his substitute and the Chairman of the Drafting Committee shall designate a member of the Drafting Committee. When serving on the General Committee, the Vice-

Chairman of the Committee of the Whole or member of the Drafting Committee shall not have the right to vote if he is of the same delegation as another member of the General Committee.

Functions
Rule 13
The General Committee shall assist the President in the general conduct of the business of the Conference and, subject to the decisions of the Conference, shall ensure the co-ordination of its work. It shall also exercise powers conferred upon it by rule 63.

IV. Secretariat
Duties of the Secretary-General
Rule 14
1. The Secretary-General of the United Nations shall be the Secretary-General of the Conference. He, or his representative, shall act in that capacity in all meetings of the Conference and its committees.

2. The Secretary-General shall appoint an Executive Secretary of the Conference and shall provide and direct the staff required by the Conference and its committees.

Duties of the secretariat
Rule 15
The secretariat of the Conference shall, in accordance with these rules:

(*a*) Interpret speeches made at meetings;

(*b*) Receive, translate, reproduce and distribute the documents of the Conference;

(*c*) Publish and circulate the official documents of the Conference;

(*d*) Prepare and circulate records of public meetings;

(*e*) Make and arrange for the keeping of sound recordings of meetings;

(*f*) Arrange for the custody and preservation of the documents of the Conference in the archives of the United Nations;

(*g*) Generally perform all other work that the Conference may require.

Statements by the secretariat
Rule 16
In the exercise of the duties referred to in rules 14 and 15, the Secretary-General or any other member of the staff designated for that purpose may, at any time, make either oral or written statements concerning any question under consideration.

V. Conduct of business
Quorum
Rule 17
The President may declare a meeting open and permit the debate to proceed when representatives of at least one third of the States participating in the Conference are present. The presence of representatives of two thirds of the States so participating shall be required for any decision to be taken.

Speeches
Rule 18
1. No one may address the Conference without having previously obtained the permission of the President. Subject to rules 19, 20 and 23 to 25, the President shall call upon speakers in the order in which they signify their desire to speak. The secretariat shall be in charge of drawing up a list of such speakers. The President may call a speaker to order if his remarks are not relevant to the subject under discussion.

2. The Conference may limit the time allowed to each speaker and the number of times each representative may speak on a question. Before a decision is taken, two representatives may speak in favour of, and two against, a proposal to set such limits. When the debate is limited and a speaker exceeds the allotted time, the President shall call him to order without delay.

Precedence
Rule 19
The chairman or rapporteur of a committee, or the representative of a sub-committee or working group, may be accorded precedence for the purpose of explaining the conclusions arrived at by his committee, subcommittee or working group.

Points of order
Rule 20
During the discussion of any matter, a representative of a participating State may at any time raise a point of order, which shall be decided immediately by the President in accordance with these rules. A representative of a participating State may appeal against the ruling of the President. The appeal shall be put to the vote immediately, and the President's ruling shall stand unless overruled by a majority of such representatives present and voting. A representative may not, in raising a point of order, speak on the substance of the matter under discussion.

Closing of the list of speakers
Rule 21
During the course of a debate the President may announce the list of speakers and, with the consent of the Conference, declare the list closed.

Right of reply
Rule 22
1. Notwithstanding rule 21, the President shall accord the right of reply to any delegation that requests it.

2. Replies made pursuant to the present rule shall be made at the end of the last meeting of the day, or at the conclusion of the consideration of the relevant issue if that is sooner.

3. The number of interventions in exercise of the right of reply for any delegation at a given meeting should be limited to two per issue.

4. The first intervention in the exercise of the right of reply, for any delegation on any issue at a given meeting, shall be limited to five minutes and the second intervention shall be limited to three minutes.

Adjournment of debate
Rule 23
During the discussion of any matter, a representative may move the adjournment of the debate on the question under discussion. In addition to the proposer of the motion, two representatives may speak in favour of, and two against, the adjournment, after which the motion shall be put immediately to the vote.

Closure of debate
Rule 24
A representative may at any time move the closure of the debate on the question under discussion, whether or not any other representative has signified his wish to speak. Permission to speak on the closure of the debate

shall be accorded only to two speakers opposing the closure, after which the motion shall be put immediately to the vote.

Suspension or adjournment of the meeting
Rule 25

During the discussion of any matter, a representative may move the suspension or the adjournment of the meeting. Such motions shall not be debated, but shall be put immediately to the vote.

Order of motions
Rule 26

Subject to rule 20, the motions indicated below shall have precedence in the following order over all proposals or other motions before the meeting:

(a) To suspend the meeting;
(b) To adjourn the meeting;
(c) To adjourn the debate on the question under discussion;
(d) To close the debate on the question under discussion.

Basic proposal
Rule 27

The draft articles on the law of treaties between States and international organizations or between international organizations, adopted by the International Law Commission, shall constitute the basic proposal for consideration by the Conference.

Articles of the basic proposal requiring substantive consideration
Rule 28

1. The Conference shall decide which of the draft articles of the basic proposal referred to in rule 27 require substantive consideration. These draft articles shall be referred to the Committee of the Whole and all other draft articles shall be referred directly to the Drafting Committee.
2. After such a decision is taken by the Conference:
(a) The Committee of the Whole may decide, at the request of a representative, to give substantive consideration to a particular article of the basic proposal that was referred directly to the Drafting Committee;
(b) The Drafting Committee itself may decide, where necessary, to transfer particular draft articles of the basic proposal to the Committee of the Whole for substantive consideration.

Other proposals and amendments
Rule 29

Other proposals and amendments thereto shall normally be submitted in writing to the Executive Secretary of the Conference, who shall circulate copies to all delegations. As a general rule, no proposal shall be considered at any meeting of the Conference unless copies of it have been circulated to all delegations not later than the day preceding the meeting. The President may, however, permit the consideration of amendments, even though these amendments have not been circulated or have only been circulated on the same day.

Decisions on competence
Rule 30

Subject to rule 20, any motion calling for a decision on the competence of the Conference to discuss any matter or to adopt a proposal submitted to it shall be put to the vote before the matter is discussed or a decision is taken as to the proposal in question.

Withdrawal of proposals and motions
Rule 31

A proposal may be withdrawn by its proposer at any time before voting on it has commenced, provided that it has not been amended. A proposal or a motion that has thus been withdrawn may be reintroduced.

Reconsideration of proposals
Rule 32

When a proposal has been adopted or rejected it may not be reconsidered unless the Conference, by a two-thirds majority of the representatives of participating States present and voting, so decides. Permission to speak on the motion to reconsider shall be accorded only to two speakers from representatives of participating States opposing the motion, after which it shall be put immediately to the vote.

Invitations to technical advisers
Rule 33

The Conference may invite to one or more of its meetings any person whose technical advice it may consider useful for its work.

VI. Decision-taking
Decision-taking rights
Rule 34

Decision-taking rights shall be exercised only by States participating in the Conference. In decision-taking by vote each State represented at the Conference shall have one vote.

Majority required
Rule 35

1. Decisions of the Conference on all matters of substance shall be taken by a two-thirds majority of the representatives present and voting.
2. Decisions of the Conference on matters of procedure shall be taken by a majority of the representatives present and voting.
3. If the question arises whether a matter is one of procedure or of substance, the President shall rule on the question. An appeal against this ruling shall be put to the vote immediately and the President's ruling shall stand unless overruled by a majority of the representatives present and voting.

Meaning of the phrase "representatives present and voting"
Rule 36

For the purposes of these rules, the phrase "representatives present and voting" means representatives present and casting an affirmative or negative vote. Representatives who abstain from voting shall be considered as not voting.

Method of voting
Rule 37

Except as provided in rule 43, the Conference shall normally vote by show of hands or by standing, but any representative may request a roll-call. The roll-call shall be taken in the English alphabetical order of the names of the States participating in the Conference, beginning with the delegation whose name is drawn by lot by the President.

Conduct during voting
Rule 38

The President shall announce the commencement of voting, after which no representative shall be permitted to intervene until the result of the vote has been announced, except on a point of order in connection with the process of voting.

Explanation of vote

Rule 39

Representatives may make brief statements consisting solely of explanation of their votes, before the voting has commenced or after the voting has been completed. The representative of a State sponsoring a proposal or motion shall not speak in explanation of vote thereon, except if it has been amended.

Division of proposals

Rule 40

A representative of a participating State may move that parts of a proposal shall be voted on separately. If objection is made to the request for division, the motion for division shall be voted upon. If the motion for division is carried, those parts of the proposal that are subsequently approved shall be put to the vote as a whole. If all operative parts of the proposal have been rejected, the proposal shall be considered to have been rejected as a whole.

Voting on amendments

Rule 41

When an amendment is moved to a proposal, the amendment shall be voted on first. When two or more amendments are moved to a proposal, the Conference shall first vote on the amendment furthest removed in substance from the original proposal and then on the amendment next furthest removed therefrom, and so on until all the amendments have been put to the vote. Where, however, the adoption of one amendment necessarily implies the rejection of another amendment, the latter amendment shall not be put to the vote. If one or more amendments are adopted, the amended proposal shall then be voted upon. A motion is considered an amendment to a proposal if it merely adds to, deletes from or revises part of the proposal. Unless specified otherwise, the word "proposal" in these rules shall be considered as including amendments.

Voting on proposals

Rule 42

If two or more proposals relate to the same question, the Conference shall, unless it decides otherwise, vote on the proposals in the order in which they have been submitted. The Conference may, after each vote on a proposal, decide whether to vote on the next proposal.

Elections

Rule 43

All elections shall be held by secret ballot unless otherwise decided by the Conference.

Rule 44

1. If, when one person or one delegation of a participating State is to be elected, no candidate obtains in the first ballot a majority of the votes of the representatives present and voting, a second ballot restricted to the two candidates obtaining the largest number of votes shall be taken. If in the second ballot the votes are equally divided, the President shall decide between the candidates by drawing lots.

2. In the case of a tie in the first ballot among three or more candidates obtaining the largest number of votes, a second ballot shall be held. If a tie results among more

than two candidates, the number shall be reduced to two by lot and the balloting, restricted to them, shall continue in accordance with the preceding paragraph.

Rule 45

When two or more elective places are to be filled at one time under the same conditions, those candidates, not exceeding the number of such places, obtaining in the first ballot a majority of the votes of the representatives present and voting shall be elected. If the number of candidates obtaining such majority is less than the number of persons or delegations to be elected, there shall be additional ballots to fill the remaining places, the voting being restricted to the candidates obtaining the greatest number of votes in the previous ballot, to a number not more than twice the places remaining to be filled, provided that, after the third inconclusive ballot, votes may be cast for any eligible person or delegation. If three such unrestricted ballots are inconclusive, the next three ballots shall be restricted to candidates who obtained the greatest number of votes in the third of the unrestricted ballots, to a number not more than twice the places remaining to be filled, and the following three ballots thereafter shall be unrestricted, and so on until all the places have been filled.

Equally divided votes

Rule 46

If a vote is equally divided on matters other than elections, the proposal or motion shall be regarded as rejected.

VII. Committees

Committee of the Whole

Rule 47

The Conference shall establish a Committee of the Whole, which may set up sub-committees or working groups. The Committee of the Whole shall have as its officers a Chairman, a Vice-Chairman and a Rapporteur.

Drafting Committee

Rule 48

1. The Conference shall establish a Drafting Committee consisting of 15 members representing participating States, including its Chairman who shall be elected by the Conference in accordance with rule 6. The other 14 members of the Committee shall be appointed by the Conference on the proposal of the General Committee. The Rapporteur of the Committee of the Whole participates *ex officio*, without a vote, in the work of the Drafting Committee.

2. The Drafting Committee shall consider draft articles of the basic proposal referred to it directly pursuant to paragraph 1 of rule 28. It shall also consider any draft articles referred to it by the Committee of the Whole after initial consideration by that Committee. The Drafting Committee shall furthermore prepare drafts and give advice on drafting as requested by the Conference or by the Committee of the Whole. It shall also co-ordinate and review the drafting of all texts adopted and shall report, as appropriate, either to the Conference or to the Committee of the Whole.

Officers

Rule 49

Except as otherwise provided in rule 6, each committee, sub-committee and working group shall elect its own officers from among representatives of participating States.

Quorum
Rule 50

1. The Chairman of the Committee of the Whole may declare a meeting open and permit the debate to proceed when representatives of at least one quarter of the States participating in the Conference are present. The presence of representatives of a majority of the States so participating shall be required for any decision to be taken.

2. A majority of the representatives on the General, Drafting or Credentials Committees or any sub-committee or working group shall constitute a quorum.

Officers, conduct of business and decision-taking
Rule 51

The rules contained in chapters II, V (except rule 17) and VI above shall be applicable, *mutatis mutandis*, to the proceedings of committees, sub-committees and working groups, except that:

(a) The Chairmen of the General, Drafting and Credentials Committees and the chairman of any sub-committee or working group may exercise the right to vote;

(b) Decisions of committees, sub-committees and working groups shall be taken by a majority of the representatives of States present and voting, except that the reconsideration of a proposal or an amendment shall require the majority established by rule 32.

VIII. Languages and records
Languages of the Conference
Rule 52

Arabic, Chinese, English, French, Russian and Spanish shall be the languages of the Conference.

Interpretation
Rule 53

1. Speeches made in a language of the Conference shall be interpreted into the other such languages.

2. A representative may speak in a language other than a language of the Conference if the delegation concerned provides for interpretation into one such language.

Records and sound recordings of meetings
Rule 54

1. Summary records of the plenary meetings of the Conference and of the meetings of the Committee of the Whole shall be kept in the languages of the Conference. As a general rule, they shall be circulated as soon as possible, simultaneously in all the languages of the Conference, to all representatives, who shall inform the secretariat within five working days after the circulation of the summary record of any changes they wish to have made.

2. The secretariat shall make sound recordings of meetings of the Conference, the Committee of the Whole and the Drafting Committee. Such recordings shall be made of meetings of other committees, sub-committees or working groups when the body concerned so decides.

Languages of official documents
Rule 55

Official documents shall be made available in the languages of the Conference.

IX. Public and private meetings
Plenary meetings and meetings of committees
Rule 56

The plenary meetings of the Conference and the meetings of committees shall be held in public unless the body concerned decides otherwise. All decisions taken by the plenary of the Conference at a private meeting shall be announced at an early public meeting of the plenary.

Meetings of sub-committees or working groups
Rule 57

As a general rule meetings of a sub-committee or working group shall be held in private.

Communiqués on private meetings
Rule 58

At the close of a private meeting, the chairman of the organ concerned may issue a communiqué to the press through the Executive Secretary.

X. Other participants and observers
Representatives of the United Nations Council for Namibia
Rule 59

Representatives designated by the United Nations Council for Namibia may participate in the deliberations of the Conference, the Committee of the Whole and other committees, sub-committees or working groups, in accordance with the relevant resolutions and decisions of the General Assembly.

Representatives of the United Nations and of the organizations that have received an invitation from the General Assembly in subparagraph 2 (e) of its resolution 39/86
Rule 60

1. Except as otherwise provided in the present rules, representatives designated by the United Nations or by organizations referred to in subparagraph 2 *(e)* of General Assembly resolution 39/86, that have traditionally been invited to participate as observers at legal codification conferences convened under the auspices of the United Nations, shall participate in the Conference in the following capacity:

(a) To participate in public and private meetings of the Conference, the Committee of the Whole, sub-committees and working groups, as well as in the process leading to general agreement;

(b) To submit documents for circulation;

(c) To intervene in the debates;

　—To exercise the right of reply in accordance with rule 22;

　—To explain their positions on any matter on which a decision has been or is to be taken;

(d) To submit substantive proposals, which as such may only be put to the vote subject to rule 63 if a formal request is made by a State to that effect. If the proposal has been circulated in writing, the formal request shall be circulated in the same manner;

(e) To submit procedural motions, including those referred to in rules 23, 24 and 25, which may not be put to the vote unless supported by a State.

2. Representatives of the organizations participating in the Conference in accordance with paragraph 1 of this rule may not:

(a) Object to any procedural motion put forward by a representative of a participating State;

(b) Prevent on their own the achievement of general agreement or participate in any vote.

3. Delegations of the organizations referred to in paragraph 1 shall be seated in alphabetical order following the seating of delegations of States.

*Representatives of organizations that have received
a standing invitation from the General Assembly
to participate in the sessions and the work of all
international conferences convened under its auspices
in the capacity of observers in accordance with
General Assembly resolutions 3237(XXIX) and 31/152*
Rule 61

Representatives designated by organizations that have
received a standing invitation from the General Assembly
in accordance with General Assembly resolutions
3237(XXIX) of 22 November 1974 and 31/152 of 20
December 1976 to participate in the sessions and the work
of all international conferences convened under its auspices
have the right to participate as observers, without the
right to vote, in the deliberations of the Conference, the
Committee of the Whole and, as appropriate, other committees, sub-committees or working groups.

Representatives of national liberation movements
Rule 62

Representatives designated by national liberation
movements invited to the Conference may participate
as observers, without the right to vote, in the deliberations of the Conference, the Committee of the Whole
and, as appropriate, other committees, sub-committees
or working groups.

XI.   Promotion of general agreement
Promotion of general agreement
Rule 63

1.   The Conference shall, both at the plenary and at
the Committee of the Whole stages, make every effort
to reach general agreement on matters of substance, particularly on the final results of the work of the Conference, and there shall be no voting on such matters
until all efforts to that end have been exhausted.

2.   In endeavouring to reach general agreement, all
possible means shall be used. The officers of the Conference shall chair as appropriate, co-ordinate and supervise meetings with a view to enhancing the prospects
of reaching general agreement.

3.   If, in the consideration of any matter of substance,
no general agreement appears to be attainable, the President of the Conference shall inform the General Committee that efforts to reach general agreement have
failed. The General Committee shall thereupon consider
the matter and may recommend that it be decided by
a vote, indicating the date of the vote, and place the question before the plenary or the Committee of the Whole
as the case may be.

XII.   Amendments to the rules of procedure
Method of amendment
Rule 64

These rules of procedure may be amended by a decision of the Conference taken by a two-thirds majority
of the representatives of participating States present and
voting.

ANNEX II
**List of draft articles of the basic proposal, for which
substantive consideration is deemed necessary***

1.   Article 2[†] "Use of terms"
2.   Article 3 "International agreements not within
the scope of the present articles"
3.   Article 5 "Treaties constituting international
organizations and treaties adopted within an
international organization"

4.   Article 6 "Capacity of international organizations to conclude treaties"
5.   Article 7 "Full powers and powers"
6.   Article 9 "Adoption of the text"
—paragraph 2
7.   Article 11 "Means of expressing consent to be
bound by a treaty"
—paragraph 2 (arts. 14.3, 16, 18 and 19.2 are
closely related to this paragraph)
8.   Article 19 "Formulation of reservations"
9.   Article 20 "Acceptance of and objection to
reservations"
10.   Article 27 "Internal law of States, rules of international organizations and observance of
treaties"
11.   Article 30 "Application of successive treaties
relating to the same subject-matter"
—paragraph 6
12.   Article 36 *bis* "Obligations and rights arising for
States members of an international organization
from a treaty to which it is a party"
13.   Article 38 "Rules in a treaty becoming binding
on third States or third organizations through
international custom"
14.   Article 45 "Loss of a right to invoke a ground
for invalidating, terminating, withdrawing from
or suspending the operation of a treaty"
15.   Article 46 "Provisions of internal law of a State
and rules of an international organization regarding competence to conclude treaties"
—paragraph 2
—paragraph 3
—paragraph 4
16.   Article 56 "Denunciation of or withdrawal from
a treaty containing no provision regarding termination, denunciation or withdrawal"
17.   Article 61 "Supervening impossibility of
performance"
18.   Article 62 "Fundamental change of
circumstances"
19.   Article 65 "Procedure to be followed with respect
to invalidity, termination, withdrawal from or
suspensions of the operation of a treaty"
—paragraph 3
20.   Article 66 "Procedures for arbitration and
conciliation"
21.   Article 73 "Cases of succession of States, responsibility of a State or of an international organization, outbreak of hostilities, termination of the
existence of an organization and termination of
participation by a State in the membership of
an organization"
22.   Article 75 "Case of an aggressor State"
23.   Article 77 "Functions of depositaries"
24.   Annex "Arbitration and conciliation procedures
established in application of article 66"

*It is understood that if certain changes to the articles listed
were approved by the Conference, consequential changes
might have to be introduced in other draft articles.

†It is noted that since draft article 2 sets out definitions,
its provisions should not be considered separately but in conjunction with the substantive consideration of other articles
to which those definitions are closely related.

ANNEX III
Draft final clauses
(Based on those of the 1969 Vienna Convention
on the Law of Treaties[4])

FINAL PROVISIONS

Article 81
Signature

The present Convention shall be open for signature until . . . (date, month, year) at the Federal Ministry for Foreign Affairs of the Republic of Austria, and subsequently, until . . . (date, month, year), at the United Nations Headquarters, New York by:

(*a*)All States;

(*b*)Namibia, represented by the United Nations Council for Namibia;

(*c*)International organizations invited to participate in the United Nations Conference on the Law of Treaties between States and International Organizations or between International Organizations.

Article 82
Ratification or act of formal confirmation

The present Convention is subject to ratification by States and by Namibia, represented by the United Nations Council for Namibia, and to acts of formal confirmation by international organizations. The instruments of ratification and those relating to acts of formal confirmation shall be deposited with the Secretary-General of the United Nations.

Article 83
Accession

1. The present Convention shall remain open for accession by any State, by Namibia, represented by the United Nations Council for Namibia, and by any international organization which has the capacity to conclude treaties.

2. An instrument of accession of an international organization shall contain a declaration that it has the capacity to conclude treaties.

3. The instruments of accession shall be deposited with the Secretary-General of the United Nations.

Article 84
Entry into force

1. The present Convention shall enter into force on the thirtieth day following the date of deposit of the . . . instrument of ratification or accession by States or by Namibia, represented by the United Nations Council for Namibia.

2. For each State or for Namibia, represented by the United Nations Council for Namibia, ratifying or acceding to the Convention after the condition specified in paragraph 1 has been fulfilled, the Convention shall enter into force on the thirtieth day after deposit by such State or by Namibia of its instrument of ratification or accession.

3. For each international organization depositing an instrument relating to an act of formal confirmation or an instrument of accession, the Convention shall enter into force on the thirtieth day after such deposit, provided that it shall not so enter into force before the Convention enters into force pursuant to paragraph 1.

Article 85
Authentic texts

The original of the present Convention, of which the Arabic, Chinese, English, French, Russian and Spanish texts are equally authentic, shall be deposited with the Secretary-General of the United Nations.

IN WITNESS WHEREOF the undersigned Plenipotentiaries, being duly authorized by their respective Governments, and duly authorized representatives of the United Nations Council for Namibia and of international organizations have signed the present Convention.

DONE AT VIENNA this . . . day of . . . one thousand nine hundred and eighty-six.

General Assembly resolution 40/76

11 December 1985   Meeting 112   Adopted without vote

Approved by Sixth Committee (A/40/952) without vote, 25 November (meeting 46); draft by Chairman (A/C.6/40/L.16), orally revised; agenda item 139.

Relations between States and international organizations

In 1985, ILC[5] resumed consideration of the relations between States and international organizations, which it had last studied in 1983.[6] It had before it the second report by the Special Rapporteur on the topic, Leonardo Díaz-González (Venezuela),[7] in which he examined the notion of an international organization and possible approaches to the scope of the future draft articles on the topic, as well as the question of the legal personality of such organizations and the legal powers deriving from it. Also before ILC was a supplementary study[8] prepared, at its request, by the Secretariat on the basis of information received from the legal counsels of the specialized agencies and the International Atomic Energy Agency, on their practice concerning their status, privileges and immunities.

The Commission concluded that the Special Rapporteur might consider submitting in 1986 concrete suggestions on the possible scope of the draft articles, as well as a schematic outline of the subject-matter to be covered by them.

The General Assembly, in **resolution 40/75**, recommended that ILC continue work on the topic.

Registration and publication of treaties by the United Nations

During 1985, some 503 international agreements and 446 subsequent actions were received by the Secretariat for registration or filing and recording. In addition, there were 310 registrations of formalities concerning agreements for which the Secretary-General performs depositary functions.

The texts of international agreements registered or filed and recorded are published in the United Nations *Treaty Series* in the original languages, with translations into English and French where necessary. In 1985, the following volumes of the *Treaty Series* covering treaties registered or filed in 1975, 1976, 1977 and 1978 were issued:

990, 1004, 1005, 1024, 1027, 1032, 1040, 1047, 1050, 1051, 1052, 1056, 1059, 1064, 1065, 1067, 1068, 1070, 1071, 1072, 1073, 1074, 1076, 1083, 1087.

Elimination of the backlog in publication

In November 1985, the Secretary-General submitted to the General Assembly his third biennial report[9] on progress made in eliminating, by 1990, the backlog in publishing the United Nations *Treaty Series*.

The report reviewed the progress made since his last report in 1983[10] and discussed the status of the *Treaty Series* as well as that of the *Cumulative Index* and the *Monthly Statement of Treaties and International Agreements Registered or Filed and Recorded with the Secretariat*. As the plan stood in 1985, no new additional resources were being requested.

On 18 December, the Assembly took note of the Secretary-General's report (**resolution 40/252, section IX**).

Multilateral treaties

New multilateral treaties concluded under United Nations auspices

The following treaties, concluded under United Nations auspices, were deposited with the Secretary-General during 1985:[11]

International Convention against Apartheid *in Sports*, adopted by the General Assembly on 10 December 1985 (**resolution 40/64 G**)
European Agreement on Main International Railway Lines (AGC), concluded at Geneva on 31 May 1985
Protocol to the 1979 Convention on Long-Range Transboundary Air Pollution on the Reduction of Sulphur Emissions or their Transboundary Fluxes by at least 30 per cent, concluded at Helsinki on 8 July 1985 (see also p. 800)
Vienna Convention for the Protection of the Ozone Layer, concluded at Vienna on 22 March 1985 (see also p. 804)
Regulation No. 63: Uniform provisions concerning the approval of mopeds with regard to noise; Regulation No. 64: Uniform provisions concerning the approval of vehicles equipped with temporary-use spare wheels/tyres, both annexed to the *Agreement concerning the Adoption of Uniform Conditions of Approval and Reciprocal Recognition of Approval for Motor Vehicle Equipment and Parts*, done at Geneva on 20 March 1958

Multilateral treaties deposited with the Secretary-General

The number of multilateral treaties for which the Secretary-General performed depositary functions stood at 334 at the end of 1985. During the year, 124 signatures were affixed to treaties for which the Secretary-General performed depositary functions and 278 instruments of ratification, accession, acceptance and approval or notifications were transmitted to him. In addition, he received 310 communications from States expressing observations or declarations and reservations made at the time of signature, ratification or accession.

The following multilateral treaties,[11] in respect of which the Secretary-General acts as depositary, came into force during 1985:

Regulation No. 63: Uniform provisions concerning the approval of mopeds with regard to noise; Regulation No. 64: Uniform provisions concerning the approval of vehicles equipped with temporary-use spare wheels/tyres, both annexed to the *Agreement concerning the Adoption of Uniform Conditions of Approval and Reciprocal Recognition of Approval for Motor Vehicle Equipment and Parts*, done at Geneva on 20 March 1958
International Coffee Agreement, 1983, adopted by the International Coffee Council on 16 September 1982
International Tropical Timber Agreement, 1983, concluded at Geneva on 18 November 1983
International Sugar Agreement, 1984, concluded at Geneva on 5 July 1984

REFERENCES

[1]YUN 1984, p. 1108, GA res. 39/86, 13 Dec. 1984. [2]YUN 1982, p. 1396. [3]A/C.6/40/10. [4]YUN 1969, p. 730. [5]A/40/10. [6]YUN 1983, p. 1128. [7]A/CN.4/391 & Add.1 & Add.1/Corr.2. [8]A/CN.4/L.383 & Add.1-3. [9]A/C.5/40/49. [10]YUN 1983, p. 1129. [11]*Multilateral Treaties Deposited with the Secretary-General: Status as at 31 December 1985* (ST/LEG/SER.E/4), Sales No. E.86.V.3.

OTHER PUBLICATIONS

Statement of Treaties and International Agreements, registered or filed and recorded with the Secretariat during 1985, ST/LEG/SER.A/455-466 (monthly); *Statement of Treaties and International Agreements*, registered or filed and recorded with the Secretariat, *Cumulative Index No. 13* (vols. 801-850), I: Treaties Nos. 11046 to 12187 (registered); II: Treaties Nos. 665 to 684 (filed and recorded).

Chapter VI

International economic law

Legal aspects of international economic law continued to be examined in 1985 by the United Nations Commission on International Trade Law (UNCITRAL) and by the General Assembly's Sixth (Legal) Committee.

In December, the Assembly noted with satisfaction UNCITRAL's adoption of the Model Law on International Commercial Arbitration and recommended that all States give it due consideration (resolution 40/72). It also recommended that UNCITRAL continue work on the topics in its work programme (40/71), and decided to consider further, in 1986, legal aspects of the new international economic order (40/67), and, in 1988, action to be taken on a series of draft articles on most-favoured-nation clauses (40/65).

Topics related to this chapter. Development policy and international economic co-operation: proposed new international economic order. Industrial development: industrial co-operation contracts.

General aspects

Report of UNCITRAL

At its eighteenth session, held at Vienna, Austria, from 3 to 21 June 1985, UNCITRAL[1] considered a draft model law on international commercial arbitration, means of international payments, and training and assistance programmes. It noted current United Nations activities relating to co-ordination of trade law and legal aspects of technology transfer, and examined legal problems arising from electronic funds transfers.

In addition, the Commission considered a report of its Working Group on International Contract Practices (eighth session, Vienna, 3-13 December 1984), which in 1984[2] it had asked to prepare uniform rules on liability of operators of transport terminals, and two reports[3] of its Working Group on the New International Economic Order (sixth session, Vienna, 10-20 September 1984;[4] seventh session, New York, 8-19 April 1985), which had continued to study a draft legal guide on drawing up international contracts for construction of industrial works.

The Secretary-General reported to the General Assembly in October[5] that on 25 September the Trade and Development Board of the United Nations Conference on Trade and Development[6] had considered and taken note of the 1985 UNCITRAL report.

GENERAL ASSEMBLY ACTION

On 11 December, the General Assembly, on the recommendation of the Sixth Committee, adopted **resolution 40/71** without vote.

Report of the United Nations Commission on International Trade Law

The General Assembly,

Having considered the report of the United Nations Commission on International Trade Law on the work of its eighteenth session,

Recalling that the object of the Commission is the promotion of the progressive harmonization and unification of international trade law,

Recalling, in this regard, its resolution 2205(XXI) of 17 December 1966, as well as all its other resolutions relating to the work of the Commission,

Recalling also its resolutions 3201(S-VI) and 3202(S-VI) of 1 May 1974, 3281(XXIX) of 12 December 1974 and 3362(S-VII) of 16 September 1975,

Reaffirming its conviction that the progressive harmonization and unification of international trade law, in reducing or removing legal obstacles to the flow of international trade, especially those affecting the developing countries, would significantly contribute to universal economic co-operation among all States on a basis of equality, equity and common interest and to the elimination of discrimination in international trade and, thereby, to the well-being of all peoples,

Having regard for the need to take into account the different social and legal systems in harmonizing and unifying international trade law,

Stressing the value of participation by States at all levels of economic development, including developing countries, in the process of harmonizing and unifying international trade law,

1. *Takes note with appreciation* of the report of the United Nations Commission on International Trade Law on the work of its eighteenth session;

2. *Commends* the Commission for the progress made in its work and for having reached decisions by consensus;

3. *Calls upon* the Commission to continue to take account of the relevant provisions of the resolutions concerning the new international economic order, as adopted by the General Assembly at its sixth and seventh special sessions, and reaffirms the importance, in particular for developing countries, of the work carried out by the Working Group on the New International Economic Order on a legal guide on the drawing up of international contracts for construction of industrial works;

4. *Notes with particular satisfaction* the completion and adoption by the Commission of the Model Law on International Commercial Arbitration;

5. *Welcomes* the work of the Commission on the legal implications of automated data processing on the flow of international trade as an activity of vital importance to States at all levels of economic development, including developing countries, and in this connection:

(a) Commends the Commission for its recommendation on the legal value of computer records which, in conjunction with the preparatory report submitted to the Commission by the Secretary-General, aids in clarifying the legal issues;

(b) Calls upon Governments and international organizations to take action, where appropriate, in conformity with the recommendation of the Commission so as to ensure legal security in the context of the widest possible use of automated data processing in international trade;

6. *Reaffirms* the mandate of the Commission, as the core legal body within the United Nations system in the field of international trade law, to co-ordinate legal activities in this field in order to avoid duplication of effort and to promote efficiency, consistency and coherence in the unification and harmonization of international trade law, and, in this connection, recommends that the Commission, through its secretariat, should continue to maintain close co-operation with the other international organs and organizations, including regional organizations, active in the field of international trade law;

7. *Reaffirms also* the importance, in particular for the developing countries, of the work of the Commission concerned with training and assistance in the field of international trade law and the desirability for it to sponsor symposia and seminars, in particular those organized on a regional basis, to promote such training and assistance, and, in this connection:

(a) Expresses its appreciation to those Governments, regional organizations and institutions that have collaborated with the secretariat of the Commission in organizing regional seminars and symposia in the field of international trade law;

(b) Welcomes the initiatives being undertaken by the Commission and its secretariat to collaborate with other organizations and institutions in the organization of regional seminars;

(c) Invites Governments, international organizations and institutions to assist the secretariat of the Commission in financing and organizing regional seminars and symposia, in particular in developing countries;

(d) Invites Governments, relevant United Nations organs, organizations, institutions and individuals to make voluntary contributions to allow the resumption of the programme of the Commission for the award of fellowships on a regular basis to candidates from developing countries to enable them to participate in such symposia and seminars;

8. *Stresses* the importance of bringing into effect the conventions emanating from the work of the Commission for the global unification and harmonization of international trade law;

9. *Recommends* that the Commission should continue its work on the topics included in its programme of work;

10. *Expresses its appreciation* of the important role played by the International Trade Law Branch of the Office of Legal Affairs of the Secretariat, as the substantive secretariat of the Commission, in assisting in the implementation of the work programme of the Commission.

General Assembly resolution 40/71

11 December 1985   Meeting 112   Adopted without vote

Approved by Sixth Committee (A/40/935) by consensus, 14 November (meeting 38); 31-nation draft (A/C.6/40/L.6); agenda item 135.
Sponsors: Argentina, Australia, Austria, Belgium, Brazil, Canada, Cyprus, Czechoslovakia, Egypt, Finland, France, Germany, Federal Republic of, Greece, Guyana, Hungary, Italy, Jamaica, Japan, Kenya, Libyan Arab Jamahiriya, Morocco, Netherlands, Nigeria, Philippines, Romania, Senegal, Singapore, Spain, Sweden, Turkey, Yugoslavia.
Meeting numbers. GA 40th session: 6th Committee 3-5, 37, 38; plenary 112.

REFERENCES

[1]A/40/17. [2]YUN 1984, p. 1114. [3]A/CN.9/259, A/CN.9/262. [4]YUN 1984, p. 575. [5]A/C.6/40/L.5. [6]A/40/15, vol. II.

International trade law

Unification of trade law

International commercial arbitration

In June 1985, UNCITRAL[1] adopted the Model Law on International Commercial Arbitration, intended for use in modernizing and harmonizing related national laws and practices. The draft text had been prepared by its Working Group on International Contract Practices during five sessions held between 1982 and 1984, and examined by the Commission and its Drafting Group.

The Commission had before it in 1985 two reports of the Secretary-General on the draft text of a model law as completed by the Working Group in 1984:[2] one contained an analytical compilation of comments by Governments and international organizations,[3] and the other an analytical commentary.[4]

The Model Law—the text of which was annexed to the 1985 UNCITRAL report to the Assembly[1]— comprised 36 articles in chapters dealing with general provisions, arbitration agreement, composition of arbitral tribunal, jurisdiction of arbitral tribunal, conduct of arbitral proceedings, making of award and termination of proceedings, recourse against award, and recognition and enforcement of awards.

GENERAL ASSEMBLY ACTION

On 11 December, the General Assembly, on the recommendation of the Sixth Committee, adopted **resolution 40/72** without vote.

**Model Law on International Commercial
Arbitration of the United Nations
Commission on International Trade Law**
The General Assembly,
Recognizing the value of arbitration as a method of settling disputes arising in international commercial relations,
Convinced that the establishment of a model law on arbitration that is acceptable to States with different legal, social and economic systems contributes to the development of harmonious international economic relations,

Noting that the Model Law on International Commercial Arbitration was adopted by the United Nations Commission on International Trade Law at its eighteenth session, after due deliberation and extensive consultation with arbitral institutions and individual experts on international commercial arbitration,

Convinced that the Model Law, together with the Convention on the Recognition and Enforcement of Foreign Arbitral Awards and the Arbitration Rules of the United Nations Commission on International Trade Law recommended by the General Assembly in its resolution 31/98 of 15 December 1976, significantly contributes to the establishment of a unified legal framework for the fair and efficient settlement of disputes arising in international commercial relations,

1. *Requests* the Secretary-General to transmit the text of the Model Law on International Commercial Arbitration of the United Nations Commission on International Trade Law, together with the *travaux préparatoires* from the eighteenth session of the Commission, to Governments and to arbitral institutions and other interested bodies, such as chambers of commerce;

2. *Recommends* that all States give due consideration to the Model Law on International Commercial Arbitration, in view of the desirability of uniformity of the law of arbitral procedures and the specific needs of international commercial arbitration practice.

General Assembly resolution 40/72

| 11 December 1985 | Meeting 112 | Adopted without vote |

Approved by Sixth Committee (A/40/935) by consensus, 14 November (meeting 38); 26-nation draft (A/C.6/40/L.7); agenda item 135.
Sponsors: Argentina, Australia, Austria, Brazil, Canada, Cyprus, Czechoslovakia, Egypt, Finland, France, Germany, Federal Republic of, Greece, Guyana, Hungary, Italy, Jamaica, Japan, Kenya, Netherlands, Nigeria, Philippines, Senegal, Singapore, Spain, Sweden, United States.
Meeting numbers. GA 40th session: 6th Committee 3-5, 37, 38; plenary 112.

In **resolution 40/71** on the report of UNCITRAL, the Assembly also expressed satisfaction at the completion and adoption of the Model Law.

International payments

Draft convention on international bills of exchange and international promissory notes

UNCITRAL's Working Group on International Negotiable Instruments, entrusted with improving the draft convention it had drawn up in 1981[5] on international bills of exchange and international promissory notes, held two sessions in 1985 (thirteenth, New York, 7-18 January;[6] fourteenth, Vienna, 9-20 December[7]) and completed, in December, its deliberations on and revision of the draft convention.

In June, the Commission[1] had agreed that, in the light of the progress made in solving major controversial issues—such as the concepts of holder and protected holder, the effect of forged endorsements and the liability of the transferor by mere delivery or by endorsement—it was reasonable to request the Group to complete

consideration of all remaining issues and to submit a draft for UNCITRAL consideration in 1986.

Electronic data processing in international trade

In 1985, UNCITRAL[1] continued consideration of legal problems arising out of the use of electronic data processing in international trade.

It had before it a secretariat report on the legal value of computer records,[8] which noted that there were fewer problems than might have been expected globally in using computer-stored data as evidence in litigation; a more serious legal obstacle to the use of computers and computer-to-computer telecommunications in international trade arose out of requirements that documents be signed or that they be in paper-based form.

The Commission recommended to Governments that they review legal requirements with a view to eliminating obstacles to admission of computer records as evidence in litigation, facilitating the recording and transmission of trade-transaction documents in computer-readable form, and permitting the use of electronic means of authentication on trade-related documents.

As regards preparation of a guide on legal problems arising from electronic funds transfers, UNCITRAL examined in 1985 a report of the Secretary-General[9] containing chapters of the draft guide additional to those considered the previous year,[10] noted a link between the guide and legal security of computer records, and suggested that the guide might include a chapter on evidence. It requested the Secretary-General to send the draft guide to Governments and interested international organizations for comment, and asked the secretariat, in co-operation with the UNCITRAL Study Group on International Payments, to submit to UNCITRAL in 1986 a revised draft for possible adoption.

In **resolution 40/71**, the Assembly welcomed UNCITRAL's work on the legal implications of automated data processing on the flow of international trade, commended it for its recommendation on the legal value of computer records, and called on Governments and international organizations to act on the recommendation.

Most-favoured-nation clauses

In response to a 1983 General Assembly request,[11] the Secretary-General submitted a report in September 1985[12] containing comments received as at 31 August—from four Member States, two United Nations organs, a specialized agency, the International Atomic Energy Agency and two other international organizations—on the draft articles on most-favoured-nation clauses adopted by the International Law Commission in 1978,[13] on the procedure for completing work on the topic, and on the forum for future discussion.

GENERAL ASSEMBLY ACTION

On 11 December, the General Assembly, on the recommendation of the Sixth Committee, adopted **resolution 40/65** without vote.

Consideration of the draft articles on most-favoured-nation clauses

The General Assembly,

Recalling its resolution 33/139 of 19 December 1978 relating to the report of the International Law Commission on the work of its thirtieth session, in particular section II of that resolution, as well as its resolutions 35/161 of 15 December 1980, 36/111 of 10 December 1981 and 38/127 of 19 December 1983, entitled "Consideration of the draft articles on most-favoured-nation clauses",

Reaffirming its appreciation of the high quality of the work done by the International Law Commission in elaborating a series of draft articles on most-favoured-nation clauses,

Bearing in mind the importance of facilitating international trade and the development of economic co-operation among all States on the basis of equality, mutual advantage and non-discrimination in the establishment of the new international economic order,

Bearing in mind also the complexity of codification or progressive development of the international law on most-favoured-nation clauses at a time of rapid development of new forms of economic co-operation, notably those in favour of developing countries,

Noting from the report of the Secretary-General that a limited number of comments have been received, which seems to indicate that most Member States are not yet in a position to decide how further to proceed in the consideration of the draft articles on most-favoured-nation clauses,

Considering that sufficient time should be given to Governments for a thorough study of the draft articles and of the questions related to the clauses in order that they may express themselves on the action that should be taken regarding the draft articles,

1. *Calls upon* Member States, interested organs of the United Nations and interested intergovernmental organizations to review the questions related to the most-favoured-nation clauses and the draft articles thereon so that the General Assembly, at its forty-third session, may decide on the action to be taken on the draft articles;

2. *Requests* the Secretary-General to reiterate his invitation to Member States and interested organs of the United Nations, as well as interested intergovernmental organizations, to submit or bring up to date, not later than 31 March 1988, any written comments and observations which they deem appropriate on the substance of the draft articles;

3. *Also requests* the Secretary-General to invite Member States to comment on the most appropriate procedure for completing work on most-favoured-nation clauses and on the forum for future discussion, bearing in mind the suggestions and proposals made in the Sixth

Committee, including the suggestion to establish a working group of the Sixth Committee after one of the existing working groups accomplishes its mandate;

4. *Further requests* the Secretary-General to submit to the General Assembly at its forty-third session a report containing the comments and observations received pursuant to paragraphs 2 and 3 above with a view to taking a final decision on the procedure to be followed;

5. *Decides* to include in the provisional agenda of its forty-third session the item entitled "Consideration of the draft articles on most-favoured-nation clauses".

General Assembly resolution 40/65

11 December 1985   Meeting 112   Adopted without vote

Approved by Sixth Committee (A/40/977) without vote, 27 November (meeting 48); 7-nation draft (A/C.6/40/L.20); agenda item 127.

Sponsors: Bulgaria, Czechoslovakia, German Democratic Republic, Hungary, Mongolia, Poland, Viet Nam.

Meeting numbers. GA 40th session: 6th Committee 46-48; plenary 112.

In explanation of position, Belgium—on behalf of the 10 member States of the European Economic Community as well as of Portugal and Spain—stated that the draft articles as a whole were not completely in harmony with the development of current international trade practices, but they could accept a resolution postponing the study of the problem until such practices were well established.

Training and assistance

In 1985, UNCITRAL continued to co-operate in holding or participating in regional seminars. The UNCITRAL secretariat organized—in co-operation with the Chamber of Commerce of Bogotá and the Iberoamerican Association of Chambers of Commerce, and with the support of the secretariat of the Organization of American States—a regional seminar on the work of UNCITRAL and international trade law (Bogotá, Colombia, 22-23 April). It also participated in a regional seminar on the international sale of goods (Dubrovnik, Yugoslavia, 11-23 March), organized by the Inter-University Centre of Postgraduate Studies in that city.

In **resolution 40/71**, the Assembly reaffirmed the importance of training and assistance in international trade law, particularly for developing countries; it invited Governments, international organizations, United Nations bodies and individuals to help finance and organize such seminars, as well as to make contributions to enable resumption of UNCITRAL fellowships for participation in them by candidates from developing countries.

REFERENCES

[1]A/40/17. [2]YUN 1984, p. 1112. [3]A/CN.9/263 & Add.1,2. [4]A/CN.9/264. [5]YUN 1981, p. 1254. [6]A/CN.9/261. [7]A/CN.9/273. [8]A/CN.9/265. [9]A/CN.9/266 & Add.1,2. [10]YUN 1984, p. 1113. [11]YUN 1983, p. 1135, GA res. 38/127, 19 Dec. 1983. [12]A/40/444. [13]YUN 1978, p. 945.

Legal aspects of the new international economic order

The United Nations continued to consider in 1985 the new international economic order (NIEO), with UNCITRAL and the Sixth Committee dealing with the legal aspects.

UNCITRAL consideration. UNCITRAL's Working Group on the New International Economic Order, at its seventh session (New York, 8-19 April),[1] continued to discuss the draft legal guide, prepared by the secretariat, on drawing up international contracts for construction of industrial works.

Asking the Working Group to continue its work expeditiously, UNCITRAL[2] noted a secretariat suggestion[3] that a more detailed examination of the issues involved in procurement and tendering than was possible in the legal guide itself might be valuable. It also took note of the secretariat's intention to submit proposals on enhancing the value of the guide by preparing annexes dealing, for instance, with legal issues related to joint ventures arising in the context of industrial contracts.

GENERAL ASSEMBLY ACTION

The Secretary-General submitted a report in August, with a later addendum,[4] containing the views of eight Member States on the 1984 study[5] by the United Nations Institute for Training and Research on the progressive development of the principles and norms of international law relating to NIEO.

The Sixth Committee considered two draft resolutions on the topic. One submitted by Cuba[6] would have had the Assembly establish a 20-member *ad hoc* group of experts, which would meet up to two weeks annually beginning in 1986, to consider States' proposals with a view to preparing a set of norms to facilitate the early initiation of NIEO. Cuba subsequently joined in sponsoring the second draft, later adopted, and withdrew its proposal.

On 11 December, the Assembly, on the recommendation of the Sixth Committee, adopted **resolution 40/67** by recorded vote.

Progressive development of the principles and norms of international law relating to the new international economic order

The General Assembly,

Bearing in mind that, in accordance with the Charter of the United Nations, the General Assembly is called upon to initiate studies and make recommendations for the purpose of encouraging the progressive development of international law and its codification,

Recalling its resolutions 3201(S-VI) and 3202(S-VI) of 1 May 1974, containing the Declaration and the Pro-

gramme of Action on the Establishment of a New International Economic Order, 3281(XXIX) of 12 December 1974, containing the Charter of Economic Rights and Duties of States, 3362(S-VII) of 16 September 1975 on development and international economic co-operation and 35/56 of 5 December 1980, the annex to which contains the International Development Strategy for the Third United Nations Development Decade,

Recalling also its resolutions 34/150 of 17 December 1979 and 35/166 of 15 December 1980, entitled "Consolidation and progressive development of the principles and norms of international economic law relating in particular to the legal aspects of the new international economic order", and its resolutions 36/107 of 10 December 1981, 37/103 of 16 December 1982, 38/128 of 19 December 1983, and 39/75 of 13 December 1984, entitled "Progressive development of the principles and norms of international law relating to the new international economic order",

Bearing in mind the urgent need to adopt measures to reactivate the process of international economic co-operation and the negotiations undertaken for that purpose, particularly in view of the economic difficulties encountered by the developing countries,

Considering the close link between the establishment of a just and equitable international economic order and the existence of an appropriate legal framework,

Recognizing the need for a systematic and progressive development of the principles and norms of international law relating to the new international economic order,

Aware, however, that the period of time available for consideration of the analytical study submitted to the General Assembly at its thirty-ninth session by the United Nations Institute for Training and Research has been relatively short and that so far only a limited number of Member States have been able to submit their views and comments thereon pursuant to paragraph 2 of resolution 39/75,

Convinced that a sufficient number of views and comments from Member States would be necessary for a proper consideration of the manner by which further work on the subject may be carried out,

1. *Urges* Member States that have not done so to submit, not later than 30 June 1986, their views and comments with respect to the study, including proposals concerning further action and procedures to be adopted within the framework of the Sixth Committee with regard to the consideration of the analytical study;

2. *Recommends* that the consideration of the most appropriate procedure for completing the elaboration of the process of progressive development of the relevant principles and norms of international law, and of the forum which would be entrusted with the task, be undertaken by the General Assembly at its forty-first session, with a view to making a final decision after taking into account all the proposals and suggestions made by Member States on the matter;

3. *Decides* to include in the provisional agenda of its forty-first session the item entitled "Progressive development of the principles and norms of international law relating to the new international economic order".

General Assembly resolution 40/67

11 December 1985   Meeting 112   125-0-19 (recorded vote)

Approved by Sixth Committee (A/40/978) by vote (76-0-17), 26 November (meeting 47); 27-nation draft (A/C.6/40/L.17); agenda item 130.

Sponsors: Barbados, Burkina Faso, Chile, Congo, Cuba, Egypt, Equatorial Guinea, India, Jamaica, Kenya, Liberia, Malaysia, Mexico, Morocco, Pakistan, Panama, Paraguay, Philippines, Romania, Samoa, Senegal, Thailand, Tunisia, Venezuela, Viet Nam, Zaire, Zambia.
Meeting numbers. GA 40th session: 6th Committee 44-47; plenary 112.

Recorded vote in Assembly as follows:

In favour: Afghanistan, Algeria, Angola, Antigua and Barbuda, Argentina, Austria, Bahamas, Bahrain, Bangladesh, Benin, Bhutan, Bolivia, Brazil, Brunei Darussalam, Bulgaria, Burkina Faso, Burma, Burundi, Byelorussian SSR, Cameroon, Cape Verde, Central African Republic, Chad, Chile, China, Colombia, Comoros, Congo, Costa Rica, Cuba, Cyprus, Czechoslovakia, Democratic Kampuchea, Djibouti, Dominican Republic, Ecuador, Egypt, El Salvador, Equatorial Guinea, Ethiopia, Fiji, Finland, Gabon, German Democratic Republic, Ghana, Greece, Guatemala, Guinea, Guinea-Bissau, Guyana, Haiti, Honduras, Hungary, India, Indonesia, Iran, Iraq, Ireland, Ivory Coast, Jamaica, Jordan, Kenya, Kuwait, Lao People's Democratic Republic, Lebanon, Lesotho, Liberia, Libyan Arab Jamahiriya, Madagascar, Malawi, Malaysia, Maldives, Mali, Malta, Mauritania, Mauritius, Mexico, Mongolia, Morocco, Mozambique, Nepal, Netherlands, Nicaragua, Niger, Nigeria, Oman, Pakistan, Panama, Papua New Guinea, Paraguay, Peru, Philippines, Poland, Qatar, Romania, Rwanda, Saint Lucia, Samoa, Sao Tome and Principe, Saudi Arabia, Senegal, Sierra Leone, Singapore, Somalia, Sri Lanka, Sudan, Suriname, Swaziland, Syrian Arab Republic, Thailand, Togo, Trinidad and Tobago, Tunisia, Turkey, Ukrainian SSR, USSR, United Arab Emirates, United Republic of Tanzania, Uruguay, Venezuela, Viet Nam, Yemen, Yugoslavia, Zaire, Zambia.

Against: None.
Abstaining: Australia, Belgium, Canada, Denmark, France, Germany, Federal Republic of, Grenada, Iceland, Israel, Italy, Japan, Luxembourg, New Zealand, Norway, Portugal, Spain, Sweden, United Kingdom, United States.

Asserting in explanation of its abstention that disagreements on substantive issues persisted, the United States said nothing had happened during the preceding year to make the topic more ripe for consideration at the legal level.

In a related action, the Assembly reaffirmed, by **resolution 40/71**, the importance, particularly for developing countries, of the Working Group's activities on the legal guide.

REFERENCES
[1]A/CN.9/262. [2]A/40/17. [3]A/CN.9/268. [4]A/40/446 & Add.1 & Add.1/Corr.1. [5]YUN 1984, p. 1115. [6]A/C.6/40/L.9.

Chapter VII

Other legal questions

In 1985, the International Law Commission (ILC), at its thirty-seventh session at Geneva from 6 May to 26 July, continued work on the progressive development and codification of international law; the General Assembly recommended in December that it continue work on all the topics in its current programme (resolution 40/75).

The twenty-first session of the International Law Seminar was held at Geneva. Other seminars and training courses were offered in 1985 as part of the United Nations Programme of Assistance in the Teaching, Study, Dissemination and Wider Appreciation of International Law. The Assembly urged all potential donors to make voluntary contributions to the Programme's financing (40/66).

By resolution 40/60, the Assembly welcomed the progress made in strengthening the co-operation between the United Nations and the Asian-African Legal Consultative Committee.

International Law Commission

ILC work programme

The 1985 ILC session (Geneva, 6 May–26 July)[1] was devoted mainly to considering draft articles on the following aspects of international law: draft Code of Offences against the Peace and Security of Mankind (see p. 1163); State responsibility (see p. 1176); status of the diplomatic courier and the diplomatic bag not accompanied by courier (see p. 1174); and jurisdictional immunities of States and their property (see p. 1175). It also continued work on relations between States and international organizations (second part of the topic) (see p. 1189) and non-navigational uses of international watercourses (see p. 1170).

The Commission decided to continue work in 1986 on all topics on its current programme, bearing in mind the desirability of achieving maximum progress in preparing draft articles on some topics before the term of its current membership concluded that year. It therefore hoped to complete the first reading of draft articles on the diplomatic courier and the diplomatic bag and on jurisdictional immunities of States, with a possibility of giving similar treatment to parts two and three of the draft articles on State responsibility.

The Secretary-General, in September,[2] transmitted to the General Assembly the draft articles which had been provisionally adopted by ILC in 1985 on State responsibility, status of the diplomatic courier and diplomatic bag not accompanied by courier and jurisdictional immunities of States and their property.

Throughout 1985, ILC continued to co-operate with several other juridical bodies, namely the Arab Commission for International Law, the Asian-African Legal Consultative Committee (see p. 1200), the European Committee on Legal Co-operation and the Inter-American Juridical Committee. Such co-operation included ILC representation at meetings of those bodies or their sending observers to the ILC session.

GENERAL ASSEMBLY ACTION

On the recommendation of the Sixth (Legal) Committee, the General Assembly, on 11 December 1985, adopted **resolution 40/75** without vote.

Report of the International Law Commission
The General Assembly,

Having considered the report of the International Law Commission on the work of its thirty-seventh session,

Emphasizing the need for the progressive development of international law and its codification in order to make it a more effective means of implementing the purposes and principles set forth in the Charter of the United Nations and in the Declaration on Principles of International Law concerning Friendly Relations and Co-operation among States in accordance with the Charter of the United Nations and to give increasing importance to its role in relations among States,

Recognizing the importance of referring legal and drafting questions to the Sixth Committee, including topics which might be submitted to the International Law Commission, and of enabling the Sixth Committee and the Commission further to enhance their contributions to the progressive development of international law and its codification,

Recalling the need to keep under review those topics of international law which, given their new or renewed interest for the contemporary international community, may be suitable for progressive development and codification of international law and therefore may be included in the future programme of work of the International Law Commission,

1. *Takes note* of the report of the International Law Commission on the work of its thirty-seventh session;

2. *Expresses its appreciation* to the International Law Commission for the work accomplished at that session;

3. *Recommends* that, taking into account the comments of Governments, whether in writing or expressed orally in debates in the General Assembly, the Interna-

tional Law Commission should continue its work on the topics in its current programme, bearing in mind the clear desirability of achieving as much progress as possible in the preparation of draft articles on specific topics before the conclusion of the term of office of the present membership;

4. *Expresses its satisfaction* with the conclusions and intentions of the International Law Commission concerning its procedures and methods of work, as reflected in paragraphs 297 to 306 of its report;

5. *Reaffirms* its previous decisions concerning the increased role of the Codification Division of the Office of Legal Affairs of the Secretariat and those concerning the documentation of the International Law Commission;

6. *Appeals* to Governments and, as appropriate, to international organizations to respond as fully and expeditiously as possible to the requests of the International Law Commission for comments, observations and replies to questionnaires and for materials on topics in its programme of work;

7. *Reaffirms its wish* that the International Law Commission continue to enhance its co-operation with intergovernmental legal bodies whose work is of interest for the progressive development of international law and its codification;

8. *Expresses the wish* that seminars will continue to be held in conjunction with sessions of the International Law Commission and that an increasing number of participants from developing countries will be given the opportunity to attend those seminars and appeals to States that can do so to make the voluntary contributions that are urgently needed for the holding of the seminars;

9. *Requests* the Secretary-General to forward to the International Law Commission, for its attention, the records of the debate on the report of the Commission at the fortieth session of the General Assembly and to prepare and distribute a topical summary of the debate.

General Assembly resolution 40/75

11 December 1985   Meeting 112   Adopted without vote

Approved by Sixth Committee (A/40/961) by consensus, 26 November (meeting 47); 62-nation draft (A/C.6/40/L.19); agenda item 138.
Sponsors: Algeria, Angola, Argentina, Australia, Austria, Belgium, Brazil, Bulgaria, Canada, Cape Verde, Chile, China, Cyprus, Ecuador, Egypt, Ethiopia, France, German Democratic Republic, Germany, Federal Republic of, Greece, Guyana, India, Iraq, Ireland, Italy, Jamaica, Japan, Jordan, Kenya, Kuwait, Lesotho, Libyan Arab Jamahiriya, Madagascar, Mongolia, Morocco, New Zealand, Niger, Nigeria, Norway, Oman, Pakistan, Paraguay, Peru, Philippines, Qatar, Romania, Saudi Arabia, Senegal, Spain, Sri Lanka, Sudan, Suriname, Syrian Arab Republic, Thailand, Tunisia, Turkey, Uruguay, Venezuela, Yemen, Yugoslavia, Zaire, Zambia.
Meeting numbers. GA 40th session: 6th Committee 23-36, 46, 47; plenary 112.

UN Programme for the teaching and study of international law

International Law Seminar

In accordance with a 1984 General Assembly wish,[3] the twenty-first session of the International Law Seminar—for advanced students and junior professors or government officials dealing with international law—was held at Geneva from 3 to 21 June, with 24 participants, all of different nationalities and mostly from developing countries.[1] In addition, one holder of a fellowship from the United Nations Institute for Training and

Research (UNITAR) and two observers were admitted to the Seminar. Participants followed the work of the 1985 ILC session and heard lectures given by its members and by others. As in the past, none of the costs of the Seminar fell on the United Nations. Argentina, Austria, Denmark, Finland and the Federal Republic of Germany made financial contributions, thus allowing 17 participants from developing countries to receive fellowships. Since the first Seminar in 1965,[4] fellowships have been awarded to 230 of the total of 471 participants, representing 113 nationalities.

The Commission[1] drew the attention of the international community to the fact that the shortage of funds might make the holding of the 1986 Seminar difficult.

Other activities

A number of additional training courses were offered in 1985 as part of the United Nations Programme of Assistance in the Teaching, Study, Dissemination and Wider Appreciation of International Law.[5] Under the annual joint United Nations/UNITAR fellowship programme, 18 middle-grade government legal officers and young international legal experts took courses at The Hague Academy of International Law (Netherlands) and attended seminars organized by UNITAR. Several fellows also received practical training at legal offices of the United Nations and related organizations.

UNITAR reported that no country in Asia and the Pacific had offered to host a regional training and refresher course in international law, scheduled for December 1985; it noted that, in order to hold such courses annually for the benefit of developing countries, it would be necessary to alleviate some of the financial burden on anticipated host countries.

The Secretary-General reported that, in 1985, Japan contributed $10,000 to the Hamilton Shirley Amerasinghe Memorial Fellowship, established in 1981[6] for study and research in the law of the sea; that there was adequate income from the fund to award the fellowship; and that the guidelines for its awarding and administration were being sent out to United Nations information centres, universities and others.

GENERAL ASSEMBLY ACTION

On 11 December 1985, the General Assembly, on the recommendation of the Sixth Committee, adopted **resolution 40/66** without vote.

United Nations Programme of Assistance in the Teaching, Study, Dissemination and Wider Appreciation of International Law
The General Assembly,
Taking note with appreciation of the report of the Secretary-General on the implementation of the United

Nations Programme of Assistance in the Teaching, Study, Dissemination and Wider Appreciation of International Law and the recommendations made by the Secretary-General and adopted by the Advisory Committee on the United Nations Programme of Assistance in the Teaching, Study, Dissemination and Wider Appreciation of International Law, which are contained in that report,

Considering that international law should occupy an appropriate place in the teaching of legal disciplines at all universities,

Noting with appreciation the efforts made by States at the bilateral level to provide assistance in the teaching and study of international law,

Convinced, nevertheless, that States and international organizations and institutions should be encouraged to give further support to the Programme and to increase their activities to promote the teaching, study, dissemination and wider appreciation of international law, in particular those activities which are of special benefit to persons from developing countries,

Recalling its resolutions 2464(XXIII) of 20 December 1968, 2550(XXIV) of 12 December 1969, 2838(XXVI) of 18 December 1971, 3106(XXVIII) of 12 December 1973, 3502(XXX) of 15 December 1975, 32/146 of 16 December 1977, 36/108 of 10 December 1981 and 38/129 of 19 December 1983, in which it stated that in the conduct of the Programme it was desirable to use as far as possible the resources and facilities made available by Member States, international organizations and others, as well as its resolution 34/144 of 17 December 1979, in which it also expressed the hope that, in appointing lecturers for the seminars to be held within the framework of the fellowship programme in international law sponsored jointly by the United Nations and the United Nations Institute for Training and Research, account would be taken of the need to secure representation of major legal systems and balance among various geographical regions,

Noting with regret that the 1985 United Nations Institute for Training and Research regional training and refresher course in international law intended for Asian and Pacific countries could not take place for lack of a host country, and considering the difficulties which the Institute may encounter in finding host countries for the organization of future regional courses,

Noting that the fund of the Hamilton Shirley Amerasinghe Fellowship on the Law of the Sea has already become operational,

1. *Authorizes* the Secretary-General to carry out in 1986 and 1987 the activities specified in his report, including the provision of:

(*a*) A minimum of fifteen fellowships each in 1986 and 1987, at the request of Governments of developing countries;

(*b*) A minimum of one scholarship each in 1986 and 1987 under the Hamilton Shirley Amerasinghe Fellowship on the Law of the Sea to be financed by the fund of voluntary contributions made specifically for the Fellowship;

(*c*) Assistance in the form of a travel grant for one participant from each developing country who will be invited to the regional courses to be organized in 1986 and 1987;

and to finance the above activities from provisions in the regular budget and also from voluntary financial contributions which would be received as a result of the requests set out in paragraphs 9, 10 and 11 below;

2. *Expresses its appreciation* to the Secretary-General for his constructive efforts to promote training and assistance in international law within the framework of the United Nations Programme of Assistance in the Teaching, Study, Dissemination and Wider Appreciation of International Law in 1984 and 1985, in particular for the organization of the twentieth and twenty-first sessions of the International Law Seminar, held at Geneva from 4 to 22 May 1984 and from 3 to 21 June 1985, respectively, and the participation of the Office of Legal Affairs of the Secretariat and its Codification Division in the activities related to the conduct of the fellowship programme in international law sponsored jointly by the United Nations and the United Nations Institute for Training and Research;

3. *Expresses its appreciation* to the United Nations Institute for Training and Research for its participation in the Programme, particularly in the organization of regional courses and in the conduct of the fellowship programme in international law sponsored jointly by the United Nations and the Institute;

4. *Expresses its appreciation* to the United Nations Educational, Scientific and Cultural Organization for its participation in the Programme, in particular for the efforts it has made to support the teaching of international law;

5. *Also expresses its appreciation* to the Government of the Republic of Cameroon and to the International Relations Institute of Cameroon for providing host facilities for the regional training and refresher course for African countries held at Yaoundé from 12 to 24 November 1984;

6. *Further expresses its appreciation* to the Hague Academy of International Law for the valuable contributions it has made to the Programme by enabling international law fellows under the sponsorship of the United Nations and the United Nations Institute for Training and Research to attend its annual international law courses and by providing facilities for seminars organized under the fellowship programme in international law in conjunction with the Academy courses and for its constructive efforts in organizing the regional training and refresher courses held at Brasilia in 1983, at Cairo in 1984 and at Rabat in 1985;

7. *Notes with appreciation* the contributions made by the Hague Academy of International Law to the teaching, study, dissemination and wider appreciation of international law, and calls upon Member States and interested organizations to give favourable consideration to the appeal of the Academy for a continuation of and, if possible, an increase in their financial contributions in order to enable the Academy to carry on with the above-mentioned activities;

8. *Urges* all Governments to encourage the inclusion of courses on international law in the programmes of legal studies offered at institutions of higher learning;

9. *Requests* the Secretary-General to continue to publicize the Programme and periodically to invite Member States, universities, philanthropic foundations and other interested national and international institutions and organizations, as well as individuals, to make voluntary contributions towards the financing of the Programme or otherwise to assist in its implementation and possible expansion;

10. *Reiterates its request* to Member States and to interested organizations and individuals to make volun-

tary contributions towards the financing of the Programme, in particular for the International Law Seminar and the Hamilton Shirley Amerasinghe Fellowship on the Law of the Sea, and expresses its appreciation to those Member States, institutions and individuals that have made voluntary contributions for this purpose;

11. *Urges* in particular all Governments to make voluntary contributions with a view to covering the amount of $30,000 needed for the financing of the daily subsistence allowance for up to twenty-five participants in each regional course organized by the United Nations Institute for Training and Research, thus alleviating the burden on prospective host countries and making it possible for the Institute to continue organizing one regional course per year;

12. *Requests* the Secretary-General to report to the General Assembly at its forty-second session on the implementation of the Programme during 1986 and 1987 and, following consultations with the Advisory Committee on the United Nations Programme of Assistance in the Teaching, Study, Dissemination and Wider Appreciation of International Law, to submit recommendations regarding the execution of the Programme in subsequent years;

13. *Decides* to include in the provisional agenda of its forty-second session the item entitled "United Nations Programme of Assistance in the Teaching, Study, Dissemination and Wider Appreciation of International Law".

General Assembly resolution 40/66

11 December 1985   Meeting 112   Adopted without vote

Approved by Sixth Committee (A/40/1010) without vote, 5 December (meeting 53); draft by Chairman (A/C.6/40/L.30); agenda item 128.
Meeting numbers. GA 40th session: 6th Committee 50, 51, 53; plenary 112.

Co-operation between the United Nations and the Asian-African Legal Consultative Committee

In response to the Assembly's 1984 request,[7] the Secretary-General submitted in October 1985 a report[8] on co-operation between the United Nations and the Asian-African Legal Consultative Committee—an organization to which the Assembly had accorded permanent observer status in 1980.[9]

In 1985, the Committee transmitted to the Secretary-General studies it had prepared on the possible wider use of the International Court of Justice in settling legal disputes[10] (see Chapter I of this section) and on strengthening the role of the United Nations through rationalization of functional modalities, with special reference to the General Assembly[11] (see Chapter IV of this section).

GENERAL ASSEMBLY ACTION

On 9 December 1985, the General Assembly adopted **resolution 40/60** without vote.

Co-operation between the United Nations and the Asian-African Legal Consultative Committee

The General Assembly,

Recalling its resolutions 36/38 of 18 November 1981, 37/8 of 29 October 1982, 38/37 of 5 December 1983 and 39/47 of 10 December 1984,

Having considered the report of the Secretary-General on the state of co-operation between the United Nations and the Asian-African Legal Consultative Committee,

Having heard the report of the Secretary-General of the Asian-African Legal Consultative Committee on the steps taken by the Committee to ensure continuing, close and effective co-operation between the two organizations,

1. *Takes note with appreciation* of the report of the Secretary-General;

2. *Notes with satisfaction* the further progress achieved towards strengthening the existing co-operation between the United Nations and the Asian-African Legal Consultative Committee;

3. *Takes note with appreciation* of the study on the strengthening of the role of the United Nations prepared by the Asian-African Legal Consultative Committee on the occasion of the fortieth anniversary of the United Nations, as well as the study on the role of the International Court of Justice and other efforts of the Committee in the continuation of its programme of support to the work of the United Nations in several areas;

4. *Requests* the Secretary-General to submit to the General Assembly at its forty-first session a report on co-operation between the United Nations and the Asian-African Legal Consultative Committee;

5. *Decides* to include in the provisional agenda of its forty-first session the item entitled "Co-operation between the United Nations and the Asian-African Legal Consultative Committee".

General Assembly resolution 40/60

9 December 1985   Meeting 108   Adopted without vote

23-nation draft (A/40/L.37 & Add.1); agenda item 31.
Sponsors: Australia, Bangladesh, China, Cyprus, Egypt, India, Indonesia, Iran, Iraq, Japan, Jordan, Libyan Arab Jamahiriya, Malaysia, Nepal, New Zealand, Oman, Pakistan, Philippines, Qatar, Sierra Leone, Sri Lanka, Sudan, Thailand.

REFERENCES

[1]A/40/10. [2]A/40/447. [3]YUN 1984, p. 1117, GA res. 39/85, 13 Dec. 1984. [4]YUN 1965, p. 624. [5]A/40/893. [6]YUN 1981, p. 139. [7]YUN 1984, p. 1119, GA res. 39/47, 10 Dec. 1984. [8]A/40/743. [9]YUN 1980, p. 469, GA res. 35/2, 13 Oct. 1980. [10]A/40/682. [11]A/40/726 & Corr.1.

PUBLICATIONS

Yearbook of the International Law Commission 1985, vol. I: *Summary Records of the Meetings of the Thirty-seventh Session, 6 May–26 July 1985* (A/CN.4/SER.A/1985), Sales No. E.86.V.4; vol. II: *Part One: Documents of the Thirty-seventh Session & Part Two: Report of the Commission to the General Assembly on the Work of Its Thirty-seventh Session* (A/CN.4/SER.A/1985/Add.1, Parts 1 & 2), Sales No. E.86.V.5 (Parts I & II).

Administrative and budgetary questions

United Nations financing

A United Nations programme budget for 1986-1987 containing appropriations of $1,663,341,500 was adopted by the General Assembly in December 1985 (resolution 40/253 A). This was $54,387,500 above the $1,608,954,000 in final appropriations for 1984-1985, also approved by the Assembly in that same month (40/239 A). Excluding inflation and foreign exchange-rate movements, the real budgetary growth between the two bienniums was calculated at 0.4 per cent.

Most of the budget was to be financed by assessed contributions from Member States. Assembly-approved estimates of income from other sources totalled $294,345,500 for 1984-1985 (resolution 40/239 B) and $317,465,600 for 1986-1987 (40/253 B).

The Committee on Contributions proposed a new scale of assessments for contributions from Member States, which was approved by the Assembly (resolution 40/248). The new scale was for the years 1986, 1987 and 1988.

Following consideration of a report by the Secretary-General on the financial emergency of the Organization, which pointed out that the short-term deficit was expected to exceed $390 million as at 31 December 1985, the Assembly again urged all Member States to meet their financial obligations (resolution 40/241 A).

UN budget

Budget for 1984-1985

Revised appropriations

In December, the General Assembly approved the final budget appropriations for the biennium 1984-1985 in the amount of $1,608,954,000. This was a reduction of $2,597,200 from the amount of $1,611,551,200 which the Assembly had approved in 1984.[1]

Reporting to the Assembly on programme budget performance for the biennium,[2] the Secretary-General noted that there was a net increase of $3,105,400, 0.24 per cent of the net amount voted by the Assembly at its previous session. There had been a decrease of $4,547,900 in expenditure requirements, but this was more than offset by a reduction of $7,653,300 in income.

The details of the expenditure requirements cited by the Secretary-General included increases of $2.9 million resulting from variations in operational rates of exchange and $897,000 in consequence of decisions of policy-making organs; decreases were of the order of a $2.2-million savings due to lower-than-anticipated inflation and $6.2 million in other changes. These "other changes" reflected a number of factors, such as variances between actual and standard salary and common staff costs, and variances between actual and assumed vacancy rates.

The Secretary-General also submitted, in an amendment[3] to the performance report, a separate estimate of the expenditures anticipated to be required for the implementation at New York of the General Service job classification exercise (see p. 1241). This estimate was $1,950,700.

An analysis of the Secretary-General's report by the Advisory Committee on Administrative and Budgetary Questions (ACABQ)[4] was issued in December 1985. It summarized the information provided by the Secretary-General concerning: expenditures (as above); the changes resulting from rates of exchange and inflation; those resulting from decisions of policy-making organs (including an increase of $1.1 million for servicing the 1985 meetings of the Programme and Budget Committee of the new Industrial Development Board of the United Nations Industrial Development Organization (UNIDO) and of the Board itself, and a decrease of $1.4 million relating to activities of the political affairs, trusteeship and decolonization bodies; and other changes.

Decreases in the "other changes" category reflected higher-than-anticipated vacancy rates in New York, publishing and travel savings, delays in recruitment and variations between actual costs and standard rates. Increases in this category were the result of salary and common staff costs, temporary assistance, general operating expenses, insurance costs and compensatory payments. The increase related to the budgets for administration and management, UNIDO and the International Court of Justice (ICJ).

ACABQ noted that the reason for the additional net requirement of $3.1 million was the reduction in income. An overall saving had in fact been achieved in the expenditure sections. It recommended that the Assembly approve the revised estimates for 1984-1985.

GENERAL ASSEMBLY ACTION

On the recommendation of the Fifth (Administrative and Budgetary) Committee, the Assembly, on 18 December 1985, adopted by recorded vote **resolution 40/239 A**, based on the Secretary-General's figures, including $1,950,700 for job classification costs. (Although consideration of the exercise had been postponed, its effective date would remain 1 January 1985; see p. 1241.)

Final budget appropriations for the biennium 1984-1985

The General Assembly

Resolves that for the biennium 1984-1985:

1. The amount of $1,611,551,200 appropriated by its resolution 39/237 A of 18 December 1984 shall be decreased by $2,597,200 as follows:

Section	Amount appropriated by resolution 39/237 A	Increase or (decrease)	Final appropriation
	(US dollars)		
PART I. *Overall policy-making, direction and co-ordination*			
1. Overall policy-making, direction and co-ordination	40,173,400	(1,706,600)	38,466,800
Total, PART I	40,173,400	(1,706,600)	38,466,800
PART II. *Political and Security Council affairs; peace-keeping activities*			
2A. Political and Security Council affairs; peace-keeping activities	82,267,900	(1,045,900)	81,222,000
2B. Department for Disarmament Affairs	9,316,500	(36,300)	9,280,200
Total, PART II	91,584,400	(1,082,200)	90,502,200
PART III. *Political affairs, trusteeship and decolonization*			
3. Political affairs, trusteeship and decolonization	28,696,500	(2,175,100)	26,521,400
Total, PART III	28,696,500	(2,175,100)	26,521,400
PART IV. *Economic, social and humanitarian activities*			
4. Policy-making organs (economic and social activities)	3,936,000	(673,800)	3,262,200

Section	Amount appropriated by resolution 39/237 A	Increase or (decrease)	Final appropriation
	(US dollars)		
5A. Office of the Director-General for Development and International Economic Co-operation	3,772,200	(225,900)	3,546,300
5B. Centre for Science and Technology for Development	3,995,200	126,100	4,121,300
5C. Regional Commissions Liaison Office	620,900	60,500	681,400
6. Department of International Economic and Social Affairs	50,056,800	(399,700)	49,657,100
7. Department of Technical Co-operation for Development	18,100,400	368,900	18,469,300
8. Office of Secretariat Services for Economic and Social Matters	3,926,600	(32,200)	3,894,400
9. Transnational corporations	9,783,500	(755,200)	9,028,300
10. Economic Commission for Europe	22,784,800	712,300	23,497,100
11. Economic and Social Commission for Asia and the Pacific	34,998,000	(1,076,100)	33,921,900
12. Economic Commission for Latin America and the Caribbean	43,210,300	(2,267,800)	40,942,500
13. Economic Commission for Africa	46,358,100	(360,100)	45,998,000
14. Economic and Social Commission for Western Asia	27,302,800	(373,000)	26,929,800
15. United Nations Conference on Trade and Development	51,577,500	(447,100)	51,130,400
16. International Trade Centre	7,892,300	(251,700)	7,640,600
17. United Nations Industrial Development Organization	74,323,300	4,367,900	78,691,200
18. United Nations Environment Programme	9,976,300	38,700	10,015,000
19. United Nations Centre for Human Settlements (Habitat)	8,816,900	(391,100)	8,425,800
20. International drug control	5,451,600	24,500	5,476,100
21. Office of the United Nations High Commissioner for Refugees	28,484,400	596,900	29,081,300
22. Office of the United Nations Disaster Relief Co-ordinator	4,794,000	382,800	5,176,800
23. Human rights	10,310,000	934,800	11,244,800
24. Regular programme of technical co-operation	32,932,900	(504,200)	32,428,700
Total, PART IV	503,404,800	(144,500)	503,260,300
PART V. *International justice and law*			
25. International Court of Justice	9,049,700	940,200	9,989,900
26. Legal activities	15,040,700	(1,903,700)	13,137,000
Total, PART V	24,090,400	(963,500)	23,126,900
PART VI. *Public information*			
27. Public information	70,170,600	(990,700)	69,179,900
Total, PART VI	70,170,600	(990,700)	69,179,900
PART VII. *Common support services*			
28. Administration and management	303,456,500	8,531,600	311,988,100
29. Conference and library services	266,603,700	(2,624,400)	263,979,300
Total, PART VII	570,060,200	5,907,200	575,967,400
PART VIII. *Special expenses*			
30. United Nations bond issue	16,769,100	(143,000)	16,626,100
Total, PART VIII	16,769,100	(143,000)	16,626,100

Section	Amount appropriated by resolution 39/237 A	Increase or (decrease) (US dollars)	Final appropriation
PART IX. *Staff assessment*			
31. Staff assessment	244,735,600	(527,800)	244,207,800
Total, PART IX	244,735,600	(527,800)	244,207,800
PART X. *Capital expenditures*			
32. Construction, alteration, improvement and major maintenance of premises	20,366,200	(171,000)	20,195,200
Total, PART X	20,366,200	(171,000)	20,195,200
PART XI. *Special grants*			
33. Grant to the United Nations Institute for Training and Research	1,500,000	(600,000)	900,000
Total, PART XI	1,500,000	(600,000)	900,000
GRAND TOTAL	1,611,551,200	(2,597,200)	1,608,954,000

2. The Secretary-General shall be authorized to transfer credits between sections of the budget with the concurrence of the Advisory Committee on Administrative and Budgetary Questions;

3. The total net provision made under the various sections of the budget for contractual printing shall be administered as a unit under the direction of the United Nations Publications Board;

4. The appropriations for the regular programme of technical co-operation under section 24, part IV, shall be administered in accordance with the Financial Regulations of the United Nations, except that the definition of obligations and the period of validity of obligations shall be subject to the following procedures:

(*a*) Obligations for personal services established in the current biennium shall be valid for the succeeding biennium, provided that appointments of the experts concerned are effected by the end of the current biennium and that the total period to be covered by obligations established for these purposes against the resources of the current biennium shall not exceed twenty-four work-months;

(*b*) Obligations established in the current biennium for fellowships shall remain valid until liquidated, provided that the fellow has been nominated by the requesting Government and accepted by the Organization and that a formal letter of award has been issued to the requesting Governments;

(*c*) Obligations in respect of contracts or purchase orders for supplies or equipment recorded in the current biennium will remain valid until payment is effected to the contractor or vendor, unless they are cancelled;

5. In addition to the appropriations voted under paragraph 1 above, an amount of $19,000 is appropriated for each year of the biennium 1984-1985 from the accumulated income of the Library Endowment Fund for the purchase of books, periodicals, maps and library equipment and for such other expenses of the Library at the Palais des Nations as are in accordance with the objects and provisions of the endowment;

6. If savings are realized in the liquidation of obligations for the biennium 1984-1985, such savings up to $3,100,000 and any savings arising out of the appropriation of $1,950,700 for the General Service classification exercise shall be surrendered as if regulations 4.3, 4.4 and 5.2 (*d*) of the Financial Regulations of the United Nations had not been suspended.

General Assembly resolution 40/239 A

18 December 1985   Meeting 121   125-12-10 (recorded vote)

Approved by Fifth Committee (A/40/1058) by vote (100-4-7) on revised appropriations and revised income estimates together, 16 December (meeting 66); draft prepared by Rapporteur after vote, based on Secretary-General's proposals in performance report (A/C.5/40/50 (Part II)); agenda item 115.
Meeting numbers. GA 40th session: 5th Committee 63-66; plenary 121.

Recorded vote in Assembly as follows:

In favour: Afghanistan, Algeria, Angola, Antigua and Barbuda, Argentina, Austria, Bahamas, Bahrain, Bangladesh, Barbados, Belize, Benin, Bhutan, Bolivia, Botswana, Brazil, Brunei Darussalam, Burkina Faso, Burma, Burundi, Cameroon, Canada, Cape Verde, Central African Republic, Chad, Chile, China, Colombia, Congo, Costa Rica, Cuba, Cyprus, Democratic Kampuchea, Democratic Yemen, Denmark, Djibouti, Dominican Republic, Ecuador, Egypt, El Salvador, Equatorial Guinea, Ethiopia, Fiji, Finland, Gabon, Gambia, Ghana, Greece, Grenada, Guatemala, Guinea, Guinea-Bissau, Guyana, Honduras, Iceland, India, Indonesia, Iran, Iraq, Ireland, Ivory Coast, Jamaica, Jordan, Kenya, Kuwait, Lebanon, Lesotho, Liberia, Libyan Arab Jamahiriya, Madagascar, Malawi, Malaysia, Maldives, Mali, Malta, Mauritania, Mauritius, Mexico, Morocco, Mozambique, Nepal, New Zealand, Nicaragua, Niger, Nigeria, Norway, Oman, Pakistan, Panama, Papua New Guinea, Peru, Philippines, Qatar, Rwanda, Saint Lucia, Saint Vincent and the Grenadines, Samoa, Sao Tome and Principe, Saudi Arabia, Senegal, Sierra Leone, Singapore, Solomon Islands, Somalia, Sri Lanka, Sudan, Suriname, Swaziland, Sweden, Syrian Arab Republic, Thailand, Togo, Trinidad and Tobago, Tunisia, Turkey, Uganda, United Arab Emirates, United Republic of Tanzania, Uruguay, Venezuela, Yemen, Yugoslavia, Zaire, Zambia, Zimbabwe.

Against: Bulgaria, Byelorussian SSR, Czechoslovakia, German Democratic Republic, Germany, Federal Republic of, Hungary, Japan, Poland, Ukrainian SSR, USSR, United Kingdom, United States.

Abstaining: Australia, Belgium, France, Israel, Italy, Luxembourg, Netherlands, Portugal, Romania, Spain.

The United States, speaking in explanation of its negative vote in the Fifth Committee, observed that the slight decline in expenditures did not suggest that Member States or the Secretariat had exercised budgetary restraint. Instead, they had indulged in a spending spree which had added over $100 million in expenditures. Rather than reduce assessed contributions, the Assembly had decided to add programmes. The United States was concerned at significant instances of over-budgeting, while the performance report belied the Secretariat's argument that no flexibility existed in the budget. Also, Member States had not been provided with adequate reporting on the components of common staff costs, which in many cases were higher despite the $22.4 million increase voted last year.

Belgium said it had abstained because it considered that the performance report in its current form did not provide all the information required by Member States.

Argentina agreed with a suggestion by the Chairman of ACABQ that the Secretary-General's report should include measures to enable the Assembly to consider programme budget performance in both its financial and programme aspects. The Byelorussian SSR expressed similar views.

Income sources

Final income estimates under the United Nations programme budget for 1984-1985, covering income other than that derived from assessments on Member States, were approved by the General

Assembly in December 1985 in the amount of $294,345,500. This was a decrease of $7,093,600 from the amount approved at the Assembly's previous session.[5]

This decrease resulted from a drop in income of the Organization's revenue-producing activities, mainly in the sale of postage stamps. This was attributed to the increase in the value of the dollar against the Swiss franc and the Austrian schilling, the withdrawal of speculative interest from the philatelic market and the overly optimistic assumption that a large revenue would be generated by the stamp issue of the fortieth anniversary of the United Nations.

GENERAL ASSEMBLY ACTION

On the recommendation of the Fifth Committee, the Assembly on 18 December 1985 adopted by recorded vote **resolution 40/239 B**, revising the 1984-1985 income estimates. In both the Fifth Committee and the Assembly, the appropriations and income resolutions were voted on together (see above, under resolution 40/239 A, for recorded vote in the Assembly).

Final income estimates for the biennium 1984-1985

The General Assembly

Resolves that for the biennium 1984-1985:

1. The estimates of income other than assessments on Member States in the amount of $54,542,800 approved by its resolution 39/237 B of 18 December 1984 shall be decreased by $7,093,600 as follows:

Income section	Amount approved by resolution 39/237 B	Increase or (decrease)	Final approved estimates
		(US dollars)	
PART I. *Income from staff assessment*			
1. Income from staff assessment	246,896,300	931,700	247,828,000
Total, PART I	246,896,300	931,700	247,828,000
PART II. *Other income*			
2. General income	35,617,800	633,000	36,250,800
3. Revenue-producing activities	18,925,000	(8,658,300)	10,266,700
Total, PART II	54,542,800	(8,025,300)	46,517,500
GRAND TOTAL	301,439,100	(7,093,600)	294,345,500

2. The income from staff assessment shall be credited to the Tax Equalization Fund in accordance with the provisions of General Assembly resolution 973(X) of 15 December 1955;

3. Direct expenses of the United Nations Postal Administration, services to visitors, catering and related services, garage operations, television services and the sale of publications, not provided for under the budget appropriations, shall be charged against the income derived from those activities.

General Assembly resolution 40/239 B

18 December 1985   Meeting 121   125-12-10 (recorded vote)

Approved by Fifth Committee (A/40/1058) by vote (100-4-7) on revised appropriations and revised income estimates together, 16 December (meeting 66); draft prepared by Rapporteur after vote, based on Secretary-General's proposals in performance report (A//C.5/40/50 (Part II)); agenda item 115.
Meeting numbers. GA 40th session: 5th Committee 63-66; plenary 121.

Budget for 1986-1987

The United Nations programme budget for 1986-1987, in an amount of $1,663,341,500, was adopted by the General Assembly in December 1985. An income estimate of $317,465,600 from sources other than assessments on Member States was also approved. Member States were to be assessed $1,345,875,900.

The Secretary-General initially proposed[6] a budget calling for gross expenditures of $1,742,784,500, of which $327,133,000 was to be financed from income sources other than Members' contributions. Recommendations for reductions of $16,335,700 in expenditures and $969,800 in income estimates were made by ACABQ in its first report on the proposed budget.[7]

Following a general debate in October on the budget and related matters, the Fifth Committee examined the expenditure and income sections, taking also into account revised estimates presented by the Secretary-General subsequent to his initial submission, along with the financial implications of actions taken by the Assembly during the session and ACABQ's recommendations on each of these proposed changes. The result, as recommended by the Fifth Committee and approved by the Assembly, was a gross budget $79,443,000 less than the Secretary-General's initial proposal, with income estimates $9,667,400 below the initial estimate (see below).

The programme content of the budget was reviewed by the Committee for Programme and Co-ordination (CPC)[8] and its recommendations were incorporated into the programme descriptions contained in the budget document.

The major factor in the reduction from the initial expenditure level was the elimination from the budget of section 17, which had provided for a maintenance budget for UNIDO pending its coming into being as a specialized agency. This had taken place on 21 June 1985, when UNIDO's Constitution had entered into force (see ECONOMIC AND SOCIAL QUESTIONS, Chapter VI). The net financial result of the conversion was a reduction in the United Nations budget of $68.8 million, the Secretary-General advised the General Assembly.[9] However, he proposed, and ACABQ concurred, that the Fifth Committee recommend to the Assembly a loan of $24 million to UNIDO to meet the initial expenses of the new agency for the calendar year 1986. The Assembly took this action within the provisions of the resolution approving the programme budget for 1986-1987.

Other budget reductions from the initial level proposed by the Secretary-General, in amounts of over $1 million, were the appropriations for political and Security Council affairs and peacekeeping ($3.7 million), the Department of International Economic and Social Affairs ($1.7 million), the regional commissions for Asia and the Pacific, Latin America and the Caribbean, Africa and Western Asia (totalling $14.3 million), the United Nations Environment Programme (UNEP) ($1.2 million), the United Nations Centre for Human Settlement (Habitat) ($1.5 million), the regular programme of technical co-operation ($7.4 million), administration and management (which included common staff costs) ($15 million) and staff assessment ($4.3 million).

These reductions were more than offset by increases approved by the Fifth Committee. In amounts of more than $1 million these were: political affairs, trusteeship and decolonization activities ($2.8 million), the Economic Commission for Europe (ECE) ($3.3 million), the United Nations Conference on Trade and Development (UNCTAD) ($8.2 million), the Office of the United Nations High Commissioner for Refugees (UNHCR) ($2.3 million), human rights activities ($1.9 million), ICJ ($2 million), conference servicing ($9.7 million) and construction, improvement and maintenance of premises ($18.2 million).

(For changes in the income estimates, see the following section of this Chapter, ''Income sources''.)

In his foreword to the programme budget,[6] the Secretary-General pointed out that its programmatic structure was derived from the objectives and strategies of the medium-term plan for 1984-1989 adopted in 1982.[10] He referred to several elements involved in the budget preparation: the establishment of priorities; the review process for determining termination of programme elements; and the exercise of maximum restraint. He also presented an overview of the methodology for preparing the programme budget. The Secretary-General noted that priority concerns had included the problems faced by the least developed countries (LDCs) and the critical situation in sub-Saharan Africa. In consequence, higher than average growth was proposed for the regional commissions.

The Secretary-General suggested that further economies could be achieved if the calendar and pattern of conferences were rationalized by biennial scheduling of meetings, shortening of their duration and selecting as the venue of meetings the headquarters of the unit responsible for substantive servicing.

Finally, the Secretary-General pointed out that his budget proposals represented a real growth of 0.4 per cent over the previous biennium (real growth excludes inflation, foreign exchange-rate movements and non-recurrent expenditures for such matters as special conferences). Also, he added, it should be kept in mind that in terms of the capacity of the Organization to deliver its programme of work, substantial resources were expected to become available from other sources than the regular budget.

Addressing the Fifth Committee, the Secretary-General drew attention to the current financial situation of the United Nations and, in particular, to the detrimental effect that withholding contributions and delaying assessed payments had on the functioning of the Organization. The financing of the Organization's activities, he believed, required agreement on three fundamental points: the level and content of the budget, the scale of assessments and the payment of assessed contributions. Lasting consensus had not been reached on any of those points. He noted that political differences remained concerning the amount of the budget and the content of programmes and he emphasized that increasingly late payment of assessed contributions was serving to aggravate the financial emergency of the Organization.

The Chairman of ACABQ, presenting that body's first report on the 1986-1987 programme budget in October to the Fifth Committee, commented on, among other things, the methodology used in reflecting estimates for non-recurrent items in the budget and stressed the need to re-examine the practice of excluding some non-recurrent items from the proposed budget. Non-recurrent costs were estimated at $83.4 million for 1984-1985 and 1986-1987. The draft programme budget illustrated the complexity of programme budgeting in the United Nations; it did not include full requirements under a number of sections, for which revised estimates would be discussed separately. The Committee had been informed that these revised estimates would increase the overall real growth rate as calculated by the Secretariat from 0.4 per cent to nearly 0.6 per cent.

The Chairman went on to say that a major negative revision of the 1986-1987 estimates would take place with the conversion of UNIDO into a specialized agency (see above). The largest increase could occur as a result of construction projects for two regional commissions at an estimated cost of $58.9 million in 1986-1987. While the strength of the United States dollar had resulted in recent years in negative budget revisions, it was probable that if the September 1985 currency situation continued to the end of the current Assembly session, additional requirements of about $45 million to $50 million would arise.

Programme budget implications during the fortieth session of the General Assembly, and implications of recommendations of the International

Civil Service Commission and the United Nations Joint Staff Pension Board would also affect the estimates, the ACABQ Chairman said. Furthermore, the financial implications of legislative decisions were so unpredictable that it was impossible to estimate exactly the additional amount the Secretariat might request.

He added that the persistent impression gained from a regular exchange of views with the heads of the agencies in the common system was that of increasing difficulty in obtaining sufficient funds for implementing work programmes, whether under assessed or extrabudgetary contributions. Assessed contributions were barely keeping up with inflation, with no growth for most programmes.

The Chairman of CPC said that in accordance with its mandate his Committee had concentrated on the programme aspects of the proposed budget. However, it had been unable to avoid considering the financial aspects as well, since the two were linked.

Among the most important items on CPC's 1985 agenda were problems relating to cross-organizational programme analysis (COPA). For that reason, particular attention had been paid to future areas for COPA, marine affairs, the general approach to COPA and analysis of the activities of the United Nations system in economic and technical co-operation among developing countries. There was general agreement that such analyses were useful tools which could help the Committee make all United Nations activities more effective.

As far as the choice of subjects for future analysis was concerned, CPC had considered four: environment, science and technology for development, women and development, and transport.

On 26 July 1985, the Economic and Social Council adopted **resolution 1985/76**, by sections III and IV of which it endorsed the conclusions and recommendations of CPC at its 1985 session, noted improvements in the format of the proposed programme budget for 1986-1987 and reiterated that the medium-term plan constituted the principal policy directive of the United Nations and should continue to serve as the framework for the biennial budget (see p. 1040). By **resolution 40/240** the General Assembly also approved the recommendations of CPC. (See Chapter II of this section.)

On 17 December, the Fifth Committee approved the programme expenditures, taking recorded votes on 30 sections and sub-sections and approving five sections without vote.

A total of 11,174 established posts were approved in conjunction with the final appropriations for expenditure and income sections of the budget. Approved temporary posts numbered 249.

The budget adopted by the Assembly was set out in three resolutions, detailing appropriations (**resolution 40/253 A**), income estimates (**40/253 B**) and the financing of 1986 appropriations (**40/253 C**) (see below). Other resolutions relating to the budget biennium concerned unforeseen costs (**40/254**) and financing of the Working Capital Fund (**40/255**).

In addition, by a 12-part resolution (**40/252**) on questions relating to the proposed programme budget for the 1986-1987 biennium, the General Assembly took action on the following items: the *Yearbook of the United Nations* (see p. 386), a telephone system at United Nations Headquarters (p. 1266), the catering operation at Headquarters (p. 1262), the United Nations Office at Nairobi, Kenya (p. 1262), accommodations at Bangkok (p. 652) and the headquarters of the Economic Commission for Africa (ECA) at Addis Ababa (p. 642), the venue of the Committee on Economic, Social and Cultural Rights in 1988 (p. 879), the inclusion of Portuguese among the official working languages of ECA (p. 640), eliminating the backlog in the publication of the United Nations *Treaty Series* (p. 1190), the 1986 budget estimates for the United Nations Computing Centre (p. 1264), staffing resources of the News Service of the Department of Political and Security Council Affairs (p. 387) and supporting staff appeals procedures (p. 1251).

In another action, the Assembly, on 18 December 1985, by **decision 40/470** suspended its fortieth (1985) session, deciding to resume it at a date to be announced for the purpose of considering several of its agenda items, including the proposed programme budget for the 1986-1987 biennium.

Appropriations

The $1,663,341,500 in appropriations approved by the General Assembly under the expenditure sections of the 1986-1987 budget were divided among major areas as follows: common support services, 36.7 per cent; economic, social and humanitarian affairs, 27.8 per cent; staff assessment, 16.5 per cent; political and Security Council affairs and peace-keeping, 5.6 per cent; public information, 4.6 per cent; overall policy-making, direction and co-ordination, 2.8 per cent; buildings and maintenance, 1.8 per cent; international justice and law, 1.6 per cent; trusteeship and decolonization, 1.5 per cent; United Nations bond issue and special grants, 1.1 per cent.

GENERAL ASSEMBLY ACTION

The expenditures sections of the 1986-1987 budget, comprising the appropriations for the biennium, were adopted by recorded vote by the Assembly on 18 December, as **resolution 40/253 A**, on the recommendation of the Fifth Committee.

Budget appropriations for the biennium 1986-1987

The General Assembly

Resolves that for the biennium 1986-1987:

1. Appropriations totalling $US 1,663,341,500 are hereby voted for the following purposes:

Section	(US dollars)
PART I. *Overall policy-making, direction and co-ordination*	
1. Overall policy-making, direction and co-ordination	45,090,200
Total, PART I	45,090,200
PART II. *Political and Security Council affairs; peace-keeping activities*	
2A. Political and Security Council affairs; peace-keeping activities	83,786,600
2B. Disarmament affairs activities	9,853,500
Total, PART II	93,640,100
PART III. *Political affairs, trusteeship and decolonization*	
3. Political affairs, trusteeship and decolonization	25,606,800
Total, PART III	25,606,800
PART IV. *Economic, social and humanitarian activities*	
4. Policy-making organs (economic and social activities)	2,526,100
5A. Office of the Director-General for Development and International Economic Co-operation	3,814,000
5B. Centre for Science and Technology for Development	4,230,300
5C. Regional Commissions Liaison Office	665,100
6. Department of International Economic and Social Affairs	54,160,700
7. Department of Technical Co-operation for Development	20,218,300
8. Office of Secretariat Services for Economic and Social Matters	4,387,700
9. Transnational corporations	10,078,000
10. Economic Commission for Europe	26,767,900
11. Economic and Social Commission for Asia and the Pacific	34,818,400
12. Economic Commission for Latin America and the Caribbean	45,293,700
13. Economic Commission for Africa	48,166,300
14. Economic and Social Commission for Western Asia	33,707,500
15. United Nations Conference on Trade and Development	60,135,300
16. International Trade Centre	8,041,300
18. United Nations Environment Programme	10,142,400
19. United Nations Centre for Human Settlements (Habitat)	8,610,400
20. International Drug Control	6,291,200
21. Office of the United Nations High Commissioner for Refugees	34,485,200
22. Office of the United Nations Disaster Relief Co-ordinator	5,708,300
23. Human rights	11,675,400
24. Regular programme of technical co-operation	29,277,200
Total, PART IV	463,200,700
PART V. *International justice and law*	
25. International Court of Justice	10,500,800
26. Legal activities	15,896,500
Total, PART V	26,397,300
PART VI. *Public information*	
27. Public information	75,668,900
Total, PART VI	75,668,900
PART VII. *Common support services*	
28. Administration and management	321,993,400
29. Conference and library services	288,823,600
Total, PART VII	610,817,000
PART VIII. *Special expenses*	
30. United Nations bond issue	16,758,600
Total, PART VIII	16,758,600
PART IX. *Staff assessment*	
31. Staff assessment	275,416,800
Total, PART IX	275,416,800

Section	(US dollars)
PART X. *Capital expenditures*	
32. Construction, alteration, improvement and major maintenance of premises	30,145,100
Total, PART X	30,145,100
PART XI. *Special grants*	
33. Grant to the United Nations Institute for Training and Research	600,000
Total, PART XI	600,000
GRAND TOTAL	1,663,341,500

2. The Secretary-General shall be authorized to transfer credits between sections of the budget with the concurrence of the Advisory Committee on Administrative and Budgetary Questions;

3. The total net provision made under the various sections of the budget for contractual printing shall be administered as a unit under the direction of the United Nations Publications Board;

4. The appropriations for the regular programme of technical co-operation under part IV, section 24, shall be administered in accordance with the Financial Regulations of the United Nations, except that the definition of obligations and the period of validity of obligations shall be subject to the following procedures:

(*a*) Obligations for personal services established in the current biennium shall be valid for the succeeding biennium, provided that appointments of the experts concerned are effected by the end of the current biennium, and that the total period to be covered by obligations established for these purposes against the resources of the current biennium shall not exceed twenty-four work-months;

(*b*) Obligations established in the current biennium for fellowships shall remain valid until liquidated, provided that the fellow has been nominated by the requesting Government and accepted by the Organization, and that a formal letter of award has been issued to the requesting Government;

(*c*) Obligations in respect of contracts or purchase orders for supplies or equipment recorded in the current biennium shall remain valid until payment is effected to the contractor or vendor, unless they are cancelled;

5. In addition to the appropriations voted under paragraph 1 above, an amount of $19,000 is appropriated for each year of the biennium 1986-1987 from accumulated income of the Library Endowment Fund for the purchase of books, periodicals, maps and library equipment and for such other expenses of the Library at the Palais des Nations as are in accordance with the objects and provisions of the endowment;

6. In addition to the appropriations voted under paragraphs 1 and 5 above, an amount of $24 million is specially appropriated for the year 1986 to finance a loan to the United Nations Industrial Development Organization. This amount shall be placed in a special account in order to meet the expenses of the initial operations of the new agency for the calendar year 1986, in accordance with General Assembly resolution 34/96, paragraph 8, of 13 December 1979. The special account will be credited with repayments made by the United Nations Industrial Development Organization.

General Assembly resolution 40/253 A

18 December 1985   Meeting 122   127-10-11 (recorded vote)

Approved by Fifth Committee (A/40/1069) by recorded vote (83-11-10), 17 December (meeting 70); agenda item 116.

Meeting numbers. GA 40th session: 5th Committee 11, 14-23, 25-28, 30-36, 38-43, 47-52, 56-70; plenary 122.

Recorded vote in Assembly as follows:

In favour: Afghanistan, Algeria, Angola, Antigua and Barbuda, Argentina, Australia, Austria, Bahamas, Bahrain, Bangladesh, Barbados, Belize, Benin, Bhutan, Bolivia, Botswana, Brazil, Brunei Darussalam, Burkina Faso, Burma, Burundi, Cameroon, Canada, Cape Verde, Central African Republic, Chad, Chile, China, Colombia, Congo, Costa Rica, Cuba, Cyprus, Democratic Kampuchea, Democratic Yemen, Denmark, Djibouti, Dominican Republic, Ecuador, Egypt, El Salvador, Equatorial Guinea, Ethiopia, Fiji, Finland, Gabon, Gambia, Ghana, Greece, Guatemala, Guinea, Guinea-Bissau, Guyana, Haiti, Honduras, Iceland, India, Indonesia, Iran, Iraq, Ireland, Ivory Coast, Jamaica, Jordan, Kenya, Kuwait, Lebanon, Lesotho, Liberia, Libyan Arab Jamahiriya, Madagascar, Malawi, Malaysia, Maldives, Mali, Malta, Mauritania, Mauritius, Mexico, Morocco, Mozambique, Nepal, New Zealand, Nicaragua, Niger, Nigeria, Norway, Oman, Pakistan, Panama, Papua New Guinea, Paraguay, Peru, Philippines, Qatar, Rwanda, Saint Vincent and the Grenadines, Samoa, Sao Tome and Principe, Saudi Arabia, Senegal, Sierra Leone, Singapore, Solomon Islands, Somalia, Sri Lanka, Sudan, Suriname, Swaziland, Sweden, Syrian Arab Republic, Thailand, Togo, Trinidad and Tobago, Tunisia, Turkey, Uganda, United Arab Emirates, United Republic of Tanzania, Uruguay, Vanuatu, Venezuela, Yemen, Yugoslavia, Zaire, Zambia, Zimbabwe.

Against: Bulgaria, Byelorussian SSR, Czechoslovakia, German Democratic Republic, Hungary, Israel, Poland, Ukrainian SSR, USSR, United States.

Abstaining: Belgium, France, Germany, Federal Republic of, Italy, Japan, Luxembourg, Netherlands, Portugal, Romania, Spain, United Kingdom.

Explaining its negative vote in the Fifth Committee, the USSR said the total appropriations were excessive; the contributions of Member States were still being spent in a wasteful and ineffective manner and on activities which were not the proper work of the United Nations and frequently contravened the provisions of the Charter. It would not pay for costs related to the United Nations bond issue or for posts or activities which contravened Charter provisions. The Charter did not authorize financing of technical assistance from the regular budget, which should be on a purely voluntary basis. Mongolia said it had abstained on the sections pertaining to technical assistance and the United Nations Institute for Training and Research (UNITAR), considering that financing for such activities should come from voluntary contributions.

The United States said that while the growth in programmes financed from the regular budget was relatively modest, it was still unacceptable at a time when many national budgets were frozen or were declining in nominal or real terms. No real attempt had been made to absorb the effect of exchange-rate fluctuations and inflation and the budget continued to finance programmes which the United States legislature had prohibited. It also objected to the continued add-ons to the budget approved at the current session. Although the budget had much to recommend it, the total resources requested were excessive and the United States had therefore voted against it.

Israel said it had voted against the resolution. It would be absurd, it said, to expect it to support the funding of vicious, politically biased anti-Israel activities with resources that ought to be used to promote the economic and social well-being of developing countries.

The United Kingdom welcomed signs of budgetary restraint, but pointed out that figures submitted by the Secretary-General did not represent the final bill, which included non-recurrent items, in other words, non-optional extras, a trend which should be be considered. In that light, the United Kingdom had abstained in the vote.

France also abstained; the method of calculating the rate of real growth was based on an inaccurate distinction between recurrent and non-recurrent expenditure and did not take exchange-rate factors duly into account. More refined instruments were needed to exercise more intelligent control over expenditures, programmes should be scrutinized more closely, priorities must be better defined, budgetary procedures rationalized to ensure better co-ordination and avoid programme duplication, better use must be made of instruments for programme evaluation, and budgetary terminology and format should be improved.

Japan, which abstained, was concerned that the Secretary-General's figures did not reflect real growth because of the way non-recurrent costs had been treated; a more rigorous approach to such costs would be necessary. Japan was disappointed that the new form of statements of programme budget implications had not been used to rationalize priorities and programmatic content. It had reservations with respect to many instances of the transfer of extrabudgetary activities to the regular budget. It was also concerned over the continuing trend towards ''grade creep'' and excessive upgradings of posts. It joined Italy in expressing concern over the many instances in which ACABQ's recommendations had been set aside.

Italy and the Federal Republic of Germany, also abstaining, criticized continual requests for additional budget appropriations for administrative costs, rising conference servicing costs and activities for which, in the view of the Federal Republic of Germany, there was no proper mandate and which had far-reaching implications. Spain felt that greater efforts should have been made to achieve budget austerity.

Australia said it had voted in favour of the budget in recognition of the Secretary-General's efforts to contain budget growth. Among its concerns were unacceptably high staff-related costs, reclassification of posts, non-essential travel to unnecessary meetings and the fact that the proportion of administrative costs continued to rise at the expense of substantive programmes.

Canada, which also voted in favour, called for a redefinition of the concept of non-recurrent costs in more conventional terms, greater restraint regarding add-ons, and elimination of programmes which had become obsolete or were of marginal usefulness, with redeployment of resources from them to programmes of higher priority.

Iceland, speaking on behalf of the five Nordic countries, expressed concern that the budget simply would not be implemented because of the practice of withholding parts of assessed contributions and because of the poor pattern of payments of those assessments.

Financial implications

The Secretary-General's initial budget proposals called for gross expenditures of $1,742,784,500. The total approved by the Fifth Committee was $1,608,954,000. (Increases and decreases in amounts of over $1 million are described in the section immediately above.)

The Fifth Committee, on 17 December, voted separately, in second reading, on each budget section, as shown in the table below.

UN PROGRAMME BUDGETS, 1984-1985 AND 1986-1987
(appropriations and income estimates in thousands of US dollars)

PART/SECTION/SUBSECTION	1984-1985		1986-1987				
	Appropriations	Established posts	Initial estimates	Appropriations	Established posts	Real growth (percentage)	Vote
PART I. *Overall policy-making, direction and co-ordination*							
1. Overall policy-making, direction and co-ordination	40,173.4	226	44,983.4	45,090.2	224	1.1	103-2-0
A. Policy-making organs	—	47	17,766.0	—	47	0.5	—
B. Executive direction and management	—	179	27,217.4	—	177	1.4	—
PART II. *Political and Security Council affairs; peace-keeping activities*							
2A. Political and Security Council affairs; peace-keeping activities	82,267.9	775	87,523.4	83,786.6	768	-1.0	101-2-2
A. Policy-making organs	—	—	957.6	—	—	42.4	—
B. Department of Political and Security Council Affairs	—	94	11,850.6	—	87	-1.5	—
C. Secretariat of the Third United Nations Conference on the Law of the Sea	—	30	6,231.4	—	30	—	—
D. Special missions	—	559	57,694.2	—	559	-1.6	—
E. United Nations Relief and Works Agency for Palestine Refugees in the Near East	—	92	10,789.6	—	92	-0.5	—
2B. Disarmament Affairs activities	9,316.5	57	9,463.4	9,853.5	57	1.3	99-3-4
A. Policy-making organs	—	—	342.1	—	—	-2.9	—
B. Department for Disarmament Affairs	—	57	9,121.3	—	57	1.5	—
PART III. *Political affairs, trusteeship and decolonization*							
3. Political affairs, trusteeship and decolonization	28,696.5	131	22,794.9	25,606.8	133	0.7	97-2-5
A. Policy-making organs	—	—	1,977.3	—	—	-3.1	—
B. Department of Political Affairs, Trusteeship and Decolonization	—	60	8,030.2	—	62	3.8	—
C. Namibia	—	33	8,659.4	—	33	-0.8	—
D. Centre against *Apartheid*	—	38	4,128.0	—	38	-0.4	—
E. Office of the Co-ordinator of the Programme of Assistance to the Kampuchean People	—	—	—	—	—	—	—
PART IV. *Economic, social and humanitarian activities*							
4. Policy-making organs (economic and social activities)	3,936.0	—	2,596.9	2,526.1	—	0.8	104-1-1
A. Economic and Social Council and its functional commissions and committees and other recurrent meetings	—	—	1,348.3	—	—	4.1	—
B. Special conferences	—	—	1,248.6	—	—	—	—
5A. Office of the Director-General for Development and International Economic Co-operation	3,772.2	27	4,027.5	3,814.0	26	-4.1	101-2-0
5B. Centre for Science and Technology for Development	3,995.2	32	4,457.8	4,230.3	32	-0.1	no vote
5C. Regional Commissions Liaison Office	620.9	6	704.5	665.1	6	1.8	104-1-2
6. Department of International Economic and Social Affairs	50,056.8	520	55,874.1	54,160.7	522	0.3	no vote
7. Department of Technical Co-operation for Development	18,100.4	199	20,086.1	20,218.3	207	4.6	84-14-8
8. Office of Secretariat Services for Economic and Social Matters	3,926.6	39	4,585.7	4,387.7	39	1.7	98-1-8
9. Transnational corporations	9,783.5	83	10,793.2	10,078.0	83	-3.5	105-1-0
10. Economic Commission for Europe	22,784.8	233	23,462.0	26,767.9	233	-0.1	no vote
11. Economic and Social Commission for Asia and the Pacific	34,998.0	554	40,418.5	34,818.4	560	1.9	95-1-11
12. Economic Commission for Latin America	43,210.3	586	49,006.3	45,293.7	591	1.4	95-1-11
13. Economic Commission for Africa	46,358.1	618	51,829.4	48,166.3	626	1.6	96-1-10
14. Economic Commission for Western Asia	27,302.8	313	35,049.7	33,707.5	313	0.1	96-2-10
15. United Nations Conference on Trade and Development	51,577.5	454	51,945.9	60,135.3	454	-0.2	105-2-0
16. International Trade Centre	7,892.3	—	8,100.7	8,041.3	—	-0.5	98-8-1
17. United Nations Industrial Development Organization	74,323.3	—	77,933.0	—	—	—	no vote
18. United Nations Environment Programme	9,976.3	104	11,375.7	10,142.4	106	0.9	85-21-0
19. United Nations Centre for Human Settlements (Habitat)	8,816.9	87	10,141.2	8,610.4	88	0.5	96-2-9
20. International drug control	5,451.6	59	5,665.3	6,291.2	59	0.1	96-7-2
21. Office of the United Nations High Commissioner for Refugees	28,484.4	290	32,154.1	34,485.2	290	1.7	95-11-0
22. Office of the United Nations Disaster Relief Co-ordinator	4,794.0	36	5,187.1	5,708.3	36	0.1	no vote
23. Human rights	10,310.0	80	9,776.8	11,675.4	81	6.1	104-2-0
24. Regular programme of technical co-operation	32,932.9	—	36,637.0	29,277.2	—	0.0	86-14-6

PART/SECTION/SUBSECTION	1984-1985		1986-1987				
	Appropri-ations	Estab-lished posts	Initial estimates	Appropri-ations	Estab-lished posts	Real growth (percent-age)	Vote
PART V. *International justice and law*							
25. International Court of Justice	9,049.7	41	8,503.5	10,500.8	41	7.1	97-2-8
26. Legal activities	15,040.7	108	16,627.3	15,896.5	108	-2.0	no vote
A. Policy-making organs	—	2	2,479.8	—	2	-4.5	—
B. Special meetings and conferences	—	—	77.3	—	—	—	—
C. Office of Legal Affairs	—	106	14,070.2	—	106	-1.6	—
PART VI. *Public information*							
27. Public information	70,170.6	750	76,439.3	75,668.9	751	-1.1	83-4-20
A. Headquarters	—	319	48,800.1	—	318	-2.3	—
B. Geneva	—	35	3,473.3	—	35	—	—
C. Information Service, Vienna	—	11	917.8	—	13	42.6	—
D. Information centres	—	385	23,248.1	—	385	0.1	—
PART VII. *Common support services*							
28. Administration, management and general services	303,456.5	2,084	337,031.8	321,993.4	2,019	0.2	81-9-15
29. Conference and library services	266,603.7	2,495	279,152.1	288,823.6	2,515	0.8	83-5-18
PART VIII. *Special expenses*							
30. United Nations bond issue	16,769.1	—	16,758.6	16,758.6	—	—	92-11-0
PART IX. *Staff assessment*							
31. Staff assessment	244,735.6	—	279,705.4	275,416.8	—	0.9	92-14-0
PART X. *Capital expenditures*							
32. Construction, alteration, improvement and major maintenance of premises	20,366.2	—	11,992.9	30,145.1	—	41.1	88-2-16
PART XI. *Special grants*							
33. United Nations Institute for Training and Research	1,500.0	—	—	600.0	—	—	83-14-10
TOTAL APPROPRIATIONS (gross)	1,611,551.2	10,987	1,742,784.5	1,663,341.5	10,968	0.1	83-11-10

INCOME SECTION	Income estimates	Estab-lished posts	Initial income estimates	Approved income estimates	Estab-lished posts	Real growth (percent-age)	Vote
1. Income from staff assessment	246,896.3	—	283,700.6	279,485.5	—	—	92-13-0
2. General income	35,617.8	—	36,428.7	28,570.0	—	—	no vote
3. Revenue-producing activities	18,925.0	211	7,003.7	9,410.1	194	—	no vote
TOTAL INCOME ESTIMATES	301,439.1	211	327,133.0	317,465.6	194	—	92-13-0
GRAND TOTAL NET BUDGET	1,310,112.1	10,776	1,415,651.5	1,345,875.9	10,774	0.1	—

NOTES:

1984-1985: Appropriations: Approved by the General Assembly on 18 December 1984 (resolution 39/237 A). *Income estimates:* Approved by the General Assembly on 18 December 1984 (resolution 39/237 B). *Established posts:* Number of established (non-temporary) staff posts authorized under the 1984-1985 regular budget.

1986-1987: Initial estimates: Contained in the Secretary-General's proposed programme budget (A/40/6 (vol. I)). *Appropriations:* Approved by the General Assembly on 18 December 1985 (resolution 40/253 A). *Approved income estimates:* Approved by the General Assembly on 18 December 1985 (resolution 40/253 B). *Established posts:* Number of established (non-temporary) staff posts authorized under the 1986-1987 regular budget. *Real growth:* Percentage increase (or decrease) in appropriations from 1984-1985 to 1986-1987, excluding inflation and non-recurrent items, as calculated by the United Nations Secretariat. *Vote:* Totals of recorded section-by-section votes (in favour–against–abstaining) in the Fifth Committee during the second reading of the budget and the Committee vote on the appropriations as a whole, 17 December 1985; the vote in the Assembly on the appropriation resolution was 127-10-11. Dashes in the final column indicate subsections not put separately to the vote; "no vote" refers to sections approved without vote.

SOURCE for subsection appropriations (1986-1987), established posts (1984-1985 and 1986-1987) and real growth: A/40/6/Add.1.

The Fifth Committee also approved appropriations covering the financial implications of decisions taken at the current Assembly session. These decisions concerned, among other things: the situation in Afghanistan and its implications for international peace and security; the question of Namibia; the international campaign against traffic in drugs; the International Conference on the Relationship between Disarmament and Development; preparation of a study on the climatic and physical effects of nuclear war, including nuclear winter; the situa-tion in Kampuchea; South Africa's *apartheid* policies; the United Nations Conference for the Promotion of International Co-operation in the Peaceful Uses of Nuclear Energy; preparation work for bringing the Common Fund for Commodities into operation; the World Conference to Review and Appraise the Achievements of the United Nations Decade for Women; the Special Committee to Investigate Israeli Practices Affecting the Human Rights of the Population of the Occupied Territories; the question of Palestine; and a grant to UNITAR.

Financing appropriations for 1986

GENERAL ASSEMBLY ACTION

Acting on the recommendation of the Fifth Committee, the General Assembly on 18 December 1985 adopted by recorded vote **resolution 40/253 C**, specifying the amounts to be obtained from each of the major income sources in order to finance appropriations during the first year of the 1986-1987 biennium (see "Appropriations" above). Member States were to be assessed $700,434,350 for 1986, net of staff assessment. Income for the year, other than staff assessment and the income from the repayment of the loan to UNIDO, was set at $18,990,050.

Financing of appropriations for the year 1986
The General Assembly
Resolves that for the year 1986:

1. Budget appropriations totalling $US 860,098,850, consisting of $US 831,670,750, being one half of the appropriations approved for the biennium 1986-1987 under paragraph 1 of resolution A above, and $24 million for 1986 only under paragraph 6 of resolution A above, together with revised income other than staff assessment for 1984-1985 decreased by $US 8,025,300, revised appropriations for 1984-1985 decreased by $US 2,597,200, and the reimbursement of $US 1 million being the commitment entered upon in 1984 under the terms of resolution 38/226 A, paragraph 6, of 20 December 1983, shall be financed in accordance with regulations 5.1 and 5.2 of the Financial Regulations of the United Nations as follows:

(a) $18,990,050 being half of the estimated income, other than staff assessment and the income from the repayment of the loan to the United Nations Industrial Development Organization, approved for the biennium 1986-1987 under resolution B above;

(b) $841,108,800 being the assessment on Member States in accordance with General Assembly resolution 40/248 of 18 December 1985 on the scale of assessments for the years 1986, 1987 and 1988;

2. There shall be set off against the assessment on Member States, in accordance with the provisions of General Assembly resolution 973(X) of 15 December 1955, their respective share in the Tax Equalization Fund in the total amount of $US 140,674,450 consisting of:

(a) $139,742,750 being half of the estimated income from staff assessment approved for the biennium 1986-1987 under resolution B above;

(b) $931,700 being the increase in the revised income from staff assessment for the biennium 1984-1985.

General Assembly resolution 40/253 C

18 December 1985   Meeting 122   126-11-11 (recorded vote)

Approved by Fifth Committee (A/40/1069) by recorded vote (83-11-10), 17 December (meeting 70); agenda item 116.
Meeting numbers. GA 40th session: 5th Committee 11, 14-23, 25-28, 30-36, 38-43, 47-52, 56-70; plenary 122.

Recorded vote in Assembly as follows:

In favour: Afghanistan, Algeria, Angola, Antigua and Barbuda, Argentina, Australia, Austria, Bahamas, Bahrain, Bangladesh, Barbados, Belize, Benin, Bhutan, Bolivia, Botswana, Brazil, Brunei Darussalam, Burkina Faso, Burma, Burundi, Cameroon, Canada, Cape Verde, Central African Republic, Chad, Chile, China, Colombia, Congo, Cuba, Cyprus, Democratic Kampuchea, Democratic Yemen, Denmark, Djibouti, Dominican Republic, Ecuador, Egypt, El Salvador, Equatorial Guinea, Ethiopia, Fiji, Finland, Gabon, Gambia, Ghana, Greece, Guatemala, Guinea, Guinea-Bissau, Guyana, Haiti, Honduras, Iceland, India, Indonesia, Iran, Iraq, Ireland, Ivory Coast, Jamaica, Jordan, Kenya, Kuwait, Lebanon, Lesotho, Liberia, Libyan Arab Jamahiriya, Madagascar, Malawi, Malaysia, Maldives, Mali, Malta, Mauritania, Mauritius, Mexico, Morocco, Mozambique, Nepal, New Zealand, Nicaragua, Niger, Nigeria, Norway, Oman, Pakistan, Panama, Papua New Guinea, Paraguay, Peru, Philippines, Qatar, Rwanda, Saint Vincent and the Grenadines, Samoa, Sao Tome and Principe, Saudi Arabia, Senegal, Sierra Leone, Singapore, Solomon Islands, Somalia, Sri Lanka, Sudan, Suriname, Swaziland, Sweden, Syrian Arab Republic, Thailand, Togo, Trinidad and Tobago, Tunisia, Turkey, Uganda, United Arab Emirates, United Republic of Tanzania, Uruguay, Vanuatu, Venezuela, Yemen, Yugoslavia, Zaire, Zambia, Zimbabwe.

Against: Bulgaria, Byelorussian SSR, Czechoslovakia, German Democratic Republic, Hungary, Israel, Mongolia, Poland, Ukrainian SSR, USSR, United States.

Abstaining: Belgium, France, Germany, Federal Republic of, Italy, Japan, Luxembourg, Netherlands, Portugal, Romania, Spain, United Kingdom.

Income sources

The appropriations approved by the General Assembly in December 1985 under the 1986-1987 budget were to be financed from three main income sources: assessments on Member States (see "Budget contributions" below); staff assessment (an income tax levied by the United Nations on staff salaries); and sales revenues (mainly from postage stamps). The remainder was to come from miscellaneous sources classified as "general income", about half of which consisted of reimbursement for services provided to specialized agencies and others.

GENERAL ASSEMBLY ACTION

Estimates of income for the 1986-1987 biennium, other than Members' assessments, in a total amount of $317,465,600, were approved by the General Assembly on 18 December 1985 when it adopted **resolution 40/253 B** by recorded vote. The approval procedure was the same as that for appropriations (see above), involving proposals by the Secretary-General, analysis by ACABQ and a recommendation by the Fifth Committee.

Income estimates for the biennium 1986-1987
The General Assembly
Resolves that for the biennium 1986-1987:

1. Estimates of income other than assessments on Member States totalling $US 317,465,600 are approved as follows:

Income section	(US dollars)
PART I. *Income from staff assessment*	
1. Income from staff assessment	279,485,500
Total, PART I	279,485,500
PART II. *Other income*	
2. General income	28,570,000
3. Revenue-producing activities	9,410,100
Total, PART II	37,980,100
GRAND TOTAL	317,465,600

2. The income from staff assessment shall be credited to the Tax Equalization Fund in accordance with the provisions of General Assembly resolution 973(X) of 15 December 1955;

3. Direct expenses of the United Nations Postal Administration, services to visitors, catering and related

services, garage operations, television services and the sale of publications, not provided for under the budget appropriations, shall be charged against the income derived from those activities;

4. Income from the repayment of the loan to the United Nations Industrial Development Organization, for which $24 million was specially appropriated under paragraph 6 of resolution A above, shall be credited to income section 2 (General income) in 1987.

General Assembly resolution 40/253 B

18 December 1985   Meeting 122   137-10 (recorded vote)

Approved by Fifth Committee (A/40/1069) by recorded vote (93-11-0), 17 December (meeting 70); agenda item 116.

Meeting numbers. GA 40th session: 5th Committee 11, 14-23, 25-28, 30-36, 38-43, 47-52, 56-70; plenary 122.

Recorded vote in Assembly as follows:

In favour: Afghanistan, Algeria, Angola, Antigua and Barbuda, Argentina, Australia, Austria, Bahamas, Bahrain, Bangladesh, Barbados, Belgium, Belize, Benin, Bhutan, Bolivia, Botswana, Brazil, Brunei Darussalam, Burkina Faso, Burma, Burundi, Cameroon, Canada, Cape Verde, Central African Republic, Chad, Chile, China, Colombia, Congo, Cuba, Cyprus, Democratic Kampuchea, Democratic Yemen, Denmark, Djibouti, Dominican Republic, Ecuador, Egypt, El Salvador, Equatorial Guinea, Ethiopia, Fiji, Finland, France, Gabon, Gambia, Germany, Federal Republic of, Ghana, Greece, Guatemala, Guinea, Guinea-Bissau, Guyana, Haiti, Honduras, Iceland, India, Indonesia, Iran, Iraq, Ireland, Italy, Ivory Coast, Jamaica, Japan, Jordan, Kenya, Kuwait, Lebanon, Lesotho, Liberia, Libyan Arab Jamahiriya, Luxembourg, Madagascar, Malawi, Malaysia, Maldives, Mali, Malta, Mauritania, Mauritius, Mexico, Morocco, Mozambique, Nepal, Netherlands, New Zealand, Nicaragua, Niger, Nigeria, Norway, Oman, Pakistan, Panama, Papua New Guinea, Paraguay, Peru, Philippines, Portugal, Qatar, Romania, Rwanda, Saint Vincent and the Grenadines, Samoa, Sao Tome and Principe, Saudi Arabia, Senegal, Sierra Leone, Singapore, Solomon Islands, Somalia, Spain, Sri Lanka, Sudan, Suriname, Swaziland, Sweden, Syrian Arab Republic, Thailand, Togo, Trinidad and Tobago, Tunisia, Turkey, Uganda, United Arab Emirates, United Kingdom, United Republic of Tanzania, Uruguay, Vanuatu, Venezuela, Yemen, Yugoslavia, Zaire, Zambia, Zimbabwe.

Against: Bulgaria, Byelorussian SSR, Czechoslovakia, German Democratic Republic, Hungary, Israel, Poland, Ukrainian SSR, USSR, United States.

Abstaining: None.

Unforeseen expenditures

GENERAL ASSEMBLY ACTION

As recommended by the Fifth Committee, the General Assembly on 18 December 1985, adopted **resolution 40/254** by recorded vote. By this action, it authorized the Secretary-General to meet unforeseen and extraordinary expenses, under specified limitations. The provisions were substantially the same as in the corresponding resolution for 1984-1985, adopted in 1983,[11] except for a small increase in allowable extra costs for ICJ.

Unforeseen and extraordinary expenses for the biennium 1986-1987

The General Assembly

1. *Authorizes* the Secretary-General, with the prior concurrence of the Advisory Committee on Administrative and Budgetary Questions and subject to the Financial Regulations of the United Nations and the provisions of paragraph 3 below, to enter into commitments in the biennium 1986-1987 to meet unforeseen and extraordinary expenses arising either during or subsequent to that biennium, provided that the concurrence of the Advisory Committee shall not be necessary for:

(*a*) Such commitments, not exceeding a total of $US 2 million in any one year of the biennium 1986-1987, as the Secretary-General certifies relate to the maintenance of peace and security;

(*b*) Such commitments as the President of the International Court of Justice certifies relate to expenses occasioned by:

(i) The designation of *ad hoc* judges (Statute of the Court, Article 31), not exceeding a total of $250,000;

(ii) The appointment of assessors (Statute, Article 30), or the calling of witnesses and the appointment of experts (Statute, Article 50), not exceeding a total of $75,000;

(iii) The holding of sessions of the Court away from The Hague (Statute, Article 22), not exceeding a total of $100,000;

(*c*) Such commitments, in an amount not exceeding $300,000, in the biennium 1986-1987, as the Secretary-General certifies are required for interorganizational security measures pursuant to General Assembly resolution 36/235, section IV, of 18 December 1981;

2. *Resolves* that the Secretary-General shall report to the Advisory Committee on Administrative and Budgetary Questions and to the General Assembly at its forty-first and forty-second sessions all commitments made under the provisions of the present resolution, together with the circumstances relating thereto, and shall submit supplementary estimates to the Assembly in respect of such commitments;

3. *Decides* that if, as a result of a decision of the Security Council, commitments relating to the maintenance of peace and security should arise in an estimated total exceeding $10 million either before the forty-first session or between the forty-first and forty-second sessions of the General Assembly, a special session of the Assembly shall be convened by the Secretary-General to consider the matter.

General Assembly resolution 40/254

18 December 1985   Meeting 122   139-8 (recorded vote)

Approved by Fifth Committee (A/40/1069) by recorded vote (96-9-0), 17 December (meeting 70); agenda item 116.

Meeting numbers. GA 40th session: 5th Committee 70; plenary 122.

Recorded vote in Assembly as follows:

In favour: Afghanistan, Algeria, Angola, Antigua and Barbuda, Argentina, Australia, Austria, Bahamas, Bahrain, Bangladesh, Barbados, Belgium, Belize, Benin, Bhutan, Bolivia, Botswana, Brazil, Brunei Darussalam, Burkina Faso, Burma, Burundi, Cameroon, Canada, Cape Verde, Central African Republic, Chad, Chile, China, Colombia, Congo, Costa Rica, Cuba, Cyprus, Democratic Kampuchea, Democratic Yemen, Denmark, Djibouti, Dominican Republic, Ecuador, Egypt, El Salvador, Equatorial Guinea, Fiji, Finland, France, Gabon, Gambia, Germany, Federal Republic of, Ghana, Greece, Guatemala, Guinea, Guinea-Bissau, Guyana, Haiti, Honduras, Iceland, India, Indonesia, Iran, Iraq, Ireland, Israel, Italy, Ivory Coast, Jamaica, Japan, Jordan, Kenya, Kuwait, Lebanon, Lesotho, Liberia, Libyan Arab Jamahiriya, Luxembourg, Madagascar, Malawi, Malaysia, Maldives, Mali, Malta, Mauritania, Mauritius, Mexico, Morocco, Mozambique, Nepal, Netherlands, New Zealand, Nicaragua, Niger, Nigeria, Norway, Oman, Pakistan, Panama, Papua New Guinea, Paraguay, Peru, Philippines, Portugal, Qatar, Romania, Rwanda, Saint Vincent and the Grenadines, Samoa, Sao Tome and Principe, Saudi Arabia, Senegal, Sierra Leone, Singapore, Solomon Islands, Somalia, Spain, Sri Lanka, Sudan, Suriname, Swaziland, Sweden, Syrian Arab Republic, Thailand, Togo, Trinidad and Tobago, Tunisia, Turkey, Uganda, United Arab Emirates, United Kingdom, United Republic of Tanzania, United States, Uruguay, Vanuatu, Venezuela, Yemen, Yugoslavia, Zaire, Zambia, Zimbabwe.

Against: Bulgaria, Byelorussian SSR, Czechoslovakia, German Democratic Republic, Hungary, Poland, Ukrainian SSR, USSR.

Financing the Working Capital Fund

GENERAL ASSEMBLY ACTION

Establishment of the Working Capital Fund at a level of $100 million during 1986-1987 was authorized by the General Assembly on 18 December 1985 by **resolution 40/255**, adopted, by recorded vote, as recommended by the Fifth Committee. The provisions of this resolution corresponded to those approved in 1983 for the previous biennium.[12] As in the past, the Fund was to be used to finance appropriations pending the receipt of Members' contributions, and to pay unforeseen costs.

Working Capital Fund for the biennium 1986-1987

The General Assembly

Resolves that:

1. The Working Capital Fund shall be established for the biennium 1986-1987 in the amount of $US 100 million;

2. Member States shall make advances to the Working Capital Fund in accordance with the scale adopted by the General Assembly for contributions of Member States to the budget for the year 1986;

3. There shall be set off against this allocation of advances:

(a) Credits to Member States resulting from transfers made in 1959 and 1960 from surplus account to the Working Capital Fund in an adjusted amount of $1,025,092;

(b) Cash advances paid by Member States to the Working Capital Fund for the biennium 1984-1985 under General Assembly resolution 38/238 of 20 December 1983;

4. Should the credits and advances paid by any Member State to the Working Capital Fund for the biennium 1984-1985 exceed the amount of that Member State's advance under the provisions of paragraph 2 above, the excess shall be set off against the amount of the contributions payable by the Member State in respect of the biennium 1986-1987;

5. The Secretary-General is authorized to advance from the Working Capital Fund:

(a) Such sums as may be necessary to finance budgetary appropriations pending the receipt of contributions; sums so advanced shall be reimbursed as soon as receipts from contributions are available for the purpose;

(b) Such sums as may be necessary to finance commitments which may be duly authorized under the provisions of the resolutions adopted by the General Assembly, in particular resolution 40/254 of 18 December 1985 relating to unforeseen and extraordinary expenses; the Secretary-General shall make provision in the budget estimates for reimbursing the Working Capital Fund;

(c) Such sums as, together with net sums outstanding for the same purpose, do not exceed $200,000, to continue the revolving fund to finance miscellaneous self-liquidating purchases and activities; advances in excess of the total of $200,000 may be made with the prior concurrence of the Advisory Committee on Administrative and Budgetary Questions;

(d) With the prior concurrence of the Advisory Committee on Administrative and Budgetary Questions, such sums as may be required to finance payments of advance insurance premiums where the period of insurance extends beyond the end of the biennium in which payment is made; the Secretary-General shall

make provision in the budget estimates of each biennium, during the life of the related policies, to cover the charges applicable to each biennium;

(e) Such sums as may be necessary to enable the Tax Equalization Fund to meet current commitments pending the accumulation of credits; such advances shall be repaid as soon as credits are available in the Tax Equalization Fund;

6. Should the provision in paragraph 1 above prove inadequate to meet the purposes normally related to the Working Capital Fund, the Secretary-General is authorized to utilize, in the biennium 1986-1987, cash from special funds and accounts in his custody, under the conditions approved in General Assembly resolution 1341(XIII) of 13 December 1958, or the proceeds of loans authorized by the Assembly.

General Assembly resolution 40/255

18 December 1985   Meeting 122   124-11-13 (recorded vote)

Approved by Fifth Committee (A/40/1069) by recorded vote (81-11-12), 17 December (meeting 70); agenda item 116.

Meeting numbers. GA 40th session: 5th Committee 70; plenary 122.

Recorded vote in Assembly as follows:

In favour: Afghanistan, Algeria, Angola, Antigua and Barbuda, Argentina, Australia, Austria, Bahamas, Bahrain, Bangladesh, Barbados, Belize, Benin, Bhutan, Bolivia, Botswana, Brazil, Brunei Darussalam, Burkina Faso, Burma, Burundi, Cameroon, Canada, Cape Verde, Chad, Chile, China, Colombia, Congo, Costa Rica, Cuba, Cyprus, Democratic Kampuchea, Democratic Yemen, Denmark, Djibouti, Dominican Republic, Ecuador, Egypt, El Salvador, Equatorial Guinea, Ethiopia, Fiji, Finland, Gabon, Gambia, Ghana, Guatemala, Guinea, Guinea-Bissau, Guyana, Haiti, Honduras, Iceland, India, Indonesia, Iran, Iraq, Ivory Coast, Jamaica, Japan, Jordan, Kenya, Kuwait, Lebanon, Lesotho, Liberia, Libyan Arab Jamahiriya, Madagascar, Malawi, Malaysia, Maldives, Mali, Malta, Mauritania, Mauritius, Mexico, Morocco, Mozambique, Nepal, New Zealand, Nicaragua, Niger, Nigeria, Norway, Oman, Pakistan, Panama, Papua New Guinea, Paraguay, Peru, Philippines, Qatar, Rwanda, Saint Vincent and the Grenadines, Samoa, Sao Tome and Principe, Saudi Arabia, Senegal, Sierra Leone, Singapore, Solomon Islands, Somalia, Sri Lanka, Sudan, Suriname, Swaziland, Sweden, Syrian Arab Republic, Thailand, Togo, Trinidad and Tobago, Tunisia, Uganda, United Arab Emirates, United Republic of Tanzania, Uruguay, Vanuatu, Venezuela, Yemen, Yugoslavia, Zaire, Zambia, Zimbabwe.

Against: Bulgaria, Byelorussian SSR, Czechoslovakia, German Democratic Republic, Hungary, Mongolia, Poland, Spain, Ukrainian SSR, USSR, United States.

Abstaining: Belgium, France, Germany, Federal Republic of, Greece, Ireland, Israel, Italy, Luxembourg, Netherlands, Portugal, Romania, Turkey, United Kingdom.

REFERENCES
[1]YUN 1984, p. 1122, GA res. 39/237 A, 18 Dec. 1984. [2]A/C.5/40/50 (Parts I & II), Add.1, Add.2 (Parts I & II), Add.3 & Corr.1, Add.4, Add.5 (Parts I & II), Add.6-36. [3]A/C.5/40/50 (Part II). [4]A/40/1050. [5]YUN 1984, p. 1124, GA res. 39/237 B, 18 Dec. 84. [6]A/40/6, Vols. I & II. [7]A/40/7 & Add.1-18. [8]A/40/38. [9]A/C.5/40/48. [10]YUN 1982, p. 1430, GA res. 37/234, 21 Dec. 1982. [11]YUN 1983, p. 1153, GA res. 38/237, 20 Dec. 1983. [12]*Ibid.*, p. 1154, GA res. 38/238, 20 Dec. 1983.

Assessment of contributions

Scale of assessments

GENERAL ASSEMBLY ACTION

In accordance with a 1984 decision,[1] by which the General Assembly had decided to postpone action on the scale of assessments of Members' contributions to the United Nations budget until 1985, the Assembly took up the question at its resumed thirty-ninth session (9-12 April).

Following informal consultations in early 1985 on 1984 recommendations by the Committee on Contributions[2] on ways to make Members' assessments more closely reflect their capacity to pay, the Fifth Committee again considered the item in April. On 12 April, on the recommendation of the Fifth Committee, the Assembly adopted **resolution 39/247 B** without vote.

The General Assembly,

Recalling its resolutions 31/95 A and B of 14 December 1976, 34/6 B of 25 October 1979, 36/231 A of 18 December 1981, 37/125 B of 17 December 1982 and 38/33 of 25 November 1983,

Taking into account the views expressed in the Fifth Committee during the debate on the report of the Committee on Contributions and having considered the report and the recommendations contained therein,

Reconfirming that the real capacity to pay of Member States is the fundamental criterion for determining the scale of assessments,

Deeply concerned, in general, by the persistent serious economic and financial situation in the world and, in particular, by the external indebtedness and other serious economic problems which continue to affect adversely the capacity to pay of developing countries,

Conscious of the problem of Member States whose national income is mostly generated by the export of one or a few products,

Noting with appreciation the efforts of the Committee on Contributions,

1. *Decides* that, in the preparation of the next scale of assessments:

(a) The ten-year statistical base period should be maintained;

(b) The upper limit of the low per capita income allowance formula shall be raised from $2,100 to $2,200;

(c) In the redistribution of the burden of relief, the Committee on Contributions should apply a limit to the relief burden borne by Member States to take into account their developmental status and developmental requirements;

(d) The individual rates of assessments of the least developed countries should not exceed the present level;

(e) The Committee on Contributions should develop a methodology to take into account the problem of the serious economic and financial situation in the world, in pursuance of the deliberations mentioned in paragraph 54 of its report;

(f) Scheme III, as defined in paragraph 49 of the report of the Committee on Contributions, should be used to limit the variations of individual rates of assessment between successive scales after pertinent modifications in the light of the views expressed by Member States in the Fifth Committee, particularly in respect of rates below the level of 1 per cent;

2. *Takes note* of the intention of the Committee on Contributions to continue to study and examine subjects indicated in its report, including the study on comparative methods of assessment mentioned in paragraph 66;

3. *Requests* the Committee on Contributions to examine the conceptual feasibility of supplementing the present methodology so that each Member State may be assigned a relevant base relief gradient on the basis of its national income and, if possible, to report to the General Assembly at its fortieth session;

4. *Also requests* the Committee on Contributions to intensify its co-operation with other international organizations engaged in the development and collection of statistics and appeals to Member States to continue to co-operate with the United Nations Statistical Office by submitting national statistics on time;

5. *Requests* the Secretary-General to provide the Committee on Contributions with the facilities it requires to carry out its work, including supplementary assistance if necessary.

General Assembly resolution 39/247 B

12 April 1985   Meeting 107   Adopted without vote

Approved by Fifth Committee (A/39/844/Add.1) without vote, 11 April (meeting 58); draft by Chairman following informal consultations (A/C.5/39/L.34), orally revised; agenda item 115.
Meeting numbers. GA 39th session: 5th Committee 57, 58; plenary 107.

A number of Members explained that, while they had participated in the consensus, they had objections to certain provisions of the decision. The United States objected to the increase, from $2,100 to $2,200 in the per capita limit for the LDCs discount and the continuation of the 10-year base period. Paragraph 1 implied that developing countries, no matter how prosperous, should not share fully in the costs of providing discounts to LDCs; purported to benefit LDCs without changing any assessments; invited the Committee to devise a scale even more complicated than the current one; and limited the responsiveness of the assessment mechanism to changes in world economic conditions. Paragraph 3 complicated the scale by adding a subsidy based on the total national income. The United States opposed the text's approval and was unable to participate in any decision to do so.

Spain was dissatisfied that the resolution provided for numerous exceptions to the principle of real capacity to pay as the fundamental criterion for determining the scale. Canada felt that the Assembly seemed embarked on a course that increasingly departed from an objective determination of the capacity to pay and said that some subparagraphs of paragraph 1 represented distortions of that principle.

Paragraphs 1 and 3 did not meet the Nordic countries expectations, said Finland, which spoke on their behalf. Finland was also concerned that the recent discussion of the scale reflected a weakening of support for the United Nations and might jeopardize its credibility.

Egypt, speaking for the members of the Group of 77, said the Group would have preferred, among other things, that the resolution spell out more clearly the economic difficulties facing the world today, especially the developing countries. Further, they felt the current methodology was inadequate to measure the real capacity to pay.

Morocco hoped the Committee on Contributions would find some additional formula which took account of the developing countries' difficulties. Mexico added that the current formula had led to an increase in the shares of the developing countries as a group at a time when their capacity to pay had declined; it was clear that the use of national income and per capita gross national product statistics alone did not adequately reflect Member States' real capacity to pay. Poland said the problem of its over-assessment must be resolved.

Kuwait said the increase in the assessment rates of those countries which shared in the burden of relief was unduly high, and a specific limit must be imposed. The Committee on Contributions must work to avoid excessive variations of individual rates between scales and refine methodology to take account of countries' economic situations.

Singapore endorsed an understanding whereby a distinction must be made between developed and developing countries in apportioning the burden of relief, to take account of the latter countries' development responsibilities. That was why a limit on the burden was being requested for the developing countries, he said.

The Libyan Arab Jamahiriya felt it was not logical that certain developing countries should be required to bear increases of more than 25 per cent over their apportionment under the previous scale. In Bangladesh's view, the text sought to benefit only LDCs whose economies would show an increase in national income, rather than those with stagnant or declining economies.

Saudia Arabia felt that current methodology unfairly overstated the real capacity to pay of some States while understating that of others. It interpreted paragraph 3 to mean that the study called for must be initiated at the June session of the Committee and, if possible, completed in time for the Assembly session which opened in September.

Report of the Committee on Contributions. The Committee on Contributions held its forty-fifth session in New York from 3 June to 3 July 1985. In its report[3] to the Assembly, it set forth a proposed new scale of assessments for the financial years 1986, 1987 and 1988. The Committee also described the methodology it had used in determining the scale, following guidelines approved by the Assembly in April 1985 (see above).

The Committee reported that it had considered proposals to incorporate in the current assessment scale methodology indicators regarding debt, international reserves and terms of trade. Among its conclusions were the following: the data on debt suffered from incomparability and the deficiencies would have to be resolved before a systematic incorporation of that information in the assessment scale would be feasible; a similar problem, as well as one of relevance of data, existed with reference to data on international reserves; nevertheless, the overall problem of indebtedness, particularly for developing countries, must be taken into account in developing a new scale of assessments.

The Committee decided on a pragmatic formula for the 1986-1988 scale, without prejudice to the future position it might adopt on the basis of more comprehensive and systematic information. The formula combined two approaches: to take debt as a ratio of export earnings and to rank countries accordingly; and to rank countries using the ratio of debt to national income. The combined approach used a weighting of 80 for debt/export earnings and 20 for debt/national income. The Committee also dealt with the questions of which countries should benefit, where to establish the cut-off point and the nature of the relief deduction to be made. The final decision was to make deductions of 10, 7.5, 5 and 2.5 per cent of debt from national income according to whether the countries' weighted average ratio exceeded a specified percentage. The Committee further decided that the relief of debt should be deducted from national rather than assessable income, and it took action, as requested by the Assembly, to limit excessive variations of individual rates of assessment between successive scales.

The Committee examined statistical information on national income and related statistics; it reviewed, on a country-by-country basis, data on national income estimates in national currencies, rates of exchange used for conversion and the derivation of national income from other aggregates such as gross domestic product or net material product. It decided to correct data for Argentina, Egypt, Iran, Iraq and Yugoslavia. It also decided to review at its next session what type of exchange rate should be used for countries with a multiple exchange-rate system.

In the proposed new scale of assessments there were 78 Member States assessed at 0.01 per cent, 11 States at 0.02 per cent and five at 0.03 per cent. A total of 94 Member States, or 59 per cent of the membership, were thus assessed at or below 0.03 per cent. The assessment rates of the Group of 77 as a whole increased from 9.34 per cent to 9.67 per cent as a result of the increase in rates of assessment of the member States of the Organization of Petroleum Exporting Countries from the current 3.3 per cent to a proposed 3.63 per cent.

GENERAL ASSEMBLY ACTION

The General Assembly, on the recommendation of the Fifth Committee, by **resolution 40/248** of 18 December adopted the scale of assessments proposed by the Committee on Contributions for the financial years 1986, 1987 and 1988. On the same date, the Assembly also decided, without vote, on the recommendation of the Fifth Committee, to adopt **decision 40/464** by which it agreed to continue in 1986 the negotiations on the methodology for elaborating future scales of assessments. The decision was based on an oral proposal by the Fifth Committee Chairman.

Scale of assessments for the apportionment of the expenses of the United Nations

The General Assembly

Resolves that:

1. The scale of assessments for the contributions of Member States to the United Nations budget for the financial years 1986, 1987 and 1988 shall be as follows:

Member State	Per cent	Member State	Per cent
Afghanistan	0.01	Greece	0.44
Albania	0.01	Grenada	0.01
Algeria	0.14	Guatemala	0.02
Angola	0.01	Guinea	0.01
Antigua and Barbuda	0.01	Guinea-Bissau	0.01
Argentina	0.62	Guyana	0.01
Australia	1.66	Haiti	0.01
Austria	0.74	Honduras	0.01
Bahamas	0.01	Hungary	0.22
Bahrain	0.02	Iceland	0.03
Bangladesh	0.02	India	0.35
Barbados	0.01	Indonesia	0.14
Belgium	1.18	Iran (Islamic Republic of)	0.63
Belize	0.01	Iraq	0.12
Benin	0.01	Ireland	0.18
Bhutan	0.01	Israel	0.22
Bolivia	0.01	Italy	3.79
Botswana	0.01	Jamaica	0.02
Brazil	1.40	Japan	10.84
Brunei Darussalam	0.04	Jordan	0.01
Bulgaria	0.16	Kenya	0.01
Burkina Faso	0.01	Kuwait	0.29
Burma	0.01	Lao People's Democratic	
Burundi	0.01	Republic	0.01
Byelorussian Soviet		Lebanon	0.01
Socialist Republic	0.34	Lesotho	0.01
Cameroon	0.01	Liberia	0.01
Canada	3.06	Libyan Arab Jamahiriya	0.26
Cape Verde	0.01	Luxembourg	0.05
Central African Republic	0.01	Madagascar	0.01
Chad	0.01	Malawi	0.01
Chile	0.07	Malaysia	0.10
China	0.79	Maldives	0.01
Colombia	0.13	Mali	0.01
Comoros	0.01	Malta	0.01
Congo	0.01	Mauritania	0.01
Costa Rica	0.02	Mauritius	0.01
Côte d'Ivoire[a]	0.02	Mexico	0.89
Cuba	0.09	Mongolia	0.01
Cyprus	0.02	Morocco	0.05
Czechoslovakia	0.70	Mozambique	0.01
Democratic Kampuchea	0.01	Nepal	0.01
Democratic Yemen	0.01	Netherlands	1.74
Denmark	0.72	New Zealand	0.24
Djibouti	0.01	Nicaragua	0.01
Dominica	0.01	Niger	0.01
Dominican Republic	0.03	Nigeria	0.19
Ecuador	0.03	Norway	0.54
Egypt	0.07	Oman	0.02
El Salvador	0.01	Pakistan	0.06
Equatorial Guinea	0.01	Panama	0.02
Ethiopia	0.01	Papua New Guinea	0.01
Fiji	0.01	Paraguay	0.02
Finland	0.50	Peru	0.07
France	6.37	Philippines	0.10
Gabon	0.03	Poland	0.64
Gambia	0.01	Portugal	0.18
German Democratic		Qatar	0.04
Republic	1.33	Romania	0.19
Germany, Federal		Rwanda	0.01
Republic of	8.26	Saint Christopher and	
Ghana	0.01	Nevis	0.01

Member State	Per cent	Member State	Per cent
Saint Lucia	0.01	Turkey	0.34
Saint Vincent and the		Uganda	0.01
Grenadines	0.01	Ukrainian Soviet Socialist	
Samoa	0.01	Republic	1.28
Sao Tome and Principe	0.01	Union of Soviet Socialist	
Saudi Arabia	0.97	Republics	10.20
Senegal	0.01	United Arab Emirates	0.18
Seychelles	0.01	United Kingdom of Great	
Sierra Leone	0.01	Britain and Northern	
Singapore	0.10	Ireland	4.86
Solomon Islands	0.01	United Republic of	
Somalia	0.01	Tanzania	0.01
South Africa	0.44	United States of America	25.00
Spain	2.03	Uruguay	0.04
Sri Lanka	0.01	Vanuatu	0.01
Sudan	0.01	Venezuela	0.60
Suriname	0.01	Viet Nam	0.01
Swaziland	0.01	Yemen	0.01
Sweden	1.25	Yugoslavia	0.46
Syrian Arab Republic	0.04	Zaire	0.01
Thailand	0.09	Zambia	0.01
Togo	0.01	Zimbabwe	0.02
Trinidad and Tobago	0.04		
Tunisia	0.03		100.00

2. In accordance with rule 160 of the rules of procedure of the General Assembly, the scale of assessments given in paragraph 1 above shall be reviewed by the Committee on Contributions in 1988, when a report shall be submitted to the Assembly for consideration at its forty-third session;

3. Notwithstanding the terms of regulation 5.5 of the Financial Regulations of the United Nations, the Secretary-General shall be empowered to accept, at his discretion and after consultation with the Chairman of the Committee on Contributions, a portion of the contributions of Member States for the calendar years 1986, 1987 and 1988 in currencies other than United States dollars;

4. In accordance with rule 160 of the rules of procedure of the General Assembly, States which are not Members of the United Nations but which participate in certain of its activities shall be called upon to contribute towards the 1986, 1987 and 1988 expenses of such activities on the basis of the following rates:

Non-member State	Per cent
Democratic People's Republic of Korea	0.05
Holy See	0.01
Liechtenstein	0.01
Monaco	0.01
Nauru	0.01
Republic of Korea	0.20
San Marino	0.01
Switzerland	1.12
Tonga	0.01
Tuvalu	0.01

[a] Prior to 1986, appeared in English alphabetical listings as the Ivory Coast.

General Assembly resolution 40/248

18 December 1985   Meeting 122   109-15-27 (recorded vote)

Approved by Fifth Committee (A/40/1066) by recorded vote (80-13-25), 17 December (meeting 69); draft by Committee on Contributions (A/40/11); agenda item 122.

Meeting numbers. GA 40th session: 5th Committee 4-7, 9-14, 16, 69; plenary 1, 4, 12, 17, 28, 122.

Recorded vote in Assembly as follows:

In favour: Afghanistan, Algeria, Angola, Antigua and Barbuda, Argentina, Australia, Austria, Bahamas, Bangladesh, Barbados, Belize, Benin, Bhutan, Bolivia, Botswana, Brazil, Bulgaria, Burkina Faso, Burma, Burundi, Byelorussian SSR, Cameroon, Canada, Cape Verde, Central African Republic, Chad, Chile, China, Congo, Costa Rica, Cuba, Czechoslovakia, Democratic Kampuchea, Democratic Yemen, Djibouti, Egypt, El Salvador, Equatorial Guinea, Ethiopia, Fiji, Gabon, Gambia, German Democratic Republic, Ghana, Guatemala, Guinea, Guinea-Bissau, Guyana, Haiti, Honduras, Hungary, India, Iraq, Ivory Coast,

Jamaica, Jordan, Kenya, Lao People's Democratic Republic, Lebanon, Lesotho, Liberia, Libyan Arab Jamahiriya, Madagascar, Malawi, Maldives, Mali, Malta, Mauritania, Mauritius, Mexico, Mongolia, Morocco, Mozambique, Nepal, New Zealand, Nicaragua, Niger, Nigeria, Pakistan, Panama, Papua New Guinea, Peru, Poland, Romania, Rwanda, Samoa, Sao Tome and Principe, Senegal, Sierra Leone, Somalia, Sri Lanka, Sudan, Suriname, Swaziland, Thailand, Togo, Tunisia, Uganda, Ukrainian SSR, USSR, United Republic of Tanzania, Uruguay, Vanuatu, Viet Nam, Yemen, Yugoslavia, Zaire, Zambia, Zimbabwe.

Against: Bahrain, Colombia, Ecuador, Iran, Kuwait, Philippines, Qatar, Saudi Arabia, Singapore, Spain, Syrian Arab Republic, Turkey, United Arab Emirates, United States, Venezuela.

Abstaining: Belgium, Brunei Darussalam, Cyprus, Denmark, Dominican Republic, Finland, France, Germany, Federal Republic of, Greece, Iceland, Indonesia, Ireland, Israel, Italy, Japan, Luxembourg, Malaysia, Netherlands, Norway, Oman, Paraguay, Portugal, Saint Vincent and the Grenadines, Solomon Islands, Sweden, Trinidad and Tobago, United Kingdom.

Among those Member States voting against the new scale of assessments were many who considered the increases to be unjust, such as Ecuador, Kuwait, Singapore, the Syrian Arab Republic, Turkey and the United Arab Emirates. Colombia believed the scale was inconsistent in its treatment of Member States. Doubts on the data used (Indonesia), on the guidelines (Sweden), or on the methodology (Japan, Singapore, Trinidad and Tobago, United States and Venezuela) were expressed by several States which abstained on or voted against the text.

Japan had reservations on the use of what it said was an over-complicated methodology that relied on non-comparable data, different accounting methods and different exchange-rate systems, and did not adequately reflect the different status of Members. Italy doubted whether the incorporation into the methodology of indicators related to indebtedness was advisable.

Singapore believed that the methodology did not correct distortions in statistics provided by the centrally planned economies which, despite high growth rates, had been given substantial reductions in their contributions, and complained that no distinction was made between developed and developing countries in the distribution of the burden of relief. Algeria also had serious reservations about the relief burden distribution formulas.

Italy, Malaysia, the Philippines and Venezuela considered that the scale did not reflect capacity to pay.

Belgium, on behalf of the 10 European Community members, said the scale was based on a methodology for assessing real capacity to pay that in itself lacked objectivity and technical exactitude.

Bahrain, Brunei Darussalam, Iran, Kuwait, the Libyan Arab Jamahiriya and Oman objected to their assessments, pointing out that their economies depended on a single non-renewable resource. Qatar said it found its increase unacceptable.

Iran said the scale did not reflect the true performances of national economies or make sufficient allowance for adverse economic trends, and no generally applicable procedure had been used to assess the impact of inflation.

Iceland and India looked forward to a comparative study on alternative methodologies at the next session.

Norway regretted the conflicting instructions, inspired more by national self-interest than a sense of responsibility towards the United Nations, that had crept into resolutions on the scale of assessments in recent years.

Among the speakers supporting the resolution were Algeria, Austria, Bangladesh, Brazil, Guatemala, Iraq, Kenya, Mexico, Morocco and Thailand. While expressing some reservations, they generally supported the efforts of the Committee on Contributions and expressed the hope that the Committee would pursue its efforts to improve the methodology and devise a fair and universally acceptable scale of assessments.

Budget contributions in 1985

Of the $858.1 million in contributions for the United Nations regular budget payable at 1 January 1985, $615.7 million had been collected from Member States by 31 December, leaving $242.4 million outstanding (see table, "Status of contributions to the UN regular budget"). Of the amount payable, assessments for 1985, due early in the year, totalled $691.9 million; the remaining $166.2 million related to previous years.

In addition, nine non-member States were assessed a total of $1.4 million for their share of the United Nations activities in which they participated (see table "Assessment of non-member States for 1985 expenses of UN activities in which they participated").

Budget assessments of Members and non-members were in accordance with scales for 1983-1985 approved by the General Assembly in 1982.[4]

The continuing shortfall in collections was again dealt with in 1985 by the Secretary-General in a report[5] to the Assembly on the Organization's financial situation (see below).

At the resumption of the Assembly's 1984 session, in April 1985, the Secretary-General, in a letter of 9 April,[6] informed the Assembly President that 13 Members—the Central African Republic, Chad, the Comoros, El Salvador, Equatorial Guinea, the Gambia, Guinea-Bissau, Mauritania, Paraguay, Romania, Saint Lucia, South Africa and Zaire—were more than two years in arrears in the payment of their budget contributions. In addenda of 11 April and 16 September, the Secretary-General reported that Chad, El Salvador, Equatorial Guinea, Paraguay, Romania, Saint Lucia and Zaire had made payments bringing their arrears below the two-year limit to maintain voting privileges, as specified in Article 19 of the United Nations Charter.

STATUS OF CONTRIBUTIONS TO THE UN REGULAR BUDGET
(amounts in US dollars)

Member State	1985 scale of assessments (per cent)	Collections in 1985	Contributions outstanding as at 31 Dec. 1985	Net assessment for 1986	Member State	1985 scale of assessments (per cent)	Collections in 1985	Contributions outstanding as at 31 Dec. 1985	Net assessment for 1986
Afghanistan	0.01	65,814	—	70,043	India	0.36	2,370,828	46,151	2,451,521
Albania	0.01	75,000	617	70,043	Indonesia	0.13	855,587	—	980,608
Algeria	0.13	855,587	—	980,608	Iran	0.58	25,685	7,475,520	4,412,737
Angola	0.01	84,303	138,588	70,043	Iraq	0.12	789,772	—	840,521
Antigua and Barbuda	0.01	80,000	36,414	70,043	Ireland	0.18	1,184,659	—	1,260,781
Argentina	0.71	270,894	8,943,964	4,342,694	Israel	0.23	1,341,784	3,008,007	1,540,957
Australia	1.57	10,332,858	—	11,627,212	Italy	3.74	24,614,576	—	26,546,463
Austria	0.75	4,936,078	—	5,183,216	Ivory Coast	0.03	479,115	—	140,087
Bahamas	0.01	65,814	—	70,043	Jamaica	0.02	74,880	65,814	140,087
Bahrain	0.01	65,814	—	140,087	Japan	10.32	67,920,430	—	75,927,084
Bangladesh	0.03	197,443	—	140,087	Jordan	0.01	65,814	—	70,043
Barbados	0.01	98,137	—	70,043	Kenya	0.01	65,814	—	70,043
Belgium	1.28	9,705,351	—	8,265,126	Kuwait	0.25	1,645,360	—	2,031,261
Belize	0.01	—	65,814	70,043	Lao People's Democratic Republic	0.01	65,814	123,803	70,043
Benin	0.01	59,169	130,783	70,043	Lebanon	0.02	101,937	131,629	70,043
Bhutan	0.01	—	65,814	70,043	Lesotho	0.01	48,090	17,724	70,043
Bolivia	0.01	128,952	112,600	70,043	Liberia	0.01	66,513	101,178	70,043
Botswana	0.01	65,814	—	70,043	Libyan Arab Jamahiriya	0.26	2,499,705	2,430,355	1,821,130
Brazil	1.39	9,766,329	15,977,892	9,806,082	Luxembourg	0.06	394,887	—	350,217
Brunei Darussalam	0.03	219,099	—	280,174	Madagascar	0.01	168,944	—	70,043
Bulgaria	0.18	1,207,122	745,894	1,120,695	Malawi	0.01	65,814	—	70,043
Burkina Faso	0.01	129,867	58,849	70,043	Malaysia	0.09	592,329	—	700,434
Burma	0.01	65,814	—	70,043	Maldives	0.01	78,597	65,814	70,043
Burundi	0.01	172,597	66,600	70,043	Mali	0.01	23,089	127,217	70,043
Byelorussian SSR	0.36	2,429,121	1,837,674	2,381,477	Malta	0.01	65,814	—	70,043
Cameroon*	0.01	(3,763)	153,639	70,043	Mauritania	0.01	111,773	114,818	70,043
Canada	3.08	20,270,827	—	21,433,292	Mauritius	0.01	4,083	61,731	70,043
Cape Verde	0.01	58,834	130,783	70,043	Mexico	0.88	5,779,909	11,757	6,233,867
Central African Republic	0.01	84,324	128,992	70,043	Mongolia	0.01	64,975	60,188	70,043
Chad	0.01	263,335	—	70,043	Morocco	0.05	329,072	—	350,217
Chile	0.07	460,701	—	490,304	Mozambique	0.01	65,814	—	70,043
China	0.88	5,717,882	4,326,660	5,533,432	Nepal	0.01	65,814	—	70,043
Colombia	0.11	—	723,958	910,565	Netherlands	1.78	11,714,958	—	12,187,559
Comoros	0.01	101,597	148,469	70,043	New Zealand	0.26	1,711,173	—	1,681,044
Congo	0.01	74,530	—	70,043	Nicaragua	0.01	40,000	207,066	70,043
Costa Rica	0.02	141,046	43,050	140,087	Niger	0.01	—	145,821	70,043
Cuba	0.09	697,657	505,854	630,390	Nigeria	0.19	2,171,805	422,015	1,330,826
Cyprus	0.01	65,814	—	140,087	Norway	0.51	3,356,533	—	3,782,346
Czechoslovakia	0.76	4,938,170	2,482,681	4,903,041	Oman	0.01	65,814	—	140,087
Democratic Kampuchea	0.01	71,200	176,896	70,043	Pakistan	0.06	414,579	—	420,261
Democratic Yemen	0.01	65,814	—	70,043	Panama	0.02	131,629	—	140,087
Denmark	0.75	4,936,078	—	5,043,128	Papua New Guinea	0.01	65,814	—	70,043
Djibouti	0.01	35,100	205,723	70,043	Paraguay	0.01	71,200	176,896	140,087
Dominica	0.01	—	161,454	70,043	Peru	0.07	387,268	1,167,402	490,304
Dominican Republic	0.03	59,381	332,967	210,130	Philippines	0.09	342,299	579,034	700,434
Ecuador	0.02	143,952	28,060	210,130	Poland	0.72	10,264,000	7,070,037	4,482,781
Egypt	0.07	—	460,701	490,304	Portugal	0.18	1,184,659	—	1,260,781
El Salvador	0.01	71,200	192,590	70,043	Qatar	0.03	—	197,443	280,174
Equatorial Guinea	0.01	71,200	183,129	70,043	Romania	0.19	500,000	3,645,456	1,330,826
Ethiopia	0.01	65,814	—	70,043	Rwanda	0.01	65,814	—	70,043
Fiji	0.01	65,814	—	70,043	Saint Christopher and Nevis	0.01	73,419	63,901	70,043
Finland	0.48	3,159,090	—	3,502,173	Saint Lucia	0.01	44,527	206,539	70,043
France	6.51	42,845,156	4,357,157	44,617,669	Saint Vincent and the Grenadines	0.01	49,360	16,454	70,043
Gabon	0.02	201,979	129,327	210,130	Samoa	0.01	199,090	65,814	70,043
Gambia	0.01	21,248	198,932	70,043	Sao Tome and Principe	0.01	64,959	65,824	70,043
German Democratic Republic	1.39	8,752,427	3,805,423	9,315,778	Saudi Arabia	0.86	5,660,037	—	6,794,214
Germany, Federal Republic of	8.54	56,205,474	—	57,855,878	Senegal	0.01	942	64,872	70,043
Ghana	0.02	131,629	—	70,043	Seychelles	0.01	65,814	—	70,043
Greece	0.40	2,632,575	—	3,081,912	Sierra Leone	0.01	—	147,639	70,043
Grenada	0.01	122,460	61,431	70,043	Singapore	0.09	592,329	—	700,434
Guatemala	0.02	—	261,566	140,087	Solomon Islands	0.01	—	65,814	70,043
Guinea	0.01	—	65,814	70,043	Somalia	0.01	67,512	65,814	70,043
Guinea-Bissau	0.01	39,100	206,964	70,043	South Africa	0.41	—	24,484,504	3,081,912
Guyana	0.01	—	82,823	70,043	Spain	1.93	12,702,174	—	14,218,818
Haiti	0.01	202,123	29,314	70,043	Sri Lanka	0.01	65,814	—	70,043
Honduras	0.01	33,804	32,010	70,043	Sudan	0.01	64,939	65,844	70,043
Hungary	0.23	1,775,197	1,219,574	1,540,957	Suriname	0.01	130,783	—	70,043
Iceland	0.03	197,443	—	210,130					

Member State	1985 scale of assessments (per cent)	Collections in 1985	Contributions outstanding as at 31 Dec. 1985	Net assessment for 1986	Member State	1985 scale of assessments (per cent)	Collections in 1985	Contributions outstanding as at 31 Dec. 1985	Net assessment for 1986
Swaziland	0.01	58,630	34,984	70,043	United Republic of Tanzania	0.01	140,242	67,907	71,909
Sweden	1.32	8,687,498	—	8,755,431	United States	25.00	123,886,104	85,515,049	210,277,200
Syrian Arab Republic	0.03	586,858	—	280,174	Uruguay	0.04	547,133	—	280,174
Thailand	0.08	526,515	—	630,390	Vanuatu	0.01	65,814	—	70,043
Togo	0.01	130,558	86,222	70,043	Venezuela	0.55	4,016,584	—	4,202,607
Trinidad and Tobago	0.03	197,433	10	280,174	Viet Nam	0.02	130,000	239,236	70,043
Tunisia	0.03	197,443	—	210,130	Yemen	0.01	83,510	—	70,043
Turkey	0.32	—	4,687,213	2,385,563	Yugoslavia	0.46	3,018,148	3,027,591	3,221,999
Uganda	0.01	—	130,783	70,043	Zaire	0.01	255,600	58,237	70,043
Ukrainian SSR	1.32	8,906,778	5,858,844	8,965,560	Zambia	0.01	65,814	—	70,043
USSR	10.54	71,119,264	40,783,134	71,444,305	Zimbabwe	0.02	90,668	158,631	140,087
United Arab Emirates	0.16	2,092,527	—	1,260,781					
United Kingdom	4.67	30,735,312	—	34,041,110	Total	100.04	615,688,143	242,431,180	735,608,914

*Including assessments for 1983 and 1984.

SOURCE: ST/ADM/SER.B/282, ST/ADM/SER.B/283.

When the Assembly opened its regular 1985 session, on 17 September, the Secretary-General reported[7] that the Central African Republic, the Comoros, the Gambia, Guinea-Bissau, Mauritania and South Africa were more than two years in arrears. In addenda of 20, 23 and 26 September and 8 October, he reported that all the above Members but South Africa had paid enough to reduce arrears below the two-year limit. South Africa would have had to pay $21,364,300 to remove itself from that category.

This information was conveyed by the President to the Assembly, which took note of it at both its resumed and regular sessions in 1985, without adopting a formal decision.

ASSESSMENT OF NON-MEMBER STATES FOR 1985 EXPENSES
OF UN ACTIVITIES IN WHICH THEY PARTICIPATED

(amounts in US dollars)

Non-member State	Rate of assessment	Amount
Democratic People's Republic of Korea	0.05	28,689
Holy See	0.01	2,191
Liechtenstein	0.01	5,761
Monaco	0.01	65
Nauru	0.01	1,745
Republic of Korea	0.18	153,185
San Marino	0.01	832
Switzerland	1.10	1,205,693
Tonga	0.01	1,745
Total		1,399,906

NOTE: Activities, conferences and subsidiary bodies for which non-member States were assessed were: ICJ, Economic and Social Commission for Asia and the Pacific, ECE, international drug control, UNCTAD, World Conference to Review and Appraise the Achievements of the United Nations Decade for Women, Seventh United Nations Congress on the Prevention of Crime and the Treatment of Offenders, Preparatory Commission for the International Sea-Bed Authority and for the International Tribunal for the Law of the Sea—third and resumed third sessions, UNHCR, Intergovernmental Committee on Science and Technology for Development, Third United Nations Regional Cartographic Conference for the Americas, United Nations Group of Experts on Geographical Names—eleventh session.

SOURCE: ST/ADM/SER.B/291.

Under Article 19 of the Charter of the United Nations, a Member in arrears to the extent of contributions due for the preceding two full years shall have no vote in the Assembly, but the Assembly could permit such a Member to vote if it was satisfied that failure to pay was due to conditions beyond the State's control.

CUMULATIVE WITHHOLDINGS OF ASSESSED CONTRIBUTIONS
BY MEMBER STATES

(estimated as at end of 1985 financial periods;
in thousands of US dollars)

Member State	Regular budget	UNEF/ UNDOF*	UNIFIL†
Albania	0.6	22.5	22.2
Algeria	—	—	266.0
Benin	—	11.0	10.7
Bulgaria	706.4	66.9	363.4
Byelorussian SSR	1,837.7	672.8	4,241.0
China	4,277.1	—	—
Cuba	—	—	226.7
Czechoslovakia	1,994.4	390.6	8,926.9
Democratic Kampuchea	70.6	22.5	—
Democratic Yemen	—	6.4	10.7
France	4,357.1	—	—
German Democratic Republic	3,602.4	1,180.4	15,288.9
Hungary	1,162.9	—	645.2
Iraq	—	117.6	248.4
Israel	12.6	—	—
Lao People's Democratic Republic	—	—	10.7
Libyan Arab Jamahiriya	—	243.7	505.2
Mongolia	59.0	6.7	22.2
Poland	2,794.8	—	11,832.4
Romania	781.2	—	—
South Africa	24,484.5	3,157.5	4,616.3
Syrian Arab Republic	—	33.6	62.1
Ukrainian SSR	5,858.8	2,509.7	15,745.7
USSR	40,783.1	22,447.1	146,310.3
United States	6,904.1	8.3	26.8
Viet Nam	13.2	20.3	57.9
Yemen	—	10.6	10.7
Total	99,700.5	30,928.2	209,450.4

*Estimated withholdings relating to the second United Nations Emergency Force (UNEF) from its inception in 1972 to the completion of its liquidation and from the inception of UNDOF in 1974 to 31 December 1985.

†Estimated cumulative withholdings from the inception of UNIFIL on 19 March 1978 to 31 December 1985.

SOURCE: A/C.5/40/16.

REFERENCES

[1]YUN 1984, p. 374, GA dec. 39/456, 18 Dec. 1984. [2]Ibid., p. 1126. [3]A/40/11 & Add.1. [4]YUN 1982, p. 1418, GA res. 37/125 A, 17 Dec. 1982. [5]A/C.5/40/16. [6]A/39/883 & Add.1,2. [7]A/40/645 & Add.1-5.

Financial situation

Financial emergency

On 3 October 1985,[1] the Secretary-General reported to the General Assembly on the financial situation of the Organization, as requested by the Assembly in 1984.[2]

The Secretary-General advised the Assembly that the short-term deficit projected to 31 December 1985 was estimated at $390.7 million, an increase of $28.1 million, or almost 8 per cent, compared with the actual deficit at 31 December 1984. Most of this increase was due to non-payment of assessments on peace-keeping operations; it corresponded to approximately 38 per cent of the total assessed contributions for 1985 for both regular budget activities and peace-keeping activities. Current peace-keeping activities remained in operation only because the troop-contributing Member States continued to bear the full burden of the deficit.

As for the regular budget, the shortfall in payments—amounting to $116.3 million—resulted in an immediate cash shortage in respect of the day-to-day cash needs of the Organization, essentially payroll and payments to vendors. To meet those obligations, the Organization had used the $100 million Working Capital Fund, as well as funds available in the Special Account and, on occasion, had resorted to borrowing temporarily from peace-keeping funds. Funds realized from the suspension of financial regulations requiring unspent appropriations to be returned to Members had also been used for this purpose (see section below).

As at 30 September 1985, the Secretary-General reported, 50 Members had fully paid and 33 Members had partially paid their 1985 assessed contributions. Twenty-two Members had not yet paid for 1985, but were not in arrears for prior years; the remaining 54 Members, about one third of the membership, were in arrears not only for 1985 but for previous years as well.

Eighteen Member States had withheld payment towards certain specific items in the regular budget; projected to 31 December 1985, these withholdings amounted to $99.7 million, virtually equalling the current level of the Working Capital Fund. The Secretary-General also listed withholdings from peace-keeping activities. As for the General Fund cash flow, he said the closing balance in June 1985 was about 40 per cent lower than the comparable amount at the end of June 1984.

The Secretary-General reviewed and analysed eight options to alleviate the financial difficulties, namely: prompt payment of assessed contributions; an increase in the Working Capital Fund; borrowing in the open market; borrowing from Member States;

suspension of financial regulations requiring the return of unspent appropriations to Members; application of credits to Members not in arrears; issuance of long-term bonds; and assessment of contributions on a biennial basis. He suggested an increase in the Working Capital Fund from the current level of $100 million to $150 million. In conclusion, he stated that the primary means of resolving the Organization's financial difficulties, and the one which would result in the lowest cost to Member States, would be the prompt payment by every Member, early in the year, of its assessed contributions. Experience in this regard, he added, had been discouraging.

The Secretary-General's report was considered by ACABQ,[3] which concurred that the root cause of the financial problem was late payments and withholdings. It was not in favour of an increase in the Working Capital Fund, but recommended that the Secretary-General report on the actual situation in 1986, after the exclusion from the budget of resources relating to UNIDO.

GENERAL ASSEMBLY ACTION

On the recommendation of the Fifth Committee, the General Assembly on 18 December 1985 adopted **resolution 40/241 A**, without vote.

The General Assembly,

Having considered the report of the Secretary-General on the analysis of the financial situation of the United Nations and the related report of the Advisory Committee on Administrative and Budgetary Questions,

Recalling its resolutions 3049 A (XXVII) of 19 December 1972, 3538(XXX) of 17 December 1975, 32/104 of 14 December 1977, 35/113 of 10 December 1980, 36/116 B of 10 December 1981, 37/13 of 16 November 1982, 38/228 B of 20 December 1983 and 39/239 B of 18 December 1984,

Mindful of the report of the Negotiating Committee on the Financial Emergency of the United Nations and of the views expressed by Member States thereon at the thirty-second session of the General Assembly,

Reiterating earlier appeals to Member States, without prejudice to their position of principle, to make voluntary contributions to the Special Account referred to in annex V to the report of the Secretary-General on the analysis of the financial situation of the United Nations,

Noting with concern that the short-term deficit of the Organization is expected to exceed $390 million as at 31 December 1985,

Concerned at the increasingly precarious financial situation of peace-keeping operations and, in particular, its adverse impact on developing-country troop contributors,

Noting also with concern that delays and partial payment of assessed contributions continue to create serious cash-flow problems for the Organization,

Considering the possibility that for many Member States administrative considerations, including a calendar difference between the national fiscal year and that of the Organization, may be responsible for the delay in the payment of assessed contributions,

Taking note of the views expressed in the Fifth Committee,

1. *Reaffirms* its commitment to seek a comprehensive and generally acceptable solution to the financial problems of the United Nations, based on the principle of collective financial responsibility of Member States and in strict compliance with the Charter of the United Nations;

2. *Urges* all Member States to meet their financial obligations;

3. *Renews its appeal* to all Member States to make their best efforts to overcome constraints to the prompt payment early each year of full assessed contributions and of advances to the Working Capital Fund;

4. *Expresses its appreciation* to all Member States which pay their assessed contributions in full within thirty days of the receipt of the Secretary-General's communication, in accordance with regulation 5.4 of the Financial Regulations of the United Nations;

5. *Requests* the Secretary-General, in addition to his official communications to the permanent representatives of Member States, to approach, as and when appropriate, the Governments of Member States for the purpose of encouraging expeditious payment in full of assessed contributions, in compliance with regulation 5.4 of the Financial Regulations of the United Nations;

6. *Invites* Member States also to provide, in response to the Secretary-General's official communication and consistent with regulation 5.4 of the Financial Regulations of the United Nations, information regarding their expected pattern of payments, in order to facilitate the financial planning by the Secretary-General;

7. *Requests* the Negotiating Committee on the Financial Emergency of the United Nations to keep the financial situation of the Organization under review and to report, as and when appropriate, to the General Assembly;

8. *Requests* the Secretary-General to submit to the General Assembly at its forty-first session detailed information relating to the extent, rate of increase and composition of the deficit of the Organization, the pattern of payments of Member States, the cash-flow situation and voluntary contributions received from Member States and other sources pursuant to Assembly resolutions 2053 A (XX) of 15 December 1965 and 3049 A (XXVII) of 19 December 1972;

9. *Decides* to include in the provisional agenda of its forty-first session the item entitled "Financial emergency of the United Nations".

General Assembly resolution 40/241 A

18 December 1985   Meeting 121   Adopted without vote

Approved by Fifth Committee (A/40/1060) without vote, 16 December (meeting 67); 12-nation draft (A/C.5/40/L.13, part A); agenda item 118.
Sponsors: Bangladesh, Canada, Denmark, Finland, Ghana, Iceland, Ireland, Nigeria, Norway, Pakistan, Sweden, Trinidad and Tobago.
Meeting numbers. GA 40th session: 5th Committee 37, 45-47, 50, 67; plenary 121.

Suspension of financial regulations in respect of budget surpluses

In his report to the General Assembly in October 1985[1] on the financial emergency of the Organization (see above), the Secretary-General described the results of suspension of the provisions of financial regulations 4.3, 4.4 and 5.2 *(d)* (requiring unspent appropriations to be returned

to Members). By late 1984, $25.8 million had been realized for the 1980-1981 and 1982-1983 bienniums. It was estimated that the suspension of the regulations would eventually yield a further $17.6 million; however, that amount would only be realized in 1987. The funds realized, he said, were fully utilized to meet the day-to-day cash needs of the Organization. The suspension of the regulations for the 1984-1985 biennium, he concluded, would help to alleviate cash flow difficulties but would not constitute a solution to the fundamental problem.

Commenting on the report, ACABQ[3] recommended that the above-mentioned financial regulations be suspended in respect of regular budget surpluses arising at the end of the 1984-1985 biennium.

GENERAL ASSEMBLY ACTION

On 18 December 1985, on the recommendation of the Fifth Committee, the Assembly adopted **resolution 40/241 B**, by recorded vote.

The General Assembly,

Having considered the various options to alleviate the financial difficulties of the United Nations, summarized in section IV of the report of the Secretary-General, as well as the related report of the Advisory Committee on Administrative and Budgetary Questions,

1. *Decides* to accept the recommendation of the Advisory Committee on Administrative and Budgetary Questions in paragraph 14 of its report that the provisions of regulations 4.3, 4.4 and 5.2 *(d)* of the Financial Regulations of the United Nations be suspended in respect of regular budget surpluses arising at the end of the biennium 1984-1985;

2. *Recommends* that the Secretary-General continue to study various options to alleviate the financial difficulties of the Organization, taking into account the views expressed by Member States at the fortieth session of the General Assembly.

General Assembly resolution 40/241 B

18 December 1985   Meeting 121   132-12-2 (recorded vote)

Approved by Fifth Committee (A/40/1060) by recorded vote (105-11-3), 16 December (meeting 67); 12-nation draft (A/C.5/40/L.13, part B), orally revised; agenda item 118.
Sponsors: Bangladesh, Canada, Denmark, Finland, Ghana, Iceland, Ireland, Nigeria, Norway, Pakistan, Sweden, Trinidad and Tobago.
Meeting numbers. GA 40th session: 5th Committee 37, 45-47, 50, 67; plenary 121.

Recorded vote in Assembly as follows:

In favour: Afghanistan,[a] Algeria, Angola, Antigua and Barbuda, Argentina, Australia, Austria, Bahamas, Bahrain, Bangladesh, Barbados, Belgium, Belize, Benin, Bhutan, Bolivia, Botswana, Brazil, Brunei Darussalam, Burkina Faso, Burma, Burundi, Cameroon, Canada, Cape Verde, Central African Republic, Chad, Chile, China, Colombia, Congo, Cyprus, Democratic Kampuchea, Democratic Yemen, Denmark, Djibouti, Dominican Republic, Ecuador, Egypt, El Salvador, Equatorial Guinea, Ethiopia, Fiji, Finland, France, Gabon, Gambia, Germany, Federal Republic of, Ghana, Greece, Guatemala, Guinea, Guinea-Bissau, Guyana, Honduras, Iceland, India, Indonesia, Iran, Ireland, Israel, Italy, Ivory Coast, Jamaica, Jordan, Kenya, Kuwait, Lebanon, Lesotho, Liberia, Libyan Arab Jamahiriya, Luxembourg, Madagascar, Malawi, Malaysia, Maldives, Mali, Malta, Mauritania, Mauritius, Mexico, Morocco, Mozambique, Nepal, Netherlands, New Zealand, Nicaragua, Niger, Nigeria, Norway, Oman, Pakistan, Panama, Papua New Guinea, Peru, Philippines, Portugal, Qatar, Rwanda, Saint Lucia, Saint Vincent and the Grenadines, Samoa, Sao Tome and Principe, Saudi Arabia, Senegal, Sierra Leone, Singapore, Solomon Islands, Somalia, Spain, Sri Lanka, Sudan, Suriname, Swaziland, Sweden, Syrian Arab Republic, Thailand, Togo, Trinidad and Tobago, Tunisia, Turkey, Uganda, United Arab Emirates, United Kingdom, United Republic of Tanzania, Uruguay, Venezuela, Yemen, Yugoslavia, Zaire, Zambia, Zimbabwe.

Against: Bulgaria, Byelorussian SSR, Cuba, Czechoslovakia, German Democratic Republic, Hungary, Mongolia, Poland, Ukrainian SSR, USSR, United States, Viet Nam.

Abstaining: Japan, Romania.

[a]Later advised the Secretariat that it had intended to vote against.

The German Democratic Republic felt that the resolution should have been deleted; it believed the Committee should not take decisions that might prejudice future discussion of the subject. The USSR said it was opposed to the practice of suspending the Financial Regulations.

Australia said it had voted in favour, but with some reservations; the solutions proposed in the text were no longer adequate and some reference to the need for greater budgetary restraint should have been included.

Issue of special postage stamps

By **resolution 40/242** of 18 December 1985, the General Assembly decided, in order to enhance the liquidity of the Organization and alleviate its financial difficulties, to place at the disposal of the Secretary-General one half of the revenue from the issue of a special United Nations postage stamp on the social and economic crisis in Africa and asked him to explore the possibility of other revenue-producing activities (see Chapter IV of this section)

Impact of inflation and monetary instability

In response to a 1984 General Assembly request,[4] the Secretary-General submitted to the Assembly a study[5] of the additional amounts required in the regular budget resulting from inflation and monetary instability over the last four bienniums in the developed countries where United Nations organizations had their headquarters.

The Secretary-General stated that the task of obtaining an estimate had been approached by taking as a starting-point the 1984-1985 revised appropriations for activities in New York, Geneva and Vienna and recalculating them at 1978-1979 exchange rates and price levels.

The result of this exercise indicated that had there been no inflation nor changes in exchange rates since 1978-1979, the net revised appropriations for the biennium 1984-1985 in respect of the three duty stations would have been $771.9 million, rather than $1,064.6 million. The difference of $292.7 million represented an increase of $355.4 million attributable to inflation and a reduction of $62.7 million due to the difference in exchange rates. The Secretary-General added that these calculations were strictly theoretical and such con-

clusions as might be drawn from them could be no firmer than the assumptions on which the recosting was based.

With respect to the Assembly's 1984 request[4] for a comparison of real, net and growth increases and increases due to inflation during the last four bienniums, the Secretary-General said the methodology used in preparing the programme budget did not lend itself to such comparisons. However, he did present a comparison of increases in budget levels with real growth as measured at the revised appropriation stage of each biennium, concluding from that exercise that the actual rate of growth in dollar levels exceeded the rate of real growth by a large margin, as the combined effects of currency fluctuations, inflation and changes in non-recurrent items were greater than the effects of real growth.

On 14 December 1985,[6] the Secretary-General submitted to the Fifth Committee revised estimates for the programme budget for the 1986-1987 biennium based on the latest currency exchange and inflation rates at various duty stations.

GENERAL ASSEMBLY ACTION

On 18 December 1985, on the recommendation of the Fifth Committee, the General Assembly adopted, without vote, **resolution 40/249**.

Impact of inflation and monetary instability on the regular budget of the United Nations

The General Assembly,

Recalling its resolution 39/240 of 18 December 1984,

1. *Takes note* of the report of the Secretary-General on the impact of inflation and monetary instability on the regular budget of the United Nations;

2. *Decides* to consider this item again at a future session.

General Assembly resolution 40/249

18 December 1985   Meeting 122   Adopted without vote

Approved by Fifth Committee (A/40/1064) without objection, 17 December (meeting 70); draft by Cuba (A/C.5/40/L.11), orally amended by Denmark; agenda item 119 (b).

Meeting numbers. GA 40th session: 5th Committee 59, 65, 70; plenary 122.

REFERENCES

[1]A/C.5/40/16. [2]YUN 1984, p. 1130, GA res. 39/239 B, 18 Dec. 1984. [3]A/40/831. [4]YUN 1984, p. 1133, GA res. 39/240, 18 Dec. 1984. [5]A/C.5/40/65. [6]A/C.5/40/91.

Accounts and auditing

Accounts for 1984

The 1984 accounts and financial statements of seven United Nations development and humanitarian assistance programmes were accepted by the General Assembly at its 1985 session along with the audit opinions on those programmes by the United Nations Board of Auditors. The Assembly also concurred with the observations of ACABQ on the subject. These actions were taken with the adoption of **resolution 40/238**, adopted without vote on 18 December on the recommendation of the Fifth Committee, which had also approved the text without vote.

The programmes for which financial reports and audited financial statements were submitted were: the United Nations Development Programme,[1] the United Nations Children's Fund,[2] the United Nations Relief and Works Agency for Palestine Refugees in the Near East,[3] UNITAR,[4] the voluntary fund administered by UNHCR,[5] the United Nations Fund for Population Activities[6] and the United Nations Industrial Development Fund.[7]

The Board of Auditors made recommendations and observations on various aspects of the financial management of these programmes. ACABQ commented on the Board's recommendations in its report of 16 September[8] before they were reviewed by the Fifth Committee. Among the topics considered were procurement practices, project management, inventory control, contractual arrangements for experts and consultants and programme delivery.

Financial reports and audited financial statements, and reports of the Board of Auditors

The General Assembly,

Having considered the financial reports and audited financial statements for the period ended 31 December 1984 of the United Nations Development Programme, the United Nations Children's Fund, the United Nations Relief and Works Agency for Palestine Refugees in the Near East, the United Nations Institute for Training and Research, the voluntary funds administered by the United Nations High Commissioner for Refugees, the United Nations Fund for Population Activities and the United Nations Industrial Development Fund, the audit opinions of the Board of Auditors and the report of the Advisory Committee on Administrative and Budgetary Questions,

Taking into account the views expressed by delegations during the debate in the Fifth Committee, particularly in support of measures for the efficient and sound financial management and control of the United Nations family of organizations,

1. *Accepts* the financial reports and audited financial statements and the audit opinions of the Board of Auditors;

2. *Concurs* with the observations and comments made by the Advisory Committee on Administrative and Budgetary Questions in its report;

3. *Requests* the Board of Auditors and the Advisory Committee on Administrative and Budgetary Questions to continue to pay close attention to the efficiency of the financial procedures and controls, the accounting system and related administrative and management areas in accordance with regulation 12.5 of the Financial Regulations of the United Nations;

4. *Requests* the Board of Auditors to submit to the General Assembly in future, in a separate, concise document, a synthesis of the main observations of common interest as related to paragraph 3 above;

5. *Also requests* the Board of Auditors and the Advisory Committee on Administrative and Budgetary Questions to keep under review the financial reserves held by United Nations organizations reported on to the General Assembly and to report to the Assembly accordingly;

6. *Further requests* the executive heads of the organizations and programmes concerned within the United Nations system to take such remedial action in areas falling within their competence as may be required by the observations and comments made by the Board of Auditors in its reports and to report thereon to the Board;

7. *Renews its invitation* to the governing bodies of the organizations concerned to consider each year at their regular sessions the remedial action taken by the respective executive heads in response to the observations and comments made by the Board of Auditors in its reports;

8. *Further requests* the Board of Auditors to include in its annual reports comments on the measures taken to comply with its previous recommendations.

General Assembly resolution 40/238

18 December 1985   Meeting 121   Adopted without vote

Approved by Fifth Committee (A/40/789) without vote, 15 October (meeting 14); draft by Chairman (A/C.5/40/L.3), orally revised; agenda item 114.
Meeting numbers. GA 40th session: 5th Committee 3-9, 14; plenary 121.

REFERENCES

[1]A/40/5/Add.1. [2]A/40/5/Add.2. [3]A/40/5/Add.3. [4]A/40/5/Add.4. [5]A/40/5/Add.5. [6]A/40/5/Add.7. [7]A/40/5/Add.9 [8]A/40/635.

Chapter II

United Nations programmes

Efforts to improve United Nations programme planning, budgeting and evaluation were continued during 1985. The Committee for Programme and Co-ordination (CPC) devoted the main part of its 1985 session to an examination of the programme elements of the proposed United Nations programme budget for 1986-1987. CPC also continued its work of analysing, evaluating and reviewing programmes of the Organization. Its recommendations were endorsed by the Economic and Social Council in resolution 1985/76 which, in turn, was endorsed by the General Assembly in resolution 40/240.

The Joint Inspection Unit (JIU) presented 13 reports during 1985. The majority of these were thematic. The General Assembly, by resolution 40/259, asked United Nations organs, after considering the JIU reports, to submit to it the results of their review, and asked JIU to evaluate its own activities and to report in 1987.

The annual report on administrative and budgetary co-ordination in the United Nations system, prepared by the Advisory Committee on Administrative and Budgetary Questions (ACABQ), provided comparative data on the specialized agencies and the United Nations. The data covered regular budgets, net contributions of Member States, established posts, regular budget contributions to technical co-operation activities, extrabudgetary funds, working capital funds, scales of assessment and collection of contributions. By resolution 40/250 the Assembly called for maximum standardization and comparability in the budgetary and administrative practices of all organizations concerned and a greater co-ordination of staff regulations.

Topics related to this chapter. Development policy and international economic co-operation: economic co-operation among developing countries—co-ordination in the United Nations system. Operational activities for development: inter-agency co-operation—programme evaluation; technical co-operation through UNDP—UNDP programme planning; other technical co-operation—Department of Technical Co-operation for Development. Institutional arrangements: co-ordination in the United Nations system. United Nations financing.

Programme planning and budgeting

The proposed programme budget for the 1986-1987 biennium was the main item before CPC at its twenty-fifth session, held from 29 April to 1 June 1985 at United Nations Headquarters[1] (see also p. 1040).

Other matters discussed included the improvement of the process of programme budgeting, the experience gained in providing statements of programme budget implications to the General Assembly in 1984, co-operation and co-ordination activities between the Food and Agriculture Organization of the United Nations and the Economic and Social Commission for Asia and the Pacific, aspects of co-ordination and rationalization of the activities of the United Nations Industrial Development Organization (UNIDO), questions relating to decentralization for improving the overall functioning of the Organization, cross-organizational programme analysis (COPA), in-depth evaluation of the drug control programme and the triennial reviews of the implementation of CPC recommendations on the programmes on transnational corporations (TNCs) and on manufactures.

The Committee also took note of a JIU report[2] on the question of reporting to the Economic and Social Council (see p. 1045). Consideration of other JIU reports (a 1984 report[3] on publications policy and practice in the United Nations system and two 1983 reports[4] on field offices of the United Nations Development Programme (UNDP) and the evaluation system of UNDP) was deferred for lack of time.

CPC decided to transmit directly to the Economic and Social Council, without discussion, the annual overview report of the Administrative Committee on Co-ordination (ACC).[5] It took similar action on the ACC report[6] concerning the establishment of a register of development activities. The Committee noted that it did not discuss these reports owing to the constraints of time. CPC also called for improvement of the work of the joint CPC/ACC meetings (see p. 1042) and requested the Secretary-General to take measures to that end.

In its conclusions and recommendations, CPC agreed that its concern regarding the inadequacy of the length of its sessions should be brought to the attention of the Economic and Social Council when that body considered the calendar of conferences for 1986-1987.

(For details of CPC recommendations and conclusions on the proposed programme budget and on evaluation of programmes, see sections below; see also p. 1206.).

ECONOMIC AND SOCIAL COUNCIL ACTION

On 26 July 1985, the Economic and Social Council, on the recommendation of its Third (Programme and Co-ordination) Committee endorsed the conclusions and recommendations set forth in CPC's 1985 report in part I of a seven-part resolution (**resolution 1985/76**), adopted without vote. The Council re-emphasized the importance of the programming and co-ordination functions of CPC, the main subsidiary organ of the Council and the General Assembly for planning, programming and co-ordination. It requested the Secretary-General to secure the follow-up and implementation by United Nations organizations of CPC's conclusions and recommendations, once approved by the Council and/or the Assembly. The Council also welcomed CPC's decision to discuss at its 1986 session the improvement of its work and the duration of its sessions.

Parts II through VII of the resolution were related to other aspects of CPC's work in 1985. Part II dealt with improving the instruments for programming and co-ordination, namely COPAs, in-depth evaluations and triennial reviews of implementation. Part III was concerned with the proposed programme budget for 1986-1987 (see below).

Under part IV, the Council endorsed CPC's conclusions and recommendations on COPAs (see p. 1044) and suggested that CPC should consider the Secretary-General's report on recurrent publications of the United Nations, with a view to identifying duplication and undue overlap (see p. 1262).

The Council, by part V of the resolution, decided to choose at its 1986 organizational session a topic for the next cross-organizational review of the medium-term plans of the organizations of the United Nations system, to be considered at its mid-1987 session.

Part VI dealt with the 1984 JIU report[2] on reporting to the Economic and Social Council (see p. 1045); the Council endorsed CPC's recommendation that the Secretary-General report in 1986 on the expert bodies within the United Nations system.

By part VII of the resolution, the Council took note of the annual overview report of ACC for 1984/85,[5] asking that body to continue to improve

the report and inviting it to proceed with the technical design for the establishment of a register of development activities (see also p. 1039).

The Economic and Social Council also took note of the report on the Joint Meetings of CPC and ACC (see p. 1042), which included conclusions reached concerning co-ordination of relief efforts in Africa and technical co-operation among developing countries, and on which the Council adopted **resolution 1985/77**.

Taking note of CPC's comments on the proposed programme budget for 1986-1987, the Council, by **resolution 1985/78**, affirmed the view that the use of consultant services was excessive and asked the Secretary-General to provide CPC with information on the reasons why particular tasks could not be carried out by regular staff.

GENERAL ASSEMBLY ACTION

On 18 December 1985, the General Assembly, on the recommendation of the Fifth (Administrative and Budgetary) Committee, adopted without vote **resolution 40/240**.

Programme planning

The General Assembly,

Recalling its resolutions 32/197 of 20 December 1977, 33/118 of 19 December 1978, 34/224 of 20 December 1979, 35/9 of 3 November 1980, 36/228 of 18 December 1981, 37/234 of 21 December 1982, 38/227 of 20 December 1983 and 39/238 of 18 December 1984,

Having considered the report of the Committee for Programme and Co-ordination on the work of its twenty-fifth session and the first report of the Advisory Committee on Administrative and Budgetary Questions on the proposed programme budget for the biennium 1986-1987,

Having considered also the proposed programme budget for the biennium 1986-1987,

Having considered further chapter VI, sections C and D, of the report of the Economic and Social Council,

Noting also the intensive discussion in the Fifth Committee of the General Assembly on programme planning,

1. *Approves* those conclusions and recommendations made by the Committee for Programme and Co-ordination at its twenty-fifth session not otherwise decided upon in the context of the consideration by the General Assembly of the proposed programme budget for the biennium 1986-1987, nor dealt with by the Economic and Social Council in its resolution 1985/78;

2. *Endorses* Economic and Social Council resolutions 1985/76, 1985/77 and 1985/78 of 26 July 1985;

3. *Takes note with satisfaction* of the qualitative improvements in the presentation of the programme aspects of the proposed programme budget for the biennium 1986-1987, in particular the expansion of programmatic coverage and further refinements in the output citations;

4. *Requests* the Secretary-General to continue his efforts to improve the analytical procedure leading to a more transparent presentation of all sections of the programme budget;

5. *Reiterates* the importance of the programme planning and budgeting cycle and, in that context, the necessity of reinforcing the monitoring and evaluation capacity of the United Nations so as to provide Member States with a basis for more informed decision-making;

6. *Requests* the Secretary-General to submit to the General Assembly at its forty-first session, through the Committee for Programme and Co-ordination at its twenty-sixth session, a report on the further experience gained in the implementation of General Assembly resolution 38/227 A, section II, paragraph 7;

7. *Decides* that the relevant conclusions and recommendations of the Committee for Programme and Co-ordination, as well as the related portions of its report, should be brought to the attention of its Main Committees for information;

8. *Requests* the Secretary-General to issue the regulations and rules governing programme planning, the programme aspects of the budget, the monitoring of implementation and the methods of evaluation in the same format as the Financial Regulations and Rules of the United Nations, and to annex to the regulations and rules the text of the resolutions and decisions on programme planning adopted by the General Assembly at its thirty-seventh, thirty-eighth and thirty-ninth sessions;

9. *Endorses* the decision of the Committee for Programme and Co-ordination to include in the provisional agenda of its twenty-sixth session an item on the improvement of the work of the Committee under its mandate, *inter alia*, with a view to its consideration of future programme budgets and medium-term plans, as well as to enhance the instruments of co-ordination, and considers this decision a positive step towards enhancing the effectiveness of the Committee as the main subsidiary organ of the Economic and Social Council and the General Assembly for planning, programming and co-ordination.

General Assembly resolution 40/240

18 December 1985   Meeting 121   Adopted without vote

Approved by Fifth Committee (A/40/1059) without vote, 16 December (meeting 67); draft by Vice-Chairman (A/C.5/40/L.18), based on informal consultations; agenda item 117.

Meeting numbers. GA 40th session: 5th Committee 11, 14-23, 25-28, 30-36, 38-43, 47-51, 56-61, 63, 67; plenary 121.

Taking action at its resumed thirty-ninth session on a programme planning item, held over for consideration from December 1984[7], the Assembly on 12 April 1985 adopted without vote **decision 39/460**. It thereby took note of the information and assurance provided by the Under-Secretary-General for Administration and Management in his statement before the Fifth Committee on 26 October 1984 concerning one of the guidelines for statements to be provided by the Secretary-General on programme implications of draft resolutions. The Under-Secretary-General had stated that in section II, paragraph 7, the word "section" had erroneously been changed to "sections" in the process of editing the Assembly's 1983 resolutions[8] on programme planning. He had assured the Committee that, in the interpretation and practical application of the resolution, the Secretariat would respect the wording of the agreed text.

Barbados had introduced the text[9] which, it stated, had been formulated in an open-ended contact group, replacing a text recommended by the Fifth Committee.[10]

Following adoption of the decision, the United States said that its participation in the consensus should not be taken to imply any agreement with the contents of the Under-Secretary-General's statement, which attempted to construe an agreement among delegations which, in the understanding of the United States, implied the use of the words "relevant sections", not "relevant section". Italy, speaking for the 10 members of the European Community, said they had agreed to the decision in a spirit of compromise but wished to stress their position that the decision did not imply any approval on their part of the interpretation given by the Under-Secretary-General to the relevant provisions of the Assembly's 1983 resolution.

Brazil welcomed the Under-Secretary-General's assurance and trusted that the matter would be treated as a clear mandate for the Secretary-General to act in the way indicated.

Financial Rules of the United Nations

In an October 1984 report[11] the Secretary-General issued proposed revisions to the United Nations Financial Rules required as a result of the restructuring of the economic and social sectors of the United Nations under a 1977 General Assembly resolution.[12] ACABQ had made a number of suggestions which were reflected in a corrigendum to the Secretary-General's report.

The Assembly's Fifth Committee had recommended, before the Assembly suspended its thirty-ninth (1984) session in December,[13] that the Assembly adopt a draft decision taking note of the revisions to the Financial Rules.

At its resumed thirty-ninth session, on 12 April 1985, the Assembly adopted **decision 39/461**, by which it took note of the amendments to the Financial Rules of the United Nations promulgated by the Secretary-General in his report.

Proposed programme budget for 1986-1987

At its 1985 session, CPC examined in detail the proposed programme budget for 1986-1987. In an introductory statement, the Assistant Secretary-General for Programme Planning and Co-ordination cited improvements in the current budget presentation. Among these were: the presentation for the first time of financial, common and conference services in programmatic terms; an increase in the number of sections in which priorities were designated; the designation of priorities in some areas of common services; more precision in output citations; and an attempt to identify those outputs with at least 50 per cent of their funding from extrabudgetary resources.

The programmatic approach, together with a number of management-enhancing measures, had translated into an overall real growth rate of 0.4 per cent, the Assistant Secretary-General said. However, aggregate growth figures should be considered with caution, since regular budgetary resources represented only a part of the Organization's total resources for the delivery of its output. Overall guidance for the preparation of the proposed programme budget had been provided by the Programme Planning and Budgeting Board.

Committee members expressed satisfaction with the improvements in the format and content of the proposed programme budget, but raised a number of questions. These concerned, among other things, the widespread use of consultants, the proposed reclassification of posts in a number of sections, and what was seen as a disproportionate growth of administrative costs relative to the growth in substantive programme areas.

Other points of concern were the elimination of activities mandated by the General Assembly without prior recourse to that body; the need for proper monitoring of programme performance and the important function of the Central Monitoring Unit in that regard; and the decentralization of activities from central units to the regional commissions.

In its report[1] to the General Assembly, CPC made a number of general recommendations on the 1986-1987 budget, as well as specific recommendations on individual budget sections. Among the general recommendations and conclusions were: that the Assembly should reiterate its 1984 request[14] to intergovernmental bodies reporting to the Assembly's Second (Economic and Financial) Committee to adjust their cycle of meetings to conform to that Committee's biennial programme of work; that the proposed use of consultant services were excessive and not conducive to an optimum utilization of regular staff resources; and that the Secretary-General should submit a report in 1986 on the results of in-house consultations on the establishment, updating, access to, use and integrity of the mailing lists and registers maintained by the United Nations.

Noting that it had received a proposal to request the Secretary-General to compile information on activities in various fields of human resources development under way or planned by United Nations organs and programmes, CPC decided that, in view of time constraints, it would consider the proposal at its 1986 session.

ECONOMIC AND SOCIAL COUNCIL ACTION

By section III of **resolution 1985/75**, the Economic and Social Council, on 26 July 1985, noted with satisfaction the improvements in the format and timeliness of submission of the proposed programme budget, reaffirmed the importance of monitoring and evaluation in the programme planning and budgeting cycle and urged the Secretary-General to refine further the methods used in those exercises, and reiterated that the medium-term plan should continue to serve as the framework for the formulation of the biennial budget. The Council recognized that the Secretary-General should keep the issue of decentralization under review and report to CPC on the better distribution of responsibilities between global and regional entities.

GENERAL ASSEMBLY ACTION

The General Assembly, with the adoption of **resolution 40/240** on 18 December, also noted with satisfaction the qualitative improvements in the proposed budget, in particular the expansion of programmatic coverage and further refinements in the output citations. Among other things, it asked the Secretary-General to report in 1986, through CPC, on experience gained in following the guidelines set out by the Assembly in 1983[8] in preparing the programmatic implications of draft resolutions it was considering.

REFERENCES
[1]A/40/38 & Corr.1 & Add.1. [2]YUN 1984, p. 978. [3]*Ibid.*, p. 367. [4]YUN 1983, pp. 473 & 460. [5]E/1985/57. [6]E/AC.51/1985/7. [7]YUN 1984, p. 1138. [8]YUN 1983, p. 1165, GA res. 38/227 A, 20 Dec. 1983. [9]A/39/L.48. [10]A/39/840. [11]A/C.5/39/21 & Corr.1. [12]YUN 1977, p. 438, GA res. 32/197, 20 Dec. 1977. [13]YUN 1984, p. 1139. [14]*Ibid.*, p. 986, GA res. 39/217, 18 Dec. 1984.

Programme evaluation

At its 1985 session, CPC conducted an in-depth evaluation of the drug control programme within the United Nations system (see p. 1014). It recommended, among other things, that the role, function and programme of work of the United Nations Narcotics Laboratory should be reviewed to determine whether certain of its functions should be decentralized to national or regional laboratories. Also, the Division of Narcotic Drugs should be strengthened with additional technical capacity so as to deal more effectively with areas such as drug demand reduction, and it should pay special attention to the countries in which the capacity for national intervention and control was limited or non-existent. The General Assembly, CPC recommended, should again request specialized agencies that had not already done so to develop specific drug control programmes and activities to be undertaken by member Governments.

Examining the triennial review on the TNC programme,[1] CPC commended the implementation of recommendations it had made in 1979.[2] In connection with this review, the Committee reiterated its position that there should be no hierarchy of mandates and that its recommendations, as approved by the Economic and Social Council and the General Assembly, should be given equal weight with those of other intergovernmental bodies (see also p. 618).

With respect to the triennial review[3] of the mineral resources programme (see p. 677), CPC decided to defer consideration of the Secretary-General's report until 1986. It took up his report[4] on the manufactures programme, noting that this was the first triennial review of this activity (see p. 602).

Discussing future areas for COPA, CPC agreed that the areas selected should be of high priority to Member States and should be areas where there might be a need for improved co-ordination and co-operation within the United Nations system (see p. 1044).

In a follow-up to the COPA in the field of marine affairs, CPC took note of information from the Secretary-General[5] and recommended that the International Maritime Organization and the United Nations Conference on Trade and Development (UNCTAD) should continue efforts to co-ordinate their work (see p. 681).

CPC then discussed the scope and general approach of the COPA of economic and social research and policy analysis[6] which was in preparation. It felt some concern about the manageability of the study, but believed that analysis of the subject was particularly important and accepted the approach proposed. CPC instructed that the analysis should include an examination of the research activities of the United Nations system in relation to legislative mandates, but should not be confused with an evaluation or make suggestions on future orientation of research activities. It should put more emphasis on existing arrangements for co-operation and co-ordination and on areas for improvement in that respect than on apparent duplications in research activities and research products. The analysis should be prepared in a manner that would enable CPC to draw specific conclusions and recommendations.

On the question of a COPA of United Nations activities in the area of economic and technical co-operation among developing countries, CPC considered that the report[7] of the Secretary-General on this matter, while comprehensive and containing much useful information, was too optimistic in its conclusions concerning co-ordination of the work of the system in this area. It recommended that the system should give greater attention in its work programmes to the implementation of existing mandates for promoting economic and technical co-operation (see also p. 426).

JIU also issued evaluation reports in 1985, transmitted to the Assembly by the Secretary-General. The first[8] was concerned with the status of internal evaluation in organizations of the United Nations system and was the third in a series. The report contained brief summaries of the current status of evaluation in 24 organizations of the system, citing progress and new developments. A summary assessment was made for each organization, together with recommendations for 10 of them. The organizations were: the United Nations, the United Nations Children's Fund, the United Nations Centre for Human Settlements, UNIDO, UNCTAD, the International Trade Centre, UNDP, the United Nations Environment Programme, the United Nations Fund for Population Activities, the Office of the United Nations High Commissioner for Refugees, the World Food Programme, the International Atomic Energy Agency (IAEA) and all the specialized agencies except the International Monetary Fund and the World Bank affiliates.

The second report[9] was the third study of developments, patterns and problems in system-wide evaluation; it reviewed current progress in integrating and using evaluation. It was found that evaluation was being actively used in a more systematic way in almost all organizations of the United Nations system, particularly through built-in self-evaluation, but for in-depth evaluations as well. Central evaluation units remained small despite increased work-loads, spending half their time on in-depth studies and reporting and leaving little time for evaluation system oversight and needed expansion of system coverage. Organizations needed to maintain clear standards to ensure evaluation quality. Long-term development efforts were needed to ensure that timely, relevant information on performance was provided to meet programme decision-making needs organization-wide. It was recommended that organizations expand evaluation coverage and strengthen design, monitoring and training efforts, and provide evaluation quality control, co-operative efforts and adequate central evaluation unit staffing.

Joint Inspection Unit

The 1985 work programme of JIU covered five broad areas of sectoral interest to the system: restructuring of the economic and social sectors, development co-operation; management and co-ordination; personnel; and evaluation. In its August 1985 report[10] JIU described how its work programme was drawn up to achieve a degree of balance among sectors and to select studies which were both timely and of importance to the system.

During 1985, JIU issued 13 reports. These reports inspected, reviewed or evaluated selected programmes of the United Nations system. They were issued subsequently as General Assembly or Economic and Social Council documents. The reports were the subject of written comments by the Secretary-General or by ACC and were considered by Main Committees of the Assembly, by the Economic and Social Council, and by the UNDP Governing Council, as appropriate.

Two of the reports concerned specific organizational entities: the Economic and Social Commission for Asia and the Pacific;[11] and the United Nations information centres.[12] The other reports were thematic. They dealt with management issues with light of the changing use of computers in United Nations organizations at Geneva[13] (see p. 1265); United Nations development system support to the implementation of the Buenos Aires Plan of Action on Technical Co-operation among Developing Countries[14] (see p. 490); the United Nations Transport and Communications Decade in Africa[15] (see p. 632); contribution of the United Nations system to the conservation and management of cultural and natural heritage in Africa;[16] United Nations technical co-operation in the Caribbean[17] (see p. 662); problems in implementing the medium-term plan of recruitment (1983-1985) for the United Nations Secretariat;[18] a follow-up on staff costs in the United Nations Secretariat;[19] reform of the United Nations;[20] status of internal evaluation in organizations of the United Nations system[21] (see above); evaluation in the United Nations system[22] (see above); and a follow-up on organization and methods for official travel in the United Nations.[23]

The activities of JIU from 1 July 1984 to 30 June 1985 were described in its seventeenth report to the General Assembly;[24] the second half of 1985 was covered in its 1985-1986 report.[25]

The work programme of JIU for 1985 was transmitted to the General Assembly in February by a note[26] of the Secretary-General.

During the year, JIU officers met with the executive heads of several participating organizations in order to intensify relations. Contact was also maintained with ACABQ, the International Civil Aviation Organization, the International Civil Service Commission, the Panel of External Auditors, ACC's Consultative Committee on Administrative Questions and the management and audit units of several secretariats.

In accordance with procedures established by the General Assembly in 1977,[27] the Secretary-General provided information in a September 1985 report[28] on the status of implementation of past JIU recommendations of interest to the Assembly. The report dealt with recommendations on: the conservation and management of the cultural and natural heritage in Asia and the Pacific;[29] management of the Office for Projects Execution of UNDP;[30] the Office of Secretariat Services for

Economic and Social Matters;[31] publications policy and practice in the United Nations system;[32] reporting to the Economic and Social Council;[33] competitive examinations in the United Nations;[34] co-operation between and management of libraries of the United Nations system;[35] and common services of United Nations organizations at the Vienna International Centre.[36]

At its 1985 session, CPC considered two JIU reports and the comments of the Secretary-General thereon. The 1984 JIU report[37] on drug abuse control activities in the United Nations system and the Secretary-General's and executive head's comments[38] (see p. 1013) were discussed in connection with the relevant section (section 20) of the proposed programme budget for 1986-1987 and the report[39] of the Secretary-General on an in-depth evaluation of the drug control programme (see above, under "Programme evaluation", and p. 1014). The JIU report[33] and related comments on reporting to the Economic and Social Council were discussed and subsequently noted, with the suggestion that the Secretary-General should continue his efforts to bring about improvements. Discussion of JIU reports on publications policy and practice in the United Nations system,[32] on field offices of UNDP[40] and on the evaluation system of UNDP[41] was deferred to 1986.

GENERAL ASSEMBLY ACTION

On 18 December 1985, the General Assembly adopted without vote **resolution 40/259**, on the recommendation of the Fifth Committee.

Joint Inspection Unit

The General Assembly,

Taking note of the report of the Joint Inspection Unit on its activities during the period 1 July 1984 to 30 June 1985, the work programme of the Unit for 1985 and the report of the Secretary-General on the implementation of the recommendations of the Unit,

Recalling its resolution 39/242 of 18 December 1984,

Convinced that the reports presented by the Joint Inspection Unit should receive adequate attention,

Recalling further the role of the Joint Inspection Unit as contained in article 5 of its statute,

1. *Emphasizes* that, in carrying out its function, the Joint Inspection Unit shall fully respect the mandates, resolutions and decisions of the General Assembly and of the legislative organs of the other participating organizations;

2. *Requests* the Joint Inspection Unit, in accordance with its statute, to include in its reports on organizations, whenever appropriate, an evaluation of the programmes and activities of the organizations;

3. *Requests* the Joint Inspection Unit, in presenting its reports, to observe the established procedures as provided for in article 11, paragraph 2, of its statute;

4. *Decides* that each report submitted by the Joint Inspection Unit during the year, along with the comments of the Secretary-General, will be considered under the appropriate agenda item of the General Assembly;

5. *Invites* United Nations organs, after considering reports of the Joint Inspection Unit and the related comments of the Secretary-General, to submit to the General Assembly the results of their review;

6. *Invites* the Joint Inspection Unit to evaluate the results of its activities and to report thereon to the General Assembly at its forty-second session.

General Assembly resolution 40/259

18 December 1985   Meeting 122   Adopted without vote

Approved by Fifth Committee (A/40/1065) without vote, 17 December (meeting 70); draft by United States (A/C.5/40/L.23), based on informal consultations and orally revised; agenda item 120.
Meeting numbers. GA 40th session: 5th Committee 37, 46, 48, 68, 70; plenary 122.

REFERENCES

(1)E/AC.51/1985/5. (2)YUN 1979, p. 625. (3)E/AC.51/1985/9. (4)E/AC.51/1985/10. (5)E/AC.51/1985/3 & Add.1. (6)E/AC.51/1985/6. (7)E/1985/53. (8)JIU/REP/85/10; A/41/201. (9)JIU/REP/85/11; A/41/202. (10)A/40/34. (11)JIU/REP/85/1; A/40/293-E/1985/72. (12)JIU/REP/85/12; A/41/120. (13)JIU/REP/85/2; A/40/410. (14)JIU/REP/85/3; A/40/656. (15)JIU/REP/85/4; A/40/633. (16)JIU/REP/85/5; E/1986/6. (17)JIU/REP/85/6; E/1985/3/Add.2. (18)JIU/REP/85/7; A/40/673 & Corr.1. (19)JIU/REP/85/8; A/40/653. (20)JIU/REP/85/9; A/40/988 & Corr.1. (21)JIU/REP/85/10; A/41/201. (22)JIU/REP/85/11; A/41/202. (23)JIU/REP/85/13; A/41/121. (24)A/40/34. (25)A/41/34. (26)A/40/137. (27)YUN 1977, p. 1053, GA res. 32/199, 21 Dec. 1977. (28)A/40/655 & Corr.1. (29)YUN 1984, p. 626. (30)*Ibid.*, p. 441. (31)*Ibid.*, p. 990. (32)*Ibid.*, p. 367. (33)*Ibid.*, p. 978. (34)*Ibid.*, p. 1154. (35)*Ibid*, p. 1185. (36)*Ibid*, p. 1181. (37)*Ibid.*, p. 955. (38)A/40/260 & Corr.1. (39)E/AC.51/1985/8 & Corr.1. (40)YUN 1983, p. 473. (41)*Ibid.*, p. 460.

Administrative and budgetary co-ordination in the UN system

In its annual report to the General Assembly on administrative and budgetary co-ordination in the United Nations system, submitted in October 1985,[1] ACABQ provided comparative data on the specialized agencies and the United Nations. This was in accord with the Assembly's decision of December 1981[2] calling for detailed reports on the budgets of the specialized agencies and IAEA every two years, beginning in 1982; in odd-numbered years reports were confined to tabular material, supplemented as necessary by special topics.

The report contained nine tables providing comparative data on: total amounts of approved regular budgets, including supplementary estimates, 1977-1986; total net contributions of Member States actually payable under approved regular budgets, including supplementary estimates, 1977-1986; established posts, 1984-1986; regular budget contributions to technical co-operation activities, 1984-1986; extrabudgetary funds administered by the United Nations system of organizations, contributions, 1983-1984; extrabudgetary funds administered by the United Nations system or organizations, expenditures, 1983-1984; working capital funds, 1986; scales of assessment applicable in 1986; and collection of contributions, 1984-1985.

ACABQ cited in its report a number of statistics drawn from the tables. Among these: the regular budgets (or budget estimates) of the United Nations, the specialized agencies (excluding the International Fund for Agricultural Development (IFAD)) and IAEA amounted in 1986 to $1,731,875,093 of which $1,604,658,577 was to be covered by assessed contributions. Further assessed contributions for the United Nations were likely in 1986 for peace-keeping operations; for the 12-month period through October 1985, the total amount assessed for the purpose was $177 million.

Also, a total of 25,012.5 established posts for 1986 had been authorized or requested under the regular budgets of the United Nations, the specialized agencies (excluding IFAD) and IAEA. This was an increase of 0.5 per cent compared to the 1985 total of 24,881 (excluding IFAD). The breakdown was: United Nations, 11,967 posts; agencies (excluding IFAD) and IAEA, 13,045.5 posts.

The United Nations, the agencies and IAEA estimated that their regular programmes of technical co-operation in 1986 would amount to $314,072,000, of which $230,205,000 was to be provided under the regular budget of the World Health Organization. The assessed budgets of the organizations also contributed towards the support costs of projects executed by them on behalf of funding programmes or under trust fund agreements; this sum was estimated at $54.4 million.

ACABQ pointed out that total outstanding contributions as at 30 September 1985 equalled 51.4 per cent of total net contributions of Member States actually payable in respect of 1985, as compared to a corresponding figure of 52.7 per cent as at 30 September 1984.

GENERAL ASSEMBLY ACTION

On 18 December 1985, on the recommendation of the Fifth Committee, the General Assembly adopted without vote **resolutions 40/250** and **40/251**.

Administrative and budgetary co-ordination of the United Nations with the specialized agencies and the International Atomic Energy Agency

The General Assembly,

Recalling its previous resolutions on this subject, in particular resolution 36/229 of 18 December 1981 by which it expressed its concern with the need for effective administrative and budgetary co-ordination within the framework of the United Nations system,

Convinced of the importance of such co-ordination by the organizations of the system,

Realizing the need to avoid duplication of efforts and proliferation of organs for the more effective use of the resources of the United Nations and the specialized agencies,

Concurring with the opinion expressed by the Advisory Committee on Administrative and Budgetary Questions in its report on the subject submitted to the General Assembly at its thirty-ninth session, that co-ordination among the agencies with a view to harmonizing their budgetary practices is of primary importance and that further efforts at standardization and harmonization should be encouraged,

1. *Recommends* that further efforts be made to achieve the maximum possible standardization and comparability in the budgetary and administrative practices of all organizations concerned;

2. *Invites* the International Civil Service Commission, in co-operation with the United Nations Joint Staff Pension Board and other appropriate bodies of the United Nations system, taking into account the relevant reports of the Joint Inspection Unit and the opinions expressed thereon in the Fifth Committee, to pursue its efforts to achieve a greater co-ordination of staff regulations;

3. *Invites* the Secretary-General and the executive heads of the specialized agencies and the International Atomic Energy Agency to submit to the General Assembly, at its forty-first session, their comments on the matters referred to in this resolution.

General Assembly resolution 40/250

18 December 1985   Meeting 122   Adopted without vote

Approved by Fifth Committee (A/40/1064) without vote, 17 December (meeting 70); draft by Chairman (A/C.5/40/L.12); agenda item 119.
Meeting numbers. GA 40th session: 5th Committee 55, 59, 65, 70; plenary 122.

Report of the Advisory Committee on Administrative and Budgetary Questions on the administrative and budgetary co-ordination of the United Nations with the specialized agencies and the International Atomic Energy Agency

The General Assembly

1. *Takes note with appreciation* of the report of the Advisory Committee on Administrative and Budgetary Questions on the administrative and budgetary co-ordination of the United Nations with the specialized agencies and the International Atomic Energy Agency;

2. *Refers* to the organizations concerned the report of the Advisory Committee as well as the comments and observations made in the course of its consideration in the Fifth Committee;

3. *Transmits* the report of the Advisory Committee to the Board of Auditors, the Panel of External Auditors, the Committee for Programme and Co-ordination and the Joint Inspection Unit for their information.

General Assembly resolution 40/251

18 December 1985   Meeting 122   Adopted without vote

Approved by Fifth Committee (A/40/1064) without vote, 17 December (meeting 70); draft by Chairman (A/C.5/40/L.24); agenda item 119 *(a)*.
Meeting numbers. GA 40th session: 5th Committee 55, 59, 65, 70; plenary 122.

Reform of the United Nations system

JIU report. In December 1985,[3] the Secretary-General transmitted to the General Assembly the report[4] of the JIU entitled "Some reflections on reform of the United Nations". From an analysis of problems confronting the United Nations system, the report called for an examination of the *raison d'être* of the institution and suggested changes that would, in the author's opin-

ion, enable the United Nations to address more meaningfully a number of issues of international concern. In this regard the report focused on three areas (including related issues of structure, administration and management): peace and security; negotiation of economic problems leading to complementarity among national economic strategies; and an integrated approach to economic and social development.

The thesis underlying the report, the author pointed out, was that serious thought about a reform of the United Nations system was now indispensable and that it should lead to the conception of a third-generation world organization genuinely in keeping with the needs of the modern world.

In summary, the conclusions of the report— described as "indications for further research"— set forth the following considerations and proposals.

The structures of the current system rested on three fallacious notions: that the maintenance of peace could be achieved through an institution, that the development of the poor countries could be achieved through a sectoral approach and that negotiations among 159 States were possible without a prior definition of agreed negotiation structures.

In the current political context it was unrealistic to believe that sovereign States could deal in common with activities outside the limited sphere where a broad consensus existed. The basic role of a world organization could only be the determined search for a better or different type of consensus which would lead towards the far-off ideals set forth in the Charter. Further reform could not be focused on modifying the structures of a political United Nations; it was not possible to propose other structures that would be an improvement on the Security Council. On the contrary, reform should focus on the transformation of the structures that supported development and on the institution of a genuine world economic forum. The aim would be to build up an "economic United Nations" side by side with the political United Nations.

On one front, the reform should be a total recasting at system level of all structures concerned with development in order to constitute regional or subregional development agencies or enterprises. On the other front, the reform should be to set up a world forum to deal essentially with economic problems. The developing countries should not continue to be left out of the discussion at the negotiating table. Thought should be given to replacing the current dual forums of the Economic and Social Council and UNCTAD by a more restricted council of the type envisaged in the original Charter, which set the Council's membership at 18. If this "economic security council" were to have 23 members, the major States and the main regions of the world could be represented on it. The secretariats of the United Nations and the major agencies could be reorganized under the authority of one or more commissions made up of independent persons of distinction.

The JIU report to the Assembly covering its work for the second half of 1985[5] stated that the majority of the Inspectors had disassociated themselves from the report, with the exception of chapter II ("Managerial shortcomings or structural shortcomings"), as they had, among other reasons, judged the report's main thesis to advocate a remodelling

of the mechanisms relating to the forum of negotiations that was inherently political, rather than administrative, in nature. The scope of the report, they believed, thus fell outside both the letter and spirit of the JIU mandate.

Action by ACC. At its October 1985 session, ACC requested[6] its Organizational Committee to prepare draft comments, for consideration at its first 1986 session, on the JIU report on reform of the United Nations.

REFERENCES

[1]A/40/769 & Corr.1. [2]YUN 1981, p. 1315, GA res. 36/229, 18 Dec. 1981. [3]A/40/988 & Corr.1 & Add.1. [4]JIU/REP/85/9. [5]A/41/34. [6]ACC/1985/DEC/16-29 (dec. 1985/22).

Chapter III

United Nations officials

The Secretary-General, in his 1985 annual report on the work of the Organization (see p. 3), stated that he had repeatedly emphasized the need to explore all avenues for utilizing resources in the most efficient manner and to provide an equitable role for women in the Secretariat. The management-improvement measures he had initiated were being pursued on a continuing basis.

The General Assembly in 1985 also took action on several personnel questions, such as the status of women in the Secretariat and in the regional commissions, job classification, recruitment, career development and other conditions of service.

Personnel questions were dealt with in several resolutions. The Assembly welcomed continuing efforts to improve the status of women staff members and noted the Secretary-General's decision to reappoint a Co-ordinator for the Improvement of the Status of Women in the Secretariat (resolution 40/258 B). It asked the regional commissions to incorporate women's concerns in their work programmes (40/105). Continuing its efforts to balance the geographical representation of staff, the Assembly asked the Secretary-General to develop and apply a new recruitment plan for 1986-1987 with specific targets for unrepresented and underrepresented countries, as well as to take other recruitment measures to bring States within their desirable ranges of representation (40/258 A). With regard to job classification of the General Service category in New York, the Assembly deferred a decision on the plan being carried out by the Secretary-General but decided, by decision 40/466, that the effective date of the classification exercise would be 1 January 1985.

As in previous years, the General Assembly acted on issues affecting working conditions, salaries and benefits, based on recommendations of the International Civil Service Commission (ICSC), which in turn consulted the participating intergovernmental organizations in the United Nations system.

In December, the Assembly, by resolution 40/244, approved several recommendations of ICSC, including approval of the range for the margin between the net remuneration (net base salary and post adjustment) of the United Nations and that of the best-paid national civil service, and requested ICSC to develop further the methodology for calculating the margin and re-examine the scope of the education grant. It also asked ICSC to carry out, in co-operation with the United Nations Joint Staff Pension Board, a comparative study of the levels of pension benefits and the ratios of pensions to salaries under the United Nations pension scheme and that of the comparator country (40/245). The Assembly also dealt with some aspects of conditions of service of non-Secretariat officials (40/256).

The Economic and Social Council instructed the Secretary-General on the use of consultant services (resolution 1985/78), asking him to report on reasons why particular tasks could not be carried out by existing regular staff. The Assembly deferred until 1986 consideration of the Secretary-General's report on the use of experts, consultants and participants in *ad hoc* expert groups, involving former staff members aged 55 or more (decision 40/456).

The Assembly approved the observations of the Advisory Committee on Administrative and Budgetary Questions (ACABQ) on the need to streamline the appeals procedures (resolution 40/252, section XII); requested the Secretary-General to do so and to continue to study the feasibility of establishing an office of Ombudsman (40/258 A); and deferred again its consideration of the feasibility of establishing a single administrative tribunal for the common system (decision 40/465).

The Secretary-General was asked to provide, in future reports on use of air travel, information on all United Nations expenditures for first class air travel (decision 40/455). Some amendments were made to the Staff Rules (40/468) and Staff Regulations (40/467).

Personnel management

The General Assembly took decisions in 1985 on a number of personnel management problems, on the basis of information provided by the Secretary-General and such bodies as ICSC, ACABQ, the Administrative Committee on Co-ordination (ACC) and the Joint Inspection Unit (JIU). Written comments were submitted to the Fifth (Administrative and Budgetary) Committee by representatives of United Nations staff, including the Co-ordination Committee for Independent Staff Unions and Associations of the United Nations System (CCISUA) and the Federation of International Civil Servants' Associations (FICSA). The issues were management improvement, staff composition, career development, personnel policies, field staff and privileges and immunities.

On 18 December, the Assembly adopted three resolutions on personnel questions: **resolution 40/258 A** on the composition of the Secretariat; **40/258 B** on improvement of the status of women in the Secretariat; and **40/258 C** on respect for the privileges and immunities of officials of the United Nations.

On the same date, the Assembly adopted **resolution 40/244** on the work of ICSC, section IV of which called for strengthening the regulation of the conditions of service of the organizations participating in the United Nations common system.

Staff composition

The Secretary-General, in his annual report[1] on the composition of the Secretariat, covering the period 1 July 1984 to 30 June 1985, presented information on nationality, sex and type of appointment (contract). On 30 June, he stated, staff members appointed for a year or more numbered 15,278, of whom 11,850 were paid from the regular budget and 3,428 from extrabudgetary sources.

During the reporting year, the Secretary-General said, substantial progress was made towards the achievement of an equitable geographical balance. The proportion of appointments from unrepresented and underrepresented Member States rose to 54.6 per cent of posts subject to geographical distribution.

Three States, formerly unrepresented, were represented: Papua New Guinea, Saint Christopher and Nevis, and Saint Lucia. Ten States were currently within their range. Between mid-1984 and mid-1985, 229 appointments were made to posts subject to geographical distribution. Of these, 125 were of nationals of Member States underrepresented or not represented at the beginning of the reporting year. Of that figure, 45 were successful candidates in national competitive examinations, which continued to be the best way of recruiting from target Member States, the Secretary-General said.

In response to Assembly concerns about the need to increase the representation of developing countries in senior and policy-making posts, the Secretary-General provided tables with data on posts at the D-1 and D-2 levels and above.

The report also described major recruitment measures undertaken. These included the establishment of targets for appointment of women and of nationals of unrepresented or underrepresented Member States, competitive examina-

tions for entry-level candidates and improvement of vacancy announcements.

In another report,[2] the Secretary-General submitted to the Assembly a list showing the name, functional title, nationality and grade of all staff members holding an appointment for one year or more on 30 June 1985.

On another subject, the Secretary-General, who was asked by the Assembly in 1984[3] to study ways of applying the population factor as one of the criteria for determining desirable ranges in seeking equitable geographical distribution of staff, indicated some of the problems that might arise from such a procedure.

The population factor was one of three weighted factors used in the construction of desirable ranges in seeking an equitable geographical distribution of staff (the other two factors being membership and contribution). The Secretary-General concluded that any change in the application of the population factor would have to be considered in the context of whatever other changes Member States might propose during a review of the scale of contributions to be undertaken in 1986. Since any significant change in the size of the base figure would affect the size or weight of the other factors and might lead to a change in the minimum desirable ranges, no change should be introduced for calculating the ranges from January 1986, except for changes in the contribution factor resulting from any changes the Assembly might make in the assessed contributions of individual Member States.

ICSC, in its annual report,[4] emphasized the importance of appropriate recruitment measures for technical co-operation personnel, stressed the potential benefits of recruitment missions, recommended active participation of senior field staff in the recruitment process, and reiterated the need for adequate training in interviewing techniques for staff involved in the selection process. It agreed to request the organizations in the common system: to harmonize their recruitment efforts, to develop recruitment sources for technical assistance personnel on as wide a geographical basis as possible, to provide forecasts of recruitment requirements, to make full use of national recruitment services and keep them informed of programmes in their countries, to help establish training programmes for the newly established services, and to recommend that their member States consider special measures to facilitate the secondment of their nationals, consider conclusion of agreements on the transfer of pension rights to enable their nationals to move freely between government service and service with the common system, and consider using reimbursable loan agreements for short technical assignments in order to obtain candidates whose career commitments would otherwise preclude service with the system. It also recommended that the organizations make full use of United Nations Volunteers, the associate experts scheme, retired persons and non-governmental organizations (NGOs) to develop their rosters.

JIU, in a report transmitted to the Assembly in September,[5] discussed problems of implementing the medium-term plan of recruitment, 1983-1985, formulated by the Office of Personnel Services (OPS) in 1982. The results of the plan suggested that its major goals—to raise the level of representation of all unrepresented and underrepresented countries to the lower limit of their desirable ranges and to improve representation of women—would not be attained.

In its recommendations, JIU suggested that the Assembly might wish to consider reviewing and modifying the existing system of ranges so that the current respective mid-points would become the upper levels, with the lower levels being 10 per cent below but not less than 5.75 posts (recommendation I). The Secretary-General should be asked to take the suggested system of desirable ranges and distribution of all the geographical posts into consideration when preparing the 1986 study of desirable ranges; statistical data should include the number and grade of geographical posts to which each country and each region was entitled (II). OPS should be made directly responsible to the Secretary-General for the implementation of recruitment plans; internal guidelines should explicitly state OPS's authority and thus strengthen it (III). OPS should indicate in its reports the departments that did not comply with the established targets and the reasons therefor (IV), additional efforts should be made to ensure equitable distribution in all departments, offices or units (V) and Governments, especially of unrepresented and underrepresented countries, should be encouraged to be more active in the recruitment process (VI).

Commenting on the JIU report, the Secretary-General considered[6] that the recommendation with respect to the mid-point of each Member State's range and the publication of data by region, country and grade would not be feasible. He indicated his general agreement with recommendations III, IV and V and stated that in large measure they were already being implemented, although, with reference to recommendation IV, he noted that a geographical balance must be approached flexibly to accommodate the particular situation in each department, office and regional commission and their programme needs. He stated that he intended to continue his recruitment efforts vigorously during the period of the next plan to improve both geographical distribution and the number and level of distribution of women.

The staff representatives of the Secretariat, in a document[7] submitted to the Fifth Committee in November, drew attention to the need to develop special recruitment measures in conjunction with more flexible personnel arrangements to facilitate the entry of disabled persons into the international civil service. They urged that specific targets be set for this purpose.

GENERAL ASSEMBLY ACTION

On 18 December, the Assembly, on the recommendation of the Fifth Committee, adopted **resolution 40/258 A**, without vote.

Composition of the Secretariat

The General Assembly,

Reaffirming its previous resolutions on personnel questions, in particular resolution 39/245 of 18 December 1984,

Concerned that the targets set in the 1983-1985 medium-term plan of recruitment were not achieved,

Recalling Article 101, paragraph 3, of the Charter of the United Nations, which states that:

"The paramount consideration in the employment of the staff and in the determination of the conditions of service shall be the necessity of securing the highest standards of efficiency, competence and integrity. Due regard shall be paid to the importance of recruiting the staff on as wide a geographical basis as possible",

1. *Reiterates its request* to the Secretary-General to strengthen the role and emphasize the authority of the Office of Personnel Services of the Department of Administration and Management in recruitment and other personnel matters throughout the Secretariat and to report thereon to the General Assembly at its forty-first session;

2. *Requests* the Secretary-General to develop and apply a second medium-term plan of recruitment for the period 1986-1987 with specific targets for recruitment from unrepresented and underrepresented countries with a view to bringing all Member States within their desirable ranges and to make special efforts to increase the number of staff recruited from Member States below the mid-point of their desirable ranges in order to bring them towards their mid-point;

3. *Further requests* the Secretary-General to continue to ensure the representation of developing countries and other countries in senior and policy-formulating posts, with due regard to equitable geographical distribution and in accordance with the relevant resolutions of the General Assembly;

4. *Requests* the Secretary-General to submit to the General Assembly at its forty-first session proposals for the review of the system of desirable ranges with a view to achieving a balanced application of all factors relevant to the calculation of the desirable ranges, including the population factor, taking into account the views of Member States expressed at the current session;

5. *Requests* the Secretary-General to speed up the recruitment process by setting strict time-limits for the departments and offices concerned to complete the recruitment procedures;

6. *Takes note* of the proposal of the Secretary-General to introduce, on an experimental basis, a competitive

examination at the P-3 level for candidates with the required qualifications and experience and requests him to submit a report thereon to the General Assembly at its forty-first session, taking into account the comments of the Advisory Committee on Administrative and Budgetary Questions and the views of Member States expressed at the current session;

7. *Further requests* the Secretary-General, in his efforts to guarantee to staff members a just and expeditious resolution of disputes and grievances, to streamline the appeals procedures and continue the study on the feasibility of establishing an office of Ombudsman, and to report thereon to the General Assembly at its forty-first session;

8. *Approves* the introduction, in accordance with the recommendation of the International Civil Service Commission, of after-service health insurance coverage for former locally recruited staff who participated in the medical expense assistance plan in appendix E to the Staff Rules of the United Nations, on the understanding that the Secretary-General will present to the General Assembly at its forty-first session the financial implications of reformulating the scheme to make it comparable to other health insurance schemes of the common system.

General Assembly resolution 40/258 A

18 December 1985   Meeting 122   Adopted without vote

Approved by Fifth Committee (A/40/1067) by consensus (parts A-C together), 17 December (meeting 69); draft by Nigeria (A/C.5/40/L.16, part A), based on informal consultations and orally revised; agenda item 123.
Meeting numbers. GA 40th session: 5th Committee 42, 43, 46, 47, 49-51, 53-55, 57, 59, 62-64, 69; plenary 122.

The Assembly, by **resolution 40/20**, called on organizations of the United Nations system to ensure that their personnel and recruitment policies provided for equitable representation of Africa at their headquarters and in regional and field operations. In section III of **resolution 40/244**, the Assembly welcomed ICSC's recommendations on introducing special measures for the recruitment of women (see p. 1238) and those on the development of recruitment sources, including national recruitment services.

International Civil Service Commission

The International Civil Service Commission held two sessions in 1985: its twenty-first in London from 11 to 29 March, and its twenty-second in New York from 8 to 26 July. It examined issues arising from Assembly decisions and resolutions, as well as those stemming from its own statute. Its eleventh annual report[4] covered various aspects of conditions of service in all staff categories, including salaries, post adjustment, health insurance, support for dependent disabled children, conditions of staff in the field and pensionable remuneration.

Several bodies in the United Nations common system, including those of staff representatives, commented on the recommendations and decisions of ICSC.

Two Inspectors of JIU submitted a report, transmitted to the Assembly in September,[8] which was a follow-up report to a 1984 JIU report[9] on staff costs in the United Nations Secretariat. They made recommendations for a review of the system of remuneration for the Professional and higher categories, on defining ICSC's mandate, on revising the methodology for comparison purposes, and on a review of staff activities. The Secretary-General commented on JIU's recommendations in November.[10]

FICSA, in October,[11] expressed concern that on several occasions the Fifth Committee had changed ICSC recommendations or decisions without hearing the staff and other parties concerned; it attached the utmost importance to consultations with representatives of the executive heads and staff. FICSA commented on ICSC views on pensionable remuneration and conditions of service of the Professional and higher categories, special measures for the recruitment of women and the use of competitive examinations.

CCISUA transmitted its comments[12] to the Fifth Committee in November. It was convinced of the need for a core of career service personnel whose conditions of service were stable over time and determined with technical objectivity, free from considerations of politics. It expressed concern at unprecedented attacks in recent discussions on the conditions of service not only on the international civil service but on the organizations and institutions of the international system itself. CCISUA offered its comments on safeguarding acquired rights, pensions and pensionable remuneration, professional remuneration, the education grant, housing, long-service awards, the status of women and conditions in the field. It also commented on JIU's report on staff costs.

The Secretary-General transmitted in November[13] a statement[14] adopted by ACC at a 4 July special session called[15] to discuss and set out its position on personnel questions. It commented on issues considered by ICSC and by the United Nations Joint Staff Pension Board, in particular the further development of the methodology for defining the comparison elements for determining remuneration, the need to utilize consultative mechanisms and the procedures to be followed when the Assembly disagreed with a recommendation of ICSC or the Board. ACC also presented its views on the JIU report.

The views of the above bodies on the various issues are presented elsewhere in this chapter under the specific subjects.

ACABQ,[16] commenting on the Secretary-General's statement[17] on the administrative and financial implications ($1,110,900) of ICSC's recommendations and decisions, concurred with his stated intention to deal with the additional costs in the context of the budget performance reports for the 1984-1985 biennium, and to reflect the saving ($25,888,200) for 1986-1987 in revised estimates to be presented for recosting that biennium's budget at December 1985 exchange rates and projected inflation rates.

GENERAL ASSEMBLY ACTION

On 18 December 1985, the Assembly, on the recommendation of the Fifth Committee, adopted **resolution 40/244**, without vote.

United Nations common system: report of the International Civil Service Commission

The General Assembly,

Having considered the eleventh annual report of the International Civil Service Commission and other reports related thereto,

Reaffirming the importance of maintaining and developing further a single unified international civil service through the application of common personnel standards, methods and arrangements,

I

1. *Takes note* of the action taken by the International Civil Service Commission in response to General Assembly resolutions 39/27 of 30 November 1984 and 39/69 of 13 December 1984;

2. *Approves* the range of 110 to 120, with a desirable mid-point of 115, for the margin between the net remuneration of officials in the Professional and higher categories of the United Nations in New York and that of officials in comparable positions in the United States federal civil service, on the understanding that the margin would be maintained at a level around the desirable mid-point of 115 over a period of time;

3. *Requests* the Commission:

(a) To develop further the methodology for calculating the margin based on net remuneration, taking into account the views expressed at the current session, and to study the possibility of calculating the margin as specified in paragraph 2 above based on a comparison of net remuneration for both services in New York and to report thereon to the General Assembly at its forty-first session;

(b) To further elaborate procedures for the operation of the post adjustment system within the approved range of the margin of net remuneration, which would enable the Commission to maintain the margin at a level around the desirable mid-point of 115 over a period of time, and to report thereon to the Assembly at its forty-first session;

4. *Also requests* the Commission to continue its studies of the post adjustment system as it relates to United Nations officials posted outside the base city of the system, the effects of exchange-rate fluctuations and the possibility of eliminating post adjustment at the base city of the system, and to report thereon to the General Assembly no later than at its forty-second session;

II

Approves the recommendations of the International Civil Service Commission contained in paragraphs 180 and 181 of its report concerning support by organizations of the United Nations common system for staff with dependent disabled children;

III

1. *Welcomes* the recommendations of the International Civil Service Commission contained in paragraph 245 of its report concerning the introduction of special measures for the recruitment of women, is cognizant of the contents of paragraphs 246 and 247 of the same report and requests the Commission to report to the General Assembly at its forty-first session on the progress made in this regard;

2. *Welcomes further* the recommendations of the Commission contained in paragraph 252 of its report concerning the development of recruitment sources, including national recruitment services;

3. *Requests* the Commission:

(a) To undertake a study of the mobility of Professional staff in the United Nations common system, including the frequency and average length of their assignments at different duty stations;

(b) To re-examine the scope of the education grant in relation to the purpose for which it was originally approved;

4. *Also requests* the Commission to re-examine the question of the mandatory age of separation from service of staff of organizations of the common system and to report thereon to the General Assembly at its forty-first session;

IV

1. *Requests* the Secretary-General in his capacity as Chairman of the Administrative Committee on Co-ordination and, through him, the other executive heads of organizations participating in the United Nations common system, to promote endeavours to maintain and strengthen the common system for the regulation and co-ordination of the conditions of service;

2. *Also requests* the executive heads of participating organizations, through the Secretary-General, to inform their respective governing bodies of the present resolution;

3. *Urges* Member States to ensure that their representatives in organizations of the United Nations common system are informed about the positions taken by them in the General Assembly on matters relating to the conditions of service;

4. *Expresses its concern* over actions taken by some of the participating organizations which have led to disparities in the United Nations common system;

5. *Requests* the International Civil Service Commission to report in detail to the General Assembly at future sessions on the consideration and implementation of the decisions and recommendations of the Commission by organizations of the United Nations common system.

General Assembly resolution 40/244

18 December 1985   Meeting 121   Adopted without vote

Approved by Fifth Committee (A/40/1061) without vote, 14 December (meeting 63); draft by Vice-Chairman (A/C.5/40/L.7), based on informal consultations and orally revised; agenda item 124.

Meeting numbers. GA 40th session: 5th Committee 29, 30, 37, 38, 42, 44-48, 50, 53, 63; plenary 121.

Status of women in the Secretariat

The Secretary-General reported in November 1985[18] that, while the percentage of Professional women in posts subject to geographical distribution had reached 23.1 per cent by mid-1985, women staff members continued to be confined to the lower salary ranks. As of 30 June, only four of the 26 assistant secretaries-general were female. At the next highest (D-2) level, 3.3 per cent of staff in geographical posts were women. Nearly three out of every four Professional women were found in service-oriented occupations, and their distribution in geographic posts was extremely uneven compared to that of men: 35 per cent were from North America and the Caribbean and 26.7 per cent from Western Europe, while only 3.7 per cent were from Eastern Europe.

As part of an action programme he had established, the Secretary-General decided to set 30 per cent of all Professional appointments (both language and geographical posts) as an overall target for recruitment of women during the 1986-1987 biennium. OPS would be responsible for sub-targets by level and by department to fulfil the overall target. The action programme—covering the areas of recruitment of Professionals, career development in all categories, training, conditions of service and grievance and discrimination issues—had been developed by the Co-ordinator for the Improvement of the Status of Women in the Secretariat, a post established on an experimental basis early in 1985. The first phase of the programme, to be concluded by 30 June 1986, was to lead to concrete policy recommendations, timetables and procedural changes. During the second phase, the following year, the policies and procedures would be implemented and a final report submitted.

In a decision adopted in October,[19] ACC stated that the organizations of the United Nations system were committed to address actively the problem of women's status and to increase their participation in decision-making and substantive programme areas. It asked its Consultative Committee on Administrative Questions (CCAQ) (Personnel and General Administrative Questions) to convene a meeting of senior recruitment staff to recommend measures for inter-agency co-operation in the recruitment of women and to examine measures to facilitate their interorganizational mobility.

The representatives of the Secretariat staff union and associations observed, in a document[7] presented to the Fifth Committee, that the number of appointments and rate of promotion of women had remained stagnant or declined. While women constituted 43.8 per cent of all staff, 82.6 per cent of them were in the General Service and related categories. The current two-tiered structure of the international civil service only exacerbated their unequal opportunities for advancement. Measures should include the establishment of departmental targets for promotion and recruitment and monitoring of the progress achieved.

Reporting in 1985,[4] ICSC considered that, while special recruitment measures were essential in effecting any significant change in Professional women's status, their success was largely dependent on the institutional and attitudinal climate of the organizations, which should give priority to recruitment at senior levels, impress on Governments their commitment to employ more women, and work with them to develop recruitment sources. It should be recommended to the organizations that they convene a meeting of their recruitment heads to discuss common prospection procedures and strategies. They should actively explore recruitment sources—i.e. national women's bureaux, university alumnae, NGOs, fellowship recipients, experts and United Nations Volunteers—to broaden their supply of women candidates from unrepresented and underrepresented States, and try to expand their supply of candidates for posts in occupations not usually identified with women through contacts with professional associations and universities. The need for professional women in technical co-operation programmes should be stressed. Organizations should introduce sensitizing courses for effecting behavioural change, and ensure that women's concerns were adequately reflected in in-service training programmes. Those that had not done so should be requested to establish a staff/management body to set goals for the advancement of women staff.

Both FICSA[11] and CCISUA[12] welcomed ICSC's proposals for improving the status of women. FICSA observed that recruitment could not be separated from forward-looking social policy and proper career development, with adequate support services, counselling, flexible personnel policy and career planning opportunities all given equal priority, and it urged that the question remain on ICSC's agenda.

The need for women to participate actively in the planning, formulation, decision-making and appraisal processes was also stressed by the World Conference to Review and Appraise the Achievements of the United Nations Decade for Women: Equality, Development and Peace (Nairobi, Kenya, 15-26 July).[20] The Forward-looking Strategies for the Advancement of Women, adopted at that Conference (see p. 938), stated that all organizations of the system should take measures to achieve the participation of women on equal terms with men at all levels by the year 2000, by preparing action plans, setting targets and assigning co-ordinators to improve their status. (See also p. 960.)

GENERAL ASSEMBLY ACTION

On 18 December 1985, the General Assembly, on the recommendation of the Fifth Committee, adopted **resolution 40/258 B** without vote.

Improvement of the status of women in the Secretariat

The General Assembly,

Recalling Article 8 of the Charter of the United Nations, which states:

"The United Nations shall place no restrictions on the eligibility of men and women to participate in any capacity and under conditions of equality in its principal and subsidiary organs",

Further recalling Article 101, paragraph 3, of the Charter of the United Nations, which states:

"The paramount consideration in the employment of the staff and in the determination of the conditions of service shall be the necessity of securing the highest standards of efficiency, competence and integrity. Due regard shall be paid to the importance of recruiting the staff on as wide a geographical basis as possible",

Recalling article 8 of the Convention on the Elimination of All Forms of Discrimination against Women, which calls upon States parties to "take all appropriate measures to ensure to women, on equal terms with men and without any discrimination, the opportunity to represent their Governments at the international level and to participate in the work of international organizations",

Reaffirming its relevant resolutions on the need to increase both the overall number of women in posts subject to geographical distribution and the proportion of women at the senior and policy-making levels of the Organization,

Noting the recommendations contained in paragraph 358 of the Nairobi Forward-looking Strategies for the Advancement of Women with respect to the recruitment, promotion and career development of women by all bodies and organizations of the United Nations system,

Convinced that women should have equal opportunity to serve the international community at all levels of responsibility and that progress in this regard can only be achieved through commitment at the highest levels of the organizations demonstrated through accountable management practices,

1. *Welcomes* the continuing efforts of the Secretary-General to improve the status of women in the Secretariat and, in particular, the action programme and work plans set out in the report of the Secretary-General on the improvement of the status of women in the Secretariat, and his providing all necessary assistance for the effective carrying out of all these tasks;

2. *Takes note* of the Secretary-General's decision to reappoint during the biennium 1986-1987, on a temporary basis, a Co-ordinator for the Improvement of the Status of Women in the Secretariat of the United Nations;

3. *Requests* the Secretary-General to take the necessary measures to increase the number of women in posts subject to geographical distribution with a view to achieving, to the extent possible, an overall participation rate of 30 per cent of the total by 1990, without prejudice to the principle of equitable geographical distribution of posts;

4. *Reiterates* that the functions of the Co-ordinator should not duplicate those of the Office of Personnel Services and stresses that the latter Office shall continue to exercise overall responsibility and implement all directives of the General Assembly and policies of the Secretary-General on personnel matters, including the implementation of all policies on the improvement of the status of women in the Secretariat, in particular the action programme and work plans set out in the report of the Secretary-General;

5. *Requests* the Secretary-General to report to the General Assembly at its forty-first session on the progress made in implementing the action programme and relevant resolutions of the General Assembly;

6. *Reiterates its request* to Member States to continue to support the efforts of the United Nations and the specialized agencies and related organizations to increase the proportion of women in the Professional category and above by, *inter alia*, nominating more women candidates.

General Assembly resolution 40/258 B

18 December 1985	Meeting 122	Adopted without vote

Approved by Fifth Committee (A/40/1067) by consensus (parts A-C together), 17 December (meeting 69); draft by Nigeria (A/C.5/40/L.16, part B), based on informal consultations; agenda item 123.

Meeting numbers. GA 40th session: 5th Committee 42, 43, 46, 47, 49-51, 53-55, 57, 59, 62-64, 69; plenary 122.

By section III of **resolution 40/244**, the Assembly welcomed ICSC's recommendations concerning the introduction of special measures for the recruitment of women and observed that it was cognizant of the recommendations on establishing staff/management bodies to set goals for advancing the status of women and of ICSC's request that organizations report to it in 1986 on progress made on its recommendations.

Women's programme officers posts at regional commissions

The Secretary-General reported to the General Assembly in November 1985,[21] in response to its 1984 request,[22] on his reassessment of the regional commissions' work programmes with a view to incorporating women's concerns in them. Noting that the commissions had carried on a variety of activities to that end, ranging from specific projects to general policy development and implementation, he described the main initiatives taken in each of the five commissions with regard to women's posts. With a view to allocating sufficient budgetary resources to staff to regularize all their senior women's programme officers posts by the end of the United Nations Decade for Women (1976-1985), he had included requests in the 1986-1987 budget for a P-3, P-4 and P-5 post as well as redeployment of a P-5 post for senior women's programme officers in the regional commissions. (See also ECONOMIC AND SOCIAL QUESTIONS, Chapters VIII and XIX.)

GENERAL ASSEMBLY ACTION

On 13 December 1985, the General Assembly, on the recommendation of the Third (Social, Humanitarian and Cultural) Committee, adopted **resolution 40/105**, without vote.

Incorporation of the interests of women in the work programmes of the regional commissions

The General Assembly,

Recalling its resolution 39/127 of 14 December 1984, in particular the reference to the incorporation of women's concerns in the overall programme of work of each regional commission and to the regularization of senior women's programme officers posts,

Convinced that further efforts are needed to ensure adequate consideration of women's concerns within the regional commissions,

Recognizing the important contribution the senior women's programme officers can make to the integration of women in development at the national and regional levels,

1. *Takes due note* of the report of the Secretary-General on measures taken by the regional commissions to incorporate women's concerns at all levels in their overall work programmes and to establish senior women's programme officers posts;

2. *Expresses deep concern* at the inadequate response of the regional commissions to the need to incorporate the interests of women in their economic and social policies and programmes;

3. *Stresses* that the integration of women in economic development as well as in social development is essential to the well-being of society;

4. *Invites* the executive secretaries of the five regional commissions to propose to their governing bodies measures for reassessing all individual work programmes in order to incorporate women's concerns at all levels in their overall work programmes for the biennium 1988-1989, taking into account the roles and responsibilities of the regional commissions in developing and implementing the system-wide, medium-term plan for women and development and the Nairobi Forward-looking Strategies for the Advancement of Women;

5. *Requests* the Secretary-General to take into account the important role of the regional commissions in promoting the advancement of women when formulating the system-wide, medium-term plan for women and development and when implementing the Forward-looking Strategies;

6. *Also requests* the Secretary-General to report to the General Assembly at its forty-first session:

(a) On the progress made in implementing paragraphs 5 and 6 of its resolution 39/127;

(b) On the measures proposed by the five regional commissions to incorporate women's concerns at all levels in their overall work programmes for the biennium 1988-1989, as outlined in paragraph 4 above.

General Assembly resolution 40/105

13 December 1985   Meeting 116   Adopted without vote

Approved by Third Committee (A/40/1008) without vote, 21 November (meeting 48); 8-nation draft (E/C.5/40/L.41); agenda item 12.

Sponsors. Bahamas, Barbados, Canada, Indonesia, Kenya, Nepal, Norway, Phillipines.

Career development

United Nations organizations continued in 1985 to focus attention on various methods for career development of the staff, such as human resources planning, recruitment policies, promotions, competitive examinations, assessment of training needs and job classification.

ICSC, in its annual report,[4] expressed agreement with the position taken by the organizations on the need for a dynamic staff-training programme, including on-the-job training. It reiterated that job classification could provide the appropriate structure for career development. Career development for General Service and related staff should be organized mainly by occupational groups and career paths established among groups in each organization at each duty station to facilitate horizontal as well as vertical mobility. Career development could be assisted by establishing profiles of staff, adequate performance appraisal, exchange of vacancy notices, recruiting at the lower levels, limited use of personal promotions and filling of higher-level vacancies by promotion within the organization.

In a follow-up status report[23] to his 1984 report[24] on his efforts to establish a new career development system, the Secretary-General informed the Assembly that work on the project had begun in January 1985, focusing on compiling the necessary information and developing the methodology for the design of some of its major components, which he expected to be completed by the end of 1986, and the system itself was expected to come into operation in 1987. Progress had been made defining career paths, standardizing post qualification requirements, utilizing existing data bases, developing a systematic rotation and mobility scheme, identifying training needs and designing a training component, and redesigning the performance evaluation system. This was a major personnel reform project, he concluded, and might take more time than originally scheduled.

Staff representatives, commenting on career development issues,[7] stated that the Secretariat must accept long-term planning, including goals and programmes to strengthen the career staff. There should be sufficient opportunities and an effective career development plan, which were lacking. They noted with alarm that junior Professional posts continued to diminish and grade-creep continued to be one of the few mechanisms for advancement; career possibilities for General Service staff were even more limited, they said. They also felt that further refinements of the competitive examination process were desirable, the most important of which was the co-ordination of the examination system within the context of career development, training and recognition of meritorious service.

With regard to competitive examinations,[4] ICSC was of the opinion that that positive experience of the United Nations deserved more attention, and their extension as a recruitment method to other organizations of the system should be considered, upholding such examinations as a useful and objective tool for recruitment, especially for the junior levels.

The opinion was expressed by FICSA[11] that, while there were some positive elements in competitive examinations for recruitment, they should not be the only deciding factor. As to their use in General Service promotions to the Professional category, the system currently applied needed to be considerably improved and FICSA did not support their use in their current form for that purpose.

Reporting in November[25] on the competitive examination system in the Secretariat, the Secretary-General agreed that they were a fair, effective and successful recruitment mechanism, and for the most part appointments at the P-1 and P-2 levels were currently made on the basis of such examinations. He reported on the results of external and internal examinations and their costs, evaluated their results, and outlined some improvements being made. He recommended that recruitment at the P-3 level through national competitive examinations be introduced on an experimental basis in 1986.

Commenting on the Secretary-General's report, ACABQ[26] said it appeared that the cost per candidate of those recruited at the P-1 and P-2 levels was very high; in view of uncertainties involving format and contents of the examination and what posts might be earmarked, it felt it was premature to extend national examinations to the P-3 level.

The General Assembly, by section III of **resolution 40/244**, called on ICSC to study the mobility of Professional staff in the common system, including the frequency and average length of their assignments at different duty stations.

Job classification

Classification of posts in the General Service and related categories, begun in 1982, was continued on the basis of the standards established by ICSC in 1983, the Secretary-General reported in December 1985.[27] Work at the first stage was carried out by two OPS classification officers, operating independently, and at the next stage reviewed by a joint staff/management body, the Classification Review Group. The Group submitted recommendations on the classification levels of 3,065 posts, all but 300 of which were accepted by the Assistant Secretary-General for Personnel Services. The matter was further reviewed by the Joint Advisory Committee, the staff/management body at Headquarters, and its findings were approved with some minor modifications. The new arrangement, the report said, represented a major policy change from the principle of rank-in-person to rank-in-post as the basis for classification. Extensive consultations with staff representatives were undertaken on questions of future consequences, such as the impact on career development and promotion procedures.

The Secretary-General stated in the report that provision was included in his initial budget proposals for 1986-1987 for all classifications within the General Service category. The proposed reclassification of 11 posts from General Service to the P-1/P-2 level would require an additional $118,000.

In a related document,[7] staff representatives expressed the view that too little importance had been attached to reconciling job classification to other aspects of administration, such as organizational planning, budgeting and career development.

GENERAL ASSEMBLY ACTION

On 18 December 1985, the General Assembly, acting on a recommendation of the Fifth Committee, adopted **decision 40/466**.

Job classification of the General Service and related categories in New York

At its 122nd plenary meeting, on 18 December 1985, the General Assembly, on the recommendation of the Fifth Committee, having considered the report of the Secretary-General on job classification of the General Service and related categories in New York, decided:

(a) To defer a decision on job classification of the General Service and related categories in New York;

(b) To consider the question at its forty-first session, or if possible before the session, on the basis of the recommendations of the Advisory Committee on Administrative and Budgetary Questions and any observations that may be made by the International Civil Service Commission;

(c) To ensure that social justice should be done in the matter;

(d) That the effective date of the implementation of the results of the classification exercise should be 1 January 1985.

General Assembly decision 40/466

Adopted by vote

Approved by Fifth Committee (A/40/1067), sub-paras. *(a)-(c)* without vote, sub-para. *(d)* by recorded vote (67-25-7), 14 December (meeting 64); oral proposal by Chairman; agenda item 123.
Meeting numbers. GA 40th session: 5th Committee 63, 64; plenary 122.

Though the first three subparagraphs were adopted together without vote, a recorded vote was taken on subparagraph *(d)* of the decision in both the Assembly and the Fifth Committee.

The Assembly adopted it by 103 votes to 22, with 15 abstentions; the Fifth Committee by 67 to 25, with 7 abstentions (the recorded vote was requested by the United States). Before the Assembly adopted subparagraphs *(a)* to *(c)*, it agreed following informal discussions to add the phrase "or if possible before the session" in subparagraph *(b)*.

Among the reasons advanced in the Committee by some of those voting against retroactive implementation were: Belgium, which said all the elements needed for consideration were not known; Bulgaria and New Zealand, which did not want to prejudice a decision on job classification taken in 1986; France, the Federal Republic of Germany and the Netherlands, which desired the views of ACABQ and ICSC first; Italy, which felt that a precedent might be set; and Japan, which did not object to retroactivity but said the financial implications required Fifth Committee approval. Ireland said its negative vote did not reflect its attitude towards the possible retroactive implementation of the exercise. For procedural reasons, Romania voted against, and Turkey voted for, the proposal.

Explaining their votes in favour: Cameroon, Denmark and Jordan said the parameters were known and they wished to support the General Service staff; Algeria felt it would compensate for the fact that the Assembly had not yet taken a decision on the job classification exercise; Canada said the provision would be in the interests of social justice, a point also made by Bangladesh, Cuba, Guinea, Guinea-Bissau, Madagascar, Peru, Spain and Yemen. Argentina, which abstained, and Barbados, which did not participate in the vote, said the specific date should have been kept separate from the substantive issue. Canada, Cuba and Tunisia said their affirmative votes were not meant to prejudice any decision ACABQ might take.

The General Assembly on 18 December, on the recommendation of the Fifth Committee, adopted **decision 40/469**, without vote; it recalled its request to the Secretary-General in 1984[3] to implement a JIU recommendation calling for a study of the situation of staff in the General Service category, and asked him to report on the study at the Assembly's 1986 session. The decision was also approved without vote in the Fifth Committee, on 17 December, on an oral proposal by Nigeria.

Consideration by the ICSC. Under article 13 of its statute, ICSC was required to establish job classification standards for all categories of staff in fields of work common to several of the organizations in the common system, including jobs in the General Service category.

In 1985, the Commission reviewed a report on the implementation during 1981 to 1983 of its 1980 "Master Standard",[28] the first tier of a three-tiered system of job classification standards. The report provided an overall analysis as well as the results and status for each organization. In the absence of statistics reflecting the distribution of different types of work in the common system, ICSC expressed concern that the Common Classification of Occupational Groups, set up to enable the development of such statistics, had not been fully implemented but concluded that the Master Standard was being generally applied throughout the system. It promulgated Tier-II standards for financial management specialists and for public information specialists, noting in the case of the latter, however, the absence of positions at the P-1 level for inclusion in the Standard and stressed the importance of P-1 as an entry level for all occupations.

ICSC decided to promulgate a supplement to the Master Standard to be used when grading the content of project jobs, as well as a job description format to provide guidance in gathering information needed to grade such posts. It provided guidance on methods to be used in developing classification standards for the General Service and related categories at Vienna, agreeing to delay a salary survey scheduled for 1986 to allow for completion of the exercise, and reviewed and approved for promulgation the proposed standard for those categories at Addis Ababa, Ethiopia, which had reduced the number of grade levels from nine to seven. It also decided to develop classification standards for the General Service at Baghdad, Iraq, and Santiago, Chile, and postponed consideration of an uncompleted project by CCAQ to develop such standards for small and medium-sized field offices.

Staff representation

The General Assembly in 1984[29] had requested ICSC to take the necessary measures to suspend implementation of a 9.6 per cent increase in the post adjustment index at the base city, New York. The Assembly's request was challenged by Secretariat members in groups of cases brought before both the United Nations Administrative Tribunal and the Administrative Tribunal of the International Labour Organisation (ILO) in June and July 1985.

In September 1985,[8] the Secretary-General transmitted to the Assembly a JIU report on staff costs and on some aspects of the use of human and financial resources in the United Nations Secretariat, a follow-up report to one on that subject it had submitted in 1984.[30] It discussed several of the staff associations in the Secretariat, and stated that staff activities involved too many people, who devoted too much of their working time to problems not directly related to the terms of reference of staff bodies. The main thrust of staff activities was directed at getting higher salaries and new financial benefits, and it was not surprising that staff bodies were supported by the Administration, which was equally interested in salaries and other benefits. Demands were cultivated by staff representatives who spread false expectations among the staff, affecting morale, and who also tried to equate staff bodies with trade unions and claimed the right of staff members to strike. Staff bodies were threatening to put the General Assembly and the Secretariat in confrontation by putting pressure on Assembly delegates in order to achieve their goals. Under the circumstances, JIU recommended (recommendation 4) that the Assembly, or a special committee, look into the entire range of staff activities and take a firm position to improve the situation. For this purpose, the Secretary-General should be asked to undertake a comprehensive review of the matter, taking into account the views of all those concerned.

Commenting on the JIU report,[10] the Secretary-General said that its assessment of staff activities lacked balance. He could not accept the observations regarding the relationship between the Administration and the staff on the salary issue, as it was normal for employee representatives to seek improved conditions of service, and said that the Inspectors were unduly harsh in contending that representatives spread false expectations among the staff, affecting morale and efficiency, and that there were no grounds for questioning the propriety of staff members appealing decisions which they considered prejudicial to their interests. He said he would continue periodically to review staff-management relations with the aim of improving the effectiveness of the Organization.

FICSA,[11] in accordance with a 1980 Assembly resolution,[31] and CCISUA[12] submitted documents to the Fifth Committee in which they held that the Inspectors' arguments were based on wrong premises and distorted facts and that no valid conclusions could be drawn from their report and it could not serve as a basis for serious discussion. The staff unions and associations of the Secretariat declared[7] that the unstated objective of the attack was to place restraints on freedom of association and undermine the confidence of Member States in the Secretariat. The Inspectors had criticized the staff for questioning before the Administrative Tribunal the Assembly's request to suspend the post adjustment increase, which was tantamount to saying that legal rights were permissible as long as they were not exercised.

Field staff

In 1985,[4] ICSC continued its study of issues relating to conditions of service of United Nations staff in the field, including the uniform application of allowances and benefits at field locations, the pre-departure allowance and the conditions of service faced by staff in Lebanon. It also received reports from organizations on problems of communications, employment opportunities for spouses and shipment of personal effects.

In regard to payment of pre-departure allowances, ICSC drew to the attention of the system's organizations the irregularity that had occurred in their interpretation of ICSC's decision on such reimbursement. Pre-departure expenses should be reimbursed only upon transfer and upon separation of a staff member from service. Further, ICSC could not agree to review extension of the current scheme to cover locations other than in the field in the context of field conditions. Its

secretariat, however, was requested to study and report on the need for pre-departure expenses to be reimbursed at other duty stations outside the context of field issues.

Concerning the situation of staff serving in Lebanon, ICSC recognized that a special situation existed, calling for an *ad hoc* remedy. Therefore, it decided: staff in the Professional and higher categories as well as other internationally recruited staff in specified duty stations in Lebanon should receive an incentive of $550 per month, at an estimated annual cost of $147,000; General Service staff should receive an incentive equivalent to 20 per cent of their base net salary, at an estimated annual cost of $75,000; the ICSC Chairman should keep the issue under review to determine if a change in service conditions occurred and, as soon as an improvement in conditions occurred, he would decide on an appropriate course of action.

Staff representatives observed[7] that instead of concentrating on purely financial incentives, greater flexibility in granting annual leave, in creating or improving commissary facilities and in using pouch facilities would make service in extremely difficult duty stations easier to bear. In addition, field staff encountered difficulties in finding adequate housing and in paying for their children's education; an immediate rise to age 25 was urged as the age-limit for the allowance for dependent children when they continued in an education programme. Field service should be recognized and rewarded with provisions for accelerated promotion, eligibility for training and counselling, and well-defined career paths.

Certain field conditions had improved over the past several ICSC sessions, according to CCISUA,[12] which had removed some impediments to mobility and recognized the special character of field work, as evidenced by the special arrangements adopted for Lebanon. Housing and educational expenses continued to be a major problem. CCISUA supported the attempt to improve the after-service health insurance scheme for locally recruited staff.

In December, the General Assembly, by **resolution 40/244**, requested ICSC to continue its studies of the post adjustment system as it related to United Nations officials posted outside the system's base city, the effects of exchange-rate fluctuations and the possibility of eliminating post adjustment at the base city, and to report to the Assembly thereon before its 1987 session.

Travel

In October, the Secretary-General submitted his annual report[32] on implementation of various resolutions regulating the standards of accommodation for air travel. He noted all exceptions made to those rules—including details of, resultant additional costs of, and reasons for such exceptions—and the savings achieved through use of economy and other air fares, for the period from 1 July 1984 to 30 June 1985. Although 60 exemptions were granted, total savings during the period were estimated at $298,500.

Representatives of the Secretary-General, meeting with ACABQ, stated that estimated savings had decreased from the 1984 level because of a reduction in travel and the wider use of business class for trips of more than nine hours. In its report[33] to the Assembly, ACABQ expressed the opinion that the practice of reporting hypothetical savings should be discontinued; instead, the report should emphasize the total additional costs incurred by the Organization as a result of exceptions to the current rules. It recommended that future reports on the matter be submitted to it for review, after which it would report to the Assembly as necessary.

The host country announced travel restrictions applicable to United Nations staff members from a number of countries (see p. 1180).

GENERAL ASSEMBLY ACTION

In December, on the recommendation of the Fifth Committee, the General Assembly adopted without vote **decision 40/455**.

Standards of accommodation for air travel

At its 121st plenary meeting, on 18 December 1985, the General Assembly, on the recommendation of the Fifth Committee:

(a) Took note of the report of the Secretary-General on standards of accommodation for air travel and the related report of the Advisory Committee on Administrative and Budgetary Questions;

(b) Endorsed the recommendation of the Advisory Committee contained in paragraph 2 of its report;

(c) Decided that future annual reports submitted to the General Assembly on this subject should include information on all expenditures by the United Nations for first class air travel.

General Assembly decision 40/455

Adopted without vote

Approved by Fifth Committee (A/40/1058) without vote, 14 December (meeting 65); draft by United States (A/C.5/40/L.10); agenda item 115.
Meeting numbers. GA 40th session: 5th Committee 63, 65; plenary 121.

Staff Rules

In July 1985, the Secretary-General submitted his annual report[34] containing the texts of provisional staff rules and amendments made to the Staff Rules of the United Nations since the previous report in 1984.[35] The changes concerned, among other things, amendments occasioned by granting staff status to language teachers, revising educational reimbursement scales and education grant entitlements, a new policy on the non-resident's allowance, deductions

of contributions to a staff representative body, establishment of a Joint Appeals Board at Nairobi and other duty stations, compensation for overtime work, clarifying the meaning of joint staff-management machinery, revised scales of pensionable remuneration and separation payments, and revised salary scales, dependency allowances and language allowances.

In a November addendum[36] to his report, the Secretary-General reported on corrections and editorial improvements to the French text of the Rules to make it more consistent with the English.

On 18 December, on the recommendation of the Fifth Committee, the Assembly adopted without vote **decision 40/468**, taking note of the reports of the Secretary-General on amendments to the Staff Rules.

Staff Regulations

The Secretary-General in November[36] proposed an amendment to the Staff Regulations of the United Nations to bring the wording of a paragraph into line with fact, replacing the term "annual budget" with "programme budget".

In addition, he proposed that amendments of an editorial nature be made to the French text of the Staff Regulations, which required the authority of the Assembly, to reflect proper terminology or usage.

GENERAL ASSEMBLY ACTION

In December, on the recommendation of the Fifth Committee, the General Assembly adopted without vote **decision 40/467**.

Amendments to the Staff Regulations of the United Nations

At its 122nd plenary meeting, on 18 December 1985, the General Assembly, on the recommendation of the Fifth Committee, having considered the report of the Secretary-General on amendments to the Staff Regulations and Rules, decided:

(a) That the last sentence of paragraph 5 of annex I to the Staff Regulations of the United Nations should be amended to replace the term "annual budget" by the term "programme budget";

(b) That the French text of regulations 3.3 (a), (e) and (f), 6.2, 8.1 (b), 8.2 and paragraphs 7 and 9 and the title of the first table of annex I to the Regulations should be amended as proposed by the Secretary-General to reflect the proper terminology and usage.

General Assembly decision 40/467

Adopted without vote

Approved by Fifth Committee (A/40/1067) without vote, 17 December (meeting 69); oral proposal by Nigeria; agenda item 123 (c).

Privileges and immunities

In October 1985,[37] the Secretary-General submitted, on behalf of ACC, a report on personnel of organizations in the United Nations system who were under detention or who had been reported missing, and on measures to safeguard staff security and encourage respect for the privileges and immunities of United Nations officials. During the period 1 September 1984 to 31 August 1985, 89 such cases of arrest and detention or disappearance had been reported to the United Nations Security Co-ordinator. In 72 of those cases, the organizations concerned were able to exercise the right of functional protection under international agreements or were successful in obtaining the release of the detainee. Of the remaining 17 cases, 16 related to locally employed members of the United Nations Relief and Works Agency for Palestine Refugees in the Near East and one to a locally recruited staff member of the United Nations Educational, Scientific and Cultural Organization in Afghanistan. The release or amnesty of detained staff members in Afghanistan, Ethiopia and Lebanon was a positive indication of the seriousness with which Member States had accepted Assembly recommendations. The Secretary-General would continue his efforts to secure full compliance with the relevant international instruments.

A list of staff members currently detained, missing, imprisoned or executed over the past 12 years was presented to the Fifth Committee in November[7] by United Nations staff representatives. They pointed out that a major problem was the growing number of acts of violence against United Nations staff.

GENERAL ASSEMBLY ACTION

On 18 December, on the recommendation of the Fifth Committee, the General Assembly adopted **resolution 40/258 C**, without vote.

> **Respect for the privileges and immunities of officials of the United Nations and the specialized agencies and related organizations**
> *The General Assembly,*
> *Recalling* Articles 100 and 105 of the Charter of the United Nations,
> *Reaffirming* its previous resolutions, in particular resolution 39/244 of 18 December 1984,
> *Reiterating* the obligation of the staff in the conduct of their duties to observe fully the laws and regulations of Member States,
> 1. *Takes note with concern* of the report submitted to the General Assembly by the Secretary-General on behalf of the Administrative Committee on Co-ordination;
> 2. *Deplores* the increasing number of cases involving the abduction and detention of United Nations officials, experts and military personnel by armed groups and individuals;
> 3. *Calls upon* all Member States that currently have United Nations officials under arrest or detention to review these cases and to co-ordinate efforts with the Secretary-General to resolve each case with all due speed;

> 4. *Calls upon* the staff of the United Nations and the specialized agencies and related organizations to comply with the obligations resulting from the Staff Regulations and Rules of the United Nations, in particular regulation 1.8, and from the equivalent provisions governing the staff of the other agencies;
> 5. *Calls upon* the Secretary-General, as chief administrative officer of the United Nations, to continue personally to act as the focal point in promoting and ensuring the observance of the privileges and immunities of officials of the United Nations and the specialized agencies and related organizations, and to take all necessary measures to implement the mandates of the General Assembly as reflected in paragraphs 7 and 8 of resolution 39/244.

General Assembly resolution 40/258 C

18 December 1985   Meeting 122   Adopted without vote

Approved by Fifth Committee (A/40/1067) by consensus (parts A-C together), 17 December (meeting 69); draft by Nigeria (A/C.5/40/L.16, part C), based on informal consultations and orally amended by Jordan; agenda item 123.
Meeting numbers. GA 40th session: 5th Committee 42, 43, 46, 47, 49-51, 53-55, 57, 59, 62-64, 69; plenary 122.

REFERENCES
[1]A/40/652. [2]A/C.5/40/L.2. [3]YUN 1984, p. 1152, GA res. 39/245, 18 Dec. 1984. [4]A/40/30 and Corr.1. [5]A/40/673 & Corr.1. [6]A/40/673/Add.1. [7]A/C.5/40/59 & Corr.1. [8]A/40/653. [9]YUN 1984, p. 1154. [10]A/40/653/Add.1. [11]A/C.5/40/26. [12]A/C.5/40/44. [13]A/C.5/40/41. [14]ACC/1985/DEC/14-15 (dec. 1985/14); ACC/1985/DEC/16-29 (dec. 1985/21 A). [15]ACC/1985/DEC/1-13 (dec. 1985/4). [16]A/40/7/Add.12. [17]A/C.5/40/45 & Corr.1. [18]A/C.5/40/30. [19]ACC/1985/DEC/16-29 (dec. 1985/21 C). [20]A/CONF.116/28/Rev.1. [21]A/40/838. [22]YUN 1984, p. 1171, GA res. 39/127, 14 Dec. 1984. [23]A/C.5/40/27. [24]YUN 1984, p. 1156. [25]A/C.5/40/39. [26]A/40/7/Add.13. [27]A/C.5/40/84 & Corr.1. [28]YUN 1981, p. 1159. [29]YUN 1984, p. 1160, GA res. 39/27, 30 Nov. 1984. [30]YUN 1984, p. 1159. [31]YUN 1980, p. 1196, GA res. 35/213, 17 Dec. 1980. [32]A/C.5/40/22 & Corr.1. [33]A/40/830. [34]A/C.5/40/5. [35]YUN 1984, p. 1157. [36]A/C.5/40/5/Add.1. [37]A/C.5/40/25.

Staff costs

Salaries and allowances

Salaries

In 1985, ICSC[1] continued to advise the General Assembly on staff salaries and allowances, and decided, among other things, that the remuneration in New York should continue to remain at its current level of post adjustment and that immediate measures should be taken to ensure equivalence of purchasing power between New York and other duty stations, pending Assembly action. Based on ICSC recommendations, the Assembly, in December, approved the range of 110 to 120, with a desirable mid-point level of around 115, for the margin between the net remuneration of officials in the Professional and higher categories in New York and officials in comparable positions in the comparator service—the

United States federal civil service (resolution 40/244, section I). The Commission had reported that the level of the margin currently stood at 121.3.

In addition, the Assembly requested ICSC to develop further the methodology for calculating the margin based on net remuneration; to elaborate procedures for the operation of the post adjustment system within the approved range, which would enable ICSC to maintain the margin at the desirable mid-point level over a period of time; and to continue studying the post adjustment system. ACC[2] was convinced that the Assembly should request ICSC to elaborate without delay a methodology for the objective definition and practical application of the proposed range for the margin under varying circumstances; until that time, it believed that the decision could be taken on the operation of the post adjustment system.

The Commission's recommendations to the Assembly took into account the suggestions made by its subsidiary body, the Advisory Committee on Post Adjustment Questions (tenth session, Vienna, 7-17 May), on such matters as the maintenance of equivalence of purchasing power between New York and other duty stations, the operation of the post adjustment system within a defined margin range, problems relating to duty stations with low or negative post adjustments, separation of the effects of inflation and currency fluctuation within the post adjustment system, and the methodology for cost-of-living surveys.

In other 1985 developments, ICSC reiterated its 1984 recommendation[3] on introducing a long-service step in the salary scale for the Professional category—with updated financial implications of $300,000 per annum—and advised the Assembly that it might wish to make representation to the governing bodies of WHO and ILO, which had introduced such a step, to consider harmonizing practices within the United Nations common system. On a related matter, the Secretary-General[4] informed the Assembly that all organizations were proceeding to implement the ICSC recommendation to grant a long-service step, effective 1 January 1985, to those General Service and other locally recruited staff members who had completed 20 years of service within the common system and five years of service at the top of the grade.

The Commission conducted a survey—at Geneva and London, respectively—of best prevailing conditions of service of the General Service and related categories and recommended a new salary scale for each duty station. After consulting with the other executive heads of agencies with staff at Geneva, the Secretary-General reported in November[4] that he had decided to implement the revised scales there as of 1 April 1985.

In the same report, the Secretary-General also gave estimated financial implications of ICSC-proposed measures relating to net remuneration, health insurance, support of staff with disabled dependants, and conditions of service in the field. ACABQ[5] subsequently commented on the Secretary-General's estimates, without specific recommendations for changes.

In its comments to the Assembly, FICSA[6] proposed re-examination of the post adjustment system, adding that the margin calculation should take into account expatriation, constraints of work, and developments in the comparator civil service. FICSA proposed using the average remuneration at each grade to measure the evolution of the margin between the remuneration of the comparator service and that of the United Nations system. It also proposed that ICSC be asked to reconsider its decision to exclude the difference in length of service from the total compensation comparison, to measure the evolution of the margin on the basis of total compensation, to use average remuneration for each grade instead of step one, and to include expatriate benefits in the total compensation comparison.

Asserting that the only valid measure for comparison was that of total compensation and that the average remuneration should be used as a point of reference, CCISUA[7] declared that the hasty determination of a range amounted to transforming the margin from a reference point to an arbitrary limit and unduly tied the salary and post adjustment systems of the United Nations to the internal policies of the comparator.

JIU report on staff costs. In a follow-up to its 1984 report[3] on staff costs in the United Nations Secretariat, JIU underlined in its 1985 report, transmitted to the General Assembly in September,[8] that its 1984 conclusions and recommendations remained valid. The application of what it termed the inadequate methodology used by ICSC resulted in unjustified costs to Member States. The introduction of a number of elements, such as career difference, for example, tended to narrow the margin artificially. The comparison of the two systems should be based on the net one with total compensation comparison being avoided until it was further developed, if necessary (recommendation 3). The JIU Inspectors suggested that the Assembly establish a special committee to assist ICSC in reviewing objectively all aspects of the United Nations system of remuneration for Professional and higher-level staff (recommendation 1), take a definitive position on the ICSC mandate, confirm the validity of the Noblemaire Principle (whereby salaries in the Professional and higher categories were based on the best-paid national civil service), and define the margin, or range for the margin, and instruct ICSC to act only within the limits of the mandate (recommendation 2). A fourth recommendation concerned staff activities (see p. 1242).

Commenting on the report, the Secretary-General[9] rejected the Inspectors' assertions of a link between the pensionable remuneration of General Service staff and the New York post adjustment index and their comments on the supportive relationship between the Administration and the staff on the salary issue. ICSC asserted that JIU intervention in the policy matters within its province threatened to undermine its authority and introduced elements of uncertainty and confusion of responsibilities with regard to the common system—a view shared by ACC,[2] as well as by CCISUA[7] and FICSA.[6]

Allowances

Following a comprehensive review of after-service health-care coverage, undertaken pursuant to a 1983 Assembly request,[10] ICSC recommended in 1985[1] that after-service health insurance, under a contributory scheme, should be provided to locally recruited General Service staff at field stations covered under appendix E of the Staff Rules of the United Nations (which described a medical expense assistance plan for such staff at designated United Nations offices). It endorsed the principle that eligibility criteria for after-service health insurance should ensure that staff with identical qualifications were eligible under the various organizations' schemes, and expressed the hope that retired staff would be consulted on such schemes, including cost-sharing. Representatives of CCISUA, the Federation of Associations of Former International Civil Servants (FAFICS) and FICSA felt that uniform eligibility criteria for after-service health insurance should be established among all organizations.

As regards another 1983 Assembly request for a study of the issue of mandatory health insurance,[11] ICSC considered that, while health insurance should be mandatory, the exact application of that concept should be left to the organizations to determine.

Assuming that active and former staff members would pay the equivalent of 1.5 per cent of their respective net salary or pension and the organization would pay the remaining part, the Secretary-General estimated[4] that the ICSC recommendation would entail an expenditure of $420,000 for 1986-1987, $340,000 relating to the improved benefit structure for all concerned and $80,000 to the introduction of after-service coverage.

ICSC reaffirmed[1] its view that there was no current need for changing the criteria for application of the education grant and that such grant should continue to be an expatriate benefit. On 18 December, by section III of **resolution 40/244**, the General Assembly requested the Commission to re-examine the scope of the grant in relation to the purpose for which it was originally approved.

As regards support to staff with dependent disabled children, ICSC made a series of recommendations, including waiving the lower age-limit for the payment of the special education grant for such children, extending to 28 the age-limit in exceptional cases, and reimbursement of expenses relating to special education-grant travel, local transportation costs or rehabilitation equipment, extending the limit for reimbursement of medical expenses. It asked organizations to provide more information to locally recruited field staff concerning disabilities and to assist them in preparing submissions for benefits. On 18 December, the Assembly approved the ICSC recommendations by section II of **resolution 40/244**.

In March 1985, the Secretary-General[12] issued to staff members a revised administrative instruction concerning new policies implemented on the ICSC recommendations on conditions of service in the field, as they related to the financial incentive for Professionals serving at specified duty stations, home-leave travel and sick-leave entitlements for personnel at duty stations with difficult conditions of life and work, additional education-grant travel, and shipment of personal effects, among other field service–related issues (see p. 1243).

Pensions

In 1985, the principal of the United Nations Joint Staff Pension Fund, providing retirement, death, disability and related benefits for staff upon cessation of their services with the United Nations, increased from $3,500,632,266 to $4,122,009,634, with the number of its participants reaching 54,013. Investment income during the year amounted to $595,766,141 ($591,449,433 net). From that amount, the Fund paid $342,043,844 in benefits, including 8,092 retirement benefits amounting to $177,491,059. In addition, it paid 8,115 early and deferred retirement benefits, 2,817 widows'/widowers' benefits, 4,397 children's benefits, 501 disability benefits and 43 secondary dependants' benefits. In the course of the year, it also paid 3,389 withdrawal or other lump-sum settlements.

The 21-member Pension Board (see APPENDIX III), charged with administering the Fund, held its thirty-fourth session from 29 July to 9 August at Montreal, Canada.[13] The Board reviewed the method of calculating the lump-sum commutation of benefits, the questions of imposing ceilings on the amount of such commutations and on the highest level of pensions, and the operation of the two-track pension adjustment system and compensatory and interim measures for participants whose pensionable remuneration had been lowered as at 1 January 1985 through the adoption of the ICSC-recommended scale of pensionable remuneration.[14] The Board discussed the management of the investments (see p. 1250) and the actuarial valuation of the Fund as at 31 December 1984. Among other things, it recommended to the Assembly that the United Nations Industrial Development Organization, which was converted to a specialized agency in the course of 1985 (see p. 591), be admitted to the Fund as of 1 January 1986 in order to ensure continued participation in the Fund by the staff, pending the formal admission process.

Responding to a 1984 Assembly request,[15] ICSC and the Pension Board discussed the methodology for determining pensionable remuneration for the Professional and higher categories and for monitoring the level of such remuneration, and re-examined the adjustment procedure between comprehensive reviews. Views of FICSA,[6] CCISUA[7] and FAFICS were heard in ICSC, which, in view of the state of flux in the retirement scheme of the comparator (United States) civil service, suggested a further review of the methodology, following receipt of the details of the new United States scheme, for report to the Assembly in 1986; it noted that because of the freezing of the New York post adjustment, the adjustment procedure as regards pensionable remuneration in between comprehensive reviews would automatically not be applied in 1986. Bearing in mind the adverse effect on the pension system of freezing pensionable remuneration scales, the Pension Board, nevertheless, accepted the continued suspension of the adjustment procedure in 1986. The Board believed that a review should cover both the methodology recommended by ICSC in 1984 and possible alternative approaches, and that a decision on a benefit adjustment system contained in article 54 (*b*) of the Regulations of the Fund should follow that on the methodology.

ACABQ[16] concurred with or had no objection to most of the Board's recommendations, among them, increasing the rate of pension contribution to 22.5 per cent (from 21.75 per cent) effective 1 January 1986 for the reason that a delay in reducing the imbalance might require more extensive corrective measures in future. In a statement transmitted to the Assembly by the Secretary-General,[2] ACC also supported the increase in contributions as of 1986, and considered it urgent to institute a system for adjusting pensionable remuneration to avoid undue erosion of benefits and to ensure a continued adequate income for the Fund.

In December, the Secretary-General submitted[17] to the Assembly, at the request of the Secretary-General of the International Telecommunication Union (ITU) and the Director-General of the United Nations Educational, Scientific and Cultural Organization (UNESCO), the text of resolutions on the pension system adopted by those agencies' legislative bodies. ITU, in its resolution, expressed its anxiety about the level of benefits and the Fund's future, hoped the measures to be adopted to restore the actuarial balance would not further reduce the level of benefits, and stressed the importance of introducing equitable interim measures to safeguard acquired rights. UNESCO expressed the hope that the Assembly would adopt the interim measures recommended by ICSC in 1984 and, commenting on a proposal to increase the Board's membership to 33, stated that UNESCO should have three seats. (The Board at its July/August session had invited member organizations to express their views on the composition of the Board so that it might submit recommendations to the Assembly at a future session.)

GENERAL ASSEMBLY ACTION

On 18 December 1985, the General Assembly, on the recommendation of the Fifth Committee, adopted **resolution 40/245**, without vote. Sections III through VI were approved without change as proposed by the Pension Board; sections I and II resulted from informal consultations on the Board's recommended text.

Report of the United Nations Joint Staff Pension Board

The General Assembly,

Recalling its resolution 39/246 of 18 December 1984,

Having considered the report of the United Nations Joint Staff Pension Board for 1985 to the General Assembly and to the member organizations of the United Nations Joint Staff Pension Fund, chapter II of the report of the International Civil Service Commission and the related report of the Advisory Committee on Administrative and Budgetary Questions,

Welcoming the improvement in the actuarial situation of the Fund as revealed by the valuation as at 31 December 1984,

I

Pensionable remuneration for the Professional and higher categories

1. *Takes note* of chapter II of the report of the International Civil Service Commission and section III.C.5 of the report of the United Nations Joint Staff Pension Board;

2. *Requests* the International Civil Service Commission, in co-operation with the United Nations Joint Staff Pension Board, to:

(*a*) Carry out a comparative study of the levels of pension benefits and the ratios of pensions to salaries under the United Nations pension scheme and that of the comparator country;

(*b*) Complete its review of the methodology for the determination of pensionable remuneration for the Professional and higher categories, for monitoring the level of pensionable remuneration and for adjustment of pensionable remuneration in between comprehensive reviews, taking into account the margin range established for net remuneration, the views expressed at the current session, including those concerning the evolution of the levels of pensionable remuneration and pensions in recent years and the different characteristics of the two services, and to submit its recommendations to the General Assembly at its forty-first session;

3. *Defers* until its forty-first session further consideration of the recommendation of the United Nations Joint Staff Pension Board regarding amendment of article 54 *(b)* of the Regulations of the United Nations Joint Staff Pension Fund contained in the Board's report for 1984 and in the mean time extends the suspension of the operation of the adjustment procedure in the said article;

II
Amendments to the Regulations of the United Nations Joint Staff Pension Fund and review of the pension adjustment system

1. *Decides* that the maximum retirement benefit payable to a participant at the Under-Secretary-General, Assistant Secretary-General or equivalent level separating on or after 1 April 1986 shall not exceed 60 per cent of the pensionable remuneration for his level applicable on the date of separation, provided, however, that the amount so calculated shall not be less than the maximum benefit payable at the standard annual rate to a participant at the D-2 level retiring on the same date and provided further that a participant who has accrued a higher benefit by 31 March 1986 by virtue of his participation up to that date shall retain his said higher benefit;

2. *Decides* that the benefit payable to a participant in the Professional or higher categories whose pensionable remuneration was lowered as at 1 January 1985 shall not be less than an amount calculated in accordance with supplementary article C of the Regulations of the United Nations Joint Staff Pension Fund, which appears in the annex to the present resolution;

3. *Requests* the United Nations Joint Staff Pension Board to study further the method of calculating the lump-sum commutation, bearing in mind the views expressed in the Fifth Committee, and to report thereon to the General Assembly at its forty-first session;

4. *Requests* the United Nations Joint Staff Pension Board, with a view to eliminating or reducing significantly inequalities of benefits payable to participants who have already separated or will separate in the near future, compared to benefits payable to those who will separate later on, to:

(a) Take steps to implement, if possible with effect from 1 July 1986, such measures as are within its competence;

(b) Recommend to the General Assembly at its forty-first session such additional measures as would require Assembly action;

5. *Defers* until its forty-first session further consideration of the question of the rate of contribution to the United Nations Joint Staff Pension Fund, and requests the United Nations Joint Staff Pension Board to submit to the General Assembly at that session its recommendations on additional economy measures, with a view to eliminating the need for any future increase in the liabilities of Member States;

6. *Requests* the United Nations Joint Staff Pension Board to review the pension adjustment system and, in particular, to consider lowering the extent by which the local currency equivalent of the United States dollar track could exceed the local track, and to report thereon to the General Assembly at its forty-first session;

7. *Amends*, with effect from 1 January 1986, the Regulations of the United Nations Joint Staff Pension Fund, as set forth in the annex to the present resolution, incorporating any consequential changes in the cross-references in the Regulations, without retroactive effect, except that supplementary article C of the said Regulations shall be applicable with effect from 1 January 1985, pursuant to General Assembly resolution 39/246, section II, paragraph 3, and article 28 *(d)* shall be applicable with effect from 1 April 1986;

8. *Requests* the United Nations Joint Staff Pension Board to examine the question of the rate of contributions that should be payable in respect of the contributory service from 1 April 1986 of the participants affected by the decision in paragraph 1 of the present section, and to make specific recommendations to the General Assembly at its forty-first session for the amendment, if necessary, with effect from 1 April 1986, of article 25 of the Regulations of the United Nations Joint Staff Pension Fund;

III
Composition of the United Nations Joint Staff Pension Board

Invites the competent organs of the member organizations of the United Nations Joint Staff Pension Fund to review the size and composition of the United Nations Joint Staff Pension Board, taking into account, where practicable, the views expressed at the current session, and to submit their conclusions to the General Assembly, through the United Nations Joint Staff Pension Board, in time to enable the Assembly to take a decision on the matter no later than at its forty-second session;

IV
Admission of the United Nations Industrial Development Organization to membership in the United Nations Joint Staff Pension Fund

Recalling its resolution 34/96 of 13 December 1979 on transitional arrangements relating to the establishment of the United Nations Industrial Development Organization as a specialized agency,

Decides that the United Nations Industrial Development Organization shall be admitted to membership in the Fund with effect from 1 January 1986, in accordance with article 3 *(c)* of the Regulations of the Fund;

V
Emergency Fund

Authorizes the United Nations Joint Staff Pension Board to supplement the voluntary contributions to the Emergency Fund, for a further period of one year, by an amount not exceeding $100,000;

VI
Administrative expenses

Approves expenses, chargeable directly to the United Nations Joint Staff Pension Fund, totalling $16,995,700 (net) for the biennium 1986-1987 and additional expenses of $173,300 (net) for 1985 for the administration of the Fund.

ANNEX
Amendments to the Regulations of the United Nations
Joint Staff Pension Fund

Article 28
Retirement benefit

Insert the following text as paragraph *(d)* and relet-ter existing paragraphs *(d)* to *(g)* as *(e)* to *(h)*:

" *(d)* (i) However, except as provided in (ii) below, the benefit otherwise payable at the standard annual rate in accordance with the applicable provisions of *(b)* or *(c)* above to a participant at the level of Under-Secretary-General, Assistant Secretary-General or their equivalent level who separates from service on or after 1 April 1986, shall not exceed, as at the time of the participant's separation, the greater of:

"*a.* 60 per cent of his pensionable remuneration on the date of separa-tion; or

"*b.* The maximum benefit payable under the same provisions of paragraphs *(b)* or *(c)* above to a participant at the level D-2 (top step for the preceding five years) with 35 years of con-tributory service, separating on the same date as the participant.

"(ii) However, the benefit payable to a partici-pant to whom the provisions of (i) above are applicable shall not be less than the benefit that would have been payable to him at the standard annual rate if he had separated from service on 31 March 1986."

Article 40
Effect of re-entry into participation

Replace subparagraph *(c)* (ii) by the following text:

"(ii) Subject to *(d)* below, a retirement, early retirement or deferred retirement benefit, as the case may be, under article 28, 29 or 30, based on the length of such additional con-tributory service; provided, however, that such benefit may not be commuted into a lump sum, in whole or in part, and shall not be subject to any minimum provisions."

Add the following article:

"*Supplementary article C*
"Transitional measures

"*(a)* Effective 1 January 1985, notwithstanding the provisions of article 1 *(h)*, the final average remuneration of a participant in the Professional or higher categories who was in contributory service on 31 December 1984, had at least 36 completed calen-dar months of such service as of that date and whose pensionable remuneration was lowered by the scale of pensionable remuneration effective 1 January 1985, shall be calculated under both article 1 *(h)* and paragraph *(b)* of this article, with the participant being entitled to that method of calculation which results in the higher benefit at the standard annual rate.

"*(b)* (i) The highest final average remuneration to which the participant would have been entitled in accordance with article 1 *(h)* if he had separated from service on 31 December 1984 or on any later date preceding his actual date of separation shall be ap-plied to his contributory service up to and including

the date on which that final average remuneration was first attained in his case; and

"(ii) The final average remuneration calculated in accordance with article 1 *(h)* shall be applied to his contributory service after such date;

"(iii) The benefit payable at the standard annual rate under the provisions of article 28 *(b)* or *(c)* shall be calculated by adding to the benefit based on the contributory service in (i) above the benefit based on the contributory service in (ii) above, subject to arti-cle 28 *(d)* where applicable.

"*(c)* Nevertheless, and notwithstanding the pro-visions of article 28 *(d)*, the benefit payable to a par-ticipant at the standard annual rate in accordance with paragraph *(b)* above shall not be less than the benefit to which he would have been entitled if he had separated on the date the highest final average remuneration was first attained in his case."

General Assembly resolution 40/245

18 December 1985   Meeting 121   Adopted without vote

Approved by Fifth Committee (A/40/1057) without vote, 16 December (meeting 67); draft by Vice-Chairman (A/C.5/40/L.15), based on informal consultations; agenda item 125.

Meeting numbers. GA 40th session: 5th Committee 29, 37, 38, 44-46, 48, 50, 53, 67; plenary 121.

In a related action, the Assembly, by section III of **resolution 40/244**, requested ICSC to re-examine, and report to it in 1986 on, the man-datory retirement age of staff.

Pension Fund investments

The Pension Board, in its annual report to the Assembly,[13] noted that as at 31 March 1985 the market value of the Fund's assets was $3,926 million, with an investment return of 8.1 per cent for the preceding year. Its investment portfolio consisted of 54 per cent in equity, 33 per cent in bonds, 10 per cent in real estate–related investments, and 3 per cent in short-term cash equivalents. Global diver-sification remained the investment principle, and $1,902 million, or 50 per cent of the Fund's long-term investments, was placed in markets outside the United States; funds were invested in 23 dif-ferent currencies and in 21 different equity markets. Of the $676 million in development-related in-vestments, 78 per cent had been made through inter-national and regional development institutions.

The Secretary-General, in his annual report[18] on the Pension Fund's investments for the year ended 31 March 1985, noted that over the preceding 35 years the book value of the portfolio had risen from $13 million to $3,502 million, a compound increase of 17.7 per cent a year. By 30 June 1985, development-related investments had reached $744 million, as compared with $636 million a year before. ACABQ[16] had no com-ments to make on the matter.

On 18 December, the General Assembly, acting without vote on a recommendation of the Fifth Committee, took note of the Secretary-General's report by **decision 40/457**.

REFERENCES

(1)A/40/30 & Corr.1. (2)A/C.5/40/41. (3)YUN 1984, p. 1160. (4)A/C.5/40/45 & Corr.1. (5)A/40/7/Add.12. (6)A/C.5/40/26. (7)A/C.5/40/44. (8)A/40/653. (9)A/40/653/Add.1. (10)YUN 1983, p. 1175, GA res. 38/232, 20 Dec. 1983. (11)*Ibid.*, p. 1196, GA res. 38/235, 20 Dec. 1983. (12)ST/AI/280/Rev.2. (13)A/40/9. (14)YUN 1984, p. 1163. (15)*Ibid.*, p. 1164, GA res. 39/246, 18 Dec. 1984. (16)A/40/848. (17)A/C.5/40/73; A/C.5/40/74. (18)A/C.5/40/24.

UN Administrative Tribunal

Appeals system for staff

In 1985, ACABQ[1] informed the General Assembly that there was an urgent need to simplify administrative procedures so as to reduce the number, and financial impact, of cases requiring full-scale formal review. It noted Administrative Tribunal decisions in which damages were awarded to applicants not on the merits of their case but because of delays in the administration of justice, failure to observe prescribed procedure and general dissatisfaction with the manner in which an administrative decision had been reached. Each case filed cost the Organization an average of $24,000, not to mention considerable distraction from normal duties, resulting in the diminished ability of the Secretariat to carry out its assigned tasks.

ACABQ recommended that the Secretary-General be asked to analyse the problem and report on specific steps taken or envisaged to remedy it, focusing on simplifying rules and procedures to facilitate the staff's understanding of its rights and obligations, identifying the aspects of staff administration giving rise to an inordinate number of appeals, and streamlining the appeals procedures.

Staff representatives, presenting their views in November,[2] stated that, in view of the increasing number of litigations resulting from the abuse of authority by executive heads and their disregard of personnel directives, the Assembly might consider whether delegation of authority should continue to be given without ensuring that such authority was properly exercised.

GENERAL ASSEMBLY ACTION

On 18 December 1985, the General Assembly adopted **section XII of resolution 40/252**, without vote.

Appeals system for staff

[*The General Assembly . . .*]

Approves the observations and recommendations of the Advisory Committee on Administrative and Budgetary Questions as contained in paragraphs 67 to 72 of chapter I of its first report on the proposed programme budget for the biennium 1986-1987.

General Assembly resolution 40/252, section XII

18 December 1985   Meeting 122   Adopted without vote

Approved by Fifth Committee (A/40/1069) without objection, 19 November (meeting 41); oral proposal by Chairman; agenda item 116.

Activities of the Tribunal

In 1985, the United Nations Administrative Tribunal met in annual plenary session in New York on 7 November, and held two panel sessions—20 May to 14 June (Geneva) and 14 October to 8 November (New York). As in previous years, it submitted a note to the General Assembly President outlining its activities for the year.[3]

During the year, the Tribunal delivered 18 judgements in cases brought by current or former staff members against the Secretary-General, and one judgement in a case by a staff member of the Food and Agriculture Organization of the United Nations against the Secretary of the Joint Staff Pension Board, with respect to claims arising from labour contracts of the international civil service.

It also continued consideration of the harmonization of its statute, rules and practices with those of the ILO Administrative Tribunal, the other of the two existing tribunals of the common system; an informal meeting of the members and secretariats of the two tribunals was envisaged in 1986. Information exchange with the World Bank counterpart was under consideration.

The Assembly's Committee on Applications for Review of Administrative Tribunal Judgements held its twenty-fifth and twenty-sixth sessions in New York, from 28 to 31 January and on 12 and 13 September, respectively.

In its comments to the Assembly, FICSA[4] objected to statements in the 1985 JIU report on staff costs[5] (see pp. 1242 and 1246) critical of the appellate procedures. FICSA said the JIU Inspectors had challenged the staff's right to appeal against decisions affecting them adversely, challenged the independence of the Tribunal, interfered in pending cases, and questioned the nature of the awards of the Tribunal. The Secretary-General, in his comments[6] on the JIU report, said he considered it improper for any individual or organ to address the Tribunal in respect of pending cases, or to question its competence.

Feasibility of establishing a single tribunal

On 18 December 1985, on the recommendation of the Fifth Committee, the Assembly adopted **decision 40/465**, by which it decided to defer until its 1986 session consideration of the Secretary-General's report,[7] originally issued in 1984,[8] on the feasibility of establishing a single administrative tribunal for the entire common system. The decision was approved without vote, as it had been in Committee on 14 December, on an oral proposal by the Chairman.

Feasibility of establishing an Ombudsman's office

In a November 1985 report to the General Assembly,[9] prepared in response to its 1984 request,[10] the Secretary-General expressed the belief that it was feasible to establish an office of Ombudsman in the United Nations if the Ombudsman was given adequate staff support. While specific proposals would be submitted to the Assembly in 1986, he envisaged the Ombudsman to have access to all levels of the Administration. Noting that the existing panels on discrimination and other grievances provided the staff serving away from headquarters with direct personal access to a mediator, the Secretary-General felt that arrangements should be made to enable those staff members to approach the Ombudsman through a local representative. In making those observations, the Secretary-General discussed the experiences of the offices of Ombudsman already functioning, in UNESCO, WHO, IMF and the World Bank, and experiences of similar panels of part-time ombudsmen or mediators in other units within the United Nations system.

Staff representatives[2] believed that the International Court of Justice should select the Ombudsman, who would maintain complete independence and impartiality and be accountable to the Assembly. They reiterated a proposal that a separate office for the administration of justice be created within the Executive Office of the Secretary-General, and, to reduce the backlog of appeals, suggested granting the Administrative Review Unit of the Office of Personnel authority to settle small claims.

On 18 December, the General Assembly, in **resolution 40/258 A**, requested the Secretary-General, in his efforts to guarantee to staff members a just and expeditious resolution of disputes and grievances, to streamline the appeals procedures and continue to study the feasibility of establishing an office of Ombudsman.

REFERENCES

[1]A/40/7. [2]A/C.5/40/59 & Corr.1. [3]A/INF.40/7.
[4]A/C.5/40/26. [5]A/40/653. [6]A/40/653/Add.1. [7]A/40/471.
[8]YUN 1984, p. 1168. [9]A/C.5/40/38. [10]YUN 1984, p. 1152,
GA res. 39/245, 18 Dec. 1984.

Other UN officials

Conditions of service and compensation

In 1985, the General Assembly took up consideration—which it had deferred in 1983[1] and 1984[2]—of conditions of service and compensation for the Chairman and Vice-Chairman of ICSC and for the Chairman of ACABQ, taking into account the relevant parts of the 1983 report[3] of the Secretary-General and the related 1984 ACABQ report.[4] In paragraph 11 of its report, ACABQ had concurred with the Secretary-General's suggestion on reimbursing those officials for the actual cost of educating their children, subject to a ceiling of $4,500 per school year, and providing one related travel per year per child from the place of scholastic attendance outside the country of the duty station to the duty station.

On 18 December 1985, the General Assembly, on the recommendation of the Fifth Committee, adopted **resolution 40/256** without vote.

Conditions of service and compensation for officials, other than Secretariat officials, serving the General Assembly

The General Assembly,

Recalling its resolution 35/221 of 17 December 1980 on the conditions of service and compensation for officials, other than Secretariat officials, serving the General Assembly,[5]

Having considered those aspects of the report of the Secretary-General on which action was deferred by the General Assembly at its thirty-eighth and thirty-ninth sessions and the related report of the Advisory Committee on Administrative and Budgetary Questions,

Affirming the principle that the conditions of service for the Chairman and Vice-Chairman of the International Civil Service Commission and for the Chairman of the Advisory Committee on Administrative and Budgetary Questions shall be separate and distinct from those of officials of the Secretariat of the United Nations,

1. *Decides* that the annual compensation of the two full-time members of the International Civil Service Commission and of the Chairman of the Advisory Committee on Administrative and Budgetary Questions shall remain at its current level, i.e. $82,056 with an additional allowance of $5,000 for the Chairman of the Commission and the Chairman of the Advisory Committee;

2. *Approves* the recommendation of the Advisory Committee on Administrative and Budgetary Questions in paragraph 11 of its report with regard to the Chairman and Vice-Chairman of the International Civil Service Commission and the Chairman of the Advisory Committee and decides that the other conditions of service for these officials shall remain unchanged;

3. *Decides* that the compensation and other conditions of service of the full-time members of the International Civil Service Commission and of the Chairman of the Advisory Committee on Administrative and Budgetary Questions shall next be reviewed at the forty-fifth session of the General Assembly and that, pending such review, the annual compensation shall be adjusted in accordance with the procedure approved in General Assembly resolution 35/221, paragraph 3.

General Assembly resolution 40/256

18 December 1985   Meeting 122   Adopted without vote

Approved by Fifth Committee (A/40/1069) without vote, 14 December (meeting 65); 8-nation draft (A/C.5/40/L.8); agenda item 116.
Sponsors: Bangladesh, Cameroon, Guinea-Bissau, India, Jamaica, Nigeria, Pakistan, Zambia.
Financial implications: ACABQ, A/39/7/Add.1; S-G, A/C.5/38/27.

Also in December, the Assembly, by **resolutions 40/257 A-C**, took action on conditions of service and compensation for members of the International Court of Justice.

Experts and consultants

The Committee for Programme and Co-ordination, at its April-June 1985 session,[6] reiterated that the use of consultant services proposed for future years was excessive and not conducive to an optimum use of regular staff resources, and again called the Assembly's attention to the issue; it also recommended that the resources allocated for the programming of specific consultant services should be used for those purposes.

ECONOMIC AND SOCIAL COUNCIL ACTION

On 26 July 1985, the Economic and Social Council, on the recommendation of its Third (Programme and Co-ordination) Committee, adopted **resolution 1985/78**, without vote.

Hiring and use of consultant services
The Economic and Social Council,

Taking note of the relevant parts of the general conclusions and recommendations of the Committee for Programme and Co-ordination on the proposed programme budget for the biennium 1986-1987 as contained in its report on its twenty-fifth session,

Affirming that the use of consultant services is excessive and not conducive to an optimum utilization of regular staff resources,

Noting the importance of taking into account the appropriate competence, knowledge and expertise of the consultants,

Noting also the desirability of having as wide a geographical basis as possible in the hiring of consultants,

Recognizing the urgent need to address these and other related concerns regarding the hiring and use of consultant services by the United Nations and to take appropriate action,

1. *Requests* the Secretary-General to take into careful consideration the comments made on this question by Member States at the twenty-fifth session of the Committee for Programme and Co-ordination and at the sec-

ond regular session of 1985 of the Economic and Social Council;

2. *Also requests* the Secretary-General to continue to provide adequate information to the Committee for Programme and Co-ordination on the reasons why particular tasks could not be carried out by existing regular staff;

3. *Further requests* the Secretary-General to submit, through the Committee for Programme and Co-ordination and the Economic and Social Council, a detailed report on this question, including, *inter alia*, comments on the implementation of the existing guidelines on the hiring and use of consultant services by the United Nations, to the General Assembly at its forty-first session for consideration.

Economic and Social Council resolution 1985/78

26 July 1985   Meeting 52   Adopted without vote

Approved by Third Committee (E/1985/141) without vote, 19 July (meeting 20); draft by Bangladesh (E/1985/C.3/L.6), orally revised; agenda item 19.

Report of the Secretary-General. In a December 1985 report[7] on the use of experts, consultants and participants in *ad hoc* expert groups, the Secretary-General stated that during 1984 there were 440 cases in which 389 former staff members aged 55 or older were re-engaged throughout the Secretariat at all duty stations.

The interim measure instituted by the Assembly in 1982[8] limiting the annual emolument to $12,000 for United Nations Joint Staff Pension Fund beneficiaries did not affect the re-engagement of former staff members under letters of appointment (contract) exceeding six months, which automatically made them Fund participants again and suspended their benefits. Of the 440 cases, 267 received remuneration of less than $12,000, and 173 received more. The Secretary-General continued to believe that the application of the $12,000 limit to former staff performing language functions was not in the interests of the United Nations as it deprived the Organization of the use of valuable experience.

On 18 December, the General Assembly, by **decision 40/456**, adopted, without vote, on the recommendation of the Fifth Committee, decided to defer until its 1986 regular session consideration of the Secretary-General's report.

REFERENCES

[1]YUN 1983, p. 1199, GA res. 38/234, sect. XVII, 20 Dec. 1983. [2]YUN 1984, p. 1170, GA res. 39/236, sect. V, 18 Dec. 1984. [3]YUN 1983, p. 1199. [4]YUN 1984, p. 1170. [5]YUN 1980, p. 1178, GA res. 35/221, 17 Dec. 1980. [6]A/40/38 & Corr.1 & Add.1. [7]A/C.5/40/40. [8]YUN 1982, p. 1489, GA res. 37/237, sect. VIII, 21 Dec. 1982.

Chapter IV

Other administrative and management questions

During 1985, in a major step to improve the administrative and financial efficiency of the United Nations, the General Assembly decided to establish a group of high-level intergovernmental experts to conduct a review with a view to identifying measures that might be taken to that end (resolution 40/237). That decision was in addition to a number of other Assembly actions resulting from the yearly review of administrative and management issues relating to conferences and meetings, documentation, premises, information systems, telecommunications and postal administration. Besides authorizing certain subsidiary organs to meet during its 1985 session (decision 40/403), the Assembly approved a draft calendar of meetings for 1986 and 1987, reaffirmed principles governing the scheduling of conferences and meetings, and called for more efficient use of conference-servicing resources and for a review of the question of providing summary records (resolution 40/243). It also urged that, in the interests of efficiency and economy, discussions on unified conference services at the Vienna International Centre be resumed (decision 40/405).

Efforts to co-ordinate and enhance United Nations information systems continued during the year, and implementation of recommendations to modernize library operations, as recommended by the Joint Inspection Unit (JIU), was in progress. Meanwhile, JIU submitted to the Assembly recommendations for the effective management of computers and related new technologies increasingly used by the United Nations system. The Secretary-General reported on his decision against a United Nations–owned communications satellite in favour of leased communications facilities, and the Assembly approved his proposal for a new telephone system at Headquarters (resolution 40/252, section II). It also approved the 1986 budget estimates of the International Computing Centre (40/252, section X).

The Assembly took note of the new catering arrangements at Headquarters and the virtual completion of the construction of additional United Nations offices and conference facilities at Nairobi, Kenya (40/252, sections III and IV). It also decided on the disposition of revenues from the sale of a special postage stamp on the social and economic crisis in Africa (40/242).

Topics related to this chapter. Institutional machinery. Institutional arrangements.

Review of UN administrative and financial matters

In 1985, at a special session held in October by the General Assembly to commemorate the fortieth anniversary of the United Nations, Member States took the opportunity to take stock of the Organization's past performance and potentialities and to propose improvements (see p. 403). Among the proposals put forward was a text introduced by Japan on behalf of 12 sponsors and adopted by the Assembly as resolution 40/237, recommending the establishment of an 18-member group of high-level intergovernmental experts to identify measures to improve the efficiency of the administrative and financial functioning of the United Nations.

Also during the year, the Secretary-General transmitted to the Assembly a JIU report containing some reflections on reform of the United Nations (see p. 1231).

GENERAL ASSEMBLY ACTION

On 18 December 1985, the General Assembly adopted **resolution 40/237** without vote.

Review of the efficiency of the administrative and financial functioning of the United Nations
The General Assembly,
Recalling the purposes and principles of the Charter of the United Nations,
Recognizing that the Organization is based on the principle of the sovereign equality of all its Members,
Mindful of the vital role of the United Nations in the maintenance of international peace and security and in the promotion of development and international co-operation,
Convinced that the improvement of the efficiency of the administrative and financial functioning of the United Nations could help it to attain the purposes and implement the principles of the Charter,
Considering the unanimous support for the United Nations, expressed by heads of State or Government or their special envoys and by the representatives of Member States during the commemoration of the fortieth anniversary of the United Nations,
Noting that all participants stressed the need to promote confidence in the United Nations and enhance the political will of Member States to render more positive support to the Organization,
Reaffirming the necessity of securing, in the employment of the Secretariat staff, the highest standards of efficiency, competence and integrity, and the importance

of recruiting the staff based on the principle of equitable geographical distribution,

Noting with appreciation the efforts of the Secretary-General, as the chief administrative officer of the Organization, to improve the efficiency and effectiveness of the Secretariat,

Bearing in mind the work of the relevant subsidiary organs of the General Assembly,

Taking fully into account the views expressed during the fortieth session,

1. *Expresses its conviction* that an overall increase in efficiency would further enhance the capacity of the United Nations to attain the purposes and implement the principles of the Charter of the United Nations;

2. *Decides* to establish a Group of High-level Intergovernmental Experts to Review the Efficiency of the Administrative and Financial Functioning of the United Nations with a term of one year, to carry out in full accordance with the principles and provisions of the Charter the following tasks:

(a) To conduct a thorough review of the administrative and financial matters of the United Nations, with a view to identifying measures for further improving the efficiency of its administrative and financial functioning, which would contribute to strengthening its effectiveness in dealing with political, economic and social issues;

(b) To submit to the General Assembly, before the opening of its forty-first session, a report containing the observations and recommendations of the Group;

3. *Requests* the President of the General Assembly, in consultation with the regional groups, to appoint as soon as possible the members of the Group of High-level Intergovernmental Experts with due regard to equitable geographical distribution;

4. *Decides* that the Group will consist of eighteen members, and requests the Secretary-General to convene a meeting of the Group as soon as possible to enable it to elect its officers;

5. *Requests* the Secretary-General to provide the Group with the necessary staff and services;

6. *Also requests* the Secretary-General to provide full assistance to the Group, in particular by submitting his views and providing information necessary to conduct the review;

7. *Invites* the relevant subsidiary organs of the General Assembly to submit to the Group, through their chairmen, information and comments on matters pertaining to their work;

8. *Decides* to include in the provisional agenda of its forty-first session an item entitled "Review of the efficiency of the administrative and financial functioning of the United Nations: report of the Group of High-level Intergovernmental Experts to Review the Efficiency of the Administrative and Financial Functioning of the United Nations".

General Assembly resolution 40/237

18 December 1985   Meeting 121   Adopted without vote

12-nation draft (A/40/L.42/Rev.1); agenda item 39.
Sponsors: Australia, Austria, Bangladesh, Barbados, Canada, Finland, Jamaica, Japan, New Zealand, Norway, Samoa, Sweden.
Financial implications. 5th Committee, A/40/1063; S-G, A/C.5/40/95.
Meeting numbers. GA 40th session: 5th Committee 68, 69; plenary 121.

Among the States explaining their positions, Brazil felt that the text tended to imply that the United Nations capacity to attain the purposes of the Charter and implement its principles depended on the increased efficiency of its administrative and financial functioning. If the United Nations lacked effectiveness, Brazil stated, it was due not to management's shortcomings but rather to the conflicting and sometimes irreconcilable goals and policies of Member States. In Peru's opinion, the momentum for improvement should come from Members' own efforts and determination rather than from outside, and should be aimed at making the Organization not only more efficient but also more equitable, independent and democratic.

Mexico said it failed to see the link between improved administrative and financial efficiency and full compliance with Charter purposes and principles; what was required was the political will to go beyond rhetoric and take action. Also, Mexico said, the Group should be unanimous in its recommendations, none of which should jeopardize the principle of equal sovereignty of States, and the independence and effectiveness of the United Nations should in no way be undermined by pressure, financial or otherwise. The factors responsible for the Organization's problems, Democratic Yemen said, were the lack of political will to arrive at solutions and failure to heed resolutions.

Singapore agreed with Democratic Yemen, but stressed that since the text's intent was to improve efficiency, and since such improvement could only help to rebuild United Nations prestige and credibility, it supported the resolution and called on other small States to do likewise. Solomon Islands saw the resolution as a move towards greater efficiency, economy and achievement, in view of what it said were rising personnel costs and increasing numbers of conferences and seminars, among the ever-growing expenditures.

The Syrian Arab Republic said it would have preferred the Group's mandate to be more clearly defined; it was imperative to appoint the Group on an equitable geographic and political basis, with a fair representation of the Group of 77 developing countries.

Argentina believed that the resolution's purpose would not be achieved without the full agreement and co-operation of all Members. Burundi, speaking for the African Group, noted that the resolution had been submitted in a difficult context, where problems believed to be uniquely financial and administrative could ultimately lead to extreme politicization. Burundi emphasized that all studies mandated by the resolution should be in strict accord with Charter principles and that any reform should take account of the principle of sovereign equality of States.

Cuba, along with Mexico, Saudi Arabia and Uruguay, shared the understanding that the Group's work would focus exclusively on administrative and financial matters.

Conferences and meetings

In 1985, the 22-member Committee on Conferences convened in New York for an organizational meeting on 11 February and for a substantive session from 26 to 30 August.[1] At the organizational meeting, the Committee decided on its programme of work for 1985-1986 and adopted a biennial approach to its work in compliance with General Assembly resolutions of 1983[2] and 1984.[3] Accordingly, in 1985 the Committee concentrated on matters relating to the pattern of conferences and the efficient use of conference-servicing resources, deferring to 1986 matters relating to the control and limitation of documentation.

The Committee recommended Assembly consideration of a draft resolution on the pattern of conferences and a draft calendar of conferences and meetings for 1986-1987 (see below).

Calendar of meetings

Pursuant to a 1984 General Assembly request,[4] the Committee on Conferences[1] in 1985 studied in depth the existing provisions relating to the pattern of conferences. It took into account the modifications it had proposed in 1983[5] intended to update the basic conference-servicing provisions adopted by the Assembly in 1976.[6] It examined the related questions of improved utilization of conference-servicing resources and the frequency of planning missions for meetings or conferences held away from United Nations Headquarters (see p. 1259).

The Committee considered a Secretariat report on current procedures for implementing that provision of a 1979 Assembly decision[7] stating that no subsidiary organ of the Assembly should be permitted to meet at Headquarters during a regular Assembly session, unless explicitly authorized by the Assembly. The report noted that a number of requests for exceptions were received each year, for which detailed substantive reasons were not normally given. It was agreed that the Chairman, having received a request for an exception to that provision, which should contain details of why the meeting was necessary, would circulate it to Committee members; on the basis of their replies, and if necessary a Committee decision, he would advise the Assembly President.

In addition, the Committee reviewed its own procedures for examining proposals with conference-servicing implications put forward at Assembly sessions, as required by a 1980 Assembly resolution.[8] It agreed to examine any such proposal before action on it was taken by the Main Committee concerned, to allow timely submission of the resulting observations to that Main Committee, as well as to the Advisory Committee on Administrative and Budgetary Questions (ACABQ) and to the Fifth (Administrative and Budgetary) Committee for their consideration.

Following extensive consultations, the Committee reached consensus on a draft resolution containing proposals to serve as a framework for more accurate forecasting of conference-servicing needs.

GENERAL ASSEMBLY ACTION

Acting on the recommendation of the Fifth Committee, the General Assembly adopted **resolution 40/243** on 18 December 1985: section I, by recorded vote, and the resolution as a whole, without vote.

Pattern of conferences
The General Assembly,

Recalling its resolutions 1202(XII) of 13 December 1957, 1851(XVII) of 19 December 1962, 1987(XVIII) of 17 December 1963, 2116(XX) of 21 December 1965, 2239(XXI) of 20 December 1966, 2361(XXII) of 19 December 1967, 2478(XXIII) of 21 December 1968, 2609(XXIV) of 16 December 1969, 2693(XXV) of 11 December 1970, 2834(XXVI) of 17 December 1971, 2960(XXVII) of 13 December 1972, 3350(XXIX) and 3351(XXIX) of 18 December 1974, 3491(XXX) of 15 December 1975, 31/140, section I, of 17 December 1976, 38/32 C of 25 November 1983 and 39/68 C of 13 December 1984,

I

Having considered the report of the Committee on Conferences,

1. *Takes note with appreciation* of the report of the Committee on Conferences;

2. *Approves* the draft calendar of conferences and meetings of the United Nations for the biennium 1986-1987 as submitted by the Committee on Conferences;

3. *Authorizes* the Committee on Conferences to make any adjustments in the calendar of conferences and meetings for the biennium 1986-1987 that may become necessary as a result of action and decisions taken by the General Assembly at its fortieth session;

4. *Reaffirms* the general principle that, in drawing up the schedule of conferences and meetings, United Nations bodies shall plan to meet at their respective established headquarters, with the following exceptions:

(a) The regular sessions of the Governing Council of the United Nations Development Programme shall be held alternately at United Nations Headquarters and at the United Nations Office at Geneva;

(b) The sessions of the International Law Commission shall be held at the United Nations Office at Geneva;

(c) The sessions of the United Nations Commission on International Trade Law may be held, subject to the provision in General Assembly resolution 2205(XXI), section II, paragraph 6, of 17 December 1966, alternately at United Nations Headquarters and at the United Nations Office at Vienna;

(d) The second regular session of the Economic and Social Council may be held at the United Nations Office at Geneva provided that the closing date falls at least six weeks before the opening of the regular session of the General Assembly;

(e) The functional commissions of the Economic and Social Council shall meet at their established headquarters unless the Council designates another place to achieve a more rational pattern of the work programme, taking into account any recommendation of the commission concerned and in consultation with the Secretary-General;

(f) The regular sessions of the Economic and Social Commission for Asia and the Pacific, the Economic Commission for Latin America and the Caribbean, the Economic Commission for Africa and the Economic and Social Commission for Western Asia, as well as meetings of their subsidiary bodies, may be held away from their headquarters when the commission concerned so decides, subject, in the case of regular sessions of the commissions, to the approval of the Economic and Social Council and the General Assembly;

(g) The International Civil Service Commission shall hold its regular annual session at United Nations Headquarters and, if more than one session is required in any one year, may accept an invitation from one of its participating organizations to hold its other session or sessions at the headquarters of that particular organization;

(h) The sessions of the Legal Sub-Committee of the Committee on the Peaceful Uses of Outer Space shall be held alternately at United Nations Headquarters and the United Nations Office at Geneva;

(i) The Conference on Disarmament shall meet at the United Nations Office at Geneva;

5. *Decides* that United Nations bodies may hold sessions away from their established headquarters when a Government issuing an invitation for a session to be held within its territory has agreed to defray, after consultation with the Secretary-General as to their nature and possible extent, the actual additional costs directly or indirectly involved;

6. *Reaffirms* its instruction to all its subsidiary organs to complete their reports for the following session of the General Assembly no later than 1 September and, where necessary, to report to the Assembly in addenda to the reports of the organs concerned any activity undertaken after the adoption of such reports;

7. *Decides* that no subsidiary organ of the General Assembly may meet at United Nations Headquarters during a regular session of the Assembly unless explicitly authorized by the Assembly;

8. *Requests* the Secretary-General to continue to provide interpretation services for informal meetings on an *ad hoc* basis in accordance with established practice;

9. *Authorizes* the Secretary-General to apply maximum overprogramming of meetings whenever possible to achieve better utilization of conference resources;

10. *Requests* the Committee on Conferences and the Secretary-General to take account of the following principles in drawing up the draft calendar of conferences and meetings:

(a) The biennial calendar of conferences and meetings approved by the General Assembly shall govern the meetings programme during the period concerned;

(b) All United Nations meetings shall be conducted within the resources allocated by the General Assembly for that purpose;

(c) Between sessions of the General Assembly, departures from the calendar may, in special or unusual circumstances, be approved by the Committee on Conferences provided that changes affecting the subsequent year of the biennium shall be approved by the Assembly;

(d) Subsidiary organs of the General Assembly shall not, without the approval of the Assembly, create new standing bodies or *ad hoc* sessional or inter-sessional bodies that require additional resources, and other principal organs of the United Nations should make similar decisions with regard to their respective subsidiary bodies, if they have not already done so;

(e) An adequate interval of time, to be determined by the body concerned, shall be allowed between sessions of a body to permit Member States to derive maximum benefit from the activities and to provide sufficient time for the preparation of future activities;

(f) United Nations bodies shall meet at their respective established headquarters, subject to the exceptions to this principle approved by the General Assembly;

(g) The capacity of the documentation services of the Secretariat to process and issue in time the documentation required for the sessions of all scheduled organs should be taken into account;

(h) No more than one special conference of the United Nations shall be convened at the same time;

(i) In any given year, no more than five special conferences should be convened, unless the General Assembly specifically decides otherwise;

11. *Requests* the Secretary-General to ensure the most rational and effective use of all United Nations conference centres and facilities;

12. *Requests* the Committee on Conferences to continue its periodic examination of the rules governing conference planning;

II

1. *Urges* all United Nations bodies to increase their efforts to ensure that their requests for conference-servicing resources correspond accurately to their requirements;

2. *Further urges* those bodies to plan their work well in advance in order to make full use of the conference-servicing resources allocated to them and so that any unused conference-servicing resources can be reassigned to ensure their most effective utilization;

3. *Requests* subsidiary organs of the General Assembly to include in their reports to the Assembly a statement on the progress made in response to the relevant provisions of Assembly resolution 39/68 B of 13 December 1984 on the rational and efficient utilization of conference-servicing resources;

4. *Urges* intergovernmental bodies reporting to the Second Committee of the General Assembly that have not yet adjusted their meeting cycles to conform to that Committee's biennial programme of work to do so as soon as possible;

5. *Requests* the Secretary-General to review the composition and frequency of planning missions for meetings and conferences held away from Headquarters, in particular those sent to cities where United Nations conference facilities already exist;

6. *Also requests* the Secretary-General to report to the Committee on Conferences at its substantive session of 1986 on the results of that review concerning planning missions sent in 1985 and, as far as possible, in 1986;

III

1. *Decides* that the Committee on Conferences should review the question of the provision of summary records at its substantive session in 1986;

2. *Also decides* that the present experimental arrangements for summary records, established by the General Assembly in its resolution 37/14 C of 16 November 1982, should remain in effect until the

Assembly, upon the recommendation of the Committee on Conferences, takes further action.

General Assembly resolution 40/243

18 December 1985   Meeting 121   Adopted without vote
                                                        Sect. I, 131-1-17 (recorded vote)

Approved by Fifth Committee (A/40/847) without vote, 1 November (meeting 24); draft by Committee on Conferences (A/40/32); agenda item 121.
Financial implications. 5th Committee, A/40/974; S-G, A/C.5/40/34.
Meeting numbers. GA 40th session: 5th Committee 9, 10, 14, 15, 17, 18, 22, 24, 52; plenary 121.

Recorded vote in Assembly as follows:

In favour: Afghanistan, Algeria, Angola, Antigua and Barbuda, Argentina, Austria, Bahamas, Bahrain, Bangladesh, Barbados, Belize, Benin, Bolivia, Botswana, Brazil, Brunei Darussalam, Bulgaria, Burkina Faso, Burma, Burundi, Byelorussian SSR, Cameroon, Cape Verde, Central African Republic, Chad, Chile, China, Colombia, Congo, Costa Rica, Cuba, Cyprus, Czechoslovakia, Democratic Kampuchea, Democratic Yemen, Djibouti, Dominican Republic, Ecuador, Egypt, El Salvador, Equatorial Guinea, Ethiopia, Fiji, Finland, Gabon, Gambia, German Democratic Republic, Ghana, Greece, Guatemala, Guinea, Guinea-Bissau, Guyana, Honduras, Hungary, India, Indonesia, Iran, Iraq, Ireland, Ivory Coast, Jamaica, Jordan, Kenya, Kuwait, Lao People's Democratic Republic, Lebanon, Lesotho, Liberia, Libyan Arab Jamahiriya, Madagascar, Malawi, Malaysia, Maldives, Mali, Malta, Mauritania, Mauritius, Mexico, Mongolia, Morocco, Mozambique, Nepal, New Zealand, Nicaragua, Niger, Nigeria, Oman, Pakistan, Panama, Papua New Guinea, Peru, Philippines, Poland, Qatar, Romania, Rwanda, Saint Lucia, Saint Vincent and the Grenadines, Samoa, Sao Tome and Principe, Saudi Arabia, Senegal, Sierra Leone, Singapore, Solomon Islands, Somalia, Spain, Sri Lanka, Sudan, Suriname, Swaziland, Syrian Arab Republic, Thailand, Togo, Trinidad and Tobago, Tunisia, Turkey, Uganda, Ukrainian SSR, USSR, United Arab Emirates, United Republic of Tanzania, Uruguay, Venezuela, Viet Nam, Yemen, Yugoslavia, Zaire, Zambia, Zimbabwe.

Against: United States.

Abstaining: Australia, Belgium, Canada, Denmark, France, Germany, Federal Republic of, Grenada, Iceland, Israel, Italy, Japan, Luxembourg, Netherlands, Norway, Portugal, Sweden, United Kingdom.

Before the Fifth Committee approved the text, an oral amendment was proposed by the United States to delete subparagraph 4 *(f)* of section I. The United States view was that meetings of regional commissions away from their headquarters were not an efficient use of resources, which could be better spent on their development programmes. The amendment was rejected by a recorded vote of 81 to 2, with 23 abstentions. Argentina stated that meeting away from headquarters, a long-standing practice, helped to spread awareness of United Nations economic and social activities and allow commissions to observe conditions in developing countries at first hand.

Citing other exceptions to the general rule, Austria believed the whole issue of the meeting cycle of the commissions should have been given proper consideration in the Committee on Conferences. Canada, Cuba, Belgium (speaking for the 10 members of the European Economic Community), New Zealand and Sweden felt that the subparagraph should be interpreted in the light of paragraph 5, which stipulated that no additional costs to the United Nations should be incurred by any departure from the general rule. Japan considered it essential to review the application of existing rules on a continuing basis, particularly in relation to the availability of conference facilities.

A related oral amendment by the United States to the calendar of conferences—to change the venue of the 1986 session of the Economic Commission for Latin America and the Caribbean from Mex-

ico City to Santiago, the subject of Economic and Social Council **decision 1985/188**—was rejected by a recorded vote of 83 to 7, with 15 abstentions. Austria, Italy and Liberia said they could not support the United States amendment because conference facilities at Santiago did not appear to be adequate. France, the Netherlands and New Zealand said that what was really at issue was the question of additional costs incurred when commission sessions were held away from the headquarters, and they could therefore not support the amendment.

A USSR oral proposal was also rejected—by a recorded vote of 72 to 31, with 1 abstention—which would have left the venue of the March 1986 session of the International Civil Service Commission (ICSC) to be determined, rather than to be held at Nairobi; if a participating organization, i.e. a specialized agency, did not invite ICSC to meet at its headquarters, it should meet in New York, the USSR said. Algeria felt that challenging the consensus reached in the Committee on Conferences would not be constructive. Nigeria said ICSC had accepted an invitation from the United Nations Environment Programme (UNEP), which it interpreted to be a participating organization as referred to in paragraph 4 *(g)*, so there was no basis for the Soviet amendment.

Calendar for 1985

Between 11 February and 27 June, and during its August session, the Committee on Conferences[1] considered seven requests for departures from the approved calendar of conferences and meetings for 1985,[9] as amended by subsequent resolutions and decisions of the 1984 General Assembly session and decisions of the Economic and Social Council at its 1985 organizational (February) session.[10] Six of those requests were approved by the Committee: the addition of the Conference on the Emergency Situation in Africa; a change in venue for the Board of Trustees of the United Nations Voluntary Fund for Victims of Torture; a resumed session of the Commission on the Status of Women acting as the Preparatory Body for the World Conference to Review and Appraise the Achievements of the United Nations Decade for Women; a change of dates and venue of the Advisory Board on Disarmament Studies; extension of the session of the General Conference of the United Nations Industrial Development Organization (UNIDO); and holding meetings of the Committee on Negotiations with Intergovernmental Agencies during the Assembly session.

The Committee did not approve a request for a change of venue, from New York to Geneva, of the Preparatory Committee for the International Conference on the Relationship between Disarmament and Development.

The Committee later informed the Assembly President, by letters of 12,[11] 17[12] and 19

September[13] and 26 November,[14] of a number of requests from subsidiary organs to meet in New York during the 1985 Assembly session in order to fulfil their mandates. The Committee did not object, on the understanding that the meetings requested would be accommodated as facilities and services became available so as not to disrupt Assembly activities. The meetings, including those requested in the first two letters as endorsed by the General Committee in September,[15] were authorized by the Assembly decision below.

GENERAL ASSEMBLY ACTION

Acting on the recommendations of the General Committee and the Committee on Conferences, the General Assembly adopted without vote **decision 40/403.**

Meetings of subsidiary organs during the fortieth session

At its 3rd and 96th plenary meetings, on 20 September and 29 November 1985, the General Assembly, on the recommendations of the Committee on Conferences and of the General Committee, decided that the following subsidiary organs should be authorized to hold meetings during the fortieth session:

(a) *Ad Hoc* Committee on the Indian Ocean;

(b) Advisory Committee on the United Nations Educational and Training Programme for Southern Africa;

(c) Committee of Trustees of the United Nations Fund for South Africa;

(d) Committee on Relations with the Host Country;

(e) Committee on the Exercise of the Inalienable Rights of the Palestinian People;

(f) Committee on the Review and Appraisal of the Implementation of the International Development Strategy for the Third United Nations Development Decade;

(g) Special Committee against *Apartheid;*

(h) Special Committee to Investigate Israeli Practices Affecting the Human Rights of the Population of the Occupied Territories;

(i) United Nations Council for Namibia;

(j) Working Group on the Financing of the United Nations Relief and Works Agency for Palestine Refugees in the Near East.

General Assembly decision 40/403

Adopted without vote

Approved by General Committee (A/40/250) without vote, 18 September (meeting 1); proposals by Committee on Conferences (A/40/663, A/40/940); agenda item 8.

Calendar for 1986-1987

At its August session, the Committee on Conferences recommended for General Assembly approval a draft calendar of conferences and meetings for the biennium 1986-1987, drawn up as at 30 August 1985 and annexed to the Committee's report.[1] The Assembly in December approved the draft calendar—by section I of **resolution 40/243** on the pattern of conferences—and authorized the Committee to make any adjustments that might become necessary as a result of Assembly decisions at its current session.

During consideration by the Fifth Committee of the draft calendar and draft resolution, two oral amendments to the calendar were proposed, one by the USSR and the other by the United States. Both were rejected by recorded vote (see p. 1258).

Referring to item 61 of the calendar for 1986, Cameroon said its offer to host the 1986 session of the Economic Commission for Africa (ECA) at Yaoundé was to enable ECA members to witness at first hand the problems confronting the region as exemplified by Cameroon, and should not be regarded as a precedent.

Israel said that, had separate votes been taken on items, it would have voted against inclusion of the three entries in each of the draft calendars for 1986 and 1987 for meetings of the Economic and Social Commission for Western Asia and the Committee on the Exercise of the Inalienable Rights of the Palestinian People.

Conference and meeting services

In response to a 1984 General Assembly request,[3] the Committee on Conferences[1] resumed in 1985 its examination of the effective use of conference resources, including the shortening of sessions. The discussion, based on a Secretariat report containing statistics of 1984 meetings of United Nations organs in New York and at Geneva, encompassed the sources of wastage, namely, cancellations and the late starting and early ending of meetings, and the continuing policy of overprogramming, which entailed a measure of underutilization. Consideration was given to proposals that the Committee negotiate for a reduction of services for subsidiary organs that had made insufficient use of them in the past and that it ask those that had not utilized 75 per cent or more of their allocations in the preceding three years to consider whether all their allocations for 1986 were necessary.

The Committee also considered the matter of planning missions undertaken prior to meetings or conferences to be held away from Headquarters. It examined for this purpose a Secretariat paper on missions undertaken in 1984, indicating the criteria used to determine their need as well as data on their composition, destination and cost.

The measures recommended by the Committee for the improved use of conference-servicing resources and for the further review of planning missions were adopted by the Assembly on 18 December as embodied in section II of **resolution 40/243.**

Earlier, on 14 December, the Fifth Committee, having considered the Secretary-General's consolidated statement[16] of programme budget implications of conference-servicing costs for the proposed 1986-1987 budget (see Chapter I of this section) and the related ACABQ recommendation,[17] approved by a recorded vote of 71 to 12, with 12 abstentions, additional appropriations of $3,400,000 for such costs in 1986. Of that amount, $3 million was for Headquarters and $400,000 for Geneva, reduced from $4,448,200 and $711,000, respectively, which had been requested by the Secretary-General.

In the opinion of ACABQ, there was no need to act on the request for $601,700 for Vienna; the amount was provisional, pending experience in operating interim conference-servicing arrangements agreed upon between the United Nations and UNIDO (see below). Additional appropriations could be considered in 1986.

Also in December, by **decision 40/421**, the Assembly deferred to its 1986 session consideration of the Secretary-General's report on draft standard rules of procedure for United Nations conferences (see p. 1181).

Unified conference services at the Vienna International Centre

In a September 1985 report,[18] the Secretary-General proposed a number of budgetary transfers and related administrative adjustments in the proposed 1986-1987 budget, aimed at pooling the conference-servicing resources at the Vienna International Centre into a unified conference service under the administrative responsibility of the United Nations. The report was submitted in response to two Assembly actions: one calling for such a service,[9] based on a recommendation of the Committee on Conferences; the other,[19] on a JIU recommendation endorsed by ACABQ.[20] These actions were taken in anticipation of the conversion of UNIDO to a specialized agency (see p. 591).

Under existing arrangements, conference services at Vienna were provided to United Nations entities sharing the Centre, including UNIDO, in translation, terminology, references, meetings planning and servicing, editorial and documents control, publications and distribution, and interpretation. These services were under UNIDO management and administration, in keeping with Department of Conference Services (DCS) guidelines. The International Atomic Energy Agency (IAEA) maintained a separate conference service, but informal co-operative arrangements were in force with some of its servicing units: printing and reproduction services were charged directly to the user; capital costs were shared in proportion to services received in the preceding year. In addition, DCS maintained a limited in-session reproduction capacity.

JIU recommendation 5 had called for: continuing the existing UNIDO/United Nations joint conference service after UNIDO became a specialized agency; formalizing the co-operative arrangements with IAEA; and pooling the other IAEA conference-servicing units into a single conference structure after application of the principles and criteria for future common services set forth by JIU in 1984.[20] In addition, the Secretary-General saw advantage in linking the Vienna conference service with its counterpart services in New York and Geneva through the world-wide communications network under United Nations control.

The Secretary-General's proposals for a unified conference service included the transfer of some $12.8 million budgeted under UNIDO and Administrative services, Vienna, to section 29 of the budget (Conference services, Vienna); redeployment of some $1.6 million of that amount for the conversion of temporary-assistance interpreter posts into established posts; and additional appropriations totalling $66,700 to upgrade posts to bring the level of the proposed service to a division.

The Secretary-General stated that a draft of his report had been submitted to UNIDO and IAEA for review. While the IAEA comments had been taken into account, UNIDO had expressed strong reservations about the immediate establishment of the proposed unified service.

Commenting on the Secretary-General's report, ACABQ[21] noted that, in the absence of an agreed approach by the parties involved, it appeared doubtful that the Secretary-General's proposals could be implemented as they stood. Affirming its continued belief in the idea of unified conference services at Vienna for both economy and efficiency, it recommended that the Assembly request the Secretary-General urgently to resume discussions with UNIDO to resolve outstanding differences in time for a further report at the Assembly's current session.

GENERAL ASSEMBLY ACTION

Acting without vote on the recommendation of the Fifth Committee, the General Assembly adopted **decision 40/405.**

Unified conference services and other joint services for the United Nations organizations at the Vienna International Centre

At its 19th plenary meeting, on 2 October 1985, the General Assembly, on the recommendation of the Fifth Committee, recalling section IV of its resolution 39/242 of 18 December 1984, and mindful of the desirability of unified conference services and other joint services at Vienna:

(a) Requested the Secretary-General, on an urgent basis, to resume discussions on unified conference services and other joint services with the Director-General of the United Nations Industrial Development Organization with a view to resolving outstanding differences in time for a further report to be submitted to the Assembly later at its fortieth session;

(b) Requested the Secretary-General to communicate to the relevant bodies of the United Nations Industrial Development Organization its concern that no action should be taken by that organization that would either preclude further discussions by the Secretary-General and the Director-General on unified conference services and other joint services or prejudge the outcome of such discussions.

General Assembly decision 40/405

Adopted without vote

Approved by Fifth Committee (A/40/695) without objection, 1 October (meeting 5); draft by ACABQ (A/40/684), orally modified; agenda items 119, 120.

Pursuant to the foregoing decision, consultations took place at Vienna, from 14 to 16 October, between senior officials of the United Nations, UNIDO and IAEA. No agreement was reached on the need to proceed at once with setting up a unified conference service. It was agreed, however, that the conference-servicing requirements and facilities of the three Vienna-based organizations be analysed systematically in a comprehensive study, to be carried out jointly by them for submission to policy-making organs in 1987 so that conclusions could be reflected in the organizations' 1988-1989 budgets. In the interim, the United Nations would continue to provide translators and supporting staff to UNIDO, and UNIDO would operate a translation/documents service jointly servicing the United Nations and UNIDO. A joint UNIDO/United Nations meetings and interpretation service, to be operated by the United Nations, would be set up, consisting of the current Meetings Planning Unit and four interpreters and an additional 16 interpreter posts. IAEA indicated its interest in a common interpreters service.

The Secretary-General set out these arrangements in a November 1985 report,[22] in which he reiterated that a unified conference service, under United Nations responsibility, would provide maximum economy and efficiency to Member States.

REFERENCES

[1]A/40/32. [2]YUN 1983, p. 1201, GA res. 38/32 D, 25 Nov. 1983. [3]YUN 1984, p. 1174, GA res. 39/68 B, 13 Dec. 1984. [4]*Ibid.*, p. 1173, GA res. 39/68 C, 13 Dec. 1984. [5]YUN 1983, p. 1201. [6]YUN 1976, p. 908, GA res. 31/140, 17 Dec. 1976. [7]YUN 1979, p. 440, GA dec. 34/401, sect. V, 29 Nov. 1979. [8]YUN 1980, p. 1225, GA res. 35/10 A, 3 Nov. 1980. [9]YUN 1984, p. 1175, GA res. 39/68 A, 13 Dec. 1984. [10]A/AC.172/102. [11]A/40/632. [12]A/40/648. [13]A/40/663. [14]A/40/940. [15]A/40/250. [16]A/C.5/40/92. [17]A/40/7/Add.1-18, annex, paras. 51-55. [18]A/C.5/40/7. [19]YUN 1984, p. 1145, GA res. 39/242, sect. IV, 18 Dec. 1984. [20]*Ibid.*, p. 1181. [21]A/40/684. [22]A/C.5/40/48.

Documents and publications

Publications policy

In May 1985,[1] the Committee for Programme and Co-ordination (CPC) deferred to its 1986 session consideration of a 1984 JIU report on publications policy and practice in the United Nations system,[2] together with the related comments of the Secretary-General, the Administrative Committee on Co-ordination (ACC) and ACABQ.

A follow-up notice on the JIU recommendations was included in the Secretary-General's report to the General Assembly in September 1985[3] on implementation of JIU recommendations on various topics. The Secretary-General stated that implementation of the recommendations to improve both the approach to sales and free distribution and the information available to management had taken place, was under way or was under discussion by the Publications Board, the interdepartmental Secretariat body which established publications policy and monitored its implementation. The question of the relevancy of recurrent publications, recommended for examination by intergovernmental bodies, was the subject of a report currently before CPC (see below).

The matter of setting up publications committees at main office locations and in large author departments for quality control would be pursued; an alternative proposed by JIU was deemed impractical—to entrust that task to a single publications director. The other recommendations on improving quality were under discussion by the Publications Board, as well as by the Inter-agency Meeting on Language Arrangements, Documentation and Publications, which was also studying the recommendations on co-operation and consultation among organizations concerning information gathering, publications preparation and distribution, publications quality and appeal in relation to target readerships, future programmes and new production technologies.

The Secretary-General noted that the recommendations to reduce the quantity of published material were addressed to governing bodies and, to a large extent, duplicated earlier proposals.

As to the recommendations on making publications more effective in disseminating knowledge of the United Nations system and on integrating certain Department of Public Information audio-visual productions with United Nations publications, ways of realizing the first were being studied and the second being implemented within existing resources.

In March 1985, revised guidelines were issued on the Organization's policy towards copyrighting, granting permission to reproduce or translate its publications and documents or extracts therefrom, and using material copyrighted in the name of others in United Nations publications or documents.[4]

Documents limitation

In 1985, two categories of documentation—summary records and recurrent publications—were reviewed in an effort to keep their production within reasonable limits. The policies laid down by the General Assembly on the control and limitation of documentation were set forth by the Secretary-General in a note of 9 May,[5] which took account of policy decisions adopted by the Assembly from 1958 to 1984.

The Assembly in 1984 had requested[6] the Committee on Conferences to examine further the relative suitability of summary records as currently prepared and of the abbreviated summary records prepared experimentally. Thus in 1985, the Committee reported,[7] it had asked United Nations organs entitled to such records for their views on the matter. In the expectation of receiving more replies than it had at the time of its August session, the Committee decided to pursue the matter in 1986.

Responding to a CPC request that all recurrent publications of the United Nations should be examined in the light of the criteria set out by the Assembly in 1983,[8] the Secretary-General submitted a report[9] in April 1985 on the results of such an examination. The data, annexed to the report, included a list of all recurrent publications by title, when it was first published, periodicity, average preparation time, justification, number of copies and sales record. The report was to assist CPC in its examination of such publications for the proposed 1986-1987 budget. The report noted that no recurrent publication had yet been recommended for termination.

It was also noted that one of the criteria, namely, whether a publication contributed to promoting the Organization's principles and purposes, was not susceptible of a judgement based on quantifiable data; such a judgement fell within the competence of the author department or CPC. Whether a publication met the criteria of usefulness to the end-user, of filling a need, or of offering a high standard of analysis or data required reactions from end-users. Consequently, and in connection with a JIU recommendation to obtain feedback,[2] reader surveys had been undertaken by several author departments, including regional commissions. Such surveys were encouraged, not only by the Publications Board but also as a standard element of the Organization's internal evaluation system.

Owing to constraints of time, CPC on 25 May 1985[1] deferred consideration of the Secretary-General's report to 1986. The Economic and Social Council, by section IV of **resolution 1985/76** of 26 July, suggested that the report be considered in the context of CPC's discussion of the cross-organizational programme analysis of economic and social research and policy analysis (see p. 1044), with a view to identifying duplication and undue overlaps.

REFERENCES

[1]A/40/38. [2]YUN 1984, p. 367. [3]A/40/655 & Corr.1. [4]ST/AI/189/Add.9/Rev.1. [5]A/INF/40/1. [6]YUN 1984, p. 1176, GA res. 39/68 D, 13 Dec. 1984. [7]A/40/32. [8]YUN 1983, p. 1206, GA res. 38/32 E, 25 Nov. 1983. [9]E/AC.51/1985/14.

UN premises

Headquarters

Catering

On 31 March 1985, at the expiration of the contract for the catering operation at United Nations Headquarters, the financial arrangements for the operation were revised to provide that the contractor operate the facilities for a one-year period for its own account, beginning on 1 April 1985. Traditionally, the catering operation had been financed by the United Nations but managed by the contractor for the account of the United Nations; consequently, fluctuations in expenses and variations in sales had a direct, and often adverse, impact on the United Nations.

In an October report,[1] the Secretary-General stated that close monitoring revealed no discernible difference in the quality of services. He also stated that proposals for a new three-year contract, beginning on 1 April 1986, were being solicited.

Acting on the recommendation of ACABQ[2] and the Fifth Committee,[3] the General Assembly, on 18 December 1985, took note of the Secretary-General's report. The action was recorded in **section III of resolution 40/252**, adopted without vote.

Telephone system

In 1985, the Secretary-General proposed to acquire a new telephone system at United Nations Headquarters that, in the long term, would be cost effective (for details, including General Assembly action, see p. 1266).

Addis Ababa and Bangkok

In 1985, the Secretary-General submitted two reports concerning the headquarters premises of the Economic Commission for Africa at Addis Ababa, Ethiopia. One report[4] gave the status of the construction of additional conference facilities, approved by the General Assembly in 1984;[5] the other[6] set forth proposals for modification, refurbishing and repair of the existing main conference room, as well as for building maintenance.

The Secretary-General also submitted a progress report[7] on the construction project to expand the conference facilities of the Economic and Social Commission for Asia and the Pacific at Bangkok, Thailand, also approved in 1984.[8]

(For details, including Assembly action, see ECONOMIC AND SOCIAL QUESTIONS, Chapter VIII.)

Nairobi

Construction

A final progress report—the last of those submitted by the Secretary-General in accordance with a 1980 request of the General Assembly[9]—was submitted in October 1985[10] on the construction and office space requirements for the United Nations Office at Nairobi. According to the report, the United Nations complex (Gigiri complex) was virtually completed. The remaining task of supervising the completion of two underground water-storage tanks, the installation of the closed-circuit television surveillance systems and the construction of a fire-engine house was transferred on 30 September 1985 to the Common Services Unit (see below). It was estimated that all outstanding items would be completed by the end of the year.

Additional to the original construction project, a number of items were approved from within existing resources: one office block; the visitors' and tours' pavilion; furniture for the coffee lounges; film projectors, spotlights and loudspeakers for the main conference rooms; electronic voting systems; landscaping and fence reinforcements; upgrading of the interpretation booths and equipment; security-checking and television surveillance equipment; a fire-engine; a mini-van; three patrol cars; and spare parts for electrical and mechanical equipment.

Of the $27,078,200 that had been appropriated, a balance of $401,200 remained unencumbered as at 31 July 1985. The Secretary-General proposed to use it for the rehabilitation of oxidation ponds, generators, zoning and metering of the conference and cafeteria lighting systems, renovation of bridge links, road repairs, lobby improvements and other miscellaneous items. On their completion, expected before the end of 1986, he would close the Nairobi construction account. The balance and its disposition were noted by ACABQ.[11]

On 18 December 1985, acting without vote on the recommendation of the Fifth Committee,[3] the General Assembly took note of the Secretary-General's report; the decision became **section IV of resolution 40/252**.

Common services

As proposed by the Secretary-General in 1983,[12] the United Nations Common Services Unit (UNCS) at Nairobi was set up on 1 July 1984 to provide a number of common services—utilities, security, local transportation of staff and management of buildings and grounds—to the United Nations offices at the Gigiri complex. Those offices included UNEP headquarters and the United Nations Centre for Human Settlements (UNCHS), as well as the regional offices of the United Nations Children's Fund, the International Civil Aviation Organization, and the United Nations Educational, Scientific and Cultural Organization which moved to the premises on 25 October 1985.

When the original estimates were prepared, only six months' experience had been gained in maintaining the new Gigiri complex and a review of its maintenance and operations requirements had been

undertaken too late to be reflected in the 1986-1987 budget. Consequently, ACABQ[13] recommended an amount of $3,243,700 for common services (a maintenance level) pending revised estimates based on the review.

The revised estimates, submitted by the Secretary-General on 14 October 1985,[14] totalled $4,446,400. Approval of that amount would require an additional appropriation of $1,202,700.

The report on estimates indicated that the rental rate of $66 per square metre arrived at in 1984[15] had been accepted by all tenants, resulting in an estimated rental income of $2,119,800. A reduced rental rate remained applicable to UNEP. Discussions had been held to determine whether certain services performed by UNEP and UNCHS could become joint services to be entrusted to UNCS.

ACABQ[11] recommended a $242,400 reduction in the Secretary-General's estimates, proposing $133,800 ($52,200 less) for a P-3 engineer post, six new temporary local-level posts and common staff costs; $364,400 ($100,000 less) for equipment rental and maintenance, including transportation; $110,000 ($36,600 less) for miscellaneous services; and $200,000 ($53,600 less) for furniture and equipment. This reduced the revised estimates from $4,446,400 to $4,204,000. Given the $3,243,700 already appropriated, the total required was $960,300.

This appropriation was part of the revised estimates under section 28 (Administration and management) of the proposed 1986-1987 budget approved in first reading by the Fifth Committee[3] on 20 November 1985 by a recorded vote of 79 to 9, with 17 abstentions.

Vienna

In 1985, the General Assembly considered proposals by the Secretary-General for unifying the conference services at the Vienna International Centre (see p. 1260).

REFERENCES
[1]A/C.5/40/17. [2]A/40/7/Add.1-18, annex, para. 14. [3]A/40/1069. [4]A/C.5/40/31/Rev.1. [5]YUN 1984, p. 620, GA res. 39/236, sect. III, 18 Dec. 1984. [6]A/C.5/40/36. [7]A/C.5/40/29. [8]YUN 1984, p. 628, GA res. 39/236, sect. XI, 18 Dec. 1984. [9]YUN 1980, p. 1239, GA res. 35/222, 17 Dec. 1980. [10]A/C.5/40/14. [11]A/40/7/Add.8. [12]YUN 1983, p. 1208. [13]A/40/7. [14]A/C.5/40/19. [15]YUN 1984, p. 1180.

Information systems, computers and telecommunication

Co-ordination of information systems

In 1985, the Administrative Committee on Coordination reported[1] on continuing efforts to improve the co-ordination and compatibility of United

Nations information systems through its Advisory Committee for the Co-ordination of Information Systems (ACCIS). For the short term, those efforts concentrated on three specific projects: setting up a register of United Nations development activities; preparing a telecommunications map and formulating standards for documents transmission; and compiling an inventory of accessible data bases and conducting a survey of dissemination policies.

At ACC's request, ACCIS convened a special session on 14 and 15 January to consider the final design, scope and problems of the Register of Development Activities for presentation to CPC. Called for in 1982 by the Economic and Social Council[2] and the General Assembly,[3] the proposal for the Register was formulated by an ACCIS technical panel and presented to ACC in 1984.[4] The special session estimated the cost to each organization participating in the Register and the cost of merging all information in a central processing unit and making it available to end-users, identified as governmental units of member States and planning, programming and operational units of United Nations organizations.

On 25 May, following introduction of ACC's report on the Register,[5] CPC decided to transmit it to the Economic and Social Council. The Council took note of it on 26 July by section VII of **resolution 1985/76**, and invited ACC to proceed with the technical design for the establishment and operation of the Register and to submit to CPC a progress report, including information on cost, funding, assessment of usefulness and agency participation.

At its third session (Geneva, 23 and 24 September),[6] ACCIS, in addition to reviewing further work on the Register, examined a report on the outcome of an experiment in the use of commercial communication systems to interconnect United Nations offices at Geneva, Nairobi, New York, Paris, Rome, Tokyo, Vienna and the offices of the regional commissions. Undertaken by its technical panel on computer-based communication services, the experiment raised the question of transmission standards, which the panel was to pursue, along with its task of preparing a telecommunications map showing existing telecommunications links (including telex), especially with developing countries. In connection with the development of a telecommunications network for the United Nations system, ACCIS welcomed the decision of the International Telecommunication Union (ITU) to study the question of the use of such a common network by the United Nations and interested specialized agencies.

ACCIS also considered the question of access to information about United Nations serial publications, currently maintained in the central data base operated by the International Serials Data System (ISDS) in Paris—a world-wide network responsible for the creation and maintenance of a register of world serial publications—but not directly accessible by end-users. ACCIS agreed to serve as the channel for requests for such information and, for that purpose, would maintain a subfile of United Nations serials at ISDS. The question of access to information on serials in machine-readable form was to be examined by the technical panel on data base access, which had also been entrusted with compiling an inventory of publicly available data bases and of current practice and policy on their availability, including access by member States, and with formulating guidelines governing access to data bases within the United Nations system.

In January, ACCIS published the *Directory of United Nations Data Bases and Information Systems,* listing over 600 selected data bases, information systems and information services operated by 38 organizations. It also continued publication of the bimonthly *ACCIS Newsletter.*

ACCIS regrouped its work for 1986-1987 under three subprogrammes: information resources of the United Nations system; tools for improving system-wide information infrastructure; and basic co-ordination services. An item on a clearing-house on office information management was added.

On 29 October,[7] ACC revised the structure of ACCIS by designating the chairmen of its technical panels *ex officio* members of the Steering Committee and inviting that Committee to appoint a vice-chairman for ACCIS.

Other activities. The United Nations continued during 1985 to operate several information systems concerned with special aspects of development. These included the Industrial and Technological Information Bank of UNIDO and the International Referral System for sources of environmental information of UNEP (see pp. 608 and 800).

Budget of the International Computing Centre

In October 1985,[8] the Secretary-General submitted to the Fifth Committee the 1986 budget estimates for the International Computing Centre (ICC) at Geneva, as reviewed by the United Nations and 13 other participating organizations and programmes using and financing ICC services. The United Nations share was $1,420,000 against a total of $5,365,500.

In recommending acceptance of the estimated amount, ACABQ[9] noted that its recommendation had no impact on the resources already approved by the Fifth Committee under the relevant section of the proposed 1986-1987 programme budget in respect of United Nations usage of ICC.

On 18 December 1985, on the recommendation of the Fifth Committee,[10] the General Assembly approved, by **section X of resolution 40/252**, the ICC budget estimates for 1986.

Library operations

In his annual report on implementation of JIU recommendations,[11] the Secretary-General stated that, with respect to the 1984 recommendations concerning library operations in the United Nations system,[12] measures for management improvement and new technology (recommendations 2 and 3) were being introduced at the Dag Hammarskjöld Library at Headquarters. Pending determination by ACC of the feasibility of establishing an inter-library panel by the system's organizations (recommendation 1), specific areas delineated as possible foci of a practical, co-operative work programme for the panel had been undertaken by the Library, including development of a common indexing vocabulary and bibliographic control over system-wide documentation, training of library staff, microform programmes and closer working relationships with international library organizations.

Within its limited resources, the United Nations Library at Geneva, as a first step towards modernizing its facilities (recommendation 4), had begun to enter into the United Nations Bibliographic Information System (UNBIS)—the computer catalogue of the Dag Hammarskjöld Library—documents produced at Geneva; entry of monographs and articles received would follow. Further modernization, however, required additional resources.

Computer use

In July 1985, the Secretary-General transmitted to the General Assembly a JIU report[13] on management issues involved in the changing use of computers in organizations of the United Nations system at Geneva. JIU stated that the policy framework developed over the past 20 years for the system-wide computer and information system activities had three interrelated aims: to promote effective international information exchange, especially for development co-operation; to develop co-ordinated or at least compatible system-wide information systems; and to use computerized systems to improve operations.

In this context, JIU surveyed the applications, initiatives, opportunities and problems encountered in the use of new computer technologies in eight major areas: substantive data bases, substantive analysis, technical co-operation, communication, records management and archives, word processing, printing and publications, and administrative and management systems. Limited to 17 United Nations entities at Geneva, the survey found a sharp increase in computer use (from four computers in 1977 to 427 in mid-1984 and from 132 computer terminals to 1,867 in the same period) and computerized systems throughout the substantive, administrative and support activities of the organizations surveyed, against a background of extremely rapid and continuing changes in office technology.

JIU outlined eight recommendations, calling for each organization to set up a central mechanism (a unit, committee or individual) at a sufficiently high level and with adequate management and technical expertise, for planning and controlling of overall information systems development; to require periodic reports on systems development policy, specific services improved, processes streamlined and savings achieved; to develop and maintain a well-rounded computer training programme; and, in recruiting, to require a high degree of skill in both computer and management systems (recommendations 1, 2, 4 and 5).

It was also recommended that ACCIS set up an informal inter-agency computer working group at Geneva to share information on computerized systems development and explore opportunities for co-operation (recommendation 3). The Office of the United Nations High Commissioner for Refugees and the International Trade Centre UNCTAD/GATT should strengthen the professional staffing of their computer units (recommendation 6). It was suggested that the Secretary-General ensure a clear-cut process for overall United Nations information systems development, reassess the adequacy and centralized-decentralized balance of management services and computer systems staffing in major duty stations, and determine the staffing needs of the Management Systems Service at Geneva, based on a survey of user requirements (recommendation 7). ACC was to develop and present to ITU a proposal to extend to the specialized agencies the telecommunications arrangements currently granted only to the United Nations (recommendation 8).

Telecommunication

Communications satellite

In keeping with a Committee on Information recommendation approved in 1984,[14] the Secretary-General, in April 1985,[15] presented to the Committee a report on the acquisition by the United Nations of its own communications satellite. The report was requested in the light of the Secretary-General's 1984 proposals to enhance the United Nations communications system.[16] The proposals provided for interconnecting the main United Nations offices and certain subsidiary offices with reliable multi-purpose telecommunication circuits for exclusive United Nations use 24 hours daily. The network would include United Nations–owned earth stations operating on leased satellite circuits primarily for use by peace-keeping missions.

As approved by the Assembly, the proposals were in the process of being implemented and were expected to become operational, on a staggered basis, during the second half of 1985. A complementary upgrading of communications facilities at Headquarters was also taking place (see below).

The report stated that, given the heavy cost, as well as the legal and technical difficulties inherent in a United Nations–owned and –operated satellite system, the Secretary-General had decided, for the time being at least, on the use of leased communications circuitry, combined with arrangements for using existing satellite facilities.

The enhanced system would serve as the framework on which an even more comprehensive one would eventually be built. As the regional telecommunications centres matured and procedures developed, regional systems might be extended. Direct, exclusive-use circuitry could be established between the United Nations information centres and the appropriate regional communications hub, facilitating information exchange and rapid information dissemination.

Following examination of the Secretary-General's report, the Committee recommended[17] to the Assembly that the Secretary-General's assessment be noted and that the acquisition of a United Nations-owned communications satellite be re-examined, should circumstances permit. The attention of the pertinent United Nations organs should be drawn to the 1984 findings of ITU against such acquisition,[18] especially as concerned the problem, given the heavy satellite traffic and absence of proper orbital locations, of positioning a United Nations satellite in the geostationary orbit.

Telephone system

In a September 1985 report,[19] the Secretary-General proposed to purchase a new telephone system at United Nations Headquarters. The proposal was born out of developments in the United States telephone industry, in particular the break-up on 1 January 1984 of the American Telephone and Telegraph Company, which had made it financially and operationally advantageous to own, rather than to lease, telephones and related circuits and switching equipment. Seventeen companies in seven different countries had been invited to submit proposals for consideration by the United Nations.

The proposal called for the acquisition of a digital Private Automated Branch Exchange, a switching system capable of servicing 7,500 telephone lines, to be located at Headquarters. The purchase would include internal lines, instruments and other equipment that were currently being rented. However, 1,000 outside lines would continue to be rented to handle incoming and outgoing calls. Savings would result not only from the lower cost of toll calls but, more significantly, from a reduction in the number of rented circuits and telephones.

The Secretary-General proposed that the acquisition be financed through a lease/purchase agreement over 60 months at a cost of $9,438,000, paid in five annual payments starting in 1987, covering principal and interest. Annually, $100,000 would be required for normal costs related to office moves. At the end of the one-year warranty period, a maintenance and installation contract would annually cost $535,000.

The total cost of the system over its expected 13-year life was estimated at $28,130,000; that of purchasing and operating it (including rented circuits) over the five-year acquisition period, $14,862,500—resulting in savings, respectively, of $32,409,000 and $4,022,900 over costs that would be incurred if the existing system were maintained. For 1986, costs would be $3,255,000; for 1987, they would be $2,626,800—a total requirement of $5,881,800 for the 1986-1987 biennium.

ACABQ[20] said it was clear that significant savings would result. Assured that the system would be adequate for the foreseeable future, was currently available and did not depend on further new technology, ACABQ accepted the proposal and reduced by $8,400 the amount already appropriated in the 1986-1987 budget for telephone rental and installation. The Fifth Committee[10] approved this reduced appropriation, along with other associated revised estimates under the same budget section 28, on 20 November 1985, by a recorded vote of 79 to 9, with 17 abstentions, and, without objection, recommended Assembly approval of the Secretary-General's proposal for the acquisition of a telephone system at Headquarters, as detailed in his report.

Acting without vote on that recommendation, the Assembly on 18 December approved the proposal, embodied in **section II of resolution 40/252.**

REFERENCES

[1]E/1985/57. [2]YUN 1982, p. 1506, ESC res. 1982/71, 10 Nov. 1982. [3]*Ibid.*, p. 624, GA res. 37/226, 20 Dec. 1982. [4]YUN 1984, p. 1182. [5]E/AC.51/1985/7. [6]ACC/1985/23. [7]ACC/1985/DEC/16-29 (dec. 1985/26). [8]A/C.5/40/15. [9]A/40/7/Add.1-18, annex, para. 44. [10]A/40/1069. [11]A/40/655 & Corr.1. [12]YUN 1984, p. 1185. [13]A/40/410. [14]YUN 1984, p. 356, GA res. 39/98 A, 14 Dec. 1984. [15]A/AC.198/95. [16]YUN 1984, p. 1183. [17]A/40/21. [18]YUN 1984, p. 1184. [19]A/C.5/40/11 & Corr.1. [20]A/40/7/Add.4.

UN Postal Administration

In 1985, gross revenue of the United Nations Postal Administration from the sale of philatelic items at United Nations Headquarters and at overseas offices totalled more than $5.5 million. Revenue from the sale of stamps for philatelic purposes was retained by the United Nations; that from stamps used for postage from Headquarters was retained by the United States Postal Service under an agreement between the United Nations and the United States. Similarly, revenue from stamps used for postage from the United Nations Office at Geneva and from the Vienna International Centre was retained by the Swiss and Austrian postal authorities, respectively, in accordance with agreements between the Organization and Switzerland and Austria.

Five commemorative stamp issues, three souvenir sheets, two souvenir cards, six definitive stamps, three postal cards and one pre-stamped envelope were released during the year.

The first issue, on the "ILO—Turin Centre", was released on 1 February in denominations of 23 United States cents, 0.80 and 1.20 Swiss francs (SwF), and 7.50 Austrian schillings (S), together with a souvenir card.

The second issue, on the theme of "United Nations University—Research, Training, Knowledge", was released on 15 March, in denominations of 50 cents, SwF 0.50 and 0.80, and S 8.50.

The third issue, marking the "40th Anniversary of the United Nations", was released on 26 June in denominations of 22 and 45 cents, SwF 0.50 and 0.70, and S 6.50 and 8.50. Three souvenir sheets, in denominations of 67 cents, SwF 1.20 and S 15, were also released.

The fourth issue was a group of 16 stamps in the commemorative "Flag Series"—the sixth group in that series, released on 20 September in denominations of 22 cents each.

The fifth and final issue, on the theme of "Child Survival", was released on 22 November, in denominations of 22 and 33 cents, SwF 0.50 and 1.20, and S 4.50 and 6. A souvenir card accompanied the issue.

On 10 May, six definitives were issued in denominations of 22 cents and $3, SwF 0.20 and 1.20, and S 4.50 and 15. A 22-cent pre-stamped envelope was issued on the same date, along with postal cards at SwF 0.50 and 0.70, and S 4.

First-day covers for the various issues in 1985 were serviced in the numbers indicated below:

ILO—Turin Centre	310,924
United Nations University	279,074
40th Anniversary of the United Nations	873,063
Flag Series	1,774,193
Child Survival	664,151
Definitives:	
22 cents and $3	88,613
SwF 0.20 and 1.20	103,165
S 4.50 and 15	142,687
22-cent envelope	28,600
SwF 0.50 postal card	34,700
SwF 0.70 postal card	34,700
S 4 postal card	53,450

Special postage stamps

In response to a 1984 General Assembly resolution,[1] the Secretary-General reported on the project of issuing special postage stamps on the critical social and economic crisis in Africa. This was part of an overall analysis of the financial situation of the United Nations.[2]

The Secretary-General stated that a special postage stamp on the crisis had been approved and was scheduled for issuance on 31 January 1986. Total gross sales were estimated at $1.2 million, or $600,000 net after deduction of expenses. As stipulated by the same resolution,[1] one half of the net revenue would be earmarked for implementing the objectives set forth in the Declaration on the Critical Economic Situation in Africa;[3] the other half would be placed in a United Nations special account.

ACABQ took note of this information when it reviewed the Secretary-General's analysis as a whole.[4]

GENERAL ASSEMBLY ACTION

Acting without vote on the recommendation of the Fifth Committee, the General Assembly adopted **resolution 40/242** on 18 December 1985.

Issue of special postage stamps

The General Assembly,

Having considered the report of the Secretary-General on the analysis of the financial situation of the United Nations and the related report of the Advisory Committee on Administrative and Budgetary Questions,

Recalling its resolution 39/239 A of 18 December 1984,

Recognizing that, pending a comprehensive settlement of the differences which have given rise to the financial emergency of the Organization, partial or interim steps could enhance the liquidity of the Organization and alleviate its financial difficulties to some extent,

Noting with satisfaction that the project on the issue of special postage stamps on the social and economic crisis in Africa is well under way,

1. *Decides,* in accordance with its resolution 39/239 A, to place one half of the revenue earned therefrom at the disposal of the Secretary-General for the implementation of objectives as detailed in the Declaration on the Critical Economic Situation in Africa, adopted by the General Assembly on 3 December 1984, and to place the remaining half in a special account;

2. *Requests* the Secretary-General to take all necessary steps to economize on the operational expenses of the project on the issue of special postage stamps with a view to increasing the net revenue and to submit a financial report to the General Assembly at its forty-first session;

3. *Also requests* the Secretary-General to explore the possibility of having recourse to other feasible revenue-producing activities that could be undertaken by the United Nations.

General Assembly resolution 40/242

18 December 1985   Meeting 121   Adopted without vote

Approved by Fifth Committee (A/40/1060) without vote, 16 December (meeting 67); 32-nation draft (A/C.5/40/L.14); agenda item 118.

Sponsors: Algeria, Bangladesh, Barbados, Burkina Faso, Cape Verde, Chile, Costa Rica, Ghana, Guinea-Bissau, Honduras, India, Indonesia, Jamaica, Lebanon, Libyan Arab Jamahiriya, Malaysia, Mali, Morocco, Nigeria, Oman, Pakistan, Panama, Peru, Philippines, Senegal, Sierra Leone, Sweden, Thailand, Trinidad and Tobago, Tunisia, Turkey, Yugoslavia.

Meeting numbers. GA 40th session: 5th Committee 46, 47, 50, 67; plenary 121.

REFERENCES

[1]YUN 1984, p. 1187, GA res. 39/239 A, 18 Dec. 1984. [2]A/C.5/40/16. [3]YUN 1984, p. 470, GA res. 39/29, annex, 3 Dec. 1984. [4]A/40/831.

PART TWO

Intergovernmental organizations
related to the United Nations

International Atomic Energy Agency (IAEA)

In 1985, the International Atomic Energy Agency (IAEA) continued its activities to increase the contributions of atomic energy to peace, health and prosperity all over the world and to ensure that its assistance was not used for military purposes. Emphasis continued to be placed on safeguards, the safety of nuclear power stations, nuclear fuel-cycle services and the management of nuclear wastes, and on the provision of technical assistance to member States, especially developing countries.

At the end of 1985, 129 non-nuclear-weapon States were parties to the Treaty on the Non-Proliferation of Nuclear Weapons[a] (Non-Proliferation Treaty (NPT)) (Belize, Bhutan, Brunei Darussalam, Democratic People's Republic of Korea, Guinea, Kiribati and Seychelles having become parties during the year). Three nuclear-weapon States were also parties. On 10 June, the safeguards agreement relating to the offer by the USSR to place some of its peaceful nuclear installations under IAEA safeguards entered into force. In September, China announced that it was willing to place some of its civilian installations under IAEA safeguards at an appropriate time.

The Agency's efforts to increase nuclear safety and radiation protection were concentrated on developing radiation protection guidelines and helping member States to apply them. In addition, IAEA continued to provide a forum for the exchange of scientific information and to support research on radiation protection.

The development phase of the Nuclear Safety Standards (NUSS) programme was completed, and emphasis switched to implementing the 60 NUSS documents. The International Nuclear Safety Advisory Group held its first two meetings.

The Agency also continued to contribute to preparations for the United Nations Conference for the Promotion of International Co-operation in the Peaceful Uses of Nuclear Energy, scheduled for 1987.

The twenty-ninth session of the IAEA General Conference was held at Vienna, Austria, from 23 to 27 September. The Conference again demanded that South Africa immediately submit all its nuclear installations and facilities to Agency safeguards, and it called on member States which had not done so to end all nuclear co-operation with South Africa and to stop purchasing Namibian uranium. On the consequences of the 1981 Israeli military attack on an Iraqi nuclear research reactor,[b] the Conference took note of Israel's statement that it would not attack nuclear facilities devoted to peaceful purposes, and called on Israel to place all its nuclear facilities under IAEA safeguards. The Conference also approved the appointment by the Board of Governors of Hans Blix (Sweden) as IAEA Director General for a further four-year term beginning on 1 December 1985.

The Board met four times during 1985, once in February and June and twice in September at Vienna.

The membership of IAEA remained at 112 throughout 1985.

Agency safeguards responsibilities

As at 31 December 1985, 129 non-nuclear-weapon States and three nuclear-weapon States (USSR, United Kingdom, United States) had become party to NPT. There were 163 safeguards agreements in force with 96 States. Safeguards were applied in four nuclear-weapon States (France, USSR, United Kingdom, United States), pursuant to voluntary-offer agreements or to safeguards transfer agreements. Safeguards were also applied in 41 non-nuclear-weapon States under agreements concluded pursuant to NPT or to NPT and the Treaty for the Prohibition of Nuclear Weapons in Latin America (Treaty of Tlatelolco), and in one non-nuclear-weapon State pursuant to the Tlatelolco Treaty. During 1985, an amendment to an existing safeguards agreement with Spain entered into force, enabling Spain to place under IAEA safeguards any new peaceful nuclear facility it might acquire.

Safeguards under other agreements were in force with nine non-nuclear-weapon States not party to either NPT or the Tlatelolco Treaty—Argentina, Brazil, Chile, Cuba, India, Israel, Pakistan, South Africa and Spain. Safeguards were applied in eight of those States, as well as in the Democratic People's Republic of Korea and Viet Nam (both party to NPT).

At the end of 1985, safeguards applied by IAEA in non-nuclear-weapon States covered material in 172 power reactors, 177 research reactors and critical assemblies, 6 conversion, 37 fuel fabrication, 6 reprocessing and 5 enrichment plants, and 486 other installations.

[a]YUN 1968, p. 17, GA res. 2373(XXII), annex, 12 June 1968.
[b]YUN 1981, p. 275.

Technical assistance

During 1985, technical assistance in the form of expert services, equipment, fellowships and training courses was provided to 81 countries and regions. A total of 615 fellows underwent individual training, and 926 participants attended 60 training courses and study tours. A total of 121 technical officers provided support to 833 ongoing projects and undertook 418 assignments. Net expenditure on technical assistance reached $33.7 million.

Income to the IAEA Technical Assistance and Co-operation Fund (TACF), derived from voluntary contributions of member States and additional income, reached $25.2 million (a 13 per cent increase over 1984). Extrabudgetary funds exceeded $7.4 million, decreasing for the second consecutive year. UNDP and in-kind resources at IAEA's disposal increased to $2.6 million and $2.8 million respectively.

Programme emphasis varied from region to region. Agriculture was the leading sector for Africa and Latin America, and also for the programme as a whole. Industry and hydrology ranked first in Asia and the Pacific, nuclear safety in Europe and nuclear materials prospecting in the Middle East.

The contribution of developing countries to the technical co-operation programme continued to grow, with these countries providing 13.2 per cent of TACF resources. They provided 33 fellowships (worth $263,100) and 570 of the 1,483 experts and lecturers at IAEA training courses. Thirty-nine of the 60 training courses and 109 of the 638 places of study were in developing countries.

Nuclear power

At the end of 1985, there were 374 nuclear power plants in operation, with a total capacity of some 250,000 megawatts (electrical), accounting for 15 per cent of the world's electricity generation. Thirty-two new plants came on line during the year, which was marked by the start-up of the Super Phénix in France, of THTR-300 (thorium high temperature reactor) in the Federal Republic of Germany, and of India's fast breeder test reactor.

IAEA continued to help strengthen nuclear power planning in developing member States, through advisory missions, training courses and guidebooks. An Agency seminar attended by some 80 participants from 29 member States (including 18 developing countries) discussed the financing of nuclear power programmes; the participants concluded that IAEA could play a useful role by providing commercial lenders with objective information on the technical viability of nuclear power, and that the Agency's involvement in financial feasibility studies would carry considerable weight with lenders and export credit agencies.

Three interregional training courses in nuclear power planning were held (in Argentina and the United States). Regarding manpower and infrastructure, training activities continued to focus on the organization of courses at training centres in member States, emphasizing management tools and methods in the planning, construction and operational phases of projects. A seminar and three national courses on project management were held (in the Republic of Korea and Yugoslavia) to initiate continuous training in that subject. In the area of quality assurance and control, IAEA organized two interregional courses (in Argentina and the Federal Republic of Germany) and national courses for Iran, the Republic of Korea, Turkey and Yugoslavia.

The Agency continued to collect and disseminate information on nuclear technology and the technical aspects of nuclear power plants, and to publish guidebooks, reports and manuals.

Environment

In 1985, IAEA continued to carry out its waste management programme. Concerning handling, treatment, conditioning and storage of radioactive wastes, a research co-ordination meeting was held on the performance of solidified high-level waste forms and engineered barriers under repository conditions. A training course on radioactive waste management was held at Saclay, France, and a code of practice on that topic was issued.

An advisory group reviewed international standards and criteria for the underground disposal of high-level wastes. The code of practice on the management of wastes from the mining and milling of uranium and thorium ores was revised, and the revised texts sent to member States for comment.

In the area of disposal of radioactive waste at sea, a group of senior experts in radiation protection and waste management reached a consensus on principles for the exemption of radiation sources and practices from regulatory control. Preparations were made to publish a document on the subject in 1986.

Among material published in 1985 on environmental aspects of nuclear energy were the sixteenth annual edition of waste management research abstracts, five reports on the technology of waste handling, treatment and storage, a report on decontaminating nuclear facilities, some 30 reports on underground disposal of radioactive waste, and two reports relating to the disposal of radioactive material at sea.

Nuclear safety

In 1985, with the 60 documents in the NUSS series of safety codes and guides for nuclear power plants completed, activities aimed at helping member States to implement the NUSS documents—for example, by organizing training courses or producing supporting manuals—were intensified.

Activities relating to nuclear installation safety emphasized operational aspects. Among such activities were missions of operational safety review teams (OSART) to Brazil, France, Pakistan and the Philippines. Created in 1983, the OSART programme aims at further enhancing the safety of nuclear power plants. Each team carries out a thorough evaluation of the safety strengths and weaknesses of a given plant, and exchanges experience with the plant managers. France was the first industrialized country to receive an OSART mission, of which two types exist: missions to developing countries to provide an operational safety review service, and missions to industrialized countries to train review participants from developing countries.

Research reactor safety missions reviewed seven installations in Egypt, Pakistan, Turkey, Viet Nam and Yugoslavia.

A meeting was held in September in collaboration with the Nuclear Energy Agency of the Organisation for Economic Co-operation and Development to review lessons from significant incidents reported to IAEA's incident reporting system, which by the end of 1985 was receiving input from 22 countries.

Under the Agency's radiation protection programme, work continued on the elaboration of guidelines for implementing the system of dose limitation set forth in the revised Basic Safety Standards for Radiation Protection; guidelines were elaborated for the design of radiation protection systems, for operational radiation protection and for radiation monitoring. The proceedings of the 1984 IAEA/WHO symposium on the assessment of radioactive contamination in man were published.

Radiation protection services were provided to five countries with developing nuclear programmes. Missions visited Jordan, Kenya and Mali to advise on the establishment of national radiation protection services, and Algeria, Bolivia, Morocco and Tunisia in connection with technical assistance projects.

Safety information was disseminated world-wide through publications and various training courses; 89 technical co-operation projects concerning radiation protection were handled and 18 missions visited developing member States; fellowships in radiation protection were arranged for 62 persons from developing countries. The sixth international training course on the physical protection of nuclear facilities and materials, held at Albuquerque, United States, was attended by 25 participants from 17 member States.

Nuclear information

The International Nuclear Information System, with 74 participating countries and 14 international organizations, had enlarged its bibliographic data base on nuclear literature to 966,500 records by the end of 1985.

To commemorate the twenty-fifth anniversary of the journal *Nuclear Fusion*, IAEA produced a special issue reviewing the major nuclear fusion activities over the previous 25 years.

Life sciences

In collaboration with WHO and other international organizations, IAEA continued to render assistance to member States—particularly to developing ones—with the application of nuclear techniques in medicine, biology and health-related environmental research. It also continued to promote greater reliability and accuracy in radiation dosimetry for medical and industrial purposes.

An international symposium on nuclear medicine and medical applications of nuclear techniques in developing countries was held at Vienna in co-operation with WHO. An Agency seminar held in Kenya reviewed current nuclear techniques for the radiation sterilization of local medical supplies in developing countries of Africa and the Middle East.

Co-ordinated research programmes carried out by IAEA dealt with optimizing nuclear medicine procedures for the diagnosis and treatment of thyroid disorders; the quality control of assays of thyroid-related hormones; quality control of liver imaging procedures; maintenance of nuclear instruments in Asia and the Pacific and in Latin America; quality control of nuclear medicine equipment; promotion of nuclear techniques for radiation-sterilization of tissue grafts for clinical use in Asia and the Pacific; application of nuclear techniques in immunoprophylaxis and in the diagnosis of parasitic diseases; the evaluation of the use of monoclonal antibodies in radioimmunoassays as a means of achieving improvements in the diagnosis of schistosomiasis, malaria and filariasis; nuclear-related techniques in occupational health studies; and toxic elements in foodstuffs. Research co-ordination meetings evaluated the results of research programmes on radiation-induced chromosomal aberrations as a biological monitor in accidental over-exposure situations; on the radiation treatment of sewage sludge for disinfection and safe reutilization; on dietary intakes of nutritionally important trace elements; and on the relationship between hair mineral concentrations and internal body burdens.

Training provided by IAEA included a train-the-trainers course on radioimmunoassay held in China, with 16 trainees from South-East Asia; workshops on the quality control of nuclear medicine instruments held in Chile, Indonesia and Mexico; a regional dosimetry calibration workshop conducted at the Agency's Dosimetry Laboratory with the co-operation of the Hungarian Office of Measures; study tours on dosimetry in the Federal Republic of Germany, Hungary, Sweden and USSR; and a training course on neutron activation analysis held in India.

An IAEA/WHO technical co-operation project on the use of brachytherapy in treating cancer of the cervix continued; a third training/demonstration course held in Egypt was attended by specialists from Egypt, Kenya and the Sudan.

Physical sciences and laboratories

The Agency continued to promote exchange of information and to assist member States with the application of nuclear techniques in experimental physics, analytical and radiation chemistry, non-destructive testing, radiation processing, industrial process control, geology, mining and hydrology.

In the area of industrial applications of nuclear technology, co-ordinated research programmes were initiated on the radiation-induced modification of polymers for industrial and medical applications, and on the radiation-induced degradation of organic materials in nuclear environments. A research co-ordination meeting on nuclear techniques in mineral exploration, mining and processing showed that a significant degree of co-operation had been achieved among the countries participating in the co-ordinated research programme. Research programmes on the development of a new technology for technetium-99m generator systems and the development of new, more specific radiopharmaceuticals continued. As part of its efforts to promote the transfer of nuclear technologies employed in industry and chemistry, the Agency supported 116 technical co-operation projects in 44 countries.

Within the isotope hydrology programme, IAEA supported 41 technical co-operation projects in 34 countries; these projects dealt with the use of isotope techniques in solving hydrological problems in the development of water resources, water pollution, geothermal studies and sediment dynamics.

Four co-ordinated research programmes on isotope hydrology continued—one in the Far East financed by Australia, two in Latin America financed by the Federal Republic of Germany and Italy, and one covering eight countries in different parts of the world.

A regional seminar on the use of isotope techniques in arid and semi-arid lands, held at Adana, Turkey, was attended by 64 participants from 18 Middle East and North African countries.

The Agency continued to provide nuclear and atomic data services to member States and to co-ordinate the activities of a world-wide network of data centres. During 1985, it received more than 700 requests from 45 member States for experimental and evaluated data, data processing computer codes and publications.

In the framework of efforts to promote the transfer of nuclear data technology to developing member States, the Agency held an interregional training course on basic and applied nuclear physics. It continued to provide equipment, fellowships and experts for an interregional project on nuclear data techniques and instrumentation designed to train nuclear scientists in developing countries, and, at IAEA headquarters, it provided to three fellows from developing countries training in nuclear data compilation and computer processing.

The International Centre for Theoretical Physics (Trieste, Italy), jointly operated by IAEA and UNESCO, continued to address physics problems both of immediate practical relevance and of a more fundamental nature through colleges, workshops and other activities relating to physical processes and mathematical modelling. Over 2,500 scientists visited the Centre during 1985, staying for a total of almost 2,100 man-months; 60 per cent were from developing countries, and they accounted for 80 per cent of the total man-months. Under its associate membership scheme, the Centre welcomed 123 associates from 58 developing countries. Approximately 300 researchers from federal institutes in 50 developing countries visited the Centre.

The main areas of research and training-for-research in 1985 were physics and energy, fundamental physics, physics and technology, physics of the environment and of natural resources, physics and development, and mathematics. A summer workshop on high-energy physics and cosmology was attended by 144 researchers, 100 of whom were from developing countries. During the same period, a research workshop on condensed matter was attended by 243 scientists. A conference on south-south and south-north co-operation in science, hosted by the Centre and organized by the Third World Academy of Sciences, was opened by the United Nations Secretary-General and attended by nearly 200 scientists.

The IAEA Laboratory at Seibersdorf, Austria, continued to provide practical support to the Agency's agricultural biotechnology, life sciences, physical sciences and safeguards programmes. It also continued to promote the transfer of advanced techniques to developing member States through co-ordinated research, assistance with technical co-operation projects, and the training of young scientists and technicians. Agricultural work focused on fertilizers, plant breeding, animal production and pest control. Medical programmes included studies of trace elements in the human body. The Safeguards Analytical Laboratory analysed nuclear fuel-cycle samples collected by IAEA safeguards inspectors.

The International Laboratory of Marine Radioactivity in Monaco, with the collaboration of UNEP and UNESCO, continued to carry out research related to radiation protection aspects of waste management in the marine environment. These included provision of technical support for marine radioactivity monitoring and investigations, data collection for evaluating radiological impacts of radio-nuclide releases into the marine environment and participation in international marine pollution monitoring and research.

Food and agriculture

Under a joint programme with FAO, IAEA continued to help developing member States to improve their agriculture and food production through the application of isotopes, ionizing radiation and related techniques. The establishment of the International Consultative Group on Food Irradiation and the world-wide interest in irradiation for food preservation led to a further increase in related activities, especially the organization of advisory group and task force meetings on the various problems impeding the widespread commercial use of the process.

Assistance to member States continued through 150 technical co-operation projects and 423 research contracts and agreements. Projects on insect eradication in Egypt, Nigeria and Peru continued.

Secretariat

At the end of 1985, the IAEA secretariat had 1,942 staff members—715 in the Professional and higher categories (drawn from 79 countries), 1,091 in the General Service category and 136 in the Maintenance and Operatives Service category.

Budget

The regular budget total for 1986 was $118,756,000, of which $108,972,179 was to be financed from contributions made by member States on the basis of the 1986 scale of assessment, $4,458,000 from income from work for others and $5,325,821 from other miscellaneous income. The target for voluntary contributions to the IAEA technical assistance and co-operation programme in 1985 was set at $26 million; at the end of the year, member States had pledged $23,255,051 in support of the programme. During 1985, a total of $14,598,893 was offered in extrabudgetary contributions from member States, the United Nations and other international organizations.

Annex I.   MEMBERSHIP OF THE INTERNATIONAL
ATOMIC ENERGY AGENCY AND CONTRIBUTIONS

(Membership as at 31 December 1985; contributions as assessed for 1985 and 1986)

MEMBER	CONTRIBUTION FOR 1985 Percentage	CONTRIBUTION FOR 1985 Net amount (in US dollars)	CONTRIBUTION FOR 1986 Percentage	CONTRIBUTION FOR 1986 Net amount (in US dollars)	MEMBER	CONTRIBUTION FOR 1985 Percentage	CONTRIBUTION FOR 1985 Net amount (in US dollars)	CONTRIBUTION FOR 1986 Percentage	CONTRIBUTION FOR 1986 Net amount (in US dollars)
Afghanistan	0.00717	6,260	0.007	6,496	Democratic People's Republic of Korea	0.03427	29,934	0.034	31,113
Albania	0.00717	6,260	0.007	6,496	Denmark	0.76624	669,239	0.766	696,726
Algeria	0.08510	74,328	0.085	77,396	Dominican Republic	0.01978	17,273	0.020	17,981
Argentina	0.47511	414,960	0.475	431,480	Ecuador	0.01347	11,767	0.014	12,239
Australia	1.60497	1,401,782	1.605	1,459,358	Egypt	0.04885	42,663	0.049	44,315
Austria	0.76624	669,239	0.766	696,726	El Salvador	0.00717	6,260	0.007	6,496
Bangladesh	0.02284	19,951	0.023	20,659	Ethiopia	0.00717	6,260	0.007	6,496
Belgium	1.31504	1,148,557	1.315	1,195,733	Finland	0.48667	425,055	0.487	442,515
Bolivia	0.00717	6,260	0.007	6,496	France	6.66840	5,824,177	6.670	6,063,402
Brazil	0.89515	781,823	0.896	814,154	Gabon	0.02071	18,088	0.021	18,831
Bulgaria	0.11937	104,261	0.119	108,509	German Democratic Republic	1.41858	1,238,992	1.419	1,289,885
Burma	0.00748	6,535	0.007	6,771	Germany, Federal Republic of	8.74968	7,641,971	8.751	7,955,859
Byelorussian SSR	0.37277	325,576	0.373	338,949	Ghana	0.01418	12,386	0.014	12,858
Cameroon	0.00717	6,260	0.007	6,496	Greece	0.25882	226,073	0.259	235,276
Canada	3.15817	2,758,345	3.159	2,871,642	Guatemala	0.01379	12,042	0.014	12,514
Chile	0.05002	43,692	0.050	45,344	Haiti	0.00717	6,260	0.007	6,496
China	0.76464	667,836	0.758	688,368	Holy See	0.01035	9,044	0.010	9,415
Colombia	0.07603	66,404	0.076	69,000	Hungary	0.17788	155,358	0.177	160,786
Costa Rica	0.01347	11,767	0.014	12,239					
Cuba	0.06106	53,332	0.061	55,456					
Cyprus	0.00717	6,260	0.007	6,496					
Czechoslovakia	0.77660	678,283	0.777	706,143					
Democratic Kampuchea	0.00717	6,260	0.007	6,496					

MEMBER	CONTRIBUTION FOR 1985 Percentage	Net amount (in US dollars)	CONTRIBUTION FOR 1986 Percentage	Net amount (in US dollars)	MEMBER	CONTRIBUTION FOR 1985 Percentage	Net amount (in US dollars)	CONTRIBUTION FOR 1986 Percentage	Net amount (in US dollars)
Iceland	0.03106	27,132	0.031	28,246	Philippines	0.06421	56,079	0.064	58,203
India	0.27569	240,790	0.274	249,286	Poland	0.57428	501,578	0.571	518,334
Indonesia	0.08982	78,447	0.090	81,515	Portugal	0.11977	104,605	0.120	108,853
Iran	0.37966	331,594	0.380	345,046	Qatar	0.03106	27,132	0.031	28,246
Iraq	0.07762	67,792	0.078	70,624	Republic of				
Ireland	0.18638	162,786	0.186	169,474	Korea	0.11780	102,888	0.118	107,136
Israel	0.23816	208,006	0.238	216,551	Romania	0.13197	115,260	0.132	119,744
Italy	3.83122	3,346,189	3.832	3,483,631	Saudi Arabia	0.88014	768,719	0.880	800,293
Ivory Coast	0.01978	17,273	0.020	17,981	Senegal	0.00717	6,260	0.007	6,496
Jamaica	0.01369	11,956	0.014	12,428	Sierra Leone	0.00717	6,260	0.007	6,496
Japan	10.57210	9,233,670	10.574	9,612,938	Singapore	0.05831	50,930	0.058	53,054
Jordan	0.00717	6,260	0.007	6,496	South Africa	0.27261	238,101	0.272	247,541
Kenya	0.00717	6,260	0.007	6,496	Spain	1.97774	1,727,357	1.978	1,798,306
Kuwait	0.25887	226,094	0.259	235,379	Sri Lanka	0.00748	6,535	0.007	6,771
Lebanon	0.01379	12,042	0.014	12,514	Sudan	0.00738	6,449	0.007	6,685
Liberia	0.00717	6,260	0.007	6,496	Sweden	1.34611	1,175,689	1.346	1,223,980
Libyan Arab					Switzerland	1.12865	985,768	1.129	1,026,259
Jamahiriya	0.26922	235,137	0.269	244,797	Syrian Arab				
Liechtenstein	0.01035	9,044	0.010	9,415	Republic	0.01978	17,273	0.020	17,981
Luxembourg	0.06213	54,263	0.062	56,492	Thailand	0.05476	47,825	0.055	49,713
Madagascar	0.00717	6,260	0.007	6,496	Tunisia	0.01978	17,273	0.020	17,981
Malaysia	0.05949	51,959	0.059	54,083	Turkey	0.21353	186,499	0.213	194,050
Mali	0.00717	6,260	0.007	6,496	Uganda	0.00717	6,260	0.007	6,496
Mauritius	0.00717	6,260	0.007	6,496	Ukrainian SSR	1.34611	1,175,689	1.346	1,223,980
Mexico	0.58346	509,597	0.583	530,129	USSR	10.79990	9,432,635	10.802	9,820,073
Monaco	0.01035	9,044	0.010	9,415	United Arab				
Mongolia	0.00717	6,260	0.007	6,496	Emirates	0.16567	144,699	0.166	150,643
Morocco	0.03388	29,591	0.034	30,770	United Kingdom	4.78385	4,178,215	4.785	4,349,832
Namibia*	—	—	—	—	United Republic				
Netherlands	1.82242	1,591,700	1.823	1,657,078	of Tanzania	0.00717	6,260	0.007	6,496
New Zealand	0.26922	235,137	0.269	244,797	United States	25.88663	22,609,380	25.891	23,538,047
Nicaragua	0.00717	6,260	0.007	6,496	Uruguay	0.02757	24,084	0.028	25,028
Niger	0.00717	6,260	0.007	6,496	Venezuela	0.35341	308,667	0.354	321,411
Nigeria	0.12371	108,052	0.124	112,536	Viet Nam	0.01497	13,072	0.015	13,544
Norway	0.51773	452,186	0.518	470,761	Yugoslavia	0.29745	259,797	0.297	270,416
Pakistan	0.04372	38,186	0.044	39,602	Zaire	0.00738	6,449	0.007	6,685
Panama	0.01347	11,767	0.014	12,239	Zambia	0.00717	6,260	0.007	6,496
Paraguay	0.00717	6,260	0.007	6,496					
Peru	0.04688	40,946	0.047	42,598	Total	100.00000	87,340,000	100.000	90,922,899

*United Nations organizations were requested by the General Assembly in resolution 36/121 D of 10 December 1981 "to grant a waiver of the assessment of Namibia during the period in which it is represented by the United Nations Council for Namibia".

Annex II.   OFFICERS AND OFFICES OF THE INTERNATIONAL ATOMIC ENERGY AGENCY

BOARD OF GOVERNORS

(For period October 1985–September 1986)

OFFICERS

Chairman: Artati Sudirdjo (Indonesia).
Vice-Chairmen: Bo Aler (Sweden), Mieczyslaw Sowinski (Poland).

MEMBERS

Algeria, Argentina, Australia, Brazil, Canada, China, Czechoslovakia, Ecuador, Egypt, Finland, France, German Democratic Republic, Germany, Federal Republic of, Greece, Guatemala, India, Indonesia, Italy, Ivory Coast, Japan, Jordan, Malaysia, Mexico, Mongolia, Morocco, Norway, Pakistan, Peru, Poland, Republic of Korea, Sweden, Sudan, USSR, United Kingdom, United States.

MAIN COMMITTEES OF THE BOARD OF GOVERNORS

ADMINISTRATIVE AND BUDGETARY COMMITTEE
   Participation in the Administrative and Budgetary Committee is open to all members of the Board of Governors.

TECHNICAL ASSISTANCE COMMITTEE
   Participation in the Technical Assistance Committee is open to all members of the Board of Governors.

SCIENTIFIC ADVISORY COMMITTEE (until 30 September 1985)
K. Beckurts (Federal Republic of Germany), D. Beninson (Argentina), A. Bennini (Algeria), Floyd L. Culler (United States), H. Dunster (United Kingdom), G. Fernández

de la Garza (Mexico), L. Gutiérrez Jodra (Spain), J. Jennekens (Canada), Malu wa Kalenga (Zaire), J. Minczewski (Poland), H. Murata (Japan), R. Ramanna (India), I. Ursu (Romania), A. Vasiliev (USSR), G. Vendryes (France).

SCIENTIFIC ADVISORY COMMITTEE (from 1 October 1985)
D. Beninson (Argentina), D. Berenyi (Hungary), H. Böhm (Federal Republic of Germany), Z. Y. Chen (China), Floyd L. Culler (United States), H. Dunster (United Kingdom), A. A. R. El Agib (Sudan), G. Fernández de la Garza (Mexico), L. Gutiérrez Jodra (Spain), J. Jennekens (Canada), Malu wa Kalenga (Zaire), A. Oyama (Japan), R. Ramanna (India), M. F. Troyanov (USSR), I. Ursu (Romania), G. Vendryes (France).

SENIOR SECRETARIAT OFFICERS

Director General: Hans Blix.
Deputy Director General for Safeguards: Peter Tempus.
Deputy Director General for Nuclear Energy and Safety: Leonard Konstantinov.

Deputy Director General for Administration: Nelson F. Sievering, Jr.
Deputy Director General for Technical Co-operation: Carlos Vélez Ocón.
Deputy Director General for Research and Isotopes: Maurizio Zifferero.

HEADQUARTERS AND LIAISON OFFICE

HEADQUARTERS
International Atomic Energy Agency
Vienna International Centre
Wagramerstrasse 5, P.O. Box 100
A-1400 Vienna, Austria
  Cable address: INATOM VIENNA
  Telephone: (222) 2360
  Telex: 1-12645

LIAISON OFFICE
International Atomic Energy Agency
  Liaison Office at the United Nations
United Nations Headquarters, Room DC1-1155
New York, N.Y. 10017, United States
  Telephone: (212) 963-6010, 963-6011, 963-6012

Chapter II

International Labour Organisation (ILO)

In 1985, the International Labour Organisation (ILO) continued activities in its six major programme areas: promotion of policies to create employment and satisfy basic human needs; development of human resources; improvement of working and living conditions and environment; promotion of social security; strengthening of industrial relations and tripartite (government/employer/worker) co-operation; and the advancement of human rights in the social and labour fields. The main instruments of action continued to be standard-setting, technical co-operation activities, research and publishing.

At year's end, ILO membership stood at 150, Viet Nam having withdrawn on 1 June.

Meetings

The seventy-first session of the International Labour Conference, held at Geneva from 7 to 27 June 1985, was attended by some 2,000 delegates and advisers from 141 countries. The Conference had before it the annual report of the ILO Governing Body, the report of the Director-General, focusing on industrial relations and tripartism, and the twenty-first special report on the effect of *apartheid* on labour and employment in South Africa.

The Conference adopted International Labour Conventions and Recommendations on occupational health services and on labour statistics. It held a first discussion on safety in the use of asbestos with a view to adopting instruments on that subject in 1986.

A tripartite Conference committee again examined the application of ILO Conventions and Recommendations by member States, and reviewed the application of ILO standards concerning labour inspection.

After considering equal employment opportunities and treatment for men and women, the Conference called on member States to overcome discrimination against women. Resolutions were also adopted on the most urgent problems of Africa, particularly food security, on statistics of productivity, and on safety in the use of dangerous substances and processes in industry.

The Inland Transport Committee (eleventh session, Geneva, 23-31 January) adopted two sets of conclusions: one on the working and social conditions of boatmen in domestic and international inland navigation, including legal protection and repatriation, as well as occupational safety and health in connection with the application of new technologies; and the other on occupational safety and health in road transport. The Committee also adopted 10 resolutions relating to different aspects of the transport industry and to future ILO activities.

The Advisory Committee on Technology (first session, Geneva, 15-19 April) noted that ILO was mandated to analyse the social dimensions of technology and to contribute to international initiatives, such as the proposed United Nations global information network (see p. 709). The Committee agreed that ILO should continue its work on new technologies and on blending them with traditional ones.

The Advisory Committee on Salaried Employees and Professional Workers (ninth session, Geneva, 17-25 April) adopted conclusions on problems specific to employees in commerce and offices—employment; working hours; temporary, part-time and home work; and remuneration—and on occupational hazards and diseases. Resolutions adopted by the Committee concerned the rights of salaried inventors and authors; personnel information systems and data privacy; freedom of association for professional and managerial staff; multinational enterprises in commerce; integration of young diploma-holders into various professions; the attention given within ILO to certain occupational groups; and future ILO work relating to salaried employees and professional workers.

Achievement of full employment and improvement of working conditions were the main themes of the Forestry and Wood Industries Committee (first session, Geneva, 18-26 September); its four resolutions were on freedom of association, pollution, multinational enterprises and future activities.

A Joint Meeting on Employment and Conditions of Work in Health and Medical Services (Geneva, 8-15 October) adopted conclusions on employment, labour-management relations, remuneration, ethical problems, working hours, and occupational health and safety. It also adopted resolutions on ILO activities in health and medical services, freedom of association and the right to collective bargaining, and equal rights and opportunities.

At the Third Tripartite Technical Meeting for the Leather and Footwear Industry (Geneva, 4-12

December), two sets of conclusions were adopted: one on manpower development, training and retraining; and the other on the impact of structural and technological changes on employment and income. The Meeting also adopted a series of resolutions on the rights of young workers, women workers and working mothers, occupational health and safety, the observance of international labour standards, working conditions and the right to organize and bargain collectively.

The Tenth Asian Regional Conference (Jakarta, Indonesia, 4-13 December), attended by some 300 delegates and advisers from 30 countries, discussed Asia's response to economic recession and adopted conclusions on vocational training, rehabilitation of the disabled, and standards. The Conference called for the combating of restrictive trade practices, improved productivity, preventing industrial accidents and promoting trade union rights.

Working environment

The 1976 International Programme for the Improvement of Working Conditions and Environment (PIACT) continued to encourage and assist member States in promoting occupational safety and health and improving general working conditions. Among key points in a 1984 ILO Conference resolution was the need for tripartite involvement in policy formulation and implementation.

PIACT sought to improve working conditions in sectors often falling outside the scope of legislation and other traditional protective measures. An innovative training package on working conditions and productivity in small enterprises was tested in courses held in India and the Philippines. Other activities included national seminars in Argentina on working conditions and environment problems in various industries; an advisory mission to Algeria to discuss future co-operation; support for national employers' programmes in Argentina, Malaysia, Pakistan and the Philippines, and, in collaboration with the United Nations Environment Programme (UNEP), for regional employers' programmes in Africa and the Caribbean; and major projects by the United Nations Development Programme (UNDP) in Indonesia and Thailand.

Several activities were rapidly organized in response to industrial accidents at Bhopal, India, and elsewhere. A mission was undertaken to advise the Indian Government on the establishment of a major accident hazard control system. An Asian Regional Workshop on Major Hazards and Their Control in Industry was held at Bombay in November. A Tripartite *Ad Hoc* Meeting of Consultants on Methods of Prevention of Major Hazards in Industry (Geneva, 15-21 October) made recommendations on training, information

dissemination, the preparation of a manual and a code of practice on the prevention of major hazards, and the creation of a list of international consultants to advise Governments, employers and workers.

Training activities included the production of video films for training rural workers and the completion of a training manual on better working conditions and environment, prepared in collaboration with the Swedish Joint Industrial Safety Council. Technical contributions were made to training courses and seminars in China, India, Madagascar, Malawi, the Niger and Tunisia.

Technical co-operation projects completed in 1985 provided assistance to institutions in Algeria, India and United Republic of Tanzania. Other projects were in progress in Greece, India, Indonesia, Iran, Poland, Singapore and Thailand.

Collaboration with the World Health Organization (WHO) and other United Nations agencies regarding working health continued, and included participation in the UNEP/WHO/ILO International Programme on Chemical Safety as well as close IAEA/WHO/ILO co-operation concerning the protection of workers against ionizing radiations.

In 1985, the International Occupational Safety and Health Information Centre added two national centres to its network, bringing the total to 50.

Information dissemination activities were stepped up. The Clearing-House for the Dissemination of Information on Conditions of Work published two issues of *Conditions of Work: A Cumulative Digest*, containing fact sheets on laws and practices relating to the introduction of new technology, and bibliographies on home work and child labour.

World Employment Programme

The World Employment Programme (WEP), through action-oriented research, technical advisory services and other field activities, addressed the employment and development problems of such underprivileged groups as the rural poor and workers of the rapidly growing urban informal sector. Guided by the Declaration of Principles and Programme of Action adopted at the 1976 World Employment Conference, WEP continued to account for approximately one third of ILO technical co-operation activities, mainly in special works programmes, manpower and employment planning, labour market information, appropriate technology, rural development, women workers, refugees and population. Advisory missions at the country and regional levels remained important programme elements. The WEP regional employment teams in Africa, Asia and Latin America continued to carry out much of the Programme's activities, providing advisory services and training courses to a large number of countries.

Field activities

In 1985, ILO spent over $90 million on technical co-operation activities (an increase of about 8.3 per cent over 1984) to promote employment, develop human resources and social institutions, and improve living and working conditions.

Most of this expenditure ($38.9 million) con-

tinued to be financed by UNDP. The ILO regular programme provided $10.6 million, while expenditure funded from multi-bilateral arrangements and other special programmes increased to $35.5 million. Activities financed by the United Nations Fund for Population Activities (UNFPA) accounted for $5.3 million.

A breakdown of expenditure on technical co-operation by activity and source of funds, and by country, territory, region or organization, is shown in the tables below.

ASSISTANCE IN 1985 BY ACTIVITY AND SOURCE OF FUNDS
(Excluding programme support costs; in US dollars)

Activity	Regular budget	UNDP*	Trust funds (including UNFPA)	Total
Employment and development	2,415,124	10,986,352	18,650,695	32,052,171
Training	2,770,051	20,283,098	7,796,783	30,849,932
Sectoral activities	638,752	3,934,435	6,618,451	11,191,638
Workers' activities	1,067,043	37,485	2,880,570	3,985,098
Working conditions and environment	1,119,671	1,959,514	285,530	3,364,715
Industrial relations and labour administration	1,201,866	1,092,068	927,442	3,221,376
Personnel, budget and finance, internal administration	—	95	1,090,648	1,090,743
Social security	267,910	284,183	411,690	963,783
Employers' activities	409,044	—	553,474	962,518
Promotion of equality	351,303	43,056	452,667	847,026
Regional and other services	—	—	603,630	603,630
Labour information and statistics	169,682	229,490	—	399,172
International labour standards	248,188	—	138,785	386,973
Programming and management	—	30,466	268,707	299,173
International Institute for Labour Studies	—	15	80,329	80,344
Total	10,658,634	38,880,257	40,759,401	90,298,292

*Includes projects for which ILO acted as executing and associated agency.

COUNTRIES, TERRITORIES, REGIONS AND ORGANIZATIONS AIDED BY ILO IN 1985

COUNTRY, TERRITORY OR OTHER	No. of experts provided	No. of fellowships awarded	EXPENDITURES ON AID GIVEN BY SOURCE OF FUNDS (in US dollars)				
			ILO regular programme	UNDP*	UNFPA	Trust funds	Total
Afghanistan	1	—	—	(10,616)	—	—	(10,616)
African National Congress	—	—	—	3,959	—	—	3,959
Algeria	11	55	28,963	1,212,743	—	53,267	1,294,973
Angola	6	1	—	381,873	—	—	381,873
Antigua	2	3	15,436	162,956	—	—	178,392
Argentina	1	36	145,155	248,488	—	—	393,643
Australia	—	2	—	—	—	—	—
Austria	1	—	—	—	—	—	—
Bahamas	1	3	23,536	84,718	—	48,265	156,519
Bahrain	1	2	5,012	81,134	—	—	86,146
Bangladesh	28	8	70,775	1,431,964	221,695	540,590	2,265,024
Barbados	1	3	66,634	—	—	41,340	107,974
Belize	1	2	4,563	13,218	—	—	17,781
Benin	14	33	34,432	1,132,563	—	140,073	1,307,068
Bhutan	—	—	—	842	—	—	842
Bolivia	1	9	7,999	186,168	—	—	194,167
Botswana	16	4	38,394	15,058	—	616,088	669,540
Brazil	11	30	10,953	815,397	—	134,464	960,814
British Virgin Islands	1	—	—	—	—	6,818	6,818
Bulgaria	—	4	6,720	1,454	—	—	8,174
Burkina Faso	10	6	47,945	572,705	—	512,212	1,132,862
Burma	21	10	15,177	1,111,333	—	68,531	1,195,041
Burundi	17	8	11,011	551,766	—	901,655	1,464,432
Cameroon	20	13	25,250	717,962	201,354	174,214	1,118,780
Canada	—	3	—	—	—	—	—
Cape Verde	10	3	—	224,381	—	2,360,165	2,584,546
Caribbean islands	—	—	115,999	79,415	—	36,033	231,447

		EXPENDITURES ON AID GIVEN BY SOURCE OF FUNDS (in US dollars)				
COUNTRY, TERRITORY OR OTHER	No. of experts provided	No. of fellowships awarded	ILO regular programme	UNDP*	UNFPA	Trust funds	Total
Cayman Islands	—	1	10,153	(393)	—	—	9,760
Central African Republic	7	7	43,568	249,629	—	—	293,197
Chad	4	1	—	27,148	—	—	27,148
Chile	—	24	19,621	3,700	—	—	23,321
China	1	33	261,450	—	—	—	261,450
Colombia	1	17	33,946	228,158	35,243	—	297,347
Comoros	2	—	26,190	—	—	—	26,190
Congo	13	22	—	937,192	92	111,984	1,049,268
Cook Islands	—	—	4,062	—	—	—	4,062
Costa Rica	3	18	46,881	97,204	—	156,745	300,830
Cuba	—	9	54,118	(6,920)	—	—	47,198
Cyprus	3	5	35,286	70,707	—	7,230	113,223
Democratic Yemen	6	12	15,188	14,152	8,955	312,812	351,107
Djibouti	4	3	—	19,630	—	—	19,630
Dominica	—	1	—	—	—	159,084	159,084
Dominican Republic	2	7	46,800	126,217	—	86	173,103
Ecuador	1	11	37,652	227,220	—	31,429	296,301
Egypt	20	102	22,928	354,904	64,121	787,419	1,229,372
El Salvador	1	6	37,043	28,491	—	—	65,534
Equatorial Guinea	6	1	8,746	133,421	—	—	142,167
Ethiopia	32	42	2,062	1,007,651	—	664,079	1,673,792
Fiji	5	4	28,198	—	16,636	373,753	418,587
France	—	1	—	—	—	—	—
Gabon	7	10	29,932	479,250	—	115,597	624,779
Gambia	12	14	—	226,095	—	387,737	613,832
Ghana	—	19	22,591	10,839	—	128,034	161,464
Greece	1	21	1,389	9,917	—	78,242	89,548
Grenada	1	1	21,952	20,973	—	—	42,925
Guatemala	1	7	16,098	(2,333)	145,582	—	159,347
Guinea	4	12	23,130	58,254	152,841	30,024	264,249
Guinea-Bissau	10	8	28,085	492,724	—	47,647	568,456
Guyana	1	1	7,671	68,627	—	—	76,298
Haiti	8	5	57,013	382,273	—	251,165	690,451
Honduras	4	9	12,035	175,518	—	1,673	189,226
Hong Kong	—	1	—	20,775	—	—	20,775
Hungary	—	1	12,056	—	—	—	12,056
India	21	89	354,362	632,176	337,371	553,040	1,876,949
Indonesia	32	39	78,176	1,528,256	—	650,835	2,257,267
Iran	12	13	2,126	842,669	—	—	844,795
Iraq	11	9	3,557	350,356	—	254,090	608,003
Ireland	—	1	—	—	—	—	—
Israel	1	—	—	—	—	—	—
Italy	—	195	—	—	—	—	—
Ivory Coast	8	8	8,640	110,137	—	354,689	473,466
Jamaica	2	6	15,019	99,938	60,573	—	175,530
Japan	—	1	—	—	—	—	—
Jordan	2	17	—	203,978	13,257	—	217,235
Kenya	9	22	—	366,466	40,557	686,503	1,093,526
Kiribati	—	—	740	29,692	18,855	—	49,287
Kuwait	—	2	—	2,222	—	8,370	10,592
Lao People's Democratic Republic	12	9	—	1,181,767	—	11,335	1,193,102
Lebanon	—	—	3,326	—	—	—	3,326
Lesotho	6	7	10,575	87,881	—	395,401	493,857
Liberia	2	20	16,672	172,819	25,818	—	215,309
Libyan Arab Jamahiriya	6	21	1,771	347,413	—	23,822	373,006
Madagascar	12	86	32,336	335,613	—	163,678	531,627
Malawi	12	10	36,432	622,866	—	34,429	693,727
Malaysia	4	51	27,796	70,715	153,584	17,430	269,525
Maldives	2	2	3,315	254,943	—	—	258,258
Mali	14	13	14,895	40,345	158,041	639,316	852,597
Malta	—	—	14,062	—	—	—	14,062
Marshall Islands	1	—	—	—	—	—	—
Mauritania	14	6	47,848	577,398	—	213,506	838,752
Mauritius	7	2	—	70,336	—	67,193	137,529
Mexico	7	13	62,899	275,952	—	65,173	404,024
Mongolia	—	—	280	(12,063)	—	—	(11,783)
Morocco	8	24	11,269	100,833	—	(25)	112,077
Mozambique	6	3	6,457	251,003	—	167,975	425,435
Namibia	3	10	58,559	411,106	—	273,212	742,877
National liberation movements†	—	7	147,458	(3,555)	—	158,437	302,340
Nepal	14	31	39,824	1,537,563	105,380	1,250,063	2,932,830
Netherlands Antilles	4	2	6,651	117,417	—	—	124,068
Nicaragua	4	6	30,101	36,490	100,336	70,440	237,367
Niger	13	20	14,114	655,356	—	353,208	1,022,678
Nigeria	17	21	37,691	1,029,869	75,998	—	1,143,558
Niue	—	—	—	4,120	—	—	4,120
Occupied Arab territories	1	16	3,991	—	—	—	3,991

COUNTRY, TERRITORY OR OTHER	No. of experts provided	No. of fellowships awarded	ILO regular programme	UNDP*	UNFPA	Trust funds	Total
				EXPENDITURES ON AID GIVEN BY SOURCE OF FUNDS (in US dollars)				
Oman	—	4	—	—	—	—	—
Pakistan	11	44	79,406	628,508	102,105	709,644	1,519,663
Panama	2	5	22,488	85,880	—	9,857	118,225
Papua New Guinea	3	—	17,904	—	14,113	3,940	35,957
Paraguay	3	6	22,620	91,895	—	35,746	150,261
Peru	7	14	48,937	230,261	—	153,731	432,929
Philippines	6	34	355,626	193,481	—	224,557	773,664
Poland	—	10	—	69,185	—	—	69,185
Portugal	1	44	74,514	126,466	—	—	200,980
Republic of Korea	—	7	11,910	—	—	—	11,910
Romania	—	—	1,210	—	—	—	1,210
Rwanda	9	7	15,252	141,830	—	1,350,930	1,508,012
Saint Christopher and Nevis	—	3	2,036	(1,089)	—	—	947
Saint Lucia	—	1	10,268	—	—	—	10,268
Saint Vincent and the Grenadines	1	1	3,175	4,325	—	—	7,500
Samoa	—	1	2,935	—	19,510	—	22,445
Sao Tome and Principe	1	2	35,036	(3,471)	18,779	—	50,344
Saudi Arabia	2	21	5,083	50,761	—	—	55,844
Senegal	12	12	28,726	531,188	—	722,883	1,282,797
Seychelles	1	2	—	7,545	2,500	—	10,045
Sierra Leone	2	5	—	—	21,921	453,716	475,637
Singapore	1	11	10,000	30,483	—	—	40,483
Solomon Islands	—	—	—	8,111	—	—	8,111
Somalia	5	12	8,993	139,294	122,103	222,757	493,147
Spain	—	32	—	—	—	—	—
Sri Lanka	16	28	21,456	1,272,091	47,424	104,304	1,445,275
Sudan	23	34	38,691	332,616	149,530	1,438,919	1,959,756
Suriname	2	5	—	137,108	—	—	137,108
Swaziland	2		24,410	86,134	—	2,200	112,744
Sweden	—	3	—	—	—	—	—
Syrian Arab Republic	1	7	—	1,004	120,132	—	121,136
Thailand	25	49	120,423	685,718	—	320,600	1,126,741
Togo	14	5	11,195	904,120	—	292,956	1,208,271
Tokelau	—	—	—	17,950	—	—	17,950
Tonga	1	1	32,662	6,501	29,843	—	69,006
Trinidad and Tobago	2	8	4,656	8,202	—	52,596	65,454
Trust Territory of the Pacific Islands	—	—	979	—	12	—	991
Tunisia	3	3	109,651	43,558	—	17,369	170,578
Turkey	3	12	72,051	93,385	22,049	—	187,485
Turks and Caicos Islands	1	2	2,220	30,117	—	—	32,337
Uganda	17	22	6,563	824,086	—	214,737	1,045,386
United Arab Emirates	—	—	5,825	28,837	—	—	34,662
United Kingdom	—	3	—	—	—	—	—
United Republic of Tanzania	11	59	66,105	253,124	—	918,219	1,237,448
United States	—	2	—	—	—	—	—
Uruguay	—	141	32,080	134,336	—	—	166,416
Vanuatu	1	—	16,908	42,688	—	—	59,596
Venezuela	1	15	68,290	70,056	—	—	138,346
Yemen	—	3	4,907	—	—	—	4,907
Zaire	9	25	18,625	629,512	—	4,000	652,137
Zambia	11	10	92,355	—	142,630	311,122	546,107
Zimbabwe	11	15	120,832	270,552	16,971	16,686	425,041
Geneva headquarters	—	1	—	—	—	—	—
Subtotal	823	2,187	4,357,743	35,018,929	2,765,911	23,272,044	65,414,627
INTERCOUNTRY REGIONAL PROJECTS							
Africa	—	—	1,445,323	907,796	388,087	4,120,426	6,861,632
Asia	—	—	1,932,256	1,349,747	581,510	1,424,210	5,287,723
Europe	—	—	7,778	135,356	—	120,378	263,512
Inter-America	—	—	1,594,841	207,626	235,538	1,621,949	3,659,954
Middle East	—	—	252,905	7,500	303,924	62,721	627,050
Subtotal	—	—	5,233,103	2,608,025	1,509,059	7,349,684	16,699,871
INTERREGIONAL PROJECTS	—	—	1,067,788	1,253,303	985,947	4,876,756	8,183,794
Total	823	2,187	10,658,634	38,880,257	5,260,917	35,498,484	90,298,292

NOTE: Figures in parentheses indicate negative adjustment to figures previously reported.
*Includes projects for which ILO acted as executing and associated agency.
†Liberation movements of South Africa.

Educational activities

In 1985 vocational training remained the largest single component of the ILO technical co-operation programme. Approximately 65 projects in urban areas and 40 in rural areas were operational during the year, while some 20 projects were completed. Major vocational training projects were concluded in the Dominican Republic, Honduras, Nigeria and Thailand. New projects included those started in Madagascar, the Netherlands Antilles, the Niger and the Sudan.

The International Institute for Labour Studies at Geneva, an ILO centre for advanced labour and social studies, held its twentieth international internship course on active labour policy development from 22 April to 7 June. Attended by 21 participants from 15 countries in Africa, the Americas and Europe, the course dealt with economic changes and developments in labour matters; technological, demographic and educational aspects of labour policy; comparative industrial relations; the role of ILO in formulating and implementing labour policy; human rights; and the environment and labour policy.

The Institute organized at Geneva from 7 to 11 October a seminar on labour-management relations and social security in the European Community for 30 participants from the Colegios Oficiales de Graduados Sociales, members of the General Council of Madrid, Spain.

The Institute, in collaboration with Brazil, organized from 14 to 31 October at Brasilia a course for participants from seven Portuguese-speaking countries on the major issues concerning labour (employment, training, working conditions, industrial relations, international labour standards).

In collaboration with the All-Union Trade Union Council and the United Nations Institute for Training and Research, the Institute organized at Baku, USSR, from 21 to 31 October a workshop on the participation of women in rural development, which brought together 20 participants from English-speaking Africa, Asia and the West Indies.

In 1985, the ILO International Centre for Advanced Technical and Vocational Training at Turin, Italy, conducted 81 courses and seminars attended by 1,578 participants from 137 countries, and administered, executed and monitored 613 individual fellowships in 68 countries.

Increased demand came for the training of trainers and managers, particularly in the small enterprises, energy, rural development and transport sectors. Management courses and seminars represented 25 per cent of the Centre's total activity.

Seminars and workshops implemented either partly or wholly in the field included: management of agricultural co-operatives (New Delhi, India, on behalf of Italy's multi-bilateral programme); low-cost audio-visual aids (Thailand, in collaboration with the Friedrich Ebert Stiftung); training methodology for instructors from meteorological training centres (Buenos Aires, Argentina, carried out at the request of the World Meteorological Organization); production of low-cost visual aids (Morocco, in collaboration with the Friedrich Ebert Stiftung); supervisory development of harbours (India, in collaboration with ILO Maritime Services); management of welfare facilities for women workers in Africa (Zimbabwe, organized within the framework of PIACT); technical and pedagogical upgrading (Spain, on behalf of its Ministry of Labour); and a seminar for trainers in the energy/power sector (Bangkok, Thailand, in collaboration with the ILO Regional Office for Asia and the Pacific).

Publications

Published ILO research covered a wide range of topical social and labour questions. New volumes issued in 1985 included: *The Cost of Social Security*, eleventh international inquiry, 1978-1980; *Directory of African Technology Institutions; Employment and Poverty in a Troubled World; How to Read a Balance Sheet* (second revised edition); *ILO Thesaurus: Labour, Employment and Training Terminology* (third edition); *Improving Working Conditions in Small Enterprises in Developing Asia; Introduction to Working Conditions and Environment; Management Self-Development*, a guide for managers, organizations and institutions; *Occupational Hazards from Non-Ionising Electromagnetic Radiation; Rehabilitation Approaches to Drug and Alcohol Dependence; Safety and Health in Coal Mines*, an ILO code of practice; *Small-Scale Paper-Making; Technological Change: The Tripartite Response, 1982-85; Technology and Employment in Industry: A Case-Study Approach* (third revised and enlarged edition); *The Trade Union Situation and Industrial Relations in Spain; The Trade Union Situation and Industrial Relations in Yugoslavia; Visual Display Units: Job Content and Stress in Office Work; Women Workers in Multinational Enterprises in Developing Countries;* and *Working Women in Socialist Countries: The Fertility Connection.*

The second volume of *World Labour Report* was published, surveying the main labour issues in the world; the forty-fifth (1985) issue of the *Year Book of Labour Statistics* also appeared. Regular periodicals and technical series included the bimonthly *International Labour Review*, the quarterly *Social and Labour Bulletin* and the biannual *Legislative Series*.

Secretariat

As at 31 December 1985, the total number of full-time staff under permanent, fixed-term and short-term appointments at ILO headquarters and elsewhere was 2,838. Of these, 1,357 were in the Professional and higher categories (drawn from 116 nationalities) and 1,481 were in the General Service or Maintenance categories. Of the Professional staff, 588 were assigned to technical co-operation projects.

Budget

The International Labour Conference in June 1985 adopted a budget of $253.1 million for 1986-1987.

MAIN CATEGORIES OF EXPENDITURE IN 1985

	Amount (in US dollars)
Staff costs	76,697,647
Operational activities	10,666,138
General operating expenses	10,161,403
Contractual services	6,579,856
Travel on official business	5,548,608
Acquisition of furniture and equipment	4,502,214
Fellowships, grants and contributions	4,102,996
Acquisition and improvement of premises	2,678,970
Supplies and materials	1,486,050
Joint activities within the UN system	773,483
Total	123,197,365

Annex I. MEMBERSHIP OF THE INTERNATIONAL LABOUR ORGANISATION AND CONTRIBUTIONS

(Membership as at 31 December 1985; contributions as assessed for 1986)

MEMBER	CONTRIBUTION Percentage	Gross amount (in US dollars)	MEMBER	CONTRIBUTION Percentage	Gross amount (in US dollars)	MEMBER	CONTRIBUTION Percentage	Gross amount (in US dollars)
Afghanistan	0.01	12,657	Germany, Federal			Norway	0.51	645,507
Algeria	0.13	164,541	Republic of	8.47	10,720,479	Pakistan	0.06	75,942
Angola	0.01	12,657	Ghana	0.02	25,314	Panama	0.02	25,314
Antigua and Barbuda	0.01	12,657	Greece	0.40	506,280	Papua New Guinea	0.01	12,657
Argentina	0.70	885,990	Grenada	0.01	12,657	Paraguay	0.01	12,657
Australia	1.56	1,974,492	Guatemala	0.02	25,314	Peru	0.07	88,599
Austria	0.74	936,618	Guinea	0.01	12,657	Philippines	0.09	113,913
Bahamas	0.01	12,657	Guinea-Bissau	0.01	12,657	Poland	0.71	898,647
Bahrain	0.01	12,657	Guyana	0.01	12,657	Portugal	0.18	227,826
Bangladesh	0.03	37,971	Haiti	0.01	12,657	Qatar	0.03	37,971
Barbados	0.01	12,657	Honduras	0.01	12,657	Romania	0.19	240,483
Belgium	1.27	1,607,439	Hungary	0.23	291,111	Rwanda	0.01	12,657
Belize	0.01	12,657	Iceland	0.03	37,971	Saint Lucia	0.01	12,657
Benin	0.01	12,657	India	0.36	455,652	San Marino	0.01	12,657
Bolivia	0.01	12,657	Indonesia	0.13	164,541	Sao Tome and Principe	0.01	12,657
Botswana	0.01	12,657	Iran	0.57	721,449	Saudi Arabia	0.85	1,075,845
Brazil	1.38	1,746,666	Iraq	0.12	151,884	Senegal	0.01	12,657
Bulgaria	0.18	227,826	Ireland	0.18	227,826	Seychelles	0.01	12,657
Burkina Faso	0.01	12,657	Israel	0.23	291,111	Sierra Leone	0.01	12,657
Burma	0.01	12,657	Italy	3.71	4,695,747	Singapore	0.09	113,913
Burundi	0.01	12,657	Ivory Coast	0.03	37,971	Solomon Islands	0.01	12,657
Byelorussian SSR	0.36	455,652	Jamaica	0.02	25,314	Somalia	0.01	12,657
Cameroon	0.01	12,657	Japan	10.23	12,948,111	Spain	1.91	2,417,487
Canada	3.05	3,860,385	Jordan	0.01	12,657	Sri Lanka	0.01	12,657
Cape Verde	0.01	12,657	Kenya	0.01	12,657	Sudan	0.01	12,657
Central African Republic	0.01	12,657	Kuwait	0.25	316,425	Suriname	0.01	12,657
Chad	0.01	12,657	Lao People's			Swaziland	0.01	12,657
Chile	0.07	88,599	Democratic			Sweden	1.31	1,658,067
China	0.87	1,101,159	Republic	0.01	12,657	Switzerland	1.09	1,379,613
Colombia	0.11	139,227	Lebanon	0.02	25,314	Syrian Arab Republic	0.03	37,971
Comoros	0.01	12,657	Lesotho	0.01	12,657	Thailand	0.08	101,256
Congo	0.01	12,657	Liberia	0.01	12,657	Togo	0.01	12,657
Costa Rica	0.02	25,314	Libyan Arab Jamahiriya	0.26	329,082	Trinidad and Tobago	0.03	37,971
Cuba	0.09	113,913	Luxembourg	0.06	75,942	Tunisia	0.03	37,971
Cyprus	0.01	12,657	Madagascar	0.01	12,657	Turkey	0.32	405,024
Czechoslovakia	0.75	949,275	Malawi	0.01	12,657	Uganda	0.01	12,657
Democratic Kampuchea	0.01	12,657	Malaysia	0.09	113,913	Ukrainian SSR	1.31	1,658,067
Democratic Yemen	0.01	12,657	Mali	0.01	12,657	USSR	10.45	13,226,565
Denmark	0.74	936,618	Malta	0.01	12,657	United Arab Emirates	0.16	202,512
Djibouti	0.01	12,657	Mauritania	0.01	12,657	United Kingdom	4.63	5,860,191
Dominica	0.01	12,657	Mauritius	0.01	12,657	United Republic of		
Dominican Republic	0.03	37,971	Mexico	0.87	1,101,159	Tanzania	0.01	12,657
Ecuador	0.02	25,314	Mongolia	0.01	12,657	United States	25.00	31,642,500
Egypt	0.07	88,599	Morocco	0.05	63,285	Uruguay	0.04	50,628
El Salvador	0.01	12,657	Mozambique	0.01	12,657	Venezuela	0.54	683,478
Equatorial Guinea	0.01	12,657	Namibia	0.01	12,657	Yemen	0.01	12,657
Ethiopia	0.01	12,657	Nepal	0.01	12,657	Yugoslavia	0.46	582,222
Fiji	0.01	12,657	Netherlands	1.76	2,227,632	Zaire	0.01	12,657
Finland	0.48	607,536	New Zealand	0.26	329,082	Zambia	0.01	12,657
France	6.46	8,176,422	Nicaragua	0.01	12,657	Zimbabwe	0.02	25,314
Gabon	0.02	25,314	Niger	0.01	12,657			
German Democratic			Nigeria	0.19	240,483	Total	100.00	126,570,000
Republic	1.38	1,746,666						

Annex II.   OFFICERS AND OFFICES OF THE INTERNATIONAL LABOUR ORGANISATION
(As at 31 December 1985)

MEMBERSHIP OF THE GOVERNING BODY OF THE INTERNATIONAL LABOUR OFFICE

Chairman: Jean-Jacques Oechslin (France), Employers' Group.
Vice-Chairmen: Kassa Kebede (Ethiopia), Government group; Gerd Muhr (Federal Republic of Germany), Workers' Group.

REGULAR MEMBERS

Government members

Algeria, Angola, Argentina, Brazil,* Burkina Faso, Canada, China,* Ethiopia, Finland, France,* Germany, Federal Republic of,* Ghana, Hungary, India,* Indonesia, Iraq, Italy,* Jamaica, Japan,* Mongolia, Nicaragua, Pakistan, Ukrainian SSR, USSR,* United Kingdom,* United States,* Venezuela, Zimbabwe.

Employers' members

W. Durling (Panama), J. Escobar Padrón (Colombia), Daniel J. Flunder (United Kingdom), Henri Georget (Niger), A. Katz (United States), Wolf-Dieter Lindner (Federal Republic of Germany), Marwan Nasr (Lebanon), Jean-Jacques Oechslin (France), Tom D. Owuor (Kenya), Aurelio Periquet (Philippines), Najib Said (Tunisia), Naval H. Tata (India), Johan von Holten (Sweden), Koh Yoshino (Japan).

Workers' members

N. Adiko (Ivory Coast), Youcef Briki (Algeria), Irving Brown (United States), S. Crean (Australia), J. J. Delpino (Venezuela), Kanti Mehta (India), R. Mercier (Canada), J. Morton (United Kingdom), Gerd Muhr (Federal Republic of Germany), Alfonso

Sánchez Madariaga (Mexico), A. M. Soubbotine (USSR), John Svenningsen (Denmark), Yoshikazu Tanaka (Japan); 1 vacant seat.

DEPUTY MEMBERS

Government deputy members

Australia, Austria, Benin, Bolivia, Botswana, Burundi, Cuba, Cyprus, Czechoslovakia, Djibouti, Iran, Libyan Arab Jamahiriya, Mexico, Norway, Sao Tome and Principe, Spain, Thailand, Yugoslavia.

Employers' deputy members

Agil Al-Jassem (Kuwait), R. H. Brillinger (Canada), Sidney B. Chambers (Jamaica), M. Eurnekian (Argentina), A. Gharbaoui (Morocco), C. Hak (Netherlands), N. Kouadio (Ivory Coast), J. M. Lacasa Aso (Spain), Munga-wa-Nyasa (Zaire), G. C. Okogwu (Nigeria), J. W. Rowe (New Zealand), J. Santos Neves (Brazil), Lucia Sasso-Mazzufferi (Italy), Fanuel C. Sumbwe (Zambia).

Workers' deputy members

R. A. Baldassini (Argentina), Marc Blondel (France), A. Chiroma (Nigeria), V. David (Malaysia), M. Diop (Senegal), Heribert Maier (Austria), Democrito T. Mendoza (Philippines), A. Mohamed (Niger), Agus Sudono (Indonesia), Jozsef Timmer (Hungary), Raffaele Vanni (Italy), Frank Walcott (Barbados), Wang Jiachong (China), Newstead L. Zimba (Zambia).

*Member holding a non-elective seat as a State of chief industrial importance.

SENIOR OFFICIALS OF THE INTERNATIONAL LABOUR OFFICE

Director-General: Francis Blanchard.
Deputy Directors-General: Bertil Bolin, Surendra K. Jain, David Taylor.
Assistant Directors-General: Faisal M. Abdel-Rahman, Vladimir Chkounaev, Fuyao Jin, Shigeru Nakatani, Franz von Mutius, Francis Wolf.

Director of the International Centre for Advanced Technical and Vocational Training: Julio Galer.

Director of the International Institute for Labour Studies: Elimane Kane.

HEADQUARTERS, REGIONAL, LIAISON AND OTHER OFFICES

HEADQUARTERS

International Labour Office
4 Route des Morillons
CH-1211 Geneva 22, Switzerland
 Cable address: INTERLAB GENEVE
 Telephone: (022) 99-61-11
 Telex: 22271 BIT CH
 Facsimile: (022) 98-86-85

REGIONAL OFFICES

International Labour Organisation Regional
 Office for Africa
P.O. Box 2788
Addis Ababa, Ethiopia
 Cable address: INTERLAB ADDIS ABABA

International Labour Organisation Regional
 Office for Arab States
CH-1211 Geneva 22, Switzerland
 Cable address: INTERLAB GENEVE

International Labour Organisation Regional
 Office for Latin America and the Caribbean
Apartado Postal 3638
Lima 1, Peru
 Cable address: INTERLAB LIMA

International Labour Organisation Regional
 Office for Asia and the Pacific
P.O. Box 1759
Bangkok 2, Thailand
 Cable address: INTERLAB BANGKOK

REGIONAL OFFICES *(cont.)*

International Labour Organisation Regional
 Office for Europe
CH-1211 Geneva 22, Switzerland
 Cable address: INTERLAB GENEVE

LIAISON OFFICES

International Labour Organisation Liaison
 Office with the European Communities and
 the Benelux
40 Rue Aimé Smekens
B-1040 Brussels, Belgium

International Labour Organisation Liaison
 Office with the United Nations
300 East 44th Street, 18th floor
New York, N.Y. 10017, United States

International Labour Organisation Liaison
 Office with the United Nations Economic
 Commission for Latin America and the Caribbean
Casilla 52353, Correo Central
Santiago, Chile

OTHER OFFICES

International Labour Organisation Office
01-Boîte Postale 3960
Abidjan 01, Ivory Coast

International Labour Organisation Office
Boîte Postale 226
16000 Alger-Gare, Algeria

OTHER OFFICES *(cont.)*

International Labour Organisation Office
P.K. 407
Ankara, Turkey

International Labour Organisation Office
Boîte Postale 683
101-Antananarivo, Madagascar

International Labour Organisation Office
2 Dongqijie Sanlitun
Beijing, China

International Labour Organisation Office
Hohenzollernstrasse 21
D-5300 Bonn 2, Federal Republic of Germany

International Labour Organisation Office
Caixa Postal 04/401-403
70312-Brasilia DF, Brazil

International Labour Organisation Office
Avenida Julio A. Roca 620 (3o piso)
1067 Buenos Aires, Argentina

International Labour Organisation Office
9 Taha Hussein Street
11561 Zamalek
Cairo, Egypt

International Labour Organisation Office
P.O. Box 1505
Colombo, Sri Lanka

OTHER OFFICES *(cont.)*

International Labour Organisation Office
Boîte Postale 414
Dakar, Senegal

International Labour Organisation Office
P.O. Box 9212
Dar es Salaam, United Republic of Tanzania

International Labour Organisation Office
P.O. Box 2061, Ramna
Dhaka, Bangladesh

International Labour Organisation Office
P.O. Box 1047
Islamabad, Pakistan

International Labour Organisation Office
P.O. Box 75
Jakarta 10002, Indonesia

International Labour Organisation Office
Boîte Postale 7248
Kinshasa 1, Zaire

International Labour Organisation Office
P.O. Box 20275 SAFAT
13063 Kuwait, Kuwait

International Labour Organisation Office
P.O. Box 2331
Lagos, Nigeria

International Labour Organisation Office
Vincent House, Vincent Square
London SW1P 2NB, England

International Labour Organisation Office
P.O. Box 32181
Lusaka, Zambia

International Labour Organisation Office
Alberto Aguilera, 15 Ddo 1
28015 Madrid, Spain

International Labour Organisation Office
P.O. Box 7587 ADC/MIA
Metro Manila, Philippines

International Labour Organisation Office
Apartado Postal 12-992
Delegación Benito Juárez
Mexico, D.F. 03000, Mexico

International Labour Organisation Office
Petrovka 15, Apt. 23
103 031, Moscow, USSR

International Labour Organisation Office
7 Sardar Patel Marg
New Delhi 110021, India

International Labour Organisation Office
75 Albert Street, Suite 202
Ottawa, Ontario K1P 5E7, Canada

OTHER OFFICES *(cont.)*

International Labour Organisation Office
205 Boulevard Saint-Germain
F-75340 Paris Cedex 07, France

International Labour Organisation Office
P.O. Box 1201
Port of Spain, Trinidad

International Labour Organisation Office
Villa Aldobrandini
Via Panisperna 28
I-00184 Rome, Italy

International Labour Organisation Office
Apartado Postal 10170, Correo Central
San José 1000, Costa Rica

International Labour Organisation Office
P.O. Box 14500
Government Buildings
Suva, Fiji

International Labour Organisation Office
5th floor, Nippon Press Center Building
2-1, Uchisaiwai-cho 2-Chome
Chiyoda-Ku
Tokyo 100, Japan

International Labour Organisation Office
1750 New York Avenue, N.W., Suite 330
Washington, D.C. 20006, United States

International Labour Organisation Office
Boîte Postale 13
Yaoundé, Cameroon

International Labour Organisation Office for Iran
CH-1211 Geneva 22, Switzerland

INSTITUTE

International Institute for Labour Studies
4 Route des Morillons
CH-1211 Geneva 22, Switzerland

TRAINING CENTRES

African Regional Labour Administration
  Centre (ARLAC)
P.O. Box 6097
Harare, Zimbabwe

African Regional Labour Administration
  Centre (CRADAT)
Boîte Postale 1055
Yaoundé, Cameroon

Centre interafricain pour le développement de la
  formation professionnelle (CIADFOR)
01 BP 3771
Abidjan 01, Ivory Coast

Jobs and Skills Programme for Africa
  (JASPA)
P.O. Box 2532
Addis Ababa, Ethiopia

TRAINING CENTRES *(cont.)*

Southern African Team for Employment Promotion
  (SATEP)
P.O. Box 32181
Lusaka, Zambia

Asian and Pacific Regional Project for
  Strengthening Labour Administration (ARPLA)
c/o ILO Regional Office for Asia
  and the Pacific
P.O. Box 1759
Bangkok 2, Thailand

Asian and Pacific Regional Skill Development
  Programme (APSDEP)
P.O. Box 1423
Islamabad, Pakistan

Asian Regional Team for Employment
  Promotion (ARTEP)
P.O. Box 643
New Delhi 110001, India

Labour and Population Team for Asia and
  the Pacific (LAPTAP)
P.O. Box 1759
Bangkok 10501, Thailand

Caribbean Labour Administration Centre (CLAC)
Verona House (1st floor)
Bank Hall, St. Michael, Barbados

Inter-American Labour Administration Centre
  (CIAT)
Apartado Postal 3638 OIT
Lima 1, Peru

Inter-American Centre of Research and
  Documentation on Vocational Training
  (CINTERFOR)
Casilla de Correo 1761
Montevideo, Uruguay

Latin American Centre for Occupational
  Safety and Health (CLASET)
Rua Capote Valente 710 Pinheiros
CEP 05409
São Paulo, SP, Brazil

Regional Employment Programme for Latin
  America and the Caribbean (PREALC Panama)
Apartado 6314
Panamá 5, Panama

Regional Employment Programme for Latin
  America and the Caribbean (PREALC Santiago)
Casilla de Correo 618
Santiago, Chile

International Centre for Advanced Technical
  and Vocational Training
125 Corso Unità d'Italia
I-10127 Turin, Italy

Chapter III

Food and Agriculture Organization of the United Nations (FAO)

The twenty-third biennial session of the Conference of the Food and Agriculture Organization of the United Nations (FAO) was held at Rome, Italy, from 9 to 28 November 1985 and marked FAO's fortieth anniversary.

The Conference reviewed the world food situation and noted that cereal production was expected to reach a record level in 1985, and that cereal stocks, forecast at 21 per cent of expected consumption, provided an adequate safeguard for world food security. However, it expressed concern regarding unduly low commodity prices and continuing widespread undernutrition in Africa. The region had experienced an annual decline in per capita food and agricultural production of nearly 2 per cent in the early 1980s, largely as a consequence of drought. Despite rising food imports, per capita supplies had steadily declined. The Conference drew the attention of the international community to the need for a long-term development effort in Africa, although emergency aid would still be necessary.

The Conference noted that the recent economic and agricultural situation had also been discouraging in Latin America and the Caribbean since the early 1980s. Per capita incomes had declined in the region, debt-service ratios had reached more than 40 per cent of export earnings and inflation rates had soared. Agricultural production per capita and exports had also fallen. In the Near East, declining agricultural production in some countries, combined with a rising demand for food, had led to greatly increased food imports. Progress had been achieved in China and the Far East with annual agricultural production increasing by between 7 and 8 per cent and by nearly 4 per cent, respectively, in the early 1980s.

The Conference approved a World Food Security Compact, which reaffirmed the objectives of world food security (increased production, stability of supplies and adequate access to food by all), called for action to achieve those objectives, and provided a clearly defined moral commitment for action by Governments, non-governmental organizations and individuals.

The Conference stressed the importance of the protection and conservation of forests and grasslands in temperate and tropical regions and the need for government intervention to prevent the blind exploitation of land leading to their destruction. In addition, an International Code of Conduct on the Distribution and Use of Pesticides was adopted.

On 11 November, the Conference admitted two new members to FAO—Cook Islands and Solomon Islands—bringing its membership to 158. Lassaad Ben Osman was appointed Independent Chairman of the FAO Council—FAO's governing body between sessions of the Conference—for a two-year term.

Funding

FAO funds come from three main sources: contributions by member nations, national trust funds and the United Nations Development Programme (UNDP).

The regular programme, financed by members according to a scale of contributions set by the Conference, supports field work and enables FAO to advise Governments, to provide a neutral forum for discussing issues related to food and agriculture and to provide the international farming community with information.

In 1985, slightly less than half the expenditure under FAO field programmes was funded by UNDP. National trust funds provided a similar share of that expenditure, while just under 10 per cent was provided by FAO's regular programme budget through the Technical Co-operation Programme, which allows FAO to respond quickly to unforeseen demands for emergency assistance and for training, investment project preparation and specialized advice.

UNDP funding rose to $120 million in 1985 from $110 million in 1984. Programme growth, however, was sustained by trust fund financing, both bilateral and unilateral, which, since 1983, had exceeded that of UNDP. Total FAO field programme expenditure rose by about 5 per cent in 1985.

Activities in 1985

Agricultural Rehabilitation Programme for Africa. Three successive years of drought in sub-Saharan Africa had produced the worst food crisis in the history of the continent; countless people died of starvation and 150 million were still considered to be at serious risk at the end of 1985. Cereal production in 1984 was more than 20 per cent below the average for the five years before 1982 and, even before the drought struck, one in every five Africans was dependent on imported grain.

Despite rain in most areas, there was an acute shortage of seed and food stocks at all points in the marketing chain were depleted.

Early in 1985, the FAO Director-General launched the Agricultural Rehabilitation Programme for Africa (ARPA), the aim of which was to rebuild African agriculture following the drought. A special donors' meeting was held at Rome on 29 March 1985 to mobilize international funding for ARPA. In addition, FAO reallocated $22.5 million (including $15 million of savings) from the regular programme budget.

ARPA, which initially covered 229 projects in 21 countries and totalled $216 million, comprised 260 projects in 25 countries, amounting to $245 million, by the end of the year. The projects—crop production and protection, irrigation and water supply, loss prevention, storage and processing, extension and training, livestock and pastures, fisheries and forestry—were all designed to produce concrete results within three years.

Agricultural development. As part of its effort to assist developing countries to improve their capacity to feed their people and to promote agricultural development generally, FAO allocated 6 per cent of regular programme and 16 per cent of field programme expenditures to research-related work. At any given time, more than 250 field projects with significant research components were under way. Countries were assisted to formulate research policies, set priorities, strengthen agricultural research institutions, and promote closer links between research and extension. During 1985, review and programming missions were sent to Burundi, Chad, Egypt, Guinea, Iraq, Liberia, Mali, Mauritania, the Niger, Panama and Sao Tome and Principe. Training courses in management and administration for research directors were held in Cameroon, Colombia and Nepal.

The field programme also included more than 150 projects with substantial planning components in 1985. FAO continued to respond to requests from member nations for assistance in formulating new laws, international agreements and the terms of foreign participation in exploiting resources. For example, Ethiopia was helped to prepare comprehensive regulations for the rational management of water resources, legal consultancies were provided to Guyana, Samoa and Tonga, and the Sudan received assistance on land-use planning legislation. In addition, an FAO study on drafting land use legislation for developing countries was completed.

In the area of appropriate farm-power development, FAO in 1985 helped more than a dozen countries to develop agricultural mechanization strategies. The assistance covered all aspects of agricultural mechanization, from basic hand-tools, through animal draught power and equipment, to mechanical power technology.

In an effort to promote economic and technical co-operation among developing countries, FAO in 1985 sponsored a consultation at Arusha, United Republic of Tanzania, which led to the formation of an Association of Agricultural Development Planners to provide for continuing exchanges of experience. In Latin America and the Caribbean, the members of the Organization of Eastern Caribbean States exchanged expertise on training in fisheries law and administration and, in Trinidad and Tobago, FAO conducted a training programme in the use of audio-visual communications for watershed management, which expertise was shared with other nations of the region. FAO also assisted Turkey in promoting technical co-operation with other countries of the Near East and North Africa in forest road network planning and construction, wood-based industries, leather technology, and artificial insemination and dairy cattle-breeding management.

In 1985, the FAO Investment Centre, which assisted developing countries to attract investment for agricultural development, helped to formulate 47 investment projects which were approved by international financing institutions, for total investments of $1,747 million; $931 million of that amount was in external loans, the balance being provided by the recipient Governments.

Rural development. As the lead agency in the United Nations system for rural development, FAO supported the Declaration of Principles and the Programme of Action adopted by the 1979 World Conference on Agrarian Reform and Rural Development (WCARRD).[a] In 1985, it organized follow-up meetings for member Governments in Africa and Asia and the Pacific, and inter-agency consultations on rural development in the Near East and Latin America and the Caribbean. Two inter-agency WCARRD follow-up missions were also organized—to Costa Rica and Uganda—to review past development strategies, identify shortcomings and recommend policy changes to help alleviate rural poverty. The relationship between rural poverty and land tenure was a particular focus during the year, with activities including a round table on trends in land ownership and use rights in Africa (Nairobi, Kenya), and an expert consultation on the socio-economic implications of fragmented holdings in the Near East (Baghdad, Iraq). Extension services in more than 70 countries received assistance, with FAO concentrating on improving the effectiveness of extension and training in serving the needs of rural groups that had been neglected in the past, especially small-scale farmers, women, young people and the disabled.

[a]YUN 1979, p. 500.

Improving nutrition among rural populations was an important part of FAO's overall rural development activities in 1985. National-level analyses of nutritional requirements for different household members based on their activities were undertaken in the Ivory Coast and Rwanda. The results confirmed that women, with their multiple roles as farmers and home-makers, had special nutritional requirements which must not be overlooked in rural development strategies.

During the year, 15 national workshops and seminars on nutrition training and education were held in Africa, Latin America and the Caribbean, Asia and the Pacific, and the Near East.

FAO also participated in the 10-year strategy against vitamin-A deficiency and nutritional blindness, launched by the World Health Organization in October 1985 (see Chapter V of this section).

Food security. The World Food Security Compact, proposed by the FAO Director-General in 1984,[b] was approved by the FAO Conference in November 1985 (see above).

Throughout 1985, the FAO Global Information and Early Warning System for Food and Agriculture monitored developments in food demand and supply at global and national levels. On the basis of recommendations of an expert consultation on supplies of food and food aid requirements held in March, and in view of continued food shortages in many African countries, the System stepped up its monitoring activities and issued special monthly reports covering crop information and the provision of emergency food aid. In addition, crop-assessment missions were sent to a number of drought-stricken African countries.

The FAO Food Security Assistance Scheme (FSAS) increased its emphasis on training and technical assistance for national grain boards, and on establishing early warning systems as part of national food security programmes. Total FSAS trust fund contributions amounted to $6.1 million, compared with $5.8 million in 1984.

At its April 1985 session, the FAO Committee on World Food Security considered ways to improve the contribution of food aid to food security, and agreed on measures to improve delivery of supplies in emergencies and on using food aid for development.

Land and water management. Following the 1984 publication of FAO's global study on land resources for populations of the future,[c] a modified methodology for national application, which permitted the use of detailed inputs on irrigation, erosion hazards and the potential for animal production, as well as cultural and socio-economic factors, was used in a pilot project in Kenya. In total, more than 20 countries began national follow-up studies using that approach, including Bangladesh,

Ethiopia, Malaysia, Mozambique, the Philippines and Thailand. Through its Interdepartmental Group for Land-use Planning, FAO began to develop a geographic information system to link its 47 land-use related data bases, and feasibility studies were begun on incorporating a mapping computer into the system.

Because past work on water resource management in the developing world had centred on large-scale irrigation and drainage systems which had often been poorly managed and maintained, FAO concentrated on training in the improved use of water resources and the development of small-scale irrigation infrastructure. The reuse of irrigation waste water gained importance as a water management technique. A project in Egypt demonstrated that cotton and wheat could be irrigated with waste water without decreasing production, by storing run-off water, mixing it with fresh water and reusing it for irrigation.

Crops. Cereals and food legumes, which supplied the largest share of the world's total calories, continued to be a primary focus of FAO activities in increasing food and agricultural production during 1985. Africa again received the largest share of FAO assistance.

More emphasis was placed on demonstrations at the farm level to familiarize farmers with improved production methods and to use their knowledge of local conditions to develop appropriate technologies. For example, improved techniques for cultivating wheat and legumes were demonstrated on farms in Kenya and the United Republic of Tanzania. Projects were also under way in Ethiopia to assist small-scale farmers in the use of improved varieties of wheat and barley, and in Morocco to teach agricultural extension workers to organize on-farm demonstrations of better wheat-planting methods.

As part of its work in rice—the world's most important staple food and the mainstay of the diet of more than 50 per cent of the total population— FAO shared technical expertise in rice improvements through the International Rice Commission, developing integrated farming systems such as rice with fish, rice with small animals and rice with mushrooms, improving pest-control techniques and increasing the productivity of small-scale farmers.

During the year, FAO operated more than 120 projects with a significant horticulture component. Horticultural crops could ensure readily available food supplies, improve diets that were poor or incomplete because of domination by a single staple food, and provide a valuable source of income. In East Africa, a regional project was under way to

[b]YUN 1984, p. 1208.
[c]*Ibid.*, p. 1209.

identify traditional fruits and vegetables that could be improved with limited supplies of inputs. In Rwanda and Senegal, projects were attempting to intensify the propagation of improved varieties of sweet potato, cassava, okra and amaranth, and small-scale farmers in Djibouti were increasing vegetable production in newly irrigated areas.

Although oil-palms made a major contribution to edible oil supplies in the developing world, both production and processing practices were often inefficient and could result in losses up to 40 per cent of potential production. With FAO assistance, 10 of the most important palm-oil-producing countries in Africa met (Abidjan, Ivory Coast, March) to establish the African Oil Palm Development Association.

In Vanuatu, where cyclones severely damaged coconut plantations in January 1985, an FAO project helped to replant the coconut groves, using improved varieties.

In 1985, FAO formulated 40 projects to improve seed production, many of them in the 24 countries included in ARPA. By the end of the year, more than half of the projects were being implemented. In the Gambia, a project helped the Government to improve production of ground-nut, barley, sorghum and millet seed, while Botswana was provided with almost 300 tonnes of seed to ensure adequate planting in the autumn season. In addition, 18 seed project formulation missions were organized for other countries and 60,000 seed samples were dispatched to 85 countries. Seven regional and nine national seminars and workshops to provide training in improved seed production were held in 1985, with a total of nearly 400 participants.

FAO's Fertilizer Programme assisted 19 developing countries—12 in Africa, 6 in Asia and the Pacific, and 1 in Latin America and the Caribbean—to increase crop production, particularly food crops grown by small-scale farmers, through effective use of mineral fertilizers and organic materials. Contracts for research on integrated plant nutrition systems, combining the application of mineral and organic fertilizers, were awarded to national institutions in India and Indonesia.

To encourage small-scale farmers to make better use of fertilizers, FAO started a system of block demonstrations. Voluntary groups of farmers received intensive assistance in implementing new techniques in order to show their effectiveness to others. In Bangladesh, farmers participating in such demonstrations achieved an average paddy yield of 6.7 tonnes a hectare, as against the national average of 2.4 tonnes.

FAO plant protection activities centred on weed management and control, and the reduction of damage caused by pests and diseases through the use of efficient and environmentally sound practices. In Ethiopia and the Gambia, a new planting technique was introduced which significantly reduced damage caused by the parasite *Striga* and other weeds. Millet yields on test plots were 50 to 100 per cent higher than average, and the technique was expected to produce progressively higher yields as weed growth was further reduced, an important result for 17 African countries where *Striga* reduced yields of maize, millet and sorghum crops by as much as 40 per cent.

While the return of the rains to Africa in 1985 signalled an easing of one crisis, it brought another in the form of serious army-worm outbreaks, which were reported from Yemen to Zimbabwe. FAO provided spraying equipment, pesticide and training in the control of the pest to eight countries in the region.

During the year, FAO also helped control locust outbreaks in Botswana, Brazil, Trinidad and the United Republic of Tanzania, and grasshopper infestations in Mali and Mauritania.

Through the International Board for Plant Genetic Resources, jointly sponsored by FAO, UNDP and the World Bank, FAO continued to collect, evaluate and conserve plant genetic resources. In 1985, the Board provided laboratory equipment to 23 gene banks in 19 countries and produced a set of standards to assist countries in upgrading national gene banks. Technical and financial support was provided to gene banks under construction at Beijing, China, and Karadj, Iran.

Livestock. In 1985, special attention was given to improved production of small animals, such as chickens, ducks, goats and rabbits, whose short reproductive cycles and dietary adaptability made them ideal for rearing in the rapidly changing and often harsh conditions of the developing world. In Tunisia, an FAO project introduced a new crossbreed of goat whose milk yield was 40 per cent above that of indigenous breeds. In addition, the project gave one goat to each primary school in the area to familiarize children with their care.

FAO also continued to help increase the productivity of larger animals for both meat and milk. Through the International Meat Development Scheme, livestock evaluation missions visited Cameroon and Guinea-Bissau to prepare projects for international funding. The FAO Dairy Training Programme, funded by Denmark and Finland, trained over 1,000 people in interregional, regional and national seminars held throughout the developing world.

FAO was also active in promoting the use of crop residues and agro-industrial by-products for animal feed, for example by solidifying molasses from sugar refining in West Africa into easily transportable feed blocks. The molasses available annually in the four West African sugar-producing countries could supply 1.4 million head of cattle for three months, enough to carry them through the dry season.

In the area of animal health, preparatory work was completed in 1985 on the African rinderpest campaign, due to start in 1986. Five subregional training courses, on diagnosis, vaccine production and quality control, and the repair of equipment, brought together specialists from 28 countries. A manual for rinderpest campaign workers and two films on rinderpest recognition and control were produced. Latin America and the Caribbean were entirely free of African swine-fever in 1985 as a result of regional assistance and 21 emergency projects provided by FAO. An FAO project funded by Italy continued to support measures to protect against reintroduction.

As part of its work to conserve genetic resources, FAO built up regional data banks on animal genetic types to assist breeding experiments and preserve endangered species. In 1985, pilot projects were completed in Africa, Asia and Latin America. In June, an expert consultation brought together animal geneticists to develop a standard format and methodology for collecting and recording animal genetic characteristics. In addition, possible locations for regional data banks were identified for funding by international financing institutions; the data banks would complement efforts to establish gene banks complete with cryogenic storage facilities.

Fisheries. During 1985, 240 FAO projects in fisheries development were under way at global, regional and national levels, with priority being given to improving the lot of small-scale fishermen. Projects included: an island-by-island study in Cape Verde to identify the special needs of small-scale fishermen and to be used as a guide in formulating a wide range of fisheries development projects; a follow-up project in Mauritania to assist inshore fishermen to improve artisanal boat-building; and, in Haiti, an investigation of the potential production of artisanal fishermen, completed in February 1985, which led to a training project.

Aquaculture (fish farming) development was one of five programmes of action adopted by the 1984 World Conference on Fisheries Management and Development.[d] Activities in 1985 included a regional training course in aquaculture development (Bouaké, Ivory Coast); projects in Barbados and Morocco to help establish fish culture programmes and train local staff; and a weed control programme in Egypt.

Agreement was reached in 1985 between FAO and Sweden on a programme to integrate aquaculture into rural development. The first project was to develop aquaculture in Zambia in conjunction with an existing rural development programme, whereby villagers would be assisted to construct small fish-ponds to supplement other farming activities.

Forests. FAO declared 1985 the International Year of the Forest to highlight the importance of forestry resources to agricultural production and to rally support for their conservation and management. The choice of 1985 was particularly appropriate since it coincided with the Ninth World Forestry Congress, held at Mexico City in July, with the theme of forest resources in the integral development of society.

FAO's short-term objectives for the Year were: to focus world attention on the need for forest conservation and protection; to raise political and public awareness; to draw attention to factors threatening forest resources; and to mobilize people to participate in forest-oriented activities during 1985. World Food Day (16 October) featured the role of forestry development in food security as one of its main themes.

As part of an integrated approach to forest assessment, FAO began mapping the tree and shrub vegetation of Africa. Existing national maps were updated and complemented by the use of Landsat images. A comprehensive framework for classifying Asian vegetation was devised as the first step towards widening the study to include tropical Asia in 1986.

The first of eight manuals on watershed management was published in 1985. When completed, the series would cover watershed survey and planning, slope treatment measures, revegetation and soil treatment measures, roadway protection, landslide prevention, gully control, torrent control and water harvesting.

Although an estimated 11 million hectares of tropical forest land was deforested each year, almost twice as much land in arid and semi-arid regions was rendered useless by the advance of the desert. In June, FAO organized a meeting on desertification control in arid-zone forestry (Saltillo, Mexico). Thirty experts from 21 countries collaborated on the development of a strategy to increase the use of trees and woody vegetation in arid zones, both to stop the advance of the desert and to help provide desperately needed fuel, fodder, food and income.

The conservation of forest genetic resources was cited as an area of primary importance by the FAO Commission on Plant Genetic Resources (Rome, March). As part of its effort to co-ordinate a global programme of forest genetic resource conservation, FAO helped to establish a network of national centres to rescue seeds from arid-zone forests and conserve their qualities before the trees were destroyed by land-use pressure.

[d]*Ibid.,* p. 1210.

Special relief operations. The FAO Office for Special Relief Operations (OSRO), which responded to requests for emergency assistance, mainly through the provision of agricultural inputs, veterinary and feed supplies, small tools and equipment, as well as transport and storage facilities, continued to be the focal point of the FAO/World Food Programme (WFP) Task Force on Africa. Projects were under way in 17 African countries and accounted for more than 70 per cent of OSRO's total budget of $8.7 million for 1985.

OSRO projects were also in operation in Viet Nam, where typhoons destroyed more than 400,000 hectares of cultivated land, swept away 50,000 homes and destroyed long stretches of road and railway; they provided vegetable seeds to permit the immediate resumption of production and bridge the food gap until the next rice harvest. In Nicaragua, where irregular rainfall resulted in widespread failure of maize and bean crops, an OSRO project supplied 250 tonnes of bean seeds.

Information. The *Fifth World Food Survey*, released in 1985, provided a comprehensive picture of the world food and nutritional situation as it changed in the 1960s and 1970s, and its causes and policy implications. The *Survey* noted that although the percentage of undernourished people in the world declined in the 1970s for the first time in four decades, the total number of the hungry continued to increase. Among interventions considered by the *Survey* to integrate nutritional considerations into agricultural and rural development programmes were improved income distribution, food subsidies, direct nutritional intervention programmes and nutritional education.

Other global-level analyses published in 1985 included a study on agricultural price policies, commodity studies on the world market situation and outlook for tomato products, and a compendium of prices of hides, skins and derived products. A statistical baseline study of African countries affected by drought, prepared in connection with ARPA, was expanded to cover all of Africa.

As part of its effort to help developing countries to develop their own statistical capabilities and infrastructures, FAO in 1985 established national demonstration and training centres in Chile and the Sudan. A workshop on improving statistics on women in agriculture (Rome, October) trained statisticians from 11 countries in how to introduce gender breakdowns in agricultural surveys.

In addition, more than 150 technical manuals were published in 1985.

World Food Programme. During 1985, WFP, which was created in 1963 to channel food surpluses to developing countries, had a total of 366 projects valued at $3,570 million under way in 91 countries. It provided more than 1.4 million tonnes of food aid to Africa alone, almost one third the total amount delivered. In sub-Saharan Africa, more than $2,270 million in development assistance was committed to help build long-term stability and sustainable increases in food and agricultural production.

In other parts of the world, food aid was provided to over 2 million refugees in Pakistan and $58 million in food was committed to Bangladesh to support projects to build rural roads and waterworks. In Latin America, food was used in a number of countries to help small-scale farmers in co-operative rural development projects and to improve dairy development.

Secretariat

At the end of 1985, the number of staff employed by FAO at its headquarters was 3,459, of whom 1,257 were in the Professional and higher categories. Field project personnel and those in regional and country offices numbered 3,492, 1,835 in the Professional and higher categories and 1,657 in the General Service category. Of the 328 associate experts working with the FAO, 36 were at headquarters and 292 in the field or regional and country offices. In addition, WFP employed 138 Professional and higher category staff and 192 General Service personnel at headquarters and 208 staff in the field.

Budget

The November 1985 session of the FAO Conference approved a budget of $437 million for 1986-1987.

Annex I.   MEMBERSHIP OF THE FOOD AND AGRICULTURE ORGANIZATION AND CONTRIBUTIONS

(Membership as at 31 December 1985; contributions as assessed for 1986 and 1987)

MEMBER	CONTRIBUTION Percent-age	CONTRIBUTION Net amount (in US dollars)	MEMBER	CONTRIBUTION Percent-age	CONTRIBUTION Net amount (in US dollars)	MEMBER	CONTRIBUTION Percent-age	CONTRIBUTION Net amount (in US dollars)
Afghanistan	0.01	22,910	Angola	0.01	22,910	Australia	1.90	4,352,900
Albania	0.01	22,910	Antigua and Barbuda	0.01	22,910	Austria	0.91	2,084,810
Algeria	0.16	366,560	Argentina	0.86	1,970,260	Bahamas	0.01	22,910

MEMBER	CONTRIBUTION Percentage	Net amount (in US dollars)	MEMBER	CONTRIBUTION Percentage	Net amount (in US dollars)	MEMBER	CONTRIBUTION Percentage	Net amount (in US dollars)
Bahrain	0.01	22,910	Guatemala	0.02	45,820	Paraguay	0.01	22,910
Bangladesh	0.04	91,640	Guinea	0.01	22,910	Peru	0.08	183,280
Barbados	0.01	22,910	Guinea-Bissau	0.01	22,910	Philippines	0.11	252,010
Belgium	1.55	3,551,050	Guyana	0.01	22,910	Poland	0.87	1,993,170
Belize	0.01	22,910	Haiti	0.01	22,910	Portugal	0.22	504,020
Benin	0.01	22,910	Honduras	0.01	22,910	Qatar	0.04	91,640
Bhutan	0.01	22,910	Hungary	0.28	641,480	Republic of Korea	0.22	504,020
Bolivia	0.01	22,910	Iceland	0.04	91,640	Romania	0.23	526,930
Botswana	0.01	22,910	India	0.43	985,130	Rwanda	0.01	22,910
Brazil	1.68	3,848,880	Indonesia	0.16	366,560	Saint Christopher and		
Bulgaria	0.22	504,020	Iran	0.70	1,603,700	Nevis	0.01	22,910
Burkina Faso	0.01	22,910	Iraq	0.14	320,740	Saint Lucia	0.01	22,910
Burma	0.01	22,910	Ireland	0.22	504,020	Saint Vincent and the		
Burundi	0.01	22,910	Israel	0.28	641,480	Grenadines	0.01	22,910
Cameroon	0.01	22,910	Italy	4.52	10,355,320	Samoa	0.01	22,910
Canada	3.72	8,522,520	Ivory Coast	0.04	91,640	Sao Tome and Principe	0.01	22,910
Cape Verde	0.01	22,910	Jamaica	0.02	45,820	Saudi Arabia	1.04	2,382,640
Central African Republic	0.01	22,910	Japan	12.46	28,545,860	Senegal	0.01	22,910
Chad	0.01	22,910	Jordan	0.01	22,910	Seychelles	0.01	22,910
Chile	0.08	183,280	Kenya	0.01	22,910	Sierra Leone	0.01	22,910
China	1.06	2,428,460	Kuwait	0.30	687,300	Solomon Islands	0.01	22,910
Colombia	0.13	297,830	Lao People's Democratic			Somalia	0.01	22,910
Comoros	0.01	22,910	Republic	0.01	22,910	Spain	2.33	5,338,030
Congo	0.01	22,910	Lebanon	0.02	45,820	Sri Lanka	0.01	22,910
Cook Islands	0.01	22,910	Lesotho	0.01	22,910	Sudan	0.01	22,910
Costa Rica	0.02	45,820	Liberia	0.01	22,910	Suriname	0.01	22,910
Cuba	0.11	252,010	Libyan Arab Jamahiriya	0.31	710,210	Swaziland	0.01	22,910
Cyprus	0.01	22,910	Luxembourg	0.07	160,370	Sweden	1.59	3,642,690
Czechoslovakia	0.92	2,107,720	Madagascar	0.01	22,910	Switzerland	1.33	3,047,030
Democratic Kampuchea	0.01	22,910	Malawi	0.01	22,910	Syrian Arab Republic	0.04	91,640
Democratic People's			Malaysia	0.11	252,010	Thailand	0.10	229,100
Republic of Korea	0.06	137,460	Maldives	0.01	22,910	Togo	0.01	22,910
Democratic Yemen	0.01	22,910	Mali	0.01	22,910	Tonga	0.01	22,910
Denmark	0.91	2,084,810	Malta	0.01	22,910	Trinidad and Tobago	0.04	91,640
Djibouti	0.01	22,910	Mauritania	0.01	22,910	Tunisia	0.04	91,640
Dominica	0.01	22,910	Mauritius	0.01	22,910	Turkey	0.39	893,490
Dominican Republic	0.04	91,640	Mexico	1.06	2,428,460	Uganda	0.01	22,910
Ecuador	0.02	45,820	Mongolia	0.01	22,910	United Arab Emirates	0.19	435,290
Egypt	0.08	183,280	Morocco	0.06	137,460	United Kingdom	5.64	12,921,240
El Salvador	0.01	22,910	Mozambique	0.01	22,910	United Republic of		
Equatorial Guinea	0.01	22,910	Namibia	0.01	22,910	Tanzania	0.01	22,910
Ethiopia	0.01	22,910	Nepal	0.01	22,910	United States	25.00	57,275,000
Fiji	0.01	22,910	Netherlands	2.15	4,925,650	Uruguay	0.05	114,550
Finland	0.58	1,328,780	New Zealand	0.31	710,210	Vanuatu	0.01	22,910
France	7.86	18,007,260	Nicaragua	0.01	22,910	Venezuela	0.66	1,512,060
Gabon	0.02	45,820	Niger	0.01	22,910	Viet Nam	0.02	45,820
Gambia	0.01	22,910	Nigeria	0.23	526,930	Yemen	0.01	22,910
Germany, Federal			Norway	0.62	1,420,420	Yugoslavia	0.55	1,260,050
Republic of	10.31	23,620,210	Oman	0.01	22,910	Zaire	0.01	22,910
Ghana	0.02	45,820	Pakistan	0.07	160,370	Zambia	0.01	22,910
Greece	0.48	1,099,680	Panama	0.02	45,820	Zimbabwe	0.02	45,820
Grenada	0.01	22,910	Papua New Guinea	0.01	22,910	Total	100.00	229,100,000

Annex II. MEMBERS OF THE COUNCIL OF THE FOOD AND AGRICULTURE ORGANIZATION

Holding office until 31 December 1986: Austria, Brazil, Bulgaria, Canada, Colombia, Congo, Cuba, Czechoslovakia, Democratic Yemen, Gambia, Lebanon, Mexico, Sao Tome and Principe, Trinidad and Tobago, Tunisia, Uganda, United States.

Holding office until conclusion of twenty-fourth session of the FAO Conference, November 1987: Afghanistan, Australia, Denmark, Ecuador, Egypt, France, India, Italy, Liberia, Pakistan, Philippines, Saudi Arabia, Senegal, United Kingdom, United Republic of Tanzania, Zimbabwe.

Holding office until 31 December 1988: Argentina, Bangladesh, Cameroon, China, Germany, Federal Republic of, Indonesia, Iraq, Japan, Malaysia, Nicaragua, Niger, Thailand, Turkey, Venezuela, Yugoslavia, Zambia.

Annex III. OFFICERS AND OFFICES OF THE FOOD AND AGRICULTURE ORGANIZATION

OFFICERS

OFFICE OF THE DIRECTOR-GENERAL
Director-General: Edouard Saouma.
Deputy Director-General: D. J. Walton.
Executive Director, World Food Programme: James Charles Ingram.

DEPARTMENTS
Assistant Director-General, Administration and Finance Department: Dean K. Crowther.

Assistant Director-General, Agriculture Department: D. F. R. Bommer.
Assistant Director-General, Development Department: R. S. Lignon.
Assistant Director-General, Forestry Department: M. A. Flores Rodas.
Assistant Director-General, Department of General Affairs and Information: P. Savary.
Assistant Director-General, Economic and Social Department: N. Islam.
Assistant Director-General, Fisheries Department: A. Lindquist, a.i.

REGIONAL REPRESENTATIVES OF THE DIRECTOR-GENERAL
Assistant Director-General and Regional Representative for Africa: J. A. C. Davies.
Assistant Director-General and Regional Representative for Asia and the Pacific:
   S. S. Puri.
Assistant Director-General and Regional Representative for Latin America and
   the Caribbean: M. E. Jalil.

Assistant Director-General and Regional Representative for the Near East: S.
   Jum'a.
Regional Representative for Europe: A. Bozzini.

HEADQUARTERS AND REGIONAL OFFICES

HEADQUARTERS

Food and Agriculture Organization
Via delle Terme di Caracalla
00100 Rome, Italy
   Cable address: FOODAGRI ROME
   Telephone: 57971
   Telex: 610181 FAO I

REGIONAL AND OTHER OFFICES

Food and Agriculture Organization Regional
   Office for Africa
P.O. Box 1628
Accra, Ghana

REGIONAL AND OTHER OFFICES *(cont.)*

Food and Agriculture Organization Regional
   Office for Asia and the Pacific
Maliwan Mansion, Phra Atit Road
Bangkok 10200, Thailand

Food and Agriculture Organization Regional
   Office for the Near East
Via delle Terme di Caracalla
00100 Rome, Italy

Food and Agriculture Organization Regional
   Office for Europe
Via delle Terme di Caracalla
00100 Rome, Italy

REGIONAL AND OTHER OFFICES *(cont.)*

Food and Agriculture Organization Regional
   Office for Latin America and the Caribbean
Avenida Santa Maria 6700
(Casilla 10095)
Santiago, Chile

Food and Agriculture Organization Liaison
   Office with the United Nations
United Nations Headquarters, Room DC1-1125
New York, N.Y. 10017, United States

Food and Agriculture Organization Liaison
   Office for North America
1001 22nd Street, N.W., Suite 300
Washington, D.C. 20437, United States

Chapter IV

United Nations Educational, Scientific and Cultural Organization (UNESCO)

The United Nations Educational, Scientific and Cultural Organization (UNESCO) continued throughout 1985 its activities aimed at promoting co-operation among nations through education, natural and social sciences, culture and communication.

After the withdrawal of Singapore and the United Kingdom on 31 December 1985, membership of UNESCO decreased to 158.

The twenty-third session of the UNESCO General Conference was held at Sofia, Bulgaria, from 8 October to 9 November. It was attended by 1,646 delegates from 154 member States, and by representatives from an associate member, two non-member States, liberation movements, United Nations bodies, and intergovernmental and non-governmental organizations (NGOs), for a total of 1,872 participants.

Education

In 1985 UNESCO continued to focus on education for development. Its major programmes were on: education for all; the formulation and application of education policies; and education, training and society.

Under the programme on education for all, a project in Latin America and the Caribbean continued. Attempting to eradicate illiteracy in the region by the year 2000, activities were aimed at implementing a plan of action adopted in 1984 by an intergovernmental regional committee for this project. With regard to the Regional Programme for the Eradication of Illiteracy in Africa, efforts centred on establishing inter-ministerial bodies and on preparing national plans linking adult literacy with the universalization and renewal of primary education.

The fourth International Conference on Adult Education (Paris, 19-29 March) was attended by 341 participants and observers from 122 member States, eight international organizations and 59 NGOs. Progress made since the third such Conference (Tokyo, 1972)[a] was assessed, and the many functions of adult education were set out in nine recommendations.

UNESCO provided support for the training of some 200 specialists from 12 countries on interaction between adult education and work, and awarded travel grants to 125 officials responsible

for workers' co-operative and trade union education in 52 member States. Some 18,000 copies of the quarterly newsletter *Adult Education—Information Notes* were distributed in the six official languages.

Regarding education in rural areas, training activities in educational strategies and approaches to educational innovations, science and technology teaching, low-cost educational materials and in-service training involved over 200 participants from 60 countries, including 15 least developed countries. These were complemented by technical missions to assist member States in revising educational content and methods and identifying innovative measures for educational reform in rural areas. In view of the need to include teacher training courses in higher agricultural education institutions, training was provided to 135 specialists from 59 countries. Seminars on improving higher agricultural education were organized in Africa, the Arab States, Asia and the Pacific, Europe, and Latin America and the Caribbean, involving 178 participants from 64 countries.

Activities for disabled persons included organizing mobile teams to train educators and parents in Asia and the Pacific, advisory support to 30 member States, technical support to a subregional project for special education in eastern and southern Africa, and organization of meetings in Chile, China, Costa Rica, Ecuador, India, Italy and Jordan.

Action to promote equality of educational opportunity for girls and women included assistance to six member States on educational and vocational guidance, support to activities in various member States in the field of literacy for women, and the launching of an international survey on the representation at the professional level of women in higher education. Other activities in favour of particular groups aimed at migrant workers, refugees and national liberation movements.

Under the programme on the formulation and application of educational policies, the fifth Regional Conference of Ministers of Education and Those Responsible for Economic Planning in Asia and the Pacific (Bangkok, Thailand, 4-11 March)

[a]YUN 1972, p. 759.

reviewed the development of education in the region and discussed priorities for educational development. It adopted a declaration and 29 recommendations focusing on improving the quality of education at both formal and non-formal levels, the specific needs of the Pacific States, and regional co-operation. The Conference was immediately followed by the third session of the Advisory Committee on Regional Co-operation in Education in Asia and the Pacific, which elaborated further measures to implement the recommendations.

Training activities in this area included 25 national training courses held with the assistance of the International Institute for Educational Planning, and 10 clusters of training materials published in English, French and Spanish. UNESCO also organized 30 advisory missions to assist member States in preparing sector studies and educational projects. Other activities sought to promote educational sciences.

Under the programme on education, training and society, 100 specialists from Africa and Asia and the Pacific received in-service training in the application of evaluation techniques to programmes designed to integrate productive work into the general education process; advisory services provided to seven member States sought to improve the introduction of productive work in secondary schools. An interregional symposium for Africa and Asia (Nairobi, Kenya, May), attended by 20 participants, made recommendations on the content, methods and programmes of training for teachers of national languages and mother tongues. Various activities were aimed at improving the teaching of science and technology, promoting physical education and sport, and integrating training and research activities.

Natural sciences

UNESCO continued contributing to international co-operation in science and technology for development during the year. Over 3,000 specialists, mainly from developing countries, were trained in basic sciences, informatics and biotechnology, in collaboration with national universities and institutions and NGOs. The education of engineers and technicians continued to receive high priority, as did activities relating to new and renewable sources of energy, with emphasis on the development of learning packages in both areas.

The importance of informatics for development, and the imbalance in equipment and informatics application between developed and developing countries, led UNESCO to launch an Intergovernmental Informatics Programme, with the goals of accelerating the training of specialists, facilitating the introduction of informatics in education, encouraging research in and through informatics,

and helping in the production of software for education and research. During the 1984-1985 biennium, about 1,200 specialists from 67 member States were involved in informatics training activities, and some 20 research and training pilot projects were implemented.

Two new networks were launched, the International Network of Centres for Computer Applications and the International Network on Earthquake Engineering, with the objective of increasing international co-operation in research and training and offering assistance to developing countries.

The second Conference of Ministers Responsible for the Application of Science and Technology to Development in Latin America and the Caribbean (Brasilia, Brazil, 20-26 August) was attended by 420 delegates from 25 countries, observers from two countries, and representatives from United Nations bodies and NGOs. It adopted recommendations aimed at harnessing local scientific and technological resources for the development of the region, especially in the rural areas.

The International Geological Correlation Programme, involving some 4,000 scientists from 130 countries, continued to stimulate international collaboration in the earth sciences through its 47 research projects in 116 countries. The geology for development project continued to focus on studying pre-Cambrian Africa, and multidisciplinary regional projects were begun to analyse the geological structure and mineral potential of the continent. The programme on geological applications of remote sensing continued stimulating research on geological interpretation of data from second-generation space-borne sensors, with its two projects focusing on areas of Africa and Latin America. Activities concerning natural hazards included a project on assessment and mitigation of earthquake risk in the Arab region. Missions were sent to various areas affected by natural hazards, including one to the Nevado del Ruiz volcano (Colombia), which subsequently erupted disastrously.

Under the Man and the Biosphere programme, implementation began of the Biosphere Reserve Action Plan, adopted in 1984 to expand the network of biosphere reserves and maintain research and training activities. Syntheses were produced of the results of pilot research projects, such as the integrated projects on arid lands based in Kenya and Tunisia. New comparative studies on tropical soil biology and fertility and on responses of savannahs to stress were launched in 1985, in co-operation with the International Union of Biological Sciences.

The International Hydrological Programme entered its twenty-first year of operation, with some 10,000 specialists world-wide contributing to its 61 projects. Twenty-eight post-graduate courses and numerous short courses, seminars and symposia were sponsored, often jointly with scientific NGOs. Pilot projects on the rational use and conservation of water resources in rural areas were under way in some 10 Arab countries, in the Sahel States of Africa and in Latin America.

The Intergovernmental Oceanographic Commission continued its programmes, which included ocean dynamics and climate, ocean science in relation to living and non-living resources, marine pollution research and monitoring, ocean mapping, ocean observation and warning systems, and marine data and information exchange.

UNESCO activities in marine sciences in 1985 enabled some 400 specialists to increase their knowledge in this field. An interregional project on research and training with a view to the integrated management of coastal systems received extrabudgetary resources, making it possible to execute various pilot projects concerning coral reefs, mangrove areas, coastal lagoons and coastal ecosystems.

Other activities dealt with urban systems and urbanization, the natural heritage, and environmental education and information.

Social sciences

In 1985, UNESCO continued emphasizing the development of social and human sciences.

To achieve greater decentralization, a regional social science unit, attached to the Regional Centre for Higher Education, was established in Latin America and the Caribbean. In collaboration with the social science networks of the region, the unit launched five regional research projects and organized four specialized meetings and two training courses.

A meeting on philosophy teaching and research in Latin America and the Caribbean (Lima, Peru, 24-28 June) was attended by 13 experts from the region. Round tables on the philosophers Al-Ghazali and Maimonides were held in December at UNESCO headquarters. The organization continued to provide financial support for the publication of the journal *Diogenes*.

The major thrust of population activities was to provide technical support to 35 national projects, mainly in training, research and planning of communication strategies. In this connection, UNESCO collaborated with regional broadcasting organizations, such as the Asia-Pacific Institute for Broadcasting Development, the Arab States Broadcasting Union and the Asociación Interamericana de Radiodifusión. Other activities dealt with the socioeconomic aspects of migration, both internal and international.

Activities for youth continued to promote the development of sport, particularly for youth in rural areas; to expand voluntary work among young people; and to examine the circumstances, in particular youth unemployment, which led young people to become socially deprived. The World Congress on Youth, organized in co-operation with the Spanish Government (Barcelona, 8-15 July), brought together 608 participants and observers from 120 member States and 96 NGOs. Discussion focused on: youth, education and work; youth and cultural development; and young people, mutual understanding and international co-operation. The Congress adopted the Barcelona Statement, to serve as a framework for future action.

On the issues of prejudice, intolerance, racism and *apartheid*, activities included meetings and studies on the phenomenon of slavery and slave trade, analysis of South African radio broadcasting, particularly programmes for neighbouring African States, a study on the access of Africans to research and advanced training in South Africa, and research on national social policies and immigration.

UNESCO continued to analyse human rights violations and the conditions for peace. With the collaboration of the International Peace Research Institute (Oslo, Norway), an international symposium was held in October on the different interpretations of the causes and consequences of conflicts. Volumes IV (1983) and V (1984) of the *UNESCO Yearbook on Peace and Conflict Studies* were published. The 1985 UNESCO Prize for Peace Education was awarded to General Indar Jit Rikhye (India) and the Georg Eckert Institute for International Research on School Textbooks (Federal Republic of Germany). Support was given to various institutions to train young professors and researchers on human rights.

The status of women programme included studies and dissemination of information on the role of women in society, efforts to incorporate women's concerns in development planning, and activities to enhance the role of women in the media. An international advisory group of experts met in Paris (25-28 June) to assist UNESCO in its efforts to improve the status of women.

Culture

Implementation of international campaigns for the safeguarding of cultural heritage was pursued throughout 1985. Two new campaigns were launched: one to safeguard the ancient monuments and sites of Paharpur Vihara and Bagerhat (Bangladesh), the other for the restoration of the architectural heritage of Guatemala. Activities were carried out in each of the 29 international campaigns in progress; preparation for nine others was undertaken.

The World Heritage Committee, established under the 1972 Convention concerning the Protection of the World Cultural and Natural Heritage, held its ninth session (Paris, 2-6 December). It inscribed

30 additional sites on the World Heritage List, thus raising to 216 the number of cultural and natural properties (situated in 55 countries) protected by the Convention, to which 88 States were parties at the end of 1985. Efforts continued to promote public awareness of the Convention's objectives and to encourage contributions to the World Heritage Fund, which supports training activities and restoration work on World Heritage sites.

Studies continued on African, Latin American, Caribbean, Arab, Asian, European and Arctic cultures. Four volumes of the *General History of Africa* were published in English, three volumes in French and Spanish, two in Portuguese and one in Arabic. Literary works from Africa, Asia and Latin America were translated and published in the *UNESCO Collection of Representative Works*, and in the European series the Nordic countries received increasing attention. The quarterly *Museum* was produced in English, French, Russian and Spanish with a circulation of 17,000 copies. The fifteenth UNESCO travelling exhibition, on Slavonic art, accompanied by a video production, was mounted. Five records in the UNESCO collection of traditional music were issued.

Regarding artistic creativity, a meeting was held in Budapest, Hungary, on the recognition and protection of young talent in cinema, dance and music. An international consultation attended by 20 member States (Venice, Italy, 24-26 June) analysed the role of major art exhibitions and international events to promote contemporary art. International experimental workshops studied the urban extension of historic centres, and the industrial design of medical equipment and hospital premises. The UNESCO/International Music Council Prize for Music was awarded to Paul Collaer (Belgium), Witold Lutoslawski (Poland) and Olivier Messiaen (France).

Communications

In 1985, UNESCO continued its efforts to improve the national and international flow of information, primarily by strengthening developing countries' communication infrastructure, training of communication personnel, production of communication equipment and improvement of media content. It also continued to study the role of communication in society, in particular the socio-cultural impact of new technologies. Under this programme, a series of comparative research studies were carried out, and a geographically-based planning consultation was held in India, covering Africa, the Arab States and Asia and the Pacific.

Further consultations were held on a new world information and communication order (see p. 373), seen as an evolving and continuing process, as well as on plurality in information, the contribution of the media to international understanding, human rights and peace, and the watch-dog role of the press. A summary of previous work on the right to communicate was prepared to help define the emphasis of future activities on that theme.

The Intergovernmental Council of the International Programme for the Development of Communication (IPDC) (sixth session, Paris, 4-11 March) approved financial contributions to 38 projects for communication development. During this session, the first IPDC-UNESCO Prize for Rural Communication, set up in 1984,[b] was awarded to the Kheda Communication Project of India. IPDC continued to support regional news agencies, regional broadcasting unions and media training. Advisory missions were organized to assist in preparing national plans for the development of community radio, news agencies, television and regional newspapers, and in the formulation of national book and communications policies.

Training programmes and materials on communications continued to expand, with the participation of national, regional and subregional institutions. More than 2,500 persons received initial or further training. A special project, PACBROAD, was launched to provide radio production training to Pacific island broadcasters. Support was provided to the establishment or reinforcement of more than 30 local newspapers in Africa. Community radio stations were set up in Burundi, Ghana, Maldives, Sri Lanka and Tonga. Community video was assisted in Nepal and in Trinidad and Tobago.

Assistance was provided to a number of Latin American countries to organize national reading campaigns using the media. Workshops were held in the Dominican Republic and in Africa on the production of reading materials. Other activities included: seminars on children's books (Arab Gulf States) and on young people's reading habits (Vienna, Austria); the launching of a regional programme for publications in Braille in Latin America; and an innovative study in China to explore problems in distributing reading material to new literates in rural areas. Training in the book profession, emphasizing management, production, editing and design, was provided to some 300 trainees.

General Information Programme

The General Information Programme continued to provide assistance to member States on scientific and technical information, documentation, libraries and archives. It also aimed at strengthening national capabilities for handling information through the development of telecommunication technologies and information systems.

The Programme continued promoting development of library and information services and systems; integrated library and information services were

bYUN 1984, p. 1217.

put into operation through two national projects. The Regional Network for the Exchange of Information and Experience in Science and Technology in Asia and the Pacific developed considerably, with 17 member States and 80 associated centres co-operating within the system at the end of 1985. A meeting on resource-sharing in southern and central Africa was convened in the United Republic of Tanzania to identify to what extent the countries of that region could assist each other in acquiring, processing and distributing information. Other activities included training courses, production and dissemination of technical publications and periodicals, and projects aimed at introducing modern technologies and establishing data bases.

Action for development

Activities continued under the programme on principles, methods and strategies of action for development. In 1984-1985, 1,396 fellowships and 293 study grants were awarded. Of these, 716 were in education, 360 in natural sciences, 147 in general information, 113 in communications, 62 in culture and 61 in social and human sciences. In addition, 312 conventional-type fellowships were awarded and training opportunities made available to 464 candidates, enabling them to take part in courses and seminars organized by NGOs, training and research institutions and foundations, making maximum use of training facilities in developing countries.

Two agreements to execute pilot projects were signed. The first was concluded with the French National Commission for UNESCO to extend cultural relations between nationals of developing countries who had emigrated to industrialized countries of Western Europe and the populations of the host countries. The second, concluded with the Congo, dealt with the development of its Mayombé region.

Other activities included training seminars, development studies and publication of technical reports. Meetings of experts examined the role of families in development in Africa (Bujumbura, Burundi, 21-25 January), social and cultural dimensions of development in integrated planning (Paris, 22-26 April), women's concerns and development planning (San Marino, 1-4 July), youth unemployment (Paris, 18-20 September), and analysis of development planning methods (Nairobi, 2-6 December).

Technical assistance

Participation Programme

At 31 December 1985, allocations approved by the Director-General under the UNESCO Par-

ticipation Programme, through which member States and organizations participate in technical assistance activities, amounted to $14,712,904.

The amounts (in United States dollars) by sector and by region were as follows:

Sector	Allocation
Education	3,731,553
Culture	3,696,968
Natural sciences	2,669,280
Social sciences	1,483,354
General Information Programme	1,366,030
Communication	858,064
Training abroad and national commissions	736,447
Programme support	171,208
Total	**14,712,904**

Region	
Africa	4,279,291
Latin America and the Caribbean	2,822,564
Asia and the Pacific	2,376,004
Europe	2,259,640
Arab States	1,502,835
Interregional	1,472,570
Total	**14,712,904**

SOURCE: UNESCO 1984-1985: report of the Director-General.

Extrabudgetary programmes

Amounts obligated in 1985 in respect of projects for which UNESCO served as executing agency, financed by UNDP, UNFPA and other extrabudgetary sources, totalled $80.3 million as shown below:

Source	Amount (in thousands of US dollars)
UNDP	33,584
Donated funds	10,897
Self-benefiting funds	9,570
Special accounts and voluntary contributions	6,872
UNFPA	6,869
Other United Nations sources	5,990
World Bank technical assistance	3,103
Associate experts	1,931
Regional banks and funds	1,496
Total	**80,312**

Sector	
Education	37,124
Natural sciences	19,301
Culture	10,701
Communication	6,774
Social and human sciences	2,737
General Information Programme	2,198
Other	1,477
Total	**80,312**

Region	
Africa	26,071
Asia and the Pacific	17,658
Arab States	16,516
Latin America and the Caribbean	9,010
Interregional and global	8,602
Europe	2,455
Total	**80,312**

Secretariat

As at 31 December 1985, the number of full-time staff employed by UNESCO on permanent, fixed-term and short-term appointments was 3,171 drawn from 135 nationalities. Of these, 1,234 were in the Professional or higher categories and 1,937 were in the General Service and Maintenance Worker categories.

Of the Professional staff, 379 were serving in the field, as were 437 General Service and Maintenance Worker staff.

Budget

The 1985 session of the UNESCO General Conference approved a budget of $307,223,000 for 1986-1987. However, after the withdrawal from the organization of two member States, the Executive Board adjusted the budget to $289,339,000. The level of the Working Capital Fund was fixed at $15,000,000 and the total assessment on member States (after reducing miscellaneous income) at $255,850,980. Amounts allocated (in thousands of United States dollars) are shown in the table below:

UNESCO REGULAR BUDGET

	Amount
Programme operations and services	209,305
Programme support services	28,607
General policy and direction	25,516
Common services	24,410
General administrative services	24,128
Appropriation reserve	15,610
Capital expenditure	1,055
Negative provision for currency fluctuation	(39,291)*
Total	289,339

*This amount was subsequently increased to a positive provision of $1,814,227 after savings of $2,337,647 and a supplementary appropriation of $38,768,000.

Annex I.   MEMBERSHIP OF THE UNITED NATIONS EDUCATIONAL, SCIENTIFIC AND CULTURAL ORGANIZATION AND CONTRIBUTIONS

(Membership as at 31 December 1985; annual contributions as assessed for 1986 and 1987)

MEMBER	CONTRIBUTION Percent-age	CONTRIBUTION Amount (in US dollars)	MEMBER	CONTRIBUTION Percent-age	CONTRIBUTION Amount (in US dollars)	MEMBER	CONTRIBUTION Percent-age	CONTRIBUTION Amount (in US dollars)
Afghanistan	0.01	18,249	Democratic Yemen	0.01	18,249	Kuwait	0.29	529,221
Albania	0.01	18,249	Denmark	0.71	1,295,679	Lao People's Demo-		
Algeria	0.14	255,486	Dominica	0.01	18,249	cratic Republic	0.01	18,249
Angola	0.01	18,249	Dominican Republic	0.03	54,747	Lebanon	0.01	18,249
Antigua and Barbuda	0.01	18,249	Ecuador	0.03	54,747	Lesotho	0.01	18,249
Argentina	0.61	1,113,189	Egypt	0.07	127,743	Liberia	0.01	18,249
Australia	1.64	2,992,836	El Salvador	0.01	18,249	Libyan Arab		
Austria	0.73	1,332,177	Equatorial Guinea	0.01	18,249	Jamahiriya	0.26	474,474
Bahamas	0.01	18,249	Ethiopia	0.01	18,249	Luxembourg	0.05	91,245
Bahrain	0.02	36,498	Fiji	0.01	18,249	Madagascar	0.01	18,249
Bangladesh	0.02	36,498	Finland	0.49	894,201	Malawi	0.01	18,249
Barbados	0.01	18,249	France	6.29	11,478,621	Malaysia	0.10	182,490
Belgium	1.17	2,135,133	Gabon	0.03	54,747	Maldives	0.01	18,249
Belize	0.01	18,249	Gambia	0.01	18,249	Mali	0.01	18,249
Benin	0.01	18,249	German Democratic			Malta	0.01	18,249
Bhutan	0.01	18,249	Republic	1.31	2,390,619	Mauritania	0.01	18,249
Bolivia	0.01	18,249	Germany, Federal			Mauritius	0.01	18,249
Botswana	0.01	18,249	Republic of	8.16	14,891,184	Mexico	0.88	1,605,912
Brazil	1.38	2,518,362	Ghana	0.01	18,249	Monaco	0.01	18,249
Bulgaria	0.16	291,984	Greece	0.43	784,707	Mongolia	0.01	18,249
Burkina Faso	0.01	18,249	Grenada	0.01	18,249	Morocco	0.05	91,245
Burma	0.01	18,249	Guatemala	0.02	36,498	Mozambique	0.01	18,249
Burundi	0.01	18,249	Guinea	0.01	18,249	Namibia*	—	—
Byelorussian SSR	0.34	620,466	Guinea-Bissau	0.01	18,249	Nepal	0.01	18,249
Cameroon	0.01	18,249	Guyana	0.01	18,249	Netherlands	1.72	3,138,828
Canada	3.02	5,511,198	Haiti	0.01	18,249	New Zealand	0.24	437,976
Cape Verde	0.01	18,249	Honduras	0.01	18,249	Nicaragua	0.01	18,249
Central African Republic	0.01	18,249	Hungary	0.22	401,478	Niger	0.01	18,249
Chad	0.01	18,249	Iceland	0.03	54,747	Nigeria	0.19	346,731
Chile	0.07	127,743	India	0.34	620,466	Norway	0.53	967,197
China	0.78	1,423,422	Indonesia	0.14	255,486	Oman	0.02	36,498
Colombia	0.13	237,237	Iran	0.62	1,131,438	Pakistan	0.06	109,494
Comoros	0.01	18,249	Iraq	0.12	218,988	Panama	0.02	36,498
Congo	0.01	18,249	Ireland	0.18	328,482	Papua New Guinea	0.01	18,249
Costa Rica	0.02	36,498	Israel	0.22	401,478	Paraguay	0.02	36,498
Cuba	0.09	164,241	Italy	3.74	6,825,126	Peru	0.07	127,743
Cyprus	0.02	36,498	Ivory Coast	0.02	36,498	Philippines	0.10	182,490
Czechoslovakia	0.69	1,259,181	Jamaica	0.02	36,498	Poland	0.63	1,149,687
Democratic Kampuchea	0.01	18,249	Japan	10.71	19,544,679	Portugal	0.18	328,482
Democratic People's			Jordan	0.01	18,249	Qatar	0.04	72,996
Republic of Korea	0.05	91,245	Kenya	0.01	18,249	Republic of Korea	0.20	364,980

| MEMBER | CONTRIBUTION | | MEMBER | CONTRIBUTION | | MEMBER | CONTRIBUTION | |
	Percent-age	Amount (in US dollars)		Percent-age	Amount (in US dollars)		Percent-age	Amount (in US dollars)
Romania	0.19	346,731	Suriname	0.01	18,249	Uruguay	0.04	72,996
Rwanda	0.01	18,249	Swaziland	0.01	18,249	Venezuela	0.59	1,076,691
Saint Christopher and			Sweden	1.24	2,262,876	Viet Nam	0.01	18,249
Nevis	0.01	18,249	Switzerland	1.11	2,025,639	Yemen	0.01	18,249
Saint Lucia	0.01	18,249	Syrian Arab			Yugoslavia	0.45	821,205
Saint Vincent and the			Republic	0.04	72,996	Zaire	0.01	18,249
Grenadines	0.01	18,249	Thailand	0.09	164,241	Zambia	0.01	18,249
Samoa	0.01	18,249	Togo	0.01	18,249	Zimbabwe	0.02	36,498
San Marino	0.01	18,249	Tonga	0.01	18,249			
Sao Tome and Principe	0.01	18,249	Trinidad and Tobago	0.04	72,996	Total	70.10	127,925,490
Saudi Arabia	0.96	1,751,904	Tunisia	0.03	54,747			
Senegal	0.01	18,249	Turkey	0.34	620,466	ASSOCIATE		
Seychelles	0.01	18,249	Uganda	0.01	18,249	MEMBER		
Sierra Leone	0.01	18,249	Ukrainian SSR	1.26	2,299,374			
Singapore†	—	—	USSR	10.08	18,394,992	British Virgin Islands	0.01	18,249
Somalia	0.01	18,249	United Arab Emirates	0.18	328,482	Netherlands Antilles	0.01	18,249
Spain	2.00	3,649,800	United Kingdom†	—	—			
Sri Lanka	0.01	18,249	United Republic of			Total	0.02	36,498
Sudan	0.01	18,249	Tanzania	0.01	18,249			

*Assessment remained suspended in 1984.

†Withdrew from UNESCO on 31 December 1985.

Annex II. OFFICERS AND OFFICES OF THE UNITED NATIONS EDUCATIONAL, SCIENTIFIC AND CULTURAL ORGANIZATION

(As at 31 December 1985)

MEMBERS OF THE EXECUTIVE BOARD

Chairman: Ivo Margan (Yugoslavia).

Vice-Chairmen: Camille Aboussouan (Lebanon), Ian Christie Clark (Canada), Ben Kufakunesu Jambga (Zimbabwe), Elsa D. R. Kelly (Argentina), Mizuo Kuroda (Japan), Guennady V. Ouranov (USSR).

Members: Eid Abdo (Syrian Arab Republic), Paul Yao Akoto (Ivory Coast), Bashir Bakri (Sudan), Alphonse Blagué (Central African Republic), Léon Louis Boissier-Palun (Benin), Hilaire Bouhoyi (Congo), Mohamed Brahimi El-Mili (Algeria), Aurelio Caicedo Ayerbe (Colombia), Dimitri Cosmadopoulos (Greece), Buyantyn Dashtseren (Mongolia), Georges-Henri Dumont (Belgium), Mohamed Fathallah El-Khatib (Egypt), Pierre Foulani (Niger), Walter Gehlhoff (Federal Republic of Germany), Miguel Gonzalez Avelar (Mexico), Gisèle Halimi (France), Reuben H. Harris (Antigua and Barbuda), Abdul Aziz Hussein (Kuwait), Attiya Inayatullah (Pakistan), Andri Isaksson (Iceland), Siegfried Kaempf (German Democratic Republic), A. Majeed Khan (Bangladesh), Edward Victor Luckhoo (Guyana), Abdelsalam A. Majali (Jordan), N'Tji Idriss Mariko (Mali), Milan Milanov (Bulgaria), Adamou Ndam Njoya (Cameroon), Musa Justice Nsibande (Swaziland), Maria Luisa Paronetto Valier (Italy), Luis Manuel Peñalver (Venezuela), Jean Ping (Gabon), Guy A. Rajaonson (Madagascar), Swaran Singh (India), Preciosa Soliven (Philippines), Sheilah Marguerite Solomon (Trinidad and Tobago), Alemayehu Teferra (Ethiopia), Iba Der Thiam (Senegal), Doddy Achdiat Tisna Amidjaja (Indonesia), Birgitta Ulvhammar (Sweden), José Israel Vargas (Brazil), Alberto Wagner de Reyna (Peru), Edward Gough Whitlam (Australia), Zhao Fusan (China).

PRINCIPAL OFFICERS OF THE SECRETARIAT

Director-General: Amadou Mahtar M'Bow.

Deputy Director-General: Jean Knapp.

Assistant Directors-General: Chikh Békri, Abdul-Razzak Kaddoura, Julio Labastida, Henri Lopes, Makaminan Makagiansar, George F. Saddler, Sema Tanguiane.

HEADQUARTERS AND OTHER OFFICE

HEADQUARTERS
UNESCO House
7 Place de Fontenoy
75700 Paris, France
  Cable address: UNESCO PARIS
  Telephone: (1)45.68.10.00
  Telex: 204461

NEW YORK OFFICE
United Nations Educational, Scientific and
  Cultural Organization
2 United Nations Plaza
New York, N.Y. 10017, United States
  Cable Address: UNESCORG NEWYORK
  Telephone: (212) 963-5995

Chapter V

World Health Organization (WHO)

The thirty-eighth World Health Assembly met at Geneva from 6 to 20 May 1985 and endorsed a zero-growth programme budget for the 1986-1987 biennium. With the addition of extrabudgetary funds, the World Health Organization (WHO) would have almost $1 billion to support health activities in its member States. The proportion to be allocated to country and regional activities was to rise to 70 per cent in 1986-1987, and the introduction of regional programme budget policies was endorsed, to ensure that the focus was kept on mainstream health activities to foster the attainment of health for all by the year 2000, as set out in the 1982 plan of action.[a]

The Health Assembly decided that emergency health relief to drought- and famine-stricken African countries should be linked to co-operation in their long-term health and socio-economic development. It also decided to strengthen WHO's co-operation with countries collaborating among themselves for health development, to increase the involvement of non-governmental organizations in health-for-all strategies, and to support the development of health-for-all leaders within the health sector and outside it. The Assembly also considered the topics of women, health and development; the epidemiological situation with regard to malaria; and the prevention of disability, including deafness.

Brunei Darussalam on 25 March 1985 became a WHO member, bringing its membership to 166 and one associate member.

Co-ordination with other organizations

WHO continued to participate in the emergency assistance being provided by the United Nations system, particularly in the critical situation in Africa, and it concentrated increasingly on promoting the preparedness and capacity of member States to cope with health emergencies and natural disasters. In connection with International Youth Year (see p. 978), the theme of World Health Day (7 April) was "Healthy Youth: Our Best Resource". Attention focused on the health needs of young people and on the mobilization and active participation of youth in promoting primary health care.

Health system infrastructure

In November a WHO consultative group assessed the current status of the organization of health systems in countries and the support being provided by WHO, and identified priority areas and activities requiring concerted action. Strengthening overall national health system organization to implement primary health care was one of the main subjects discussed by the UNICEF/WHO Joint Committee on Health Policy at its twenty-fifth session, in January. An interregional meeting (Ottawa, Canada, June) on developing and strengthening logistic support to primary health care stressed the need to plan the development and maintenance of health facilities and also the need for hospital support at the primary health care level. A first interregional meeting on community involvement in health development took place at Brioni, Yugoslavia, in June.

Health promotion and care

General health protection

Progress reviews were made in preparation for the July World Conference to Review and Appraise the Achievements of the United Nations Decade for Women (see p. 937). Discussion of the Director-General's report on women, health and development in WHO governing bodies led to the provision of a framework for WHO's implementation of the forward-looking strategies—that emerged from the Conference—for the advancement of women in 1986-2000.

The prevention and management of malnutrition continued to be accorded highest priority, with particular reference in 1985 to vitamin-A deficiency and related blindness. In the area of accident prevention, attention was given to falls of elderly people, burn injuries, spinal cord injuries, accidents in domestic settings, traffic safety, and accidents and violent deaths among adolescents. The first global liaison meeting on accident and injury prevention was convened at Geneva, whose target—to be evaluated annually—was for as many countries as possible to have introduced and enforced legislation related to the wearing of seat-belts in motor vehicles by the year 2000.

Health of specific population groups

A November WHO interregional meeting at Geneva reiterated that maternal mortality and morbidity were found to be related to the organization of services for appropriate referral, quality of care and its supervision, and the integration of primary health care with traditional community perceptions

[a]YUN 1982, p. 1538.

and attitudes towards pregnancy and delivery care. In many parts of the world, maternal mortality rates were 200 to 500 times higher than in more privileged countries. WHO emphasized research, development and evaluation of appropriate technologies for use by traditional birth attendants, such as risk profiles and delivery kits. The report was published of a symposium on fetal diagnosis of congenital disorders, with descriptions of such diagnostic approaches as amniocentesis, fetoscopy, ultrasound examination, and cytogenetic or biochemical analysis of chorionic villi.

To examine the nature and magnitude of child abuse in the context of the role of the family, child labour, sexual abuse and child prostitution, vagrant children and children in war, an international conference was convened at Berne, Switzerland, in December under the joint sponsorship of WHO and the Council for International Organizations of Medical Sciences. Workshops were held with participants from four regions in 1985 as a means of analysing and meeting the reproductive health needs of adolescents.

The Special Programme of Research, Development and Research Training in Human Reproduction responded to member States' requests by studying the feasibility, in national contexts, of integrating family planning within maternal and child health services. In 1985 three projects were successfully completed: in the Republic of Korea, on the effectiveness of integrated programmes when co-ordinated by nurse midwives; in Bangladesh, on the important role of village practitioners in expanding family planning services and in promoting the use of contraceptive methods; and in Chile, on continuing the use of intra-uterine devices and oral contraceptives.

Mid-year reports to WHO indicated unusually high prevalence rates for occupational and work-related diseases, which were frequently found to be superimposed on existing serious health problems such as malnutrition and parasitic diseases, thus confirming the rationale for WHO's stress on developing workers' health programmes within the health services infrastructure. The first International Conference on the Health Hazards and Biological Effects of Welding Fumes and Gases (Copenhagen, Denmark, February) was organized jointly by the Commission of the European Communities, WHO, the Danish Welding Institute and the International Agency for Research on Cancer. The Conference considered experimental and epidemiological studies of the effects of welding fumes and gases and made recommendations on the reduction of exposure and the development of monitoring, educational and health assessment programmes.

Environmental health

For the approaching mid-point of the 1981-1990 International Drinking Water Supply and Sanitation Decade on 31 December 1985, the Executive Board reviewed WHO's programme and evaluated progress towards adequate water supply and sanitation. The second and third volumes of the WHO *Guidelines for Drinking-water Quality* were published in 1985, and considerable activity followed on the part of member States to put drinking-water standards into effect and to take the requisite surveillance and corrective measures.

Against the background of innumerable individual cases of poisoning and industrial accidents endangering communities, the Fourth General Meeting of the World Federation of Associations of Clinical Toxicology Centres and Poison Control Centres, convened in October at WHO headquarters jointly by the Commission of the European Communities and the UNEP/ILO/WHO International Programme on Chemical Safety, concluded that harmonization of data on poisoning and the standard of services provided by poison centres could be enhanced through greater international collaboration. National workshops and regional courses continued to be organized, based on WHO guidelines, on the assessment of pollution sources and environmental health impact assessment.

By the end of 1985, the first edition of the *Codex Alimentarius* (standards and codes of hygienic and technological practice defined by a joint FAO/WHO Commission) was completed with the publication of additional volumes. Jointly with FAO, WHO also continued to support the work of expert groups on pesticide residues and collaborated with member States in the FAO/WHO food contamination monitoring programme, a health-related activity of UNEP's Global Environmental Monitoring System.

Diagnostic, therapeutic and rehabilitative technology

In line with increasing interest in the assessment of health technology and with a view to developing and using appropriate technologies, a global programme for appropriate medical health care technology was established in July at the Danish Hospital Institute, a WHO collaborating centre.

WHO purchased 40 X-ray machines for its basic radiological system, to be installed in 10 countries in the Eastern Mediterranean region. Three copiously illustrated manuals were either published or prepared for publication in Arabic, English, French and Spanish, on radiographic interpretation for general practitioners, and darkroom and radiographic techniques.

At a conference convened by WHO (Nairobi, Kenya, November), 92 experts from Governments and national regulatory authorities, industry, and organizations of patients and consumers, as well as teachers and providers of health care, reached agreement on making the world-wide use of drugs more rational. The responsibility of Governments and the importance of the essential drug concept were affirmed, and WHO's support and leadership role was delineated.

Disease prevention and control

Immunization

Data available in July showed that thanks to the Expanded Programme on Immunization, of which UNICEF was a major supporter, 40 per cent of children in the developing countries (excluding China) had received the full course of DPT (diphtheria, pertussis and tetanus) and poliomyelitis vaccines, compared with 5 per cent when the Programme was launched in 1974. Immunization against those diseases and measles and tuberculosis was saving the lives of about 800,000 infants yearly.

Malaria

The overall world malaria situation in 1985 showed no real general improvement. Of the total world population, 48 per cent (2,266 million people) lived in areas where malaria risk persisted but organized control was being pursued, and 8 per cent (398 million) were living in areas (mainly in tropical Africa) where malaria endemicity remained basically unchanged. About 95 million clinical cases occurred each year with 240 million people becoming infected.

Other parasitic diseases

After 10 years of the Onchocerciasis (river blindness) Control Programme in the Volta River basin region, the disease had been brought under control in 90 per cent of the area by the use of insecticides to control the blackfly population responsible for transmission.

Diarrhoeal diseases

The second International Conference on Oral Rehydration Therapy was held in Washington, D.C., in December 1985 under the joint sponsorship of the United States Agency for International Development, WHO and UNICEF. Participants from 90 countries learned of the progress made since the first conference three years earlier. In Bangladesh, for example, 2.6 million leaflets describing oral rehydration—a method of preventing dehydration caused by diarrhoea—were distributed through the primary school system. A 1985 evaluation showed that about 88 per cent of primary school children were involved with the follow-up activity.

Acute respiratory infections

Ten health systems research projects on the feasibility and impact on mortality of strategies for the control of acute respiratory infections and 11 etiological and epidemiological research projects had been continued or initiated in 1985. These activities had given encouraging preliminary results. A project in the United Republic of Tanzania, for example, showed that one year after implementing

intervention strategies a 19.5 per cent overall reduction of mortality in children under 5 years of age was observed by comparison with a control area.

Zoonoses

The Joint FAO/WHO Expert Committee on Brucellosis (sixth meeting, Geneva, November) made recommendations in the context of health for all to guide communities in controlling and where possible eliminating brucellosis from domestic animals, protecting people and treating them when protection failed.

Sexually transmitted diseases

WHO developed training modules to enable a large number of health care personnel to carry out control activities in regard to sexually transmitted diseases, and closer collaboration in research was undertaken to economize scarce resources, accelerate the development of better and simpler diagnostic tools, and identify an immunizing agent against syphilis and the endemic treponematoses. To co-ordinate global surveillance activities and to assess the international health implications of acquired immune deficiency syndrome (AIDS), consultations, meetings and workshops were organized and a network of collaborating centres was established by WHO following an April international conference on AIDS held at Atlanta, Georgia, under joint United States/WHO sponsorship.

Cancer

WHO developed a method for setting priorities for cancer control programmes by providing a structure and terminology for comparisons of cost effectiveness. A November meeting reviewed the approaches and impediments to reducing mortality from cervical cancer (about 500,000 new cases each year), and formulated strategies to encourage early detection, adequate cytological services and appropriate therapy. Data for 1960-1980 on cancer mortality from 28 countries, representing 75 per cent of the population of the developed world, showed an increase of 19 per cent in cancer deaths among males and a decrease of 2 per cent among females. A dramatic rise in mortality was registered for lung cancer (76 per cent for men and 135 per cent for women).

Other non-communicable diseases

The annual meeting in Moscow in June/July of the principal investigators in WHO's Country-wide Integrated Programme for the Prevention of Non-Communicable Diseases decided that greater emphasis should be placed on nutrition and reviewed a draft manual containing guidelines on monitoring and evaluation.

Secretariat

As at 31 December 1985, the total number of full-time staff employed by WHO stood at 4,477 on permanent and fixed-term contracts. Of these, 1,438 staff members, drawn from 124 nationalities, were in the Professional and higher categories, and 3,039 were in the General Service category. Of the total number of staff, 108 were in posts financed by UNDP, UNEP, UNFPA and the United Nations Fund for Drug Abuse Control.

Budget

The thirty-sixth (1983) World Health Assembly had approved an effective budget of $520.1 million for 1984-1985.[b]

The thirty-eighth Assembly approved a working budget of $554 million for the 1986-1987 biennium, divided into allocations for WHO's work programme as follows: health system infrastructure, 32.6 per cent; health promotion and care, 18.5 per cent; disease prevention and control, 15.5 per cent; programme support, 21.8 per cent; and direction, co-ordination and management, 11.6 per cent.

INTEGRATED INTERNATIONAL HEALTH PROGRAMME OBLIGATIONS BY SOURCE OF FINANCING FOR THE TWO-YEAR PERIOD 1984-1985

Source	Amount (in US dollars)
Regular budget	520,100,000
Pan American Health Organization	139,095,000
International Agency for Research on Cancer	20,960,000
Other sources	
Voluntary Fund for Health Promotion	95,491,000
Tropical diseases research	64,136,000
Onchocerciasis Control Programme	41,000,000
Sasakawa Health Trust Fund	6,500,000
United Nations sources	
UNICEF	60,000
UNDP	36,718,000
UNEP	965,000
UNFDAC	59,000
UNFPA	39,333,000
UNHCR	142,000
Trust funds	14,740,000
Special Account for Servicing Costs	10,295,000
Total	990,131,000

[b]YUN 1983, p. 1250.

SERVICES AND CO-OPERATION EXTENDED BY WHO IN THE TWO-YEAR PERIOD 1984-1985, BY REGION AND COUNTRY OR TERRITORY

(in US dollars)

	Regular budget	Other sources	Total		Regular budget	Other sources	Total
Africa				*Africa* (cont.)			
Algeria	396,000	930,800	1,326,800	Seychelles	455,400	—	455,400
Angola	1,399,400	1,787,200	3,186,600	Sierra Leone	920,900	9,600	930,500
Benin	986,300	121,600	1,107,900	Swaziland	586,700	599,200	1,185,900
Botswana	684,300	327,600	1,011,900	Togo	928,900	—	928,900
Burkina Faso	1,363,100	594,200	1,957,300	Uganda	1,283,900	246,800	1,530,700
Burundi	1,237,500	284,200	1,521,700	United Republic of			
Cameroon	807,300	—	807,300	Tanzania	1,373,600	119,600	1,493,200
Cape Verde	888,800	—	888,800	Zaire	1,741,600	10,900	1,752,500
Central African Republic	1,158,200	558,500	1,716,700	Zambia	1,408,000	1,104,800	2,512,800
Chad	1,245,000	1,014,700	2,259,700	Zimbabwe	1,669,000	184,900	1,853,900
Comoros	1,319,800	43,200	1,363,000	Inter-country			
Congo	853,200	298,600	1,151,800	programmes	27,660,700	46,267,600	73,928,300
Equatorial Guinea	824,600	—	824,600				
Ethiopia	2,831,300	1,432,000	4,263,300	Subtotal	76,290,700	61,512,900	137,803,600
Gabon	750,000	—	750,000	*The Americas*			
Gambia	869,500	819,200	1,688,700				
Ghana	981,700	621,000	1,602,700	Antigua and Barbuda	—	159,300	159,300
Guinea	1,346,400	777,300	2,123,700	Argentina	1,271,200	1,506,300	2,777,500
Guinea-Bissau	999,600	202,900	1,202,500	Bahamas	360,000	306,000	666,000
Ivory Coast	789,700	10,000	799,700	Barbados	86,400	522,400	608,800
Kenya	1,161,900	193,800	1,355,700	Belize	471,300	220,800	692,100
Lesotho	944,800	12,200	957,000	Bolivia	358,100	2,335,800	2,693,900
Liberia	1,120,200	—	1,120,200	Brazil	1,407,600	8,455,700	9,863,300
Madagascar	869,900	485,000	1,354,900	Canada	45,000	46,400	91,400
Malawi	927,900	384,600	1,312,500	Chile	783,500	824,500	1,608,000
Mali	1,332,100	216,000	1,548,100	Colombia	1,230,700	3,281,400	4,512,100
Mauritania	1,051,400	418,500	1,469,900	Costa Rica	741,800	1,599,600	2,341,400
Mauritius	400,600	85,000	485,600	Cuba	777,200	882,000	1,659,200
Mozambique	1,325,200	268,100	1,593,300	Dominica	—	330,900	330,900
Namibia	547,500	—	547,500	Dominican Republic	526,600	2,621,800	3,148,400
Niger	1,334,500	894,300	2,228,800	Ecuador	1,733,800	1,023,000	2,756,800
Nigeria	2,471,400	—	2,471,400	El Salvador	984,200	1,101,800	2,086,000
Réunion	67,400	—	67,400	French Guiana	—	52,900	52,900
Rwanda	1,464,200	—	1,464,200	Grenada	—	108,100	108,100
St. Helena	58,500	—	58,500	Guatemala	737,900	3,528,000	4,265,900
Sao Tome and Principe	541,800	96,500	638,300	Guyana	973,800	27,200	1,001,000
Senegal	911,000	92,500	1,003,500				

	Regular budget	Other sources	Total
The Americas (cont.)			
Haiti	990,800	2,423,100	3,413,900
Honduras	688,200	1,712,100	2,400,300
Jamaica	783,400	1,321,400	2,104,800
Mexico	829,200	4,055,900	4,885,100
Netherlands Antilles	65,600	15,100	80,700
Nicaragua	508,000	2,071,000	2,579,000
Panama	876,700	1,498,600	2,375,300
Paraguay	287,600	3,054,000	3,341,600
Peru	605,500	3,714,600	4,320,100
Saint Lucia	—	239,100	239,100
Saint Vincent and the Grenadines	—	220,700	220,700
Suriname	337,900	534,700	872,600
Trinidad and Tobago	807,300	723,200	1,530,500
United States	417,500	70,400	487,900
Uruguay	489,400	494,200	983,600
Venezuela	854,500	2,295,400	3,149,900
West Indies	553,500	896,300	1,449,800
Inter-country programmes	21,990,400	81,178,300	103,168,700
Subtotal	43,574,600	135,452,000	179,026,600
South-East Asia			
Bangladesh	6,348,000	4,521,200	10,869,200
Bhutan	642,000	860,800	1,502,800
Burma	4,123,000	5,174,200	9,297,200
Democratic People's Republic of Korea	1,327,400	39,400	1,366,800
India	9,920,000	9,234,600	19,154,600
Indonesia	7,113,000	3,320,100	10,433,100
Maldives	770,500	142,600	913,100
Mongolia	1,491,100	430,800	1,921,900
Nepal	4,492,000	3,753,300	8,245,300
Sri Lanka	3,264,000	1,678,700	4,942,700
Thailand	3,824,000	303,400	4,127,400
Inter-country programmes	11,351,300	6,667,800	18,019,100
Subtotal	54,666,300	36,126,900	90,793,200
Europe			
Albania	33,100	—	33,100
Austria	24,800	—	24,800
Belgium	20,600	—	20,600
Bulgaria	92,400	—	92,400
Czechoslovakia	24,800	—	24,800
Denmark	20,600	—	20,600
Finland	20,600	—	20,600
France	27,600	—	27,600
German Democratic Republic	30,400	—	30,400
Germany, Federal Republic of	27,600	—	27,600
Greece	30,400	—	30,400
Hungary	36,000	—	36,000
Iceland	20,600	—	20,600
Ireland	24,800	—	24,800
Italy	30,400	—	30,400
Luxembourg	15,100	—	15,100
Malta	24,800	—	24,800
Monaco	3,000	—	3,000
Morocco	462,000	1,823,000	2,285,000
Netherlands	24,800	—	24,800
Norway	20,600	—	20,600
Poland	45,600	—	45,600
Portugal	72,000	206,800	278,800
Romania	45,600	—	45,600
San Marino	3,000	—	3,000
Spain	30,400	—	30,400
Sweden	20,600	—	20,600
Switzerland	20,600	—	20,600
Turkey	525,800	161,300	687,100
USSR	60,700	—	60,700

	Regular budget	Other sources	Total
Europe (cont.)			
United Kingdom	27,600	—	27,600
Yugoslavia	37,200	—	37,200
Inter-country programmes	18,869,700	7,814,000	26,683,700
Subtotal	20,773,800	10,005,100	30,778,900
Eastern Mediterranean			
Afghanistan	4,534,100	1,307,600	5,841,700
Bahrain	139,500	31,700	171,200
Cyprus	568,000	—	568,000
Democratic Yemen	3,313,000	1,941,900	5,254,900
Djibouti	708,300	120,000	828,300
Egypt	1,898,600	336,800	2,235,400
Iran	469,000	—	469,000
Iraq	687,300	187,900	875,200
Israel	453,000	—	453,000
Jordan	1,140,900	1,642,600	2,783,500
Kuwait	126,400	107,400	233,800
Lebanon	1,140,000	206,600	1,346,600
Libyan Arab Jamahiriya	109,000	2,036,200	2,145,200
Oman	864,600	1,163,200	2,027,800
Pakistan	2,930,300	248,200	3,178,500
Qatar	64,000	67,800	131,800
Saudi Arabia	165,700	5,637,000	5,802,700
Somalia	4,167,600	715,500	4,883,100
Sudan	3,138,600	538,500	3,677,100
Syrian Arab Republic	1,749,400	—	1,749,400
Tunisia	1,700,000	182,500	1,882,500
United Arab Emirates	55,300	104,000	159,300
Yemen	3,180,100	8,468,500	11,648,600
Inter-country programmes	14,843,000	2,978,300	17,821,300
Subtotal	48,145,700	28,022,200	76,167,900
Western Pacific			
American Samoa	115,000	—	115,000
Australia	100,000	—	100,000
China	4,242,800	2,476,600	6,719,400
Cook Islands	400,000	74,700	474,700
Democratic Kampuchea	500,000	900	500,900
Fiji	1,528,300	138,300	1,666,600
French Polynesia	70,000	—	70,000
Guam	80,000	—	80,000
Hong Kong	110,000	23,000	133,000
Japan	100,000	—	100,000
Kiribati	570,000	—	570,000
Lao People's Democratic Republic	1,430,000	767,100	2,197,100
Macau	50,000	—	50,000
Malaysia	1,195,100	334,000	1,529,100
New Zealand	60,000	—	60,000
Niue	58,000	—	58,000
Papua New Guinea	2,205,800	531,800	2,737,600
Philippines	1,758,400	175,700	1,934,100
Republic of Korea	1,544,300	267,500	1,811,800
Samoa	720,000	116,600	836,600
Singapore	516,000	404,600	920,600
Solomon Islands	745,000	263,800	1,008,800
Tokelau	20,000	—	20,000
Tonga	772,000	32,200	804,200
Trust Territory of the Pacific Islands	620,000	164,500	784,500
Tuvalu	75,000	55,500	130,500
Vanuatu	800,000	469,200	1,269,200
Viet Nam	3,751,400	3,188,600	6,940,000
Inter-country programmes	14,483,000	7,314,300	21,797,300
Subtotal	38,620,100	16,798,900	55,419,000
Total	282,071,200	287,918,000	569,989,200

NOTE: For assistance rendered by WHO in 1984-1985, by sector and region, see YUN 1984, p. 1226.

Annex I. MEMBERSHIP OF THE WORLD HEALTH ORGANIZATION AND CONTRIBUTIONS

(Membership as at 31 December 1985; contributions as assessed for 1986-1987)

MEMBER	CONTRIBUTION Percent- age	CONTRIBUTION Amount* (in US dollars)	MEMBER	CONTRIBUTION Percent- age	CONTRIBUTION Amount* (in US dollars)
Afghanistan	0.01	49,145	Ireland	0.18	884,630
Albania	0.01	49,145	Israel	0.22	1,056,650
Algeria	0.13	663,470	Italy	3.67	18,159,515
Angola	0.01	49,145	Ivory Coast	0.03	122,875
Antigua and Barbuda	0.01	49,145	Jamaica	0.02	98,295
Argentina	0.70	3,219,110	Japan	10.13	51,038,145
Australia	1.54	7,789,640	Jordan	0.01	49,145
Austria	0.74	3,587,680	Kenya	0.01	49,145
Bahamas	0.01	49,145	Kiribati	0.01	49,145
Bahrain	0.01	73,715	Kuwait	0.24	1,277,785
Bangladesh	0.03	122,875	Lao People's Democratic		
Barbados	0.01	49,145	Republic	0.01	49,145
Belgium	1.26	5,946,730	Lebanon	0.02	73,725
Benin	0.01	49,145	Lesotho	0.01	49,145
Bhutan	0.01	49,145	Liberia	0.01	49,145
Bolivia	0.01	49,145	Libyan Arab Jamahiriya	0.25	1,228,660
Botswana	0.01	49,145	Luxembourg	0.06	270,310
Brazil	1.36	6,708,455	Madagascar	0.01	49,145
Brunei Darussalam	0.03	172,010	Malawi	0.01	49,145
Bulgaria	0.18	835,495	Malaysia	0.09	466,890
Burkina Faso	0.01	49,145	Maldives	0.01	49,145
Burma	0.01	49,145	Mali	0.01	49,145
Burundi	0.01	49,145	Malta	0.01	49,145
Byelorussian SSR	0.35	1,670,980	Mauritania	0.01	49,145
Cameroon	0.01	49,145	Mauritius	0.01	49,145
Canada	3.02	14,819,015	Mexico	0.86	4,251,140
Cape Verde	0.01	49,145	Monaco	0.01	49,145
Central African Republic	0.01	49,145	Mongolia	0.01	49,145
Chad	0.01	49,145	Morocco	0.05	245,730
Chile	0.07	344,025	Mozambique	0.01	49,145
China	0.86	4,005,450	Nepal	0.01	49,145
Colombia	0.11	589,745	Netherlands	1.75	8,502,310
Comoros	0.01	49,145	New Zealand	0.25	1,179,520
Congo	0.01	43,145	Nicaragua	0.01	49,145
Cook Islands	0.01	49,145	Niger	0.01	49,145
Costa Rica	0.02	98,295	Nigeria	0.19	933,775
Cuba	0.09	442,320	Norway	0.50	2,531,020
Cyprus	0.01	73,715	Oman	0.01	73,715
Czechoslovakia	0.75	3,513,975	Pakistan	0.06	294,880
Democratic Kampuchea	0.01	49,145	Panama	0.02	98,295
Democratic People's			Papua New Guinea	0.01	49,145
Republic of Korea	0.05	245,730	Paraguay	0.01	73,715
Democratic Yemen	0.01	72,145	Peru	0.07	344,025
Denmark	0.74	3,563,115	Philippines	0.09	466,890
Djibouti	0.01	49,145	Poland	0.71	3,292,830
Dominica	0.01	49,145	Portugal	0.18	884,630
Dominican Republic	0.03	147,440	Qatar	0.03	172,010
Ecuador	0.02	122,860	Republic of Korea	0.18	909,200
Egypt	0.07	344,025	Romania	0.19	933,775
El Salvador	0.01	49,145	Rwanda	0.01	49,145
Equatorial Guinea	0.01	49,145	Saint Christopher and Nevis	0.01	49,145
Ethiopia	0.01	49,145	Saint Lucia	0.01	49,145
Fiji	0.01	49,145	Saint Vincent and the Grenadines	0.01	49,145
Finland	0.47	2,359,010	Samoa	0.01	49,145
France	6.39	31,647,460	San Marino	0.01	49,145
Gabon	0.02	122,860	Sao Tome and Principe	0.01	49,145
Gambia	0.01	49,145	Saudi Arabia	0.84	4,398,545
German Democratic Republic	1.36	6,536,470	Senegal	0.01	49,145
Germany, Federal Republic of	8.38	40,496,585	Seychelles	0.01	49,145
Ghana	0.02	73,725	Sierra Leone	0.01	49,145
Greece	0.39	2,014,980	Singapore	0.09	466,890
Grenada	0.01	49,145	Somalia	0.01	49,145
Guatemala	0.02	98,295	Solomon Islands	0.01	49,145
Guinea	0.01	49,145	South Africa	0.40	2,039,570
Guinea-Bissau	0.01	49,145	Spain	1.89	9,534,330
Guyana	0.01	49,145	Sri Lanka	0.01	49,145
Haiti	0.01	49,145	Sudan	0.01	49,145
Honduras	0.01	49,145	Suriname	0.01	49,145
Hungary	0.22	1,056,650	Swaziland	0.01	49,145
Iceland	0.03	147,440	Sweden	1.29	6,192,450
India	0.35	1,695,545	Switzerland	1.08	5,356,930
Indonesia	0.13	663,470	Syrian Arab Republic	0.03	172,010
Iran	0.57	2,924,185	Thailand	0.08	417,740
Iraq	0.12	589,755	Togo	0.01	49,145

MEMBER	CONTRIBUTION Percent-age	Amount* (in US dollars)	MEMBER	CONTRIBUTION Percent-age	Amount* (in US dollars)
Tonga	0.01	49,145	Vanuatu	0.01	49,145
Trinidad and Tobago	0.03	172,010	Venezuela	0.54	2,776,745
Tunisia	0.03	147,440	Viet Nam	0.02	73,725
Turkey	0.31	1,572,675	Yemen	0.01	49,145
Uganda	0.01	49,145	Yugoslavia	0.45	2,211,580
Ukrainian SSR	1.29	6,241,550	Zaire	0.01	49,145
USSR	10.34	50,006,400	Zambia	0.01	49,145
United Arab Emirates	0.16	835,475	Zimbabwe	0.02	98,295
United Kingdom	4.58	22,975,790			
United Republic of Tanzania	0.01	59,145	ASSOCIATE MEMBER		
			Namibia	0.01	49,145
United States	25.00	125,576,525			
Uruguay	0.04	196,585	Total	100.00	494,813,100

*Adjusted to take into account the actual amounts paid to staff as reimbursement for taxes levied by member countries on the WHO emoluments of their nationals.

Annex II.   OFFICERS AND OFFICES OF THE WORLD HEALTH ORGANIZATION
(As at 31 December 1985)

OFFICERS OF THE THIRTY-EIGHTH WORLD HEALTH ASSEMBLY

President: Dr. S. Surjaningrat (Indonesia).
Vice Presidents: Dr. Aleya H. Ayoub (Egypt), Dr. W. Chinchón (Chile), D. S. Katopola (Malawi), Dr. E. Nakamura (Japan), Dr. Barbro Westerholm (Sweden).
Chairman, Committee A: Dr. D. G. Makuto (Zimbabwe).
Chairman, Committee B: R. Rochon (Canada).

*MEMBERS OF THE EXECUTIVE BOARD**

Chairman: Dr. G. Tadesse.
Vice-Chairmen: Dr. A. A. El Gamal, A. Grimsson, Dr. U. Sudsukh.
Rapporteurs: M. K. Bah, Dr. Sung Woo Lee.

Members were designated by: Argentina, Australia, Belgium, Canada, Cuba, Cyprus, Democratic Yemen, Djibouti, Ecuador, Egypt, Equatorial Guinea, Ethiopia, Germany, Federal Republic of, Ghana, Guinea, Hungary, Iceland, Indonesia, Ivory Coast, Kenya, Lesotho, Malta, Nepal, Panama, Poland, Republic of Korea, Syrian Arab Republic, Thailand, Tonga, United Kingdom, Venezuela.

*The Board consists of 31 persons designated by as many member States which have been elected for such purpose by WHO.

SENIOR OFFICERS OF THE SECRETARIAT

Director-General: Dr. Halfdan Mahler.
Deputy Director-General: Dr. T. Adeoye Lambo.
Assistant Directors-General: Warren W. Furth, Dr. J. Hamon, Dr. S. K. Litvinov, Dr. Lu Rushan, Dr. F. Partow.
Director, Regional Office for Africa: Dr. G. L. Monekosso.

Director, Regional Office for the Americas (Pan American Sanitary Bureau): Dr. C. Guerra de Macedo.
Director, Regional Office for South-East Asia: Dr. U Ko Ko.
Director, Regional Office for Europe: Dr. J. E. Asvall.
Director, Regional Office for the Eastern Mediterranean: Dr. Hussein A. Gezairy.
Director, Regional Office for the Western Pacific: Dr. Hiroshi Nakajima.

HEADQUARTERS AND OTHER OFFICES

HEADQUARTERS
World Health Organization
Avenue Appia
1211 Geneva 27, Switzerland
   Cable address: UNISANTE GENEVA
   Telephone: 91 21 11
   Telex: 27821

LIAISON OFFICE WITH THE
UNITED NATIONS
World Health Organization
2 United Nations Plaza
New York, N.Y. 10017, United States
   Cable address: UNSANTE NEWYORK
   Telephone: (212) 963-6001
   Telex: 234292

REGIONAL OFFICE FOR THE EASTERN
MEDITERRANEAN
World Health Organization
P.O. Box 1517
Alexandria, Egypt
   Cable address: UNISANTE ALEXANDRIA
   Telephone: 802318, 807843
   Telex: 54028, 54684

REGIONAL OFFICE FOR AFRICA
World Health Organization
P.O. Box No. 6
Brazzaville, Congo
   Cable address: UNISANTE BRAZZAVILLE
   Telephone: 81 38 60-65
   Telex: 5217, 5364

REGIONAL OFFICE FOR EUROPE
World Health Organization
8 Scherfigsvej
DK-2100 Copenhagen O, Denmark
   Cable address: UNISANTE COPENHAGEN
   Telephone: 29 01 11
   Telex: 15348

REGIONAL OFFICE FOR THE WESTERN
PACIFIC
World Health Organization
P.O. Box 2932
Manila 2801, Philippines
   Cable address: UNISANTE MANILA
   Telephone: 59 20 41, 59 37 21
   Telex: 27652, 40365, 63260

REGIONAL OFFICE FOR SOUTH-EAST ASIA
World Health Organization
World Health House
Indraprastha Estate, Mahatma Gandhi Road
New Delhi 110002, India
   Cable address: WHO NEWDELHI
   Telephone: 27 01 81 88
   Telex: 3165095, 3165031

REGIONAL OFFICE FOR THE AMERICAS/
PAN AMERICAN SANITARY BUREAU
World Health Organization
525 23rd Street, N.W.
Washington, D.C. 20037, United States
   Cable address: OFSANPAN WASHINGTON
   Telephone: (202) 861-3200
   Telex: 248338, 440057, 64152, 892744

Chapter VI

International Bank for Reconstruction and Development (World Bank)

During the fiscal year 1 July 1984 to 30 June 1985, the International Bank for Reconstruction and Development (World Bank) and its affiliate, the International Development Association (IDA), continued to help developing countries to raise their standards of living by channelling financial resources to them from developed countries.

Lending commitments by the Bank, credit approvals from IDA, and investment commitments by a second affiliate, the International Finance Corporation (IFC), amounted to $15,324 million—a decline of $894 million from the previous fiscal year.

Membership in the Bank rose to 149 in 1985, with the admission of Tonga on 13 September.

Lending operations

In fiscal year 1985, the World Bank made 131 loans amounting to $11,358.3 million to 44 countries, a decline of $589 million from fiscal 1984. This brought the cumulative total of loan commitments by the Bank since its inception in 1946 to $112,921.8 million.

WORLD BANK LOANS APPROVED BY REGION/COUNTRY AND PURPOSE
1 JULY 1984–30 JUNE 1985
(in millions of US dollars)

REGION/COUNTRY	Agriculture and rural development	Development finance companies	Education	Energy	Industry	Non-project	Population, health and nutrition	Small-scale enterprises	Technical assistance	Telecommunications	Transportation	Urbanization	Water supply and sewerage	Total
Eastern and southern Africa														
Botswana	10.7	—	—	—	—	—	—	—	—	—	—	—	—	10.7
Kenya	—	—	—	—	—	—	—	—	—	32.6	—	—	—	32.6
Malawi	—	—	—	—	6.4	—	—	—	—	—	—	—	—	6.4
Seychelles	—	—	—	—	—	—	—	—	—	—	6.2	—	—	6.2
Swaziland	—	—	—	—	—	—	—	—	—	—	8.6	—	—	8.6
Zimbabwe	—	10.0	—	—	—	—	—	—	—	—	—	—	—	10.0
Subtotal	10.7	10.0	—	—	6.4	—	—	—	—	32.6	14.8	—	—	74.5
Western Africa														
Cameroon	33.8	—	—	—	—	—	—	—	—	—	125.0	—	—	158.8
Ivory Coast	31.3	—	—	—	—	—	—	—	—	—	110.0	—	—	141.3
Nigeria	—	—	—	—	—	—	34.0	—	13.0	—	—	—	72.0	119.0
Subtotal	65.1	—	—	—	—	—	34.0	—	13.0	—	235.0	—	72.0	419.1
East Asia and Pacific														
China	17.0	—	—	268.0	97.0	—	—	—	—	—	277.6	—	—	659.6
Indonesia	501.7	—	225.0	50.0	—	—	85.0	—	—	—	111.0	—	—	972.7
Malaysia	37.7	—	—	—	—	—	—	52.1	—	—	—	—	—	89.8
Papua New Guinea	9.7	—	—	—	—	—	—	—	—	—	—	—	—	9.7
Philippines	250.0	—	—	—	—	—	—	—	—	4.0	—	—	—	254.0
Republic of Korea	25.0	222.0	—	—	50.0	—	—	111.0	—	—	—	53.0	95.0	556.0
Thailand	—	—	—	85.0	—	—	—	—	—	—	—	27.5	—	112.5
Subtotal	841.1	222.0	225.0	403.0	147.0	—	85.0	163.1	—	4.0	388.6	80.5	95.0	2,654.3
South Asia														
India	200.0	—	—	974.0	300.0	—	—	—	—	—	200.0	—	—	1,674.0
Pakistan	—	—	—	433.0	—	—	—	—	—	—	—	—	—	433.0
Sri Lanka	38.0	—	—	—	—	—	—	—	—	—	24.0	—	—	62.0
Subtotal	238.0	—	—	1,407.0	300.0	—	—	—	—	—	224.0	—	—	2,169.0
Europe, the Middle East and North Africa														
Algeria	—	—	—	—	—	—	—	—	—	—	—	—	262.0	262.0
Cyprus	7.0	—	—	—	—	—	—	—	—	—	—	—	—	7.0
Egypt	207.0	—	19.3	—	—	—	—	—	—	—	37.0	—	—	263.3

REGION/COUNTRY Europe, the Middle East and North Africa (cont.)	Agriculture and rural development	Development finance companies	Education	Energy	Industry	Non-project	Population, health and nutrition	Small-scale enterprises	Technical assistance	Telecommunications	Transportation	Urbanization	Water supply and sewerage	Total
Hungary	80.0	—	—	47.2	122.5	—	—	—	—	—	75.0	—	—	324.7
Jordan	—	—	—	—	—	—	13.5	—	—	—	30.0	28.0	30.0	101.5
Morocco	100.0	25.1	27.1	27.0	—	—	28.4	—	—	—	—	—	—	207.6
Oman	—	—	—	—	—	—	—	—	23.0	—	—	—	—	23.0
Portugal	—	—	—	—	—	—	—	—	—	—	66.0	—	—	66.0
Tunisia	37.0	54.0	—	—	—	—	—	50.0	—	—	—	—	—	141.0
Turkey	300.0	—	57.7	142.0	55.1	—	—	—	—	—	134.5	9.2	—	698.5
Yugoslavia	75.0	—	—	217.5	—	—	—	—	—	—	—	—	—	292.5
Subtotal	806.0	79.1	104.1	433.7	177.6	—	41.9	50.0	—	23.0	342.5	37.2	292.0	2,387.1
Latin America and the Caribbean														
Argentina	—	—	—	180.0	—	—	—	—	—	—	—	—	—	180.0
Brazil	222.7	—	72.0	712.0	—	—	—	300.0	—	—	200.0	—	16.3	1,523.0
Chile	56.0	—	—	—	—	—	—	—	11.0	—	140.0	80.0	—	287.0
Colombia	—	90.0	—	130.0	—	300.0	—	40.0	—	—	—	—	147.5	707.5
Costa Rica	—	—	—	—	—	80.0	—	—	3.5	—	—	—	—	83.5
Dominican Republic	—	—	5.8	—	—	—	—	—	—	—	—	—	—	5.8
Ecuador	—	—	—	—	—	—	—	—	8.0	—	—	—	—	8.0
Guatemala	—	—	—	44.6	—	—	—	—	—	—	—	—	—	44.6
Honduras	—	—	—	—	—	—	—	—	—	—	—	6.9	—	6.9
Jamaica	—	—	—	—	—	55.0	—	—	9.0	—	—	—	—	64.0
Mexico	90.0	105.0	81.0	—	—	—	—	—	—	—	322.0	—	—	598.0
Panama	—	—	—	51.0	—	—	—	—	—	—	—	—	—	51.0
Peru	—	—	27.0	—	4.0	—	—	—	—	—	—	—	—	31.0
Uruguay	60.0	—	—	4.0	—	—	—	—	—	—	—	—	—	64.0
Subtotal	428.7	195.0	185.8	1,121.6	4.0	435.0	—	340.0	31.5	—	662.0	86.9	163.8	3,654.3
Total	2,389.6	506.1	514.9	3,365.3	635.0	435.0	160.9	553.1	44.5	59.6	1,866.9	204.6	622.8	11,358.3
NUMBER OF LOANS	34	6	9	23	7	3	5	5	5	3	18	6	7	131

Agriculture and rural development

In its continued commitment to agriculture and rural development, the Bank made 34 loans in fiscal 1985 amounting to $2,389.6 million to 22 countries. Indonesia received $501.7 million, of which $160 million helped support the planning of transmigration and other development programmes in the Other Islands, promote the welfare of transmigrants and other local people through better physical planning of settlements and improve the quality and economic viability of the transmigration programme. Turkey received $300 million to finance a portion of the imported inputs, capital goods, training and consultant services needed to support the Government's agricultural-sector adjustment programme. Of $250 million provided to the Philippines, $150 million went to support the Government's short-term economic stabilization programme and a medium-term programme of agricultural policy and institutional reform.

Development finance companies

The Bank made six loans totalling $506.1 million in fiscal 1985 to assist development finance companies in six countries. The Republic of Korea received $222 million to support ongoing financial reforms and to provide credit to cover foreign-exchange costs of industrial equipment imported by private firms seeking to acquire, build, modernize or replace productive assets. Mexico received $105 million for a second mining-development project which would finance evaluation exploration, mine development and mine exploitation, strengthen the capabilities of the major institutions supporting small and medium-scale mining enterprises and improve co-ordination. A loan of $90 million was made to development finance companies in Colombia to channel term financing towards efficient investment projects in the industrial sector and to assist the Government in strengthening ongoing financial-sector reforms.

Education

During fiscal 1985, the Bank granted nine loans totalling $514.9 million for education projects in eight countries. Indonesia received two loans totalling $225 million to assist in the training of its own university teachers and researchers through the development of new graduate-level programmes and to raise the quality of general secondary education. A loan of $81 million went to Mexico to support the National Agency for Professional Technical Education in implementing the second phase of its technical-training programme for skilled workers and technicians. Brazil received $72 million to finance the foreign-exchange costs in 1984-1986 of its programme for support of science and technology development.

Energy

Twenty-three energy projects—in oil, gas, coal and power—were assisted in 15 countries during fiscal 1985 at a cost of $3,365.3 million. Four loans totalling $974 million were made to India, of which $300 million helped meet the electricity demand in the western region of the country by installing two 500-megawatt generating units at the Chandrapur thermal power plant in Maharashtra State. Brazil received two loans totalling $712 million, of which $400 million assisted the Government to reverse the financial deterioration of the power sector by constructing transmission facilities included in the 1985-1992 transmission-expansion programmes of two major electricity companies. Pakistan received four loans totalling $433 million; $178 million supported the Government's reforms in the energy sector and assisted in the implementation of its core energy-investment programme for 1986/87.

Industry

The Bank made seven loans for the industrial sector amounting to $635 million during fiscal 1985. The largest loans included $300 million to India for the establishment of a gas-based petrochemical-manufacturing facility near Bombay; $73 million (out of a total of $122.5 million) to Hungary to increase and diversify the production of fine chemicals, particularly pharmaceuticals, thus increasing the country's foreign-exchange earnings; and $97 million to China for the rehabilitation and modernization of selected fertilizer facilities.

Non-project

Three non-project loans totalling $435 million were made during the fiscal year. Colombia received $300 million to support the first phase of its trade-policy reforms, Costa Rica received $80 million to support its structural adjustment and economic recovery programme, and Jamaica received $55 million as a third loan in support of its programme of structural adjustment aimed at achieving export development and economic deregulation.

Population, health and nutrition

Five loans amounting to $160.9 million were made to four countries in fiscal 1985. Indonesia received two loans totalling $85 million, of which $46 million helped to support a population project aimed at strengthening the activities of the National Family Planning Co-ordinating Board and assisting the Ministry of Population and Environment. A loan of $34 million was granted to Nigeria to expand and improve the delivery of primary health and family-planning services, including immunization, in Sokoto State. In Morocco, $28.4 million assisted the Ministry of Public Health in shifting emphasis from an urban-based, hospital-oriented health system to a more cost-effective system of primary care.

Small-scale enterprises

Five loans totalling $553.1 million were granted for small-scale enterprises during fiscal year 1985. Brazil received $300 million for a development-banking project which would provide funds for larger, privately controlled industrial enterprises to export, expand or reorient production for export and for small and medium-sized enterprises. The Republic of Korea received $111 million to provide credit, technical assistance and training, tailored to the needs of small and medium-sized industries. Malaysia received $52.1 million to help develop small-scale enterprises by increasing the availability of institutional credit and by expanding and improving technical assistance.

Technical assistance

During fiscal 1985, five countries received loans for technical assistance amounting to $44.5 million. Nigeria received $13 million to help improve the quality and reliability of its management-information system, upgrade its statistical system and introduce methods to monitor the progress of public-sector activities. A loan of $11 million to Chile helped improve its ability to guide the economy by improving economic policy execution. Jamaica received $9 million to help the Government implement, monitor and sustain its structural adjustment effort.

The largest element of technical assistance continued to be that financed as a component of loans for other purposes. During the year, these technical assistance components totalled $1,148.4 million in 203 operations, compared with $1,093.2 million in the same number of operations in fiscal 1984. Among the larger amounts of technical assistance financed as components of Bank loans were $143.9 million of a $160 million transmigration loan to Indonesia, and $13.6 million of a $56 million agricultural loan to Chile.

The Bank continued to serve as executing agency for projects financed by the United Nations Development Programme (UNDP). At the end of fiscal 1985, the number of projects in progress stood at 123 for a total allocation of $174.7 million. Among the larger new UNDP-financed projects were feasibility and engineering studies for agricultural and transportation projects in Bangladesh, a study of alternative modes of vocational training in eight Arab States, and preparation of an investment project to strengthen economic management in Papua New Guinea.

The Bank's technical co-operation was extended to Arab oil-producing developing countries in Europe, the Middle East and North Africa, on a reimbursable basis when the annual programme exceeded one staff-year of Bank input and on a non-reimbursable basis in response to *ad hoc* requests for programmes requiring less than one staff-year. In fiscal 1985, about 34 staff-years of reimbursable technical assistance were provided by the Bank, some 94 per cent to Saudi Arabia. The Bank also provided non-reimbursable technical assistance to Kuwait for manpower planning and to the United Arab Emirates for an education-sector survey.

Telecommunications

The Bank made three loans for telecommunications projects totalling $59.6 million in fiscal 1985. Kenya received $32.6 million to expand and modernize existing telecommunications infrastructure. A loan of $23 million went to Oman to expand local, domestic long-distance and international telephone facilities as well as to provide first-time telephone service to about 37 rural communities. The Philippines received $4 million to promote and support the sound regulatory, institutional and financial development of the telecommunications sector.

Transportation

Eighteen loans totalling $1,866.9 million were made to 16 countries during fiscal 1985 for the development of transportation systems. Mexico received two loans totalling $322 million, of which $300 million financed investment and operational and financial improvements to the railway system. Of two loans to China totalling $277.6 million, $235 million was for upgrading and electrifying more than 600 kilometres of railway lines, and for modernizing a passenger-coach factory. A loan of $200 million was granted to India to upgrade major highways in six states. Other loans were for rail, port and highway improvement.

Urban development

In fiscal 1985, six countries received loans totalling $204.6 million for urban projects. Chile received $80 million to support a programme in the Ministry of Housing and Urbanism through a package of policy improvements, housing construction, studies and technical assistance. A loan of $53 million was made to the Republic of Korea to improve traffic and transport conditions in Seoul.

Water supply and sewerage

Seven loans totalling $622.8 million were made to six countries in fiscal 1985 for water supply and sewerage. Algeria received $262 million to help expand water production and distribution levels required by some 2.1 million inhabitants of Oran and Constantine. Two loans totalling $147.5 million were granted to Colombia, $129 million of which supported a project which would continue the Bank's efforts to provide essential water-supply and sewerage infrastructure for Bogotá. Water service for about 5 million people in Seoul would be improved and capacity to serve 1.1 million more by 1991 would be provided through a $95 million loan to the Republic of Korea.

Economic Development Institute

Fiscal 1985 was the first year of the Economic Development Institute's (EDI) five-year plan designed to strengthen its work on development policy issues and place more emphasis on national economic management, sectors, public enterprises and projects. To promote these objectives, EDI organized a wide range of senior policy seminars, mostly for Africa. Training courses and seminars emphasized policy issues and efforts were initiated to produce more training materials dealing with such issues.

Of 82 courses and seminars held (17 in the United States and 65 elsewhere), 49 were direct training for senior and middle-level officials. Some 2,800 participants—about 45 per cent from smaller or poorer countries—benefited from EDI training.

New courses and seminars were given on education-sector management, population and development, agriculture-sector planning and agricultural marketing, mostly for sub-Saharan Africa. Other new direct training efforts were on food policy, entrepreneurial development, and management of city growth, technology and technical assistance.

Concerted efforts were made to increase the quantity, and improve the quality, of EDI's training materials. In fiscal 1985, EDI produced in final form 30 course notes, 20 case-studies, seven comprehensive collections of readings, five seminar papers and 16 audio-visual modules (mostly on water and sanitation).

In addition to organizing joint activities with training institutions in developing countries, EDI also supported them by contributing staff for courses and seminars organized and directed by them and by advising them on their planning, financing and administration. Substantial assistance in planning was provided in fiscal 1985 to agencies in Indonesia, Morocco and Nigeria. The first major EDI-led review of an overseas training institution, the Eastern and Southern African Management Institute, was completed; its recommendations were used as the basis for management improvements and the provision of external aid.

The EDI programme of seminars for trainers in developing-country institutions was growing rapidly, concentrating on Asia and Latin America. In fiscal 1985, 18 such seminars, including several case-writing workshops, were given in a variety of sectors.

Co-financing by national and international aid agencies for programmes directed or co-directed by EDI had grown from about $900,000 in fiscal 1983 to nearly $2.5 million in fiscal 1985. These funds were for regional and world-wide training activities; for national programmes, the training components of Bank loans were expected to become an increasingly important source of finance. A vocational training loan to Morocco, for example, contained funds for a major training programme developed with EDI assistance.

Co-financing

Despite a difficult market environment which continued to limit the availability of co-financing with export-credit agencies and commercial banks, the flow of funds to developing countries was maintained through co-financing with the World Bank. The Bank's contribution during fiscal 1985 amounted to $4,749.3 million for 104 projects, an increase of more than $100 million over fiscal 1984. Of this total, co-financing with official development agencies remained by far the largest source—$2,453.5 million in 87 projects. This form of co-financing provided development-oriented lending, highly concessional terms and long maturities. During fiscal 1985, private co-financing amounted to $922 million for five projects.

In sub-Saharan Africa, where increased financial support was needed to support policy reforms, about half the funds committed to the Special Facility for sub-Saharan Africa took the form of special joint financing, thus providing a substantial supplement to the flows provided by direct contributors.

Special Action Programme

The Special Action Programme (SAP), initiated as the Special Assistance Programme in February 1983[a] for a two-year period, was intended to strengthen the Bank's ability to assist developing countries to adjust to the current economic environment. It was composed of financial measures, combined with policy advice.

In March 1985, the Executive Directors assessed the progress achieved and agreed that SAP had been highly successful. Some effects of SAP were readily quantifiable: for instance, incremental disbursements to 44 countries during the period fiscal 1984-1986 were estimated at about $4.5 billion, almost double the estimate made when SAP was launched. The Executive Directors also agreed to a recommendation not to extend SAP formally.

Financing activities

During fiscal 1985, the World Bank borrowed the equivalent of $11,085.8 million, consisting of new medium- and long-term borrowings plus incremental short-term discount-rate and Central Bank Facility borrowings outstanding on 30 June 1985. The total was made up of $3,486.8 million in United States dollars, $2,090.4 million in Japanese yen, $1,952.7 million in Swiss francs, $1,659.3 million in deutsche mark, $758.8 million in Netherlands guilders, $364.5 million in pounds sterling, $304.4 million in Canadian dollars, $221 million in European currency units, $83.6 million in Austrian schillings, $51.2 million in Italian lire, $50.5 million in Belgian francs, $29.4 million in Norwegian kroner, $17.4 million in Danish kroner and $15.8 million in Luxembourg francs.

Of the 121 medium- and long-term borrowing operations conducted by the Bank, 100 were in the private sector and accounted for $8,513 million, or 77 per cent of the total funds borrowed. The other medium- and long-term issues, totalling $1,863 million, or 17 per cent of the funds raised, were placed with official sources. Short-term borrowings outstanding as at 30 June amounted to $3,458 million.

As at 30 June 1985, the Bank's outstanding obligations totalled $50,319 million—an increase of $5,290 million over fiscal 1984—denominated in 20 different currencies and currency units.

During fiscal 1985, the Bank continued to engage in currency swaps as a means of increasing its access to low nominal-cost currencies. It executed 50 currency-swap transactions aggregating $1,360 million—$887 into Swiss francs, $268 into deutsche mark, $96 million into Netherlands guilders and $109 million into Japanese yen.

Capitalization

For the fiscal year ending 30 June 1985, the value of the Bank's capital stock was expressed on the basis of the special drawing right (SDR) in terms of United States dollars as computed by the International Monetary Fund on 28 June, when the value of the SDR was set at $0.998281. The subscribed capital of the Bank, as at 30 June, totalled SDR 58,948 million, an increase of SDR 4,633 million from fiscal 1984.

Income, expenditures and reserves

The Bank's gross revenues, generated primarily from loans and investments, increased by $874 million or 19 per cent, to a total of $5,529 million in fiscal 1985. Net income was a record $1,137 million; the 90 per cent increase over the preceding year was primarily a result of high returns on the Bank's liquidity and low borrowing costs.

Expenditures totalled $4,392 million, up 8.3 per cent from the previous fiscal year. Administrative costs amounted to $355 million, up by $25 million.

The Bank's General Reserve amounted to $3,727 million at the end of fiscal 1985.

Secretariat

As at 30 June 1985, the staff of the World Bank numbered 5,866, of whom 2,920 were staff in the Professional or higher categories, drawn from 112 nationalities.

[a]YUN 1983, p. 1259.

STATEMENT OF INCOME AND EXPENSES

(for the fiscal year ended 30 June 1985)

	Amount (in thousands of US dollars)
Income	
Income from investments*	2,019,138
Income from loans	
Interest	3,238,737
Commitment charges	239,144
Front-end fees	10,062
Other income†	21,671
Total income	5,528,752

	Amount (in thousands of US dollars)
Expenses	
Administrative expenses‡	354,820
Interest on borrowings	3,932,867
Bond issuance and other financial expenses	64,873
Contributions to special programmes	39,065
Total expenses	4,392,560
Net income	1,137,127

*Includes net gains of $338,721,000 resulting from sales of investments.

†Includes net gains of $16,485,000 resulting from repurchases of obligations of the Bank prior to maturity.

‡All administrative expenses of the Bank and IDA and a portion of those of IFC are paid by the Bank. The administrative expenses are net of a management fee of $273,180,000 charged to IDA and of a service and support fee of $2,975,000 charged to IFC.

Annex I. MEMBERS OF THE WORLD BANK, SUBSCRIPTIONS AND VOTING POWER
(As at 30 June 1985)

MEMBER	Amount (in SDRs)	Percentage of total	Number of votes	Percentage of total	MEMBER	Amount (in SDRs)	Percentage of total	Number of votes	Percentage of total
	SUBSCRIPTION		**VOTING POWER**			**SUBSCRIPTION**		**VOTING POWER**	
Afghanistan	30,000	0.05	550	0.09	Haiti	58,900	0.10	839	0.13
Algeria	475,500	0.81	5,005	0.80	Honduras	11,000	0.02	360	0.06
Antigua and Barbuda	2,000	*	270	0.04	Hungary	420,300	0.71	4,453	0.71
Argentina	583,100	0.99	6,081	0.97	Iceland	68,000	0.12	930	0.15
Australia	1,273,700	2.16	12,987	2.07	India	2,300,200	3.90	23,252	3.71
Austria	546,900	0.93	5,719	0.91	Indonesia	777,700	1.32	8,027	1.28
Bahamas	17,100	0.03	421	0.07	Iran	158,000	0.27	1,830	0.29
Bahrain	56,600	0.10	816	0.13	Iraq	95,600	0.16	1,206	0.19
Bangladesh†	124,200	0.21	1,492	0.24	Ireland	270,100	0.46	2,951	0.47
Barbados	51,900	0.09	769	0.12	Israel	110,800	0.19	1,358	0.22
Belgium	1,432,100	2.43	14,571	2.33	Italy	1,984,200	3.37	20,092	3.21
Belize	3,900	0.01	289	0.05	Ivory Coast	83,400	0.14	1,084	0.17
Benin	10,000	0.02	350	0.06	Jamaica	44,600	0.08	696	0.11
Bhutan†	900	*	259	0.04	Japan	4,083,000	6.93	41,080	6.56
Bolivia	26,400	0.04	514	0.08	Jordan	23,300	0.04	483	0.08
Botswana	33,100	0.06	581	0.09	Kenya	131,500	0.22	1,565	0.25
Brazil	1,079,400	1.83	11,044	1.76	Kuwait	645,100	1.09	6,701	1.07
Burkina Faso†	10,000	0.02	350	0.06	Lao People's Democratic				
Burma†	59,100	0.10	841	0.13	Republic	10,000	0.02	350	0.06
Burundi	15,000	0.03	400	0.06	Lebanon	9,000	0.02	340	0.05
Cameroon†	20,000	0.03	450	0.07	Lesotho	36,200	0.06	612	0.10
Canada	2,178,200	3.70	22,032	3.52	Liberia	21,300	0.04	463	0.07
Cape Verde	1,600	*	266	0.04	Libyan Arab Jamahiriya	195,100	0.33	2,201	0.35
Central African Republic	10,000	0.02	350	0.06	Luxembourg	82,500	0.14	1,075	0.17
Chad	10,000	0.02	350	0.06	Madagascar	21,900	0.04	469	0.07
Chile†	124,000	0.21	1,490	0.24	Malawi†	15,000	0.03	400	0.06
China	2,348,200	3.98	23,732	3.79	Malaysia	425,000	0.72	4,500	0.72
Colombia	117,500	0.20	1,425	0.23	Maldives	26,200	0.04	512	0.08
Comoros	1,600	*	266	0.04	Mali	17,300	0.03	423	0.07
Congo	10,000	0.02	350	0.06	Malta	16,300	0.03	413	0.07
Costa Rica	13,100	0.02	381	0.06	Mauritania	10,000	0.02	350	0.06
Cyprus	78,800	0.13	1,038	0.17	Mauritius	67,800	0.12	928	0.15
Democratic Kampuchea	21,400	0.04	464	0.07	Mexico	636,000	1.08	6,610	1.06
Democratic Yemen	33,600	0.06	586	0.09	Morocco	261,200	0.44	2,862	0.46
Denmark	513,600	0.87	5,386	0.86	Mozambique	27,200	0.05	522	0.08
Djibouti†	3,100	0.01	281	0.04	Nepal	53,300	0.09	783	0.12
Dominica†	1,600	*	266	0.04	Netherlands	1,511,700	2.56	15,367	2.45
Dominican Republic	58,900	0.10	839	0.13	New Zealand	331,300	0.56	3,563	0.57
Ecuador†	36,800	0.06	618	0.10	Nicaragua	9,100	0.02	341	0.05
Egypt	344,400	0.58	3,694	0.59	Niger†	10,000	0.02	350	0.06
El Salvador	14,100	0.02	391	0.06	Nigeria	294,100	0.50	3,191	0.51
Equatorial Guinea	6,400	0.01	314	0.05	Norway†	241,000	0.41	2,660	0.42
Ethiopia	53,300	0.09	783	0.12	Oman†	19,200	0.03	442	0.07
Fiji	48,100	0.08	731	0.12	Pakistan†	251,900	0.43	2,769	0.44
Finland	372,600	0.63	3,976	0.63	Panama	21,600	0.04	466	0.07
France	3,426,000	5.81	34,510	5.51	Papua New Guinea	24,600	0.04	496	0.08
Gabon	12,000	0.02	370	0.06	Paraguay	38,600	0.07	636	0.10
Gambia	5,300	0.01	303	0.05	Peru	93,800	0.16	1,188	0.19
Germany, Federal Republic of	3,434,700	5.83	34,597	5.52	Philippines	359,800	0.61	3,848	0.61
Ghana	85,600	0.15	1,106	0.18	Portugal	132,400	0.22	1,574	0.25
Greece	94,500	0.16	1,195	0.19	Qatar	109,600	0.19	1,346	0.21
Grenada	1,700	*	267	0.04	Republic of Korea	316,300	0.54	3,413	0.54
Guatemala	16,700	0.03	417	0.07	Romania	200,100	0.34	2,251	0.36
Guinea	71,300	0.12	963	0.15	Rwanda†	17,400	0.03	424	0.07
Guinea-Bissau	2,700	*	277	0.04	Saint Christopher				
Guyana†	57,900	0.10	829	0.13	and Nevis	2,500	*	275	0.04

MEMBER	SUBSCRIPTION Amount (in SDRs)	SUBSCRIPTION Percentage of total	VOTING POWER Number of votes	VOTING POWER Percentage of total	MEMBER	SUBSCRIPTION Amount (in SDRs)	SUBSCRIPTION Percentage of total	VOTING POWER Number of votes	VOTING POWER Percentage of total
Saint Lucia	2,900	*	279	0.04	Togo	15,000	0.03	400	0.06
Saint Vincent and the Grenadines	1,300	*	263	0.04	Trinidad and Tobago	66,700	0.11	917	0.15
Samoa	26,700	0.05	517	0.08	Tunisia	37,300	0.06	623	0.10
Sao Tome and Principe	1,400	*	264	0.04	Turkey	340,800	0.58	3,658	0.58
Saudi Arabia	1,121,200	1.90	11,462	1.83	Uganda	33,300	0.06	583	0.09
Senegal	36,200	0.06	612	0.10	United Arab Emirates†	98,000	0.17	1,230	0.20
Seychelles	1,100	*	261	0.04	United Kingdom	3,537,600	6.00	35,626	5.69
Sierra Leone	15,000	0.03	400	0.06	United Republic of Tanzania†	35,000	0.06	600	0.10
Singapore	32,000	0.05	570	0.09	United States	12,317,700	20.90	123,427	19.70
Solomon Islands	28,300	0.05	533	0.09	Uruguay	51,800	0.09	768	0.12
Somalia	18,900	0.03	439	0.07	Vanuatu	32,300	0.05	573	0.09
South Africa	571,300	0.97	5,963	0.95	Venezuela	756,000	1.28	7,810	1.25
Spain	913,500	1.55	9,385	1.50	Viet Nam	54,300	0.09	793	0.13
Sri Lanka	211,000	0.36	2,360	0.38	Yemen	45,500	0.08	705	0.11
Sudan	60,000	0.10	850	0.14	Yugoslavia†	150,900	0.26	1,759	0.28
Suriname	16,200	0.03	412	0.07	Zaire	264,300	0.45	2,893	0.46
Swaziland	44,000	0.07	690	0.11	Zambia†	115,100	0.20	1,401	0.22
Sweden	736,700	1.25	7,617	1.22	Zimbabwe†	81,700	0.14	1,067	0.17
Syrian Arab Republic	123,300	0.21	1,483	0.24					
Thailand	311,100	0.53	3,361	0.54	Total	58,947,600	100.00‡	626,476	100.00‡

NOTE: Tonga became a member on 13 September 1985.

*Less than 0.005 per cent.

†Amounts aggregating the equivalent of $60,712,000, in current United States dollars, had been received from members on account of increases in subscriptions, which were in process of completion: Bangladesh $7,579,000, Bhutan $7,000, Burkina Faso $117,000, Burma $3,780,000, Cameroon $111,000, Chile $2,850,000, Djibouti $4,000, Dominica $2,000, Ecuador $311,000, Guyana $224,000, Malawi $174,000, Niger $40,000, Norway $10,118,000, Oman $163,000, Pakistan $18,066,000, Rwanda $1,358,000, United Arab Emirates $1,082,000, United Republic of Tanzania $130,000, Yugoslavia $4,885,000, Zambia $3,592,000, Zimbabwe $6,119,000.

‡May differ from the sum of the individual percentages because of rounding.

Annex II. EXECUTIVE DIRECTORS AND ALTERNATES OF THE WORLD BANK
(As at 30 June 1985)

Appointed Director	Appointed Alternate	Casting the vote of
James B. Burnham	Hugh W. Foster	United States
Kenji Yamaguchi	Toshihiro Yamakawa	Japan
Nigel L. Wicks	Richard Manning	United Kingdom
Reinhard Münzberg	Michael von Harpe	Federal Republic of Germany
Bruno de Maulde	Francis Mayer	France

Elected Director	Elected Alternate	Casting the votes of
Fawzi Hamad Al-Sultan (Kuwait)	Mohammad Al-Shawi (Saudi Arabia)	Bahrain, Egypt, Iraq, Jordan, Kuwait, Lebanon, Maldives, Oman, Pakistan, Qatar, Saudi Arabia, Syrian Arab Republic, United Arab Emirates, Yemen
Frank Potter (Canada)	George L. Reid (Barbados)	Antigua and Barbuda, Bahamas, Barbados, Belize, Canada, Dominica, Grenada, Guyana, Ireland, Jamaica, Saint Christopher and Nevis, Saint Lucia, Saint Vincent and the Grenadines
Jacques de Groote (Belgium)	Oral Akman (Turkey)	Austria, Belgium, Hungary, Luxembourg, Turkey
C. R. Krishnaswamy Rao Sahib (India)	Gholam Kibria (Bangladesh)	Bangladesh, Bhutan, India, Sri Lanka
Leonor Filardo de González (Venezuela)	María Antonieta Domínguez (Honduras)	Costa Rica, El Salvador, Guatemala, Honduras, Mexico, Nicaragua, Panama, Spain, Suriname, Venezuela
Xu Naijiong (China)	Yang Guanghui (China)	China
Mario Draghi (Italy)	Rodrigo M. Guimarães (Portugal)	Greece, Italy, Malta, Portugal
Ronald H. Dean (Australia)	You Kwang Park (Republic of Korea)	Australia, New Zealand, Papua New Guinea, Republic of Korea, Samoa, Solomon Islands, Vanuatu
Ferdinand van Dam (Netherlands)	Riza Sapunxhiu (Yugoslavia)	Cyprus, Israel, Netherlands, Romania, Yugoslavia
Pekka Korpinen (Finland)	Per Taxell (Sweden)	Denmark, Finland, Iceland, Norway, Sweden
Phaichitr Uathavikul (Thailand)	Shashi N. Shah (Nepal)	Burma, Fiji, Indonesia, Lao People's Democratic Republic, Malaysia, Nepal, Singapore, Thailand, Viet Nam
Edgar Gutiérrez-Castro (Colombia)	Guillermo A. Rivera (Dominican Republic)	Brazil, Colombia, Dominican Republic, Ecuador, Haiti, Philippines

Elected Director	Elected Alternate	Casting the votes of
Astère Girukwigomba (Burundi)	Mitiku Jembere (Ethiopia)	Botswana, Burundi, Ethiopia, Gambia, Guinea, Kenya, Lesotho, Liberia, Malawi, Mozambique, Nigeria, Seychelles, Sierra Leone, Sudan, Swaziland, Trinidad and Tobago, Uganda, United Republic of Tanzania, Zambia, Zimbabwe
Mourad Benachenhou (Algeria)	Salem Mohamed Omeish (Libyan Arab Jamahiriya)	Afghanistan, Algeria, Democratic Yemen, Ghana, Iran, Libyan Arab Jamahiriya, Morocco, Tunisia
Nicéphore Soglo (Benin)	André Milongo (Congo)	Benin, Burkina Faso, Cameroon, Cape Verde, Central African Republic, Chad, Comoros, Congo, Djibouti, Equatorial Guinea, Gabon, Guinea-Bissau, Ivory Coast, Madagascar, Mali, Mauritania, Mauritius, Niger, Rwanda, Sao Tome and Principe, Senegal, Somalia, Togo, Zaire
Carlos Corti* (Uruguay)	Félix Alberto Camarasa (Argentina)	Argentina, Bolivia, Chile, Paraguay, Peru, Uruguay

NOTE: Democratic Kampuchea and South Africa did not participate in the 1984 regular election of Executive Directors.

*Resigned 30 June 1985; succeeded by Kenneth Coates (Uruguay).

Annex III.   PRINCIPAL OFFICERS AND OFFICES OF THE WORLD BANK
(As at 1 July 1985)

PRINCIPAL OFFICERS*

President: A. W. Clausen.
Senior Vice-President, Finance: Moeen A. Qureshi.
Senior Vice-President, Operations: Ernest Stern.
Vice-President: Warren C. Baum.
Vice-President, External Relations: Jose Botafogo G.
Vice-President, Energy and Industry: Jean-Loup Dherse.
Vice-President, Pension Fund: K. Georg Gabriel.
Vice-President and Controller: Hans C. Hittmair.
Regional Vice-President, South Asia: W. David Hopper.
Vice-President, Operations Policy: S. Shahid Husain.
Regional Vice-President, Eastern and Southern Africa: Edward V. K. Jaycox.
Director-General, Operations Evaluation: Shiv S. Kapur.

Regional Vice-President, East Asia and Pacific: Attila Karaosmanoglu.
Regional Vice-President, Latin America and the Caribbean: A. David Knox.
Vice-President, Economics and Research: Anne O. Krueger.
Vice-President, Co-financing: Teruyuki Ohuchi.
Vice-President, Personnel and Administration: Martijn J. W. M. Paijmans.
Vice-President and Treasurer: Eugene H. Rotberg.
Vice-President and General Counsel: Ibrahim F. I. Shihata.
Vice-President and Secretary: Timothy T. Thahane.
Regional Vice-President, Western Africa: Wilfried P. Thalwitz.
Regional Vice-President, Europe, Middle East and North Africa: Willi A. Wapenhans.
Vice-President, Financial Policy, Planning and Budgeting: D. Joseph Wood.

*The World Bank and IDA had the same officers and staff.

HEADQUARTERS AND OTHER OFFICES

HEADQUARTERS
The World Bank
1818 H Street, N.W.
Washington, D.C. 20433, United States
   Cable address: INTBAFRAD WASHINGTONDC
   Telephone: (202) 477-1234
   Telex: RCA 248423 WORLDBK
          WUI 64145 WORLDBANK

NEW YORK OFFICE
The World Bank Mission to the United Nations
747 Third Avenue, 26th floor
New York, N.Y. 10017, United States
   Cable address: INTBAFRAD NEWYORK
   Telephone: (212) 963-6008

EUROPEAN OFFICE
The World Bank
66 Avenue d'Iéna
75116 Paris, France
   Cable address: INTBAFRAD PARIS
   Telephone: (1) 4723-54-21
   Telex: 842-620628

LONDON OFFICE
The World Bank
New Zealand House, 15th Floor, Haymarket
London, SW1 Y4TE, England
   Cable address: INTBAFRAD LONDON
   Telephone: (01) 930-8511
   Telex: 919462

GENEVA OFFICE
The World Bank
ITC Building
54 Rue de Montbrillant
(P.O. Box 104)
1211 Geneva 20 CIC, Switzerland
   Telephone: (22) 33 21 20
   Telex: 28883

TOKYO OFFICE
The World Bank
Kokusai Building, Room 916
1-1 Marunouchi 3-chome, Chiyoda-ku
Tokyo 100, Japan
   Cable address: INTBAFRAD TOKYO
   Telephone: (03) 214-5001
   Telex: 781-26838

REGIONAL MISSION IN EASTERN AND
   SOUTHERN AFRICA
The World Bank
Reinsurance Plaza, 5th and 6th floors
Taifa Road
(P.O. Box 30577)
Nairobi, Kenya
   Cable address: INTBAFRAD NAIROBI
   Telephone: (254-2) 338868, 24391
   Telex: 22022

REGIONAL MISSION IN WESTERN AFRICA
The World Bank
Immeuble Shell, 64 Avenue Lamblin
(Boîte Postale 1850)
Abidjan 01, Ivory Coast
   Cable address: INTBAFRAD ABIDJAN
   Telephone: (225) 44 22 27, 32 90 06, 44 20 38
   Telex: 28132

REGIONAL MISSION IN THAILAND
The World Bank
Udom Vidhya Building, 956 Rama IV Road
Sala Daeng
Bangkok 5, Thailand
   Cable address: INTBAFRAD BANGKOK
   Telephone: (66-2) 235-5300-8
   Telex: 82817

Chapter VII

International Finance Corporation (IFC)

The International Finance Corporation (IFC), established in 1956 as an affiliate of the International Bank for Reconstruction and Development (World Bank), is a multilateral development institution that promotes private investment and assists private enterprises in its developing member countries. Its capital resources are provided by its 127 member States—including 106 developing countries—which collectively determine its policies and activities.

During the fiscal year ending 30 June 1985, the first year of IFC's current five-year programme, the IFC Board of Directors approved 75 investments in 38 developing countries and one regional project in Africa, totalling $937.2 million. Of that amount, $609.3 million was to be invested for IFC's own account and $327.9 million would be syndicated, or sold, to other investors. Compared to the 1984 fiscal year, the total approved investments increased by $241.6 million, from $695.6 million, and investments net of syndications rose $218.3 million, from $391 million. Of the total dollar amount, $875.9 million was for loans and $61.3 million for equity or equity-like investments. Of the latter, $7.4 million was approved for the exercise-of-rights issues by firms in which IFC already had equity investments. Four of the loans, which totalled $37.3 million, involved the restructuring of existing obligations.

IFC estimated that the total capital costs of projects it would help to finance would be more than $2,767.6 million. In other words, for every dollar invested by IFC for its own account, others would invest about $3.50.

All loans reflected market rates. The typical United States fixed-rate loan was priced at 13.25 per cent for a period of seven to eight years with a grace period of four years. The maturities of IFC loans, set to conform to the nature and needs of each project, ranged from eight to 12 years.

During the year, IFC invested in China for the first time. It also approved investments in five countries in which it had not invested during the previous three years. Thirty-three investments, with a total value of $258.9 million, were located in countries with a per capita income below $805. Early in the fiscal year, at the request of IFC's management, the Board of Directors approved the use of lending at variable rates. During the year, more than 20 per cent of the loans were priced at variable rates, with 34 per cent of United States dollar–denominated loans so priced.

Supplementing its loans, equity and equity-like instruments, IFC also provided a broad range of other financial services, including underwritings, guarantees and stand-by arrangements. Up to one third of the staff effort was expended for technical assistance activities. These services were generally provided free of charge. However, to bring itself in line with market practices, IFC began to charge fees for special service activities; such fees generated about $2.6 million in income for IFC during fiscal year 1985.

Equity from a special line of financing established with Saudi Arabia in 1983 was called upon to help fill a financing gap in two projects: a battery-manufacturing business in Yemen and an oil palm plantation in the Philippines.

The Corporation continued aggressively to seek out commercial banks and other financial institutions to join in loan syndications and parallel financing. During the year, some $327.9 million in loans by IFC was syndicated with 36 such institutions, in line with the IFC objective of placing about one third of its loans in the international financial markets. Included among the year's activities was a $50-million underwriting for a Latin American export finance bank for which IFC, together with the Goldman Sachs International Corporation, was the leading underwriter. This medium-term floating-rate note issue was the first for a Latin American private-sector firm, since the debt crisis began in 1982, involving new money from international capital markets.

The Board of Directors had approved in 1984 a five-year financial and operational plan covering the fiscal years 1985 to 1989. The programme, dependent on a proposed $650-million capital increase, targeted an annual growth rate of about 7 per cent in both the number and the dollar volume in real terms of projects approved by the Board. Thus, during the five years covered, IFC expected to undertake more than 400 new investments and commit about $4,000 million of its own funds (or $7,300 million inclusive of syndications to commercial financial institutions) in business ventures with total capital costs exceeding $30 billion. During 1985, IFC achieved the objectives established for the first year of the programme.

The five-year programme set out a number of new initiatives, responding to the priority needs of developing member countries. These included corporate restructuring assistance provided to about 30 companies to restructure their operations to reflect economic policy adjustments made by their Governments. In four cases completed in 1985, IFC provided $40.3 million in loans and quasi-equity investments. Concerning African initiatives, IFC during the year approved $60.4 million in financing for 15 projects in sub-Saharan Africa. In May 1985, after informal discussions in a number of African capitals, it entered into a funding agreement with the United Nations Development Programme to study the possibility of establishing an African Project Development Facility to help African entrepreneurs develop new business ventures. IFC also began discussions with private companies and public agencies on the creation of an African Management Services Facility, which would contribute experienced management to African enterprises. With regard to energy, IFC diversified its activities in oil and gas exploration and development, particularly encouraging independent oil companies to expand activities in developing countries. One oil exploration project in Colombia and two energy development projects in Chile and Pakistan were approved. Concerning financial markets and institutional development, IFC expanded into a number of new areas, helping to establish an insurance company in Indonesia, underwriting a Eurodollar bond issue, providing a line of equity to an intermediary on an agency basis and setting up new investment banks with the participation of similar developing-country institutions. It also promoted the formation of national and multi-country equity investment trusts to encourage equity flows.

While continuing to borrow most of its funds from the World Bank, IFC for the first time supplemented them by borrowing from private capital markets. By the end of May 1985, it had carried out two $50-million fixed-rate borrowings at favourable rates. Later in the year, it raised $29 million through a private placement. In June 1984, the Board of Directors had approved for submission to the Board of Governors a resolution proposing to increase IFC's authorized shares from 650,000 to 1,300,000. During the 1985 fiscal year, 104 member countries, representing 70.6 per cent of the total voting shares and 82 per cent of the membership, ratified the resolution. It was expected that the 75 per cent of the voting shares required for ratification would be reached early in fiscal year 1986.

During the 1985 fiscal year, Mozambique and Hungary joined the IFC, bringing its membership to 127.

IFC COMMITMENTS BY TYPE OF BUSINESS
(as at 30 June 1985)

Sector	Amount (in millions of US dollars)
Chemicals and petrochemicals	377.58
Development finance	160.13
Energy and mining	80.59
Capital markets	60.85
Agribusiness	59.30
Automotive/vehicles	39.40
Guarantee facility	38.00
Pulp, paper and timber	36.56
Tourism	27.90
Manufacturing	20.29
Textiles	18.12
Cement and construction materials	14.46
Iron and steel	4.05
Total	937.23

IFC INVESTMENTS
(1 July 1984–30 June 1985)

Recipient	Sector	Amount (in thousands of US dollars)
Argentina	Capital markets	2,050
	Chemicals and petrochemicals	49,310
	Agribusiness	12,000
Bangladesh	Manufacturing	1,970
	Capital markets	2,000
Brazil	Iron and steel	4,050
	Pulp, paper and timber	32,570
	Chemicals and petrochemicals	8,000
Cameroon	Agribusiness	2,180
Chile	Chemicals and petrochemicals	55,000
	Mining	18,700
China	Automotive/vehicles	17,020
Colombia	Development finance	18,000
	Capital markets	30
	Energy	5,000
Egypt	Manufacturing	4,640
	Capital markets	1,860
Fiji	Tourism	6,800
Guyana	Pulp, paper and timber	1,700
India	Automotive/vehicles	15,620
	Capital markets	5,610
	Cement, construction materials and manufacturing	13,450
Indonesia	Capital markets	360
	Cement and construction materials	830
Ivory Coast	Agribusiness	2,550
Jamaica	Development finance	7,300
	Agribusiness	3,540
Kenya	Agribusiness	8,840
	Tourism	3,600
Madagascar	Textiles	6,650
Malawi	Pulp, paper and timber	2,290
Mauritania	Agribusiness	1,200
Morocco	Agribusiness	4,580
	Development finance	40,000
Nigeria	Tourism	2,500
Pakistan	Energy and mining	39,900
Panama	Capital markets	37,500
Paraguay	Agribusiness	800
Peru	Energy and mining	16,800
Philippines	Agribusiness	10,110
	Guarantee facility	38,000*
Portugal	Development finance	230
Republic of Korea	Capital markets	5,540
	Manufacturing	1,700
Somalia	Manufacturing	620
Sri Lanka	Capital markets	3,960
Swaziland	Capital markets	1,630
	Textiles	2,430
Thailand	Energy and mining	190
	Chemicals and petrochemicals	270
	Cement and construction materials	180
Trinidad and Tobago	Chemicals and petrochemicals	265,000
Tunisia	Textiles	2,260

Recipient	Sector	Amount (in thousands of US dollars)
Turkey	Capital markets	310
	Automotive/vehicles	6,760
Uruguay	Agribusiness	8,900
Yemen	Manufacturing	360
	Agribusiness	4,500
Yugoslavia	Development finance	90,600
	Manufacturing	11,000
Zaire	Tourism	15,000
	Textiles	6,780
	Agribusiness	100
Africa region	Development finance	4,000
Total		937,230†

*Contractor bonding facility.
†Includes bonding facility.

Financial operations

IFC's total operating income in fiscal year 1985 was $172.7 million, or $21.6 million higher than in the previous year. Reflecting in part the Corporation's increased business activities, administrative expenses increased by $6.5 million over the previous year, to $51.5 million. Net income amounted to $28.3 million, all of which was added to accumulated earnings.

STATEMENT OF INCOME AND EXPENDITURE
(for fiscal year ending 30 June 1985)

Income	Amount (in thousands of US dollars)
Income from deposits and securities	15,157

Income	Amount (in thousands of US dollars)
Income from loan and equity investments	
Interest	131,770
Dividends and profit participations	14,418
Commitment fees	4,786
Realized gain on equity sales	4,565
Other investment fees	2,580
Other operating income (expense)	(579)
Total income	172,697
Expenditure	
Charges on borrowings	63,508
Administrative expenses*	51,458
Total expenditure	114,966
Income from operations	57,731
Provision for losses	(29,396)
Net income—transferred to accumulated earnings	28,335

*The World Bank charges IFC an annual service and support fee which for the year ending 30 June 1985 was fixed at $2,975,000.

Capital and accumulated earnings

The net income of $28.3 million was allocated to accumulated earnings, bringing the total to $258.4 million. With paid-in capital of $545.8 million, net worth reached $804.2 million, up from $774.3 million at the end of the previous fiscal year.

Secretariat

At the end of the fiscal year, IFC had a total staff of 433, drawn from 70 countries, including 54 developing countries.

Annex I.   MEMBERS OF THE INTERNATIONAL FINANCE CORPORATION,
SUBSCRIPTIONS AND VOTING POWER
(As at 30 June 1985)

MEMBER	SUBSCRIPTION Amount (in thousands of US dollars)	Percentage of total	VOTING POWER Number of votes	Percentage of total	MEMBER	SUBSCRIPTION Amount (in thousands of US dollars)	Percentage of total	VOTING POWER Number of votes	Percentage of total
Afghanistan	111	0.02	361	0.06	Denmark	4,779	0.88	5,029	0.87
Argentina	9,821	1.80	10,071	1.74	Djibouti	21	*	271	0.05
Australia	12,191	2.23	12,441	2.15	Dominica	11	*	261	0.05
Austria	5,085	0.93	5,335	0.92	Dominican Republic	306	0.06	556	0.10
Bangladesh	2,328	0.43	2,578	0.45	Ecuador	674	0.12	924	0.16
Barbados	93	0.02	343	0.06	Egypt	3,124	0.57	3,374	0.58
Belgium	13,723	2.51	13,973	2.42	El Salvador	11	*	261	0.05
Belize	26	*	276	0.05	Ethiopia	33	0.01	283	0.05
Bolivia	490	0.09	740	0.13	Fiji	74	0.01	324	0.06
Botswana	29	0.01	279	0.05	Finland	4,043	0.74	4,293	0.74
Brazil	10,169	1.86	10,419	1.80	France	29,528	5.41	29,778	5.16
Burkina Faso	245	0.04	495	0.09	Gabon	429	0.08	679	0.12
Burma	666	0.12	916	0.16	Gambia	35	0.01	285	0.05
Burundi	100	0.02	350	0.06	Germany, Federal Republic of	33,204	6.08	33,454	5.79
Cameroon	490	0.09	740	0.13	Ghana	1,306	0.24	1,556	0.27
Canada	20,952	3.84	21,202	3.67	Greece	1,777	0.33	2,027	0.35
Chile	2,328	0.43	2,578	0.45	Grenada	21	*	271	0.05
China	4,154	0.76	4,404	0.76	Guatemala	306	0.06	556	0.10
Colombia	2,083	0.38	2,333	0.40	Guinea	134	0.02	384	0.07
Congo	67	0.01	317	0.05	Guinea-Bissau	18	*	268	0.05
Costa Rica	245	0.04	495	0.09	Guyana	368	0.07	618	0.11
Cyprus	551	0.10	801	0.14	Haiti	306	0.06	556	0.10

MEMBER	SUBSCRIPTION Amount (in thousands of US dollars)	Percentage of total	VOTING POWER Number of votes	Percentage of total	MEMBER	SUBSCRIPTION Amount (in thousands of US dollars)	Percentage of total	VOTING POWER Number of votes	Percentage of total
Honduras	184	0.03	434	0.08	Peru	1,777	0.33	2,027	0.35
Hungary	1,364	0.25	1,614	0.28	Philippines	3,247	0.59	3,497	0.61
Iceland	11	*	261	0.05	Portugal	2,144	0.39	2,394	0.41
India	19,788	3.63	20,038	3.47	Republic of Korea	2,450	0.45	2,700	0.47
Indonesia	7,351	1.35	7,601	1.32	Rwanda	306	0.06	556	0.10
Iran	372	0.07	622	0.11	Saint Lucia	19	*	269	0.05
Iraq	67	0.01	317	0.05	Samoa	9	*	259	0.04
Ireland	332	0.06	582	0.10	Saudi Arabia	9,251	1.69	9,501	1.65
Israel	550	0.10	800	0.14	Senegal	707	0.13	957	0.17
Italy	19,114	3.50	19,364	3.35	Seychelles	7	*	257	0.04
Ivory Coast	913	0.17	1,163	0.20	Sierra Leone	83	0.02	333	0.06
Jamaica	1,103	0.20	1,353	0.23	Singapore	177	0.03	427	0.07
Japan	25,546	4.68	25,796	4.47	Solomon Islands	11	*	261	0.05
Jordan	429	0.08	679	0.12	Somalia	83	0.02	333	0.06
Kenya	1,041	0.19	1,291	0.22	South Africa	4,108	0.75	4,358	0.75
Kuwait	4,533	0.83	4,783	0.83	Spain	6,004	1.10	6,254	1.08
Lebanon	50	0.01	300	0.05	Sri Lanka	1,838	0.34	2,088	0.36
Lesotho	18	*	268	0.05	Sudan	111	0.02	361	0.06
Liberia	83	0.02	333	0.06	Swaziland	184	0.03	434	0.08
Libyan Arab Jamahiriya	55	0.01	305	0.05	Sweden	6,923	1.27	7,173	1.24
Luxembourg	551	0.10	801	0.14	Syrian Arab Republic	72	0.01	322	0.06
Madagascar	111	0.02	361	0.06	Thailand	2,818	0.52	3,068	0.53
Malawi	368	0.07	618	0.11	Togo	368	0.07	618	0.11
Malaysia	3,921	0.72	4,171	0.72	Trinidad and Tobago	1,059	0.19	1,309	0.23
Maldives	4	*	254	0.04	Tunisia	919	0.17	1,169	0.20
Mali	116	0.02	366	0.06	Turkey	3,063	0.56	3,313	0.57
Mauritania	55	0.01	305	0.05	Uganda	735	0.13	985	0.17
Mauritius	429	0.08	679	0.12	United Arab Emirates	1,838	0.34	2,088	0.36
Mexico	6,004	1.10	6,254	1.08	United Kingdom	37,900	6.94	38,150	6.61
Morocco	2,328	0.43	2,578	0.45	United Republic of Tanzania	724	0.13	974	0.17
Mozambique	182	0.03	432	0.07	United States	146,661	26.87	146,911	25.44
Nepal	306	0.06	556	0.10	Uruguay	919	0.17	1,169	0.20
Netherlands	14,458	2.65	14,708	2.55	Vanuatu	25	*	275	0.05
New Zealand	923	0.17	1,173	0.20	Venezuela	7,106	1.30	7,356	1.27
Nicaragua	184	0.03	434	0.08	Viet Nam	166	0.03	416	0.07
Niger	67	0.01	317	0.05	Yemen	184	0.03	434	0.08
Nigeria	5,575	1.02	5,825	1.01	Yugoslavia	2,879	0.53	3,129	0.54
Norway	4,533	0.83	4,783	0.83	Zaire	1,929	0.35	2,179	0.38
Oman	306	0.06	556	0.10	Zambia	1,286	0.24	1,536	0.27
Pakistan	4,411	0.81	4,661	0.81	Zimbabwe	546	0.10	796	0.14
Panama	344	0.06	594	0.10					
Papua New Guinea	490	0.09	740	0.13	Total	545,784	100.00†	577,534	100.00†
Paraguay	123	0.02	373	0.06					

*Less than 0.005 per cent.

†May differ from the sum of the individual percentages because of rounding.

Annex II.   EXECUTIVE DIRECTORS AND ALTERNATES
OF THE INTERNATIONAL FINANCE CORPORATION
(As at 1 July 1985)

Appointed Director	Appointed Alternate	Casting the vote of
James B. Burnham	Hugh W. Foster	United States
Timothy P. Lankester	Richard Manning	United Kingdom
Reinhard Münzberg	Michael von Harpe	Federal Republic of Germany
Bruno de Maulde	Francis Mayer	France
Kenji Yamaguchi	Toshihiro Yamakawa	Japan

Elected Director	Elected Alternate	Casting the votes of
Fawzi Hamad Al-Sultan (Kuwait)	Mohammed Al-Shawi (Saudi Arabia)	Egypt, Iraq, Jordan, Kuwait, Lebanon, Maldives, Oman, Pakistan, Saudi Arabia, Syrian Arab Republic, United Arab Emirates, Yemen
Frank Potter (Canada)	George L. Reid (Barbados)	Barbados, Belize, Canada, Dominica, Grenada, Guyana, Ireland, Jamaica, Saint Lucia
Jacques de Groote (Belgium)	Oral Akman (Turkey)	Austria, Belgium, Hungary, Luxembourg, Turkey
C. R. Krishnaswamy Rao Sahib (India)	Gholam Kibria (Bangladesh)	Bangladesh, India, Sri Lanka
Mario Draghi (Italy)	Rodrigo M. Guimarães (Portugal)	Greece, Italy, Portugal

Appointed Director	Appointed Alternate	Casting the vote of
Leonor Filardo de González (Venezuela)	María Antonieta Domínguez (Honduras)	Costa Rica, El Salvador, Guatemala, Honduras, Mexico, Nicaragua, Panama, Spain, Venezuela
Pekka Korpinen (Finland)	Per Taxell (Sweden)	Denmark, Finland, Iceland, Norway, Sweden
Ferdinand van Dam (Netherlands)	Riza Sapunxhiu (Yugoslavia)	Cyprus, Israel, Netherlands, Yugoslavia
Edgar Gutiérrez-Castro (Colombia)	Guillermo A. Rivera (Dominican Republic)	Brazil, Colombia, Dominican Republic, Ecuador, Haiti, Philippines
Ronald H. Dean (Australia)	You Kwang Park (Republic of Korea)	Australia, New Zealand, Papua New Guinea, Republic of Korea, Samoa, Solomon Islands, Vanuatu
Phaichitr Uathavikul (Thailand)	Sashi N. Shah (Nepal)	Burma, Fiji, Indonesia, Malaysia, Nepal, Singapore, Thailand, Viet Nam
Astère Girukwigomba (Burundi)	Mitiku Jembere (Ethiopia)	Botswana, Burundi, Ethiopia, Gambia, Guinea, Kenya, Lesotho, Liberia, Malawi, Mozambique, Nigeria, Seychelles, Sierra Leone, Sudan, Swaziland, Trinidad and Tobago, Uganda, United Republic of Tanzania, Zambia, Zimbabwe
Kenneth Coates (Uruguay)	Felix Alberto Camarasa (Argentina)	Argentina, Bolivia, Chile, Paraguay, Peru, Uruguay
Nicéphore Soglo (Benin)	André Milongo (Congo)	Burkina Faso, Cameroon, Congo, Djibouti, Gabon, Guinea-Bissau, Ivory Coast, Madagascar, Mali, Mauritania, Mauritius, Niger, Rwanda, Senegal, Somalia, Togo, Zaire
Mourad Benachenhou (Algeria)	Salem Mohamed Omeish (Libyan Arab Jamahiriya)	Afghanistan, Ghana, Iran, Libyan Arab Jamahiriya, Morocco, Tunisia
Xu Naijiong (China)	Yang Guanghui (China)	China

NOTE: South Africa did not participate in the 1984 regular election of Executive Directors.

Annex III.   PRINCIPAL OFFICERS AND OFFICES OF THE INTERNATIONAL FINANCE CORPORATION
(As at 1 July 1985)

PRINCIPAL OFFICERS

President: A. W. Clausen.*
Executive Vice-President: William S. Ryrie.
Vice-President, Corporate Affairs and Development: Francisco J. Alejo.
Vice-President, Investment Operations: Judhvir Parmar.
Vice-President, Portfolio and Financial Management: Hilary P. Reddy.†
Vice-President and General Counsel: Jose E. Camacho.
Vice-President, Engineering: Makarand V. Dehejia.
Vice-President and Special Adviser: Sven K. Riskaer.
Vice-President and Special Adviser: Jose M. Ruisanchez.
Secretary: Timothy T. Thahane.*

Director, Department of Investments, Africa I: Andre G. Hovaguimian.‡
Director, Department of Investments, Africa II: M. Azam K. Alizai.
Director, Department of Investments, Asia I: Torstein Stephansen.#
Director, Department of Investments, Asia II: Wilfried Kaffenberger.#
Director, Department of Investments, Europe and Middle East: Douglas Gustafson.
Director, Department of Investments, Latin America and Caribbean I: Helmut Paul.
Director, Department of Investments, Latin America and Caribbean II: Daniel F. Adams.

Director, Capital Markets: David Gill.
Manager, Caribbean Projects Development Facility: Hugh Henry-May.
Director, Corporate Promotion and Syndications: Giovanni Vacchelli.
Economic Adviser and Director, Development Department: Richard Richardson.
Deputy Director, Engineering: David B. Minch (Acting).
Director, Financial Management and Planning: Richard H. Frank.
Deputy General Counsel: Walter F. Norris.
Director, Management Systems and Accounting: Roswitha J. Klement-Francis
Manager, Personnel and Administration: John H. Stewart.
Special Representative, Middle East: Cherif Hassan.
Special Representative, Far East: Naokado Nishihara.
Special Representative, London: Hans Pollan.
Special Representative, Paris: Gunter H. Kreuter.‡
   Regional Mission in East Asia: Vijay K. Chaudhry.
   Regional Mission in Eastern Africa: V. S. Raghavan.
   Regional Mission in India: Athishdam Tharmaratnam.
   Regional Mission in Indonesia: Peter L. F. Edmonds.
   Regional Mission in Western Africa: Jean-Olivier Fraisse.
Special Adviser: James M. Kearns.

*Held the same position in the World Bank.
†Effective 3 September 1985.
‡Effective 1 September 1985.
#Effective 1 October 1985.

HEADQUARTERS AND OTHER OFFICES

HEADQUARTERS
International Finance Corporation
1818 H Street, N. W.
Washington, D. C. 20433, United States
  Cable address: CORINTFIN WASHINGTONDC
  Telephone: (202) 477-1234
  Telex: ITT 440098, RCA 248423, WU 64145

NEW YORK OFFICE
International Finance Corporation
747 Third Avenue, 26th floor
New York, N. Y. 10017, United States
  Cable address: CORINTFIN NEWYORK
  Telephone: (212) 754-6008

EUROPEAN OFFICE
International Finance Corporation
New Zealand House, 15th floor
Haymarket, London SW1 Y4TE, England
  Cable address: CORINTFIN LONDON
  Telephone: (01) 930-8741
  Telex: 851-919462

PARIS OFFICE
International Finance Corporation
66 avenue d'Iéna
75116 Paris, France
  Cable address: CORINTFIN PARIS
  Telephone: (1) 4 723-54-21
  Telex: 842-620628

TOKYO OFFICE
International Finance Corporation
5-1 Nibancho, Chiyoda-ku
Tokyo 102, Japan
  Cable address: SPCORINTFIN TOKYO
  Telephone: (03) 261-3626
  Telex: 781-26554

REGIONAL MISSION IN EAST ASIA
World Bank Group
Central Bank of the Philippines
Manila, Philippines
  Cable address: CORINTFIN MANILA
  Telephone: 59-99-35
  Telex: 742-40541

REGIONAL MISSION IN EASTERN AFRICA
International Finance Corporation
Reinsurance Plaza, 5th Floor
Taifa Road
(P. O. Box 30577)
Nairobi, Kenya
  Cable address: CORINTFIN NAIROBI
  Telephone: 24726
  Telex: 963-22022

REGIONAL MISSION IN INDIA
International Finance Corporation
55 Lodi Estate
(P. O. Box 416)
New Delhi 110003, India
  Cable address: CORINTFIN NEWDELHI
  Telephone: 697-905
  Telex: 953-3161493

REGIONAL MISSION IN INDONESIA
International Finance Corporation
Jl. Rasuna Said, Kav. B-10
Suite 301
(P. O. Box 324/JKT)
Kuningan, Jakarta 12940
Indonesia
  Cable address: CORINTFIN JAKARTA
  Telephone: 516069
  Telex: 796-44456

REGIONAL MISSION IN THE MIDDLE EAST
International Finance Corporation
3 Elbergas Street, Garden City
Cairo, Egypt
  Cable address: IFCAI CAIRO
  Telephone: 982914
  Telex: 927-93110

REGIONAL MISSION IN WESTERN AFRICA
International Finance Corporation
Immeuble Alpha 2000, rue Gourgas
01-P. O. Box 1748
Abidjan-01, Ivory Coast
  Cable address: CORINTFIN ABIDJAN
  Telephone: 32-65-97, 33-11-51
  Telex: 969-23533

Chapter VIII

International Development Association (IDA)

Established in 1960 as an affiliate of the International Bank for Reconstruction and Development (World Bank), the International Development Association (IDA) promotes economic development primarily in the poorer developing countries. It provides assistance for the same purposes as the Bank but on easier terms. Though legally and financially distinct from the Bank, IDA shares the same staff.

The funds used by IDA—called credits to distinguish them from World Bank loans—come mostly from subscriptions in convertible currencies from members, general replenishments from its more industrialized and developed members, and transfers from the Bank's net earnings.

IDA assistance during fiscal year 1985 (1 July 1984 to 30 June 1985) concentrated on the very poor countries—those with an annual per capita gross national product of less than $791 (in 1983 dollars). More than 50 countries were eligible under that criterion. Credits are interest-free, with a service charge, to cover administrative costs, of 0.75 per cent on disbursed and 0.5 per cent on undisbursed balances. After an initial grace period of 10 years, the credits are then repayable over 50 years.

Unlike the Bank, which may lend to public and private entities with government guarantees, IDA lends only to Governments. In the case of revenue-producing projects, IDA credits are re-lent by the Governments on terms reflecting the local cost of capital. Therefore, IDA terms assist Governments to finance economic development without distorting the local credit structure.

At the end of fiscal 1985, IDA resources totalled $33,295 million.

The bulk of IDA funds for lending is provided by its Part I (industrial) member countries and several Part II (developing) countries under a series of replenishment agreements. The IDA Deputies met (Seoul, Republic of Korea, October 1985) to review the role of IDA and its future direction in the context of a mid-term review, to be undertaken in 1986, of the seventh replenishment of its resources;[a] they discussed the marked deterioration in the economies of the poorest countries, especially in Africa. At the same time, the planned lending by IDA to the poorest countries had been sharply curtailed because of the lower volume of resources made available under the seventh replenishment as compared with the sixth. As a result, investments in those countries in infrastructure, social sectors and productive activity were deferred, with a resulting adverse impact on long-term growth and the living standards of the poor. These concerns added urgency to the negotiations for the eighth replenishment and led to a commitment by the Deputies to complete the negotiations by the time of the 1986 annual meetings.

Membership of IDA rose to 134 in 1985 after the admission of Hungary on 29 April and Tonga on 23 October.

Special Facility for sub-Saharan Africa

During fiscal year 1985, the World Bank published a report on the problems of, and prospects for, sustained development in sub-Saharan Africa, and proposed a joint programme of action designed to address the long-term constraints on development in the region. The report called for the creation of a special assistance facility in support of reform programmes undertaken by African Governments.

A recent review by the Bank showed that there were 21 countries where structural reforms were ongoing or where there were reasonable prospects that such programmes could be put in place in the next two years. For those 21 countries, net disbursements of official assistance declined from $5.4 billion a year during 1980-1982 to $4.5 billion in 1983. In the absence of special action, they were expected to decline further to about $3.7 billion a year during 1985-1987. Programmes of structural adjustment and economic reform could not be effective given such a declining rate of external finance. The Special Facility, therefore, represented a crucial component of the joint programme of action.

In May 1985, the Bank's Executive Directors authorized IDA to act as administrator of, and to accept contributions to, the Facility. This action followed an agreement, reached on 1 February, between 14 countries and the Bank to mobilize additional resources of over $1.1 billion, to be committed over a three-year period, in Special Facility operations. As of 30 June 1985, resources expected for such operations totalled more than $1.2 billion.

Funds from the Special Facility were to be used to provide credits to IDA-eligible countries in sub-Saharan Africa that had undertaken, or were committed to undertake, appropriate medium-term programmes of policy reform. The credits, which were to be made on IDA terms, would help finance quick-disbursing lending operations in support of struc-

[a]YUN 1984, p. 1242.

tural and sectoral adjustment, rehabilitation and emergency reconstruction. All operations would be approved and administered by Bank staff, and would be subject to approval by IDA's Executive Directors.

Lending operations (credits)

By 30 June 1985, IDA had made cumulative net commitments totalling $36,682.1 million. Commitments in fiscal 1985 amounted to $3,028.1 million, of which $1,390.1 million went to seven countries in South Asia and $711.5 million to 15 countries in eastern and southern Africa. India was the largest borrower with six credits amounting to $672.9 million, followed by China with five credits ($442.3 million) and Bangladesh with four ($266 million).

IDA CREDITS APPROVED BY REGION/COUNTRY AND PURPOSE
1 JULY 1984–30 JUNE 1985
(including IDA share of joint Bank/IDA operations; in millions of US dollars)

REGION/COUNTRY	Agriculture and rural development	Development finance companies	Education	Energy	Industry	Non-project	Population, health and nutrition	Small-scale enterprises	Technical assistance	Telecommunications	Transportation	Urban development	Water supply and sewerage	Total
Eastern and southern Africa														
Burundi	—	—	—	12.3	—	—	—	—	—	—	18.1	—	—	30.4
Djibouti	—	—	5.0	—	—	—	—	—	—	—	—	5.0	—	10.0
Ethiopia	52.0	—	70.0	—	—	—	—	—	4.0	40.0	—	—	—	166.0
Kenya	—	—	—	—	—	—	—	—	—	—	—	—	6.0	6.0
Lesotho	—	—	10.0	—	—	—	3.5	—	—	—	—	—	—	13.5
Madagascar	12.0	40.0	—	—	—	—	—	—	—	—	—	—	15.0	67.0
Malawi	23.8	—	—	—	—	—	—	—	—	—	—	15.0	—	38.8
Mozambique	—	—	—	—	—	45.0	—	—	—	—	—	—	—	45.0
Rwanda	11.5	—	—	—	—	—	—	—	4.8	—	—	—	—	16.3
Somalia	20.6	—	—	—	—	—	—	—	—	—	—	—	—	20.6
Sudan	25.5	—	—	12.0	—	—	—	—	—	—	—	—	—	37.5
Uganda	10.0	—	—	33.9	—	—	—	—	—	—	—	—	28.0	71.9
United Republic of Tanzania	—	—	—	8.0	—	—	—	—	10.0	—	27.0	—	—	45.0
Zaire	27.4	—	—	—	—	—	—	—	9.0	—	55.0	—	—	91.4
Zambia	32.1	—	—	—	—	—	—	—	—	—	20.0	—	—	52.1
Subtotal	214.9	40.0	85.0	66.2	—	45.0	3.5	—	27.8	40.0	120.1	20.0	49.0	711.5
Western Africa														
Benin	—	—	—	—	—	—	—	—	5.0	—	—	—	—	5.0
Burkina Faso	13.7	—	21.6	—	—	—	26.6	—	—	—	—	—	—	61.9
Cape Verde	—	4.0	—	—	—	—	—	—	—	—	—	—	—	4.0
Central African Republic	—	—	—	—	—	—	—	—	8.0	—	—	—	—	8.0
Equatorial Guinea	9.3	—	—	—	—	—	—	—	—	—	—	—	—	9.3
Ghana	—	—	—	—	—	60.0	—	—	—	—	40.0	22.0	—	122.0
Guinea	—	—	—	8.0	—	—	—	—	9.5	—	—	—	—	17.5
Guinea-Bissau	—	—	—	—	—	10.0	—	—	6.0	—	—	—	—	16.0
Liberia	—	—	—	2.6	—	—	—	—	—	—	—	—	5.0	7.6
Mali	19.5	—	—	—	—	—	—	—	—	—	—	—	—	19.5
Mauritania	7.5	5.3	—	—	—	16.4	—	—	—	—	—	—	—	29.2
Niger	9.3	—	—	7.5	—	—	—	—	—	—	—	—	—	16.8
Sao Tome and Principe	—	—	—	—	—	5.0	—	—	—	—	—	—	—	5.0
Senegal	—	—	—	—	—	—	—	—	—	—	—	—	24.0	24.0
Togo	—	—	12.4	—	—	27.8	—	—	6.2	—	—	—	—	46.4
Subtotal	59.3	9.3	34.0	18.1	—	119.2	26.6	—	34.7	—	40.0	22.0	29.0	392.2
East Asia and the Pacific														
China	187.3	—	145.0	—	—	—	—	—	—	—	30.0	—	80.0	442.3
Samoa	—	2.0	—	—	—	—	—	—	—	—	—	—	—	2.0
Solomon Islands	—	—	—	—	—	—	—	—	—	—	2.0	—	—	2.0
Subtotal	187.3	2.0	145.0	—	—	—	—	—	—	—	32.0	—	80.0	446.3
South Asia														
Bangladesh	48.0	—	78.0	110.0	—	30.0	—	—	—	—	—	—	—	266.0
Bhutan	—	—	—	—	9.0	—	—	—	—	—	—	—	—	9.0
Burma	14.5	—	—	—	—	—	—	—	—	—	17.8	—	—	32.3
India	534.9	—	—	—	—	—	—	—	—	—	—	138.0	—	672.9
Nepal	7.2	—	8.4	—	—	—	—	7.5	—	22.0	47.5	—	—	92.6
Pakistan	192.8	—	52.5	—	—	—	—	—	—	—	—	—	—	245.3
Sri Lanka	72.0	—	—	—	—	—	—	—	—	—	—	—	—	72.0
Subtotal	869.4	—	138.9	110.0	9.0	30.0	—	7.5	—	22.0	65.3	138.0	—	1,390.1

REGION/COUNTRY Europe, the Middle East and North Africa	Agriculture and rural development	Development finance companies	Education	Energy	Industry	Non-project	Population, health and nutrition	Small-scale enterprises	Technical assistance	Telecommunications	Transportation	Urban development	Water supply and sewerage	Total
Democratic Yemen	5.0	—	—	—	—	—	—	—	—	—	14.4	—	—	19.4
Yemen	10.0	8.0	—	—	—	—	—	—	4.7	—	—	—	—	22.7
Subtotal	15.0	8.0	—	—	—	—	—	—	4.7	—	14.4	—	—	42.1
Latin America and the Caribbean														
Grenada	5.0	—	—	—	—	—	—	—	—	—	—	—	—	5.0
Guyana	8.8	—	—	—	—	—	—	—	—	—	—	—	—	8.8
Haiti	—	—	10.0	22.1	—	—	—	—	—	—	—	—	—	32.1
Subtotal	13.8	—	10.0	22.1	—	—	—	—	—	—	—	—	—	45.9
Total	1,359.7	59.3	412.9	216.4	9.0	194.2	30.1	7.5	67.2	62.0	271.8	180.0	158.0	3,028.1
NUMBER OF CREDITS	41	5	10	10	1	7	2	1	10	2	10	4	6	109

Agriculture and rural development

As in previous years, in fiscal 1985 credits for agriculture and rural development accounted for the largest amount of IDA lending—44.9 per cent. Forty-one credits worth $1,359.7 million were committed in 25 countries.

Of credits totalling $534.9 million made to India, $165 million assisted in the expansion and improvement of social forestry activities in several states. China received four credits amounting to $187.3 million, of which $75 million helped increase the production of crops and other agricultural products in west-central Anhui province by developing rural infrastructure and agricultural support services and improving the planning and management of irrigation and flood-control schemes.

Other credits went to agricultural research and development, agro-industry, irrigation and drainage, fisheries, forestry, livestock, training and technical assistance.

Development finance companies

IDA extended five credits totalling $59.3 million in fiscal 1985 to assist development finance companies. A credit of $40 million went to Madagascar to support policy reforms designed to enhance the efficiency and productivity of the industrial sector and to increase the capacity of selected industrial enterprises to produce basic consumption goods for the domestic market and for export.

Other credits helped finance investments in small and medium-scale industrial enterprises, training and technical assistance in Cape Verde, Mauritania, Samoa and Yemen.

Education

Ten countries received credits totalling $412.9 million for education projects during fiscal 1985.

China received $145 million to promote policy and institutional changes in the engineering and economic/finance education subsector in some 35 universities. A $78-million credit to Bangladesh supported a long-term investment programme in primary education.

Other credits were committed to improve access to, and the quality of, primary and secondary education, teacher-training programmes, curriculum development and educational materials.

Energy

Nine countries received credits totalling $216.4 million for energy-related projects in fiscal 1985.

A credit of $110 million supported the Bangladesh Oil and Gas Corporation in its efforts to expand gas supplies and strengthen its management capability. Uganda was granted two credits totalling $33.9 million to rehabilitate turbo-generator units, strengthen and upgrade transmission lines, provide financial-policy and institutional assistance to the Uganda Electricity Board and technical assistance to the new Energy Department and to support government efforts to attract oil companies to explore for hydrocarbons.

Industry

A credit of $9 million was extended to Bhutan for the construction of a calcium-carbide plant, which was expected to enhance the country's ability to generate foreign-exchange earnings for economic development.

Non-project

IDA committed $194.2 million for seven non-project credits during fiscal year 1985. Ghana received $60 million to finance imports for the primary-production sectors of agriculture, mining, manufacturing and transportation in support of the Government's economic recovery programme. A $45-million credit to Mozambique helped support priority economic-rehabilitation needs within the context of the Government's economic action programme for 1984-1986. Bangladesh received $30 million to assist in the rehabilitation of flood-damaged facilities.

Population, health and nutrition

Two countries received credits totalling $30.1 million for projects in population, health and nutrition. A credit of $26.6 million was granted to Burkina Faso to improve the quality and accessibility of health and family planning services for over 50 per cent of the population and to immunize about 60 per cent of children through the age of four against major childhood communicable diseases. Lesotho received $3.5 million for a project aimed at strengthening the organization and management of the Ministry of Health and manpower development and training, as well as improving health care coverage and family planning services.

Small-scale enterprises

Nepal was extended a credit of $7.5 million to finance private industrial enterprises through the Nepal Industrial Development Corporation, for the establishment of an import-export facility, and for studies on industrial and export incentives and tourism promotion.

Technical assistance

Credits totalling $67.2 million were awarded to 10 countries for technical assistance in fiscal year 1985. The United Republic of Tanzania received $10 million for its programme to revise policies and institutional arrangements in the agricultural sector by providing the capacity to analyse policy alternatives and to monitor and supervise parastatal performance. A $9.5-million credit was granted to Guinea to improve its economic management through a three-year, first-phase programme of technical assistance and staff training focused on macro-economic management, investment choice and procurement, and control of public finance and external debt. Zaire's Ministry of Primary and Secondary Education received $9 million to improve its planning, management and administrative capability in order to provide enhanced education services.

Other technical assistance credits were for macro-economic management, public investment programming, budget preparation and execution and public finance management and statistics.

Telecommunications

Two credits totalling $62 million were granted for telecommunications projects. Ethiopia received $40 million for a sixth project comprising the capital investment part of the Ethiopian Telecommunications Authority's development programme for 1984-1988, which was designed to increase the availability of services and to improve service quality. A credit of $22 million financed a fourth project in Nepal to strengthen the Nepal Telecommunications Corporation, expand local telephone facilities in Kathmandu and other urban areas and provide first-time telephone service to some 90 rural communities.

Transportation

IDA granted 10 credits totalling $271.8 million for transportation projects during fiscal 1985.

A credit of $55 million to Zaire financed a sixth highway project to consolidate the country-wide bridge, road and ferry rehabilitation and maintenance programmes and strengthen the administration and training capabilities of the agency in charge of the main road network. Nepal received $47.5 million to complete an all-weather, east-west highway. A credit of $40 million supported a three-year rehabilitation/maintenance programme for Ghana's trunk roads, a bridge rehabilitation programme, a three-year pilot feeder-road programme and the rehabilitation of 105 kilometres of the Accra–Kumasi highway. China received $30 million towards a first highway project to improve the quality of future construction works, increase the cost-effectiveness of highway investments, support a highway research programme and provide for training. The United Republic of Tanzania received $27 million to assist in the rehabilitation and modernization of the port of Dar es Salaam, and to provide technical assistance and training for the Tanzania Harbours Authority.

Urban development

In fiscal 1985, four credits totalling $180 million were granted for urban development. India received $138 million for land infrastructure servicing and slum upgrading to benefit half a million people in the Bombay metropolitan region. A $22-million credit to Ghana strengthened the institutions responsible for infrastructure maintenance and urban services in Accra and removed transport bottle-necks there. A credit of $15 million to Malawi helped to reorient future housing development towards a market-based system. Djibouti received $5 million to help upgrade low-income areas.

Water supply and sewerage

Six countries received credits totalling $158 million for water supply and sewerage in fiscal 1985. Of that amount, $80 million went to China to provide water-supply facilities and develop and strengthen systems, institutions and technology; safe drinking-water would be provided to some 6 million people in five provinces and Beijing. A $28-million credit went to Uganda to help finance the rehabilitation of the water-supply and sanitation facilities in seven major towns. Madagascar received $15 million to restore essential facilities damaged by a cyclone in April 1984, support institutional arrangements for the co-ordination of reconstruction efforts and develop measures to minimize the potential damage from natural disasters.

Secretariat

The principal officers, staff, headquarters and other offices of IDA are the same as those of the World Bank (see Chapter VI of this section).

STATEMENT OF INCOME AND EXPENSES
(for the fiscal year ended 30 June 1985)

	Amount *(in thousands of US dollars)*
Income	
Income from development credits:	
Service charges	157,944
Commitment charges	28,750
Income from investments	22,595
Total income	209,289
Expenses	
Management fee to World Bank	273,180
Operating loss (income less expenses)	(63,891)
Translation adjustments for fiscal year	(692)
Net loss	(64,583)

Annex I.   MEMBERS OF THE INTERNATIONAL DEVELOPMENT ASSOCIATION, SUBSCRIPTIONS, VOTING POWER AND SUPPLEMENTARY RESOURCES
(As at 30 June 1985)

MEMBER	TOTAL SUBSCRIPTIONS AND SUPPLEMENTARY RESOURCES — Amount *(in thousands of US dollars)*	Percent-age of total	VOTING POWER — Number of votes	Percent-age of total
Part I members				
Australia	675,530	1.87	72,274	1.43
Austria	248,293	0.69	32,697	0.65
Belgium	378,401	1.05	58,076	1.15
Canada	1,817,440	5.03	170,303	3.37
Denmark	364,939	1.01	48,303	0.96
Finland	196,551	0.54	28,073	0.56
France	1,802,750	4.99	188,726	3.74
Germany, Federal Republic of	4,275,051	11.84	355,673	7.04
Iceland	4,107	0.01	11,895	0.24
Ireland	31,425	0.09	13,702	0.27
Italy	755,797	2.09	123,671	2.45
Japan	5,589,552	15.48	403,763	7.99
Kuwait	562,799	1.56	57,762	1.14
Luxembourg	16,577	0.05	12,646	0.25
Netherlands	803,608	2.22	96,098	1.90
New Zealand	27,290	0.08	13,410	0.27
Norway	359,446	1.00	45,465	0.90
South Africa	51,060	0.14	16,408	0.32
Sweden	994,622	2.75	117,110	2.32
United Arab Emirates	136,464	0.38	15,942	0.32
United Kingdom	3,421,152	9.47	337,949	6.69
United States	11,893,836	32.93	961,854	19.04
Subtotal	34,406,690	95.27	3,181,800	63.00
Part II members				
Afghanistan	1,144	0.01	13,557	0.27
Algeria	4,424	0.01	18,481	0.37
Argentina	45,416	0.13	81,053	1.60
Bangladesh	5,903	0.02	31,373	0.62
Belize	204	*	1,764	0.03
Benin	514	*	1,861	0.04
Bhutan	51	*	510	0.01

MEMBER	TOTAL SUBSCRIPTIONS AND SUPPLEMENTARY RESOURCES — Amount *(in thousands of US dollars)*	Percent-age of total	VOTING POWER — Number of votes	Percent-age of total
Part II members (cont.)				
Bolivia	1,121	0.01	13,748	0.27
Botswana	175	*	11,706	0.23
Brazil	62,242	0.17	87,977	1.74
Burkina Faso	542	*	9,720	0.19
Burma	2,258	0.01	18,729	0.37
Burundi	842	*	12,667	0.25
Cameroon	1,085	*	7,771	0.15
Cape Verde	82	*	516	0.01
Central African Republic	542	*	9,720	0.19
Chad	533	*	3,354	0.07
Chile	3,758	0.01	18,741	0.37
China	33,014	0.09	96,173	1.90
Colombia	8,189	0.02	23,784	0.47
Comoros	86	*	5,774	0.11
Congo	537	*	6,685	0.13
Costa Rica	217	*	7,844	0.16
Cyprus	843	*	13,959	0.28
Democratic Kampuchea	1,085	*	7,826	0.15
Democratic Yemen	1,311	0.01	10,591	0.21
Djibouti	165	*	532	0.01
Dominica	84	*	3,186	0.06
Dominican Republic	504	*	12,628	0.25
Ecuador	878	*	13,552	0.27
Egypt	5,633	0.02	28,424	0.56
El Salvador	348	*	6,244	0.12
Equatorial Guinea	338	*	1,967	0.04
Ethiopia	591	*	12,988	0.26
Fiji	592	*	2,130	0.04
Gabon	533	*	2,093	0.04
Gambia	292	*	10,644	0.21
Ghana	2,501	0.01	15,362	0.30
Greece	8,029	0.02	21,242	0.42
Grenada	101	*	10,186	0.20
Guatemala	453	*	11,367	0.22

MEMBER	TOTAL SUBSCRIPTIONS AND SUPPLEMENTARY RESOURCES		VOTING POWER		MEMBER	TOTAL SUBSCRIPTIONS AND SUPPLEMENTARY RESOURCES		VOTING POWER	
	Amount (in thousands of US dollars)	Percent- age of total	Number of votes	Percent- age of total		Amount (in thousands of US dollars)	Percent- age of total	Number of votes	Percent- age of total
Part II members (cont.)					*Part II members* (cont.)				
Guinea	1,132	0.01	13,557	0.27	Paraguay	330	*	8,124	0.16
Guinea-Bissau	143	*	528	0.01	Peru	1,804	0.01	854	0.02
Guyana	890	*	12,859	0.25	Philippines	5,504	0.02	16,583	0.33
Haiti	867	*	13,959	0.28	Republic of Korea	12,429	0.03	16,650	0.33
Honduras	344	*	12,218	0.24	Rwanda	853	*	12,667	0.25
Hungary	8,958	0.02	21,070	0.42	Saint Lucia	169	*	10,445	0.21
India	50,727	0.14	163,194	3.23	Saint Vincent and the				
Indonesia	12,182	0.03	52,936	1.05	Grenadines	71	*	514	0.01
Iran	5,814	0.02	15,455	0.31	Samoa	96	*	7,537	0.15
Iraq	843	*	9,407	0.19	Sao Tome and Principe	71	*	514	0.01
Israel	2,388	0.01	9,386	0.19	Saudi Arabia	1,218,770	3.37	132,754	2.63
Ivory Coast	1,085	*	7,771	0.15	Senegal	1,849	0.01	17,424	0.34
Jordan	393	*	12,218	0.24	Sierra Leone	819	*	12,667	0.25
Kenya	1,847	0.01	16,021	0.32	Solomon Islands	93	*	518	0.01
Lao People's					Somalia	811	*	10,506	0.21
Democratic Republic	535	*	11,723	0.23	Spain	64,105	0.18	57,788	1.14
Lebanon	479	*	8,562	0.17	Sri Lanka	3,307	0.01	22,506	0.45
Lesotho	174	*	10,487	0.21	Sudan	1,106	*	14,005	0.28
Liberia	867	*	13,959	0.28	Swaziland	348	*	11,073	0.22
Libyan Arab Jamahiriya	1,105	*	7,771	0.15	Syrian Arab Republic	1,038	*	7,651	0.15
Madagascar	1,029	*	702	0.01	Thailand	3,393	0.01	22,506	0.45
Malawi	831	*	12,667	0.25	Togo	830	*	12,667	0.25
Malaysia	2,859	0.01	20,584	0.41	Trinidad and Tobago	1,376	0.01	770	0.02
Maldives	33	*	11,212	0.22	Tunisia	1,598	0.01	2,793	0.06
Mali	950	*	12,307	0.24	Turkey	6,207	0.02	23,450	0.46
Mauritania	542	*	6,685	0.13	Uganda	1,779	0.01	16,021	0.32
Mauritius	976	*	14,360	0.28	United Republic of				
Mexico	27,638	0.08	24,428	0.48	Tanzania	1,831	0.01	16,021	0.32
Morocco	3,863	0.01	24,417	0.48	Vanuatu	194	*	1,761	0.03
Mozambique	1,367	0.01	774	0.02	Viet Nam	1,603	0.01	8,889	0.18
Nepal	556	*	12,984	0.26	Yemen	477	*	11,468	0.23
Nicaragua	409	*	10,896	0.22	Yugoslavia	19,176	0.05	29,446	0.58
Niger	550	*	12,839	0.25	Zaire	3,196	0.01	12,164	0.24
Nigeria	3,645	0.01	4,057	0.08	Zambia	2,905	0.01	19,730	0.39
Oman	366	*	12,221	0.24	Zimbabwe	4,242	0.02	1,324	0.03
Pakistan	11,315	0.03	49,173	0.97	Subtotal	1,708,221	4.73	1,870,313	37.00
Panama	25	*	5,657	0.11					
Papua New Guinea	954	*	13,050	0.26	Total	36,114,911	100.00†	5,052,113	100.00†

NOTE: Tonga became a member on 23 October 1985.

*Less than 0.005 per cent.

†May differ from the sum of the individual percentages because of rounding.

Annex II.   EXECUTIVE DIRECTORS AND ALTERNATES OF THE INTERNATIONAL DEVELOPMENT ASSOCIATION (As at 30 June 1985)

Appointed Director	*Appointed Alternate*	*Casting the vote of*
James B. Burnham	Hugh W. Foster	United States
Kenji Yamaguchi	Toshihiro Yamakawa	Japan
Reinhard Münzberg	Michael von Harpe	Federal Republic of Germany
Nigel L. Wicks	Richard Manning	United Kingdom
Bruno de Maulde	Francis Mayer	France

Elected Director	*Elected Alternate*	*Casting the votes of*
Fawzi Hamad Al-Sultan (Kuwait)	Mohammad Al-Shawi (Saudi Arabia)	Egypt, Iraq, Jordan, Kuwait, Lebanon, Maldives, Oman, Pakistan, Saudi Arabia, Syrian Arab Republic, United Arab Emirates, Yemen
Pekka Korpinen (Finland)	Per Taxell (Sweden)	Denmark, Finland, Iceland, Norway, Sweden
Frank Potter (Canada)	George L. Reid (Barbados)	Belize, Canada, Dominica, Grenada, Guyana, Ireland, Saint Lucia, Saint Vincent and the Grenadines
C. R. Krishnaswamy Rao Sahib (India)	Gholam Kibria (Bangladesh)	Bangladesh, Bhutan, India, Sri Lanka
Astère Girukwigomba (Burundi)	Mitiku Jembere (Ethiopia)	Botswana, Burundi, Ethiopia, Gambia, Guinea, Kenya, Lesotho, Liberia, Malawi, Mozambique, Nigeria, Sierra Leone, Sudan, Swaziland, Trinidad and Tobago, Uganda, United Republic of Tanzania, Zambia, Zimbabwe

Elected Director	Elected Alternate	Casting the votes of
Nicéphore Soglo (Benin)	André Milongo (Congo)	Benin, Burkina Faso, Cameroon, Cape Verde, Central African Republic, Chad, Comoros, Congo, Djibouti, Equatorial Guinea, Gabon, Guinea-Bissau, Ivory Coast, Madagascar, Mali, Mauritania, Mauritius, Niger, Rwanda, Sao Tome and Principe, Senegal, Somalia, Togo, Zaire
Edgar Gutiérrez-Castro (Colombia)	Guillermo A. Rivera (Dominican Republic)	Brazil, Colombia, Dominican Republic, Ecuador, Haiti, Philippines
Phaichitr Uathavikul (Thailand)	Shashi N. Shah (Nepal)	Burma, Fiji, Indonesia, Lao People's Democratic Republic, Malaysia, Nepal, Thailand, Viet Nam
Ferdinand van Dam (Netherlands)	Riza Sapunxhiu (Yugoslavia)	Cyprus, Israel, Netherlands, Yugoslavia
Jacques de Groote (Belgium)	Oral Akman (Turkey)	Austria, Belgium, Hungary, Luxembourg, Turkey
Mario Draghi (Italy)	Rodrigo M. Guimarães (Portugal)	Greece, Italy
Leonor Filardo de González (Venezuela)	María Antonieta Domínguez (Honduras)	Costa Rica, El Salvador, Guatemala, Honduras, Mexico, Nicaragua, Panama, Spain
Ronald H. Dean (Australia)	You Kwang Park (Republic of Korea)	Australia, New Zealand, Papua New Guinea, Republic of Korea, Samoa, Solomon Islands, Vanuatu
Carlos Corti* (Uruguay)	Félix Alberto Camarasa (Argentina)	Argentina, Bolivia, Chile, Paraguay, Peru
Mourad Benachenhou (Algeria)	Salem Mohamed Omeish (Libyan Arab Jamahiriya)	Afghanistan, Algeria, Democratic Yemen, Ghana, Iran, Libyan Arab Jamahiriya, Morocco, Tunisia
Xu Naijiong (China)	Yang Guanghui (China)	China

NOTE: Democratic Kampuchea and South Africa did not participate in the 1984 regular election of Executive Directors.
*Resigned 30 June 1985; succeeded by Kenneth Coates (Uruguay).

Annex III. HEADQUARTERS AND OTHER OFFICES

HEADQUARTERS
International Development Association
1818 H Street, N.W.
Washington, D.C. 20433, United States
Cable address: INDEVAS WASHINGTONDC
Telephone: (202) 477-1234
Telex: RCA 248423 INDEVAS
        WUI 64145 INDEVAS

NEW YORK OFFICE
International Development Association
747 Third Avenue, 26th floor
New York, N.Y. 10017, United States
Cable address: INDEVAS NEWYORK
Telephone: (212) 963-6008

EUROPEAN OFFICE
International Development Association
66 avenue d'Iéna
75116 Paris, France
Cable address: INDEVAS PARIS
Telephone: (1) 4723-54-21
Telex: 842-620628

LONDON OFFICE
International Development Association
New Zealand House, 15th floor, Haymarket
London SW1 Y4TE, England
Cable address: INDEVAS LONDON
Telephone: (01) 930-8511
Telex: 919462

GENEVA OFFICE
International Development Association
ITC Building
54 rue de Montbrillant
(P.O. Box 104)
1211 Geneva 20 CIC, Switzerland
Telephone: (22) 33 21 20
Telex: 28883

TOKYO OFFICE
International Development Association
Kokusai Building, Room 916
1-1 Marunouchi 3-chome, Chiyoda-ku
Tokyo 100, Japan
Cable address: INDEVAS TOKYO
Telephone: (03) 214-5001
Telex: 781-26838

REGIONAL MISSION IN EASTERN
  AND SOUTHERN AFRICA
International Development Association
Reinsurance Plaza, 5th and 6th floors
Taifa Road
(P.O. Box 30577)
Nairobi, Kenya
Cable address: INDEVAS NAIROBI
Telephone: (254-2) 338868, 24391
Telex: 22022

REGIONAL MISSION IN WESTERN AFRICA
International Development Association
Immeuble Shell, 64 avenue Lamblin
(Boîte postale 1850)
Abidjan 01, Ivory Coast
Cable address: INDEVAS ABIDJAN
Telephone: (225) 44 22 27, 32 90 06, 44 20 38
Telex: 28132

REGIONAL MISSION IN THAILAND
International Development Association
Udom Vidhya Building, 956 Rama IV Road
Sala Daeng
Bangkok 5, Thailand
Cable address: INDEVAS BANGKOK
Telephone: (66-2) 235-5300-8
Telex: 82817

Chapter IX

International Monetary Fund (IMF)

The world economy during 1985 presented a mixed picture. Inflation receded further, world output increased at a moderate pace and interest rates declined significantly. At the same time, the slow-down in industrial countries—particularly in the United States—was sharper than expected, world trade was sluggish, protectionist pressures intensified, real primary commodity prices declined steeply, and the developing world experienced a set-back in its efforts to achieve growth with adjustment.

The 3 per cent rate of growth recorded for world output in 1985 represented a considerable slow-down from the 4.5 per cent rate of the previous year. The slow-down in the growth of industrial countries' output led to a marked deceleration in the growth of world trade and, in combination with plentiful supplies, a sharp fall in real primary product prices. As a result, the export earnings of developing countries stagnated and their debt ratios, which had begun to recede in 1984, rose again in 1985 to reach record levels.

In the second half of the year, steps were taken to address these imbalances to reduce the risks and uncertainties in global economic prospects. An agreement reached in New York on 22 September among the Group of Five (France, Federal Republic of Germany, Japan, United Kingdom, United States) set forth their policy intentions to achieve increased and more balanced growth as well as exchange rate relationships that better reflected underlying economic fundamentals. Studies of the functioning of the international monetary system, conducted by the Group of 10 (industrial countries) and the Group of 24 (developing countries), recognized that the role of the International Monetary Fund (IMF) in the system would be conditioned by members' views of how the system was expected to evolve. Both groups agreed that surveillance of exchange rate policies was central to the role of IMF and that it should be strengthened. However, the reports differed on other issues: while the Group of 10 urged that IMF should keep its lending in line with its quota resources, ensure effective conditionality and step up its co-operation with the World Bank, the Group of 24 called for an increase in special drawing right (SDR) allocations, a liberalization of the conditions attached to IMF-supported economic programmes, and greater voting power in IMF for developing countries. The reports were

discussed at the twenty-fifth meeting of the Interim Committee of the Boards of Governors of the International Monetary Fund (Seoul, Republic of Korea, 6 and 7 October).

The debt situation and strategy

An important aspect of the Fund's activities was the handling of international debt problems. The aggregate current account deficit of the capital importing developing countries was reduced from about $100 billion in 1981 to some $25 billion in 1984/85. On the whole, external debt was serviced and principal restructured in an orderly fashion, while total external payments arrears were reduced in 1985 for the first time in recent years. Notwithstanding the progress that had been achieved by 1985, developing countries remained vulnerable to a number of developments in the world economy—a slow-down in world trade, low oil and commodity prices, declining commercial bank financing and greater protectionism in industrial countries. In some heavily indebted countries, income per capita remained below pre-1982 levels.

In response to these difficulties, the United States Secretary of the Treasury, James A. Baker III, at the annual meetings of the World Bank and IMF (Seoul, Republic of Korea, October 1985), proposed an initiative to reinforce the debt strategy in ways that would permit debtor countries to achieve both growth and balance-of-payments viability. The initiative—known as the Baker Plan—was endorsed by the IMF Managing Director and the World Bank President in a joint statement issued in December 1985.

IMF-World Bank collaboration

In 1985, IMF and the World Bank continued to strengthen their collaboration. Bank staff participated in IMF missions to 17 countries, while IMF staff participated in Bank missions on 18 occasions. There were 44 instances of parallel or overlapping IMF and Bank missions.

For many countries where structural reforms were important, their economic programmes were supported by both IMF arrangements and World Bank loans. IMF-Bank collaboration to mobilize commercial bank financing became particularly close and was an element in five of nine commercial bank loan packages concluded or agreed to in 1985.

Access to IMF resources

An important aspect of membership in IMF is the access of members to its resources. Under the Fund's policy of enlarged access, in operation since 1981 and subject to annual review since 1983, a member with a stand-by or extended arrangement with IMF was permitted to obtain, subject to certain conditions, a larger amount of resources from the Fund relative to its quota, and for longer periods, than could be obtained from IMF ordinary resources. The bulk of the resources for the enlarged access policy were made available under medium-term borrowing arrangements with members that had strong balance-of-payments positions, principally Saudi Arabia.

In that context, the Fund's short-term borrowing arrangements for SDR 3 billion with the Bank for International Settlements (BIS), Japan and the National Bank of Belgium were extended effective 26 April 1985. The extensions were to hold until 31 December 1985 in the cases of BIS and Japan and until 28 February 1986 in the case of the National Bank of Belgium.

On 9 December 1985, the IMF Executive Board resolved that the enlarged access policy should be continued in 1986, with modest reductions in access limits. Access would be subject to annual limits of 90 or 110 per cent of quota (previously 95 or 115 per cent), three-year limits of 270 or 330 per cent of quota (previously 280 or 345 per cent), and cumulative limits of 400 or 440 per cent of quota (previously 408 or 450 per cent), depending on the seriousness of a member's balance-of-payments needs and the strength of its adjustment efforts.

Other IMF facilities

In October 1985, the Interim Committee of the IMF Board of Governors agreed to permit the SDR 2.7 billion in expected receipts from loan repayments during 1985-1991 to a Trust Fund established in 1976[a] to be used to provide concessional balance-of-payments assistance to low-income developing countries. The Fund was terminated in 1981 and its responsibilities confined to the receipt and disposition of interest and loan repayments through a special disbursement account.

On 3 May 1985, the IMF Executive Board reviewed its 1981 decision[b] allowing the compensatory financing facility to be used to compensate for temporary increases in cereal import costs. The decision was extended for another four years, with a provision that it be reviewed by the Executive Board not later than 13 May 1987.

Financial assistance

The level of financial assistance by the Fund declined to SDR 4 billion in 1985 from SDR 7.3 billion in 1984. The decline followed three years of high levels of assistance in response to the needs of some heavily indebted member countries. To some extent, it also reflected the progress made by several countries to strengthen their external positions. All purchases in 1985 were made by developing countries. Reserve tranche drawings—which were not included in purchases and were not subject to conditionality or repurchase requirements—fell in 1985 to SDR 200 million from SDR 800 million in 1984.

As of 31 December 1985, there were 29 stand-by arrangements (typically made over a one-year period) and three extended arrangements (usually made over three years), with an aggregate approved value of SDR 9.9 billion and an undrawn balance of SDR 4.7 billion. Purchases made in support of economic adjustment programmes under stand-by and extended arrangements accounted for 78 per cent of total drawings in 1985, compared with 88 per cent in 1984.

SDR activity

Total transfers of SDRs increased to SDR 15.9 billion in 1985 from SDR 15.7 billion in 1984. As a result of transferring SDR 6.4 billion to its members and receiving SDR 4.5 billion from them, IMF saw its SDR holdings decline by SDR 1.9 billion. SDR transfers among members and official institutions authorized to hold SDRs declined to SDR 5 billion in 1985 from SDR 5.8 billion in 1984. This reflected a decline in the volume of transactions "by agreement"—voluntary transfers of SDRs in exchange for currencies—to SDR 2.6 billion from SDR 3 billion the previous year, and of transactions "with designation" to SDR 1.9 billion from SDR 2.3 billion in 1984. Under transactions with designation, participants with sufficiently strong international financial positions were designated by IMF to exchange their usable currencies for SDRs of participants in need of balance-of-payments assistance.

Although the volume of total SDR acquisitions by members against payment of foreign exchange increased to a record level of SDR 4.2 billion in 1985, transactions by agreement registered a lower volume due to the increase in the amount of SDRs that members acquired from IMF to pay charges (SDR 1.6 billion in 1985, compared with SDR 450 million in 1984). For the third consecutive year, transactions by agreement exceeded transactions with designation.

Policy on arrears

Owing to difficulties that many member countries faced in meeting their payment obligations, IMF experienced some prolonged delays in repayments during 1984 and 1985. Accordingly, the Executive Board in March 1985 decided to exclude

[a]YUN 1976, p. 999.
[b]YUN 1981, p. 1447.

from the Fund's current income the charges receivable from members that were overdue by six months or more. As a result, IMF incurred a net deficit of SDR 30 billion in the financial year ended 30 April 1985, after a net surplus of SDR 73 billion in 1983/84.

In addition to the change in its accounting procedures, IMF adopted several related decisions during the year, as part of an overall policy with respect to members in protracted arrears. In February, it was decided that a member's right to purchase under stand-by and extended arrangements would be suspended when it had overdue financial obligations to the Fund.

Publications

Publications issued by IMF in 1985 included the *Annual Report of the Executive Board*, the *Annual Report on Exchange Arrangements and Exchange Restrictions, Balance of Payments Statistics* (monthly and *Yearbook*), *Direction of Trade Statistics* (monthly and *Yearbook*), *Government Finance Statistics Yearbook, International Financial Statistics* (monthly, *Yearbook* and two supplements) and the *World Economic Outlook*.

Periodicals included the quarterlies *Staff Papers* and *Finance and Development* (published jointly with the World Bank), the *IMF Survey* (published 23 times a year) and the monthly *IMF Memorandum*. Also published were explanatory pamphlets on the workings of IMF and papers on subjects of interest to the international financial community.

Membership

During 1985, membership of IMF rose to 149 with the admission of Tonga on 13 September.

Secretariat

As at 31 December 1985, the total full-time staff of IMF—including permanent, fixed-term and temporary employees—was 1,780, drawn from 102 nationalities.

PURCHASES AND REPURCHASES IN 1985
(in millions of SDRs)

	Purchases	Repurchases
World	4,198.6	3,641.2
Developing countries	4,198.6	3,641.2
Africa	1,025.0	766.5
Central African Republic	11.0	9.5
Chad	7.0	3.5
Equatorial Guinea	5.4	6.9
Ethiopia	—	31.0
Gambia	—	2.8
Ghana	120.0	—
Guinea-Bissau	—	0.9
Ivory Coast	60.4	97.6
Kenya	123.1	69.7
Liberia	—	6.9
Madagascar	29.0	33.0

	Purchases	Repurchases
Africa (cont.)		
Malawi	23.0	16.0
Mali	13.0	4.5
Mauritania	9.6	12.4
Mauritius	35.5	47.8
Morocco	215.1	143.2
Mozambique	13.2	—
Niger	15.5	—
Senegal	55.6	40.9
Sierra Leone	—	4.4
Somalia	34.6	8.8
South Africa	70.0	—
Sudan	—	4.9
Swaziland	—	1.0
Togo	15.0	8.4
Uganda	—	64.2
United Republic of Tanzania	—	4.8
Zaire	169.0	103.8
Zambia	—	18.7
Zimbabwe	—	20.9
Asia	992.0*	1,623.6*
Bangladesh	91.0	68.7
Burma	6.9	13.5
Fiji	4.8	5.1
India	—	174.8
Indonesia	—	264.9
Lao People's Democratic Republic	—	6.4
Malaysia	—	155.7
Nepal	10.3	3.9
Pakistan	88.6	149.2
Papua New Guinea	—	6.6
Philippines	318.0	162.0
Republic of Korea	135.9	361.8
Samoa	1.7	1.4
Solomon Islands	—	0.4
Sri Lanka	—	35.9
Thailand	335.0	213.5
Europe	255.0	834.0
Cyprus	—	3.2
Hungary	—	88.3
Romania	—	172.9
Turkey	—	247.5
Yugoslavia	255.0	322.1
Middle East	63.4	13.7
Democratic Yemen	—	1.9
Egypt	—	11.8
Jordan	57.4	—
Yemen	6.0	—
Western hemisphere	1,863.2	403.4*
Argentina	984.5	—
Belize	4.8	—
Bolivia	—	18.2
Brazil	—	64.5
Chile	195.6	21.4
Costa Rica	34.0	—
Dominica	—	1.5
Dominican Republic	76.9	32.2
Ecuador	84.4	—
El Salvador	—	26.6
Grenada	—	2.1
Guatemala	—	47.8
Guyana	—	1.0
Haiti	—	11.8
Honduras	—	16.7
Jamaica	51.0	61.3
Mexico	295.8	—
Nicaragua	—	9.0
Panama	35.0	28.3
Peru	—	49.3
Saint Lucia	—	1.7
Saint Vincent and the Grenadines	—	0.7
Uruguay	101.2	9.5

*Differs from the sum of individual figures because of rounding.

SOURCE: *International Financial Statistics Yearbook, 1986.*

CURRENCIES DRAWN AND REPURCHASES BY
CURRENCY OF REPURCHASE IN 1985
(in millions of SDRs)

	Currencies drawn	Repurchases by currency of repurchase
World	4,198.6	3,641.2*
Industrial countries	1,776.7	2,156.3*
Australian dollars	—	16.5
Austrian schillings	—	36.3
Belgian francs	—	40.8
Canadian dollars	—	57.2
Danish kroner	—	18.6
Deutsche mark	80.2	158.6
Finnish markkaa	—	10.2
French francs	70.0	106.3
Irish pounds	4.0	10.7
Italian lire	15.0	90.4
Japanese yen	290.0	77.5
Netherlands guilders	—	68.9
Norwegian kroner	11.0	35.3
Pounds sterling	4.8	148.9
Spanish pesetas	11.0	3
Swedish kronor	6.9	31.1
United States dollars	1,283.8	1,210.4
Developing countries	267.6	315.1
Africa	0.9	13.3*
Algerian dinars	—	10.4
Botswana pula	0.9	0.3
Burundi francs	—	0.3
Rwanda francs	—	0.3
Tunisian dinars	—	1.9
Asia	88.4	25.8*
Chinese yuan	15.0	20.3
Indonesian rupiahs	60.4	—
Singapore dollars	13.0	5.6
Europe	2.0	9.7*
Greek drachmae	—	6.4
Maltese liri	2.0	3.2
Middle East	156.1	231.5
Kuwaiti dinars	1.0	16.0
Qatar riyals	0.8	3.4
Rials Omani	1.0	3.1
Saudi Arabian riyals	148.9	196.2
United Arab Emirates dirhams	4.4	12.7

	Currencies drawn	Repurchases by currency of repurchase
Western hemisphere	20.2	34.8
Paraguayan guaraníes	—	0.7
Trinidad and Tobago dollars	0.4	12.2
Venezuelan bolívares	19.8	21.9
SDRs	2,154.3	1,169.9

*Differs from the sum of individual figures because of rounding.

SOURCE: *International Financial Statistics Yearbook, 1986.*

STAND-BY AND EXTENDED ARRANGEMENTS
(as at 31 December 1985; in thousands of SDRs)

Member	Amount agreed	Undrawn balance
Stand-by arrangements	4,789,125	2,514,794
Argentina	1,419,000	709,500
Bangladesh	180,000	144,000
Belize	7,125	1,185
Central African Republic	15,000	14,000
Costa Rica	54,000	20,000
Dominican Republic	78,500	17,075
Ecuador	105,500	21,100
Equatorial Guinea	9,200	3,800
Ivory Coast	66,200	26,480
Jamaica	115,000	100,000
Kenya	85,200	—
Madagascar	29,500	6,500
Mali	22,860	16,360
Mauritania	12,000	2,400
Mauritius	49,000	21,000
Morocco	200,000	190,000
Nepal	18,650	8,400
Niger	13,480	10,784
Panama	90,000	55,000
Philippines	615,000	212,000
Republic of Korea	280,000	240,000
Senegal	76,600	21,000
Somalia	22,100	20,100
Thailand	400,000	250,000
Togo	15,360	3,360
Uruguay	122,850	87,750
Yugoslavia	300,000	135,000
Zaire	162,000	33,000
Zambia	225,000	145,000
Extended arrangements	5,070,375	2,145,250
Brazil	4,239,375	1,496,250
Chile	750,000	625,000
Malawi	81,000	24,000

Annex I.   MEMBERSHIP OF THE INTERNATIONAL MONETARY FUND, QUOTAS AND VOTING POWER
(As at 3 January 1986)

	QUOTA		VOTING POWER			QUOTA		VOTING POWER	
MEMBER	Amount (in millions of SDRs)	General and SDR Departments percentage of total*	Number of votes†	General and SDR Departments percentage of total	MEMBER	Amount (in millions of SDRs)	General and SDR Departments percentage of total*	Number of votes†	General and SDR Departments percentage of total
Afghanistan	86.70	0.10	1,117	0.12	Benin	31.30	0.04	563	0.06
Algeria	623.10	0.70	6,481	0.70	Bhutan	2.50	0.002	275	0.03
Antigua and Barbuda	5.00	0.01	300	0.03	Bolivia	90.70	0.10	1,157	0.12
Argentina	1,113.00	1.25	11,380	1.22	Botswana	22.10	0.02	471	0.05
Australia	1,619.20	1.81	16,442	1.77	Brazil	1,461.30	1.64	14,863	1.60
Austria	775.60	0.87	8,006	0.86	Burkina Faso	31.60	0.04	566	0.06
Bahamas	66.40	0.07	914	0.10	Burma	137.00	0.15	1,620	0.17
Bahrain	48.90	0.05	739	0.08	Burundi	42.70	0.05	677	0.07
Bangladesh	287.50	0.32	3,125	0.34	Cameroon	92.70	0.10	1,177	0.13
Barbados	34.10	0.04	591	0.06	Canada	2,941.00	3.29	29,660	3.19
Belgium	2,080.40	2.33	21,054	2.26	Cape Verde	4.50	0.01	295	0.03
Belize	9.50	0.01	345	0.04	Central African Republic	30.40	0.03	554	0.06

MEMBER	QUOTA Amount (in millions of SDRs)	QUOTA General and SDR Departments percentage of total*	VOTING POWER Number of votes†	VOTING POWER General and SDR Departments percentage of total	MEMBER	QUOTA Amount (in millions of SDRs)	QUOTA General and SDR Departments percentage of total*	VOTING POWER Number of votes†	VOTING POWER General and SDR Departments percentage of total
Chad	30.60	0.03	556	0.06	Morocco	306.60	0.34	3,316	0.36
Chile	440.50	0.49	4,655	0.50	Mozambique	61.00	0.07	860	0.09
China	2,390.90	2.68	24,159	2.60	Nepal	37.30	0.04	623	0.07
Colombia	394.20	0.44	4,192	0.45	Netherlands	2,264.80	2.54	22,898	2.46
Comoros	4.50	0.01	295	0.03	New Zealand	461.60	0.52	4,866	0.52
Congo	37.30	0.04	623	0.07	Nicaragua	68.20	0.08	932	0.10
Costa Rica	84.10	0.09	1,091	0.12	Niger	33.70	0.04	587	0.06
Cyprus	69.70	0.08	947	0.10	Nigeria	849.50	0.95	8,745	0.94
Democratic Kampuchea	25.00	0.03	500	0.05	Norway	699.00	0.78	7,240	0.78
Democratic Yemen	77.20	0.09	1,022	0.11	Oman	63.10	0.07	881	0.09
Denmark	711.00	0.80	7,360	0.79	Pakistan	546.30	0.61	5,713	0.61
Djibouti	8.00	0.01	330	0.04	Panama	102.20	0.11	1,272	0.14
Dominica	4.00	0.004	290	0.03	Papua New Guinea	65.90	0.07	909	0.10
Dominican Republic	112.10	0.13	1,371	0.15	Paraguay	48.40	0.05	734	0.08
Ecuador	150.70	0.17	1,757	0.19	Peru	330.90	0.37	3,559	0.38
Egypt	463.40	0.52	4,884	0.52	Philippines	440.40	0.49	4,654	0.50
El Salvador	89.00	0.10	1,140	0.12	Portugal	376.60	0.42	4,016	0.43
Equatorial Guinea	18.40	0.02	434	0.05	Qatar	114.90	0.13	1,399	0.15
Ethiopia	70.60	0.08	956	0.10	Republic of Korea	462.80	0.52	4,878	0.52
Fiji	36.50	0.04	615	0.07	Romania	523.40	0.59	5,484	0.59
Finland	574.90	0.64	5,999	0.64	Rwanda	43.80	0.05	688	0.07
France	4,482.80	5.02	45,078	4.85	Saint Christopher and Nevis	4.50	0.01	295	0.03
Gabon	73.10	0.08	981	0.11	Saint Lucia	7.50	0.01	325	0.03
Gambia	17.10	0.02	421	0.05	Saint Vincent and the Grenadines	4.00	0.004	290	0.03
Germany, Federal Republic of	5,403.70	6.05	54,287	5.84	Samoa	6.00	0.01	310	0.03
Ghana	204.50	0.23	2,295	0.25	Sao Tome and Principe	4.00	0.004	290	0.03
Greece	399.90	0.45	4,249	0.46	Saudi Arabia	3,202.40	3.59	32,274	3.47
Grenada	6.00	0.01	310	0.03	Senegal	85.10	0.10	1,101	0.12
Guatemala	108.00	0.12	1,330	0.14	Seychelles	3.00	0.003	280	0.03
Guinea	57.90	0.06	829	0.09	Sierra Leone	57.90	0.06	829	0.09
Guinea-Bissau	7.50	0.01	325	0.03	Singapore	92.40	0.10	1,174	0.13
Guyana	49.20	0.06	742	0.08	Solomon Islands	5.00	0.01	300	0.03
Haiti	44.10	0.05	691	0.07	Somalia	44.20	0.05	692	0.07
Honduras	67.80	0.08	928	0.10	South Africa	915.70	1.03	9,407	1.01
Hungary	530.70	0.59	5,557	0.60	Spain	1,286.00	1.44	13,110	1.41
Iceland	59.60	0.07	846	0.09	Sri Lanka	223.10	0.25	2,481	0.27
India	2,207.70	2.47	22,327	2.40	Sudan	169.70	0.19	1,947	0.21
Indonesia	1,009.70	1.13	10,347	1.11	Suriname	49.30	0.06	743	0.08
Iran	660.00	0.74	6,850	0.74	Swaziland	24.70	0.03	497	0.05
Iraq	504.00	0.56	5,290	0.57	Sweden	1,064.30	1.19	10,893	1.17
Ireland	343.40	0.38	3,684	0.40	Syrian Arab Republic	139.10	0.16	1,641	0.18
Israel	446.60	0.50	4,716	0.51	Thailand	386.60	0.43	4,116	0.44
Italy	2,909.10	3.26	29,341	3.15	Togo	38.40	0.04	634	0.07
Ivory Coast	165.50	0.19	1,905	0.20	Tonga	3.25	0.003	282	0.03
Jamaica	145.50	0.16	1,705	0.18	Trinidad and Tobago	170.10	0.19	1,951	0.21
Japan	4,223.30	4.73	42,483	4.57	Tunisia	138.20	0.15	1,632	0.18
Jordan	73.90	0.08	989	0.11	Turkey	429.10	0.48	4,541	0.49
Kenya	142.00	0.16	1,670	0.18	Uganda	99.60	0.11	1,246	0.13
Kuwait	635.30	0.71	6,603	0.71	United Arab Emirates	202.60	0.23	2,276	0.24
Lao People's Democratic Republic	29.30	0.03	543	0.06	United Kingdom	6,194.00	6.94	62,190	6.68
Lebanon	78.70	0.09	1,037	0.11	United Republic of Tanzania	107.00	0.12	1,320	0.14
Lesotho	15.10	0.02	401	0.04	United States	17,918.30	20.06	179,433	19.29
Liberia	71.30	0.08	963	0.10	Uruguay	163.80	0.18	1,888	0.20
Libyan Arab Jamahiriya	515.70	0.58	5,407	0.58	Vanuatu	9.00	0.01	340	0.04
Luxembourg	77.00	0.09	1,020	0.11	Venezuela	1,371.50	1.54	13,965	1.50
Madagascar	66.40	0.07	914	0.10	Viet Nam	176.80	0.20	2,018	0.22
Malawi	37.20	0.04	622	0.07	Yemen	43.30	0.05	683	0.07
Malaysia	550.60	0.62	5,756	0.62	Yugoslavia	613.00	0.69	6,380	0.69
Maldives	2.00	0.002	270	0.03	Zaire	291.00	0.33	3,160	0.34
Mali	50.80	0.06	758	0.08	Zambia	270.30	0.30	2,953	0.32
Malta	45.10	0.05	701	0.08	Zimbabwe	191.00	0.21	2,160	0.23
Mauritania	33.90	0.04	589	0.06					
Mauritius	53.60	0.06	786	0.08	Total	89,305.05	100.00‡	930,300	100.00‡
Mexico	1,165.50	1.31	11,905	1.28					

*All members were participants in the SDR Department.

†Voting power varies on certain matters pertaining to the General Department with use of the Fund's resources in that Department.

‡May differ from the sum of the individual percentages because of rounding.

Annex II. EXECUTIVE DIRECTORS AND ALTERNATES OF THE INTERNATIONAL MONETARY FUND
(As at 3 January 1986)

Appointed Director	Appointed Alternate	Casting the vote of
Charles H. Dallara	Mary K. Bush	United States
T. P. Lankester	Michael Foot	United Kingdom
Guenter Grosche	Bernd Goos	Federal Republic of Germany
Bruno de Maulde	Sylvain de Forges	France
Hirotake Fujino	Masahiro Sugita	Japan
Yusuf A. Nimatallah	Jobarah E. Suraisry	Saudi Arabia

Elected Director	Elected Alternate	Casting the votes of
Pedro Pérez (Spain)	Guillermo Ortiz (Mexico)	Costa Rica, El Salvador, Guatemala, Honduras, Mexico, Nicaragua, Spain, Venezuela
J. J. Polak (Netherlands)	J. de Beaufort Wijnholds (Netherlands)	Cyprus, Israel, Netherlands, Romania, Yugoslavia
Jacques de Groote (Belgium)	Heinrich G. Schneider (Austria)	Austria, Belgium, Hungary, Luxembourg, Turkey
Marcel Massé (Canada)	Luke Leonard (Ireland)	Antigua and Barbuda, Bahamas, Barbados, Belize, Canada, Dominica, Grenada, Ireland, Jamaica, Saint Christopher and Nevis, Saint Lucia, Saint Vincent and the Grenadines
Salvatore Zecchini (Italy)	Nikolaos Coumbis (Greece)	Greece, Italy, Malta, Portugal
Mohamed Finaish (Libyan Arab Jamahiriya)	Tariq Alhaimus (Iraq)	Bahrain, Democratic Yemen, Iraq, Jordan, Kuwait, Lebanon, Libyan Arab Jamahiriya, Maldives, Oman, Pakistan, Qatar, Somalia, Syrian Arab Republic, United Arab Emirates, Yemen
C. R. Rye (Australia)	Antonio V. Romuáldez (Philippines)	Australia, New Zealand, Papua New Guinea, Philippines, Republic of Korea, Samoa, Seychelles, Solomon Islands, Vanuatu
Hans Lundström (Sweden)	Henrik Fugmann (Denmark)	Denmark, Finland, Iceland, Norway, Sweden
Arjun K. Sengupta (India)	A. S. Jayawardena (Sri Lanka)	Bangladesh, Bhutan, India, Sri Lanka
Alexandre Kafka (Brazil)	Hernando Arias (Panama)	Brazil, Colombia, Dominican Republic, Ecuador, Guyana, Haiti, Panama, Suriname, Trinidad and Tobago
E. I. M. Mtei (United Republic of Tanzania)	Ahmed Abdallah (Kenya)	Botswana, Burundi, Ethiopia, Gambia, Guinea, Kenya, Lesotho, Liberia, Malawi, Mozambique, Nigeria, Sierra Leone, Sudan, Swaziland, Uganda, United Republic of Tanzania, Zambia, Zimbabwe
J. E. Ismael (Indonesia)	Jaafar Ahmad (Malaysia)	Burma, Fiji, Indonesia, Lao People's Democratic Republic, Malaysia, Nepal, Singapore, Thailand, Viet Nam
Huang Fanzhang (China)	Jiang Hai (China)	China
Fernando L. Nebbia (Argentina)	Brian Jensen (Peru)	Argentina, Bolivia, Chile, Paraguay, Peru, Uruguay
Ghassem Salehkhou (Iran)	Omar Kabbaj (Morocco)	Afghanistan, Algeria, Ghana, Iran, Morocco, Tunisia
Abderrahmane Alfidja (Niger)	Mawakani Samba (Zaire)	Benin, Burkina Faso, Cameroon, Cape Verde, Central African Republic, Chad, Comoros, Congo, Djibouti, Equatorial Guinea, Gabon, Guinea-Bissau, Ivory Coast, Madagascar, Mali, Mauritania, Mauritius, Niger, Rwanda, Sao Tome and Principe, Senegal, Togo, Zaire

NOTE: Democratic Kampuchea, Egypt, South Africa and Tonga did not participate in the 1984 regular election of Executive Directors.

Annex III. PRINCIPAL OFFICERS AND OFFICES OF THE INTERNATIONAL MONETARY FUND

(As at 3 January 1986)

PRINCIPAL OFFICERS

Managing Director: Jacques de Larosière.
Deputy Managing Director: Richard D. Erb.
Counsellor: C. David Finch.*
Counsellor: Walter O. Habermeier.*
Economic Counsellor: William C. Hood.*
Counsellor: L. A. Whittome.*
Director, Administration Department: Graeme F. Rea.
Director, African Department: Alassane D. Ouattara.
Director, Asian Department: Tun Thin.
Director, Central Banking Department: J. B. Zulu.
Director, European Department: L. A. Whittome.
Director, Exchange and Trade Relations Department: C. David Finch.
Director, External Relations Department: Azizali F. Mohammed.
Director, Fiscal Affairs Department: Vito Tanzi.

Director, IMF Institute: Gérard M. Teyssier.
Director, Legal Department: François P. Gianviti.
Director, Middle Eastern Department: A. Shakour Shaalan.
Director, Research Department: William C. Hood.
Secretary, Secretary's Department: Leo Van Houtven.
Treasurer, Treasurer's Department: Walter O. Habermeier.
Director, Western Hemisphere Department: Eduardo Wiesner.
Director, Bureau of Computing Services: Warren N. Minami.
Director, Bureau of Language Services: Andrew J. Beith.
Director, Bureau of Statistics: Werner Dannemann.
Director, Office in Europe (Paris): Aldo Guetta.
Director, Office in Geneva: Carlos A. Sansón.
Internal Auditor: Robert Noë.
Special Representative to the United Nations: Jan-Maarten Zegers.

*Alphabetical listing.

HEADQUARTERS AND OTHER OFFICES

HEADQUARTERS

International Monetary Fund
700 19th Street N.W.
Washington, D.C. 20431, United States
  Cable address: INTERFUND WASHINGTONDC
  Telephone: (202) 623-7000
  Telex: (RCA) 248331 IMF UR, (FTCC) 82983 IMF UF,
    (ITT) 440040 FUND UI, (MCI) 64111 IMF UW,
    (TRT) 197677 FUND UT

OTHER OFFICES

International Monetary Fund
Office in Europe
64-66 avenue d'Iéna
75116 Paris, France
  Cable address: INTERFUND PARIS
  Telephone: 723-54-21
  Telex: 610712 INTERFUND PARIS

International Monetary Fund
Office in Geneva
58, rue de Moillebeaux
1209 Geneva, Switzerland
  Cable address: INTERFUND GENEVA
  Telephone: 34-30-30
  Telex: 23503 IMF CH

International Monetary Fund Office
United Nations Headquarters, Room DC1-1146
New York, N.Y. 10017, United States
  Telephone: (212) 963-6009

Chapter X

International Civil Aviation Organization (ICAO)

The International Civil Aviation Organization (ICAO) facilitates the safety, regularity and efficiency of civil air transport. As an intergovernmental regulatory organization in international civil aviation, its objectives are set down in annexes to the Convention on International Civil Aviation (Chicago, United States, 1944) which prescribe standards, recommended practices and procedures for facilitating civil aviation operations.

ICAO estimated total traffic of the world's scheduled airlines to be over 166 billion tonne-kilometres during 1985, an increase of 5.2 per cent over 1984. The airlines carried over 890 million passengers at a load factor of 66 per cent, 1 percentage point above 1984. Air freight remained at around 39 billion tonne-kilometres and airmail traffic at around 4.3 billion tonne-kilometres.

During the year, the ICAO Council held three regular sessions. It also convened a two-day extraordinary session at the request of Iran, following a notification by Iraq that it was not responsible for the safety of international flights operating within Iranian airspace. The Council urged the parties involved to assure the safety and regularity of international civil aviation along designated international air traffic service routes.

During 1985, membership of ICAO rose to 156 with the admission of Brunei Darussalam on 3 January, the Comoros on 14 February and Solomon Islands on 11 May.

Activities in 1985

Air navigation

During 1985, ICAO's efforts in air navigation continued to be directed towards updating and implementing ICAO Specifications and Regional Plans. The Specifications consisted of International Standards and Recommended Practices contained in 17 technical annexes to the Chicago Convention, and of Procedures for Air Navigation Services (PANS) contained in three PANS documents. Regional Plans set forth air navigation facilities and services required for international air navigation in the nine ICAO regions.

The Specifications in seven annexes and in one PANS document were amended. Amendments were also made to Regional Plans.

Seven air navigation meetings covering a wide range of subjects recommended changes to ICAO Specifications. To facilitate the implementation of the provisions of annexes and PANS, ICAO made available guidance material in the form of new and revised technical manuals and circulars.

ICAO regional offices assisted States in implementing Regional Plans. Their work was supplemented by that of experts sent to advise on installing new facilities and services and on operating existing ones.

During the year, special attention was given to: aircraft airworthiness and operations; environmental protection; transport of dangerous goods; helicopter operations; accident investigation and prevention; personnel licensing and training; aviation medicine; aerodromes; telecommunications; rules of the air and air traffic services; search and rescue; meteorology; aeronautical charts and information services; audio-visual training aids; and safeguarding international civil aviation against acts of unlawful interference.

Air transport

ICAO continued in 1985 its programmes of economic studies, collecting and publishing air transport statistics, and promoting greater facilitation in international air transport.

The Third Air Transport Conference (Montreal, Canada, 22 October–7 November) approved 23 recommendations on various aspects of regulatory policies governing scheduled and non-scheduled services, unilateral measures affecting international air transport, the role of Governments in the tariff field, rules and conditions associated with international tariffs and tariff enforcement.

The panel on route facility costs (Montreal, June/July) completed its work on a manual on route air navigation facility economics and considered developments concerning implementation of the World Area Forecast System. Workshops were held on airport and route facility economics (Bangkok, Thailand, September), aviation forecasting and economic planning (Mexico City, November), and statistics (Dakar, Senegal, December). A facilitation area meeting discussed problems in eastern and southern

Africa (Arusha, United Republic of Tanzania, November).

ICAO publications in 1985 included a study of air passenger and freight transport development in Africa, the regular series of digests of civil aviation statistics, the yearbook on world civil aviation statistics, a second edition of the definition of a scheduled international air service, a revised edition of the manual on air traffic forecasting, a study of regional differences in fares, rates and costs for international air transport in 1983 and a survey of international air transport fares and rates in 1984.

ICAO continued to co-operate closely with other international organizations such as the International Air Transport Association, the Airport Associations Co-ordinating Council, the Customs Co-operation Council, the World Tourism Organization and the Universal Postal Union. It also continued to provide secretariat services to three independent regional civil aviation bodies—the African Civil Aviation Commission, the European Civil Aviation Conference and the Latin American Civil Aviation Commission.

Following a 1982 conference to amend the 1956 Danish and Icelandic joint financing agreements for air navigation services in Greenland and the Faeroe Islands, and in Iceland, the two agreements as amended were provisionally applied from 1 January 1983. By the end of 1985, the protocols of amendment had been accepted by 13 countries.

Legal matters

The Legal Committee did not meet in 1985. However, the ICAO secretariat submitted to the Council in March a preliminary study which had been requested the previous year in connection with a draft instrument on the interception of civil aircraft.[a] The Council concluded that no new rules should be drafted relating to the aftermath of the landing of an intercepted aircraft pending the entry into force of an amendment (article 3 *bis*), embodied in a Protocol, to the Chicago Convention which reaffirmed the principle that every State must refrain from resorting to the use of weapons against civil aircraft in flight. In December, the Council decided that the item should remain on the general work programme of the Legal Committee with the understanding that no work should be undertaken pending the entry into force of article 3 *bis*.

Also in December, the Council had before it two reports which were to be referred to the Legal Committee for consideration: one on the United Nations Convention on the Law of the Sea—implications, if any, for the application of the Chicago Convention, its annexes and other international air law instruments; and the other on liability of air traffic control agencies. The Council also considered a model clause on aviation security for bilateral air agreements, prepared by the ICAO secretariat, and decided to send it to States and international organizations for their comments.

The Committee on Unlawful Interference with International Civil Aviation and Its Facilities held 12 meetings in 1985. It continued reviewing proposals to amend Specifications on security—safeguarding international civil aviation against acts of unlawful interference. On 19 December, on the recommendation of the Committee, the ICAO Council adopted an amendment to the Specifications in question.

In addition, the Committee considered proposals for a new comprehensive work programme as well as recommendations for a formal review of its terms of reference to enable it to play a more effective role in assisting the Council in matters pertaining to aviation security. Its recommendations were approved by the Council on 3 December.

The Committee also studied proposals for a consolidation of all ICAO Assembly resolutions in force pertaining to aviation security. On 16 December, the Council approved the text of a consolidated statement proposed by the Committee and decided to present it to the 1986 session of the Assembly for approval.

The following conventions and protocols on international air law concluded under ICAO auspices were ratified or adhered to during 1985:

Convention on International Recognition of Rights in Aircraft (Geneva, 1948)
  Grenada, Uruguay
Convention on Offences and Certain Other Acts Committed on Board Aircraft (Tokyo, 1963)
  Antigua and Barbuda, Malaysia
Convention for the Suppression of Unlawful Seizure of Aircraft (The Hague, 1970)
  Antigua and Barbuda, Malaysia
Protocol to Amend the Convention for the Unification of Certain Rules relating to International Carriage by Air signed at Warsaw on 12 October 1929, as amended by the Protocol done at The Hague on 28 September 1955 (Guatemala City, 1971) (not in force)
  Italy
Convention for the Suppression of Unlawful Acts against the Safety of Civil Aviation (Montreal, 1971)
  Antigua and Barbuda, Bahamas, Malaysia, Venezuela
Additional Protocol No. 1 to Amend the Convention for the Unification of Certain Rules relating to International Carriage by Air signed at Warsaw on 12 October 1929 (Montreal, 1975) (not in force)
  Italy

[a]YUN 1984, p. 1256.

Additional Protocol No. 2 to Amend the Convention for the Unification of Certain Rules relating to International Carriage by Air signed at Warsaw on 12 October 1929, as amended by the Protocol done at The Hague on 28 September 1955 (Montreal, 1975) (not in force)

Italy

Additional Protocol No. 3 to Amend the Convention for the Unification of Certain Rules relating to International Carriage by Air signed at Warsaw on 12 October 1929, as amended by the Protocols done at The Hague on 28 September 1955 and at Guatemala City on 8 March 1971 (Montreal, 1975) (not in force)

Italy

Montreal Protocol No. 4 to Amend the Convention for the Unification of Certain Rules relating to International Carriage by Air signed at Warsaw on 12 October 1929, as amended by the Protocol done at The Hague on 28 September 1955 (Montreal, 1975) (not in force)

Italy

Technical assistance

During 1985, ICAO provided technical assistance to 89 States; in 52 of these, there were resident missions consisting of one or more experts. In addition to resident expertise, assistance was provided in the form of equipment, fellowships and scholarships and through short missions by experts.

Ten new large-scale projects, each costing more than $500,000, for which ICAO was to be the executing agency, were approved by the Administrator of the United Nations Development Programme (UNDP). Three large-scale projects were financed under trust fund assistance.

ICAO employed 597 experts (some in two or more programmes) from 50 countries during all or part of 1985, 386 on assignments under UNDP and 218 on trust fund projects (including seven under the associate experts programme). There were also 29 United Nations Volunteers. The number of experts in the field at the end of 1985 was 282, compared with 331 at the end of 1984.

A total of 1,177 fellowships were awarded in 1985 (1,106 in 1984), of which 1,135 were implemented.

Equipment purchases and sub-contracts continued to represent a substantial proportion of the technical assistance programme. Forty-three Governments or organizations had registered with ICAO under the Civil Aviation Purchasing Service. The total for equipment and sub-contracts committed during 1985 amounted to some $13 million.

The following countries and Territories were aided:

Africa: Angola, Benin, Botswana, Burundi, Cameroon, Cape Verde, Central African Republic, Chad, Congo, Equitorial Guinea, Ethiopia, Gabon, Ghana, Guinea, Guinea-Bissau, Ivory Coast, Kenya, Lesotho, Liberia, Madagascar, Malawi, Mali, Mauritania, Mauritius, Mozambique, Niger, Nigeria, Rwanda, Senegal, Seychelles, Sierra Leone, Swaziland, Togo, Uganda, United Republic of Tanzania, Zaire, Zambia, Zimbabwe.

Americas: Antigua and Barbuda, Argentina, Bahamas, Bolivia, Brazil, Cayman Islands, Chile, Colombia, Ecuador, Honduras, Netherlands Antilles, Panama, Peru, Trinidad and Tobago, Turks and Caicos Islands, Uruguay, Venezuela.

Asia/Pacific: Afghanistan, Bangladesh, Brunei, Burma, China, Democratic People's Republic of Korea, India, Indonesia, Kiribati, Lao People's Democratic Republic, Malaysia, Maldives, Nepal, Pakistan, Philippines, Republic of Korea, Singapore, Sri Lanka, Thailand, Vietnam.

Europe, Mediterranean and Middle East: Algeria, Democratic Yemen, Djibouti, Egypt, Greece, Iraq, Jordan, Kuwait, Lebanon, Libyan Arab Jamahiriya, Morocco, Oman, Poland, Qatar, Saudi Arabia, Somalia, Sudan, Syrian Arab Republic, Yemen.

Included in the above were the following, aided under trust fund arrangements: Argentina, Bolivia, Brunei, Cape Verde, Iraq, Ivory Coast, Jordan, Libyan Arab Jamahiriya, Nigeria, Peru, Saudi Arabia, Trinidad and Tobago, Venezuela, Yemen.

Secretariat

As at 31 December 1985, the total number of staff members employed in the ICAO secretariat stood at 875: 320 in the Professional and higher categories drawn from 73 nationalities, and 555 in the General Service and related categories. Of the total, 215 persons were employed in regional offices. In addition, there were 249 in the Professional category serving as technical experts on UNDP field projects.

Budget

Revised appropriations for the 1985 financial year totalled $39,179,000. Modifications were approved by the ICAO Council and are reflected below (in United States dollars):

	Appropriations	Revised appropriations	Actual obligations
Meetings	318,000	323,000	322,061
Secretariat	27,600,000	29,006,700	29,006,617
General services	4,123,000	4,301,000	4,300,519
Equipment	416,000	719,700	719,644
Other budgetary provisions	132,000	66,700	66,639
Contingencies	4,328,000	4,761,900	—
Total	36,917,000	39,179,000	34,415,480

Annex I.   MEMBERSHIP OF THE INTERNATIONAL CIVIL AVIATION ORGANIZATION AND CONTRIBUTIONS

(Membership as at 31 December 1985; contributions as assessed for 1985)

MEMBER	CONTRIBUTION Percentage	CONTRIBUTION Net amount (in US dollars)	MEMBER	CONTRIBUTION Percentage	CONTRIBUTION Net amount (in US dollars)	MEMBER	CONTRIBUTION Percentage	CONTRIBUTION Net amount (in US dollars)
Afghanistan	0.06	18,074	Greece	0.47	141,583	Paraguay	0.06	18,074
Algeria	0.17	51,211	Grenada	0.06	18,074	Peru	0.11	33,136
Angola	0.06	18,074	Guatemala	0.06	18,074	Philippines	0.28	84,347
Antigua and Barbuda	0.06	18,074	Guinea	0.06	18,074	Poland	0.49	147,608
Argentina	0.69	207,856	Guinea-Bissau	0.06	18,074	Portugal	0.25	75,310
Australia	1.64	494,034	Guyana	0.06	18,074	Qatar	0.06	18,074
Austria	0.59	177,732	Haiti	0.06	18,074	Republic of Korea	0.59	177,732
Bahamas	0.06	18,074	Honduras	0.06	18,074	Romania	0.19	57,236
Bahrain	0.06	18,074	Hungary	0.16	48,198	Rwanda	0.06	18,074
Bangladesh	0.06	18,074	Iceland	0.06	18,074	Saint Lucia	0.06	18,074
Barbados	0.06	18,074	India	0.52	156,645	Saint Vincent and the		
Belgium	1.16	349,438	Indonesia	0.31	93,384	Grenadines	0.06	18,074
Benin	0.06	18,074	Iran	0.45	135,558	Sao Tome and Principe	0.06	18,074
Bolivia	0.06	18,074	Iraq	0.19	57,236	Saudi Arabia	0.71	213,880
Botswana	0.06	18,074	Ireland	0.19	57,236	Senegal	0.06	18,074
Brazil	1.53	460,897	Israel	0.33	99,409	Seychelles	0.06	18,074
Brunei Darussalam	0.06	18,074	Italy	3.20	963,968	Sierra Leone	0.06	18,074
Bulgaria	0.14	42,174	Ivory Coast	0.06	18,074	Singapore	0.59	177,732
Burkina Faso	0.06	18,074	Jamaica	0.06	18,074	Solomon Islands	0.06	18,074
Burma	0.06	18,074	Japan	9.02	2,717,185	Somalia	0.06	18,074
Burundi	0.06	18,074	Jordan	0.12	36,149	South Africa	0.56	168,694
Cameroon	0.06	18,074	Kenya	0.06	18,074	Spain	1.92	578,381
Canada	2.92	879,620	Kiribati	0.06	18,074	Sri Lanka	0.06	18,074
Cape Verde	0.06	18,074	Kuwait	0.33	99,409	Sudan	0.06	18,074
Central African Republic	0.06	18,074	Lao People's Democratic			Suriname	0.06	18,074
Chad	0.06	18,074	Republic	0.06	18,074	Swaziland	0.06	18,074
Chile	0.15	45,186	Lebanon	0.17	51,211	Sweden	1.12	337,389
China	0.56	168,694	Lesotho	0.06	18,074	Switzerland	1.20	361,488
Colombia	0.21	63,260	Liberia	0.06	18,074	Syrian Arab Republic	0.07	21,087
Comoros	0.06	18,074	Libyan Arab Jamahiriya	0.23	69,285	Thailand	0.30	90,372
Congo	0.06	18,074	Luxembourg	0.06	18,074	Togo	0.06	18,074
Costa Rica	0.06	18,074	Madagascar	0.06	18,074	Tonga	0.06	18,074
Cuba	0.10	30,124	Malawi	0.06	18,074	Trinidad and Tobago	0.08	24,099
Cyprus	0.06	18,074	Malaysia	0.18	54,223	Tunisia	0.06	18,074
Czechoslovakia	0.56	168,694	Maldives	0.06	18,074	Turkey	0.28	84,347
Democratic Kampuchea	0.06	18,074	Mali	0.06	18,074	Uganda	0.06	18,074
Democratic People's			Malta	0.06	18,074	USSR	9.69	2,919,016
Republic of Korea	0.06	18,074	Mauritania	0.06	18,074	United Arab Emirates	0.18	54,223
Democratic Yemen	0.06	18,074	Mauritius	0.06	18,074	United Kingdom	5.12	1,542,349
Denmark	0.64	192,794	Mexico	0.97	292,203	United Republic of		
Djibouti	0.06	18,074	Monaco	0.06	18,074	Tanzania	0.06	18,074
Dominican Republic	0.06	18,074	Morocco	0.10	30,124	United States	25.00	7,531,000
Ecuador	0.06	18,074	Mozambique	0.06	18,074	Uruguay	0.06	18,074
Egypt	0.16	48,198	Nauru	0.06	18,074	Vanuatu	0.06	18,074
El Salvador	0.06	18,074	Nepal	0.06	18,074	Venezuela	0.61	183,756
Equatorial Guinea	0.06	18,074	Netherlands	1.93	581,393	Viet Nam	0.06	18,074
Ethiopia	0.06	18,074	New Zealand	0.35	105,434	Yemen	0.06	18,074
Fiji	0.06	18,074	Nicaragua	0.06	18,074	Yugoslavia	0.46	138,570
Finland	0.42	126,521	Niger	0.06	18,074	Zaire	0.06	18,074
France	5.96	1,795,390	Nigeria	0.23	69,285	Zambia	0.06	18,074
Gabon	0.06	18,074	Norway	0.48	144,595	Zimbabwe	0.06	18,074
Gambia	0.06	18,074	Oman	0.06	18,074			
Germany, Federal			Pakistan	0.26	78,322			
Republic of	7.07	2,129,767	Panama	0.06	18,074	Total*	100.30	30,214,372†
Ghana	0.06	18,074	Papua New Guinea	0.06	18,074			

   *Includes assessments for Brunei Darussalam, the Comoros, Saint Vincent and the Grenadines, Solomon Islands and Tonga which became contracting States after current rates were established.

   †Not equal to the sum of individual figures because of rounding.

Annex II.   OFFICERS AND OFFICES OF THE INTERNATIONAL CIVIL AVIATION ORGANIZATION
(As at 31 December 1985)

ICAO COUNCIL

OFFICERS
President: Assad Kotaite (Lebanon).
First Vice-President: S. Ahmad (Pakistan).
Second Vice-President: S. D. Faye (Senegal).
Third Vice-President: O. Vodicka (Czechoslovakia).
Secretary: Yves Lambert (France).

MEMBERS
Algeria, Argentina, Australia, Belgium, Brazil, Canada, China, Colombia, Czecho-slovakia, Egypt, France, Germany, Federal Republic of, Guatemala, India, Indonesia, Iraq, Italy, Jamaica, Japan, Kenya, Lebanon, Madagascar, Mexico, Nigeria, Norway, Pakistan, Senegal, Spain, USSR, United Kingdom, United Republic of Tanzania, United States, Venezuela.

PRINCIPAL OFFICERS OF THE SECRETARIAT

Secretary-General: Yves Lambert.
Director, Air Navigation Bureau: D. W. Freer.
Director, Air Transport Bureau: R. A. Bickley.

Director, Legal Bureau: Michael Milde.
Director, Technical Assistance Bureau: M. J. Challons.
Chief, Public Information Office: Eugene Sochor.

HEADQUARTERS AND REGIONAL OFFICES

HEADQUARTERS
International Civil Aviation Organization
1000 Sherbrooke Street West, Suite 400
Montreal, Quebec, Canada H3A 2R2
  Cable address: ICAO MONTREAL
  Telephone: (514) 285-8219
  Telex: 05-24513
  Facsimile: (514) 288-4772

AFRICAN OFFICE
International Civil Aviation Organization
Boîte Postale 2356
Dakar, Senegal
  Cable address: ICAOREP DAKAR
  Telephone: (221) 21-54-52, 22-47-86
  Telex: 3348 ICAO SG
  Facsimile: (221) 22-69-26

EASTERN AFRICAN OFFICE
International Civil Aviation Organization
P.O. Box 46294
Nairobi, Kenya
  Cable address: ICAOREP NAIROBI
  Telephone: (402) 333 930, 520-600 (ext. 3000-3030)
  Telex: KE 25295
  Facsimile: (402) 520-199

NORTH AMERICAN AND CARIBBEAN OFFICE
International Civil Aviation Organization
Apartado Postal 5-377
C.P. 11590
Mexico 5, D.F., Mexico
  Cable address: ICAOREP MEXICO
  Telephone: (905) 250-3211
  Telex: 1777598 ICAOME
  Facsimile: (905) 254-4274

SOUTH AMERICAN OFFICE
International Civil Aviation Organization
Apartado 4127
Lima 100, Peru
  Cable address: ICAOREP LIMA
  Telephone: 51-5414, 51-5325, 51-5497
  Telex: 25689 PE ICAO
  Facsimile: 51-5497 (Ext. 39)

ASIA AND PACIFIC OFFICE
International Civil Aviation Organization
P.O. Box 614
Bangkok, Thailand
  Cable address: ICAOREP BANGKOK
  Telephone: (02) 258-0226
  Telex: 87969 ICAOBKK TH
  Facsimile: (02) 258-9198

EUROPEAN OFFICE
International Civil Aviation Organization
3 *bis*, Villa Emile-Bergerat
92522 Neuilly-sur-Seine (Cedex)
France
  Cable address: ICAOREP PARIS
  Telephone: (1) 46-37-96-96
  Telex: 610075 (for ICAOREP)
  Facsimile: (1) 46-24-09-14

MIDDLE EAST OFFICE
International Civil Aviation Organization
16 Hassan Sabri
Zamalek
Cairo, Egypt
  Cable address: ICAOREP CAIRO
  Telephone: (202) 3401463, 3401532, 3418163
  Telex: 92459 ICAOR UN
  Facsimile: (202) 3405344

Chapter XI

Universal Postal Union (UPU)

The Universal Postal Union (UPU), established at
Berne, Switzerland, in 1874 for the reciprocal exchange of postal services between nations, is one
of the oldest international intergovernmental
organizations. Its aim is to promote the organization and improvement of postal services and to further the development of international collaboration
in this sphere. It also participates in various forms
of postal technical assistance requested by its member
States.

In 1985, UPU membership rose to 168 following
the admission of Brunei Darussalam on 15 January.

Activities of UPU organs

Universal Postal Congress

The Universal Postal Congress, composed of all
member States, is the supreme legislative authority
of UPU and normally meets every five years. The
most recent Congress (the nineteenth) took place
at Hamburg, Federal Republic of Germany, in 1984
and the twentieth was scheduled to meet at
Washington, D.C., in 1989.

The work of the Congress consists mainly of examining and revising the Acts of the Union based
on proposals submitted by member States, the Executive Council or the Consultative Council for Postal
Studies, and of making administrative arrangements
for UPU activities. The Acts in force since 1 July
1981 were those of the 1979 Rio de Janeiro (Brazil)
Congress. The Acts of the 1984 Hamburg Congress
were to enter into force in 1986.

Executive Council

At its 1985 session, held at Berne from 22 April
to 3 May, the 40-member Executive Council—which
carries out the work of UPU between Congress sessions by maintaining close contact with postal administrations, exercising control over the International Bureau (the UPU secretariat), promoting
technical assistance and working with the United
Nations and other organizations—considered administrative matters and examined studies concerning international mail referred to it by the 1984
Congress.

Among other questions reviewed by the Council were: a decision to reconstitute the CCC-UPU
(Customs Co-operation Council–Universal Postal
Union) Contact Committee; rate-fixing for letter-post
items; transit charges and terminal dues; basic airmail
conveyance rates; maximizing air conveyance of mail;

land and sea rates for parcel post; and customs treatment of postal items.

Consultative Council for Postal Studies

The 35-member Consultative Council for Postal
Studies continued in 1985 its studies of various
technical, economic and operational problems affecting postal administrations of UPU member
States, including matters of particular interest to
new and developing countries.

The annual meeting of the Council (Berne, 7-
17 October) dealt mainly with the launching of
studies on the 1984-1989 work programme and the
implementation of selected means of action. Activities were also initiated in connection with the
1984 Declaration of Hamburg, which stressed that
UPU must "actively participate in strengthening the
international postal service as a whole and in improving the standard and speed of international mail
circulation and postal exchanges". During the year,
work continued on preparing the fifth edition of
the *Multilingual Vocabulary of the International Postal
Service*. The Council also dealt with technical co-
operation, international high-speed mail and computers in the postal service.

International Bureau

Under the general supervision of the Government of the Swiss Confederation, the International
Bureau—the UPU secretariat—continued to serve
the postal administrations of member States as an
organ for liaison, information and consultation.

During 1985, the Bureau was responsible for collecting, co-ordinating, publishing and disseminating
international postal service information. At the request of postal administrations, it also conducted
inquiries and acted as a clearing-house for settling
certain accounts between them.

As at 31 December 1985, the number of permanent and temporary staff members employed by
the UPU secretariat was 141—59 in the Professional
and higher categories (drawn from 48 countries)
and 82 in the General Service category. Also, as
French remained the sole official UPU language,
16 officials were employed in the Arabic, English,
Portuguese, Russian and Spanish translation services.

Technical co-operation

The year 1985 marked the end of the five-year
period for which the 1979 Congress had set policy

guidelines for technical assistance. Technical co-operation provided by UPU was financed for the most part by the United Nations Development Programme (UNDP); UNDP/UPU project expenditures amounted to almost $2 million. Several regional projects in Africa, Asia and the Pacific, and Latin America received assistance in the form of expert and consultant services, training fellowships or equipment.

UPU participated in the programming work concerning countries which had submitted their programmes to the June session of the UNDP Governing Council. Of the six national programmes approved, two included assistance to the postal services of Bhutan and Guatemala. Other projects were approved for Botswana, Guinea, Kuwait, Madagascar, Nepal and Zaire, and revised for Bangladesh, Cape Verde, Chad, the Congo, Greece, Guatemala, Haiti, the Ivory Coast, Jordan, Liberia, the Niger, the Philippines, Qatar and Senegal.

Regional and interregional programmes concerning postal services were carried out under UNDP in Africa, Asia and the Pacific, the Caribbean and Latin America.

Technical co-operation among developing countries (TCDC) was the subject of special attention from UPU during the year. At its May/June session, the High-level Committee on the Review of TCDC (see p. 489), noting that the 1978 Buenos Aires Plan of Action for Promoting and Implementing TCDC[a] had not produced the anticipated results, took some organizational and logistical decisions. Subsequently, the UNDP Governing Council approved $1.5 million to finance the promotion of TCDC.

Assistance was also provided through the UPU Special Fund and the regular budget. Total expenditures from these two sources in 1985 amounted to approximately $995,000. In addition, 14 countries provided training fellowships and donated postal materials or equipment to postal administrations in Africa, Asia and Latin America.

UPU continued its programme of technical assistance subject to payment, by which member States could finance assistance themselves by funds on deposit.

Budget

Under UPU's self-financing system, contributions are payable in advance by member States based on the following year's budget. At its 1985 session, the Executive Council approved a budget of $24,743,000 Swiss francs for 1986 (see table).

Income	Amount (in Swiss francs)
Contributions from member States	21,381,360
Taken from reserve funds	1,000,000
Contribution allocated by UNDP for support of technical co-operation projects	1,315,200
Sale of publications	467,000
Other	579,440
Total	24,743,000*

Expenditure	
Staff	19,517,100
Overheads	5,225,900
Total	24,743,000*

*Equal to $11,838,755 on the basis of 2.09 Swiss francs = $US 1.00.

Each member State chooses its class of contribution, on a scale of 0.5 to 50 units. For 1986, the Executive Council fixed the amount of the contributory unit at 21,840 Swiss francs on the basis of a total of 979 units. The following table gives assessments by class of contribution:

CLASS OF CONTRIBUTION	ASSESSMENTS	
	Swiss francs	US dollar equivalent*
50 units	1,092,000	522,500
40 units	—	—
35 units	—	—
25 units	546,000	261,250
20 units	—	—
15 units	327,600	156,750
10 units	218,400	104,500
5 units	109,200	52,250
3 units	65,520	31,350
1 unit	21,840	10,450
0.5 unit	10,920	5,225

*Calculated on the basis of 2.09 Swiss francs = $US 1.00.

[a]YUN 1978, p. 467.

Annex I. MEMBERSHIP OF THE UNIVERSAL POSTAL UNION AND CLASS OF CONTRIBUTION
(Membership as at 31 December 1985; contributions as assessed for 1986)

Member	Class of contri-bution;* no. of units	Member	Class of contri-bution;* no. of units	Member	Class of contri-bution;* no. of units	Member	Class of contri-bution;* no. of units	Member	Class of contri-bution;* no. of units	Member	Class of contri-bution;* no. of units
Afghanistan	0.5	Bahamas	1	Bhutan	0.5	Burkina		Canada	50	China	25
Albania	1	Bahrain	1	Bolivia	0.5	Faso	0.5	Cape Verde	0.5	Colombia	3
Algeria	5	Bangladesh	10	Botswana	0.5	Burma	3	Central		Comoros	0.5
Angola	1	Barbados	1	Brazil	25	Burundi	0.5	African		Congo	1
Argentina	15	Belgium	15	Brunei		Byelorussian		Republic	0.5	Costa Rica	1
Australia	25	Belize	1	Darussalam	1	SSR	3	Chad	0.5	Cuba	3
Austria	5	Benin	0.5	Bulgaria	3	Cameroon	1	Chile	5	Cyprus	1

Member	Class of contribution;* no. of units	Member	Class of contribution;* no. of units	Member	Class of contribution;* no. of units	Member	Class of contribution;* no. of units	Member	Class of contribution;* no. of units	Member	Class of contribution;* no. of units
Czechoslovakia	10	German Democratic Republic	15	Jordan	1	Nauru	1	Saint Vincent and the Grenadines	1	Tunisia	5
Democratic Kampuchea	1	Germany, Federal Republic of	50	Kenya	3	Nepal	3	San Marino	1	Turkey	5
Democratic People's Republic of Korea	5	Ghana	3	Kiribati	1	Netherlands	15	Sao Tome and Principe	0.5	Tuvalu	1
		Greece	3	Kuwait	10	Netherlands Antilles	1	Saudi Arabia	25	Uganda	0.5
Democratic Yemen	0.5	Grenada	1	Lao People's Democratic Republic	0.5	New Zealand	15	Senegal	1	Ukrainian SSR	10
Denmark	10	Guatemala	3	Lebanon	0.5	Nicaragua	1	Seychelles	1	USSR	25
Djibouti	0.5	Guinea	0.5	Lesotho	0.5	Niger	1	Sierra Leone	0.5	United Arab Emirates	1
Dominica	1	Guinea-Bissau	0.5	Liberia	1	Nigeria	10	Singapore	1	United Kingdom	50
Dominican Republic	1	Guyana	1	Libyan Arab Jamahiriya	5	Norway	10	Solomon Islands	1	United Kingdom Overseas Territories	5
Ecuador	1	Haiti	0.5	Liechtenstein	1	Oman	1	Somalia	0.5		
Egypt	10	Honduras	1	Luxembourg	3	Pakistan	15	Spain	25	United Republic of Tanzania	0.5
El Salvador	1	Hungary	5	Madagascar	3	Panama	1	Sri Lanka	5	United States	50
Equatorial Guinea	0.5	Iceland	1	Malawi	0.5	Papua New Guinea	1	Sudan	0.5	Uruguay	3
Ethiopia	0.5	India	25	Malaysia	3	Paraguay	1	Suriname	1	Vanuatu	1
Fiji	1	Indonesia	10	Maldives	1	Peru	3	Swaziland	1	Vatican	1
Finland	10	Iran	5	Mali	0.5	Philippines	1	Sweden	15	Venezuela	3
France	50	Iraq	3	Malta	1	Poland	5	Switzerland	15	Viet Nam	1
Gabon	1	Ireland	10	Mauritania	1	Portugal	5	Syrian Arab Republic	1	Yemen	0.5
Gambia	0.5	Israel	3	Mauritius	1	Qatar	5	Thailand	3	Yugoslavia	5
		Italy	25	Mexico	10	Republic of Korea	10	Togo	0.5	Zaire	3
		Ivory Coast	3	Monaco	1	Romania	3	Tonga	1	Zambia	3
		Jamaica	1	Mongolia	1	Rwanda	0.5	Trinidad and Tobago	1	Zimbabwe	3
		Japan	50	Morocco	5	Saint Lucia	1				
				Mozambique	1						

NOTE: The UPU official nomenclature differs from that of the United Nations.

*For amount of contributions from members, see table under BUDGET above.

Annex II.   ORGANS, OFFICERS AND OFFICE OF THE UNIVERSAL POSTAL UNION

EXECUTIVE COUNCIL
(Elected to hold office until the twentieth (1989) Universal Postal Congress)

Chairman: Federal Republic of Germany.
Vice-Chairmen: Benin, Jordan, Mexico, USSR.
Secretary-General: Adwaldo Cardoso Botto de Barros, Director-General of the International Bureau.
Members: Algeria, Australia, Belgium, Benin, Brazil, Cameroon, Chile, Colombia, Egypt, Ethiopia, France, Gabon, Germany, Federal Republic of, Honduras, Hungary, India, Iraq, Ireland, Ivory Coast, Japan, Jordan, Lebanon, Madagascar, Mexico, New Zealand, Nigeria, Norway, Pakistan, Peru, Poland, Portugal, Romania, Saudi Arabia, Senegal, Switzerland, Thailand, USSR, United States, Uruguay, Zambia.

CONSULTATIVE COUNCIL FOR POSTAL STUDIES
(Elected to hold office until the twentieth (1989) Universal Postal Congress)

Chairman: Tunisia.
Vice-Chairman: Canada.
Secretary-General: Adwaldo Cardoso Botto de Barros, Director-General of the International Bureau.
Members: Algeria, Argentina, Australia, Austria, Bangladesh, Belgium, Brazil, Canada, China, Cuba, Egypt, Finland, France, Germany, Federal Republic of, India, Indonesia, Italy, Japan, Kenya, Morocco, Netherlands, New Zealand, Pakistan, Spain, Sri Lanka, Sudan, Switzerland, Thailand, Tunisia, USSR, United Kingdom, United Republic of Tanzania, United States, Yugoslavia, Zimbabwe.

INTERNATIONAL BUREAU

OFFICERS

Director-General: Adwaldo Cardoso Botto de Barros.
Deputy Director-General: Félix Cicéron.
Assistant Directors-General: Jaime Ascandoni, Abdel Kader Baghdadi, El Mostafa Gharbi.

HEADQUARTERS

Bureau international de l'Union postale universelle
Weltposstrasse 4
Berne, Switzerland
    Postal address: Union postale universelle
                  Case postale
                  3000 Berne 15 (Suisse)

    Cable address: UPU BERNE
    Telephone: (31) 43 22 11
    Telex: 912761 UPU CH
    Facsimile: 31 43 22 10

Chapter XII

International Telecommunication Union (ITU)

As at 31 December 1985, 160 countries were members of the International Telecommunication Union (ITU). There were no new admissions during 1985.

Administrative Council

The fortieth session of the Administrative Council of ITU was held from 1 to 17 July 1985 at ITU headquarters, Geneva. It reviewed administrative and financial matters, considered the report of the Independent Commission for World-wide Telecommunications Development, and decided to establish, within the framework of ITU, a Centre for Telecommunications Development at Geneva. The Council also constituted a group of experts to work on the separation of the existing ITU Convention into two separate instruments: a Constitution containing the provisions of fundamental character; and a Convention comprising the other provisions which by definition might require periodic revision.

Administrative radio conferences

The first session of the World Administrative Radio Conference (WARC) on the use of the geostationary-satellite orbit and the planning of space services utilizing it (Geneva, 8 August–15 September 1985) adopted, for submission to its second (1988) session, a technical report covering in-service networks of fixed-satellite services, planning, guidelines for regulatory procedures for space services and frequency bands, inter-service sharing considerations, feeder links and satellite sound-broadcasting systems for individual reception. It also established guidelines for inter-sessional work to be carried by the ITU technical secretariats.

A Regional Administrative Radio Conference for services in certain parts of the MF (medium frequency) band in Region 1 (Africa and Europe) (Geneva, 25 February–15 March) adopted a regional agreement incorporating frequency assignment plans for stations of the maritime mobile service and of the aeronautical radio-navigation service (radio-beacons).

Another Regional Administrative Radio Conference (Geneva, 4-13 March) adopted a regional agreement for radio-beacons in the European maritime area in the frequency band 283.5-315 kilohertz.

Two other Regional Administrative Radio Conferences were held during 1985: one for the African broadcasting area (Geneva, 12 and 13 August), to abrogate certain parts of the 1963 Geneva Agreement on Very High Frequency (VHF)/Ultra-High Frequency (UHF) Broadcasting;[a] and the other for the European broadcasting area (Geneva, 12 and 13 August), to revise certain parts of the 1961 Stockholm Broadcasting Agreement.[b]

International consultative committees

During 1985, the International Radio Consultative Committee (CCIR) made important progress in the study of television and sound broadcasting topics, fixed satellite systems and mobile communications. Meetings of 13 final study groups were held (Geneva, 16 September–20 November) to prepare proposals for the sixteenth (1986) CCIR plenary assembly. The meetings, which were attended by 1,079 participants from 47 countries, many for more than one study group, resulted in 875 new or revised texts for presentation to the assembly. CCIR also prepared the technical bases for Regional Administrative Radio Conferences for the Americas and Africa, to be held in 1986, and completed inter-sessional technical studies for the WARC on high frequency (HF) broadcasting, the next session of which was planned for 1987.

The International Telegraph and Telephone Consultative Committee (CCITT) held the first series of meetings of the new study period which began after the 1984 CCITT plenary assembly.[c] The CCITT secretariat focused its activities mainly on preparing recommendations to appear in the CCITT book (Red Book), published in 1985.

International Frequency Registration Board

The major activities of the International Frequency Registration Board (IFRB) during 1985 included completion of work resulting from the 1979 WARC, and follow-up action on decisions of the 1984 Regional Administrative Conference for FM (frequency modulation) sound broadcasting in VHF bands in Region 1 and in certain countries in Region 3 (Asia and Australasia), and on deci-

[a]YUN 1963, p. 659.
[b]YUN 1961, p. 651.
[c]YUN 1984, p. 1264.

sions of the first (1984) session of the WARC for HF broadcasting. IFRB also organized international monitoring programmes and prepared and participated in the 1985 WARC on the geostationary-satellite orbit (see above).

Other IFRB activities included the examination and recording in the Master International Frequency Register of frequency assignment notices received from member countries, and follow-up actions to the following conferences: the 1961 European VHF/UHF Broadcasting Conference; the 1963 African VHF/UHF Broadcasting Conference; the 1975 Regional (Regions 1 and 3) Administrative LF(low frequency)/MF Broadcasting Conference; the 1981 Regional (Region 2—the Americas) Administrative Radio Conference for MF sound broadcasting; the 1983 WARC for mobile services; the 1983 Regional (Region 2) Administrative Radio Conference for planning the broadcasting satellite service; and the 1984 Regional (Region 1 and certain countries of Region 3) Administrative Radio Conference for FM sound broadcasting in the frequency band 87.5-108 megahertz.

Technical co-operation

In 1985, the rate of implementation of ITU technical assistance activities showed a slight but consistent upturn, as the volume of resources available to the United Nations Development Programme (UNDP), the major contributor to ITU technical co-operation activities, levelled out. Under ITU programmes of technical co-operation in developing countries, 584 expert missions were carried out, 834 fellows were trained abroad and equipment valued at $7,212,617 was delivered, mainly to telecommunication training centres. Total assistance amounted to some $26.3 million.

The following countries and territories were aided:

Africa: Algeria, Angola, Benin, Burundi, Cameroon, Central African Republic, Chad, Djibouti, Egypt, Equatorial Guinea, Gambia, Guinea, Ivory Coast, Lesotho, Madagascar, Malawi, Mauritania, Morocco, Mozambique, Rwanda, Sao Tome and Principe, Senegal, Somalia, Sudan, Swaziland, Togo, Tunisia, Uganda, Zaire, Zimbabwe.

The Americas: Bermuda, Brazil, Chile, Colombia, Ecuador, Guyana, Haiti, Honduras, Netherlands Antilles, Nicaragua, Panama, Peru, Suriname, Trinidad and Tobago, Uruguay.

Asia and the Pacific: Afghanistan, Bangladesh, Burma, China, India, Indonesia, Iran, Lao People's Democratic Republic, Malaysia, Mongolia, Nepal, Pakistan, Papua New Guinea, Republic of Korea, Samoa, Singapore, Sri Lanka, Thailand, Tokelau, Tonga, Trust Territory of the Pacific Islands, Vanuatu.

Europe and the Middle East: Albania, Bulgaria, Cyprus, Czechoslovakia, Democratic Yemen, Greece, Hungary, Jordan, Kuwait, Poland, Qatar, Romania, Saudi Arabia, Yemen.

The main objectives of ITU technical co-operation continued to be: promoting development of regional telecommunications networks in Africa, the Americas, Asia, the Pacific, the Middle East and the Mediterranean Basin; strengthening telecommunication technical and administrative services in developing countries; and vocational training.

ITU continued to promote development of regional telecommunication networks and their integration into the world-wide telecommunication system, in accordance with objectives established by the World Plan Committee and regional plan committees.

The Pan-African Telecommunications Network (PANAFTEL), with its basic structure designed to interconnect countries without transit beyond the continent, made steady progress in 1985. Most of the network was installed, with the sole exception of the Central African subregion. UNDP financed two regional projects for PANAFTEL, one for its continued implementation and operation, and the other for its maintenance. Action was taken at the regional level to encourage countries to adopt national plans for the improvement of maintenance; by the end of 1985, some 25 countries were participating in that common effort.

Co-ordination activities continued during 1985 on a project for a Regional African Satellite Communication System for the development of Africa. Action was taken towards undertaking a feasibility study on the implementation of a regional telecommunication satellite system. An Inter-Agency Co-ordination Committee, with overall responsibility for the project, drew up a structure for the study and identified sources of financing.

In the Americas, several projects were under way during the year to strengthen national telecommunication technical and administrative services. While there was no ITU-executed project aimed at the development of a regional network, ITU continued to foster the development of the network by supporting national and regional organizations responsible for such activities. Technical meetings were held with the Association of Telecommunication Organizations of the Andean Subregional Agreement on a project for an Andean satellite, and activities were initiated with the Caribbean Association of National Telecommunications Organizations.

Activities related to developing a regional telecommunication network in Asia and the Pacific were mostly pursued by the countries on a bilateral basis. However, during 1985, ITU provided assistance to countries in planning and development activities, as well as in improving operation of existing networks through a number of UNDP-funded projects. Through a regional project, ITU assisted least developed countries (LDCs) of the region to upgrade their telecommunication services in rural areas. Progress was achieved in computer-aided network planning, installation of pilot radio-relay systems and rural concentrator equipment and preparing master plans for telecommunication development. As part of a UNDP/ITU regional project on transit and transport for LDCs, ITU provided equipment to upgrade maritime communication services in Maldives.

Assistance to countries in the South Pacific was provided through a regional project, which aimed to provide reliable telecommunication services for the island countries in the area. Technical backstopping was also provided to a number of investment projects funded by the European Economic Community, two of which were completed, resulting in the commissioning of satellite earth stations in Kiribati and Papua New Guinea.

Activities in Europe, the Middle East and the Mediterranean Basin continued at the regional level, under the MEDARABTEL and European regional projects, and the GULFVISION project. The third phase of the MEDARABTEL project was extended for six months, until the end of 1986, with a new activity to co-ordinate network operation in the MEDARABTEL region. Main achievements included a microwave field survey carried out on the Sudanese part of the Egypt-Sudan microwave link and the convening of the Fourth Consultative Meeting on Submarine Cables. In 1985, two ARABSAT satellites were launched which covered the whole Arab world. The GULFVISION project provided assistance through a study on television/radio propagation in the Gulf area, the results of which would enable the countries of the region to make the best use of the allocated bands for television and sound/FM broadcasting services.

The main objective of the European regional project was to provide the economic sectors of the countries concerned with a more effective international telecommunications infrastructure through the introduction of new and appropriate technologies as well as modern tools and methods for management and operations. In Albania, assistance continued under a pilot project on telecommunications development. The contract for the Albanian portion of the Albania-Greece microwave link was signed by ITU at the end of 1985.

Training activities

Under the course development in telecommunications project in 1985, 172 people attended training development workshops, and more than 150 new courses were made available. By year's end, some 425 courses were available and some 450 projects were under development. Japan contributed to the project with a gift of 15 microcomputers and associated peripherals and software.

Publications

Publications issued by ITU in either trilingual or separate English, French and Spanish editions during 1985 included:

> *Report on the Activities of the Union, 1984*
> *Financial Operating Report for 1984*
> *Twenty-fourth Report by the International Telecommunication Union on Telecommunication and the Peaceful Uses of Outer Space*, Information Booklet No. 33
> *List of International Telephone Routes*, 25th ed., 1985
> *Table of International Telex Relations and Traffic*, 1985
> *Table of Rates for Telegrams*, 1985
> *Yearbook of Common Carrier Telecommunication Statistics*, 12th ed., 1985
> *List of Ship Stations*, 25th ed., 1985, and Supplement Nos. 1-3
> *List of Coast Stations*, vols. I and II, 10th ed., 1985
> *List of International Monitoring Stations (List VIII)*, 6th ed., 1985
> *Catalogue of Telecommunication Training Opportunities*, Issue No. 3, 1985
> *Directory of Training Centres*, Issue No. 3, 1985
> *CODEVTEL Course Catalogue*
> *Tentative High Frequency Broadcasting Schedules*, 1985
> *IFRB Handbook on Radio Regulatory Procedures*, parts I-VII
> *International Frequency List*, 11th ed., 1985
> *Joint IFRB/CCIR Booklet on National Frequency Management*
> *Sound Tape Recording, Television Tape Recording and Film Techniques for the International Exchange of Programmes*
> *CCIR Handbook on Satellite Communications*
> *CCITT Red Book*, VIIIth Plenary Assembly, Malaga-Torremolinos, 1984, vols. II-IV & VI-IX & Annex B
> *Primary Sources of Energy for the Power Supply of Remote Telecommunication Systems* (GAS 4)
> *World Plan Book* (Washington, 1985)
> *Instructions for the International Telephone Service*, 1985

Secretariat

As at 31 December 1985, the total staff of ITU numbered 742 officials (excluding staff on short-term contracts). Of these, nine were elected officials, 578 had permanent contracts and 155 had fixed-term contracts; 63 nationalities were represented in those posts subject to geographical distribution.

Budget

The following budget for 1985 was adopted by the Administrative Council in 1984:

	Amount (in Swiss francs)
Income	
Contribution by members and private operating agencies	95,958,000
Contribution by UNDP for technical co-operation administrative expenses	10,175,000
Sales of publications	13,665,000
Miscellaneous	335,000
Total	120,133,000
Expenditure	
Administrative Council	768,000
Common headquarters expenditure	79,496,000
Conferences and meetings	15,144,000
Miscellaneous	885,000
Total general expenses	96,293,000

	Amount (in Swiss francs)
Expenditure (cont.)	
Technical co-operation	10,175,000
Publications	13,665,000
Total	120,133,000

Each member of ITU chooses the class of contribution in which it wishes to be included and pays in advance its annual contributory share to the budget on the basis of the budgetary provision (see Annex I below).

As at the end of 1985, the total of units for members was 393. The contributory unit for 1985 was 221,400 Swiss francs; the unit for 1986 was to be 232,200 Swiss francs.

Annex I. MEMBERSHIP OF THE INTERNATIONAL TELECOMMUNICATION UNION AND CONTRIBUTIONS

(Membership as at 31 December 1985; contributions as assessed for 1986)

MEMBER	CONTRIBUTION Class of contribution; no. of units	In Swiss francs*	MEMBER	CONTRIBUTION Class of contribution; no. of units	In Swiss francs*	MEMBER	CONTRIBUTION Class of contribution; no. of units	In Swiss francs*
Afghanistan	0.125	29,025	El Salvador	0.250	58,050	Maldives	0.125	29,025
Albania	0.250	58,050	Equatorial Guinea	0.125	29,025	Mali	0.125	29,025
Algeria	1.000	232,200	Ethiopia	0.125	29,025	Malta	0.250	58,050
Angola	0.250	58,050	Fiji	0.250	58,050	Mauritania	0.250	58,050
Argentina	3.000	696,600	Finland	5.000	1,161,000	Mauritius	0.250	58,050
Australia	18.000	4,179,600	France	30.000	6,966,000	Mexico	1.000	232,200
Austria	1.000	232,200	Gabon	0.500	116,100	Monaco	0.250	58,050
Bahamas	0.500	116,100	Gambia	0.125	29,025	Mongolia	0.250	58,050
Bahrain	0.500	116,100	German Democratic Republic	3.000	696,600	Morocco	1.000	232,200
Bangladesh	0.125	29,025	Germany, Federal Republic of	30.000	6,966,000	Mozambique	0.250	58,050
Barbados	0.250	58,050				Namibia†	—	—
Belgium	5.000	1,161,000	Ghana	0.250	58,050	Nauru	0.125	29,025
Belize	0.125	29,025	Greece	1.000	232,200	Nepal	0.125	29,025
Benin	0.250	58,050	Grenada	0.125	29,025	Netherlands	10.000	2,322,000
Bolivia	0.250	58,050	Guatemala	0.250	58,050	New Zealand	2.000	464,400
Botswana	0.500	116,100	Guinea	0.125	29,025	Nicaragua	0.500	116,100
Brazil	3.000	696,600	Guinea-Bissau	0.125	29,025	Niger	0.125	29,025
Brunei Darussalam	0.500	116,100	Guyana	0.250	58,050	Nigeria	2.000	464,400
Bulgaria	1.000	232,200	Haiti	0.125	29,025	Norway	5.000	1,161,000
Burkina Faso	0.125	29,025	Honduras	0.250	58,050	Oman	0.500	116,100
Burma	0.500	116,100	Hungary	1.000	232,200	Pakistan	2.000	464,400
Burundi	0.125	29,025	Iceland	0.250	58,050	Panama	0.500	116,100
Byelorussian SSR	0.500	116,100	India	10.000	2,322,000	Papua New Guinea	0.500	116,100
Cameroon	0.500	116,100	Indonesia	1.000	232,200	Paraguay	0.500	116,100
Canada	18.000	4,179,600	Iran	1.000	232,200	Peru	0.250	58,050
Cape Verde	0.125	29,025	Iraq	0.250	58,050	Philippines	1.000	232,200
Central African Republic	0.125	29,025	Ireland	2.000	464,400	Poland	2.000	464,400
Chad	0.125	29,025	Israel	1.000	232,200	Portugal	1.000	232,200
Chile	1.000	232,200	Italy	10.000	2,322,000	Qatar	0.500	116,100
China	10.000	2,322,000	Ivory Coast	1.000	232,200	Republic of Korea	1.000	232,200
Colombia	1.000	232,200	Jamaica	0.250	58,050	Romania	0.500	116,100
Comoros	0.125	29,025	Japan	30.000	6,966,000	Rwanda	0.125	29,025
Congo	0.500	116,100	Jordan	0.500	116,100	Saint Vincent and the Grenadines	0.125	29,025
Costa Rica	0.250	58,050	Kenya	0.250	58,050	San Marino	0.250	58,050
Cuba	0.500	116,100	Kuwait	1.000	232,200	Sao Tome and Principe	0.125	29,025
Cyprus	0.250	58,050	Lao People's Democratic Republic	0.500	116,100	Saudi Arabia	10.000	2,322,000
Czechoslovakia	2.000	464,400	Lebanon	0.250	58,050	Senegal	1.000	232,200
Democratic Kampuchea	0.500	116,100	Lesotho	0.125	29,025	Sierra Leone	0.125	29,025
Democratic People's Republic of Korea	0.250	58,050	Liberia	0.250	58,050	Singapore	1.000	232,200
Democratic Yemen	0.125	29,025	Libyan Arab Jamahiriya	1.500	348,300	Somalia	0.125	29,025
Denmark	5.000	1,161,000	Liechtenstein	0.500	116,100	South Africa	1.000	232,200
Djibouti	0.125	29,025	Luxembourg	0.500	116,100	Spain	3.000	696,600
Dominican Republic	0.500	116,100	Madagascar	0.250	58,050	Sri Lanka	0.500	116,100
Ecuador	0.500	116,100	Malawi	0.125	29,025	Sudan	0.125	29,025
Egypt	1.000	232,200	Malaysia	3.000	696,600	Suriname	0.250	58,050
						Swaziland	0.250	58,050

MEMBER	CONTRIBUTION		MEMBER	CONTRIBUTION		MEMBER	CONTRIBUTION	
	Class of contribution; no. of units	In Swiss francs*		Class of contribution; no. of units	In Swiss francs*		Class of contribution; no. of units	In Swiss francs*
Sweden	10.000	2,322,000	Uganda	0.125	29,025	Vatican City State	0.250	58,050
Switzerland	10.000	2,322,000	Ukrainian SSR	1.000	232,200	Venezuela	2.000	464,400
Syrian Arab Republic	0.500	116,100	USSR	30.000	6,966,000	Viet Nam	0.500	116,100
Thailand	1.500	348,300	United Arab Emirates	1.000	232,200	Yemen	0.250	58,050
Togo	0.250	58,050	United Kingdom	30.000	6,966,000	Yugoslavia	1.000	232,200
Tonga	0.125	29,025	United Republic of			Zaire	0.500	116,100
Trinidad and Tobago	1.000	232,200	Tanzania	0.125	29,025	Zambia	0.250	58,050
Tunisia	1.000	232,200	United States	30.000	6,966,000	Zimbabwe	0.500	116,100
Turkey	1.000	232,200	Uruguay	0.500	116,100	Total	393.000	91,254,600

NOTE: The ITU nomenclature differs from that of the United Nations.

*For the equivalent amounts in United States dollars, the rate of exchange that was to be applicable on 1 January 1986 was Swiss francs 2.09 = $US 1.00.

†Exempt from payment until it accedes to independence.

Annex II.   OFFICERS AND OFFICES OF THE INTERNATIONAL TELECOMMUNICATION UNION

ADMINISTRATIVE COUNCIL, INTERNATIONAL FREQUENCY REGISTRATION BOARD AND PRINCIPAL OFFICERS

PRINCIPAL OFFICERS OF THE UNION
Secretary-General: Richard E. Butler.
Deputy Secretary-General: Jean Jipguep.

ITU ADMINISTRATIVE COUNCIL
Algeria, Argentina, Australia, Benin, Brazil, Cameroon, Canada, China, Colombia, Egypt, Ethiopia, France, German Democratic Republic *(Vice-Chairman)*, Germany, Federal Republic of, India, Indonesia, Italy, Japan, Kenya, Kuwait, Lebanon, Mexico, Morocco, Nigeria, Pakistan, Peru, Philippines *(Chairman)*, Romania, Saudi Arabia, Senegal, Spain, Sweden, Switzerland, Thailand, USSR, United Kingdom, United Republic of Tanzania, United States, Venezuela, Yugoslavia, Zambia.

INTERNATIONAL FREQUENCY REGISTRATION BOARD
Chairman: Gary C. Brooks (Canada).
Vice-Chairman: Vladimir V. Kozlov (USSR).
Members: William H. Bellchambers (United Kingdom), Abderrazak Berrada (Morocco), Yoshitaka Kurihara (Japan).

OFFICERS OF THE INTERNATIONAL CONSULTATIVE COMMITTEES
Director, International Radio Consultative Committee (CCIR): Richard C. Kirby (United States).
Director, International Telegraph and Telephone Consultative Committee (CCITT): Theodor Irmer (Federal Republic of Germany).

HEADQUARTERS

General Secretariat of the International Telecommunication Union
Place des Nations
1211 Geneva 20, Switzerland
Cable address: BURINTERNA GENEVA
Telephone: (22) 99 51 11
Telex: 421000 UIT CH
Telefax: (Groups 2 and 3) (22) 33 72 56

Chapter XIII

World Meteorological Organization (WMO)

The membership of the World Meteorological Organization (WMO) increased to 159, comprising 154 States and five Territories, when Solomon Islands was admitted on 5 June 1985.

During the year, WMO carried out its activities in accordance with the programmes and budget adopted in 1983 for the period 1984-1987 by its highest body, the World Meteorological Congress, which meets at least once every four years. The 36-member Executive Council meets annually to supervise the implementation of programmes and regulations.

Activities in 1985

World Weather Watch

The World Weather Watch (WWW), the basic programme of WMO, continued to provide in 1985 global observational data and processed information required by member States for operational and research purposes. Its essential elements were the Global Data-Processing System (GDPS), which provided for processing, storage and retrieval of data and made available processed information; the Global Observing System (GOS), which obtained observational data; and the Global Telecommunication System (GTS), which offered telecommunication facilities for rapid collection, exchange and distribution of observational data and processed information.

During 1985, the main activities of GOS continued under its two sub-systems, one surface-based and the other space-based, which were directed to improving the operations of GOS at the global, regional and national levels. The surface-based sub-system provided conventional basic data from observational networks of stations on land and sea, as well as aircraft meteorological observations. Within the space-based sub-system, meteorological satellites in both near-polar-orbiting and geostationary systems took direct observations. Those satellite systems made a major contribution to operations and research in meteorology, hydrology and other environmental activities by providing additional data on vertical profiles of temperature and humidity; temperature of sea, land and cloud-top surfaces; wind field derived from cloud displacement; cloud amounts; and snow and ice cover.

With regard to GDPS, a number of WWW data-processing centres installed new-generation electronic computers, improving their capability to analyse and forecast products to be exchanged globally and regionally. Those products were used to prepare routine weather forecasts as well as severe-weather warnings by various national meteorological services. GTS comprised more than 280 point-to-point circuits in addition to radio broadcasts and satellite dissemination systems. In 1985, progress was achieved in its operation by the introduction of medium-speed transmission techniques and by upgrading a number of radio circuits to satellite/cable circuits.

Ocean affairs

Marine meteorology continued to receive close attention in 1985, as the demand for marine meteorological information increased. The Commission for Marine Meteorology took action on a number of issues, including ways of improving data coverage of the world's oceans, using the latest advances in marine telecommunications, satellite systems and automation techniques, and maintenance of high standards of marine meteorological services. The Commission continued work on implementation of the WMO Wave Programme, development of a guide to applications of marine climatology, training seminars on marine meteorological services for developing countries, development of a digital sea-ice data bank, and preparation of the Marine Meteorology Programme, part of the Second WMO Long-Term Plan. Operational oceanographic data exchanged through GTS were extensively used for both operational and research purposes, such as climate studies.

Aviation

In June, the Executive Council expressed strong support for an expanded Aviation Meteorology Programme and took measures to strengthen its activities. A revision of the WMO Technical Regulations, where they applied to services for aviation, was undertaken in view of their importance for implementing the World Area Forecast System. A number of activities were further developed within the WMO Aeronautical Meteorology Programme to help member States establish and operate aeronautical meteorological services required to ensure safety, efficiency and economy of air navigation.

Tropical Cyclone Programme

Efforts begun in 1980 to strengthen the WMO Tropical Cyclone Programme continued with work on a number of projects for transfer of technology and provision of advice to countries on improving their protective systems. At the regional level, progress was made in five tropical cyclone basins on improving or formulating tropical cyclone operational plans. Those plans provided for effective forecasting and warning systems through regional co-ordination and co-operation, including clearly defined sharing of responsibilities for the various components. Substantial progress was made in improving those warning systems and related community preparedness measures, such as the application of information from meteorological satellites, the establishment of flood forecasting systems and the training of personnel.

World Climate Programme

The World Climate Programme, established in 1979, continued to aid nations in applying climate information to human activities, to improve the knowledge of climate processes and to warn nations of man-made changes that might affect the well-being of humanity. To meet those objectives, the responsibilities were divided among four components: the World Climate Applications Programme (WCAP), the World Climate Data Programme (WCDP), the World Climate Impact Studies Programme (WCIP) and the World Climate Research Programme (WCRP).

Within WCAP, attention continued to be given to the priority areas of food, water and energy, along with work in urban climate and human health. As in previous years, the main effort in agrometeorology was directed towards assistance to agrometeorological services in developing countries to strengthen their capability to provide comprehensive services to agriculture. To this end, short- and medium-term agrometeorological missions of experts were provided to developing countries. The WMO Commission for Climatology, meeting in December 1985, allocated to its working groups and rapporteurs the responsibility for data management, statistical methods in the application of climatological data, energy, urban and building climatology, air pollution, human biometeorology, tourism and recreation, transport and economic planning, climatological maps and aspects of education and training.

The primary objective of WCDP was to ensure the timely availability of reliable climate data, in an acceptable format, to support climate application impact studies and research.

Activities under WCIP were carried out by the United Nations Environment Programme (UNEP), in co-operation with WMO, on reducing the vulnerability of food systems to climate, assessing the impact of man-induced climatic changes and improving the methodology for climate impact studies.

In October 1985, WMO, UNEP and the International Council of Scientific Unions (ICSU) sponsored an International Conference on the Assessment of the Role of Carbon Dioxide and of Other Greenhouse Gases in Climate Variations and Associated Impacts. The Conference concluded that the increase in "greenhouse" gases would probably produce global temperature increases during the first half of the next century. An International Scientific Advisory Group on Greenhouse Gases was set up to maintain a continuous assessment.

WCRP was conducted jointly by WMO and ICSU to determine the extent to which climate could be predicted and the extent of man's influence on climate. Research initially focused on three areas: the physical basis and feasibility of predicting short-term climate anomalies (on a time scale of one to three months); interannual variability, particularly resulting from interaction with the tropical oceans (on a time scale of a few years); and long-term climate and climate trends (on a time scale of 10 to 100 years).

Research and development

The WMO Research and Development Programme involved research activities on the possibilities of predicting environmental conditions important to the well-being of humanity. The activities included weather prediction research and tropical meteorology. The responsibility for promoting and co-ordinating such activities lay with the WMO Commission for Atmospheric Sciences (CAS). The second session of the CAS Working Group on Short- and Medium-range Weather prediction Research (Belgrade, Yugoslavia, August) examined the work done so far and the future strategy for implementing such research. Special efforts were made to ensure the transfer of methodology and experience in weather prediction to all WMO members in an effective and economic way. As requested by the Executive Council, a thorough review of all aspects of the annual progress reports on numerical weather Prediction was undertaken. The report for 1984, the twelfth in a series, was compiled and distributed.

In tropical meteorology, continued efforts were made to implement the components of the WMO Tropical Meteorology Programme. The CAS Working Group on Tropical Meteorology reviewed the status of 12 specific priority projects within the programme and gave guidance on further implementation, including the organization of workshops. Under the tropical cyclone component, an International Workshop on Tropical Cyclones

(Bangkok, Thailand, 25 November–5 December), with 80 specialists, researchers and forecasters, examined forecasting and research trends of tropical cyclones. Under the monsoon component, the WMO/CAS Project on Long-term Asian Summer Monsoon Studies continued to be implemented, with activity centres in the India Meteorological Department (New Delhi) and the Malaysian Meteorological Service (Kuala Lumpur) functioning during 1985. Both centres intensified research on numerical modelling of the monsoon. The New Delhi centre hosted the first WMO Regional Workshop on the Asian Summer Monsoon (4-8 November).

Progress was also made on other long-term projects: a multi-level numerical model for the tropics (India and Japan serving as activity centres); radiation flux studies in the tropics with pilot studies conducted in Australia and India; and moisture budget studies and their agricultural application, with the activity centre at Niamey, Niger.

In the environment field, WMO activities focused on the Environmental Pollution Monitoring and Research Programme. Under its Background Air Pollution Monitoring Network (BAPMoN), a total of 95 countries were operating and/or preparing 17 baselines, 22 continental stations and 172 regional stations. Collaboration continued with the International Atomic Energy Agency (IAEA) laboratories in Monaco and Vienna and with WMO data centres in Czechoslovakia and the United States. WMO co-sponsored a Symposium on Integrated Global Monitoring of the State of the Biosphere, held at Tashkent, USSR, at which assessing and forecasting the state of all environmental compartments of the biosphere were discussed. The WMO-led Working Group on the Interchange of Pollutants between the Atmosphere and the Oceans of the Group of Experts on the Scientific Aspects of Marine Pollution reported on the transport and deposit of contaminants (mainly heavy metals) into the Mediterranean, with recommendations for monitoring and transport modelling within a pilot project to start in 1986 under the Long-term Programme for Pollution Monitoring and Research in the Mediterranean.

The major effort within WMO on atmospheric ozone resided in its Global Ozone Research and Monitoring Project. The project aimed at improving the world-wide ground-based data collecting network for ozone (the Global Ozone Observing System), studying the distribution and changes of non-CO_2 "greenhouse" gases and participating in the ongoing efforts to assess ozone change. Atmospheric CO_2 was monitored by WMO under a separate programme. WMO co-ordinated, organized or otherwise participated in international assessments of the state of the ozone layer in co-operation with other international and national agencies.

The main objectives of the WMO Cloud Physics and Weather Modification Programme were to promote sound scientific foundations for weather modification based on cloud physics and other investigations, and to provide the rationale underlying all aspects of weather modification. WMO continued to provide advice on weather modification to member States and to other international organizations.

Hydrology and water resources development

The Hydrology and Water Resources Programme promoted world-wide co-operation in the evaluation of water resources and assisted in their development through the co-ordination of hydrological networks and services, including data collection and processing, forecasting and warnings, and supply of meteorological and hydrological data for design purposes. The three components of the programme were: the Operational Hydrology Programme; applications and services to water resources; and co-operation with water-related programmes of other international organizations.

The Operational Hydrology Programme, which provided the framework for all scientific and technical aspects of the activities in hydrology, comprised: the measurement of basic hydrological elements from networks of stations, and the collection, transmission, storage, retrieval and publication of basic hydrological data; hydrological forecasting; and improvement of relevant techniques in network design, standardization of instruments and methods of observation, data transmission and processing, supply of meteorological data for design purposes and hydrological forecasting. The emphasis of the programme fell on its Hydrological Operational Multipurpose Subprogramme, the aims of which were to provide an international and systematic framework of the integration of techniques and procedures for collecting and processing hydrological data. A large part of the activities in hydrology and water resources was carried out through the Commission for Hydrology, which meets quadrennially (it last met at Geneva, August/September 1984), operating through working groups of experts. For implementation of the Programme during the period 1984-1987, it established three working groups composed of 18 rapporteurs and appointed 10 individual rapporteurs.

A programme on applications and services to water resources included technical support for water-related activities such as the Tropical Cyclone Programme and the World Climate Programme. The hydrological activities under the former programme focused on completion of the hydrological component of the Typhoon Operational Experiment. Under the World Climate Programme, studies continued with respect to climate variability and its impact on water-resource systems.

Education and training

Progress in the Education and Training Programme was maintained throughout the year. The main activities were the awarding of fellowships; the strengthening of regional meteorological training centres; the organization and co-sponsorship of courses, seminars and workshops; the preparation of training publications and other training aids; surveys of training needs; provision of advice and information on education and training; and collaboration with other organizations.

More than 780 participants, mainly from developing countries, benefited from training events organized by WMO. Under fellowship funds from various sources administered by WMO in 1985, a total of 536 fellows were being trained; of that number, 312 completed training and 224 would continue in 1986. Eighteen training events were organized during 1985 in regional or national training institutions of 16 member countries. The topics covered different areas of meteorology and operational hydrology and were tailored to meet the express needs of countries. In addition, WMO co-sponsored or jointly supported 17 training events in 1985 along with other organizations and agencies within and outside the United Nations system, universities and education and training institutions in member countries.

Technical co-operation

The Technical Co-operation Programme continued to form one of the major activities in 1985. Assistance was provided through the United Nations Development Programme (UNDP), the Voluntary Co-operation Programme (VCP), funds-in-trust arrangements and the regular WMO budget. Under UNDP, assistance was provided in 1985 to 89 countries at a value of $13.5 million, compared to $11.8 million for 1984. Developing countries received aid to develop their meteorological and hydrological services and to train personnel at all levels, by means of experts or fellowships for training abroad and support for training seminars. Advice was given in fields ranging from specialized subjects, such as the interpretation and utilization of satellite data, to general advice on the establishment, organization and operation of national meteorological and hydrological services. With water resources of vital importance to developing countries, assistance in that field was also provided. In 1985, under UNDP sectoral support in meteorology and operational hydrology, missions to 14 countries were undertaken at the request of UNDP resident representatives or government authorities to provide advice on the requirements for and application of meteorological information in various sectors of the national economy.

VCP was maintained by voluntary contributions of members, either in the form of equipment and services or cash. Support in 1985 was given mainly to the Global Observing System element of WWW, and for establishing or updating automatic picture transmission/weather facsimile and upper-air stations. Many long-term fellowships for training of meteorological personnel were also awarded. The total value of the aid provided under VCP for 1985 was approximately $6.5 million.

Under the regular budget of WMO, 38 fellowships were awarded in 1985, and financial support was also provided for participants in special training courses, technical conferences and study tours. Seven trust fund projects were being implemented in 1985; four were funded by the countries receiving the assistance and three by other countries. Thirteen United Nations Volunteers served in WMO-executed projects during the year. One of the pressing problems of the meteorological and hydrological services of developing countries was the need for qualified personnel. Under the Technical Co-operation Programme, 536 fellows received meteorological or hydrological training—211 under UNDP, 207 under VCP, 85 under the regular budget and 33 under trust funds.

Secretariat

As at 31 December 1985, the total number of full-time staff employed by WMO (excluding 52 professionals on technical assistance projects) on permanent and fixed-term contracts stood at 295. Of these, 137 were in the Professional and higher categories (drawn from 49 nationalities) and 158 in the General Service and related categories.

Budget

The year 1985 was the second year of the ninth financial period (1984-1987), for which the Ninth (1983) WMO Congress established a maximum expenditure of $77.5 million. It had authorized additional expenditures for increases in salaries and allowances consequent upon similar increases approved by the United Nations. Also, additional expenditures of no more than $500,000 were authorized, to provide for circumstances such as losses from changes in currency exchange rates and to meet unforeseen programme activities of an urgent character.

The regular budget for 1985 amounted to $19,480,000. The 1985 budget for technical co-operation activities, financed from overhead allocations and other extrabudgetary sources, amounted to an additional $2,339,400.

At its June 1985 session, the Executive Council approved a regular budget of $18,028,000 for 1986. To that amount, supplementary estimates of $5,641,500 were added later in the year.

Annex I.   MEMBERSHIP OF THE WORLD
            METEOROLOGICAL ORGANIZATION AND CONTRIBUTIONS
            (Membership as at 31 December 1985; contributions as assessed for 1986)

	CONTRIBUTION			CONTRIBUTION			CONTRIBUTION	
MEMBER	Percent-age	Net amount (in US dollars)	*MEMBER*	Percent-age	Net amount (in US dollars)	*MEMBER*	Percent-age	Net amount (in US dollars)
Afghanistan	0.03	4,728	German Democratic			Panama	0.07	11,032
Albania	0.03	4,728	Republic	1.38	217,488	Papua New Guinea	0.03	4,728
Algeria	0.10	15,760	Germany, Federal			Paraguay	0.03	4,728
Angola	0.06	9,456	Republic of	6.25	985,000	Peru	0.23	36,248
Argentina	1.10	173,360	Ghana	0.09	14,184	Philippines	0.29	45,704
Australia	1.70	267,920	Greece	0.32	50,432	Poland	1.08	170,208
Austria	0.64	100,864	Guatemala	0.07	11,032	Portugal	0.24	37,824
Bahamas	0.03	4,728	Guinea	0.03	4,728	Qatar	0.07	11,032
Bahrain	0.03	4,728	Guinea-Bissau	0.03	4,728	Republic of Korea	0.18	28,368
Bangladesh	0.04	6,304	Guyana	0.03	4,728	Romania	0.33	52,008
Barbados	0.03	4,728	Haiti	0.03	4,728	Rwanda	0.03	4,728
Belgium	1.26	198,576	Honduras	0.03	4,728	Saint Lucia	0.03	4,728
Belize	0.03	4,728	Hungary	0.42	66,192	Sao Tome and Principe	0.03	4,728
Benin	0.03	4,728	Iceland	0.07	11,032	Saudi Arabia	0.42	66,192
Bolivia	0.08	12,608	India	1.27	200,152	Senegal	0.03	4,728
Botswana	0.03	4,728	Indonesia	0.45	70,920	Seychelles	0.03	4,728
Brazil	1.36	214,133	Iran	0.47	74,072	Sierra Leone	0.03	4,728
Brunei	0.03	4,728	Iraq	0.10	15,760	Singapore	0.09	14,184
Bulgaria	0.29	45,704	Ireland	0.24	37,824	Solomon Islands*	—	—
Burkina Faso	0.03	4,728	Israel	0.25	39,400	Somalia	0.03	4,728
Burma	0.07	11,032	Italy	2.80	441,280	South Africa†	0.66	104,016
Burundi	0.03	4,728	Ivory Coast	0.07	11,032	Spain	1.49	234,824
Byelorussian SSR	0.45	70,920	Jamaica	0.07	11,032	Sri Lanka	0.08	12,608
Cameroon	0.03	4,728	Japan	5.41	852,616	Sudan	0.07	11,032
Canada	2.80	441,280	Jordan	0.03	4,728	Suriname	0.03	4,728
Cape Verde	0.03	4,728	Kenya	0.03	4,728	Swaziland	0.03	4,728
Central African Republic	0.03	4,728	Kuwait	0.18	28,368	Sweden	1.36	214,336
Chad	0.03	4,728	Lao People's Democratic			Switzerland	1.14	179,664
Chile	0.25	39,400	Republic	0.03	4,728	Syrian Arab Republic	0.12	18,912
China	2.75	433,400	Lebanon	0.07	11,032	Thailand	0.23	36,248
Colombia	0.24	37,824	Lesotho	0.03	4,728	Togo	0.03	4,728
Comoros	0.03	4,728	Liberia	0.03	4,728	Trinidad and Tobago	0.07	11,032
Congo	0.03	4,728	Libyan Arab Jamahiriya	0.16	25,216	Tunisia	0.07	11,032
Costa Rica	0.07	11,032	Luxembourg	0.09	14,184	Turkey	0.45	70,920
Cuba	0.07	31,520	Madagascar	0.03	4,728	Uganda	0.03	4,728
Cyprus	0.03	4,728	Malawi	0.03	4,728	Ukrainian SSR	1.50	236,400
Czechoslovakia	0.88	138,688	Malaysia	0.26	40,976	USSR	10.42	1,642,192
Democratic Kampuchea	0.03	4,728	Maldives	0.03	4,728	United Kingdom	5.32	838,432
Democratic People's			Mali	0.03	4,728	United Republic of Tanzania	0.03	4,728
Republic of Korea	0.07	11,032	Malta	0.03	4,728	United States	24.71	3,894,296
Democratic Yemen	0.03	4,728	Mauritania	0.03	4,728	Uruguay	0.19	29,944
Denmark	0.73	115,048	Mauritius	0.03	4,728	Vanuatu	0.03	4,728
Djibouti	0.03	4,728	Mexico	0.86	135,536	Venezuela	0.54	85,104
Dominica	0.03	4,728	Mongolia	0.03	4,728	Viet Nam	0.07	11,032
Dominican Republic	0.07	11,032	Morocco	0.13	20,488	Yemen	0.03	4,728
Ecuador	0.07	11,032	Mozambique	0.06	9,456	Yugoslavia	0.51	80,376
Egypt	0.30	47,280	Nepal	0.03	4,728	Zaire	0.07	11,032
El Salvador	0.03	4,728	Netherlands	1.36	214,336	Zambia	0.06	9,456
Ethiopia	0.03	4,728	New Zealand	0.44	69,344	Zimbabwe	0.03	4,728
Fiji	0.03	4,728	Nicaragua	0.03	4,728			
Finland	0.51	80,376	Niger	0.03	4,728	British Caribbean Territories	0.03	4,728
France	5.34	841,584	Nigeria	0.24	37,824	French Polynesia	0.03	4,728
Gabon	0.04	6,304	Norway	0.59	92,984	Hong Kong	0.03	4,728
Gambia	0.03	4,728	Oman	0.03	4,728	Netherlands Antilles	0.03	4,728
			Pakistan	0.16	25,216	New Caledonia	0.03	4,728
						Total	100.0	15,764,525

*Became a member on 5 June 1985.

†Suspended by the Seventh (1975) WMO Congress from exercising the rights and privileges of a member.

Annex II.   OFFICERS AND OFFICE OF THE WORLD METEOROLOGICAL ORGANIZATION

MEMBERS OF THE WMO EXECUTIVE COUNCIL

President: R. L. Kintanar (Philippines).
First Vice-President: Ju. A. Izrael (USSR).
Second Vice-President: Zou Jingmeng (China).
Third Vice-President: J. P. Bruce (Canada).

Members (one seat vacant): S. P. Adhikary (Nepal), L.-K. Ahialegbedzi (Togo), S. Alaimo (Argentina), M. A. Badran (Egypt), A. Bensari (Morocco), C. E. Berridge* (British Caribbean Territories), M. Boulama (acting) (Niger), C. M. Contreras Viñals (acting) (Spain), S. K. Das (India), Workineh Degefu* (Ethiopia),

MEMBERS OF THE WMO EXECUTIVE COUNCIL (cont.)

J. Djigbenou (Ivory Coast), H. Gonzales Pacheco (acting) (Peru), J. González Montoto (Cuba), C. A. Grezzi* (Uruguay), R. E. Hallgren (United States), J. T. Houghton (acting) (United Kingdom), E. J. Jatila (Finland), S. A. A. Kazmi* (Pakistan), J. P. N. Labrousse (France), U. B. Lifiga (acting) (United Republic of Tanzania), G. Mankedi (Congo), L. A. Mendes Victor* (Portugal), A. D. Moura (Brazil), A. Nania (Italy), H. Reiser (acting) (Federal Republic of Germany), V. Richter (Czechoslovakia), R. M. Romaih (Saudi Arabia), V. A. Simango (Zambia), E. Uchida (acting) (Japan), Ho Tong Yuen* (Malaysia), J. W. Zillman (Australia).

NOTE: The Executive Council is composed of four elected officers, the six Presidents of the regional associations (indicated by an asterisk), who are *ex-officio* members, and 26 elected members. Members serve in their personal capacities, not as representatives of Governments.

SENIOR MEMBERS OF THE WMO SECRETARIAT

Secretary-General: G. O. P. Obasi.
Deputy Secretary-General: D. K. Smith.
Director, Assistant to the Secretary-General: R. Czelnai.
Director, World Weather Watch Department: G. K. Weiss.
Director, Research and Development Programmes Department: A. Zaitsev.
Director, Hydrology and Water Resources Department: J. Nemec.
Director, Technical Co-operation Department: G. Gosset.
Director, Education and Training Department: M. J. Connaughton.
Director, Administration Department: J. K. Murithi.

Director, Languages, Publications and Conferences Department: A. W. Kabakibo.
Director, World Climate Programme Department: T. D. Potter.
Director, World Climate Research Programme: P. Morel.
Regional Director for Africa: S. Chacowry.
Regional Director the Americas: G. Lizano Vindas.
Regional Director for Asia and the South-West Pacific: K. Rajendram.
Special Assistant to the Secretary-General: A. K. Elamly.
Executive Assistant to the Secretary-General: J. B. L. Breslin.

PRESIDENTS OF REGIONAL ASSOCIATIONS AND TECHNICAL COMMISSIONS

REGIONAL ASSOCIATIONS

I. Africa: Workineh Degefu (Ethiopia).
II. Asia: S. A. A. Kazmi (Pakistan).
III. South America: C. A. Grezzi (Uruguay).

IV. North and Central America: C. E. Berridge (British Caribbean Territories).
V. South-West Pacific: Ho Tong Yuen (Malaysia).
VI. Europe: L. A. Mendes Victor (acting) (Portugal).

TECHNICAL COMMISSIONS

Aeronautical Meteorology: J. Kastelein (Netherlands).
Agricultural Meteorology: A. Kassar (Tunisia).
Atmospheric Sciences: F. Mesinger (Yugoslavia).
Basic Systems: J. R. Neilon (United States).

Climatology: J. L. Rasmussen (United States).
Hydrology: O. Starosolszky (Hungary).
Instruments and Methods of Observation: S. Huovila (Finland).
Marine Meteorology: F. G#rard (France).

HEADQUARTERS

World Meteorological Organization
41, Avenue Giuseppe-Motta
Case postale No. 5
1211 Geneva 20, Switzerland
Cable address: METEOMOND GENEVA
Telephone: 7 30 8111
Telex: 23260

Chapter XIV

International Maritime Organization (IMO)

In 1985, the International Maritime Organization (IMO) held the fourteenth regular session of its biennial Assembly from 11 to 21 November at its headquarters in London. The Assembly re-elected Chandrika Prasad Srivastava as IMO Secretary-General for a fourth consecutive four-year term, beginning on 1 January 1986. The 28 resolutions adopted by the Assembly aimed at preventing marine pollution and improving maritime safety, and included one calling for better security in port and on board ships. The Assembly also adopted the budget and work programme of IMO for 1986-1987 and approved the long-term work plan of the organization up to 1992. It also established a technical co-operation fund of $1.2 million, the interest to be used for IMO's technical co-operation activities.

Membership of IMO as at 31 December 1985 remained at 127 and one associate member.

Activities in 1985

At its June session, the IMO Council, the organization's governing body between Assembly sessions, chose Shen Zhaoqi (China) as the winner of the International Maritime Prize for 1984. The Prize is awarded annually to the individual or organization judged to have made the most significant contribution to IMO's work and objectives.

The theme for World Maritime Day, which was celebrated at IMO headquarters on 26 September, was "Maritime search and rescue".

World Maritime University

Members of the inaugural class of the World Maritime University—68 students from 39 countries—graduated from their two-year course on 9 July 1985. The University was established under the auspices of IMO in 1983 at Malmö, Sweden, to provide advanced training for senior personnel, mainly from developing countries, involved in maritime administration, technical management of shipping companies and maritime education. On 10 December, the second class—70 students from 48 countries—also graduated from the University.

On 7 October, the Dalian Marine College in China became the first official branch of the University. It was envisaged that other colleges around the world would also be recognized as branches and would offer specialized short-term courses developed and operated under the University's guidance.

Search and rescue

The International Convention on Maritime Search and Rescue (SAR), 1979, entered into force on 22 June 1985. The Convention facilitates co-operation between Governments and between those participating in SAR operations at sea by establishing an international SAR plan.

Prevention of pollution

Meeting at IMO headquarters (23-27 September), the contracting parties to the Convention on the Prevention of Marine Pollution by Dumping of Wastes and Other Matter (London Dumping Convention) adopted a resolution on environmental hazards caused by disposal at sea of persistent plastics and other synthetic materials. Another resolution called for suspension of all dumping at sea of low-level radioactive wastes to permit time for further consideration of issues which would provide a broader basis for an informed judgement of proposals to amend the Convention's annexes.

Amendments to annex II of the International Convention for the Prevention of Pollution from Ships, 1973, as modified by the 1978 Protocol (MARPOL 73/78), were adopted by the Marine Environment Protection Committee in December 1985. The amendments, dealing with noxious liquid substances carried in bulk, took into account technological changes made since 1973 and made the annex's implementation easier and more effective. It was agreed that the amendments were to enter into force on 7 April 1987 under MARPOL's "tacit acceptance" procedure and that the implementation of the annex would be deferred from 2 October 1986 (three years after MARPOL's entry into force) to 7 April 1987.

Amendments to the International Bulk Chemical Code and the Bulk Chemical Code were also adopted by the Committee in December 1985. The amendments, extending coverage of the two Codes to pollution as well as safety aspects, were to enter into force on 7 April 1987.

Liability for maritime claims

The conditions for entry into force of the Convention on Limitation of Liability for Maritime

Claims, 1976, were fulfilled on 1 November 1985. The Convention, raising the amount of compensation available for loss of life, personal injury or property damage (including damage to other ships or harbour works), was to enter into force on 1 December 1986.

Publications

Among publications issued by IMO during 1985 were: *Medical First Aid Guide*; the 1984 amendments to MARPOL 73/78;[a] *Code of Safe Practice for Diving Systems; IMO/ILO Guidelines for Packing Cargo in Freight Containers or Vehicles; Proceedings of the IMO/UNDP International Seminar on Reception Facilities for Wastes; Testing and Evaluation of Life-Saving Appliances*; and *Fire Test Procedures*.

Secretariat

As at 31 December 1985, the IMO secretariat employed 251 full-time staff members (excluding those on technical assistance projects). Of these, 87 were in the Professional and higher categories and 164 were in the General Service and related categories. There were 27 Professional and 10 General Service staff employed on technical assistance projects.

Budget

In November 1985, the IMO Assembly adopted a budget of $30,059,000 for the 1986-1987 biennium, with $14,480,000 allocated to 1986 and $15,579,000 to 1987.

[a]YUN 1984, p. 1275.

Annex I. MEMBERSHIP OF THE INTERNATIONAL MARITIME ORGANIZATION AND CONTRIBUTIONS

(Membership as at 31 December 1985; contributions as assessed for 1985)

MEMBER	CONTRIBUTION Percentage of total	Net amount (in US dollars)	MEMBER	CONTRIBUTION Percentage of total	Net amount (in US dollars)	MEMBER	CONTRIBUTION Percentage of total	Net amount (in US dollars)
Algeria	0.36	36,384	Ghana	0.07	6,698	Philippines	0.82	83,111
Angola	0.05	4,687	Greece	7.90	800,804	Poland	0.82	82,807
Argentina	0.63	63,724	Guatemala	0.02	2,176	Portugal	0.40	40,879
Australia	0.62	63,178	Guinea	0.02	2,176	Qatar	0.10	10,017
Austria	0.12	11,938	Guinea-Bissau	0.02	2,176	Republic of Korea	1.56	158,316
Bahamas	0.74	74,586	Guyana	0.02	2,176	Romania	0.65	65,631
Bahrain	0.02	2,176	Haiti	0.02	2,176	Saint Lucia	0.02	2,176
Bangladesh	0.11	10,785	Honduras	0.09	8,753	Saint Vincent and		
Barbados	0.02	2,176	Hungary	0.07	7,206	the Grenadines	0.05	4,778
Belgium	0.68	68,463	Iceland	0.06	6,539	Saudi Arabia	0.95	96,268
Benin	0.02	2,176	India	1.52	153,903	Senegal	0.02	2,176
Brazil	1.41	143,330	Indonesia	0.47	47,338	Seychelles	0.02	2,176
Brunei Darussalam	0.02	2,176	Iran	0.56	56,587	Sierra Leone	0.02	2,176
Bulgaria	0.34	34,374	Iraq	0.29	29,654	Singapore	1.51	152,467
Burma	0.05	4,936	Ireland	0.10	10,390	Somalia	0.02	2,176
Cameroon	0.04	4,168	Israel	0.18	18,114	Spain	1.70	172,305
Canada	0.99	100,337	Italy	2.26	229,270	Sri Lanka	0.19	19,345
Cape Verde	0.02	2,176	Ivory Coast	0.06	5,726	Sudan	0.05	4,665
Chile	0.16	16,081	Jamaica	0.02	2,176	Suriname	0.02	2,176
China	2.16	219,058	Japan	9.70	982,855	Sweden	0.92	93,599
Colombia	0.14	13,845	Jordan	0.02	2,176	Switzerland	0.21	21,307
Congo	0.02	2,176	Kenya	0.02	2,176	Syrian Arab Republic	0.04	3,762
Costa Rica	0.02	2,176	Kuwait	0.62	63,011	Thailand	0.17	17,075
Cuba	0.27	27,057	Lebanon	0.13	12,840	Togo	0.02	2,176
Cyprus	1.52	154,443	Liberia	13.85	1,403,282	Trinidad and Tobago	0.02	2,176
Czechoslovakia	0.13	13,180	Libyan Arab Jamahiriya	0.28	28,334	Tunisia	0.09	8,753
Democratic Kampuchea	0.02	2,176	Madagascar	0.04	4,258	Turkey	0.79	79,600
Democratic Yemen	0.02	2,176	Malaysia	0.42	42,979	USSR	6.16	624,534
Denmark	1.25	126,711	Maldives	0.06	5,591	United Arab Emirates	0.22	22,698
Djibouti	0.02	2,176	Malta	0.33	33,347	United Kingdom	3.76	380,946
Dominica	0.02	2,176	Mauritania	0.02	2,176	United Republic of		
Dominican Republic	0.02	2,176	Mauritius	0.02	2,176	Tanzania	0.04	3,829
Ecuador	0.12	11,802	Mexico	0.42	42,653	United States	5.01	507,096
Egypt	0.23	22,992	Morocco	0.12	12,298	Uruguay	0.07	6,788
El Salvador	0.02	2,176	Mozambique	0.02	2,176	Venezuela	0.31	31,677
Equatorial Guinea	0.02	2,176	Nepal	0.02	2,176	Viet Nam	0.09	8,798
Ethiopia	0.02	2,176	Netherlands	1.16	117,674	Yemen	0.02	2,176
Fiji	0.02	2,176	New Zealand	0.15	15,461	Yugoslavia	0.69	69,596
Finland	0.57	57,987	Nicaragua	0.02	2,176	Zaire	0.04	4,416
France	2.36	238,965	Nigeria	0.15	15,381			
Gabon	0.05	4,687	Norway	4.03	407,930			
Gambia	0.02	2,176	Oman	0.02	2,176	*Associate Member*		
German Democratic			Pakistan	0.17	16,849			
Republic	0.46	46,218	Panama	8.33	843,623	Hong Kong	0.65	65,998
Germany, Federal			Papua New Guinea	0.02	2,176			
Republic of	1.76	177,919	Peru	0.23	23,195	Total*	100.02	10,134,655

*Includes assessment for Brunei Darussalam which became a member after current rates were established.

Annex II.   OFFICERS AND OFFICES OF THE INTERNATIONAL MARITIME ORGANIZATION
(As at 31 December 1985)

IMO COUNCIL AND MARITIME SAFETY COMMITTEE

IMO COUNCIL
Chairman: W. A. O'Neill (Canada).
Members: Algeria, Argentina, Bangladesh, Brazil, Bulgaria, Canada, Chile, China, Cuba, Egypt, France, Gabon, Germany, Federal Republic of, Ghana, Greece, India, Indonesia, Italy, Japan, Kuwait, Lebanon, Liberia, Morocco, Netherlands, Nigeria, Norway, Saudi Arabia, Spain, Trinidad and Tobago, USSR, United Kingdom, United States.

MARITIME SAFETY COMMITTEE
Chairman: E. Jansen (Norway).

Membership in the Maritime Safety Committee is open to all IMO member States.

OFFICERS AND OFFICES

PRINCIPAL OFFICERS OF IMO SECRETARIAT
Secretary-General: Chandrika Prasad Srivastava.
Assistant Secretary-General: T. A. Mensah.
Secretary, Maritime Safety Committee: Y. Sasamura.

HEADQUARTERS
International Maritime Organization
4 Albert Embankment
London SE1 7SR, England
    Cable address: INTERMAR LONDON, SE1
    Telephone: (01) 735-7611
    Telex: 23588

Chapter XV

World Intellectual Property Organization (WIPO)

During 1985, membership of the World Intellectual Property Organization (WIPO) increased to 112 with the admission of Angola (15 April), Nicaragua (5 May) and Bangladesh (11 May). The number of States party to the Paris Convention for the Protection of Industrial Property rose to 97 with the admission of Mongolia. The number of States party to the Berne Convention for the Protection of Literary and Artistic Works remained at 76. Barbados became party to the Nice Agreement concerning the International Classification of Goods and Services for the Purposes of the Registration of Marks, raising membership of the Nice Union to 33. Barbados and Italy deposited their instruments of accession to the Patent Co-operation Treaty (PCT), bringing PCT Union membership to 39. At the end of the year, total membership in WIPO and its various Unions, taken together, was 127.

Seventeen intergovernmental Unions in the two main fields of intellectual property were administered by WIPO in 1985. They were founded on the multilateral treaties, conventions and agreements listed below in order of adoption:

Industrial property: Paris Convention for the Protection of Industrial Property; Madrid Agreement for the Repression of False or Deceptive Indications of Source on Goods; Madrid Agreement concerning the International Registration of Marks; The Hague Agreement concerning the International Deposit of Industrial Designs; Nice Agreement concerning the International Classification of Goods and Services for the Purposes of the Registration of Marks; Lisbon Agreement for the Protection of Appellations of Origin and Their International Registration; Locarno Agreement establishing an International Classification for Industrial Designs; Patent Co-operation Treaty; Strasbourg Agreement concerning the International Patent Classification (IPC); Trademark Registration Treaty; Vienna Agreement establishing an International Classification of the Figurative Elements of Marks; Budapest Treaty on the International Recognition of the Deposit of Microorganisms for the Purposes of Patent Procedure; Nairobi Treaty on the Protection of the Olympic Symbol.

Copyright and neighbouring rights: Berne Convention for the Protection of Literary and Artistic Works; Rome Convention for the Protection of Performers, Producers of Phonograms and Broadcasting Organizations; Geneva Convention for the Protection of Producers of Phonograms against Unauthorized Duplication of Their Phonograms; Brussels Convention relating to the Distribution of Programme-Carrying Signals Transmitted by Satellite.

At the sixteenth series of meetings, held at Geneva in September/October 1985, the governing bodies of WIPO and the Unions administered by it approved reports on activities and the programme and budget for 1986-1987.

The WIPO General Assembly unanimously appointed Arpad Bogsch as the Director General of WIPO for a further period of six years.

Activities in 1985

Development co-operation activities

During 1985, WIPO co-operated with most developing countries and with intergovernmental organizations in their development projects relating to intellectual property, by providing assistance in the preparation of legislation, or establishment or modernization of national or regional institutions, including patent documentation and information services.

Two WIPO permanent programmes, supervised by intergovernmental permanent committees, provided the framework for development co-operation relating to industrial property and to copyright and neighbouring rights.

Regarding industrial property, WIPO organized a workshop on patents in the service of development (Harare, Zimbabwe), a high-level policy planning meeting on industrial property in Africa (Lomé, Togo), a national industrial property seminar (Baghdad, Iraq), a high-level workshop on industrial property in the Arab countries (Geneva), a regional workshop on invention development and innovation (Manila, Philippines), a regional workshop on licensing and other industrial property transfer arrangements (Bombay, India), an interregional seminar on industrial strategy and the patent system (Seoul, Republic of Korea), a high-level meeting of government officials of South Pacific countries to consider co-operation in industrial property (Suva, Fiji), a meeting for the English-speaking Caribbean countries, Haiti and Suriname to consider co-operation in industrial property (Bridgetown, Barbados), a workshop on classification, search and examination of patent applications in chemistry for the Andean countries (Caracas, Venezuela), an Ibero-American meeting on the establishment of an international patent documentation centre in the Spanish language (Madrid, Spain), a meeting of vice-ministers and a meeting of heads of industrial property offices of the Central American isthmus countries (Guatemala City) and a symposium on industrial property for judges of the same countries (San José, Costa Rica), a national workshop on patent documents as a source of technological information (Havana and Cienfuegos, Cuba), and a meeting of directors of industrial property offices of Argentina, Chile, Paraguay and Uruguay (Asunción, Paraguay).

Medals and prizes for inventors and promoters of innovation were awarded by WIPO at national and international exhibitions or contests and special ceremonies held in Belgium, Bulgaria, China, India, the Ivory Coast, Japan, Paraguay, the Philippines, the Republic of Korea, Switzerland, Uruguay, the USSR and Zaire.

Continuing a programme started in 1975, 410 state-of-the-art search reports on technology disclosed in patent documents and related literature were provided to developing countries free of charge under agreements concluded between WIPO and contributing industrial property offices in developed countries. Most of the reports were prepared by the patent offices of Australia, Austria, Finland, the German Democratic Republic, the Federal Republic of Germany, Japan, Sweden and the USSR.

Development co-operation activities in copyright and neighbouring rights included training courses at Brasilia, Brazil, and Nanjing, China; a seminar for Central American and Caribbean States, at Mexico City, and seminars at Cairo, Egypt, and Cotonou, Benin; and a workshop at Zomba, Malawi.

WIPO training programmes continued to grow, with 239 fellowships granted in 1985 to nationals of 83 developing countries in industrial property and 60 fellowships to nationals from 48 developing countries in copyright, in addition to individuals recommended by various organizations. In the industrial property sector, 22 countries—including seven developing countries—three intergovernmental organizations and two non-governmental organizations provided individual and group training. Concerning copyright, 12 countries (seven developing) and one national organization provided such training.

Industrial property

The first consultative meeting on the revision of the Paris Convention for the Protection of Industrial Property took place at Geneva in June 1985, to revise the Convention by introducing new provisions and changing existing ones to meet the needs of developing countries more effectively. The proposed changes included giving full recognition to inventors' certificates, a form of protection existing in several socialist countries.

At Geneva in July, an expert committee discussed harmonizing certain provisions in laws to protect inventions.

Another expert committee met at Geneva in February and December to advise on proposals contained in a memorandum drawn up by the International Bureau—the WIPO secretariat—on a possible treaty on the international registration of marks. The memorandum highlighted the limited territorial scope of the Madrid Agreement on the subject, the reasons for its lack of attractiveness for member States of the Paris Union not party to the Agreement, and the need to seek solutions acceptable to the greatest number of countries and to devise a simple, inexpensive system for users. The memorandum also set out likely differences between the Madrid Agreement and a new treaty which would coexist with it. It was decided that the International Bureau would draw up a detailed outline of a new treaty and would study its financial aspects and links with regional systems.

The Bureau published the text of the first version of a draft treaty on protecting intellectual property in respect of integrated circuits (popularly called "microchips"). It also published *Industrial Property Protection of Biotechnological Inventions* which analysed several related basic issues.

Work continued on updating IPC and other classifications concerning industrial designs or registration of trade and service marks.

During 1985, 7,305 international applications were filed under PCT in 28 receiving offices. The *PCT Gazette* was published fortnightly and special issues were put out in March and December to consolidate general information. The total number of registrations of marks under the Madrid Agreement was 8,961. To that figure should be added 4,736 renewals under the Agreement's Nice and Stockholm Acts. Registrations and renewals therefore totalled 13,697, compared to 13,043 in 1984. The total number of changes recorded in the International Register of Marks was 15,610, as compared with 17,501 in 1984.

Copyright and neighbouring rights

Activities in copyright and neighbouring rights included the convening, jointly with the United Nations Educational, Scientific and Cultural Organization, of a group of experts on the copyright aspects of protecting computer software (Geneva, February/March), an expert group on the copyright aspects of direct broadcasting by satellite (Paris, March), and a committee of governmental experts on model provisions for national laws on publishing contracts for literary works (Paris, December). Two other meetings were held in Paris—the Executive Committee of the Berne Union and the Intergovernmental Committee of the International Convention for the Protection of Performers, Producers of Phonograms and Broadcasting Organizations.

Publications

The International Bureau continued to issue regularly the following publications, in various languages: *Copyright, Industrial Property, International Designs Bulletin, Les Marques internationales, WIPO Newsletter, PCT Gazette, Les Appellations d'origine, Intellectual Property in Asia and the Pacific, Industrial Property Laws and Treaties* and *Copyright Laws and Treaties*.

Secretariat

As at 31 December 1985, WIPO employed 288 full-time staff members. Of those, 99 were in the Professional and higher categories (drawn from 40 member States) and 189 were in the General Service category. In addition, 91 experts were employed by WIPO on technical assistance projects during the year.

Budget

The principal sources of the WIPO budget—approximately 87 million Swiss francs for the 1984-1985 biennium—are ordinary and special contributions from member States and income derived from international registration services (primarily under PCT and the Madrid Agreement).

Ordinary contributions are paid on the basis of a class-and-unit system by members of the Paris, Berne, Nice, Locarno, IPC and Vienna Unions and by WIPO member States not belonging to any of the Unions.

States members of the six Unions are placed in seven classes (I to VII) to determine the amounts of their ordinary contributions. WIPO States not members of any of the Unions are placed in three classes (A, B or C) for the same purpose. States in Class I or A pay the highest contributions of their group and those in Class VII or C the lowest. The class in which a State is placed is decided solely by the State and the rights of each are the same, irrespective of the class.

The contribution class for each member State of WIPO and of the Paris or Berne Unions, together with the amount of the ordinary contribution of each State, is given in Annex I below (the class indicated for the Paris Union also applies to the Nice, Locarno, IPC and Vienna Unions). Members of one or more Unions do not pay separate contributions to WIPO; the Unions themselves contribute towards the costs of WIPO's International Bureau and programme of legal-technical assistance.

The amounts of ordinary contributions payable for 1986 are given in the table below.

Income and expenditure

Summary figures for income and expenditure for the biennium 1984-1985 are as follows:

	In thousands of Swiss francs	Equivalent in thousands of US dollars*
Income		
Contributions	40,065	19,170
Income from registration services	40,908	19,573
Publications and miscellaneous	8,416	4,027
Total	89,389	42,770
Expenditure		
Staff	55,449	26,531
Publications	4,538	2,171
Buildings†	9,759	4,669
Travel	2,732	1,307
Meetings	1,179	564
Other	13,093	6,265
Total	86,750	41,507

*At the United Nations rate of exchange for December 1985: 2.09 Swiss francs = $US 1.00.

†Includes maintenance, rental and amortization of the building loan.

CONTRIBUTION SCALES FOR 1986
(1.68 Swiss francs = $US 1.00: United Nations rate as at 31 December 1986)

	In Swiss francs	Equivalent in US dollars		In Swiss francs	Equivalent in US dollars
WIPO*			V	67,782	40,346
Class			VI	40,670	24,208
A	85,000	50,595	VII	13,556	8,069
B	22,500	15,178	**NICE UNION**		
C	8,500	5,059	*Class*		
PARIS UNION			I	51,880	30,881
Class			II	†	†
I	565,059	336,345	III	31,129	18,529
II	†	†	IV	20,752	12,352
III	339,037	201,808	V	10,375	6,176
IV	226,024	134,538	VI	6,226	3,706
V	113,010	67,268	VII	2,075	1,235
VI	67,809	40,363	**LOCARNO UNION**		
VII	22,602	13,454	*Class*		
BERNE UNION			I	20,013	11,913
Class			II	†	†
I	338,912	201,733	III	12,008	7,148
II	271,129	161,386	IV	8,005	4,765
III	203,347	121,040	V	4,003	2,383
IV	135,565	80,693	VI	2,401	1,429
			VII	†	†

IPC UNION Class	In Swiss francs	Equivalent in US dollars	VIENNA UNION Class	In Swiss francs	Equivalent in US dollars
I	272,846	162,408	I	5,085	3,027
II	†	†	II	†	†
III	163,708	97,445	III	3,051	1,816
IV	109,138	64,963	IV	†	†
V	†	†	V	†	†
VI	32,742	19,489	VI	610	363
VII	10,914	6,496	VII	203	121

NOTE: There were no contributions to the PCT Union for 1986.

*The amounts indicated are payable by those States members of WIPO which are not members of any of the Unions (see Annex I).

†No State currently belonged to this class.

Annex I. MEMBERSHIP OF THE WORLD INTELLECTUAL PROPERTY ORGANIZATION AND UNIONS ADMINISTERED TO WHICH CONTRIBUTIONS ARE PAYABLE

(As at 31 December 1985; ordinary contributions payable in 1986)

STATE OR OTHER	MEMBER							CLASS W	P	B	In Swiss francs	Equivalent in US dollars*
Algeria	W	P	—	N	—	—	—	—	VI	—	74,035	44,068
Angola	W	—	—	—	—	—	—	C	—	—	8,500	5,059
Argentina	W	P	B	—	—	—	—	—	VI	VI	108,479	64,570
Australia	W	P	B	N	—	IPC	—	—	III	III	737,221	438,822
Austria	W	P	B	N	—	IPC	—	—	IV	VI	396,584	236,061
Bahamas	W	P	B	—	—	—	—	—	VII	VII	36,158	21,522
Bangladesh	W	—	—	—	—	—	—	C	—	—	8,500	5,059
Barbados	W	P	B	N	—	—	—	—	VII	VII	38,233	22,757
Belgium	W	P	B	N	—	IPC	—	—	III	III	737,221	438,822
Benin	W	P	B	N	—	—	—	—	VII	VII	38,233	22,757
Brazil	W	P	B	—	—	IPC	—	—	IV	IV	470,727	280,194
Bulgaria	W	P	B	—	—	—	—	—	VI	VI	108,479	64,570
Burkina Faso	W	P	B	—	—	—	—	—	VII	VII	36,158	21,522
Burundi	W	P	—	—	—	—	—	—	VII	—	22,602	13,453
Byelorussian SSR	W	—	—	—	—	—	—	C	—	—	8,500	5,059
Cameroon	W	P	B	—	—	—	—	—	VII	VI	63,272	37,661
Canada	W	P	B	—	—	—	—	—	III	III	542,384	322,847
Central African Republic	W	P	B	—	—	—	—	—	VII	VII	36,158	21,522
Chad	W	P	B	—	—	—	—	—	VII	VII	36,158	21,522
Chile	W	—	B	—	—	—	—	—	—	VI	40,670	24,208
China	W	P	—	—	—	—	—	—	III	—	339,037	201,807
Colombia	W	—	—	—	—	—	—	C	—	—	8,500	5,059
Congo	W	P	B	—	—	—	—	—	VII	VII	36,158	21,522
Costa Rica	W	—	B	—	—	—	—	—	—	VII	13,556	8,069
Cuba	W	P	—	—	—	—	—	—	VI	—	67,809	40,362
Cyprus	W	P	B	—	—	—	—	—	VII	VII	36,158	21,522
Czechoslovakia	W	P	B	N	LO	IPC	—	—	IV	IV	499,484	297,311
Democratic People's Republic of Korea	W	P	—	—	—	—	—	—	VII	—	22,602	13,453
Denmark	W	P	B	N	LO	IPC	—	—	IV	IV	499,484	297,311
Dominican Republic	—	P	—	—	—	—	—	—	VI	—	67,809	40,362
Egypt	W	P	B	—	—	IPC	—	—	VI	VII	114,107	67,920
El Salvador	W	—	—	—	—	—	—	C	—	—	8,500	5,059
Fiji	W	—	B	—	—	—	—	—	—	VII	13,556	8,069
Finland	W	P	B	N	LO	IPC	—	—	IV	IV	499,484	297,311
France	W	P	B	N	LO	IPC	VA	—	I	I	1,253,795	746,306
Gabon	W	P	B	—	—	—	—	—	VII	VII	36,158	21,522
Gambia	W	—	—	—	—	—	—	C	—	—	8,500	5,059
German Democratic Republic	W	P	B	N	LO	IPC	—	—	III	V	613,664	365,276
Germany, Federal Republic of	W	P	B	N	—	IPC	—	—	I	I	1,228,697	731,367
Ghana	W	P	—	—	—	—	—	—	VII	—	22,602	13,453
Greece	W	P	B	—	—	—	—	—	V	VI	153,680	91,476
Guatemala	W	—	—	—	—	—	—	C	—	—	8,500	5,059
Guinea	W	P	B	—	—	—	—	—	VII	VII	36,158	21,522
Haiti	W	P	—	—	—	—	—	—	VII	—	22,602	13,453
Holy See	W	P	B	—	—	—	—	—	VII	VII	36,158	21,522
Honduras	W	—	—	—	—	—	—	C	—	—	8,500	5,059
Hungary	W	P	B	N	LO	—	—	—	V	VI	168,058	100,034
Iceland	—	P	B	—	—	—	—	—	VII	VII	36,158	21,522
India	W	—	B	—	—	—	—	—	—	IV	135,565	80,693
Indonesia	W	P	—	—	—	—	—	—	VI	—	67,809	40,362
Iran	—	P	—	—	—	—	—	—	VI	—	67,809	40,362
Iraq	W	P	—	—	—	—	—	—	VI	—	67,809	40,362
Ireland	W	P	B	N	LO	IPC	—	—	IV	IV	499,484	297,311
Israel	W	P	B	N	—	IPC	—	—	VI	VI	147,447	87,766

STATE OR OTHER	MEMBER							CLASS			CONTRIBUTION In Swiss francs	Equivalent in US dollars*
								W	P	B		
Italy	W	P	B	N	LO	IPC	—	—	III	III	749,229	445,969
Ivory Coast	W	P	B	—	—	—	—	—	VII	VI	63,272	37,661
Jamaica	W	—	—	—	—	—	—	C	—	—	8,500	5,059
Japan	W	P	B	—	—	IPC	—	—	I	II	1,109,034	660,139
Jordan	W	P	—	—	—	—	—	—	VII	—	22,602	13,453
Kenya	W	P	—	—	—	—	—	—	VI	—	67,809	40,362
Lebanon	—	P	B	N	—	—	—	—	VI	VI	114,705	68,276
Libyan Arab Jamahiriya	W	P	B	—	—	—	—	—	VI	VI	108,479	64,570
Liechtenstein	W	P	B	N	—	—	—	—	VII	VII	38,233	22,757
Luxembourg	W	P	B	N	—	IPC	VA	—	VII	VII	49,350	29,374
Madagascar	—	P	B	—	—	—	—	—	VII	VI	63,272	37,661
Malawi	W	P	—	—	—	—	—	—	VII	—	22,602	13,453
Mali	W	P	B	—	—	—	—	—	VII	VII	36,158	21,522
Malta	W	P	B	—	—	—	—	—	VII	VII	36,158	21,522
Mauritania	W	P	B	—	—	—	—	—	VII	VII	36,158	21,522
Mauritius	W	P	—	—	—	—	—	—	VII	—	22,602	13,453
Mexico	W	P	B	—	—	—	—	—	IV	IV	361,589	215,231
Monaco	W	P	B	N	—	IPC	—	—	VII	VII	49,147	29,254
Mongolia	W	P	—	—	—	—	—	—	VII	—	22,602	13,453
Morocco	W	P	B	N	—	—	—	—	VI	VI	114,705	68,276
Netherlands	W	P	B	N	LO	IPC	VA	—	III	III	752,280	447,785
New Zealand	W	P	B	—	—	—	—	—	V	V	180,792	107,614
Nicaragua	W	—	—	—	—	—	—	C	—	—	8,500	5,059
Niger	W	P	B	—	—	—	—	—	VII	VII	36,158	21,522
Nigeria	—	P	—	—	—	—	—	—	VI	—	67,809	40,362
Norway	W	P	B	N	LO	IPC	—	—	IV	IV	499,484	297,311
Pakistan	W	—	B	—	—	—	—	—	—	VI	40,670	24,208
Panama	W	—	—	—	—	—	—	C	—	—	8,500	5,059
Peru	W	—	—	—	—	—	—	C	—	—	8,500	5,059
Philippines	W	P	B	—	—	—	—	—	VI	VI	108,479	64,570
Poland	W	P	B	—	—	—	—	—	V	VI	153,680	91,476
Portugal	W	P	B	N	—	IPC	—	—	IV	V	423,696	252,199
Qatar	W	—	—	—	—	—	—	B	—	—	25,500	15,178
Republic of Korea	W	P	—	—	—	—	—	—	VI	—	67,809	40,362
Romania	W	P	B	—	—	—	—	—	VI	VI	108,479	64,570
Rwanda	W	P	B	—	—	—	—	—	VII	VII	36,158	21,522
San Marino	—	P	—	—	—	—	—	—	VI	—	67,809	40,362
Saudi Arabia	W	—	—	—	—	—	—	A	—	—	85,000	50,595
Senegal	W	P	B	—	—	—	—	—	VII	VI	63,272	37,661
Somalia	W	—	—	—	—	—	—	C	—	—	8,500	5,059
South Africa	W	P	B	—	—	—	—	—	IV	IV	361,589	215,231
Spain	W	P	B	N	LO	IPC	—	—	IV	II	635,048	378,004
Sri Lanka	W	P	B	—	—	—	—	—	VII	VII	36,158	21,522
Sudan	W	P	—	—	—	—	—	—	VII	—	22,602	13,453
Suriname	W	P	B	N	—	IPC	—	—	VII	VII	49,147	29,254
Sweden	W	P	B	N	LO	IPC	VA	—	III	III	752,280	447,785
Switzerland	W	P	B	N	LO	IPC	—	—	III	III	749,229	445,969
Syrian Arab Republic	—	P	—	—	—	—	—	—	VI	—	67,809	40,362
Thailand	—	—	B	—	—	—	—	—	—	VII	13,556	8,069
Togo	W	P	B	—	—	—	—	—	VII	VII	36,158	21,522
Trinidad and Tobago	—	P	—	—	—	—	—	—	VI	—	67,809	40,362
Tunisia	W	P	B	N	—	—	VA	—	VI	VI	115,315	68,639
Turkey	W	P	B	—	—	—	—	—	VI	VI	108,479	64,570
Uganda	W	P	—	—	—	—	—	—	VII	—	22,602	13,453
Ukrainian SSR	W	—	—	—	—	—	—	C	—	—	8,500	5,059
USSR	W	P	—	N	LO	IPC	—	—	I	—	909,798	541,546
United Arab Emirates	W	—	—	—	—	—	—	B	—	—	25,500	15,178
United Kingdom	W	P	B	N	—	IPC	—	—	I	I	1,228,697	731,367
United Republic of Tanzania	W	P	—	—	—	—	—	—	VII	—	22,602	13,453
United States	W	P	—	N	—	IPC	—	—	I	—	889,785	529,633
Uruguay	W	P	B	—	—	—	—	—	VII	VII	36,158	21,522
Venezuela	W	—	B	—	—	—	—	—	—	V	67,782	40,346
Viet Nam	W	P	—	—	—	—	—	—	VII	—	22,602	13,453
Yemen	W	—	—	—	—	—	—	C	—	—	8,500	5,059
Yugoslavia	W	P	B	N	LO	—	—	—	VI	VI	117,106	69,705
Zaire	W	P	B	—	—	—	—	—	VI	VI	108,479	64,570
Zambia	W	P	—	—	—	—	—	—	VII	—	22,602	13,453
Zimbabwe	W	P	B	—	—	—	—	—	VII	VII	36,158	21,522
Total	112	97	76	33	15	27	5				22,783,000	13,561,239

NOTE: Membership in WIPO is indicated by "W"; in the Paris Union by "P"; in the Berne Union by "B"; in the Nice Union by "N"; in the Locarno Union by "LO"; in the Strasbourg (IPC) Union by "IPC"; in the Vienna Union by "VA". The class indicated for the Paris Union applies equally to the Nice, Locarno, IPC and Vienna Unions. Five States were members of Unions to which contributions are not payable and therefore are not included in this table.

*Calculated on the basis of the United Nations rate of exchange for December 1986: 1.68 Swiss francs = $US 1.00.

Annex II.   OFFICERS AND OFFICES OF THE WORLD INTELLECTUAL PROPERTY ORGANIZATION
(As at 31 December 1985)

CO-ORDINATION COMMITTEE

OFFICERS
Chairman: Adolfo Loredo Hill (Mexico).
First Vice-Chairman: Jacek Szomanski (Poland).
Second Vice-Chairman: J. H. A. Gariepy (Canada).

MEMBERS
Algeria, Angola, Argentina, Australia, Austria, Brazil, Bulgaria, Canada, Chile, China, Colombia, Cuba, Czechoslovakia, Denmark, Egypt, France, German Democratic Republic, Germany, Federal Republic of, Hungary, India, Indonesia, Italy, Ivory Coast, Japan, Mexico, Morocco, Netherlands, Nicaragua, Nigeria, Philippines, Poland, Saudi Arabia, Senegal, Sweden, Switzerland, Tunisia, Turkey, USSR, United Kingdom, United Republic of Tanzania, United States, Uruguay, Venezuela, Yugoslavia, Zaire, Zimbabwe.

SENIOR OFFICERS OF THE INTERNATIONAL BUREAU

Director General: Arpad Bogsch.
Deputy Directors General: Klaus Pfanner, Marino Porzio, Lev Efremovich Kostikov.
Legal Counsel: Gust Ledakis.
Director, Public Information and Copyright Department: Claude Masouyé.
Director, Development Co-operation and External Relations Bureau:
  Ibrahima Thiam (Africa).
  Laksmanathan Kadirgamar (Asia and the Pacific).
  Enrique Pareja (Latin America and the Caribbean).
  Kamil Idris (Arab countries).
Director, Developing Countries (Copyright) Division: Shahid Alikhan.
Director, Industrial Property Division: Ludwig Baeumer.
Director, Patent Co-operation Treaty Division: François Curchod.
Director, Patent Information and Classifications Division: Paul Claus.
Director, Copyright Law Division: Mihaly Ficsor.
Director, Administrative Division: Thomas A. J. Keefer.
Director, Public Information Division: Roger Harben.

HEADQUARTERS AND OTHER OFFICE

HEADQUARTERS
World Intellectual Property Organization
34 Chemin des Colombettes
1211 Geneva 20, Switzerland
  Cable address: WIPO Geneva *or* OMPI Genève
  Telephone: (22) 999-111
  Telex: 22376 OMPI CH
  Facsimile: (41-22) 335428

LIAISON OFFICE WITH THE UNITED NATIONS IN NEW YORK
World Intellectual Property Organization
2 United Nations Plaza, Room 560
New York, N.Y. 10017, United States
  Telephone: (212) 963-6813
  Telex: 420544 UNH UI

Chapter XVI

International Fund for Agricultural Development (IFAD)

The International Fund for Agricultural Development (IFAD) completed its eighth year of operations in 1985, during which it continued to provide concessional assistance for financing agricultural projects in developing countries. The Fund aimed at increasing food production, reducing malnutrition and alleviating rural poverty. It concentrated on low-income, food-deficit countries, which received most of IFAD's lending, and on the poorest farmers, aiming at providing them with the necessary production means and institutional support. Particular emphasis was given to: simplifying project design; restoring agricultural capacity to sub-Saharan countries; and ways of reducing the costs of technical assistance, project administration and recurrent expenditures. IFAD also gave special attention to the issues of women in development, co-operation with non-governmental organizations and the environment.

The IFAD Executive Board held three regular sessions in 1985 (April, September, December), approving 17 projects and 23 technical assistance grants, and deferring the ninth session of the Governing Council, made up of the entire membership, until January 1986. The Board convened a special session in May, at which it endorsed a proposal for an IFAD Special Programme for sub-Saharan African countries affected by drought and desertification. The seventh and eighth (suspended) meetings of members of the consultation on the second replenishment of IFAD's resources were held in February/March and May, respectively. All meetings were held at Rome, Italy.

Membership of IFAD remained at 139 countries. Of these, 20 were in Category I (developed countries), 12 in Category II (oil-exporting developing countries) and 107 in Category III (other developing countries).

Since 1979, approved loans have been denominated in special drawing rights (SDRs), an international unit of account. Dollar figures in this chapter are based on the SDR/United States dollar conversion rate at 31 December 1985 (SDR 1 = $1.09842). However, approximate amounts in United States dollars for loans approved since 1979 have been based on the SDR/United States dollar exchange rate at the time of loan negotiations.

Following approval of the 17 new projects in 1985, the total assistance provided by the Fund to some 87 member countries since 1978 amounted to SDR 1,897.3 million, of which SDR 1,808.7 million was committed for 177 projects and SDR 88.6 million for technical assistance grants.

Of the 177 loans provided since 1978, 63 were for projects in Africa, 48 in Asia, 33 in Latin America and the Caribbean, and 33 in the Near East and North Africa. Most loans (67.3 per cent) were made on highly concessional terms, with a service charge of 1 per cent per annum, a 50-year maturity period and a 10-year grace period. Another 26.2 per cent of the loans were made available on intermediate terms (at 4 per cent, 20 years maturity and a five-year grace period) and the remaining 6.5 per cent on ordinary terms (8 per cent, 15-18 years maturity and a three-year grace period). The Fund paid particular attention to the needs of the poorest countries: 67.3 per cent of all loans in the period 1978-1985 went to 55 countries with a per capita income below $300 in 1976 prices, or about $520 in 1985 prices.

Resources

Initial resources and contributions to the first replenishment had brought to IFAD about $2.1 billion to cover operations from 1978-1983. Because of delay in concluding negotiations on the second replenishment of resources, the first had to be stretched over four years (1981-1984) instead of three years. As the 1985 consultations on the second replenishment produced no agreement, because one important member was unable to join in the consensus, it was decided to suspend the consultations until January 1986.

Under these circumstances, IFAD adopted in 1985 a number of extraordinary measures to raise additional resources. It launched the Special Programme for sub-Saharan Africa, with a three-year target of voluntary contributions of $300 million. Under an agreement with the Belgian Government in regard to the Survival Fund for the Third World,[a] it mobilized $8.25 million for three projects in Ethiopia, Kenya and Somalia. After a call for advance contributions

---

[a]YUN 1984, p. 1285.

to the second replenishment, IFAD received $66 million in pledges and $46 million in payments from 61 member countries during 1985. Members' contributions to the first replenishment stood at $947,827,233 at 31 December 1985 (see ANNEX I, below).

Investments

At the end of 1985, IFAD liquid assets totalled $668.5 million. Of this amount, $22.2 million was held on demand deposit and $354.2 million (53 per cent) was held on deposit with, or in obligations issued by, commercial banks, while the balance of $292.1 million was in bonds or similar securities issued or guaranteed by member Governments. While the maximum maturity for any of these investments was five years, the average length of the investment portfolio was 35.7 months.

During the year, IFAD increased the percentage of its portfolio of bonds and similar obligations issued by member developing countries. As of 31 December 1985, the Fund had a total of $244.8 million or 35.6 per cent of total liquid assets deposited with banks of developing countries or in bonds or similar securities issued by developing country Governments and international development institutions.

The downward trend of interest rates on most major currencies which began in late 1984 continued through 1985. Consequently, the average rate of return for 1985 was approximately 9.68 per cent versus 11.06 per cent for 1984.

Activities in 1985

The 17 new loans approved by IFAD in 1985 totalled SDR 126.3 million ($138.9 million), while the 23 technical assistance grants came to SDR 10.6 million (about $11.7 million), bringing the total financial assistance provided in 1985 to SDR 136.9 million ($150.6 million), a 38 per cent reduction over 1984 in real terms. Difficulties in resource mobilization forced the Fund to cut back loans, and 1985 represented the lowest level of operations in its history.

In the face of these constraints, IFAD sought to reduce the size of loans (without affecting the quality or leverage of the project) and to mobilize more resources from co-financing agencies. Thirteen of the projects approved in 1985 were initiated by IFAD and 4 by other donors. The Fund's share in total project cost was 21.2 per cent, while those of external donors and recipients were 49 and 29.8 per cent respectively. IFAD effectiveness in mobilizing resources was reflected in its lower share in total project cost in 1985 as compared with the average for 1978-1985 (28 per cent).

In 1985, six projects were approved for Africa, involving loans of SDR 49.8 million, and dealing with agricultural development, rehabilitation of drought-affected areas, small-scale irrigation and smallholder food crops.

The four projects approved for Asia, for SDR 38.7 million, emphasized agricultural development, livestock development, agricultural credit and rural development. For Latin America and the Caribbean, a small farmers development project and one for agricultural credit, for SDR 7.7 million, were approved.

The five projects approved in the Near East and North Africa were for artisanal fisheries development, livestock health services, agricultural development, agricultural extension and rainfed agricultural development, and involved loans of SDR 30.9 million.

The Fund continued to support agricultural research, project preparation and training. In 1985, support for agricultural research programmes of international and regional centres totalled $6.9 million; IFAD financed 13 research programmes, including two new programmes at the International Institute of Tropical Agriculture at Ibadan, Nigeria, and at the International Irrigation Management Institute at Kandy, Sri Lanka.

The Fund continued its special programming missions, which analysed in depth carefully selected member countries and aimed at directing financial assistance to the most needy of the rural poor. The three missions launched in 1985 went to Angola, Bhutan and Bolivia.

The tables on p. 1367 indicate the projects and technical assistance grants approved in 1985.

Income and expenditure

Total revenue for 1985 was $78.7 million, consisting of $66 million of investment income and $12.7 million from interest and service charges on loans. Total expenses for the year amounted to $20.7 million, compared with a budget of $26.2 million. The excess of revenue over expenses for the year was $58 million.

Secretariat

At the end of December 1985, the IFAD secretariat totalled 174, of whom 82 were executive or technical staff (Professional category and above)—drawn from 44 countries—and 92 were support staff (General Service category).

TECHNICAL ASSISTANCE GRANTS

Recipient	Amount (in thousands of US dollars)	Recipient	Amount (in thousands of US dollars)
CGIAR*-supported international centres		*Other agricultural research centres*	
International Crops Research Institute for the Semi-Arid Tropics, Hyderabad, India	250	Scientific, Technical and Research Commission of OAU, Ouagadougou, Burkina Faso	800
International Institute of Tropical Agriculture, Ibadan, Nigeria	750	International Centre for Insect Physiology and Ecology, Nairobi, Kenya	800
International Potato Centre, Lima, Peru	400	International Irrigation Management Institute, Kandy, Sri Lanka	1,683
International Food Policy Research Institute, Washington, D.C.	250		
International Centre for Tropical Agriculture, Cali, Colombia	500	Subtotal	3,283
International Livestock Centre for Africa, Addis Ababa, Ethiopia	500	*Other technical assistance grants*	
International Rice Research Institute, Los Baños, Philippines	600		
West African Rice Development Association, Monrovia, Liberia	400	Scientific, Technical and Research Commission of OAU, Ouagadougou, Burkina Faso	1,450
Subtotal	3,650	Total	8,383

*Consultative Group on International Agricultural Research.

PROJECT LOANS APPROVED AND TECHNICAL ASSISTANCE GRANTED DURING 1985

		Loan		Technical assistance
Country	Purpose	Amount (in millions of SDRs)	Amount* (in millions of US dollars)	Amount* (in thousands of US dollars)
Bangladesh	Minor crops agricultural development	—	—	150
Belize	Toledo small farmers' development†	2.10	2.15	—
Bhutan	Tashigang and Mongar area development	4.45	4.75	—
Bolivia	Guadalquivir agricultural development	—	—	300
Djibouti	Artisanal fisheries development	1.15	1.10	—
Equatorial Guinea	Agricultural development on the mainland	1.65	1.55	750
Ethiopia	Rehabilitation programme for drought-affected areas	13.05	12.50	290
Guinea	Gueckedou agricultural development	5.05	5.00	—
Haiti	Rehabilitation of small irrigation schemes	—	—	80
Indonesia	Smallholder cattle development†	11.60	12.00	—
Lesotho	Rural enterprises development	—	—	230
Mauritania	Small-scale irrigation	3.50	3.40	—
Nepal	Small farmer development	15.15	14.50	100
Nigeria	Multi-state agricultural development	12.05	12.00	—
Pakistan	Malakand area development	—	—	180
Panama	Agricultural credit‡	5.60	6.00	—
Somalia	Livestock health services	5.90	6.30	—
Sri Lanka	Kegalle rural development	7.50	8.00	—
Sudan	Western savannah	9.45	10.00	—
Syrian Arab Republic	National agricultural extension‡	7.55	7.50	—
Tunisia	Sidi Bouzid rainfed agricultural development‡	6.05	6.00	—
United Republic of Tanzania	Southern highlands smallholder food crops	14.50	15.00	—
Yemen	Southern uplands rural women development	—	—	150
Zambia	Traditional food crops	—	—	125
Total		126.30	127.75	2,355

*Dollar equivalent based on SDR/United States dollar exchange rate at the time of loan negotiations.

NOTE: Loans are on highly concessional terms except for those marked †, which are on intermediate terms, and ‡, which are on ordinary terms.

Annex I. MEMBERSHIP OF THE INTERNATIONAL FUND FOR AGRICULTURAL DEVELOPMENT AND CONTRIBUTIONS PLEDGED AND PAID
(As at 31 December 1985)

MEMBER	INITIAL CONTRIBUTIONS (in US dollar equivalent) Pledged	Paid	FIRST REPLENISHMENT CONTRIBUTIONS (in US dollar equivalent) Pledged	Paid	MEMBER	INITIAL CONTRIBUTIONS (in US dollar equivalent) Pledged	Paid	FIRST REPLENISHMENT CONTRIBUTIONS (in US dollar equivalent) Pledged	Paid
Category I					*Category I* (cont.)				
Australia	5,445,882	5,445,882	6,102,791	6,102,791	Ireland	823,699	823,699	789,801	789,801
Austria	4,800,000	4,800,000	4,331,784	4,331,784	Italy	25,000,000	25,000,000	38,700,000	38,700,000
Belgium	10,928,515	10,928,515	9,238,284	9,238,284	Japan	55,000,000	55,000,000	63,235,478	63,235,478
Canada	23,571,428	23,571,428	30,000,000	30,000,000	Luxembourg	351,494	351,494	258,777	258,777
Denmark	7,500,000	7,500,000	6,688,963	6,688,963	Netherlands	39,101,083	39,101,083	35,462,094	35,462,094
Finland	2,214,022	2,214,022	4,428,044	4,428,044	New Zealand	1,005,025	1,005,025	1,047,136	1,047,136
France	17,000,000	17,000,000	30,592,000	30,592,000	Norway	17,150,396	17,150,396	23,923,186	23,923,186
Germany, Federal Republic of	55,000,000	55,000,000	47,487,805	47,487,805	Spain	2,000,000	2,000,000	2,000,000	2,000,000
					Sweden	15,171,504	15,171,504	19,562,005	19,562,005

MEMBER	INITIAL CONTRIBUTIONS (in US dollar equivalent)		FIRST REPLENISHMENT CONTRIBUTIONS (in US dollar equivalent)	
	Pledged	Paid	Pledged	Paid
Category I (cont.)				
Switzerland	10,679,612	10,679,612	13,805,825	13,805,825
United Kingdom	26,011,561	26,011,561	18,643,247	18,643,247
United States	200,000,000	200,000,000	180,000,000	180,000,000
Subtotal	518,754,221	518,754,221	536,297,220	536,297,220
Category II				
Algeria	10,000,000	10,000,000	15,580,000	15,580,000
Gabon	500,000	500,000	801,000	801,000
Indonesia	1,250,000	1,250,000	1,909,000	1,909,000
Iran	124,750,000	41,583,333	—	—
Iraq	20,000,000	20,000,000	31,099,000	31,099,000
Kuwait	36,000,000	36,000,000	56,041,000	56,041,000
Libyan Arab Jamahiriya	20,000,000	20,000,000	—	—
Nigeria	26,000,000	26,000,000	40,459,000	40,459,000
Qatar	9,000,000	9,000,000	13,980,000	13,980,000
Saudi Arabia	105,500,000	105,500,000	155,618,000	155,618,000
United Arab Emirates	16,500,000	16,500,000	25,680,000	25,680,000
Venezuela	66,000,000	66,000,000	38,489,000	38,489,000
Subtotal	435,500,000	352,333,333	379,656,000	379,656,000
Category III				
Afghanistan	8,696	8,696	—	—
Angola	—	—	—	—
Argentina	30	30	900,000	900,000
Bangladesh*	241,935	241,935	621,806	621,806
Barbados	1,000	1,000	—	—
Belize	—	—	—	—
Benin	10,000	10,000	10,000	10,000
Bhutan	—	—	1,000	1,000
Bolivia	—	—	50,000	
Botswana	—	—	15,000	15,000
Brazil	—	—	9,862,954	9,862,954
Burkina Faso	10,000	10,000	—	—
Burundi	—	—	89,518	—
Cameroon	50,000	50,000	52,903	52,903
Cape Verde	1,000	1,000	—	—
Central African Republic	2,667	2,667	7,936	7,936
Chad	—	—	—	—
Chile	50,000	50,000	—	—
China	787,500	787,500	1,300,000	1,300,000
Colombia	—	—	—	—
Comoros	26,452	13,226	—	—
Congo	—	—	120,160	120,160
Costa Rica	—	—	—	—
Cuba	—	—	99,197	99,197
Cyprus	25,000	25,000	12,000	12,000
Democratic Yemen	—	—	50,000	50,000
Djibouti	—	—	3,000	3,000
Dominica	—	—	10,987	10,987
Dominican Republic	25,000	25,000	—	—
Ecuador	25,047	25,047	50,946	50,946
Egypt*	94,488	94,488	141,732	141,732
El Salvador	40,000	40,000	—	—
Equatorial Guinea	—	—	—	—
Ethiopia	23,623	23,623	23,623	23,623
Fiji	10,000	10,000	10,000	10,000
Gambia	—	—	—	—
Ghana	100,000	100,000	—	—
Greece	150,000	150,000	200,000	200,000
Grenada	—	—	—	—
Guatemala	—	—	—	—
Guinea	1,112,594	1,112,594	60,000	60,000
Guinea-Bissau	—	—	10,000	10,000
Guyana	—	—	30,000	30,000
Haiti	16,470	16,470	13,530	13,530
Honduras	25,000	25,000	50,000	50,000
India*	5,000,000	5,000,000	6,500,000	6,500,000
Israel	150,000	150,000	150,000	—
Ivory Coast	—	—	—	—
Jamaica	4,480	4,480	15,000	15,000

MEMBER	INITIAL CONTRIBUTIONS (in US dollar equivalent)		FIRST REPLENISHMENT CONTRIBUTIONS (in US dollar equivalent)	
	Pledged	Paid	Pledged	Paid
Category III (cont.)				
Jordan*	30,000	30,000	75,000	75,000
Kenya*	488,182	488,182	851,807	851,807
Lao People's Democratic Republic	10,000	10,000	—	—
Lebanon	—	—	25,000	25,000
Lesotho	15,000	15,000	50,000	50,000
Liberia	10,000	10,000	10,000	10,000
Madagascar	—	—	—	—
Malawi	5,000	5,000	18,365	18,365
Maldives	—	—	—	—
Mali	—	—	10,000	10,000
Malta	—	—	—	—
Mauritania	—	—	—	—
Mauritius	—	—	—	—
Mexico	5,000,000	5,000,000	6,503,166	6,503,166
Morocco*	222,943	222,943	89,899	89,899
Mozambique	28,853	28,853	86,559	86,559
Nepal	5,000	5,000	5,000	5,000
Nicaragua	28,571	28,571	—	—
Niger	40,000	40,000	40,000	40,000
Oman	—	—	—	—
Pakistan*	812,695	812,695	1,097,206	1,097,206
Panama	—	—	25,000	25,000
Papua New Guinea	20,000	20,000	—	—
Paraguay	—	—	—	—
Peru	—	—	60,000	60,000
Philippines*	250,000	250,000	245,101	245,101
Portugal	—	—	—	—
Republic of Korea	158,725	158,725	276,694	276,694
Romania	442,565	442,565	—	—
Rwanda	—	—	14,499	14,499
Saint Lucia	—	—	—	—
Saint Vincent and the Grenadines†	—	—	—	—
Samoa	10,000	10,000	—	—
Sao Tome and Principe	—	—	—	—
Senegal	10,000	10,000	13,226	13,226
Seychelles	5,000	1,667	—	—
Sierra Leone	18,296	18,296	18,430	18,430
Solomon Islands	—	—	10,000	10,000
Somalia	10,000	10,000	—	—
Sri Lanka*	783,473	783,473	1,000,000	1,000,000
Sudan	10,000	10,000	10,000	10,000
Suriname	—	—	—	—
Swaziland	—	—	8,980	8,980
Syrian Arab Republic*	90,000	90,000	127,226	—
Thailand	100,000	100,000	100,000	100,000
Togo	8,000	8,000	4,000	4,000
Tonga	—	—	—	—
Tunisia	65,963	65,963	300,000	300,000
Turkey	8,575	8,575	17,454	17,454
Uganda	143	143	53,572	53,572
United Republic of Tanzania	18,282	18,282	38,941	38,941
Uruguay	—	—	—	—
Viet Nam	52,632	52,632	—	—
Yemen	50,000	50,000	—	—
Yugoslavia	17,263	17,263	134,909	134,909
Zaire	30,000	6,053	—	—
Zambia	32,205	32,205	92,687	92,687
Zimbabwe	—	—	—	—
Subtotal	16,878,348	16,837,842	31,874,013	31,457,269
Total	971,132,569	887,925,396	947,827,233	947,410,489
Special contributions				
OPEC Fund	—	—	20,000,000	20,000,000
Others	101,157	101,157	—	—

NOTE: According to article 4, section 2 (c), of the Agreement establishing IFAD, members' initial contributions are payable in cash or promissory notes, either in a single sum or in three annual instalments. Contributions have been translated on the basis of International Monetary Fund exchange rates as at 31 December 1985.

*Arrangements were concluded or were under negotiation with these member States to utilize all or part of their non-convertible currency contributions in the Fund's operations.

†Had not completed the required membership formalities.

Annex II.   OFFICERS AND OFFICES OF THE
            INTERNATIONAL FUND FOR AGRICULTURAL DEVELOPMENT
            (As at 31 December 1985)

EXECUTIVE BOARD

Chairman: Idriss Jazairy.

MEMBERS
Category I: Belgium, Denmark, Germany, Federal Republic of, Italy, Japan, United States. *Alternates:* Canada, Finland, France, Netherlands, United Kingdom.

Category II: Algeria, Iraq, Kuwait, Nigeria, Saudi Arabia, Venezuela. *Alternates:* Gabon, Indonesia, Iran, Libyan Arab Jamahiriya, Qatar, United Arab Emirates.

Category III: Brazil, Cameroon, Kenya, Mexico, Pakistan, Philippines. *Alternates:* Colombia, Cuba, Egypt, Ghana, India, Sri Lanka.

SENIOR SECRETARIAT OFFICERS

President: Idriss Jazairy.
Vice-President: Donald S. Brown.
Assistant President, Head of Economic and Planning Department: Vacant.
Assistant President, Head of Project Management Department: Moise Mensah.
Assistant President, Head of General Affairs Department: Vacant.

Controller, Financial Services Division: Desmond Saldanha.
Treasurer, Financial Services Division: My Huynh Cong.
Chief, Personnel Services Division: Alan Prien.
Director, Legal Services Division: Mohammed Nawaz.

HEADQUARTERS AND OTHER OFFICE

HEADQUARTERS
International Fund for Agricultural Development
107 Via del Serafico
00142 Rome, Italy
  Cable address: IFAD ROME
  Telephone: (6) 54591
  Telex: 614160, 614162

LIAISON OFFICE WITH THE UNITED NATIONS IN NEW YORK
International Fund for Agricultural Development
Room S-2955
United Nations Headquarters
New York, N.Y. 10017, United States
  Telephone: (212) 963-4245, 4246, 4248, 0058, 0059, 0060

Chapter XVII

Interim Commission for the International Trade Organization (ICITO) and the General Agreement on Tariffs and Trade (GATT)

The United Nations Conference on Trade and Employment, held at Havana, Cuba, between November 1947 and March 1948, drew up a charter for an International Trade Organization (ITO) and established an Interim Commission for the International Trade Organization (ICITO). Since the charter itself was never accepted, ITO was not established. However, while drawing up the charter, the Preparatory Committee's members negotiated on tariffs among themselves, and also drew up the General Agreement on Tariffs and Trade (GATT). The Agreement—a multilateral treaty embodying reciprocal rights and obligations—is the only multilateral instrument that lays down agreed rules for international trade. It entered into force on 1 January 1948 with 23 contracting parties. Since then, ICITO has provided the GATT secretariat.

As at 31 December 1985, the number of contracting parties to GATT stood at 90. One other country, Tunisia, had acceded provisionally. The contracting parties conducted about 85 per cent of all international trade while 31 other countries applied the rules of GATT.

Multilateral trade negotiations

The multilateral work programme pursued within GATT during 1985 had two distinct strands—the continuation of work resulting from the conclusion of the Tokyo Round of multilateral trade negotiations in 1979,[a] and the work programme set out by the 1982 GATT Ministerial Meeting.[b] These programmes were undertaken amidst intensified discussions and debates by contracting parties on the question of holding a new round of multilateral trade negotiations.

Implementation of the Tokyo Round agreements

The agreements of the Tokyo Round, the seventh "round" of multilateral trade negotiations in the 38-year history of GATT, provided an improved framework for the conduct of world trade and were adopted as an integral part of the rules of GATT.

Tariff negotiations during the Tokyo Round resulted in agreement on import duty reductions to be effected in eight annual cuts by the industrialized countries. On 1 January 1985, the sixth of such cuts was máde. By the end of the year, tariff cuts negotiated under this Round, for both industrial and agricultural goods, covered trade worth some $300 billion.

In 1985, the GATT Committee on Tariff Concessions continued compiling tariff schedules in loose-leaf form to allow an easier reference to changes made during rounds of tariff negotiations. By the end of the year, 37 out of a total of 62 national tariff schedules were available in this form. The Committee was also concerned with the upcoming implementation of the new Harmonized Commodity Description and Coding System developed by the Customs Co-operation Council at Brussels, Belgium. The System, which would facilitate the analysis of trade statistics and monitor and protect the value of tariff concessions, would serve as a single standard for the classification of traded goods. The introduction of the System presented GATT with the need for negotiations where the change from current nomenclatures disturbed the balance of concessions already negotiated in tariff rounds and other past negotiations.

The Committee on Subsidies and Countervailing Measures continued to oversee the implementation of a code providing a mechanism for international surveillance and dispute settlement and aiming to ensure that the use of subsidies by any signatory did not harm the trading interests of others. It considered panel reports on complaints by the United States on alleged subsidies by the European Communities (EC) on exports of wheat flour and pasta products, and by EC concerning a section of a 1984 United States Trade and Tariff Act relating to countervailing and anti-dumping action on imported wine. It also established a panel to rule on the wine industry complaint.

The Committee on Anti-Dumping Practices continued to examine national laws and legislation. ("Dumped" goods were broadly defined as imports which were sold at prices below those charged by the producer in his domestic market.) During the year, the Committee adopted a number of recommendations by the *Ad Hoc* Group on the Implementation of the Anti-Dumping Code.

[a]YUN 1979, p. 1328.
[b]YUN 1982, p. 1598.

The Committee on Government Procurement continued to examine laws, procedures and regulations and made further progress in renegotiating the Agreement on Government Procurement. It reviewed the follow-up of a 1984 panel report on a United States complaint against EC practices relating to the treatment of value-added taxes.[c] It also published a practical guide to the Agreement intended for the business community. A Working Party on Computer Procurement submitted its recommendations to the Committee at the end of the year.

Implementation of the Agreement on Technical Barriers to Trade—commonly known as the "Standards Code"—is monitored by the Committee on Technical Barriers to Trade. In 1985, it released a list of products covered by notifications under the Agreement for the use of national standards bodies. It also discussed technical questions relating to testing and inspection procedures.

As recommended by the Committee on Trade in Civil Aircraft, a further 32 categories of products were, as of 1 January 1985, added to the duty-free coverage of the Agreement on Trade in Civil Aircraft, and the Committee discussed the measures taken by member Governments to implement this extension of the Agreement. Attention was also given to the question of export credits for civil aircraft sales.

Throughout the year, the International Meat Council, which oversees the Arrangement regarding Bovine Meat, continued to discuss and analyse the bovine meat market situation. The 26 signatories to this Arrangement—one of two multilateral agreements relating to trade in agricultural products negotiated during the Tokyo Round (the other covered dairy products)—accounted for some 90 per cent of the world's exports of fresh, chilled and frozen beef and veal (excluding intra-EC trade) and about 60 per cent of both world imports and world production.

In May 1985, the International Dairy Products Council, supervisor of the International Dairy Arrangement, adopted decisions, in the aftermath of EC's sales of "old" butter,[d] aimed at contributing to greater stability in dairy markets by reducing excess supplies and stimulating demand in response to lower prices. A report on the world market for dairy products was published in December.

Work also continued during the year in committees overseeing the agreements on customs valuation and import licensing.

Ministerial work programme

GATT continued in 1985 to implement the multilateral work programme set out by the 1982 GATT Ministerial Meeting. The ministerial declaration had called for efforts to achieve a comprehensive understanding on safeguards—the right of GATT contracting parties to impose temporary trade restrictions on imports which seriously injured a domestic industry or threatened to do so. Consultations held during the year revealed some convergence of views on a number of safeguard issues, and the contracting parties called on the Safeguards Committee to continue its work.

The Committee on Trade in Agriculture, established by the Ministerial Meeting, continued considering its 1984 recommendations to achieve greater liberalization of trade in agriculture.[e] In November 1985, the contracting parties decided that the Committee should pursue its examination of all the approaches referred to in the recommendations and of the way they could be elaborated as a basis for possible future negotiations.

The Committee on Trade and Development held further consultations with a number of countries to review their trading policies in relation to Part IV of the General Agreement dealing with special treatment for developing countries. Consultations covering trade in tropical products and barriers affecting the trading prospects of the least developed countries were also continued. The Committee undertook a review of the operation of the "Enabling Clause"—which provides the legal basis in GATT for preferences to developing countries, as in the case of the GSP (generalized system of preferences) programmes—and on prospects for increasing trade between developed and developing countries.

Other aspects of the ministerial work programme included the examination of quantitative restrictions and other non-tariff measures with a view to eliminating those not in conformity with GATT, and a review of the adequacy and effectiveness of the Tokyo Round agreements and obstacles to their acceptance by non-signatories.

Other GATT activities

Contracting parties session

The year 1985 was marked by discussions aimed at strengthening the trading system and restoring the credibility of trade rules. It was a sign to the outside world—especially the business community—that the 90 contracting parties were moving together to overcome problems facing world trade and use the opportunities that negotiations could offer for growth and development.

In November 1985, at a session held at the senior official level, GATT contracting parties reviewed progress made in implementing the 1982

[c]YUN 1984, p. 1289.
[d]*Ibid.*, p. 1290.
[e]*Ibid.*

ministerial work programme and dealt with questions relating to changes in the trading environment. They decided—as they had already discussed earlier at a special session held from 30 September to 2 October—to establish a preparatory committee to determine the objectives, subject-matter and participation in a new round of multilateral trade negotiations. The preparatory committee was to begin its work in January 1986 under the chairmanship of the GATT Director-General.

Council of Representatives

The Council of Representatives, GATT's highest body between sessions of the contracting parties, held two meetings in 1985 to review developments in the trading system. Three new dispute panels were set up during the year and several reports were adopted or considered further.

Consultative Group of Eighteen

At its three meetings held in 1985, the Consultative Group of Eighteen—a high-level forum for discussing problems facing international trade—considered practical steps which could be taken to further trade liberalization and enhance the integrity of the trading system. These discussions were closely linked with the decision taken later in the year by the contracting parties to begin preparations for a new round of multilateral trade negotiations.

Balance-of-payments restrictions

During 1985, the GATT Committee on Balance-of-Payments Import Restrictions held full consultations with Colombia, Israel and Portugal. Consultations under a simplified procedure took place with Brazil, Egypt, Ghana, Pakistan, Sri Lanka, Tunisia and Turkey.

Textiles Arrangement

The Arrangement regarding International Trade in Textiles, known as the Multifibre Arrangement (MFA), regulating most of the $15 billion worth of textiles and clothing which MFA member countries in the developing world exported to those in the developed world, was extended a second time in 1981[f] until 31 July 1986. By the end of 1985, the Protocol extending MFA had been accepted by 43 signatories representing 52 countries. In 1985, the Textiles Committee conducted its fourth annual review of the current extension and discussed the question of renewing the Arrangement. It also stressed the need for more liberal treatment of textiles and clothing in line with the objectives of trade liberalization to which the proposed round of multilateral trade negotiations was addressed.

Technical assistance

In 1985, the GATT secretariat's Technical Co-operation Division organized missions to, or seminars in, the following developing countries: Cameroon, China (twice), Costa Rica, Haiti, Jamaica, Malaysia, Republic of Korea, Thailand, Turkey (twice) and Uruguay. GATT officials also participated in seminars sponsored by regional organizations.

Training programme

The year 1985 marked the thirtieth anniversary of the GATT commercial policy training courses. From 1955 to the end of 1985, a total of 954 officials from 112 countries and 10 regional organizations had attended courses. A course in French and one in English were given in 1985.

International Trade Centre

Established by GATT in 1964, and jointly operated by GATT and the United Nations Conference on Trade and Development since 1968, the International Trade Centre continued to provide trade information and trade promotion advisory services to developing countries. The Centre's work was directed at assisting developing countries to formulate and implement trade promotion programmes and activities and to become self-reliant. The value of its technical co-operation programme in 1985 was estimated at $15.1 million.

Publications

Publications issued in 1985 included the annual volumes of *GATT Activities, International Trade* and *Basic Instruments and Selected Documents*, and the newsletter *GATT Focus*, issued six times a year. Also published was *The World Market for Dairy Products (1985)* in book form.

Secretariat

As at 31 December 1985, the GATT secretariat employed 295 staff members—130 in the Professional and higher categories and 165 in the General Service category. They were drawn from 44 nationalities.

Financial arrangements

Member countries of GATT contribute to the budget in accordance with a scale assessed on the basis of each country's share in the total trade of the contracting parties and associated Governments. The budget for 1985 was 57,540,000 Swiss francs. The scale of contributions for 1985 is given below. (The United Nations rate of exchange for December 1985 was SwF 2.09 = $US 1.00.)

[f]YUN 1981, p. 1484.

Annex I. CONTRACTING PARTIES TO THE GENERAL AGREEMENT ON TARIFFS AND TRADE AND SCALE OF CONTRIBUTIONS FOR 1985
(As at 31 December 1985)

Contracting party	CONTRIBUTION Percent-age	Net contribution (in Swiss francs)	Contracting party	CONTRIBUTION Percent-age	Net contribution (in Swiss francs)
Argentina	0.52	293,800	Malawi	0.12	67,800
Australia	1.43	807,950	Malaysia	0.77	435,050
Austria	1.10	621,500	Maldives	0.12	67,800
Bangladesh	0.12	67,800	Malta	0.12	67,800
Barbados	0.12	67,800	Mauritania	0.12	67,800
Belgium	3.18	1,796,700	Mauritius	0.12	67,800
Belize	0.12	67,800	Netherlands	4.34	2,452,100
Benin	0.12	67,800	New Zealand	0.34	192,100
Brazil	1.39	785,350	Nicaragua	0.12	67,800
Burkina Faso	0.12	67,800	Niger	0.12	67,800
Burma	0.12	67,800	Nigeria	1.03	581,950
Burundi	0.12	67,800	Norway	1.01	570,650
Cameroon	0.12	67,800	Pakistan	0.26	146,900
Canada	4.26	2,406,900	Peru	0.20	113,000
Central African Republic	0.12	67,800	Philippines	0.41	231,650
Chad	0.12	67,800	Poland	0.78	440,700
Chile	0.25	141,250	Portugal	0.44	248,600
Colombia	0.25	141,250	Republic of Korea	1.48	836,200
Congo	0.12	67,800	Romania	0.72	406,800
Cuba	0.32	180,800	Rwanda	0.12	67,800
Cyprus	0.12	67,800	Senegal	0.12	67,800
Czechoslovakia	1.00	565,000	Sierra Leone	0.12	67,800
Denmark	1.02	576,300	Singapore	1.09	615,850
Dominican Republic	0.12	67,800	South Africa	1.17	661,050
Egypt	0.33	186,450	Spain	1.58	892,700
Finland	0.82	463,300	Sri Lanka	0.12	67,800
France	6.71	3,791,150	Suriname	0.12	67,800
Gabon	0.12	67,800	Sweden	1.70	960,500
Gambia	0.12	67,800	Switzerland	1.72	971,800
Germany, Federal Republic of	10.23	5,779,950	Thailand	0.51	288,150
Ghana	0.12	67,800	Togo	0.12	67,800
Greece	0.43	242,950	Trinidad and Tobago	0.19	107,350
Guyana	0.12	67,800	Turkey	0.44	248,600
Haiti	0.12	67,800	Uganda	0.12	67,800
Hungary	0.54	305,100	United Kingdom	7.67	4,333,550
Iceland	0.12	67,800	United Republic of Tanzania	0.12	67,800
India	0.73	412,450	United States	14.88	8,407,200
Indonesia	1.16	655,400	Uruguay	0.12	67,800
Ireland	0.55	310,750	Yugoslavia	0.75	423,750
Israel	0.47	265,550	Zaire	0.12	67,800
Italy	4.93	2,785,450	Zambia	0.12	67,800
Ivory Coast	0.16	90,400	Zimbabwe	0.12	67,800
Jamaica	0.12	67,800	*Associated Governments*		
Japan	8.62	4,870,300			
Kenya	0.12	67,800	Democratic Kampuchea	0.12	67,800
Kuwait	0.63	355,950	Tunisia	0.17	96,050
Luxembourg	0.28	158,200			
Madagascar	0.12	67,800	Total	100.00	56,500,000

Annex II. OFFICERS AND OFFICE OF THE GENERAL AGREEMENT ON TARIFFS AND TRADE
(As at 31 December 1985)

OFFICERS

OFFICERS OF THE CONTRACTING PARTIES*

Chairman of the Contracting Parties: Kazuo-Chiba (Japan).
Vice-Chairmen of the Contracting Parties: Abdel-Bari Hamza (Egypt), Gustavo Adolfo Vargas (Nicaragua), Jean-Louis Wolzfeld (Luxembourg).
Chairman of the Council of Representatives: Kun Park (Republic of Korea).
Chairman of the Committee on Trade and Development: Osvaldo López-Noguerol (Argentina).

SENIOR OFFICERS OF THE SECRETARIAT

Director-General: Arthur Dunkel.
Deputy Directors-General: Madan G. Mathur, William B. Kelly.

SENIOR OFFICERS OF THE
INTERNATIONAL TRADE CENTRE UNCTAD/GATT
Executive Director: Göran M. Engblom.
Deputy Executive Director: Said T. Harb.

*Elected at the end of the November 1985 session of contracting parties to hold office until the end of the next session.

HEADQUARTERS

GATT Secretariat
Centre William Rappard
Rue de Lausanne 154
1211 Geneva 21, Switzerland
Cable address: GATT GENEVA
Telephone: (022) 39 51 11
Telex: 28787 GATT CH

Appendices

Roster of the United Nations

(As at 31 December 1985)

MEMBER	DATE OF ADMISSION	MEMBER	DATE OF ADMISSION	MEMBER	DATE OF ADMISSION
Afghanistan	19 Nov. 1946	Germany, Federal Republic of	18 Sep. 1973	Peru	31 Oct. 1945
Albania	14 Dec. 1955	Ghana	8 Mar. 1957	Philippines	24 Oct. 1945
Algeria	8 Oct. 1962	Greece	25 Oct. 1945	Poland	24 Oct. 1945
Angola	1 Dec. 1976	Grenada	17 Sep. 1974	Portugal	14 Dec. 1955
Antigua and Barbuda	11 Nov. 1981	Guatemala	21 Nov. 1945	Qatar	21 Sep. 1971
Argentina	24 Oct. 1945	Guinea	12 Dec. 1958	Romania	14 Dec. 1955
Australia	1 Nov. 1945	Guinea-Bissau	17 Sep. 1974	Rwanda	18 Sep. 1962
Austria	14 Dec. 1955	Guyana	20 Sep. 1966	Saint Christopher and Nevis	23 Sep. 1983
Bahamas	18 Sep. 1973	Haiti	24 Oct. 1945	Saint Lucia	18 Sep. 1979
Bahrain	21 Sep. 1971	Honduras	17 Dec. 1945	Saint Vincent and the Grenadines	16 Sep. 1980
Bangladesh	17 Sep. 1974	Hungary	14 Dec. 1955	Samoa	15 Dec. 1976
Barbados	9 Dec. 1966	Iceland	19 Nov. 1946	Sao Tome and Principe	16 Sep. 1975
Belgium	27 Dec. 1945	India	30 Oct. 1945	Saudi Arabia	24 Oct. 1945
Belize	25 Sep. 1981	Indonesia[2]	28 Sep. 1950	Senegal	28 Sep. 1960
Benin	20 Sep. 1960	Iran (Islamic Republic of)	24 Oct. 1945	Seychelles	21 Sep. 1976
Bhutan	21 Sep. 1971	Iraq	21 Dec. 1945	Sierra Leone	27 Sep. 1961
Bolivia	14 Nov. 1945	Ireland	14 Dec. 1955	Singapore[4]	21 Sep. 1965
Botswana	17 Oct. 1966	Israel	11 May 1949	Solomon Islands	19 Sep. 1978
Brazil	24 Oct. 1945	Italy	14 Dec. 1955	Somalia	20 Sep. 1960
Brunei Darussalam	21 Sep. 1984	Ivory Coast (Côte d'Ivoire)[3]	20 Sep. 1960	South Africa	7 Nov. 1945
Bulgaria	14 Dec. 1955	Jamaica	18 Sep. 1962	Spain	14 Dec. 1955
Burkina Faso	20 Sep. 1960	Japan	18 Dec. 1956	Sri Lanka	14 Dec. 1955
Burma	19 Apr. 1948	Jordan	14 Dec. 1955	Sudan	12 Nov. 1956
Burundi	18 Sep. 1962	Kenya	16 Dec. 1963	Suriname	4 Dec. 1975
Byelorussian Soviet Socialist Republic	24 Oct. 1945	Kuwait	14 May 1963	Swaziland	24 Sep. 1968
Cameroon	20 Sep. 1960	Lao People's Democratic Republic	14 Dec. 1955	Sweden	19 Nov. 1946
Canada	9 Nov. 1945	Lebanon	24 Oct. 1945	Syrian Arab Republic[1]	24 Oct. 1945
Cape Verde	16 Sep. 1975	Lesotho	17 Oct. 1966	Thailand	16 Dec. 1946
Central African Republic	20 Sep. 1960	Liberia	2 Nov. 1945	Togo	20 Sep. 1960
Chad	20 Sep. 1960	Libyan Arab Jamahiriya	14 Dec. 1955	Trinidad and Tobago	18 Sep. 1962
Chile	24 Oct. 1945	Luxembourg	24 Oct. 1945	Tunisia	12 Nov. 1956
China	24 Oct. 1945	Madagascar	20 Sep. 1960	Turkey	24 Oct. 1945
Colombia	5 Nov. 1945	Malawi	1 Dec. 1964	Uganda	25 Oct. 1962
Comoros	12 Nov. 1975	Malaysia[4]	17 Sep. 1957	Ukrainian Soviet Socialist Republic	24 Oct. 1945
Congo	20 Sep. 1960	Maldives	21 Sep. 1965	Union of Soviet Socialist Republics	24 Oct. 1945
Costa Rica	2 Nov. 1945	Mali	28 Sep. 1960	United Arab Emirates	9 Dec. 1971
Cuba	24 Oct. 1945	Malta	1 Dec. 1964	United Kingdom of Great Britain and Northern Ireland	24 Oct. 1945
Cyprus	20 Sep. 1960	Mauritania	27 Oct. 1961	United Republic of Tanzania[5]	14 Dec. 1961
Czechoslovakia	24 Oct. 1945	Mauritius	24 Apr. 1968	United States of America	24 Oct. 1945
Democratic Kampuchea	14 Dec. 1955	Mexico	7 Nov. 1945	Uruguay	18 Dec. 1945
Democratic Yemen	14 Dec. 1967	Mongolia	27 Oct. 1961	Vanuatu	15 Sep. 1981
Denmark	24 Oct. 1945	Morocco	12 Nov. 1956	Venezuela	15 Nov. 1945
Djibouti	20 Sep. 1977	Mozambique	16 Sep. 1975	Viet Nam	20 Sep. 1977
Dominica	18 Dec. 1978	Nepal	14 Dec. 1955	Yemen	30 Sep. 1947
Dominican Republic	24 Oct. 1945	Netherlands	10 Dec. 1945	Yugoslavia	24 Oct. 1945
Ecuador	21 Dec. 1945	New Zealand	24 Oct. 1945	Zaire	20 Sep. 1960
Egypt[1]	24 Oct. 1945	Nicaragua	24 Oct. 1945	Zambia	1 Dec. 1964
El Salvador	24 Oct. 1945	Niger	20 Sep. 1960	Zimbabwe	25 Aug. 1980
Equatorial Guinea	12 Nov. 1968	Nigeria	7 Oct. 1960		
Ethiopia	13 Nov. 1945	Norway	27 Nov. 1945		
Fiji	13 Oct. 1970	Oman	7 Oct. 1971		
Finland	14 Dec. 1955	Pakistan	30 Sep. 1947		
France	24 Oct. 1945	Panama	13 Nov. 1945		
Gabon	20 Sep. 1960	Papua New Guinea	10 Oct. 1975		
Gambia	21 Sep. 1965	Paraguay	24 Oct. 1945		
German Democratic Republic	18 Sep. 1973				

(footnotes on next page)

(footnotes for preceding page)

[1]Egypt and Syria, both of which became Members of the United Nations on 24 October 1945, joined together—following a plebiscite held in those countries on 21 February 1958—to form the United Arab Republic. On 13 October 1961, Syria, having resumed its status as an independent State, also resumed its separate membership in the United Nations; it changed its name to the Syrian Arab Republic on 14 September 1971. The United Arab Republic continued as a Member of the United Nations and reverted to the name of Egypt on 2 September 1971.

[2]On 20 January 1965, Indonesia informed the Secretary-General that it had decided to withdraw from the United Nations. On 19 September 1966, it notified him of its decision to resume participation in United Nations activities. On 28 September 1966, the General Assembly took note of that decision and the President invited the representatives of Indonesia to take their seats in the Assembly.

[3]On 6 November 1985, Côte d'Ivoire requested that its name no longer be translated into different languages (see p. 392). However, for ease of reference, "Ivory Coast" has been used throughout this volume.

[4]On 16 September 1963, Sabah (North Borneo), Sarawak and Singapore joined with the Federation of Malaya (which became a United Nations Member on 17 September 1957) to form Malaysia. On 9 August 1965, Singapore became an independent State and on 21 September 1965 it became a Member of the United Nations.

[5]Tanganyika was admitted to the United Nations on 14 December 1961, and Zanzibar on 16 December 1963. Following ratification, on 26 April 1964, of the Articles of Union between Tanganyika and Zanzibar, the two States became represented as a single Member: the United Republic of Tanganyika and Zanzibar; it changed its name to the United Republic of Tanzania on 1 November 1964.

Appendix II

Charter of the United Nations and Statute of the International Court of Justice

Charter of the United Nations

NOTE: The Charter of the United Nations was signed on 26 June 1945, in San Francisco, at the conclusion of the United Nations Conference on International Organization, and came into force on 24 October 1945. The Statute of the International Court of Justice is an integral part of the Charter.

Amendments to Articles 23, 27 and 61 of the Charter were adopted by the General Assembly on 17 December 1963 and came into force on 31 August 1965. A further amendment to Article 61 was adopted by the General Assembly on 20 December 1971, and came into force on 24 September 1973. An amendment to Article 109, adopted by the General Assembly on 20 December 1965, came into force on 12 June 1968.

The amendment to Article 23 enlarges the membership of the Security Council from 11 to 15. The amended Article 27 provides that decisions of the Security Council on procedural matters shall be made by an affirmative vote of nine members (formerly seven) and on all other matters by an affirmative vote of nine members (formerly seven), in-cluding the concurring votes of the five permanent members of the Security Council.

The amendment to Article 61, which entered into force on 31 August 1965, enlarged the membership of the Economic and Social Council from 18 to 27. The subsequent amendment to that Article, which entered into force on 24 September 1973, further increased the membership of the Council from 27 to 54.

The amendment to Article 109, which relates to the first paragraph of that Article, provides that a General Conference of Member States for the purpose of reviewing the Charter may be held at a date and place to be fixed by a two-thirds vote of the members of the General Assembly and by a vote of any nine members (formerly seven) of the Security Council. Paragraph 3 of Article 109, which deals with the con-sideration of a possible review conference during the tenth regular ses-sion of the General Assembly, has been retained in its original form in its reference to a "vote of any seven members of the Security Coun-cil", the paragraph having been acted upon in 1955 by the General Assembly, at its tenth regular session, and by the Security Council.

WE THE PEOPLES
OF THE UNITED NATIONS
DETERMINED
to save succeeding generations from the scourge of war, which twice in our lifetime has brought untold sorrow to mankind, and
to reaffirm faith in fundamental human rights, in the dignity and worth of the human person, in the equal rights of men and women and of nations large and small, and
to establish conditions under which justice and respect for the obliga-tions arising from treaties and other sources of international law can be maintained, and
to promote social progress and better standards of life in larger freedom,

AND FOR THESE ENDS
to practice tolerance and live together in peace with one another as good neighbours, and
to unite our strength to maintain international peace and security, and
to ensure, by the acceptance of principles and the institution of methods, that armed force shall not be used, save in the common interest, and
to employ international machinery for the promotion of the economic and social advancement of all peoples,

HAVE RESOLVED TO
COMBINE OUR EFFORTS TO
ACCOMPLISH THESE AIMS
Accordingly, our respective Governments, through representatives assembled in the city of San Francisco, who have exhibited their full powers found to be in good and due form, have agreed to the present Charter of the United Nations and do hereby establish an international organization to be known as the United Nations.

Chapter I
PURPOSES AND PRINCIPLES

Article 1
The Purposes of the United Nations are:

1. To maintain international peace and security, and to that end: to take effective collective measures for the prevention and removal of threats to the peace, and for the suppression of acts of aggression or other breaches of the peace, and to bring about by peaceful means, and in conformity with the principles of justice and international law, adjustment or settlement of international disputes or situations which might lead to a breach of the peace;

2. To develop friendly relations among nations based on respect for the principle of equal rights and self-determination of peoples, and to take other appropriate measures to strengthen universal peace;

3. To achieve international co-operation in solving international prob-lems of an economic, social, cultural, or humanitarian character, and in promoting and encouraging respect for human rights and for fun-damental freedoms for all without distinction as to race, sex, language, or religion; and

4. To be a centre for harmonizing the actions of nations in the at-tainment of these common ends.

Article 2
The Organization and its Members, in pursuit of the Purposes stated in Article 1, shall act in accordance with the following Principles.

1. The Organization is based on the principle of the sovereign equality of all its Members.

2. All Members, in order to ensure to all of them the rights and benefits resulting from membership, shall fulfil in good faith the obliga-tions assumed by them in accordance with the present Charter.

3.   All Members shall settle their international disputes by peaceful means in such a manner that international peace and security, and justice, are not endangered.

4.   All Members shall refrain in their international relations from the threat or use of force against the territorial integrity or political independence of any state, or in any other manner inconsistent with the Purposes of the United Nations.

5.   All Members shall give the United Nations every assistance in any action it takes in accordance with the present Charter, and shall refrain from giving assistance to any state against which the United Nations is taking preventive or enforcement action.

6.   The Organization shall ensure that states which are not Members of the United Nations act in accordance with these Principles so far as may be necessary for the maintenance of international peace and security.

7.   Nothing contained in the present Charter shall authorize the United Nations to intervene in matters which are essentially within the domestic jurisdiction of any state or shall require the Members to submit such matters to settlement under the present Charter; but this principle shall not prejudice the application of enforcement measures under Chapter VII.

Chapter II
MEMBERSHIP

Article 3

The original Members of the United Nations shall be the states which, having participated in the United Nations Conference on International Organization at San Francisco, or having previously signed the Declaration by United Nations of 1 January 1942, sign the present Charter and ratify it in accordance with Article 110.

Article 4

1.   Membership in the United Nations is open to all other peace-loving states which accept the obligations contained in the present Charter and, in the judgment of the Organization, are able and willing to carry out these obligations.

2.   The admission of any such state to membership in the United Nations will be effected by a decision of the General Assembly upon the recommendation of the Security Council.

Article 5

A Member of the United Nations against which preventive or enforcement action has been taken by the Security Council may be suspended from the exercise of the rights and privileges of membership by the General Assembly upon the recommendation of the Security Council. The exercise of these rights and privileges may be restored by the Security Council.

Article 6

A Member of the United Nations which has persistently violated the Principles contained in the present Charter may be expelled from the Organization by the General Assembly upon the recommendation of the Security Council.

Chapter III
ORGANS

Article 7

1.   There are established as the principal organs of the United Nations: a General Assembly, a Security Council, an Economic and Social Council, a Trusteeship Council, an International Court of Justice, and a Secretariat.

2.   Such subsidiary organs as may be found necessary may be established in accordance with the present Charter.

Article 8

The United Nations shall place no restrictions on the eligibility of men and women to participate in any capacity and under conditions of equality in its principal and subsidiary organs.

Chapter IV
THE GENERAL ASSEMBLY

Composition

Article 9

1.   The General Assembly shall consist of all the Members of the United Nations.

2.   Each Member shall have not more than five representatives in the General Assembly.

Functions and powers

Article 10

The General Assembly may discuss any questions or any matters within the scope of the present Charter or relating to the powers and functions of any organs provided for in the present Charter, and, except as provided in Article 12, may make recommendations to the Members of the United Nations or to the Security Council or to both on any such questions or matters.

Article 11

1.   The General Assembly may consider the general principles of co-operation in the maintenance of international peace and security, including the principles governing disarmament and the regulation of armaments, and may make recommendations with regard to such principles to the Members or to the Security Council or to both.

2.   The General Assembly may discuss any questions relating to the maintenance of international peace and security brought before it by any Member of the United Nations, or by the Security Council, or by a state which is not a Member of the United Nations in accordance with Article 35, paragraph 2, and, except as provided in Article 12, may make recommendations with regard to any such questions to the state or states concerned or to the Security Council or to both. Any such question on which action is necessary shall be referred to the Security Council by the General Assembly either before or after discussion.

3.   The General Assembly may call the attention of the Security Council to situations which are likely to endanger international peace and security.

4.   The powers of the General Assembly set forth in this Article shall not limit the general scope of Article 10.

Article 12

1.   While the Security Council is exercising in respect of any dispute or situation the functions assigned to it in the present Charter, the General Assembly shall not make any recommendation with regard to that dispute or situation unless the Security Council so requests.

2.   The Secretary-General, with the consent of the Security Council, shall notify the General Assembly at each session of any matters relative to the maintenance of international peace and security which are being dealt with by the Security Council and shall similarly notify the General Assembly, or the Members of the United Nations if the General Assembly is not in session, immediately the Security Council ceases to deal with such matters.

Article 13

1.   The General Assembly shall initiate studies and make recommendations for the purpose of:

a.   promoting international co-operation in the political field and encouraging the progressive development of international law and its codification;

b.   promoting international co-operation in the economic, social, cultural, educational, and health fields, and assisting in the realization of human rights and fundamental freedoms for all without distinction as to race, sex, language, or religion.

2.   The further responsibilities, functions and powers of the General Assembly with respect to matters mentioned in paragraph 1(b) above are set forth in Chapters IX and X.

Article 14

Subject to the provisions of Article 12, the General Assembly may recommend measures for the peaceful adjustment of any situation, regardless of origin, which it deems likely to impair the general welfare or friendly relations among nations, including situations resulting from a violation of the provisions of the present Charter setting forth the Purposes and Principles of the United Nations.

Article 15

1. The General Assembly shall receive and consider annual and special reports from the Security Council; these reports shall include an account of the measures that the Security Council has decided upon or taken to maintain international peace and security.

2. The General Assembly shall receive and consider reports from the other organs of the United Nations.

Article 16

The General Assembly shall perform such functions with respect to the international trusteeship system as are assigned to it under Chapters XII and XIII, including the approval of the trusteeship agreements for areas not designated as strategic.

Article 17

1. The General Assembly shall consider and approve the budget of the Organization.

2. The expenses of the Organization shall be borne by the Members as apportioned by the General Assembly.

3. The General Assembly shall consider and approve any financial and budgetary arrangements with specialized agencies referred to in Article 57 and shall examine the administrative budgets of such specialized agencies with a view to making recommendations to the agencies concerned.

Voting

Article 18

1. Each member of the General Assembly shall have one vote.

2. Decisions of the General Assembly on important questions shall be made by a two-thirds majority of the members present and voting. These questions shall include: recommendations with respect to the maintenance of international peace and security, the election of the non-permanent members of the Security Council, the election of members of the Economic and Social Council, the election of members of the Trusteeship Council in accordance with paragraph 1(c) of Article 86, the admission of new Members to the United Nations, the suspension of the rights and privileges of membership, the expulsion of Members, questions relating to the operation of the trusteeship system, and budgetary questions.

3. Decisions on other questions, including the determination of additional categories of questions to be decided by a two-thirds majority, shall be made by a majority of the members present and voting.

Article 19

A Member of the United Nations which is in arrears in the payment of its financial contributions to the Organization shall have no vote in the General Assembly if the amount of its arrears equals or exceeds the amount of the contributions due from it for the preceding two full years. The General Assembly may, nevertheless, permit such a Member to vote if it is satisfied that the failure to pay is due to conditions beyond the control of the Member.

Procedure

Article 20

The General Assembly shall meet in regular annual sessions and in such special sessions as occasion may require. Special sessions shall be convoked by the Secretary-General at the request of the Security Council or of a majority of the Members of the United Nations.

Article 21

The General Assembly shall adopt its own rules of procedure. It shall elect its President for each session.

Article 22

The General Assembly may establish such subsidiary organs as it deems necessary for the performance of its functions.

Chapter V
THE SECURITY COUNCIL

Composition

Article 23[1]

1. The Security Council shall consist of fifteen Members of the United Nations. The Republic of China, France, the Union of Soviet Socialist Republics, the United Kingdom of Great Britain and Northern Ireland, and the United States of America shall be permanent members of the Security Council. The General Assembly shall elect ten other Members of the United Nations to be non-permanent members of the Security Council, due regard being specially paid, in the first instance to the contribution of Members of the United Nations to the maintenance of international peace and security and to the other purposes of the Organization, and also to equitable geographical distribution.

2. The non-permanent members of the Security Council shall be elected for a term of two years. In the first election of the non-permanent members after the increase of the membership of the Security Council from eleven to fifteen, two of the four additional members shall be chosen for a term of one year. A retiring member shall not be eligible for immediate re-election.

3. Each member of the Security Council shall have one representative.

Functions and powers

Article 24

1. In order to ensure prompt and effective action by the United Nations, its Members confer on the Security Council primary responsibility for the maintenance of international peace and security, and agree that in carrying out its duties under this responsibility the Security Council acts on their behalf.

2. In discharging these duties the Security Council shall act in accordance with the Purposes and Principles of the United Nations. The specific powers granted to the Security Council for the discharge of these duties are laid down in Chapters VI, VII, VIII, and XII.

3. The Security Council shall submit annual and, when necessary, special reports to the General Assembly for its consideration.

Article 25

The Members of the United Nations agree to accept and carry out the decisions of the Security Council in accordance with the present Charter.

Article 26

In order to promote the establishment and maintenance of international peace and security with the least diversion for armaments of the world's human and economic resources, the Security Council shall be responsible for formulating, with the assistance of the Military Staff Committee referred to in Article 47, plans to be submitted to the Members of the United Nations for the establishment of a system for the regulation of armaments.

---

[1]Amended text of Article 23 which came into force on 31 August 1965. (The text of Article 23 before it was amended read as follows:

1. The Security Council shall consist of eleven Members of the United Nations. The Republic of China, France, the Union of Soviet Socialist Republics, the United Kingdom of Great Britain and Northern Ireland, and the United States of America shall be permanent members of the Security Council. The General Assembly shall elect six other Members of the United Nations to be non-permanent members of the Security Council, due regard being specially paid, in the first instance to the contribution of Members of the United Nations to the maintenance of international peace and security and to the other purposes of the Organization, and also to equitable geographical distribution.

2. The non-permanent members of the Security Council shall be elected for a term of two years. In the first election of non-permanent members, however, three shall be chosen for a term of one year. A retiring member shall not be eligible for immediate re-election.

3. Each member of the Security Council shall have one representative.)

Voting

Article 27 [2]

1. Each member of the Security Council shall have one vote.

2. Decisions of the Security Council on procedural matters shall be made by an affirmative vote of nine members.

3. Decisions of the Security Council on all other matters shall be made by an affirmative vote of nine members including the concurring votes of the permanent members; provided that, in decisions under Chapter VI, and under paragraph 3 of Article 52, a party to a dispute shall abstain from voting.

Procedure

Article 28

1. The Security Council shall be so organized as to be able to function continuously. Each member of the Security Council shall for this purpose be represented at all times at the seat of the Organization.

2. The Security Council shall hold periodic meetings at which each of its members may, if it so desires, be represented by a member of the government or by some other specially designated representative.

3. The Security Council may hold meetings at such places other than the seat of the Organization as in its judgment will best facilitate its work.

Article 29

The Security Council may establish such subsidiary organs as it deems necessary for the performance of its functions.

Article 30

The Security Council shall adopt its own rules of procedure, including the method of selecting its President.

Article 31

Any Member of the United Nations which is not a member of the Security Council may participate, without vote, in the discussion of any question brought before the Security Council whenever the latter considers that the interests of that Member are specially affected.

Article 32

Any Member of the United Nations which is not a member of the Security Council or any state which is not a Member of the United Nations, if it is a party to a dispute under consideration by the Security Council, shall be invited to participate, without vote, in the discussion relating to the dispute. The Security Council shall lay down such conditions as it deems just for the participation of a state which is not a Member of the United Nations.

Chapter VI
PACIFIC SETTLEMENT OF DISPUTES

Article 33

1. The parties to any dispute, the continuance of which is likely to endanger the maintenance of international peace and security, shall, first of all, seek a solution by negotiation, enquiry, mediation, conciliation, arbitration, judicial settlement, resort to regional agencies or arrangements, or other peaceful means of their own choice.

2. The Security Council shall, when it deems necessary, call upon the parties to settle their dispute by such means.

Article 34

The Security Council may investigate any dispute or any situation which might lead to international friction or give rise to a dispute, in order to determine whether the continuance of the dispute or situation is likely to endanger the maintenance of international peace and security.

Article 35

1. Any Member of the United Nations may bring any dispute, or any situation of the nature referred to in Article 34, to the attention of the Security Council or of the General Assembly.

2. A state which is not a Member of the United Nations may bring to the attention of the Security Council or of the General Assembly any dispute to which it is a party if it accepts in advance, for the purposes of the dispute, the obligations of pacific settlement provided in the present Charter.

3. The proceedings of the General Assembly in respect of matters brought to its attention under this Article will be subject to the provisions of Articles 11 and 12.

Article 36

1. The Security Council may, at any stage of a dispute of the nature referred to in Article 33 or of a situation of like nature, recommend appropriate procedures or methods of adjustment.

2. The Security Council should take into consideration any procedures for the settlement of the dispute which have already been adopted by the parties.

3. In making recommendations under this Article the Security Council should also take into consideration that legal disputes should as a general rule be referred by the parties to the International Court of Justice in accordance with the provisions of the Statute of the Court.

Article 37

1. Should the parties to a dispute of the nature referred to in Article 33 fail to settle it by the means indicated in that Article, they shall refer it to the Security Council.

2. If the Security Council deems that the continuance of the dispute is in fact likely to endanger the maintenance of international peace and security, it shall decide whether to take action under Article 36 or to recommend such terms of settlement as it may consider appropriate.

Article 38

Without prejudice to the provisions of Articles 33 to 37, the Security Council may, if all the parties to any dispute so request, make recommendations to the parties with a view to a pacific settlement of the dispute.

Chapter VII
ACTION WITH RESPECT TO THREATS TO THE PEACE, BREACHES OF THE PEACE, AND ACTS OF AGGRESSION

Article 39

The Security Council shall determine the existence of any threat to the peace, breach of the peace, or act of aggression and shall make recommendations, or decide what measures shall be taken in accordance with Articles 41 and 42, to maintain or restore international peace and security.

Article 40

In order to prevent an aggravation of the situation, the Security Council may, before making the recommendations or deciding upon the measures provided for in Article 39, call upon the parties concerned to comply with such provisional measures as it deems necessary or desirable. Such provisional measures shall be without prejudice to the rights, claims, or position of the parties concerned. The Security Council shall duly take account of failure to comply with such provisional measures.

Article 41

The Security Council may decide what measures not involving the use of armed force are to be employed to give effect to its decisions, and it may call upon the Members of the United Nations to apply such measures. These may include complete or partial interruption of economic relations and of rail, sea, air, postal, telegraphic, radio, and other means of communication, and the severance of diplomatic relations.

---

[2]Amended text of Article 27 which came into force on 31 August 1965. (The text of Article 27 before it was amended read as follows:

1. Each member of the Security Council shall have one vote.

2. Decisions of the Security Council on procedural matters shall be made by an affirmative vote of seven members.

3. Decisions of the Security Council on all other matters shall be made by an affirmative vote of seven members including the concurring votes of the permanent members; provided that, in decisions under Chapter VI, and under paragraph 3 of Article 52, a party to a dispute shall abstain from voting.)

Article 42

Should the Security Council consider that measures provided for in Article 41 would be inadequate or have proved to be inadequate, it may take such action by air, sea, or land forces as may be necessary to maintain or restore international peace and security. Such action may include demonstrations, blockade, and other operations by air, sea, or land forces of Members of the United Nations.

Article 43

1. All Members of the United Nations, in order to contribute to the maintenance of international peace and security, undertake to make available to the Security Council, on its call and in accordance with a special agreement or agreements, armed forces, assistance, and facilities, including rights of passage, necessary for the purpose of maintaining international peace and security.

2. Such agreement or agreements shall govern the numbers and types of forces, their degree of readiness and general location, and the nature of the facilities and assistance to be provided.

3. The agreement or agreements shall be negotiated as soon as possible on the initiative of the Security Council. They shall be concluded between the Security Council and Members or between the Security Council and groups of Members and shall be subject to ratification by the signatory states in accordance with their respective constitutional processes.

Article 44

When the Security Council has decided to use force it shall, before calling upon a Member not represented on it to provide armed forces in fulfilment of the obligations assumed under Article 43, invite that Member, if the Member so desires, to participate in the decisions of the Security Council concerning the employment of contingents of that Member's armed forces.

Article 45

In order to enable the United Nations to take urgent military measures, Members shall hold immediately available national air-force contingents for combined international enforcement action. The strength and degree of readiness of these contingents and plans for their combined action shall be determined, within the limits laid down in the special agreement or agreements referred to in Article 43, by the Security Council with the assistance of the Military Staff Committee.

Article 46

Plans for the application of armed force shall be made by the Security Council with the assistance of the Military Staff Committee.

Article 47

1. There shall be established a Military Staff Committee to advise and assist the Security Council on all questions relating to the Security Council's military requirements for the maintenance of international peace and security, the employment and command of forces placed at its disposal, the regulation of armaments, and possible disarmament.

2. The Military Staff Committee shall consist of the Chiefs of Staff of the permanent members of the Security Council or their representatives. Any Member of the United Nations not permanently represented on the Committee shall be invited by the Committee to be associated with it when the efficient discharge of the Committee's responsibilities requires the participation of that Member in its work.

3. The Military Staff Committee shall be responsible under the Security Council for the strategic direction of any armed forces placed at the disposal of the Security Council. Questions relating to the command of such forces shall be worked out subsequently.

4. The Military Staff Committee, with the authorization of the Security Council and after consultation with appropriate regional agencies, may establish regional sub-committees.

Article 48

1. The action required to carry out the decisions of the Security Council for the maintenance of international peace and security shall be taken by all the Members of the United Nations or by some of them, as the Security Council may determine.

2. Such decisions shall be carried out by the Members of the United Nations directly and through their action in the appropriate international agencies of which they are members.

Article 49

The Members of the United Nations shall join in affording mutual assistance in carrying out the measures decided upon by the Security Council.

Article 50

If preventive or enforcement measures against any state are taken by the Security Council, any other state, whether a Member of the United Nations or not, which finds itself confronted with special economic problems arising from the carrying out of those measures shall have the right to consult the Security Council with regard to a solution of those problems.

Article 51

Nothing in the present Charter shall impair the inherent right of individual or collective self-defence if an armed attack occurs against a Member of the United Nations, until the Security Council has taken measures necessary to maintain international peace and security. Measures taken by Members in the exercise of this right of self-defence shall be immediately reported to the Security Council and shall not in any way affect the authority and responsibility of the Security Council under the present Charter to take at any time such action as it deems necessary in order to maintain or restore international peace and security.

Chapter VIII
REGIONAL ARRANGEMENTS

Article 52

1. Nothing in the present Charter precludes the existence of regional arrangements or agencies for dealing with such matters relating to the maintenance of international peace and security as are appropriate for regional action, provided that such arrangements or agencies and their activities are consistent with the Purposes and Principles of the United Nations.

2. The Members of the United Nations entering into such arrangements or constituting such agencies shall make every effort to achieve pacific settlement of local disputes through such regional arrangements or by such regional agencies before referring them to the Security Council.

3. The Security Council shall encourage the development of pacific settlement of local disputes through such regional arrangements or by such regional agencies either on the initiative of the states concerned or by reference from the Security Council.

4. This Article in no way impairs the application of Articles 34 and 35.

Article 53

1. The Security Council shall, where appropriate, utilize such regional arrangements or agencies for enforcement action under its authority. But no enforcement action shall be taken under regional arrangements or by regional agencies without the authorization of the Security Council, with the exception of measures against any enemy state, as defined in paragraph 2 of this Article, provided for pursuant to Article 107 or in regional arrangements directed against renewal of aggressive policy on the part of any such state, until such time as the Organization may, on request of the Governments concerned, be charged with the responsibility for preventing further aggression by such a state.

2. The term enemy state as used in paragraph 1 of this Article applies to any state which during the Second World War has been an enemy of any signatory of the present Charter.

Article 54

The Security Council shall at all times be kept fully informed of activities undertaken or in contemplation under regional arrangements or by regional agencies for the maintenance of international peace and security.

Chapter IX
INTERNATIONAL ECONOMIC AND SOCIAL CO-OPERATION

Article 55

With a view to the creation of conditions of stability and well-being which are necessary for peaceful and friendly relations among nations based on respect for the principle of equal rights and self-determination of peoples, the United Nations shall promote:

a. higher standards of living, full employment, and conditions of economic and social progress and development;
b. solutions of international economic, social, health, and related problems; and international cultural and educational co-operation; and
c. universal respect for, and observance of, human rights and fundamental freedoms for all without distinction as to race, sex, language, or religion.

Article 56
All Members pledge themselves to take joint and separate action in co-operation with the Organization for the achievement of the purposes set forth in Article 55.

Article 57
1. The various specialized agencies, established by intergovernmental agreement and having wide international responsibilities, as defined in their basic instruments, in economic, social, cultural, educational, health, and related fields, shall be brought into relationship with the United Nations in accordance with the provisions of Article 63.
2. Such agencies thus brought into relationship with the United Nations are hereinafter referred to as specialized agencies.

Article 58
The Organization shall make recommendations for the co-ordination of the policies and activities of the specialized agencies.

Article 59
The Organization shall, where appropriate, initiate negotiations among the states concerned for the creation of any new specialized agencies required for the accomplishment of the purposes set forth in Article 55.

Article 60
Responsibility for the discharge of the functions of the Organization set forth in this Chapter shall be vested in the General Assembly and, under the authority of the General Assembly, in the Economic and Social Council, which shall have for this purpose the powers set forth in Chapter X.

Chapter X
THE ECONOMIC AND SOCIAL COUNCIL

Composition

Article 61[3]
1. The Economic and Social Council shall consist of fifty-four Members of the United Nations elected by the General Assembly.
2. Subject to the provisions of paragraph 3, eighteen members of the Economic and Social Council shall be elected each year for a term of three years. A retiring member shall be eligible for immediate re-election.
3. At the first election after the increase in the membership of the Economic and Social Council from twenty-seven to fifty-four members, in addition to the members elected in place of the nine members whose term of office expires at the end of that year, twenty-seven additional members shall be elected. Of these twenty-seven additional members, the term of office of nine members so elected shall expire at the end of one year, and of nine other members at the end of two years, in accordance with arrangements made by the General Assembly.
4. Each member of the Economic and Social Council shall have one representative.

Functions and powers

Article 62
1. The Economic and Social Council may make or initiate studies and reports with respect to international economic, social, cultural, educational, health, and related matters and may make recommendations with respect to any such matters to the General Assembly, to the Members of the United Nations, and to the specialized agencies concerned.
2. It may make recommendations for the purpose of promoting respect for, and observance of, human rights and fundamental freedoms for all.

3. It may prepare draft conventions for submission to the General Assembly, with respect to matters falling within its competence.
4. It may call, in accordance with the rules prescribed by the United Nations, international conferences on matters falling within its competence.

Article 63
1. The Economic and Social Council may enter into agreements with any of the agencies referred to in Article 57, defining the terms on which the agency concerned shall be brought into relationship with the United Nations. Such agreements shall be subject to approval by the General Assembly.
2. It may co-ordinate the activities of the specialized agencies through consultation with and recommendations to such agencies and through recommendations to the General Assembly and to the Members of the United Nations.

Article 64
1. The Economic and Social Council may take appropriate steps to obtain regular reports from the specialized agencies. It may make arrangements with the Members of the United Nations and with the specialized agencies to obtain reports on the steps taken to give effect to its own recommendations and to recommendations on matters falling within its competence made by the General Assembly.
2. It may communicate its observations on these reports to the General Assembly.

Article 65
The Economic and Social Council may furnish information to the Security Council and shall assist the Security Council upon its request.

Article 66
1. The Economic and Social Council shall perform such functions as fall within its competence in connexion with the carrying out of the recommendations of the General Assembly.
2. It may, with the approval of the General Assembly, perform services at the request of Members of the United Nations and at the request of specialized agencies.
3. It shall perform such other functions as are specified elsewhere in the present Charter or as may be assigned to it by the General Assembly.

Voting

Article 67
1. Each member of the Economic and Social Council shall have one vote.
2. Decisions of the Economic and Social Council shall be made by a majority of the members present and voting.

Procedure

Article 68
The Economic and Social Council shall set up commissions in economic and social fields and for the promotion of human rights, and such other commissions as may be required for the performance of its functions.

---

[3]Amended text of Article 61, which came into force on 24 September 1973. (The text of Article 61 as previously amended on 31 August 1965 read as follows:
1. The Economic and Social Council shall consist of twenty-seven Members of the United Nations elected by the General Assembly.
2. Subject to the provisions of paragraph 3, nine members of the Economic and Social Council shall be elected each year for a term of three years. A retiring member shall be eligible for immediate re-election.
3. At the first election after the increase in the membership of the Economic and Social Council from eighteen to twenty-seven members, in addition to the members elected in place of the six members whose term of office expires at the end of that year, nine additional members shall be elected. Of these nine additional members, the term of office of three members so elected shall expire at the end of one year, and of three other members at the end of two years, in accordance with arrangements made by the General Assembly.
4. Each member of the Economic and Social Council shall have one representative.)

Article 69

The Economic and Social Council shall invite any Member of the United Nations to participate, without vote, in its deliberations on any matter of particular concern to that Member.

Article 70

The Economic and Social Council may make arrangements for representatives of the specialized agencies to participate, without vote, in its deliberations and in those of the commissions established by it, and for its representatives to participate in the deliberations of the specialized agencies.

Article 71

The Economic and Social Council may make suitable arrangements for consultation with non-governmental organizations which are concerned with matters within its competence. Such arrangements may be made with international organizations and, where appropriate, with national organizations after consultation with the Member of the United Nations concerned.

Article 72

1. The Economic and Social Council shall adopt its own rules of procedure, including the method of selecting its President.

2. The Economic and Social Council shall meet as required in accordance with its rules, which shall include provision for the convening of meetings on the request of a majority of its members.

Chapter XI
DECLARATION REGARDING NON-SELF-GOVERNING TERRITORIES

Article 73

Members of the United Nations which have or assume responsibilities for the administration of territories whose peoples have not yet attained a full measure of self-government recognize the principle that the interests of the inhabitants of these territories are paramount, and accept as a sacred trust the obligation to promote to the utmost, within the system of international peace and security established by the present Charter, the well-being of the inhabitants of these territories, and, to this end:

a. to ensure, with due respect for the culture of the peoples concerned, their political, economic, social, and educational advancement, their just treatment, and their protection against abuses;

b. to develop self-government, to take due account of the political aspirations of the peoples, and to assist them in the progressive development of their free political institutions, according to the particular circumstances of each territory and its peoples and their varying stages of advancement;

c. to further international peace and security;

d. to promote constructive measures of development, to encourage research, and to co-operate with one another and, when and where appropriate, with specialized international bodies with a view to the practical achievement of the social, economic, and scientific purposes set forth in this Article; and

e. to transmit regularly to the Secretary-General for information purposes, subject to such limitation as security and constitutional considerations may require, statistical and other information of a technical nature relating to economic, social, and educational conditions in the territories for which they are respectively responsible other than those territories to which Chapters XII and XIII apply.

Article 74

Members of the United Nations also agree that their policy in respect of the territories to which this Chapter applies, no less than in respect of their metropolitan areas, must be based on the general principle of good-neighbourliness, due account being taken of the interests and well-being of the rest of the world, in social, economic, and commercial matters.

Chapter XII
INTERNATIONAL TRUSTEESHIP SYSTEM

Article 75

The United Nations shall establish under its authority an international trusteeship system for the administration and supervision of such territories as may be placed thereunder by subsequent individual agreements. These territories are hereinafter referred to as trust territories.

Article 76

The basic objectives of the trusteeship system, in accordance with the Purposes of the United Nations laid down in Article 1 of the present Charter, shall be:

a. to further international peace and security;

b. to promote the political, economic, social, and educational advancement of the inhabitants of the trust territories, and their progressive development towards self-government or independence as may be appropriate to the particular circumstances of each territory and its peoples and the freely expressed wishes of the peoples concerned, and as may be provided by the terms of each trusteeship agreement;

c. to encourage respect for human rights and for fundamental freedoms for all without distinction as to race, sex, language, or religion, and to encourage recognition of the interdependence of the peoples of the world; and

d. to ensure equal treatment in social, economic, and commercial matters for all Members of the United Nations and their nationals, and also equal treatment for the latter in the administration of justice, without prejudice to the attainment of the foregoing objectives and subject to the provisions of Article 80.

Article 77

1. The trusteeship system shall apply to such territories in the following categories as may be placed thereunder by means of trusteeship agreements:

a. territories now held under mandate;

b. territories which may be detached from enemy states as a result of the Second World War; and

c. territories voluntarily placed under the system by states responsible for their administration.

2. It will be a matter for subsequent agreement as to which territories in the foregoing categories will be brought under the trusteeship system and upon what terms.

Article 78

The trusteeship system shall not apply to territories which have become Members of the United Nations, relationship among which shall be based on respect for the principle of sovereign equality.

Article 79

The terms of trusteeship for each territory to be placed under the trusteeship system, including any alteration or amendment, shall be agreed upon by the states directly concerned, including the mandatory power in the case of territories held under mandate by a Member of the United Nations, and shall be approved as provided for in Articles 83 and 85.

Article 80

1. Except as may be agreed upon in individual trusteeship agreements, made under Articles 77, 79, and 81, placing each territory under the trusteeship system, and until such agreements have been concluded, nothing in this Chapter shall be construed in or of itself to alter in any manner the rights whatsoever of any states or any peoples or the terms of existing international instruments to which Members of the United Nations may respectively be parties.

2. Paragraph 1 of this Article shall not be interpreted as giving grounds for delay or postponement of the negotiation and conclusion of agreements for placing mandated and other territories under the trusteeship system as provided for in Article 77.

Article 81

The trusteeship agreement shall in each case include the terms under which the trust territory will be administered and designate the authority which will exercise the administration of the trust territory. Such authority, hereinafter called the administering authority, may be one or more states or the Organization itself.

Article 82

There may be designated, in any trusteeship agreement, a strategic area or areas which may include part or all of the trust territory to which the agreement applies, without prejudice to any special agreement or agreements made under Article 43.

Article 83

1.   All functions of the United Nations relating to strategic areas, including the approval of the terms of the trusteeship agreements and of their alteration or amendments, shall be exercised by the Security Council.

2.   The basic objectives set forth in Article 76 shall be applicable to the people of each strategic area.

3.   The Security Council shall, subject to the provisions of the trusteeship agreements and without prejudice to security considerations, avail itself of the assistance of the Trusteeship Council to perform those functions of the United Nations under the trusteeship system relating to political, economic, social, and educational matters in the strategic areas.

Article 84

It shall be the duty of the administering authority to ensure that the trust territory shall play its part in the maintenance of international peace and security. To this end the administering authority may make use of volunteer forces, facilities, and assistance from the trust territory in carrying out the obligations towards the Security Council undertaken in this regard by the administering authority, as well as for local defence and the maintenance of law and order within the trust territory.

Article 85

1.   The functions of the United Nations with regard to trusteeship agreements for all areas not designated as strategic, including the approval of the terms of the trusteeship agreements and of their alteration or amendment, shall be exercised by the General Assembly.

2.   The Trusteeship Council, operating under the authority of the General Assembly, shall assist the General Assembly in carrying out these functions.

Chapter XIII
THE TRUSTEESHIP COUNCIL

Composition

Article 86

1.   The Trusteeship Council shall consist of the following Members of the United Nations:
   a.   those Members administering trust territories;
   b.   such of those Members mentioned by name in Article 23 as are not administering trust territories; and
   c.   as many other Members elected for three-year terms by the General Assembly as may be necessary to ensure that the total number of members of the Trusteeship Council is equally divided between those Members of the United Nations which administer trust territories and those which do not.

2.   Each member of the Trusteeship Council shall designate one specially qualified person to represent it therein.

Functions and powers

Article 87

The General Assembly and, under its authority, the Trusteeship Council, in carrying out their functions, may:
   a.   consider reports submitted by the administering authority;
   b.   accept petitions and examine them in consultation with the administering authority;
   c.   provide for periodic visits to the respective trust territories at times agreed upon with the administering authority; and
   d.   take these and other actions in conformity with the terms of the trusteeship agreements.

Article 88

The Trusteeship Council shall formulate a questionnaire on the political, economic, social, and educational advancement of the inhabitants of each trust territory, and the administering authority for each trust territory within the competence of the General Assembly shall make an annual report to the General Assembly upon the basis of such questionnaire.

Voting

Article 89

1.   Each member of the Trusteeship Council shall have one vote.

2.   Decisions of the Trusteeship Council shall be made by a majority of the members present and voting.

Procedure

Article 90

1.   The Trusteeship Council shall adopt its own rules of procedure, including the method of selecting its President.

2.   The Trusteeship Council shall meet as required in accordance with its rules, which shall include provision for the convening of meetings on the request of a majority of its members.

Article 91

The Trusteeship Council shall, when appropriate, avail itself of the assistance of the Economic and Social Council and of the specialized agencies in regard to matters with which they are respectively concerned.

Chapter XIV
THE INTERNATIONAL COURT OF JUSTICE

Article 92

The International Court of Justice shall be the principal judicial organ of the United Nations. It shall function in accordance with the annexed Statute, which is based upon the Statute of the Permanent Court of International Justice and forms an integral part of the present Charter.

Article 93

1.   All Members of the United Nations are *ipso facto* parties to the Statute of the International Court of Justice.

2.   A state which is not a Member of the United Nations may become a party to the Statute of the International Court of Justice on conditions to be determined in each case by the General Assembly upon the recommendation of the Security Council.

Article 94

1.   Each Member of the United Nations undertakes to comply with the decision of the International Court of Justice in any case to which it is a party.

2.   If any party to a case fails to perform the obligations incumbent upon it under a judgment rendered by the Court, the other party may have recourse to the Security Council, which may, if it deems necessary, make recommendations or decide upon measures to be taken to give effect to the judgment.

Article 95

Nothing in the present Charter shall prevent Members of the United Nations from entrusting the solution of their differences to other tribunals by virtue of agreements already in existence or which may be concluded in the future.

Article 96

1.   The General Assembly or the Security Council may request the International Court of Justice to give an advisory opinion on any legal question.

2.   Other organs of the United Nations and specialized agencies, which may at any time be so authorized by the General Assembly, may also request advisory opinions of the Court on legal questions arising within the scope of their activities.

Chapter XV
THE SECRETARIAT

Article 97

The Secretariat shall comprise a Secretary-General and such staff as the Organization may require. The Secretary-General shall be appointed by the General Assembly upon the recommendation of the Security Council. He shall be the chief administrative officer of the Organization.

Article 98

The Secretary-General shall act in that capacity in all meetings of the General Assembly, of the Security Council, of the Economic and Social Council, and of the Trusteeship Council, and shall perform such other functions as are entrusted to him by these organs. The Secretary-General shall make an annual report to the General Assembly on the work of the Organization.

Article 99

The Secretary-General may bring to the attention of the Security Council any matter which in his opinion may threaten the maintenance of international peace and security.

Article 100

1. In the performance of their duties the Secretary-General and the staff shall not seek or receive instructions from any government or from any other authority external to the Organization. They shall refrain from any action which might reflect on their position as international officials responsible only to the Organization.
2. Each Member of the United Nations undertakes to respect the exclusively international character of the responsibilities of the Secretary-General and the staff and not to seek to influence them in the discharge of their responsibilities.

Article 101

1. The staff shall be appointed by the Secretary-General under regulations established by the General Assembly.
2. Appropriate staffs shall be permanently assigned to the Economic and Social Council, the Trusteeship Council, and, as required, to other organs of the United Nations. These staffs shall form a part of the Secretariat.
3. The paramount consideration in the employment of the staff and in the determination of the conditions of service shall be the necessity of securing the highest standards of efficiency, competence, and integrity. Due regard shall be paid to the importance of recruiting the staff on as wide a geographical basis as possible.

Chapter XVI
MISCELLANEOUS PROVISIONS

Article 102

1. Every treaty and every international agreement entered into by any Member of the United Nations after the present Charter comes into force shall as soon as possible be registered with the Secretariat and published by it.
2. No party to any such treaty or international agreement which has not been registered in accordance with the provisions of paragraph 1 of this Article may invoke that treaty or agreement before any organ of the United Nations.

Article 103

In the event of a conflict between the obligations of the Members of the United Nations under the present Charter and their obligations under any other international agreement, their obligations under the present Charter shall prevail.

Article 104

The Organization shall enjoy in the territory of each of its Members such legal capacity as may be necessary for the exercise of its functions and the fulfilment of its purposes.

Article 105

1. The Organization shall enjoy in the territory of each of its Members such privileges and immunities as are necessary for the fulfilment of its purposes.

2. Representatives of the Members of the United Nations and officials of the Organization shall similarly enjoy such privileges and immunities as are necessary for the independent exercise of their functions in connexion with the Organization.
3. The General Assembly may make recommendations with a view to determining the details of the application of paragraphs 1 and 2 of this Article or may propose conventions to the Members of the United Nations for this purpose.

Chapter XVII
TRANSITIONAL SECURITY ARRANGEMENTS

Article 106

Pending the coming into force of such special agreements referred to in Article 43 as in the opinion of the Security Council enable it to begin the exercise of its responsibilities under Article 42, the parties to the Four-Nation Declaration, signed at Moscow, 30 October 1943, and France, shall, in accordance with the provisions of paragraph 5 of that Declaration, consult with one another and as occasion requires with other Members of the United Nations with a view to such joint action on behalf of the Organization as may be necessary for the purpose of maintaining international peace and security.

Article 107

Nothing in the present Charter shall invalidate or preclude action, in relation to any state which during the Second World War has been an enemy of any signatory to the present Charter, taken or authorized as a result of that war by the Governments having responsibility for such action.

Chapter XVIII
AMENDMENTS

Article 108

Amendments to the present Charter shall come into force for all Members of the United Nations when they have been adopted by a vote of two thirds of the members of the General Assembly and ratified in accordance with their respective constitutional processes by two thirds of the Members of the United Nations, including all the permanent members of the Security Council.

Article 109 [4]

1. A General Conference of the Members of the United Nations for the purpose of reviewing the present Charter may be held at a date and place to be fixed by a two-thirds vote of the members of the General Assembly and by a vote of any nine members of the Security Council. Each Member of the United Nations shall have one vote in the conference.
2. Any alteration of the present Charter recommended by a two-thirds vote of the conference shall take effect when ratified in accordance with their respective constitutional processes by two thirds of the Members of the United Nations including all the permanent members of the Security Council.
3. If such a conference has not been held before the tenth annual session of the General Assembly following the coming into force of the present Charter, the proposal to call such a conference shall be

---

[4] Amended text of Article 109 which came into force on 12 June 1968.
(The text of Article 109 before it was amended read as follows:

1. A General Conference of the Members of the United Nations for the purpose of reviewing the present Charter may be held at a date and place to be fixed by a two-thirds vote of the members of the General Assembly and by a vote of any seven members of the Security Council. Each Member of the United Nations shall have one vote in the conference.
2. Any alteration of the present Charter recommended by a two-thirds vote of the conference shall take effect when ratified in accordance with their respective constitutional processes by two thirds of the Members of the United Nations including all the permanent members of the Security Council.
3. If such a conference has not been held before the tenth annual session of the General Assembly following the coming into force of the present Charter, the proposal to call such a conference shall be placed on the agenda of that session of the General Assembly, and the conference shall be held if so decided by a majority vote of the members of the General Assembly and by a vote of any seven members of the Security Council.)

placed on the agenda of that session of the General Assembly, and the conference shall be held if so decided by a majority vote of the members of the General Assembly and by a vote of any seven members of the Security Council.

Chapter XIX
RATIFICATION AND SIGNATURE

Article 110

1.   The present Charter shall be ratified by the signatory states in accordance with their respective constitutional processes.

2.   The ratifications shall be deposited with the Government of the United States of America, which shall notify all the signatory states of each deposit as well as the Secretary-General of the Organization when he has been appointed.

3.   The present Charter shall come into force upon the deposit of ratifications by the Republic of China, France, the Union of Soviet Socialist Republics, the United Kingdom of Great Britain and Northern Ireland, and the United States of America, and by a majority of the other signatory states. A protocol of the ratifications deposited shall thereupon be drawn up by the Government of the United States of America which shall communicate copies thereof to all the signatory states.

4.   The states signatory to the present Charter which ratify it after it has come into force will become original Members of the United Nations on the date of the deposit of their respective ratifications.

Article 111

The present Charter, of which the Chinese, French, Russian, English, and Spanish texts are equally authentic, shall remain deposited in the archives of the Government of the United States of America. Duly certified copies thereof shall be transmitted by that Government to the Governments of the other signatory states.

IN FAITH WHEREOF the representatives of the Governments of the United Nations have signed the present Charter.

DONE at the city of San Francisco the twenty-sixth day of June, one thousand nine hundred and forty-five.

Statute of the International Court of Justice

Article 1

THE INTERNATIONAL COURT OF JUSTICE established by the Charter of the United Nations as the principal judicial organ of the United Nations shall be constituted and shall function in accordance with the provisions of the present Statute.

Chapter I
ORGANIZATION OF THE COURT

Article 2

The Court shall be composed of a body of independent judges, elected regardless of their nationality from among persons of high moral character, who possess the qualifications required in their respective countries for appointment to the highest judicial offices, or are jurisconsults of recognized competence in international law.

Article 3

1.   The Court shall consist of fifteen members, no two of whom may be nationals of the same state.

2.   A person who for the purposes of membership in the Court could be regarded as a national of more than one state shall be deemed to be a national of the one in which he ordinarily exercises civil and political rights.

Article 4

1.   The members of the Court shall be elected by the General Assembly and by the Security Council from a list of persons nominated by the national groups in the Permanent Court of Arbitration, in accordance with the following provisions.

2.   In the case of Members of the United Nations not represented in the Permanent Court of Arbitration, candidates shall be nominated by national groups appointed for this purpose by their governments under the same conditions as those prescribed for members of the Permanent Court of Arbitration by Article 44 of the Convention of The Hague of 1907 for the pacific settlement of international disputes.

3.   The conditions under which a state which is a party to the present Statute but is not a Member of the United Nations may participate in electing the members of the Court shall, in the absence of a special agreement, be laid down by the General Assembly upon recommendation of the Security Council.

Article 5

1.   At least three months before the date of the election, the Secretary-General of the United Nations shall address a written request to the members of the Permanent Court of Arbitration belonging to the states which are parties to the present Statute, and to the members of the national groups appointed under Article 4, paragraph 2, inviting them to undertake, within a given time, by national groups, the nomination of persons in a position to accept the duties of a member of the Court.

2.   No group may nominate more than four persons, not more than two of whom shall be of their own nationality. In no case may the number of candidates nominated by a group be more than double the number of seats to be filled.

Article 6

Before making these nominations, each national group is recommended to consult its highest court of justice, its legal faculties and schools of law, and its national academies and national sections of international academies devoted to the study of law.

Article 7

1.   The Secretary-General shall prepare a list in alphabetical order of all the persons thus nominated. Save as provided in Article 12, paragraph 2, these shall be the only persons eligible.

2.   The Secretary-General shall submit this list to the General Assembly and to the Security Council.

Article 8

The General Assembly and the Security Council shall proceed independently of one another to elect the members of the Court.

Article 9

At every election, the electors shall bear in mind not only that the persons to be elected should individually possess the qualifications required, but also that in the body as a whole the representation of the main forms of civilization and of the principal legal systems of the world should be assured.

Article 10

1.   Those candidates who obtain an absolute majority of votes in the General Assembly and in the Security Council shall be considered as elected.

2.   Any vote of the Security Council, whether for the election of judges or for the appointment of members of the conference envisaged in Article 12, shall be taken without any distinction between permanent and non-permanent members of the Security Council.

3.   In the event of more than one national of the same state obtaining an absolute majority of the votes both of the General Assembly and of the Security Council, the eldest of these only shall be considered as elected.

Article 11

If, after the first meeting held for the purpose of the election, one or more seats remain to be filled, a second and, if necessary, a third meeting shall take place.

Article 12

1. If, after the third meeting, one or more seats still remain unfilled, a joint conference consisting of six members, three appointed by the General Assembly and three by the Security Council, may be formed at any time at the request of either the General Assembly or the Security Council, for the purpose of choosing by the vote of an absolute majority one name for each seat still vacant, to submit to the General Assembly and the Security Council for their respective acceptance.

2. If the joint conference is unanimously agreed upon any person who fulfils the required conditions, he may be included in its list, even though he was not included in the list of nominations referred to in Article 7.

3. If the joint conference is satisfied that it will not be successful in procuring an election, those members of the Court who have already been elected shall, within a period to be fixed by the Security Council, proceed to fill the vacant seats by selection from among those candidates who have obtained votes either in the General Assembly or in the Security Council.

4. In the event of an equality of votes among the judges, the eldest judge shall have a casting vote.

Article 13

1. The members of the Court shall be elected for nine years and may be re-elected; provided, however, that of the judges elected at the first election, the terms of five judges shall expire at the end of three years and the terms of five more judges shall expire at the end of six years.

2. The judges whose terms are to expire at the end of the above-mentioned initial periods of three and six years shall be chosen by lot to be drawn by the Secretary-General immediately after the first election has been completed.

3. The members of the Court shall continue to discharge their duties until their places have been filled. Though replaced, they shall finish any cases which they may have begun.

4. In the case of the resignation of a member of the Court, the resignation shall be addressed to the President of the Court for transmission to the Secretary-General. This last notification makes the place vacant.

Article 14

Vacancies shall be filled by the same method as that laid down for the first election, subject to the following provision: the Secretary-General shall, within one month of the occurrence of the vacancy, proceed to issue the invitations provided for in Article 5, and the date of the election shall be fixed by the Security Council.

Article 15

A member of the Court elected to replace a member whose term of office has not expired shall hold office for the remainder of his predecessor's term.

Article 16

1. No member of the Court may exercise any political or administrative function, or engage in any other occupation of a professional nature.

2. Any doubt on this point shall be settled by the decision of the Court.

Article 17

1. No member of the Court may act as agent, counsel, or advocate in any case.

2. No member may participate in the decision of any case in which he has previously taken part as agent, counsel, or advocate for one of the parties, or as a member of a national or international court, or of a commission of enquiry, or in any other capacity.

3. Any doubt on this point shall be settled by the decision of the Court.

Article 18

1. No member of the Court can be dismissed unless, in the unanimous opinion of the other members, he has ceased to fulfil the required conditions.

2. Formal notification thereof shall be made to the Secretary-General by the Registrar.

3. This notification makes the place vacant.

Article 19

The members of the Court, when engaged on the business of the Court, shall enjoy diplomatic privileges and immunities.

Article 20

Every member of the Court shall, before taking up his duties, make a solemn declaration in open court that he will exercise his powers impartially and conscientiously.

Article 21

1. The Court shall elect its President and Vice-President for three years; they may be re-elected.

2. The Court shall appoint its Registrar and may provide for the appointment of such other officers as may be necessary.

Article 22

1. The seat of the Court shall be established at The Hague. This, however, shall not prevent the Court from sitting and exercising its functions elsewhere whenever the Court considers it desirable.

2. The President and the Registrar shall reside at the seat of the Court.

Article 23

1. The Court shall remain permanently in session, except during the judicial vacations, the dates and duration of which shall be fixed by the Court.

2. Members of the Court are entitled to periodic leave, the dates and duration of which shall be fixed by the Court, having in mind the distance between The Hague and the home of each judge.

3. Members of the Court shall be bound, unless they are on leave or prevented from attending by illness or other serious reasons duly explained to the President, to hold themselves permanently at the disposal of the Court.

Article 24

1. If, for some special reason, a member of the Court considers that he should not take part in the decision of a particular case, he shall so inform the President.

2. If the President considers that for some special reason one of the members of the Court should not sit in a particular case, he shall give him notice accordingly.

3. If in any such case the member of the Court and the President disagree, the matter shall be settled by the decision of the Court.

Article 25

1. The full Court shall sit except when it is expressly provided otherwise in the present Statute.

2. Subject to the condition that the number of judges available to constitute the Court is not thereby reduced below eleven, the Rules of the Court may provide for allowing one or more judges, according to circumstances and in rotation, to be dispensed from sitting.

3. A quorum of nine judges shall suffice to constitute the Court.

Article 26

1. The Court may from time to time form one or more chambers, composed of three or more judges as the Court may determine, for dealing with particular categories of cases; for example, labour cases and cases relating to transit and communications.

2. The Court may at any time form a chamber for dealing with a particular case. The number of judges to constitute such a chamber shall be determined by the Court with the approval of the parties.

3. Cases shall be heard and determined by the chambers provided for in this Article if the parties so request.

Article 27

A judgment given by any of the chambers provided for in Articles 26 and 29 shall be considered as rendered by the Court.

Article 28

The chambers provided for in Articles 26 and 29 may, with the consent of the parties, sit and exercise their functions elsewhere than at The Hague.

Article 29

With a view to the speedy dispatch of business, the Court shall form annually a chamber composed of five judges which, at the request of the parties, may hear and determine cases by summary procedure. In addition, two judges shall be selected for the purpose of replacing judges who find it impossible to sit.

Article 30

1.   The Court shall frame rules for carrying out its functions. In particular, it shall lay down rules of procedure.

2.   The Rules of the Court may provide for assessors to sit with the Court or with any of its chambers, without the right to vote.

Article 31

1.   Judges of the nationality of each of the parties shall retain their right to sit in the case before the Court.

2.   If the Court includes upon the Bench a judge of the nationality of one of the parties, any other party may choose a person to sit as judge. Such person shall be chosen preferably from among those persons who have been nominated as candidates as provided in Articles 4 and 5.

3.   If the Court includes upon the Bench no judge of the nationality of the parties, each of these parties may proceed to choose a judge as provided in paragraph 2 of this Article.

4.   The provisions of this Article shall apply to the case of Articles 26 and 29. In such cases, the President shall request one or, if necessary, two of the members of the Court forming the chamber to give place to the members of the Court of the nationality of the parties concerned, and, failing such, or if they are unable to be present, to the judges specially chosen by the parties.

5.   Should there be several parties in the same interest, they shall, for the purpose of the preceding provisions, be reckoned as one party only. Any doubt upon this point shall be settled by the decision of the Court.

6.   Judges chosen as laid down in paragraphs 2, 3 and 4 of this Article shall fulfil the conditions required by Articles 2, 17 (paragraph 2), 20, and 24 of the present Statute. They shall take part in the decision on terms of complete equality with their colleagues.

Article 32

1.   Each member of the Court shall receive an annual salary.

2.   The President shall receive a special annual allowance.

3.   The Vice-President shall receive a special allowance for every day on which he acts as President.

4.   The judges chosen under Article 31, other than members of the Court, shall receive compensation for each day on which they exercise their functions.

5.   These salaries, allowances, and compensation shall be fixed by the General Assembly. They may not be decreased during the term of office.

6.   The salary of the Registrar shall be fixed by the General Assembly on the proposal of the Court.

7.   Regulations made by the General Assembly shall fix the conditions under which retirement pensions may be given to members of the Court and to the Registrar, and the conditions under which members of the Court and the Registrar shall have their travelling expenses refunded.

8.   The above salaries, allowances, and compensation shall be free of all taxation.

Article 33

The expenses of the Court shall be borne by the United Nations in such a manner as shall be decided by the General Assembly.

Chapter II
COMPETENCE OF THE COURT

Article 34

1.   Only states may be parties in cases before the Court.

2.   The Court, subject to and in conformity with its Rules, may request of public international organizations information relevant to cases before it, and shall receive such information presented by such organizations on their own initiative.

3.   Whenever the construction of the constituent instrument of a public international organization or of an international convention adopted thereunder is in question in a case before the Court, the Registrar shall so notify the public international organization concerned and shall communicate to it copies of all the written proceedings.

Article 35

1.   The Court shall be open to the states parties to the present Statute.

2.   The conditions under which the Court shall be open to other states shall, subject to the special provisions contained in treaties in force, be laid down by the Security Council, but in no case shall such conditions place the parties in a position of inequality before the Court.

3.   When a state which is not a Member of the United Nations is a party to a case, the Court shall fix the amount which that party is to contribute towards the expenses of the Court. This provision shall not apply if such state is bearing a share of the expenses of the Court.

Article 36

1.   The jurisdiction of the Court comprises all cases which the parties refer to it and all matters specially provided for in the Charter of the United Nations or in treaties and conventions in force.

2.   The states parties to the present Statute may at any time declare that they recognize as compulsory *ipso facto* and without special agreement, in relation to any other state accepting the same obligation, the jurisdiction of the Court in all legal disputes concerning:

a.   the interpretation of a treaty;

b.   any question of international law;

c.   the existence of any fact which, if established, would constitute a breach of an international obligation;

d.   the nature or extent of the reparation to be made for the breach of an international obligation.

3.   The declarations referred to above may be made unconditionally or on condition of reciprocity on the part of several or certain states, or for a certain time.

4.   Such declarations shall be deposited with the Secretary-General of the United Nations, who shall transmit copies thereof to the parties to the Statute and to the Registrar of the Court.

5.   Declarations made under Article 36 of the Statute of the Permanent Court of International Justice and which are still in force shall be deemed, as between the parties to the present Statute, to be acceptances of the compulsory jurisdiction of the International Court of Justice for the period which they still have to run and in accordance with their terms.

6.   In the event of a dispute as to whether the Court has jurisdiction, the matter shall be settled by the decision of the Court.

Article 37

Whenever a treaty or convention in force provides for reference of a matter to a tribunal to have been instituted by the League of Nations, or to the Permanent Court of International Justice, the matter shall, as between the parties to the present Statute, be referred to the International Court of Justice.

Article 38

1.   The Court, whose function is to decide in accordance with international law such disputes as are submitted to it, shall apply:

a.   international conventions, whether general or particular, establishing rules expressly recognized by the contesting states;

b.   international custom, as evidence of a general practice accepted as law;

c.   the general principles of law recognized by civilized nations;

d.   subject to the provisions of Article 59, judicial decisions and the teachings of the most highly qualified publicists of the various nations, as subsidiary means for the determination of rules of law.

2.   This provision shall not prejudice the power of the Court to decide a case *ex aequo et bono*, if the parties agree thereto.

Chapter III
PROCEDURE

Article 39

1.   The official languages of the Court shall be French and English. If the parties agree that the case shall be conducted in French, the

judgment shall be delivered in French. If the parties agree that the case shall be conducted in English, the judgment shall be delivered in English.

2. In the absence of an agreement as to which language shall be employed, each party may, in the pleadings, use the language which it prefers; the decision of the Court shall be given in French and English. In this case the Court shall at the same time determine which of the two texts shall be considered as authoritative.

3. The Court shall, at the request of any party, authorize a language other than French or English to be used by that party.

Article 40

1. Cases are brought before the Court, as the case may be, either by the notification of the special agreement or by a written application addressed to the Registrar. In either case the subject of the dispute and the parties shall be indicated.

2. The Registrar shall forthwith communicate the application to all concerned.

3. He shall also notify the Members of the United Nations through the Secretary-General, and also any other states entitled to appear before the Court.

Article 41

1. The Court shall have the power to indicate, if it considers that circumstances so require, any provisional measures which ought to be taken to preserve the respective rights of either party.

2. Pending the final decision, notice of the measures suggested shall forthwith be given to the parties and to the Security Council.

Article 42

1. The parties shall be represented by agents.

2. They may have the assistance of counsel or advocates before the Court.

3. The agents, counsel, and advocates of parties before the Court shall enjoy the privileges and immunities necessary to the independent exercise of their duties.

Article 43

1. The procedure shall consist of two parts: written and oral.

2. The written proceedings shall consist of the communication to the Court and to the parties of memorials, counter-memorials and, if necessary, replies; also all papers and documents in support.

3. These communications shall be made through the Registrar, in the order and within the time fixed by the Court.

4. A certified copy of every document produced by one party shall be communicated to the other party.

5. The oral proceedings shall consist of the hearing by the Court of witnesses, experts, agents, counsel, and advocates.

Article 44

1. For the service of all notices upon persons other than the agents, counsel, and advocates, the Court shall apply direct to the government of the state upon whose territory the notice has to be served.

2. The same provision shall apply whenever steps are to be taken to procure evidence on the spot.

Article 45

The hearing shall be under the control of the President or, if he is unable to preside, of the Vice-President; if neither is able to preside, the senior judge present shall preside.

Article 46

The hearing in Court shall be public, unless the Court shall decide otherwise, or unless the parties demand that the public be not admitted.

Article 47

1. Minutes shall be made at each hearing and signed by the Registrar and the President.

2. These minutes alone shall be authentic.

Article 48

The Court shall make orders for the conduct of the case, shall decide the form and time in which each party must conclude its arguments, and make all arrangements connected with the taking of evidence.

Article 49

The Court may, even before the hearing begins, call upon the agents to produce any document or to supply any explanations. Formal note shall be taken of any refusal.

Article 50

The Court may, at any time, entrust any individual, body, bureau, commission, or other organization that it may select, with the task of carrying out an enquiry or giving an expert opinion.

Article 51

During the hearing any relevant questions are to be put to the witnesses and experts under the conditions laid down by the Court in the rules of procedure referred to in Article 30.

Article 52

After the Court has received the proofs and evidence within the time specified for the purpose, it may refuse to accept any further oral or written evidence that one party may desire to present unless the other side consents.

Article 53

1. Whenever one of the parties does not appear before the Court, or fails to defend its case, the other party may call upon the Court to decide in favour of its claim.

2. The Court must, before doing so, satisfy itself, not only that it has jurisdiction in accordance with Articles 36 and 37, but also that the claim is well founded in fact and law.

Article 54

1. When, subject to the control of the Court, the agents, counsel, and advocates have completed their presentation of the case, the President shall declare the hearing closed.

2. The Court shall withdraw to consider the judgment.

3. The deliberations of the Court shall take place in private and remain secret.

Article 55

1. All questions shall be decided by a majority of the judges present.

2. In the event of an equality of votes, the President or the judge who acts in his place shall have a casting vote.

Article 56

1. The judgment shall state the reasons on which it is based.

2. It shall contain the names of the judges who have taken part in the decision.

Article 57

If the judgment does not represent in whole or in part the unanimous opinion of the judges, any judge shall be entitled to deliver a separate opinion.

Article 58

The judgment shall be signed by the President and by the Registrar. It shall be read in open court, due notice having been given to the agents.

Article 59

The decision of the Court has no binding force except between the parties and in respect of that particular case.

Article 60

The judgment is final and without appeal. In the event of dispute as to the meaning or scope of the judgment, the Court shall construe it upon the request of any party.

Article 61

1. An application for revision of a judgment may be made only when it is based upon the discovery of some fact of such a nature as to be a decisive factor, which fact was, when the judgment was given, unknown to the Court and also to the party claiming revision, always provided that such ignorance was not due to negligence.

2. The proceedings for revision shall be opened by a judgment of the Court expressly recording the existence of the new fact, recognizing

that it has such a character as to lay the case open to revision, and declaring the application admissible on this ground.

3. The Court may require previous compliance with the terms of the judgment before it admits proceedings in revision.

4. The application for revision must be made at latest within six months of the discovery of the new fact.

5. No application for revision may be made after the lapse of ten years from the date of the judgment.

Article 62

1. Should a state consider that it has an interest of a legal nature which may be affected by the decision in the case, it may submit a request to the Court to be permitted to intervene.

2. It shall be for the Court to decide upon this request.

Article 63

1. Whenever the construction of a convention to which states other than those concerned in the case are parties is in question, the Registrar shall notify all such states forthwith.

2. Every state so notified has the right to intervene in the proceedings; but if it uses this right, the construction given by the judgment will be equally binding upon it.

Article 64

Unless otherwise decided by the Court, each party shall bear its own costs.

Chapter IV
ADVISORY OPINIONS

Article 65

1. The Court may give an advisory opinion on any legal question at the request of whatever body may be authorized by or in accordance with the Charter of the United Nations to make such a request.

2. Questions upon which the advisory opinion of the Court is asked shall be laid before the Court by means of a written request containing an exact statement of the question upon which an opinion is required, and accompanied by all documents likely to throw light upon the question.

Article 66

1. The Registrar shall forthwith give notice of the request for an advisory opinion to all states entitled to appear before the Court.

2. The Registrar shall also, by means of a special and direct communication, notify any state entitled to appear before the Court or international organization considered by the Court, or, should it not be sit-

ting, by the President, as likely to be able to furnish information on the question, that the Court will be prepared to receive, within a time limit to be fixed by the President, written statements, or to hear, at a public sitting to be held for the purpose, oral statements relating to the question.

3. Should any such state entitled to appear before the Court have failed to receive the special communication referred to in paragraph 2 of this Article, such state may express a desire to submit a written statement or to be heard; and the Court will decide.

4. States and organizations having presented written or oral statements or both shall be permitted to comment on the statements made by other states or organizations in the form, to the extent, and within the time limits which the Court, or, should it not be sitting, the President, shall decide in each particular case. Accordingly, the Registrar shall in due time communicate any such written statements to states and organizations having submitted similar statements.

Article 67

The Court shall deliver its advisory opinions in open court, notice having been given to the Secretary-General and to the representatives of Members of the United Nations, of other states and of international organizations immediately concerned.

Article 68

In the exercise of its advisory functions the Court shall further be guided by the provisions of the present Statute which apply in contentious cases to the extent to which it recognizes them to be applicable.

Chapter V
AMENDMENT

Article 69

Amendments to the present Statute shall be effected by the same procedure as is provided by the Charter of the United Nations for amendments to that Charter, subject however to any provisions which the General Assembly upon recommendation of the Security Council may adopt concerning the participation of states which are parties to the present Statute but are not Members of the United Nations.

Article 70

The Court shall have power to propose such amendments to the present Statute as it may deem necessary, through written communications to the Secretary-General, for consideration in conformity with the provisions of Article 69.

Appendix III

Structure of the United Nations

General Assembly

The General Assembly is composed of all the Members of the United Nations.

SESSIONS
Resumed thirty-ninth session: 9-12 April and 16 September 1985.
Fortieth session:[1] 17 September–18 December 1985 (suspended).

OFFICERS
Resumed thirty-ninth session
President: Paul John Firmino Lusaka (Zambia).
Vice-Presidents: Bahrain, Bangladesh, Bolivia, Bulgaria, Chad, China, Cuba, Cyprus, Djibouti, France, Ghana, Guatemala, Iceland, Italy, Malaysia, Morocco, Togo, USSR, United Kingdom, United States, Yemen.

Fortieth session
President: Jaime de Piniés (Spain).[a]
Vice-Presidents:[b] Bahamas, Barbados, Burkina Faso, China, Costa Rica, Cyprus, Democratic Yemen, France, Gabon, Kenya, Lesotho, Malta, Pakistan, Philippines, Qatar, Romania, Senegal, Tunisia, USSR, United Kingdom, United States.

[a]Elected on 17 September 1985 (decision 40/302).
[b]Elected on 17 September 1985 (decision 40/303).

The Assembly has four types of committees: (1) Main Committees; (2) procedural committees; (3) standing committees; (4) subsidiary and *ad hoc* bodies. In addition, it convenes conferences to deal with specific subjects.

Main Committees

Seven Main Committees have been established as follows:

Political and Security Committee (disarmament and related international security questions) (First Committee)
Special Political Committee
Economic and Financial Committee (Second Committee)
Social, Humanitarian and Cultural Committee (Third Committee)
Trusteeship Committee (including Non-Self-Governing Territories) (Fourth Committee)
Administrative and Budgetary Committee (Fifth Committee)
Legal Committee (Sixth Committee)

The General Assembly may constitute other committees, on which all Members of the United Nations have the right to be represented.

OFFICERS OF THE MAIN COMMITTEES
Resumed thirty-ninth session

Fifth Committee[a]
Chairman: Ernest Besley Maycock (Barbados).
Vice-Chairmen: Mihail Bushev (Bulgaria), Otto Ditz (Austria).
Rapporteur: Ali Achraf Mojtahed (Iran).

[a]The only Main Committee to meet at the resumed session.

Fortieth session[a]

[a]Chairmen elected by the Main Committees; announced by the Assembly President on 17 September 1985 (decision 40/304).

First Committee
Chairman: Ali Alatas (Indonesia).
Vice-Chairmen: Carlos Lechuga Hevia (Cuba), Adeito Nzengeya Bagbeni (Zaire).
Rapporteur: Yannis Souliatis (Greece).

Special Political Committee
Chairman: Keijo Korhonen (Finland).
Vice-Chairmen: Jaroslav Cesar (Czechoslovakia), Kwam Kouassi (Togo).
Rapporteur: Raimundo González (Chile).

Second Committee
Chairman: Omer Birido (Sudan).
Vice-Chairmen: Soemadi D. M. Brotodiningrat (Indonesia), Inga Ericksson (Sweden).
Rapporteur: Jorge Lago Silva (Cuba).

Third Committee
Chairman: Endre Zador (Hungary).
Vice-Chairmen: Alphons Hamer (Netherlands), Abdullah Zawawi Mohamed (Malaysia).
Rapporteur: Paul Désiré Kaboré (Burkina Faso).

Fourth Committee
Chairman: Javier Chamorro Mora (Nicaragua).
Vice-Chairmen: Bouba Diallo (Mali), V. F. Skofenko (Ukrainian SSR).
Rapporteur: Stefano Stefanini (Italy).

Fifth Committee
Chairman: Tommo Monthe (Cameroon).
Vice-Chairmen: Hans Erik Kastoft (Denmark), Adnan A. Yonis (Iraq).
Rapporteur: Falk Meltke (German Democratic Republic).

Sixth Committee
Chairman: Riyadh Al-Qaysi (Iraq).
Vice-Chairmen: Roberto Herrera Cáceres (Honduras), Bernd Mützelburg (Federal Republic of Germany).
Rapporteur: Molefi Pholo (Lesotho).

Procedural committees

General Committee
The General Committee consists of the President of the General Assembly, as Chairman, the 21 Vice-Presidents and the Chairmen of the seven Main Committees.

Credentials Committee
The Credentials Committee consists of nine members appointed by the General Assembly on the proposal of the President.

Fortieth session
Botswana, Brazil, Burundi, Canada *(Chairman)*, China, Papua New Guinea, Suriname, USSR, United States.[a]

[a]Appointed on 17 September 1985 (decision 40/301).

---

[1]The fortieth session of the General Assembly resumed in 1986 from 28 April to 9 May, on 20 June and on 15 September.

Standing committees

The two standing committees consist of experts appointed in their individual capacity for three-year terms.

Advisory Committee on Administrative and Budgetary Questions

Members:

To serve until 31 December 1985: Traian Chebeleu (Romania); Mohamed Malloum Fall (Mauritania); Mohammad Samir Mansouri (Syrian Arab Republic); C. S. M. Mselle, *Chairman* (United Republic of Tanzania); Christopher R. Thomas (Trinidad and Tobago).

To serve until 31 December 1986: Henrik Amneus (Sweden); Ma Longde (China); Andrew Robin Murray (United Kingdom); Samuel Pinheiro-Guimarães (Brazil);[a] Banbit A. Roy (India); Yukio Takasu (Japan).

To serve until 31 December 1987: Even Fontaine-Ortiz (Cuba); Jobst Holborn (Federal Republic of Germany); Virginia C. Housholder (United States);[b] I. V. Khalevinski (USSR); Rachid Lahlou (Morocco).[c]

[a]Resigned in September 1985; Luiz Sergio Gama Figueira (Brazil) was appointed by the General Assembly on 26 September (decision 40/305 A) to fill the resultant vacancy.

[b]Resigned effective 31 December 1985; Richard Nygard (United States) was appointed by the General Assembly on 18 December (decision 40/305 C) to fill the resultant vacancy.

[c]Resigned in November 1985; Noureddine Sefiani (Morocco) was appointed by the General Assembly on 27 November (decision 40/305 B) to fill the resultant vacancy.

On 18 December 1985 (decision 40/305 C), the General Assembly appointed the following five members for a three-year term beginning on 1 January 1986 to fill the vacancies occurring on 31 December 1985: Ahmad Fathi Al-Masri (Syrian Arab Republic), Traian Chebeleu (Romania), C. S. M. Mselle (United Republic of Tanzania), Oluseye D. Oduyemi (Nigeria), Christopher R. Thomas (Trinidad and Tobago).

Committee on Contributions

Members:

To serve until 31 December 1985: Andrzej Abraszewski (Poland); Mohammed Sadiq Al-Mahdi (Iraq); Hamed Arabi El-Houderi (Libyan Arab Jamahiriya); Richard Vognild Hennes (United States); Zoran Lazarevic (Yugoslavia); Yasuo Noguchi (Japan).

To serve until 31 December 1986: Marco Antônio Diniz Brandão (Brazil);[a] Leoncio Fernández Maroto (Spain); Lance Louis E. Joseph (Australia); Atilio Norberto Molteni, *Vice-Chairman* (Argentina); Oluseye D. Oduyemi (Nigeria); Omar Sirry (Egypt).

To serve until 31 December 1987: Amjad Ali, *Chairman* (Pakistan); Ernesto Battisti (Italy); Javier Castillo Ayala (Mexico); A. S. Chistyakov (USSR); Dominique Souchet (France); Wang Liansheng (China).

[a]Resigned in December 1985; Gilberto Vergne Saboia (Brazil) was appointed by the General Assembly on 18 December (decision 40/318) for a one-year term beginning on 1 January 1986 to fill the resultant vacancy.

On 18 December 1985 (decision 40/318), the General Assembly appointed the following six members for a three-year term beginning on 1 January 1986 to fill the vacancies occurring on 31 December 1985: Andrzej Abraszewski (Poland), John Fox (United States), Elias M. C. Kazembe (Zambia), Yasuo Noguchi (Japan), Adnan A. Yonis (Iraq), Assen Iliev Zlatanov (Bulgaria).

Subsidiary, *ad hoc* and related bodies

The following subsidiary, *ad hoc* and related bodies were in existence or functioning in 1985, or were established during the General Assembly's fortieth session, held from 17 September to 18 December 1985. (For other related bodies, see p. 1421.)

Ad Hoc Committee of the General Assembly for the Announcement of Voluntary Contributions to the 1986 Programme of the United Nations High Commissioner for Refugees

As soon as practicable after the opening of each regular session of the General Assembly, an *ad hoc* committee of the whole of the Assembly meets, under the chairmanship of the President of the session, to enable Governments to announce pledges of voluntary contributions to the programme of UNHCR for the following year. Also invited to announce their pledges are States which are members of specialized agencies but not Members of the United Nations. In 1985, the *Ad Hoc* Committee met on 15 November.

Ad Hoc Committee of the General Assembly for the Announcement of Voluntary Contributions to the United Nations Relief and Works Agency for Palestine Refugees in the Near East

As soon as practicable after the opening of each regular session of the General Assembly, an *ad hoc* committee of the whole of the Assembly meets, under the chairmanship of the President of the session, to enable Governments to announce pledges of voluntary contributions to the programme of UNRWA for the following year. Also invited to announce their pledges are States which are members of specialized agencies but not Members of the United Nations. In 1985, the *Ad Hoc* Committee met on 11 November.

Ad Hoc Committee of the International Conference on Kampuchea

The *Ad Hoc* Committee of the International Conference on Kampuchea held six meetings between 17 January and 12 September 1985, at United Nations Headquarters.

Members: Belgium, Japan, Malaysia, Nepal, Nigeria, Peru, Senegal, Sri Lanka, Sudan, Thailand.

Chairman: Massamba Sarré (Senegal).
Vice-Chairman: Edmonde Dever (Belgium).
Rapporteur: Zain Azraai (Malaysia).

Ad Hoc Committee of the Whole to Review the Implementation of the Charter of Economic Rights and Duties of States

The *Ad Hoc* Committee of the Whole to Review the Implementation of the Charter of Economic Rights and Duties of States,[2] composed of all States Members of the United Nations, met at United Nations Headquarters from 25 March to 18 April 1985.

Chairman: Porfirio Muñoz-Ledo (Mexico).
Vice-Chairmen: Tamas Foldeak (Hungary), Habib M. Kaabachi (Tunisia).

Ad Hoc Committee on the Drafting of an International Convention against Apartheid in Sports

The *Ad Hoc* Committee on the Drafting of an International Convention against *Apartheid* in Sports, which was to consist of 25 members, had a membership of 24 in 1985. It held two meetings during the year, at United Nations Headquarters, on 18 January and 26 August.

With the General Assembly's adoption on 10 December 1985 of the International Convention against *Apartheid* in Sports (see p. 165), the *Ad Hoc* Committee fulfilled its mandate.

Members: Algeria, Barbados, Canada, Congo, German Democratic Republic, Ghana, Guinea, Haiti, Hungary, India, Indonesia, Jamaica, Malaysia, Nepal, Nigeria, Peru, Philippines, Somalia, Sudan, Syrian Arab Republic, Trinidad and Tobago, Ukrainian SSR, United Republic of Tanzania, Yugoslavia.

Chairman: Ernest Besley Maycock (Barbados).
Vice-Chairmen: Hari Bhakta Joshi (Nepal), Shani O. Lweno (United Republic of Tanzania), Janos Matus (Hungary).
Rapporteur: Raymond Wolfe (Jamaica).

Ad Hoc Committee on the Drafting of an International Convention against the Recruitment, Use, Financing and Training of Mercenaries

The *Ad Hoc* Committee on the Drafting of an International Convention against the Recruitment, Use, Financing and Training of Mercenaries, held its fifth session at United Nations Headquarters from 8 April to 3 May 1985.

---

[2]YUN 1974, p. 403, GA res. 3281(XXIX), 12 Dec. 1974.

Members: Algeria, Angola, Bangladesh, Barbados, Bulgaria, Canada, Cuba, Democratic Yemen, Ethiopia, France, German Democratic Republic, Germany, Federal Republic of, Haiti, India, Italy, Jamaica, Japan, Mongolia, Nigeria, Portugal, Senegal, Seychelles, Spain, Suriname, Togo,[a] Turkey, Ukrainian SSR, USSR, United Kingdom, United States, Uruguay, Viet Nam,[b] Yugoslavia, Zaire, Zambia.

[a]Until 31 December 1985, when it withdrew in accordance with a schedule of rotation agreed on by the Group of African States. On 11 December 1985 (decision 40/315), the General Assembly confirmed the appointment by its President of Benin, effective 1 January 1986, to fill the resultant vacancy.

[b]Appointed by the President of the thirty-ninth session of the General Assembly, as stated in his communication of 3 September 1985 to the Secretary-General.

Chairman: Harley S. L. Moseley (Barbados).
Vice-Chairmen: Abdallah Baali (Algeria), B. I. Tarasyuk (Ukrainian SSR), Tullio Treves (Italy).
Rapporteur: Hameed Mohamed Ali (Democratic Yemen).

Ad Hoc Committee on the Implementation of the Collective Security Provisions of the Charter of the United Nations

The *Ad Hoc* Committee on the Implementation of the Collective Security Provisions of the Charter of the United Nations, established in 1983, had not been constituted by the end of 1985. On 16 December, the General Assembly requested its President to appoint 54 Member States and on the basis of consultation already conducted to constitute the Committee's membership on the basis of equitable geographical representation and including the permanent members of the Security Council.

Ad Hoc Committee on the Indian Ocean

The *Ad Hoc* Committee on the Indian Ocean, continuing the preparatory work for the Conference on the Indian Ocean (to be convened no later than 1988 at Colombo, Sri Lanka), held three sessions during 1985—from 28 January to 8 February, from 25 March to 4 April and from 1 to 12 July—with two additional meetings on 19 November and 5 December, all at United Nations Headquarters.

Members: Australia, Bangladesh, Bulgaria, Canada, China, Democratic Yemen, Djibouti, Egypt, Ethiopia, France, German Democratic Republic, Germany, Federal Republic of, Greece, India, Indonesia, Iran, Iraq, Italy, Japan, Kenya, Liberia, Madagascar, Malaysia, Maldives, Mauritius, Mozambique, Netherlands, Norway, Oman, Pakistan, Panama, Poland, Romania, Seychelles, Singapore, Somalia, Sri Lanka, Sudan, Thailand, Uganda, USSR, United Arab Emirates, United Kingdom, United Republic of Tanzania, United States, Yemen, Yugoslavia, Zambia.

Sweden, a major maritime user of the Indian Ocean, continued to participate in the meetings as an observer.

Chairman: Nissanka Wijewardane (Sri Lanka).
Vice-Chairmen: Manuel dos Santos (Mozambique); Wilhelm Grundmann (German Democratic Republic); Izhar Ibrahim (Indonesia) (until 1 July), Samsi Abdullah (Indonesia) (from 1 July); John Okely (Australia).
Rapporteur: André Tahindro (Madagascar).

Ad Hoc Committee on the World Disarmament Conference

The 40-member *Ad Hoc* Committee on the World Disarmament Conference held two sessions in 1985, at United Nations Headquarters: the first from 22 to 25 April; and the second from 15 to 19 July.

Members: Algeria, Argentina, Austria, Belgium, Brazil, Bulgaria, Burundi, Canada, Chile, Colombia, Czechoslovakia, Egypt, Ethiopia, Hungary, India, Indonesia, Iran, Italy, Japan, Lebanon, Liberia, Mexico, Mongolia, Morocco, Netherlands, Nigeria, Pakistan, Peru, Philippines, Poland, Romania, Spain, Sri Lanka, Sweden, Tunisia, Turkey, Venezuela, Yugoslavia, Zaire, Zambia.

The USSR participated in the work of the *Ad Hoc* Committee, while China, France, the United Kingdom and the United States maintained contact with it through its Chairman, pursuant to a 1973 General Assembly resolution.[3]

Chairman: Nissanka Wijewardane (Sri Lanka).
Vice-Chairmen:[a] Kazimierz Tomaszewski (Poland).
Rapporteur: Arturo Laclaustra (Spain).

[a]Two posts remained vacant.

WORKING GROUP
Members: Burundi, Egypt, Hungary, India, Iran, Italy, Mexico, Peru, Poland, Spain *(Chairman)*, Sri Lanka.

Advisory Committee for the International Youth Year

The 24-member Advisory Committee for the International Youth Year held its fourth and final session at Vienna, Austria, from 25 March to 3 April 1985.

Members: Algeria, Chile, Costa Rica, Democratic Yemen, Germany, Federal Republic of, Guatemala, Guinea, Indonesia, Ireland, Jamaica, Japan, Lebanon, Morocco, Mozambique, Netherlands, Nigeria, Norway, Poland, Romania, Rwanda, Sri Lanka, USSR, United States, Venezuela.

Chairman: Nicu Ceauscescu (Romania).
Vice-Chairmen: Edmund Bartlett (Jamaica), Hocine Oussedik (Algeria), Mr. Soenaryo (Indonesia).
Rapporteur: Manfred Gerwinat (Federal Republic of Germany).

Advisory Committee on the United Nations Educational and Training Programme for Southern Africa

Members: Byelorussian SSR, Canada, Denmark, India, Japan, Liberia, Nigeria, Norway, United Republic of Tanzania, United States, Venezuela, Zaire, Zambia.

Chairman: Tom Eric Vraalsen (Norway).
Vice-Chairman: Love Kunda M'tesa (Zambia).

Advisory Committee on the United Nations Programme of Assistance in the Teaching, Study, Dissemination and Wider Appreciation of International Law

The Advisory Committee on the United Nations Programme of Assistance in the Teaching, Study, Dissemination and Wider Appreciation of International Law held its twentieth session on 30 October 1985 at United Nations Headquarters.

Members (until 31 December 1987): Barbados, Cyprus, France, Ghana, Libyan Arab Jamahiriya, Netherlands, Romania, Sierra Leone, Syrian Arab Republic, Turkey, USSR, United Kingdom, Venezuela.

Chairman: Yaw Konadu-Yiadom (Ghana).

Board of Auditors

The Board of Auditors consists of three members appointed by the General Assembly for three-year terms.

Members:
To serve until 30 June 1986: Senior President of the Audit Office of Belgium.
To serve until 30 June 1987: Chairman of the Commission of Audit of the Philippines.
To serve until 30 June 1988: Auditor-General of Ghana.

On 18 December 1985 (decision 40/319), the General Assembly appointed the Senior President of the Audit Office of France for a three-year term beginning on 1 July 1986.

Collective Measures Committee

Established in 1950 under the General Assembly's "Uniting for Peace" resolution,[4] the Collective Measures Committee reported three times to the Assembly. In noting the third report, to its ninth (1954) session, the Assembly directed the Committee to remain in a position to pursue such further studies as it may deem desirable to strengthen the capability of the United Nations to maintain peace and to report to the Security Council and to the Assembly as appropriate.[5]

---

[3]YUN 1973, p. 18, res. 3183(XXVIII), 18 Dec. 1973.
[4]YUN 1950, p. 194, res. 377(V), part A, para. 11, 3 Nov. 1950.
[5]YUN 1954, p. 23, res. 809(IX), 4 Nov. 1954.

Members: Australia, Belgium, Brazil, Burma, Canada, Egypt, France, Mexico, Philippines, Turkey, United Kingdom, United States, Venezuela, Yugoslavia.

Commission on Human Settlements

The Commission on Human Settlements (p. 1415) reports to the General Assembly through the Economic and Social Council.

Committee for Programme and Co-ordination

The Committee for Programme and Co-ordination (p. 1415) is the main subsidiary organ of the Economic and Social Council and of the General Assembly for planning, programming and co-ordination; it reports to both.

Committee for the United Nations Population Award

The Committee for the United Nations Population Award is composed of: *(a)* 10 representatives of United Nations Member States elected by the Economic and Social Council for a three-year period, with due regard for equitable geographical representation and the need to include Member States that had made contributions for the Award; *(b)* the Secretary-General and the UNFPA Executive Director, to serve *ex officio;* and *(c)* five individuals eminent for their significant contributions to population-related activities, selected by the Committee, to serve as honorary members in an advisory capacity for a renewable three-year term.

In 1985, the Committee held six meetings between 24 January and 2 May, at United Nations Headquarters.

Members (until 31 December 1985): Australia, Bangladesh, Burundi, China, Colombia, Egypt, Japan, Mexico, Tunisia, Yugoslavia.
Ex-officio members: The Secretary-General and the UNFPA Executive Director.
Honorary members (until 31 December 1985): Kenneth K. S. Dadzie, Nobusuke Kishi, Alva Myrdal, Raúl Prebisch, Robert E. Turner III.

Chairman: Anwarul Karim Chowdhury (Bangladesh).

On 30 May and 26 July 1985 (decisions 1985/160 and 1985/204), the Economic and Social Council elected the following 10 members for a three-year term beginning on 1 January 1986 to fill the vacancies occurring on 31 December 1985: Burundi, Colombia, Ecuador, Japan, Mexico, Pakistan, Spain, Sudan, Tunisia, Yugoslavia.

Committee of Trustees of the United Nations Trust Fund for South Africa
Members: Chile, Morocco, Nigeria, Pakistan, Sweden.

Chairman: Anders Ferm (Sweden).
Vice-Chairman: Joseph N. Garba (Nigeria).

Committee on Applications for Review of Administrative Tribunal Judgements

In 1985, the Committee on Applications for Review of Administrative Tribunal Judgements held two sessions, at United Nations Headquarters: its twenty-fifth from 28 to 31 January; and its twenty-sixth on 12 and 13 September.

Members (until 16 September 1985) (based on the composition of the General Committee at the General Assembly's thirty-ninth session): Bahrain, Bangladesh, Barbados, Bolivia, Brazil, Bulgaria, Chad, China, Cuba, Cyprus, Djibouti, France, German Democratic Republic, Ghana, Guatemala, Guinea, Iceland, Italy, Malaysia, Morocco, New Zealand, Papua New Guinea, Somalia, Togo, USSR, United Kingdom, United States, Yemen, Zambia.

Chairman: Gunter Goerner (German Democratic Republic).
Rapporteur: Franklin D. Berman (United Kingdom) (twenty-fifth session); David M. Edwards (United Kingdom) (twenty-sixth session).

Members (from 17 September 1985) (based on the composition of the General Committee at the General Assembly's fortieth session): Bahamas, Barbados, Burkina Faso, Cameroon, China, Costa Rica, Cyprus, Democratic Yemen, Finland, France, Gabon, Hungary, Indonesia, Iraq, Kenya, Lesotho, Malta, Nicaragua, Pakistan, Philippines,

Qatar, Romania, Senegal, Spain, Sudan, Tunisia, USSR, United Kingdom, United States.

Committee on Arrangements for a Conference for the Purpose of Reviewing the Charter

All Members of the United Nations are members of the Committee on Arrangements for a Conference for the Purpose of Reviewing the Charter.

The Committee, established in 1955, last met in 1967, following which the General Assembly decided to keep it in being.[6]

Committee on Conferences

The Committee on Conferences consists of 22 Member States appointed by the President of the General Assembly on the basis of equitable geographical balance, to serve for a three-year term.

Members (until 31 December 1986): Algeria, Austria, Bahamas, Bulgaria, Byelorussian SSR, Chile, Cyprus, France, Germany, Federal Republic of, Honduras, Indonesia, Italy, Japan, Kenya, Mexico, Nigeria, Senegal, Sri Lanka, Tunisia, USSR, United Kingdom, United States.

Chairman: Bernards A. N. Mudho (Kenya).
Vice-Chairmen: J. D. Ariyaratne (Sri Lanka), P. G. Belyaev (Byelorussian SSR), Fernando Danus (Chile).
Rapporteur: Otto Ditz (Austria).

Committee on Information

In 1985, the 69-member Committee on Information held, at United Nations Headquarters, an organizational session from 19 to 21 March and its seventh session from 17 June to 5 July and on 29 August.

Members: Algeria, Argentina, Bangladesh, Belgium, Benin, Brazil, Bulgaria, Burundi, Chile, China, Colombia, Congo, Costa Rica, Cuba, Cyprus, Denmark, Ecuador, Egypt, El Salvador, Ethiopia, Finland, France, German Democratic Republic, Germany, Federal Republic of, Ghana, Greece, Guatemala, Guinea, Guyana, India, Indonesia, Italy, Ivory Coast, Japan, Jordan, Kenya, Lebanon, Mexico, Mongolia, Morocco, Netherlands, Niger, Nigeria, Pakistan, Peru, Philippines, Poland, Portugal, Romania, Singapore, Somalia, Spain, Sri Lanka, Sudan, Syrian Arab Republic, Togo, Trinidad and Tobago, Tunisia, Turkey, Ukrainian SSR, USSR, United Kingdom, United Republic of Tanzania, United States, Venezuela, Viet Nam, Yemen, Yugoslavia, Zaire.

Chairman: Willi Schlegel (German Democratic Republic).
Vice-Chairmen: Melchior Bwakira (Burundi), Q. A. M. A. Rahim (Bangladesh), Ernesto Rodríguez-Medina (Colombia).
Rapporteur: Pablo Barrios (Spain).

Committee on Relations with the Host Country
Members: Bulgaria, Canada, China, Costa Rica, Cyprus, France, Honduras, Iraq, Ivory Coast, Mali, Senegal, Spain, USSR, United Kingdom, United States (host country).

Chairman: Constantine Moushoutas (Cyprus).
Vice-Chairmen: Bulgaria, Canada, Ivory Coast.
Rapporteur: Emilia Castro de Barish (Costa Rica).

Committee on the Development and Utilization of New and Renewable Sources of Energy

The Committee on the Development and Utilization of New and Renewable Sources of Energy, open to the participation of all States as full members, did not meet in 1985.

Committee on the Exercise of the Inalienable Rights of the Palestinian People
Members: Afghanistan, Cuba, Cyprus, German Democratic Republic, Guinea, Guyana, Hungary, India, Indonesia, Lao People's Democratic Republic, Madagascar, Malaysia, Mali, Malta, Nigeria, Pakistan, Romania, Senegal, Sierra Leone, Tunisia, Turkey, Ukrainian SSR, Yugoslavia.

---

[6]YUN 1967, p. 291, res. 2285(XXII), 5 Dec. 1967.

Chairman: Massamba Sarré (Senegal).
Vice-Chairmen: Oscar Oramas-Oliva (Cuba), Mohammad Farid Zarif (Afghanistan).
Rapporteur: Victor J. Gauci (Malta) (until 28 October 1985), George Agius (Malta) (from 29 October).

WORKING GROUP
Members: Afghanistan, Cuba, German Democratic Republic, Guinea, Guyana, India *(Vice-Chairman)*, Malta *(Chairman)*, Pakistan, Senegal, Tunisia, Turkey, Ukrainian SSR; Palestine Liberation Organization.

Committee on the Peaceful Uses of Outer Space
The 53-member Committee on the Peaceful Uses of Outer Space held its twenty-eighth session at United Nations Headquarters from 17 to 28 June 1985.

Members: Albania, Argentina, Australia, Austria, Belgium, Benin, Brazil, Bulgaria, Burkina Faso, Cameroon, Canada, Chad, Chile, China, Colombia, Czechoslovakia, Ecuador, Egypt, France, German Democratic Republic, Germany, Federal Republic of, Hungary, India, Indonesia, Iran, Iraq, Italy, Japan, Kenya, Lebanon, Mexico, Mongolia, Morocco, Netherlands, Niger, Nigeria, Pakistan, Philippines, Poland, Portugal, Romania, Sierra Leone, Sudan, Sweden, Syrian Arab Republic, Turkey, USSR, United Kingdom, United States, Uruguay, Venezuela, Viet Nam, Yugoslavia.

Chairman: Peter Jankowitsch (Austria).
Vice-Chairman: Teodor Marinescu (Romania).
Rapporteur: Henrique Rodrigues Valle (Brazil).

LEGAL SUB-COMMITTEE
The Legal Sub-Committee, a committee of the whole, held its twenty-fourth session at United Nations Headquarters from 18 March to 4 April 1985.

Chairman: Ludek Handl (Czechoslovakia).

SCIENTIFIC AND TECHNICAL SUB-COMMITTEE
The Scientific and Technical Sub-Committee, a committee of the whole, held its twenty-second session at United Nations Headquarters from 11 to 22 February 1985.

Chairman: J. H. Carver (Australia).

Committee on the Review and Appraisal of the Implementation of the International Development Strategy for the Third United Nations Development Decade
The Committee on the Review and Appraisal of the Implementation of the International Development Strategy for the Third United Nations Development Decade, open to the participation of all States as full members, resumed its session (begun in 1984) in 1985 at United Nations Headquarters, from 6 to 14 May and from 9 to 24 September, thereby completing its work.

Chairman: Kenneth K. S. Dadzie (Ghana).
Vice-Chairmen: Oscar R. de Rojas (Venezuela); Per Jodahl (Sweden) (until 14 May), Krister Kumlin (Sweden) (from 14 May); Konstantin Kolev (Bulgaria).
Rapporteur: Yousif Gewaily (Qatar).

Disarmament Commission
In 1985, the Disarmament Commission, composed of all the Members of the United Nations, held a series of meetings between 6 and 31 May and an organizational meeting on 2 December, all at United Nations Headquarters.

Chairman: Mansur Ahmad (Pakistan).
Vice-Chairmen: Bahamas, Byelorussian SSR, Cameroon, German Democratic Republic, Greece, Iran, Mexico, Morocco.
Rapporteur: Arturo Laclaustra (Spain).

Group of High-level Intergovernmental Experts to Review the Efficiency of the Administrative and Financial Functioning of the United Nations
On 18 December 1985, the General Assembly established a Group of High-level Intergovernmental Experts, for a term of one year, to conduct a review of the administrative and financial functioning of the United Nations, with a view to improving its efficiency. The Group, to consist of 18 members appointed by the Assembly President with due regard to equitable geographical distribution, had not been constituted by the end of 1985.

High-level Committee on the Review of Technical Co-operation among Developing Countries
In 1985, the High-level Committee on the Review of Technical Co-operation among Developing Countries, composed of all States participating in UNDP, held its fourth session at United Nations Headquarters from 28 May to 3 June and on 5 June.

President: Hamed Zeghal (Tunisia).
Vice-Presidents: Oscar R. de Rojas (Venezuela), Peter Marx (German Democratic Republic), Faruq S. Ziada (Iraq).
Rapporteur: Saviour F. Borg (Malta).

Intergovernmental Committee on Science and Technology for Development
The Intergovernmental Committee on Science and Technology for Development, open to the participation of all States as full members, held its seventh session at United Nations Headquarters from 28 May to 7 June 1985.

Chairman: Lars Anell (Sweden).
Vice-Chairmen: Francisco de Lima e Silva (Brazil), Mumtaz Ali Kazi (Pakistan), Nicholas Dlamini Kitikiti (Zimbabwe).
Rapporteur: Andrzej J. Wilk (Poland).

ADVISORY COMMITTEE ON SCIENCE
AND TECHNOLOGY FOR DEVELOPMENT
The 28-member Advisory Committee on Science and Technology for Development held its fifth session at United Nations Headquarters from 4 to 13 February 1985.

Members:
To serve until 31 December 1986: Oscar Aguero Wood (Chile); Umberto Colombo, *Chairman* (Italy); Etienne Cracco (Belgium); Djibril Fall (Senegal); Essam El Din Galal (Egypt); Henri Hogbe-Nlend, *Vice-Chairman* (Cameroon); Mumtaz Ali Kazi, *Vice-Chairman* (Pakistan); Lydia Makhubu (Swaziland); James Mullin, *Rapporteur* (Canada); Tiberiu Muresan (Romania); Keichi Oshima (Japan); Francisco R. Sagasti (Peru); M. S. Swaminathan (India);[a] José Israel Vargas, *Vice-Chairman* (Brazil).
To serve until 31 December 1987: Saleh Abdulrahman Al-Athel (Saudi Arabia); Lars Anell (Sweden); Ang How-Ghee (Singapore); Sadak Ben Jamaa, *Vice-Chairman* (Tunisia); I. D. Ivanov, *Vice-Chairman* (USSR); Ernst Keller (Switzerland); Stefen Kwiatkowski (Poland); Manlio D. Martínez (Honduras); Abdou Dioffo Moumouni (Niger); V. Nyathi (Zimbabwe); Sanga Sabhasri (Thailand); Yannis Tsividis (Greece); Lawrence A. Wilson (Trinidad and Tobago); Xu Zhaoxiang (China).

[a]Resigned on 2 January 1985; on 28 May, the Intergovernmental Committee appointed Yash Pal (India) to fill the resultant vacancy.

Interim Committee of the General Assembly
The Interim Committee of the General Assembly, on which each Member of the United Nations has the right to appoint one representative, was originally established by the Assembly in 1947 to function between the Assembly's regular sessions. It was re-established in 1948 for a further year and in 1949[7] for an indefinite period. The Committee has not met since 1961.[8]

International Civil Service Commission
The International Civil Service Commission consists of 15 members who serve in their personal capacity as individuals of recognized competence in public administration or related fields, particularly in personnel management. They are appointed by the General Assembly, with due regard for equitable geographical distribution, for four-year terms.

---

[7]YUN 1948-49, p. 411, res. 295(IV), 21 Nov. 1949.
[8]YUN 1961, p. 705.

The Commission held two sessions in 1985: its twenty-first in London from 11 to 29 March; and its twenty-second at United Nations Headquarters from 8 to 26 July.

Members:
To serve until 31 December 1985: Michel Auchère (France); Ralph Enckell (Finland); Masao Kanazawa (Japan);[a] Helmut Kitschenberg (Federal Republic of Germany); Antônio Fonseca Pimentel (Brazil).
To serve until 31 December 1986: Richard M. Akwei, *Chairman* (Ghana); Moulaye El Hassen (Mauritania);[b] Dayton W. Hull (United States);[b] Jiri Nosek (Czechoslovakia);[b] Carlos S. Vegega, *Vice-Chairman* (Argentina).
To serve until 31 December 1988: Amjad Ali (Pakistan); Michael O. Ani (Nigeria);[a] Omar Sirry (Egypt); V. V. Tsybukov (USSR); M. A. Vellodi (India).

[a]Died on 23 March and in December 1985, respectively; the resultant vacancies were not filled in 1985.
[b]Resigned effective October 1985; on 18 December (decision 40/322), the General Assembly appointed Turkia Daddah (Mauritania), André Xavier Pirson (Belgium) and Karel Houska (Czechoslovakia), respectively, for a one-year term beginning on 1 January 1986, to fill the resultant vacancies.

On 18 December 1985 (decision 40/322), the General Assembly appointed the following members for a four-year term beginning on 1 January 1986 to fill the vacancies occurring on 31 December 1985: Genichi Akatani (Japan), Michel Auchère (France), Claudia Cooley (United States), Antônio Fonseca Pimentel (Brazil), Alexis Stephanou (Greece).

ADVISORY COMMITTEE ON POST ADJUSTMENT QUESTIONS
The Advisory Committee on Post Adjustment Questions consists of six members, of whom five are chosen from the geographical regions of Africa, Asia, Latin America, Eastern Europe, and Western Europe and other States; and one, from ICSC, who serves *ex officio* as Chairman. Members are appointed by the ICSC Chairman to serve for four-year terms.
The Advisory Committee held its tenth session at Vienna, Austria, from 7 to 17 May 1985.

Members:
To serve until 31 December 1985: Nana Wereko Ampem II (also known as Emmanuel Noi Omaboe) (Ghana).
To serve until 31 December 1986: Carmen McFarlane (Jamaica), Hugues Picard (France).
To serve until 31 December 1987: A. F. Revenko (USSR).
To serve until 31 December 1988: Saw Swee Hock (Singapore).[a]
Ex-officio member: Jiri Nosek, *Chairman* (Czechoslovakia).[b]

[a]Appointed in April 1985.
[b]Resigned effective October 1985; ICSC appointed Carlos S. Vegega (Argentina) to serve as Chairman of the Advisory Committee.

International Law Commission
The International Law Commission consists of 34 persons of recognized competence in international law, elected by the General Assembly to serve in their individual capacity for a five-year term. Vacancies occurring within the five-year period are filled by the Commission.
The Commission held its thirty-seventh session at Geneva from 6 May to 26 July 1985.

Members (until 31 December 1986): Richard Osuolale A. Akinjide (Nigeria); Riyadh Al-Qaysi (Iraq); Gaetano Arangio-Ruiz (Italy);[a] Mikuin Leliel Balanda (Zaire); Julio Barboza (Argentina); Boutros Boutros-Ghali (Egypt); Carlos Calero Rodrigues (Brazil); Jorge Castañeda (Mexico); Leonardo Díaz-González (Venezuela); Khalafalla El Rasheed Mohamed-Ahmed, *First Vice-Chairman* (Sudan); Constantin Flitan, *Rapporteur* (Romania); Laurel B. Francis (Jamaica); Huang Jiahua (China);[a] Jorge Enrique Illueca (Panama); Andreas J. Jacovides (Cyprus); Satya Pal Jagota, *Chairman* (India); Abdul G. Koroma (Sierra Leone); José Manuel Lacleta Muñoz (Spain); Ahmed Mahiou (Algeria); Chafic Malek (Lebanon); Stephen C. McCaffrey (United States); Frank X. J. C. Njenga (Kenya); Motoo Ogiso (Japan); Syed Sharifuddin Pirzada (Pakistan); Edilbert Razafindralambo (Madagascar); Paul Reuter (France); Willem Riphagen (Netherlands); Emmanuel J. Roukounas (Greece);[a] Sir Ian Sinclair, *Second Vice-*

Chairman (United Kingdom); Sompong Sucharitkul (Thailand); Doudou Thiam (Senegal); Christian Tomuschat (Federal Republic of Germany);[a] N. A. Ushakov (USSR); Alexander Yankov (Bulgaria).

[a]Elected on 8 May 1985 to fill four vacancies that arose in 1984.

Investments Committee
The Investments Committee consists of nine members appointed by the Secretary-General, after consultation with the United Nations Joint Staff Pension Board and ACABQ, subject to confirmation by the General Assembly. Members serve for three-year terms.

Members:
To serve until 31 December 1985: Aloysio de Andrade Faria, Braj Kumar Nehru *(Chairman)*, Stanislaw Raczkowski.
To serve until 31 December 1986: David Montagu, Yves Oltramare, Emmanuel Noi Omaboe (also known as Nana Wereko Ampem II).
To serve until 31 December 1987: Jean Guyot, George Johnston, Michiya Matsukawa.

In addition, during 1985, Ahmed Abdullatif and Juergen Reimnitz served in an *ad hoc* consultative capacity.

On 18 December 1985 (decision 40/320), the General Assembly confirmed the appointment by the Secretary-General of Aloysio de Andrade Faria, Braj Kumar Nehru and Stanislaw Raczkowski as members for a three-year term beginning on 1 January 1986.

Joint Advisory Group on the International Trade Centre UNCTAD/GATT
The Joint Advisory Group was established in accordance with an agreement between UNCTAD and GATT with effect from 1 January 1968, the date on which their joint sponsorship of the International Trade Centre commenced.
Participation in the Group is open to all States members of UNCTAD and to all Contracting Parties to GATT.
The Group held its eighteenth session at Geneva from 15 to 22 April 1985.

Chairman: Wilbert Kumalija Chagula (United Republic of Tanzania).
Vice-Chairmen: J. Jachim (Czechoslovakia), M. Olarreaga (Uruguay).
Rapporteur: K. Ilander (Finland).

TECHNICAL COMMITTEE
Following a two-year experiment, in which meetings of the Technical Committee and the Group were combined in a single meeting (the Group's annual session), with the session attended by both technical experts and officials dealing with policy matters, the Group decided in 1985 that this would become a permanent arrangement. The Committee thereby ceased to exist.

Joint Inspection Unit
The Joint Inspection Unit consists of not more than 11 Inspectors appointed by the General Assembly from candidates nominated by Member States following appropriate consultations, including consultations with the President of the Economic and Social Council and with the Chairman of ACC. The Inspectors, chosen for their special experience in national or international administrative and financial matters, with due regard for equitable geographical distribution and reasonable rotation, serve in their personal capacity for five-year terms.

Members:
To serve until 31 December 1985:[a] Maurice Bertrand (France); Alfred Nathaniel Forde (Barbados); Moustapha Ould Khalifa (Mauritania); Earl D. Sohm (United States); Miljenko Vukovic (Yugoslavia).
To serve until 31 December 1987: A. S. Efimov, *Vice-Chairman* (USSR); Mohamed Salah Eldin Ibrahim, *Chairman* (Egypt); Nasser Kaddour (Syrian Arab Republic); Siegfried Schumm (Federal Republic of Germany); Norman Williams (Panama).
To serve until 31 December 1989: Kahono Martohadinegoro (Indonesia).[b]

[a]Members to fill the vacancies occurring on 31 December 1985 were appointed by the General Assembly in 1984 (YUN 1984, p. 1317).
[b]Appointed on 9 April 1985 (decision 39/305 C) to fill a vacancy created in 1984.

Negotiating Committee on the Financial Emergency
of the United Nations

Established in 1975 by the General Assembly[9] to consist of 54 Member States appointed by its President on the basis of equitable geographical balance, the Negotiating Committee on the Financial Emergency of the United Nations has a membership of 48. It has not met since 1976.[10]

Members: Argentina, Austria, Bangladesh, Bolivia, Burkina Faso, Canada, Chad, Colombia, Cuba, Ecuador, Egypt, Finland, France, Gabon, German Democratic Republic, Germany, Federal Republic of, Ghana, Greece, Grenada, India, Indonesia, Iran, Ireland, Italy, Jamaica, Japan, Jordan, Kenya, Kuwait, Libyan Arab Jamahiriya, Malawi, Mexico, Morocco, Nigeria, Pakistan, Philippines, Poland, Spain, Sudan, Swaziland, Sweden, Trinidad and Tobago, Tunisia, Turkey, USSR, United Kingdom, United States, Venezuela.

Office of the United Nations High Commissioner
for Refugees (UNHCR)

EXECUTIVE COMMITTEE OF THE HIGH
COMMISSIONER'S PROGRAMME

The Executive Committee held two sessions in 1985, at Geneva: its resumed thirty-fifth on 24 January and its thirty-sixth from 7 to 18 October.

Members: Algeria, Argentina, Australia, Austria, Belgium, Brazil, Canada, China, Colombia, Denmark, Finland, France, Germany, Federal Republic of, Greece, Holy See, Iran, Israel, Italy, Japan, Lebanon, Lesotho, Madagascar, Morocco, Netherlands, Nicaragua, Nigeria, Norway, Sudan, Sweden, Switzerland, Thailand, Tunisia, Turkey, Uganda, United Kingdom, United Republic of Tanzania, United States, Venezuela, Yugoslavia, Zaire; Namibia (represented by the United Nations Council for Namibia).

Resumed thirty-fifth session
Chairman: F. Mebazaa (Tunisia).
Vice-Chairman: K. Chiba (Japan).
Rapporteur: I. Uusitalo (Finland).

Thirty-sixth session
Chairman: K. Chiba (Japan).
Vice-Chairman: H. Charry-Samper (Colombia).
Rapporteur: E. E. E. Mtango (United Republic of Tanzania).

United Nations High Commissioner for Refugees: Poul Hartling.
Deputy High Commissioner: William Richard Smyser.

On 10 December 1985 (decision 40/310), the General Assembly elected Jean-Pierre Hocké as High Commissioner for a three-year term beginning on 1 January 1986.

SUB-COMMITTEE OF THE WHOLE
ON INTERNATIONAL PROTECTION

The Sub-Committee of the Whole on International Protection held its tenth meeting at Geneva on 30 September and on 1 and 4 October 1985.

Chairman: F. Mebazaa (Tunisia).

SUB-COMMITTEE ON
ADMINISTRATIVE AND FINANCIAL MATTERS

The Sub-Committee on Administrative and Financial Matters, which is composed of all members of the Executive Committee, held its fifth meeting at Geneva concurrently with the tenth meeting of the Sub-Committee of the Whole on International Protection.

Chairman: K. Chiba (Japan).

Panel for Inquiry and Conciliation

The Panel for Inquiry and Conciliation was created by the General Assembly in 1949[11] to consist of qualified persons, designated by United Nations Member States, each to serve for a term of five years. Information concerning the Panel's composition had from time to time

been communicated to the Assembly and the Security Council; the last consolidated list was issued by the Secretary-General in a note of 20 January 1961.

Panel of External Auditors

The Panel of External Auditors consists of the members of the United Nations Board of Auditors and the appointed external auditors of the specialized agencies and IAEA.

Panel of Military Experts

The General Assembly's "Uniting for Peace" resolution[12] called for the appointment of military experts to be available, on request, to United Nations Member States wishing to obtain technical advice on the organization, training and equipment of elements within their national armed forces which could be made available, in accordance with national constitutional processes, for service as a unit or units of the United Nations upon the recommendation of the Security Council or the Assembly.

Preparatory Committee for the Fortieth
Anniversary of the United Nations

The Preparatory Committee for the Fortieth Anniversary of the United Nations (observed in 1985), consisting of the members of the General Committee of the General Assembly's thirty-eighth (1983) session and open to the participation of all Member States on an equal basis, held eight meetings between 19 February and 11 September 1985, thereby completing its work.

Chairman: Paul John Firmino Lusaka (Zambia).
Vice-Chairmen: Miguel A. Albornoz (Ecuador), Jaroslav César (Czechoslovakia), Faruq S. Ziada (Iraq).
Rapporteur: Peter David Lee (Canada).

Preparatory Committee for the International Conference on
the Relationship between Disarmament and Development

In 1985, the Preparatory Committee for the International Conference on the Relationship between Disarmament and Development (to be held in 1986), which was to be composed of 54 members, had a membership of 52. It met at United Nations Headquarters from 29 July to 9 August 1985.

Members:[a] Afghanistan, Argentina, Australia, Austria, Bahamas, Bangladesh, Bolivia, Brazil, Bulgaria, Cameroon, Canada, China, Colombia, Congo, Cuba, Czechoslovakia, France, German Democratic Republic, Germany, Federal Republic of, Ghana, Greece, India, Indonesia, Iran, Italy, Jamaica, Kenya, Mexico, Mongolia, Netherlands, Nigeria, Norway, Pakistan, Philippines, Portugal, Romania, Rwanda, Senegal, Spain, Sri Lanka, Sudan, Swaziland, Sweden, Syrian Arab Republic, Togo, Uganda, USSR, United Kingdom, Uruguay, Venezuela, Yugoslavia, Zambia.

[a]Appointed by the President of the thirty-ninth session of the General Assembly, as stated in his communication of 8 July 1985 to the Secretary-General; on 16 December, the Assembly authorized additional sessions open to all States.

Chairman: Muchkund Dubey (India).
Vice-Chairmen: Dietmar Hucke (German Democratic Republic), Martin Huslid (Norway), Oscar Oramas-Oliva (Cuba).
Rapporteur: Bernards A. N. Mudho (Kenya).

Preparatory Committee for the United Nations Conference
for the Promotion of International Co-operation
in the Peaceful Uses of Nuclear Energy

In 1985, the Preparatory Committee for the United Nations Conference for the Promotion of International Co-operation in the Peaceful Uses of Nuclear Energy (rescheduled for 1987), which was to be composed of 70 Member States and, on an equal footing, other Member States which might express interest in participating in the Committee's work, had a membership of 66. It held its sixth session at Vienna, Austria, from 21 October to 1 November 1985.

---

[9]YUN 1975, p. 957, res. 3538(XXX), 17 Dec. 1975.
[10]YUN 1976, pp. 889 and 1064.
[11]YUN 1948-49, p. 416, res. 268 D (III), 28 Apr. 1949.
[12]YUN 1950, p. 194, res. 377(V), part A, para. 10, 3 Nov. 1950.

Members: Algeria, Argentina, Australia, Austria, Belgium, Brazil, Bulgaria, Byelorussian SSR, Cameroon, Canada, Chile, China, Colombia, Costa Rica, Cuba, Czechoslovakia, Denmark, Ecuador, Egypt, Finland, France, German Democratic Republic, Germany, Federal Republic of, Ghana, Greece, Guatemala, Hungary, India, Indonesia, Iran, Iraq, Ireland, Italy, Ivory Coast, Japan, Libyan Arab Jamahiriya, Malaysia, Mauritania, Mexico, Morocco, Netherlands, Niger, Nigeria, Norway, Pakistan, Peru, Philippines, Poland, Romania, Saudi Arabia, Senegal, Spain, Sri Lanka, Sweden, Syrian Arab Republic, Thailand, Turkey, Ukrainian SSR, USSR, United Arab Emirates, United Kingdom, United States, Uruguay, Venezuela, Yugoslavia, Zaire.

Chairman: Novak Pribicevic (Yugoslavia).
Vice-Chairmen: Juan Carlos Beltramino (Argentina), Essam El-Din Hawas (Egypt), Zdenek Kamis (Czechoslovakia), Jan Kronholm (Sweden), Suror Merza Mahmoud (Iraq), Jorge Morelli Pando (Peru), Frans J. A. Terwisscha van Scheltinga (Netherlands), Kobina Wudu (Ghana).
Rapporteur: Enny Soeprapto (Indonesia).

Preparatory Committee of the Whole for the Special Session of the General Assembly on the Critical Economic Situation in Africa

On 2 December 1985, the General Assembly established a committee of the whole to undertake preparations for a special session of the Assembly on the critical economic situation in Africa, scheduled for May 1986. The Preparatory Committee did not meet in 1985.

Special Committee against *Apartheid*

The Special Committee against *Apartheid* has a membership of 18. Additional members remained to be appointed by the end of 1985 in pursuance of a 1979 General Assembly request[13] to increase that number.

Members: Algeria, German Democratic Republic, Ghana, Guinea, Haiti, Hungary, India, Indonesia, Malaysia, Nepal, Nigeria, Peru, Philippines, Somalia, Sudan, Syrian Arab Republic, Trinidad and Tobago, Ukrainian SSR.

Chairman: Joseph N. Garba (Nigeria).
Vice-Chairmen: Uddhav Deo Bhatt (Nepal), Serge Elie Charles (Haiti), G. I. Oudovenko (Ukrainian SSR).
Rapporteur: Bhaskar Kumar Mitra (India).

SUB-COMMITTEE ON PETITIONS AND INFORMATION
Members: Algeria *(Chairman)*, German Democratic Republic, Nepal, Somalia, Trinidad and Tobago.

SUB-COMMITTEE ON THE IMPLEMENTATION OF UNITED NATIONS RESOLUTIONS AND COLLABORATION WITH SOUTH AFRICA
Members: Ghana *(Chairman)*, Hungary, India, Peru, Sudan.

Special Committee on Enhancing the Effectiveness of the Principle of Non-Use of Force in International Relations

The 35-member Special Committee on Enhancing the Effectiveness of the Principle of Non-Use of Force in International Relations met at United Nations Headquarters between 28 January and 22 February 1985.

Members: Belgium, Benin, Bulgaria, Cuba,[a] Cyprus, Ecuador,[a] Egypt, Finland, France, Germany, Federal Republic of, Greece, Guinea, Hungary, India, Iraq, Italy, Japan, Mexico,[a] Mongolia, Morocco, Nepal, Nicaragua,[b] Panama,[b] Peru,[b] Poland, Romania, Senegal, Somalia, Spain, Togo, Turkey, Uganda, USSR, United Kingdom, United States.

[a]Withdrew from membership with effect from 31 December 1985, as stated in a letter of 10 December to the General Assembly President from the Chairman of the Latin American Group. On 11 December (decision 40/314), the Assembly confirmed the appointment by its President of Argentina, Brazil and Chile, effective 1 January 1986, to fill the resultant vacancies.
[b]Replaced Argentina, Brazil and Chile, in accordance with a system of rotation agreed upon by the Latin American States when the Special Committee was constituted.

Chairman: P. Sreenivasa Rao (India).
Vice-Chairmen: Carlos Bernal (Mexico), Kari Hakapaa (Finland), Gyula Szelei-Kiss (Hungary).
Rapporteur: Mohammed Loulichki (Morocco).

Special Committee on Peace-keeping Operations

The 33-member Special Committee on Peace-keeping Operations did not meet in 1985.

Members: Afghanistan, Algeria, Argentina, Australia, Austria, Canada, Denmark, Egypt, El Salvador, Ethiopia, France, German Democratic Republic, Guatemala, Hungary, India, Iraq, Italy, Japan, Mauritania, Mexico, Netherlands, Nigeria, Pakistan, Poland, Romania, Sierra Leone, Spain, Thailand, USSR, United Kingdom, United States, Venezuela, Yugoslavia.

WORKING GROUP
Members: Argentina, Canada, Egypt, France, Hungary, India, Japan, Mexico, Nigeria, Pakistan, USSR, United Kingdom, United States.

Special Committee on the Charter of the United Nations and on the Strengthening of the Role of the Organization

The 47-member Special Committee on the Charter of the United Nations and on the Strengthening of the Role of the Organization met at United Nations Headquarters between 4 and 29 March 1985.

Members: Algeria, Argentina, Barbados, Belgium, Brazil, China, Colombia, Congo, Cyprus, Czechoslovakia, Ecuador, Egypt, El Salvador, Finland, France, German Democratic Republic, Germany, Federal Republic of, Ghana, Greece, Guyana, India, Indonesia, Iran, Iraq, Italy, Japan, Kenya, Liberia, Mexico, Nepal, New Zealand, Nigeria, Pakistan, Philippines, Poland, Romania, Rwanda, Sierra Leone, Spain, Tunisia, Turkey, USSR, United Kingdom, United States, Venezuela, Yugoslavia, Zambia.

Chairman: Moritaka Hayashi (Japan).
Vice-Chairmen: Ridha Bouabid (Tunisia), Domingo S. Cullen (Argentina), Andrzej Kakolecki (Poland).
Rapporteur: Johan Swinnen (Belgium).

Special Committee on the Situation with regard to the Implementation of the Declaration on the Granting of Independence to Colonial Countries and Peoples

Members:[a] Afghanistan, Bulgaria, Chile, China, Congo, Cuba, Czechoslovakia, Ethiopia, Fiji, India, Indonesia, Iran, Iraq, Ivory Coast, Mali, Sierra Leone, Sweden, Syrian Arab Republic, Trinidad and Tobago, Tunisia, USSR, United Republic of Tanzania, Venezuela, Yugoslavia.

[a]Australia informed the General Assembly President on 9 January 1985 of its decision to withdraw from membership.

Chairman: Abdul G. Koroma (Sierra Leone).
Vice-Chairmen: Jan Lundvik (Sweden), Oscar Oramas-Oliva (Cuba), Jiri Pulz (Czechoslovakia).
Rapporteur: Ahmad Farouk Arnouss (Syrian Arab Republic).

SUB-COMMITTEE ON PETITIONS, INFORMATION AND ASSISTANCE
Members: Afghanistan, Bulgaria, Congo, Cuba, Czechoslovakia *(Chairman)*, Indonesia, Iran, Iraq, Mali, Sierra Leone, Sweden, Syrian Arab Republic, Tunisia, United Republic of Tanzania.

SUB-COMMITTEE ON SMALL TERRITORIES
Members: Afghanistan, Bulgaria, Chile, Cuba, Czechoslovakia, Ethiopia, Fiji, India, Indonesia, Iran, Iraq, Ivory Coast, Mali, Sweden *(Rapporteur)*, Trinidad and Tobago, Tunisia *(Chairman)*, United Republic of Tanzania, Venezuela, Yugoslavia.

WORKING GROUP
In 1985, the Working Group of the Special Committee, which functions as a steering committee, consisted of: Congo, Iran; the five officers of the Special Committee; and the Chairman and the Rapporteur of the Sub-Committee on Small Territories.

[13]YUN 1979, p. 201, res. 34/93 R, 17 Dec. 1979.

Special Committee to Investigate Israeli Practices Affecting the Human Rights of the Population of the Occupied Territories
Members: Senegal, Sri Lanka *(Chairman)*, Yugoslavia.

Special Committee to Select the Winners of the United Nations Human Rights Prize

The Special Committee to Select the Winners of the United Nations Human Rights Prize was established pursuant to a 1966 resolution of the General Assembly[14] recommending that a prize or prizes in the field of human rights be awarded not more often than at five-year intervals. Prizes were awarded for the third time on 11 December 1978.[15]

Members: The President of the General Assembly, the President of the Economic and Social Council, the Chairman of the Commission on Human Rights, the Chairman of the Commission on the Status of Women and the Chairman of the Sub-Commission on Prevention of Discrimination and Protection of Minorities.

United Nations Administrative Tribunal
Members:
To serve until 31 December 1985: Mutuale Tshikankie, *President* (Zaire); Roger Pinto (France); Samarendranath Sen, *First Vice-President* (India).
To serve until 31 December 1986: Arnold Wilfred Geoffrey Kean, *Second Vice-President* (United Kingdom); Herbert K. Reis (United States).
To serve until 31 December 1987: Luis María de Posadas Montero (Uruguay); Endre Ustor (Hungary).

On 18 December 1985 (decision 40/321), the General Assembly appointed Ahmed Osman (Egypt), Roger Pinto (France) and Samarendranath Sen (India) for a three-year term beginning on 1 January 1986 to fill the vacancies occurring on 31 December 1985.

United Nations Capital Development Fund

The United Nations Capital Development Fund was set up as an organ of the General Assembly to function as an autonomous organization within the United Nations framework, with the control of its policies and operations to be exercised by a 24-member Executive Board elected by the Assembly from Members of the United Nations or members of the specialized agencies or of IAEA. The chief executive officer of the Fund, the Managing Director, exercises his functions under the general direction of the Executive Board, which reports to the Assembly through the Economic and Social Council.

EXECUTIVE BOARD

The UNDP Governing Council (p. 1419) acts as the Executive Board of the Fund—and the UNDP Administrator as its Managing Director—in conformity with measures the General Assembly adopted provisionally in 1967[16] and reconfirmed yearly until 1980.[17] In 1981 the Assembly decided that UNDP continue to provide the Fund with, among other things, all headquarters administrative support services;[18] the Fund thus continued to operate under the same arrangements, which remained unchanged in 1985.

Managing Director: F. Bradford Morse (UNDP Administrator).

United Nations Children's Fund (UNICEF)

EXECUTIVE BOARD

The Executive Board of UNICEF (p. 1418) reports to the Economic and Social Council and, as appropriate, to the General Assembly.

United Nations Commission on International Trade Law (UNCITRAL)

The United Nations Commission on International Trade Law consists of 36 members elected by the General Assembly, in accordance with a formula providing equitable geographical representation and adequate representation of the principal economic and legal systems of the world. Members serve for six-year terms.

The Commission held its eighteenth session at Vienna, Austria, from 3 to 21 June 1985.

Members:
To serve until the day preceding the Commission's regular annual session in 1986: Cuba, Cyprus, Czechoslovakia, Germany, Federal Republic of, Guatemala, Hungary, India, Iraq, Italy, Kenya, Peru, Philippines, Senegal, Sierra Leone, Spain, Trinidad and Tobago, Uganda, United States, Yugoslavia.
To serve until the day preceding the Commission's regular annual session in 1989: Algeria, Australia, Austria, Brazil, Central African Republic, China, Egypt, France, German Democratic Republic, Japan, Mexico, Nigeria, Singapore, Sweden, USSR, United Kingdom, United Republic of Tanzania.

Chairman: Roland Loewe (Austria).
Vice-Chairmen: L. G. Paes de Barros Leaes (Brazil), Ivan Szasz (Hungary), H. Z. Tang (China).
Rapporteur: E. E. E. Mtango (United Republic of Tanzania).

On 10 December 1985 (decision 40/313), the General Assembly elected the following for a six-year term beginning on the first day of the regular annual session in 1986 (23 June) to fill the vacancies occurring the day before: Argentina, Chile, Cuba, Cyprus, Czechoslovakia, Hungary, India, Iran, Iraq, Italy, Kenya, Lesotho, Libyan Arab Jamahiriya, Netherlands, Sierra Leone, Spain, United States, Uruguay, Yugoslavia.

WORKING GROUP ON
INTERNATIONAL CONTRACT PRACTICES

The Working Group on International Contract Practices, which is composed of all States members of UNCITRAL, did not meet in 1985.

WORKING GROUP ON
INTERNATIONAL NEGOTIABLE INSTRUMENTS

The Working Group on International Negotiable Instruments held two sessions in 1985: its thirteenth at United Nations Headquarters from 7 to 18 January; and its fourteenth at Vienna, Austria, from 9 to 20 December.

Members: Australia, Cuba, Czechoslovakia, Egypt, France, India, Japan, Mexico, Nigeria, Sierra Leone, Spain, USSR, United Kingdom, United States.

Chairman: Willem Vis (Netherlands).[a]
Rapporteur: G. O. Adebanjo (Nigeria).

[a]Elected in his personal capacity.

WORKING GROUP ON THE
NEW INTERNATIONAL ECONOMIC ORDER

The Working Group on the New International Economic Order, which is composed of all States members of UNCITRAL, held its seventh session at United Nations Headquarters from 8 to 19 April 1985.

Chairman: Leif Sevon (Finland).[a]
Rapporteur: Jelena Vilus (Yugoslavia).

[a]Elected in his personal capacity.

United Nations Conciliation Commission for Palestine
Members: France, Turkey, United States.

United Nations Conference on Trade and Development (UNCTAD)

Members of UNCTAD are Members of the United Nations or members of the specialized agencies or of IAEA.

TRADE AND DEVELOPMENT BOARD

The Trade and Development Board is a permanent organ of UNCTAD. Its membership is drawn from the following list of UNCTAD members.

Part A. Afghanistan, Algeria, Angola, Bahrain, Bangladesh, Benin, Bhutan, Botswana, Brunei Darussalam,[a] Burkina Faso, Burma, Burundi, Cameroon, Cape Verde, Central African Republic, Chad, China, Comoros, Congo, Democratic Kampuchea, Democratic People's Republic of Korea, Democratic Yemen, Djibouti, Egypt, Equatorial Guinea, Ethiopia, Fiji,

---

[14]YUN 1966, p. 458, res. 2217 A (XXI), annex, 19 Dec. 1966.
[15]YUN 1978, p. 721.
[16]YUN 1967, p. 372, res. 2321(XXII), 15 Dec. 1967.
[17]YUN 1980, p. 607, dec. 35/422, 5 Dec. 1980.
[18]YUN 1981, p. 469, res. 36/196, 17 Dec. 1981.

Gabon, Gambia, Ghana, Guinea, Guinea-Bissau, India, Indonesia, Iran, Iraq, Israel, Ivory Coast, Jordan, Kenya, Kuwait, Lao People's Democratic Republic, Lebanon, Lesotho, Liberia, Libyan Arab Jamahiriya, Madagascar, Malawi, Malaysia, Maldives, Mali, Mauritania, Mauritius, Mongolia, Morocco, Mozambique, Namibia, Nepal, Niger, Nigeria, Oman, Pakistan, Papua New Guinea, Philippines, Qatar, Republic of Korea, Rwanda, Samoa, Sao Tome and Principe, Saudi Arabia, Senegal, Seychelles, Sierra Leone, Singapore, Solomon Islands, Somalia, South Africa, Sri Lanka, Sudan, Swaziland, Syrian Arab Republic, Thailand, Togo, Tonga, Tunisia, Uganda, United Arab Emirates, United Republic of Tanzania, Vanuatu, Viet Nam, Yemen, Yugoslavia, Zaire, Zambia, Zimbabwe.

Part B. Australia, Austria, Belgium, Canada, Cyprus, Denmark, Finland, France, Germany, Federal Republic of, Greece, Holy See, Iceland, Ireland, Italy, Japan, Liechtenstein, Luxembourg, Malta, Monaco, Netherlands, New Zealand, Norway, Portugal, San Marino, Spain, Sweden, Switzerland, Turkey, United Kingdom, United States.

Part C. Antigua and Barbuda, Argentina, Bahamas, Barbados, Belize, Bolivia, Brazil, Chile, Colombia, Costa Rica, Cuba, Dominica, Dominican Republic, Ecuador, El Salvador, Grenada, Guatemala, Guyana, Haiti, Honduras, Jamaica, Mexico, Nicaragua, Panama, Paraguay, Peru, Saint Christopher and Nevis,[a] Saint Lucia, Saint Vincent and the Grenadines, Suriname, Trinidad and Tobago, Uruguay, Venezuela.

Part D. Albania, Bulgaria, Byelorussian SSR, Czechoslovakia, German Democratic Republic, Hungary, Poland, Romania, Ukrainian SSR, USSR.

[a]Became a member of UNCTAD after the sixth (1983) session of the Conference. By decision of the Board, subsequently included in Parts A and C, respectively, for the purpose of elections, pending approval by the Conference at its seventh (1987) session.

BOARD MEMBERS AND SESSIONS

The membership of the Board is open to all UNCTAD members. Those wishing to become members of the Board communicate their intention to the Secretary-General of UNCTAD for transmittal to the Board President, who announces the membership on the basis of such notifications.

The Board held the following sessions in 1985, at Geneva: its thirtieth from 18 to 29 March (first part) and on 2 May (second part); its fourteenth special session from 10 to 15 and on 27 June; and its thirty-first session from 16 to 27 September.

Members: Afghanistan, Algeria, Angola, Argentina, Australia, Austria, Bahrain, Bangladesh, Barbados, Belgium, Benin, Bhutan,[a] Bolivia, Brazil, Bulgaria, Burkina Faso, Burma, Burundi, Byelorussian SSR, Cameroon, Canada, Central African Republic, Chad, Chile, China, Colombia, Congo, Costa Rica, Cuba, Cyprus, Czechoslovakia, Democratic People's Republic of Korea, Democratic Yemen, Denmark, Dominican Republic, Ecuador, Egypt, El Salvador, Ethiopia, Finland, France, Gabon, German Democratic Republic, Germany, Federal Republic of, Ghana, Greece, Grenada, Guatemala, Guinea, Guyana, Haiti, Honduras, Hungary, India, Indonesia, Iran, Iraq, Ireland, Israel, Italy, Ivory Coast, Jamaica, Japan, Jordan, Kenya, Kuwait, Lebanon, Liberia, Libyan Arab Jamahiriya, Liechtenstein, Luxembourg, Madagascar, Malaysia, Mali, Malta, Mauritania, Mauritius, Mexico, Mongolia, Morocco, Namibia,[b] Nepal, Netherlands, New Zealand, Nicaragua, Nigeria, Norway, Oman, Pakistan, Panama, Papua New Guinea, Peru, Philippines, Poland, Portugal, Qatar, Republic of Korea, Romania, Saudi Arabia, Senegal, Sierra Leone, Singapore, Somalia, Spain, Sri Lanka, Sudan, Suriname, Sweden, Switzerland, Syrian Arab Republic, Thailand, Togo, Trinidad and Tobago, Tunisia, Turkey, Uganda, Ukrainian SSR, USSR, United Arab Emirates, United Kingdom, United Republic of Tanzania, United States, Uruguay, Venezuela, Viet Nam, Yemen, Yugoslavia, Zaire, Zambia.

[a]Became a member on 16 September 1985.
[b]Became a member on 18 September 1985.

OFFICERS (BUREAU) OF THE BOARD
Thirtieth session
President: Julio A. Lacarte Muró (Uruguay).
Vice-Presidents: Karim E. Al-Shakar (Bahrain), Moncef Benattia (Tunisia), Gerald P. Carmen (United States), Sergio Cattani (Italy), Kazuo Chiba (Japan), Hans V. Ewerlof (Sweden), Edouard Francisque (Haiti), Maung Maung Gyi (Burma), M. S. Pankine (USSR), Willi Schild (German Democratic Republic).
Rapporteur: Adikwu F. Okoh (Nigeria).

Fourteenth special session
President: Julio A. Lacarte Muró (Uruguay).
Vice-Presidents: Karim E. Al-Shakar (Bahrain), Moncef Benattia (Tunisia), Gerald P. Carmen (United States), Gervais Charles (Haiti), V. N. Cheklin (USSR), Kazuo Chiba (Japan), Hans V. Ewerlof (Sweden), Maung Maung Gyi (Burma), O. Hlavacek (Czechoslovakia), M. Martinez (Italy).
Rapporteur: Adikwu F. Okoh (Nigeria).

Thirty-first session
President: Martin J. Huslid (Norway).
Vice-Presidents: Ghaleb Z. Barakat (Jordan), A. Betancourt Roa (Cuba), F. Isak Bihi (Somalia), Gerald P. Carmen (United States), W. Carrasco-Fernández (Chile), F. Furulyas (Hungary), P.-L. Girard (Switzerland), M. Soumahoro (Ivory Coast), N. Vejjajiva (Thailand), J.-L. Wolzfeld (Luxembourg).
Rapporteur: M. Outkine (USSR).

SUBSIDIARY ORGANS OF THE
TRADE AND DEVELOPMENT BOARD

The main committees of the Board are open to the participation of all interested UNCTAD members, on the understanding that those wishing to attend a particular session of one or more of the main committees communicate their intention to the Secretary-General of UNCTAD during the preceding regular session of the Board. On the basis of such notifications, the Board determines the membership of the main committees.

COMMITTEE ON COMMODITIES

In 1985, the Committee on Commodities held three sessions, at Geneva: its second special session from 21 to 25 January; its third special session from 3 to 7 and on 12 June; and its eleventh session from 2 to 13 December.

Members: Algeria, Argentina, Australia, Austria, Bahrain, Bangladesh, Belgium, Bolivia, Brazil, Bulgaria, Burkina Faso, Burma, Burundi, Cameroon, Canada, Central African Republic, Chad, Chile, China, Colombia, Costa Rica, Cuba, Czechoslovakia, Democratic People's Republic of Korea, Democratic Yemen, Denmark, Dominican Republic, Ecuador, Egypt, El Salvador, Ethiopia, Finland, France, Gabon, German Democratic Republic, Germany, Federal Republic of, Ghana, Greece, Guatemala, Guinea, Haiti, Honduras, Hungary, India, Indonesia, Iran, Iraq, Ireland, Israel, Italy, Ivory Coast, Jamaica, Japan, Jordan, Kenya, Kuwait, Liberia, Libyan Arab Jamahiriya, Madagascar, Malaysia, Malta, Mauritius, Mexico, Morocco, Netherlands, New Zealand, Nicaragua, Nigeria, Norway, Pakistan, Panama, Peru, Philippines, Poland, Qatar, Republic of Korea, Romania, Rwanda, Saudi Arabia, Senegal, Somalia, Spain, Sri Lanka, Sudan, Sweden, Switzerland, Syrian Arab Republic, Thailand, Togo, Trinidad and Tobago, Tunisia, Turkey, Uganda, USSR, United Kingdom, United Republic of Tanzania, United States, Uruguay, Venezuela, Viet Nam, Yemen, Yugoslavia, Zaire.

Second and third special sessions
Chairman: R. Rasmusson (Sweden).
Vice-Chairmen: L. Denisov (USSR); K. Fraterman (Netherlands) (second special session), J. Bartlett (United Kingdom) (third special session); G. García de González (Cuba); J. R. Odzaga (Gabon); Djunaedi Sutisnawinata (Indonesia).
Rapporteur: K. Shenkoru (Ethiopia).

Eleventh session
Chairman: S. Alfarargi (Egypt).
Vice-Chairmen: A. Aggrey-Orleans (Ghana), W. A. Bastiaanse (Netherlands), J. M. Maldonado Muñoz (Honduras), M. Yaqub Malik (Pakistan), J. Strebski (Poland).
Rapporteur: Pierre Annoye (Belgium).

COMMITTEE ON TUNGSTEN

The Committee on Tungsten held its seventeenth session at Geneva from 11 to 15 November 1985.

Members: Argentina, Australia, Austria, Belgium, Bolivia, Brazil, Canada, China, Cyprus, France, Gabon, Germany, Federal Republic of, Italy, Japan, Mexico, Netherlands, Peru, Poland, Portugal, Republic of Korea, Romania, Rwanda, Spain, Sweden, Thailand, Turkey, USSR, United Kingdom, United States.

Chairman: A. Klum (Sweden).
Vice-Chairman/Rapporteur: Walter Goode (Australia).

PERMANENT GROUP ON SYNTHETICS AND SUBSTITUTES

The Permanent Group on Synthetics and Substitutes did not meet in 1985.

Members: Argentina, Brazil, Canada, Chad, Egypt, France, Germany, Federal Republic of, Indonesia, Italy, Japan, Malaysia, Mexico, Netherlands, Nigeria, Philippines, Poland, Senegal, Sri Lanka, Sudan, Uganda, USSR, United Kingdom, United States, Viet Nam.

PERMANENT SUB-COMMITTEE ON COMMODITIES

The Permanent Sub-Committee on Commodities, whose membership is identical to that of the Committee on Commodities, held its fourth session at Geneva from 14 to 22 January 1985.

Chairman: Ibrahima Sy (Senegal).
Vice-Chairmen: Emile M'Lingui Keffa (Ivory Coast), Jean Poswick (Belgium), Carola Sanchez-Peña de Lorenz (Bolivia), Jerzy Strebski (Poland), Djunaedi Sutisnawinata (Indonesia).
Rapporteur: Inga Magistad (Norway).

COMMITTEE ON ECONOMIC CO-OPERATION AMONG DEVELOPING COUNTRIES

The Committee on Economic Co-operation among Developing Countries held its fourth session at Geneva from 18 to 29 November 1985.

Members: Algeria, Argentina, Australia, Austria, Bahrain, Bangladesh, Belgium, Benin, Bolivia, Brazil, Bulgaria, Burma, Cameroon, Canada, Central African Republic, Chile, China, Colombia, Costa Rica, Cuba, Czechoslovakia, Democratic People's Republic of Korea, Democratic Yemen, Denmark, Dominican Republic, Ecuador, Egypt, El Salvador, Ethiopia, Finland, France, Gabon, German Democratic Republic, Germany, Federal Republic of, Ghana, Greece, Guatemala, Guyana, Haiti, Honduras, Hungary, India, Indonesia, Iran, Iraq, Ireland, Israel, Italy, Ivory Coast, Jamaica, Japan, Jordan, Kenya, Kuwait, Lebanon, Liberia, Libyan Arab Jamahiriya, Madagascar, Malaysia, Malta, Mauritius, Mexico, Morocco, Netherlands, New Zealand, Nicaragua, Nigeria, Norway, Oman, Pakistan, Panama, Peru, Philippines, Poland, Qatar, Republic of Korea, Romania, Saudi Arabia, Senegal, Singapore, Somalia, Spain, Sri Lanka, Sudan, Suriname, Sweden, Switzerland, Syrian Arab Republic, Thailand, Togo, Trinidad and Tobago, Tunisia, Turkey, Uganda, USSR, United Arab Emirates, United Kingdom, United Republic of Tanzania, United States, Uruguay, Venezuela, Viet Nam, Yemen, Yugoslavia, Zaire, Zambia.

Chairman: Hamida Redouane (Algeria).
Vice-Chairmen: Sergio Cerda (Argentina), Helmut Koinzer (Federal Republic of Germany), Yeboah Konadu (Ghana), Juan López-de-Chicheri (Spain), Parameswaran Nagaratnam (Sri Lanka).
Rapporteur: Helfred Bemme (German Democratic Republic).

COMMITTEE ON INVISIBLES AND FINANCING RELATED TO TRADE

In 1985, the Committee on Invisibles and Financing related to Trade held its eleventh session at Geneva from 18 to 22 February (first part) and from 25 February to 8 March (second part).

Members: Algeria, Argentina, Australia, Austria, Bahrain, Bangladesh, Belgium, Bolivia, Brazil, Bulgaria, Burkina Faso, Burundi, Cameroon, Canada, Central African Republic, Chad, Chile, China, Colombia, Costa Rica, Cuba, Czechoslovakia, Democratic People's Republic of Korea, Democratic Yemen, Denmark, Dominican Republic, Ecuador, Egypt, El Salvador, Ethiopia, Finland, France, German Democratic Republic, Germany, Federal Republic of, Ghana, Greece, Guatemala, Guinea, Honduras, Hungary, India, Indonesia, Iran, Iraq, Ireland, Israel, Italy, Ivory Coast, Jamaica, Japan, Jordan, Kenya, Kuwait, Lebanon, Liberia, Libyan Arab Jamahiriya, Madagascar, Malaysia, Mali, Malta, Mexico, Morocco, Netherlands, New Zealand, Nicaragua, Nigeria, Norway, Pakistan, Panama, Peru, Philippines, Poland, Qatar,

Republic of Korea, Romania, Saudi Arabia, Senegal, Somalia, Spain, Sri Lanka, Sudan, Sweden, Switzerland, Syrian Arab Republic, Thailand, Trinidad and Tobago, Tunisia, Turkey, Uganda, USSR, United Kingdom, United Republic of Tanzania, United States, Uruguay, Venezuela, Viet Nam, Yemen, Yugoslavia, Zaire, Zimbabwe.

Chairman: Jiri Vetrovsky (Czechoslovakia).
Vice-Chairmen: Leonard J. Edwards (Canada); Ulrich Fahr (Federal Republic of Germany) (first part), Alice Dress (United States) (second part); Ashok Goenka (India) (first part), V. K. S. Nair (India) (second part); Saad Kanouni (Morocco) (first part), Mohammed Sbihi (Morocco) (second part); Mohammed Mourad (Egypt) (first part), Abouzaid Omar (Egypt) (second part).
Rapporteur: Alejandro Abreu Pepper (Venezuela).

COMMITTEE ON MANUFACTURES

The Committee on Manufactures did not meet in 1985.

Members: Algeria, Argentina, Australia, Austria, Bahrain, Bangladesh, Belgium, Bolivia, Brazil, Bulgaria, Burkina Faso, Cameroon, Canada, Central African Republic, Chile, China, Colombia, Costa Rica, Cuba, Czechoslovakia, Democratic People's Republic of Korea, Democratic Yemen, Denmark, Dominican Republic, Ecuador, Egypt, El Salvador, Ethiopia, Finland, France, German Democratic Republic, Germany, Federal Republic of, Ghana, Greece, Guatemala, Haiti, Honduras, Hungary, India, Indonesia, Iran, Iraq, Ireland, Israel, Italy, Ivory Coast, Jamaica, Japan, Jordan, Kenya, Kuwait, Liberia, Libyan Arab Jamahiriya, Madagascar, Malaysia, Mali, Malta, Mauritius, Mexico, Morocco, Netherlands, New Zealand, Nicaragua, Nigeria, Norway, Pakistan, Panama, Peru, Philippines, Poland, Qatar, Republic of Korea, Romania, Saudi Arabia, Senegal, Singapore, Somalia, Spain, Sri Lanka, Sudan, Sweden, Switzerland, Syrian Arab Republic, Thailand, Trinidad and Tobago, Tunisia, Turkey, USSR, United Kingdom, United Republic of Tanzania, United States, Uruguay, Venezuela, Viet Nam, Yemen, Yugoslavia, Zaire.

COMMITTEE ON SHIPPING

The Committee on Shipping did not meet in 1985.

Members: Algeria, Argentina, Australia, Bahrain, Bangladesh, Belgium, Benin, Bolivia, Brazil, Bulgaria, Burkina Faso, Cameroon, Canada, Central African Republic, Chile, China, Colombia, Costa Rica, Cuba, Cyprus, Czechoslovakia, Democratic People's Republic of Korea, Democratic Yemen, Denmark, Dominican Republic, Ecuador, Egypt, El Salvador, Ethiopia, Finland, France, Gabon, German Democratic Republic, Germany, Federal Republic of, Ghana, Greece, Guatemala, Guinea, Honduras, Hungary, India, Indonesia, Iran, Iraq, Israel, Italy, Ivory Coast, Jamaica, Japan, Jordan, Kenya, Kuwait, Lebanon, Liberia, Libyan Arab Jamahiriya, Madagascar, Malaysia, Malta, Mauritius, Mexico, Morocco, Netherlands, New Zealand, Nicaragua, Nigeria, Norway, Oman,[a] Pakistan, Panama, Peru, Philippines, Poland, Portugal, Qatar, Republic of Korea, Romania, Saudi Arabia, Senegal, Somalia, Spain, Sri Lanka, Sudan, Sweden, Switzerland, Syrian Arab Republic, Thailand, Trinidad and Tobago, Tunisia, Turkey, Uganda, USSR, United Arab Emirates, United Kingdom, United Republic of Tanzania, United States, Uruguay, Venezuela, Viet Nam, Yemen, Yugoslavia, Zaire.

[a]Declared elected by the Trade and Development Board on 18 March 1985, raising the Committee's membership to 101.

WORKING GROUP ON INTERNATIONAL SHIPPING LEGISLATION

The Working Group on International Shipping Legislation, whose membership is identical to that of the Committee on Shipping, held its eleventh session at Geneva from 14 to 22 October 1985.

Chairman: J. R. Perrett (United Kingdom).
Vice-Chairmen: M. B. Nasrah (Egypt), R. Richter (German Democratic Republic), W. W. Sturms (Netherlands), Djunaedi Sutisnawinata (Indonesia), Gustavo Adolfo Vargas (Nicaragua).
Rapporteur: Sergio Cerda (Argentina).

COMMITTEE ON TRANSFER OF TECHNOLOGY

The Committee on Transfer of Technology did not meet in 1985.

Members: Algeria, Argentina, Australia, Austria, Bahrain, Bangladesh, Belgium, Bolivia, Brazil, Bulgaria, Burkina Faso, Cameroon, Canada, Chile, China, Colombia, Costa Rica, Cuba, Czechoslovakia, Democratic People's Republic of Korea, Democratic Yemen, Denmark, Dominican Republic,[a] Ecuador, Egypt, El Salvador, Ethiopia, Finland, France, German Democratic Republic, Germany, Federal Republic of, Ghana, Greece, Guatemala, Haiti, Honduras, Hungary, India, Indonesia, Iran, Iraq, Ireland, Israel, Italy, Ivory Coast, Jamaica, Japan, Jordan, Kenya, Kuwait, Liberia, Libyan Arab Jamahiriya, Madagascar, Malaysia, Malta, Mauritius, Mexico, Morocco, Netherlands, New Zealand, Nicaragua, Nigeria, Norway, Pakistan, Panama, Peru, Philippines, Poland, Qatar, Republic of Korea, Romania, Saudi Arabia, Senegal, Sierra Leone, Somalia, Spain, Sri Lanka, Sudan, Sweden, Switzerland, Syrian Arab Republic, Thailand, Trinidad and Tobago, Tunisia, Turkey, USSR, United Arab Emirates, United Kingdom, United Republic of Tanzania, United States, Uruguay,[a] Venezuela, Viet Nam, Yemen, Yugoslavia, Zaire.

[a]Declared elected by the Trade and Development Board on 18 March 1985, raising the Committee's membership to 96.

SPECIAL COMMITTEE ON PREFERENCES
The Special Committee on Preferences, which is open to the participation of all UNCTAD members, held its thirteenth session at Geneva from 10 to 19 April 1985.

Chairman: Ibrahima Sy (Senegal).
Vice-Chairmen: M. Baati (Tunisia), M. Costantino (Italy), D. Dwoskin (United States), Vicente Montemayor Cantú (Mexico), T. Syquia (Philippines).
Rapporteur: K. Trepczynski (Poland).

United Nations Council for Namibia
Members: Algeria, Angola, Australia, Bangladesh, Belgium, Botswana, Bulgaria, Burundi, Cameroon, Chile, China, Colombia, Cyprus, Egypt, Finland, Guyana, Haiti, India, Indonesia, Liberia, Mexico, Nigeria, Pakistan, Poland, Romania, Senegal, Turkey, USSR, Venezuela, Yugoslavia, Zambia.

President: Paul John Firmino Lusaka (Zambia).
Vice-Presidents: Hocine Djoudi (Algeria); Ignac Golob (Yugoslavia); A. Coskun Kirca (Turkey) (until 3 April 1985), Ilter Turkmen (Turkey) (from 3 April); Natarajan Krishnan (India); Noel G. Sinclair (Guyana).

United Nations Commissioner for Namibia: Brajesh Chandra Mishra.[a]

[a]Reappointed by the General Assembly on 17 December 1985 (decision 40/317) for a one-year term beginning on 1 January 1986.

COMMITTEE ON THE UNITED NATIONS FUND FOR NAMIBIA
Members: Australia, Finland, India, Nigeria, Romania, Senegal, Turkey, Venezuela *(Vice-Chairman/Rapporteur)*, Yugoslavia, Zambia; the President of the Council *(ex-officio Chairman)*.

STANDING COMMITTEE I
Members: Algeria, Cameroon *(Chairman)*, China, Colombia, Finland, Haiti, Indonesia, Nigeria, Poland, Senegal, Turkey *(Vice-Chairman)*, USSR, Venezuela, Zambia.

STANDING COMMITTEE II
Members: Algeria,[a] Angola, Australia, Bangladesh, Botswana, Bulgaria, Chile, Colombia, Cyprus, Egypt,[a] Finland, Guyana, Liberia *(Vice-Chairman)*, Mexico, Pakistan *(Chairman)*, Romania, Zambia.

[a]Membership approved by the Council on 28 March and 10 January 1985, respectively.

STANDING COMMITTEE III
Members: Algeria, Angola, Australia, Belgium, Bulgaria *(Chairman)*, Burundi, Colombia, Cyprus, Egypt, India, Mexico *(Vice-Chairman)*, Nigeria, Pakistan, Romania, Venezuela, Yugoslavia, Zambia.

STEERING COMMITTEE
In 1985, the Steering Committee consisted of the Council's President and five Vice-Presidents, the chairmen of its three standing committees and the Vice-Chairman/Rapporteur of the Committee on the United Nations Fund for Namibia.

United Nations Development Fund for Women (UNIFEM)
The United Nations Development Fund for Women entered into autonomous association with UNDP on 1 July 1985.

The Director of the Fund, to have the authority to conduct all matters related to its mandate, was to be appointed by the UNDP Administrator, who is accountable for its management and operations.

CONSULTATIVE COMMITTEE
A Consultative Committee to advise the UNDP Administrator on all policy matters affecting the Fund's activities was to be composed of five Member States designated by the General Assembly President with due regard for the financing of the Fund from voluntary contributions and to equitable geographical distribution. Each State member of the Committee, to serve for a three-year term, was to designate a person with expertise in development co-operation activities, including those benefiting women.

On 18 December 1985 (decision 40/324), the Assembly noted the appointment by its President of India, Kenya and Norway as members of the Consultative Committee for a three-year term beginning on 1 January 1986; two posts remained vacant.

United Nations Development Programme (UNDP)

GOVERNING COUNCIL
The Governing Council of UNDP (p. 1419) reports to the Economic and Social Council and through it to the General Assembly.

United Nations Environment Programme (UNEP)

GOVERNING COUNCIL
The Governing Council of UNEP consists of 58 members elected by the General Assembly for three-year terms.

Seats on the Governing Council are allocated as follows: 16 to African States, 13 to Asian States, 6 to Eastern European States, 10 to Latin American States, and 13 to Western European and other States.

The Governing Council, which reports to the Assembly through the Economic and Social Council, held its thirteenth session at Nairobi, Kenya, from 14 to 24 May 1985.

Members:
To serve until 31 December 1985: Argentina, Australia, Cameroon, Chile, China, Finland, France, Hungary, Indonesia, Italy, Ivory Coast, Lesotho, Nigeria, Papua New Guinea, Peru, Philippines, Saudi Arabia, Uganda, Yugoslavia.
To serve until 31 December 1986: Algeria, Austria, Belgium, Brazil, Germany, Federal Republic of, Haiti, Japan, Kuwait, Malaysia, Nepal, Norway, Rwanda, Sudan, Togo, Ukrainian SSR, USSR, United States, Venezuela, Zaire.
To serve until 31 December 1987: Botswana, Bulgaria, Canada, Colombia, Ghana, India, Jamaica, Jordan, Kenya, Libyan Arab Jamahiriya, Malta, Mexico, Niger, Oman, Panama, Poland, Sri Lanka, Tunisia, Turkey, United Kingdom.

President: Emil Salim (Indonesia).
Vice-Presidents: A. Kantschev (Bulgaria), D. Miller (Canada), A. Waligo (Uganda).
Rapporteur: Jorge Enrique Illueca (Panama).

Executive Director of UNEP: Mostafa Kamal Tolba.
Deputy Executive Director: Joseph C. Wheeler.

On 17 December 1985 (decision 40/316), the General Assembly elected the following for a three-year term beginning on 1 January 1986 to fill 17 of the 19 vacancies occurring on 31 December 1985: Argentina, Australia, Barbados, Chile, China, Congo, Denmark, France, Indonesia, Netherlands, Nigeria, Papua New Guinea, Swaziland, Syrian Arab Republic, Thailand, Uganda, Zambia; no further elections were held in 1985 to fill the remaining seats.

COMMITTEE OF PERMANENT REPRESENTATIVES
On 23 May 1985, the UNEP Governing Council established an open-ended Committee of Permanent Representatives, consisting of permanent representatives to UNEP and/or Government-designated officials, to consider administrative and budgetary and programme matters, and

to review progress in implementing the programme and Council decisions. It was to meet with the Executive Director three times a year, as well as six weeks prior to the fourteenth (1987) Council session.

INTERGOVERNMENTAL INTER-SESSIONAL
PREPARATORY COMMITTEE ON THE ENVIRONMENTAL
PERSPECTIVE TO THE YEAR 2000 AND BEYOND

The 30-member Intergovernmental Inter-sessional Preparatory Committee on the Environmental Perspective to the Year 2000 and Beyond, which reports to the UNEP Governing Council, held two sessions in 1985, at Nairobi, Kenya: its second on 22 and 23 May; and its third on 2 and 3 December.

Members: Algeria, Argentina, Austria, Bangladesh, Botswana,[a] Brazil, Cameroon,[a] Canada, Chile, China, Denmark, Germany, Federal Republic of, Greece, India, Indonesia, Ivory Coast, Jamaica, Japan, Kenya, Malawi, Malaysia, Mexico, Morocco, Netherlands, Poland, Saudi Arabia, Senegal,[a] Switzerland, Ukrainian SSR, USSR.

[a]Replaced by Nigeria, Zaire and Zimbabwe on 24 May 1985, following a request by the African Group for a change in its membership.

Chairman: Kishan K. S. Rana (India).
Vice-Chairmen: J. Richard Gaechter (Switzerland), Ahmed A. Haggag (Egypt), Carlos Negri (Chile).
Rapporteur: V. S. Dolmatov (USSR).

SPECIAL COMMISSION ON THE ENVIRONMENTAL
PERSPECTIVE TO THE YEAR 2000 AND BEYOND

The Special Commission on the Environmental Perspective to the Year 2000 and Beyond—also known as the World Commission on Environment and Development—consists of 22 members, 14 from developing countries and 8 from developed countries, serving in their individual capacity, selected by the Commission's Chairman and Vice-Chairman.

In 1985, the Commission met at Jakarta, Indonesia, from 27 to 31 March; at Oslo, Norway, from 21 to 28 June; and at São Paolo and Brasilia, Brazil, from 25 October to 4 November.

Members: Susanna Agnelli (Italy); Saleh Abdulrahman Al-Athel (Saudi Arabia); Gro Harlem Brundtland, *Chairman* (Norway); Bernard T. G. Chidzero (Zimbabwe); Lamine Fadika (Ivory Coast);[a] Pablo Gonzalez Casanova (Mexico); Volker Hauff (Federal Republic of Germany); Mansour Khalid, *Vice-Chairman* (Sudan); Istvan Lang (Hungary); Ma Shijun (China);[a] Margarita Marino de Botero (Colombia); Paulo Nogueira-Neto (Brazil);[a] Saburo Okita (Japan); Shridath S. Ramphal (Guyana); William D. Ruckelshaus (United States); Mohamed Sahnoun (Algeria); Emil Salim (Indonesia); Bukar Shaib (Nigeria); Nagendra Singh (India); Vladimir Sokolov (USSR);[a] Janez Stanovnik (Yugoslavia);[a] Maurice F. Strong (Canada).[a]

[a]Selected in 1985.

United Nations Financing System for Science and Technology for Development

The United Nations Financing System for Science and Technology for Development finances, at the request of Governments, a broad range of activities intended to strengthen the endogenous scientific and technological capacities of developing countries. Its policy-making body is the Intergovernmental Committee on Science and Technology for Development (p. 1397) and the overall supervision of its management is entrusted to the UNDP Administrator, who was to be accountable to an Executive Board responsible for the System's operation and conduct. The Administrator, in consultation with the Director-General for Development and International Economic Co-operation, reports annually to the Intergovernmental Committee.

EXECUTIVE BOARD

The Executive Board was to be composed of 21 directors elected by the Intergovernmental Committee for three-year terms, one third to be drawn from developed countries and two thirds from developing countries reflecting an appropriate balance between donors and recipients.

The Board had not been constituted by the end of 1985.

United Nations Fund for Population Activities (UNFPA)

The United Nations Fund for Population Activities, a subsidiary organ of the General Assembly, plays a leading role within the United Nations system in promoting population programmes and in providing assistance to developing countries at their request in dealing with their population problems. It operates under the overall policy guidance of the Economic and Social Council and under the financial and administrative policy guidance of the Governing Council of UNDP.

Executive Director: Rafael M. Salas.
Deputy Executive Director: Heino E. Wittrin.

United Nations Industrial Development Organization (UNIDO)

INDUSTRIAL DEVELOPMENT BOARD

The Industrial Development Board, the principal organ of UNIDO, consisted of 45 States elected by the General Assembly, on the basis of equitable geographical distribution, to serve for three-year terms. States eligible for election to the Board were those which were Members of the United Nations or members of the specialized agencies or of IAEA.

The Board reported annually to the Assembly through the Economic and Social Council.

The Board's membership was drawn from the following four groups of States:

List A. 18 of the following States: Afghanistan, Algeria, Angola, Bahrain, Bangladesh, Benin, Bhutan, Botswana, Brunei Darussalam, Burkina Faso, Burma, Burundi, Cameroon, Cape Verde, Central African Republic, Chad, China, Comoros, Congo, Democratic Kampuchea, Democratic People's Republic of Korea, Democratic Yemen, Djibouti, Egypt, Equatorial Guinea, Ethiopia, Fiji, Gabon, Gambia, Ghana, Guinea, Guinea-Bissau, India, Indonesia, Iran, Iraq, Israel, Ivory Coast, Jordan, Kenya, Kuwait, Lao People's Democratic Republic, Lebanon, Lesotho, Liberia, Libyan Arab Jamahiriya, Madagascar, Malawi, Malaysia, Maldives, Mali, Mauritania, Mauritius, Mongolia, Morocco, Mozambique, Nepal, Niger, Nigeria, Oman, Pakistan, Papua New Guinea, Philippines, Qatar, Republic of Korea, Rwanda, Sao Tome and Principe, Saudi Arabia, Senegal, Seychelles, Sierra Leone, Singapore, Solomon Islands, Somalia, South Africa, Sri Lanka, Sudan, Swaziland, Syrian Arab Republic, Thailand, Togo, Tunisia, Uganda, United Arab Emirates, United Republic of Tanzania, Vanuatu, Viet Nam, Yemen, Yugoslavia, Zaire, Zambia, Zimbabwe.
List B. 15 of the following States: Australia, Austria, Belgium, Canada, Cyprus, Denmark, Finland, France, Germany, Federal Republic of, Greece, Iceland, Ireland, Italy, Japan, Liechtenstein, Luxembourg, Malta, Monaco, Netherlands, New Zealand, Norway, Portugal, Spain, Sweden, Switzerland, Turkey, United Kingdom, United States.
List C. 7 of the following States: Antigua and Barbuda, Argentina, Bahamas, Barbados, Belize, Bolivia, Brazil, Chile, Colombia, Costa Rica, Cuba, Dominica, Dominican Republic, Ecuador, El Salvador, Grenada, Guatemala, Guyana, Haiti, Honduras, Jamaica, Mexico, Nicaragua, Panama, Paraguay, Peru, Saint Christopher and Nevis, Saint Lucia, Saint Vincent and the Grenadines, Suriname, Trinidad and Tobago, Uruguay, Venezuela.
List D. 5 of the following States: Albania, Bulgaria, Byelorussian SSR, Czechoslovakia, German Democratic Republic, Hungary, Poland, Romania, Ukrainian SSR, USSR.

The Industrial Development Board held its nineteenth session at Vienna, Austria, from 13 to 31 May 1985.

BOARD MEMBERS
To serve until 31 December 1985: Austria, Belgium, Bulgaria, Chad, Chile, Finland, Indonesia, Italy, Libyan Arab Jamahiriya, Peru, Rwanda, Sudan, Switzerland, Uganda, USSR.
To serve until 31 December 1986: Argentina, Brazil, Democratic Yemen, France, Ghana, Hungary, India, Japan, Malawi, Netherlands, Norway, Pakistan, Romania, United Arab Emirates, United States.
To serve until 31 December 1987: Australia, China, Czechoslovakia, Ecuador, Germany, Federal Republic of, Iraq, Ivory Coast, Lesotho, Mexico, Philippines, Sierra Leone, Spain, Turkey, United Kingdom, Venezuela.

President: E. Ivan (Hungary).
Vice-Presidents: M. A. Manouan (Ivory Coast), Domingo L. Siazon, Jr. (Philippines), A. Thabault (France).
Rapporteur: C. Abad Ortiz (Ecuador).

Executive Director of UNIDO: Abd-El Rahman Khane.
Deputy Executive Director: Philippe Jacques Farlan Carré.

PERMANENT COMMITTEE

The Permanent Committee, which has the same membership as the Industrial Development Board, did not meet in 1985.

On 21 June 1985, the Constitution of UNIDO as a specialized agency entered into force. For the remainder of the year, the new agency existed side by side with the former subsidiary body, under transitional arrangements approved by the General Assembly.[19] On 31 December, however, these transitional arrangements came to an end, and on 1 January 1986 UNIDO achieved independent status as a specialized agency.

United Nations Institute for Disarmament Research (UNIDIR)

BOARD OF TRUSTEES

The Secretary-General's Advisory Board on Disarmament Studies, composed in 1985 of 24 eminent persons selected on the basis of their personal expertise and taking into account the principle of equitable geographical representation, functions as the Board of Trustees of UNIDIR; the Director of UNIDIR reports to the General Assembly and is an *ex-officio* member of the Advisory Board when it acts as the Board of Trustees.

Members: Oluyemi Adeniji (Nigeria); Hadj Benabdelkader Azzout (Algeria); Rolf Björnerstedt, *Chairman* (Sweden); O. N. Bykov (USSR); James E. Dougherty (United States); Omran El-Shafei (Egypt); Constantin Ene (Romania); Edgar Faure (France); Alfonso García Robles (Mexico); Ignac Golob (Yugoslavia); A. C. Shahul Hameed (Sri Lanka); Bjorn Inge Kristvik (Norway);[a] Carlos Lechuga Hevia (Cuba); Liang Yufan (China); Sir Ronald Mason (United Kingdom); Akira Matsui (Japan); William Eteki Mboumoua (Cameroon); Manfred Mueller (German Democratic Republic); Carlos Ortiz de Rozas (Argentina); Maharajakrishna K. Rasgotra (India); Friedrich Ruth (Federal Republic of Germany); Amada Segarra (Ecuador);[b] Agha Shahi (Pakistan); Tadeusz Strulak (Poland).

[a]Appointed on 12 March 1985.
[b]Appointed on 21 September 1984.

Director of UNIDIR: Liviu Bota.

United Nations Institute for Training and Research (UNITAR)

The Executive Director of UNITAR, in consultation with the Board of Trustees of the Institute, reports through the Secretary-General to the General Assembly and, as appropriate, to the Economic and Social Council and other United Nations bodies.

BOARD OF TRUSTEES

The Board of Trustees of UNITAR is composed of: *(a)* not less than 11 and not more than 30 members, which may include one or more officials of the United Nations Secretariat, appointed on a broad geographical basis by the Secretary-General, in consultation with the Presidents of the General Assembly and the Economic and Social Council; and *(b)* four *ex-officio* members.
The Board held its twenty-third session at United Nations Head-quarters from 9 to 11 September 1985.

Members:
To serve until 31 December 1985: Ole Algard (Norway); Stephane Hessel (France); Johan Kaufmann (Netherlands); Porfirio Muñoz-Ledo (Mexico); Olara Otunnu (Uganda); José Luis Pardos (Spain); Taieb Slim, *Vice-Chairman* (Tunisia); Anders I. Thunborg (Sweden); B. S. Vaganov (USSR).
To serve until 31 December 1986: Margaret Joan Anstee (Secretariat); William H. Barton, *Chairman* (Canada); Roberto E. Guyer (Argentina); Mohamed Omar Madani (Saudi Arabia); Donald O. Mills

(Jamaica); Pei Monong (China); Shizuo Saito (Japan); Agha Shahi (Pakistan); Ali A. Treiki (Libyan Arab Jamahiriya); Victor Umbricht (Switzerland); Anton Vratusa (Yugoslavia).
To serve until 31 December 1987: Siméon Aké (Ivory Coast); Adhemar M. A. d'Alcantara (Belgium); Alan L. Keyes (United States); Umberto La Rocca (Italy); K. Natwar-Singh (India); Klaus Törnudd (Finland); Rüdiger von Wechmar (Federal Republic of Germany).
Ex-officio members: The Secretary-General, the President of the General Assembly, the President of the Economic and Social Council and the Executive Director of UNITAR.

Executive Director of UNITAR: Michel Doo Kingué.

United Nations Joint Staff Pension Board

The United Nations Joint Staff Pension Board is composed of 21 members, as follows:

Six appointed by the United Nations Staff Pension Committee (two from members elected by the General Assembly, two from those appointed by the Secretary-General, two from those elected by participants).
Fifteen appointed by Staff Pension Committees of other member organizations of the United Nations Joint Staff Pension Fund, as follows: two each by WHO, FAO, UNESCO; and one each by ILO, ICAO, IAEA, WMO, IMO, ITU, ICITO/GATT, WIPO, IFAD.

The Board held its thirty-fourth session at Montreal, Canada, from 29 July to 9 August 1985.

Members:
United Nations
Representing the General Assembly: Representatives: Jobst Holborn (Federal Republic of Germany); Yukio Takasu (Japan). Alternates: Eduardo César Añón Noceti (Uruguay); Sol Kuttner (United States); Mario Majoli, *Second Vice-Chairman* (Italy); Michael George Okeyo (Kenya).
Representing the Secretary-General: Representatives: J. Richard Foran (Canada); Louis-Pascal Nègre (Mali). Alternates: Paul C. Szasz (United States); Raymond Gieri (United States); Matias de la Mota (Spain); Anthony J. Miller (Australia).
Representing the Participants: Representatives: Susanna H. Johnston (United States); Bruce C. Hillis (Canada). Alternates: Gualtiero Fulcheri (Italy); Sergio Zampetti (Italy); Anders Tholle (Denmark).
International Labour Organisation
Representing the Governing Body: Representative: William M. Yoffee (United States). Alternate: J. Mainwaring (Canada).
Observer: Aamir Ali, *Chairman* (India).[a]
World Health Organization
Representing the Executive Head: Representative: Warren W. Furth (United States). Alternates: Dr. David E. Barmes (Australia); Herbert R. Crockett (Canada); Dr. Susan E. Holck (United States); John E. Morgan (Australia); Robert L. Munteanu (Romania).
Representing the Participants: Representative: Dr. Alain Vessereau (France). Alternates: Ram L. Rai (India); Vincent Bambinelli (United States); Maggy Melloni (France); David Payne (United Kingdom); Hans-Walter Schmidtkunz (Federal Republic of Germany).
Food and Agriculture Organization of the United Nations
Representing the Governing Body: Representative: Michael Metelits (United States).
Representing the Executive Head: Representative: Mohsen Bel Hadj Amor (Tunisia).
Observer: Aurelio Marcucci, *First Vice-Chairman* (Italy).[a]
United Nations Educational, Scientific and Cultural Organization
Representing the Executive Head: Representative: George F. Saddler (United States). Alternate: Gilles de Leiris (United States).

---

[19]YUN 1979, p. 622, res. 34/96, 13 Dec. 1979.

Representing the Participants: Representative: Alastair McLurg (United Kingdom). Alternate: Yvette D'Silva (France).

International Civil Aviation Organization
Representing the Participants: Representative: Alain R. Minot (Canada). Alternate: René Pouliot (Canada).
Observer: Shelton E. Jayasekera, *Rapporteur* (Sri Lanka).[a]

International Atomic Energy Agency
Representing the Executive Head: Representative: Dieter Goethel (Federal Republic of Germany).

World Meteorological Organization
Representing the Executive Head: Representative: Jeremia M. K. Murithi (Kenya).

International Maritime Organization
Representing the Participants: Representative: Francis J. Frere Van Tongerlooy (Belgium).

International Telecommunication Union
Representing the Governing Body: Representative: P. A. Gagné (Canada).

Interim Commission for the International Trade Organization/General Agreement on Tariffs and Trade
Representing the Governing Body: Representative: Elizabeth Michaud (France). Alternate: G. A. Stünzi (Switzerland).

World Intellectual Property Organization
Representing the Participants: Representative: Gilles Frammery (France).

International Fund for Agricultural Development
Representing the Governing Body: Representative: Y. Hamdi (Egypt).

[a]The *Yearbook* lists only those observers who were officers.

STANDING COMMITTEE OF THE PENSION BOARD
Members (elected at the Board's thirty-fourth session):

United Nations (Group I)
Representing the General Assembly: Representative: Mario Majoli. Alternates: Eduardo César Añón Noceti, Jobst Holborn, Sol Kuttner, Michael George Okeyo, Yukio Takasu.
Representing the Secretary-General: Representative: J. Richard Foran. Alternates: Louis-Pascal Nègre, Paul C. Szasz, Raymond Gieri, Victor Elissejev, Matias de la Mota.
Representing the Participants: Representative: Susanna H. Johnston. Alternates: Bruce C. Hillis, Gualtiero Fulcheri, Sergio Zampetti, Anders Tholle.

Specialized agencies (Group II)
Representing the Governing Body: Representative: J. A. Lozada, Jr. (IAEA). Alternates: E. Biskup (WMO), P. A. Gagné (ITU), P. Anders (IMO).
Representing the Executive Head: Representative: Aamir Ali (ILO). Alternates: Niall MacCabe (ILO), Franz Von Mutius (ILO).
Representing the Participants: Representative: Dr. Alain Vessereau (WHO). Alternates: Vincent Bambinelli (WHO), David Payne (WHO), Ram L. Rai (WHO), Maggy Melloni (WHO), Hans-Walter Schmidtkunz (WHO).

Specialized agencies (Group III)
Representing the Governing Body: Representative: Y. Hamdi (IFAD). Alternates: Elizabeth Michaud (ICITO/GATT), E. Biskup (WIPO), A. Zerhouni (ICAO).
Representing the Executive Head: Representative: Mohsen Bel Hadj Amor (FAO). Alternates: Maria Grazia Iuri (FAO), Victor E. Orebi (FAO), Giorgio Eberle (FAO), Takashi Kubo (FAO), Tullia P. Rothe (FAO).
Representing the Participants: Representative: Alastair McLurg (UNESCO). Alternate: Yvette D'Silva (UNESCO).

COMMITTEE OF ACTUARIES
The Committee of Actuaries consists of five members, each representing one of the five geographical regions of the United Nations.

Members: Ajibola O. Ogunshola (Nigeria), *Region I* (African States); Kunio Takeuchi (Japan), *Region II* (Asian States); Evgeny M. Chetyrkin (USSR), *Region III* (Eastern European States); Dr. Gonzalo Arroba (Ecuador), *Region IV* (Latin American States); Robert J. Myers (United States), *Region V* (Western European and other States).

United Nations Relief and Works Agency for Palestine Refugees in the Near East (UNRWA)

ADVISORY COMMISSION OF UNRWA
The Advisory Commission of UNRWA met at Vienna, Austria, on 29 August 1985.

Members: Belgium, Egypt, France, Japan, Jordan *(Chairman)*, Lebanon, Syrian Arab Republic, Turkey, United Kingdom, United States.

WORKING GROUP ON THE FINANCING OF UNRWA
Members: France, Ghana *(Vice-Chairman)*, Japan, Lebanon, Norway *(Rapporteur)*, Trinidad and Tobago, Turkey *(Chairman)*, United Kingdom, United States.

Commissioner-General of UNRWA: Olof Rydbeck.[a]
Deputy Commissioner-General: Robert S. Dillon.

[a]Retired effective 31 October 1985; Giorgio Giacomelli was appointed by the Secretary-General in consultation with the members of the Advisory Commission on 13 May 1985 to fill the resultant vacancy.

United Nations Scientific Advisory Committee
Established by the General Assembly in 1954 as a seven-member advisory committee on the International Conference on the Peaceful Uses of Atomic Energy (1955), the United Nations Scientific Advisory Committee was so renamed and its mandate revised by the Assembly in 1958,[20] retaining its original composition. The Committee has not met since 1956.[21]

Members: Brazil, Canada, France, India, USSR, United Kingdom, United States.

United Nations Scientific Committee on the Effects of Atomic Radiation
The 20-member United Nations Scientific Committee on the Effects of Atomic Radiation held its thirty-fourth session at Vienna, Austria, from 10 to 14 June 1985.

Members: Argentina, Australia, Belgium, Brazil, Canada, Czechoslovakia, Egypt, France, Germany, Federal Republic of, India, Indonesia, Japan, Mexico, Peru, Poland, Sudan, Sweden, USSR, United Kingdom, United States.

Chairman: T. Kumatori (Japan).
Vice-Chairman: A. Kaul (Federal Republic of Germany).
Rapporteur: A. Hidayatalla (Sudan).

United Nations Special Fund
(to provide emergency relief and development assistance)

BOARD OF GOVERNORS
The activities of the United Nations Special Fund were suspended, *ad interim*, in 1978 by the General Assembly, which assumed the functions of the Board of Governors of the Fund. In 1981,[22] the Assembly decided to continue performing those functions, within the context of its consideration of the item on development and international economic co-operation, pending consideration of the question in 1983. However, no action was taken in 1983, 1984 or 1985.

United Nations Special Fund for Land-locked Developing Countries
On 17 December 1985 (decision 40/448 A), the General Assembly, on the recommendation of the UNDP Governing Council, requested the Secretary-General to take the necessary steps to dissolve the United Nations Special Fund for Land-locked Developing Countries by 31 December 1986.

[20]YUN 1958, p. 31, res. 1344(XIII), 13 Dec. 1958.
[21]YUN 1956, p. 108.
[22]YUN 1981, p. 418, dec. 36/424, 4 Dec. 1981.

United Nations Staff Pension Committee

The United Nations Staff Pension Committee consists of three members elected by the General Assembly, three appointed by the Secretary-General and three elected by the participants in the United Nations Joint Staff Pension Fund. The term of office of the elected members is three years, or until the election of their successors.

Members:
Elected by Assembly (to serve until 31 December 1985): *Members:* Sol Kuttner *(Chairman)*, Mario Majoli, Michael George Okeyo. *Alternates:* Eduardo César Añón Noceti, Jobst Holborn, Yukio Takasu.
Appointed by Secretary-General (to serve until further notice): *Members:* J. Richard Foran, Louis-Pascal Nègre, Paul C. Szasz. *Alternates:* Raymond Gieri, Victor Elisseev, Matias de la Mota.
Elected by Participants (to serve until 31 December 1985): *Members:* Susanna H. Johnston, Bruce C. Hillis. *Alternates:* Gualtiero Fulcheri, Sergio Zampetti, Anders Tholle.

On 18 December 1985 (decision 40/323), the General Assembly elected the following for a three-year term beginning on 1 January 1986 to fill the vacancies occurring on 31 December 1985: *Members:* Sol Kuttner, Mario Majoli, Michael George Okeyo; *Alternates:* Jobst Holborn, Miguel A. Ortega, Yukio Takasu.

United Nations University

COUNCIL OF THE UNITED NATIONS UNIVERSITY

The Council of the United Nations University, the governing board of the University, consists of: *(a)* 24 members appointed jointly by the Secretary-General and the Director-General of UNESCO, in consultation with the agencies and programmes concerned including UNITAR, who serve in their personal capacity for six-year terms; *(b)* the Secretary-General, the Director-General of UNESCO and the Executive Director of UNITAR, who are *ex-officio* members; and *(c)* the Rector of the University, who is normally appointed for a five-year term.

In 1985, the Council held two sessions: its twenty-fifth from 8 to 12 July at Mexico City; and its twenty-sixth from 9 to 13 December in Tokyo.

Members:
To serve until 2 May 1986: Ungku Abdul Aziz, *Vice-Chairman* (Malaysia); Elise M. Boulding (United States); Satish Chandra (India); Donald E. U. Ekong (Nigeria); André Louis Jaumotte, *Vice-Chairman* (Belgium); Reimut Jochimsen (Federal Republic of Germany); F. S. C. P. Kalpage (Sri Lanka); Sir John Kendrew (United Kingdom); Shizuo Saito (Japan); Charles Valy Tuho (Ivory Coast); Víctor Luis Urquidi, *Chairman* (Mexico).
To serve until 2 May 1989: Bakr Abdullah Bakr, Vice-Chairman (Saudi Arabia); Bashir Bakri (Sudan); Marie-Thérèse Basse (Senegal); André Blanc-Lapierre (France); Jozsef Bognar (Hungary); Mercedes B. Concepción, *Vice-Chairman* (Philippines); Helga Gyllenberg (Finland);[a] Walter Joseph Kamba (Zimbabwe); Gerald Cecil Lalor (Jamaica);[a] Maria de Lourdes Pintasilgo, *Vice-Chairman* (Portugal); Y. M. Primakov (USSR); Alberto Wagner de Reyna (Peru); Zhao Dihua (China).
Ex-officio members: The Secretary-General, the Director-General of UNESCO and the Executive Director of UNITAR.

Rector of the United Nations University: Mr. Soedjatmoko.[b]

[a]Appointed in May 1985.
[b]Reappointed for a two-year term beginning on 1 September 1985.

The Council maintained four standing committees during 1985: the Committee on Finance and Budget; the Committee on Institutional and Programmatic Development; the Committee on Statutes, Rules and Guidelines; and the Committee on the Report of the Council.

United Nations Voluntary Fund for Indigenous Populations

On 13 December 1985, the General Assembly established the United Nations Voluntary Fund for Indigenous Populations to provide financial assistance to representatives of indigenous communities and organizations who would not otherwise be able to participate in the meetings of the Working Group on Indigenous Populations, a subsidiary of the Sub-Commission on Prevention of Discrimination and Protection of Minorities.

BOARD OF TRUSTEES

The Board of Trustees to advise the Secretary-General in his administration of the Fund was to consist of five members with relevant experience on issues affecting indigenous populations, appointed in their personal capacity by the Secretary-General for a three-year term. At least one member was to be a representative of a widely recognized organization of indigenous people.

The Board had not been constituted by the end of 1985.

United Nations Voluntary Fund for Victims of Torture

BOARD OF TRUSTEES

The Board of Trustees to advise the Secretary-General in his administration of the United Nations Voluntary Fund for Victims of Torture consists of five members with wide experience in the field of human rights, appointed in their personal capacity by the Secretary-General with due regard for equitable geographical distribution and in consultation with their Governments.

The Board held its fourth session from 15 to 19 April 1985 at United Nations Headquarters.

Members (to serve until 31 December 1985): Hans Danelius, *Chairman* (Sweden); Elizabeth Odio Benito (Costa Rica); Waleed M. Sadi (Jordan); Ivan Tosevski (Yugoslavia); Amos Wako (Kenya).

World Food Council

The World Food Council, at the ministerial or plenipotentiary level, functions as an organ of the United Nations and reports to the General Assembly through the Economic and Social Council. It consists of 36 members, nominated by the Economic and Social Council and elected by the Assembly according to the following pattern: nine members from African States, eight from Asian States, seven from Latin American States, four from socialist States of Eastern Europe and eight from Western European and other States. Members serve for three-year terms.

During 1985, the World Food Council held its eleventh session from 10 to 13 June in Paris. It was preceded by a preparatory meeting held at Rome, Italy, from 29 April to 2 May.

Members:
To serve until 31 December 1985: Australia, Bangladesh, Ecuador, Ethiopia, German Democratic Republic, Germany, Federal Republic of, Ghana, Nicaragua, Nigeria, USSR, United Arab Emirates, Venezuela.
To serve until 31 December 1986: Argentina, Burundi, Central African Republic, Chile, Finland, France, Hungary, Iraq, Italy, Japan, Morocco, Pakistan.
To serve until 31 December 1987: Brazil, Bulgaria, Canada, China, Ivory Coast, Kenya, Mexico, Sri Lanka, Thailand, Turkey, United States, Zambia.

President: Eugene F. Whelan (Canada).
Vice-Presidents: Pedro Antonio Blandón (Nicaragua), Karl Friedrich Gebhardt (German Democratic Republic), Saihou Sabally (Gambia).
Rapporteur: Reaz Rahman (Bangladesh).

Executive Director: Maurice J. Williams.
Deputy Executive Director: Diogo A. N. de Gaspar.[a]

[a]Resigned effective 31 March 1985.

On 30 May 1985 (decision 1985/160), the Economic and Social Council nominated the following 14 States, 12 of which were to be elected by the General Assembly, for a three-year term beginning on 1 January 1986 to fill the vacancies occurring on 31 December 1985: Antigua and Barbuda, Australia, Bangladesh, Cyprus, Dominican Republic, German Democratic Republic, Germany, Federal Republic of, Guinea, Honduras, India, Mali, Somalia, Syrian Arab Republic, USSR. All but India and the Syrian Arab Republic were elected by the Assembly on 10 December 1985 (decision 40/311).

Conferences

Seventh United Nations Congress on the Prevention of Crime and the Treatment of Offenders

The Seventh United Nations Congress on the Prevention of Crime and the Treatment of Offenders was held at Milan, Italy, from 26 August to 6 September 1985. Participating were the following 123 States and the United Nations Council for Namibia:

Afghanistan, Algeria, Argentina, Australia, Austria, Bangladesh, Belgium, Benin, Bolivia, Botswana, Brazil, Bulgaria, Burkina Faso, Burundi, Byelorussian SSR, Cameroon, Canada, Cape Verde, Central African Republic, Chad, Chile, China, Colombia, Comoros, Costa Rica, Cuba, Czechoslovakia, Democratic Yemen, Denmark, Djibouti, Dominican Republic, Egypt, Ethiopia, Finland, France, Gabon, Gambia, German Democratic Republic, Germany, Federal Republic of, Ghana, Greece, Guatemala, Guinea, Guinea-Bissau, Haiti, Holy See, Hungary, India, Indonesia, Iran, Iraq, Ireland, Israel, Italy, Jamaica, Japan, Jordan, Kenya, Kuwait, Lebanon, Libyan Arab Jamahiriya, Liechtenstein, Madagascar, Malawi, Malaysia, Maldives, Mali, Malta, Mauritania, Mexico, Monaco, Mongolia, Morocco, Mozambique, Nepal, Netherlands, New Zealand, Nicaragua, Niger, Nigeria, Norway, Pakistan, Panama, Peru, Philippines, Poland, Portugal, Qatar, Republic of Korea, Romania, Rwanda, Samoa, San Marino, Sao Tome and Principe, Saudi Arabia, Senegal, Seychelles, Sierra Leone, Somalia, Spain, Sri Lanka, Sudan, Swaziland, Sweden, Switzerland, Syrian Arab Republic, Thailand, Togo, Turkey, Uganda, Ukrainian SSR, USSR, United Arab Emirates, United Kingdom, United Republic of Tanzania, United States, Uruguay, Venezuela, Yemen, Yugoslavia, Zaire, Zambia, Zimbabwe.

President: Mino Martinazzoli (Italy).
First Vice-President: Jan Pjescak (Czechoslovakia).
Vice-Presidents: Argentina, Botswana, Canada, Chile, China, Cuba, Egypt, Ethiopia, Finland, France, Germany, Federal Republic of, Guatemala, India, Indonesia, Mali, Poland, Saudi Arabia, Seychelles, Spain, Thailand, USSR, United Kingdom, Zaire.
Rapporteur-General: Yoshio Suzuki (Japan).

Chairmen of committees:
Committee I: Hassan B. Jallow (Gambia).
Committee II: Manuel López-Rey y Arrojo (Bolivia).
Credentials Committee: V. Esposito (Italy).

United Nations Conference on Conditions for Registration of Ships

The second and third parts of the United Nations Conference on Conditions for Registration of Ships were held at Geneva from 28 January to 15 February and from 8 to 19 July 1985. Participating were the following 102 States:

Algeria, Angola,[a] Argentina, Australia, Austria, Bahamas, Bangladesh, Belgium, Benin,[a] Bolivia, Brazil, Bulgaria, Byelorussian SSR, Cameroon, Canada, Chile, China, Colombia, Congo,[a] Costa Rica,[b] Cuba, Cyprus, Czechoslovakia, Democratic People's Republic of Korea, Democratic Yemen, Denmark, Djibouti,[a] Dominican Republic,[b] Ecuador, Egypt, El Salvador,[b] Ethiopia,[a] Finland, France, Gabon, German Democratic Republic, Germany, Federal Republic of, Ghana, Greece, Guatemala, Guinea,[a] Haiti,[b] Hungary, India, Indonesia, Iran, Iraq, Israel, Italy, Ivory Coast, Jamaica,[a] Japan, Jordan, Kenya, Kuwait, Lebanon, Liberia, Libyan Arab Jamahiriya, Madagascar, Malaysia, Malta, Mauritania, Mexico, Morocco, Netherlands, New Zealand, Nicaragua, Nigeria, Norway, Oman, Pakistan, Panama, Peru, Philippines, Poland, Portugal,[a] Qatar, Republic of Korea, Saudi Arabia, Senegal, Singapore, Somalia, Spain, Sri Lanka, Sudan, Sweden, Switzerland, Thailand, Trinidad and Tobago, Tunisia, Turkey, Ukrainian SSR, USSR, United Kingdom, United Republic of Tanzania, United States, Uruguay, Vanuatu, Venezuela, Yemen, Yugoslavia, Zaire.

[a]Participated in the third part only.
[b]Participated in the second part only.

President: Lamine Fadika (Ivory Coast).
Vice-Presidents: Australia, Bolivia, China, Czechoslovakia, Egypt, France, Indonesia, Japan, Lebanon, Liberia, Norway, Peru, Poland, United States.
Rapporteur: Jean Evelyn George (Trinidad and Tobago).

Chairmen of committees:
General Committee: Lamine Fadika (Ivory Coast).
First Committee: Krzysztof Dabrowski (Poland).
Second Committee: Rudi Okken (Netherlands) (second part), I. G. Lochhead (Canada) (third part).
Drafting Committee: Yashwant Sinha (India) (second part), D. Soysa (Sri Lanka) (third part).
Credentials Committee: G. A. Mathas (Gabon).

World Conference to Review and Appraise the Achievements of the United Nations Decade for Women: Equality, Development and Peace

The World Conference to Review and Appraise the Achievements of the United Nations Decade for Women: Equality, Development and Peace was held at Nairobi, Kenya, from 15 to 26 July 1985. Participating were the following 157 States, as well as the Special Committee against *Apartheid* and the United Nations Council for Namibia:

Afghanistan, Albania, Algeria, Angola, Antigua and Barbuda, Argentina, Australia, Austria, Bahrain, Bangladesh, Barbados, Belgium, Belize, Benin, Bhutan, Botswana, Brazil, Bulgaria, Burkina Faso, Burundi, Byelorussian SSR, Cameroon, Canada, Cape Verde, Central African Republic, Chad, Chile, China, Colombia, Comoros, Congo, Costa Rica, Cuba, Cyprus, Czechoslovakia, Democratic Kampuchea, Democratic People's Republic of Korea, Democratic Yemen, Denmark, Djibouti, Dominica, Dominican Republic, Ecuador, Egypt, El Salvador, Equatorial Guinea, Ethiopia, Fiji, Finland, France, Gabon, Gambia, German Democratic Republic, Germany, Federal Republic of, Ghana, Greece, Grenada, Guatemala, Guinea, Guinea-Bissau, Guyana, Haiti, Holy See, Honduras, Hungary, Iceland, India, Indonesia, Iran, Iraq, Ireland, Israel, Italy, Ivory Coast, Jamaica, Japan, Jordan, Kenya, Kiribati, Kuwait, Lao People's Democratic Republic, Lesotho, Liberia, Libyan Arab Jamahiriya, Luxembourg, Madagascar, Malawi, Malaysia, Maldives, Mali, Malta, Mauritania, Mauritius, Mexico, Mongolia, Morocco, Mozambique, Nepal, Netherlands, New Zealand, Nicaragua, Niger, Nigeria, Norway, Oman, Pakistan, Panama, Papua New Guinea, Paraguay, Peru, Philippines, Poland, Portugal, Republic of Korea, Romania, Rwanda, Saint Christopher and Nevis, Saint Lucia, Saint Vincent and the Grenadines, Samoa, San Marino, Sao Tome and Principe, Saudi Arabia, Senegal, Seychelles, Sierra Leone, Solomon Islands, Somalia, Spain, Sri Lanka, Sudan, Suriname, Swaziland, Sweden, Switzerland, Syrian Arab Republic, Thailand, Togo, Trinidad and Tobago, Tunisia, Turkey, Uganda, Ukrainian SSR, USSR, United Arab Emirates, United Kingdom, United Republic of Tanzania, United States, Uruguay, Vanuatu, Venezuela, Viet Nam, Yemen, Yugoslavia, Zaire, Zambia, Zimbabwe.

President: Margaret Kenyatta (Kenya).
Vice-President for Co-ordination: Tom Eric Vraalsen (Norway).
Vice-Presidents: Australia, Austria, Bangladesh, Burundi, Chad, Chile, Costa Rica, Cuba, Czechoslovakia, Ecuador, France, German Democratic Republic, Germany, Federal Republic of, Greece, India, Indonesia, Iraq, Ireland, Japan, Liberia, Mali, Nicaragua, Syrian Arab Republic, Thailand, Tunisia, USSR, United Republic of Tanzania, Venezuela, Zambia.
Rapporteur-General: Elena Lagadinova (Bulgaria).

Presiding officers of committees:
First Committee: Cecilia López (Colombia).
Second Committee: Rosario G. Manalo (Philippines).
Credentials Committee: Achyut Bhandari (Bhutan).

Security Council

The Security Council consists of 15 Member States of the United Nations, in accordance with the provisions of Article 23 of the United Nations Charter as amended in 1965.

MEMBERS
Permanent members: China, France, USSR, United Kingdom, United States.

Non-permanent members: Australia, Burkina Faso, Denmark, Egypt, India, Madagascar, Peru, Thailand, Trinidad and Tobago, Ukrainian SSR.

On 17 October 1985 (decision 40/306), the General Assembly elected Bulgaria, the Congo, Ghana, the United Arab Emirates and Venezuela for a two-year term beginning on 1 January 1986, to replace Burkina Faso, Egypt, India, Peru and the Ukrainian SSR, whose terms of office were to expire on 31 December 1985.

PRESIDENTS

The presidency of the Council rotates monthly, according to the English alphabetical listing of its member States. The following served as Presidents during 1985:

Month	Member	Representative
January	France	Claude de Kémoularia
February	India	Natarajan Krishnan
March	Madagascar	Blaise Rabetafika
April	Peru	Javier Arias Stella
May	Thailand	Siddi Savetsila
		Birabhongse Kasemsri
June	Trinidad and Tobago	Errol Mahabir
		D. H. N. Alleyne
		Hamid Mohammed
July	Ukrainian SSR	G. I. Oudovenko
August	USSR	O. A. Troyanovsky
September	United Kingdom	Sir Geoffrey Howe
		Sir John Adam Thomson
October	United States	Vernon A. Walters
		Herbert S. Okun
November	Australia	Richard Arthur Woolcott
December	Burkina Faso	Léandre Bassolé

Collective Measures Committee

The Collective Measures Committee (p. 1395) reports to both the General Assembly and the Security Council.

Military Staff Committee

The Military Staff Committee consists of the chiefs of staff of the permanent members of the Security Council or their representatives. It met fortnightly throughout 1985; the first meeting was held on 4 January and the last on 20 December.

Standing committees

Each of the two standing committees of the Security Council is composed of representatives of all Council members:

Committee of Experts (to examine the provisional rules of procedure of the Council and any other matters entrusted to it by the Council)
Committee on the Admission of New Members

In addition, the Council maintains an *ad hoc* Committee on Council Meetings Away from Headquarters.

Ad hoc bodies

Ad Hoc Committee established under resolution 507(1982)
Members: France *(Chairman)*, Guyana,[a] Jordan,[a] Uganda.[a]

[a]Not Council members in 1985.

Ad Hoc Sub-Committee on Namibia
The *Ad Hoc* Sub-Committee on Namibia consists of all the members of the Security Council. It did not meet in 1985.

Committee of Experts established by the Security Council at its 1506th meeting
(on the question of micro-States)
The Committee of Experts consists of all the members of the Security Council. The chairmanship is rotated monthly in the English alphabetical order of the member States.
The Committee did not meet in 1985.

Security Council Commission established under resolution 446(1979)
(to examine the situation relating to settlements in the Arab territories occupied since 1967, including Jerusalem)
Members:[a] Bolivia, Portugal *(Chairman)*, Zambia.

[a]Not Council members in 1985.

Security Council Commission of Investigation established under resolution 571(1985)
On 20 September 1985, the Security Council decided to send immediately to Angola a commission of investigation, comprising three Council members, to evaluate the damage resulting from South Africa's invasion.

Members: Australia, Egypt *(Chairman)*, Peru.

Security Council Committee established by resolution 421(1977) concerning the question of South Africa
The Committee consists of all the members of the Security Council.

PEACE-KEEPING OPERATIONS AND SPECIAL MISSIONS

United Nations Truce Supervision Organization (UNTSO)
Chief of Staff: Lieutenant-General Emmanuel Alexander Erskine.

United Nations Disengagement Observer Force (UNDOF)
Force Commander: Major-General Carl-Gustav Stahl (until 31 May 1985), Major-General Gustav Hägglund (from 1 June).

United Nations Interim Force in Lebanon (UNIFIL)
Force Commander: Lieutenant-General William Callaghan.

United Nations Peace-keeping Force in Cyprus (UNFICYP)
Acting Special Representative of the Secretary-General in Cyprus: James Holger.
Force Commander: Major-General Günther G. Greindl.

United Nations Military Observer Group in India and Pakistan (UNMOGIP)
Chief Military Observer: Brigadier-General Thor A. Johnsen.

United Nations Transition Assistance Group (UNTAG)
Authorized by the Security Council in 1978,[23] the United Nations Transition Assistance Group had not been emplaced in Namibia by the end of 1985.

Special Representative of the Secretary-General: Martti Ahtisaari.
Commander-designate: Lieutenant-General Dewan Prem Chand.

[23]YUN 1978, p. 915, res. 435(1978), 29 Sep. 1978.

Economic and Social Council

The Economic and Social Council consists of 54 Member States of the United Nations, elected by the General Assembly, each for a three-year term, in accordance with the provisions of Article 61 of the United Nations Charter as amended in 1965 and 1973.

MEMBERS
To serve until 31 December 1985: Algeria, Botswana, Bulgaria, Congo, Djibouti, Ecuador, German Democratic Republic, Lebanon, Luxembourg, Malaysia, Mexico, Netherlands, New Zealand, Saudi Arabia,

Sierra Leone, Suriname, Thailand, United States.

To serve until 31 December 1986: Argentina, Canada, China, Costa
Rica, Finland, Guyana, Indonesia, Papua New Guinea, Poland,
Rwanda, Somalia, Sri Lanka, Sweden, Uganda, USSR, United
Kingdom, Yugoslavia, Zaire.

To serve until 31 December 1987: Bangladesh, Brazil, Colombia,
France, Germany, Federal Republic of, Guinea, Haiti, Iceland, India,
Japan, Morocco, Nigeria, Romania, Senegal, Spain, Turkey,
Venezuela, Zimbabwe.

On 17 October 1985 (decision 40/307), the General Assembly elected
the following 18 States for a three-year term beginning on 1 January
1986 to fill the vacancies occurring on 31 December 1985: Australia,
Belgium, Byelorussian SSR, Djibouti, Egypt, Gabon, German
Democratic Republic, Iraq, Italy, Jamaica, Mozambique, Pakistan,
Panama, Peru, Philippines, Sierra Leone, Syrian Arab Republic, United
States.

SESSIONS

Organizational session for 1985: United Nations Headquarters, 5-8
February and 22 March.

First regular session of 1985: United Nations Headquarters, 7-31 May
and 20 June.

Second regular session of 1985: Geneva, 3-26 July.

Resumed second regular session of 1985: United Nations Headquarters, 12 December.

OFFICERS

President: Tomohiko Kobayashi (Japan).

Vice-Presidents: Ivan Garvalov (Bulgaria), Henri A. M. Guda (Suriname),
Rabah Hadid (Algeria), Krister Kumlin (Sweden).

Subsidiary and other related organs

SUBSIDIARY ORGANS

In addition to three regular sessional committees, the Economic and
Social Council may, at each session, set up other committees or working groups, of the whole or of limited membership, and refer to them
any items on the agenda for study and report.

Other subsidiary organs reporting to the Council consist of functional commissions, regional commissions, standing committees, expert bodies and *ad hoc* bodies.

The inter-agency Administrative Committee on Co-ordination also
reports to the Council.

Sessional bodies

SESSIONAL COMMITTEES

Each of the sessional committees of the Economic and Social Council consists of the 54 members of the Council.

First (Economic) Committee. Chairman: Rabah Hadid (Algeria). *Vice-
Chairmen:* Pekka Juhani Huhtaniemi (Finland), Nandini Ranasinghe
(Sri Lanka).

Second (Social) Committee. Chairman: Ivan Garvalov (Bulgaria). *Vice-
Chairmen:* Bassy Camara (Guinea), Alphons C. M. Hamer
(Netherlands).

Third (Programme and Co-ordination) Committee. Chairman: Henri
A. M. Guda (Suriname). *Vice-Chairmen:* Soemadi D. M. Brotodiningrat (Indonesia), Günter Schumann (German Democratic Republic).

SESSIONAL WORKING GROUP OF GOVERNMENTAL EXPERTS
ON THE IMPLEMENTATION OF THE INTERNATIONAL
COVENANT ON ECONOMIC, SOCIAL AND CULTURAL RIGHTS

The Sessional Working Group of Governmental Experts on the Im-
plementation of the International Covenant on Economic, Social and
Cultural Rights, which was to consist of 15 members elected by the
Council from among the States parties to the Covenant, met at United
Nations Headquarters from 22 April to 9 May 1985.

Members:

To serve until 31 December 1985:[a] France, Kenya, Peru, USSR.

To serve until 31 December 1986: Denmark, German Democratic
Republic, Japan, Mexico,[b] Tunisia.

To serve until 31 December 1987:[a] Bulgaria, Ecuador,[b] Senegal,[b] Spain.

[a]One seat allocated to a member from Asian States remained unfilled in 1985.
[b]Elected on 8 February 1985 (decision 1985/111).

Chairman: Ulrich Kords (German Democratic Republic).

Vice-Chairmen: Hisami Kurokochi (Japan), Miguel Ruiz-Cabañas (Mexico), Philippe Texier (France).

Rapporteur: Sidaty Aidara (Senegal).

On 30 May 1985 (decision 1985/160), the Economic and Social Council elected France, Iraq, Peru and the USSR for a three-year term beginning on 1 January 1986 to fill four of the five vacancies occurring on
31 December 1985; no further elections were held in 1985 to fill the
remaining seat, allocated to a member from African States.

On 28 May 1985 (decision 1985/162), the Council decided that the
Group's 1986 Bureau be constituted as follows: Chairman — Latin
American States; Vice-Chairmen — African States, Eastern European
States, Western European and other States; Rapporteur — Asian States.

Also on 28 May, the Council decided to rename the Group "Committee on Economic, Social and Cultural Rights" (see p. 1417).

Functional commissions

Commission for Social Development

The Commission for Social Development consists of 32 members,
elected for four-year terms by the Economic and Social Council according to a specific pattern of equitable geographical distribution.

The Commission held its twenty-ninth session at Vienna, Austria,
from 18 to 27 February 1985.

Members:

To serve until 31 December 1986: Argentina, Austria, Byelorussian
SSR, Central African Republic, Cyprus, Ecuador, Finland, Ghana,
India, Liberia, Togo.

To serve until 31 December 1987: Canada, El Salvador, France, Haiti,
Kenya, Malaysia, Mongolia, Morocco, Romania, USSR, United
States.

To serve until 31 December 1988:[a] Chile, Denmark, Italy, Mali,[b]
Netherlands, Panama, Poland, Thailand, Zimbabwe.

[a]One seat allocated to a member from Asian States remained unfilled in 1985.
[b]Elected on 8 February 1985 (decision 1985/111).

Chairman: Luvsandanzangyn Ider (Mongolia).

Vice-Chairmen: Pekka Harttila (Finland), María Teresa Infante Barros
(Chile), A. V. Lioutsko (Byelorussian SSR).

Rapporteur: Folly Glidjito Akakpo (Togo).

Commission on Human Rights

The Commission on Human Rights consists of 43 members, elected
for three-year terms by the Economic and Social Council according
to a specific pattern of equitable geographical distribution.

The Commission held its forty-first session at Geneva from 4
February to 15 March 1985.

Members:

To serve until 31 December 1985: Bangladesh, Colombia, Costa Rica,
Cyprus, Finland, India, Ireland, Libyan Arab Jamahiriya, Mozam-
bique, Netherlands, Nicaragua, Ukrainian SSR, USSR, United
Republic of Tanzania.

To serve until 31 December 1986: Brazil, Cameroon, France, German
Democratic Republic, Jordan, Kenya, Mauritania, Mexico, Philip-
pines, Senegal, Spain, Syrian Arab Republic, United States,
Yugoslavia.

To serve until 31 December 1987: Argentina, Australia, Austria,
Bulgaria, China, Congo, Gambia, Germany, Federal Republic of,
Japan, Lesotho, Liberia, Peru, Sri Lanka, United Kingdom,
Venezuela.

Chairman: Abu Sayeed Chowdhury (Bangladesh).

Vice-Chairmen: Héctor Charry Samper (Colombia), Paul Bamela Engo
(Cameroon), I. S. Khmel (Ukrainian SSR).

Rapporteur: Karl Borchard (Federal Republic of Germany).

On 30 May 1985 (decision 1985/160), the Economic and Social Council elected the following 14 members for a three-year term beginning on 1 January 1986 to fill the vacancies occurring on 31 December 1985: Algeria, Bangladesh, Belgium, Byelorussian SSR, Colombia, Costa Rica, Cyprus, Ethiopia, India, Ireland, Mozambique, Nicaragua, Norway, USSR.

AD HOC WORKING GROUP OF EXPERTS
(established by Commission on Human
Rights resolution 2(XXIII) of 6 March 1967)
Members: Mikuin Leliel Balanda (Zaire); Annan Arkyin Cato, *Chairman/Rapporteur* (Ghana); Humberto Díaz-Casanueva (Chile); Felix Ermacora (Austria); Branimir M. Jankovic, *Vice-Chairman* (Yugoslavia); Mulka Govinda Reddy (India).

GROUP OF THREE ESTABLISHED UNDER THE
INTERNATIONAL CONVENTION ON THE SUPPRESSION
AND PUNISHMENT OF THE CRIME OF *APARTHEID*
The Group of Three held its eighth session at Geneva from 28 January to 1 February 1985.

Members: Mexico, Senegal, Ukrainian SSR.

Chairman/Rapporteur: I. S. Khmel (Ukrainian SSR).

SUB-COMMISSION ON PREVENTION OF
DISCRIMINATION AND PROTECTION OF MINORITIES
The Sub-Commission consists of 26 members elected by the Commission on Human Rights from candidates nominated by Member States of the United Nations, in accordance with a scheme to ensure equitable geographical distribution. Members serve in their individual capacity as experts, rather than as governmental representatives, each for a three-year term.
The Sub-Commission held its thirty-eighth session at Geneva from 5 to 30 August 1985.

Members (until March 1987): Miguel Alfonso Martínez (Cuba); Awn Shawkat Al Khasawneh (Jordan); Murlidhar Chandrakant Bhandare (India); Marc Bossuyt (Belgium); Abu Sayeed Chowdhury (Bangladesh); Erica-Irene A. Daes, *Chairman* (Greece); Driss Dahak (Morocco); Jules Deschênes (Canada); George Dove-Edwin (Nigeria); Enzo Giustozzi (Argentina); Gu Yijie (China); Aidiid Abdillahi Ilkahanaf (Somalia); Louis Joinet (France); Ahmed Mohamed Khalifa (Egypt); Antonio Martínez Báez, *Vice-Chairman* (Mexico); Dumitru Mazilu, *Vice-Chairman* (Romania); Chama L. C. Mubanga-Chipoya, *Rapporteur* (Zambia); John P. Roche (United States); Kwesi B. S. Simpson (Ghana); V. N. Sofinsky (USSR); Masayuki Takemoto, *Vice-Chairman* (Japan); Ivan Tosevski (Yugoslavia); Antonio Jose Uribe Portocarrero (Colombia); Rodrigo Valdez Baquero (Ecuador); Benjamin Charles George Whitaker (United Kingdom); Fisseha Yimer (Ethiopia).

Working Group
(established by resolution 2(XXIV) of 16 August 1971
of the Sub-Commission on Prevention of Discrimination
and Protection of Minorities pursuant to Economic and
Social Council resolution 1503(XLVIII))
The Working Group on Communications concerning human rights held its fourteenth session at Geneva from 22 July to 2 August 1985.

Members: Murlidhar Chandrakant Bhandare (India); Marc Bossuyt, *Chairman/Rapporteur* (Belgium); Antonio Martínez Báez (Mexico); V. N. Sofinsky (USSR); Fisseha Yimer (Ethiopia).

Working Group
(established on 21 August 1974 by resolution 11(XXVII)
of the Sub-Commission on Prevention of Discrimination
and Protection of Minorities)
The Working Group on Slavery held its eleventh session at Geneva from 29 July to 2 August 1985.

Members: Abu Sayeed Chowdhury, *Chairman/Rapporteur* (Bangladesh); Jules Deschênes (Canada); Dumitru Mazilu (Romania); Chama L. C. Mubanga-Chipoya (Zambia); Rodrigo Valdez Baquero (Ecuador).

Working Group on Detention
The Working Group on Detention met at Geneva between 12 and 22 August 1985.

Members: Miguel Alfonso Martínez (Cuba); Murlidhar Chandrakant Bhandare (India); John Carey, *Chairman/Rapporteur* (United States); Driss Dahak (Morocco); Dumitru Mazilu (Romania).

Working Group on Indigenous Populations
The Working Group on Indigenous Populations held its fourth session at Geneva from 29 July to 2 August and on 23 August 1985.

Members: Miguel Alfonso Martínez (Cuba); Erica-Irene A. Daes, *Chairman/Rapporteur* (Greece); Gu Yijie (China); Kwesi B. S. Simpson (Ghana); Ivan Tosevski (Yugoslavia).

WORKING GROUP OF GOVERNMENTAL
EXPERTS ON THE RIGHT TO DEVELOPMENT
The Working Group of Governmental Experts on the Right to Development did not meet in 1985.

Members: Luís Aguirre Gallardo (Panama), Juan Alvarez Vita (Peru), Peter L. Berger (United States), D. V. Bykov (USSR), K. L. Dalal (India), Paul J. I. M. de Waart (Netherlands), Georges Gautier (France), Riyadh Aziz Hadi (Iraq), Julio Heredia Pérez (Cuba), Irina Kolarova (Bulgaria), Fatma Z. Ksentini (Algeria), Ahmed Saker (Syrian Arab Republic), Alioune Sène (Senegal), Kongit Sinegiorgis (Ethiopia), Danilo Turk (Yugoslavia).

WORKING GROUP ON ENFORCED
OR INVOLUNTARY DISAPPEARANCES
During 1985, the mandate of the Working Group on Enforced or Involuntary Disappearances was extended for one year by a Commission on Human Rights resolution of 11 March, as approved by the Economic and Social Council on 30 May (decision 1985/142).
The Working Group held three sessions in 1985: its sixteenth at Buenos Aires, Argentina, from 5 to 14 June; its seventeenth at Geneva from 9 to 13 September; and its eighteenth at Geneva from 4 to 13 December.

Members: Jonas Kwami Dotse Foli (Ghana); Agha Hilaly (Pakistan); Ivan Tosevski, *Chairman/Rapporteur* (Yugoslavia); Toine F. van Dongen (Netherlands); Luis Alberto Varela Quirós (Costa Rica).

WORKING GROUPS
(to study situations revealing a consistent
pattern of gross violations of human rights)

Working Group established by Commission on
Human Rights decision 1984/114 of 6 March 1984:
Members: Ghaleb Z. Barakat, *Chairman/Rapporteur* (Jordan); Leandro Despouy (Argentina);[a] Todor Dichev (Bulgaria); Francis Mahon Hayes (Ireland); E. E. E. Mtango (United Republic of Tanzania).

[a]Replaced Roberto Bianchi (Argentina), who was unable to attend the Group's 1985 meetings.

Working Group established by Commission on
Human Rights decision 1985/106 of 5 March 1985:
Members: Carlton Anyangwe (Cameroon), Todor Dichev (Bulgaria), Francis Mahon Hayes (Ireland), Jorge Montaño (Mexico), Hisham Muhaisen (Jordan).

WORKING GROUP (OPEN-ENDED)

Working Group established by Commission on
Human Rights resolution 1984/24 of 8 March 1984
(to draft a convention on the rights of the child):
Chairman/Rapporteur: Adam Lopatka (Poland).

Commission on Narcotic Drugs
The Commission on Narcotic Drugs consists of 40 members, elected for four-year terms by the Economic and Social Council from among the Members of the United Nations and members of the specialized

agencies and the parties to the Single Convention on Narcotic Drugs, 1961, with due regard for the adequate representation of *(a)* countries which are important producers of opium or coca leaves, *(b)* countries which are important in the manufacture of narcotic drugs, and *(c)* countries in which drug addiction or the illicit traffic in narcotic drugs constitutes an important problem, as well as taking into account the principle of equitable geographical distribution.

The Commission held its thirty-first session at Vienna, Austria, from 11 to 20 February 1985.

Members:

To serve until 31 December 1985: Argentina, Australia, Austria, Bahamas, Belgium, Bulgaria, Hungary, India, Ivory Coast, Japan, Malaysia, Mexico, Nigeria, Panama, Republic of Korea, Senegal, Turkey, USSR, United Kingdom, Zaire.
To serve until 31 December 1987: Algeria, Brazil, Canada, Colombia, Finland, France, German Democratic Republic, Germany, Federal Republic of, Greece, Iran, Italy, Madagascar, Morocco, Netherlands, Pakistan, Peru, Sri Lanka, Thailand, United States, Yugoslavia.

Chairman: Maurice Randrianame (Madagascar).
First Vice-Chairman: Mairaj Husain (Pakistan).
Second Vice-Chairman: Juhana Idanpaan-Heikkila (Finland).
Rapporteur: Luis Guillermo Thornberry Lumbreras (Peru).

On 30 May 1985 (decision 1985/160), the Economic and Social Council elected the following 20 members for a four-year term beginning on 1 January 1986 to fill the vacancies occurring on 31 December 1985: Argentina, Australia, Belgium, Bulgaria, China, Ecuador, Hungary, Indonesia, Japan, Malaysia, Mali, Mexico, Nigeria, Senegal, Spain, Turkey, USSR, United Kingdom, Venezuela, Zambia.

SUB-COMMISSION ON ILLICIT DRUG TRAFFIC AND
RELATED MATTERS IN THE NEAR AND MIDDLE EAST

During 1985, the Sub-Commission held two sessions: its nineteenth at Vienna, Austria, on 7 February; and its twentieth at Teheran, Iran, from 11 to 18 September.

Members: Afghanistan, Iran, Pakistan, Sweden, Turkey.

Chairman: Erdem Erner (Turkey).
Vice-Chairman: Mairaj Husain (Pakistan) (nineteenth session), Dr. S. H. Fakhr (Iran) (twentieth session).

MEETING OF OPERATIONAL HEADS
OF NATIONAL NARCOTICS LAW ENFORCEMENT
AGENCIES, FAR EAST REGION (HONLEA)

A meeting to co-ordinate regional activities against illicit drug traffic, convened annually in one of the region's capitals, is open to any country or territory in the region approved by the Commission, as well as to observers from the Association of South-East Asian Nations, the Colombo Plan Bureau, the Customs Co-operation Council, the International Criminal Police Organization and the International Narcotics Control Board. Any interested Government outside the region may be invited by the Secretary-General to send an observer at its own expense.

The twelfth meeting of HONLEA was held at Colombo, Sri Lanka, from 4 to 8 November 1985.

Commission on the Status of Women

The Commission on the Status of Women consists of 32 members, elected for four-year terms by the Economic and Social Council according to a specific pattern of equitable geographical distribution.

The Commission was designated by the Council as the preparatory body for the World Conference to Review and Appraise the Achievements of the United Nations Decade for Women (p. 1409), held in July 1985.

The Commission did not hold a regular session in 1985.

Members:

To serve until 31 December 1986: Australia, Czechoslovakia, Indonesia, Kenya, Liberia, Mexico, Philippines, Sierra Leone, USSR, United Kingdom, United States.
To serve until 31 December 1987: China, Cuba, Denmark, Ecuador, German Democratic Republic, Germany, Federal Republic of, Nicaragua, Pakistan, Togo, Zambia.

To serve until 31 December 1988: Brazil, Byelorussian SSR, Canada, France, Greece, India, Japan, Mauritius, Sudan, Tunisia, Venezuela.

Population Commission

The Population Commission consists of 27 members, elected for four-year terms by the Economic and Social Council according to a specific pattern of equitable geographical distribution.

The Commission held its twenty-third session at United Nations Headquarters from 19 to 28 February 1985.

Members:

To serve until 31 December 1985: Bolivia, China, Japan, Mexico, Sudan, USSR, United Kingdom, United States, Zambia.
To serve until 31 December 1987: Bulgaria, Costa Rica, Egypt, France, India, Malaysia, Nigeria, Sweden, Togo.
To serve until 31 December 1988: Brazil, Cameroon, Colombia, Germany, Federal Republic of, Mauritius, Netherlands, Thailand, Turkey, Ukrainian SSR.

Chairman: R. P. Kapoor (India).
Vice-Chairmen: A. A. Kadejo (Nigeria), Vladimir Kalaydjiev (Bulgaria), Victor Hugo Morgan (Costa Rica).
Rapporteur: Anita Melin (Sweden).

On 30 May 1985 (decision 1985/160) the Economic and Social Council elected the following nine members for a four-year term beginning on 1 January 1986 to fill the vacancies occurring on 31 December 1985: Burundi, China, Cuba, Iran, Malawi, Mexico, USSR, United Kingdom, United States.

Statistical Commission

The Statistical Commission consists of 24 members, elected for four-year terms by the Economic and Social Council according to a specific pattern of equitable geographical distribution.

The Commission held its twenty-third session at United Nations Headquarters from 25 February to 6 March 1985.

Members:

To serve until 31 December 1985: Argentina, France, Ireland, Libyan Arab Jamahiriya, Nigeria, Spain, Togo, USSR.
To serve until 31 December 1987: Bulgaria, China, Cuba, Czechoslovakia, Ghana, Kenya, Pakistan, United States.
To serve until 31 December 1988: Brazil, Finland, India, Japan, Mexico, New Zealand, Ukrainian SSR, United Kingdom.

Chairman: Thomas Patrick Linehan (Ireland).
Vice-Chairmen: Jessé de Souza Montello (Brazil), Vladimir Micka (Czechoslovakia), Kiron Chandra Seal (India).
Rapporteur: Emmanuel Oti Boateng (Ghana).

On 30 May 1985 (decision 1985/160) the Economic and Social Council elected the following eight members for a four-year term beginning on 1 January 1986 to fill the vacancies occurring on 31 December 1985: Argentina, Egypt, France, Germany, Federal Republic of, Spain, Togo, USSR, Zambia.

WORKING GROUP ON INTERNATIONAL
STATISTICAL PROGRAMMES AND CO-ORDINATION

The Working Group consists of the Bureau of the Statistical Commission; the representatives to the Commission of the two major contributors to the United Nations budget, unless they are already represented in the Bureau; and one representative to the Commission from a developing country from among members of each of the following: ECA, ECLAC, ESCAP and ESCWA, unless they are also already represented in the Bureau. Members serve two-year terms.

The Working Group held its eleventh session at Geneva from 2 to 4 September 1985.

Members: Jessé de Souza Montello (Brazil); M. A. Korolev (USSR); Thomas Patrick Linehan, *Chairman* (Ireland); Vladimir Micka (Czechoslovakia); Emmanuel Oti Boateng (Ghana); Kiron Chandra Seal (India); Dorothy M. Tella (United States).

Regional commissions

Economic and Social Commission for Asia and the Pacific (ESCAP)

The Economic and Social Commission for Asia and the Pacific held its forty-first session at Bangkok, Thailand, from 19 to 29 March 1985.

Members: Afghanistan, Australia, Bangladesh, Bhutan, Brunei Darussalam,[a] Burma, China, Democratic Kampuchea, Fiji, France, India, Indonesia, Iran, Japan, Lao People's Democratic Republic, Malaysia, Maldives, Mongolia, Nauru, Nepal, Netherlands, New Zealand, Pakistan, Papua New Guinea, Philippines, Republic of Korea, Samoa, Singapore, Solomon Islands, Sri Lanka, Thailand, Tonga, Tuvalu,[b] USSR, United Kingdom, United States, Vanuatu, Viet Nam.
Associate members: Cook Islands, Guam, Hong Kong, Kiribati, Niue, Trust Territory of the Pacific Islands.

Switzerland, not a Member of the United Nations, participates in a consultative capacity in the work of the Commission.

[a]Became a full member on 18 February 1985.
[b]Became a full member in January 1985.

Chairman: Prakash Chandra Lohani (Nepal).
Vice-Chairmen: Yusuf bin Haji Mohd. Noor (Malaysia), John Giheno (Papua New Guinea), M. H. M. Naina Marikar (Sri Lanka), Jonati Mavoa (Fiji), Mayumi Moriyama (Japan), M. Munir-Uz-Zaman (Bangladesh), Qian Qichen (China), P. A. Sangma (India), Siddhi Savetsila (Thailand), Soo-Ik Sohn (Republic of Korea), Soubanh Srithirath (Lao People's Democratic Republic), Vicente B. Valdepenas, Jr. (Philippines), D. Zagasbaldan (Mongolia).
Rapporteur: Rosalinda V. Tirona (Philippines).

Following are the main subsidiary and related bodies of the Commission:
Advisory body: Advisory Committee of Permanent Representatives and Other Representatives Designated by Members of the Commission.
Legislative bodies: Committee on Agricultural Development; Committee on Development Planning; Committee on Industry, Technology, Human Settlements and the Environment; Committee on Natural Resources; Committee on Population; Committee on Shipping, and Transport and Communications; Committee on Social Development; Committee on Statistics; Committee on Trade.
Subsidiary bodies: Governing Board, Asian and Pacific Centre for Transfer of Technology;[a] Governing Board, Regional Co-ordination Centre for Research and Development of Coarse Grains, Pulses, Roots and Tuber Crops in the Humid Tropics of Asia and the Pacific; Governing Council, Regional Mineral Resources Development Centre.
Related intergovernmental bodies: Asian and Pacific Development Centre; Committee for Co-ordination of Joint Prospecting for Mineral Resources in Asian Offshore Areas; Committee for Co-ordination of Joint Prospecting for Mineral Resources in South Pacific Offshore Areas; Interim Committee for Co-ordination of Investigations of the Lower Mekong Basin; Typhoon Committee.
Regional institution: Statistical Institute for Asia and the Pacific.
Intergovernmental meeting convened by ESCAP: Special Body on Land-locked Countries.

[a]Formerly the Regional Centre for Technology Transfer; its statute was adopted by ESCAP on 29 March 1985.

Economic and Social Commission for Western Asia (ESCWA)

The Economic Commission for Western Asia held its twelfth session at Baghdad, Iraq, on 24 and 25 April 1985.
On 26 July, the Economic and Social Council changed the name of ECWA to Economic and Social Commission for Western Asia.

Members: Bahrain, Democratic Yemen, Egypt, Iraq, Jordan, Kuwait, Lebanon, Oman, Qatar, Saudi Arabia, Syrian Arab Republic, United Arab Emirates, Yemen; Palestine Liberation Organization.

Chairman: Ali Ahmad Al-Ansari (Qatar).
Vice-Chairmen: Jaweed Al-Ghoseini (Palestine Liberation Organization), Muhammad Al-Khadim Al-Wajih (Yemen).
Rapporteur: Sayed Al-Masri (Egypt).

The Commission's one main subsidiary organ, the Technical Committee, composed of all ESCWA members, reviews the Commission's programme of work.

Economic Commission for Africa (ECA)

The Economic Commission for Africa meets in annual session at the ministerial level known as the Conference of Ministers.

The Commission held its twentieth session (eleventh meeting of the Conference of Ministers) at Addis Ababa, Ethiopia, from 25 to 29 April 1985.

Members: Algeria, Angola, Benin, Botswana, Burkina Faso, Burundi, Cameroon, Cape Verde, Central African Republic, Chad, Comoros, Congo, Djibouti, Egypt, Equatorial Guinea, Ethiopia, Gabon, Gambia, Ghana, Guinea, Guinea-Bissau, Ivory Coast, Kenya, Lesotho, Liberia, Libyan Arab Jamahiriya, Madagascar, Malawi, Mali, Mauritania, Mauritius, Morocco, Mozambique, Niger, Nigeria, Rwanda, Sao Tome and Principe, Senegal, Seychelles, Sierra Leone, Somalia, South Africa,[a] Sudan, Swaziland, Togo, Tunisia, Uganda, United Republic of Tanzania, Zaire, Zambia, Zimbabwe.

Switzerland, not a Member of the United Nations, participates in a consultative capacity in the work of the Commission.

[a]On 30 July 1963, the Economic and Social Council decided that South Africa should not take part in the work of ECA until conditions for constructive co-operation had been restored by a change in South Africa's racial policy (YUN 1963, p. 274, res. 974 D IV (XXXVII)).

Chairman: Bernard T. G. Chidzero (Zimbabwe).
First Vice-Chairman: Etienne Ntsama (Cameroon).
Second Vice-Chairman: Ali Oubouzar (Algeria).
Rapporteur: Cheikh Hamidou Kane (Senegal).

The Commission has established the following principal legislative organs:

Conference of Ministers; sectoral ministerial conferences, each assisted by an appropriate committee of technical officials; Council of Ministers of each Multinational Programming and Operational Centre, assisted by its committee of officials; Technical Preparatory Committee of the Whole.

The Commission has also established the following subsidiary bodies:

Joint Conference of African Planners, Statisticians and Demographers (a standing technical body); Governing Council, African Institute for Economic Development and Planning; Institut de formation et de recherche démographiques; Intergovernmental Committee of Experts for Science and Technology Development; Joint Intergovernmental Regional Committee on Human Settlements and Environment; Regional Institute for Population Studies.

Economic Commission for Europe (ECE)

The Economic Commission for Europe held its fortieth session at Geneva from 16 to 27 April 1985.

Members: Albania, Austria, Belgium, Bulgaria, Byelorussian SSR, Canada, Cyprus, Czechoslovakia, Denmark, Finland, France, German Democratic Republic, Germany, Federal Republic of, Greece, Hungary, Iceland, Ireland, Italy, Luxembourg, Malta, Netherlands, Norway, Poland, Portugal, Romania, Spain, Sweden, Switzerland, Turkey, Ukrainian SSR, USSR, United Kingdom, United States, Yugoslavia.

The Holy See, Liechtenstein and San Marino, which are not Members of the United Nations, participate in a consultative capacity in the work of the Commission.

Chairman: Athanasios Petropoulos (Greece).
Vice-Chairman: Stefan Murin (Czechoslovakia).
Rapporteurs: Jan Bielawski (Poland), Leo D'Aes (Belgium).

Following are the principal subsidiary bodies of the Commission:
Chemical Industry Committee; Coal Committee; Committee on Agricultural Problems; Committee on Electric Power; Committee on Gas; Committee on Housing, Building and Planning; Committee on

the Development of Trade; Committee on Water Problems; Conference of European Statisticians; Inland Transport Committee; Meeting of Government Officials Responsible for Standardization Policies; Senior Advisers to ECE Governments on Environmental Problems; Senior Advisers to ECE Governments on Science and Technology; Senior Economic Advisers to ECE Governments; Steel Committee; Timber Committee.

Other subsidiary bodies are: Senior Advisers to ECE Governments on Energy; Working Party on Engineering Industries and Automation.

Ad Hoc meetings of experts are convened for sectors of activity not dealt with by these principal bodies.

Economic Commission for Latin America and the Caribbean (ECLAC)

The Economic Commission for Latin America and the Carribbean did not meet in 1985.

Members: Antigua and Barbuda, Argentina, Bahamas, Barbados, Belize, Bolivia, Brazil, Canada, Chile, Colombia, Costa Rica, Cuba, Dominica, Dominican Republic, Ecuador, El Salvador, France, Grenada, Guatemala, Guyana, Haiti, Honduras, Jamaica, Mexico, Netherlands, Nicaragua, Panama, Paraguay, Peru, Portugal, Saint Christopher and Nevis, Saint Lucia, Saint Vincent and the Grenadines, Spain, Suriname, Trinidad and Tobago, United Kingdom, United States, Uruguay, Venezuela.
Associate members: British Virgin Islands, Montserrat, Netherlands Antilles, United States Virgin Islands.

Switzerland, not a Member of the United Nations, participates in a consultative capacity in the work of the Commission.

The Commission has established the following principal subsidiary bodies:

Caribbean Development and Co-operation Committee; Central American Economic Co-operation Committee and its Inter-agency Committee; Committee of High-level Government Experts; Committee of the Whole; Technical Committee, Latin American Institute for Economic and Social Planning.

The Latin American Demographic Centre forms part of the ECLAC system as an autonomous institution.

Standing committees

Commission on Human Settlements

The Commission on Human Settlements consists of 58 members elected by the Economic and Social Council for three-year terms according to a specific pattern of equitable geographical distribution; it reports to the General Assembly through the Council.

The Commission held its eighth session at Kingston, Jamaica, from 29 April to 10 May 1985.

Members:
To serve until 31 December 1985: Algeria, Canada, Colombia, Cuba, France, German Democratic Republic, Hungary, Indonesia, Lebanon, Libyan Arab Jamahiriya, Malaysia, Netherlands, Nigeria, Norway, Papua New Guinea, Peru, Sierra Leone, Sweden, Uganda.
To serve until 31 December 1986: Bulgaria, Central African Republic, Finland, Gabon, Ghana, Guinea, Haiti, Honduras, Iraq, Japan, Nicaragua, Pakistan, Philippines, Rwanda, Spain, Turkey, USSR, United Republic of Tanzania, United States, Venezuela.
To serve until 31 December 1987:[a] Bangladesh, Botswana, Burundi, Chile, Cyprus, Germany, Federal Republic of, Greece, India, Jamaica, Jordan, Kenya, Lesotho, Mexico, Norway,[b] Sri Lanka, Tunisia, Ukrainian SSR.

[a]Two seats allocated to one member each from Eastern European States and from Western European and other States remained unfilled in 1985.
[b]Elected on 30 May 1985 (decision 1985/160).

Chairman: Bruce Golding (Jamaica).
Vice-Chairmen: Istvan Geczi (Hungary), Najet Khantouche (Tunisia), B. C. Perera (Sri Lanka).
Rapporteur: Nicholas Loukidis (Greece).

On 30 May 1985 (decision 1985/160), the Economic and Social Council elected the following for a three-year term beginning on 1 January 1986 to fill 17 of the 19 vacancies occurring on 31 December 1985: Bolivia, Canada, Congo, Dominican Republic, France, Hungary, Indonesia, Italy, Malawi, Malaysia, Morocco, Netherlands, Nigeria, Panama, Poland, Swaziland, Sweden. No further elections were held in 1985 to fill the remaining two seats, allocated to members from Asian States.

Commission on Transnational Corporations

The Commission on Transnational Corporations consists of 48 members, elected from all States for three-year terms by the Economic and Social Council according to a specific pattern of geographical distribution.

In 1985, the Commission held its eleventh session from 10 to 19 April and reconvened its special session, open to the participation of all States, from 17 to 21 June, both at United Nations Headquarters.

Members:
To serve until 31 December 1985: Bahamas, Brazil, Central African Republic, Cuba, Cyprus, Indonesia, Kenya, Mexico, Netherlands, Nigeria, Norway, Thailand, Uganda, USSR, United Kingdom, United States.
To serve until 31 December 1986: Bangladesh, China, Colombia, Costa Rica, Czechoslovakia, Egypt, France, German Democratic Republic, Germany, Federal Republic of, Guinea, Japan, Morocco, Philippines, Switzerland, Togo, Trinidad and Tobago.
To serve until 31 December 1987: Algeria, Argentina, Bulgaria, Cameroon, Canada, Ghana, India, Iraq, Italy, Jamaica, Mauritius, Pakistan, Republic of Korea, Turkey, Ukrainian SSR, Venezuela.
Expert advisers (to serve through the twelfth (1986) session): Thomas J. Bata (Canada), Friedrich Dribbusch (Federal Republic of Germany), Wim Kok (Netherlands), Celso Lafer (Brazil), Luis Enrique Marius (Uruguay/Italy), Elias J. Mashasi (United Republic of Tanzania), Charles Albert Michalet (France), Zuhayr Mikdashi (Lebanon), Alassane Dramane Ouattara (Burkina Faso), Brian Price (United Kingdom), John Bower Rhodes (United States), David Sycip (Philippines), Teng Weizao (China), V. P. Trepelkov (USSR), Nat Weinberg (United States), Eduardo White (Argentina).

Eleventh session
Chairman: Konstantin Kolev (Bulgaria).
Vice-Chairmen: Even Fontaine-Ortiz (Cuba), Gonzalo G. Santos, Jr. (Philippines), Ibrahima Kalil Touré (Guinea).
Rapporteur: Marino Baldi (Switzerland).

Reconvened special session
Chairman: Miguel Marín-Bosch (Mexico).
Vice-Chairmen: Irtiza Husain (Pakistan), Jürgen Kühn (Federal Republic of Germany), Wolfgang Sproete (German Democratic Republic).
Rapporteur: Raouf A. Saad (Egypt).

On 30 May 1985 (decision 1985/160), the Economic and Social Council elected the following for a three-year term beginning on 1 January 1986 to fill 15 of the 16 vacancies occurring on 31 December 1985: Antigua and Barbuda, Benin, Brazil, Cuba, Cyprus, Indonesia, Kenya, Mexico, Netherlands, Nigeria, Norway, Swaziland, USSR, United Kingdom, United States. No further election was held in 1985 to fill the remaining seat, allocated to a member from Asian States.

INTERGOVERNMENTAL WORKING GROUP
OF EXPERTS ON INTERNATIONAL
STANDARDS OF ACCOUNTING AND REPORTING

The Intergovernmental Working Group of Experts on International Standards of Accounting and Reporting (p. 1417) reports to the Commission on Transnational Corporations.

Committee for Programme and Co-ordination

The Committee for Programme and Co-ordination is the main subsidiary organ of the Economic and Social Council and of the General Assembly for planning, programming and co-ordination and reports directly to both. It consists of 21 members nominated by the Council and elected by the Assembly for three-year terms according to a specific pattern of equitable geographical distribution.

During 1985, the Committee held, at United Nations Headquarters, an organizational meeting on 1 April and its twenty-fifth session from 29 April to 1 June.

Members:

To serve until 31 December 1985: Argentina, Chile, Ethiopia, France, Nigeria, USSR, United States.

To serve until 31 December 1986: Brazil, Cameroon, Egypt, India, Indonesia, Japan, Liberia.

To serve until 31 December 1987: Bangladesh, Byelorussian SSR, Germany, Federal Republic of, Netherlands, Trinidad and Tobago, United Kingdom, Yugoslavia.

Chairman: Miodrag Cabric (Yugoslavia).

Vice-Chairmen: Jan Berteling (Netherlands), Anwarul Karim Chowdhury (Bangladesh), Deryck Lance Murray (Trinidad and Tobago).

Rapporteur: Oluseye D. Oduyemi (Nigeria).

On 30 May 1985 (decision 1985/160), the Economic and Social Council nominated the following nine Member States of the United Nations, seven of which were to be elected by the General Assembly, for a three-year term beginning on 1 January 1986 to fill the vacancies occurring on 31 December 1985: Argentina, Benin, Bolivia, Chile, France, Peru, USSR, United States, Zambia. All but Bolivia and Chile were elected by the Assembly on 10 December 1985 (decision 40/312).

Committee on Natural Resources

The Committee on Natural Resources consists of 54 members, elected by the Economic and Social Council for four-year terms in accordance with the geographical distribution of seats in the Council.

The Committee held its ninth session at United Nations Headquarters from 8 to 17 April 1985.

Members:

To serve until 31 December 1986:[a] Algeria, Australia, Bolivia, Burkina Faso, Central African Republic, Czechoslovakia, Denmark, France, German Democratic Republic, Germany, Federal Republic of, Hungary, Italy, Liberia, Mexico, Norway, Pakistan, Philippines, Spain, Thailand, Turkey, Uganda, United States, Yugoslavia, Zimbabwe.

To serve until 31 December 1988:[b] Argentina,[c] Bangladesh, Botswana, Brazil, Burundi, Canada, Chile, China, Colombia, Ecuador, Egypt, Ghana, Greece, India, Japan, Kenya, Libyan Arab Jamahiriya, Malaysia, Morocco, Netherlands, Sudan, Ukrainian SSR, USSR, Uruguay, Venezuela.

[a]Three seats allocated to members from Asian States remained unfilled in 1985.
[b]Two seats allocated to one member each from Latin American States and from Western European and other States remained unfilled in 1985.
[c]Elected on 8 February 1985 (decision 1985/111).

Chairman: Rodolfo del Rosario (Philippines).

Vice-Chairmen: Reinder J. Brolsma (Netherlands), Mary Carrasco (Bolivia), Vaclav Oklestek (Czechoslovakia).

Rapporteur: Philip Maingi Mwanzia (Kenya).

Committee on Negotiations with Intergovernmental Agencies

The Committee on Negotiations with Intergovernmental Agencies met at United Nations Headquarters on 14 and from 18 to 20 November 1985 to negotiate a relationship agreement between the United Nations and UNIDO.

Members:[a] Algeria, Argentina, Bangladesh, Botswana, Brazil, Bulgaria, Colombia, Congo, Ecuador, France, German Democratic Republic, Germany, Federal Republic of, Guinea, India, Japan, Mexico, Morocco, Netherlands, Nigeria, Poland, Somalia, Thailand, USSR, United Kingdom, United States, Venezuela, Yugoslavia, Zaire, Zimbabwe.

[a]Appointed by the President of the Economic and Social Council, as stated in his letter of 24 July 1985 to the Secretary-General.

Chairman: Anwarul Karim Chowdhury (Bangladesh).

Committee on Non-Governmental Organizations

The Committee on Non-Governmental Organizations consists of 19 members, elected by the Economic and Social Council for a four-year term according to a specific pattern of equitable geographical representation.

In 1985, the Committee met at United Nations Headquarters from 11 to 22 March and on 8 May, and at Geneva on 4 July.

Members (until 31 December 1986): Chile, Costa Rica, Cuba, Cyprus, France, Ghana, India, Kenya, Libyan Arab Jamahiriya, Nicaragua, Nigeria, Pakistan, Rwanda, Sweden, Thailand, USSR, United Kingdom, United States, Yugoslavia.

Chairman: Emilia Castro de Barish (Costa Rica).
Vice-Chairman: Alexandros N. Vikis (Cyprus).
Rapporteur: Ashur Fartas (Libyan Arab Jamahiriya).

Expert bodies

Ad Hoc Group of Experts on International Co-operation in Tax Matters

The membership of the *Ad Hoc* Group of Experts on International Co-operation in Tax Matters—to consist of 25 members drawn from 15 developing and 10 developed countries, appointed by the Secretary-General to serve in their individual capacity—remained at 24 in 1985, with one member from a developing country still to be appointed.

The *Ad Hoc* Group, which normally meets biennially, held its third meeting at Geneva from 9 to 20 December 1985.

Members: Maurice Hugh Collins, *Chairman* (United Kingdom); Jean François Court (France); Ton Dekker (Netherlands); Francisco O. N. Dornelles, *Vice-Chairman* (Brazil); Hussein M. El Baroudy (Egypt); Mordecai S. Feinberg (United States); José Ramón Fernández-Pérez (Spain); Antonio H. Figueroa (Argentina); Mayer Gabay (Israel); R. R. Khosla, *Vice-Chairman* (India); Marwan Koudsi (Syrian Arab Republic); Felipe Lamarca (Chile); Daniel Luthi (Switzerland); Mohamed Medaghri-Alaoui (Morocco); Thomas Menck (Federal Republic of Germany); Canute R. Miller (Jamaica); Muhammad Wasim Mirza (Pakistan); Alberto Navarro Rodríguez (Mexico); Isaac O. Oni, *Rapporteur* (Nigeria); Alfred Philipp (Austria); Rainer Söderholm (Finland); Sikuan Sutanto (Indonesia); Tetsuo Takikawa (Japan); André Titty (Cameroon).

Committee for Development Planning

The Committee for Development Planning is composed of 24 experts representing different planning systems. They are appointed by the Economic and Social Council, on nomination by the Secretary-General, to serve in their personal capacity for a term of three years.

The Committee held its resumed twenty-first session at United Nations Headquarters from 20 to 23 April 1985.

Members (until 31 December 1986):[a] Ismail Sabri Abdalla (Egypt); Abdlatif Y. Al-Hamad (Kuwait); Gerassimos D. Arsenis (Greece); Sir Kenneth Berrill (United Kingdom); Bernard T. G. Chidzero (Zimbabwe); Jean-Pierre Cot (France); Hernando de Soto (Peru); Celso Furtado (Brazil); Armin Gutowski (Federal Republic of Germany); Huan Xiang (China); Shinichi Ichimura (Japan); V. N. Kirichenko (USSR); Robert S. McNamara (United States); Joseph Elenga Ngamporo (Congo); G. O. Nwankwo (Nigeria); Jozef Pajestka, *Vice-Chairman* (Poland); I. G. Patel (India); Shridath S. Ramphal, *Chairman* (Guyana); Luis A. Rojo (Spain); Mohammad Sadli (Indonesia); Rehman Sobhan (Bangladesh); Janez Stanovnic (Yugoslavia).

[a]Gerald K. Helleiner (Canada) and P. Göran Ohlin, *Rapporteur* (Sweden) resigned on 19 February and 1 January 1985, respectively; no replacements were appointed in 1985.

Committee of Experts on the Transport of Dangerous Goods

The Committee of Experts on the Transport of Dangerous Goods is composed of experts from countries interested in the international transport of dangerous goods. The experts are made available by their Governments at the request of the Secretary-General. The membership, to be increased to 15 in accordance with a 1975 resolution of the Economic and Social Council,[24] was 10 in 1985. The Committee did not meet during the year.

---

[24]YUN 1975, p. 734, res. 1973(LIX), 30 July 1975.

Members:[a] Canada, France, Germany, Federal Republic of, Italy, Japan, Norway, Poland, USSR, United Kingdom, United States.

[a]Iran, Iraq and Thailand had expressed interest in participating in the Committee's work following the Council's 1975 resolution; however, having been inactive for many years, they are no longer considered members.

The Committee may alter, as required, the composition of its subsidiary bodies. In addition, any Committee member may participate in the work of and vote in those bodies provided such member notify the United Nations Secretariat of the intention to do so.

GROUP OF EXPERTS ON EXPLOSIVES

The Group of Experts on Explosives held its twenty-fifth session at Geneva from 16 to 20 September 1985.

Chairman: R. R. Watson (United Kingdom).

GROUP OF RAPPORTEURS OF THE COMMITTEE OF
EXPERTS ON THE TRANSPORT OF DANGEROUS GOODS

The Group of Rapporteurs of the Committee of Experts on the Transport of Dangerous Goods held its thirty-third session at Geneva from 5 to 16 August 1985.

Chairman: L. Andronov (USSR).

Committee on Crime Prevention and Control

The Committee on Crime Prevention and Control consists of 27 members elected for four-year terms by the Economic and Social Council, according to a specific pattern of equitable geographical representation, from among experts nominated by Member States.

The Committee did not meet in 1985.

Members:

To serve until 31 December 1986: André Bissonnette (Canada), Dusan Cotic (Yugoslavia), Ahmed Mohamed Khalifa (Egypt), A. Y. Kudryavtsev (USSR), Robert Linke (Austria),[a] Manuel López-Rey y Arrojo (Bolivia), Charles Alfred Lunn (Barbados), Jorge Arturo Montero-Castro (Costa Rica), Mphanza Patrick Mvunga (Zambia), Amadou Racine Ba (Mauritania), Simone Andrée Rozes (France), Yoshio Suzuki (Japan), Mervyn Patrick Wijesinha (Sri Lanka), Wu Han (China).

To serve until 31 December 1988: Mohamed Aboulashi (Morocco), David Faulkner (United Kingdom), Ronald L. Gainer (United States), Jozsef Godony (Hungary), Aura Guerra de Villaláz (Panama), A. R. Khandker (Bangladesh), Abdul Meguid Ibrahim Kharbit (Kuwait), Farouk A. Mourad (Saudi Arabia), Bertin Pandi (Central African Republic), Aregba Polo (Togo), Miguel A. Sánchez Méndez (Colombia), Abdel Aziz Abdalla Shiddo (Sudan), Bo Svensson (Sweden).

[a]Died; Ronald Miklau (Austria) was elected by the Economic and Social Council on 30 May 1985 (decision 1985/160) to fill the resultant vacancy.

Committee on Economic, Social and Cultural Rights

On 28 May 1985, the Economic and Social Council decided to change the name of its Sessional Working Group of Governmental Experts on the Implementation of the International Covenant on Economic, Social and Cultural Rights (p. 1411) to Committee on Economic, Social and Cultural Rights.

The Committee was to consist of 18 experts serving in their personal capacity, elected by the Council from among persons nominated by States parties to the Covenant. The experts were to have recognized competence in the field of human rights, with due consideration given to equitable geographical distribution and to the representation of different forms of social and legal systems. Members were to serve for four-year terms, except that at the first election, to be held in 1986, nine were to be chosen by lot to serve for two years.

United Nations Group of Experts on Geographical Names

The United Nations Group of Experts on Geographical Names represents various geographical/linguistic divisions, of which there were 17 in 1985, as follows: Africa Central; Africa East; Africa West; Arabic; Asia East (other than China); Asia South-East and Pacific South-West; Asia South-West (other than Arabic); China; Dutch- and German-speaking; East Central and South-East Europe; India; Latin America; Norden; Romano-Hellenic; Union of Soviet Socialist Republics; United Kingdom; United States of America and Canada.

The Group of Experts did not meet in 1985.

Ad hoc bodies

Ad Hoc Committee on the Preparations for the Public Hearings on the Activities of Transnational Corporations in South Africa and Namibia

The *Ad Hoc* Committee on the Preparations for the Public Hearings on the Activities of Transnational Corporations in South Africa and Namibia, which was to be composed of five States, had four members in 1985.

The *Ad Hoc* Committee met at United Nations Headquarters from 16 to 18 January and on 14 and 15 February 1985, thereby completing its work.

Members: Bangladesh, Cuba, German Democratic Republic, Nigeria.

Chairman/Rapporteur: Chiedu I. Osakwe (Nigeria).

Commission on the Status of Women acting as the Preparatory Body for the World Conference to Review and Appraise the Achievements of the United Nations Decade for Women

The Commission on the Status of Women (p. 1413) acting as the Preparatory Body for the World Conference to Review and Appraise the Achievements of the United Nations Decade for Women (p. 1409) held its third (final) session at Vienna, Austria, from 4 to 13 March and at United Nations Headquarters from 29 April to 7 May 1985.

Chairman: Rosario G. Manalo (Philippines).
Vice-Chairmen: Irene Bwalya Chiwele (Zambia), Dagmar Molkova (Czechoslovakia), Ivan Peñaherrera (Ecuador).
Rapporteur: Helen Ware (Australia).

Intergovernmental Working Group of Experts on International Standards of Accounting and Reporting

The Intergovernmental Working Group of Experts on International Standards of Accounting and Reporting, which reports to the Commission on Transnational Corporations (p. 1415), consists of 34 members, elected for three-year terms by the Economic and Social Council according to a specific pattern of equitable geographical distribution. Each State elected appoints an expert with appropriate experience in accounting and reporting.

The Group held its third session at United Nations Headquarters from 11 to 22 March 1985.

Members:

To serve until 31 December 1985:[a] Algeria, Cyprus, Ecuador, Germany, Federal Republic of, India, Italy, Japan, Morocco, Panama, Saint Lucia, Tunisia, Uganda, United Kingdom, United States.

To serve until 31 December 1987:[b] Barbados, Brazil, Canada, China, Egypt, France, Malaysia, Norway, Pakistan, Spain, Swaziland, Zaire, Switzerland.

[a]The seats allocated to one member from Asian States and two members from Eastern European States remained unfilled in 1985.
[b]The seats allocated to two members from African States, one member from Eastern European States and one member from Latin American States remained unfilled in 1985.

Chairman: Irtiza Husain (Pakistan).
Vice-Chairmen: John Bagnall (Canada), Mohamed Adel El-Safty (Egypt).
Rapporteur: Spyros Christou (Cyprus).

On 26 July 1985 (decision 1985/204), the Economic and Social Council elected the following for a three-year term beginning on 1 January 1986 to fill 8 of the 17 vacancies occurring on 31 December 1985: Cyprus, Germany, Federal Republic of, India, Italy, Japan, Nigeria, United Kingdom, United States. No further elections were held in 1985 to fill the remaining seats, allocated to three members from African States, one member from Asian States, two members from Eastern European States and three members from Latin American States.

Administrative Committee on Co-ordination

The Administrative Committee on Co-ordination held four sessions in 1985: an organizational session at United Nations Headquarters on 11 and 12 February; its first session at Geneva on 22 and 23 April; a special session at Geneva on 4 July; and its second session at United Nations Headquarters on 28 and 29 October.

The membership of ACC, under the chairmanship of the Secretary-General of the United Nations, includes the executive heads of ILO, FAO, UNESCO, WHO, the World Bank, IMF, ICAO, UPU, ITU, WMO, IMO, WIPO, IFAD, IAEA and the secretariat of the Contracting Parties to GATT.

Also take part in the work of ACC are the United Nations Director-General for Development and International Economic Co-operation; the Under-Secretaries-General for International Economic and Social Affairs, for Administration and Management, and for Technical Co-operation for Development; and the executive heads of UNCTAD, UNDP, UNEP, UNFPA, UNHCR, UNICEF, UNIDO, UNITAR, UNRWA and WFP.

ACC has established subsidiary bodies on organizational, administrative and substantive questions.

Other related bodies

Intergovernmental Committee on Science and Technology for Development

The Intergovernmental Committee on Science and Technology for Development (p. 1397) reports annually to the General Assembly through the Economic and Social Council.

International Research and Training Institute for the Advancement of Women (INSTRAW)

The International Research and Training Institute for the Advancement of Women, a body of the United Nations financed through voluntary contributions, functions under the authority of a Board of Trustees.

BOARD OF TRUSTEES

Prior to the General Assembly's endorsement of the INSTRAW statute on 9 April 1985, the Board of Trustees was composed of a President appointed by the Secretary-General; 10 members serving in their individual capacity, appointed by the Economic and Social Council on the nomination of the Secretary-General; and *ex-officio* members. Members served for three-year terms, with a maximum of two terms.

The Board, which reported annually to the Council, held its fifth session at Havana, Cuba, from 28 January to 1 February 1985.

Members (until 30 June 1985):
To serve until 30 June 1985: Gulzar Bano (Pakistan); Ester Boserup (Denmark); Vilma Espín de Castro, *Presiding Officer* (Cuba); Vida Tomsic (Yugoslavia).
To serve until 30 June 1986: Suad Ibrahim Eissa (Sudan); María Lavalle Urbina (Mexico); Helen Arnopoulos Stamiris, *Vice-Presiding Officer* (Greece).
To serve until 30 June 1987: Daniela Colombo (Italy); Zhor Lazrak (Morocco); Achie Sudiarti Luhulima, *Rapporteur* (Indonesia)

President (until 30 June 1985): Delphine Tsanga (Cameroon).

According to the statute of INSTRAW, approved by the Economic and Social Council in 1984[25] and endorsed by the General Assembly on 9 April 1985, the Board of Trustees was to be composed of 11 members serving in their individual capacity, appointed by the Economic and Social Council on the nomination of States; and *ex-officio* members. Members were to serve for three-year terms, with a maximum of two terms. The Board, which was to elect its own officers, including its President, was to report periodically to the Council and where appropriate to the Assembly.

On 30 May 1985 (decision 1985/160), the Economic and Social Council appointed the following five members for a three-year term beginning on 1 July 1985 to fill the vacancies occurring on 30 June and the additional seat: Fabiola Cuvi Ortiz (Ecuador), Ingrid Eide (Norway), Elena Atanassova Lagadinova (Bulgaria), Lin Shangzhen (China), Victoria N. Okobi (Nigeria).

Members (from 1 July 1985):
To serve until 30 June 1986: Suad Ibrahim Eissa (Sudan), María Lavalle Urbina (Mexico), Helen Arnopoulos Stamiris (Greece).

To serve until 30 June 1987: Daniela Colombo (Italy), Zhor Lazrak (Morocco), Achie Sudiarti Luhulima (Indonesia).
To serve until 30 June 1988: Fabiola Cuvi Ortiz (Ecuador), Ingrid Eide (Norway), Elena Atanassova Lagadinova (Bulgaria), Lin Shangzhen (China), Victoria N. Okobi (Nigeria).

Ex-officio members: The Director of the Institute, and representatives of the Secretary-General, each of the regional commissions and the host country (Dominican Republic).
Director of the Institute: Dunja Pastizzi-Ferencic.

Office of the United Nations High Commissioner for Refugees (UNHCR)

The United Nations High Commissioner for Refugees (p. 1399) reports annually to the General Assembly through the Economic and Social Council.

United Nations Capital Development Fund

EXECUTIVE BOARD

The Executive Board of the United Nations Capital Development Fund (p. 1401) reports annually to the General Assembly through the Economic and Social Council.

United Nations Children's Fund (UNICEF)

EXECUTIVE BOARD

The UNICEF Executive Board consists of 41 members elected by the Economic and Social Council from Member States of the United Nations or members of the specialized agencies or of IAEA, for three-year terms.

In 1985, the Executive Board held a series of meetings between 15 and 26 April and (with its composition as of 1 August) organizational meetings on 11 and 14 June, all at United Nations Headquarters.

Members (until 31 July 1985):
To serve until 31 July 1985: Algeria, Bahrain, Bangladesh, Burkina Faso, Central African Republic, Chad, Chile, France, Hungary, Italy, Japan, Madagascar, Mexico, Nepal, Netherlands, Panama, Somalia, Swaziland, USSR, United Kingdom, United States.
To serve until 31 July 1986: Australia, Canada, China, Colombia, Cuba, Finland, Germany, Federal Republic of, Lesotho, Thailand, Yugoslavia.
To serve until 31 July 1987: Belgium, Benin, Bhutan, Denmark, India, Indonesia, Niger, Romania, Switzerland, Venezuela.

Chairman: Richard Manning (Australia).
First Vice-Chairman: Jassim Buallay (Bahrain).
Second Vice-Chairman: Mihaly Simai (Hungary).
Third Vice-Chairman: Bernadette Palle (Burkina Faso).
Fourth Vice-Chairman: Martti Ahtisaari (Finland).

On 30 May 1985 (decision 1985/160), the Economic and Social Council elected the following 21 members for a three-year term beginning on 1 August 1985 to fill the vacancies occurring on 31 July: Argentina, Bangladesh, Brazil, Bulgaria, Chile, Congo, Djibouti, Ethiopia, France, Gabon, Italy, Japan, Mali, Mexico, Netherlands, Oman, Pakistan, Tunisia, USSR, United Kingdom, United States.

Members (from 1 August 1985):
To serve until 31 July 1986: Australia, Canada, China, Colombia, Cuba, Finland, Germany, Federal Republic of, Lesotho, Thailand, Yugoslavia.
To serve until 31 July 1987: Belgium, Benin, Bhutan, Denmark, India, Indonesia, Niger, Romania, Switzerland, Venezuela.
To serve until 31 July 1988: Argentina, Bangladesh, Brazil, Bulgaria, Chile, Congo, Djibouti, Ethiopia, France, Gabon, Italy, Japan, Mali, Mexico, Netherlands, Oman, Pakistan, Tunisia, USSR, United Kingdom, United States.

Chairman: Anwarul Karim Chowdhury (Bangladesh).
First Vice-Chairman: Gaetano Zucconi (Italy).

---

[25]YUN 1984, p. 902, dec. 1984/124, 24 May 1984.

Second Vice-Chairman: Poliana Cristescu (Romania).
Third Vice-Chairman: Berhanu Dinka (Ethiopia).
Fourth Vice-Chairman: Hector Terry Molinert (Cuba).

Executive Director of UNICEF: James P. Grant.

COMMITTEE ON ADMINISTRATION AND FINANCE
The Committee on Administration and Finance is a committee of the whole of the UNICEF Executive Board.

Chairman: Hisami Kurokochi (Japan) (until 31 July), A. P. Maruping (Lesotho) (from 1 August).
Vice-Chairman: A. P. Maruping (Lesotho) (until 31 July), Erik Fiil (Denmark) (from 1 August).

PROGRAMME COMMITTEE
The Programme Committee is a committee of the whole of the UNICEF Executive Board.

Chairman: Anwarul Karim Chowdhury (Bangladesh) (until 31 July), Gabriel Restrepo (Colombia) (from 1 August).
Vice-Chairman: Gabriel Restrepo (Colombia) (until 31 July), Mohammed Said Al-Mohamed (Oman) (from 1 August).

UNICEF/WHO Joint Committee on Health Policy
The UNICEF/WHO Joint Committee on Health Policy consists of: six members of the UNICEF Executive Board, among whom are the chairmen of the Executive Board and the Programme Committee who serve *ex officio;* and six members of the WHO Executive Board.
The Joint Committee, which meets biennially, held its twenty-fifth session at Geneva from 28 to 30 January 1985.

Members:
UNICEF ex-officio members: Anwarul Karim Chowdhury (Bangladesh); Richard Manning, *Chairman* (Australia).
Elected by UNICEF: Dr. John J. Hutchings, *Rapporteur* (United States); R. P. Khosla (India); Anna Liisa Korhonen (Finland); Hector Terry Molinert (Cuba).
Appointed by WHO: M. K. Bah (Guinea); Dr. J. M. Borgoño, *Rapporteur* (Chile); Dr. A. A. El Gamal (Egypt); J. F. Isakov (USSR); Dr. D. N. Regmi (Nepal); Dr. G. Rifai (Syrian Arab Republic).

United Nations Conference on Trade and Development (UNCTAD)

TRADE AND DEVELOPMENT BOARD
The Trade and Development Board (p. 1401) reports to UNCTAD; it also reports annually to the General Assembly through the Economic and Social Council.

United Nations Development Programme (UNDP)

GOVERNING COUNCIL
The Governing Council of UNDP consists of 48 members, elected by the Economic and Social Council from Member States of the United Nations or members of the specialized agencies or of IAEA. Twenty-seven seats are allocated to developing countries as follows: 11 to African countries, 9 to Asian countries and Yugoslavia, and 7 to Latin American countries. Twenty-one seats are allocated to economically more advanced countries as follows: 17 to Western European and other countries, and 4 to Eastern European countries. The term of office is three years, one third of the members being elected each year.
In 1985, the Governing Council held, at United Nations Headquarters, an organizational meeting on 19 and 22 February, a special meeting on preparations for the fourth programming cycle from 19 to 22 February, and its thirty-second session from 3 to 29 June.

Members:
To serve until 31 December 1985: Australia, Belgium, Brazil, Canada, Central African Republic, Chad, Denmark, Finland, France, German Democratic Republic, Lesotho, Mauritania, Nepal, Philippines, United Republic of Tanzania, Yugoslavia.
To serve until 31 December 1986: Argentina, Bahrain, Bangladesh, Ethiopia, Gambia, Germany, Federal Republic of, Hungary, India, Jamaica, Netherlands, Norway, Poland, Switzerland, Togo, Turkey, Venezuela.

To serve until 31 December 1987: Austria, Benin, Chile, China, Cuba, Italy, Japan, Mexico, Pakistan, Saudi Arabia, Swaziland, Sweden, Tunisia, USSR, United Kingdom, United States.

President: Wlodzimierz Natorf (Poland).
Vice-Presidents: Lloyd M. H. Barnett (Jamaica), Thabo Makeka (Lesotho), C. Richard Mann (Canada), M. S. Mukherjee (India).

On 30 May 1985 (decision 1985/160), the Economic and Social Council elected the following 16 members for a three-year term beginning on 1 January 1986 to fill the vacancies occurring on 31 December 1985: Belgium, Brazil, Bulgaria, Burundi, Cameroon, Canada, Cape Verde, Denmark, France, Indonesia, Kuwait, Malawi, Mauritius, New Zealand, Republic of Korea, Spain.

Administrator of UNDP: F. Bradford Morse.
Associate Administrator: G. Arthur Brown.

BUDGETARY AND FINANCE COMMITTEE
The Budgetary and Finance Committee, a committee of the whole, held a series of meetings at United Nations Headquarters between 3 and 29 June 1985.

Chairman: C. Richard Mann (Canada).
Rapporteur: D. Mondal (Bangladesh).

COMMITTEE OF THE WHOLE
In accordance with its 1983 decision,[26] the Governing Council resolved itself into a Committee of the Whole and held meetings between 3 and 7 June 1985 to consider matters related to programme management. The President of the Governing Council acted as presiding officer.

United Nations Environment Programme (UNEP)

GOVERNING COUNCIL
The Governing Council of UNEP (p. 1404) reports to the General Assembly through the Economic and Social Council.

United Nations Industrial Development Organization (UNIDO)

INDUSTRIAL DEVELOPMENT BOARD
The Industrial Development Board (p. 1405), the principal organ of UNIDO, reports annually to the General Assembly through the Economic and Social Council.

United Nations Institute for Training and Research (UNITAR)
The Executive Director of UNITAR (p. 1406) reports to the General Assembly and, as appropriate, to the Economic and Social Council.

United Nations Research Institute for Social Development (UNRISD)

BOARD OF DIRECTORS
The Board of Directors of UNRISD reports to the Economic and Social Council through the Commission for Social Development.
The Board consists of:

The Chairman, appointed by the Secretary-General: Paul-Marc Henry (France);
Seven members, nominated by the Commission for Social Development and confirmed by the Economic and Social Council (to serve until 30 June 1985):[a] Gustavo Esteva (Mexico), Vera Nyitrai (Hungary), Achola Pala Okeyo (Kenya), K. N. Raj (India), Eugene B. Skolnikoff (United States); (to serve until 30 June 1987): Ulf Hannerz (Sweden);
Eight other members, as follows: a representative of the Secretary-General, the Director of the Latin American Institute for Economic and Social Planning, the Director of the Asian and Pacific Development Centre, the Director of the African Institute for Economic Development and Planning, the Executive Secretary of ESCWA, the

---

[26]YUN 1983, p. 1365.

Director of UNRISD *(ex officio)*, and the representatives of two of the following specialized agencies appointed as members and observers in annual rotation: ILO and FAO (members); UNESCO and WHO (observers).

[a]A seat left vacant in 1984 by the appointment of Paul-Marc Henry (France) as Chairman remained unfilled.

On 30 May 1985 (decision 1985/160), the Economic and Social Council confirmed the nomination by the Commission for Social Development of the following four members for terms beginning on 1 July to fill the vacancies occurring on 30 June: for a four-year term, Ismail Sabri Abdalla (Egypt), Louis Emerij (Netherlands), Sally Weaver (Canada); for a two-year term, Gustavo Esteva (Mexico). The Council also nominated Sartaj Aziz (Pakistan) and Vida Cok (Yugoslavia) for a four-year term beginning on 1 July 1985.

Director of the Institute: Enrique Oteiza.

United Nations Special Fund

BOARD OF GOVERNORS
The Board of Governors of the United Nations Special Fund (p. 1407) reports annually to the General Assembly through the Economic and Social Council.

United Nations University

COUNCIL OF THE UNITED NATIONS UNIVERSITY
The Council of the United Nations University (p. 1408), the governing board of the University, reports annually to the General Assembly, to the Economic and Social Council and to the UNESCO Executive Board through the Secretary-General and the UNESCO Director-General.

World Food Council

The World Food Council (p. 1408), an organ of the United Nations at the ministerial or plenipotentiary level, reports to the General Assembly through the Economic and Social Council.

World Food Programme

COMMITTEE ON FOOD AID POLICIES AND PROGRAMMES
The Committee on Food Aid Policies and Programmes, the governing body of WFP, consists of 30 members, of which 15 are elected by the Economic and Social Council and 15 by the FAO Council, from Member States of the United Nations or from members of FAO. Members serve for three-year terms.

The Committee reports annually to the Economic and Social Council, the FAO Council and the World Food Council.

The Committee held two sessions during 1985, at Rome, Italy: its nineteenth from 20 to 31 May; and its twentieth from 30 September to 10 October.

Members:
To serve until 31 December 1985:
   Elected by Economic and Social Council: Burkina Faso, Colombia, Mexico, Sweden, United Kingdom.
   Elected by FAO Council: Cuba, France, Germany, Federal Republic of, Nigeria, Zambia.
To serve until 31 December 1986:
   Elected by Economic and Social Council: Egypt *(First Vice-Chairman),* Hungary, India, Italy, Norway *(Chairman).*
   Elected by FAO Council: Australia, Bangladesh, Canada, Saudi Arabia, United States.
To serve until 31 December 1987:
   Elected by Economic and Social Council: Belgium *(Second Vice-Chairman),* Denmark, Japan, Lesotho, Pakistan.
   Elected by FAO Council: Brazil, Congo, Kenya, Netherlands, Thailand.

On 30 May 1985 (decision 1985/160), the Economic and Social Council elected Argentina, Cape Verde, Colombia, Finland and the United Kingdom; and, on 28 November, the FAO Council elected Ethiopia, France, the Federal Republic of Germany, Sao Tome and Principe, and Venezuela, all for a three-year term beginning on 1 January 1986 to fill the vacancies occurring on 31 December 1985.

Executive Director of WFP: James Charles Ingram.
Deputy Executive Director: Salahuddin Ahmed.

Conference

Third United Nations Regional Cartographic Conference for the Americas

The Third United Nations Regional Cartographic Conference for the Americas was held at United Nations Headquarters from 19 February to 1 March 1985. Participating were the following 45 States:

Argentina, Bahamas, Benin, Brazil, Brunei Darussalam, Burma, Canada, Central African Republic, Chile, China, Colombia, Costa Rica, Cuba, Ecuador, Equatorial Guinea, Ethiopia, Finland, France, Germany, Federal Republic of, Ghana, Guatemala, India, Jamaica, Japan, Jordan, Kuwait, Libyan Arab Jamahiriya, Malaysia, Mexico, Nepal, Netherlands, Nigeria, Norway, Panama, Peru, Poland, Republic of Korea, Saint Lucia, Sweden, Uganda, USSR, United Kingdom, United States, Uruguay, Venezuela.

President: César Durán Abad (Ecuador).
First Vice-President: Giampiero Bellucci Casunatti (Mexico).
Second Vice-President: Luis Polanco Gallardo (Chile).
Rapporteur: Wayne Miller (United States).

Chairmen of technical committees:
   Committee I: Richard Groot (Canada).
   Committee II: Giampiero Bellucci Casunatti (Mexico).
   Committee III: Paulo César Teixeira Trino (Brazil).
   Committee IV: Rupert B. Southard (United States).

Trusteeship Council

Article 86 of the United Nations Charter lays down that the Trusteeship Council shall consist of the following:

Members of the United Nations administering Trust Territories;
Permanent members of the Security Council which do not administer Trust Territories;
As many other members elected for a three-year term by the General Assembly as will ensure that the membership of the Council is equally divided between United Nations Members which administer Trust Territories and those which do not.[a]

[a]During 1985, only one Member of the United Nations was an administering member of the Trusteeship Council, while four permanent members of the Security Council continued as non-administering members. Therefore, the parity called for by Article 86 of the Charter was not maintained.

MEMBERS
Member administering a Trust Territory: United States.
Non-administering members: China, France, USSR, United Kingdom.

SESSION
Fifty-second session: United Nations Headquarters, 13 May–11 July 1985.

OFFICERS
President: Peter M. Maxey (United Kingdom).
Vice-President: Laurent Rapin (France).

United Nations Visiting Mission to the Trust Territory of the Pacific Islands, 1985

Members: André Rocher (France); Sir Richard Stratton, *Chairman* (United Kingdom).

International Court of Justice

Judges of the Court

The International Court of Justice consists of 15 Judges elected for nine-year terms by the General Assembly and the Security Council.

The following were the Judges of the Court serving in 1985, listed in the order of precedence:

Judge	Country of nationality	End of term[a]
Nagendra Singh, *President*[b]	India	1991
Guy Ladreit de Lacharrière, *Vice-President*[b]	France	1991
Manfred Lachs	Poland	1994
Platon D. Morozov[c]	USSR	1988
José María Ruda	Argentina	1991
Taslim Olawale Elias	Nigeria	1994
Shigeru Oda	Japan	1994
Roberto Ago	Italy	1988
José Sette Câmara	Brazil	1988
Stephen M. Schwebel	United States	1988
Sir Robert Y. Jennings	United Kingdom	1991
Kéba Mbaye	Senegal	1991
Mohammed Bedjaoui	Algeria	1988
Ni Zhengyu	China	1994
Jens Evensen	Norway	1994

[a]Term expires on 5 February of the year indicated.
[b]Elected by the Court on 14 February 1985 for a three-year term.
[c]Resigned on 23 August 1985; Nikolai K. Tarasov (USSR) was elected on 9 December by the General Assembly (decision 40/309) and the Security Council (resolution 570(1985) of 12 September 1985 and decision of 9 December) to fill the resultant vacancy.

Registrar: Santiago Torres Bernárdez.
Deputy Registrar: Eduardo Valencia-Ospina.

Chamber formed in the case concerning the
Frontier Dispute (Burkina Faso/Mali)

On 3 April 1985, in accordance with Article 26, paragraph 2, of its Statute, the Court constituted a Chamber to deal with the case concerning the *Frontier Dispute (Burkina Faso/Mali)*.

Members: Mohammed Bedjaoui *(President)*, Manfred Lachs, José María Ruda.
Ad hoc members:[a] F. Luchaire, G. Abi-Saab.

[a]Appointed by Burkina Faso and Mali, respectively, in accordance with Article 31 of the Court's Statute.

Chamber of Summary Procedure
(as constituted by the Court on 14 February 1985)

Members: Nagendra Singh *(ex officio)*, Guy Ladreit de Lacharrière *(ex officio)*, José María Ruda, Kéba Mbaye, Ni Zhengyu.
Substitute members: Sir Robert Y. Jennings, Jens Evensen.

Parties to the Court's Statute

All Members of the United Nations are *ipso facto* parties to the Statute of the International Court of Justice. Also parties to it are the following non-members: Liechtenstein, San Marino, Switzerland.

States accepting the compulsory jurisdiction of the Court

Declarations made by the following States, a number with reservations, accepting the Court's compulsory jurisdiction (or made under the Statute of the Permanent Court of International Justice and deemed to be an acceptance of the jurisdiction of the International Court) were in force at the end of 1985:[a]

Australia, Austria, Barbados, Belgium, Botswana, Canada, Colombia, Costa Rica, Democratic Kampuchea, Denmark, Dominican Republic, Egypt, El Salvador, Finland, Gambia, Haiti, Honduras, India, Japan, Kenya, Liberia, Liechtenstein, Luxembourg, Malawi, Malta, Mauritius, Mexico, Netherlands, New Zealand, Nicaragua, Nigeria, Norway, Pakistan, Panama, Philippines, Portugal, Senegal,[b] Somalia, Sudan, Swaziland, Sweden, Switzerland, Togo, Uganda, United Kingdom, Uruguay.

[a]The United States and Israel withdrew their declarations of acceptance on 8 October and 21 November 1985, respectively.
[b]Filed its declaration of acceptance on 3 May 1985.

United Nations organs and specialized and related agencies authorized to request advisory opinions from the Court

Authorized by the United Nations Charter to request opinions on any legal question: General Assembly, Security Council.

Authorized by the General Assembly in accordance with the Charter to request opinions on legal questions arising within the scope of their activities: Economic and Social Council, Trusteeship Council, Interim Committee of the General Assembly, Committee on Applications for Review of Administrative Tribunal Judgements, ILO, FAO, UNESCO, WHO, World Bank, IFC, IDA, IMF, ICAO, ITU, WMO, IMO, WIPO, IFAD, IAEA.

Committees of the Court

BUDGETARY AND ADMINISTRATIVE COMMITTEE
Members: Nagendra Singh *(ex officio)*, Guy Ladreit de Lacharrière *(ex officio)*, Taslim Olawale Elias, José Sette Câmara, Stephen M. Schwebel.

COMMITTEE ON RELATIONS
Members: Platon D. Morozov (until 23 August 1985), Mohammed Bedjaoui, Jens Evensen.

LIBRARY COMMITTEE
Members: José María Ruda, Shigeru Oda, Sir Robert Y. Jennings, Ni Zhengyu.

RULES COMMITTEE
Members: Manfred Lachs, Platon D. Morozov (until 23 August 1985), Shigeru Oda, Roberto Ago, José Sette Câmara, Sir Robert Y. Jennings, Kéba Mbaye.

Other United Nations-related bodies

The following bodies are not subsidiary to any principal organ of the United Nations but were established by an international treaty instrument or arrangement sponsored by the United Nations and are thus related to the Organization and its work. These bodies, often referred to as "treaty organs", are serviced by the United Nations Secretariat and may be financed in part or wholly from the Organization's regular budget, as authorized by the General Assembly, to which most of them report annually.

Committee on the Elimination of Discrimination against Women

The Committee on the Elimination of Discrimination against Women was established under the Convention on the Elimination of All Forms of Discrimination against Women.[27] It consists of 23 experts elected

by the States parties to the Convention to serve in their personal capacity, with due regard for equitable geographical distribution and for representation of the different forms of civilization and principal legal systems. Members serve for four-year terms.

The Committee, which reports annually to the General Assembly through the Economic and Social Council, held its fourth session at Vienna, Austria, from 21 January to 1 February 1985.

Members:
To serve until 15 April 1986: A. P. Biryukova (USSR); Irene R. Cortes, *Vice-Chairman* (Philippines); Farida Abou El-Fetouh (Egypt); Guan

[27]YUN 1979, p. 898, GA res. 34/180, annex, article 17, 18 Dec. 1979.

Minqian (China); Luvsandanzangyn Ider (Mongolia); Zagorka Ilic (Yugoslavia); Vinitha Jayasinghe (Sri Lanka); Raquel Macedo de Sheppard (Uruguay); Landrada Mukayiranga (Rwanda); Vesselina Peytcheva (Bulgaria); Maria Regent-Lechowicz (Poland); Lucy Smith, *Vice-Chairman* (Norway).

To serve until 15 April 1988: Desirée P. Bernard, *Chairman* (Guyana); Marie Caron (Canada); Elizabeth Evatt (Australia); Aída González Martínez (Mexico); Chryssanthi Laiou-Antoniou (Greece); Alma Montenegro de Fletcher (Panama); Maria Margarida de Rego da Costa Salema Moura Ribeiro (Portugal); Edith Oeser, *Rapporteur* (German Democratic Republic); Kongit Sinegiorgis, *Vice-Chairman* (Ethiopia); Esther Véliz Díaz de Villalvilla (Cuba); Margareta Wadstein (Sweden).

Committee on the Elimination of Racial Discrimination

The Committee on the Elimination of Racial Discrimination was established under the International Convention on the Elimination of All Forms of Racial Discrimination.[28] It consists of 18 experts elected by the States parties to the Convention to serve in their personal capacity, with due regard for equitable geographical distribution and for representation of the different forms of civilization and principal legal systems. Members serve for four-year terms.

The Committee, which reports annually to the General Assembly through the Secretary-General, held two sessions in 1985: its thirty-first at United Nations Headquarters from 4 to 22 March; and its thirty-second at Geneva from 5 to 23 August.

Members:

To serve until 19 January 1986: Jean-Marie Apiou (Burkina Faso); Oladapo Olusola Fafowora (Nigeria);[a] Abdel Moneim M. Ghoneim (Egypt); George O. Lamptey, *Vice-Chairman* (Ghana); Karl Josef Partsch, *Rapporteur* (Federal Republic of Germany); Emmanuel J. Roukounas (Greece); Agha Shahi (Pakistan); Michael E. Sherifis, *Vice-Chairman* (Cyprus); Luis Valencia Rodríguez, *Chairman* (Ecuador).

To serve until 19 January 1988: Nikola Cicanovic (Yugoslavia); John J. Cremona (Malta); Nicolás de Pierola y Balta (Peru); Matey Karasimeonov, *Vice-Chairman* (Bulgaria); Kjell Oberg (Sweden); Shanti Sadiq Ali (India); Song Shuhua (China); G. B. Starushenko (USSR); Mario Jorge Yutzis (Argentina).

[a]Resigned by a letter of 27 June 1985; the appointment of Hamzat Ahmadu (Nigeria) was approved by the Committee on 5 August to fill the resultant vacancy.

Conference on Disarmament

The Conference on Disarmament, the multilateral negotiating forum on disarmament, reports annually to the General Assembly and is serviced by the United Nations Secretariat. It was composed of 40 members in 1985.

The Conference met at Geneva in 1985 from 5 February to 23 April and from 11 June to 30 August.

Members: Algeria, Argentina, Australia, Belgium, Brazil, Bulgaria, Burma, Canada, China, Cuba, Czechoslovakia, Egypt, Ethiopia, France, German Democratic Republic, Germany, Federal Republic of, Hungary, India, Indonesia, Iran, Italy, Japan, Kenya, Mexico, Mongolia, Morocco, Netherlands, Nigeria, Pakistan, Peru, Poland, Romania, Sri Lanka, Sweden, USSR, United Kingdom, United States, Venezuela, Yugoslavia, Zaire.

The presidency, which rotates in English alphabetical order among the members, was held by the following in 1985: February, United States; March, Venezuela; April and the recess between the first and second parts of the 1985 session, Yugoslavia; June, Zaire; July, Algeria; August and the recess until the 1986 session, Argentina.

Human Rights Committee

The Human Rights Committee was established under the International Covenant on Civil and Political Rights.[29] It consists of 18 experts elected by the States parties to the Covenant to serve in their personal capacity for four-year terms.

The Committee, which reports annually to the General Assembly through the Economic and Social Council, held three sessions in 1985: its twenty-fourth at United Nations Headquarters from 25 March to

12 April; its twenty-fifth at Geneva from 8 to 26 July; and its twenty-sixth at Geneva from 21 October to 8 November.

Members:

To serve until 31 December 1986: Néjib Bouziri (Tunisia); Joseph A. L. Cooray (Sri Lanka); Vojin Dimitrijevic (Yugoslavia); Roger Errera (France); Bernhard Graefrath, *Rapporteur* (German Democratic Republic); Birame Ndiaye, *Vice-Chairman* (Senegal); Torkel Opsahl (Norway); Julio Prado Vallejo, *Vice-Chairman* (Ecuador); Christian Tomuschat, *Vice-Chairman* (Federal Republic of Germany).

To serve until 31 December 1988: Andrés Aguilar (Venezuela); Rosalyn Higgins (United Kingdom); Rajsoomer Lallah (Mauritius); Andreas V. Mavrommatis, *Chairman* (Cyprus); A. P. Movchan (USSR); Fausto Pocar (Italy); Alejandro Serrano Caldera (Nicaragua); S. Amos Wako (Kenya); Adam Zielinski (Poland).

International Narcotics Control Board (INCB)

The International Narcotics Control Board, established under the Single Convention on Narcotic Drugs, 1961, as amended by the 1972 Protocol, consists of 13 members, elected by the Economic and Social Council for five-year terms, three from candidates nominated by WHO and 10 from candidates nominated by Members of the United Nations and parties to the Single Convention.

The Board held two sessions in 1985, at Vienna, Austria: its thirty-seventh from 13 to 24 May; and its thirty-eighth from 8 to 25 October.

Members:

To serve until 1 March 1987: Dr. Ramón de la Fuente Muñiz (Mexico);[a] Betty C. Gough, *President* (United States); S. Oguz Kayaalp (Turkey)[a,b]; Paul Reuter (France); Dr. Bror Anders Rexed (Sweden); Adolf-Heinrich von Arnim (Federal Republic of Germany); Sir Edward Williams, *Rapporteur* (Australia).

To serve until 1 March 1990: Sahibzada Raoof Ali Khan (Pakistan); Dr. Cai Zhi-ji (China); Dr. John C. Ebie, *First Vice-President* (Nigeria);[a] Dr. Diego Garcés-Giraldo (Colombia); Ben J. A. Huyghe-Braeckmans (Belgium); Dr. Mohsen Kchouk, *Second Vice-President* (Tunisia).

[a]Elected from candidates nominated by WHO.
[b]Elected on 8 February 1985 (decision 1985/111) to fill a vacancy created in 1984.

Preparatory Commission for the International Sea-Bed Authority and for the International Tribunal for the Law of the Sea

The Preparatory Commission for the International Sea-Bed Authority and for the International Tribunal for the Law of the Sea was established by the Third United Nations Conference on the Law of the Sea. It consists of States, Namibia (represented by the United Nations Council for Namibia), self-governing associated States, territories enjoying full internal self-government and international organizations which have signed or acceded to the United Nations Convention on the Law of the Sea. As of 31 December 1985, the Commission had 159 members.

In 1985, the Commission held its third session at Kingston, Jamaica, from 11 March to 4 April and meetings at Geneva from 12 August to 4 September.

Members: Afghanistan, Algeria, Angola, Antigua and Barbuda, Argentina, Australia, Austria, Bahamas, Bahrain, Bangladesh, Barbados, Belgium, Belize, Benin, Bhutan, Bolivia, Botswana, Brazil, Brunei Darussalam, Bulgaria, Burkina Faso, Burma, Burundi, Byelorussian SSR, Cameroon, Canada, Cape Verde, Central African Republic, Chad, Chile, China, Colombia, Comoros, Congo, Cook Islands, Costa Rica, Cuba, Cyprus, Czechoslovakia, Democratic Kampuchea, Democratic People's Republic of Korea, Democratic Yemen, Denmark, Djibouti, Dominica, Dominican Republic, Egypt, El Salvador, Equatorial Guinea, Ethiopia, European Economic Community, Fiji, Finland, France, Gabon, Gambia, German Democratic Republic, Ghana, Greece, Grenada, Guatemala, Guinea, Guinea-Bissau, Guyana, Haiti, Honduras, Hungary, Iceland, India, Indonesia, Iran, Iraq, Ireland, Italy, Ivory Coast, Jamaica, Japan, Kenya, Kuwait, Lao People's Democratic Republic, Lebanon, Lesotho, Liberia, Libyan

---

[28]YUN 1965, p. 443, GA res. 2106 A (XX), annex, article 8, 21 Dec. 1965.
[29]YUN 1966, p. 427, GA res. 2200 A (XXI), annex, part IV, 16 Dec. 1966.

Arab Jamahiriya, Liechtenstein, Luxembourg, Madagascar, Malawi, Malaysia, Maldives, Mali, Malta, Mauritania, Mauritius, Mexico, Monaco, Mongolia, Morocco, Mozambique, Namibia (United Nations Council for), Nauru, Nepal, Netherlands, New Zealand, Nicaragua, Niger, Nigeria, Niue, Norway, Oman, Pakistan, Panama, Papua New Guinea, Paraguay, Philippines, Poland, Portugal, Qatar, Republic of Korea, Romania, Rwanda, Saint Christopher and Nevis, Saint Lucia, Saint Vincent and the Grenadines, Samoa, Sao Tome and Principe, Saudi Arabia, Senegal, Seychelles, Sierra Leone, Singapore, Solomon Islands, Somalia, South Africa, Spain, Sri Lanka, Sudan, Suriname, Swaziland, Sweden, Switzerland, Thailand, Togo, Trinidad and Tobago, Tunisia, Tuvalu, Uganda, Ukrainian SSR, USSR, United Arab Emirates, United Republic of Tanzania, Uruguay, Vanuatu, Viet Nam, Yemen, Yugoslavia, Zaire, Zambia, Zimbabwe.

Chairman: Joseph S. Warioba (United Republic of Tanzania).
Vice-Chairmen: Algeria, Australia, Brazil, Cameroon, Chile, China, France, India, Iraq, Japan, Liberia, Nigeria, Sri Lanka, USSR.
Rapporteur-General: Kenneth O. Rattray (Jamaica).

CREDENTIALS COMMITTEE
Members: Austria, China, Colombia, Costa Rica, Hungary, Ireland, Ivory Coast, Japan, Somalia.
Chairman: Karl Wolf (Austria).

GENERAL COMMITTEE
The General Committee consists of the Commission's Chairman, the 14 Vice-Chairmen, the Rapporteur-General and the 20 officers of the four Special Commissions.

SPECIAL COMMISSIONS
The four Special Commissions are each composed of all the members of the Commission.

Special Commission 1 (on the problem of land-based producers)
Chairman: Hasjim Djalal (Indonesia).
Vice-Chairmen: Austria, Cuba, Romania, Zambia.

Special Commission 2 (on the Enterprise)
Chairman: Lennox Ballah (Trinidad and Tobago).
Vice-Chairmen: Canada, Mongolia, Senegal, Yugoslavia.

Special Commission 3 (on the mining code)
Chairman: Hans H. M. Sondaal (Netherlands).
Vice-Chairmen: Gabon, Mexico, Pakistan, Poland.

Special Commission 4 (on the International Tribunal for the Law of the Sea)
Chairman: Günter Goerner (German Democratic Republic).
Vice-Chairmen: Colombia, Greece, Philippines, Sudan.

Principal members of the United Nations Secretariat

(as at 31 December 1985)

Secretariat

The Secretary-General: Javier Pérez de Cuéllar

Executive Office of the Secretary-General
Under-Secretary-General, Chef de Cabinet: Virendra Dayal

Office of the Director-General for Development and International Economic Co-operation
Director-General: Jean L. Ripert

Office of the Under-Secretaries-General for Special Political Affairs
Under-Secretaries-General: Diego Cordovez, Brian E. Urquhart
Assistant Secretary-General: Fou-Tchin Liu

Office for Special Political Questions
Under-Secretary-General, Co-ordinator, Special Economic Assistance Programmes: Abdulrahim Abby Farah

Office of the Under-Secretary-General for Political and General Assembly Affairs
Under-Secretary-General: William B. Buffum
Assistant Secretary-General in charge of preparations for the fortieth anniversary of the United Nations: Robert G. Muller

Office of Secretariat Services for Economic and Social Matters
Assistant Secretary-General: Sotirios Mousouris

Office for Field Operational and External Support Activities
Assistant Secretary-General: James O. C. Jonah

Office of Legal Affairs
Under-Secretary-General, the Legal Counsel: Carl-August Fleischhauer

Department of Political and Security Council Affairs
Under-Secretary-General: Viacheslav A. Ustinov
Assistant Secretary-General, Centre against Apartheid: Iqbal A. Akhund

Department of Political Affairs, Trusteeship and Decolonization
Under-Secretary-General: Rafeeuddin Ahmed
Assistant Secretary-General: Najmuddine S. Rifai

Department for Disarmament Affairs
Under-Secretary-General: Jan Martenson

Department of International Economic and Social Affairs
Under-Secretary-General: Shuaib Uthman Yolah
Assistant Secretary-General for Development Research and Policy Analysis: P. Göran Ohlin
Assistant Secretary-General for Programme Planning and Co-ordination: Luis Maria Gomez
Assistant Secretary-General for Social Development and Humanitarian Affairs: Leticia R. Shahani
Assistant Secretary-General for Special Assignments: Vladimir S. Pozharski

Department of Technical Co-operation for Development
Under-Secretary-General: Xie Qimei
Assistant Secretary-General: Margaret Joan Anstee

Economic and Social Commission for Asia and the Pacific
Under-Secretary-General, Executive Secretary: Shah A. M. S. Kibria

Economic and Social Commission for Western Asia
Under-Secretary-General, Executive Secretary: Mohammed Said Nabulsi

Economic Commission for Africa
Under-Secretary-General, Executive Secretary: Adebayo Adedeji

Economic Commission for Europe
Under-Secretary-General, Executive Secretary: Klaus Aksel Sahlgren

Economic Commission for Latin America and the Caribbean
Under-Secretary-General, Executive Secretary: Norberto Gonzalez

Centre for Science and Technology for Development
Assistant Secretary-General, Executive Director: Amilcar F. Ferrari

United Nations Centre for Human Settlements
Under-Secretary-General, Executive Director: Arcot Ramachandran
Assistant Secretary-General, Deputy Administrator: Sumihiro Kuyama

United Nations Centre on Transnational Corporations
Assistant Secretary-General, Executive Director: Peter Hansen

Department of Administration and Management
Under-Secretary-General: Patricio Ruedas

OFFICE OF FINANCIAL SERVICES
Assistant Secretary-General, Controller: J. Richard Foran

OFFICE OF PERSONNEL SERVICES
Assistant Secretary-General: Louis-Pascal Nègre
Assistant Secretary-General, Co-ordinator for the Improvement of the Status of Women in the Secretariat: Mercedes Pulido de Briceño

OFFICE OF GENERAL SERVICES
Assistant Secretary-General: Alice Weil

Department of Conference Services
Under-Secretary-General for Conference Services and Special Assignments: Eugeniusz Wyzner

Department of Public Information
Under-Secretary-General: Yasushi Akashi

United Nations Office at Geneva
Under-Secretary-General, Director-General of the United Nations Office at Geneva: Erik Suy
Assistant Secretary-General, Personal Representative of the Secretary-General, Secretary-General of the Conference on Disarmament: Miljan Komatina

Centre for Human Rights
Assistant Secretary-General: Kurt Herndl

United Nations Office at Vienna
Under-Secretary-General, Director-General of the United Nations Office at Vienna: Mowaffak Allaf

International Court of Justice Registry
Assistant Secretary-General, Registrar: Santiago Torres Bernárdez

Secretariats of subsidiary organs, special representatives and other related bodies

International Trade Centre UNCTAD/GATT
Assistant Secretary-General, Executive Director: Goran M. Engblom

Office of the Special Representative of the Secretary-General for Co-ordinating Kampuchean Humanitarian Assistance Programmes
Under-Secretary-General, Senior Adviser to the Secretary-General: Sir Robert Jackson
Assistant Secretary-General, Special Representative of the Secretary-General: Tatsuro Kunugi

Office of the Special Representative of the Secretary-General for Emergency Operations in Ethiopia
Assistant Secretary-General, Special Representative of the Secretary-General: Michael Priestley

Office of the Special Representative of the Secretary-General for Humanitarian Affairs in South-East Asia
Under-Secretary-General, Special Representative of the Secretary-General: Rafeeuddin Ahmed

Office of the Special Representative of the Secretary-General for Namibia
Under-Secretary-General, Special Representative of the Secretary-General: Martti Ahtisaari

Office of the Special Representative of the Secretary-General for the Law of the Sea
Under-Secretary-General, Special Representative of the Secretary-General: Satya N. Nandan

Office of the Special Representative of the Secretary-General for United Nations Emergency Operations in the Sudan
Special Representative of the Secretary-General: Winston Prattley

Office of the United Nations Commissioner for Namibia
Assistant Secretary-General, Commissioner for Namibia: Brajesh Chandra Mishra

Office of the United Nations Disaster Relief Co-ordinator
Under-Secretary-General, Disaster Relief Co-ordinator: M'Hamed Essaafi

Office of the United Nations High Commissioner for Refugees
Under-Secretary-General, High Commissioner: Poul Hartling
Assistant Secretary-General, Deputy High Commissioner: William Richard Smyser

United Nations Children's Fund
Under-Secretary-General, Executive Director: James P. Grant
Assistant Secretary-General, Deputy Executive Director, Operations: Karl-Eric Knutsson
Assistant Secretary-General, Deputy Executive Director, Programmes: Richard Jolly
Assistant Secretary-General, Deputy Executive Director for External Relations: Varindra T. Vittachi

United Nations Conference for the Promotion of International Co-operation in the Peaceful Uses of Nuclear Energy
Assistant Secretary-General, Secretary-General of the Conference: Amrik S. Mehta

United Nations Conference on Trade and Development
Assistant Secretary-General, Deputy Secretary-General of the Conference, Officer-in-Charge: Alister McIntyre
Assistant Secretary-General, Deputy Secretary-General of the Conference: Yves Berthelot
Assistant Secretary-General, Assistant Secretary-General of the Conference: Johannes Pronk

United Nations Development Programme
Administrator: F. Bradford Morse
Associate Administrator: G. Arthur Brown
Assistant Administrator, Bureau for Finance and Administration: Pierre Vinde
Assistant Administrator, Bureau for Special Activities: Paul Thyness
Assistant Administrator and Director, Bureau for Programme Policy and Evaluation: Horst P. Wiesebach
Executive Director, United Nations Fund for Population Activities: Rafael M. Salas
Deputy Executive Director, United Nations Fund for Population Activities: Heino E. Wittrin
Assistant Executive Director, United Nations Fund for Population Activities: Nafis I. Sadik
Assistant Administrator and Regional Director, Regional Bureau for Africa: Pierre-Claver Damiba
Assistant Administrator and Regional Director, Regional Bureau for Arab States: Mustapha Zaanouni
Assistant Administrator and Regional Director, Regional Bureau for Asia and the Pacific: Andrew J. Joseph
Assistant Administrator and Regional Director, Regional Bureau for Latin America and the Caribbean: Hugo Navajas-Mogro
Assistant Administrator and Director, European Office, Geneva: Aldo Romano Ajello

United Nations Disengagement Observer Force
Assistant Secretary-General, Force Commander: Major-General Gustav Hägglund

United Nations Environment Programme
Under-Secretary-General, Executive Director: Mostafa Kamal Tolba
  Assistant Secretary-General, Deputy Executive Director: Joseph Wheeler
  Assistant Secretary-General, Assistant Executive Director, Office of the Environment Programme: Gennady N. Golubev
  Assistant Secretary-General, Assistant Executive Director, Office of the Environment Fund and Administration: Rudolf Schmidt

United Nations Fund for Drug Abuse Control
Assistant Secretary-General, Executive Director: Giuseppe di Gennaro

United Nations Industrial Development Organization
Under-Secretary-General, Executive Director: Abd-El Rahman Khane
  Assistant Secretary-General, Deputy Executive Director: Philippe Jacques Farlan Carré

United Nations Institute for Training and Research
Under-Secretary-General, Executive Director: Michel Doo Kingué

United Nations Interim Force in Lebanon
Assistant Secretary-General, Force Commander: Lieutenant-General William Callaghan

United Nations Office for Emergency Operations in Africa
Director: F. Bradford Morse
Under-Secretary-General, Executive Co-ordinator: Maurice F. Strong

United Nations Peace-keeping Force in Cyprus
Assistant Secretary-General, Force Commander: Major-General Günther G. Greindl

Acting Special Representative of the Secretary-General: James Holger

United Nations Relief and Works Agency for Palestine Refugees in the Near East
Under-Secretary-General, Commissioner-General: Giorgio Giacomelli
  Assistant Secretary-General, Deputy Commissioner-General: Robert S. Dillon

United Nations Truce Supervision Organization
Assistant Secretary-General, Chief of Staff: Lieutenant-General Emmanuel Alexander Erskine

United Nations University
Under-Secretary-General, Rector: Mr. Soedjatmoko
  Assistant Secretary-General, Director, World Institute for Development Economics Research: Lalith R. U. Jayawardena

World Food Council
Assistant Secretary-General, Executive Director: Maurice J. Williams

On 31 December 1985, the total number of staff of the United Nations holding permanent, probationary and fixed-term appointments with service or expected service of a year or more was 26,007. Of these, 8,766 were in the Professional and higher categories and 17,241 were in the General Service, Manual Worker and Field Service categories. Of the same total, 23,618 were regular staff serving at Headquarters or other established offices and 2,389 were assigned as project personnel to technical co-operation projects. In addition, UNRWA had some 16,700 local area staff.

Agenda of United Nations principal organs in 1985

This appendix lists the items on the agenda of the General Assembly, the Security Council, the Economic and Social Council and the Trusteeship Council during 1985. For the Assembly and the Economic and Social Council, the column headed "Allocation" indicates the assignment of each item to plenary meetings or committees.

Agenda item titles have been shortened by omitting mention of reports following the subject of the item. Thus, "Question of Cyprus: report of the Secretary-General" has been shortened to "Question of Cyprus". Where the subject-matter of the item is not apparent from its title, the subject is identified in square brackets; this is not part of the title.

General Assembly

Agenda items considered at the resumed thirty-ninth session
(9-12 April and 16 September 1985)

Item No.	Title	Allocation
2.	Minute of silent prayer or meditation.	Plenary
11.	Report of the Security Council.	Plenary
12.	Report of the Economic and Social Council.	1
17.	Appointments to fill vacancies in subsidiary organs and other appointments:	
	(g) Appointment of one member of the Joint Inspection Unit;	Plenary
	(i) Confirmation of the appointment of the Secretary-General of the United Nations Conference on Trade and Development.	Plenary
25.	The situation in Central America: threats to international peace and security and peace initiatives.	Plenary
38.	Launching of global negotiations on international economic co-operation for development.	Plenary
41.	Observance of the quincentenary of the discovery of America.	Plenary
42.	Question of Cyprus.	2
43.	Implementation of the resolutions of the United Nations.	Plenary
44.	Consequences of the prolongation of the armed conflict between Iran and Iraq.	Plenary
80.	Development and international economic co-operation:	
	(c) Trade and development.	3
81.	Operational activities for development:	
	(j) Liquidation of the United Nations Emergency Operation Trust Fund and allocation of the remaining balance.	3
92.	International Research and Training Institute for the Advancement of Women.	4
93.	United Nations Decade for Women: Equality, Development and Peace:	
	(b) Preparations for the World Conference to Review and Appraise the Achievements of the United Nations Decade for Women.	5
109.	Programme budget for the biennium 1984-1985.	5th
110.	Programme planning.	6
115.	Scale of assessments for the apportionment of the expenses of the United Nations.	5th
140.	Celebration of the one-hundred-and-fiftieth anniversary of the emancipation of slaves in the British Empire.	Plenary

Agenda of the fortieth session
(first part, 17 September–18 December 1985)

Item No.	Title	Allocation
1.	Opening of the session by the Chairman of the delegation of Zambia.	Plenary
2.	Minute of silent prayer or meditation.	Plenary

---

[1]Allocated to the plenary and Second, Third, Fourth and Fifth Committees at the first part of the session in 1984 but considered only in plenary meetings at the resumed session; also considered in conjunction with item 92.
[2]Not allocated and consideration deferred to the fortieth session.
[3]Allocated to the Second Committee at the first part of the session in 1984 but considered in plenary meetings at the resumed session.
[4]Allocated to the Third Committee at the first part of the session in 1984 but considered in plenary meetings at the resumed session; considered only in conjunction with item 12.
[5]Allocated to the Third Committee at the first part of the session in 1984 but considered in plenary meetings at the resumed session.
[6]Allocated to the Fifth Committee at the first part of the session in 1984 but considered in plenary meetings at the resumed session.

Item No.	Title	Allocation
3.	Credentials of representatives to the fortieth session of the General Assembly:	
	(a) Appointment of the members of the Credentials Committee;	Plenary
	(b) Report of the Credentials Committee.	Plenary
4.	Election of the President of the General Assembly.	Plenary
5.	Election of the officers of the Main Committees.	Plenary
6.	Election of the Vice-Presidents of the General Assembly.	Plenary
7.	Notification by the Secretary-General under Article 12, paragraph 2, of the Charter of the United Nations.	Plenary
8.	Adoption of the agenda and organization of work.	Plenary
9.	General debate.	Plenary
10.	Report of the Secretary-General on the work of the Organization.	Plenary
11.	Report of the Security Council.	Plenary
12.	Report of the Economic and Social Council.	Plenary, 2nd, 3rd, 4th, 5th, 6th
13.	Report of the International Court of Justice.	Plenary
14.	Report of the International Atomic Energy Agency.	Plenary
15.	Elections to fill vacancies in principal organs:	
	(a) Election of five non-permanent members of the Security Council;	Plenary
	(b) Election of eighteen members of the Economic and Social Council;	Plenary
	(c) Election to fill a casual vacancy on the International Court of Justice.	Plenary
16.	Elections to fill vacancies in subsidiary organs and other elections:	
	(a) Election of nineteen members of the Governing Council of the United Nations Environment Programme;	Plenary
	(b) Election of twelve members of the World Food Council;	Plenary
	(c) Election of seven members of the Committee for Programme and Co-ordination;	Plenary
	(d) Election of the members of the Board of Governors of the United Nations Special Fund for Land-locked Developing Countries;	Plenary
	(e) Election of nineteen members of the United Nations Commission on International Trade Law;	Plenary
	(f) Election of the United Nations High Commissioner for Refugees.	Plenary
17.	Appointments to fill vacancies in subsidiary organs and other appointments:	
	(a) Appointment of members of the Advisory Committee on Administrative and Budgetary Questions;	5th
	(b) Appointment of members of the Committee on Contributions;	5th
	(c) Appointment of a member of the Board of Auditors;	5th
	(d) Confirmation of the appointment of members of the Investments Committee;	5th
	(e) Appointment of members of the United Nations Administrative Tribunal;	5th
	(f) Appointment of members of the International Civil Service Commission;	5th
	(g) Appointment of members and alternate members of the United Nations Staff Pension Committee;	5th
	(h) Appointment of the members of the Consultative Committee on the United Nations Development Fund for Women;	Plenary
	(i) Confirmation of the appointment of the Executive Director of the United Nations Special Fund for Land-locked Developing Countries;	Plenary
	(j) Appointment of the United Nations Commissioner for Namibia;	Plenary
	(k) Confirmation of the appointment of the Secretary-General of the United Nations Conference on Trade and Development;	Plenary
	(l) Appointment of a member of the Special Committee on the Situation with regard to the Implementation of the Declaration on the Granting of Independence to Colonial Countries and Peoples.	Plenary
18.	Implementation of the Declaration on the Granting of Independence to Colonial Countries and Peoples.	Plenary, 4th
19.	Admission of new Members to the United Nations.	Plenary
20.	Return or restitution of cultural property to the countries of origin.	Plenary
21.	The situation in Central America: threats to international peace and security and peace initiatives.	Plenary
22.	The situation in Kampuchea.	Plenary
23.	Question of the Falkland Islands (Malvinas).	Plenary, 4th[7]
24.	Co-operation between the United Nations and the Organization of the Islamic Conference.	Plenary
25.	Co-operation between the United Nations and the Organization of African Unity.	Plenary
26.	Co-operation between the United Nations and the League of Arab States.	Plenary
27.	International Year of Peace.	Plenary
28.	The situation in Afghanistan and its implications for international peace and security.	Plenary
29.	Armed Israeli aggression against the Iraqi nuclear installations and its grave consequences for the established international system concerning the peaceful uses of nuclear energy, the non-proliferation of nuclear weapons and international peace and security.	Plenary

[7]Hearings of organizations and individuals having an interest in the question.

Item No.	*Title*	*Allocation*
30.	Critical economic situation in Africa.	Plenary
31.	Co-operation between the United Nations and the Asian-African Legal Consultative Committee.	Plenary
32.	Question of the Comorian island of Mayotte.	Plenary
33.	Question of Palestine.	Plenary
34.	Question of Namibia.	Plenary, 4th[8]
35.	Policies of *apartheid* of the Government of South Africa.	Plenary, SPC[7]
36.	Law of the sea.	Plenary
37.	United Nations Conference for the Promotion of International Co-operation in the Peaceful Uses of Nuclear Energy.	Plenary
38.	The situation in the Middle East.	Plenary
39.	Commemoration of the fortieth anniversary of the United Nations.	Plenary
40.	Question of peace, stability and co-operation in South-East Asia.	Plenary
41.	Launching of global negotiations on international economic co-operation for development.	Plenary
42.	Question of equitable representation on and increase in the membership of the Security Council.	Plenary
43.	Observance of the quincentenary of the discovery of America.	Plenary
44.	Question of Cyprus.	9
45.	Implementation of the resolutions of the United Nations.	Plenary
46.	Consequences of the prolongation of the armed conflict between Iran and Iraq.	Plenary
47.	Celebration of the one-hundred-and-fiftieth anniversary of the emancipation of slaves in the British Empire.	Plenary
48.	Economic and social consequences of the armaments race and its extremely harmful effects on world peace and security.	1st
49.	Implementation of General Assembly resolution 39/51 concerning the signature and ratification of Additional Protocol I of the Treaty for the Prohibition of Nuclear Weapons in Latin America (Treaty of Tlatelolco).	1st
50.	Cessation of all test explosions of nuclear weapons.	1st
51.	Urgent need for a comprehensive nuclear-test-ban treaty.	1st
52.	Establishment of a nuclear-weapon-free zone in the region of the Middle East.	1st
53.	Establishment of a nuclear-weapon-free zone in South Asia.	1st
54.	Convention on Prohibitions or Restrictions on the Use of Certain Conventional Weapons Which May Be Deemed to Be Excessively Injurious or to Have Indiscriminate Effects.	1st
55.	Conclusion of an international convention on the strengthening of the security of non-nuclear-weapon States against the use or threat of use of nuclear weapons.	1st
56.	Conclusion of effective international arrangements to assure non-nuclear-weapon States against the use or threat of use of nuclear weapons.	1st
57.	Prevention of an arms race in outer space.	1st
58.	Implementation of General Assembly resolution 39/60 on the immediate cessation and prohibition of nuclear-weapon tests.	1st
59.	Implementation of the Declaration on the Denuclearization of Africa.	1st
60.	Prohibition of the development and manufacture of new types of weapons of mass destruction and new systems of such weapons.	1st
61.	Review and implementation of the Concluding Document of the Twelfth Special Session of the General Assembly:	
	(a) World Disarmament Campaign;	1st
	(b) United Nations programme of fellowships on disarmament;	1st
	(c) Implementation of General Assembly resolution 39/63 C on a nuclear-arms freeze;	1st
	(d) Consideration of guidelines for confidence-building measures;	1st
	(e) Freeze on nuclear weapons;	1st
	(f) Convention on the Prohibition of the Use of Nuclear Weapons;	1st
	(g) Third special session of the General Assembly devoted to disarmament;	1st
	(h) Disarmament and international security.	1st
62.	Reduction of military budgets.	1st
63.	Chemical and bacteriological (biological) weapons.	1st
64.	Israeli nuclear armament.	1st
65.	Review of the implementation of the recommendations and decisions adopted by the General Assembly at its tenth special session:	
	(a) Report of the Disarmament Commission;	1st
	(b) Report of the Conference on Disarmament;	1st
	(c) Status of multilateral disarmament agreements;	1st
	(d) Advisory Board on Disarmament Studies;	1st

[8]Hearings of organizations.
[9]The General Committee made no recommendation regarding the allocation of this item.

Item No.	Title	Allocation
	(e) Cessation of the nuclear-arms race and nuclear disarmament;	1st
	(f) Non-use of nuclear weapons and prevention of nuclear war;	1st
	(g) Prohibition of the nuclear neutron weapon;	1st
	(h) Prevention of nuclear war;	1st
	(i) Bilateral nuclear-arms negotiations;	1st
	(j) United Nations Institute for Disarmament Research;	1st
	(k) Comprehensive programme of disarmament;	1st
	(l) Disarmament Week;	1st
	(m) Implementation of the recommendations and decisions of the tenth special session;	1st
	(n) Review and appraisal of the implementation of the Declaration of the 1980s as the Second Disarmament Decade.	1st
66.	Implementation of the Declaration of the Indian Ocean as a Zone of Peace.	1st
67.	World Disarmament Conference.	1st
68.	General and complete disarmament:	
	(a) Further measures in the field of disarmament for the prevention of an arms race on the sea-bed, the ocean floor and in the subsoil thereof;	1st
	(b) Study on the naval arms race;	1st
	(c) Study on concepts of security;	1st
	(d) Study of the question of nuclear-weapon-free zones in all its aspects;	1st
	(e) Study on conventional disarmament;	1st
	(f) Military research and development;	1st
	(g) Review of the role of the United Nations in the field of disarmament;	1st
	(h) Prohibition of the production of fissionable material for weapons purposes;	1st
	(i) Curbing the naval arms race: limitation and reduction of naval armaments and extension of confidence-building measures to seas and oceans;	1st
	(j) Prohibition of the development, production, stockpiling and use of radiological weapons.	1st
69.	Relationship between disarmament and development:	
	(a) Reallocation and conversion of resources, through disarmament measures, from military to civilian purposes;	1st
	(b) Relationship between disarmament and development;	1st
	(c) International Conference on the Relationship between Disarmament and Development.	1st
70.	Question of Antarctica.	1st
71.	Strengthening of security and co-operation in the Mediterranean region.	1st
72.	Review of the implementation of the Declaration on the Strengthening of International Security.	1st
73.	Implementation of the collective security provisions of the Charter of the United Nations for the maintenance of international peace and security.	1st
74.	Effects of atomic radiation.	SPC
75.	Report of the Special Committee to Investigate Israeli Practices Affecting the Human Rights of the Population of the Occupied Territories.	SPC
76.	International co-operation in the peaceful uses of outer space:	
	(a) Report of the Committee on the Peaceful Uses of Outer Space;	SPC
	(b) Implementation of the recommendations of the Second United Nations Conference on the Exploration and Peaceful Uses of Outer Space.	SPC
77.	Comprehensive review of the whole question of peace-keeping operations in all their aspects.	SPC
78.	Questions relating to information.	SPC
79.	United Nations Relief and Works Agency for Palestine Refugees in the Near East.	SPC
80.	International co-operation to avert new flows of refugees.	SPC
81.	Israel's decision to build a canal linking the Mediterranean Sea to the Dead Sea.	SPC
82.	Question of the Malagasy islands of Glorieuses, Juan de Nova, Europa and Bassas da India.	SPC
83.	Question of the composition of the relevant organs of the United Nations.	SPC
84.	Development and international economic co-operation:	
	(a) International Development Strategy for the Third United Nations Development Decade;	2nd
	(b) Review of the implementation of the Charter of Economic Rights and Duties of States;	2nd
	(c) Trade and development;	2nd
	(d) Science and technology for development;	2nd
	(e) Economic and technical co-operation among developing countries;	2nd
	(f) Environment;	2nd
	(g) Human settlements;	2nd
	(h) International Year of Shelter for the Homeless;	2nd
	(i) Effective mobilization and integration of women in development;	2nd
	(j) Implementation of the Substantial New Programme of Action for the 1980s for the Least Developed Countries;	2nd
	(k) New international human order: moral aspects of development;	2nd
	(l) Long-term trends in economic development;	2nd
	(m) Immediate measures in favour of the developing countries;	2nd
	(n) New and renewable sources of energy;	2nd
	(o) Development of the energy resources of developing countries.	2nd

Item No.	Title	Allocation

85. Operational activities for development:
    (a) Operational activities of the United Nations system; — 2nd
    (b) United Nations Development Programme; — 2nd
    (c) United Nations Capital Development Fund; — 2nd
    (d) United Nations Volunteers programme; — 2nd
    (e) United Nations technical co-operation activities; — 2nd
    (f) Liquidation of the United Nations Emergency Operation Trust Fund and allocation of the remaining balance. — 2nd

86. Training and research: United Nations Institute for Training and Research. — 2nd

87. Special economic and disaster relief assistance: special programmes of economic assistance. — 2nd

88. Implementation of the Programme of Action for the Second Decade to Combat Racism and Racial Discrimination. — 3rd

89. International Youth Year: Participation, Development, Peace. — Plenary,[10] 3rd

90. World social situation:
    (a) World social situation; — 3rd
    (b) Popular participation in its various forms as an important factor in development and in the full realization of all human rights. — 3rd

91. National experience in achieving far-reaching social and economic changes for the purpose of social progress. — 3rd

92. United Nations Decade for Women: Equality, Development and Peace:
    (a) Implementation of the Programme of Action for the Second Half of the United Nations Decade for Women; — 3rd
    (b) World Conference to Review and Appraise the Achievements of the United Nations Decade for Women: Equality, Development and Peace; — 3rd
    (c) United Nations Development Fund for Women; — 3rd
    (d) Prevention of prostitution. — 3rd

93. Importance of the universal realization of the right of peoples to self-determination and of the speedy granting of independence to colonial countries and peoples for the effective guarantee and observance of human rights. — 3rd

94. Elimination of all forms of racial discrimination:
    (a) Report of the Committee on the Elimination of Racial Discrimination; — 3rd
    (b) Status of the International Convention on the Elimination of All Forms of Racial Discrimination; — 3rd
    (c) Status of the International Convention on the Suppression and Punishment of the Crime of *Apartheid*. — 3rd

95. Policies and programmes relating to youth. — 3rd

96. Question of aging. — 3rd

97. Implementation of the World Programme of Action concerning Disabled Persons and United Nations Decade of Disabled Persons. — 3rd

98. Crime prevention and criminal justice:
    (a) Report of the Seventh United Nations Congress on the Prevention of Crime and the Treatment of Offenders; — 3rd
    (b) Implementation of the recommendations of the Sixth United Nations Congress on the Prevention of Crime and the Treatment of Offenders; — 3rd
    (c) Implementation of the conclusions of the Seventh United Nations Congress on the Prevention of Crime and the Treatment of Offenders. — 3rd

99. International Research and Training Institute for the Advancement of Women. — 3rd

100. Elimination of all forms of discrimination against women:
    (a) Report of the Committee on the Elimination of Discrimination against Women; — 3rd
    (b) Status of the Convention on the Elimination of All Forms of Discrimination against Women. — 3rd

101. Elimination of all forms of religious intolerance. — 3rd

102. Human rights and scientific and technological developments. — 3rd

103. Question of a convention on the rights of the child. — 3rd

104. International Covenants on Human Rights:
    (a) Report of the Human Rights Committee; — 3rd
    (b) Status of the International Covenant on Economic, Social and Cultural Rights, the International Covenant on Civil and Political Rights and the Optional Protocol to the International Covenant on Civil and Political Rights; — 3rd
    (c) Reporting obligations of States parties to United Nations conventions on human rights. — 3rd

105. Office of the United Nations High Commissioner for Refugees:
    (a) Report of the High Commissioner; — 3rd
    (b) Assistance to refugees in Africa. — 3rd

106. International campaign against traffic in drugs. — 3rd

107. Alternative approaches and ways and means within the United Nations system for improving the effective enjoyment of human rights and fundamental freedoms. — 3rd

---

[10]Meetings designated United Nations World Conference for the International Youth Year.

Item No.	Title	Allocation
108.	New international humanitarian order.	3rd
109.	Information from Non-Self-Governing Territories transmitted under Article 73 *e* of the Charter of the United Nations.	4th
110.	Activities of foreign economic and other interests which are impeding the implementation of the Declaration on the Granting of Independence to Colonial Countries and Peoples in Namibia and in all other Territories under colonial domination and efforts to eliminate colonialism, *apartheid* and racial discrimination in southern Africa.	4th
111.	Implementation of the Declaration on the Granting of Independence to Colonial Countries and Peoples by the specialized agencies and the international institutions associated with the United Nations.	4th
112.	United Nations Educational and Training Programme for Southern Africa.	4th
113.	Offers by Member States of study and training facilities for inhabitants of Non-Self-Governing Territories.	4th
114.	Financial reports and audited financial statements, and reports of the Board of Auditors:	
	(a) United Nations Development Programme;	5th
	(b) United Nations Children's Fund;	5th
	(c) United Nations Relief and Works Agency for Palestine Refugees in the Near East;	5th
	(d) United Nations Institute for Training and Research;	5th
	(e) Voluntary funds administered by the United Nations High Commissioner for Refugees;	5th
	(f) United Nations Fund for Population Activities;	5th
	(g) United Nations Industrial Development Fund.	5th
115.	Programme budget for the biennium 1984-1985.	5th
116.	Proposed programme budget for the biennium 1986-1987.	5th
117.	Programme planning.	5th
118.	Financial emergency of the United Nations.	5th
119.	Administrative and budgetary co-ordination of the United Nations with the specialized agencies and the International Atomic Energy Agency:	
	(a) Report of the Advisory Committee on Administrative and Budgetary Questions;	5th
	(b) Impact of inflation and monetary instability on the regular budget of the United Nations;	5th
	(c) Feasibility of establishing a single administrative tribunal.	5th
120.	Joint Inspection Unit.	5th
121.	Pattern of conferences.	5th
122.	Scale of assessments for the apportionment of the expenses of the United Nations.	5th
123.	Personnel questions:	
	(a) Composition of the Secretariat;	5th
	(b) Respect for the privileges and immunities of officials of the United Nations and the specialized agencies and related organizations;	5th
	(c) Other personnel questions.	5th
124.	United Nations common system.	5th
125.	United Nations pension system.	5th
126.	Financing of the United Nations peace-keeping forces in the Middle East:	
	(a) United Nations Disengagement Observer Force;	5th
	(b) United Nations Interim Force in Lebanon;	5th
	(c) Review of the rates of reimbursement to the Governments of troop-contributing States.	5th
127.	Consideration of the draft articles on most-favoured-nation clauses.	6th
128.	United Nations Programme of Assistance in the Teaching, Study, Dissemination and Wider Appreciation of International Law.	6th
129.	Measures to prevent international terrorism which endangers or takes innocent human lives or jeopardizes fundamental freedoms and study of the underlying causes of those forms of terrorism and acts of violence which lie in misery, frustration, grievance and despair and which cause some people to sacrifice human lives, including their own, in an attempt to effect radical changes.	6th
130.	Progressive development of the principles and norms of international law relating to the new international economic order.	6th
131.	Development and strengthening of good-neighbourliness between States.	6th
132.	Peaceful settlement of disputes between States.	6th
133.	Draft Code of Offences against the Peace and Security of Mankind.	6th
134.	Report of the Special Committee on Enhancing the Effectiveness of the Principle of Non-Use of Force in International Relations.	6th
135.	Report of the United Nations Commission on International Trade Law on the work of its eighteenth session.	6th
136.	Consideration of effective measures to enhance the protection, security and safety of diplomatic and consular missions and representatives.	6th
137.	Report of the *Ad Hoc* Committee on the Drafting of an International Convention against the Recruitment, Use, Financing and Training of Mercenaries.	6th
138.	Report of the International Law Commission on the work of its thirty-seventh session.	6th
139.	Preparation for the United Nations Conference on the Law of Treaties between States and International Organizations or between International Organizations.	6th

Item No.	Title	Allocation
140.	Report of the Committee on Relations with the Host Country.	6th
141.	Report of the Special Committee on the Charter of the United Nations and on the Strengthening of the Role of the Organization.	6th
142.	Draft Body of Principles for the Protection of All Persons under Any Form of Detention or Imprisonment.	6th
143.	Draft standard rules of procedure for United Nations conferences.	6th
144.	Torture and other cruel, inhuman or degrading treatment or punishment.	3rd
145.	International co-operation in the peaceful exploitation of outer space under conditions of its non-militarization.	1st
146.	Solemn appeal to States in conflict to cease armed action forthwith and to settle disputes between them through negotiations, and to States Members of the United Nations to undertake to solve situations of tension and conflict and existing disputes by political means and to refrain from the threat or use of force and from any intervention in the internal affairs of other States.	Plenary
147.	International relief to Mexico.	Plenary
148.	Draft Declaration on Social and Legal Principles relating to the Protection and Welfare of Children, with Special Reference to Foster Placement and Adoption Nationally and Internationally.	6th
149.	International relief to Colombia.	Plenary

Security Council

Agenda items considered during 1985

Item No.[11]   Title

1. Letter dated 28 January 1985 from the Chargé d'affaires a.i. of the Permanent Mission of Chad to the United Nations addressed to the President of the Security Council (complaint against the Libyan Arab Jamahiriya).

2. The situation in the Middle East.

3. The situation between Iran and Iraq.

4. The question of South Africa.

5. Letter dated 6 May 1985 from the Permanent Representative of Nicaragua to the United Nations addressed to the President of the Security Council (complaint against the United States).

6. The situation in Namibia.

7. The situation in Cyprus.

8. Complaint by Angola against South Africa.

9. Letter dated 17 June 1985 from the Permanent Representative of Botswana to the United Nations addressed to the President of the Security Council (complaint against South Africa).

10. Date of elections to fill a vacancy in the International Court of Justice.

11. The situation in the occupied Arab territories.

12. United Nations for a better world and the responsibility of the Security Council in maintaining international peace and security.

13. Letter dated 26 September 1985 from the Permanent Representative of Botswana to the United Nations addressed to the President of the Security Council (complaint against South Africa).

14. Letter dated 1 October 1985 from the Permanent Representative of Tunisia to the United Nations addressed to the President of the Security Council (complaint against Israel).

15. The Middle East problem including the Palestinian question.

16. Election of a member of the International Court of Justice.

17. Letter dated 6 December 1985 from the Chargé d'affaires a.i. of the Permanent Mission of Nicaragua to the United Nations addressed to the President of the Security Council (complaint against the United States).

18. Letter dated 16 December 1985 from the Permanent Representative of the United States of America to the United Nations addressed to the President of the Security Council (terrorist attacks at the Rome and Vienna airports).

19. Complaint by Lesotho against South Africa.

Economic and Social Council

Agenda of the organizational session for 1985
(5-8 February and 22 March 1985)

Item No.	Title	Allocation
1.	Election of the Bureau.	Plenary
2.	Adoption of the agenda and other organizational matters.	Plenary

---

[11]Numbers indicate the order in which items were taken up in 1985.

Item No.	Title	Allocation
3.	Basic programme of work of the Council for 1985 and 1986.	Plenary
4.	Resumed session of the Committee on the Review and Appraisal of the Implementation of the International Development Strategy for the Third United Nations Development Decade.	Plenary
5.	Elections to subsidiary bodies of the Council and confirmation of representatives on the functional commissions and on the Sessional Working Group of Governmental Experts on the Implementation of the International Covenant on Economic, Social and Cultural Rights.	Plenary
6.	Provisional agenda for the first regular session of 1985 and other organizational matters.	Plenary

Agenda of the first regular session of 1985
(7-31 May and 20 June 1985)

Item No.	Title	Allocation
1.	Adoption of the agenda and other organizational matters.	Plenary
2.	Implementation of the Programme of Action for the Second Decade to Combat Racism and Racial Discrimination.	Plenary
3.	Implementation of the International Covenant on Economic, Social and Cultural Rights.	12
4.	Convention on the Elimination of All Forms of Discrimination against Women.	Plenary
5.	Activities for the advancement of women; United Nations Decade for Women: Equality, Development and Peace.	Plenary
6.	International Covenant on Civil and Political Rights.	Plenary
7.	Assistance to the drought-stricken areas of Ethiopia.	Plenary
8.	Non-governmental organizations.	Plenary
9.	University for Peace.	Plenary
10.	Population questions.	1st
11.	Statistical questions.	1st
12.	Transport of dangerous goods.	1st
13.	Cartography.	1st
14.	Public administration and finance.	1st
15.	Transnational corporations.	1st
16.	Human rights.	2nd
17.	Social development.	2nd
18.	Narcotic drugs.	2nd
19.	Elections and nominations.	Plenary
20.	Consideration of the provisional agenda for the second regular session of 1985.	Plenary

Agenda of the second regular session of 1985
(3-26 July 1985; resumed 12 December)

Item No.	Title	Allocation
1.	Opening of the session.	Plenary
2.	Adoption of the agenda and other organizational matters.	Plenary
3.	General discussion of international economic and social policy, including regional and sectoral developments.	Plenary
4.	Review of the immediate and longer-term aspects of the critical economic situation in Africa and the follow-up of the response by the international community and the United Nations system.	Plenary
5.	Report of the United Nations High Commissioner for Refugees.	Plenary
6.	Permanent sovereignty over national resources in the occupied Palestinian and other Arab territories.	Plenary
7.	United Nations University.	Plenary
8.	Regional co-operation.	1st
9.	Transnational corporations.	1st
10.	Food problems.	1st
11.	Natural resources.	1st
12.	Industrial development co-operation.[13]	1st
13.	Trade and development.	1st
14.	International co-operation on the environment.	1st
15.	International co-operation in the field of human settlements.	1st

[12]Allocated to the Sessional Working Group of Governmental Experts on the Implementation of the International Covenant on Economic, Social and Cultural Rights.
[13]Only item considered at the resumed session, at a plenary meeting.

Item No.	Title	Allocation
16.	Science and technology for development.	1st
17.	Special economic, humanitarian and disaster relief assistance.	3rd
18.	Operational activities for development.	3rd
19.	International co-operation and co-ordination within the United Nations system.	3rd
20.	Proposed programme budget for the biennium 1986-1987.	3rd
21.	Implementation of the Declaration on the Granting of Independence to Colonial Countries and Peoples by the specialized agencies and the international institutions associated with the United Nations.	3rd
22.	Countries stricken by desertification and drought.	1st
23.	Calendar of conferences and meetings for 1986-1987.	3rd
24.	Elections.	Plenary

Trusteeship Council

Agenda of the fifty-second session
(13 May–11 July 1985)

Item No.	Title

1. Adoption of the agenda.

2. Report of the Secretary-General on credentials.

3. Election of the President and the Vice-President.

4. Examination of the annual report of the Administering Authority for the year ended 30 September 1984: Trust Territory of the Pacific Islands.

5. Examination of petitions listed in the annex to the agenda.

6. Arrangements for the dispatch of a periodic visiting mission to the Trust Territory of the Pacific Islands, 1985.

7. Offers by Member States of study and training facilities for inhabitants of Trust Territories.

8. Dissemination of information on the United Nations and the International Trusteeship System in Trust Territories.

9. Co-operation with the Committee on the Elimination of Racial Discrimination.

10. Decade for Action to Combat Racism and Racial Discrimination.

11. Attainment of self-government or independence by the Trust Territories and the situation in Trust Territories with regard to the implementation of the Declaration on the Granting of Independence to Colonial Countries and Peoples.

12. Co-operation with the Special Committee on the Situation with regard to the Implementation of the Declaration on the Granting of Independence to Colonial Countries and Peoples.

13. Adoption of the report of the Trusteeship Council to the Security Council.

Appendix V

United Nations Information Centres and Services

(As at 31 December 1985)

ACCRA. United Nations Information Centre
Gamal Abdel Nasser/Liberia Roads
(P.O. Box 2339)
Accra, Ghana
>*Serving:* Ghana, Sierra Leone

ADDIS ABABA. United Nations Information
Service, Economic Commission for Africa
Africa Hall
(P.O. Box 3001)
Addis Ababa, Ethiopia
>*Serving:* Ethiopia

ALGIERS. United Nations Information Centre
19 Avenue Chahid El-Quali Mustapha Sayed
(Boîte Postale 823)
Algiers, Algeria
>*Serving:* Algeria

ANKARA. United Nations Information Centre
197 Ataturk Bulvari
(P.K. 407)
Ankara, Turkey
>*Serving:* Turkey

ANTANANARIVO. United Nations Information
Centre
22 Rue Rainitovo Antsahavola
(Boîte Postale 1348)
Antananarivo, Madagascar
>*Serving:* Madagascar

ASUNCION. United Nations Information
Centre
Casilla de Correo 1107
Asunción, Paraguay
>*Serving:* Paraguay

ATHENS. United Nations Information Centre
36 Amalia Avenue
GR-105, 58 Athens, Greece
>*Serving:* Cyprus, Greece, Israel

BAGHDAD. United Nations Information Serv-
ice, Economic and Social Commission for
Western Asia
Amiriya, Airport Street
(P.O. Box 27)
Baghdad, Iraq
>*Serving:* Iraq

BANGKOK. United Nations Information Serv-
ice, Economic and Social Commission for
Asia and the Pacific
United Nations Building
Rajdamnern Avenue
Bangkok 10200, Thailand
>*Serving:* Democratic Kampuchea, Lao
People's Democratic Republic, Malaysia,
Singapore, Thailand, Viet Nam

BEIRUT. United Nations Information Centre
Apt. No. 1, Fakhoury Building
Montée Bain Militaire, Ardati Street
(P.O. Box 4656)
Beirut, Lebanon
>*Serving:* Jordan, Kuwait, Lebanon, Syrian
Arab Republic

BELGRADE. United Nations Information Centre
Svetozara Markovica 58
(P.O. Box 157)
Belgrade, Yugloslavia YU-11001
>*Serving:* Albania, Yugoslavia

BOGOTA. United Nations Information Centre
Calle 72 No. 12-65 (piso 2)
(Apartado Aéreo 058964)
Bogotá 2, Colombia
>*Serving:* Colombia, Ecuador, Venezuela

BRAZZAVILLE. United Nations Information
Centre
S.22 Avenue Pointe-Hollandaise
(Boîte Postale 465)
Mpila-Brazzaville, Congo
>*Serving:* Congo

BRUSSELS. United Nations Information Centre and Liaison Office
108 Rue d'Arlon
1040 Brussels, Belgium
>*Serving:* Belgium, Luxembourg,
Netherlands; liaison with EEC

BUCHAREST. United Nations Information Centre
16 Aurel Vlaicu Street
(P.O. Box 1-701)
Bucharest, Romania
>*Serving:* Romania

BUENOS AIRES. United Nations Information
Centre
Junín 1940 (1er piso)
1113 Buenos Aires, Argentina
>*Serving:* Argentina, Uruguay

BUJUMBURA. United Nations Information
Centre
Avenue de la Poste 7
Place de l'Indépendance
(Boîte Postale 2160)
Bujumbura, Burundi
>*Serving:* Burundi

CAIRO. United Nations Information Centre
1 Osiris Street
Tagher Building (Garden City)
(P.O. Box 262)
Cairo, Egypt
>*Serving:* Egypt, Saudi Arabia, Yemen

COLOMBO. United Nations Information
Centre
202-204 Bauddhaloka Mawatha
(P.O. Box 1505)
Colombo 7, Sri Lanka
>*Serving:* Sri Lanka

COPENHAGEN. United Nations Information
Centre
37 H. C. Andersens Boulevard
DK-1553 Copenhagen V, Denmark
>*Serving:* Denmark, Finland, Iceland, Nor-
way, Sweden

DAKAR. United Nations Information Centre
9 Allées Robert Delmas
(Boîte Postale 154)
Dakar, Senegal
>*Serving:* Cape Verde, Gambia, Guinea,
Guinea-Bissau, Ivory Coast, Mauritania,
Senegal

DAR ES SALAAM. United Nations Informa-
tion Centre
Samora Machel Avenue
Matasalamat Building (1st floor)
(P.O. Box 9224)
Dar es Salaam, United Republic of Tanzania
>*Serving:* United Republic of Tanzania

DHAKA. United Nations Information Centre
House 12, Road 6
Dhanmandi
(G.P.O. Box 3658, Dhaka 100)
Dhaka, Bangladesh
>*Serving:* Bangladesh

GENEVA. United Nations Information Service,
United Nations Office at Geneva
Palais des Nations
1211 Geneva 10, Switzerland
>*Serving:* Bulgaria, Hungary, Poland,
Spain, Switzerland

HARARE. United Nations Information Centre
Dolphin House
123 Moffat Street/Union Avenue
(P.O. Box 4408)
Harare, Zimbabwe
>*Serving:* Zimbabwe

ISLAMABAD. United Nations Information
Centre
House No. 26
88th Street, Ramna 6/3
(P.O. Box 1107)
Islamabad, Pakistan
>*Serving:* Pakistan

JAKARTA. United Nations Information Centre
Gedung Dewan Pers (5th floor)
32-34 Jalan Kebon Sirih
Jakarta, Indonesia

Serving: Indonesia

KABUL. United Nations Information Centre
Shah Mahmoud Ghazi Watt
(P.O. Box 5)
Kabul, Afghanistan

Serving: Afghanistan

KATHMANDU. United Nations Information Centre
Pulchowk, Patan
(P.O. Box 107, Pulchowk)
Kathmandu, Nepal

Serving: Nepal

KHARTOUM. United Nations Information Centre
Al Qasr Avenue, Street No. 15
Block 3, House No. 3
Khartoum East
(P.O. Box 1992)
Khartoum, Sudan

Serving: Somalia, Sudan

KINSHASA. United Nations Information Centre
Bâtiment Deuxième République
Boulevard du 30 Juin
(Boîte Postale 7248)
Kinshasa, Zaire

Serving: Zaire

LAGOS. United Nations Information Centre
17 Kingsway Road, Ikoyi
(P.O. Box 1068)
Lagos, Nigeria

Serving: Nigeria

LA PAZ. United Nations Information Centre
Edificio Naciones Unidas
Plaza Isabel La Católica
Ex-Clínica Santa Isabel
Planta Baja
(Apartado Postal 686)
La Paz, Bolivia

Serving: Bolivia

LIMA. United Nations Information Centre
Mariscal Blas Cerdeña 450
San Isidro
(P. O. Box 11199)
Lima, Peru

Serving: Peru

LISBON. United Nations Information Centre
Rua Latino Coelho No. 1
Edificio Aviz, BI-1-10º
1000 Lisbon, Portugal

Serving: Portugal

LOME. United Nations Information Centre
107 Boulevard Circulaire
(Boîte Postale 911)
Lomé, Togo

Serving: Benin, Togo

LONDON. United Nations Information Centre
20 Buckingham Gate
London SW1E 6LB, England

Serving: Ireland, United Kingdom

LUSAKA. United Nations Information Centre
P.O. Box 32905
Lusaka, Zambia

Serving: Botswana, Malawi, Swaziland, Zambia

MANAGUA. United Nations Information Centre
Bolonia, de Plaza España 2 cuadras abajo
(P.O. Box 3260)
Managua, Nicaragua

Serving: Nicaragua

MANAMA. United Nations Information Centre
King Faisal Road, Gufool
(P.O. Box 26004)
Manama, Bahrain

Serving: Bahrain, Qatar, United Arab Emirates

MANILA. United Nations Information Centre
NEDA Building (ground floor)
106 Amorsolo Street
Legaspi Village, Makati
(P.O. Box 7285 (ADC), MIA Road, Pasay City)
Metro Manila, Philippines

Serving: Philippines

MASERU. United Nations Information Centre
Corner Kingsway and Hilton Roads
 opposite Sanlam Centre
(P.O. Box 301)
Maseru, 100 Lesotho

Serving: Lesotho

MEXICO CITY. United Nations Information Centre
Presidente Masaryk 29 (7º piso)
11570 México, D.F., Mexico

Serving: Cuba, Dominican Republic, Mexico

MONROVIA. United Nations Information Centre
LBDI Building
Tubman Boulevard
(P.O. Box 274)
Monrovia, Liberia

Serving: Liberia

MOSCOW. United Nations Information Centre
4/16 Ulitsa Lunacharskogo
Moscow 121002, USSR

Serving: Byelorussian SSR, Ukrainian SSR, USSR

NAIROBI. United Nations Information Centre
Electricity House
Harambee Avenue
(P.O. Box 30218)
Nairobi, Kenya

Serving: Kenya, Seychelles, Uganda

NEW DELHI. United Nations Information Centre
55 Lodi Estate
New Delhi 110 003, India

Serving: Bhutan, India

OUAGADOUGOU. United Nations Information Centre
218 Rue de la Gare
Secteur No. 3
(Boîte Postale 135)
Ouagadougou, Burkina Faso

Serving: Burkina Faso, Chad, Mali, Niger

PANAMA CITY. United Nations Information Centre
Urbanización Obarrio
Calle 54 y Avenida Tercera Sur, Casa No. 17
(P.O. Box 6-9083 El Dorado)
Panama City, Panama

Serving: Panama

PARIS. United Nations Information Centre
4 et 6 Avenue de Saxe
75700 Paris, France

Serving: France

PORT MORESBY. United Nations Information Centre
Credit House (3rd floor)
Musgrave Street, Ela Beach
(P.O. Box 472)
Port Moresby, Papua New Guinea

Serving: Papua New Guinea, Solomon Islands

PORT OF SPAIN. United Nations Information Centre
15 Keate Street
(P.O. Box 130)
Port of Spain, Trinidad

Serving: Antigua and Barbuda, Bahamas, Barbados, Belize, Dominica, Grenada, Guyana, Jamaica, Netherlands Antilles, Saint Christopher and Nevis, Saint Lucia, Saint Vincent and the Grenadines, Suriname, Trinidad and Tobago

PRAGUE. United Nations Information Centre
Panska 5
11000 Prague 1, Czechoslovakia

Serving: Czechoslovakia, German Democratic Republic

RABAT. United Nations Information Centre
Angle Charia Ibnouzaid et Zankat Roundanat, No. 6
(Casier ONU)
Rabat, Morocco

Serving: Morocco

RANGOON. United Nations Information Centre
28A Manawhari Road
(P.O. Box 230)
Rangoon, Burma

Serving: Burma

RIO DE JANEIRO. United Nations Information Centre
Rua Cruz Lima 19, Grupo 201
22230 Rio de Janeiro, RJ Brazil

Serving: Brazil

ROME. United Nations Information Centre
Palazzetto Venezia
Piazza San Marco 50
Rome, Italy

Serving: Holy See, Italy, Malta

SAN SALVADOR. United Nations Information Centre
Edificio Escalón (2º piso)
Paseo General Escalón y 87 Avenida Norte
Colonia Escalón
(Apartado Postal 2157)
San Salvador, El Salvador

Serving: El Salvador

SANTIAGO. United Nations Information Service, Economic Commission for Latin America and the Caribbean
Edificio Naciones Unidas
Avenida Dag Hammarskjold
(Casilla 179-D)
Santiago, Chile

Serving: Chile

SYDNEY. United Nations Information Centre
National Mutual Centre
44 Market Street (16th floor)
(P.O. Box 4045, Sydney, N.S.W. 2001)
Sydney, N.S.W. 2000, Australia

Serving: Australia, Fiji, Kiribati, Nauru, New Zealand, Samoa, Tonga, Tuvalu, Vanuatu

TEHERAN. United Nations Information Centre
Avenue Gandhi, 43 Street No. 3
(P.O. Box 1555)
Teheran, Iran

Serving: Iran

TOKYO. United Nations Information Centre
Shin Aoyama Building Nishikan (22nd floor)
1-1 Minami Aoyama 1-chome, Minato-ku
Tokyo 107, Japan

Serving: Japan, Trust Territory of the Pacific Islands

TRIPOLI. United Nations Information Centre
Muzaffar Al Aftas Street
Hay El-Andalous
(P.O. Box 286)
Tripoli, Libyan Arab Jamahiriya

Serving: Libyan Arab Jamahiriya

TUNIS. United Nations Information Centre
61 Boulevard Bab-Benat
(Boîte Postale 863)
Tunis, Tunisia

Serving: Tunisia

VIENNA. United Nations Information Service, United Nations Office at Vienna
Vienna International Centre
Wagramerstrasse 5
(P.O. Box 500, A-1400 Vienna)
A-1220 Vienna, Austria

Serving: Austria, Federal Republic of Germany

WASHINGTON, D.C. United Nations Information Centre
1889 F Street, N.W.
Washington, D.C. 20006, United States

Serving: United States

YAOUNDE. United Nations Information Centre
Immeuble Kamden
Rue Joseph Clère
(Boîte Postale 836)
Yaoundé, Cameroon

Serving: Cameroon, Central African Republic, Gabon

Indexes

Using the subject index

The designations employed and the presentation of entries in the subject index do not imply the expression of any opinion by the Department of Public Information of the United Nations. The index contains four types of entries:

Subject terms, including geographical names, are in bold face and, in most cases, are based on the subject descriptors used in the United Nations Bibliographical Information System (UNBIS), published in the *UNBIS Thesaurus* (United Nations Publication: Sales No. E.85.I.20). In order to minimize subentries, the index lists broad and narrow terms in their separate alphabetical positions; for example, "human rights", "racial discrimination" and "right to development". Subjects pertaining to the United Nations or the system as a whole, such as "contributions (UN)", "finances (UN)" and "staff (UN/UN system)", are indexed separately, with cross-references under "United Nations".

NAMES of organizations and subsidiary bodies, conferences, United Nations Secretariat departments and offices, programmes, and special decades and observances, are given in full in capitals and small capitals and are alphabetized in either of two ways: (1) Names of bodies, units and programmes that are part of the United Nations, names of subsidiary bodies of specialized agencies and of their affiliated institutions, and titles of special decades and observances, are indexed under their key word: APARTHEID, SPEC. CT. AGAINST; DEVELOPMENT DECADE, 3RD UN; LAW OF THE SEA, 3RD UN CF. ON THE; MARITIME DAY, WORLD; TECHNICAL CO-OPERATION FOR DEVELOPMENT, DEPARTMENT OF. (2) Names of specialized agencies and of non–United Nations organizations are alphabetized under the first word of their title: INTER-AMERICAN CS. ON HUMAN RIGHTS; WORLD METEOROLOGICAL ORGANIZATION.

Names of publications are italicized, with only those receiving relatively extensive treatment in *Yearbook* articles, such as *Development Forum* and the *World Economic Survey 1985*, being listed.

Cross-references are not given to entries in close proximity; for example, there is a cross-reference to "economic development" under "development" but not to "development assistance".

Bodies/subjects/topics are listed only when substantive information is given.

Abbreviations

In addition to the abbreviations contained in the list on p. xvi, the subject index uses the following:

CD	Conference on Disarmament
cf(s).	conference(s)
cl(s).	council(s)
cs(s).	commission(s)
ct(s).	committee(s)
DC	Disarmament Commission
DG	Director-General
mtg(s).	meeting(s)
sess.	session
SCPDPM	Sub-Commission on Prevention of Discrimination and Protection of Minorities of the Commission on Human Rights
spec.	special
UNCLS	United Nations Conference on the Law of the Sea
UNJSPB	United Nations Joint Staff Pension Board

Subject index

Page numbers in bold-face type indicate resolutions and decisions

accident/injury prevention, 1302 (WHO); industrial, 457 (ILO)

accounting, *see* accounts (UN); *and under* transnational corporations

ACCOUNTING AND REPORTING, AD HOC INTERGOVERNMENTAL WORKING GROUP OF EXPERTS ON INTERNATIONAL STANDARDS OF (TNCs Cs.), members/officers, 1417; sess., 617-18, **618** (Cs./ESC)

accounts (UN) *(1984)*, 1222-23, **1223** (ACABQ/Auditors Board/GA); *see also* organizational entries

Achille Lauro, see under hijacking

acquired immune deficiency syndrome (AIDS), 1304 (WHO)

Aden, Gulf of: regional seas programme (UNEP), 816

ad hoc committee . . . *for specific ct., see key word(s) of title*

ADMINISTRATION AND MANAGEMENT, DEPARTMENT OF (SECRETARIAT), Under-S-G/Assistants/offices, 1424

administrative and budgetary questions: co-ordination, 1230, **1230-31** (GA); review, 1254, **1254-55**, 1255 (GA/JIU/S-G)

ADMINISTRATIVE AND BUDGETARY QUESTIONS, ADVISORY CT. ON, 1230-31, members, 1394; officials, conditions of service/compensation, 1252, **1252-53** (ACABQ/GA); report, 1230, **1231** (GA)

ADMINISTRATIVE AND FINANCIAL FUNCTIONING OF THE UN, GROUP OF HIGH-LEVEL INTERGOVERNMENTAL EXPERTS TO REVIEW THE EFFICIENCY OF THE: establishment, 1254, **1255** (GA); structure, 1397

administrative and management questions (UN/UN system), 1254-67; personnel, 1233-45; *see also* Secretariat (UN); staff (UN/UN system); *and under* pensions

Administrative Ct. on Co-ordination, *see* Co-ordination, Administrative Ct. on

ADMINISTRATIVE TRIBUNAL, ILO, 1242

ADMINISTRATIVE TRIBUNAL, UN, 1242, 1251; appeals system, 1251, **1251** (ACABQ/GA); judgements, 1169, 1251; members, 1401; Ombudsman, proposed, **1236**, 1262 (GA/S-G); single tribunal, feasibility, 1251 (GA)

ADMINISTRATIVE TRIBUNAL JUDGEMENTS, CT. ON APPLICATIONS FOR REVIEW OF (GA), 1251; members/officers, 1396

adoption/foster placement, *see under* Children, draft Declaration on . . .

adult education, 1295 (UNESCO); *see also under* education

Afghanistan: & GA credentials, 396, **397** (Credentials Ct./GA); human rights violations, 905-9 (communications, 906-7; ESC, **906**, 906; GA, **907-8**, 908-9; SCPDPM, 906; Spec. Rapporteur, 905-6, 907); industrial planning, 607 (DTCD/UNIDO); refugee assistance, 232,

238, 859 (Human Rights Cs.), 994, 1009 (GA/UNHCR)

Afghanistan situation, 232-39 (communications, 232-37; GA, **237-38**, 238-39; S-G, 237, 398); & Iran, 237 (S-G); & Pakistan border incidents, 232-37 (communications); proximity talks, 232, 237, 398 (S-G Spec. Representative); self-determination, 232, **238** (GA), 859 (Human Rights Cs.)

Africa, 8, 9 (S-G), 126-204, 625-44 (ECA), 1278 (ILO), 1292 (WFP), 1309 (World Bank, *table*), 1318 (IFC), 1346 (ITU/UNDP), 1366 (IFAD)

& aging persons, 984, **988**

agricultural development, 1288 (FAO)

& children, UNICEF programme, 966-67; expenditures, 965 *(table)*

civil aviation, technical assistance, 1340 (ICAO)

development policy/economic co-operation, 626-29 (ECA/ESC); planning, 627-28; 2nd Spec. Memorandum, 626; *see also under* Africa, Lagos Plan of Action

disasters, 499 (S-G/UNDRO)

drought/desertification, effects of, 11 (S-G), 805-7 (ESC, 806; GA, **806-7**; OAU, 806; S-G, 805-6); regional action, 626 (ECA); relief assistance, 537 (GA/UNDP/UNDRO/Islamic Cf.); 2nd Ministerial Cf. for joint policy, 806, **807** (GA); UNICEF, 689; *see also country names; regional entries*

drug abuse, 1026 (INCB); illicit drug traffic, 1026, **1026-27** (ESC/INCB)

economic/social trends, *Survey*, 1324-25 (ESC)

education, 1295, 1299 (UNESCO); Cf. on Higher Learning: Mbabane Action Programme, 638 (ECA)

energy situation in, 637 (ECA), 690 (UNIDO)

& environmental issues, 639 (ECA/UNEP); Cf. on, 639, 793; education/training, 820 (UNEP); industry-related, 819 (UNEP); marine/coastal, Convention on management, 110; & youth, workshop, 793; *see also* Sudano-Sahelian region

food and agriculture, crisis in, 500, **501-2** (ACC/GA), 637-38 (ECA), 970 (UNICEF); aid, 698 (WFC), 702 (WFP); co-ordination, 702 (WFP); FAO/WFP Task Force, 702; production, 701 (ESC)

health/health-related issues, 774 (UNU), 965 *(table)*, 966-67 (UNICEF)

human rights violations, 898-905; *see also country names; subject entries*

human settlements, 639; & environment, Jt. Regional Ct., 628

industrial development, 598 (IDDA/UNIDO), 601 (UNIDO), 635-36 (ECA/IDDA); & manpower develop-

ment, 604 (ECA/UNIDO); planning, 607-8 (IDDA/UNIDO); technical co-operation, 635 (IDDA); *see also* Africa, Industrial Development Decade for

information, UNESCO Programme, 1299

LDCs, 434, 629-30 (ESC, **629-30**, 630; Intergovernmental Ct./Cf. of Ministers, 629)

migrant workers, welfare of, 735, **735-36** (ESC)

Multinational Programming and Operational Centres, 624, 627; directors of, appointment, 643, **643** (ESC)

natural resources, 636-37 (ECA), 785, 786 (UNU); sea-bed exploration/water resources, 637 (ECA)

population, 638-39 (ECA); information network (POPIN), 638; publication, 638; regional institutes, 638-39; UNFPA allocation, 764 *(table)*

refugee assistance, 996-97; food aid, 698 (WFC); UNHCR expenditures, 994, 994 *(table)*; *see also* Africa, 2nd International Cf. on Assistance to; southern African student refugees

science and technology, 785 (UNU Spec. Ct.)

technical co-operation, 468, 1299 (UNESCO)

trade & finance, 630-31; external debt, 631; information/training, 630 (ECA/ITC); preferential trade area, 630-31, **631** (GA/ECA); promotion/facilitation, 561 (ITC), 630 (ECA)

& transnational corporations, 620 (ECA/TNCs Centre); training programme, 622 (TNCs Centre), 630 (ECA)

transport/communications: air, 632 (S-G); link with Europe, 634 (ECA/ECE/ESC); remote sensing, 633-34 (ECA mission); satellite communications system, proposed, 633 (Inter-Agency Ct.); *see also* Africa, Transport and Communications Decade in; Zaire

UNDP programmes, 500

UN Space Applications Programmes, 102

volunteer programmes, 487, 488 (UNV); Domestic Development Services, 500 (UNV)

see also country names and organizational and subject entries

AFRICA, AGRICULTURAL REHABILITATION PROGRAMME FOR, 1287-88 (FAO)

Africa, critical economic situation, 11 (S-G), 498-504 (ACC/CPC, 499-500; communications, 501; ESC, **501-2**, 502-3; GA, **503**, 504; JUNIC, 499; S-G, 498-99; UNDP, 500-1), 626 (ECA); & children, 966 (UNICEF); debt problems, 498, 499, **502** (ESC), 544; Declaration *(1984)*, 498, 501, **503**, 504 (GA); famine in, 499 (S-G);

Africa, critical economic situation *(cont.)*
food crisis, 499, 500 (ACC), **501-2**
(ESC/S-G); information dissemination,
504 (GA); & nutrition, 775 (ACC Sub-
Ct.); Priority Recovery Programme
(OAU), **202** (GA), 499, 501 (ESC), **503**
(GA); & spec. postage stamps, 504
(GA); 2nd Spec. Memorandum (ECA),
498, 503, 625

Africa, critical situation in: GA spec.
sess., proposed, 499, **502** (ESC/OAU);
Preparatory Ct. of the Whole for,
establishment, **503** (GA), 1396 (OAU),
1400; spec. postage stamp, 1267, **1267**
(ACABQ/GA/S-G)

AFRICA, DECLARATION ON THE
DENUCLEARIZATION OF *(1964)*: implementation, 59, **59-60**, 60 (DC/GA),
119, 143, 204 (GA)

AFRICA, EMERGENCY TASK FORCE, UN: &
UNHCR, 997

AFRICA, FAO/WFP TASK FORCE ON, 702;
& Office for Special Relief Operations
projects, 1292

AFRICA, INDUSTRIAL DEVELOPMENT
DECADE FOR *(1980-1990)*: implementation, 635-36 (ECA/UNIDO), 635; ESC,
636, 636; IDDA, 635); financing, 635,
636 (ECA/ESC), 600 (UNIDO)

AFRICA, INTERNATIONAL ACTION FOR
RELAUNCHING THE INITIATIVE FOR
LONG-TERM DEVELOPMENT AND
ECONOMIC GROWTH IN: 2ND SPEC.
MEMORANDUM (ECA CF. OF
MINISTERS), 498, 503 (ESC&S-G), 625

AFRICA, INTERNATIONAL CF. ON THE
EMERGENCY SITUATION IN (Mar.), 201
(S-G), 496, 498-99

AFRICA, *1980* LAGOS PLAN OF ACTION
FOR THE IMPLEMENTATION OF THE
MONROVIA STRATEGY FOR THE
ECONOMIC DEVELOPMENT OF (OAU),
498, 672 (ESC)

AFRICA, MINISTERIAL REGIONAL CF. ON
SECURITY, DISARMAMENT AND
DEVELOPMENT IN (OAU): Lomé Declara-
tion/Action Plan, 14; & nuclear armaments, 59

AFRICA, REGIONAL PROGRAMME FOR THE
ERADICATION OF ILLITERACY IN
(UNESCO), 1295

AFRICA, 2ND INTERNATIONAL CF. ON
ASSISTANCE TO REFUGEES IN (ICARA
II): Declaration/Action Programme, 997;
follow-up, 997-99 (ESC, 998; GA, **998-99**,
999; OAU, 997-98; S-G, 998;
UNDP/UNHCR, 997)

AFRICA, 2ND REGIONAL CF. ON DEVELOP-
MENT AND UTILIZATION OF MINERAL
RESOURCES IN: Lusaka Action Pro-
gramme, 636

AFRICA, SPEC. EMERGENCY ASSISTANCE
FUND FOR DROUGHT AND FAMINE IN
(OAU): establishment, 499, **502** (ESC),
807 (S-G/GA)

AFRICA, STATISTICAL TRAINING PRO-
GRAMME FOR, 640

AFRICA, TRANSPORT AND COMMUNICA-
TIONS DECADE IN *(1978-1988)*, 631-33
(ESC, 632-33, **633**, 633; GA, 633; JIU,
632; S-G, 631-32); Phase I *(1978-1983)*,
631; Phase II *(1984-1988)*, 631-32 (S-G);
UNIDO activities, 614

AFRICA, TRUST FUND TO COMBAT

POVERTY AND HUNGER IN (UNDP): ex-
penditures/income, 500

AFRICA, UN OFFICE FOR EMERGENCY
OPERATIONS IN, **202** (S-G/GA), 456, 499,
504 (GA), 997 (UNHCR); Director/Under-
S-G, 1425; establishment, 496

AFRICA, UN REGIONAL CENTRE FOR
PEACE AND DISARMAMENT IN, 94-95
(GA, **94**, 94; OAU, 94; S-G, 94-95)

AFRICA, PRIORITY PROGRAMME FOR
ECONOMIC RECOVERY *(1986-1990)*
(OAU), 499, **501** (ESC), **503**, 504 (GA)

AFRICA LIBERATION DAY, 1079, 1092

AFRICA ASSOCIATION FOR PUBLIC AD-
MINISTRATION AND MANAGEMENT, 638

AFRICAN CENTRAL BANKS: ROUND TABLE
OF GOVERNORS OF, & OFFICIALS OF
INTERNATIONAL FINANCE INSTITUTIONS,
631

AFRICAN CENTRE OF METEOROLOGICAL
APPLICATIONS FOR DEVELOPMENT, 627;
establishment/composition, 628 (ECA)

AFRICAN DEVELOPMENT, UN TRUST FUND
FOR, 627; 5th biennial pledging cf., 627

AFRICAN DEVELOPMENT BANK: & African
Industrial Development Fund, 636 (ECA);
road construction, 538

AFRICAN INSTITUTE FOR ECONOMIC
DEVELOPMENT AND PLANNING, 628-29
(ECA, 628; ESC, **628**, 628-29), 1414

AFRICAN INSTITUTE FOR HIGHER
TECHNICAL TRAINING AND RESEARCH,
638

AFRICAN MINISTERIAL CONFERENCE ON
THE ENVIRONMENT: Cairo Programme,
639 (ECA), **790**, 793 (UNEP Cl.); desertification control, 807-8; & youth, 793

AFRICAN MINISTERS OF FINANCE, CF. OF:
proposed establishment, 630, 631 (ECA)

AFRICAN MINISTERS OF INFORMATION, CF.
OF: 1st extraordinary sess., 403; resolu-
tions on *apartheid*, 128-29, 173, on
Namibia, 1094

AFRICAN MINISTERS OF SOCIAL AFFAIRS:
4th Cf. of (ECA/OAU), 638; regional co-
operation, 731

AFRICAN MINISTERS OF TRADE, 8TH CF.
OF, 620, 630

AFRICAN MONETARY FUND: proposed
establishment, 630 (ECA)

AFRICAN NATIONAL CONGRESS OF SOUTH
AFRICA: assistance/support, 170
(UNDP/UNIDO); death sentences, 163-64
(communications, 164; GA, **160**, 162;
SC, 164); detentions, **160**, 162 (*Apart-
heid* Ct./GA); financing, New York office
161, 170 (GA); observer, Review Cf. on
Women's Decade, 938

African News Agency, Pan, *see* Pan African
News Agency

AFRICAN OIL PALM DEVELOPMENT
ASSOCIATION: establishment, 1290 (FAO)

AFRICAN PLANNERS, STATISTICIANS AND
DEMOGRAPHERS, JOINT CF. OF, 1414

AFRICAN REGIONAL CONFERENCE ON
AGING, 984, 988 (GA)

AFRICAN REGIONAL INSTITUTE FOR THE
PREVENTION OF CRIME AND THE
TREATMENT OF OFFENDERS, 739 (7th
UN Congress)

AFRICAN REHABILITATION INSTITUTE FOR
DISABLED PERSONS, 638

AFRICAN REMOTE SENSING COUNCIL, 633-
34; Plenipotentiaries Cf., 634

AFRICAN SATELLITE COMMUNICATION
SYSTEM, REGIONAL, 633 (Inter-Agency
Co-ordinating Ct.), 1346

AFRICAN WOMEN, INTERNATIONAL CT.
FOR DEVELOPMENT PROJECTS FOR:
establishment, 967

AFRICAN WORKSHOP ON YOUTH FOR THE
ENVIRONMENT, 793 (UNEP)

AGING, INTERNATIONAL PLAN OF ACTION
ON (Vienna): implementation, 984-85
(GA, **988-89**; ESC, 985, **985-86**; S-G/
Social Development Cs., 984-85)

AGING, UN TRUST FUND FOR: contributions, 986-87, **988** (GA/S-G); financial
viability, 985, **986** (GA/S-G)

AGING, WORLD ASSEMBLY ON *(1982)*, 984

aging persons, 763 (ECE/UNFPA), 984-89;
accident prevention, 1302 (WHO); co-
operation in UN, 987 (S-G); elderly
women, 987 (NGO Ct.), 987, **988** (GA/
S-G); information network, 986, **987**
(GA/S-G); & population structure, 770,
771 (ESC/S-G); publications, 986; socio-
economic factors, 769, **770** (Population
Cs./ESC); technical co-operation, 985,
986, 986 (GA/S-G/UNFPA); world situation, study, 984 (DIESA), 986 (S-G)

agrarian reform and rural development, *see
under* rural development

agreements, *see subject entries*; treaties

AGRICULTURAL BIOMETEOROLOGY, INTER-
AGENCY GROUP ON, 805

agricultural commodities, 569-70; *see
also* names of individual commodities

agricultural development, 1288 (FAO); environmental aspects, *1985* UNEP report,
791-92; IDA credits, 1324-25 *(table)*,
1325; IFAD, 1365-66, 1367 *(tables)*;
World Bank loans, 1309-10 *(table)*, 1310;
see also food; International Fund for
Agricultural Development; rural
development

AGRICULTURAL DEVELOPMENT PLANNERS,
ASSOCIATION OF: establishment, 497
(FAO)

agricultural machinery, 609 (IDDA/
UNIDO), 613; 3rd Consultation, preparations, 613 (ESCAP)

AGRICULTURAL PROBLEMS, CT. ON (ECE),
656-57

agriculture: mechanization, 1288 (FAO);
nuclear technology, 1272 (IAEA); pest
control, mtg. on, 802 (China/FAO/UNEP);
produce standardization, 657 (ECE);
research, 1366 (IFAD); trade, 698, **700**
(GA/WFC), 1371 (GATT)

AGRICULTURE, CT. ON TRADE IN (GATT),
698, **700** (GA/WFC), 1371

agro-industries: intergovernmental mtg.
on, 604 (UNIDO); technical co-operation,
609-10 (UNIDO); *see also* fisheries; food
industry; leather industry; packaging industry; textiles; wood products industry

agrometeorology: & remote sensing, 101
(European Space Agency/FAO/WMO)

AGRONOMIC STUDIES, INTERNATIONAL IN-
STITUTE FOR ADVANCED MEDITERRA-
NEAN, 679 (FAO)

aircraft, *see* civil aircraft

air navigation, 1338 (ICAO); airlines, world
traffic, 1338; mtgs./safety issues, 1338
(ICAO); services, joint finance
agreements, 1339; Specifications &
Regional Plans, 1338 (ICAO)

AIR NAVIGATION SERVICES, PROCEDURES FOR, 1338

air pollution: 657 (ECE); & forests, 657; & motor vehicles, 657; sulphur emissions, Protocol, 657

AIR POLLUTION, ECE CONVENTION ON LONG-RANGE TRANSBOUNDARY *(1979)*: Executive Body, 3rd sess., 657; Protocol on Financing, adoption, 657, **790** (GA); Protocol on the Reduction of Sulphur Emissions, 657 (signatures/ratification, 800); Working Group on Nitrogen Oxides, established, 657

AIR POLLUTION MONITORING NETWORK, BACKGROUND, 804 (UNEP/WMO); 723 (IAEA/WMO)

air transport, 1338-39 (ICAO); conventions/protocols, 1339-40 *(list)*; international co-operation, 1339; publications, 1339 (ICAO); regional css., 1338; route facility issues, 1338-39; & terrorist attacks, 1167, **1168** (GA/S-G); *see also* air navigation; International Civil Aviation Organization

AIR TRANSPORT CF., THIRD, 1338

Albania: human rights violations, 912 (SCPDPM); microwave link with Greece, 1347; telecommunications development, 1347

alcohol: & drugs, 1013, 1028

Algeria: economic growth, 626; industrial planning, 607 (UNIDO); refugees in, 1004; water supply loans, 1312 (World Bank)

aluminium, 614, 615 (UNIDO)

Amerasinghe (Hamilton Shirley) Fellowship on the Law of the Sea, *see under* law of the sea

American-Arab Anti-Discrimination Ct., *see under* terrorism, international

American Samoa, **1141-42** (GA); information to UN, 1082

Americas, 205-19; civil aviation, technical assistance, 1340 (ICAO); drug traffic/production, 1027; industrial development, 601 (UNIDO); quincentenary anniversary observance, 205 (GA); refugees, 994, 995-96 *(table)*, 1007 (UNHCR); telecommunications training, 1346 (ITU); UNICEF programme, 965 *(table)*, 967; *see also* Andean Pact subregion; *country, organizational and regional entries*

amnesty, *see under* human rights: promotion/protection

amphetamines, 1028; schedules of, review, 1029; *see also* psychotropic substances

Andean Pact subregion; drug traffic, 1027; ecosystems protection, 798, 812 (UNEP trust fund); food/agriculture, 663 (ECLAC); land management, training, 811; telecommunications, 1346

ANDEAN SUBREGIONAL AGREEMENT, ASSOCIATION OF TELECOMMUNICATION ORGANIZATIONS OF THE, 1346

Angola: admission to WIPO, 1359; *1984* Lusaka Understanding, 177, 179, 181 (communications); refugees in, 1004; & South Africa, 180-89 (communications, 181, 189; GA, **132**, **160**, 189, **858**; Human Rights Cs., 181, 862; SC, 181-82, **182-83**, 183-85, **185**, 185-86, **187**, 186-88, **188-89**; Namibia Cl., 180; S-G, 185);

UNICEF aid to, 967; *see also* Namibia: "linkage" issue

ANGOLA, SC CS. OF INVESTIGATION: appointment, **185**, **187**, 187-88, **189** (SC); members, 1410

Anguilla, **1142-43** (GA); information to UN, 1082

animals: feeds, 1290-91 (FAO); genetic resources, 1291 (FAO); *see also* livestock; *and under* nature conservation/protection

Antarctica: disarmament, 28 (GA); S-G study, 389-91 (communications, 389; GA, **389-90**, 391)

ANTARCTIC TREATY *(1959)*, parties to, 100 *(list)*; & South Africa, 204, **390** (GA); 13th Consultative Mtg., 389 (communication)

ANTI-DUMPING CODE, AD HOC GROUP ON IMPLEMENTATION OF THE (GATT), 1370

ANTI-DUMPING PRACTICES, CT. ON (GATT), 1370; *see also* international trade

apartheid, 10 (S-G), 126-35
  general aspects, 127-32 (*Apartheid* Ct., 127-28; communications, 128-29; GA, **129-31**, **131-33**, 133-34; Human Rights Cs., 128-29)
  & genocide, 898-99 (*Ad Hoc* Working Group/Human Rights Cs.)
  hearings, 134 (*Apartheid* Ct./GA)
  information dissemination, **377**, **382**, 383 (GA/Information Ct.)
  international action against, 134-35 (*Apartheid* Ct., 134-135; GA, **131**, 135)
  labour/employment under, 1278 (ILO)
  mtgs./missions/observances, 174-76 (*Apartheid* Ct.)
  national liberation movements, aid to, 169-71 (*Apartheid*/Colonial Countries Cts., 170; ESC/Human Rights Cs., 170; GA, **132**, **161**, 170-71; UNDP/UNIDO, 170); *see also* South Africa, UN Trust Fund for
  & NGOs, 171-74 (*Apartheid* Ct.), **173**, 174 (GA/*Apartheid* Ct.)
  postage stamps, 172
  publications, 172 (*Apartheid* Ct./Centre)
  public information, 172-74 (*Apartheid* Ct., 172-74; Colonial Countries Ct./Human Rights Cs./Namibia Cl., 173; GA, **152**, **173-74**, 174)
  & sports, 164-69 (*Apartheid* Ct., 164-65; GA, **130**, **165**); draft convention, 165-69 (*Ad Hoc* Ct., 165; GA, **164-68**, 169); UN mission, 175
  & TNCs: applicability of *Apartheid* Convention, 901, **902** (Group of Three/Human Rights Cs./GA)
  UNESCO activities, 1297
  victims of, UNCHS assistance, 830, 900 (SCPDPM)
  women/children under, 175 (*Apartheid* Ct. mission)
  see also country names; Namibia; racial discrimination; South Africa; southern Africa; *and under* women

APARTHEID, CENTRE AGAINST (Secretariat), 172

APARTHEID, INTERNATIONAL CF. ON WOMEN AND CHILDREN UNDER, 175

APARTHEID, INTERNATIONAL CONVENTION ON THE SUPPRESSION AND PUNISHMENT OF THE CRIME OF *(1973)*, 900-3

(GA, **901-2**, 902-3; Group of Three, 900-1; Human Rights Cs., 901); accessions/ratifications, 901, **902** (GA/S-G); Group of Three (8th sess.), 1412 (members)

APARTHEID, RACISM AND RACIAL DISCRIMINATION, ROUND TABLE ON INTERNATIONAL LEGAL ISSUES RELATING TO, **838** (GA)

APARTHEID, SPEC. CT. AGAINST, 126-27, **129** (GA); Chairman, *1985* missions, 174-75; members/officers, 1400; Sub-Ct. on Petitions and Information, members, 1400; Sub-Ct. on the Implementation of UN Resolutions and Collaboration with South Africa, members, 1400; work programme/spec. allocation for, **176-77**, 178 (GA)

APARTHEID, TRUST FUND FOR PUBLICITY AGAINST, 172, **173** (*Apartheid* Ct./GA)

APARTHEID PROPAGANDA, MEDIA WORKSHOP ON COUNTERING, 172, 175; participants/recommendations, 172

APARTHEID IN SPORTS, AD HOC CT. ON THE DRAFTING OF AN INTERNATIONAL CONVENTION AGAINST, 165; members/officers, 1394; Working Group, 165

APARTHEID IN SPORTS, INTERNATIONAL CONVENTION AGAINST: adoption, 165-69 (*Ad Hoc* Ct., 165; GA, **165-66**, 169), **166-69** *(text)*

aquaculture (fish farming), *see under* fisheries; Zambia

ARAB GULF PROGRAMME FOR UN DEVELOPMENT ORGANIZATIONS: development aid, 461 *(table)*; desertification/drought aid, 810; & UNICEF, 969, 974 *(table)*

ARAB INDUSTRIAL DEVELOPMENT ORGANIZATION: & UNIDO, 610

Arab-Israeli conflict, *see* Lebanon; Middle East situation; Palestine question

Arab States: communications, 1298 (UNESCO); environment, training, 820 (UNEP); Fez Summit Cf., *1982*, 264; industrial development, 601 (UNIDO); & Israel, 293-305; mass communications, 370 (ITU/UNESCO); & Middle East situation, 285; regional seas programme, 816 (UNEP); remote sensing, 1297 (UNESCO); & social welfare policies, 731; technical co-operation, 468-69 (UNDP), 1299 (UNESCO), 1311-12 (World Bank); & TNCs, 620 (ECWA/TNCs Centre); UNICEF programmes, 969; volunteer programmes, 487 (UNV); *see also country names*; Economic Commission for Western Asia; League of Arab States; Middle East; Western Asia

ARAB STATES, EXTRAORDINARY SUMMIT CF. (Casablanca), 264; communiqué, circulation, 399; & Iran-Iraq conflict, 250

Arab States, League of, *see* League of Arab States

arbitrary executions, *see* summary executions

Arbitration Rules, *see under* International Commercial Arbitration

Argentina: flood measures, 547 (UNDRO); & human rights violations, 912 (ESC); IAEA safeguards, 1271; natural resources exploration, 669 (UNRFNRE); *see also* Beagle Channel dispute; Falkland Islands (Malvinas)

arid/semi-arid lands: economic analysis, 818-19; isotope techniques, seminar, 1274 (IAEA); _see also_ desertification

arms race, 6 (S-G); bilateral negotiations, **46**, 46-47 (GA); economic/social consequences of, 88-89, report (communications, 88; GA, **88-89**, 89); & environment, 817 (UNEP); & international security Declaration, **118** (GA); in outer space, 78-82 (_Ad Hoc_ Ct./CD/COPUOS, 79; GA, 79-80, **80-81**), 101, **107** (COPUOS/GA); on sea-bed, 115 (GA); UNIDIR study, 79, **80** (GA); _see also_ conventional weapons; disarmament; disarmament and development; environmental modification; nuclear disarmament; Sea-Bed and the Ocean Floor . . ., Treaty on

ARMS RACE AND THE ENVIRONMENT, ADVISORY GROUP ON THE: 2nd mtg., 817 (Stockholm International Peace Research Institute/UNEP)

arts, 1298 (UNESCO), 1360 (WIPO); conventions on protection of artists/performers, 1359 _(list)_

Aruba: IPF for, 470 (UNDP Cl.)

asbestos: safety in use, 1278 (ILO)

Asia: agricultural development, 1366 (IFAD); conservation, wildlife, 813 (IUCN/UNEP); drug abuse/traffic, 1027-28; energy conservation, 607 (UNIDF); radio services, 385; UNICEF programmes, 965 _(table)_, 968-69

ASIA, MINISTERIAL-LEVEL CF. ON THE ENVIRONMENT IN (ESCAP): Declaration/Framework, 650

Asia and the Pacific, 644-53; civil aviation, technical assistance, 1340 (ICAO); colonialism Declaration, seminar, 1060 (Colonial Countries Ct.); cultural/natural heritage, conservation, 1229 (JIU); development policy & regional cooperation, 645 (ESCAP); disability issues, 776 (ESCAP); economic/social trends, _Survey_, 645 (ESC); education, 1295-1301 (UNESCO); environment, 650 (ESCAP), 796 (UNEP); food aid, 702 (WFP); generalized system of preferences project, 556-57 (UNCTAD); human rights, 889, 905-12; industrial development, 601-2 (UNIDO); information network, 1299 (UNESCO); mass communication, 685 (ITU/UNESCO); nuclear medicine, 411 (IAEA/WHO); nuclear technology, 648 (ESCAP); political/security questions, 220-32; population, 650 (ESCAP Population Ct.), 764 _(table)_; technical co-operation, 469 (UNDP), 646 (ESCAP/ECDC/TCDC), 1299 (UNESCO); technology transfer, 649 (ESCAP); telecommunications, 1346, 1346-47 (ITU); & TNCs, 620, 622, 647 (TNCs Centre/ESCAP); trade information, 646; trade promotion, 561 (ITC), 646, (ITC/ESCAP); UNICEF programme, 963 _(table)_, 968-69; volunteer programmes, 487 (UNV); World Bank loans, 1309 _(table)_; _see also_ Economic and Social Commission for Asia and the Pacific; South-East Asia; Western Asia; _and country names; organizational, regional and subject entries_

ASIA AND THE PACIFIC, ADVISORY CT. ON REGIONAL CO-OPERATION IN EDUCATION IN (UNESCO): 3rd sess., 1296

ASIA AND THE PACIFIC, 5TH REGIONAL CF. OF MINISTERS OF EDUCATION AND THOSE RESPONSIBLE FOR ECONOMIC PLANNING IN (UNESCO), 1295-96

ASIA AND THE PACIFIC, FERTILIZER ADVISORY, DEVELOPMENT AND INFORMATION NETWORK FOR (ESCAP/FAO/UNIDO), 648-49

ASIA AND THE PACIFIC, STATISTICAL INSTITUTE FOR, 651

ASIA AND THE PACIFIC, TECHNOLOGY ATLAS FOR (ESCAP), 649

ASIA AND THE PACIFIC, TECHNOLOGY FOR DEVELOPMENT IN: Tokyo Programme (ESCAP), 644, 649

ASIA AND THE PACIFIC, TRANSPORT AND COMMUNICATIONS DECADE FOR _(1985-1994)_: Declaration launching, 647; implementation, 647

ASIAN-AFRICAN CF. (BANDUNG), 30TH ANNIVERSARY COMMEMORATIVE MTG.: Declaration, 403; on _apartheid_, 128; on colonialism Declaration, 1060; on disarmament, 14; on economic co-operation, 412; on Namibia, 1094

ASIAN-AFRICAN LEGAL CONSULTATIVE CT.: co-operation with UN, 1200, **1200** (GA/S-G); & refugee protection, 1010

ASIAN FORUM OF ENVIRONMENTAL JOURNALISTS (ESCAP): establishment, 650

ASIAN AND PACIFIC CENTRE FOR TRANSFER OF TECHNOLOGY (ESCAP): adoption of statute, 649; functions/organization/headquarters, 649; Technical Advisory Ct., 1st sess., 649

ASIAN AND PACIFIC DEVELOPMENT CENTRE, 645

ASIAN AND PACIFIC MINISTERIAL CF. ON SOCIAL WELFARE AND SOCIAL DEVELOPMENT, 3RD, 649

ASIAN REGION, _1982_ SEMINAR ON NATIONAL, LOCAL AND REGIONAL ARRANGEMENTS FOR THE PROMOTION AND PROTECTION OF HUMAN RIGHTS IN THE: report, 889 (Human Rights Cs.)

ASIAN REGIONAL CF., 10TH (ILO), 1279

ASIA-PACIFIC CALL FOR ACTION ON POPULATION AND DEVELOPMENT (ESCAP), 650

ASSOCIATION OF SOUTH-EAST ASIAN NATIONS: drug abuse/traffic, 1028; & Kampuchea situation, 222, 224; nuclear-free zone (proposed), 58; & South-East Asia security, 229, 230; UNIDO study, 608

ASTRONAUTICAL FEDERATION, INTERNATIONAL, 103

asylum, right of, _see under_ refugees

atmosphere, _see_ air pollution; climate; nuclear-weapon tests in; ozone layer

ATMOSPHERIC SCIENCES, CS. FOR, 1351 (WMO); numerical weather prediction, 1351

atomic energy, _see_ nuclear energy

ATOMIC RADIATION, UN SCIENTIFIC CT. ON THE EFFECTS OF, 388, **388** (GA); members/officers, 1407; _see also_ radiation, effects of

AUDIO-VISUAL MATTERS, _AD HOC_ WORKING GROUP ON (JUNIC), 387; _see also_ radio/visual services

auditing, _see_ accounts (UN)

AUDITORS, BOARD OF: financial reports, 1223, **1223** (ACABQ/GA); members, 1395

AUDITORS, PANEL OF EXTERNAL: members, 1399

Australia: drug abuse, 1028; withdrawal from Colonial Countries Ct., 1060

Austria: & UN Postal Administration, 1266

automation, _see under_ engineering industries

aviation, _see_ WMO programmes, 1287; _see also_ air transport

Azania, Pan Africanist Congress of, _see_ Pan Africanist Congress of Azania

BABY FOOD ACTION NETWORK, INTERNATIONAL, 969

BACTERIOLOGICAL (BIOLOGICAL) AND TOXIN WEAPONS, CONVENTION ON THE PROHIBITION OF THE DEVELOPMENT, PRODUCTION AND STOCKPILING OF, AND ON THEIR DESTRUCTION: parties, 100

bacteriological (biological) weapons: Geneva Protocol _1925_, parties, 100; _see also_ chemical weapons

balance of payments, 411-12; restrictions, 1372 (GATT); _see also_ exports; international trade

BALANCE-OF-PAYMENTS IMPORT RESTRICTIONS, CT. ON (GATT), 1372

Balkans: disaster prevention in, 547 (UNDRO); nuclear-weapon-free zones (proposed), 57

BANANAS, 2ND PREPARATORY MTG. ON: proposed, 567 (UNCTAD)

Bandung Cf., 30th Anniversary Mtg., _see_ Asian-African Cf. (Bandung), 30th Anniversary Commemorative Mtg.

Bangladesh: admission to WIPO, 1359; cyclone in, 541, **542**, 542 (GA/UNDP/UNDRO); diarrhoeal diseases, 1304 (WHO); education, 1325 (IDA); energy, 1325 (IDA); family planning, 968 (UNICEF/World Bank), 1303 (WHO); fertilizers, use of, 1290 (FAO); flood damage credits, 1326 (IDA); monuments, safeguarding, 1297 (UNESCO); nutrition, 968 (UNICEF/WHO); rice bran plant, 610 (UNCDF/UNIDO)

BANK FOR INTERNATIONAL SETTLEMENTS, 1330

BANK OF CENTRAL AFRICAN STATES: new member, 512

bantustanization, _see under_ South Africa

Barbados: admission to Nice Union & PCT Union, 1359 (WIPO)

Barcelona Convention for the Mediterranean Action Plan, _see under_ Mediterranean

Barcelona Statement, _see under_ Youth, World Congress on

Bassas da India, _see_ Malagasy islands

bauxite, 614, 615 (UNIDO)

Beagle Channel dispute, 109

Beirut, Observer Group in, _see_ Truce Supervision Organization, UN

Belgium: & IFAD 3rd World Fund, 1365; & UNRFNRE co-financing, 669

Belize: accession to NPT, 1277

Benin: DTCD project, 486; spec. economic/disaster relief assistance, 504-6 (GA, 505, **505-6**; S-G, 504-5, 505); LDC classification, 504; natural resources exploration, 669 (UNRFNRE); Nigerian aliens in, 504; refugees in, 1004; UN Information Centre, 381, 385 (GA/Information Ct./S-G)

Bermuda, 1143-44 (GA); information to UN, 1082

Berne Convention for the Protection of Literary and Artistic Works, *see* Literary and Artistic Works, Berne Convention for the Protection of

BERNE UNION: contributions to WIPO, 1362 *(table)*; Executive Ct., 1360; members, 1359, 1362-63 *(table)*

Bhutan: accession to NPT, 1271; industry, credit for, 1325 (IDA)

Bikini, nuclear testing, compensation for, *see under* Marshall Islands

bilharzia: control, 801 (UNEP/Egypt)

bills of exchange, draft convention, *see under* international payments

biological sciences, *see* life sciences

BIOLOGICAL SCIENCES, INTERNATIONAL UNION OF, 1296

biological weapons, *see* bacteriological weapons

BIOMASS, SOLAR AND WIND ENERGY, REGIONAL NETWORK ON (ESCAP), 648

biomass energy, 648 (ESCAP), 689 (UNCTAD), 692 (UNDP/UNIDO), 693 (UNEP)

biosphere, 5 (S-G); *1984* Action Plan, implementation, 813, (UNEP Cl.); *1983* Congress, proceedings, 813; global monitoring, Symposium, 1352 (WMO); reserves network, 813 1296 (UNESCO)

BIOSPHERE RESERVE SCIENTIFIC ADVISORY PANEL: establishment/mtg., 813

biotechnology: inventions, protection, 1360 (WIPO); UNU regional programmes, 774-75; *see also* genetic engineering

birth control, *see* family planning

blindness: & nutritional deficiency, 775 (ACC Sub-Ct.), 1289 (FAO/WHO), 1302 (WHO); regional action plans, 776

Bolivia: spec. economic assistance, 527 (GA/Venezuela)

Bonn Economic Declaration, *see under* Economic Summit

Botswana: refugees in, 192, 997 (UN mission), 1004; seed production, 1290 (FAO); & South Africa, 178, 189-93 (communications, 189-90; GA, 193, **858**; SC, 190-91, **191-92**, 192, **192-93**; UN mission, 193)

boundaries, *see under* continental shelf; exclusive economic zones

BOVINE MEAT, ARRANGEMENT REGARDING (GATT), 1371

brain drain (reverse transfer of technology), 489 (TCDC High-level Ct.), 718-20 (GA, **720**, 720; Inter-Agency Group on Reverse Transfer of Technology, 719-20; UNCTAD, 720); *see also* technology, reverse transfer of

Brazil: energy loans, 1311 (World Bank); education, 1310 (World Bank); & IAEA safeguards, 1271; ILO training course, 1283; small-scale enterprises, 1311 (World Bank); urban children, 971 (UNICEF)

breast-feeding, 969, 971 (UNICEF)

British Commonwealth, *see under* Commonwealth States

British Virgin Islands, 1144-45 (GA); information to UN, 1082

broadcasting, 1345 (ITU); *see also* direct broadcast satellites; radio broadcasting; television broadcasting

brucellosis, 774 (UNU), 1304 (FAO/WHO Expert Ct.)

BRUCELLOSIS, JOINT FAO/WHO EXPERT CT. ON: 6th mtg., 121

Brunei Darussalam: accession to NPT, 1271; admission to ESCAP, 645, **651** (ESC), to ICAO, 1338, to WHO, 1302, to UPU, 1342

budget (UN), *1984-1985*, 1201-4

appropriations, revised, 1201-4 (ACABQ, 1201-2; GA, **1202-3**, 1203; S-G, 1201), 1209-10 *(table)*

income sources, 1203-4, **1204** (GA), 1210 *(table)*

budget (UN), *1986-1987*, 1204-13

appropriations, 1206-9, **1206-7**, 1207 (GA), 1209-10 *(table)*

financing *(1986)*, 1211, **1211** (GA)

income sources, 1210 *table*, 1211, **1211-12** (GA)

unforeseen expenses, 1211, **1211** (GA)

Working Capital Fund, financing, 1212-13, **1213** (GA)

see also contributions (UN); financial situation (UN); programmes (UN)

Buenos Aires Plan of Action for Promoting and Implementing TCDC *1978*, *see under* technical co-operation among developing countries

building materials industry, 611 (UNIDO); energy use in, 826 (UNCHS); 1st Consultation (UNCHS/UNIDO), 604, 611, 831

Burkina Faso (Upper Volta): 486 (DTCD); family planning/health, 1326 (IDA); & Mali frontier dispute, 198, 1157 (ICJ)

Burma: nutrition programmes, 968 (UNICEF/WHO)

Burundi: Information Centre, Director, 385 (S-G); refugees in, 1004

Cameroon: industrial planning, 607 (UNIDO); refugees in, 1004; UN Information Centre, Director, 385 (S-G)

Canada: drug traffic, 1027 (INCB)

cancer, 1180 (IAEA/WHO), 1304 (WHO); & environment, 802 (UNEP)

CANCER, INTERNATIONAL AGENCY FOR RESEARCH ON, 802

cannabis: abuses of, 1026, 1027; cultivation, 1027, 1028

Cape Verde: CILSS aid to, 810; fisheries development, 1291 (FAO); industrial development project, 605 (UNIDO); spec. economic assistance, 506-7 (GA, **506-7**; S-G, 506); wind energy project, 810 (UNSO/Denmark)

Capital Development Fund, UN, *see* Development Fund, UN Capital

capital goods industry, 662 (ECLAC), 667 (ESCWA); & energy technology, 2nd Consultation, 604, 615; follow-up, 690 (UNIDO)

capital punishment, 866, **866** (S-G/GA); abolition, proposed Protocol to Civil/Political Rights Covenant, 866-67, **867** (Human Rights Cs./ESC); *see also* summary executions

CARIBBEAN, CONSULTATIVE GROUP FOR ECONOMIC DEVELOPMENT IN, 470 (UNDP)

CARIBBEAN ASSOCIATION OF NATIONAL TELECOMMUNICATIONS ORGANIZATIONS, 1346

CARIBBEAN DEVELOPMENT AND CO-OPERATION CT., 661, 1415

Caribbean region: agricultural development, 1366 (IFAD); disaster preparedness/prevention, 547 (UNDRO); economic co-operation, 470 (UNDP); human rights training, **891** (GA/UNITAR); industrial management, 607 (UNIDO); literacy programmes, 1295 (UNESCO); radio unit, **382**; regional seas programme (UNEP), 816; social science research, 1297 (UNESCO); technical co-operation, 662 (JIU/S-G), 1299 (UNESCO); telecommunications, 1346 (ITU); *see also country names*; Economic Commission for Latin America and the Caribbean; *and regional and subject entries*

CARIBBEAN STATES, ORGANIZATION OF EASTERN, 1288 (FAO)

CARTAGENA CONSENSUS: & economic co-operation, 412 (communication); & Latin America economic crisis; 3rd Ministerial Mtg./Follow-up Machinery, Final Communiqué, 661

CARTOGRAPHIC CF. FOR THE AMERICAS, 3RD UN REGIONAL *(1985)*: 683 (ESC/S-G); Ct. chairmen, 1420; officers/participants, 1420; resolutions, 683

cartography, 486 (DTCD), 683; 4th Cf. *(1989)*, 683 (ESC/S-G); desertification, mapping, 808 (UNEP); publications, 683; World Map project, 683

cassava: processing plant, 610 (UNIDO); protein enrichment of, expert mtgs., 598 (UNIDO)

cattle, *see* livestock

Cayman Islands, 1145-46 (GA); information to UN, 1082

censuses, *see under* demographic activities; Household Survey Capability Programme, National; statistics

Central Africa: investment promotion, 606 (UNIDO); Mineral Resources Centre, 636 (ECA); regional seas programme (UNEP), 816

CENTRAL AFRICAN CUSTOMS AND ECONOMIC UNION: industrial training, 602-3 (UNIDO); members, 512

Central African Republic: spec. economic assistance, 507-8 (GA, **507-8**; S-G, 507); refugees, 1004

Central America: peace/security issues, 206-9; refugee assistance/protection, 1007, 1009 (UNHCR); *see also* Americas; Caribbean region; *country names; subject entries*

CENTRAL AMERICA, CONTADORA ACT ON PEACE AND CO-OPERATION IN, 206-9 (communications, 206-8; SC, 206, **214**; S-G, 207); *ad hoc* follow-up cts., 206; Group members, 205; Support Group, 207 (S-G)

CENTRAL AMERICA AND PANAMA, PERMANENT CT. OF HOUSING AND DEVELOPMENT FOR, 832-33

Central America situation, 205-8 (communications, 205-7; GA, 208; OAS, 208; S-G, 207-8); agreements on economic/political/refugee/security matters, 207; "Declaration of San Salvador", 206; Lima Declaration, 206; *see also country names*

cereals, *see* grains

Chad: displaced persons/refugees, emergency assistance, 509, 999-1000 (GA, **999-1000**, 1000; UNDRO/UNICEF/ NGOs, 999); interim plan, *1986-1988*, 509; & Libyan Arab Jamahiriya, 195-96 (SC); ODA flows, OECD report, 508; spec. economic assistance, 508-9 (GA, **509**; S-G, 508-9); & UN representation, 397

CHARTER, CT. ON ARRANGEMENTS FOR A CF. FOR THE PURPOSE OF REVIEWING THE, 1396

CHARTER OF THE UN, 1379-88 *(text)*

CHARTER OF THE UN, AD HOC CT. ON IMPLEMENTATION OF THE COLLECTIVE SECURITY PROVISIONS OF THE, 119-21 (GA, **120**, 120-21; S-G, 119-20); members, 1395

CHARTER OF THE UN, SPEC. CT. ON THE, AND ON THE STRENGTHENING OF THE ROLE OF THE ORGANIZATION, 1177, **1178-79** (GA); members/officers, 1400; Working Group, 1177

CHEMICAL CODE, BULK: amendments, 1356 (IMO)

CHEMICAL CODE, INTERNATIONAL BULK: amendments, 1356 (IMO)

chemical industries, 655-57; Periodic Survey, 655 (Group of Experts); safety in, 1279; technical co-operation, 610-12 (UNIDO); *see also* building materials; fertilizer industry; pesticides; petro-chemical industry; pharmaceutical industry

CHEMICAL INDUSTRY CT. (ECE), 655

CHEMICAL SAFETY, INTERNATIONAL PRO-GRAMME ON, 802, 1279 (ILO/UNEP/ WHO); *see also under* toxic substances

chemicals, harmful: international trade in, 802 (*Ad Hoc* Expert Group); publication, 821; *see also* environmental monitoring; pesticides; toxic substances

CHEMICALS (IN PARTICULAR PESTICIDES) IN INTERNATIONAL TRADE, AD HOC WORKING GROUP OF EXPERTS FOR THE EXCHANGE OF INFORMATION ON POTENTIALLY HARMFUL: mtgs., 802

chemical weapons, 7 (S-G); convention (proposed), 70-73 (*Ad Hoc* Ct./CD, 70-71; communications, 71; GA, **71-72**, 72, **72-73**, 73); *1925* Geneva Protocol, parties, 100; use of (alleged), 70, 71 (com-munications); *see also* Iran-Iraq conflict; Kampuchea situation

CHEMICAL WEAPONS, AD HOC CT. ON, 70-71, **72** (GA); working groups, 71

Chicago Convention, *see* International Civil Aviation, Convention on *(1944)*

child, rights of: draft convention, 929-30 (ESC, **929**; GA, 929, **929-930**; Human Rights Cs./Working Group, 929)

CHILD, RIGHTS OF THE, WORKING GROUP ON THE, 1412

CHILD DEVELOPMENT, NATIONAL IN-STITUTE OF PUBLIC CO-OPERATION AND (India): Maurice Pate Memorial Award to, 963

CHILD LABOUR IN ALL PARTS OF THE WORLD, SEMINAR ON WAYS TO ELIMINATE THE EXPLOITATION OF, 930 (ILO/S-G)

children, 962-76; abuse of, 967 (UNICEF), 1303 (WHO); commemorative stamp, 1267; disabled, 776 (UNESCO/UNICEF);

education, 970 *(table)*, 971-72 (UNICEF); essential drugs, 966 *(table)*, 971 (UNICEF/WHO); health, expenditures, 967 *(table)*; immunization *(UCI-1990)*, 11 (S-G), 963, **964** (GA), 970 (UNICEF), 971; nutrition, 970 *(table)*, 972 (UNICEF/ WHO); primary health care, 966, 970-71 (UNICEF); publication, 976; sale of/labour, 871, 930 (SCPDPM), 971, 976 (UNICEF/ILO); sexual exploitation, 871 (Working Group on Slavery); survival & development, 494-95 (UNCDF), 966, 970 *(table)*; welfare, urban areas, 969, 971 (UNICEF); *see also* infant feeding

CHILDREN, DRAFT DECLARATION ON SOCIAL AND LEGAL PRINCIPLES RELATING TO PROTECTION AND WELFARE OF, WITH SPECIAL REFERENCE TO FOSTER PLACEMENT AND ADOPTION NATIONALLY AND IN-TERNATIONALLY, 976 (GA)

CHILDREN'S FUND, UN, 962-76, 1419
accounts *(1983)*, 974 (UNICEF Board); *(1984)*, 975 (ACABQ/Auditors Board/GA/UNICEF Board)

award to Water Resources Association, 972

contributions, 973, 973-74 *(table)*

Executive Director, 1419, 1424; Deputies, 1424

financial plan *(1985-1988)*, 973 (UNICEF Board)

40th anniversary, preparations, 964, **964-65** (GA)

Greeting Card Operation, 975 (UNICEF Board)

headquarters arrangements, 975 (ACABQ/UNICEF Board)

income/expenditures, total, 973-75 (ACABQ/UNICEF Board)

information, 964

inter-agency co-operation, 975-76

Joint Ct. with WHO, 963, members, 1419

Maurice Pate Memorial Award *(1985)*, 963; commitment, 966 *(table)*

medium-term plan *(1984-1987)*, 963 (UNICEF Board)

& NGO Ct. for, 964

policy review, 963 (UNICEF Board)

programme policy decisions, 963-65

programmes, 965-69; expenditures/com-mitments: regional/interregional, 965-66 *(tables)*, 966-69; sectoral, 969-73, 970 *(table)*

CHILDREN'S FUND, UN, EXECUTIVE BOARD, 962-63, 1418-19 (members/of-ficers); Administration & Finance Ct., 962, 1419 (members/officers); Pro-gramme Ct., 962, 1419 (members/of-ficers); working group, mandate renewed, 963

Chile: birth control, 1303 (WHO); GA credentials, 396, **397** (Credentials Ct./GA); energy production, 614 (UNIDO); human rights violations, 913-16 (ESC/SCPDPM, 913; GA, **914-16**, 916; Human Rights Cs., 913; Spec. Rap-porteur, 913-14, 916); & IAEA safeguards, 1271; states of emergency, 854 (Human Rights Cs.); technical assistance, 1311 (World Bank); urban development, 1312

(World Bank); *see also* Beagle Channel dispute

China: agricultural development, 1325 (IDA); & drug control, 1028; economic trends, 428 (*1985 World Economic Survey*), 430 (UNCTAD *Report*); educa-tion, 1325 (IDA); energy resources development, 692 (UNIDO); fertilizer in-dustry loans, 1311 (World Bank); food production, 1287 (FAO Cl.); highway development, 1326 (IDA); & IAEA safeguards, 1271; IFC investment, 1317; import management, 646 (ESCAP/ITC); information projects, 799 (UNEP); & Maritime University, branch established, 1356; & non-metallic minerals, 611 (UNIDO); transportation, 1312 (World Bank); water supply, 1327 (IDA); *see also* Viet Nam

civil aircraft: export credits, 1371 (GATT); non-use of force against, amendment/ conventions, 1339 (ICAO); *see also* air navigation; air transport; International Convention on Civil Aviation

CIVIL AIRCRAFT, CT. ON TRADE IN (GATT), 1371

civil and political rights, 852-53 (S-G); state of siege/emergency, 854, **854** (ESC/Human Rights Cs./SCPDPM); *see also* capital punishment; conscientious objectors; detainees; disappearance of persons; freedom of movement; freedom of speech; prisoners; prostitu-tion; self-determination of peoples; slavery; *and country names*

CIVIL AND POLITICAL RIGHTS, INTERNA-TIONAL COVENANT/OPTIONAL PRO-TOCOL *(1966)*: accessions/ratifications, 853 (S-G); implementation, 853-54 (ESC/Human Rights Cs./Ct., 853; GA, 853-54)

civil aviation, *see* air navigation; air transport; civil aircraft

CIVIL AVIATION, CONVENTION FOR THE SUPPRESSION OF UNLAWFUL ACTS AGAINST THE SAFETY OF, **1170** (SC)

Civil Aviation, International Convention on *(1944)*, *see* International Civil Aviation, Convention on *(1944)*

CIVIL AVIATION PURCHASING SERVICE, 1340

Civilian Persons, Convention on Protection of, in Time of War (4th Geneva Conven-tion), *see under* Geneva Conventions

Civil Service Commission, International, *see* International Civil Service Cs.

climate: & agriculture, 805; & carbon monoxide effects, 805, 1351 (WMO); cloud physics, 1252 (WMO); food/ agriculture, 1351 (WMO); glacier inven-tory, 804 (UNEP); impact studies, 804-5 (UNEP), 1351 (WMO); monitoring, 804 (WMO/UNEP); & nuclear war, effects on, 39, **39-40** (S-G/GA)

CLIMATE IMPACT STUDIES PROGRAMME, WORLD (UNEP), 804-5 (UNEP Cl.); joint mtg. with International Council of Scien-tific Unions/UNEP/WMO, 805; publica-tions, 805; Scientific Advisory Ct., 4th mtg., 805

CLIMATOLOGY, CS. FOR (WMO), 1351

CLIMATE PROGRAMME, WORLD (WMO): implementation, 805 (UNEP Cl.), 1351

(International Council of Scientific Unions/WMO/UNEP); components, 1351

clothing industry, 609 (UNIDO); *see also* textile industry

coal: development, 684 (S-G); DTCD projects, 689; trade, Working Party on, 656 (ECE)

COAL COMMITTEE (ECE): 81st sess., 656

COARSE GRAINS, PULSES, ROOTS AND TUBER CROPS IN THE HUMID TROPICS OF ASIA AND THE PACIFIC, REGIONAL CO-ORDINATION CENTRE: Governing Board, 3rd sess., 649

cocaine, abuse of, 1027 (INCB); production/traffic, 1026, 1028 (INCB)

COCAINE AND HEROINE ANALYSIS, EXPERT GROUP ON, 1015

COCOA AGREEMENT, *1980* INTERNATIONAL: proposed successor, 569

COCOA CONFERENCE, UN: 3rd part, 569

coconuts: cyclone damage, 1290 (FAO)

codeine: medical need for, 1019

Code of Conduct, Intergovernmental Working Group on, *see under* transnational corporations

Codex Alimentarius, 1303

Collective Measures Ct. (GA), 1395-96; *see also* Peace, Uniting for

Colombia: development finance, 1310 (World Bank); trade policy reforms, 1311 (World Bank); UNICEF projects, 968; volcanic eruption, aid for, 545-46 (GA, **546**; UNDP Administrator, 545-46), 702 (WFP), 775 (UNDRO); water supply/ sewerage loans, 1312 (World Bank)

colonial countries, 1059-83

information dissemination, 1064 (GA), 1079-81 (Colonial Countries Ct./Sub-Ct. on Petitions, 1079; GA, **1080**, 1080-81); NGO role, 1079-80; publications, **1080** (GA)

mercenaries, recruitment/training, **858**, 862 (GA/Human Rights Cs.); use of, **1063** (GA)

military activities in, **1062-63** (GA), 1077-79 (Colonial Countries Ct., 1077; GA, **1077-79**, 1079)

COLONIAL COUNTRIES AND PEOPLES, DECLARATION ON THE GRANTING OF INDEPENDENCE TO *(1960)*

implementation, **119**, **1064-65**, 1065-66 (GA); foreign interests impeding, **1073-77** (Colonial Countries Ct., 1073; GA, **1073-76**, 1076-77); by international organizations, 1066-73 (Colonial Countries Ct., 1069; ESC, **1066-68**, 1068-69; GA, **1069-72**, 1072-73; ESC President/S-G, 1066)

25th anniversary observance, 1060-64 (Colonial Countries Ct., 1060; communications, 1060-61; GA, 1061, **1061-63**, 1063-64); DPI action/regional seminars, 1060; GA spec. mtg., 1061; UN Postal Administration, 1060

COLONIAL COUNTRIES AND PEOPLES, SPEC. CT. ON THE SITUATION WITH REGARD TO THE IMPLEMENTATION OF THE DECLARATION ON THE GRANTING OF INDEPENDENCE TO, 1059, 1060, **1070** (GA); co-operation with TC, 1089; extraordinary sess. (Tunis), **382** (GA), 1060; members/officers, 1400; membership withdrawal, 1060; Sub-Ct. on Petitions, Information and Assistance, 1060, 1400;

Sub-Ct. on Small Territories, 1060, 1400; Working Group, 1400

commercial arbitration, *see* international commercial arbitration

committee . . . *for specific ct., see key word(s) of title*

commodities, 561 (ITC), 565-71 (GA, 567-68; Commodities Ct./UNCTAD, 566-67; UNCTAD *Report/World Economic Survey*, 565); international economic classifications, 1032-33, **1033** (ESC/Statistical Cs.); UNCTAD survey, 566 (Commodities Ct.); *see also* metals; minerals; *names of individual products*

COMMODITIES, CT. ON (TDB), 566; members/officers, 1402; spec. sess. (2nd & 3rd), 566

COMMODITIES, COMMON FUND FOR:

Agreement Establishing *(1980)*, 567, 568, **700** (GA); financing, 568 (S-G); First Account, 567; Preparatory Cs., 568; Second Account, contributions, 568; signatures/ratifications, 568 (GA/S-G)

COMMODITIES, INTEGRATED PROGRAMME FOR (UNCTAD), **699** (GA)

COMMODITIES, PERMANENT SUB-CT. ON (TDB), 565, 1403

COMMODITY DESCRIPTION AND CODING SYSTEM, HARMONIZED, 558, 1370

COMMONWEALTH STATES: & *apartheid*, 127, 128; & Cyprus, 254; communiqué, circulation to UN, 403; drug abuse/traffic, 1017, 1024; economic co-operation, 413; Media Workshop on *Apartheid*, 172, 175; & South Africa, 172-73, 180; Southern Africa, Accord on, 138

COMMUNICATION, INTERNATIONAL PROGRAMME FOR THE DEVELOPMENT OF, 369, **372** (GA); Intergovernmental Cl., 369-70, **372** (GA), 1298 (UNESCO); IPDC/UNESCO Prize, 1298; Spec. Account, 370

communications, 1298 (UNESCO); fellowships, 1299 (UNESCO); infrastructures, **379**, **380** (GA/Information Ct.); regional activities, 1298 (UNESCO); technical co-operation, 1299 *(tables)*; *see also* mass communication; new world information and communication order; public information; radio broadcasting; telecommunications

COMMUNICATIONS, WORKING GROUP ON (SCPDPM): members, 1412

communications satellites, 633 (ECA); seminar, 101 (COPUOS/USSR); & UN acquisition, 374, **380** (GA/S-G); *see also* satellites; telecommunications

Comorian island of Mayotte, status, 198-200 (communications, 199-200; GA, **199-200**, 200, **858**; S-G, 198)

Comoros: admission to ICAO, 1338; economic assistance, 509-10 (GA, **510**; S-G, 509-10); external trade balance, 510

COMPUTER APPLICATIONS, INTERNATIONAL NETWORK OF CENTRES FOR, 1296

COMPUTER PROCUREMENT, WORKING PARTY ON (GATT), 1371

computer technology, 613 (UNIDO), 826-27 (UNCHS), 831 (UNCHS/UNESCO), 1360 (UNESCO/WIPO); housing finance software, 826 (UNCHS); as management tool, 607 (UNIDO); UNESCO projects, 1296; urban data management, 826 (UNCHS); *see also* information systems

COMPUTING CENTRE, INTERNATIONAL, budget, 1264 (ACABQ/GA-S-G)

CONFERENCES, CT. ON, 1256, **1256** (GA); members/officers, 1396

conferences/meetings (UN), 1256-61

calendars: *1985*, 1258-59 (Ct. on Cfs., 1258-59; GA, **1259**); *1986-1987*, 1259-60 (Ct. on Cfs./GA)

pattern of, 1256-58 (Ct. on Cfs., 1256; GA, **1256-58**, 1258)

rules of procedure (draft), consideration deferred, 1181 (GA/S-G)

services, 1259-60 (ACABQ/Ct. on Cfs./GA); Under-S-G, 1424; Vienna Centre, 1260-61 (ACABQ/JIU/S-G, 1260; GA, **1260-61**, 1261)

see also documentation (UN); *geographic and subject entries*

CONFERENCE SERVICES, DEPARTMENT OF, 1260; Under-S-G, 1424

Congo, 1299 (UNESCO); disaster preparedness, 547 (UNDRO); natural resources exploration, 669-70 (UNRFNRE)

conscientious objectors, rights, 873 (Human Rights Cs./S-G)

conservation, 812-13; national strategies, 801 (UNEP Cl.); wetlands as waterfowl habitats, Convention on, 813; *see also* biosphere; ecosystems; wild flora/fauna; *and under* wildlife

CONSERVATION OF MIGRATORY SPECIES OF WILD ANIMALS, CONVENTION ON: Cf. of parties to, 1st mtg., **790** (GA), 813 (UNEP Cl.); interim trust fund, 813; Standing Ct./Scientific Cl. established, 813

CONSERVATION OF NATURE AND NATURAL RESOURCES, INTERNATIONAL UNION FOR, 812; endangered species/protected areas, projects, 812

CONSERVATION STRATEGY, WORLD *(1980)*: implementation, UNEP co-ordinating role, 812

construction industry, 826 (UNCHS); *see also* building materials industry

consular relations: Vienna Convention on *(1963)*/Optional Protocols, States parties, 1172

consultants, *see* United Nations: experts/consultants

consumer protection, 571, **571** (GA); guidelines, **571-74** *(text)*

Contadora Act/Group on Peace and Co-operation in Central America, *see* Central America, Contadora Act on Peace and Co-operation in

container transport, *see* multimodal transport

continental shelf

definition, 109 (S-G), 113 (S-G Office)

delimitation: Libyan Arab Jamahiriya & Malta, 109 (S-G), 1156 (ICJ); & Tunisia, 1155-56 (ICJ)

CONTRACT PRACTICES, WORKING GROUP ON INTERNATIONAL (UNCITRAL): members/officers, 1401

contributions (UN), 1213-20 (Contributions Ct., 1214; GA, **1214**, 1214-15)

non-members' assessments, 1219 *(table)*

scale of assessments, 1214-17 (Contributions Ct., 1215; GA, **1214**, 1214-15, **1215-16**, **1216-17**, 1217)

status, 1218-19 *(table)*

contributions (UN) *(cont.)*
  withholdings, Members' cumulative,
    1219 *(table)*
CONTRIBUTIONS, AD HOC CTS. OF THE
  GA FOR ANNOUNCEMENT OF, *see*
  Palestine Refugees in the Near East, *Ad
  Hoc* Ct. . . .; Refugees, *Ad Hoc* Ct. . . .
CONTRIBUTIONS, CT. ON (GA), 1215;
  members, 1394
conventional weapons, 6 (S-G), 76-78;
  follow-up study, 77, **77-78** (GA); *1980*
  Convention/Protocols, ratification, 78, **78**
  (GA/S-G); regional initiatives, 76, **76-77**,
  77 (GA/S-G); *see also* disarmament
  conventions, *see* multilateral treaties;
  treaties; *and under subject entries*
Cook Islands: admission to FAO, 1287
co-operative movements, *see under* social
  development
CO-ORDINATION, ADMINISTRATIVE CT. ON,
  1039-40; bodies on specific subjects,
  1040; Joint Mtgs. with CPC, 1042-44;
  members, 1418; reports, *1983/84*, 1039,
  1040, **1042** (CPC/ESC), 1224 (CPC); subsidiary bodies, 1039-40; & UNCHS participation, 832-33 (Human Settlements
  Cs., 831-32; S-G, 832)
CO-ORDINATION, CT. FOR PROGRAMME
  AND, 1040-42, 1224-25, **1225** (ESC),
  1396; Joint Mtgs. with ACC, 1042-44;
  members/officers, 1415-16; work pro-
  gramme/organization, **1041**, 1042
  (ESC/GA)
co-ordination in the UN system, 1038-45
  (ACC, 1039-40; CPC, 1040; GA, **1038-39**)
  administrative/budgetary, 1230, **1230-31**
    (ACABQ/GA)
  cross-organizational programme
    analyses, **1041**, 1044 (CPC/ESC/S-G),
    1227-28 (CPC)
  Joint Mtgs. of ACC/CPC, 1042-44 (CPC,
    1043; ESC, **1043-44**); review, 1042-43
    (CPC, 1043; ESC, **1042-43**)
  medium-term plans, **1041**, 1044
    (ACC/ESC)
  see also programmes (UN)
copyright/neighbouring rights, 1360
  (WIPO); conventions, 1359 *(list)*; publications, 1361; training programmes, 1360;
  see also industrial property; Literary and
  Artistic Works, Berne Convention for the
  Protection of (WIPO); patents
Costa Rica: border incident, 208 (OAS);
  refugees in, 1007; World Bank projects,
  1311; *see also* Central America situation;
  Nicaragua
Côte d'Ivoire, *see* Ivory Coast
COUNCIL FOR MUTUAL ECONOMIC
  ASSISTANCE : environmental monitoring,
  801 (UNEP); & International Register of
  Potentially Toxic Chemicals co-operation,
  803
crime, 738-57; congresses on, proposed
  change in procedures, 742 (ESC/S-G);
  regional/interregional institutes, 738; **741**
  (GA/Milan Action Plan); technical co-
  operation, 738, 739 (Milan Action Plan/
  7th Congress), 740, **741** (GA/S-G); *see
  also* Social Defence, UN Trust Fund for;
  Social Defence Research Institute, UN
CRIME AND THE TREATMENT OF OF-
  FENDERS, 6TH UN CONGRESS ON THE
  PREVENTION OF: Caracas Declaration,
  739, **741** (GA/S-G)

CRIME AND THE TREATMENT OF OF-
  FENDERS, 7TH UN CONGRESS ON THE
  PREVENTION OF : Action Plan, 738, 738-
  42 (GA, **740-42**, 742; S-G, 739-40); Cf.
  S-G, 738; Cts., chairmen, 1409; officers,
  1409; participants/observers, 738, 1409;
  preparatory mtgs., 738; resolutions, 638
  (ECA), 738-39
CRIME PREVENTION AND CONTROL, CT.
  ON (ESC): members/sess., 1417
CRIME PREVENTION AND CRIMINAL
  JUSTICE IN THE CONTEXT OF DEVELOP-
  MENT AND A NEW INTERNATIONAL
  ECONOMIC ORDER, GUIDING PRIN-
  CIPLES FOR, **741**, 742 (GA/7th UN
  Congress)
CRIMES AGAINST INTERNATIONALLY PRO-
  TECTED PERSONS, INCLUDING
  DIPLOMATIC AGENTS, CONVENTION ON
  THE PREVENTION AND PUNISHMENT OF
  (1973), States parties, 1167, **1170**
    (SC/S-G), 1172
criminal justice: & development, Guiding
  Principles, 742 (7th Congress/GA);
  discrimination in, 739 (7th UN Con-
  gress); & juveniles, Standard Minimum
  Rules (Beijing Rules), 746, **746-56** (GA/
  S-G); UN standards for, 757 (GA/7th
  Congress); & victims, Declaration on
  basic principles for, **742-44** (GA); *see
  also* judiciary system; prisoners/de-
  tainees; summary executions; terrorism;
  torture and other cruel treatment;
  women
CRIMINAL POLICE ORGANIZATION, INTER-
  NATIONAL: & drug control, 1013, **1021**
    (GA)
crops, 1289-90 (FAO); *see also* grains;
  plants; seeds
cross-organizational programme analyses,
  see under co-ordination in the UN
  system
Cuba: industrial management, 607; &
  IAEA safeguards, 1271; synthetic drugs
  programme, 612 (UNIDO); UNICEF project, 967-68; *see also* Angola; Namibia
  question
CULTURAL AND NATURAL HERITAGE, IN-
  TERNATIONAL CONVENTION CONCERN-
  ING THE PROTECTION OF THE WORLD
  (UNESCO) *(1972)*: implementation,
  1297-98; States parties, 1298; World
  Heritage List, 1298
CULTURAL AND TECHNICAL CO-
  OPERATION, AGENCY FOR: & co-
  operation with UN, 1055, **1055** (GA)
cultural development, 759; Berne
  Centenary, 759 (S-G); World Decade for,
  proposed, 759 (ACC/UNESCO
  DG)
cultural heritage/property: protection,
  242 (communications); restitution, 757-
  59 (GA, **758-59**, 759; S-G/UNESCO DG,
  757-58)
CULTURAL PROPERTY, INTERGOVERNMEN-
  TAL CT. FOR PROMOTING THE RETURN
  OF, TO ITS COUNTRIES OF ORIGIN OR
  ITS RESTITUTION IN CASE OF ILLICIT
  APPROPRIATION, 757-58
CULTURAL PROPERTY, UNESCO CONVEN-
  TION ON THE MEANS OF PROHIBITING
  AND PREVENTING THE ILLICIT IMPORT,
  EXPORT AND TRANSFER OF OWNERSHIP
  OF: States parties, 721, **758** (GA)

culture, 1297-98, 1299 (UNESCO); & colonial Territories, **1062** (GA); & development, agreements, 1299 (UNESCO); &
  multi-ethnic societies, 785 (UNU); protection of, 1297-98 (World Heritage Ct.);
  publications, 1298; technical assistance,
  1299 *(tables)*; *see also* arts; music
CUSTOMS CO-OPERATION COUNCIL
  (GATT), 1370; Commodity Descrip-
  tion/Coding System, 1370 (GATT)
CUSTOMS CO-OPERATION COUNCIL, CON-
  TACT CT. (UPU): reconstitution, 1342
customs formalities, 1371; *1982* Convention on Harmonization of Frontier Controls of Goods, entry into force, 655
CYCLONE PROGRAMME, TROPICAL (WMO),
  648, 723; strengthening, 1351
cyclones, 541, 648 (ESCAP); disaster
  prevention steps, 547 (UNDRO);
  forecasting, 1352 (WMO); *see also*
  typhoons
CYCLONES, INTERNATIONAL WORKSHOP
  ON TROPICAL, 1351-52
Cyprus: emergency medical service, 257;
  food aid, 257 (WFP); humanitarian
  assistance, 256-57 (UNFICYP); human
  rights in, 913 (Human Rights Cs.); &
  UNDP, 257
CYPRUS, CT. ON MISSING PERSONS IN:
  appointment, ICRC representative, 252,
  913 (S-G); resumption, 255 (S-G)
CYPRUS, UN PEACE-KEEPING FORCE IN,
  256-58; casualties, 257; Civilian Police,
  257 (S-G), 257 *(table)*; Commander,
  1410, 1425; composition, 257 *(table)*;
  continuation *(Dec. 1985)*, 252-54 (SC,
  252-53, **254**; S-G, 802), *(June 1986)*,
  255-56 (SC, **255**, 255-56; S-G, 254-55);
  contributions, 258 *(table)*; financing, 258
  (S-G); humanitarian functions, Co-
  ordinator, 257; S-G Spec. Representative
  (Acting), 1410, 1425
Cyprus question, 4 (S-G), 251-58 (communications, 252, 254, 254-55; GA, 256;
  SC, 252-54, **254**, 254, **255**, 255-56; S-G,
  251-52, 252); & S-G good offices, 398

DAG HAMMARSKJÖLD LIBRARY, 1265 (S-G)
DAIRY PRODUCTS CL., INTERNATIONAL,
  1371; & Dairy Arrangement (GATT),
  1371
DAIRY TRAINING PROGRAMME (FAO), 1290
dangerous goods, *see* explosives; toxic
  substances
DANGEROUS GOODS, CT. OF EXPERTS ON
  THE TRANSPORT OF, 585, 588;
  members/officers, 1416-17; Explosives,
  Group of Experts on, Chairman, 1417;
  Group of Rapporteurs, 1417
  (members/officers)
data processing, electronic: in natural
  resources exploration, 671, **671**
    (DTCD/ESC/S-G)
Dead Sea canal project, *see*
  Mediterranean–Dead Sea canal project
debt problems, 7-8 (S-G), 575-77, 1330
  (IMF/World Bank); in LDCs, 436 (S-G),
  443, **448**, 576 (SNPA review); *see also
  under* Africa; developing countries; Latin
  America
decolonization, *see* colonial countries
deforestation, 818 (ACC); assessment
  mtg., 818

Democratic Kampuchea: GA credentials, 228-29, 396, **397** (Credentials Ct./GA); *see also* Kampuchea situation

Democratic People's Republic of Korea: accession to NPT, 1271; & IAEA safeguards, 1271; *see also* Korean question

Democratic Yemen: desertification control, 808 (UNEP); flood relief, 517-18 (GA, **528**; S-G, 527-28)

demographic activities: data analysis, 769 (Population Cs.); DTCD/UNFPA projects, 486; regional training institutes, 638-39 (ECA); statistics, 486 (DTCD), 663-64 (ECLAC), 1033 (Statistical Cs.); *see also* population

Denmark: co-operation with UNICEF, 971; desertification assistance, 810; slum upgrading, 826 (UNCHS)

DESERTIFICATION, INTER-AGENCY WORKING GROUP ON (ACC), 808 (UNEP Cl.), **809** (GA)

DESERTIFICATION, PLAN OF ACTION TO COMBAT *(1977)*: implementation, 807-9 (African Cf., 807-8; Consultative Group, 808; GA, **809**; UNEP Cl., 808-9); financing, 808 (S-G), **809** (GA); *see also under* Sudano-Sahelian region

DESERTIFICATION ASSESSMENT AND MAPPING METHODOLOGY AND DATA BASE (FAO/UNEP), 808 (expert mtg.)

desertification control, 805-7 (ESC, 806; GA, **806-7**, 807; OAU, 806; S-G, 805-6); impact on foreign trade, **807** (GA); information, 808; mapping, 808; Ministerial Cf., 806, **807** (GA); publications, 808; symposium on, 538; *see also* Africa; East Africa; Sudano-Sahelian region

DESERTIFICATION CONTROL, CONSULTATIVE GROUP FOR, 808 (UNEP Cl.), **809** (GA)

DESERTIFICATION INFORMATION CAMPAIGN (UNEP), 808

detainees: detention on mental illness grounds, draft principles/guidelines, 865, **865** (GA/SCPDPM); detention without charge/trial, 865-66 (Human Rights Cs.); protection of, draft Principles, 863 (GA/Working Group); & unacknowledged detention, draft declaration, 865 (SCPDPM/Working Group); *see also* capital punishment; prisoners; territories occupied by Israel; torture

DETENTION, WORKING GROUP ON (SCPDPM), 862; members, 1412

DETENTION OR IMPRISONMENT, DRAFT BODY OF PRINCIPLES FOR THE PROTECTION OF ALL PERSONS UNDER ANY FORM OF, 863 (GA/Working Group)

deterrence: study, 98 (Advisory Board); *see also* disarmament

developing countries, 7-8 (S-G); agrometeorology services, 1351 (WMO); capital flows, 411 (CDP working group), 621-22 (TNCs Centre); coercive economic actions against, 422-23 (GA, **422-23**, 423; S-G, 422); debt problems, 7-8 (S-G), 419 (Ct. on Development Strategy), 575-77 (CDP, 575-76; GA, 577; TDB, 576-77); economic trends, 428, 429 (surveys); energy co-operation, 689; energy resources, 685-87; human resources development, 780-81; & IAEA,

technical assistance to, 1272; industrial co-operation, 604-5 (ECA/IDB/UNIDO); industrial production, redeployment, 605-6 (IDB/UNIDO); insurance, 579-80 (Ct. on Invisibles); & international economic security, 421-22 (GA, **421**, 422; ESC, 421); SDR activity, 1331, 1332-34 *(tables)*; & trade, 554-55 (UNCTAD *Report*), 558-59 (Spec. Ct. on Preferences/TDB); & world economy, 1330 (Group of 24); *see also* debt problems; economic co-operation among developing countries; global system of trade preferences among developing countries; international trade; island developing countries; land-locked developing countries; least developed countries; technical co-operation among developing countries

DEVELOPING COUNTRIES, INTEGRATED PROGRAMME OF INTERNATIONAL CO-OPERATION FOR THE MOBILIZATION OF PERSONAL SAVINGS IN, 579 (DIESA)

DEVELOPING COUNTRIES, MTG. OF GOVERNMENTAL EXPERTS ON CO-OPERATIVE EXCHANGE OF SKILLS AMONG, 492-93 (High-level Ct./TDB), 688-89

DEVELOPING COUNTRIES, 3RD INTERNATIONAL SYMPOSIUM ON THE MOBILIZATION OF PERSONAL SAVINGS IN, 579 (ESC)

DEVELOPING COUNTRIES, WORKING PARTY ON TRADE EXPANSION AND REGIONAL ECONOMIC INTEGRATION AMONG: energy co-operation, 689

DEVELOPING COUNTRIES AFFLICTED BY DROUGHT, FAMINE AND MALNUTRITION, UNDP TRUST FUND FOR, establishment, 481 (GA/S-G), 495

developing island countries, *see* island developing countries

development
administration/finance, 431-32 (DTCD/Experts' Mtg., 431; ESC, **431-32**; projects/funding, 431; publications, 432

& culture, 1299 (UNESCO)

& disarmament, 6 (S-G); *see also under* disarmament

education, 432 (GA/JUNIC), 1299 (UNESCO)

environment/population/resources, inter-relationship, 430 (CCSQ/GA)

information systems on aspects of, 1264

long-term trends, 415-17 (ESC, **415-16**; GA, **416-17**, 417; S-G, 415)

moral aspects of, 423-24 (GA, **423-24**; S-G, 423)

planning, 430-31 (CDP/ESC); publication, 432; *see also* Development Planning, Ct. for

social aspects, 486 (DTCD), **725-26** (ESC)

see also new international economic order; rural development; social development; *and under* disarmament; women in development

DEVELOPMENT, DECLARATION ON SOCIAL PROGRESS AND *(1969)*: implementation, 727-28 (ESC, **727-28**; Cs. for Social Development/GA, 728)

Development, Department of Technical Co-operation for, *see* Technical Co-operation for Development, Department of

development, operational activities for, 456-95

contributions, 462-63 (communications/DIEC DG, 462; GA, 462-63); & IFAD replenishments, **458**, 460, 462 (GA); UN Pledging Cf., 456, 463 *(table)*; to World Bank/IFAD, drop in, 457, 462

co-ordination in UN, 463 (CCSQ(OPS)), 472-73 (ACC, 472-73; JIU, 473; UNDP Administrator/Cl., 472); at country level, 472-73 (ACC, 472-73; JIU, 473; UNDP, 472); evaluation, 464 (CCSQ(OPS)/UNDP)

expenditures, 461-62 (UNDP Administrator); by executing body, 461 *(table)*

general aspects, 456-58 (ACC, 457; DIEC DG, 456-57; GA, **457-58**; S-G, 458)

policy review *(1986)*, 457, **458** (ACC/GA)

procurement practices, 475 (Inter-Agency Unit/UNDP Cl.)

UNDP activities, 464-68; *see also* technical co-operation; *and country, organizational and subject entries*

development, right to: proposed declaration, 879-81 (ESC, **880**, 880; GA, 880-81, **884**; Human Rights Cs./S-G, 879)

DEVELOPMENT, RIGHT TO, WORKING GROUP OF GOVERNMENTAL EXPERTS ON, 879, **880** (ESC), 881, **884** (GA); members, 1412; *1986* sess., postponed, 881 (GA)

DEVELOPMENT, ROUND TABLE ON HUMAN DIMENSIONS OF, 781

DEVELOPMENT, UN TRUST FUND FOR AFRICAN, *see* African Development, UN Trust Fund for

DEVELOPMENT ACTIVITIES, REGISTER OF, **1042**, 1264 (ACC/ESC)

DEVELOPMENT ACTIVITIES, UN PLEDGING CONFERENCE FOR *(1985)*, 456, 463 *(table)*, 464

development and international economic co-operation, 7-8 (S-G), 410-18 (ACC/CDP, 411; communications, 412-13; ESC, **413-14**; GA, **414**, 414-15; S-G, 412); global negotiations, proposed, 417-18 (GA); long-term trends, 415-17 (ACC, 411; ESC, **415-16**, 416; GA, **416-17**, 417; S-G, 415); *World Economic Survey*, 411-12; *see also* new international economic order

DEVELOPMENT AND INTERNATIONAL ECONOMIC CO-OPERATION, OFFICE OF THE DG FOR (Secretariat): activities 456-58 (DG, 456-57; GA, **457-58**); DG, 1423

development assistance, official, 412 *(World Economic Survey)*, 415 (S-G), 456 (DIEC DG), 576 (UNCTAD), 577 (TDB), 578 (CDP/*World Economic Survey*); 702 (WFP); *see also* development, operational activities for; development finance; Development Programme, UN; Special Fund, UN; technical co-operation

Development Centre, Asian and Pacific (ESCAP), *see* Asian and Pacific Development Centre

DEVELOPMENT DECADE, CT. ON THE REVIEW AND APPRAISAL OF THE IMPLEMENTATION OF THE INTERNATIONAL DEVELOPMENT STRATEGY FOR THE 3RD UN, 418; members/officers, 1397; resumed sess., 420, **420** (ESC)

DEVELOPMENT DECADE, 3RD UN *(1980s)*:
International Development Strategy, implementation, 418-20 (Ct. on Strategy,
418-19; ESC, 420, **420**; GA, 420; S-G,
415); & ODA targets, 419

DEVELOPMENT ECONOMICS RESEARCH,
WORLD INSTITUTE FOR: activities, inauguration of, 785; Board, 785; Director,
785, 1425; Trust Fund, 786 (UNU)

DEVELOPMENT EDUCATION, *AD HOC*
WORKING GROUP ON (JUNIC), 432

development finance, 577-79 (CDP, 577-
78; Ct. on Invisibles, 578; GA, 578-79);
companies for, 1310; & foreign direct investment, 578 (Ct. on Invisibles), 621-22
(TNCs Centre/Cs.); IDA credits, 1324-25;
IDA/IFAD replenishment, 462-63 (GA);
see also debt problems; exports; savings

Development Forum, **382**, 384 (DPI/GA);
financial support, *Development
Business* and World Bank, *382*, 387,
388 (ACC/GA/Information Ct./JUNIC)

DEVELOPMENT FUND, UN CAPITAL, 493-95
(UNDP Administrator/Cl.); contributions,
493-94, 494 *(table)*, 494 (UN Pledging
Cf.); Executive Board, 1401, 1418; joint
financing agreements, 494-95; Managing
Director, 1401; programme resources,
493; project expenditures, 493, 494
(table)

DEVELOPMENT OBJECTIVES, TASK FORCE
ON LONG-TERM (ACC), **417** (GA)

DEVELOPMENT PLANNING, CT. FOR, 430-
31; working groups, mtgs. cancellation,
431 (ESC); members/officers, 1416

DEVELOPMENT PROGRAMME, UN, 464-85,
1404

accounts *(1984)*, 481-82 (ACABQ/Auditors
Board, 482-83; GA, 483)

Administrator, 1419

advisory services, short-term, establishment, 474 (CCSQ(OPS)/UNDP)

audit reports *(1983)*, 482 (UNDP Ad-
ministrator/Cl.)

budgets: *(1984-1985)*, revised, 478
(ACABQ/UNDP Cl.); *1986-1987*, 479
(ACABQ/UNDP Cl.); *see also* financial
situation; support costs *below*

country/intercountry programmes, 467-68
(UNDP Administrator); IPFs, 470-72
(CCSQ(OPS)), 472; ESC, 471-72;
UNDP Administrator, 470-71; UNDP
Cl., 471)

& exchange rates, 482-83 (UNDP Ad-
ministrator/Cl.)

financial regulations, 482 (UNDP Ad-
ministrator/Cl.)

financial situation, 475-78 (Auditors'
Board/UNDP Administrator); contributions, 475, 476-78 *(table)*; field programme expenditures, 465, 475; in-
come/expenditures, 475; *1984*
situation, review, 479 (UNDP Cl.); UN
Pledging Cf., 463, 463 *(table)*, 464

Information: UNDP Division of,
strengthening, 474 (UNDP Ad-
ministrator/Cl.); budgetary aspects,
479 (ACABQ)

job classification, 483 (ACABQ/UNDP)

Operational Reserve, increase in, 471,
480 (UNDP Cl.)

procurement, 475 (Inter-Agency
Unit/UNDP)

programme planning/management:
evaluation, 473 (ACC/Central Evaluation Office/UNDP); 4th programme
cycle *(1987-1991)*, preparations, 473-74
(UNDP Cl.)

projects execution, 474-75 (UNDP Cl./Ad-
ministrator); expenditures, 475; Office
for, 474; personnel for, 483-84
(ACC/UNDP Cl.)

Resident Representatives, 2nd Global
Mtg. of, 464

spec. funds, 466 (UNDP)

Spec. Programme Resources, 471
(UNDP Cl.), 479-80 (UNDP Cl.);
allocations for TCDC, 474, 480
(UNDP); field programme, expenditures, 475

structure, 1419-20; bureaux, ad-
ministrators/directors, 1424

support costs: reimbursement, 483
(UNDP Cl.); sectoral, 481 (UNDP Cl.)

technical co-operation, 464-67 (GA, 467;
UNDP Administrator, 464-66; UNDP
Cl., 466-67)

trust funds, 481-82 (GA/UNDP Cl.);
allocations from UN Emergency Trust
Fund, 481 (GA/S-G); closures, 481
(GA); new, 481

DEVELOPMENT PROGRAMME, UN, GOV-
ERNING CL., 466-67 (ESC, 466; GA,
467): Administrator's report, 464-66,
1419; Cts., 1419; documentation, 484-85
(UNDP Cl.); members/officers, 1419

diarrhoeal diseases, 967 (UNICEF), 970
(UNICEF), 1304 (UNICEF/WHO); *see also*
oral rehydration therapy

diplomacy, 9 (S-G)

diplomatic bags and couriers: draft articles, 1174-75 (ILC/Spec. Rapporteur/S-G)

diplomatic relations, 1172-76; Vienna
Convention *(1961)*, States parties, 1172;
see also consular relations

diplomats, protection of, 1172-74 (communications, 1173; GA, **1173-74**); S-G,
1172-73); conventions/protocols, status,
1167, **1168** (S-G/GA), 1172; *see also* host
country relations (UN/United States)

direct broadcast satellites, *see* communications satellites

DISABLED PEOPLES' INTERNATIONAL: 2nd
World Congress, 776

disabled persons, 775-80

advisory services, 775 (CSDHA/DTCD)

education, 1295 (UNESCO)

employment, UN, **778**, 779 (GA), 779
(inter-agency mtg.)

human rights of, 931 (Spec. Rap-
porteur/SCPDPM), 776

publication, 776

refugees, 776

rehabilitation and disability prevention,
775

vocational rehabilitation/employment, ILO
Convention, 775-76

DISABLED PERSONS, INTERNATIONAL YEAR
OF *(1981)*: national cts., 776 (S-G); Trust
Fund for, 777, **777** (CSDHA/ESC)

DISABLED PERSONS, UN DECADE OF
(1983-1992), World Action Programme:
implementation, 775-79 (CSDHA/S-G,

775-76; ESC, 777, **777**; GA, 777, **778-
79**); inter-agency co-operation, 776; national cts., 776; & NGOs, 776; Voluntary
Trust Fund for, **778-79**, 779-80

DISABLEMENT, INTERNATIONAL INITIATIVE
AGAINST AVOIDABLE, 775

disappearance of persons, 870-72 (communications, 871; ESC, 871; GA, **871-72**;
Human Rights Cs., 870; Working Group,
870-71); *see also* Guatemala

DISAPPEARANCES, WORKING GROUP ON
ENFORCED OR INVOLUNTARY, 871; man-
date extended, 870, 871, **871** (ESC/
Human Rights Cs./GA); members, 1412

disarmament, 6-7, (S-G), 13-100

agreements: compliance/verification, 23-
25 (GA, **23**, 23-24, **24**, 24-25);
multilateral, parties/signatories, 100
(S-G), 100 *(list)*

comprehensive programme (proposed),
33-34 (CD/Ad Hoc Ct., 33-34; GA, **34**)

& development, 87-88 (S-G); *see also*
Disarmament and Development, International Cf. on Relationship between

fellowships, UN programme, 97-98 (GA,
97-98, 98; S-G, 97)

general & complete, 13-14 (communications, 14; S-G, 13-14), 26 (DC)

international co-operation, *1979* Declaration: implementation, 20, **20-22**, 22
(GA)

& international security, 26-29 (GA/S-G,
26, **26-27**, 27); compliance with SC
resolutions, **27-28**, 28 (GA); studies:
on security concepts, 28-29 (Group of
Experts, 28; GA, **28-29**, 29), on deterrence, 29 (Group of Experts)

military budgets, 82-85 (communications,
83; DC/Working Group, 82-83; GA,
83-84, 84); reduction procedures 84-
85 (Experts Group, 84; GA, **84-85**,
85); expenditures, annual report, 84
(S-G)

military capabilities, information, **85-86**,
86 (GA)

military research/development, 86-87 (Experts Group/S-G)

naval arms race, 25, 29-32; proposed
negotiations, 29-30 (DC, 29; GA, 29,
29-30); study, 29-31 (GA, **30-31**, 31;
Governmental Experts Group, 29-30)

publications, 13, 70

regional centre, establishment, 94-95

research studies, 98-100 (Advisory
Board/S-G, 98; GA, **98-99**, 99;
UNIDIR, 100)

spec. sessions, 15-20; GA 10th (1st,
1978), implementation, 17-20 (GA, **17-
20**); GA 12th (2nd, *1982*), 20, 20; 3rd
spec. sess., 20, **20**

UN role in, 25, **25-26** (DC/GA)

World Cf. on, proposed, 31-33 (*Ad Hoc*
Ct., 32-33; GA, **33**)

see also arms race; bacteriological
(biological) weapons; chemical
weapons; conventional weapons;
deterrence; nuclear disarmament;
nuclear-weapon-free zones; nuclear
weapons; outer space: arms race;
radiological weapons; weapons of
mass destruction; zones of peace

DISARMAMENT, AD HOC CT. ON THE COMPREHENSIVE PROGRAMME OF, **33**, 33-34 (GA)

DISARMAMENT, CF. ON, 16, **16-17**, 17 (GA); *ad hoc* bodies, re-establishment, 16; members/structure, 1422; proposed membership increase, 16

DISARMAMENT AFFAIRS, UN DEPARTMENT FOR (Secretariat): & fellowship programme, 97; Under-S-G, 1423; & World Campaign, 95

DISARMAMENT AND DEVELOPMENT, GROUP OF GOVERNMENTAL EXPERTS ON THE RELATIONSHIP BETWEEN *(1981)*: recommendations, 87 (S-G)

DISARMAMENT AND DEVELOPMENT, INTERNATIONAL CF. ON THE RELATIONSHIP BETWEEN *(1986)*: preparations, 87-89 (Preparatory Ct., 87; GA, **87-88**); S-G of, appointment, 88

DISARMAMENT AND DEVELOPMENT, PREPARATORY CT. FOR THE INTERNATIONAL CF. ON THE RELATIONSHIP BETWEEN, 87, **87** (GA); change of venue, 1258 (Ct. on Cfs.)

DISARMAMENT CAMPAIGN, WORLD: implementation, 92-94 (GA, **92-93**, 93; S-G, 92); financing, 93, **93-94** (GA); & mass media role, **382**, 383 (GA/Information Ct.), 384 (DPI); regional activities, 92 (S-G), 94-95, **95**, 95 (GA/S-G)

DISARMAMENT COMMISSION, 15, **15-16** (GA); Ct. of the Whole, 15; members/officers, 1397

DISARMAMENT CONFERENCE, AD HOC CT. ON THE WORLD: 32-33; mandate renewed, 32, **33** (GA); members/officers, 1395; Working Group, members, 1395

DISARMAMENT DECADE, 2ND: Declaration of the 1980s, review/appraisal, 22-23 (DC, 22; GA, 22, **22-23**)

DISARMAMENT IN EUROPE, CF. ON CONFIDENCE- AND SECURITY-BUILDING MEASURES AND, 119 (GA)

DISARMAMENT RESEARCH, UN INSTITUTE FOR, 99-100 (S-G); Board of Trustees, 99, 1406 (members); Director, 1406

DISARMAMENT STUDIES, ADVISORY BOARD ON, 99, **99**; as UNIDIR Board of Trustees, 99

DISARMAMENT WEEK: mass media role, **382** (GA/Information Ct.), 384 (DPI); observance, 95-97 (GA, **95-96**, 96-97; S-G, 95)

Disarmament Yearbook, United Nations, 93

disaster preparedness/prevention, *see under* disasters

disaster relief, *see under* disasters

DISASTER RELIEF, UN TRUST FUND FOR GENERAL, 535, 537

DISASTER RELIEF ASSISTANCE, UN TRUST FUNDS FOR, 535-36; contributions, 535 *(table)*; expenditures, 535-36 *(table)*

DISASTER RELIEF CO-ORDINATOR, OFFICE OF THE UN, 534-35 (S-G); financing, Trust Funds/UN budget, 535-36; publication, 535; Under-S-G (Co-ordinator), 1424

disasters, 534-37; co-ordination in UN system, 536-37 (S-G); human settlements planning, 831 (UNCHS/UNDRO/UNEP); preparedness/prevention, 546-47 (UNDP/UNDRO); technical

assistance, 547; UNIDO assistance, 599; UN Supply Depot, 547; *see also* Africa, critical situation in; drought-stricken areas; earthquakes; floods; typhoons; *and country names and regional entries*

discrimination, *see* indigenous populations; minorities; nazism/fascism; racial discrimination; religious freedom

DISCRIMINATION BASED ON RELIGION OR BELIEF, *1981* DECLARATION ON ELIMINATION OF ALL FORMS OF INTOLERANCE AND OF, 845 (Human Rights Cs.), **847** (GA); *see also* religious freedom

DISCRIMINATION AND PROTECTION OF MINORITIES, SUB-CS. ON PREVENTION OF: Bureau, inter-sess. mtgs., 887; future work/programme review, 887 (Human Rights Cs./SCPDPM/Working Group); members, 1412; report, 887 (ESC); Working Groups, 1412

diseases: & nutrition, 774-75; occupational/work-related, 1303 (WHO); prevention/control, 1304 (WHO); research/training, 1273 (IAEA/WHO); *see also* immunization; *names of diseases; and under* children

DISEASES, COUNTRY-WIDE INTEGRATED PROGRAMME FOR THE PREVENTION OF NON-COMMUNICABLE (WHO), 1304

DISENGAGEMENT OBSERVER FORCE, UN, 262, 314-15 (SC, 315, **315**; S-G, 314); appropriations, 262, 316-18 (ACABQ, 316-17, GA, **317-18**, 318; S-G, 316); Commander, 315 (SC/S-G), 1410, 1424; composition, 313, 315 *(table)*; contributions, 316, **318** (GA/S-G), 319-20 *(table)*; headquarters, proposed relocation, 316 (ACABQ/S-G); new field service post, proposed, 316 (ACABQ/S-G); suspension of financial regulations, 316, **318-19**, 319 (GA); troop contributors' reimbursement, 316 (GA); & UNTSO, 262, 313; *see also* Golan Heights; Syrian Arab Republic

displaced persons, *see* refugees/displaced persons *and under* Palestine refugees

disputes, peaceful settlement of, 118, 121, **121-22** (GA), 1160-61 (GA, **1160-61**, 1161; Spec. Ct./Working Group, 1160); *see also* international relations: non-use of force in

Djibouti: census, aid on, 511 (DTCD); economic assistance, 511, **511** (GA/S-G); geothermal exploration, 686 (UNDP); IDA/WFP/World Bank action, 509; port of, 511 (UNCTAD/UNDP); refugee assistance, 1000, **1000-1** (GA/UNHCR); refugees in, 511, 1000; urban development, 1326 (IDA); *see also* East Africa: drought-stricken areas; Ethiopia

documentation (UN): limitation/control, 1261-62 (CPC/ESC/S-G); *see also* publications

DOSIMETRY LABORATORIES, SECONDARY STANDARD, 1274 (IAEA/WHO)

dosimetry radiation: workshops, 1273-74 (IAEA)

drinking-water: & adult/child diseases, 680; consumer protection guidelines, **573** (GA); health hazards, 815 (UNEP); WHO programme, 1303; *see also* water supply

DRINKING WATER SUPPLY AND SANITATION DECADE, INTERNATIONAL *(1981-1990)*: implementation, 680-81 (ESC, 680-81; GA, **681**, 681; S-G, 680), 815, 816 (UNEP); information/communications, allocations, 474, 680 (UNDP); publication, 1303; WHO projects, 1303

Drought Control in the Sahel, Permanent Inter-State Ct. on, *see* Sahel, Permanent Inter-State Ct. on Drought Control in the

DROUGHT AND DESERTIFICATION, INTERNATIONAL SYMPOSIUM ON, 538 (UNSO)

DROUGHT AND DEVELOPMENT, INTERGOVERNMENTAL AUTHORITY FOR: action plan, 539 (UNDP/UNSO); agreement on establishment, 538-39, **539** (GA/mtgs.); headquarters, 539; members, 810

Drought and Famine in Africa, Spec. Emergency Assistance Fund for, *see* Africa, Spec. Emergency Assistance Fund for Drought and Famine in

drought-stricken areas: effects of, 537 (GA/S-G/UNDP/UNDRO); appeal for funds, 499-500 (Cf. on Africa emergency); *see also country names*; desertification; East Africa; Sahel; Sudano-Sahelian region

DRUG ABUSE CONTROL, AD HOC INTER-AGENCY MTG. ON CO-ORDINATION IN MATTERS OF INTERNATIONAL (ACC), 1016-17

DRUG ABUSE CONTROL, UN FUND FOR, 1015-16; contributions, 1016 (7th UN Congress on Crime), 1016 *(table)*; Executive Director, 1425; programme budget, 1015; technical co-operation, 1015

DRUG ABUSE CONTROL STRATEGY, INTERNATIONAL: implementation, 1014-15 (GA, **1015**; Narcotic Drugs Cs., 1015; S-G, 1014-15)

DRUG ABUSE AND ILLICIT TRAFFICKING, INTERNATIONAL CF. ON (Vienna, *1987*), 1016-19 (Ad Hoc Inter-Agency Mtg., 1016-17; ESC, 1017; GA, **1017-18**, 1018-19; S-G, 1016-17)

drugs of abuse, 10 (S-G), 1012-28; & alcohol, 1013, 1028; co-ordination in UN, 1013, 1014, 1030 (Ad Hoc Inter-Agency Mtg./JIU/S-G), 1227 (CPC); "designer", 1013 (INCB), 1020; illicit traffic, 10 (S-G), 739 (7th UN Congress on Crime); international control, 1013-22 (CPC/JIU, 1013-14; CPC/S-G, 1014; GA, **1020-22**; INCB, 1013); law enforcement, 1022-23 (ESC, **1022-23**; Narcotic Drugs Cs., 1022); licit uses, 1019-20 (ESC, **1019-20**; Expert Group/Narcotic Drugs Cs., 1019); prevention education, **1019** (ESC); traditional, 1016; *see also* narcotic drugs; psychotropic substances

DRUG SMUGGLING BY AIR AND SEA, EXPERT GROUP ON COUNTERMEASURES TO, 1015

DRUG TRAFFIC AND RELATED MATTERS IN THE NEAR AND MIDDLE EAST, SUB-COMMISSION ON ILLICIT, 1020, 1025-26; members/officers, 1413

EARTHQUAKE ENGINEERING, INTERNATIONAL NETWORK ON (UNESCO), 1296

earthquakes, 543-45; & human set-
tlements planning, 831 (UNCHS/
UNDRO/UNEP); risk mitigation, 547
(Italy/UNDRO); _see also_ Mexico; Yemen

Earthwatch, _see under_ Environmental
Monitoring System, Global

East Africa: drought-stricken areas,
assistance, 538-39 (GA, **539**, 539; S-G,
538-39); & ocean energy resources, 637
(ECA); food supplies, 1290-90 (FAO); Intergovernmental Authority established,
538-39, **539** (GA/S-G); IDA credits, 1324
(table); regional seas programme
(UNEP), 816; _see also country names_

East Asia, 220-31; IDA credits, 1324
(table); refugees, 1007-8; regional seas
programme (UNEP), 816; _see also_ Asia
and the Pacific; _country names_; South-
East Asia

EASTERN AFRICAN REGION, REGIONAL
SEAS TRUST FUND FOR THE: establishment, 798 (UNEP Cl.)

eastern and southern Africa: Mineral
Resources Development Centre, 636
(ECA); Preferential Trade Area, 608
(UNIDO/UNIDO study), 630-31, **631**
(ECA/GA)

Eastern Europe: economic trends, 428,
429 (surveys); technical co-operation,
560 (UNCTAD/USSR); trade preferences,
560 (TDB); _see also country names_

eastern Mediterranean region, _see_ Arab
States; Middle East; Western Asia

East Timor, 1136-37 (communications,
1136-37; GA, 1137; Human Rights Cs./
S-G, 1137); humanitarian assistance, 1137
(ICRC/UNICEF); Indonesia-Portugal talks,
1137 (S-G); information to UN, 1082,
1137 (communication)

East-West trade: chemical products, 655
(ECE); expansion, 554; _Survey_, 654
(ECE); _see also_ international trade: countries having different economic and
social systems

**economic and social affairs: trends/
policy**, 427-30 (UNCTAD _Report_, 429-30;
World Economic Survey, 428-29); inter-
agency co-ordination, 430 (ACC/GA);
research/policy, 1228 (cross-
organizational programme analysis)

ECONOMIC AND SOCIAL AFFAIRS, DEPART-
MENT OF INTERNATIONAL: officials, 1423

ECONOMIC AND SOCIAL COMMISSION FOR
ASIA AND THE PACIFIC, 644-53; cf.
facilities, expansion, 652-53 (ACABQ/S-G,
652; GA, **652**, 652-53); Executive
Secretary, 1423; headquarters/41st
sess. 644; legislative cts., functions, 652;
membership, terms of reference, 651,
651 (ESC/ESCAP); members/officers, 645,
1414; Pacific Operations Centre,
establishment, 651; publications, 645,
653; restructuring, JIU proposals, 651-52
(ESC/S-G); subsidiary bodies, 645, 1414;
technical co-operation, 646; UN accommodation, Bangkok, 652, **652** (GA/S-G);
work programme, _1986-1987_, 651

ECONOMIC AND SOCIAL COMMISSION FOR
WESTERN ASIA: Executive Secretary,
1423; members/officers, 1414; _see also_
Economic Commission for Western Asia

ECONOMIC AND SOCIAL COUNCIL, 7 (S-G),
1045-58, 1410-20
ad hoc/related bodies, 1417-20
agenda: _(1985)_, 1056; 1432-33 _(list)_
calendar of cfs./mtgs., 1056 (ESC)
documentation, limitation, 1056
(Secretariat); discontinuance of summary records, 1056, **1056-57** (ESC)
expert bodies, 1416-17
functional css./subsidiaries, 1410-13
& GA: 2nd Ct. biennial work programme, 1058 (GA)
& intergovernmental organizations, **1055**
(GA)
members/officers/sessions, 1410-11
publications, 1057
& NGOs, consultative status, 1046-54;
applications/reclassification requests,
1046-47 (Ct. on NGOs, 1046; ESC,
1046-47, 1047); categories/roster, 1047-
54 _(lists)_; withdrawal of, **1047** (ESC)
regional css., structure, 1414-15; _see also_
Economic and Social Commission for
Asia and the Pacific; Economic Commission for Africa; Economic Commission for Europe; Economic Commission for Latin America and the
Caribbean; Economic Commission for
Western Asia
related bodies, 1418-20
report _(1985)_, 1057 (GA)
reporting procedures: JIU study _(1984)_,
1045-46 (CPC/ESC/S-G)
resolutions/decisions, financial implications, 1057 (ACABQ/ESC/GA/S-G)
sessional cts., members/officers, 1411;
subsidiary bodies, 1411
standing cts., 1415-16
work programme _(1985-1986)_, 1055-56

ECONOMIC AND SOCIAL INFORMATION,
UN TRUST FUND FOR, **381** (GA)

ECONOMIC AND SOCIAL MATTERS, OFFICE
OF SECRETARIAT SERVICES FOR: Assistant S-G, 1423

Economic and Social Planning, Latin
American Institute for, _see_ Latin
American Institute for Economic and
Social Planning

economic and social policy: surveys/
trends, 428-30 _(World Economic
Survey)_

economic and social questions, 4-5, 7-8
(S-G), 496-1058

economic assistance: spec. programmes,
497, **497** (GA/S-G); _see also country
names_; development assistance; disaster
relief; emergency humanitarian
assistance

ECONOMIC ASSISTANCE, COUNCIL FOR
MUTUAL: & economic co-operation, 412;
& toxic chemicals, co-operation with
UNEP, 803

ECONOMIC COMMISSION FOR AFRICA,
624-44; Executive Secretary, 1423;
facilities, expansion, 642, **642** (GA/S-G);
institutions sponsored by, 642;
legislative/subsidiary organs, 1414;
members/officers, 1414; Multinational
Programming and Operational Centres,
627, 643; sess., change of venue, 641;
technical co-operation, 626-27; work programme, 641; working language, 640-41
(ACABQ/S-G, 641; ESC, **641-42**; GA, **641**)

ECONOMIC COMMISSION FOR EUROPE,
653-59; Executive Secretary, 1423; 40th
sess., 653; members/officers, 1414; principal organs/subsidiary bodies, 653,
1414-15; publications, 653, 659; Senior
Economic Advisers, 21st sess., 654;
work programme, 658

ECONOMIC COMMISSION FOR LATIN
AMERICA AND THE CARIBBEAN, 659-64;
cfs./mtgs., 659-60; Ct. of High-Level
Government Experts, 659-60; Ct. of the
Whole, 18th sess., 659, 660; Executive
Secretary, 1423; members/associates,
1309; _1986_ sess. venue, 664 (ESC/S-G);
publications, 660, 664; rules of procedure, 664 (ESC); Statistics Division,
664; subsidiary bodies, 1415; technical
co-operation, 662

ECONOMIC COMMISSION FOR WESTERN
ASIA, 665-68; Executive Secretary, 1423;
members/officers, 1414; name change,
665 (ESC); secretariat, staff vacancies
665; subsidiary organ (Technical Ct.),
665, 1414; technical co-operation, 666;
work programme, 665; _see also_
Economic and Social Commission for
Western Asia

Economic Community of the Great Lakes
Countries (Africa), _see_ Great Lakes
Countries, Economic Community of the

economic co-operation, _see_ development
and international economic co-operation

**economic co-operation among develop-
ing countries**, 425-27 (GA, **450**; S-G,
427; UNCTAD, 425-26); co-ordination in
UN, 426-27 (ACC/CPC Joint Mtgs., 427;
CPC, 426-27; ESC, 427; GA/S-G, 427,
450; UNCTAD, 425-26); mandates/pro-
grammes, S-G report, 426-27, 1228
(CPC/cross-organizational programme
analysis); trade & regional integration,
425-26 (ECDC Working Party); _see also_
global system of trade preferences
among developing countries (proposed);
regional css.; technical co-operation
among developing countries

ECONOMIC CO-OPERATION AMONG
DEVELOPING COUNTRIES, CT. ON, 426
(TDB); members/officers, 1403; Working
Party on Trade Expansion, 425-26

ECONOMIC CO-OPERATION AND DEVELOP-
MENT, ORGANISATION FOR: Declaration
on Investment & Multinational Enterprises, 617

economic development, _see_ developing
countries; _and entries following_
development

ECONOMIC DEVELOPMENT INSTITUTE
(WORLD BANK), 1312; water resources
development, 679

ECONOMIC INTEGRATION AMONG
DEVELOPING COUNTRIES, WORKING
PARTY ON TRADE EXPANSION AND
REGIONAL (UNCTAD), 425-26; proposed
name change, 426

economic planning, _see_ development
planning

ECONOMIC RIGHTS AND DUTIES OF
STATES, AD HOC CT. OF THE WHOLE
TO REVIEW THE IMPLEMENTATION OF
THE CHARTER OF, 424-25, **425**;
members/officers, 1394

ECONOMIC RIGHTS AND DUTIES OF
STATES, CHARTER OF _(1974)_: implemen-

tation, 424-25 (*Ad Hoc* Ct./communications, 424; GA, **425**, 425; S-G, 424)

economics: international classifications, 1032-33, **1033** (ESC/Statistical Cs.)

economic, social and cultural rights, 875-83; general aspects, 875-77 (GA, **875-76**, 876-77; Human Rights Cs., 875; S-G, 875); *see also* development, right to; education, right to; food, right to; trade union rights; *and under* human rights

ECONOMIC, SOCIAL AND CULTURAL RIGHTS, CT. ON: establishment, **892** (GA); venue of meeting, **879** (GA); *see also under* Economic, Social and Cultural Rights, Sessional Working Group of Governmental Experts . . .

ECONOMIC, SOCIAL AND CULTURAL RIGHTS, INTERNATIONAL COVENANT ON (*1966*): accessions/ratifications, 876, 891 (S-G); implementation, 876-77 (ESC, 878; GA, 877, **892**; Sessional Working Group, 876-77)

ECONOMIC, SOCIAL AND CULTURAL RIGHTS, SESSIONAL WORKING GROUP OF GOVERNMENTAL EXPERTS ON THE IMPLEMENTATION OF THE INTERNATIONAL COVENANT ON, 876-77; Bureau, 879 (ESC), 1411 (members/officers); composition/organization/administration, 878-79 (ESC, 878, **878-79**; GA, 877; Human Rights Cs./S-G, 878); renamed, **878** (ESC), 1411, 1417; provisional agenda (*1986*), 879 (ESC)

ECONOMIC SUMMIT, 10TH (Bonn): on aid to Africa, 501 (communication); & world economy, 412 (Declaration)

economic surveys, 428-29; Africa, 626 (ESC); Asia and the Pacific, 645 (ESC); Europe, 830-31 (ESC); Latin America, 660 (ESC); Western Asia, 665-66 (ESC); *see also Trade and Development Report, 1985; World Economic Survey 1985*

economic zones, *see* exclusive economic zones

ECOSYSTEM CONSERVATION GROUP: UNEP co-ordinating role, 812

ecosystems, 804-17; atmosphere, 804-5; freshwater, 814-15; lithosphere, 812; mountain, 812 (UNEP); terrestrial, 805-14; in tropics, photosynthesis potential, 814; *see also* acid rain; climate; desertification; forests; marine environment; nature conservation; ozone layer; regional seas programme; soil management; tropical forests; wildlife

Ecuador: natural resources exploration, 669, 670 (UNRFNRE); trade promotion, 561 (ITC)

education, 1295-96 (UNESCO); fellowships, 1299 (UNESCO); IDA credits, 1324-25 *(table)*, 1325; ILO activities, 1283; primary, joint programme, 971-72 (UNESCO/UNICEF); Mbabane Action Programme (ECA), 638; right to, 882, **884** (GA); technical co-operation, 1299 (UNESCO); World Bank loans, 1309-10 *(table)*, 1310; *see also* children; human resources; southern Africa; Trust Territory of the Pacific Islands; vocational training; youth

EDUCATION, 4TH INTERNATIONAL CF. ON ADULT, 1295 (UNESCO); 3rd *1972* Cf., 1295

EDUCATIONAL PLANNING, INTERNATIONAL INSTITUTE FOR, 1296

Egypt: Palestine refugees in, 357-58 (UNRWA) & Sudan microwave link, 1347 (ITU); *see also* hijacking: Egyptian aircraft; Middle East

elderly persons, *see* aging persons

electricity: seminar/mtgs., 656 (ECE); supply projects, 690 (DTCD)

ELECTRIC POWER, CT. ON (ECE), 656

electronic data processing, *see under* computer technology

electronics: technical assistance, 613 (UNIDO); *see also* micro-electronics

El Salvador: inclusion in LDC list, 434-35, **435**

elections in, 208 (S-G)

emergency economic situation, 664 (ESC)

human rights violations, 916-20 (GA, **918-20**, 920; Human Rights Cs./ESC/SCPDPM, 917; Spec. Representative, 916, 917-19); Spec. Representative, mandate extended, 917 (Human Rights Cs./ESC)

kidnapping incident, 207

see also Central America situation

EMERGENCY OPERATION TRUST FUND, UN: liquidation/fund allocations, 481 (GA/S-G), 548-49 (S-G)

emergency relief/assistance, 547-50; *see also country names*; disaster relief; Special Fund, UN

EMPLOYEES AND PROFESSIONAL WORKERS, ADVISORY CT. ON SALARIED (ILO), 1278

employment, 654 (ECE), 1279 (ILO); *apartheid* effects, 1278 (ILO); & development, 1279; equal opportunities in, 1278 (ILO); in health & medical services, 1278 (ILO); right to, **884** (GA); technical co-operation (ILO), 1280, 1280-82 *(tables)*; worker rights & ILO, 734 (communications); *see also* labour; migrant workers; social security; working conditions

EMPLOYMENT AND CONDITIONS OF WORK IN HEALTH AND MEDICAL SERVICES, JOINT MTG. ON (ILO), 1278

EMPLOYMENT PROGRAMME, WORLD (ILO): implementation, 1279-80

energy, 637 (ECA), 648 (ESCAP), 656 (ECA), 663 (ECLAC), 667 (ESCWA); conservation, 607 (UNIDO); consumption/exploration, 685 (S-G); DTCD projects, 485, 486; & environment, 819; equipment related to, 614 (UNIDO); IDA credits, 1324-25 *(table)*, 1325; planning/management, 689 (DTCD), 785 (UNU); rural projects, 687 (UNU); statistics/publication, 695, 1032; technical co-operation, 689-90 (DTCD/UNIDO); technology transfer, 717 (UNCTAD); World Bank affiliate, proposed, 685, 686 (S-G); World Bank loans, 1309-10 *(table)*, 1311; *see also* nuclear energy

ENERGY, *AD HOC* INTER-AGENCY GROUP ON NEW AND RENEWABLE SOURCES OF (ACC), 691-92

ENERGY, CT. ON DEVELOPMENT AND UTILIZATION OF NEW AND RENEWABLE

SOURCES OF, 691 (ACC/S-G), 693 (GA); members, 1396

energy, new and renewable sources of (non-conventional): assessment programme (UNDP/World Bank), 686; co-ordination in UN, 691-92 (ACC Inter-Agency Group); information networks on, strengthening, 692; Nairobi Action Programme, implementation, 691-93 (ACC, 691-92; Ct. on, 691; GA, 693; S-G, 691; UNDP/UNIDO/UNU, 692; UNEP, 692-93) *see also* nuclear energy

ENERGY ACCOUNT, UNDP, 686-87 (Governing Cl.); project expenditures, 687 *(table)*

ENERGY CO-OPERATION AMONG ECONOMIC CO-OPERATION AND INTEGRATION ORGANIZATIONS, EXPERT GROUP ON: conclusions, 691 (Working Party on Trade Expansion)

ENERGY RESEARCH GROUP (UNU), 687

ENERGY RESOURCES, CENTRE ON SMALL (UNDP/UNITAR), 692, 782

energy resources development, 685-88 (GA, **688**, 688; S-G, 684-87; UNU, 688); in industry, 690 (UNIDO); power alcohol technology, 689 (UNCTAD); technology transfer, 688-90 (DTCD, 689-90; ESC, 690; UNCTAD, 689); *see also* coal; gas; electric power; geothermal exploration; natural gas; nuclear energy; petroleum technology; solar power

ENERGY SECTOR MANAGEMENT ASSISTANCE PROGRAMME (UNDP/World Bank), 686

ENERGY SYSTEMS ASSOCIATION, INTEGRATED RURAL, 687 (UNU)

Enewetak, nuclear testing, compensation for, *see under* Marshall Islands

engineering industries, 635 (ECA/IDDA); industrial robots, 613 (UNIDO); Seminar on uses of powder metallurgy (ECE), 656; technical co-operation, 612-13 (UNDP/UNIDO); *see also* agricultural machinery; computer technology; energy: equipment related to; metalworking and machine tools; *and under* transport

ENGINEERING INDUSTRIES AND AUTOMATION, WORKING PARTY ON (ECE), 656

environment, 639 (ECA), 650 (ESCAP), 657 (ECE), 663 (ECLAC), 667 (ESCWA), 788-821, 1272 (IAEA) accounting, mtgs., 819; & *apartheid*, 818 (UNEP Cl.); chemical accidents, 791, 796, 802; co-ordination in UN, **789**, 794 (ACC/GA/UNEP Cl.); cross organizational programme analysis, 794-95 (CPC/UNEP); & development, **437**, 818-19 (GA/UNEP Cl.); *see also under* development; education/training, 820-21 (UNEP Cl.); proposed mtg. on, 820 (UNEP Cl.); emerging issues, update on, 792 (UNEP Cl.); & human settlements, 819-20 (ESCWA/UNCHS/UNEP); & industry, 819 (UNEP)

environment *(cont.)*
international co-operation in, 789-91 (GA, **789-90**, 790-91; UNEP Cl., 789)
international instruments, **789-90**, 800 (GA/UNEP Executive Director)
management of, UNEP projects, 795-96
monitoring, 803-4
NGO/UNEP co-operation, 796
& population & agricultural technology, 791-92 (UNEP Executive Director)
public information, 798-99; *see also* environmental information networks
regional activities, 793-94 (UNEP Cl.); information on, 794
state of, 791-92; future reports on, 792; national reports, 792; *1984* report, follow-up, 792 (UNEP Cl.); *1985* report, 791-92
statistics, 1032 (Statistical Office)
trust fund establishment, 798
in work place, 1279 (ILO)
see also arms race, environmental aspects; climate; desertification; ecosystems; human settlements; marine environment; material remnants of war; natural resources; radioactive waste management; regional seas programme
Environment, African Ministerial Cf. on the, *see* African Ministerial Conference on the Environment
ENVIRONMENT, CT. OF INTERNATIONAL DEVELOPMENT INSTITUTIONS ON THE, 819; Declaration on policies/procedures, 819 (UNEP Cl.)
ENVIRONMENT, INTERNATIONAL PROGRAMME FOR THE IMPROVEMENT OF WORKING CONDITIONS AND, 1279
ENVIRONMENT, SCIENTIFIC CT. ON PROBLEMS OF THE, 801; & Carbon Unit, 801
ENVIRONMENTAL EDUCATION PROGRAMME, INTERNATIONAL (UNEP/UNESCO), 850
environmental health, 773-74 (UNEP, 773-74; FAO/WHO, 774); 1303 (WHO); *see also under* environmental monitoring
environmental information networks:
Global Resource Information Data Base, 792, 800 (UNEP Cl.), establishment, 798, 801 (Advisory Ct.); International Referral System for sources of environmental information (INFOTERRA), 800-1; & science/technology, proposed extension to, 710, 711 (ACC Task Force/Intergovernmental Ct./S-G); publications/seminars, 801
environmental law: impact assessment, 800 (Experts Group); international instruments, 800: Register of treaties, revision, 800; *see also* marine environment; natural resources; ozone layer
ENVIRONMENTAL LAW, MONTEVIDEO PROGRAMME FOR THE DEVELOPMENT AND PERIODIC REVIEW OF *(1981)*: implementation, 800
ENVIRONMENTAL LAW, WORKING GROUP OF EXPERTS ON, 800 (UNEP Cl.)
ENVIRONMENTAL LAW AND MACHINERY UNIT, 800
ENVIRONMENTAL LIAISON CENTRE, 796
ENVIRONMENTAL MODIFICATION TECHNIQUES, CONVENTION ON THE PROHIBITION OF MILITARY OR ANY OTHER

HOSTILE USE OF: parties to/signatories, 100 (S-G/*list*)
environmental monitoring, 1352 (WMO); Earthwatch, 799-800; health-related, 803-4 (FAO/UNEP/WHO); indicators, 791 (UNEP Cl.); integration methodology, 801 (UNEP/UNESCO/WMO); & long-range transport, 804 (UNEP); national conservation strategies, 801 (UNEP); *see also* air pollution; biosphere; chemicals; oceans; ozone layer; regional seas programme; toxic substances
ENVIRONMENTAL MONITORING SYSTEM, GLOBAL, 774 (UNEP/WHO), 791, 800; 10th anniversary, 798
ENVIRONMENTAL PERSPECTIVE TO THE YEAR 2000 AND BEYOND (UNEP), preparations: 792-93 (Preparatory Ct./World Cs./UNEP Cl.); Intergovernmental Inter-sessional Preparatory Ct. on, 792, 1405 (members/officers); trust fund for, closure of, 798; World Cs., 792, 1405 (members/sess.)
ENVIRONMENTAL PROBLEMS, SENIOR ADVISERS TO ECE GOVERNMENTS ON, 657
ENVIRONMENT AND DEVELOPMENT, INTERNATIONAL INSTITUTE FOR, 796; data reports, 791 (Earthscan media unit, 794
ENVIRONMENT AND DEVELOPMENT, WORLD CS. ON (SPECIAL CS.): members, 1405; name change, from Spec. Cs. to, **789**, 792 (GA/UNEP Cl.); secretariat/work plan, establishment, 792
ENVIRONMENT AND DEVELOPMENT FOR NGOS, GLOBAL MTG. ON, 796
ENVIRONMENT DAY, WORLD, 796, 798, 799
ENVIRONMENT PROBLEMS, INTERNATIONAL SCIENTIFIC COUNCIL ON GEOLOGY AND, 812
ENVIRONMENT PROGRAMME, UN, 788-93, 1404-5
clearing-house mechanism, 795-96 (UNEP Cl.)
co-ordination with/among Governments, 795; Ct. established, 795
Executive Director/Deputies, 1404, 1425
Fund, 796-98; accounts *(1984-1985)*, 797 (Auditors Bd.); additional funding sources, 798 (UNEP Cl.); contributions, **790**, 796 (GA/UNEP Cl.), 797 *(table)*; programme budgets, *1984-1985*, 797, *1986-1987* (ACABQ/UNEP), 797-98, *1988-1989*, 798; Trust Funds, 798
Governing Cl., 788-89, **789** (ESC/GA), 1419; biennial cycle of sess., **789**, 799 (GA/UNEP Cl.); members/officers, 1404; *1987* sess./agenda, 799
Information Advisory Ct.: 1st mtg., 798
Information Service reform, 799 (UNEP Cl.); *see also* environmental information networks
& NGOs, 796
Permanent Representatives, Ct. of: establishment, 793; members, 1404-5
& UNCHS, discontinuance of joint mtgs., 795 (GA/UNEP Cl.)
Equatorial Guinea: economic assistance, 511-13 (GA, **513**; S-G, 511-12); human rights advisory services, 894-95 (ESC, **894-95**; UN mission, 895), 895 (mtgs.);

member of Central African Bank/Customs & Economic Union, 512; S-G mission, 511-13
Ethiopia: agricultural development, 1288 (FAO); biofuel programme, 692 (UNIDO); displaced persons, 1001, **1001-2** (GA/UNHCR); desertification/drought assistance, 810 (UNSO); drought, 539-41 (ESC, **540-41**, 541; GA, **541**, Office for Emergency Operations in Africa, Director, 540; S-G, 539-40); refugees in, 1001 (UNHCR); Relief/Rehabilitation Commissioner, 540, **541** (GA); & Somalia, 198 (communication); telecommunications, 1326 (IDA); *see also* East Africa
ETHIOPIA, OFFICE OF THE SPEC. REPRESENTATIVE OF THE S-G FOR EMERGENCY OPERATIONS IN: Assistant S-G, 540, **541** (GA), 1424
ETHNIC STUDIES, INTERNATIONAL CENTRE FOR, 785-86
Europa, *see* Malagasy islands
Europe: drug traffic, 1028 (INCB); economic co-operation, regional, 654-55; economic trends, *Survey*, 653-54 (ESC); energy conservation, 607, 690 (UNIDO); human rights violations, 912; industry, 602 (UNIDO), 607 (UNIDO); radio service unit, **380**, 385 (GA/Information Ct.); refugees in, 996 *(table)*, 1007; standardization, 658 (ECE Experts Group); technical assistance, 469-70 (UNDP); telecommunications, 1345 (ITU); trade & economic co-operation, 559-60 (UNCTAD), 1299 (UNESCO); & TNCs, 620 (ECE/TNCs Centre); *see also country names*; Economic Commission for Europe; Gibraltar, Strait of; *regional and subject entries*
EUROPE, CF. ON SECURITY AND CO-OPERATION IN, **119** (GA); Helsinki Final Act, implementation, 620 (ECE); Madrid Mtg., Concluding Document, 653, 655; *see also* peace and security, international
EUROPEAN COMMUNITIES: accession, Spain, 1146; & Central America, 207; dairy/meat exports, 1371 (GATT); & Iran-Iraq conflict, 250; & International Register of Potentially Toxic Chemicals Legal File, 803; ILO seminar, 1283; & Kampuchea situation, 222; & Lebanon, 302, 308; & Middle East, 263, 286; & Namibia, 1094; & South Africa, 159; subsidies, dispute settlement, 1370 (GATT); telecommunications services, 1347
EUROPEAN SPACE AGENCY, 101, 102; & space transportation, 104
exchange rates, *see* international monetary and financial system
exclusive economic zones: & Law of the Sea Convention, 112; Namibia, 115, **1108** (GA), 1125 (Colonial Countries Ct.); national legislation, 109 (S-G); *see also* continental shelf; fisheries
experts, 1272, 1274 (IAEA), 1339 (ICAO); ILO expenditures, 1280-82 *(table)*; *see also subject entries*; United Nations: experts/consultants
EXPLOSIVES, GROUP OF EXPERTS ON: Chairman, 1417
explosives, transport of, *see* dangerous goods, transport of

exports: & earnings shortfalls, 579 (TDB); promotion, 561 (ITC); proposed compensatory facility, 579 (Expert Group/TDB); subsidies, 822 (GATT); *see also* international trade; trade promotion

external debt, *see* debt problems

extradition: laws/treaties, modernizing/developing, 739 (7th UN Crime Congress)

extra-legal executions, *see* summary executions

Falkland Islands (Malvinas), 1132-36 (communications, 1132-34; Colonial Countries Ct./S-G, 1134; GA, **1134-35**, 1135-36); information to UN, 1082; petitions, 1136 (GA); S-G mission, 1136

family planning, 763 (UNFPA); contraceptive research, 766 (UNDP); IDA credits, 1274; & maternal/child health, 763, 766 (UNFPA); research, 765-66 (UNDP/ UNFPA); Spec. Programmes, funding, 766 (UNDP/UNFPA); UNFPA allocations, 764 *(table)*; UNICEF programme, 968; World Bank loans, 1311

FAMINE AND MALNUTRITION, TRUST FUND FOR COUNTRIES AFFLICTED BY: allocations from UN Emergency Fund, 547-48; *see also* hunger/malnutrition

Far East Region, Meeting of Operational Heads of National Narcotics Law Enforcement Agencies, *see under* narcotics law enforcement agencies

fascism, *see* nazism/fascism

FAUNA AND FLORA, CONVENTION ON INTERNATIONAL TRADE IN ENDANGERED SPECIES OF WILD: implementation, 813 (UNEP); Cf. of parties to, 5th mtg., 813; UNEP Trust Fund, 798

Federated States of Micronesia, *see* Micronesia, Federated States of

fellowships: civil aviation, 1340 (ICAO); copyright/industrial property, 1360 (WIPO); DTCD programme, 486; disarmament, 96-97 (GA, **96-97**, 97; S-G, 96); human rights, 894 (S-G); human settlements, 826 (UNCHS); industrial development, 602 (UNIDO); IAEA, 1272; ILO expenditures on, 1280-82 *(table)*; international law, 1198 (UN/UNITAR); meteorology, 1353 (WMO); mineral resources exploration, 675 (DTCD); nuclear technology, 1274 (IAEA); space applications, 102 (UN Programme); in Trust Territories 1088 (S-G/TC); UNCITRAL, 1194; UNESCO projects, 1299; UNU programme, 786; *see also regional and subject entries*

fertility: & contraceptive use, **770** (ESC); decline in, 650 (ESCAP); migration effects on, 761 (Population Cs.); *see also* family planning; human reproduction

fertilizer industry, 611-12 (UNIDO); ECE seminar, 656

FERTILIZER INFORMATION HANDLING, REGIONAL CONSULTATION ON COMPUTERIZED (ESCAP/FAO/UNIDO), 609

FERTILIZER PROGRAMME (FAO), 1290

fertilizers, 648-49 (ESCAP), 655-56 (ECE), 1290 (FAO); nitrogenous fixation project, 604 (UNIDO)

fibres, *see* jute; textiles

filariasis, 1273 (IAEA)

finances (UN), 1201-23; *see also* accounts (UN); Auditors, Board of; budget (UN); contributions (UN); financial situation (UN)

FINANCIAL EMERGENCY OF THE UN, NEGOTIATING CT. ON THE, members, 1399

financial policy, *see* debt problems; development finance; insurance; international monetary and financial system; public finance

financial situation (UN), 1220-22 (ACABQ/S-G, 1220; GA, **1220-21**); currency instability/inflation, effects of, 1222, **1222** (S-G/GA); postage stamps, revenue from, 1222 (S-G); suspension of financial regulations, 1221, **1221-22**, 1222 (ACABQ/S-G/GA); *see also* contributions (UN)

fisheries, 609 (UNIDO), 1291 (FAO); aquaculture, 1291 (FAO); Ist Consultation, preparations, 609 (FAO/UNIDO); UNIDO study, 608; zones, extent of, 109 (S-G)

FISHERIES MANAGEMENT AND DEVELOPMENT, WORLD CF. ON *(1984)*: implementation, **700** (FAO Cf.), 1291

fissionable materials: prohibition of production, **43**, 43-44 (GA)

floods, 541-43; *see also* Bangladesh; Madagascar; Viet Nam

food, 697-706; consumer protection, **573** (GA guidelines); contamination control, training on, 802 (FAO/UNEP/USSR); coordination, 698, **700** (GA/WFC); as human right, study, 881 (Human Rights Cs./SCPDPM); production, 701 (GA), 1275 (IAEA); technology transfer, 717; world situation, 697, 698 (WFC); *see also* grains; names of food products

food aid, 701-3 (CFA, 701-2; ESC, **703**; GA, **703**, 703; WFP, 702); development assistance, 702, 704 *(table)*; emergency operations, 702, 704 *(table)*; *see also* commodities

FOOD AID CONVENTION *(1980)*: contributions to WFP, 703, 705-6 *(table)*

FOOD AID POLICIES AND PROGRAMMES, CT. ON, 697, **699**, 701-2; 10th annual review, 702; projects approved, 702-3; *see also* Food Programme, World

food and agriculture, 637-38 (ECA/FAO/ S-G), 648-49 (ESCAP/FAO), 663 (ECLAC), 667 (ESCWA), 1275 (IAEA/FAO), 1287-94 (FAO); IFAD replenishment, 637 (ECA), **700**, 701 (GA); world situation, 697-701 (ESC, 699; GA, **699-700**, 700-1; WFC, 698-99); WFC Executive Director, 697-98); *see also under* Africa

FOOD AND AGRICULTURE, GLOBAL INFORMATION AND EARLY WARNING SYSTEM IN (FAO), 1289, **1345** (GA)

FOOD AND AGRICULTURE ORGANIZATION OF THE UN, 1287-94; budget, 1292; Cf., 1287; Cl., 1287 (Chairman), 1294 (members); contributions, 1292-94 *(table)*; 40th anniversary, 1287; funding, 1287; headquarters/field offices, 1294; Investment Centre, 1288; members, 1287, 1292-93 *(table)*; officers/departments, 1293 *(list)*; publications, 1292; regional representatives, 1294; secretariat, 1292; Spec. Relief Opera-

tions Office, 1292; Technical Co-operation Programme, 1287

FOOD CONFERENCE, WORLD *(1974)*: 10th anniversary mtg., 697, **699** (CFA/GA)

FOOD COUNCIL, WORLD, 698-99, **699**, 1420; Executive Director/Deputy, 1408, 1425; members/officers, 1408; reports, 697-98

FOOD DATA SYSTEMS, INTERNATIONAL NETWORK OF (UNU), 774

FOOD DAY, WORLD, 1291

food industry, 609-10 (UNIDO); round table on co-operation in food-processing, 604 (UNIDO); training programmes, 603 (UNIDO); & UNFDAC, 610

FOOD IRRADIATION, INTERNATIONAL CONSULTATIVE GROUP ON: establishment, 1275

food problems, 697-701 (ESC, 699; GA, **699-700**, 700-1; WFC, 698-99; & health, 1303 (FAO/WHO); information/early warning system, 697, **700** (GA), 701 (CFA), 1289; national strategies, 698, **699** (GA/WFC); relief operations, 1292 (FAO); security, 11 (S-G), **700** (GA); trade, 698-99, **699** (GA/WFC); world situation, 697, 698 (WFC); *World Food Survey*, 1292 (FAO); *see also* agriculture; hunger

FOOD PROCESSING INDUSTRY, 2ND CONSULTATION ON THE, WITH SPEC. EMPHASIS ON VEGETABLE OILS AND FATS, 609-10

FOOD PROGRAMME, WORLD, 701-3, 1292 (FAO); Executive Director/Deputy, 1420, 1425; Food Aid Ct. (governing body), 701-2, 1420 (members); pledging targets/contributions *(1987-1988)*, 703, **703** (ESC/GA), 705-6, 706 *(tables)*; UN/FAO Joint Task Force on Relationship Problems, 702; & UNDP, 702; & UNHCR, 702

FOOD RESERVE, INTERNATIONAL EMERGENCY, contributions, 702, 705 *(table)*; targets, 703

food security, 1289; *see also* food problems

FOOD SECURITY, CT. ON WORLD (FAO), 1289

FOOD SECURITY ASSISTANCE SCHEME (FAO), 1289

FOOD SECURITY COMPACT, WORLD: approval, 1289 (FAO Cf.), 882 (SCPDPM)

Food Survey, Fifth World, 1292 (FAO)

force, non-use of in international relations, *see under* peace and security, international

foreign trade, *see* international trade

FOREST, INTERNATIONAL YEAR OF THE *(1985)*, 812, 1291

forestry: & desertification control, 1291 (FAO); remote sensing applications, 657 (ECE/FAO)

FORESTRY AND WOOD INDUSTRIES COMMITTEE (ILO), 1278

FORESTRY CONGRESS, NINTH WORLD *(1985)*, 812, 1291

forests, 657 (ECE), 1291 (FAO); air pollution effects on, 804; environmental monitoring, pilot project, **790** (GA), 801 (UNEP/UNESCO/WMO); genetic resources, 1291 (FAO); protection of, 101 (UN/FAO cf.), 812 (UNEP Executive Director); & remote sensing, 101

forests *(cont.)*
(FAO/UN); tree-planting projects, 796
(NGOs/UNEP); watershed management,
1291 (FAO); *see also* deforestation;
tropical forests; tropical timber
foundries, 615 (UNIDO)
Fouta Djallon massif, *see under* Guinea
France: UNIFIL battalion, 305; & UN-
RFNRE co-financing, 669-70; *see also*
Comorian island of Mayotte; Malagasy
islands; Mururoa Atoll
freedom of movement, *see under* human
rights
freedom of speech, *see under* human
rights
FREQUENCY REGISTER, MASTER INTERNA-
TIONAL (ITU), 1346; *see also* radio
broadcasting: frequency allocation
freshwater ecosystems, 814-15 (UNEP);
see also ecosystems; water resources
management
front-line States (Angola, Botswana,
Mozambique, United Republic of Tanzania, Zambia, Zimbabwe), 170-80;
assistance to, **1067** (ESC), **1071** (GA);
see also Namibia; South Africa; *and
under names of States*
fuels, coal; energy; gas; oil
fuelwood, 688 (GA), 691 (S-G), 693
(UNEP); *see also* forestry; forests

Gambia: desertification assistance, 810;
economic assistance, 513-15 (GA, **514-15**;
S-G, 514); seed production, 1290 (FAO)
GAS, CT. ON (ECE): 31st sess., 656
Gaza Strip: development projects, 282
(UNDP/UNIDO), 326, 349, **349**, **350**
(ESC/GA); refugees in, 366-67 (GA, **367**,
367; S-G, 366-67); *see also* Palestinians,
assistance to; territories occupied by
Israel
GENERAL AGREEMENT ON TARIFFS AND
TRADE, 1370-73; Cl. of Representatives,
1372; Consultative Group of Eighteen,
1371; Contracting Parties, 1371-72 (sess.);
contributions, 1373 *(table)*; financing,
1372; headquarters, 1373; members,
1370, 1373 *(table)*; officers, 1373;
publications, 1372; secretariat, 1370,
1372; spec. sess., 1372; Technical Co-
operation Division/training programme,
1372; work programme, 1371
GENERAL ASSEMBLY, 1393-1409
Main Cts.: officers, 1393
procedural cts. (Credentials/General): officers, 1393
publications, 398
rationalization of procedures, 397-98
(GA/S-G/Spec. Ct.)
standing cts. (ACABQ/Contributions):
members, 1394
strengthening effectiveness of, 8-9 (S-G);
2nd Ct., biennial work programme,
1057-58 (GA)
subsidiary/*ad hoc*/related bodies,
1393-1408
GENERAL ASSEMBLY (39th sess., resumed):
agenda, 395, 1426; dates/officers, 1393
GENERAL ASSEMBLY (40th sess.): agenda,
395, **395-96** (GA), 1426-32 *(list)*; dates/of-
ficers, 1393; publications, 398; representatives' credentials, 396-97 (Credentials

Ct., 396-97; GA, **397**); suspension, 395,
395 (GA); work organization, 396, **396**
(GA)
GENERAL ASSEMBLY, INTERIM CT. OF THE,
1397
GENERAL ASSEMBLY AFFAIRS, OFFICE OF
THE UNDER-S-G FOR POLITICAL AND:
Under-S-G/Assistant S-G, 1423
generalized system of preferences, 558-
59 (Spec. Ct.); "Enabling Clause", 1371;
regional office 558; technical co-
operation, 558-59 (UNCTAD/UNDP); *see
also* trade preferences
genetic resources: plants/animals, 814
(FAO/UNEP)
GENEVA CONVENTIONS *(1949)/*ADDITIONAL
PROTOCOLS *(1977)*: & El Salvador, 916;
& Israel, 262, **266**, **338** (GA), 925; infor-
mation dissemination, 377; & Iran-Iraq
conflict, 244; & Lebanon situation, 298;
& Namibia question, **1109** (GA); &
South African freedom fighters, 176; *see
also under* territories occupied by Israel
Geneva Protocol *(1925)*, *see under*
bacteriological (biological) weapons
genocide: conventions, 928; *1978* study,
proposed update, 928, **928**
(GA/SCPDPM/Spec. Rapporteur)
GEOGRAPHICAL NAMES, UN GROUP OF
EXPERTS ON: divisions, 1417
GEOLOGICAL CORRELATION PROGRAMME,
INTERNATIONAL, 1296 (UNESCO)
geology: & the environment, 812
geosphere-biosphere programme, 104
geostationary orbit, 380 (GA/ITU); legal
aspects, 105, **106** (COPUOS/GA);
technical aspects 104, **106** (COPUOS/
GA/ITU); *see also* communications
satellites
geothermal energy, 669 (UNRFNRE/
United States), 670 (UNDP), **671** (ESC),
686-87 (UNDP Energy Account), 690
(DTCD)
Ghana: IDA credit, 1326; industrial planning, 607 (UNIDO); mineral resources
exploration, 675 (DTCD); transportation,
1326 (IDA); urban development, 1326
(IDA)
Gibraltar, 1146, **1147** (communications/
Colonial Countries Ct./GA); information
to UN, 1082
Gibraltar, Strait of: Europe-Africa link,
634, **634**, 655 (ECA/ECE/ESC)
GLACIER MONITORING SERVICE, WORLD
(UNEP): Inventory, 804
global economic negotiations, *see under*
development and international economic
co-operation
Global Information and Early Warning
System in Food and Agriculture, *see*
Food and Agriculture, Global Information
and Early Warning System in (FAO)
**global system of trade preferences
among developing countries**, 559
(UNCTAD)
Glorieuses, *see* Malagasy islands
Golan Heights: administration of, 340-43
(GA, **266**, 267-68, **340-41**, 341, **341-42**,
342-43; Human Rights Cs./S-G, 340);
alleged nuclear-missile deployment in,
263 (communication); educational in-
stitutions in, **333**, 343 (GA); & *1949*
Geneva Convention, **266** (GA); *see also*
Disengagement Observer Force, UN

gold: exploration, 669, 670 (UNRFNRE),
675 (DTCD)
good-neighbourliness between States, *see
under* States'
GOVERNMENT PROCUREMENT, CT. ON
(GATT), 1371
grains: contributions through IEFR, 705
(table); import costs, IMF compensatory
financing, 1331; world production, 1287
(FAO); *see also* Coarse Grains, Pulses,
Roots and Tuber Crops . . ., Regional Co-
ordinating Centre; Food Reserve, International Emergency
GREAT LAKES COUNTRIES, ECONOMIC
COMMUNITY OF THE: industrial planning, 608 (UNIDO)
Greece: civil aviation, 1340 (ICAO)
GROUP OF 77: 9th annual mtg., on Africa
economic situation, 501; proposal on
restrictive business practices, 564
Guam, 1147-48 (GA); hearings, 1148; information to UN, 1082
Guatemala: architectural heritage, restoration, 1297 (UNESCO); disappearances,
920, 921, **923** (GA/Human Rights Cs.);
elections in, 922, **923** (GA/SCPDPM);
human rights violations, 920-23 (ESC,
921; GA, **922-24**, 924; Human Rights
Cs., 921; SCPDPM, 921-22; Spec. Rapporteur, 920-21, 922); political situation,
207 (communication); refugees from,
920, 922; Spec. Rapporteur, mandate extended, 921 (ESC/Human Rights Cs.)
Guinea: accession to NPT, 1271; economic
assistance, 486 (DTCD); & Fouta Djallon
massif, 516; pharmaceutical industry in,
612 (IDDA/UNIDO); spec. economic
assistance, 515-16 (GA, **515-16**, 516; UN
agencies, 516); technical assistance, 1326
(IDA); *see also* maritime boundaries
Guinea-Bissau: spec. economic
assistance, 516-18 (GA, **517-18**; S-G
review mission, 516-17); *see also*
maritime boundaries
GULF CO-OPERATION COUNCIL: Supreme
Cl. communiqué, circulation, 403; &
Iran-Iraq conflict, 250 (Ministerial Cl.);
Middle East, 286 (communication)
Guyana: energy resources development,
692 (UNIDO)

Habitat, *see* Human Settlements, UN Centre for
Habitat News, 826
Haiti: human rights advisory services, 895
(Centre/Human Rights Cs./S-G); natural
resources exploration, 669 (UNRFNRE);
spec. economic assistance, UN mission,
528-29 (GA/S-G)
HAZARDOUS WASTES, *AD HOC* WORKING
GROUP OF EXPERTS ON ENVIRONMEN-
TALLY SOUND MANAGEMENT OF: Cairo
guidelines, adoption, 803
health, 773-75, 1278 (ILO), 1302-4 (WHO);
co-ordination, 1302; & environment, proposed UNEP report, 792; IDA credits for,
1324-25 *(table)*, 1326; maternal, 1302-3;
monitoring, UNEP/WHO programme,
803, 803-4 (FAO/UNEP); system infrastructure, 1302 (WHO); technology,
1303 (WHO); World Bank loans, 1309-10
(table), 1311; *see also* children; disabled

persons; diseases; environmental health; nutrition; primary health care

HEALTH AND MEDICAL SERVICES, JOINT MTG. ON EMPLOYMENT AND CONDITIONS OF WORK IN (ILO), 1278

HEALTH DAY, WORLD, 1302

HEALTH FOR ALL BY THE YEAR 2000, GLOBAL STRATEGY FOR: UNICEF/WHO collaboration, 976

HEALTH HAZARDS AND BIOLOGICAL EFFECTS OF WELDING FUMES AND GASES, INTERNATIONAL CF. ON (1st), 1303 (Denmark/EC/WHO)

HEALTH POLICY, UNICEF/WHO JOINT CT. ON, 1302

health services: region/country, 1305-6 *(table)*; workers' programmes, 1303

heroin, abuse of/traffic in, 1026, 1027, 1028

hides/skins, 566 (UNCTAD); *see also* leather industry

highways, *see* roads

hijacking, 3 (S-G), 1169, **1170** (SC); *Achille Lauro*, 272, 291-92 (communications, 291; SC, 291-92); aircraft, 1339 (ICAO); at Beirut Airport, 304-5 (communications); conventions, 1339; of Egyptian aircraft, 292; *see also* terrorism, international

Holy See: consultative status in ECE, 1414; letter on Lebanon situation, 302; papal visit to UN Office (Nairobi), 798; UN assessment, 1216 (GA), 1219 *(table)*

HOMELESS, INTERNATIONAL YEAR OF SHELTER FOR THE *(1987)*, 827-30 (CCSQ(PROG), 828, 829; GA, **829-30**, 830; Human Settlements Cs., 828; S-G, 828-29); *Bulletin*, 828; contributions, 824, 828, **829** (GA); follow-up sess., 828, **830**, 830 (Human Settlements Cs./GA); geographic representation, 828; projects/regional activities, 650 (ESCAP), 828 (UNCHS)

Honduras: disaster prevention, UNDRO mission, 547; elections in, 206; refugees in, 920, 1007; *see also* Central America situation; Nicaragua

horticulture, 1289-90 (FAO)

HOSTAGES, INTERNATIONAL CONVENTION AGAINST THE TAKING OF *(1979)*, 3 (S-G); parties to, 1167 (S-G), **1170** (SC)

hostage-taking, 1169-70, **1170** (SC)

HOST COUNTRY, CT. ON RELATIONS WITH THE, 1180, **1181** (GA); members/officers, 1396

host country relations (UN/United States), 1180-81 (Ct., 1180; GA, **1180-81**)

HOUSEHOLD SURVEY CAPABILITY PROGRAMME, NATIONAL, 651 (ESCAP), 1034-35 (Statistical Cs.)

housing: building/building technology, 658 (ECE); financing, 659 (ECE); & population, world censuses, 1015, **1034** (ESC/Statistical Cs.); UNEP/WHO project, 820; *see also* Homeless, International Year of Shelter for the; human settlements

HOUSING, WORKING PARTY ON (ECE), 658

HOUSING, BUILDING AND PLANNING, CT. ON (ECE), 657-58

HOUSING FINANCE SOFTWARE, 826 (UNCHS)

human environment, *see under* environment

HUMAN EXPOSURE ASSESSMENT LOCATIONS: UNEP/WHO programme, 803

humanitarian assistance, 927, **928** (GA/Human Rights Cs.); *see also* disasters; Kampuchea situation; mass exoduses; refugees

HUMANITARIAN ISSUES, INDEPENDENT CS. ON INTERNATIONAL, 896, **897** (GA/S-G)

humanitarian order, new international, *see* human rights: new international humanitarian order

HUMAN REPRODUCTION, SPEC. PROGRAMME OF RESEARCH, DEVELOPMENT AND RESEARCH TRAINING IN (WHO), 1303 (WHO); Policy & Co-ordination Ct., 766; UNFPA allocations, 766 (UNDP); *see also* family planning; fertility

human resources, 638 (ECA), 780-87; development, 780-81 (GA, **781**; S-G, 781; UNDP Cl. 780-81), 1227 (CPC); industrialization, 598, 602; Round Table, 781; training/research, 781-82 (UNITAR), 785-86 (UNU); *see also* brain drain; manpower development; Peace, University for; Training and Research, UN Institute for; Transfer of Knowledge through Expatriate Nationals; University, UN; vocational training

human rights, 10-11 (S-G), 835-935

advancement, 882-85 (GA, **883-85**, 885; S-G, 882-83)

advisory services, 893 (Human Rights Cs./S-G); & UNITAR/Human Rights Centre, 893; *see also under* Bolivia; Equatorial Guinea; Haiti; Uganda

force, use of by legal authorities, 866 (SCPDPM/S-G)

freedom of movement, study, 872 (Human Rights Cs./SCPDPM)

freedom of speech, 871-72 (Human Rights Cs.)

force, use of by legal authorities, 866 (SCPDM/S-G)

& individual & international law: status of, 931-32 (Spec. Rapporteur/SCPDPM)

international instruments, 889-93; list of, addition to, 889 (SCPDPM); reporting obligations, 889-91 (GA, **890-91**; S-G, 889-90); & UNITAR, **890** (GA); *see also* civil and political rights; economic, social and cultural rights; Human Rights, International Covenants on; Human Rights, Universal Declaration of

& judicial system, independence of: final report, 873 (SCPDPM/Spec. Rapporteur)

legal institutions, strengthening of: technical assistance, 896 (S-G)

new international humanitarian order (proposed), 896-97, **897** (GA/S-G)

non-citizens: draft declaration, adoption, 850-52 (GA, **850-52**, 852; Working Group, 850); **850-51** *(text)*

& peace, 119 (GA), 933-35 (GA, **934-35**, 935; SCPDPM, 933-34)

& popular participation, S-G study, 881-82 (GA, **882**, 882; Human Rights Cs., 881; S-G, 882)

promotion/protection: amnesty, role in, 873 (SCPDPM/Spec. Rapporteur);

draft declaration/body of principles, responsibility for, 896, **896** (ESC/Human Rights Cs./Spec. Rapporteur); national institutions for, 885-86 (GA, 885, **886**; S-G, 885); regional arrangements, 850-51 (Human Rights Cs.)

public information, 887-89 (GA, **887-89**; Human Rights Cs., 888; S-G, 887-88)

& science & technology, 932-33 (GA, **932-33**, 933; Human Rights Cs./S-G, 932); & computerized personal files, draft guidelines, 933 (CCAQ/SCPDPM); hazardous technologies, 934 (SCPDPM)

see also apartheid; child, rights of the; civil and political rights; conscientious objection; development, right to; disabled persons; food, right to; prisoners, treatment of; racism and racial discrimination; self-determination; youth; *and under country names*; criminal justice; refugees: protection; women

HUMAN RIGHTS, CENTRE FOR (Division of Human Rights): Assistant S-G, 1424

HUMAN RIGHTS, CS. ON, 886-87, 1411-12; *Ad Hoc* Expert Group, members, 1412; members/officers, 1411; report, 886 (ESC); *1986* sess., organization, 886 (ESC); Working Groups, 1412; *see also* Discrimination and Protection of Minorities, Sub-Cs. on Prevention of; *and under Apartheid*, International Convention on

Human Rights, Division of, *see* Human Rights, Centre for

HUMAN RIGHTS, INTERNATIONAL COVENANTS ON *(1966)*, 891-93 (GA, **891-93**; Human Rights Cs., 891; S-G, 891)

HUMAN RIGHTS, UNIVERSAL DECLARATION OF *(1948)*, 10 (S-G); personalized version of, 890, **890** (GA/Human Rights Cs.)

HUMAN RIGHTS CT., 853, 853-54 (GA); members/sess., 1422; official records, publication, **892** (GA)

HUMAN RIGHTS PRIZE, SPEC. CT. TO SELECT THE WINNERS OF THE UN: members, 1401

human rights violations, 898-929; general aspects, 898 (ESC/GA); mass exoduses, 927, **927-28**, 928 (GA/Human Rights Cs.); and peace, 1297 (UNESCO); working groups on, members, 1412; *see also* genocide *and country names*

human settlements, 639 (ECA), 650 (ESCAP), 657-58 (ECE), 668 (ESCWA), 822-34; Asian bank (proposed), 823; co-ordination in UN system, 831-32 (GA, **832**; S-G, 832); cross-organizational programme analysis, 833 (GA, **832**, 833; Human Settlements Cs., 833); & environment, 819-20 (UNCHS/UNEP); finance mobilization, **823**, 824 (GA/Human Settlements Cs.); Habitat Cf. (10th anniversary), 822 (Human Settlements Cs.); information, 826; & microcomputer/software applications, 826-27; planning/strategies, 823 (UNCHS); political/economic/social issues, 830-31; regional co-ordination, 832-33; technical advisory services, 827; technical co-operation, 827 (UNCHS/UNDP); trilingual thesaurus, 827; World

human settlements *(cont.)*
Habitat Day, 822; *see also under* Africa; *apartheid*; construction; Homeless, International Year of Shelter for the; housing; territories occupied by Israel
HUMAN SETTLEMENTS, CS. ON, 822-23 (ESC, 822; GA, **822-23**, 823), 1396; Executive Director/Deputy Administrator, 1424; members/officers, 1415; *1985* sess., 822; sess., biennial cycle, 833-34 (GA, **833-34**); UNCHS, 833); themes, future sess., 834
Human Settlements, Global Report on, 825-26
HUMAN SETTLEMENTS, UN CENTRE FOR (HABITAT), 825-27; co-ordination in UN, 831-32 (GA, **832**; Human Settlements Cs./S-G, 832); extrabudgetary resources, 824; & NGOs, 827; programme/budget, 827; technical co-operation, 827; & UNEP, joint mtgs., **832**, 833 (GA/Human Settlements Cs./UNEP)
HUMAN SETTLEMENTS AND ENVIRONMENT, JOINT INTERGOVERNMENTAL REGIONAL CT. ON: 3rd mtg., 628, 639
HUMAN SETTLEMENTS FOUNDATION, UN HABITAT AND, 824-25; accounts, *1984-1985*, 825; contributions, **823**, 824 (GA/Human Settlements Cs.), 825 *(table)*
Hungary: admission to IDA, 1323, to IFC, 1318; industrial loans, 1311 (World Bank)
hunger: elimination, 698 (WFC); *see also* food; malnutrition
HYDROLOGICAL PROGRAMME, OPERATIONAL (UNESCO/WMO): Multi-purpose Subprogramme, 1352; 3rd phase *(1984-1989)*, 1296-97, 1352
hydrology, 679 (UNESCO); IAEA projects, 1274; technical co-operation, 1353 (WMO)
HYDROLOGY, CS. FOR, 1352
HYDROLOGY AND WATER RESOURCES PROGRAMME (WMO), 1352
hydropower, 690 (UNIDO), 692 (UNDP)
hygiene: standards and codes, FAO/WHO publication, 1303

illiteracy: eradication, 1295 (UNESCO); UNICEF/UNESCO/World Bank programmes, 971-72
immunization, 1304 (WHO); World Bank loans, 1311; *see also under* children
IMMUNIZATION, EXPANDED PROGRAMME ON, 1304 (WHO)
imports: national operations, 562 (ITC)
India: agricultural development, 1325 (IDA); Bhopal chemical accident in *(1984)*, 791, 796, 802, 1279 (ILO); Child Development Institute, Maurice Pate Award, 963; desertification control, 808 (UNEP); & drug traffic, 1028; economy & opiates production, 1019 (Expert Group); energy loans, 1311 (World Bank); food security, study, 698 (UNRISD), 970 (UNICEF); & IAEA safeguards, 1271; industrial planning, 607 (UNIDO); transportation loans, 1312 (World Bank); urban development, 1326 (IDA)
INDIA AND PAKISTAN, UN MILITARY OBSERVER GROUP IN: Chief, 1410

Indian Ocean:
marine affairs co-operation, cf. (phase 1), 682
zone of peace: Cf. on (proposed), 89-91 (*Ad Hoc* Ct., 89-90; communications, 90; GA **90-91**, 91); Declaration *(1971)*, implementation, 89, **90-91** (*Ad Hoc* Ct./GA)
see also Malagasy islands
INDIAN OCEAN, *AD HOC* CT. ON THE, 89-90, **91** (GA); members/officers, 1395
indigenous populations, 847-48 (ESC/Human Rights Cs./SCPDPM/Working Group); voluntary fund, establishment, 847-48 (ESC, 847, **848**; GA, **848**, 848; Human Rights Cs., 847); *see also* minorities
INDIGENOUS POPULATIONS, UN VOLUNTARY FUND FOR: Board of Trustees, 511
INDIGENOUS POPULATIONS, WORKING GROUP ON (SCPDPM), 847; members, 1412
Indo-China: refugees in, 1007-8 (UNHCR); *see also country names; subject entries*
Indonesia: education loans, 1310 (World Bank); family planning loans, 1311 (World Bank); rural development/transmigration programmes, 1310 (World Bank); UN Information Centre, reopened, 385; *see also* East Timor
INDUSTRIAL AND TECHNOLOGICAL INFORMATION BANK, 608-9; Inquiry Service, 609; publication, 609; regional activities, 609; review of, 608-9 (advisory group mtg.); & technology transfer, role in, 608, 718 (UNIDO Executive Director)
industrial development, 591-615, 635-36 (ECA), 647 (ESCAP), 662-63 (ECLAC), 667 (ESCWA)
co-operation, 603-5; System of Consultations, 603-4; trade aspects, 605 (UNCTAD/UNIDO expert group); *see also* developing countries
financing, resource mobilization, 606 (4th General Cf./GA)
international bank, proposed, 599
investment promotion, 606
management, 606-51; expenditures, 606 (UNDP/UNIDO)
& manpower development, 638 (ECA)
planning, 607-8 (DTCD/UNDP/UNIDO); expenditures, 607
production, redeployment/restructuring, 605-6 (IDB/UNIDO Cf.)
publications, 603, 608, 609, 615
studies, 608 (UNIDO)
technical co-operation, 600-3 (CPC, 602; S-G, 600-1; UNIDO Executive Director, 602); projects/expenditures, 600-2 (CPC/S-G/UNIDO), 601 *(table)*; training programmes, 602-3 (UNIDO)
technology, 608; *see also* technology, transfer of
see also names of specific industries
INDUSTRIAL DEVELOPMENT BOARD, 592, 597; Chairman/members, 1405-6, 1419-20; Permanent Ct., 597, 1406 (members/officers)
Industrial Development Decade for Africa *(1980-1990)*, *see* Africa, Industrial Development Decade for
INDUSTRIAL DEVELOPMENT FIELD ADVISERS PROGRAMME, SENIOR: Junior

Professional Officers programme, 603; strengthening, 603 (IDB/UNDP)
INDUSTRIAL DEVELOPMENT FUND, UN, 599-600 (Board of Auditors/GA/IDB); budgetary resources, 600 (S-G/UNIDO); contributions, 599-600 *(table)*; projects, 599
INDUSTRIAL DEVELOPMENT ORGANIZATION, UN, 591-600, 1405-6
Committee on the Negotiation of a Relationship Agreement, 592
Constitution, signatures/ratifications, 591-92 (communications, 592)
conversion into specialized agency: budgetary aspects, 596-97 (ACABQ/GA/S-G); UN/UNIDO relationship agreement, 591-97 (ESC, 592, **592-93**, **593**; GA, **593**, **593-96** *(text)*; IDB/UNIDO General Cf., 592)
co-ordination in UN system, 598 (CPC/S-G)
Director-General, appointment, 591
Executive Director, 1406, 1425; Deputy, 1425
financial questions, 599-600; *see also* Industrial Development Fund, UN
programme budget, *1986-1987*, 597, 599, 600, 602 (GA/IDB)
Programme & Budget Ct., 598
& UNDP draft relationship agreement, 592
& WIPO reservations, 592
INDUSTRIAL DEVELOPMENT ORGANIZATION, UN: 2ND GENERAL CF. *(1975)*: Declaration/Action Plan, 591
INDUSTRIAL DEVELOPMENT ORGANIZATION, UN: 4TH GENERAL CF. *(1984)*: follow-up, 598-99 (IDB)
INDUSTRIAL INQUIRY SERVICE, 609
industrialization: role of energy in, 690 (UNIDO); & social development, 598 (UNIDO studies)
industrial property, 1360 (WIPO); development co-operation, 1359-60; fellowships, 1360 (WIPO); international instruments, 1359 *(list)*; publications, 1360; *see also* marks; patents; trade marks
INDUSTRIAL PROPERTY, PARIS CONVENTION FOR THE PROTECTION OF: accessions, 1359; mtg. on revision of, 1360; *see also* Paris Union
industrial robots, *see under* engineering industries
INDUSTRIAL SERVICES, SPECIAL, 600, 603; project expenditures, 603
industry, 655-56 (ECE); accident prevention, 724 (IAEA/UNDRO), 1279 (ILO); consultations, future, 597 (OECD/UNIDO), 604; environmental impact of, 819; IDA credits, 1325, 1325-26 *(table)*; UNEP activities, 819; World Bank loans, 1309-10 *(table)*, 1311; world trends in, 604 (UNIDO Executive Director); *see also* agro-industries; capital goods industry; chemical industries; engineering industries; metallurgical industries; metals; small-scale industry
INDUSTRY, TECHNOLOGY, HUMAN SETTLEMENTS AND THE ENVIRONMENT, CT. ON (ESCAP), 647, 517
infants, *see* breast-feeding
INFORMATICS PROGRAMME, INTERGOVERNMENTAL (UNESCO), 1296

information, 369-88; co-ordination in UN system, 386-88 (ACC, 388; GA/Information Ct., 387; JUNIC, 386-87); global flow of, 1298-99 (UNESCO); human settlements, 826-27 (UNCHS); *see also* mass communication; new world information and communication order; public information
INFORMATION, CT. ON, 369; members/officers, 1396; recommendations, 369, **376** (GA), **377-82** *(text)*
INFORMATION, DIVISION OF (UNDP): strengthening, 474 (UNDP Cl.)
Information, UN Trust Fund for Economic and Social, *see* Economic and Social Information, UN Trust Fund for
Information Bank, Industrial and Technological, *see* Industrial and Technological Information Bank
information centres/services (UN), 381, 385-86 (GA/Information Ct./S-G), 1435-37 *(list)*; new, **381**, 385 (GA/S-G)
INFORMATION COMMITTEE, JOINT UN, **377**, 386-87 (GA); *Ad Hoc* Working Group on Audio-Visual Matters, 387; & Africa, 499
Information Data Base, Global Resource, *see under* environmental information networks
INFORMATION PROGRAMME, GENERAL (UNESCO), 1298-99, 1299 *(tables)*
INFORMATION REFERRAL SYSTEM, 488 (UNDP)
information systems, 827 (UNCHS); **1273** (IAEA), 1298-99 (UNESCO); bibliographic, 1264; co-ordination in UN, 1263-64 (ACC/CPC, 1263-64); desertification control, 808; development, 1264; environment, 800-1; food/agriculture, **700** (GA); genetic resources, 814 (UNEP); industry/technology, 608-9; international trade, 557 (UNCTAD), 561 (ITC)
INFORMATION SYSTEM, UN BIBLIOGRAPHIC, 1265
INFORMATION SYSTEMS, ADVISORY CT. FOR CO-ORDINATION OF, 1264 (ACC/ESC); publications, 1264
INFOTERRA, *see under* environmental information networks
inland transport, 1278 (ILO); *see also* dangerous goods, transport of; railways; road transport/roads
INLAND TRANSPORT CT. (ECE), 655
INLAND TRANSPORT CT. (ILO), 1278
inland water transport, 647 (ESCAP)
INQUIRY AND CONCILIATION, PANEL FOR (GA), 1399
insurance, 579-80 (Ct. on Invisibles)
intellectual property: international instruments, 1359 *(list)*; publication, 1361; *see also* copyright/neighbouring rights
INTERGOVERNMENTAL AGENCIES, CT. ON NEGOTIATIONS WITH: members, appointment of, 592, **592**, 1416 (ESC/S-G); & UN/UNIDO relationship agreement, **592-93** (ESC)
intergovernmental organizations, 1271-1373; co-operation with UN, 398-403; & ICSC, 1233; *see also names of organizations*
INTERNATIONAL ATOMIC ENERGY AGENCY, 1271-77; administrative/budgetary coordination, 1230, **1230-31** (ACABQ/GA); annual report, 693-94, **694** (DG/GA);

Board of Governors, 1271, 1276 *(list)*; budget, 1275; cts., 1277; contributions, 1275-76 *(table)*; DG/Deputies, 1271, 1277; General Cf., 1271; headquarters/liaison office, 1277; members, 1271, 1275-76 *(table)*; secretariat, 1275, 1277; technical co-operation, 1272, 1275
INTERNATIONAL BANK FOR RECONSTRUCTION AND DEVELOPMENT (World Bank), 1309-16; capitalization, 1313; co-financing, 1313; Economic Development Institute, 1312; Executive Directors/alternates, 1315-16; financing activities, 1314; headquarters/field offices, 1316; & IMF, 1330; income/expenditures/reserves, 1313, 1314 *(table)*; lending operations, 1309-12, 1309-10 *(table)*; members, 1309, 1314-15 *(table)*; principal officers, 1316; secretariat, 1313; Spec. Action Programme, 1313; subscriptions/voting power, 1314-15 *(table)*; technical co-operation, 1311-12; as UNDP executing agency, 1311
international civil aviation, *see* air navigation; air transport; civil aviation; hijacking
INTERNATIONAL CIVIL AVIATION, CONVENTION ON (CHICAGO CONVENTION, *1944*): amendment, 1339 (ICAO); annexes (Standards/Recommended Practices), 1337; application to Law of the Sea Convention, 1339 (ICAO Legal Ct.)
INTERNATIONAL CIVIL AVIATION AND ITS FACILITIES, CT. ON UNLAWFUL INTERFERENCE WITH, 1339
INTERNATIONAL CIVIL AVIATION ORGANIZATION, 1338-42; Assembly, 1339; budget, 1340 *(table)*; contributions, 1341 *(table)*; conventions, 1339-40 *(list)*; Cl., 1338, 1342: headquarters/regional offices, 1342; Legal Ct., 1339; members, 1338, 1341 *(table)*; officers, 1342; publications, 1339; secretariat, 1340, 1342; technical co-operation, 1340
INTERNATIONAL CIVIL SERVANTS' ASSOCIATION, FEDERATION OF, 1234; *see also* staff (UN/UN system)
international civil service, 9 (S-G), 1233-45; *see also* pensions; privileges and immunities; staff (UN/UN system)
INTERNATIONAL CIVIL SERVICE COMMISSION, 1236-37 (GA, **1237**; ACC/CCISUA/FICSA/JIU, 1236); budget, revised estimates, *1984-1985*, 1236-37 (ACABQ/S-G); members, 1397-98; officials, allowances/compensation, 1252, **1252-53** (ACABQ/GA/S-G)
INTERNATIONAL COMMERCIAL ARBITRATION, MODEL LAW ON: adoption, **1192** (GA); *see also under* international trade law
INTERNATIONAL CONTRACT PRACTICES, WORKING GROUP ON (UNCITRAL), 1191; Chairman/members, 1401
INTERNATIONAL CONTRACT PRACTICES IN INDUSTRY, WORKING GROUP OF EXPERTS ON (ECE), 655
INTERNATIONAL COMMITTEE OF THE RED CROSS: & East Timor, 1137; & Guatemala, 922, **923** (GA); & Iran-Iraq conflict, 244, 245, 246; & Lebanon, 297, 301, **303** (S-G/GA), 548; & prisoner exchanges, *1983* accord with PLO, 337 (Human Rights Cs.); & UNDOF, 314

INTERNATIONAL COURT OF JUSTICE, 1156-59
advisory opinions, organs authorized to request, 1421; UN Administrative Tribunal judgement, review of, 1157
cases, 1156-57, 1421; *see also* continental shelf: delimitation; Mali & Burkina Faso; Nicaragua
Chamber of Summary Procedure, 1421
cts., 1421
compulsory jurisdiction, States accepting, 1421
organizational questions: conditions of service, 1157-59 (ACABQ/S-G, 1157-58; GA, **1158-59**, 1159); emoluments, 1157, **1158** (ACABQ/GA/S-G); pension plan, 1157-58, **1158** (ACABQ/GA-S/G); terms, 1421 *(list)*
publications, 1159
Registrar/Deputy, 1421, 1424
reports, 1156 (GA)
Statute, 1388-92 *(text)*; parties to, 1421
International Criminal Police Organization, *see* Criminal Police Organization, International
INTERNATIONAL DEVELOPMENT ASSOCIATION, 1323-29; Executive Director/alternates, 1328-29; headquarters/field offices, 1329; income/expenses, 1329 *(table)*; lending operations, 1324-25 *(table)*, 1325-27; members, 1323, 1327-28 *(table)*; replenishments (7th, 8th), 458, 463, 1323; secretariat, 1327; Spec. Facility, 1323-24; subscriptions/supplementary resources/voting power, 1327-28 *(table)*; technical assistance, 1326
International Development Strategy, *see under* Development Decade, 3rd UN
International Economic and Social Affairs, Department of, *see* Economic and Social Affairs, Department of International
international economic law, 1191-96; *see also* Economic Rights and Duties of States, Charter of; international trade law; new international economic order
international economic relations, 409-55; & economic security, 421, **421-22** (ESC/GA); *see also country names, and appropriate organizational and topical entries*
International Emergency Food Reserve, *see* Food Reserve, International Emergency
international finance, 575-80; *see also* debt servicing; development finance; international monetary and financial system; taxation
INTERNATIONAL FINANCE CORPORATION, 1317-22; borrowing policy, 1318; capital/reserves, 1319; commitments, 1318 *(table)*; Directors/alternates, 1320-21; expenditures/income, 1319, 1319 *(table)*; five-year plan, *1985-1989*, 1317-18; headquarters/field offices, 1322; investments, 1318-19 *(table)*; members, 1318, 1319-20 *(table)*; principal officers, 1321; secretariat, 1319; subscriptions/voting power, 1319-20 *(table)*; technical assistance, 1317-18
INTERNATIONAL FREQUENCY REGISTRATION BOARD, 1345-46
INTERNATIONAL FUND FOR AGRICULTURAL DEVELOPMENT, 1365-69; budget, 1366; contributions, 1367-68 *(table)*; Executive

International Fund for Agricultural Development *(cont.)*
  Board, 1365, 1369; Governing Cl., 1365; headquarters/liaison office, 1369; investments, 1366; members, 1365, 1367-68 *(table)*; officers, 1369; president, appointment, 1284; project loans, 1365, 1367 *(table)*; replenishments, **458**, 460 (GA), **700**, 701 (GA/WFC), 1365, 1365-66; resources, 1365-66; secretariat, 1366; technical assistance grants, 1366, 1367 *(table)*
INTERNATIONAL LABOUR ORGANISATION, 1278-86; budget, 1284 *(table)*; commemorative stamp (Turin Centre), 564; communication on, 1044; contributions, 1284 *(table)*; DG, 1285; Governing Body (International Labour Office), 1278, 1285 (members/officers); headquarters/other offices, 1285-86 *(list)*; International Labour Cf., 1278; mtgs., 1278-79; members, 1278, 1284 *(table)*; publications, 1283; secretariat, 1283-84; technical co-operation, 1280, 1280-82 *(tables)*
international law: fellowships/seminars, 1198, **1199-1200** (GA/UN/UNITAR); & individual rights, 931-32 (Spec. Rapporteur); & international organizations, 1177-81; publications, 1200; *see also* Asian-African Legal Consultative Ct.; diplomatic relations; international economic law; international trade law; international watercourses; law of the sea; treaties; *and under* international organizations; States
INTERNATIONAL LAW, ADVISORY CT. ON THE UN PROGRAMME OF ASSISTANCE IN THE TEACHING, STUDY, DISSEMINATION AND WIDER APPRECIATION OF: Chairman/members, 1395
INTERNATIONAL LAW, HAGUE ACADEMY OF, 1198, **1199** (GA)
INTERNATIONAL LAW, UN PROGRAMME OF ASSISTANCE IN THE TEACHING, STUDY, DISSEMINATION AND WIDER APPRECIATION OF, 1198-1200 (ILC/UNITAR, 1198; GA, **1198-1200**); seminars/training, 1198 (S-G/UN/UNITAR)
INTERNATIONAL LAW COMMISSION, 1197 (S-G), **1197-98** (GA); & juridical bodies, 1197; members, 1398; publications, 1200
INTERNATIONAL LAW SEMINAR, 1198, **1199**
INTERNATIONAL MARITIME ORGANIZATION, 1356-58; Assembly (14th biennial), 1356; budget, 1357; contributions, 1357 *(table)*; Conventions, 1356-57; Cl., 1356, 1358; headquarters, 1358; Maritime Safety Ct., 1358; members, 1356, 1357 *(table)*; officers, 1358; publications, 1357; secretariat, 1357; S-G, re-election, 1356; technical co-operation fund, establishment, 1356
international monetary and financial system, 412 (ESC), 575-80, 1330; exchange rates, 575 (CDP/UNCTAD *Report*); liquidity, 575 (CDP/UNCTAD *Report*); publications, 581; studies, 1330 (Group of *10*/Group of *24*/IMF Interim Ct.); *see also* debt problems; development finance; international trade; investment; taxation; trade-related finance
INTERNATIONAL MONETARY FUND, 1330-36; arrears policy, 1331-32; currencies drawn/repurchased, 1332, 1333 *(tables)*;

Directors/alternates, 1335 *(list)*; field offices/headquarters, 1336; Interim Ct., 1330; Managing Director/principal officers, 1336; members, 1332, 1333-34 *(table)*; publications, 1332; quotas/voting power, 1333-34 *(table)*; secretariat, 1332; SDR activity, 1331; stand-by arrangements, 1331, 1333 *(table)*; & World Bank, 1330
INTERNATIONAL NEGOTIABLE INSTRUMENTS, WORKING GROUP ON (UNCITRAL), 1193; Chairman/members, 1401
international organizations: implementation of Declaration on Granting Independence to Colonial Countries and Peoples, 1066-73; relations with States, 1189 (GA/ILC/Spec. Rapporteur); & treaties involving, *1986* UN Cf. preparations, 1182-89; *see also* intergovernmental organizations; non-governmental organizations; specialized agencies; *and under* Colonial Countries and Peoples, Declaration on . . .; treaties
international payments: bills of exchange/promissory notes, draft convention, 1193 (UNCITRAL Working Group); *see also* international trade law
INTERNATIONAL PAYMENTS, STUDY GROUP ON (UNCITRAL), 1193
international peace and security, *see* peace and security, international
INTERNATIONAL PLANNED PARENTHOOD FEDERATION: recipient, UN Population Award, 771
INTERNATIONAL POLICE ASSOCIATION: consultative status with ESC, withdrawal, 559, **1047** (ESC/NGOs Ct.)
international relations: legal aspects, 1160-71; non-use of force in, proposed treaty, 1162-63 (communications, 1162; GA, **1162-63**, 1180; Spec. Ct./Working Group, 1162); *see also* diplomatic relations; disputes, peaceful settlement of; peace and security, international; *and* appropriate topical entries
INTERNATIONAL RELATIONS, SPEC. CT. ON ENHANCING THE EFFECTIVENESS OF THE PRINCIPLE OF NON-USE OF FORCE IN, 1162; members/officers, 1400; Working Group, re-establishment, 1162
international rivers, *see* international watercourses
international security, *see* peace and security, international
INTERNATIONAL TELECOMMUNICATION UNION, 1345-49; Administrative Cl., 1345, 1349 (members); administrative radio cfs., 1345; budget, 1347-48 *(table)*; consultative cts., 1345; contributions, 1348-49 *(table)*; headquarters, 1349; International Frequency Registration Board, 1345-46, 1349 (members); members, 1345, 1348-49 *(table)*; principal officers, 1268; publications, 1347; secretariat, 1347; technical co-operation, 1346-47
international trade, 7-8, 411-12 *(World Economic Survey)*, 551-75, 630 (ECA), 646 (ESCAP), 655 (ECE), 661-62 (ECLAC), 666 (ESCWA), 1370-72 (GATT) anti-dumping practices, 1371 (GATT) contract practices, 655 (ECE) co-operation in and related issues, 552-54 (ACC/CDP/UNCTAD *Report*, 552;

ESC, 552-53; GA, **553-54**, 554; S-G, 553)
countries having different economic and social systems, 559-60 (TDB/UNCTAD); technical co-operation, 560 (UNDP/USSR)
Data Base on Trade Measures, 557
& government procurement, 1371
industrial collaboration, 605 (Ad Hoc UNCTAD/UNIDO Expert Group)
promotion/facilitation, 560-63; *see also* International Trade Centre; trade facilitation
protectionism/structural adjustment, 7 (S-G), 429, 555 (*World Economic Survey*), 556-57 (GA, 557; TDB, 556-57); UNCTAD VI implementation, 557 (TDB); *see also* developing countries, economic measures against
publications, 574-75, 1372
restrictive business practices, 563-65 (GA, 565, **565**; Intergovernmental Expert Group, 562; UN review cf., 563-65)
safeguards on restrictions, 1371 (GATT)
in services, 557 (TDB)
standardization policies, 658 (ECE expert group)
subsidies/countervailing measures, 1370 (GATT)
trade policy, 554-56 (UNCTAD *Report*/ *World Economic Survey*)
trading system: review, 556 (GA/UNCTAD)
& TNCs, role in, 1322-23 (TNCs Centre)
see also agriculture; commodities; exports; General Agreement on Tariffs and Trade; multilateral trade negotiations; *and entries beginning with* trade
INTERNATIONAL TRADE CENTRE (UNCTAD/ GATT), 561-62 (JAG/TDB); Executive Director, 1424; expenditures/trust funds, 562; Market News Service, expansion, 561; staff, 562; technical co-operation, 562, 1372
INTERNATIONAL TRADE CENTRE, JOINT ADVISORY GROUP ON THE, 562; members/officers, 1398; Technical Ct., 1398
international trade law, 1192-94; commercial arbitration, Model Law, 1192-93 (GA, **1192-93**, 1193; UNCITRAL, 1192); electronic data processing, **1192**, 1193 (GA/S-G/UNCITRAL); industrial contracts, draft legal guide, 1193 (UNCITRAL Working Group); international payments, draft convention, 1193 (UNCITRAL); most-favoured-nation clauses, 1193-94 (GA, **1194**, 1194; S-G, 1193-94); training/assistance programmes, 1194 (GA/UNCITRAL); *see also* new international economic order: legal aspects
INTERNATIONAL TRADE LAW, UN COMMISSION ON, 1191 (GA, 1191, **1191**; S-G/ UNCITRAL, 1191); members/officers, 1401; Working Groups, 1401 (chairmen/members)
INTERNATIONAL TRADE PROCEDURES, WORKING PARTY ON FACILITATION OF (ECE), 655
international treaties and agreements, *see* treaties/agreements

International Trusteeship System, *see* Trusteeship System, international

international watercourses: non-navigational uses, draft articles, 1170-71 (GA, 1171; ILC/Spec. Rapporteur, 1170); *see also* inland water transport

International Water Resources Association, *see* Water Resources Association, International

INTER-PARLIAMENTARY CONFERENCE (74th): & *apartheid*, 128 (communication); & colonial countries, 1061; & economic co-operation, 413; & Falkland Islands (Malvinas), 1134 (communication); & Namibia, 1094; & youth, 982

investment/pre-investment: promotion, 606 (UNIDO): & TNCs, 621-22 (TNCs Centre)

INVESTMENT CO-OPERATION PROGRAMME (UNIDO), 606

INVESTMENT PROMOTION SERVICES (UNIDO), 606

INVESTMENTS COMMITTEE: members, 1398

Invisibles and Financing related to Trade, Ct. on (TDB), *see* Trade, Ct. on Invisibles and Financing related to

iodine: deficiency diseases, 775; proposed action plan & consultative group, 775

Iran: Afghan refugees in, 1009 (GA/UNHCR); human rights violations, 909-12 (communication, 910; ESC, **911**; GA, **910-11**, 912-13; Human Rights Cs., 909; SCPDPM, 909-10; Spec. Representative, 909, 910); *see also* Afghanistan situation

Iran-Iraq conflict, 239-50 (communications, 239-42, 242-44, 250; GA, 250; SC, 240, 241; S-G, 242); air/naval traffic interference, 248-49, 250 (communications); attacks on civilian areas, chemical weapons, alleged use, 247-50 (communications, 247, 248-50; GA, 250; medical specialist, 247-49; SC, 248); international flights, safety of, 1338 (ICAO extraordinary sess.); nuclear power plants, alleged attacks, 249 (communications); & prisoners of war, 244-47 (communications, 244, 245, 246-47; SC, 245-46; S-G, 244-45); S-G area visits, 239, 242, 398

Iraq: & Israel, attack on nuclear facility *(1981)*, 293-95 (communications/IAEA/S-G, 293; GA, **293-94**, 294-95)

iron and steel industry, 614-15 (UNIDO); 4th Consultation, preparations, 614; 3rd Consultation, follow-up, 615; mini-plants, guidelines, 605 (UNIDO); *see also* steel

IRON AND STEEL INDUSTRY, ENVIRONMENTAL CONSULTATIVE CT. ON THE (UNEP), 819

IRON ORE, 4TH PREPARATORY MTG. ON, 570; statistical issues, 570 (expert group)

irrigation, 679 (FAO); *see also* floods; water resources

Islamic Conference, Organization of the, *see* Organization of the Islamic Conference

island developing countries: & SNPA review, 441-42, **447** (GA); South Pacific Forum, statement on, 532

Israel: economic/financial/military aid to, 266; & GA credentials, 271, 397 (Credentials Ct./GA); & human rights, 925-27 (Human Rights Cs./SCPDPM); & IAEA safeguards, 64 (S-G), 65 (UNIDIR

study), 1271; & Iraq nuclear installations, 66 (GA); & nuclear armament, 64-66 (GA, **65**, 65-66; S-G/UNIDIR, 64-65); *see also* Iraq; Lebanon situation; Middle East situation; Palestine question; territories occupied by Israel; *and under* South Africa

ISRAELI PRACTICES AFFECTING THE HUMAN RIGHTS OF THE POPULATION OF THE OCCUPIED TERRITORIES, SPEC. CT. TO INVESTIGATE, 326, 329, **332** (GA); facilities provided by S-G, implementation of *1984* request, 329, **333-34** (GA/S-G); members, 1401; *see also* territories occupied by Israel

Italy: & admission to Patent Co-operation Treaty Union, 1359

Ivory Coast: industrial development training, 603 (IDDA/UNIDO); official name change (Côte d'Ivoire), 392

Jamaica: export development, 1311 (World Bank); non-project, 1311 (World Bank)

Japan: economic trends, 428, 429 (surveys); ODA targets, 462

Jerusalem, 280-81 (communications, 280; GA, **280-81**, 281); Medical Hospice, closing, 281, 328, **334** (communications/GA); university, proposed, 361-62 (GA, **361**, 363; S-G, 361)

JOINT INSPECTION UNIT: members, 1398; work programme, 1228-29 (CPC/S-G), **1229-30** (GA); *see also* subject entries

Joint Staff Pension Board, UN, *see* Pension Board, UN Joint Staff

Joint United Nations Information Committee, *see* Information Committee, Joint UN

Jordan: aid to Palestinians in, 282 (UNICEF); Mediterranean–Dead Sea canal project, effects of, 351 (UNEP), 352 (UN mission); refugees in, 357 (UNRWA); solar energy equipment, 614 (UNIDO); *see also* Middle East situation

JOURNALIST ATTACHMENT PROGRAMME (UNEP), 798-99

journalists/broadcasters: DPI training programme, 380, 384 (GA/S-G), 387 (JUNIC)

Juan de Nova, *see* Malagasy islands

judicial system, independence, *see under* human rights

JUDICIARY, BASIC PRINCIPLES ON THE INDEPENDENCE OF THE, 757 (GA/7th UN Crime Congress)

jute/jute products, 561 (ITC); regional seminar (ESCAP), 646

JUTE ORGANIZATION, INTERNATIONAL, 561

JUVENILE JUSTICE, UN STANDARD MINIMUM RULES FOR THE ADMINISTRATION OF (Beijing Rules), 746-56 (GA, **746-47**; S-G, 746), **747-56** *(text)*; *see also* youth: juvenile prisoners

KAMPUCHEA, *AD HOC* COMMITTEE OF THE INTERNATIONAL CONFERENCE ON, 225-26, **227** (GA); members/officers, 1394; missions, 225

KAMPUCHEAN HUMANITARIAN ASSISTANCE PROGRAMMES, OFFICE OF THE SPEC.

REPRESENTATIVE OF THE S-G FOR CO-ORDINATING, 1424

Kampuchea situation, 221-28 (*Ad Hoc* Ct., 225-26; communications, 221-25; ESC, 225; GA, **226-28**, 228; S-G, 226); chemical weapons, alleged use, 222 (communication); humanitarian assistance, 226, **227** (GA/S-G), 1008 (contributions); & human rights violations, 913 (ESC/Human Rights Cs.); refugees/displaced persons, 1008 (S-G/UNHCR); & self-determination, 860-61 (ESC, **860-61**, 861; Human Rights Cs., 860); & S-G Spec. Representative, 226; S-G visits, 226; *see also* Democratic Kampuchea

Kenya: & environmental issues, 796 (NGOs/UNEP); 820 (UNEP/WHO); fuelwood project, 693 (UNEP); natural resources exploration, 670 (UNRFNRE); refugees in, 1004; telecommunications loans, 1312 (World Bank)

Kiribati: accession to NPT, 1271; economic assistance, UN mission, 529-30 (ESC/GA/S-G); satellite station, 1347

Korea, Democratic People's Republic of, *see* Democratic People's Republic of Korea

Korea, Republic of, *see* Republic of Korea

Korean question, 220-21 (communication, 221; UN Command, 220-21)

Kuwait: & Iran-Iraq conflict: assassination attempt, 243 (communication); freedom of navigation, 249 (communication); regional seas programme (UNEP), 816

labour: educational activities, 1202-3 (ILO); managers, environmental training, 820 (ILO/UNEP); occupational health services, 1278 (ILO); publications, 1203; statistics, ILO Convention, 1278; *see also* *apartheid*; employment; International Labour Organisation; technical and vocational training; trade unions; working conditions

LABOUR CONVENTIONS AND RECOMMENDATIONS, INTERNATIONAL, 1278

LABOUR STUDIES, INTERNATIONAL INSTITUTE FOR (ILO), 1283

Lagos Plan of Action, *see* Africa, *1980* Lagos Plan of Action for the Implementation of the Monrovia Strategy . . .

land-locked developing countries, 451-55 (GA, **452-53**, 453-54; UNCTAD, 451-52); & SNPA, **444-45**, 447 (GA); transit/transport issues, 451, 452 (TDB); *see also* Zaire

LAND-LOCKED DEVELOPING COUNTRIES, *AD HOC* GROUP OF EXPERTS TO STUDY WAYS AND MEANS OF IMPROVING TRANSIT-TRANSPORT INFRASTRUCTURES AND SERVICES FOR, 451

LAND-LOCKED DEVELOPING COUNTRIES, UN SPECIAL FUND FOR: Board of Governors/Executive Director, 455 (GA); contributions, 454 *(table)*; dissolution, 451, **454-55** (GA/UNDP), 1407

LAND-LOCKED STATES, CONVENTION ON TRANSIT TRADE OF *(1965)*, 451

land management, 811-12 (UNEP), 1289 (FAO); *see also* soil management

land-mines, *see* material remnants of war

LAND-USE PLANNING, INTERGOVERNMEN-
TAL GROUP FOR (FAO), 1289
LANGUAGE ARRANGEMENTS, DOCUMENTA-
TION AND PUBLICATIONS, INTER-
AGENCY MTG. ON, 1261 (JIU/S-G)
Lao People's Democratic Republic:
dispute with Thailand, 231-32 (com-
munications): & Mekong River Basin
Ct., 646
Latin America: agricultural development,
1288 (FAO), 1366 (IFAD); colonialism
Declaration, seminar, 1060 (Colonial
Countries Ct.); communications, 1298
(UNESCO); culture, 1298 (UNESCO);
data flows, 1322 (TNCs Centre); debt
crisis, 660 (ECLAC), 660, 661 (Cartagena
Consensus/ECLAC); development
policy/co-operation, 659 (ECLAC/Latin
American Institute for Economic and
Social Planning); economic crisis in, expert mtg., 660; economic/social trends,
428 *(World Economic Survey)*; education, 1295 (UNESCO); energy, 782
(UNDP/UNITAR); environmental activities,
819 (ECLAC/UNEP); food projects, 1292
(WFP); human rights violations, 912-25;
IFC investment, 1317; illiteracy programmes, 1295 (UNESCO); international
trade law, 1194 (UNCITRAL); natural
sciences, 1296 (UNESCO); publication,
660; social movements, 786 (UNU);
social sciences, 1297 (UNESCO);
technical co-operation, 1299 (UNESCO);
volunteer programme, 607 (UNV); *see
also country names;* Economic Commission for Latin America and the Caribbean; *and regional and subject entries*
Latin America, *1967* Treaty for the Prohibition of Nuclear Weapons in, *see* Nuclear
Weapons in Latin America, Treaty for
the Prohibition of
LATIN AMERICA, 2ND MTG. OF OFFICIALS
RESPONSIBLE FOR EXTERNAL TRADE IN,
661-62
LATIN AMERICA, 2ND REGIONAL EXPERT
GROUP MTG. ON CAPITAL GOODS IN,
615 (UNIDO), 662
Latin America and the Caribbean, 659-
64; agricultural development, 1288
(FAO); biotechnology programme, 774
(UNU); development policy, 661; & disarmament, Lima Declaration, 83; &
economic co-operation, Lima Declaration, 413; economic trends, *Survey,
1984,* 660; education, 820 (UNEP); environmental issues, 793-94 (UNEP Cl.);
food/agriculture, 663 (ECLAC/FAO); food
production, 1287 (FAO Cl.); human settlements, 832-33 (ECLAC/Human Settlements Cs.); IDA credits, 1325 *(table);*
micro-electronics network, establishment, 608 (UNIDO); non-project loans,
1311 (World Bank); technical co-
operation, 465-66, 470 (UNDP), 662
(JIU/S-G); & TNCs, 620 (ECLAC/TNCs
Centre); trade promotion, 561 (ITC);
UNICEF programmes, 965 *(table),* 967-
68; World Bank loans, 1310 *(table)*
LATIN AMERICA AND THE CARIBBEAN, EN-
VIRONMENTAL TRAINING NETWORK FOR,
793-94 (UNEP Cl.)
LATIN AMERICA AND THE CARIBBEAN, 5TH
CF. OF MINISTERS OF HEADS OF PLAN-
NING OF, 661

LATIN AMERICA AND THE CARIBBEAN, 4TH
INTERGOVERNMENTAL REGIONAL MTG.
ON THE ENVIRONMENT IN, 793
LATIN AMERICA AND THE CARIBBEAN,
REGIONAL BUREAU FOR (UNDP): & aid
to Colombia, 545-46; Director, 1424
LATIN AMERICAN AND THE CARIBBEAN,
REGIONAL CENTRE FOR HIGHER
EDUCATION IN (UNESCO), 1297
LATIN AMERICA AND THE CARIBBEAN,
REGIONAL MICRO-ELECTRONICS NET-
WORK FOR (ECLAC/Latin American
Economic System/UNIDO): establish-
ment, 663
LATIN AMERICA AND THE CARIBBEAN, 2ND
CF. OF MINISTERS RESPONSIBLE FOR
THE APPLICATION OF SCIENCE AND
TECHNOLOGY TO DEVELOPMENT IN
(UNESCO), 1296
LATIN AMERICAN DEMOGRAPHIC CENTRE,
1415; Demographic Unit established,
663
LATIN AMERICAN ECONOMIC SYSTEM: data
flows, 621 (TNCs Centre); & Nicaragua,
215; transport activities, 662
LATIN AMERICAN ENERGY ORGANIZATION:
memorandum on energy co-operation,
690 (UNIDO)
LATIN AMERICAN INSTITUTE FOR
ECONOMIC AND SOCIAL PLANNING: ad-
visory/research/training, 661; Joint Plan-
ning Unit for the Caribbean, establish-
ment, 661; name change, 659 (ECLAC);
Technical Ct., 6th sess., 661
LATIN AMERICAN INTEGRATION ASSOCIA-
TION, 662
LATIN AMERICAN MINING AGENCY: 1st GA
of, 663
LATIN AMERICAN ORGANIZATION FOR
HOUSING AND DEVELOPMENT OF
HUMAN SETTLEMENTS: co-operation
with Human Settlements Cs., 832
LATIN AMERICAN SEMINAR ON FOOD
SCIENCES AND TECHNOLOGY, 5TH
(ECLAC), 663
law, *see* adoption law; international law; international trade law
law of the sea, 109-15 (ESC, 115; GA,
113-14, 114-15; S-G, 109-10)
Amerasinghe Fellowship, contributions,
1198 (S-G), **1199, 1200** (GA)
communications, 111
information system, 113
medium-term plan *(1984-1989),* 114 (GA)
Preparatory Cs., 110-11, **114;** Spec. Css.,
111-12
publications, 113, 115
S-G, Office of Spec. Representative:
functions, 112-13
treaties, 113
see also exclusive economic zone; land-
locked developing countries; marine
affairs; territorial sea; *and under* sea;
sea-bed
LAW OF THE SEA, INTERNATIONAL
TRIBUNAL FOR THE: Declaration, 110,
114 (GA/Preparatory Cs.); draft procedural rules, 112 (Spec. Cs. *4);* Creden-
tials/General Cts., 1423 (officers);
members/officers, 1422; Spec. Css., 1423
(members/officers)
LAW OF THE SEA, OFFICE OF THE SPEC.
REPRESENTATIVE OF THE S-G FOR THE,
112-13; S-G/Assistant S-G, 1424

LAW OF THE SEA, 3RD UN CF. ON THE,
109, **114** (GA)
LAW OF THE SEA, UN CONVENTION ON
THE *(1982),* 109-10, **114** (GA/S-G); &
naval arms race, 30 (expert study);
ratifications/signatures, 109, **114** (GA)
Law of the Sea Bulletin, 113
LEAD AND ZINC STUDY GROUP, INTERNA-
TIONAL, 569, 570
LEAGUE OF ARAB STATES: co-operation
with UN, 399-401 (GA, **399-401,** 401;
S-G, 399); & Iran-Iraq conflict, 245; &
Palestine, 268 (GA); participation in SC,
274; & refugee protection, 1010; &
social development, joint mtg. with UN,
731
LEAGUE OF NATIONS, 3 (S-G)
LEAGUE OF RED CROSS SOCIETIES: &
IYDP, 774
least developed countries, 433-51; com-
modities, **444** (GA); debt problems, 436
(S-G), **443, 448** (GA); disaster aid, **442,
447** (GA); energy resources, **446,** 688
(GA); environment, **441, 447** (GA); exports, 436 (S-G), **443-44, 449-50**
(GA/ITC), 562 (ITC); food/agriculture,
438-40, 445 (GA); human resources, **445**
(GA); identification, 433-34 (CDP, 433;
ESC, 433-34, **434;** GA, 126); industrial
development, **440-41, 446** (GA), 605
(GA/IDB/UNCTAD/UNIDO); infrastructures, **441, 447** (GA); inter-agency consultations, 434-35 (ACC); investments/
pre-investment, **441** (GA); natural
resources/energy, **440** (GA); ODA targets,
436 (S-G), **437** (GA); resources mobilization, **447-48;** statistics, spec. problems,
1036-37 (ACC/Statistical Cs.); support
measures, international, **442-44** (GA);
technical assistance, **443, 448-49** (GA),
583 (UNCTAD); technology, **444** (GA);
telecommunications, 1347 (ITU/UNDP);
trade, **442** (GA); & trade preferences,
558 (Special Ct.); transport/communica-
tions, **444** (GA); *see also under* Africa:
least developed countries
LEAST DEVELOPED COUNTRIES, INTER-
GOVERNMENTAL GROUP ON (UNCTAD),
434-35, **437** (GA), 605
LEAST DEVELOPED COUNTRIES, SPEC.
MEASURES FUND FOR THE (UNDP),
435-36; contributions/expenditures, 435
LEAST DEVELOPED COUNTRIES, SUBSTAN-
TIAL NEW PROGRAMME OF ACTION
FOR THE 1980S FOR THE, implementa-
tion: ESCAP, 646; follow-up ar-
rangements, **444-45** (GA), **450-51** (GA);
global review, *1990,* **438** (GA); mid-term
review, 434-51 (ACC, 434-35; GA, **436-
51,** 451; S-G, 436; UNCTAD, 434; UNDP,
435-36); UNCDF projects, 493, 495;
UNIDO country reviews, 605
LEAST DEVELOPED COUNTRIES, 3RD MTG.
OF MULTILATERAL AND BILATERAL
FINANCIAL AND TECHNICAL ASSISTANCE
INSTITUTIONS WITH REPRESENTATIVES
OF (UNCTAD), 434, 435 (ACC)
LEATHER AND FOOTWEAR INDUSTRY, 3RD
TRIPARTITE TECHNICAL MTG. FOR (ILO),
1278-79
LEATHER AND LEATHER PRODUCTS IN-
DUSTRY PANEL (8th sess.), 610
leather industry: technical co-operation/
missions, 610; *see also* hides/skins

Lebanon: emergency aid, 548 (NGOs), 548-49 (UN bodies); industrial sector, 598 (UNIDO), 599 (IDB); reconstruction/development, 548-50 (ESC, **549-50**; GA, **550**; S-G, 548-49); refugee assistance, 548 (UNRWA), 1009 (UNHCR); S-G Trust Fund, 548; UNDRO mission, 549; UNICEF programmes, 282-84, 548, 549, 969

Lebanon, Inter-Agency Working Group on Assistance to: UNIDO participation, 598

Lebanon, Office of the UN Co-ordinator of Assistance for the Reconstruction and Development of, 548, 549; resumption of functions, **550** (GA)

Lebanon, UN Interim Force in, 305-11 (communications, 305-6, 308; SC, 302-3, 307, **307**, 307-8, **309-10**; S-G, 306-7, 308-9, 310-11); casualties/prisoners, 306, 308, 309; Commander, 309, 1410, 1425; composition, 305, 320; contributions, 320, **322**, 323-24 *(table)*; co-operation with ICRC/UNICEF/UNRWA, 306, 309; Financial Regulations, suspension, 321, **322-23** (ACABQ/GA); financing, 320-23 (ACABQ, 320-21; GA, **321-22**, 322; S-G, 320); future prospects, 306-7, 309 (S-G); troop contributors' reimbursement, review, 324-26 (ACABQ, 325; GA, **325-26**, 326; S-G, 324-25); & UNTSO, 305, 310

Lebanon Reconstruction and Development Programme, 548 (S-G); UN Co-ordinator, absence of, 161, **550** (GA)

Lebanon situation, 295-305 (communications, 297-98, 301-2, 304-5; SC, 298-301, 302-3, **303**, 303-4; S-G, 295-97)

Beirut area, 297 (Observer Group Beirut/UNTSO), 302 (communication), 311 (UNRWA Commissioner-General); proposed airport isolation, 304-5 (communications)

cf. on military aspects (Naqoura, *8 Nov. 1984*–Jan. *1985*), 295, 296 (S-G)

& human rights violations, 927, **927** (ESC/Human Rights Cs.)

Israel Defence Forces, unilateral redeployment, 295-97 (S-G)

1949 Israel-Lebanon General Armistice Agreement, 296

peace-keeping operation, 305-11; *see also* Lebanon, UN Interim Force in

prisoners/detainees, transfers of, 301-2, 304 (communications), 870 (Human Rights Cs.)

refugees in, 311-13 (communications, 311-12; GA, 313; SC, **303**, 313; UNRWA, 311-13); administrative/financial services, UNRWA sub-office established (Cyprus), 312; casualties/incidents, 311 (UNRWA Commissioner-General); emergency operations, 312 (UNRWA); food rations, 312-13 (UNRWA); hospitals/medical services/schools, 313 (UNRWA); unemployment, 313 (UNESCO/UNRWA)

Under-S-G visits, 297, 306-7, 309

Legal Affairs, Office of (Secretariat): Under-S-G, 1423

legal questions, 1155-1758; & civil aviation, 1339-40

Lesotho: economic assistance, 518-19 (S-G); industrial development project,

605 (UNIDO); population/health, 1326 (IDA); refugees in, 1005 (UNHCR); & South Africa, 178, 193-96 (GA, 196; SC, 194-195, **195-96**); *see also* southern Africa: student refugees in

liberation movements, *see* national liberation movements

Liberia: spec. economic assistance, 519-20 (GA/review mission/S-G); UNDP projects, 520

libraries (UN), *see* United Nations: library management

Library, Dag Hammarskjöld, *see* Dag Hammarskjöld Library

Libyan Arab Jamahiriya: & Egypt, 259; iron and steel plants, 615 (UNIDO); & United States, 258-59; *see also* Chad; continental shelf: delimitation

Liechtenstein: consultative status in ECE, 1414

life sciences, 1273-74 (IAEA)

Lima Declaration: on disarmament, 83; on economic co-operation, 413; on Falkland Islands (Malvinas) question, 1134 (communication)

liner conferences, 585

Liner Conferences, Convention on Code of Conduct for *(1974)*, 585; States parties, 587

literacy, 971 (UNICEF), 1298 (UNESCO)

Literary and Artistic Works, Berne Convention for the Protection of (WIPO), accessions, 1359; *1986* centenary, 759 (S-G/WIPO DG)

lithosphere, *see under* ecosystems

livestock, 1290-91 (FAO); genetic resources, 814 (FAO/UNEP)

Living Standards Measurement Study, 1035 (Statistical Cs.)

Locarno Union: agreements, 1359 *(list)*; contributions to WIPO, 1361 *(table)*; members, 1362-63 *(table)*

machinery, *see under* agricultural machinery

Madagascar: cyclones/floods, assistance, 542-43 (GA, **543**, 543; S-G, 542-43); development finance, 1325 (IDA); energy equipment, 614 (UNIDO); science/technology cs., proposed, 638 (ECA); water supply, 1327

Madrid Agreement, *see* Marks, Madrid Agreement concerning the International Registration of; *and under* marks

Maghreb countries, 807 (GA)

Malagasy islands (Glorieuses, Juan de Nova, Europa, Bassas da India), 200 (GA)

malaria, 1273 (IAEA), 1304 (WHO)

Malawi: housing, 1326 (IDA); mineral survey, 675 (UNRFNRE)

Malaysia: industrial planning, 607 (UNIDO); small-scale enterprise loans, 1311 (World Bank)

Maldives: maritime communications, 1347 (ITU)

Mali: & Burkina Faso, frontier dispute, 198, 1157 (ICJ); mineral resources, 675 (UNRFNRE)

malnutrition: joint UNICEF/WHO programme, 968; prevention, 1303 (WHO);

& urban children, 971 (UNICEF); *see also* famine; hunger

Malta, *see* continental shelf: delimitation

Malvinas, *see* Falkland Islands (Malvinas)

Management Systems Services (Geneva), 1265

Man-made Fibres, International Cf. on, 612

manpower development: industrial, 602 (UNIDO), 1279 (ILO); nuclear power, 1272 (IAEA); trade promotion, 561-62 (ITC); *see also* brain drain; human resources

manufactures, 582 (TDB Working Party); technical co-operation, evaluation, 602 (CPC/S-G)

Manufactures, Ct. on (TDB), 582; members, 1403

Mar del Plata Action Plan, *see* water resources development

Mariana Islands, *see* Northern Mariana Islands

marijuana, *see* cannabis

marine affairs, 113 (ESCAP); cross-organizational programme analysis, 1228 (CPC); & Law of the Sea Convention, 109-10 (S-G), 113 (S-G Spec. Representative)

marine environment: & law of the sea, 113; Montreal Guidelines, 815 *(Ad Hoc Expert Group)*, 1275 (IAEA/UNEP/UNESCO); protection, 110 (S-G), 815-16 *(Ad Hoc Expert Group/UNEP Cl.)*; radioactive wastes, 694 (IAEA), 816 (UNEP); *see also* Africa; oceans; regional seas programme; ships

Marine Environment, Ad Hoc Working Group of Experts on Protection of the, against Pollution from Land-Based Sources: Montreal Guidelines, 815 (UNEP Cl.)

Marine Environment Protection Committee (IMO), 1356

Marine Mammals, Global Plan of Action for the Conservation, Management and Utilization of (FAO/UNEP), 682-83; consultative mtgs., 683; co-ordination in UN, 683; projects, 683

marine pollution: & chemicals, 815 (Joint Expert Group), 1356; dumping of wastes, 1356 (IMO); & Japan, 1087; land-based, impact, 815 (UNEP); prevention, 110; reference methods, development of, 815 (FAO/UNEP)

Marine Pollution, Joint Group of Experts on Scientific Aspects of, 815, 1352

Marine Pollution by Dumping of Wastes and Other Matter, Convention on the Prevention of *(1975)*, 1086-87 (TC); Contracting Parties, mtg., 110, 694, 1356

Marine Radioactivity, International Laboratory of (IAEA), 1275

marine resources, 681-83 (CPC-S-G, 682; ESC, **682**, 682; IMO/UNCTAD, 681-82); publications, 683; *see also under* Namibia: natural resources

marine sciences, 1297 (UNESCO)

maritime affairs, 1356-57 (IMO); conventions, 1356-57; fraud, 588 (Ad Hoc Group); publication, 585; safety, 110; technical co-operation, 587, 1356 (IMO); training, 587-88; transport statistics, 663 maritime affairs *(cont.)* (DIESA/ECLAC); *see also relevant subject entries*

maritime boundaries, delimitation, 109; & Guinea & Guinea-Bissau, 109; *see also* continental shelf

MARITIME CLAIMS, CONVENTION ON LIMITATION AND LIABILITY FOR *(1976)*, 1356-57

MARITIME DAY, WORLD (IMO), 1356

MARITIME FRAUD, AD HOC INTERGOVERNMENTAL GROUP TO CONSIDER MEANS OF COMBATING ALL ASPECTS OF, INCLUDING PIRACY, 588

maritime law, *see under* continental shelf; law of the sea; maritime boundaries, delimitation; shipping; ships

MARITIME PRIZE, INTERNATIONAL: *1984* award, 1356

MARITIME SEARCH AND RESCUE, INTERNATIONAL CONVENTION ON *(1979)*: status, 110, 1356

maritime transport, 585-86; technical assistance/training, 587; total volume, 585 *(1985 Review)*; *see also* International Maritime Organization; multimodal transport; ports; shipping; ships

MARITIME UNIVERSITY, WORLD (IMO), 1356; official branch, 1356

marks: conventions/agreements, 1359 *(list)*; Madrid Agreement, 1360; Nice Agreement, 1360; proposed treaty on registration of, 1360; registrations, total, 1360

MARKS, MADRID AGREEMENT CONCERNING THE INTERNATIONAL REGISTRATION OF, 1359, 1360

Marshall Islands: nuclear testing, compensation for, 1087 (TC); public finance, 1085 (TC); TC Mission, 1087-88; *see also* Trust Territory of the Pacific Islands

mass communication, 369-73 (communications, 371; GA, **371-73**, 373; Information Ct., 370-71; ITU/UNESCO, 369-70); *see also* communication; new world information and communication order; public information

mass exoduses, *see under* human rights violations

MASS MEDIA, DECLARATION ON FUNDAMENTAL PRINCIPLES CONCERNING THE CONTRIBUTION OF THE, TO THE PROMOTION OF HUMAN RIGHTS AND TO COUNTERING RACIALISM, APARTHEID AND INCITEMENT TO WAR (UNESCO), **373** (GA)

material remnants of war, 817-18 (GA, **817**, 818; S-G, 817)

maternal and child health, 966 (UNICEF), 1303 (WHO); *see also* children; family planning

Mauritania: abolition of slavery, 871-72 (ESC, 873; Human Rights Cs., 871-72; SCPDPM/Working Group, 872); desertification assistance, 810 (UNSO); interim report, 872 (SCPDPM expert); LDC classification, 520; spec. economic assistance, 520-22 (GA, **521-22**, 522; S-G, 520-21);

Mayotte, *see* Comorian island of Mayotte

MEAT COUNCIL, INTERNATIONAL, 1371 (GATT); & Bovine Meat Arrangement, 1371

MEAT DEVELOPMENT SCHEME, INTERNATIONAL, 1290 (FAO)

medical ethics, *see under* detainees

MEDICAL SCIENCES, COUNCIL FOR INTERNATIONAL ORGANIZATIONS OF: & adolescent health, joint cf. with WHO, 1303

MEDICINE, ADVISORY PANEL ON PREVENTIVE, 612

MEDITERRANEAN ACTION PLAN, *1978* BARCELONA CONVENTION FOR THE, 547 (UNCHS/UNDRO/UNEP/UNESCO); & UNCHS, 831

Mediterranean-Dead Sea canal project, 262, 351-52 (GA, **352**, 352; S-G, 351-52; UNEP Cl., 351, 818); UN mission, 352

Mediterranean region: civil aviation, technical assistance, 1340 (ICAO); disaster prevention, 547 (UNDRO); economic co-operation among, 654-55; human rights violations, 912; political issues, 251-60; pollution monitoring, 1352 (WMO); population, UNFPA allocation, 764-65 *(table)*; regional seas programme (UNEP), 816; security/co-operation in, 259-60 (communications, 259; GA, **259-60**, 260; SC, 260); telecommunications, 1347 (ITU); transport development, 655; *see also* country names

meeting records (UN/UN system), *see under* documentation (UN)

meetings (UN), *see* conferences/meetings (UN)

MEKONG BASIN, INTERIM CT. FOR CO-ORDINATION OF INVESTIGATIONS OF THE LOWER (ESCAP), 646; plenary sess., 222, 646; work programme, 646

Members (UN), *see under* United Nations

mental illness, *see under* detainees

mercenaries: draft convention, 1165-66 (Ad Hoc Ct., 1165; communications, 1384; GA, **1165-66**, 1166); recruitment/financing, 861 (Human Rights Cs.); training/transit, 1166 (GA); *see also* colonial countries; Namibia question

MERCENARIES, AD HOC CT. ON THE DRAFTING OF AN INTERNATIONAL CONVENTION AGAINST THE RECRUITMENT, USE, FINANCING AND TRAINING OF, 1165, **1166** (GA); members/officers, 1165, 1394-95; Working Groups, 1165

metallurgical industries, 614-15; computerized maintenance, expert mtg., 614 (UNIDO); technical co-operation, 614 (UNDP/UNIDO); *see also* aluminium; bauxite; foundries; iron and steel industry; metals: non-ferrous

metals, 570-71 (UNCTAD) exploration, 669, 670 (UNRFNRE) non-ferrous, 614, 615 (TNCs/UNCTAD/UNIDO); 1st Consultation, preparations, 615, *see also names of individual metals*

metalworking/machine tools, 613 (UNIDO)

meteorology: & aviation, 1350 (WMO); education/training, 1353 (WMO); & environmental pollution, 1352 (WMO); marine activities, 1350; research/development, 1351-52 (WMO); technical co-operation, 1353 (WMO); *see also* climate; Hydrology and Water Resources Programme; World Meteorological Organization; *and under* weather

METEOROLOGY, CS. FOR MARINE, 1350

Mexico: development finance, 1310 (World Bank); & drug control, 1027 (INCB); earthquakes in, 543-45 (GA, **544**, **544-45**; S-G, 544; UNDP/UNDRO, 544), 544 (DTCD role); education loans, 1310 (World Bank); geothermal drilling, 670 (UNRFNRE); population education, 763 (UNFPA); refugees in, 920 (Human Rights Cs.), 1007 (UNHCR); transportation loans, 1312 (World Bank)

MICROBIAL STRAIN DATA NETWORK WORKING GROUP, 814

MICROBIOLOGICAL RESOURCES CENTRES, 814 (UNEP)

MICROBIOLOGY, 7TH INTERNATIONAL CF. ON GLOBAL IMPACTS OF APPLIED, 814

micro-electronics, 607, 608 (UNIDO), 663 (ECLAC)

Micronesia, *see* Trust Territory of the Pacific Islands

Micronesia, Federated States of: public finance, 1085 (TC); *see also* Trust Territory of the Pacific Islands

MICRO-ORGANISMS, WORLD DATA CENTRE FOR, 814 (UNEP)

MICRO-STATES, CT. OF EXPERTS ON (SC): members, 1410

microwave technology, 1347 (ITU)

Middle East: civil aviation, technical assistance, 1340 (ICAO); human rights violations, 925-27; population, UNFPA allocation, 764-65 *(table)*; radio/television services, **380**, 385 (GA/Information Ct.); refugees/displaced persons, 994, 996 *(table)*, 1009; telecommunications, 1346, 1347 (ITU); UNICEF, 965-66 *(table)*, 969; volunteer programmes, 487 (UNV); World Bank loans, 1309-10 *(table)*, 1311-12; *see also* Arab States; Economic Commission for Western Asia; nuclear-weapon-free zones; Western Asia

Middle East situation, 263-72 (communications, 263-64; GA, **264-66**, 266-67); Arab Peace Plan *(1982)*, 264, **265** (communication/GA); *1978* Camp David accords, 860 (Human Rights Cs.); GA resolutions, voting procedures, 271 (S-G/UN Legal Counsel); compliance with GA/SC resolutions, **265-66** (GA); Jordan accord *(11 Feb.)*, 263, 264, 273 (communications/S-G); proposed peace cf., 268-70 (communication, 268; GA, **266**, **268-69**, 269-70; Human Rights Cs., 270; Palestinian Rights Ct., 268; S-G, 340); *see also* Disengagement Observer Force, UN; Golan Heights; Jerusalem; Lebanon, UN Interim Force in; Lebanon situation; Palestine question; Palestine refugees; territories occupied by Israel

migrant workers: in Africa, 735, **735-36** (ESC); discrimination against, 848, 849 (CRD/communication/GA); draft convention on protection of, 734 (S-G), 848-49 (GA, **849**, 849; Human Rights Cs., 848; Working Group, 848-49); welfare of, 734, **734-35** (ESC/GA), 848 (S-G)

MIGRANT WORKERS AND THEIR FAMILIES, WORKING GROUP ON THE DRAFTING OF AN INTERNATIONAL CONVENTION ON THE PROTECTION OF THE RIGHTS OF ALL, 848-49, **849** (GA)

migration: flows, effects of, 761, **770** (ESC/Population Cf.)

MIGRATION, INTERGOVERNMENTAL CT. FOR: & brain drain, co-operation with ILO, 719

Migratory Species of Wild Animals, Convention on the Conservation of, *see under* wild animals

military expenditures, *see under* disarmament

MILITARY EXPERTS, PANEL OF, 1399; *see also* Peace, Uniting for

MILITARY STAFF COMMITTEE (SC), 1410

milk/milk products: proposed co-operative system, 604 (UNIDO)

Mineral Resources Development Centre, Central African, *see under* Central Africa

Mineral Resources Development Centre, Eastern and Southern African, *see under* eastern and southern Africa

minerals, 570, 675-77; cross-organizational programme analysis, 1228 (CPC); evaluation, deferred, 677 (CPC/S-G), 1228; exploitation/processing, 675-76 (ESC, **676**; S-G, 675-76); non-metallic, 611, 675, 676 (S-G); nuclear techniques, 1274 (IAEA); statistics, 1032 (Statistical Cs.); surveys, 636 (ECA); technical co-operation, 675 (DTCD/UNRFNRE); *see also* metals; mining; *and names of minerals*

MINERALS, FIRST WORLD CONGRESS ON NON-METALLIC, 611

mining, 663 (ECLAC); effects of nationalization, 675 (S-G); small-scale, **676-77** (ESC); in Namibia, 1123-24; *see also* natural resources: offshore mining; seabed mining

minorities: draft declaration on rights of, 850-51 (GA/Human Rights Cs./Working Group)

missing persons, *see* Cyprus, Ct. on Missing Persons in; disappearance of persons

monetary policy, *see* international monetary and financial system

Mongolia: admission to Paris Union, 1359; steel plant in, 615 (UNIDO)

MONITORING AND ASSESSMENT RESEARCH CENTRE: & Global Environmental Monitoring System/UNEP, 791, 801

Monrovia Strategy for the Economic Development of Africa, Lagos Plan of Action for the Implementation of the, *see* Africa, *1980* Lagos Plan of Action for the Implementation of the Monrovia Strategy for the Economic Development of

monsoons: WMO activities, 1352

Montevideo Programme, *see* Environmental Law, Montevideo Programme for the Development and Periodic Review of

Montserrat, **1148-49** (GA); information to UN, 1082

MOON AND OTHER CELESTIAL BODIES, AGREEMENT GOVERNING THE ACTIVITIES OF STATES ON THE *(1979)*, parties/signatories, 100 (S-G)

Morocco: & primary health care, 1311 (World Bank); refugees in, 1005 (UNHCR); *see also* Western Sahara

mortality, 760 (Population Cs.), **770**, 771 (ESC/S-G)

motor vehicles, 826 (ILO/UNCHS); multilateral treaties on, 1190; seat belts,

1302 (WHO); technical assistance, 614 (UNIDO)

MOTORWAY, TRANS-EUROPEAN NORTH-SOUTH, 655 (ECE); *see also* road transport/roads

Mozambique: admission to IFC, 1318; IDA credit, 1326; refugees in, 1005; & South Africa, Nkomati Accord *(1984)*, 179, 196; spec. economic assistance, 522-24 (GA, **523-24**; S-G, 522-23)

MULTIFIBRE ARRANGEMENT (TEXTILES, ARRANGEMENT REGARDING INTERNATIONAL TRADE IN), 1371

multilateral trade negotiations, 1370-71 8th round, preparatory ct. (GATT), 1372 Tokyo Round, 7th: implementation, 1370 (GATT); review, 1371

multilateral treaties: disarmament, parties/signatories, 100 (S-G); publications, 1190; S-G as depositary, 1190, 1190 *(list)*; treaties deposited (new), 1190 *(list)*; *see also subject entries; and under* States; treaties/agreements

multimodal transport: training, 587

Mururoa Atoll: nuclear tests, 48

MUSIC, UNESCO/INTERNATIONAL MUSIC COUNCIL PRIZE FOR: award, 1298

Namibia, 1090-1131

foreign economic interests, 1122-25 (GA, **1109**); investment, 1122-23 (Colonial Countries Ct./Human Rights Cs./S-G, 1123; GA, **1108**, 1123)

international assistance, 1095 (Colonial Countries Ct.), 1127-31 (GA, **1128-29**; Nationhood Programme/Institute, 1130-31; UNDP/specialized agencies, 1131; UN Namibia Fund, 1129-30); *see also* Namibia, UN Fund for; Southern Africa, UN Educational and Training Programme for

Nationhood Programme, 1130-31 (ESC, 1130; GA, 1130-31)

natural resources: exploitation/protection, 1093, 1094 (communications), 1123-25 (Colonial Countries Ct./Human Rights Cs., 1123; GA, **1075**, **1108-9**, 1125; Namibia Cl., 1092, 1124-25); marine, **1074**, **1108**

postage stamp, **1118** (GA)

refugees: assistance, 830 (Human Settlements Cs.); outflow, **1078** (GA), 1095 (Colonial Countries Ct.); *see also* southern Africa: student refugees in

self-determination, 860-61 (Human Rights Cs.), 1096 (ESC), 1112 (GA)

social conditions/labour exploitation, 1095 (Colonial Countries Ct.), 1125-26 (Namibia Cl.)

territorial sea, expansion of/economic zone, proclamation, **1075** (GA)

TNCs in, 1092 (Namibia Cl.), 1094 (communication); reference book distribution, **1117**, 1119 (GA), 1123 (GA/S-G); *see also under* South Africa

uranium, 1093 (communication), 1102 (SC), **1109**, 1114, 1125 (GA)

vocational training, 1119-20; Centre (Angola), 1120, 1130

see also South West Africa People's Organization

NAMIBIA, AD HOC SUB-CT. ON (SC): members, 1410

NAMIBIA, CF. ON THE INTENSIFICATION OF INTERNATIONAL ACTION FOR THE INDEPENDENCE OF, 1092

NAMIBIA, DECREE NO. 1 FOR THE PROTECTION OF THE NATURAL RESOURCES OF: implementation, 1092, **1114** (GA), 1124 (Namibia Cl.), 1119 (Namibia Commissioner), 1125 (GA)

NAMIBIA, INTERNATIONAL CF. FOR THE IMMEDIATE INDEPENDENCE OF *(1986)*, **1115**, **1118** (GA)

NAMIBIA, OFFICE OF THE UN COMMISSIONER FOR, 1119-20; appointment of Commissioner, 1120 (GA/S-G), 1404, 1424; regional offices, 1119-20

NAMIBIA, UN CL. FOR, 1091-93, **1107** (GA); membership in international organizations, **1068** (ESC); members/officers, 1404; missions, 1093; participation in UN Cf. on Women, 936; Standing Cts./Steering Ct., 1404; Vienna mtgs., 1091-92; work programme, **1113-15**, 1115 (GA)

NAMIBIA, UN FUND FOR, 1127-30 (GA, **1128-29**, 1129; Namibia Cl., 1127); Ct. on, 1404 (members); contributions, **1129**, 1129-30, 1130 *(table)*; missions, 1129-30; programme expenditures, 1127

NAMIBIA, UN INSTITUTE FOR, 1131

NAMIBIA, WEEK OF SOLIDARITY WITH THE PEOPLE OF, 1092, 1116 (Namibia Cl.)

NAMIBIA DAY, 1092, 1116 (Namibia Cl.), **1118** (GA)

NAMIBIAN PEOPLE, INTERNATIONAL CF. IN SUPPORT OF THE STRUGGLE OF THE, FOR INDEPENDENCE *(1983)*: Action Programme/Declaration, implementation, 140 (Human Rights Cs.)

Namibia question, 1091-1122 (Colonial Countries Ct., 1095; communications, 1093-94; ESC, 1096; GA, **1104-9**, **1109-11**, 1111-12; Human Rights Cs., 1095-96; Namibia Cl., 1091-93; SC, 1096-97, **1097-98**, 1098-1101, 1101-4; S-G, 1095; Vienna Action Programme, 1091-92)

cfs./seminars/symposia, 1092

GA spec. sess., proposed, **1121**, 1121-22 (GA)

information dissemination, 1114-19 (Colonial Countries Ct./Vienna Declaration, 1116; GA, **1116-19**, 1119; Namibia Cl., 1115-16); publications, 1116

interim government in, 202 (S-G), **856**, **1068** (ESC), **1071** (GA), 1091 (Vienna Declaration); 1094 (communication), **1097** (SC), **1105**, 1108, 1112 (GA); installation (Windhoek, *17 June*), **857** (GA), 1102 (SC), 1125 (Namibia Cl.)

& "linkage", 1091 (Vienna Declaration), 1093 (Namibia Cl.), 1094 (communication), 1095 (S-G), 1102 (SC), **1106**, **1111** (GA)

mercenaries, use of, 1096, **1107**, 1108 (Human Rights Cs./GA)

missions, 1093, **1113** (Namibia Cl./GA)

political/military aspects, 1120-21 (Colonial Countries Ct./Human Rights Cs., 1121; GA, **1121**, 1121-22; Namibia Cl./Vienna Declaration, 1120)

Multi-Party Cf. of South West Africa/Namibia, 1093, 1095 (S-G/Vienna Declaration)

Namibia question *(cont.)*
political prisoners/detainees, 1092, 1095 (Colonial Countries Ct.), 1096 (Human Rights Cs.)
& self-determination, **857**, 860-61 (GA/Human Rights Cs.), 1091 Vienna Declaration); *see also* self-determination of peoples
UN settlement plan: compliance, 1091-92 (Vienna Declaration), 1093 (Namibia Cl. mission), 1095 (S-G), 1096 (ESC), **1097-98** (SC), **1105** (GA); & proportional representation, 1101 (SC), 1105 (GA)
UN Transition Assistance Group: Commander-designate/S-G Spec. Representative, 1410, 1424
Vienna plenary mtgs.: Declaration/Action Programme, 1091-92, **1107** (GA)
Walvis Bay/offshore islands, **1065**, **1109**, **1114**, (GA); Colonial Countries Ct., 1095
see also Angola; self-determination of peoples; South Africa; southern Africa; South West Africa People's Organization

narcotic drugs, 10 (S-G)
conventions/treaties, 1013 (INCB), 1028-29 (ESC); States parties, 1028-29
illicit traffic, 1020-28 (GA, **1020-22**; INCB/Narcotic Drugs Cs., 1020); Declaration, 959 *(text)*; draft convention, 1023-25 (ESC, **1024**; GA, **1024-25**; S-G, 1024); law enforcement, 1022-23 (ESC, **1022-23**, **1023**; INCB/ Narcotic Drugs Cs., 1022); regional activities, 1027-28; & 7th UN Congress on Crime, 1022, 1024, **1025**
publications, 1030
raw materials for licit use, 1019, **1019-20** (Cs./ESC)
WHO activities, 1028, 1029
see also amphetamines; cannabis; cocaine; heroin; opium; psychotropic substances; *and under* drugs of abuse
NARCOTIC DRUGS, CS. ON, 1012, 1015, **1015**, 1030 (ESC/GA/S-G), 1029-30, 1412-13; agenda/documentation, 1030 (ESC); members/officers/sess., 1413; 9th spec. sess., 1030, **1030**; subsidiary bodies, 1020, 1413
NARCOTIC DRUGS, DIVISION OF: proposed strengthening, 1227 (CPC)
NARCOTIC DRUGS, SINGLE CONVENTION ON *(1961)*, 1013 (S-G), 1028-29 (Narcotic Drugs Cs./GA); Protocol *(1972)*, States parties, 1028
NARCOTICS CONTROL BOARD, INTERNATIONAL, 1012, 1030; members/Chairman, 1422; reports *(1984, 1985)*, 1013 (ESC)
NARCOTICS LABORATORY (UN Division of Narcotic Drugs), 1012, 1016, 1227 (CPC)
NARCOTICS LAW ENFORCEMENT AGENCIES, FAR EAST REGION, MEETING OF OPERATIONAL HEADS OF NATIONAL, 1020, 1028, 1413
NATIONAL ACCOUNTS, UN SYSTEM OF: revision, 1032 (S-G/Statistical Cs./Inter secretariat Working Group); & System of Statistical Balances of the National Economy, 1032
NATIONAL HOUSEHOLD SURVEY CAPABILITY PROGRAMME: implementation, 1034-35 (ACC/Statistical Cs.)

national liberation movements:
assistance, 201, **1067** (ESC), **1063**, **1071**, **1072** (GA), 1066 (S-G); observer status in international organizations, **1068** (ESC); & UN anniversary sess., 403; *see also under* apartheid and names of movements/organizations
natural resources, 485, 486 (DTCD), 636-37 (ECA), 647-48 (ESCAP), 663 (ECLAC), 669-83
co-ordination in UN, 674, **674** (ESC/S-G)
exploration, 669-71 (UNDP, 670; UN-RFNRE, 669-70); electronic data processing in, 671, **671** (ESC/S-G)
& offshore mining, sharing, 816 (UNEP)
oil/gas deposits, 685 (S-G)
permanent sovereignty over, 672-73 (ESC, **672**; GA, 673; S-G/TNCs Cs., 672); *see also under* Namibia
publication, 675
subsurface space, utilization, 674 (Natural Resources Ct./S-G)
see also energy resources; geothermal energy; marine resources; metals; minerals; water resources; *and under* sea-bed
NATURAL RESOURCES, CT. ON (ESC), 669, 673-74; agenda/report, 673-74 (ESC); members/officers, 1416; rationalization of work, 669, **673** (ESC); secretariat services for, 669, **673**
NATURAL RESOURCES, CT. ON (ESCAP): 12th sess., 647-48
NATURAL RESOURCES EXPLORATION, UN REVOLVING FUND FOR, 669-71; budget, approval, 670 (UNDP); co-financing arrangements, 669-70, **671** (ESC); contributions, 670-71 (ESC, **671**; UNDP, 670), 670 *(table)*; Director, appointment, 670; expenditures, 670 *(table)*
NATURAL RESOURCES IN AFRICA, INSTITUTE FOR (UNU): proposed establishment, 785
natural sciences, 1296-97 (UNESCO); fellowships, 1299; technical assistance, 1299 *(tables)*
NATURE AND NATURAL RESOURCES, INTERNATIONAL UNION FOR CONSERVATION OF, 812
nature conservation: habitats, protection, 813; *see also* conservation; cultural and natural heritage; wild flora and fauna; wildlife
NAVAL ARMS RACE, NAVAL FORCES AND NAVAL ARMS SYSTEMS, GROUP OF GOVERNMENTAL EXPERTS TO CARRY OUT A COMPREHENSIVE STUDY ON THE, 30-31; *see also* disarmament: naval arms race
navigation, international, *see* air navigation; inland water transport; international watercourses
nazism/fascism: measures against, 842-45 (GA, **842-44**, 844; Human Rights Cs., 842; S-G/communications, 842); victory over, 40th anniversary, 844-45 (CERD/Human Rights, 844; communications, 844; ESC, 844-45, **845**)
Near and Middle East: drug traffic, 1025-26 (INCB/Narcotic Drugs Cs.)
Near East: agricultural development, 1288 (FAO), 1366 (IFAD); food production, 1287 (FAO Cl.)

neighbouring rights, *see* copyright
neighbouring States, *see under* States
Nepal: highway development, 1326 (IDA); industrial development, 1326 (IDA); medicinal plants, drugs from, 605 (UNIDO); national conservation strategy, 812 (IUCN/UNEP/United States); telecommunications, 1326 (IDA)
Netherlands: contributions to peacekeeping forces, 122
Netherlands Antilles: IPF for, 470 (UNDP Cl.)
neutron weapons (enhanced radiation weapons): proposed convention on prohibition, 44, **44** (GA)
New Caledonia, 1081 (Colonial Countries Ct./communication)
new international economic order, 7 (S-G), 420-21; & OAU co-operation, **202**, 421 (GA); & human rights, 881, **884** (GA); legal aspects, 420-21, 1195-96 (GA, 1195, **1195-96**; S-G/UNCITRAL Working Group, 1195; UNITAR study, 1195)
NEW INTERNATIONAL ECONOMIC ORDER, WORKING GROUP ON THE (UNCITRAL), 1191, 1195; Chairman/members, 1401
new international human order (proposed), *see* development: moral aspects
news agencies, 370 (UNESCO); technology workshop, **380** (GA/Information Ct.); *see also* names of agencies
Newspaper Supplement, World, **382**, 387 (GA/Information Ct.)
NEWS SERVICE OF THE DEPARTMENT OF POLITICAL AND SECURITY COUNCIL AFFAIRS, 387, **387** (GA)
new world information and communication order (proposed), 373-74 (GA, **373**, 374, **376-79**; Information Ct., 374; UNESCO, 373-74); second *(1986)* round table, **373**, 374 (GA/UNESCO)
New Zealand: drug abuse, 1028; information to UN, 1082; *see also* Tokelau
Nicaragua, 208-19; admission to WIPO, 1359; & Costa Rica, 208-10 (communications); crop failures, 1292 (FAO); economic assistance, 530-31, **531** (GA/ S-G); & Honduras, 210-11 (communications); & United States, 211-19 (communications, 212-13, 215-16; ICJ, 1156-57; SC, **212-13**, 213-18, **218**, 218-19); *see also* Central America situation
NICE AGREEMENT CONCERNING INTERNATIONAL CLASSIFICATION OF GOODS AND SERVICES FOR THE PURPOSES OF THE REGISTRATION OF MARKS: accession, 1359
NICE UNION: contribution to WIPO, 1361 *(table)*; members, 1359, 1362-63 *(table)*
nickel: 1st Preparatory Mtg., 570; International Study Group established, 570; UN Cf. on, 113, 570
Nigeria: & illicit drug traffic, oil glut effect on, 626, 1026; refugees in, 1005; World Bank project, 1311
Nkomati Accord, *see under* Mozambique
non-aligned countries: & African economic crisis, 501; & Angola, 182; & Antarctica, 389; & Cyprus, 254; & Mayotte, 197; & Mediterranean security, 259;
NON-ALIGNED COUNTRIES, CF. OF FOREIGN MINISTERS OF: & Angola, 180; & Chad-Libyan Arab Jamahiriya dispute, 197; circulation of documents, 403;

& colonialism, 1061; & disarmament, 14; drug abuse/illicit traffic, 1017, 1024; Economic Declaration, 413; & Falkland Islands (Malvinas), 1134; on Indian Ocean, 90; on Kampuchea, 226; on Malagasy islands, 200; & Mayotte, 198-99; & Middle East, 274; on Namibia, 1094; on New Caledonia, 1081; on nuclear power, 695; on Puerto Rico, 1081; on South Africa nuclear collaboration, 59; & Western Sahara, 1138

NON-ALIGNED COUNTRIES, CO-ORDINATING BUREAU OF: & Angola, 182; & Central America situation, 215-16 (communication); Extraordinary Ministerial Mtg., 501; & Lebanon, 298 (communication); & South Africa, 155

NON-ALIGNED COUNTRIES, MEETING OF MINISTERS AND HEADS OF DELEGA-TIONS OF: & Angola, 183; circulation of documents, 403; & Middle East situation, 285

NON-ALIGNED NEWS AGENCIES, POOL OF: co-operation with DPI, 376, **378-79**, 384, (GA/Information Ct); 4th cf., 378 (GA/Information Ct.)

non-citizens, human rights of, *see under* human rights

non-conventional energy sources, *see* biomass energy; geothermal energy; *and under* energy, new and renewable sources of

non-ferrous metals, *see* metals

NON-GOVERNMENTAL LIAISON SERVICES (GENEVA/NEW YORK): & development education, 432; financial situation, **382** (GA), 387 (Information Ct./JUNIC)

non-governmental organizations, 9 (S-G)
& aging persons, 987
& *apartheid*, **173**, 174 (*Apartheid* Ct./GA)
& colonial countries, assistance to, 1079 (Colonial Countries Ct./Sub-Ct.)
& disabled persons, 776
environmental issues: co-operation with UNEP, 796
& ESC, consultative status with, 1046-51, 1047-54 (*lists*); applications/reclassifications, 1046-47 (Ct. of NGOs, 1046; ESC, **1046-47**, 1047); withdrawal, **1047** (ESC)
& IFAD co-operation, 1365
& LDCs, **450** (GA)
& Palestine question, 273-74, **916** (GA); in SC mtg., 274; proposed cf., 268
& UN bodies/specialized agencies, consultative status with, 1051-54 (*list*)
& UN Decade of Disabled Persons, publicizing, 776

NON-GOVERNMENTAL ORGANIZATIONS, CT. ON, 1046, **1046** (ESC); members/officers, 1416

non-nuclear-weapon States: & IAEA safeguards agreements, 1271-72; international arrangements (negative security arrangements), proposed, 67-68 (*Ad Hoc* Ct./CD, 67; GA, **67-68**, 68); security guarantees, proposed convention, **68-69**, 69-70 (GA)

NON-NUCLEAR-WEAPON STATES, AD HOC WORKING GROUP ON EFFECTIVE INTERNATIONAL ARRANGEMENTS TO ASSURE, AGAINST THE USE OR THREAT OF USE OF NUCLEAR WEAPONS, 67, **68** (GA)

non-project sector: IDA credits, 1324-25 *(table)*, 1326; World Bank loans, 1309-10 *(table)*, 1311

non-proliferation, 56-67; *see also* non-nuclear-weapon States; nuclear-weapon-free zones

NON-PROLIFERATION OF NUCLEAR WEAPONS, *1968* TREATY ON THE: parties to, 57, 100

NON-PROLIFERATION OF NUCLEAR WEAPONS, 3RD REVIEW CF. OF THE PARTIES TO THE TREATY ON THE: Final Document/Declaration, 56-58 (GA, **57**, 57-58; Preparatory Ct., 57); participants/observers, 56

Non-Self-Governing Territories, 840, **841** (CERD/GA), 1082-83; information to UN, 1082 *(list)*, 1082-83, **1083** (GA); scholarships, 1082, **1082** (GA/S-G); UN visiting missions, 1083 (Colonial Countries Ct./GA); *see also* colonial countries; self-determination of peoples; Trust Territory of the Pacific Islands *and names of Territories*

non-use of force, *see under* international relations

North Africa: agricultural development, 1366 (IFAD); UNICEF programme, 965 *(table)*, 969; World Bank projects, 1311

NORTH ATLANTIC TREATY ORGANIZATION: Cl. communiqué on disarmament, 14

Northern Mariana Islands: & war claims, 1086 (TC); *see also* Trust Territory of the Pacific Islands

Norway: IYDP Trust Fund, 780

nuclear disarmament, 35-70; bilateral negotiations (Geneva), 6 (S-G), 44-47 (communications, 45; GA, **45**, 45-46, **46**, 46-47); proposed subsidiary body, 40, **42** (CD/GA); verification measures, 7 (S-G); *see also* non-nuclear-weapon States; non-proliferation; nuclear war

nuclear energy, 693-94, **694** (GA/IAEA/S-G); environmental aspects, 693, 1272 (IAEA); incidents/accidents, 694; industrial applications, 1274 (IAEA); peaceful uses, 7 (S-G), 694-96 (Cf. on); technology transfer, 1274 (IAEA)

NUCLEAR ENERGY, PREPARATORY CT. FOR THE UN CF. FOR THE PROMOTION OF INTERNATIONAL CO-OPERATION IN THE PEACEFUL USES OF, 694-95, **696** (GA); members/officers, 1399-1400; 6th/7th sess., 695, **696** (GA); Working Group established, 695

NUCLEAR ENERGY, UN CF. FOR THE PROMOTION OF INTERNATIONAL CO-OPERATION IN THE PEACEFUL USES OF *(1987)*: date, 695, **696** (GA/Preparatory Ct.); IAEA, 1271; preparations, 694-96 (communications, 695; **695-96**; Preparatory Ct., 694-95); regional activities, 695; S-G, 1424

NUCLEAR ENERGY AGENCY (OECD): & plant safety, 1273

nuclear fusion: journal on, 25th anniversary issue, 1273 (IAEA)

NUCLEAR INFORMATION SYSTEM, INTERNATIONAL, 1273

nuclear medicine, 1273-74 (IAEA); *see also* diseases

nuclear non-proliferation, *see* non-proliferation; nuclear-weapon-free zones; zones of peace

nuclear power, 693-94 (IAEA DG/S-G), 1272 (IAEA)
& developing countries, planning for, 693-94, 1272 (IAEA)
facilities, protection, IAEA training course, 1273; *see also* Iraq
industrial applications, 1274 (IAEA)
plants: accidents/incidents, 694 (IAEA DG), 1273 (IAEA); financing, 693 (IAEA DG), 1272 (IAEA); safety, 694 (IAEA DG), 1273 (IAEA review teams); world-wide capacity, 684 (S-G), 693, 1272 (IAEA)
safeguards agreements, 1271 (IAEA)
sources, for spacecraft, 103, **106**, **107** (COPUOS/GA/Working Group); legal aspects, 104-5, **106** (COPUOS/GA/Working Group)
technical co-operation, 1272 (IAEA)
training course, 6th international, 1273
see also under outer space

NUCLEAR SAFETY ADVISORY GROUP: 1st mtg., 694, 1271

NUCLEAR SAFETY STANDARDS: programme implementation, 1271, 1272-73 (IAEA)

nuclear war:
biologic/climatic effects of, 39-40 (GA, **39-40**, 40; S-G, 39), 1372 (UNU)
prevention, 35-38 (CD/DC, 35; GA, 36, **36-37**, 37, **37-38**; S-G, 35-36)

NUCLEAR WAR, INTERNATIONAL PHYSICIANS FOR THE PREVENTION OF: *1985* Nobel Peace Prize, 35

nuclear-weapon-free zones, 7 (S-G), 58-59 (communications, 58; Expert Group study, 58; GA, **58-59**, 59; S-G, 58); Africa, 59-60 (communications, 59; DC/S-G, 59; GA, 59, **59-60**); Balkans (proposed), 58; Europe, 58; Latin America, **62-63**, 63 (GA); Middle East (proposed), 63-64 (GA, **63-64**, 64; S-G, 63); South Asia (proposed), 66-67 (GA, **66-67**, 67; S-G, 66); South Pacific, 58; *see also* Indian Ocean; Israel; Sea-Bed and the Ocean Floor . . ., Treaty on; South Africa; zones of peace

NUCLEAR-WEAPON-FREE ZONES, GROUP OF GOVERNMENTAL EXPERTS ON: comprehensive study, 58, **58-59** (GA)

nuclear weapons, 3, 6 (S-G)
fissionable material for, prohibition of production, **43**, 43-44
freeze (proposed), **53-54**, 54, **54-55**, 55, **55-56**
neutron bomb (enhanced radiation weapons): prohibition of, **44**, 44 (GA)
prohibition of use of: draft convention, 38, **38**, (GA), 38-39 *(text)*; non-first-use of, 35, **36** (GA)
& South Africa, 61, **62**; *see also* South Africa: nuclear capability
strategic/intermediate-range, bilateral negotiations on: Geneva summit, 43-45 (communications, 44; GA, **44**, 44-45), **45**, 45-46 (GA)
see also non-nuclear-weapon States; Non-Proliferation of Nuclear Weapons, Treaty on the; Sea-Bed and the Ocean Floor . . ., Treaty on; *and under* nuclear war

NUCLEAR WEAPONS IN LATIN AMERICA, TREATY FOR THE PROHIBITION OF (Treaty of Tlatelolco, 1967): parties to, 100; Protocol I, application, **62-63**, 63

Nuclear Weapons in Latin America, Treaty for the Prohibition of *(cont.)* (GA); Protocol II, 62; & safeguards agreements, 1271

nuclear-weapon tests, 47-53; *ad hoc* ct., proposed establishment, 47-49 (CD, 47; GA, **49**); cessation/prohibition, implementation of GA resolution, **50-51**, 51 (GA); & Mururoa Atoll, 48; proposed treaty on, 47-49 (CD, 47; communications, 47-48; GA, 48, **48-49**, 49, **49-50**, 50, **51-52**, 52-53); unilateral moratorium, 47 (CD), 47-48 (communication), **50** (GA); verification measures, 47 (*Ad Hoc* Scientific Experts), **52** (GA)

NUCLEAR WEAPON TESTS IN THE ATMOSPHERE, IN OUTER SPACE AND UNDER WATER, TREATY BANNING (1963): conversion to comprehensive treaty (proposed), 47, **49** (GA); parties to, 100

nutrition: and health, 774-75 (ACC, 775; UNICEF/UNU/WHO, 774-75), 962 (UNICEF), 1289 (FAO); IDA credits, 1324-25 *(table)*; publications, 775; vitamin/mineral deficiencies, ACC support programme, 1039; *see also* children; food; infants; malnutrition

NUTRITION, SUB-CT. ON (ACC), 774, 775; Advisory Group, 775

NUTRITION SUPPORT PROGRAMME, UNICEF/WHO JOINT, 972

OCCUPATIONAL SAFETY AND HEALTH INFORMATION CENTRE (ILO), 1279; *see also* working conditions

Oceania: refugee assistance, 996 *(table)*, 1007 (UNHCR)

OCEAN MINING ASSOCIATES, 110

OCEANOGRAPHIC COMMISSION, INTERGOVERNMENTAL, 1297 (UNESCO)

oceans, 1297 (UNESCO), 1350 (WMO); global monitoring, proposed programme, 815 (UNEP); mining, 110-11 (Preparatory Cs.); radioactive wastes, 1272 (IAEA); resources development, 115 (ESC); *see also* sea; sea-bed

OCEANS AND COASTAL AREAS PROGRAMME ACTIVITY CENTRE (UNEP), 815

oil, 685 (S-G), 689-90 (DTCD), 691 (S-G), 693 (UNEP); commercial consumption, 685 (S-G); *see also* petroleum

Oman: telecommunications aid, 1312 (World Bank)

ONCHOCERCIASIS CONTROL PROGRAMME (WHO), 1304, 1305 *(table)*

OPIATE RAW MATERIALS, EXPERT GROUP ON REDUCTION OF EXCESSIVE STOCKS OF, 1015, 1019

opiates, 1013, 1019; raw material stocks/production, 1019

opium: abuse of, 1026; cultivation, 1019, 1020 (INCB); traffic in, 1028

oral rehydration therapy, 966, 968 (UNICEF); Cf. on, 1304

ORGANISATION FOR ECONOMIC CO-OPERATION AND DEVELOPMENT: financial resources allocation, 597 (Development Centre/UNIDO experts mtg.); trade co-operation, 555 (UNCTAD *Report*)

ORGANIZATION OF AFRICAN UNITY, 201-4 (ESC, 202; GA, **202-4**, 204; S-G, 201-2);

& Africa economic situation, 499, 501; & Angola & Botswana, 179-80; Assembly sess., 201-2 (S-G), 499, 805; & Chad-Libyan Arab Jamahiriya dispute, 197; & Mayotte, 198; & Middle East, 264; & Namibia, 1094; & refugees, 192, **194** (GA), 1010; & regional disarmament centre, 94, 204; & Western Sahara, 204; *see also* Africa, critical economic situation in

ORGANIZATION OF AMERICAN STATES: & Costa Rica border incident, 208; & humid tropics, 819 (UNEP); & refugee protection, 1010

ORGANIZATION OF THE ISLAMIC CONFERENCE: & African disaster relief, 537; & *apartheid*, 128; & colonialism Declaration, 1060; co-operation with UN, 401-2 (communications/S-G, 20-21; GA, **402**); economic co-operation, 412 (communication); & Iran-Iraq conflict, 244-45, 249 (Islamic Peace Ct.); & Israel, 264, 271; & Mayotte, 198; & Middle East, 268, 286; & Namibia, 1094; & nuclear-weapon-free zones, 58; & refugee protection, 1010

ORGANIZATION OF PETROLEUM EXPORTING COUNTRIES: oil glut effects, 626

outer space, 101-8 applications, UN programme: implementation, 101-2, **107** (GA) co-ordination in UN system, 102-3 (ACC/COPUOS/S-G), **106** (GA) definition/delimitation, 105, **106** (COPUOS/GA); Working Group, 105 exploration, impact on mankind: study, 371 information service, proposed, 103, **106** international co-operation, 101, **105-8**, 108 (GA) legal aspects, 104-5, **106** (COPUOS/GA) nuclear power sources, for spacecraft 103, **106** (COPUOS/GA); legal aspects, 104-5, **106** (COPUOS/GA) publications, 108 scientific/technical aspects, 103-4, **106-7** (COPUOS/GA) systems in, implications, 103 treaties/conventions, **106**, 108; ratifications, 108; States parties, 100 *(list)* *see also* arms race; communications satellites; geostationary orbit; remote sensing

OUTER SPACE, CONVENTION ON REGISTRATION OF OBJECTS LAUNCHED INTO: parties, 108; *see also* space objects

OUTER SPACE, CT. ON THE PEACEFUL USES OF, 101, **106** (GA) Legal Sub-Ct., 104, **106** (COPUOS/GA); Chairman, 1397; Working Group on remote sensing, re-establishment, 104 members/officers, 1397 revitalization, proposed, 104 Scientific and Technical Sub-Ct., 101, **107** (COPUOS/GA); Chairman, 1397; Working Group on Nuclear Power Sources, 103

OUTER SPACE, 2ND UN CF. ON THE EXPLORATION AND PEACEFUL USES OF: implementation, 103, **107**, **108** (COPUOS/GA/S-G)

OUTER SPACE ACTIVITIES, 7TH INTER-AGENCY MTG. ON (ACC), 102-3 (COPUOS/S-G)

ozone layer: chlorofluorocarbons, proposed protocol on, 804 (*ad hoc* steering ct./UNEP Executive Director); modification/impact of, 804 (UNEP Co-ordinating Ct.); seminar, 804

OZONE LAYER, AD HOC WORKING GROUP OF LEGAL AND TECHNICAL EXPERTS FOR THE ELABORATION OF A GLOBAL FRAMEWORK CONVENTION FOR THE PROTECTION OF THE, 804

OZONE LAYER, CO-ORDINATING COMMITTEE ON THE (UNEP), 804

OZONE LAYER, VIENNA CONVENTION FOR THE PROTECTION OF THE: adoption, **790**, 804 (GA/UNEP Cl.); signatures, 804

OZONE RESEARCH AND MONITORING PROJECT, GLOBAL (WMO), 1352

PACIFIC ENERGY DEVELOPMENT PROGRAMME, 648

Pacific Islands, Trust Territory of the, *see* Trust Territory of the Pacific Islands

Pacific Ocean, *see* Oceania; South Pacific

PACIFIC OPERATIONS CENTRE (ESCAP), 651; headquarters, Vanuatu, 532; Pacific Liaison Office/UNDP Advisory Team, 646, 651

Pacific region, 651 (ESCAP); broadcast training project (PACBROAD), 1298 (UNESCO); & debt servicing, 555 (UNCTAD *Report*); growth rates, 428 (*World Economic Survey*); industrial development, 601-2 (UNIDO); *see also country names*

packaging industry, 610 (UNIDO)

Pakistan: energy loans, 1311 (World Bank); energy technology, 690 (DTCD); genetic engineering, cattle, 814 (FAO/UNEP); human rights, 912 (SCPDPM); & IAEA safeguards, 1271; industrial development, 607 (UNIDO); refugees in, 994, 996 *(table)*, 1009 (UNHCR/World Bank); UNICEF programme, 965 *(table)*, 968; *see also* Afghanistan situation

Palau: & IYY, 1085; public finance, 1085 (TC); *see also* Trust Territory of the Pacific Islands

PALESTINE, INTERNATIONAL CF. ON THE QUESTION OF (1983): Declaration/Action Programme, implementation, 273, **276** (GA/Palestinian Rights Ct.), 278 (Human Rights Cs.); *see also* Middle East situation: proposed peace cf.

PALESTINE, UN CONCILIATION CS. FOR, **354**, 358, 359 (GA); co-operation with Palestinian Rights Ct., 273-74, **276** (GA); members, 1401

PALESTINE, UN SEMINARS ON THE QUESTION OF (10th, 11th, 12th), 273

PALESTINE LIBERATION ORGANIZATION: accord with Jordan, 263, 264, 273 (communications); as representative of Palestinians, **265** (GA); raid on Tunisia headquarters, 285-91 (communications, 285-87; ICAO, 285; SC, 287, **287**, 287-90; S-G, 290-91)

Palestine question, 272-78 (communications, 272-73; GA, 276, **276-77**, 277, **277-78**, 278; Human Rights Cs., 278; Palestinian Rights Ct., 273-74; SC, 274-

76); public information, 278-80
(DPI/Palestinian Rights Ct., 278-79; GA,
279, 279-80, **380**, 384); regional
seminars/symposia, 273-74 (Palestinian
Rights Ct.); terrorist attacks, 272-73; *see
also* Jerusalem; Lebanon situation; Middle East situation; territories occupied by
Israel

Palestine refugees/displaced persons,
353-68
assistance, 357-58 (GA, **358**; UNRWA,
357-58)
education/training, 360-61 (UNRWA), 362
(GA); scholarships, 362-63 (GA, **362-
63**; S-G/UNRWA, 362); UN agencies,
362; universities, 362 (GA); *see also*
Jerusalem: university, proposed
food aid, 359-60 (Commissioner-General,
359; GA, 359, **360**; S-G, 360)
property rights, 363-64 (GA, **363**, 364;
S-G, 363)
protection, 364-66 (GA, **364-65**, 365-66;
S-G, 364)
repatriation, 358-59 (Commissioner-
General/Conciliation Cs./S-G, 358; GA,
354, **358-59**, 359)
see also Lebanon situation: refugees in
PALESTINE REFUGEES IN THE NEAR EAST,
AD HOC CT. OF THE GA FOR THE AN-
NOUNCEMENT OF VOLUNTARY CON-
TRIBUTIONS TO THE UN RELIEF AND
WORKS AGENCY FOR: mtg., **1394**
PALESTINE REFUGEES IN THE NEAR EAST,
UN RELIEF AND WORKS AGENCY FOR,
353-57 (Commissioner-General, 353-54;
GA, **354**, 354)
Advisory Cs., 356-57; members, 1407
Commissioner-General, 354, 355, 1407,
1425; Deputy, 1407, 1425; spec.
report, 355
compensation claims, 357
field/headquarters/liaison offices, 353;
proposed headquarters relocation,
354
financing, 354-57 (Advisory Cs., 356-57;
Commissioner-General, 354-55; GA,
357; Working Group, 355-56); contributions, 355 (Working Group), 356;
expenditures, 354-55, 356; income,
354;
staff: arrests/detention, 353; & financial
crisis, 356; total, 361, 1425
Working Group on the Financing of the,
355-56, **357** (GA); members, 1407
PALESTINIAN PEOPLE, CT. ON THE EXER-
CISE OF THE INALIENABLE RIGHTS OF
THE, 273, **276** (GA); co-operation with
DPI, 278; members/officers, 1396-97;
Working Group, members, 1397
PALESTINIAN PEOPLE, INTERNATIONAL DAY
OF SOLIDARITY WITH THE, observance,
279 (DPI)
PALESTINIAN RIGHTS, DIVISION FOR
(Secretariat), **277-78**, 278 (GA); NGO
symposia/mtgs., 273-74
Palestinians: agriculture/health, 283
(FAO/WHO); assistance to, 281-85 (ACC,
281-82; ECWA/FAO/WHO, 283; ESC,
283, 284; GA, **284**, 285; S-G, 281-82;
UNDP/UNIDO, 282; UNICEF, 282-83);
child health, 283 (UNICEF); co-
ordination in UN, Geneva mtg., 282,
284 (GA/S-G); science/technology, 283

(ECWA/Science & Technology Centre);
self-determination, **265**, 278 (GA), 860
(Human Rights Cs.); S-G mtg. (Geneva,
5-6 July), 282, **283**, **284** (ESC/GA);
small-scale industries, training, 603
(UNIDO); *see also* territories occupied
by Israel

palm-oil producing countries, 1290
PAN-AFRICAN DOCUMENTATION AND IN-
FORMATION SYSTEM, 627-28 (ECA);
Regional Technical Ct., 627-28
PAN AFRICANIST CONGRESS OF AZANIA:
assistance/support, 162 (UNDP/UNIDO);
New York office, financing **161**, 170
(GA); observer, UN Women's Cf., 937
PAN AFRICAN NEWS AGENCY, 173; &
Namibia, 1094
PAN-AFRICAN TELECOMMUNICATIONS
UNION: co-operation with the European
Space Agency, 102
PAN AMERICAN CENTRE FOR HUMAN
ECOLOGY AND HEALTH, 774 (WHO)
PAN AMERICAN HEALTH ORGANIZATION: &
child survival, 967 (WHO/UNICEF)
Papua New Guinea: chemical accident,
802; refugees in, 1007 (UNHCR)
Paraguay: & state of siege, 854
(SCPDPM/S-G); 924 (SCPDPM)
parasitic diseases, 1273 (IAEA), 1304
(WHO)
Paris Convention for the Protection of In-
dustrial Property, *see* Industrial Property,
Paris Convention for the Protection of
PARIS UNION: contribution to WIPO, 1347
(table); & Madrid Agreement, 1360;
members, 1362-63 *(table)*
PATENT CO-OPERATION TREATY: accessions, 1359; publications, 1360, 1361
PATENT CO-OPERATION UNION: contributions to WIPO, 1361 *(table)*; members,
1359, 1362-63 *(table)*
PATENT DOCUMENTATION CENTRE, INTER-
NATIONAL (Spanish): proposed establishment, 1359
patents, 1359-60 (WIPO); agreements,
1359 *(list)*; *see also* copyright; industrial
property; marks: registrations; trade
marks
pattern of conferences (UN), *see under*
conferences/meetings (UN)
peace, 1297 (UNESCO); education for, 786-
87; *Yearbooks on (1983, 1984)*, 1297;
see also peace and security, international; *and under* human rights
PEACE, DECLARATION ON THE RIGHT OF
PEOPLES TO, implementation, 125, **125**
(communication/GA)
PEACE, INTERNATIONAL YEAR OF *(1986)*, 6
(S-G), 122-25 (ACC, 123; communications, 123; GA, 122, **123-24**; S-G, 122-
23); Proclamation, **123-24** *(text)*; programme of, 123 (S-G), **124** (GA), 831
(Human Settlements Cs.)
"PEACE, UNITING FOR", *1948* GA resolution: Collective Measures Ct./expert
panel, 1410
PEACE, UNIVERSITY FOR, 786-87, **787**
(ESC)
peace and security, international, 5-6,
1177 (S-G), 116-25
draft code of offences against, 1163-65
(GA, **1164**, 1165; ILC, 1163-64; S-G,
1164)

1970 Declaration, implementation, 116-19
(communications, 116-17; GA, **117-19**,
119; S-G, 116)
& non-use of force, 118 (GA)
& UN anniversary sess., **118**
UN Charter provisions, implementation,
119-21 (GA, **120**, 120-21; S-G, 119)
see also disarmament; disputes,
peaceful settlement of; international
relations; United Nations: strengthening role of
PEACE EDUCATION, UNESCO PRIZE FOR
(1985), 1297
peace-keeping operations (UN), 5 (S-G),
316-26; comprehensive review, 122, **122**
(GA); publication, 122; *see also under*
Cyprus, UN Peace-keeping Force in;
Disengagement Observer Force, UN;
Lebanon, UN Interim Force in; Truce
Supervision Organization, UN
PEACE-KEEPING OPERATIONS, SPEC. CT.
ON: mandate reaffirmed, **122** (GA);
members/Working Group, 1400
PEACE RESEARCH INSTITUTE, STOCKHOLM
INTERNATIONAL: & arms race impact on
environment, 813
PENSION BOARD, UN JOINT STAFF, 1247;
members, 1406-7; Actuaries Ct., 1407;
Standing Ct., 1406
PENSION COMMITTEE, UN STAFF:
members, 1408
PENSION FUND, UN JOINT STAFF, 1247,
1248
administrative expenses/composition,
1249 (GA)
admission of UNIDO to membership,
1249 (GA)
Emergency Fund, contributions, **1249**
investments, 1247, 1250 (ACABQ/
GA/S-G/
Regulations, amendments to, **1250**, 1250
(GA)
pensions (UN system), 1247-51
adjustments, review of, 1248 (ICSC/Pen-
sion Board), **1249** (GA)
pensionable remuneration, 1247-50 (GA,
1248, **1248-49**; ACABQ/Board/ICSU/
S-G, 1247-48)
Peru: & forest assessment, 819 (OAU/
UNEP); presidential inauguration, Lima
Declaration, 83, 206; & UNFDAC/UNIDO
co-operation, 610
pest control, 1289, 1290 (FAO)
pesticide industry, 612 (UNIDO); *see also*
chemicals; plants
PESTICIDES, INTERNATIONAL CODE OF
CONDUCT ON THE DISTRIBUTION AND
USE OF: adoption of, 774 (FAO Cf.),
1287 (FAO Cl.)
PESTS AND PESTICIDES, 4TH INTERNA-
TIONAL MTG. ON PERCEPTION AND
MANAGEMENT OF, 802
petrochemical industry, 612 (UNIDO);
man-made fibres, 612; 3rd Consultation,
604, 612; UNIDO study, 608; *see also*
fertilizers
petroleum industry: & environment, 819;
exploration, symposium on financing,
686; exports/production, 685 (S-G)
PETROLEUM INDUSTRY ENVIRONMENTAL
CONSERVATION ASSOCIATION, INTERNA-
TIONAL: review on environmental
management, 819

pharmaceutical industry, 612 (UNIDO); supply sources, directory, 612 (UNIDO/ WHO); 3rd Consultation, preparations, 612

PHARMACEUTICAL INDUSTRY, AD HOC PANEL OF EXPERTS ON CONTRACTUAL ARRANGEMENTS IN THE, 612

pharmaceuticals: consumer protection, **571-74** (GA guidelines); technology transfer, 707, 717 (UNCTAD/UNFSSTD/ WHO); *see also under* drugs

Philippines: agricultural policy, loan, 1310 (World Bank); education, 972 (UNICEF); refugee centre, 831 (UNCHS/UNHCR); telecommunications loans, 1312 (World Bank); UNIDO project, 611

philosophy: UNESCO projects, 1297

photosynthesis: & bioproductivity, 814; publications, 814

physical sciences, 1274-75 (IAEA)

PHYSICS, INTERNATIONAL CENTRE FOR THEORETICAL, 1274 (IAEA/UNESCO)

piracy, *see under* refugees: protection of

Pitcairn, **1149** (GA); information to UN, 1082

Planners, Statisticians and Demographers, Joint Cf. of African (ECA), *see* African Planners, Statisticians and Demographers, Joint Cf. of

planning, *see* development planning; programmes (UN)

PLANT GENETIC RESOURCES, CS. ON (FAO), 1291

PLANT GENETIC RESOURCES, INTERNATIONAL UNDERTAKING ON, 814 (FAO/UNEP); Cs., 814 (FAO)

PLANT GENETIC RESOURCES, INTERNATIONAL BOARD FOR (FAO/UNDP), 814; FAO/UNEP, 1290

PLANT PROTECTION, REGIONAL CENTRE FOR TRAINING IN (Yaoundé), 802

plants: genetic resources, 814; & photosynthesis, 814; protection, 802; publications, 814; weed control, 1290 (FAO)

Poland: UN Information Centre, **381**, 385, 386 (GA/Information Ct./S-G); & transborder data flows, TNCs Centre report, 621

Police Association, International, *see* International Police Association

POLITICAL AFFAIRS, TRUSTEESHIP AND DECOLONIZATION, DEPARTMENT OF (Secretariat): Under-S-G, 1423

POLITICAL AND GENERAL ASSEMBLY AFFAIRS, OFFICE OF THE UNDER-S-G FOR (Secretariat): officials, 1423

POLITICAL AND SECURITY COUNCIL AFFAIRS, DEPARTMENT OF (Secretariat): officials, 1423

POLITICAL QUESTIONS, OFFICE FOR SPECIAL (Secretariat): Co-ordinator, 1423

pollutants, 801-5; long-range transport of, monitoring, 804 (ECE); WMO activities, 1350

POLLUTANTS BETWEEN THE ATMOSPHERE AND THE OCEANS, INTERCHANGE OF, 1352 (WMO Working Group)

pollution control: assessment, WHO guidelines, 774, 801 (University of London); *see also under* air pollution; marine pollution; ships; water pollution

poppy: cultivation, 1026, 1027; *see also* opiates; opium

popular participation, *see under* social development

population, 639-40 (ECA), 650 (ESCAP), 663-64 (ECLAC), 668 (ESCWA), 760-72 (UNFPA), 1297 (UNESCO), 1309-10, *(table)*, 1311 (World Bank loans), 1325-26 *(table)*, 1326 (IDA credits)
  data collection, expenditure, 763, 764 *(table)*; evaluation, 766
  & development, 769, **770** (ESC/Population Cs.); evaluation, 766; planning, UNFPA expert mtg., 763
  education/communication, 763, 764 *(table)*
  & environment, 791 (UNEP Executive Director)
  publications, 772
  spec. programmes, 763, 764 *(table)*, 766
  technical co-operation, **770** (ESC); & DIESA/DTCD co-ordination, 760 (S-G), **770** (ESC)
  trends/policies, 769, **769-70** (ESC/Population Cs.); formulation/evaluation, 764 *(table)*; programme evaluations, 557
  world situation, 4 (S-G), 771 (ESC/S-G); changing structure, 761 (Population Cs.), 770, **770-71** (ESC/Population Cs./S-G)
  see also aging persons; demographic activities; family planning; fertility; migration; women and society; youth; *and regional entries*

POPULATION, INTERNATIONAL CF. ON *(1984)*: DIESA/DTCD Steering Ct. on, 761; follow-up, 760-62 (ACC, 761; ESC, **762**, 762; Population Cs., 760-61; S-G, 760; UNDP/UNFPA, 761)

POPULATION ACTIVITIES, UN FUND FOR, 762-69; accounts *(1984)*, 768 (Auditors Board/GA); allocations by executing agency/major function, 763, 764 *(tables)*; audited accounts *(1983)*, 768 (UNDP Cl.); budget *(1986-1987)*, 766-67 (ACABQ/UNDP/UNFPA); contributions, 767, 767-68 *(table)*; country/region/territory projects, 764-65 *(table)*, 765 (UNDP); Executive Director/Deputy, 1405; governing body (UNDP Cl.), 760; programme planning/evaluation, 766 (UNDP/ UNFPA Executive Director); staffing, 768-69 (ACABQ/UNDP Cl.); strengthening (UNDP/Steering Ct.); work programmes *(1986-1989)*, 766 (UNDP/ UNFPA Executive Director)

POPULATION AND HOUSING CENSUS PROGRAMME, WORLD: *1980* census, implementation, 1034 (Statistical Cs.); *1990* census, 1034, **1034** (ESC/Statistical Cs.)

POPULATION AND THE URBAN FUTURE, *1986* CF. ON (UNCHS/UNFPA), 826

POPULATION AWARD, UN, 771-72; Ct. for, 771, 1396 (Chairman/members); recipient, 771; Trust Fund, 771-72

POPULATION COMMISSION (ESC): 760, 769; agenda/documentation, 769 (ESC/Population Cs.); members/officers, 1413; work programme, 769, **769-70** (ESC/Population Cs.)

POPULATION CONFERENCE, WORLD, *(1974)* ACTION PLAN: implementation, 772 (Population Cs.)

POPULATION INFORMATION NETWORK, 638 (ECA), 769, **770** (ESC/Population Cs.)

POPULATION STUDIES, REGIONAL INSTITUTE FOR, 638, 639

ports, 587 (UNCTAD), 647 (ESCAP)

Portugal: NSGT information to UN, 1082-83; Portuguese as ECA official language, **640-41**, 641 (ESC); *see also* East Timor

postage stamps (UN), *see* Africa, critical economic situation; Africa, critical situation in; United Nations Postal Administration

Postal Service, Multilingual Vocabulary of the International: 5th edition, 1342

postal services, 1342-44 (UPU); & TCDC, 1343; *see also* Universal Postal Union

PREFERENCES, SPEC. CT. ON (TDB), 558; members/officers, 1404

PREFERENTIAL TRADE AREA FOR EASTERN AND SOUTHERN AFRICA: UNIDO study, 608

premises (UN), 1262-63
  Addis Ababa (ECA), 1262 (ACABQ/S-G)
  Bangkok (ESCAP), proposed expansion, 1262 (S-G)
  & communications interconnection, proposed, 1264 (Advisory Ct. for the Co-ordination of Information Systems)
  headquarters: catering, 1262 (ACABQ/GA/S-G); telephone system, 1262, 1266 (ACABQ/GA/S-G)
  Nairobi, common services (UNCHS/ UNEP), 1263 (ACABQ/GA/S-G); construction, 1262-63 (ACABQ/GA/S-G)
  see also United Nations: Vienna International Centre

PRICE STATISTICS PROGRAMME, INTERNATIONAL: Phase V, International Comparison Project, 1032 (ACC/Statistical Cs.)

primary health care: promotion, 1302 (UNICEF/WHO Ct.); *see also* children; diseases; health; nutrition; *and under* drugs

prisoners:
  alternatives to prison/social resettlement, 739 (7th UN Crime Congress)
  treatment: conduct of law enforcement officials, 739 (7th UN Congress), 742 (GA), 862-64 (GA, **863-64**; S-G, 862-63; Working Group, 863); Standard Minimum Rules for treatment of *(1955)*: implementation, 739 (7th UN Congress)
  see also detention; summary executions; torture and other cruel treatment; women; youth; *and under* territories occupied by Israel

PRISONERS, MODEL AGREEMENT ON THE TRANSFER OF FOREIGN, 757 (GA/7th UN Congress)

prisoners of war, *see under* Geneva Conventions

privileges and immunities, 1244-45, **1245** (ACC/GA), 1245 *(list)*; study, 1189

PRIVILEGES AND IMMUNITIES OF THE UNITED NATIONS, CONVENTION ON, 1180

Programme and Co-ordination, Ct. for, *see* Co-ordination, Ct. for Programme and

programmes (UN), 1224-32
  budget *(1986-1987)*, proposed, 1226-27 (CPC, 1226-27; ESC/GA, 1227); cross-organizational programme analysis, 1227-28 (CPC)

planning, 1224-26 (CPC, 1224-25; ESC, 1225; GA, **1225-26**, 1226) & specialized agencies' administrative/budgetary co-ordination, 1230-32 (ACABQ, 1230; GA, **1230-31**) & UN financial rules, 1226 (GA/S-G) *see also* co-ordination in the UN system; Joint Inspection Unit

prostitution, 871 (Human Rights Cs.); prevention/rehabilitation, 649 (ESCAP); *see also* slavery/slavery-like practices; *and under* women

PROSTITUTION OF OTHERS, *1949* CONVENTION FOR THE SUPPRESSION OF THE TRAFFIC IN PERSONS AND OF THE EXPLOITATION OF THE, 871, 958 (Human Rights Cs./Working Group)

protectionism, *see under* international trade

psychotropic substances, 1013 (INCB), 1022 (Operational Heads of National Narcotics Law Enforcement Agencies, Far East Region), 1028, 1029, **1029** (ESC/INCB/Narcotic Drugs Cs.)

PSYCHOTROPIC SUBSTANCES, *1971* CONVENTION ON, 1013 (INCB), 1029; accession (China), 1028; illicit traffic, **1023** (ESC); ratifications, **1025** (GA)

public accounting, *see* accounts (UN)

public administration and finance, 431-32 (ESC, **431-32**); DTCD/UNDP projects, 431, 486; Expert Mtg., 431 (S-G); *see also* taxation

PUBLIC ADMINISTRATION AND FINANCE, 7TH MTG. OF EXPERTS ON THE UN PROGRAMME IN, 431, **431** (ESC/S-G)

publications policy (UN), 1208 (Publications Board/S-G); & copyright, revised guidelines, 1261

public information (UN system), 374-84 (GA, **375-83**, 383-84; Information Ct., 374-75); co-ordination in the UN system, 386-88 (ACC, 388; GA, **378**; Information Ct., 387; JUNIC, 386-87); *see also* Development Forum; news agencies; new world information and communication order; Radio and Visual Services Division; *and subject entries*

PUBLIC INFORMATION, DEPARTMENT OF (Secretariat), **376**, 384-85 (GA/Information Ct./S-G); data collection, evaluation, **381**, 384 (GA/Information Ct./S-G); fellowships/training, 380, 384; liaison services, **382** (GA); official languages, **380** (GA/Information Ct.); staff, geographical distribution, **381**, 384; Under-S-G, 384, 1424; *see also* Information Centres (UN); Radio and Visual Services Division; *Yearbook of the United Nations*

Puerto Rico, 1081 (Colonial Countries Ct.)

racial discrimination/racism, 835-42; global study *(1988)*, authorization, **838**; S-G study, 837; *see also* apartheid; minorities

RACIAL DISCRIMINATION, CT. ON THE ELIMINATION OF, 839-40, **840-41** (GA); co-operation with TC, 1089; members/officers, 1422

RACIAL DISCRIMINATION, INTERNATIONAL CONVENTION ON THE ELIMINATION OF ALL FORMS OF *(1965)*: accessions/

ratifications, 839, **839** (GA/S-G); implementation, 839-42 (CERD, 839-40; communications, 840; GA, **840-41**, 841-42); reporting obligations, 839 (CERD)

RACIAL DISCRIMINATION, INTERNATIONAL DAY FOR THE ELIMINATION OF: observance, 175 (*Apartheid* Ct.), 840 (communication)

RACIAL DISCRIMINATION, 2ND DECADE FOR ACTION TO COMBAT RACISM AND *(1983-1993)*: Action Programme, implementation, 835-39 (CERD, 836; ESC, 836, **836**; GA, **837-38**, 838; Human Rights Cs., 835-36; S-G, 835; Spec. Rapporteur, 836-37); seminar, **838** (GA), 838-39; S-G study, 837; Trust Fund for, contributions, **837** (GA)

radiation: dosimetry workshop, 1274 (IAEA); effects of, 388-89 (GA, **388-89**; UNSCEAR, 388); protection services, 1273 (IAEA); training/missions, 1273 (IAEA); symposium *(1984)*, proceedings, 1273 (IAEA/WHO)

RADIATION, UN SCIENTIFIC CT. ON THE EFFECTS OF ATOMIC, 388, **388** (GA); members/officers, 1407

RADIATION PROTECTION, BASIC SAFETY STANDARDS FOR (IAEA/ILO/WHO), 1273

radioactive waste management, 694 (IAEA DG), 1272 (IAEA); sea disposal, 1272 (IAEA); *see also* marine environment; oceans; *and under* Trust Territory of the Pacific Islands

RADIO AND VISUAL SERVICES DIVISION (DPI): restructuring, proposed, **382** (GA), 385 (ACABQ/S-G)

radio broadcasting, **379** (GA), 1345 (ITU); administrative cfs., 1345 (ITU); agreements, revisions, 1345; consultative cts., 1345 (ITU); frequency allocation, 1345-46 (ITU); regional organizations, 370 (UNESCO), **380**, 385 (GA/Information Ct.); short-wave networks, **381** (GA), 385; space services, ITU regulations, **107**

RADIO CONFERENCE, WORLD ADMINISTRATIVE, 1345 (ITU); *1979* Cf., implementation, 1345-46; criteria on orbit use, 104 (COPUOS)

RADIO CONSULTATIVE COMMITTEE, INTERNATIONAL, 1345 (ITU); *1986* plenary assembly, preparations, 1345

radiological weapons, 72, **72-73** (CD/GA); stockpiling, 72, **73-74** (CD/GA)

RAILWAY LINES, EUROPEAN AGREEMENT ON MAIN INTERNATIONAL: signature, 655

railways, 614 (UNIDO), 647 (ESCAP), 655 (ECE)

raw materials: UNIDO projects, 605; *see also* natural resources

RED CRESCENT SOCIETIES, 329; IYDP implementation, 776; UNICEF support, 282

Red Cross, International Ct. of the, *see* International Committee of the Red Cross

Red Cross Societies, League of, *see* League of Red Cross Societies

Red Sea: regional seas programme (UNEP), 816

refugees/displaced persons, 11 (S-G), 990-1011
assistance, UNHCR programmes, 994-96; development-oriented, 991, **991** (Executive Ct./GA); contributions, 992, 993 *(table)*; emergency food aid, 702,

991 (WFP); General/Spec. Programmes, expenditures, 994-95, 995-96 *(tables)*; UNCHS/UNHCR co-operation, 831

co-operation in the UN, 991, **992** (GA/UNHCR)

Handbook for Emergencies, 995

international co-operation to avert new flows of, 1011, **1011** (Expert Group/GA)

international instruments, accessions/ratifications, 1010-11 (GA)

legal principles, 1010

Nansen Medal, award, 990

& NGOs, 991, **992**

protection of, 1009-11 (UNHCR); anti-piracy programme, 1009; military attacks on camps, 1009; & *non-refoulement*, 1009, 1010 (GA); strengthening, 1010 (Executive Ct./GA); & women, **992**, 1010 (GA/UNHCR)

publications/films, 995, 1011

resettlement mechanisms, 991, 995 (Executive Ct.)

social conditions of, 736 (UNRISD)

see also human rights violations: mass exoduses; Palestine refugees; *and country names and regional entries*

REFUGEES, *AD HOC* CT. OF THE GA FOR THE ANNOUNCEMENT OF VOLUNTARY CONTRIBUTIONS TO THE *1986* PROGRAMME OF THE UN HIGH COMMISSIONER FOR, 992; mtg., 1394

REFUGEES, EXECUTIVE CT. OF THE PROGRAMME OF THE UN HIGH COMMISSIONER FOR, 990; Administrative and Financial Matters, Sub-Ct. on, 1399 (Chairman); International Protection, Sub-Ct. of the Whole on, 1399 (Chairman); members/officers, 1399

REFUGEES, GROUP OF GOVERNMENTAL EXPERTS ON INTERNATIONAL CO-OPERATION TO AVERT NEW FLOWS OF, 928 (GA), 1011

REFUGEES, OFFICE OF THE UN HIGH COMMISSIONER FOR, 991-96; accounts, voluntary funds *(1984)*, 993 (ACABQ/Auditors Board/Executive Ct./S-G); contributions, 992 (*Ad Hoc* Ct./Executive Ct.), 993 *(table)*; expenditures, General/Spec. Programmes, 994-95, 995-96 *(table)*; programme policy, **990-92** (Executive Ct./GA); South-East Asia operations, 1008-9 (JIU/S-G)

REFUGEES, UN HIGH COMMISSIONER FOR, 990, 993, **994** (GA); Deputy, 1414; report, **991-92** (GA)

Refugees in Africa, 2nd International Cf. on Assistance to, *see* Africa, 2nd International Cf. on Assistance to Refugees in

Refugees in the Near East, UN Relief and Works Agency for Palestine, *see* Palestine Refugees in the Near East, UN Relief and Works Agency for

regional commissions: co-operation among, 624-25 (ESC/S-G); executive secretaries, mtg., 624-25; & TNCs, joint units, 619-20; water resources, education/training, 679; & women, posts for, 1239, **1239-40** (GA/S-G); *see also* names of regional css.

regional seas programme (UNEP), 816-17 *(list)*; Trust Fund, 798

RELIEF OPERATIONS, FAO OFFICE FOR SPECIAL, 1292

religious freedom: 845-47 (communication, 845; GA, **846-47**; Human Rights Cs., 845; SCPDPM, 846); *1984* Seminar, 845-46, **846** (GA/Human Rights Cs.)

remote sensing: applications, 101-2 (UN Programme); centre, 712 (DTCD/ UNFSSTD); geological, 1296 (UNESCO); legal principles (draft), 104, **206** (COPUOS/GA/Working Group); scientific/technical aspects, 103, **106** (COPUOS/GA)

Republic of Korea: audio-visual training, contribution for, 370; development finance, 1310 (World Bank); & energy development, 689 (UNCTAD); family planning, 1303 (WHO); small-scale enterprises, 1311 (World Bank); urban development, 1312 (World Bank); water supply/sewerage, 1312 (World Bank); *see also* Korean question

respiratory infections, 1304 (WHO)

restrictive business practices, *see under* international trade

RESTRICTIVE BUSINESS PRACTICES, INTERGOVERNMENTAL GROUP OF EXPERTS ON (UNCTAD), 563

RESTRICTIVE BUSINESS PRACTICES, SET OF MULTILATERALLY AGREED EQUITABLE PRINCIPLES AND RULES FOR THE CONTROL OF *(1980)*: UN review Cf., 563-65 (GA, 565, **565**; Intergovernmental Group, 563)

RICE COMMISSION, INTERNATIONAL, 1289 (FAO)

rice production, 1289; research projects, 773

rights of the child, *see* child, rights of

right to development, *see* development, right to

right to education, *see under* education

right to food, *see under* food

rinderpest: *1986* campaign, preparations, 1291 (FAO)

rivers: transport of carbons/minerals through, 801 (Scientific Ct./UNEP); Zambezi Action Plan, management of, 814 (inter-agency mtg.), 815; *see also* water problems; water resources

road transport/roads, 646 (ESCAP), 655 (ECE); *see also* motor vehicles

robots, industrial, *see* engineering industries

rubber, 569 (UNCTAD)

RUBBER AGREEMENT, INTERNATIONAL NATURAL *(1979)*: UN Cf. on, 569

RUBBER ORGANIZATION, INTERNATIONAL NATURAL, 569

rules of origin, *see under* generalized system of trade preferences

RURAL COMMUNICATION, INTERNATIONAL PROGRAMME FOR THE DEVELOPMENT OF COMMUNICATION—UNESCO PRIZE FOR: award, 1298

rural development, 432-33 (ACC, 432-33; GA/SNPA/UNCTAD, 433), 486 (DTCD); education, 1295 (UNESCO); energy systems, 687 (UNU); & FAO, 432, 1288-89; IDA credits, 1324-25 *(table)*, 1325; social aspects, 730-31 (ESC/S-G); UNCDF projects, 493; World Bank loans, 1309-10 *(table)*, 1310; *see also*

agricultural development; *and entries under* women

RURAL DEVELOPMENT, TASK FORCE ON (ACC), 432-33 (CCSQ(PROG))

RURAL DEVELOPMENT, WORLD CF. ON AGRARIAN REFORM AND *(1979)*: Action Programme/Declaration, follow-up, 1288

Rwanda: gold exploration, 678 (UNRFNRE); refugees in, 1005 (UNHCR)

Sahel: drought, 191, 537; *see also* Sudano-Sahelian region

SAHEL, INSTITUT DU, 810 (UNDP/UNSO)

SAHEL, PERMANENT INTER-STATE CT. ON DROUGHT CONTROL IN THE, **807** (GA), 810 (UNDP/UNSO); members, 537, 810

St. Helena, **1149-50** (GA); & Ascensión military facilities, 1150; information to UN, 1082

Saint Lucia: natural resources exploration, 669, 670

sanitation: UNCHS programme, 828; UNICEF projects, 967, 972-73; *see also* Drinking Water Supply and Sanitation Decade, International; water supply

San Marino: consultative status in ECE, 1414

Sao Tome and Principe: spec. economic assistance, 524 (S-G/UN system)

satellites: direct broadcasting by, 1360 (UNESCO/WIPO); spacing of, study, 103 (COPUOS); *see also* communications satellites; geostationary orbit; remote sensing

Saudi Arabia: balance-of-payments position, 1331 (IMF); co-operation with IFC, 1317; petrochemical products, tariffs, 666

savings: co-operation programme, 579 (DIESA); mobilization symposium, 579 (ESC)

schistosomiasis, 1273 (IAEA)

science, *see* life sciences; natural sciences; physical sciences; social sciences; *and under* science and technology *and* technological *and* technology entries

science and technology, 638 (ECA), 649 (ESCAP), 659 (ECE), 663 (ECLA), 667 (ESCWA), 707-20, 1298 (UNESCO)
  Advance Technology Alert System, 716 (Centre/Intergovernmental Ct.); *ATAS Bulletin*, 716
  co-ordination in UN the system, 716-17 (ACC Task Force/Intergovernmental Ct.)
  financing, 711-14; *see also* Science and Technology for Development, UN Financing System for
  & human rights, 932, **932-33** (GA/Human Rights Cs./S-G); *see also under* human rights
  information network, 709-11 (ACC, 709; Advisory Ct., 710; GA, 711, **715**; Intergovernmental Ct., 710-11; S-G, 709-10); 709 (UNU), 716 (Centre), 1299 (UNESCO)
  institutional arrangements, 714-15; *see also names of bodies*
  national focal points, registry update, 714 (Centre/S-G), 715 (Centre)
  operational activities, 711-12 (UNFSSTD)
  publications, 711, 716
  resources mobilization, 713, 715 (Ad-

visory Ct./specialists' panel), 716 (Centre)
  Vienna Programme of Action, *1979*: implementation, mid-term review, 707-9 (ACC Task Force, 716; Advisory Ct., 709, 715; GA, 709, **715**; Intergovernmental Ct., 709; S-G, 708-9)
  see also brain drain; technology transfer

SCIENCE AND TECHNOLOGY FOR DEVELOPMENT, ACC TASK FORCE, 716-17

SCIENCE AND TECHNOLOGY FOR DEVELOPMENT, ADVISORY CT. ON, 715; members, 1397

SCIENCE AND TECHNOLOGY FOR DEVELOPMENT, CENTRE FOR, 716 (Intergovernmental Ct./S-G); Executive Director, 1423; publications, 716

SCIENCE AND TECHNOLOGY FOR DEVELOPMENT, INTERGOVERNMENTAL CT. ON, 707; work methods, 714-15 (ESC, 715; GA, **715**), 1418; members/officers, 1397

SCIENCE AND TECHNOLOGY FOR DEVELOPMENT, UN FINANCING SYSTEM FOR, 711-14 (DIEC DG/UNDP); contributions/expenditures, 713, 713-14 *(tables)*; Executive Board, 1405; financial situation, long-term arrangements, 712-13 (GA, 712, **713**); S-G/working group, 712); projects, 711-12

SCIENCES, THIRD WORLD ACADEMY OF: cf. on co-operation in science, 1274

SCIENTIFIC ADVISORY COMMITTEE, UN, members, 1407

SCIENTIFIC AND TECHNOLOGICAL INFORMATION, INTERGOVERNMENTAL PROGRAMME FOR CO-OPERATION IN THE FIELD OF (UNESCO), 710 (S-G)

SCIENTIFIC KNOWLEDGE, COMMUNICATION CENTRE OF (UNU), 710

SCIENTIFIC UNIONS, INTERNATIONAL CL. FOR: & climate, joint mtg. with UNEP/WMO, 805; & space activities, environmental effects, 103 (Ct. on Space Research)

sea: peaceful uses of, study, 30-31 (Expert Group); salvage & assistance, convention on, 110; *see also* law of the sea; oceans; regional seas programme

SEA, INTERNATIONAL CONVENTION FOR THE SAFETY OF LIFE AT *(1974)*: 110

sea, law of the, *see* law of the sea

Sea, UN Convention on the Law of the, *see* Law of the Sea, UN Convention on the

sea-bed: artistic treasures, recovery, 115; claims, negotiations, 111 (Preparatory Cs.); mining, 110-11 (Preparatory Cs.), draft regulations for, 112, land-based producers, 112 (Preparatory Cs.); pioneer investors: applications, registration, 111 (communications); *see also under* arms race

SEA-BED AND THE OCEAN FLOOR AND IN THE SUBSOIL THEREOF, TREATY ON THE PROHIBITION OF THE EMPLACEMENT OF NUCLEAR WEAPONS AND OTHER WEAPONS OF MASS DESTRUCTION ON THE *(1971)*: parties to, 32, 100; proposed broadening, 32, **32** (CD/GA)

SEA-BED AUTHORITY, INTERNATIONAL, 110, 111 (Preparatory Cs.); Enterprise (operational arm), 112 (Spec. Cs. 2); organizational matters, Geneva mtg., 111 (Preparatory Cs.)

SEA-BED AUTHORITY, PREPARATORY CS. FOR THE INTERNATIONAL: Cts., 1423; members/officers, 1422-23; Spec. Css., 1423

Second World War, *see* World War II

SECRETARIAT (UN), 9 (S-G); composition/principal members, 1423-25; *see also* administrative and management questions; pensions (UN system); staff (UN/UN system); *and names of departments and offices (under key word)*

SECRETARY-GENERAL (UN): annual report, 3-11; Executive Office, 1423; good offices missions, 398; *see also under* multilateral treaties

SECURITY, GROUP OF GOVERNMENTAL EXPERTS TO CARRY OUT A COMPREHENSIVE STUDY OF CONCEPTS OF, 28, **28** (GA)

SECURITY COUNCIL, 5-6 (S-G), 392-94
ad hoc bodies, 1410
agenda, 393-94 (GA/S-G), 407 *(list)*
Cts., 1410
mtgs., 392-93; away from headquarters, Ct. on, 1410
members, 394, 1409-10
membership, proposed increase/representation, deferred, 394 (GA)
peace/security issues: effectiveness in, **119**, 393 (GA/S-G)
peace-keeping operations/special missions, 1410
Presidents, 513
publication, 394
reports: *1983-1984*, 394 (GA); *1984-1985*, 394 (GA)

Security Council, Repertoire of the Practice of the: updating, 1179

SECURITY COUNCIL AFFAIRS, DEPARTMENT OF POLITICAL AND (Secretariat): Under-S-G/Assistant, 1423

seeds: production, 1290 (FAO)

SEISMIC EVENTS, *AD HOC* GROUP OF EXPERTS TO CONSIDER INTERNATIONAL CO-OPERATIVE MEASURES TO DETECT AND IDENTIFY, 47; *see also* nuclear-weapon tests: verification measures

seismic monitoring: 47, **52** (*Ad Hoc* Group/GA); workshop (Oslo), 47

self-determination of peoples, **119** (GA), 127 (Human Rights Cs.), **855-58**, 858-59 (GA); universal realization of the right to, 854-55, **855** (GA/S-G); *see also* Afghanistan; colonial countries; Kampuchea; Namibia; Non-Self-Governing Territories; Palestinians; South Africa; Western Sahara

Senegal: refugees in, 1005

sexually transmitted diseases, 1304 (WHO)

Seychelles: housing development, 826 (UNCHS); party to NPT, 1271

shelter, *see under* Homeless, International Year of Shelter for the; housing

shipping, 586-87, 647 (ESCAP); international legislation, 587 (UNCTAD Shipping Division/Working Group); technical assistance/training, 587-88 (UNCTAD/UNDP); *see also* land-locked developing countries: transit/transport issues; liner

conferences; maritime transport; multimodal transport; ports

SHIPPING, AND TRANSPORT AND COMMUNICATIONS, CT. ON (ESCAP), 646-47; & Ports & Inland Waterways Wing, 647

SHIPPING, CT. ON (TDB): members, 1403

SHIPPING LEGISLATION, WORKING GROUP ON INTERNATIONAL (TDB), 587; members/officers, 1403

SHIPS, INTERNATIONAL CONVENTION FOR PREVENTION OF POLLUTION FROM *(1973)*: amendments, 1356 (IMO); *1978* Protocol *(MARPOL 73/78)*, 1356 (IMO)

SHIPS, UN CF. ON CONDITIONS FOR REGISTRATION OF, 110, 586-87 (GA, **586**; S-G, 586); Cts., 1409 (members); draft composite text, 586-87 (GA, **586-87**, 587); officers/participants, 1409

Sierra Leone: economic assistance, 524-25 (GA, 524, **525**; S-G, 524); industrial planning project, 607 (UNIDO)

SILK, REGIONAL CONSULTATIVE GROUP ON (ESCAP): mtg., 646

silver: exploration, 669, 670 (UNRFNRE)

Singapore: withdrawal from UNESCO, 1295

slavery/slavery-like practices, 871-72 (Human Rights Cs./Working Group, 871); conventions, 871; emancipation from, 150th anniversary (British Empire), 391, 871 (GA); *see also* Mauritania; prostitution; *and under* children

SLAVERY, WORKING GROUP ON (SCPDPM), 871; members, 1412

SLAVERY IN ALL ITS FORMS, WORLD DAY FOR THE ABOLITION OF, proposed, 871

slums/squatter settlements: rehabilitation, 826 (UNCHS); UNICEF programmes, 968

small-scale industry: IDA credits, 1324-25 *(table)*, 1326; World Bank loans, 1309-10 *(table)*, 1311

social defence, *see entries under* crime

SOCIAL DEFENCE, UN TRUST FUND FOR, 757

SOCIAL DEFENCE RESEARCH INSTITUTE, UN, 757

social development, 638 (ECA), 649-50 (ESCAP), 663 (ECLAC), 667-68 (ESCWA), 721-38
& aging persons, 984-85 (CSDHA/Social Development Cs.)
co-operatives, role in, 732-33, **733** (ESC/S-G)
co-ordination in UN, 722 (S-G)
economic/social aspects, 725, **725-26** (ESC); Declaration *(1969)*, implementation, 727-28, 728 (Cs./ECA/GA); UN role in, **726-27**, 727 (GA)
evaluation of UN activities, 731, **733** (CPC/ESC)
& family, impact on, 729, **730** (GA/S-G)
national experience in achieving, 728-29 (ESC, **728-29**, 504; GA, **729**, 729; S-G, 728)
& popular participation, 736 (UNRISD); *see also under* human rights
publications, 738
research, 736 (UNRISD)
world situation, *1985 Report*, 721-25 (ESC, **722-23**, 498; GA, **723-25**, 500; S-G, 722)

SOCIAL DEVELOPMENT, CS. FOR (ESC), 721, 736-38; agenda/documentation, 737

(ESC); cf. documents, distribution, 737, **737** (ESC); members/officers, 1411; report, 737 (ESC); trust funds, income/expenditures, 737; work programmes, **736-37** (ESC), 737 (GA)

SOCIAL DEVELOPMENT, INTERNATIONAL VOLUNTEER DAY FOR ECONOMIC AND: observance, 727 (GA)

SOCIAL DEVELOPMENT, UN RESEARCH INSTITUTE FOR, 736 (Social Development Cs.); Board of Directors/Chairman, 1419-20; Director, 1420; finances, 736

SOCIAL DEVELOPMENT AND HUMANITARIAN AFFAIRS, CENTRE FOR (DIESA); & Action Plan on Aging, 985 (GA/S-G)

social sciences, 1297 (UNESCO); publications/seminars/studies, 1299; technical assistance, 1297 *(tables)*

social security: ILO assistance, 1278, 1280 *(table)*; ILO seminar, 461

social statistics, 1033; *see also under* housing; migration; population; *subject entries*

social welfare: co-operatives, 732-33, **733** (ESC/S-G); income distribution, 733 (S-G/Social Development Cs.); integration policies, 732 (S-G/Social Development Cs.); policies/programmes, 649 (ESCAP), 731-36; regional/interregional, 731-32 (ESC, **731-32**, 732; S-G, 731); *see also* employment; migrant workers

soil management, 811-12 (UNEP); training/workshops, 811 (UNEP); *see also* desertification; land management

SOILS POLICY, WORLD *(1982)*: Action Plan, implementation, 811-12 (UNEP Cl.)

solar energy, 648 (ESCAP), 687 (DTCD)

SOLAR ENERGY TECHNOLOGY, ABSTRACTS OF SELECTED, 687

Solomon Islands: admission to FAO, 1287, to ICAO, 1338, to WMO, 1350

Somalia: refugee assistance, 1002, **1002-3** (GA/WFP); refugees in, 1002; UNDP/UNEP aid, 810 *passim*; *see also* East Africa: drought-stricken areas; Ethiopia

South Africa, African National Congress of, *see* African National Congress of South Africa

SOUTH AFRICA, FREEDOM CHARTER OF: 30th anniversary observance, 176

SOUTH AFRICA, INTERNATIONAL DAY OF SOLIDARITY WITH THE STRUGGLING PEOPLE OF: observance, 176

South Africa, relations with:
arms embargo, **61** (GA), 144-45 (*Apartheid*/Colonial Countries Cts., 144; communication, 144; GA, **130**, **132**, 145; Namibia Cl./Vienna Declaration, 144; S-G, 144-45)
boycotts: academic/consular/cultural/sports, **132** (GA), 137, 138 (*Apartheid* Ct.)
economic relations, 145-46 (*Apartheid* Ct./Human Rights Cs., 145; communication, 146; GA, **130**, **132**, 146)
general aspects, 135-38 (*Apartheid* Ct., 135-36; Colonial Countries Ct./Human Rights Cs., 136; communications, 137-38; ESC, 137; GA, **130**, **132**, 136-37; Namibia Cl./Vienna Declaration, 136)
& IAEA: safeguards agreements, 1271

South Africa, relations with *(cont.)*
& IMF/World Bank, 150-51 (Colonial Countries Ct., 150-51; Human Rights Cs./Namibia Cl./Vienna Declaration, 150; ESC, 151; GA, **131**, 151, **1071**)
investments/loans, 146-47 (*Apartheid* Ct., 146-47; GA, **130**, **132**, 147, **1074-75**; Human Rights Cs./SC, 147)
& Israel, 151-52 (*Apartheid* Ct., 151-52; GA, **131**, **151-52**, 152), **266** (SC); Declaration on Alliance between, 152
military/nuclear collaboration, 62 (GA), 141-44 (*Apartheid* Ct., 141-42; Colonial Countries Ct./Human Rights Cs., 143; communications, 143; GA, **130**, **132**, 143, **858**; Human Rights Cs., 904; Namibia Cl./Vienna Declaration, 142-43; SC, 143; S-G, 142)
& neighbouring States, 178-80 (*Apartheid* Ct., 178-79; Colonial Countries Ct./Human Rights Cs., 179; communications, 179-80; ESC, 180; GA, **130**, **132**, 180, **1077**; Namibia Cl., 179); *see also country names*
nuclear capability, 59-62 (communications/DC Working Group II/S-G, 59; GA, **60**, **60-61**, 61-62), **119**; in nuclear materials/equipment, **1074** (GA); *see also under* Israel
oil embargo, 146 (Colonial Countries Ct./Human Rights Cs., 146; GA, **130**, **132**, 146); Cf. on, 146 (Maritime Trade Unions)
sanctions, 138-41 (*Apartheid* Ct., 138-39; Colonial Countries Ct., 139-40; GA, **130**, **132**, 141; Human Rights Cs., 140; Namibia Cl./Vienna Declaration, 139; SC, 140); *1986* World Cf. on, 137 (OAU), **140-41** (GA)
& TNCs, 147-50 (ESC, **148-49**, 149; GA, **130**, 150; Human Rights Cs., 148; TNCs Cs., 147-48); list, review/update, 904-5 (Human Rights Cs./SCPDPM/ Spec. Rapporteur); & non-collaboration by, 616 (TNCs Cs.); number operating in, 150; public hearings, preparations, 149-50 (*Ad Hoc* Ct./TNCs Centre, 149-50; ESC, 150; GA, **130**, 150; S-G, 150)
see also apartheid
SOUTH AFRICA, SECURITY CL. CT. CONCERNING THE QUESTION OF: members, 1410
South Africa, situation in, 152-65
bantustans, 152, 154, 159 (*Apartheid* Ct.), 161 (GA), **857**, 862 (GA/Human Rights Cs.)
constitution, 137 (communication), **132**, 161 (GA), **857-58**, 862 (GA/Human Rights Cs.)
emergency, state of, 152-61 (*Apartheid* Ct., 152-54; CERD, 159; communications, 159-60; GA, **160-61**, 161, **858**; Human Rights Cs., 154; SC, 154-55, **155**, 155-56, 156-57, **158**, 158-59)
foreign support, 904-5 (Human Rights Cs./S-G/Spec. Rapporteur)
human rights violations, 899-901 (*Ad Hoc* Working Group, 899-900; ESC, **900-1**, 901)
national liberation movements, assistance to, 169-71 (*Apartheid*/Colonial Countries Cts./Human Rights

Cs., 170; ESC, 170; GA, **132**, **161**, 170-71; UNDP/UNIDO, 170)
political prisoners/detainees, 161-63 (*Apartheid* Ct., 161-62; Colonial Countries Ct., 162-63; communications, 159, 162, 163; GA, **160**, 161, **173**, **858**; Human Rights Cs., 163, 862; Namibia Cl./Vienna Declaration, 162; SC, **158**, 163); Day of Solidarity with, 163 (communication), 176
Sharpeville massacre, 25th anniversary observance, 156, 176
Soweto, *1976* uprising, 137 (communication)
& trade union rights, 154 (ESC/Human Rights Cs.), 905-6 (*Ad Hoc* Working Group, 859; ESC, **905-6**)
see also apartheid; colonial countries; Namibia; national liberation movements; non-governmental organizations; nuclear safeguards; self-determination of peoples; *and regional and subject entries*
SOUTH AFRICA, UN TRUST FUND FOR, 171-72 (GA, **171-72**; S-G, 171); contributions, 171 *(table)*; Trustees Ct., members/officers, 1396
SOUTH AFRICA AND ISRAEL, INTERNATIONAL CF. ON THE ALLIANCE BETWEEN *(1983)*: Declaration, 152
SOUTH AFRICA AND NAMIBIA, AD HOC CT. ON THE PREPARATIONS FOR THE PUBLIC HEARINGS ON THE ACTIVITIES OF TNCS IN, 149; Chairman/members, 1417; expert Panel, appointment, 149, 150 (GA); & report of TNCs Cs., 1055 (ESC)
SOUTH AFRICA AND NAMIBIA, INTERNATIONAL DAY OF SOLIDARITY WITH THE STRUGGLE OF WOMEN IN: observance, 176
SOUTH AFRICAN POLITICAL PRISONERS, INTERNATIONAL DAY OF SOLIDARITY WITH, 163 (communication); observance, 176
South America: endangered animal species in, 813 (IUCN/UNEP)
South Asia: proposed regional seas programme, 817; refugee assistance, 996 *(table)*; UNICEF programmes, 965 *(table)*; World Bank loans, 1309 *(table)*; *see also* nuclear-weapon-free zones; *and country names and regional entries*
South-East Asia, 229-32
international security in, 229-31 (communications, 229-30; GA, 230-31); *see also* Viet Nam: dispute with China; Lao People's Democratic Republic: dispute with Thailand
refugee assistance, 996 *(table)*, 1007 (S-G/UNHCR), 1008-9 (JIU); *see also under* Viet Nam
zone of peace (proposed), 226, **227** (GA/S-G)
see also Indo-China; Kampuchea situation; Mekong Basin, Interim Ct. for . . . Lower; *and country names*
SOUTH-EAST ASIA, OFFICE OF THE SPEC. REPRESENTATIVE OF THE S-G FOR HUMANITARIAN AFFAIRS IN: Under-S-G, 1424
South-East Asian Nations, Association of, *see* Association of South-East Asian Nations

South-East Pacific: regional seas programme (UNEP), 816
southern Africa, 202 (S-G), 1079 (Colonial Countries Ct.); & disabled, leadership development, 776; IDA credits, 1324 *(table)*; student refugees in, 1005-6, **1006-7** (GA); *see also* Angola; *apartheid*; Botswana; Lesotho; Mozambique; Namibia question; self-determination of peoples; South Africa, relations with: & neighbouring States
SOUTHERN AFRICA, AD HOC WORKING GROUP OF EXPERTS ON: emergency mtgs. (Geneva), 900; human rights progress report, 898-900 (ESC, **899-900**, 900; Human Rights Cs., 899)
SOUTHERN AFRICA, UN EDUCATIONAL AND TRAINING PROGRAMME FOR, 200-1 (GA, **201**; S-G, 200-1); Advisory Ct., members/officers, 1395; assistance to Namibia, **1129**, 1131 (GA/S-G); contributions, 200 (S-G), 201 *(table)*
SOUTHERN AFRICAN DEVELOPMENT CO-ORDINATION CONFERENCE, 179 (Colonial Countries Ct.), **132**, 180 (GA); co-operation with UN, 643, **644** (GA/S-G), 644 (mtgs./members); desertification/drought assistance, 808 (UNEP Cl.); energy assistance, 690 (DTCD); UNIDO study, 608
South Pacific: conservation, Cf. on., 813; energy resources, 687 (UNDP); Nuclear-Free-Zone Treaty/Protocols, 58 (signatures, 58); regional seas programme, 816; telecommunications, 1347 (ITU/UNDP)
SOUTH PACIFIC COMMISSION: Subregional Mtg. on Women, 649
SOUTH PACIFIC FORUM: & economic co-operation, 413; & island developing countries, 530, 532; & Micronesia, 1085; & New Caledonia, 1081; nuclear-weapon-free zone, 58; & radioactive wastes/nuclear tests, 48, 694
SOUTH PACIFIC REGIONAL ENVIRONMENT PROGRAMME: draft convention on radioactive dumping, 694
SOUTH WEST AFRICA PEOPLE'S ORGANIZATION: international assistance, 170 (Colonial Countries Ct./UNDP), **1070** (GA), 1127 (Namibia Fund), 1127, **1129** (GA/Namibia Cl.); missions, 1091, 1093 (Namibia Cl.); New York office, **1114** (GA), 1119; participation in SC, 1091, 1097; as representative of Namibia, **857**, **1078**, **1106**, **1107** (GA); transit camps/settlements, *Apartheid* Ct. visit, 175; & UN 40th anniversary, 129, 403; *see also* Namibia
South-West Asia: refugee expenditures, 996 *(table)*, 1009 (UNHCR)
space, *see* outer space *and following entries*
Space Agency, European, *see* European Space Agency
SPACE APPLICATIONS PROGRAMME (UN), 101-3 (COPUOS 202; GA, **107**; S-G/UN Expert, 102); budget/contributions, 102; co-ordination, 102-3 (ACC, 102-3; COPUOS, 102; GA, **106**); *1986* proposals, 102, **107** (COPUOS/GA); seminars/training, 101-2; *see also* geostationary orbit; remote sensing

SPACE COMMUNICATIONS, INTERNATIONAL SYSTEM AND ORGANIZATION OF (INTERSPUTNIK): COPUOS observer status, 101, **107** (COPUOS/GA)

space objects: launchings, notifications of, 108; & nuclear power sources, legal aspects, 104-5, **106** (COPUOS/GA/Working Group); Treaty, 108

SPACE RESEARCH, CT. ON, 103

space transportation, 101, **107** (COPUOS/GA)

Spain: accession to EC, 1146; & IAEA safeguards agreement, 1271; information to UN, 1083; *see also* Gibraltar; Western Sahara

special committee, *see under key word(s) of title*

special drawing rights, *see under* International Monetary Fund

special economic, humanitarian and disaster relief assistance: general aspects, 497, **497** (GA/S-G); *see also country names*; disaster relief; emergency relief/assistance

SPECIAL FUND, UN (development assistance/emergency relief): Board of Governors, 1407, 1420

Special Fund for Land-locked Developing Countries (UN), *see* Land-locked Developing Countries, UN Special Fund for

specialized agencies, 7 (S-G); administrative/budgetary co-ordination, 1230, **1230-31** (ACABQ/GA); & NGOs, consultative status with, 1051-54 *(list)*; *see also* colonial countries; Namibia; privileges and immunities

SPECIAL POLITICAL AFFAIRS, OFFICE OF THE UNDER-SECRETARIES-GENERAL FOR (Secretariat), 1423; Middle East visits of Under-S-G, 306, 309

SPECIAL POLITICAL QUESTIONS, OFFICE FOR (Secretariat): officials, 1423

sports, *see under apartheid*; South Africa

Sri Lanka: drug traffic, 1028

staff (UN/UN system), 1234-53

allowances, 1247 (ICSC/GA); & mandatory health insurance, 1247 (GA)

arrests/detentions, 1244-45; *see also* privileges and immunities

career development, 1240-41 (ICSC/S-G); competitive examinations, 1240-41 (ACABQ/FICSA/GA/ICSC/S-G)

composition, 1234-36 (GA, **1235-36**, 1236; ICSC, 1234-35; JIU, 1235; S-G, 1234)

field personnel, 1243 (CCISUA/GA/ICSC)

job classification, 1241-42 (GA, **1241**, 1241-42; ICSC, 1242; S-G, 1241)

recruitment, 1233 (S-G); & disabled, 1235; medium-term plan, 1235 (JIU/Office of Personnel Services/S-G)

Regulations, amendments, 1244, **1244** (GA/S-G)

representation, 1242-43 (JIU, 1242-43; CCISUA/FICSA/S-G, 1243)

rules, 1244 (GA/S-G)

salaries, 1245-47 (GA/ICSC/S-G, 1245-46; CCISUA/FICSA, 1246; JIU, 1246-47)

total, 1425

travel: accommodations, 1243-45, **1245** (ACABQ/GA/S-G); restrictions, 1244, 1180 (Host Country Ct.)

women, status of, 1237-40 (GA, **1238-39**, 1239; CCISUA/FICSA/ICSC, 1238; S-G, 1237-38); appointment of Co-ordinator, 1238, **1239** (GA/S-G); in regional css., 1239, **1239-40** (GA/S-G)

see also Administrative Tribunal, UN; International Civil Service Commission; pensions (UN system); privileges and immunities

STAFF UNIONS AND ASSOCIATIONS OF THE UN SYSTEM, CO-ORDINATING CT. FOR INDEPENDENT, 1233

States: good-neighbourliness between, 1161-62 (GA, **1161**, 1161; Sub-Ct., 1161); & international law, 1175-76; jurisdictional immunity, draft articles, 1175 (ILC/Spec. Rapporteur); liability, draft articles, 1175-76 (ILC/Spec. Rapporteur); & non-interference in internal affairs, 936 (GA); relations between and international organizations, 1189 (GA/ILC/Spec. Rapporteur); responsibility, 1176 (ILC/Spec. Rapporteur); *see also* disputes, peaceful settlement of; treaties/agreements

STATES, DECLARATION ON PRINCIPLES OF INTERNATIONAL LAW CONCERNING FRIENDLY RELATIONS AND CO-OPERATION AMONG, IN ACCORDANCE WITH THE CHARTER OF THE UN, 260

STATISTICAL ACTIVITIES, SUB-CT. ON (ACC), 1031-32

STATISTICAL COMMISSION (ESC): agenda/documentation *(1987)*, 1031; members, 1413; report, 1031 (ESC); Working Group on International Programmes/Co-ordination, 1413

STATISTICAL OFFICE (Secretariat), 1036

STATISTICAL PROGRAMMES AND CO-ORDINATION, WORKING GROUP ON INTERNATIONAL, 1031, 1037; members, 1413

statistics, 485, 486 (DTCD/Statistical Office), 608 (UNIDO), 640 (ECA), 650-51 (ESCAP), 659 (ECE), 664 (ECLAC), 668 (ESCWA), 1031-37; aviation, 1339 (ICAO); co-ordination in the UN system, 1036-37 (ACC Sub-Ct.); economic, 1032-33; publication policy, 1037; publications, 1037 *(list)*; social/demographic, 1033-36; technical co-operation, 1036 (ACC/S-G); *see also organizational and subject entries*

steel, 656 (ECE); statistics, ECE Working Party, 656; tubes, ECE seminar, 656; *see also* iron and steel industry

STEEL COMMITTEE (ECE): 53rd sess., 656

student refugees, *see under* southern Africa

sub-Saharan Africa, 498 (S-G); economy, 419 (Ct. on Strategy); food aid, 702 (WFP); public administration, 431, **431** (ESC/S-G); Spec. Facility, financing, 460-61, 1313, 1323-24 (IDA/World Bank); Spec. Programme for, 461, 1365 (IFAD); & UNDP field offices, proposed strengthening, 501; volunteer programme, 487 (UNV)

SUB-SAHARAN AFRICA, SPEC. PROGRAMME FOR (IFAD), 1365

SUBSIDIES AND COUNTERVAILING MEASURES, CT. ON (GATT), 1370

Sudan: cattle, conservation, 814 (FAO/UNEP); desertification control, 808 (African Cf.); & Egypt microwave link,

1347 (ITU); refugee assistance, 995, 1003, **1003-4** (GA/S-G/UNHCR); refugees in, 1003; S-G Spec. Representative, 1424; UNICEF programmes, 969

SUDANO-SAHELIAN ACTIVITIES, UN TRUST FUND FOR: contributions, 538 *(table)*, **811** (GA); expenditures, 538 *(table)*; UNSO allocations/pledges, 809-10

SUDANO-SAHELIAN OFFICE, UN, 537-38 (UNDP), 809-10

Sudano-Sahelian region, 537-38 (ESC/GA, 538; UNDP/UNSO, 537)

desertification control, *1977* Action Plan, 809-11 (GA, 810, **811**; UNDP/UNEP, 810; UNSO, 809-10)

drought-related assistance: medium- and long-term programme, implementation, **807**, 810 (GA/UNDP/UNSO)

Permanent Inter-State Ct. on Drought Control in the Sahel, **807** (GA), 810 (UNSO)

see also desertification

sugar, 569-70

SUGAR AGREEMENT, INTERNATIONAL *(1984)*: in force, 569

SUGAR ORGANIZATION, INTERNATIONAL: Cl., 569-70

summary executions, 739 (7th UN Congress), 867-69 (ESC, 867, **867-68**; GA, **868-69**; Spec. Rapporteur, 867); *see also* capital punishment

Suriname: & alleged summary executions, 867 (Spec. Rapporteur)

Swaziland: economic assistance, 525, 525-26 (GA/S-G/UN bodies); 4th Development Plan, 525; *1984* cyclone/flood damage, 525, 526; refugees in, 1005, 1006 (UNHCR)

Sweden: & biotechnology research, 774-75; & Indian Ocean Ct., 1395

Switzerland: consultative status in ECA, 1414, in ECLAC, 1415, in ESCAP, 1414; & UN Postal Administration, 1266

SYNTHETICS AND SUBSTITUTES, PERMANENT GROUP ON (TDB): members, 1403

Syrian Arab Republic: aid to Palestinians in, 283 (FAO/UNICEF); & Israel, 313-14 (communications); refugee assistance, 161 (UNHCR); *see also* Disengagement Observer Force, UN; Golan Heights; *and under* Lebanon

SYSTEM OF STATISTICAL BALANCES OF THE NATIONAL ECONOMY, *see under* National Accounts, UN System of

Tanzania, United Republic of, *see* United Republic of Tanzania

TARIFF CONCESSIONS, CT. ON (GATT), 1370

TAR SANDS, INFORMATION CENTRE FOR HEAVY CRUDE AND, 782 (UNDP/UNITAR)

TAR SANDS, 3RD INTERNATIONAL CF. ON HEAVY CRUDE AND, 692, 782 (UNDP/UNITAR)

taxation: co-operation on tax evasion, 580 (*Ad Hoc* Expert Group); UN Convention *(1979)*, 580 (*Ad Hoc* Expert Group)

TAX MATTERS, *AD HOC* GROUP OF EXPERTS ON INTERNATIONAL CO-OPERATION IN, 580; members, 1416

technical and vocational training, 603 (UNIDO)

TECHNICAL AND VOCATIONAL TRAINING, INTERNATIONAL CENTRE FOR ADVANCED (ILO), 603 (UNIDO), 1283

TECHNICAL ASSISTANCE AND CO-OPERATION FUND (IAEA), 1272

technical co-operation, 464-73 (UNDP), 485-93 (DTCD/UN), 500 (S-G), 558-59 (UNCTAD/UNDP), 560 (UNCTAD), 561-62 (ITC), 600-3, (UNIDO), 622-23 (TNCs Centre), 646 (ESCAP), 662 (ECLAC), 666 (ECWA), 827 (UNCHS), 1272, 1273, 1275 (IAEA), 1272 (FAO/IAEA), 1280 (ILO), 1280-82 *(tables)*, 1287 (FAO), 1299 (UNESCO), 1309-10 *(table)*, 1311-12 (World Bank), 1325-26 *(table)*, 1326 (IDA), 1340 (ICAO), 1342-43 (UPU); 1346-47 (ITU), 1353 (WMO), 1356 (IMO), 1359-60 (WIPO), 1367 (IFAD), 1372 (GATT)

administrative/budgetary co-ordination, 1230 (ACABQ)

aging persons, programmes for, 986-87, **988** (GA/Trust Fund)

crime prevention, UN activities, 738, **741** (GA/Milan Action Plan)

development administration, 431 (DTCD)

drug abuse control, 1015-16 (GA/UNFDAC), 1016 *(table)*

energy, 689-90 (DTCD)

health, expenditures, 461

human rights, 893 (Human Rights Cs./S-G)

labour, 1280 (ILO)

mineral resources exploration, 675 (DTCD/UNRFNRE), 1274 (IAEA)

population activities, 769, **770** (ESC/Population Cs.)

statistics, 1036 (ACC/DTCD/S-G/Working Group)

UNDP expenditures, 461 *(table)*, 461-62 (UNDP Administrator)

UN programmes, 485-86; *see also* names of individual programmes; subject entries

see also development, operational activities for; development assistance; Development Programme, UN; *and under specific economic and social sectors*

technical co-operation among developing countries, 488-94 (ACC, 490-91; ESC/JIU/UNDP Cl., 235; GA, **491**; High-level Ct., 489; UNDP Administrator, 488-89), 646 (ESCAP); Information Referral System, 488 (UNDP Administrator); & IPFs, 492 (High-Level Ct./UNDP Cl.); *1978* Buenos Aires Action Plan, 426-27 (CPC), 1039 (ACC/JIU); skilled workers, exchanges of, 492-93 (Expert Mtg./High-level Ct./UNCTAD); Spec. Programme Resources, allocations, 491-92 (High-level Ct./UNDP Cl.); Spec. Unit, 488 (activities), 492 (staffing); *see also* economic co-operation among developing countries; *and subject entries*

TECHNICAL CO-OPERATION AMONG DEVELOPING COUNTRIES, HIGH-LEVEL CT. ON THE REVIEW OF, 489-89 (ESC/UNDP Cl.), **491** (GA); members/officers, 1397

TECHNICAL CO-OPERATION FOR DEVELOPMENT, DEPARTMENT OF (Secretariat), 485-86 (GA/S-G/UNDP Cl.); project ex-

penditures, 485-86; Under-S-G/Assistant, 1423

Technological Information Bank, Industrial and, *see* Industrial and Technological Information Bank

TECHNOLOGICAL INFORMATION EXCHANGE SYSTEM, 718

TECHNOLOGICAL INFORMATION PILOT SYSTEM: preparatory stage, 711 (UNFSSTD)

TECHNOLOGIES, INTERNATIONAL SYMPOSIUM ON CLEAN, 819

technology: nuclear, 1272 (IAEA); *see also* Industrial and Technological Information Bank; science and technology

TECHNOLOGY, ADVISORY CT. ON , 1278

TECHNOLOGY, ADVISORY SERVICE ON TRANSFER OF, 717 (TDB)

TECHNOLOGY, CT. ON TRANSFER OF (TDB): members, 1403-4

TECHNOLOGY, INTER-AGENCY GROUP ON REVERSE TRANSFER OF, 719-20, **720** (GA)

TECHNOLOGY, 3RD MTG. OF GOVERNMENTAL EXPERTS ON THE REVERSE TRANSFER OF, 719, **720** (GA)

TECHNOLOGY, UN CF. ON AN INTERNATIONAL CODE OF CONDUCT ON THE TRANSFER OF *(1978)*: 6th sess., 689, 717

TECHNOLOGY ALERT SYSTEM, ADVANCE, 716 (Centre for Science and Technology)

technology transfer, 608 (IDB), 614 (UNIDO), 649 (ESCAP), 688-89 (S-G), 717-19 (TDB/UNCTAD, 717-18; UNIDO, 718); Advisory Service on, 581 (UNCTAD); draft code of conduct, 689, 718-19 (GA, **718**; UN Cf., 718); publication, 719 (TDB Ct. on, members, 1403; UNCTAD studies, 717-18; *see also* brain drain

TECHNOLOGY TRANSFER REGISTRIES, 10TH MTG. OF HEADS OF, 608, 718

telecommunications, 370, 1346-47 (ITU); IDA credits, 1324-25 *(table)*, 1326; news exchanges, tariff reductions, **373** (GA/UNESCO); training activities, 1347 (ITU); World Bank loans, 1309-10 *(table)*, 1312; *see also* International Telecommunication Union; mass communications; Radio and Visual Services Division; *regional entries*

TELECOMMUNICATIONS DEVELOPMENT, CENTRE FOR: proposed establishment, 370, 1345

TELECOMMUNICATIONS DEVELOPMENT, INDEPENDENT CS. FOR WORLD-WIDE, 370, 1345

TELECOMMUNICATIONS NETWORK, PAN-AFRICAN, 1346

TELECOMMUNICATIONS SATELLITE ORGANIZATION, INTERNATIONAL: observer status in COPUOS, 101, **107** (COPUOS/GA)

TELECOMMUNICATION STUDIES, MULTINATIONAL SCHOOL OF ADVANCED (ITU), 370

TELEGRAPH AND TELEPHONE CONFERENCE, WORLD ADMINISTRATIVE *(1988)*: preparatory mtgs., 370 (ITU)

TELEGRAPH AND TELEPHONE CONSULTATIVE COMMITTEE, INTERNATIONAL, 1345

television broadcasting, 1345 (International Radio Consultative Committee), 1347 (ITU); regional units, **380**, 385

(GA/S-G); *see also* communications satellites; Radio and Visual Services Division

terrestrial ecosystems, *see* ecosystems

territorial sea: extension (Namibia), 1125 (Colonial Countries Ct.); in Law of the Sea Convention, 109 (S-G)

territories occupied by Israel, 326-35 (communications, 326-28; GA, **332-34**, 334; Human Rights Cs., 328-29; Israeli Practices Ct., 329; SC, 329-32; S-G, 329)

cultural property/religious sites, **333** (GA)

detainees/prisoners, 335-38 (communications, 335-36; GA, **337**, 337-38; Human Rights Cs., 336-37; Israeli Practices Ct., 337; S-G, 337); release/detention of Ziyad Abu Eain, 337, **337**, 337-38 (GA/S-G)

economic practices, 346-48 (ESC, **346-47**, 347; GA, **347**, 347-48; S-G, 346; UNCTAD, 347); development projects, 348-49 (ESC, **348**, 348-49; GA, **349**, 349; S-G, 348); economic resources, study, 346 (S-G); S-G seminar on, 344

educational institutions, 350-52 (communications, 349-51; GA, **351**, 351; S-G/UNESCO, 350); S-G seminar, 350

4th Geneva Convention *(1949)*, compliance, 334-35 (GA, **335**, 335; Human Rights Cs., 334)

human rights violations, 329 (Israeli Practices Ct.), **333** (GA), 869, 925-27 (Human Rights Cs.)

human settlements in, 345, 830-31 (GA/UNCHS)

information dissemination, **380** (GA)

living conditions, 344-46 (ECWA/S-G, 344; GA, **344-45**, 345-46); *1987* seminar on, **345** (GA)

officials: assassination attempts, action on, 344 (S-G); expulsion, 343-44 (GA, **343-44**, 344; S-G, 343)

SC Cs., 1410

S-G seminar, **344** (ESC/S-G), 350 (S-G)

settlements policy, 338-40 (communications, 338-40; GA, **333**, 339-40; Israeli Practices Ct., 339)

workers, conditions of, **333** (GA)

see also Gaza Strip; Golan Heights; Jerusalem; Lebanon situation; Mediterranean–Dead Sea canal project; Palestinians; West Bank

terrorism, international, 3, 10-11 (S-G), 272 (communications/SC), 738 (Milan Action Plan), 739 (7th UN Congress); *Ad Hoc* Ct. on, *1979* recommendations, 1166, **1168**; attack on American-Arab Anti-Discrimination Ct., 292; conventions on, status, 1167 (S-G); information dissemination, **381**, 1169 (GA); prevention of, measures for, 1166-70 (communications, 1166-67; GA, 1167, **1167-68**, 1168-69; SC, 1169-70, **1170**, 1170; S-G, 1167); at Rome/Vienna airports, 292-93 (communications, 292-93; SC/S-G, 292); *see also* diplomats, protection of; hijacking; Hostages, International Convention against the Taking of

textiles, 609 (UNIDO)

Textiles, Arrangement regarding International Trade in, *see* Multifibre Arrangement

TEXTILES COMMITTEE (GATT), 1372

Thailand: Anti-Piracy Programme, implementation, 1008, 1009; Displaced Persons Ct., 1008-9; mineral exploration, 675 (UNRFNRE); pulp/paper-making, 611 (UNIDO); refugees in, 1007-8 (UNHCR); UNFDAC projects, 1014 (S-G); *see also under* Kampuchea situation; Lao People's Democratic Republic

THIRD WORLD, SURVIVAL FUND FOR THE (Belgium/IFAD), 1365

timber, *see* forests; tropical forests; tropical timber; wood products industry

TIMBER COMMITTEE (ECE), 657

tin: exploration, 675

Tokelau, 1150, 1150-51 (Colonial Countries Ct./GA); information to UN, 1082

Tokyo Round, *see* multilateral trade negotiations

Tonga: admission to IDA, 1323, to IMF, 1332

TORTURE, UN VOLUNTARY FUND FOR VICTIMS OF, 864, 864-65 (GA/Human Rights Cs./S-G); Board of Trustees, 864, 1408 (members); balance/projects, 864

torture and other cruel treatment, 863-65; Convention against, status, 863-64 (GA, 863, 863-64; Human Rights Cs./S-G, 863); Spec. Rapporteur, appointment, 863 (ESC/Human Rights Cs.); victims of, 864 (S-G); *see also* capital punishment; detainees; prisoners

tourism, 590 (ESC/S-G)

TOURISM ORGANIZATION, WORLD: Acapulco Document/Manila Declaration, 590, 590 (GA/S-G); co-operation with ICAO, 1339

TOXIC CHEMICALS, INTERNATIONAL REGISTER OF POTENTIALLY, 802-3 (UNEP Cl.); *Bulletin*, 803; co-operation with international organizations, 803; hazard control, 802-3 (Legal File); publications, 803; Query-Response Service, 802

TOXICOLOGY CENTRES AND POISON CONTROL CENTRES, WORLD FEDERATION OF ASSOCIATIONS OF, 774; 4th General Mtg., 1303

toxic substances, 773-74 (UNEP/WHO); chemical accidents, 594, 796, 802, 1303 (WHO); & food contamination, 1303 (FAO/WHO); information exchange, 802 (International Register); *see also under* environmental monitoring

trade: & standardization, 659 (ECE); *see also* international trade

TRADE, AGREEMENT ON TECHNICAL BARRIERS TO ("Standards Code"), 1371

TRADE, CT. ON DEVELOPMENT OF (ECE): 34th sess., 655

TRADE, CT. ON INVISIBLES AND FINANCING RELATED TO (TDB), 575, 578, 579-80; members/officers, 1403

TRADE, CT. ON TECHNICAL BARRIERS TO (GATT), 1371

TRADE AND DEVELOPMENT, CT. ON (GATT), 1371

TRADE AND DEVELOPMENT, UN CF. ON, 7 (S-G), 581-84; calendar of mtgs., 583 (Interim Ct./TDB); medium-term plan/programme budget, 582 (CPC, 582-83; Working Party, 582); mtgs., servicing, 584; members, 1401; officials, 1424; Programme Co-ordination & Evaluation

Unit, establishment, 582 (CPC); S-G, appointment/confirmation, 581, 584 (GA/S-G), 584 (GA); structure, 1401-4; technical co-operation, 583

TRADE AND DEVELOPMENT, UN CF. ON (UNCTAD VII-*1987*): 581, 582, 583 (GA/TDB)

TRADE AND DEVELOPMENT BOARD (UNCTAD), 581, 581-82, 582 (GA), 1401-2, 1419; mtgs., scheduling of, 583-84 (ESC/TDB working group); members/sess./officers, 1402 (Bureau); subsidiary organs, 1402-4; Working Party on the Medium-term Plan and the Programme Budget, 582, 583; *see also* Commodities, Ct. on; Commodities, Permanent Sub-Ct. on; Developing Countries, Ct. on Economic Co-operation among; Manufactures, Ct. on; Preferences, Spec. Ct. on; Shipping, Ct. on; Shipping Legislation, Working Group on International; Ships, UN Cf. on Conditions for Registration of; Synthetics and Substitutes, Permanent Group on; Technology, Ct. on Transfer of; Trade, Ct. on Invisibles and Financing related to; Tungsten, Ct. on

Trade and Development Report, 1985 (UNCTAD *Report*), 429-30; commodities, 565; & debt problems, 576; exchange rates, 575; & trade policy, 552, 554-55

TRADE AND PRODUCTION GOODS CLASSIFICATION, COMBINED, 1033

Trade Centre, International, *see* International Trade Centre

TRADE EXPANSION AND REGIONAL ECONOMIC INTEGRATION AMONG DEVELOPING COUNTRIES, WORKING PARTY ON, 425-26 (ECDC Ct.); proposed name change, 426, 689

TRADE FACILITATION, UNCTAD SPECIAL PROGRAMME ON (FALPRO), 562-63; publication, 563 (ECE/FALPRO)

TRADE FAIR, 4TH ASIA-PACIFIC INTERNATIONAL, 646

TRADE IMPACT ANALYSIS MODEL: UNIDO study, 608

trade law, *see* international trade law

TRADE MEASURES, DATA BASE ON (UNCTAD), 557

trade negotiations, *see* international trade; multilateral trade negotiations

trade policy, *see* international trade

trade preferences, 557-59; rules of origin, 558 (Special Ct.), 559 (Working Group); *see also* generalized system of preferences; global system of trade preferences among developing countries (proposed); Preferences, Spec. Ct. on

trade promotion, 561-63 (ITC/JAG); *see also* International Trade Centre

trade-related finance, 579-80; *see also* exports; insurance; taxation

trade restrictions, *see* international trade: protectionism, restrictive business practices

TRADE UNION COUNCIL, ALL-UNION: workshop with UNITAR, 1283

trade unions: infringement of rights, 904, 904-5 (ESC/*Ad Hoc* Working Group); *see also under* South Africa

training and research, 785-86 (UNITAR/UNU); commercial policy, GATT programme, 1372; diplomacy, 782

(UNITAR); international law, 782 (UNITAR); public administration, 782 (UNITAR); telecommunications, 1346; & working conditions, 1279 (ILO), 1280 *(table)*; *see also country names*; fellowships; human resources; manpower development; vocational training

TRAINING AND RESEARCH, UN INSTITUTE FOR, 781-85 (DIEC DG/S-G); accounts *(1984)*, 782-83 (ACABQ/Auditors Board, 738; GA, 783); Board of Trustees, 736-37, 737 (GA), 1406 (members); contributions, 738, 738 (GA), 738 *(table)*; Executive Director, 1406, 1419, 1425; expenditures/income *(1985)*, 782 *(table)*; financing, 783, 783 (GA), 783 (S-G/UN Pledging Cf.); long-term financing, 783-85 (GA, 784, 784-85; S-G, 783-84)

TRAINMAR, interregional maritime programme, 554 (Ct. on Shipping/UNCTAD)

transboundary air pollution, *see* air pollution

transboundary water pollution, *see* water problems

TRANSFER OF KNOWLEDGE THROUGH EXPATRIATE NATIONALS, 484, 489 (TCDC/UNDP)

transfer of technology, *see* technology transfer

Transition Assistance Group, UN, *see under* Namibia question

TRANSIT SYSTEM, NORTHERN CORRIDOR: Agreement, implementation, 563

transnational corporations, 616-23, 647 (ESCAP), 667 (ESCWA)

accounting and reporting standards, 617-18 (Cs., 618; ESC, 618; Intergovernmental Expert Group, 617-18); studies (Centre), 618

bilateral/international/regional arrangements, 617 (Centre/Cs.)

code of conduct (draft), 616-17 (Cs., 616; ESC, 616; Expert Group Mtg., 647 (Centre/ESCAP); & natural resources sovereignty, 672, 672 (Cs./ESC)

& CPC *1979* recommendations: implementation, 1227-28 (CPC)

definition, 616-17 (Centre/Cs.)

& environmental impact, 621 (Centre/UNEP)

information system, 619 (Centre/Cs.)

& international economic relations, studies, 621-22

publications, 623

& regional css., joint units, 619-20

research programmes, 621-22 (Centre/Cs.)

technical co-operation, 622-23 (Centre/Cs.); financing, 1324 (Centre Trust Fund/UNDP)

transborder data flows, 621 (Centre/Cs.)

see also under colonial countries; international trade; Namibia; South Africa; *and regional entries*

TRANSNATIONAL CORPORATIONS, Cs. ON: co-operation with Information Ct., 375, 380 (GA/Information Ct.); members/officers, 1415; reconvened spec. sess., 1317, 1415 (officers)

TRANSNATIONAL CORPORATIONS, UN CENTRE ON (Secretariat), 618-23 (Cs./S-G, 618; ESC, 618-19, 619); Executive Director, 1424

Transnational Corporations in South Africa and Namibia, Ad Hoc Ct. on the Preparations for the Public Hearings on the Activities of, *see* South Africa and Namibia, Ad Hoc Ct. on the Preparations for the Public Hearings on the Activities of Transnational Corporations in

transport, 585-90, 655 (ECE), 662 (ECLAC), 646-47 (ESCAP), 666-67 (ESCWA); environmental impact of, 819 (UNEP); equipment, 614 (UNIDO); IDA credits, 1324-25 *(table)*, 1326; maritime, 662 (ECLAC); water-related, 614 (UNIDO); World Bank loans, 1309-10 *(table)*, 1312; *see also* Africa, Transport and Communications Decade in; air transport; Asia and the Pacific, Transport and Communications Decade for; inland transport; maritime transport; motor vehicles; multimodal transport; ports; railways; road transport/roads; shipping; space transportation

TRANSPORT AND COMMUNICATIONS, MTG. OF MINISTERS RESPONSIBLE FOR (ESCAP), 646

transport of dangerous goods, 588-90 (ESC, **588-89**, 589; S-G, 588); European Agreement on carriage by road, 655; publications, 590; *see also* dangerous goods

TRANSPORT OF DANGEROUS GOODS, CT. OF EXPERTS ON THE, 588; proposed enlargement, 588, **589** (ESC/S-G); Explosives, Group of Experts on, 588; Group of Rapporteurs of the, 588

treaties/agreements, 1182-90; publications, 1190; registration/publication, 1189; *see also* multilateral treaties; States

TREATIES BETWEEN STATES AND INTERNATIONAL ORGANIZATIONS OR BETWEEN INTERNATIONAL ORGANIZATIONS, UN CF. ON THE LAW OF *(1986)*, 1182-89; draft rules of procedure/annexes, **1182-89**; preparations, 1182, **1182** (GA)

Treaty Series (UN), 1189; backlog, 1190 (GA/S-G)

Tropical Cyclone Programme (WMO), *see* cyclones

tropical forests, **790**, 812 (GA/UNEP Executive Director), 1291 (FAO); research/training, 812 (FAO/UNEP/UNESCO); UN Year of, proposed, 812

TROPICAL FORESTS ACTION PLAN, 812

tropical products: trade consultations, 1371 (GATT)

tropical timber, 570, 812 (UNEP)

TROPICAL TIMBER AGREEMENT, INTERNATIONAL *(1983)*, 812 (UNEP); ratifications/signatures, 570

TROPICAL TIMBER COUNCIL, INTERNATIONAL, 570

TRUCE SUPERVISION ORGANIZATION, UN, 270-71 (S-G); Chief of Staff, 1410, 1425; Observer Groups (Beirut, Egypt), 271

Trusteeship and Decolonization, Department of Political Affairs, *see* Political Affairs, Trusteeship and Decolonization, Department of

TRUSTEESHIP COUNCIL, 1084, 1089, 1420; agenda, 1434 *(list)*; & CERD, 1089; & Colonial Countries Ct., 1089

TRUSTEESHIP SYSTEM, INTERNATIONAL, 1084-89

Trust Territory of the Pacific Islands (Micronesia), 1084-89 (Colonial Countries Ct./TC, 1084; GA, 1084-85); claims, 1084 (TC); economic conditions, 1085-86 (Colonial Countries Ct./TC); education, 1086 (TC); fellowships/scholarships, 1088 (S-G/TC); hearings/petitions, 1088 (GA/TC); information dissemination, 1089 (S-G/TC); nuclear testing, compensation for, 1087 (TC); politics/government, 1085 (Colonial Countries Ct./TC); population, 1084 *(1984)*; radioactive waste management, 1087 (TC); self-determination, 1085 (Colonial Countries Ct./communication/TC); social conditions, 1086 (TC); Visiting Mission, 1087, **1087** (GA/TC), 1087-88 (report), 1420 (Chairman/members); *see also* Marshall Islands; Micronesia, Federated States of; Northern Mariana Islands; Palau

tungsten, 571 (UNCTAD); market situation, working group, 571

TUNGSTEN, CT. ON (TDB), 569, 570-71; members/officers, 1402-3

Tunisia: desertification control, 808 (UNEP); & GATT, provisional accession, 1370; livestock production, 1290 (FAO); refugees in, 1005 (UNHCR); *see also* continental shelf: delimitation; Palestine Liberation Organization: raid on Tunisia headquarters

Turkey: agricultural development, 1288 (FAO), 1310 (World Bank); drug control projects, 1014 (S-G/UNFDAC); *see also* Cyprus

Turks and Caicos Islands, **1151-52** (GA); information to UN, 1082

Tuvalu: admission to ESCAP, 645, **651** (ESC); review mission, 531-32 (ESC, 532; S-G, 531-32); in South Pacific Forum statement, 532

TYPHOON COMMITTEE, 650 (ESCAP/WMO)

TYPHOON OPERATIONAL EXPERIMENT, 1352 (WMO)

typhoons: forecasting, 650; *see also* cyclones; monsoons

Uganda: developments in, 997; drought aid, 517 (GA); economic assistance, 526-27 (GA, **527**, 527; S-G/UN system, 526-27); energy projects, 1325 (IDA); human rights advisory services, 895 (Human Rights Cs./S-G); internal situation, 527; national conservation strategy, 812 (Ecosystem Conservation Group/IUCN/UNDP); refugee settlements, 831 (UNCHS/UNHCR); refugees in, 1005 (UNHCR); UNCTAD/UNDP projects, 527; water supply/sewerage, 1327 (IDA); *see also* East Africa: drought-stricken areas assistance

UN Chronicle, **382**, 385; spec. anniversary issue, 403

Union of Soviet Socialist Republics, *see* communications satellites; Eastern Europe; nuclear disarmament

United Kingdom: NSGT information to UN, 1082; withdrawal from UNESCO, 1295; *see also* Falkland Islands (Malvinas); Gibraltar

UNITED NATIONS
anniversary (40th): commemoration, 3, 8

(S-G), 396, 403-8 (ACC, 404; commemorative stamp, 1267; communications, 404, 406-8; GA, **406**, 406; Preparatory Ct., 404-5; S-G, 403); draft declarations, 404-5 (Preparatory Ct.); GA Presidents' mtg., 403; public information, 374, 387, 403-4; theme, 403

annual report on work of (S-G), 3-11

Charter, 1379-88 *(text)*

computer use in, 1265 (JIU)

Correspondents Association: & DPI, **382** (GA/Information Ct.)

diplomatic missions to: & host country relations, 1180, **1180** (Ct. on Host Country/GA)

experts/consultants, use of, 1127 (CPC/GA), 1253, **1253** (ESC/S-G)

Geneva Office: Director/Assistant, 1424

Headquarters: communications satellite, 1265-66 (GA/Information Ct./S-G); UN/US Agreement on, 1181, **1182** (GA/S-G); *see also* premises (UN)

institutional arrangements, 1038-58

& intergovernmental organizations, 398-403

library management, 1265 (JIU/S-G), 1229 (JIU)

members, 392; dates of admission/roster, 1377-78

officials, 1233-53; Geneva Office, 1424; *see also* staff (UN/UN system)

organs/subsidiary bodies: agenda (principal organs), 1426-34 *(lists)*; composition, 408 (GA)

rationalization of procedures, 397-98 (GA/S-G/Spec. Ct.)

reform of system, proposed, 1231-32 (ACC/JIU)

related bodies ("treaty organs"), 1421-23

resolutions, implementation, 1179-80 (GA)

strengthening role of, 4-5, 1177 (S-G), 1177-80 (ACC/communications, 1179; Charter Ct./Working Group, 1177; GA, **1178-79**, 1179; JIU, 1178; SC, 1177-78)

structure, 1393-1425

universality of, 4 (S-G)

Vienna International Centre: DG, 1424; unified cf. services, 1260-61 (ACABQ/JIU/S-G, 1260; GA, **1260-61**, 1261)

see also accounts (UN); administrative and management questions (UN/UN system); budget (UN); conferences/meetings (UN); contributions (UN); co-ordination in the UN system; documentation (UN); finances (UN); financial situation (UN); host country relations; information centres/offices; pensions (UN system); premises (UN); privileges and immunities; programmes (UN)

United Nations . . . *for specific bodies see key word(s) of title*

UNITED NATIONS, PREPARATORY CT. FOR THE 40TH ANNIVERSARY OF THE, 404-6, **406**, (GA); members/officers, 1399

UNITED NATIONS DAY *(24* Oct.), 116

United Nations Disengagement Observer Force, *see* Disengagement Observer Force, UN

UNITED NATIONS EDUCATIONAL, SCIENTIFIC AND CULTURAL ORGANIZATION,

1295-1301; budget, 1300 *(table)*; contributions, 1300-1 *(table)*; DG/Assistants, 1301; Executive Board, 1301 *(list)*; extrabudgetary programmes, 1299 *(tables)*; General Cf., 370, 1295; General Information Programme, 1298-99; headquarters/ New York office, 1301; members, 1295, 1300-1 *(table)*; Participation Programme, 1299 *(table)*; secretariat, 1300; technical co-operation, 1300 *(tables)*

United Nations Model Double Taxation Convention between Developed and Developing Countries *(1979)*, see under taxation

United Nations Organs, Repertory of Practice of: updating, 553

UNITED NATIONS POSTAL ADMINISTRATION, 1266-67; revenue agreements, 1266; spec. postage stamps, 1267, **1267** (ACABQ/GA/S-G)

United Nations Special Fund (development assistance/emergency relief), see Special Fund, UN (development assistance/ emergency relief)

United Nations system of organizations, *see appropriate organizational and topical entries*

United Nations Truce Supervision Organization, see Truce Supervision Organization, UN

UNITED NATIONS UNIVERSITY, 785-86; commemorative stamp, 1267; contributions, 786 *(table)*; Cl., 786; finances, 786; headquarters, 786; publications, 786

UNITED NATIONS UNIVERSITY, CL., 1420; members, 1408; Rector, 1408, 1425; Standing Cts., 1408

United Republic of Tanzania: desertification control, 808 (UNEP); refugees in, 1005 (UNHCR); respiratory infections, 587 (WHO); technical assistance, 1326 (IDA); transportation, 1326 (IDA); UNSO assistance, eligibility, 639, **811** (GA/ UNEP)

United States: & drug control, 1027 (INCB); NSGT information to UN, 1082; & UNRFNRE co-financing, 669; *see also* Guam; Libyan Arab Jamahiriya; Nicaragua

United States Virgin Islands, 1152-53 (GA); information to UN, 1082

Universal Declaration of Human Rights, *see* Human Rights, Universal Declaration of

UNIVERSAL POSTAL UNION, 1342-44; budget, 1343 *(tables)*; Consultative Cl. for Postal Studies, 1342, 1344; contributions, 1343-44 *(tables)*; Executive Cl., 1342, 1344; headquarters, 1344; International Bureau (secretariat), 1342, 1344; members, 1342, 1343-44 *(table)*; publication, 1342; Special Fund, 1343; technical co-operation, 1342-43; Universal Postal Congress, 1342

uranium: waste management, 1272 (IAEA); *see also* radioactive waste management; *and under* Namibia

urban development/planning: housing & population cf., 826; IDA credits, 1324-25 *(table)*, 1326; World Bank loans, 1309-10 *(table)*, 1312

URBAN FUTURE, CF. ON POPULATION AND THE *(1986)*: 826 (UNCHS/UNFPA)

Uruguay: human rights violations, 925, 926 (ESC/Human Rights Cs.)

Vanuatu: cyclone damage, 532, 1290 (FAO); economic assistance, 532-33 (GA, **532-33**; S-G, 532); ESCAP/UNCTAD/ UNDP projects, 532; inclusion in LDC list, 433 (CDP/GA)

vegetable oils and fats: processing/production, 1290 (FAO); & trade barrier impact on, 610 (GATT/UNCTAD/UNIDO); *see also names of edible oils*

Venezuela, see under Bolivia

Vienna International Centre, *see under* United Nations

Viet Nam: & dispute with China, 231 (communications); & IAEA safeguards, 1271; Orderly Departure Programme (UNHCR), 994, 995; refugees, 994; typhoon relief, 1292 (FAO); withdrawal from ILO, 456; *see also* Kampuchea situation

VOCATIONAL REHABILITATION AND EMPLOYMENT (DISABLED PERSONS) CONVENTION (ILO), 775-76

vocational training, 776, 1279, 1283 (ILO)

VOLUNTEERS, UN, 486-88; Domestic Development Services, 488 (UNDP Cl.); International Day, 488, **488** (GA/UNDP Cl.); posts/volunteers, 486; project expenditures, 487, 487 *(table)*; Spec. Voluntary Fund, contributions, 487 *(table)*; in WMO projects, 1353

Walvis Bay, *see under* Namibia question

war, *see* material remnants of war; nuclear war; World War II

WARSAW TREATY OF FRIENDSHIP, CO-OPERATION AND MUTUAL ASSISTANCE: Political Consultative Ct., & nuclear weapons, 14; States parties, 117

waste management, see radioactive waste management

WATER DEVELOPMENT PROJECTS, WORKING GROUP ON LARGE-SCALE, 815

WATERFOWL HABITAT, CONVENTION ON WETLANDS OF INTERNATIONAL IMPORTANCE ESPECIALLY AS: Task Force, 813

WATERFOWL RESEARCH BUREAU, INTERNATIONAL, 813

WATER IN INDUSTRIAL PROCESSES, SEMINAR ON RATIONAL USES OF, 656 (ECE)

water problems, 656 (ECE); co-operation among Danube States, declaration, 656 (ECE); *see also* drinking-water; sanitation

WATER PROBLEMS, CT. ON (ECE), 656

WATER QUALITY AND QUANTITY, GROUP ON ASPECTS OF (ECE), 656

water resources: co-ordination in UN, 648, 679-80 (ACC Group/ESC/Natural Resources Ct.); development, 648 (ESCAP), 677-81 (ESC/S-G), 815 (UNEP); exploration, 486 (DTCD); high-level experts' mtg., proposed, 679, **679** (ESC); lake basins, 814-15; management, 1289 (FAO); Mar del Plata Action Plan *(1977)*, implementation, 677-79 (ESC, **678-79**; S-G, 677-78); mtgs./seminars, 815; national plans/

bodies, 677; sharing, agreements, 677; study, 815; *see also* hydrology

WATER RESOURCES, INTERSECRETARIAT GROUP FOR (ACC), 679; ESCAP participation, 648

WATER RESOURCES ASSOCIATION, INTERNATIONAL: Crystal Drop Award, 972

WATER RESOURCES MANAGEMENT, INTERNATIONAL TRAINING CENTRE FOR: 8th sess., 815

WATER RESOURCES PROJECTS, INTERREGIONAL SEMINAR ON ASSESSMENT AND EVALUATION OF MULTIPLE-OBJECTIVE, 815

water supply, 815 (UNEP/WHO), 967, 972-73 (UNICEF); IDA credits, 1324-25 *(table)*, 1327; World Bank loans, 1309-10 *(table)*, 1312; *see also under* drinking-water; hydrology

watercourses, *see* inland water transport; international watercourses

weapons, *see* arms race; conventional weapons; disarmament

weapons/systems of mass destruction: prohibition (proposed), 74-76; *see also* bacteriological (biological) weapons; chemical weapons; nuclear weapons; radiological weapons

WEAPONS WHICH MAY BE DEEMED TO BE EXCESSIVELY INJURIOUS OR TO HAVE INDISCRIMINATE EFFECTS, CONVENTION ON PROHIBITIONS OR RESTRICTIONS ON THE USE OF CERTAIN CONVENTIONAL/PROTOCOLS, 76, 78, **78** (GA/S-G); States parties, 78, 100 *(list)*

weather: modification, WMO Programme, 1352; prediction, 1351 (WMO); *see also* climate; meteorology

WEATHER WATCH, WORLD (Global Observing System/Global Data-processing System/Global Telecommunications), 1350 (WMO)

welfare, *see* social welfare

West Africa: animal feed production, 1290-91 (FAO); IDA credits, 1324 *(table)*; mass communications project, 370 (ITU); railway equipment, 614 (UNIDO); regional seas programme (UNEP), 816

WEST AFRICAN STATES, ECONOMIC COMMUNITY OF: desertification control, **807** (GA); industrial planning, 608 (UNIDO)

West Bank: situation in, 326-28; UNDP/ UNIDO projects, 282; refugees in, 367-68 (communications, 367-68; GA, **368**, 368; S-G, 368); WHO programmes, 283; *see also under* Palestine refugees; territories occupied by Israel

Western Asia, 665-68; debt problems, 666; development policy/co-operation, 666; economic/social trends, *Survey*, 665-66 (ESC); political/security issues, 232-50; technical co-operation, 466 (UNDP), 666 (ESCWA); transport publication, 667; urbanization, environmental impact of, 667 (ESCWA); *see also* Afghanistan; Democratic Yemen; Economic Commission for Western Asia; Iran-Iraq conflict; Yemen *and under subject entries*

Western Sahara, 1137-41 (Colonial Countries Ct./communications/S-G, 1138; GA, **1138-39**, 1139-40); information to UN, 1083; & OAU, 1138 (S-G); petitions,

Western Sahara *(cont.)*
hearings, 1140-41; self-determination, **858**, 862 (GA/Human Rights Cs.)
wheat, *see* grains
WILD ANIMALS, CONVENTION ON THE CONSERVATION OF MIGRATORY SPECIES OF: Cf. of parties, 1st mtg., 813; participants/organs established, 813; trust fund, 813
WILD FAUNA AND FLORA, CONVENTION ON INTERNATIONAL TRADE IN ENDANGERED SPECIES OF, 813
wildlife, 813; endangered animal species, 813 (UNEP)
WILDLIFE FUND, WORLD: structure, 812
women, 831 (Human Settlements Cs.), 936-61, 1296 (UNESCO); elderly, question of: cf. on, 987 (NGO Ct.), **989** (GA); health concerns, 963, 967 (UNICEF); publications, 944, 952
WOMEN, CS. ON THE STATUS OF, 936, **941** (GA); members/officers, 1413; as Preparatory Body for UN Decade Review Cf., 942-43, 1417 (members/officers)
WOMEN, CT. ON THE ELIMINATION OF DISCRIMINATION AGAINST, 960, **960** (ESC); members, 1421
WOMEN, CONVENTION ON THE ELIMINATION OF ALL FORMS OF DISCRIMINATION AGAINST *(1979)*: implementation, 640 (ECA), 960-61 (Ct. on Discrimination, 960; ESC, **960-61**; GA, **961**); accessions/ratifications/signatures, 961 (GA/S-G)
WOMEN, INTERNATIONAL RESEARCH AND TRAINING INSTITUTE FOR THE ADVANCEMENT OF, 952-54 (Board of Trustees, 952-53; GA, **954**); Board of Trustees, 952, **953** (ESC), 1418 (members/President); contributions, **952** *(table)*; Director, 1418; official languages, Arabic proposed, 953 (Board of Trustees); programme, 953; statute, 954, **954** (GA); UN Trust Fund for, **954**
women, status of, 952-59, 1297 (UNESCO)
in agriculture, statistics workshop, 1292 (FAO)
under *apartheid*, 956-57 (*Apartheid* Ct., 956; GA/S-G, 957)
& criminal justice system, 739 (7th UN Congress)
& domestic violence, 744-45, **745-46** (GA/S-G)
elderly, 952 (GA)
information dissemination, **377** (GA)
in LDCs, **446** (GA)
& peace, **955-56** (GA)
& population, **957** (ESC)
& prostitution, 938 (Review Cf.), 957-58 (GA, **958**; Human Rights Cs., 958; SCPDPM/S-G, 957; Working Group on Slavery, 958); *see also* prostitution
refugees, 958-59 (GA/S-G/UNHCR)
research/training, 952-53 (INSTRAW)
situation in Arab territories, 958 (S-G)
& society, **954-55** (GA)
in UN Secretariat, 959 (S-G), 1237-40 (CCISUA/FICSA/ICSC, 1238; GA, **1238-39**; S-G, 1237-38); Co-ordinator for, appointment, 1238, **1239** (GA/S-G); in regional css., 1239, **1239-40** (GA/S-G)

& water resources, 975 (INSTRAW/UNICEF)
see also Nairobi Forward-looking Strategies *under* Women, UN Decade for
WOMEN, UN DECADE FOR *(1976-1985)*, 11 (S-G)
Action Programme, Second Half: implementation, 649 (ESCAP), 936 (Review Cf.)
Review Cf., 937-42; Cts., 1409 (officers); draft resolutions/declaration, 938-39; inaugural ceremonies, 937 (S-G); Nairobi Forward-looking Strategies, 937-38, **940-42** (GA); officers, 937; participants & observers, 937, 1409; preparations, 639 (ECA), 649 (ESCAP), 667-68 (ESCWA), 942-44 (ACC, 944; Cs. on Status of Women, 942-43; ESC, **943**; GA, **943**, 944; S-G, 943; UNEP, 944); resolution of appreciation, 938, **942** (GA)
Review Cf.: follow-up, 944 (CCSQ(PROG)/GA)
Voluntary Fund renamed, 949; *see* Women, UN Development Fund for
WOMEN, UN DEVELOPMENT FUND FOR, 949-52 (ACABQ/UNDP, 950; GA, **951-52**, 952; S-G, 949-50); association with UNDP, 949 (S-G), 1404; Consultative Ct., 950, 952 (GA), 1404 (members); contributions/pledges, 950, 950-51 *(table)*; income/expenditures, 950; publication, 952
WOMEN AND CHILDREN UNDER *APARTHEID*, INTERNATIONAL CF. ON, 956-57
women and development, 486 (DTCD/UNDP Cl.), 639-40, **640** (ECA/ESC), 667 (ESCWA), 944-47 (GA, **945-46**, 946; S-G, 944-45; UNDP, 946-47; UNIDO, 946), 1297 (UNESCO)
co-ordination in UN, 948-49, **949** (ESC/S-G)
& employment opportunities, 1278 (ILO)
food/agriculture, **700** (GA)
integration in industrial development, 946 (IDB/UNIDO)
operational activities, 947 (TCDC/UNDP)
population programmes, 760, 763 (Population Cs./UNFPA)
in rural areas: *1984* Interregional Seminar, 947-48 (GA, **947-48**, 948; S-G, 947), 1283 (ILO)
World Survey on role of, 936, 939 (Review Cf.), 944-45, 946 (GA/S-G)
WOMEN IN DEVELOPMENT, MINISTERIAL CF. OF NON-ALIGNED AND OTHER DEVELOPING COUNTRIES ON THE ROLE OF, 945
WOMEN IN SOUTH AFRICA AND NAMIBIA, INTERNATIONAL DAY OF SOLIDARITY WITH THE STRUGGLE OF, 176, 956 (*Apartheid* Ct.)
WOMEN OF SOUTH AFRICA AND NAMIBIA, INTERNATIONAL CT. OF SOLIDARITY WITH THE STRUGGLE OF, 956
WOMEN'S YEAR, INTERNATIONAL *(1975)*, 937
wood products industry, 610 (UNIDO), 1278 (ILO)
WORK, CLEARING-HOUSE FOR THE DISSEMINATION OF INFORMATION ON CONDITIONS OF, 1279
working conditions: health/medical services, 1278; maritime, 1283 (ILO); oc-

cupational safety, 1279 (ILO/WHO); publication, 1279; radiation protection (IAEA/ILO/WHO), 1279; technical cooperation, 1279, 1280 *(table)*; *see also under* employment
WORKING CONDITIONS AND ENVIRONMENT, INTERNATIONAL PROGRAMME FOR: implementation, 1279 (ILO)
World Bank, *see* International Bank for Reconstruction and Development
World Bank Economic Development Institute, *see* Economic Development Institute (World Bank)
World Disarmament Campaign, *see* Disarmament Campaign, World
World Economic Survey 1985 (DIESA), 411-12, 428-29; on commodity prices, 565; development finance, 578; financial policy, 575; format, review of, 1045; & international trade, 555
world economy, 427-30 (*World Economic Survey*/UNCTAD *Report*), 1330 (IMF)
World Employment Programme, *see* Employment Programme, World
World Food Council, *see* Food Council, World
WORLD HEALTH ORGANIZATION, 1302-8; Assembly (38th), 1302, 1308; budgets, 1302, 1305 *(tables)*; contributions, 1307-8 *(tables)*; co-ordination in the UN system, 1302; Executive Board, 1308 *(list)*; headquarters/regional offices, 1308; members, 1302, 1307-8 *(table)*; officers, 1308; secretariat, 1305; technical co-operation, 1305-6 *(tables)*
WORLD HERITAGE COMMITTEE, 1297-98; *see also* cultural heritage/property: protection
WORLD INTELLECTUAL PROPERTY ORGANIZATION, 1359-64; awards, 1360; budget, 1359, 1361; contributions, 1362-63 *(tables)*; contribution scales, 1361-62 *(table)*; Co-ordination Ct., 1364; DG, reappointment, 1359; expenditures/income, 1361 *(table)*; headquarters/liaison office, 1364; International Bureau (secretariat), 1360, 1361, 1364 (officers); members, 1359, 1362-63 *(table)*; publications, 1360, 1361; technical co-operation, 1359-60
WORLD METEOROLOGICAL ORGANIZATION, 1350-55; budget, 1353; Congress (9th), 1350; contributions, 1354 *(table)*; Executive Cl. (Executive Ct.), 1350, 1354-55; headquarters, 1355; members, 1350, 1354 *(table)*; regional associations/technical css., 1355; secretariat, 1353, 1355 (members); technical co-operation, 1353
World Newspaper Supplement, see Newspaper Supplement, World
WORLD WAR II: 40th anniversary, 117 (communications), 845-46, **846** (ESC); *see also under* nazism/fascism: measures against
World Weather Watch, *see* Weather Watch, World

Yearbook of the United Nations, 386, **386** (ACABQ/GA/S-G)
Yemen: desertification control, ESCWA/FAO/UNEP mission, 667; earthquake

relief, 545 (GA/S-G/Social Development Cs.); refugee assistance, 1009 (UNHCR)

youth, 663 (ECLAC), 762-63 (UNFPA), 976-84; communication channels with UN, implementation of guidelines, 980-82 (GA, **981-82**; S-G, 980-81); co-ordination/information, 977, **978** (ESC/S-G); & crime, 739 (7th UN Congress); in development & society, 649 (ESCAP), 982-83 (ESC, **982**; GA, 982, **983**; Social Development Cs., 982); education/training, 982, **983-84** (GA/Inter-Parliamentary Cf.); & environment, 793, 820 (UNEP/IUCN), 977 (UNEP); & human rights, 930-31 (ESC/GA/Human Rights Cs./SCPDPM); information dissemination, **377**; juvenile prisoners, protection of, 864 (SCPDPM); & NGOs, 981 (S-G); & population structure, **771** (ESC); publications, 984; situation in the 1980s, 976-77 (ESC, **977**; S-G, 976-77; Social Develop-

ment Cs., 977); UNESCO programmes, 1297; world population, 976-77 (S-G); *see also* Juvenile Justice, UN Standard Minimum Rules for the Administration of

YOUTH, DECLARATION ON THE PROMOTION AMONG, OF THE IDEALS OF PEACE, MUTUAL RESPECT AND UNDERSTANDING BETWEEN PEOPLES: 20th anniversary, 978, **979** (ESC)

YOUTH, WORLD CONGRESS ON (SPAIN/UNESCO), 978, **979**, 1297; Barcelona statement, 1297

YOUTH YEAR, ADVISORY CT. FOR THE INTERNATIONAL, 978, **979** (GA); members/officers, 1395

YOUTH YEAR, INTERNATIONAL: PARTICIPATION, DEVELOPMENT, PEACE: & ECLAC Regional Plan, 663; follow-up guidelines, **977** (ESC), 978 (Advisory Ct.), **980**, 980 (GA); Trust Fund for, proposed name

change, 979 (S-G); UN Cf. on, 978-80 (ACC/communications, 979; Advisory Ct., 978; GA **979-80**, 980; S-G, 978-79)

Zaire: 1st development plan, 486 (DTCD); refugees in, 1005 (UNHCR); technical assistance, 1326 (IDA); transport/trade problems, **634-35** (GA); transportation, 1326 (IDA)

ZAMBEZI ACTION PLAN, 814, 815 (UNEP)

Zambia: aquaculture development, 1291 (FAO/Sweden); refugees in, 1005, 1006 (UNHCR)

Zimbabwe: refugees in, 1005 (UNHCR)

zinc, *see* Lead and Zinc Study Group, International

zones of peace (proposed), *see under* Indian Ocean; South-East Asia

Index of names

Page numbers in bold-face type indicate resolutions and decisions

Abad Ortiz, C., 1406
Abbas, Abul, 291
Abdalla, Ismail Sabri, 1416, 1420
Abdallah, Ahmed, 1335
Abdel-Rahman, Faisal M., 1285
Abdo, Eid, 1301
Abdullah, Samsi, 1395
Abdullatif, Ahmed, 1398
Abi-Saab, Georges Michel, 1157, 1421
Aboulashi, Mohamed, 1417
Aboussouan, Camille, 1301
Abraszewski, Andrzej, 1394
Abu Eain, Ziyad, 262, 326, 337, **337**, 926
Adams, Daniel F., 1321
Adebanjo, G. O., 1401
Adedeji, Adebayo, 1423
Adeniji, Oluyemi, 1406
Adhikary, S. P., 1354
Adiko, N., 1285
Aggrey-Orleans, A., 1402
Agius, George, 1397
Agnelli, Susanna, 1405
Ago, Roberto, **1156**, 1421
Aguero Wood, Oscar , 1397
Aguilar, Andrés, 909, 1422
Aguirre Gallardo, Luís, 1412
Ahialegbedzi, L.-K., 1354
Ahmad, Jaafar, 1335
Ahmad, Mansur, 67, 1397
Ahmad, S., 1342
Ahmadu, Hamzat, 1422
Ahmed, Rafeeuddin, 226, 1137, 1423, 1424
Ahmed, Salahuddin, 1420
Ahtisaari, Martti, 1410, 1418, 1424
Aidara, Sidaty, 1411
Aimé, Jean-Claude, 297
Akakpo, Folly Glidjito, 1411
Akashi, Yasushi, 1424
Akatani, Genichi, 1398
Aké, Siméon, 1406
Akhund, Iqbal A., 1423
Akinjide, Richard Osuolale A., 1398
Akman, Oral, 1315, 1320, 1329
Akoto, Paul Yao, 1301
Akwei, Richard M., 1398
Alaimo, S., 1354
Al-Ansari, Ali Ahmad, 1414
Alatas, Ali, 31, 1393
Al-Athel, Saleh Abdulrahman, 1397, 1405
Albornoz, Miguel A., 1399
Alcalay, Glenn H., 1088
Alejo, Francisco J., 1321
Aler, Bo, 1276
Alfarargi, Saad, 79, 1402
Alfidja, Abderrahmane, 1335
Algard, Ole, 1406
Al-Ghoseini, Jaweed, 1414
Alhaimus, Tariq, 1335
Al-Hamad, Abdlatif Y., 1416
Ali, Aamir, 1406, 1407
Ali, Amjad, 1394, 1398
Ali, Hameed Mohamed, 1395
Ali Khan, Sahibzada Raoof, 1422
Alikhan, Shahid, 1364
Alizai, M. Azam K., 1321

Al-Jassem, Agil, 1285
Al Khasawneh, Awn Shawkat, 1412
Allaf, Mowaffak, 1424
Allen, Woody, 135
Alleyne, D. H. N., 1410
Al-Mahdi, Mohammed Sadiq, 1394
Al-Masri, Ahmad Fathi, 1394
Al-Masri, Sayed, 1414
Al-Mohamed, Mohammed Said, 1419
Al-Qaysi, Riyadh, 1393, 1398
Al-Shakar, Karim E., 1402
Al-Shawi, Mohammad, 1315, 1320, 1328
Al-Sultan, Fawzi Hamad, 1315, 1320, 1328
Alvarez Vita, Juan, 1412
Al-Wajih, Muhammad Al-Khadim, 1414
Amneus, Henrik, 1394
Ampem II, Nana Wereko, 1398
Anders, P., 1407
Anderson, David R., 1088
Andronov, L., 1417
Anell, Lars, 1397
Ang How-Ghee, 1397
Ani, Michael O., 1398
Anjain, Jeton, 1088
Annoye, Pierre, 1402
Añón Noceti, Eduardo César, 1406, 1407, 1408
Anstee, Margaret Joan, 1406, 1423
Anyangwe, Carlton, 1412
Apiou, Jean-Marie, 1422
Arafat, Yasser, 264, 285, 288, 291, 329, 842,
     1094, 1167
Arangio-Ruiz, Gaetano, 1398
Arias, Hernando, 1335
Arias Stella, Javier, 1410
Ariyaratne, J. D., 1396
Arnouss, Ahmad Farouk, 1400
Arns, Cardinal Paulo Evaristo, 990
Arroba, Dr. Gonzalo, 1407
Arsenis, Gerassimos D., 1416
Ascandoni, Jaime, 1344
Asvall, Dr. J. E., 1308
Aten, Erhart, 1088
Auchère, Michel, 1398
Ayoub, Dr. Aleya H., 1308
Aziz, Sartaj, 1420
Aziz, Ungku Abdul, 1408
Azraai, Zain, 1394
Azzout, Hadj Benabdelkader, 1406

Baali, Abdallah, 1395
Baati, M., 1404
Badran, M. A., 1354
Baeumer, Ludwig, 1364
Bagbeni, Adeito Nzengeya, 1393
Baghdadi, Abdel Kader, 1344
Bagnall, John, 1417
Bah, M. K., 1308, 1419
Baker III, James A., 1330
Bakr, Bakr Abdullah, 1408
Bakri, Bashir, 1301, 1408
Balanda, Mikuin Leliel, 1398, 1412
Baldassini, R. A., 1285
Baldi, Marino, 1415
Ballah, Lennox, 1423

Balos, Ataji, 1088
Bambinelli, Vincent, 1406, 1407
Bano, Gulzar, 1418
Barakat, Ghaleb Z., 1402, 1412
Barboza, Julio, 1176, 1398
Barmes, Dr. D., 1406
Barnett, Lloyd M. H., 1419
Barre, Siad, 198
Barrios, Pablo, 1396
Bartlett, Edmund, 1395
Bartlett, J., 1402
Barton, William H., 1406
Basse, Marie-Thérèse, 1408
Bassolé, Léandre, 1410
Bastiaanse, W. A., 1402
Bastid, S., 1156
Bata, Thomas J., 1415
Beckurts, K., 1276
Bedjaoui, Mohammed, 1156, **1156**, 1157, 1421
Bedor, J. Roman, 1088
Beith, Andrew J., 1335
Békri, Chikh, 1301
Bel Hadj Amor, Mohsen, 1406, 1407
Bellchambers, William H., 1349
Bellucci Casunatti, Giampiero, 1420
Beltramino, Juan Carlos, 1400
Belyaev, P. G., 1396
Bemme, Helfred, 1403
Benachenhou, Mourad, 1316, 1321, 1329
Benattia, Moncef, 1402
Beninson, D., 1276
Ben Jamaa, Sadak, 1397
Bennini, A., 1276
Bensari, A., 1354
Berezovoy, Anatoly Nicolaevich, 798
Berger, Peter L., 1412
Berman, Franklin D., 1396
Bernal, Carlos, 1400
Bernard, Desirée P., 1422
Bernyi, D., 1276
Berrada, Abderrazak, 1349
Berridge, C. E., 1354, 1355
Berrill, Sir Kenneth, 1416
Berteling, Jan, 1416
Berthelot, Yves, 1424
Bertrand, Maurice, 1398
Betancourt Roa, A., 1402
Betts, Alexander Jacob, 1136
Bhandare, Murlidhar Chandrakant, 1412
Bhandari, Achyut, 1409
Bhatt, Uddhav Deo, 1400
Biadi-Llah, Mr., 1140
Bickley, R. A., 1342
Bielawski, Jan, 1414
Bihi, F. Isak, 1402
Biko, Steve, 136
bin Haji Mohd. Noor, Yusuf, 1414
Birido, Omer, 1393
Biryukova, A. P., 1421
Biskup, E., 1407
Bissonnette, André, 1417
Björnerstedt, Rolf, 86, 1406
Blagué, Alphonse, 1301

Blanchard, Francis, 1285
Blanc-Lapierre, André, 1408
Blandón, Pedro Antonio, 1408
Blix, Hans, **694**, 1271, 1277
Blondel, Marc, 1285
Boateng, Emmanuel Oti, 1413
Boesak, Allan, 159, 162
Bognar, Jozsef, 1408
Bogsch, Arpad, 1359, 1364
Böhm, H., 1276
Boissier-Palun, Léon Louis, 1301
Bolin, Bertil, 1285
Bommer, D. F. R., 1293
Borchard, Karl, 1411
Borg, Saviour F., 1397
Borgoño, Dr. J. M., 1419
Boserup, Ester, 1418
Bossuyt, Marc, 867, **867**, 871, 1412
Bota, Liviu, 1406
Botafogo G., Jose, 1316
Botha, P. W., 153, 1096
Botto de Barros, Adwaldo Cardoso, 1344
Bouabid, Ridha, 1400
Bouhoyi, Hilaire, 1301
Boulama, M., 1354
Boulding, Elise M., 1408
Boutros-Ghali, Boutros, 1398
Bouziri, Néjib, 1422
Bozzini, A., 1294
Brahimi El-Mili, Mohamed, 1301
Breslin, J. B. L., 1355
Briki, Youcef, 1285
Brillinger, R. H., 1285
Brolsma, Reinder J., 1416
Brooks, Gary C., 1349
Brotodiningrat, Soemadi D. M., 1393, 1411
Brown, Donald S., 1369
Brown, G. Arthur, 1419, 1424
Brown, Irving, 1285
Bruce, J. P., 1354
Brundtland, Gro Harlem, 1405
Brunner, Alois, 314
Buallay, Jassim, 1418
Buffum, William B., 1423
Burnham, James B., 1315, 1320, 1328
Burrows, Vinie, 134
Bush, Mary K., 1335
Bushev, Mihail, 1393
Butler, Richard E., 74, 1349
Bwakira, Melchior, 1396
Bykov, O. N., 1406, 1412

Cabric, Miodrag, 1416
Cáceres, Roberto Herrera, 1161
Caicedo Ayerbe, Aurelio, 1301
Cai Zhi-ji, Dr., 1422
Calero Rodrigues, Carlos, 1398
Callaghan, Lt.-Gen. William, 1410, 1425
Camacho, Jose E., 1321
Camara, Bassy, 1411
Camarasa, Felix Alberto, 1321, 1329
Carey, John, 1412
Carmen, Gerald P., 1402
Caron, Marie, 1422
Carrasco, Mary, 1416
Carrasco-Fernández, W., 1402
Carré, Philippe Jacques Farlan, 1406, 1425
Cars, Hans Christian, 84
Carver, J. H., 1397
Castañeda, Jorge, 1398
Castillo Ayala, Javier, 1394
Castro de Barish, Emilia, 1396, 1416
Cato, Annan Arkyin, 1412

Cattani, Sergio, 1402
Ceauscescu, Nicu, 1395
Cerda, Sergio, 1403
César, Jaroslav, 1393, 1399
Chacowry, S., 1355
Chagula, Wilbert Kumalija, 1398
Chaiklin, Seth, 1088
Challons, M. J., 1342
Chambers, Sidney B., 1285
Chamorro Mora, Javier, 1393
Chandra, Satish, 1408
Chapman, Frank, 134
Charles, Gervais, 1402
Charles, Serge Elie, 1400
Charry Samper, Héctor, 1399, 1411
Chaudhry, Vijay K., 1321
Chebeleu, Traian, 1394
Cheek, John E., 1136
Cheikh, Biadillah Mohamed, 1141
Cheklin, V. N., 1402
Chen, Z. Y., 1276
Chetyrkin, E. M., 1407
Chiba, Kazuo, 1373, 1399, 1402
Chidzero, Bernard T. G., 1405, 1414, 1416
Chikana, Rev. Frank, **155**
Chinchón, Dr. W., 1308
Chiroma, A., 1285
Chistyakov, A. S., 1394
Chiwele, Irene Bwalya, 1417
Chkounaev, Vladimir, 1285
Chowdhury, Abu Sayeed, 1411, 1412
Chowdhury, Anwarul Karim, 1396, 1416, 1418, 1419
Christou, Spyros, 1417
Cicanovic, Nikola, 1422
Cicéron, Félix, 1344
Clark, Ian Christie, 1301
Clark, Roger, 1088
Claus, Paul, 1364
Clausen, A. W., 1316, 1321
Clifton, D. L., 1136
Coates, Kenneth, 1316, 1321, 1329
Cok, Vida, 1420
Collaer, Paul, 1298
Collett, Alec, 353
Collins, Maurice Hugh, 1416
Colombo, Daniela, 1418
Colombo, Umberto, 1397
Colville of Culross, Viscount, 920
Concepción, Mercedes B., 1408
Connaughton, M. J., 1355
Contreras Viñals, C. M., 1354
Cooley, Claudia, 1398
Cooray, Joseph A. L., 1422
Cordovez, Diego, 237, 1423
Cortes, Irene R., 1421
Corti, Carlos, 1329
Cosmadopoulos, Dimitri, 1301
Costantino, M., 1404
Cot, Jean-Pierre, 1416
Cotic, Dusan, 1417
Coumbis, Nikolaos, 1335
Court, Jean François, 1416
Cracco, Etienne, 1397
Crean, S., 1285
Cremona, John J., 1422
Cristescu, Poliana, 1419
Crockett, H., 1406
Crowther, Dean K., 1293
Cruse, Ossie, 1088
Cruz, Fernando, 895
Cruz, Jose R., 1088
Cullen, Domingo S., 1400
Culler, Floyd L., 1276

Curchod, François, 1364
Cuvi Ortiz, Fabiola, 1418
Czelnai, R., 1355

Dabrowski, Krzysztof, 1409
Daddah, Turkia, 1398
Dadzie, Kenneth K. S., 552, 584, **584**, 1396, 1397
Daes, Erica-Irene A., 896, 931, 1412
D'Aes, Leo, 1414
Dahak, Driss, 1412
Dahlman, Ola, 47
Dalal, K. L., 1412
d'Alcantara, Adhemar M. A., 1406
Dallara, Charles H., 1335
Damiba, Pierre-Claver, 1424
Danelius, Hans, 1408
Dannemann, Werner, 1335
Danus, Fernando, 1396
Das, S. K., 1354
Dashtseren, Buyantyn, 1301
David, Paul, **155**
David, V., 1285
Davies, J. A. C., 1294
Dayal, Virendra, 1423
Dean, Ronald H., 1315, 1321, 1329
de Andrade Faria, Aloysio, 1398
de Beaufort Wijnholds, J., 1335
de Forges, Sylvain, 1335
de Gaspar, Diogo A. N., 1408
Degefu, Workineh, 1354, 1355
de González, Leonor Filardo, 1321
de Groote, Jacques, 1315, 1320, 1329, 1335
Dehejia, Makarand V., 1321
de Kémoularia, Claude, 1410
Dekker, Ton, 1416
de Lacharrière, Guy Ladreit, **1156**, 1421
de la Fuente Muñiz, Dr. Ramón, 1422
de la Mota, Matias, 1406, 1407, 1408
de Larosière, Jacques, 1335
de Leiris, Gilles, 1407
de Lima e Silva, Francisco, 1397
Delpino, J. J., 1285
del Rosario, Rodolfo, 1416
de Maciello, Susan Couttes, 1136
de Maulde, Bruno, 1315, 1320, 1328, 1335
Denisov, L., 1402
Denktas, Rauf R., 251, 252, 253, 254, 255
de Pierola y Balta, Nicolás, 1422
de Posadas Montero, Luis María, 1401
de Rojas, Oscar R., 1397
Deschênes, Jules, 850, 1412
de Soto, Hernando, 1416
de Souza Montello, Jessé, 1413
Despouy, Leandro, 854, 931, 1412
Dever, Edmonde, 1394
de Waart, Paul J. I. M., 1412
Dherse, Jean-Loup, 1316
Diallo, Bouba, 1393
Díaz-Casanueva, Humberto, 1412
Díaz-González, Leonardo, 1189, 1398
Dichev, Todor, 1412
di Gennaro, Giuseppe, 1425
Dillon, Robert S., 1407, 1425
Dimitrijevic, Vojin, 1422
Diniso, Oupa Moses, 162
Diniz Brandao, Marco Antônio, 1394
Dinka, Berhanu, 1419
Diop, M., 1285
Ditz, Otto, 1393, 1396
Djalal, Hasjim, 1423
Djigbenou, J., 1355
Djoudi, Hocine, 1404

Dolmatov, V. S., 1405
Domínguez, Dr. Manuel, 247, 248
Domínguez, María Antonieta, 1315, 1321, 1329
Doo Kingué, Michel, 1406, 1425
Dornelles, Francisco O. N., 1416
dos Santos, Manuel, 1395
Dougherty, James E., 1406
Dove-Edwin, George, 1412
Draghi, Mario, 1315, 1320, 1329
Dress, Alice, 1403
Dribbusch, Friedrich, 1415
D'Silva, Y., 1407
Dubey, Muchkund, 1399
Dumont, Georges-Henri, 1301
Dunkel, Arthur, 1373
Dunster, H., 1276
Durán Abad, César, 1420
Dwoskin, D., 1404

Eberle, G., 1407
Ebie, Dr. John C., 1422
Ebrahim, Gora, 1097
Edmonds, Peter L. F., 1321
Edwards, David M., 1396
Edwards, Leonard J., 1403
Efimov, A. S., 1398
Eide, Asbjorn, 836, 881
Eide, Ingrid, 1418
Eissa, Suad Ibrahim, 1418
Ekong, Donald E. U., 1408
El Agib, A. A. R., 1276
Elamly, A. K., 1355
El Baroudy, Hussein M., 1416
El-Fetouh, Farida Abou, 1421
El Gamal, Dr. A. A. A., 1308, 1419
El Hassen, Moulaye, 1398
El-Houderi, Hamed Arabi, 1394
Elias, Tasim Olawale, **1156**, 1421
Elissejev, V., 1407, 1408
El-Khani, Abdallah Fikri, 1156, **1156**
El-Khatib, Mohamed Fathallah, 1301
El-Mahmud-Okereke, Noel Enuma, 134
El-Safty, Mohamed Adel, 1417
El-Shafei, Omran, 1406
Emerij, Louis, 1420
Emil, Salim, 1404
Enckell, Ralph, 1398
Ene, Constantin, 1406
Engblom, Göran M., 1373, 1424
Engo, Paul Bamela, 25, 1411
Erb, Richard D., 1335
Ericksson, Inga, 1393
Ermacora, Felix, 905, 1412
Erner, Erdem, 1413
Errera, Roger, 1422
Erskine, Lt.-Gen. Emmanuel Alexander, 1410, 1425
Ertekun, Necati Munir, 252
Espiell, Héctor Gros, 894
Espín de Castro, Vilma, 1418
Esposito, V., 1409
Essaafi, M'Hamed, 1424
Esteva, Gustavo, 1419, 1420
Eurnekian, M., 1285
Evatt, Elizabeth, 1422
Evensen, Jens, 1170, 1421
Ewerlof, Hans V., 1402

Fadika, Lamine, 1405, 1409
Fafowora, Oladapo Olusola, 1422
Fahr, Ulrich, 1403
Fakhr, Dr. S. H., 1413

Fall, Djibril, 1397
Fall, Mohamed Malloum, 1394
Farah, Abdulrahim Abby, 1423
Fartas, Ashur, 1416
Faulkner, David, 1417
Faulkner, Douglas, 1088
Faure, Edgar, 1406
Faye, S. D., 1342
Feinberg, Mordecai S., 1416
Ferm, Anders, 28, 1396
Fernández, Oscar, 895
Fernández de la Garza, G., 1276
Fernández Maroto, Leoncio, 1394
Fernández-Pérez, José Ramón, 1416
Ferrari, Amilcar F., 1423
Ficsor, Mihaly, 1364
Figueira, Luiz Sergio Gama, 1394
Figueroa, Antonio H., 1416
Fiil, Erik, 1419
Filardo de González, Leonor, 1315, 1329
Finaish, Mohamed, 1335
Finch, C. David, 1335
Finney, Albert, 135
Fleischhauer, Carl-August, 1423
Flitan, Constantin, 1398
Flores Rodas, M. A., 1293
Fofange, Mr., 1140
Foldeak, Tamas, 1394
Foli, Jonas Kwami Dotse, 895, 1412
Fontaine-Ortiz, Even, 1394, 1415
Foot, Michael, 1335
Foran, J. Richard, 1406, 1407, 1408, 1424
Forde, Alfred Nathaniel, 1398
Foster, Hugh W., 1315, 1320, 1328
Foster, Wendell, 134
Foulani, Pierre, 1301
Fox, John, 1394
Fraisse, Jean-Olivier, 1321
Frammery, G., 1407
Francis, Laurel B., 1398
Francisque, Edouard, 1402
Frank, Richard H., 1321
Fraterman, K., 1402
Freer, D. W., 1342
Frere Van Tongerlooy, Francis J., 1407
Fugmann, Henrik, 1335
Fujino, Hirotake, 1335
Fulcheri, Gualtiero, 1406, 1407, 1408
Furtado, Celso, 1416
Furth, Warren W., 1308, 1406
Furulyas, F., 1402

Gabay, Mayer, 1416
Gabriel, K. Georg, 1316
Gaechter, J. Richard, 1405
Gagné, P. A., 1407
Gainer, Ronald L., 1417
Galal, Essam El Din, 1397
Garba, Joseph N., 1396, 1400
Garcés-Giraldo, Dr. Diego, 1422
García de González, G., 1402
García Robles, Alfonso, 34, 1406
Gariepy, J. H. A., 1364
Garvalov, Ivan, 1411
Gauci, Victor J., 1397
Gautier, Georges, 1412
Gebhardt, Karl Friedrich, 1408
Geczi, Istvan, 1415
Gehlhoff, Walter, 1301
George, Jean Evelyn, 1409
Gérard, F., 1355
Gerwinat, Manfred, 1395
Gewaily, Yousif, 1397

Gezairy, Dr. Hussein A., 1308
Gharbaoui, A., 1285
Gharbi, El Mostafa, 1344
Ghoneim, Abdel Moneim M., 1422
Giacomelli, Giorgio, 354, 1425
Gianviti, François P., 1335
Gieri, Raymond, 1406, 1407, 1408
Giheno, John, 1414
Gill, David, 1321
Girard, P.-L., 1402
Girukwigomba, Astère, 1316, 1321, 1328
Giustozzi, Enzo, 1412
Godony, Jozsef, 1417
Goenka, Ashok, 1403
Goerner, Günter, 1396, 1423
Goethel, Dieter, 1407
Golding, Bruce, 1415
Golob, Ignac, 1404, 1406
Golubev, Gennady N., 1425
Gomez, Luis Maria, 1423
Gonzales Pacheco, H., 1355
Gonzalez, Norberto, 1423
González, Raimundo, 1393
Gonzalez Avelar, Miguel, 1301
Gonzalez Casanova, Pablo, 1405
Gonzalez Martínez, Aida, 1422
González Montoto, J., 1355
Goode, Walter, 1403
Goos, Bernd, 1335
Gorbachev, Mikhail S., 117
Gosset, G., 1355
Gough, Betty C., 1422
Graefrath, Bernhard, 1422
Grant, James P., 1419, 1424
Green, Roger, 134
Greindl, Maj.-Gen. Günther G., 1410, 1425
Grezzi, C. A., 1355
Grimsson, A., 1308
Groot, Richard, 1420
Grosche, Guenter, 1335
Grundmann, Wilhelm, 1395
Guan Minqian, 1421
Guda, Henri A. M., 1411
Guerra de Macedo, Dr. C., 1308
Guerra de Villaláz, Aura, 1417
Guetta, Aldo, 1335
Guimarães, Rodrigo M., 1315, 1320, 1329
Gumede, Archie, **155**
Gusmão, Kay Rala Xanana, 1136
Gustafson, Douglas, 1321
Gutiérrez-Castro, Edgar, 1315, 1321, 1329
Gutiérrez Jodra, L., 1276
Gutowski, Armin, 1416
Guyer, Roberto E., 1406
Gu Yijie, 1412
Guyot, Jean, 1398
Gyi, Maung Maung, 1402
Gyllenberg, Helga, 1408

Habermeier, Walter O., 1335
Habré, Hissein, 196, 197
Hadi, Riyadh Aziz, 1412
Hadid, Rabah, 1411
Haggag, Ahmed A., 1405
Hägglund, Maj.-Gen. Gustav, 315, 1410, 1424
Hak, C., 1285
Hakapaa, Kari, 1400
Halimi, Gisèle, 1301
Hallgren, R. E., 1355
Hamdi, Y., 1407
Hameed, A. C. Shahul, 1406
Hamer, Alphons C. M., 1393, 1411
Hamm, Lawrence, 134

Hamon, Dr. J., 1308
Hamza, Abdel-Bari, 1373
Handl, Ludek, 1397
Hannerz, Ulf, 1419
Hansen, Peter, 1424
Harb, Said T., 1373
Harben, Roger, 1364
Harris, Reuben H., 1301
Hartling, Poul, 990, 993, **994**, 1399, 1424
Harttila, Pekka, 1411
Hassan, Cherif, 1321
Hassan II, King, 845, 979
Hauff, Volker, 1405
Hawas, Essam El-Din, 1400
Hayashi, Moritaka, 1400
Hayes, Francis Mahon, 1412
Helleiner, Gerald K., 1416
Heng Samrin, 229, 230
Hennes, Richard Vognild, 1394
Henry, Paul-Marc, 1419
Henry-May, Hugh, 1321
Hepburn, Davidson L., 59
Heredia Pérez, Julio, 1412
Herndl, Kurt, 1424
Herrera Cáceres, Roberto, 1393
Hessel, Stephane, 1406
Hidayatalla, A., 1407
Higgins, Rosalyn, 1422
Hilaly, Agha, 1412
Hillis, Bruce C., 1406, 1407, 1408
Hittmair, Hans C., 1316
Hlavacek, O., 1402
Hock, Saw Swee, 1398
Hocké, Jean-Pierre, 990, 993, 1399
Hogbe-Nlend, Henri, 1397
Holborn, Jobst, 1394, 1406, 1407, 1408
Holck, Dr. S. E., 1406
Holger, James, 1410, 1425
Hood, William C., 1335
Hopper, W. David, 1316
Ho Tong Yuen, 1355
Houghton, J. T., 1355
Housholder, Virginia C., 1394
Houska, Karel, 1398
Hovaguimian, Andre G., 1321
Howe, Sir Geoffrey, 1410
Huang Fanzhang, 1335
Huang Jiahua, 1398
Huan Xiang, 1416
Hucke, Dietmar, 1399
Huhtaniemi, Pekka Juhani, 1411
Hull, Dayton W., 1398
Huovila, S., 1355
Husain, Irtiza, 1415, 1417
Husain, Mairaj, 1413
Husain, S. Shahid, 1316
Huslid, Martin J., 1399, 1402
Hussein, Abdul Aziz, 1301
Hussein, King, 264, 268, 274
Hutchings, Dr. John J., 1419
Huyghe-Braeckmans, Ben J. A., 1422

Ibrahim, Gora, 134
Ibrahim, Izhar, 1395
Ibrahim, Mohamed Salah Eldin, 1398
Ichimura, Shinichi, 1416
Idanpaan-Heikkila, Juhana, 1413
Ider, Luvsandanzangyn, 1411, 1422
Idris, Kamil, 1364
Ignac, Golob, 1404
Ilander, K., 1398
Ilic, Zagorka, 1422
Ilkahanaf, Aidiid Abdillahi, 1412

Illueca, Jorge Enrique, 1398, 1404
Inayatullah, Attiya, 1301
Infante Barros, María Teresa, 1411
Ingram, James Charles, 1293, 1420
Irmer, Theodor, 1349
Isakov, J. F., 1419
Isaksson, Andri, 1301
Islam, N., 1293
Ismael, J. E., 1335
Ismail, Yvonne, 134
Iuri, M. G., 1407
Ivan, E., 1406
Ivanov, I. D., 1397
Izrael, Ju. A., 1354

Jachim, J., 1398
Jackson, Sir Robert, 1424
Jacovides, Andreas J., 1398
Jagota, Satya Pal, 1398
Jain, Surendra K., 1285
Jalil, M. E., 1294
Jallow, Hassan B., 1409
Jambga, Ben Kufakunesu, 1301
Jankovic, Branimir M., 1412
Jankowitsch, Peter, 1397
Jansen, E., 1358
Jasset, Essop, **155**
Jaumotte, André Louis, 1408
Jayasekera, Shelton E., 1407
Jayasinghe, Vinitha, 1422
Jayawardena, A. S., 1335
Jayawardena, Lalith R. U., 1425
Jaycox, Edward V. K., 1316
Jazairy, Idriss, 1369
Jembere, Mitiku, 1316, 1321, 1328
Jennekens, J., 1276
Jennings, Sir Robert Y., **1156**, 1421
Jensen, Brian, 1335
Jiang Hai, 1335
Jiménez de Aréchaga, Eduardo, 1156, **1156**
Jin Fuyao, 1285
Jipguep, Jean, 1349
Jochimsen, Reimut, 1408
Jodahl, Per, 1397
John, Ismael, 1088
John Paul II, Pope, 302, 798, 845, 979
Johnsen, Brig.-Gen. Thor A., 1410
Johnston, George, 1398
Johnston, Susanna H., 1406, 1407, 1408
Joinet, Louis, 866, 873, 933, 1412
Jolly, Richard, 1424
Jonah, James O. C., 1423
Joseph, Andrew J., 1424
Joseph, Lance Louis E., 1394
Joshi, Hari Bhakta, 1394
Jum'a, S., 1294

Kaabachi, Habib M., 1394
Kabakibo, A. W., 1355
Kabbaj, Omar, 1335
Kaboré, Paul Désiré, 1393
Kaddour, Nasser, 1398
Kaddoura, Abdul-Razzak, 1301
Kadejo, A. A., 1413
Kadirgamar, Laksmanathan, 1364
Kaempf, Siegfried, 1301
Kaffenberger, Wilfried, 1321
Kafka, Alexandre, 1335
Kakolecki, Andrzej, 1400
Kalaydjiev, Vladimir, 1413
Kalpage, F. S. C. P., 1408
Kamba, Walter Joseph, 1408

Kamis, Zdenek, 1400
Kanazawa, Masao, 1398
Kane, Cheikh Hamidou, 1414
Kane, Elimane, 1285
Kanouni, Saad, 1403
Kantschev, A., 1404
Kapoor, R. P., 1413
Kapur, Shiv S., 1316
Karaosmanoglu, Attila, 1316
Karasimeonov, Matey, 1422
Kasemsri, Birabhongse, 1410
Kassar, A., 1355
Kastelein, J., 1355
Kastoft, Hans Erik, 1393
Katopola, D. S., 1308
Kaufmann, Johan, 1406
Kaul, A., 1407
Kayaalp, S. Oguz, 1422
Kazembe, Elias M. C., 1394
Kazi, Mumtaz Ali, 1397
Kazmi, S. A. A., 1355
Kchouk, Dr. Mohsen, 1422
Kean, Arnold Wilfred Geoffrey, 1401
Kearns, James M., 1321
Kebede, Kassa, 1285
Keefer, Thomas A. J., 1364
Keller, Ernst, 1397
Kelly, Elsa D. R., 1301
Kelly, William B., 1373
Kendrew, Sir John, 1408
Kenyatta, Margaret, 937, 1409
Keyes, Alan L., 1406
Khalevinski, I. V., 1394
Khalid, Mansour, 1405
Khalifa, Ahmed Mohamed, 904, 1412, 1417
Khan, A. Majeed, 1301
Khandker, A. R., 1417
Khane, Abd-El Rahman, 1406, 1425
Khantouche, Najet, 1415
Kharbit, Abdul Meguid Ibrahim, 1417
Khmel, I. S., 1411, 1412
Khosla, R. R., 1416, 1419
Khumalo, Duma Joshua, 162
Kibria, Gholam, 1315, 1320, 1328
Kibria, Shah A. M. S., 1423
Kikine, Sam, **155**
Kintanar, R. L., 1354
Kirby, Richard C., 1349
Kirca, A. Coskun, 1404
Kirichenko, V. N., 1416
Kishi, Nobusuke, 1396
Kitikiti, Nicholas Dlamini, 1397
Kitschenberg, Helmut, 1398
Klement-Francis, Roswitha J., 1321
Klinghoffer, Leon, 272, 291, 292
Klum, A., 1403
Knapp, Jean, 1301
Knox, A. David, 1316
Knutsson, Karl-Eric, 1424
Kobayashi, Tomohiko, 1411
Koinzer, Helmut, 1403
Kok, Wim, 1415
Ko Ko, Dr. U, 1308
Kolarova, Irina, 1412
Kolev, Konstantin, 1397, 1415
Komatina, Miljan, 1424
Konadu, Yeboah, 1403
Konadu-Yiadom, Yaw, 1395
Konstantinov, Leonard, 1277
Kooijmans, Peter H., 863
Koray, Ozer, 252, 253, 254, 255, 256
Kords, Ulrich, 1411
Korhonen, Anna Liisa, 1419
Korhonen, Keijo, 1393

Korolev, M. A., 1413
Koroma, Abdul G., 1398, 1400
Korpinen, Pekka, 1315, 1321, 1328
Kostikov, Lev Efremovich, 1364
Kotaite, Assad, 1342
Kouadio, N., 1285
Kouassi, Kwam, 1393
Koudsi, Marwan, 1416
Kozlov, Vladimir V., 1349
Kreuter, Gunter H., 1321
Krishnan, Natarajan, 1404, 1410
Kristvik, Bjorn Inge, 1406
Kronholm, Jan, 1400
Krueger, Anne O., 1316
Ksentini, Fatma Z., 1412
Kubo, T., 1407
Kudryavtsev, A. Y., 1417
Kühn, Jürgen, 1415
Kumatori, T., 1407
Kumlin, Krister, 1397, 1411
Kunugi, Tatsuro, 1424
Kurihara, Yoshitaka, 1349
Kuroda, Mizuo, 1301
Kurokochi, Hisami, 1411, 1419
Kuttner, Sol, 1406, 1407, 1408
Kuyama, Sumihiro, 1424
Kwiatkowski, Stefen, 1397
Kyprianou, Spyros, 251, 252, 253, 255, 256

Labastida, Julio, 1301
Labrousse, J. P. N., 1355
Lacarte Muró, Julio A., 1402
Lacasa Aso, J. M., 1285
Lachs, Manfred, 1421, **1156**, 1157
Laclaustra, Arturo, 1395, 1397
Lacleta Muñoz, José Manuel, 1398
Lafer, Celso, 1415
Lagadinova, Elena Atanassova, 1409, 1418
Lago Silva, Jorge, 1393
Lahlou, Rachid, 1394
Laiou-Antoniou, Chryssanthi, 1422
Lallah, Rajsoomer, 913, 914, 1422
Lalor, Gerald Cecil, 1408
Lamarca, Felipe, 1416
Lambert, Yves, 1342
Lambo, Dr. T. Adeoye, 1308
Lamptey, George O., 1422
Lang, Istvan, 1405
Lankester, Timothy P., 1320, 1335
Lara Bonilla, Rodrigo, 1027
La Rocca, Umberto, 1406
Lavalle Urbina, María, 1418
Lazarevic, Zoran, 1394
Lazrak, Zhor, 1418
Leaes, L. G. Paes de Barros, 1401
Lechuga Hevia, Carlos, 1393, 1406
Ledakis, Gust, 1364
Lee, Peter David, 1399
Lee, Dr. Sung Woo, 1308
Leonard, Luke, 1335
Leutwiler, Fritz, 147
Liang Yufan, 1406
Lifiga, U. B., 1355
Lignon, R. S., 1293
Lindquist, A., 1293
Linehan, Thomas Patrick, 1413
Linke, Robert, 1417
Lin Shangzhen, 1418
Lioutsko, A. V., 1411
Litvinov, Dr. S. K., 1308
Liu, Fou-Tchin, 1423
Lizano Vindas, G., 1355
Lochhead, I. G., 1409

Loewe, Roland, 1401
Lohani, Prakash Chandra, 1414
Lopatka, Adam, 1412
Lopes, Henri, 1301
López, Cecilia, 1409
López-de-Chicheri, Juan, 1403
López-Noguerol, Osvaldo, 1373
López-Rey y Arrojo, Manuel, 1409, 1417
Loredo Hill, Adolfo, 1364
Loukidis, Nicholas, 1415
Loulichki, Mohammed, 1400
Lowery, Evelyn, 134
Lozada, J. A. Jr., 1407
Luchaire, François, 1157, 1421
Luckhoo, Edward Victor, 1301
Luhulima, Achie Sudiarti, 1418
Lundström, Hans, 1335
Lundvik, Jan, 1400
Lunn, Charles Alfred, 1417
Lu Rushan, Dr., 1308
Lusaka, Paul John Firmino, 1399, 1404
Luthi, Daniel, 1416
Lutoslawski, Witold, 1298
Lweno, Shani O., 1394

Maalainine, Mohamed Taquiollah, 1141
MacCabe, N., 1407
Macedo de Sheppard, Raquel, 1422
MacMichael, David, 216
Madani, Mohamed Omar, 1406
Magistad, Inga, 1403
Mahabir, Errol, 1410
Mahiou, Ahmed, 1398
Mahler, Dr. Halfdan, 1308
Mahmoud, Suror Merza, 1400
Maier, Heribert, 1285
Mainwaring, J., 1406
Majali, Abdelsalam A., 1301
Majoli, Mario, 1406, 1407, 1408
Makagiansar, Makaminan, 1301
Makatini, Mfanafuthi J., 185, 187, 1097
Makeka, Thabo, 1419
Makhele, M. V., **195**
Makhubu, Lydia, 1397
Maksoud, Clovis, 1097
Makuto, Dr. D. G., 1308
Maldonado Muñoz, J. M., 1402
Malek, Chafic, 1398
Malik, M. Yaqub, 1402
Maloise, Malesela Benjamin, 127, **160**, 163, 164, **164**
Ma Longde, 1394
Malu wa Kalenga, 1276
Manalo, Rosario G., 1409, 1417
Mandela, Nelson, 132, 135, 153, **155**, 157, **158**, 159, **160**, 162, 163, **173**, **857**, 900
Mandela, Winnie, 153, 159
Mankedi, G., 1355
Mann, C. Richard, 1419
Manning, Richard, 1315, 1320, 1328, 1418, 1419
Manouan, M. A., 1406
Mansouri, Mohammad Samir, 1394
Marcucci, Aurelio, 1406
Margan, Ivo, 1301
Marikar, M. H. M. Naina, 1414
Mariko, N'Tji Idriss, 1301
Marín-Bosch, Miguel, 1415
Marinescu, Teodor, 1397
Marino de Botero, Margarita, 1405
Marius, Luis Enrique, 1415
Martenson, Jan, 88, 1423
Martinazzoli, Mino, 1409

Martínez, Manlio D., 1397
Martínez, Miguel Alfonso, 1402, 1412
Martínez Báez, Antonio, 1412
Martínez Cobo, José R., 847
Martohadinegoro, Kahono, 1398
Maruping, A. P., 1419
Marx, Peter, 1397
Mashasi, Elias J., 1415
Ma Shijun, 1405
Mason, Sir Ronald, 1406
Masouyé, Claude, 1364
Massé, Marcel, 1335
Mathas, G. A., 1409
Mathur, Madan G., 1373
Matsui, Akira, 1406
Matsukawa, Michiya, 1398
Matus, Janos, 1394
Mavoa, Jonati, 1414
Mavrommatis, Andreas V., 1422
Maxey, Peter M., 1420
Maycock, Ernest Besley, 1393, 1394
Mayer, Francis, 1315, 1320, 1328
Mazilu, Dumitru, 931, 1412
Mbaye, Kéba, **1156**, 1156, 1421
Mboumoua, William Eteki, 1406
M'Bow, Amadou Mahtar, 1301
McBurney, Raúl Milton, 1136
McCaffrey, Stephen C., 1170, 1398
McFarlane, Carmen, 1398
McIntyre, Alister, 1424
McLurg, A., 1407
McNamara, Robert S., 1416
Mebazaa, F., 1399
Medaghri-Alaoui, Mohamed, 1416
Mehta, Amrik S., 1424
Mehta, Kanti, 1285
Melin, Anita, 1413
Melloni, M., 1406, 1407
Meltke, Falk, 1393
Menck, Thomas, 1416
Mendes Victor, L. A., 1355
Mendoza, Democrito T., 1285
Mensah, Moise, 1369
Mensah, T. A., 1358
Mercier, R., 1285
Mesinger, F., 1355
Messiaen, Olivier, 1298
Metelits, M., 1406
Michalet, Charles Albert, 1415
Michaud, E., 1407
Micka, Vladimir, 1413
Mikdashi, Zuhayr, 1415
Miklau, Ronald, 1417
Milanov, Milan, 1301
Milde, Michael, 1342
Miller, A., 1406
Miller, Canute R., 1416
Miller, D., 1404
Miller, Wayne, 1420
Mills, Donald O., 1406
Milongo, André, 1316, 1321, 1329
Minami, Warren N., 1335
Minch, David B., 1321
Minczewski, J., 1276
Minot, A. R., 1407
Mirza, Muhammad Wasim, 1416
Mishra, Brajesh Chandra, 1120, 1404, 1424
Mitra, Bhaskar Kumar, 1400
Mkhatshwa, Rev. Simangaliso, 134
M'Lingui Keffa, Emile, 1403
Mnumzana, Neo, 194, 1097
Mohamed, A., 1285
Mohamed, Abdullah Zawawi, 1393

Mohamed-Ahmed, Khalafalla El Rasheed, 1398
Mohammed, Azizali F., 1335
Mohammed, Hamid, 1410
Mohammed, Ismael **155**
Mojtahed, Ali Achraf, 1393
Mokgesi, Francis Don, 162
Mokoena, Aubrey, **155**
Mokoena, Reid Melebu, 162
Molinert, Hector Terry, 1419
Molkova, Dagmar, 1417
Molteni, Atilio Norberto, 1394
Mondal, D., 1419
Monekosso, Dr. G. L., 1308
Montagu, David, 1398
Montaño, Jorge, 1412
Montemayor Cantú, Vicente, 1404
Montenegro de Fletcher, Alma, 1422
Montero-Castro, Jorge Arturo, 1417
Monthe, Tommo, 1393
Morel, P., 1355
Morgan, J., 1406
Morgan, Victor Hugo, 1413
Moriyama, Mayumi, 1414
Morozov, Platon D., **1156**, 1421
Morse, F. Bradford, 1401, 1419, 1424, 1425
Morton, J., 1285
Moseley, Harley S. L., 1395
Mosler, Hermann, **1156**, 1156
Mothopeng, Zephania, **160**, 162, 163, **173**, **857**, 900
Moumouni, Abdou Dioffo, 1397
Moura, A. D., 1355
Mourad, Farouk A., 1417
Mourad, Mohammed, 1403
Moura Ribeiro, Maria Margarida de Rego da Costa Salema, 1422
Moushoutas, Constantine, 1396
Mousouris, Sotirios, 1423
Movchan, A. P., 1422
Mselle, C. S. M., 1394
Mtango, E. E. E., 1399, 1401, 1412
Mtei, E. I. M., 1335
M'tesa, Love Kunda, 1395
Mubanga-Chipoya, Chama L. C., 872, 1412
Mudho, Bernards A. N., 1396, 1399
Mueller, Manfred, 1406
Mueshihange, Peter, 185, 187
Muhaisen, Hisham, 1412
Muhr, Gerd, 1285
Mukayiranga, Landrada, 1422
Mukherjee, M. S., 1419
Muller, Robert G., 1423
Mullin, James, 1397
Munga-wa-Nyasa, 1285
Munir-Uz-Zaman, M., 1414
Muñoz-Ledo, Porfirio, 1394, 1406
Munteanu, R. L., 1406
Münzberg, Reinhard, 1315, 1320, 1328
Murata, H., 1276
Muresan, Tiberiu, 1397
Murin, Stefan, 1414
Murithi, J. K., 1355, 1407
Murray, Andrew Robin, 1394
Murray, Deryck Lance, 1416
Mutuale Tshikankie, 1401
Mützelburg, Bernd, 1393
Mvunga, Mphanza Patrick, 1417
Mwanzia, Philip Maingi, 1416
Myers, Robert J., 1407
My Huynh Cong, 1369
Myrdal, Alva, 1396

Nabors, Jovita, 1088
Nabulsi, Mohammed Said, 1423
Nagaratnam, Parameswaran, 1403
Naidoo, M. J., **155**
Nair, V. K. S., 1403
Nakajima, Dr. Hiroshi, 1308
Nakamura, Dr. E., 1308
Nakatani, Shigeru, 1285
Nandan, Satya N., 1424
Nania, A., 1355
Nansen, Fridtjof, 990
Nasrah, M. B., 1403
Natorf, Wlodzimierz, 1419
Natwar-Singh, K., 1406
Naudé, Beyers, 134
Navajas-Mogro, Hugo, 1424
Navarro Rodríguez, Alberto, 1416
Nawaz, Mohammed, 1369
Ndiaye, Birame, 1422
Nebbia, Fernando L., 1335
Nègre, Louis-Pascal, 1406, 1407, 1408, 1424
Negri, Carlos, 1405
Nehru, Braj Kumar, 1398
Neilon, J. R., 1355
Nelson, George B., 798
Nemec, J., 1355
Ngamporo, Joseph Elenga, 1416
Ngcobo, Isaac, **155**
Nimatallah, Yusuf A., 1335
Nishihara, Naokado, 1321
Ni Zhengyu, 1421
Njenga, Frank X. J. C., 1398
Njikelana, Sisa, **155**
Njoya, Adamou Ndam, 1301
Nkondo, Curtis, **155**
Noë, Robert, 1335
Noguchi, Yasuo, 1394
Nogueira-Neto, Paulo, 1405
Norris, Walter F., 1321
Nosek, Jiri, 1398
Nsibande, Musa Justice, 1301
Ntsama, Etienne, 1414
Nujoma, Sam, 1094, 1097
Nwankwo, G. O., 1416
Nyathi, V., 1397
Nygard, Richard, 1394
Nyitrai, Vera, 1419

Obasi, G. O. P., 1355
Oberg, Kjell, 1422
Oda, Shigeru, 1156, **1156**, 1421
Odeh, Alex, 292
Odio Benito, Elizabeth, 1408
Oduyemi, Oluseye D., 1394, 1416
Odzaga, J. R., 1402
Oechslin, Jean-Jacques, 1285
Oeser, Edith, 1422
Ogiso, Motoo, 1398
Ogunshola, Ajibola O., 1407
Ohlin, P. Göran, 1416, 1423
Ohuchi, Teruyuki, 1316
Okely, John, 1395
Okeyo, Achola Pala, 1419
Okeyo, Michael George, 1406, 1407, 1408
Okita, Saburo, 1405
Okken, Rudi, 1409
Oklestek, Vaclav, 1416
Okobi, Victoria N., 1418
Okogwu, G. C., 1285
Okoh, Adikwu F., 1402
Okun, Herbert S., 1410
Olarreaga, M., 1398
Oltramare, Yves, 1398

Omaboe, Emmanuel Noi, 1398
Omar, Abouzaid, 1403
Omar, Mansour, 1140
Omeish, Salem Mohamed, 1316, 1321, 1329
O'Neill, W. A., 1358
Oni, Isaac O., 1416
Opsahl, Torkel, 1422
Oramas-Oliva, Oscar, 1397, 1399, 1400
Orebi, V. E., 1407
Orr, Dr. Wendy, 162
Ortega, Miguel A., 1408
Ortiz, Guillermo, 1335
Ortiz de Rozas, Carlos, 1406
Osakwe, Chiedu I., 1417
Oshima, Keichi, 1397
Osman, Ahmed, 1401
Osman, Lassaad Ben, 1287
Oteiza, Enrique, 1420
Otunnu, Olara, 1406
Ouattara, Alassane Dramane, 1335, 1415
Oubouzar, Ali, 1414
Oudovenko, G. I., 1400, 1410
Ould Khalifa, Moustapha, 1398
Ouranov, Guennady V., 1301
Oussedik, Hocine, 1395
Outkine, M., 1402
Oyama, A., 1276

Paijmans, Martijn J. W. M., 1316
Pajestka, Jozef, 1416
Pal, Yash, 1397
Palle, Bernadette, 1418
Pandi, Bertin, 1417
Pando, Jorge Morelli, 1400
Pankine, M. S., 1402
Pardos, José Luis, 1406
Pareja, Enrique, 1364
Park, Kun, 1373
Park, You Kwang, 1315, 1321, 1329
Parmar, Judhvir, 1321
Partow, Dr. F., 1308
Partsch, Karl Josef, 1422
Pastizzi-Ferencic, Dunja, 1418
Pastor Ridruejo, José Antonio, 916
Patel, I. G., 1416
Paul, Helmut, 1321
Payi, Clarence Lucky, 162
Payne, D., 1406, 1407
Pei Monong, 1406
Peñaherrera, Ivan, 1417
Peñalver, Luis Manuel, 1301
Pepper, Alejandro Abreu, 1403
Perera, B. C., 1415
Pérez, Pedro, 1335
Pérez de Cuéllar, Javier, 1423
Perrett, J. R., 1403
Petersen, Glenn, 1088
Petropoulos, Athanasios, 1414
Peytcheva, Vesselina, 1422
Pfanner, Klaus, 1364
Philipp, Alfred, 1416
Pholo, Molefi, 1393
Picard, Hugues, 1398
Pilloud, Claude, 252, 912
Pimentel, Antônio Fonseca, 1398
Ping, Jean, 1301
Pinheiro-Guimarães, Samuel, 1394
Pintasilgo, Maria de Lourdes, 1408
Pinto, Roger, 1401
Pirson, André Xavier, 1398
Pirzada, Syed Sharifuddin, 1398
Pjescak, Jan, 1409
Pocar, Fausto, 1422

Polak, J. J., 1335
Polanco Gallardo, Luis, 1420
Pollan, Hans, 1321
Polo, Aregba, 1417
Pol Pot, 222, 223, 228, 229, 860
Porzio, Marino, 1364
Poswick, Jean, 1403
Potter, Frank, 1315, 1320, 1328
Potter, T. D., 1355
Pouliot, R., 1407
Pozharski, Vladimir S., 1423
Prado Vallejo, Julio, 1422
Prattley, Winston, 1424
Prebisch, Raúl, 1396
Prem Chand, Lt.-Gen. Dewan, 1410
Pribicevic, Novak, 1400
Price, Brian, 1415
Prien, Alan, 1369
Priestley, Michael, 1424
Primakov, Y. M., 1408
Pronk, Johannes, 1424
Pulido de Briceño, Mercedes, 1424
Pulz, Jiri, 1400
Puri, S. S., 1294

Qian Qichen, 1414
Quass, Susan, 1088
Quentin-Baxter, Robert Q., 1175
Qureshi, Moeen A., 1316
Qweta, Thomazile, **155**

Rabetafika, Blaise, 1410
Rachid, Ahmed, 1141
Racine Ba, Amadou, 1417
Raczkowski, Stanislaw, 1398
Raghavan, V. S., 1321
Rahim, Q. A. M. A., 1396
Rahman, Reaz, 1408
Rai, Ram L., 1406, 1407
Raj, K. N., 1419
Rajaonson, Guy A., 1301
Rajendram, K., 1355
Ramachandran, Arcot, 1424
Ramanna, R., 1276
Ramashamula, Theresa, 162
Ramgobin, Mewa, **155**
Ramphal, Shridath S., 1405, 1416
Rana, Kishan K. S., 1405
Ranasinghe, Nandini, 1411
Randrianame, Maurice, 1413
Rao, P. Sreenivasa, 1400
Rapin, Laurent, 1420
Rasgotra, Maharajakrishna K., 1406
Rasmussen, J. L., 1355
Rasmusson, R., 1402
Rattray, Kenneth O., 1423
Razafindralambo, Edilbert, 1398
Rea, Graeme F., 1335
Reagan, Nancy, 1027
Reddy, Hilary P., 1321
Reddy, Mulka Govinda, 1412
Redouane, Hamida, 1403
Regent-Lechowicz, Maria, 1422
Regmi, Dr. D. N., 1419
Reid, George L., 1315, 1320, 1328
Reimnitz, Juergen, 1398
Reis, Herbert K., 1401
Reiser, H., 1355
Restrepo, Gabriel, 1419
Reuter, Paul, 1398, 1422
Revenko, A. F., 1398
Rexed, Dr. Bror Anders, 1422

Rhodes, John Bower, 1415
Richardson, Richard, 1321
Richter, R., 1403
Richter, V., 1355
Rifai, Dr. G., 1419
Rifai, Najmuddine S., 1423
Rikhye, Gen. Indar Jit, 1297
Ripert, Jean L., 1423
Riphagen, Willem, 1176, 1398
Riskaer, Sven K., 1321
Rivera, Guillermo A., 1315, 1321, 1329
Roche, John P., 1412
Rocher, André, 1420
Rochon, R., 1308
Rodrigues Valle, Henrique, 1397
Rodríguez-Medina, Ernesto, 1396
Roff, Susanne R., 1088
Rojo, Luis A., 1416
Romaih, R. M., 1355
Romano Ajello, Aldo, 1424
Romuáldez, Antonio V., 1335
Rotberg, Eugene H., 1316
Rothe, T., 1407
Roukounas, Emmanuel J., 1398, 1422
Rowe, J. W., 1285
Roy, Banbit A., 1394
Rozes, Simone Andrée, 1417
Ruckelshaus, William D., 1405
Ruda, José Maria, **1156**, 1156, 1157, 1421
Ruedas, Patricio, 1424
Ruisanchez, Jose M., 1321
Ruiz-Cabañas, Miguel, 1411
Ruth, Friedrich, 1406
Rydbeck, Olof, 354, **354**, 1407
Rye, C. R., 1335
Ryrie, William S., 1321

Saad, Raouf A., 1415
Sabally, Saihou, 1408
Sabhasri, Sanga, 1397
Saddler, George F., 1301, 1407
Sadi, Waleed M., 1408
Sadik, Nafis I., 1424
Sadiq Ali, Shanti, 1422
Sadli, Mohammad, 1416
Sagasti, Francisco R., 1397
Sahib, C. R. Krishnaswamy Rao, 1315, 1320,
   1328
Sahlgren, Klaus Aksel, 1423
Sahnoun, Mohamed, 1405
Saito, Shizuo, 1406, 1408
Saker, Ahmed, 1412
Salas, Rafael M., 1405, 1424
Saldanha, Desmond, 1369
Salehkhou, Ghassem, 1335
Salim, Emil, 1404, 1405
Saloojee, Cassim, **155**
Samba, Mawakani, 1335
Sánchez Madariaga, Alfonso, 1285
Sánchez Méndez, Miguel A., 1417
Sanchez-Peña de Lorenz, Carola, 1403
Sangma, P. A., 1414
Sansón, Carlos A., 1335
Santos, Gonzalo G., Jr., 1415
Santos Neves, J., 1285
Saouma, Edouard, 1293
Sapunxhiu, Riza, 1315, 1321, 1329
Sarré, Massamba, 1394, 1397
Sasamura, Y., 1358
Sasso-Mazzufferi, Lucia, 1285
Savary, P., 1293
Savetsila, Siddi, 1410, 1414
Sbihi, Mohammed, 1403

Schild, Willi, 1402
Schlegel, Willi, 1396
Schmidt, Rudolf, 1425
Schmidtkunz, H., 1406, 1407
Schneider, Heinrich G., 1335
Schumann, Günter, 1411
Schumm, Siegfried, 1398
Schwebel, Stephen M., 1156, **1156**, 1421
Seal, Kiron Chandra, 1413
Sefatsa, Mojalefa Reginald, 162
Sefiani, Noureddine, 1394
Segarra, Amada, 1406
Sen, Samarendranath, 1401
Sène, Alioune, 1412
Sengupta, Arjun K., 1335
Serrano Caldera, Alejandro, 1422
Sette Câmara, José, 1156, **1156**, 1421
Sevon, Leif, 1401
Sewpershad, George, **155**
Shah, Shashi N., 1315, 1321, 1329
Shahani, Leticia R., 738, 1423
Shahi, Agha, 1406, 1422
Shahin, Abdul Aziz, 337
Shaib, Bukar, 1405
Shakour Shaalan, A., 1335
Shenkoru, K., 1402
Shen Zhaoqi, 1356
Sherifis, Michael E., 1422
Shiddo, Abdel Aziz Abdalla, 1417
Shihata, Ibrahim F. I., 1316
Siazon, Domingo L., Jr., 591, 1406
Sievering, Nelson F., Jr., 1277
Sihanouk, Samdech Norodom, 222, 223, **227**,
   229
Silbanus, Pedrus T., 1088
Simai, Mihaly, 1418
Simango, V. A., 1355
Simpson, Kwesi B. S., 1412
Sinclair, Sir Ian, 1398
Sinclair, Noel G., 1404
Sinegiorgis, Kongit, 1412, 1422
Singh, Nagendra, **1156**, 1405, 1421
Singh, Swaran, 1301
Singham, A. W., 1112
Singhvi, L. M., 873
Sinha, Yashwant, 1409
Sirry, Omar, 1394, 1398
Sisulu, Albertina, **155**
Skofenko, V. F., 1393
Skolnikoff, Eugene B., 1419
Slim, Taieb, 1406
Smith, D. K., 1355
Smith, Lucy, 1422
Smith, Teresa K., 1140
Smyser, William Richard, 1399, 1424
Sobhan, Rehman, 1416
Sochor, Eugene, 1342
Söderholm, Rainer, 1416
Soedjatmoko, Mr., 1408, 1425
Soenaryo, Mr., 1395
Soeprapto, Enny, 1400
Sofinsky, V. N., 1412
Soglo, Nicéphore, 1316, 1321, 1329
Sohm, Earl D., 1398
Sohn, Soo-Ik, 1414
Sokolov, Vladimir, 1405
Solenberger, Robert R., 1088
Soliven, Preciosa, 1301
Solomon, Sheilah Marguerite, 1301
Sondaal, Hans H. M., 1423
Song Shuhua, 1422
Soubbotine, A. M., 1285
Souchet, Dominique, 1394
Souliatis, Yannis, 1393

Soumahoro, M., 1402
Southard, Rupert B., 1420
Sowinski, Mieczyslaw, 1276
Soysa, D., 1409
Sproete, Wolfgang, 1415
Srithirath, Soubanh, 1414
Srivastava, Chandrika Prasad, 1356, 1358
Stahl, Maj.-Gen. Carl-Gustav, 315, 1410
Stamiris, Helen Arnopoulos, 1418
Stanovnic, Janez, 1405, 1416
Starosolszky, O., 1355
Starushenko, G. B., 1422
Stefanini, Stefano, 1393
Stephanou, Alexis, 1398
Stephansen, Torstein, 1321
Stern, Ernest, 1316
Stewart, John H., 1321
Stratton, Sir Richard, 1420
Strebski, Jerzy, 1402, 1403
Strong, Maurice F., 500, 1405, 1425
Strulak, Tadeusz, 1406
Stunzi, G. A., 1407
Sturms, W. W., 1403
Subrahmanyam, K., 29
Sucharitkul, Sompong, 1175, 1398
Sudirdjo, Artati, 1276
Sudono, Agus, 1285
Sudsukh, Dr. U., 1308
Sugita, Masahiro, 1335
Sumbwe, Fanuel C., 1285
Suraisry, Jobarah E., 1335
Surjaningrat, Dr. S., 1308
Sutanto, Sikuan, 1416
Sutisnawinata, Djunaedi, 1402, 1403
Suy, Erik, 1424
Suzuki, Yoshio, 1409, 1417
Svenningsen, John, 1285
Svensson, Bo, 1417
Swaminathan, M. S., 1397
Swinnen, Johan, 1400
Sy, Ibrahima, 1403, 1404
Sycip, David, 1415
Syquia, T., 1404
Szasz, Ivan, 1401
Szasz, Paul C., 1406, 1407, 1408
Szelei-Kiss, Gyula, 1400
Szomanski, Jacek, 1364

Tadesse, Dr. G., 1308
Tahindro, André, 1395
Takasu, Yukio, 1394, 1406, 1407, 1408
Takemoto, Masayuki, 1412
Takeuchi, Kunio, 1407
Takikawa, Tetsuo, 1416
Talbot, Karen, 134
Tambo, Oliver, 159, 190, 193
Tanaka, Yoshikazu, 1285
Tang, H. Z., 1401
Tanguiane, Sema, 1301
Tanzi, Vito, 1335
Tarasov, Nikolai K., 1421
Tarasyuk, B. I., 1395
Taxell, Per, 1315, 1321, 1328
Taylor, David, 1285
Teehan, Ronald Franquez, 1148
Teferra, Alemayehu, 1301
Tella, Dorothy M., 1413
Tempus, Peter, 1277
Teng Weizao, 1415
Terwisscha van Scheltinga, Frans J. A., 1400
Tewid, Leslie, 1088
Texier, Philippe, 1411
Teyssier, Gérard M., 1335

Thabault, A., 1406
Thahane, Timothy T., 1316, 1321
Thalwitz, Wilfried P., 1316
Tharmaratnam, Athishdam, 1321
Thiam, Doudou, 1163, 1398
Thiam, Iba Der, 1301
Thiam, Ibrahima, 1364
Thin, Tun, 1335
Tholle, Anders, 1406, 1407, 1408
Thomas, Christopher R., 1394
Thomson, Sir John Adam, 1410
Thornberry Lumbreras, Luis Guillermo, 1413
Thunborg, Anders I., 1406
Thyness, Paul, 1424
Timmer, Jozsef, 1285
Tinca, Gheorghe, 83
Tirona, Rosalinda V., 1414
Tisna Amidjaja, Doddy Achdiat, 1301
Titty, André, 1416
Toivo ja Toivo, Andimba, 1101
Tolba, Mostafa Kamal, 1404, 1425
Tomaszewski, Kazimierz, 1395
Tomita, Shigeaki, 670
Tomsic, Vida, 1418
Tomuschat, Christian, 1398, 1422
Törnudd, Klaus, 58, 1406
Torres Bernárdez, Santiago, 1421, 1424
Tosevski, Ivan, 1408, 1412
Touré, Ibrahima Kalil, 1415
Treiki, Ali A., 1406
Trepczynski, K., 1404
Trepelkov, V. P., 1415
Treves, Tullio, 1395
Trino, Paulo César Teixeira, 1420
Troyanov, M. F., 1276
Troyanovsky, O. A., 1410
Tsanga, Delphine, 1418
Tsividis, Yannis, 1397
Tsybukov, V. V., 1398
Tuho, Charles Valy, 1408
Turbanski, Stanislaw, 71
Turk, Danilo, 1412
Turkmen, Ilter, 1404
Turner, Robert E., III, 1396
Tutu, Bishop Desmond, 134, 155

Uathavikul, Phaichitr, 1315, 1321, 1329
Uchida, E., 1355
Ulvhammar, Birgitta, 1301
Umbricht, Victor, 1406
Uribe Portocarrero, Antonio Jose, 1412
Urquhart, Brian, 306, 309, 1423
Urquidi, Víctor Luis, 1408
Ursu, I., 1276
Ushakov, N. A., 1398
Ustinov, Viacheslav A., 1423
Ustor, Endre, 1401
Uusitalo, I., 1399

Vacchelli, Giovanni, 1321
Vaganov, B. S., 1406
Valdepenas, Vicente B., Jr., 1414
Valdez Baquero, Rodrigo, 1412
Valencia Rodríguez, Luis, 1422
Valencia-Ospina, Eduardo, 1421
Valier, Maria Luisa Paronetto, 1301
Valticos, N., 1156, **1156**
van Dam, Ferdinand, 1315, 1321, 1329
van Dongen, Toine F., 1412
Van Houtven, Leo, 1335
Vanni, Raffaele, 1285
Varela Quirós, Luis Alberto, 1412

Vargas, Gustavo Adolfo, 1373, 1403
Vargas, José Israel, 1301, 1397
Vasiliev, A., 1276
Vegega, Carlos S., 1398
Vejjajiva, N., 1402
Vélez Ocón, Carlos, 1277
Véliz Díaz de Villalvilla, Esther, 1422
Vellodi, M. A., 1398
Vendryes, G., 1276
Vergne Saboia, Gilberto, 1394
Vessereau, Dr. Alain, 1406, 1407
Vikis, Alexandros N., 1416
Vilus, Jelena, 1401
Vinde, Pierre, 1424
Vis, Willem, 1401
Vittachi, Varindra T., 1424
Vodicka, O., 1342
Volio Jiménez, Fernando, 894, 914
von Arnim, Adolf-Heinrich, 1422
von Harpe, Michael, 1315, 1320, 1328
von Mutius, Franz, 1285, 1407
von Roemer, Beatrice, 134
von Wechmar, Rüdiger, 1406
Vraalsen, Tom Eric, 1395, 1409
Vratusa, Anton, 1406
Vukovic, Miljenko, 1398

Wadstein, Margareta, 1422
Wagner de Reyna, Alberto, 1301, 1408
Wako, S. Amos, 867, **868**, **869**, 1408, 1422
Walcott, Frank, 1285
Waligo, A., 1404
Walters, Vernon A., 1410
Walton, D. J., 1293
Wang Jiachong, 1285
Wang Liansheng, 1394
Wapenhans, Willi A., 1316
Ware, Helen, 1417
Warioba, Joseph S., 1423
Watson, R. R., 1417
Weaver, Sally, 1420
Weddey, Goukouni, 197
Weil, Alice, 1424
Weinberg, Nat, 1415
Weisgall, Jonathan M., 1088
Weiss, G. K., 1355
Westerholm, Dr. Barbro, 1308
Wheeler, Joseph C., 1404, 1425
Whelan, Eugene F., 1408
Whitaker, Ben Charles George, 928, 1412
White, Eduardo, 1415
Whitlam, Edward Gough, 1301
Whittome, L. A., 1335
Wicks, Nigel L., 1315, 1328
Wiesebach, Horst P., 1424
Wiesner, Eduardo, 1335
Wijesinha, Mervyn Patrick, 1417
Wijewardane, Nissanka, 1395
Wilk, Andrzej J., 1397
Williams, Sir Edward, 1422
Williams, Maurice J., 1408, 1425
Williams, Norman, 1398
Wilson, Lawrence A., 1397
Wittrin, Heino E., 1405, 1424
Wolf, Francis, 1285
Wolf, Karl, 1423
Wolfe, Raymond, 1394
Wolzfeld, Jean-Louis, 1373, 1402
Wonder, Stevie, 135
Wood, D. Joseph, 1316
Wood, William, 1088
Woods, Jeanne M., 134
Woolcott, Richard Arthur, 1410

Wudu, Kobina, 1400
Wu Han, 1417
Wurth, Paul, 252, 912
Wyzner, Eugeniusz, 1424

Xie Qimei, 1423
Xulu, Sipho Bridget, 162
Xu Naijiong, 1315, 1321, 1329
Xu Zhaoxiang, 1397

Yakimetz, Vladimir Victorovich, 1157
Yamaguchi, Kenji, 1315, 1320, 1328
Yamakawa, Toshihiro, 1315, 1320, 1328
Yang Guanghui, 1315, 1321, 1329

Yankov, Alexander, 1175, 1398
Yimer, Fisseha, 1412
Yoffee, W., 1406
Yolah, Shuaib Uthman, 1423
Yonis, Adnan A., 1393, 1394
Yutzis, Mario Jorge, 1422

Zaanouni, Mustapha, 1424
Zador, Endre, 1393
Zagasbaldan, D., 1414
Zaitsev, A., 1355
Zampetti, Sergio, 1406, 1407, 1408
Zarif, Mohammad Farid, 1397
Zecchini, Salvatore, 1335

Zegers, Jan-Maarten, 1335
Zeghal, Hamed, 1397
Zerhouni, A., 1407
Zerouali, Breika, 1140
Zhao Dihua, 1408
Zhao Fusan, 1301
Ziada, Faruq S., 1397, 1399
Zielinski, Adam, 1422
Zifferero, Maurizio, 1277
Zillman, J. W., 1355
Zimba, Newstead L., 1285
Zlatanov, Assen Iliev, 1394
Zou Jingmeng, 1354
Zucconi, Gaetano, 1418
Zulu, J. B., 1335

Index of resolutions and decisions

General Assembly

Thirty-ninth session

Resolution No.	Page
39/213	
Res. B	586
39/247	
Res. B	1214
39/248	571
39/249	954

Decision No.	Page
39/305	
Dec. C	1398
39/324	
Dec. B	584
39/454	
Dec. B	417
Dec. C	395, 417
39/457	394
39/458	481
39/459	943
39/460	394, 1226
39/461	1226
39/462	208, 395
39/463	395
39/464	395
39/465	395
39/466	250, 395
39/467	395

Fortieth session

Resolution No.	Page
40/1	544
40/2	
Res. A	397
Res. B	397
40/3	123
40/4	402
40/5	399
40/6	294
40/7	226
40/8	694
40/9	121
40/10	124
40/11	125
40/12	237
40/13	546
40/14	979
40/15	983
40/16	983
40/17	981
40/18	45
40/19	758
40/20	202
40/21	1134
40/22	837
40/23	729
40/24	855
40/25	855
40/26	839
40/27	902
40/28	840
40/29	987
40/30	988

Resolution No.	Page
40/31	778
40/32	740
40/33	746
40/34	742
40/35	756
40/36	745
40/37	740
40/38	954
40/39	961
40/40	503
40/41	1141
40/42	1147
40/43	1143
40/44	1144
40/45	1145
40/46	1148
40/47	1151
40/48	1142
40/49	1152
40/50	1138
40/51	1083
40/52	1073
40/53	1069
40/54	201
40/55	1082
40/56	1061
40/57	1064
40/58	1080
40/59	
Res. A	317
Res. B	318
40/60	1200
40/61	1167
40/62	199
40/63	113
40/64	
Res. A	129
Res. B	160
Res. C	140
Res. D	173
Res. E	151
Res. F	176
Res. G	165
Res. H	171
Res. I	131
40/65	1194
40/66	1198
40/67	1195
40/68	1160
40/69	1164
40/70	1162
40/71	1191
40/72	1192
40/73	1173
40/74	1165
40/75	1197
40/76	1182
40/77	1180
40/78	1178
40/79	62
40/80	
Res. A	48
Res. B	49
40/81	51
40/82	63
40/83	66
40/84	78
40/85	68

Resolution No.	Page
40/86	67
40/87	80
40/88	50
40/89	
Res. A	59
Res. B	60
40/90	74
40/91	
Res. A	83
Res. B	84
40/92	
Res. A	71
Res. B	72
Res. C	73
40/93	65
40/94	
Res. A	76
Res. B	58
Res. C	77
Res. D	75
Res. E	28
Res. F	31
Res. G	43
Res. H	55
Res. I	29
Res. J	32
Res. K	85
Res. L	23
Res. M	57
Res. N	26
Res. O	25
40/95	695
40/96	
Res. A	276
Res. B	277
Res. C	279
Res. D	268
40/97	
Res. A	1104
Res. B	1109
Res. C	1113
Res. D	1116
Res. E	1128
Res. F	1121
40/98	726
40/99	882
40/100	723
40/101	954
40/102	955
40/103	958
40/104	951
40/105	1239
40/106	947
40/107	942
40/108	940
40/109	846
40/110	865
40/111	934
40/112	932
40/113	929
40/114	874
40/115	891
40/116	890
40/117	998
40/118	991
40/119	993
40/120	1024
40/121	1020

Resolution No.	Page
40/122	1017
40/123	886
40/124	883
40/125	888
40/126	897
40/127	864
40/128	863
40/129	1015
40/130	849
40/131	848
40/132	1002
40/133	1001
40/134	1000
40/135	1003
40/136	999
40/137	907
40/138	1006
40/139	918
40/140	923
40/141	910
40/142	928
40/143	868
40/144	850
40/145	914
40/146	862
40/147	870
40/148	842
40/149	927
40/150	88
40/151	
Res. A	27
Res. B	93
Res. C	53
Res. D	92
Res. E	54
Res. F	38
Res. G	95
Res. H	97
Res. I	20
40/152	
Res. A	36
Res. B	46
Res. C	41
Res. D	34
Res. E	96
Res. F	15
Res. G	39
Res. H	44
Res. I	20
Res. J	17
Res. K	98
Res. L	22
Res. M	16
Res. N	18
Res. O	24
Res. P	42
Res. Q	37
40/153	90
40/154	33
40/155	87
40/156	
Res. A	389
Res. B	390
Res. C	390
40/157	259
40/158	117
40/159	120
40/160	388

GENERAL ASSEMBLY,
  40th SESSION *(cont.)*

Resolution No.	Page
40/161	
Res. A	337
Res. B	335
Res. C	339
Res. D	332
Res. E	343
Res. F	340
Res. G	351
40/162	106
40/163	122
40/164	
Res. A	375
Res. B	371
40/165	
Res. A	354
Res. B	357
Res. C	358
Res. D	362
Res. E	367
Res. F	360
Res. G	358
Res. H	363
Res. I	364
Res. J	368
Res. K	361
40/166	1011
40/167	352
40/168	
Res. A	264
Res. B	341
Res. C	280
40/169	349
40/170	284
40/171	681
40/172	590
40/173	421
40/174	1055
40/175	806
40/176	703
40/177	1038
40/178	414
40/179	1035
40/180	593
40/181	699
40/182	425
40/183	452
40/184	718
40/185	422
40/186	631
40/187	586
40/188	218
40/189	581
40/190	634
40/191	720
40/192	565
40/193	715
40/194	713
40/195	643
40/196	491
40/197	817
40/198	
Res. A	809
Res. B	811
40/199	795, 833
40/200	789
40/201	344
40/202	
Res. A	822
Res. B	833
Res. C	832

Resolution No.	Page
40/203	829
40/204	945
40/205	436
40/206	424
40/207	416
40/208	688
40/209	807
40/210	964
40/211	457
40/212	488
40/213	781
40/214	784
40/215	528
40/216	513
40/217	507
40/218	509
40/219	521
40/220	525
40/221	539
40/222	505
40/223	510
40/224	514
40/225	517
40/226	506
40/227	511
40/228	541
40/229	550
40/230	543
40/231	542
40/232	523
40/233	532
40/234	531
40/235	515
40/236	497
40/237	1254
40/238	1223
40/239	
Res. A	1202
Res. B	1204
40/240	1225
40/241	
Res. A	1220
Res. B	1221
40/242	1267
40/243	1256
40/244	1237
40/245	1248
40/246	
Res. A	321
Res. B	322
40/247	325
40/248	1216
40/249	1222
40/250	1230
40/251	1231
40/252	
section I	386
section II	1266
section III	1262
section IV	1263
section V	652
section VI	642
section VII	879
section VIII	641
section IX	1190
section X	1264
section XI	387
section XII	1251
40/253	
Res. A	1207
Res. B	1211
Res. C	1211

Resolution No.	Page
40/254	1212
40/255	1213
40/256	1252
40/257	
Res. A	1158
Res. B	1158
Res. C	1158
40/258	
Res. A	1235
Res. B	1239
Res. C	1245
40/259	1229

Decision No.	Page
40/301	1393
40/302	1393
40/303	1393
40/304	1393
40/305	
Dec. A	1394
Dec. B	1394
Dec. C	1394
40/306	1410
40/307	1411
40/308	584
40/309	1421
40/310	1399
40/311	1408
40/312	1416
40/313	1401
40/314	1400
40/315	1395
40/316	1404
40/317	1404
40/318	1394
40/319	1395
40/320	1398
40/321	1401
40/322	1398
40/323	1408
40/324	1404
40/401	396
40/402	395
40/403	1259
40/404	406
40/405	1260
40/406	1155
40/407	134
40/408	230
40/409	1112
40/410	1136
40/411	1150
40/412	1149
40/413	1146
40/414	1149
40/415	1077
40/416	394
40/417	3
40/418	394
40/419	1161
40/420	863
40/421	1260
40/422	976
40/423	1057
40/424	80
40/425	880
40/426	935
40/427	881
40/428	99
40/429	200
40/430	408
40/431	1057

Decision No.	Page
40/432	347
40/433	150
40/434	606
40/435	633
40/436	1058
40/437	415
40/438	420
40/439	557
40/440	568
40/441	800, 810, 816
40/442	946
40/443	433
40/444	693
40/445	553
40/446	480
40/447	480
40/448	
Dec. A	454, 1407
Dec. B	455
Dec. C	455
40/449	458
40/450	481
40/451	783
40/452	527
40/453	527
40/454	520, 529, 530, 532
40/455	1244
40/456	1253
40/457	1250
40/458	1057
40/459	417
40/460	394
40/461	871
40/462	1057
40/463	597
40/464	1216
40/465	1251
40/466	1241
40/467	1244
40/468	1244
40/469	1242
40/470	394

Security Council

Resolution No.	Page
560(1985)	155
561(1985)	307
562(1985)	212
563(1985)	315
564(1985)	303
565(1985)	253
566(1985)	1097
567(1985)	182
568(1985)	191
569(1985)	158
570(1985)	1421
571(1985)	185
572(1985)	192
573(1985)	287
574(1985)	187
575(1985)	309
576(1985)	315
577(1985)	188
578(1985)	255
579(1985)	1170
580(1985)	195

Economic and Social Council

Organizational session, 1985

Decision No.	Page
1985/101	845, 1055
1985/102	806
1985/103	418
1985/104	1024
1985/105	853
1985/106	583
1985/107	1042
1985/108	431
1985/109	641, 1056
1985/110	434
1985/111	1411, 1416, 1422
1985/112	641

First regular session, 1985

Resolution No.	Page
1985/1	540
1985/2	787
1985/3	770
1985/4	762
1985/5	769
1985/6	957
1985/7	1033
1985/8	1034
1985/9	589
1985/10	431
1985/11	1026
1985/12	1022
1985/13	1023
1985/14	1019
1985/15	1029
1985/16	1019
1985/17	878
1985/18	961
1985/19	836
1985/20	737
1985/21	722
1985/22	733
1985/23	977
1985/24	734
1985/25	420
1985/26	731
1985/27	982
1985/28	985
1985/29	730
1985/30	978
1985/31	725
1985/32	728
1985/33	866
1985/34	727

Resolution No.	Page
1985/35	777
1985/36	736
1985/37	854
1985/38	848
1985/39	894
1985/40	867
1985/41	867
1985/42	929
1985/43	904
1985/44	845
1985/45	953
1985/46	949

Decision No.	Page
1985/113	1046
1985/114	1047
1985/115	1054
1985/116	420
1985/117	853
1985/118	769
1985/119	762
1985/120	771
1985/121	769
1985/122	1031
1985/123	588
1985/124	683
1985/125	683
1985/126	579
1985/127	149
1985/128	1030
1985/129	1013
1985/130	1030
1985/131	1017
1985/132	877
1985/133	737
1985/134	742
1985/135	730
1985/136	737
1985/137	847
1985/138	898
1985/139	925
1985/140	899
1985/141	836
1985/142	1412
1985/143	872
1985/144	863
1985/145	917
1985/146	921
1985/147	906
1985/148	909
1985/149	880
1985/150	913
1985/151	886
1985/152	896
1985/153	887
1985/154	886
1985/155	859
1985/156	912

Decision No.	Page
1985/157	925
1985/158	943
1985/159	552
1985/160	1396, 1408, 1411, 1412, 1413, 1415, 1416, 1417, 1418, 1419, 1420
1985/161	879
1985/162	1411
1985/163	1056
1985/164	943

Second regular session, 1985

Resolution No.	Page
1985/47	676
1985/48	676
1985/49	
Res. A	678
Res. B	679
1985/50	671
1985/51	671
1985/52	672
1985/53	674
1985/54	673
1985/55	673
1985/56	549
1985/57	283
1985/58	348
1985/59	1066
1985/60	651
1985/61	636
1985/62	628
1985/63	629
1985/64	735
1985/65	633
1985/66	643
1985/67	640
1985/68	640
1985/69	665
1985/70	634
1985/71	618
1985/72	148
1985/73	703
1985/74	592
1985/75	682
1985/76	1041
1985/77	1043
1985/78	1253
1985/79	1030
1985/80	501

Decision No.	Page
1985/165	786
1985/166	673

Decision No.	Page
1985/167	680
1985/168	680
1985/169	598
1985/170	636
1985/171	581
1985/172	789
1985/173	822
1985/174	344
1985/175	715
1985/176	806
1985/177	346
1985/178	415
1985/179	416
1985/180	421
1985/181	413
1985/182	626, 645, 654, 660, 665
1985/183	412, 552
1985/184	530, 532, 538
1985/185	998
1985/186	466, 490
1985/187	348
1985/188	664
1985/189	641
1985/190	664
1985/191	625, 634, 652, 655, 662
1985/192	616
1985/193	616
1985/194	616
1985/195	618
1985/196	699
1985/197	697
1985/198	590, 1046
1985/199	701
1985/200	1056
1985/201	1030
1985/202	1056
1985/203	503
1985/204	1396, 1417
1985/205	1057

Resumed second regular session, 1985

Resolution No.	Page
1985/81	593

Trusteeship Council

Fifty-second session

Resolution No.	Page
2179(LII)	1087

NOTE: Numbers in italics indicate that the text is summarized rather than reprinted in full.

How to obtain previous volumes of the *Yearbook*

All previous volumes of the *Yearbook of the United Nations* are available in microfiche from the United Nations Sales Section, Room DC2-0853, United Nations, New York, N.Y. 10017 (Microfiche). Please write or telephone 212-963-2940 for further information. Various volumes prior to the 1979 *Yearbook* are available in limited supply as well. Please write to the Sales Section, United Nations, New York, N.Y. 10017, or the Sales Unit, Palais des Nations, 1211 Geneva 10, Switzerland.

The 1985 *Yearbook* is sold and distributed in the United States and Canada by Kluwer Academic Publishers, 101 Philip Drive, Norwell, Massachusetts 02061; in all other countries by Kluwer Academic Publishers Group, P.O. Box 322, 3300 AH Dordrecht, The Netherlands.

Yearbook of the United Nations, 1985
Volume 39

Compiled by the Yearbook Section of the Department of Public Information, United Nations, New York. Although the *Yearbook* is based on official sources, it is not an official record.

Chief Editor: James A. Beresford Lubin.

Senior Editors/Writers: Hiroko Kimura, Christine B. Koerner.

Editors/Writers: Eliane Freeman, Kathryn Gordon, Donald Paneth, Juanita J. B. Phelan.

Contributing Editors/Writers: J. K. Anderson, Elizabeth G. Baldwin, Edoardo Bellando, Ruth Seligman, Alexander Taukatch.

Copy Editor: Alison M. Koppelman.

Indexer: Elaine P. Adam.

Editorial Assistants/Production Staff/Typesetters: Sunita Chabra, Georgina Kettles, Minnie N. Roque, Joyce B. Rosenblum, Leonard M. Simon.